Crockford's

Clerical Directory

2006/2007

Crockford's

Clerical Directory

2006/2007

Ninety-ninth edition
First issue 1858

A Directory of the Clergy
of the Church of England
the Church in Wales
the Scottish Episcopal Church
the Church of Ireland

CHURCH HOUSE
PUBLISHING

Crockford's Clerical Directory published December 2005 for The Archbishops' Council by:
Church House Publishing
Church House
Great Smith Street
London SW1P 3NZ

Please send any corrections to the Compiler, Crockford (address as above), Tel (020) 7898 1012
Fax (020) 7898 1769 E-mail crockford@c-of-e.org.uk

ISBN 0 7151 1001 2 (hardback)
0 7151 1002 0 (paperback)

Jacket and cover design by Visible Edge Ltd

Typeset by
RefineCatch Ltd,
Bungay, Suffolk

Printed by
William Clowes Ltd,
Beccles, Suffolk

CONTENTS

INDEX TO ADVERTISEMENTS

Advertisements can be found on the following pages:

The inclusion of advertisements is for purposes of information and is not to be taken as implying acceptance of the objects of the advertiser by the publishers or proprietors.

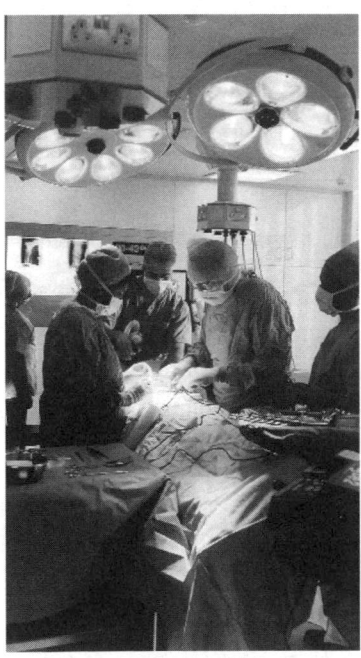

Simply the best way to buy your next car
autosave®
Only autosave can offer a unique car buying package complete with 20 years of experience selling cars directly to the Church, its members, charities, schools and organisations.
VALUE
Because of the relationships we have built with all manufacturers over the many years we have been operating, we are able to pass on substantial discounts on both new and used cars.The reduced costs could mean money in the bank for you or the choice of a better model for the same budget.
CONVENIENCE
Whether you contact autosave through our easy to navigate website, where you will find an extensive selection of cars to choose from, or by telephone, our advisors are ready to help, provide impartial advice and provide you with the most stress free car purchase you will ever make - we will even deliver the car to your door!
PEACE OF MIND
Free delivery nationwide on all new and used vehicles. All vehicles come fully prepared, complete with our 'total peace of mind package' that includes a 120 point vehicle inspection, with a parts and labour warranty and a full HPi check allows you to be rest assured.
CHOICE
As a completely independent company, autosave can offer any make and model of car from any manufacturer to ensure our customers buy the car they want and that best suits their requirement.
FREE MOTORIST INFORMATION PACK
Phone now for your free copy. An informative motoring guide completely free!
autosave
autosave offer a typical saving of over £3000 on nearly new vehicles such as this Vauxhall Corsa
www.autosave.co.uk
0114 255 4040
www.autosave.co.uk
autosave Limited, London House, Little London Road, Sheffield S8 0UH
email:helpline@autosave.co.uk
Savings correct at time of going to press.

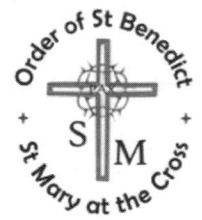

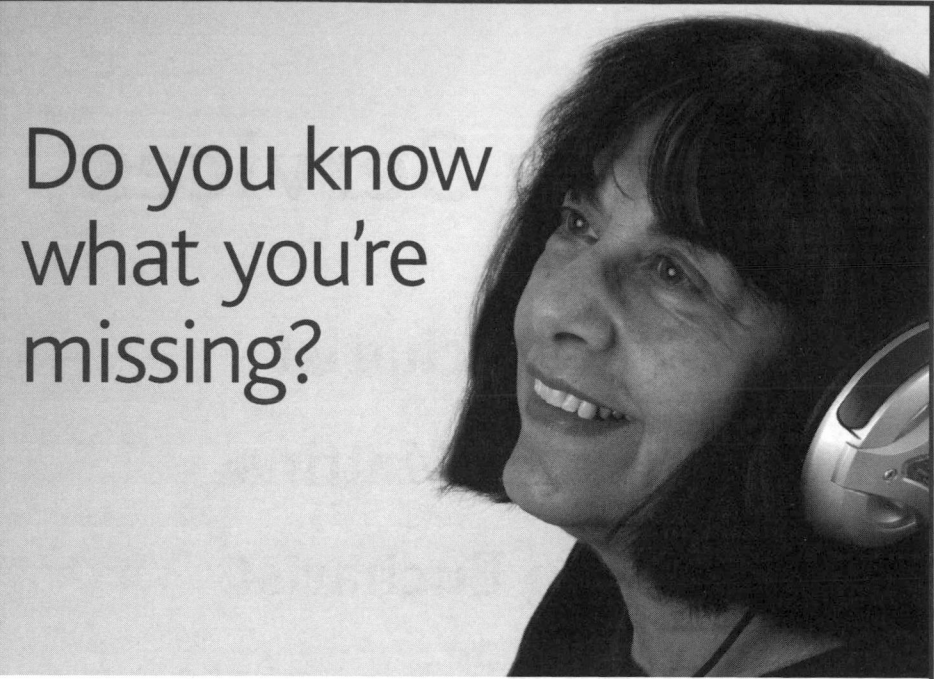

INTRODUCTION

This, the ninety-ninth edition of *Crockford's Clerical Directory*, provides details as at 1 August 2005 of more than 26,000 clergy and deaconesses in the Church of England (including the Diocese in Europe), the Church in Wales, the Scottish Episcopal Church, and the Church of Ireland. It also includes in the main biographical section those Michaelmas ordinands of whom we were notified in advance.

First published in 1858, the publication of *Crockford* now spans almost one and a half centuries. The Oxford University Press purchased the copyright for *Crockford* in 1921, publishing thirty-six editions before transferring ownership to the Church Commissioners and the Central Board of Finance, on economic grounds, sixty years later. This is the second edition under the sole ownership of the Archbishops' Council.

The publishing, design, advertising, selling and distribution of the directory are carried out by Church House Publishing in partnership with the *Crockford* Department, who are responsible for the actual compilation of the text. The information that generates the biographical entries is stored on a database, which is updated daily. Much of this information is obtained from the direct link with the Church Commissioners' central clergy pay-roll. Any alterations to this pay-roll (for example, changes of address or appointment) are automatically reflected on the *Crockford* database. However, approximately one-third of the clergy are not on the central pay-roll. These are principally non-stipendiary ministers, those engaged in some form of ministry outside the parochial system (such as hospital, university, prison or service chaplains) and those serving in Wales, Scotland and Ireland. In maintaining the records of these clergy, we continue to rely greatly on the assistance of bishops' secretaries and diocesan offices, and information contained in diocesan directories, year books and the Church Press. We are also grateful for the help provided by the central authorities of the Church in Wales, the Scottish Episcopal Church, the Church of Ireland, the Ministry of Defence, the Hospital Chaplaincies Council, and our various overseas contacts.

A tremendous amount of help has come from the clergy themselves. We are enormously grateful to all those who have provided us with information, and have helped to minimize omissions and errors. For reasons of time, space and consistency, we are unable to include all the information clergy request us to publish, and we apologise that it has not been possible to respond to each letter individually. We are also grateful to Richard Christmas, Ruth Shobande and Angela Florence, who have been responsible for most of the work in compiling the directory, and have coped with a rush of last-minute correspondence.

We are always glad to be informed of amendments to entries, and we particularly appreciate any information about clergy whose addresses are not currently known to us (see list on p. 1240). Information relating to omissions or amendments should be sent to the *Crockford* Department; requests for archival information from earlier editions should be addressed in writing to Lambeth Palace Library; and requests for other information should be addressed to the Church of England Enquiry Centre.

Crockford Department
Church House
Great Smith Street
London SW1P 3NZ

Tel (020) 7898 1012
E-mail crockford@c-of-e.org.uk
Website www.cofe.anglican.org

The Librarian
Lambeth Palace Library
Lambeth Palace
London SE1 7JU

Fax (020) 7928 7932

Church of England Enquiry Centre
Church House
Great Smith Street
London SW1P 3NZ

Tel (020) 7898 1445
E-mail feedback@c-of-e.org.uk

JOHN CROCKFORD

John Crockford, publisher (?1823–1865) is best remembered for his association with the clerical directory that bears his name. He was the eldest child of a Somerset schoolmaster and his wife, John and Hannah Crockford; and by 1841 he was working as an attorney's clerk in Taunton, Somerset. John Crockford Sr was described in 1869 as Gentleman, of Rowbarton near Taunton. By his early twenties he was in business as a printer and publisher at 29 Essex Street, Strand; and it was from that address that *Crockford* was first published in 1858. On 6 December of the same year, John Crockford moved to new business premises at 346 Strand and 19 Wellington Street North.

His private address at that time was 16 Oakley Square, Hampstead Road; though by 1865 he had moved to 10 Park Road, Haverstock Hill.

Crockford's business association of more than two decades with Edward William Cox (1809–1879) had begun in 1843, when the *Law Times* first appeared. Both men are claimed as publisher – Crockford by Boase in *Modern English Biography*; Cox by the *Athenaeum* and by *Notes and Queries*. There is similar lack of agreement over other publications, such as the ill-fated *Critic*. "[Crockford] tried to establish a literary paper, the *Critic*. To this he brought all his great ability, but after fifteen years he gave it up in despair" (*Notes and Queries*): whereas the *Dictionary of National Biography* has it that Cox became "proprietor of . . . two other papers called respectively 'The Critic' and 'The Royal Exchange'."

The truth appears to be that the two men, who shared the same business address in Essex Street, were joint founders of a number of projects. Cox – the elder, more established and richer man – was often the financier and named publisher, with Crockford as the manager of the undertaking. Each had his own specialities: Cox, called to the bar in 1843, and successively Recorder of Helston & Falmouth (1857–1868) and of Portsmouth (1868–1879), was no doubt the leader in the establishment of the *Law Times*, to which, in *DNB*'s words, he "thenceforth devoted . . . the larger portion of his time and attention." But the legend which has arisen that Cox, restrained by professional ethics from using his own name, chose, almost at random, the name of one of his clerks to bear the title of his new clerical directory in 1858 – thus, in the words of the first postwar editor (probably Newman) bestowing "a more than tomb-stone meed of remembrance" – cannot be substantiated. As the jubilee account of the *Field* notes, Crockford was an equal partner in the success of the joint enterprises: "It was John Crockford who purchased the paper for Mr Cox. He obtained it from Mr Benjamin Webster for a trifling sum . . . In a short time the net profits amounted to 20,000*l*. a year. The management was placed under Crockford's control. He was a splendid man of business" (*Notes and Queries*).

The first *Clerical Directory* (1858), "A Biographical and Statistical Book of Reference for facts relating to the clergy and the Church", seems to have been assembled in a very haphazard fashion, with names added "as fast as they could be obtained", out of alphabetical order and with an unreliable index. By 1860 the *Directory* had become a very much more useful work of reference; and by 1917, with the absorption of its only serious rival, the *Clergy List*, reigned supreme.

No more than glimpses survive of Crockford's personality, and those mostly from the account of him given by John C. Francis, in the *Field* jubilee article already referred to. "I had occasion to call upon him a short time before his death, when we joined in a hearty laugh over his former furious attacks upon the *Athenaeum*. 'Dilke's Drag' he used to call it, and would accuse it of 'vulgar insolence and coxcombry' and 'the coarsest vulgarity'. As we parted he said, 'You have the *Athenaeum* to be proud of, and we have the *Field*.'"

John Crockford died suddenly at his home on 13 January 1865, at the age of 41. He left a widow, Annie (née Ellam) whom he married on 24 December 1847 at St Pancras Old Church. A daughter, Florence Annie, was born in St Pancras in 1852. (Florence married Arthur Brownlow in 1875 and had a son called Frederick.) His very brief will, proved 6 February 1865 at the Principal Probate Registry, left everything to his widow. His personal effects were valued at less than £1,000, but the family must have lived in some style, since one of the witnesses to the will was the resident coachman. Crockford's widow moved to 4 Upper Eton Place, Tavistock Hill, and died there on 26 July 1868.

BRENDA HOUGH

A request from the *Dictionary of National Biography* for a notice of the life of John Crockford led to the preparation of this article, a shorter version of which appeared in *The Dictionary of National Biography: Missing Persons*, 1993. For the information from the 1841 Census, and the record of Crockford's daughter Florence, we are indebted to Mr Ken Rhoades, of Kent.

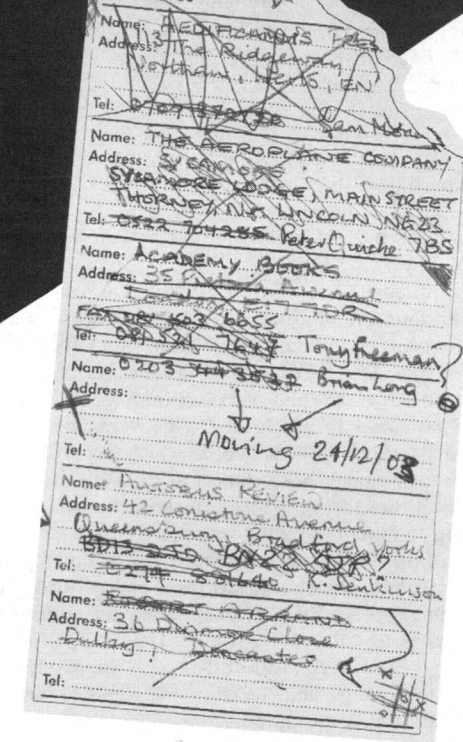

A USER'S GUIDE TO *CROCKFORD*

Who is included in Crockford?
Crockford includes details of over 26,000 clergy and deaconesses of the Church of England, the Church in Wales, the Scottish Episcopal Church and the Church of Ireland. Clergy currently serving overseas qualify for inclusion if they have trained or have been licensed in this country (see **Overseas clergy**). Clergy who have died since the last edition are listed on p. 1242. Generally, clergy who have resigned their offices (but not their orders) are included unless they are known to have been received into another Church. A small number of clergy are excluded at their own request.

Readers and lay workers are not included: please consult diocesan directories. The *Who's Who* section of *The Church of England Year Book* (published annually by Church House Publishing and covering most aspects of the life and institutions of the Church of England) lists members of General Synod and principal members of staff of the Church's central organizations.

Addresses and telephone numbers
Where more than one telephone number is given, the first will normally relate to the address shown.

Addressing the clergy
See p. *31*.

Appointment details in the *Biographies* section
These reflect the legal pastoral situation prevailing at 1 August 2005, the date of the compilation of this edition of *Crockford*. Conventional districts, proprietary chapels and local ecumenical projects are also recorded. Benefice names are only recorded once in a biographical entry when they apply to successive appointments.

Crockford does not record group ministries, informal local arrangements, areas of special responsibility, emeritus appointments (except as reflected in the style of address), licence or permission to officiate when held in conjunction with another appointment from the same diocese, commissary appointments, examining chaplaincies, or secular appointments (except for educational or charitable posts).

Appointments held before ordination are not included (apart from service as a deaconess) unless they straddle the date of ordination.

Archbishops overseas
The presiding (arch-)bishop or metropolitan of each of the provinces of the Anglican Communion is listed in the main *Biographies* section, cross-referenced as appropriate, together with the Moderator of each of the united churches.

Archdeaconries
See *Archdeaconries, deaneries and rural deans* on p. 970.

Archdeacons
Look up the place name in *Biographies*: this is cross-referenced to a personal name.

Bishops (diocesan, area, suffragan, and provincial episcopal visitors)
Look up the place name in *Biographies*: this is cross-referenced to a personal name. See also p. 921, which lists the diocesan, area, suffragan and assistant bishops by diocese, as well as provincial episcopal visitors.

Bishops (assistant)
See *Bishops in England, Wales, Scotland and Ireland* on p. 921.

Bishops in the House of Lords
See p. 924.

Bishops overseas
See *Bishops of Anglican dioceses overseas* on p. 1213, and *Bishops of united churches* on p. 1234. Further information about the Anglican Communion can be found in *The Church of England Year Book.*

Bishops and archbishops, former
A list of former archbishops and bishops (diocesan and suffragan) will be found on p. 925.

Boundaries, provincial and diocesan
Maps of England and Wales, Scotland and Ireland, showing provincial and diocesan boundaries and cathedral cities, will be found on pp. 1246–49.

Cathedral clergy
See *Cathedrals* on p. 963 for full-time cathedral clergy. The list does not include honorary appointments.

Chapel Royal
See *Royal Peculiars* on p. 965.

Christian names
The name by which a person prefers to be known, if not the first Christian name, is underlined (for example, SMITH, David John prefers to be called John). Names 'in religion' or names not part of a person's legal name are shown in parentheses.

Church: how to find the names of clergy responsible for a particular church
Look up the place name in the appropriate *Benefices and churches* section, see pp. 978–1189: if the entry is in bold type, the names of all clergy are listed and can be cross-referenced in the *Biographies* section; if the place name is not in bold type, the name of the benefice is given where the names of all clergy will be found.

Church: how to find the names of clergy responsible for a particular church when there is a vacancy
If the benefice is vacant, the telephone number of the clergy house is usually given in the appropriate *Benefices and churches* section to enable contact to be made with a new incumbent or priest-in-charge. The deanery reference (e.g. *Guildf 2*) following the benefice name cross-refers to *Archdeaconries, deaneries and rural deans* on p. 970 by means of which the name of the rural dean responsible for the vacant benefice can be found.

College chaplains
See p. 1207 for chaplains at universities, colleges of further education, colleges of higher education, sixth-form colleges, and schools.

Corrections
Please send notice of any corrections to:
Crockford Compiler, Church House, Great Smith Street, London SW1P 3NZ
Tel (020) 7898 1012 Fax (020) 7898 1769 E-mail crockford@c-of-e.org.uk

Crockford
The full title is *Crockford's Clerical Directory*. *Crockford* (not *Crockford's*) is an accepted abbreviation. See also the biography of John Crockford on p. *23*.

Deaconesses
See separate section on p. 915.

Deacons
See *Biographies* section.

Deaneries
See rural or area deans below.

Deans
Look up the place name in *Biographies*: this is cross-referenced to a personal name. See also *Cathedrals* on p. 963, and *Royal Peculiars* on p. 965.

Diocesan offices
Details of the diocesan offices in England, Wales, Scotland and Ireland can be found on p. 966.

E-mail addresses
These are provided where known. See after the telephone and/or fax number.

Europe, chaplains in
See *Chaplains of the Diocese of Gibraltar in Europe* on pp. 1190–92.

Fax numbers
The exchange number is only given if different from that of the preceding telephone number.

Hospital chaplains
Whole-time and part-time hospital chaplains are listed under their NHS trusts on p. 1197. Cross-references have been inserted for individual hospitals.

Lay workers
Lay workers are not included in *Crockford*: please consult diocesan directories.

London churches
See *English benefices and churches* on p. 978. City and Guild churches are listed under LONDON CITY CHURCHES and LONDON GUILD CHURCHES. In other cases, see under church name (e.g. LANGHAM PLACE (All Souls), WESTMINSTER (St Matthew)).

Married or single?
Crockford does not provide information on marital status. However, we have included the form of address Miss, Mrs or Ms where requested. Where there has been a change of surname, a cross-reference may be found from the previous name.

Non-stipendiary clergy
Non-stipendiary clergy are listed in the main *Biographies* section.

Ordination courses
See *Theological colleges and courses* on p. 1211.

Overseas clergy
Clergy who are on the *Crockford* database and who are currently serving overseas qualify for inclusion. Service overseas has in the past been recorded simply by country, though higher office (e.g. as bishop or archdeacon) has also been noted. Other eligible appointments are now being added on request.

Overseas addresses and telephone numbers are given as required by a user in the UK, and include the international access and country codes, as well as the area code. If dialling from within the country concerned, the user will need to omit the international access and country codes, and dial zero immediately before the area code.

Patronage
The patron of each benefice is listed under the benefice name in *English benefices and churches* on p. 978.

Prison chaplains
See p. 1195.

Proprietary chapels
See *English benefices and churches* on p. 978.

Provincial episcopal visitors
Look up the place name in *Biographies*: this is cross-referenced to a personal name. See also p. 921, which lists the diocesan, area, suffragan and assistant bishops and provincial episcopal visitors.

Provosts
Look up the place name in *Biographies*: this is cross-referenced to a personal name. See also *Cathedrals* on p. 963.

Queen's Chaplains
See *Royal Peculiars* on p. 965.

Readers
Readers are not included in *Crockford*: please consult diocesan directories.

Religious orders
For members of religious orders where the Christian name alone is commonly used (e.g. Brother Aidan) a cross-reference is provided to the surname. Names 'in religion' not forming part of a person's legal name will be shown in parentheses. Details of religious communities are provided in *The Church of England Year Book.*

Retired clergy
The description 'rtd' does not imply that ministry has ceased, only that clergy so described are now in receipt of a pension. All eligible appointments are now recorded.

Rural or area deans
See *Archdeaconries, deaneries and rural deans* on p. 970. To find who is the rural dean of a particular church, look up the place or benefice name in the appropriate *Benefices* section: the deanery reference (e.g. *Guildf 2*) following the benefice name cross-refers to *Archdeaconries, deaneries and rural deans* on p. 970 where the name of the rural dean responsible can be found.

School chaplains
See p. 1209 for chaplains in schools.

Service chaplains
See p. 1193.

Sixth-form colleges
See p. 1208.

Theological colleges and courses
See p. 1211.

University chaplains
See p. 1207.

© Andy Stonehouse, S2 Design 2005

HOW TO ADDRESS THE CLERGY

In offering the advice below, we do not intend to imply that other practices are necessarily to be discouraged (for example, the use of Father as in 'Father Smith'). A good deal depends on circumstances, and, where a personal preference is known, it is usually good practice to follow it.

The following notes show acceptable current usage

(a) on an envelope or formal listing
(b) in starting a social letter or in speech, and
(c) when referring to a member of the clergy

Category (a) is not open to much variation, owing to the formality of the context, but categories (b) and (c) will often vary according to circumstances. It is always acceptable to use the appropriate Christian name in place of initials (for example, the Revd Alice Smith). In the absence of any style or title conferred by a post, all deacons and priests are styled 'The Reverend', and all who have been consecrated bishop are styled 'The Right Reverend'.

For abbreviations, see paragraph 13 below.

1 **Deacons and Priests**

(a) The Reverend A B Smith
(b) Mr/Mrs/Miss/Ms Smith (unless it is known that some other style is preferred – the title Vicar or Rector is acceptable only if the person so addressed really is the incumbent of the parish where you live or worship)
(c) The Reverend A B Smith at the first mention, and Mr/Mrs/Miss/Ms Smith thereafter

Notes 1 The form 'Reverend Smith' or 'The Reverend Smith' should *never* be used this side of the Atlantic. If the Christian name or initials are not known, the correct forms are
(a) The Reverend—Smith, *or* The Reverend Mr/Mrs/Miss/Ms Smith
(b) Mr/Mrs/Miss/Ms Smith
(c) The Reverend Mr/Mrs/Miss/Ms Smith at the first mention, and Mr/Mrs/Miss/Ms Smith thereafter

2 There is no universally accepted way of addressing an envelope to a married couple of whom both are in holy orders. We recommend the style 'The Reverend A B and the Reverend C D Smith'.

2 **Prebendaries**

(a) The Reverend Prebendary A B Smith
(b) Prebendary Smith
(c) Prebendary Smith

3 **Canons (both Residentiary and Honorary)**

(a) The Reverend Canon A B Smith
(b) Canon Smith
(c) Canon Smith

4 **Archdeacons**

(a) The Venerable the Archdeacon of X
(b) Archdeacon, *or more formally* Mr Archdeacon
(c) The Archdeacon of X at the first mention, and the Archdeacon thereafter

Notes 1 In the case of an archdeacon (or dean/provost, bishop, or archbishop) in office, the style above is to be preferred. The personal name should be used only for the purpose of identification.

2 For an archdeacon emeritus, the correct forms are
(a) The Venerable A B Smith
(b) Archdeacon
(c) Archdeacon Smith

5 **Deans and Provosts**

(a) The Very Reverend the Dean/Provost of X
(b) Dean/Provost, *or more formally* Mr Dean/Provost
(c) The Dean/Provost of X at the first mention, and the Dean thereafter (see also note 1 to paragraph 4 above)

6 **Bishops, Diocesan and Suffragan**

(a) The Right Reverend the Bishop of X, *or* The Right Reverend the Lord Bishop of X
(b) Bishop, *or more formally* My Lord
(c) The Bishop of X at the first mention, and the Bishop thereafter (see also note 1 to paragraph 4 above)

Notes 1 The use of 'Lord' before 'Bishop' is diminishing. It is a matter of individual preference whether it should be used.
2 The Bishop of London is a Privy Councillor, and has the style 'The Right Reverend and Right Honourable the Lord Bishop of London'.
3 The Bishop of Meath and Kildare is styled 'The Most Reverend'.

7 **Assistant and Retired Bishops**

(a) The Right Reverend A B Smith
(b) Bishop
(c) Bishop Smith

8 **Archbishops**

(a) The Most Reverend the Lord Archbishop of X
(b) Archbishop, *or more formally* Your Grace
(c) The Archbishop of X at the first mention, and the Archbishop thereafter (see also note 1 to paragraph 4 above)

Notes 1 The Archbishops of Canterbury and York, being Privy Councillors, also have 'Right Honourable' included in their style (for example, The Most Reverend and Right Honourable the Lord Archbishop of Canterbury).
2 The presiding bishop of the Scottish Episcopal Church is the Primus, and the correct forms are
(a) The Most Reverend the Primus
(b) Primus
(c) Primus
3 A retired archbishop properly reverts to the status of bishop, but may be given as a courtesy the style of an archbishop.

9 **Chaplains to the Armed Services**

(a) The Reverend A B Smith RN (*or* CF *or* RAF)
(b) Padre, *or* Padre Smith
(c) The Padre, *or* Padre Smith

10 **Titled Clerics**

Where a member of the clergy also holds a temporal title, this is always preceded in writing by the ecclesiastical one.

Barons (other than retired archbishops)
(a) The Reverend the Lord Smith of Y
(b) Lord Smith
(c) The Reverend the Lord Smith at the first mention, and Lord Smith thereafter

Baronets
(a) The Reverend Sir Alan Smith Bt
(b) Sir Alan Smith or Sir Alan
(c) The Reverend Sir Alan Smith at the first mention, and Sir Alan Smith thereafter

Knights
An ordained priest may be appointed to an order of knighthood, but will not normally receive the accolade or title. The appropriate designation will follow the name or

ecclesiastical title (for example, The Right Reverend the Bishop of X, KCVO). If he was knighted *before* he was ordained, he will retain his title.

11 **Ordained Members of Religious Orders**

(a) The Reverend Alan/Alice Smith XYZ; The Reverend Brother Alan/Sister Alice XYZ
(b) Father, Father Smith, *or* Father Alan; Brother Alan/Sister Alice
(c) The Reverend Alan/Alice Smith; Father Alan Smith; Father Smith; Brother Alan/ Sister Alice

Notes 1 A name 'in religion', shown in parentheses in the biographical entry, should be used in preference to the baptismal name or initials. Sometimes the surname is not used. In this Directory, however, the entry will be found under the surname, whether it is normally used or not, and, if appropriate, a cross-reference is given under the Christian name.
2 Some orders use 'Brother' and 'Sister' for lay and ordained members without distinction, along with Christian names.
3 It is customary to specify the religious order by giving the appropriate letters after the name.

12 **Academics**

When a member of the clergy holds more than one title, the ecclesiastical one is normally used.

Professor	(a)	The Reverend Canon A B Smith
also Canon	(b)	Canon Smith, *or* Professor Smith, according to context
	(c)	Canon Smith, *or* Professor Smith, according to context
Canon	(a)	The Reverend Canon A B Smith (degree)
also Doctor	(b)	Canon Smith, *or* Dr Smith, according to context
	(c)	Canon Smith, *or* Dr Smith, according to context

13 **Abbreviations**

The following abbreviations are in common use

Reverend:	Revd *or* Rev
Father:	Fr
Right Reverend:	Rt Revd *or* Rt Rev
Prebendary:	Preb
Venerable:	Ven

Reverend, Right Reverend, Very Reverend, Most Reverend and Venerable, whether abbreviated or not, should always be preceded by the definite article.

ABBREVIATIONS USED IN CROCKFORD'S CLERICAL DIRECTORY

A

AAAI	Associate, Institute of Administrative Accountants
AB	Bachelor of Arts (USA)
ABEng	Associate Member of the Association of Building Engineers
ABIA	Associate, Bankers' Institute of Australasia
ABIPP	Associate, British Institute of Professional Photography
ABIST	Associate, British Institute of Surgical Technology
ABM	Advisory Board of Ministry (now Ministry Division)
ABPsS	Associate, British Psychological Society (now see AFBPsS)
ABSM	Associate, Birmingham and Midland Institute School of Music
ACA	Associate, Institute of Chartered Accountants
ACC	Anglican Consultative Council
ACCA	Associate, Chartered Association of Certified Accountants (formerly AACCA)
ACCM	Advisory Council for the Church's Ministry (now Ministry Division)
ACCS	Associate, Corporation of Secretaries
ACCTS	Association for Christian Conferences, Teaching, and Service
ACE	Associateship of the College of Education
	Member, Association of Conference Executives
ACF	Army Cadet Force
ACGI	Associate, City and Guilds of London Institute
ACIArb	Associate, Chartered Institute of Arbitrators
ACIB	Associate, Chartered Institute of Bankers (formerly AIB)
ACIBS	Associate, Chartered Institute of Bankers in Scotland
ACII	Associate, Chartered Insurance Institute
ACIOB	Associate, Chartered Institute of Building
ACIPA	Associate, Chartered Institute of Patent Agents
ACIPD	Associate, Chartered Institute of Personnel and Development
ACIS	Associate, Institute of Chartered Secretaries and Administrators
ACIT	Associate, Chartered Institute of Transport
ACMA	Associate, Chartered Institute of Management Accountants (formerly ACWA)
ACMI	Associate, Chartered Management Institute (formerly AIMgt)
ACORA	Archbishops' Commission on Rural Areas
ACP	Associate, College of Preceptors
ACS	Additional Curates Society
ACSM	Associate, Camborne School of Mines
ACT	Australian Capital Territory
	Australian College of Theology
ACTVR	Advanced Certificate in Television and Radio
ACUPA	Archbishops' Commission on Urban Priority Areas
ACertC	Advanced Certificate in Counselling
ACertCM	Archbishop of Canterbury's Certificate in Church Music
AD	Area Dean
ADC	Advanced Diploma in Counselling
ADCM	Archbishop of Canterbury's Diploma in Church Music
ADEDC	Advanced Diploma in Education of the Deaf and Partially Hearing Children
ADFM	Advanced Diploma in Farm Management
ADMT	Advanced Diploma in Ministerial Theology
ADPS	Advanced Diploma in Pastoral Studies
ADTPS	Advanced Diploma in Theology and Pastoral Studies
ADUT	Advanced Diploma in Urban Theology
ADipR	Archbishop's Diploma for Readers
AEdRD	Associateship in Educational Research and Development
AFAIM	Associate Fellow, Australian Institute of Management
AFBPsS	Associate Fellow, British Psychological Society (formerly ABPsS)
AFC	Air Force Cross
AFIMA	Associate Fellow, Institute of Mathematics and its Applications
AFOM	Associate, Faculty of Occupational Medicine
AGSM	Associate, Guildhall School of Music and Drama
AHSM *or* AHA	Associate, Institute of Health Service Management (formerly Administrators)
AIA	Associate, Institute of Actuaries
AIAS	Associate, Incorporated Association of Architects and Surveyors
AIAT	Associate, Institute of Animal Technicians
AIDS	Acquired Immunity Deficiency Syndrome
AIFST	Associate, Institute of Food Science and Technology
AIGCM	Associate, Incorporated Guild of Church Musicians
AIIM	Associate, Institute of Investment Management
AIL	Associate, Institute of Linguists
AIMLS	Associate, Institute of Medical Laboratory Sciences
AIMSW	Associate, Institute of Medical Social Work
AIMarE	Associate, Institute of Marine Engineering
AIMgt	Associate, Institute of Management (now see ACMI)
AIPM	Associate, Institute of Personnel Management (now see ACIPD)
AITI	Associate, Institute of Taxation in Ireland
AKC	Associate, King's College London
ALA	Associate, Library Association
ALAM	Associate, London Academy of Music
ALBC	Associate, London Bible College
ALCD	Associate, London College of Divinity
ALCM	Associate, London College of Music
ALSM	Associate, Lancashire School of Music
AM	Albert Medal
	Master of Arts (USA)
AMA	Associate, Museums Association
AMASI	Associate Member of the Architects and Surveyors Institute
AMCST	Associate, Manchester College of Science and Technology
AMCT	Associate, Manchester College of Technology
AMIBF	Associate Member, Institute of British Foundrymen
AMIC	Associate Member, Institute of Counselling
AMICME	Associate Member, Institute of Cast Metal Engineers
AMIDHE	Associate Member, Institute of Domestic Heating Engineers
AMIEHO	Associate Member, Institution of Environmental Health Officers
AMIM	Associate Member, Institute of Metals
AMIMMM	Associate Member, Institute of Materials, Minerals and Mining
AMIMinE	Associate Member, Institute of Mining Engineers
AMITD	Associate Member, Institute of Training and Development (now see ACIPD)
AMIW	Associate Member, Institute of Welfare (formerly AMIWO)
AMInstT	Associate Member, Institute of Transport
AMInstTA	Associate Member, Institute of Transport Administration
AMRSH	Associate Member, Royal Society of Health
AMSIA	Associate Member, Society of Investment Analysts
AMusLCM	Associate in Music, London College of Music
AMusTCL	Associate in Music, Trinity College of Music London
ANC	African National Congress
ANCA	Advanced National Certificate in Agriculture
AO	Officer, Order of Australia
APhS	Associate, Philosophical Society of England
ARAM	Associate, Royal Academy of Music
ARCA	Associate, Royal College of Art
ARCIC	Anglican-Roman Catholic International Commission
ARCM	Associate, Royal College of Music
ARCO	Associate, Royal College of Organists
ARCO(CHM)	Associate, Royal College of Organists with Diploma in Choir Training
ARCS	Associate, Royal College of Science
ARCST	Associate, Royal College of Science and Technology (Glasgow)
ARCT	Associate, Royal Conservatory of Music Toronto
ARCUK	Architects' Registration Council of the United Kingdom
ARHistS	Associate, Royal Historical Society
ARIAM	Associate, Royal Irish Academy of Music
ARMCM	Associate, Royal Manchester College of Music
ARPS	Associate, Royal Photographic Society
ARSM	Associate, Royal School of Mines
AS	Associate in Science (USA)
ASCA	Associate, Society of Company and Commercial Accountants

ASSP	Society of All Saints Sisters of the Poor
ASVA	Associate, Incorporated Society of Valuers and Auctioneers
ATC	Air Training Corps
ATCL	Associate, Trinity College of Music London
ATD	Art Teacher's Diploma
ATI	Associate, Textile Institute
ATII	Associate Member, Institute of Taxation
ATL	Association of Teachers and Lecturers
ATPL	Airline Transport Pilot's Licence
ATV	Associated Television
ATh(SA)	Associate in Theology (South Africa)
AVCM	Associate, Victoria College of Music
Ab	(Diocese of) Aberdeen and Orkney
Aber	Aberdeen
Abp	Archbishop
Abth	Aberystwyth
AcDipEd	Academic Diploma in Education
Ad	Advanced
AdCertEd	Advanced Certificate of Education
AdDipCrim	Advanced Diploma in Criminology
AdDipEd	Advanced Diploma in Education
AdDipPTS	Advanced Diploma Pastoral and Theological Studies
AdDipTh	Advanced Diploma in Theology
Admin	Administration
	Administrative
	Administrator
Adn	Archdeacon
Adnry	Archdeaconry
Adv	Adviser
	Advisory
Agric	Agricultural
	Agriculture
Aid	Aidan
	Aidan's
alt	alternate
Andr	Andrew
	Andrew's
	Andrews
Angl	Anglican
	Anglicans
Ant	Anthony
	Anthony's
Appt	Appointment
Arg	(Diocese of) Argyll and The Isles
Arm	(Diocese of) Armagh
Assn	Association
Assoc	Associate
Asst	Assistant
Aug	Augustine
	Augustine's
Aus	Australian
Aux	Auxiliaries
	Auxiliary

B

b	Born
B & W	(Diocese of) Bath and Wells
B or Bapt	Baptist
	Baptist's
BA	Bachelor of Arts
BA(Econ)	Bachelor of Arts in Economics
BA(Ed)	Bachelor of Arts in Education
BA(QTS)	Bachelor of Arts (Qualified Teacher Status)
BA(Theol)	Bachelor of Arts in Theology
BAI	Bachelor of Engineering (also see BE and BEng)
BAO	Bachelor of Obstetrics
BASc	Bachelor of Applied Science
BAdmin	Bachelor of Administration
BAgr	Bachelor of Agriculture
BAppSc(OT)	Bachelor of Applied Science (Occupational Therapy)
BArch	Bachelor of Architecture
BBA	Bachelor of Business Administration
BBC	British Broadcasting Corporation
BBS	Bachelor of Business Studies
BC	British Columbia (Canada)
BCA	Bachelor of Commerce and Administration
BCC	British Council of Churches (now CTBI)
BCL	Bachelor of Civil Law
BCMS	Bible Churchmen's Missionary Society (now Crosslinks)
BCh or BChir	Bachelor of Surgery (also see BS and ChB)
BCom *or* BComm	Bachelor of Commerce
BCombStuds	Bachelor of Combined Studies
BD	Bachelor of Divinity
BDA	Bachelor of Dramatic Art
BDQ	Bachelor of Divinity Qualifying Examination
BDS	Bachelor of Dental Surgery
BDSc	Bachelor of Dental Science
BE	Bachelor of Engineering (also see BAI and BEng)
BEM	British Empire Medal
BEcon	Bachelor of Economics (USA)
BEd	Bachelor of Education
BEdSt	Bachelor of Educational Studies
BEng	Bachelor of Engineering (also see BAI and BE)
BFA	Bachelor of Fine Arts
BFBS	British and Foreign Bible Society
BHSc	Bachelor of Health Sciences
BIE	Bachelor of Industrial Engineering (USA)
BL	Bachelor of Law
BLib	Bachelor of Librarianship
BLitt	Bachelor of Letters
BM	Bachelor of Medicine (also see MB)
BM, BCh	Conjoint degree of Bachelor of Medicine, Bachelor of Surgery
BMMF	Bible and Medical Missionary Fellowship (now Interserve)
BMU	Board for Mission and Unity
BMedSci	Bachelor of Medical Science
BMet	Bachelor of Metallurgy
BMin	Bachelor of Ministry
BMus	Bachelor of Music (also see MusB and MusBac)
BMusEd	Bachelor of Music Education
BN	Bachelor of Nursing
BNC	Brasenose College
BPaed	Bachelor of Paediatrics
BPh or BPhil	Bachelor of Philosophy
BPharm	Bachelor of Pharmacy
BPhil(Ed)	Bachelor of Philosophy (Education)
BRE	Bachelor of Religious Education (USA)
BRF	Bible Reading Fellowship
BS	Bachelor of Science (also see BSc)
	Bachelor of Surgery (also see BCh, BChir and ChB)
BSB	Brotherhood of St Barnabas
BSE	Bachelor of Science in Engineering (also see BScEng)
BSEd	Bachelor of Science in Education (USA)
BSP	Brotherhood of St Paul
BSS	Bachelor of Social Studies
BSSc	Bachelor of Social Science (also see BSocSc)
BSW	Bachelor of Social Work
BSc	Bachelor of Science (also see BS)
BSc(Econ)	Bachelor of Science in Economics
BSc(Soc)	Bachelor of Science (Sociology)
BScAgr	Bachelor of Science in Agriculture
BScEcon	Bachelor of Science in Economics
BScEng	Bachelor of Science in Engineering (also see BSE)
BScFor	Bachelor of Science in Forestry
BScTech	Bachelor of Technical Science
BSocAdmin	Bachelor of Social Administration
BSocSc	Bachelor of Social Science (also see BSSc)
BT	Bachelor of Teaching
BTEC HNC	Business and Technician Education Council Higher National Certificate
BTEC NC	Business and Technician Education Council National Certificate
BTEC ND	Business and Technician Education Council National Diploma
BTS	Bachelor of Theological Studies
BTech	Bachelor of Technology
BTh *or* BTheol	Bachelor of Theology (also see STB)
BVM&S	Bachelor of Veterinary Medicine and Surgery
BVSc	Bachelor of Veterinary Science
BVetMed	Bachelor of Veterinary Medicine (also see VetMB)
Ball	Balliol
Ban	(Diocese of) Bangor
Barn	Barnabas
	Barnabas's
Bart	Bartholomew
	Bartholomew's
Bd	Board
Bedf	Bedford
Belf	Belfast
BesL	Bachelier es Lettres
Bibl	Biblical
Birm	(Diocese of) Birmingham
Blackb	(Diocese of) Blackburn
Bp	Bishop
Br	British
Bradf	(Diocese of) Bradford
Bre	(Diocese of) Brechin
Brig	Brigadier
Bris	(Diocese of) Bristol
Bt	Baronet

C

C	Curate
c	Consecrated
C & O	(Diocese of) Cashel and Ossory (united dioceses of Cashel, Waterford, Lismore, Ossory, Ferns and Leighlin)
C of E	Church of England
C of S	Church of Scotland
C&G	City and Guilds
C, C & R	(Diocese of) Cork, Cloyne and Ross
C-in-c	Curate-in-charge
c/o	Care of
CA	Church Army
	Member, Institute of Chartered Accountants of Scotland
CA(Z)	Member, Institute of Chartered Accountants of Zimbabwe
CACP	Certificate in Advanced Counselling Practice
CACTM	Central Advisory Council for the Ministry (now Ministry Division)
CANDL	Church and Neighbourhood Development in London
CANP	Certificate in Advanced Nursery Practices
CAP	Certificat d'aptitude de la Prêtrise
CARA	Care and Resources for people affected by AIDS/HIV
CARE	Christian Action Research and Education
CASA	Anglican Church of the Southern Cone of America
CASS	Certificate in Applied Social Studies

CB	Companion, Order of the Bath
CBE	Commander, Order of the British Empire
CBIM	Companion, British Institute of Management
CBTS	Certificate in Biblical and Theological Studies
CBiol	Chartered Biologist
CCBI	Council of Churches for Britain and Ireland (now see CTBI)
CCC	Corpus Christi College
	Council for the Care of Churches
CCCS	Commonwealth and Continental Church Society
CCSk	Certificate in Counselling Skills
CCT	Certificate in Clinical Teaching
CCWA	Churches Community Work Alliance
CChem	Chartered Chemist
CD	Canadian Forces Decoration
	Conventional District (also see ED)
CDipAF	Certified Diploma in Accounting and Finance
CECD	Church of England Council for the Deaf
CECM	Certificate of Education for the Church's Ministry
CECS	Church of England Children's Society (now known as the Children's Society)
CEIR	Certificate in Economics and Industrial Relations
CEMS	Church of England Men's Society
CETD	Certificate in the Education of the Deaf
CEng	Chartered Engineer
CF	Chaplain to the Forces
CFTV	Certificate in Film and Television
CGA	Community of the Glorious Ascension
CGLI	City and Guilds of London Institute
CGeol	Chartered Geologist
CH	Companion of Honour
CIO	Church Information Office
CIPFA	Chartered Institute of Public Finance and Accountancy
CITC	Church of Ireland Theological College
CJGS	Community of the Companions of Jesus the Good Shepherd
CLCE	Certificate for Leadership in Christian Education
CLJ	Commander, Order of St Lazarus of Jerusalem
CM	Carnegie Medal
CMBHI	Craft Member, British Horological Institute
CMD	Cambridge Mission to Delhi (now see USPG)
CME	Continuing Ministerial Education
CMG	Companion, Order of St Michael and St George
CMIWSc	Certificate, Institute of Wood Science
CMJ	Church's Ministry among Jewish People
CMS	Church Mission Society (formerly Church Missionary Society)
CMath	Chartered Mathematician
CNAA	Council for National Academic Awards
CNI	Companion, Nautical Institute
COPEC	Conference on Politics, Economics and Community
CORAT	Christian Organizations Research and Advisory Trust
CORE	City Outreach through Renewal Evangelism
CP	Community Priest
CPA	Chartered Patent Agent (formerly FCIPA)
CPAS	Church Pastoral Aid Society
CPC	Certificate of Professional Competence (Road Transport)
CPES	Certificate in Post Excavation Studies
CPEng	Chartered Professional Engineer (of Institution of Engineers of Australia)
CPFA	Member Chartered Institute of Public Finance and Accountancy (formerly IPFA)
CPM	Colonial Police Medal
CPPS	Certificate of Proficiency in Pastoral Studies
CPS	Certificate in Pastoral Studies
CPSS	Certificate in Pastoral and Social Studies
CPTS	Certificate in Pastoral and Theological Studies
CPhys	Chartered Physicist of the Institute of Physics
CPsychol	Chartered Member, British Psychological Society
CQSW	Certificate of Qualification in Social Work
CR	Community of the Resurrection (Mirfield)
CSA	Community of St Andrew
CSD	Co-operative Secretaries Diploma
	Community of St Denys
CSF	Community of St Francis
CSG	Company of the Servants of God
CSMV	Community of St Mary the Virgin
CSP	Community of St Peter
CSS	Certificate in Social Service
CSSM	Children's Special Service Mission
CSWG	Community of the Servants of the Will of God
CSocSc	Certificate in Social Science
CTBI	Churches Together in Britain and Ireland (formerly CCBI)
CTBS	Certificate of Theology and Biblical Studies
CTM	Certificate in Theology for Ministry
CUF	Church Urban Fund
CVO	Commander, Royal Victorian Order
CWME	Commission on World Mission and Evangelism
CWWCh	Certificate of Women's Work in the Church
CY	Church and Youth
CYCW	Certificate in Youth and Community Work
CYFA	Church Youth Fellowships Association
Cam	Cambridge
Can	Canon
Cand	Candidate
	Candidate's
	Candidates'
Cant	(Diocese of) Canterbury
Capt	Captain
Carl	(Diocese of) Carlisle
Cath	Catharine/Catherine
	Catharine's/Catherine's
Cathl	Cathedral
Cdre	Commodore
Cen	Centre
	Center
	Central
Cert	Certificat(e)
CertBibKnowl	Certificate of Bible Knowledge
CertCS	Certificate in Christian Studies
CertCT	Certificate in Ceramic Technology
CertCYW	Certificate in Community and Youth Work
CertEd	Certificate of Education
CertFAI	Certificate in French, Arabic and Islamic Studies
CertFE	Certificate of Further Education
CertFT	Certificate in Family Therapy
CertHE	Certificate in Higher Education
CertHist	Certificate in History
CertMBiol	Certificate of Microbiology
CertMS	Certificate in Management Studies
CertMan	Certificate in Management
CertMin	Certificate in Ministry
CertPSC	Certificate in Professional Studies in Counselling
CertRE	Certificate in Religious Education
CertRK	Certificate in Religious Knowledge
CertRS	Certificate in Religious Studies
CertSS	Certificate in Social Studies
CertTESLA	Certificate in Teaching English as a Second Language to Adults
CertTESOL	Certificate in Teaching English to Speakers of Other Languages
CertTS	Certificate in Timber Surveying
CertYS	Certificate in Youth Service
Ch	Christ
	Christ's
	Church
Ch Ch	Christ Church
ChB	Bachelor of Surgery (also see BCh, BChir and BS)
Chan	Chancellor
Chapl	Chaplain
	Chaplaincies
	Chaplaincy
	Chaplains
Chas	Charles
	Charles's
Chelmsf	(Diocese of) Chelmsford
Chelt	Cheltenham
Ches	(Diocese of) Chester
Chich	(Diocese of) Chichester
Chmn	Chairman
	Chairwoman
Chpl	Chapel
Chr	Christian
	Christians
Chris	Christopher
	Christopher's
Chrys	Chrysostom
	Chrysostom's
Chu	Churchill
Cl-in-c	Cleric-in-charge
Clem	Clement
	Clement's
Cllr	Councillor/Counsellor
Clogh	(Diocese of) Clogher
Co	Company
	County
	Counties
Co-ord	Co-ordinator
	Co-ordinating
Col	Colonel
Coll	College
Colleg	Collegiate
Comdr	Commander
Comdr OM (Italy)	Commander, Order of Merit of the Italian Republic
Commn	Commission
Commr	Commissioner
Comp	Comprehensive
Conf	Confederation
	Conference
Conn	(Diocese of) Connor
Corp	Corporation
Coun	Council
Cov	(Diocese of) Coventry
Cttee	Committee
Cust	Custodian
	Custody
Cuth	Cuthbert
	Cuthbert's
Cypr	Cyprian
	Cyprian's

D

d	Ordained Deacon
D & D	(Diocese of) Down and Dromore
D & G	(Diocese of) Dublin and Glendalough
D & R	(Diocese of) Derry and Raphoe

D&C	Dean and Chapter
DA	Diploma in Anaesthetics (England)
	Diploma in Art (Scotland)
DAA	Diploma in Archive Administration
DAC	Diploma in Adult Counselling
DACE	Diploma in Adult and Continuing Education
DAES	Diploma in Advanced Educational Studies
DAM	Diploma in Archives Management
DAPC	Diploma in Advanced Psychological Counselling
DASAE	Diploma of Advanced Study in Adult Education
DASE	Diploma in the Advanced Study of Education
DASHE	Diploma in Advanced Studies in Higher Education
DASS	Diploma in Applied Social Studies
DASSc	Diploma in Applied Social Science
DATh	Diploma of the Arts in Theology
DArch	Doctor of Architecture
DB	Bachelor of Divinity (USA)
DBE	Dame Commander, Order of the British Empire
DBF	Diocesan Board of Finance
DBMS	Diploma in Biblical and Mission Studies
DBO	Diploma of the British Orthoptic Society
DBP	Diocesan Board of Patronage
DBRS	Diploma in Biblical and Religious Studies
DBS	Diploma in Biblical Studies
DBTS	Diploma in Biblical and Theological Studies
DC	District of Columbia (USA)
DCAe	Diploma of the College of Aeronautics
DCC	Diploma in Crisis Counselling of the Institute of Counselling
DCCD	Diploma in Church and Community Development
DCE	Diploma in Careers Education
DCEG	Diploma in Careers Education and Guidance
DCG	Diploma in Careers Guidance
DCH	Diploma in Child Health
DCHC	Diploma in Counselling and Hospital Chaplaincy
DCL	Doctor of Civil Law
DCM	Diploma in Christian Ministry
DCMus	Diploma in Church Music
DCR	Diploma of the College of Radiographers
DCR, MU	Diploma of the College of Radiographers in Medical Ultra Sound
DCYW	Diploma in Community and Youth Work
DChemEng	Diploma in Chemical Engineering
DClinPsych	Diploma in Clinical Psychology
DCnL	Doctor of Canon Law
DD	Doctor of Divinity
DDPH	Diploma in Dental Public Health
DEHC	Diploma in the Education of Handicapped Children
DEd	Doctor of Education (also see EdD)
DEng	Doctor of Engineering
DFC	Distinguished Flying Cross
DFM	Distinguished Flying Medal (Canada)
DGA	Diploma in Government Administration
DGM	Diploma in Geriatric Medicine
DHA	District Health Authority
DHL	Doctor of Humane Letters
DHRK	Diploma in Humanities and Religious Knowledge
DHSA	Diploma in Health Services Administration
DHSc	Doctor of Health Science
DHistA	Diploma in the History of Art
DHumLit	Doctor of Humane Letters
DIC	Diploma of Membership of Imperial College London
DIH	Diploma in Industrial Health
DIL	Diploma of the Institute of Linguists
DIS	Diploma in Industrial Studies
DIT	Diploma in Interpreting and Translating
DL	Deputy Lieutenant
DLA	Diploma in Liturgy and Architecture
DLC	Diploma of Loughborough College
DLIS	Diploma in Library and Information Studies
DLLP	Diploma in Law and Legal Practice
DLO	Diploma in Laryngology and Otology
DLSc	Doctor of Legal Science
DLitt	Doctor of Letters (also see LittD)
DLitt et Phil	Doctor of Letters and Philosophy
DMA	Diploma in Municipal Administration
DMEd	Diploma of Management in Education
DMS	Diploma in Management Studies
DMS(Ed)	Diploma in Management Studies (Education)
DMU	Diploma in Medical Ultrasound
DMin	Doctor of Ministry
DMinTh	Doctor of Ministry and Theology
DMusEd	Diploma in Music Education
DN	Diploma in Nursing
DNM	Diploma in Nuclear Medicine
DOE	Department of the Environment
DOMS	Diploma in Ophthalmic Medicine and Surgery
DON	Diploma in Ophthalmic Nursing
DPA	Diploma in Public Administration
DPH	Diploma in Public Health
DPM	Diploma in Psychological Medicine
DPMSA	Diploma in Philosophy of Medicine, Society of Apothecaries
DPS	Diploma in Pastoral Studies
DPSA	Diploma in Public and Social Administration
DPSE	Diploma in Professional Studies in Education
DPSN	Diploma in Professional Studies in Nursing
DPST	Diploma in Pastoral and Social Theology
DPhil	Doctor of Philosophy (also see PhD)
DProf	Doctor in Professional Studies
DRBS	Diploma in Religious and Biblical Studies
DRCOG	Diploma of the Royal College of Obstetricians and Gynaecologists
DRI	Diploma in Radionuclide Imaging
DRSAMD	Diploma of the Royal Scottish Academy of Music and Drama
DRSS	Diploma in Religious and Social Studies
DSC	Distinguished Service Cross
DSCE	Diploma in Social and Community Education
DSM	Distinguished Service Medal
DSO	Companion, Distinguished Service Order
DSPT	Diploma in Social and Pastoral Theology
DSRS	Diploma in Social and Religious Studies
DSS	Diploma in Social Studies
DST	Doctor of Sacred Theology (also see STD)
DSc	Doctor of Science (also see ScD)
DSc(Eng)	Doctor of Science in Engineering
DSocSc	Doctor of Social Science
DTI	Department of Trade and Industry
DTM	Diploma in Tropical Medicine
DTM&H	Diploma in Tropical Medicine and Hygiene
DTPH	Diploma in Tropical Public Health
DTPS	Diploma in Theological and Pastoral Studies
DTech	Doctor of Technology
DTh	Doctor of Theology (also see ThD)
DUP	Docteur de l'Université de Paris
DUniv	Doctor of the University
Darw	Darwin
Dav	David
	David's
Dep	Deputy
Dept	Department
DèS	Docteur ès sciences
DèsL	Docteur ès lettres
Det	Detention
Dio	Diocese
Dioc	Diocesan
Dip	Diploma
DipAD	Diploma in Art and Design
DipADO	Diploma of the Association of Dispensing Opticians
DipAE	Diploma in Adult Education
DipAI	Diploma in Artificial Insemination
DipAdEd	Diploma in Advanced Education
DipAgr	Diploma in Agriculture
DipApTh	Diploma in Applied Theology
DipArch	Diploma in Architecture
DipBA	Diploma in Business Administration
DipBBSS	Diploma in Bilingual Business and Secretarial Studies
DipBS	Diploma in Business Studies
DipC&G	Diploma in Counselling and Guidance
DipC&S	Diploma in Counselling and Supervision
DipCACP	Diploma in Cognitive Approaches to Counselling and Psychotherapy
DipCOT	Diploma of the College of Occupational Therapists
DipCSM	Diploma of the Cork School of Music
DipCart	Diploma in Cartography
DipCombStuds	Diploma in Combined Studies
DipDA	Diploma in Dramatic Art
DipEE	Diploma in Electrical Engineering
DipEED	Diploma in Environmental Engineering and Design
DipEH	Diploma in Environmental Health
DipEd	Diploma in Education
DipEdAdmin	Diploma in Educational Administration
DipEurHum	Diploma in European Humanities
DipFD	Diploma in Funeral Directing
DipFE	Diploma in Further Education
DipFL	Diploma in Foreign Languages
DipG&C	Diploma in Guidance and Counselling
DipGD	Diploma in Graphic Design
DipGL	Diploma in German Language
DipHCM	Diploma in Hotel and Catering Management
DipHE	Diploma in Higher Education

DipHSM	Diploma in Health Services Management
DipHSW	Diploma in Health and Social Welfare
DipHV	Diploma in Health Visiting
DipHum	Diploma in Humanities
DipInfSc	Diploma in Information Science
DipInstAM	Diploma of the Institute of Administrative Management
DipInstBM	Diploma of the Institution of Merchanting (Builders)
DipInstHSM	Diploma of the Institute of Health Service Management
DipInstM	Diploma of the Institute of Marketing
DipLaw	Diploma in Law
DipM	Diploma in Marketing
DipMM	Diploma in Mission and Ministry
DipMMin	Diploma in Management for Ministry
DipMaths	Postgraduate Diploma in Mathematics
DipMechE	Diploma in Mechanical Engineering
DipMgt	Diploma in Management
DipMin	Diploma in Ministry
DipN	Diploma in Nursing
DipNCTD	Diploma of the National College of Teachers of the Deaf
DipOAS	Diploma in Oriental and African Studies
DipOHS	Diploma in Occupational Health and Safety
DipOT	Diploma in Occupational Therapy
DipP&C	Diploma in Psychology and Counselling
DipPE	Diploma in Physical Education
DipPS	Diploma in Pastoral Studies
DipPSA	Diploma in Public and Social Administration
DipPSE	Diploma in Personal and Social Education
DipPhil	Diploma in Philosophy
DipPsychP&C	Diploma in Psychodynamic Psychotherapy and Counselling
DipRAM	Diploma of the Royal Academy of Music
DipRCM	Diploma of the Royal College of Music
DipRD	Diploma in Reading Development
DipRE	Diploma in Religious Education
DipREBT	Diploma in Rational Emotive Behaviour Therapy and Counselling
DipREM	Diploma in Rural Estate Management
DipRIPH&H	Diploma of the Royal Institute of Public Health and Hygiene
DipRK	Diploma in Religious Knowledge
DipRS	Diploma in Religious Studies
DipRSAMDA	Diploma of the Royal Scottish Academy of Music and Dramatic Art
DipSC	Diploma in Student Counselling
DipSM	Diploma in Sales Marketing of the Managing and Marketing Sales Association
DipSS	Diploma in Social Studies
DipSoc&CtyEd	Diploma in Social and Community Education
DipSocSc	Diploma in Social Sciences
DipTE	Diploma in Transportation Engineering
DipTLSA	Diploma in Teaching Literacy Skills to Adults
DipTM	Diploma in Training Management
DipTS	Diploma in Transport Studies
DipTSM	Diploma in the Techniques of Safety Management
DipTT	Diploma in Travel and Tourism

DipTh	Diploma in Theology
DipVG	Diploma in Vocational Guidance
DipYESTB	Diploma of the Youth Employment Service Training Board
DipYL	Diploma in Youth Leadership
DipYS	Diploma in Youth Service
Dip Psych	Diploma in Psychology
Dipl-Reg	Diplom-Regiesseur für Musiktheater
Dir	Director
Distr	District
Div	Divinity
Div Test	Divinity Testimonium
DivCert	Divinity Certificate
Dn	Deacon
Dn-in-c	Deacon-in-charge
Dom	Domestic
Down	Downing
Dr	Doctor
Dr rer nat	Doctor of Natural Science
DrTheol	Doctor of Theology (Germany)
Dss	Deaconess
dss	Admitted Deaconess
Dub	Dublin
Dur	(Diocese of) Durham

E

E	East
	Eastern
EAMTC	East Anglian Ministerial Training Course
EC	Emergency Commission
ED	Ecclesiastical District (also see CD)
	Efficiency Decoration
EMMTC	East Midlands Ministry Training Course
EN(G)	Enrolled Nurse (General)
EN(M)	Enrolled Nurse (Mental)
ERD	Emergency Reserve Decoration
ESC	Ecole Superieure de Commerce
ESMI	Elderly, Sick and Mentally Infirm
Ecum	Ecumenical
	Ecumenics
	Ecumenism
Ed	Editor
	Editorial
EdD	Doctor of Education (also see DEd)
EdM	Master of Education (USA) (also see MEd)
Edin	(Diocese of) Edinburgh
Edm	Edmund
	Edmund's
Educn	Education
	Educational
Edw	Edward
	Edward's
Eliz	Elizabeth
	Elizabeth's
Em	Emanuel
	Emmanuel
Emb	Embassy
EngD	Doctor of Engineering
EngTech	Engineering Technician
Episc	Episcopal
	Episcopalian
Eur	(Diocese of) Gibraltar in Europe
	Europe
	European
EurIng	European Engineer
Ev	Evangelist
	Evangelist's
	Evangelists
Evang	Evangelical
	Evangelism
Ex	(Diocese of) Exeter
Ex Dioc Cert	Exeter Diocesan Certificate
Exam	Examining
Exec	Executive
Exor	Executor
Ext	Extension

F

F&HE	Further and Higher Education
FAA	Fellow, Institution of Administrative Accountants
FACC	Fellow, American College of Cardiology
FACOG	Fellow, American College of Obstetricians and Gynaecologists
FADO	Fellow, Association of Dispensing Opticians
FAEB	Fellow, Academy of Environmental Biology (India)
FAHA	Fellow, Australian Academy of the Humanities
FAIM	Fellow, Australian Institute of Management
FAIWCW	Fellow, Australian Institute of Welfare and Community Workers
FASI	Fellow, Architects' and Surveyors' Institute
FBA	Fellow, British Academy
FBCO	Fellow, British College of Ophthalmic Opticians (Optometrists)
FBCS	Fellow, British Computer Society
FBCartS	Fellow, British Cartographic Society
FBDO	Fellow, Association of British Dispensing Opticians
FBEng	Fellow, Association of Building Engineers
FBIM	Fellow, British Institute of Management (formerly MBIM)
FBIS	Fellow, British Interplanetary Society
FBIST	Fellow, British Institute of Surgical Technologists
FBOA	Fellow, British Optical Association
FBPICS	Fellow, British Production and Inventory Control Society
FBPsS	Fellow, British Psychological Society
FBS	Fellow, Burgon Society
FCA	Fellow, Institute of Chartered Accountants
FCCA	Fellow, Chartered Association of Certified Accountants (formerly FACCA)
FCFI	Fellow, Clothing and Footwear Institute
FCIArb	Fellow, Chartered Institute of Arbitrators
FCIB	Fellow, Chartered Institute of Bankers
	Fellow, Corporation of Insurance Brokers
FCII	Fellow, Chartered Insurance Institute
FCILA	Fellow, Chartered Institute of Loss Adjusters
FCIM	Fellow, Chartered Institute of Marketing (formerly FInstM)
FCIOB	Fellow, Chartered Institute of Building
FCIPD	Fellow, Chartered Institute of Personnel and Development
FCIS	Fellow, Institute of Chartered Secretaries and Administrators
FCIT	Fellow, Chartered Institute of Transport
FCMA	Fellow, Institute of Cost and Management Accountants
FCMI	Fellow, Chartered Management Institute (formerly FIMgt)
FCO	Foreign and Commonwealth Office
FCOptom	Fellow, College of Optometrists
FCP	Fellow, College of Preceptors
FCollP	Ordinary Fellow, College of Preceptors
FDS	Fellow in Dental Surgery

FDSRCPSGlas	Fellow in Dental Surgery, Royal College of Physicians and Surgeons of Glasgow
FDSRCS	Fellow in Dental Surgery, Royal College of Surgeons of England
FE	Further Education
FEPA	Fellow, Evangelical Preachers' Association
FEng	Fellow, Royal Academy (formerly Fellowship) of Engineering
FFA	Fellow, Institute of Financial Accountants
FFAEM	Fellow, Faculty of Accident and Emergency Medicine
FFARCS	Fellow, Faculty of Anaesthetists, Royal College of Surgeons of England
FFChM	Fellow, Faculty of Church Music
FFDRCSI	Fellow, Faculty of Dentistry, Royal College of Surgeons in Ireland
FFHom	Fellow, the Faculty of Homoeopathy
FFOM	Fellow, Faculty of Occupational Medicine
FFPHM	Fellow, Faculty of Public Health Medicine
FGA	Fellow, Gemmalogical Association
FGCM	Fellow, Guild of Church Musicians
FGMS	Fellow, Guild of Musicians and Singers
FGS	Fellow, Geological Society of London
FHA	Fellow, Institute of Hospital Administrators (now see FHSM)
FHCIMA	Fellow, Hotel Catering and Institutional Management Association
FHSM	Fellow, Institute of Health Services Management
FIA	Fellow, Institute of Actuaries
FIBD	Fellow, Institute of British Decorators
FIBMS	Fellow, Institute of Biomedical Sciences
FIBiol	Fellow, Institute of Biology
FICE	Fellow, Institution of Civil Engineers
FICM	Fellow, Institution of Commercial Managers
FICS	Fellow, International College of Surgeons
FIChemE	Fellow, Institution of Chemical Engineers
FIDiagE	Fellow, Institute of Diagnostic Engineers
FIED	Fellow, Institution of Engineering Designers
FIEE	Fellow, Institution of Electrical Engineers (formerly FIERE)
FIEEE	Fellow, Institute of Electrical and Electronics Engineers (NY)
FIFF	Fellow, Institute of Freight Forwarders
FIFireE	Fellow, Institution of Fire Engineers
FIHT	Fellow of the Institution of Highways and Transportation
FIHospE	Fellow, Institute of Hospital Engineering
FIIM	Fellow, Institution of Industrial Managers (formerly FIPlantE)
FIL	Fellow, Institute of Linguists
FILEx	Fellow, Institute of Legal Executives
FIMA	Fellow, Institute of Mathematics and its Applications
FIMEMME	Fellow, Institution of Mining Electrical and Mining Mechanical Engineers
FIMI	Fellow, Institute of the Motor Industry
FIMLS	Fellow, Institute of Medical Laboratory Sciences
FIMM	Fellow, Institution of Mining and Metallurgy (now see FIMMM)
FIMMM	Fellow, Institute of Materials, Minerals and Mining
FIMS	Fellow, Institute of Management Specialists
FIMSSA	Fellow, Institute of Mine Surveyors of South Africa
FIMarE	Fellow, Institute of Marine Engineers
FIMechE	Fellow, Institution of Mechanical Engineers
FIMgt	Fellow, Institute of Management (now see FCMI)
FINucE	Fellow, Institution of Nuclear Engineers
FIOSH	Fellow, Institute of Occupational Safety and Health
FIPD	Fellow, Institute of Personnel Development
FIPEM	Fellow, Institute of Physics and Engineering in Medicine
FIPM	Fellow, Institute of Personnel Management (now see FCIPD)
FIQA	Fellow, Institute of Quality Assurance
FISM	Fellow, Institute of Supervisory Management
FIST	Fellow, Institute of Science and Technology
FIStructE	Fellow, Institution of Structural Engineers
FITD	Fellow, Institute of Training and Development (now see FCIPD)
FIWSc	Fellow, Institute of Wood Science
FInstAM	Fellow, Institute of Administrative Management
FInstD	Fellow, Institute of Directors
FInstE	Fellow, Institute of Energy
FInstMC	Fellow, Institute of Measurement and Control
FInstP	Fellow, Institute of Physics
FInstSMM	Fellow, Institute of Sales and Marketing Management
FInstTT	Fellow, Institute of Travel and Tourism
FKC	Fellow, King's College London
FLA	Fellow, Library Association
FLAME	Family Life and Marriage Education
FLCM	Fellow, London College of Music
FLIA	Fellow, Life Insurance Association
FLS	Fellow, Linnean Society
FMA	Fellow, Museums Association
FNI	Fellow, Nautical Institute
FPS	Fellow, Pharmaceutical Society of Great Britain
FPhS	Fellow, Philosophical Society of England
FRACI	Fellow, Royal Australian Chemical Institute
FRAI	Fellow, Royal Anthropological Institute
FRAM	Fellow, Royal Academy of Music
FRAS	Fellow, Royal Asiatic Society
	Fellow, Royal Astronomical Society
FRAeS	Fellow, Royal Aeronautical Society
FRCA	Fellow, Royal College of Anaesthetists
FRCGP	Fellow, Royal College of General Practitioners
FRCM	Fellow, Royal College of Music
FRCO	Fellow, Royal College of Organists
FRCOG	Fellow, Royal College of Obstetricians and Gynaecologists
FRCOphth	Fellow, Royal College of Ophthalmologists
FRCP	Fellow, Royal College of Physicians
FRCP(C)	Fellow, Royal College of Physicians of Canada
FRCPEd	Fellow, Royal College of Physicians Edinburgh
FRCPGlas	Fellow, Royal College of Physicians and Surgeons, Glasgow (also see FRCSGlas)
FRCPath	Fellow, Royal College of Pathologists
FRCPsych	Fellow, Royal College of Psychiatrists
FRCR	Fellow, Royal College of Radiologists
FRCS	Fellow, Royal College of Physicians and Surgeons of England
FRCSE or FRCSEd	Fellow, Royal College of Surgeons of Edinburgh
FRCSGlas	Fellow, Royal College of Physicians and Surgeons, Glasgow (also see FRCPGlas)
FRCSI	Fellow, Royal College of Surgeons in Ireland
FRCVS	Fellow, Royal College of Veterinary Surgeons
FREng	Fellow, Royal Academy of Engineering
FRGS	Fellow, Royal Geographical Society
FRHS	Fellow, Royal Horticultural Society
FRHistS	Fellow, Royal Historical Society
FRIAS	Fellow, Royal Incorporation of Architects of Scotland
FRIBA	Fellow, Royal Institute of British Architects
FRICS	Fellow, Royal Institution of Chartered Surveyors (formerly FLAS and FSI)
FRIN	Fellow, Royal Institute of Navigation
FRINA	Fellow, Royal Institution of Naval Architects
FRIPHH	Fellow, Royal Institute of Public Health and Hygiene
FRMetS	Fellow, Royal Meteorological Society
FRS	Fellow, Royal Society
FRSA	Fellow, Royal Society of Arts
FRSAI	Fellow, Royal Society of Antiquaries of Ireland
FRSC	Fellow, Royal Society of Canada
	Fellow, Royal Society of Chemistry (formerly FRIC)
FRSCM	Hon Fellow, Royal School of Church Music
FRSE	Fellow, Royal Society of Edinburgh
FRSH	Fellow, Royal Society for the Promotion of Health
FRSL	Fellow, Royal Society of Literature
FRSM	Fellow, Royal Society of Medicine
FRTPI	Fellow, Royal Town Planning Institute
FSA	Fellow, Society of Antiquaries
FSAScot	Fellow, Royal Society of Antiquaries of Scotland
FSCA	Fellow, Royal Society of Company and Commercial Accountants
FSJ	Fellowship of St John the Evangelist
FSR	Fellowship Diploma of the Society of Radiographers
FSS	Fellow, Royal Statistical Society
FTC	Flying Training Command
	Full Technological Certificate, City and Guilds of the London Institute
FTCD	Fellow, Trinity College Dublin
FTCL	Fellow, Trinity College of Music London
FTII	Fellow, Institute of Taxation

FVCM	Fellow, Victoria College of Music
FWeldI	Fellow, Institute of Welding
Fell	Fellow
Fitzw	Fitzwilliam
Foundn	Foundation
Fran	Francis
	Francis's

G

G&C	Gonville and Caius
GB	Great Britain
GBSM	Graduate of the Birmingham School of Music
GCMG	Knight Grand Cross, Order of St Michael and St George
GCVO	Knight Grand Cross, Royal Victorian Order
GDipGP	Graduate Diploma in Gestalt Psychotherapy
GFS	Girls' Friendly Society
GGSM	Graduate Diploma of the Guildhall School of Music and Drama
GIBiol	Graduate of the Institute of Biology
GIFireE	Graduate of the Institute of Fire Engineers
GIMechE	Graduate of the Institution of Mechanical Engineers
GIPE	Graduate of the Institution of Production Engineers
GInstP	Graduate of the Institute of Physics
GLCM	Graduate Diploma of the London College of Music
GM	George Medal
GNSM	Graduate of the Northern School of Music
GRIC	Graduate Membership, Royal Institute of Chemistry
GRNCM	Graduate of the Royal Northern College of Music
GRSC	Graduate of the Royal School of Chemistry
GRSM	Graduate of the Royal Schools of Music
GSM	(Member of) Guildhall School of Music and Drama
GTCL	Graduate Diploma of Trinity College of Music, London
Gabr	Gabriel
	Gabriel's
Gd	Good
Gen	General
Geo	George
	George's
Gib	Gibraltar
Glam	Glamorgan
Glas	(Diocese of) Glasgow and Galloway
	Glasgow
Glos	Gloucestershire
Glouc	(Diocese of) Gloucester
Gov	Governor
Gp	Group
Gr	Grammar
Grad LI	Graduate of the Landscape Institute
GradCertEd(FE)	Graduate Certificate in Education (Further Education)
GradDipEd	Postgraduate Diploma of Education (Australia)
GradDipPhys	Graduate Diploma in Physiotherapy
GradDipRE	Postgraduate Diploma in Religious Education (Australia)
GradIEE	Graduate of the Institution of Electrical Engineers
GradIMI	Graduate of the Institute of the Motor Industry
GradIPM	Graduate of the Institute of Personnel Management
GradInstT	Graduate of the Institute of Transport
Greg	Gregory
	Gregory's
Gt	Great
Gtr	Greater
Guildf	(Diocese of) Guildford

H

H	Holy
H&FE	Higher and Further Education
HA	Health Authority
HDipEd	Higher Diploma in Education
HDipHV	Higher Diploma in Health Visit Studies
HDipRE	Higher Diploma in Religious Education
HE	Higher Education
HIV	Human Immunodeficiency Virus
HM	Her (or His) Majesty
HMI	Her (or His) Majesty's Inspector (or Inspectorate)
HMS	Her (or His) Majesty's Ship
HNC	Higher National Certificate
HND	Higher National Diploma
HND(IMechE)	Higher National Diploma, Institution of Mechanical Engineers
HQ	Headquarters
HTC	Higher Technical Certificate
HTV	Harlech Television
HVCert	Health Visitor's Certificate
Hatf	Hatfield
Hd	Head
Heref	(Diocese of) Hereford
Hertf	Hertford
Hist	Historic
	Historical
	History
Ho	House
Hon	Honorary
	Honourable
HonDLaws	Honorary Doctor of Laws
HonFChS	Honorary Fellow, Society of Chiropodists
HonLMStJ	Honorary Life Member, St John's Ambulance Association
HonRCM	Honorary Member, Royal College of Music
Hosp	Hospital

I

I	Incumbent
IAAP	International Association for Analytical Psychology
IBA	Independent Broadcasting Authority
ICF	Industry Churches Forum (formerly Industrial Christian Fellowship)
ICM	Irish Church Missions
ICS	Intercontinental Church Society
IDC	Inter-Diocesan Certificate
IDWAL	Inter-Diocesan West Africa Link
IEAB	Igreja Episcopal Anglicana do Brasil
IEng	Incorporated Engineer (formerly TEng(CEI))
IFES	International Fellowship of Evangelical Students
ILEA	Inner London Education Authority
IMinE	Institution of Mining Engineers
INSEAD	Institut Européen d'Administration des Affaires
IPFA	Member, Chartered Institute of Public Finance and Accountancy
ISO	Imperial Service Order
IT	Information Technology
ITV	Independent Television
IVF	Inter-Varsity Fellowship of Evangelical Unions (now see UCCF)
IVS	International Voluntary Service
Imp	Imperial
Inc	Incorporated
Ind	Industrial
	Industry
Info	Information
Insp	Inspector
Inst	Institut
	Institute
	Institution
Intercon	Intercontinental
Internat	International
Interpr	Interpretation
Is	Island
	Islands
	Isle
	Isles

J

JCD	Doctor of Canon Law
JCL	Licentiate in Canon Law
JD	Doctor of Jurisprudence
JEM	Jerusalem and the East Mission (now see JMECA)
JMECA	Jerusalem and Middle East Church Association (formerly JEM)
JP	Justice of the Peace
Jas	James
	James's
Jes	Jesus
Jo	John
	John's
Jos	Joseph
	Joseph's
Jt	Joint
Jun	Junior

K

K	King
	King's
K, E & A	(Diocese of) Kilmore, Elphin and Ardagh
KA	Knight of St Andrew, Order of Barbados
KBE	Knight Commander, Order of the British Empire
KCB	Knight Commander, Order of the Bath
KCMG	Knight Commander, Order of St Michael and St George
KCVO	Knight Commander, Royal Victorian Order
KPM	King's Police Medal
Kath	Katharine/Katherine
	Katharine's/Katherine's
Kt	Knight

L

L & K	(Diocese of) Limerick and Killaloe (united dioceses of Limerick, Ardfert, Aghadoe, Killaloe, Kilfenora, Clonfert, Kilmacduagh and Emly)
LASI	Licentiate, Ambulance Service Institute
LBIPP	Licentiate, British Institute of Professional Photography
LCC	London County Council
LCL	Licentiate in Canon Law
LCP	Licentiate, College of Preceptors
LCST	Licentiate, College of Speech Therapists
LDS	Licentiate in Dental Surgery
LDSRCSEng	Licentiate in Dental Surgery of the Royal College of Surgeons of England
LDiv	Licentiate in Divinity
LEA	Local Education Authority
LEP	Local Ecumenical Project
LGCM	Lesbian and Gay Christian Movement
LGSM	Licentiate, Guildhall School of Music and Drama
LHSM	Licentiate, Institute of Health Services Management
LICeram	Licentiate, Institute of Ceramics
LIMA	Licentiate, Institute of Mathematics and its Applications
LLA	Lady Literate in Arts
LLAM	Licentiate, London Academy of Music and Dramatic Art
LLB	Bachelor of Laws

LLCM	Licentiate, London College of Music
LLD	Doctor of Laws
LLM	Master of Laws
LMH	Lady Margaret Hall
LMPA	Licentiate Master, Photographers' Association
LNSM	Local Non-stipendiary Minister (or Ministry)
LOROS	Leicestershire Organization for the Relief of Suffering
LRAM	Licentiate, Royal Academy of Music
LRCP	Licentiate, Royal College of Physicians
LRCPI	Licentiate, Royal College of Physicians of Ireland
LRCSEng	Licentiate of the Royal College of Surgeons in England
LRIC	Licenciate, Royal Institute of Chemistry
LRPS	Licentiate, Royal Photographic Society
LRSC	Licentiate, Royal Society of Chemistry
LRSM	Licentiate Diploma of the Royal Schools of Music
LSE	London School of Economics and Political Science
LSHTM	London School of Hygiene and Tropical Medicine
LSIAD	Licentiate, Society of Industrial Artists and Designers
LSMF	Licentiate, State Medical Faculty
LST	Licentiate in Theology (also see LTh)
LSocEth	Licence en Sociologie-Ethnologie
LTCL	Licentiate, Trinity College of Music London
LTh	Licentiate in Theology (also see LST)
LVCM	Licentiate, Victoria College of Music
LVO	Lieutenant, Royal Victorian Order
LWCMD	Licentiate, Welsh College of Music and Drama
Lamp	Lampeter
Lanc	Lancaster
Laur	Laurence
	Laurence's
Lawr	Lawrence
	Lawrence's
Ld	Lord
Ldr	Leader
Lect	Lecturer
Leic	(Diocese of) Leicester
Leon	Leonard
	Leonard's
LèsL	Licencié ès lettres
Lib	Librarian
	Library
Lic	Licence
	Licensed
	Licentiate
LicIM&C	Licentiate, Institute of Measurement and Control
LicTh	Licence in Theology
Lich	(Diocese of) Lichfield
Linc	(Diocese of) Lincoln
Lit	Literature
LittD	Doctor of Letters (also see DLitt)
Liturg	Liturgical
Liv	(Diocese of) Liverpool
Llan	(Diocese of) Llandaff
Lon	(Diocese of) London
Loughb	Loughborough
Lt	Lieutenant
	Little
Ltd	Limited

M

M & K	(Diocese of) Meath and Kildare
MA	Master of Arts
MA(Ed)	Master of Arts in Education
MA(MM)	Master of Arts in Mission and Ministry
MA(TS)	Master of Arts in Theological Studies
MA(Theol)	Master of Arts in Theology
MAAIS	Member, Association of Archaeological Illustrators and Surveyors
MAAR	Member, American Academy of Religion
MAAT	Member, Association of Accounting Technicians
MACC	Member, Australian College of Chaplains
MACE	Member, Australian College of Educators
MACT	Member, Association of Corporate Treasurers
MAE	Member, Academy of Experts
MAJA	Member, Association of Jungian Analysts
MAMIT	Member, Associate of Meat Inspectors Trust
MAPsS	Member, Australian Psychological Society
MASCH	Member, Australian Society of Clinical Hypnotherapists
MASI	Member, Architects and Surveyors Institute
MAT	Master of Arts and Teaching (USA)
MATA	Member, Animal Technicians' Association
MATCA	Member, Air Traffic Control Association
MArAd	Master of Archive Administration
MArch	Master of Architecture
MB	Bachelor of Medicine (also see BM)
MB,BS or MB,ChB	Conjoint degree of Bachelor of Medicine, Bachelor of Surgery
MBA	Master of Business Administration
MBAC	Member, British Association for Counselling
MBAOT	Member, British Association of Occupational Therapists (formerly MAOT)
MBAP	Member, British Association of Psychotherapists
MBASW	Member, British Association of Social Workers
MBATOD	Member, British Association of Teachers of the Deaf
MBC	Metropolitan (or Municipal) Borough Council
MBCO	Member, British College of Optometrists
MBCS	Member, British Computer Society
MBChA	Member, British Chiropody Association
MBE	Member, Order of the British Empire
MBES	Member, Biological Engineering Society
MBEng	Member, Association of Building Engineers
MBHI	Member, British Horological Institute
MBKSTS	Member, British Kinematograph, Sound and Television Society
MBPsS	Member, British Psychological Society
MC	Military Cross
MCA	Member, Institute of Chartered Accountants
MCB	Master in Clinical Biochemistry
MCCDRCS	Member in Clinical Community Dentistry, Royal College of Surgeons
MCD	Master of Civic Design
MCE	Master of Civil Engineering
MCIArb	Member, Chartered Institute of Arbitrators
MCIBS	Member, Chartered Institute of Bankers in Scotland
MCIBSE	Member, Chartered Institute of Building Service Engineers
MCIEH	Member, Chartered Institute of Enviromental Health (formerly MIEH)
MCIH	Member, Chartered Institute of Housing (formerly MIH)
MCIJ	Member, Chartered Institute of Journalists
MCIM	Member, Chartered Institute of Marketing (formerly MInstM)
MCIMA	Member, Chartered Institute of Management Accountants
MCIOB	Member, Chartered Institute of Building
MCIPD	Member, Chartered Institute of Personnel and Development
MCIPS	Member, Chartered Institute of Purchasing and Supply
MCIT	Member, Chartered Institute of Transport
MCIWEM	Member, Chartered Institution of Water and Enviromental Management
MCL	Master of Canon Law
MCMI	Member, Chartered Management Institute (formerly MIMgt)
MCS	Master of Christian Studies
MCSD	Member, Chartered Society of Designers
MCSP	Member, Chartered Society of Physiotherapy
MCST	Member, College of Speech Therapists
MCT	Member, Association of Corporate Treasurers
MCThA	Member, Clinical Theology Association
MChOrth	Master of Orthopaedic Surgery
MChS	Member, Society of Chiropodists
MChemA	Master in Chemical Analysis
MCollP	Member, College of Preceptors
MCom	Master of Commerce
MCommH	Master of Community Health
MD	Doctor of Medicine
MDiv	Master of Divinity
ME	Master of Engineering (also see MEng)
MEHS	Member, Ecclesiastical History Society
MEd	Master of Education
MEng	Master of Engineering
MFA	Master of Fine Art
MFBA	Member, Freshwater Biological Association
MFCM	Member, Faculty of Community Medicine
MFOM	Member, Faculty of Occupational Medicine
MGDSRCSEng	Membership in General Dental Surgery, Royal College of Surgeons of England
MHCIMA	Member, Hotel Catering and Institutional Management Association
MHSA	Member, Hymn Society of America
MHSGBI	Member, Hymn Society of Great Britain and Ireland
MHSM	Member, Institute of Health Services Management
MHort (RHS)	Master of Horticulture, Royal Horticultural Society
MHums	Master of Humanities
MIA	Malawi Institute of Architects
MIAAP	Member, International Association for Analytical Psychology
MIAAS	Member, Incorporated Association of Architects and Surveyors
MIAM	Member, Institute of Administrative Management
MIAP	Member, Institution of Analysts and Programmers
MIAT	Member, Institute of Asphalt Technology

MIBC	Member, Institute of Business Counsellors
MIBCO	Member, Institution of Building Control Officers
MIBF	Member, Institute of British Foundrymen
MIBiol	Member, Institute of Biology
MICA	Member, International Cartographic Association
MICAS	Member, Institute of Chartered Accountants of Scotland
MICE	Member, Institution of Civil Engineers (formerly AMICE)
MICFM	Member, Institute of Charity Fundraising Managers
MICFor	Member, Institute of Chartered Foresters
MICS	Member, Institute of Chartered Shipbrokers
MIChemE	Member, Institution of Chemical Engineers
MICorrST	Member, Institution of Corrosion Science and Technology
MIDPM	Member, Institute of Data Processing Management
MIE	Member, Institute of Engineers and Technicians
MIEAust	Member, Institute of Engineers and Technicians Australia
MIED	Member, Institute of Engineering Designers
MIEE	Member, Institution of Electrical Engineers (formerly AMIEE & MIERE)
MIEEE	Member, Institute of Electrical and Electronics Engineers (NY)
MIEEM	Member, Institute of Ecology and Environmental Management
MIEleclE	Corporate Member, Institution of Electrical and Electronics
	Incorporated Engineers
MIEx	Member, Institute of Export
MIFA	Member, Institute of Field Archaeologists
MIGasE	Member, Institution of Gas Engineers
MIHE	Member, Institute of Health Education
MIHEEM	Member, Institute of Healthcare Engineering and Estate Management
MIHT	Member, Institution of Highways and Transportation
MIHospE	Member, Institute of Hospital Engineers
MIIExE	Member, Institute of Incorporated Executive Engineers
MIIM	Member, Institution of Industrial Managers
MIInfSc	Member, Institute of Information Scientists
MIL	Member, Institute of Linguists
MILT	Member, Institute of Logistics and Transport
MIM	Member, Institute of Metals (formerly Institution of Metallurgists)
MIMA	Member, Institute of Management Accountants
	Member, Institute of Mathematics and its Applications
MIMC	Member, Institute of Management Consultants
MIMI	Member, Institute of the Motor Industry
MIMM	Member, Institution of Mining and Metallurgy (now see MIMMM)
MIMMM	Member, Institute of Materials, Minerals and Mining
MIMarE	Member, Institute of Marine Engineers
MIMechE	Member, Institution of Mechanical Engineers (formerly AMIMechE)
MIMfgE	Member, Institution of Manufacturing Engineers
MIMgt	Member, Institute of Management (now see MCMI)
MIMunE	Member, Institution of Municipal Engineers
MINucE	Member, Institute of Nuclear Engineers
MIOSH	Member, Institution of Occupational Safety and Health
MIOT	Member, Institute of Operating Theatre Technicians
MIPI	Member, Institute of Private Investigators
MIPM	Member, Institute of Personnel Management (now see MCIPD)
MIPR	Member, Institute of Public Relations
MIProdE	Member, Institution of Production Engineers
MIQA	Member, Institute of Quality Assurance
MISE	Member, Institute of Sales Engineers
MISM	Member, Institute of Supervisory Management
MISW	Member, Institute of Social Welfare
MIStructE	Member, Institute of Structural Engineers
MITD	Member, Institute of Training and Development (now see MCIPD)
MITE	Member, Institution of Electrical and Electronics Technician Engineers
MITMA	Member, Institute of Trade Mark Agents
MITPA	Member, International Tax Planning Association
MITSA	Member, Institute of Trading Standards Administration
MITT	Member, Institute of Travel and Tourism
MIW	Member, Institute of Welfare (formerly MIWO)
MInstAM	Member, Institute of Administrative Management
MInstC(Glas)	Member, Institute of Counselling (Glasgow)
MInstD	Member, Institute of Directors
MInstE	Member, Institute of Energy
MInstGA	Member, Institute of Group Analysis
MInstP	Member, Institute of Physics
MInstPC	Member, Institute of Psychotherapy and Counselling
MInstPI	Member, Institute of Patentees and Inventors
MInstPS	Corporate Member, Institute of Purchasing and Supply
MInstPkg	Member, Institute of Packaging
MInstTA	Member, Institute of Transport Administration
ML	Master of Leadership
MLL	Master of Laws
MLS	Master of Library Studies
MLib	Master of Librarianship
MLitt	Master of Letters
MM	Military Medal
MMCET	Martyrs' Memorial and Church of England Trust
MMS	Member, Institute of Management Services
MMedSc	Master of Medical Science
MMet	Master of Metallurgy
MMin	Master of Ministry
MMinTheol	Master in Ministry and Theology
MMus	Master of Music (also see MusM)
MN	Master of Nursing
MNAAL	Member, North American Academy of Liturgy
MNFSH	Member, National Federation of Spiritual Healers
MOD	Ministry of Defence
MPA	Master of Public Administration
MPH	Master of Public Health
MPS	Master of Professional Studies
MPhil	Master of Philosophy
MPhys	Master of Physics
MPsychSc	Master of Psychological Science
MRAC	Member, Royal Agricultural College
MRAeS	Member, Royal Aeronautical Society
MRCGP	Member, Royal College of General Practitioners
MRCO	Member, Royal College of Organists
MRCOG	Member, Royal College of Obstetricians and Gynaecologists
MRCP	Member, Royal College of Physicians
MRCPath	Member, Royal College of Pathologists
MRCPsych	Member, Royal College of Psychiatrists
MRCS	Member, Royal College of Surgeons
MRCSE	Member, Royal College of Surgeons of Edinburgh
MRCVS	Member, Royal College of Veterinary Surgeons
MRHS	Member, Royal Horticultural Society
MRIA	Member, Royal Irish Academy
MRICS	Member, Royal Institution of Chartered Surveyors
MRIN	Member, Royal Institute of Navigation
MRINA	Member, Royal Institution of Naval Architects
MRIPHH	Member, Royal Institute of Public Health and Hygiene
MRPharmS	Member, Royal Pharmaceutical Society (formerly MPS)
MRSC	Member, Royal Society of Chemistry (formerly MRIC)
MRSH	Member, Royal Society for the Promotion of Health
MRSL	Member, Order of the Republic of Sierra Leone
MRST	Member, Royal Society of Teachers
MRTPI	Member, Royal Town Planning Institute
MRTvS	Member, Royal Television Society
MRelSc	Master of Religious Science
MS	Master of Science (USA)
	Master of Surgery
MSAICE	Member, South African Institution of Civil Engineers
MSAPP	Member, Society of Advanced Psychotherapy Practitioners
MSE	Master of Science in Engineering (USA)
	Minister (or Ministers) in Secular Employment
MSERT	Member, Society of Electronic and Radio Technicians
MSGT	Associate Member, Society of Glass Technology
MSHAA	Member, Society of Hearing Aid Audiologists
MSI	Member, Securities Institute
MSIAD	Member, Society of Industrial Artists and Designers
MSOSc	Member, Society of Ordained Scientists
MSOTS	Member, Society for Old Testament Study
MSR	Member, Society of Radiographers
MSSCLE	Member, Society for the Study of the Crusades and the Latin East

MSSCh	Member, School of Surgical Chiropody
MSSTh	Member, Society for the Study of Theology
MSSc	Master of Social Science (also see MSocSc)
MSTSD	Member, Society of Teachers of Speech and Drama
MSW	Master of Social Work
MSacMus	Master of Sacred Music
MSc	Master of Science
MSc(Econ)	Master of Science in Economics
MScRel	Maitrise es Sciences Religieuses
MSci	Master of Natural Sciences
MSoc	Maitrise en Sociologie
MSocSc	Master of Social Sciences (also see MSSc)
MSocWork	Master of Social Work (USA)
MSt	Master of Studies
MTD	Master of Transport Design
MTS	Master of Theological Studies
MTech	Master of Technology
MTh or MTheol	Master of Theology (also see STM and ThM)
MU	Mothers' Union
MVI	Member, Victoria Institute
MVO	Member, Royal Victorian Order
Magd	Magdalen/Magdalene
	Magdalen's/Magdalene's
Man	(Diocese of) Manchester
Man Dir	Managing Director
Mansf	Mansfield
Marg	Margaret
	Margaret's
Matt	Matthew
	Matthew's
Mert	Merton
MesL	Lettres Modernes
Metrop	Metropolitan
Mgt	Management
Mich	Michael
	Michael's
	Michael and All Angels
Midl	Midlands
Mil	Military
Min	Minister
	Ministries
	Ministry
	Minor
Minl	Ministerial
Miss	Mission
	Missions
	Missionary
Missr	Missioner
Mon	(Diocese of) Monmouth
Mor	(Diocese of) Moray, Ross and Caithness
Mt	Mount
MusB or MusBac	Bachelor of Music (also see BMus)
MusD or MusDoc	Doctor of Music
MusM	Master of Music (also see MMus)

N

N	North
	Northern
NACRO	National Association for the Care and Rehabilitation of Offenders
NASA	National Aeronautics and Space Administration (USA)
NC(BS)	National Certificate in Business Studies (Irish Republic)
NCA	National Certificate in Agriculture
NCEC	National Christian Education Council
NCTJ	National Certificate for the Training of Journalists
NDA	National Diploma in Agriculture
NDAD	National Diploma in Art and Design
NDD	National Diploma in Design
NDFOM	National Diploma in Farm Organisation and Management
NDH	National Diploma in Horticulture
NDN	National District Nurse Certificate
NDTJ	National Diploma in the Training of Journalists
NE	North East
NEBSS	National Examinations Board for Supervisory Studies
NEOC	North East Oecumenical Course (formerly North East Ordination Course)
NHS	National Health Service
NIDA	National Institute of Dramatic Art
NJ	New Jersey
NNEB	National Nursery Examination Board
NS	Nova Scotia (Canada)
NSM	Non-stipendiary Minister (or Ministry)
NSPCC	National Society for the Prevention of Cruelty to Children
NSW	New South Wales (Australia)
NT	New Testament
NTMTC	North Thames Ministerial Training Course
NUI	National University of Ireland
NUU	New University of Ulster
NW	North West/Northwestern
NWT	North West Territories (Canada)
NY	New York (USA)
NZ	New Zealand
Nat	National
Nath	Nathanael/Nathaniel
	Nathanael's/Nathaniel's
Newc	(Diocese of) Newcastle
Nic	Nicholas/Nicolas
	Nicholas's/Nicolas's
Nor	(Diocese of) Norwich
Northn	Northampton
Nottm	Nottingham
Nuff	Nuffield

O

OAM	Medal of the Order of Australia
OBE	Officer, Order of the British Empire
OBI	Order of British India
OCF	Officiating Chaplain to the Forces
OGS	Oratory of the Good Shepherd
OH	Ohio
OHP	Order of the Holy Paraclete
OLM	Ordained Local Minister (or Ministry)
OM	Order of Merit
OM(Ger)	Order of Merit of Germany
OMF	Overseas Missionary Fellowship
ONC	Ordinary National Certificate
OND	Ordinary National Diploma
OSB	Order of St Benedict
OSJM	Prelate, Order of St John of Malta
OSP	Order of St Paul
OStJ	The Most Venerable Order of the Hospital of St John of Jerusalem
OT	Old Testament
Offg	Officiating
Offic	Officiate
Ord	Ordained
	Ordinands
	Ordination
Org	Organizer
	Organizing
Ox	(Diocese of) Oxford

P

P	Patron(s)
	Priest
p	Ordained Priest
P in O	Priest in Ordinary
P-in-c	Priest-in-charge
PACTA	Professional Associate, Clinical Theology Association
PBS	Pengeran Bintang Sarawak (Companion of the Order of the Star, Sarawak)
PC	Perpetual Curate
	Privy Counsellor
PCC	Parochial Church Council
PCVG	Postgraduate Certificate of Vocational Guidance
PDATS	Postgraduate Diploma in Applied Theological Studies
PEV	Provincial Episcopal Visitor
PGCE	Postgraduate Certificate in Education
PGCPT	Postgraduate Certificate in Pastoral Theology
PGCTh	Postgraduate Certificate in Theology
PGCertEBD	Postgraduate Certificate in Emotional and Behavioural Disorders
PGD	Postgraduate Diploma
PGDE	Postgraduate Diploma in Education
PGDHE	Postgraduate Diploma in Healthcare Ethics
PGDPT	Postgraduate Diploma in Pastoral Theology
PGDTMM	Postgraduate Diploma in the Theology of Mission and Ministry
PGDTheol	Postgraduate Diploma in Theology
PGDipESL	Postgraduate Diploma in English as a Second Language
PM	Priest Missioner
PO	Post Office
PPAC	Post Professional Award in Counselling
PQCSW	Post-Qualifying Certificate in Social Work
PV	Priest Vicar
Par	Parish
	Parishes
Paroch	Parochial
Past	Pastoral
Patr	Patrick
	Patrick's
	Patronage
Pemb	Pembroke
Penn	Pennsylvania (USA)
Perm	Permission
Pet	(Diocese of) Peterborough
	Peter
	Peter's
Peterho	Peterhouse
PhB	Bachelor of Philosophy
PhC	Pharmaceutical Chemist
PhD	Doctor of Philosophy (also see DPhil)
PhD(Educ)	Doctor of Philosophy in Education
PhL	Licentiate of Philosophy
Phil	Philip
	Philip's
plc	public limited company
Poly	Polytechnic
Portsm	(Diocese of) Portsmouth
Pre-Th	Pre-Theological
Preb	Prebendary
Prec	Precentor
Prep	Preparatory
Pres	President
Prin	Principal
Pris	Prison
	Prisons
Prof	Professor
	Professorial
Progr	Program
	Programme
	Programmes
Prop	Proprietary
Prov	Province
	Provincial
Pt	Point

Q

QC	Queen's Counsel
QFSM	Queen's Fire Service Medal for Distinguished Service

QGM	Queen's Gallantry Medal
QHC	Honorary Chaplain to The Queen
QN	Queen's Nurse
QPM	Queen's Police Medal
QSM	Queen's Service Medal
QSO	Queen's Service Order of New Zealand
QUB	The Queen's University of Belfast
QVRM	Queen's Volunteer Reserve Medal
Qld	Queensland
Qu	Queen
	Queen's
	Queens'

R

R	Rector
	Royal
R and D	Research and Development
R of O	Reserve of Officers
R&SChTrust	Rochester and Southwark Church Trust
RAAF	Royal Australian Air Force
RAChD	Royal Army Chaplains' Department
RAD or RADD	Royal Association in Aid of Deaf People (formerly Deaf and Dumb)
RADA	Royal Academy of Dramatic Art
RADICLE	Residential and Drop-in Centre London Enterprises
RAEC	Royal Army Educational Corps
RAF	Royal Air Force
RAFVR	Royal Air Force Volunteer Reserve
RAM	(Member) Royal Academy of Music
RAN	Royal Australian Navy
RANSR	Royal Australian Naval Strategic Reserve
RAuxAF	Royal Auxiliary Air Force
RC	Roman Catholic
RCA	Royal College of Art
RCAF	Royal Canadian Air Force
RCM	Royal College of Music
RCN	Royal Canadian Navy
	Royal College of Nursing
RCNT	Registered Clinical Nurse Teacher
RCPS	Royal College of Physicians and Surgeons
RCS	Royal College of Surgeons of England
RCSE	Royal College of Surgeons of Edinburgh
RD	Royal Navy Reserve Decoration
	Rural Dean
RE	Religious Education
RFN	Registered Fever Nurse
RGN	Registered General Nurse
RHV	Registered Health Visitor
RIA	Royal Irish Academy
RIBA	(Member) Royal Institute of British Architects (formerly ARIBA)
RLSMD	Royal London School of Medicine and Dentistry
RM	Registered Midwife
RMA or RMC	Royal Military Academy (formerly College), Sandhurst
RMCM	Royal Manchester College of Music
RMCS	Royal Military College of Science, Shrivenham
RMN	Registered Mental Nurse
RN	Registered Nurse (Canada)
	Royal Navy
RN(MH)	Registered Nurse (for the mentally handicapped)
RNIB	Royal National Institute for the Blind
RNLI	Royal National Lifeboat Institution
RNMH	Registered Nurse for the Mentally Handicapped
RNR	Royal Naval Reserve
RNT	Registered Nurse Tutor
RNVR	Royal Naval Volunteer Reserve
RNZN	Royal New Zealand Navy
RS	Religious Studies
RSCM	(Member) Royal School of Church Music
RSCN	Registered Sick Children's Nurse
RTCert	Certified Reality Therapist
RTE	Radio Telefis Eireann
RVC	Royal Veterinary College
RVO	Royal Victorian Order
Reg	Registered
Relig	Religion(s)
	Religious
Relns	Relations
Rem	Remand
Rep	Representative
Res	Residence
	Resident
	Residential
	Residentiary
Resp	Responsibility
Resurr	Resurrection
Revd	Reverend
Rich	Richard
	Richard's
Ripon	Ripon and Leeds
Rob	Robinson
Roch	(Diocese of) Rochester
Rt	Right
Rtd or rtd	Retired

S

S	South
	Southern
S & B	(Diocese of) Swansea and Brecon
S & M	(Diocese of) Sodor and Man
S'wark	(Diocese of) Southwark
S'well	(Diocese of) Southwell
SA	Salvation Army
SAMS	South American Mission Society
SAP	(Member) Society of Analytical Psychologists
SCM	State Certified Midwife
	Student Christian Movement
SE	South East
SEITE	South East Institute for Theological Education
SEN	State Enrolled Nurse
SHARE	Shelter Housing and Renewal Experiment
SMF	Society for the Maintenance of the Faith
SNTS	Society for New Testament Studies
SOAS	School of Oriental and African Studies
SOMA	Sharing of Ministries Abroad
SOSc	Society of Ordained Scientists
SPCK	Society for Promoting Christian Knowledge
SPG	Society for the Propagation of the Gospel (now see USPG)
SRCh	State Registered Chiropodist
SRD	State Registered Dietician
SRN	State Registered Nurse
SROT	State Registered Occupational Therapist
SRP	State Registered Physiotherapist
SS	Saints
	Saints'
	Sidney Sussex
SSB	Society of the Sisters of Bethany
SSC	Secretarial Studies Certificate
	Societas Sanctae Crucis (Society of the Holy Cross)
	Solicitor before the Supreme Court (Scotland)
SSEES	School of Slavonic and East European Studies
SSF	Society of St Francis
SSJ	Society of St John of Jerusalem
SSJE	Society of St John the Evangelist
SSM	Society of the Sacred Mission
STB	Bachelor of Theology (also see BTh)
STD	Doctor of Sacred Theology (also see DST)
STETS	Southern Theological Education and Training Scheme
STL	Reader (or Professor) of Sacred Theology
STM	Master of Theology (also see MTh or MTheol and ThM)
STV	Scottish Television
STh	Scholar in Theology (also see ThSchol)
	Student in Theology
SW	South West
SWJ	Servants with Jesus
SWMTC	South West Ministry Training Course
Sacr	Sacrist
	Sacristan
Sarum	(Diocese of) Salisbury
Sav	Saviour
	Saviour's
ScD	Doctor of Science (also see DSc)
Sch	School
Sec	Secretary
Selw	Selwyn
Sem	Seminary
Sen	Senior
Sheff	(Diocese of) Sheffield
Shep	Shepherd
So	Souls
	Souls'
Soc	Social
	Society
Southn	Southampton
Sqn Ldr	Squadron Leader
St	Saint
St Alb	(Diocese of) St Albans
	St Alban
	St Alban's
St And	(Diocese of) St Andrews, Dunkeld and Dunblane
St As	(Diocese of) St Asaph
St D	(Diocese of) St Davids
St E	(Diocese of) St Edmundsbury and Ipswich
Ste	Sainte
Steph	Stephen
	Stephen's
Sub	Substitute
Succ	Succentor
Suff	Suffragan
Supt	Superintendent
Syn	Synod

T

T, K & A	(Diocese of) Tuam, Killala and Achonry
TA	Territorial Army
TAVR	Territorial and Army Volunteer Reserve
TC	Technician Certificate
TCD	Trinity College, Dublin
TCert	Teacher's Certificate
TD	Team Deacon
	Territorial Efficiency Decoration
TDip	Teacher's Diploma
TEAR	The Evangelical Alliance Relief
TEM	Territorial Efficiency Medal
TEng	Senior Technician Engineer
TISEC	Theological Institute of the Scottish Episcopal Church
TM	Team Minister (or Ministry)
TP	Team Priest
TR	Team Rector
TS	Training Ship
TSB	Trustee Savings Bank
TV	Team Vicar
	Television
TVS	Television South
Tas	Tasmania
Tech	Technical
	Technology
temp	temporarily

Th	Theologian
	Theological
	Theology
ThA	Associate of Theology
ThB	Bachelor of Theology (USA)
ThD	Doctorate in Theology (also see DTh)
ThDip	Theology Diploma (Australia)
ThL	Theological Licentiate
ThM	Master of Theology (also see MTh or MTheol and STM)
ThSchol	Scholar in Theology (also see STh)
Thos	Thomas

U

UAE	United Arab Emirates
UCCF	Universities and Colleges Christian Fellowship of Evangelical Unions (formerly IVF)
UCD	University College, Dublin
UEA	University of East Anglia
UED	University Education Diploma
UK	United Kingdom
UKRC	United Kingdom Register of Counsellors
UMCA	Universities' Mission to Central Africa (now see USPG)
UMIST	University of Manchester Institute of Science and Technology
UNISA	University of South Africa
UPA	Urban Priority Area (or Areas)
URC	United Reformed Church
US or USA	United States (of America)
USCL	United Society for Christian Literature
USPG	United Society for the Propagation of the Gospel (formerly SPG, UMCA, and CMD)
UWE	University of the West of England
UWIST	University of Wales Institute of Science and Technology
Univ	University

V

V	Vicar
	Virgin
	Virgin's
VRD	Royal Naval Volunteer Reserve Officers' Decoration
VRSM	Volunteer Reserves Service Medal
Ven	Venerable
VetMB	Bachelor of Veterinary Medicine (also see BVetMed)
Vic	Victoria (Australia)
Vin	Vincent
	Vincent's
Voc	Vocational
	Vocations

W

W	West
	Western
w	with
W/Cdr	Wing Commander
WCC	World Council of Churches
WEC	Worldwide Evangelism Crusade
WEMTC	West of England Ministerial Training Course
WMMTC	West Midlands Ministerial Training Course
WRAF	Women's Royal Air Force
Wadh	Wadham
Wakef	(Diocese of) Wakefield
Westf	Westfield
Westmr	Westminster
Wilts	Wiltshire
Win	(Diocese of) Winchester
Wm	William
Wolfs	Wolfson
Wolv	Wolverhampton
Worc	(Diocese of) Worcester

Y

YMCA	Young Men's Christian Association
YOI	Young Offender Institution

Bringing *Healing and Hope* to the vulnerable
and disadvantaged in the lands of the Bible.

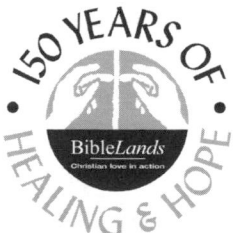

A

AAGAARD, Angus Robert. b 64. Moray Ho Coll of Educn CQSW86. Ripon Coll Cuddesdon BTh93. **d** 93 **p** 94. C Taunton St Andr *B & W* 93-97; TV Southampton (City Cen) *Win* 97-01; TR N Lambeth *S'wark* from 01. *St Anselm's Vicarage, 286 Kennington Road, London SE11 5DU* Tel (020) 7735 3415 *or* 7735 3403 Mobile 07810-646644 E-mail angus.aagaard@virgin.net

ABAYOMI-COLE, Bimbisara Alfred (Bimbi). b 58. CCC Ox BA80 MA85. Trin Coll Bris BA94. **d** 94 **p** 95. C Deptford St Pet *S'wark* 94-98; V Crofton St Paul *Roch* from 98. *St Paul's Vicarage, 2 Oakwood Road, Orpington BR6 8JH* Tel and fax (01689) 852939 E-mail bimbiabayomi_cole@hotmail.com

ABBEY, Canon Anthony James. b 36. Selw Coll Cam BA59 MA63 ARCO61. Ely Th Coll 59. **d** 61 **p** 62. C Wanstead St Mary *Chelmsf* 61-63; C Laindon w Basildon 63-67; R Sandon 67-76; V Epping St Jo 76-92; Hon Can Chelmsf Cathl 85-01; P-in-c Doddinghurst and Mountnessing 92-01; rtd 01; Perm to Offic *Worc* from 01. *Canons Piece, 2 The Squires, Blackminster, Evesham WR11 7XN* Tel (01386) 834119 E-mail anthony@canonspiece.fsnet.co.uk

ABBOTT, Barry Joseph. b 59. Sunderland Univ BA98 MCIEH. NEOC 89. **d** 92 **p** 93. NSM Bishopwearmouth Ch Ch *Dur* 92-98; NSM Silksworth 98-00; P-in-c Lumley 00-04; AD Chester-le-Street 02-04; P-in-c Whickham from 04. *The Rectory, Church Chare, Whickham, Newcastle upon Tyne NE16 4SH* Tel 0191-488 7397 Mobile 07801-074909

ABBOTT, Charles Peter. b 25. Maryland Univ 60. Pecusa Ord Course. **d** 62 **p** 62. USA 62-66; C Oxhey St Matt *St Alb* 66-70; Asst Chapl Alleyn's Foundn Dulwich 70-72; C Dulwich St Barn *S'wark* 70-72; V Southway *Ex* 72-78; V Whitgift w Adlingfleet and Eastoft *Sheff* 78-79; rtd 86. *1 St Augustine's Close, Cooden Drive, Bexhill-on-Sea TN39 3AZ*

ABBOTT, Christopher Ralph. b 38. Univ of Wales (Lamp) BA59. Wells Th Coll 59. **d** 61 **p** 62. C Camberwell St Giles *S'wark* 61-67; C Portsea St Mary *Portsm* 67-70; V Portsea St Cuth 70-87; P-in-c Gt Milton *Ox* 87-88; P-in-c Lt Milton 87-88; R Gt w Lt Milton and Gt Haseley 88-93; R Chailey *Chich* 93-00; Chapl Chailey Heritage Hosp Lewes 95-00; rtd 00; Perm to Offic *Chich* from 01; Chapl SSB from 02; Hon C Purbrook *Portsm* from 03. *6 Winchfield Crescent, Havant PO9 3SP* Tel (023) 9247 7376 E-mail christopherabbott@jonty.fsnet.co.uk

ABBOTT, David John. b 52. CertEd. St Jo Coll Nottm. **d** 87 **p** 88. C Biddulph *Lich* 87-90; C Tunbridge Wells St Jas *Roch* 90-92; TV Tunbridge Wells St Jas w St Phil 92-98; V Sunnyside w Bourne End *St Alb* from 98; RD Berkhamsted from 04. *The Vicarage, Ivy House Lane, Berkhamsted HP4 2PP* Tel (01442) 865100 E-mail ssvicarage@yahoo.co.uk

ABBOTT, David Robert. b 49. Edin Univ BD72 Birm Univ DipTh73. Qu Coll Birm 72. **d** 74 **p** 75. C Kirkby *Liv* 74-78; C Ditton St Mich 78-80; R Ashton-in-Makerfield H Trin from 80. *The Rectory, North Ashton, Wigan WN4 0QF* Tel (01942) 727241

ABBOTT, Miss Geraldine Mary. b 33. SRN55 SCM58 Open Univ BA77 Lon Univ MTh85. Oak Hill Th Coll BA82. **dss** 86 **d** 87 **p** 94. Tutor Oak Hill Th Coll 86-96; St Alb St Paul *St Alb* 86-94; Hon Par Dn 87-94; Hon C from 94. *2 Wheatleys, St Albans AL4 9UE* Tel (01727) 860869

ABBOTT, Mrs Kathleen Frances. b 60. STETS 96. **d** 99 **p** 00. NSM St Helens *Portsm* 99-02; P-in-c Wootton from 02. *The Rectory, 32 Church Road, Wootton Bridge, Ryde PO33 4PX* Tel and fax (01983) 882213 E-mail kath.abbott@btinternet.com

ABBOTT, Canon Nigel Douglas Blayney. b 37. Open Univ BA87. Bps' Coll Cheshunt 58. **d** 61 **p** 62. C Northampton St Mich *Pet* 61-64; C Wanstead St Mary *Chelmsf* 64-66; Chapl St Jo Sch Tiffield 66-69; V Earls Barton *Pet* 69-73; V Cov H Trin *Cov* 73-80; Provost St Jo Cathl Oban *Arg* 80-86; R Oban St Jo 80-86; TR Hemel Hempstead *St Alb* 86-96; RD Hemel Hempstead 94-96; Chmn BSR 94-00; R Much Hadham 96-02; Hon Can St Alb 96-02; rtd 02; Perm to Offic *Ely* from 03. *1 Cambridge Road, Ely CB7 4HJ* Tel (01353) 662256 E-mail ndbabbot@waitrose.com

ABBOTT, Peter John. b 48. S Glam Inst HE CQSW86. St Mich Coll Llan 94. **d** 96 **p** 97. C Neath w Llantwit *Llan* 96-98; C Merthyr Tydfil Ch Ch 98-00; P-in-c Llangeinor w Nantymoel and Wyndham 00-02; V Cwm Ogwr 02-03; TV Ebbw Vale *Mon* from 03. *1 Brecon Heights, Victoria, Ebbw Vale NP23 8WP* Tel (01495) 306403

ABBOTT, Stephen Anthony. b 43. K Coll Cam BA65 MA69 Edin Univ BD68 Harvard Univ ThM69. Edin Th Coll 66. **d** 69 **p** 70. C Deal St Leon *Cant* 69-72; Chapl K Coll Cam 72-75; C Cambridge St Matt *Ely* 75-76; Asst Chapl Bris Univ and Hon C Clifton St Paul 77-80; Perm to Offic *Bris* 81-04; P-in-c Mangotsfield from 04. *The Vicarage, St James Place, Mangotsfield, Bristol BS16 9JA* Tel 0117-956 0510 E-mail stephen.abbott@withleigh.freeserve.co.uk

ABBOTT, Stephen John. b 62. Qu Mary Coll Lon LLB83. Linc Th Coll BTh92. **d** 92 **p** 93. C E Dereham and Scarning *Nor* 92-95; TV Penistone and Thurlstone *Wakef* 95-97; R Brandon and Santon Downham w Elveden *St E* 97-00; P-in-c Gt Barton 00-04; rtd 04; Perm to Offic *St E* from 04. *10 Meadowlands, Woolpit, Bury St Edmunds IP30 9SE* Tel (01359) 241614 Mobile 07742-396523 E-mail sj.abbott@lineone.net

ABBOTT, Mrs Valerie Ann. b 45. Keele Univ BA68. Trin Coll Bris MLitt00. **d** 00 **p** 01. NSM Knowle St Martin *Bris* 00-01; NSM Brislington St Chris and St Cuth 01-04; NSM Mangotsfield from 04. *The Vicarage, St James Place, Mangotsfield, Bristol BS16 9JA* Tel 0117-956 0510 Mobile 07979-997968 E-mail val.abbott@btinternet.com

ABDY, John Channing. b 38. Nottm Univ BA63. Cuddesdon Coll 63. **d** 65 **p** 66. C Leagrave *St Alb* 65-69; C N Mymms 69-72; V Kings Walden 72-79; V S Woodham Ferrers *Chelmsf* 79-85; V Walthamstow St Pet 85-91; V Burrington and Churchill *B & W* from 91. *The Parsonage, Bristol Road, Langford, Bristol BS40 5JE* Tel (01934) 852295

ABECASSIS, Joanna Margaret. b 54. Girton Coll Cam BA75 MA79 PhD81. WEMTC 99. **d** 02 **p** 03. C Tavistock and Gulworthy *Ex* from 02. *32 Plym Crescent, Tavistock PL19 9HX* Tel (01822) 615501 E-mail joanna@abecassis.freeserve.co.uk

ABEL, David John. b 31. S'wark Ord Course 71. **d** 74 **p** 75. NSM Crowhurst *S'wark* 74-85; NSM Lingfield and Crowhurst 85-92; Perm to Offic *S'wark* 92-98; *Chich* from 98; *St E* from 03. *Balcombe Mill, Mill Lane, Balcombe, Haywards Heath RH17 6QT* Tel (01444) 811121

ABELL, Canon Brian. b 37. Nottm Univ BA61 DipEd Leeds Univ MA95. Cuddesdon Coll 61. **d** 63 **p** 64. C Lightcliffe *Wakef* 63-66; C-in-c Mixenden CD 66-68; Lect Linc Coll of Tech 68-69; Chapl Trent Coll Nottm 70-74; V Thorner *Ripon* 74-82; V Far Headingley St Chad 82-86; Deputation Appeals Org CECS 86-89; V Masham and Healey *Ripon* 89-00; Hon Can Ripon Cathl 99-00; rtd 00; Perm to Offic *Ripon* from 00. *Manor Garth, 1 Manor Road, Harrogate HG2 0HP* Tel and fax (01423) 526112 E-mail brian.abell@virgin.net

ABELL, George Derek. b 31. Selw Coll Cam BA54 MA68. Qu Coll Birm 54. **d** 56 **p** 57. C Stoke upon Trent *Lich* 56-60; C Wolverhampton 60-64; R Bridgnorth St Mary *Heref* 64-70; P-in-c Oldbury 64-70; Australia 70-73; R Withington w Westhide and Weston Beggard *Heref* 73-81; R Withington w Westhide 81-83; P-in-c Sutton St Nicholas w Sutton St Michael 76-81; R 81-83; Preb Heref Cathl 82-83; V Basing *Win* 83-88; rtd 88; Perm to Offic *Heref* 88-04. *25 Eastfield Court, Church Street, Faringdon SN7 8SL* Tel (01367) 240731

ABELL, Peter John. b 45. Chich Th Coll 67. **d** 70 **p** 71. C Churchdown St Jo *Glouc* 70-74; Chapl RAF 74-98; R Kilkhampton w Morwenstow *Truro* from 98. *The Rectory, East Road, Kilkhampton, Bude EX23 9QS* Tel and fax (01288) 321314 E-mail rectorkilkstow@aol.com

ABERDEEN AND ORKNEY, Bishop of. *See* CAMERON, The Most Revd Andrew Bruce

ABERDEEN AND ORKNEY, Dean of. *See* STRANRAER-MULL, The Very Revd Gerald Hugh

ABERDEEN, Provost of. *See* KILGOUR, The Very Revd Richard Eifl

ABERNETHY, Canon Alan Francis. b 57. QUB BA78 BD89. CITC. **d** 81 **p** 82. C Dundonald *D & D* 81-84; C Lecale Gp 84-86; I Helen's Bay 86-90; I Ballyholme from 90; Preb Down Cathl from 00; Dioc Dir of Ords from 04. *Ballyholme Rectory, 3 Ward Avenue, Bangor BT20 5JW* Tel (028) 9127 7901 Fax 9146 6357 E-mail ballyholme@btinternet.com

ABERNETHY, David Terence Phillips (Terry). b 42. St D Coll Lamp 61. **d** 65 **p** 66. C Abergele *St As* 65-72; Bermuda 72-84; V Beaulieu and Exbury and E Boldre *Win* from 84. *The Rectory,*

Palace Lane, Beaulieu, Brockenhurst SO42 7YG Tel and fax (01590) 612242 E-mail t.abernethy@beaulieu-rectory.org.uk

ABINGTON, David John Barringer. b 48. EAMTC 91. **d** 94 **p** 95. C Newport w Longford and Chetwynd *Lich* 94-96; C Newport w Longford, Chetwynd and Forton 96-98; R Adderley, Ash, Calverhall, Ightfield etc 98-02; R Brading w Yaverland *Portsm* from 02. *The Vicarage, Mall Road, Brading, Sandown PO36 0DE* Tel (01983) 407262 Mobile 07855-086978

ABLETT, Edwin John. b 37. Clifton Th Coll 64. **d** 67 **p** 68. C Sneinton St Chris w St Phil *S'well* 67-70; R High and Gd Easter w Margaret Roding *Chelmsf* 70-73; SAMS Chile 73-75; C Gt Baddow *Chelmsf* 75-78; V Newchapel *Lich* 78-82; V S Westoe *Dur* 82-86; V Tibshelf *Derby* 86-00; rtd 00; Perm to Offic *St D* from 00. *22 Dolaufan, Burry Port SA16 0RD* Tel (01554) 834709 E-mail johnablett@copihue.wanadoo.co.uk

ABLETT, Mrs Jennifer Vera. b 46. Dioc OLM tr scheme 97. **d** 00 **p** 01. OLM Henley, Claydon and Barham *St E* from 00. *10 Phillipps Road, Barham, Ipswich IP6 0AZ* Tel (01473) 830205

ABRAHAM, Brian. b 42. **d** 00 **p** 01. OLM Burscough Bridge *Liv* from 00. *4 Mere Court, Burscough, Ormskirk L40 0TQ* Tel (01704) 892547

ABRAHAM, Canon David Alexander. b 37. AKC61. **d** 62 **p** 63. C Oswestry St Oswald *Lich* 62-63; C Gt Wyrley 63-65; C Sprowston *Nor* 65-67; V Ormesby w Scratby 67-81; R Oxborough w Foulden and Caldecote 81-87; R Cockley Cley w Gooderstone 81-87; V Didlington 81-87; R Gt and Lt Cressingham w Threxton 81-87; R Hilborough w Bodney 81-87; P-in-c Nor St Giles 87-96; Chapl Asst Norfolk and Nor Hosp 87-91; V Thorpe St Matt *Nor* 96-00; Hon Can Nor Cathl 95-00; rtd 00; Perm to Offic *Nor* from 00. *170 Desmond Drive, Old Catton, Norwich NR6 7JW* Tel (01603) 402797

ABRAHAM, Estelle Pamela. b 46. C F Mott Coll of Educn TCert69. **d** 04 **p** 05. OLM Bolton Breightmet St Jas *Man* from 04. *6 Barchester Avenue, Bolton BL2 5EF* Tel (01204) 412830 E-mail pam.abraham@ntlworld.com

ABRAHAM, Canon John Callis Harford. b 31. Univ of W Aus BA52. Westcott Ho Cam 53. **d** 55 **p** 56. C Wigan St Anne *Liv* 55-57; Australia 57-67 and from 68; C Northam Perth 57-60; R Wongan Hills 60-62; Vice-Warden Wollaston Th Coll and R Graylands 63-67; P-in-c City Beach 66-67; Lic to Offic *Birm* 67-68; R Applecross Perth 68-76; Can Perth 71-84; R Leeming 76-79; Chapl Home Miss 79-81; R Wembley 81-89; R Albany 90-94; Can Bunbury 92-94; rtd 94. *10 Royston Park, Pioneer Street, Albany, W Australia 6330* Tel (0061) (8) 9841 1809

ABRAHAM, Richard James. b 42. Liv Univ BA63. Ridley Hall Cam 64. **d** 66 **p** 67. C Warrington St Ann *Liv* 66-70; C Golborne 70-73; V Bickershaw 73-78; V Ewerby w Evedon *Linc* 78-82; R Kirkby Laythorpe w Asgarby 78-82; R Kirkby Laythorpe 82-03; rtd 03. *23 Londesborough Way, Metheringham, Lincoln LN4 3HW*

ABRAHAMS, Peter William. b 42. Southn Univ BA77. Sarum Th Coll 77. **d** 78 **p** 79. C Bitterne Park *Win* 78-82; C Old Brumby *Linc* 82-84; V Mitcham Ascension *S'wark* 84-91; TV Riverside *Ox* from 91. *The Vicarage, Mill Street, Colnbrook, Slough SL3 0JJ* Tel and fax (01753) 682156 *or* tel 687654 E-mail frapeter@aol.com

ABRAM, Paul Robert Carrington. b 36. Keble Coll Ox BA62 MA65. Chich Th Coll 60. **d** 62 **p** 63. C Redcar *York* 62-65; CF 65-89; V Salcombe *Ex* 89-96; Miss to Seafarers from 89; rtd 96; Chapl to The Queen from 96; Chapl St Pet-ad-Vincula at HM Tower of Lon from 96; Dep P in O from 96. *1 The Green, HM Tower of London, London EC3N 4AB* Tel (020) 7488 5689 Fax 7702 2214

ABREY, Mark Evans John. b 66. Ripon Coll Cuddesdon BTh93. **d** 93 **p** 94. C W Derby St Mary *Liv* 93-97; P-in-c Anfield St Marg 97-01; Chapl R Liverpool Children's NHS Trust 97-99; P-in-c Chadlington and Spelsbury, Ascott under Wychwood *Ox* 01-05; V Chase from 05; P-in-c Ascott under Wychwood from 05. *The Vicarage, Church Road, Chadlington, Chipping Norton OX7 3LY* Tel (01608) 676572 E-mail mark@abreys.com

ABREY, Philip James. b 51. N Ord Course 82. **d** 85 **p** 86. NSM Hindley All SS *Liv* 85-90; C Caversham St Pet and Mapledurham etc *Ox* 90-00; Min Caversham Park LEP 90-00; Co Ecum Officer (Berks) 96-00; Perm to Offic *Cov* from 01; Chapl HM Pris The Mount from 02. *HM Prison, The Mount, Molyneux Avenue, Bovingdon, Hemel Hempstead HP3 0NZ* Tel (01442) 834363 E-mail philip.abrey@hmps.gsi.gov.uk

ABSALOM, Alexander James David Edward. b 69. St Jo Coll Dur BA91. Cranmer Hall Dur 92. **d** 94 **p** 95. C Cranham Park *Chelmsf* 94-98; Perm to Offic *Sheff* 98-05; Miss Priest Philadelphia St Thos from 05. *6 Gilpin Street, Sheffield S6 3BL* Tel 0114-241 9560

ABSALOM, Hugh Pryse. b 10. Fitzw Ho Cam BA31 MA36 Lon Univ BD56. **d** 36 **p** 37. C Abergavenny H Trin *Mon* 36-39; C Torquay St Luke *Ex* 39-43; Chapl RAFVR 43-49; Canada 49-52; C Brixham *Ex* 52-53; V Friday Bridge *Ely* 53-57; V Coldham 53-57; V Lucton w Eyton *Heref* 57-61; C-in-c Croft w Yarpole 57-61; Chapl and Master Lucton Sch 57-61; Chapl St Hild Coll Dur 61-73; Chapl and Sen Lect St Hild's Tr Coll Dur 61-73; R Walton W w Talbenny and Haroldston W *St D* 73-77; rtd 77. *Bush House Nursing Home, Pembroke Road, Pembroke SA71 4RJ*

ABSOLON, Michael John. b 33. St Jo Coll Cam BA54 MA59 Lon Hosp BChir57 MB57 FRCS FRCOPhth. Wycliffe Hall Ox 95. **d** 96 **p** 97. NSM Micheldever and E Stratton, Woodmancote etc *Win* 96-98; NSM Chipping Campden w Ebrington *Glouc* 98-99 and from 00; Perm to Offic 99-00. *Oakham House, Ebrington, Chipping Campden GL55 6NL* Tel (01386) 593123

ABUJA, Bishop of. *See* AKINOLA, The Most Revd Peter Jasper

ABULEMOI, Joseph Oriho. *See* CHOUFAR, Joseph Oriho Abulemoi

ACARNLEY, Rita Kay. b 57. Girton Coll Cam BA79 MA83 Newc Univ MA94 St Jo Coll Dur BA98. Cranmer Hall Dur 96. **d** 99 **p** 00. NSM Humshaugh w Simonburn and Wark *Newc* 99-00; Tutor TISEC and Prov Local Collaborative Min Officer Scotland 00-03; R Stonehaven *Bre* from 03; R Catterline from 03; P-in-c Muchalls from 03. *St Ternan's Rectory, Muchalls, Aberdeen AB39 3PP* Tel (01569) 730625 E-mail ritaacarnley@dunelm.org.uk

ACCRA, Bishop of. *See* AKROFI, The Most Revd Justice Ofei

ACHESON, Denise. **d** 05. C Ballyholme *D & D* from 05. *34 Beverley Gardens, Bangor BT20 4NQ* Tel (028) 9127 1922 E-mail deniseacheson@hotmail.com

ACHESON, James Malcolm. b 48. BNC Ox BA70 MA73. Sarum & Wells Th Coll 83. **d** 85 **p** 86. C Highgate St Mich *Lon* 85-88; TV Tisbury *Sarum* 88-94; Offg Chapl RAF 88-94; R Storrington *Chich* from 94. *The Rectory, Rectory Road, Storrington, Pulborough RH20 4EF* Tel (01903) 742888

ACHESON, Canon Russell Robert. b 16. Univ Coll Ox BA39 MA45 DipTh47. Wells Th Coll 45. **d** 47 **p** 48. C Bedminster Down *Bris* 47-49; Youth Chapl 49-54; Chapl Bris Univ 55-66; V Clifton St Paul 57-66; Hon Can Bris Cathl 64-66; V Much Wenlock w Bourton *Heref* 66-79; P-in-c Hughley w Church Preen 69-79; RD Condover 72-78; P-in-c Harley w Kenley 73-75; Preb Heref Cathl 74-79; P-in-c Shipton 76-79; P-in-c Easthope w Long Stanton 76-79; Warden of Readers 78-83; Can Res Heref Cathl 79-83; rtd 83; Perm to Offic *Heref* from 83; Perm to Offic *Ban* from 97. *1 Penras Terrace, Newborough, Llanfairpwll-gwyngyll LL61 6RS* Tel (01248) 440325

ACHONRY, Dean of. *Vacant*

ACHURCH, Peter William Hammond. b 37. ACT DipTh87 Tabor Coll (Australia) DipC&G98. Ridley Coll Melbourne 82 St Barn Coll Adelaide 85. **d** 82 **p** 84. Australia 82-00; C Port Lincoln 82-84; P-in-c Elliston w Lock and Wuddina 86; R 87-89; Par P Leigh Creek 89-93; TV Madeley *Heref* from 00. *Sutton Hill Vicarage, 1 Spencer Drive, Sutton Hill, Telford TF7 4JY* Tel (01952) 680004

ACKERLEY, Glyn James. b 57. HNC83 Kent Univ MA04. Cranmer Hall Dur 84. **d** 87 **p** 88. C Tonbridge SS Pet and Paul *Roch* 87-90; R Willingham *Ely* 90-94; R Rampton 90-94; V Chatham St Phil and St Jas *Roch* from 94. *The Vicarage, 139 Sussex Drive, Walderslade, Chatham ME5 0NR* Tel (01634) 861108 *or* 862498 E-mail glynackerley@blueyonder.co.uk

ACKERMAN, David Michael. b 71. Westmr Coll Ox BTh95 Brighton Univ PGCE98. Pontificium Institutum Internationale Angelicum Rome STB01 MA02. **d** 01 **p** 02. In RC Ch 01-04; C Fairford and Kempsford w Whelford *Glouc* from 05. *The Parsonage, High Street, Kempsford, Fairford GL7 4ET* Tel (01285) 810507 Mobile 07916-348719 E-mail dmackerman@hotmail.com

ACKFORD, Christopher Mark. b 60. Univ Coll Lon BDS83 K Coll Lon MSc89. Ripon Coll Cuddesdon 02. **d** 04 **p** 05. C Bracknell *Ox* from 04. *4 Micheldever Way, Bracknell RG12 0XX* Tel (01344) 452608 Mobile 07780-554032 E-mail mark@ackford.freeserve.co.uk

ACKLAM, Leslie Charles. b 46. Birm Univ BEd71. Ripon Coll Cuddesdon 78. **d** 80 **p** 81. C Chingford St Anne *Chelmsf* 80-83; C Spalding *Linc* 83-85; V Spalding St Paul 85-93; P-in-c Linc St Faith and St Martin w St Pet from 93; Chapl Linc Univ from 96. *165C Carholme Road, Lincoln LN1 1RU* Tel (01522) 887827 E-mail leslie.acklam@ntlworld.com

ACKLAND, Canon John Robert Warwick. b 47. **d** 82 **p** 83. NSM Shooters Hill Ch Ch *S'wark* 82-88; NSM Mottingham St Andr 82-94; NSM Woolwich St Thos 94-96; NSM Bellingham St Dunstan 96-03; Hon Chapl S'wark Cathl 98-03; P-in-c Perry Hill St Geo w Ch Ch and St Paul 03-04; V from 04; Hon Can S'wark Cathl from 05. *The Vicarage, 2A Vancouver Road, London SE23 2AF* Tel (020) 8699 7676 *or* 8699 7202 E-mail johnackland1@compuserve.com

ACKROYD, David Andrew. b 66. Coll of Ripon & York St Jo BA90 St Jo Coll Dur BA97. Cranmer Hall Dur 94. **d** 97 **p** 98. C Lilleshall and Sheriffhales *Lich* 97-01; Asst Chapl R Wolv Hosps NHS Trust 01-02; C Ogley Hay *Lich* 02-03. *Address temp unknown* E-mail revandy@tinyworld.co.uk

ACKROYD, Dennis. b 36. Cranmer Hall Dur 67. **d** 70 **p** 71. C Newcastle w Butterton *Lich* 70-73; C Horsell *Guildf* 73-77; P-in-c Moreton and Woodsford w Tincleton *Sarum* 77-82; R 82-86; RD Dorchester 79-85; R Ewhurst *Guildf* 86-94; V Cleckheaton

St Luke and Whitechapel *Wakef* 94-02; rtd 02; Perm to Offic *Sarum* from 03. *17 Charles Street, Weymouth DT4 7JG* Tel (01305) 778122

ACKROYD, Eric. b 29. Leeds Univ BA51 Liv Univ MA71 Leic Univ MA(Ed)86. St Jo Coll Dur DipTh54. **d** 55 **p** 56. C Newland St Jo *York* 55-58; Succ Birm Cathl *Birm* 58-60; Chapl K Sch Bruton 61-66; Lect Kirkby Fields Coll of Educn Liv 67-72; Sen Lect Nene Coll of HE Northn 72-85; rtd 85. *40 Lumbertubs Lane, Northampton NN3 6AH* Tel (01604) 717848

ACKROYD, John Michael. b 32. Lon Univ BSc53. Ripon Hall Ox 71. **d** 73 **p** 74. C Keighley *Bradf* 73-76; TV 76-81; V Keighley All SS 81; V Whalley *Blackb* 81-97; Chapl Calderstones Hosp Clitheroe 81-93; Chapl Calderstones NHS Trust 93-97; rtd 97; Perm to Offic *Blackb* from 97. *1 Calder Vale, Whalley, Clitheroe BB7 9SR* Tel (01254) 823943

ACKROYD, Peter Michael. b 60. Jes Coll Cam BA82 MA86 Fontainebleau MBA87 Edin Univ PhD02. Wycliffe Hall Ox BA93 DipTh94 MA00. **d** 94 **p** 95. C Denton Holme *Carl* 94-97; Sec Proclamation Trust 97-00; V Wootton *St Alb* from 02. *The Vicarage, Church Road, Wootton, Bedford MK43 9HF* Tel (01234) 768391 E-mail ackroyds@lineone.net

ACKROYD, Ruth. b 49. **d** 04 **p** 05. NSM Hoole *Ches* from 04. *Strathmore, Ashby Place, Hoole, Chester CH2 3AG* Tel (01244) 344529

ACKROYD, William Lancelot. b 1900. Egerton Hall Man 31. **d** 33 **p** 34. C Salford Ch Ch *Man* 33-35; C Pendlebury St Jo 35-37; R Ardwick St Thos 37-42; V Bolton SS Simon and Jude 42-45; Gen Sec BFBS 45-47; R Old Trafford St Jo *Man* 47-53; V S Petherwin w Trewen *Truro* 53-60; V St Germans 60-64; V Eastleach w Southrop *Glouc* 64-68; rtd 68; C Stokenham w Sherford *Ex* 69-71; Perm to Offic *Truro* 72-03. *Elysian, Linden Avenue, Port St Mary, Isle of Man IM9 5ER*

ACONLEY, Carole Ann. b 51. Hull Univ BTh01. NEOC 99. **d** 02 **p** 03. NSM Langtoft w Foxholes, Butterwick, Cottam etc *York* from 02. *Hawthorn Farm, Langtoft, Driffield YO25 3BT* Tel (01377) 267219 E-mail caroleaconley1@tinyworld.com

ACREMAN, John. b 53. Oak Hill Th Coll 86. **d** 88 **p** 89. C Iver *Ox* 88-92; R Hook Norton w Gt Rollright, Swerford etc from 92. *The Rectory, Hook Norton, Banbury OX15 5QQ* Tel (01608) 737223 E-mail acreman@xalt.co.uk

ACWORTH, The Ven Richard Foote. b 36. SS Coll Cam BA62 MA65. Cuddesdon Coll 61. **d** 63 **p** 64. C Fulham St Etheldreda *Lon* 63-64; C Langley All SS and Martyrs *Man* 64-66; C Bridgwater St Mary w Chilton Trinity *B & W* 66-69; V Yatton 69-81; V Yatton Moor 81; P-in-c Taunton St Jo 81-84; P-in-c Taunton St Mary 81-85; V 85-93; Preb Wells Cathl 87-93; Adn Wells, Can Res and Preb Wells Cathl 93-03; rtd 03. *Corvedale Cottage, Ganes Terrace, Croscombe, Wells BA5 3QJ* Tel (01749) 342242

ACWORTH, Richard John Philip. b 30. Ch Ch Ox BA52 MA56 Paris Univ DèsL70. **d** 63 **p** 63. In RC Ch 63-67; C Walthamstow St Mary w St Steph *Chelmsf* 68-70; P-in-c Lt Sampford 70-76; P-in-c Gt Sampford 74-76; Lect Bath Coll of HE 76-77; Lect Th Derby Lonsdale Coll *Derby* 77-83; Derbyshire Coll of HE 83-88; P-in-c Newton Tracey, Alverdiscott, Huntshaw etc *Ex* 88-96; TR Newton Tracey, Horwood, Alverdiscott etc 96-98; RD Torrington 94-97; rtd 98; Perm to Offic *Portsm* from 98. *91 Oaklands Road, Havant PO9 2RL* Tel (023) 9245 0567

ADAIR, Raymond. b 33. Ripon Hall Ox 70. **d** 72 **p** 73. C Knottingley *Wakef* 72-75; C Sandal St Helen 75-77; V Sandal St Cath 77-87; V Brownhill 87-97; rtd 97; Perm to Offic *Wakef* from 99. *15 Chestnut Fold, Upper Lane, Netherton, Wakefield WF4 4HW* Tel (01924) 274640

ADAIR, William Matthew. b 52. Open Univ BA. CITC 77. **d** 77 **p** 78. C Portadown St Mark *Arm* 77-78; Asst Chapl Miss to Seamen 78-80; C Lisburn Ch Ch Cathl *Conn* 80-84; I Kildress w Altedesert *Arm* 84-92; I Portadown St Columba from 92; Dioc Sec Min of Healing 95-99. *St Columba's Rectory, 81 Loughgall Road, Portadown, Craigavon BT62 4EG* Tel (028) 3833 2746

ADAM, Canon David. b 36. Kelham Th Coll 54. **d** 59 **p** 60. C Auckland St Helen *Dur* 59-63; C Owton Manor CD 63-67; V Danby *York* 67-90; Can and Preb York Minster 89-90; V Holy Is *Newc* 90-03; rtd 03; Perm to Offic *Newc* from 03. *The Old Granary, Warren Mill, Belford NE70 7EE* Tel (01668) 214770

ADAM, Gordon Angus James. b 62. SSC. SEITE 97. **d** 00 **p** 01. NSM Kentish Town St Silas and H Trin w St Barn *Lon* 00-03; NSM Boxmoor St Jo *St Alb* from 03. *167 Long Chaulden, Hemel Hempstead HP1 2JH* Tel and fax (01442) 246538 Mobile 07721-020334 E-mail gaja1962@aol.com

ADAM, Canon John Marshall William. b 09. Oriel Coll Ox BA31 MA36. Wycliffe Hall Ox 31. **d** 33 **p** 34. C Endcliffe *Sheff* 33-35; Chapl Sheff Cathl 35-36; India 36-39; Chapl Sheff Cathl *Sheff* 39-42; V Paddock *Wakef* 42-46; Home Sec Miss Coun of Ch Assembly 46-55; R Friern Barnet St Jas *Lon* 55-63; V Preston St Jo *Blackb* 63-69; Hon Can Blackb Cathl 64-74; RD Preston 67-70; V Broughton 69-74; rtd 74; Perm to Offic *Blackb* from 74. *7 Caton Green Road, Brookhouse, Lancaster LA2 9JL* Tel (01524) 770030

ADAM, Lawrence. b 38. N Ord Course 82. **d** 82 **p** 83. C Thornton-le-Fylde *Blackb* 82-86; Dioc Video Production Co-ord 85-97; P-in-c Scorton 86-91; C W Burnley All SS 91-97; P-in-c Ashton St Jas *Man* 97-99; TV Ashton 00-03; rtd 03; Perm to Offic *Ches* from 03. *23 Dryden Avenue, Cheadle SK8 2AW*

ADAM (née YATES), Mrs Lindsay Anne. b 69. Selw Coll Cam BA91 MA95 Barrister 92 K Coll Lon DipTh96. Ripon Coll Cuddesdon BTh99. **d** 99 **p** 00. C Bampton w Clanfield *Ox* 99-02; Chapl Pemb Coll Cam from 02. *The Rectory, 40 Church Lane, Girton, Cambridge CB3 0JP* Tel and fax (01223) 276235 *or* tel 338100 E-mail cha@pem.cam.ac.uk *or* laa@luxmundi.co.uk

ADAM, Michael MacIntosh. b 48. Sarum & Wells Th Coll. **d** 84 **p** 85. C Stamford Hill St Thos *Lon* 84-87; rtd 88; Perm to Offic *Lon* from 88. *Flat 1, 112 Millfields Road, London E5 0AP*

ADAM, Canon Peter James Hedderwick. b 46. Lon Univ BD73 MTh76 Dur Univ PhD81. Ridley Coll Melbourne ThL69. **d** 70 **p** 71. Australia 70-72, 73-74 and from 82; C Ivanhoe St Jas 70-72; C Rosanna 72; Hon C Holborn St Geo w H Trin and St Bart *Lon* 72-73; C Essendon St Thos and Tutor Ridley Coll 73-74; Tutor St Jo Coll Dur 75-82; Hon C Dur St Cuth *Dur* 75-82; P-in-c Carlton St Jude 82-88; V 88-01; Adn Melbourne 88-91; Chapl Melbourne Univ 95-01; Can Melbourne from 96; Prin Ridley Coll from 01. *160 The Avenue, Parkville, Vic, Australia 3053* Tel (0061) (3) 9207 4800 Fax 9387 5099 E-mail principal@ridley.unimelb.edu.au

ADAM, William Jonathan. b 69. Man Univ BA91 Univ of Wales (Cardiff) LLM03. Westcott Ho Cam 92 Bossey Ecum Inst Geneva Cert Ecum Studies 94. **d** 94 **p** 95. C Beaconsfield *Ox* 94-97; C Witney 97-98; TV 98-02; P-in-c Girton *Ely* from 02; Dioc Ecum Officer from 02. *The Rectory, 40 Church Lane, Girton, Cambridge CB3 0JP* Tel (01223) 276235 Fax as telephone E-mail wja@luxmundi.co.uk

ADAMS, Mrs Alison Mary. b 51. Girton Coll Cam MA73 Birm Univ BMus76 CertEd77 Sheff Univ MPhil93. EMMTC 94. **d** 97 **p** 98. NSM Burbage w Aston Flamville *Leic* from 97; Dir Bloxham Project from 00. *Nibelheim, 29 Leicester Lane, Desford, Leicester LE9 9JJ* Tel (01455) 823674 E-mail admin@bloxhamproject.org.uk

ADAMS, Anthony John. b 42. St Jo Coll Nottm 83. **d** 85 **p** 86. C Wellesbourne *Cov* 85-89; R Weddington and Caldecote 89-01; P-in-c Butlers Marston and the Pillertons w Ettington from 01; P-in-c Alderminster and Halford from 01; P-in-c Tredington and Darlingscott w Newbold on Stour from 04. *The Vicarage, Warwick Road, Ettington, Stratford-upon-Avon CV37 7SH* Tel (01789) 748137 E-mail stour.dene5@btinternet.com

ADAMS, Anthony Paul. b 41. St Alb and Ox Min Course 95. **d** 98 **p** 99. NSM Banbury St Hugh *Ox* 98-01; P-in-c Wootton w Glympton and Kiddington 01-04; P-in-c Broughton and Duddon *Carl* from 04. *The Vicarage, Broughton-in-Furness LA20 6HS* Tel (01229) 716305 E-mail adamsfamily2@btinternet.com

ADAMS, Brian Hugh. b 32. Pemb Coll Ox BA54 MA57 Lon Univ DipTh56. Sarum & Wells Th Coll 77. **d** 79 **p** 80. Hon C Crediton *Ex* 79-81; Chapl St Brandon's Sch Clevedon 81-85; C Street w Walton *B & W* 86-88; RD Glastonbury 86-92 and 93-97; V Baltonsborough w Butleigh and W Bradley 88-97; rtd 97; Perm to Offic *B & W* from 97. *Manor Cottage, Weir Lane, Yeovilton, Yeovil BA22 8EU* Tel (01935) 840462 E-mail adamsbj@eurobell.co.uk

ADAMS, Brian Peter. b 47. FInstD FRSA Avery Hill Coll CertEd70 Lon Univ CertRS92 DipRS93. S'wark Ord Course 90. **d** 93 **p** 94. NSM Tonbridge SS Pet and Paul *Roch* 93-99; P-in-c Chatham St Mary w St Jo from 99. *The Rectory, 65 Maidstone Road, Chatham ME4 6DP* Tel (01634) 843632 Mobile 07778-777824 E-mail b.adams@cableinet.co.uk

ADAMS, Mrs Celia. b 39. R Holloway Coll Lon BSc60 Cam Univ CertEd61. Sarum & Wells Th Coll 86. **d** 88 **p** 94. NSM Canley *Cov* 88-91; NSM Cov N Deanery 91-92; C Coventry Caludon 92-97; Asst to Dioc Dir of Educn 92-93; Asst Chapl Geo Eliot Hosp NHS Trust Nuneaton 97-01; rtd 01; Perm to Offic *Ban* and *Cov* from 01. *22 Frankwell Street, Tywyn LL36 9EW* Tel (01654) 711604

ADAMS, The Ven Charles Alexander. b 29. MBE73 CBE82 JP. AKC59. **d** 60 **p** 61. C Bishopwearmouth St Mich w St Hilda *Dur* 60-63; C Ox SS Phil and Jas *Ox* 63-66; C Tunbridge Wells St Barn *Roch* 66-68; St Vincent from 68; Miss to Seafarers from 68; Can Kingstown Cathl from 73; Adn St Vincent & The Grenadines 76-98; rtd 98. *St Mary's Rectory, Bequia, Northern Grenadines, Windward Islands* Tel (001784) 458 3234 Fax 457 3532 E-mail caadams@caribsurf.com

ADAMS, Capt Christopher John. b 40. **d** 98 **p** 99. C Luton St Fran *St Alb* from 98. *91 Byron Road, Lewsey, Luton LU4 0HX* Tel (01582) 529373

ADAMS, David. *See* ADAMS, John David Andrew

ADAMS, David James. b 58. Trin Coll Bris 95. **d** 97 **p** 98. C Wirksworth *Derby* 97-00; P-in-c Seale and Lullington 00-02; R Seale and Lullington w Coton in the Elms 02-05; CF from 05. *c/o MOD Chaplains (Army)* Tel (01980) 615804 Fax 615800

ADAMS, David John Anthony. b 46. QUB BSc70 DipArch72. Bris Sch of Min 81. **d** 84 **p** 85. NSM Sea Mills *Bris* 84-97; C Henbury 97-00; V Longwell Green from 00. *The Vicarage, 85 Bath Road, Longwell Green, Bristol BS30 9DF* Tel 0117-932 3714 Mobile 07803-330727 E-mail djadams@surfaid.org

ADAMS, Denis Leslie. b 23. Ox NSM Course 78. **d** 81 **p** 82. NSM Reading All SS *Ox* 81-82; C Wargrave 82-83; C Skegness and Winthorpe *Linc* 83-85; V Gainsborough St Jo 85-89; rtd 89; Perm to Offic *Linc* 89-01. *4 Collum Gardens, Ashby, Scunthorpe DN16 2SY* Tel (01724) 842554

ADAMS, Donald John. b 46. St Jo Coll Nottm 86. **d** 88 **p** 89. C Byfleet *Guildf* 88-93; P-in-c E Molesey St Mary 93-03; Perm to Offic *S'wark* 96-03; rtd 03. *The Harnhill Centre, Harnhill Manor, Cirencester GL7 5PX* Tel (01285) 852009 E-mail cada.adams@virgin.net

ADAMS, Douglas George. b 39. St Luke's Coll Ex CertEd69 MEd87 ALBC65. SW Minl Tr Course 86. **d** 89 **p** 90. NSM Bude Haven and Marhamchurch *Truro* 89-93; P-in-c St Mewan 93-04; P-in-c Mevagissey and St Ewe 00-04; Chapl Mt Edgcumbe Hospice 93-96; rtd 04; Perm to Offic *Truro* from 05. *9 Arundel Terrace, Bude EX23 8LS* Tel (01288) 353842 E-mail douglasadams@tiscali.co.uk

ADAMS, Gillian. *See* WILTON, Mrs Gillian Linda

ADAMS, Godfrey Bernard. b 47. Local Minl Tr Course. **d** 93 **p** 94. OLM Saddleworth *Man* from 93. *11 Springmeadow Lane, Uppermill, Oldham OL3 6EP* Tel (01457) 875126 E-mail godfreyadams@compuserve.com

ADAMS, Hubert Theodore. b 28. FCA. OLM course 96. **d** 98 **p** 99. OLM Blurton *Lich* from 98. *12 Earls Road, Trentham, Stoke-on-Trent ST4 8DG* Tel (01782) 641383

ADAMS, Ian Robert. b 57. R Holloway Coll Lon BA79. Ridley Hall Cam 95. **d** 97 **p** 98. C Thame *Ox* 97-04; Ldr mayBe from 04. *33A Vicarage Road, Oxford OX1 4RD* Tel (01865) 723544 Mobile 07753-635688 E-mail gailian@waitrose.com

ADAMS, James Michael. b 49. Man Univ LLB71 Lon Univ PGCE79. St Jo Coll Nottm DipTh. **d** 82 **p** 83. C Luton St Mary *St Alb* 82-85; TV Cove St Jo *Guildf* 85-92; V Chislehurst Ch Ch *Roch* from 92. *Christ Church Vicarage, 62 Lubbock Road, Chislehurst BR7 5JX* Tel (020) 8467 3185 *or* tel and fax 8325 3557 E-mail michaeladams@fish.co.uk

ADAMS, Mrs Jayne Maxine. b 57. Westhill Coll Birm CertEd78. WMMTC 94. **d** 97 **p** 98. NSM Cotteridge *Birm* 97-99; NSM Nechells 99-05; NSM Bournville from 05. *40 Middle Park Drive, Northfield, Birmingham B31 2FL* Tel 0121-476 0206 E-mail jane@adamsj21.freeserve.co.uk

ADAMS, John. b 38. Lon Univ DipEd66 Open Univ BA79. Linc Th Coll 68. **d** 70 **p** 71. C Skipton H Trin *Bradf* 70-72; C Bassingham *Linc* 72-73; Chapl St Piers Hosp Sch Lingfield 73-74; Hon C Keighley *Bradf* 76-79; P-in-c Bredenbury and Wacton w Grendon Bishop *Heref* 79-84; P-in-c Edwyn Ralph and Collington w Thornbury 79-84; P-in-c Pencombe w Marston Stannett and Lt Cowarne 79-84; V Macclesfield St Jo *Ches* 84-87; R Wimblington *Ely* 87-90; V Manea 87-90; R Hallaton w Horninghold, Allexton, Tugby etc *Leic* 90-96; P-in-c Moulton *Linc* 96-97; V 97-03; rtd 03; Perm to Offic *Linc* from 03. *17 Linden Drive, Burgh le Marsh, Skegness PE24 5BP* Tel (01754) 810366

ADAMS, Canon John Christopher Ronald. b 29. St Paul's Coll Grahamstown. **d** 55 **p** 56. Rhodesia 55-66; C Northolt Park St Barn *Lon* 67-68; C W Brompton St Mary 68-69; Zimbabwe 69-98; rtd 98; Perm to Offic *S'wark* from 01. *The College of St Barnabas, Blackberry Lane, Lingfield RH7 6NJ* Tel (01342) 870544

ADAMS, John David Andrew. b 37. TCD BA60 MA64 BD69 Div Test61 Reading Univ MEd74. **d** 62 **p** 63. C Belfast St Steph *Conn* 62-65; Asst Master Lacunza Academy Spain 65-67; Asst Master Tower Ramparts Sch Ipswich 67-70; Asst Master Robert Haining Sch Surrey 70-74; Hd Master St Paul's Secondary Sch Addlestone 74-82; Hd Master Weydon Secondary Sch Farnham 82-98; NSM Bourne *Guildf* 80-99; NSM The Bourne and Tilford from 99; Chapl to The Queen from 94; Consultant to Secondary Schs from 98. *Brookside Farm, Oast House Crescent, Farnham GU9 0NP* Tel (01252) 726888 E-mail j.david_adams@ntworld.com

ADAMS, John Mark Arthur. b 67. Reading Univ BSc89. St Jo Coll Nottm MA98. **d** 99 **p** 00. C Skegby *S'well* 99-02; C Bletchley *Ox* from 02. *14 Hamilton Lane, Bletchley, Milton Keynes MK3 5LU* Tel (01908) 366083 Mobile 07712-674824 E-mail rev-mark@ntlworld.com

ADAMS, John Peter. b 42. Lon Univ BD69. Oak Hill Th Coll 65. **d** 70 **p** 71. C Whitnash *Cov* 70-73; Hon Asst Chapl Basle *Eur* 73-74; Chapl Davos 74-75; Chapl Düsseldorf 75-76; C Gt Baddow *Chelmsf* 77-80; Miss Eur Chr Miss 80-91; Perm to Offic *Chelmsf* 80-91; Hon Asst Chapl Vienna *Eur* 90-91; Asst Chapl Zürich 91-95; P-in-c Harmondsworth *Lon* 95-99; TV Shebbear, Buckland Filleigh, Sheepwash etc *Ex* 99-02; rtd 02; Perm to Offic *Ex* from 02. *The Leas, Kingscott, Torrington EX38 7JW* Tel (01805) 622161 E-mail john@adams1100.freeserve.co.uk

ADAMS, John Richard. b 38. St D Coll Lamp BA62 Lich Th Coll 62. **d** 64 **p** 65. C Falmouth K Chas *Truro* 64-68; C Bath Twerton-on-Avon *B & W* 68-72; C Milton *Win* 72-79; P-in-c Weymouth St Edm *Sarum* 79-90; V 90-95; Chapl Westhaven Hosp Weymouth 79-94; P-in-c The Winterbournes and Compton Valence 95-03; rtd 03. *1 Manor Barn, Bothenhampton, Bridport DT6 4BJ* Tel (01308) 422808

ADAMS, Jonathan Henry. b 48. St Andr Univ MA73. Cranmer Hall Dur 73. **d** 76 **p** 77. C Upperby St Jo *Carl* 76-78; C Sunderland St Chad *Dur* 78-82; Soc Resp Officer 83-91; TV Willington *Newc* 91-96; Local Min Development Officer 91-96; P-in-c Byker St Silas 96-01; Perm to Offic from 01. *5A Tunstall Vale, Sunderland SR2 7HP* Tel 0191-525 1881 E-mail jonathan@openroad.fsnet.co.uk

ADAMS, Margaret Anne. *See* FREEMAN, Mrs Margaret Anne

ADAMS, Mark. *See* ADAMS, John Mark Arthur

ADAMS, Martin Philip. b 57. Open Univ BA99. Sarum & Wells Th Coll 88. **d** 90 **p** 91. C Sandringham w W Newton *Nor* 90-93; P-in-c Docking w The Birchams and Stanhoe w Barwick 93-95; V Docking, the Birchams, Stanhoe and Sedgeford 95-97; V Orrell *Liv* 97-03; R Aughton St Mich from 03; Dir Dioc OLM Scheme from 03. *The Rectory, 10 Church Lane, Aughton, Ormskirk L39 6SB* Tel and fax (01695) 423204 E-mail rev.martin@btopenworld.com

ADAMS, Michael. *See* ADAMS, James Michael

ADAMS, Canon Michael John. b 48. St Jo Coll Dur BA77. Ripon Coll Cuddesdon 77. **d** 79 **p** 80. C Falmouth K Chas *Truro* 79-81; C St Buryan, St Levan and Sennen 81-83; P-in-c Lanlivery w Luxulyan 83-84; V 84-88; V St Agnes 88-99; V Newquay from 99; RD Powder 90-96; Hon Can Truro Cathl from 03; Perm to Offic *Ex* from 94. *20 St Michael's Road, Newquay TR7 1RA* Tel and fax (01637) 872096 E-mail vicar@st-michaels-newquay.org.uk

ADAMS, Nigel David. b 40. Sarum & Wells Th Coll 86. **d** 88 **p** 89. C Tile Hill *Cov* 88-91; C Coventry Caludon 91-92; TV 92-97; Asst Chapl HM YOI Onley 92-95; Sub Chapl HM Pris Birm 95-01; P-in-c Nuneaton St Mary *Cov* 97-01; rtd 01; Perm to Offic *Ban* and *Cov* from 01; AD Ystumaner *Ban* from 05. *22 Frankwell Street, Tywyn LL36 9EW* Tel (01654) 711604

ADAMS, Olugboyega Adeoye. b 55. Illinois Univ BSc81 Univ of Kansas MSc82 Lon Univ PhD93. EMMTC 99. **d** 02 **p** 03. C Glenfield *Leic* from 02. *8 Lynmouth Close, Glenfield, Leicester LE3 8RW* Tel 0116-287 8224 E-mail oluadams@ukgateway.net

ADAMS, Peter. Bris Univ CertEd52 Lon Univ AdDipEd72. Oak Hill Th Coll 91. **d** 91 **p** 92. NSM Towcester w Easton Neston *Pet* 91-95; Perm to Offic *Ex* from 94. *3 Copperwood Close, Ashburton, Newton Abbot TQ13 7JQ* Tel (01364) 654261

ADAMS, Canon Peter. b 37. K Coll Lon AKC65 Trin Coll Cam MA70. St Boniface Warminster 65. **d** 66 **p** 67. C Clapham H Trin *S'wark* 66-70; Chapl Trin Coll Cam 70-75; Warden Trin Coll Cen Camberwell 75-83; V Camberwell St Geo *S'wark* 75-83; RD Camberwell 80-83; P-in-c W Dulwich All SS and Em 83-85; V 85-92; V Addington 92-02; Hon Can S'wark Cathl 99-02; rtd 03. *26 Mansfield Road, South Croydon CR2 6HN* Tel (020) 8680 3191 E-mail canon.adams@talk21.com

ADAMS, Peter Anthony. b 48. K Coll Lon BD70 AKC70 MTh72. **d** 72 **p** 74. Lic to Offic *Eur* 72-73; C Ashford *Cant* 73-79; P-in-c Ramsgate H Trin 79-86; P-in-c Ramsgate St Geo 84-86; R Ramsgate H Trin and St Geo from 86. *Holy Trinity Rectory, Winterstoke Way, Ramsgate CT11 8AG* Tel (01843) 593593

ADAMS, Peter Harrison. b 41. Tyndale Hall Bris 63. **d** 68 **p** 69. C Kendal St Thos *Carl* 68-71; C W Bromwich Gd Shep w St Jo *Lich* 71-75; R Aldham *Chelmsf* 76-81; R Marks Tey 76-81; R Marks Tey w Aldham and Lt Tey 81-85; NSM Colchester St Jo from 85; Dioc Missr from 85. *4 St Jude's Gardens, St John's Estate, Colchester CO4 4PP* Tel (01206) 854041 E-mail peter@through-faith-missions.org

ADAMS, Raymond William. b 58. Reading Univ BA79. Oak Hill Th Coll BA85. **d** 85 **p** 86. C Blackpool St Thos *Blackb* 85-88; C Padiham 88-90; TV Rodbourne Cheney *Bris* 90-02; RD Cricklade 97-99; V Haydon Wick from 02. *The Vicarage, 54 Furlong Close, Swindon SN25 1QP* Tel (01793) 634258 E-mail r.adams4@ntlworld.com

ADAMS, Richard. *See* ADAMS, John Richard

ADAMS, Richard John. b 48. Leeds Univ BA70. St Alb and Ox Min Course 94. **d** 97 **p** 98. C N Hinksey and Wytham *Ox* 97-01; V Fence-in-Pendle and Higham *Blackb* from 01. *The Vicarage, 12 Wheatcroft Avenue, Fence, Burnley BB12 9QL* Tel (01282) 617316 E-mail richard@gwyneth.net

ADAMS, Robin Thomas. b 54. QUB BSc76. Oak Hill Th Coll BA79. **d** 79 **p** 80. C Magheralin *D & D* 79-82; C Coleraine *Conn* 82-86; I Belfast St Aid 86-89; USA from 89; I Tecumseh St Pet 89-97; V Ch of the Word from 98. *14215 Lee Highway, Gainsville, VA 20155, USA* Tel (001) (703) 754 9673 E-mail theword@erols.com

ADAMS, Roger Charles. b 36. Em Coll Cam BA60 MA64. Tyndale Hall Bris 60. **d** 62 **p** 63. C Longfleet *Sarum* 62-65; C Uphill *B & W* 66-71; R Ramsden Crays w Ramsden Bellhouse

Chelmsf 71-78; SW Area Sec BFBS 78-84; P-in-c Plymouth St Aug *Ex* 84-85; TV Plymouth Em w Efford 85-90; V Paignton Ch Ch 90-01; rtd 01; Perm to Offic *Ex* from 01. *171 Elburton Road, Plymouth PL9 8HY* Tel (01752) 407287

ADAMS, Ms Ruth Helen. b 73. St Jo Coll Dur BA94 CITC BTh97. **d** 97 **p** 98. C Drumragh w Mountfield *D & R* 97-99; Chapl Trin Coll Cam from 00. *Trinity College, Cambridge CB2 1TQ* Tel (01223) 338472 E-mail rha20@cam.ac.uk

ADAMS, Stephen Paul. b 56. Ex Univ BSc78. Sarum & Wells Th Coll 85. **d** 87 **p** 88. C Swansea St Nic *S & B* 87-88; C Llwynderw 88-91; R Badby w Newham and Charwelton w Fawsley etc *Pet* 91-97; R Abington from 97; RD Northn from 01. *The Rectory, 5 Abington Park Crescent, Northampton NN3 3AD* Tel (01604) 631041 Fax as telephone
E-mail stephen@abingtonrectory.fsnet.co.uk

ADAMS (née DABIN), Susan. b 51. NTMTC 96. **d** 00 **p** 01. NSM Hullbridge *Chelmsf* 00-03; NSM Ashingdon w S Fambridge from 03. *49 Crouch Avenue, Hullbridge, Hockley SS5 6BS* Tel (01702) 231825

ADAMS, Theo. *See* ADAMS, Hubert Theodore

ADAMS, William Thomas. b 47. Ches Coll of HE CertEd69 Open Univ BA74 Leic Univ MA91. EAMTC 97. **d** 00 **p** 01. NSM Helmdon w Stuchbury and Radstone etc *Pet* 00-03; NSM Astwell Gp 03-05; R from 05. *Brookdale, Mill Road, Whitfield, Brackley NN13 5TQ* Tel (01280) 850683
E-mail will.adams@tesco.net

ADAMSON, Anthony Scott. b 49. Newc Univ BA70. St Jo Coll Dur 75. **d** 78 **p** 79. C High Elswick St Paul *Newc* 78-86; C Benwell 86-92; V Tweedmouth from 92; P-in-c Scremerston from 02; P-in-c Spittal from 02; RD Norham 00-03; AD from 03. *The Vicarage, Main Street, Tweedmouth, Berwick-upon-Tweed TD15 2AW* Tel (01289) 306409
E-mail ktadamson@tweedmouth.freeserve.co.uk

ADAMSON, Arthur John. b 38. Keble Coll Ox BA61 MA65. Tyndale Hall Bris 61. **d** 63 **p** 64. C Redhill H Trin *S'wark* 63-66; Chapl Trent Park Coll of Educn 66-69; C Enfield Ch Ch Trent Park *Lon* 66-70; Ind Chapl *S'wark* 70-74; V Battersea St Geo w St Andr 70-74; R Reedham *Nor* 74-80; Min Beighton and Moulton 75-80; P-in-c Cantley w Limpenhoe and Southwood 77-80; R Oulton St Mich 80-90; Chapl Lothingland Hosp 80-90; R Laceby *Linc* 90-98; R Laceby and Ravendale Gp 98-03; rtd 03. *24 Mill Lane, Cottesmore, Oakham LE15 7DL* Tel (01572) 812816 E-mail ajaca@compuserve.com *or* ajohnadamson@aol.com

ADAMSON, Paul. b 35. Leeds Univ BA58. Coll of Resurr Mirfield. **d** 60 **p** 61. C Southwick St Columba *Dur* 60-63; Br Guiana 63-66; Guyana 66-75; C Benwell St Jas *Newc* 75-77; V Cowgate 77-83; V Prudhoe 83-93; TV N Tyne and Redesdale 93-98; TR 98-00; RD Bellingham 98-00; rtd 00; Perm to Offic *Newc* from 01. *11 Carham Close, Corbridge NE45 5NA* Tel (01434) 633274

ADAN, Howard Keith. b 62. **d** 01 **p** 02. C Amsterdam w Den Helder and Heiloo *Eur* 01-04; Asst Chapl from 04; Angl Chapl Amsterdam Airport Schiphol from 04. *Korvet 14, 1186 WE Amstelveen, The Netherlands* Tel (0031) (20) 453 9085 Fax 453 9086

ADDENBROOKE, Peter Homfray. b 38. Trin Coll Cam BA59 MA68 Ex Univ PGCE60. Lich Th Coll 61. **d** 63 **p** 64. C Bakewell *Derby* 63-67; C Horsham *Chich* 67-73; P-in-c Colgate 73-98; Adv for Past Care and Counselling 73-93; rtd 98; Perm to Offic *Chich* from 99. *Oaks, Forest Road, Colgate, Horsham RH12 4SZ* Tel (01293) 851362

ADDIS, Arthur Lewis. b 11. TD. Worc Ord Coll 62. **d** 64 **p** 65. C Highcliffe w Hinton Admiral *Win* 64-66; R W Dean w E Grimstead *Sarum* 66-70; V Stratford sub Castle 70-79; rtd 79; Perm to Offic *Sarum* from 79. *Abbeyfield House, 33 Manor Road, Salisbury SP1 1JT* Tel (01722) 500328

ADDISON, Bernard Michael Bruce. b 31. Cam Univ MA73. St Steph Ho Ox 58. **d** 61 **p** 62. C Paddington St Sav *Lon* 61-64; C Primrose Hill St Mary w Avenue Road St Paul 64-66; C Claremont St Sav S Africa 66-69; C Sydney St Jas Australia 70-72; C Catford St Andr *S'wark* 72-73; Chapl Ch Coll Cam 73-78; Chapl Bonn w Cologne *Eur* 79-82; R Kegworth *Leic* 82-89; V Market Harborough 89-94; rtd 94; Spain from 94. *Calle Madrid 28, Piso 4, PTA 8, 46700 Gandia, Valencia, Spain* Tel (0034) (96) 287 8798

ADDISON, David John Frederick. b 37. Museums Assn Dip 73 K Coll Dur BA60 DipEd62 Birm Univ MA79 Bris Univ MLitt93. Wells Th Coll 64. **d** 66 **p** 71. C Rastrick St Matt *Wakef* 66-67; Perm to Offic *Bradf* 67-71; Hon C Manningham St Luke 71-73; Perm to Offic *Glouc* 77-79; Hon C Bisley w Oakridge 79-81; V Newland and Redbrook w Clearwell 81-02; Chapl R Forest of Dean Coll 89-02; rtd 02; Perm to Offic *Glouc* from 02 and *Mon* from 04. *28 Patterson Way, Monmouth NP25 5BS* Tel (01600) 719530

ADDISON, Philip Ives. b 29. K Coll Dur 49. Ely Th Coll 59. **d** 61 **p** 62. C Waltham Cross *St Alb* 61-64; C Bedford St Paul 64-66; Chapl Bedford N Wing Hosp 64-66; Chapl RN 66-70; V Foleshill St Laur *Cov* 70-74; C-in-c Halsham *York* 74-78; V Owthorne and Rimswell w Withernsea 74-99; Chapl Withernsea Hosp 74-99; rtd 99; Perm to Offic *York* from 99. *10 Park Avenue, Beverley HU17 7AT* Tel (01482) 872714

ADDISON SMITH, Canon Anthony Cecil. b 18. Keble Coll Ox BA48 MA53. Linc Th Coll 48. **d** 49 **p** 50. C Berwick H Trin *Newc* 49-52; V Middlesbrough St Chad *York* 52-58; V Saltburn-by-the-Sea 58-64; R Long Marston 64-66; V Easingwold w Raskelf 66-78; RD Easingwold 70-77; Can and Preb York Minster 76-83; V Selby Abbey 78-83; rtd 83; Perm to Offic *Ox* 83-85 and from 87; C Cookham 85-86; C Hambleden Valley 87. *5 Tierney Court, Marlow SL7 2BL* Tel (01628) 483288

ADDLEY, David Bernard. b 41. St Paul's Cheltenham CertEd64 Leic Univ DipEd69 Bradf Univ MSc73. Ox Min Course 91. **d** 92 **p** 93. NSM Claydon w Mollington *Ox* 92-94; NSM Ironstone 94-03; P-in-c Aston Cantlow and Wilmcote w Billesley *Cov* from 03; Perm to Offic *Pet* from 95. *The Vicarage, Church Road, Wilmcote, Stratford-upon-Avon CV37 9XD* Tel 07941-728652 (mobile) Fax (01789) 292376

ADEKANYE, Joseph (Kehinde). b 47. Lon Bible Coll DipRS82 Liv Inst of Educn MA98. Immanuel Coll Ibadan DipTh72 Oak Hill Th Coll BA84. **d** 72 **p** 73. Nigeria 72-80 and from 84; Lect Abp Vining Coll of Th Akure from 94; Perm to Offic *Liv* 97-00. *Archbishop Vining College, PO Box 3, Akure, Nigeria* Tel (00234) (34) 233031

ADEMOLA, Canon Ade. b 62. Goldsmiths' Coll Lon BA91 N Lon Univ MA94. NTMTC 95. **d** 98 **p** 99. NSM Lt Ilford St Barn *Chelmsf* 98-02; V Leyton Em from 02; Can Ibadan from 03. *Emmanuel Vicarage, 149 Hitcham Road, London E17 8HL* Tel (020) 8539 2200 Mobile 07941-029084
E-mail orison@ntlworld.com

ADENEKAN, Latiff. b 38. **d** 04. OLM Tulse Hill H Trin and St Matthias *S'wark* from 04. *32 Dalmore Road, London SE21 8HB*

ADENEY, Harold Walter. b 14. OBE76. Qu Coll Cam BA35 MB BChir38 MA53. Trin Coll Bris. **d** 75 **p** 76. Burundi 75-82; Perm to Offic *St Alb* 83-98 and *Nor* 92-05. *Eckling Grange Residential Home, Norwich Road, Dereham NR20 3BB* Tel (01362) 690239

ADEY, John Douglas. b 33. Man Univ BSc54. Coll of Resurr Mirfield 56. **d** 58 **p** 59. C Forton *Portsm* 58-64; C Northolt St Mary *Lon* 64-67; V Snibston *Leic* 67-72; V Outwood *Wakef* 72-78; V Clifton 78; V Upton Priory *Ches* 79-81; V Hyde St Thos 81-82; V Newton in Mottram 82-89; R Roos and Garton w Tunstall, Grimston and Hilston *York* 89-92; C Woodchurch *Ches* 92-95; C Coppenhall 95-98; rtd 98; Perm to Offic *Portsm* from 98. *90A Winter Road, Southsea PO4 9BX* Tel (023) 9273 4116

ADEY HUISH, Helen Louise. b 59. Bris Univ BA81 Qu Coll Cam PhD87. St Alb and Ox Min Course 01. **d** 04 **p** 05. NSM Banbury *Ox* from 04. *Hilary's, Shenington, Banbury OX15 6NH* Tel and fax (01295) 670387 E-mail adey-hui@fish.co.uk

ADFIELD, Richard Ernest. b 31. Oak Hill Th Coll 62. **d** 64 **p** 65. C Bedworth *Cov* 64-67; V Whitehall Park St Andr Hornsey Lane *Lon* 67-77; V Kensington St Helen w H Trin 77-86; V Turnham Green Ch Ch 86-92; rtd 92; Perm to Offic *Chich* 92-02; Chapl Brighton and Sussex Univ Hosps NHS Trust 02-03; Chapl Whittington Coll Felbridge from 03. *363 Hangleton Road, Hove BN3 7LQ* Tel (01273) 732538

✠ADIE, The Rt Revd Michael Edgar. b 29. CBE94. St Jo Coll Ox BA52 MA56 Surrey Univ DUniv95. Westcott Ho Cam 52. **d** 54 **p** 55 **c** 83. C Pallion *Dur* 54-57; Abp's Dom Chapl *Cant* 57-60; V Sheff St Mark Broomhall *Sheff* 60-69; RD Hallam 66-69; R Louth w Welton-le-Wold *Linc* 69-75; P-in-c N w S Elkington 69-75; TR Louth 75-76; V Morton w Hacconby 76-83; Adn Linc 77-83; Can and Preb Linc Cathl 77-83; Bp Guildf 83-94; rtd 95; Perm to Offic *Portsm* from 95; Hon Asst Bp Portsm from 95; Hon Asst Bp Chich from 96. *Greenslade, Froxfield, Petersfield GU32 1EB* Tel (01730) 827266

ADKINS, Peter Vincent Alexander (Alex). b 44. Lanc Univ BA71 Lon Inst of Educn CertEd78. Kelham Th Coll 63. **d** 69 **p** 70. SSM 67-73; Tutor Kelham Th Coll 71-73; Jerusalem 73-75; Hon C Cambridge St Giles w St Pet *Ely* 76-78; Hon C Northolt St Mary *Lon* 81-83; P-in-c Hanworth St Geo 83-86; R 86-88; Adult Educn Officer 83-86; Burford Priory 89-93; Warden Edw King Ho *Linc* 93-04; Gen Preacher from 93; Hon Succ Linc Cathl 99-04; rtd 04. *4 Holly Cottages, Main Street, Horsington, Woodhall Spa LN10 5EX* Tel (01526) 388448
E-mail alexad@tiscali.co.uk

ADLAM, Keith Richard. b 44. STETS 00. **d** 03 **p** 04. NSM Binstead *Portsm* from 03; NSM Havenstreet St Pet from 03. *23 Queen's Road, Ryde PO33 3BG* Tel (01983) 616903 Fax 810270 E-mail kejo@jakaranda75.freeserve.co.uk

ADLEY, Ernest George. b 38. Leeds Univ BA61. Wells Th Coll 62. **d** 64 **p** 65. C Bideford *Ex* 64-67; C Yeovil St Mich *B & W* 67-70; V Taunton Lyngford 70-79; R Skegness and Winthorpe *Linc* 79-91; R Wantage Downs *Ox* 91-03; rtd 03; Perm to Offic *Ox* from 04. *13 Pixton Close, Didcot OX11 0BX* Tel (01235) 210395

ADLINGTON, David John. b 51. AKC73. K Coll Lon 70 St Aug Coll Cant 73. **d** 74 **p** 75. C Clapham St Paul *S'wark* 74-77; C

Bethnal Green St Matt *Lon* 77-80; P-in-c Stepney St Pet w St Benet 80-84; PV and Succ S'wark Cathl *S'wark* 84-87; PV and Succ Llan Cathl *Llan* 88-91; Dioc Dir of Educn 91-00; V St Hilary 91-94; TV Cowbridge 94-95; C Whitchurch 95-00; P-in-c Folkestone St Mary and St Eanswythe *Cant* 00-02; V from 02; Hon Min Can Cant Cathl from 01. *The Vicarage, Priory Gardens, Folkestone CT20 1SW* Tel (01303) 252947

ADMAN, Fayaz. b 63. Pakistan Adventist Sem Sheikhupura BA94. St Thos Th Coll Karachi 97. **d** 98 **p** 99. Pakistan 98-04; C S Rochdale *Man* from 04. *St Peter's Vicarage, Church Road, Rochdale OL16 5NW* Tel (01706) 656536 E-mail revfadman_bpchp_dop@hotmail.com

ADNETT, Roy Gumley. b 14. Tyndale Hall Bris 39. **d** 42 **p** 43. C Blackb Ch Ch *Blackb* 42-44; C Denton Holme *Carl* 44-46; V Constable Lee *Man* 46-49; R Peldon w Gt and Lt Wigborough *Chelmsf* 49-55; V Chilcompton *B & W* 55-80; RD Midsomer Norton 78-81; R Chilcompton w Downside and Stratton on the Fosse 80-81; rtd 81; Perm to Offic *Leic* 81-96. *Bosbury, St James Close, Pangbourne, Reading RG8 7AP* Tel 0118-984 3781

ADOYO, Miss Eugeniah Ombwayo. b 54. Lon Bible Coll 84 Westmr Coll Ox BA86 MPhil90. **dss** 82 **d** 91 **p** 91. Kenya 82-94; Internat Sec Crosslinks 94-97; Hon C Hatcham St Jas *S'wark* 94-97; C S'wark Ch Ch and Chapl S Lon Ind Miss 97-02; TV Plaistow and N Canning Town *Chelmsf* from 02. *St Philip's Vicarage, 19 Abbey Street, London E13 8DT* Tel (020) 7474 4596

ADSETTS, Ms Marilyn Ann. b 47. St Jo Coll York CertEd69 Leeds Univ BEd70 Spurgeon's Coll Lon MTh00. EAMTC 98. **d** 00 **p** 01. C Rushmere *St E* 00-03; V Rhymney *Mon* from 03. *The Vicarage, Lawn Terrace, Rhymney NP22 5LL* Tel and fax (01685) 840500 E-mail mbygrace@aol.com

ADU-BOACHIE, Francis. b 60. Oak Hill Th Coll DipTh95. **d** 95 **p** 96. C Stonebridge St Mich *Lon* 95-01; V Wembley St Jo from 01. *The Vicarage, 3 Crawford Avenue, Wembley HA0 2HX* Tel (020) 8902 0273 E-mail francis@adu-boachie.freeserve.co.uk

ADYERI, James Joloba. b 58. Redcliffe Coll 96 Chelt & Glouc Coll of HE BA99. United Th Coll Bangalore 91. **d** 84 **p** 85. Uganda 85-88, 89-91, 92-96 and from 99; India 88-89 and 91-92; Perm to Offic *Glouc* 96-99. *PO Box 84, Mityana, Uganda* Tel (00256) (46) 23 36

AFFLECK, John. b 20. Liv Univ LLB48. K Coll Lon 68 St Aug Coll Cant 71. **d** 71 **p** 72. C Hutton *Chelmsf* 71-74; P-in-c Hawkchurch, Fishpond, Bettiscombe, Marshwood etc *Sarum* 74-80; R Marshwood Vale 80-86; rtd 86; Perm to Offic *Sarum* from 86. *23 St Nicholas Hospital, St Nicholas Road, Salisbury SP1 2SW* Tel (01722) 334659

AFFLECK, Stuart John. b 47. AKC69. St Aug Coll Cant. **d** 70 **p** 71. C Prittlewell St Mary *Chelmsf* 70-75; Asst Chapl Charterhouse Sch Godalming 75-78; Chapl 78-80; Warden Pilsdon Community 80-94; Perm to Offic *S'wark* from 03. *3 Chislehurst Road, Richmond TW10 6PW*

AGAR, George. b 40. Edin Univ BSc63 Ox Univ PGCE64. N Ord Course 92. **d** 94 **p** 95. Hd Biddulph High Sch Stoke-on-Trent 94-96; NSM Sandbach *Ches* 94-99; NSM Hartford from 99. *128 Middlewich Road, Sandbach CW11 1FH* Tel (01270) 760191 E-mail geohil.agar@virgin.net

AGASSIZ, David John Lawrence. b 42. St Pet Hall Ox BA64 MA68 Imp Coll Lon PhD94. Ripon Hall Ox 64. **d** 66 **p** 67. C Southampton St Mary Extra *Win* 66-71; V Enfield St Jas *Lon* 71-80; P-in-c Grays Thurrock *Chelmsf* 80-83; P-in-c Grays All SS 81-84; P-in-c Lt Thurrock St Mary 81-84; P-in-c W Thurrock 81-83; P-in-c Grays SS Pet and Paul, S Stifford and W Thurrock 83-84; TR Grays Thurrock 84-90; Hon Can Chelmsf Cathl 90-93; Dioc Development Rep 90-93; Perm to Offic 93-94; Kenya 98-00; Perm to Offic *S'wark* from 02. *23 St James's Road, Gravesend DA11 0HF* Tel (01474) 332193 E-mail david@agassiz.worldonline.co.uk

AGBELUSI, Dele Omotayo. b 51. Ahmadu Bello Univ Zaria MSc81. Immanuel Coll Ibadan DipTh85 Oak Hill Th Coll BA99. **d** 86 **p** 87. Nigeria 86-96; C Edmonton All SS w St Mich *Lon* 97-99; V Hornsey Ch Ch from 99. *Christ Church Vicarage, 32 Crescent Road, London N8 8AX* Tel (020) 8340 1656 *or* 8340 1566 E-mail agbelusi@aol.com

AGER, David George. b 52. Lon Univ BA73 Solicitor 77. SW Minl Tr Course 01. **d** 04 **p** 05. NSM Bradford w Oake, Hillfarrance and Heathfield *B & W* from 04. *14 Morgans Rise, Bishops Hull, Taunton TA1 5HW* Tel (01823) 335424 Mobile 07887-893918 E-mail ager@talk21.com

AGGETT, Miss Vivienne Cecilia. b 33. Sarum & Wells Th Coll 86. **d** 88 **p** 94. C Binley *Cov* 88-91; C Hednesford *Lich* 91-96; rtd 96; Perm to Offic *Cov* from 98 and *Lich* from 04; Asst Chapl Gtr Athens *Eur* from 01. *Balsi, Andros, Greece 84503* Tel (0033) (282) 41102

AGGREY, Solomon Samuel. b 49. BSc76. Immanuel Coll Ibadan MA84. **d** 80 **p** 82. Nigeria 80-88; Miss Partner CMS from 88; C Gorton Em and Gorton St Jas *Man* 93-95. *Address temp unknown*

AGNEW, Kenneth David. b 33. Jes Coll Cam BA58 MA62. Clifton Th Coll 58. **d** 60 **p** 61. C Lozells St Silas *Birm* 60-63; C Skellingthorpe *Linc* 63-68; C Birchwood 68-72; R Willand *Ex* 72-00; RD Cullompton 89-95; rtd 00; Perm to Offic *B & W* from 01. *Eastgate, 14 Limington Road, Ilchester, Yeovil BA22 8LX* Tel (01935) 842010

AGNEW, Kevin Raymond Christopher. b 59. Chich Th Coll. **d** 94 **p** 95. C Eastbourne St Mary *Chich* 94-98; V Roughey from 98. *Roffey Vicarage, 52 Shepherds Way, Horsham RH12 4LX* Tel (01403) 265333

AGNEW, Stephen Mark. b 54. Univ of Wales (Ban) BSc76 Southn Univ BTh81. Sarum & Wells Th Coll 76. **d** 79 **p** 80. C Wilmslow *Ches* 79-84; V Crewe St Jo 84-90; Chapl Bromsgrove Sch 90-99; V Claines St Jo *Worc* from 99. *The Vicarage, Claines Lane, Worcester WR3 7RN* Tel (01905) 754772 Mobile 07762-250749 E-mail revsmagnew@yahoo.com

AHON, Ahon Bol Nyuar. b 62. **d** 01 **p** 03. Uganda 01-03; Hon Chapl Birm Cathl *Birm* from 03. *44C Braithwaite Road, Birmingham B11 1LA* Tel 0121-242 0450 Mobile 07956-165426 E-mail de_nyuar@yahoo.com

AHRENS, Irene Karla Elisabeth. b 40. Berlin Univ Bonn Univ PhD69 Lon Bible Coll BA92 K Coll Lon MTh93. SEITE 93. **d** 95 **p** 96. NSM Kew St Phil and All SS w St Luke *S'wark* 95-99; Asst Chapl Berlin *Eur* from 00. *Wildpfad 26, 14193 Berlin, Germany* Tel (0049) (30) 8972 7027 *or* 8256 5300 E-mail iahrens@compuserve.com

AIDLEY, Jessica-Jil Stapleton. b 42. Westf Coll Lon BSc67 UEA PhD73 PGCE84. **d** 99 **p** 00. OLM High Oak, Hingham and Scoulton w Wood Rising *Nor* 99-04; Perm to Offic *Mon* 04-05; NSM Rockfield and Dingestow Gp from 05. *The Yew Tree, Lydart, Monmouth NP25 4RH* Tel (01600) 713075 E-mail j.aidley@btopenworld.com

AIKEN, Nicholas John. b 58. Sheff Univ BA. Wycliffe Hall Ox 80. **d** 82 **p** 83. C Ashtead *Guildf* 82-86; Dioc Youth Officer 86-93; R Wisley w Pyrford from 93; RD Woking from 03. *The Rectory, Aviary Road, Woking GU22 8TH* Tel (01932) 352914 E-mail rector@wisleywithpyrford.org

AIKEN, Simon Mark. b 62. St Andr Univ MTh85. Ripon Coll Cuddesdon 86. **d** 88 **p** 89. C Burnley St Matt w H Trin *Blackb* 88-91; C Heyhouses on Sea 91-94; V Musbury 94-99; V Longridge from 99. *The Vicarage, Church Street, Longridge, Preston PR3 3WA* Tel (01772) 783281 *or* 786240 Fax 786240 E-mail simon_preston_lancs@yahoo.co.uk

AINGE, Canon David Stanley. b 47. Brasted Place Coll 68 Lon Univ DipTh74. Oak Hill Th Coll 70. **d** 73 **p** 74. C Bitterne *Win* 73-77; C Castle Church *Lich* 77-79; P-in-c Becontree St Alb *Chelmsf* 79-89; P-in-c Becontree St Jo 85-89; TR Becontree S 89-91; RD Barking and Dagenham 86-91; V Leyton St Mary w St Edw 91-96; P-in-c Leyton St Luke 91-96; V Leyton St Mary w St Edw and St Luke 96-03; RD Waltham Forest 94-00; R Gt Dunmow and Barnston from 03; Hon Can Chelmsf Cathl from 97. *The Vicarage, The Charters, Church End, Dunmow CM6 2SJ* Tel (01371) 872504 E-mail davidsainge@hotmail.com

AINSCOUGH, Malcolm Ralph. b 52. Liv Univ BEd76 Liv Inst of Educn DASE85. St Mich Coll Llan DipTh87. **d** 87 **p** 88. C Fleur-de-Lis *Mon* 87-90; C Chepstow 90-91; TV Cwmbran 91-95; V Newport St Steph and H Trin 95-03; R Hasland *Derby* from 03; V Temple Normanton from 03. *The Rectory, 49 Churchside, Hasland, Chesterfield S41 0JX* Tel (01246) 232486 E-mail ainscoughm@fsmail.net

AINSLEY, Canon Anthony Dixon. b 29. Oriel Coll Ox BA52 MA57 Univ of S Africa BA74. St Steph Ho Ox 53. **d** 55 **p** 56. C Burnley St Cath *Blackb* 55-60; S Africa 60-80; Adn All SS 73-80; Can St Jo Cathl Umtata 73-80; Hon Can from 81; Chapl Bordeaux w Riberac, Cahors, Duras etc *Eur* 81; V Blackpool St Steph *Blackb* 81-94; rtd 94; Perm to Offic *Bradf* 94-99. *187A Filey Road, Scarborough YO11 3AE*

AINSLEY, Peter Dixon. b 32. OBE87. St Steph Ho Ox 58. **d** 60 **p** 61. C Bury St Thos *Man* 60-62; Chapl RN 62-87; Chapl HM Pris Liv 87-88; Chapl HM Pris Garth 88-95; rtd 95; Perm to Offic *Blackb* and *Liv* from 95. *21 Ridge Close, Southport PR9 8JU*

AINSWORTH, Mrs Janina. b 50. **d** 05. NSM E Farnworth and Kearsley *Man* from 05. *The Rectory, Walkden Road, Worsley, Manchester M28 2WH* Tel 0161-790 2362 E-mail jan@ainsworths.org.uk

AINSWORTH, Mark John. b 64. Lon Univ MTh92. Wycliffe Hall Ox 86. **d** 89 **p** 90. C Chipping Barnet w Arkley *St Alb* 89-93; USA from 93. *270 Bent Road, Wyncote, PA 19095, USA* Tel (001) (215) 517 8568 E-mail mjaec@earthlink.net

AINSWORTH, Canon Michael Ronald. b 50. K Coll Lon LLB71 LLM72 Trin Hall Cam BA74 MA79. Westcott Ho Cam 72. **d** 75 **p** 76. C Scotforth *Blackb* 75-78; Chapl St Martin's Coll of Educn 78-82; Chapl N Ord Course 82-89; R Withington St Chris *Man* 89-94; TR Worsley from 94; AD Eccles from 00; Hon Can Man Cathl from 04. *The Rectory, Walkden Road, Worsley, Manchester M28 2WH* Tel 0161-790 2362 E-mail michael.ainsworth@i12.com

AINSWORTH, Paul Henry. b 46. JP. Man Poly BA81. N Ord Course 85. **d** 88 **p** 89. NSM Salterhebble All SS *Wakef* 88-92; C Golcar 92-96; TV Moor Allerton *Ripon* from 96. *St Stephen's Vicarage, Tynwald Drive, Leeds LS17 5DR* Tel 0113-268 7338 E-mail p.ainsworth@virgin.net *or* vicar@ststephensmoortown.org.uk

AINSWORTH, Peter. b 34. Lon Univ BD57. Coll of Resurr Mirfield 69. **d** 70 **p** 71. C Leeds St Wilfrid *Ripon* 70-74; TV Tong *Bradf* 74-77; V Fairweather Green 77-94; rtd 94; Perm to Offic *Wakef* 94-02 and *York* from 03. *34 Dulverton Hall, Esplanade, Scarborough YO11 2AR* Tel (01723) 340134

AINSWORTH-SMITH, Canon Ian Martin. b 41. Selw Coll Cam BA64 MA68. Westcott Ho Cam 64. **d** 66 **p** 67. C Mill Hill Jo Keble Ch *Lon* 66-69; USA 69-71; C Purley St Mark *S'wark* 71-73; Chapl St Geo Hosp Lon 73-94; Chapl St Geo Healthcare NHS Trust Lon from 94; Hon Can S'wark Cathl *S'wark* from 95. *St George's Hospital, Blackshaw Road, London SW17 0QT* Tel (020) 7223 5302, 8725 3071 *or* 8672 1255
E-mail ian.ainsworth-smith@stgeorges.nhs.uk

AIPO RONGO, Bishop of. *See* AYONG, The Most Revd James Simon

AIRD, Donald Allan Ross. b 33. BSc84. AKC55. **d** 56 **p** 57. C N Wembley St Cuth *Lon* 56-59; C Sidmouth, Woolbrook and Salcombe Regis *Ex* 59-62; Youth Chapl *Ely* 62-68; V Swaffham Bulbeck 62-69; V Preston Ascension *Lon* 69-79; V St Marylebone St Mark Hamilton Terrace 79-95; rtd 95; Perm to Offic *Worc* from 95. *1 Mews Cottages, 81 Albert Road South, Malvern WR14 3DX* Tel (01684) 569603

AIRD, Robert Malcolm. b 31. Lon Univ BSc54. Westcott Ho Cam 75. **d** 77 **p** 78. C Burnham *B & W* 77-79; P-in-c Taunton Lyngford 79-84; V 84-87; R Dulverton and Brushford 87-94; rtd 96. *Arran Cottage, East Street, Chulmleigh EX18 7DD* Tel (01769) 581042

AIRD, Wendy Elizabeth. b 41. SEITE. **d** 00 **p** 01. NSM Streatham Immanuel and St Andr *S'wark* from 00. *85A Clarence Avenue, London SW4 8LQ* Tel (020) 8671 2592 Mobile 07711-301813

AIREY, Robert William. b 54. OLM course 96. **d** 99 **p** 00. OLM Holcombe *Man* from 99. *4 Pine Street, Haslingden, Rossendale BB4 5ND* Tel (01706) 224743

AIREY, Simon Christopher. b 60. Trin Coll Bris BA87. **d** 87 **p** 88. C Wilton *B & W* 87-90; Chapl Scargill Ho 90-93; TV Kingswood *Bris* 93-96; Asst P Nether Springs Northumbria Community 96-98 and 02-03; C Bath Abbey w St Jas *B & W* 98-02; C Nailsea Ch Ch w Tickenham from 03. *37 Nightingale Gardens, Nailsea, Bristol BS48 2BH* E-mail si4pope@hotmail.com

AISBITT, Joanne. *See* LISTER, Mrs Joanne

AISBITT, Michael. b 60. St Pet Coll Ox BA81 MA84. Westcott Ho Cam 81. **d** 84 **p** 85. C Norton St Mary *Dur* 84-87; C Kirkleatham *York* 87-90; V S Bank 90-96; R Whitby 96-97; TR Whitby w Aislaby and Ruswarp 97-00; R Attleborough w Besthorpe *Nor* from 00; RD Thetford and Rockland from 03. *The Rectory, Surrogate Street, Attleborough NR17 2AW* Tel (01953) 453185

AISBITT, Osmond John. b 35. St Chad's Coll Dur BA57 DipTh61. **d** 61 **p** 62. C Ashington *Newc* 61-64; C Blyth St Mary 64-68; V Cleckheaton St Jo *Wakef* 68-75; V Horbury 75-78; V Horbury w Horbury Bridge 78-97; rtd 97; Perm to Offic *Carl* 97-00 and from 02; P-in-c Nerja and Almuécar *Eur* 00-02. *8 Stonecross Gardens, Ulverston LA12 7HA* Tel (01229) 585622

AITCHISON, Charles Baillie. b 45. New Coll Dur BEd85 Bede Coll Dur TCert67 Newc Univ DAES74 ACP69. LNSM course 85. **d** 93 **p** 98. NSM Peebles *Edin* from 93; NSM Innerleithen from 93. *45 Whitehaugh Park, Peebles EH45 9DB* Tel (01721) 729750 *or* tel and fax 724008

AITKEN, Christopher William Mark. b 53. Dur Univ BA75. Westcott Ho Cam 76. **d** 79 **p** 80. C Finchley St Mary *Lon* 79-82; C Radlett *St Alb* 82-85; V Sprowston *Nor* 85-90; R Beeston St Andr 85-90; R Sprowston w Beeston 90-93; Chapl Sherborne Sch 93-04; Hd Master St Lawr Coll Ramsgate from 04. *Headmaster's House, St Lawrence College, College Road, Ramsgate CT11 7AE* Tel (01843) 572900
E-mail cwmaitken@talk21.com *or* hm@slcuk.com

AITKEN, Leslie St John Robert. b 41. Open Univ BA75. Cranmer Hall Dur 62. **d** 65 **p** 66. C Worc St Barn w Ch Ch *Worc* 65-69; C Halesowen 69-73; P-in-c Wyche 73-80; R Blackley St Pet *Man* 80-99; Chapl Booth Hall Hosp Man 80-89; R Sutton, Huttoft and Anderby *Linc* from 99. *The Vicarage, Huttoft Road, Sutton-on-Sea, Mablethorpe LN12 2RU* Tel (01507) 441169

AITKEN, Valerie Anne. b 46. STETS 01. **d** 04 **p** 05. NSM Perivale *Lon* from 04. *22 Woodfield Road, London W5 1SH* Tel (020) 8997 6819 Mobile 07779-340050
E-mail valerie.aitken2@btinternet.com

AITKEN, William Stuart. b 35. FCFI MSIAD CertEd. Cant Sch of Min 79. **d** 82 **p** 83. NSM Roch 82-86; C Orpington All SS 86-88; R Burham and Wouldham 88-96; Dioc Communications Officer 88-96; rtd 96; Perm to Offic *Roch* from 96. *18 Commissioners Road, Rochester ME2 4EB* Tel (01634) 715892

AITON, Janice Haran. MA79 Jordanhill Coll Glas PGCE80. TISEC 98. **d** 01 **p** 02. C St Andrews St Andr *St And* 01-04; I Dunboyne Union *M & K* from 04. *The Rectory, Ballygoran, Maynooth, Co Kildare, Irish Republic* Tel (01353) (1) 285430

AITON, Canon Robert Neilson. b 36. Univ of Wales BA59 DipEd60. Chich Th Coll 74. **d** 76 **p** 77. C E Grinstead St Swithun *Chich* 76-83; R Lavant 83-90; Chapl St Barn Hospice Worthing 90-95; V Durrington *Chich* 90-01; Can and Preb Chich Cathl from 99; rtd 01; Lic to Offic *Chich* from 01. *Fieldings, Joys Croft, Chichester PO19 4NJ* Tel (01243) 781728
E-mail maiton@talk21.com

✠**AJETUNMOBI, The Rt Revd Jacob Ademola.** b 48. Middx Univ BA93. Igbaja Sem Nigeria BTh73 Lon Bible Coll BA80. **d** 83 **p** 83 **c** 99. Bp's Chapl and V Ilesa St Marg Nigeria 83-88; Chapl to Nigerian Students in UK (CMS) 88-99; Miss Partner CMS 88-99; Bp Ibadan S from 99. *59 Milton Avenue, London NW10 8PL,* or *c/o Bishopscourt, PO Box 166, Ibadan, Nigeria* Tel and fax (020) 8969 2379 Fax (00234) (22) 810 1413
E-mail jacajet@aol.com

AKEHURST, Peter Russell. b 16. Reading Univ BSc38 Trin Hall Cam. Wycliffe Hall Ox. **d** 48 **p** 49. C Tonbridge SS Pet and Paul *Roch* 48-51; C Kennington St Mark *S'wark* 51; S Africa 51-70; R Didsbury St Jas *Man* 70-74; V Totland Bay *Portsm* 75-81; rtd 81; Perm to Offic *Bris* 86-89; Perm to Offic *Ox* 89-90 and from 99. *20 Emmbrook Court, Woolacombe Drive, Reading RG6 5TZ* Tel 0118-986 2946

✠**AKINOLA, The Most Revd Peter Jasper.** b 44. Virginia Th Sem MTS81 Hon DD93. **d** 78 **p** 79 **c** 89. V Abuja St Jas Nigeria 78-79; V Suleja St Jas 81-84; Prov Missr 84-89; Bp Abuja from 89; Abp Prov III from 97; Primate All Nigeria from 00. *PO Box 212, ADCP, Abuja, Nigeria* Tel (00234) (9) 523 6928 *or* 523 0989 Mobile 90-805853 Fax (9) 523 0986
E-mail abuja@anglican.skannet.com.ng

AKKER, Derek Alexander. b 46. Bradf Univ MA83. N Ord Course 85. **d** 88 **p** 89. C Mossley *Man* 88-90; C Bury St Pet 90-92; V Lever Bridge 92-97; TV Wolstanton *Lich* 97-99; V Hattersley *Ches* from 99. *St Barnabas' Vicarage, Hattersley Road East, Hyde SK14 3EQ* Tel 0161-368 2795

AKRILL, Dean. b 71. York Univ BA97. Ripon Coll Cuddesdon BTh00. **d** 00 **p** 01. C Swinton *Sheff* 00-01; C Wath-upon-Dearne 01-04; V Mosbrough from 04. *The Vicarage, 25 Kelgate, Mosborough, Sheffield S20 5EJ* Tel 0114-248 6518

✠**AKROFI, The Most Revd Justice Ofei.** b 42. Cen Connecticut State Univ USA BSc72 MEd73 Hon DHL00. Yale Div Sch MDiv76. **d** 76 **p** 76 **c** 96. Chapl Adisadel Coll Accra Ghana 76-78; Chapl Ridge Ch 78-81; Dean Accra 82-96; Bp Accra from 96; Abp W Africa from 03. *Bishopscourt, PO Box GP 8, Accra, Ghana* Tel (00233) (21) 662292 *or* 663595 Fax 668822
E-mail bishopakrofi@yahoo.com

ALASAUKKO-OJO, Tuomas. b 78. Helsinki Univ MTh06. **d** 05. C Helsinki *Eur* from 05. *Rastilantie 5 B 16, Helsinki FI-00980, Finland* Tel (00358) (50) 309 9132
E-mail assistant-curate@anglican.fi

ALBAN-JONES, Timothy Morris. b 64. MBE03. Warwick Univ BA85. Ripon Coll Cuddesdon 85. **d** 88 **p** 89. C Tupsley *Heref* 88-93; TV Ross 93-00; P-in-c Soham *Ely* 00-01; P-in-c Wicken 00-01; V Soham and Wicken from 02. *The Vicarage, Cross Green, Soham, Ely CB7 5DU* Tel (01353) 720423
E-mail vicar@soham.org.uk

ALBERS, Johannes Reynoud (Joop). b 47. Hogeschool Holland BTh92 Amsterdam Univ MTh. EAMTC 99. **d** 00 **p** 01. C Voorschoten *Eur* 00-02; C Amsterdam w Den Helder and Heiloo 02-04; Asst Chapl from 04. *Dorpsweg 134, 1697 KH Schellinkhout, The Netherlands* Tel (0031) (22) 950 1611
E-mail joopalbers@quicknet.nl

ALBON, Lionel Frederick Shapland. b 31. CEng MIMechE60. St Alb Minl Tr Scheme 80. **d** 83 **p** 84. NSM Bromham w Oakley *St Alb* 83-88; NSM Bromham w Oakley and Stagsden 88-89; Ind Chapl 89-96; rtd 96; Lic to Offic *St Alb* from 96. *Greenways, 43 High Street, Stagsden, Bedford MK43 8SG* Tel (01234) 825754

ALBY, Harold Oriel. b 45. Witwatersrand Univ BA68 MA77. Sarum Th Coll 68. **d** 71 **p** 72. S Africa 71-89; C Germiston St Boniface 71-74; C Johannesburg Cathl 74-75; R Ermelo w Pet Retief 57-78; R Potchefstroom 78-82; R Boksburg 82-89; P-in-c Forton *Portsm* 89-96; V Milton from 96. *St James's Vicarage, 287 Milton Road, Southsea PO4 8PG* Tel (023) 9273 2786

ALCOCK, Edwin James. b 31. AKC57. **d** 58 **p** 59. C Old St Pancras w Bedford New Town St Matt *Lon* 58-62; C Hillingdon St Andr 62-81; V N Acton St Gabr 81-01; rtd 01; Perm to Offic *Lon* from 02. *17 Westfields Road, London W3 0AX* Tel (020) 8896 2748

ALCOCK, Mrs Linda Mary. b 45. St Gabr Coll Lon TCert67. St Alb and Ox Min Course 96. **d** 99 **p** 00. OLM Shires' Edge *Ox* from 99. *Copperfields, Swan Lane, Great Bourton, Banbury OX17 1QR* Tel (01295) 750744

ALDCROFT, Malcolm Charles. b 44. Leeds Univ MA94. N Ord Course 79. **d** 82 **p** 83. NSM Alverthorpe *Wakef* 82-85; NSM Horbury Junction 85-93; Sub Chapl HM Pris and YOI New Hall 94-97; Sub Chapl HM Pris Wakef 96-97; R Cupar and Ladybank Ladybank *St And* 97-05; Chapl Stratheden Hosp Fife 97-05; Dioc Miss Officer and Min Development Co-ord *Mor* from 05; Hon C Arpafeelie from 05. *St John's Rectory, Arpafeelie, North Kessock, Inverness IV1 3XD* Tel (01463) 811316 E-mail malcolm@aldcroft.freeserve.co.uk

ALDEN, Andrew Michael. b 65. Bris Univ BA88 Ex Univ PGCE89 Lon Univ MA98. Wycliffe Hall Ox 01. **d** 03 **p** 04. C Weston-super-Mare St Paul *B & W* from 03. *Somerset House, 20 Addiscombe Road, Weston-super-Mare BS23 4LT* Tel (01934) 621120 E-mail andrewmalden@aol.com

ALDEN, Mrs Pamela Ann (Pat). b 42. St Gabr Coll Lon TCert67. Dioc OLM tr scheme 99. **d** 02 **p** 03. OLM Camberwell St Giles w St Matt *S'wark* from 02. *189 Upland Road, London SE22 0DG* Tel (020) 8693 5207 Mobile 07710-283710 Fax (020) 8693 6408 E-mail pat@alphaplus.co.uk

ALDER, Mrs Anne-Louise. b 63. STETS 99. **d** 02 **p** 03. C Cowes H Trin and St Mary *Portsm* 02-05; C Cowes St Faith from 05. *St Faith's Vicarage, St Faith's Road, Cowes PO31 7HH* Tel and fax (01983) 289533 E-mail louise.alder@lineone.net

ALDER, Eric Reginald Alfred. b 23. St Luke's Coll Ex 47 Lon Univ BA55 Cam Inst of Educn 64. Chich Th Coll 70. **d** 71 **p** 72. C Deal St Leon w Sholden *Cant* 71-80; P-in-c Woodnesborough 80-83; P-in-c Worth 80-83; P-in-c Staple 80-83; V Woodnesborough w Worth and Staple 83-90; rtd 90; Perm to Offic *Cant* from 90. *3 Hackington Terrace, Canterbury CT2 7HE* Tel (01227) 766783

ALDERMAN, Canon John David. b 49. Man Univ BA71 Lon Inst of Educn PGCE72 Selw Coll Cam BA79 MA80. Ridley Hall Cam 77. **d** 80 **p** 81. C Hartley Wintney, Elvetham, Winchfield etc *Win* 80-83; V Bursledon 83-92; R Dibden 92-05; Hon Can Win Cathl 01-05; AD Lyndhurst 04-05; Patr Sec CPAS from 05. *3 Riversleigh Road, Leamington Spa CV32 6BG* Tel (01926) 431203 E-mail gillianandjohn@tiscali.co.uk

ALDERSLEY, Ian. b 42. FIBMS68. Wycliffe Hall Ox 89. **d** 91 **p** 92. C Allestree *Derby* 91-94; R Brailsford w Shirley and Osmaston w Edlaston from 94; P-in-c Yeaveley from 05. *The Rectory, Church Lane, Brailsford, Derby DE6 3BX* Tel (01335) 360362 E-mail ian@aldersley.fsbusiness.co.uk

ALDERSON, Albert George. b 22. K Coll Lon 46. **d** 50 **p** 51. C Whitworth w Spennymoor *Dur* 50-54; V S Shields St Fran 54-69; P-in-c 69-72; V S Shields St Jude 69-72; R Penshaw 72-79; P-in-c Bilsdale Midcable *York* 79-80; P-in-c Hawnby w Old Byland 79-80; P-in-c Scawton w Cold Kirby 79-80; R Upper Ryedale 80-91; rtd 91; Perm to Offic *York* from 91. *c/o Mrs M E Potts, Chapel Garth, Old Byland, York YO62 5LG* Tel (01439) 712631

ALDERSON, Christopher Derek. b 21. AKC55. **d** 55 **p** 56. C Goring-by-Sea *Chich* 55-59; V Gt Bentley *Chelmsf* 59-67; R Lt Bentley 60-67; V Dunster *B & W* 67-82; P-in-c Brompton Regis w Upton and Skilgate 82-83; R 83-86; rtd 86; Perm to Offic *B & W* 86-90. *2 Milne Way, Newport PO30 1YF* Tel (023) 9282 1032

ALDERSON, Mrs Maureen. b 40. WMMTC 90. **d** 93 **p** 94. NSM Yardley St Cypr Hay Mill *Birm* 93-96; P-in-c 96-00; V 00-02; P-in-c Gainford *Dur* from 02; P-in-c Winston from 02. *The Vicarage, Low Green, Gainford, Darlington DL2 3DS* Tel (01325) 730261

ALDERSON, Major Robin Edward Richard. **d** 04. OLM Sternfield, Benhall, Snape etc *St E* from 04. *The Cloisters, Sandy Lane, Snape, Saxmundham IP17 1SD* Tel (01728) 688255

ALDERSON, Roger James Ambrose. b 47. Lon Univ BD70 AKC71 Man Univ 76 Liv Inst of Educn PGCE93. St Aug Coll Cant. **d** 71 **p** 72. C Lawton Moor *Man* 71-75; C Barton w Peel Green 75-76; R Heaton Norris St Thos 76-85; V Bedford Leigh 85-92; V Cleadon Park *Dur* from 99. *St Cuthbert's Vicarage, 218 Sunderland Road, South Shields NE34 6AT* Tel 0191-456 2875 Mobile 07710-722817

ALDERTON-FORD, Jonathan Laurence. b 57. Nottm Univ BTh85. St Jo Coll Nottm 82. **d** 85 **p** 86. C Gaywood, Bawsey and Mintlyn *Nor* 85-87; C Herne Bay Ch Ch *Cant* 87-90; Min Bury St Edmunds St Mary *St E* 90-91; Min Moreton Hall Estate CD 91-94; V Bury St Edmunds Ch Ch from 94. *18 Heldhaw Road, Bury St Edmunds IP32 7ER* Tel (01284) 769956 *or* tel and fax 725391 E-mail ccmh@iname.com *or* revdjonathanford@minister.com

ALDIS, John Arnold. b 43. Univ of Wales (Cardiff) BA65 Lon Univ BD67. Clifton Th Coll 65. **d** 69 **p** 70. C Tonbridge SS Pet and Paul *Roch* 69-72; C St Marylebone All So w SS Pet and Jo *Lon* 72-77; Overseas Service Adv CMS 77-80; C Welling *Roch* 77-80; V Leic H Trin w St Jo *Leic* 80-89; Hon Can Leic Cathl 88-89; V W Kowloon St Andr Hong Kong 89-99; Sen Chapl Protestant Ch Oman 00-01; V Watford *St Alb* from 02. *St Mary's Vicarage, 14 Cassiobury Drive, Watford WD17 3AB* Tel (01923) 254005 Mobile 0772-632991 Fax (01923) 229274 E-mail jcaldis@btopenworld.com

ALDIS, Miss Rosemary Helen. b 40. Southn Univ BSc62 Ox Univ Inst of Educn DipEd63 Keele Univ MSc67. All Nations Chr Coll MA99. **d** 05. NSM Gabalfa *Llan* from 05. *94 Glendower Court, Velindre Road, Cardiff CF14 2TZ* Tel (029) 2062 6337 E-mail aldisrosemary@omf.net

ALDOUS, Alexander Charles Victor. b 56. Southn Univ BA81 K Alfred's Coll Win PGCE83. S Dios Minl Tr Scheme 91. **d** 94 **p** 95. Chapl Oundle Sch 94-97; Chapl Benenden Sch 98-01; Chapl Oakham Sch from 02. *75 Station Road, Oakham LE15 6QT* Tel (01572) 723941 *or* 758591 E-mail aa@oakham.rutland.sch.uk

ALDOUS, John Herbert. b 37. Portsm Poly CQSW83. Bp Otter Coll 94. **d** 96 **p** 00. NSM Gosport Ch Ch *Portsm* 96-00; NSM Rowner 00-02; R Sabie St Pet S Africa from 02. *St Peter's Rectory, PO Box 71, Sabie, 1260 South Africa*

ALDRIDGE, Mrs Anne Louise. b 59. Nottm Univ BEd80. EAMTC 96. **d** 99 **p** 00. NSM Milton *Ely* 99-04; Deputy Chapl Team Ldr Cam Univ Hosps NHS Foundn Trust from 04. *Addenbrooke's Hospital, Hills Road, Cambridge CB2 2QQ* Tel (01223) 245151 Fax 216520 E-mail r.aldridge@ntlworld.com

ALDRIDGE, Christopher John. b 35. Trin Hall Cam BA57 MA61. Ripon Hall Ox 59. **d** 60 **p** 61. C Coalville *Leic* 60-64; P-in-c Clifton St Fran *S'well* 64-72; V Gospel Lane St Mich *Birm* 72-90; V Selly Oak St Mary 90-00; rtd 00; Perm to Offic *Birm* from 00. *22 Woodlands Road, Sparkhill, Birmingham B11 4HE* Tel 0121-449 6196 E-mail cja-kfa@fish.co.uk

ALDRIDGE, Harold. b 35. Keble Coll Ox BA61 MA71. Chich Th Coll 60. **d** 62 **p** 63. C Notting Hill All SS w St Columb *Lon* 62-65; C Kensington St Mary Abbots w St Geo 65-69; Chapl Beech Hill Sch Macclesfield 69-82; TV Staveley and Barrow Hill *Derby* 82-86; P-in-c Longford 86-89; P-in-c Radbourne 86-89; P-in-c Dalbury, Long Lane and Trusley 86-89; V Braddan *S & M* 89-94; rtd 97. *Anfield Hey Residential Home, 46 Victoria Road, Douglas, Isle of Man IM2 4HQ* Tel (01624) 624147

ALDRIDGE, Canon Harold John. b 42. Lon Univ DipTh67. Oak Hill Th Coll 65. **d** 69 **p** 70. C Rawtenstall St Mary *Man* 69-72; CMJ 72-76; C Woodford Wells *Chelmsf* 76-79; TV Washfield, Stoodleigh, Withleigh etc *Ex* 79-86; V Burton *Ches* 86-90; P-in-c Shotwick 90; V Burton and Shotwick from 91; Dioc Clergy Widows and Retirement Officer from 91; RD Wirral S from 96; Hon Can Ches Cathl from 98; Chapl Clatterbridge Hosp Wirral 86-91; Chapl Wirral Hosp NHS Trust 91-97; Chapl Wirral and W Cheshire Community NHS Trust 97-03; Chapl Cheshire and Wirral Partnership NHS Trust from 03. *The Vicarage, Vicarage Lane, Burton, Neston CH64 5TJ* Tel 0151-336 4070

ALDRIDGE, Mark Richard. b 58. Oak Hill Th Coll BA89. **d** 89 **p** 90. C Combe Down w Monkton Combe and S Stoke *B & W* 89-90; C Woodside Park St Barn *Lon* 90-94; P-in-c Cricklewood St Gabr and St Mich 94-99; V 99-04; Min Oak Tree Angl Fellowship from 04. *41 South Parade, London W4 1JS* Tel (020) 8742 7764 E-mail marka@oaktree.org.uk

ALEXANDER, David Graham. b 61. Ridley Hall Cam 87. **d** 89 **p** 90. C New Barnet St Jas *St Alb* 89-93; C Northwood H Trin *Lon* 93-95; V Stopsley *St Alb* from 95. *The Vicarage, 702 Hitchin Road, Luton LU2 7UJ* Tel (01582) 729194 Fax 450375 E-mail stopsley@aol.com

ALEXANDER, Douglas Keith. b 45. Ripon Coll Cuddesdon 87. **d** 89 **p** 90. C Thorpe St Matt *Nor* 89-92; P-in-c Lakenham St Alb 92-97; Chapl Nor City Coll of F&HE 92-97; TV Barnham Broom 97-00; TV Barnham Broom and Upper Yare 00-04; TR from 04. *The Rectory, The Street, Reymerston, Norwich NR9 4AG* Tel and fax (01362) 858377 Mobile 07876-572724 E-mail doug.alexander@btinternet.com

ALEXANDER, James Crighton. b 43. Qu Coll Cam BA65 MA69. Cuddesdon Coll 68. **d** 68 **p** 69. C Much Wenlock w Bourton *Heref* 68-72; V Oakington *Ely* from 72; P-in-c Dry Drayton 85-95. *The Vicarage, 99 Water Lane, Oakington, Cambridge CB4 5AL* Tel (01223) 232396 E-mail liesl@free2live.org.uk

ALEXANDER, Canon James Douglas. b 27. Linc Th Coll 57. **d** 58 **p** 59. C Frodingham *Linc* 58-61; V Alvingham w N and S Cockerington 61-65; V Keddington 61-65; R Gunhouse w Burringham 65-70; R Peterhead *Ab* 70-76; R Aberdeen St Mary 76-95; Miss to Seafarers from 76; Can St Andr Cathl *Ab* from 79; Chapl HM Pris Aber from 82; P-in-c Cove Bay *Ab* 85-90; rtd 95; Dioc Supernumerary *Ab* from 95. *21 Whitehall Road, Aberdeen AB25 2PP* Tel (01224) 643202

ALEXANDER, Jane Louise. *See* MacLAREN, Mrs Jane Louise

ALEXANDER, Julius Erik Louis. b 66. Guildf Co Coll of Tech BTEC NC84 BTEC HNC86. Wycliffe Hall Ox 89. **d** 92 **p** 93. C Hoole *Ches* 92-94; C Offerton 94-98; TV Upper Holloway *Lon* 98-03; Asst Chapl Southn Univ Hosps NHS Trust from 03. *Trust Management Offices, Southampton General Hospital, Tremona Road, Southampton SO16 6YD* Tel (023) 8077 7222 E-mail jalexander@blueyonder.co.uk

ALEXANDER, Canon Loveday Constance Anne. b 47. Somerville Coll Ox BA69 MA78 DPhil78. N Ord Course 98. **d** 99 **p** 00. NSM Alderley Edge *Ches* from 99; Can Th Ches Cathl from 03; Perm to Offic *Sheff* from 00. *5 Nevill Road, Bramhall, Stockport SK7 3ET* Tel 0161-439 7946 E-mail l.c.alexander@sheffield.ac.uk

ALEXANDER, Michael George. b 47. Open Univ BA90 DipEd91. Sarum & Wells Th Coll 74. **d** 77 **p** 78. C Wednesfield *Lich* 77-80; C Tettenhall Wood 80-83; Distr Min 83-85; Dioc Adv in Adult and Youth Educn *Derby* 85-89; V Hazlewood 85-89; V Turnditch 85-89; Par Educn Adv (Laity Development) 89-96; Dioc Laity Development Adv 96-00; Dioc Dir Studies Bp's Centres of Learning 96-00; P-in-c Ticknall, Smisby and Stanton-by-Bridge 00-01; P-in-c Barrow-on-Trent w Twyford and Swarkestone 00-01; V Ticknall, Smisby and Stanton by

Bridge etc from 01; RD Melbourne from 02. *The Vicarage, 7 Church Lane, Ticknall, Derby DE73 7JU* Tel (01332) 862549 E-mail mike.alexander@ticvic.fsnet.co.uk

ALEXANDER, Norman William. b 27. Chich Th Coll 54. **d** 56 **p** 57. C Hatcham St Cath *S'wark* 56-59; C Horley 59-61; V Markington and S Stainley *Ripon* 61-69; R Mutford w Rushmere w Gisleham w N Cove w Barnby *Nor* 69-74; R W Winch 74-81; V Frensham *Guildf* 81-84; V Hemsby *Nor* 84-89; RD Flegg (Gt Yarmouth) 87-89; rtd 89; Perm to Offic *Nor* 98-03. *14 Fitton Road, St Germans, King's Lynn PE34 3AU* Tel (01553) 617513

ALEXANDER, Peter John. b 36. CQSW73 DMA74. Oak Hill Th Coll 92. **d** 95 **p** 96. NSM Aspenden, Buntingford and Westmill *St Alb* 95-02; rtd 02; Perm to Offic *Nor* from 02. *Dellgate, 4 The Dell, Bodham, Holt NR25 6NG* Tel (01263) 588126

ALEXANDER, Mrs Rachel Clare. b 57. EAMTC 96. **d** 99 **p** 00. NSM Mattishall w Mattishall Burgh, Welborne etc *Nor* 99-02; Perm to Offic 02-03; NSM Rugby St Matt *Cov* 03-04. *Minstrels, 50 Dereham Road, Mattishall, Dereham NR20 3NS* Tel (01362) 858655 E-mail rachel@ralexander.fsnet.co.uk

ALEXANDER, Robert. b 37. Lon Univ LLB60 St Cath Coll Ox BA62. St Steph Ho Ox 60. **d** 63 **p** 64. C Kensington St Mary Abbots w St Geo *Lon* 63-68; C Notting Hill 71-74; TV 74-79; Australia from 79; rtd 02. *302/27 Neutral Street, North Sydney, NSW, Australia 2060* Tel and fax (0061) (2) 9954 0543 E-mail robalexand@bigpond.com

ALEXANDER, Sarah Louise. b 72. Wycliffe Hall Ox 02. **d** 04 **p** 05. C Enfield Ch Ch Trent Park *Lon* from 04. *2 Chalk Lane, Cockfosters, Barnet EN4 9JQ* Tel 07889-146141 (mobile) E-mail sarah-alex1@yahoo.co.uk

ALEXANDER, Wilfred Robert Donald. b 35. TCD BA58 MA80. **d** 63 **p** 63. C Raheny w Coolock *D & G* 63-67; Min Can St Patr Cathl Dublin 65-67; Hon C Herne Hill St Paul *S'wark* 68-70; Asst Master Gosforth Gr Sch 71-76; Hon C Long Benton St Mary *Newc* 74-76; Chapl St Mary and St Anne's Sch Abbots Bromley 76-80; V Cauldon *Lich* 80-83; V Waterfall 80-83; P-in-c Calton 80-83; P-in-c Grindon 80-83; V Blackb St Luke w St Phil *Blackb* 83-89; V Rainhill *Liv* 89-92; R Croft w Southworth 92-99; C Croft w Southworth and Newchurch 99-01; rtd 01. *16 Hawkshaw Close, Birchwood, Warrington WA3 7NF* Tel (01925) 851472

ALEXANDER-YATES, Tristan Nathaniel. b 66. SEITE 99. **d** 03 **p** 04. NSM Eltham H Trin *S'wark* from 03. *St Kentigern House, 31 Fairfield Grove, London SE7 8UA* Tel (020) 8853 2257 Mobile 07970-016009 E-mail tristalex@aol.com

ALFORD, John. b 35. Nottm Univ BSc58 NDA59 DipEd76. Qu Coll Birm 74. **d** 77 **p** 78. NSM Edgmond *Lich* 77-87; C Cheadle 87-88; C Cheadle w Freehay 88-89; P-in-c Wootton Wawen *Cov* 89-95; P-in-c Grafham *Ely* 95-00; P-in-c Ellington 95-00; P-in-c Easton 95-00; P-in-c Spaldwick w Barham and Woolley 95-00; V 00-01; rtd 01; Perm to Offic *Ely* from 01. *4 Armstrong Close, Perry, Huntingdon PE28 0DF* Tel (01480) 812075 E-mail margaretalford@aol.com

ALFORD, Mrs Rosalie Grace. b 40. Bedf Coll Lon BA61 Lon Univ PGCE62. STETS 95. **d** 98 **p** 99. NSM Wadhurst *Chich* from 98; NSM Stonegate from 98. *Content, 1 Ingoldsby Cottages, Faircrouch Lane, Wadhurst TN5 6PP* Tel (01892) 782974

ALKER, Canon Adrian. b 49. Wadh Coll Ox BA70 Lanc Univ MA71. Ripon Coll Cuddesdon 77. **d** 79 **p** 80. C W Derby St Mary *Liv* 79-83; Dioc Youth Officer *Carl* 83-88; V Sheff St Mark Broomhill *Sheff* from 88; Dioc Dir of In-Service Tr from 90; Hon Can Sheff Cathl from 05. *St Mark's Vicarage, 4 St Mark's Crescent, Sheffield S10 2SG* Tel and fax 0114-267 0362 E-mail alker@stmarkssheffield.co.uk

ALLABY, Miss Mary Dorothea. b 60. Bedf Coll Lon BA82 W Sussex Inst of HE PGCE83. Trin Coll Bris DipHE90 ADPS92. **d** 92 **p** 94. Par Dn Ipsley *Worc* 92-94; C 94-96; TV Bloxwich *Lich* 96-02; V Trent Vale 02-03. *Address withheld by request* E-mail mary@allaby.freeserve.co.uk

ALLABY, Simon Arnold Kenworthy. b 65. St Chad's Coll Dur BA88. Trin Coll Bris 88. **d** 90 **p** 91. C Preston on Tees *Dur* 90-93; C Chester le Street 93-99; R Ardingly *Chich* from 99. *The Rectory, Church Lane, Ardingly, Haywards Heath RH17 6UR* Tel (01444) 892332

ALLAIN CHAPMAN, Ms Justine Penelope Heathcote. b 67. K Coll Lon BA88 PGCE89 Nottm Univ MDiv93. Linc Th Coll 91. **d** 93 **p** 94. Par Dn Forest Hill *S'wark* 93-94; C 94-96; TV Clapham Team 96-01; V Clapham St Paul 02-04; Dir Miss & Past Studies SEITE from 04; Perm to Offic *Cant* from 04. *SEITE Ground Floor Offices, Sun Pier House, Medway Street, Chatham ME4 4HF* Tel (01634) 846683 E-mail j.allain-chapman@seite.co.uk

ALLAN, Andrew John. b 47. Westcott Ho Cam 76. **d** 79 **p** 80. C Whitstable All SS w St Pet *Cant* 79-84; C Whitstable 84-86; P-in-c Littlebourne 86-87; P-in-c Ickham w Wickhambreaux and Stodmarsh 86-87; R Littlebourne and Ickham w Wickhambreaux etc from 87. *The Vicarage, Church Road, Littlebourne, Canterbury CT3 1UA* Tel (01227) 721233

ALLAN, Canon Archibald Blackie. b 35. Edin Th Coll 57. **d** 60 **p** 61. C Aberdeen St Jo *Ab* 60-63; R 82-00; Chapl St Paul's Cathl Dundee *Bre* 63-68; P-in-c Aberdeen St Clem *Ab* 68-76; Vice-Provost St Andr Cathl 76-82; Can 88-00; Hon Can from 01; rtd 00. *32 Craigiebuckler Terrace, Aberdeen AB15 8SX* Tel (01224) 316636

ALLAN, Donald James. b 35. Sarum & Wells Th Coll 63. **d** 65 **p** 66. C Royton St Paul *Man* 65-71; V Middleton Junction 71-78; P-in-c Finmere w Mixbury *Ox* 78-83; R Finmere w Mixbury, Cottisford, Hardwick etc 83; Chapl Westcliff Hosp 83-87; V Westcliff St Andr *Chelmsf* 83-87; R Goldhanger w Lt Totham 87-01; rtd 01; P-in-c St Goran w Caerhays *Truro* from 01. *The Vicarage, Gorran, St Austell PL26 6HN* Tel (01726) 844457 E-mail donald.allan2@btinternet.com

ALLAN, Jeanette Winifred. b 40. ALA63. St And Dioc Tr Course 79. **dss** 81 **d** 86 **p** 94. NSM Hillfoot's TM 81-86; NSM Bridge of Allan *St And* 86-88; NSM Dunblane 88-98; R Glenrothes from 98. *St Luke's Rectory, 60 Ninian Quadrant, Glenrothes KY7 4HP* Tel (01592) 759764 E-mail revdjallan@aol.com

ALLAN, John. *See* ALLAN, Andrew John

ALLAN, John William. b 58. St Olaf Coll Minnesota BA80 Birm Univ 86. Trin Lutheran Sem Ohio MDiv84 Qu Coll Birm 90. **d** 91 **p** 92. In Lutheran Ch (USA) 84-86; C Newport w Longford and Chetwynd *Lich* 91-94; P-in-c Longdon 94-01; Local Min Adv (Wolverhampton) 94-01; V Alrewas from 01; V Wychnor from 01; RD Lich from 04. *The Vicarage, Church Road, Alrewas, Burton-on-Trent DE13 7BT* Tel (01283) 790486 E-mail john.allan@lichfield.anglican.org

ALLAN, Peter Burnaby. b 52. Clare Coll Cam BA74 MA78 St Jo Coll Dur BA82. Cranmer Hall Dur 80. **d** 83 **p** 84. C Chaddesden St Mary *Derby* 83-86; C Brampton St Thos 86-89; TV Halesworth w Linstead, Chediston, Holton etc *St E* 89-94; TR Trunch *Nor* 94-03; R Ansley and Arley *Cov* from 03. *The Vicarage, 60 Birmingham Road, Ansley, Nuneaton CV10 9PS* Tel (024) 7639 6403 *or* 7639 6036 E-mail peter@allan49.fsworld.co.uk

ALLAN, Peter George. b 50. Wadh Coll Ox BA72 MA76. Coll of Resurr Mirfield 72. **d** 75 **p** 76. C Stevenage St Geo *St Alb* 75-78; Chapl Wadh Coll and C Ox St Mary V w St Cross and St Pet *Ox* 78-82; CR from 85. *House of the Resurrection, Stocks Bank Road, Mirfield WF14 0BN* Tel (01924) 494318

ALLANDER, William Edward Morgell Kidd. b 15. TCD BA37 MA40. CITC 37. **d** 38 **p** 39. C Knock *D & D* 38-43; Hd of Trin Coll Miss Belf 43-46; Lic to Offic *Lon* 46-51; C Foleshill St Laur *Cov* 53-55; P-in-c Wood End 55-57; V 57-64; V Atherstone 64-73; I Rathcooney Union *C, C & R* 73-88; rtd 88. *12 Richmond Estate, Blackrock, Cork, Irish Republic* Tel (00353) (21) 429 3352 Fax 429 3642 E-mail wallander@eircom.net

ALLARD, John Ambrose. b 30. Bps' Coll Cheshunt 63. **d** 65 **p** 66. C Leigh-on-Sea St Marg *Chelmsf* 65-69; P-in-c Rawreth w Rettendon 69-70; R 70-72; V Barkingside St Fran 73-84; V E Ham St Geo 84-86; V St Osyth 86-95; rtd 95; Perm to Offic *Nor* and *St E* 97-02; Hon C Stonehaven *Bre* from 03; Hon C Muchalls from 03. *18 Greystone Place, Newtonhill, Stonehaven AB39 3UL* Tel (01569) 731767

ALLARD, Roderick George. b 44. Lon Univ BA77 Sheff Poly MSc88 Loughb Coll of Educn CertEd96. N Ord Course 97. **d** 99 **p** 00. NSM Charlesworth and Dinting Vale *Derby* from 99. *16 Springmeadow, Charlesworth, Glossop SK13 5HP* Tel (01457) 866278 Mobile 07798-843283

ALLARDICE, Alexander Edwin. b 49. SRN. Chich Th Coll 73. **d** 76 **p** 77. C Rugeley *Lich* 76-79; C Felixstowe St Jo *St E* 79-81; TV Ipswich St Fran 81-87; C Lostwithiel *Truro* 87-90; C Boconnoc w Bradoc 87-90; C St Veep 87-90; C St Winnow 87-90; R Lostwithiel, St Winnow w St Nectan's Chpl etc 90-97; R Mevagissey and St Ewe 97-99; rtd 99; Perm to Offic *Truro* from 99. *4 Pensylva, St Austell PL25 4RW* Tel (01726) 77695 Fax as telephone E-mail alex.allardice@classicfm.net

ALLBERRY, William Alan John. b 49. Ch Coll Cam BA70 MA71. Ripon Coll Cuddesdon 84. **d** 86 **p** 87. C Brixton St Matt *S'wark* 86-90; V Wandsworth St Paul 90-98; R Esher *Guildf* from 98; RD Emly from 01. *The Rectory, 4 Esher Place Avenue, Esher KT10 8PY* Tel and fax (01372) 462611 E-mail william.allberry@btopenworld.com

ALLBUTT, Mavis Miriam. **d** 98 **p** 99. OLM Meir *Lich* from 98. *16 Sorrento Grove, Meir Hay, Stoke-on-Trent ST3 5XZ* Tel (01782) 599653

ALLCHIN, Canon Arthur Macdonald (Donald). b 30. Ch Ch Ox BA51 MA55 BLitt56 Univ of Wales 93. Bucharest Th Inst Hon DD77 Cuddesdon Coll 54. **d** 56 **p** 57. C Kensington St Mary Abbots w St Geo *Lon* 56-60; Lib Pusey Ho 60-69; Warden Community of Sisters of the Love of God Ox 68-73; Can Res and Lib Cant Cathl *Cant* 73-87; Hon Prov Can Cant Cathl from 88; Dir St Theosevia Cen for Chr Spirituality 87-94; Hon Prof Univ of N Wales Ban from 93; rtd 94; Lic to Offic *Cant* 94-97; Perm to Offic *Ban* from 97. *1 Trem yr Wyddfa, Bangor LL57 2ER* Tel (01248) 353744

ALLCHIN, Miss Maureen Ann. b 50. Edge Hill Coll of HE CertEd71 Sussex Univ MA93. S Dios Minl Tr Scheme 88. **d** 91 **p** 94. Hd Past Faculty Steyning Gr Sch 79-92; NSM Southwick St Mich *Chich* 91-92; C Storrington 93-95; TV Bridport *Sarum*

from 95. *The Vicarage, King's Head Hill, Bradpole, Bridport DT6 3DZ* Tel (01308) 458788 Fax 421048 E-mail maureen.allchin@btopenworld.com

ALLCOCK, Jeremy Robert. b 63. Trin Coll Bris BA92. **d** 92 **p** 93. C Walthamstow St Luke *Chelmsf* 92-96; V E Ham St Paul 96-05; V Paddington St Steph w St Luke *Lon* from 05. *St Stephen's Vicarage, 25 Talbot Road, London W2 5JF* Tel (020) 7792 2283 E-mail jeme6@aol.com

ALLCOCK, Peter Michael. b 37. Oak Hill Th Coll 65. **d** 68 **p** 69. C Upper Tulse Hill St Matthias *S'wark* 68-71; C Dunkeswell and Dunkeswell Abbey *Ex* 71-72; P-in-c Luppitt and Monkton 72-75; V Okehampton w Inwardleigh 75-80; TV Solihull *Birm* 80-85; V Highbury New Park St Aug *Lon* 85-99; V E and W Horndon w Lt Warley and Childerditch *Chelmsf* 99-02; rtd 02; Perm to Offic *Birm* and *Cov* from 03. *10 Arden Close, Balsall Common, Coventry CV7 7NY* Tel (01676) 533968 E-mail pma946078@aol.com

ALLDRIT, Nicolas Sebastian Fitz-Ansculf. b 41. St Edm Hall Ox BA63 MA69 DPhil69. Cuddesdon Coll 72. **d** 72 **p** 73. C Limpsfield and Titsey *S'wark* 72-81; Tutor Linc Th Coll 81-96; Sub-Warden 88-96; R Witham Gp *Linc* from 97. *The Rectory, 15 Hillview Road, South Witham, Grantham NG33 5QW* Tel (01572) 767240

ALLEN, Andrew Stephen. b 55. MPS Nottm Univ BPharm77. St Steph Ho Ox 78. **d** 81 **p** 82. C Gt Ilford St Mary *Chelmsf* 81-83; C Luton All SS w St Pet *St Alb* 83-86; TV Chambersbury 86-91; TV Brixham w Churston Ferrers and Kingswear *Ex* 91-01; TR from 01. *The Rectory, 16 Holwell Road, Brixham TQ5 9NE* Tel (01803) 851570 *or* tel and fax 855675 E-mail andallen@hotmail.com

ALLEN, Ms Beverley Carole. b 52. Ch Ch Coll Cant CertEd74 Open Univ BA91. Sarum Th Coll 93. **d** 96 **p** 97. NSM Ruislip Manor St Paul *Lon* from 96. *10 Shipley Mill Close, Stone Cross, Pevensey BN24 5PY* Tel (01323) 740283 E-mail revbev@tiscali.co.uk

ALLEN, Brian. *See* ALLEN, Frank Brian

ALLEN, Brian. b 58. Oak Hill NSM Course 90. **d** 93 **p** 94. NSM W Norwood St Luke *S'wark* 93-02; NSM Gipsy Hill Ch Ch from 02. *76 Bradley Road, London SE19 3NS* Tel (020) 8771 4282

ALLEN, Brian Stanley. b 24. Roch Th Coll 65. **d** 67 **p** 68. C Roch 67-74; P-in-c Drypool St Jo *York* 74-80; TV Drypool 80; V Marlpool *Derby* 80-87; rtd 87; Perm to Offic *York* from 90. *22 Sycamore Terrace, York YO30 7DN* Tel (01904) 653418

ALLEN, Miss Charlotte. b 79. St Jo Coll Dur BA00 Anglia Poly Univ MA03. Westcott Ho Cam 00. **d** 03 **p** 04. C Southwick *Chich* from 03. *1 Church House Close, Southwick, Brighton BN42 4WQ* Tel (01273) 592787 E-mail charlie.allen@dunelm.org.uk

ALLEN, Christopher Dennis. b 50. Fitzw Coll Cam BA73 MA77. Cuddesdon Coll 74. **d** 76 **p** 77. C Kettering St Andr *Pet* 76-79; C Pet H Spirit Bretton 79-82; R Bardney *Linc* 82-87; V Knighton St Mary Magd *Leic* from 87. *The Vicarage, Church Lane, Leicester LE2 3WG* Tel 0116-270 5730 E-mail callen@leicester.anglican.org

ALLEN, Christopher Leslie. b 56. Leeds Univ BA78. St Jo Coll Nottm 79. **d** 80 **p** 81. C Birm St Martin *Birm* 80-85; Tr and Ed Pathfinders 85-89; Hd 89-92; Midl Youth Dept Co-ord CPAS 85-89; Hon C Selly Park St Steph and St Wulstan *Birm* 86-92; V Hamstead St Bernard 92-95; NSM Kidderminster St Mary and All SS w Trimpley etc *Worc* from 03. *17 Alder Avenue, Kidderminster DY10 2LD* Tel and fax (01562) 820702 Mobile 07956-303037 E-mail chris.allen@ukonline.co.uk

ALLEN, David. b 38. Llan Dioc Tr Scheme. **d** 76 **p** 77. C Fairwater *Llan* 76-84; Chapl Bp of Llan High Sch 84-97; Lic to Offic *Llan* from 84. *1 Kenley Close, Llandaff, Cardiff CF5 2PA* Tel (029) 2056 0252

ALLEN, David Edward. b 70. Van Mildert Coll Dur BSc91. Ripon Coll Cuddesdon BA94. **d** 95 **p** 96. C Grantham *Linc* 95-99; C W Hampstead St Jas *Lon* 99-01; C Kilburn St Mary w All So and W Hampstead St Jas 01-02; V Finsbury St Clem w St Barn and St Matt from 02; Chapl Moorfields Eye Hosp NHS Trust from 04. *St Clement's Vicarage, King Square, London EC1V 8DA* Tel (020) 7251 0706 E-mail davideallen@blueyonder.co.uk

ALLEN, Derek. b 57. MCIOB89. **d** 99 **p** 00. OLM Bacup Ch Ch *Man* 99-04; OLM Bacup and Stacksteads from 04. *180 New Line, Bacup OL13 9RU* Tel (01706) 875960 E-mail allen.newline@cwcom.net

ALLEN, Canon Francis Arthur Patrick. b 26. Em Coll Saskatoon Div Test52. **d** 51 **p** 52. Canada 51-57; C Bishopwearmouth St Nic *Dur* 57-59; Japan 59-63; Hon Can Kobe from 63; V Kingston upon Hull St Matt *York* 63-67; Australia from 67; rtd 91. *136 High Street, Morpeth, NSW, Australia 2321* Tel (0061) (2) 4934 7049

ALLEN, Frank Brian. b 47. K Coll Lon BD AKC71. **d** 71 **p** 72. C Leam Lane *Dur* 71-74; C Tynemouth Ch Ch *Newc* 74-78; Chapl Preston Hosp N Shields 74-78; Chapl Newc Poly *Newc* 78-84; V Newc St Hilda 84-88; Chapl Nottm Mental Illness and Psychiatric Unit 88-89; Chapl for Mental Health Newc Mental Health Unit 89-94; Chapl Newc City Health NHS Trust 94-96; Chapl Team Leader from 96; Visiting Fell Newc Univ *Newc* from 96. *Trust Chaplaincy Centre, St Nicholas Hospital, Gosforth, Newcastle upon Tyne NE3 3XT* Tel 0191-273 6666 ext 28465 Fax 232 2840 E-mail brian_allen63@hotmail.com *or* brian.allen@nmht.nhs.uk

ALLEN, The Ven Geoffrey Gordon. b 39. Sarum Th Coll 64. **d** 66 **p** 67. C Langley Marish *Ox* 66-70; Miss to Seamen 70-82; Chapl Rotterdam w Schiedam *Eur* 78-82; Asst Chapl The Hague 84-93; Chapl Voorschoten 84-93; Can Brussels Cathl from 89; Adn NW Eur and Chapl E Netherlands 93-04; P-in-c Haarlem 95-02; rtd 04. *Hans Brandts Buyslaan 22, 6952 BK Dieren, The Netherlands* Tel (0031) (313) 412533 E-mail geoffrey@archdeacon.demon.nl

ALLEN, Giles David. b 70. RCM BMus91. Coll of Resurr Mirfield 92. **d** 95 **p** 96. C Palmers Green St Jo *Lon* 95-99; V Lund *Blackb* from 99. *Lund Vicarage, Church Lane, Clifton, Preston PR4 0ZE* Tel (01772) 683617 E-mail giles@lund18.freeserve.co.uk

ALLEN, Gordon Richard. b 29. St Jo Coll Dur BA54 DipTh55 MA58. **d** 55 **p** 56. C N Meols *Liv* 55-58; Uganda 58-63; V Lathom *Liv* 64-68; USA from 68; rtd 94. *237 Emery's Bridge Road, South Berwick, ME 03908, USA*

ALLEN, Hugh Edward. b 47. Sarum & Wells Th Coll 79. **d** 81 **p** 82. C Frome St Jo *B & W* 81-85; R Old Cleeve, Leighland and Treborough 85-97; RD Exmoor 92-97; P-in-c The Stanleys *Glouc* 97-99. *3 Norden's Meadow, Wiveliscombe, Taunton TA4 2JW* Tel (01984) 623078

ALLEN, Mrs Jacqueline Lesley. b 54. EMMTC 99. **d** 02 **p** 03. NSM Huthwaite *S'well* from 02. *63 Main Street, Huthwaite, Sutton-in-Ashfield NG17 2LQ* Tel (01623) 479680 Mobile 07956-050446 E-mail jackie@serv77.netscapeonline.com

ALLEN, Jamie. *See* ALLEN, Timothy James

ALLEN, Mrs Jane Rosemary. b 39. Cartrefle Coll of Educn BA83 PGCE84. St As & Ban Minl Tr Course 99. **d** 00 **p** 01. C Llandudno *Ban* 00-05; TV from 05. *The Wyngarth, 11 Abbey Road, Llandudno LL30 2EE* Tel (01492) 860531 E-mail revmil@hotmail.com

ALLEN, John Catling. b 25. Leeds Univ BA50. Coll of Resurr Mirfield 50. **d** 52 **p** 53. C Knowle H Nativity *Bris* 52-54; C De Beauvoir Town St Pet *Lon* 54-57; C Beckenham St Barn *Roch* 57-60; V Orpington St Andr 60-66; V Linc St Jo *Linc* 66-84; C Tynemouth Ch Ch w H Trin *Newc* 85-87; C N Shields 87-89; rtd 89; Hon C Gt and Lt Torrington and Frithelstock *Ex* from 89. *7 St Barnabas, The Beauchamp Community, Newland, Malvern WR13 5AX* Tel (01684) 899390

ALLEN, John Clement. b 32. K Coll Lon 54. **d** 58 **p** 59. C Middlesbrough St Martin *York* 58-60; C Northallerton w Kirby Sigston 60-64; V Larkfield *Roch* 64-70; R Ash 70-79; R Ridley 70-79; RD Cobham 76-79; R Chislehurst St Nic 79-97; rtd 97; Perm to Offic *Sarum* from 97. *The Peppergarth, 9 Lane Fox Terrace, Penny Street, Sturminster Newton DT10 1DE* Tel (01258) 473754

ALLEN, The Very Revd John Edward. b 32. Univ Coll Ox BA56 MA63 Fitzw Coll Cam BA68. Westcott Ho Cam 66. **d** 68 **p** 69. C Deal St Leon *Cant* 68-71; P-in-c Clifton St Paul *Bris* 71-78; Chapl Bris Univ 71-78; P-in-c Chippenham St Andr w Tytherton Lucas 78-82; Provost Wakef 82-97; rtd 97; Perm to Offic *York* from 98. *The Glebe Barn, Main Street, Sawdon, Scarborough YO13 9DY* Tel (01723) 859854

ALLEN, John Michael. b 27. Cuddesdon Coll 71. **d** 72 **p** 73. C Shrewsbury St Giles *Lich* 72-75; V Hengoed w Gobowen 75-82; V Burghill *Heref* 82-85; RD Heref Rural 83-85; TV Bracknell *Ox* 85-92; rtd 92; Perm to Offic *Heref* 93-05. *4 Denehyrst Court, York Road, Guildford GU1 4EA* Tel (01483) 569623

ALLEN, Mrs Kathleen. b 46. N Ord Course 88. **d** 91 **p** 94. NSM Colne H Trin *Blackb* 91-94; NSM Colne Ch Ch 94-98; NSM Colne and Villages from 98. *St Mary's Vicarage, Burnley Road, Trawden, Colne BB8 8PN* Tel and fax (01282) 864046 E-mail kathleen@k-allen.fsnet.co.uk

ALLEN, Malcolm. b 60. Open Th Coll BA00. Trin Coll Bris 94. **d** 96 **p** 97. C Skirbeck H Trin *Linc* 96-00; TV Cheltenham St Mark *Glouc* from 00. *St Barnabas' Vicarage, 152 Alstone Lane, Cheltenham GL51 8HL* Tel and fax (01242) 694203 E-mail malcolmallen@blueyonder.co.uk

ALLEN, Michael Edward Gerald. b 26. Selw Coll Cam BA50 MA53. Chich Th Coll 50. **d** 52 **p** 53. C Farncombe *Guildf* 52-56; R Bentley 56-60; V Baswich *Lich* 60-75; V Highbrook and W Hoathly *Chich* 75-91; RD Cuckfield 77-88; rtd 91; Perm to Offic *Chich* from 91. *Flat 2, 13 St John's Road, Eastbourne BN20 7NQ* Tel (01323) 728240

ALLEN, Michael Stephen. b 37. Nottm Univ BA60. Cranmer Hall Dur 60. **d** 62 **p** 63. C Sandal St Helen *Wakef* 62-66; Hon C Tile Cross *Birm* 66-70; V 72-84; Hon C Bletchley *Ox* 70-72; Vice-Prin Aston Tr Scheme 84-91; Hon C Boldmere *Birm* 85-91; P-in-c Easton w Colton and Marlingford *Nor* 91-93; Local Min Officer 91-93; Dioc Adv in Adult Educn *S'well* 93-02; rtd 02; Perm to Offic *S'well* from 02. *8 Grenville Rise, Arnold, Nottingham NG5 8EW* Tel 0115-967 9515 E-mail msa@amd.fsnet.co.uk

ALLEN, Noel Stephen (Brother Noel). b 38. OAM05. Kelham Th Coll 58. **d** 63 **p** 64. C Nuneaton St Mary *Cov* 63-67; Brotherhood of Gd Shep Australia from 67; P-in-c Tennant Creek 68-75; C Darwin Cathl 75-81; R Alice Springs 81-85; R Fred's Pass 85-89; Can Darwin 86-89; Chapl Qu Eliz Hosp from 90. *12 Francis Street, Peterhead, S Australia 5016* Tel (0061) (8) 8242 2645 E-mail nsallen@esc.net.au *or* noel.allen@nwahs.sa.gov.au

ALLEN, Patricia. *See* LEWER ALLEN, Mrs Patricia

ALLEN, Patrick Charles Benedict. b 55. Ex Univ 79. St Steph Ho Ox 83 SSC87. **d** 86 **p** 87. C Bethnal Green St Matt w St Jas the Gt *Lon* 86-90; C Kenton 90-92; V Plumstead St Nic *S'wark* 92-94; In RC Ch 94-97; Asst to RD Battersea 97-98; P-in-c Lavender Hill Ascension 97-00; P-in-c Battersea St Pet and St Paul 97-98; P-in-c Battersea St Phil w St Bart 98-00; V Lavender Hill Ascension etc from 00. *The Clergy House, Pountney Road, London SW11 5TU* Tel and fax (020) 7228 5340 *or* tel 7622 1929 E-mail patrickallen@clergyhouse.fsnet.co.uk

ALLEN, Peter Henry. b 34. Nottm Univ BA66. Kelham Th Coll 58. **d** 66 **p** 67. C Salisbury St Martin *Sarum* 66-70; C Melksham 70-73; C Paignton Ch Ch *Ex* 73-76; P-in-c W Holloway St Dav *Lon* 76-77; V Barnsbury St Dav w St Clem 77-84; P-in-c Brentford St Faith 84-87; TV Brentford 87-91; TV Catford (Southend) and Downham *S'wark* 91-01; rtd 01. *17 Mayfield Road, Belvedere DA17 6DX* Tel 07939-580266 (mobile)

ALLEN, Peter John. b 34. Leic Coll of Educn CertEd74 Leic Univ BEd75 MA79. EAMTC 89. **d** 92 **p** 93. NSM Ketton w Tinwell *Pet* 92-94; NSM Easton on the Hill, Collyweston w Duddington etc 94-96; Chapl St Pet Via del Mar Chile 96-99; NSM Culworth w Sulgrave and Thorpe Mandeville etc *Pet* 00-04; rtd 04. *18 Scythe Road, Daventry NN11 0WN* Tel (01327) 300596 E-mail peterjallen@tinyworld.co.uk

ALLEN, Canon Peter John Douglas. b 35. Jes Coll Cam BA61 MA64 PGCE67. Westcott Ho Cam 60. **d** 62 **p** 63. C Wyken *Cov* 62-65; USA 65-66; Chapl Jes Coll Cam 66-72; Chapl K Sch Cant 72-87; Hon Min Can Cant Cathl *Cant* 73-87; Second Master and Sen Chapl Sedbergh Sch Cumbria 87-93; P-in-c Edin St Ninian *Edin* from 93; Prec and Can St Mary's Cathl from 94; Tutor Edin Th Coll 94-01; Chapl Edin Academy from 99; Chapl Fettes Coll Edin from 02. *12A Grosvenor Crescent, Edinburgh EH12 5EL* Tel 0131-337 0027 E-mail pa@cathedral.net

ALLEN, Peter Richard. b 62. Qu Coll Birm BA04. **d** 04 **p** 05. C Hackenthorpe *Sheff* from 04. *5 Grassington Drive, Hackenthorpe, Sheffield S12 4NE* Tel 0114-248 9941 E-mail prallen3@yahoo.co.uk

ALLEN, Philip Gerald. b 48. Lon Univ DipTh71. Trin Coll Bris 71. **d** 73 **p** 74. C Portsea St Luke *Portsm* 73-75; C-in-c 75-79; C Southsea St Jude 75-79; P-in-c Gatten St Paul 79-85; V from 85. *St Paul's Vicarage, St Paul's Crescent, Shanklin PO37 7AW* Tel (01983) 862027

ALLEN, Richard James. b 46. Wells Th Coll 69. **d** 71 **p** 72. C Upholland *Liv* 71-75; TV 76-79; TV Padgate 79-85; V Weston-super-Mare St Andr Bournville *B & W* 85-93; V Williton from 93; Chapl Taunton and Somerset NHS Trust from 93. *The Vicarage, 16 Bridge Street, Williton, Taunton TA4 4NR* Tel (01984) 632626 E-mail vicar@dickallen.freeserve.co.uk

ALLEN, Richard John Slaney. b 54. **d** 00 **p** 01. NSM Tooting All SS *S'wark* 00-04; Asst Chapl SW Lon and St George's Mental Health NHS Trust 03-05; NSM Streatham Ch Ch *S'wark* from 05; NSM Streatham Hill St Marg from 05. *9 Roman Rise, London SE19 1JG* Tel (020) 8761 3968

ALLEN, Richard Lee. b 41. Liv Inst of Educn TCert67. N Ord Course 80. **d** 83 **p** 84. NSM Colne Ch Ch *Blackb* 83-90; P-in-c Trawden 91-98; NSM Colne and Villages from 98; Chapl Burnley Health Care NHS Trust 99-03; Chapl E Lancs Hosps NHS Trust from 03. *St Mary's Vicarage, Burnley Road, Trawden, Colne BB8 8PN* Tel and fax (01282) 864046

ALLEN, Roger Charles Brews. b 44. Solicitor 77 Loughb Univ BTech66. LNSM course 89. **d** 92 **p** 93. OLM S Elmham and Ilketshall *St E* 92-95; OLM Bungay H Trin w St Mary from 95. *33A Earsham Street, Bungay NR35 1AF* Tel (01986) 896927 E-mail rallen@zetnet.co.uk

ALLEN, Roy Vernon. b 43. Open Univ BA81 Birm Univ MA84. Sarum Th Coll 67. **d** 70 **p** 71. C Hall Green Ascension *Birm* 70-74; V Temple Balsall 74-78; P-in-c Smethwick St Steph 78-81; V Smethwick St Mich 78-81; V Smethwick SS Steph and Mich 81-86; V Marston Green from 86. *The Vicarage, Elmdon Road, Birmingham B37 7BT* Tel 0121-779 2492 E-mail roy_v_allen@hotmail.com

ALLEN, Canon Steven. b 49. Nottm Univ BA73. St Jo Coll Nottm 73. **d** 75 **p** 76. C Gt Horton *Bradf* 75-80; V 89-02; V Upper Armley *Ripon* 80-89; RD Bowling and Horton *Bradf* 98-02; Hon Can Bradf Cathl from 00; Dioc Tr Officer from 02. *48 Toller Grove, Bradford BD9 5NP* Tel (01274) 482059 E-mail steve.allen@bradford.anglican.org

ALLEN, Stuart Philip. b 73. St Cath Coll Ox BA95. Oak Hill Th Coll BA02. **d** 02 **p** 03. C Burford w Fulbrook, Taynton, Asthall etc *Ox* from 02. *6 Orchard Row, Fulbrook, Burford OX18 4BT* Tel (01993) 824484 E-mail stuartpallen@yahoo.co.uk

ALLEN, Mrs Susan Rosemary. b 47. Warwick Univ BSc68 Trevelyan Coll Dur PGCE69. Sarum Th Coll 93. **d** 96 **p** 97. C Goldsworth Park *Guildf* 96-01; TV Hemel Hempstead *St Alb* from 01. *33 Craigavon Road, Hemel Hempstead HP2 6BA* Tel (01442) 270585 E-mail revsue@fish.co.uk

ALLEN, Thomas Davidson. b 49. QUB BA. CITC 81. **d** 84 **p** 85. C Magheralin w Dollingstown *D & D* 84-86; I Kilwarlin Upper w Kilwarlin Lower 86-91; I Maghera w Killelagh *D & R* 91-03; I Donaghcloney w Waringstown *D & D* from 03. *The Rectory, 54 Banbridge Road, Waringstown, Craigavon BT66 7QD* Tel (028) 3888 1218 E-mail tallen@talk21.com

ALLEN, Thomas Henry. b 42. N Ord Course 87. **d** 90 **p** 91. C Upholland *Liv* 90-93; TV Walton-on-the-Hill from 93. *51 Queens Drive, Walton, Liverpool L4 6SF* Tel 0151-521 5276 E-mail vicar@staidanswalton.org.uk

ALLEN, Timothy James. b 71. Warwick Univ BA93. Ripon Coll Cuddesdon BTh99. **d** 99 **p** 00. C Nuneaton St Mary *Cov* 99-02; V Seend, Bulkington and Poulshot *Sarum* 02-03. *Address temp unknown* E-mail jamie@boofuls.co.uk

ALLEN, Tom Giles. b 57. Hull Univ BA78 Westhill Coll Birm 84. Carl and Blackb Dioc Tr Inst. **d** 98 **p** 99. C Mirfield *Wakef* 98-01; V Oakworth *Bradf* from 01. *The Vicarage, 18 Sunhurst Drive, Oakworth, Keighley BD22 7RG* Tel (01535) 648496

ALLEN, Zachary Edward. b 52. Warwick Univ BA74. Ripon Coll Cuddesdon 78. **d** 81 **p** 82. C Bognor *Chich* 81-84; C Rusper and Roughey 84-86; TV Carl H Trin and St Barn *Carl* 86-90; Chapl Strathclyde Ho Hosp Carl 86-90; V Findon w Clapham and Patching *Chich* 90-01; V Rustington from 01. *The Vicarage, Claigmar Road, Rustington, Littlehampton BN16 2NL* Tel (01903) 784749

ALLEYNE, Sir John Olpherts Campbell, Bt. b 28. Jes Coll Cam BA50 MA55. **d** 55 **p** 56. C Southampton St Mary w H Trin *Win* 55-58; Chapl Cov Cathl *Cov* 58-62; Chapl Clare Hall Cam 62-66; Chapl Bris Cathl *Bris* 66-68; Area Sec (SW England) Toc H 68-71; V Speke All SS *Liv* 71-73; TR Speke St Aid 73-76; R Win St Matt *Win* 76-93; rtd 93; Perm to Offic *Guildf* from 93. *2 Ash Grove, Guildford GU2 8UT* Tel (01483) 573824

ALLFORD, Judith Mary. b 55. Sheff Univ BA Lon Univ BD. Trin Coll Bris 77. **dss** 86 **d** 87 **p** 94. Par Dn Deptford St Jo w H Trin *S'wark* 87-91; Asst Chapl Dulwich Hosp 91-93; Asst Chapl K Coll Hosp Lon 91-95; Asst Chapl King's Healthcare NHS Trust 93-95; Chapl St Pet's Hosp NHS Trust Chertsey from 95. *St Peter's Hospital, Guildford Road, Chertsey KT16 0PZ* Tel (01932) 872000 ext 3324 E-mail shirley.sikora@stph.tr.sthames.nhs.uk

ALLIES, Lorna. **d** 05. OLM Thurton *Nor* from 05. *Gull Meadow, Gull Lane, Framingham Earl, Norwich NR14 7PH* Tel (01508) 493867

ALLIN, Philip Ronald. b 43. Reading Univ MA96 Birm Univ CQSW. Lich Th Coll 71. **d** 71 **p** 72. C Sutton in Ashfield St Mary *S'well* 71-74; Chapl to Sutton Cen 74-76; Lic to Offic 74-76; P-in-c Grove 76-77; R Ordsall 76-80; V Mansfield St Mark 81-83; TR Hermitage and Hampstead Norreys, Cold Ash etc *Ox* 83-96; OCF 83-96; Chapl Nine o'clock Service *Sheff* 96-03; rtd 03. *352 Crookesmoor Road, Sheffield S10 1BH* Tel 0114-266 4463

ALLINGTON, Andrew William. b 57. ACA81 Sheff Univ BA78. Cranmer Hall Dur BA95. **d** 95 **p** 96. C Clifton *York* 95-99; P-in-c Stainforth *Sheff* 99-02; V from 02. *The Vicarage, Field Road, Stainforth, Doncaster DN7 5AQ* Tel (01302) 841295 E-mail allingtonandrew@hotmail.com

ALLINGTON-SMITH, Canon Richard. b 28. Lon Univ BA49 MA52. Wells Th Coll 54. **d** 56 **p** 57. C Milton next Gravesend Ch Ch *Roch* 56-61; R Cuxton 61-67; V Rainham 67-79; V Gt Yarmouth *Nor* 79-89; TR 89-91; Hon Can Nor Cathl 86-98; rtd 91; P-in-c Nor St Andr *Nor* 91-98; Perm to Offic from 98. *14 Yare Court, 22A Yarmouth Road, Norwich NR7 0EF* Tel (01603) 437185

ALLINSON, Capt Paul Timothy. b 63. CA Tr Coll 82 Edin Th Coll 89. **d** 91 **p** 92. C Peterlee *Dur* 91-94; C Shadforth and Sherburn w Pittington 94-97; P-in-c Byers Green 97-04; P-in-c Seaton Carew from 04; Dioc Children's Adv from 94. *The Vicarage, 5 Crawford Street, Seaton Carew, Hartlepool TS25 1UT* Tel 07888-726535 (mobile) E-mail revdpaul@lineone.net

ALLISON, Elliott Desmond. b 36. Univ of S Africa BA64 K Coll Lon MTh74. S Africa Federal Th Coll. **d** 69 **p** 70. *Flat 1, 20 Southview Gardens, Worthing BN11 5JA*

ALLISON, James Timothy. b 61. Man Univ BSc83. Oak Hill Th Coll BA89. **d** 89 **p** 90. C Walkden Moor *Man* 89-93; Chapl Huddersfield Univ *Wakef* 93-98; V Erringden from 98. *The Vicarage, Brier Hey Lane, Mytholmroyd, Hebden Bridge HX7 5PJ* Tel (01422) 883130 E-mail erringden@aol.com

ALLISON, Keith. b 34. Dur Univ BA59. Ely Th Coll 59. **d** 61 **p** 62. C Sculcoates *York* 61-64; C Stainton-in-Cleveland 64-65; C Leeds St Pet *Ripon* 65-70; V Micklefield *York* 70-74; V Appleton-le-Street w Amotherby 74-78; P-in-c Barton le Street 77-78; P-in-c Salton 77-80; R Amotherby w Appleton and Barton-le-Street 78-82; Chapl Lister Hosp Stevenage 82-90; P-in-c

St Ippolyts *St Alb* 82-85; V 85-90; Chapl Hitchin Hosp 86-90; Chapl Shotley Bridge Gen Hosp 90-94; Chapl NW Dur HA 90-94; Sen Chapl N Dur Acute Hosps NHS Trust 94-98; Sen Chapl N Dur Healthcare NHS Trust 98-00; rtd 00. *2 Middlewood Road, Lanchester, Durham DH7 0HL* Tel (01207) 529046

ALLISON, Michael John. b 33. Leeds Univ BSc97 ATI58. Wilson Carlile Coll 05. **d** 05. NSM Windhill *Bradf* from 05. *33 Busy Lane, Shipley BD18 1DX* Tel (01274) 587194 E-mail mjohn.allison@shipley33.freeserve.co.uk

ALLISTER, The Ven Donald Spargo. b 52. Peterho Cam BA74 MA77. Trin Coll Bris 74. **d** 76 **p** 77. C Hyde St Geo *Ches* 76-79; C Sevenoaks St Nic *Roch* 79-83; V Birkenhead Ch Ch *Ches* 83-89; R Cheadle 89-02; RD Cheadle 99-02; Adn Ches from 02. *The Rectory, Chester Road, Delamere, Northwich CW8 2HS* Tel (01606) 882184 Fax 301911 E-mail donald.allister@chester.anglican.org

ALLISTON, Cyril John. b 11. Fitzw Ho Cam BA33 MA37. Cuddesdon Coll 33. **d** 35 **p** 36. C Boyne Hill *Ox* 35-37; C Hessle *York* 37-39; Chapl S African Ch Railway Miss 40-50; C-in-c Miri Sarawak 50-52; R Jesselton and Adn N Borneo 52-59; Can Kuching 55-59; R Somersham w Pidley and Colne *Ely* 60-63; V Penponds *Truro* 63-70; R Hermanus St Pet S Africa 71-76; rtd 76. *Flat 4, Kogelpark, Kleinmond, 7195 South Africa* Tel (0027) (28) 271 3168

ALLMAN, Mrs Susan. b 56. Bris Univ BA77. WEMTC 93. **d** 96 **p** 97. NSM Henleaze *Bris* 96-99; C Southmead 99-02; V Two Mile Hill St Mich from 02. *St Michael's Vicarage, Two Mile Hill, Bristol BS15 1BE* Tel 0117-967 1371

ALLMARK, Leslie. b 48. Open Univ BA90. Man OLM Scheme 98. **d** 01 **p** 02. OLM Halliwell St Luke *Man* from 01. *75 Crosby Road, Bolton BL1 4EJ* Tel (01204) 845795 E-mail leslie@lallmark.freeserve.co.uk

ALLON-SMITH, Roderick David. b 51. Leic Univ BA PhD Cam Univ MA. Ridley Hall Cam 79. **d** 82 **p** 83. C Kinson *Sarum* 82-86; V Westwood *Cov* 86-96; RD Cov S 92-96; P-in-c Radford Semele 96-04; Dioc Dir Par Development and Evang 01-03; Dioc Missr *Dur* from 04. *5 Beechways, Durham DH1 4LG* Tel 0191-384 4330 E-mail allonsmith@bigfoot.com

ALLPORT, David Jack. b 55. Ox Univ BA MEd. Qu Coll Birm 78. **d** 80 **p** 81. C Abingdon w Shippon *Ox* 80-83; C-in-c Woodgate Valley CD *Birm* 83-91; Perm to Offic *Lich* from 91. *122 Cherry Tree Avenue, Walsall WS5 4JL* Tel (01922) 640059

ALLRED, Frank. b 23. Tyndale Hall Bris 62. **d** 64 **p** 65. C Halliwell St Pet *Man* 64-67; V Ravenhead *Liv* 67-75; R Chadwell *Chelmsf* 75-82; TV Heworth H Trin *York* 82-86; rtd 87; Perm to Offic *York* from 87. *12 Viking Road, Bridlington YO16 6TW* Tel (01262) 677321

ALLSO, Michael Neal. b 48. FRICS72 MCIArb73 MAE00. SW Minl Tr Course 95. **d** 98 **p** 99. NSM Ex St Thos and Em *Ex* 98-01; NSM Colyton, Southleigh, Offwell, Widworthy etc 01-03; NSM Colyton, Musbury, Southleigh and Branscombe 03-04; C Widecombe-in-the-Moor, Leusdon, Princetown etc from 04. *The Vicarage, Widecombe-in-the-Moor, Newton Abbot TQ13 7TF* Tel (01364) 621334 E-mail frmichaelallso@aol.com

ALLSOP, Anthony James. b 37. AKC62. **d** 63 **p** 64. C Leytonstone St Marg w St Columba *Chelmsf* 63-68; V Gt Ilford St Alb 68-80; V Gainsborough St Jo *Linc* 80-85; V Hockerill *St Alb* 85-02; Chapl Herts and Essex Hosp Bp's Stortford 85-95; Chapl Essex and Herts Community NHS Trust 95-01; Chapl N Essex Mental Health Partnership NHS Trust 01-02; rtd 02; Perm to Offic *Ches* from 03. *63 Longdown Road, Congleton CW12 4QH* Tel (01260) 280628

ALLSOP, Mrs Beryl Anne. b 45. EMMTC 94. **d** 97 **p** 98. NSM Clipstone *S'well* 97-00; NSM Blidworth w Rainworth from 00. *The Vicarage, 2 Kirks Croft, Blidworth, Mansfield NG21 0QU* Tel (01623) 792306 E-mail beryl@faithfulfish.co.uk

ALLSOP, David George. b 48. Wycliffe Hall Ox. **d** 99 **p** 00. C Chenies and Lt Chalfont, Latimer and Flaunden *Ox* 99-02; P-in-c from 02. *The Rectory, Chenies, Rickmansworth WD3 6ER* Tel (01923) 284433 Mobile 07818-441431 E-mail dgaera@aol.com

ALLSOP, Patrick Leslie Fewtrell. b 52. Fitzw Coll Cam BA74 MA78. Ripon Coll Cuddesdon BA78 MA83. **d** 79 **p** 80. C Barrow St Matt *Carl* 79-82; Chapl Eton Coll 82-88; Chapl K Sch Roch 89-02; Hon PV Roch Cathl *Roch* 89-97; Chapl St Paul's Sch Barnes from 02. *St Paul's School, Lonsdale Road, London SW13 9JT* Tel (020) 8748 9162

ALLSOP, Peter William. b 33. Kelham Th Coll 58. **d** 58 **p** 59. C Woodford St Barn *Chelmsf* 58-61; C Upholland *Liv* 61-65; V Wigan St Geo 65-71; P-in-c Marham *Ely* 71-72; TV Fincham 72-76; V Trawden *Blackb* 76-90; C Marton 90-92; C S Shore H Trin 92-98; rtd 98; Perm to Offic *Blackb* from 98. *31 Lomond Avenue, Blackpool FY3 9QL* Tel (01253) 696624 E-mail peter.w.allsop@amserve.net

ALLSOPP, The Ven Christine. b 47. Aston Univ BSc68. S Dios Minl Tr Scheme 86. **d** 89 **p** 94. C Caversham St Pet and Mapledurham etc *Ox* 89-94; C Bracknell 94; TV 94-98; P-in-c Bourne Valley *Sarum* 98-00; TR 00-05; RD Alderbury 99-05; Can and Preb Sarum Cathl 02-05; Adn Northn *Pet* from 05; Can Pet Cathl from 05. *11 The Drive, Northampton NN1 4RZ* Tel (01604) 714015 Fax 792016 E-mail archdeacon@aofn.wanadoo.co.uk

ALLSOPP, Mark Dennis. b 66. Cuddesdon Coll 93. **d** 96 **p** 97. C Hedworth *Dur* 96-98; C Gt Aycliffe 98-00; TV Gt Aycliffe and Chilton 00-04; P-in-c Kirklevington *York* from 04; P-in-c High and Low Worsall from 04; Chapl HM YOI Kirklevington Grange from 04. *49 Ash Grove, Kirklevington, Yarm TS15 9NQ* Tel (01642) 782245 E-mail mark@dallsopp.fsworld.co.uk

ALLSOPP, Mrs Patricia Ann. b 48. St Mary's Coll Chelt CertEd69. Qu Coll Birm. **d** 00 **p** 01. C Upton-on-Severn, Ripple, Earls Croome etc *Worc* 00-04; P-in-c Finstall 04-05; V from 05. *The Vicarage, 15 Finstall Road, Bromsgrove B60 2EA* Tel (01527) 872459 E-mail tricia@easynet.co.uk

ALLSOPP, Stephen Robert. b 50. BSc71 MSc72 PhD75. Mon Dioc Tr Scheme 81. **d** 84 **p** 85. NSM Trevethin *Mon* 84-88; Asst Chapl K Sch Roch from 88; Hon PV Roch Cathl *Roch* from 89; Chapl K Prep Sch Roch from 99. *33 St Margarets Street, Rochester ME1 1UF* Tel (01634) 409878 E-mail stephen@theallsopps.freeserve.co.uk

ALLSWORTH, Peter Thomas. b 44. St Mich Coll Llan 93. **d** 93 **p** 94. C Prestatyn *St As* 93-96; V Esclusham from 96. *The Vicarage, Vicarage Hill, Rhostyllen, Wrexham LL14 4AR* Tel (01978) 354438

ALLTON, Canon Paul Irving. b 38. Man Univ BA60. **d** 63 **p** 64. C Kibworth Beauchamp *Leic* 63-66; C Reading St Mary V *Ox* 66-70; R Caston *Nor* 70-75; R Caston w Griston, Mert and Thompson 70-75; P-in-c Sturston w Thompson and Tottington 70-75; V Holme-next-the-Sea 75-80; V Hunstanton St Mary w Lt Ringstead 75-80; V Hunstanton St Mary w Ringstead Parva, Holme etc 80-85; RD Heacham and Rising 81-85; Hon Can Nor Cathl 85-93; TR Lowestoft and Kirkley 85-93; TR Keynsham *B & W* 93-96; TR Gaywood *Nor* 96-01; rtd 01; Perm to Offic *Nor* from 01. *Chalk Bank, Herrings Lane, Burnham Market, King's Lynn PE31 8DW* Tel (01328) 738341

ALLUM, Jeremy Warner. b 32. Wycliffe Hall Ox 60. **d** 62 **p** 63. C Hornchurch St Andr *Chelmsf* 62-67; P-in-c W Derby St Luke *Liv* 67-69; V 69-75; P-in-c Boulton *Derby* 75-90; RD Melbourne 86-90; V Hathersage 90-98; rtd 98; Perm to Offic *Derby* from 98. *32 Sandown Avenue, Mickleover, Derby DE3 0QQ* Tel (01332) 231253

ALLWOOD, Linda Angela Fredrika. b 76. Newc Univ BA00. Cranmer Hall Dur 01. **d** 03 **p** 04. C Northampton St Giles *Pet* from 03. *18 The Avenue, Cliftonville, Northampton NN1 5BT* Tel (01604) 632489 Mobile 07939-001160 E-mail linda_allwood@hotmail.com

ALLWRIGHT, Mrs Janet Margaret. b 40. Oak Hill Th Coll 87. **d** 90 **p** 94. NSM Galleywood Common *Chelmsf* 90-93; NSM Downham w S Hanningfield 93-99; Chapl HM Pris Bullwood Hall 98-03; TV Canvey Is *Chelmsf* from 03. *St Katherine's House, 17 The Ridings, Canvey Island SS8 9QZ* Tel (01268) 681318 E-mail revdjanet@supanet.com

ALMOND, Kenneth Alfred. b 36. EMMTC 76 Linc Th Coll 78. **d** 79 **p** 80. C Boston *Linc* 79-82; V Surfleet 82-87; RD Elloe W 86-96; V Spalding St Jo w Deeping St Nicholas 87-98; rtd 98; Perm to Offic *Linc* from 99. *1 Buckingham Close, Fishtoft, Boston PE21 9QB* Tel and fax (01205) 352805 E-mail ken.hilary@btopenworld.com

ALP, Mrs Elaine Alison. b 54. Oak Hill Th Coll 87. **d** 00. Dn-in-c Blackb St Mich w St Jo and H Trin *Blackb* 00-02; Par Dn Fleetwood St Nic from 02. *15 Leighton Avenue, Fleetwood FY7 8BP* Tel (01253) 777775

ALPIAR, Ronald. b 29. Pemb Coll Cam BA52. Ely Th Coll 52. **d** 54 **p** 55. C Plaistow St Andr *Chelmsf* 54-56; SSF 54-57; rtd 79. *84 Dudsbury Road, Ferndown BH22 8RG* Tel (01202) 590314

ALSBURY, Colin. b 56. Ch Ch Ox BA77 MA81. Ripon Coll Cuddesdon 77. **d** 80 **p** 81. C Oxton *Ches* 80-84; V Crewe All SS and St Paul 84-92; Ind Chapl 92-95; V Kettering St Andr *Pet* 95-02; V Frome St Jo *B & W* from 02; V Woodlands from 02. *St John's Vicarage, Vicarage Close, Frome BA11 1QL* Tel (01373) 472853 E-mail colin.alsbury@zetnet.co.uk

ALSOP, Eric George. b 12. Liv Univ BA. Dorchester Miss Coll 34. **d** 37 **p** 38. C Grimsby All SS *Linc* 37-39; Chapl RAF 39-58; Asst Chapl-in-Chief RAF 58-67; QHC 65-67; V Over *Ely* 67-69; P-in-c Bodiam *Chich* 69-72; V Burwash Weald 72-77; rtd 77; Perm to Offic *Chich* 77-00; *Cant* from 90; *St Alb* from 00. *4 Windsor Road, Barton-le-Clay, Bedford MK45 4LX* Tel (01582) 881444

ALTHAM, Donald. b 40. Liv Univ BA62. N Ord Course 87. **d** 90 **p** 91. NSM Ramsbottom St Jo and St Paul *Man* 90-96; NSM Holcombe 99-04; NSM Walmersley from 04; NSM Bircle from 04; Chapl Asst Burnley Health Care NHS Trust 93-03; Chapl Asst E Lancs Hosps NHS Trust from 03. *387 Whalley Road, Ramsbottom, Bury BL0 0ER* Tel (01706) 822025

✠**ALVAREZ-VELAZQUEZ, The Rt Revd David Andres.** b 41. Inter American Univ Puerto Rico BA62 Caribbean Cen of Advanced Studies. NY Th Sem MDiv65. **d** 65 **p** 65 **c** 87. Puerto Rico from 65; C St Mich 65; Chapl Episc Cathl Sch 65-67; R

St Mark 67-70; R St Jo Cathl 70-79; R Trujillo Alto St Hilda 79-87; Bp Puerto Rico from 87. *PO Box 902, Saint Just Station, Saint Just, 00978, Puerto Rico* Tel (001) (787) 761 9800 Mobile 376 4125 Fax 761 0320 E-mail iep@spiderlinkpr.net

ALVEY, Martyn Clifford. b 53. EMMTC 96. **d** 99 **p** 00. NSM Burton Joyce w Bulcote and Stoke Bardolph *S'well* 99-02; C Worksop St Jo from 02; AD Worksop from 04. *27 Sunnyside, Worksop S81 7LN* Tel (01909) 473998 E-mail alvey@fish.co.uk

AMAT-TORREGROSA, Gabriel José. b 42. R Superior Coll of Music Madrid MA63. Bapt Th Sem Ruschlikon Zürich 64. **d** 71 **p** 72. Spain 71-98; Asst Chapl Zürich *Eur* from 98. *Lettenmattstrasse 33, 8903 Birmendsdorf, Switzerland* Tel (0041) (1) 737 4187 Fax 252 6042

AMBANI, Stephen Frederick. b 45. Univ of Wales (Lamp) BA90. St Jo Coll Nottm 86 CA Tr Coll Nairobi 70. **d** 83 **p** 83. Kenya 83-93; C Glan Ely *Llan* 93-95; C Whitchurch 95-97; V Nantymoel w Wyndham 97-99; V Tonyrefail w Gilfach Goch and Llandyfodwg 99-03; V Tonyrefail w Gilfach Goch 04; rtd 05. *96 High Street, Tonyrefail, Porth CF39 8PL* Tel (01443) 670330

AMBROSE, James Field. b 51. Newc Univ BA73. Cranmer Hall Dur DipTh80. **d** 80 **p** 81. C Barrow St Geo w St Luke *Carl* 80-83; C Workington St Jo 83-85; Ch Radio Officer BBC Radio Shropshire 85-88; R Montford w Shrawardine and Fitz *Lich* 85-88; Chapl RAF 88-92; Voc and Min Adv CPAS 92-99; TV Syston *Leic* from 99. *The Vicarage, 25 Ling Dale, East Goscote, Leicester LE7 8XW* Tel 0116-260 5938 E-mail jambrose@leicester.anglican.org

AMBROSE, John George. b 30. Lon Univ BD Ox Univ PGCE. **d** 74 **p** 75. C Rayleigh *Chelmsf* 74-79; V Hadleigh St Barn 79-95; rtd 95; Perm to Offic *Chelmsf* from 95. *9 Fairview Gardens, Leigh-on-Sea SS9 3PD* Tel (01702) 474632

AMBROSE, Thomas. b 47. Sheff Univ BSc69 PhD73 Em Coll Cam BA77 MA84. Westcott Ho Cam 75. **d** 78 **p** 79. C Morpeth *Newc* 78-81; C N Gosforth 81-84; R March St Jo *Ely* 84-93; RD March 89-93; P-in-c Witchford w Wentworth 93-99; Dioc Dir of Communications 93-99; Chapl K Sch Ely 94-96; V Trumpington *Ely* from 99. *The Vicarage, Grantchester Road, Trumpington, Cambridge CB2 2LH* Tel and fax (01223) 841262 Mobile 07711-263083 E-mail tom.ambrose@ely.anglican.org

AMELIA, Alison. b 67. Hull Univ BA03 St Jo Coll Dur BA05. Cranmer Hall Dur 03. **d** 05. C Nunthorpe *York* from 05. *15 Ripon Road, Nunthorpe, Middlesbrough TS7 0HX* Tel (01642) 325993 E-mail aamelia333@yahoo.com

AMES, Jeremy Peter. b 49. K Coll Lon BD71 AKC71. **d** 72 **p** 73. C Kennington St Jo *S'wark* 72-75; Chapl RN 75-04; rtd 04; Master St Nic Hosp Salisbury from 04. *The Master's House, St Nicholas Hospital, St Nicholas Road, Salisbury SP1 2SW* Tel (01722) 336874 E-mail cyberjpa@aol.com

AMES, Reginald John. b 27. Bps' Coll Cheshunt 51. **d** 54 **p** 55. C Edmonton St Alphege *Lon* 54-58; C Mill Hill Jo Keble Ch 58-60; P-in-c Northwood Hills St Edm 61-64; V 64-92; rtd 92; Hon C Moffat *Glas* 92-01. *Oakbank, Lochwood, Beattock, Moffat DG10 9PS* Tel (01683) 300381

AMES-LEWIS, Richard. b 45. Em Coll Cam BA66 MA70. Westcott Ho Cam 76. **d** 78 **p** 79. C Bromley St Mark *Roch* 78-81; C Edenbridge 81-84; V 84-91; P-in-c Crockham Hill H Trin 84-91; P-in-c Barnes St Mary *S'wark* 91-97; TR Barnes 97-00; RD Richmond and Barnes 94-00; TR E Dereham and Scarning *Nor* from 00; P-in-c Swanton Morley w Beetley w E Bilney and Hoe from 02; RD Dereham in Mitford from 03. *The Vicarage, 1 Vicarage Meadows, Dereham NR19 1TW* Tel (01362) 693680 *or* 693143 E-mail rameslew@fish.co.uk

AMEY, Graham George. b 44. Lon Univ BD70. Tyndale Hall Bris 67. **d** 71 **p** 72. C Hornsey Rise St Mary *Lon* 71-74; C St Helens St Helen *Liv* 74-79; V Liv All So Springwood 79-91; V Whiston 91-02; V Aigburth from 02. *St Anne's Vicarage, 389 Aigburth Road, Liverpool L17 6BH* Tel 0151-727 1101

AMEY, John Mark. b 59. Ripon Coll Cuddesdon 98. **d** 00 **p** 01. C Winchmore Hill St Paul *Lon* 00-04; V Sutton *Ely* from 04; R Witcham w Mepal from 04; Chapl ATC from 03. *The Vicarage, 7 Church Lane, Sutton, Ely CB6 2RQ* Tel (01353) 778645 Mobile 07905-122090 E-mail mark.amey@ely.anglican.org

AMIS, Ronald. b 37. Linc Th Coll 74. **d** 76 **p** 77. C Grantham w Manthorpe *Linc* 76-78; C Grantham 78-79; P-in-c Holbeach Hurn 79-81; V Long Bennington w Foston 81-91; V Corby Glen 91-93; RD Grantham 90-92; rtd 93; Perm to Offic *Pet* 93-03. *11 Green Street, Great Gonerby, Grantham NG31 8LD*

AMOAKO-ADU, Canon Seth Yaw. b 60. **d** 86 **p** 87. Koforidua 86-05; C Cottingham *York* from 05. *10 Kingtree Avenue, Cottingham HU16 4DD* Tel (01482) 840896

AMOR, Peter David Card. b 28. AKC53. **d** 54 **p** 55. C St Margaret's-on-Thames *Lon* 54; C Leighton Buzzard *St Alb* 54-58; C Toxteth Park St Agnes *Liv* 58-62; C-in-c Aldershot Ascension CD *Guildf* 62-65; V Bingley H Trin *Bradf* 65-72; V The Collingbournes *Sarum* 72-75; R The Collingbournes and Everleigh 75-77; V Thorpe *Guildf* 77-85; P-in-c Monks Risborough *Ox* 85-89; R 89-94; rtd 94; Perm to Offic *Ox* from 97. *1 Culverton Hill, Princes Risborough HP27 0DZ* Tel (01844) 345236

AMOS, Canon Alan John. b 44. OBE79. K Coll Lon BD66 MTh67 AKC67. St Steph Ho Ox 68. **d** 69 **p** 70. C Hoxton H Trin w St Mary *Lon* 69-72; Lebanon 73-82; Lect Liturg Studies Westcott Ho Cam 82-85; Vice-Prin 85-89; Prin Cant Sch of Min 89-94; Co-Prin SEITE 94-96; Hon PV Roch Cathl *Roch* from 95; Hon Can from 05; Chapl Medway NHS Trust from 96. *Medway Hospital, Windmill Road, Gillingham ME7 5NY* Tel (01634) 830000 ext 3561 Fax 815811

AMOS, Brother. *See* YONGE, James Mohun

AMOS, Colin James. b 62. Univ of Wales (Lamp) BA83 Univ of Wales (Cardiff) CQSW85. Ridley Hall Cam 93. **d** 93 **p** 94. C Aberdare *Llan* 93-96; V Port Talbot St Theodore from 96. *St Theodore's Vicarage, Talbot Road, Port Talbot SA13 1LB* Tel (01639) 883935 Fax 760104 E-mail fr.amos@ntlworld.com

AMOS, Patrick Henry. b 31. Roch Th Coll 63. **d** 65 **p** 66. C Strood St Nic *Roch* 65-68; C Polegate *Chich* 68-71; V Horam 71-83; R Chiddingly w E Hoathly 83-93; rtd 93; Perm to Offic *Cant* and *Roch* from 93; Clergy Widows' Officer (Maidstone Adnry) *Cant* from 95. *20 Fauchons Close, Bearsted, Maidstone ME14 4BB* Tel (01622) 736725

AMYES, Emma Charlotte. b 65. Redcliffe Coll BA01. Ridley Hall Cam. **d** 04 **p** 05. C Hucclecote *Glouc* from 04. *18 Millfields, Hucclecote, Gloucester GL3 3NH* Tel (01452) 371003 Mobile 07866-808635 E-mail emma.amyes@virgin.net

AMYES, Geoffrey Edmund. b 74. Bris Univ BSc96 Cam Univ BTh04. Ridley Hall Cam 01. **d** 04 **p** 05. C Hucclecote *Glouc* from 04. *18 Millfields, Hucclecote, Gloucester GL3 3NH* Tel (01452) 371003 Mobile 07792-519910 E-mail g.amyes@virgin.net

AMYS, Richard James Rutherford. b 58. Trin Coll Bris BA90. **d** 90 **p** 91. C Whitnash *Cov* 90-93; P-in-c Gravesend H Family w Ifield *Roch* 93-95; R 95-99; R Eastington, Frocester, Haresfield etc *Glouc* from 99. *The Rectory, Mill End Lane, Eastington, Stonehouse GL10 3SG* Tel and fax (01453) 822437 Mobile 07796-956050 E-mail richardjramys@aol.com

ANAN, Gabriel Jaja. b 48. Univ of E Lon MA96 MCIT92 Regents Th Coll BA92. NTMTC 00. **d** 03 **p** 04. NSM Victoria Docks St Luke *Chelmsf* from 03. *41 Camel Road, London E16 2DE* Tel (020) 7473 6003 Mobile 07734-707887 E-mail gabriel58@hotmail.com

ANAND, Jessie Nesam Nallammal. b 54. Madurai Univ BSc75 BEd76 Annamalai Univ MA84. Tamilnadu Th Sem BD91 New Coll Edin MTh94 EMMTC 02. **d** 03 **p** 04. NSM Birstall and Wanlip *Leic* 03-05; NSM Emmaus Par Team from 05. *St Alban's House, Weymouth Street, Leicester LE4 6FN* Tel 0116-266 1002 Mobile 07811-189358 E-mail jessieanand@yahoo.co.uk

ANAND, The Very Revd Sekar Anand Asir. b 53. Madurai Univ BSc75 Serampore Univ BD79 New Coll Edin MTh93 Annamalai Univ MA99. **d** 80 **p** 81. India 80-91 and 95-00; C Nayaith St Jo 80-82; R Tuticorin St Paul 82-84; Sec Tirunelveli Children's Miss 84-91; C Edin St Pet *Edin* 91-92; Hon C Burmantofts St Steph and St Agnes *Ripon* 92-93; C Edin St Mark *Edin* 93-95; Provost Palayamcottai Cathl 95-99; C Leic Resurr *Leic* from 00. *St Alban's Vicarage, Weymouth Street, Leicester LE4 6FN* Tel 0116-266 1002 E-mail anandjessie@yahoo.co.uk

ANCRUM, John. b 28. Clifton Th Coll 55. **d** 58 **p** 59. C Branksome St Clem *Sarum* 58-61; C Sparkhill St Jo *Birm* 61-63; V Tibshelf *Derby* 63-70; Canada 70-74; P-in-c Salwarpe *Worc* 74-75; P-in-c Tibberton w Bredicot and Warndon 75-76; P-in-c Hadzor w Oddingley 76-78; Lic to Offic *Chelmsf* 78-81; Chapl HM Pris Stafford 81-82; Chapl HM Pris Dartmoor 82-89; Lic to Offic *Ex* 88-89; rtd 89; Perm to Offic *Ex* from 89. *14 Merrivale View Road, Dousland, Yelverton PL20 6NS*

ANDAYI, Elphas Ombuna. b 57. St Phil Th Coll Maseno 78. **d** 79 **p** 81. Kenya 79-98 and from 99; Provost Butere 92-97; C Sparkhill w Greet and Sparkbrook *Birm* 98-99. *PO Box 199, Bukura, Kenya* Tel (00254) (333) 20038 Fax 20412

ANDERS, Mrs Erika Gertrud. b 45. ACT 88 St Jo Coll Nottm 99. **d** 92 **p** 02. C Proserpine St Paul Australia 92; NSM Hamburg *Eur* from 99. *Niendorfer Kirchenweg 5C, 22459 Hamburg, Germany* Tel (0049) (40) 582850 Mobile 162-700 0404 Fax (40) 582841

ANDERS, Jonathan Cyril. b 36. Wycliffe Hall Ox 69. **d** 71 **p** 72. C Prescot *Liv* 71-74; C-in-c 74-76; R Wavertree St Mary 76-81; V Aigburth 81-01; rtd 01; Perm to Offic *Liv* from 03. *3 Silverleigh, Liverpool L17 5BL* Tel 0151-728 9997

ANDERS, Roger John. b 38. Man Univ LLB61. N Ord Course 91. **d** 94 **p** 95. NSM New Mills *Derby* 94-97; NSM Buxton w Burbage and King Sterndale 97-98; NSM Adderley, Ash, Calverhall, Ightfield etc *Lich* 98-03; R from 03. *The Rectory, Moreton Say, Market Drayton TF9 3RS* Tel (01630) 638110 Fax as telephone E-mail anders@u.genie.co.uk

ANDERSEN, Paul John. b 49. Univ of Alabama BA. Protestant Th Sem Virginia MDiv77. **d** 77 **p** 83. USA 77-82; Belize 82-84; Chapl Zagreb *Eur* 84-85; Chapl Belgrade 85-86; USA 86-89; India 89-91; Sierra Leone 92-93; Chapl Valletta *Eur* 94-96; Chapl Skopje 96-98; NSM Worcester St Luke USA 98-00; NSM S Barre Ch Ch 00-02; R Milford Trin Ch from 02. *23 Dana Park, Hopedale, MA 01747-1919, USA* E-mail paulandersen@earthlink.net

ANDERSON, Albert Geoffrey (Geoff). b 42. Ex Univ BA65 MA67. Qu Coll Birm. **d** 75 **p** 76. C Helsby and Ince *Ches* 75-77; C Helsby and Dunham-on-the-Hill 77-78; TV Gleadless *Sheff* 78-85; V Thorpe Hesley 85-92; R Ribbesford w Bewdley and Dowles *Worc* 92-03; rtd 03. *2 Waterworks Road, Worcester WR1 3EX* Tel (01905) 612634 E-mail ga@priest.com

ANDERSON, Alice Calder. b 50. Moray Ho Coll of Educn DipEd76 Dip Counselling 99. Local Minl Tr Course 90. **d** 93 **p** 95. NSM Edin St Barn *Edin* from 93. *35 Polton Court, Bonnyrigg EH19 3HF* Tel 0131-663 7078

ANDERSON, Mrs Ann. b 57. Cranmer Hall Dur 01. **d** 03 **p** 04. C Chester le Street *Dur* from 03. *107 Rydal Road, Chester le Street DH2 3DS* Tel 0191-388 4642

ANDERSON, Preb Brian Arthur. b 42. Sarum Th Coll 75. **d** 78 **p** 79. C Plymouth St Jas Ham *Ex* 78-80; Org Sec CECS *B & W, Ex* and *Truro* 80-89; TV Saltash *Truro* 89-94; RD E Wivelshire 91-94; P-in-c St Breoke and Egloshayle 94-96; R 96-02; RD Trigg Minor and Bodmin 95-02; P-in-c Torpoint from 02; P-in-c Antony w Sheviock from 02; Preb St Endellion from 99. *The Rectory, Sheviock, Torpoint PL11 3EH* Tel (01503) 230622 Mobile 07710-231219 E-mail shevrec@tesco.net

ANDERSON, Brian Glaister. b 35. K Coll Lon 57. **d** 79 **p** 79. Chapl St Fran Sch Hooke 79; C Croydon St Jo *Cant* 80-83; Dep Chapl HM Youth Cust Cen Glen Parva 83-84; Chapl HM YOI Hewell Grange 84-89; Chapl HM Rem Cen Brockhill 84-89; Chapl HM Pris Parkhurst 89-96; rtd 96. *The Garden Flat, 126A High Street, Portsmouth PO1 2HW* Tel (023) 9236 9441 Mobile 07900-272006 E-mail brianders@ntlworld.com

ANDERSON, David. b 19. Selw Coll Cam BA41 MA45. Wycliffe Hall Ox 47. **d** 49 **p** 50. C Bishopwearmouth St Gabr *Dur* 49-52; Tutor St Aid Birkenhead 52-56; Chapl Heswall Nautical Sch 52-53; Nigeria 56-62; Prin Wycliffe Hall Ox 62-69; Sen Lect Wall Hall Coll Aldenham 70-74; Prin Lect 74-84; rtd 84; Perm to Offic *Dur* 84-02. *16 Manor Park, Borrowash, Derby DE72 3LP* Tel (01332) 664426

ANDERSON, David Graham. b 33. MICE MIStructE. St Mich Coll Llan 85. **d** 88 **p** 89. C Llanishen and Lisvane *Llan* 88-90; C Fazeley *Lich* 90-94; Perm to Offic *Heref* 96-01; rtd 98; Perm to Offic *Llan* from 01. *12 Brockhill Way, Penarth CF64 5QD* Tel (029) 2070 9780

ANDERSON, David Lee. b 75. Westmr Coll Ox BTh96. Ripon Coll Cuddesdon MTh99. **d** 98 **p** 99. C Balderton *S'well* 98-02; V Harworth from 02. *The Vicarage, Tickhill Road, Harworth, Doncaster DN11 8PD* Tel (01302) 744157

ANDERSON, David Richard. b 58. Lanc Univ BEd79. EAMTC 96. **d** 99 **p** 00. C N Walsham w Antingham *Nor* 99-02; R Stalham, E Ruston, Brunstead, Sutton and Ingham from 02; P-in-c Smallburgh w Dilham w Honing and Crostwight from 05. *The Vicarage, Camping Field Lane, Stalham, Norwich NR12 9DT* Tel (01692) 580250 E-mail revdanderson@bigfoot.com

ANDERSON, Digby Carter. b 44. Reading Univ BA Brunel Univ MPhil73 PhD77. **d** 85 **p** 86. NSM Luton St Sav *St Alb* from 85. *17 Hardwick Place, Woburn Sands, Milton Keynes MK17 8QQ* Tel (01908) 584526

ANDERSON, Donald Whimbey. b 31. Trin Coll Toronto BA54 MA58 LTh57 STB57 ThD71. **d** 56 **p** 57. Canada 57-59, 75-88 and from 96; Japan 59-74; Philippines 74-75; Dir Ecum Affairs ACC 88-96; rtd 96. *Conference on the Religious Life, 31 Island View Drive, RR1, Little Britain ON, Canada K0M 2C0* Tel (001) (705) 786 3330 Fax as telephone E-mail da@ecunet.org

ANDERSON, Francis Hindley. b 20. Ch Coll Cam BA43 MA47. Wycliffe Hall Ox. **d** 44 **p** 45. C Surbiton St Matt *S'wark* 44-48; C Loughborough All SS *Leic* 48-50; C Pimlico St Pet w Westmr Ch Ch *Lon* 50-59; V Upper Chelsea St Sav 59-91; rtd 92; P-in-c Linchmere *Chich* 93-96; C Lynchmere and Camelsdale 96-97; Perm to Offic *Guildf* 96-97 and *Chich* from 97. *35 Oaklands, Haslemere GU27 3RD* Tel (01428) 642133

ANDERSON, Geoff. *See* ANDERSON, Albert Geoffrey

ANDERSON, Canon Gordon Fleming. b 19. TCD BA41 MA46. **d** 42 **p** 43. C Drumholm *D & R* 42-46; C Clooney 46-47; I Termonamongan 47-57; P-in-c Cumber Lower 57-61; I 61-72; I Cumber Lower w Banagher 72-94; Can Derry Cathl 76-94; Preb Howth St Patr Cathl Dublin 86-94; rtd 94. *Woodlands, 85 Dunboe Road, Ardiclave, Coleraine BT51 4JR*

ANDERSON, Gordon Stuart. b 49. St Jo Coll Nottm. **d** 82 **p** 83. C Hattersley *Ches* 82-86; C Dagenham *Chelmsf* 86-91; TV Mildenhall *St E* 91-01; V Southminster *Chelmsf* from 01. *The Vicarage, Burnham Road, Southminster CM0 7ES* Tel (01621) 772300 Mobile 07759-550990 E-mail gandr42@btinternet.com

ANDERSON, Graeme Edgar. b 59. Poly of Wales BSc82. St Jo Coll Nottm MTh02. **d** 02 **p** 03. C Brislington St Luke *Bris* from 02. *119 Birchwood Road, Bristol BS4 4RB* Tel 0117-373 0293 Mobile 07840-926736 E-mail graemeandjudy@hotmail.com

ANDERSON, Hugh Richard Oswald. b 35. Roch Th Coll 68. **d** 70 **p** 71. C Minehead *B & W* 70-76; C Darley w S Darley *Derby* 76-80; R Hasland 80-94; V Temple Normanton 80-94; rtd 94; Perm to Offic *Derby* from 94. *32 Barry Road, Brimington, Chesterfield S43 1PX* Tel (01246) 551020

ANDERSON, James. b 36. Magd Coll Ox BA59 MA64 Leeds Univ MA00. **d** 02 **p** 03. NSM Holme and Seaton Ross Gp *York* from 02. *Lincoln Flats Farmhouse, Foggathorpe, Selby YO8 6PZ* Tel and fax (01430) 860106

ANDERSON, James Frederick Wale. b 34. G&C Coll Cam BA58 MA62. Cuddesdon Coll 60. **d** 62 **p** 63. C Leagrave *St Alb* 62-65; C Eastleigh *Win* 65-70; R Sherfield-on-Loddon 70-86; P-in-c Stratfield Saye w Hartley Wespall 75-86; R Sherfield-on-Loddon and Stratfield Saye etc 86-87; R Newton Valence, Selborne and E Tisted w Colemore 87-99; rtd 99; Chapl Surrey Hants Borders NHS Trust 01-04; Hon C Farnham *Guildf* 01-04. *1 Potter's Gate, Farnham GU9 7EJ* Tel (01252) 710728

ANDERSON, Canon James Raffan. b 33. FRSA90 Edin Univ MA54. Edin Th Coll 56. **d** 58 **p** 59. Chapl St Andr Cathl *Ab* 58-59; Prec St Andr Cathl 59-62; CF (TA) 59-67; Chapl Aber Univ *Ab* 60-62; Chapl Glas Univ *Glas* 62-69; Chapl Lucton Sch 69-71; Chapl Barnard Castle Sch 71-74; Asst Dir of Educn *Blackb* 74-78; P-in-c Whitechapel 74-78; Bp's Officer for Min *Cov* 78-87; Hon Can Cov Cathl 83-87; Miss Sec Gen Syn Bd for Miss and Unity 87-92; rtd 92; Perm to Offic *Blackb* from 98. *Eccles Moss Farm, Bleasdale Road, Whitechapel, Preston PR3 2ER* Tel and fax (01995) 641280 E-mail jamesanders@onetel.com

ANDERSON (née FLAHERTY), Mrs Jane Venitia. b 68. Oak Hill Th Coll DipHE91 BA92. **d** 93 **p** 94. C Timperley *Ches* 93-97; C Cheshunt *St Alb* 97-99; P-in-c N Springfield *Chelmsf* from 99. *The Vicarage, St Augustine's Way, Beardsley Drive, Springfield, Chelmsford CM1 6GX* Tel (01245) 466160

ANDERSON, Jeremy. *See* ANDERSON, Brian Glaister

ANDERSON, Jeremy Dudgeon. b 41. Edin Univ BSc63. Trin Coll Bris 75. **d** 77 **p** 78. C Bitterne *Win* 77-81; TV Wexcombe *Sarum* 81-91; Evang Enabler (Reading Deanery) *Ox* 91-96; V Epsom Common Ch Ch *Guildf* 96-00; C Kinson *Sarum* from 00. *80 Pine Vale Crescent, Bournemouth BH10 6BJ* Tel (01202) 520778

ANDERSON, Mrs Joanna Elisabeth. b 53. St Andr Univ MTh75. EMMTC 85. **d** 88 **p** 95. Par Dn Crosby *Linc* 88-92; Warden Iona Community *Arg* 92-95; R S Trin Broads *Nor* 95-02; Dir Body, Mind, Spirit Project from 02; Public Preacher *Nor* from 02. *1 Church Cottages, Ranworth, Norwich NR13 6HS* Tel (01603) 270680

ANDERSON, John Michael. b 17. Madras Univ BA38. St Aug Coll Cant 59. **d** 60 **p** 61. C Smethwick St Alb *Birm* 60-62; C Stockland Green 62-65; C Braunstone *Leic* 65-69; Trinidad and Tobago 69-73; V Leic St Sav *Leic* 74-82; rtd 82; Perm to Offic *Leic* 82-97. *3 St Mary's Avenue, Braunstone, Leicester LE3 3FT* Tel 0116-225 0378

ANDERSON, John Robert. b 75. QUB BD96 TCD MPhil98. CITC 96. **d** 98 **p** 99. C Magherafelt *Arm* 98-02; C Ballymena w Ballyclug *Conn* 02-05; I Billy w Derrykeighan from 05. *26 Castlewood Park, Dervock, Ballymoney BT53 8DA* Tel (028) 2074 1241

ANDERSON, Canon Keith Bernard. b 36. Qu Coll Cam BA60 MA64. Tyndale Hall Bris 60. **d** 62 **p** 63. C Bootle St Leon *Liv* 62-65; Lect Can Warner Mem Coll Buye Burundi 66-73; Lect Mweya United Th Sem 74; Dir Studies Dio Nakuru Kenya 74-77; Dir RE Dio Mt Kenya E 78-83; Hon Can Mt Kenya E from 82; P-in-c Newnham and Doddington w Wychling *Cant* 83-88; Chapl Cannes w Grasse *Eur* 88-94; Dir and Chapl Mulberry Ho High Ongar 94-95; TV Horley *S'wark* 96-01; rtd 01; Perm to Offic *S'wark* 01-05. *93 Rusper Road, Horsham RH12 4BJ* Tel (01403) 262185 E-mail kb.anderson@virgin.net

ANDERSON, Canon Keith Edward. b 42. Fitzw Coll Cam BA77 MA83 MRCS83. Ridley Hall Cam 74. **d** 77 **p** 78. C Goodmayes All SS *Chelmsf* 77-80; Chapl Coll of SS Mark and Jo Plymouth *Ex* 80-87; RD Plymouth Moorside 83-86; V Northampton H Sepulchre w St Andr and St Lawr *Pet* 87-98; RD Northn 92-98; Adv for Min Willesden *Lon* 98-03; Adv for Ord Min Development *Win* from 03; Can Res Win Cathl from 03. *Church House, 9 The Close, Winchester SO23 9LS* Tel (01962) 844644 *or* 624805 E-mail keith.anderson@chsewinchester.clara.net

ANDERSON, Kenneth. b 38. G&C Coll Cam BA62 MA66. Westcott Ho Cam 63. **d** 65 **p** 66. C Nor St Steph *Nor* 65-68; Chapl Norfolk and Nor Hosp 65-68; C Wareham w Arne *Sarum* 68-71; Chapl Sherborne Sch 71-83; Zimbabwe 83-94; Chapl Trevelyan and Van Mildert Coll *Dur* 95-04; Dioc Voc Adv 95-04; rtd 04. *39 Hallgarth Street, Durham DH1 3AT* Tel 0191-383 0628 *or* 374 3770

ANDERSON, Martin Edward. b 73. Humberside Univ BA95 St Jo Coll Dur BA02. Cranmer Hall Dur 99. **d** 02 **p** 03. C Gt Aycliffe and Chilton *Dur* from 02. *20 Haslewood Road, Newton Aycliffe DL5 4XF* Tel (01325) 313699 E-mail martin.anderson@durham.anglican.org

ANDERSON, Canon Michael Garland. b 42. Clifton Th Coll 62. **d** 66 **p** 67. C Fareham St Jo *Portsm* 66-69; C Worting *Win* 69-74; V Hordle from 74; RD Lyndhurst 82-00; Hon Can Win Cathl from 92. *The Vicarage, Stopples Lane, Hordle, Lymington SO41 0HX* Tel (01425) 614428 E-mail canon.m.g.anderson@ukgateway.net

ANDERSON, Canon Michael John Austen. b 35. AKC60. **d** 66 **p** 67. C Southall Ch Redeemer *Lon* 66-69; C Hampstead Garden

Suburb 69-73; V S Mimms St Giles 73-80; V The Brents and Davington w Oare and Luddenham *Cant* 80-86; V Margate All SS 86-00; Hon Can Cant Cathl 97-00; rtd 00; Perm to Offic *Cant* from 01. *Camwa Ash, Bull Lane, Boughton under Blean, Faversham ME13 9AH* Tel (01227) 752352 Mobile 07885-211863

ANDERSON, Nicholas Patrick. b 53. Lanc Univ BA87. Allen Hall 79. **d** 81 **p** 82. In RC Ch 81-89; C Gt Crosby St Faith *Liv* 89-92; C Walton-on-the-Hill 92-95; V Pemberton St Fran Kitt Green 95-04; V Rainhill from 04. *St Ann's Vicarage, View Road, Prescot L35 0LE* Tel 0151-426 4666

ANDERSON, Olaf Emanuel. b 64. Univ of Qld BA88. St Fran Coll Brisbane 84. **d** 87 **p** 88. Australia 87-90 and from 94; Hon C Woolloongabba 87; C Cleveland 88-90; C Petersfield *Portsm* 91-93; P-in-c Goodna 94-00; R New Farm 00-02. *Address temp unknown* E-mail olaf.anderson@docnet.org.au

ANDERSON, Mrs Pearl Ann. b 46. St Andr Univ MA68 MCIPD74. Cant Sch of Min 90. **d** 93 **p** 00. Par Dn Epping St Jo *Chelmsf* 93-95; Adv to Coun for Soc Resp *Roch* and *Cant* 95-02; Asst Chief Exec Ch in Soc *Roch* and *Cant* from 02; Hon C Biddenden and Smarden from 00. *1 Gibbs Hill, Headcorn, Ashford TN27 9UD* Tel (01622) 890043 *or* 755014 Fax 693531 E-mail pearlaanderson@btopenworld.com *or* pearl@churchinsociety.org

ANDERSON, Peter John. b 44. Nottm Univ BA65 BA73 Ex Univ CertEd66. St Jo Coll Nottm. **d** 74 **p** 75. C Otley *Bradf* 74-77; TV Marfleet *York* 77-84; V Greasbrough *Sheff* 84-95; I Clonmel Union *C, C & R* 95-02; I Rathcooney Union 95-02; Chapl Cannes *Eur* from 02. *Résidence Kent, 4 avenue Général Ferrié, 06400 Cannes, France* Tel (0033) (4) 93 94 54 61 E-mail pjhmander@yahoo.net

ANDERSON, Peter Scott. b 49. Nottm Univ BTh72 CertEd. Kelham Th Coll 68. **d** 74 **p** 75. C Sheff St Cecilia Parson Cross *Sheff* 74-77; C Leytonstone St Marg w St Columba *Chelmsf* 77-81; P-in-c Forest Gate St Edm 81-89; V 89-90; P-in-c Plaistow 90-94; V Willesden Green St Andr and St Fran *Lon* from 94. *The Clergy House, St Andrew's Road, London NW10 2QS* Tel (020) 8459 2670 E-mail peter@scottanderson.freeserve.co.uk

ANDERSON, Philip Gregory. b 80. Keble Coll Ox BA01. Ripon Coll Cuddesdon BA04. **d** 05. C Prescot *Liv* from 05. *St Mary's House, 2 West Street, Prescot L34 1LQ* Tel 07773-582920 (mobile) E-mail philipanderson@merseymail.com

ANDERSON, Canon Roderick Stephen. b 43. Cant Univ (NZ) BSc63 PhD67 New Coll Ox BA72. Wycliffe Hall Ox 70. **d** 73 **p** 74. C Bradf Cathl *Bradf* 73-75; C Allerton 76-78; V Cottingley 78-94; RD Airedale 88-95; Hon Can Bradf Cathl from 94; V Heaton St Barn from 94. *The Vicarage, Parsons Road, Heaton, Bradford BD9 4AY* Tel (01274) 496712 *or* 499354 E-mail rod@kiwityke.org.uk

ANDERSON, Canon Rosemary Ann. b 36. Ex Univ BA59. N Ord Course 83. **dss** 86 **d** 87 **p** 94. Oldham St Paul *Man* 86-87; Hon Par Dn 87-89; Bp's Adv for Women's Min 88-99; Par Dn Roughtown 93-94; P-in-c 94-99; Hon Can Man Cathl 96-99; rtd 99; Perm to Offic *Man* 99-03. *11E Rhodes Hill, Lees, Oldham OL4 5EA* Tel 0161-620 1549

ANDERSON, Scott. *See* ANDERSON, Peter Scott

ANDERSON, Stuart. b 31. Dur Univ BA52. Linc Th Coll 52. **d** 54 **p** 55. C Billingham St Cuth *Dur* 54-57; C Fulham St Etheldreda *Lon* 57-61; New Zealand from 61. *3 Arataki Road, Havelock North, Hawkes Bay, New Zealand* Tel (0064) (6) 877 8567

ANDERSON, Timothy George. b 59. Ealing Coll of HE BA82. Wycliffe Hall Ox 83. **d** 86 **p** 87. C Harold Wood *Chelmsf* 86-90; C Whitfield *Derby* 90-95; P-in-c Wolverhampton St Luke *Lich* 95-98; V 98-01; I Dundonald *D & D* from 01. *St Elizabeth's Rectory, 26 Ballyregan Road, Dundonald, Belfast BT16 1HY* Tel (028) 9048 3153 *or* 9048 2644

ANDERSON, Timothy James Lane. b 59. Pemb Coll Ox BA80 MA90. St Jo Coll Nottm Dip Th Studies 92. **d** 93 **p** 94. C Reigate St Mary *S'wark* 93-95; Perm to Offic *S'well* from 95. *3 Dale Lane, Beeston, Nottingham NG9 4EA* Tel 0115-922 4773

ANDERSON-MacKENZIE, Janet Melanie. b 70. Edin Univ BSc93 PhD97. WEMTC 01. **d** 04 **p** 05. C Woolavington w Cossington and Bawdrip *B & W* 04-05; C Wellington and Distr from 05. *11 John Grinter Way, Wellington TA21 9AR* E-mail janet@clergy.plus.com

ANDERTON, David Edward. b 60. Leeds Poly BSc92. St Jo Coll Nottm 02. **d** 04 **p** 05. C Daybrook *S'well* from 04. *5 Blake Close, Arnold, Nottingham NG5 6NB* Tel 0115-926 8517 Mobile 07751-269412 E-mail d.anderton1@btinternet.com

ANDERTON, David Ernest. b 36. CEng68 MIMechE68. Dioc OLM tr scheme 97. **d** 00 **p** 01. OLM Eccleston Ch Ch *Liv* from 00. *16 Croxteth Drive, Rainford, St Helens WA11 8JZ* Tel (01744) 637600 Mobile 07751-038014

ANDERTON, Frederic Michael. b 31. Pemb Coll Cam MA57 Jung Inst Zürich Dip Analytical Psychology 86 IAAP. Westcott Ho Cam 64. **d** 66 **p** 67. C St John's Wood *Lon* 66-69; C All Hallows by the Tower etc 70-77; C St Giles Cripplegate w St Bart Moor Lane etc 77-82; C Zürich *Eur* 82-86; Perm to Offic *Lon* from 94; rtd 96. *61 Brassey Road, Winchester SO22 6SB* Tel (01962) 856326 Fax 852851 E-mail robin.anderton@lineone.net

ANDERTON, Peter. b 45. Sarum & Wells Th Coll 80. **d** 82 **p** 83. C Adel *Ripon* 82-86; P-in-c Dacre w Hartwith 86-90; P-in-c Thornthwaite w Thruscross and Darley 88-90; V Dacre w Hartwith and Darley w Thornthwaite 90-91; V Owton Manor *Dur* 91-02; V Torrisholme *Blackb* 02-03; P-in-c Hunslet St Mary *Ripon* 03; V Hunslet w Cross Green from 03. *The Vicarage, Church Street, Hunslet, Leeds LS10 2QY* Tel 0113-271 9661 *or* 270 4659 E-mail fr.peter@ntlworld.com

ANDREW, Brian. b 31. Oak Hill Th Coll 75. **d** 77 **p** 78. C Broadwater St Mary *Chich* 77-81; R Nettlebed w Bix and Highmore *Ox* 81-87; V Shenstone *Lich* 87-96; rtd 96; Perm to Offic *Ex* from 97 and *Derby* from 01. *18 Shaldon Drive, Littleover, Derby DE23 6HZ* Tel (01332) 768259

ANDREW, David Neil. b 62. Down Coll Cam BA83 MA87 PhD88. Ridley Hall Cam 93. **d** 93 **p** 94. C Heatherlands St Jo *Sarum* 93-98; P-in-c White Waltham w Shottesbrooke *Ox* from 98. *The Vicarage, Waltham Road, White Waltham, Maidenhead SL6 3JD* Tel (01628) 822000

ANDREW, David Shore. b 39. Liv Univ BA61 CertEd62. OLM course 97. **d** 99 **p** 00. NSM Birkenshaw w Hunsworth *Wakef* from 99. *448 Oxford Road, Gomersal, Cleckheaton BD19 4LD* Tel (01274) 873339

ANDREW, Donald. b 35. Tyndale Hall Bris 63. **d** 66 **p** 67. C Croydon Ch Ch Broad Green *Cant* 66-69; C Ravenhead *Liv* 69-72; Scripture Union 72-77; V Rushen *S & M* 77-82; TR Heworth H Trin *York* 82-00; rtd 00; Perm to Offic *York* from 05. *60 Viking Road, Bridlington YO16 6TW* Tel (01262) 601273

ANDREW, Frank. b 17. St D Coll Lamp BA49 Ely Th Coll 50. **d** 51 **p** 52. C Howden *York* 51-55; V Mosbrough *Sheff* 55-59; C-in-c Greenhill CD 59-65; V Greenhill 65-69; R March St Jo *Ely* 69-77; R March St Mary 71-77; RD March 73-77; R Catworth Magna 77-83; R Covington 77-83; R Tilbrook 77-83; rtd 83; Perm to Offic *Chich* from 83. *11 Romney Close, Seaford BN25 3TR* Tel (01323) 897352

ANDREW, Jeremy Charles Edward. b 68. St Jo Coll Dur BA01. Cranmer Hall Dur 98. **d** 01. C Newquay *Truro* 01-04; P-in-c Perranzabuloe from 04. *The Vicarage, Cocks, Perranporth TR6 0AT* Tel (01872) 573375

ANDREW, John. b 60. St Mich Coll Llan 98. **d** 00 **p** 01. C Oystermouth *S & B* from 00. *83 Castle Acre, Mumbles, Swansea SA3 5TH* Tel (01792) 405310

ANDREW, Canon John Gerald Barton. b 31. OBE. Keble Coll Ox BA55 MA58 Cuttington Univ Coll Liberia Hon DD76 Kentucky Sem Hon DD76 Nashotah Ho Wisconsin Hon DD77 Gen Th Sem NY Hon DD96. Cuddesdon Coll 54. **d** 56 **p** 57. C Redcar *York* 56-59; USA 59-60 and 72-96; Abp's Dom Chapl *York* 60-61; Abp's Dom Chapl *Cant* 61-65; Abp's Sen Chapl 65-69; Six Preacher Cant Cathl 67-72; V Preston St Jo *Blackb* 69-72; RD Preston 70-72; R St Thos Fifth Avenue 72-96; rtd 96; Perm to Offic *B & W* 97-99. *414 East 52nd Street, New York, NY 10022, USA* Tel (001) (212) 355 0064

ANDREW, Jonathan William. b 50. Univ Coll Ox MA78 FCA80. Ripon Coll Cuddesdon 02. **d** 04 **p** 05. NSM Hersham *Guildf* from 04. *Orchard, 6 Westacres, Esher KT10 9JE* Tel (01372) 464380 Mobile 07968-765188 E-mail jandrewesher@hotmail.com

ANDREW, Michael Paul. b 51. SSC Leic Univ CertEd73. Chich Th Coll 80. **d** 83 **p** 84. C Par *Truro* 83-86; Hon Chapl Miss to Seamen 86; P-in-c Salford Ordsall St Clem *Man* 86-91; P-in-c Hammersmith St Jo *Lon* 91-04. *45 Tintagel Crescent, Plymouth PL2 3TS* Tel (01752) 299286 Mobile 07712-816680 E-mail father.paul@compuserve.com

ANDREW, Philip John. b 62. Nottm Univ BSc84. St Jo Coll Nottm MTh02. **d** 02 **p** 03. C Reading Greyfriars *Ox* from 02. *26 Prospect Street, Reading RG1 7YG* Tel 0118-959 9930 E-mail phil.andrew@greyfriars.org.uk

ANDREW, Ronald Arthur. b 27. Sarum Th Coll 64. **d** 65 **p** 66. C Darwen St Cuth *Blackb* 65-69; C Padiham 69-71; V Colne H Trin 71-76; V Adlington 76-85; V Goosnargh w Whittingham 85-92; rtd 92; Perm to Offic *Blackb* from 92. *1 Greystone Drive, Fence, Burnley BB12 9PJ* Tel (01282) 617532

ANDREW, Sydney William. b 55. Cranmer Hall Dur 82. **d** 85 **p** 86. C Horncastle w Low Toynton *Linc* 85-88; V Worlaby 88-93; V Bonby 88-93; V Elsham 88-93; rtd 93; Lic to Offic *Linc* 93-95; Hon C Brocklesby Park 95-04; Hon C Croxton 96-04; Hon C Caistor Gp from 04. *10 Bentley Lane, Grasby, Barnetby DN38 6AW* Tel (01652) 628586 E-mail bridget.revdoc@clara.co.uk

ANDREW, Canon William Hugh. b 32. Selw Coll Cam BA56 MA60. Ridley Hall Cam 56. **d** 58 **p** 59. C Woking St Mary *Guildf* 58-61; C Farnborough 61-64; V Gatten St Paul *Portsm* 64-71; R Weymouth St Mary *Sarum* 71-76; V Heatherlands St Jo 76-82; Can and Preb Sarum Cathl 81-86; R Alderbury and W Grimstead 82-86; Perm to Offic *Bris* 86-88; Communications Dir Bible Soc 86-94; Communications Consultant 94-97; Hon C The Lydiards *Bris* 88-94; C W Swindon and the Lydiards 94-96; Hon C 96-98; rtd 96; Perm to Offic *Win* from 98. *31 Charnock Close, Hordle, Lymington SO41 0GU* Tel (01425) 627220

ANDREWES, Nicholas John. b 64. Southn Univ BA87 La Sainte Union Coll PGCE88. Cranmer Hall Dur BTh93. **d** 96 **p** 97. C Dovecot *Liv* 96-00; TV Pendleton *Man* 00-03; P-in-c Lower Crumpsall w Cheetham St Mark from 03. *26 Saltire Gardens, Salford M7 4BG* Tel and fax 0161-792 3123
E-mail nick.andrewes@virgin.net

ANDREWES UTHWATT, Henry. b 25. Jes Coll Cam BA49 MA51. Wells Th Coll 49. **d** 51 **p** 52. C Fareham H Trin *Portsm* 51-55; C Haslemere *Guildf* 55-59; C Wimbledon *S'wark* 59-61; V W Wimbledon Ch Ch 61-73; V Yeovil St Jo w Preston Plucknett *B & W* 73-76; TR Yeovil 76-82; V Burrington and Churchill 82-90; RD Locking 87-90; rtd 90; Perm to Offic *B & W* from 90; Chapl Partis Coll Bath from 91; Chapl Bath and West Community NHS Trust from 91. *71 Mount Road, Bath BA2 1LJ* Tel (01225) 482220

ANDREWS, Anthony Brian. b 33. Lon Univ BA54 AKC58. Coll of Resurr Mirfield 56. **d** 58 **p** 59. C Haggerston St Columba *Lon* 58-60; C N Hammersmith St Kath 60-63; V Goldthorpe *Sheff* 63-74; V Notting Hill St Mich and Ch Ch *Lon* from 74. *St Michael's Vicarage, 35 St Lawrence Terrace, London W10 5SR* Tel (020) 8969 0776 *or* 8428 7091 Fax 8969 0805
E-mail a.b.a@btinternet.com *or* archangel@supanet.com

ANDREWS, Anthony Frederick. b 25. K Coll Lon 54. **d** 55 **p** 56. C Kentish Town St Jo *Lon* 55-58; C Belmont 58-60; R Evershot, Frome St Quinton, Melbury Bubb etc *Sarum* 60-66; CF 66-69; C Bridgwater St Mary w Chilton Trinity *B & W* 69-70; R Cossington 70-73; C Highworth w Sevenhampton and Inglesham etc *Bris* 75-84; P-in-c Bishopstone w Hinton Parva 84-88; rtd 88. *Burford House, Highworth, Swindon SN6 7AD* Tel (01793) 762796

ANDREWS, Anthony John. b 35. S'wark Ord Course 75. **d** 80 **p** 81. NSM Cheam *S'wark* 80-83; C Epsom St Martin *Guildf* 83-86; V Barton *Portsm* 86-89; Chapl Northwick Park and St Mark's NHS Trust Harrow 90-98; C Regent's Park St Mark *Lon* 98-00; rtd 00; Perm to Offic *Lon* from 00. *112 Albury Drive, Pinner HA5 3RG*

ANDREWS, Benjamin. b 75. St Steph Ho Ox 97. **d** 00 **p** 01. C Whitchurch *Llan* 00-03; C Newton Nottage 03-05; C Cardiff St Mary and St Steph w St Dyfrig etc from 05. *St Paul's Vicarage, Llanmaes Street, Cardiff CF11 7LR* Tel (029) 2022 8707 E-mail frbenandrews@aol.com

ANDREWS, Canon Brian Keith. b 39. Keble Coll Ox BA62 MA69. Coll of Resurr Mirfield 62. **d** 64 **p** 65. C Is of Dogs Ch Ch and St Jo w St Luke *Lon* 64-68; C Hemel Hempstead *St Alb* 68-71; TV 71-79; V Abbots Langley from 79; RD Watford 88-94; Hon Can St Alb from 94. *The Vicarage, High Street, Abbots Langley WD5 0AS* Tel (01923) 263013 *or* tel and fax 261795
E-mail brianandrews@abbotslangley.u-net.com

ANDREWS, Canon Christopher Paul. b 47. Fitzw Coll Cam BA70 MA73. Westcott Ho Cam 69. **d** 72 **p** 73. C Croydon St Jo *Cant* 72-75; C Gosforth All SS *Newc* 75-79; TV Newc Epiphany 80-87; RD Newc Cen 82-87; V Alnwick and Chapl Alnwick Infirmary 87-96; R Grantham *Linc* from 96; Can and Preb Linc Cathl from 04; Chapl United Lincs Hosps NHS Trust 99-01. *The Rectory, 4 Church Street, Grantham NG31 6RR* Tel (01476) 563710 *or* 572932 E-mail chris-p-andrews@hotmail.com

ANDREWS, Clive Frederick. b 43. St Jo Coll Nottm 81. **d** 83 **p** 84. C Leic St Jas *Leic* 83-86; Ind Chapl 86-90; Hon TV Melton Gt Framland 89-90; TV Clifton *S'well* 90-92; P-in-c Gamston w Eaton and W Drayton 92-94; R from 94; P-in-c Elkesley w Bothamsall from 92; Chapl Bramcote Sch Notts from 92. *The Vicarage, 3 Maple Drive, Elkesley, Retford DN22 8AX* Tel (01777) 838293 E-mail cliveand@waitrose.com

ANDREWS, Edward Robert. b 33. St Mich Coll Llan 62. **d** 64 **p** 65. C Kingswinford St Mary *Lich* 64-69; Chapl RAF 69-88; R St Just-in-Roseland w Philleigh *Truro* 88-99; rtd 99. *2 Ingleside, Gunsdown Villas, Station Road, South Molton EX36 3EA* Tel (01769) 572386

ANDREWS, Frances. b 24. EMMTC 73. **dss** 78 **d** 87 **p** 94. Porchester *S'well* 78-86; Asst Chapl Nottm City Hosp 86-88; Hon C Gedling *S'well* 88-92; NSM Epperstone 92-95; NSM Gonalston 92-95; NSM Oxton 92-95; rtd 95; Perm to Offic *S'well* from 95. *1 Cromford Avenue, Carlton, Nottingham NG4 3RU* Tel 0115-961 3857

ANDREWS, Preb John Colin. b 47. Open Univ BA93. Sarum & Wells Th Coll 78. **d** 80 **p** 81. C Burnham *B & W* 80-84; V Williton 84-92; P-in-c Ashwick w Oakhill and Binegar 92-02; Dioc Communications Officer from 92; TV Yatton Moor from 02; Preb Wells Cathl from 04. *Cherry Tree House, Ham Lane, Kingston Seymour, Clevedon BS21 6XE* Tel (01934) 830208
E-mail john.andrews@bathwells.anglican.org

ANDREWS, Preb John Douglas. b 19. Keble Coll Ox BA39 MA44. Chich Th Coll 40. **d** 42 **p** 43. C S Bermondsey St Aug *S'wark* 42-44; C Lambeth St Jo w All SS 44-46; C Towcester w Easton Neston *Pet* 46-50; C Shrewsbury H Cross *Lich* 50-52; V Ettingshall 52-59; V Walsall St Andr 59-68; V Penkhull 68-80; P-in-c Ellenhall w Ranton 80-86; P-in-c Chebsey 80-86; Preb Lich Cathl 81-86; rtd 86; Perm to Offic *Heref* and *Lich* 86-01; *York* from 01. *28 Dulverton Hall, Esplanade, Scarborough YO11 2AR* Tel (01723) 340128

ANDREWS, John Elfric. b 35. Ex Coll Ox BA59 MA63. Wycliffe Hall Ox 59. **d** 61 **p** 62. C Pittville All SS *Glouc* 61-66; Cand Sec Lon City Miss 66-92; Lic to Offic *S'wark* 66-92; R Kingham w Churchill, Daylesford and Sarsden *Ox* 92-99; rtd 99; Perm to Offic *St E* from 01. *4 St George's Road, Felixstowe IP11 9PL* Tel (01394) 283557 E-mail john.andrew@care4free.net

ANDREWS, John Francis. b 34. Jes Coll Cam BA58 MA62. S'wark Ord Course 78. **d** 81 **p** 82. NSM Norwood All SS *Cant* 81-82; NSM Upper Norwood All SS w St Marg 82-85; NSM Upper Norwood All SS *S'wark* 85-87; NSM Dulwich St Barn 89-92; NSM S Dulwich St Steph 92-95; Perm to Offic *S'wark* from 95 and *Sarum* from 01. *6 Kennington Square, Wareham BH20 4JR* Tel (01929) 555311

ANDREWS, John George William. b 42. Qu Coll Birm 65. **d** 68 **p** 69. C Smethwick St Matt w St Chad *Birm* 68-71; CF 71-97; P-in-c Lyme Regis *Sarum* 97-98; TV Golden Cap Team 98-03; rtd 03. *North Gate House, Stapledon Lane, Ashburton, Newton Abbot TQ13 7AE*

ANDREWS, John Robert. b 42. Nottm Coll of Educn CertEd63 FRSA92 FCMI92. **d** 04 **p** 05. OLM Farewell *Lich* from 04. *1 Chaseley Gardens, Burntwood WS7 9DJ* Tel (01543) 674354 Mobile 07711-246656
E-mail johnrobert.andrews@btinternet.com

ANDREWS, Mrs Judith Marie. b 47. Avery Hill Coll CertEd68. Dioc OLM tr scheme 97. **d** 00 **p** 01. OLM Wilford Peninsula *St E* from 00. *Hillside, Tower Hill, Hollesley, Woodbridge IP12 3QX* Tel (01394) 411642
E-mail judith.andrews@btopenworld.com

ANDREWS, Keith. b 47. St Mich Coll Llan 79. **d** 81 **p** 82. C Penarth w Lavernock *Llan* 81-85; V Nantymoel w Wyndham 85-91; RD Bridgend 89-93; R Coychurch w Llangan and St Mary Hill 91-98; V Caerau St Cynfelin from 98. *The Vicarage, Cymmer Road, Caerau, Maesteg CF34 0YR* Tel (01656) 736500

ANDREWS, Morey Alisdair Christopher. b 66. Leic Poly BSc91 MRICS91. St Jo Coll Nottm MA99. **d** 99 **p** 00. C Yate New Town *Bris* 99-02; C Downend from 02. *15 Glendale Road, Downend, Bristol BS16 6EQ* Tel 0117-956 8859
E-mail moreyandrews@onetel.com

ANDREWS, Paul Douglas. b 54. Univ of Wales (Abth) BLib76 PhD99. St Alb and Ox Min Course. **d** 00 **p** 01. NSM Kempston and Biddenham *St Alb* 00-03; C Leighton Buzzard w Eggington, Hockliffe etc from 03. *St Michael's Vicarage, 4 Warneford Way, Leighton Buzzard LU7 4PX* Tel (01525) 370524
E-mail p.d.andrews@btinternet.com

ANDREWS, Peter Alwyne. b 44. Lon Univ BSc67. Westcott Ho Cam 70. **d** 73 **p** 74. C Barnoldswick w Bracewell *Bradf* 73-76; C Maltby *Sheff* 76-78; V Bradf St Oswald Chapel Green *Bradf* 78-85; V Hanwell St Thos *Lon* from 85. *St Thomas's Vicarage, 182 Boston Road, London W7 2AD* Tel (020) 8567 5280 Fax 8567 1061 E-mail thomashanwell@btinternet.com

ANDREWS, Peter Douglas. b 52. SEN72 SRN78. St Steph Ho Ox 86. **d** 88 **p** 89. C Perry Barr *Birm* 88-92; TV Swindon New Town *Bris* 92-98; V Streatham St Pet *S'wark* from 98. *St Peter's Vicarage, 113 Leigham Court Road, London SW16 2NS* Tel (020) 8769 2922

ANDREWS, Raymond Cyril. b 50. SEITE 00. **d** 03 **p** 04. C E Dulwich St Jo *S'wark* from 03. *11 Hinckley Road, London SE15 4HZ* Tel 07930-694221 (mobile)
E-mail andrewsrandrews@aol.com

ANDREWS, Richard John. b 57. Bris Univ BA78 CertEd79. Ripon Coll Cuddesdon 82. **d** 84 **p** 85. C Kidderminster St Mary and All SS, Trimpley etc *Worc* 84-87; Hon C Derby Cathl *Derby* 87-89; Chapl Derbyshire Coll of HE 87-89; V Chellaston *Derby* 89-93; V Spondon from 93; TR Dunstable *St Alb* from 05. *The Rectory, 8 Furness Avenue, Dunstable LU6 3BN* Tel (01582) 703271 *or* 477401 E-mail rector@dunstableparish.org.uk

ANDREYEV, Michael. b 62. Hatf Coll Dur BA85. Wycliffe Hall Ox BA93 MA03. **d** 96 **p** 97. C Surbiton Hill Ch Ch *S'wark* 96-01; NSM Stapenhill w Cauldwell *Derby* 02-03; P-in-c from 03. *3 Stapenhill Road, Burton-on-Trent DE15 9AF* Tel (01283) 530320 E-mail michael.andreyev@ukonline.co.uk

ANGEL, Andrew Richard. b 67. St Pet Coll Ox BA89 Lon Inst of Educn PGCE90 Surrey Univ MA94. St Jo Coll Nottm PhD04. **d** 02 **p** 03. C Dartford Ch Ch *Roch* from 02. *102 Chastilian Road, Dartford DA1 3LG* Tel (01322) 229103
E-mail revandyangel@hotmail.com

ANGEL, Gervais Thomas David. b 36. Ch Ch Ox BA59 MA62 Bris Univ MEd78 Lon Univ PGCE72. Wycliffe Hall Ox 57. **d** 61 **p** 62. C Aberystwyth St Mich *St D* 61-65; Tutor Clifton Th Coll 65-71; Dean of Studies Trin Coll Bris 71-81; Dir of Studies 81-90; Area Sec (W and SW) SAMS 90-02; NSM Stoke Gifford *Bris* 92-02; rtd 02; Perm to Offic *Bris* from 02. *82 Oak Close, Little Stoke, Bristol BS34 6RD* Tel (01454) 618081 Mobile 07967-441426 Fax 0117-904 8588
E-mail gervais.angel@blueyonder.co.uk

ANGEL, Robin Alan. b 41. St Mich Coll Llan. **d** 89 **p** 90. C Whitchurch *Llan* 89-94; V Aberpergwm and Blaengwrach 94-01;

V Caerau w Ely 01-03; V Porth w Trealaw from 03. *St Paul's Vicarage, 70 Birchgrove Street, Porth CF39 9UU* Tel (01443) 682401

ANGELL, Geoffrey. b 63. St Jo Coll Nottm. **d** 01 **p** 02. C Daventry, Ashby St Ledgers, Braunston etc *Pet* 01-04; C Oakham, Hambleton, Egleton, Braunston and Brooke from 04. *The Vicarage, 67 Church Street, Langham, Oakham LE15 7JE* Tel (01572) 722969 E-mail revgeoff@artangells.com

ANGELO, Brother. *See* DEACON, Donald

ANGIER, Patrick John Mark. b 61. Leic Univ BSc83. Trin Coll Bris. **d** 03 **p** 04. C Stratford-upon-Avon, Luddington etc *Cov* from 03. *2 St John's Close, Stratford-upon-Avon CV37 9AB* Tel (01789) 268836 Mobile 07971-923668 E-mail patrick.angier@btinternet.com

ANGLE, John Edwin George. b 42. Lon Bible Coll BD65 Liv Univ AdDipEd73 Univ of Wales MEd75 UWE Dip Educn Mgt 85. WEMTC 92. **d** 94 **p** 95. NSM Clevedon St Andr and Ch Ch *B & W* 94-97; NSM Worle 97-98; P-in-c Camelot Par 98-01; R from 01; Warden of Readers Wells Adnry from 02. *The Rectory, 6 The Close, North Cadbury, Yeovil BA22 7DX* Tel (01963) 440469 E-mail johnangle@onetel.com

ANGOVE, Ms Helen Teresa. b 71. Bath Univ BEng93. Ripon Coll Cuddesdon BTh97. **d** 97 **p** 98. C Bridgwater St Mary, Chilton Trinity and Durleigh *B & W* 97-01; P-in-c Elstree *St Alb* 01-03; USA from 03. *500 S Madison Avenue, Apartment #3, Pasadena, CA 91101, USA* Tel (001) (626) 793 7386 E-mail htangove@yahoo.com

ANGUS, Canon Edward. b 39. Man Univ BA60. Qu Coll Birm DipTh61. **d** 62 **p** 63. C Chorley St Geo *Blackb* 62-65; C S Shore H Trin 65-68; R Bretherton 68-76; V Altham w Clayton le Moors 76-90; V Preesall 90-04; RD Garstang 96-01; Hon Can Blackb Cathl 98-04; rtd 04. *14 Lazenby Avenue, Fleetwood FY7 8QH* Tel (01253) 686817

ANGWIN, Richard Paul. b 25. ACA49 FCA60 AKC56. **d** 56 **p** 57. C Clacton St Jas *Chelmsf* 56-59; V Brightlingsea 59-69; V Wanstead H Trin Hermon Hill 69-75; Chapl Wanstead Hosp Lon 69-75; Chapl Halstead Hosp 75-87; V Halstead St Andr *Chelmsf* 75-78; P-in-c Greenstead Green 75-78; V Halstead St Andr w H Trin 78-79; V Halstead St Andr w H Trin and Greenstead Green 79-87; RD Halstead and Coggeshall 84-87; rtd 87; Perm to Offic *Lich* from 88. *2 Seckham Road, Lichfield WS13 7AN* Tel (01543) 250848 E-mail skypilot@sagainternet.co.uk

ANKER, George William. b 10. AKC51. **d** 51 **p** 52. C Richmond H Trin and Ch Ch *S'wark* 51-54; C Battersea St Pet 54-57; C Shere *Guildf* 57-62; C Leatherhead 62-68; V Brockley Hill St Sav *S'wark* 68-72; C Sanderstead All SS 72-76; rtd 76; Perm to Offic *S'wark* from 76. *The College of St Barnabas, Blackberry Lane, Lingfield RH7 6NJ* Tel (01342) 870260

ANKER, Malcolm. b 39. Univ of Wales BA61. Bps' Coll Cheshunt 61. **d** 63 **p** 64. C Marfleet *York* 63-66; C Cottingham 66-69; V Skirlaugh w Long Riston 69-74; V Elloughton and Brough w Brantingham 74-84; V Tadcaster 84-86; V Tadcaster w Newton Kyme 86-91; V Oatlands *Guildf* 91-05; rtd 05. *10 Pegasus Close, Haslemere GU27 3SZ* Tel (01428) 651630

ANKER-PETERSEN, Robert Brian. b 52. Aber Univ MTh88. Wycliffe Hall Ox BA79 MA88. **d** 93 **p** 94. C Perth St Ninian *St And* 93-96; Bp's Researcher on Ch's Min of Healing from 93; Dir Bield Retreat and Healing Cen from 93; Dioc Dir of Healing from 97. *Blackruthven House, Tibbermore, Perth PH1 1PY* Tel (01738) 583238 Fax 583828 E-mail robin@bieldatblackruthven.org.uk

ANKERS, Charles William (Bill). b 42. FIMI. NEOC 89. **d** 93 **p** 95. NSM York St Luke *York* 93-95; C Kexby w Wilberfoss 95-98; Asst Chapl HM Pris Full Sutton 95-98; V Norton juxta Malton *York* from 98. *The Vicarage, 80 Langton Road, Norton, Malton YO17 9AE* Tel (01653) 692741

ANKETELL, Jeyarajan. b 41. Lon Univ BSc62 PhD67 MInstP. Coll of Resurr Mirfield 69. **d** 73 **p** 74. Asst Chapl Newc Univ *Newc* 73-75; Asst Chapl Lon Univ *Lon* 75-77; Teacher from 78; Lic to Offic *S'wark* 81-83; Chasetown High Sch from 85; NSM Lich St Mary w St Mich *Lich* 86-96; NSM Lich St Mich w St Mary and Wall from 96. *7 Wissage Lane, Lichfield WS13 6DQ* Tel (01543) 268897

ANN-MARIA, Sister. *See* STUART, Sister Ann-Marie Lindsay

ANNANCY, Felix. b 62. Hull Univ DipTh87. **d** 87 **p** 88. C Fenton *Lich* 87-88; Ghana 88-98 and from 00; C Stalybridge St Paul *Ches* 98-00; Perm to Offic *Man* from 00. *c/o St Crispin's Rectory, 2 Hart Road, Manchester M14 7LE*

ANNAS, Geoffrey Peter. b 53. Sarum & Wells Th Coll. **d** 83 **p** 84. C S'wark H Trin w St Matt *S'wark* 83-87; TV Walworth 87-94; Warden Pemb Coll Miss Walworth 87-94; V Southampton Thornhill St Chris *Win* from 94. *St Christopher's Vicarage, 402 Hinkler Road, Southampton SO19 6DF* Tel (023) 8044 8537

ANNE, Sister. *See* PROUDLEY, Sister Anne

ANNIS, Herman North. b 28. Lich Th Coll 62. **d** 64 **p** 65. C Kilburn St Aug *Lon* 64-67; C Toxteth Park St Agnes *Liv* 67-70; V 70-82; V Hempton and Pudding Norton *Nor* 82-84; P-in-c Sculthorpe w Dunton and Doughton 82-84; V Northampton H Trin *Pet* 84-95; rtd 95; Hon C Brighton St Bart *Chich* 95-99. *2 rue de la Liberté, 53500 St Denis-de-Gastines, France* Tel (0033) (2) 43 00 69 66

ANNIS, Jennifer Mary. b 49. Middx Univ BA95. Oak Hill Th Coll 92. **d** 95 **p** 97. NSM Digswell and Panshanger *St Alb* 95-97; NSM Codicote 97-98 and 99-00; Tanzania 98-99; Chapl ATC from 99. *Glanafon, Trecwn, Haverfordwest SA62 5XT* Tel (01348) 840689

ANNIS, Rodney James. b 43. Ex Univ BA75 MA79 PhD86. Ripon Coll Cuddesdon 75. **d** 76 **p** 77. C Brixham *Ex* 76-77; Asst Chapl Ex Univ 77-80; Chapl Ex Sch 77-80; C Boston *Linc* 80-84; Chapl Trin Hall Cam 84-87; Chapl St Edw K and Martyr Cam *Ely* 84-87; V Bush Hill Park St Steph *Lon* from 87. *St Stephen's Vicarage, 43A Village Road, Enfield EN1 2ET*

ANNON, Jacqueline. **d** 01 **p** 02. OLM Tooting All SS *S'wark* 01-04. *31 Hamilton Road, London SE27 9RZ* Tel (020) 8473 2456

ANNS, Pauline Mary. *See* HIGHAM, Mrs Pauline Mary

ANSAH, Canon Kwesi Gyebi Ababio (George). b 54. DipSM87. Simon of Cyrene Th Inst 90 Oak Hill Th Coll DipHE93 BTh97. **d** 93 **p** 94. C Peckham St Mary Magd *S'wark* 93-96; V W Dulwich Em from 96; Hon Can Kumasi from 04. *Emmanuel Vicarage, 94 Clive Road, London SE21 8BU* Tel (020) 8670 2793 E-mail kgyebiababio@easicom.com

ANSCOMBE, John Thomas. b 51. Ex Univ BA72. Cranmer Hall Dur. **d** 74 **p** 75. C Upper Armley *Ripon* 74-77; C Leeds St Geo 78-81; Exec Producer Scripture Union 81-96; Hon C Beckenham Ch Ch *Roch* from 82. *22 Hawthornedene Road, Bromley BR2 7DY* Tel and fax (020) 8462 4831 Mobile 07720-876487 E-mail john_anscombe@hotmail.com

ANSELL, Antony Michael. b 40. St Jo Coll Nottm 78. **d** 80 **p** 81. C Harrow Weald St Mich *Lon* 80-84; Hon C Ches Square St Mich w St Phil 86-88; Hon C Mayfair Ch Ch 88-02; Perm to Offic *Win* from 02. *Fullerton Mill, Fullerton, Andover SP11 7LA* Tel (01264) 861076 Mobile 07855-943615 E-mail a.ansell@andover.co.uk

ANSELL, Howard. b 36. St Jo Coll Cam BA59 MA62. NW Ord Course 73. **d** 76 **p** 77. C Chapeltown *Sheff* 76-79; V Worsbrough St Thos and St Jas 79-83; R Lt Waltham *Chelmsf* 83-00; P-in-c Gt Leighs 92-00; P-in-c Lt Leighs 95-00; rtd 00; Perm to Offic *Linc* from 00. *5 Roselea Avenue, Welton, Lincoln LN2 3RT* Tel (01673) 860508

ANSELL, John Christopher. b 49. Sarum & Wells Th Coll 79. **d** 81 **p** 82. C Dartford St Alb *Roch* 81-84; C Leybourne and Larkfield 84-88; TV Mortlake w E Sheen *S'wark* 88-98; V Mitcham SS Pet and Paul from 98. *The Vicarage, 11 Vicarage Gardens, Mitcham CR4 3BL* Tel (020) 8648 1566 E-mail jsansell@hotmail.com *or* mitchamparishchurch@uk2.net

ANSELL, Mrs Mandy. b 47. **d** 04 **p** 05. OLM Rockland St Mary w Hellington, Bramerton etc *Nor* from 04. *44 The Street, Rockland St Mary, Norwich NR14 7AH* Tel (01508) 538654 E-mail ansell44@tiscali.co.uk

ANSELL, Philip Harding. b 67. LMH Ox BA89 Rob Coll Cam BA92. Ridley Hall Cam. **d** 93 **p** 94. C Rainham w Wennington *Chelmsf* 93-97; C Rodbourne Cheney *Bris* 97-01; V Moseley St Agnes *Birm* from 01. *St Agnes' Vicarage, 5 Colmore Crescent, Birmingham B13 9SJ* Tel and fax 0121-449 0368

ANSELL, Stuart Adrian. b 59. Ripon Coll Cuddesdon DipMin95 St Alb Minl Tr Scheme 81. **d** 97 **p** 98. C Cheadle w Freehay *Lich* 97-00; P-in-c Silverdale 00-03; V from 03; V Keele from 03. *21 Pepper Street, Silverdale, Newcastle ST5 6QJ* Tel (01782) 616804

ANSELM, Brother. *See* SMYTH, Robert Andrew Laine

ANSON (née DRAX), Mrs Elizabeth Margaret. b 57. St Jo Coll Nottm DipMin93. **d** 94 **p** 95. C Kimberworth *Sheff* 94-95; C Doncaster St Mary 95-97; rtd 97. *164 Park Avenue, Princes Avenue, Hull HU5 3EY* Tel (01482) 343169

ANSON, Harry. b 35. FInstFF79. St Jo Coll Nottm 83. **d** 88 **p** 03. NSM Ayr *Glas* 88-93; Hon Chapl Miss to Seamen 91-93; rtd 94. *Fairview, Balbinny, Aberlemno, Forfar DD8 3PF* Tel and fax (01307) 830446 Mobile 07790-470660 E-mail h2avro@hotmail.com

ANSTEY, Nigel John. b 55. Cranmer Hall Dur 84. **d** 87 **p** 88. C Plumstead St Jo w St Jas and St Paul *S'wark* 87-91; TV Ipswich St Fran *St E* 91-97; TV Walthamstow *Chelmsf* from 97. *St Luke's Vicarage, 17A Greenleaf Road, London E17 6QQ* Tel (020) 8520 2885 E-mail nigel@theansteys.freeserve.co.uk

ANSTICE, John Neville. b 39. Lon Univ BSc63. Cuddesdon Coll 69. **d** 71 **p** 72. C Stonebridge St Mich *Lon* 71-74; Chapl Woodbridge Sch 74-76; TV Droitwich *Worc* 76-80; P-in-c Salwarpe 76-79; Perm to Offic *Chich* from 80; rtd 99. *10 Selham Close, Crawley RH11 0EH* Tel (01293) 535654

ANTANANARIVO, Bishop of. *See* RABENIRINA, The Most Revd Remi Joseph

ANTELL, Roger Howard. b 47. Lon Univ BD71 Warwick Univ MSc79 Ox Univ MTh99. Ripon Coll Cuddesdon 97. **d** 99 **p** 00. C Ashchurch *Glouc* 99-03; R Stoke Prior, Wychbold and Upton

Warren *Worc* from 03. *The Rectory, Fish House Lane, Stoke Prior, Bromsgrove B60 4JT* Tel (01527) 832501 E-mail roger.antell@btinternet.com

ANTHAPURUSHA, b 53. Bangalore Univ BA77 Jnana Deepa Vidyapeeth Poona BPh80 Delhi Univ MA83 MPhil84 Serampore Th Coll BD87. Bp's Coll Calcutta 85. **d** 87 **p** 88. India 87-99; Bethany Chr Trust Edin 01-02; C Bistre *St As* from 02. *11 Bron yr Eglwys, Mynydd Isa, Mold CH7 6YQ* Tel (01352) 753465 E-mail apurusha@bronyreglwys.fsnet.co.uk

ANTHONY, Gerald Caldecott. b 18. Down Coll Cam BA41 MA44. Wycliffe Hall Ox 41. **d** 43 **p** 44. C Roxeth Ch Ch *Lon* 43-47; C Harlington 47-49; R Grays Inn Road St Bart 49-51; P-in-c Ernesettle *Ex* 51-55; V S Lambeth All SS and St Barn *S'wark* 55-58; Chapl Parkstone Sea Tr Sch Poole 58-64; Chapl HMS Ganges 64-65; P-in-c Bulmer *York* 65-66; R 66-72; V Broughton-in-Furness w Woodland *Carl* 72-75; P-in-c Seathwaite w Ulpha 73-75; V Broughton and Duddon 75-83; rtd 83; Perm to Offic *Worc* from 83. *2 Coppice Close, Malvern WR14 1LE* Tel (01886) 832930 Fax 830930 E-mail gacoppice@talk21.com

ANTHONY, Ian Charles. b 47. NW Ord Course 76. **d** 79 **p** 80. NSM Lt Lever *Man* from 79. *36 Meadow Close, Little Lever, Bolton BL3 1LG* Tel (01204) 791437

ANTHONY, Miss Sheila Margaret. b 52. Wycliffe Hall Ox BTh04. **d** 04 **p** 05. C Bideford, Northam, Westward Ho, Appledore etc *Ex* from 04. *61 Hanson Park, Northam, Bideford EX39 3SB* Tel (01237) 479339

ANTHONY MARY, Father. *See* HIRST, Anthony Melville

ANTOINE, Emma Louise. b 72. Newc Univ BA96. Westcott Ho Cam 02. **d** 05. C Easthampstead *Ox* from 05. *162 Hicks Farm Rise, High Wycombe HP13 7SG* Tel (01494) 526265 E-mail eantoine@fish.co.uk

ANTONY-ROBERTS, Gelert Roderick. b 43. Southn Univ BEd78 Reading Univ MA84. Sarum & Wells Th Coll 88. **d** 90 **p** 91. C Alton St Lawr *Win* 90-94. *Address temp unknown*

ap GWILYM, Gwynn. b 50. Univ of Wales (Ban) BA71 MA76. Wycliffe Hall Ox BA84 MA89 MPhil00. **d** 84 **p** 85. C Ynyscynhaearn w Penmorfa and Porthmadog *Ban* 84-86; R Penegoes and Darowen w Llanbryn-Mair 86-97; R Mallwyd w Cemais, Llanymawddwy, Darowen etc 97-02; P-in-c Penyfai *Llan* from 02. *The Vicarage, Pen-y-Fai, Bridgend CF31 4LS* Tel (01656) 652849

ap IORWERTH, Geraint. b 50. Univ of Wales (Lamp) DipTh72 Univ of Wales (Cardiff) DPS73 MPhil90 Open Univ BA78. Burgess Hall Lamp 69 Westmr Past Foundn 73 St Mich Coll Llan 73. **d** 74 **p** 75. C Holyhead w Rhoscolyn *Ban* 74-78; R Pennal w Corris and Esgairgeiliog from 78; Co-Founder and Ldr Order of Sancta Sophia from 87. *The Rectory, Pennal, Machynlleth SY20 9JS* Tel (01654) 791216 Fax as telephone E-mail apennal@ouvip.com

APPELBE, Canon Frederick Charles. b 52. TCD DipTh87. CITC 87. **d** 87 **p** 88. C Waterford w Killea, Drumcannon and Dunhill *C & O* 87-90; C Taney *D & G* 90-92; I Rathmichael from 92; Can Ch Ch Cathl Dublin from 02. *Rathmichael Rectory, Shankill, Co Dublin, Irish Republic* Tel and fax (00353) (1) 282 2803 Mobile 87-248 2410 E-mail rathmichael@dublin.anglican.org

APPLEBY, Anthony Robert Nightingale. b 40. K Coll Lon AKC62. St Boniface Warminster 62. **d** 63 **p** 64. C Cov St Mark *Cov* 63-67; CF 67-95; R Dulverton and Brushford *B & W* 95-02; rtd 02. *9 Ashleigh Park, Bampton, Tiverton EX16 9LF* Tel (01398) 331122

APPLEBY, David. b 60. St Jo Coll Dur BA04. Cranmer Hall Dur 02. **d** 04 **p** 05. C W Acklam *York* from 04. *37 Lambourne Drive, Marton-in-Cleveland, Middlesbrough TS7 8QF* Tel (01642) 314504 E-mail jdha@fish.co.uk

APPLEBY, Janet Elizabeth. b 58. Bris Univ BSc80 MSc81 Newc Poly BA90. Cranmer Hall Dur 01. **d** 03 **p** 04. C Newc H Cross *Newc* from 03. *2A Lanercost Drive, Newcastle upon Tyne NE5 2DE* Tel 0191-274 9574 E-mail janet.appleby@dunelm.org.uk

APPLEBY, Miss Janet Mohr. b 32. Lon Univ TCert53 BA79 Sussex Univ MA(Ed)74. Chich Th Coll 90. **d** 91 **p** 95. NSM Rottingdean *Chich* 91-95; NSM Stantonbury and Willen *Ox* 95-02; Perm to Offic from 02. *38 Darwin Close, Milton Keynes MK5 6FF* Tel (01908) 526737

APPLEBY, Ms Jennie. b 58. Southlands Coll Lon CertEd81. Cranmer Hall Dur 01. **d** 03 **p** 04. C Marton-in-Cleveland *York* from 03. *37 Lambourne Drive, Marton-in-Cleveland, Middlesbrough TS7 8QF* Tel (01642) 314504 E-mail jdha@fish.co.uk

APPLEBY, Mrs Melanie Jayne. b 65. RGN86. Ripon Coll Cuddesdon 01. **d** 03 **p** 04. C Reddish *Man* from 03. *49 Ilkley Crescent, Reddish, Stockport SK5 6HG* Tel 0161-442 2094 Mobile 07876-191572 E-mail melanieappleby@hotmail.com

APPLEFORD, Kenneth Henry. b 30. Portsm Dioc Tr Course 91. **d** 92. NSM Portsea St Mary *Portsm* 92-00; rtd 00. *124 Stride Avenue, Portsmouth PO3 6HN* Tel (023) 9281 4685

APPLEFORD, Canon Patrick Robert. b 25. Trin Coll Cam BA49 MA54. Chich Th Coll 50. **d** 52 **p** 53. C Poplar All SS w St Frideswide *Lon* 52-58; Chapl Bps' Coll Cheshunt 58-61; Educn Sec USPG 61-66; Dean Lusaka 66-72; P-in-c Sutton St Nicholas w Sutton St Michael *Heref* 73-75; Dir of Educn *Chelmsf* 75-90; Can Chelmsf Cathl 78-90; rtd 90; Perm to Offic *Chelmsf* from 90. *35 Sowerberry Close, Chelmsford CM1 4YB* Tel (01245) 443508

APPLEGARTH, Anthony Edgar. b 44. Chich Th Coll 82. **d** 84 **p** 85. C Cannington, Otterhampton, Combwich and Stockland *B & W* 84-86; C Bridgwater St Mary, Chilton Trinity and Durleigh 86-89; R Stogursey w Fiddington 89-00; P-in-c Devonport St Mark Ford *Ex* 00-02; V from 02. *St Mark's Vicarage, Cambridge Road, Plymouth PL2 1PU* Tel (01752) 565534

APPLEGATE, The Ven John. b 56. Bris Univ BSc78. Trin Coll Bris DipHE81 PhD85. **d** 84 **p** 85. C Collyhurst *Man* 84-87; Asst Chapl Monsall Hosp 84-87; C Broughton St Jas w St Clem and St Matthias 87-94; R Broughton St Jo 94-96; TR Broughton 96-02; AD Salford 97-02; Research Fell and Lect Man Univ from 00; Bp's Adv Hosp Chapl from 02; Adn Bolton from 02. *45 Rudgwick Drive, Bury BL8 1YA* Tel 0161-761 6117 Fax 763 7973 E-mail archdeacon@rudgwickdr.fsnet.co.uk

APPLETON, Mrs Bonita. b 55. St Jo Coll Nottm 91. **d** 93 **p** 94. C Camberley St Paul *Guildf* 93-96; TV Cove St Jo 96-03; Dioc Par Resources Officer from 03. *Diocesan House, Quarry Street, Guildford GU1 3XG* Tel (01483) 790330 E-mail bonnie.appleton@cofeguildford.org.uk

APPLETON, John Bearby. b 42. Linc Th Coll 74. **d** 76 **p** 77. C Selby Abbey *York* 76-79; C Epsom St Barn *Guildf* 79-82; V Linc All SS *Linc* 82-94; rtd 02. *33 South End, Osmotherley, Northallerton DL6 3BN*

APPLETON, Canon Ronald Percival. b 15. St Pet Hall Ox BA36 MA40. Ridley Hall Cam 36. **d** 38 **p** 39. C Hunsingore w Cowthorpe *Ripon* 38-39; C High Harrogate Ch Ch 39-42; C Bromley SS Pet and Paul *Roch* 42-44; R Knockholt 44-53; V Bromley Common St Luke 53-62; V Winchcombe, Gretton, Sudeley Manor etc *Glouc* 62-86; RD Winchcombe 63-86; Hon Can Glouc Cathl 80-86; rtd 86; Perm to Offic *Glouc* 86-97; Perm to Offic *Worc* from 97. *1 Abbey Croft, Pershore WR10 1JQ* Tel (01386) 553023

APPLETON, Timothy Charles. b 36. Selw Coll Cam BA60 MA65 K Coll Lon PhD67 Cam Univ ScD81. S'wark Ord Course 69. **d** 72 **p** 73. NSM Harston w Hauxton *Ely* 72-76; Lect Cam Univ 73-88; Lic to Offic *Ely* 76-79 and from 84; P-in-c Gt w Lt Eversden 79-84; Chapl and Cllr Bourn Hall Clinic from 88. *44 Eversden Road, Harlton, Cambridge CB3 7ET* Tel (01223) 262226 Fax 264332 E-mail tca@ifc.co.uk

APPLIN, David Edward. b 39. Oak Hill Th Coll 63. **d** 65 **p** 66. C Ox St Clem *Ox* 65-69; C Felixstowe SS Pet and Paul *St E* 69-71; Lic to Offic *Win* 71-91; Travelling Sec Rwanda Miss 71-74; Home Sec 74-77; Gen Sec 77-81; Dir Overseas Personnel Dept TEAR Fund 82-87; Overseas Dir 87-92; Hon C Kempshott *Win* 91-92; R Awbridge w Sherfield English 92-97; Exec Dir Samaritan's Purse Internat from 95. *Flat 4, 25 Christchurch Road, St Cross, Winchester SO23 9SU* Tel (01962) 865678

APPS, Anthony Howard. b 22. Ch Coll Cam BA47 MA51. **d** 49 **p** 50. C Poplar All SS w St Frideswide *Lon* 49-55; V Mile End Old Town H Trin 55-66; V Myddleton Square St Mark 66-82; rtd 82; Perm to Offic *York* from 82. *18 Longworth Way, Guisborough TS14 6DG* Tel (01287) 637939

APPS, Bryan Gerald. b 37. Univ of Wales (Lamp) BA59 St Cath Coll Ox BA61 MA65. Wycliffe Hall Ox 59. **d** 61 **p** 62. C Southampton St Alb *Win* 61-65; C Andover w Foxcott 65-69; P-in-c Freemantle 69-72; R 73-78; V Pokesdown All SS 78-03; rtd 03; Hon C Bournemouth St Pet w St Swithun, H Trin etc *Win* from 03. *14 Bartlett Drive, Bournemouth BH7 7JT* Tel (01202) 418360 E-mail bryanapps@talk21.com

APPS, David Ronald. b 34. Univ of Wales (Lamp) BA57. Sarum Th Coll 57. **d** 59 **p** 60. C Southbourne St Chris *Win* 59-62; C Weeke 62-67; V Alton All SS 67-80; V Charlestown *Truro* 80-97; Miss to Seamen 80-97; rtd 99. *12 Walnut Close, Exminster, Exeter EX6 8SZ* Tel (01392) 823672

APPS, Canon Michael John (Brother Bernard). b 28. Pemb Coll Cam BA52 MA56. Cuddesdon Coll 53. **d** 55 **p** 56. C Spalding *Linc* 55-58; SSF from 58; Perm to Offic *Chelmsf* 59-63 and 67-69; P-in-c Plaistow 63-67; Australia 69-75; Guardian St Nic Friary Harbledown 77-78; Guardian Hilfield Friary Dorchester 78-89; Can and Preb Sarum Cathl *Sarum* 81-89; Perm to Offic *Lon* 93-96 and from 99; *Cant* 03-05. *The Friary, Hilfield, Dorchester DT2 7BE* Tel (01300) 341345 Fax 341293

APTED, Peter John. b 43. Middx Univ MA01. NTMTC 95. **d** 98 **p** 99. NSM Feltham *Lon* 98-01; TV Horsham *Chich* from 01. *St Leonard's Vicarage, Cambridge Road, Horsham RH13 5ED* Tel (01403) 266903 E-mail peter@revapted.freeserve.co.uk

APTHORP, The Ven Arthur Norman. b 24. Pemb Coll Cam BA47 MA50. Chich Th Coll 48. **d** 50 **p** 51. C Henfield *Chich* 50-52; C Hove All SS 52-56; Australia from 56; R Narembeen 57-60; R Boulder 60-66; R Northam 66-72; R Kalgoorlie and

Boulder 72-78; Hon Can Perth 73-77 and 79-89; R Dianella 78-82; R Merredin 82-89; Adn of the Country (Perth) 82-87; Adn of the Goldfields 87-89; rtd 89. *2 Brookton Highway, Brookton, W Australia 6306* Tel (0061) (8) 9642 1046

AQUILINA, Ivan Dominic. b 66. Univ of Malta BA95 BA97 Educn Division Malta PGCE96 Leeds Univ MA02. Coll of Resurr Mirfield 98. **d** 00 **p** 01. C Leam Lane *Dur* 00-01; C Jarrow 01-04; C St Marylebone All SS *Lon* from 04. *6 Margaret Street, London W1W 8RQ* Tel (020) 7636 6952 Mobile 07947-139263 E-mail fatheraquilina@btinternet.com

ARANZULLA, John Paul. b 71. G&C Coll Cam BA94 Oak Hill Th Coll BA01. K Coll Lon 01. **d** 04 **p** 05. C Muswell Hill St Jas w St Matt *Lon* from 04. *31A Kings Avenue, London N10 1PA* E-mail aranzulla@bigfoot.com

ARBER, Gerald Kenneth. b 37. Open Univ BA87. Oak Hill NSM Course 81. **d** 84 **p** 85. NSM Romford St Edw *Chelmsf* 84-95; NSM Cranham from 95. *5 Hill Grove, Romford RM1 4JP* Tel (01708) 750070

ARBERY, Canon Richard Neil. b 25. AKC49. **d** 50 **p** 51. C Pemberton St Jo *Liv* 50-55; V Roundthorn *Man* 55-59; V Hindley All SS *Liv* 59-78; Chapl HM Youth Cust Cen Hindley 70-84; Asst Chapl HM YOI Hindley 84-90; RD Wigan *Liv* 75-89; Hon Can Liv Cathl 77-92; V Wigan St Andr 78-92; rtd 92; Perm to Offic *Liv* from 92. *11 Gillan Road, Wigan WN6 7HQ* Tel (01942) 491734

ARCH, Ian Michael. b 75. Univ Coll Dur MSc97 Peterho Cam BA02. Westcott Ho Cam 00. **d** 03. C Bromborough *Ches* from 03. *193 Allport Road, Wirral CH62 6BA* Tel 0151-334 4181 E-mail ian.arch@dunelm.org.uk

ARCHER, Alan Robert. b 38. AKC56. Lich Th Coll 65. **d** 68 **p** 69. C Lower Mitton *Worc* 68-71; C Foley Park 71-74; V Warndon 74-79; P-in-c Clifton upon Teme 79-81; P-in-c Lower Sapey 79-81; P-in-c The Shelsleys 79-81; V Malvern Wells and Wyche 81-83; TV Braunstone *Leic* 83-91; P-in-c Bemerton *Sarum* 91-03; Dioc Link Officer for ACUPA 92-94; rtd 03. *15 Summerfield Road, Stourport-on-Severn DY13 9BE* Tel (01299) 822983

ARCHER, David John. b 69. Ridley Hall Cam. **d** 05. C Abingdon *Ox* from 05. *33 Mattock Way, Abingdon OX14 2PQ* Tel (01235) 555083

ARCHER, Graham John. b 58. Lanc Univ BSc79. St Jo Coll Nottm 82. **d** 85 **p** 86. C Ipswich St Matt *St E* 85-89; C Walton 89-95; P-in-c 95-99; Chapl Local Health Partnerships NHS Trust 96-99; P-in-c Portswood Ch Ch *Win* 99-05; V from 05; P-in-c Portswood St Denys from 00. *The Vicarage, 36 Brookvale Road, Southampton SO17 1QR* Tel (023) 8055 4277 E-mail vicar@highfield.org.uk

ARCHER, John Thomas. b 28. Birm Coll of Commerce GIMechE68 Birm Poly CQSW83. EMMTC 79. **d** 80 **p** 81. NSM Derby St Thos *Derby* 80-86; V Edlington *Sheff* 87-98; rtd 98; Perm to Offic *Lich* from 04. *Little Croft, 20 Adderley, Cheadle, Stoke-on-Trent ST10 2NJ* Tel (01538) 751541

ARCHER, Keith Malcolm. b 40. Man Univ BA61 MA80 Magd Coll Cam BA67 MA72. Ridley Hall Cam 66. **d** 68 **p** 69. C Newland St Jo *York* 68-72; Hon C Kersal Moor *Man* 72-79; Ind Chapl 72-93; V Weaste from 93. *The Vicarage, 43 Derby Road, Salford M6 5YD* Tel 0161-736 5819 E-mail keitharcher@weaste.in2home.co.uk

ARCHER, Michael James. b 67. St Jo Coll Dur BA90 St Edm Coll Cam PhD95. Ridley Hall Cam CTM92. **d** 94 **p** 95. C Littleover *Derby* 94-97; C Edgware *Lon* 97-98; TV 98-01; P-in-c Bletchley *Ox* from 01. *101 Whalley Drive, Bletchley, Milton Keynes MK3 6HX* Tel (01908) 630305

ARCHER, Michael John. b 37. Trin Coll Bris 76. **d** 78 **p** 79. C Kinson *Sarum* 78-81; C Harpenden St Nic *St Alb* 81-88; P-in-c Rashcliffe and Lockwood *Wakef* 88-00; rtd 00; Perm to Offic *Truro* from 02. *Seaview Cottage, Porthallow, Helston TR12 6PW* Tel (01326) 280502

ARCHER, Neill John. b 61. UEA BA82. NTMTC 96. **d** 99 **p** 00. C Ripley *Derby* 99-02; C Forster Tuncurry Australia 02-03; Perm to Offic *Lon* 03-04; P-in-c Malmesbury w Westport and Brokenborough *Bris* from 04. *The Vicarage, Holloway, Malmesbury SN16 9BA* Tel (01666) 823126 Mobile 07946-540720 E-mail neilljarcher@tiscali.co.uk

ARCHER, Ms Sarah Elizabeth. b 66. Charing Cross Hosp Medical Sch MB, BS89 Heythrop Coll Lon MA03 MRCGP95. Ripon Coll Cuddesdon BA99. **d** 00 **p** 01. C Dulwich St Barn *S'wark* 00-03; C Shepherd's Bush St Steph w St Thos *Lon* from 03. *The Parsonage, 1 Commonwealth Avenue, London W12 7QR* Tel (020) 8743 7100 Mobile 07717-718569 E-mail searcher@fish.co.uk

ARCUS, Jeffrey. b 40. NW Ord Course 72. **d** 75 **p** 76. C Halliwell St Thos *Man* 75-78; C Walmsley 78-81; P-in-c Bury Ch King 81-82; TV Bury Ch King w H Trin 82-93; V Ramsbottom St Jo and St Paul from 93; C Edenfield and Stubbins from 04. *St Paul's Vicarage, Maple Grove, Ramsbottom, Bury BL0 0AN* Tel (01706) 821036

ARDAGH-WALTER, Christopher Richard. b 35. Univ of Wales (Lamp) BA58. Chich Th Coll 58. **d** 60 **p** 61. C Heavitree *Ex* 60-64; C Redcar *York* 64-67; C King's Worthy *Win* 67-69; C-in-c Four Marks CD 70-73; V Four Marks 73-76; P-in-c Eling, Testwood and Marchwood 76-78; TR Totton 76-84; R The Sherbornes w Pamber 84-88; V Froyle and Holybourne 88-95; C Verwood *Sarum* 95-97; rtd 97; Perm to Offic *Win* from 98 and *Ox* from 01. *2 Bunkers Hill, Newbury RG14 6TF* Tel (01635) 41128 E-mail ctaw@a-walter.freeserve.co.uk

✠**ARDEN, The Rt Revd Donald Seymour.** b 16. CBE81. Leeds Univ BA37. Coll of Resurr Mirfield 37. **d** 39 **p** 40 **c** 61. C Hatcham St Cath *S'wark* 39-40; C Potten End w Nettleden *St Alb* 41-43; S Africa 44-61; Can Zululand 59-61; Bp Nyasaland 61-64; Bp S Malawi 71-81; Abp Cen Africa 71-80; Asst Bp Willesden *Lon* 81-94; Hon Asst Bp Lon from 94; P-in-c Uxbridge St Marg 81-86; rtd 86; Hon C N Harrow St Alb *Lon* from 86. *6 Frobisher Close, Pinner HA5 1NN* Tel (020) 8866 6009 Fax 8868 8013 E-mail ardendj@yahoo.co.uk

ARDFERT AND AGHADOE, Archdeacon of. *Vacant*

ARDILL, Robert William Brian. b 40. QUB BSc63 PhD67 SOSc. Ox NSM Course 80 St Jo Coll Nottm 84. **d** 83 **p** 85. NSM Sunninghill *Ox* 83-84; Hon Chapl R Holloway Coll *Lon* 83-84; C Lenton *S'well* 85-87; Perm to Offic *Leic* 92-95; C Harpenden St Nic *St Alb* 95-00; R N Tawton, Bondleigh, Sampford Courtenay etc *Ex* from 00. *The Rectory, Essington Close, North Tawton EX20 2EX* Tel (01837) 82645 E-mail brian.ardill@onetel.net

ARDING, Richard. b 52. ACIB84. Oak Hill Th Coll 90. **d** 92 **p** 93. C Bromley Common St Aug *Roch* 92-96; V Wilmington from 96. *The Vicarage, 1 Curate's Walk, Dartford DA2 7BJ* Tel (01322) 220561 E-mail richardarding@btopenworld.com

ARDIS, Edward George. b 54. Dur Univ BA76. CITC 76. **d** 78 **p** 79. C Dublin Drumcondra w N Strand and St Barn *D & G* 78-81; C Dublin St Bart w Leeson Park 81-84; I Ardamine w Kiltennel, Glascarrig etc *C & O* 84-89; Can Tuam Cathl *T, K & A* 89-03; Dean Killala 89-03; I Killala w Dunfeeny, Crossmolina etc 89-94; I Killala w Dunfeeny, Crossmolina, Kilmoremoy etc 94-03; Dir of Ords 95-03; I Dublin Irishtown w Donnybrook *D & G* from 03. *St Mary's Rectory, 4 Ailesbury Grove, Donnybrook, Dublin 4, Irish Republic* Tel (00353) (1) 269 2090 E-mail donnybrook@dublin.anglican.org

ARDLEY, Annette Susan. b 68. SEITE 01. **d** 04 **p** 05. C Barham w Bishopsbourne and Kingston *Cant* from 04. *19 Heathfield Way, Barham, Canterbury CT4 6QH* Tel (01227) 833820 E-mail nettie@ardley185.fsnet.co.uk

ARENS, Johannes. b 69. Heythrop Coll Lon MTh97. **d** 96 **p** 97. Old Catholic Ch Germany 96-04; TV Harrogate St Wilfrid *Ripon* from 04. *St Wilfrid's House, 23 Azerley Grove, Harrogate HG3 2SY* Tel (01423) 709432 E-mail johannes.arens@gmx.net

ARGENTINA, Bishop of. *See* VENABLES, The Most Revd Gregory James

ARGLES, Mrs Christine. b 57. Bris Univ BA00. Trin Coll Bris 00. **d** 02 **p** 03. C Nailsea Ch Ch w Tickenham *B & W* 02-05; Chapl Weston Area Health Trust from 05. *Weston General Hospital, Grange Road, Uphill, Weston-super-Mare BS23 4TQ* Tel (01934) 636363 Mobile 07763-476127 Fax 619275 E-mail chrisargles@aol.com

ARGUILE, Canon Roger Henry William. b 43. Dur Univ LLB64 Keble Coll Ox BA70 MA75. St Steph Ho Ox 69 Ripon Hall Ox 70. **d** 71 **p** 72. C Walsall *Lich* 71-76; TV Blakenall Heath 76-83; TV Stafford 83-95; P-in-c St Neots *Ely* 95-97; V from 97; Hon Can Ely Cathl from 01; RD St Neots from 02. *The Vicarage, Church Street, St Neots PE19 2BU* Tel (01480) 472297 E-mail roger.arguile@snpc.freeserve.co.uk

ARGYLE, Douglas Causer. b 17. St Jo Coll Cam BA39 MA43. Ridley Hall Cam 39. **d** 41 **p** 42. C Somercotes *Derby* 41-44; CF (EC) 44-47; Chapl Repton Sch Derby 47-59; Chapl Gresham's Sch Holt 59-74; P-in-c Eastleach w Southrop *Glouc* 74-82; rtd 82; Perm to Offic *Glouc* from 82. *East Lynn, London Road, Fairford GL7 4AR* Tel (01285) 713235

ARGYLE, Edward Charles. b 55. Edith Cowan Univ (Aus) BSocSc99. St Barn Coll Adelaide 77 ACT DipTh80. **d** 80 **p** 80. Australia 80-83 and from 94; C Whitford 80-82; C Gt Yarmouth *Nor* 83-85; I Kilcooley w Littleon, Crohane and Fertagh *C & O* 85-94; Can Ossory and Leighlin Cathls 90-94; NY USA 92; Min Cranbrook w Mt Barker from 95; R Albany from 02. *Peel Place, Collie Street, PO Box 5520, Albany, W Australia 6332* Tel (0061) (8) 9842 6215 *or* 9841 5015 Mobile 428-514119 Fax 9841 3360 E-mail eargyle@telstra.easymail.com.au

ARGYLL AND THE ISLES, Bishop of. *See* SHAW, The Rt Revd Alexander Martin

ARGYLL AND THE ISLES, Dean of. *See* FLATT, The Very Revd Roy Francis Ferguson

ARKELL, Kevin Paul. b 53. Preston Poly BTh86 Leeds Univ MA95. Sarum & Wells Th Coll 84. **d** 86 **p** 87. C S Petherton w the Seavingtons *B & W* 86-88; P-in-c Gt Harwood St Bart *Blackb* 88-90; V 90-95; TR Darwen St Pet w Hoddlesden 95-03; Acting RD Darwen 97-98; AD Blackb and Darwen 98-03; P-in-c Pokesdown All SS *Win* from 03. *All Saints' Vicarage, 14 Stourwood Road, Bournemouth BH6 3QP* Tel and fax (01202) 423747 Mobile 07971-800083 E-mail kevin.arkell@ntlworld.com

ARLOW, Canon William James. b 26. Edin Th Coll 59. **d** 59 **p** 60. C Ballymacarrett St Patr *D & D* 59-61; Cen Adv on Chr Stewardship to Ch of Ireland 61-66; I Newry St Patr 66-70; I Belfast St Donard 70-74; Dep Sec Irish Coun of Chs 74-75; Sec 75-79; Can for Ecum Affairs Belf Cathl from 79; Treas 85-89; P-in-c Ballyphilip w Ardquin 86-89; rtd 89; Lic to Offic *D & D* from 90. *13 Ashford Park, Bangor BT19 6DD* Tel (028) 9146 9758 E-mail william.arlow@talk21.com

ARMAGH, Archbishop of. *See* EAMES, The Most Revd and Rt Hon Lord

ARMAGH, Archdeacon of. *See* HOEY, The Ven Raymond George

ARMAGH, Dean of. *See* CASSIDY, The Very Revd Herbert

ARMAN, Canon Brian Robert. b 54. St Jo Coll Dur BA77. Cranmer Hall Dur 74. **d** 78 **p** 79. C Lawrence Weston *Bris* 78-82; C Bishopston 82-88; R Filton from 88; P-in-c Horfield St Greg 03-05; Hon Can Bris Cathl from 01. *The Rectory, Station Road, Bristol BS34 7BX* Tel 0117-979 1128

ARMES, John Andrew. b 55. SS Coll Cam BA77 MA81 Man Univ PhD96. Sarum & Wells Th Coll 77. **d** 79 **p** 80. C Walney Is *Carl* 79-82; Chapl to Agric 82-86; TV Greystoke, Matterdale and Mungrisdale 82-86; TV Watermillock 82-86; TV Man Whitworth *Man* 86-88; TR 88-94; Chapl Man Univ 86-94; P-in-c Goodshaw and Crawshawbooth 94-98; AD Rossendale 94-98; R Edin St Jo *Edin* from 98. *1 Ainslie Place, Edinburgh EH3 6AR* Tel 0131-225 5004 *or* 229 7565 Fax 229 2561 E-mail johnarmes@btconnect.com

ARMFELT, Julian Roger. b 31. K Coll Cam BA53. Wells Th Coll 54. **d** 56 **p** 58. C Stocksbridge *Sheff* 56-57; C Cantley 57-59; P-in-c Clayton w Frickley 59-61; C Eglingham *Newc* 61-63; V Alkborough w Whitton *Linc* 63-64; C Corringham 69-73; TV Fincham *Ely* 73-75; V Freckleton *Blackb* 75-79; P-in-c Sherburn *York* 79-80; P-in-c W and E Heslerton w Knapton 79-80; P-in-c Yedingham 79-80; R Sherburn and W and E Heslerton w Yedingham 80-83; TV York All SS Pavement w St Crux and St Martin etc 83-84; P-in-c York St Mary Bishophill Junior w All SS 83-84; C Howden 84-86; P-in-c Laughton w Throapham *Sheff* 86-88; rtd 88; Perm to Offic *Newc* 88-02. *29 Dulverton Hall, Esplanade, Scarborough YO11 2AR* Tel (01723) 340129

ARMITAGE, Bryan Ambrose. b 28. K Coll Lon AKC55 BD58. **d** 56 **p** 57. C High Harrogate St Pet *Ripon* 56-59; S Africa 59-61; Uganda 61-73; Chapl Sutton Valence Sch Kent 73-75; Chapl Qu Ethelburga's Sch Harrogate 76-91; V Weaverthorpe w Helperthorpe, Luttons Ambo etc *York* 91-99; Chapl Qu Ethelburga's Coll York from 99. *5 York Road, Harrogate HG1 2QA* Tel (01423) 536547

ARMITAGE, Richard Norris. b 51. AKC. St Aug Coll Cant 73. **d** 74 **p** 75. C Chapelthorpe *Wakef* 74-77; C W Bromwich All SS *Lich* 77-82; P-in-c Ketley 82-83; V Oakengates 82-83; V Ketley and Oakengates 83-89; V Evesham *Worc* 89-96; V Evesham w Norton and Lenchwick from 96; RD Evesham from 00. *The Vicarage, 5 Croft Road, Evesham WR11 4NE* Tel (01386) 446219 *or* 442213 Fax 761214 E-mail allsaintsevesham@tiscali.co.uk

ARMITAGE, Susan. b 46. Th Ext Educn Coll 91. **d** 92 **p** 95. Pretoria Corpus Christi S Africa 92-97; C Fawley *Win* 97-00; C Chandler's Ford 00-04; TV Wylye and Till Valley *Sarum* from 04. *The Vicarage, Chapel Lane, Shrewton, Salisbury SP3 4BX* Tel (01980) 620580 E-mail sue.armitage@dial.pipex.com

ARMITSTEAD, Margaretha Catharina Maria. b 65. Free Univ of Amsterdam MA89. St Alb and Ox Min Course 00. **d** 03 **p** 04. C Littlemore *Ox* from 03. *20 Vicarage Close, Littlemore, Oxford OX4 4PL* Tel (01865) 779885 Mobile 07761-549548 E-mail mail@armistead34.free-online.co.uk

ARMITT, Andy John. b 68. Moorlands Bible Coll 88 Trin Coll Bris BA00. **d** 00 **p** 01. C Millhouses H Trin *Sheff* 00-03; R Bisley and W End *Guildf* from 03. *The Rectory, Clews Lane, Bisley, Woking GU24 9DY* Tel and fax (01483) 473377 Mobile 07811-909782 E-mail andyarmitt@hotmail.com

ARMSON, Canon John Moss. b 39. Selw Coll Cam BA61 MA64 St Andr Univ PhD65. Coll of Resurr Mirfield 64. **d** 66 **p** 67. C Notting Hill St Jo *Lon* 66-69; Chapl and Fell Down Coll Cam 69-73; Chapl Westcott Ho Cam 73-76; Vice-Prin 76-82; Prin Edin Th Coll 82-89; Can St Mary's Cathl *Edin* 82-89; Can Res Roch Cathl *Roch* 89-01; rtd 01; Hengrave Community of Reconciliation from 01. *Mill Bank, Rowlestone, Hereford HR2 0DS* Tel (01981) 241046 E-mail j.armson@virgin.net *or* j.armson@hengravehallcentre.org.uk

ARMSTEAD, Geoffrey Malcolm. b 32. K Coll Lon BD56 AKC56 Nottm Univ AdDipEd73. St Boniface Warminster 56. **d** 57 **p** 57. C Weymouth H Trin *Sarum* 57-60; C Mortlake w E Sheen *S'wark* 60-63; Chapl Em Sch Wandsworth 63-74; Dep Hd Master Harriet Costello Sch 74-91; Acting Hd Master 91-92; Perm to Offic *Win* 74-92 and from 01; V Win St Bart 92-01; rtd 01. *Polecat Cottage, Polecat Corner, Tunworth, Basingstoke RG25 2LA* Tel (01256) 471650 E-mail geoffrey@armsteadg.freeserve.co.uk

ARMSTEAD, Gordon. b 33. Oak Hill Th Coll DPS74. **d** 74 **p** 75. C Woodside *Ripon* 74-76; C Heaton Ch Ch *Man* 76-79; Australia 79-81; R Levenshulme St Mark *Man* 81-86; V Borth and Eglwys-fach w Llangynfelyn *St D* 86-92; rtd 93; Perm to Offic *Blackb* 93-99; *Derby* from 99. *4 School Lane, Ripley, Derby DE5 3GT* Tel (01773) 741642

ARMSTRONG, Adrian Christopher. b 48. LSE BSc70 K Coll Lon PhD80. EAMTC 84. **d** 87 **p** 88. NSM Linton *Ely* 87-95; P-in-c N and S Muskham *S'well* 95-00; P-in-c Averham w Kelham 95-00; Perm to Offic *B & W* 01-02; Hon C Wiveliscombe w Chipstable, Huish Champflower etc from 02. *Cridlands Barn, Brompton Ralph, Taunton TA4 2RU* Tel (01984) 632191 E-mail wheelievicar@aol.com

ARMSTRONG, Alexander Milford. b 57. Local Minl Tr Course 87 96. **d** 95 **p** 95. NSM Livingston LEP *Edin* 95-97; C Cleator Moor w Cleator *Carl* 97-98; C Frizington and Arlecdon 97-98; C Crosslacon 98-99; V Westfield St Mary from 99. *St Mary's Vicarage, Salisbury Street, Workington CA14 3TA* Tel and fax (01900) 603227 E-mail amvarmstrong@hotmail.com

ARMSTRONG, The Very Revd Christopher John. b 47. Nottm Univ BTh75. Kelham Th Coll 72. **d** 75 **p** 76. C Maidstone All SS w St Phil and H Trin *Cant* 76-79; Chapl St Hild and St Bede Coll *Dur* 79-84; Abp's Dom Chapl and Dir of Ords *York* 85-91; V Scarborough St Martin 91-01; Dean Blackb from 01. *The Deanery, Preston New Road, Blackburn BB2 6PS* Tel (01254) 52502 *or* 51491 Fax 689666 E-mail dean@blackburn.anglican.org

ARMSTRONG, Christopher John Richard. b 35. Fribourg Univ LTh60 Ch Coll Cam BA64 MA68 PhD79. Edin Th Coll 74. **d** 59 **p** 59. In RC Ch 59-71; Lect Aber Univ *Ab* 68-74; C Ledbury *Heref* 74-76; P-in-c Bredenbury and Wacton w Grendon Bishop 76-79; P-in-c Edwyn Ralph and Collington w Thornbury 76-79; P-in-c Pencombe w Marston Stannett and Lt Cowarne 76-79; R Cherry Burton *York* 79-80; Tutor Westcott Ho Cam 80-85; V Bottisham *Ely* 85-89; P-in-c Lode and Longmeadow 85-89; P-in-c Cropthorne w Charlton *Worc* 89-93; Dioc Local Min Sec 89-93; R Aberdaron w Rhiw and Llanfaelrhys etc *Ban* 93-99; rtd 99; Perm to Offic *Heref* and *Ban* from 99. *Rowlstone Mill, Pontrilas, Hereford HR2 0DP* Tel (01981) 240346

ARMSTRONG, Colin John. b 32. St Cath Soc Ox BA59 MA65. Wells Th Coll 59. **d** 61 **p** 62. C Acomb St Steph *York* 61-64; C Newland St Jo 64-67; Chapl and Tutor All SS Coll Tottenham 67-78; Chapl and Tutor Middx Poly *Lon* 78-85; rtd 97; Perm to Offic *St E* from 97. *Mead House, The Street, Preston St Mary, Sudbury CO10 9NQ* Tel (01787) 248218 E-mail armsuff@waitrose.com

ARMSTRONG, Eileen. **d** 95 **p** 96. NSM *M & K* from 95. *Hennigan, Nobber, Co Meath, Irish Republic* Tel (00353) (46) 905 2314

ARMSTRONG, John Edwin. b 51. Leic Univ CertEd73 BEd74 Homerton Coll Cam AEdRD87. Ridley Hall Cam CTM93. **d** 93 **p** 94. C Gt Wilbraham *Ely* 93-96; P-in-c Bassingbourn 96-02; V 02-04; P-in-c Whaddon 96-02; V 02-04; P-in-c Southam *Cov* from 04; P-in-c Ufton from 04. *The Rectory, Park Lane, Southam, Leamington Spa CV47 0JA* Tel (01926) 812413 E-mail revarmstrong@yahoo.com

ARMSTRONG, John Gordon. b 64. Man Poly BSc86 MSc91 Man Univ MA03. Wycliffe Hall Ox 95. **d** 97 **p** 98. C Pennington *Man* 97-01; P-in-c Holcombe from 01; P-in-c Hawkshaw Lane from 01. *The Rectory, 12 Carrwood Hey, Ramsbottom, Bury BL0 9QT* Tel and fax (01706) 822312 E-mail john.armstrong4@tesco.net

ARMSTRONG, Canon John Hammond. b 24. MBE98. Dur Univ BA47 DipTh49. **d** 49 **p** 50. C Bishopwearmouth St Gabr *Dur* 49-52; C Cockfield w Staindrop 52-54; V Skipwith *York* 54-59; V Thorganby 54-59; V N Ferriby 59-63; R Sutton upon Derwent 63-71; Dioc Stewardship Adv 63-75; P-in-c York All SS and St Crux w St Sav etc 71-72; R 72-76; P-in-c York St Denys 74-76; TR York All SS Pavement w St Crux and St Denys 76-77; TR York All SS Pavement w St Crux and St Martin etc 77-91; Can and Preb York Minster 72-97; RD City of York 76-86; rtd 91; Perm to Offic *York* from 91. *20 Hempland Avenue, Stockton Lane, York YO31 1DE* Tel (01904) 421312

ARMSTRONG, Mrs Margaret Betty. b 48. SRN70 RSCN71. Westcott Ho Cam CTM92. **d** 92 **p** 94. NSM Linton *Ely* 92-95; NSM Shudy Camps 92-95; NSM Castle Camps 92-95; NSM Bartlow 92-95; NSM N and S Muskham and Averham w Kelham *S'well* 95-00; P-in-c Lydeard St Lawrence w Brompton Ralph etc *B & W* from 01. *Cridlands Barn, Brompton Ralph, Taunton TA4 2RU* Tel (01984) 623191 E-mail wheelievicar@aol.com

ARMSTRONG, Maurice Alexander. b 62. Ulster Poly BA84 TCD DipTh87. CITC 84. **d** 87 **p** 88. C Portadown St Mark *Arm* 87-90; I Sixmilecross w Termonmaguirke 90-95; I Richhill 95-01; I Tempo and Clabby *Clogh* from 01. *The Rectory, Clabby, Fivemiletown BT75 0RD* Tel (028) 8952 1697

ARMSTRONG, Nicholas Paul. b 58. Bris Univ BSc79. Trin Coll Bris DipHE93. **d** 93 **p** 94. C Filey *York* 93-97; P-in-c Alveley and Quatt *Heref* 97-98; R from 98. *The Rectory, Alveley, Bridgnorth WV15 6ND* Tel and fax (01746) 780326 E-mail nicka@fish.co.uk

ARMSTRONG, Canon Robert Charles (Robin). b 24. TCD BA46 HDipEd52 MA57. CITC 47. **d** 47 **p** 48. C Belfast St Luke *Conn*

48-50; Warden Gr Sch Dub 50-59; Succ St Patr Cathl Dublin 50-59; I Dublin Finglas *D & G* 59-67; I Dun Laoghaire 67-94; Dir of Ords (Dub) 74-84; USPG Area Sec 77-94; Can Ch Ch Cathl Dublin 84-88; Treas 88-94; rtd 94. *1 Glenageary Terrace, Dun Laoghaire, Co Dublin, Irish Republic* Tel (00353) (1) 284 6941

ARMSTRONG, Samuel David. b 48. BD MTh. **d** 86 **p** 87. C Cambridge H Trin w St Andr Gt *Ely* 86-89; V Cambridge St Martin 89-00; I Carrigaline Union *C, C & R* from 00. *The Rectory, Carrigaline, Co Cork, Irish Republic* Tel (00353) (21) 437 2224

ARMSTRONG, Samuel George. b 39. Ox Univ Inst of Educn TCert65 CYCW65 AdCertEd71 Open Univ BA72 Reading Univ MSc89. S Dios Minl Tr Scheme 90. **d** 93 **p** 94. NSM N Tadley St Mary *Win* from 93. *The Cedars, Blakes Lane, Tadley, Basingstoke RG26 3PU* Tel 0118-981 6593
E-mail sammie@armstrongsg.freeserve.co.uk

ARMSTRONG, Mrs Susan Elizabeth. b 45. **d** 05. OLM Tilstock, Edstaston and Whixall *Lich* from 05. *Tarragon Cottage, Shrewsbury Street, Prees, Whitchurch SY13 2DH* Tel (01948) 840039 E-mail suearmstrong@tesco.net

ARMSTRONG, Mrs Valri. b 50. Man Univ BA73. **d** 04. OLM Stoke by Nayland w Leavenheath and Polstead *St E* from 04. *Orchid House, 38 Bramble Way, Leavenheath, Colchester CO6 4UN* Tel (01206) 262814
E-mail mrsvarmstrong@hotmail.co.uk

ARMSTRONG, William. b 29. Sarum Th Coll 52. **d** 54 **p** 55. C Hebburn St Cuth *Dur* 54-55; C Ferryhill 55-57; C Gateshead H Trin 57-60; V Cassop cum Quarrington 60-66; Australia 66-81; Asst Dir of Educn *Liv* 81-90; V Aintree St Pet 81-88; TV Speke St Aid 88-90; rtd 90. *10 Blenheim Court, Horn Lane, Woodford Green IG8 9AQ* Tel (020) 8504 1874

ARMSTRONG-MacDONNELL, Mrs Vivienne Christine. b 42. Open Univ BA89 Ex Univ MEd01 Lambeth MA05. Ripon Coll Cuddesdon 88. **d** 90 **p** 94. C Crediton and Shobrooke *Ex* 90-93; Dioc Adv in Adult Tr 93-00; rtd 00; Perm to Offic *Ex* from 00. *Strand House, Woodbury, Exeter EX5 1LZ* Tel and fax (01395) 232790 E-mail viv.a-macdonnell@tiscali.co.uk

ARNDT, Miss Sarah. b 76. Univ of Wales (Abth) BTh98. St Jo Coll Nottm 98. **d** 00 **p** 01. C Flint *St As* 00-02. *14 Erw Gaer, Moss, Wrexham LL11 6DF* Tel (01978) 750384

ARNESEN, Christopher Paul. b 48. Lon Univ BA70. Sarum & Wells Th Coll 78. **d** 80 **p** 81. C Dalton-in-Furness *Carl* 80-83; C Ranmoor *Sheff* 83-86; R Distington *Carl* 86-93; TV Sheff Manor *Sheff* 93-97; Mental Health Chapl Sheff Care Trust 98-04; Perm to Offic *Sheff* from 04. *21 Horndean Road, Sheffield S5 6UJ* E-mail paul.arnesen@arnies.org.uk

ARNESEN, Raymond Halfdan (Brother Ælred). b 25. Qu Coll Cam BA49 MA54. Linc Th Coll 50. **d** 52 **p** 53. C Newc St Fran *Newc* 52-55; SSF 55-66; Cistercian Monk from 66; Ewell Monastery 66-04; rtd 95. *44 Amwell Road, Cambridge CB4 2UL*

ARNOLD, Adrian Paul. b 69. St Steph Ho Ox. **d** 01 **p** 02. C Staincliffe and Carlinghow *Wakef* 01-04; V New Cantley *Sheff* from 04. *St Hugh's House, Levet Road, Cantley, Doncaster DN4 6JQ* Tel (01302) 535739 Mobile 07951-873597
E-mail frarnold@aparnold.freeserve.co.uk

ARNOLD, Brother. *See* NODDER, Thomas Arthur

ARNOLD, David Alun. b 78. St Andr Univ MTheol00. Coll of Resurr Mirfield 01. **d** 03 **p** 04. C Ribbleton *Blackb* 03-05; C Hawes Side and Marton Moss from 05. *1 Dugdale Court, Squires Gate Lane, Blackpool FY4 3RW* Tel (01253) 768545 Mobile 07786-168261

ARNOLD, Derek John. b 59. Wycliffe Hall Ox 01. **d** 03 **p** 04. C St Jo in Bedwardine *Worc* from 03. *16 Heron Close, Worcester WR2 4BW* Tel (01905) 339053 Mobile 07789-631346
E-mail curate@stjohninbedwardine.co.uk

ARNOLD, Elisabeth Anne Truyens. b 44. TCert66. LNSM course 88. **d** 91 **p** 94. OLM Ipswich St Thos *St E* 91-00; Chapl Dioc Min Course 00-01; OLM Tutor from 01. *66 Bromeswell Road, Ipswich IP4 3AT* Tel (01473) 257406

ARNOLD, Ernest Stephen. b 27. **d** 64 **p** 65. C Aberavon *Llan* 64-68; V Ferndale 68-74; Cyprus 81-85; rtd 94; Perm to Offic *Portsm* from 94. *Barn Cottage, Apse Manor Road, Shanklin PO37 7PN* Tel (01983) 866324

ARNOLD, Miss Frances Mary. b 64. R Holloway Coll Lon BA86 Hatf Coll Dur PGCE90. Westcott Ho Cam 01. **d** 04 **p** 05. C Biggleswade *St Alb* from 04. *St Andrew's House, 46 Wilsheres Road, Biggleswade SG18 0DN* Tel (01767) 314240

ARNOLD, Graham Thomas. b 62. Aston Tr Scheme 87 Ripon Coll Cuddesdon 89. **d** 92 **p** 93. C Margate St Jo *Cant* 92-95; TV Whitstable 95-00. *62B Crawthew Grove, London SE22 9AB* Tel (020) 8693 2323

ARNOLD, Jennifer Anne. b 54. Univ Coll Lon BSc75 MB, BS78 FRCR85. Qu Coll Birm 00. **d** 02 **p** 03. C Aston SS Pet and Paul *Birm* from 02. *68 Manor Road, Aston, Birmingham B6 6QT* Tel 0121-326 7390 Mobile 07754-449266
E-mail arnolds68@btopenworld.com

ARNOLD, The Very Revd John Robert. b 33. OBE02. SS Coll Cam BA57 MA61 Lambeth DD99. Westcott Ho Cam 58. **d** 60 **p** 61. C Millhouses H Trin *Sheff* 60-63; Chapl and Lect Southn Univ *Win* 63-72; Gen Sec Gen Syn Bd for Miss and Unity 72-78; Hon Can Win Cathl *Win* 74-78; Dean Roch 78-89; Dean Dur 89-02; rtd 03; Perm to Offic *Cant* from 02. *26 Hawks Lane, Canterbury CT1 2NU* Tel (01227) 764703

ARNOLD, Jonathan Allen. b 69. St Pet Coll Ox BA92 MA99 K Coll Lon PhD04 LTCL89 LRAM94. Ripon Coll Cuddesdon 03. **d** 05. NSM Chalgrove w Berrick Salome *Ox* from 05. *4 School Yard, Stadhampton, Oxford OX44 7TT* Tel (01865) 400194
E-mail jonathan.arnold@fish.co.uk

✠**ARNOLD, The Rt Revd Keith Appleby.** b 26. Trin Coll Cam BA50 MA55. Westcott Ho Cam 50. **d** 52 **p** 53 **c** 80. C Haltwhistle *Newc* 52-55; C Edin St Jo *Edin* 55-61; R 61-69; CF (TA) 58-62; V Kirkby Lonsdale w Mansergh *Carl* 69-73; RD Berkhamsted *St Alb* 73-80; TR Hemel Hempstead 73-80; Suff Bp Warw *Cov* 80-90; Hon Can Cov Cathl 80-90; rtd 90; Hon Asst Bp Ox from 97. *9 Dinglederry, Olney MK46 5ES* Tel (01234) 713044

ARNOLD, Michael John. b 44. Rhodes Univ BA68 St Edm Hall Ox BA72 MA77. St Jo Coll Nottm 93. **d** 98 **p** 98. Asst Chapl St Jo Coll Johannesburg S Africa 98-99; Chapl from 01; Chapl Clayesmore Sch Blandford 98-01. *St John's College, St David's Road, Houghton Estate, Johannesburg, 2198 South Africa* Tel (0027) (11) 648 9932 *or* 648 1350 Mobile (0) 72 3134315 Fax 487 2227 E-mail arnoldmj@hotmail.com

ARNOLD, Norman. *See* ARNOLD, Victor Norman

ARNOLD, Richard Nicholas. b 54. AKC76. S'wark Ord Course 76. **d** 77 **p** 78. C Nunhead St Antony *S'wark* 77-80; C Walworth 80-82; P-in-c Streatham Hill St Marg 82-84; V 84-89; P-in-c Oseney Crescent St Luke *Lon* 89-93; P-in-c Kentish Town St Jo 89-93; P-in-c Kentish Town St Benet and All SS 89-93; V Kentish Town from 93; AD S Camden from 00. *Kentish Town Vicarage, 43 Lady Margaret Road, London NW5 2NH* Tel (020) 7485 4231 Mobile 07802-730974 Fax (020) 7482 7222
E-mail fr.arnold@lineone.net

ARNOLD, Canon Roy. b 36. St D Coll Lamp BA62 DipTh63. **d** 63 **p** 64. C Brislington St Luke *Bris* 63-66; C Ches St Mary *Ches* 67-70; V Brinnington w Portwood 71-75; V Sale St Paul 75-82; R Dodleston 82-84; V Sheff St Oswald *Sheff* 84-90; Dioc Communications Officer 84-97; Chapl w the Deaf 90-97; Hon Can Sheff Cathl 95-97; rtd 97; Perm to Offic *Ches* from 97. *49 Crossfield Road, Bollington, Macclesfield SK10 5EA* Tel (01625) 575472

ARNOLD, Ms Sonja Marie. b 63. Wycliffe Hall Ox BTh98. **d** 98 **p** 99. Assoc V Hammersmith St Simon *Lon* from 98; Dean of Women's Min Kensington Area from 02. *Flat 2, 176 Holland Road, London W14 8AH* Tel (020) 7603 8475 *or* 7603 1418
E-mail sarnold@stsimonsw14.com

ARNOLD, Victor Norman. b 45. Oak Hill Th Coll 91. **d** 94 **p** 95. NSM Chigwell and Chigwell Row *Chelmsf* 94-98; C W Ham 98-04; C Hornchurch St Andr from 04. *Spring Cottage, 6 Spring Grove, Loughton IG10 4QA* Tel (020) 8508 6572
E-mail norman@ediblehedge.freeserve.co.uk

ARNOTT, Preb David. b 44. Em Coll Cam BA66. Qu Coll Birm 68. **d** 69 **p** 70. C Charlton St Luke w St Paul *S'wark* 69-73; C S Beddington St Mich 73-78; Chapl Liv Poly *Liv* 78-82; V Bridgwater St Fran *B & W* 86-02; Preb Wells Cathl 00-02; V Yealmpton and Brixton *Ex* from 02; RD Ivybridge from 03. *The Vicarage, Bowden Hill, Yealmpton, Plymouth PL8 2JX* Tel and fax (01752) 880979

ARNOTT, Eric William. b 12. Cranmer Hall Dur 67. **d** 68 **p** 69. C Gosforth St Nic *Newc* 68-71; C Wooler 71-74; TV Wooler Gp 74-78; rtd 78. *21 Folly Mill Lodge, South Street, Bridport DT6 3QS* Tel (01308) 426761

ARRAND, The Ven Geoffrey William. b 44. K Coll Lon BD66 AKC66. **d** 67 **p** 68. C Washington *Dur* 67-70; C S Ormsby w Ketsby, Calceby and Driby *Linc* 70-73; TV Gt Grimsby St Mary and St Jas 73-79; TR Halesworth w Linstead and Chediston *St E* 79-80; TR Halesworth w Linstead, Chediston, Holton etc 80-85; R Hadleigh w Layham and Shelley 85-94; Dean Bocking 85-94; RD Hadleigh 86-94; Hon Can St E Cathl from 91; Adn Suffolk from 94. *Glebe House, The Street, Ashfield, Stowmarket IP14 6LX* Tel (01728) 685497 Fax 685969
E-mail archdeacon.geoffrey@stedmundsbury.anglican.org

ARRANDALE, Richard Paul Matthew. b 63. BA87. Chich Th Coll 87. **d** 90 **p** 91. C E Grinstead St Swithun *Chich* 90-94; C Crawley 94. *Address temp unknown*

ARRIDGE, Leonard Owen. b 22. Univ of Wales (Ban) BA51. St Deiniol's Hawarden 64. **d** 67 **p** 68. Tutor Ches Coll of HE 67-79; Hon C Hope *St As* 67-69; Hon C Wrexham 69-79; Min Can Ban Cathl *Ban* 79-87; C Ban Cathl Par 79-87; rtd 87; Perm to Offic *Ban* from 87. *8 Ffordd Islwyn, Bangor LL57 1AR* Tel (01248) 362233

ARSCOTT, Barry James. b 36. AKC59. **d** 60 **p** 61. C Walthamstow St Andr *Chelmsf* 60-65; P-in-c Leyton St Luke 65-67; V 67-77; P-in-c Lt Ilford St Barn 77-86; V 86-01; rtd 01. *232 Fencepiece Road, Ilford IG6 2ST* Tel (020) 8502 6853

ARTHINGTON, Sister Muriel. b 23. **dss** 67 **d** 87. St Etheldreda's Children's Home Bedf 64-84; Hon Par Dn Bedford St Paul *St Alb* 87-94; rtd 97; Assoc Sister CSA from 03; Perm to Offic

St Alb from 94 and *Ox* from 03. *Paddock House, 6 Linford Lane, Willen, Milton Keynes MK15 9DL* Tel (01908) 661554

ARTHUR, Graeme Richard. b 52. Univ of NSW BCom78. Linc Th Coll 93. **d** 93 **p** 94. C Witney *Ox* 93-97; R Westcote Barton w Steeple Barton, Duns Tew etc from 97. *The Rectory, 29 Enstone Road, Westcote Barton, Chipping Norton OX7 7AA* Tel (01869) 340510 E-mail graeme@arfa.clara.net

ARTHUR, Canon Ian Willoughby. b 40. Lon Univ BA63 BA66 PGCE64 Lambeth STh94 Kent Univ MA98. Ripon Coll Cuddesdon 78. **d** 80 **p** 81. C Kempston Transfiguration *St Alb* 80-83; R Potton w Sutton and Cockayne Hatley 83-96; P-in-c Sharnbrook and Knotting w Souldrop 96-04; RD Sharnbrook 97-04; Hon Can St Alb 99-04; rtd 04; Perm to Offic *St Alb* from 04. *35 London Road, Chipping Norton OX7 5AX* Tel (01608) 646839 E-mail iwarthur@supanet.com

ARTHUR, Mrs Joan Diane. b 42. St Alb and Ox Min Course. **d** 00 **p** 01. NSM High Wycombe *Ox* from 00. *34 Hithercroft Road, High Wycombe HP13 5LS* Tel (01494) 534582 Mobile 07961-840420 Fax (01494) 523311

ARTHUR, Kenneth Paul. b 64. Univ of Wales (Cardiff) BScEcon86 Roehampton Inst PGCE87. St Steph Ho Ox BTh05. **d** 00 **p** 01. C Bodmin w Lanhydrock and Lanivet *Truro* 00-02; P-in-c Treverbyn from 02; P-in-c Boscoppa from 02; RD St Austell from 05. *The Vicarage, Treverbyn Road, Stenalees, St Austell PL26 8TL* Tel (01726) 851923

ARTHY, Ms Nicola Mary. b 64. St Jo Coll Ox BA85 MA93. SEITE. **d** 00 **p** 01. C Guildf H Trin w St Mary *Guildf* 00-01; C Farncombe 01-04; P-in-c Toddington, Stanton, Didbrook w Hailes etc *Glouc* 04-05; TV Winchcombe from 05. *St Martha's, 22 Delavale Road, Winchcombe, Cheltenham GL54 5HN* Tel (01242) 603109 Mobile 07944-721835 E-mail nikkiarthy@tesco.net

ARTLEY, Clive Mansell. b 30. St Jo Coll Dur BA56 Leeds Univ MA(Theol)01. Cranmer Hall Dur DipTh58. **d** 58 **p** 59. C Eston *York* 58-61; R Burythorpe w E Acklam and Leavening 61-64; CF 64-73; Teacher 73-93; Perm to Offic *York* from 73; rtd 93. *56 High Street, Castleton, Whitby YO21 2DA* Tel (01287) 660470

ARTLEY, Miss Pamela Jean. b 47. Worc Coll of Educn CertEd68 Hull Univ MEd91. NEOC 99. **d** 02 **p** 03. NSM Bridlington Priory *York* 02-05; P-in-c Nafferton w Wansford from 05. *The Vicarage, 3 Middle Street, Nafferton, Driffield YO25 4JS* E-mail pjartley@fish.co.uk

ARTUS, Stephen James. b 60. Man Poly BA82 W Midl Coll of Educn PGCE84. St Jo Coll Nottm MA95. **d** 95 **p** 96. C Altrincham St Geo *Ches* 95-99; P-in-c Norton 99-05; V from 05. *The Vicarage, Windmill Hill, Runcorn WA7 6QE* Tel (01928) 715225 E-mail stephen@nortonvicarage.fsnet.co.uk

ARUNDEL, Canon Michael. b 36. Qu Coll Ox BA60 MA64. Linc Th Coll 60. **d** 62 **p** 63. C Hollinwood *Man* 62-65; C Leesfield 65-69; R Newton Heath All SS 69-80; RD N Man 75-80; P-in-c Eccles St Mary 80-81; TR Eccles 81-91; R Man St Ann 91-01; Hon Can Man Cathl 82-01; rtd 01. *20 Kiln Brow, Bromley Cross, Bolton BL7 9NR* Tel (01204) 591156

ARVIDSSON, Carl Fredrik. b 66. Regents Th Coll 88 Chich Th Coll 92. **d** 92 **p** 93. C Southsea H Spirit *Portsm* 92-94; C Botley, Curdridge and Durley 94-96; P-in-c Ringwould w Kingsdown *Cant* 96-97; R 97-01; Hon Min Can Cant Cathl from 01; Sen Chapl K Sch Cant from 01. *The King's School, Canterbury CT1 2ER* Tel (01227) 595613 E-mail chaplainkings@aol.com

ASAJU, Prof Emmanuel Dapo Folorunsho. b 61. Ilorin Univ Nigeria BA83 MA85 PhD03. Lagos Angl Dioc Sem 98. **d** 98 **p** 99. V Iba Epiphany Nigeria 98-00; V Ketu Transfiguration 00-02; Perm to Offic *Birm* from 03. *6 Durban Gardens, Dagenham RM10 9XU* Tel 07986-694940 (mobile) E-mail dapoasaju@yahoo.co.uk

ASBRIDGE, Preb John Hawell. b 26. Dur Univ BA47. Bps' Coll Cheshunt 47. **d** 49 **p** 50. C Barrow St Geo *Carl* 49-52; C Fort William *Arg* 52-54; C Lon Docks St Pet w Wapping St Jo *Lon* 54-55; C Kilburn St Aug 55-59; V Northolt Park St Barn 59-66; V Shepherd's Bush St Steph w St Thos 66-96; Preb St Paul's Cathl 89-96; rtd 96. *Crystal Glen, The Old Mineral Line, Roadwater, Watchet TA23 0RL* Tel (01984) 640211

ASBRIDGE, Nigel Henry. b 58. Bris Univ BA80. Chich Th Coll 87. **d** 89 **p** 90. C Tottenham St Paul *Lon* 89; C W Hampstead St Jas 89-94; P-in-c Hornsey H Innocents 94-04; P-in-c Stroud Green H Trin 02-04; Nat Chapl-Missr Children's Soc from 04. *The Children's Society, Edward Rudolf House, Margery Street, London WC1X 0JL* Tel (020) 7841 4567 E-mail nigelasbridge@hotmail.com

ASBURY, William. b 35. Sheff Univ CertEd61 Liv Univ MA89. All Nations Chr Coll 57. **d** 97 **p** 98. NSM Southport Ch Ch *Liv* 97-00; Town Cen Chapl 97-00; Perm to Offic from 00. *Address temp unknown*

ASH, Arthur Edwin. b 44. St Jo Coll Nottm 85. **d** 87 **p** 88. C Attleborough *Cov* 87-91; V Garretts Green *Birm* 91-02; rtd 02; Perm to Offic *Birm* from 02. *1 Margetts Close, Kenilworth CV8 1EN* Tel (01926) 853547 E-mail aash@tinyworld.co.uk

ASH, Brian John. b 32. ALCD62. **d** 62 **p** 63. C Plymouth St Andr *Ex* 62-66; Area Sec CMS *Cant* and *Roch* 66-73; V Bromley Common St Aug *Roch* 73-97; rtd 97; Perm to Offic *Chelmsf* 97-00. *The Vines, 95 Green Lane, Leigh-on-Sea SS9 5QU* Tel (01702) 523644 E-mail brian.ash@zen.co.uk

ASH, Christopher Brian Garton. b 53. Trin Hall Cam MA76. Wycliffe Hall Ox BA92. **d** 93 **p** 94. C Cambridge H Sepulchre *Ely* 93-97; P-in-c Lt Shelford 97-02; R 02-04; Dir Cornhill Tr Course from 04. *The Cornhill Training Course, 140-148 Borough High Street, London SE1 1LB* Tel (020) 7407 0562 E-mail cbga@proctrust.org.uk

ASH, David Nicholas. b 61. Southlands Coll Lon BA82. Wycliffe Hall Ox BTh03. **d** 03 **p** 04. C Walsall *Lich* from 03. *164 Birmingham Road, Walsall WS1 2NJ* Tel (01922) 641330 E-mail revdavidash@fish.co.uk

ASH, Canon Nicholas John. b 59. Bath Univ BSc81 Nottm Univ BTh88. Linc Th Coll 85. **d** 88 **p** 89. C Hersham *Guildf* 88-93; P-in-c Flookburgh *Carl* 93-97; Dioc Officer for Stewardship 94-97; TV Cartmel Peninsula 97-98; Dir of Ords 97-03; P-in-c Dalston 98-00; P-in-c Wreay 98-00; P-in-c Raughton Head w Gatesgill 98-00; V Dalston w Cumdivock, Raughton Head and Wreay 01-03; Can Res Portsm Cathl *Portsm* from 03. *32 Woodville Drive, Porstmouth PO1 2TG* Tel (023) 9242 3797 E-mail nickash405@hotmail.com

ASHBRIDGE, Miss Kathleen Mary. b 30. Alnwick Tr Coll CertEd51. **d** 03 **p** 04. NSM Caldbeck, Castle Sowerby and Sebergham *Carl* from 03. *Sharpe House, Caldbeck, Wigton CA7 8EX* Tel (01697) 478205

ASHBURNER, David Barrington. b 26. Ch Coll Cam BA51 MA55. Wycliffe Hall Ox 51. **d** 53 **p** 54. C Coalville *Leic* 53-56; C Leic H Apostles 56-58; V Bucklebury w Marlston *Ox* 58-70; V Belton *Leic* 70-75; P-in-c Osgathorpe 73-75; R Belton and Osgathorpe 75-79; V Frisby-on-the-Wreake w Kirby Bellars 79-82; V Uffington w Woolstone and Baulking *Ox* 82-91; P-in-c Shellingford 83-91; RD Vale of White Horse 87-91; rtd 91; Perm to Offic *Glouc* and *Ox* from 91. *7 Stonefern Court, Stow Road, Moreton-in-Marsh GL56 0DW* Tel (01608) 650347

✠**ASHBY, The Rt Revd Godfrey William Ernest Candler.** b 30. Lon Univ AKC54 BD54 PhD69. **d** 55 **p** 56 **c** 80. C St Helier *S'wark* 55-57; S Africa 57-88 and from 95; Can Grahamstown Cathl 69-75; Dean and Adn Grahamstown 75-80; Bp St John's 80-85; Prof Div Witwatersrand Univ 85-88; Asst Bp Johannesburg 85-88; Asst Bp Leic 88-95; P-in-c Newtown Linford 92-95; Hon Can Leic Cathl 93-95; rtd 95; Asst Bp George from 95. *PO Box 2685, Knysna, 6570 South Africa* Tel (0027) (445) 827059

ASHBY, Mrs Judith Anne Stuart. b 53. Man Univ BSc74 MSc76 Ox Brookes Univ PGCE99. STETS 96. **d** 99 **p** 00. NSM Swindon Ch Ch *Bris* 99-05; P-in-c Cricklade w Latton from 05. *57 Greywethers Avenue, Swindon SN3 1QG* Tel (01793) 330851 E-mail judith.ashby@ntlworld.com

ASHBY, Kevin Patrick. b 53. Jes Coll Ox BA76 MA80. Wycliffe Hall Ox 76. **d** 78 **p** 79. C Market Harborough *Leic* 78-82; C Horwich H Trin *Man* 82-84; C Horwich 84; TV 84-90; R Billing *Pet* 90-01; RD Northn 98-01; R Buckingham *Ox* from 01; AD Buckingham from 04. *The Rectory, 39 Fishers Field, Buckingham MK18 1SF* Tel (01280) 813178 Fax 820901 E-mail kevinp.ashby@virgin.net

ASHBY, Mrs Linda. b 48. Dartford Coll of Educn CertEd70. **d** 03 **p** 04. OLM N w S Wootton *Nor* from 03. *4 Melford Close, South Wootton, King's Lynn PE30 3XH* Tel (01553) 672893 E-mail linda@loobylin.freeserve.co.uk

ASHBY, Peter George. b 49. Univ of Wales (Cardiff) BSc(Econ)70 Nottm Univ DipTh71. Linc Th Coll 70. **d** 73 **p** 74. C Bengeo *St Alb* 73-75; Chapl Hatf Poly 76-79; C Apsley End 80; TV Chambersbury 80-82; Zimbabwe 82-87; Adn N Harare 84-87; V Eskdale, Irton, Muncaster and Waberthwaite *Carl* 87-93; TR Sedgley All SS *Worc* 93-99; TV Tettenhall Regis *Lich* 99-04; V W Bromwich St Jas w St Paul from 04. *St James's Vicarage, 23 Rowley View, West Bromwich B70 8QR* Tel 0121-553 3538

ASHCROFT, Mrs Ann Christine. b 46. Cov Coll of Educn TCert68. N Ord Course 82. **d** 87 **p** 94. Chapl Trin High Sch Man 86-91; Burnage St Nic *Man* 86-95; Hon Par Dn 87-95; Dio Adv Man Coun for Educn 91-95; TV Wareham and Chapl Purbeck Sch *Sarum* 95-02; TR By Brook *Bris* from 02. *The Rectory, The Street, Yatton Keynell, Chippenham SN14 7BA* Tel (01249) 782663 E-mail bybrook.parishoffice@btopenworld.com

ASHCROFT, Canon Mark David. b 54. Worc Coll Ox BA77 MA82 Fitzw Coll Cam BA81. Ridley Hall Cam 79. **d** 82 **p** 83. C Burnage St Marg *Man* 82-85; CMS 86-96; Kenya 86-96; R Harpurhey Ch Ch *Man* from 96; R Harpurhey St Steph from 96; AD N Man from 00; Hon Can Man Cathl from 04. *95 Church Lane, Manchester M9 5BG* Tel 0161-205 4020

ASHDOWN, Andrew William Harvey. b 64. K Coll Lon BD88 AKC88. Sarum & Wells Th Coll 88. **d** 90 **p** 91. C Cranleigh *Guildf* 90-94; V Ryhill *Wakef* 94-98; P-in-c Denmead *Portsm* 98-99; V 99-05; S Asia Regional Officer USPG from 05; Hon C Tadley S and Silchester *Win* from 05. *St Mary's House,*

10 Romans Field, Silchester, Reading RG7 2QH Tel 0118-970 2353 *or* (020) 7928 8681 Fax (020) 7928 2371 E-mail andrewa@uspg.org.uk

ASHTDOWN, Anthony Hughes. b 37. AKC63. **d** 64 **p** 65. C Tettenhall Regis *Lich* 64-67; P-in-c Bassaleg *Mon* 67-70; Rhodesia 70-77; P-in-c Longton St Jas *Lich* 77-78; P-in-c Longton St Jo 77-78; R Longton 78-80; TR Cove St Jo *Guildf* 80-87; Chapl Lisbon *Eur* 87-90; V Wanstead H Trin Hermon Hill *Chelmsf* 90-00; Perm to Offic *Chich* from 00; rtd 02. *49 Broyle Road, Chichester PO19 4BA* Tel (01243) 532405

ASHDOWN, Barry Frederick. b 42. St Pet Coll Ox BA65 MA69. Ridley Hall Cam 66. **d** 68 **p** 69. C Shipley St Pet *Bradf* 68-71; C Rushden w Newton Bromswold *Pet* 71-74; R Haworth *Bradf* 74-82; V Ore Ch Ch *Chich* 82-87; C Southwick St Mich 91-93. *Address temp unknown*

ASHDOWN, Philip David. b 57. Imp Coll Lon BSc79 NW Univ Chicago MS80 Cranfield Inst of Tech PhD85 ARCS79 CMath MIMA87. Ripon Coll Cuddesdon 91. **d** 93 **p** 94. C Houghton le Spring *Dur* 93-96; C Stockton and Chapl Stockton Campus Dur Univ 96-02; V Stockton St Pet *Dur* from 02. *St Peter's Vicarage, 11 Lorne Court, Stockton-on-Tees TS18 3UB* Tel (01642) 670981 E-mail philip.ashdown@durham.anglican.org

ASHE, Canon Francis John. b 53. Sheff Univ BMet74. Ridley Hall Cam 77. **d** 79 **p** 80. C Ashtead *Guildf* 79-82; S Africa 82-87; R Wisley w Pyrford *Guildf* 87-93; V Godalming 93-01; TR from 01; RD Godalming 96-02; Hon Can Guildf Cathl from 03. *The Rectory, Westbrook Road, Godalming GU7 1ET* Tel and fax (01483) 860594 E-mail john.ashe@dsl.pipex.com *or* john.ashe@godalming.org.uk

ASHE, Francis Patrick Bellesme. b 15. St Jo Coll Cam BA37 MA41. Westcott Ho Cam 37. **d** 40 **p** 41. C Woolwich St Mary w H Trin *S'wark* 40-44; Greece 44-46; Youth Chapl *S'wark* 46-50; V Blindley Heath 49-56; V Otley *Bradf* 56-64; V Leamington Priors St Mary *Cov* 64-72; R Church Stretton *Heref* 72-74; Chmn Admin Project Vietnam Orphanage 75-81; rtd 80; Perm to Offic *Guildf* from 81. *62 Busbridge Lane, Godalming GU7 1QQ* Tel (01483) 422435

ASHENDEN, Canon Gavin Roy Pelham. b 54. Bris Univ LLB76 Oak Hill Th Coll BA80 Heythrop Coll Lon MTh89 Sussex Univ DPhil98. **d** 80 **p** 81. C Bermondsey St Jas w Ch Ch *S'wark* 80-83; TV Sanderstead All SS 83-89; Chapl and Lect Sussex Univ *Chich* from 89; Can and Preb Chich Cathl from 03. *The Meeting House, Sussex University, Southern Ring Road, Falmer, Brighton BN1 9RH* Tel (01273) 678217 Fax 678918 E-mail g.ashenden@sussex.ac.uk

ASHFORTH, David Edward. b 37. Lon Univ BSc ARCS59 Birm Univ DipTh61. Qu Coll Birm. **d** 61 **p** 62. C Scarborough St Columba *York* 61-65; C Northallerton w Kirby Sigston 65-67; V Keyingham 67-73; Chapl Imp Coll *Lon* 73-89; V Balderstone *Blackb* 89-01; Dir Post-Ord Tr 89-01; rtd 01; Perm to Offic *Ripon* from 02. *Sunnyholme Cottage, Preston under Scar, Leyburn DL8 4AH* Tel (01969) 622438 E-mail d.ashforth@btinternet.com

ASHLEY, Brian. b 36. S'wark Ord Course 75. **d** 77 **p** 78. NSM Horsell *Guildf* from 77. *5 Birtley House, 38 Claremont Avenue, Woking GU22 7SG* Tel (01483) 761232 E-mail brianthebusiness@onetel.com

ASHLEY, Brian Christenson. b 33. Roch Th Coll 68. **d** 70 **p** 71. C New Sleaford *Linc* 70-72; Min Basegreen CD 72-74; TV Gleadless *Sheff* 74-77; R Dinnington 77-85; RD Laughton 82-85; V Mosbrough 85-88; P-in-c Curbar and Stoney Middleton *Derby* 88-91; rtd 91; Perm to Offic *Pet* from 95. *15 Eliot Close, Saxon Fields, Kettering NN16 9XR* Tel (01536) 524457

ASHLEY, Clive Ashley. b 54. Croydon Coll of Art and Design LSIAD75 Lon Hosp SRN80 E Ham Coll of Tech FE TCert82 NE Lon Poly NDN83. Aston Tr Scheme 81 Cranmer Hall Dur 84. **d** 86 **p** 87. C Withington St Paul *Man* 86-89; Asst Chapl Freeman Hosp Newc 89-92; Chapl St Rich and Graylingwell Hosps Chich 92-98; Chapl Bognor Regis War Memorial Hosp 95-98; Chapl and Bereavement Cllr R W Sussex Trust 98-01; R New Fishbourne *Chich* from 01; P-in-c Appledram from 01. *The Rectory, 31 Caspian Close, Fishbourne, Chichester PO18 8AY* Tel (01243) 783364 Mobile 07747-155119 E-mail clive.ashley@tesco.net

ASHLEY, John Michael. b 28. Worc Coll Ox BA51 MA54. Linc Th Coll 50. **d** 54 **p** 55. Australia 54-60; C Anderby w Cumberworth *Linc* 60-66; P-in-c Huttoft 60-61; V 61-66; R Woolsthorpe 66-93; R W w E Allington and Sedgebrook 66-93; CF (TAVR) 79-93; rtd 93; Perm to Offic *Linc* 93-99. *35 Gregory Close, Harlaxton, Grantham NG32 1JG* Tel (01476) 561846

ASHLEY, Ms Rosemary Clare. b 60. Dur Univ BA82 Birkbeck Coll Lon MSc01 Brunel Univ MPhil05. Wycliffe Hall Ox 02. **d** 05. C Leyton St Cath and St Paul *Chelmsf* from 05. *114 Hainault Road, London E11 1EL* Tel (020) 8558 7294 Mobile 07984-618534 E-mail rosyashley@hotmail.com

ASHLEY-ROBERTS, James. b 53. Lon Univ BD77. Oak Hill Th Coll 75 Wycliffe Hall Ox 79. **d** 80 **p** 81. C Gt Warley Ch Ch *Chelmsf* 80-83; C E Ham St Paul 83-85; TV Holyhead w Rhoscolyn w Llanfair-yn-Neubwll *Ban* 85-88; R 88-91; V Penrhyndeudraeth w Llanfrothen w Beddgelert 91-97; V Ffestiniog w Blaenau Ffestiniog 97-01. *11 Simon's Close, Crowborough TN6 2XU*

ASHLING, Raymond Charles. b 32. Dur Univ BA58. Linc Th Coll 58. **d** 60 **p** 61. C Halifax St Aug *Wakef* 60-63; C Farlington *Portsm* 63-65; Rhodesia 65-71; Chapl Rishworth Sch Ripponden 71-75; Lesotho 75-85; V Somercotes *Linc* 85-88; Ethiopia 88-89; R Gt w Lt Snoring w Kettlestone and Pensthorpe *Nor* 89-94; rtd 94. *14 Abbey Court, Norwich NR1 2AW*

ASHMAN, Peter Nicholas. b 52. CSS81 SEN73. Sarum & Wells Th Coll 87. **d** 89 **p** 90. C Stafford *Lich* 89-93; R Dymchurch w Burmarsh and Newchurch *Cant* 93-99; R Lyminge w Paddlesworth, Stanford w Postling etc from 99. *The Rectory, Rectory Lane, Lyminge, Folkestone CT18 8EG* Tel (01303) 862432 E-mail p.ashman@btinternet.com

ASHMAN, Mrs Vanessa Mary. b 53. Dioc OLM tr scheme 00. **d** 03 **p** 04. OLM Lyminge w Paddlesworth, Stanford w Postling etc *Cant* from 03. *The Rectory, Rectory Lane, Lyminge, Folkestone CT18 8EG* Tel and fax (01303) 862432 E-mail vanessa.ashman@btinternet.com

ASHTON, Anthony Joseph. b 37. Oak Hill Th Coll 62. **d** 65 **p** 66. C Crookes St Thos *Sheff* 65-68; C Heeley 68-73; V Bowling St Steph *Bradf* 73-78; R Chesterfield H Trin *Derby* 78-92; rtd 93; Perm to Offic *Derby* 93-00. *19 High Park, Stafford ST16 1BL* Tel (01785) 223943

✠**ASHTON, The Rt Revd Cyril Guy.** b 42. Lanc Univ MA86. Oak Hill Th Coll 64. **d** 67 **p** 68 **c** 00. C Blackpool St Thos *Blackb* 67-70; Voc Sec CPAS 70-74; V Lancaster St Thos *Blackb* 74-91; Lanc Almshouses 76-90; Dioc Dir of Tr *Blackb* 91-00; Hon Can Blackb Cathl 91-00; Suff Bp Doncaster *Sheff* from 00. *Bishop's House, 3 Farrington Court, Wickersley, Rotherham S66 1JQ* Tel (01709) 730130 Fax 730230 E-mail m.powell1@virgin.net

ASHTON, David. b 52. Sarum Th Coll 93. **d** 96 **p** 97. NSM St Leonards Ch Ch and St Mary *Chich* 96-98; NSM Upper St Leonards St Jo 98-99; C Uckfield 99-02; V Langney from 02. *St Richard's Rectory, 7 Priory Road, Eastbourne BN23 7AX* Tel (01323) 761158

ASHTON, David William. b 51. Reading Univ BA74 Lanc Univ PGCE75. Wycliffe Hall Ox 79. **d** 82 **p** 83. C Shipley St Pet *Bradf* 82-85; C Tadley St Pet *Win* 85-88; V Sinfin *Derby* 88-91; Chapl Sophia Antipolis *Eur* 91-94; P-in-c Swanwick and Pentrich *Derby* 95-00; V 00-02; RD Alfreton 95-02; Chapl S Derbyshire Acute Hosps NHS Trust from 02. *Chaplaincy Services, Derby City General Hospital, Uttoxeter Road, Derby DE22 3NE* Tel (01332) 340131 E-mail david.ashton@sdah-tr.trent.nhs.uk

ASHTON, Grant. *See* ASHTON, William Grant

✠**ASHTON, The Rt Revd Jeremy Claude.** b 30. Trin Coll Cam BA53 MA57. Westcott Ho Cam 53. **d** 55 **p** 56 **c** 76. C Bury St Mary *Man* 55-60; CF (TA) 57-60; CF (TA - R of O) 60-70; Papua New Guinea 60-86; Asst Bp Papua 76-77; Bp Aipo Rongo 77-86; rtd 86; Australia from 86. *38 Urquhart Street, Castlemaine, Vic, Australia 3450* Tel and fax (0061) (3) 5472 1074

ASHTON, Miss Joan Elizabeth. b 54. Eaton Hall Coll of Educn CertEd76. Cranmer Hall Dur 91. **d** 93 **p** 94. Par Dn Darnall-cum-Attercliffe *Sheff* 93-94; C Hillsborough and Wadsley Bridge 94-96; P-in-c Stainforth 96-98; P-in-c Arksey 98-03; Asst Chapl Doncaster R Infirmary and Montagu Hosp NHS Trust 98-01; Asst Chapl Doncaster and Bassetlaw Hosps NHS Trust 01-04; Co-ord Chapl Services Rotherham Gen Hosps NHS Trust from 04. *Rotherham District General Hospital, Moorgate Road, Rotherham S60 2UD* Tel (01709) 820000 E-mail joan.ashton@rothgen.nhs.uk

ASHTON, Ms Lesley June. b 49. York Univ BA89. NEOC 00. **d** 04 **p** 05. C Roundhay St Edm *Ripon* from 04. *1 Gledhow Grange View, Leeds LS8 1PH* Tel 0113-268 9797 E-mail lesley.ashton1@ntlworld.com

ASHTON, Mrs Margaret Lucie. b 40. St Jo Coll Nottm DPS79. **dss** 83 **d** 87 **p** 94. Billericay and Lt Burstead *Chelmsf* 83-99; NSM 87-99; rtd 99; Hon C Fordingbridge and Breamore and Hale etc *Win* from 01. *3 Stephen Martin Gardens, Fordingbridge SP6 1RF* Tel (01425) 656205 E-mail peterdashton@onetel.com

ASHTON, Neville Anthony. b 45. Sarum & Wells Th Coll 78. **d** 80 **p** 81. C Hattersley *Ches* 80-82; C Lancaster Ch Ch w St Jo and St Anne *Blackb* 82-84; R Church Kirk from 84. *Church Kirk Rectory, 434 Blackburn Road, Accrington BB5 0DE* Tel (01254) 236946

ASHTON, Nigel Charles. b 49. SW Minl Tr Course. **d** 78 **p** 79. NSM St Stephen by Saltash *Truro* 78-94; Perm to Offic *Ex* from 95. *9 Bunn Road, Exmouth EX8 5PP* Tel (01395) 224345

ASHTON, Canon Peter Donald. b 34. Lon Univ BD62. ALCD61. **d** 62 **p** 63. C Walthamstow St Mary *Chelmsf* 62-68; V Girlington *Bradf* 68-73; Dir Past Studies St Jo Coll Nottm 73-80; TR Billericay and Lt Burstead *Chelmsf* 80-99; Chapl Mayflower Hosp Billericay 80-99; Chapl St Andr Hosp Billericay 80-93; Chapl Thameside Community Healthcare NHS Trust 93-99; RD Basildon *Chelmsf* 89-99; Hon Can Chelmsf Cathl 92-99; rtd 99; Hon C Fordingbridge and Breamore and Hale etc *Win* from

01. *3 Stephen Martin Gardens, Fordingbridge SP6 1RF* Tel (01425) 656205 E-mail peterdashton@onetel.com

ASHTON, Preb Samuel Rupert. b 42. Sarum & Wells Th Coll. **d** 83 **p** 84. C Ledbury w Eastnor *Heref* 83-86; R St Weonards w Orcop, Garway, Tretire etc 86-98; RD Ross and Archenfield 91-95 and 96-98; Preb Heref Cathl from 97; P-in-c Cradley w Mathon and Storridge 98-99; R from 99. *The Rectory, Cradley, Malvern WR13 5LQ* Tel (01886) 880438

ASHTON, Stephen Robert. b 55. BA BPhil Lon Univ MA99 FRSA03 FGMS03. Sarum & Wells Th Coll. **d** 84 **p** 85. C Penzance St Mary w St Paul *Truro* 84-86; C Tewkesbury w Walton Cardiff *Glouc* 86-89; P-in-c Newton Heath St Wilfrid and St Anne *Man* 89-92; V Breage w Germoe *Truro* 92-94. *20 Tregarrick Close, Helston TR13 8YA* Tel (01326) 563127 E-mail sashton44@hotmail.com

ASHTON, William Grant. b 57. St Chad's Coll Dur BA79. Oak Hill Th Coll BA85. **d** 85 **p** 86. C Lancaster St Thos *Blackb* 85-89; CF from 89. *c/o MOD Chaplains (Army)* Tel (01980) 615804 Fax 615800

ASHWELL, Anthony John. b 42. St Andr Univ BSc65. Sarum & Wells Th Coll 86. **d** 88 **p** 89. C Plymstock *Ex* 88-91; C Axminster, Chardstock, Combe Pyne and Rousdon 91-92; TV 92-95; C Crediton and Shobrooke 95-97; TV Bride Valley *Sarum* from 97; P-in-c Symondsbury from 05; RD Lyme Bay from 03. *The Vicarage, Litton Cheney, Dorchester DT2 9AG* Tel (01308) 482302 E-mail anthonyashwell@aol.com

ASHWIN, Canon Vincent George. b 42. Worc Coll Ox BA65. Coll of Resurr Mirfield 65. **d** 67 **p** 68. C Shildon *Dur* 67-70; C Newc St Fran *Newc* 70-72; R Mhlosheni Swaziland 72-75; R Manzini 75-79; V Shildon *Dur* 79-85; V Fenham St Jas and St Basil *Newc* 85-97; RD Newc W 89-97; V Haydon Bridge and Beltingham w Henshaw 97-04; RD Hexham 97-02; Hon Can Newc Cathl 00-04; rtd 04; Perm to Offic *S'well* from 04. *83 Westgate, Southwell NG25 0LS* Tel (01636) 813975 E-mail vincentashwin@tiscali.co.uk

ASHWIN-SIEJKOWSKI, Piotr Jan (Peter). b 64. Warsaw Univ PhD97. Coll of Resurr Mirfield 98. **d** 91 **p** 92. Poland 92-98; C Tile Hill *Cov* 99-01; Chapl and Lect Univ Coll Chich 01-04; TV Richmond St Mary w St Matthias and St Jo *S'wark* from 04. *19 Old Deer Park Gardens, Richmond TW9 2TM* Tel (020) 8940 8359 E-mail piotr-ashwin@fsmail.net

ASHWORTH, Canon David. b 40. Nottm Univ BPharm62. Linc Th Coll 63. **d** 65 **p** 66. C Halliwell St Thos *Man* 65-69; C Heywood St Jas 69-72; C-in-c Heywood St Marg CD 72-78; V Hale *Ches* 78-87; V Hale and Ashley 87-96; RD Bowdon 87-95; Hon Can Ches Cathl from 94; V Prestbury from 96; RD Macclesfield 98-03. *The Vicarage, Prestbury, Macclesfield SK10 4DG* Tel (01625) 829288 *or* 827625 E-mail david@ashworth39.freeserve.co.uk

ASHWORTH, Edward James. b 33. Clifton Th Coll 60. **d** 63 **p** 64. C Spitalfields Ch Ch w All SS *Lon* 63-65; C Pennycross *Ex* 65-69; C Blackb Ch Ch *Blackb* 69-72; V Camerton H Trin W Seaton *Carl* 72-79; V Tunstead *Man* 79-97; rtd 97; Perm to Offic *Man* from 00. *187 Bacup Road, Rossendale BB4 7NW* Tel (01706) 222805

ASHWORTH, James Nigel. b 55. York Univ BA77. Cranmer Hall Dur 93. **d** 93 **p** 94. C Rothwell *Ripon* 93-96; Chapl Campsfield Ho Oxon 96-99; Hon C Akeman *Ox* 96-99; V Kemsing w Woodlands *Roch* from 99. *The Vicarage, High Street, Kemsing, Sevenoaks TN15 6NA* Tel (01732) 761351 E-mail nigelashworth@btinternet.com

ASHWORTH, John Russell. b 33. Lich Th Coll 57. **d** 60 **p** 61. C Castleford All SS *Wakef* 60-62; C Luton St Sav *St Alb* 63-67; V Clipstone *S'well* 67-70; V Bolton-upon-Dearne *Sheff* 70-82; V Thornhill Lees *Wakef* 82-98; rtd 98; Perm to Offic *Wakef* from 99. *Walsingham, 2 Vicarage Road, Savile Town, Dewsbury WF12 9PD* Tel (01924) 461269

ASHWORTH, Keith Benjamin. b 33. NW Ord Course 76. **d** 79 **p** 80. C Pennington *Man* 79-83; P-in-c Bolton St Bede 83-88; V 88-95; V Hillock 95-01; rtd 01; Perm to Offic *Man* from 01. *52 Longsight Lane, Bolton BL2 3JS* Tel (01204) 302833

ASHWORTH, Martin. b 41. AKC63. **d** 64 **p** 65. C-in-c Wythenshawe Wm Temple Ch CD *Man* 64-71; R Haughton St Anne 71-83; V Prestwich St Marg from 83. *St Margaret's Vicarage, 2 St Margaret's Road, Prestwich, Manchester M25 5QB* Tel 0161-773 2698

ASHWORTH, Nigel. *See* ASHWORTH, James Nigel

ASHWORTH, Timothy. b 52. Worc Coll of Educn CertEd74. Trin Coll Bris DipHE79 Oak Hill Th Coll BA81. **d** 82 **p** 83. C Tonbridge St Steph *Roch* 82-85; C-in-c Whittle-le-Woods *Blackb* 85-90; Chapl Scargill Ho 90-96; V Ingleton w Chapel le Dale *Bradf* 96-03; TV Yate New Town *Bris* from 03. *22 Hampden Close, Yate, Bristol BS37 5UW* Tel (01454) 319416 E-mail timashworth@lineone.net

ASHWORTH, Mrs Vivien. b 52. Worc Coll of Educn CertEd73. Trin Coll Bris DipHE81 Oak Hill Th Coll BA82. **dss** 82 **d** 87 **p** 94. Tonbridge St Steph *Roch* 82-85; Whittle-le-Woods *Blackb* 85-90; Hon Par Dn 87-90; Chapl Scargill Ho 90-96; Hon C Ingleton w Chapel le Dale *Bradf* 96-03; Dioc Youth Adv 96-01; Hon C Yate New Town *Bris* from 03; Sub Chapl HM Pris Ashfield from 04. *22 Hampden Close, Yate, Bristol BS37 5UW* Tel (01454) 319416 E-mail viv.ashworth@lineone.net

ASIR, Jebamani Sekar Anand. *See* ANAND, The Very Revd Sekar Anand Asir

ASKEW, Miss Alison Jane. b 57. Dur Univ BA78 PGCE79. S Dios Minl Tr Scheme 93. **d** 95 **p** 96. NSM Kingsclere *Win* 95-96; Asst Chapl N Hants Hosps NHS Trust 95-99; Chapl from 99; Sen Chapl from 04. *6 Worcester Block, North Hampshire Hospital, Basingstoke RG24 9NA* Tel (01256) 473202

ASKEW, Canon Dennis. b 30. Open Univ BA76. Kelham Th Coll 45 Lich Th Coll 55. **d** 58 **p** 59. C Garforth *Ripon* 58-61; C Seacroft 61-64; V Holland Fen *Linc* 64-69; R Folkingham w Laughton 69-77; V Aswarby w Swarby 69-77; R Osbournby w Scott Willoughby 69-77; R Pickworth w Walcot 69-77; V Threckingham 69-77; P-in-c Newton w Haceby 72-77; P-in-c Aunsby w Dembleby 72-77; R S Lafford 77-87; Can and Preb Linc Cathl from 86; R Ruskington 87-96; rtd 96; Perm to Offic *Linc* from 96. *Langford House, 4 Hereford Close, Sleaford NG34 8TP* Tel (01529) 305645

ASKEW, Peter Timothy. b 68. Ridley Hall Cam 00. **d** 02 **p** 03. C Bilton *Ripon* from 02; Chapl St Aid Sch Harrogate from 05. *59 Coppice Way, Harrogate HG1 2DJ* Tel (01423) 566983 Mobile 07754-046029 E-mail peteaskew@hotmail.com *or* peteraskew@btopenworld.com

ASKEW, Canon Reginald James Albert. b 28. CCC Cam BA51 MA55. Linc Th Coll 55. **d** 57 **p** 58. C Highgate St Mich *Lon* 57-61; Lect and Vice-Prin Wells Th Coll 61-69; PV Wells Cathl *B & W* 61-69; V Paddington Ch Ch *Lon* 69-73; Member Corrymeela Community from 71; Prin Sarum & Wells Th Coll 73-87; Chmn S Dios Minl Tr Scheme 73-87; Can and Preb Sarum Cathl *Sarum* 75-87; Dean K Coll Lon 88-93; rtd 93; Perm to Offic *B & W* from 93 and *Lon* 93-96. *Carters Cottage, North Wootton, Shepton Mallet BA4 4AF* Tel (01749) 890728

ASKEW, Preb Richard George. b 35. BNC Ox BA59 MA63. Ridley Hall Cam 62. **d** 64 **p** 65. C Chesham St Mary *Ox* 64-66; C Mossley Hill St Matt and St Jas *Liv* 66-67; Chapl Ox Pastorate 67-72; Asst Chapl BNC Ox 67-71; R Ashtead *Guildf* 72-83; RD Leatherhead 80-83; Can Res and Treas Sarum Cathl *Sarum* 83-90; Dioc Adv on Miss and Min *B & W* 83-90; R Bath Abbey w St Jas 90-00; Preb Wells Cathl 92-00; Perm to Offic *Sarum* 00-01; TV Cley Hill Warminster 01-04; rtd 04. *Easter Cottage, 133 Foxholes, Crockerton, Warminster BA12 7DB* Tel (01985) 219367 E-mail askew.easter@btinternet.com

ASKEW, Sydney Derek. b 29. Roch Th Coll 66. **d** 68 **p** 69. C Kirkstall *Ripon* 68-73; V Markington w S Stainley and Bishop Thornton 73-94; rtd 94; Perm to Offic *Ripon* from 95. *6 Mallorie Close, Ripon HG4 2QE* Tel (01765) 603309

ASKEY, Gary Simon. b 64. K Coll Lon LLB99 Univ Coll Lon LLM00. St Steph Ho Ox 88. **d** 91 **p** 92. SSM 87-99; Prior SSM Priory Kennington 96-98; C Middlesbrough All SS *York* 91-94; Sub-Chapl HM Pris Holme Ho 92-94; C Whitby 94-96; Missr Whitby Miss and Seafarer's Trust 94-96; Lic to Offic *S'wark* 96-03; Hon C Angell Town St Jo 98-03. *115 Metro Central Heights, Newington Causeway, London SE1 6BB* Tel (020) 7407 6131 E-mail simon@askey.gs

ASKEY, John Stuart. b 39. Chich Th Coll 63. **d** 66 **p** 67. C Feltham *Lon* 66-69; C Epsom Common Ch Ch *Guildf* 69-72; C Chesterton Gd Shep *Ely* 72-74; R Stretham w Thetford 74-93; Dioc Spirituality Officer 75-98; Dioc Youth Officer 80-99; P-in-c Brinkley, Burrough Green and Carlton 93-97; P-in-c Westley Waterless 93-97; P-in-c Dullingham 93-97; P-in-c Stetchworth 93-97; R Raddesley Gp 97-99; Chapl Gothenburg w Halmstad, Jönköping etc *Eur* 99-04; rtd 04. *165 Lewes Road, Brighton BN2 3LD*

ASKEY, Mrs Susan Mary. b 44. Leeds Univ MA00. N Ord Course 99. **d** 99 **p** 00. C Golcar *Wakef* 99-02; P-in-c Drighlington from 02. *The Vicarage, Back Lane, Drighlington, Bradford BD11 1LS* Tel 0113-285 2402 E-mail susanaskey@virgin.net

ASKEY, Thomas Cyril. b 29. Sheff Univ BSc50 Man Univ MA(Theol)81 ACIPA58 MITMA76. NW Ord Course 70. **d** 73 **p** 74. NSM Gawsworth *Ches* 73-76; Perm to Offic 76-80; rtd 81; Perm to Offic *Derby* from 99. *Park Cottage, Nether End, Baslow, Bakewell DE45 1SR* Tel (01246) 583780

ASPDEN, Peter George. b 28. Univ of Wales (Lamp) BA50. Ely Th Coll 52. **d** 53 **p** 54. C Morecambe St Barn *Blackb* 53-55; C Marton 55-58; V Tockholes 58-63; P-in-c St Annes St Marg 63-66; V 66-75; V Lancaster Ch Ch 75-79; R Eccleston 79-94; rtd 94; Perm to Offic *Liv* from 94 and *Blackb* from 05. *21 Glencoyne Drive, Southport PR9 9TS* Tel (01704) 214066 E-mail revpgandema@tiscali.co.uk

ASPINALL, Philip Norman. b 51. Cam Univ MA ATI. WMMTC 86. **d** 89 **p** 90. NSM Cov E *Cov* 89-98. *139 Wiltshire Court, Nod Rise, Mount Nod, Coventry CV5 7JP* Tel (024) 7646 7509

ASQUITH, Barbara Rosemary. b 37. **d** 03 **p** 04. OLM S Ossett *Wakef* from 03. *115 Teall Street, Ossett WF5 0HS* Tel (01924) 271302 Mobile 07754-859247

ASQUITH, Eric Lees. b 24. St Aid Birkenhead 55. **d** 56 **p** 57. C Hanging Heaton *Wakef* 56-59; V Netherthong 59-68; rtd 89. *15 Heycroft Way, Nayland, Colchester CO6 4LN* Tel (01206) 262593

ASQUITH, Michael John. b 60. St D Coll Lamp BA82 MPhil91 Ch Ch Coll Cant PGCE83. Cant Sch of Min 91. **d** 94 **p** 95. C S Ashford Ch Ch *Cant* 94-98; P-in-c Weldon w Deene *Pet* 98-00; P-in-c Corby Epiphany w St Jo from 98. *64 South Road, Corby NN17 1XD* Tel (01536) 203671 Fax 262491 E-mail mikeasq@aol.com

ASQUITH, Rosemary. *See* ASQUITH, Barbara Rosemary

ASSON, Geoffrey Ormrod. b 34. Univ of Wales (Ban) BA54 St Cath Coll Ox BA56 MA61. St Steph Ho Ox 54. **d** 57 **p** 58. C Aberdare *Llan* 57-59; C Roath 59-61; R Hagworthingham w Asgarby and Lusby *Linc* 61-65; P-in-c Mavis Enderby w Raithby 62-65; V Friskney 65-69; R S Ormsby w Ketsby, Calceby and Driby 69-74; R Harrington w Brinkhill 69-74; R Oxcombe 69-74; R Ruckland w Farforth and Maidenwell 69-74; R Somersby w Bag Enderby 69-74; R Tetford and Salmonby 69-74; P-in-c Belchford 71-74; P-in-c W Ashby 71-74; V Riverhead w Dunton Green *Roch* 75-80; R Kington w Huntington *Heref* 80-82; RD Kington and Weobley 80-86; P-in-c Almeley 81-82; P-in-c Knill 81-82; P-in-c Old Radnor 81-82; R Kington w Huntington, Old Radnor, Kinnerton etc 82-86; V Mathry w St Edren's and Grandston etc *St D* 86-97; Bp's Rural Adv and Tourist Officer 91-95; rtd 96. *Sincerity, St Dogmaels, Cardigan SA43 3JZ* Tel (01239) 615591

ASTILL, Cyril John. b 33. Lon Univ DipTh64. Oak Hill Th Coll 62. **d** 65 **p** 66. C Carl St Jo *Carl* 65-68; C St Helens St Helen *Liv* 68-71; V Blackb Sav *Blackb* 71-85; P-in-c Blackb Ch Ch w St Matt 81-83; TR N Ferriby *York* 85-97; V 97-99; rtd 99; P-in-c Burton Agnes w Harpham and Lowthorpe etc *York* 99-03. *235 South Gyle Road, Edinburgh EH12 9EJ* Tel 0131 334 2943

ASTIN, Alfred Ronald. b 18. St Pet Hall Ox BA43 MA45. Ridley Hall Cam. **d** 47 **p** 48. C Weaste *Man* 47-50; C Harpurhey Ch Ch 50-51; V Leesfield 51-57; V Earlham St Anne *Nor* 57-70; V Sheringham 70-84; rtd 84; Perm to Offic *Nor* 84-99. *c/o The Revd T R Astin, 1 Cowslip Crescent, Thatcham RG18 4DE* Tel (01635) 869940

ASTIN, Howard Keith. b 51. Warwick Univ LLB DipHE. Trin Coll Bris 83. **d** 83 **p** 84. C Kirkheaton *Wakef* 83-88; V Bowling St Jo *Bradf* from 88. *St John's Vicarage, 96 Lister Avenue, Bradford BD4 7QS* Tel (01274) 727355

ASTIN, Mrs Moira Anne Elizabeth. b 65. Clare Coll Cam BA86 MA90. Wycliffe Hall Ox BA96. **d** 95 **p** 96. C Newbury *Ox* 95-99; C Thatcham 99-01; TV 01-05; TV Woodley from 05; Angl Ecum Officer (Berks) from 03. *23 Kingfisher Drive, Woodley, Reading RG5 3LG* Tel 0118-954 5669 E-mail moira.astin@btinternet.com

ASTIN, Timothy Robin. b 58. St Edm Hall Ox BA79 Darw Coll Cam PhD82 FGS. Ox Min Course 90. **d** 93 **p** 94. NSM Reading St Jo *Ox* 93-95; NSM Newbury 95-99; NSM Beedon and Peasemore w W Ilsley and Farnborough 99-05; NSM Woodley from 05. *23 Kingfisher Drive, Woodley, Reading RG5 3LG* Tel 0118-954 5669 E-mail t.r.astin@reading.ac.uk

ASTLEY, Prof Jeffrey. b 47. Down Coll Cam BA68 MA72 Birm Univ DipTh69 Dur Univ PhD79. Qu Coll Birm 68. **d** 70 **p** 71. C Cannock *Lich* 70-73; Lect and Chapl St Hild Coll Dur 73-75; Sen Lect and Chapl SS Hild and Bede Coll Dur 75-77; Prin Lect & Hd Relig Studies Bp Grosseteste Coll 77-81; Lic to Offic *Linc* 78-81; Dir N England Inst for Chr Educn from 81. *Carter House, Pelaw Leazes Lane, Durham DH1 1TB* Tel 0191-384 1034 *or* 374 7807 Fax 384 7529 E-mail jeff.astley@durham.ac.uk

ASTON, Glyn. b 29. Univ of Wales (Abth) BA54 TCert55. Sarum & Wells Th Coll 84. **d** 79 **p** 80. Hon C Maindee *Mon* 79-85; C 85-86; V Llangwm Uchaf and Llangwm Isaf w Gwernesney etc 86-99; rtd 99; Lic to Offic *Mon* from 99. *Flat 4, 47 Caerau Road, Newport NP20 4HH*

ASTON, John Bernard. b 34. Leeds Univ BA55 PGCE56. Qu Coll Birm 72. **d** 75 **p** 76. NSM Shenstone *Lich* from 75; Chapl HM YOI Swinfen Hall 90-99; NSM Stonnall *Lich* from 00. *4 Footherley Road, Shenstone, Lichfield WS14 0NJ* Tel (01543) 480388

ASTON, John Leslie. b 47. Oak Hill Th Coll 77. **d** 80 **p** 81. C Trentham *Lich* 80-83; C Meir Heath 83-85; V Upper Tean 85-91; CF 91-02; C Andover w Foxcott *Win* 02-05; P-in-c Felixstowe SS Pet and Paul *St E* from 05. *The Vicarage, 14 Picketts Road, Felixstowe IP11 7JT* Tel (01394) 284049 E-mail john@astfam.freeserve.co.uk

ASTON, Mrs Kim Elizabeth. b 57. Colchester Inst of Educn BA78 LRAM78. SEITE 00. **d** 03 **p** 04. NSM Croydon St Jo *S'wark* 03-04; C from 05. *61 Boundary Way, Croydon CR0 5AU* Tel (01689) 843669 *or* (020) 8688 8104 E-mail astonkim@hotmail.com

ASTON, Michael James. b 48. Loughb Univ BSc70 DIS70 MBCS85. NTMTC 98. **d** 01 **p** 02. NSM Writtle w Highwood *Chelmsf* from 01. *15 Weller Grove, Chelmsford CM1 4YJ* Tel (01245) 442547 Mobile 07940-417418 E-mail mikaston@globalnet.co.uk

ASTON, Roger. b 52. Ox Poly BEd83. St Alb and Ox Min Course 96. **d** 99 **p** 00. OLM Eynsham and Cassington *Ox* from 99. *30 Meadow Way, Yarnton, Kidlington, Oxford OX5 1TA* Tel (01865) 378773

ASTON SMITH, Anthony. b 29. Trin Coll Cam BA52 MA56 PhD56 CEng MIM FIDiagE MICorrST AMIMechE. Ox NSM Course 86. **d** 93 **p** 94. NSM Ox St Giles and SS Phil and Jas w St Marg *Ox* 93-99; rtd 99; Perm to Offic *Ox* from 99. *32 Chalfont Road, Oxford OX2 6TH* Tel (01865) 557090 E-mail a.j.astonsmith@btinternet.com

ASTON, Archdeacon of. *Vacant*

ASTON, Suffragan Bishop of. *Vacant.*

ATACK, John Philip. b 49. Lanc Univ MA91. Linc Th Coll 86. **d** 88 **p** 89. C Cleveleys *Blackb* 88-92; V Appley Bridge 92-96; P-in-c Mostyn w Ffynnongroyw *St As* 99-03; P-in-c Colwyn from 03; Hon Chapl Miss to Seafarers from 01. *The Vicarage, 28 Bodelwyddan Avenue, Old Colwyn, Colwyn Bay LL29 9NP* Tel (01492) 518394 E-mail phil.atack@btopenworld.com

ATFIELD, Gladys. Univ Coll Lon BSc53 DipTh76. Gilmore Course. **dss** 79 **d** 87 **p** 94. Bexley St Mary *Roch* 79-01; Hon C 87-01; rtd 01. *7 Clarendon Mews, High Street, Bexley DA5 1JS* Tel (01322) 551741

ATHERFOLD, Mrs Evelyne Sara. b 43. Leeds Inst of Educn CertEd64. N Ord Course 82. **dss** 85 **d** 92 **p** 94. Kirk Sandall and Edenthorpe *Sheff* 85-87; NSM Fishlake w Sykehouse and Kirk Bramwith etc 87-00; P-in-c 00-03; R from 03; Chapl HM YOI Hatfield 96-03. *The Vicarage, Church Street, Fishlake, Doncaster DN7 5JW* Tel (01302) 841396

ATHERLEY, Keith Philip. b 56. St Steph Ho Ox 77. **d** 80 **p** 81. C Armley w New Wortley *Ripon* 80-82; C Harrogate St Wilfrid and St Luke 82-85; V Forcett and Stanwick w Aldbrough 85-89; CF 89-03. *Address temp unknown*

ATHERSTONE, Andrew Castell. b 74. Ch Coll Cam BA95 MA98 Wycliffe Hall Ox MSt99 DPhil01. **d** 01 **p** 02. C Abingdon *Ox* 01-05; NSM Eynsham and Cassington from 05; Research Fell Latimer Trust from 05. *44 Shakespeare Road, Eynsham, Witney OX29 4PY* Tel (01865) 731239 E-mail andrew@atherstone53.freeserve.co.uk

ATHERSTONE, Canon Castell Hugh. b 45. Natal Univ BA67 St Chad's Coll Dur DipTh69 MA79. **d** 70 **p** 70. S Africa 70-83; Dioc Stewardship Adv *Ely* 83-87; P-in-c Doddington w Benwick 83-87; R Frant w Eridge *Chich* 87-95; P-in-c Mark Cross 94-95; RD Rotherfield 90-94; V Seaford w Sutton from 95; RD Lewes and Seaford from 97; Can and Preb Chich Cathl from 02. *The Vicarage, 46 Sutton Road, Seaford BN25 1SH* Tel (01323) 893508 Fax as telephone E-mail hugh@atherstoneweb.org

ATHERTON, Graham Bryson. b 47. FTCL68 GRSM69 ARMCM69 Man Univ CertEd70. Edin Th Coll 77. **d** 79 **p** 80. C Orford St Marg *Liv* 79-82; V Warrington St Barn 82-88; V Leeds Halton St Wilfrid *Ripon* 88-95; RD Whitkirk 92-95; TR Guiseley w Esholt *Bradf* from 95. *The Rectory, The Green, Guiseley, Leeds LS20 9BB* Tel (01943) 874321 E-mail graham.atherton@ntlworld.com

ATHERTON, Henry Anthony. b 44. Univ of Wales BSc67 DipEd68 Fitzw Coll Cam BA72 MA75 Heythrop Coll Lon MTh00 FGS68. Westcott Ho Cam 70. **d** 72 **p** 73. C Leamington Priors All SS *Cov* 72-75; C Orpington All SS *Roch* 75-78; V Gravesend St Mary 78-87; Chapl St Jas Hosp Gravesend 82-87; V Bromley St Andr *Roch* from 87. *The Vicarage, 1 Lake Avenue, Bromley BR1 4EN* Tel (020) 8460 0481 Fax as telephone

ATHERTON, Canon John Robert. b 39. Lon Univ BA60 Man Univ MA74 PhD79. Coll of Resurr Mirfield 60. **d** 62 **p** 63. C Aberdeen St Marg *Ab* 62-64; C Bury St Mark *Man* 64-67; P-in-c Glas St Marg *Glas* 67-68; R Hulme St Geo *Man* 68-74; Ind Chapl 68-74; Asst Dir Wm Temple Foundn 74-79; Dir from 79; Lic to Offic 74-84; Can Res Man Cathl 84-04; rtd 04. *102 Fairview Drive, Adlington, Chorley PR6 9SB* Tel (01257) 474882 Mobile 07989-969567

ATHERTON, Lionel Thomas. b 45. Univ of Wales (Ban) BA74 St Luke's Coll Ex. St Steph Ho Ox 74. **d** 76 **p** 77. C Chenies and Lt Chalfont *Ox* 76-79; C Fleet *Guildf* 79-84; V S Farnborough 84-89; TR Alston Team *Newc* 89-96; V Chorley St Pet *Blackb* from 96; Bp's Adv on New Relig Movements from 02. *St Peter's Vicarage, Harpers Lane, Chorley PR6 0HT* Tel and fax (01257) 263423 E-mail lionelatherton@hotmail.com

ATHERTON, Paul Christopher. b 56. Chich Th Coll. **d** 82 **p** 83. C Orford St Marg *Liv* 82-86; Chapl Univ of Wales (Cardiff) *Llan* 88-89; TV Walton St Mary *Liv* 89-92; C Westmr St Matt *Lon* 92-96; C Somers Town 96-97; V Bush Hill Park St Mark from 97; Chapl N Middx Hosp NHS Trust from 97. *The Vicarage, St Mark's Road, Enfield EN1 1BE* Tel (020) 8363 2780 E-mail paul.atherton@blueyonder.co.uk

ATHERTON, Philip Andrew. b 51. Wycliffe Hall Ox. **d** 84 **p** 85. C Ox St Clem *Ox* 84-87; Lic Preacher *Man* 87-99; Ind Missr 87-99. *Address temp unknown*

ATHERTON, Timothy Edward John. b 60. Cranmer Hall Dur 83. **d** 86 **p** 87. C S Molton w Nymet St George, High Bray etc *Ex* 86-89; Canada from 89. *Box 515, Yellowknife NT, Canada, X1A 2N4* Tel (001) (867) 669 9874

ATKIN, Arthur Courtney Qu'appelle. b 19. Dur Univ BA44. Lich Th Coll 59. **d** 59 **p** 60. Chapl Bromsgrove Jun Sch 59-64; C Kidderminster St Geo *Worc* 59-60; C Bromsgrove All SS 60-64; Chapl RN 64-69; Chapl R Hosp Sch Holbrook 69-72; P-in-c Brixham *Ex* 72-74; Chapl Colston's Sch Bris 74-79; P-in-c Pitcombe w Shepton Montague and Bratton St Maur *B & W* 79-85; rtd 86; Perm to Offic *B & W* 86-93; Perm to Offic *Heref* from 93. *8 St Katherine's, High Street, Ledbury HR8 1DZ*

ATKIN, John Anthony. b 33. Glouc Th Course 70. **d** 72 **p** 73. NSM Leamington Priors All SS *Cov* 72-77; NSM Barford 77-78; NSM Barford w Wasperton and Sherbourne 78-80; P-in-c Exford w Exmoor *B & W* 80-82; P-in-c Hawkridge w Withypool 80-82; P-in-c Exford, Exmoor, Hawkridge and Withypool 82-83; R 83-92; RD Exmoor 86-92; rtd 93; Perm to Offic *B & W* from 93. *Halsgrove Farm, Withypool, Minehead TA24 7RX* Tel (01643) 83388

ATKINS, Austen Shaun. b 55. St Pet Coll Ox MA82 Selw Coll Cam MA85. Ridley Hall Cam 79. **d** 82 **p** 83. C S Mimms Ch Ch *Lon* 82-86; C Fulham St Matt 86-91; P-in-c Fulham St Dionis Parson's Green 91-03; V 03-04; C Ox St Andr *Ox* from 05. *313 Woodstock Road, Oxford OX2 7NY* Tel (01865) 513688

ATKINS, Canon David John. b 43. Lon Univ DipTh68. Kelham Th Coll 64. **d** 68 **p** 69. C Lewisham St Mary *S'wark* 68-72; Min Motspur Park 72-77; P-in-c Mitcham Ascension 77-82; V 82-83; P-in-c Downham w S Hanningfield *Chelmsf* 83-88; R 88-01; Asst RD Chelmsf 88-93; RD Chelmsf S 93-01; P-in-c W Hanningfield 90-93; Hon Can Chelmsf Cathl from 00; V Maldon All SS w St Pet from 01. *All Saints' Vicarage, Church Walk, Maldon CM9 4PY* Tel (01621) 854179

ATKINS, Dean John. b 70. Univ of Wales (Cardiff) BD93. St Steph Ho Ox 93. **d** 95 **p** 96. C Merthyr Dyfan *Llan* 95-99; V Aberaman and Abercwmboi w Cwmaman 99-01; C Roath St German from 01; Dioc Youth Officer from 01. *St Anne's, 1 North Church Street, Cardiff CF10 5HB* Tel (029) 2049 9867

ATKINS, Mrs Diana. b 31. K Coll Lon BD54 DipEd55. Qu Coll Birm 81. **dss** 83 **d** 87. De Beauvoir Town St Pet *Lon* 83-85; Gleadless *Sheff* 85-87; Par Dn 87-93; rtd 93; Perm to Offic *Sheff* from 93. *27 Stannington Glen, Sheffield S6 6NA* Tel 0114-234 0543

ATKINS, Forrest William (Bill). b 59. Ch Coll Cam MA85 Lon Univ BD84. Ridley Hall Cam 83. **d** 86 **p** 87. C Normanton *Derby* 86-90; C Stratford St Jo and Ch Ch w Forest Gate St Jas *Chelmsf* 90-97; Asst Chapl Dubai and Sharjah w N Emirates 97-03; I Mohill w Farnaught, Aughavas, Oughteragh etc *K, E & A* from 03. *St Mary's Rectory, Mohill, Co Leitrim, Irish Republic* Tel (00353) (71) 963 2959

ATKINS, Francis John. b 47. CEng MIStructE. S Dios Minl Tr Scheme. **d** 89 **p** 90. NSM Studley *Sarum* 89-92; Lic to RD Bradford from 92. *Church Cottage, 344 Frome Road, Trowbridge BA14 0EF* Tel (01225) 761757

ATKINS, Jane Elizabeth. b 51. EMMTC 98. **d** 01 **p** 02. NSM Fenn Lanes Gp *Leic* 01-05; P-in-c Ashill w Saham Toney *Nor* from 05. *The Rectory, Swaffham Road, Ashill, Thetford IP25 7BT* Tel (01760) 441191 E-mail revd.jane@ntlworld.com

ATKINS, Nicholas Steven. b 60. Oak Hill Th Coll BA88. **d** 88 **p** 89. C Shepton Mallet w Doulting *B & W* 88-91; C Combe Down w Monkton Combe and S Stoke 91-93; TV N Wingfield, Clay Cross and Pilsley *Derby* 93-98; V Essington *Lich* from 98; P-in-c Ipswich St Matt *St E* from 05. *St Matthew's Rectory, 3 Portman Road, Ipswich IP1 2ES* Tel (01473) 251630

ATKINS, Canon Paul Henry. b 38. St Mich Coll Llan 62. **d** 65 **p** 66. C Sheringham *Nor* 65-68; V Southtown 68-84; RD Flegg (Gt Yarmouth) 78-84; R Aylmerton w Runton 84-99; P-in-c Beeston Regis 98-99; P-in-c Gresham 98-99; R Aylmerton, Runton, Beeston Regis and Gresham 99-03; RD Repps 86-95; Hon Can Nor Cathl 88-03; rtd 03; Perm to Offic *Nor* from 03. *34 Regis Avenue, Beeston Regis, Sheringham NR26 8SW* Tel (01263) 820147 E-mail amdd24@dial.pipex.com

ATKINS, Peter. b 29. Edin Univ MA52. Edin Th Coll 52. **d** 54 **p** 55. C Edin Old St Paul *Edin* 54-59; P-in-c Edin St Dav 59-64; Chapl Fulbourn Hosp Cam 64-66; R Galashiels *Edin* 66-69; Perm to Offic 69-72; Divisional Dir Soc Services Brighton 72-83; Asst Dir Soc Services E Sussex from 83. *11 South Street, Lewes BN7 2BT* Tel (01273) 476230

ATKINS, Robert Brian. b 49. CIPFA78 Open Univ BA94. St Alb and Ox Min Course 94. **d** 97 **p** 98. NSM Bicester w Bucknell, Caversfield and Launton *Ox* from 97. *8 Tubb Close, Bicester OX26 2BN* Tel (01869) 253448 Mobile 07973-713149 E-mail frbob@fish.co.uk

ATKINS, Roger Francis. b 30. AKC54. **d** 55 **p** 56. C Bromley All Hallows *Lon* 55-58; C Eastleigh *Win* 58-62; Missr The Murray Australia 62-65; R Mossman 65-69; Adn Carpentaria 69-71; V Wolverley *Worc* 71-76; V S Hackney St Mich w Haggerston St Paul *Lon* 76-85; TV Gleadless *Sheff* 85-93; rtd 93; Perm to Offic *Sheff* from 93. *27 Stannington Glen, Sheffield S6 6NA* Tel 0114-234 0543

ATKINS, Shaun. *See* ATKINS, Austen Shaun

ATKINS, Timothy David. b 45. Ridley Hall Cam 71. **d** 74 **p** 75. C Stoughton *Guildf* 74-79; C Chilwell *S'well* 79-84; R Eastwood 84-91; V Finchley Ch Ch *Lon* from 91; Chapl Barnet Healthcare NHS Trust 92-01; Chapl Enfield Primary Care Trust from 01. *Christ Church Vicarage, 616 High Road, London N12 0AA* Tel (020) 8445 2377 *or* 8445 2532 Fax 8343 9406 *or* 8492 0278 E-mail christchurch@nfinchley.fsnet.co.uk

ATKINS, Timothy James. b 38. Worc Coll Ox BA62. Cuddesdon Coll 62. **d** 64 **p** 65. C Stafford St Mary *Lich* 64-67; C Loughborough St Pet *Leic* 67-69; C Usworth *Dur* 69-71; Lic to Offic *Newc* 71-76; P-in-c Slaley 76-87; P-in-c Shotley from 87. *St John's Vicarage, Snods Edge, Consett DH8 9TL* Tel (01207) 255665 E-mail timatk@snods.fsnet.co.uk

ATKINS, Timothy Samuel. b 22. DSC44. Em Coll Cam BA46 MA52. Ridley Hall Cam 47. **d** 49 **p** 50. C Melton Mowbray w Burton Lazars, Freeby etc *Leic* 49-51; C Preston St Jo *Blackb* 51-54; V Baxenden 54-58; R Mildenhall *St E* 58-63; V Bunbury *Ches* 63-87; RD Malpas 85-87; rtd 87; Perm to Offic *Ches* 87-01. *7 Fosbrooke House, Clifton Drive, Lytham St Annes FY8 5RQ*

ATKINS, William. *See* ATKINS, Forrest William

ATKINSON, Albert Edward. b 35. St Deiniol's Hawarden 79. **d** 79 **p** 80. C Ellesmere Port *Ches* 79-81; TV 81-84; P-in-c Kirkby Malzeard w Grewelthorpe and Mickley etc *Ripon* 84-88; P-in-c Fountains 88-90; R Fountains Gp 90-92; V Aysgarth and Bolton cum Redmire 92-96; rtd 96; Perm to Offic *Ripon* from 96; Hon Min Can Ripon Cathl from 01. *79 Hillshaw Park Way, Ripon HG4 1JU* Tel (01765) 607964

ATKINSON, Brian Colin. b 49. Sarum & Wells Th Coll 85. **d** 87 **p** 88. C Up Hatherley *Glouc* 87-90; R Upper Stour *Sarum* 90-95; TR Trowbridge H Trin 95-04; P-in-c Fairford and Kempsford w Whelford *Glouc* from 04; RD Fairford from 04. *The Vicarage, The Croft, Fairford GL7 4BB* Tel and fax (01285) 712467 E-mail katki01225@aol.com

ATKINSON, Christopher John. b 57. Man Univ BA80 DipTh84. Qu Coll Birm 82. **d** 85 **p** 86. C Stalybridge *Man* 85-88; P-in-c Westhall w Brampton and Stoven *St E* 88-89; P-in-c Sotterley, Willingham, Shadingfield, Ellough etc 88-90; P-in-c Hundred River Gp of Par 90-92; R Hundred River 92-97; P-in-c Eye w Braiseworth and Yaxley 97-00; P-in-c Occold 97-00; P-in-c Bedingfield 97-00; R Eye 00-03; RD Hartismere 97-03; V Bourne *Linc* from 03. *The Vicarage, Church Walk, Bourne PE10 9UQ* Tel (01778) 422412 E-mail chris_atk@yahoo.com

ATKINSON, Canon Christopher Lionel Varley. b 39. K Coll Lon 63. Chich Th Coll 65. **d** 67 **p** 68. C Sowerby Bridge w Norland *Wakef* 67-70; P-in-c Flushing *Truro* 70-73; Dioc Adv in RE 70-73; Perm to Offic *Worc* 74-78; TR Halesowen 78-88; RD Dudley 79-87; Hon Can Worc Cathl 83-88; V Cartmel *Carl* 88-97; TV Cartmel Peninsula 97-98; RD Windermere 94-98; Hon Can Carl Cathl 94-98; TR Bensham *Dur* 98-03; AD Gateshead 99-03; rtd 03; Bp's Adv Spiritual Development *Dur* from 03; Hon Can Dur Cathl from 01. *4 Attwood Place, Tow Law, Bishop Auckland DL13 4ER* Tel (01388) 731749

ATKINSON, Clive James. b 68. QUB BSc90. CITC 90. **d** 93 **p** 94. C Belfast H Trin and Ardoyne *Conn* 93-97; I Belfast Upper Falls 97-02; Chapl Vevey w Château d'Oex and Villars *Eur* from 02. *The Parsonage, Chemin de Champsavaux 1, 1807 Blonay, Vaud, Switzerland* Tel (0041) (21) 943 2239 E-mail info@allsaints.ch

ATKINSON, David. b 64. St Cuth Soc Dur BA02. Cranmer Hall Dur 02. **d** 04 **p** 05. C Dunston *Dur* from 04. *21 Park Terrace, Dunston, Gateshead NE11 9PA* Tel 0191-460 6706 E-mail david@theatkinsons.co.uk

ATKINSON, Canon David James. b 41. Lon Univ BD AKC63 Selw Coll Cam BA65 MA72. Linc Th Coll 65. **d** 66 **p** 67. C Linc St Giles *Linc* 66-70; Asst Chapl Newc Univ *Newc* 70-73; Adult Educn Officer *Lich* 73-75; P-in-c Adbaston 73-80; Dir of Educn 75-82; Preb Lich Cathl 79-82; Chapl Hull Univ *York* 82-87; Dir of Educn *Linc* 87-94; Can and Preb Linc Cathl from 89; P-in-c Bishop Norton, Wadingham and Snitterby 94-01; Perm to Offic from 01. *4 The Orchards, Middle Rasen, Market Rasen LN8 3TL* Tel (01673) 849979

✠**ATKINSON, The Rt Revd David John.** b 43. K Coll Lon BSc65 AKC65 PhD69 Bris Univ MLitt73 Ox Univ MA85 MSOSc. Trin Coll Bris and Tyndale Hall Bris 69. **d** 72 **p** 73 **c** 01. C Halliwell St Pet *Man* 72-74; C Harborne Heath *Birm* 74-77; Lib Latimer Ho Ox 77-80; Chapl CCC Ox 80-93; Fell 84-93; Visiting Lect Wycliffe Hall Ox 84-93; Can Res and Chan S'wark Cathl *S'wark* 93-96; Adn Lewisham 96-01; Suff Bp Thetford *Nor* from 01. *The Red House, 53 Norwich Road, Stoke Holy Cross, Norwich NR14 8AB* Tel (01508) 491014 Fax 492105 E-mail bishop.thetford@4frontmedia.co.uk

ATKINSON, Derek Arthur. b 31. K Coll Lon BD59 AKC59. **d** 60 **p** 61. C Ashford *Cant* 60-64; C Deal St Leon 64-68; R E w W Ogwell *Ex* 68-81; Asst Dir of RE 68-78; Dep Dir and Children's Adv 78-88; R Ogwell and Denbury 81-84; R Kenton w Mamhead and Powderham 84-88; rtd 88; Perm to Offic *Ex* 88-98. *High Trees, Fulford Road, Fulford, Stoke-on-Trent ST11 9QT* Tel (01782) 397156 E-mail derek-atkinson@lineone.net

ATKINSON, Ian. b 33. BNC Ox BA58 MA63. Coll of Resurr Mirfield 56. **d** 58 **p** 59. C Welling *S'wark* 58-62; C Camberwell St Giles 62-63; V Wandsworth Common St Mary 63-67; S Africa 67-68; C Oxted *S'wark* 68-69; Asst Chapl Ch Hosp Horsham 70-85; NSM Dalmahoy *Edin* 85-91; Asst Master Clifton Hall Sch 85-91; NSM Dunkeld *St And* 92-98; rtd 98. *2 Pinel Lodge, Druids Park, Murthly, Perth PH1 4ES* Tel (01738) 710561

ATKINSON, Canon Prof James. b 14. St Jo Coll Dur BA36 MA39 MLitt50 Univ of Munster DTh55 Hull Univ Hon DD97. **d** 37 **p** 38. C Newc H Cross *Newc* 37-41; Succ Sheff Cathl *Sheff* 41-42; Prec 42-44; V Shiregreen St Jas and St Chris 44-51; Fell Sheff Univ from 51; Can Th Leic Cathl *Leic* 54-70; Lect Th Hull Univ 56-64; Reader 64-67; Prof Bibl Studies Sheff Univ 67-79; Lic to Offic *Sheff* 68-02; Can Th Sheff Cathl 70-93; rtd 79; Latimer Ho Ox 81-84. *Leach House, Leadmill Bridge, Hathersage, Hope Valley S32 1BA* Tel (01433) 650570

ATKINSON, Canon John Dudley. b 38. ACA60 FCA71. Qu Coll Birm 63. **d** 66 **p** 67. C Bishop's Stortford St Mich *St Alb* 66-70; C Norton 70-73; V Markyate Street 73-80; R Baldock w Bygrave 80-94; RD Stevenage 83-89; TR Bride Valley *Sarum* 94-03; RD Lyme Bay 98-03; Can and Preb Sarum Cathl 02-03; rtd 03; Perm to Offic *Heref* from 04. *48 Prince Rupert Road, Ledbury HR8 2FA* Tel (01531) 632014
E-mail canonjda@btinternet.com

ATKINSON, Ms Judith Angela. b 70. Leeds Univ BA92 Fitzw Coll Cam BA95 MA02. Ridley Hall Cam 93. **d** 96 **p** 97. C Chester le Street *Dur* 96-00; Community Employment Development Worker 00-01; NSM Dunston 01-02; Perm to Offic *Birm* from 03. *73 Farquhar Road, Edgbaston, Birmingham B15 2QP* Tel 0121-452 2607
E-mail juditha_stephenb@hotmail.com

ATKINSON, Mrs Kate Bigwood. b 56. Cranmer Hall Dur 94. **d** 96 **p** 97. C Woking St Jo *Guildf* 96-00; NSM Haslemere and Grayswood 00-03; Assoc Min Nevada St Patr USA from 03. *818 Barbara Street, Incline Village, NV, USA*
E-mail revkotty@aol.com

ATKINSON, Canon Lewis Malcolm. b 34. St Jo Coll Dur. **d** 82 **p** 83. C Chapeltown *Sheff* 82-85; V Sheff St Paul 85-93; Ind Chapl 85-99; RD Ecclesfield 90-93; V Oughtibridge 93-99; RD Tankersley 96-99; Hon Can Sheff Cathl 98-99; rtd 99; Perm to Offic *Sheff* from 99. *14 Rowan Close, Chapeltown, Sheffield S35 1QE*

ATKINSON, Marianne Rose. b 39. Girton Coll Cam BA61 CertEd62 MA64. Linc Th Coll 86. **d** 88 **p** 94. C S w N Hayling *Portsm* 88-91; C Rainham *Roch* 91-92; Asst Chapl Salford R Hosps NHS Trust 92-97; Hon C Prestwich St Marg *Man* 94-97; Chapl R United Hosp Bath NHS Trust 97-00; rtd 00; Perm to Offic *B & W* 00-03 and *St E* from 03. *68 Barons Road, Bury St Edmunds IP33 2LW* Tel (01284) 752075
E-mail torrensatkinson@aol.com

ATKINSON, Megan Annice. b 37. SRN58. STETS 95. **d** 98 **p** 01. NSM Bridgemary *Portsm* 98-02; NSM Locks Heath 02-04; rtd 04; Perm to Offic *Portsm* from 05. *23 Home Rule Road, Locks Heath, Southampton SO31 6LH* Tel (01489) 575331

ATKINSON, Michael Hubert. b 33. Qu Coll Ox BA57 MA60. Ripon Hall Ox 56. **d** 58 **p** 59. C Attercliffe w Carbrook *Sheff* 58-60; Ind Chapl 60-66; C Sharrow St Andr 60-66; Ind Chapl *Pet* 66-71; Sen Ind Chapl *Cant* 71-79; Research Officer Gen Syn Bd for Soc Resp 79-87; Representation Sec USPG 88-92; TV High Wycombe *Ox* 92-97; Chapl Bucks Coll of HE 94-97; rtd 97. *7 Birch Court, Old Bridge Rise, Ilkley LS29 9HH* Tel (01943) 609891

ATKINSON, Nigel Terence. b 60. Sheff Univ BA82 St Jo Coll Dur MA96. Westmr Th Sem (USA) MDiv87 Cranmer Hall Dur 87. **d** 89 **p** 90. C Oakwood St Thos *Lon* 89-92; P-in-c Dolton *Ex* 92-95; P-in-c Iddesleigh w Dowland 92-95; P-in-c Monkokehampton 92-95; Warden Latimer Ho Ox 95-98; V Knutsford St Jo and Toft *Ches* from 98. *The Vicarage, 11 Gough's Lane, Knutsford WA16 8QL* Tel (01565) 632834 Fax 755160
E-mail nigelatk@btopenworld.com

ATKINSON, Mrs Patricia Anne. b 47. EAMTC 86. **d** 89 **p** 01. NSM Nor St Steph *Nor* 89-94; Lic to Offic from 94; Chapl Norwich Primary Care Trust from 00; Chapl Norfolk and Nor Univ Hosp NHS Trust from 01; NSM Brundall w Braydeston and Postwick *Nor* 01-02. *32 Berryfields, Brundall, Norwich NR13 5QE* Tel (01603) 714720 E-mail apatrici@fish.co.uk

ATKINSON, Peter Duncan. b 41. Univ Coll Dur BA62. Linc Th Coll 63. **d** 65 **p** 66. C Beckenham St Geo *Roch* 65-69; C Caversham *Ox* 69-75; P-in-c Millfield St Mark *Dur* 76-86; V Dedworth *Ox* 86-93; TV Aylesbury w Bierton and Hulcott 93-05; rtd 05. *24 Grimbald Road, Knaresborough HG5 8HD* Tel (01423) 866593

ATKINSON, Canon Peter Gordon. b 52. St Jo Coll Ox BA74 MA78. Westcott Ho Cam 77. **d** 79 **p** 80. C Clapham Old Town *S'wark* 79-83; P-in-c Tatsfield 83-90; R Bath H Trin *B & W* 90-91; Prin Chich Th Coll 91-94; Can and Preb Chich Cathl *Chich* 91-97; R Lavant 94-97; Can Res and Chan Chich Cathl from 97. *The Residentiary, Canon Lane, Chichester PO19 1PX* Tel (01243) 782961 E-mail peteratkinson@fastnet.co.uk

ATKINSON, Philip Charles. b 50. Hull Univ BA71 PhD76 Chorley Coll of Educn CertEd77. N Ord Course 81. **d** 84 **p** 85. NSM Bolton SS Simon and Jude *Man* 84-87; Chapl R Wolv Sch from 87. *Royal Wolverhampton School, 179 Penn Road, Wolverhampton WV3 0EQ* Tel (01902) 341230

ATKINSON, Philip Stephen. b 58. K Coll Lon BD80 AKC80 Dur Univ MA97. Ridley Hall Cam 81. **d** 83 **p** 84. C Barrow St Matt *Carl* 83-86; C Kirkby Lonsdale 86-89; R Redmarshall *Dur* 89-95; V Bishopton w Gt Stainton 89-95; C Kirkby Lonsdale *Carl* 95-97; Chapl Casterton Sch Lancs from 95; NSM Kirkby Lonsdale *Carl* from 97. *Beckside, Casterton, Kirkby Lonsdale, Carnforth LA6 2SB* Tel (01524) 279248

ATKINSON, The Ven Richard William Bryant. b 58. OBE02. Magd Coll Cam MA. Ripon Coll Cuddesdon. **d** 84 **p** 85. C Abingdon w Shippon *Ox* 84-87; TV Sheff Manor *Sheff* 87-91; TR 91-96; Hon Tutor Ripon Coll Cuddesdon 87-92; V Rotherham *Sheff* 96-02; Hon Can Sheff Cathl 98-02; Adn Leic from 02. *46 Southernhay Road, Leicester LE2 3TJ* Tel and fax 0116-270 4441 *or* tel 0116-248 7419
E-mail archdeacon.richard@chouse.leicester.anglican.org

ATKINSON, Canon Samuel Charles Donald. b 30. TCD BA54. **d** 55 **p** 56. C Belfast St Simon *Conn* 55-62; I Ballynaclough *L & K* 62-68; I Cloughjordan w Modreeny 68-87; Dioc Youth Adv (Killaloe) 75-83; Dioc Info Officer 76-88; Can Killaloe Cathl 76-82; Chan 82-96; I Cloughjordan w Borrisokane etc 87-96; rtd 96. *Dromore Lodge, Rockcorry, Co Monaghan, Irish Republic* Tel (00353) (42) 42356

ATKINSON, Simon James. b 71. St Chad's Coll Dur BA93 Ustinov Coll Dur PGCE04. St Steph Ho Ox 93. **d** 95 **p** 96. C Norton St Mary *Dur* 95-96; C Hartlepool H Trin 96-99; TV Jarrow 99-01; V Chich St Wilfrid *Chich* 01-03; Perm to Offic *Dur* from 03. *10 St Carileph Way, Bishop Auckland DL14 7GD* Tel (01388) 459589 E-mail simon@utopia101.plus.com

ATKINSON, Terence Harry. b 52. Coll of Resurr Mirfield 88. **d** 90 **p** 91. C Bottesford w Ashby *Linc* 90-93; TV Cleethorpes 93-98; C-in-c Cleethorpes St Fran CD 98-01; V Chapel St Leonards w Hogsthorpe 01-03; P-in-c Gt Grimsby St Andr w St Luke and All SS from 03. *St Andrew's Vicarage, 2A Albion Street, Grimsby DN32 7DY* Tel (01472) 348200

ATKINSON, Wendy Sybil. b 53. Man Univ BA95. N Ord Course 95. **d** 97 **p** 98. NSM Brinnington w Portwood *Ches* 97-99; C 99-01; NSM Werneth from 01. *8 Freshfield Close, Marple Bridge, Stockport SK6 5ES* Tel 0161-427 5612

ATKINSON-JONES, Mrs Susan Florence. b 64. Univ of Wales (Cardiff) BD93. St Mich Coll Llan 96. **d** 98 **p** 99. C Bargoed and Deri w Brithdir *Llan* 98-05; TV Sanderstead All SS *S'wark* from 05. *35 Audley Drive, Warlingham CR6 9AH* Tel (020) 8657 5505
E-mail susan@sanderstead-parish.org.uk

ATLING, Edwood Brian. b 46. ACIB FIMgt. Westcott Ho Cam 00. **d** 02 **p** 03. NSM Godmanchester *Ely* 02-04; P-in-c Abbots Ripton w Wood Walton from 04; P-in-c Kings Ripton from 04; P-in-c Houghton w Wyton from 04. *Blue Cedars, 70 Common Lane, Hemingford Abbots, Huntingdon PE28 9AW* Tel (01480) 493975 Mobile 07775-544679 Fax (01480) 496240
E-mail atling@btopenworld.com

ATTA-BAFFOE, Victor Reginald. b 59. Trin Coll Toronto BTh88 Episc Div Sch Cambridge (USA) MA92 Yale Univ STM93. St Nic Th Coll Ghana LTh87. **d** 88 **p** 89. Ghana 88-90 and 93-98; USA 90-93; Lect St Nic Th Coll 88-90 and 93-98; NSM Finsbury Park St Thos *Lon* from 99. *20 Great Peter Street, London SW1P 2BU* Tel (020) 7222 3704 Fax 7233 0255

ATTAWAY, Mrs Elizabeth Ann. b 36. Herts Coll CertEd56. Cant Sch of Min 93 Bp Otter Coll 57. **d** 96 **p** 97. NSM Maidstone St Paul *Cant* 96-02; NSM Boxley w Detling from 02. *1 Staplers Court, Penenden Heath, Maidstone ME14 2XB* Tel (01622) 762656 E-mail glattaway@btinternet.com

ATTFIELD, David George. b 31. Magd Coll Ox BA54 MA58 BD61 K Coll Lon MPhil72 Dur Univ MA81. Westcott Ho Cam 57. **d** 58 **p** 59. C Edgbaston St Aug *Birm* 58-61; C Ward End 61-62; Lect Div St Kath Coll Tottenham 62-64; All SS Coll Tottenham 64-68; Sen Lect St Bede Coll Dur 68-75; St Hild and St Bede Coll 75-80; TV Drypool *York* 80-86; R Newton Heath All SS *Man* 86-96; rtd 97; Perm to Offic *Dur* from 97. *19 Laburnum Avenue, Durham DH1 4HA* Tel 0191-383 0509

ATTLEY, Ronald. b 46. Open Univ BA87 Dur Univ CCSk90. Brasted Th Coll 66 Chich Th Coll 68. **d** 70 **p** 71. C Heworth St Mary *Dur* 70-73; C Hulme Ascension *Man* 73-75; Belize 76-79 and 00; V Leadgate *Dur* 79-84; Chapl HM Rem Cen Ashford 84-87; Chapl HM Pris Ashwell and Stocken 87-89; Chapl HM Pris Frankland 89-92; Chapl HM YOI Deerbolt 92-96; V Bath St Barn w Englishcombe *B & W* 96-00; V Brinnington w Portwood *Ches* from 01. *St Luke's Vicarage, Brinnington Road, Stockport SK5 8BS* Tel 0161-430 4164

ATTRILL, Norman Edmund Charles. b 16. K Coll Lon BA37. Wm Temple Coll Rugby 65 Ripon Hall Ox 67. **d** 68 **p** 69. C Portsea St Mary *Portsm* 68-72; V Sea View 72-80; rtd 81; Perm to Offic *Ox* from 83. *27 Church Street, Henley-on-Thames RG9 1SE* Tel (01491) 574268

ATTWATER, Mrs Sallyanne. b 48. Westmr Coll Ox MTh98. S Dios Minl Tr Scheme 86. **d** 94 **p** 95. Chapl Asst Eastbourne Distr Gen Hosp 94-95; Asst Chapl Princess Alice Hosp and All SS Hosp 94-95; C E Grinstead St Swithun *Chich* 95-98; P-in-c Bishop's Cannings, All Cannings etc *Sarum* from 98. *The Vicarage, The Street, Bishop's Cannings, Devizes SN10 2LD* Tel (01380) 860650 E-mail revsally@attwater.freeserve.co.uk

ATTWATER, Canon Stephen Philip. b 47. ALCM67. Linc Th Coll 85. **d** 87 **p** 88. C Warrington St Elphin *Liv* 87-90; P-in-c Eccleston St Thos 90-94; V 94-99; V Padgate from 99; AD Warrington from 05; Hon Can Liv Cathl from 05. *The Rectory, Station Road, Padgate, Warrington WA2 0PD* Tel (01925) 821555 E-mail stephen@attwater1.freeserve.co.uk

ATTWOOD, Andrew Michael. b 66. Derby Coll of Educn BEd91. Trin Coll Bris BA02. **d** 02 **p** 03. C Leamington Priors St Mary *Cov* from 02. *12 Otters Rest, Leamington Spa CV31 1AD* Tel (01926) 315399 Mobile 07884-136816 E-mail a.attwood@talk21.com

ATTWOOD, Anthony Norman. b 47. Univ of Wales (Abth) BSc(Econ)69 Hull Univ MA82. Qu Coll Birm 69. **d** 72 **p** 73. C Greenhill *Sheff* 72-75; V Elsecar 76-81; Ind Missr 81-95; TV Maltby 81-86; Ind Chapl 86-95; RD Adwick 89-95; Teesside Ind Miss *Dur* 95-99; P-in-c Swindon St Aug *Bris* 99-03; Soc Resp Adv 99-03; P-in-c Dudley St Barn *Worc* from 03; P-in-c Dudley St Thos and St Luke from 04. *St Thomas's Vicarage, King Street, Dudley DY2 8QB* Tel (01384) 252015 Mobile 07967-604435 E-mail aattwood@fish.co.uk

ATTWOOD, Preb Carl Norman Harry. b 53. Bris Univ BA74 Ox Univ BA76 MA80. Cuddesdon Coll 74. **d** 77 **p** 78. C Tupsley *Heref* 77-82; R Colwall w Upper Colwall and Coddington from 82; Perm to Offic *Worc* from 82; Bp's Voc Officer *Heref* 83-89; Chapl St Jas Sch Malvern from 86; RD Ledbury *Heref* 90-96; Preb Heref Cathl from 97. *The Rectory, Walwyn Road, Colwall, Malvern WR13 6EG* Tel (01684) 540330 Fax 540083 E-mail carl@attwoods.org

ATTWOOD, David John Edwin. b 51. Dur Univ BA76 Em Coll Cam BA73 MA77. Cranmer Hall Dur 74. **d** 77 **p** 78. C Rodbourne Cheney *Bris* 77-79; C Lydiard Millicent w Lydiard Tregoz 79-85; Dir and Lect Trin Coll Bris 85-97; V Prenton *Ches* 97-02; R Sundridge w Ide Hill and Toys Hill *Roch* from 02. *The Rectory, Chevening Road, Sundridge, Sevenoaks TN14 6AB* Tel (01959) 563749 E-mail david@attwood27.freeserve.co.uk

ATTWOOD, Leslie Thomas. b 42. Univ of W of England MA94 Cranfield Univ MBA MCIPD76. St Steph Ho Ox. **d** 83 **p** 84. C Ascot Heath *Ox* 83-86; Dioc Tr Officer *Truro* 86-88; C Wallasey St Hilary *Ches* 98-00; C Devizes St Pet *Sarum* 00-02; TV Godrevy *Truro* from 02. *The Vicarage, 43 School Lane, St Erth, Hayle TR27 4HN* Tel (01736) 753194 E-mail attwood99@lineone.net

ATTWOOD, Peter John. b 44. ACIB68. SEITE 00. **d** 03 **p** 04. NSM Langton Green *Roch* from 03. *Podlea, Colemans Hatch, Hartfield TN7 4EN* Tel (01342) 822428 Mobile 07714-026402 E-mail rev@podlea.co.uk

ATWELL, The Very Revd James Edgar. b 46. Ex Coll Ox BA68 MA73 BD94 Harvard Univ ThM70. Cuddesdon Coll 68. **d** 70 **p** 71. C E Dulwich St Jo *S'wark* 70-74; C Cambridge Gt St Mary w St Mich *Ely* 74-77; Chapl Jes Coll Cam 77-81; V Towcester w Easton Neston *Pet* 81-95; RD Towcester 83-91; Provost St E 95-00; Dean St E from 00. *The Provost's House, Bury St Edmunds IP33 1RS* Tel (01284) 754852 *or* 754933 Fax 768655 E-mail dean@burycathedral.fsnet.co.uk

ATWELL, Robert Ronald. b 54. St Jo Coll Dur BA75 Dur Univ MLitt79. Westcott Ho Cam 76. **d** 78 **p** 79. C Mill Hill Jo Keble Ch *Lon* 78-81; Chapl Trin Coll Cam 81-87; OSB 87-98; Lic to Offic *Ox* 87-97; Perm to Offic *Ely* 97-98; V Primrose Hill St Mary w Avenue Road St Paul *Lon* from 98. *St Mary's Vicarage, 44 King Henry's Road, London NW3 3RP* Tel (020) 7722 3062 *or* 7722 3238 E-mail robertatwell@smvph44.plus.com

AUCHMUTY, John Robert. b 67. ACCA. CITC 89. **d** 92 **p** 93. C Dundela St Mark *D & D* 92-96; I Eglish w Killylea *Arm* 96-01; I Killaney w Carryduff *D & D* from 01. *The Rectory, 700 Saintfield Road, Carryduff, Belfast BT8 8BU* Tel (028) 9081 2342 *or* 9081 3489 E-mail cofi@carryduff70.freeserve.co.uk

AUCKLAND, Bishop of. *See* PATERSON, The Rt Revd John Campbell

AUCKLAND, Archdeacon of. *See* JAGGER, The Ven Ian

AUDEN, Lawson Philip. b 45. Qu Coll Birm 73. **d** 78 **p** 81. C Spalding *Linc* 78-81; TV Wordsley *Lich* 81-82; TV Kidderminster St Mary and All SS, Trimpley etc *Worc* 82-87; Ind Chapl 82-87; Perm to Offic *Cov* and *Worc* 87-97; *Birm, Lich* and *Glouc* 94-97; Chapl Worcs Community Healthcare NHS Trust 91-97; P-in-c Pebworth w Dorsington and Honeybourne *Glouc* 97-99; Perm to Offic *Cov* 98-01; *B & W* from 00; Chapl Miss to Seafarers from 99; Millennium Officer *Glouc* 99-01; Perm to Offic *Glouc* from 01. *4 Penlea Court, Shirehampton, Bristol BS11 0BY* Tel 0117-982 7879 *or* (01275) 372926 E-mail philipauden@ukf.net

AUDIBERT, Mrs Janice Elizabeth. b 56. OLM course 98. **d** 99 **p** 00. OLM Oakdale *Sarum* 99-02; C from 02. *24 Blackbird Close, Poole BH17 7YA* Tel and fax (01202) 389751 E-mail janice.audibert@christ-church-creekmoor.org.uk

AULD, Jeremy Rodger. b 66. Edin Univ LLB87 Solicitor 89 Barrister 97. TISEC BD04. **d** 04. C Edin St Pet *Edin* from 04. *10 Hope Park Crescent, Edinburgh EH8 9NA* Tel 0131-667 4537 Mobile 07976-707253 E-mail jeremya@fish.co.uk

AULD, Mrs Sheila Edith. b 38. Newc Poly BA87 Univ of Northumbria at Newc MA99. NEOC 91. **d** 94 **p** 95. Project Worker Cedarwood Trust 88-02; NSM Newc St Gabr *Newc* 94-02; rtd 02; Perm to Offic *Newc* from 02. *5 Gibson Fields, Hexham NE46 1AS* Tel (01434) 602297

AUST, Arthur John. b 14. St Aug Coll Cant 62. **d** 63 **p** 64. C Dagenham *Chelmsf* 63-65; Kenya 65-67; P-in-c Skidbrooke *Linc* 67-69; R Theddlethorpe w Mablethorpe 67-71; Nigeria 71-74; S Africa 74-77; TV Clyst St George, Aylesbeare, Clyst Honiton etc *Ex* 79-81; rtd 81; Perm to Offic *Cant* from 81. *20 Campbell Road, Deal CT14 7EQ* Tel (01304) 361583

AUSTEN, Glyn Benedict. b 54. UEA BA77 MPhil80. Ripon Coll Cuddesdon BA81 MA85. **d** 82 **p** 83. C Newport w Longford and Chetwynd *Lich* 82-85; C Hawley H Trin *Guildf* 85-87; R Barnack w Ufford and Bainton *Pet* 87-03; Asst Master Stamford High Sch from 03. *31 Hillview Road, South Witham, Grantham NG33 5QW* Tel (01572) 767944 *or* (01780) 484200 Fax (01780) 484201 E-mail g.b.austen@ukf.net

AUSTEN, John. b 46. St Cath Coll Cam BA69 MA72. Qu Coll Birm DipTh70. **d** 71 **p** 72. C Thornaby on Tees *York* 71-74; C Aston St Jas *Birm* 74-82; Chapl Aston Univ 82-88; C Handsworth St Andr from 88. *151 Church Lane, Birmingham B20 2RU* Tel 0121-554 8882 Fax 551-8637 E-mail johnausten@iname.com

AUSTEN, Simon Neil. b 67. Warwick Univ BSc88. Wycliffe Hall Ox BA93 MA97 DipMin94. **d** 94 **p** 95. C Gt Chesham *Ox* 94-98; Chapl Stowe Sch 98-02; V Houghton *Carl* from 02. *The Vicarage, Houghton, Carlisle CA6 4HZ* Tel (01228) 810076 *or* 515972 E-mail simon.austen@ukgateway.net *or* office@hkchurch.co.uk

AUSTERBERRY, Preb David Naylor. b 35. Birm Univ BA58. Wells Th Coll 58. **d** 60 **p** 61. C Leek St Edw *Lich* 60-63; Iran 64-70; Chapl CMS Foxbury 70-73; V Walsall Pleck and Bescot *Lich* 73-82; R Brierley Hill 82-88; R Kinnerley w Melverley and Knockin w Maesbrook 88-99; RD Oswestry 92-95; Preb Lich Cathl 96-00; rtd 00; Perm to Offic *Heref* and *Lich* from 00. *Chad Cottage, Dovaston, Kinnerley, Oswestry SY10 8DT* Tel (01691) 682039

AUSTERBERRY, John Maurice. b 62. Birm Univ BA83. Sarum & Wells Th Coll 84. **d** 86 **p** 87. C Clayton *Lich* 86-89; Asst Chapl Withington Hosp *Man* 89-95; Chapl Tameside and Glossop NHS Trust 95-99; Chapl N Staffs Hosp NHS Trust from 99. *City General Hospital, Newcastle Road, Stoke-on-Trent ST4 6QG* Tel (01782) 715444 *or* 552252

AUSTIN, Canon Alfred George. b 36. Ridley Coll Melbourne ThL61. **d** 61 **p** 62. Australia 61-77; C Dartford St Alb *Roch* 77-79; Australia from 79; R Tatura 79-84; R W Bend 84-90; R Kyneton 90-93; Can 83-97; I Essendon Ch Ch 97-01; rtd 01. *Brocklyn, 3 Alpina Place, Kangaroo Flat, Vic, Australia 3555* Tel (0061) (3) 5447 0174

AUSTIN, Mrs Catherine Brenda. b 57. **d** 00 **p** 01. OLM Henley, Claydon and Barham *St E* from 00. *Fait Accompli, 7 Freeman Avenue, Henley, Ipswich IP6 0RZ* Tel (01473) 830100

AUSTIN, The Ven George Bernard. b 31. St D Coll Lamp BA53 Chich Th Coll 53. **d** 55 **p** 56. C Chorley St Pet *Blackb* 55-57; C Notting Hill St Clem *Lon* 57-60; Asst Chapl Lon Univ 60-61; C Dunstable *St Alb* 61-64; V Eaton Bray 64-70; V Bushey Heath 70-88; Hon Can St Alb 78-88; Adn York 88-99; Can and Preb York Minster 98-99; rtd 99; Perm to Offic *York* from 99. *North Back House, 3B Main Street, Wheldrake, York YO19 6AG* Tel (01904) 448509 Fax 448002 E-mail george.austin@virgin.net

AUSTIN, Glyn. *See* AUSTIN, Ronald Glyn

AUSTIN, Miss Jane. b 43. SRN64 SCM66. **dss** 81 **d** 87 **p** 94. Tonbridge SS Pet and Paul *Roch* 81-98; Par Dn 87-94; C 94-98; Hon Can Roch Cathl 96-98; P-in-c Meltham *Wakef* 98-01; V from 01; P-in-c Helme 00-01; RD Almondbury from 01. *The Vicarage, 150 Huddersfield Road, Meltham, Holmfirth HD9 4AL* Tel (01484) 850050 E-mail j.austin.meltham@care4free.net

✠**AUSTIN, The Rt Revd John Michael.** b 39. St Edm Hall Ox BA63. St Steph Ho Ox 62. **d** 64 **p** 65 **c** 92. C E Dulwich St Jo *S'wark* 64-68; USA 68-69; Warden Pemb Ho and Missr Walworth St Chris CD *S'wark* 69-76; TV Walworth 75-76; Soc Resp Adv *St Alb* 76-84; Dir Dioc Bd for Soc Resp *Lon* 84-92; Preb St Paul's Cathl 89-92; Suff Bp Aston *Birm* 92-05; Warden CSMV from 98; rtd 05. *Bell House, The Row, Hartest, Bury St Edmunds IP29 4DL*

AUSTIN, Leslie Ernest. b 46. Trin Coll Bris 72. **d** 74 **p** 75. C Paddock Wood *Roch* 74-79; C Upper Armley *Ripon* 79-81; V Horton *Bradf* 81-85; V Long Preston w Tosside 85-97; TR Shirwell, Loxhore, Kentisbury, Arlington, etc *Ex* from 97. *The Rectory, 2 Barnfield, Bratton Fleming, Barnstaple EX31 4RT* Tel (01598) 710807 E-mail les@austin85.freeserve.co.uk

AUSTIN, Margaret Rose. b 41. Qu Coll Birm 01. **d** 03 **p** 04. NSM Farewell *Lich* from 03; NSM Gentleshaw from 03; NSM Hammerwich from 03. *137 Highfields Road, Chasetown, Burntwood WS7 4QT* Tel (01543) 686883 E-mail margaret@austin1693.freeserve.co.uk

AUSTIN, Canon Michael Ridgwell. b 33. Lon Univ BD57 PhD69 Birm Univ MA66 FRHistS. Lon Coll of Div ALCD56. **d** 57 **p** 58. C Ward End *Birm* 57-60; PC Derby St Andr *Derby* 60-66; Lect Th Derbyshire Coll of HE 66-73; Prin Lect 73-85; Chapl Derby Cathl *Derby* 66-81; Can Res Derby Cathl 81-85; Bp's Adv on Tr *S'well* 85-88; Dir Post-Ord Tr 86-94; Can Res S'well Minster 88-94; Dioc Dir of Tr 88-94; Abps' Adv for Bps' Min 94-98; rtd 98; Perm to Offic *S'well* from 04. *7 Dudley Doy Road, Southwell NG25 0NJ* Tel (01636) 812604

AUSTIN, Ronald Glyn. b 52. Univ of Wales (Cardiff) BD90 Univ of Wales MPhil98. St Mich Coll Llan 88. **d** 90 **p** 91. C Llangynwyd w Maesteg *Llan* 90-91; C Barry All SS 91-93; V Nantymoel w Wyndham 93-97; V Pontyclun w Talygarn 97-02; Tutor St Mich Coll Llan 02-04; V Llansantffraid, Bettws and Aberkenfig *Llan* from 04. *St Bride's Rectory, Heol Persondy, Aberkenfig, Bridgend CF32 9RH* Tel (01656) 720274

AUSTIN, Mrs Susan Frances. b 47. Open Univ BA81. Cant Sch of Min 87. **d** 92 **p** 94. Chapl Ch Ch High Sch Ashford 90-94; C Gt Chart *Cant* 92-94; C Ashford 92-94; C Estover *Ex* 94-96; V Stevenage All SS Pin Green *St Alb* 96-98; P-in-c Bredgar w Bicknor and Frinsted w Wormshill etc *Cant* 00-04; rtd 04; Perm to Offic *Cant* from 04. *58 Seaway Gardens, St Marys Bay, Romney Marsh TN29 0RH* Tel (01303) 815009 E-mail susanaustin@talk21.com

AUSTRALIA, Primate of. *See* CARNLEY, The Most Revd Peter Frederick

AVANN, Canon Penelope Joyce. b 46. Trin Coll Bris DipTh71. **dss** 83 **d** 87 **p** 98. Southborough St Pet w Ch Ch and St Matt *Roch* 83-89; Par Dn 87-89; Warden Past Assts from 89; Par Dn Beckenham St Jo 89-94; C 94-02; Hon Can Roch Cathl from 94; C Green Street Green and Pratts Bottom from 02. *9 Ringwood Avenue, Orpington BR6 7SY* Tel and fax (01689) 861742 Mobile 07710-418839

AVENT, Raymond John. b 28. St D Coll Lamp BA55 Coll of Resurr Mirfield 55. **d** 57 **p** 58. C Bury H Trin *Man* 57-60; C Holborn St Alb w Saffron Hill St Pet *Lon* 60-66; C Munster Square St Mary Magd 66-67; V Tottenham St Paul 67-77; RD E Haringey 73-77; V Kilburn St Aug w St Jo 77-87; AD Westmr Paddington 79-84; R St Vedast w St Mich-le-Querne etc 87-94; rtd 94; Perm to Offic *Lon* 94-00; *Glouc* from 00. *Maryvale House, Catbrook, Chipping Campden GL55 6DE* Tel (01386) 841323 E-mail avent@campadene.fsnet.co.uk

AVERY, Richard Julian. b 52. Keble Coll Ox BA73. St Jo Coll Nottm 74. **d** 77 **p** 78. C Macclesfield St Mich *Ches* 77-80; Canada 82-83 and 87-97; C Becontree St Mary *Chelmsf* 84-87; TV Cheltenham St Mark *Glouc* 97-03; Perm to Offic from 03. *19 Porchester Road, Hucclecote, Gloucester GL3 3EE*

AVERY, Robert Edward. b 69. Magd Coll Cam BA90. Ripon Coll Cuddesdon 90. **d** 93 **p** 94. C Cen Telford *Lich* 93-96; C Cambridge Gt St Mary w St Mich *Ely* 96-99; V Tamerton Foliot *Ex* 99-03; V Tunbridge Wells K Chas *Roch* from 03. *The Vicarage, 5D Frant Road, Tunbridge Wells TN2 5SB* Tel (01892) 525455 E-mail robert.avery@btinternet.com

AVERY, Russel Harrold. b 46. JP74. ACT ThDip75 Moore Th Coll Sydney 66. **d** 77 **p** 77. Australia 77-78, 88-98 and from 02; C Prenton *Ches* 78-79; Egypt 79-82; Chapl Maisons-Laffitte *Eur* 82-88; Chapl Nord Pas de Calais 98-02; rtd 02. *1A Alliedale Close, Hornsby, NSW, Australia 2077* Tel (0061) (2) 9487 5580 *or* 9269 0844 Mobile 412-381642 E-mail rhavery@cia.com.au

AVES, Peter Colin. b 57. Qu Mary Coll Lon BSc79 CertEd80 Lon Univ BD89. Wycliffe Hall Ox 85. **d** 88 **p** 89. C Thames Ditton *Guildf* 88-90; C Chertsey 90-93; R Stockbridge and Longstock and Leckford *Win* 93-00; Chapl to the Deaf *Sarum* 00-03; TV Beaminster Area from 03. *The Vicarage, 20 Orchard Way, Mosterton, Beaminster DT8 3LT* Tel (01308) 868090 E-mail peteraves@excite.co.uk

AVESON, Ian Henry. b 55. Jes Coll Ox BA77 MA81 Univ Coll Dur PGCE78 Birkbeck Coll Lon MSc85. St Mich Coll Llan BD97. **d** 97 **p** 98. C Penarth All SS *Llan* 97-99; TV Aberystwyth *St D* from 99. *Holy Trinity Vicarage, Buarth Road, Aberystwyth SY23 1NB* Tel (01970) 617015

AVEYARD, Ian. b 46. Liv Univ BSc68 Sheff Univ MEd00. ALCD72 St Jo Coll Nottm 71. **d** 71 **p** 72. C Bradley *Wakef* 71-74; C Knowle *Birm* 74-79; P-in-c Cofton Hackett 79; P-in-c Barnt Green 79; V Cofton Hackett w Barnt Green 80-94; Dioc Dir of Reader Tr 85-94; Warden of Readers 91-94; Course Leader St Jo Coll Nottm 96-99; P-in-c Thanington *Cant* from 99; Dioc Dir of Ords from 99. *The Vicarage, 70 Thanington Road, Canterbury CT1 3XE* Tel (01227) 464516 Fax 785894 E-mail ian@iaveyard.freeserve.co.uk

AVIS, Preb Paul David Loup. b 47. Lon Univ BD70 PhD76. Westcott Ho Cam 73. **d** 75 **p** 76. C S Molton, Nymet St George, High Bray etc *Ex* 75-80; V Stoke Canon, Poltimore w Huxham and Rewe etc 80-98; Preb Ex Cathl from 93; Sub Dean Ex Cathl from 97; Gen Sec Coun for Chr Unity from 98. *Church House, Great Smith Street, London SW1P 3NZ,* or *48 Trinity Rise, London SW2 2QR* Tel (020) 7898 1470 Fax 7898 1483 E-mail paul.avis@c-of-e.org.uk

AWRE, Richard William Esgar. b 56. Univ of Wales BA78. Wycliffe Hall Ox 78. **d** 81 **p** 82. C Blackpool St Jo *Blackb* 81-84; Asst Dir of Ords and Voc Adv 84-89; C Altham w Clayton le Moors 84-89; V Longridge 89-99; V Kenilworth St Nic *Cov* from 99; RD Kenilworth from 01. *The Vicarage, 7 Elmbank Road, Kenilworth CV8 1AL* Tel (01926) 854367 *or* 857509 E-mail stnicholasken@aol.com

AXFORD, Mrs Christine Ruth. b 53. Glam Coll of Educn BEd75. STETS BTh00. **d** 00 **p** 02. NSM Yeovil w Kingston Pitney *B & W* 00-01; NSM N Hartismere *St E* from 02. *The Rectory, Oakley, Diss IP21 4BW* Tel and fax (01379) 742708 E-mail robaxford@onetel.net.uk

AXFORD, Robert Henry. b 50. Univ of Wales BEng72 CEng85. Sarum & Wells Th Coll 89. **d** 91 **p** 92. C Castle Cary w Ansford *B & W* 91-95; P-in-c Queen Camel w W Camel, Corton Denham etc 95-01; R 01-02; R N Hartismere *St E* from 02; RD Hartismere from 04. *The Rectory, Oakley, Diss IP21 4BW* Tel and fax (01379) 742708 E-mail robaxford@onetel.net.uk

AXON, Andrew John. b 76. Univ of Wales (Lamp) BTh97. Trin Coll Bris 99. **d** 01 **p** 02. C Sevenhampton w Charlton Abbots, Hawling etc *Glouc* from 01. *The Rectory, Withington, Cheltenham GL54 4BG* Tel (01242) 890242 E-mail mail@ajaxon.freeserve.co.uk

AXTELL, Ronald Arthur John. b 33. Lon Univ BSc54 St Cath Soc Ox BA58 MA62. Wycliffe Hall Ox 56. **d** 58 **p** 59. C Walton Breck *Liv* 58-61; Iran 63-78; Chapl Tehran 63-67; Chapl Kerman 67-68; Chapl Shiraz 69-78; Chr Witness to Israel Miss in Man 78-82; Perm to Offic *Man* 79-82; TV Man Resurr 82; TV Man Gd Shep 82-88; R Levenshulme St Pet 88-98; rtd 98; Perm to Offic *Man* from 98. *15 Berwick Avenue, Stockport SK4 3AA* Tel 0161-432 5943 E-mail axtell@ntlworld.com

AXTELL, Stephen Geoffrey. b 57. Open Univ BSc96. St Jo Coll Nottm 00. **d** 02 **p** 03. C Coseley Ch Ch *Worc* from 02. *12 Ribbesford Crescent, Coseley, Bilston WV14 8XU* Tel (01902) 493600 Mobile 07887-544776 E-mail saxtell@globalnet.co.uk

AYERS, Canon John. b 40. FCollP Bris Univ BEd75 Newton Park Coll Bath MEd89 FRSA94. **d** 77 **p** 78. NSM Corsham *Bris* 77-79; NSM Gtr Corsham 79-88; NSM Ditteridge 88-92; NSM Box w Hazlebury and Ditteridge from 93; Hon Can Bris Cathl from 94. *Toad Hall, Middlehill, Box, Corsham SN13 8QP* Tel (01225) 742123 E-mail johnayers@middlehill.netlineuk.net

AYERS, Paul Nicholas. b 61. St Pet Coll Ox BA82 MA86. Trin Coll Bris 83. **d** 85 **p** 86. C Clayton *Bradf* 85-88; C Keighley St Andr 88-91; V Wrose 91-97; V Pudsey St Lawr and St Paul from 97. *The Vicarage, Vicarage Drive, Pudsey LS28 7RL* Tel 0113-256 4197 *or* 257 7843

AYERS-HARRIS, Mrs Rebecca Theresa. b 70. Nottm Univ BA91 Birm Univ PGCE92. WEMTC 01. **d** 04. NSM Leominster *Heref* from 04. *1 Hillside Cottage, Kimbolton, Leominster HR6 0JA* Tel (01568) 750605

AYERST, Edward Richard. b 25. Leeds Univ BA51. Coll of Resurr Mirfield 51. **d** 53 **p** 54. C Bethnal Green St Jo w St Simon *Lon* 53-57; C Hayes St Mary 58-60; V Edmonton St Mary w St Jo 60-66; R Whippingham w E Cowes *Portsm* 66-77; V Bridgwater St Mary w Chilton Trinity *B & W* 77-84; V Durleigh 77-84; V Bridgwater St Mary, Chilton Trinity and Durleigh 84-90; Chapl to The Queen 87-95; rtd 90; Perm to Offic *B & W* from 90. *56 Maple Drive, Burham-on-Sea TA8 1DH* Tel (01278) 780701

AYERST, Gabrielle Mary. b 52. St Luke's Coll Ex BEd74. SEITE 97. **d** 00 **p** 01. NSM Surbiton St Andr and St Mark *S'wark* from 00. *Flat 3, 11 Claremont Gardens, Surbiton KT6 4TN* Tel (020) 8390 2166 E-mail gadrillea@paff.nsf.org.uk

AYKROYD, Harold Allan. b 22. DFC. Man Univ BA48. Qu Coll Birm 73. **d** 76 **p** 76. NSM Moseley St Agnes *Birm* 76-82; NSM Bournville 82-96; Perm to Offic from 96. *108 Middleton Hall Road, Birmingham B30 1DG* Tel 0121-451 1365 *or* 569 4687

AYLEN, George Richard. b 24. Chich Th Coll 48. **d** 52 **p** 53. C Cant St Greg *Cant* 52-55; C Margate All SS 55-58; V Spring Park 58-61; V Newington 61-67; V Whitstable St Pet 67-75; R Petham w Waltham and Lower Hardres w Nackington 75-78; rtd 78; Perm to Offic *Cant* 80-98. *c/o Mark Aylen Esq, Sylvan, Minstead, Lyndhurst SO43 7FY* Tel (01703) 282334

AYLETT, Graham Peter. b 59. Qu Coll Cam BA81 MA84 PhD85 St Jo Coll Dur BA88. Cranmer Hall Dur 86 All Nations Chr Coll 96. **d** 90 **p** 91. C Wilton *B & W* 90-94; C Runcorn All SS *Ches* 94-96; C Thetford *Nor* 97-98; Mongolia from 98. *c/o JCS, PO Box 49/532, Ulaanbaatar 210349, Mongolia*

AYLETT, Mrs Nicola Jane. b 63. St Anne's Coll Ox BA84 St Jo Coll Dur BA89. Cranmer Hall Dur 87 All Nations Chr Coll 96. **d** 90 **p** 94. C Wilton *B & W* 90-94; NSM Runcorn All SS *Ches* 94-96; Perm to Offic *Nor* 97-98; Mongolia from 98. *c/o JCS, PO Box 49/532, Ulaanbaatar 210349, Mongolia*

AYLING, Arnold Paul. b 38. Ball Coll Ox BA61. Wells Th Coll 65. **d** 67 **p** 68. C Weymouth H Trin *Sarum* 67-70; Chapl K Alfred Coll *Win* 70-73; Miss to Seamen 73-84; Dunkirk 73; Nigeria 74-82; S Africa 82-84; Perm to Offic *Sarum* 85-86 and *Chich* from 85; Chapl Tunbridge Wells HA 86-94; Chapl Kent and Sussex Weald NHS Trust 94-99; rtd 99. *Elmcroft, 36 The Green, Southwick, Brighton BN42 4FR* Tel (01273) 592329 Mobile 07770-967339 E-mail paul.ayling@virgin.net

AYLING, Miss Dallas Jane. b 53. Trin Coll Bris BA94. **d** 98 **p** 99. C Ellesmere Port *Ches* 98-02; TV Birkenhead Priory from 02. *10 Cavendish Road, Birkenhead CH41 8AX* Tel 0151-653 6092 E-mail revddallasayling@yahoo.co.uk

AYLING, Canon John Michael. b 37. St Cath Coll Cam BA60 MA64. Linc Th Coll 60. **d** 62 **p** 63. C Stoke upon Trent *Lich* 62-66; C Codsall 66-67; Australia 67-71; Solomon Is 71-72; Lic to Offic *St Alb* 72-91; TR Boscastle w Davidstow *Truro* 91-98; R 98-02; RD Stratton 98-02; Hon Can Truro Cathl 01-02; rtd 02; Perm to Offic *Heref* from 03. *Woodstock House, Church Street, Leominster HR6 8ED* Tel (01568) 611523 E-mail john.ayling@virgin.net

AYLING, Mrs Susan Pamela. b 48. OBE03. City of Lon Poly Dip Civil Law 68 Kent Univ DTM98. SEITE 95. **d** 98 **p** 99. NSM Oxshott *Guildf* 98-02; NSM Cuddington from 02. *114 Edenfield Gardens, Worcester Park KT4 7DY* Tel (020) 8337 6347 *or* 7438 6589 E-mail sue.ayling@btinternet.com

AYLWARD, James Gareth. b 45. St Cath Coll Cam BA68 MA72. St As Minl Tr Course 94. **d** 97 **p** 98. NSM Wrexham *St As* 97-00; V Broughton 00-05; V Broughton and Berse from 05. *The Vicarage, Bryn-y-Gaer Road, Pentre Broughton, Wrexham LL11 6AT* Tel (01978) 756210

AYNSLEY, Ernest Edgar. b 02. FRIC Dur Univ BSc23 MSc24 PhD34 DSc62. Westcott Ho Cam 42. **d** 42 **p** 43. Hon C Long Benton St Mary *Newc* 42-54; Hon C Newc St Barn and St Jude 54-57; Hon C Gosforth St Nic 57-62; Lic to Offic 63-95; Prof Chemistry Newc Univ 63-67; rtd 67. *7 Manor Court, Ulgham, Morpeth NE61 3BG* Tel (01670) 790197

AYOK-LOEWENBERG, Joseph. b 60. DipEd91. Trin Coll Bris 85. **d** 88 **p** 89. C Swanage and Studland *Sarum* 88-90; Cam Univ Miss Bermondsey 90; Crowther Hall CMS Tr Coll Selly Oak 90-91; C Barnes St Mary *S'wark* 91-92; C Earlsfield St Jo 92; CMS Uganda 92-95; P-in-c Symondsbury and Chideock *Sarum* 96-98; TV Golden Cap Team 98-01; CMS from 01; Egypt from 02. *CMS, Partnership House, 157 Waterloo Road, London SE1 8UU* Tel (020) 7928 8681 E-mail ayokloewenberg@dataxprs.com.eg

✠**AYONG, The Most Revd James Simon.** b 44. Newton Th Coll DipTh Martin Luther Sem BTh. **d** 82 **p** 84 **c** 96. Papua New Guinea from 82; Asst P Popondetta Resurr 85-86; Lect Newton Th Coll 87-88; Prin 89-93; Par P Gerehu 94-95; Bp Aipo Rongo from 95; Abp Papua New Guinea from 96. *PO Box 893, Mount Hagen, Western Highlands Province, Papua New Guinea* Tel (00675) 542 1131 *or* 542 3727 Fax 542 1181 E-mail acpnghgn@global.net.pg

AYRE, Richard. b 40. Liv Inst of Educn CertEd61 Newc Univ BPhil(Ed)88. **d** 04. OLM Chapel House *Newc* from 04. *57 Grosvenor Court, Newcastle upon Tyne NE5 1RY* Tel 0191-267 2096

AYRES, Anthony Lawrence. b 47. Trin Coll Bris 69. **d** 73 **p** 74. C Plumstead All SS *S'wark* 73-77; Hon C 77-00; Member of Counselling Team CA from 83. *37 Donaldson Road, London SE18 4JZ* Tel (020) 8856 1542

AYRES, Dean Matthew. b 68. Bris Univ BSc89 Spurgeon's Coll CertHE96. Ridley Hall Cam 00. **d** 02 **p** 03. C Epsom Common Ch Ch *Guildf* from 02. *278 The Greenway, Epsom KT18 7JF* Tel (01372) 803916 Mobile 07779-584045 E-mail dma@ntlworld.com

AZER, Ms Helen. b 77. Ch Ch Ox BA00 MA03. Wycliffe Hall Ox BTh04. **d** 04 **p** 05. C Ox St Aldate *Ox* from 04. *St Aldate's Parish Centre, 40 Pembroke Street, Oxford OX1 1BP* Tel (01865) 254816 E-mail helen.azer@staldates.org.uk

B

BAAR, Canon William Henry. b 19. Yale Univ BA42 BD45 MA48 PhD53 DD77. Seabury-Western Th Sem STM55. **d** 54 **p** 54. USA 54-86; Chapl Chicago Univ 54-60; R Glencoe St Eliz 60-66; R La Grange Em 66-86; Chapl Venice w Trieste *Eur* 86-93; Can Malta Cathl 89-93; USA from 93; R Chicago St Eliz from 99. *114 Briarwood Lakes, Oak Brook, IL 60523, USA* Tel (001) (603) 654 1893

BABB, Canon Geoffrey. b 42. Man Univ BSc64 MA74 Linacre Coll Ox BA67. Ripon Hall Ox 65. **d** 68 **p** 69. C Heywood St Luke *Man* 68-71; P-in-c Loundsley Green Ascension CD *Derby* 71-76; TV Old Brampton and Loundsley Green 76-77; TV Stafford St Mary and St Chad *Lich* 77-79; TV Stafford 79-88; Soc Resp Officer 77-88; Preb Lich Cathl 87-88; P-in-c Salford Sacred Trin *Man* 88-99; Dir CME 88-99; Hon Can Man Cathl from 89; P-in-c Wythenshawe St Martin 99; P-in-c Newall Green St Fran 99; TR Wythenshawe from 99. *St Martin's Vicarage, 2 Blackcarr Road, Manchester M23 1LX* Tel 0161-998 3408 E-mail geoff@gbabb.fsnet.co.uk

BABBAGE, Canon Stuart Barton. b 16. AM95. St Jo Coll Auckland 35 Univ of NZ BA35 MA36 K Coll Lon PhD42. Tyndale Hall Bris 37 ACT ThD50. **d** 39 **p** 40. C Havering-atte-Bower *Chelmsf* 39-41; Tutor and Lect Oak Hill Th Coll 39-41; Chapl-in-Chief RAF 42-46; Australia 46-63; Dean Sydney 47-53; Dean Melbourne 53-62; Prin Ridley Coll Melbourne 53-63; USA 63-73; V Atlanta and Austell 63-65; Visiting Prof Columbia Th Sem 63-67; Pres Conwell Th Sch Philadelphia 67-69; Vice-Pres and Dean Gordon-Conwell Th Sem 69-73; Australia from 73; Master New Coll Univ of NSW 73-82; Registrar ACT 77-92; rtd 83; Hon Can Sydney from 83. *46 St Thomas Street, Waverley, NSW, Australia 2024* Tel (0061) (2) 9665 1882

BABINGTON, Canon Gervase Hamilton. b 30. Keble Coll Ox BA57 MA57. Wells Th Coll 55. **d** 57 **p** 58. C Sheff St Geo and St Steph *Sheff* 57-60; P-in-c Manor Park CD 60-65; R Waddington *Linc* 65-81; RD Graffoe 74-81; Can and Preb Linc Cathl 77-95; V Gainsborough All SS 81-90; RD Corringham 82-87; R Walesby 90-95; rtd 95; Perm to Offic *Linc* 95-98. *15 Highfields, Nettleham, Lincoln LN2 2ST* Tel (01522) 595702

BABINGTON, Peter Gervase. b 69. Aston Univ BSc91 Birm Univ MPhil03. Cuddesdon Coll BTh98. **d** 98 **p** 99. C Salter Street and Shirley *Birm* 98-02; V Bournville from 02. *The Vicarage, 61 Linden Road, Birmingham B30 1JT* Tel 0121-472 1209 *or* 472 7215 E-mail pb@fish.co.uk

BACH, Mrs Frances Mary. b 48. Open Univ BA AIL. CITC BTh. **d** 94 **p** 95. NSM Ballynure and Ballyeaston *Conn* 94-96; C Larne and Inver 96-99; C Glynn w Raloo 96-99; I Armoy w Loughguile and Drumtullagh from 99. *The Rectory, 181 Glenshesk Road, Armoy, Ballymoney BT53 8RJ* Tel (028) 2075 1226 *or* 2082 3348

BACH, John Edward Goulden. b 40. JP. Dur Univ BA66 DipTh69. Cranmer Hall Dur 66. **d** 69 **p** 70. C Bradf Cathl *Bradf* 69-72; Chapl and Lect NUU 73-84; Chapl and Lect Ulster Univ from 84. *The Anglican Chaplaincy, 70 Hopefield Avenue, Portrush BT56 8HE* Tel (028) 2075 1226, 2032 4549 *or* 2082 3348 Fax 2032 4904 E-mail revjegbach@hotmail.com *or* jeg.bach@ulst.ac.uk

BACHELL, Kenneth George. b 22. Lon Univ BD49. K Coll Lon 55. **d** 56 **p** 57. C Bitterne Park *Win* 56-60; C-in-c Andover St Mich CD 60-64; V Andover St Mich 64-68; V Southampton St Alb 68-76; Warden Dioc Conf Ho Crawshawbooth *Man* 76-79; P-in-c Crawshawbooth 76-79; V Holdenhurst *Win* 79-83; V Froyle and Holybourne 83-87; rtd 87; Perm to Offic *Blackb* 88-98. *18 Cherrylea, Auchterarder PH3 1QG* Tel (01764) 663824

BACHMANN, Douglas Paul. b 49. **d** 75 **p** 76. USA 75-77 and from 79; C Alverstoke *Portsm* 77-79. *1141 Roxie Lane, Walnut Creek, CA 94596-1806, USA*

BACK, Esther Elaine. *See* McCAFFERTY, Mrs Esther Elaine

BACKHOUSE, Alan Eric. b 37. Keble Coll Ox BA61 MA67. Tyndale Hall Bris 61. **d** 64 **p** 65. C Burnage St Marg *Man* 64-67; C Cheadle Hulme St Andr *Ches* 67-70; V Buglawton 70-80; V New Ferry 80-87; V Tarvin 87-93; V Knypersley *Lich* 93-99; Patr Sec Ch Soc Trust 99-00; C Watford *St Alb* 99-02; rtd 02. *Perelandra, Church Pitch, Llandyssil, Montgomery SY16 6LQ* Tel (01686) 669963

BACKHOUSE, Colin. b 41. Birm Poly BA67 MCSD82. Oak Hill Th Coll 85. **d** 87 **p** 88. C Branksome St Clem *Sarum* 87-91; P-in-c Bluntisham cum Earith w Colne and Woodhurst *Ely* 91-92; R from 92. *The Rectory, Rectory Lane, Bluntisham, Huntingdon PE28 3LN* Tel (01487) 740456 E-mail colin.backhouse@ely.anglican.org

BACKHOUSE, John. b 30. Univ Coll Southn BA50. Wycliffe Hall Ox 51. **d** 53 **p** 54. C Eccleston St Luke *Liv* 53-55; C Maghull 55-58; V Lathom 58-64; Area Sec CMS 64-78; Dios Linc and Ely 64-71; Leic 72-78; Pet 72-75; Cov 75-78; V Thorpe Acre w Dishley *Leic* 78-83; R Ab Kettleby Gp 83-89; P-in-c Bitteswell 89-94; RD Guthlaxton II 90-94; rtd 94; Perm to Offic *Leic* from 94. *29 Peashill Close, Sileby, Loughborough LE12 7PT* Tel (01509) 812016

BACKHOUSE, Jonathan Roland. b 60. Jes Coll Cam BA82 MA85. Trin Coll Bris 01. **d** 03 **p** 04. C Nailsea H Trin *B & W* from 03. *26 St Mary's Grove, Nailsea, Bristol BS48 4NQ* Tel (01275) 852355 E-mail jcbackhouse@bigfoot.com

BACKHOUSE, Robert. b 35. ALCD70. **d** 70 **p** 71. C Harold Wood *Chelmsf* 70-74; Publicity Sec CPAS 74-78; rtd 00; Perm to

Offic *Sarum* from 01. *4 Silver Street, Wilton, Salisbury SP2 0HX* Tel (01722) 741358

BACON, David Gary. b 62. Leic Univ BA83 Southn Univ BTh88. Sarum & Wells Th Coll 85. **d** 88 **p** 89. C Bromley St Mark *Roch* 88-92; C Lynton, Brendon, Countisbury, Lynmouth etc *Ex* 92; TV 92-95; P-in-c Lapford, Nymet Rowland and Coldridge 95-99; P-in-c Dartford St Alb *Roch* 99-05; P-in-c Bramshaw and Landford w Plaitford *Sarum* from 05. *The Rectory, Bramshaw, Lyndhurst SO43 7JF* Tel (01794) 390256 E-mail david.bacon@tesco.net

BACON, Derek Robert Alexander. b 44. Birkbeck Coll Lon DAC87 CACP89 BA92 MSc94 Ulster Univ PhD04. TCD Div Sch 69. **d** 71 **p** 72. C Templemore *D & R* 71-73; V Choral Derry Cathl 72-73; C Heeley *Sheff* 74-76; V Sheff St Pet Abbeydale 76-82; Chapl Gt Ormond Street Hosp for Children NHS Trust 82-95; Visiting Fell Ulster Univ 95-97; Perm to Offic *Conn* from 04. *14A Heathmount, Portstewart BT55 7AP* Tel (028) 7083 4987 E-mail d.bacon@ulster.ac.uk

BACON, Eric Arthur. b 23. Qu Coll Birm 68. **d** 69 **p** 70. C Linc St Pet-at-Gowts and St Andr *Linc* 69-71; C Asterby Gp 71-74; V Anwick 74-78; V S Kyme 74-78; P-in-c Kirkby Laythorpe w Asgarby 76-78; P-in-c Ewerby w Evedon 76-78; P-in-c Burton Pedwardine 76-78; V Messingham 78-89; rtd 89; Perm to Offic *Linc* 89-01. *2 Curtois Close, Branston, Lincoln LN4 1LJ* Tel (01522) 794265

BACON, Janet Ann. b 57. Man Univ LLB78. NTMTC 95. **d** 98 **p** 99. NSM Stifford *Chelmsf* 98-01; P-in-c Sandbach Heath w Wheelock *Ches* 01-03; V from 03. *Heath Vicarage, School Lane, Sandbach CW11 2LS* Tel (01270) 768826 E-mail j.bacon@virgin.net

BACON, John Martindale. b 22. St Aid Birkenhead 54. **d** 57 **p** 58. C Bury St Paul *Man* 57-59; C-in-c Clifton Green St Thos CD 59-71; V Astley Bridge 71-87; rtd 87; Perm to Offic *Man* from 87-00 and *Blackb* from 87. *21 Lichen Close, Charnock Richard, Chorley PR7 5TT* Tel (01257) 792535 E-mail johnandcon.bacon@virgin.net

BADDELEY, The Ven Martin James. b 36. Keble Coll Ox BA60 MA64. Linc Th Coll 60. **d** 62 **p** 63. C Stretford St Matt *Man* 62-64; Lect Linc Th Coll 65-66; Tutor 66-69; Chapl 68-69; Chapl Fitzw Coll and New Hall Cam 69-74; Can Res Roch Cathl *Roch* 74-80; Hon Can 80-96; Prin S'wark Ord Course 80-94; Co-Prin SEITE 94-96; Adn Reigate *S'wark* 96-00; rtd 00; Perm to Offic *Heref* from 00 and *Worc* from 01. *2 Glendower, Fossil Bank, Upper Colwall, Malvern WR13 6PJ* Tel (01684) 569761

BADEN, Peter Michael. b 35. CCC Cam BA59 MA62. Cuddesdon Coll 58. **d** 60 **p** 61. C Hunslet St Mary and Stourton *Ripon* 60-63; Lic to Offic *Wakef* 63-64; C E Grinstead St Swithun *Chich* 65-68; V Brighton St Martin 68-74; TR Brighton Resurr 74-76; R Westbourne 76-84; V Stansted 76-84; V Copthorne 84-91; V Clifton *Carl* 91-00; R Dean 91-00; P-in-c Mosser 99-00; rtd 00; Perm to Offic *Pet* from 00; *Carl* from 01. *3 Poppyfield Court, Thrapston, Kettering NN14 4TS* Tel (01832) 734897

BADGER, Mark. b 65. Birm Univ BTh96. Qu Coll Birm 93. **d** 96 **p** 97. C Barbourne *Worc* 96-01; P-in-c Worc St Geo w St Mary Magd 01-05; Chapl R Gr Sch Worc 02-05; Chapl Thames Valley Police Force *Ox* from 05. *Tallet Cottage, Manor Farm Close, Kingham, Chipping Norton OX7 6YX* Tel 07946-529431 (mobile) E-mail revmarkb@ukonline.co.uk

BADHAM, Prof Paul Brian Leslie. b 42. Jes Coll Ox BA65 MA69 Jes Coll Cam BA68 MA72 Birm Univ PhD73. Westcott Ho Cam 66. **d** 68 **p** 69. C Edgbaston St Bart *Birm* 68-69; C Rubery 69-73; Lic to Offic *St D* from 73; Lect Th Univ of Wales (Lamp) 73-83; Sen Lect 83-88; Reader 88-91; Prof Th from 91. *University of Wales, Lampeter SA48 7ED* Tel (01570) 424708

BAGE, Damon John. b 71. Teesside Univ BA95. St Steph Ho Ox 01. **d** 03 **p** 04. C Stockton St Jo *Dur* from 03. *243 Darlington Lane, Stockton-on-Tees TS19 8AA* Tel (01642) 676323 E-mail damon_j_bage@hotmail.com

BAGLEY, Canon John Marmaduke Erskine. b 08. G&C Coll Cam BA30 MA36. Ely Th Coll 30. **d** 32 **p** 33. C Swindon New Town *Bris* 32-36; C Cambridge St Mary Less *Ely* 36-38; Chapl Jubbulpore Ch Ch 38-44; C Littleham w Exmouth *Ex* 44-46; R Huntingdon All SS w St Jo *Ely* 46-63; Chapl HM Borstal Gaynes Hall 52-55; V Ely 63-74; Chapl Ely Cathl 63-74; RD Ely 66-71; Hon Can Ely Cathl 68-74; P-in-c Chettisham 68-74; rtd 74; Perm to Offic *St E* 74-77; *Ely* from 77 and *Nor* from 91. *18 Slade Court, Runton House Close, West Runton, Cromer NR27 9RA* Tel (01263) 837685

BAGLEY, Roy Victor. b 33. **d** 03 **p** 04. OLM Chasetown *Lich* from 03. *65 Oakdene Road, Burntwood WS7 4SA* Tel (01543) 686000 E-mail roy.bagley@lineone.net

BAGNALL, Katherine Janet. b 67. Sunderland Univ BEd92. NEOC 02. **d** 05. NSM Monkwearmouth *Dur* from 05. *14 Grasmere Avenue, Gateshead NE10 0XN* Tel 0191-440 9416 E-mail kbagnall@blueyonder.co.uk

BAGOTT, Paul Andrew. b 61. Leeds Univ BA85. Westcott Ho Cam 86. **d** 88 **p** 89. C Chingford SS Pet and Paul *Chelmsf* 88-91; C Pimlico St Sav *Lon* 91-95; P-in-c Clerkenwell H Redeemer and St Mark 95-01; V Clerkenwell H Redeemer from 02; V Clerkenwell St Mark from 02. *Holy Redeemer Clergy House, 24 Exmouth Market, London EC1R 4QE* Tel and fax (020) 7837 1861 E-mail holyredeemer@freeuk.com

BAGSHAW, Paul Stanley. b 55. Selw Coll Cam BA78 MA81 Man Univ CQSW80. N Ord Course 85. **d** 88 **p** 89. Ind Missr *Sheff* 86-90; C Handsworth Woodhouse 88-90; NSM 91-93; C Newark *S'well* 93-96; P-in-c Ordsall from 96. *The Rectory, All Hallows Street, Retford DN22 7TP* Tel (01777) 702515 E-mail paul_bagshaw@yahoo.com

BAGSHAWE, John Allen. b 45. Dur Univ BA70 DipTh71. Cranmer Hall Dur 67. **d** 71 **p** 72. C Bridlington Priory *York* 71-75; C N Ferriby 75-79; V Kingston upon Hull St Matt w St Barn from 79; AD W Hull from 00. *St Matthew's Vicarage, Boulevard, Hull HU3 2TA* Tel (01482) 326573 E-mail allen@stmatthews.karoo.co.uk

BAGULEY, Henry. b 23. Qu Coll Birm 55. **d** 58 **p** 59. C Wilmslow *Ches* 58-61; V Kelsall 61-75; V New Brighton St Jas 75-88; rtd 88; Perm to Offic *Ches* from 88 and *Lich* from 93. *The Meadows, Nantwich Road, Whitchurch SY13 4AA* Tel (01948) 662692

BAGULEY, Paul. b 36. NTMTC 94. **d** 98 **p** 99. NSM N Harrow St Alb *Lon* from 98. *86 Central Avenue, Pinner HA5 5BP* Tel (020) 8866 3454 E-mail paulbaguley@waitrose.com

BAHAMAS AND THE TURKS AND CAICOS ISLANDS, Bishop of the. *See* GOMEZ, The Most Revd Drexel Wellington

BAILES, Kenneth. b 35. Dur Univ BA69 DPhil. **d** 71 **p** 72. C Redcar *York* 71-73; TV Redcar w Kirkleatham 73-74; P-in-c Appleton Roebuck w Acaster Selby 74-80; P-in-c Sutton on the Forest 80-82; R Stamford Bridge Gp 82-90; V Healaugh w Wighill, Bilbrough and Askham Richard 90-95; rtd 95; Perm to Offic *York* from 98. *The Peace Centre, Inholmes, Leeds Road, Tadcaster LS24 9LP* Tel (01937) 833752 Mobile 07764-614139 E-mail kb13@btinternet.com

BAILEY, Adrian Richard. b 57. St Jo Coll Dur 89. **d** 91 **p** 92. C Oswestry St Oswald *Lich* 91-94; C Shobnall 94-99; C Burton 94-99; Town Cen Chapl 94-99; P-in-c Shobnall 99-01; P-in-c Hengoed w Gobowen from 01; C Weston Rhyn and Selattyn from 05; Chapl Robert Jones/Agnes Hunt Orthopaedic NHS Trust from 01. *The Vicarage, Old Chirk Road, Gobowen, Oswestry SY11 3LL* Tel (01691) 661226 E-mail arb2@totalise.co.uk

BAILEY, Alan George. b 40. Open Univ BA93. Ripon Hall Ox 62. **d** 64 **p** 65. C Formby H Trin *Liv* 64-67; C Upholland 67-70; P-in-c Edgehill St Dunstan 70-74; V 74-81; RD Toxteth 78-81; Perm to Offic 81-83; Asst Chapl Liv Cathl 83-85; C Liv Our Lady and St Nic w St Anne 85-89; V Waddington *Bradf* 89-03; rtd 03. *102 Woone Lane, Clitheroe BB7 1BJ* Tel (01200) 425699

BAILEY, Andrew Henley. b 57. AKC78. Sarum & Wells Th Coll 79. **d** 80 **p** 81. C Romsey *Win* 80-83; V Bournemouth St Alb 83-93; R Milton from 93. *The Rectory, Church Lane, New Milton BH25 6QN* Tel and fax (01425) 615150 E-mail andrew@miltonrectory.freeserve.co.uk

BAILEY, Andrew John. b 37. Trin Coll Cam BA61 MA. Ridley Hall Cam 60. **d** 63 **p** 64. C Drypool *York* 63-66; C Melton Mowbray w Thorpe Arnold *Leic* 66-69; C-in-c Skelmersdale Ecum Cen *Liv* 69-79; V Langley Mill *Derby* 79-90; V Gt Faringdon w Lt Coxwell *Ox* 90-02; AD Vale of White Horse 97-01; rtd 02; Perm to Offic *Ches* from 02. *58 Manor Road, Sandbach CW11 2ND* Tel (01270) 764076 E-mail bailey@manorroad58.freeserve.co.uk

BAILEY, Canon Angela. b 61. Kent Univ BA82. Qu Coll Birm 83. **dss** 85 **d** 87 **p** 94. Reculver and Herne Bay St Bart *Cant* 85-88; Par Dn 87-88; Asst Chapl Hull Univ *York* 88-92; Sen Chapl 94-98; Perm to Offic 92-94; P-in-c Rowley w Skidby from 98; Sen Chapl E Riding Community Health Trust 98-04; Can and Preb York Minster *York* from 03. *The Rectory, 31 Old Village Road, Little Weighton, Cottingham HU20 3US* Tel (01482) 843317 E-mail angela@petermichael.karoo.co.uk

BAILEY, Anthony. b 27. Univ of Wales (Lamp) BA51. Ely Th Coll 51. **d** 53 **p** 54. C Barkingside H Trin *Chelmsf* 53-55; Chapl W Buckland Sch Barnstaple 55-59; R Machen *Mon* 59-66; Min Can Bris Cathl *Bris* 66-84; Chapl Bris Cathl Sch 66-84; Succ Bris Cathl *Bris* 68-82; P-in-c Maenclochog w Henry's Moat and Mynachlogddu etc *St D* 83-90; V 90-92; rtd 92; P-in-c Llanglydwen and Llanfyrnach *St D* 94-04. *Charing Cross, Llangolman, Clunderwen SA66 7XN* Tel (01437) 532430 Mobile 07974-557912 E-mail anthony_bailey@lineone.net

BAILEY, Bertram Arthur. b 20. Tyndale Hall Bris 65. **d** 67 **p** 68. C Bath St Luke *B & W* 67-72; C Bickenhill w Elmdon *Birm* 72-73; R N Tawton *Ex* 73-79; R N Tawton and Bondleigh 79-87; rtd 87; Perm to Offic *B & W* from 87; Clergy Retirement and Widows' Officer from 89. *4 Uphill Road South, Weston-super-Mare BS23 4SD* Tel (01934) 633552

BAILEY, Brendan John. b 61. Strathclyde Univ BSc83 K Coll Lon MA99. Ripon Coll Cuddesdon BTh93. **d** 94 **p** 95. C Purley *Ox* 94-99; R Nettlebed w Bix, Highmoor, Pishill etc from 99. *The Rectory, High Street, Nettlebed, Henley-on-Thames RG9 5DD* Tel (01491) 641575 E-mail baileybj@freeuk.com

BAILEY, Canon Brian Constable. b 36. K Coll Lon AKC62. **d** 63 **p** 64. C Mill Hill Jo Keble Ch *Lon* 63-66; C Gt Stanmore 66-69; C

Gt Marlow *Ox* 69-72; R Burghfield 72-81; R Wokingham All SS 81-96; Hon Can Ch Ch 94-96; TV Pinhoe and Broadclyst *Ex* 96-00; rtd 00; V of Close Sarum Cathl *Sarum* 00-01. *2 Rose Cottages, Maudlin Road, Totnes TQ9 5TG* Tel (01803) 865992 E-mail bcbailey@ukonline.co.uk

BAILEY, Canon David Charles. b 52. Linc Coll Ox BA75 MA78 MSc77. St Jo Coll Nottm BA79. **d** 80 **p** 81. C Worksop St Jo *S'well* 80-83; C Edgware *Lon* 83-87; V S Cave and Ellerker w Broomfleet *York* 87-97; RD Howden 91-97; V Beverley Minster from 97; P-in-c Routh from 97; Can and Preb York Minster from 98. *The Minster Vicarage, Highgate, Beverley HU17 0DN* Tel (01482) 881434 E-mail baileys_bevmin@bigfoot.com

BAILEY, Derek Gilbert. b 42. Div Hostel Dub 65. **d** 68 **p** 69. C Cork St Luke w St Ann *C, C & R* 68-72; CF from 72; Perm to Offic *York* from 98; *Sheff* 97-01 and from 03. *c/o MOD Chaplains (Army)* Tel (01980) 615804 Fax 615800

BAILEY, Derek William. b 39. Man Univ BA96. Cranmer Hall Dur 64. **d** 67 **p** 68. C Sutton *Liv* 67-69; C Chapel-en-le-Frith *Derby* 69-73; V Hadfield 73-90; R Collyhurst *Man* 90-95; V Chaddesden St Mary *Derby* 95-02; rtd 02; Perm to Offic *York* from 03. *187 Bishopthorpe Road, York YO23 1PD* Tel (01904) 628080

BAILEY, Canon Edward Ian. b 35. CCC Cam BA59 MA63 Bris Univ MA69 PhD77. United Th Coll Bangalore 59 Westcott Ho Cam 61. **d** 63 **p** 64. C Newc St Jo *Newc* 63-65; Asst Chapl Marlborough Coll 65-68; Perm to Offic *Bris* 69-70; R Winterbourne from 70; P-in-c Winterbourne Down 75-81; RD Stapleton 77-83; Chapl Frenchay Hosp Bris 79-84; Hon Can Bris Cathl *Bris* from 84; Warden of Readers 95-03; Visiting Prof Middx Univ *Lon* from 97. *The Rectory, 58 High Street, Winterbourne, Bristol BS36 1JQ* Tel (01454) 772131 *or* 776518 E-mail eibailey@csircs.freeserve.co.uk

BAILEY, Edward Peter. b 35. Nottm Univ MA93. Qu Coll Birm. **d** 62 **p** 63. C Ordsall *S'well* 62-66; C Clifton w Glapton 66-71; V Lady Bay 71-83; Relig Affairs Adv to Radio Trent 83-85; C Gedling 86-89; C Bilborough St Jo 89-00; rtd 00; Perm to Offic *York* from 00. *Cragside Cottage, 18 Egton Road, Aislaby, Whitby YO21 1SU*

BAILEY, Elizabeth. b 47. **d** 03 **p** 04. OLM Bishop's Cannings, All Cannings etc *Sarum* from 03. *Lynden, The Street, Bishop's Cannings, Devizes SN10 2LD* Tel (01380) 860400 E-mail liz@bailey-davison.com

BAILEY, Mrs Elizabeth Carmen. b 45. EAMTC 89. **d** 93 **p** 94. NSM Roughton and Felbrigg, Metton, Sustead etc *Nor* 93-95 and 99-02; NSM Gresham 95-99; P-in-c Roughton and Felbrigg, Metton, Sustead etc from 02. *5 Warren Road, Southrepps, Norwich NR11 8UN* Tel (01263) 834525 E-mail elizabeth.bailey2@btopenworld.com

BAILEY, Eric Arthur. b 14. AKC37. **d** 37 **p** 38. C S'wark St Geo *S'wark* 37-39; C Waltham Cross *St Alb* 39-41; C Diss *Nor* 41-42; Chapl CF (EC) 42-43; C Kingsbury *Birm* 44-45; V Dordon 45-52; R Londesborough *York* 52-60; P-in-c Nunburnholme 53-54; R 54-60; P-in-c Burnby 53-54; R 54-60; V Gt w Lt Ouseburn *Ripon* 60-65; V Stonegate *Chich* 65-79; rtd 79; Perm to Offic *St E* 81-88. *Hill End, Sapiston, Bury St Edmunds IP31 1RR* Tel (01359) 269638

BAILEY, Frederick Hugh. b 18. Keble Coll Ox BA40. Linc Th Coll 40. **d** 42 **p** 43. C Boultham *Linc* 42-49; Chapl Rauceby Hosp Lincs from 49; R Quarrington w Old Sleaford *Linc* 49-84; R Silk Willoughby 57-84; rtd 84; Perm to Offic *Linc* 99-02. *1 Willow Close, Scopwick, Lincoln LN4 3PJ* Tel (01522) 321127

BAILEY, Ian Arthur. b 53. **d** 01 **p** 02. NSM Clifton H Trin, St Andr and St Pet *Bris* from 01. *5 Queens Gate, Stoke Bishop, Bristol BS9 1TZ* Tel 0117-968 6251

BAILEY, Canon Ivan John. b 33. Keble Coll Ox BA57 MA65. St Steph Ho Ox 57. **d** 59 **p** 60. C Ipswich All Hallows *St E* 59-62; Clerical Sec CEMS 62-66; V Cringleford *Nor* 66-81; RD Humbleyard 73-81; R Colney 80-81; Relig Adv Anglia TV 81-91; P-in-c Kirby Bedon w Bixley and Whitlingham *Nor* 81-92; Hon Can Nor Cathl 84-98; Chapl St Andr Hosp Norwich 92-94; Chapl Mental Health Unit Nor HA 92-94; Chapl Norfolk Mental Health Care NHS Trust 94-98; rtd 98; Perm to Offic *Nor* from 98. *21 Cranleigh Rise, Norwich NR4 6PQ* Tel (01603) 453565

BAILEY, Ms Jane Rome. b 50. Univ of Wales (Ban) BA99 BTh03. Ban Ord Course 00. **d** 03 **p** 04. C Deanery of Llifon and Talybolion *Ban* from 03. *3 Harbour View, Holyhead LL65 2HL* Tel (01407) 761320 E-mail jane@deanery.fslife.com

BAILEY, John Ernest. b 32. Leeds Univ BA57. Coll of Resurr Mirfield 57. **d** 59 **p** 60. C Newbury St Nic *Ox* 59-62; Australia 62-63; V Uffington w Woolstone and Baulking *Ox* 63-70; P-in-c Gt w Lt Oakley *Pet* 70-72; TV Corby SS Pet and Andr w Gt and Lt Oakley 70-72; Chapl Cen Hosp Warw 72-94; Chapl Cen Weston and Abbeyfields 82-90; Chapl Cen Weston 90-94; Chapl S Warks Mental Health Services NHS Trust 94-96; rtd 96; Perm to Offic *Cov* from 96. *22 Hill Wootton Road, Leek Wootton, Warwick CV35 7QL* Tel (01926) 853528

✠**BAILEY, The Rt Revd Jonathan Sansbury.** b 40. Trin Coll Cam BA61 MA65. Ridley Hall Cam 62. **d** 65 **p** 66 **c** 92. C Sutton *Liv* 65-68; C Warrington St Paul 68-71; Warden Marrick Priory *Ripon* 71-76; V Wetherby 76-82; Adn Southend *Chelmsf* 82-92; Suff Bp Dunwich *St E* 92-95; Bp Derby 95-05; Clerk of the Closet 96-05; rtd 05. *26 Burleigh Way, Wickwar, Wotton-under-Edge GL12 8LR* Tel (01454) 294112

BAILEY, Joyce Mary Josephine. *See* OUTEN, Mrs Joyce Mary Josephine

BAILEY, Judith Elizabeth Anne. b 61. RGN RSCN84. Trin Coll Carmarthen 96. **d** 99 **p** 00. OLM Blyth Valley *St E* from 99. *13 Oak Way, Halesworth IP19 8EB* Tel (01986) 872747 E-mail judith.bailey@ntlworld.com

BAILEY, Justin Mark. b 55. Birm Univ BA77 Southn Univ MTh97 Wolv Poly PGCE78. Ripon Coll Cuddesdon 90. **d** 92 **p** 93. C Oakdale *Sarum* 92-96; P-in-c Milton Abbas, Hilton w Cheselbourne etc 96-05; P-in-c Piddletrenthide w Plush, Alton Pancras etc 02-05; V Piddle Valley, Hilton, Cheselbourne etc from 05. *The Vicarage, Church Lane, Piddletrenthide, Dorchester DT2 7QY* Tel (01300) 348211 E-mail jbailey2@toucansurf.com

BAILEY, Mark David. b 62. Ripon Coll Cuddesdon 87. **d** 90 **p** 91. C Leigh Park *Portsm* 90-93; C Fleet *Guildf* 93-95; TV Basingstoke *Win* 95-00; P-in-c Twyford and Owslebury and Morestead from 00. *The Vicarage, Church Lane, Twyford, Winchester SO21 1NT* Tel (01962) 712208 E-mail revd.bailey@ukgateway.net

BAILEY, Canon Mark Robert. b 60. St Paul's Cheltenham BA81. Trin Coll Bris BA89. **d** 89 **p** 90. C Heigham H Trin *Nor* 89-94; Chapl UEA 92-93; TV Cheltenham St Mary, St Matt, St Paul and H Trin *Glouc* from 94; Hon Can Glouc Cathl from 04. *100 Hewlett Road, Cheltenham GL52 6AR* Tel (01242) 582398 *or* 262306 E-mail mark.bailey@trinityuk.org

BAILEY, Martin Tristram. b 57. Oak Hill Th Coll DipHE91. **d** 91 **p** 92. C Brundall w Braydeston and Postwick *Nor* 91-95; TV Plymouth St Andr and St Paul Stonehouse *Ex* from 95; Chapl St Dunstan's Abbey Sch Plymouth from 02. *88 Durnford Street, Plymouth PL1 3QW* Tel (01752) 228114 E-mail martin@standrewschurch.org.uk

BAILEY, Nicholas Andrew. b 55. Open Univ BA84 Nottm Univ CertEd80. Ripon Coll Cuddesdon 88. **d** 90 **p** 91. C Guisborough *York* 90-92; Chapl Repton Prep Sch from 92. *Repton Preparatory School, Foremarke Hall, Milton, Derby DE65 6EJ*

BAILEY, Norman Gerald. b 25. **d** 83 **p** 84. Hon C Kingswood *Bris* 83-90; Hon C E Bris 90-97; Perm to Offic from 97. *Address temp unknown*

BAILEY, Patricia Laura. b 49. Wall Hall Coll Aldenham CertEd72. NTMTC 95. **d** 98 **p** 99. NSM Hackney Marsh *Lon* 98-01; NSM S Hackney St Jo w Ch Ch 01-04; NSM Cosby *Leic* from 04; NSM Whetstone from 04. *The Vicarage, 15 Starmer Close, Cosby, Leicester LE9 1SL* Tel 0116-284 9541 E-mail revpatbailey@bushberry.fsnet.co.uk

BAILEY, Peter. *See* BAILEY, Edward Peter

BAILEY, Canon Peter Robin. b 43. St Jo Coll Dur BA64. Trin Coll Bris 72. **d** 74 **p** 75. C Corby St Columba *Pet* 74-77; C Bishopsworth *Bris* 77-82; V Sea Mills 82-97; RD Westbury and Severnside 91-97; P-in-c Bishopston 97-98; P-in-c Bris St Andr w St Bart 97-98; TR Bishopston and St Andrews from 98; Hon Can Bris Cathl from 97. *The Vicarage, Walsingham Road, St Andrews, Bristol BS6 5BT* Tel 0117-924 8683 Fax as telephone E-mail peterandheather@blueyonder.co.uk

BAILEY, Richard William. b 38. Man Univ BSc59. Ripon Hall Ox 63. **d** 65 **p** 66. C Tonge *Man* 65-68; C Stretford St Matt 68-71; R Abbey Hey 71-80; V E Crompton 80-86; V Chadderton St Matt 86-98; R Stand 98-04; rtd 04. *Address withheld by request* E-mail bailey.ditchash@tesco.net

BAILEY, Richard William. b 47. All Nations Chr Coll DBMS75 Oak Hill Th Coll BA84. **d** 84 **p** 85. C Huyton St Geo *Liv* 84-87; V Wombridge *Lich* 87-97; P-in-c Shenstone from 97; P-in-c Stonnall from 97. *The Vicarage, St John's Hill, Shenstone, Lichfield WS14 0JB* Tel (01543) 480286 Fax 480864 E-mail ricthevic@madasafish.com

BAILEY, Robert Henry. b 45. FCA69. N Ord Course 99. **d** 02 **p** 03. NSM Dewsbury *Wakef* 02-05; NSM Kinsley w Wragby from 05; Sub Chapl HM Pris Leeds from 02. *16 Lumley Road, Dewsbury WF12 7DU* Tel (01924) 460072 Mobile 07973-697954 E-mail robertbailey.minster@btopenworld.co.uk

BAILEY, Canon Robert William. b 49. Open Univ BA91. Bernard Gilpin Soc Dur 68 Lich Th Coll 69. **d** 72 **p** 73. C Stoke *Cov* 72-75; Chapl RAF 75-99; RD Calne *Sarum* 97-98; TV Cartmel Peninsula *Carl* from 99; Hon Can Carl Cathl from 05. *The Vicarage, Priest Lane, Cartmel, Grange-over-Sands LA11 6PU* Tel and fax (01539) 536261 E-mail vicar.cartmel@virgin.net

BAILEY, Ronald William. b 12. Linc Coll Ox BA35 BSc36 MA45. Ripon Hall Ox 57. **d** 58 **p** 59. C N Stoneham *Win* 58-61; V Lamberhurst *Roch* 61-77; rtd 77. *Flat 1, 48 Southwood Avenue, Bournemouth BH6 3QB* Tel (01202) 420829

BAILEY, Simon. b 56. Man Univ MusB Nottm Univ BCombStuds. Linc Th Coll. **d** 83 **p** 84. C Armley w New Wortley *Ripon* 83-86; C Harrogate St Wilfrid and St Luke 86-90; R Harby, Long Clawson and Hose *Leic* 90-94; V Woodhall *Bradf* 94-03; RD Calverley 98-01; R N Adelaide Ch Ch Australia from

03. *Christ Church Rectory, 35 Palmer Place, North Adelaide, S Australia 5006*

BAILEY, Stephen. b 39. Leic Univ BA61. Clifton Th Coll 61. **d** 62 **p** 63. C Wellington w Eyton *Lich* 62-66; C Rainham *Chelmsf* 66-69; V Ercall Magna *Lich* 69-75; V Rowton 69-75; RD Wrockwardine 72-75; V W Bromwich Gd Shep w St Jo 75-83; P-in-c W Bromwich St Phil 80-81; V 81-83; R Chadwell *Chelmsf* 83-96; RD Thurrock 92-96; V Galleywood Common 96-04; rtd 04. *64 Bridport Way, Braintree CM7 9FJ* Tel (01376) 550859 E-mail jenniferbailey@thevicarage450.fsnet.co.uk

BAILEY, Stephen John. b 57. NE Surrey Coll of Tech HNC78. Sarum & Wells Th Coll 88. **d** 90 **p** 91. C Redhill H Trin *S'wark* 90-95; Chapl E Surrey Coll 91-93; P-in-c Betchworth *S'wark* 95-00; V from 00; P-in-c Buckland 95-00; R from 00. *The Rectory, Old Reigate Road, Betchworth RH3 7DE* Tel (01737) 842102 E-mail stephenbaileyrev@compuserve.com

BAILEY, Mrs Susan Mary. b 40. F L Calder Coll Liv CertEd61. EAMTC 89. **d** 92 **p** 94. NSM Chelmsf Cathl *Chelmsf* 92-93; NSM Needham Market w Badley *St E* 93-95; NSM Belper *Derby* 96-00; NSM Allestree St Nic and Quarndon 00-05; Chapl Morley Retreat and Conf Ho Derby 00-05; rtd 05. *28 Burleigh Way, Wickwar, Wotton-under-Edge GL12 8LR* Tel (01454) 294112 E-mail susan.m.bailey@gmail.com

BAILEY, Yvonne Mary. *See* HOBSON, Mrs Yvonne Mary

BAILIE, Alison Margaret. b 62. Leeds Univ LLB83. Trin Coll Bris BA98. **d** 98 **p** 99. C Halliwell St Pet *Man* 98-05; P-in-c Droylsden St Mary from 05. *St Mary's Rectory, Dunkirk Street, Droylsden, Manchester M43 7FB* Tel 0161-370 1569 E-mail alison@bailie.free-online.co.uk

BAILLIE, Canon Frederick Alexander. b 21. FRGS Open Univ BA75 QUB MA86 PhD87. CITC 53. **d** 55 **p** 56. C Belfast St Paul *Conn* 55-59; C Dunmurry 59-61; RAChD 57-84; I Eglantine *Conn* 61-69; I Belfast Whiterock 69-74; Hd of S Ch Miss Ballymacarrett 74-79; I Magheraculmoney *Clogh* 79-87; Dioc Communications Officer 80-86; Hon CF from 84; Can Clogh Cathl *Clogh* 85-87; rtd 87. *2 Raasay Court, Portree IV51 9TG* Tel (01478) 611376 E-mail f.baillie@amserve.com

BAILLIE, Terence John. b 46. New Coll Ox BA69 MA78 Man Univ MSc72. St Jo Coll Nottm 74. **d** 77 **p** 78. C Chadwell *Chelmsf* 77-80; C Bickenhill w Elmdon *Birm* 80-84; V Bedminster St Mich *Bris* 84-96; V Clevedon St Andr and Ch Ch *B & W* from 96. *The Vicarage, 10 Coleridge Road, Clevedon BS21 7TB* Tel (01275) 872982 E-mail terry.baillie@tesco.net

BAILY, Canon Robert Spencer Canning. b 21. G&C Coll Cam BA42 MA46. Westcott Ho Cam 42. **d** 44 **p** 45. C Sherborne w Castleton and Lillington *Sarum* 44-46; C Heacham *Nor* 46-47; C Bedford All SS *St Alb* 48-50; C-in-c Hayes St Edm CD *Lon* 50-56; R Blofield w Hemblington *Nor* 56-69; P-in-c Perlethorpe *S'well* 69-87; Dir of Educn 69-87; Hon Can S'well Minster 80-87; rtd 87; Perm to Offic *Linc* 87-02; *S'well* 87-00. *17 Ravendale Close, Grantham NG31 8BS* Tel (01476) 568614

BAIN, Alan. b 48. Thames Poly BSc72. St Jo Coll Nottm DipTh75. **d** 77 **p** 78. C Wakef St Andr and St Mary *Wakef* 77-81; V Bath Odd Down *B & W* 81-82; P-in-c Combe Hay 81-82; V Bath Odd Down w Combe Hay from 82. *The Vicarage, 39 Frome Road, Bath BA2 2QF* Tel (01225) 832838 *or* tel and fax 835228 E-mail ambain2000@yahoo.com

BAIN, Andrew John. b 55. Newc Poly BA77 Edin Univ MTh89. Edin Th Coll 86. **d** 88 **p** 89. Chapl St Mary's Cathl *Edin* 88-91; C Edin St Mary 88-91; R Edin St Jas 91-98; P-in-c Edin St Marg 93-98; Dioc Dir of Ords 95-98; R Haddington from 98. *The Rectory, Church Street, Haddington EH41 3EX* Tel (01620) 822203 *or* 823268 E-mail htrinity@fish.co.uk

BAIN, David Roualeyn Findlater (Roly). b 54. Bris Univ BA75. Ripon Coll Cuddesdon 76. **d** 78 **p** 79. C Perry Hill St Geo *S'wark* 78-81; Chapl Asst Guy's Hosp Lon 81-84; Succ S'wark Cathl *S'wark* 81-84; V Streatham St Paul 84-90; Perm to Offic *Bris* and *Lon* from 90. *The Vicarage, The Street, Olveston, Bristol BS35 4DA* Tel (01454) 616593 Fax as telephone

BAIN, The Ven John Stuart. b 55. Van Mildert Coll Dur BA77. Westcott Ho Cam 78. **d** 80 **p** 81. C Washington *Dur* 80-84; C Dunston 84-86; V Shiney Row 86-92; V Herrington 86-92; P-in-c Whitworth w Spennymoor 92-97; P-in-c Merrington 94-97; AD Auckland 96-02; V Spennymoor, Whitworth and Merrington 97-02; Hon Can Dur Cathl 98-02; Adn Sunderland from 02; P-in-c Hedworth 02-03; P-in-c from 03. *St Nicholas' Vicarage, Hedworth Lane, Boldon Colliery NE35 9JA* Tel 0191-536 2300 Fax 519 3369 E-mail archdeacon.of.sunderland@durham.anglican.org

BAIN, Lawrence John Weir. b 60. NTMTC 02. **d** 05. C Stoughton *Guildf* from 05. *12 Grange Close, Guildford GU2 9QJ* Tel (01483) 511378

BAINBRIDGE, Ms Christine Susan. b 48. St Aid Coll Dur BA70 K Coll Lon MA99. SEITE 93. **d** 96 **p** 97. C S'wark H Trin w St Matt *S'wark* 96-99; Asst to Bp Woolwich (Greenwich Area) 99-03; C Lee Gd Shep w St Pet 99-03; P-in-c Deptford St Jo w H Trin from 03. *St John's Vicarage, St John's Vale, London SE8 4EA* Tel (020) 8692 2857 E-mail christine.bainbridge@southwark.anglican.org

BAINBRIDGE, David George. b 42. Wadh Coll Ox BA63 MA67 Lon Univ CertEd67. Ridley Hall Cam 84. **d** 86 **p** 87. C Downend *Bris* 86-90; TV Yate New Town 90-01; Lee Abbey Internat Students' Club Kensington from 01; Perm to Offic *Lon* from 01. *Lee Abbey International Students' Club, 57-67 Lexham Gardens, London W8 6JJ* Tel (020) 7373 7242 *or* 7244 2709 Fax 7244 8702 E-mail warden@leeabbeylondon.com

BAINBRIDGE, John Richard. b 35. Pemb Coll Cam BA59 MA63. Clifton Th Coll 65. **d** 67 **p** 68. C Ex St Leon w H Trin *Ex* 67-70; P-in-c Penge St Paul *Roch* 70-73; Chapl Uppingham Sch 73-87; V Stevenage St Nic and Graveley *St Alb* 87-98; rtd 98. *Willowdown Cottage, 8 Laxton, Corby NN17 3AT* Tel (01780) 450308

BAINBRIDGE, Richard Densham. b 49. Ch Coll Cam BA71 MA75 Edge Hill Coll of HE PGCE72 Roehampton Inst DCCD91. S'wark Ord Course 91. **d** 94 **p** 95. C Bermondsey St Jas w Ch Ch *S'wark* 94-99; V Lee Gd Shep w St Pet from 99. *47 Handen Road, London SE12 8NR* Tel (020) 8318 2363 E-mail revrdb@yahoo.com

BAINES, Alan William. b 50. S Bank Poly BSc72. Trin Coll Bris 92. **d** 94 **p** 95. C Chenies and Lt Chalfont, Latimer and Flaunden *Ox* 94-98; V Eye *Pet* 98-05; Post Ord Tr Co-ord 00-05; TV Duston Team from 05. *The Rectory, 3 Main Road, Duston, Northampton NN5 6JB* Tel (01604) 752591 E-mail alan.baines@talk21.com

BAINES, Bernard Frederick. b 20. JP. ACP. St Jo Coll Nottm 83. **d** 84 **p** 85. NSM Nottingham All SS *S'well* 84-90; rtd 90; Perm to Offic *S'well* from 90. *18 Forest Road East, Nottingham NG1 4HH* Tel 0115-978 4191

BAINES, Derek Alfred. b 53. MCSP75. Carl and Blackb Dioc Tr Inst 99. **d** 02 **p** 03. NSM Lostock Hall *Blackb* from 02. *16 Middlefield, Leyland PR26 7AE* Tel and fax (01772) 641521 Mobile 07774-200885 E-mail baines@fish.co.uk

BAINES, Edward. *See* BAINES, Noel Edward

BAINES, John Charles. b 68. Ripon Coll Cuddesdon 00. **d** 02 **p** 03. C Morton and Stonebroom w Shirland *Derby* from 02. *Ash Tree House, 18 Wellington Park, Shirland, Alfreton DE55 6EQ* Tel (01773) 830561

BAINES, John Edmund. b 22. Down Coll Cam BA47 MA50 Lon Univ BD51. New Coll Lon. **d** 58 **p** 59. C Penistone w Midhope *Wakef* 58-60; V Batley St Thos 60-69; V Cawthorne 69-89; rtd 89; Perm to Offic *Wakef* from 90. *3 Huskar Close, Silkstone, Barnsley S75 4SX* Tel (01226) 791088

BAINES, Keith. b 46. **d** 99 **p** 00. OLM Atherton and Hindsford *Man* 99-02; OLM Atherton and Hindsford w Howe Bridge 02-05; TV from 05. *6 Marton Drive, Atherton, Manchester M46 9WA* Tel (01942) 897668 E-mail baines1@supanet.com

✠BAINES, The Rt Revd Nicholas. b 57. Bradf Univ BA80. Trin Coll Bris BA87. **d** 87 **p** 88 **c** 03. C Kendal St Thos *Carl* 87-91; C Leic H Trin w St Jo *Leic* 91-92; V Rothley 92-00; RD Goscote 96-00; Adn Lambeth *S'wark* 00-03; Area Bp Croydon from 03. *53 Stanhope Road, Croydon CR0 5NS* Tel (020) 8681 5496 Fax 8686 2074 E-mail nick.baines@southwark.anglican.org

BAINES, Noel Edward (Ted). b 29. St Jo Coll Dur BSc52 DipTh54 MA62. **d** 54 **p** 55. C Rainham *Chelmsf* 54-58; C Surbiton Hill Ch Ch *S'wark* 58-61; V Southborough St Matt *Roch* 61-67; V Beckenham St Jo 67-74; Hd RE Taunton Manor High Sch Caterham 74-83; Keston Coll 85-91; Perm to Offic *Roch* 74-91; Hon C Bromley Ch Ch 91-98; Hon C New Beckenham St Paul from 98; rtd 94; Perm to Offic *Roch* from 98. *10 Bromley Avenue, Bromley BR1 4BQ* Tel (020) 8460 8256 Fax as telephone E-mail xfz73@dial.pipex.com

BAIRD, Agnes Murry (Nancy). Man Univ CertEd70. EAMTC 93. **d** 96 **p** 97. NSM Bramford *St E* 96-98; NSM Haughley w Wetherden and Stowupland from 98. *32 Maple Road, Stowupland, Stowmarket IP14 4DG* Tel (01449) 674734 E-mail nbaird@fish.co.uk

BAIRD, Paul Drummond. b 48. Newc Univ CertEd71 Open Univ BA85. Ripon Coll Cuddesdon 88. **d** 90 **p** 91. C Chandler's Ford *Win* 90-93; V Hythe 93-03; P-in-c Compton and Otterbourne from 03. *The Rectory, Kiln Lane, Otterbourne, Winchester SO21 2EJ* Tel (01962) 713400 E-mail paulbaird@aol.com

BAIRD, Robert Douglas. b 21. ERD56. Cam Univ MA64. Ripon Coll Cuddesdon. **d** 85 **p** 86. NSM Charlbury w Shorthampton *Ox* 85-87; Asst Chapl HM Pris Grendon and Spring Hill 85; Lic to Offic *Ox* 87-91; Perm to Offic from 91. *Glebe House, Ibstone, High Wycombe HP14 3XZ* Tel (01491) 638642 E-mail robert@baird1921.freeserve.co.uk

BAIRD, Canon William Stanley. b 33. TCD BA54 Div Test. **d** 56 **p** 57. C Carlow *C & O* 56-59; I Dunganstown *D & G* 59-64; C Knock *D & D* 64-69; P-in-c Kilwarlin Upper w Kilwarlin Lower 69-71; I 71-72; Warden Ch Min of Healing (Ireland) 72-79; I Dublin Drumcondra w N Strand *D & G* 79-91; Dir of Ords (Dub) 84-99; Can Ch Ch Cathl Dublin 88-99; I Swords w Donabate and Kilsallaghan 91-99; rtd 99. *5 Weavers Way, Wheaton Hall, Dublin Road, Drogheda, Co Louth, Irish Republic* Tel (00353) (41) 984 6645

BAISLEY, George. b 45. Sarum & Wells Th Coll 78. **d** 80 **p** 81. C Glouc St Geo w Whaddon *Glouc* 80-83; R Welford w Weston and Clifford Chambers 83-87; Chapl Myton Hamlet Hospice 87-91; Chapl Warw Univ *Cov* 87-91; R Berkswell 91-03; RD Kenilworth 96-01; Chapl Bromley Coll 03-04; P-in-c Doddington, Newnham and Wychling *Cant* from 04; P-in-c Teynham w Lynsted and Kingsdown from 04; P-in-c Norton from 04. *The Vicarage, The Street, Doddington, Sittingbourne ME9 0BH* Tel (01795) 886265 Mobile 07941-507063 E-mail george@baisley.co.uk

BAKER, Alan. b 42. Liv Univ BA64. Carl Dioc Tr Inst 93. **d** 96 **p** 97. NSM Flookburgh *Carl* 96-97; NSM Cartmel Peninsula from 97; Perm to Offic *Blackb* from 98. *1 Church View, Priest Lane, Cartmel, Grange-over-Sands LA11 6PU* Tel (01539) 536551

BAKER, Albert George. b 30. Qu Coll Birm. **d** 61 **p** 62. C Merton St Mary *S'wark* 61-64; C Limpsfield and Titsey 64-65; C Chapel-en-le-Frith *Derby* 65-68; R Odd Rode *Ches* 68-76; V Holme Cultram St Mary *Carl* 76-78; R Blofield w Hemblington *Nor* 78-94; rtd 94. *240 Raedwald Drive, Bury St Edmunds IP32 7DN* Tel (01284) 701802

BAKER, Alicia Mary. b 63. Trin Coll Bris BA03. **d** 03 **p** 04. C E Ham St Paul *Chelmsf* from 03. *St Paul's Church, 227 Burges Road, London E6 2EU* E-mail aliciabakeruk@hotmail.com

BAKER, Angela Mary. b 42. **d** 91. Par Dn Battersea St Sav and St Geo w St Andr *S'wark* 91-94; C 94-96; C Battersea Fields 96-02; rtd 02. *Finches, Ide Hill, Sevenoaks TN14 6JW* Tel (01732) 750470

BAKER, Mrs Ann Christine. b 49. Edin Univ BEd71. Carl and Blackb Dioc Tr Inst 98. **d** 01 **p** 02. NSM St Bees *Carl* 01-04; P-in-c Eskdale, Irton, Muncaster and Waberthwaite from 04. *Eskdale Vicarage, Boot, Holmrook CA19 1TF* Tel (019467) 23242 E-mail j.baker@can-online.org.uk

BAKER, Anne-Marie Clare. *See* BIRD, Mrs Anne-Marie Clare

BAKER, Anthony Peter. b 38. Hertf Coll Ox BA59 MA63. Clifton Th Coll 60. **d** 63 **p** 64. C Ox St Ebbe w St Pet *Ox* 63-66; C Welling *Roch* 66-70; V Redland *Bris* 70-79; Lect Tyndale Hall Bris 70-71; Lect Trin Coll Bris 71-77; V Beckenham Ch Ch *Roch* 79-94; Chapl Beckenham Hosp 79-94; V Hove Bp Hannington Memorial Ch *Chich* 94-03; rtd 03; Perm to Offic *Chich* from 04. *12 Paradise Close, Eastbourne BN20 8BT* Tel (01323) 438783

BAKER, Miss Barbara Ann. b 36. Linc Th Coll 85. **d** 87 **p** 94. Par Dn Hornchurch St Andr *Chelmsf* 87-94; C 94-97; rtd 97; Perm to Offic *Chelmsf* from 97. *120 Devonshire Road, Hornchurch RM12 4LN* Tel (01708) 477759

BAKER, Canon Bernard George Coleman. b 36. Lon Univ BD61. Oak Hill Th Coll 61. **d** 63 **p** 64. C Broadwater St Mary *Chich* 63-66; Tanzania 66-84 and 96-01; BCMS Miss P and Chapl Morogoro Em Ch 66-79; V Moshi St Marg 79-84; Hon Can Morogoro from 77; Hon Can Mt Kilimanjaro from 82; C-in-c Ryde St Jas Prop Chpl *Portsm* 84-96; Crosslinks 96-01; Asst P Ruaha Cathl and Teacher Amani Chr Tr Cen 96-01; rtd 01; Perm to Offic *Ex* from 02. *104 Merafield Road, Plympton, Plymouth PL7 1SJ* Tel (01752) 339879

BAKER (formerly BARTON), Mrs Caroline Janet. b 61. Ex Univ BA83 Lon Univ 86. Westcott Ho Cam 93. **d** 96 **p** 97. C Ivybridge w Harford *Ex* 96-02; P-in-c Torquay St Luke from 02; Dioc Adv in Adult Tr from 02. *St Luke's Vicarage, 1 Mead Road, Torquay TQ2 6TE* Tel (01803) 690539

BAKER, Charles Edward. b 47. **d** 87 **p** 88. NSM Dublin Clontarf *D & G* 87-90; NSM Delgany 90-94; NSM Dublin Sandford w Milltown 94-97; NSM Dublin St Patr Cathl Gp from 97. *12 Aranleigh Vale, Rathfarnham, Dublin 14, Irish Republic* Tel (00353) (1) 494 6465

BAKER, Prof Christopher James. b 54. St Cath Coll Cam BA75 MA78 PhD78 CEng83 FICE96 FIHT95. EMMTC 85. **d** 88 **p** 89. NSM Matlock Bath *Derby* 88-95; NSM Matlock Bath and Cromford 95; NSM Beeston *S'well* 95-98; Perm to Offic *Lich* 98-00; NSM Lich St Mich w St Mary and Wall from 00. *28 Grosvenor Close, Lichfield WS14 9SR* Tel (01543) 256320 *or* 262211 E-mail cjsmbaker@aol.com

BAKER, Christopher Peter. b 64. St Cuth Soc Dur BA95 Heythrop Coll Lon MA02 Greenwich Univ PGCE96. SEITE 99. **d** 02 **p** 03. C Kennington St Mark *S'wark* from 02. *73 Baytree Road, London SW2 5RR* Tel (020) 7274 6907 Fax as telephone

BAKER, Christopher Richard. b 61. Man Univ BA83 PhD02 Southn Univ BTh90 Heythrop Coll Lon MTh92. Sarum & Wells Th Coll 86. **d** 89 **p** 93. C Dulwich St Barn *S'wark* 89-92; Tutor Sarum & Wells Th Coll 92-94; Dir Chr Tr Milton Keynes *Ox* 94-98; Stantonbury and Willen 95-98; Dir Tr OLM 98-99; Development Officer Wm Temple Foundn 01-04; Research Dir from 04. *Luther King House, Brighton Grove, Rusholme, Manchester M14 5JP* Tel 0161-249 2502 Fax 256 1142 E-mail temple@wtf.org.uk

BAKER, David. b 63. SW Minl Tr Course 99. **d** 02. NSM Parkham, Alwington, Buckland Brewer etc *Ex* from 02. *4 Ashley Terrace, Bideford EX39 3AL* Tel (01237) 473453 E-mail bakerbuzz@hotmail.com

BAKER, David Ayshford. b 66. St Aid Coll Dur BA88 Univ of Wales (Cardiff) Dip Journalism 89. Wycliffe Hall Ox BTh97. **d** 97 **p** 98. C Chadwell Heath *Chelmsf* 97-01; C Surbiton Hill Ch Ch *S'wark* from 01. *181 Elgar Avenue, Surbiton KT5 9JX* Tel (020) 8399 1503 E-mail emmanueltolworth@onetel.com

BAKER, David Clive. b 47. Sarum & Wells Th Coll 76. **d** 78 **p** 79. C Shirley *Birm* 78-82; R Wainfleet All SS w St Thos *Linc* 82-83; P-in-c Wainfleet St Mary 82-83; P-in-c Croft 82-83; R The Wainfleets and Croft 83-86; V Stirchley *Birm* 86-96; Perm to Offic 97-98; V Handsworth St Mich 98-02; Chapl Aston Univ 99-02; C Codsall *Lich* 02-05; P-in-c Coven 04-05; V Bilbrook and Coven from 05. *The New Vicarage, Church Lane, Coven, Wolverhampton WV9 5DE* Tel (01902) 790230 Mobile 07958-468819

BAKER, David Frederick. b 32. Clifton Th Coll 67. **d** 69 **p** 70. C Bilton *Ripon* 69-71; C Heworth w Peasholme St Cuth *York* 71-75; V Sand Hutton w Gate and Upper Helmsley 75-77; P-in-c Bossall w Buttercrambe 75-77; V Sand Hutton 77-80; R Preston in Holderness 80; P-in-c Sproatley 80; R Preston and Sproatley in Holderness 80-89; C Topcliffe w Dalton and Dishforth 89; V Baldersby w Dalton, Dishforth etc 89-96; rtd 96; Perm to Offic *York* and *Ripon* from 96. *Chinkoa, 15 Williamson Gardens, Ripon HG4 2QB* Tel (01765) 601822

BAKER, David John. b 27. LRAM50 GRSM51. Ely Th Coll 53. **d** 55 **p** 56. C Swanley St Mary *Roch* 55-58; C Guildf St Nic *Guildf* 58-63; Prec St Alb Abbey *St Alb* 63-67; P-in-c Colney St Pet 67-68; V 68-73; V Tattenham Corner and Burgh Heath *Guildf* 73-84; R Fetcham 84-96; rtd 96; Perm to Offic *Guildf* from 96. *1 Terra Cotta Court, Quennels Hill, Wrecclesham, Farnham GU10 4SL* Tel (01252) 734202

BAKER, David Jordan. b 35. Univ of Wales (Lamp) BA59. Ely Th Coll 59. **d** 61 **p** 62. C Spalding *Linc* 61-66; C Gainsborough All SS 66-69; V Wrawby 69-78; V Melton Ross w New Barnetby 70-78; V Linc St Pet-at-Gowts and St Andr 78-94; rtd 98; Perm to Offic *Linc* from 01. *Fartherwell, The Paddock, Canwick, Lincoln LN4 2RX* Tel (01522) 526903

BAKER, Dilly. *See* BAKER, Ms Hilary Mary

BAKER, Frank Thomas. b 36. Selw Coll Cam BA61. Coll of Resurr Mirfield. **d** 63 **p** 64. C Mackworth St Fran *Derby* 63-66; C Leeds St Pet *Ripon* 66-73; P-in-c Stanley *Dur* 73-74; R Crook 73-74; Chapl Bucharest *Eur* 74-75; C Tewkesbury w Walton Cardiff *Glouc* 75-81; Min Can Windsor 81-86; rtd 86. *15 Hartford Court, 33 Filey Road, Scarborough YO11 2TP* Tel (01723) 352466

BAKER, Frederick Peter. b 24. Bps' Coll Cheshunt 58. **d** 60 **p** 61. C Peckham St Jude *S'wark* 60-63; C Mitcham St Mark 63-66; C Northampton St Pet w Upton *Pet* 66-69; P-in-c Northampton St Lawr 69-71; V Northampton St Edm 71-78; V Spratton 78-83; R Walgrave w Hannington and Wold 83-89; rtd 89; Perm to Offic *Win* 89-98 and *Ely* from 00. *73 Five Arches, Orton Wistow, Peterborough PE2 6FQ* Tel (01733) 371349

BAKER, Canon Gerald Stothert. b 30. Univ of NZ MA54. St Jo Coll Auckland LTh56. **d** 56 **p** 57. New Zealand 56-87 and from 92; Hon Can Wellington 80-87; Adn Wairarapa 95-96; TV Kidderminster St Mary and All SS w Trimpley etc *Worc* 87-92; rtd 95. *83 Kuratawhiti Street, Greytown, New Zealand* Tel (0064) (6) 304 8367

BAKER, Gillian Devonald. b 40. S Dios Minl Tr Scheme 88. **d** 91 **p** 94. NSM Redhorn *Sarum* 91-02; NSM TV from 02; Chapl HM Pris Erlestoke 94-01. *11 The Street, Chirton, Devizes SN10 3QS* Tel (01380) 848170 Fax 840152 E-mail davidb@atlanticbridge.co.uk

BAKER, The Very Revd Graham Brinkworth. b 26. AKC54. **d** 55 **p** 56. C Wandsworth St Anne *S'wark* 55-58; Canada from 58. *1280 Tracksell Avenue, Victoria BC, Canada, V8P 2C9*

BAKER, Harry Hallas. b 16. Bps' Coll Cheshunt 51. **d** 53 **p** 54. C Killingworth *Newc* 53-58; V Mickley 58-63; V Howdon Panns 63-73; C Alnwick St Mich 73-74; C Alnwick 74-84; rtd 84; Perm to Offic *Newc* from 84. *c/o J Curtis Esq, 58 Easterly Avenue, Leeds LS8 2TD*

BAKER, Mrs Heather Elizabeth. b 48. WEMTC 94. **d** 97 **p** 98. NSM Ewyas Harold w Dulas, Kenderchurch etc *Heref* 97-98; C 98-00; C Burghill and Stretton Sugwas 00-01; P-in-c Glasbury and Llowes w Clyro and Betws *S & B* from 02. *The Vicarage, 4 The Birches, Glasbury, Hereford HR3 5NW*

BAKER, Ms Hilary Mary (Dilly). b 61. Man Univ BA83 Univ of Wales (Cardiff) CQSW86. Sarum & Wells Th Coll 86. **d** 89 **p** 94. Par Dn E Dulwich St Jo *S'wark* 89-92; Tutor Sarum & Wells Th Coll 92-94; TV Stantonbury and Willen *Ox* 94-01; Warden Scargill Ho from 01. *Scargill House, Kettlewell, Skipton BD23 5HU* Tel (01756) 760234 E-mail warden@scargillhouse.co.uk

BAKER, Hugh Crispin. b 58. Open Univ BA92. Linc Th Coll 95. **d** 95 **p** 96. C Birstall and Wanlip *Leic* 95-99; V Middlestown *Wakef* from 99; Dioc Rural Officer from 04. *The Vicarage, 2 Netherton Hall Gardens, Netherton, Wakefield WF4 4JA* Tel (01924) 278384 E-mail hugh.baker@tesco.net

BAKER, Hugh John. b 46. Birm Univ BSocSc68. Cuddesdon Coll 69. **d** 71 **p** 72. C Binley *Cov* 71-74; C Pemberton St Mark Newtown *Liv* 74-78; TV Sutton 78-90; V Hints *Lich* 90-05; V Fazeley from 90; V Canwell from 05; R Drayton Bassett from 05; Chapl S Staffs Healthcare NHS Trust from 00. *St Paul's*

Vicarage, 9 West Drive, Bonehill, Tamworth B78 3HR Tel (01827) 287701 *or* 289414
E-mail elizabethatthevicarage@supanet.com

BAKER, Iain. b 70. St D Coll Lamp BA91. Oak Hill Th Coll BA99. **d** 99 **p** 00. C Gt Clacton *Chelmsf* 99-03; V Kidsgrove *Lich* from 03. *St Thomas's Vicarage, The Avenue, Kidsgrove, Stoke-on-Trent ST7 1AG* Tel (01782) 772895 *or* 771727
E-mail ib.ib@virgin.net

BAKER, Ivon Robert. b 28. St Aug Coll Cant 59. **d** 60 **p** 61. C Sutton in Ashfield St Mary *S'well* 60-62; V Gringley-on-the-Hill 62-94; Chapl HM YOI Gringley 82-91; RD Bawtry *S'well* 85-90; rtd 94; Perm to Offic *York* from 94. *2 Willowgate, Pickering YO18 7BE* Tel (01751) 472281

BAKER, Canon James Henry. b 39. MBE02. Kelham Th Coll 62. **d** 67 **p** 68. C Sheff Arbourthorne *Sheff* 67-70; C Pemberton St Jo *Liv* 70-71; Chapl and Prec St Mary's Cathl *Edin* 71-74; R Lochgelly *St And* 74-84; P-in-c Rosyth and Inverkeithing 76-84; Can St Ninian's Cathl Perth 83-84; TR Whitehaven *Carl* 84-04; RD Calder 96-01; Hon Can Carl Cathl from 96; rtd 04. *Eskdale Vicarage, Boot, Holmrook CA19 1TF* Tel (019467) 23242
E-mail j.baker@can-online.org.uk

BAKER, Jean Margaret. b 47. Sheff Univ BSc69 DipEd70 Lon Univ BD78. All Nations Chr Coll 75 Gilmore Course 81. **dss** 82 **d** 87 **p** 97. Liv Our Lady and St Nic w St Anne *Liv* 82-87; Chapl Huyton Coll 87; Chapl St Mary and St Anne's Sch Abbots Bromley 87-91; Chapl Howell's Sch Denbigh 91-98; C Denbigh *St As* from 97. *Lle Braf, 28 Abrams Lane, Denbigh LL16 3SS* Tel (01745) 812262 E-mail margaret@smallrev.demon.co.uk

BAKER, Jenifer Marlene. b 44. Bris Univ BSc65 Univ of Wales (Swansea) PhD71 York St Jo Coll BA05. **d** 05. OLM Ruyton XI Towns w Gt and Lt Ness *Lich* from 05. *Clock Cottage, Church Street, Ruyton XI Towns, Shrewsbury SY4 1LA* Tel (01939) 260910

BAKER, John Albert. b 29. St Edm Hall Ox BA52 MA56 Lon Univ BSc68 S Bank Poly MSc76. Cuddesdon Coll 52. **d** 54 **p** 55. C Battersea St Luke *S'wark* 54-58; Hon C from 84; C Richmond St Mary 58-62; V Battersea Park All SS 62-83; Tutor Roehampton Inst 83-91; rtd 94. *44 Wroughton Road, London SW11 6BG* Tel (020) 7585 2492

BAKER, John Alfred. b 41. Dioc OLM tr scheme 99. **d** 02 **p** 03. OLM Herne *Cant* from 02. *Oakfield, 219 Canterbury Road, Herne Bay CT6 7HB* Tel (01227) 362519 Mobile 07960-107169
E-mail john-baker@kent35.fslife.co.uk

✠**BAKER, The Rt Revd John Austin.** b 28. Oriel Coll Ox BA52 MA55 BLitt55 MLitt. Lambeth DD91 Cuddesdon Coll 52. **d** 54 **p** 55 **c** 82. C Cuddesdon *Ox* 54-57; Tutor Cuddesdon Coll 54-57; C Hatch End St Anselm *Lon* 57-59; Lect K Coll Lon 57-59; Chapl CCC Ox 59-73; Lect Th Ox Univ 59-73; Can Westmr Abbey 73-82; Sub Dean Westmr 78-82; R Westmr St Marg 78-82; Chapl to Speaker of Ho of Commons 78-82; Bp Sarum 82-93; Can and Preb Sarum Cathl 82-93; rtd 93; Hon Asst Bp Win from 94. *4 Mede Villas, Kingsgate Road, Winchester SO23 9QQ* Tel (01962) 861388 Fax 843089

BAKER, John Carl. b 55. Chich Th Coll 77. **d** 80 **p** 81. C Wigan St Andr *Liv* 80-83; V Hollinfare 83-85; TV Seacroft *Ripon* 85-89; TV Bottesford w Ashby *Linc* 89-94; V Liv St Paul Stoneycroft *Liv* 94-02; V Altcar and Hightown from 02. *St Stephen's Vicarage, St Stephen's Road, Liverpool L38 0BL* Tel 0151-926 2469 E-mail revjcb@btopenworld.com

BAKER, John Reginald. b 62. Hatf Coll Dur BSc83. Wycliffe Hall Ox 86. **d** 89 **p** 90. C Amersham *Ox* 89-92; C Greenford H Cross *Lon* 92-97. *11A Lakeside Road, London W14 0DX* Tel (020) 8574 3762

BAKER, Jonathan Mark Richard. b 66. St Jo Coll Ox BA88 MPhil90. St Steph Ho Ox BA92. **d** 93 **p** 94. C Ascot Heath *Ox* 93-96; C Reading St Mark 96; P-in-c 96-99; V 99-02; P-in-c Reading H Trin 96-99; V 99-02; Prin Pusey Ho Ox from 03. *Pusey House, Oxford OX1 3LZ* Tel (01865) 278415 Fax 278416
E-mail jonathan.baker@stx.ox.ac.uk

BAKER, Canon Jonathan William. b 61. SS Coll Cam MA85. Wycliffe Hall Ox BA91. **d** 92 **p** 93. C Sanderstead All SS *S'wark* 92-96; P-in-c Scalby w Ravenscar and Staintondale *York* 96-97; V Scalby 97-04; P-in-c Hackness w Harwood Dale 96-97; V 97-04; P-in-c Scarborough St Luke 03-04; Can Res Pet Cathl *Pet* from 04. *The Chapter Office, Minster Precincts, Peterborough PE1 1XS* Tel (01733) 343342
E-mail jonathan.baker@peterborough-cathedral.org.uk

BAKER, Kenneth William. b 38. Nottm Univ DTPS95. EMMTC 92. **d** 96 **p** 97. NSM Welford w Sibbertoft and Marston Trussell *Pet* 96-99; P-in-c 98-01; P-in-c N w S Kilworth and Misterton *Leic* 01-03; P-in-c Swinford w Catthorpe, Shawell and Stanford 01-03; TR Gilmorton, Peatling Parva, Kimcote etc from 03. *The Rectory, Kilworth Road, Swinford, Lutterworth LE17 6BQ* Tel (01788) 860409

BAKER, Marc Crispin. b 75. Westmr Coll Ox BTh96. Oak Hill Th Coll 00. **d** 02 **p** 03. C Upton (Overchurch) *Ches* from 02. *43 Grafton Drive, Wirral CH49 0TX* Tel 0151-678 1235 *or* 677 1186 Fax 606 1935 E-mail office@stmupton.freeserve.co.uk

BAKER, Canon Michael Robert Henry. b 39. Keele Univ MA88. Lich Th Coll 63. **d** 66 **p** 67. C Wellingborough All SS *Pet* 66-68; C Pet All SS 68-73; V Earls Barton 73-87; RD Wellingborough 76-87; P-in-c Gt Doddington 77-82; TR Kingsthorpe w Northampton St Dav 87-95; V Towcester w Easton Neston 95-04; RD Towcester 98-03; Can Pet Cathl 85-04; rtd 04. *Magdalene Cottage, 56 Queen Street, Geddington, Kettering NN14 1AZ* Tel (01536) 741091
E-mail mikemargbaker@aol.com

BAKER, Michael William. b 38. Roch Th Coll 68. **d** 70 **p** 71. C Woodmansterne *S'wark* 70-75; TV Danbury *Chelmsf* 75-78; P-in-c Barrington *Ely* 78-90; V 90-97; P-in-c Shepreth 78-90; V 90-97; rtd 97; Perm to Offic *Nor* from 98. *The White House, Church Street, Elsing, Dereham NR20 3EB* Tel (01362) 637370

BAKER, Miles Anthony. b 71. Brunel Univ BA92. Ridley Hall Cam 99. **d** 02 **p** 03. C Paignton Ch Ch and Preston St Paul *Ex* from 02; P-in-c Upton from 05. *Upton Rectory, Furzehill Road, Torquay TQ1 3JG* Tel (01803) 211572
E-mail dawnmiles@dbaker16.fsnet.co.uk

BAKER, Canon Neville Duff. b 35. St Aid Birkenhead 60. **d** 63 **p** 64. C Stranton *Dur* 63-66; C Houghton le Spring 66-68; V Tudhoe Grange from 68; P-in-c Merrington 91-94; RD Auckland 83-94; Hon Can Dur Cathl from 90. *St Andrew's Vicarage, Barnfield Road, Spennymoor DL16 6EA* Tel (01388) 814817

BAKER, Noel Edward Lloyd. b 37. Sarum & Wells Th Coll 73. **d** 75 **p** 76. C Charlton Kings St Mary *Glouc* 75-79; V Clearwell 79-81; R Eastington and Frocester 81-97; RD Stonehouse 90-94; P-in-c Eastington and Frocester 97-98; P-in-c Standish w Haresfield and Moreton Valence etc 97-98; rtd 98; Perm to Offic *Glouc* from 00. *46 Dozule Close, Leonard Stanley, Stonehouse GL10 3NL* Tel (01453) 823569
E-mail noel_brenda@yahoo.co.uk

BAKER, Paul Anthony. b 64. St Chad's Coll Dur BA85. St Steph Ho Ox BA88 MA98. **d** 89 **p** 90. C Hartlepool St Aid *Dur* 89-93; TV Jarrow 93-98; V Sunderland Pennywell St Thos 98-04; V Darlington St Mark w St Paul from 04. *St Mark's Vicarage, 394 North Road, Darlington DL1 3BH* Tel (01325) 382400

BAKER, Peter Colin. b 43. Sarum & Wells Th Coll. **d** 82 **p** 83. C Bridgemary *Portsm* 82-86; V Ash Vale *Guildf* 86-99; P-in-c Earlham St Anne *Nor* from 99; P-in-c Earlham St Mary from 99. *The Vicarage, Bluebell Road, Norwich NR4 7LP* Tel (01603) 452922 E-mail peterbaker854@hotmail.com

BAKER, Peter Graham. b 55. MA PhD. St Steph Ho Ox. **d** 82 **p** 83. C Ches H Trin *Ches* 82-86; C Holborn St Alb w Saffron Hill St Pet *Lon* 86-91; V Golders Green 91-01; AD W Barnet 95-00; V Regent's Park St Mark from 01. *St Mark's Vicarage, 4 Regent's Park Road, London NW1 7TX* Tel (020) 7485 6340 *or* 7586 1694 E-mail petergbaker@freeuk.com

BAKER, Canon Peter Malcolm. b 21. Lich Th Coll 40. **d** 43 **p** 45. C Bedminster St Aldhelm *Bris* 43-47; C Charlton Kings H Apostles *Glouc* 47-49; C Halesowen *Worc* 49-53; CF (TA) 53-75; V Dudley St Luke *Worc* 53-59; R Hindlip w Martin Hussingtree 59-67; V Inkberrow 67-75; P-in-c Kington w Dormston 74-75; R Inkberrow w Cookhill and Kington w Dormston 75-77; P-in-c Wilden 77-80; R Mamble w Bayton 80-82; RD Stourport 80-88; R Teme Valley N 82-88; Hon Can Worc Cathl 84-88; rtd 88; Perm to Offic *Heref* from 88; Perm to Offic *Worc* from 88. *The Ryelands, Menith Wood, Worcester WR6 6UG* Tel (01584) 881227

BAKER, Robert John Kenneth. b 50. MICE79 Southn Univ BSc71. Oak Hill Th Coll 88. **d** 90 **p** 91. C Cromer *Nor* 90-94; P-in-c Pakefield 94; R from 94. *The Rectory, The Causeway, Pakefield, Lowestoft NR33 0JZ* Tel (01502) 574040

BAKER, Canon Robert Mark. b 50. Bris Univ BA73. St Jo Coll Nottm 74. **d** 76 **p** 77. C Portswood Ch Ch *Win* 76-80; R Witton w Brundall and Braydeston *Nor* 80-89; P-in-c Buckenham w Hassingham and Strumpshaw 80-86; R Brundall w Braydeston and Postwick from 89; RD Blofield 89-94; Hon Can Nor Cathl from 93. *The Rectory, 73 The Street, Brundall, Norwich NR13 5LZ* Tel (01603) 715136 E-mail bob-baker@clara.net

BAKER, Ronald Harry. b 21. Ely Th Coll 62. **d** 64 **p** 65. C Crediton *Ex* 64-66; R Thornbury 66-73; R Bradford 67-73; R Black Torrington, Bradf and Thornbury 73-77; P-in-c Broadhempston and Woodland 77-78; P-in-c Lt Hempston 77-78; P-in-c Berry Pomeroy 77-78; V Broadhempston, Woodland, Berry Pomeroy etc 78-86; rtd 86; Chapl Marseille w St Raphaël, Aix-en-Provence etc *Eur* 87-88; Perm to Offic *Ex* from 88. *95 Barton Avenue, Paignton TQ3 3HY* Tel (01803) 557462

BAKER, Ronald Kenneth. b 43. Open Univ BA80. St Jo Coll Nottm 85. **d** 87 **p** 88. C Paddock Wood *Roch* 87-90; V Ramsgate St Mark *Cant* 90-95; P-in-c Ewhurst and Bodiam *Chich* 95-98; V 98-03; rtd 03. *49 Coneyburrow Gardens, St Leonards-on-Sea TN38 9RZ* Tel (01424) 851870

BAKER, Roy David. b 36. St Aid Birkenhead 59. **d** 62 **p** 63. C Garston *Liv* 62-64; C N Meols 64-68; V Newton-le-Willows 68-73; V Crossens 73-82; V Blundellsands St Nic 82-01; rtd 01; Perm to Offic *Liv* from 03. *18 Ennerdale Road, Formby, Liverpool L37 2EA* Tel (01704) 830622

BAKER, Sarah Jane. b 59. Lon Univ MB, BS82 DRCOG87 Sheff Univ MPhil00 Coll of Ripon & York St Jo MA02. N Ord Course 99. **d** 02 **p** 03. NSM Kinsley w Wragby *Wakef* from 02. *12 Ingswell Drive, Notton, Wakefield WF4 2NF* Tel (01226) 728336 Mobile 07885-376182 E-mail sarahrekab@aol.com

BAKER, Simon Nicholas Hartland. b 57. K Coll Lon BD78 Trin Hall Cam DipTh79. Qu Coll Birm 79. **d** 81 **p** 82. C Tupsley *Heref* 81-85; V Shinfield *Ox* 85-98; Prin Berks Chr Tr Scheme 93-98; Lay Min Adv and Warden of Readers *Win* 98-02; Dir of Min Development from 02. *The Rectory, Trinity Hill, Medstead, Alton GU34 5LT* Tel (01420) 568191

BAKER, Stephen Anthony. b 55. St Luke's Coll Ex BEd80. Sarum & Wells Th Coll 88. **d** 91 **p** 92. C Guildf H Trin w St Mary *Guildf* 91-97; Chapl Guildf Coll of Tech 91-97; Chapl Eliz Coll Guernsey 97-01. *Address temp unknown*

BAKER, Stuart. b 44. MATA63 AIAT65. Spurgeon's Coll DipTh71 Bapt Tr Coll DipMin75 Ripon Coll Cuddesdon 92. **d** 93 **p** 94. C Whitchurch *Bris* 93-97; R Brightling, Dallington, Mountfield etc *Chich* from 97. *The Rectory, Brightling, Robertsbridge TN32 5HE* Tel (01424) 838281

BAKER, William Alfred Douglas. b 21. Lon Univ BSc52 MSc56. Qu Coll Birm 72. **d** 75 **p** 76. NSM Bridgnorth w Tasley *Heref* 75-78; NSM Bridgnorth, Tasley, Astley Abbotts, etc 78-97; Perm to Offic 97-00. *Address temp unknown*

BAKER, William John. b 45. FCII80. Cranmer Hall Dur 87. **d** 89 **p** 90. C Sale St Anne *Ches* 89-93; V Crewe St Andr 93-94; P-in-c Crewe St Jo 93-94; V Crewe St Andr w St Jo from 94. *St John's Vicarage, 14 Dane Bank Avenue, Crewe CW2 8AA* Tel (01270) 569000 Fax 650209 E-mail bill@revbaker.fsnet.co.uk

BAKERE, The Very Revd Ronald Duncan. b 35. TCD BA58 MA61 BD62 Ch Ch Ox MA66 FRSA68 FBIM79. **d** 59 **p** 60. C Knockbreda *D & D* 59-61; C Dublin Zion Ch *D & G* 61-63; Min Can St Patr Cathl Dublin 62-64; CF (TA) 65-67; Lect Plymouth Poly *Ex* 67-72; Prin Kuka Teachers' Coll Nigeria 73-77; Cen Org Red Cross Ex 78-81; Perm to Offic *Ex* 82-85; P-in-c Chew Magna w Dundry *B & W* 86-87; Hd RS Sir John Cass Foundn Lon 88-93; Dean Port Moresby Papua New Guinea 93-96; Visiting Prof H Spirit RC Sem 94-96; rtd 96; Perm to Offic *Lon* from 96. *12 Dumbarton Road, London SW2 5LU* Tel (020) 8674 0283

BAKKER, Gregory Kendall. b 66. California State Univ BA89. Trin Episc Sch for Min Penn MDiv92 Trin Coll Bris 99. **d** 92 **p** 93. C Tariffville USA 92-96; Lect St Phil Coll Kongwa Tanzania 96-99; C Wroughton *Bris* 00-02; TV Stratton St Margaret w S Marston etc from 02. *The Vicarage, South Marston, Swindon SN3 4SR* Tel (01793) 827021 E-mail gkbakker@hotmail.com

BAKKER (née CAMPBELL), Mrs Jane Judith. b 68. Trin Coll Bris BA01. **d** 01 **p** 02. NSM Lyddington and Wanborough and Bishopstone etc *Bris* 01-03; NSM Stratton St Margaret w S Marston etc from 03. *The Vicarage, South Marston, Swindon SN3 4SR* Tel (01793) 827021 E-mail jcampbell@fish.co.uk

BALCH, John Robin. b 37. Lon Univ BSc61 Bris Univ CertEd62. ALCD68. **d** 68 **p** 69. C Bath Walcot *B & W* 68-71; C Fulwood *Sheff* 71-76; V Erith St Paul *Roch* 76-93; RD Erith 90-93; P-in-c Fairlight *Chich* 93-94; R Fairlight, Guestling and Pett 94-01; rtd 01; Perm to Offic *Derby* from 01. *29 Whitecotes Park, Chesterfield S40 3RT* Tel (01246) 297099

BALCHIN, Michael John. b 38. Selw Coll Cam BA60 MA64. Wells Th Coll 60. **d** 62 **p** 63. C Bournemouth H Epiphany *Win* 62-65; C Bris St Mary Redcliffe w Temple etc *Bris* 65-69; R Norton sub Hamdon *B & W* 69-70; P-in-c Chiselborough w W Chinnock 69-70; R Norton sub Hamdon w Chiselborough 70-77; P-in-c Chipstable w Huish Champflower and Clatworthy 77-82; R 82-88; Perm to Offic *Ban* from 88; rtd 03. *Gartheiniog, Aberangell, Machynlleth SY20 9QG* Tel (01650) 511659

BALDOCK, Andrew Robert. b 67. St Jo Coll Dur BA00. Cranmer Hall Dur 98. **d** 00 **p** 02. C Peterlee *Dur* 00-01; C Felling 01-03; C Dur St Nic from 03. *95 Rochester Road, Durham DH1 5PN* Tel 0191-386 5605 E-mail andrew.baldock@lineone.net

BALDOCK, Charles William Martin. b 52. Nottm Univ BPharm73. St Jo Coll Nottm LTh. **d** 85 **p** 86. C Nailsea Ch Ch *B & W* 85-89; V Brampton Bierlow *Sheff* 89-00; RD Wath 95-00; Hon Can Sheff Cathl 98-00; V Dringhouses *York* from 00; RD City of York from 04; Chapl St Leon Hospice York from 02. *The Vicarage, Tadcaster Road, Dringhouses, York YO24 1QG* Tel (01904) 706120 Fax 709111 E-mail mserz@baldock13.fsnet.co.uk

BALDOCK, Canon Norman. b 29. K Coll Lon BD52 AKC52. **d** 53 **p** 54. C Cant St Pet w H Cross *Cant* 53-54; C Thornton Heath St Jude 54-58; V Ash w W Marsh 58-67; V Sheerness H Trin w St Paul 67-75; V Margate St Jo 75-94; RD Thanet 80-86; Hon Can Cant Cathl 82-94; Chapl Margate Gen Hosp 82-94; rtd 94; Perm to Offic *Cant* from 94. *9 Beach Avenue, Birchington CT7 9VS* Tel (01843) 841173

BALDOCK, Reginald David. b 48. Oak Hill Th Coll 72. **d** 75 **p** 76. C Plymouth St Jude *Ex* 75-79; C Ardsley *Sheff* 79-85; V Rawthorpe *Wakef* 85-96; C Salterhebble All SS 96-98; P-in-c Bournemouth St Jo w St Mich *Win* from 98. *The Vicarage, 13 Durley Chine Road South, Bournemouth BH2 5JT* Tel (01202) 761962 E-mail r.baldock1@ntlworld.com

BALDRY, John Netherway. b 19. Lon Univ BA53. **d** 79 **p** 80. NSM Brighton St Paul *Chich* from 79. *81 Windsor Court, Tongdean Lane, Brighton BN1 5JS* Tel (01273) 501268

BALDRY, Ralph Yorke. b 18. St Jo Coll Ox BA40 MA44. Wycliffe Hall Ox 40. **d** 41 **p** 42. C Southall H Trin *Lon* 41-45; C Oakwood St Thos 45-47; V Clay Hill St Jo 47-52; V Stonebridge St Mich 52-58; V Finchley St Luke 64-72; V Golders Green St Alb 72-80; P-in-c Golders Green St Mich 77-80; V Golders Green 80-83; rtd 84; Perm to Offic *Lon* 84-04. *4 Millbridge Mews, Hertford SG14 1HE* Tel (01992) 558734

BALDWICK, Frank Eric. b 24. Ripon Hall Ox 54. **d** 55 **p** 56. C Newark Ch Ch and Hawton *S'well* 55-58; C W Bridgford 58-60; V Oldham St Barn *Man* 60-65; R Gt Lever 65-78; V Hindsford 78-81; TV Clifton *S'well* 81-89; rtd 89; Perm to Offic *S'well* from 89. *35 Lady Bay Road, West Bridgford, Nottingham NG2 5BJ* Tel 0115-982 1273

BALDWIN, Colin Steven. b 61. Brighton Poly BA85. St Jo Coll Nottm MTh01. **d** 01 **p** 02. C Billericay and Lt Burstead *Chelmsf* 01-05; P-in-c Prittlewell St Steph from 05. *26 Eastbourne Grove, Westcliff-on-Sea SS0 0QF* Tel (01702) 352448 Mobile 07714-048450 E-mail csbald@aol.com

BALDWIN, David Frederick Beresford. b 57. Wolv Univ 91. Ripon Coll Cuddesdon DipMin95. **d** 95 **p** 96. C Uttoxeter w Bramshall *Lich* 95-97; C Uttoxeter Area 97-98; V Tilstock, Edstaston and Whixall from 98; P-in-c Prees from 03; P-in-c Fauls from 03; Rural Chapl (Salop Adnry) from 00. *The Vicarage, Tilstock, Whitchurch SY13 3JL* Tel and fax (01948) 880552 E-mail revddavidbaldwin@lichfield.net

BALDWIN, Derek Wilfred Walter. b 23. Lon Univ LTh74. ALCD56. **d** 52 **p** 53. C Sharrow St Andr *Sheff* 52-54; C Woodlands 54-56; V Shepley *Wakef* 56-59; V Earl's Heaton 59-66; Org Sec CECS *B & W*, *Ex* and *Truro* 66-72; R Morchard Bishop *Ex* 72-73; Org Sec CECS *St Alb* and *Ox* 73-77; C Portishead *B & W* 77-79; R Wymondham w Edmondthorpe *Leic* 79-80; P-in-c St Mewan *Truro* 80-81; V Crowan w Godolphin 81-83; C Cockington *Ex* 83-87; rtd 87; Perm to Offic *Ex* from 90. *53 Higher Woolbrook Park, Sidmouth EX10 9ED*

BALDWIN, Mrs Frances Mary. b 49. SRN71. SEITE 99. **d** 02 **p** 03. NSM Caterham *S'wark* from 02. *3 Hillhurst Gardens, Caterham CR3 5HX* Tel (020) 8660 7534 E-mail francesb3@btinternet.com

BALDWIN, John Charles. b 39. Bris Univ BSc61 Sussex Univ DPhil65 FBCS CEng. St Steph Ho Ox 82. **d** 83 **p** 84. C Llandaff w Capel Llanilltern *Llan* 83-90; V Ewenny w St Brides Major 90-92; Lic to Offic from 92; Hon Chapl Llan Cathl from 96; rtd 04. *60 Llantrisant Road, Llandaff, Cardiff CF5 2PX* Tel (029) 2055 4457 Fax 2038 7835 E-mail johnbaldwin@rb.churchinwales.org.uk

BALDWIN, Jonathan Michael. b 58. Chich Th Coll 92. **d** 94 **p** 95. C Crawley *Chich* 94-96; C New Shoreham 96-02; C Old Shoreham 96-02; Chapl Gatwick Airport from 02; C Crawley from 02. *18 Aldingbourne Close, Ifield, Crawley RH11 0QJ* Tel (01293) 447221

BALDWIN, Peter Alan. b 48. Bede Coll Dur BA70. Qu Coll Birm 72. **d** 73 **p** 74. C Hartlepool St Oswald *Dur* 73-75; C Darlington H Trin 75-78; OGS from 77; C-in-c Bishop Auckland Woodhouse Close CD *Dur* 78-82; V Ferryhill 82-88; P-in-c Charlestown *Man* 88-89; V Pendleton St Thos 88-89; TR Pendleton St Thos w Charlestown 89-90; TR Newton Aycliffe *Dur* 90-96; TR Gt Aycliffe 96-97; AD Sedgefield 96-99; V The Trimdons 97-99; P-in-c Bramley *Ripon* 99-00; TR 00-02; Hon C Harrogate St Wilfrid 02-03; Hon C Methley w Mickletown 03-04; Dom Chapl to Bp Horsham *Chich* from 04; P-in-c Buncton and Wiston from 05. *4 Michell Close, Horsham RH12 1JT* Tel (01403) 241597 Mobile 07967-119362 E-mail peterabaldwin5@aol.com

BALDWIN, Mrs Vivien Lindsay. b 50. DipHE99. St Alb and Ox Min Course 97. **d** 98 **p** 99. NSM Westbury w Turweston, Shalstone and Biddlesden *Ox* 98-00; C W Buckingham 00-02; P-in-c Stoneleigh w Ashow *Cov* from 02; Rural Life Officer from 02. *The Parsonage, Church Lane, Stoneleigh, Coventry CV8 3DN* Tel (024) 7641 5506 Mobile 07720-811477 E-mail viv@vivbaldwin.worldonline.co.uk

BALDWIN, William. b 48. RMN73 FRSH83. NW Ord Course 75. **d** 78 **p** 79. C Royton St Anne *Man* 78-82; V Halliwell St Thos 82-87; TR Atherton 87-99; TR Atherton and Hindsford 99-02; TV Atherton and Hindsford w Howe Bridge from 02; AD Leigh from 01. *Atherton Rectory, Bee Fold Lane, Atherton, Manchester M29 0BL* Tel (01942) 874666 Fax 876620 E-mail frbill@fsmail.net

BALE, Edward William Carre. b 22. AKC55 Leic Univ DSRS67. **d** 55 **p** 56. C Mansfield SS Pet and Paul *S'well* 55-59; C Corby St Jo *Pet* 59-61; R Corby SS Pet and Andr 61-69; V Wollaston and Strixton 69-87; rtd 88; Perm to Offic *Pet* 89-94 and *Ox* from 88. *27 The Crescent, Haversham, Milton Keynes MK19 7AN* Tel (01234) 391443 E-mail tedcarrebale@lineone.net

BALE, Kenneth John. b 34. Univ of Wales (Lamp) BA58. Qu Coll Birm. **d** 60 **p** 61. C Mitcham St Olave *S'wark* 60-63; C Warlingham w Chelsham and Farleigh 63-67; V Battersea Rise St Mark 67-85; Perm to Offic 85-88; Hon C Balham St Mary and St Jo 88-90; V S Wimbledon All SS 90-01; Dioc Adv Min of Healing 91-01; rtd 01; Perm to Offic *Sheff* from 01. *23 Selhurst Crescent, Bessacarr, Doncaster DN4 6EF* Tel (01302) 539100 Fax 371850 E-mail kbale@mistral.co.uk

BALFOUR, Andrew Crispin Roxburgh. b 49. Coll of Resurr Mirfield 93. **d** 95 **p** 96. C S Lafford *Linc* 95-99; P-in-c St Neot and Warleggan *Truro* 99-00; P-in-c Cardynham 99-00; R St Neot and Warleggan w Cardynham from 00. *The Vicarage, St Neot, Liskeard PL14 6NG* Tel (01579) 320472

BALFOUR, Hugh Rowlatt. b 54. SS Coll Cam BA76. Ridley Hall Cam 78. **d** 81 **p** 82. C Bedford Ch Ch *St Alb* 81-86; P-in-c Camberwell Ch Ch *S'wark* 86-90; V from 90. *Christ Church Vicarage, 79 Asylum Road, London SE15 2RJ* Tel (020) 7639 5662 E-mail hrbalfours@hotmail.com

BALFOUR, Mark Andrew. b 66. York Univ BA88 R Holloway Coll Lon PhD98. Trin Coll Bris BA01. **d** 02 **p** 03. C Churchdown *Glouc* from 02. *11 Chapel Hay Lane, Churchdown, Gloucester GL3 2ET* Tel (01452) 713080 E-mail thebalfours@btinternet.com

BALFOUR, Mrs Penelope Mary. b 47. St Andr Univ MA69 St Jo Coll York DipEd72. Coates Hall Edin 89 St Jo Coll Nottm 84. **d** 88 **p** 95. C Dundee St Marg *Bre* 88-94; Dioc AIDS Officer 90-94; NSM Invergowrie 94-96; C from 00; Chapl Abertay Univ 94-97; C Dundee St Marg 96-00. *10 Strathaird Place, Dundee DD2 4TN* Tel (01382) 643114

BALKWILL, Michael Robert. b 67. Univ of Wales (Lamp) BD89 Univ of Wales (Cardiff) MTh92. St Mich Coll Llan 89 Bp Tucker Coll Mukono 91. **d** 91 **p** 92. C Llanrhos *St As* 91-97; Dioc RE Adv from 94; R Llanfyllin and Bwlchycibau from 97; Perm to Offic *Ban* from 97; Dioc Co-ord Dept of Development and Tr for Miss *St As* from 99. *The Rectory, Coed Llan Lane, Llanfyllin SY22 5BW* Tel (01691) 648306

BALKWILL, Roger Bruce. b 41. Univ of Wales DipTh64 DPS66. St Mich Coll Llan 61. **d** 64 **p** 65. C Llantrisant *Llan* 64-68; C Caerphilly 68-73; Rhodesia 73-76; P-in-c Ilam w Blore Ray and Okeover *Lich* 76-81; P-in-c Albrighton 81-82; V from 82; P-in-c Beckbury 89-90; P-in-c Badger 89-90; P-in-c Ryton 89-90; P-in-c Kemberton, Sutton Maddock and Stockton 89-90; RD Shifnal 89-98; P-in-c Boningale from 97. *The Vicarage, High Street, Albrighton, Wolverhampton WV7 3EQ* Tel (01902) 372701

BALL, Alan. b 26. Qu Coll Birm 72. **d** 75 **p** 75. NSM Hamstead St Paul *Birm* 75-93; rtd 93; Perm to Offic *Portsm* from 93. *25 Tebourba Drive, Alverstoke, Gosport PO12 2NT* Tel (023) 9260 1694

BALL, Andrew Thomas. b 54. K Coll Lon BD75 AKC75. Sarum & Wells Th Coll 76. **d** 77 **p** 78. C Ribbleton *Blackb* 77-80; C Sedgley All SS *Lich* 80-84; V Pheasey 84-90; Chapl Gd Hope Distr Gen Hosp Sutton Coldfield 90-94; Chapl Gd Hope Hosp NHS Trust Sutton Coldfield from 94. *Chaplain's Office, Good Hope Hospital, Rectory Road, Sutton Coldfield B75 7RR* Tel 0121-378 2211 ext 2676 *or* 243 1948

BALL, Anthony Charles. b 46. Lon Univ BD71. Chich Th Coll 72. **d** 73 **p** 74. C Heref St Martin *Heref* 73-76; C Ealing St Pet Mt Park *Lon* 76-82; V Ruislip Manor St Paul from 82. *St Paul's Vicarage, Thurlstone Road, Ruislip HA4 0BP* Tel (01895) 633499

BALL, Anthony James. b 68. St Chad's Coll Dur BA89. NTMTC 97. **d** 00 **p** 01. NSM Madrid *Eur* 00-03; Chapl Damascus from 03. *FCO (Damascus), King Charles Street, London SW1A 2AH* E-mail anthony.ball@fco.gov.uk

BALL, Anthony Michael. b 46. Kelham Th Coll 66. **d** 70 **p** 71. C Kingswinford St Mary *Lich* 70-74; C W Bromwich All SS 74-76; P-in-c Priorslee 76-80; V 80-82; Asst Chapl HM Pris Liv 82-83; Chapl 88-95; Chapl HM Pris Lewes 83-88; Chapl HM Pris Featherstone 95-00; Chapl HM Pris The Verne from 00. *The Chaplain's Office, HM Prison, The Verne, Portland DT5 1EG* Tel (01305) 825198

BALL, Christopher Rowland. b 40. Wycliffe Hall Ox. **d** 82 **p** 83. C Heysham *Blackb* 82-86; TV Swanborough *Sarum* 86-90; R Llanyblodwel and Trefonen *Lich* 90-99; rtd 99; Perm to Offic *Lich* 01-03. *27 Wallace Lane, Forton, Preston PR3 0BA*

BALL, Canon Frank. b 21. Leeds Univ BA47. Coll of Resurr Mirfield 46. **d** 48 **p** 49. C Shiregreen St Hilda *Sheff* 48-50; C Attercliffe w Carbrook 50-53; V Handsworth Woodhouse 53-61; V Sheff St Leon Norwood 61-87; RD Ecclesfield 80-87; Hon Can Sheff Cathl 85-93; rtd 87; Gov and Chapl Shrewsbury Hosp Sheff 87-93; Perm to Offic *Sheff* from 93. *40 Seagrave Road, Sheffield S12 2JS* Tel 0114-264 4931

BALL, Geoffrey Ernest. b 49. Ox Min Course 00. **d** 03. NSM Winslow w Gt Horwood and Addington *Ox* from 03. *19 Offa's Lane, Winslow, Buckingham MK18 3JS* E-mail geoffball@btopenworld.com

BALL, George Raymond. b 15. Univ of Wales (Lamp) BA40. St Mich Coll Llan 40. **d** 42 **p** 43. C Llansamlet *S & B* 42-46; C Swansea St Nic 46-50; R Bosherston w St Twynells *St D* 50-85; rtd 85. *1 Meadow Bank, St Twynnells, Pembroke SA71 5HZ* Tel (01646) 661432

BALL, Ian Raymond. b 45. CertEd Univ of Wales MPhil. Glouc Th Course 81. **d** 85 **p** 87. NSM Churchstoke w Hyssington and Sarn *Heref* from 85; Lic to Bp Ludlow from 87; Lic to Offic *St As* from 93. *Bachaethlon Cottage, Sarn, Newtown SY16 4HH* Tel (01686) 670505 Fax as telephone E-mail iball@compuserve.com

BALL, Mrs Jane. b 68. Charlotte Mason Coll of Educn BEd91. St Steph Ho Ox 01. **d** 03 **p** 04. C Bedale and Leeming *Ripon* from 03. *The Old Grammar School, North End, Bedale DL8 1AF* Tel (01677) 423919 Mobile 07764-349957 E-mail jjball@onetel.com

BALL, John Kenneth. b 42. Lon Univ BSc64 AKC64. Linc Th Coll 69. **d** 71 **p** 72. C Garston *Liv* 71-74; C Eastham *Ches* 74-75; C Barnston 75-77; V Over St Jo 77-82; V Helsby and Dunham-on-the-Hill 82-94; RD Frodsham 88-94; P-in-c Alvanley 92-94; V Hoylake 94-98; rtd 98; P-in-c Downholme and Marske *Ripon* 00-05; C Richmond w Hudswell and Downholme and Marske from 05. *5 Belle Vue Terrace, Bellerby, Leyburn DL8 5QL* Tel (01969) 623357

✠**BALL, The Rt Revd John Martin.** b 34. Univ of Wales BA55. Tyndale Hall Bris. **d** 59 **p** 60 **c** 95. C Blackb St Jude *Blackb* 59-63; Kenya 63-79; Dep Gen Sec BCMS 79-81; Gen Sec 81-93; Gen Sec Crosslinks 93-95; Hon C Sidcup Ch Ch *Roch* 81-95; Hon Can Karamoja from 88; Asst Bp Tanzania 95-00; rtd 00; Hon Asst Bp Chelmsf from 00. *5 Hill View Road, Chelmsford CM1 7RS* Tel (01245) 268296 E-mail ball_john@onetel.com

BALL, John Roy. b 47. Fitzw Coll Cam MA71. Wycliffe Hall Ox 83. **d** 85 **p** 86. C Stockport St Mary *Ches* 85-88; C Fazeley *Lich* 88-94; Res Min Drayton Bassett 89-94; Chapl Grenoble *Eur* 94-00; P-in-c Lithuania 00-05; Asst Chapl Amsterdam w Den Helder and Heiloo from 05. *De Kuilenaar 60, 1851 RZ Heiloo, The Netherlands* E-mail jroyball@christchurch.nl

BALL, Jonathan. b 63. BNC Ox BA85 Leeds Univ BA87. Coll of Resurr Mirfield 85. **d** 88 **p** 89. C Blakenall Heath *Lich* 88-92; TV Rugeley 92-96; CF from 96; Perm to Offic *Cant* 97-99 and *Ox* from 01. *c/o MOD Chaplains (Army)* Tel (01980) 615804 Fax 615800

BALL, Mrs Judith Anne. b 48. Nottm Univ BA70 Liv Univ PGCE71. N Ord Course 98. **d** 01 **p** 02. C Upholland *Liv* from 01. *8 Beacon View Drive, Upholland, Skelmersdale WN8 0HL* Tel (01695) 622181

BALL, Kevin Harry. b 55. Linc Th Coll 92. **d** 94 **p** 95. C New Mills *Derby* 94-96; C Walthamstow St Sav *Chelmsf* 96-98; V Stocksbridge *Sheff* 98-00; C Barnsley St Mary *Wakef* 00-01; Chapl Barnsley Coll 00-01; P-in-c Sneinton St Cypr *S'well* from 01; Chapl Notts Fire and Rescue Service from 04. *St Cyprian's Vicarage, Marston Road, Nottingham NG3 7AN* Tel 0115-987 3425

BALL, Mrs Marion Elaine. b 68. Hertf Coll Ox BA90 St Jo Coll Dur BA99. Cranmer Hall Dur 97. **d** 02 **p** 03. C Kingston upon Hull H Trin *York* from 02. *67 Adelaide Street, Hull HU3 2EZ* Tel (01482) 329580 E-mail meandpj@fish.co.uk

BALL, Mark Francis. b 72. St Jo Coll Dur BA94. St Steph Ho Ox BA00. **d** 01 **p** 02. C Poulton-le-Fylde *Blackb* 01-04; TV Loughton St Jo *Chelmsf* from 04. *2 Doubleday Road, Loughton IG10 2AT* Tel 07958-982482 (mobile) E-mail thereverendmarkball@hotmail.com

✠**BALL, The Rt Revd Michael Thomas.** b 32. Qu Coll Cam BA55 MA59. **d** 71 **p** 71 **c** 80. CGA from 60; Prior Stroud Priory 64-76; C Whiteshill *Glouc* 71-76; Lic to Offic 76; P-in-c Stanmer w Falmer *Chich* 76-80; Chapl Sussex Univ 76-80; Suff Bp Jarrow *Dur* 80-90; Angl Adv Tyne Tees TV 84-90; Bp Truro 90-97; rtd 97; Perm to Offic *B & W* from 01. *Manor Lodge, Aller, Langport TA10 0QN* Tel (01458) 250495

BALL, Nicholas Edward. b 54. Man Univ BA75 Ox Univ MA85. Ripon Coll Cuddesdon 79. **d** 80 **p** 81. C Yardley Wood *Birm* 80-83; C Moseley St Mary 83-86; Chapl Cen 13 83-85; V Bartley Green 86-95; P-in-c Hall Green St Pet 95-97; Perm to Offic 00-03; Chapl Birm Children's Hosp NHS Trust from 03; Chapl Birm Heartlands and Solihull NHS Trust from 03. *5 Princethorpe Close, Shirley, Solihull B90 2LP* Tel 0121-243 1336

BALL, Norman. b 41. Liv Univ BA63 Ch Coll Liv CertEd72. Cuddesdon Coll 65. **d** 68 **p** 69. C Broseley w Benthall *Heref* 68-72; Hd RS Christleton High Sch 72-75; V Plemstall w Guilden Sutton *Ches* 75-79; Hd RS Neston Co High Sch 79-94; NSM Dodleston 86-91; NSM Buckley *St As* 91-94; TV Hawarden 94-00; rtd 00; Perm to Offic *St As* from 00. *White Cottage, Lower Mountain Road, Penyffordd, Chester CH4 0EX* Tel (01244) 661132

BALL, Peter Edwin. b 44. Lon Univ BD65 DipEd. Wycliffe Hall Ox 75. **d** 77 **p** 78. C Prescot *Liv* 77-80; R Lawford *Chelmsf* 80-99; RD Harwich 91-96; P-in-c Broomfield 99-04; V from 04. *Broomfield Vicarage, 10 Butlers Close, Chelmsford CM1 7BE* Tel (01245) 440318 E-mail brian@theworboys.freeserve.co.uk

✠**BALL, The Rt Revd Peter John.** b 32. Qu Coll Cam BA54 MA58. Wells Th Coll 54. **d** 56 **p** 57 **c** 77. C Rottingdean *Chich* 56-58; Novice SSM 58-60; CGA from 60; Prior CGA 60-77; Lic to Offic *Birm* 65-66; P-in-c Hoar Cross *Lich* 66-69; Lic to Offic *B & W* 69-77; Suff Bp Lewes *Chich* 77-84; Area Bp Lewes 84-92;

Can and Preb Chich Cathl 78-92; Bp Glouc 92-93; rtd 93; Perm to Offic *B & W* from 01. *Manor Lodge, Aller, Langport TA10 0QN* Tel (01458) 250495

BALL, Canon Peter Prior. b 25. St Jo Coll Ox BA50 MA55. Ridley Hall Cam 51. **d** 53 **p** 54. C Gt Baddow *Chelmsf* 53-56; C Farnborough *Guildf* 56-60; Chapl RN 60-76; Chapl Cannes *Eur* 76-80; Visiting Chapl (Eur & N Africa) ICS 80-86; Eur Rep SOMA UK from 86; rtd 90; Hon Can Malta Cathl *Eur* from 91. *Château d'Azur, 44 Boulevard d'Italie, Monte Carlo MC98000, Monaco* Tel and fax (00377) 93 30 40 19 E-mail pball@monaco.mc

BALL, Canon Peter William. b 30. Worc Coll Ox BA53 MA57. Cuddesdon Coll 53. **d** 55 **p** 56. C Poplar All SS w St Frideswide *Lon* 55-61; V Preston Ascension 61-68; R Shepperton 68-84; RD Staines 72-74; RD Spelthorne 74-83; Preb St Paul's Cathl 76-84; Can Res and Chan 84-90; Perm to Offic *Sarum* from 90; rtd 95. *Whittonedge, Whittonditch Road, Ramsbury, Marlborough SN8 2PX* Tel (01672) 520259 E-mail peterball@fish.co.uk

BALL, Philip John. b 52. Bris Univ BEd75 Ox Univ MTh98. Ripon Coll Cuddesdon 79. **d** 82 **p** 83. C Norton St Mich *Dur* 82-84; C Greenford H Cross *Lon* 84-88; V Hayes St Edm 88-97; AD Hillingdon 94-97; TR Bicester w Bucknell, Caversfield and Launton *Ox* from 97; AD Bicester and Islip from 00. *St Edburg's Vicarage, Victoria Road, Bicester OX26 6PQ* Tel (01869) 253222 Fax 246949 E-mail philipball@lineone.net

BALL, Philip John. b 63. Coll of Ripon & York St Jo BA91. Cranmer Hall Dur 97. **d** 99 **p** 00. C Linthorpe *York* 99-02; C Kingston upon Hull H Trin from 02. *67 Adelaide Street, Hull HU3 2EZ* Tel (01482) 329580 E-mail meandpj@fish.co.uk

BALL, Mrs Rita Enid. b 49. Sheff Univ LLB69. St Alb and Ox Min Course 94. **d** 97 **p** 98. NSM Newbury *Ox* 97-03; R Wantage Downs from 03. *The Rectory, Church Street, East Hendred, Wantage OX12 8LA* Tel (01235) 833235 E-mail ball@totalserve.co.uk

BALL, Roy. *See* BALL, John Roy

BALL, Timothy William. b 60. Trin Coll Bris 96. **d** 96 **p** 97. C Harlow St Mary and St Hugh w St Jo the Bapt *Chelmsf* 96-99; V Springfield H Trin from 99; Ind Chapl from 00. *The Vicarage, 61 Hill Road, Chelmsford CM2 6HW* Tel (01245) 353389 E-mail timmyball@tesco.net

BALL, Vernon. b 34. Ox Min Course 87. **d** 90 **p** 91. NSM Banbury *Ox* 90-99. *20 Springfield Avenue, Banbury OX16 9HT* Tel (01295) 265740

BALLANTINE, Peter Sinclair. b 46. Nottm Univ MTh85. K Coll Lon BA68 AKC68 St Jo Coll Nottm 70 Lon Coll of Div ALCD71 BD73 LTh74. **d** 73 **p** 74. C Rainham *Chelmsf* 73-77; C Wennington 73-77; TV Barton Mills *St E* 77-80; TV Barton Mills, Beck Row w Kenny Hill etc 80-82; Chapl Liv Poly *Liv* 83-86; Tr Officer Rugby Deanery *Cov* 86-97; P-in-c Churchover w Willey 86-97; P-in-c Clifton upon Dunsmore and Newton 86-97; Dir Buckingham Adnry Chr Tr Sch *Ox* 97-02; TV Stantonbury and Willen from 02. *The Rectory, The Green, Great Linford, Milton Keynes MK14 5BD* Tel (01908) 605892 Mobile 07984-902641 E-mail pballarev@aol.com

BALLANTINE, Roderic Keith. b 44. Chich Th Coll 66. **d** 69 **p** 70. C Nunhead St Antony *S'wark* 69-72; C S Hackney St Jo w Ch Ch *Lon* 72-75; P-in-c Kensal Town St Thos w St Andr and St Phil 75-79; V Stoke Newington St Andr from 79. *St Andrew's Vicarage, 106 Bethune Road, London N16 5DU* Tel (020) 8800 2900 E-mail roderic@fish.co.uk

BALLANTYNE, Jane Elizabeth. *See* KENCHINGTON, Mrs Jane Elizabeth Ballantyne

BALLARD, The Ven Andrew Edgar. b 44. Dur Univ BA66. Westcott Ho Cam 66. **d** 68 **p** 69. C St Marylebone St Mary *Lon* 68-72; C Portsea St Mary *Portsm* 72-76; V Haslingden w Haslingden Grane *Blackb* 76-82; V Walkden Moor *Man* 82-93; TR Walkden Moor w Lt Hulton 93-98; Chapl Salford Coll 82-92; AD Farnworth *Man* 90-98; P-in-c Rochdale 98-99; TR 00; Hon Can Man Cathl from 98; Adn Rochdale from 00. *57 Melling Road, Oldham OL4 1PN* Tel 0161-678 1454 Fax 678 1455 E-mail andrew.ballard@virgin.net

BALLARD, Miss Anne Christina. b 54. LRAM76 HonRCM93 ARAM94. Wycliffe Hall Ox 82. **dss** 85 **d** 87 **p** 94. Hove Bp Hannington Memorial Ch *Chich* 85-87; Chapl St Mich Sch Burton Park 87-89; Chapl RCM *Lon* 89-93; Chapl Imp Coll 89-93; Prec Ch Ch *Ox* 93-98; P-in-c Ivinghoe w Pitstone and Slapton 98-03; P-in-c Llanbadarn Fawr, Llandegley and Llanfihangel etc *S & B* from 03. *The Rectory, Rock Road, Crossgates, Llandrindod Wells LD1 6RU* Tel (01597) 851204 Mobile 07958-571914 E-mail annieballard@supanet.com

BALLARD, Charles Martin. b 29. Jes Coll Cam BA52 MA56. **d** 58 **p** 59. C Doncaster St Geo *Sheff* 58-61; V Balne 61-62; rtd 94; Perm to Offic *Ely* 95-00. *35 Abbey Road, Cambridge CB5 8HH*

BALLARD, Duncan Charles John. b 65. Sheff Univ BSc87. St Mich Coll Llan 00. **d** 02 **p** 03. C Worc St Barn w Ch Ch *Worc* from 02. *96 Hollymount, Worcester WR4 9SF* Tel (01905) 29129 E-mail st.marys@virgin.net

BALLARD, Canon Michael Arthur. b 44. Lon Univ BA66. Westcott Ho Cam 68. **d** 70 **p** 71. C Harrow Weald All SS *Lon* 70-73; C Aylesbury *Ox* 73-78; V Eastwood *Chelmsf* 78-90; RD Hadleigh 83-90; R Southchurch H Trin from 90; RD Southend-on-Sea 94-00; Hon Can Chelmsf Cathl from 89. *The Rectory, 8 Pilgrims Close, Southend-on-Sea SS2 4XF* Tel (01702) 466423

BALLARD, Nigel Humphrey. b 48. Linc Th Coll 92. **d** 94 **p** 95. C Old Brumby *Linc* 94; C Bottesford w Ashby 94-97; P-in-c Helpringham w Hale 97-01; rtd 02. *16 Princes Avenue, Hove BN3 4GD* Tel (01273) 202584

BALLARD, Canon Peter James. b 55. SS Hild & Bede Coll Dur BEd78. Sarum & Wells Th Coll 85. **d** 87 **p** 88. C Grantham *Linc* 87-90 and 91; Australia 90; V Lancaster Ch Ch *Blackb* 91-98; RD Lancaster 94-98; Can Res Blackb Cathl and Dioc Dir of Educn from 98. *Wheatfield, 7 Dallas Road, Lancaster LA1 1TN* Tel (01524) 32897 *or* (01254) 54421 Mobile 07970-923141 Fax (01524) 66095 *or* (01254) 699963 E-mail peter.ballard@blackburn.anglican.org

BALLARD, Steven Peter. b 52. Man Univ BA73 MA74 Philipps Univ Marburg DrTheol98. St Steph Ho Ox 76. **d** 78 **p** 79. C Lancaster St Mary *Blackb* 78-81; C Blackpool St Mich 81-84; V Brierfield 84-94; Perm to Offic *Carl* from 95. *1 St Catherines Court, Drovers Lane, Penrith CA11 9EJ* Tel (01768) 890976

BALLENTINE, Ian Clarke. b 46. Aston Univ BSc71 CEng. BTh. **d** 91 **p** 92. C Lurgan St Jo *D & D* 91-95; I Mallusk *Conn* from 95. *The Rectory, 6 Carwood Drive, Glengormley, Newtownabbey BT36 5LP* Tel (028) 9083 3773 *or* tel and fax 9087 9029 E-mail ian_ballentine@bigfoot.com

BALLENTYNE, Mrs Fiona Virginia Grace. b 61. ALAM80 R Holloway Coll Lon BA83 Dur Univ PGCE90. EAMTC 95. **d** 97 **p** 98. NSM Halesworth w Linstead, Chediston, Holton etc *St E* 97-98; C Sole Bay 98-00; Chapl St Felix Sch Southwold 99-00; Chapl HM YOI Castington 00-05; Chapl Northumbria Healthcare NHS Trust 00-05; Chapl HM Pris Sudbury from 05. *Chaplain's Office, HM Prison, Sudbury, Ashbourne DE6 5HW* Tel (01283) 584088 E-mail jvfb27@aol.com

BALLINGER, Francis James. b 43. AKC70. **d** 71 **p** 85. C Weston-super-Mare St Sav *B & W* 71-72; Dir Bd Soc Resp *Leic* 85-88; Hon C Bringhurst w Gt Easton 85-88; TV Melksham *Sarum* 88-93; P-in-c Coughton and Spernall, Morton Bagot and Oldberrow *Cov* 93-98; Dioc Rural Adv 93-98; R Kingstone w Clehonger, Eaton Bishop etc *Heref* 98-03; rtd 04. *4 Broxburn Road, Warminster BA12 8EX* Tel (01985) 300316 E-mail f.ballinger@midnet.com

BALLISTON THICKE, James. *See* THICKE, James Balliston

BALMER, Walter Owen. b 30. N Ord Course 83. **d** 86 **p** 87. NSM Gateacre *Liv* 86-91; NSM Hale 91-00; Perm to Offic from 00. *38 Grangemeadow Road, Liverpool L25 4SU* Tel 0151-421 1189

BALMFORTH, The Ven Anthony James. b 26. BNC Ox BA50 MA51. Linc Th Coll 50. **d** 52 **p** 53. C Mansfield SS Pet and Paul *S'well* 52-55; V Skegby 55-61; V Kidderminster St Jo *Worc* 61-65; V Kings Norton *Birm* 65-72; TR 73-79; RD Kings Norton 73-79; Hon Can Birm Cathl 75-79; Hon Can Bris Cathl *Bris* 79-90; Adn Bris 79-90; rtd 90; Perm to Offic *Glouc* from 90. *Slipper Cottage, Stag Hill, Yorkley, Lydney GL15 4TB* Tel (01594) 564016

BALOGUN, Olusegun Joseph. b 69. Ogun State Univ BSc91 Lagos Univ MSc96. Immanuel Coll Ibadan 96. **d** 98 **p** 99. Nigeria 98-02; C Mansfield St Jo *S'well* from 04. *55 Arun Dale, Mansfield Woodhouse, Mansfield NG19 9RE* Tel (01623) 620803 Mobile 07960-050923 E-mail balogun_stjohns@yahoo.co.uk

BAMBER, David Beverley. b 51. Univ of Wales (Lamp) BA75. St Steph Ho Ox 75. **d** 77 **p** 78. C Altrincham St Geo *Ches* 77-80; C Oxton 80-81; Perm to Offic *Derby* 85-87; C Staveley and Barrow Hill 87-88; C W Retford *S'well* 89-90; C E Retford 89-90 and 91-92. *Address temp unknown*

BAMBER, Patrick Herbert. b 71. Dundee Univ MA93. Wycliffe Hall Ox BTh02. **d** 02 **p** 03. C St Austell *Truro* from 02. *St Luke's House, 5 Penhaligon Way, St Austell PL25 3AR* Tel (01726) 69857 E-mail patrick_bamber@onetel.net

BAMBER, Ms Sheila Jane. b 54. Univ of Wales (Lamp) BA75 Sheff Univ MA77 Open Univ MBA94. Ripon Coll Cuddesdon 96. **d** 98 **p** 99. C Dur St Cuth *Dur* 98-01; C Sacriston and Kimblesworth 01-02; TV Dur N from 02; Dioc Dir of Educn from 04. *The Vicarage, 8 Woodland Close, Bearpark, Durham DH7 7EB* Tel 0191-373 3886 Mobile 07989-542565

BAMBERG, Robert William. b 43. Chu Coll Cam BA65 PGCE68. SW Minl Tr Course 98. **d** 01 **p** 02. NSM Kingsteignton *Ex* from 01. *11 Portland Avenue, Teignmouth TQ14 8RR* Tel (01626) 773711 E-mail sllbmbrg@aol.com

BAMFORD, Geoffrey Belk. b 35. Lon Univ BA57 Leic Coll of Educn PGCE58. Dioc OLM tr scheme 97. **d** 99 **p** 00. OLM Upper Holme Valley *Wakef* from 99. *11 Flushouse, Holmbridge, Holmfirth HD9 2QY* Tel (01484) 682532 E-mail judibamford@supanet.com

BAMFORD, Mrs Marion. b 35. K Coll Lon BA56 AKC56. N Ord Course 81. **dss** 84 **d** 90 **p** 94. Baildon *Bradf* 84-85; S Kirkby *Wakef* 85-90; Dn-in-c Brotherton 90-94; P-in-c 94-96; Chapl Pontefract Gen Infirmary 89-96; rtd 96; Perm to Offic

Wakef 96-97 and from 98; *Bradf* from 96. *170 Warren Lane, Eldwick, Bingley BD16 3BY* Tel (01274) 564925

BAMFORTH, Marvin John. b 48. N Ord Course 78. **d** 81 **p** 82. C Barnoldswick w Bracewell *Bradf* 81-84; V Cullingworth 84-88; New Zealand 88-89; V Thornton in Lonsdale w Burton in Lonsdale *Bradf* 89-98; Dioc Chapl MU 91-94; P-in-c Bentham St Jo 93-98; Cyprus from 98. *The Anglican Church of Paphos, PO Box 61083, 8130 Paphos, Cyprus* Tel (00357) (26) 952486

BAMFORTH, Stuart Michael. b 35. Hertf Coll Ox BA58 MA61. Sarum Th Coll 60. **d** 62 **p** 63. C Adel *Ripon* 62-67; V Hempton and Pudding Norton *Nor* 67-71; V Toftrees w Shereford 67-71; P-in-c Pensthorpe 67-71; P-in-c Colkirk 69-70; Lic to Offic *Derby* 72-77 and *Ripon* from 77; rtd 95; Perm to Offic *York* from 01. *52 Beverley Road, Market Weighton, York YO43 3JP* Tel (01430) 874105

BANBURY, David Paul. b 62. Coll of Ripon & York St Jo BA84. Ridley Hall Cam 85. **d** 88 **p** 89. C Blackb St Jas *Blackb* 88-90; C Preston St Cuth 90-95; P-in-c Bradf St Clem *Bradf* 95-00; V 00; CPAS Evang from 01; Perm to Offic *Cov* from 01. *6 Kingland Drive, Leamington Spa CV32 6BL* Tel (01926) 771097 *or* 458458 E-mail david@cpas.org.uk

BANDAWE, Mrs Christine. b 57. N Ord Course 01. **d** 04 **p** 05. C Middleton St Mary *Ripon* from 04. *43 Moor Flatts Avenue, Leeds LS10 3SS* Tel 0113-270 2643

BANDS, Canon Leonard Michael. b 40. Rhodes Univ BA64. St Paul's Coll Grahamstown. **d** 69 **p** 70. C Uitenhage S Africa 69-72; R Alexandria 72-75; Chapl Rhodes Univ 75-80; Chapl Dioc Sch for Girls Grahamstown 80-86; Chapl Dioc Coll Cape Town 87-94; Dean Bloemfontein 94-02; C Lockerbie *Glas* from 03; C Moffat from 03. *The Rectory, Ashgrove Terrace, Lockerbie DG11 2BQ* Tel and fax (01576) 202484 Mobile 07755-341094 E-mail michaelbands@whsmithnet.co.uk

BANFIELD, Andrew Henry. b 48. AKC71. St Aug Coll Cant 72. **d** 73 **p** 74. C Crayford *Roch* 73-76; Youth Chapl *Glouc* 77-89; Soc Services Development Officer Glos Co Coun from 89; Perm to Offic from 02. *Address temp unknown*

BANFIELD, The Ven David John. b 33. ALCD56. **d** 57 **p** 58. C Middleton *Man* 57-62; Chapl Scargill Ho 62-65; Asst Warden 65-67; V Addiscombe St Mary *Cant* 67-80; V Luton St Mary *St Alb* 80-90; Hon Can St Alb 89-90; RD Luton 89-90; Adn Bris 90-98; Hon Can Bris Cathl 90-98; rtd 98; Perm to Offic *Bris* from 98. *47 Avon Way, Stoke Bishop, Bristol BS9 1SL* Tel 0117-968 4227

BANGAY, Edward Newman. b 37. CQSW75. New Coll Lon BD60. **d** 98 **p** 98. NSM Yeovil w Kingston Pitney *B & W* 98-02; Chapl E Somerset NHS Trust 98-02; Perm to Offic *B & W* from 02. *Castle Cottage, Main Street, Mudford, Yeovil BA21 5TE* Tel (01935) 850452

BANGAY (formerly REAST), Mrs Eileen Joan. b 40. Open Univ BA93. EMMTC 81. **dss** 84 **d** 87 **p** 94. Linc St Mary-le-Wigford w St Benedict etc *Linc* 80-90; C 87-90; C Stamford All SS w St Jo 90-93; NSM Walesby 93-95; P-in-c Sutton Bridge 95-00; V 00; RD Elloe E 99-00; rtd 01; Perm to Offic *Linc* from 01. *7 Chesham Drive, Baston, Peterborough PE6 9QW* Tel (01778) 560327

BANGLADESH, Moderator of the Church of. *See* BAROI, The Rt Revd Michael

BANGOR, Archdeacon of. *See* WILLIAMS, The Ven Meurig Llwyd

BANGOR, Bishop of. *See* CROCKETT, The Rt Revd Phillip Anthony

BANGOR, Dean of. *See* HAWKINS, The Very Revd Alun John

BANISTER, Desmond Peter. b 52. K Coll Lon BA75 AKC75. St Alb and Ox Min Course 02. **d** 05. Hd Master Quainton Hall Sch Harrow from 98; NSM Hatch End St Anselm *Lon* from 05. *14 Tazewell Court, Bath Road, Reading RG1 6HQ* Tel 0118-959 4192 *or* (020) 8427 5619 E-mail dpbanister@uk2.net

BANISTER, Jane Catherine. b 67. Man Univ BA90 Anglia Poly Univ BA96. Westcott Ho Cam 94. **d** 97 **p** 98. C Addington *S'wark* 97-00; C Wisley w Pyrford *Guildf* 00-02; Lic to Offic *St Alb* from 03. *The Vicarage, Station Road, Aldbury, Tring HP23 5RS* Tel (01442) 851200 E-mail jbanister@fish.co.uk

BANISTER, Canon Martin John. b 39. Worc Coll Ox BA62 MA68. Chich Th Coll 62. **d** 64 **p** 65. C Wellingborough All Hallows *Pet* 64-67; C Heene *Chich* 67-70; V Denford w Ringstead *Pet* 70-78; P-in-c Wilshamstead *St Alb* 78-80; P-in-c Houghton Conquest 78-80; V Wilshamstead and Houghton Conquest 80-89; RD Elstow 86-89; V Waltham Cross 89-04; RD Cheshunt 00-04; Hon Can St Alb 03-04; rtd 04; Perm to Offic *St Alb* from 04. *35 Cottonmill Lane, St Albans AL1 2BT* Tel (01727) 847082

BANKS, Aleck George. b 18. Lon Univ BD42 AKC42. **d** 42 **p** 43. C Colchester St Jas, All SS, St Nic and St Runwald *Chelmsf* 42-45; C Leigh St Clem 45-51; V Bradfield 51-56; PC Becontree St Geo 56-61; V S Benfleet 61-83; rtd 83; Perm to Offic *Chelmsf* from 83 and *St E* from 85. *5 Gosford Close, Clare, Sudbury CO10 8PT* Tel (01787) 277088

BANKS, Allen James. b 48. Carl and Blackb Dioc Tr Inst 98. **d** 01 **p** 02. OLM Kells *Carl* from 01. *36 Basket Road, Whitehaven CA28 9AH* Tel (01946) 61470

BANKS, Brian William Eric. b 35. Lon Univ BD69 Birm Univ DPS70 Open Univ BA94. Wycliffe Hall Ox 63. **d** 65 **p** 66. C Swindon Ch Ch *Bris* 65-68; C Halesowen *Worc* 68-71; R Wychbold and Upton Warren 71-77; V Bengeworth 77-87; RD Evesham 81-87; R Freshwater *Portsm* 87-00; R Yarmouth 95-00; rtd 00; Perm to Offic *Sarum* from 01. *Candleford, 16 Malthouse Meadow, Portesham, Weymouth DT3 4NS* Tel (01305) 871126

BANKS, Mrs Dawn. b 56. Carl and Blackb Dioc Tr Inst 01. **d** 04 **p** 05. OLM Preesall *Blackb* 04-05; OLM Waterside Par from 05. *Squires Gate Farm, Head Dyke Lane, Pilling, Preston PR3 6SD* Tel (01253) 790250

BANKS, Geoffrey Alan. b 43. St Andr Univ MA66. N Ord Course 84. **d** 87 **p** 88. NSM Shelley and Shepley *Wakef* 87-89; C Halifax 89-91; V Holmfield 91-98; TV Upper Holme Valley from 98. *The Vicarage, Ash Grove Road, Holmfirth HD9 3JR* Tel (01484) 683131 E-mail geoff@banksvicarage.fsnet.co.uk

BANKS, John Alan. b 32. Hertf Coll Ox BA54 MA58. Westcott Ho Cam 56. **d** 58 **p** 59. C Warsop *S'well* 58-61; C Ox St Aldate w H Trin *Ox* 61-64; V Ollerton *S'well* 64-75; V Boughton 64-75; R Wollaton 75-83; RD Beeston 77-81; Lic to Offic 83-85; C Bramcote 85-86; C Arnold 86-95; rtd 95; Perm to Offic *S'well* from 95. *247 Oxclose Lane, Nottingham NG5 6FB* Tel 0115-926 6814

BANKS, Michael Lawrence. b 40. Open Univ BA72 Brunel Univ MA82. Westcott Ho Cam 84. **d** 86 **p** 87. C Cheshunt *St Alb* 86-89; Chapl HM Pris Blundeston 89-90; V Leagrave *St Alb* 90-94; V Hatfield Hyde 95-01; rtd 01; Perm to Offic *Nor* 01-03; P-in-c Barningham w Matlaske w Baconsthorpe etc 03-05. *Quarndon, Post Office Lane, Saxthorpe, Norwich NR11 7BL* Tel (01263) 587319 E-mail mbanks@tiscali.co.uk

BANKS, Canon Michael Thomas Harvey. b 35. Ushaw Coll Dur 58 Open Univ BA75. **d** 63 **p** 64. In RC Ch 63-69; C Winlaton *Dur* 69-71; P-in-c Bishopwearmouth Gd Shep 71-75; TV Melton Mowbray w Thorpe Arnold *Leic* 75-80; TR Loughborough Em 80-88; Dir of Ords 83-97; Hon Can Leic Cathl 83-87; Can Res and Chan 87-03; Assoc P Christianity S 93-95; Hon C Leic H Spirit 01-03; rtd 03; Perm to Offic *Glouc* from 04. *Harvard House, 7 Harvard Close, Moreton-in-Marsh GL56 0JT* Tel (01608) 650706

BANKS, Norman. b 54. Oriel Coll Ox BA76 MA80. St Steph Ho Ox 79. **d** 82 **p** 83. C Newc Ch Ch w St Ann *Newc* 82-87; P-in-c 87-90; V Tynemouth Cullercoats St Paul 90-00; V Walsingham, Houghton and Barsham *Nor* from 00. *The Vicarage, Church Street, Walsingham NR22 6BL* Tel (01328) 821316

BANKS, Philip Charles. b 61. NE Lon Poly BSc85 Nottm Univ BTh93 MRICS87. Linc Th Coll 90. **d** 93 **p** 94. C Chelmsf Ascension *Chelmsf* 93-94; C Brentwood St Thos 94-98; P-in-c Elmstead 98-03; V Coggeshall w Markshall from 03; Bp's Press Officer from 97; Bp's Dom Chapl 01-04. *The Vicarage, 4 Church Green, Coggeshall, Colchester CO6 1UD* Tel (01376) 561234 Mobile 07798-681886 E-mail pbanks@chelmsford.anglican.org

BANKS, Stephen John. b 65. Newc Univ BSc87. St Jo Coll Nottm MA96 DipMM97. **d** 97 **p** 98. C Sheldon *Birm* 97-00; P-in-c Austrey and Warton from 00; AD Polesworth from 02. *The Vicarage, 132 Main Road, Austrey, Atherstone CV9 3EB* Tel (01827) 839022 E-mail sbanks.home@ukgateway.net

BANKS, Susan Angela. *See* GRIFFITHS, Mrs Susan Angela

BANNARD-SMITH, Dennis Ronald. b 22. Birm Univ BSc42. St Alb Minl Tr Scheme 80. **d** 83 **p** 84. NSM Pavenham *St Alb* 83-88; NSM Odell and Pavenham 88-92; Perm to Offic from 92. *Goodly Heritage, 10 The Bury, Pavenham, Bedford MK43 7PX* Tel (01234) 822992

BANNER, John William. b 36. Open Univ BA78. Tyndale Hall Bris 61. **d** 64 **p** 65. C Bootle St Leon *Liv* 64-66; C Wigan St Jas 66-69; C Stapleton *Bris* 69-70; Australia 70-72; V Liv Ch Ch Norris Green *Liv* 72-82; V Tunbridge Wells H Trin w Ch Ch *Roch* from 82. *The Vicarage, 63 Claremont Road, Tunbridge Wells TN1 1TE* Tel (01892) 526644 Fax 529300 E-mail crossandcrown@compuserve.com

BANNER, Prof Michael Charles. b 61. Ball Coll Ox BA83 MA86 DPhil87. **d** 86 **p** 87. Fell St Pet Coll Ox 85-88; Dean Peterho Cam 88-94; Prof Moral and Soc Th K Coll Lon 94-05; NSM Balsham, Weston Colville, W Wickham etc *Ely* from 01. *Address temp unknown*

BANNISTER, Preb Anthony Peter. b 40. Ex Univ BA62. Clifton Th Coll 63. **d** 65 **p** 66. C Uphill *B & W* 65-69; C Hove Bp Hannington Memorial Ch *Chich* 69-74; V Wembdon *B & W* 74-91; Youth Chapl 80-83; RD Bridgwater 80-89; V Taunton St Jas 91-05; Preb Wells Cathl 97-05; rtd 05. *Ashe House Cottage, Ashe House, Ashe, Basingstoke RG25 3AQ* Tel (01256) 770039 E-mail apbannister@tiscali.co.uk

BANNISTER, Clifford John. b 53. Hatf Coll Dur BA76. Ripon Coll Cuddesdon 84. **d** 86 **p** 87. C Weymouth H Trin *Sarum* 86-89; TV Basingstoke *Win* 89-94; V Hedge End St Jo from 94. *The Vicarage, Vicarage Drive, Hedge End, Southampton SO30 4DU* Tel (01489) 782288 E-mail cliff.bannister@fish.co.uk

BANNISTER, Grattan Eric McGillycuddy Colm Brendon. TCD BA50 MA53. **d** 52 **p** 57. C Rainbow Hill St Barn *Worc* 57-58; C

Cork St Luke *C, C & R* 61-63; P-in-c Schull 63-75; rtd 75. *Ballydehob, Co Cork, Irish Republic*

BANNISTER, John Leslie. b 55. Lanc Univ MA99. Carl and Blackb Dioc Tr Inst 95. **d** 98 **p** 99. C Flimby and Netherton *Carl* 98-00; C Whitehaven 00-02; TV 02-04; TR from 04. *The Rectory, Autumn Garth, Harras Road, Harras Moor, Whitehaven CA28 6SG* Tel (01946) 693474 Mobile 07788-562488 E-mail johnlbannister@onetel.com

BANNISTER, Lesley. b 30. **d** 99 **p** 00. OLM Gt Cornard *St E* from 99. *58 Broom Street, Great Cornard, Sudbury CO10 0JT* Tel (01787) 372889

BANNISTER, Peter. *See* BANNISTER, Preb Anthony Peter

BANNISTER, Peter Edward. b 38. Leeds Univ BSc60. Linc Th Coll 72. **d** 74 **p** 75. C Norbury St Steph *Cant* 74-77; C Allington and Maidstone St Pet 77-80; R Temple Ewell w Lydden 80-86; TV Bracknell *Ox* 86-93; P-in-c Swallowfield 93-03; rtd 03. *15 Ryeland Street, Cross Hills, Keighley BD20 8SR* Tel (01535) 636036 E-mail peter.bannister@virgin.net

BANNISTER-PARKER, Mrs Charlotte. b 63. Trevelyan Coll Dur BA84 Dur Univ MA92 Middx Univ BA05. Westmr Past Foundn 00. **d** 05. NSM Ox St Mary V w St Cross and St Pet *Ox* from 05. *8 Belbroughton Road, Oxford OX2 6UZ* Tel (01865) 512252 E-mail charlotte@thegbps.co.uk

BANTING, David Percy. b 51. Magd Coll Cam MA74. Wycliffe Hall Ox MA79. **d** 80 **p** 81. C Ox St Ebbe w H Trin and St Pet *Ox* 80-83; Min St Jos Merry Hill CD *Lich* 83-90; V Chadderton Ch Ch *Man* 90-98; V Harold Wood *Chelmsf* from 98. *The Vicarage, 15 Athelstan Road, Harold Wood, Romford RM3 0QB* Tel (01708) 376400 *or* 342080 E-mail office@stpetersharoldwood.org

BANTING, The Ven Kenneth Mervyn Lancelot Hadfield. b 37. Pemb Coll Cam BA61 MA65. Cuddesdon Coll 64. **d** 65 **p** 66. Asst Chapl Win Coll 65-70; C Leigh Park *Portsm* 70-72; TV Hemel Hempstead *St Alb* 73-79; V Goldington 79-88; P-in-c Renhold 80-82; RD Bedford 84-87; V Portsea St Cuth *Portsm* 88-96; RD Portsm 94-96; Hon Can Portsm Cathl 95-96; Adn Is of Wight 96-03; Can Res Portsm Cathl 02-03; rtd 03; Perm to Offic *Portsm* from 03. *Furzend, 38A Bosham Hoe, Bosham PO18 8ET* Tel (01243) 572340 E-mail merlin.banting@fish.co.uk

BANYARD, Douglas Edward. b 21. S'wark Ord Course 69. **d** 71 **p** 72. NSM Selsdon St Jo w St Fran *Cant* 71-77; Perm to Offic *Portsm* from 77; Perm to Offic *Chich* from 77. *22 Lower Wardown, Petersfield GU31 4NY* Tel (01730) 261004

BANYARD, Michael George. b 47. Ch Ch Coll Cant CertEd69 Birm Univ BPhil79 Open Univ MA92. Westcott Ho Cam 01. **d** 03 **p** 04. NSM Chippenham *Ely* from 03. *The Vicarage, High Street, Chippenham, Ely CB7 5PP* Tel (01638) 721616 E-mail banyardmg1@yahoo.co.uk

BANYARD, Peter Vernon. b 35. Sarum Th Coll 57. **d** 59 **p** 60. C Southampton Maybush St Pet *Win* 59-63; C Tilbury Docks *Chelmsf* 63-65; Miss to Seamen 63-65; Namibia 65-68; V Chesterfield St Aug *Derby* 68-74; TV Grantham w Manthorpe *Linc* 74-78; TV Grantham 78-79; Chapl Warminster Sch 79-85; V Hykeham *Linc* 85-88; rtd 88; Perm to Offic *Linc* from 88. *56 Western Avenue, Lincoln LN6 7SY* Tel and fax (01522) 829026 E-mail ppbanyard@hotmail.com

BANYARD (or BRUNSKILL), Canon Sheila Kathryn. b 53. Univ of Wales (Ban) BA75 K Coll Lon MA83 Ox Univ MTh99. Cranmer Hall Dur 76. **dss** 82 **d** 92 **p** 94. Sunbury *Lon* 82-85; Asst Chapl Ch Hosp Horsham 85-90; Chapl Malvern Girls' Coll 90-95; TV Droitwich Spa *Worc* 95-00; TR from 00; RD Droitwich 99-02; Hon Can Worc Cathl from 03. *The Rectory, 205 Worcester Road, Droitwich WR9 8AS* Tel and fax (01905) 773134 *or* tel 794952 E-mail sk.banyard@virgin.net *or* droitwich.parish@virgin.net

✠**BARAHONA, The Most Revd Martin de Jesus.** **c** 92. Bp El Salvador from 92; Primate Cen America from 02. *47 Avenida Sur, 723 Col Flor Blanca, Apt Postal (01), 274 San Salvador, El Salvador* Tel (00503) 223 2252 *or* 224 6136 Fax 223 7952 E-mail anglican@saltel.net

BARBER, Ann. *See* BARBER, Mrs Margaret Ann

BARBER, Ms Annabel Ruth. b 58. Leeds Univ BSc80. NEOC 01. **d** 04 **p** 05. C Scawby, Redbourne and Hibaldstow *Linc* from 04. *The Rectory, Church Road, Waddingham, Gainsborough DN21 4ST* Tel (01673) 818551

BARBER, Charles William Walters. b 60. Pemb Coll Cam BA81 MA85. Wycliffe Hall Ox 83. **d** 86 **p** 87. C Wolverhampton St Matt *Lich* 86-90; C Hornsey Rise Whitehall Park Team *Lon* 90-94; Sub Chapl HM Pris Holloway 95; V Bowling St Steph *Bradf* 96-04. *Address temp uknown*

BARBER, Canon Christopher Albert. b 33. Ch Coll Cam BA53 MA57. Coll of Resurr Mirfield 56. **d** 58 **p** 59. C Cov St Pet *Cov* 58-61; C Stokenchurch and Cadmore End *Ox* 61-64; V Royton St Paul *Man* 64-70; V Stapleford *Ely* 70-80; RD Shelford 76-80; V Cherry Hinton St Andr 80-88; Hon Can Ely Cathl 88-98; R Cottenham 88-92; RD N Stowe 90-92; V Terrington St John 92-98; V Tilney All Saints 92-98; rtd 98; Perm to Offic *Ely* from 98; Asst Rtd Clergy and Clergy Widow(er)s' Officer from 00. *20 King Edgar Close, Ely CB6 1DP* Tel (01353) 612338

BARBER, Craig John Francis. b 71. STETS 98. **d** 02 **p** 03. NSM Brighton St Bart *Chich* 02-03; C Brighton St Geo w St Anne and St Mark from 03. *28 Henley Road, Brighton BN2 5NA* Tel (01273) 687420

BARBER, Garth Antony. b 48. Southn Univ BSc69 Lon Univ MSc79 FRAS MSOSc. St Jo Coll Nottm. **d** 76 **p** 77. C Hounslow H Trin *Lon* 76-79; Chapl City of Lon Poly 79-86; P-in-c Twickenham All Hallows 86-97; Chapl Richmond Coll 87-97; Chapl UEA *Nor* 97-02; P-in-c Kingswood *S'wark* from 02. *The Vicarage, Woodland Way, Kingswood, Tadworth KT20 6NW* Tel (01737) 832164 E-mail garth.barber@virgin.net

BARBER, Geoffrey Thomas. b 23. Univ of Wales (Lamp) BA51. Ridley Hall Cam 51. **d** 53 **p** 54. C Walthamstow St Mary *Chelmsf* 53-55; C Woking St Pet *Guildf* 56-57; V Chelsea St Jo *Lon* 57-66; V Rushden St Pet 66-75; V Leyton Em *Chelmsf* 75-81; rtd 81; Perm to Offic *Sarum* from 81. *22 Longacre Drive, Ferndown BH22 9EE* Tel (01202) 873626

BARBER, Hilary John. b 65. Aston Tr Scheme 92 Sarum Th Coll 94. **d** 96 **p** 97. C Moston St Jo *Man* 96-00; Adnry Liturg Adv from 98; R Chorlton-cum-Hardy St Clem from 00. *The Rectory, 6 Edge Lane, Manchester M21 9JF* Tel 0161-881 3063 E-mail barberhilary@hotmail.com

BARBER, John Eric Michael. b 30. Wycliffe Hall Ox 63. **d** 65 **p** 66. C Lupset *Wakef* 65-68; C Halifax St Jo Bapt 68-70; V Dewsbury St Matt and St Jo 70-80; V Perry Common *Birm* 80-95; rtd 95; Perm to Offic *Sarum* from 95. *21A Westhill Road, Weymouth DT4 9NB* Tel (01305) 786553

BARBER, Mrs Margaret Ann. b 31. GTCL52. Dalton Ho Bris 55 Sarum & Wells Th Coll 82. **dss** 83 **d** 87 **p** 94. Wimborne Minster and Holt *Sarum* 83-90; Par Dn 87-90; rtd 90; Hon Par Dn Hampreston *Sarum* 90-94; Hon C 94-02; Perm to Offic from 02. *22 Longacre Drive, Ferndown BH22 9EE* Tel (01202) 873626

BARBER, Martin John. b 35. Univ Coll Lon BA61. Linc Th Coll 61. **d** 63 **p** 64. C Stepney St Dunstan and All SS *Lon* 63-67; Chapl K Sch Bruton 67-93; rtd 93; Perm to Offic *B & W* from 93. *1 Plox Green, Bruton BA10 0EY* Tel (01749) 812290

BARBER, Michael. *See* BARBER, John Eric Michael

BARBER, Michael. b 40. Open Univ BA83. Oak Hill Th Coll 69. **d** 71 **p** 72. C Rothley *Leic* 71-74; C Leic Martyrs 74-76; V Queniborough 76-82; V Monkwearmouth All SS *Dur* 82-92; V Mirehouse *Carl* 92-05; rtd 05. *Allonby, 23 Victoria Park, Kirkcudbright DG6 4EN* Tel (01946) 693565

BARBER, Neil Andrew Austin. b 63. Ealing Coll of Educn BA85. NTMTC 94. **d** 98 **p** 98. St Mary's Chr Workers' Trust from 95; NSM Eastrop *Win* 98-01; V Normanton *Derby* from 01. *St Giles's Vicarage, 16 Browning Street, Derby DE23 8DN* Tel (01332) 767483 E-mail neil.barber@stgiles-derby.org.uk

✠**BARBER, The Rt Revd Paul Everard.** b 35. St Jo Coll Cam BA58 MA66. Wells Th Coll 58. **d** 60 **p** 61 **c** 89. C Westborough *Guildf* 60-66; V York Town St Mich 66-73; V Bourne 73-80; RD Farnham 74-79; Hon Can Guildf Cathl 80-89; Adn Surrey 80-89; Suff Bp Brixworth *Pet* 89-01; Can Pet Cathl 89-01; rtd 01; Hon Asst Bp B & W from 01. *Hillside, 41 Somerton Road, Street BA16 0DR* Tel (01458) 442916

BARBER, Philip Kenneth. b 43. St Jo Coll Dur BA65 Sheff Univ DipEd66. NW Ord Course 74. **d** 76 **p** 77. NSM Burscough Bridge *Liv* 76-84; Asst Master Ormskirk Gr Sch 76-84; P-in-c Brigham *Carl* 84-85; V 85-89; P-in-c Mosser 84-85; V 85-89; P-in-c Borrowdale 89-94; Chapl Keswick Sch 89-94; P-i-c Beetham and Educn Adv *Carl* 94-99; P-in-c Brampton and Farlam and Castle Carrock w Cumrew 99-02; P-in-c Irthington, Crosby-on-Eden and Scaleby 99-02; P-in-c Hayton w Cumwhitton 99-02; TR Eden, Gelt and Irthing 02-04; rtd 04; Perm to Offic *Carl* from 04 and *Blackb* from 05. *18 Holbeck Avenue, Morecambe LA4 6NP* Tel (01524) 401695 E-mail pbarber@crowdenlea.demon.co.uk

BARBER, Ralph Warwick. b 72. Lon Guildhall Univ BA94. Ripon Coll Cuddesdon 03. **d** 05. C Newquay *Truro* from 05. *127 Penmere Drive, Newquay TR7 1NS* Tel 07855-414421 (mobile) E-mail fatherralph@hotmail.co.uk

BARBER, Royston Henry. b 38. Univ of Wales (Abth) BD86. United Th Coll Abth 83. **d** 86 **p** 87. NSM Tywyn w Aberdyfi *Ban* 86-92; NSM Cannington, Otterhampton, Combwich and Stockland *B & W* 93-98; Perm to Offic *B & W* from 98 and *Ex* from 00. *Brambledown, Silver Street, Culmstock, Cullompton EX15 3JE* Tel (01884) 841041

BARBER, Sheila. b 50. N Ord Course 96. **d** 99 **p** 00. C Dinnington *Sheff* 99-02; V Woodhouse St Jas from 02. *St James's Vicarage, 65 Cardwell Avenue, Sheffield S13 7XB* Tel 0114-269 4146 E-mail gannow@olas.go-plus.net

BARBOUR, Mrs Jennifer Louise. b 32. JP67. Barrister-at-Law 55 St Hugh's Coll Ox BA54 MA57. Gilmore Course 80. **dss** 81 **d** 87 **p** 94. Bray and Braywood *Ox* 81-84; Hermitage and Hampstead Norreys, Cold Ash etc 84-87; Chapl Leeds Poly *Ripon* 87-92; Chapl Leeds Metrop Univ 92-95; rtd 95; NSM Shipton Moyne w Westonbirt and Lasborough *Glouc* 95-99; Perm to Offic *Bris* from 95; *Glouc* from 99; *Cov* and *Worc* from 00. *Cheriton, Aston Road, Chipping Campden GL55 6HR* Tel (01386) 840279

BARBOUR, Walter Iain. b 28. FICE65 Pemb Coll Cam BA48 MA53. Ox NSM Course 78. **d** 81 **p** 82. NSM Bray and Braywood *Ox* 81-84; NSM Thatcham 84-87; TV Moor Allerton *Ripon* 87-95; rtd 95; NSM Shipton Moyne w Westonbirt and Lasborough *Glouc* 95-98; Perm to Offic *Bris* from 95; *Glouc* 98-01; *Cov* and *Worc* from 00. *Cheriton, Aston Road, Chipping Campden GL55 6HR* Tel (01386) 840279

BARBY, Canon Sheana Braidwood. b 38. Bedf Coll Lon BA59. EMMTC 81. **dss** 84 **d** 87 **p** 94. Derby St Paul *Derby* 84-87; NSM Derby Cathl 87-03; Dioc Dir of Ords 90-97; Par Educn Adv 93-01; rtd 03; Hon Can Derby Cathl *Derby* from 96; RD Derby N 00-05. *2 Margaret Street, Derby DE1 3FE* Tel (01332) 383301 E-mail sheana@barbyr.freeserve.co.uk

BARCLAY, Ian Newton. b 33. Clifton Th Coll 58. **d** 61 **p** 62. C Cullompton *Ex* 61-63; C Ashill w Broadway *B & W* 63-66; V Chatham St Phil and St Jas *Roch* 66-69; C St Helen Bishopsgate w St Martin Outwich *Lon* 70-73; V Prestonville St Luke *Chich* 73-81; Lic to Offic 82-93; rtd 93; P-in-c Cannes *Eur* 98-02. *35 Marine Avenue, Hove BN3 4LH* E-mail barclaycan@compuserve.com

BARCLAY, Mrs Susan Molly. Wycliffe Hall Ox. **d** 87 **p** 99. Hon Par Dn March St Wendreda *Ely* 87-96; Tutor Past Studies Ridley Hall Cam from 96. *42 Greystoke Road, Cambridge CB1 8DS* Tel (01223) 246877 *or* 741058 E-mail sue.barclay@btopenworld.com

BARCROFT, Ambrose William Edgar. b 17. TCD BA40 MA46. TCD Div Sch Div Test41. **d** 41 **p** 42. C Drumachose *D & R* 41-46; Chapl RN 46-70; R Pitlochry *St And* 70-82; rtd 82; Perm to Offic *St And* from 82. *Farragon, The Terrace, Bridge of Tilt, Pitlochry PH18 5SZ* Tel (01796) 481691

BARCROFT, Ian David. b 60. UMIST BSc83 Edin Univ BD88 Glas Univ MTh01. Edin Th Coll 85. **d** 88 **p** 89. Prec St Ninian's Cathl Perth *St And* 88-92; Min Perth St Ninian 88-92; P-in-c Aberdeen St Clem *Ab* 92-97; R Hamilton *Glas* from 97. *The Rectory, 4C Auchingramont Road, Hamilton ML3 6JT* Tel and fax (01698) 429895 E-mail ian.barcroft@btopenworld.com

BARD, Canon Christopher Frederick Jesse. b 52. AKC75 Open Univ BA88. St Aug Coll Cant 75. **d** 76 **p** 77. C Billingham St Cuth *Dur* 76-79; C Egglescliffe and Chapl to Arts and Recreation *York* and *Dur* 79-81; P-in-c Epping Upland *Chelmsf* 81-95; Dioc Communications Officer 81-91; BBC Essex Relig Progs Producer from 89; TV Epping Distr from 95; Hon Can Chelmsf Cathl from 03. *The Vicarage, Epping Green, Epping CM16 6PN* Tel (01992) 572949 Fax 578892 E-mail chrisbard@hotmail.com *or* chris.bard@bbc.co.uk

BARDELL, Alan George. City Univ BSc. Guildf Dioc Min Course 89. **d** 92 **p** 93. OLM Addlestone *Guildf* from 92. *14 Dickens Drive, Addlestone KT15 1AW* Tel (01932) 847574

BARDELL, Terence Richard. b 51. **d** 01 **p** 02. OLM Coningsby w Tattershall *Linc* 01-05; C Gt Grimsby St Mary and St Jas from 05. *62A Brighowgate, Grimsby DN32 0QW*

BARDSLEY, Warren Nigel Antony. b 52. AKC74. St Aug Coll Cant 74. **d** 75 **p** 76. C Leeds St Aid *Ripon* 75-78; C Cov St Jo *Cov* 78-80; P-in-c Stoke Golding w Dadlington *Leic* 80-89; TV Swinton and Pendlebury *Man* 90-94. *Orchard House, 22 Upper Olland Street, Bungay NR35 1BH* Tel (01986) 895760

BARDWELL, Mrs Elaine Barbara. b 60. K Coll Lon BA81 AKC81. St Steph Ho Ox BA85 MA90. **dss** 86 **d** 87 **p** 95. Heref H Trin *Heref* 86-89; C 87-89; Dir Past Studies St Steph Ho Ox 89-96; V New Marston *Ox* from 96; AD Cowley from 02. *The Vicarage, 8 Jack Straws Lane, Headington, Oxford OX3 0DL* Tel (01865) 434340 E-mail elaine.bardwell@virgin.net

BARDWELL, John Edward. b 53. Jes Coll Cam BA75 MA79 Ox Univ BA85 MA90. St Steph Ho Ox 83. **d** 86 **p** 87. C Heref H Trin *Heref* 86-89; Perm to Offic *Ox* 90-96. *The Vicarage, 8 Jack Straws Lane, Headington, Oxford OX3 0DL* Tel (01865) 434340

BAREHAM, Miss Sylvia Alice. b 36. Hockerill Coll Cam CertEd59 Open Univ BA83 Ox Univ DipEd84. Ox Min Course 86. **d** 89 **p** 94. NSM N Leigh *Ox* 89-93; NSM Bampton w Clanfield 93-95; NSM Kedington *St E* 95-97; NSM Hundon w Barnardiston 95-97; NSM Haverhill w Withersfield, the Wrattings etc 95-97; NSM Stourhead from 97; Perm to Offic *Chelmsf* from 05. *St Mary's Cottage, Little Wratting, Haverhill CB9 7UQ* Tel (01440) 762303

BARFF, John Robert. b 43. Ch Coll Cam BA66 MA70 K Coll Lon MTh69. ALCD68. **d** 69 **p** 70. C Fulham St Mary N End *Lon* 69-73; CMS 73-83; Sudan 75-83; P-in-c Pilning *Bris* 83-85; P-in-c Compton Greenfield 83-85; V Pilning w Compton Greenfield 85-92; rtd 92; Perm to Offic *Bris* from 92. *10 Cote Park, Bristol BS9 2AD* Tel 0117-968 5889

BARFORD, Patricia Ann. b 47. Univ of Wales (Cardiff) BSc68 PhD73. WMMTC 95. **d** 98 **p** 99. NSM Stoke Prior, Wychbold and Upton Warren *Worc* 98-05; C Redditch H Trin from 05. *Greenfields, Church Road, Dodford, Bromsgrove B61 9BY* Tel (01527) 871614

BARGE, Mrs Ann Marina. b 42. S'wark Ord Course 89. **d** 96 **p** 97. C Ludlow, Ludford, Ashford Carbonell etc *Heref* from 96. *8 Old Street, Ludlow SY8 1NP* Tel (01584) 877307

BARGE, David Robert. b 45. S Dios Minl Tr Scheme 92. **d** 95 **p** 96. NSM Westfield *B & W* 95-00; C Frome St Jo and St Mary 00; V Frome St Mary from 01. *St Mary's House, 40 Innox Hill, Frome BA11 2LN* Tel (01373) 455996 E-mail barge@innox.fsnet.co.uk

BARGE, Marian. **d** 00. OLM Mynyddislwyn *Mon* from 00. *8 Pinewood Court, Pontllanfraith, Blackwood NP12 2PA* Tel (01495) 227208

BARGH, George Edward Norman. b 25. St Jo Coll Cam BA48 MA53 Leeds Univ LLB51. Carl Dioc Tr Course 80. **d** 83 **p** 84. NSM Ulverston St Mary w H Trin *Carl* 83-86; P-in-c Egton w Newland 86-87; P-in-c Blawith w Lowick 86-87; P-in-c Egton-cum-Newland and Lowick 87-89; rtd 90; Perm to Offic *Carl* from 90. *1 Willowdene Gardens, Old Hall Road, Ulverston LA12 7WD* Tel (01229) 588051

BARHAM, Ian Harold. b 40. Clifton Th Coll 64. **d** 66 **p** 67. C Broadwater St Mary *Chich* 66-69 and 72-76; Burundi 71-72; R Beyton and Hessett *St E* 76-79; Perm to Offic 79-81; Hon C Bury St Edmunds St Mary 81-84; Chapl St Aubyn's Sch Tiverton 84-96; Chapl Lee Abbey 96-99; rtd 00; Perm to Offic *Ex* from 00. *53 Sylvan Road, Exeter EX4 6EY* Tel (01392) 251643

BARHAM, Mrs Jennifer Mary. b 43. RN65. Oak Hill Th Coll 92. **d** 95 **p** 96. NSM Leigh-on-Sea St Aid *Chelmsf* 95-02; NSM Gt Burstead from 02; Chapl Basildon and Thurrock Gen Hosps NHS Trust 01-03. *47 Walker Drive, Leigh-on-Sea SS9 3QT* Tel (01702) 558766 E-mail jen-john@barham47.freeserve.co.uk

✠**BARHAM, The Rt Revd Kenneth Lawrence.** b 36. OBE01. Clifton Th Coll BD63. **d** 63 **p** 64 **c** 93. C Worthing St Geo *Chich* 63-65; C Sevenoaks St Nic *Roch* 65-67; C Cheltenham St Mark *Glouc* 67-70; V Maidstone St Luke *Cant* 70-79; S Area Sec Rwanda Miss 79-84; P-in-c Ashburnham w Penhurst *Chich* 84-01; Asst Bp Cyangugu (Rwanda) 93-96; Bp 96-01; rtd 01. *Rosewood, Canadia Road, Battle TN33 0LR* Tel and fax (01424) 773073 E-mail bishopken@binternet.com

BARHAM, Canon Peter. b 62. Selw Coll Cam MA83. Linc Th Coll BTh94. **d** 94 **p** 95. C Fornham All SS and Fornham St Martin w Timworth *St E* 94-97; P-in-c Cockfield w Bradfield St Clare, Felsham etc 97-01; Min Can St E Cathl 98-03; Chapl 01-03; Can Res St E Cathl from 03. *2 Abbey Precincts, Bury St Edmunds IP33 1RS* Tel and fax (01284) 701472 E-mail revpeterbarham@aol.com

BARKER, Arthur John Willoughby. b 10. Lon Coll of Div 46. **d** 48 **p** 49. C Addiscombe St Mary *Cant* 48-53; V Westgate St Jas 53-58; Warden Scargill Ho 58-61; V Dent w Cowgill *Bradf* 61-76; rtd 76; Perm to Offic *Bradf* 76-99. *Manormead, Tilford Road, Hindhead GU26 6RA* Tel (01428) 602500

BARKER, Arundel Charles. b 24. Tyndale Hall Bris 54. **d** 56 **p** 57. C Rodbourne Cheney *Bris* 56-58; V Islington St Steph w St Bart and St Matt *Lon* 58-65; R Passenham *Pet* 65-90; P-in-c Cosgrove 65-66; rtd 90; Perm to Offic *Derby* from 90. *7 Bull Farm Mews, Bull Lane, Matlock DE4 5NB* Tel (01629) 580321

BARKER, Brian Wallwork. b 26. G&C Coll Cam BA50 MA55. Wells Th Coll 51. **d** 52 **p** 53. C Bradford cum Beswick *Man* 52-55; Singapore 55-61; Malaya 62-63; Malaysia 63-64; V Ashton St Jas *Man* 65-71; R Burnage St Nic 71-85; R Heaton Reddish 85-91; rtd 91; Perm to Offic *Man* and *Ches* from 91. *105 Crossfield Road, Cheadle Hulme, Cheadle SK8 5PD* Tel 0161-486 0334

BARKER, Cameron Timothy. b 62. Rhodes Univ BA83 Nottm Univ MA(TS)96. St Jo Coll Nottm 94. **d** 96 **p** 97. C W Streatham St Jas *S'wark* 96-00; V Herne Hill from 00. *The Vicarage, 1 Finsen Road, London SE5 9AX* Tel (020) 7771 0381 E-mail cbarker@fish.co.uk

BARKER, Prof Charles Philip Geoffrey. b 50. Lon Univ MB, BS75 MS91 FRCS79 FICS92. S Dios Minl Tr Scheme 95. **d** 98 **p** 99. NSM Alverstoke *Portsm* 98-02; NSM The Lickey *Birm* from 02. *Siyabonga, 59 Beacon Hill, Rednal, Birmingham B45 9QW* Tel and fax 0121-453 4212 Mobile 07775-861216 E-mail revdocpb@compuserve.com

✠**BARKER, The Rt Revd Clifford Conder.** b 26. TD71. Oriel Coll Ox BA50 MA55. St Chad's Coll Dur DipTh52. **d** 52 **p** 53 **c** 76. C Falsgrave *York* 52-55; C Redcar 55-57; V Sculcoates 57-63; CF (TA) 58-74; P-in-c Sculcoates St Silas *York* 59-61; V Rudby in Cleveland w Middleton 63-70; RD Stokesley 65-70; V York St Olave w St Giles 70-76; RD City of York 71-75; Can and Preb York Minster 73-76; Suff Bp Whitby 76-83; Suff Bp Selby 83-91; rtd 91; Hon Asst Bp York from 95. *15 Oak Tree Close, Strensall, York YO32 5TE* Tel (01904) 490406

BARKER, David Robert. b 45. Worc Coll Ox BA67 MA70. Virginia Th Sem BD72. **d** 72 **p** 73. C Roehampton H Trin *S'wark* 72-75; Chapl Goldsmiths' Coll Lon 75-79; Min Tr Officer *Cov* 79-85; Selection Sec and Sec for Continuing Minl Educn ACCM 85-90; V Sutton Valence w E Sutton and Chart Sutton *Cant* from 90. *The Vicarage, Chart Road, Sutton Valence, Maidstone ME17 3AW* Tel (01622) 843156

BARKER, Edward. *See* BARKER, William Edward

BARKER, Gavin. *See* BARKER, James Gavin

BARKER, Gillian Ann. b 52. Portsm Univ MA02. Portsm Dioc Tr Course 91. **d** 92 **p** 98. NSM Alverstoke *Portsm* 92-95; NSM Bridgemary 95-96; Asst Chapl Portsm Hosps NHS Trust 96-98; Chapl 98-01; Chapl Ox Radcliffe Hosps NHS Trust from 01. *The Horton Hospital, Oxford Road, Banbury OX16 9AL* Tel (01295) 229104 *or* 275500 E-mail gill.barker@orh.nhs.uk

BARKER, Gordon Frank. b 43. Heriot-Watt Univ MSc75 Sheff Univ MA98. S & M Dioc Tr Inst 91. **d** 94 **p** 95. NSM Malew *S & M* 94-00; V Grain w Stoke *Roch* 00-04; Through Faith Miss Ev 00-04; P-in-c Andreas *S & M* from 04; P-in-c Jurby from 04; P-in-c Lezayre from 04. *The Rectory, Village Road, Andreas Village, Ramsey, Isle of Man IM7 4HH* Tel (01624) 880419 Mobile 07624-487228 E-mail gordon@revgfbgrainstoke.fsnet.co.uk

BARKER, Howard. *See* BARKER, Canon John Howard

BARKER, Canon Hugh Remington. b 19. Pemb Coll Cam BA41 MA45. Chich Th Coll 41. **d** 43 **p** 44. C Mill Hill St Mich *Lon* 43-48; C Welling *S'wark* 48-51; V Walworth All SS and St Steph 51-62; V Wisbech St Mary *Ely* 62-75; RD Wisbech 72-75; P-in-c Walpole St Andrew 75-77; V 77-84; P-in-c Walpole St Peter 75-77; R 77-84; RD Lynn Marshland 76-84; Hon Can Ely Cathl 81-84; rtd 84; Perm to Offic *Ely* from 84. *39 Dowgate Road, Leverington, Wisbech PE13 5DJ* Tel (01945) 585385

BARKER, James Gavin. b 33. Kelham Th Coll 54. **d** 58 **p** 59. C Greenford H Cross *Lon* 58-61; C Bournemouth St Clem w St Mary *Win* 61-66; C Pokesdown St Jas 66-70; V Stanmore 70-77; Chapl Besselsleigh Sch Abingdon 77-86; Hon C S Hinksey *Ox* 77-79; Hon C Wootton (Boars Hill) 79-86; V Southbourne St Chris *Win* 86-98; rtd 98. *11 Beaconsfield Road, Christchurch BH23 1QT* Tel (01202) 479828

BARKER, Canon John Howard. b 36. Southn Univ BA58. Ripon Coll Cuddesdon 80. **d** 82 **p** 83. C W Leigh *Portsm* 82-84; V Cosham 84-88; Bp's Dom Chapl 88-96; Hon Can Portsm Cathl 93-02; V St Helens and Sea View 96-02; rtd 02; Perm to Offic *Portsm* from 02. *Coniston Lodge, 3 Coniston Drive, Ryde PO33 3AE* Tel (01983) 618674 Mobile 07802-281797 E-mail jhbarker@netcomuk.co.uk

BARKER, John Lawrence. b 26. Middx Poly BA74 NE Lon Poly MSc84. Oak Hill NSM Course 86. **d** 88 **p** 89. NSM Prittlewell *Chelmsf* 88-91; Perm to Offic *Linc* from 91. *Rose Cottage, Back Lane, Bilsby, Alford LN13 9PT* Tel (01507) 462644

BARKER, John Stuart. b 30. Keele Univ BA55. Wells Th Coll 55. **d** 57 **p** 58. C Oswestry St Oswald *Lich* 57-60; C Portishead *B & W* 60-63; V Englishcombe 63-69; R Priston 63-69; V Chew Magna w Dundry 70-85; rtd 94. *9 West Street, Axbridge BS26 2AA* Tel (01934) 732740

BARKER, Jonathan. b 55. Hull Univ BA79. Westcott Ho Cam 79. **d** 83 **p** 84. C Sketty *S & B* 83-86; Chapl Sport and Leisure 83-86; C Swansea St Mary w H Trin 85-86; Bermuda 86-90; TV Liv Our Lady and St Nic w St Anne *Liv* 90-93; P-in-c S Shore St Pet *Blackb* 93-98; Chapl Blackpool Victoria Hosp NHS Trust 93-98; V Cleckheaton St Jo *Wakef* from 98. *St John's Vicarage, 33 Ashbourne Avenue, Cleckheaton BD19 5JH* Tel (01274) 874896 E-mail jonathanbarker@euphony.net

BARKER, Julian Roland Palgrave. b 37. Magd Coll Cam BA61 MA65. Westcott Ho Cam 61. **d** 63 **p** 64. C Stafford St Mary *Lich* 63-66; Chapl Clare Hall Cam 66-69; Chapl Clare Coll Cam 66-70; Tutor St Aug Coll Cant 70-71; TV Raveningham *Nor* 71-78; TR 78-82; V Foremark *Derby* 82-02; V Repton 82-02; P-in-c Newton Solney 01-02; V Foremark and Repton w Newton Solney 02-03; RD Repton 91-95; rtd 03. *103 Albert Bridge Road, London SW11 4PF* Tel (020) 7738 1951

BARKER, Mark. b 62. ACIB90. St Jo Coll Nottm BTh95. **d** 95 **p** 96. C Barking St Marg w St Patr *Chelmsf* 95-98; C Cranham Park 98-04; V Tonbridge St Steph *Roch* from 04. *St Stephen's Vicarage, 6 Brook Street, Tonbridge TN9 2PJ* Tel (01732) 353079 E-mail revmarkbarker@onetel.com

BARKER, Neil Anthony. b 52. St Andr Univ BSc73. Ridley Hall Cam 74. **d** 77 **p** 78. C Leic H Apostles *Leic* 77-81; C Camberley St Paul *Guildf* 81-86; R Bradfield *Ox* 86-88; R Bradfield and Stanford Dingley 88-92; R Woodmansterne *S'wark* 92-05; AD Reigate 05; Chapl Mothers' Union 96-05; TR Modbury, Bigbury, Ringmore w Kingston etc *Ex* from 05. *The Vicarage, Church Lane, Modbury, Ivybridge PL21 0QN* Tel (01548) 830260 E-mail revneil@i.am

BARKER, Canon Nicholas John Willoughby. b 49. Oriel Coll Ox BA73 BA75 MA77. Trin Coll Bris 75. **d** 77 **p** 78. C Watford *St Alb* 77-80; TV Didsbury St Jas and Em *Man* 80-86; TR Kidderminster St Geo *Worc* from 86; RD Kidderminster from 01; Hon Can Worc Cathl from 03. *The Rectory, 30 Leswell Street, Kidderminster DY10 1RP* Tel and fax (01562) 822131 E-mail nbarker@wfcsmail.com

BARKER, Philip. *See* BARKER, Prof Charles Philip Geoffrey

BARKER, Canon Roy Thomas. b 33. K Coll Lon BD57 AKC57. **d** 58 **p** 59. C Headingley *Ripon* 58-62; C Hawksworth Wood 62-66; S Africa 66-92; Sub-Dean Cape Town 73-80; Can 74-80; Dean and Adn Grahamstown 80-92; Hon Can from 92; V Southmead *Bris* 92-98; rtd 98; Perm to Offic *Bris* from 98. *7 Cleeve Avenue, Downend, Bristol BS16 6BT* Tel 0117-956 9057 E-mail roy@cleeveave.freeserve.co.uk

BARKER, Canon Timothy Reed. b 56. Qu Coll Cam BA79 MA82. Westcott Ho Cam 78. **d** 80 **p** 81. C Nantwich *Ches* 80-83; V Norton 83-88; V Runcorn All SS 88-94; Urban Officer 88-90; Dioc Communications Officer 91-98; Bp's Chapl 94-98; Hon P Asst Ches Cathl 94-98; V Spalding *Linc* from 98; RD Elloe W from 00; Can and Preb Linc Cathl from 03. *The Parsonage, 1 Halmer Gate, Spalding PE11 2DR* Tel (01775) 722772 *or* 722675 Mobile 07775-833426 Fax (01775) 710273 E-mail tim.barker@spaldingchurches.org

BARKER, William Edward. b 28. Kelham Th Coll 49. **d** 54 **p** 55. C Warsop *S'well* 54-55; C Bawtry w Austerfield 55-57; V Frizington *Carl* 57-64; V Barrow St Jas 64-70; V Applethwaite 70-93; P-in-c Troutbeck 78-93; rtd 93; Perm to Offic *Carl* from 93. *114 Burneside Road, Kendal LA9 4RZ* Tel (01539) 734787

BARKING, Area Bishop of. *See* HAWKINS, The Rt Revd David John Leader

BARKS, Jeffrey Stephen. b 45. Cranmer Hall Dur 66. **d** 71 **p** 72. C Wootton *St Alb* 71-74; C Boscombe St Jo *Win* 74-76; C Ringwood 76-80; P-in-c Spaxton w Charlynch *B & W* 80; P-in-c Enmore w Goathurst 80; P-in-c Spaxton w Goathurst, Enmore and Charlynch 80-81; R 81-92; RD Bridgwater 89-94; V Wembdon from 92. *The Vicarage, 12 Greenacre, Wembdon, Bridgwater TA6 7RD* Tel (01278) 423647 *or* 423468 E-mail stephenbarks@dsl.pipex.com

BARLEY, Ann Christine. b 47. Nottm Univ Dip Past Counselling 98. LNSM course 91. **d** 93 **p** 94. OLM Walton *St E* 93-00; OLM Walton and Trimley from 00. *13 New Road, Trimley St Mary, Felixstowe IP11 0TQ* Tel (01394) 283752 E-mail ann.carmel@lineone.net

BARLEY, Christopher James. b 56. St Steph Ho Ox BA90 MA93. **d** 93 **p** 94. C Upton cum Chalvey *Ox* 93-96; TV High Wycombe 96-01; V Swinton *Sheff* from 01. *The Vicarage, 50 Golden Smithies Lane, Swinton, Mexborough S64 8DL* Tel (01709) 582259

BARLEY, Gordon Malcolm. b 59. Aston Tr Scheme 94 Oak Hill Th Coll 96. **d** 98 **p** 99. C Walthamstow St Jo *Chelmsf* 98-02; TV Barking St Marg w St Patr from 02. *St Patrick's Vicarage, 79 Sparsholt Road, Barking IG11 7YG* Tel (020) 8594 1960 E-mail revgbarley@eggconnect.net

BARLEY, Ivan William. b 48. Loughb Univ MA01 CEng74 MIEE74. **d** 93 **p** 94. OLM Walton *St E* 93-00; OLM Walton and Trimley from 00; Dioc NSM/OLM Officer from 02. *13 New Road, Trimley St Mary, Felixstowe IP11 0TQ* Tel (01394) 283752 E-mail iwbarley@iee.org

BARLEY, Lynda Mary. b 53. York Univ BA74 PGCE75 Lon Univ MSc76 FSS77. S'wark Ord Course 93. **d** 96 **p** 97. NSM Lower Nutfield *S'wark* 96-97; NSM Littleham w Exmouth *Ex* 97-98; NSM Tedburn St Mary, Whitestone, Oldridge etc 98-00; Hd Research and Statistics Abps' Coun from 00; NSM Cullompton, Willand, Uffculme, Kentisbeare etc *Ex* from 03. *Church House, Great Smith Street, London SW1P 3NZ* Tel (020) 7898 1542 Fax 7898 1532 E-mail lynda.barley@c-of-e.org.uk

BARLEY, Victor Laurence. b 41. St Jo Coll Cam MA66 Ch Ch Ox DPhil72 FRCSEd75 FRCR76. **d** 02 **p** 03. NSM Flax Bourton *B & W* from 02; NSM Barrow Gurney from 02. *North Archway Cottage, Barrow Court, Barrow Gurney, Bristol BS48 3RW* Tel (01275) 463006 Pager 07654-630255 E-mail victor_barley@talk21.com

BARLING, Michael Keith. b 38. Oak Hill Th Coll 63. **d** 66 **p** 67. C Portman Square St Paul *Lon* 66-70; C Enfield Ch Ch Trent Park 70-74; V Sidcup St Andr *Roch* 74-78; Dir Fountain Trust 78-81; Chapl Bethany Fellowship and Roffey Place 81-88; Hon C Kennington St Mark *S'wark* 88-89; Prin Kingdom Faith Bible Coll 89-99; Pastor from 99. *Roffey Place, Horsham RH12 4RU* Tel (01293) 851543 Mobile 07818-405858 Fax (01293) 854610 E-mail church@kingdomfaith.com

BARLOW, Alan David. b 36. Worc Coll Ox BA59 MA65. Wycliffe Hall Ox 59. **d** 61 **p** 62. C Wealdstone H Trin *Lon* 61-67; V Neasden cum Kingsbury St Cath 67-73; Chapl Cranleigh Sch Surrey 73-81; Chapl Cheltenham Ladies' Coll 82-01; rtd 01; Perm to Offic Glouc from 02. *22 Moorend Road, Leckhampton, Cheltenham GL53 0EU* Tel (01242) 584668 Fax as telephone E-mail revdavid@globalnet.co.uk

BARLOW, Canon Charles William Moore. b 32. ALCM50 Man Univ BA57 Hon FGCM94 Hon RSCM98. Cuddesdon Coll 56. **d** 58 **p** 59. C Atherton *Man* 58-61; C Swinton St Pet 61-64; V Dobcross 64-76; V Dobcross w Scouthead 76-98; Hon Can Man Cathl 96-98; AD Saddleworth 97-98; rtd 99; Perm to Offic *Man* 99-03. *18 Mount Road, Marsden, Huddersfield HD7 6HP* Tel (01484) 844494

BARLOW, Clive Christopher. b 42. Linc Th Coll 67. **d** 70 **p** 71. C Surbiton St Mark *S'wark* 70-74; C Spring Park *Cant* 74-77; V Ash w Westmarsh 77-92; RD E Bridge 86-92; R Chartham from 92; RD W Bridge 95-01. *The Rectory, The Green, Chartham, Canterbury CT4 7JW* Tel (01227) 738256 Fax 732282 E-mail c.barlow@btinternet.com

BARLOW, Darren. b 65. Ridley Hall Cam CTM98. **d** 98 **p** 99. C Rayleigh *Chelmsf* 98-01; TV Billericay and Lt Burstead from 01. *The Vicarage, 7A Horace Road, Billericay CM11 1AA* Tel (01277) 656266 E-mail darren@revbarlow.freeserve.co.uk

BARLOW, David. *See* BARLOW, Alan David

BARLOW, David. b 50. Leeds Univ BA71 MA. Wycliffe Hall Ox 71. **d** 73 **p** 74. C Horninglow *Lich* 73-75; C Wednesfield St Thos 75-77; C Bloxwich 77-78; Chapl RN from 78. *Royal Naval Chaplaincy Service, Room 203, Victory Building, HM Naval Base, Portsmouth PO1 3LS* Tel (023) 9272 7903 Fax 9272 7111

BARLOW, Canon Edward Burnley. b 29. St Aid Birkenhead 56. **d** 58 **p** 59. C Lenton Abbey *S'well* 58-61; C Ipswich All SS *St E* 61-63; R Fishtoft *Linc* 63-76; V Linc St Giles 76-96; Can and Preb Linc Cathl from 92; rtd 96; Perm to Offic *Linc* 96-99. *8 Pynder Close, Washingborough, Lincoln LN4 1EX* Tel (01522) 793762

BARLOW, Paul Andrew. b 59. Imp Coll Lon BSc80 UMIST PhD84 Bolton Inst of HE PGCE85. Aston Tr Scheme 89 Chich Th Coll 91. **d** 93 **p** 94. C Hale *Guildf* 93-97; C Christchurch *Win* 97-01; P-in-c Alton All SS from 01. *All Saints' Vicarage, Queen's Road, Alton GU34 1HU* Tel (01420) 83458 E-mail paul@paulbarlow.plus.com

BARLOW, Paul Benson. b 31. Fitzw Coll Cam BA73 MA77 FRSA94. **d** 64 **p** 65. C Bath Abbey w St Jas *B & W* 64-74; Dep Hd Master Leys High Sch Redditch 74-81; Hd Master Jo Kyrle High Sch Ross-on-Wye 82-96; Perm to Offic *Heref* 82-85; Lic to Offic 85-92; NSM Walford and St John w Bishopswood, Goodrich etc 92-97; Perm to Offic from 97. *The Coach House, Hentland, Ross-on-Wye HR9 6LP*

BARLOW, Robert Mark. b 53. St Jo Coll Nottm 84. **d** 86 **p** 87. C Colwich w Gt Haywood *Lich* 86-91; R Crick and Yelvertoft w Clay Coton and Lilbourne *Pet* 91-04; Bp's Rural Officer 98-04; Chapl to Agric and Rural Life *Worc* from 04; C Martley and Wichenford, Knightwick etc from 05. *The White House, Ankerdine Hill, Knightwick, Worcester WR6 5PR* Tel (01886) 821339 Mobile 07947-600627 E-mail rbarlow@cofe-worcester.org.uk

BARLOW, Thomas Frank. b 24. WMMTC. **d** 84 **p** 85. NSM Dudley St Jas *Worc* 84-88; NSM Belbroughton w Fairfield and Clent 88-93; Perm to Offic from 93. *30 The Glebe, Belbroughton, Stourbridge DY9 9TH* Tel (01562) 730426

BARLOW, Timothy David. b 46. Univ Coll Ox BA67 MA71 Lon Univ BD71. Oak Hill Th Coll 71. **d** 71 **p** 72. C Marple All SS *Ches* 71-74; C Northwood Em *Lon* 74-78; Chapl Vevey w Château d'Oex and Villars *Eur* 78-84; Switzerland 84-89; V Chadkirk *Ches* from 89. *34 Church Lane, Romiley, Stockport SK6 4AA* Tel 0161-430 4841 E-mail timbarlow@romileylifecentre.co.uk

BARLOW, William George. b 40. Liv Univ BSc62 Univ of Wales BD65. St Mich Coll Llan 76. **d** 76 **p** 77. C Roath *Llan* 76-79; TV Cyncoed *Mon* 79-83; R Radyr *Llan* from 83; RD Llan 95-04. *The Rectory, 52 Heol Isaf, Radyr, Cardiff CF15 8DY* Tel (029) 2084 2417

BARNACLE, Ronald William. b 20. Wells Th Coll 66. **d** 66 **p** 67. C Emscote *Cov* 66-67; C Nuneaton St Nic 67-69; C Camp Hill w Galley Common 69-70; R Etton w Dalton Holme *York* 70-76; R Hinderwell w Roxby 76-78; P-in-c Buckland Newton *Sarum* 78-80; P-in-c Wootton Glanville and Holnest 78-80; P-in-c Pulham 78-80; R Radwinter w Hempstead *Chelmsf* 80-83; V Blackfordby *Leic* 83-84; rtd 84; Perm to Offic *Worc* 84-92; *Cov* from 87; *Leic* from 97. *207 Town Thorns, Brinklow Road, Easenhall, Rugby CV23 0JE* Tel (01788) 833873

BARNARD, Canon Anthony Nevin. b 36. St Jo Coll Cam BA60 MA64. Wells Th Coll 61. **d** 63 **p** 64. C Cheshunt *St Alb* 63-65; Tutor Wells Th Coll 65-66; Chapl 66-69; Vice-Prin 69-71; Dep Prin Sarum & Wells Th Coll 71-77; Dir S Dios Minl Tr Scheme 74-77; Can Res and Chan Lich Cathl *Lich* from 77; Warden of Readers 77-91; Dir of Tr 86-91. *13 The Close, Lichfield WS13 7LD* Tel (01543) 306210 *or* 306240 Fax 306109 E-mail tony.barnard@lichfield-cathedral.org

BARNARD, Catherine Elizabeth. b 54. York Univ BA76 Dur Univ BA79. Cranmer Hall Dur 77. **dss** 80 **d** 87 **p** 94. Mexborough *Sheff* 80-83; Sheff Manor 83-90; Hon Par Dn 87-90; Hon Par Dn Bolsterstone 90-94; C from 94. *The Vicarage, Stone Moor Road, Bolsterstone, Sheffield S36 3ZN* Tel and fax 0114-288 2149

BARNARD, Jonathan Dixon. b 46. St Cath Coll Cam BA68. Cuddesdon Coll 69. **d** 71 **p** 72. C Silksworth *Dur* 71-74; C Hatfield Hyde *St Alb* 74-78; TV Hitchin 78-86; TR Penrith w Newton Reigny and Plumpton Wall *Carl* 86-91; rtd 91. *4 Hallin Croft, Penrith CA11 8AA* Tel (01768) 63000

BARNARD, Kevin James. b 52. Keble Coll Ox BA77 MA79. Cranmer Hall Dur 77. **d** 79 **p** 80. C Swinton *Sheff* 79-83; TV Sheff Manor 83-90; V Bolsterstone from 90; Bp's Adv on Issues Relating to Ageing from 94. *The Vicarage, Stonemoor Road, Bolsterstone, Sheffield S36 3ZN* Tel and fax 0114-288 2149

BARNARD, Leslie William. b 24. St Cath Coll Ox BA50 MA55 Southn Univ PhD70. Cuddesdon Coll 51. **d** 51 **p** 52. C Portswood Ch Ch *Win* 51-55; V Shaw and Whitley *Sarum* 55-61; R Chilcomb w Win All SS and Chesil *Win* 61-68; Sen Lect Leeds Univ 69-83; Dioc Dir of Tr *Ripon* 70-76; Chapl Harrogate Gen Hosp 83-89; rtd 89; Perm to Offic *Ripon* from 89. *3 The Old College, Steven Way, Ripon HG4 2TQ*

BARNDEN, Saskia Gail. b 50. Waterloo Univ (Canada) BA70 Victoria Univ (BC) MA71 Indiana Univ PhD88 Westmr Coll Ox CertEd75. St Alb and Ox Min Course 97. **d** 00 **p** 01. Asst Chapl Wycombe Abbey Sch 00-01; Chapl Haberdashers' Monmouth Sch for Girls from 01. *47 Elvetham Road, Birmingham B15 2LY* Tel 0121-440 5677 *or* (01600) 711100 Mobile 07813-616574 E-mail headsec@hmsg.org

BARNES, Alan Duff. b 42. St Steph Ho Ox 75. **d** 77 **p** 78. C Wanstead H Trin Hermon Hill *Chelmsf* 77-80; C Clacton St Jas 80-82; R Cranham 82-89; V Calcot *Ox* from 89. *St Birinus' House, Langley Hill, Calcot, Reading RG31 4QX* Tel 0118-942 2828

BARNES, Canon Brian. b 42. Sussex Univ MA82. Cant Sch of Min 79. **d** 82 **p** 83. NSM Maidstone All SS and St Phil w Tovil *Cant* 82-89; C 89-92; FE Adv Gen Syn Bd of Educn 86-92; R Staplehurst *Cant* 92-02; V Hythe from 02; RD W Charing 95-99; AD Cranbrook 99-01; Hon Can Cant Cathl from 01. *St Leonard's Vicarage, Oak Walk, Hythe CT21 5DN* Tel (01303) 266217 E-mail brian.barnes@virgin.net

BARNES, Brian. b 49. St Mich Coll Llan 93. **d** 93 **p** 94. C Betws w Ammanford *St D* 93-96; V Llanwnda, Goodwick w Manorowen and Llanstinan from 96. *The Vicarage, Dyffryn, Goodwick SA64 0AN* Tel (01348) 873758

BARNES, Canon Bryan Peter. b 24. Leeds Univ BA50. Coll of Resurr Mirfield 50. **d** 52 **p** 53. C Swindon New Town *Bris* 52-59; S Rhodesia 59-65; Rhodesia 65-66; V Moorfields *Bris* 66-71; P-in-c Winterbourne Down 71-75; V Fishponds St Mary 75-87; Hon Can Bris Cathl 84-87; rtd 87; NSM Duloe w Herodsfoot *Truro* 91-95; Warden Jes Hosp Cant 95-98. *St Katharine's House, Ormond Road, Wantage OX12 8EA* Tel (01235) 772798

BARNES, Canon Charles Peter Kentish. b 19. Ch Coll Cam BA40 MA44. Ridley Hall Cam 40. **d** 42 **p** 43. C Reading St Jo *Ox* 42-45; C Sutton Coldfield H Trin *Birm* 45-49; Sub-Dean Cairo Cathl Egypt 49-52; R Wavertree St Mary *Liv* 52-56; R Maghull 56-69; R Stratford-on-Avon w Bishopton *Cov* 69-75; TR 75-81; Hon Can Cov Cathl 75-84; V Priors Hardwick, Priors Marston and Wormleighton 81-84; rtd 84; Perm to Offic *Cov* and *Glouc* from 84. *1 Capel Court, The Burgage, Prestbury, Cheltenham GL52 3EL* Tel (01242) 516591

BARNES, Christopher Charles. b 51. Victoria Univ Wellington BA79 TDip79. Trin Coll Bris. **d** 00 **p** 01. C Langport Area Chs *B & W* 00-03; P-in-c Burton and Rosemarket *St D* from 03; Chapl Miss to Seafarers Milford Haven from 03. *The Rectory, Burton, Milford Haven SA73 1NX* Tel (01646) 600877 Mobile 07932-165719 E-mail chris.barnes@ukonline.co.uk

BARNES, Colin. b 33. St Jo Coll York CertEd58. St Aid Birkenhead 61. **d** 64 **p** 65. C Eccles St Mary *Man* 64-66; C Barrow St Geo w St Luke *Carl* 66-68; V Goodshaw *Man* 68-80; P-in-c Wythenshawe St Martin 80-83; New Zealand 83-98; rtd 98; Perm to Offic *Man* from 98. *5 Worston Close, Rawtenstall, Rossendale BB4 8UP* Tel (01706) 215199

BARNES, Cyril Arthur. b 26. Edin Th Coll 47. **d** 50 **p** 51. C Aberdeen St Jo *Ab* 50-53; R Forres *Mor* 53-55; C Darrington *Wakef* 55-58; V Ripponden 58-67; V Thorpe 66-67; R Huntly *Mor* 67-83; R Aberchirder 67-83; Hon Can St Andr Cathl Inverness 71-80; Dioc Sec 71-83; R Keith 74-83; Syn Clerk 77-80; Dean Mor 80-83; rtd 83; Perm to Offic *Ab* from 83 and *Mor* from 90. *Nazareth House, 34 Claremont Street, Aberdeen AB10 6RA* Tel (01224) 594964

BARNES, David John. b 37. Lon Univ DipRS65 Kent Univ MA96. Chich Th Coll 65. **d** 68 **p** 69. C Crayford *Roch* 68-71; Chapl RAF 71-75; Chapl Sutton Valence Sch Kent 75-87; C Minster-in-Sheppey *Cant* 87-93; V Ash w Westmarsh 93-01; RD E Bridge 98-01; rtd 01; Perm to Offic *Cant* from 02. *Home Farm Cottage, School Lane, Higham, Rochester ME3 7JG* Tel and fax (01474) 822589 E-mail davidbarnes@breatheconnect.com

BARNES, David Keith. b 53. Linc Th Coll. **d** 89 **p** 90. C E Crompton *Man* 89-93; V Belfield 93-99; V Honley *Wakef* from 99. *The Vicarage, St Mary's Road, Honley, Holmfirth HD9 6AZ* Tel (01484) 661178

BARNES, Derek Ian. b 44. Leeds Univ BA66. Westcott Ho Cam 66. **d** 68 **p** 69. C Far Headingley St Chad *Ripon* 68-71; Chapl Qu Eliz Coll *Lon* 72-77; Warden Lee Abbey Internat Students' Club Kensington 77-81; Hon C Willesden Green St Gabr *Lon* 81-83; P-in-c Southall H Trin 84-98; P-in-c Southall St Geo 89-92; Perm to Offic 99-02; Chapl W Lon Mental Health NHS Trust from 02. *West London Mental Health NHS Trust, Uxbridge Road, Southall UB1 3EU* Tel (020) 8354 8354 *or* 8354 8974 E-mail derekibarnes@yahoo.com *or* derek.barnes@wlmht.nhs.uk

BARNES, Preb Donald Edward. b 26. K Coll Lon BD51 AKC51. **d** 52 **p** 53. C Willesden St Matt *Lon* 52-59; V Cricklewood St Pet 59-79; Lect Bps' Coll Cheshunt 63-68; V Belsize Park *Lon* 79-96; Preb St Paul's Cathl 84-96; AD N Camden 83-88; rtd 96; Perm to Offic *Lon* from 96. *94 Hamilton Road, London NW11 9DY* Tel (020) 8731 9860

BARNES, Duncan Christopher. b 64. Warwick Univ BA90. Trin Coll Bris BA93. **d** 93 **p** 94. C Hornchurch St Andr *Chelmsf* 93-98; V Bicker *Linc* 98-00; V Donington 98-00; TV Woughton *Ox* from 00. *2 Braunston, Woughton Park, Milton Keynes MK6 3AU* Tel (01908) 674742 E-mail dunc@classicfm.net

✠**BARNES, The Rt Revd Edwin Ronald.** b 35. Pemb Coll Ox BA58 MA62. Cuddesdon Coll 58. **d** 60 **p** 61 **c** 95. C Portsea N End St Mark *Portsm* 60-64; C Woodham *Guildf* 64-67; R Farncombe 67-78; V Hessle *York* 78-87; AD W Hull 85-87; Prin St Steph Ho Ox 87-95; Hon Can Ch Ch *Ox* 94-95; Suff Bp Richborough (PEV) *Cant* 95-01; Hon Asst Bp St Alb 96-01;

Hon Asst Bp Chelmsf 99-01; rtd 01; Hon Asst Bp Win from 01. *1 Queen Elizabeth Avenue, Lymington SO41 9HN* Tel (01590) 610133 E-mail bishedwin@aol.com

BARNES, Mrs Enid Mabel. b 38. Homerton Coll Cam Dip Teaching58. WMMTC 87. **d** 90 **p** 94. Par Dn Walsall St Paul *Lich* 90-94; C 94-96; TV Chell 96-02; rtd 02; Perm to Offic *Lich* 02-04. *10 Hind Avenue, Breaston, Derby DE72 3DG* Tel (01332) 873665 E-mail enidbarnes@hotmail.com

BARNES, Harvey Thomas. b 61. SW Minl Tr Course 02. **d** 05. C Plympton St Mary *Ex* from 05. *22 Priory Mill, Plympton, Plymouth PL7 1WR* Tel (01752) 344168

BARNES, Miss Heather Dawn. b 75. Liv Hope BA96 PGCE97. Ridley Hall Cam 03. **d** 05. C Luton Lewsey St Hugh *St Alb* from 05. *247 Leagrave High Street, Luton LU4 0NA*

BARNES, Jennifer. b 45. AdDipCrim Open Univ MA97. N Ord Course 94. **d** 96 **p** 97. C Thorne *Sheff* 96-99; C Clifton St Jas 99-01; Chapl HM Pris Featherstone 01-04; Chapl HM YOI Swinfen Hall from 04. *HM YOI Swinfen Hall, Lichfield WS14 9QS* Tel (01543) 484000

BARNES, Jeremy Paul Blissard. b 70. Southn Univ BSc92. Wycliffe Hall Ox BTh99. **d** 99 **p** 00. C Brompton H Trin w Onslow Square St Paul *Lon* 99-05; C Shadwell St Paul w Ratcliffe St Jas from 05. *The Vicarage, 16 Cannon Street Road, London E1 0BH* E-mail jez.barnes@stpaulsshadwell.org

BARNES, Canon John Barwick. b 32. AKC58. **d** 59 **p** 60. C Brentwood St Thos *Chelmsf* 59-65; R Arkesden w Wicken Bonhunt 65-71; V Gt Ilford St Mary 71-99; Hon Can Chelmsf Cathl 95-99; rtd 99; Perm to Offic *Chelmsf* from 99. *352 Henley Road, Ilford IG1 1TJ* Tel (020) 8478 1954

BARNES, John Christopher. b 43. MA ATI. Linc Th Coll 78. **d** 80 **p** 81. C Guiseley *Bradf* 80-83; TV Guiseley w Esholt 83-86; V Rawdon 86-92; R Armthorpe *Sheff* 92-98; TR Maltby 98-01; RD Doncaster 96-98; Hon Can Sheff Cathl 00-01; TR Blakenall Heath *Lich* 01-05; P-in-c Gomersal *Wakef* from 05. *The Vicarage, 404 Spen Lane, Gomersal, Cleckheaton BD19 4LS* Tel (01274) 872131 E-mail jcbjb7@aol.com

BARNES, John Seymour. b 30. Qu Coll Birm 58. **d** 61 **p** 62. C Bromsgrove St Jo *Worc* 61-64; C Kingsthorpe *Pet* 64-66; C Styvechale *Cov* 66-69; P-in-c Avon Dassett w Farnborough 69-75; P-in-c Cov St Alb 75-84; R Weddington and Caldecote 84-89; P-in-c Wilnecote *Lich* 89-90; V Bentley 90-96; rtd 96; Perm to Offic *Lich* 96-04. *10 Hind Avenue, Breaston, Derby DE72 3DG* Tel (01332) 873665

BARNES, Canon Katrina Crawford. b 52. K Coll Lon BA98 AKC98. Oak Hill Th Coll 90. **d** 93 **p** 94. NSM Bromley H Trin *Roch* 93-98; C Meopham w Nurstead 98-00; Assoc Staff Tutor SEITE 99-03; R Longfield *Roch* from 01; Bp's Adv for Ord Women's Min from 05; Hon Can Roch Cathl from 05. *The Rectory, 67 Main Road, Longfield DA3 7PQ* Tel (01474) 702201 E-mail katrina_barnes@talk21.com

BARNES, Mrs Mary Jane. b 48. St Jo Coll Nottm 97. **d** 99 **p** 00. C Harefield *Lon* 99-02; TV New Windsor *Ox* from 02. *The Vicarage, 73 Alma Road, Windsor SL4 3HD* Tel (01753) 861757 Mobile 07930-337407 E-mail mary@harefield9.fsnet.co.uk

BARNES, Matthew John. b 68. Leeds Univ MA99. St Jo Coll Nottm BA93. **d** 96 **p** 97. C Stanley *Wakef* 96-99; TV N Wingfield, Clay Cross and Pilsley *Derby* from 99. *The Vicarage, Stretton Road, Clay Cross, Chesterfield S45 9AQ* Tel (01246) 250110 Mobile 07977-976348 E-mail mjbarnes@talk21.com

BARNES, Neal Duncan. b 63. Leeds Univ BSc84 Cranfield Inst of Tech PhD92. Oak Hill Th Coll 93. **d** 95 **p** 96. C Biggleswade *St Alb* 95-99; V Anlaby St Pet *York* from 99; Hon Chapl Ambulance Service Hull from 99. *The Vicarage, Church Street, Anlaby, Hull HU10 7DG* Tel (01482) 653024 E-mail neal@anvic.karoo.co.uk

BARNES, Canon Neil. b 42. Kelham Th Coll 61 Bps' Coll Cheshunt 65. **d** 68 **p** 69. C Poulton-le-Fylde *Blackb* 68-72; C Ribbleton 72-75; V Knuzden 75-81; Chapl Prestwich Hosp Man 81-88; Chapl Salford Mental Health Services NHS Trust 88-04; Manager Chapl Services 94-04; Hon Can Man Cathl *Man* 96-04; Perm to Offic *Blackb* from 04. *Leads Cottage, Bacup Road, Cliviger, Burnley BB11 3QZ* Tel (01282) 451533 E-mail neilbarnes@bigfoot.com

BARNES, Paul. *See* BYLLAM-BARNES, Preb Paul William Marshall

BARNES, Paul Nicholas. b 58. Qu Coll Birm 89. **d** 91 **p** 92. C Weymouth H Trin *Sarum* 91-95; P-in-c Studley from 95. *The Vicarage, 340 Frome Road, Studley, Trowbridge BA14 0ED* Tel (01225) 753162

BARNES, Peter. *See* BARNES, Canon Charles Peter Kentish

BARNES, Peter Frank. b 52. St Jo Coll Nottm LTh81. **d** 81 **p** 82. C Colne St Bart *Blackb* 81-83; C Melton Mowbray w Thorpe Arnold *Leic* 83-86; P-in-c Barlestone 86-89; V Broughton and Duddon *Carl* 89-98; V Shrewsbury St Geo w Greenfields *Lich* from 98; P-in-c Bicton, Montford w Shrawardine and Fitz 98-00. *The Vicarage, St George's Street, Shrewsbury SY3 8QA* Tel (01743) 235461 E-mail peter.barnes@lineone.net

BARNES, Philip John. b 52. SEITE 01. **d** 04 **p** 05. NSM Gravesend St Mary *Roch* from 04. *69 The Fairway, Gravesend DA11 7LN* Tel (01474) 560519 E-mail philbarnes@blueyonder.co.uk

BARNES, Philip Richard. b 73. Westmr Coll Ox BTh94 Heythrop Coll Lon MA99. St Steph Ho Ox. **d** 00 **p** 01. C Ruislip St Martin *Lon* 00-03; Shrine P Shrine of Our Lady of Walsingham from 03. *The Shrine of Our Lady of Walsingham, The College, Knight Street, Walsingham NR22 6EF* Tel (01328) 824203 E-mail p.barnes@olw-shrine.org.uk

BARNES, Roland Peter. b 59. Ban Ord Course 01. **d** 03 **p** 04. NSM Bro Ddyfi Uchaf *Ban* from 03; P-in-c from 05. *Y Rheithordy, Mallwyd, Machynlleth SY20 9HJ* Tel (01650) 531650

BARNES, Stephen. b 46. Hull Univ BA69 Bris Univ DipTh71. Clifton Th Coll 69. **d** 72 **p** 73. C Girlington *Bradf* 72-74; TV Glyncorrwg w Afan Vale and Cymmer Afan *Llan* 74-79; R 79-86; V Aberavon 86-01; V Dulais Valley from 01. *The Vicarage, 86 Church Road, Seven Sisters, Neath SA10 9DT* Tel and fax (01639) 700286 E-mail sbarnes.cwmdulais@btinternet.com

BARNES, Stephen John. b 59. Univ of Wales (Cardiff) BSc80. Chich Th Coll 83. **d** 86 **p** 87. C Neath w Llantwit *Llan* 86-89; C Coity w Nolton 89-95; V Troedyrhiw w Merthyr Vale from 95. *The Vicarage, Nixonville, Merthyr Vale, Merthyr Tydfil CF48 4RF* Tel (01443) 690249

BARNES, Stephen Martin Leonard. b 60. St Steph Ho Ox. **d** 87. C N Hinksey *Ox* 87-88; In RC Ch 88-98; NSM Kingstanding St Mark *Birm* 98-04. *Address temp unknown*

BARNES, Stephen William. b 53. Man Univ BSc. St Jo Coll Nottm DipTh82. **d** 83 **p** 84. C Chadwell Heath *Chelmsf* 83-87; C Becontree St Alb 88-89; Deanery Youth Chapl 88-91; C Becontree S 89-91; TV Worth *Chich* 91-98; Chapl Willen Hospice Milton Keynes from 99. *23 White Horse Drive, Milton Keynes MK4 2AZ* Tel (01908) 508896 *or* 663636 E-mail chaplain@willen-hospice.org.uk

BARNES, Mrs Sylvia Frances. b 43. Shoreditch Coll Lon CertEd75. S Tr Scheme 92. **d** 96 **p** 97. Hon C Cusop w Blakemere, Bredwardine w Brobury etc *Heref* from 96. *Pwll Cwm, Arthur's Stone Lane, Dorstone, Hereford HR3 6AY* Tel (01981) 500252

BARNES, Thomas. *See* BARNES, Canon William Thomas

BARNES, Timothy. b 56. Birm Univ BSc78. Westcott Ho Cam 96 Lon Bible Coll 82. **d** 98 **p** 99. C Shrub End *Chelmsf* 98-02; V Leigh-on-Sea St Aid from 02. *St Aidan's Vicarage, 78 Moor Park Gardens, Leigh-on-Sea SS9 4PY* Tel (01702) 512531 E-mail timbarnes@timbo7.fsnet.co.uk

BARNES, William Joseph Athanasius. b 57. St Andr Univ MTh84 Newc Univ MA02 RGN89. Westcott Ho Cam 91. **d** 92 **p** 93. C S Bank *York* 92-95; C Northallerton w Kirby Sigston 95-97; V Dormanstown 97-01; P-in-c Netherton St Andr *Worc* from 01; P-in-c Darby End from 03. *St Andrew's Vicarage, Highbridge Road, Netherton, Dudley DY2 0HT* Tel (01384) 257097 E-mail bja.barnes@btopenworld.com

BARNES, Canon William Thomas. b 39. Dur Univ BA60. Wycliffe Hall Ox 60. **d** 62 **p** 63. C Scotforth *Blackb* 62-66; C Cleveleys 66-67; V Colne Ch Ch 67-74; V Bamber Bridge St Sav 74-04; Hon Can Blackb Cathl 00-04; rtd 04. *12 Little Close, Farington Moss, Leyland PR26 6QU* Tel (01772) 457646

BARNES-CLAY, Peter John Granger. b 43. Cam Univ CertEd69 MCollP. Chich Th Coll 72. **d** 75 **p** 82. C Earlham St Anne *Nor* 75-76; Asst Master Hewett Sch Nor 76-83; Hon C Eaton 81-83; C 83-87; R Winterton w E and W Somerton and Horsey 87-92; R Weybourne Gp 92-03; RD Holt 95-02; rtd 03; Perm to Offic *Nor* 03-05; C Smallburgh w Dilham w Honing and Crostwight from 05. *The Rectory, The Street, Honing, North Walsham NR28 9NB* Tel (01263) 824775 E-mail becketsthree@aol.com

BARNETT, Alec James Leon. b 44. Em Coll Cam BA66 MA70 PGCE71. Cuddesdon Coll 66. **d** 69 **p** 70. C Preston St Jo *Blackb* 69-72; Asst Master Hutton Grammar Sch 70-72; Asst Chapl Uppingham Sch 72-80; Hd of RE 73-80; Dir of Farmington/Ampleforth Project 79-83; C Witney *Ox* 80-84; P-in-c Lt Compton w Chastleton, Cornwell etc 84-88; Prin Ox Chr Tr Scheme 84-88; P-in-c St Michael Penkevil *Truro* 88-95; P-in-c Lamorran and Merther 88-95; Dioc Tr Officer 88-95; Chapl Strasbourg *Eur* 95-01; Abp Cant's Rep at Eur Inst from 95; Perm to Offic *Truro* from 95; rtd 01. *7 rue des Magnolias, La Croix, 17800 St Léger, France* Tel (0033) (5) 46 94 99 25 Fax 46 94 95 01 E-mail james.barnett@wanadoo.fr

BARNETT, Ann. *See* BARNETT, Miss Patricia Ann

BARNETT, David John. b 33. Magd Coll Ox BA56 BTh58 MA61. St Steph Ho Ox 56. **d** 59 **p** 60. C Styvechale *Cov* 59-62; S Africa 62-69; Rhodesia 70-76; V Colindale St Matthias *Lon* 77-90; R Finchley St Mary 90-98; rtd 98; Perm to Offic *Ex* from 98. *2 Curlew Way, Exeter EX4 4SW* Tel (01392) 431486

BARNETT, Dudley Graham. b 36. Ch Ch Ox BA62 MA65. St Steph Ho Ox 62. **d** 64 **p** 65. C Abbey Hey *Man* 64-68; V Swinton H Rood 68-90; R Old Trafford St Hilda 90-01; R Firswood and Gorse Hill 01-02; rtd 02; Perm to Offic *Man* from 02. *6A Gilda Crescent Road, Eccles, Manchester M30 9AG* Tel 0161-707 9767

BARNETT, James. *See* BARNETT, Alec James Leon
BARNETT, James Andrew McWilliam. b 76. Leeds Univ BA99. Trin Coll Bris BA01. **d** 02 **p** 03. C Bolton St Paul w Em *Man* from 02; TV Leeds St Geo *Ripon* from 05. *14 Parkside Green, Leeds LS6 4NY* Tel 07780-787694 (mobile) E-mail barnettsbarnet@yahoo.co.uk
BARNETT, John. *See* BARNETT, David John
BARNETT, Canon John Raymond. b 51. Lon Univ LLB74 BD86 Birm Univ MA98. Westcott Ho Cam 74. **d** 77 **p** 78. C Northfield *Birm* 77-81; V Hamstead St Bernard 81-91; R The Quinton 91-03; AD Edgbaston 98-03; P-in-c Langley St Jo from 03; P-in-c Langley St Mich from 03; P-in-c Oldbury from 03; P-in-c Londonderry from 04; Hon Can Birm Cathl from 01. *The Vicarage, St John's Road, Oldbury, Warley B68 9RP* Tel 0121-552 5005 Mobile 07980-947238 E-mail barnett4@jajolohe.freeserve.co.uk
BARNETT, John Richard. b 28. Open Univ BA99. Portsm Dioc Tr Course 86. **d** 88 **p** 98. NSM Droxford and Meonstoke w Corhampton cum Exton *Portsm* 88-91; NSM W Meon and Warnford 91-01; rtd 01; Perm to Offic *Chich* from 01. *5 The Croft, 10 St Annes Road, Eastbourne BN21 2DL* Tel (01323) 731711
BARNETT, Michael. *See* BARNETT, Preb Raymond Michael
BARNETT, Canon Norman. b 19. Univ of Wales BA41. St Mich Coll Llan 41. **d** 43 **p** 44. C Roath St German *Llan* 43-49; Chapl Llan Cathl 49-53; R Liss *Portsm* 53-85; RD Petersfield 70-75; Hon Can Portsm Cathl 76-85; rtd 85; Perm to Offic *Portsm* and *Sarum* from 85. *8 Lovells Mead, Marnhull, Sturminster Newton DT10 1JL* Tel (01258) 820260
BARNETT, Miss Patricia Ann. b 38. Whitelands Coll Lon CertEd. St Jo Coll Dur 75. **dss** 78 **d** 87 **p** 94. Gateacre *Liv* 78-82; Litherland St Paul Hatton Hill 82-88; Par Dn 87-88; Par Dn Platt Bridge 88-94; C 94-95; V Skelmersdale Ch at Cen 95-98; rtd 98; Perm to Offic *Liv* from 00. *93 Alder Hey Road, St Helens WA10 4DW* Tel (01744) 607609
BARNETT, Peter Geoffrey. b 46. AKC71. St Aug Coll Cant 71. **d** 72 **p** 73. C Wolverhampton *Lich* 72-77; P-in-c Caldmore 77-83; TR Bris St Agnes and St Simon w St Werburgh *Bris* 83-87; P-in-c Bris St Paul w St Barn 83-87; TR Bris St Paul's 87-94; Warden Pilsdon Community 94-04; Ewell Monastery from 04. *Ewell Monastery, Water Lane, West Malling, Maidstone ME19 6HH* Tel (01732) 843089 Fax 870279 E-mail community@ewell-monastery.co.uk
BARNETT, Preb Raymond Michael. b 31. Man Univ BA54. Wells Th Coll 54. **d** 56 **p** 57. C Fallowfield *Man* 56-59; Madagascar 59-60; V Blackrod *Man* 60-67; V Woolavington *B & W* 67-76; RD Bridgwater 72-76; V St Decumans 76-96; RD Quantock 78-86 and 93-95; Preb Wells Cathl 89-96; rtd 96; Perm to Offic *B & W* from 96. *4 Foster Close, Wells BA5 3NB* Tel (01749) 672983
BARNETT, Russell Scott. b 20. Oak Hill Th Coll 56. **d** 58 **p** 59. C Ulverston St Mary *Carl* 58-61; V Kirkdale St Paul N Shore *Liv* 61-67; V Salterhebble All SS *Wakef* 67-77; R Aikton *Carl* 77-85; R Orton St Giles 77-85; rtd 86; Perm to Offic *Carl* from 86. *5 Heath Mount, Free School Lane, Halifax HX1 2YR* Tel (01422) 349200
BARNFATHER, Thomas Fenwick. b 52. Linc Th Coll 86. **d** 88 **p** 89. C Sedgefield *Dur* 88-91; TV E Darlington 91-92; CF 92-96; V Heybridge w Langford *Chelmsf* 96-98; Chapl HM YOI Dover 98-00; Chapl HM Pris Swaleside 00-01; P-in-c Aylesham w Adisham *Cant* 01-04; Asst Dir of Ords from 02. *2 Archcliffe Fort, Archcliffe Road, Dover CT17 9EL* Tel and fax (01304) 242792 E-mail tomandrosie@home9818.freeserve.co.uk
BARNSHAW, Anthony James. b 72. St Jo Coll Nottm. **d** 05. C Kersal Moor *Man* from 05. *94 Woodward Road, Prestwich, Manchester M25 9TZ* Tel 0161-773 8892 E-mail a.barnshaw@btopenworld.com
BARNSLEY, Mrs Angela Vera. b 47. St Hild Coll Dur BA70. St Alb Minl Tr Scheme 90. **d** 93. NSM Codicote *St Alb* 93-94. *1 All Saints Road, Weymouth DT4 9EZ* Tel (01305) 770406
BARNSLEY, Anna. *See* BARNSLEY, Mrs Valerie Anne
BARNSLEY, David Edward. b 75. Ox Brookes Univ BSc97. Oak Hill Th Coll BA03. **d** 03 **p** 04. C Kilnhurst *Sheff* from 03. *30 Buckthorn Close, Swinton, Mexborough S64 8QY* Tel (01709) 577453 E-mail davidb@rnsley.freeserve.co.uk
BARNSLEY, Canon Melvyn. b 46. Dur Univ BA67 CertEd. St Chad's Coll Dur 64. **d** 71 **p** 72. C Cov St Thos *Cov* 71-74; C Cov St Jo 71-75; V New Bilton 75-82; R Stevenage St Andr and St Geo *St Alb* from 82; RD Stevenage 89-99; Hon Can St Alb from 00. *The Rectory, Cuttys Lane, Stevenage SG1 1UP* Tel (01438) 351631
BARNSLEY, Mrs Valerie Anne (Anna). b 48. Sussex Univ BEd71. WMMTC 91. **d** 94 **p** 95. NSM Tettenhall Regis *Lich* 94-99; Perm to Offic from 99. *The Retreat, Clive Road, Pattingham, Wolverhampton WV6 7BU* Tel (01902) 701713
BARNSTAPLE, Archdeacon of. *See* GUNN-JOHNSON, The Ven David Allan
✠**BAROI, The Rt Revd Michael.** Bp Dhaka and Moderator Ch of Bangladesh from 03. *St Thomas's Church, 54 Johnson Road, Dhaka-1, Bangladesh* Tel and fax (00880) (2) 238218 E-mail cob@citecho.net *or* cbdacdio@bangla.net
BARON, Noel Spencer Peter. b 15. K Coll Cam BA39 MA42. Linc Th Coll 40. **d** 41 **p** 42. C Welwyn Garden City *St Alb* 41-43; C Welwyn 43-48; V Holcombe Rogus w Hockworthy *Ex* 48-52; V W Malvern *Worc* 52-83; rtd 83; Perm to Offic *Heref* from 85; *Glouc* from 98. *Brindley, 21 The Crescent, Colwall, Malvern WR13 6QN* Tel (01684) 540477
BARON, Peter Murray. b 56. New Coll Ox MA78. Cranmer Hall Dur 91. **d** 93 **p** 94. C Monkseaton St Pet *Newc* 93-95; C Guildf St Sav *Guildf* 96-98; V Northwood H Trin *Lon* 98-04. *Address temp unknown*
BARON, Thomas Michael. b 63. St Steph Ho Ox 85. **d** 88 **p** 89. C Hartlepool St Paul *Dur* 88-92; Chapl Asst Hartlepool Gen Hosp 89-92; Asst Chapl Whittington Hosp Lon 92-95; Chapl Enfield Community Care NHS Trust 95-01; Chapl Chase Farm Hosps NHS Trust 95-99; Chapl Barnet and Chase Farm Hosps NHS Trust from 99; Chapl Barnet, Enfield and Haringey Mental Health Trust from 01; Chapl Enfield Primary Care Trust from 01. *The Chaplaincy, Chase Farm Hospital, The Ridgeway, Enfield EN2 8JL* Tel (020) 8375 1078 *or* 8882 1195 E-mail frtom.baron@btinternet.com
BARON, Mrs Vanessa Lillian. b 57. City Univ BSc79 Fitzw Coll Cam MA85 SRN79. Ridley Hall Cam 83. **dss** 86 **d** 87 **p** 94. Roxbourne St Andr *Lon* 86-89; Par Dn 87-89; NSM Roxeth 92-95; Lic Preacher from 95; Asst Chapl Harrow Sch 95-04; Chapl St Paul's Girls' Sch Hammersmith from 04. *2 Kennet House, Harrow Park, Harrow HA1 3JE* Tel (020) 8872 8182 *or* 7603 2288 E-mail vbaron@spgs.org
BARR, John. *See* BARR, Michael John Alexander
BARR, John Gourlay Crichton. b 23. Edin Univ BL46. Edin Dioc NSM Course 81. **d** 84 **p** 85. NSM Edin St Mark *Edin* 84-91; rtd 91; NSM Brechin *Bre* from 92. *Grove House, 22 St Andrew Street, Brechin DD9 6JJ* Tel (01356) 624412
BARR (née HAYTER), Mary Elizabeth. b 58. Jes Coll Ox BA80 CertEd81 MA84 Qu Coll Ox DPhil85. Ridley Hall Cam 84. **dss** 86 **d** 87 **p** 94. Chapl Cam Univ Pastorate 86-91; Cambridge H Trin w St Andr Gt *Ely* 86-87; Par Dn 87-91; Perm to Offic 91-92; Perm to Offic *Ex* 92-94; NSM Torquay St Luke 94-97; NSM Gt Malvern St Mary *Worc* from 97; Chapl Worcs Community Healthcare NHS Trust 99-01; Chapl Worcs Community and Mental Health Trust from 01. *Priory Vicarage, Clarence Road, Malvern WR14 3EN* Tel and fax (01684) 563707 *or* 561020 E-mail jmbarr@ukonline.co.uk *or* office@greatmalvernpriory.org.uk
BARR, Michael John Alexander. b 60. Qu Coll Ox BA82 MA86 Pemb Coll Cam BA86 MA90. Ridley Hall Cam 84. **d** 87 **p** 88. C Earley St Pet *Ox* 87-89; C Cambridge Gt St Mary w St Mich *Ely* 89-92; Chapl Girton Coll Cam 90-92; P-in-c Torquay St Luke *Ex* 92-97; Dioc Communications Officer 92-97; P-in-c Gt Malvern St Mary *Worc* 97-99; V from 99; RD Malvern from 01. *Priory Vicarage, Clarence Road, Malvern WR14 3EN* Tel and fax (01684) 563707 *or* 561020 E-mail jmbarr@ukonline.co.uk *or* office@greatmalvernpriory.org.uk
BARR, Norma Margaret. b 41. Trin Coll Bris BA99. **d** 00 **p** 01. C Aberdour *St And* 01-03; P-in-c Pontiac Grace Ch USA from 03. *Grace Rectory, 410E Torrance Avenue, Pontiac, IL 61764, USA* Tel (001) (815) 842 1743 Fax 844 3331 E-mail norma.m@ukgateway.net
BARR, The Very Revd William Norman Cochrane. b 20. TCD BA44 MA50 BD50. CITC 45. **d** 46 **p** 46. C Ballymena *Conn* 46-52; C Belf Cathl 52-54; R Duneane w Ballyscullion 54-58; Bp's Dom Chapl 56-71; P-in-c Belfast Whiterock 58-61; I Derriaghy w Colin 61-90; Can Conn Cathl 80-82; Dean Conn 82-90; rtd 90. *45 Killeaton Crescent, Dunmurry, Belfast BT17 9HB* Tel (028) 9062 1746 E-mail wncbarr@btinternet.com
BARRACLOUGH, Mrs Barbara Amanda Juliet. b 61. Stirling Univ BA83 Ches Coll of HE MA00. N Ord Course 97. **d** 00 **p** 01. C Lupset *Wakef* 00-04; V W Ardsley from 04. *Woodkirk Vicarage, 1168 Dewsbury Road, Dewsbury WF12 7JL* Tel (01924) 472375 Mobile 07808-382016 Fax (01924) 475758 E-mail amanda.barraclough@blueyonder.co.uk
BARRACLOUGH, Dennis. b 35. St Jo Coll York CertEd58 Lambeth STh68 LCP62 FCP74. Ripon Hall Ox 66. **d** 68 **p** 69. C Woodhouse *Wakef* 68-71; V Gildersome 71-83; V Kirkburton 83-00; RD Kirkburton 92-98; rtd 00; Perm to Offic *Wakef* from 00. *8 Clough Park, Fenay Bridge, Huddersfield HD8 0JH* Tel (01484) 325515
BARRACLOUGH, Canon Owen Conrad. b 32. Pemb Coll Cam BA55 MA59. Westcott Ho Cam 56. **d** 57 **p** 58. C Chippenham St Andr w Tytherton Lucas *Bris* 57-62; V Harringay St Paul *Lon* 62-70; Bp's Chapl for Community Relns *Cov* 70-77; P-in-c Baginton 72-77; V Swindon Ch Ch *Bris* 77-97; Chapl Princess Marg Hosp Swindon 77-89; Hon Can Bris Cathl *Bris* 87-97; rtd 98; Perm to Offic *Bris* from 98 and *Glouc* 98-01; Jt P-in-c Staverton w Boddington and Tredington etc *Glouc* 01-04; NSM

Twigworth, Down Hatherley, Norton, The Leigh etc from 04. *Robin Hollow, 10A Church Road, St Marks, Cheltenham GL51 7AN* Tel (01242) 230855

BARRALL, John Henry. b 31. BEd. Bps' Coll Cheshunt. **d** 61 **p** 62. C Digswell *St Alb* 61-65; C Aldershot St Mich *Guildf* 65-70; TV Hemel Hempstead *St Alb* 70-82; Perm to Offic 83-91; R Meppershall w Campton and Stondon 91-98; rtd 98; Perm to Offic *Ely* from 99 and *St Alb* from 01; OCF 97-03. *10 Caldecote Road, Ickwell, Biggleswade SG18 9EH* Tel (01767) 627407 E-mail john@barrall.fsnet.co.uk

BARRAND, George William (Bill). b 33. HNC55. Lon Coll of Div 59. **d** 62 **p** 63. C Bucknall and Bagnall *Lich* 62-65; C Parr *Liv* 65-69; Australia from 70; rtd 98. *2/20 Riversdale Road, Yarra Junction, Vic, Australia 3797* Tel (0061) (3) 5967 2592

BARRATT, The Ven Anthony John. b 19. Glas Univ MRCVS. Bible Churchmen's Coll Bris. **d** 49 **p** 50. C Slough *Ox* 49-52; SAMS Miss Cholchol Falkland Is 52-64; Hon Can Port Stanley 57-64; SAMS Miss Asuncin Paraguay 64-70; Argentina 70-84; Adn Tucuman 73-84; rtd 84. *Couchill Villa, Couchill Farm Lane, Seaton EX12 3AL* Tel (01297) 21118

BARRATT, Mrs Elizabeth June. b 32. ACP65. Trin Coll Bris 75. **dss** 78 **d** 87 **p** 94. W Kilburn St Luke w St Simon and St Jude *Lon* 78-87; Par Dn 87-94; C 94-98; rtd 98; Hon C Kensal Rise St Mark and St Martin *Lon* from 99. *68A Bathhurst Gardens, London NW10 5HY* Tel (020) 8968 5951

BARRATT, Peter. b 29. Down Coll Cam BA53 MA57. Ridley Hall Cam 53. **d** 55 **p** 56. C Bebington *Ches* 55-58; C-in-c Cam St Martin CD *Ely* 58-61; V Cambridge St Martin 61-68; V Rawtenstall St Mary *Man* 68-83; AD Rossendale 80-83; V Bosley and N Rode w Wincle and Wildboarclough *Ches* 83-94; rtd 94; Perm to Offic *Ches* from 94. *10 Snab Wood Close, Little Neston, Neston CH64 0UP* Tel 0151-336 6641

BARRATT, Philip Norman. b 62. Aston Tr Scheme 87 St Steph Ho Ox 89 Coll of Resurr Mirfield 90. **d** 92 **p** 93. C Heywood St Luke w All So *Man* 92-96; V Thornham St Jas from 96. *St James's Vicarage, 120 Shaw Road, Rochdale OL16 4SQ* Tel (01706) 645256 Mobile 07775-646733 E-mail pn.barratt@zen.co.uk

BARRELL, Adrian Edward. b 36. Keble Coll Ox BA59. Ely Th Coll 59. **d** 62 **p** 63. C Plymouth St Jas Ham *Ex* 62-66; C Bideford 66-70; V Walkhampton 70-80; rtd 01. *Cartref, Dousland, Yelverton PL20 6PA* Tel (01822) 852612

BARRETT, Alan. b 48. Southn Univ BA69. Wycliffe Hall Ox 74. **d** 77 **p** 78. C Conisbrough *Sheff* 77-80; C Lower Homerton St Paul *Lon* 80-81; C-in-c Hounslow Gd Shep Beavers Lane CD 81-87; R Langdon Hills *Chelmsf* 87-97; P-in-c Tamworth *Lich* 97-03; V from 03; RD Tamworth 99-04. *The Vicarage, Hospital Street, Tamworth B79 7EE* Tel and fax (01827) 62446 *or* tel 68339 E-mail alan.barrett@breathemail.net

BARRETT, Alastair David. b 75. Fitzw Coll Cam BA97 MA01 Birm Univ BD00. Qu Coll Birm MA01. **d** 01 **p** 02. C Sutton Coldfield St Chad *Birm* 01-04; C Langley St Jo from 04; C Langley St Mich from 04; C Oldbury from 04; C Londonderry from 04. *St Mark's Vicarage, 15 St Mark's Road, Smethwick B67 6QF* Tel 0121-429 1149 E-mail alastair.barrett@btopenworld.com

BARRETT, Mrs Alexandra Mary. b 75. Clare Coll Cam BA96 MA99. Westcott Ho Cam 00. **d** 03 **p** 04. C Godmanchester *Ely* from 03. *59 London Road, Godmanchester, Huntingdon PE29 2HZ* Tel (01480) 450852 Mobile 07790-673546 E-mail allyb@fish.co.uk

BARRETT, Arthur. *See* BARRETT, Kenneth Arthur Lambart

BARRETT, Christopher Paul. b 49. AKC71 St Aug Coll Cant 71. **d** 72 **p** 73. C Tupsley *Heref* 72-75; C Ex St Thos *Ex* 75-79; R Atherington and High Bickington 79-83; V Burrington 79-83; Asst Dir of Educn 79-87; P-in-c Sticklepath 83-85; P-in-c Barnstaple 83-85; TV 85-90; V Whipton 90-99; TV Ex St Thos and Em from 99. *St Andrew's Vicarage, 78 Queens Road, Exeter EX2 9EW* Tel (01392) 439501

BARRETT, Clive. b 55. Ox Univ BA76 MA80 CertEd77 Leeds Univ PhD98. St Steph Ho Ox 80. **d** 83 **p** 84. C Wakef Cathl *Wakef* 83-87; Asst Chapl Leeds Univ *Ripon* 87-97; Dioc Development Rep 89-92; P-in-c Middleton St Cross from 98. *St Cross Vicarage, Middleton Park Avenue, Leeds LS10 4HT* Tel 0113-271 6398 Mobile 07966-540699 E-mail clivebarrett@hotmail.com

BARRETT, David Brian. b 27. Clare Coll Cam BA48 MA50 BD69 Columbia Univ (NY) PhD65. Union Th Sem (NY) STM63 PhD65 Ridley Hall Cam 52. **d** 54 **p** 55. Succ Bradf Cathl *Bradf* 54-56; CMS 57-92; Kenya 57-62 and 65-85; USA 62-63; Guatemala 63-65; Research Sec ACC 70-87; Lic to Offic *Lon* 70-87; USA from 87; rtd 92. *2503 Prestwick Circle, Richmond, VA 23294, USA* Tel (001) (804) 747 7455 Fax 358 0504

BARRETT, Canon Derek Leonard. b 25. St Fran Coll Brisbane ThL57. **d** 57 **p** 58. Australia 57-63; C Ramsgate St Geo *Cant* 64-65; C Putney St Mary *S'wark* 65-67; V Kidderminster St Jo *Worc* 67-77; V Stourbridge St Thos 77-90; RD Stourbridge 83-89; Hon Can Worc Cathl 87-90; rtd 90; Perm to Offic *Glouc*; *Worc* from 90. *Lotty Leven, Crystal Waters, M/S 16, Maleny, Qld, Australia 4552*

BARRETT, Gary John. b 46. Sarum & Wells Th Coll 87. **d** 90 **p** 91. NSM Guernsey St Peter Port *Win* 90-97; Chapl Eliz Coll Guernsey 93-97; P-in-c Westham *Chich* 97-98; V from 98. *The Vicarage, 6 Rattle Road, Westham, Pevensey BN24 5DE* Tel (01323) 762294

BARRETT, Graham Crichton. b 51. IEng76 FIMEMME78. Linc Th Coll 88. **d** 90 **p** 91. C Torpoint *Truro* 90-94; Dio Youth and Voc Officer 94-95; C St Columb Major w St Wenn 94-95; P-in-c St Issey w St Petroc Minor 95-00; Dioc Children's Adv 95-00. *Address temp unknown*

BARRETT, John Joseph James. b 38. Lon Univ BD65. Sarum & Wells Th Coll. **d** 78 **p** 78. C Danbury *Chelmsf* 78-80; Ind Chapl 80-89; C Dovercourt 80-83; TV Dovercourt and Parkeston 83-89; V Rubery *Birm* 89-04; rtd 04. *4 Arran Hill, Thrybergh, Rotherham S65 4BH* Tel (01709) 850288 E-mail rev.barrett@btinternet.com

BARRETT, Jonathan Murray. b 68. Oak Hill Th Coll BA98. **d** 98 **p** 99. C Pennycross *Ex* 98-02; TV Plymouth Em, St Paul Efford and St Aug from 02. *28A Sefton Avenue, Plymouth PL4 7HB* Tel (01752) 661797

BARRETT, Canon Kenneth. b 42. Univ of Wales (Lamp) BA64. St Steph Ho Ox 65. **d** 67 **p** 68. C Poulton-le-Fylde *Blackb* 67-69; C S Shore H Trin 69-72; V Brierfield 72-83; V Chorley St Geo from 83; Hon Can Blackb Cathl from 03. *St George's Vicarage, Letchworth Place, Chorley PR7 2HJ* Tel (01257) 263064

BARRETT, Kenneth Arthur Lambart. b 60. CITC BTh94. **d** 97 **p** 98. C Seagoe *D & D* 97-00; I Dublin Booterstown *D & G* 00-04; I Dublin Mt Merrion 00-04; I Boyle and Elphin w Aghanagh, Kilbryan etc *K, E & A* from 04; I Taunagh w Kilmactranny, Ballysumaghan etc from 04. *The Rectory, Riverstown, Co Sligo, Irish Republic* Tel and fax (00353) (71) 916 5368 *or* tel 966 3000 E-mail boyle@elphin.anglican.org

BARRETT, Canon Kenneth Sydney. b 26. Roch Th Coll 60. **d** 62 **p** 63. C Wollaton *S'well* 62-65; C Hucknall Torkard 65-67; Australia from 67; Can Bunbury 76-92; rtd 92. *PO Box 818, 2 Loxton Street, Mandurah, W Australia 6210* Tel (0061) (8) 9581 2519 Fax as telephone E-mail joykenb@iinet.net.au

BARRETT, Mrs Marion Lily. b 54. Ex Univ BA01 SRN75. SW Minl Tr Course 91. **d** 94 **p** 95. C St Mawgan w St Ervan and St Eval *Truro* 94-97; C St Breoke and Egloshayle 97-98; Asst Chapl R Cornwall Hosps Trust 98-99; Chapl 00-05; R St Mewan w Mevagissey and St Ewe *Truro* from 05. *The Rectory, St Mewan Lane, St Mewan, St Austell PL26 7DP* Tel (01726) 72679 E-mail marionstmewan@btinternet.com

BARRETT, Paul. *See* BARRETT, Christopher Paul

✠**BARRETT, The Rt Revd Peter Francis.** b 56. TCD BA78 MA81 MPhil84. CITC 78. **d** 81 **p** 82 **c** 03. C Drumachose *D & R* 81-83; C Dublin St Ann *D & G* 83-85; I Conwal Union w Gartan *D & R* 85-90; I Belfast St Geo *Conn* 90-94; Chapl TCD 94-98; Min Can St Patr Cathl Dublin 94-96; Succ 96-98; Dean Waterford *C & O* 98-03; I Waterford w Killea, Drumcannon and Dunhill 98-03; Bp C & O from 03. *Knocknabooley, Stoneyford, Co Kilkenny, Irish Republic* Tel (00353) (56) 772 8818 *or* 776 1910 E-mail bishop@cashel.anglican.org

BARRETT, Mrs Rachel Jeanne Alexandra. b 56. Ex Univ BA78 PGCE79. SW Minl Tr Course 92. **d** 95 **p** 96. NSM Ex St Mark *Ex* 95-96; NSM Ex St Mark, St Sidwell and St Matt 96-00; Chapl St Margaret's Sch Ex 00-05; Chapl Derby High Sch from 05. *Derby High School, Hillsway, Littleover, Derby DE23 3DT* Tel (01332) 514267 Fax 516085

BARRETT, Ronald Reginald. b 30. Roch Th Coll 61. **d** 64 **p** 65. C Spring Park *Cant* 64-66; C Thornton Heath St Jude 66-68; V Greengates *Bradf* 68-73; V Shelf 73-79; V Embsay w Eastby 79-87; V Farndon and Coddington *Ches* 87-92; rtd 92; Perm to Offic *Bradf* from 92. *12 Craigmore Drive, Ben Rhydding, Ilkley LS29 8PG* Tel (01943) 609713

BARRETT, Stephen David Norman. b 54. Aber Univ BSc75 Edin Univ BD78. Edin Th Coll 75. **d** 78 **p** 79. C Ardrossan *Glas* 78-80; R Peterhead *Ab* 80-81; Chapl HM Pris Peterhead 80-81; R Renfrew *Glas* 81-87; R Bishopbriggs 87-94; Chapl HM Pris Glas (Barlinnie) 87-94; Chapl Stobhill Gen Hosp 87-94; P-in-c Port Glas 94-99; R from 99. *St Mary's Rectory, Bardrainney Avenue, Port Glasgow PA14 6HB* Tel (01475) 707444

BARRIBAL, Richard James Pitt. b 45. Trin Coll Bris DipTh80. **d** 80 **p** 81. C Northampton St Giles *Pet* 80-82; V Long Buckby w Watford 82-86; Perm to Offic from 86; Perm to Offic *Leic* from 00. *45 Knights End Road, Great Bowden, Market Harborough LE16 7EY* Tel (01858) 431495 Fax 468852 E-mail richard.barribal@lineone.net

BARRIE, John Arthur. b 38. K Coll Lon 58 Bps' Coll Cheshunt 59. **d** 63 **p** 64. C Southgate St Mich *Lon* 63-66; CF 66-88; Sen CF 88-93; Chapl Guards Chpl Lon 88-92; QHC 91-93; P-in-c Heref H Trin *Heref* 93-96; P-in-c Breinton 95-96; V St Marylebone St Mark Hamilton Terrace *Lon* from 96; Ecum Adv (Two Cities Area) from 99. *St Mark's Vicarage, 114 Hamilton Terrace, London NW8 9UT* Tel (020) 7328 4373 *or* 7624 4065 E-mail john.barrie1@btopenworld.com

BARRINGTON, Dominic Matthew Jesse. b 62. Hatf Coll Dur BA84 MSc85 LTCL. Ripon Coll Cuddesdon BA94 MA98 Ch

Div Sch of Pacific MTS95. **d** 95 **p** 96. C Mortlake w E Sheen *S'wark* 95-98; Chapl St Chad's Coll Dur 98-03; P-in-c Kettering SS Pet and Paul *Pet* from 03. *The Rectory, Church Walk, Kettering NN16 0DJ* Tel and fax (01536) 513385 Mobile 07720-704953 E-mail dominic@peterandpaul.org.uk

✠**BARRINGTON-WARD, The Rt Revd Simon.** b 30. KCMG01. Magd Coll Cam BA53 MA57. Wycliffe Coll Toronto Hon DD Westcott Ho Cam 54. **d** 56 **p** 57 **c** 85. Chapl Magd Coll Cam 56-60; Nigeria 60-63; Fell and Dean of Chpl Magd Coll Cam 63-69; Prin Crowther Hall CMS Tr Coll Selly Oak 69-74; Gen Sec CMS 75-85; Hon Can Derby Cathl *Derby* 75-85; Chapl to The Queen 84-85; Bp Cov 85-97; rtd 97; Hon Fell Magd Coll Cam from 87; Hon Asst Chapl from 98; Hon Asst Bp Ely from 97. *4 Searle Street, Cambridge CB4 3DB* Tel (01223) 740460 E-mail sb292@cam.ac.uk

BARRODALE, Canon George Bryan. b 44. Univ of Wales (Ban) DipTh DipMin88. St Mich Coll Llan 67. **d** 69 **p** 70. C Maindee *Mon* 69-72; TV Merthyr Tydfil and Cyfarthfa *Llan* 72-76; R Cotgrave *S'well* 76-00; P-in-c Owthorpe 76-00; CF (TA) 76-86; RD Bingham *S'well* 94-00; Hon Can S'well Minster from 97; V Beeston from 00. *The Vicarage, Middle Street, Beeston, Nottingham NG9 1GA* Tel 0115-925 4571 E-mail bbarrodale@aol.com

BARRON, Arthur Henry. b 45. Solicitor 72. SEITE 99. **d** 02 **p** 03. NSM Addiscombe St Mary Magd w St Martin *S'wark* from 02; Chapl Asst St Mary's NHS Trust Paddington from 05. *23 Little Woodcote Lane, Purley CR8 3PZ* Tel (020) 8763 0934 Mobile 07710-275977 E-mail art_barron@hotmail.com

BARRON, Kurt Karl. b 60. Chich Th Coll BTh92. **d** 92 **p** 93. C Bulwell St Mary *S'well* 92-97; TV Southend *Chelmsf* 97-01; P-in-c Mansfield St Lawr *S'well* from 01. *St Lawrence's Vicarage, 3 Shaw Street, Mansfield NG18 2NP* Tel (01623) 623698

BARRON, Leslie Gill. b 44. ACII69. Lich Th Coll 67. **d** 70 **p** 71. C Bishopwearmouth Ch Ch *Dur* 70-72; C Bishopwearmouth St Mary V w St Pet CD 72-75; C Harton 75-77; V Lumley 77-88; P-in-c Hendon and Sunderland 88-90; R Hendon 90-94; P-in-c Ushaw Moor 94-95; V Bearpark and Ushaw Moor 95-04. *34 Brecongill Close, Hartlepool TS24 8PH*

BARRON, Richard Davidson. b 51. Lon Univ BSc74. Trin Coll Bris 75. **d** 78 **p** 79. C Bradley *Wakef* 78-81; C Heworth H Trin *York* 81-82; TV 82-89; Chapl York Distr Hosp 82-86; R Greenhithe St Mary *Roch* from 89. *The Rectory, Mounts Road, Greenhithe DA9 9ND* Tel (01322) 382031 E-mail rbarron@smgreenhithe.freeserve.co.uk

BARRON, Canon Victor Robert. b 45. Lon Bible Coll DipTh68 St Luke's Coll Ex CertEd70. Trin Coll Bris 76. **d** 78 **p** 79. C Rainham *Chelmsf* 78-81; V Easton H Trin w St Gabr and St Lawr *Bris* 81-82; V Easton H Trin w St Gabr and St Lawr and St Jude 82-89; TR Kinson *Sarum* 89-00; RD Poole 94-00; Can and Preb Sarum Cathl 98-00; rtd 00; Perm to Offic *Sarum* from 00. *April Cottage, 159 Middlehill Road, Wimborne BH21 2HJ* Tel and fax (01202) 848236 E-mail vicbarron@onetel.com

BARROW, Paul. b 48. **d** 04 **p** 05. NSM Ches H Trin *Ches* from 04. *1 Haslin Crescent, Christleton, Chester CH3 6AN* Tel (01244) 332002

BARRY, Colin Lionel. Open Univ BSc94. Bp Attwell Tr Inst 85. **d** 96 **p** 97. NSM Arbory *S & M* from 96. *80 Ballanorris Crescent, Ballabeg, Castletown, Isle of Man IM9 4ER* Tel (01624) 823080

BARRY, Ms Jacqueline Françoise. Univ of Bordeaux II LSocEth86 MSoc87 York Univ PGCE91. Ridley Hall Cam. **d** 99 **p** 00. C Sydenham H Trin *S'wark* 99-03; C Paddington Em Harrow Road *Lon* from 03; C W Kilburn St Luke w St Simon and St Jude from 03. *Emmanuel Vicarage, 44C Fermoy Road, London W9 3NH* Tel (020) 8969 0438 E-mail jackie.barry@lineone.net

BARRY, Canon John. b 15. TCD BA38 BA37 TCD MA41. CITC 38. **d** 38 **p** 39. C Belfast St Matt *Conn* 38-41; C Dundela St Mark *D & D* 41-45; I Dunluce *Conn* 45-49; I Hillsborough *D & D* 49-83; Can Belf Cathl 56-64; Chan Down Cathl *D & D* 64-73; Preb St Patr Cathl Dublin 73-83; rtd 83. *16 West Park, Lisburn BT28 2BQ* Tel (028) 9267 0664

BARRY, Canon Jonathan Peter Oulton. b 47. TCD BA70 MA73 Hull Univ BA73 QUB PhD84. Ripon Hall Ox 73. **d** 74 **p** 75. C Dundela St Mark *D & D* 74-79; I Ballyphilip w Ardquin 79-85; Dioc Info Officer 80-90; I Comber from 85; Preb St Audoen St Patr Cathl Dublin from 01. *The Rectory, 12 Windmill Hill, Comber, Newtownards BT23 5WH* Tel and fax (028) 9187 2283 E-mail comber@down.anglican.org

BARRY, Keith Gordon. b 67. TCD BA92. CITC 92. **d** 94 **p** 95. C Templemore *D & R* 94-97; V Choral Derry Cathl 94-97; CF from 97. *c/o MOD Chaplains (Army)* Tel (01980) 615804 Fax 615800

BARRY, Nicholas Brian Paul. b 61. Leic Univ BA83. St Steph Ho Ox 84. **d** 87 **p** 88. C St John's Wood *Lon* 87-90; Chapl RAF from 90. *Chaplaincy Services (RAF), HQ, Personnel and Training Command, RAF Innsworth, Gloucester GL3 1EZ* Tel (01452) 712612 ext 5164 Fax 510828

BARSLEY, Canon Margaret Ann. b 39. Totley Hall Coll CertEd60. EMMTC 79. **dss** 83 **d** 87 **p** 94. Kirton in Holland *Linc* 83-89; NSM 87-89; NSM Skirbeck Quarter 89-96; P-in-c Swineshead 96-99; V 99-04; RD Holland W 97-04; Can and Preb Linc Cathl from 00; rtd 04. *44 Sentance Crescent, Kirton, Boston PE20 1XF* E-mail margaret@churchlane8539.freeserve.co.uk

BARTER, Christopher Stuart. b 49. Chich Th Coll. **d** 84 **p** 85. C Margate St Jo *Cant* 84-88; R Whitwood *Wakef* 88-95; Chapl Castleford, Normanton and Distr Hosp 88-95; P-in-c Ravensthorpe *Wakef* 95-98; AIDS Cllr W Yorks HA 95-98; TV Gt Yarmouth *Nor* 98-02; R Somersham w Pidley and Oldhurst *Ely* from 02. *The Rectory, Rectory Lane, Somersham, Huntingdon PE28 3EL* Tel (01487) 840676 E-mail chrisbarter@talk21.com

BARTER, The Very Revd Donald. b 34. St Fran Coll Brisbane ThL69 ACT ThSchol74. **d** 69 **p** 70. Australia 69-90 and from 93; C Townsville 69-72; R Mareeba 72-76; R Ingham 76-81; Adn of the W and R Mt Isa 81-86; Dean Townsville 86-90; Chapl Miss to Seamen 86-90; Chapl HM Police Service 88-90; Appeals Dir SPCK 90-93; Lic to Offic *Leic* 90-93; Asst to Dean St Jas Cathl 94-00. *6 Sixth Avenue, South Townsville, Qld, Australia 4810* Tel and fax (0061) (7) 4772 7036 Mobile 414-989593 E-mail donbarter@optusnet.com.au

BARTER, Geoffrey Roger. b 41. Bris Univ BSc63. Clifton Th Coll 65. **d** 67 **p** 68. C Normanton *Derby* 67-70; C Rainham *Chelmsf* 70-75; V Plumstead St Jo w St Jas and St Paul *S'wark* 75-82; V Frogmore *St Alb* 82-01; rtd 01; Perm to Offic *Chich* from 02. *45 West Front Road, Pagham, Bognor Regis PO21 4SZ* Tel (01243) 262522

BARTER, Leonard Reginald Treseder. **d** 95. OLM St Stythians w Perranarworthal and Gwennap *Truro* from 95. *1 Valandrucia, Foundry, Stithians, Truro TR3 7BU* Tel (01209) 860341

BARTER, Susan Kathleen. b 53. Open Univ MBA97. Ridley Hall Cam 01. **d** 03 **p** 04. C Happisburgh, Walcott, Hempstead w Eccles etc *Nor* from 03. *Atherstone House, Lighthouse Lane, Happisburgh, Norwich NR12 0QA* Tel (01692) 652248 Mobile 07778-063644 E-mail susan@thecoastalgroup.co.uk

BARTHOLOMEW, Craig Gerald. b 61. UNISA BTh82 Potchefstroom Univ MA92 Bris Univ PhD97. Wycliffe Hall Ox BA84 MA88. **d** 86 **p** 87. S Africa 86-92; C Pinetown Ch Ch 87-89; Lect Geo Whitefield Coll Cape Town 89-92; Research Fell Glos Univ 97-04; Perm to Offic *Glouc* from 98. *Gisela's Cottage, Lyday Close, Oakridge, Stroud GL6 7NU* Tel (01285) 760590 Mobile 07788-413755 E-mail cbartholomew@chelt.ac.uk

BARTHOLOMEW, David Grant. b 50. Univ of Wales (Lamp) BA77 Brighton Poly DMS78. Chich Th Coll 91. **d** 93 **p** 94. C Petersfield *Portsm* 93-96; R Etton w Helpston and Maxey *Pet* 96-98; R Burghclere w Newtown and Ecchinswell w Sydmonton *Win* from 98. *The Rectory, Well Street, Burghclere, Newbury RG20 9HS* Tel (01635) 278470 E-mail davidrectory@aol.com

BARTLAM, Alan Thomas. b 51. Bris Univ BEd74. Linc Th Coll 88. **d** 90 **p** 91. C Longdon-upon-Tern, Rodington, Uppington etc *Lich* 90-92; C Tilstock and Whixall 92-95; V Tilstock, Edstaston and Whixall 95-98; R Bewcastle, Stapleton and Kirklinton etc *Carl* from 98. *Stapleton Rectory, Roweltown, Carlisle CA6 6LD* Tel (01697) 748660 E-mail alanbartlam@stapletonrectory.freeserve.co.uk

BARTLE, Alan. b 45. Ridley Hall Cam 82. **d** 84 **p** 85. C Ely 84-88; V 87-93; V Chettisham 87-93; V Prickwillow 87-93; P-in-c Thorney Abbey 93-95. *Address temp unknown*

BARTLE, Canon David Colin. b 29. Em Coll Cam BA53 MA57. Ridley Hall Cam 53. **d** 55 **p** 56. C Birm St Martin *Birm* 55-57; C Boscombe St Jo *Win* 57-60; V Lowestoft St Jo *Nor* 60-70; P-in-c Thetford St Cuth w H Trin 70-72; P-in-c Thetford St Mary 70-72; P-in-c Thetford St Pet w St Nic 70-72; TR Thetford 72-75; P-in-c Kilverstone 70-75; P-in-c Croxton 70-75; Teacher Bournemouth Sch 75-83; R Brantham w Stutton *St E* 83-90; RD Samford 86-90; P-in-c Roxwell *Chelmsf* 90-93; Dioc Dir of Ords 90-93; Dioc Lay Min Adv 90-93; Hon Can Chelmsf Cathl 91-93; rtd 93; Perm to Offic *Win* 93-98; Chapl R Bournemouth and Christchurch Hosps NHS Trust 98-00. *40 Blue Waters Drive, Paignton TQ4 6JE* Tel (01803) 843456 E-mail dbartle8@aol.com

BARTLE, Canon Reginald Stephen. b 24. K Coll Lon AKC51 BD52. **d** 52 **p** 53. C Penge Ch Ch w H Trin *Roch* 52-55; SAMS 55-79; Chile 55-70; Adn Chile 64-70; Hon Can Chile from 64; NW Area Sec SAMS 70-73; Home Sec 73-79; C Tunbridge Wells St Jas *Roch* 80-83; rtd 83; Perm to Offic *St D* 84-94; *Chelmsf* 94-00; *S'wark* 00-01; *Cant* 01-03. *24 Bromley College, London Road, Bromley BR1 1PE* Tel (020) 8460 7128

BARTLE-JENKINS, Canon Leonard Christmas. b 13. Univ of Wales (Lamp) BA35. Lich Th Coll 35. **d** 38 **p** 39. C Fleur-de-Lis *Mon* 38-41; C Trevethin 41-47; V Llangattock-vibon-Avel 47-55; V Bassaleg 55-74; Can St Woolos Cathl 64-82; RD Bassaleg 67-82; R Michaelston-y-Fedw and Rudry 74-82; rtd 82; Lic to Offic *Mon* from 82; Perm to Offic *Llan* from 82. *c/o Mrs C Judd, 13 Grove Road, Bridgend CF31 3EF*

BARTLE-JENKINS, Paul. b 43. Bris & Glouc Tr Course. **d** 84 **p** 86. NSM Bris St Agnes and St Simon w St Werburgh *Bris* 84-87; NSM Bris St Paul's from 87. *188A Henleaze Road, Westbury-on-Trym, Bristol BS9 4NE* Tel 0117-962 0286 E-mail fatherpaul00@hotmail.com

BARTLES-SMITH, The Ven Douglas Leslie. b 37. St Edm Hall Ox BA61 MA65. Wells Th Coll 61. **d** 63 **p** 64. C Westmr St Steph w St Jo *Lon* 63-68; P-in-c Camberwell St Mich w All So w Em *S'wark* 68-72; V 72-75; V Battersea St Luke 75-85; RD Battersea 81-85; Adn S'wark 85-04; rtd 04; Chapl to The Queen from 96; Perm to Offic *Lich* from 04. *18 Vane Road, Shrewsbury SY3 7HB* Tel (01743) 363282

BARTLETT, Alan Bennett. b 58. G&C Coll Cam BA81 MA85 Birm Univ PhD87 St Jo Coll Dur BA90. Cranmer Hall Dur 88. **d** 91 **p** 92. C Newc H Cross *Newc* 91-94; C Newburn 94-96; Tutor Cranmer Hall Dur from 96. *Cranmer Hall, St John's College, 3 South Bailey, Durham DH1 3RJ* Tel 0191-334 3849 E-mail a.b.bartlett@durham.ac.uk

BARTLETT, Anthony Martin. b 43. Cranmer Hall Dur 74. **d** 77 **p** 78. C Heworth St Mary *Dur* 77-80; V Cleadon 80-84; CF (TA) 81-90; Prec Dur Cathl *Dur* 85-87; V Harton 87-95; P-in-c Hendon 95-96; R 96-97; V Greenlands *Blackb* from 01. *St Anne's House, Salmesbury Avenue, Blackpool FY2 0PR* Tel (01253) 353900 E-mail bcressell@aol.com

BARTLETT, David John. b 36. Pemb Coll Ox BA61. Linc Th Coll 63. **d** 65 **p** 66. C Wollaton *S'well* 65-70; V Woodthorpe 70-83; V Farnsfield 83-01; P-in-c Kirklington w Hockerton 83-01; RD S'well 83-93; Chapl Rodney Sch Kirklington 83-01; rtd 01; Perm to Offic *S'well* from 01. *6 De Havilland Way, Farndon Road, Newark NG24 4RF* Tel (01636) 651582

BARTLETT, David William. b 59. Trin Coll Bris 89. **d** 91 **p** 92. C Frinton *Chelmsf* 91-95; TV Eston w Normanby *York* 95-96; Assoc P Worksop St Jo *S'well* 96-01; TV Trunch *Nor* from 01. *The Rectory, Clipped Hedge Lane, Southrepps, Norwich NR11 8NS* Tel (01263) 833404 E-mail revdb@beeb.net

BARTLETT, George Frederick. b 34. Clifton Th Coll 61. **d** 64 **p** 65. C Branksome St Clem *Sarum* 64-71; V Gt Baddow *Chelmsf* 71-72; Perm to Offic *Win* 81-87; rtd 99. *8 Glencarron Way, Southampton SO16 7EF* Tel (023) 8032 5162 E-mail george.bartlett@cwcom.net

BARTLETT, Prof John Raymond. b 37. BNC Ox BA59 MA62 BLitt62 TCD MA70 LittD94. Linc Th Coll 61. **d** 63 **p** 64. C W Bridgford *S'well* 63-66; Lect Div TCD 66-86; Assoc Prof Bibl Studies 86-92; Fell 75-92; Prof Past Th 90-01; Prin CITC 89-01; Treas Ch Ch Cathl Dublin *D & G* 86-88; Prec 88-01; rtd 01. *102 Sorrento Road, Dalkey, Co Dublin, Irish Republic* Tel (00353) (1) 284 7786 E-mail jrbartlett@eircom.net

BARTLETT, Kenneth Vincent John. b 36. OBE93. Oriel Coll Ox BA61 BTh63. Ripon Hall Ox 61. **d** 63 **p** 64. C Paddington St Jas *Lon* 63-67; Lic to Offic from 67; rtd 01. *25 Tudor Road, Kingston-upon-Thames KT2 6AS* Tel (020) 8541 0378 E-mail shaa4949@aol.com

BARTLETT, Canon Maurice Edward. b 33. G&C Coll Cam BA59 MA63. Wells Th Coll 59. **d** 60 **p** 61. C Batley All SS *Wakef* 60-64; Bp's Dom Chapl 64-66; Dir of Ords 64-66; Asst Chapl HM Pris Wakef 64-66; V Allerton *Liv* 66-81; V Lancaster St Mary *Blackb* 81-97; Sub-Chapl HM Pris Lanc 81-97; Hon Can Blackb Cathl 87-97; rtd 97. *Waverley House, West Common, Bowness-on-Solway, Carlisle CA7 5AG*

BARTLETT, Michael Fredrick. b 52. Ex Univ BA74 Liv Univ BPhil75 Ox Univ BA79 MA. Ripon Coll Cuddesdon 76 Ven English Coll Rome 78. **d** 79 **p** 80. C Kirkby *Liv* 79-82; C Wordsley *Lich* 82-83; TV 83-88; Chapl Wordsley Hosp 82-88; TV Redditch, The Ridge *Worc* 88-05; TR Redditch Ch the K from 05. *St Luke's Rectory, 69 Evesham Road, Redditch B97 4JX* Tel (01527) 545521

BARTLETT, Preb Michael George. b 35. S Dios Minl Tr Scheme 84. **d** 87 **p** 88. NSM Wimborne Minster and Holt *Sarum* 87-90; C Charlestown *Truro* 90-91; R St Endellion w Port Isaac and St Kew from 91; Preb St Endellion from 91. *The Rectory, St Endellion, Port Isaac PL29 3TP* Tel (01208) 880442

BARTLETT, Canon Richard Charles. b 68. St Kath Coll Liv BA90 Surrey Univ MA01. Westcott Ho Cam 91. **d** 94 **p** 95. C Wareham *Sarum* 94-98; Assoc V Ealing All SS *Lon* 98-02; Chapl Twyford C of E High Sch Acton 98-02; USPG Brazil 02-05; Hon Can Brasilia Cathl from 05; V Northwood H Trin *Lon* from 05. *Holy Trinity Vicarage, Gateway Close, Northwood HA6 2RW* Tel (01923) 825732 E-mail richard.bartlett@london.anglican.org

BARTON, Andrew Edward. b 53. MRSC St Jo Coll Ox MA77 DPhil80. Ridley Hall Cam 87. **d** 90 **p** 91. C Ringwood *Win* 90-94; R Baughurst, Ramsdell, Wolverton w Ewhurst etc from 95; Lect K Alfred's Coll Win 95-98. *The Rectory, Wolverton, Tadley RG26 5RU* Tel and fax (01635) 298008 Mobile 07778-771651 E-mail andrew.e.barton@ntlworld.com

BARTON, Anne. *See* BARTON, Margaret Anne

BARTON, Canon Arthur Michael. b 33. CCC Cam BA57 MA61. Wycliffe Hall Ox 57. **d** 59 **p** 60. Min Can Bradf Cathl *Bradf* 59-61; C Maltby *Sheff* 61-63; V Silsden *Bradf* 63-70; V Moor Allerton *Ripon* 70-81; TR 81-82; V Wetherby 82-98; Chapl HM YOI Wetherby 82-89; RD Harrogate *Ripon* 88-95; Hon Can Ripon Cathl 89-98; rtd 98; Perm to Offic *Ripon* from 98. *22 Ash Road, Harrogate HG2 8EG* Tel (01423) 870799 E-mail teambarton@aol.com

BARTON, The Ven Charles John Greenwood. b 36. ALCD63. **d** 63 **p** 64. C Cant St Mary Bredin *Cant* 63-66; V Whitfield w W Langdon 66-75; V S Kensington St Luke *Lon* 75-83; AD Chelsea 80-83; Chief Broadcasting Officer for C of E 83-90; Adn Aston *Birm* 90-03; Can Res Birm Cathl 90-02; P-in-c Bickenhill 02-03; rtd 03; Perm to Offic *Cant* from 03. *3 Stuart Court, Puckle Lane, Canterbury CT1 3LA* Tel (01227) 379688 Mobile 07976-747535 E-mail venjb@globalnet.co.uk

BARTON, Dale. b 49. Selw Coll Cam BA71 MA76. Linc Th Coll 71. **d** 73 **p** 74. C Gosforth All SS *Newc* 73-77; Lesotho 77-81; Dep Warden CA Hostel Cam 82-83; C Shepton Mallet w Doulting *B & W* 83-88; TV Preston St Steph *Blackb* 88-96; V 96-99; Bp's Adv on Inter-Faith Relns from 99. *5 Vincent Court, Blackburn BB2 4LD* Tel (01254) 672744 E-mail st.barton@ukonline.co.uk

BARTON, David Gerald Story. b 38. Selw Coll Cam BA62 MA66. Cuddesdon Coll 63. **d** 65 **p** 66. C Cowley St Jas *Ox* 65-67; C Hambleden 67-70; Hon C Hammersmith St Jo *Lon* 72-77; Hon C Paddington St Jas 77-81; Hd Master Soho Par Sch 81-88; Hon C Westmr St Jas 81-92; RE Project Officer Lon Dioc Bd for Schs 88-92; Dioc Schs Adv *Ox* 93-99; rtd 00. *254 Iffley Road, Oxford OX4 1SE* Tel (01865) 240059 E-mail david.barton@dial.appleinter.net

BARTON, Edward. b 23. **d** 75 **p** 76. C Budock *Truro* 75-79; P-in-c St Stithians w Perranarworthal 79-80; V St Stythians w Perranarworthal and Gwennap 80-82; rtd 88; Perm to Offic *Truro* from 98. *Riverside, 5 Riviera Terrace, Malpas, Truro TR1 1SR* Tel (01872) 271686

BARTON, Eric Alfred. b 13. Clifton Th Coll 38. **d** 40 **p** 41. C Stratford New Town St Paul *Chelmsf* 40-42; C S Mimms Ch Ch *Lon* 42-44; V Holloway St Mary Magd 45-48; V Ripon H Trin *Ripon* 48-53; V Clifton *York* 53-59; R Haworth *Bradf* 59-61; V Buttershaw St Paul 61-70; V Nailsea Ch Ch *B & W* 70-82; rtd 82; Perm to Offic *Ex* from 82. *22 Woolbrook Rise, Sidmouth EX10 9UD* Tel (01395) 514841

BARTON, Canon Geoffrey. b 27. Oriel Coll Ox BA48 MA52. Chich Th Coll 49. **d** 51 **p** 52. C Arnold *S'well* 51-53; C E Retford 53-54; V Mirfield Eastthorpe St Paul *Wakef* 54-60; V Boroughbridge w Roecliffe *Ripon* 60-73; V Aldborough w Boroughbridge and Roecliffe 73; P-in-c Farnham w Scotton and Staveley and Copgrove 73-74; R 74-77; Chapl Roundway Hosp Devizes 77-92; Can and Preb Sarum Cathl *Sarum* 86-92; rtd 92; Perm to Offic *Sarum* from 01. *4B Willow House, Downlands Road, Devizes SN10 5EA* Tel (01380) 725311

BARTON (née MACDONALD), Helen Maria. b 56. Lon Bible Coll BA83 St Jo Coll Dur MA04 St Mary's Coll Strawberry Hill PGCE98. Cranmer Hall Dur 01. **d** 03 **p** 04. C Wisley w Pyrford *Guildf* 03-04; C Lanchester *Dur* from 04. *1 Briardene, Durham DH1 4QU* Tel 0191-386 0201 E-mail hmbarton@fsmail.net

BARTON, Mrs Jean Valerie. b 42. Wycliffe Hall Ox BTh01. **d** 02 **p** 03. NSM Harwell w Chilton *Ox* from 02. *Woodside, Drayton Road, Sutton Courtenay, Abingdon OX14 4HA* Tel (01235) 523702 E-mail pj1barton@ad.com

BARTON, John. *See* BARTON, The Ven Charles John Greenwood

BARTON, Canon John. b 25. MBE91. Keble Coll Ox BA48 MA50. Ely Th Coll 48. **d** 50 **p** 51. C Worksop St Anne *S'well* 50-53; C Harrogate St Wilfrid *Ripon* 53-56; V Beeston Hill H Spirit 56-60; Chapl Stanley Royd & Pinderfields Hosps Wakef 60-72; RD Wakef 68-72; Chapl Jo Radcliffe Hosp & Radcliffe Infirmary 72-90; Chapl Chu Hosp Ox 72-89; Hon Can Ch Ch *Ox* 77-94; RD Cowley 89-94; rtd 90; Perm to Offic *Ox* 94-01; Perm to Offic *Roch* from 01. *150A Longlands Road, Sidcup DA15 7LF* Tel (020) 8300 7073

BARTON, Prof John. b 48. Keble Coll Ox BA69 MA73 Mert Coll Ox DPhil74 St Cross Coll Ox DLitt88. **d** 73 **p** 73. Jun Research Fell Mert Coll Ox 73-74; Lect St Cross Coll Ox 74-89; Fell 74-91; Chapl 79-91; Lect Th Ox Univ 74-89; Reader 89-91; Oriel and Laing Prof of Interpr of H Scrip from 91; Fell Oriel Coll Ox from 91; Can Th Win Cathl *Win* from 91. *11 Withington Court, Abingdon OX14 3QA* Tel (01235) 525925 E-mail johnbarton@oriel.ox.ac.uk

BARTON, Canon John Christopher Peter. b 28. Trin Hall Cam BA51 MA56. Ridley Hall Cam 51. **d** 53 **p** 54. C Erith St Paul *Roch* 53-56; C Cockfosters Ch Ch CD *Lon* 56-64; V Welling *Roch* 64-75; P-in-c Malmesbury w Westport *Bris* 75-84; P-in-c Charlton w Brokenborough and Hankerton 80-84; V Malmesbury w Westport and Brokenborough 84-94; Hon Can Kigezi from 92; rtd 94; Perm to Offic *B & W* from 94. *Orchard House, Orchard Road, Crewkerne TA18 7AF* Tel (01460) 72536

BARTON, Canon John Michael. b 40. TCD BA62 Div Test. **d** 63 **p** 64. C Coleraine *Conn* 63-68; C Portadown St Mark *Arm* 68-71; I Carnteel and Crilly 71-83; I Derryloran 83-97; Bp's C Acton and Drumbanagher from 97; Can Arm Cathl from 94; Treas 98-01; Chan from 01. *Drumbanagher Vicarage, 128 Tandragee Road, Newry BT35 6LW* Tel (028) 3082 1298

BARTON, Mrs Margaret Ann Edith. b 48. Newc Univ BA71. EMMTC 95. **d** 98 **p** 99. NSM Castle Bytham w Creeton *Linc* 98-04; P-in-c Corby Glen from 04. *Blanchland House, Swinstead Road, Corby Glen, Grantham NG33 4NU* Tel (01476) 550763

BARTON, Margaret Anne. b 54. St Anne's Coll Ox BA76 MA80 DPhil81 Selw Coll Cam BA89 MA94. Ridley Hall Cam 87. **d** 90

p 94. Par Dn Burley Ville *Win* 90-94; Chapl K Alfred Coll 94-98; Dioc Development and Research Officer for Liturg Matters 99-01; NSM Baughurst, Ramsdell, Wolverton w Ewhurst etc 99-01; Asst Chapl Gen Synod 96-00; rtd 01. *The Rectory, Wolverton, Tadley RG26 5RU* Tel (01635) 298008 Fax as telephone E-mail rev.anne.barton@ntlworld.com

BARTON, Michael. *See* BARTON, Canon Arthur Michael

BARTON, Patrick. **d** 05. C Arm St Mark *Arm* from 05. *6 Ashley Avenue, Armagh BT60 1HD* Tel (028) 3752 2389 E-mail patdebbarton@hotmail.com

BARTON, Peter. *See* BARTON, Canon John Christopher Peter

BARTON, Canon Samuel David. b 45. DipTh. **d** 84 **p** 85. C Ballywillan *Conn* 84-86; I Aghadowey w Kilrea *D & R* 86-92; Bp's C Fahan Lower and Upper from 92; Dioc Educn Co-ord from 94; Dioc Communications Officer from 98; Can Raphoe Cathl from 98. *The Rectory, Cahir O'Doherty Avenue, Buncrana, Co Donegal, Irish Republic* Tel (00353) (74) 936 1154 Fax 936 3726 E-mail dco@derry.anglican.org *or* sbarton@iol.ie

BARTON, Prof Stephen Christian. b 52. Macquarie Univ (NSW) BA75 DipEd75 Lanc Univ MA78 K Coll Lon PhD92. Cranmer Hall Dur 91. **d** 93 **p** 94. NSM Neville's Cross St Jo CD *Dur* 93-00; NSM Dur St Marg and Neville's Cross St Jo from 00. *1 Briardene, Durham DH1 4QU* Tel 0191-386 0201 E-mail s.c.barton@durham.ac.uk

BARTON, Stephen William. b 50. St Jo Coll Cam BA73 MA76 Leeds Univ MPhil81. Coll of Resurr Mirfield 75. **d** 77 **p** 78. C Horton *Bradf* 77-80; USPG 80-92; Bangladesh 81-92; TV Southampton (City Cen) *Win* 92-98; Chapl Manager Birm Women's Healthcare NHS Trust from 99. *The Chaplaincy, Birmingham Women's Hospital, Edgbaston, Birmingham B15 2TG* Tel 0121-472 1377 ext 4208 Fax 627 2602

BARTON, Timothy Charles. b 47. Sarum & Wells Th Coll 73. **d** 76 **p** 77. C Upholland *Liv* 76-80; V Dalton from 80. *88 Lyndhurst Avenue, Skelmersdale WN8 6UH* Tel (01695) 733148

BARTON, Trevor James. b 50. St Alb Minl Tr Scheme 79. **d** 87 **p** 88. NSM Hemel Hempstead *St Alb* from 87. *46 Crossfell Road, Hemel Hempstead HP3 8RQ* Tel and fax (01442) 251537 E-mail trevorbarton@hotmail.com

BARWELL, Brian Bernard Beale. b 30. Preston Poly CertEd79. AKC59 St Boniface Warminster 59. **d** 60 **p** 61. C Heywood St Jas *Man* 60-63; V Smallbridge 63-69; V Farington *Blackb* 69-72; C-in-c Blackb St Luke w St Phil 72-75; C Standish 75-76; Lic to Offic 76-92; rtd 92; Perm to Offic *Blackb* from 92. *70 Claytongate, Coppull, Chorley PR7 4PS* Tel (01257) 794251

BARZEY, Ms Michele Alison Lesley. b 63. Trin Coll Bris BA94. **d** 94. C Gravelly Hill *Birm* 94-96; Perm to Offic from 00. *6 Topcliffe House, Yatesbury Avenue, Birmingham B35 6DU* Tel 0121-730 3094

BASAVARAJ, Mrs Patricia Margaret. b 37. SRN61 SCM62. **d** 00. OLM Verwood *Sarum* from 00. *Hope Cottage, Church Hill, Verwood BH31 6HT* Tel (01202) 822920

BASFORD HOLBROOK, Colin Eric. b 42. St Steph Ho Ox 73. **d** 75 **p** 76. C Dovecot *Liv* 75-78; V Hollinfare 79-83; CMS 83-88; Cyprus 83-91; Chapl Athens w Kifissia, Patras, Thessaloniki etc *Eur* 91-93; Chapl Athens w Patras, Thessaloniki and Voula 93-94; rtd 02. *PO Box 42786, Larnaca 6503, Cyprus* Tel (00357) (24) 620864

BASH, Anthony. b 52. Bris Univ LLB73 LLM76 Glas Univ BD89 Clare Hall Cam PhD96. Westcott Ho Cam 94. **d** 96 **p** 97. C Kingston upon Hull H Trin *York* 96-99; V N Ferriby 99-04; Chapl and Fell Univ Coll Dur from 05. *University College, The Castle, Palace Green, Durham DH1 3RW* Tel 0191-334-3800 *or* 334 4116

BASHFORD, Richard Frederick. b 36. Lon Univ DipTh68. Clifton Th Coll. **d** 68 **p** 69. C Bedworth *Cov* 68-71; C Lower Homerton St Paul *Lon* 71-75; V Bordesley Green *Birm* 75-81; R Birm Bishop Latimer w All SS from 81. *The Vicarage, 28 Handsworth New Road, Birmingham B18 4PT* Tel 0121-554 2221 E-mail domusmariae@blueyonder.co.uk

BASHFORD, Robert Thomas. b 49. Ch Coll Cam BA70 CertEd72 MA74 Lon Univ BD84 MPhil89. Oak Hill Th Coll 86. **d** 88 **p** 89. C Frinton *Chelmsf* 88-91; C Galleywood Common 91-96; V Clapham *St Alb* 96-02; P-in-c Westgate St Jas *Cant* from 02. *St James's Vicarage, Orchard Gardens, Margate CT9 5JT* Tel (01843) 832380

BASHFORTH, Alan George. b 64. Ex Univ MA. Ripon Coll Cuddesdon BTh96. **d** 96 **p** 97. C Calstock *Truro* 96-98; C St Ives 98-01; V St Agnes and Mithian w Mount Hawke from 01. *The Vicarage, 6 Penwinnick Parc, St Agnes TR5 0UQ* Tel (01872) 553391

BASINGSTOKE, Suffragan Bishop of. *See* WILLMOTT, The Rt Revd Trevor

BASKERVILLE, John. b 45. Open Univ BA78. Sarum & Wells Th Coll 92. **d** 93 **p** 94. C Wanstead St Mary w Ch Ch *Chelmsf* 93-96; C Chingford SS Pet and Paul 96-98; V Felkirk w Brierley *Wakef* 98-04; rtd 04. *131 Howard Road, Upminster RM14 2UQ* Tel (01708) 641242 Mobile 07710-209469

BASKERVILLE, Philip Duncan. b 58. St Chad's Coll Dur BSc79 Oriel Coll Ox PGCE80. Trin Coll Bris BA87. **d** 88 **p** 89. C Roby *Liv* 88-93; Kenya 93-97; C Barnston *Ches* from 98; Chapl St Andr Sch Turi Kenya from 05. *PO Private Bag, Molo 20106, Kenya* Tel (00254) (360) 21013 E-mail chaplain@turimail.co.ke

BASON, Brian Vaudrey. b 27. Leeds Univ BA49 Lon Univ BD69 AMusTCL97. Coll of Resurr Mirfield 49. **d** 51 **p** 52. C Haggerston St Aug w St Steph *Lon* 51-55; C Bow w Bromley St Leon 55-56; V Audenshaw St Hilda *Man* 56-89; Audenshaw High Sch 89-92; rtd 92; Perm to Offic *Ches* from 89; *Man* 89-95 and from 99. *78 Windsor Road, Denton, Manchester M34 2HE* Tel 0161-320 4408

BASS, Colin Graham. b 41. Liv Univ BSc62 Fitzw Ho Cam BA64 MA68. Ox NSM Course 84. **d** 87 **p** 88. Dir of Studies Leighton Park Sch Reading 87-97; NSM Earley St Pet *Ox* 87-92; NSM Reading Deanery from 92. *9 Bramley Close, Reading RG6 7PL* Tel 0118-966 3732 E-mail colin.bass@lineone.net

BASS, George Michael. b 39. Ely Th Coll 62. **d** 65 **p** 66. C Romaldkirk *Ripon* 65-68; C Kenton Ascension *Newc* 68-71; CF 71-94; Chapl Northumbria Healthcare NHS Trust 95-02; rtd 02; Perm to Offic *Newc* from 02. *35 Kelso Drive, North Shields NE29 9NS* Tel 0191-258 2514

BASS, Marguerite Rowena. b 61. St Jo Coll Nottm. **d** 05. C Wellingborough All SS *Pet* from 05. *29 Northfield Avenue, Ringstead, Kettering NN14 4DX* Tel (01933) 460213

BASS, Mrs Rosemary Jane. b 38. Linc Th Coll 76. **dss** 79 **d** 87 **p** 94. Bedford All SS *St Alb* 79-84; Leavesden All SS 84-94; Par Dn 87-94; C 94-95; V Luton St Andr 95-01; rtd 01; Perm to Offic *St Alb* from 01. *41 Darlow Drive, Biddenham, Bedford MK40 4AY* Tel and fax (01234) 219812

BASSETT, John Edmund. b 33. St Aid Birkenhead 63. **d** 66 **p** 67. C Guiseley *Bradf* 66-67; C Stechford *Birm* 67-71; C Ross *Heref* 71-72; P-in-c Brampton Abbotts 73-75; P-in-c Weston under Penyard 73-75; P-in-c Hope Mansell 73-75; TR Halesworth w Linstead and Chediston *St E* 75-78; R Laceby *Linc* 78-83; V Sale St Paul *Ches* 83-88; P-in-c Southport All SS *Liv* 88-94; P-in-c Southport All So 88-94; V Southport All SS and All So 94-98; P-in-c Aspull 98-99; V Aspull and New Springs 99-02; rtd 02; Hon C Pool w Arthington *Ripon* 02-03; Hon C Lower Wharfedale from 03. *The Vicarage, Old Pool Bank, Pool in Wharfedale, Otley LS21 1EJ* Tel 0113-284 3706

BASSETT, Mrs Rosemary Louise. b 42. STETS. **d** 00 **p** 01. NSM The Winterbournes and Compton Valence *Sarum* 00-03; P-in-c from 03. *The Rectory, Martinstown, Dorchester DT2 9JZ* Tel (01305) 889466 E-mail rose_trevor@trbassett.freeserve.co.uk

BASTEN, Richard Henry. b 40. Codrington Coll Barbados 60. **d** 63 **p** 64. Br Honduras 63-67; Barbados 68-72; C Hartlepool H Trin *Dur* 72-73; Chapl Bedstone Coll 73-88; C Clun w Chapel Lawn *Heref* 73-77; P-in-c Clungunford 77-78; R Clungunford w Clunbury and Clunton, Bedstone etc 78-88; R Rowde and Poulshot *Sarum* 88-95; rtd 95; Perm to Offic *Glouc* from 95. *41 Bewley Way, Churchdown, Gloucester GL3 2DU* Tel (01452) 859738

BASTIDE, Derek. b 44. Dur Univ BA65 Reading Univ DipEd66 Sussex Univ MA77. Chich Th Coll 76. **d** 77 **p** 78. Hon C Lewes All SS, St Anne, St Mich and St Thos *Chich* 77-84; Prin Lect Brighton Poly 80-92; Prin Lect Brighton Univ from 92; P-in-c Hamsey *Chich* from 84. *The Rectory, Offham, Lewes BN7 3PX* Tel (01273) 474356

BASTOCK, Kenneth William. b 22. Launde Abbey 75. **d** 76 **p** 77. C Glen Parva and S Wigston *Leic* 76-80; V Orton-on-the-Hill w Twycross etc 80-92; rtd 92; Perm to Offic *Leic* from 92. *18 Beech Road, Oadby, Leicester LE2 5QL* Tel 0116-271 0454

BASTON, Canon Caroline. b 56. Birm Univ BSc78 CertEd79. Ripon Coll Cuddesdon 87. **d** 89 **p** 94. Par Dn Southampton Thornhill St Chris *Win* 89-94; C 94-95; R Win All SS w Chilcomb and Chesil from 95; Dioc Communications Officer 95-98; Dioc Dir of Ords from 99; Hon Can Win Cathl from 00. *All Saints' Rectory, 19 Petersfield Road, Winchester SO23 0JD* Tel (01962) 853777 Fax 841714 E-mail caroline.baston@ukgateway.net

BATCHELOR, Alan Harold. b 30. Bris Univ BA54 Hull Univ MA63 Dip Personnel Mgt 68 LSE. Linc Th Coll 54. **d** 56 **p** 57. C Kingston upon Hull St Alb *York* 56-60; C Attercliffe w Carbrook *Sheff* 60-62; India 63-87; Ind Chapl *Ripon* 87-95; C Kirkstall 92-95; rtd 95; Perm to Offic *Ripon* from 01. *16 Moor Grange Rise, Leeds LS16 5BP* Tel 0113-226 9671

BATCHELOR, John Millar. CITC 76. **d** 78 **p** 79. C Belfast All SS *Conn* 78-80; I Eglish w Killylea *Arm* 80-96; I Ballyhalbert w Ardkeen *D & D* 96-01; rtd 01. *Rhone Brae, 102 Eglish Road, Dungannon BT70 1LB* Tel (028) 8775 0177 E-mail jm_batchelor@lineone.net

BATCHELOR, Martin John. b 67. Plymouth Poly BSc91. St Jo Coll Nottm Dip Th Studies 94 MA95. **d** 95 **p** 96. C Brecon St Mary and Battle w Llanddew *S & B* 95-97; Min Can Brecon Cathl 95-97; C Sketty 97-00; TV Hawarden *St As* from 00. *102A Hawarden Way, Mancot, Deeside CH5 2EW* Tel (01244) 539901 E-mail martin_batchelor@bigfoot.com

BATCHFORD, Philip John. b 71. Sheff Univ BA99. Ridley Hall Cam 00. **d** 02 **p** 03. C Sheff St Mary Bramall Lane *Sheff* from 02; V Netherthorpe St Steph from 05. *The Vicarage, 115 Upperthorpe Road, Sheffield S6 3EA* Tel 0114-276 7130

BATCOCK, Neil Gair. b 53. UEA BA74. Westcott Ho Cam 94. **d** 96 **p** 97. C Barton upon Humber *Linc* 96-99; TV Totnes w Bridgetown, Berry Pomeroy etc *Ex* from 99. *The Vicarage, Week, Dartington, Totnes TQ9 6JL* Tel (01803) 868304 E-mail gair2@aol.com

BATE, Dylan Griffin. b 48. Glam Poly HNC71. Mon Dioc Tr Scheme 91. **d** 94 **p** 95. NSM Fleur-de-Lis *Mon* 94-96; NSM Bedwellty 96-97; C Pontypool 97-99; C Tenby *St D* 99-02; R Begelly w Ludchurch and Crunwere from 02. *The Rectory, New Road, Begelly, Kilgetty SA68 0YG* Tel (01834) 812348

BATE, Preb Lawrence Mark. b 40. Univ Coll Ox BA63. Coll of Resurr Mirfield 65. **d** 67 **p** 68. C Benwell St Jas *Newc* 67-69; C Monkseaton St Pet 69-72; TV Withycombe Raleigh *Ex* 72-84; RD Aylesbeare 81-84; R Alphington 84-00; RD Christianity 95-99; TV Heavitree w Ex St Paul 00-02; TV Heavitree and St Mary Steps from 02; Preb Ex Cathl from 02. *Chapple Court, Kenn, Exeter EX6 7UR* Tel (01392) 833485 *or* 201021 E-mail morleybate@freeuk.com

BATE, Michael Keith. b 42. Lich Th Coll 67. **d** 69 **p** 70. C W Bromwich St Jas *Lich* 69-73; C Thornhill *Wakef* 73-76; V Wrenthorpe 76-82; V Upper Gornal *Lich* 82-93; V Upper Gornal *Worc* 93-05; TV Gornal and Sedgley from 05; Chapl Burton Road Hosp Dudley 82-94; Chapl Dudley Gp of Hosps NHS Trust 94-00. *St Peter's Vicarage, 35 Eve Lane, Dudley DY1 3TY* Tel (01902) 883467 E-mail mbate@surefish.co.uk

BATE, Stephen Donald. b 58. Sheff Univ BSc79 Cov Univ PhD92 CEng97 MIEE97. **d** 05. OLM Whitnash *Cov* from 05. *73 Golf Lane, Whitnash, Leamington Spa CV31 2QB* Tel (01926) 334134 Mobile 07773-583356 E-mail sbate@aol.com

BATEMAN, James Edward. b 44. Lon Univ BSc65 Bris Univ DipTh74. Trin Coll Bris 71. **d** 74 **p** 75. C Woodlands *Sheff* 74-77; C Rushden w Newton Bromswold *Pet* 77-84; R Vange *Chelmsf* 84-94; V Southminster 94-01; P-in-c Nazeing and Roydon 01-03; Warden Stacklands Retreat Ho W Kingsdown from 03. *Stacklands Retreat House, West Kingsdown, Sevenoaks TN15 6AN* Tel (01474) 852247 E-mail warden@stacklands.org.uk

BATEMAN, Kenneth William. b 34. ACII58. N Ord Course 85. **d** 88 **p** 89. Hon C Pilling *Blackb* 88-91; Chapl Lanc Moor Hosp 88-92; Chapl Lanc Priority Services NHS Trust 92-95; C Kirkby Lonsdale *Carl* 91-95; NSM 95-98; rtd 95; Perm to Offic *Carl* from 98. *Greenside, Barbon, Carnforth LA6 2LT* Tel (015242) 76318

BATEMAN, Martyn Henry. b 31. Jes Coll Cam BA54 MA58. Clifton Th Coll 54. **d** 56 **p** 57. C Heatherlands St Jo *Sarum* 56-59; C New Malden and Coombe *S'wark* 59-60; Iran 60-62; V Charsfield *St E* 62-69; R Monewden and Hoo 62-69; V Wickham Market 69-82; Hon Can St E Cathl 80-85; V Felixstowe SS Pet and Paul 82-85; TR Lydford, Brent Tor, Bridestowe and Sourton *Ex* 85-92; RD Tavistock 90-92; rtd 92; Perm to Offic *Mor* from 01. *Ardochy, Whitebridge, Inverness IV2 6UR* Tel (01456) 486273

BATEMAN, Patrick John. b 64. St Jo Coll Nottm 99. **d** 01 **p** 02. C Wallington H Trin *S'wark* 01-05; P-in-c Chipstead from 05. *The Rectory, Starrock Lane, Chipstead, Coulsdon CR5 3QD* Tel (01737) 552157 Mobile 07764-171400 E-mail patrickbateman@blueyonder.co.uk

BATEMAN, Richard William. b 36. AKC61. **d** 62 **p** 63. C Pennywell St Thos and Grindon St Oswald CD *Dur* 62-66; Trinidad and Tobago 66-70; R Etherley *Dur* 70-77; Ind Chapl *Roch* 77-83; Hon C Chatham St Steph 78-83; Chapl RN 79-83; V Kemsing w Woodlands *Roch* 83-90; P-in-c Petham and Waltham w Lower Hardres etc *Cant* 90-98; P-in-c Elmsted w Hastingleigh 98; rtd 01. *Stoneyridge, Waddem Hall Lane, Petham, Canterbury CT4 5PX* Tel (01227) 709318 *or* 700440

BATEMAN-CHAMPAIN, John Nicholas. b 30. G&C Coll Cam BA53 DipRS85. S'wark Ord Course 85. **d** 85 **p** 86. C Harpenden St Jo *St Alb* 85-88; V Northaw 88-97; rtd 97; Perm to Offic *Guildf* from 97. *Littleworth, Surrey Gardens, Effingham, Leatherhead KT24 5HF* Tel (01483) 282461 E-mail nickchampain@aol.com

BATES, Derek Alvin. b 27. St Mich Coll Llan 57. **d** 59 **p** 60. C Bishop's Cleeve *Glouc* 59-63; V Shebbear *Ex* 67-71; R Buckland Filleigh 67-71; R Highampton w Sheepwash 71; R Coates *Ely* 72-80; R Clovelly *Ex* 80-92; V Woolfardisworthy and Buck Mills 80-92; rtd 92; Perm to Offic *Ex* from 92. *Two Old Road, Shepherds Meadow, Abbotsham, Bideford EX39 5BP*

✠**BATES, The Rt Revd Gordon.** b 34. Kelham Th Coll 54. **d** 58 **p** 59 **c** 83. C New Eltham All SS *S'wark* 58-62; Asst Youth Chapl *Glouc* 62-64; Youth Chapl *Liv* 65-69; Chapl Liv Cathl 65-69; V Huyton St Mich 69-73; Can Res and Prec Liv Cathl 73-83; Dir of Ords 73-83; Suff Bp Whitby *York* 83-99; rtd 99; Hon Asst Bp Carl from 99; NSM Kirkby Lonsdale from 03; Perm to Offic *Blackb* from 99 and *Liv* from 01. *2 Loyne Park, Whittington, Carnforth LA6 2NL* Tel (015242) 72010

BATES, James. b 46. Linc Th Coll 73. **d** 75 **p** 76. C Ewell *Guildf* 75-77; C Farncombe 77-80; V Pet St Mary Boongate *Pet* 80-92; V Kingston All SS w St Jo *S'wark* 92-05; P-in-c Win St Cross w St Faith *Win* from 05; Master St Cross Hosp from 05. *The Master's Lodge, St Cross Hospital, Winchester SO23 9SD* Tel (01962) 852888 E-mail masterstcross@aol.com

BATES, Michael. b 33. Dur Univ BSc57 Hull Univ Ad Dip Maths Educn 84. Clifton Th Coll 57. **d** 59 **p** 60. C Drypool St Columba w St Andr and St Pet *York* 59-62; C Cheadle *Ches* 62-67; V Newbottle *Dur* 67-75; Chapl Nat Coal Bd 68-75; Teacher Bilton Grange High Sch Hull 76-88; Tutor Wilberforce Coll Hull 88-94; Hon C Kingston upon Hull H Trin *York* 81-96; rtd 96; Perm to Offic *York* from 96. *5 Fernland Close, Brough HU15 1DQ* Tel (01482) 669023

BATES, Miss Phyllis Edith. b 29. S'wark Ord Course 80. **dss** 83 **d** 87 **p** 94. Registrar S'wark Ord Course 83-89; Fulham St Dionis Parson's Green *Lon* 83-87; Hon Par Dn 87-94; rtd 89; NSM Hammersmith St Paul *Lon* from 94; Perm to Offic *S'wark* from 89. *26 St Dionis Road, London SW6 4TT* Tel (020) 7731 6935

BATES, Robert John. b 50. FRICS81. EAMTC 99. **d** 02 **p** 03. NSM Pet St Mary Boongate *Pet* 02-05; C Ketton, Collyweston, Easton-on-the-Hill etc from 05. *The Rectory, 38 West Street, Stamford PE9 2QB* Tel (01780) 482226 E-mail rev.bobbates@virgin.net

BATES, Mrs Rosemary Eileen Hamilton. b 45. Ripon Coll Cuddesdon 87. **d** 89 **p** 94. Par Dn Brackley St Pet w St Jas *Pet* 89-94; C 94-95; P-in-c N Hinksey and Wytham *Ox* 95-04; rtd 04. *9 High Street, Balsham, Cambridge CB1 6DJ* Tel (01223) 892245 E-mail revrosie@rosiebates.com

BATES, Stuart Geoffrey. b 61. Univ of Wales (Lamp) BA82. St Steph Ho Ox 83. **d** 85 **p** 86. C Bromley St Mark *Roch* 85-88; C Westmr St Matt *Lon* 88-89; C Gt Ilford St Mary *Chelmsf* 89-95; V Crofton Park St Hilda w St Cypr *S'wark* from 95. *St Hilda's Vicarage, 35 Buckthorne Road, London SE4 2DG* Tel (020) 8699 1277

BATES, William Frederic. b 49. St Jo Coll Dur BSc72 BA74 MA97. Cranmer Hall Dur. **d** 75 **p** 76. C Knutsford St Jo and Toft *Ches* 75-78; C Ripley *Derby* 78-80; R Nether and Over Seale 81-93; V Lullington 81-93; V Allestree St Nic from 93; Bp's Adv on New Relig Movements from 99; P-in-c Quarndon from 00. *The Vicarage, 4 Lawn Avenue, Allestree, Derby DE22 2PE* Tel (01332) 550224 E-mail will@bates4.wanadoo.co.uk

BATES, William Hugh. b 33. Keble Coll Ox BA56 MA59. Westcott Ho Cam 59. **d** 60 **p** 61. C Horsforth *Ripon* 60-63; Tutor St Chad's Coll Dur 63-70; V Bishop Wilton *York* 70-76; RD Pocklington 74-76; V Pickering 76-82; Prin NEOC 79-94; P-in-c Crayke w Brandsby and Yearsley *York* 82-94; P-in-c Stillington and Marton w Moxby 82-94; rtd 94; Perm to Offic *York* from 94. *Jessbrook Cottage, Bugthorpe, York YO41 1QG* Tel (01759) 368402

BATESON, Canon Geoffrey Frederick. b 27. K Coll Lon BD51 AKC51. **d** 52 **p** 53. C Tynemouth Cullercoats St Paul *Newc* 52-56; C Gosforth All SS 56-60; V Monkseaton St Pet 60-68; V Newc St Geo 68-77; RD Newc 75-77; R Morpeth 77-89; Chapl St Geo and Cottage Hosp Morpeth 77-89; Hon Can Newc Cathl *Newc* 80-89; rtd 89; Perm to Offic *York* from 91. *1 Netherby Close, Sleights, Whitby YO22 5HD* Tel (01947) 810997

BATESON, Canon James Howard. b 36. Qu Mary Coll Lon BSc57 MSOSc88. EMMTC 85. **d** 87 **p** 88. NSM W Bridgford *S'well* 87-88; NSM Wilford Hill 88-95; Dioc Officer for NSMs 94-04; P-in-c Kilvington and Staunton w Flawborough 96-04; Hon Can S'well Minster 99-04; rtd 04; Perm to Offic *S'well* from 04. *45 Stamford Road, West Bridgford, Nottingham NG2 6GD* Tel and fax 0115-923 1820 E-mail h_bateson@primeuk.net

BATESON, Keith Nigel. b 43. **d** 00 **p** 01. OLM Wonersh w Blackheath *Guildf* from 00. *Advent Cottage, Blackheath Lane, Wonersh, Guildford GU5 0PN* Tel (01483) 892753 E-mail k.bateson@handbag.com

BATESON, Tracey Jane. b 74. St Mark & St Jo Coll Lon BEd96. Trin Coll Bris BA03. **d** 04 **p** 05. C Holdenhurst and Iford *Win* from 04. *19 Colemore Road, Bournemouth BH7 6RZ* Tel (01202) 431993 Mobile 07977-012292 E-mail tracey-j@fish.co.uk

BATEY, Canon Herbert Taylor. b 22. Qu Coll Ox BA46 MA48. Linc Th Coll 48. **d** 48 **p** 49. C Dalton-in-Furness *Carl* 48-50; C Egremont 50-52; V Cleator Moor w Cleator 52-59; Chapl St Bees Sch Cumbria 59-64; Chapl Culham Coll Abingdon 64-68; Prin Lect 68-75; P-in-c Culham *Ox* 68-75; Vice-Prin Coll of Ripon and York St Jo 75-92; Hon Can Ripon Cathl *Ripon* 85-92; rtd 87; Perm to Offic *Ripon* from 92. *29 College Road, Ripon HG4 2HE* Tel (01765) 607096

BATEY, William Abbott. b 20. Cranmer Hall Dur 62. **d** 63 **p** 64. C Appleby and Murton cum Hilton *Carl* 63-66; R Moresby 66-77; P-in-c Arnside 77-85; V 85-90; rtd 90; Perm to Offic *Carl* from 90. *33 Greengate, Levens, Kendal LA8 8NF* Tel (01539) 566791

BATH, David James William. b 43. Oak Hill NSM Course 87. **d** 89 **p** 90. NSM Henley *Ox* 89-90; Gen Manager Humberside Gd News Trust 90-96; NSM Anlaby St Pet *York* 96-04; P-in-c Anlaby Common St Mark from 04. *St Mark's Vicarage, 1055 Anlaby Road, Hull HU4 7PP* Tel (01482) 351977 E-mail davidjwbath@hotmail.com

BATH AND WELLS, Bishop of. *See* PRICE, The Rt Revd Peter Bryan

BATH, Archdeacon of. *See* PIGGOTT, The Ven Andrew John

BATHURST, Bishop of. *See* HURFORD, The Rt Revd Richard Warwick

BATLEY-GLADDEN, Dane Christopher. b 68. St Steph Ho Ox 96. **d** 99 **p** 00. C Hendon St Alphage *Lon* 99-01; C-in-c Grahame Park St Aug CD from 01. *St Augustine's House, Great Field, London NW9 5SY* Tel (020) 8205 1979 Fax 8205 6127 E-mail frdane@dcbg.org.uk

BATSLEER, Canon Albert. b 21. Selw Coll Cam BA46 MA54. Cuddesdon Coll 46. **d** 48 **p** 49. C Leic St Phil *Leic* 48-50; C Hope St Jas *Man* 50-52; V Heap Bridge 52-56; V Glossop *Derby* 56-65; R Staveley 65-72; V Riddings 72-81; RD Alfreton 76-81; V New Mills 81-85; RD Glossop 81-83; Hon Can Derby Cathl 81-85; rtd 85; Perm to Offic *Pet* 95-04. *16 Oak Court, 1 Mauldeth Road, Manchester M20 4NE* Tel 0161-224 7387

BATSON, David Frederick Edward. b 38. K Coll Lon AKC61 BD69 FSAScot97. St Boniface Warminster. **d** 62 **p** 63. C Southport H Trin *Liv* 62-64; Asst Chapl Hurstpierpoint Coll 64-65; C Cleator Moor w Cleator *Carl* 65-66; Asst Master K Geo V Sch Southport 66-67; NSM Leigh w Bransford *Worc* 68-79; Hon Asst Chapl Convent of H Name Malvern Link 68-72; Prin Soc Work Tr Dept Dumfries and Galloway Coun 84-94; Lect and Tutor Langside Coll Glas 95-97; Lect Soc Studies Dumfries and Galloway Coll from 96; Visiting Lect Paisley Univ from 02; Perm to Offic *Glas* from 03. *Kindar House, New Abbey, Dumfries DG2 8DB* Tel (01387) 850514 Fax 850556

BATSON, John Gordon Kemp. b 38. Kelham Th Coll 60 Bps' Coll Cheshunt 64. **d** 65 **p** 66. C Lamorbey H Redeemer *Roch* 65-69; Trinidad and Tobago 69-74; V Borough Green *Roch* 74-83; V Perry Street 83-92; V Yalding w Collier Street 92-97; V Woodnesborough w Worth and Staple *Cant* 97-03; rtd 03; Perm to Offic *Cant* from 03. *21 Selsea Avenue, Herne Bay CT6 8SB* Tel (01227) 368780 E-mail johnbatson01@hotmail.com

BATSON, Lee Paul. b 77. R Holloway Coll Lon BA99 MA00 Selw Coll Cam BA03. Westcott Ho Cam 01. **d** 04 **p** 05. C Saffron Walden w Wendens Ambo, Littlebury etc *Chelmsf* from 04. *42 De Vigier Avenue, Saffron Walden CB10 2BN* Tel (01799) 500815 E-mail curate.saffronwalden@ntlworld.com

BATSON, Paul Leonard. b 47. Southn Univ BTh79. Sarum & Wells Th Coll 73. **d** 75 **p** 76. C Chesham St Mary *Ox* 75-79; Dioc Youth Adv *Newc* 79-85; V Earley St Pet *Ox* 85-93; Perm to Offic *Sarum* from 01. *Maple Cottage, 78 Murhill, Limpley Stoke, Bath BA2 7FB* Tel (01225) 722721

BATSON, William Francis Robert (Bob). b 43. Nottm Univ Dip Town Planning 69 St Jo Coll Dur BA72. **d** 73 **p** 74. C Eastwood *S'well* 73-77; R Long Marton w Dufton and w Milburn *Carl* 77-79; V Flimby 79-85; TR Raveningham *Nor* 85-91; R Kinver and Enville *Lich* 91-00; V Ledsham w Fairburn *York* from 00. *The Vicarage, 11 Main Street, Ledston, Castleford WF10 2AA* Tel (01977) 556946 E-mail bob@ledvic.fsnet.co.uk

BATSTONE, Bruce. b 70. Bris Univ BA92. St Steph Ho Ox 98. **d** 00 **p** 01. C Leigh-on-Sea St Marg *Chelmsf* 00-03; C Old St Pancras *Lon* from 03; Chapl Camden and Islington Community Health NHS Trust from 03. *33 Crowndale Road, London NW1 1TN* Tel (020) 7387 4193 E-mail fr.bruce@posp.co.uk

BATT, Canon Joseph William. b 39. Keele Univ BA62 DipSS62. Ripon Hall Ox 63. **d** 64 **p** 65. C Bushbury *Lich* 64-68; C Walsall 68-71; Nigeria 71-75; Hon Can Oke-Osun from 94; Area Sec CMS *Guildf* and *Chich* 75-84; V Ottershaw *Guildf* 84-04; rtd 04. *8 Parkwood Road, Shipley BD18 4SS* Tel (01274) 589775 E-mail jbatt@fish.co.uk

BATT, Kenneth Victor. b 41. Wycliffe Hall Ox 68. **d** 71 **p** 72. C Yateley *Win* 71-76; R The Candover Valley 76-82; R Durrington *Sarum* 82-89; V Kempshott *Win* 89-00; P-in-c Bournemouth H Epiphany 00-05; V from 05. *The Vicarage, 81 Castle Lane West, Bournemouth BH9 3LH* Tel (01202) 512481

BATTE, Mrs Kathleen. b 47. Homerton Coll Cam TCert68. NEOC 91. **d** 94 **p** 95. NSM Newc St Gabr *Newc* 94-96; NSM Wilford Hill *S'well* 96-99; P-in-c Cinderhill 99-05; Bp's Adv for Self-Supporting Min from 05. *10 Bracey Rise, West Bridgford, Nottingham NG2 7AX* Tel 0115-923 4503 E-mail kath.batte@talk21.com

BATTEN, Graham John. b 39. Open Univ BA81 Univ of Wales (Cardiff) DipTh65. St D Coll Lamp 65. **d** 66 **p** 67. C Llangynwyd w Maesteg *Llan* 66-70; C St Andrews Major w Michaelston-le-Pit 70-72; Chapl RN 72-91; Asst Chapl of the Fleet 91-94; V Dover St Mary *Cant* 94-00; rtd 00; Perm to Offic *B & W* from 01. *Parsonage House, Tower Hill Road, Crewkerne TA18 8BJ* Tel (01460) 271069

BATTEN, Stuart William. b 73. Univ of Wales (Abth) BD94 MTh96. Trin Coll Bris 96. **d** 98 **p** 99. C Northolt W End St Jos *Lon* 98-01; TV Hucknall Torkard *S'well* from 01. *St Peter and Paul's Vicarage, Ruffs Drive, Hucknall, Nottingham NG15 6JG* Tel 0115-963 3640 E-mail stuart.batten@btinternet.com

BATTERSBY, David George Sellers. b 32. AKC57. St Boniface Warminster 57 Lambeth STh80. **d** 58 **p** 59. C Glas St Marg *Glas* 58-60; C Burnley St Pet *Blackb* 60-62; V Warton St Paul 62-71; Chapl K Wm's Coll Is of Man 71-91; C Ashchurch *Glouc* 91-97; rtd 97; Perm to Offic *Glouc* and *Worc* from 97, *Ox* from 03. *Shill Brook Cottage, Buckland Road, Bampton OX18 2AA* Tel (01993) 851414 E-mail dgsb@fan.com

BATTERSBY, Paul Clifford. b 49. Bede Coll Dur TCert70 St Jo Coll Dur BA74. Cranmer Hall Dur. **d** 75 **p** 76. C Sunderland St Chad *Dur* 75-78; Argentina 78-81; P-in-c Holme and Dioc Youth Officer *Carl* 81-85; Nat Officer for Youth Work Gen Syn Bd of Educn 85-92; TR Darwen St Pet w Hoddlesden *Blackb* 92-94; Soc Resp Officer 95-99; V Witton 99-03; V Leyland St Ambrose from 03. *St Ambrose Vicarage, 85 Moss Lane, Leyland, Preston PR25 4XA* Tel (01772) 462204 E-mail email@reverend.co.uk

BATTERSBY, Simon Charles. b 64. Wycliffe Hall Ox BTh01. **d** 01 **p** 02. C Askern *Sheff* 01-03; Chapl Bethany Sch Goudhurst from 03. *Providence Cottage, Curtisden Green, Goudhurst, Cranbrook TN17 1LD* Tel and fax (01580) 211579 Mobile 07956-576737 E-mail pastasimon@hotmail.com

BATTERSHELL, Mrs Anne Marie. b 33. Ox Poly BEd83. St Alb and Ox Min Course 95. **d** 98 **p** 99. NSM Goring w S Stoke *Ox* 98-01; NSM Brafferton w Pilmoor, Myton-on-Swale etc *York* 01-03; rtd 03; Perm to Offic *Wakef* from 04. *26 Winterbutlee Grove, Todmorden OL14 7QU* Tel (01706) 839848 E-mail revanne@battershell.fsnet.co.uk

BATTEY, Alexander Robert Fenwick. b 77. St Andr Univ MA99. Ripon Coll Cuddesdon BA05. **d** 05. C Whitby w Aislaby and Ruswarp *York* from 05. *19 Eskdale Road, Whitby YO22 4JH* Tel (01947) 820386

BATTIN (née WEBB), Mrs Frances Mary. b 52. WEMTC 92. **d** 95 **p** 96. NSM Inkberrow w Cookhill and Kington w Dormston *Worc* 95-98; Asst Chapl HM Pris Brockhill 98-03; Perm to Offic *Worc* from 03. *Collitts Forge, Upper Moor, Pershore WR10 2JR* Tel (01386) 860467

BATTISON, Mark Richard. b 62. EMMTC 01. **d** 04 **p** 05. NSM Leic St Jas *Leic* from 04. *44 Hidcote Road, Oadby, Leicester LE2 5PE* Tel 0116-271 1951 Fax 271 7719 Mobile 07717-200777 E-mail markb@onetel.com

BATTLE, Dean of. *See* EDMONDSON, The Very Revd John James William

BATTMAN, John Brian. b 37. ALCD61. **d** 61 **p** 62. C Fulham Ch Ch *Lon* 61-64; Argentina 64-69; Paraguay 69-76; Adn Paraguay 70-76; Ext Sec SAMS 77-80; V Romford Gd Shep Collier Row *Chelmsf* 80-92; V Werrington *Pet* 92-02; rtd 02; Perm to Offic *St E* from 02. *1 Butley Close, Ipswich IP2 9TR* Tel (01473) 680141 E-mail jnbattman@aol.com

BATTY, John Ivan. b 35. Clifton Th Coll 59. **d** 62 **p** 63. C Clayton *Bradf* 62-67; V Toxteth Park St Clem *Liv* 67-73; R Darfield *Sheff* 73-90; Chapl Düsseldorf *Eur* 90-95; V The Marshland *Sheff* 95-00; rtd 00; Perm to Offic *Sheff* and *Linc* from 00. *4 St Lawrence Way, Tallington, Stamford PE9 4RH* Tel and fax (01780) 740151

BATTY, Mark Alan. b 56. BSc. Ripon Coll Cuddesdon. **d** 82 **p** 83. C Bottesford w Ashby *Linc* 82-86; V Scunthorpe All SS 86-95; P-in-c N Wolds Gp 95-97; V from 97. *The Vicarage, St Barnabas Road, Barnetby DN38 6JE* Tel (01652) 688182

BATTY, Stephen Roy. b 58. Chich Th Coll 88. **d** 90 **p** 91. C Wimborne Minster and Holt *Sarum* 90-94; P-in-c Yetminster w Ryme Intrinseca and High Stoy 94-02; V Branksome St Aldhelm from 02; Perm to Offic *Win* from 02. *The Vicarage, St Aldhelm's Road, Poole BH13 6BT* Tel (01202) 764420

BATTYE, Canon John Noel. b 42. TCD BA64 MA73. CITC 66. **d** 66 **p** 67. C Drumglass *Arm* 66-69; C Ballynafeigh St Jude *D & D* 70-73; Chapl Pemb Coll Cam 73-78; Bp's C Knocknagoney *D & D* 78-80; I Cregagh from 80; Preb Castleknock St Patr Cathl Dublin from 94. *St Finnian's Rectory, 3 Upper Knockbreda Road, Belfast BT6 9QH* Tel (028) 9079 3822

BATTYE, Ms Lisa Katherine. b 55. Man Univ BN78 MA(Theol)96 RM79 Man Poly Dip Counselling 84 Liv Univ MTh00. N Ord Course 96. **d** 99 **p** 00. C Clifton *Man* 99-02; R Kersal Moor from 02. *St Paul's Rectory, 1 Moorside Road, Salford M7 3PJ* Tel 0161-792 5362 E-mail lisa@battye.fsbusiness.co.uk

BATY, Edward. b 30. Open Univ BA77 UEA PhD88 MRICS59. St Aid Birkenhead 60. **d** 62 **p** 63. C Acomb St Steph *York* 62-64; Succ Chelmsf Cathl *Chelmsf* 64-67; V Becontree St Cedd 67-71; R Hope Bowdler w Eaton-under-Heywood *Heref* 71-79; R Rushbury 71-79; P-in-c Cardington 71-79; R Fincham *Ely* 79-82; OCF 79-94; R Long Stanton w St Mich *Ely* 82-94; P-in-c Lolworth 85-88; CF(V) 86-95; rtd 95; Perm to Offic *Guildf* from 95. *25 Martindale Avenue, Camberley GU15 1BB* Tel (01276) 20315

BAUDAINS, Mrs Geraldine Louise. b 58. SW Minl Tr Course 02. **d** 05. NSM Jersey All SS *Win* from 05; NSM Jersey St Simon from 05. *Le Chataignier, La Rue du Flicquet, St Martin, Jersey JE3 6BP* Tel (01534) 855556 E-mail baudains@jerseymail.co.uk

BAUERSCHMIDT, John Crawford. b 59. Kenyon Coll Ohio BA81. Gen Th Sem (NY) MDiv84. **d** 84 **p** 85. USA 84-87 and from 92; Lib Pusey Ho 87-91. *120 South New Hampshire, Covington, LA 70433, USA*

BAUGHAN, Mrs Emma Louise Langley. b 70. Bris Univ BA93 MA98. STETS 01. **d** 03. C Horfield H Trin *Bris* from 03. *31 Rosling Road, Bristol BS7 8SX* Tel 0117-951 9771 Mobile 07974-658619 E-mail emmalang@aol.com

BAUGHEN, Andrew Jonathan. b 64. Lon Guildhall Univ BA87. Wycliffe Hall Ox BTh94. **d** 94 **p** 95. C Battersea Rise St Mark *S'wark* 94-97; P-in-c Clerkenwell St Jas and St Jo w St Pet *Lon* 97-00; V from 00. *St James's Church, Clerkenwell Close, London EC1R 0EA* Tel (020) 7251 1190 E-mail vicar@jc-church.org

✠**BAUGHEN, The Rt Revd Michael Alfred.** b 30. Lon Univ BD55. Oak Hill Th Coll 51. **d** 56 **p** 57 **c** 82. C Hyson Green *S'well* 56-59; C Reigate St Mary *S'wark* 59-61; Ord Cand Sec CPAS 61-64; R Rusholme H Trin *Man* 64-70; TV St Marylebone All So w SS Pet and Jo *Lon* 70-75; R 75-82; AD Westmr St Marylebone 78-82; Preb St Paul's Cathl 79-82; Bp Ches 82-96; rtd 96; Hon Asst Bp Lon from 96; Perm to Offic *S'wark* 97-02. *99 Brunswick Quay, London SE16 7PX* Tel (020) 7237 0167

BAULCOMB, Canon Geoffrey Gordon. b 46. K Coll Lon BD86 AKC68. **d** 69 **p** 70. C Crofton Park St Hilda w St Cypr *S'wark* 69-74; TV Padgate *Liv* 74-79; R Whitton and Thurleston w Akenham *St E* 79-03; Hon Can St E Cathl 03; rtd 03; Perm to Offic *St E* from 03. *Greenlands, 39 Filching Road, Eastbourne BN20 8SE* Tel (01323) 641746 E-mail geoffreybaulcomb@hotmail.com

✠**BAVIN, The Rt Revd Timothy John.** b 35. Worc Coll Ox BA59 MA61. Cuddesdon Coll 59. **d** 61 **p** 62 **c** 74. S Africa 61-69 and 73-85; C Uckfield *Chich* 69-71; V Brighton Gd Shep Preston 71-73; Dean and Adn Johannesburg 73-74; Bp Johannesburg 74-85; Bp Portsm 85-95; OGS from 87; Community of Our Lady and St John from 96; Perm to Offic *Win* from 96; rtd 98. *Alton Abbey, Abbey Road, Beech, Alton GU34 4AP* Tel (01420) 562145 *or* 563575 Fax 561691

BAVINGTON, John Eduard. b 68. Loughb Univ BEng91. Trin Coll Bris BA99. **d** 99 **p** 00. C W Ealing St Jo w St Jas *Lon* 99-02; V Bradf St Clem *Bradf* from 02. *St Clement's Vicarage, 294A Barkerend Road, Bradford BD3 9DF* Tel (01274) 665109

BAWTREE, Andrew James. b 66. Univ of Wales BD91 Nottm Univ MA95 Ch Ch Coll Cant PGCE92. St Jo Coll Nottm 94. **d** 96 **p** 97. C Hoddesdon *St Alb* 96-99; USA from 99. *Trinity Church, 515 Yancey Street, South Boston, VA 24592, USA* Tel (001) (804) 572 4513

BAWTREE, Canon Robert John. b 39. Oak Hill Th Coll 62. **d** 67 **p** 68. C Foord St Jo *Cant* 67-70; C Boscombe St Jo *Win* 70-73; C Kinson *Sarum* 73-75; TV Bramerton w Surlingham *Nor* 76-82; R Arborfield w Barkham *Ox* 82-91; V Hildenborough *Roch* 91-04; RD Tonbridge 95-01; Hon Can Roch Cathl from 02; rtd 04; Hon C Camelot Par *B & W* from 04. *Four Posts, Long Street, Galhampton, Yeovil BA22 7AZ* Tel (01963) 440356

BAXANDALL, Peter. b 45. Tyndale Hall Bris 67. **d** 70 **p** 72. C Kidsgrove *Lich* 70-71; C St Helens St Mark *Liv* 71-75; C Ardsley *Sheff* 76-77; Rep Leprosy Miss E Anglia 77-86; P-in-c March St Wendreda *Ely* 86-87; R from 87; RD March from 93. *St Wendreda's Rectory, 21 Wimblington Road, March PE15 9QW* Tel (01354) 653377 Fax as telephone E-mail peter.baxandall@ely.anglican.org

BAXENDALE, John Richard. b 48. Cranmer Hall Dur 89. **d** 91 **p** 92. C Carl St Jo *Carl* 91-94; C Dalston 94-95; P-in-c Monton *Man* 95-96; TV Eccles 96-04; V Clifton from 04. *St Anne's Vicarage, 237 Manchester Road, Manchester M27 6PP* Tel 0161-794 1939

BAXENDALE, Paul Gordon. b 70. Leeds Univ BA91. Ridley Hall Cam 93. **d** 96 **p** 97. C Kendal St Thos *Carl* 96-01; P-in-c Burton and Holme from 01. *St James's Vicarage, Glebe Close, Burton, Carnforth LA6 1PL* Tel (01524) 781391

BAXENDALE, Rodney Douglas. b 45. Ex Univ BA66. Linc Th Coll 78. **d** 80 **p** 81. C Maidstone All SS and St Phil w Tovil *Cant* 80-83; Chapl RN 83-03. *17 Valletort Road, Plymouth PL1 5PH* Tel (01752) 500573 E-mail thebaxendales@blueyonder.co.uk

BAXTER, Anthony. b 54. SEITE 99. **d** 02. NSM Romford Ascension Collier Row *Chelmsf* from 02. *54 South Drive, Brentwood CM14 5DL* Tel (01277) 210937 Mobile 07909-984675 Fax (01277) 211926 E-mail tonybaxter54@aol.com

BAXTER, Brian Raymond. b 31. Tyndale Hall Bris. **d** 58 **p** 59. C Heworth H Trin *York* 58-61; C Belper *Derby* 61-65; R Leverton *Linc* 65-67; C Mile Cross *Nor* 74-76; C Farnborough *Guildf* 76-79; Ldr Southgate Chr Project Bury St Edmunds 79-84; Chapl W Suffolk Hosp 79-81; R Ringsfield w Redisham, Barsham, Shipmeadow etc *St E* 82-88; V Nor Heartsease St Fran *Nor* 88-91; rtd 91; Perm to Offic *Nor* from 91. *22A Gurney Close, Norwich NR5 0HB* Tel (01603) 748588

BAXTER, David. *See* BAXTER, Canon Richard David

BAXTER, David Norman. b 39. Open Univ BA87. Kelham Th Coll 59. **d** 64 **p** 65. C Tonge Moor *Man* 64-68; Chapl RN 68-84; P-in-c Becontree St Pet *Chelmsf* 84-85; TV Becontree W 85-86; TR 86-94; Spain from 94; rtd 99. *C/ Vidal i Barraquer, 10, Escalera B, 1-2, 08870 Sitges, Barcelona, Spain* Tel (0034) 93 894 6151 Fax 894 3800 E-mail dnbaxter@teleline.es

BAXTER, Dennis Alexander. b 56. Sheff Univ BA96. St Mich Coll Llan 03. **d** 05. C Tenby *St D* from 05. *The Vicarage, Penally, Tenby SA70 7PN* Tel (01834) 842035 Mobile 07963-467702 E-mail aarowkosky2@aol.com

BAXTER (née AVIS), Mrs Elizabeth Mary. b 49. Leeds Metrop Univ BA93. N Ord Course 81. **dss** 84 **d** 87 **p** 94. Leeds St Marg and All Hallows *Ripon* 84-93; Par Dn 87-93; Chapl Abbey Grange High Sch 85-93; Par Dn Topcliffe *York* 93-94; C 94-96; C Thirsk from 96; Jt Dir H Rood Ho Cen for Health and Past Care from 93; Perm to Offic *Ripon* from 93; *Dur* and *Newc* from 94; *Bradf* and *Sheff* from 95; *Wakef* from 97. *Holy Rood House, 10 Sowerby Road, Sowerby, Thirsk YO7 1HX* Tel (01845) 522580 Fax 527300 E-mail holyroodhouse@centrethirsk.fsnet.co.uk

BAXTER, Harold Leslie. b 11. Roch Th Coll 62. **d** 64 **p** 65. C Corsham *Bris* 64-67; C Bath Lyncombe *B & W* 67-70; V Shapwick w Ashcott 70-88; P-in-c Burtle 75-88; V Shapwick w Ashcott and Burtle 88-95; rtd 96; Perm to Offic *Truro* from 97. *Tredole, Prussia Cove Lane, Rosudgeon, Penzance TR20 9AX* Tel (01736) 762133

BAXTER, Jane Elizabeth. b 51. EAMTC 98. **d** 01 **p** 02. C Clare w Poslingford, Cavendish etc *St E* 01-04; P-in-c Lyddington w Stoke Dry and Seaton etc *Pet* from 04. *The Rectory, 4 Windmill Way, Lyddington, Oakham LE15 9LY* Tel (01572) 822717 E-mail revjanebaxter@tesco.net

BAXTER, John Richard. b 44. ACII66. STETS 96. **d** 99 **p** 00. NSM Banstead *Guildf* 99-03; TV Surrey Weald from 03. *High Lea, 54 The Street, Capel, Dorking RH5 5LE* Tel (01306) 711260 Mobile 07974-692334 E-mail johnbaxter@eastewell.freeserve.co.uk

BAXTER, Leslie. *See* BAXTER, Harold Leslie

BAXTER, Peter James. b 29. St Chad's Coll Dur BA53 DipTh55. **d** 55 **p** 56. C Stanground *Ely* 55-58; C Paddington St Mich w All SS *Lon* 58; C Woodston *Ely* 59-62; R Eynesbury 62-89; rtd 89. *c/o Wellers Solicitors, Tenison House, Tweedy Road, Bromley BR1 3NF*

BAXTER, Canon Richard David. b 33. Kelham Th Coll 53. **d** 57 **p** 58. C Carl St Barn *Carl* 57-59; C Barrow St Matt 59-64; V Drighlington *Wakef* 64-73; V Penistone 73-80; V Carl St Aid and Ch Ch *Carl* 80-86; Can Res Wakef Cathl *Wakef* 86-97; Prec from 86; Vice-Provost 92-97; rtd 97; Perm to Offic *Carl* from 97; Hon V Choral Carl Cathl from 04. *20 Summerfields, Dalston, Carlisle CA5 7NW* Tel and fax (01228) 710496 E-mail canondavidbaxter@btinternet.com

BAXTER, Stanley Robert. b 31. Leeds Univ MA90 FRSA96 MInstD97 FRSH99. Chich Th Coll 79. **d** 80 **p** 81. In Lutheran Ch 71-79; C Far Headingley St Chad *Ripon* 80-82; P-in-c Leeds St Marg and All Hallows 82-93; P-in-c Leeds All Hallows w Wrangthorn 85-87; P-in-c Topcliffe *York* 93-95; NSM 95-96; NSM Thirsk from 96; Dir Leeds Cen for Urban Th Studies 88-93; Assoc Chapl Leeds Univ *Ripon* 91-93; Jt Dir H Rood Ho Cen for Health and Past Care from 93; Perm to Offic *Dur* and *Newc* from 94; *Bradf* and *Sheff* from 95; *Wakef* from 97; Mental Health Chapl Hambleton and Richmondshire Primary Care Trust from 03. *Holy Rood House, 10 Sowerby Road, Sowerby, Thirsk YO7 1HX* Tel (01845) 522580 *or* 522004 Fax 527300 E-mail holyroodhouse@centrethirsk.fsnet.co.uk

BAXTER, Stuart. b 43. Liv Univ BA65 Nottm Univ PGCE66. Cuddesdon Coll 66. **d** 70 **p** 71. C Kirkby *Liv* 70-73; C Ainsdale 73-76; Sierra Leone 77-83; CMS 83-84; V Nelson in Lt Marsden *Blackb* 84-92; V Lostock Hall 92-99; P-in-c Hatton *Derby* 99-04; Asst Chapl HM Pris Sudbury 99-03; Asst Chapl HM Pris Foston Hall from 03. *The Chaplaincy, HM Prison Foston Hall, Foston, Derby DE65 5DN* Tel (01283) 584325

BAXTER, Terence Hugh. b 48. Leeds Poly BSc74. N Ord Course 89. **d** 92 **p** 93. NSM Guiseley w Esholt *Bradf* 92-04; NSM Weston w Denton from 04; NSM Leathley w Farnley, Fewston and Blubberhouses from 04. *The Rectory, Stainburn Lane, Leathley, Otley LS21 2LF* E-mail terry.baxter@tesco.net

BAYCOCK, Philip Louis. b 33. Wells Th Coll 64. **d** 66 **p** 67. C Kettering SS Pet and Paul *Pet* 66-68; C St Peter-in-Thanet *Cant* 68-72; V Bobbing w Iwade 72-73; Perm to Offic 73-76; V Thanington w Milton 77-84; R Chagford w Gidleigh and Throwleigh *Ex* 84-01; rtd 01; Perm to Offic *Ex* from 01. *7 Grove Meadow, Sticklepath, Okehampton EX20 2NE* Tel (01837) 840617 E-mail louisb@care4free.net

BAYES, Frederick Alan. b 60. Imp Coll Lon BSc81. St Jo Coll Dur BA92 Cranmer Hall Dur 93. **d** 93 **p** 94. C Talbot Village *Sarum* 93-97; Chapl St Hild and St Bede Coll *Dur* 97-03; Bp's Adv in Interfaith Matters 02-03; V Penllergaer *S & B* from 03. *The Vicarage, 16 Swansea Road, Penllergaer, Swansea SA4 9AQ* Tel (01792) 892603

BAYES, Paul. b 53. Birm Univ BA75. Qu Coll Birm 76. **d** 79 **p** 80. C Tynemouth Cullercoats St Paul *Newc* 79-82; Chapl Qu Eliz Coll *Lon* 82-87; Chapl Chelsea Coll 85-87; TV High Wycombe *Ox* 87-90; TR 90-94; TR Totton *Win* 95-04; AD Lyndhurst 00-04; Nat Miss and Evang Adv Abps' Coun from 04. *Church House, Great Smith Street, London SW1P 3NZ* Tel (020) 7898 1502 Fax 7898 1431 E-mail paul.bayes@c-of-e.org.uk

BAYFORD, Mrs Daphne Jean. b 32. Lon Univ TCert53. Qu Coll Birm 84. **d** 87 **p** 94. NSM Brinklow *Cov* 87-95; NSM Harborough Magna 87-95; NSM Monks Kirby w Pailton and Stretton-under-Fosse 87-95; Perm to Offic from 95 and *Leic* from 97. *Warwick House, 36 Lutterworth Road, Pailton, Rugby CV23 0QE* Tel (01788) 832797

BAYFORD, Terence Michael. b 48. Westmr Coll Ox MTh96. Wilson Carlile Coll 70 N Ord Course 97. **d** 99 **p** 00. Dep Chapl HM Pris Wakef 99-01; NSM Alverthorpe *Wakef* 99-01; Chapl HM Pris Moorland from 01; Perm to Offic *Wakef* from 01. *HM Prison Moorland, Bawtry Road, Hatfield Woodhouse, Doncaster DN7 6BW* Tel (01302) 523000 ext 3131

BAYLDON, Roger. b 38. MBE74 TD99. **d** 04. OLM Parkstone St Pet and St Osmund w Branksea *Sarum* from 04. *37 Blake Dene Road, Poole BH14 8HF* Tel and fax (01202) 730683 Mobile 07831-272773 E-mail r.bayldon@btinternet.com *or* roger@bayldon.com

BAYLEY, Anne Christine. b 34. OBE86. MB, ChB58 FRCS66 FRCSEd86 Girton Coll Cam BA55. St Steph Ho Ox 90. **d** 91 **p** 94. NSM Wembley Park St Aug *Lon* 91-97; Perm to Offic *York* from 97. *Michaelmas Barn, Farndale, Kirkbymoorside, York YO62 7LA* Tel and fax (01751) 433445

BAYLEY, David Francis. b 47. **d** 99 **p** 00. OLM Wriggle Valley *Sarum* 99-04; NSM Weaverthorpe w Helperthorpe, Luttons Ambo etc *York* from 04. *Chapel House, Back Lane, West Lutton, Malton YO17 8TF* Tel (01944) 738446 Mobile 07817-023108 E-mail revdavid@yetminster1.fsnet.co.uk

BAYLEY, Canon John Benson. b 39. K Coll Cam BA60 MA64. Qu Coll Birm 61. **d** 63 **p** 64. C Clee *Linc* 63-68; V Gainsborough H Trin 68-73; P-in-c Linc St Mich 73-75; P-in-c Linc St Pet in Eastgate w St Marg 73-75; P-in-c Linc St Mary Magd w St Paul 73-75; R Linc Minster Gp 75-02; Can and Preb Linc Cathl 75-02; Hon PV 77-02; rtd 02. *16 Bexmore Drive, Streethay, Lichfield WS13 8LB*

BAYLEY, Michael John. b 36. CCC Cam BA60 MA64 Sheff Univ DSS67 PhD73. Linc Th Coll 60. **d** 62 **p** 63. C Leeds Gipton Epiphany *Ripon* 62-66; NSM Sheff St Mark Broomhill *Sheff* 67-93; C Sheff St Mary w Highfield Trin 93-95; C Sheff St Mary Bramall Lane 95-00; rtd 00. *27 Meadowbank Avenue, Sheffield S7 1PB* Tel 0114-258 5248

BAYLEY, Oliver James Drummond. b 49. Mansf Coll Ox MA PGCE. St Jo Coll Nottm 81. **d** 83 **p** 84. C Bath Weston St Jo w Kelston *B & W* 83-88; P-in-c Bathampton 88-93; P-in-c Claverton 92-93; R Bathampton w Claverton 93-96; Chapl Dauntsey's Sch Devizes 96-02; rtd 02; Perm to Offic *Win* from 01. *80 Adelaide Road, Southampton SO17 2HW* Tel (023) 8055 7582

BAYLEY, Raymond. b 46. Keble Coll Ox BA68 MA72 Dur Univ DipTh69 Ex Univ PhD86. St Chad's Coll Dur 68. **d** 69 **p** 70. C Mold *St As* 69-74; C Llandaff w Capel Llanilltern *Llan* 74; PV Llan Cathl 74-77; V Cwmbach 77-80; Dir Past Studies St Mich Coll Llan 80-84; V Ynysddu *Mon* 84-86; V Griffithstown 86-92; V Rhosymedre *St As* 92-96; Warden and R Ruthin w Llanrhydd from 96; Warden of Readers from 02. *The Cloisters, School Road, Ruthin LL15 1BL* Tel (01824) 702068 E-mail othniel@amserve.net

BAYLIS (née LOFTS), Mrs Sally Anne. b 55. Kent Univ BA78 K Coll Lon MA80 Nottm Univ PGCE93. St Jo Coll Nottm 01. **d** 03 **p** 04. C Gedling *S'well* from 03. *7 Berkeley Avenue, Nottingham NG3 5BU* Tel and fax 0115-962 1077 E-mail k.baylis@ntlworld.com

BAYLISS, Geoffrey Brian Tudor. b 60. R Holloway Coll Lon BSc83 Univ of Wales (Swansea) PGCE85. EAMTC 96. **d** 99 **p** 00. NSM Panfield and Rayne *Chelmsf* 99-04; TV Halstead Area from 04. *The Vicarage, Church Road, Gosfield, Halstead CO9 1UD* Tel (01787) 273434 E-mail geoff@bayliss41.freeserve.co.uk

BAYLISS, Grant David. b 75. Ex Univ BA96. Ripon Coll Cuddesdon BA99. **d** 03 **p** 04. C Prestbury and All SS *Glouc* from 03. *8 Boulton Road, Cheltenham GL50 4RZ* Tel (01242) 238601 E-mail gdbayliss@ukonline.co.uk

BAYLOR, Nigel Peter. b 58. NUI BA80 TCD DipTh84 MPhil88. **d** 84 **p** 86. C Carrickfergus *Conn* 84-87; C Dundela St Mark *D & D* 87-89; I Galloon w Drummully *Clogh* 89-94; Adult Educn Adv 91-94; I Carnmoney *Conn* 94-03; I Jordanstown from 03. *The Rectory, 120A Circular Road, Jordanstown, Newtownabbey BT37 0RH* Tel (028) 9086 2119 E-mail nigel.baylor@ukgateway.net

BAYLY, Samuel Niall Maurice. b 36. TCD BA64 MA. CITC Div Test65. **d** 65 **p** 66. C Belfast St Matt *Conn* 65-68; Miss to Seamen 68-69; C Belfast St Pet *Conn* 69-74; I Belfast Ch Ch 74-02. *81 Dunluce Avenue, Belfast BT9 7AW* Tel (028) 9066 8732

BAYMAN, Ann Bernette. b 45. **d** 04. OLM Westleton w Dunwich *St E* from 04; OLM Darsham from 04; OLM Middleton cum Fordley and Theberton w Eastbridge from 04; OLM Yoxford, Peasenhall and Sibton from 04. *Seadrift, St James's Street, Dunwich, Saxmundham IP17 3DT* Tel (01728) 648545 Mobile 07884-072944 E-mail anniebayman@webtribe.net

BAYNE, Canon David William. b 52. St Andr Univ MA75. Edin Th Coll 88. **d** 90 **p** 91. C Dumfries *Glas* 90-92; P-in-c 92-93; R 93-99; Chapl Dumfries and Galloway R Infirmary 92-99; Chapl Crichton R Hosp Dumfries 92-99; Chapl HM Pris Dumfries 96-99; P-in-c Castle Douglas *Glas* from 99; Can St Mary's Cathl from 99. *The Rectory, 68 St Andrew Street, Castle Douglas DG7 1EN* Tel and fax (01556) 503818 E-mail dwbayne@aol.com

BAYNE, Mrs Felicity Meriel. b 47. WEMTC 91. **d** 94 **p** 95. NSM Cheltenham Ch Ch *Glouc* 94-98; NSM Leckhampton St Pet from 98. *Hamfield House, Ham Road, Charlton Kings, Cheltenham GL52 6NG* Tel (01242) 237074

BAYNE-JARDINE, Anthea Mary. *See* GRIGGS, Mrs Anthea Mary

BAYNES, Mrs Clare. b 57. Reading Univ BA79. St Alb and Ox Min Course 01. **d** 04. NSM Chambersbury *St Alb* from 04. *4 Pilgrim Close, Park Street, St Albans AL2 2JD* Tel (01727) 875524 E-mail clare@simonbaynes.fsnet.co.uk

BAYNES, Matthew Thomas Crispin. b 62. UEA BA83 Qu Coll Cam BA86 MA91. Westcott Ho Cam 85. **d** 87 **p** 88. C Southgate Ch Ch *Lon* 87-90; C Gt Berkhamsted *St Alb* 90-95; V Coseley Ch Ch *Worc* 95-99; R Bredon w Bredon's Norton from 99; RD Pershore from 05. *The Rectory, Bredon, Tewkesbury GL20 7LT* Tel (01684) 772237 E-mail matthew@tcbaynes.fsnet.co.uk

BAYNES, Simon Hamilton. b 33. New Coll Ox BA57 DipTh58 MA62. Wycliffe Hall Ox 57. **d** 59 **p** 60. C Rodbourne Cheney *Bris* 59-62; Japan 63-80; C Keynsham *B & W* 80-84; P-in-c Winkfield *Ox* 84-85; V Winkfield and Cranbourne 85-99; rtd 99; Lic to Offic *Ox* 99-02; Hon C Thame from 02. *23 Moorend Lane, Thame OX9 3BQ* Tel (01844) 213673 E-mail baynes@psa-online.com

BAYNES, Timothy Francis de Brissac. b 29. Ely Th Coll 59. **d** 61 **p** 62. C Hockerill *St Alb* 61-65; C Mansfield Woodhouse *S'well* 65-67; Ind Chapl *Man* 67-94; P-in-c Miles Platting St Jo 67-72; rtd 94; Perm to Offic *Man* 94-97. *46 Kirkbie Green, Kendal LA9 7AJ* Tel (01539) 740605

BAYNES, William Hendrie. b 39. Adelaide Univ BA60. S'wark Ord Course 77. **d** 79 **p** 80. C Notting Hill All SS w St Columb *Lon* 79-85; Perm to Offic 86-87 and 99-00; Hon C Paddington St Sav 88-98; Asst Chapl St Mary's NHS Trust Paddington 94-99; Convenor Lon NSMs/MSE *Lon* from 95; Hon C Paddington St Jas from 00. *39E Westbourne Gardens, London W2 5NR* Tel and fax (020) 7727 9530 *or* tel 7727 9522 E-mail will.baynes@london.anglican.org

BAYNHAM, Matthew Fred. b 57. BNC Ox BA78 Birm Univ MPhil00. Wycliffe Hall Ox 80. **d** 83 **p** 84. C Yardley St Edburgha *Birm* 83-87; TV Bath Twerton-on-Avon *B & W* 87-93; V Reddal Hill St Luke *Worc* 93-00; RD Dudley 98-00; Chapl Bp Grosseteste Coll Linc 00-05; Assoc Chapl Liv Univ *Liv* from 05. *Fronnant, Nanternis, New Quay SA45 9RW* Tel (01545) 560500

BAYS, Mrs Helen Margaret. b 48. Kent Univ BA69 RGN71 RHV73. STETS 97. **d** 00 **p** 01. NSM Calne and Blackland *Sarum* 00-02; NSM Sampford Peverell, Uplowman, Holcombe Rogus etc *Ex* from 02. *14 Stockton Hill, Dawlish EX7 9LP* Tel (01626) 862860 E-mail hbays@fish.co.uk

BAZELY, William Francis. b 53. Sheff Univ BEng75. St Jo Coll Nottm 78. **d** 81 **p** 82. C Huyton St Geo *Liv* 81-84; TV Netherthorpe *Sheff* 84-92; Chapl Lambeth Healthcare NHS Trust 92-98; Chapl Guy's and St Thos' Hosps NHS Trust Lon 98-01; C Rotherham *Sheff* 01-03; Chapl Rotherham Gen Hosps NHS Trust 01-03; Chapl Rotherham Priority Health Services NHS Trust 01-03; Sen Chapl Norfolk Mental Health Care NHS Trust from 03. *34 Woodcock Road, Norwich NR3 3TX* Tel (01603) 421345 Mobile 07786-734519 E-mail bill_bazely@hotmail.com

✠**BAZLEY, The Rt Revd Colin Frederick.** b 35. St Pet Coll Ox BA57 MA61. Tyndale Hall Bris 57. **d** 59 **p** 60 **c** 69. C Bootle St Leon *Liv* 59-62; SAMS Miss Chile 62-00; Adn Cautin and Malleco 67-69; Asst Bp Cautin and Malleco 69-75; Asst Bp Santiago 75-77; Bp Chile 77-00; Primate CASA 77-83; Primate Iglesia Anglicana del Cono Sur 89-95; rtd 00; Hon Asst Bp Ches from 00; Warden of Readers from 00. *121 Brackenwood Road, Higher Bebington, Wirral CH63 2LU* Tel 0151-608 1193 Mobile 07866-391333 E-mail colin@colbarb.fsnet.co.uk

BAZLINTON, Stephen Cecil. b 46. Lon Univ BDS RCS LDS. Ridley Hall Cam 78. **d** 85 **p** 86. NSM Stebbing w Lindsell *Chelmsf* 85-04; NSM Stebbing and Lindsell w Gt and Lt Saling from 04. *St Helens, High Street, Stebbing, Dunmow CM6 3SE* Tel (01371) 856495 E-mail revbaz@care4free.co.uk

BEACH, Jonathan Mark. b 67. Essex Univ BSc89. Trin Coll Bris BA94. **d** 94 **p** 95. C Oulton Broad *Nor* 94-97; Chapl RAF from 97; Perm to Offic *Nor* 98-00. *Chaplaincy Services (RAF), HQ, Personnel and Training Command, RAF Ainsworth, Gloucester GL3 1EZ* Tel (01452) 712612 ext 5164 Fax 510828

BEACH, Mark Howard Francis. b 62. Kent Univ BA83 Nottm Univ MA95. St Steph Ho Ox 85. **d** 87 **p** 88. C Beeston *S'well* 87-90; C Hucknall Torkard 90-93; R Gedling 93-01; R Netherfield 96-01; Bp's Chapl *Wakef* 01-03; TR Rugby St Andr

Cov from 03. *The Rectory, Church Street, Rugby CV21 3PH* Tel (01788) 542936 *or* 565609 Mobile 07930-577248 E-mail mark.beach@zetnet.co.uk

BEACH, Stephen John. b 58. Man Univ BA81 BD88 Didsbury Coll of Educn PGCE82. N Ord Course 92. **d** 93 **p** 94. C Harwood *Man* 93-97; TV Westhoughton and Wingates 97-01; P-in-c Devonport St Budeaux *Ex* 01-02; V from 02. *St Budeaux Vicarage, Agaton Road, Plymouth PL5 2EW* Tel (01752) 361019 *or* 351087 E-mail steph.beach@xalt.co.uk

BEACHAM, Peter Martyn. b 44. Ex Coll Ox BA65 MA70 Lon Univ MPhil67 FSA92 MRTPI69. Sarum Th Coll 70. **d** 73 **p** 74. NSM Ex St Martin, St Steph, St Laur etc *Ex* 73-74; NSM Cen Ex 74-90; Perm to Offic from 99. *Bellever, Barrack Road, Exeter EX2 6AB* Tel (01392) 435074

BEACOM, Canon Thomas Ernest. b 12. TCD BA33 MA40 BD40. **d** 36 **p** 36. C Limerick St Lawr w H Trin and St Jo *L & K* 36-38; C Seapatrick *D & D* 38-44; P-in-c Belfast St Kath *Conn* 44-58; I 58-82; Dioc Registrar 63-82; Can Belf Cathl 66-82; rtd 82. *4955-41 Avenue, Drayton Valley AB, Canada, T7A 1V4* Tel (001) (780) 542 3488

BEACON, Canon Ralph Anthony. b 44. Univ of Wales (Ban) DipTh70. St Mich Coll Llan 70. **d** 71 **p** 72. C Neath w Llantwit *Llan* 71-74; TV Holyhead w Rhoscolyn *Ban* 74-78; R Llanenddwyn w Llanddwywe, Llanbedr w Llandanwg 78-99; V Harlech and Llanfair-juxta-Harlech etc from 99; RD Ardudwy 89-01; AD from 01; Hon Can Ban Cathl 91-97; Can Cursal 97-03; Can and Preb Ban Cathl from 03. *The Rectory, Môn Dirion, Ffordd Uchaf, Harlech LL46 2SS* Tel (01766) 781336 Mobile 07713-421858

BEACON, Mrs Stephanie Kathleen Nora. b 49. Univ of Wales (Ban) BA70 PGCE71. NW Ord Course 94. **d** 96 **p** 97. NSM Llanenddwyn w Llanddwywe, Llanbedr w Llandanwg *Ban* 96-98; C Ardudwy 98-99; P-in-c Llanenddwyn w Llanddwywe, Llanbedr w Llandanwg 99-01; R from 01. *The Rectory, Môn Dirion, Ffordd Uchaf, Harlech LL46 2SS* Tel (01766) 781336 Mobile 07713-421858

BEADLE, David Alexander. b 37. St And Dioc Tr Course. **d** 88 **p** 89. NSM St Andrews St Andr *St And* from 88. *48 Clayton Caravan Park, St Andrews KY16 9YB* Tel (01334) 870001 E-mail dabeadle@lineone.net

BEADLE, Canon Janet Mary. b 52. Philippa Fawcett Coll CertEd74. EAMTC 91. **d** 94 **p** 95. C Kingston upon Hull H Trin *York* 94-98; V Ness Gp *Linc* from 98; Bp's Adv in Women's Min from 00; Can and Preb Linc Cathl from 03. *The Vicarage, 10 Church Street, Thurlby, Bourne PE10 0EH* Tel (01778) 422475 E-mail janet.beadle@talk21.com

BEADLE, Mrs Lorna. b 40. NEOC DipHE95. **d** 95 **p** 96. NSM Ashington *Newc* from 95; Chapl Mothers' Union from 02. *9 Arundel Square, Ashington NE63 8AW* Tel (01670) 816467

✠**BEAK, The Rt Revd Robert Michael Cawthorn.** b 25. OBE90. Lon Bible Coll DipTh51. **d** 53 **p** 54 **c** 84. C Tunbridge Wells St Jo *Roch* 53-55; BCMS 55-56 and 84-89; Kenya 56-69 and 84-89; R Heanton Punchardon *Ex* 70-84; Offg Chapl RAF 70-80; RD Barnstaple *Ex* 77-81; R Heanton Punchardon w Marwood 79-84; Preb Ex Cathl 82-84; Asst Bp Mt Kenya E 84-89; rtd 90; Hon Asst Bp Derby from 91. *Ashcroft Cottage, Butts Road, Ashover, Chesterfield S45 0AX* Tel (01246) 590048

BEAK, Stephen Robert. b 64. City Univ BSc86. Wycliffe Hall Ox BTh94. **d** 94 **p** 95. C Lache cum Saltney *Ches* 94-97; C Howell Hill *Guildf* 97-01; NSM Woking St Mary 01-05; V from 05. *Bethany House, West Hill Road, Woking GU22 7UJ* Tel (01483) 761269 E-mail stephen.beak@ntlworld.com

BEAKE, Christopher Martyn Grandfield. b 36. K Coll Lon BA60 AKC60. **d** 61 **p** 62. C Berwick H Trin *Newc* 61-66; V Tynemouth H Trin W Town 66-78; V Hanslope w Castlethorpe *Ox* 78-01; rtd 01. *8 Radstone Road, Brackley NN13 5GB* Tel (01280) 706543

BEAKE, Canon Stuart Alexander. b 49. Em Coll Cam BA72 MA76. Cuddesdon Coll 72. **d** 74 **p** 75. C Hitchin St Mary *St Alb* 74-76; C Hitchin 77-79; TV Hemel Hempstead 79-85; Bp's Dom Chapl *S'well* 85-87; V Shottery St Andr *Cov* 87-00; RD Fosse 93-99; Dioc Dir of Ords 96-00; Hon Can Cov Cathl 98-00; Can Res and Sub-Dean Cov Cathl from 00. *109 Beechwood Avenue, Coventry CV5 6FQ* Tel (024) 7667 8752 *or* 7652 1230 E-mail sabeake@msn.com *or* stuart.beake@coventrycathedral.org.uk

BEAKEN, Robert William Frederick. b 62. SS Paul & Mary Coll Cheltenham BA83 Lambeth STh90 MA01 FSAScot01. Ripon Coll Cuddesdon 85 Ven English Coll & Pontifical Gregorian Univ Rome 87. **d** 88 **p** 89. C Forton *Portsm* 88-92; C Shepshed *Leic* 92-94; V Colchester St Barn *Chelmsf* 94-02; P-in-c Gt and Lt Bardfield from 02. *The Vicarage, Braintree Road, Great Bardfield, Braintree CM7 4RN* Tel (01371) 810267 E-mail robert@webform.com

BEAL, David Michael. b 61. Nottm Univ BTh89. St Jo Coll Nottm 86. **d** 89 **p** 90. C Marton *Blackb* 89-92; C Darwen St Pet w Hoddlesden 92-93; TV 93-97; R Itchingfield w Slinfold *Chich* from 97. *The Rectory, The Street, Slinfold, Horsham RH13 0RR* Tel (01403) 790197

BEAL, Malcolm. b 31. Bris Univ BA52. Ridley Hall Cam 57. **d** 59 **p** 60. C Keynsham w Queen Charlton *B & W* 59-62; C Speke All SS *Liv* 62-65; Uganda 65-74; V Salford Priors *Cov* 74-83; R Jersey St Clem *Win* 83-97; rtd 97; Perm to Offic *Ex* from 97 and *B & W* from 03. *3 Redwoods Close, Hemyock, Cullompton EX15 3QQ* Tel (01823) 680853 E-mail mmbeal@lineone.net

BEALES, Christopher Leader Day. b 51. St Jo Coll Dur BA72. Cranmer Hall Dur DipTh75. **d** 76 **p** 77. C Upper Armley *Ripon* 76-79; Ind Chapl 76-79; Ind Chapl *Dur* 79-84; Sen Chapl 82-84; Sec Ind Cttee of Gen Syn Bd for Soc Resp 85-91; Sec Inner Cities Relig Coun (DOE) 92-94; Dir Churches' Regional Commn in the NE *Newc & Dur* 94-97; Consultant Dir 98; C Thamesmead *S'wark* 99-01. *169 Westmount Road, London SE9 1XY* Tel (020) 8859 6733 E-mail chris@c-beales.freeserve.co.uk

BEALES, John David. b 55. SS Hild & Bede Coll Dur BA77 Univ of W Aus DipEd79 Nottm Univ DipTh82. St Jo Coll Nottm DPS83. **d** 83 **p** 84. Australia 83-89 and 95-00; C Scarborough 83-86; Dioc Youth Chapl Perth 86-89; Dir Educn and Tr Philo Trust 89-90; NSM Nottingham St Nic *S'well* 89-95; Dir Evang Melbourne 95-00; Perm to Offic *Chelmsf* 99-01. *52 Wellesley Road, Colchester CO3 3HF* Tel (01206) 530934 E-mail davidbeales@ntlworld.com

BEALING, Andrew John. b 42. Sarum Th Coll 67. **d** 69 **p** 70. C Auckland St Andr and St Anne *Dur* 69-73; P-in-c Eastgate and Rookhope 73-76; V Frosterley 76-85; V Rekendyke from 85; Chapl S Tyneside Distr Hosp 90-93; Chapl S Tyneside Healthcare Trust from 93; Chapl Miss to Seafarers from 02. *The Vicarage, St Jude's Terrace, South Shields NE33 5PB* Tel 0191-455 2338

BEALING, Mrs Patricia Ramsey. b 39. Lightfoot Ho Dur IDC63. **dss** 63 **d** 87 **p** 94. Rekendyke *Dur* 85-87; Par Dn 87-94; C from 94; Chapl S Tyneside Distr Hosp 88-93; Chapl S Tyneside Healthcare Trust from 93. *The Vicarage, St Jude's Terrace, South Shields NE33 5PB* Tel 0191-455 2338

BEAMENT, Canon Owen John. b 41. MBE01. Bps' Coll Cheshunt 61. **d** 64 **p** 65. C Deptford St Paul *S'wark* 64-68; C Peckham St Jo 69-73; C Vauxhall St Pet 73-74; V Hatcham Park All SS from 74; Hon Can S'wark Cathl from 97. *All Saints Vicarage, 22 Erlanger Road, London SE14 5TG* Tel (020) 7639 3497 E-mail owenbeament@aol.com

BEAMER, Neville David. b 40. Univ of Wales (Lamp) BA62 Jes Coll Ox BA65 MA70. Wycliffe Hall Ox 64. **d** 65 **p** 66. C Hornchurch St Andr *Chelmsf* 65-68; C Warwick St Mary *Cov* 68-72; V Holton-le-Clay *Linc* 72-75; P-in-c Stoneleigh w Ashow *Cov* 75-79; P-in-c Baginton 77-79; V Fletchamstead 79-86; Warden Whatcombe Ho Blandford Forum 86-90; R Jersey St Lawr and V Jersey Millbrook St Matt *Win* 90-95; V Yateley 95-03; P-in-c Eversley 98-03; R Yateley and Eversley 03-05; RD Odiham 95-04; rtd 05. *8 Aintree Road, Stratford-upon-Avon CV37 9FL* Tel (01789) 263435 E-mail nevillebeamer@aol.com

BEAMISH, Canon Frank Edwin. b 28. TCD BA49 MA. TCD Div Sch. **d** 50 **p** 52. C Templecorran *Conn* 50-53; C Drumglass *Arm* 53-61; I Caledon w Brantry 61-94; Preb Arm Cathl from 88; Treas Arm Cathl from 92; rtd 94. *214 Killylea Road, Caledon BT68 4TN* Tel (028) 3756 8609

BEAN, Alan Evison. b 13. Ch Coll Cam BA35 MA39. Ely Th Coll 35. **d** 36 **p** 37. C Hendon St Ignatius *Dur* 36-40; Perm to Offic *Ox* 41-50; CF 42-45; SSJE from 47; India 50-55 and 57-64; Lic to Offic *Ox* 55-02. *St John's Home, St Mary's Road, Oxford OX4 1QE*

BEAN, Douglas Jeyes Lendrum. b 25. Worc Coll Ox BA50 MA53. Ely Th Coll 50. **d** 51 **p** 52. C Croydon Woodside *Cant* 51-54; Min Can Windsor 54-59; V Reading St Laur *Ox* 59-68; Chapl HM Borstal Reading 61-68; RD Reading *Ox* 65-68; Min Can St Paul's Cathl *Lon* 68-72; Hon Min Can from 72; V St Pancras w St Jas and Ch Ch 72-93; PV Westmr Abbey 75-80; rtd 93; Perm to Offic *Lon* from 99. *3 Bishop Street, London N1 8PH* Tel (020) 7226 8340

BEAN, James Corey. b 35. Centenary Coll New Jersey BA58 Long Is Univ MS74. Seabury-Western Th Sem LTh61. **d** 61 **p** 62. USA 61-79 and from 90; Chapl Wiesbaden *Eur* 79-90. *968 High Street, Box 490, Pomeroy, WA 99347, USA* Tel (001) (509) 843 1871

BEAN, Canon John Victor. b 25. Down Coll Cam BA47 MA51. Sarum Th Coll 48. **d** 50 **p** 51. C Milton *Portsm* 50-55; C Fareham SS Pet and Paul 55-59; V St Helens 59-66; V Cowes St Mary 66-91; RD W Wight 68-72; Hon Can Portsm Cathl 70-91; P-in-c Cowes St Faith 77-80; C-in-c Gurnard All SS CD 78-91; Chapl to The Queen 80-95; rtd 91; Perm to Offic *Portsm* from 91. *Magnolia, 23 Seldon Avenue, Ryde PO33 1NS* Tel (01983) 812516 Fax as telephone

BEAN, Kevin Douglas. b 54. Edin Univ BD78. Edin Th Coll 75. **d** 81 **p** 82. USA 81-88 and from 89; C Edin St Marg *Edin* 88-89; C Edin Old St Paul 88-89. *54 Robert Road, Marblehead, MA 01945, USA*

BEANE, Andrew Mark. b 72. St Jo Coll Nottm BA02. **d** 02 **p** 03. C Thorpe St Matt *Nor* from 02. *15 Stanley Avenue, Norwich NR7 0BE* Tel (01603) 439113 E-mail andrewbeane@onetel.com

BEANEY, John. b 47. Trin Coll Bris DipHE79. **d** 79 **p** 80. C Bromley Ch Ch *Roch* 79-84; V Broadheath *Ches* from 84; Chapl Altrincham Gen Hosp 91-94; Chapl Trafford Healthcare NHS Trust 94-98. *The Vicarage, Lindsell Road, West Timperley, Altrincham WA14 5NX* Tel 0161-928 4820
E-mail johnbeaney@broadheath99.freeserve.co.uk

BEARCROFT, Bramwell Arthur. b 52. Homerton Coll Cam BEd82. EAMTC 87. **d** 90 **p** 91. Chapl and Hd RS Kimbolton Sch Cambs 88-94; NSM Tilbrook *Ely* 90-94; NSM Covington 90-94; NSM Catworth Magna 90-94; NSM Keyston and Bythorn 90-94; NSM Cary Deanery *B & W* 94-02; Hd Master Hazlegrove Sch 94-02. *Clé de Tève, Devillac, 47210 Lot et Garonne, France* Tel (0033) (5) 53 71 46 24
E-mail jenniferbearcroft@hotmail.com

BEARD, Christopher Robert. b 47. Chich Th Coll 81. **d** 83 **p** 84. C Chich St Paul and St Pet *Chich* 83-86; TV Ifield 86-91; V Haywards Heath St Rich 91-99; P-in-c Donnington from 99; Chapl St Wilfrid's Hospice Eastbourne from 99. *The Vicarage, 34 Graydon Avenue, Donnington, Chichester PO19 8RF* Tel (01243) 776395

BEARD, Laurence Philip. b 45. Lon Univ BA68. Trin Coll Bris 88. **d** 90 **p** 91. C Trentham *Lich* 90-94; V Wolverhampton St Matt 94-01; P-in-c Hartshill *Cov* from 01. *The New Vicarage, Church Road, Hartshill, Nuneaton CV10 0LY* Tel (024) 7639 2266
E-mail lpbeard@talk21.com

BEARD, Robert John Hansley. b 61. St Andr Univ BD85. Ripon Coll Cuddesdon 86 Ch Div Sch of the Pacific (USA) 87. **d** 88 **p** 89. C Sheff Manor *Sheff* 88-91; C Rotherham 91-94; V Sheff St Pet Abbeydale 94-02; Assoc Chapl Sheff Hallam Univ 95-98; Bp's Adv on Interfaith Issues 96-02; Intercultural Regeneration Development Worker *Simunye* from 02. *18 Arnside Road, Sheffield S8 0UX* Tel 0114-255 6335
E-mail arjay61@hotmail.com

BEARDALL, Raymond. b 32. St Jo Coll Nottm 70. **d** 72 **p** 73. C Ilkley All SS *Bradf* 72-74; C Seasalter *Cant* 74-79; V Farndon *S'well* 79-84; R Thorpe 79-84; V Blidworth 84-97; rtd 97; Perm to Offic *S'well* from 03. *4 Winster Avenue, Ravenshead, Nottingham NG15 9DD* Tel (01623) 408205
E-mail raymond.beardall@ntlworld.com

BEARDMORE, John Keith. b 42. FCP85 Bris Univ BEd74 K Coll Lon MA90. **d** 77 **p** 78. NSM Maindee *Mon* from 77. *16 Hove Avenue, Newport NP19 7QP* Tel (01633) 263272

BEARDSHAW, David. b 37. JP. DPS. Wells Th Coll 65. **d** 67 **p** 68. C Wood End *Cov* 67-69; C Stoke 70-73; V Whitley 73-77; Dioc Educn Officer 77-87; P-in-c Offchurch 87-93; Warden Offa Retreat Ho 87-93; rtd 93. *188 Ashington Grove, Coventry CV3 4DB*

BEARDSLEY, Christina. b 51. Sussex Univ BA73 St Jo Coll Cam PhD99. Westcott Ho Cam 76. **d** 78 **p** 79. C Portsea N End St Mark *Portsm* 78-85; V Catherington and Clanfield 85-00; Chapl Worthing and Southlands Hosps NHS Trust 00-01; Asst Chapl Chelsea and Westmr Healthcare NHS Trust 01-04; Chapl from 04. *403 Mile Oak Road, Portslade, Brighton BN41 2RD* Tel (01273) 413696 *or* (020) 8746 8083
E-mail chaplaincy@chelwest.nhs.uk

BEARDSLEY, Nigel Andrew. b 61. Sheff Hallam Univ BSc88 Nottm Univ MA00. EMMTC 97. **d** 00 **p** 01. C Bath Bathwick *B & W* 00-05; Chapl RN from 05. *Royal Navy Chaplaincy Service, Room 203, Victory Building, HM Naval Base, Portsmouth PO1 3LS* Tel (023) 9272 7900
E-mail beardsley@lanj.freeserve.co.uk

BEARDSMORE, Alan. b 45. Wycliffe Hall Ox 67. **d** 70 **p** 71. C Prittlewell St Mary *Chelmsf* 70-72; C Epsom St Martin *Guildf* 72-78; P-in-c Burbage and Savernake Ch Ch *Sarum* 78-79; P-in-c E Grafton, Tidcombe and Fosbury 78-79; TV Wexcombe 79-80; Chapl RN 80-83; TV Haverhill w Withersfield, the Wrattings etc *St E* 83-87; V Gt Barton 87-95; V Eaton *Nor* from 95. *The Vicarage, 210 Newmarket Road, Norwich NR4 7LA* Tel (01603) 250915 E-mail ab@eatonparish.com *or* office@eatonparish.com

BEARDSMORE, John. b 19. Kelham Th Coll 46. **d** 51 **p** 51. C Caldmore *Lich* 51-53; C Otley *Bradf* 53-55; V Burley in Wharfedale 55-69; V Bromley H Trin *Roch* 69-70; V Buttershaw St Paul *Bradf* 70-88; rtd 88; Perm to Offic *Bradf* from 88. *41 Nab Wood Grove, Shipley BD18 4HR* Tel (01274) 596197

BEARE, The Very Revd William. b 33. TCD BA58 DipCSM77. **d** 59 **p** 60. C Waterford St Patr *C & O* 59-62; C Cork H Trin w Shandon St Mary *C, C & R* 62-64; I Rathcormac 64-68; I Marmullane w Monkstown 68-76; Dioc C 76-82; I Stradbally w Ballintubbert, Coraclone etc *C & O* 82-99; Can Ossory and Leighlin Caths 88-90; Chan 90-92; Prec 92-99; Preb Stagonil St Patr Cathl Dublin from 95; Dean Lismore *C & O* from 99; I Lismore w Cappoquin, Kilwatermoy, Dungarvan etc from 99. *The Deanery, The Mall, Lismore, Co Waterford, Irish Republic* Tel and fax (00353) (58) 54105 Mobile 87-233 1508

BEARN, Hugh William. b 62. Man Univ BA84. Cranmer Hall Dur 86. **d** 89 **p** 90. C Heaton Ch Ch *Man* 89-92; Chapl RAF Coll Cranwell 92-96; V Tottington *Man* from 96. *St Anne's Vicarage, Chapel Street, Tottington, Bury BL8 4AP* Tel (01204) 883713

BEARPARK, Canon John Michael. b 36. Ex Coll Ox BA59 MA63. Linc Th Coll 59. **d** 61 **p** 62. C Bingley H Trin *Bradf* 61-64; C Baildon 64-67; V Fairweather Green 67-77; Chapl Airedale Gen Hosp 77-94; V Steeton 77-94; Hon Can Bradf Cathl 89-01; V Bentham St Marg 94-01; P-in-c Bentham St Jo 99-01; RD Ewecross 94-00; rtd 01; Perm to Offic *Bradf* from 01. *31 Northfields Crescent, Settle BD24 9JP* Tel (01729) 822712

BEASLEY, Canon Arthur James. b 12. Hertf Coll Ox BA33 MA38. Ridley Hall Cam 34. **d** 36 **p** 37. C Harpurhey Ch Ch *Man* 36-39; C Flixton St Mich 39-42; P-in-c Stand 42-43; R Moss Side Ch Ch 43-48; Chapl Man R Infirmary 43-48; V Heaton Ch Ch *Man* 48-81; Hon Can Man Cathl 72-81; rtd 81; Perm to Offic *Man* from 81. *40 Chorley New Road, Lostock, Bolton BL6 4AL* Tel (01204) 494450

BEASLEY, Noel Michael Roy. b 68. Imp Coll Lon BSc91 Oriel Coll Ox DPhil96 St Jo Coll Dur BA98. Cranmer Hall Dur. **d** 99 **p** 00. C Newport w Longford, Chetwynd and Forton *Lich* 99-03; Chapl Westcott Ho Cam from 03. *Westcott House, Jesus Lane, Cambridge CB5 8BP* Tel (01223) 741000

BEASLEY, Canon Walter Sydney. b 33. Nottm Univ BA57. Linc Th Coll 57. **d** 59 **p** 60. C Harworth *S'well* 59-64; V Forest Town 64-70; R Bulwell St Mary 70-97; Hon Can S'well Minster 85-97; rtd 97; Perm to Offic *S'well* from 04. *3 Clayton's Drive, Nottingham NG7 2PF* Tel 0115-970 2717 Mobile 07889-350442

BEATER, David MacPherson. b 41. Chich Th Coll 66. **d** 69 **p** 70. C Withington St Crispin *Man* 69-72; C Lightbowne 72-74; V Prestwich St Hilda 74-81; V Northfleet *Roch* 81-85; C Bickley 86-90; TV Stanley *Dur* 90-97; SSF 97-01; C Seaton Hirst *Newc* 01-05; rtd 05. *7 Ferndown, Minnis Road, Birchington CT7 9QE*

BEATON, Mark Timothy. b 61. Univ of Wales (Ban) BA83. Trin Coll Bris 03. **d** 05. C Swindon St Jo and St Andr *Bris* from 05. *Church House, Raleigh Avenue, Swindon SN3 3DZ* Tel (01793) 480078 E-mail mark.beaton@tesco.net

BEATTIE, David George. **d** 04. Aux Min Belfast H Trin and St Silas *Conn* from 04. *Address temp unkown*

BEATTIE, Ian David. b 36. Univ of NZ BA58. St Jo Coll Auckland LTh60. **d** 60 **p** 61. New Zealand 60-64 and from 71; C Shirley St Jo *Cant* 64-65; V S Wimbledon St Andr *S'wark* 65-71. *1/148A Tasman Street, Nelson 7001, New Zealand* Tel (0064) (3) 546 7507

BEATTIE, Margaret. *See* BREWSTER, Margaret

BEATTIE, Canon Noel Christopher. b 41. TCD BTh65 Cranfield Inst of Tech MSc86. **d** 68 **p** 69. C Belfast H Trin *Conn* 68-70; C Belfast St Bart 70-73; C Doncaster St Mary *Sheff* 73-77; TV Northampton Em *Pet* 77-88; Ind Chapl 85-88; Ind Chapl *Linc* 88-92; Ind Chapl *Roch* 92-04; Hon Can Roch Cathl from 00; rtd 04. *6 Oaks Road, Church Stretton SY6 7AX* Tel (01694) 725530
E-mail noelbt@globalnet.co.uk

BEATTY, Robert Harold. b 27. W Ontario Univ BA48 Keble Coll Ox BA55 MA58 McGill Univ Montreal PhD62. **d** 51 **p** 52. Canada 51, 55-57 and 58-67; Perm to Offic *Ox* 52-55; Tutor Bps' Coll Cheshunt 57-58; C W Byfleet *Guildf* 67-71; C Oseney Crescent St Luke w Camden Square St Paul *Lon* 71-72; R Cosgrove *Pet* 72-83; V Hebburn St Oswald *Dur* 83-93; rtd 93; Perm to Offic *Dur* and *Newc* from 93. *60 Briarwood Avenue, Gosforth, Newcastle upon Tyne NE3 5DB* Tel 0191-285 2429

BEAUCHAMP, Anthony Hazlerigg Proctor. b 40. Trin Coll Cam BA62 MA66 MICE68. St Jo Coll Nottm 73. **d** 75 **p** 76. C New Humberstone *Leic* 75-77; C-in-c Polegate *Chich* 77-80; Chapl Bethany Sch Goudhurst 80-86; Chapl Luckley-Oakfield Sch Wokingham 86-88; Chapl Clayesmore Sch Blandford 89-93; R Kirby-le-Soken w Gt Holland *Chelmsf* 93-00; Asst P Wetheral w Warwick *Carl* 00-01; rtd 01; Perm to Offic *Carl* from 00; *Chich* from 01. *2 Stelvio Cottages, 17 Beachy Head Road, Eastbourne BN20 7QP* Tel (01323) 732743

BEAUCHAMP, Gerald Charles. b 55. Hull Univ BA78 K Coll Lon MA96. Coll of Resurr Mirfield 78. **d** 80 **p** 81. C Hatcham St Cath *S'wark* 80-83; S Africa 83-86; C Ealing St Steph Castle Hill *Lon* 86-88; P-in-c Brondesbury St Anne w Kilburn H Trin 88-89; V 89-93; Chapl Kilburn Coll 88-93; C Chelsea St Luke and Ch Ch *Lon* 93-96; V W Brompton St Mary w St Pet 96-04; AD Chelsea 02-04; SSJE from 04. *Monastery of St John the Evangelist, 980 Memorial Drive, Cambridge, MA 02138-5717, USA* Tel (001) (617) 876 3037 E-mail gerald@ssje.org

BEAUCHAMP, John Nicholas. b 57. Wycliffe Hall Ox 92. **d** 94 **p** 95. C Ipswich St Jo *St E* 94-97; TV Beccles St Mich 97-05; P-in-c from 05. *Hillcrest, 17 Upper Grange Road, Beccles NR34 9NU* Tel (01502) 712317

BEAUCHAMP, Julian Thomas Proctor. b 68. Ex Univ BA91. Oak Hill Th Coll BA05. **d** 05. C Cheadle *Ches* from 05. *39C Oakfield Avenue, Cheadle SK8 1EF* Tel 0161-428 5696 Mobile 07974-397022 E-mail jtpb1@tiscali.co.uk

BEAUMONT, Canon Brian Maxwell. b 34. Nottm Univ BA56. Wells Th Coll 58. **d** 59 **p** 60. C Clifton *S'well* 59-62; C E Stoke w Syerston 62; C Edgbaston St Geo *Birm* 62-65; V Smethwick St Alb 65-70; V Blackb H Trin *Blackb* 70-77; Asst Dir RE 70-73; Dir RE 73-92; Hon Can Blackb Cathl 73-77 and 92-99; Can Res 77-92; V Goosnargh w Whittingham 92-99; Bp's Adv for Rural

Areas 92-99; rtd 99; Perm to Offic *Blackb* from 00. *14 Green Drive, Barton, Preston PR3 5AT* Tel (01772) 861131

BEAUMONT, Mrs Jane. b 56. Ches Coll of HE BTh. N Ord Course 01. **d** 04 **p** 05. NSM Chadkirk *Ches* from 04. *Highgate, Sandy Lane, Higher Chisworth, Glossop SK13 5SA* Tel (01457) 853053

BEAUMONT, Canon John Philip. b 32. Leeds Univ BA55. Coll of Resurr Mirfield 55. **d** 57 **p** 58. C Leeds St Marg *Ripon* 57-60; C Wellingborough All Hallows *Pet* 60-64; Chapl HM Borstal Wellingborough 64-70; V Wellingborough St Andr *Pet* 64-70; V Finedon 70-96; Can Pet Cathl 80-96; RD Higham 83-87; rtd 96; Perm to Offic *Pet* from 96. *9 Warren Bridge, Oundle, Peterborough PE8 4DQ* Tel (01832) 273863 E-mail john@beaumont.plus.com

BEAUMONT, John William. b 19. MBE48. RMC 38. Qu Coll Birm 48. **d** 51 **p** 52. C Portsea N End St Mark *Portsm* 51-54; C-in-c Leigh Park St Fran CD 54-59; V S w N Hayling 59-74; R Droxford 74-86; R Meonstoke w Corhampton cum Exton 78-86; rtd 86; Perm to Offic *Portsm* from 86. *134 The Dale, Widley, Waterlooville PO7 5DF* Tel (023) 9237 7492

BEAUMONT, Stephen Martin. b 51. K Coll Lon BD73 AKC74. St Aug Coll Cant 73. **d** 74 **p** 75. C Benwell St Jas *Newc* 74-77; Asst Chapl Marlborough Coll 77-81; R Ideford, Luton and Ashcombe *Ex* 81-84; Bp's Dom Chapl 81-84; Chapl Taunton Sch 85-91; Chapl Haileybury Coll 92-00; Second Chapl and Hd Div Tonbridge Sch from 00. *Tonbridge School, High Street, Tonbridge TN9 1JP* Tel (01732) 365555

BEAUMONT, Terence Mayes. b 41. Lon Univ BA63 Nottm Univ DipTh69. Linc Th Coll 68. **d** 71 **p** 72. C Hitchin St Mary *St Alb* 71-74; C Harpenden St Nic 75-79; V Stevenage St Pet Broadwater 79-87; V St Alb St Mich from 87. *St Michael's Vicarage, St Michael's Street, St Albans AL3 4SL* Tel (01727) 835037

BEAUMONT, Mrs Veronica Jean. b 38. Ox Min Course CBTS93. **d** 93 **p** 94. NSM High Wycombe *Ox* 93-03; NSM W Wycombe w Bledlow Ridge, Bradenham and Radnage from 03; Fundraising Manager (Oxon) Children's Soc from 95. *Edgehill, Upper Stanley Road, High Wycombe HP12 4DB* Tel (01494) 523697 E-mail veronica.beaumont@virgin.net

BEAUMONT OF WHITLEY, The Revd and Rt Hon Lord (Timothy Wentworth). b 28. Ch Ch Ox BA52 MA56. Westcott Ho Cam 54. **d** 55 **p** 56. Asst Chapl Hong Kong Cathl 55-59; Hon C Westmr St Steph w St Jo *Lon* 60-63; Lic to Offic 63-73; Hon C Balham Hill Ascension *S'wark* 85-86; P-in-c Richmond St Luke 86-87; P-in-c N Sheen St Phil and All SS 86-87; V Kew St Phil and All SS w St Luke 87-91; Perm to Offic from 91; rtd 93. *40 Elms Road, London SW4 9EX* Tel and fax (020) 7498 8664 E-mail beaumontt@parliament.uk

BEAVAN, Canon Edward Hugh. b 43. Ex Coll Ox BA70 MA74 Solicitor 66. Cuddesdon Coll 69. **d** 71 **p** 72. C Ashford St Hilda *Lon* 71-74; C Newington St Mary *S'wark* 74-76; R Sandon *Chelmsf* 76-86; V Thorpe Bay 86-98; P-in-c Bradwell on Sea 98-05; P-in-c St Lawrence 98-05; V Burnham from 05; Ind Chapl from 98; RD Maldon and Dengie from 00; Hon Can Chelmsf Cathl from 02. *The Vicarage, 2A Church Road, Burnham-on-Crouch CM0 8DA* Tel (01621) 782071 E-mail hugh@beavan.go-plus.net

BEAVER, William Carpenter. b 45. Colorado Coll BA Wolfs Coll Ox DPhil76. Ox NSM Course 79. **d** 82 **p** 83. NSM Kennington St Jo w St Jas *S'wark* 82-95; NSM Avonmouth St Andr *Bris* 96-97; NSM Bris St Mary Redcliffe w Temple etc from 95; NSM St Andr Holborn *Lon* from 01; Dir Communications for C of E 97-02; Dir Communications for Br Red Cross 02-04; Speech Writer to the Ld Mayor of Lon from 04. *The Mansion House, Mansion House Street, London EC4N 8BH* Tel (020) 7626 2500 E-mail william.beaver@corpoflondon.gov.uk

BEAVIS, Adrian Neill. b 74. Worc Coll Ox BA97. Wycliffe Hall Ox MTh00. **d** 00 **p** 01. C E Twickenham St Steph *Lon* from 00. *308 Richmond Road, Twickenham TW1 2PD* Tel (020) 8892 8869 *or* 8892 5258 E-mail adrian@st-stephens.org.uk

BEAVIS, Mrs Sandra. **d** 98. NSM Southbourne w W Thorney *Chich* from 98. *Lavande, Gordon Road, Southbourne, Emsworth PO10 8AZ* Tel (01243) 371853 E-mail s.lavande@tesco.net

BEAZLEY, Prof John Milner. b 32. DRCOG59 MRCOG62 FRCOG73 FACOG89 Man Univ MB, ChB57 MD64. St Deiniol's Hawarden 83. **d** 86 **p** 87. NSM W Kirby St Bridget *Ches* 86-89; NSM Newton 89-92; NSM Hayton w Cumwhitton *Carl* 92-98; rtd 99; Perm to Offic *Carl* from 99. *High Rigg, Faugh, Heads Nook, Carlisle CA8 9EA* Tel (01228) 70353

BEAZLEY, Miss Margaret Sheila Elizabeth Mary. b 32. Nor City Coll CertEd59. St Alb Minl Tr Scheme 86. **d** 89 **p** 94. NSM Ware St Mary *St Alb* from 89. *38 Fanshawe Crescent, Ware SG12 0AS* Tel (01920) 462349

BEBBINGTON, Ms Julia. b 69. Man Univ BA98 St Jo Coll Dur MA00. Cranmer Hall Dur. **d** 00 **p** 01. C Langley and Parkfield *Man* 00-04; V Cowgate *Newc* from 04. *St Peter's Vicarage, Druridge Drive, Newcastle upon Tyne NE5 3LP* Tel 0191-286 9913 E-mail jbebbing@fish.co.uk

BECK, Alan. b 28. AKC50. **d** 53 **p** 54. C N Harrow St Alb *Lon* 53-56; C Northolt St Mary 56-59; C Loughborough All SS *Leic* 59-61; V Crookham *Guildf* 61-69; V Puriton *B & W* 69-78; P-in-c Pawlett 74-78; V Puriton and Pawlett 78-79; P-in-c Staplegrove 79-84; R 84-88; rtd 88; Perm to Offic *B & W* 88-97. *Redwing, Creech Heathfield, Taunton TA3 5EG* Tel (01823) 443030

BECK, Amanda Ruth. b 68. Liv Univ BA91 Birm Univ BD93. Qu Coll Birm 91. **d** 94 **p** 95. C W Derby Gd Shep *Liv* 94-99; Asst Chapl Voorschoten *Eur* 99-02; P-in-c Kingston Vale St Jo *S'wark* from 03. *St John's Vicarage, Robin Hood Lane, London SW15 3PY* Tel (020) 8546 4079 E-mail mandy.beck@iname.com

BECK, Mrs Gillian Margaret. b 50. Sheff Univ CertEd71 Nottm Univ BTh78. Linc Th Coll 74. **dss** 78 **d** 87. Gt Grimsby St Mary and St Jas *Linc* 78-83; St Paul's Cathl *Lon* 84-87; Hon Par Dn St Botolph Aldgate w H Trin Minories 87-88; Par Dn Monkwearmouth St Andr *Dur* 88-94; C 94-97; NSM Eppleton and Hetton le Hole 97-04. *The Rectory, South Street, West Rainton, Houghton le Spring DH4 6PA* Tel 0191-584 3263 E-mail mgtbex@zoom.co.uk

BECK, John Edward. b 28. ARCM52 FRCO59 St Jo Coll Ox BA56 MA59. Wells Th Coll 56. **d** 58 **p** 59. C Dursley *Glouc* 58-61; C Glouc St Paul 61-63; S Rhodesia 63-65; Rhodesia 65-70; C Cheltenham Ch Ch *Glouc* 70-77; C Cirencester 77-93; rtd 93; Perm to Offic *Glouc* from 93. *25 Bowling Green Road, Cirencester GL7 2HD* Tel (01285) 653778

BECK, Michael Leonard. b 50. K Coll Lon BD77 AKC77. Linc Th Coll 77. **d** 78 **p** 79. C Gt Grimsby St Mary and St Jas *Linc* 78-83; Min Can and Succ St Paul's Cathl *Lon* 83-88; V Monkwearmouth St Andr *Dur* 88-96; TR Monkwearmouth 97; R Eppleton and Hetton le Hole 97-04; AD Houghton 97-04; P-in-c Lyons 00-04; P-in-c W Rainton from 04; P-in-c E Rainton from 04; Dir Reader Min from 04. *The Rectory, South Street, West Rainton, Houghton le Spring DH4 6PA* Tel 0191-584 3263 E-mail mgtbex@zoom.co.uk

BECK, The Very Revd Peter John. b 48. Mert Coll Ox BA69 MA73. Sarum Th Coll 69. **d** 72 **p** 73. C Banbury *Ox* 72-75; TV 75-78; Dioc Youth and Community Officer 75-78; P-in-c Linc St Mary-le-Wigford w St Benedict etc *Linc* 78-81; City Cen Chapl 78-81; New Zealand from 81; TV Glenfield 81-85; V Mt Albert St Luke 86-93; Adn Waitemata 87-93; V Auckland St Matt 93-00; Adn Auckland 98-00; Hon Asst P Wellington Cathl 00-02; Dir Vaughan Park Retreat Cen 02; Dean Christchurch from 02; V Gen from 03. *25 Springfield Road, St Albans, Christchurch, New Zealand* Tel (0064) (3) 377 6095 *or* 366 0046 Mobile 21-654445 E-mail beckwest@paradise.net.nz *or* peterbeck@xtra.co.nz

BECK, Roger William. b 48. Chich Th Coll 79. **d** 81 **p** 82. C St Marychurch *Ex* 81-85; TV Torre 85-88; V Torquay St Jo and Ellacombe 88-94; C Plympton St Mary from 94. *27 Pinewood Close, Plympton, Plymouth PL7 2DW* Tel (01752) 336393

BECK, Mrs Sandra Veronica. b 52. St Jo Coll Nottm 97. **d** 00 **p** 01. NSM Digswell and Panshanger *St Alb* 00-04; NSM Codicote from 04. *48 Grange Rise, Codicote, Hitchin SG4 8YR* Tel (01438) 820191 E-mail beck@colinsandie.freeserve.co.uk

BECK, Canon Stephen. b 16. St Pet Hall Ox BA44 MA45. Westcott Ho Cam 45. **d** 47 **p** 48. C Portsea N End St Mark *Portsm* 47-56; RAChD 56-59; V Moseley St Agnes *Birm* 59-83; RD Moseley 71-81; Hon Can Birm Cathl 76-83; rtd 83; Perm to Offic *Ban* from 83. *Artro View, Moelfre Terrace, Llanbedr LL45 2DQ* Tel (01341) 23545

BECKERLEG, Barzillai. b 20. Selw Coll Cam BA43 MA46. Westcott Ho Cam 42. **d** 44 **p** 45. C Golders Green St Alb *Lon* 44-48; Chapl St Jo Coll Dur 48-52; Lic to Offic *Dur* 49-52; V Battersea St Mary *S'wark* 52-58; V Wentworth *Sheff* 58-59; Hd Master Newc Cathl Choir Sch 59-62; Prec Newc Cathl *Newc* 59-62; R Duncton *Chich* 62-64; R Burton w Coates 62-64; V Kippington *Roch* 64-75; R E Bergholt *St E* 75-79; Chapl St Mary's Sch Wantage 79-85; rtd 85; Perm to Offic *Truro* from 85; *Roch* 86-93; *Chich* from 93; *S'wark* and *Roch* from 00. *1 The Briary, Bexhill-on-Sea TN40 2ET* Tel (01424) 215115

BECKETT, George. b 26. Scawsby Coll of Educn CertEd76 Sheff Univ BEd77 Hull Univ MEd84. **d** 91 **p** 92. NSM Hatfield *Sheff* from 91. *10 Norman Drive, Hatfield, Doncaster DN7 6AQ* Tel (01302) 841091

BECKETT, Graham. b 49. St As Minl Tr Course 95. **d** 99 **p** 00. NSM Hawarden *St As* 99-01; C from 01. *Hillview, Church Lane, Ewloe, Deeside CH5 3BF* Tel (01244) 535269

BECKETT, John Adrian. b 61. Bris Univ BVSc85. Trin Coll Bris. **d** 00 **p** 01. C Harrogate St Mark *Ripon* 00-04; P-in-c Sevenhampton w Charlton Abbots, Hawling etc *Glouc* from 04. *The Rectory, Station Road, Andoversford, Cheltenham GL54 4LA* Tel (01242) 820230

BECKETT, Michael Shaun. b 55. ACA79. Oak Hill Th Coll BA88. **d** 88 **p** 89. C Cambridge St Barn *Ely* 88-93; P-in-c Cambridge St Paul 93-94; V from 94. *St Paul's Vicarage, 15 St Paul's Road, Cambridge CB1 2EZ* Tel (01223) 354186 *or* 315832 Fax 576899 E-mail office@centrestpauls.org

BECKETT, Mrs Patricia Anne. b 44. **d** 00 **p** 01. NSM Cheddleton *Lich* from 00. *5 Deepdale Close, Milton, Stoke-on-Trent ST6 8XF* Tel (01782) 542703

BECKETT, Canon Stanley. b 20. Linc Th Coll. **d** 64 **p** 65. C Barnston *Ches* 64-71; V Daresbury 71-87; Hon Can Ches Cathl 82-87; P-in-c Aston by Sutton 86-87; Hon C 87-90; rtd 87; Hon C Grappenhall *Ches* 90-98; Perm to Offic *Linc* from 98. *82, Fairfields, Holbeach, Spalding PE12 7JE* Tel (01406) 490191

BECKHAM, John Francis. b 25. Bps' Coll Cheshunt 65. **d** 67 **p** 68. C Leytonstone St Jo *Chelmsf* 67-70; C Colchester St Mary V 70-73; R Lawford 73-80; V Gt w Lt Chesterford 80-90; rtd 90; Perm to Offic *St E* from 91. *North Barn, Reckford Road, Westleton, Saxmundham IP17 3BE* Tel (01728) 648969

BECKINSALE, Mrs Pamela Rachel. b 46. Man Univ BSc69. Cant Sch of Min 88. **d** 91 **p** 94. NSM Sittingbourne St Mich *Cant* 91-96; Perm to Offic 96-98; Lic to Offic from 98; Hon Chapl N Kent Health Care NHS Trust 96-98; Chapl Thames Gateway NHS Trust from 98. *8 Glovers Crescent, Bell Road, Sittingbourne ME10 4DU* Tel (01795) 471632

BECKLEY, Peter William (Pedr). b 52. Lon Univ BSc73 CertEd. Trin Coll Bris 76. **d** 79 **p** 80. C Plymouth St Jude *Ex* 79-83; C Ecclesall *Sheff* 83-88; V Greystones from 88. *The Vicarage, 1 Cliffe Farm Drive, Sheffield S11 7JW* Tel 0114-266 7686

BECKLEY, Simon Richard. b 38. Lon Univ BA61. Oak Hill Th Coll 58. **d** 63 **p** 64. C Watford St Luke *St Alb* 63-67; C New Ferry *Ches* 67-70; C Chadderton Ch Ch *Man* 70-73; V Friarmere 73-80; V Tranmere St Cath *Ches* 80-03; Chapl Wirral Community Healthcare NHS Trust 80-97; Chapl Wirral and W Cheshire Community NHS Trust 97-03; rtd 03. *162 Heathbank Avenue, Wirral CH61 4YG* Tel 0151-648 7767

BECKWITH, Ian Stanley. b 36. Nottm Univ BA58 Selw Coll Cam CertEd59 Westmr Coll Ox MTh96. Linc Th Coll 78. **d** 79 **p** 80. NSM Linc Cathl *Linc* 79-85; Sen Lect Bp Grosseteste Coll Linc 80-86; NSM Wallingford w Crowmarsh Gifford etc *Ox* 91-97; OLM Tr Officer (Berks) 96-02; P-in-c Gt Coxwell w Buscot, Coleshill etc 97-02; rtd 02; Perm to Offic *Heref* from 02. *2 Affcot Mill, Affcot, Church Stretton SY6 6RL* Tel (01694) 781667

BECKWITH, Canon John Douglas. b 33. AKC57. **d** 58 **p** 65. C Streatham St Leon *S'wark* 58-59; Lic to Offic *Ripon* 59-60; Nigeria 60-62; C Bedale *Ripon* 62-63; C Mottingham St Andr *S'wark* 64-69; Chapl Gothenburg w Halmstad and Jönköping *Eur* 69-70; Chapl to Suff Bp Edmonton 70-77; Dir of Ords *Lon* 70-77; V Brookfield St Anne, Highgate Rise 77-88; Can Gib Cathl *Eur* 84-88; Hon Can Gib Cathl 88-05; P-in-c Bladon w Woodstock *Ox* 88-93; P-in-c Wootton and Kiddington w Asterleigh 88; C Kidlington w Hampton Poyle 93-94; Perm to Offic *Lon* from 94 and *Eur* from 98; rtd 98. *4 St James Close, Bishop Street, London N1 8PH* Tel and fax (020) 7226 6672 Mobile 07710-277124 E-mail malbis@dircon.co.uk

BECKWITH, John James. b 53. UMIST BSc74 Newc Univ PGCE88. **d** 02 **p** 03. OLM Bothal and Pegswood w Longhirst *Newc* 02-04; C Morpeth from 04. *5 Coquetdale Close, Pegswood, Morpeth NE61 6YG* Tel (01670) 505076 E-mail parish@morpeth43.freeserve.co.uk

BECKWITH, Roger Thomas. b 29. St Edm Hall Ox BA52 MA56 BD85 Lambeth DD92. Ripon Hall Ox 51 Tyndale Hall Bris 52 Cuddesdon Coll 54. **d** 54 **p** 55. C Harold Wood *Chelmsf* 54-57; C Bedminster St Luke w St Silas *Bris* 57-59; Tutor Tyndale Hall Bris 59-63; Lib Latimer Ho Ox 63-73 and from 94; Warden 73-94; Lect Wycliffe Hall Ox 71-94; Hon C Wytham *Ox* 88-90; Hon C N Hinksey and Wytham 90-96; rtd 94; Hon C Ox St Mich w St Martin and All SS *Ox* 97-03; Perm to Offic from 03. *310 Woodstock Road, Oxford OX2 7NR* Tel (01865) 557340

BEDDINGTON, Peter Jon. b 36. ACP68 DipEd81. NW Ord Course 71. **d** 74 **p** 75. C Bury St Pet *Man* 74-77; Hon C Bury Ch King 77-82; Hon C Elton All SS from 82. *18 Throstle Grove, Bury BL8 1EB* Tel 0161-764 3292

BEDEAU (née MILLS), Mrs Melina. b 40. Local Minl Tr Course. **d** 00 **p** 04. NSM W Bromwich St Phil *Lich* 00-03; NSM W Bromwich Gd Shep w St Jo from 03. *4 Jervoise Street, West Bromwich B70 9LY* Tel 0121-553 6833

BEDELL, Anthony Charles John. b 59. Worc Coll Ox BA81 ACA84. Linc Th Coll BTh90. **d** 90 **p** 91. C Newbold w Dunston *Derby* 90-94; C Bedford Leigh *Man* 94-98; V Blackb St Luke w St Phil *Blackb* 98-03; Min Partnership Development Officer *Pet* 03; L'Arche Bognor Community 03-04; Perm to Offic *Chich* from 03. *113 Beaconsfield Road, Wick, Littlehampton BN17 6LL* Tel (01903) 726941

BEDFORD, Christopher John. b 40. CEng68 MIStructE68. **d** 05. OLM Chobham w Valley End *Guildf* from 05. *23 Swallow Rise, Knaphill, Woking GU21 2LG* Tel (01483) 480127 E-mail ahbedford@hotmail.com

BEDFORD, The Ven Colin Michael. b 35. ALCD60. **d** 61 **p** 62. C Woking St Mary *Guildf* 61-63; C Guildf St Sav 63-65; C Morden *S'wark* 65-69; V Toxteth Park St Philemon *Liv* 69-75; P-in-c Toxteth Park St Gabr 69-75; P-in-c Toxteth Park St Jas and St Matt 69-75; P-in-c Prince's Park St Paul 70-75; P-in-c Toxteth Park St Cleopas 73-78; TR Toxteth St Philemon w St Gabr 75-89; TR Toxteth St Philemon w St Gabr and St Cleopas 89-91; R Edgware *Lon* 91-98; TR 98-00; Can Akoko from 96; Adn Ondo from 99; rtd 00; Perm to Offic *Liv* from 01. *44 Arbour Street, Southport PR8 6SQ* Tel (01704) 535811

BEDFORD, Michael Anthony. b 38. Reading Univ BSc59 Heythrop Coll Lon MA00. **d** 01 **p** 02. NSM Ruislip St Martin *Lon* from 01. *7 Chandos Road, Eastcote, Pinner HA5 1PR* Tel (020) 8866 4332 E-mail mabedford@tesco.net

BEDFORD, Richard Derek Warner. b 27. Clare Coll Cam BA52. ALCD54. **d** 54 **p** 55. C Wallington H Trin *S'wark* 54-57; C Sanderstead All SS 57; C Weybridge *Guildf* 57-59; C Addlestone 59-62; C-in-c New Haw CD 62-66; V Epsom Common Ch Ch 66-81; R Walton-on-the-Hill 81-87; Asst Chapl Burrswood Home of Healing 87-92; rtd 92; Perm to Offic *Chich* from 92; Perm to Offic *Roch* from 92. *2 Lealands Close, Groombridge, Tunbridge Wells TN3 9ND* Tel (01892) 864550

BEDFORD, Archdeacon of. *See* HUGHES, The Ven Paul Vernon

BEDFORD, Suffragan Bishop of. *See* INWOOD, The Rt Revd Richard Neil

BEDWELL, Stanley Frederick. b 20. MPS42. Ox NSM Course 77. **d** 80 **p** 81. NSM Farnham Royal *Ox* 80-81; NSM Farnham Royal w Hedgerley from 81. *18 Ingleglen, Farnham Common, Slough SL2 3QA* Tel (01753) 644522

BEEBEE, Meyrick Richard Legge. St Alb and Ox Min Course 99. **d** 02 **p** 03. NSM Gerrards Cross and Fulmer *Ox* from 02. *Oak House, 86 Fulmer Road, Gerrards Cross SL9 7EG* Tel (01753) 882524 E-mail mbeebee@aol.com

BEEBY, Lawrence Clifford. b 28. S'wark Ord Course 70. **d** 73 **p** 74. C Notting Hill St Jo *Lon* 73-74; C Sunbury 74-76; C-in-c Hounslow Gd Shep Beavers Lane CD 76-80; Chapl Botleys Park Hosp Chertsey 80-96; rtd 96; Perm to Offic *Guildf* 96-99 and *Lon* from 96. *54 Bingley Road, Sunbury-on-Thames TW16 7RB* Tel (01932) 788922

BEECH, Miss Ailsa. b 44. N Co Coll Newc TDip65. Trin Coll Bris 78. **dss** 80 **d** 87 **p** 94. Pudsey St Lawr and St Paul *Bradf* 80-88; Par Dn 87-88; C Attleborough *Cov* 88-89; Par Dn Cumnor *Ox* 89-92; Asst Chapl Walsgrave Hosp Cov 92-94; Asst Chapl Walsgrave Hosps NHS Trust 94-96; Chapl 96-00; Chapl Univ Hosps Coventry and Warks NHS Trust 00-04; rtd 04; Perm to Offic *York* from 04. *Oxenby, Whitby Road, Pickering YO18 7HL* Tel (01751) 472689 E-mail ailsab@btopenworld.com

BEECH, Mrs Charmian Patricia. b 45. RGN66 RHV70 TCert74. St As Minl Tr Course 99. **d** 02 **p** 03. C Connah's Quay *St As* 02-04; P-in-c Hodnet w Weston under Redcastle *Lich* from 04; Dioc Child Protection Officer from 04. *The Rectory, Abbots Way, Hodnet, Market Drayton TF9 3NQ* Tel (01630) 685491 E-mail charmian.beech@virgin.net

BEECH, Derek Charles. b 49. EMMTC 99. **d** 02 **p** 03. NSM Horsley and Denby *Derby* from 02. *39 Brook Street, Heage, Belper DE56 2AG* Tel (01773) 850168 Mobile 07967-582661

BEECH, Frank Thomas. b 36. Tyndale Hall Bris 64. **d** 66 **p** 67. C Penn Fields *Lich* 66-70; C Attenborough w Chilwell *S'well* 70-74; P-in-c 74-75; P-in-c Attenborough 75-76; V 76-84; V Worksop St Anne 84-03; Chapl Welbeck Coll 84-03; rtd 04; Perm to Offic *S'well* from 04. *43 Bescar Lane, Ollerton, Newark NG22 9BS* Tel 07743-592012 (mobile) E-mail frank.beech@lineone.net

BEECH, John. b 41. St Jo Coll Nottm. **d** 83 **p** 83. C York St Paul *York* 83-84; P-in-c Bubwith w Ellerton and Aughton 84-85; P-in-c Thorganby w Skipwith and N Duffield 84-85; V Bubwith w Skipwith 85-87; V Acomb H Redeemer 87-00; P-in-c Westleigh St Pet *Man* 00-01; rtd 01. *6 Parkfield, Stillington, York YO60 1JW* E-mail jobe@cwcom.net

BEECH, John Thomas. b 38. St Aid Birkenhead 64. **d** 67 **p** 68. C Burton St Paul *Lich* 67-70; Chapl RN 70-85; V Ellingham and Harbridge and Ibsley *Win* 85-94; Chapl Whiteley Village *Guildf* 94-03; rtd 03. *10 Friars Walk, Barton-on-Sea, New Milton BH25 7DA*

BEECH, Peter John. b 34. Bps' Coll Cheshunt 58. **d** 61 **p** 62. C Fulham All SS *Lon* 61-64; S Africa 64-67; V S Hackney St Mich *Lon* 68-71; P-in-c Haggerston St Paul 68-71; V S Hackney St Mich w Haggerston St Paul 71-75; V Wanstead H Trin Hermon Hill *Chelmsf* 75-89; P-in-c St Mary-at-Latton 89-90; V 90-99; rtd 99; Perm to Offic *Ely* from 99. *9 Fitzgerald Close, Ely CB7 4QB* Tel (01353) 666269

BEECHAM, Clarence Ralph. b 35. S'wark Ord Course. **d** 83 **p** 84. NSM Leigh-on-Sea St Jas *Chelmsf* 83-86. *27 Scarborough Drive, Leigh-on-Sea SS9 3ED* Tel (01702) 574923

BEECROFT, Benjamin Harold. b 77. Trin Coll Bris BA98. **d** 00 **p** 01. C Stapleford *S'well* 00-04; C Warfield *Ox* from 04. *2 Dorset Vale, Warfield, Bracknell RG42 3JL* Tel (01344) 310659

BEECROFT, Mrs Christine Mary. b 62. RGN85. Trin Coll Bris BA97 MA99. **d** 98 **p** 99. C Roxeth *Lon* 98-00; Perm to Offic *S'well* 00-02; C Stapleford 02-04; NSM Warfield *Ox* from 04. *2 Dorset Vale, Warfield, Bracknell RG42 3JL* Tel (01344) 310659 E-mail christine.beecroft@ntlworld.com

BEEDELL, Trevor Francis. b 31. ALCD65. **d** 65 **p** 66. C Walton *St E* 65-68; R Hartshorne *Derby* 68-79; RD Repton 74-79; V Doveridge 79-86; Chapl HM Det Cen Foston Hall 79-80; Dioc Dir of Chr Stewardship *Derby* 79-97; rtd 97; Perm to Offic *Derby* from 97. *185 High Lane West, West Hallam, Ilkeston DE7 6HP* Tel 0115-932 5589

BEEDON, David Kirk. b 59. Birm Univ BA89 MPhil93. Qu Coll Birm 86. **d** 89 **p** 90. C Cannock *Lich* 89-92; V Wednesbury St Bart 92-99; R Lich St Mich w St Mary and Wall from 99. *St Michael's Rectory, St Michael Road, Lichfield WS13 6SN* Tel and fax (01543) 262420 *or* 262211 E-mail dkbeedon@aol.com

BEEK, Canon Michael Peter. b 27. Em Coll Cam BA50 MA55. Linc Th Coll 50. **d** 52 **p** 53. C Mitcham St Barn *S'wark* 52-55; C Talbot Village *Sarum* 55-58; V Higham and Merston *Roch* 58-66; R Gravesend St Geo and St Jas 66-74; RD Gravesend 70-74; Hon Can Roch Cathl 73-92; RD Tunbridge Wells 74-83; R Speldhurst w Groombridge 74-77; P-in-c Ashurst 77; R Speldhurst w Groombridge and Ashurst 77-83; V Bromley SS Pet and Paul 83-92; rtd 92; Perm to Offic *Nor* from 92 and *St E* from 97; RD Hartismere *St E* 93-97. *18 Henry Ward Road, Harleston IP20 9EZ* Tel (01379) 854003

BEER, Mrs Janet Margaret. b 43. Goldsmiths' Coll Lon CertEd64. Oak Hill Th Coll 83. **dss** 86 **d** 87 **p** 94. London Colney St Pet *St Alb* 86-97; Hon C 87-97; Chapl St Alb High Sch for Girls 87-89; Chapl Middx Univ *Lon* 94-97; NSM Northaw and Cuffley *St Alb* from 97. *Northaw Vicarage, 58 Hill Rise, Cuffley, Potters Bar EN6 4RG* Tel (01707) 874126 E-mail jan.beer@ntlworld.com

BEER, The Ven John Stuart. b 44. Pemb Coll Ox BA65 MA70 Fitzw Coll Cam MA78. Westcott Ho Cam 69. **d** 71 **p** 72. C Knaresborough St Jo *Ripon* 71-74; Chapl Fitzw Coll and New Hall Cam 74-80; Fell Fitzw Coll 77-80; Bye-Fell from 01; P-in-c Toft w Caldecote and Childerley *Ely* 80-83; R 83-87; P-in-c Hardwick 80-83; R 83-87; V Grantchester 87-97; Dir of Ords, Post-Ord Tr and Student Readers from 88; Hon Can Ely Cathl from 89; Adn Huntingdon 97-04; Acting Adn Wisbech 02-04; Adn Ely from 04. *St Botolph's Rectory, 1A Summerfield, Cambridge CB3 9HE* Tel and fax (01223) 350424 E-mail archdeacon.ely@ely.anglican.org

BEER, Michael Trevor. b 44. Chich Th Coll 66. **d** 69 **p** 70. C Leagrave *St Alb* 69-73; St Vincent 73-74; C Thorley w Bishop's Stortford H Trin *St Alb* 74-80; V London Colney St Pet 80-97; V Northaw and Cuffley from 97. *Northaw Vicarage, 58 Hill Rise, Cuffley, Potters Bar EN6 4RG* Tel (01707) 874126

BEER, Nigel David. b 62. Portsm Poly BSc84. St Jo Coll Nottm Dip Th Studies 92 MA93. **d** 93 **p** 94. C Rastrick St Matt *Wakef* 93-96; C Bilton *Ripon* 96-98; TV Moor Allerton from 98. *73 The Avenue, Leeds LS17 7NP* Tel 0113-267 8487 E-mail nbeer@lineone.net

BEER, William Barclay. b 43. ACT ThA68 St Steph Ho Ox. **d** 71 **p** 72. C St Marychurch *Ex* 71-76; V Pattishall w Cold Higham *Pet* 76-82; V Northampton St Benedict 82-85; V Chislehurst Annunciation *Roch* from 85. *The Vicarage, 2 Foxhome Close, Chislehurst BR7 5XT* Tel (020) 8467 3606 Fax as telephone E-mail wbeer@lineone.net

BEESLEY, Michael Frederick. b 37. K Coll Cam BA59. Westcott Ho Cam 60. **d** 61 **p** 64. C Eastleigh *Win* 61-69; rtd 02. *24 Charmouth Grove, Poole BH14 0LP* Tel (01202) 773471

BEESLEY, Ramon John. b 27. Magd Coll Ox BA51 MA55. Wycliffe Hall Ox 51. **d** 53 **p** 56. C Gerrards Cross *Ox* 53-54; Asst Chapl Embley Park Sch Romsey 54-58; Perm to Offic *Win* 54-58; Asst Master Farnham Sch 58-62; Perm to Offic *Guildf* 58-62; Perm to Offic *Win* from 63; Hd Science Gore Sch New Milton 63-69; Dep Hd Applemore Sch Dibden Purlieu 69-74; Hd Master Bellemoor Sch Southn 74-84; rtd 84. *Wayfarers, Burley, Ringwood BH24 4HW* Tel (01425) 402284

BEESON, Christopher George. b 48. Man Univ BSc70. Qu Coll Birm 72. **d** 75 **p** 76. C Flixton St Mich *Man* 75-78; C Newton Heath All SS 78-80; R Gorton St Jas 80-90; Dioc Communications Officer *Blackb* 91-92; C Ribbleton 92-93; rtd 93; Perm to Offic *Blackb* from 93. *24 Arnold Close, Ribbleton, Preston PR2 6DX* Tel (01772) 702675 E-mail cbeeson@cix.co.uk

BEESON, The Very Revd Trevor Randall. b 26. OBE97. K Coll Lon MA76 FKC87 Southn Univ Hon DLitt99. **d** 51 **p** 52. C Leadgate *Dur* 51-54; C Norton St Mary 54-56; C-in-c Stockton St Chad CD 56-60; V Stockton St Chad 60-65; C St Martin-in-the-Fields *Lon* 65-71; V Ware St Mary *St Alb* 71-76; Can Westmr Abbey 76-87; Treas 78-82; R Westmr St Marg 82-87; Chapl to Speaker of Ho of Commons 82-87; Dean Win 87-96; rtd 96; Perm to Offic *Win* from 96. *69 Greatbridge Road, Romsey SO51 8FE* Tel (01794) 514627

BEESTON, Andrew Bernard. b 41. RMN64 RGN67. NEOC 99. **d** 01 **p** 02. NSM Cullercoats St Geo *Newc* from 01. *21 Deepdale Road, Cullercoats, North Shields NE30 3AN* Tel 0191-259 0431 E-mail abeeston@ukf.net

BEET, Duncan Clive. b 65. Ridley Hall Cam 98. **d** 01 **p** 02. C Northampton Em *Pet* 01-04; P-in-c Mears Ashby and Hardwick and Sywell etc from 04. *The Vicarage, 46 Wellingborough Road, Mears Ashby, Northampton NN6 0DZ* Tel (01604) 812907

BEETHAM, Anthony. b 32. Lon Univ BSc53. Ox NSM Course. **d** 75 **p** 76. Dir Chr Enquiry Agency 88-97; NSM Ox St Clem *Ox* 75-02; rtd 02; Perm to Offic *Ox* from 03. *44 Rose Hill, Oxford OX4 4HS* Tel (01865) 770923

BEETON, David Ambrose Moore. b 39. Chich Th Coll 62. **d** 65 **p** 66. C Forest Gate St Edm *Chelmsf* 65-71; V Rush Green 71-81; V Coggeshall w Markshall 81-02; rtd 02; Perm to Offic *Nor* from 03. *Le Strange Cottages, 2 Hunstanton Road, Heacham, King's Lynn PE31 7HH* Tel (01485) 572150

BEETY, Arthur Edward. b 38. Sheff Univ BA60. Cant Sch of Min 92. **d** 95 **p** 96. NSM Cobham w Luddesdowne and Dode *Roch* from 95. *The Old Forge, 4 The Street, Cobham, Gravesend DA12 3BN* Tel (01474) 816684 E-mail arthur.beety@btinternet.com

BEEVER, Miss Alison Rosemary. b 59. Man Univ BA80. Linc Th Coll 88. **d** 90 **p** 94. Par Dn Watford Ch Ch *St Alb* 90-94; C 94-96; V Tilehurst St Cath *Ox* 96-01; P-in-c Cen Ex 01-04; Dioc Dir of Ords 01-04; rtd 04. *The Rectory, 3 Spicer Road, Exeter EX1 1SX* Tel (01392) 272450

BEEVERS, Preb Colin Lionel. b 40. K Coll Lon BSc62 PhD66 CEng70 MIEE70 MBIM73. Sarum & Wells Th Coll 87. **d** 89 **p** 90. C Ledbury w Eastnor *Heref* 89-93; C Lt Marcle 89-93; Asst Dir of Tr 92-96; P-in-c Kimbolton w Hamnish and Middleton-on-the-Hill 93-96; P-in-c Bockleton w Leysters 93-96; P-in-c Ledbury w Eastnor 96-98; P-in-c Much Marcle 96-98; TR Ledbury 98-05; RD Ledbury 96-02; Preb Heref Cathl 02-05; Chapl Herefordshire Primary Care Trust 96-05; rtd 05. *55 Lion Court, Sansome Place, Worcester WR1 1UT* Tel (01905) 24132 E-mail annandcolin.beevers@virgin.net

BEEVERS, Reginald. b 22. Dur Univ BA48. Qu Coll Birm 48. **d** 50 **p** 51. C Stockton H Trin *Dur* 50-52; C Esh 52-53; C-in-c Peterlee CD 53-57; V Peterlee 57-60; Chapl Worc R Infirmary 60-63; Lic to Offic *Man* 63-65; Chapl Hulme Gr Sch Oldham 63-65; Chapl Guy's Hosp Lon 65-70; Chapl Liv Coll 70-81; R Hatch Beauchamp w Beercrocombe, Curry Mallet etc *B & W* 81-88; rtd 88; P-in-c Oare w Culbone *B & W* 90-93; Perm to Offic 93-99. *18 Abbey Close, Curry Rivel, Langport TA10 0EL* Tel (01458) 253676

BEGBIE, Jeremy Sutherland. b 57. Edin Univ BA77 Aber Univ BD80 PhD87 LRAM80 ARCM77 MSSTh. Ridley Hall Cam 80. **d** 82 **p** 83. C Egham *Guildf* 82-85; Chapl Ridley Hall Cam 85-87; Dir Studies 87-92; Vice-Prin 93-00; Assoc Prin from 00; Hon Reader St Andr Univ from 00. *Ridley Hall, Ridley Hall Road, Cambridge CB3 9HG* Tel (01223) 741075 *or* 360995 Fax 741081 E-mail jb215@cam.ac.uk

BEGGS, Norman Lindell. b 32. N Lon Poly CQSW77. S Dios Minl Tr Scheme 86. **d** 89 **p** 90. NSM Milborne St Andrew w Dewlish *Sarum* 89-92; C 92-95; C Piddletrenthide w Plush, Alton Pancras etc 92-95; C Puddletown and Tolpuddle 92-95; rtd 95; Perm to Offic *Sarum* from 95. *Wallingford House, Dewlish, Dorchester DT2 7LX* Tel (01258) 837320

BEGLEY, Frank William. b 18. Univ of Wales (Lamp) BA48. **d** 49 **p** 50. C Ebbw Vale *Mon* 49-55; C Richmond St Jo *S'wark* 55-57; Tanganyika 57-63; C-in-c Boxmoor St Fran Hammerfield CD *St Alb* 64-66; Guyana 66-70; C Roath *Llan* 70-74; V Cardiff St Dyfrig and St Samson 74-83; R Llanwenarth Ultra *Mon* 83-87; rtd 87; Perm to Offic *Llan* from 87. *24 St Teilo's Court, Sturminster Road, Roath, Cardiff CF23 5AX* Tel (029) 2048 9375

BEGLEY, Mrs Helen. b 59. Kingston Poly BA81. N Ord Course 87. **d** 89 **p** 94. Par Dn Leeds H Trin *Ripon* 89-90; Chapl to the Deaf 89-96; Par Dn Leeds City 91-94; C 94-96; Chapl to the Deaf (Wilts) *Sarum* 96-03; C Upper Wylye Valley from 03. *The Vicarage, Green Lane, Codford, Warminster BA12 0NY* Tel (01985) 850019 E-mail begley@avonrd.freeserve.co.uk

BEHENNA, Preb Gillian Eve. b 57. CertEd78. St Alb Minl Tr Scheme 82. **dss** 85 **d** 87 **p** 94. Chapl to the Deaf *Sarum* 85-90; Chapl with Deaf People *Ex* 90-04; Preb Ex Cathl 02-04; Chapl w Deaf Community *Bris* from 05. *1 Saxon Way, Bradley Stoke, Bristol BS32 9AR* Tel (01454) 202483 Mobile 07715-707137 E-mail gill@signsofgod.fsnet.co.uk

BEHREND, Michael Christopher. b 60. St Jo Coll Cam BA82 MA86 PGCE83. Oak Hill Th Coll DipHE95. **d** 97 **p** 98. C Hensingham *Carl* 97-02; TV Horwich and Rivington *Man* from 02. *St Catherine's House, Richmond Street, Horwich, Bolton BL6 5QT* Tel (01204) 697162

BELCHER, Mrs Catherine Jane Allington. b 53. Charlotte Mason Coll of Educn CertEd75. EAMTC 02. **d** 05. NSM Norwich St Mary Magd w St Jas *Nor* from 05. *70 Mill Hill Road, Norwich NR2 3DS* E-mail revkatebelcher@yahoo.co.uk

BELCHER, David John. b 44. Ch Ch Ox BA65 MA69. Cuddesdon Coll 68. **d** 70 **p** 71. C Gateshead St Mary *Dur* 70-73; C Stockton St Pet 73-76; Lic to Offic *Lich* 76-81; P-in-c W Bromwich Ch Ch 81-85; P-in-c W Bromwich Gd Shep w St Jo 85-89; V 89-95; RD W Bromwich 90-94; R Bratton, Edington and Imber, Erlestoke etc *Sarum* 95-03; rtd 03; Hon C Smestow

Vale *Lich* from 03. *The Vicarage, 59 Six Ashes Road, Bobbington, Stourbridge DY7 5BZ* Tel (01384) 221580

BELCHER, Canon Derek George. b 50. Univ of Wales LLM04 MEd86 Lon Univ PGCE82 MRSH73 MBIM82. Chich Th Coll 74. **d** 77 **p** 78. C Newton Nottage *Llan* 77-81; PV Llan Cathl 81-87; V Margam 87-01; Hon Can Llan Cathl from 97; RD Margam 99-01; TR Cowbridge from 01. *The Rectory, 85 Broadway, Llanblethian, Cowbridge CF71 7EY* Tel (01446) 771625 Mobile 07796-170671 E-mail derek@cowbridge.plus.com *or* rector@cowbridgeparish.com

BELCHER, Frederick William. b 30. Kelham Th Coll 50 Chich Th Coll 53. **d** 54 **p** 55. C Catford St Laur *S'wark* 54-58; C-in-c Plumstead Wm Temple Ch Abbey Wood CD 58-62; V Eltham Park St Luke 62-64; Lic to Offic 65-81; NSM Charminster and Stinsford *Sarum* 88-94; Perm to Offic from 94; rtd 95. *Little Mead, North Street, Charminster, Dorchester DT2 9QZ* Tel (01305) 260688

BELFAST, Dean of. *See* McKELVEY, The Very Revd Robert Samuel James Houston

BELHAM, John Edward. b 42. K Coll Lon BSc65 AKC65 PhD70. Oak Hill Th Coll 69. **d** 72 **p** 73. C Cheadle Hulme St Andr *Ches* 72-75; C Cheadle 75-83; R Gressenhall w Longham w Wendling etc *Nor* from 83. *The Rectory, Bittering Street, Gressenhall, Dereham NR20 4EB* Tel (01362) 860211

BELHAM, Michael. b 23. Lon Univ BScEng50. **d** 67 **p** 68. C Northwood Hills St Edm *Lon* 67-69; C Hendon St Mary 69-73; V Tottenham H Trin 73-78; V Hillingdon St Jo 78-85; P-in-c Broughton *Ox* 85; R Broughton w N Newington and Shutford 85-90; Chapl Horton Gen Hosp 85-90; rtd 90; Perm to Offic *Pet* from 90; *Ox* 90-00; *B & W* from 01; Sec DBP *Ox* 95-01. *14 Holly Court, Frome BA11 2SQ* Tel (01373) 462941 E-mail michael-belham@supanet.com

BELING, David Gibson. b 30. Fitzw Ho Cam BA54 MA58. **d** 56 **p** 57. C Radipole *Sarum* 56-59; C Broadwater St Mary *Chich* 59-61; R W Knighton w Broadmayne *Sarum* 61-73; V Paignton St Paul Preston *Ex* 73-91; rtd 91; Perm to Offic *Ex* from 91. *51 Manor Road, Paignton TQ3 2HZ*

BELITHER, John Roland. b 36. Oak Hill Th Coll 83. **d** 86 **p** 87. NSM Bushey Heath *St Alb* 86-91; V Marsh Farm from 91. *The Vicarage, 40 Purway Close, Luton LU3 3RT* Tel (01582) 575757

BELL, Adrian Christopher. b 48. AKC70. St Aug Coll Cant 70. **d** 71 **p** 72. C Sheff St Aid w St Luke *Sheff* 71-74; C Willesborough w Hinxhill *Cant* 74-78; P-in-c Wormshill 78; P-in-c Hollingbourne w Hucking 78-82; P-in-c Leeds w Broomfield 79-82; V Hollingbourne and Hucking w Leeds and Broomfield 82-84; V Herne Bay Ch Ch 84-91; R Washingborough w Heighington and Canwick *Linc* 91-01; R Fakenham w Alethorpe *Nor* from 01. *The Rectory, Gladstone Road, Fakenham NR21 9BZ* Tel and fax (01328) 862268 E-mail adrian.bell4@btopenworld.com

BELL, Alan. b 29. Handsworth Coll Birm 55 Linc Th Coll 64. **d** 65 **p** 65. C Spilsby w Hundleby *Linc* 65-67; R Ludford Magna w Ludford Parva 67-76; V Burgh on Bain 68-76; V Kelstern, Calcethorpe and E Wykeham 68-76; Clerical Org Sec CECS 76-78; rtd 94. *116 The Birches, Crawley RH10 1RZ* Tel (01293) 407195

BELL, Alan John. b 47. Liv Univ BA68. Ridley Hall Cam 69. **d** 72 **p** 73. C Speke St Aid *Liv* 72-77; P-in-c Halewood 77-81; R Wavertree St Mary 81-88; Chapl Mabel Fletcher Tech Coll and Olive Mt Hosp 81-88; R Fakenham w Alethorpe *Nor* 88-00; RD Burnham and Walsingham 92-00; TR Stockport SW *Ches* from 00; RD Stockport from 05. *St George's Vicarage, 7 Corbar Road, Stockport SK2 6EP* Tel 0161-456 0918 *or* 480 2453 E-mail vicaralanbell@aol.com

BELL, Allan McRae. b 49. Moray Ho Teacher Tr Coll Edin CertEd80 E Lon Univ BA90. S'wark Ord Course 86. **d** 92 **p** 95. NSM Bow H Trin and All Hallows *Lon* 91-93; NSM R Foundn of St Kath in Ratcliffe 93-95; USA 95-97; Chapl Univ of California 95-96; P-in-c Bolinas St Aidan 96-97. *177 Well Street, London E9 6QU* Tel (020) 8985 1978

BELL, Andrew Thomas. b 58. Ripon Coll Cuddesdon 93. **d** 95 **p** 96. C Leighton Buzzard w Eggington, Hockliffe etc *St Alb* 95-98; TV Schorne *Ox* from 98. *The Vicarage, Church Street, North Marston, Buckingham MK18 3PH* Tel (01296) 670298

BELL, Anthony Lawson. b 47. AKC72. St Aug Coll Cant 71. **d** 72 **p** 73. C Peterlee *Dur* 72-77; C-in-c Stockton St Jas CD 82-89; P-in-c Byers Green 89-96; Ind Chapl Teesside 89-96; P-in-c Ault Hucknall *Derby* 96-99; V Ault Hucknall and Scarcliffe from 99. *The Vicarage, 59 The Hill, Glapwell, Chesterfield S44 5LX* Tel (01246) 850371 Fax 857530 E-mail glapwell@tonybell.co.uk *or* glapwell@btconnect.com

BELL, Antony Fancourt. b 28. Magd Coll Ox BA51 MA58. Wells Th Coll 54. **d** 56 **p** 57. C Clapham H Trin *S'wark* 56-59; C Gillingham *Sarum* 59-61; R Stanway *Chelmsf* 61-94; RD Dedham and Tey 81-91; rtd 94. *Walsingham House, Ilchester Road, Charlton Mackrell, Somerton TA11 6AN* Tel (01458) 223657

BELL, Arthur Francis. b 17. Leeds Univ BA39. Bps' Coll Cheshunt 40. **d** 41 **p** 42. C Bedford H Trin *St Alb* 41-43; C Chesterfield St Mary and All SS *Derby* 43-45; C Barrowhill 45-46; C Westbury-on-Trym H Trin *Bris* 46-48; C Knowle H Nativity 48-50; R Priston *B & W* 50-61; V Englishcombe 55-61; R Charlcombe 61-85; rtd 85; Perm to Offic *B & W* from 86. *Waterhouse, Waterhouse Lane, Monkton Combe, Bath BA2 7JB* Tel (01225) 720271

BELL, Arthur James. b 33. Ch Coll Cam BA57 MA60. Coll of Resurr Mirfield 57. **d** 59 **p** 60. C New Cleethorpes *Linc* 59-63; C Upperby St Jo *Carl* 63-66; P-in-c Wabasca Canada 67-72 and 77-83; Perm to Offic *Ely* 73-75; Lic to Offic *Carl* 75-76; Warden Retreat of the Visitation Rhandirmwyn 83-99; Perm to Offic *Dur* from 00. *Burnside, 22 Rose Terrace, Stanhope, Bishop Auckland DL13 2PE* Tel (01388) 526514

BELL, Barnaby. *See* BELL, Simon Barnaby

BELL, Bede. *See* BELL, William Wealands

BELL, Brian Thomas Benedict. b 64. Newc Poly BA87 Dip French Studies 91 Newc Univ PGCE88 Univ of Northumbria at Newc MA93. Coll of Resurr Mirfield BA97. **d** 97 **p** 98. C Tynemouth Cullercoats St Paul *Newc* 97-01; V Horton from 01. *St Benedict's Vicarage, Brierley Road, Blyth NE24 5AU* Tel (01670) 367035 E-mail frbrian@ourladyandbenedict.fsnet.co.uk

BELL, Catherine Ann. *See* MOSS, Mrs Catherine Ann

BELL, Canon Charles William. b 43. TCD Div Test 66 BA66 MA69. CITC 64. **d** 67 **p** 68. C Newtownards *D & D* 67-70; C Larne and Inver *Conn* 70-74; C Ballymena w Ballyclug 74-80; Bp's C Belfast Ardoyne 80-88; Bp's C Belfast Ardoyne w H Redeemer 88-89; I Eglantine from 89; Dioc Info Officer (S Conn) from 89; Preb Conn Cathl from 04. *All Saints' Rectory, 16 Eglantine Road, Lisburn BT27 5RQ* Tel (028) 9266 2634 Fax 9266 8651 E-mail rector@eglantine.org

BELL, Colin Ashworth. b 52. FCCA83. Westcott Ho Cam 89. **d** 91 **p** 92. C Lytham St Cuth *Blackb* 91-93; C Whittle-le-Woods 93-97; V Stalybridge H Trin and Ch Ch *Ches* from 97. *The Vicarage, 277 Mottram Road, Stalybridge SK15 2RT* Tel 0161-303 1984 *or* 304 9308 E-mail pastors@holytrinitystalybridge.co.uk

BELL, Colin Douglas. b 65. QUB DipTh90 BTh94 TCD MPhil96. CITC 94. **d** 96 **p** 97. C Dundonald *D & D* 96-98; C Knock 98-00; I Lack *Clogh* 00-02; I Rathcoole *Conn* from 02. *7 Oaklands Meadow, Newtownabbey BT37 0XN* Tel (028) 9086 7714

BELL, Cyril John. b 22. Lon Univ BA48. Wycliffe Hall Ox 52. **d** 53 **p** 54. C Monkwearmouth St Pet *Dur* 53-56; Ch of S India 56-60; Hon C Westlands St Andr *Lich* 66-71; Lic to Offic *Ches* 71-82; Perm to Offic 82-90 and from 91; Perm to Offic *Lich* 90-97. *49 Delamere Road, Nantwich CW5 7DF* Tel (01270) 628910

BELL, David James. b 62. QUB BSc84 BTh. **d** 91 **p** 92. C Ballyholme *D & D* 91-94; C Coleraine *Conn* 94-00; I Ardtrea w Desertcreat *Arm* from 00. *Tullyhogue Rectory, 50 Lower Grange Road, Cookstown BT80 8SL* Tel and fax (028) 8676 1163 E-mail bell.david@talk21.com

BELL, Canon David Owain. b 49. Dur Univ BA69 Nottm Univ DipTh70 Fitzw Coll Cam BA72 MA80. Westcott Ho Cam 70. **d** 72 **p** 73. C Houghton le Spring *Dur* 72-76; C Norton St Mary 76-78; P-in-c Worc St Clem *Worc* 78-84; R 84-85; R Old Swinford Stourbridge 85-97; RD Stourbridge 90-96; Hon Can Worc Cathl from 96; TR Kidderminster St Mary and All SS w Trimpley etc from 97. *The Vicarage, 22 Roden Avenue, Kidderminster DY10 2RF* Tel (01562) 823265 E-mail dowainbell@yahoo.co.uk

BELL, Canon Donald Jon. b 50. Sarum & Wells Th Coll 73. **d** 76 **p** 77. C Jarrow *Dur* 76-80; C Darlington St Cuth w St Hilda 80-83; V Wingate Grange 83-89; V Sherburn w Pittington 89-95; AD Dur from 93; R Shadforth 94-95; P-in-c Dur St Cuth 95-97; V 97-02; R Witton Gilbert 97-02; TR Dur N from 02; Chapl Dur and Darlington Fire and Rescue Brigade from 95; Hon Can Dur Cathl from 01. *St Cuthbert's Vicarage, 1 Aykley Court, Durham DH1 4NW* Tel and fax 0191-386 4526 Mobile 07973-829491 E-mail aread@djonbell.freeserve.co.uk

BELL, Dorothy Jane. b 53. Teesside Univ BSc93. Cranmer Hall Dur 01. **d** 03 **p** 04. C Washington *Dur* from 03. *38 Brancepeth Road, Washington NE38 0LA* Tel 0191-483 2360

BELL, Edwin Lucius Wyndham. b 19. Worc Coll Ox BA41 MA45. Westcott Ho Cam 41. **d** 43 **p** 44. C Croydon St Jo *Cant* 43-50; CF 50-54; V Bapchild w Tonge and Rodmersham *Cant* 54-63; P-in-c Murston 54-56; V Maidstone St Paul 63-78; P-in-c Nonington w Barfreystone 78-85; P-in-c Womenswold 78-85; rtd 85; Perm to Offic *Cant* 85-05. *Manormead, Tilford Road, Hindhead GU26 6RA* Tel (01428) 602500

BELL, Evelyn Ruth. b 52. Univ of Wales (Cardiff) BSc(Econ). St Alb and Ox Min Course 97. **d** 00 **p** 01. C Waltham Cross *St Alb* 00-03; Chapl HM Pris Edmunds Hill from 03. *HM Prison Edmunds Hill, Stradishall, Newmarket CB8 9YN* Tel (01440) 743595 E-mail eve.bell@hmps.gsi.gov.uk

BELL, Canon Francis William Albert. b 28. TCD BA52 MA57 BD57. **d** 53 **p** 54. C Belfast St Mich *Conn* 53-55; C Belfast All SS 55-61; C Ballynafeigh St Jude *D & D* 61-63; P-in-c Ballyhalbert 63-71; P-in-c Ardkeen 67-71; I Ballyhalbert w Ardkeen 71-95; Miss to Seamen 71-95; Can Belf Cathl 89-95; rtd 95. *Stationbanks, 18 Kilmore Road, Crossgar, Downpatrick BT30 9HJ* Tel (028) 4483 1665

BELL, Mrs Glynis Mary. b 44. Leeds Univ BA66. St Alb and Ox Min Course 99. **d** 02 **p** 03. OLM Newport Pagnell w Lathbury and Moulsoe *Ox* from 02. *6 Kipling Drive, Newport Pagnell MK16 8EB* Tel (01908) 612971

BELL, Godfrey Bryan. b 44. Oak Hill Th Coll 72. **d** 75 **p** 76. C Penn Fields *Lich* 75-79; R Dolton *Ex* 79-89; R Iddesleigh w Dowland 79-89; R Monkokehampton 79-89; R Tollard Royal w Farnham, Gussage St Michael etc *Sarum* 89-96; TV Washfield, Stoodleigh, Withleigh etc *Ex* from 96. *The Vicarage, 3 Court Gardens, Stoodleigh, Tiverton EX16 9PL* Tel (01398) 351373 E-mail gomar@stoodleigh.freeserve.co.uk

BELL, Graham Dennis Robert. b 42. K Coll Lon BSc63 AKC63 Nottm Univ MTh73 ALCM76 Lambeth STh01. Tyndale Hall Bris 65. **d** 68 **p** 69. C Stapleford *S'well* 68-71; C Barton Seagrave *Pet* 71-73; C Barton Seagrave w Warkton 73-76; Perm to Offic *Nor* 76-82; V Wickham Market *St E* 82-86; V Wickham Market w Pettistree and Easton 86-98; R Thrapston *Pet* from 98. *The Rectory, 48 Oundle Road, Thrapston, Kettering NN14 4PD* Tel (01832) 732393 E-mail graham@bellgood.fsnet.co.uk

BELL, Canon Jack Gorman. b 23. Lon Univ BSc48. Oak Hill Th Coll 51. **d** 53 **p** 54. C Blackpool Ch Ch *Blackb* 53-55; C Chadderton Ch Ch *Man* 55-59; R Man St Jerome w Ardwick St Silas 59-69; V Mosley Common 69-89; Hon Can Man Cathl 87-89; rtd 89; Perm to Offic *Carl* from 89. *36 Sandgate, Kendal LA9 6HT* Tel (01539) 725807

✠**BELL, The Rt Revd James Harold.** b 50. St Jo Coll Dur BA72 St Pet Hall Ox BA74 MA78. Wycliffe Hall Ox 72. **d** 75 **p** 76 **c** 04. Hon C Ox St Mich w St Martin and All SS *Ox* 75-76; Chapl and Lect BNC Ox 76-82; R Northolt St Mary *Lon* 82-93; AD Ealing 91-93; Adv for Min Willesden 93-97; Dioc Dir of Min and Tr *Ripon* 97-99; Dioc Dir of Miss 99-04; Can Res Ripon Cathl 97-99; Hon Can from 99; Suff Bp Knaresborough from 04. *Thistledown, Main Street, Exelby, Bedale DL8 2HD* Tel (01677) 423525 E-mail bishop.knaresb@btinternet.com

BELL, James Samuel. b 40. MBE71. RMA 59 St Chad's Coll Dur BA69. Coll of Resurr Mirfield 71. **d** 72 **p** 73. C Lambeth St Phil *S'wark* 72-74; C N Lambeth 74; P-in-c Invergordon St Ninian *Mor* 74-77; P-in-c Dornoch 74-77; P-in-c Brora 74-77; V Pet H Spirit Bretton *Pet* 77-83; P-in-c Marholm 82-83; Sen Chapl Tonbridge Sch 83-00; rtd 00. *Clocktower House, Edderton, Tain IV19 1LJ* Tel (01862) 821305

BELL, Jane. *See* BELL, Dorothy Jane

BELL, Canon Jeffrey William. b 37. Buckingham Univ MA94. Sarum Th Coll 60. **d** 63 **p** 64. C Northampton St Matt *Pet* 63-66; C Portishead *B & W* 66-68; C Digswell *St Alb* 68-72; V Pet St Jude *Pet* 72-79; V Buckingham *Ox* 79-93; RD Buckingham 84-88 and 89-90; V Portsea N End St Mark *Portsm* 93-03; Hon Can Portsm Cathl 00-03; rtd 03; Hon C The Bourne and Tilford *Guildf* from 03. *All Saints' Vicarage, Tilford, Farnham GU10 2DA* Tel (01252) 792333 E-mail thebells2000@hotmail.com

BELL, Jennifer Kathryn. b 77. Harper Adams Univ Coll BSc99. CITC BTh04. **d** 04 **p** 05. C Belfast St Anne *Conn* from 04; Asst Chapl R Group of Hosps Health and Soc Services Trust from 04; Asst Chapl Belfast City Hosp Health and Soc Services Trust from 04. *260 Merville Garden Village, Newtownabbey BT37 9TT* Tel (028) 9085 2587

BELL, John. *See* BELL, Cyril John

BELL, John. *See* BELL, Canon Donald Jon

BELL, John Christopher. b 33. TCD BA56 MA66. TCD Div Sch Div Test. **d** 56 **p** 57. C Newtownards *D & D* 56-59; C Willowfield 59-62; I Carrowdore 62-70; I Drumbo 70-98; Chapl Young Offender Cen Belf 79-98; Can Down Cathl *D & D* 87-98; Treas 91-98; rtd 98. *Ashwell House, 6 Ballywillin Road, Crossgar, Downpatrick BT30 9LE* Tel (028) 4483 1907

BELL, John Edward. b 34. Cranmer Hall Dur. **d** 67 **p** 68. C Harraby *Carl* 67-70; C Dalton-in-Furness 70-72; V Pennington 72-75; V Carl St Herbert w St Steph 75-84; V Wreay 84-85; rtd 99; Perm to Offic *Carl* from 01. *189 Brampton Road, Carlisle CA3 9AX* Tel (01228) 522746

BELL, John Holmes. b 50. Sheff City Coll of Educn CertEd71. Oak Hill Th Coll DipHE79 BA80. **d** 80 **p** 81. C Leic St Phil *Leic* 80-83; C Portswood Ch Ch *Win* 83-86; TV S Molton w Nymet St George, High Bray etc *Ex* 86-01; V Stoke Fleming, Blackawton and Strete from 01. *Church House, 6 Glebe Park, Stoke Fleming, Dartmouth TQ6 0RD* Tel (01803) 771050 E-mail john@ding-dong.fsnet.co.uk

BELL, Karl Edwin. b 33. Minnesota Univ BA56. Seabury-Western Th Sem MDiv61. **d** 61 **p** 62. USA 61-71 and 76-92; Venezuela 71-76; Chapl Wiesbaden *Eur* from 92. *St Augustine of Canterbury, Frankfurterstrasse 3, 65189 Wiesbaden, Germany* Tel (0049) (611) 306674 Fax 372270 E-mail bell@wiesbaden.netsurf.de

BELL, Kenneth Murray. b 30. Sarum & Wells Th Coll 75. **d** 74 **p** 76. Perm to Offic *Guildf* 74-76; C Hartley Wintney and Elvetham *Win* 76-77; C Hartley Wintney, Elvetham, Winchfield etc 77-80; V Fair Oak 80-95; rtd 96; Perm to Offic *Win* from 96. *12 Hill Meadow, Overton, Basingstoke RG25 3JD* Tel (01256) 770890 E-mail keny12@talk21.com

BELL, Kevin David. b 58. Newc Univ MA93. Selly Oak Coll CPS87 Aston Tr Scheme 78 Sarum & Wells Th Coll 80. **d** 83 **p** 84. C Weoley Castle *Birm* 83-87; C Acocks Green 87-89; CF from 89; Perm to Offic *Guildf* 97-00. *c/o MOD Chaplains (Army)* Tel (01980) 615804 Fax 615800

BELL, Canon Nicholas Philip Johnson. b 46. St Jo Coll Dur BSc69 Nottm Univ DipTh72. St Jo Coll Nottm 70. **d** 73 **p** 74. C Chadderton Ch Ch *Man* 73-77; C Frogmore *St Alb* 77-81; V Bricket Wood 81-91; RD Aldenham 87-91; V Luton St Mary from 91; Hon Can St Alb from 01. *The Vicarage, 48 Crawley Green Road, Luton LU2 0QX* Tel (01582) 728925 Fax as telephone E-mail nickbell@stmarysluton.org

BELL, Owain. *See* BELL, Canon David Owain

BELL, Paul Joseph. b 35. Dur Univ BA56 DipEd57. Trin Coll Bris 77. **d** 77 **p** 78. Burundi 77-81; C Highbury Ch Ch w St Jo and St Sav *Lon* 82-85; V Middleton w E Winch *Nor* 85-95; P-in-c Barningham w Matlaske w Baconsthorpe etc 95-99; R 99-02; rtd 02; Perm to Offic *Portsm* from 02. *21 Hurst Point View, Totland Bay PO39 0AQ* Tel (01983) 756180

BELL, Philip Harold. b 19. Leeds Univ BA45 K Alfred's Coll Win PGCE69. Coll of Resurr Mirfield 38. **d** 44 **p** 45. C Barrow St Matt *Carl* 44-49; C Lewisham St Jo Southend *S'wark* 50-56; Tristan da Cunha 56-61; R Crawley w Littleton *Win* 61-72; V Holdenhurst 72-78; P-in-c Hilperton w Whaddon *Sarum* 78-84; P-in-c Staverton 78-84; R Hilperton w Whaddon and Staverton etc 85-86; rtd 86; Perm to Offic *Sarum* from 86 and *Cov* from 92. *31 Duxford Close, Bowerhill, Melksham SN12 6XN* Tel (01225) 709732 E-mail phildil@talk21.com

BELL, Reginald Leslie. b 13. Trin Coll Bris 72. **d** 74 **p** 75. NSM Stoke Bishop *Bris* 74-75 and 78-94; NSM Horfield H Trin 75-77; Perm to Offic from 94. *September Cottage, 14 Pitch and Pay Lane, Bristol BS9 1NH* Tel 0117-968 1510

BELL, Richard Herbert. b 54. Univ Coll Lon BSc75 PhD79 Tubingen Univ DrTheol91. Wycliffe Hall Ox BA82 MA87. **d** 83 **p** 84. C Edgware *Lon* 83-86; W Germany 86-90; Lect Th Nottm Univ 90-97; Sen Lect from 97; Perm to Offic *S'well* 92-01. *14 Anderson Crescent, Beeston, Nottingham NG9 2PT* Tel 0115-917 4955 *or* 951 5858 E-mail richard.bell@nottingham.ac.uk

BELL, Robert Clarke. b 30. Roch Th Coll 63. **d** 65 **p** 66. C Leeds All SS *Ripon* 65-67; C Claxby w Normanby-le-Wold *Linc* 67-69; R Newark St Leon *S'well* 69-71; V Gosberton Clough *Linc* 71-74; P-in-c Quadring 73-74; Chapl to the Deaf 74-85; V Harmston and Coleby 85-94; RD Graffoe 92-94; rtd 94; Perm to Offic *Blackb* 94-05 and *Carl* 94-98. *Terrace House Farm, Gainsborough Road, Knaith, Gainsborough DN21 5PE*

BELL, Robert Mason. b 35. Lon Coll of Div 66. **d** 68 **p** 69. C Burgess Hill St Andr *Chich* 68-78; R Lewes St Jo sub Castro 78-00; rtd 00. *10 Rufus Close, Lewes BN7 1BG* Tel (01273) 470561

BELL, Ross K. b 64. Bradf and Ilkley Coll BA87. Aston Tr Scheme 89 Westcott Ho Cam 91. **d** 94 **p** 95. C W Bromwich All SS *Lich* 94-98; TV Cen Wolverhampton 98-02; Chapl Bilston Street Police Station from 04. *2 St Anne's Road, Wolverhampton WV10 6SP* Tel 07976-157022 (mobile) E-mail rotinkerbell@aol.com

BELL, Mrs Shena Margaret. b 49. EAMTC. **d** 00 **p** 01. C Earls Barton *Pet* 00-04; P-in-c Raunds from 04; P-in-c Stanwick w Hargrave from 04. *The Vicarage, High Street, Raunds, Wellingborough NN9 6HS* Tel (01933) 461509 E-mail shena.bell@virgin.net

BELL, Simon Barnaby. b 48. Bris Univ CertEd70. Sarum & Wells Th Coll 87. **d** 89 **p** 90. C Ewyas Harold w Dulas *Heref* 89-90; C Ewyas Harold w Dulas, Kenderchurch etc 90-93; P-in-c Clungunford w Clunbury and Clunton, Bedstone etc 93-01; R from 01. *The Rectory, Clungunford, Craven Arms SY7 0PN* Tel (01588) 660342

BELL, Canon Stuart Rodney. b 46. Ex Univ BA67. Tyndale Hall Bris 69. **d** 71 **p** 72. C Henfynyw w Aberaeron and Llanddewi Aberarth *St D* 71-74; V 81-88; V Llangeler 74-80; TR Aberystwyth from 88; Chapl Univ of Wales (Abth) from 94; Ev St Teilo Trust from 95; Can St D Cathl from 01. *The Rectory, Laura Place, Aberystwyth SY23 2AU* Tel and fax (01970) 617184 *or* tel 625080

BELL, Terrance James. b 63. Toronto Univ BA92. Trin Coll Toronto MDiv97. **d** 97 **p** 98. C Wedmore w Theale and Blackford *B & W* 97-01; C Hampstead St Jo *Lon* from 01; Chapl Eden Hall Marie Curie Hospice from 01. *3 Holly Bush Vale, London NW3 6TX* Tel (020) 7433 1115 E-mail vestry@hampsteadparishchurch.org.uk *or* t5@fish.co.uk

BELL, Timothy John Keeton. b 59. All Nations Chr Coll. Trin Coll Bris BA02. **d** 02 **p** 03. C Saltford w Corston and Newton

St Loe *B & W* from 02; Chapl Bath Spa Univ Coll from 04. *2 Fenton Close, Saltford, Bristol BS31 3AT* Tel (01225) 873027 E-mail tim@tmpsbell.fsnet.co.uk

BELL, William Wealands. b 63. York Univ BA86 Dur Univ PGCE87 Leeds Univ BA99. Coll of Resurr Mirfield 97. **d** 99 **p** 00. C Jarrow *Dur* 99-02; Novice CR 02-04; Chapl Aldenham Sch Herts from 04. *3 The Orchard, Aldenham School, Aldenham Road, Elstree, Borehamwood WD6 3RL* Tel (01923) 851636 *or* 856111 E-mail wealandsbell@hotmail.com *or* wwb@aldenham.com

BELL-RICHARDS, Douglas Maurice. b 23. St Steph Ho Ox 59. **d** 61 **p** 62. C Chipping Campden *Glouc* 61-62; C Thornbury 62-67; V Dymock w Donnington 67-75; V Fairford 75-91; rtd 91. *5 Palace Yard, Hereford HR4 9BJ* Tel (01432) 341070

BELLAMY, Charles Gordon. b 15. St Chad's Coll Dur BA42. St Deiniol's Hawarden 36. **d** 42 **p** 43. C Howdon Panns *Newc* 42-44; C Byker St Ant 44-46; C Horton 46-50; C Sighill 50-56; V Burnley St Matt w H Trin *Blackb* 56-67; V Overton 67-80; rtd 80; Hon C Monkseaton St Mary *Newc* 80-94; Hon C Tynemouth Cullercoats St Paul 94-96; Perm to Offic from 96. *60 Davison Avenue, Whitley Bay NE26 1SH* Tel 0191-251 3355

BELLAMY, David Quentin. b 62. Univ of Wales (Cardiff) BMus84 Univ of Wales (Ban) MA93. Ripon Coll Cuddesdon 87 Ch Div Sch of the Pacific (USA). **d** 90 **p** 91. C Rhyl w St Ann *St As* 90-94; V Llay 94-04; V Prestatyn from 04. *The Vicarage, 109 High Street, Prestatyn LL19 9AR* Tel (01745) 853780 E-mail quentinbellamy@cwcom.net

BELLAMY, Mrs Dorothy Kathleen. b 33. Gilmore Course 74. **dss** 82 **d** 87 **p** 94. Feltham *Lon* 82-84; Twickenham St Mary 84; Hampton St Mary 84-85; Hampton Wick 85-87; Par Dn 87-88; Par Dn Teddington St Mark and Hampton Wick St Jo 88-90; Par Dn Westbury *Sarum* 90-94; C 94-96; rtd 97; NSM Freshwater *Portsm* from 97; NSM Yarmouth from 97. *1 Meadows Close, Brighstone, Newport PO30 4BQ* Tel (01983) 740508

BELLAMY, John Stephen. b 55. Jes Coll Ox BA77 MA81. St Jo Coll Nottm. **d** 84 **p** 85. C Allerton *Liv* 84-87; C Southport Ch Ch 87-89; Bp's Dom Chapl 89-91; V Birkdale St Jas from 91. *St James's Vicarage, 26 Lulworth Road, Southport PR8 2BQ* Tel (01704) 566255 Fax 564907 E-mail jsbellamy@onetel.com

BELLAMY, Mervyn Roger Hunter. b 47. Sussex Univ CertEd Heythrop Coll Lon MA04. St Mich Coll Llan 81. **d** 81 **p** 82. C Frecheville and Hackenthorpe *Sheff* 81-85; V Shiregreen St Hilda 85-94; RD Ecclesfield 93-94; R Rawmarsh w Parkgate 94-01; P-in-c King's Sutton and Newbottle and Charlton *Pet* from 01. *The Vicarage, Church Avenue, King's Sutton, Banbury OX17 3RD* Tel (01295) 811364

BELLAMY, Peter Charles William. b 38. Birm Univ MA70 PhD79 Dip Past Counselling 65 Dip Child Psychology75. K Coll Lon AKC61. **d** 62 **p** 63. C Allestree *Derby* 62-65; Chapl All SS Hosp Birm 65-73; Chapl St Pet Coll of Educn Saltley 73-78; Chapl Qu Eliz Psychiatric Hosp Birm 78-90; Lect Past Psychology Birm Univ 79-92; Manager HIV Services Birm Cen HA 90-92; Commr for Public Health Cen and S Birm HA 92-96; Research Fell Birm Univ *Birm* 97-02; Local Min Development Adv *Heref* 01-04; rtd 04. *Orchard House, Diddlebury, Craven Arms SY7 9DH* Tel (01584) 841511 E-mail petejan.diddlebury@virgin.net

BELLAMY, Robert John. b 40. Ripon Hall Ox 64. **d** 66 **p** 67. C Fishponds St Jo *Bris* 66-70; C Oldland 70-74; P-in-c Coalpit Heath 74-76; TV Cannock *Lich* 90-96; Perm to Offic 96-98 and 03-04; Hon C Longdon 98-03; Hon C Shareshill from 04. *10 Meadowlark Close, Hednesford, Cannock WS12 1UE* Tel (01543) 876809 E-mail robert.jbellamy@virgin.net

BELLAMY, Roger. *See* BELLAMY, Mervyn Roger Hunter

BELLAMY, Stephen. *See* BELLAMY, John Stephen

BELLAMY-KNIGHTS, Peter George. b 41. Leic Univ BSc63 Man Univ MSc67 PhD70 Lon Univ BD03 CMath91 FIMA91 CEng94 FRAeS98. Man OLM Scheme 03. **d** 04 **p** 05. NSM Man Cathl *Man* from 04. *113 Old Hall Lane, Manchester M14 6HL* Tel 0161-224 2702

BELLENES, Peter Charles. b 49. Pontifical Univ Salamanca DipPhil68 Thurrock Coll Essex CQSW72. Linc Th Coll 79. **d** 81 **p** 90. C Penistone *Wakef* 81-82; Hon C Liskeard, St Keyne, St Pinnock, Morval etc *Truro* 89-91; Hon C Menheniot 91-99; P-in-c Marldon *Ex* 99-03; TV Totnes w Bridgetown, Berry Pomeroy etc from 03. *The Vicarage, 1 Love Lane Close, Marldon, Paignton TQ3 1TH* Tel and fax (01803) 557294 E-mail pbellenes@aol.com

BELLENGER, Peter John Russell. b 74. New Coll Ox BA96 MA02 St Jo Coll Dur BA03. Cranmer Hall Dur 01. **d** 04 **p** 05. C Tollington *Lon* from 04. *St Mark's Vicarage, 1 Moray Road, London N4 3LD* Tel 08456-447533 Fax (020) 7589 3390

BELLINGER, Canon Denys Gordon. b 29. Sheff Univ BA49. Westcott Ho Cam 51. **d** 53 **p** 54. C Ribbleton *Blackb* 53-56; C Lancaster St Mary 56-58; V Colne H Trin 58-68; V Scotforth 68-93; RD Lancaster 82-89; Hon Can Blackb Cathl 86-93; rtd 93; Perm to Offic *Blackb* from 93. *40 Yewlands Drive, Garstang, Preston PR3 1JP* Tel (01995) 601539

BELLINGER, Richard George. b 47. Univ of Wales (Abth) BSc(Econ)69. S Dios Minl Tr Scheme 91. **d** 94 **p** 95. NSM Guernsey St Steph *Win* 94-96; NSM Guernsey St Martin from 96. *La Maison des Vinaires, Rue des Vinaires, St Peter's, Guernsey GY7 9EZ* Tel (01481) 63203 Fax 66989

BELLIS, Huw. b 72. Univ of Wales (Lamp) BA94. Westcott Ho Cam 96. **d** 98 **p** 99. C Merrow *Guildf* 98-02; TV Tring *St Alb* from 02. *The Vicarage, Station Road, Aldbury, Tring HP23 5RS* Tel (01442) 851200 E-mail hbellis@fish.co.uk

BELOE, Mrs Jane. STETS. **d** 04 **p** 05. NSM Shedfield *Portsm* from 04. *Roughay Cottage, Popes Lane, Upham, Southampton SO32 1JB* Tel (01489) 860452

BELOE, Robert Francis. b 39. Sarum Th Coll. **d** 65 **p** 71. C Nor Heartsease St Fran *Nor* 65-66; C Edmonton St Mary w St Jo *Lon* 68-70; C St Marylebone Ch Ch w St Paul 70-74; P-in-c Wicken *Ely* 74-76; V 76-00; rtd 00; Perm to Offic *Ely* from 00. *29 Juniper Drive, Ely CB7 4TT* Tel (01353) 667704

BELSHAW, Patricia Anne. b 47. **d** 05. OLM Leyland St Jas *Blackb* from 05. *9 The Laund, Leyland, Preston PR26 7XX* Tel (01772) 453624

BEMENT, Peter James. b 43. Univ of Wales (Cardiff) BA64 PhD69. Wycliffe Hall Ox 92. **d** 94 **p** 95. C Hubberston *St D* 94-97; V Llandeilo Fawr and Taliaris from 97. *The Vicarage, 10 Carmarthen Road, Llandeilo SA19 6RS* Tel (01558) 822421

BENCE, Canon Graham Edwin. b 16. Lon Univ BA54. Sarum Th Coll 64. **d** 65 **p** 66. C Clacton St Jas *Chelmsf* 65-68; R Barlborough *Derby* 68-86; RD Bolsover 70-73; RD Bolsover and Staveley 73-78; Hon Can Derby Cathl 78-86; rtd 86; Perm to Offic *Lich* from 87. *Flat 3, 4 Quarry Place, Shrewsbury SY1 1JN* Tel (01743) 233533

BENCE, Helen Mary. b 44. Leic Univ BA65 PGCE66. EMMTC 93. **d** 97 **p** 98. NSM Humberstone *Leic* 97-02; NSM Thurnby Lodge 01-02; TV Oadby from 03. *The Grange, 126 Shanklin Drive, Leicester LE2 3QB* Tel 0116-270 7820 E-mail helenbence@leicester.freeserve.co.uk

BENCE, Norman Murray. b 34. Ripon Hall Ox 63. **d** 63 **p** 64. C Eling *Win* 63-66; Australia 66 and 75; NSM Holdenhurst and Iford *Win* from 81. *72 Corhampton Road, Bournemouth BH6 5PB* Tel (01202) 421992 Fax 420154

BENDELL, David James. b 38. S'wark Ord Course. **d** 87 **p** 88. NSM Surbiton Hill Ch Ch *S'wark* from 87. *3 Pine Walk, Surbiton KT5 8NJ* Tel (020) 8399 7143 E-mail dbendell@aol.com

BENDING, Richard Clement. b 47. Southn Univ BSc68. Ridley Hall Cam 87. **d** 89 **p** 90. Par Dn St Neots *Ely* 89-92; V Buckden 92-99; P-in-c Hail Weston 97-99; P-in-c Terrington St John 99-02; P-in-c Tilney All Saints 99-02; P-in-c Wiggenhall St Germans and Islington 99-02; P-in-c Wiggenhall St Mary Magd 99-02; V E Marshland 02-05; rtd 05; Perm to Offic *Nor* from 05. *Dawn Cottage, Newgate Green, Cley, Holt NR25 7TT* Tel (01263) 741603 E-mail rcbending@hotmail.com

BENEDICT, Brother. *See* WINSPER, Arthur William

BENFIELD, Paul John. b 56. Newc Univ LLB77 Southn Univ BTh89 Barrister-at-Law (Lincoln's Inn) 78. Chich Th Coll 86. **d** 89 **p** 90. C Shiremoor *Newc* 89-92; C Hexham 92-93; TV Lewes All SS, St Anne, St Mich and St Thos *Chich* 93-97; R Pulborough 97-00; V Fleetwood St Nic *Blackb* from 00. *St Nicholas' Vicarage, Highbury Avenue, Fleetwood FY7 7DJ* Tel and fax (01253) 874402 E-mail benfield@btinternet.com

BENFORD, Brian. b 47. Sheff Univ BA Hull Univ MEd PhD88. N Ord Course 82. **d** 85 **p** 86. NSM Stocksbridge *Sheff* 85-90; NSM Gawber *Wakef* 90-02. *Address temp unknown*

BENFORD, Steven Charles. b 61. Leic Univ MB, ChB86. NEOC 97. **d** 00 **p** 01. NSM Northallerton w Kirby Sigston *York* 00-04; P-in-c York St Luke from 04. *79 Burton Stone Lane, York YO30 6BZ* Tel (01904) 641058 E-mail benford@doctors.org.uk

BENGE, Charles David. b 40. Cranmer Hall Dur 63. **d** 68 **p** 69. C Millfield St Mark *Dur* 68-72; C Hensingham *Carl* 72-75; TV Maghull *Liv* 75-82; V Bootle St Leon 82-97; NSM Ormskirk 97-01; rtd 01; Perm to Offic *Liv* from 03. *26 Drummersdale Lane, Scarisbrick, Ormskirk L40 9RB* Tel (01704) 880956

BENGE, Ian Roger. b 48. STETS 98. **d** 01 **p** 02. NSM Langney *Chich* 01-04; C W Burnley All SS *Blackb* from 04; Miss P Wellfield Methodist and Angl Ch Sch from 04. *Wellfield Church House, 11 Clover Crescent, Burnley BB12 0EX* Tel (01282) 432204 Fax 427981 Mobile 07709-746450 E-mail revianbenge@btopenworld.com

BENIAMS, Alec Charles. b 28. AKC52. **d** 53 **p** 54. C Gosforth All SS *Newc* 53-56; C Cullercoats St Geo 56-58; C Eltham St Jo *S'wark* 58-59; C-in-c Lynemouth St Aid CD *Newc* 59-61; CF (TA) 60-67; V Lynemouth *Newc* 61-63; V Whittingham 63-67; V Willington 67-71; CF (TA - R of O) from 67; V Haydon Bridge *Newc* 71-85; R Yardley Hastings, Denton and Grendon etc *Pet* 85-90; rtd 90; Perm to Offic *Newc* from 90. *12 Dickson Drive, Highford Park, Hexham NE46 2RB* Tel (01434) 600226

BENIANS, Martin Ackland. b 19. St Jo Coll Cam BA41 MA45. Ridley Hall Cam 59. **d** 59 **p** 60. C Headstone St Geo *Lon* 59-62;

R Rackheath and V Salhouse *Nor* 62-89; rtd 89; Perm to Offic *Nor* from 89. *26 Victoria Street, Sheringham NR26 8JZ* Tel (01263) 822563

BENISON, Canon Brian. b 41. K Coll Lon 61. Bps' Coll Cheshunt 63. **d** 66 **p** 67. C Tynemouth Ch Ch *Newc* 66-70; C Gosforth All SS 70-72; TV Cullercoats St Geo 73-81; V Denton 81-93; V Blyth St Mary 93-04; RD Bedlington 98-03; Chapl Cheviot and Wansbeck NHS Trust 93-98; Chapl Northumbria Healthcare NHS Trust 98-04; Hon Can Newc Cathl *Newc* from 01; rtd 04. *64 Monks Wood, North Shields NE30 2UA* Tel 0191-257 1031 E-mail revbenison@aol.com

BENJAMIN, Adrian Victor. b 42. Wadh Coll Ox BA66 MA68. Cuddesdon Coll 66. **d** 68 **p** 69. C Gosforth All SS *Newc* 68-71; C Stepney St Dunstan and All SS *Lon* 71-75; V Friern Barnet All SS from 75; Relig Ed ITV Oracle from 83. *All Saints' Vicarage, 14 Oakleigh Park South, London N20 9JU* Tel (020) 8445 4654 *or* 8445 8388 Mobile 07889-83298 Fax 8445 6831 E-mail allsaints@mcmail.com

✠**BENN, The Rt Revd Wallace Parke.** b 47. UCD BA69 Lon Univ DipTh71. Trin Coll Bris 69. **d** 72 **p** 73 **c** 97. C New Ferry *Ches* 72-76; C Cheadle 76-82; V Audley *Lich* 82-87; V Harold Wood *Chelmsf* 87-97; Chapl Harold Wood Hosp Chelmsf 87-96; Area Bp Lewes *Chich* from 97; Can Chich Cathl from 97. *Bishop's Lodge, 16A Prideaux Road, Eastbourne BN21 2NB* Tel (01323) 648462 Fax 641514 E-mail lewes@clara.net

BENNELL, Canon Richard. b 25. Leeds Univ BA45 DipEd45. Coll of Resurr Mirfield 46. **d** 48 **p** 49. C Bedminster *Bris* 48-51; C Brislington St Anne 51-56; V Fishponds St Jo 56-68; V Knowle St Martin 68-73; TR Knowle 73-80; RD Brislington 73-79; Hon Can Bris Cathl 76-91; Chapl St Monica Home Westbury-on-Trym 80-91; rtd 91; Perm to Offic *Bris* from 91. *1B Cooper Road, Bristol BS9 3QZ* Tel 0117-962 2364

BENNET, Mark David. b 62. SS Coll Cam BA84 MA92 Anglia Poly Univ MA04 ACA89. Westcott Ho Cam 98. **d** 01 **p** 02. C Chapel Allerton *Ripon* from 01; TV Gt Parndon *Chelmsf* from 05. *Great Parndon Rectory, Perry Road, Harlow CM18 7NP* Tel (01279) 432626 E-mail markbennet@btinternet.com

BENNETT, Alan Robert. b 31. Roch Th Coll 62. **d** 64 **p** 65. C Asterby w Goulceby *Linc* 64-67; C St Alb St Pet *St Alb* 67-70; R Banham *Nor* 70-72; CF 72-77; P-in-c Colchester St Mary Magd *Chelmsf* 77; TV Colchester St Leon, St Mary Magd and St Steph 77-81; R Colne Engaine 81-88; P-in-c Stoke Ferry w Wretton *Ely* 88-89; V 89-96; V Whittington 88-96; rtd 96; Hon C Wimbotsham w Stow Bardolph and Stow Bridge etc *Ely* 96-00; Perm to Offic from 00. *34 West Way, Wimbotsham, King's Lynn PE34 3PZ* Tel (01366) 385958

BENNETT, Canon Alan William. b 42. Sarum Th Coll 65. **d** 68 **p** 69. C Fareham H Trin *Portsm* 68-71; C Brighton St Matthias *Chich* 71-73; C Stanmer w Falmer and Moulsecoomb 73-75; C Moulsecoomb 76; V Lower Sandown St Jo *Portsm* 76-80; V Soberton w Newtown 80-87; R Aston Clinton w Buckland and Drayton Beauchamp *Ox* from 87; RD Wendover 94-04; Hon Can Ch Ch from 03. *The Rectory, New Road, Aston Clinton, Aylesbury HP22 5JD* Tel and fax (01296) 631626 E-mail alanbennett@s-michaels.org.uk

BENNETT, Alexander Steven Frederick. b 69. Hull Univ BA91. Westcott Ho Cam 93. **d** 95 **p** 96. C Whitton and Thurleston w Akenham *St E* 95-99; OGS from 99; C Oswestry *Lich* 99-01; V Oswestry H Trin 01-04; CF from 04. *c/o MOD Chaplains (Army)* Tel (01980) 615804 Fax 615800 E-mail asfb@clara.co.uk

BENNETT, Anthony. b 31. Qu Coll Birm 72. **d** 74 **p** 74. C Hobs Moat *Birm* 74-76; C Hill 76-79; R Grendon 79-82; R Upwell Ch Ch *Ely* 82-86; R Welney 82-86; P-in-c Coates 86-88; R 88-93; rtd 93; Perm to Offic *Ely* from 93. *21 Fosbrooke House, 8 Clifton Drive, Lytham St Annes FY8 5RQ*

BENNETT, Anton Wayne. b 69. SW Poly Plymouth BSc90. Westcott Ho Cam 00. **d** 02 **p** 03. C Pendleton *Man* 02-05; R Abberton, The Flyfords, Naunton Beauchamp etc *Worc* from 05. *The Rectory, Church End, Bishampton, Pershore WR10 2LT* Tel (01386) 462648 E-mail father.anton@virgin.net

BENNETT, Arnold Ernest. b 29. K Coll Lon BD59 AKC53. **d** 54 **p** 55. C S w N Hayling *Portsm* 54-59; C Stevenage *St Alb* 59-64; R N w S Wootton *Nor* 64-74; V Hykeham *Linc* 74-85; V Heckfield w Mattingley and Rotherwick *Win* 85-99; rtd 99; Perm to Offic *Win* from 99. *24 Cricket Green, Hartley Wintney, Basingstoke RG27 8PP* Tel (01252) 843147

BENNETT, Arthur Harling. b 22. Ripon Hall Ox 70. **d** 71 **p** 72. C Standish *Blackb* 71-74; TV Darwen St Pet w Hoddlesden 75-79; V Whitechapel 79-89; V Whitechapel w Admarsh-in-Bleasdale 89-90; rtd 90; Perm to Offic *Blackb* from 90. *1 Eden Gardens, Longridge, Preston PR3 3WF* Tel (01772) 784924

BENNETT, Avril Elizabeth Jean. b 63. BEd. **d** 00 **p** 01. NSM Dublin Crumlin w Chapelizod *D & G* 00-03; NSM Tallaght from 03. *17 Ardeevin Court, Lucan, Co Dublin, Irish Republic* Tel (00353) (1) 628 2353

BENNETT, Ben. *See* BENNETT, Stuart

BENNETT, Bernard Michael. b 27. Leeds Univ CertEd52 DipPE54. St Aid Birkenhead 55. **d** 58 **p** 59. C Hemsworth *Wakef* 58-60; C Chapelthorpe 60-62; V Birkenhead St Bede w All SS *Ches* 62-71; V Latchford St Jas 71-75; Chapl HM Pris Appleton Thorn 75-82; V Appleton Thorn and Antrobus *Ches* 75-86; Chapl HM Rem Cen Risley 81-84; rtd 86; Perm to Offic *Ches* from 86-01 and *Blackb* 91-03. *8 Hanover Close, Prenton CH43 1XR* Tel 0151-652 8968

BENNETT, Charles William. b 38. LTh. St Jo Coll Auckland 60. **d** 63 **p** 64. New Zealand 63-80 and from 81; C Tauranga 63-68; V Clive 68-71; C Cathl 71-74; V Waipaoa 74-79; C N Walsham w Antingham *Nor* 80-81; V Waipaoa 81-82; V Te Puke 82-87; V Dannevirke and P-in-c Woodville 87-91; V Westshore 91-93; Min Enabler from 94. *59 McGrath Street, Napier, New Zealand* Tel (0064) (6) 835 9924 Fax 835 9920 E-mail w.bennett@clear.net.nz

BENNETT, Christopher Ian. b 75. TCD BA98 BTh00. CITC 97. **d** 00 **p** 01. C Larne and Inver *Conn* 00-03; C Holywood *D & D* from 03. *30 Abbots Wood, Holywood BT18 9PL* Tel (028) 9042 4319 Mobile 07980-885991 E-mail bennett@holywoodparishchurch.co.uk

BENNETT, Clifford Orford. b 32. St Mich Coll Llan 73. **d** 75 **p** 76. C Holywell *St As* 75-79; V Pontblyddyn 79-99; rtd 99. *4 Bryn Teg, Brynford, Holywell CH8 8AP* Tel (01352) 719028

BENNETT, David Edward. b 35. Fitzw Ho Cam BA56 MA60 Lon Univ PGCE. Wells Th Coll 58. **d** 60 **p** 61. C Lightcliffe *Wakef* 60-62; NE Area Sec Chr Educn Movement 62-68; Gen Insp RE Nottm Co Coun 68-00; Hon C Holme Pierrepont w Adbolton *S'well* 71-85; NSM Radcliffe-on-Trent and Shelford etc 85-00; rtd 00; Perm to Offic *S'well* from 04. *The Old Farmhouse, 65 Main Street, Gunthorpe, Nottingham NG14 7EY* Tel 0115-966 3451

BENNETT, Donovan Harry. b 27. Qu Mary Coll Lon BScEng52 FGS61 AMICE61 CEng61 FICE72. Moray Ord Course 88. **d** 92 **p** 93. Hon C Dingwall *Mor* 92-93; Hon C Strathpeffer 92-93; Hon C Inverness St Mich 93-95; Assoc Chapl Raigmore Hosp NHS Trust Inverness 94-96; P-in-c Grantown-on-Spey *Mor* 96-99; Can St Andr Cathl Inverness 98-00; Perm to Offic from 99. *8 Brewster Drive, Forres IV36 2JW* Tel (01479) 872866

BENNETT, Edwin James. b 23. St Barn Coll Adelaide ThL47 STh52. **d** 47 **p** 48. Australia 47-74; V Oldham St Barn *Man* 74-78; V Alderney *Win* 78-84; V Hatherden w Tangley, Weyhill and Penton Mewsey 84-89; rtd 89; Perm to Offic *Win* from 89. *Kalgoorlie, 35 Hatherden Road, Charlton, Andover SP10 4AP* Tel (01264) 356358

BENNETT, Garry Raymond. b 46. K Coll Lon 66 St Aug Coll Cant 69. **d** 70 **p** 71. C Mitcham St Mark *S'wark* 70-73; C Mortlake w E Sheen 73-75; TV 76-78; V Herne Hill St Paul 78-88; P-in-c Ruskin Park St Sav and St Matt 82-88; V Herne Hill 89; Sen Dioc Stewardship Adv *Chelmsf* 89-94; TR Southend 94-98; Chapl Herne Hill Sch S'wark from 98; Perm to Offic *St D* from 00. *Hendre House, Llandeloy, Haverfordwest SA62 6LW* Tel (01348) 831160 Fax 837244

BENNETT, Geoffrey Kenneth. b 56. Ex Univ MA01. Oak Hill Th Coll. **d** 89 **p** 90. C Ipswich St Matt *St E* 89-92; R St Ruan w St Grade and Landewednack *Truro* 92-98; V Budock from 98; P-in-c Mawnan from 03. *The Vicarage, School Lane, Budock Water, Falmouth TR11 5DJ* Tel (01326) 376422 E-mail g.k.bennett@amserve.net

BENNETT, George Darley. b 21. ACIS47. **d** 66 **p** 67. Zambia 66-76; R Hulland, Atlow and Bradley *Derby* 76-78; P-in-c Hulland, Atlow, Bradley and Hognaston 76-78; R 78-86; RD Ashbourne 81-86; rtd 87; Perm to Offic *Derby* from 87. *11 Freemantle Road, Mickleover, Derby DE3 9HW* Tel (01332) 510212

BENNETT, Canon George Edward. b 51. Univ of Wales (Abth) BA72. St Steph Ho Ox 73. **d** 76 **p** 77. C Clifton All SS w Tyndalls Park *Bris* 76-78; C Clifton All SS w St Jo 78-82; Chapl Newbury and Sandleford Hosps 82-93; TV Newbury *Ox* 82-93; V Llwynderw *S & B* from 93; RD Clyne from 98; Hon Can Brecon Cathl 00-02; Can Res Brecon Cathl from 02. *Llwynderw Vicarage, Fairwood Road, West Cross, Swansea SA3 5JP* Tel (01792) 401903

BENNETT, Graham Eric Thomas. b 53. Sarum & Wells Th Coll 88. **d** 90 **p** 91. C Baswich *Lich* 90-94; C Codsall 94-00; P-in-c Willenhall St Steph 00-05; V from 05. *St Stephen's Vicarage, 27 Wolverhampton Street, Willenhall WV13 2PS* Tel and fax (01902) 605239 E-mail grahambennett@tinyworld.co.uk

BENNETT, Handel Henry Cecil. b 33. MCIM. Cant Sch of Min 79. **d** 82 **p** 83. NSM St Margarets-at-Cliffe w Westcliffe etc *Cant* 82-85; Dir Holy Land Chr Tours 85-94; Holy Land Consultant F T Tours 95-96; Sen Travel Consultant Raymond Cook Chr Tours from 96; Perm to Offic *St Alb* 85-99 and *Ex* from 99. *Camps Bay, 2 Victoria Road, Sidmouth EX10 8TZ* Tel and fax (01395) 514211 Mobile 07774-981569

BENNETT, Helen Anne. b 69. Coll of Ripon & York St Jo BEd91 Bris Univ BA01. Trin Coll Bris 99. **d** 01 **p** 02. C Beverley Minster *York* 01-05; P-in-c Liv Ch Ch Norris Green *Liv* from 05. *9 Kingsland Crescent, Liverpool L11 7AN* Tel 0151-474 1444 E-mail habennett@bigfoot.com

BENNETT, Canon Ian Frederick. b 30. Ch Coll Cam BA54 MA62. Westcott Ho Cam 61. **d** 63 **p** 64. C Hemel Hempstead *St Alb* 63-68; Asst Chapl Man Univ *Man* 69-73; Sen Chapl 73-79; C Chorlton upon Medlock 69-73; P-in-c 73-79; TR Man Whitworth 79; Dioc Tr Officer *Birm* 79-88; Hon Can Birm Cathl 86-88; Can Res Newc Cathl *Newc* 88-98; Dioc Dir of Min and Tr 90-98; Dir Post-Ord Tr 97-98; rtd 98; Perm to Offic *Newc* from 98. *21 Otterburn Avenue, Gosforth, Newcastle upon Tyne NE3 4RR* Tel 0191-285 1967

BENNETT, John David. b 58. Ox Univ BA79 MA83. Westcott Ho Cam 81. **d** 83 **p** 84. C Taunton St Andr *B & W* 83-86; Chapl Trowbridge Coll *Sarum* 86-90; Asst P Studley 86-90; V Yeovil H Trin *B & W* 90-95; R Yeovil H Trin w Barwick 95-02; R Sprowston w Beeston *Nor* from 02. *The Vicarage, 2 Wroxham Road, Norwich NR7 8TZ* Tel (01603) 426492

BENNETT, John Seccombe. b 59. Wye Coll Lon BSc81 Leic Poly CertEd84. Trin Coll Bris. **d** 00 **p** 01. C Llanrhian w Llanhywel and Carnhedryn etc *St D* 00-01; C Dewisland 01-02; TV from 02; Chapl St D Cathl from 00. *The Vicarage, Llanrhian, Haverfordwest SA62 5BG* Tel (01348) 831354

BENNETT, Joyce Mary. b 23. OBE79. Westf Coll Lon BA44 DipEd45 K Coll Lon DipTh61 Hong Kong Univ Hon DSocSc84. **d** 62 **p** 71. Hong Kong 62-83; NSM St Martin-in-the-Fields *Lon* 84-87; Perm to Offic *Ox* from 87; Perm to Offic *Lon* 87-88 and from 99. *The Cornerstone, 72 The Crescent, High Wycombe HP13 6JP* Tel (01494) 539016

BENNETT, Lee. b 70. RGN93 Leeds Univ BA00. Coll of Resurr Mirfield 97. **d** 00 **p** 01. C Hemsworth *Wakef* 00-03; V Huddersfield All SS and St Thos 03-04; Assoc P Athersley from 04; Assoc P Monk Bretton from 04. *St Paul's Vicarage, Burton Road, Barnsley S71 2HQ* Tel (01226) 203159 E-mail frlee.bennett@bigfoot.com

BENNETT, Mark Ian. b 61. K Coll Cam BA83 MA86. Trin Coll Bris BA94 PGDTheol00. **d** 94 **p** 95. C Selly Park St Steph and St Wulstan *Birm* 94-97; C Harrow Trin St Mich *Lon* 97-99; Hon C Redland *Bris* 99-00; Chapl United Bris Healthcare NHS Trust 00; TV Drypool *York* from 00. *Victoria Dock Vicarage, 22 Corinthian Way, Hull HU9 1UF* Tel (01482) 610584 Mobile 07866-680535 E-mail mark@thebennetts.karoo.co.uk

BENNETT, Michael John. b 43. K Coll Lon AKC66. St Boniface Warminster 66. **d** 67 **p** 68. C Chester le Street *Dur* 67-71; C Portland All SS w St Pet *Sarum* 71-74; Chapl Portland Hosp Weymouth 74-85; V Portland St Jo *Sarum* 74-85; R Alveley and Quatt *Heref* 85-92; Dep Chapl HM YOI Glen Parva 93-95; TV Wrexham *St As* 95-99; V Llansantffraid-ym-Mechain and Llanfechain 99-05; C Rhyl w St Ann from 05. *122 Rhuddlan Road, Rhyl LL18 2RD* Tel (01745) 342949

BENNETT, Nigel John. b 47. Oak Hill Th Coll 66. **d** 71 **p** 72. C Tonbridge St Steph *Roch* 71-75; C Heatherlands St Jo *Sarum* 75-79; P-in-c Kingham w Churchill, Daylesford and Sarsden *Ox* 79; R 80-85; Chapl Blue Coat Sch Reading from 85. *13 Wilmington Close, Woodley, Reading RG5 4LR* Tel 0118-969 9223 E-mail revnjb@hotmail.com *or* njb@blue-coat.readingsch.uk

BENNETT, Osmond Shirley. b 36. Oriel Coll Ox BA67. Ripon Hall Ox 64. **d** 68 **p** 69. C Stocking Farm *Leic* 68-71; C Thurcaston 71-72; V Leic St Marg 72-82; V Leic St Marg and All SS 83-89; R Houghton-on-the-Hill, Keyham and Hungarton 89-00; rtd 00. *48 Wide Lane, Hathern, Loughborough LE12 5LN* Tel (01509) 553644

BENNETT, Paul. b 55. Southn Univ BTh94. St Steph Ho Ox 95. **d** 97 **p** 98. C Willingdon *Chich* 97-00; C Hangleton 00-04; R Letchworth *St Alb* from 04. *St Michael's Rectory, 39 South View, Letchworth Garden City SG6 3JJ* Tel (01462) 684822 E-mail rectory@letchworthparish.fsnet.co.uk *or* fr.paul@cwcom.net

BENNETT, Paul John. b 47. Univ of Wales (Cardiff) DPS89. St Mich Coll Llan 88 Llan Dioc Tr Scheme 79. **d** 85 **p** 86. NSM Ystrad Rhondda w Ynyscynon *Llan* 85-89; C Tylorstown w Ynyshir 89-93; V Llanwynno 93-02; V Aberdare St Fagan from 02. *St Fagan's Vicarage, Windsor Street, Trecynon, Aberdare CF44 8LL* Tel (01656) 881435

BENNETT, Paul Jonathan. b 61. Ex Univ BA85. Ripon Coll Cuddesdon 85. **d** 87 **p** 88. C Henleaze *Bris* 87-91; P-in-c Swindon All SS 91-94; V Swindon All SS w St Barn 94-96; V Patrick, Foxdale and German St Jo *S & M* 96-00. *60 Teign View Road, Bishopsteignton, Teignmouth TQ14 9SZ* Tel (01626) 774474 E-mail pbennett1961@yahoo.co.uk

BENNETT, Paul William. b 61. DCR92. Linc Th Coll 95. **d** 95 **p** 96. C Thornton-le-Fylde *Blackb* 95-00; V Wesham 00-03; P-in-c Treales 00-03; V Wesham and Treales from 03. *The Vicarage, Mowbreck Lane, Wesham, Preston PR4 3HA* Tel (01772) 682206

BENNETT, Peter Hugh. b 22. K Coll Lon 46. **d** 50 **p** 51. C Newington Transfiguration *York* 50-53; C Bottesford *Linc* 53-57; V Tile Hill *Cov* 58-64; V Hillmorton 64-76; R Beaudesert w Henley-in-Arden 76-81; P-in-c Ullenhall cum Aspley 76-81; R Beaudesert and Henley-in-Arden w Ullenhall 81-87; rtd 87; Perm to Offic *Cov* from 87. *20 Avon Crescent, Stratford-upon-Avon CV37 7EY* Tel (01789) 296278

BENNETT, Miss Rachel Elizabeth. b 56. W Sussex Inst of HE CertEd79. **d** 04. NSM Littlehampton and Wick *Chich* 04-05; C Durrington from 05. *26 Vancouver Close, Worthing BN13 2SH* Tel (01903) 693075 E-mail rachelbennett@beeb.net

BENNETT, Richard Edward Stuart. b 24. St Jo Coll Ox BA49 MA55. Wells Th Coll 50. **d** 51 **p** 52. C Twerton *B & W* 51-56; V Gt Staughton *Ely* 56-63; Chapl HM Youth Cust Cen Gaynes Hall 56-63; R Camerton *B & W* 63-80; R Dunkerton 63-80; R Camerton w Dunkerton, Foxcote and Shoscombe 80-88; RD Midsomer Norton 86-88; rtd 88; Perm to Offic *B & W* 88-94. *Xlendi, 21 King's Oak Meadow, Clutton, Bristol BS39 5SU*

BENNETT, Robert Geoffrey. b 43. FCA. **d** 05. OLM Woking St Jo *Guildf* from 05. *10 Barricane, Woking GU21 7RB* Tel (01483) 722832

BENNETT, Roger Sherwood. b 35. Nottm Univ BA56. Wells Th Coll 58. **d** 59 **p** 60. C Mansfield Woodhouse *S'well* 59-60; C Spalding *Linc* 60-63; V Gedney 63-69; Chapl RNR 65-68; Chapl RN 69-90; V Amport, Grateley, Monxton and Quarley *Win* 90-95; rtd 96; Perm to Offic *Win* from 96. *Le Reduit, School Lane, Nether Wallop, Stockbridge SO20 8EH* Tel (01264) 782336

BENNETT, Roy Donald. b 40. Nottm Univ MA97. St Jo Coll Nottm 78. **d** 80 **p** 81. C Fletchamstead *Cov* 80-83; C Bedworth 83-87; P-in-c Studley 87-93; Chapl Univ Hosp Nottm 93-96; Chapl Qu Medical Cen Nottm 94-96; Chapl Bassetlaw Hosp and Community Services NHS Trust 96-01; Chapl Doncaster and Bassetlaw Hosps NHS Trust 01-02; rtd 02; Perm to Offic *Sarum* from 03. *21 High Street, Puddletown, Dorchester DT2 8RT* Tel (01305) 848144

BENNETT, Shirley. *See* BENNETT, Osmond Shirley

BENNETT (née FORD), Ms Simone Louise. b 70. Warwick Univ BA92. Westcott Ho Cam 00. **d** 02 **p** 03. C Stockingford *Cov* 02-03; C Didsbury Ch Ch *Man* from 03; C Withington St Chris from 03. *46 Trenant Road, Salford M6 7ES* Tel and fax 0161-736 3856 Mobile 07946-548366 E-mail simone.bennett@virgin.net

BENNETT, Stuart (Ben). b 61. St Jo Coll Nottm BA02. **d** 02 **p** 03. C Consett *Dur* from 02. *Church House, 1C Aynsley Terrace, Consett DH8 5LX* Tel (01207) 590731 E-mail stubennett@bigfoot.com

BENNETT, Ms Toni Elizabeth. b 56. Worc Coll of Educn BA81 Sheff Poly 87. St Jo Coll Nottm MA94. **d** 96 **p** 97. C Heanor *Derby* 96-00; TV Bedworth *Cov* from 00. *2 Bryony Close, Bedworth CV12 0GG* Tel (024) 7664 4693 E-mail bnntoni1@aol.com

BENNETT, William Leslie. b 52. TCD Div Sch DipTh90. **d** 90 **p** 91. C Carrickfergus *Conn* 90-93; I Lisnaskea *Clogh* 93-00; I Newcastle w Newtownmountkennedy and Calary *D & G* from 00. *The Rectory, Church Lane, Newcastle, Greystones, Co Wicklow, Irish Republic* Tel (00353) (1) 281 9300 E-mail revwilliambennett@eircom.net

BENNETT-REES, Catherine Mary. b 77. LMH Ox BA99 Selw Coll Cam BA02. Ridley Hall Cam 02. **d** 04 **p** 05. NSM Cambridge H Trin *Ely* from 04. *Holy Trinity Church, Market Street, Cambridge CB2 3NZ* Tel (01344) 626041 Mobile 07740-859447 E-mail catbennettrees@hotmail.com

BENNETT-SHAW, Miss Anne Elizabeth. b 38. **d** 02 **p** 03. OLM Upper Wylye Valley *Sarum* from 02. *5 Hospital of St John, Heytesbury, Warminster BA12 0HW* Tel (01985) 840339 E-mail bennettshaw@bt.internet.com

✠BENNETTS, The Rt Revd Colin James. b 40. Jes Coll Cam BA63 MA67. Ridley Hall Cam 63. **d** 65 **p** 66 **c** 94. C Tonbridge St Steph *Roch* 65-69; Chapl Ox Pastorate 69-79; C Ox St Aldate w H Trin *Ox* 69-73; Asst Chapl Jes Coll Ox 73-75; Chapl 75-78; P-in-c Ox St Andr *Ox* 79; V 80-90; RD Ox 84-89; Can Res Ches Cathl and Dioc Dir of Ords *Ches* 90-94; Area Bp Buckm *Ox* 94-98; Bp Cov from 98. *The Bishop's House, 23 Davenport Road, Coventry CV5 6PW* Tel (024) 7667 2244 Fax 7671 3271 E-mail bishcov@btconnect.com

BENNETTS, Gordon Vivian. b 15. TD62. Open Univ BA78. **d** 77 **p** 78. NSM Phillack w Gwithian and Gwinear *Truro* 77-79; NSM Redruth 79-80; NSM Redruth w Lanner 80-82; Chapl Tehidy Hosp Camborne 82-87; Lic to Offic *Truro* from 82; Chapl Duchy Hosp Truro 87-02. *66 Tregolls Road, Truro TR1 1LD* Tel (01872) 241857

BENNETTS, John Barrington. b 32. **d** 92 **p** 93. NSM Falmouth K Chas *Truro* 92-04; rtd 04; Perm to Offic *Truro* from 04. *39 Budock Terrace, Falmouth TR11 3NE* Tel (01326) 314961 *or* 312111 E-mail kcmvestry@onetel.com

BENNETTS, Ms Rachel Mary. b 69. Homerton Coll Cam BEd91. Trin Coll Bris BA01. **d** 02 **p** 03. C Wroughton *Bris* from 02. *21 Anthony Road, Wroughton, Swindon SN4 9HN* Tel (01793) 813929 Mobile 07881-563215 E-mail racheagle@yahoo.co.uk

BENNETTS, William Rawling. b 28. Univ of W Aus BSc48 BA54 Adelaide Univ DipEd56. Cuddesdon Coll 56. **d** 58 **p** 59. C Portsea St Mary *Portsm* 58-60; Australia from 60; rtd 93. *8 Kapok Court, Parkwood, W Australia 6147* Tel (0061) (8) 9354 3536

BENNIE, Stanley James Gordon. b 43. Edin Univ MA65. Coll of Resurr Mirfield 66. **d** 68 **p** 69. C Ashington *Newc* 68-70; Prec St Andr Cathl Inverness *Mor* 70-74; Itinerant Priest 74-81; R Portsoy *Ab* 81-84; R Buckie 81-84; R Stornoway *Arg* from 84; R Eorropaidh 84-95; Miss to Seafarers from 84. *St Peter's House, 10 Springfield Road, Stornoway HS1 2PT* Tel (01851) 703609 *or* 08453-458564 E-mail gm4ptq@btinternet.com *or* stornoway@argyll.anglican.org

BENNISON, Philip Owen. b 42. Dur Univ BA64. Coll of Resurr Mirfield 64. **d** 66 **p** 67. C Guisborough *York* 66-67; C S Bank 67-71; C Thornaby on Tees St Paul 71-72; TV Thornaby on Tees 72-74; R Skelton in Cleveland 74-78; R Upleatham 75-78; Chapl Freeman Hosp Newc 78-84; V Ashington *Newc* 84-93; Chapl N Tees Health NHS Trust Stockton-on-Tees 93-02; P-in-c Newton Flowery Field *Ches* from 02; P-in-c Hyde St Thos from 02. *St Stephen's Vicarage, 154 Bennett Street, Hyde SK14 4SS* Tel and fax 0161-368 3333 E-mail philip_bennison@hotmail.com

BENNISON, Timothy Paul. b 63. Aber Univ BD94. Edin Th Coll 95. **d** 97 **p** 98. C St Andr Cathl *Ab* 97-00; Asst Chapl Aberdeen Univ 97-00; P-in-c Aberdeen St Jas *Ab* 00-03; Dioc Miss 21 Co-ord 00-03. *127 Don Street, Woodside, Aberdeen AB24 2SA* Tel (01224) 488064 Mobile 07050-395100 E-mail t.bennison@runbox.com

BENOY, Stephen Michael. b 66. Clare Coll Cam BA87 MA90. Trin Coll Bris BA93. **d** 96 **p** 97. C New Malden and Coombe *S'wark* 96-02; Kingston Borough Youth Project 00-02; V Kettering Ch the King *Pet* from 02. *The Vicarage, Deeble Road, Kettering NN15 7AA* Tel (01536) 512828 E-mail steve.benoy@virgin.net

BENSON, Christopher Hugh. b 53. Bath Academy of Art BA75 Keble Coll Ox BA78 MA87. Chich Th Coll 78. **d** 80 **p** 81. C Heavitree w Ex St Paul *Ex* 80-83; P-in-c Broadclyst 83-85; TV Pinhoe and Broadclyst 85-90; V Kingsteignton from 90; Chapl Plymouth Univ 92-95; RD Newton Abbot and Ipplepen from 01. *The Vicarage, Daws Meadow, Kingsteignton, Newton Abbot TQ12 3UA* Tel (01626) 354915 E-mail chrishbenson@hotmail.com

BENSON, David. *See* BENSON, John David

BENSON, Gareth Neil. b 47. HNC71 Jordan Hill Coll Glas FE TCert80. St And NSM Tr Scheme 77. **d** 81 **p** 82. NSM Glenrothes *St And* 81-88; NSM Kirkcaldy from 88; NSM Kinghorn from 88; P-in-c from 04. *The Rectory, 1 Longbraes Gardens, Kirkcaldy KY2 5YJ* Tel (01592) 204208 *or* 568518 E-mail g-benson@iat.ac.uk

BENSON, George Patrick (Paddy). b 49. Ch Ch Ox BA70 Lon Univ BD77 Open Univ MPhil94. All Nations Chr Coll 78 St Jo Coll Nottm 89. **d** 91 **p** 92. C Upton (Overchurch) *Ches* 91-95; V Barnston from 95; RD Wirral N from 98. *The Vicarage, 87 Barnston Road, Heswall, Wirral CH61 1BW* Tel 0151-648 1776 *or* 648 2404 Fax 648 2407 E-mail muhunjia@aol.com

BENSON, Mrs Hilary Christine. b 51. Man Univ BA72 Hughes Hall Cam PGCE73. Trin Coll Bris DipHE83. **dss** 84 **d** 87 **p** 94. Starbeck *Ripon* 84-86; Birm St Martin w Bordesley St Andr *Birm* 86-91; NSM 87-91; NSM Brandwood 91-97; Chapl Birm Univ 92-97; Chapl St Edw Sch Ox 97-00; Chapl Qu Anne's Sch Caversham from 00. *Queen Anne's School, Henley Road, Caversham, Reading RG4 6DX* Tel 0118-947 1582 *or* 954 5026 E-mail saintbede@ntlworld.com

BENSON, John David. b 36. St Aid Birkenhead 58. **d** 61 **p** 62. C Kingston upon Hull St Martin *York* 61-65; C Marfleet 65-68; V Ingleby Greenhow 68-72; P-in-c Kildale 68-72; Asst Youth Chapl 68-72; Dioc Youth Chapl *Sheff* 72-78; V Thorne 78-91; V Totley 91-98; rtd 98; Perm to Offic *Sheff* from 98. *14 Ash Hill Crescent, Hatfield, Doncaster DN7 6HY* Tel (01302) 846359

BENSON, John Patrick. b 51. Univ of Wales (Ban) BSc72. Trin Coll Bris 83. **d** 85 **p** 86. C Stoke Damerel *Ex* 85-88; P-in-c Petrockstowe, Petersmarland, Merton and Huish 88; TV Shebbear, Buckland Filleigh, Sheepwash etc 89-94; RD Torrington 93-94; P-in-c Newport, Bishops Tawton and Tawstock 94-97; TV Barnstaple from 97. *The Vicarage, 40 Chichester Road, Newport, Barnstaple EX32 9EH* Tel (01271) 372733

BENSON, The Very Revd John Patrick. b 52. Ch Coll Cam BA73 MA76 PhD76. Trin Coll Bris 78. **d** 81 **p** 82. C Walmley *Birm* 81-84; C Chadkirk *Ches* 84-86; Singapore from 87; V St Geo Singapore 87-95; Dir of Tr from 95; Dean Cambodia from 95. *Anglican Retreat Centre, 41 Ceylon Road, Singapore 429630* Tel (0065) 447 4416 Fax 447 0842

BENSON, Nicholas Henry. b 53. Man Univ BSc75 Leeds Univ MSc77. Trin Coll Bris 81. **d** 84 **p** 85. C Starbeck *Ripon* 84-86; C Birm St Martin w Bordesley St Andr *Birm* 86-91; Chapl to the Markets 86-91; V Brandwood 91-97; Perm to Offic *Ox* 99-01; NSM Reading St Jo from 01. *Hillside, 2 Henley Road, Caversham, Reading RG4 6DS* Tel 0118-954 5026 E-mail saintbede@ntlworld.com

BENSON, Paddy. *See* BENSON, George Patrick

BENSON, Peter Leslie. b 60. Leeds Univ BA81. Westcott Ho Cam 81. **d** 85 **p** 86. C Kippax w Allerton Bywater *Ripon* 85-88; C Potternewton 88-91; Asst Chapl St Jas Univ Hosp Leeds 91-94; Chapl Dewsbury Health Care NHS Trust 94-98; P-in-c Batley St Thos *Wakef* 98-99; V from 99. *The Vicarage, 16 Stockwell Drive, Batley WF17 5PA* Tel (01924) 473901 Mobile 07985-054318 E-mail peter@plbenson.f2s.com

BENSON, Philip Steven. b 59. ACertCM79 LLCM80 Ulster Univ BSc81. S Dios Minl Tr Scheme 88. **d** 92 **p** 93. Producer Relig Broadcasting Dept BBC 91-94; NSM W Ealing St Jo w St Jas *Lon* 92-94; Lic to Offic *Ches* from 94; Relig Progr Producer BBC Man from 94. *4 Cranford Avenue, Knutsford WA16 0EB* Tel (01565) 652513 Fax 641695 E-mail pt@fish.co.uk

BENSON, Mrs Rachel Candia. b 43. JP76. TCD MA66 Lon Univ PGCE67 DipRS87. S'wark Ord Course 84. **d** 87 **p** 94. NSM Putney St Marg *S'wark* 87-97; NSM Sand Hutton *York* from 97; NSM Whitwell w Crambe, Flaxton and Foston from 97. *Grange Farm, Westow, York YO60 7NJ* Tel (01653) 658296 Fax 658456

BENSON, Richard John. b 55. Birm Coll of Educn CertEd78. Ripon Coll Cuddesdon DipMin94. **d** 94 **p** 95. C Alford w Rigsby *Linc* 94-97; R Partney Gp from 97. *The Rectory, Partney, Spilsby PE23 4PG* Tel (01790) 753570

BENSON, Steven. *See* BENSON, Philip Steven

BENT, David Michael. b 55. Leeds Univ BSc77. Trin Coll Bris BA94. **d** 96 **p** 97. C Gorleston St Andr *Nor* 96-00; TR Brinsworth w Catcliffe and Treeton *Sheff* 00-03; TR Rivers Team from 03. *The Vicarage, 61 Whitehill Lane, Brinsworth, Rotherham S60 5JR* Tel (01709) 363850 E-mail david.bent@btinternet.com

BENT, Mrs Helen Margaret. b 56. Sheff Univ BMus77 Trent Poly PGCE78 Suffolk Poly BA00. EAMTC 97. **d** 98 **p** 99. C Gorleston St Mary *Nor* 98-00; C Brightside w Wincobank *Sheff* 00-04; Bp's Adv in Music and Worship from 05. *The Vicarage, 61 Whitehill Lane, Brinsworth, Rotherham S60 5JR* Tel (01709) 363850 E-mail helen@thebents.co.uk

BENT, Michael Charles. b 31. Kelham Th Coll 51. **d** 55 **p** 56. C Wellingborough St Mary *Pet* 55-60; New Zealand 60-85, 89-94 and from 96; Papua New Guinea 94-96; Adn Taranaki 76-85; Dean H Trin Cathl Suva Fiji 85-89; Can St Pet Cathl Hamilton 90-94. *34 Brooklands Road, New Plymouth, New Zealand* Tel (0064) (6) 753 5507 E-mail miro@clear.net.nz

BENTALL, Mrs Jill Margaret. b 44. MCSP66. S Dios Minl Tr Scheme 91. **d** 94 **p** 95. NSM Knights Enham *Win* 94-02; C Andover w Foxcott from 02. *Old Farm Cottage, 102 Charlton, Andover SP10 4AN* Tel (01264) 365643

BENTHAM, John William. b 58. Loughb Univ BSc80 Nottm Univ LTh85. St Jo Coll Nottm DipPS85. **d** 85 **p** 86. C Burmantofts St Steph and St Agnes *Ripon* 85-88; C Horsforth 88-90; P-in-c Nottingham St Sav *S'well* 90-92; V 92-98; Chapl Nottm Univ from 98. *51 Chaworth Road, West Bridgford, Nottingham NG2 7AE* Tel 0115-846 1054 *or* 846 6037 E-mail john.bentham@nottingham.ac.uk

BENTHAM, Philip John (Ben). b 55. Hull Univ BA83 PGCE85. Trin Coll Bris MA96. **d** 96 **p** 97. C Wrockwardine Deanery *Lich* 96-00; Zimbabwe from 00. *Address temp unknown*

✠**BENTLEY, The Rt Revd David Edward.** b 35. Leeds Univ BA56. Westcott Ho Cam 58. **d** 60 **p** 61 **c** 86. C Bris St Ambrose Whitehall *Bris* 60-62; C Guildf H Trin w St Mary *Guildf* 62-66; R Headley All SS 66-73; R Esher 73-86; RD Emly 77-82; Hon Can Guildf Cathl 80-86; Chmn Dioc Coun Soc Resp 80-86; Suff Bp Lynn *Nor* 86-93; Chmn Cand Cttee ACCM 87-91; ABM 91-93; Bp Glouc 93-03; rtd 04; Hon Asst Bp Lich from 04. *19 Gable Croft, Lichfield WS14 9RY* Tel (01543) 419376

BENTLEY, Edward John. b 35. Bris Univ BA61. Tyndale Hall Bris 58. **d** 63 **p** 64. C Wolverhampton St Luke *Lich* 63-66; BCMS 66-72; C Cheltenham St Mark *Glouc* 72-78; V Wallasey St Nic *Ches* 78-02; rtd 02; Perm to Offic *Ches* from 02. *8 Caithness Drive, Wallasey CH45 7PW* Tel 0151-637 1923

BENTLEY, Frank Richard. b 41. K Coll Lon BD67 AKC67. **d** 68 **p** 69. C Feltham *Lon* 68-72; P-in-c Bethnal Green St Bart 72-77; R Bow w Bromley St Leon 77-88; P-in-c Mile End Old Town H Trin 77-88; P-in-c Bromley All Hallows 77-88; AD Tower Hamlets 83-88; TR E Ham w Upton Park St Alb *Chelmsf* 88-97; P-in-c Petersham *S'wark* from 97; Chapl HM Pris Latchmere Ho from 97. *The Vicarage, Bute Avenue, Richmond TW10 7AX* Tel (020) 8940 8435 *or* 8588 4000

BENTLEY, The Ven Frank William Henry. b 34. AKC57. **d** 58 **p** 59. C Shepton Mallet *B & W* 58-62; R Kingsdon w Podymore-Milton 62-66; P-in-c Yeovilton 62-66; P-in-c Babcary 64-66; V Wiveliscombe 66-76; RD Tone 73-76; V St Jo in Bedwardine *Worc* 76-84; P-in-c Worc St Mich 82-84; RD Martley and Worc W 80-84; Hon Can Worc Cathl 81-84; Adn Worc and Can Res Worc Cathl 84-99; rtd 99; Perm to Offic *Worc* from 04; Chapl to The Queen 94-04. *96 Comer Road, Worcester WR2 5HY* Tel (01905) 330429 E-mail f.bentley@virgin.net

BENTLEY, Graham John. b 29. S'wark Ord Course 77. **d** 80 **p** 81. NSM Merton St Mary *S'wark* 80-83; C Balham St Mary 83-84; C Wimbledon 85-86; V Raynes Park St Sav 86-95; rtd 95; Perm to Offic *Guildf* from 95. *61 Clarence Road, Fleet, Aldershot GU51 3RY* Tel (01252) 682464

BENTLEY, Ian Robert. b 55. Sheff Univ BA76 Sheff City Poly PGCE78. St Jo Coll Dur 95. **d** 95 **p** 96. C Mattishall w Mattishall Burgh, Welborne etc *Nor* 95-98; R Ditchingham, Hedenham and Broome from 98; R Earsham w Alburgh and Denton from 98. *The Rectory, School Road, Earsham, Bungay NR35 2TF* Tel (01986) 892147 E-mail ian@revbentley.freeserve.co.uk

BENTLEY, Ian Ronald. b 51. BA79. Oak Hill Th Coll 76. **d** 79 **p** 80. C Northwood Em *Lon* 79-85; C St Marylebone All So w SS Pet and Jo 85-88; C Langham Place All So 88-91; V Eynsham and Cassington *Ox* 91-05; V Chineham *Win* from 05. *The Vicarage, 1 Hartswood, Chineham, Basingstoke RG24 8SJ* Tel (01256) 474285

BENTLEY, Lesley. b 55. RMN80 Univ of Wales (Lamp) BA76 Nottm Univ MTh82. St Jo Coll Nottm DPS83. **dss** 82 **d** 87 **p** 94. Mickleover St Jo *Derby* 82-84; Thornton *Liv* 84-89; Par Dn 87-89; Dir Diaconal Mins 89-92; Par Dn Farnworth 92-94; C 94-95; V Westbrook St Phil 95-01; Hon Can Liv Cathl 99-01; V Bilton *Ripon* 01-03; TR from 03; Initial Minl Educn Officer from 03. *Bilton Vicarage, Bilton Lane, Harrogate HG1 3DT* Tel (01423) 527811 E-mail lesley_bentley@btopenworld.com

BENTLEY, Paul. b 48. Sarum & Wells Th Coll DipTh93. **d** 93 **p** 94. C Ex St Dav *Ex* 93-96; P-in-c Marlpool *Derby* 96-01; V 01-02; Chapl Derbyshire Community Health Services 96-00; Chapl Amber Valley Primary Care Trust 00-02; Chapl Mansfield Distr Primary Care Trust from 02. *The Pilgrim Centre, Mansfield Community Hospital, Stockwell Gate, Mansfield NG18 5QJ* Tel (01623) 785011 E-mail paul.bentley@mansfield-pct.nhs.uk *or* revpaulb@aol.com

BENTLEY, Richard. *See* BENTLEY, Frank Richard

BENTLEY, William. Univ Coll Dur BA39 DipTh40 MA42. St Andr Whittlesford 40. **d** 41 **p** 42. C Chester le Street *Dur* 41-46; C Bishopwearmouth St Mich 46-49; V Auckland St Pet 49-59; R Hartlepool St Hilda 59-82; Chapl St Hilda's Hosp Hartlepool 59-82; rtd 82. *4 Lindisfarne, High Shincliffe, Durham DH1 2PH* Tel 0191-384 9876

BENTON, John Anthony. b 27. Ex Coll Ox BA48 MA52. Sarum Th Coll 49. **d** 50 **p** 51. C N Keyham *Ex* 50-52; C Tavistock and Gulworthy 52-55; C Heavitree 55-56; R Lower Gravenhurst *St Alb* 56-61; V Silsoe 56-61; V Upper Gravenhurst 56-61; C Port Elizabeth St Cuth S Africa 61-63; R Port Elizabeth St Sav 64-68; R Moretonhampstead *Ex* 68-74; RD Moreton 73-74; R Holsworthy w Cookbury and Hollacombe 74-80; TR Withycombe Raleigh 80-92; RD Aylesbeare 84-89; rtd 92; Perm to Offic *Ex* from 92. *38 Wreford's Close, Exeter EX4 5AY* Tel (01392) 211428

BENTON, Canon Michael John. b 38. Lon Univ BSc60 FRSA93 MSOSc. Sarum & Wells Th Coll 72. **d** 74 **p** 74. Sen Lect K Alfred Coll *Win* 74-76; NSM Weeke 74-76; C Bursledon 76-78; R Over Wallop w Nether Wallop 78-83; Dir of Educn 79-96; R Win St Lawr and St Maurice w St Swithun 83-90; Hon Can Win Cathl 89-03; P-in-c Kingsclere 96-03; Chapl to The Queen from 98; rtd 03; Perm to Offic *Win* from 03. *South Lodge, Auchterarder House, Auchterarder PH3 1ER* Tel (01764) 662991

BENTON-EVANS, Martin James William. b 69. K Coll Lon BA90 Anglia Poly Univ PGCE97. Ripon Coll Cuddesdon BTh03. **d** 03 **p** 04. C Ivybridge w Harford *Ex* from 03. *12 Buddle Close, Ivybridge PL21 0JU* Tel (01752) 691742 Mobile 07915-650434 E-mail jim@benton-evans1.demon.co.uk

BENWELL, John Desmond. Jes Coll Cam BA54 MA58 Sheff Univ DSS58 Lon Univ CASS59. St Jo Coll Nottm CertCS89. **d** 89 **p** 89. Somalia 89-90; Chapl Fontainebleau *Eur* 91-93; Hon C Portswood Ch Ch *Win* 93-99; rtd 99; Perm to Offic *Win* from 04. *14 Furzedown Road, Southampton SO17 1PN* Tel (023) 8055 7622

BENWELL, Michael Patrick. b 55. Jes Coll Cam BA77 Glas Univ PhD80. Sarum & Wells Th Coll BTh92. **d** 92 **p** 93. C Eastleigh *Win* 92-95; Chapl Leeds Metrop Univ *Ripon* 95-99; TV Seacroft from 99. *St Luke's Vicarage, Stanks Lane North, Leeds LS14 5AS* Tel 0113-273 1302 E-mail benwell@ndirect.co.uk

BENZIES, Neil Graham. Bede Coll Dur. Cranmer Hall Dur 93. **d** 95 **p** 96. NSM Stockton St Pet *Dur* from 95. *62 Fairwell Road, Stockton-on-Tees TS19 7HX* Tel (01642) 582322

BERDINNER, Clifford. b 24. SS Mark & Jo Coll Plymouth BA88 Ex Univ MPhil95. **d** 64 **p** 65. C Leic St Pet *Leic* 64-67; R Heather 67-72; NSM Totnes and Berry Pomeroy *Ex* 86-91; NSM Totnes, Bridgetown and Berry Pomeroy etc 91-94; rtd 89; Perm to Offic *Ex* from 89. *Little Croft, 30 Droridge, Dartington, Totnes TQ9 6JQ* Tel (01803) 732518

BERESFORD, Charles Edward. b 45. St Jo Coll Nottm. **d** 86 **p** 87. C Bushbury *Lich* 86-90; TV Glascote and Stonydelph 90-98; TR N Wingfield, Clay Cross and Pilsley *Derby* from 98. *The Rectory, St Lawrence Road, North Wingfield, Chesterfield S42 5HX* Tel (01246) 851181
E-mail rev-ceb@north-wingfield.freeserve.co.uk

BERESFORD, Canon Eric Brian. b 57. Liv Univ BSc78. Wycliffe Hall Ox BA82 MA86. **d** 82 **p** 83. C Upton (Overchurch) *Ches* 82-85; Canada from 85; Asst Prof Ethics McGill Univ Montreal 88-96; Consultant Ethics and Interfaith Relns Gen Syn 96-04; President Atlantic Sch of Th Halifax NS from 05; Consultant Ethics ACC 99-05; Hon Can Montreal from 99. *Atlantic School of Theology, 660 Francklyn Street, Halifax NS, Canada, B3H 3B5* Tel (001) (902) 423 6801
E-mail eberesford@astheology.ns.ca

BERESFORD, Mrs Florence. b 33. Cranmer Hall Dur 75. **dss** 78 **d** 87 **p** 94. Eighton Banks *Dur* 78-86; Lobley Hill 86-87; Par Dn 87-90; Par Dn Chester le Street 90-91; rtd 91. *Gilead, 39 Picktree Lodge, Chester-le-Street DH3 4DH* Tel 0191-388 7425

BERESFORD, Peter Marcus de la Poer. b 49. Cranmer Hall Dur 74. **d** 77 **p** 78. C Walney Is *Carl* 77-80; C Netherton 80-83; TV Wednesfield *Lich* 83-88; TV Rugby St Andr *Cov* 88-97; Chapl Rugby Hosps 88-97; R Barby w Kilsby *Pet* from 97. *The Rectory, Barby, Rugby CV23 8TZ* Tel (01788) 890252

BERESFORD-DAVIES, Thomas. b 14. Univ of Wales (Lamp) BD67. **d** 42 **p** 43. C Glouc St Mary de Lode and St Nic *Glouc* 42-46; C Langley Marish *Ox* 46; C Glouc St Jas *Glouc* 46-48; V Church Honeybourne w Cow Honeybourne 48-51; P-in-c Pauntley w Upleadon 51-62; V Twigworth w Down Hatherley 63-85; rtd 85; P-in-c Glouc St Mark *Glouc* 86-87; Perm to Offic from 87. *Islwyn, Tewkesbury Road, Twigworth, Gloucester GL2 9PQ* Tel (01452) 730362

BERESFORD JONES, Gareth Martin. b 70. Ex Univ BA93 Fitzw Coll Cam BTh01. Westcott Ho Cam 98. **d** 01 **p** 02. C Sidcup St Jo *Roch* 01-05; Chapl Ealing Hosp NHS Trust from 05. *36 Speldhurst Road, London E9 7EH* Tel (020) 8985 4453
E-mail gmbj27@btconnect.com

BERESFORD-PEIRSE, Mark de la Poer. b 45. Qu Coll Birm 73. **d** 76 **p** 77. C Garforth *Ripon* 76-79; C Beeston 79-83; V Barton and Manfield w Cleasby 83-90; V Pannal w Beckwithshaw 90-01; Dioc Chapl MU from 91; R W Tanfield and Well w Snape and N Stainley from 01. *The Rectory, Main Street, West Tanfield, Ripon HG4 5JJ* Tel (01677) 470321

BERG, John Russell. b 36. MBE78. Sarum Th Coll 57. **d** 60 **p** 61. C Ipswich St Aug *St E* 60-64; C Whitton and Thurleston w Akenham 64-65; Miss to Seafarers 65-04; Hong Kong 65-68; Japan 68-04; rtd 01; Perm to Offic *St E* from 04. *23 Old Maltings Court, Old Maltings Approach, Melton, Woodbridge IP12 1AE* Tel (01394) 383748 E-mail jrberg@tiscali.co.uk

BERG, Canon Paul Michael. b 31. Lon Univ BA53. Oak Hill Th Coll 54. **d** 56 **p** 57. C Woodford Wells *Chelmsf* 56-60; V Tittensor *Lich* 60-65; V Rainham *Chelmsf* 65-74; R Wennington 65-74; V Clifton Ch Ch w Em *Bris* 74-97; Hon Can Bris Cathl 82-97; RD Clifton 87-93; rtd 97; Perm to Offic *B & W* from 97. *32 Old Farm Road, Nether Stowey, Bridgwater TA5 1PE* Tel (01278) 733032
E-mail langham@ision.co.uk

BERGER, Otto. b 19. CEng FIMechE. Oak Hill Th Coll. **d** 83 **p** 84. NSM Dovercourt and Parkeston *Chelmsf* 83-93; Perm to Offic from 93. *Address temp unkown*

BERGQUIST, Anders Karim. b 58. Peterho Cam BA79 MA83 PhD90. St Steph Ho Ox BA85 MA90. **d** 86 **p** 87. C Abbots Langley *St Alb* 86-89; Hon C Cambridge St Mary Less *Ely* 89-97; Tutor Westcott Ho Cam 89-95; Vice-Prin 95-97; Can Res St Alb 97-02; Minl Development Officer 97-02; V St John's Wood *Lon* from 02. *St John's House, St John's Wood High Street, London NW8 7NE* Tel (020) 7722 4378 *or* 7586 3864
E-mail vicar.stjohnswood@london.anglican.org

BERKSHIRE, Archdeacon of. *See* RUSSELL, The Ven Norman Atkinson

BERMUDA, Archdeacon of. *See* DOUGHTY, The Ven Andrew William

BERMUDA, Bishop of. *See* RATTERAY, The Rt Revd Alexander Ewen

BERNARD, Brother. *See* APPS, Canon Michael John

BERNARDI, Frederick John. b 33. JP75. Chich Th Coll 55. **d** 58 **p** 59. C Blackb St Luke *Blackb* 58-60; C Ribbleton 60-63; V Brinsley w Underwood *S'well* 63-66; Barbados 67-71; V Sparkbrook St Agatha *Birm* 71-77; P-in-c Sparkbrook Ch Ch 73-75; V Haywards Heath St Wilfrid *Chich* 77-80; TR 80-87; Chapl Madrid *Eur* 87-90; NSM Tooting All SS *S'wark* 90-91; V Hanger Hill Ascension and W Twyford St Mary *Lon* 91-95; rtd 95; Perm to Offic *Chich* from 95. *42 Woodlands Way, Southwater, Horsham RH13 9HZ* Tel (01403) 733335
E-mail stella@knights-templar.org.uk *or* john@bernardi.co.uk

BERNERS-WILSON (or SILLETT), Mrs Angela Veronica Isabel. b 54. St Andr Univ MTh76. Cranmer Hall Dur 77. **dss** 79 **d** 87 **p** 94. Southgate Ch Ch *Lon* 79-82; St Marylebone Ch Ch 82-84; Ind Chapl 82-84; Chapl Thames Poly *S'wark* 84-91; Chapl Bris Univ *Bris* 91-95; C Bris St Mich and St Paul 94-95; P-in-c Colerne w N Wraxall 95-01; R 01-04; Chapl Bath Univ *B & W* from 04. *Chaplain's House, The Avenue, Claverton Down, Bath BA2 7AX* Tel (01225) 386193
E-mail abw@colrec.freeserve.co.uk

BERRETT, Canon Paul Graham. b 49. St Chad's Coll Dur BA70. St Steph Ho Ox 71. **d** 74 **p** 75. C Hockerill *St Alb* 74-77; C Leighton Buzzard 77-81; C Leighton Buzzard w Eggington, Hockliffe etc 81-83; V Bournemouth St Fran *Win* from 83; Hon

Can Win Cathl from 05. *St Francis's Vicarage, Charminster Road, Bournemouth BH8 9SH* Tel (01202) 529336 *or* tel and fax 511845 E-mail saintfrancis@ukonline.co.uk

BERRIDGE, Grahame Richard. b 38. S'wark Ord Course 71. **d** 72 **p** 73. NSM S Beddington St Mich *S'wark* 72-75; NSM Merton St Jas 75-81; Perm to Offic from 81. *11 Cedar Walk, Kingswood, Tadworth KT20 6HW* Tel (01737) 358882

BERRIMAN, Brinley John. b 50. Univ Coll Lon BSc71. SW Minl Tr Course 95. **d** 98 **p** 99. NSM St Ives and Halsetown *Truro* 98-00; P-in-c Lanteglos by Camelford w Advent from 00. *The Rectory, Trefrew, Camelford PL32 9TP* Tel (01840) 211040 E-mail brin@dreckly.net

BERRIMAN, Gavin Anthony. b 60. S'wark Ord Course 87. **d** 90 **p** 91. C Greenwich St Alfege w St Pet and St Paul *S'wark* 90-94; V Lee St Aug from 94. *St Augustine's Vicarage, 336 Baring Road, London SE12 0DU* Tel (020) 8857 4941

BERROW, Philip Rees. b 36. St D Coll Lamp 58. **d** 62 **p** 63. C Neath w Llantwit *Llan* 62-66; CF 67-87; R Welford w Weston and Clifford Chambers *Glouc* 87-94; P-in-c Badminton w Lt Badminton, Acton Turville etc 94-03; rtd 03. *The Moorings, 4 Dunstone Park Road, Paignton TQ3 3NG* Tel (01803) 665113 E-mail prberrow@hotmail.com

BERRY, Canon Adrian Charles. b 50. Mert Coll Ox BA71 MA78. Cuddesdon Coll 72. **d** 75 **p** 76. C Prestbury *Glouc* 75-79; C Cirencester 79-83; V Cam w Stinchcombe 83-88; Dioc Ecum Officer 83-95; P-in-c Twyning 88-95; R Leckhampton St Pet 95-02; Dioc Min Development Officer *Llan* from 02; P-in-c Wenvoe and St Lythans from 02; Can Llan Cathl from 02. *The Rectory, 2 Port Road, Wenvoe, Cardiff CF5 6DF* Tel (029) 2059 3392

BERRY, Alan Peter. b 36. NW Ord Course 74. **d** 77 **p** 78. NSM Headingley *Ripon* 77-78; NSM Chapel Allerton 78-91; Perm to Offic from 91. *17 High Street, Spofforth, Harrogate HG3 1BQ* Tel (01937) 590503 E-mail apeterberry@btinternet.com

BERRY, Anthony Nigel. b 53. Lon Bible Coll BA80. Sarum & Wells Th Coll 84. **d** 87 **p** 88. NSM Howell Hill *Guildf* 87-90; C 90; C Farnham 90-93; R Abinger cum Coldharbour from 93; Dioc Tr Officer for Past Assts from 94. *The Rectory, Abinger Lane, Abinger Common, Dorking RH5 6HZ* Tel (01306) 730746 E-mail revanberry@aol.com

BERRY, David Llewellyn Edward. b 39. St Jo Coll Cam BA61 MA65. Wells Th Coll 64. **d** 66 **p** 67. C Poplar All SS w St Frideswide *Lon* 66-69; C Ellesmere Port *Ches* 69-73; V Brafferton w Pilmoor and Myton-on-Swale *York* 73-79; P-in-c Thormanby 78-79; R Skelton w Upleatham 79-87; V Barrow St Aid *Carl* 87-97; Chapl Rotterdam *Eur* 97-99; rtd 99; Perm to Offic *Carl* from 04. *2 The Croft, Warcop, Appleby-in-Westmorland CA16 6PH* Tel (01768) 342175

BERRY, Mrs Eleanor Shields. b 48. Derby Univ BEd95. EMMTC 01. **d** 04 **p** 05. NSM Morley w Smalley and Horsley Woodhouse *Derby* from 04. *5 Gilbert Close, Spondon, Derby DE21 7GP* Tel (01332) 675265 E-mail es.berry@ukonline.co.uk

BERRY, Prof Frank John. b 47. Lon Univ BSc72 PhD75 DSc88 FRSC84. Qu Coll Birm 96. **d** 99 **p** 00. Prof Inorganic Chemistry Open Univ from 91; NSM Rednal *Birm* 99-04; NSM Birm St Martin w Bordesley St Andr from 04. *44 Middle Park Road, Selly Oak, Birmingham B29 4BJ* Tel 0121-475 2718

BERRY, Miss Heather Evelyn. b 45. Lon Univ BA67 Ex Univ PGCE68. Dioc OLM tr scheme 98. **d** 00 **p** 01. OLM Gaywood *Nor* from 00. *12 Kent Road, King's Lynn PE30 4AF* Tel (01553) 764098

BERRY, Ian Thomas Henry. b 73. QUB BSc94. CITC BTh98. **d** 98 **p** 99. C Bangor Abbey *D & D* 98-02; I Monaghan w Tydavnet and Kilmore *Clogh* from 02. *The Rectory, Clones Road, Monaghan, Irish Republic* Tel (00353) (47) 81136 E-mail monaghan@clogher.anglican.org

BERRY, John. b 41. Dur Univ BA62. Oak Hill Th Coll 63. **d** 65 **p** 66. C Burnage St Marg *Man* 65-68; C Middleton 68-70; Travelling Sec IVF 70-73; V Derby St Pet *Derby* 73-76; P-in-c Derby Ch Ch and H Trin 73-76; V Derby St Pet and Ch Ch w H Trin 76-81; Bp's Officer for Evang *Carl* 81-86; P-in-c Bampton and Mardale 81-86; TR N Wingfield, Pilsley and Tupton *Derby* 86-89; Evang Sec Evang Alliance 89-92; V Guernsey H Trin *Win* 92-98; TR Broadwater St Mary *Chich* from 98. *The Rectory, 8 Sompting Avenue, Worthing BN14 8HN* Tel (01903) 823996

BERRY, Paul Edward. b 56. N Ord Course 91. **d** 94 **p** 95. C Halliwell St Luke *Man* 94-98; TV Horwich and Rivington from 98. *St Elizabeth's Vicarage, Cedar Avenue, Horwich, Bolton BL6 6HT* Tel (01204) 669120 E-mail st.liz@xalt.co.uk

BERRY, The Very Revd Peter Austin. b 35. Keble Coll Ox BA59 BTh61 MA63 Birm Univ Hon DD97. St Steph Ho Ox 59. **d** 62 **p** 63. C Cov St Mark *Cov* 62-66; Dioc Community Relns Officer 64-70; C Cov Cathl 66-73; Can Res Cov Cathl 73-86; Vice-Provost Cov Cathl 77-86; Bp's Adv for Community Relns 77-86; Provost Birm 86-99; rtd 99; Perm to Offic *Cov* from 99 and *Birm* from 00. *Reed Lodge, D5 Kenilworth Court, Hagley Road, Birmingham B16 9NU* Tel 0121-454 0021

BERRY, Mrs Philippa Raines. b 51. Man Univ BA72 Univ of Wales (Cardiff) CertEd73. St Jo Coll Nottm 82. **d** 95 **p** 96. NSM Leic H Apostles *Leic* 95-04; P-in-c from 04. *The Vicarage, 281 Fosse Road South, Leicester LE3 1AE* Tel 0116-282 4336 E-mail pipberry@hotmail.com

BERRY, Sister Susan Patricia (Sister Sue). b 49. Bris Univ BA70 Hughes Hall Cam PGCE72. Qu Coll Birm 77. **dss** 86 **d** 87 **p** 94. Chapl Barn Fellowship Whatcombe Ho 86-89; Chapl Lee Abbey 89-91; NSM Thatcham *Ox* 93-95; CSF from 95; Perm to Offic *B & W* 96-97 and from 98; Chapl Guy's and St Thos' Hosps NHS Trust Lon 97-98; Perm to Offic *S'wark* 97-98. *Community of St Francis, Compton Durville, South Petherton TA13 5ES* Tel (01460) 240473 Fax 242360

BERRY, Timothy Hugh. b 50. Reading Univ BA72. Oak Hill NSM Course 81. **d** 84 **p** 85. NSM Swanley St Paul *Roch* 84-88; C Gorleston St Andr *Nor* 88-93; V Grain w Stoke *Roch* 93-95; rtd 95. *26 Cyclamen Road, Swanley BR8 8HJ* Tel (01322) 613385

BERRY-DAVIES, Charles William Keith. b 48. MIOT71. Linc Th Coll. **d** 83 **p** 84. C Hythe *Cant* 83-86; Chapl RAF from 86; Perm to Offic *Linc* 93-96. *Chaplaincy Services (RAF), HQ, Personnel and Training Command, RAF Innsworth, Gloucester GL3 1EZ* Tel (01452) 712612 ext 5164 Fax 510828

BERRYMAN, William Arthur David. b 47. Lon Univ BD69 St Pet Coll Ox CertEd71. Sarum & Wells Th Coll 75. **d** 76 **p** 77. Asst Master Preston Sch Yeovil 76-80; Hon C Yeovil St Mich *B & W* 76-80; C Ex St Dav and Chapl Ex Coll 80-83; Chapl RN 83-89; V Highertown and Baldhu *Truro* 89-95; TR Cov E *Cov* 95-97; TR The Abbey and P-in-c Leic St Paul *Leic* 97-01; R Banchory and P-in-c Kincardine O'Neil *Ab* 01-05; P-in-c Beeston *Ripon* from 05. *Beeston Vicarage, 16 Town Street, Beeston, Leeds LS11 8PN* Tel 0113-270 5529

BERSON, Alan Charles. b 31. Univ of Michigan BA52 MA53 Lon Univ PhD62. St Steph Ho Ox 63. **d** 65 **p** 66. C Leeds St Pet *Ripon* 65-68; C St Giles-in-the-Fields *Lon* 68; Lic to Offic 69-80; Perm to Offic 80-88; rtd 96. *74 Ridgmount Gardens, London WC1E 7AX* Tel and fax (020) 7636 1990

BERSWEDEN, Judith Anne. b 63. St Jo Coll Dur BA84. Ripon Coll Cuddesdon BA91. **d** 92 **p** 94. Par Dn Mirfield *Wakef* 92-94; NSM Robert Town 94-97; NSM Roberttown w Hartshead 97-00; NSM Alderbury Deanery from 00; Chapl Bp Wordsworth Sch Salisbury from 01. *The Rectory, Winterslow, Salisbury SP5 1RE* Tel (01980) 862231 E-mail judith.bersweden@breathemail.net

BERSWEDEN, Nils Herry Stephen. b 57. Newc Univ BSc78. Ripon Coll Cuddesdon 88. **d** 90 **p** 91. C Mirfield *Wakef* 90-93; P-in-c Purlwell 93-94; P-in-c Robert Town 94-97; V Roberttown w Hartshead 97-00; P-in-c Winterslow *Sarum* 00-01; TV Clarendon from 01. *The Rectory, Winterslow, Salisbury SP5 1RE* Tel (01980) 862231 E-mail nils.bersweden@breathemail.net

BERTRAM, Canon Richard Henry. b 27. TCD BA50 MA64. CITC 50. **d** 53 **p** 54. C Sligo Cathl *K, E & A* 53-56; C Dublin Booterstown *D & G* 56-58; I Stranorlar w Meenglas and Kilteevogue *D & R* 58-65; I Dublin St Cath w St Jas *D & G* 65-73; I Dublin Irishtown 73-74; I Dublin Irishtown w Donnybrook 74-02; Can Ch Ch Cathl Dublin 86-02; Treas 95-02; rtd 02. *Glencoe, The Harbour, North Beach, Greystones, Co Wicklow, Irish Republic* Tel (00353) (1) 287 5320

BESSANT, Brian Keith. b 32. Roch Th Coll 65. **d** 67 **p** 68. C Chatham St Wm *Roch* 67-70; C Cove St Jo *Guildf* 71-74; V Frimley Green 74-97; rtd 97; Perm to Offic *Guildf* from 97. *14 Tay Close, Farnborough GU14 9NB* Tel (01252) 376530

BESSANT, Canon Idwal Brian. b 39. Cardiff Coll of Art ATD62. St Mich Coll Llan 65. **d** 68 **p** 69. C Llantwit Major and St Donat's *Llan* 68-73; R Llangammarch w Garth, Llanlleonfel etc *S & B* 73-77; V Crickhowell 77-78; CMS Miss 78-83; Cyprus 80-83; V Crickhowell w Cwmdu and Tretower *S & B* 83-91; RD Crickhowell 86-91; V Llanwrtyd w Llanddulas in Tir Abad etc 91-04; Can Res Brecon Cathl 98-04; RD Builth 02-04; rtd 04. *10 Bronant, Talgarth, Brecon LD3 0HF*

BESSANT, Simon David. b 56. Sheff Univ BMus77 MA00. St Jo Coll Nottm. **d** 81 **p** 82. C Litherland St Jo and St Jas *Liv* 81-84; C Holloway Em w Hornsey Road St Barn *Lon* 84-86; C Holloway St Mark w Em 86-91; V Blackb Redeemer *Blackb* 91-98; Acting RD Blackb 97-98; Dir Miss and Evang from 98; Dir CME from 02. *1 Swallowfields, Blackburn BB1 8NR* Tel (01254) 580176 Fax 279883 E-mail s.d.bessant@dial.pipex.com

BESSENT, Stephen Lyn. b 53. Bris Univ BA75. Wycliffe Hall Ox 75. **d** 77 **p** 78. C Patchway *Bris* 77-80; TV Swindon St Jo and St Andr 80-83; TV Eston w Normanby *York* 83-90; V Cogges *Ox* 90-94; P-in-c S Leigh 90-94; V Cogges and S Leigh 94-01; P-in-c Alphington *Ex* from 01. *The Rectory, Rectory Drive, Alphington, Exeter EX2 8XJ* Tel (01392) 437662

BEST, Miss Karen Belinda. b 62. Qu Coll Birm 92. **d** 94 **p** 95. C Southall Green St Jo *Lon* 94-97; C Northolt Park St Barn 97-00; V Gillingham St Barn *Roch* from 00. *The Vicarage, 1 St Barnabas Close, Gillingham ME7 4BU* Tel (01634) 851010 E-mail kbest36310@aol.com

BEST, Canon Raymond. b 42. Sarum & Wells Th Coll 71. **d** 74 **p** 75. C Whorlton *Newc* 74-78; C Seaton Hirst 78-83; C Benwell St Jas 83-85; TV Benwell 85-89; V Walker 89-00; P-in-c Byker

St Martin 96-99; Hon Can Newc Cathl from 97; V Haltwhistle and Greenhead from 00; AD Hexham from 02. *The Vicarage, Edens Lawn, Haltwhistle NE49 0AB* Tel (01434) 320215 E-mail canonbest@aol.com

BESTELINK, Canon William Meindert Croft. b 48. Hull Univ BA70 FRSA78. Cuddesdon Coll 71. **d** 73 **p** 74. C Holt *Nor* 73-74; C E Dereham w Hoe 74-76; C Thorpe 76-80; R Colby w Banningham and Tuttington 80-90; R Felmingham 80-90; R Suffield 80-90; P-in-c Roydon St Remigius 90-04; P-in-c Scole, Brockdish, Billingford, Thorpe Abbots etc 02-04; P-in-c Gillingham w Geldeston, Stockton, Ellingham etc from 04; RD Redenhall 00-03; Dioc Rural Officer from 99; Hon Can Nor Cathl from 02. *The Rectory, 60 The Street, Geldeston, Beccles NR34 0LN* Tel (01502) 712255 Mobile 07966-549638 E-mail wmcbestelink@hotmail.com

BESTLEY, Peter Mark. b 60. Qu Coll Cam MA Univ of Wales (Cardiff) MPhil92. St Mich Coll Llan 89. **d** 92 **p** 93. C Hampton All SS *Lon* 92-95; Chapl W Middx Univ Hosp NHS Trust 95-99; Hon C Bracknell *Ox* from 04. *5 The Elms, Warfield Park, Bracknell RG42 3RP* Tel (01344) 886080

BESWETHERICK, Andrew Michael. b 55. Ex Univ BEd80. S'wark Ord Course 87. **d** 90 **p** 91. Dep Hd Maze Hill Sch Greenwich 88-98; NSM Blackheath St Jo *S'wark* from 90; Hd Sixth Form Rosemary Sch Islington from 98. *112 Charlton Road, London SE7 7EY* Tel (020) 8853 0853

BESWICK, Canon Gary Lancelot. b 38. ALCD63. **d** 63 **p** 64. C Walthamstow St Mary *Chelmsf* 63-67; C Laisterdyke *Bradf* 67-70; V Idle H Trin 70-78; Area Sec (NW England) SAMS 78-92; Area Sec (N Thames) 92-97; Hon Can N Argentina from 87; R Gt Smeaton w Appleton Wiske and Birkby etc *Ripon* 97-03; rtd 03. *17 Gustory Road, Crantock, Newquay TR8 5RG* Tel (01637) 831361

BESWICK, Mrs Jane. b 62. **d** 04. OLM Radcliffe St Andr *Man* from 04. *12 Cobden Street, Radcliffe, Manchester M26 4HR* Tel 0161-724 4633 E-mail j.beswick@tiscali.co.uk

BESWICK, Joseph Hubert. b 25. Birm Univ MB, ChB48 Lon Univ DipTh58. **d** 59 **p** 60. Lic to Offic *S'well* 59-00. *38 Hallams Lane, Beeston, Nottingham NG9 5FH* Tel 0115-925 6719

BETSON, Stephen. b 53. Sarum & Wells Th Coll 89. **d** 91 **p** 92. C Sittingbourne St Mich *Cant* 91-95; V Fairweather Green *Bradf* 95-01; R Hockwold w Wilton *Ely* from 01; R Weeting from 01. *The Rectory, 25 South Street, Hockwold, Thetford IP26 4JG* Tel (01842) 828469 E-mail betson1@tesco.net

BETTELEY, John Richard. b 46. Sarum & Wells Th Coll 81. **d** 83 **p** 84. C Auchterarder *St And* 83-85; C Dunblane 83-85; Chapl RAF 85-89; R Callander *St And* 89-94; P-in-c Aberfoyle 89-94; P-in-c Doune 89-94; R Ballachulish *Arg* 94-04; R Glencoe 94-04; R Onich 94-04; Dioc Youth Officer 94-01; Syn Clerk 99-04; Can St Jo Cathl Oban 99-04; Can Cumbrae 99-04; R Aboyne *Ab* from 04; R Ballater from 04; R Braemar from 04. *Glenmoriston, 7 Invercauld Road, Ballater AB35 5RP* Tel (01339) 755726 Mobile 07713-914602 E-mail upper.deeside@virgin.net

BETTERIDGE, Simon Frank. b 66. St Jo Coll Nottm. **d** 00 **p** 01. C Studley *Cov* 00-02; C Leamington Priors St Paul 02-04; Chapl Univ Hosps Coventry and Warks NHS Trust from 04. *49 Wathen Road, Leamington Spa CV32 5UY* Tel (01926) 451439 Mobile 07867-527291 E-mail porters88@yahoo.co.uk

BETTIS, Canon Margaret Jean. b 42. Gilmore Ho 72. **dss** 77 **d** 87 **p** 94. Kenya 77-79; Tutor Crowther Hall CMS Tr Coll Selly Oak 79-82; Hodge Hill *Birm* 82-87; Par Dn 87; Par Dn Flitwick *St Alb* 87-93; P-in-c Westoning w Tingrith 93-94; V 94-04; Hon Can St Alb 97-04; rtd 04; Perm to Offic *St Alb* from 04 and *Glouc* from 05. *19 Bathurst Road, Cirencester GL7 1SA* Tel (01285) 658695

BETTRIDGE, Canon Graham Winston. b 39. Kelham Th Coll 60. **d** 65 **p** 66. C Burley in Wharfedale *Bradf* 65-67; C Baildon 67-70; V Harden and Wilsden 70-81; TR Kirkby Lonsdale *Carl* from 81; Hon Can Carl Cathl from 89; Chapl Cumbria Constabulary from 96. *The Rectory, Vicarage Lane, Kirkby Lonsdale, Carnforth LA6 2BA* Tel (01524) 271320 *or* 72044

BETTS, Alan John. b 55. Portsm Poly BSc77 St Martin's Coll Lanc PGCE81. St Jo Coll Nottm 93. **d** 93 **p** 94. C Cannock *Lich* 93-01; P-in-c Endon w Stanley 01-04; V Bagnall w Endon from 04. *St Luke's Vicarage, Leek Road, Endon, Stoke-on-Trent ST9 9BH* Tel (01782) 502166

BETTS, Canon Anthony Clive. b 40. Wells Th Coll 63. **d** 65 **p** 66. C Leeds All Hallows w St Simon *Ripon* 65-67; C Wetherby 67-70; C Adel 70-73; V Leeds All SS 73-79; V Leeds Richmond Hill 79-84; R Knaresborough 84-03; TR 03-05; RD Harrogate 95-98; Hon Can Ripon Cathl from 04; rtd 05. *1 Bilsdale Close, Romanby, Northallerton DL7 8FT* Tel (01609) 760378 E-mail tonybetts@bettst.freeserve.co.uk

BETTS, Canon Anthony Percy. b 26. Lon Univ BD52. ALCD52. **d** 52 **p** 53. C Guildf St Sav *Guildf* 52-56; C Hanworth St Geo *Lon* 56-59; V Derby St Aug *Derby* 59-74; RD Derby 71-74; V Bracebridge *Linc* 74-83; R Fenny Bentley, Kniveton, Thorpe and Tissington *Derby* 83-91; RD Ashbourne 86-91; Hon Can Derby Cathl 87-91; rtd 91; Perm to Offic *Derby* from 91. *Otterbourne House, Windley, Belper DE56 2LP* Tel (01773) 550677

BETTS, David John. b 38. Lon Univ BSc61. Oak Hill Th Coll 63. **d** 65 **p** 66. C Slough *Ox* 65-70; C Welling *Roch* 70-75; V Swanley St Paul 75-93; R Nottingham St Nic *S'well* 93-98; TV Canford Magna *Sarum* 98-04; rtd 04. *290 Rempstone Road, Wimborne BH21 1SZ* Tel (01202) 840537

BETTS, Canon Edmund John. b 51. St Chad's Coll Dur BA72 Lanc Univ MA81. Qu Coll Birm 75. **d** 76 **p** 77. C Leagrave *St Alb* 76-79; Asst Chapl R Albert Hosp Lanc 79-81; Chapl Lea Castle Hosp and Kidderminster Gen Hosp 81-86; Prov Officer Educn for Min Ch in Wales 86-88; Exec Sec for Min 88-90; TR Haverhill w Withersfield, the Wrattings etc *St E* 90-97; V Haverhill w Withersfield from 97; RD Clare from 91; Hon Can St E Cathl from 02; CUF Link Officer from 02. *The Rectory, 10 Hopton Rise, Haverhill CB9 7FS* Tel and fax (01440) 708768 E-mail edmund.betts@talk21.com

BETTS, George William John. b 23. Ex Univ BA51. Westcott Ho Cam 51. **d** 53 **p** 54. C Wallsend St Luke *Newc* 53-54; C Benwell St Jas 54-56; C Plumstead St Jas w St Jo *S'wark* 56; C Peckham St Andr w All SS 56; C Eltham St Jo 57-60; C Findon *Chich* 60-67; Rhodesia 67-68; C Sherborne w Castleton and Lillington *Sarum* 68-69; C Brookfield St Anne, Highgate Rise *Lon* 69; rtd 88. *72 Westmount Road, London SE9 1JE* Tel (020) 8850 2116

BETTS, Ivan Ringland. b 38. TCD BA61 MA67. **d** 62 **p** 63. C Ballyholme *D & D* 62-65; C Dundela St Mark 65-69; Miss to Seamen 69-73; Sudan 69-71; Trinidad and Tobago 71-73; C Drumglass *Arm* 73-81; I Augher w Newtownsaville and Eskrahoole *Clogh* 81-86; Bp's C Ballymacarrett St Martin *D & D* 86-02; rtd 02. *56 Norwood Drive, Belfast BT4 2EB* Tel (028) 9065 0723 E-mail ibetts@compuserve.com

BETTS, Mrs Patricia Joyce. b 43. St Kath Coll Lon CertEd64 FRSA96. S Dios Minl Tr Scheme 90. **d** 96 **p** 97. NSM Bath Widcombe *B & W* 96-00; P-in-c 00-05; Perm to Offic from 05. *Hunters Lodge, North Road, Bath BA2 6HP* Tel (01225) 464918 E-mail candpbetts@aol.com

BETTS, Paul Robert. b 31. Lon Univ BSc51. Oak Hill Th Coll 53. **d** 56 **p** 57. C Plymouth St Jude *Ex* 56-59; C Cheltenham St Mark *Glouc* 59-63; V Finchley St Paul Long Lane *Lon* 63-76; Warden St Columba Cen Cam 76-79; R Datchworth w Tewin *St Alb* 79-96; rtd 96; Perm to Offic *Ex* from 96. *2 Penny Close, Exminster, Exeter EX6 8SU* Tel (01392) 824403

BETTS, Richard Alan. b 56. ACA83 UEA BA77. Sarum & Wells Th Coll 93. **d** 93 **p** 94. C Mile Cross *Nor* 93-97; TV Dorchester *Sarum* from 97. *St George's Vicarage, 59 Fordington High Street, Dorchester DT1 1LB* Tel (01305) 262394 E-mail richard@betts39.fsnet.co.uk

BETTS, Steven James. b 64. York Univ BSc86. Ripon Coll Cuddesdon 87. **d** 90 **p** 91. C Bearsted w Thurnham *Cant* 90-94; Bp's Chapl *Nor* 94-97; V Old Catton from 97; RD Nor N 01-05; Bp's Officer for Ord and Initial Tr from 05. *Emmaus House, 65 The Close, Norwich NR1 4DH* Tel (01603) 628103 E-mail stevenbetts@norwich.anglican.org *or* s-s.betts@ukgateway.net

BEVAN, Alan John. b 29. Bris Univ BA54. Oak Hill Th Coll 54. **d** 56 **p** 59. C Penn Fields *Lich* 56-57; C Corsham *Bris* 58-61; C Wath-upon-Dearne w Adwick-upon-Dearne *Sheff* 61-68; C Darfield 68-71; C Drypool St Columba w St Andr and St Pet *York* 71-79; Chapl HM Pris Wandsworth 79-83; Chapl HM Pris Kirkham 83-86; rtd 86; Perm to Offic *Ex* from 86. *c/o the Revd J Ancrum, 14 Merrivale Road, Dousland, Yelverton PL20 6NS*

BEVAN, Bryan David. Lon Univ BD60 MA70 CertEd65 DipEd66 MPhil84. Lambeth STh62 St Aug Coll Cant 62. **d** 64 **p** 66. C E Dereham w Hoe *Nor* 64-65; C Hove All SS *Chich* 65-67; Lect St Mich Coll Salisbury 67-70; The Coll Bedf from 70. *4A De Parys Lodge, De Parys Avenue, Bedford MK40 2TZ* Tel (01234) 343622

BEVAN, Canon Charles Joseph Godfrey. b 22. TCD BA44 MA52. **d** 45 **p** 46. C Dublin St Geo *D & G* 45-49; I Rathvilly *C & O* 49-59; I Carbury *M & K* 59-64; I Drogheda St Pet w Ballymakenny, Beaulieu etc *Arm* 64-90; I Drogheda w Ardee, Collon and Termonfeckin 90-95; Miss to Seamen 64-95; Can Arm Cathl *Arm* 83-95; Chan 88-92; Prec 92-95; rtd 95. *13 St Peter's Place, Drogheda, Co Louth, Irish Republic* Tel (00353) (98) 414 4622

BEVAN, David Graham. b 34. Univ of Wales (Lamp) BA54 LTh56. Gen Th Sem (NY) MDiv57. **d** 57 **p** 58. C Llanelli *St D* 57-60; CF 60-76; rtd 99. *148 Bromley Heath Road, Bristol BS16 6JJ* Tel 0117-956 0946

BEVAN, Gordon Richard. b 26. NW Ord Course. **d** 75 **p** 76. C Spondon *Derby* 75-80; R Upper Langwith w Langwith Bassett etc 80-94; TV E Scarsdale 94-96; rtd 96; Perm to Offic *Derby* from 96. *8 Whaley Common, Langwith, Mansfield NG20 9HY* Tel (01623) 742413

BEVAN, Hubert Basil Henry. b 24. Univ of Wales (Lamp) BA52 LTh54 MTh75 PhD78. **d** 54 **p** 55. C Knighton and Heyope *S & B* 54-60; C Toxteth Park St Marg *Liv* 60-61; V Walsall St Mary and All SS Palfrey *Lich* 61-64; R Sunderland *Dur* 64-66; V Hendon St Paul 64-66; V Gilfach Goch w Llandyfodwg *Llan*

66-73; R Cregina *S & B* 73-78; V Bettws Disserth w Llansantffraed in Elwell 73-78; V Glascwm and Rhulen 76-78; R Llanferres, Nercwys and Eryrys *St As* 78-80; Tutor St Deiniol's Lib Hawarden 79-89; V Treuddyn and Nercwys and Eryrys *St As* 80-85; R Llanfynydd 85-89; rtd 89. *Bryn Heulog, Bryniau Duon, Old Llandegfan, Menai Bridge LL59 5PP*

BEVAN, Janet Mary. *See* MOORE, Ms Janet Mary

BEVAN, Noel Haden. b 34. St Aid Birkenhead 61. **d** 63 **p** 64. C Girlington *Bradf* 63-66; C Worksop St Jo *S'well* 66-68; V Everton w Mattersey 68-70; R Everton and Mattersey w Clayworth 70-77; TV Barton Mills *St E* 77-80; TV Barton Mills, Beck Row w Kenny Hill etc 80-85; TV Mildenhall 85-86; P-in-c Sternfield w Benhall and Snape 86-89; R 89-98; rtd 98. *6 Benhall Green, Saxmundham IP17 1HU* Tel (01728) 604169

BEVAN, Paul John. b 49. Bris Sch of Min 84. **d** 87. NSM Bishopsworth *Bris* 87-96. *10 Brookdale Road, Headley Park, Bristol BS13 7PZ* Tel 0117-964 6330

BEVAN, Peter John. b 54. K Coll Lon BA76 AKC76 MA86. St Steph Ho Ox BA79. **d** 80 **p** 81. C Brighouse *Wakef* 80-83; C Chapelthorpe 83-86; V Scholes 86-95; V Potters Bar *St Alb* from 95. *The Vicarage, 15 The Walk, Potters Bar EN6 1QN* Tel (01707) 644539 *or* 645080

BEVAN, Philip Frank. b 41. Brasted Th Coll 63 Chich Th Coll 65. **d** 67 **p** 68. C Walton St Mary *Liv* 67-71; Bahamas 71-78; P-in-c Long Is SS Pet and Paul 71-73; R Nassau St Matt 73-78; Perm to Offic *Lon* and *S'wark* from 00. *5 Dunstable Road, Richmond TW9 1UH* Tel (020) 8940 3622 Mobile 07970-961539 E-mail fr.philip@btinternet.com

BEVAN, Canon Richard Justin William. b 22. LTh42 St Chad's Coll Dur BA45 DTh72 PhD80. St Aug Coll Cant 39. **d** 45 **p** 46. C Stoke upon Trent *Lich* 45-49; Chapl Aberlour Orphanage 49-51; Lic to Offic *Mor* 49-51; Lic to Offic *Blackb* 51-52; C Church Kirk 52-56; C Whalley 56-61; R Dur St Mary le Bow w St Mary the Less *Dur* 61-64; Chapl Dur Univ 61-74; V Dur St Oswald 64-74; P-in-c Dur St Mary le Bow w St Mary the Less 64-67; R 67-74; R Grasmere *Carl* 74-82; Can Res, Lib and Treas Carl Cathl 82-89; Vice-Dean Carl 86-89; Chapl to The Queen 86-93; rtd 89; Perm to Offic *Carl* from 89. *Beck Cottage, West End, Burgh-by-Sands, Carlisle CA7 6BT* Tel (01228) 576781

BEVAN, Rodney. b 57. Leeds Univ BA80 Keele Univ PGCE81 Open Univ MA99. St Jo Coll Dur 97. **d** 99 **p** 00. C Ogley Hay *Lich* 99-03; TV Rossendale Middle Valley *Man* 03-04; TR from 04. *St Anne's Vicarage, Ashworth Road, Rossendale BB4 9JE* Tel (01706) 221889 E-mail rjdr@uk.packardbell.org

BEVER, Canon Michael Charles Stephen. b 44. Selw Coll Cam BA66 MA70. Cuddesdon Coll. **d** 69 **p** 70. C Steeton *Bradf* 69-72; C Northampton St Mary *Pet* 72-74; Niger 75-79; P-in-c Elmstead *Chelmsf* 80-83; V 83-85; V Bocking St Pet 85-96; P-in-c Odiham *Win* from 96; Hon Can Awka from 93. *The Vicarage, The Bury, Odiham, Hook RG29 1ND* Tel and fax (01256) 703896 E-mail mcsb@ozala.fsnet.co.uk

BEVERIDGE, Mrs Freda Joy. b 38. Qu Mary Coll Lon BA59 Lon Inst of Educn PGCE60. Ripon Coll Cuddesdon 83. **dss** 85 **d** 87 **p** 94. Ox St Giles and SS Phil and Jas w St Marg *Ox* 85-88; Par Dn 87-88; Par Dn Woughton 88-94; C 94-95; TR 95-97; C Woodham *Guildf* 97-00; rtd 00; Perm to Offic *Sarum* from 01. *Moonraker Cottage, 27 New Road, Chiseldon, Swindon SN4 0LY* Tel (01793) 741064

BEVERIDGE, Simon Alexander Ronald. b 61. Nottm Univ BA84. Chich Th Coll 84. **d** 87 **p** 88. C Braunton *Ex* 87-90; TV N Creedy 90-93; Chapl RN from 93. *Royal Naval Chaplaincy Service, Room 203, Victory Building, HM Naval Base, Portsmouth PO1 3LS* Tel (023) 9272 7903 Fax 9272 7111

BEVERLEY, David John. b 46. Univ of Wales (Lamp) BA68. Linc Th Coll 71. **d** 73 **p** 74. C Cov E *Cov* 73-76; C Immingham *Linc* 76-84; V Bracebridge Heath 84-86; Ind Chapl 86-97; P-in-c Scunthorpe Resurr 97-01; V 01-02; R Trentside E from 02. *The Vicarage, Mirfield Road, Scunthorpe DN15 8AN* Tel (01724) 842196 E-mail davejbev@aol.com

BEVERLEY, Suffragan Bishop of (Provincial Episcopal Visitor). *See* JARRETT, The Rt Revd Martyn William

BEVINGTON, Canon Colin Reginald. b 36. ALCD63. **d** 63 **p** 64. C Devonport St Budeaux *Ex* 63-65; C Attenborough w Chilwell *S'well* 65-68; R Benhall w Sternfield *St E* 68-74; P-in-c Snape w Friston 73-74; V Selly Hill St Steph *Birm* 74-81; P-in-c Selly Oak St Wulstan 80-81; V Selly Park St Steph and St Wulstan 81-88; Dioc Adv on Miss *St E* 88-95; Dioc and Co Ecum Officer 88-99; Hon Can St E Cathl 93-00; Bp's Dom Chapl and Personal Asst 95-99; R Holbrook, Freston, Woolverstone and Wherstead 99-00; RD Samford 99-00; rtd 01; Perm to Offic *St E* from 01. *44 Thorney Road, Capel, Ipswich IP9 2LH* Tel (01473) 310069 E-mail bevington@capel19.freeserve.co.uk

BEVINGTON, David John. b 51. Ch Coll Cam BA72 MA76. Trin Coll Bris 73. **d** 76 **p** 77. C Tulse Hill H Trin *S'wark* 76-79; C Galleywood Common *Chelmsf* 79-82; TV Hanley H Ev *Lich* 82-90; TV Hemel Hempstead *St Alb* 90-99; V Calbourne w Newtown *Portsm* from 99; V Shalfleet from 99. *The Vicarage, 4 Manor Green, Shalfleet, Newport PO30 4QT* Tel (01983) 531238 E-mail dbevington@lineone.net

BEVIS, Anthony Richard. b 34. Chich Th Coll 87. **d** 87 **p** 89. NSM Hamble le Rice *Win* 87-94; NSM Woolston from 94; Chapl Southn Community Services NHS Trust 90-01; Chapl Southn City Primary Care Trust from 01. *Lynwood, High Street, Hamble, Southampton SO31 4HA* Tel (023) 8045 3102 *or* 8047 2258

BEVIS, Derek Harold. b 23. FCIS. **d** 90 **p** 91. OLM Guildf Ch Ch *Guildf* 90-98; rtd 98; Perm to Offic *Guildf* from 99. *94 Wodeland Avenue, Guildford GU2 4LD* Tel (01483) 561968

BEWES, Anthony Charles Neill. b 71. Birm Univ BA93. Wycliffe Hall Ox 96. **d** 99 **p** 00. C Sevenoaks St Nic *Roch* 99-05; Team Ldr Titus Trust from 05. *45 Lonsdale Road, Oxford OX2 7ES* Tel (01865) 553625 E-mail anthony@bewes.com

BEWES, Helen Catherine. *See* SCAMMAN, Mrs Helen Catherine

BEWES, Preb Richard Thomas. b 34. OBE05. Em Coll Cam BA58 MA61. Ridley Hall Cam 57. **d** 59 **p** 60. C Beckenham Ch Ch *Roch* 59-65; V Harold Wood *Chelmsf* 65-74; V Northwood Em *Lon* 74-83; R St Marylebone All So w SS Pet and Jo 83-88; P-in-c Portman Square St Paul 87-88; R Langham Place All So 88-04; Preb St Paul's Cathl 88-04; rtd 04. *50 Curzon Road, London W5 1NF* Tel (020) 8998 1723

BEWLEY, Albert Latham. b 38. Leeds Univ BA61. Ely Th Coll 61. **d** 63 **p** 64. C Wigan St Mich *Liv* 63-65; C Caister *Nor* 65-69; R W Lynn 69-76; V Lakenham St Jo 76-97; rtd 97; Perm to Offic *Nor* from 97. *37 St Mary's Road, Poringland, Norwich NR14 7SR* Tel (01508) 492685

BEWLEY, Robin John. b 63. St Jo Coll Ox BA86 MA95 Fitzw Coll Cam BA99 PhD05. Ridley Hall Cam. **d** 00 **p** 01. NSM Histon and Impington *Ely* 00-04; C Harborne Heath *Birm* from 04. *55 Albert Road, Harborne, Birmingham B17 0AP* Tel 0121-426 2548 Mobile 07733-346631 E-mail rob@thebewleys.co.uk

BEYNON, Malcolm. b 36. Univ of Wales (Lamp) BA56 Univ of Wales (Swansea) DipSocSc59 Univ of Wales (Cardiff) PGCE71. St Mich Coll Llan 56. **d** 59 **p** 60. C Aberavon *Llan* 59-62; C Whitchurch 63-68; V Llanwynno 68-73; Chapl Old Hall Sch Wellington Shropshire 74-75; Chapl Nevill Holt Sch Market Harborough 75-82; Chapl Denstone Coll Prep Sch Uttoxeter 82-93; V Dale and St Brides w Marloes *St D* 93-01; rtd 01. *22 Ostrey Bank, St Clears, Carmarthen SA33 4AH*

BEYNON, Nigel David. b 68. Collingwood Coll Dur BSc90. Ridley Hall Cam BA94. **d** 95 **p** 96. C Fulham St Matt *Lon* 95-98; Assoc V St Helen Bishopsgate w St Andr Undershaft etc from 98; Student Team Ldr from 01. *12 Merrick Square, London SE1 4JB* Tel (020) 7378 0229 *or* 7283 2231 E-mail n.beynon@st-helens.org.uk

BEYNON, Vincent Wyn. b 54. CertEd76 Lambeth STh97 Anglia Poly Univ MA04. St Mich Coll Llan 78. **d** 81 **p** 82. C Llantrisant *Llan* 81-83; C Caerphilly 84-85; R Gelligaer 85-88; TV Gtr Corsham *Bris* 88-97; R Potton w Sutton and Cockayne Hatley *St Alb* from 97; RD Biggleswade from 01. *The Rectory, Hatley Road, Potton, Sandy SG19 2RP* Tel (01767) 260782 E-mail wynbeynon@biggleswadedeanery.org

BIANCHI, Mrs Margaret Ruth. b 56. St Mary's Coll Dur BA77. Cranmer Hall Dur 78. **dss** 80 **d** 91 **p** 94. Chester le Street *Dur* 80-83; W Pelton 83-91; NSM 91-95; Perm to Offic from 95. *8 Lindisfarne, Washington NE38 7JR* Tel 0191-417 0852

BIANCHI, Robert Frederick. b 56. St Jo Coll Dur BA77. Cranmer Hall Dur 78. **d** 80 **p** 81. C Chester le Street *Dur* 80-83; C W Pelton 83-86; P-in-c 86-95; Perm to Offic from 95. *8 Lindisfarne, Washington NE38 7JR* Tel 0191-417 0852

BIBBY, Canon Frank. b 37. ACP60 K Coll Lon BD64 AKC64. **d** 65 **p** 66. C Upholland *Liv* 65-67; Lect Birm Coll of Educn 67-72; V Prestwich St Gabr *Man* 72-76; Dir of Ords 72-76; V Hope St Jas 76-86; AD Salford 82-86; R Prestwich St Mary 86-02; Hon Can Man Cathl 96-02; AD Radcliffe and Prestwich 99-02; rtd 02; Perm to Offic *Man* from 02. *65 Leyton Drive, Bury BL9 9TS* Tel 0161-766 3123

BIBBY, Paul Benington. b 27. Magd Coll Cam BA51 MA56. Westcott Ho Cam 55. **d** 57 **p** 58. C Flixton St Mich *Man* 57-60; C Woolwich St Mary w H Trin *S'wark* 60-62; V Hurst *Man* 62-69; Hd of Cam Ho Camberwell 69-76; R Shepton Mallet *B & W* 76-81; P-in-c Doulting w E and W Cranmore and Downhead 78-81; R Shepton Mallet w Doulting 81-82; Sen Chapl Eton Coll 82-87; R Hambleden Valley *Ox* 87-93; rtd 93; Perm to Offic *Nor* from 94. *Vine Cottage, Cross Lane, Stanhoe, King's Lynn PE31 8PS* Tel (01485) 518291

BICK, David Jim. b 33. ALCD59 LTh74. **d** 59 **p** 60. C Glouc St Cath *Glouc* 59-61; C Coleford w Staunton 61-63; R Blaisdon w Flaxley 63-72; V Coaley 72-83; P-in-c Arlingham 80-83; P-in-c Frampton on Severn 80-83; Hon C Saul w Fretherne and Framilode 83-84; Perm to Offic from 84; rtd 98. *St Joseph's, Prinknash Park, Cranham, Gloucester GL4 8EU* Tel (01452) 812973

BICKERSTETH, Anthony Cyril. b 33. K Coll Lon 54. Bps' Coll Cheshunt 55. **d** 58 **p** 59. C Middlesbrough St Oswald *York* 58-61; S Africa 61-64; V Stillington w Marton and Farlington *York* 64-68; V Stoke Newington Common St Mich *Lon* 68-74; V

Nayland w Wiston *St E* 74-82; R Tolleshunt Knights w Tiptree *Chelmsf* 82-87; rtd 87; Perm to Offic *Chelmsf* 87-90. *42 Roman Road, Colchester CO1 1UP* Tel (01206) 544517

BICKERSTETH, David Craufurd. b 50. Wycliffe Hall Ox 71. **d** 75 **p** 76. C Beverley Minster *York* 75-79; C Farnborough *Guildf* 79-81; P-in-c Dearham *Carl* 81-85; V 85-86; R Gosforth w Nether Wasdale and Wasdale Head 86-93; P-in-c Harraby 93-97; V Maryport 98-04; TR Maryport, Netherton and Flimby from 04; Dioc Chapl Mothers' Union 94-97. *The Vicarage, Church Street, Maryport CA15 6HE* Tel (01900) 813077 E-mail david.bickersteth@btinternet.com

BICKERSTETH, Edward Piers. b 56. R Agric Coll Cirencester DipREM78 MRICS80. Wycliffe Hall Ox 89. **d** 91 **p** 92. NSM Bebington *Ches* 91-92; C 92-94; Proclamation Trust 94-98; P-in-c Arborfield w Barkham *Ox* 98-02; R from 02. *The Rectory, Church Lane, Arborfield, Reading RG2 9HZ* Tel 0118-976 0285

✠**BICKERSTETH, The Rt Revd John Monier.** b 21. KCVO89. Ch Ch Ox BA49 MA53. Wells Th Coll 48. **d** 50 **p** 51 **c** 70. C Moorfields *Bris* 50-54; C-in-c Hurst Green CD *S'wark* 54-62; V Chatham St Steph *Roch* 62-70; Hon Can Roch Cathl 68-70; Suff Bp Warrington *Liv* 70-75; Bp B & W 75-87; ChStJ and Sub-Prelate from 77; Clerk of the Closet 79-89; rtd 87. *Beckfords, Newtown, Tisbury, Salisbury SP3 6NY* Tel (01747) 870479

BICKERSTETH, Simon Craufurd. b 77. St Jo Coll Dur BA98. Wycliffe Hall Ox 99. **d** 01 **p** 02. C Windermere *Carl* from 01. *Burnthwaite, 24 Kendal Road, Bowness-on-Windermere, Windermere LA23 3EW* Tel (01539) 444301 Mobile 07752-853148 E-mail simon.bickersteth@btinternet.com

BICKNELL, Jonathan Richard. b 62. Wycliffe Hall Ox. **d** 00 **p** 01. C Chesham Bois *Ox* 00-02. *210 High Street, Berkhamsted HP4 1AG* Tel (01442) 872447

BICKNELL (née RIDING), Mrs Pauline Alison. b 61. SEN82. Oak Hill Th Coll BA90. **d** 90 **p** 96. Par Dn Moor Allerton *Ripon* 90-93; Par Dn Leeds St Aid 93-94; C 94-96; C Rothwell 96-99; TV Drypool *York* 99-05; P-in-c Slyne w Hest *Blackb* from 05. *The Vicarage, Summerfield Drive, Slyne, Lancaster LA2 6AQ* Tel (01524) 822128 E-mail pauline@bicknells.freeserve.co.uk

BIDDELL, Canon Christopher David. b 27. Ch Coll Cam BA48 MA52. Ridley Hall Cam 51. **d** 51 **p** 52. C Hornchurch St Andr *Chelmsf* 51-54; Succ S'wark Cathl *S'wark* 54-56; P-in-c Wroxall *Portsm* 56-61; R Bishop's Waltham 62-75; RD Bishop's Waltham 69-74; V Stockport St Geo *Ches* 75-86; Hon Can Ches Cathl 81-86; Can Res 86-93; RD Stockport 85-86; Vice-Dean Ches 91-93; rtd 93; P-in-c Duncton *Chich* 95-98; P-in-c Tillington 95-98; P-in-c Up Waltham 95-98; Perm to Offic from 98. *3 Park Terrace, Tillington, Petworth GU28 9AE* Tel (01798) 342008

BIDDER, John. b 19. Cuddesdon Coll. **d** 62 **p** 63. C Birstall *Leic* 62-65; R Croft 65-71; R Witcham w Mepal *Ely* 71-80; R Coates 80-85; rtd 85; Perm to Offic *Blackb* from 86. *Carinya, 83 Main Street, Nether Kellett, Carnforth LA6 1EF* Tel (01524) 734993

BIDDINGTON, Terence Eric. b 56. MCollP83 Hull Univ BA77 Trin & All SS Coll Leeds PGCE78 Leeds Univ PhD86 Nottm Univ BTh88 Man Univ MA(Theol)96. Linc Th Coll 85. **d** 88 **p** 89. C Harpenden St Jo *St Alb* 88-90; Chapl Keele Univ *Lich* 90-93; Freelance Th Educator and Asst Lect Keele Univ 94-99; Assoc Min Betley and Keele 90-93; Asst Dir Cornerstone St Aug *Man* 95-96; Mental Health Advocate Stockport 96-98; Dir and Sen Advocate Stockport MIND from 98; Perm to Offic *Man* 99-01; P-in-c Heaton Norris Ch w All SS 01-02; C Heatons 02-03; Asst Chapl Man Mental Health Partnership 01-03; Chapl Man Univ *Man* from 03; Chapl Man Metrop Univ from 03. *St Anne's Rectory, St Anne's Drive, Denton, Manchester M34 3EB* Tel 0161-336 2374 *or* 0161-275 2894 E-mail tbjp2000@fish.co.uk

BIDDLE, Nicholas Lawrence. b 71. K Coll Lon BA94 Leeds Univ MA98. Coll of Resurr Mirfield 96. **d** 98 **p** 99. C Bedford St Andr *St Alb* 98-01; Bp's Dom Chapl and Research Asst *Chich* 01-04; P-in-c Brighton Gd Shep Preston from 04. *The Good Shepherd Vicarage, 272 Dyke Road, Brighton BN1 5AE* Tel (01273) 882987 Mobile 07790-287280 E-mail n.biddle@ntlworld.com

BIDDLE, Miss Rosemary. b 44. CertEd67. St Jo Coll Dur 76. **dss** 79 **d** 87 **p** 94. Sheldon *Birm* 79-83; Burntwood *Lich* 83-87; Par Dn 87-89; Par Dn Gt Wyrley 89-94; C 94-99; rtd 99; Perm to Offic *Lich* from 00. *8 Brook Lane, Great Wyrley, Walsall WS6 6BQ* Tel (01922) 419032

BIDDLECOMBE, Francis William. b 30. St Mich Coll Llan 57. **d** 59 **p** 60. C Llangynwyd w Maesteg *Llan* 59-62; C Roath 62-65; V Llanddewi Rhondda w Bryn Eirw 65-71; V Berse and Southsea *St As* 71-79; P-in-c Teme Valley S *Worc* 79-85; rtd 92; Perm to Offic *Heref* from 92; Perm to Offic *Worc* from 92. *Four Winds, New Road, Highley, Bridgnorth WV16 6NN* Tel (01746) 861746 E-mail francis@sagainternet.co.uk

BIDE, Mrs Mary Elizabeth. b 53. St Anne's Coll Ox BA74 MA78. S Dios Minl Tr Scheme 91. **d** 94 **p** 95. NSM Gt Bookham *Guildf* 94-95; C 95-98; Past Tutor Dioc Min Course 97-03; P-in-c Frimley Green 98-01; V Frimley Green and Mytchett 02-03; Prec Ch Ch *Ox* from 03. *Christ Church, Oxford OX1 1DP* Tel (01865) 276214 E-mail mary.bide@christ-church.oxford.ac.uk

BIDEN, Neville Douglas. b 31. S'wark Ord Course 76. **d** 79 **p** 80. C Ash *Guildf* 79-82; NSM Surbiton St Andr and St Mark *S'wark* 87-91; Chapl Asst Long Grove Hosp Epsom 90-91; C Coulsdon St Jo *S'wark* 91-96; rtd 96; Perm to Offic *Heref* 95-97; *Guildf* from 97; *Win* from 01. *5 Taylor Drive, Bramley, Tadley RG26 5XB* Tel (01256) 880459 E-mail rev.nev@virgin.net

BIDGOOD, Julian Paul. b 71. Sussex Univ BA92. Oak Hill Th Coll BA03. **d** 03 **p** 04. C Ox St Ebbe w H Trin and St Pet *Ox* from 03. *81 Marlborough Road, Oxford OX1 4LX* Tel (01865) 765755 *or* 240438 Mobile 07779-296511 E-mail julianbidgood@hotmail.com

BIELBY, Elaine Elizabeth. b 57. Surrey Univ MSc83. Ripon Coll Cuddesdon 96. **d** 98 **p** 99. C Marton-in-Cleveland *York* 98-01; P-in-c Welton w Melton from 01; Tr Officer E Riding from 01. *St Helen's Vicarage, Cowgate, Welton, Brough HU15 1ND* Tel (01482) 666677 E-mail ebielby@fish.co.uk

BIENFAIT, Alexander. b 61. Hatf Poly BSc86. Sarum & Wells Th Coll BTh94. **d** 94 **p** 95. C Battersea St Luke *S'wark* 94-96; C Clapham Team 96-99; TV Whitstable *Cant* from 99. *St Andrew's Vicarage, 38A Saddleton Road, Whitstable CT5 4JH* Tel (01227) 263152 E-mail alex.bienfait@virgin.net

BIERBAUM, Ms Ruth Anne. b 67. RN89. Trin Coll Bris BA98. **d** 99 **p** 00. C Filey *York* 99-02; C Coxheath, E Farleigh, Hunton, Linton etc *Roch* from 02. *19 Westerhill Road, Coxheath, Maidstone ME17 4DQ* Tel (01622) 743866 Mobile 017984-803728 E-mail ruth@bierbaum.freeserve.co.uk

BIGGAR, Prof Nigel John. b 55. Worc Coll Ox BA76 MA88 Chicago Univ AM80 PhD86 Regent Coll Vancouver MCS81. **d** 90 **p** 91. Lib Latimer Ho Ox 85-91; Asst Lect Chr Ethics Wycliffe Hall Ox 87-94; Chapl Oriel Coll Ox 90-99; Prof Th Leeds Univ *Ripon* 99-04; Prof Th TCD from 04; Can Ch Ch Cathl Dublin *D & G* from 05. *School of Religions and Theology, Arts Building, Trinity College, Dublin 2, Irish Republic* Tel (00353) (1) 608 3397 **or** 608 1297 E-mail biggarn@tcd.ie

BIGGIN, Ronald. b 20. NW Ord Course 70. **d** 73 **p** 74. C Thelwall *Ches* 73-79; V 79-87; rtd 87; NSM Lt Leigh and Lower Whitley *Ches* 90-93; Perm to Offic from 93. *12 Wilmslow Crescent, Thelwall, Warrington WA4 2JE* Tel (01925) 261531

BIGGS, David James. b 55. St Jo Coll Auckland LTh82. **d** 81 **p** 82. New Zealand 81-86; C Stevenage St Andr and St Geo *St Alb* 86-89; TV Moulsecoomb *Chich* 89-99; C Brighton St Pet w Chpl Royal 99-02; P-in-c from 02. *4 Parochial Mews, Princes Street, Brighton BN2 1WF* Tel (01273) 774492

BIGGS, George Ramsay. b 45. Liv Univ BA67 Qu Coll Cam BA73. Westcott Ho Cam 72. **d** 74 **p** 75. C Lee St Aug *S'wark* 74-78; TV Eling, Testwood and Marchwood *Win* 78; TV Totton 78-93; V E and W Wellow 93-98; V E w W Wellow and Sherfield English from 98; Hosp Chapl Adv (Bournemouth Adnry) from 02. *Wellow Vicarage, 1 The Beeches, West Wellow, Romsey SO51 6RN* Tel (01794) 323562

BIGGS, Laurence John. b 60. Leeds Univ BSc81. Trin Coll Bris DipHE94. **d** 94 **p** 95. C St Alb St Paul *St Alb* 94-99; V Codicote from 99. *The Vicarage, 4 Bury Lane, Codicote, Hitchin SG4 8XT* Tel (01438) 820266 Fax 822007 E-mail lbiggs@enterprise.net

BIGGS, Philip John. b 51. Ripon Hall Ox 74 Ripon Coll Cuddesdon 75. **d** 77 **p** 78. C Maidstone All SS w St Phil and H Trin *Cant* 77-80; Dioc Youth Officer *Truro* 80-84; Australia from 84; Hon Chapl Miss to Seafarers from 84; Chapl St Hilda's Angl Sch Perth 84-87; R Bicton 87-91; R Mosman Park from 92; AD Claremont 98-01. *8 Vlamingh Place, Mosman Park, W Australia 6012* Tel (0061) (8) 9384 4279 *or* 9384 0108 Fax 9384 0108 E-mail bigger@opera.iinet.net.au

BIGGS, Stewart Richard. b 58. SEITE. **d** 01 **p** 02. C Tunbridge Wells St Jas w St Phil *Roch* 01-04; C Tunbridge Wells St Jas 04-05; V St Mary Cray and St Paul's Cray from 05. *The Vicarage, Main Road, Orpington BR5 3EN* Tel (01689) 827697 Mobile 07967-979559 E-mail revstewb@xalt.co.uk

BIGMORE, Graeme Paul. b 57. Univ of Wales (Cardiff) BTh95. St Mich Coll Llan 89. **d** 92 **p** 93. C Cardiff St Jo *Llan* 92-96; Cardiff City Cen Chapl 94-96; C Rhondda 96-98; V Tylorstown w Ynyshir 98-05; V Ynyshir from 05. *The Vicarage, Graig Road, Ynyshir, Porth CF39 0NS* Tel (01443) 684148

BIGNELL, Alan Guy. b 39. Lon Univ BA64. Ox NSM Course 78. **d** 81 **p** 82. NSM Upton cum Chalvey *Ox* 81-90; NSM Burnham and Slough Deanery from 90. *Little Gidding, 2 Turners Road, Slough SL3 7AN* Tel (01753) 523005 E-mail abignell@waitrose.com

BIGNELL, David Charles. b 41. EMMTC 76. **d** 79 **p** 80. C Porchester *S'well* 79-82; V Awsworth w Cossall 82-86; Bp's Ecum Officer from 84; V Edwalton from 86. *The Vicarage, Village Street, Edwalton, Nottingham NG12 4AB* Tel 0115-923 2034 E-mail office@edwaltonchurch.plus.com

BIGWOOD, Kate Elizabeth. *See* ATKINSON, Mrs Kate Bigwood

BILES, David George. b 35. AKC58 Open Univ BA75 Lambeth STh91 Leeds Univ MA96. **d** 59 **p** 60. C Cockerton *Dur* 59-62; C Winlaton 62-67; P-in-c Dipton 67-74; R Wolviston 74-89; P-in-c Thirkleby w Kilburn and Bagby *York* 89-90; V 90-00; RD Thirsk 90-91; RD Mowbray 91-00; rtd 00; Perm to Offic *York* from 00.

10 King Rudding Close, Riccall, York YO19 6RY Tel and fax (01757) 248829

BILES, Mrs Kathleen Anne. b 52. Bradf Univ BA74. St Jo Coll Nottm 98. **d** 04. C Ch Ch Cathl Stanley Falkland Is from 04. *PO Box 166, 14 Kent Road, Stanley FIQQ 1ZZ, Falkland Islands* Tel and fax (00500) 21897 E-mail kbiles@horizon.co.fk

BILES, Canon Timothy Mark Frowde. b 35. Univ of Wales DipTh64. St Mich Coll Llan 60. **d** 64 **p** 66. C Middleton St Cross *Ripon* 64-66; Chapl St Fran Sch Hooke 66-72; P-in-c Toller Porcorum w Hooke *Sarum* 72-79; P-in-c Melplash w Mapperton 74-79; P-in-c Beaminster 77-79; TR Beaminster Area 79-00; Can and Preb Sarum Cathl 83-00; RD Beaminster 84-89; rtd 00; Perm to Offic *Sarum* from 01. *36 Hound Street, Sherborne DT9 3AA* Tel (01935) 816247

BILL, Alan. b 29. K Coll Lon BD66 AKC66. **d** 67 **p** 68. C Gt Burstead *Chelmsf* 67-70; TV Thornaby on Tees *York* 71-76; R E Gilling 76-81; V Ormesby 81-91; rtd 91; Perm to Offic *Newc* from 91. *13 Wilmington Close, Tudor Grange, Newcastle upon Tyne NE3 2SF* Tel 0191-242 4467

BILL, Canon Thomas Andrew Graham. b 47. Dur Univ BA76. Cranmer Hall Dur. **d** 77 **p** 78. C Penwortham St Mary *Blackb* 77-80; C Torrisholme 80-82; P-in-c Accrington St Pet 82-89; P-in-c Haslingden St Jo Stonefold 82-89; V Skerton St Chad 89-03; R Burnley St Pet from 03; Hon Can Blackb Cathl from 03. *St Peter's Rectory, 1 Ridge Court, Burnley BB10 3LN* Tel and fax (01282) 413599 E-mail tom.bill@lineone.net

BILLAM, John. b 38. St Aid Birkenhead 63. **d** 66 **p** 67. C Wellington Ch Ch *Lich* 66-70; P-in-c Colwyn *S & B* from 03. *Melin y Cwm, Beulah, Llanwrtyd Wells LD5 4TT* Tel (01591) 620493

BILLETT, Anthony Charles. b 56. Bris Univ BEd. Wycliffe Hall Ox 82. **d** 85 **p** 86. C Waltham Abbey *Chelmsf* 85-88; C Nor St Pet Mancroft w St Jo Maddermarket *Nor* 88-91; V Stalham and E Ruston w Brunstead 91-00; R Stalham, E Ruston, Brunstead, Sutton and Ingham 00-01; R Diss from 01. *The Rectory, 26 Mount Street, Diss IP22 3QG* Tel (01379) 642072 E-mail tbillett@diss26.freeserve.co.uk

BILLETT (née RANDALL), Mrs Elizabeth Nicola. b 55. RGN75 SCM81. EAMTC 94. **d** 97 **p** 98. C Loddon, Sisland w Hales and Heckingham *Nor* 97-98; C Loddon, Sisland, Chedgrave, Hardley and Langley 98-01; TV Hempnall from 02. *The Flat, George's House, The Street, Woodton, Bungay NR35 1LZ* Tel (01508) 482366

BILLINGHURST, Richard George. b 48. St Jo Coll Cam BA70 MA74 FIA76. Ridley Hall Cam 76. **d** 79 **p** 80. C Caverswall *Lich* 79-81; C Cullompton *Ex* 81-84; R Redgrave cum Botesdale w Rickinghall *St E* 84-92; R Skellingthorpe w Doddington *Linc* from 92; RD Graffoe 94-02. *The Rectory, 50 Lincoln Road, Skellingthorpe, Lincoln LN6 5UY* Tel (01522) 682520 Mobile 07971-590378 Fax (01522) 693330 E-mail acorns@clara.co.uk

BILLINGS, Canon Alan Roy. b 42. Em Coll Cam BA65 MA69 Bris Univ PGCE66 Leic Univ MEd75. NY Th Sem DMin87 Linc Th Coll 66. **d** 68 **p** 69. C Knighton St Mary Magd *Leic* 68-72; P-in-c Sheff Gillcar St Silas *Sheff* 72-76; V Beighton 76-77; Hd RE Broadway Sch Barnsley 77-81; Perm to Offic 77-81; V Walkley 81-86; Dir Ox Inst for Ch and Soc 86-92; Perm to Offic *Ox* 86-92; Vice-Prin Ripon Coll Cuddesdon 88-92; Prin WMMTC 92-94; V Kendal St Geo *Carl* from 94; Warden of Readers 96-03; Dir Centre for Ethics and Relig Lanc Univ from 00; Hon Can Carl Cathl from 05. *St George's Vicarage, 3 Firbank, Sedbergh Road, Kendal LA9 6BE* Tel (01539) 723039 *or* 720018 Fax 737180 E-mail alanbillingsuk@yahoo.co.uk

BILLINGS, Derek Donald. b 30. Fitzw Ho Cam BA54 MA59. Tyndale Hall Bris 55. **d** 56 **p** 57. C Attenborough w Bramcote and Chilwell *S'well* 56-58; R Ashley w Silverley *Ely* 59-66; V Bottisham 66-80; R Houghton w Wyton 80-97; rtd 97; Perm to Offic *Ely* from 97. *The Limes, 59 Cambridge Street, Godmanchester, Huntingdon PE29 2AY* Tel (01480) 414244

BILLINGS, Roger Key. b 41. ACIB. Oak Hill Th Coll BA80. **d** 80 **p** 81. C Tunbridge Wells St Jas *Roch* 80-84; V Chatham St Paul w All SS 84-95; V Carterton *Ox* 95-03; TR Brize Norton and Carterton from 03; AD Witney from 03. *St John's Vicarage, 6 Burford Road, Carterton OX18 3AA* Tel (01993) 846996 *or* 842429 E-mail rkbcar@tinyonline.co.uk

BILLINGSLEY, Raymond Philip. b 48. FCMA80 Open Univ BA98 DASS98. Qu Coll Birm 87. **d** 89 **p** 90. C Yardley St Edburgha *Birm* 89-92; V Ward End 92-96; V Brymbo *St As* 96-04; V Northop from 04. *The Vicarage, Church Road, Northop, Mold CH7 6BS* Tel (01352) 840235 Mobile 08315-39896

BILLINGTON, Charles Alfred. b 30. Leeds Univ BA55. Coll of Resurr Mirfield 53. **d** 55 **p** 56. C Carl H Trin *Carl* 55-59; CR 59-64; R Man St Aid *Man* 64-66; V Gt Crosby St Faith *Liv* 66-72; R Harrold and Carlton w Chellington *St Alb* 72-80; R Tintinhull w Chilthorne Domer, Yeovil Marsh etc *B & W* 80-81; Chapl Leybourne Grange Hosp W Malling 81-85; V Walsden *Wakef* 85-88; R Llanfair Talhaearn and Llansannan etc *St As* 88-97; rtd 97. *5 Sunningdale, Abergele LL22 7UB* Tel (01745) 824563

BILLINGTON, George. b 45. St Jo Coll Nottm 92. **d** 94 **p** 95. C Accrington St Jo w Huncoat *Blackb* 94-98; C Whittle-le-Woods 98-00; V Stalmine w Pilling from 00. *St John's Vicarage, Lancaster Road, Pilling, Preston PR3 6AE* Tel (01253) 799170 E-mail george.billington@ukonline.co.uk

BILLOWES, David. b 20. Chich Th Coll. **d** 76 **p** 77. NSM Cowes St Mary *Portsm* 76-91; Chapl St Mary's Hosp Newport 82-91; rtd 91; Perm to Offic *Portsm* from 91. *45 Solent View Road, Gurnard, Cowes PO31 8JZ* Tel (01983) 297366

BILLS, Reginald. b 18. TCert47. Lich Th Coll 68 Wm Temple Coll Rugby DipTh68. **d** 70 **p** 71. C Wednesfield St Thos *Lich* 70-73; C Wolverhampton St Pet 73-79; Chapl St Pet Colleg Sch 73-79; C Wolverhampton St Andr 79-81; P-in-c Brockmoor 81-87; rtd 87. *43 Kewstoke Road, Willenhall WV12 5DY* Tel (01922) 405049

BILNEY, Kenneth Henry. b 25. FBCS. St Deiniol's Hawarden 75. **d** 75 **p** 76. Hon C Knighton St Mary Magd *Leic* 75-78; C Leic St Jas 78-80; R Leire w Ashby Parva and Dunton Bassett 80-90; rtd 90; Perm to Offic *Leic* from 90. *20 Ferndale Road, Leicester LE2 6GN* Tel 0116-257 0436

BILSTON, Barbara Bradley. b 35. Man Univ BA58 Essex Univ MA75. EAMTC 96. **d** 97 **p** 98. NSM Bacton w Wyverstone and Cotton *St E* 97-00; NSM Bacton w Wyverstone, Cotton and Old Newton etc 00-04; Asst to RD Stowmarket 04-05; RD from 05. *Boy's Hall, Ward Green, Old Newton, Stowmarket IP14 4EY* Tel and fax (01449) 781253 Mobile 07889-516674 E-mail b.b.bilston@open.ac.uk

BILTON, Canon Paul Michael. b 52. AKC74. St Aug Coll Cant 74. **d** 75 **p** 76. C Skipton Ch Ch *Bradf* 75-79; Ind Chapl *Worc* 79-81; V Greetland and W Vale *Wakef* 81-88; R Mablethorpe w Trusthorpe *Linc* 88-91; V Bradf St Wilfrid Lidget Green *Bradf* 91-04; P-in-c Bradf St Columba w St Andr 00-04; V Bradf St Wilfrid w St Columba from 04; RD Bowling and Horton from 02; Hon Can Bradf Cathl from 04. *St Wilfrid's Vicarage, St Wilfrid's Road, Bradford BD7 2LU* Tel (01274) 572504

BIMSON, Sara Margaret. b 56. St Jo Coll Nottm BA. **d** 03 **p** 04. C Maidstone St Martin *Cant* from 03. *85 Loose Road, Maidstone ME15 7DA* Tel (01622) 679432 E-mail sara.bimson@btopenworld.com

BINDING, Ms Frances Mary. b 59. York Univ BA81 Newc Poly PGCE82. WEMTC 98. **d** 02 **p** 03. C Bromyard *Heref* from 02. *12 Lower Thorn, Bromyard HR7 4AZ* Tel (01885) 482620 E-mail franbinding@lineone.net

BINDOFF, Ms Anna. b 70. Leeds Univ BA94. Ripon Coll Cuddesdon BA97. **d** 98 **p** 99. Asst Chapl New Coll Ox 98-01; Hon C Blackbird Leys *Ox* 98-01; C 01-04. *23 Brook Street, Watlington OX49 5JH* Tel (01491) 613327

BINDOFF, Stanley. b 54. Sarum & Wells Th Coll 79. **d** 82 **p** 83. C Thirsk *York* 82-86; Chapl HM YOI Northallerton 85-89; P-in-c Rounton w Welbury *York* 86-89; Chapl HM Pris Gartree 89-92; Chapl HM Pris Frankland 92-96; Chapl HM YOI Deerbolt 96-03; TR Castleford *Wakef* from 03. *The Rectory, 15 Barnes Road, Castleford WF10 5AA* Tel (01977) 733796 Pager 07693-277628 E-mail fr_stan@blueyonder.co.uk

BING, Alan Charles. b 56. St Edm Hall Ox BA78 MA91 Ex Univ MA96. Oak Hill Th Coll 89. **d** 91 **p** 92. C Fremington *Ex* 91-94; C-in-c Roundswell CD 94-97; TV Barnstaple 97-99; Chapl N Devon Coll Barnstaple 96-99; P-in-c Ulverston St Mary w H Trin *Carl* 99-04; R from 04. *The Rectory, 15 Ford Park Crescent, Ulverston LA12 7JR* Tel and fax (01229) 584331 E-mail alanbing@fish.co.uk

BINGHAM, Mrs Marie Joyce Phyllis. b 27. Glouc Sch of Min 80. **dss** 84 **d** 87 **p** 94. Glouc St Mary de Crypt w St Jo and Ch Ch *Glouc* 84-85; Glouc St Mary de Lode and St Nic 85-87; Hon C 87-95; Hon C Glouc St Mary de Crypt w St Jo and Ch Ch 94-95; Hon C Glouc St Mary de Crypt w St Jo, Ch Ch etc 95-98; Perm to Offic from 98. *Clematis Cottage, 1 Queenwood Grove, Prestbury, Cheltenham GL52 3NG* Tel (01452) 242252

BINGHAM, Norman James Frederick. b 26. Lon Univ BSc51. Tyndale Hall Bris 61. **d** 63 **p** 64. C Chell *Lich* 63-67; C Macclesfield St Mich *Ches* 67-71; P-in-c Macclesfield St Pet 71-73; V Leyton St Mary w St Edw *Chelmsf* 73-91; RD Waltham Forest 81-86; P-in-c Leyton St Luke 82-91; rtd 91; Perm to Offic *St Alb* from 91. *97 Monks Walk, Buntingford SG9 9DP* Tel (01763) 272275

BINKS, Canon Edmund Vardy. b 36. K Coll Lon BD61 AKC61 Liv Univ Hon LLD98 FRSA89. **d** 62 **p** 63. C Selby Abbey *York* 62-65; Asst Chapl Univ Coll of Ripon and York St Jo 65-83; Hd St Kath Coll Liv 83-87; Prin Univ Coll Ches 87-98; Hon Can Ches Cathl 95-98; Perm to Offic *Chich* from 98; rtd 01. *2 Lodge Close, Lewes BN7 1AR* Tel (01273) 487136

BINLEY, Miss Teresa Mary. b 37. Dalton Ho Bris 61. **d** 87 **p** 94. Par Dn Ashton-upon-Mersey St Mary *Ches* 87-92; Bp's Officer for Women in Min 87-92; C Chaddesden St Mary *Derby* 92-98; rtd 98; Perm to Offic *Derby* from 98. *27 Hindscarth Crescent, Mickleover, Derby DE3 9NN* Tel (01332) 511146

BINNEY, Mark James Gurney. b 58. K Coll Lon BD80. Qu Coll Birm 84. **d** 86 **p** 87. C Hornchurch St Andr *Chelmsf* 86-89; C Hutton 89-91; V Pheasey *Lich* 91-96; TV Wombourne w Trysull and Bobbington 96-99; V Wilnecote from 99. *The Vicarage, 64 Glascote Lane, Wilnecote, Tamworth B77 2PH* Tel (01827) 280806 Mobile 07703-359204

BINNS, David John. b 39. Moore Th Coll Sydney ThL64. **d** 64 **p** 65. Australia 64-67 and from 70; C Norbiton *S'wark* 67-69; R Adelaide St Luke 80-98; Assoc Min 98-00; rtd 00. *Unit 4/2 Spence Avenue, Myrtle Bank, S Australia 5064* Tel (0061) (8) 8338 5779 Mobile 0417-860560 E-mail djb29@ozemail.com.au

BINNS, Miss Elizabeth Ann. b 55. Man Metrop Univ BA87 RGN77. **d** 05. OLM Bury St Jo w St Mark *Man* from 05. *36 Raymond Avenue, Bury BL9 6NN* Tel 0161-764 5071 Mobile 07976-818157 E-mail elizabethbinns@aol.com

BINNS, John Richard Elliott. b 51. Cam Univ MA76 Lon Univ PhD89. Coll of Resurr Mirfield 74. **d** 76 **p** 77. C Clapham H Trin *S'wark* 76-78; C Clapham Old Town 78-80; TV Mortlake w E Sheen 80-87; V Upper Tooting H Trin 87-94; V Cambridge Gt St Mary w St Mich *Ely* from 94. *Great St Mary's Vicarage, 39 Madingley Road, Cambridge CB3 0EL* Tel (01223) 355285 *or* 741716 Fax 462914 E-mail bep21@cam.ac.uk

BINNS, Peter Rodney. b 44. St Andr Univ MA66. Ox NSM Course 72. **d** 75 **p** 76. NSM Amersham on the Hill *Ox* 75-90; NSM Wingrave w Rowsham, Aston Abbotts and Cublington 90-97; NSM Hawridge w Cholesbury and St Leonard 90-97; NSM Amersham on the Hill from 97. *16 Turnfurlong Row, Turnfurlong Lane, Aylesbury HP21 7FF* Tel (01296) 330836 Fax 337965

BINNY, John Wallace. b 46. Univ of Wales (Lamp) BA70. St Mich Coll Llan 69. **d** 71 **p** 72. C Llantrisant *Llan* 71-77; V Troedyrhiw w Merthyr Vale 77-82; R Eglwysbrewis w St Athan, Flemingston, Gileston 82-95; R Eglwysbrewis w St Athan w Gileston 95-03; V Pentyrch w Capel Llanillterne from 03. *The Vicarage, Church Road, Pentyrch, Cardiff CF15 9QF* Tel (029) 2089 0318

BIRBECK, Anthony Leng. b 33. MBE90. Linc Coll Ox BA59 MA61. Linc Th Coll 58. **d** 60 **p** 61. C Redcar *York* 60-74; Chapl Teesside Ind Miss 62-74; Can Res and Treas Wells Cathl *B & W* 74-78; NSM Wells St Thos w Horrington 89-98; rtd 98; Perm to Offic *B & W* from 98. *Beeches, Cannard's Grave Road, Shepton Mallet BA4 4LX* Tel (01749) 330382 Mobile 07802-725024 E-mail tony-birbeck@msn.com

BIRBECK, John Trevor. b 49. ACIB77. St Jo Coll Nottm 86. **d** 88 **p** 89. C Eccleshill *Bradf* 88-92; V Hurst Green and Mitton 92-03; R Rawmarsh w Parkgate *Sheff* from 03. *The Rectory, 2 High Street, Rawmarsh, Rotherham S62 6NE* Tel (01709) 527160 E-mail john.birbeck@ntlworld.com

BIRCH, Arthur James Fleet. b 14. Univ Coll Dur BA36 MA39. **d** 37 **p** 38. C W Bromwich Ch Ch *Lich* 37-41; C Wroxeter 41-43; C Crewe St Jo *Ches* 43-46; V Lostock Gralam 46-55; V Plemstall w Guilden Sutton 55-59; V Hooton 59-70; R Lymm 70-79; rtd 79; Perm to Offic *Ches* from 79. *21 Arran Drive, Frodsham WA6 6AL* Tel (01928) 733709

BIRCH, Derek. b 31. Univ of Wales (Lamp) BA58. Coll of Resurr Mirfield 58. **d** 60 **p** 61. C S Elmsall *Wakef* 60-62; C Penistone w Midhope 62-66; V Silkstone 66-89; Chapl Stainborough 76-89; P-in-c Hoyland Swaine 85-89; V Hoylandswaine and Silkstone w Stainborough 89-97; rtd 98; Perm to Offic *Wakef* from 98. *46 Pengeston Road, Penistone, Sheffield S36 6GW* Tel (01226) 761523

BIRCH, Graham James. b 62. N Ord Course BTh94. **d** 97 **p** 98. C Southport St Phil and St Paul *Liv* 97-01; P-in-c Wigan St Cath from 01. *St Catharine's Vicarage, St Catharine Terrace, Wigan WN1 3JW* Tel (01942) 731962 E-mail madrebgra@aol.com

BIRCH, Henry Arthur. b 24. St Jo Coll Dur BA48. Tyndale Hall Bris 48. **d** 49 **p** 50. C Edin St Thos *Edin* 49-51; C Surbiton Hill Ch Ch *S'wark* 51-54; R Uphill *B & W* 54-69; Australia 69-81 and from 84; S Africa 81-84; rtd 90. *9/87 Yathong Road, Carringbah, NSW, Australia 2229* Tel (0061) (2) 9525 1763

BIRCH, Janet Ann. St Alb Minl Tr Scheme 77. **dss** 80 **d** 87 **p** 94. Luton St Mary *St Alb* 80-87; Par Dn Streatley 87-91; rtd 91; NSM Aldeburgh w Hazlewood *St E* 91-01; Perm to Offic 01-03. *3 Market Cross House, Wentworth Road, Aldeburgh IP15 5BJ* Tel (01728) 453371

BIRCH, Mark Russell. b 70. Bris Univ BVSc93 Em Coll Cam BA99. Westcott Ho Cam 97. **d** 00 **p** 01. C Cirencester *Glouc* 00-03; Chapl and Fell Ex Coll Ox from 03. *Exeter College, Oxford OX1 3DP* Tel (01865) 279610 E-mail mark.birch@exeter.ox.ac.uk

BIRCH, Richard Arthur. b 51. **d** 01 **p** 02. NSM Foord St Jo *Cant* 01-04; NSM Hawkinge w Acrise and Swingfield from 04. *38 Martello Drive, Hythe CT21 6PJ* Tel (01303) 267155 E-mail richarda.birch@virgin.net

BIRCH, Shirley Anne. b 34. EMMTC 88. **d** 91 **p** 94. Hon Par Dn Melton Gt Framland *Leic* 91-93; NSM Melton Mowbray 93-01; NSM Minster-in-Sheppey *Cant* from 02. *St Peter's House, 2 St Peter's Close, Minster on Sea, Sheerness ME12 3DD* Tel (01795) 662399

BIRCHALL, John Dearman. b 70. St Andr Univ MA93. Wycliffe Hall Ox BTh99. **d** 99 **p** 00. C Purley Ch Ch *S'wark* 99-02; C Fisherton Anger *Sarum* from 02. *14 Wyndham Park, Salisbury SP1 3BA* Tel (01722) 416577 E-mail john@jssbirchall.freeserve.co.uk

BIRCHALL, Robert Gary. b 59. Sheff Univ BA81. St Jo Coll Nottm 85. **d** 88 **p** 89. C Manston *Ripon* 88-91; C Leic Martyrs *Leic* 91-94; C New Humberstone 94-95; V Burnopfield *Dur* from 95. *The Vicarage, Front Street, Burnopfield, Newcastle upon Tyne NE16 6HQ* Tel (01207) 270261 E-mail gmsr@globalnet.co.uk

BIRCHARD, Canon Thaddeus Jude. b 45. Louisiana State Univ BA66 Nottm Univ DipTh68. Kelham Th Coll 66. **d** 70 **p** 71. C Devonport St Mark Ford *Ex* 70-73; C Southend St Jo w St Mark, All SS w St Fran etc *Chelmsf* 73-76; TV Poplar *Lon* 76-80; V Paddington St Jo w St Mich 80-01; Hon Can Louisiana from 90; rtd 01; Perm to Offic *Lon* from 02. *142 Dibdin House, Maida Vale, London W9 1QG* Tel (020) 7328 2380 E-mail thaddeus@birchard.co.uk

BIRCHMORE, Brian Leonard. b 35. ALCD59. **d** 59 **p** 60. C Rusthall *Roch* 59-62; C Rainham 62-64; C Belvedere All SS 64-66; V Meopham 66-74; R Chatham St Mary w St Jo 74-75; Perm to Offic *Chelmsf* 81-83; Ind Chapl Harlow 83-89; P-in-c Bush End and Hatfield Broad Oak 83-89; P-in-c Greenstead 89-97; C All Hallows by the Tower etc *Lon* 97-01; rtd 01. *39 Elmbrook Drive, Bishop's Stortford CM23 4JB* Tel (01279) 507612

BIRD, Mrs Ann Maud. b 39. **d** 00 **p** 01. OLM W Bromwich All SS *Lich* from 00. *16 Caldwell Street, West Bromwich B71 2DN* Tel 0121-588 4335

BIRD (née BAKER), Mrs Anne-Marie Clare. b 56. Wye Coll Lon BSc78 Glas Univ MSc80. St Jo Coll Nottm 88. **d** 90 **p** 94. Par Dn Levenshulme St Pet *Man* 90-94; C 94-95; P-in-c Crumpsall 95-03; TV Keynsham *B & W* from 03. *9 Chelmer Grove, Keynsham, Bristol BS31 1QA* Tel 0117-986 1837

BIRD, Anthony Peter. b 31. St Jo Coll Ox BA54 BTh55 MA57 Birm Univ MB, ChB70. Cuddesdon Coll 55. **d** 57 **p** 58. C Stafford St Mary *Lich* 57-60; Chapl Cuddesdon Coll 60-61; Vice-Prin 61-64; C Selly Oak St Wulstan *Birm* 64-68; Lic to Offic 68-79; Prin Qu Coll Birm 74-79; Perm to Offic *Birm* from 85; rtd 96. *93 Bournbrook Road, Birmingham B29 7BX*

BIRD, Brian Edward. b 37. Rhodes Univ BA. **d** 75. S Africa 75-99; Bp's C Mt Merrion *D & D* from 99. *122 Mount Merrion Avenue, Belfast BT6 0FS* Tel and fax (028) 9029 4471

BIRD, The Ven Colin Richard Bateman. b 33. Selw Coll Cam BA56 MA61. Cuddesdon Coll 56. **d** 58 **p** 59. C St Mark's Cathl George S Africa 58-61; C Claremont St Sav 61-64; R N Suburbs Pretoria 64-66; R Tzaneen w Duiwelskloof and Phalaborwa 66-70; C Limpsfield and Titsey *S'wark* 70-75; V Hatcham St Cath 75-88; RD Deptford 80-85; Hon Can S'wark Cathl 82-88; Adn Lambeth 88-99; P-in-c Brixton Hill St Sav 91-94; rtd 00; Perm to Offic *St E* from 00; *Chelmsf* and *Nor* from 01. *32 Bristol Road, Bury St Edmunds IP33 2DL* Tel (01284) 723810 E-mail dickbird@btopenworld.com

BIRD, The Very Revd David John. b 46. St D Coll Lamp BA70 Duquesne Univ PhD87. Gen Th Sem (NY) STM74. **d** 70 **p** 71. C Kidderminster St Geo *Worc* 70-72; USA from 72; Chapl Trin Sch New York 72-78; V Rochdale Ch Ch 78-79; R New Kensington St Andr 79-89; R Washington Grace Ch 89-03; Dean Trin Cathl San Jose from 03. *Trinity Cathedral, 81 North 2nd Street, San Jose, CA 95113-1205, USA* Tel (001) (408) 293 7953 Fax 293 4993 E-mail david3933@aol.com

BIRD, Canon David Ronald. b 55. York Univ BA76. St Jo Coll Nottm 83. **d** 86 **p** 87. C Kinson *Sarum* 86-90; R Thrapston *Pet* 90-97; P-in-c Islip 94-95; RD Higham 94-97; V Northampton St Giles from 97; Can Pet Cathl from 01. *St Giles's Vicarage, 2 Spring Gardens, Northampton NN1 1LX* Tel (01604) 634060 Fax 628623 E-mail david@dbird.freeserve.co.uk

BIRD, Donald Wilfred Ray. b 27. Dur Univ BA52. Linc Th Coll 61. **d** 63 **p** 64. C E w W Barkwith *Linc* 63-65; Rhodesia 66-80; R Scotter w E Ferry *Linc* 80-92; rtd 92; Zimbabwe 94; Perm to Offic *Ban* from 97 and *Bradf* from 00. *18 Park Place, Hellifield, Skipton BD23 4HB* Tel (01729) 850310

BIRD, Douglas Norman. b 38. LNSM course 89. **d** 92 **p** 93. OLM New Bury *Man* from 92. *10 Hawthorne Avenue, Horwich, Bolton BL6 6JD* Tel (01204) 480000

BIRD, Canon Frederick Hinton. b 38. St Edm Hall Ox BA62 MA66 Univ of Wales MEd81 PhD86. St D Coll Lamp BD65. **d** 65 **p** 66. C Mynyddislwyn *Mon* 65-67; Min Can St Woolos Cathl 67-70; Chapl Anglo-American Coll Farringdon 70-71; Perm to Offic *Ox* 70-78; *Cant* 72-78 and *Mon* 76-82; V Rushen *S & M* 82-03; Can St German's Cathl from 93; rtd 03. *Conrhenny, 56 Selborne Drive, Douglas, Isle of Man IM2 3NL* Tel (01624) 621624

BIRD, Geoffrey. b 44. Dioc OLM tr scheme 97. **d** 99 **p** 00. Asst Chapl HM YOI and Remand Cen Brinsford 99; Sen Chapl 99-04; Chapl HM Pris Shepton Mallet from 04. *HM Prison, 3 Cornhill, Shepton Mallet BA4 5LU* Tel (01749) 343377

BIRD, Canon Geoffrey Neville. b 22. AKC48. St Boniface Warminster 48. **d** 49 **p** 50. C Berkeley *Glouc* 49-53; C Malden St Jo *S'wark* 53-54; C Glouc St Aldate *Glouc* 54-56; R Edge w

Pitchcombe 56-82; P-in-c Brookthorpe w Whaddon and Harescombe 76-82; R The Edge, Pitchcombe, Harescombe and Brookthorpe 82-90; Hon Can Glouc Cathl 83-90; RD Bisley 84-90; rtd 90; Perm to Offic *Glouc* from 90. *Ivycroft, Winstone, Cirencester GL7 7JZ* Tel (01285) 821664

BIRD, Graham Desmond. b 44. **d** 02. OLM Stalham, E Ruston, Brunstead, Sutton and Ingham *Nor* from 02. *Cephas House, Camping Field Lane, Stalham, Norwich NR12 9DZ* Tel (01692) 581560 E-mail gbird29714621@aol.com

BIRD, Henry John Joseph. b 37. ARCO58 Qu Coll Cam BA59 MA63. Linc Th Coll 62. **d** 64 **p** 65. C Harbledown *Cant* 64-68; C Skipton H Trin *Bradf* 68-70; V Oakworth 70-81; Chapl Abingdon Sch 81-82; P-in-c Doncaster St Geo *Sheff* 82-85; V 85-02; rtd 02. *332 Thorne Road, Doncaster DN2 5AL* Tel (01302) 326041

BIRD, Hinton. *See* BIRD, Canon Frederick Hinton

BIRD, Hugh Claud Handley. b 24. FRCGP SS Coll Cam MA MB BCh. Ridley Hall Cam. **d** 86 **p** 86. NSM Coxheath w E Farleigh, Hunton and Linton *Roch* 86-95; Perm to Offic *Cant* from 95. *The Slate Barn, Seamark Road, Brooksend, Birchington CT7 0JL* Tel (01843) 846619

BIRD, Jeffrey David. b 54. Nottm Univ BCombStuds85. Linc Th Coll 82. **d** 85 **p** 86. C Frome St Jo *B & W* 85-88; Asst Chapl HM Pris Pentonville 88-89; Chapl HM Pris Dartmoor 89-95; Chapl HM Pris Albany 95-03; Chapl HM Pris Linc from 03; Gen Preacher *Linc* from 03. *The Chaplain's Office, HM Prison, Greetwell Road, Lincoln LN2 4BD* Tel (01522) 663090 Fax 663001

BIRD, Jeremy Paul. b 56. Ex Univ BSc77 DipTh78 Hull Univ MA88. Sarum Th Coll 78. **d** 80 **p** 81. C Tavistock and Gulworthy *Ex* 80-83; Chapl Teesside Poly *York* 83-88; R Chipstable w Huish Champflower and Clatworthy *B & W* 88-93; Rural Affairs Officer 88-93; V Uffculme *Ex* 93-01; P-in-c Dawlish from 01. *The Vicarage, 13 West Cliff Road, Dawlish EX7 9EB* Tel (01626) 862021 E-mail jerry@credamus.freeserve.co.uk

BIRD, John. *See* BIRD, Henry John Joseph

BIRD, John Anthony. b 45. EMMTC 00. **d** 03 **p** 04. NSM Thringstone St Andr *Leic* from 03. *8 Buckingham Drive, Loughborough LE11 4TE* Tel (01509) 234962

BIRD, Maurice Pidding. b 19. Linc Coll Ox BA40 MA44. Cuddesdon Coll 40. **d** 42 **p** 43. C Malden St Jo *S'wark* 42-43; C Headington *Ox* 43-46; C Eastney *Portsm* 47-55; Chapl Hostel of God Clapham 55-59; R Winterton w E Somerton *Nor* 59-71; V Heigham St Barn 71-75; V Heigham St Barn w St Bart 75-82; P-in-c Edington and Imber *Sarum* 82-83; P-in-c Erlestoke and Gt Cheverell 82-83; P-in-c Edington and Imber, Erlestoke and E Coulston 83-88; rtd 88; Perm to Offic *Ripon* and *Wakef* from 88. *61 Beechwood, Woodlesford, Leeds LS26 8PQ* Tel 0113-282 0865

BIRD, Nicholas William Randle. b 70. RGN92 Univ of Cen England in Birm BSc99. NEOC 02. **d** 05. C Thirsk *York* from 05. *3 Herriot Way, Thirsk YO7 1FL* Tel (01845) 523812 E-mail nick@benbird.freeserve.co.uk

BIRD, Norman David. b 32. CQSW73. Coll of Resurr Mirfield 87. **d** 89 **p** 90. NSM Willesden Green St Andr and St Fran *Lon* 89-92; NSM Preston Ascension 93-98; rtd 98; Perm to Offic *Lon* from 99. *5 Oldfield Road, London NW10 9UD* Tel (020) 8451 4160

BIRD, Canon Peter Andrew. b 40. Wadh Coll Ox BA62 MA68. Ridley Hall Cam 63. **d** 65 **p** 66. C Keynsham w Queen Charlton *B & W* 65-68; C Strood St Nic *Roch* 68-72; TV Strood 72-79; V S Gillingham 79-89; V Westerham 89-02; Hon Can Roch Cathl 01-02; Perm to Offic from 02. *Iona Prospect View, Stanedge Road, Bakewell DE45 1DG* Tel (01629) 813087

BIRD, Rex Alan. b 30. Trin Coll Bris 54. **d** 57 **p** 58. C Wellington Ch Ch *Lich* 57-59; C St Alb St Paul *St Alb* 59-61; V Rainham *Chelmsf* 61-65; R Wennington 61-65; R Lavenham *St E* 65-75; CF (TA) from 65; RD Lavenham *St E* 72-75; Dean and V Battle *Chich* 75-84; V Castle Hedingham *Chelmsf* 84-91; R Monks Eleigh w Chelsworth and Brent Eleigh etc *St E* 91-99; rtd 99; Perm to Offic *St E* from 00. *6 Deacons Close, Lavenham, Sudbury CO10 9SZ* Tel (01787) 247657

BIRD, Richard. *See* BIRD, The Ven Colin Richard Bateman

BIRD, Canon Roger Alfred. b 49. AKC72. St Aug Coll Cant 72. **d** 73 **p** 74. C Prestatyn *St As* 73-78; R Llandysilio and Penrhos and Llandrinio etc 78-92; Dioc RE Adv from 84; Dioc Dir of Educn from 89; R Guilsfield 92-97; R Guilsfield w Pool Quay 97-02; V Guilsfield w Buttington from 02; Hon Can St As Cathl from 93; RD Pool 96-01. *The Vicarage, Guilsfield, Welshpool SY21 9NF* Tel and fax (01938) 554245 E-mail rogerb@infinnet.co.uk

BIRDSEYE, Miss Jacqueline Ann. b 55. Sussex Univ BEd78 Southn Univ BTh88 K Coll Lon MTh93. Sarum & Wells Th Coll 85. **d** 88 **p** 94. C Egham Hythe *Guildf* 88-91; C Fleet 91-92; C Shottermill 92-95; C Leavesden All SS *St Alb* 95-98; R Ashwell w Hinxworth and Newnham 98-05; R Moreton and Woodsford w Tincleton *Sarum* from 05. *The Rectory, 17 Warmwell Road, Crossways, Dorchester DT2 8BS* Tel (01305) 854046

BIRDWOOD, William Halhed. b 51. St Jo Coll Dur BA73. Sarum & Wells Th Coll 76. **d** 78 **p** 79. C Royston *St Alb* 78-82; C Thorley w Bishop's Stortford H Trin 82-89; Chapl HM Pris Ex 89-96; Chapl HM Pris Dartmoor from 96; Lic to Offic *Ex* from 89. *HM Prison Dartmoor, Princetown, Yelverton PL20 6RR* Tel (01822) 890261 Fax 890679

BIRKENHEAD, Suffragan Bishop of. *See* URQUHART, The Rt Revd David Andrew

BIRKET, Cyril. b 28. Cen Lancs Univ BA04 ACIS70. NW Ord Course 71. **d** 74 **p** 75. C Broughton *Blackb* 74-79; V Wesham 79-86; V Overton 86-96; rtd 96; Perm to Offic *Blackb* from 96. *61 Twemlow Parade, Heysham, Morecambe LA3 2AL* Tel (01524) 852870 E-mail cyril@clerical.freeserve.co.uk

BIRKETT, Mrs Joyce. b 38. WMMTC 84. **d** 87 **p** 94. Par Dn Hill *Birm* 87-91; Asst Chapl Highcroft Hosp Birm 87-91; Par Dn Rowley Regis *Birm* 91-94; C 94-96; V Londonderry 96-01; rtd 01. *83 Callowbrook Lane, Rubery, Rednal, Birmingham B45 9HP* Tel 0121-457 9759

BIRKETT, Neil Warren. b 45. Lanc Univ BEd74 Southn Univ MA84. Kelham Th Coll 65. **d** 77 **p** 77. NSM Win St Matt *Win* from 77. *Corrymeela, 132 Teg Down Meads, Winchester SO22 5NS* Tel (01962) 864910

BIRKIN, Mrs Elspeth Joyce (Joy). b 36. CertEd58. WMMTC 95. **d** 96 **p** 97. NSM Hanley Castle, Hanley Swan and Welland *Worc* 96-01; NSM Berrow w Pendock, Eldersfield, Hollybush etc 01-04; Perm to Offic from 04. *9 Hastings Road, Malvern WR14 2SS* Tel (01684) 569493

BIRKINSHAW, Ian George. b 58. Pemb Coll Ox BA81 Leeds Univ MA97 Sheff Univ PGCE82. N Ord Course 93. **d** 96 **p** 97. NSM Chapeltown *Sheff* 96-97; C Normanton *Wakef* 98-01; C York St Mich-le-Belfrey *York* from 01. *13 Hempland Drive, York YO31 1AY* Tel (01904) 427802

BIRMINGHAM, Archdeacon of. *See* OSBORNE, The Ven Hayward John

BIRMINGHAM, Bishop of. *Vacant*

BIRMINGHAM, Dean of. *See* MURSELL, The Rt Revd Alfred Gordon

BIRNIE, Ms Ruth Burdett. b 41. Glas Univ MA64 Jordanhill Coll Glas PGCE65 Leeds Univ MA73. NEOC 02. **d** 04 **p** 05. NSM Gosforth All SS *Newc* from 04. *27 Delaval Terrace, Newcastle upon Tyne NE3 4RT* Tel 0191-284 1393 E-mail ruth@birnie27.fsnet.co.uk

BIRT, David Edward. b 26. St Steph Ho Ox 86. **d** 86 **p** 87. NSM Ealing Ch the Sav *Lon* 86-99; Perm to Offic from 99. *10 Manor Court Road, London W7 3EL* Tel (020) 8579 4871

BIRT, Patrick. b 34. Glouc Th Course 71. **d** 75 **p** 75. NSM Bisley *Glouc* 75-76; NSM Whiteshill 76-81; C Stroud H Trin 81; R Ruardean 81-86; V Newbridge-on-Wye and Llanfihangel Brynpabuan *S & B* 86-88; TV Gillingham *Sarum* 88-99; rtd 99; Perm to Offic *Sarum* from 01. *Hornbeam Cottage, Green Lane, Stour Row, Shaftesbury SP7 0QD* Tel (01747) 839716

BIRT, Richard Arthur. b 43. Ch Ch Ox BA66 MA69. Cuddesdon Coll 67. **d** 69 **p** 70. C Sutton St Mich *York* 69-71; C Wollaton *S'well* 71-75; R Kirkby in Ashfield 75-80; P-in-c Duxford *Ely* 80-87; R 87-88; P-in-c Hinxton 80-87; V 87-88; P-in-c Ickleton 80-87; V 87-88; V Weobley w Sarnesfield and Norton Canon *Heref* 88-00; P-in-c Letton w Staunton, Byford, Mansel Gamage etc 88-00; rtd 00; Perm to Offic *Heref* from 00. *18 Ingestre Street, Hereford HR4 0DU*

BIRTWISTLE, Canon James. b 33. FCA66. Ely Th Coll 57. **d** 59 **p** 60. C Southport St Luke *Liv* 59-63; V Cleator Moor w Cleator *Carl* 63-70; R Letchworth *St Alb* 70-73; P-in-c Wareside 73-80; Dep Dir of Educn 77-80; Dioc Dir of Educn 80-98; Hon Can St Alb 85-98; P-in-c Hertingfordbury 88-98; rtd 98; Perm to Offic *Ex* from 99. *9 Stoneborough Lane, Budleigh Salterton EX9 6HL* Tel (01395) 442517

BIRTWISTLE, Lesley Sutherland. b 44. LLB. EMMTC 00. **d** 00 **p** 01. NSM Appleby Gp *Leic* from 00. *14 Nethercroft Drive, Packington, Ashby-de-la-Zouch LE65 1WT* Tel (01530) 833333 *or* 413309 E-mail bwistle@btinternet.com

BISASO-SEKITOLEKO, Capt Samuel. b 66. Cheltenham & Glouc Coll of HE BA99. St Paul's Coll Limuru. **d** 99 **p** 02. NSM Matson *Glouc* 99; NSM Ponders End St Matt *Lon* 01-02; NSM Brownswood Park from 02. *St John's Vicarage, 2A Gloucester Drive, London N4 2LW*

BISCOE, Clive. b 45. St Deiniol's Hawarden 85. **d** 86 **p** 87. C Llansamlet *S & B* 86-90; V Landore 90-91. *6 Hazelwood Row, Cwmavon, Port Talbot SA12 9DP*

BISH, Donald. b 26. Ripon Hall Ox. **d** 75 **p** 75. C S Gillingham *Roch* 75-79; R Wateringbury w Teston and W Farleigh 79-92; rtd 92; Perm to Offic *Cant* from 92; Perm to Offic *Roch* 92-98 and from 00. *5 Eynesford Road, Allington, Maidstone ME16 0TD* Tel (01622) 661847

BISHOP, Mrs Alice Margaret Marion. b 67. Newnham Coll Cam BA89 MA93 Lon Univ MTh92. St Steph Ho Ox 92. **d** 94. C Stepney St Dunstan and All SS *Lon* 94-99. *The Vicarage, Church Lane, Old Basing, Basingstoke RG24 7DJ* Tel (01256) 473762

BISHOP, Andrew Scott. b 70. Leeds Univ BA93 Heythrop Coll Lon MTh02. St Steph Ho Ox BTh93. **d** 96 **p** 97. C Westmr St Steph w St Jo *Lon* 96-99; C Kensington St Mary Abbots w St Geo 99-03; V Basing *Win* from 03. *The Vicarage, Church Lane, Old Basing, Basingstoke RG24 7DJ* Tel (01256) 473762 E-mail andrew_bishop@talk21.com

BISHOP, Canon Anthony John. b 43. G&C Coll Cam BA66 MA69 Lon Univ MTh69. ALCD67. **d** 69 **p** 70. C Eccleston St Luke *Liv* 69-73; C Gt Baddow *Chelmsf* 73-77; Nigeria 77-84; Lect Lon Bible Coll 84-85; TV Chigwell *Chelmsf* 85-93; P-in-c Walthamstow St Jo 93-98; V from 98; Hon Can Kano from 00. *St John's Vicarage, 18 Brookscroft Road, London E17 4LH* Tel (020) 8531 6249 E-mail bishop@fish.co.uk

BISHOP, The Ven Anthony Peter. b 46. CB01. Nottm Univ LTh74 MPhil84 ALCD71 FRSA87. St Jo Coll Nottm 71. **d** 71 **p** 72. C Beckenham St Geo *Roch* 71-75; Chapl RAF 75-91; Command Chapl RAF 91-98; Chapl-in-Chief RAF 98-01; Can and Preb Linc Cathl *Linc* 98-01; Hon C Tewkesbury w Walton Cardiff and Twyning *Glouc* 01-03; C from 03. *The Vicarage, Churchend, Twyning GL20 6DA* Tel (01684) 290765

BISHOP, Miss Cecil Marie. b 18. Lon Univ LLB40 DipTh48. St Chris Coll Blackheath 46 Gilmore Ho 56. **dss** 57 **d** 87. Jamaica 57-74; The Gambia 74-76; Lic to Offic *Ex* 76-87; rtd 78; Hon Par Dn Paignton St Jo *Ex* 87-94; Perm to Offic from 94. *5 Lancaster House, Belle Vue Road, Paignton TQ4 6HD* Tel (01803) 523522

BISHOP, Canon Christopher. b 48. St Aug Coll Cant 71. **d** 72 **p** 73. C Gt Ilford St Mary *Chelmsf* 72-75; C Upminster 75-78; Adn's Youth Chapl 77-80; Dioc Youth Officer 80-86; Chapl Stansted Airport from 86; P-in-c Manuden w Berden 86-03; P-in-c Manuden w Berden and Quendon w Rickling from 03; RD Newport and Stansted from 89; Hon Can Chelmsf Cathl from 99. *The Vicarage, 24 Mallows Green Road, Manuden, Bishops Stortford CM23 1DG* Tel (01279) 812228 E-mail chrismitre@hotmail.com

BISHOP, Craig. *See* BISHOP, Stephen Craig

BISHOP, David. b 65. St Jo Coll Nottm 01. **d** 03 **p** 04. C Boulton *Derby* from 03. *2 Rosemary Drive, Alvaston, Derby DE24 0TA* Tel (01332) 576042

BISHOP, Canon David Harold. b 28. ARIBA53 FRSA75 DipArch. Westcott Ho Cam 55. **d** 57 **p** 58. C Cannock *Lich* 57-61; C Gt Barr 61-67; V All Hallows Lon Wall *Lon* 67-80; Architectural Adv CCC 67-80; Can Res Nor Cathl *Nor* 80-92; Vice-Dean 84-92; rtd 92; Perm to Offic *Sarum* from 92. *Coneycote, 6 Coneygar Park, Bridport DT6 3BA* Tel (01308) 424673

BISHOP, David Henry Ryder. b 27. R Agric Coll Cirencester MRAC50. Tyndale Hall Bris 54. **d** 57 **p** 58. C Sevenoaks St Nic *Roch* 57-59; C Branksome St Clem *Sarum* 59-63; Chapl Jinja Uganda 64-67; Dep Sec CCCS 68; R Ox St Clem *Ox* 69-91; Zimbabwe 91-93; rtd 93; Perm to Offic *Ox* from 99. *40 Old High Street, Headington, Oxford OX3 9HN* Tel (01865) 760099 E-mail david@bishox.go-plus.net

BISHOP, Donald. b 22. Lon Univ BSc48. Qu Coll Birm 56. **d** 57 **p** 58. C Trowbridge H Trin *Sarum* 57-60; CF (TA) 58-68; V Bodicote *Ox* 60-87; P-in-c Broughton 71-85; rtd 87; Perm to Offic *Cov* 87-01 and *Wakef* from 01. *17 Westminster Road, Halifax HX3 8DH* Tel (01422) 200844

BISHOP, Huw Daniel. b 49. Univ of Wales (Lamp) BA71 DipTh73. Bp Burgess Hall Lamp CPS73. **d** 73 **p** 74. C Carmarthen St Pet *St D* 73-77; Prov Youth Chapl Wales 77-79; V Llanybydder and Llanwenog w Llanwnnen 79-80; Youth and Community Officer 80-81; Hd RS Carre's Gr Sch Sleaford 81-85; Hd RS K Sch Pet 85-92; Lic to Offic *Linc* 83-95; CF (TA) from 85; Perm to Offic *Pet* 86-92 and *Lich* 92-00. *Address temp unknown*

BISHOP, Ian Gregory. b 62. Portsm Poly BSc84 MRICS87. Oak Hill Th Coll BA91. **d** 91 **p** 92. C Purley Ch Ch *S'wark* 91-95; P-in-c Saxlingham Nethergate and Shotesham *Nor* 95-97; TR Newton Flotman, Swainsthorpe, Tasburgh, etc 98-01; V Middlewich w Byley *Ches* from 01; RD Middlewich from 05. *St Michael's Vicarage, 37 Queen's Street, Middlewich CW10 9AR* Tel (01606) 833124 E-mail ian@bishopfamily.fsnet.co.uk

BISHOP, Jeremy Simon. b 54. Nottm Univ BSc75 Yonsei Univ S Korea 84. All Nations Chr Coll 82 Wycliffe Hall Ox 89. **d** 91 **p** 92. C Macclesfield Team Par *Ches* 91-98; R Carlton Colville w Mutford and Rushmere *Nor* 98-99; V Carlton Colville and Mutford from 99. *The Rectory, Rectory Road, Carlton Colville, Lowestoft NR33 8BB* Tel (01502) 565217

BISHOP, John Baylis. b 32. Selw Coll Cam BA54 MA58. Cuddesdon Coll 54. **d** 56 **p** 57. C Middlesbrough St Oswald *York* 56-59; C Romsey *Win* 59-62; Chapl RN 62-66; P-in-c Linc St Mary-le-Wigford w St Martin *Linc* 66-67; V Linc St Faith 66-68; V Linc St Faith and St Martin w St Pet 69-71; Lic to Offic *Bris* 72-84; C Henbury 84-87; TV Bris St Agnes and St Simon w St Werburgh 87; TV Bris St Paul's 87-92; P-in-c Barrow Gurney *B & W* 92-98; P-in-c Flax Bourton 92-98; Asst Resources Adv 92-94; rtd 98. *56 Darren View, Crickhowell NP8 1DS* Tel (01873) 812167

BISHOP, John Charles Simeon. b 46. Chich Th Coll 77. **d** 79 **p** 79. SSF 66-86; P-in-c Edin St Dav *Edin* 82-86; Chapl to the Deaf *Birm* 86-99; C Portsea N End St Mark *Portsm* 99-01; Chapl to the Deaf *Linc* from 01. *220 Boultham Park Road, Lincoln LN6 7SU* Tel and fax (01522) 787136 E-mail revsimeonbishop@aol.com

BISHOP, John David. b 36. Liv Univ BEng MIMechE. EMMTC. **d** 85 **p** 86. NSM Ockbrook *Derby* from 85. *143 Victoria Avenue, Borrowash, Derby DE7 3HF* Tel (01332) 663828

BISHOP, Joy. **d** 01. NSM Penkridge Team *Lich* 01-04; NSM Baswich from 04. *21 Farmdown Road, Stafford ST17 0AP* Tel (01785) 603074

BISHOP, Keith William. b 45. SEITE 00. **d** 03 **p** 04. NSM Balham St Mary and St Jo *S'wark* from 03. *43 Magdalen Road, London SW18 3ND* Tel (020) 8870 7267 E-mail keithwilliambishop@hotmail.com

BISHOP, Mark Andrew. b 58. Down Coll Cam BA80 MA83 Barrister 81. EAMTC 99. **d** 02 **p** 03. Dep Chan *Roch* from 01; NSM Cambridge St Mary Less *Ely* from 02. *10 Wordsworth Grove, Cambridge CB3 9HH* Tel (01223) 362281 Fax 323247 E-mail markbishop@ukonline.co.uk

BISHOP, Michael George. b 27. Wycliffe Hall Ox 63. **d** 65 **p** 66. C Cheltenham St Mary *Glouc* 65-68; P-in-c Edale *Derby* 68-71; V Doveridge 71-79; Chapl HM Det Cen Foston Hall 73-79; V Cotmanhay *Derby* 79-81; Chapl Ilkeston Gen Hosp 79-81; USA 81-89; Perm to Offic *Chich* 89-02 and *Nor* from 03; rtd 92. *Cherry Tree Cottage, Gormans Lane, Colkirk, Fakenham NR21 7NP* Tel (01328) 853461

BISHOP, Philip Michael. b 47. Lon Univ BD69 AKC69. St Aug Coll Cant 70. **d** 71 **p** 72. C Mansfield Woodhouse *S'well* 71-76; C Liscard St Mary w St Columba *Ches* 76-78; V Thornton-le-Moors w Ince and Elton 78-90; V Sutton w Carlton and Normanton upon Trent etc *S'well* 90-96; P-in-c Ch Broughton w Barton Blount, Boylestone etc *Derby* 96-98; P-in-c Longford, Long Lane, Dalbury and Radbourne 96-98; R Boylestone, Church Broughton, Dalbury, etc from 98. *The Vicarage, Chapel Lane, Church Broughton, Derby DE65 5BB* Tel (01283) 585296 E-mail p.michael.bishop@ntlworld.com

BISHOP, Phillip Leslie. b 44. K Coll Lon BD66 AKC66. **d** 67 **p** 68. C Albrighton *Lich* 67-70; C St Geo-in-the-East St Mary *Lon* 70-71; C Middlesbrough Ascension *York* 71-73; P-in-c Withernwick 73-77; Ind Chapl 73-82; V Gt Ayton w Easby and Newton in Cleveland 82-89; RD Stokesley 85-89; R Guisborough from 89; Chapl S Tees Community and Mental NHS Trust 90-99; Chapl Tees and NE Yorks NHS Trust from 99; Chapl Langbaurgh Primary Care Trust from 02. *The Rectory, Church Street, Guisborough TS14 6BS* Tel and fax (01287) 632588 E-mail phillip@guisrec.fsnet.co.uk

BISHOP, Simeon. *See* BISHOP, John Charles Simeon

BISHOP, Stephen Craig. b 68. Wye Coll Lon BSc90 Man Univ MA92 Ex Univ MPhil97 Glos Univ PGCE98. Wycliffe Hall Ox 03. **d** 05. C Thornbury and Oldbury-on-Severn w Shepperdine *Glouc* from 05. *50 Park Road, Thornbury, Bristol BS35 1HR*

BISHOP, Stephen John. b 62. Hull Univ BA84 PGCE86. Ripon Coll Cuddesdon 90 Ch Div Sch of the Pacific (USA) 90. **d** 92 **p** 93. C Syston *Leic* 92-95; C Market Harborough 95-97; TV Market Harborough and The Transfiguration etc 97-00; R Six Saints circa Holt from 00; Rural Officer (Leic Adnry) from 01. *The Rectory, Rectory Lane, Medbourne, Market Harborough LE16 8DZ* Tel (01858) 565933 E-mail stephenjbishop@btopenworld.com

BISHOP, Stephen Patrick. b 60. Dioc OLM tr scheme 99. **d** 02 **p** 03. OLM Purley Ch Ch *S'wark* from 02. *Elmwood, 117 Mitchley Avenue, South Croydon CR2 9HP* Tel (020) 8651 2840 E-mail elmwood@tinyonline.co.uk

BISHOP, Miss Waveney Joyce. b 38. Westf Coll Lon BSc60. Cranmer Hall Dur DipTh72. **dss** 82 **d** 87 **p** 94. Leyton St Mary w St Edw *Chelmsf* 82-84; Bishopsworth *Bris* 84-96; Hon Par Dn 87-94; Hon C 94-96; rtd 96; Perm to Offic *Bris* 96-99 and *B & W* from 98. *14 Saxby Close, Clevedon BS21 7YF* Tel (01275) 343533

BISHTON, Gerald Arthur. b 32. MRSH76 Ruskin Coll Ox Dip Economics 56 St Pet Hall Ox BA59 MA63. Qu Coll Birm 60. **d** 61 **p** 62. C Forest Gate St Edm *Chelmsf* 61-64; Asst Chapl Lon Univ *Lon* 64-67; Chapl NE Lon Poly 68-73; Sen Lect 73-80; Chapl St Mary's Hosp Gt Ilford 68-80; Ind Chapl *Chelmsf* 80-97; P-in-c Shopland 80-89; P-in-c Sutton 80-89; P-in-c Sutton w Shopland 89-97; rtd 97; Perm to Offic *Leic* and *Pet* from 97. *32 Horsefair Close, Market Harborough LE16 9QP* Tel (01858) 466141

BISIG (née BOULNOIS), Linda Dianne. b 59. Trin Coll Bris 92. **d** 96 **p** 97. C Brampton Bierlow *Sheff* 96-99; Asst Chapl Berne w Neuchâtel *Eur* from 00. *Jubiläumsplatz 2, CH-3066 Bern, Switzerland* Tel (0041) (31) 352 8567 Fax 351 0548

BISSET, Michael Davidson. b 55. NTMTC DipTS99. **d** 99 **p** 00. C Ickenham *Lon* 99-03; P-in-c Penn *Ox* 03-04; P-in-c Tyler's Green 03-04; V Penn and Tylers Green from 04. *The Vicarage, Church Road, Penn, High Wycombe HP10 8NU* Tel (01895) 676092 E-mail mike.bisset@talk21.com

BISSET, Canon Robert McBain. b 05. Glas Univ MA30. Edin Th Coll 30. **d** 32 **p** 33. C Glas Ch Ch *Glas* 32-37; I Glas St Luke 37-41; R Lanark 41-47; R Bearsden 47-73; R Milngavie 56-73; Can St Mary's Cathl 62-73; rtd 73; Hon Can St Mary's Cathl *Glas* from 77. *Rannoch Lodge, Rannoch Drive, Cumbernauld, Glasgow G67 4EP* Tel (01236) 729273

BISSEX, Mrs Janet Christine Margaret. b 50. Westhill Coll Birm CertEd72. Trin Coll Bris 76. **dss** 86 **d** 87 **p** 94. Toxteth Park St Bede *Liv* 86-93; Par Dn 87-93; Dn-in-c Kirkdale St Mary and St Athanasius 93-94; P-in-c 94-03; C Litherland St Andr 03; TV Bootle from 04. *The Vicarage, 4 St Andrews Road, Bootle L20 5EX* Tel 0151-922 7916 Fax 944 1121 E-mail bissexj@fish.co.uk

BLACK, Canon Alexander Stevenson. b 28. Glas Univ MA53. Edin Th Coll 53. **d** 55 **p** 56. C Dumfries *Glas* 55-58; Chapl Glas Univ 58-61; C Glas St Mary 58-61; P-in-c E Kilbride 61-69; R Edin St Columba *Edin* 69-79; TV Edin St Jo 79-83; R Haddington 83-93; R Dunbar 83-93; Can St Mary's Cathl from 88; rtd 93. *3 Bass Rock View, Canty Bay, North Berwick EH39 5PJ* Tel (01620) 894771

BLACK, Anne. *See* BLACK, Mrs Elizabeth Anne

BLACK, Dominic Paul. b 70. S Bank Univ BSc95 St Jo Coll Dur BA98. Cranmer Hall Dur 95. **d** 98 **p** 99. C N Hull St Mich *York* 98-04; V N Ormesby from 04. *The Vicarage, James Street, North Ormesby, Middlesbrough TS3 6LD* Tel (01642) 271814

BLACK, Douglas John. b 58. Middx Poly BA80 CertMS84. Ridley Hall Cam 89. **d** 91 **p** 92. C Wrexham *St As* 91-01; Chapl NE Wales Inst HE 93-01; V Thelwall *Ches* from 02. *All Saints' Vicarage, Bell Lane, Thelwall, Warrington WA4 2SX* Tel (01925) 261166 E-mail revdouglasblack@aol.com

BLACK, Mrs Elizabeth Anne. b 47. Qu Coll Birm 80 Cranmer Hall Dur 81. **dss** 82 **d** 87 **p** 03. Cleadon *Dur* 82-85; S Westoe 85-88; Par Dn 87-88; Par Dn Chester le Street 88-92; Emmaus Chr Healing Trust 93-02; NE Regional Co-ord Acorn Chr Foundn from 00; NSM Barony of Burgh *Carl* from 02. *The Gables, Monkhill Road, Moorhouse, Carlisle CA5 6ER* Tel (01228) 575064 E-mail eabgables@aol.com

BLACK, Ian Christopher. b 62. Kent Univ BA85 Nottm Univ MDiv93. Linc Th Coll 91. **d** 93 **p** 94. C Maidstone All SS and St Phil w Tovil *Cant* 93-96; P-in-c The Brents and Davington w Oare and Luddenham 96-02; Hon Min Can Cant Cathl 97-02; Asst Dir Post-Ord Tr 98-02; V Whitkirk *Ripon* from 02. *Whitkirk Vicarage, 386 Selby Road, Leeds LS15 0AA* Tel 0113-264 5790 E-mail icblack@btinternet.com

BLACK, Ian Forbes. b 29. St Aid Birkenhead 55. **d** 58 **p** 59. C Bramhall *Ches* 58-61; C Witton 61-63; P-in-c Prestonpans *Edin* 63-68; R Edin Ch Ch-St Jas 68-71; Asst Chapl HM Pris Liv 71-72; Chapl HM Pris Haverigg 72-73; R Bootle w Corney *Carl* 73-75; P-in-c Whicham w Whitbeck 73-75; R Bootle, Corney, Whicham and Whitbeck 75-86; P-in-c Orton St Giles 86-89; R 89-94; P-in-c Aikton 86-89; R 89-94; rtd 94; Perm to Offic *Carl* from 98. *Solwayside, Port Carlisle, Wigton CA7 5BU* Tel (01697) 351964

BLACK (formerly NAPIER), Jennifer Beryl. b 39. S Dios Minl Tr Scheme 89. **d** 93 **p** 96. NSM Itchen Valley *Win* 93-01; Perm to Offic from 02. *Old Pump House, Kilmeston, Alresford SO24 0NL* Tel (01962) 771702

BLACK, The Very Revd Leonard Albert. b 49. Edin Th Coll 69. **d** 72 **p** 73. C Aberdeen St Marg *Ab* 72-75; Chapl St Paul's Cathl Dundee *Bre* 75-77; P-in-c Aberdeen St Ninian *Ab* 77-80; N Area Chapl Miss to Seafarers 80-03; R Inverness St Mich *Mor* from 80; R Inverness St Jo 80-87; P-in-c Balloch New Town Distr 80-87; Relig Progr Producer Moray Firth Radio 87-03; Syn Clerk and Can St Andr Cathl Inverness *Mor* 92-03; Dean Mor from 03. *St Michael's Rectory, Abban Street, Inverness IV3 8HH* Tel (01463) 224433 *or* tel and fax 233797 Mobile 07836-365719 E-mail st.michael@angelforce.co.uk

BLACK, Canon Neville. b 36. MBE97. Oak Hill Th Coll 61. **d** 64 **p** 65. C Everton St Ambrose w St Tim *Liv* 64-69; P-in-c Everton St Geo 69-71; V 71-81; P-in-c Everton St Benedict 70-72; P-in-c Everton St Chad w Ch Ch 70-72; Nat Project Officer Evang Urban Tr Project 74-81; TR St Luke in the City 81-04; Chapl Liv Women's Hosp 82-92; Chapl Liv Women's Hosp NHS Trust 92-04; Tutor N Ord Course 82-89; Dir Gp for Urban Min and Leadership *Liv* 84-95; Hon Can Liv Cathl 87-04; P-in-c Edgehill St Dunstan 98-02; rtd 05. *445 Aigburth Road, Liverpool L19 3PA* Tel 0151-427 9803 Fax 494 0736 Pager 07699-727640 E-mail neville.black@btinternet.com

BLACK, Canon Robert John Edward Francis Butler. b 41. TCD BA65 HDipEd70 DipG&C80 MA85. CITC 66. **d** 66 **p** 67. C Jordanstown *Conn* 66-68; C Dublin St Steph and St Ann *D & G* 68-73; C Stillorgan w Blackrock 73-85; Hd Master Dundalk Gr Sch *Arm* 85-96; Lic to Offic from 85; Hd Master Kilkenny Coll *C & O* from 96; Can Ossory Cathl from 96. *Kilkenny College, Kilkenny, Co Kilkenny, Irish Republic* Tel (00353) (56) 772 2213 *or* 776 1544 Fax 777 0918

BLACK, Samuel James. b 38. CITC. **d** 68 **p** 69. C Cloughfern *Conn* 68-72; C Lisburn St Paul 72-78; I Rasharkin w Finvoy 78-82; I Belfast Upper Malone (Epiphany) 82-95; I Ballymore *Arm* from 95. *The Rectory, Glebe Hill Road, Tandragee, Craigavon BT62 2EP* Tel (028) 3884 0234

BLACK, William Henry. St Deiniol's Hawarden. **d** 88 **p** 89. NSM Malahide w Balgriffin *D & G* 88-89; NSM Dublin St Ann and St Steph 89-94; C 94-00; Hon Asst Chapl Miss to Seamen 89-00; I Dublin Drumcondra w N Strand *D & G* from 00. *The Rectory, 74 Grace Park Road, Drumcondra, Dublin 9, Irish Republic* Tel and fax (00353) (1) 837 2505

BLACKALL, Mrs Margaret Ivy. b 38. St Kath Coll Lon CertEd58. EAMTC 82. **dss** 86 **d** 87 **p** 94. NSM Wickham Market w Pettistree and Easton *St E* 86-88; Par Dn Leiston 88-92; Par Dn Gt and Lt Glemham, Blaxhall etc 92-94; P-in-c 94-96; R 96-02; P-in-c Sternfield w Benhall and Snape 98-02; rtd 03; Perm to Offic *St E* from 03. *6 Orchard Place, Wickham Market, Woodbridge IP13 0RU* Tel (01728) 747326 Mobile 07850-632900 E-mail mgtblack@globalnet.co.uk

BLACKALL, Robin Jeremy McRae. b 35. Ridley Hall Cam 67. **d** 69 **p** 70. C Stowmarket *St E* 69-72; R Stanstead w Shimplingthorne and Alpheton 72-77; R Bradwell on Sea *Chelmsf* 77-79; R St Lawrence 77-79; Warden Bede Ho Staplehurst 79-81; Chapl HM Det Cen Blantyre Ho 81-82; R Edith Weston w N Luffenham and Lyndon w Manton *Pet* 86-95; P-in-c Upwell St Pet *Ely* 95-99; P-in-c Outwell 95-99; Dioc Rural Miss Officer 95-01; P-in-c Barton Bendish w Beachamwell and Shingham 99-01; P-in-c Boughton 99-01; P-in-c Wereham 99-01; rtd 01; Perm to Offic *Ely* from 01 and *Nor* from 02. *The Pightle House, Eastmoor Road, Eastmoor, Oxborough, King's Lynn PE33 9PZ* Tel (01366) 328663 Fax 328163 E-mail rjmb@globalnet.co.uk

BLACKALL, Susan Elizabeth. b 52. Qu Univ Kingston Ontario BA74 MA75 CCC Ox DPhil82. SEITE 00. **d** 03 **p** 04. NSM Eltham St Barn *S'wark* from 03. *8 Park Place House, Park Vista, London SE10 9ND* Tel (020) 8853 3302 E-mail s.blackall@research-int.com

BLACKBURN, David James. b 45. Hull Univ BA67. Trin Coll Bris DipHE87. **d** 87 **p** 88. C Bromsgrove St Jo *Worc* 87-90; V Cradley 90-01; R Kinver and Enville *Lich* from 01. *The Vicarage, Vicarage Drive, Kinver, Stourbridge DY7 6HJ* Tel (01384) 872556

BLACKBURN, Frederick John Barrie. b 28. TD73. Lich Th Coll 52. **d** 55 **p** 56. C Hebburn St Cuth *Dur* 55-58; C Bishopwearmouth St Mary V w St Pet CD 58-61; V Hunwick 61-64; CF (TA) 61-87; V Eighton Banks *Dur* 64-75; R Stella 75-87; TV Bellingham/Otterburn Gp *Newc* 87-89; rtd 89. *26 Kepier Chare, Ryton NE40 4UW* Tel and fax 0191-413 7365 Mobile 07745-028780

BLACKBURN, Helen Claire. b 55. Leeds Univ BA76 MA00 PGCE78 ARCM75. N Ord Course 96. **d** 99 **p** 00. C Sheff Cathl *Sheff* 99-01; CA from 00; Asst Chapl Cen Sheff Univ Hosps NHS Trust 01-04; Chapl from 04. *Royal Hallamshire Hospital, Glossop Road, Sheffield S10 2JF* Tel 0114-271 1900 *or* 271 5056 E-mail helen.blackburn@sth.nhs.uk

BLACKBURN, The Ven John. b 47. CB04. Open Univ BA88. St Mich Coll Llan 66. **d** 71 **p** 72. C Risca *Mon* 71-76; CF (TA) 73-76; CF 76-99; Dep Chapl Gen 99-00; Chapl Gen 00-04; Adn for the Army 99-04; QHC from 96; Hon Can Ripon Cathl *Ripon* 01-04; V Risca *Mon* from 04. *The Vicarage, 1 Gelli Crescent, Risca, Newport NP11 6QG* Tel (01633) 612307 E-mail northmanor@btinternet.com

BLACKBURN, Sister Judith Elizabeth. b 58. SEITE 99. **d** 02 **p** 03. NSM Old Ford St Paul and St Mark *Lon* 02-05; P-in-c Bethnal Green St Pet w St Thos from 05. *St Saviour's Priory, 18 Queensbridge Road, London E2 8NX* Tel (020) 7739 9976 Mobile 07855-510393 E-mail judithblackburn@aol.com

BLACKBURN, Keith Christopher. b 39. K Coll Lon BD63 AKC63. St Boniface Warminster 63. **d** 64 **p** 65. C Surbiton St Andr *S'wark* 64-66; C Battersea St Mary 67-70; Teacher Sir Walter St Jo Sch Battersea 67-70; Hon C Eltham H Trin 70-76; Hd of Ho Crown Woods Sch Eltham 70-76; Dep Hd Master Altwood C of E Sch 76-82; Lic to Offic *Ox* 76-82; Chapl and Hd Master St Geo Sch Gravesend 83-93; Hon C Fawkham and Hartley *Roch* 83-93; V Seal St Pet 93-05; rtd 05. *The Tythe Barn, St Weonards, Hereford HR2 8NT* Tel (01981) 580389 E-mail revkcb@aol.com

BLACKBURN, Peter James Whittaker. b 47. Sydney Univ BA69. Coll of Resurr Mirfield DipTh71. **d** 72 **p** 73. C Felixstowe St Jo *St E* 72-76; C Bournemouth St Pet w St Swithun, H Trin etc *Win* 76-79; R Burythorpe, Acklam and Leavening w Westow *York* 79-85; Chapl Naples Ch Ch *Eur* 85-91; Chapl Algarve 91-97. *12 rue de la Cave Forte, 49730 Parnay, France*

BLACKBURN, The Ven Richard Finn. b 52. St Jo Coll Dur BA74 Hull Univ MA97. Westcott Ho Cam 81. **d** 83 **p** 84. C Stepney St Dunstan and All SS *Lon* 83-87; P-in-c Isleworth St Jo 87-92; V Mosbrough *Sheff* 92-99; RD Attercliffe 96-99; Hon Can Sheff Cathl 98-99; Adn Sheff and Rotherham from 99; Can Res Sheff Cathl 99-05. *34 Wilson Road, Sheffield S11 8RN* Tel 0114-266 6009 *or* (01709) 309110 Fax (01709) 309107 E-mail archdeacons.office@sheffield.anglican.org

BLACKBURN, William Ross. b 67. NW Univ Illinois BA90. Trin Episc Sch for Min Penn MDiv95. **d** 95. USA 95-01; NSM St Andrews St Andr *St And* from 01. *South Bowhill Farmhouse, Peat Inn, Cupar KY15 5LL* Tel (01334) 840567 E-mail wrossblackburn@yahoo.com

BLACKBURN, Archdeacon of. *See* HAWLEY, The Ven John Andrew

BLACKBURN, Bishop of. *See* READE, The Rt Revd Nicholas Stewart

BLACKBURN, Dean of. *See* ARMSTRONG, The Very Revd Christopher John

BLACKER, Herbert John. b 36. Bris Univ BSc59. Cranmer Hall Dur. **d** 61 **p** 62. C Wednesbury St Bart *Lich* 61-63; C Chasetown 63-65; C Chigwell *Chelmsf* 65-69; TV Barnham Broom w Kimberley, Bixton etc *Nor* 69-76; R Burgh Parva w Briston 76-92; P-in-c Melton Constable w Swanton Novers 86-92; R Briston w Burgh Parva and Melton Constable 92-01; rtd 01; Perm to Offic *Nor* from 01 and *St E* from 04. *227 Church Road, Kessingland, Lowestoft NR33 7SF* Tel (01502) 740554

BLACKETT, James Gilbert. b 27. Tyndale Hall Bris 52. **d** 55 **p** 56. C Heworth H Trin *York* 55-57; C Newburn *Newc* 57-58; C Newc St Barn and St Jude 58-61; V Broomfleet *York* 61-67; V Ledsham 67-74; V Burton All SS *Lich* 74-82; V Burton All SS w Ch Ch 82-92; rtd 92; Perm to Offic *Ox* and *Pet* from 92. *103 Milford Avenue, Stony Stratford, Milton Keynes MK11 1EZ* Tel (01908) 265149

BLACKETT, Robert Peter. b 63. Dur Univ BSc85. Ripon Coll Cuddesdon BTh95. **d** 95 **p** 96. C Wigton *Carl* 95-00; R Bowness-on-Solway, Kirkbride and Newton Arlosh from 00. *The Rectory, Church Road, Kirkbride, Carlisle CA7 5HY* Tel (01697) 351256

BLACKFORD, David Walker. b 25. Univ of Wales DipTh69. **d** 70 **p** 71. C Holyhead w Rhoscolyn w Llanfair-yn-Neubwll *Ban* 70-72; Lic to Offic *Blackb* 72-80; Hon C Bassaleg *Mon* 80-85; V Treuddyn and Nercwys and Eryrys *St As* 85-90; Lic to Offic *Mon* from 99. *11 Whitechapel Walk, Undy, Magor, Newport NP26 3NS* Tel (01633) 880507

BLACKHAM, Paul. b 70. BD PhD. AKC. **d** 97 **p** 98. C Langham Place All So *Lon* from 97. *20 Holcroft Court, Clipstone Street, London W1W 5DH* Tel (020) 7580 1033 *or* 7580 3522 E-mail paul.blackham@allsouls.org

BLACKIE, Richard Footner (Brother Edmund). b 37. St Cath Coll Cam BA59 MA63 Worc Coll Ox BA59 BSc61. Ely Th Coll 60. **d** 62 **p** 63. C Saffron Walden *Chelmsf* 62-65; SSF from 66. *Society of St Francis, 42 Balaam Street, London E13 8AQ* Tel (020) 7476 5189

BLACKLEDGE, David John. b 51. Oak Hill Th Coll 89. **d** 92 **p** 93. NSM Woodford Wells *Chelmsf* from 92. *Hornbeam, 143 Monkhams Lane, Woodford Green IG8 0NW* Tel (020) 8262 7690 E-mail djblackled@aol.com

BLACKLEDGE, Philip Vincent Patrick. b 74. Edin Univ BMus92 BD02. TISEC 99. **d** 02 **p** 03. C Edin St Mary *Edin* from 02; Chapl St Mary's Cathl from 03. *8 Grosvenor Street, Edinburgh EH12 5EG* Tel 0131-346 7653 E-mail chaplain@cathedral.net

BLACKMAN, Brian David Eric. b 38. Ox NSM Course 82. **d** 85 **p** 86. NSM Reading St Luke *Ox* 85-86; NSM Reading St Luke w St Bart from 86. *13 Avebury Square, Reading RG1 5JH* Tel 0118-926 0345

BLACKMAN (née PRATT), Christine Fiona. b 60. Reading Univ BSc81. Ox Min Course 88. **d** 91 **p** 94. NSM Reading St Luke w St Bart *Ox* 91-94; NSM Earley St Pet 94-95; NSM Reading St Luke w St Bart from 95. *13 Avebury Square, Reading RG1 5JH* Tel 0118-926 0345

BLACKMAN, Clive John. b 51. Hull Univ BSc73 MSc74. Qu Coll Birm 75. **d** 78 **p** 79. C Folkestone St Sav *Cant* 78-81; Chapl Birm Univ *Birm* 81-86; V Thorpe St Matt *Nor* 86-94; R Cringleford w Colney and Bawburgh 94-98; Asst Dir Lay and Reader Tr 98-03; Chapl Nor City Coll of F&HE from 03. *13 Norvic Drive, Norwich NR4 7NN* Tel (01603) 505776 E-mail cliveblackman@norwich.anglican.org

BLACKMAN, James Bentley. b 57. SS Hild & Bede Coll Dur BEd80 Nottm Univ BTh88. Linc Th Coll 85. **d** 88 **p** 89. C Nether Hoyland St Pet *Sheff* 88-91; C Harrogate St Wilfrid and St Luke *Ripon* 91-94; V Leyburn w Bellerby 94-01; Asst Chapl S Derbyshire Community and Mental Health Trust from 01. *42 Robincroft Road, Allestree, Derby DE22 2FR* Tel (01332) 554769 E-mail cyra@blackmanj57.fsnet.co.uk

BLACKMAN, John Franklyn. b 34. LRAM70 DipRS75. S'wark Ord Course 72. **d** 75 **p** 76. NSM Cov H Trin *Cov* 75-81; Succ Cov Cathl 81-95; TV Cov E 88-95; rtd 98; Perm to Offic *Newc* 98-01. *1 Old Deanery Close, Minster Road, Ripon HG4 1LZ*

BLACKMAN, Michael Orville. b 46. Univ of W Ontario BMin80 Univ of W Indies LTh70. Codrington Coll Barbados 67. **d** 71 **p** 71. C St Jo Cathl Antigua 71-73; R H Innocents w St Sav Barbados 73-78; Hon C Westminster St Jas Canada 78-80; P-in-c St Patr Barbados 80-86; TV E Ham w Upton Park St Alb *Chelmsf* 86-91; R St Pet Barbados 91-97; V Dalton *Sheff* 97-03; P-in-c S Wimbledon All SS *S'wark* from 03; P-in-c Raynes Park St Sav from 03. *St Saviour's Vicarage, Church Walk, London SW20 9DW* Tel (020) 8542 2787

BLACKMAN, Peter Richard. b 28. Sarum Th Coll 52. **d** 55 **p** 56. C Aylestone *Leic* 55-60; V Ratby cum Groby 60-84; TR 84-93; rtd 93; Perm to Offic *Chich* from 93. *25 Turnbull Road, Chichester PO19 7LY* Tel (01243) 787299

BLACKMORE, Cuthbert. b 17. Qu Coll Birm 57. **d** 59 **p** 60. C Acomb St Steph *York* 59-62; V Hackness w Harwood Dale 62-66; V Seamer w E Ayton 66-83; rtd 84; Perm to Offic *York* from 99. *85 West Garth, Cayton, Scarborough YO11 3SD* Tel (01723) 585156

BLACKMORE, Frank Ellis. b 43. Univ of Wales (Lamp) BA66. Wells Th Coll 65. **d** 67 **p** 68. C S'wark St Geo *S'wark* 67-70; Hon C Camberwell St Giles 70-79; NSM Paddington St Sav *Lon* from 79. *65 Sutherland Avenue, London W9 2HF* Tel (020) 7289 3020

BLACKMORE, Robert Ivor. b 37. Univ of Wales (Lamp) 59 Open Univ BA78 Univ of Wales MTh94. **d** 62 **p** 63. C Llangynwyd w Maesteg *Llan* 62-65; C Dowlais 65-67; C Neath w Llantwit 67-71; V Fochriw w Deri 71-73; V Troedrhiwgarth 73-80; V Seven Sisters 80-00; rtd 02. *Cefnforest, Bethlehem, Llandeilo SA19 6YL* Tel (01550) 777543

BLACKMORE, Vernon John. b 50. Southn Univ BSc Man Univ MSc Lon Univ DipTh K Coll Lon MTh. Oak Hill Th Coll DipHE. **d** 82 **p** 83. C Ecclesall *Sheff* 82-87; Bp's Adv on Youth 85-87; Ed Lion Publishing 87-90; Dir Publications, Tr and Sales CPAS from 90; Perm to Offic *Cov* 90-98. *Write Connection, 53 Coten End, Warwick CV34 4NU* Tel (01926) 775024 Fax 410571

BLACKSHAW, Brian Martin. b 43. Lanc Univ MA74 Ch Ch Ox BA95 MA96. Ox NSM Course 87. **d** 90 **p** 91. NSM Amersham *Ox* 90-93; C Hatch End St Anselm *Lon* 93-95; V Cheshunt *St Alb* from 96. *The Vicarage, Churchgate, Cheshunt EN8 9DY* Tel (01992) 623121 E-mail brianandpatsy@cheshunt99.freeserve.co.uk

BLACKSHAW, Trevor Roland. b 36. GIMechE59. Lon Coll of Div 67. **d** 69 **p** 70. C New Catton St Luke *Nor* 69-73; C Luton Lewsey St Hugh *St Alb* 73-78; V Llandinam w Trefeglwys w Penstrowed *Ban* 78-85; Dioc Dir of Adult Educn 83-85; Consultant Dir Wholeness Through Ch Min 86-92; Midl Regional Co-ord Crosslinks 92-97; Dir and Warden Divine Healing Miss Crowhurst 97-02; rtd 02; Perm to Offic *Lich* from 04. *Mayland, 2 Balmoral Crescent, Oswestry SY11 2XG* Tel (01691) 659645 E-mail trevor@blackshawt.freeserve.co.uk

BLACKTOP, Graham Leonard. b 33. St Alb Minl Tr Scheme 82. **d** 85 **p** 86. NSM Rickmansworth *St Alb* 85-92; Perm to Offic *Sarum* from 92. *Dairy House, Wolfeton, Dorchester DT2 9QN* Tel and fax (01305) 262184

BLACKWALL, David D'Arcy Russell. b 35. Southn Univ BSc60 Imp Coll Lon DIC62. Wycliffe Hall Ox 63. **d** 65 **p** 66. C Southampton Thornhill St Chris *Win* 65-68; V Long Sutton 69-72; Chapl Ld Wandsworth Coll Hants 69-74; Hon C Odiham w S Warnborough *Win* 72-75; Chapl St Lawr Coll Ramsgate 75-95; Hd Jun Sch 95-97; Lic to Offic *Cant* 75-98; Perm to Offic *Sarum* from 98; rtd 00. *Cookwell, Back Lane, Okeford Fitzpaine, Blandford Forum DT11 0RD* Tel (01258) 860157

BLACKWELL, Geoffrey Albert. b 27. Lon Coll of Div 62. **d** 65 **p** 66. C Clifton *York* 65-69; Chapl RN 69-73; Warden St Mich Home of Healing Cleadon 73-75; V S Hetton *Dur* 75-82; CSWG 83-94; P-in-c Burpham *Chich* 95-96; rtd 96; Perm to Offic *Chich* from 96. *1 Highfield Gardens, Rustington, Littlehampton BN16 2PZ* Tel (01903) 782219

BLACKWELL, Geoffrey David. b 34. Jes Coll Ox BA57 MA61. Chich Th Coll 57. **d** 59 **p** 60. C Romford St Edw *Chelmsf* 59-62; S Africa 62-68; Chapl Westcott Ho Cam 68-73; V Forest Gate St Edm *Chelmsf* 73-81; Pilsdon Community 83-95; rtd 94; Perm to Offic *Pet* from 94. *15 Chatsfield, Werrington, Peterborough PE4 5DJ* Tel (01733) 324278

BLACKWELL, Nicholas Alfred John. b 54. Warwick Univ MA97. St Jo Coll Nottm BTh85. **d** 85 **p** 86. C Birkenhead Priory *Ches* 85-88; C Stratford-on-Avon w Bishopton *Cov* 88-91; TV Cov E 91-98; Perm to Office from 98. *74 Brays Lane, Coventry CV2 4DW* Tel (024) 7645 6175

BLACKWELL-SMYTH, Charles Peter Bernard. b 42. TCD BA64 MA71 MB73. Gen Th Sem (NY) MDiv65. **d** 65 **p** 66. C Bangor Abbey *D & D* 65-67; C Dublin Ch Ch Leeson Park *D & G* 67-69; P-in-c Carbury *M & K* 73-75; Hon C St Stephen in Brannel *Truro* 87-94; Perm to Offic from 94. *Parcgwyn, Rectory Road, St Stephen, St Austell PL26 7RL* Tel (01726) 822465

BLACOE, Canon Brian Thomas. b 36. Open Univ DipEH BA. Oak Hill Th Coll 63. **d** 66 **p** 67. C Dundonald *D & D* 66-69; C Drumcree *Arm* 69-74; I Ardtrea w Desertcreat 74-78; I Annalong *D & D* 78-95; I Knocknamuckley from 95; Can Dromore Cathl from 93; Prec from 02. *30 Mossbank Road, Ballynagarrick, Portadown BT63 5SL* Tel (028) 3883 1227 Mobile 07745-564056 Fax (028) 3883 2934 E-mail eablacoe@tiscali.co.uk

BLADE, Brian Alan. b 24. ACCS55 ASCA66. Roch Th Coll 67. **d** 69 **p** 70. C Barnehurst *Roch* 69-71; C Crayford 71-76; V

Buttershaw St Aid *Bradf* 76-80; R Etton w Helpston *Pet* 80-86; V Hardingstone and Horton and Piddington 86-90; rtd 90; Perm to Offic *Cant* and *Roch* from 90. *25 Dan Drive, Faversham ME13 7SW* Tel (01795) 531842 E-mail revbrianblade@tesco.net

BLADE, Mrs Susan Joan. b 58. SEITE. **d** 00 **p** 01. NSM Wateringbury and Teston *Roch* 00-02; Asst Chapl Maidstone and Tunbridge Wells NHS Trust 00-02; Chapl from 02. *Eagle Lodge, Mill Lane, Wateringbury, Maidstone ME18 5PE* Tel (01622) 812581

BLAGDEN, Ms Susan. b 64. Ox Min Course 89 Ripon Coll Cuddesdon DipMin99. **d** 99 **p** 00. C Grantham *Linc* 99-03; Asst Chapl Stoke Mandeville Hosp NHS Trust from 03. *Stoke Mandeville Hospital, Mandeville Road, Aylesbury HP21 8AL* Tel (01296) 315000

BLAGG, Colin. b 31. Leeds Univ BA57. Coll of Resurr Mirfield 57. **d** 59 **p** 60. C Edin Old St Paul *Edin* 59-63; R Gourock *Glas* 63-68; Chapl to the Deaf RADD Lon 68-74; Hon C Stoke Newington St Olave *Lon* 73-74; Chapl to the Deaf *Chich* 74-80; V Shoreham Beach 80-96; rtd 97; Perm to Offic *Chich* from 97. *82 Buckingham Court, Shrubbs Drive, Bognor Regis PO22 7SF*

BLAIN, Anne Sharon. b 46. RGN89. Dioc OLM tr scheme 98. **d** 01 **p** 02. OLM Tadworth *S'wark* from 01. *Watts Cottage, Watts Lane, Tadworth KT20 5RW* Tel (01737) 355347 Mobile 07811-267238 Fax (01737) 351546 E-mail breusis@aol.com

BLAIR, Mrs Catherine Jill. b 62. Nottm Univ BA84 BArch87 RIBA88. St Jo Coll Nottm MA02. **d** 02 **p** 03. C Goldsworth Park *Guildf* from 02. *52 Eastmead, Woking GU21 3BP* Tel (01483) 755351 E-mail jonnyblair@jonnyblair.fsnet.co.uk

BLAIR, Henry. *See* BLAIR, William Henry

BLAIR, John Wallace. b 48. Lon Univ BSc70 Birm Univ DipTh82. Qu Coll Birm 79. **d** 81 **p** 82. C Chorlton-cum-Hardy St Werburgh *Man* 81-83; CF 83-97; I Faughanvale *D & R* from 97. *21 Main Street, Eglinton, Londonderry BT47 3AB* Tel (028) 7181 0217

BLAIR, Jonathan Lewis. b 62. Nottm Univ BA84 ACA88. St Jo Coll Nottm. **d** 02 **p** 03. C Goldsworth Park *Guildf* from 02. *52 Eastmead, Woking GU21 3BP* Tel (01483) 755351 E-mail jonnyblair@jonnyblair.fsnet.co.uk

BLAIR, The Very Revd Patrick Allen. b 31. Trin Coll Cam BA54 MA58. Ridley Hall Cam 54. **d** 56 **p** 57. C Harwell *Ox* 56-59; Chapl Oundle Sch 59-64; Jerusalem 64-66; Sudan 67-71; Provost Khartoum 67-71; R Chester le Street *Dur* 71-77; TR Barking St Marg w St Patr *Chelmsf* 77-87; Chapl Barking Hosp 77-87; Tunisia 87-91; Cyprus 91-96; Provost Nicosia 91-96; rtd 96. *Grace Cottage, Pilley Green, Boldre, Lymington SO41 5QG* Tel (01596) 677015

BLAIR, Philip Hugh. b 39. St Edm Hall Ox BA62 MA67 Ex Univ DipEd75 PhD84. Ridley Hall Cam 62. **d** 64 **p** 65. C Camborne *Truro* 64-68; C Kenwyn 68-70; Sudan 70-73; P-in-c Probus *Truro* 73-74; P-in-c St Enoder 74-75; Perm to Offic Cyprus and the Gulf 90-94; rtd 04. *St Martin's, 121 Newland, Sherborne DT9 3DU* Tel and fax (01935) 816022 E-mail philip@philipblair.net

BLAIR, William Henry. b 66. QUB BAgr89 TCD BTh04. CITC 01. **d** 04. C Monaghan w Tydavnet and Kilmore *Clogh* from 04. *The Rectory, Glaslough, Co Monaghan, Irish Republic* Tel (00353) (47) 88277 E-mail henryblair@utvinternet.co.uk

BLAIR-BROWN, Dennis. b 17. Em Coll Saskatoon LTh52. **d** 56 **p** 56. Canada 56-63; C Lymington *Win* 63-70; V E and W Wellow 70-93; rtd 93; Perm to Offic *Sarum* from 98. *135 The Close, Salisbury SP1 2EY* Tel (01722) 334008

BLAIR-CHAPPELL, Mrs Elcineide Menezes. b 47. Sao Paulo Univ Brazil 74 Birm Poly PGCE88. WMMTC 00. **d** 03 **p** 04. NSM Erdington *Birm* from 03. *18 Kempson Avenue, Sutton Coldfield B72 1HJ* Tel 0121-682 5340

BLAIR-FISH, Canon John Christopher. b 20. Linc Coll Ox BA46 MA47. Cuddesdon Coll 48. **d** 49 **p** 50. C Mottingham St Andr *S'wark* 49-51; C Warlingham w Chelsham 51-55; V Surbiton St Mark 55-72; R Chipstead 73-89; Hon Can S'wark Cathl 79-88; rtd 89; Perm to Offic *Chich* from 93. *39 Beehive Lane, Ferring, Worthing BN12 5NR* Tel (01903) 241480 E-mail cblair@fish.co.uk

BLAKE, Colin David. b 52. Rolle Coll CertEd Ex Univ BEd Lon Univ BD. Trin Coll Bris 81. **d** 84 **p** 85. C Hucclecote *Glouc* 84-88; C Patchway and Min Bradley Stoke N CD *Bris* 88-00; TV Worle *B & W* from 00. *6 Gannet Road, Worle, Weston-super-Mare BS22 8UR* Tel (01934) 521765 E-mail colinblake1@aol.com

BLAKE, Ian Martyn. b 57. BA79. Oak Hill Th Coll 76. **d** 80 **p** 81. C Widford *Chelmsf* 80-84; C Barton Seagrave w Warkton *Pet* 84-90; V Sneinton St Chris w St Phil *S'well* 90-01; C Howell Hill w Burgh Heath *Guildf* from 01. *18 Nonsuch Walk, Cheam SM2 7NG* Tel (020) 8873 1961 Fax 8224 9961 E-mail ian-anne@blake.org

BLAKE, Mrs Margaret. b 48. Open Univ BA87. S'wark Ord Course 92. **d** 95 **p** 96. C Farnham *Guildf* 95-01; P-in-c Farncombe 01-05; R from 05. *The Rectory, 38 Farncombe Hill, Godalming GU7 2AU* Tel (01483) 416091 E-mail revmargaretblake@aol.com

BLAKE, Preb Patrick John. b 30. Univ of Wales BA51 DipEd52 St Edm Hall Ox BA54 MA58. St Mich Coll Llan 54. **d** 55 **p** 56. C Buckley *St As* 55-59; C Oystermouth *S & B* 59-63; V Cleeve *B & W* 63-71; R Bruton w Lamyatt, Wyke and Redlynch 71-83; Dioc Ecum Officer 79-84; Preb Wells Cathl 79-03; TR Yeovil 83-88; P-in-c Backwell 88-89; R 89-92; R Backwell w Chelvey and Brockley 92-95; RD Portishead 92-95; rtd 95; Perm to Offic *B & W* from 95; Clergy Retirement and Widows' Officer 96-06. *The Firs, 47 Lower Street, Merriott TA16 5NN* Tel (01460) 78932

BLAKE, Peta Ruth. b 44. Lambeth STh89 Episc Div Sch Cam Mass MA89 DMin90. Trin Coll Bris 82. **dss** 83 **d** 87. New Swindon St Barn Gorse Hill *Bris* 83-88; Par Dn 87-88; Perm to Offic 88-93. *10 Elmer Close, Malmesbury SN16 9UE* Tel (01666) 823722

BLAKE, Philip Charles. b 29. Mitchell Coll of Adv Educn (NSW) BA80 Macquarie Univ (NSW) MA86 FAIWCW88 MACC88. Oak Hill Th Coll 54. **d** 57 **p** 58. C Slough *Ox* 57-60; C Uphill *B & W* 60-62; V Branston *Lich* 62-69; Australia from 69; rtd 94. *412 Gravelly Beach Road, Gravelly Beach, Tas, Australia 7276* Tel (0061) (03) 6394 3582 Fax 6394 3112 E-mail philipblake@bigpond.com

BLAKE, Steven Robert (Max). b 53. Furzedown Coll of Educn CertEd74 Brentwood Coll of Educn BEd91. NTMTC 98. **d** 01 **p** 02. NSM Orsett and Bulphan and Horndon on the Hill *Chelmsf* from 01. *Oakfield, Victoria Road, Horndon-on-the-Hill, Stanford-le-Hope SS17 8ND* Tel (01375) 360522 E-mail maxbla@lineone.net

BLAKELEY, Julian Graham. b 60. Oak Hill Th Coll BA88. **d** 88 **p** 89. C Bedworth *Cov* 88-91; C Harlow St Mary and St Hugh w St Jo the Bapt *Chelmsf* 91-95; R Darfield *Sheff* 95-03; TR Eston w Normanby *York* from 03. *429 Normanby Road, Middlesbrough TS6 0ED* Tel (01642) 206264 E-mail julianandhelen@blakeley050682.freeserve.co.uk

BLAKELEY, Robert Daniel. b 29. Saskatchewan Univ BA63 St Pet Coll Ox BA66 MA70. Em Coll Saskatchewan LTh56. **d** 56 **p** 57. I Radisson Canada 56-59; USA 59-68 and 71-75; C New York St Alb 61-64; Asst P Brooklyn St Anne 66-68; C High Wycombe *Ox* 68-71; Chapl St Luke's Sch New Canaan 71-75; C St Marylebone St Mary *Lon* 75-82; Chapl Hill Ho Sch Knightsbridge 75-82; P-in-c Tasburgh *Nor* 82-85; P-in-c Tharston 82-85; P-in-c Forncett St Mary w St Pet 82-85; P-in-c Flordon 82-85; Hd Master and Chapl Corona Ravenscourt Sch Lon 85-92; rtd 92. *11 Harcourt Drive, Canterbury CT2 8DP* Tel (01227) 453872

BLAKELY, Denise Irene. *See* CADDOO, Mrs Denise Irene

BLAKEMAN, Mrs Janet Mary. b 36. Man Univ BA57 CertEd58. Carl Dioc Tr Course 87. **d** 90 **p** 97. NSM Wetheral w Warwick *Carl* 90-97; NSM Thornthwaite cum Braithwaite, Newlands etc 97-01; Perm to Offic from 01. *Langstrath, Greenfield Lane, Brampton CA8 1AU* Tel (01697) 72008

BLAKEMAN, Walter John. b 37. Qu Coll Birm 74. **d** 76 **p** 77. C Gnosall *Lich* 76-83; C Cheadle 83-86; Res Min Hednesford 86-90; Min Roundshaw LEP *S'wark* 90-94; TV E Scarsdale *Derby* 94-98; rtd 98. *Llandyn House, High Street, Glyn Ceiriog, Llangollen LL20 7EH* Tel (01691) 718173

BLAKESLEY, John. b 50. Keble Coll Ox BA72 MA76. St Steph Ho Ox 72. **d** 74 **p** 75. C Egremont *Carl* 74-77; C Doncaster Ch Ch *Sheff* 77-79; V Auckland St Helen *Dur* 79-94; Chapl Tindale Crescent Hosp Dur 90-94; Lect Th Dur Univ from 91; Tutor St Chad's Coll Dur 95-00; C Ch the King *Newc* 00-03; V Cambois and Sleekburn from 03. *St John's Vicarage, North View, Bedlington NE22 7ED* Tel (01670) 822309

BLAKEWAY-PHILLIPS, Richard John. b 19. St Chad's Coll Dur BA43. **d** 43 **p** 44. C Ledbury *Heref* 43-45; C Cirencester *Glouc* 45-50; C Lydney w Aylburton 50-52; R Dumbleton w Wormington 52-58; V Crawley Down All SS *Chich* 58-69; V Arrington *Ely* 69-77; R Orwell 69-77; R Wimpole 69-77; P-in-c Gt w Lt Abington 77-86; P-in-c Hildersham 77-86; rtd 86; Perm to Offic *Heref* from 86. *61 Long Row, Latchford Lane, Great Haseley, Oxford OX44 7LE*

BLAKEY, Canon Cedric Lambert. b 54. Fitzw Coll Cam BA76 MA80. St Jo Coll Nottm 77. **d** 79 **p** 80. C Cotmanhay *Derby* 79-83; C-in-c Blagreaves St Andr CD 83-89; P-in-c Sinfin Moor 84-89; V Heanor 89-97; RD Heanor 94-97; Bp's Dom Chapl 97-05; NSM Derby Cathl from 05; Hon Can from 02. *Derby Cathderal Office, 18/19 Irongate, Derby DE1 3GP* Tel (01332) 345848 E-mail c.blakey@btinternet.com

BLAKEY, William George. b 51. Southn Univ BSc72 PGCE73. Oak Hill Th Coll BA82. **d** 82 **p** 83. C Cheltenham St Mark *Glouc* 82-85; P-in-c Parkham, Alwington, Buckland Brewer etc *Ex* 85-86; R 86-94; TR 94-01; P-in-c Lundy Is 92-01; RD Hartland 89-96; TR Wareham *Sarum* from 01. *The Rectory, 19 Pound Lane, Wareham BH20 4LQ* Tel (01929) 552684 *or* 550905 E-mail bill@blakey.ctlconnect.co.uk *or* rector@warehamchurches.org.uk

BLAMEY, Mark Kendall. b 62. Bris Poly BSc84 MRICS86. Ripon Coll Cuddesdon 99. **d** 01 **p** 02. C Cowley St Jo *Ox* 01-04;

P-in-c Goring w S Stoke from 04. *The Vicarage, Manor Road, Goring, Reading RG8 9DR* Tel (01491) 872196 E-mail mark@blamey.fslife.co.uk

BLAMIRE, Jean. *See* PROSSER, Jean

BLAMIRE, Philip Gray. b 50. St Pet Coll Birm CertEd71 Wall Hall Coll Aldenham BEd76 UEA MA91. EAMTC 00. **d** 03 **p** 04. C Swaffham *Nor* from 03. *Rosewood Cottage, 50 The Street, Sporle, King's Lynn PE32 2DR* Tel (01760) 723526 E-mail philgb@lineone.net

BLAMIRE-BROWN, Charles Richard. b 21. St Cath Soc Ox BA49 MA53. Cuddesdon Coll 49. **d** 51 **p** 52. C Bedale *Ripon* 51-53; C Welwyn *St Alb* 53-58; P-in-c Tewin 58-67; R 67-75; RD Hatfield 71-75; V Chipperfield St Paul 75-86; rtd 86. *7 Willoughby Avenue, Kenilworth CV8 1DG* Tel (01926) 850808

BLANCH, Paul Frederick. b 56. St Cuth Soc Dur BA97. Chich Th Coll 83. **d** 86 **p** 87. C Chaddesden St Phil *Derby* 86-88; C Auckland St Andr and St Anne *Dur* 88-91; P-in-c Hunwick 91-94; Chapl HM Pris Edin 98-02; P-in-c Edin St Salvador *Edin* 98-00; R 00-02; P-in-c Wester Hailes St Luke 00-02; P-in-c Melton *St E* 02-03; P-in-c Ufford w Bredfield and Hasketon 02-03; R Melton and Ufford 03-05; V Meir Heath and Normacot *Lich* from 05. *St Francis's Vicarage, Sandon Road, Stoke-on-Trent ST3 7LH* Tel (01782) 393189 E-mail frpaul@meltuff.freeserve.co.uk

BLANCHARD, Christopher John. b 46. Univ of Wales (Lamp) BA70. St Mich Coll Llan 86. **d** 79 **p** 80. NSM Chepstow *Mon* 79-81; NSM Itton and St Arvans w Penterry and Kilgwrrwg etc 81-86; TV Ebbw Vale 87-89; R Llangenni and Llanbedr Ystrad Yw w Patricio *S & B* 89-98; V Chepstow *Mon* from 98. *The Vicarage, 25 Mount Way, Chepstow NP16 5NF* Tel (01291) 620980

BLANCHARD, Frank Hugh. b 30. St Jo Coll Dur BA54 DipTh55 MA62. **d** 55 **p** 56. C Bottesford *Linc* 55-58; CMS 58-65; C Kirby Grindalythe *York* 65-67; V 67-71; C N Grimston w Wharram Percy and Wharram-le-Street 65-67; V 67-71; P-in-c Thorpe Bassett 67-71; P-in-c Settrington 67-68; V Scarborough St Jas 71-79; P-in-c Scarborough H Trin 78-79; V Scarborough St Jas and H Trin 79-86; R Stockton-on-the-Forest w Holtby and Warthill 87-94; rtd 94; P-in-c Rothesay *Arg* 94-96; Perm to Offic *York* from 00. *23 Front Street, Sowerby, Thirsk YO7 1JG* Tel (01845) 574446

BLANCHARD, Mrs Jean Ann. b 43. St Alb Minl Tr Scheme 79. **dss** 85 **d** 87 **p** 94. Mill End and Heronsgate w W Hyde *St Alb* 85-92; Hon Par Dn 87-92; Par Dn Luton All SS w St Pet 92-94; C 94-95; P-in-c Skirbeck Quarter *Linc* 96-97; V 97-01; P-in-c Digby Gp from 01. *The Rectory, 1 Thomas à Becket Close, Digby, Lincoln LN4 3GA* Tel (01526) 321099

BLANCHARD, Canon Lawrence Gordon. b 36. Edin Univ MA60. Linc Th Coll 63. **d** 65 **p** 66. C Woodhouse *Wakef* 65-67; C Cannock *Lich* 67-70; Swaziland 70-76; TV Raveningham *Nor* 76-80; V Ancaster *Linc* 80-87; Dir LNSM 80-87; Can and Preb Linc Cathl 85-88; Dir of Tr CA 88-93; V Roxton w Gt Barford *St Alb* 93-98; rtd 98; Perm to Offic *St E* from 99. *The Old Post Office, Post Office Road, Knodishall, Saxmundham IP17 1UG* Tel (01728) 830580 E-mail laurie-blanchard@lineone.net

BLAND, Albert Edward. b 14. St Mich Coll Llan. **d** 62 **p** 63. C Darwen St Cuth *Blackb* 62-65; P-in-c Over Darwen St Jo 65-66; V 66-67; V Feniscowles 67-84; rtd 85; Perm to Offic *Blackb* from 85 and *Derby* from 96. *18 Royal Oak Place, Matlock Street, Bakewell DE45 1HD* Tel (01629) 813370

BLAND, Mrs Elizabeth Anne. b 63. Collingwood Coll Dur BA85. St Alb and Ox Min Course 01. **d** 04. C N Shields *Newc* from 04. *St Augustine's Vicarage, 51 Drummond Terrace, North Shields NE30 2AW* Tel 0191-259 6202 Mobile 07903-044224 E-mail seat@seatbland.freeserve.co.uk

BLAND, Jean Elspeth. b 42. K Coll Lon BA63. Glouc Sch of Min 87. **d** 90 **p** 94. Par Dn Cen Telford *Lich* 90-94; Asst Chapl HM Pris Shrewsbury 92-94; Chapl HM Pris Doncaster 94-98; C Goole *Sheff* 99; P-in-c Purleigh, Cold Norton and Stow Maries *Chelmsf* from 99. *All Saints' Rectory, The Street, Purleigh, Chelmsford CM3 6QH* Tel (01621) 826905

BLANDFORD-BAKER, Neil James. b 64. Dundee Univ BSc86 Nottm Univ BTh92. St Jo Coll Nottm DipMM93. **d** 93 **p** 94. C The Quinton *Birm* 93-96; V E Acton St Dunstan w St Thos *Lon* from 96; Dir of Ords Willesden Area from 02. *The Vicarage, 54 Perryn Road, London W3 7NA* Tel (020) 8743 4117 E-mail jamesbb@btinternet.com

BLANEY, Laurence. b 41. Lon Univ DipTh69 Open Univ BA85 Essex Univ MA88 PhD95. Oak Hill Th Coll 66. **d** 69 **p** 70. C Leyton St Mary w St Edw *Chelmsf* 69-73; P-in-c Wimbish w Thunderley 73-77; P-in-c Steeple 77-82; P-in-c Mayland 77-82; R Pitsea 82-95; R Pitsea w Nevendon 95-96; P-in-c Mayland from 96; P-in-c Steeple from 96. *The Vicarage, 31 Imperial Avenue, Mayland, Chelmsford CM3 6AH* Tel (01621) 740943 E-mail vicar.mayland@onnet.co.uk

BLANKENSHIP, Charles Everett. b 42. Santa Clara Univ BA64. Cuddesdon Coll 71. **d** 74 **p** 75. C Catford (Southend) and Downham *S'wark* 74-78; P-in-c Battersea St Phil w St Bart 78-83; V 83-85; TV Wimbledon 85-91; P-in-c Welling 91-92; V 92-99; P-in-c S Norwood St Alb from 99; RD Croydon N from 02. *The Vicarage, 6 Dagmar Road, London SE25 6HZ* Tel (020) 8653 6092 E-mail chuck@blankenship.demon.co.uk

BLANKLEY, Roger Henry. b 32. MRICS60. Clifton Th Coll 62. **d** 66 **p** 67. C Peckham St Mary Magd *S'wark* 66-69; SAMS 70-74; Brazil 74-80; R Gillingham w Geldeston, Stockton, Ellingham etc *Nor* 80-91; P-in-c Charmouth and Catherston Leweston *Sarum* 91-97; rtd 97; Perm to Offic *Cov* 98-00 and from 02; *Glouc* from 97, *Ox* from 00; Asst Area Sec SAMS 98-00. *12 Hubbard Close, Buckingham MK18 1YS* Tel (01280) 814710 E-mail mblankley@rblankley.freeserve.co.uk

BLANT, Edgar. b 18. St Chad's Coll Dur BA47 DipTh48. **d** 48 **p** 49. C Meir *Lich* 48-54; Antigua 55-85; St Kitts-Nevis 60-85; Adn St Kitts 78-85; rtd 86; Perm to Offic *Lich* 86-98. *326 Sandon Road, Stoke-on-Trent ST3 7EB* Tel (01782) 398300

BLATCHLEY, Ms Elizabeth. b 62. Wycliffe Hall Ox 01. **d** 03 **p** 04. C Northolt W End St Jos *Lon* from 03. *341 Balmoral Drive, Hayes UB4 8DL* Tel (020) 8561 1434 E-mail revbetsy@blueyonder.co.uk

BLATCHLY, Owen Ronald Maxwell. b 30. Bps' Coll Cheshunt 62. **d** 64 **p** 65. C Boxmoor St Jo *St Alb* 64-67; C Boreham Wood All SS 67-69; C Frimley *Guildf* 69-77; V Manaccan w St Anthony-in-Meneage *Truro* 77-82; R Binfield *Ox* 82-97; rtd 97; Perm to Offic *Truro* from 97. *1 Rose Cottages, East Road, Stithians, Truro TR3 7BD* Tel (01209) 860845

BLATHERWICK, Mrs Jane Lesley. b 63. St Jo Coll Nottm. **d** 05. C Arnold *S'well* from 05. *3 Ashington Drive, Arnold, Nottingham NG5 8GH* Tel 0115-922 9085

BLAY, Ian. b 65. Man Univ BA88. Westcott Ho Cam 89. **d** 91 **p** 92. C Withington St Paul *Man* 91-94; C Elton All SS 94-96; R Droylsden St Andr 96-05; Dioc Ecum Officer 98-05; R Mobberley *Ches* from 05. *The Rectory, Church Lane, Mobberley, Knutsford WA16 7RA* Tel (01565) 873218 Mobile 07879-004033 E-mail ian@blay.freeserve.co.uk

BLEAKLEY, Melvyn Thomas. b 43. K Coll Lon BD66 AKC66 Reading Univ TCert78. **d** 67 **p** 68. C Cross Heath *Lich* 67-70; TV High Wycombe *Ox* 70-77; Perm to Offic 77-00; NSM Chalfont St Giles from 00. *294 Hughenden Road, High Wycombe HP13 5PE* Tel (01494) 529315 E-mail melvyn_bleakley@hotmail.com

BLEE, Peter Michael. b 64. St Jo Coll Cam BA86. St Steph Ho Ox BTh94. **d** 94 **p** 95. C Guildf St Nic *Guildf* 94-97; C Whipton *Ex* 97-03; P-in-c Berwick w Selmeston and Alciston *Chich* from 03. *The Parsonage, Berwick, Polegate BN26 6SR* Tel (01323) 870512 E-mail pn.blee@virgin.net

BLENKIN, Hugh Linton. b 16. Trin Coll Cam BA39 MA43. Lambeth STh56 Westcott Ho Cam 39. **d** 40 **p** 41. C Hitchin St Mary *St Alb* 40-43; Prec St Alb Abbey 43-48; Chapl and Lect Hockerill Coll Bishop's Stortford 48-66; Lect St Mich Coll Salisbury 66-78; Lect Sarum Th Coll 78-83; rtd 81. *Amesbury Abbey, Amesbury, Salisbury SP4 7EX* Tel (01980) 624813

BLENNERHASSETT, Canon Richard Noel Rowland. b 09. TCD BA33 MA52. **d** 33 **p** 34. C Clonmel *C & O* 33-37; I Kilrossanty 37-39; I Kilrossanty w Stradbally and Monksland 39-45; I Knappagh *T, K & A* 45-47; I Aughaval w Burrishoole 47-68; I Aughaval w Burrishoole w Achill w Dugort 68-69; Dom Chapl to Bp Tuam 51-57; Can Tuam Cathl 52-69; Adn Tuam 56-69; Preb Kilmactalway St Patr Cathl Dublin 60-67; I Timoleague *C, C & R* 69-73; rtd 73. *The Moorings, Fenit, Tralee, Co Kerry, Irish Republic* Tel (00353) (66) 713 6198

BLEWETT, Roy. b 32. K Coll Lon BSc54 MPhil74 Leeds Inst of Educn 66 Newc Univ DipRS81. Edin Th Coll 81. **d** 82 **p** 83. C Newc St Fran *Newc* 82-85; P-in-c Cornhill w Carham 85-91; P-in-c Branxton 85-91; rtd 92; Perm to Offic *Truro* from 92. *Bryn Mawr, Lower Broad Lane, Redruth TR15 3HT* Tel (01209) 313152

BLEWETT, Timothy John. b 67. Surrey Univ BA88 Cam Univ BA92 MA92 Coll of Ripon & York St Jo MA96. Westcott Ho Cam 89. **d** 92 **p** 93. C Knaresborough *Ripon* 92-95; V Hanmer, Bronington, Bettisfield, Tallarn Green *St As* 95-98; Can Res and Can Cursal St As Cathl 98-03; Asst Dioc Dir of Ords 98-00; Dioc Dir of Ords 00-03; Dioc Officer for Min and Adv for CME 98-03; CF 03-04; P-in-c Loddington *Leic* from 04; Warden Launde Abbey from 04. *The Warden's House, Launde Abbey, Launde Road, Launde, Leicester LE7 9XB* Tel (01572) 717254 E-mail tim.blewett@virgin.net

BLICK, John Harold Leslie. b 36. Univ of Wales (Lamp) BA61. Bps' Coll Cheshunt 61. **d** 63 **p** 64. C Radlett *St Alb* 63-66; Min St Cem Miss Labrador Canada 66-71; Min Marsh Farm CD *St Alb* 71-76; R Shaw cum Donnington *Ox* 76-89; rtd 96; Perm to Offic *Mon* from 99. *Springwood, Cleddon, Trelleck NP25 4PN* Tel (01600) 860094 Fax 869045 E-mail revdjblick@aol.com

BLIGH, Philip Hamilton. b 36. Lon Univ BSc57 PhD61 MEd79 St Cath Coll Ox BA63 MInstP75. S'wark Ord Course 86. **d** 88 **p** 89. C Abington *Pet* 88-90; V Bozeat w Easton Maudit 90-99; R Hackett Australia 99-01; rtd 01; Perm to Offic *Nor* from 02. *Harmony House, 40 Cromwell Road, Cromer NR27 0BE* Tel (01263) 511385 E-mail philaud@blighp.freeserve.co.uk

BLISS, Allan Ernest Newport. b 29. K Coll Lon AKC50. St Boniface Warminster 54. **d** 54 **p** 57. C Wooburn *Ox* 54-56; C Whitley Ch Ch 56-58; C Hatcham Park All SS *S'wark* 63-68; C Sundon w Streatley *St Alb* 68-73; P-in-c Caldecote All SS 74-78; V 78-91; V Old Warden 81-91; Perm to Offic from 91; rtd 94. *6 Jubilee Gardens, Biggleswade SG18 0JW* Tel (01767) 313797

BLISS, David Charles. b 52. Aston Univ BSc75 Cranfield Inst of Tech MSc82. St Jo Coll Nottm 87. **d** 89 **p** 90. C Burntwood *Lich* 89-93; TV Aston cum Aughton w Swallownest, Todwick etc *Sheff* 93-02; V Todwick from 02; Chapl among Deaf People from 97; AD Laughton from 03. *The Rectory, 15 Rectory Gardens, Todwick, Sheffield S26 1JU* Tel (01909) 770283 Fax 774873
E-mail chaplain-adeafp-sheffield@dcbliss.freeserve.co.uk

BLISS, John Derek Clegg. b 40. Sarum Th Coll. **d** 68 **p** 69. C Wymondham *Nor* 68-73; V Easton 73-80; R Colton 73-80; USA from 80; rtd 01. *4 Edgewater Hillside, Westport, CT 06880, USA* Tel (001) (203) 222 1879 E-mail jb106600@aol.com

BLISS, Neil Humberstone. b 29. TCD BA54 MA59. Coll of Resurr Mirfield 55. **d** 57 **p** 58. C N Keyham *Ex* 57-60; C Usuthu Swaziland 61-65; P-in-c Piet Retief S Africa 65-66; R 66-67; Chapl St Chris Sch Swaziland 68-73; Chapl Waterford Kamhlaba Sch Mbabane 73-78; R Pigg's Peak 78-80; P-in-c Osmington w Poxwell *Sarum* 80-81; TV Preston w Sutton Poyntz and Osmington w Poxwell 81-84; V Ernesettle *Ex* 84-88; R S Tawton and Belstone 88-93; rtd 94. *Jordan House, Jordan, Lyme Regis DT7 3AQ* Tel (01297) 445189

BLISSARD-BARNES, Christopher John. b 36. ARCO55 Linc Coll Ox BA61 MA64. Ridley Hall Cam 61. **d** 63 **p** 64. C Woking St Paul *Guildf* 63-67; C Orpington Ch Ch *Roch* 67-71; P-in-c Heref St Jas *Heref* 71-78; Chapl Heref Gen Hosp 71-78; R Hampreston *Sarum* 78-88; TR 88-89; RD Wimborne 80-85; P-in-c Hambledon *Guildf* 89-94; R Newdigate 94-01; Warden of Readers 93-99; rtd 01; Perm to Offic *Win* from 02. *148 Olivers Battery Road South, Winchester SO22 4LF* Tel and fax (01962) 862082 E-mail cf@blissard-barnes.freeserve.co.uk

BLOCK, Robert Allen. b 62. Univ of Wales (Lamp) BA84. Coll of Resurr Mirfield 86. **d** 88 **p** 89. C Hampton *Worc* 88-91; C Notting Hill St Mich and Ch Ch *Lon* 91-96; P-in-c Hammersmith St Luke 96-02; C-in-c Hammersmith SS Mich and Geo White City Estate CD 96-02. *Swan Cottage, North Molton, South Molton EX36 3HT* Tel (01598) 740258
E-mail robertblock@zoom.co.uk

BLOCKLEY, Christopher John Hamilton. b 72. UWE LLB96 Rob Coll Cam BTh04 Barrister-at-Law (Gray's Inn) 98. Ridley Hall Cam 01. **d** 04 **p** 05. C Kingswood *Bris* from 04. *36 Elmfield, Bristol BS15 9SS* Tel 0117-967 2360 Mobile 07866-477848
E-mail chris_blockley@hotmail.com

BLODWELL, Ms Christine Maria. b 46. Open Univ BA Jo Dalton Coll Man CertEd71. N Ord Course 04. **d** 05. NSM Marple All SS *Ches* from 05. *149 Low Leighton Road, New Mills, High Peak SK22 4LR* Tel (01663) 746523 Mobile 07931-714130
E-mail cmblodwell@aol.com

BLOFELD, Thomas Guest. *See* GUEST-BLOFELD, Thomas

BLOGG, Kevin Derek. b 55. Ch Ch Coll Cant BSc82 PGCE87. Franciscan Ho of Studies. **d** 84 **p** 85. NSM Eythorne and Elvington w Waldershare etc *Cant* 89-92; Orchard Sch Cant 89-90; Harbour Sch Dover 92-93; NSM Colkirk w Oxwick w Pattesley, Whissonsett etc *Nor* 95-02; NSM Gressenhall w Longham w Wendling etc from 02; Sidestrand Hall Sch Nor from 94. *The Rectory Barn, Rectory Road, Gressenhall, Dereham NR19 2QG* Tel (01362) 861084

BLOOD, David John. b 36. G&C Coll Cam BA60 MA64. Westcott Ho Cam 60. **d** 62 **p** 63. C Rushmere *St E* 62-66; C Harringay St Paul *Lon* 66-70; Lic to Offic 71-81; rtd 01. *42 Churston Gardens, London N11 2NL*

BLOOD, Canon Michael William. b 44. AKC67. **d** 69 **p** 70. C Moseley St Agnes *Birm* 69-75; V Cotteridge from 75; Relig Progr Producer BBC Radio W Midl from 76; Hon Can Birm Cathl from 97. *118 Northfield Road, Birmingham B30 1DX* Tel 0121-458 2815 Fax 459 6909 E-mail bj@blood.u-net.com

BLOOD, Stephen John. b 28. Keble Coll Ox BA53 MA58. Coll of Resurr Mirfield 53. **d** 55 **p** 56. C Greenford H Cross *Lon* 55-58; C Forest Gate St Edm *Chelmsf* 58-61; C-in-c Ashford St Hilda CD *Lon* 61-73; V Ashford St Hilda 73-00; rtd 00; Perm to Offic *St Alb* from 00. *69 Hampstead Road, Kings Langley WD4 8BS* Tel (01923) 268453

BLOOMER, Ms Sherry Lesley. b 50. TD91. Liv Jo Moores Univ BA91 Lon Univ DN82 Wolv Poly CertEd83 RN73 RM74 RHV78 DipHV78. Westcott Ho Cam 95. **d** 97 **p** 98. C Llangollen w Trevor and Llantysilio *St As* 97-00; R Cilcain and Nannerch and Rhydymwyn 00-04; V Worc St Clem and Lower Broadheath *Worc* from 04; Chapl Univ Coll Worc from 04. *St Clement's Rectory, 124 Laugherne Road, Worcester WR2 5LT* Tel (01905) 339455 E-mail sherry@sbloomer.freeserve.co.uk

BLOOMFIELD, John Michael. b 35. Univ of Wales (Lamp) BA57. Sarum Th Coll 59. **d** 61 **p** 62. C Fordington *Sarum* 61-64; C Branksome St Aldhelm 64-66; Youth Chapl *Win* 66-69; R Win All SS w Chilcomb and Chesil 71-79; P-in-c Corsley *Sarum* 79-81; P-in-c Studland 83-86; Chapl HM Pris Dorchester 87-89; C Dorchester *Sarum* 87-89; Chapl HM Pris The Verne 89-00; rtd 00; Perm to Offic *Sarum* from 01. *Green Acres, Valley Road, Corfe Castle, Wareham BH20 5HU* Tel (01929) 480924 Fax 481699 E-mail swanbeck@aol.com

BLOOMFIELD, John Stephen. b 56. Southn Univ. Chich Th Coll 83. **d** 86 **p** 87. C Chich St Paul and St Pet *Chich* 86-89; TV Littlehampton and Wick 89-98; V Hunstanton St Edm w Ringstead *Nor* from 98. *St Edmund's Vicarage, 53 Northgate, Hunstanton PE36 6DS* Tel (01485) 532531

BLOOR, Ms Amanda Elaine. b 62. Leic Univ BA83 Open Univ PGCE96 York Univ MA02. Ripon Coll Cuddesdon 02. **d** 04 **p** 05. C Hambleden Valley *Ox* from 04. *The Vicarage, Turville, Henley-on-Thames RG9 6QU* Tel (01491) 638539
E-mail markandamanda@waitrose.com

BLOOR, Terence Bernard. b 62. Liv Univ BTh02. N Ord Course 99. **d** 02 **p** 03. C Hadley *Lich* from 02. *10 Partridge Close, Leegomery, Telford TF1 4WF* Tel (01952) 240146 Mobile 07890-980749 E-mail terry-bloor@supanet.com

BLORE, John Francis. b 49. Jes Coll Ox BA72 MA76. Wycliffe Hall Ox 73. **d** 75 **p** 76. C Waltham Abbey *Chelmsf* 75-78; C E Ham St Geo 78-81; R Colchester St Mich Myland 81-00; Chapl Oxley Parker Sch Colchester 81-00; P-in-c Halstead St Andr w H Trin and Greenstead Green *Chelmsf* 00-04; TR Halstead Area from 04; RD Hinckford from 03. *The Vicarage, Parsonage Street, Halstead CO9 2LD* Tel (01787) 472171
E-mail john@johnfblore.freeserve.co.uk

BLOUNT, Robin George. b 38. Lon Univ DipTh68. Lon Coll of Div 61 Wycliffe Hall Ox 67. **d** 68 **p** 69. C Bletchley *Ox* 68-71; C Washington *Dur* 71-74; TV Chelmsley Wood *Birm* 74-76; Ind Chapl *Worc* 76-89; Asst P Dudley St Jo 76-89; Asst P Dudley St Thos and St Luke 88-89; Ind Chapl (Eurotunnel Development) *Cant* 89-03; rtd 03; Perm to Offic *Cant* from 03. *6 Lyn Court, Shorncliffe Road, Folkestone CT20 2PE* Tel (01303) 250028 E-mail robin.blount@freeuk.com

BLOWERS, Canon Ralph Barrie. b 28. Fitzw Ho Cam BA50 MA61. Ridley Hall Cam 51. **d** 53 **p** 54. C Higher Openshaw *Man* 53-56; R Man Albert Memorial Ch 56-68; RD Cheetham 63-69; R Man Albert Memorial Ch w Newton Heath 68-69; V Normanton *Derby* 69-93; RD Derby 74-79; RD Derby S 79-89; Hon Can Derby Cathl 85-93; rtd 93; Perm to Offic *Derby* from 93. *8 Portland Close, Mickleover, Derby DE3 9BQ* Tel (01332) 517114 E-mail canonblowers@onetel.com

BLOWS, Canon Derek Reeve. b 26. Linc Coll Ox BA50 MA52 SAP75. Cuddesdon Coll 50. **d** 52 **p** 53. C Cov St Mark *Cov* 52-56; Lic to Offic *Sarum* 56-58; Chapl Warlingham Park Hosp Croydon 58-65; V Purley St Mark *S'wark* 65-70; Dir Past Care and Counselling 70-80; Hon Can S'wark Cathl 72-80; Dir Westmr Past Foundn 80-91; rtd 91; Perm to Offic *Roch* from 91. *2 Blackmoor House, Four Elms, Edenbridge TN8 6PG* Tel (01732) 700770

BLOXAM-ROSE, Canon Simon Franklyn. b 61. Southn Univ BTh MA92 PhD99 HonFLCM88. Chich Th Coll 85. **d** 88 **p** 89. C Bassaleg *Mon* 88-89; Chapl Aldenham Sch Herts 89-94; Perm to Offic *Ex* from 90; Chapl (Sen) Millfield Sch Somerset from 94; Can St Jo Pro-Cathl Katakwa from 95. *The Chaplaincy, Butleigh Road, Street BA16 0DA* Tel (01458) 447276
E-mail sbr@millfield.somerset.sch.uk

BLOXHAM, Oliver. b 27. Ely Th Coll 60. **d** 62 **p** 63. C Newc H Cross *Newc* 62-65; C Ponteland 65-69; V Dudley 69-79; P-in-c Balkwell 79-81; V 81-92; rtd 92; Perm to Offic *Newc* from 92. *23 Lambley Avenue, North Shields NE30 3SL* Tel 0191-296 1785

BLUNDELL, Catherine. b 62. St Alb and Ox Min Course 96. **d** 99 **p** 00. C Furze Platt *Ox* 99-03; TV Bracknell from 03. *St Paul's Vicarage, 58 Harmans Water Road, Bracknell RG12 9PT* Tel (01344) 422819
E-mail catherine.blundell@btinternet.com

BLUNDELL, Peter Grahame. b 61. Ealing Coll of Educn BA83. Oak Hill NSM Course 91. **d** 94 **p** 95. NSM Kensington St Barn *Lon* 94-97; Zimbabwe 97-99; Assoc Min Romford Gd Shep Collier Row *Chelmsf* 99-04; I Oak Ridges Canada from 04. *19 Waldron Crescent, Richmond Hill ON, Canada, L4E 4A3*

BLUNDEN, Jacqueline Ann. *See* MILLER, Mrs Jacqueline Ann

BLUNDEN, Jeremy Augustine. b 61. BSc CEng88. SEITE DipTM99. **d** 99 **p** 00. NSM Sydenham St Bart *S'wark* 99-01; C 01-03; V Clapham H Spirit from 03. *15 Elms Road, London SW4 9ER* Tel (020) 7622 8703
E-mail jeremy.blunden@virgin.net

BLUNSUM, Charles Michael. b 28. ACIB51 MBIM86. **d** 74 **p** 75. C Stoke Bishop *Bris* 74-79; Chapl Brunel Manor Chr Cen Torquay 79-94; rtd 94; Perm to Offic *Ex* from 94. *16A Hollywater Close, Torquay TQ1 3TN* Tel (01803) 214371

BLUNT, The Ven Paul David. b 44. Lon Univ BSc65 Leeds Univ DipTh70. Coll of Resurr Mirfield 67. **d** 70 **p** 71. C Norbury St Steph *Cant* 70-73; Canada from 73. *1234 Prestone Drive, Orleans ON, Canada, K1E 3X6* E-mail st.helen@on.aibn.com

BLYDE, Ian Hay. b 52. Liv Univ BSc74 Edin Univ BD80. Edin Th Coll 77. **d** 80 **p** 81. C Ainsdale *Liv* 80-83; Chapl Birkenhead

Sch Merseyside 83-90; V Over St Chad *Ches* 90-93; Chapl Ex Sch 93-98; Chapl St Marg Sch Ex 93-98; NSM Littleham w Exmouth *Ex* from 03. *2 Hulham Road, Exmouth EX8 3HR* Tel (01395) 267863

BLYTH, Andrew Kenneth Eric. b 63. Roehampton Inst BA86 Middx Univ PGCE87. Ridley Hall Cam 98. **d** 00 **p** 01. C Luton St Mary *St Alb* 00-04; P-in-c Walton H Trin *Ox* from 04. *The Rectory, 42 Redwood Drive, Aylesbury HP21 7TN* Tel (01296) 394906 Mobile 07905-181002 E-mail hta_vicar@yahoo.co.uk

BLYTH, Bryan Edward Perceval. b 22. Linc Coll Ox BA49 MA52. Wells Th Coll 48. **d** 50 **p** 51. C Timperley *Ches* 50-52; C Talbot Village *Sarum* 52-55; C-in-c Weymouth St Edm 55; P-in-c 56-63; Asst Dir of Educn *Chelmsf* 64-67; Hon C Mountnessing 67-68; Hon C Ingatestone w Buttsbury 67-68; Teacher Ingatestone Sec Modern Sch 67-68; Teacher Westwood Co Jun Sch 68-72; Dep Hd 72-87; Hon C Thundersley 80-84; rtd 87; Perm to Offic *Sarum* and *Win* from 98. *Greenways, 19 Chiltern Drive, New Milton BH25 7JY* Tel (01425) 611140

BLYTH, Canon Drummond Gwyn. b 26. K Coll Lon 53. **d** 54 **p** 55. C N Lynn w St Marg and St Nic *Nor* 54-59; C Sheff St Cecilia Parson Cross *Sheff* 59-62; R Carlton Colville *Nor* 62-70; V Stalham w Brunstead 70-77; P-in-c E Ruston 76-77; RD Waxham 77-89; V Stalham and E Ruston w Brunstead 77-91; Hon Can Nor Cathl 87-91; rtd 91; Perm to Offic *Nor* from 91. *Pegg's Close, 6 St Nicholas Place, Sheringham NR26 8LE* Tel (01263) 822611

BLYTH, Mrs Geraldine Anne. b 50. Llan Dioc Tr Scheme 90. **d** 94 **p** 97. C Llantrisant *Llan* 94-01; P-in-c Llanharry from 01; Chapl Pontypridd and Rhondda NHS Trust from 01. *The Rectory, Llanharry, Pontyclun CF72 9LH* Tel (01443) 223140

BLYTH, Graham. *See* BLYTH, Michael Graham

BLYTH, Ian John. b 40. Rhodes Univ BA66 Natal Univ BEd81 MEd96. **d** 82 **p** 83. S Africa 82-01; Dioc Educn Officer Natal 83-85; R Pietermaritzburg St Luke 85-87; Lic to Offic 88-01; NSM W Woodhay w Enborne, Hampstead Marshall etc *Ox* from 02. *St Laurence's Rectory, West Woodhay, Newbury RG20 0BL* Tel and fax (01488) 669233 Mobile 07900-857096 E-mail ian@blythkin.fsnet.co.uk

BLYTH, John Reddie. b 25. Wadh Coll Ox BA48 MA50. Ridley Hall Cam 48. **d** 50 **p** 51. C Southport Ch Ch *Liv* 50-52; C Enfield Ch Ch Trent Park *Lon* 52-55; V Plymouth St Jude *Ex* 55-63; E Midl Area Sec CPAS 63-70; V Parkstone St Luke *Sarum* 70-90; Chapl Uplands Sch Parkstone 70-73; rtd 90; Perm to Offic *Chich* from 90. *5 Powell Road, Newick, Lewes BN8 4LS* Tel (01825) 722011

BLYTH, Kenneth Henry. b 35. Lon Univ DipTh60. Oak Hill Th Coll 58. **d** 61 **p** 62. C St Alb St Paul *St Alb* 61-65; P-in-c Aspenden and Layston w Buntingford 65-66; R 66-72; R Washfield, Stoodleigh, Withleigh etc *Ex* 72-82; P-in-c Cruwys Morchard 72-74; RD Tiverton 76-82; V Eastbourne H Trin *Chich* 82-00; rtd 00; Perm to Offic *Ex* from 00. *Hamslade House, Bampton, Tiverton EX16 9JA*

BLYTH, Michael Graham. b 53. Jes Coll Ox BA75 MA78 Dur Univ PhD79. Qu Coll Birm 82. **d** 84 **p** 85. C Nantwich *Ches* 84-86; C Coppenhall 86-88; TV Southend *Chelmsf* 88-95; P-in-c Danbury from 95; RD Chelmsf S from 01. *St John's Rectory, 55 Main Road, Danbury, Chelmsford CM3 4NG* Tel (01245) 223140 E-mail graham@revdoc.fsnet.co.uk

BOAG, David. b 46. Edin Th Coll 69. **d** 72 **p** 73. C Edin Old St Paul *Edin* 72-75; P-in-c Edin St Andr and St Aid 75-88; Lic to Offic from 88. *7 Starch Mill, Ford Road, Haddington EH41 4AR* Tel (01620) 826839

BOAG, Michael John. b 61. Leeds Univ BA00. Coll of Resurr Mirfield 98. **d** 00 **p** 01. C Howden *York* 00-03; Min Can and Succ Windsor from 03; Chapl St Geo Sch Windsor from 03. *3 The Cloisters, Windsor Castle, Windsor SL4 1NJ* Tel (01753) 848737 E-mail succentor@stgeorges-windsor.org

BOAK, Canon Donald Kenneth. b 30. MBAOT53. S'wark Ord Course 82. **d** 85 **p** 86. C Tulse Hill H Trin and St Matthias *S'wark* 85-88; C Surbiton St Matt 88-91; Intercon Ch Soc, SAMS and Miss to Seamen 91-95; Peru 91-95; Dean Lima 93-95; rtd 95; Hon Can Peru from 95; Hon C Bournemouth St Andr *Win* 96-99; Perm to Offic *Sarum* 98-01 and *Win* from 99. *3 Hymans Way, Totton, Southampton SO40 3DL* Tel (023) 8086 8265

BOAKES, Norman. b 50. Univ of Wales (Swansea) BA71 Ox Univ MTh96. Bp Burgess Hall Lamp 71. **d** 73 **p** 74. C Swansea St Mary w H Trin *S & B* 73-78; Chapl Univ of Wales (Swansea) 76-78; Chapl K Alfred Coll *Win* 78-82; V Colbury 82-91; Chapl Ashurst Hosp 82-91; Chapl Mental Handicap Services Unit 82-91; V Southampton Maybush St Pet *Win* from 91; P-in-c Southampton St Jude from 04; Bp's Adv for Hosp Chapl 87-00; AD Southampton from 02. *Maybush Vicarage, Sedbergh Road, Southampton SO16 9HJ* Tel (023) 8070 3443 E-mail nboakes@fish.co.uk

BOAR, Alan Bennett. b 23. Sarum Th Coll 56. **d** 58 **p** 59. C E Dereham w Hoe *Nor* 58-60; C Gorleston St Andr 60-63; V Tibenham 63-67; P-in-c Tivetshall 64-67; R Beeston St Laurence w Ashmanhaugh and Hoveton 67-78; P-in-c Tunstead w Sco' Ruston 67-78; P-in-c Marsham 78-89; P-in-c Burgh 78-89; rtd 89; Perm to Offic *Nor* from 89. *20 Emelson Close, Dereham NR19 2ES* Tel (01362) 698944

BOARDMAN, Frederick Henry. b 25. Liv Univ BSc46 St Cath Soc Ox BA49 MA54 Birm Univ MEd71 PhD77. Wycliffe Hall Ox 47. **d** 50 **p** 51. C Bootle Ch Ch *Liv* 50-52; C-in-c Netherton CD 52-57; V Stechford *Birm* 57-63; Lic to Offic *Birm* 63-69 and *Liv* 71-89; Hon C Sutton *Liv* 76-89; Hon C Burtonwood 89-02; rtd 90; Perm to Offic *Liv* from 92. *Woodside, Burtonwood Road, Great Sankey, Warrington WA5 3AN* Tel (01925) 635079

BOARDMAN, Jonathan. b 63. Magd Coll Cam BA89 Magd Coll Ox MA90. Westcott Ho Cam 87. **d** 90 **p** 91. C W Derby St Mary *Liv* 90-93; Prec St Alb Abbey *St Alb* 93-96; TR Catford (Southend) and Downham *S'wark* 96-99; RD E Lewisham 99; Chapl Rome *Eur* from 99. *All Saints, via del Babuino 153, 00187 Rome, Italy* Tel (0039) (06) 3600 2171 *or* 3600 1881 E-mail j.boardman@agora.stm.it

BOARDMAN, Preb Philippa Jane. b 63. Jes Coll Cam BA85 MA89. Ridley Hall Cam 87. **d** 90 **p** 94. Par Dn Walthamstow St Mary w St Steph *Chelmsf* 90-93; C Hackney Wick St Mary of Eton w St Aug *Lon* 93-96; P-in-c Old Ford St Paul and St Mark 96-03; V from 03; Dean of Women's Min Stepney Area 94-02; Preb St Paul's Cathl from 02. *The Vicarage, St Stephen's Road, London E3 5JL* Tel (020) 8980 9020

BOCKING (Essex), Dean of. *See* NEED, The Very Revd Philip Alan

BOCKING (Suffolk), Dean of. *See* STRANACK, The Very Revd David Arthur Claude

BODDINGTON, Canon Alan Charles Peter. b 37. Lon Univ DipTh65. Oak Hill Th Coll 63. **d** 66 **p** 67. C Bedworth *Cov* 66-69; Bp's Officer for Min 69-75; Bp's Chapl for Miss 69-73; P-in-c Wroxall and Honiley 72-75; V Westwood 75-85; Asst Chapl Warw Univ 78-85; TR N Farnborough *Guildf* 85-02; RD Aldershot 88-93; Hon Can Guildf Cathl 92-02; rtd 02; Perm to Offic *Cov* from 02. *Tremar, Hathaway Lane, Stratford-upon-Avon CV37 9BJ* Tel (01789) 263643 Mobile 07866-909092

BODDY, Alan Richard. b 47. Ripon Coll Cuddesdon. **d** 84 **p** 85. C Eastcote St Lawr *Lon* 84-87; C Kensington St Mary Abbots w St Geo 87-90; Chapl HM Pris Brixton 90-91; Chapl HM Pris Send and Downview 91-92; Chapl HM Pris High Down 92-98; Chapl HM Pris Wormwood Scrubs 98-02; rtd 02; PV Westmr Abbey from 02; Perm to Offic *Lon* and *Ox* from 02. *105 Valiant House, Vicarage Crescent, London SW11 3LX*

BODDY, David. b 57. Linc Th Coll 92. **d** 92 **p** 93. C Peterlee *Dur* 92-95; C Penshaw 95-97; P-in-c Shiney Row 95-98; P-in-c Herrington 95-98; TV S Shields All SS 98-04; V Haswell, Shotton and Thornley from 04. *The Vicarage, Shotton Colliery, Durham DH6 2JW* Tel 0191-526 1156 Mobile 07971-304622 E-mail davidboddy@lineone.net

BODKIN, Thomas Patrick Joseph. b 45. Richmond Fellowship Coll Dip Human Relns 78 Open Univ BA77 BA90. St Hyacinth's Coll & RC Sem Mass 64 Franciscan Ho of Studies DipPhil67 DipTh70. **d** 80 **p** 80. In RC Ch 80-86; NSM Littlehampton and Wick *Chich* 91-93; Visiting Tutor Moral Th Chich Th Coll 92-99; TV Aldrington *Chich* 93-97; P-in-c Bishopstone 97-99. *Address temp unknown*

BODLE, Richard Talbot. b 70. Southn Univ LLB91. Wycliffe Hall Ox BTh98. **d** 98 **p** 99. C S Mimms Ch Ch *Lon* 98-02; TV Edgware from 02. *1 Beulah Close, Edgware HA8 8SP* Tel (020) 8958 9730 E-mail richard.bodle@london.anglican.org

BODMIN, Archdeacon of. *See* COHEN, The Ven Clive Ronald Franklin

BODY, Andrew. b 46. Pemb Coll Cam BA68 MA71. Ridley Hall Cam 68. **d** 70 **p** 71. C New Bury *Man* 70-73; TV Droylsden St Mary 73-78; V Low Harrogate St Mary *Ripon* 78-92; Trustee FLAME from 90; TR Redhorn *Sarum* 92-97; V Chobham w Valley End *Guildf* from 97. *Chobham Vicarage, Bagshot Road, Chobham, Woking GU24 8BY* Tel (01276) 858197 E-mail andrew@abody.freeserve.co.uk

BODY, Mrs Shuna Jane. b 67. SEITE 98. **d** 01 **p** 02. NSM Appledore w Brookland, Fairfield, Brenzett etc *Cant* from 01. *Hope Farm, Snargate, Romney Marsh TN29 9UQ* Tel (01797) 343977 Mobile 07977-981990 E-mail shunabody@hotmail.com

BODYCOMBE, Stephen John. b 58. Lanchester Poly BA. St Mich Coll Llan DipTh83. **d** 83 **p** 84. C Cardiff St Jo *Llan* 83-86; V Dinas and Penygraig w Williamstown 86-00; V Dyffryn from 00. *The Vicarage, Dyffryn, Neath SA10 7AZ* Tel (01792) 814237

BOFFEY, Ian. b 40. Glas Univ MA63. Glas NSM Course 75. **d** 75 **p** 78. NSM Dalry *Glas* 75-78; P-in-c 78-97; N Ayrshire TM from 97. *2 Kinloch Avenue, Stewarton, Kilmarnock KA3 3HF* Tel (01560) 482586 E-mail ian@boffey.evemail.net

BOGA, Bishop of. *See* NJOJO, The Rt Revd Patrice Byankya

BOGGUST, Mrs Patricia Anne. b 42. Portsm Dioc Tr Course. **d** 90 **p** 98. NSM Hook w Warsash *Portsm* 90-94; NSM Locks Heath from 94; Perm to Offic *Win* from 01. *21 Beverley Close, Park Gate, Southampton SO31 6QU* Tel (01489) 573586

BOGLE, Ms Elizabeth. b 47. York Univ BA68 Leeds Univ PGCE69. S'wark Ord Course 93. **d** 96 **p** 97. NSM E Greenwich

S'wark 96-00; NSM Hatcham St Jas from 00. *8 Waller Road, London SE14 5LA* Tel (020) 7732 9420 *or* 8305 2339 E-mail elizabethbogle@hotmail.com

BOGLE, James Main Lindam Linton. b 33. Peterho Cam BA56 MA60. Wells Th Coll 59. **d** 61 **p** 62. C Bermondsey St Anne *S'wark* 61-65; Chapl York Univ *York* 65-72; V Brayton 72-76; V Forest Hill St Aug *S'wark* 76-83; C Hatcham St Cath 83-85; Hon C 91-03; C Herne Hill St Paul 86-87; rtd 87; Perm to Offic *S'wark* from 04. *96 Grierson Road, London SE23 1NX* Tel (020) 8699 9996 E-mail james.bogle@btinternet.com

BOHAN, Kimberley. b 72. St Andr Univ MA93 Smith Coll (USA) MAT94 St Andr Univ BD99 Edin Univ MTh03. **d** 03. C Glas St Ninian *Glas* from 03. *Flat 3/2, 16 Maxwell Road, Glasgow G41 1QE* Tel 0141-429 7417 E-mail kimberley@k-bohan.freeserve.co.uk

BOHUN, Brother Roger Alexander. b 32. Lon Univ BSc58. Cuddesdon Coll 65. **d** 68 **p** 69. C Rugby St Andr *Cov* 68-74; SSF from 74; Perm to Offic *Sarum* 74-76, 88-93 and from 00; *Newc* 76-78; Tanzania 78-86; Zimbabwe 86-88 and 93-00; P-in-c Waruka Ch Distr 86-88; R Bonda Miss 93-95; P-in-c Chimanimani and Chipinge Miss Distr 96-00; rtd 00. *The Friary, Hilfield, Dorchester DT2 7BE* Tel (01300) 341345 Fax 341293

BOIT, Mervyn Hays. b 38. Univ of Wales (Lamp) BA59. St Mich Coll Llan 59. **d** 61 **p** 62. C Roath St German *Llan* 61-63; C Skewen 63-69; V Pontycymer and Blaengarw 69-03; rtd 03. *Address temp unknown*

BOLAND, Christopher Paul. b 75. Hertf Coll Ox MPhys97. Ridley Hall Cam BTh01. **d** 01 **p** 02. C Skirbeck H Trin *Linc* 01-05; P-in-c Grantham, Harrowby w Londonthorpe from 05. *The Vicarage, Edinburgh Road, Grantham NG31 9QZ* Tel (01476) 564781 Mobile 07791-702537 E-mail chrisboland@fish.co.uk

BOLAND, Geoffrey. b 56. Open Univ BA03. Oak Hill Th Coll DipHE89. **d** 89 **p** 90. C Ormskirk *Liv* 89-94; C Woodside Park St Barn *Lon* 94-99; TV Canford Magna *Sarum* from 99. *11 Plantagenet Crescent, Bournemouth BH11 9PL* Tel (01220) 573872

BOLD, Peter Edward. b 64. Sheff Univ BEng86 PhD90. Cranmer Hall Dur BA94. **d** 95 **p** 96. C Grenoside *Sheff* 95-97; Dioc Communications Officer 97-01; C Rotherham 97-01; P-in-c Brampton Bierlow from 01; V from 05. *Brampton Vicarage, Christchurch Road, Wath-upon-Dearne, Rotherham S63 6NW* Tel (01709) 873210 E-mail pebold@talk21.com

BOLE, Malcolm Dennis. b 30. Oak Hill Th Coll 65. **d** 67 **p** 68. C Bridlington Priory *York* 67-70; Rwanda 71-73; P-in-c Combe Hay *B & W* 74-81; V Bath Odd Down 74-81; P-in-c Taunton St Jas 81-84; V 84-90; R Bicknoller w Crowcombe and Sampford Brett 90-98; rtd 98; Perm to Offic *B & W* from 01. *7 Putsham Mead, Kilve, Bridgwater TA5 1DZ* Tel (01278) 741297

BOLLARD, Canon Richard George. b 39. Fitzw Ho Cam BA61 MA65 K Coll Lon BD63 AKC63. **d** 64 **p** 65. C Southampton Maybush St Pet *Win* 64-68; Chapl Aston Univ *Birm* 68-74; TR Chelmsley Wood 74-82; V Coleshill and Maxstoke 82-04; RD Coleshill 82-92; Hon Can Birm Cathl 85-04; Dioc Ecum Officer 97-02; rtd 04. *Moreton Cottage, 12 Prince Edward Road, Hereford HR4 0LG* Tel (01432) 267414

BOLLEY, Michael Francis. b 55. St Cath Coll Ox BA76 MSc77 MA92. Ripon Coll Cuddesdon 90. **d** 92 **p** 93. C Pinner *Lon* 92-95; C Eastcote St Lawr 95-99; P-in-c Southall H Trin from 99. *Holy Trinity Vicarage, Park View Road, Southall UB1 3HJ* Tel (020) 8574 3839 E-mail michael@bolley.freeserve.co.uk

BOLSTER, David Richard. b 50. BA. St Jo Coll Nottm. **d** 84 **p** 85. C Luton Lewsey St Hugh *St Alb* 84-87; V Woodside w E Hyde 87-01; V Edmonton St Aldhelm *Lon* from 01. *St Aldhelm's Vicarage, Windmill Road, London N18 1PA* Tel (020) 8807 5336 E-mail david.bolster@london.anglican.org

BOLT, David Dingley. b 18. St Jo Coll Cam LLB58 LLM85. Westcott Ho Cam 66. **d** 68 **p** 69. Malawi 68-70; C Chesterton Gd Shep *Ely* 70-71; P-in-c Gt Wilbraham 71-74; V 74-86; P-in-c Lt Wilbraham 71-74; R 74-86; RD Quy 75-81; rtd 86; Perm to Offic *Ely* from 86. *24 Warwick Road, Cambridge CB4 3HN* Tel (01223) 366361

BOLT, George Henry. b 34. MInstP75 CPhys75 Lon Univ BSc60 Bath Univ MSc75. S Dios Minl Tr Scheme 85. **d** 88 **p** 89. NSM Oldbury *Sarum* 88-89; Chapl Chippenham Tech Coll 89-90; C Kington St Michael *Bris* 90-92; P-in-c Aldenham *St Alb* 92-98; rtd 98; Perm to Offic *Ban* from 98. *Ty Capel Ffrwd, Llanfachreth, Dolgellau LL40 2NR* Tel (01341) 422006

BOLT, Mrs Mary Veronica. b 36. S Dios Minl Tr Scheme 90. **d** 93 **p** 94. NSM Aldenham *St Alb* 93-98; Sub-Chapl HM Pris The Mount 93-98; rtd 98; Perm to Offic *Ban* 98-99; P-in-c Maentwrog w Trawsfynydd 99-03. *Ty Capel Ffrwd, Llanfachreth, Dolgellau LL40 2NR* Tel (01341) 422006 E-mail mary.bolt@care4free.net

BOLTON, Christopher Leonard. b 60. St Mich Coll Llan DipTh83. **d** 83 **p** 84. C Lampeter *St D* 83-86; P-in-c Llanarth and Capel Cynon w Talgarreg etc 86-87; V from 87; RD Glyn Aeron from 02. *The Vicarage, Llanarth SA47 0NJ* Tel (01545) 580745

BOLTON, Mrs Jane Elizabeth. b 53. Leic Univ BA75. Ripon Coll Cuddesdon 95. **d** 97 **p** 98. C Sheff St Mark Broomhill *Sheff* 97-02; P-in-c Dinnington 02-04; P-in-c Laughton w Throapham 03-04; P-in-c Dinnington w Laughton and Throapham 04-05; R from 05. *The Rectory, 217 Nursery Road, Dinnington, Sheffield S25 2QU* Tel (01909) 562335

BOLTON, John. b 43. SS Paul & Mary Coll Cheltenham DipEd64. Trin Coll Bris 83. **d** 85 **p** 86. C Minehead *B & W* 85-89; R Winford w Felton Common Hill 89-98; C-in-c Locking Castle CD from 98. *The Vicarage, 78 Bransby Way, Weston-super-Mare BS24 7BW* Tel (01934) 516565 Fax 513218 E-mail john20011ccp@aol.com

BOLTON, Kelvin. b 53. Wilson Carlile Coll 88 Trin Coll Bris BA98. **d** 98 **p** 99. C Walton Breck Ch Ch *Liv* 98-01; V Goose Green from 01. *St Paul's Vicarage, Warrington Road, Wigan WN3 6QB* Tel (01942) 242984 E-mail kelvinb@whsmithnet.co.uk

BOLTON, Paul Edward. b 71. St Jo Coll Ox BA94 MA98 Peterho Cam BA97. Ridley Hall Cam 95. **d** 98 **p** 99. C Lowestoft Ch Ch *Nor* 98-01; Titus Trust from 01. *93 Morrell Avenue, Oxford OX4 1NQ* Tel (01865) 248955 E-mail paul_bolton@lineone.net

BOLTON, Peter Richard Shawcross. b 58. Warwick Univ BA79. Sarum & Wells Th Coll 80. **d** 83 **p** 84. C Beckenham St Jas *Roch* 83-86; C Bedford Leigh *Man* 86-88; V Royton St Paul 88-94; AD Tandle 93-94; P-in-c Lower Broughton Ascension 95-01; P-in-c Salford Ordsall St Clem 98-01; P-in-c Ardwick St Benedict 99-01; V Leavesden All SS *St Alb* from 01. *All Saints' Vicarage, Horseshoe Lane, Watford WD25 7HJ* Tel (01923) 672375 *or* tel and fax 661862 E-mail peterbolton@btconnect.com

BOLTON, Richard David Edward. b 52. MA. St Steph Ho Ox 79. **d** 81 **p** 82. C Rawmarsh w Parkgate *Sheff* 81-84; Chapl Wellingborough Sch 85-92; Chapl Merchant Taylors' Sch Northwood from 91; Perm to Offic *Lon* from 91; P in O from 96. *1 Askew Road, Sandy Lodge, Northwood HA6 2JE* Tel (01923) 821136 *or* 820644

BOLTON, Archdeacon of. *See* APPLEGATE, The Ven John

BOLTON, Suffragan Bishop of. *See* GILLETT, The Rt Revd David Keith

BOMFORD, Canon Rodney William George. b 43. BNC Ox BA64 DipTh66 MA68. Coll of Resurr Mirfield 67 Union Th Sem (NY) STM69. **d** 69 **p** 70. C Deptford St Paul *S'wark* 69-77; V Camberwell St Giles w St Matt 77-01; RD Camberwell 87-97; Hon Can S'wark Cathl 93-01; rtd 01. *The Manor House, Modbury, Ivybridge PL21 0RA* Tel (01548) 831277

BOMYER, Julian Richard Nicholas Jeffrey. b 55. AKC78 Sarum & Wells Th Coll 78. **d** 79 **p** 80. C Rugby St Andr *Cov* 79-84; TV 85-88; P-in-c Clifton upon Dunsmore w Brownsover 84-85; Prec Ch Ch *Ox* 88-93; V Hampton *Worc* 93-01; P-in-c Sedgeberrow w Hinton-on-the-Green 00-01; R Hampton w Sedgeberrow and Hinton-on-the-Green from 01. *St Andrew's Vicarage, Pershore Road, Evesham WR11 2PQ* Tel (01386) 446381 Fax 49224 E-mail vicar@hamptonchurch.org.uk

BOND, Alan Richard. b 49. Lon Univ BSc71 Imp Coll Lon ARCS71 MCMI75 MIMA75 CMath98. S Dios Minl Tr Scheme 80. **d** 83 **p** 84. NSM Westbourne *Chich* 83-86. *Southlyn, The Park, Castle Cary BA7 7EP*

✠**BOND, The Rt Revd Charles Derek.** b 27. AKC51. **d** 52 **p** 53 **c** 76. C Friern Barnet St Jas *Lon* 52-56; Lic to Offic *Birm* 56-58; Midl Sch Sec SCM 56-58; V Harringay St Paul *Lon* 58-62; V Harrow Weald All SS 62-72; P-in-c Pebmarsh *Chelmsf* 72-73; Adn Colchester 72-76; Suff Bp Bradwell 76-84; Area Bp Bradwell 84-92; rtd 92; Hon Asst Bp *Glouc* and *Worc* from 92. *Ambleside, 14 Worcester Road, Evesham WR11 4JU* Tel (01386) 446156 E-mail bondd46@aol.com

BOND, Charles Robert. b 25. Trin Coll Bris DipHE80. **d** 80 **p** 81. C Wythenshawe Wm Temple Ch *Man* 80-82; TV Cwmbran *Mon* 82-88; Chapl Corfu *Eur* 88-91; Chapl Playa de Las Americas Tenerife 91-93; rtd 93. *38 Birch Avenue, Alsager, Stoke-on-Trent ST7 2QY* Tel (01270) 884184

BOND, Daniel Michael. b 75. Bp Grosseteste Coll BA(QTS)97 Cam Univ BTh02. Ridley Hall Cam 99. **d** 02 **p** 03. C Ranworth w Panxworth, Woodbastwick etc *Nor* 02-05; R Acle w Fishley, N Burlingham, Beighton w Moulton from 05. *The Rectory, Norwich Road, Acle, Norwich NR13 3BU* Tel (01493) 750393 E-mail dmb40@cam.ac.uk

BOND, David. b 36. Oak Hill Th Coll 72. **d** 74 **p** 75. C Leyton St Mary w St Edw *Chelmsf* 74-78; C Slough *Ox* 78-80; V Selby St Jas *York* 80-93; P-in-c Wistow 80-82; V 82-93; RD Selby 89-93; P-in-c Northiam *Chich* 93-94; R 94-99; rtd 99; Perm to Offic *Chich* from 00. *32 Reginald Road, Bexhill-on-Sea TN39 3PH* Tel (01424) 731845

BOND, David Matthew. b 38. Leic Univ BA59 Leeds Univ PGCE67 Nottm Univ MA85. Sarum Th Coll 59. **d** 61 **p** 62. C Leic St Anne *Leic* 61-64; E England Sec SCM 64-66; Hon C Nor St Pet Mancroft *Nor* 64-67; Lect and Hd of Section Pet Regional Coll 67-96; Lect Pet Coll of Adult Educn from 96; Hon C Stamford All SS w St Pet *Linc* 74-81; Hon C Stamford All SS w St Jo from 81; Perm to Offic *Pet* from 85. *2 The Courtyard, Cotterstock, Peterborough PE8 5HD* Tel (01832) 226255

BOND, David Warner. b 32. MA BSc(Econ). Cant Sch of Min 79. **d** 82 **p** 83. NSM Otham w Langley *Cant* 82-04; Perm to Offic from 04. *6 Denton Close, Maidstone ME15 8ER* Tel (01622) 202239 Fax 205149 E-mail dwbond@bigfoot.com

BOND, Derek. *See* BOND, The Rt Revd Charles Derek

BOND, Douglas Gregory. b 39. FVCM. Edin Th Coll 74. **d** 76 **p** 77. NSM Edin St Paul and St Geo *Edin* 76-83; P-in-c Abthorpe w Slapton *Pet* 83-84; R Silverstone and Abthorpe w Slapton 84-89; V Pet St Jude 89-95; R Kislingbury and Harpole 95-04; rtd 04; Perm to Offic *Pet* from 04. *3 Mews Cottages, Meeting Lane, Towcester NN12 6JX* Tel (01327) 358861 Mobile 07802-736409 E-mail father.d@highrev.fsnet.co.uk

BOND, Gordon. b 44. Chich Th Coll 68. **d** 71 **p** 72. C Wisbech St Aug *Ely* 71-74; C Wembley Park St Aug *Lon* 74-77; C York Town St Mich *Guildf* 77-80; C Haywards Heath St Wilfrid *Chich* 80; TV 80-82; V Lower Beeding 82-86; V E Grinstead St Mary from 86; RD E Grinstead 98-04. *The Vicarage, Windmill Lane, East Grinstead RH19 2DS* Tel (01342) 323439 E-mail bond_st_mary_eg@yahoo.co.uk

BOND, Canon John Albert. b 35. LRAM55 GGSM56 St Cath Soc Ox BA61 MA65 MPhil77 Seabury-Western Th Sem BD62. Wycliffe Hall Ox 58. **d** 62 **p** 63. C Chelmsf Cathl *Chelmsf* 62-63; Succ 63-64; Prec 64-66; Lect St Osyth Coll Clacton-on-Sea 66-69; Lect Ch Ch Coll Cant 69-73; Sen Lect 73-85; Prin Lect and Hd RS Cant Ch Ch Univ Coll 85-00; Hon Min Can Cant Cathl *Cant* 70-85; Hon Can 85-00; rtd 00; Perm to Offic *Cant* from 03. *St Lawrence Priory, 136 Old Dover Road, Canterbury CT1 3NX* Tel (01227) 765575

BOND, The Very Revd John Frederick Augustus. b 45. Open Univ BA75. CITC 64. **d** 67 **p** 69. C Lisburn St Paul *Conn* 67-70; C Finaghy 70-77; I Ballynure and Ballyeaston 77-99; I Skerry w Rathcavan and Newtowncrommelin from 99; Can Conn Cathl 96-98; Prec 98-01; Dean Conn from 01. *The Rectory, 49 Rectory Gardens, Broughshane, Ballymena BT42 4LF* Tel and fax (028) 2586 1215 Mobile 07711-285728 E-mail skerry@connor.anglican.org *or* dean@connor.anglican.org

BOND, Kim Mary. *See* BURGESS, Mrs Kim Mary

BOND, Lawrence. b 53. ACIB77. Sarum & Wells Th Coll 92. **d** 92 **p** 93. C Saffron Walden w Wendens Ambo and Littlebury *Chelmsf* 92-95; TV 96-00; P-in-c Takeley w Lt Canfield 00-04; R from 04; RD Dunmow from 02. *The Rectory, Parsonage Road, Takeley, Bishop's Stortford CM22 6QX* Tel and fax (01279) 870837 E-mail lbd.littlebury@virgin.net

BOND, Linda. b 52. Nottm Univ BEd80 Lon Inst of Educn MA89 ACertCM87. EAMTC 96. **d** 99 **p** 00. C Brackley St Pet w St Jas *Pet* 99-03; C Skegness and Winthorpe *Linc* 03-04; C Skegness Gp from 04. *18 Danial Close, Skegness PE25 1RQ* Tel (01754) 610113 E-mail linda@revdbond.fsnet.co.uk

BOND, Mark Francis Wilson. b 53. Sarum & Wells Th Coll 89. **d** 91 **p** 92. C Taunton Lyngford *B & W* 91-95; V Highbridge 95-02; R Jersey St Brelade *Win* from 02. *The Rectory, La Marquanderie Hill, St Brelade, Jersey JE3 8EP* Tel (01534) 742302 E-mail bonds@jerseymail.co.uk

BOND, Norman. b 23. Wycliffe Hall Ox. **d** 70 **p** 71. C Warrington St Ann *Liv* 70-73; P-in-c 73-77; P-in-c Warrington St Pet 73-77; V Wigan St Cath 77-88; rtd 88; Perm to Offic *Carl* 88-01; *Liv* 88-98; *S & M* from 00. *5 Bradda Glen Close, Port Erin, Isle of Man IM9 6PG* Tel (01624) 832817

BOND, Paul Maxwell. b 36. TD73. Open Th Coll BA00 ACIB56. Oak Hill Th Coll 76. **d** 79 **p** 80. NSM Wisley w Pyrford *Guildf* 79-91; Org Children's Soc SW Lon 88-91; C Egham *Guildf* 91-93; C Horsell 93-94; V Rockfield and St Maughen's w Llangattock etc *Mon* 94-99; rtd 99; Hon C Islip w Charlton on Otmoor, Oddington, Noke etc *Ox* 99-01; Hon C Ray Valley 01-04. *19 Millview, Blockley Court, Blockley, Moreton-in-Marsh GL56 9AZ* Tel (01386) 701669 E-mail paul_bond@bigfoot.com

BOND, Robert. *See* BOND, Charles Robert

BOND, Mrs Susan Fraser. b 55. SS Hild & Bede Coll Dur BEd78 Leeds Univ MA00. N Ord Course 96. **d** 99 **p** 00. C Tickhill w Stainton *Sheff* 99-02; R Warmsworth from 02. *Warmsworth Rectory, 187 Warmsworth Road, Doncaster DN4 0TW* Tel (01302) 853324 E-mail sue@bond007.fslife.co.uk

BOND, Thomas James. b 18. TCD BA41 MA68. CITC 41. **d** 42 **p** 43. C Annagh w Drumaloor and Cloverhill *K, E & A* 42-44; C Sligo Cathl 44-47; I Kilgobbin *L & K* 47-49; I Bourney w Dunkerrin 49-52; I Kilkeevin w Kiltullagh *K, E & A* 52-55; I Bailieborough 55-60; I Templemichael w Clongish, Clooncumber etc 60-91; Preb Elphin Cathl 67-91; Adn Elphin and Ardagh 78-91; rtd 91. *Apartment 5, 69 Strand Road, Sandymoutn, Dublin 4, Irish Republic*

BOND-THOMAS, David Harradence. b 23. Ch Coll Cam BA44 MA51. **d** 59 **p** 60. C Langley Marish *Ox* 59-62; C Earley St Pet 62-71; P-in-c Middleton Stoney 71-77; P-in-c Bucknell 71-76; P-in-c Weston on the Green 72-76; P-in-c Chesterton w Wendlebury 76-77; V Chesterton w Middleton Stoney and Wendlebury 77-89; rtd 89; Perm to Offic *Glouc* from 89. *35 Greet Road, Winchcombe, Cheltenham GL54 5JT* Tel (01242) 603150

BONE, Janet. **d** 05. NSM Penallt and Trellech *Mon* from 05. *Ty Ffynnon, The Narth, Monmouth NP25 4QJ* Tel (01600) 860466

✠**BONE, The Rt Revd John Frank Ewan.** b 30. St Pet Coll Ox BA54 MA59 Whitelands Coll Lon PGCE71. Ely Th Coll 54. **d** 56 **p** 57 **c** 89. C Pimlico St Gabr *Lon* 56-60; C Henley *Ox* 60-63; V Datchet 63-76; RD Burnham 74-77; R Upton cum Chalvey 76-78; Adn Buckingham 77-89; Area Bp Reading 89-96; rtd 97; Hon Asst Bp Ox from 97. *4 Grove Road, Henley-on-Thames RG9 1DH* Tel (01491) 413482 E-mail jfebone@onetel.com

BONHAM, Mrs Valerie. b 47. ALA94. St Alb and Ox Min Course 94. **d** 97 **p** 98. NSM Newbury *Ox* 97-98; C Cookham 98-02; P-in-c Coleford w Holcombe *B & W* from 02. *The Vicarage, Church Street, Coleford, Radstock BA3 5NG* Tel (01373) 813382

BONHAM-CARTER, Gerard Edmund David. b 31. Lon Univ BSc53 DCAe55. S'wark Ord Course 84. **d** 87 **p** 88. NSM Wandsworth St Paul *S'wark* 87-04; Chapl R Hosp for Neuro-Disability 92-04; Perm to Offic *St E* from 87 and *S'wark* from 04. *7 Fleur Gates, Princes Way, London SW19 6QQ* Tel and fax (020) 8788 1230 E-mail gerard.bonham-carter@ukgateway.net

BONIFACE, Lionel Ernest George. b 36. Lon Coll of Div ALCD63 BD64. **d** 64 **p** 65. C Attenborough w Chilwell *S'well* 64-69; C Farndon 69-71; C Thorpe 69-71; P-in-c Mansfield St Aug 71-77; V Oughtibridge *Sheff* 77-92; Ind Chapl 79-81; P-in-c Treeton 92-93; TV Brinsworth w Catcliffe and Treeton 93-98; rtd 98; Perm to Offic *Sheff* from 99. *30 Everard Avenue, Bradway, Sheffield S17 4LZ* Tel 0114-235 0415

BONIWELL, Timothy Richard. b 51. AKC73. St Aug Coll Cant 74. **d** 75 **p** 76. C Walthamstow St Mich *Chelmsf* 75-78; C Wigmore Abbey *Heref* 78-83; C Studley and Chapl Trowbridge Coll *Sarum* 83-86; V Bath St Barn w Englishcombe *B & W* 86-95; R Tintinhull w Chilthorne Domer, Yeovil Marsh etc 95-02; V Enfield St Geo *Lon* 02-05; Chapl Convent of St Mary at the Cross Edgware from 05. *St John's House, 27 Highview Avenue, Edgware HA8 9TX* Tel (020) 8958 8980 E-mail boniwell@btinternet.com

BONNER, David Robert. b 28. ASCA66 FCIS72 FCIB74 Lon Univ DipRS78. S'wark Ord Course 74. **d** 77 **p** 78. NSM Hampton All SS *Lon* 77-84; P-in-c Twickenham All SS 84-91; rtd 91; Perm to Offic *Lon* from 91. *17 St James's Road, Hampton Hill, Hampton TW12 1DH* Tel (020) 8979 1565

BONNER, James Maxwell Campbell. b 28. Sydney Univ BSc48 DipEd49. Oak Hill Th Coll BD59. **d** 60 **p** 61. C Walthamstow St Mary *Chelmsf* 60-63; C Morden *S'wark* 63-65; Australia from 65; rtd 98. *1206/5 Albert Road, Strathfield, NSW, Australia 2135* Tel (0061) (2) 9763 7535

BONNET, Tom. b 51. Univ of Wales (Cardiff) BTh90. St Mich Coll Llan 90. **d** 90 **p** 91. C Criccieth w Treflys *Ban* 90-91; C Denio w Abererch 91-93; R Llanfachraeth 93-94; R Valley w Llanfachraeth 94-98; R Valley w Llechylched and Caergeiliog from 98; AD Llifon and Talybolion from 04. *The Rectory, London Road, Valley, Holyhead LL65 3DP* Tel and fax (01407) 741242 Mobile 07713-548941 E-mail rev@tbonnet.freeserve.co.uk

BONNEY, Canon Mark Philip John. b 57. St Cath Coll Cam BA78 MA82. St Steph Ho Ox BA84 MA89. **d** 85 **p** 86. C Stockton St Pet *Dur* 85-88; Chapl St Alb Abbey *St Alb* 88-90; Prec 90-92; V Eaton Bray w Edlesborough 92-96; R Gt Berkhamsted 96-04; RD Berkhamsted 02-04; Can Res and Treas Sarum Cathl *Sarum* from 04. *Loders, 23 The Close, Salisbury SP1 2EH* Tel (01722) 322172 E-mail treasurer@salcath.co.uk

BONNEY, Prof Richard John. b 47. Ox Univ DPhil73. **d** 96 **p** 97. NSM Knighton St Mary Magd *Leic* from 96. *7 Carisbrooke Park, Leicester LE2 3PQ* Tel 0116-212 5677 E-mail bon@leicester.anglican.org

BONNEY, Stuart Campbell. b 51. Edin Univ BD83. Edin Th Coll 81. **d** 83 **p** 84. C Edin St Luke *Edin* 83-86; C Edin St Martin 83-86; P-in-c Auchterarder *St And* 86-90; P-in-c Muthill 86-90; Dep Chapl HM Pris Leeds 90-91; Chapl HM Pris Moorland 91-96; P-in-c Bathgate *Edin* 96-01; P-in-c Linlithgow 96-01. *Circlebay Cottage, 159 Main Street, Pathhead EH37 5SQ* Tel (01875) 320336 E-mail bonney678@netscapeonline.co.uk

BONNEYWELL, Miss Christine Mary. b 57. Univ of Wales (Lamp) BA78 LTh80. Sarum & Wells Th Coll 80. **d** 81 **p** 94. C Swansea St Pet *S & B* 81-84; C Llangyfelach 84-86; Chapl Univ of Wales (Lamp) *St D* 86-90; Educn Officer Wells Cathl *B & W* 90-95; C Yeovil H Trin w Barwick 95-97; Chapl Yeovil Distr Hosp 95-97; Chapl Pilgrim Health NHS Trust Boston 97-01; Chapl United Lincs Hosps NHS Trust from 01. *The Chaplaincy, Pilgrim Hospital, Sibsey Road, Boston PE21 9QT,* or *4 Hospital Lane, Boston PE21 9BY* Tel (01205) 364801 ext 2243 *or* 355151 Fax 354395

BONSALL, Charles Henry Brash. b 42. Ex Univ BA66. Ridley Hall Cam 66. **d** 68 **p** 69. C Cheltenham St Mary *Glouc* 68-72; Sudan 72-77 and 79-83; Perm to Offic *Nor* 78; Development and Miss Sec Intercon Ch Soc 83-93; Perm to Offic *Birm* from 91; rtd 93. *3 Pakenham Road, Birmingham B15 2NE* Tel 0121-440 6143

BONSEY, Hugh Richmond Lowry. b 49. Sarum & Wells Th Coll 74. **d** 76 **p** 77. C Bris St Mary Redcliffe w Temple etc *Bris* 76-80;

TV Sutton *Liv* 80-88; P-in-c Yatton Keynell *Bris* 88-89; P-in-c Biddestone w Slaughterford 88-89; P-in-c Castle Combe 88-89; P-in-c W Kington 88-89; P-in-c Nettleton w Littleton Drew 88-89; C Westbury-on-Trym H Trin 89-90; V Peasedown St John w Wellow *B & W* 90-04; TV Wylye and Till Valley *Sarum* from 04. *The Rectory, West Street, Great Wishford, Salisbury SP2 0PQ* Tel (01722) 790363 E-mail hbonsey@blueyonder.co.uk

BONSEY, Thory Richmond. b 18. St Chad's Coll Dur 37. Cuddesdon Coll 46. **d** 47 **p** 48. C Salisbury St Martin *Sarum* 47-50; C Kingsthorpe *Pet* 50-53; PC Ashwick w Oakhill *B & W* 53-57; V Desborough *Pet* 57-61; R Teigh w Whissendine 61-67; R Ecton 67-73; V Ketton 73-77; Australia from 77; rtd 83. *PO Box 548, Heathcote, Vic, Australia 3523* E-mail tfbonsey@austarmetro.com.au

BONTING, Prof Sjoerd Lieuwe. b 24. Amsterdam Univ BSc44 MSc50 PhD52 Lon Univ BD58 SOSc. Washington Dioc Course 63. **d** 63 **p** 64. C Bethesda St Luke USA 63-65; Prof Biochemistry Nijmegen Univ 65-85; Chapl Nijmegen, Eindhoven, Arnhem, and Twenthe *Eur* 80-85; Consultant NASA USA 85-98; Asst Sunnyvale St Thos 85-90; Asst Palo Alto St Mark 90-93; Perm to Offic *Eur* from 93. *Specreyse 12, 7471 TH Goor, The Netherlands* Tel (0031) (547) 260947 E-mail s.l.bonting@wxs.nl

BOOKER, Gerald Dennis. b 30. St Pet Coll Ox BA52 MA56. Ridley Hall Cam 53 Oak Hill Th Coll 80. **d** 81 **p** 82. Hon C Hertford All SS *St Alb* 81-83; R Bramfield w Stapleford and Waterford 83-96; Chapl Herts Univ 90-96; rtd 96; Perm to Offic *St Alb* from 96. *The Garden House, Churchfields, Hertford SG13 8AE*

BOOKER, James Howard. b 57. Edin Th Coll 88. **d** 90 **p** 91. C Peterhead *Ab* 90-92; C Old Deer 90-92; C Longside 90-92; C Strichen 90-92; Bp's Chapl Peterhead 92-93; R 93-00; Miss to Seamen 92-00; Chapl HM Pris Peterhead 93-00. *Address temp unknown*

BOOKER, Mrs Margaret Katharine. b 20. MCSP42. Westcott Ho Cam 82. **dss** 83 **d** 87 **p** 94. Stansted Mountfitchet *Chelmsf* 83-95; Par Dn 87-90; NSM 90-95; rtd 90; Perm to Offic *Ely* from 95. *49 Home Farm Road, Houghton, Huntingdon PE28 2BN* Tel (01480) 469167

BOOKER, Michael Charles. b 36. LLCM57 ARCO58. Lon Coll of Div. **d** 63 **p** 64. C Royston *St Alb* 63-66; C Mildenhall *St E* 66-68; Min Can St E Cathl 68-83; Prec 70-83; Chapl Framlingham Coll 84-99; rtd 99; Perm to Offic *St E* from 99. *29 The Mowbrays, Framlingham, Woodbridge IP13 9DL* Tel (01728) 723122

BOOKER, Michael Paul Montague. b 57. Jes Coll Ox BA79 Bris Univ CertEd80. Trin Coll Bris 84. **d** 87 **p** 88. C Cant St Mary Bredin *Cant* 87-91; V Leamington Priors St Mary *Cov* 91-96; Dir Miss and Past Studies Ridley Hall Cam 96-05; P-in-c Comberton *Ely* from 05; P-in-c Toft w Caldecote and Childerley from 05. *Address temp unknown* E-mail mpmb2@cam.ac.uk

BOOKLESS, Andrew Pitcairn. b 63. Sheff Univ BA85. St Jo Coll Nottm DipMM92. **d** 92 **p** 93. C Llantrisant *Llan* 92-95; C Llangynwyd w Maesteg 95-97; V Bargoed and Deri w Brithdir from 97. *The Vicarage, Vicarage Lane, Bargoed CF81 8TR* Tel (01443) 831069

BOOKLESS, David John Charles. b 62. Jes Coll Cam MA83 PGCE. Trin Coll Bris MA91. **d** 91 **p** 92. C Southall Green St Jo *Lon* 91-99; P-in-c Southall St Geo 99-01; Nat Dir A Rocha UK (Christians in Conservation) from 01; Hon C Southall Green St Jo from 03. *13 Avenue Road, Southall UB1 3BL* Tel (020) 8571 0981 *or* 8574 5935 E-mail dave.bookless@arocha.org *or* uk@arocha.org

BOOKLESS, John Guy. b 19. Clare Coll Cam BA40 MA46 Serampore Univ MTh72. Ridley Hall Cam 47. **d** 49 **p** 50. C Toxteth Park Ch Ch *Liv* 49-50; C Fazakerley Em 50-51; Tutor Ridley Hall Cam 51-52; India 53-72; Miss Bhagalpur 53-60; Tutor Bp's Coll Calcutta 61-65; Lect United Th Coll Bangalore 66-72; C St Alb St Mich *St Alb* 73-76; C Harlow New Town w Lt Parndon *Chelmsf* 76-78; TV 78-79; V Willoughby-on-the-Wolds w Wysall *S'well* 79-85; P-in-c Widmerpool 79-85; rtd 85; Perm to Offic *S'well* 85-88; *Leic* 85-03. *7 Oakland Gardens, Bargoed CF81 8QF* Tel (01443) 832166

BOOKLESS, Mrs Rosemary. b 26. Westf Coll Lon BA47 DipEd49 Serampore Univ BD72. St Mich Ho Ox 56. **dss** 80 **d** 91 **p** 94. Willoughby-on-the-Wolds w Wysall and Widmerpool *S'well* 80-85; rtd 85; Perm to Offic *Leic* 85-89; Loughborough Em 89-91; NSM 91-95; NSM Loughborough Em and St Mary in Charnwood 95-97; Perm to Offic 97-03. *7 Oakland Gardens, Bargoed CF81 8QF* Tel (01443) 832166 E-mail rosemary@rbookless.freeserve.co.uk

BOON, Marion. *See* SIMMONS, Ms Marion

BOON, Nigel Francis. b 39. St Jo Coll Nottm. **d** 83 **p** 84. C St Helens St Helen *Liv* 83-86; V Kirkdale St Lawr 86-92; V Huyton Quarry 92-99; rtd 01. *c/o Mrs Celeste Deville, 33 Lightsfield, Oakley, Basingstoke RG23 7BL* E-mail nigelboon@aol.com

BOON, William John. b 54. Glouc Sch of Min 84. **d** 88 **p** 89. Hon C Matson *Glouc* 88-91; NSM Gt Witcombe 91; C 91-95; C Brockworth 91-96; P-in-c Sharpness w Purton and Brookend 96-99; P-in-c Slimbridge 97-99; R Sharpness, Purton, Brookend and Slimbridge from 00; RD Dursley from 02. *The Vicarage, Sanigar Lane, Newtown, Berkeley GL13 9NF* Tel (01453) 811360 E-mail bill_boon@lineone.net

BOOT, Felicity Olivia. b 43. TCert64. STETS 94. **d** 97 **p** 98. NSM Lyndhurst and Emery Down and Minstead *Win* 97-04; Chapl Southn Univ Hosps NHS Trust from 04. *The Firs, Pikes Hill, Lyndhurst SO43 7AY* Tel (023) 8079 8517 E-mail felicityboot@hotmail.com

BOOTES, Michael Charles Edward. b 35. ACP70. Sarum Th Coll 58. **d** 61 **p** 62. C Winchmore Hill St Paul *Lon* 61-64; Switzerland 64-67; C St Marylebone All SS *Lon* 67-68; OGS from 68; Chapl Kingsley St Mich Sch W Sussex 69-75; V Brandon *Dur* 75-78; Chapl Shoreham Gr Sch 78-79; C Clayton w Keymer *Chich* 80-84; TV Ovingdean w Rottingdean and Woodingdean 84-85; TR Ovingdean 85-88; V Lundwood *Wakef* 88-92; C Pontefract St Giles 92-95; P-in-c Kellington w Whitley 95-00; rtd 00; Hon C Castleford *Wakef* 00-05; Hon C Methley w Mickletown *Ripon* from 05. *The Rectory, Church Side, Methley, Leeds LS26 9BJ* Tel (01977) 557080 Mobile 07903-215210 E-mail mb@ogs.net

BOOTH, Charles. *See* BOOTH, Ewart Charles

BOOTH, Charles Robert. b 48. Leeds Univ CertEd75. N Ord Course 79. **d** 82 **p** 83. C Eccleshill *Bradf* 82-84; C Jersey St Brelade *Win* 84-88; Australia 88-90 and from 93; C Newman 88-90; V Blurton *Lich* 90-93; Chapl Frederick Irwin Angl Communion Sch Mandurah 94-98; R Spearwood from 99. *10 Fallow Crescent, Spearwood, W Australia 6163* Tel (0061) (8) 9418 1005

BOOTH, David. b 44. Coll of Resurr Mirfield 72. **d** 74 **p** 75. C Osmondthorpe St Phil *Ripon* 74-77; C Armley w New Wortley 77-79; V Leeds St Wilfrid 79-95; V Royton St Paul *Man* from 95. *St Paul's Vicarage, 2 Low Meadows, Royton, Oldham OL2 6YB* Tel 0161-624 2388

BOOTH, Derek. b 36. LTCL ALCM AKC61. **d** 62 **p** 63. C Woodchurch *Ches* 62-65; C Penrith St Andr *Carl* 65-67; C Tranmere St Paul *Ches* 67-70; C Wilmslow 70-72; V Micklehurst 73-97; C Staveley and Barrow Hill *Derby* 97-01; rtd 01; Perm to Offic *Derby* from 01. *9 Ilam Close, Inkersall, Chesterfield S43 3EW* Tel (01246) 475421

BOOTH, Eric James. b 43. Open Univ BA84. N Ord Course 86. **d** 89 **p** 90. NSM Nelson St Phil *Blackb* 89-93; NSM Fence and Newchurch-in-Pendle 93-97; NSM Padiham w Hapton and Padiham Green 97-03; rtd 03. *5 Round Hill Place, Cliviger, Burnley BB10 4UA* Tel (01282) 450708

BOOTH, Ewart Charles. b 67. LTCL85 K Coll Lon LLB88. Sarum & Wells Th Coll BTh93. **d** 93 **p** 95. NSM Tadley St Pet *Win* 93-95; C Highcliffe w Hinton Admiral 95-00; R W Parley *Sarum* from 00. *The Rectory, 250 New Road, West Parley, Ferndown BH22 8EW* Tel (01202) 873561

BOOTH, Graham Richard. b 55. Birm Univ BSocSc75. St Jo Coll Nottm 89. **d** 91 **p** 92. C Woodthorpe *S'well* 91-96; P-in-c Trowell 96-02; P-in-c Awsworth w Cossall 00-02; R Trowell, Awsworth and Cossall 02-05; Community of Aid and Hilda from 05. *The Open Gate, Marygate, Holy Island, Berwick-upon-Tweed TD15 2SD* Tel and fax (01289) 389222 E-mail g.r.booth@ntlworld.com

BOOTH, Ian George. b 64. Chich Th Coll 85 Linc Th Coll 87. **d** 88 **p** 89. C Pet St Mary Boongate *Pet* 88-90; C Hawley H Trin *Guildf* 90-94; V Willesden St Mary *Lon* 94-03; P-in-c Gosport H Trin *Portsm* 03-05; V from 05; V Gosport Ch Ch from 05; RD Gosport from 03. *9 Britannia Way, Gosport PO12 4FZ* Tel (023) 9258 0173

BOOTH, Jon Alfred. b 42. Nottm Univ BA64 Lon Univ MPhil72. Coll of Resurr Mirfield 78. **d** 80 **p** 81. C Elland *Wakef* 80-84; C Royston from 84. *The Vicarage, Church Street, Royston, Barnsley S71 4QZ* Tel (01226) 722410

BOOTH, Kenneth Neville. b 41. Otago Univ BA62 MA63 BD66 MTh69 St Andr Univ PhD74. St Jo Coll Auckland 63. **d** 65 **p** 66. New Zealand 65-69; C St Paul's Cathl Dunedin 65-69; Perm to Offic *St And* 70-71; Lect St Andr Univ 70-71; New Zealand 72-80; Lect St Jo Coll Auckland 72-80; Asst P Tamaki St Thos 73-80; Perm to Offic *Ox* 80-81; New Zealand from 81; Warden Selwyn Coll Dunedin 81-85; Lect 81-97; V Roslyn 85-97; Adn Dunedin 86-95; V Gen 92-97; Dir Coll Ho Inst of Th from 97. *30 Church Lane, Merivale, Christchurch 8001, New Zealand* Tel (0064) (3) 355 9145 Fax 355 6140 E-mail chit@cyberxpress.co.nz

BOOTH, Leonard William. b 46. K Coll Lon BD70 AKC70. **d** 71 **p** 72. C Cockerton *Dur* 72-75; C Hove St Barn *Chich* 75-77; TV Brighton Resurr 77-78; C E Grinstead St Mary 78-81; USA from 81. *254 St Joseph Avenue, Long Beach, CA 90803, USA* Tel (001) (562) 433 6531 E-mail fatherleo@fatherleo.com

BOOTH, Michael Kevin. b 47. Louvain Univ Belgium BA. St Jo Coll Nottm 88 Oscott Coll (RC) 65. **d** 71 **p** 72. In RC Ch 71-87; C N Reddish *Man* 88-89; R Heaton Norris Ch w All SS 89-99; rtd 99; Perm to Offic *Man* from 00. *3 Potter Road, Hadfield, Hyde SK13 2RA* Tel (01457) 853963

BOOTH, Paul Harris. b 49. St Jo Coll Nottm LTh79. **d** 79 **p** 80. C Thorpe Edge *Bradf* 79-82; P-in-c Frizinghall 82-83; TV Shipley St Paul and Frizinghall 83-97; rtd 97; Perm to Offic *Bradf* from 97. *3 Gilstead Court, Gilstead, Bingley BD16 3LA* Tel (01274) 551071 *or* (01535) 650526 Fax (01535) 650550 E-mail paul@gilcourt.freeserve.co.uk

BOOTH, Terrence Richard. b 44. Edith Cowan Univ (Aus) BA98. St Jo Coll Morpeth ThDip70. **d** 69 **p** 70. Australia 69-79 and from 81; C Corowa 69-71; Asst Broken Hill 72-74; P-in-c Urana/Jerilderie 74-79; C Chesterfield St Mary and All SS *Derby* 79-81; Chapl Chesterfield R Hosp 79-81; R Coolamon/Ganmain 82; RD Murrumbidgee 83-84; Chapl Bunbury Cathl Gr Sch 85-93; Chapl Edith Cowan Univ 86-92; R Casino 94-98; R Ithaca-Ashgrove 98-01; AD from 01. *286 Waterworks Road, PO Box 31, Ashgrove, Qld, Australia 4060* Tel (0061) (7) 3366 2320 Fax 3366 9793 E-mail stpaulsash@iprimus.com.au

BOOTH, Wallace. b 14. **d** 62 **p** 63. C Croydon Woodside *Cant* 62-66; V Woodnesborough 66-79; P-in-c Staple 77-79; rtd 79; Perm to Offic *Chich* from 87. *3 St Augustine's Close, Bexhill-on-Sea TN39 3AZ* Tel (01424) 214524

BOOTH, Preb William James. b 39. LVO99. TCD BA60 MA75. **d** 62 **p** 63. C Belfast St Luke *Conn* 62-64; Chapl Cranleigh Sch Surrey 65-74; Chapl Westmr Sch 74-91; Lic to Offic *Lon* 74-93; P in O 76-93; PV Westmr Abbey 87-93; Sub-Dean HM Chpls R and Dep Clerk of the Closet from 91; Sub-Almoner and Dom Chapl to The Queen from 91; Preb St Paul's Cathl *Lon* from 00. *Marlborough Gate, St James's Palace, London SW1A 1BG* Tel (020) 7930 6609

BOOTHBY, Frank. b 29. St D Coll Lamp 56. **d** 58 **p** 59. C Maghull *Liv* 58-61; C N Meols 61-64; Miss to Seamen 64; rtd 94. *7 Belsfield Drive, Hesketh Bank, Preston PR4 6YB*

BOOTHBY, Mrs Julia. b 64. St Andr Univ MTheol87. St Alb and Ox Min Course 02. **d** 04. C Welwyn w Ayot St Peter *St Alb* from 04. *Beevors House, Aldenham School, Aldenham Road, Elstree, Borehamwood WD6 3AJ* Tel (01923) 851620 E-mail juliabby@aol.com

BOOTHMAN, Ms Olive. b 31. TCD BA. **d** 94 **p** 95. NSM Clondalkin w Rathcoole *D & G* from 94. *Miley Hall, Blessington, Co Wicklow, Irish Republic* Tel (00353) (45) 865119

BOOTS, Claude Donald Roy. b 26. Roch Th Coll 67. **d** 69 **p** 70. C Midsomer Norton *B & W* 69-73; V Westfield 73-80; P-in-c Hambridge w Earnshill and Isle Brewers 80; R Ilton w Hambridge, Earnshill, Isle Brewers etc 80-91; rtd 91; Perm to Offic *B & W* from 91. *41 Furlong Close, Midsomer Norton, Bath BA3 2PR* Tel (01761) 419263 E-mail mvcdboots@ukonline.co.uk

BOOYS, Mrs Susan Elizabeth. b 56. Bris Univ BA78 LMH Ox PGCE79. St Alb and Ox Min Course 92. **d** 95 **p** 96. C Kidlington w Hampton Poyle *Ox* 95-99; TV Dorchester 99-05; TR from 05; TV Warborough 99-05; TR from 05. *The Rectory, Manor Farm Road, Dorchester-on-Thames, Wallingford OX10 7HZ* Tel and fax (01865) 340007 E-mail sue@booys.fsnet.co.uk

BOREHAM, Harold Leslie. b 37. S'wark Ord Course. **d** 72 **p** 73. C Whitton and Thurleston w Akenham *St E* 72-77; R Saxmundham 77-85; V Felixstowe SS Pet and Paul 85-96; Chapl Felixstowe Hosp 85-96; Chapl Bartlet Hosp Felixstowe 95-96; P-in-c Ramsgate St Mark *Cant* 96-01; V 01-03; Chapl E Kent NHS and Soc Care Partnership Trust 98-03; rtd 03; Perm to Offic *St E* from 03. *313 St John's Road, Colchester CO4 0JR* Tel (01206) 853769 E-mail harry@borehamclan.fsnet.co.uk

BORLEY, Mark Letchford. b 61. Lon Univ BSc83 PhD87. St Jo Coll Nottm MTh03. **d** 04. C W Swindon and the Lydiards *Bris* 04-05; C Swindon All SS w St Barn from 05; C Swindon St Aug from 05. *2 Ferndale Road, Swindon SN2 1EX* Tel (01793) 524724 Mobile 07811-124237 E-mail mark@borley.net

BORROWDALE, Geoffrey Nigel. b 61. Southn Univ BSc83 W Sussex Inst of HE PGCE94. Chich Th Coll 87. **d** 90 **p** 99. C Tilehurst St Mich *Ox* 90-91; Perm to Offic *Chich* 93-97; NSM Sunninghill *Ox* 98-99; C Bracknell 99-01; P-in-c Theale and Englefield from 01. *The Rectory, Englefield Road, Theale, Reading RG7 5AS* Tel 0118-930 2759 E-mail priest@holytrinitytheale.org.uk

BORSBEY, Alan. b 38. Linc Th Coll 71. **d** 73 **p** 73. C Bardsley *Man* 73-75; C Elton All SS 75-78; V Bury St Paul 78-96; P-in-c Bolton St Bede 96-03; rtd 03. *9 Lon Gardener, Valley, Holyhead LL65 3DN* Tel (01407) 742474

BORTHWICK, Alexander Heywood. b 36. Open Univ BA80 Surrey Univ MSc89 MBPsS90. Lich Th Coll 57. **d** 60 **p** 61. C Glas Ch Ch *Glas* 60-62; C Landore *S & B* 62-64; C Swansea St Thos and Kilvey 64-65; Br Guiana 65-66; Guyana 66-70; C Oystermouth *S & B* 70-71; USPG 71-83; Area Sec *Man* and *Liv* 71-76; Area Sec *Blackb* and *S & M* 73-76; Sch and Children's Work Sec 76-83; Chapl Tooting Bec Hosp Lon 83-91; Chapl Charing Cross Hosp Lon 92-94; Chapl Hammersmith Hosps NHS Trust 94-00; TR Catford (Southend) and Downham *S'wark* 00-04; rtd 04. *Le Roc de Brolange, 5 Brolange, 17150 Soubran, France* Tel (0033) (5) 46 48 46 23

BOSHER, Philip Ross. b 61. Sarum & Wells Th Coll 84. **d** 87 **p** 88. C Warminster St Denys *Sarum* 87-90; P-in-c Farley w Pitton and W Dean w E Grimstead 90-91; TV Alderbury Team 91-96; CF from 96. *c/o MOD Chaplains (Army)* Tel (01980) 615804 Fax 615800

BOSS, Mrs Ann. b 42. Cen Lancs Univ BA93. Carl and Blackb Dioc Tr Inst 99. **d** 02 **p** 03. NSM Scorton and Barnacre and Calder Vale *Blackb* 02-05; P-in-c Hanmer Springs New Zealand from 05. *The Vicarage, 31 Jollies Pass Road, Hanmer Springs, New Zealand 8273* Tel (0064) (3) 315 7221

BOSSOM, Peter Emery. b 28. St D Dioc Tr Course. **d** 82 **p** 83. NSM Llandysilio w Egremont and Llanglydwen etc *St D* 82-86; rtd 86; Lic to Offic *St D* 86-90. *Address temp unknown*

BOSSWARD, Eric Paul. b 63. Nottm Poly CQSW90. Trin Coll Bris BA99. **d** 99 **p** 00. C Ecclesall *Sheff* 99-01; C Netherthorpe St Steph 01-04; Co-ord Chapl HM YOI Castington from 04. *HM Young Offender Institution, Castington, Morpeth NE65 9XG* Tel (01670) 762100 E-mail eric@bossward.freeserve.co.uk

BOSTOCK, Peter Anthony. b 64. Nottm Univ BA85 Fitzw Coll Cam BA89. Westcott Ho Cam 87. **d** 90 **p** 91. C Brighton St Matthias *Chich* 90-94; C Leytonstone St Marg w St Columba *Chelmsf* 94-98; P-in-c Bishopwearmouth Gd Shep *Dur* 98-02; V Monk Bretton *Wakef* 02-03; P-in-c Ryhill from 03; P-in-c Sharlston from 03. *The Vicarage, 20 School Lane, Ryhill, Wakefield WF4 2DW* Tel (01226) 722363 Mobile 07752-886039 E-mail frpeterbostock@msn.com

BOSTON, Jonathan Bertram. b 40. Ely Th Coll 61. **d** 64 **p** 65. C Eaton *Nor* 64-70; Sen Chapl ACF Norfolk from 70; V Horsham St Faith w Newton St Faith 70-90; V Horsford 71-90; V Horsford and Horsham w Newton St Faith 90-97; P-in-c Litcham w Kempston, E and W Lexham, Mileham etc from 97. *Bevan House, Front Street, Litcham, King's Lynn PE32 2QG* Tel (01328) 700760

BOSWELL, Canon Colin John Luke. b 47. Sarum & Wells Th Coll 72. **d** 74 **p** 75. C Upper Tooting H Trin *S'wark* 74-78; C Sydenham St Phil 78-79; C St Helier 80-83; P-in-c Caterham 83-95; P-in-c Chaldon 85-95; RD Caterham 85-95; V Croydon St Jo from 95; Hon Can S'wark Cathl from 99; RD Croydon Cen from 00. *Croydon Vicarage, 22 Bramley Hill, Croydon CR2 6LT* Tel (020) 8688 1387 *or* 8688 8104 Mobile 07931-850905 E-mail croydon.parishchurch@lineone.net

BOTHAM, Arthur. b 53. St Jo Coll Nottm. **d** 00 **p** 01. C Hartley Wintney, Elvetham, Winchfield etc *Win* 00-04; TV Basingstoke from 04. *The Vicarage, 25 Tewkesbury Close, Popley, Basingstoke RG24 9DU* Tel (01256) 324734 E-mail arthur.botham@talk21.com

BOTHAM, Norman. b 29. Nottm Univ MPhil80 Lon Univ CertEd55 MRTvS84. S'wark Ord Course 63. **d** 66 **p** 67. Lect Coll SS Mark & Jo Chelsea 66-69; C Englefield Green *Guildf* 66-69; Sen Lect Shoreditch Coll Egham 69-74; C Bagshot 69-73; C-in-c Bath H Trin *B & W* 74; Asst Dir RE 74; Sen Lect Doncaster Inst of HE 74-82; Public Preacher *S'well* from 75; Hon AP Bawtry w Austerfield and Miss 75-85; Offg Chapl RAF from 85; rtd 94; Perm to Offic *Sheff* from 98. *Rufford, Mattersey Road, Ranskill, Retford DN22 8NF* Tel (01777) 818234

BOTT, Graham Paul. b 49. Staffs Univ MBA95. N Ord Course 00. **d** 03 **p** 04. NSM Rickerscote *Lich* from 03. *24 Wayfield Drive, Stafford ST16 1TR* Tel (01785) 255658

BOTT, Theodore Reginald. b 27. MBE03. Birm Univ BSc52 PhD68 DSc84 CEng58 FIChemE68. WMMTC 85. **d** 86 **p** 87. NSM Harborne St Faith and St Laur *Birm* 86-97; Perm to Offic from 97. *17 Springavon Croft, Harborne, Birmingham B17 9BJ* Tel 0121-427 4209

BOTTERILL, David Darrell. b 45. Open Univ BA. Sarum & Wells Th Coll. **d** 83 **p** 84. C Blandford Forum and Langton Long etc *Sarum* 83-86; TV Shaston 86-00; Chapl HM YOI Guys Marsh 89-91; P-in-c Portland St Jo *Sarum* from 00; Asst Chapl Dorset Community NHS Trust from 01. *St John's Vicarage, Ventnor Road, Portland DT5 1JE* Tel (01305) 820103 E-mail david.botterill@btinternet.com

BOTTING, Canon Michael Hugh. b 25. K Coll Lon BSc51 AKC K Coll Lon PGCE52. Ridley Hall Cam 54. **d** 56 **p** 57. C Onslow Square St Paul *Lon* 56-61; V Fulham St Matt 61-72; RD Hammersmith 67; V Leeds St Geo *Ripon* 72-84; RD Headingley 81-84; Hon Can Ripon Cathl 82-84; R Aldford and Bruera *Ches* 84-90; rtd 90; Jt Dir Lay Tr *Ches* 90-95; Perm to Offic from 95. *25 Woodfield Grove, Hoole, Chester CH2 3NY* Tel (01244) 321133 E-mail michael.botting@btinternet.com

BOTTING, Paul Lloyd. b 43. SSC. Brasted Th Coll 67 St Mich Coll Llan 69. **d** 71 **p** 72. C Hucknall Torkard *S'well* 71-74; C Cen Torquay *Ex* 74-76; P-in-c Sutton in Ashfield St Mich *S'well* 76; V 77-88; Chapl King's Mill Hosp Sutton-in-Ashfield 85-88; Perm to Offic *Leic* 95-97; NSM Vale of Belvoir Gp 95-97; C High Framland Par 97-01; C Waltham on the Wolds, Stonesby, Saxby etc 97-01; C Wymondham w Edmondthorpe, Buckminster etc 97-01; P-in-c High Framland Par from 01. *High Framland Rectory, 5 Croxton Lane, Harston, Grantham NG32 1PP* Tel (01476) 870188 E-mail plb@pixie-cat.fslife.co.uk

BOTTOMLEY, Gordon. b 31. Oak Hill Th Coll 51. **d** 55 **p** 56. C Kinson *Sarum* 55-58; Lic to Offic *Man* 58-63; N Area Sec BCMS 58-63; V Hemswell w Harpswell *Linc* 63-72; V Glentworth 63-72; Chapl RAF 63-71; R Bucknall and Bagnall *Lich* 72-80; TR 80-82; P-in-c Worthing H Trin *Chich* 82-88; V Camelsdale 88-96; rtd 96; Perm to Offic *Portsm* from 98. *6 Jay Close, Fareham PO14 3TA*

BOTTOMLEY, Philip. b 45. St Jo Coll Dur BA67. Cranmer Hall Dur 67. **d** 70 **p** 71. C Harlow New Town w Lt Parndon *Chelmsf* 70-74; C W Kilburn St Luke w St Simon and St Jude *Lon* 74-78; Midl Sec CMJ 78-84; Hon C Selly Park St Steph and St Wulstan *Birm* 81-84; Exec Dir CMJ USA 84-91; R Pittsburgh Epiphany 91-02; R Clarksburg Ch Ch from 02. *Christ Episcopal Church, PO Box 1492, Clarksburg, WV 26302, USA* Tel (001) (304) 622 3694 Fax 623 4855 E-mail englishreverend@verizon.net

BOTWRIGHT, Canon Adrian Paul. b 55. St Jo Coll Ox MA PGCE. Westcott Ho Cam 80. **d** 82 **p** 83. C Chapel Allerton *Ripon* 82-85; Chapl Chapel Allerton Hosp 82-85; C Bourne *Guildf* 85-88; V Weston 88-94; R Skipton H Trin *Bradf* from 94; P-in-c Embsay w Eastby from 05; Hon Can Bradf Cathl from 02. *The Rectory, Rectory Lane, Skipton BD23 1ER* Tel (01756) 793622 *or* 700773 E-mail rector@holytrinityskipton.org.uk

BOUCHER, Brian Albert. b 39. Univ of Wales (Lamp) BA61. Chich Th Coll 61. **d** 63 **p** 64. C Hoxton H Trin w St Mary *Lon* 63-67; Chapl RN 67-68; Asst Chapl Harrow Sch 68-73; Chapl 73-86; P-in-c Clerkenwell H Redeemer w St Phil *Lon* 86-91; P-in-c Myddleton Square St Mark 86-91; Chapl Hurstpierpoint Coll 92-96; rtd 96; Perm to Offic *Chich* from 01. *20 Summervale Road, Tunbridge Wells TN4 8JB* Tel (01892) 530342

BOUCHER, Geoffrey John. b 61. Warwick Univ BA82 K Coll Lon 94. Ridley Hall Cam 94. **d** 96 **p** 97. C Tavistock and Gulworthy *Ex* 96-01; P-in-c W Monkton *B & W* from 01. *The Rectory, West Monkton, Taunton TA2 8QT* Tel (01823) 412226 E-mail geoffboucher@onetel.com

BOUGHEY, Richard Keith. b 26. Man Univ MEd71. Qu Coll Birm 77. **d** 80 **p** 82. NSM Upper Tean *Lich* 80-81; NSM Stoke-upon-Trent 80-81; NSM Uttoxeter w Bramshall 82-88; rtd 88; Perm to Offic *Lich* from 88. *Kontokali, The Old Lane, Deadman's Green, Checkley, Stoke-on-Trent ST10 4NQ* Tel (01538) 722013

BOUGHTON, Mrs Elisabeth Mary Victoria. b 66. St Anne's Coll Ox BA87 MA93. Ridley Hall Cam 89. **d** 91 **p** 94. C Guildf Ch Ch *Guildf* 91-95; Chapl St Cath Sch Bramley 92-97; NSM Fetcham *Guildf* from 97; Chapl Guildf YMCA from 04. *The Rectory, 10A The Ridgeway, Fetcham, Leatherhead KT22 9AZ* Tel (01372) 372598

BOUGHTON, Canon Michael John. b 37. Kelham Th Coll 57. **d** 62 **p** 63. C Grantham St Wulfram *Linc* 62-66; C Kingsthorpe *Pet* 66-68; C Linc St Nic w St Jo Newport *Linc* 68-72; V Scunthorpe All SS 72-79; V Crowle 79-89; R Epworth 80-89; TR Bottesford w Ashby 89-02; Can and Preb Linc Cathl from 00; rtd 02. *45 Albion Crescent, Lincoln LN1 1EB* Tel (01552) 569653 E-mail mboughton@aol.com

BOUGHTON, Paul Henry. b 55. ACA80 Imp Coll Lon BScEng77 ARSM77. Ridley Hall Cam 89. **d** 91 **p** 92. C Guildf Ch Ch *Guildf* 91-96; R Fetcham from 96. *The Rectory, 10A The Ridgeway, Fetcham, Leatherhead KT22 9AZ* Tel (01372) 372598

BOULCOTT, Thomas William. b 16. Bps' Coll Cheshunt 47. **d** 49 **p** 50. C Hitchin St Mary *St Alb* 49-51; C Kempston All SS 51-54; Chapl Bedf Gen Hosp 52-54; V Newfoundpool *Leic* 54-61; V N Evington 61-73; Chapl Leic Gen Hosp 62-73; V Loppington w Newtown *Lich* 73-85; RD Wem and Whitchurch 83-85; rtd 85; Perm to Offic *Lich* 85-94. *Silver Birch, Tilley Road, Wem, Shrewsbury SY4 5HA* Tel (01939) 233602

BOULD, Preb Arthur Roger. b 32. Selw Coll Cam BA54 MA58 Wadh Coll Ox BA55 DipTh56 DipEd57 MA58. St Steph Ho Ox 54. **d** 57 **p** 58. C Wednesfield St Thos *Lich* 57-64; V Wellington Ch Ch 64-71; R Cheadle 71-88; P-in-c Freehay 84-88; R Cheadle w Freehay 88-91; Chapl Cheadle Hosp 71-91; Chapl HM Pris Moorcourt 72-82; RD Cheadle 72-91; Preb Lich Cathl 83-99; Asst to Bp Wolv 91-97; Bp Lich's Past Aux 97-99; C Stafford 97-99; rtd 99; Perm to Offic *Lich* from 00. *4 Mansell Close, Castlefields, Stafford ST16 1AG* Tel (01785) 220860 Fax as telephone

BOULD, Stephen Frederick. b 49. K Coll Lon BD78 AKC78. Sarum & Wells Th Coll 78. **d** 79 **p** 80. C Cantril Farm *Liv* 79-82; AV Hindley St Pet 82-85; Hon C Leic H Spirit *Leic* 85-88; Chapl Leic Univ 85-88; V Leic Ch Sav 88-96; P-in-c New Humberstone 94-96; TR Leic Presentation 96-98; TR Bruton and Distr *B & W* 98-05; P-in-c Folkestone St Pet *Cant* from 05. *St Peter's Vicarage, North Street, Folkestone CT19 6AL* Tel (01303) 254472 E-mail boldini@btopenworld.com

BOULLIER, Kenneth John. b 51. Lon Bible Coll 79 Trin Coll Bris DipHE84. **d** 84 **p** 85. C Heref St Pet w St Owen and St Jas *Heref* 84-87; V Nutley *Chich* 88-93; R Maresfield 88-93; New Zealand 93-97; R Nailsea H Trin *B & W* from 97. *The Rectory, 2 Church Lane, Nailsea, Bristol BS48 4NG* Tel (01275) 853227 Fax 852291 E-mail kenboullier@htnailsea.swinternet.co.uk

BOULNOIS, Linda Dianne. *See* BISIG, Linda Dianne

BOULSOVER, Philip John. b 16. ACT ThL55 Kelham Th Coll 34. **d** 40 **p** 41. C Middlesbrough St Cuth *York* 40-41; C Northallerton 41-43; C Bexhill St Pet *Chich* 43-51; Australia from 51; R Atherton 51-56; R Rockhampton 56-67; R Canberra St Luke 67-81; rtd 81. *21 Chillagoe Street, Fisher, Canberra, ACT, Australia 2611* Tel (0061) (2) 6288 7589

BOULT, Geoffrey Michael. b 56. Southn Univ BTh88 Bris Univ MA90 Birm Univ MSc97. Sarum & Wells Th Coll 77. **d** 80 **p** 81. C Newark w Hawton, Cotham and Shelton *S'well* 80-83; TV Melksham *Sarum* 83-90; P-in-c Charminster and Stinsford 90-95; Perm to Offic *Birm* 95-96; Perm to Offic *Sarum* 95-98. *Address temp unknown*

BOULTBEE, John Michael Godolphin. b 22. Oak Hill Th Coll 66. **d** 68 **p** 69. C Hawkwell *Chelmsf* 68-71; C St Keverne *Truro* 71-73; V Constantine 74-79; P-in-c St Merryn 79-81; V 81-87; rtd 87; Perm to Offic *Ex* from 87. *July Cottage, 8 Williams Close, Dawlish EX7 9SP* Tel (01626) 865761

BOULTER, Michael Geoffrey. b 32. Lon Univ BD56. Tyndale Hall Bris 53. **d** 57 **p** 58. C Tranmere St Cath *Ches* 57-60; R Cheetham Hill *Man* 60-65; R Tollard Royal w Farnham *Sarum* 65-66; Chapl Alderney Hosp Poole 66-96; V Branksome St Clem *Sarum* 66-96; rtd 96. *7 Temple Trees, 13 Portarlington Road, Bournemouth BH4 8BU* Tel (01202) 768718

BOULTER, Robert George. b 49. Man Univ BA90. St Aug Coll Cant 72. **d** 75 **p** 76. C Langley All SS and Martyrs *Man* 75-80; V Lower Kersal 80-84; Oman 84-86; Slough Community Chapl *Ox* 86-87; R Whalley Range St Marg *Man* 87-99; P-in-c from 99. *St Margaret's Rectory, Rufford Road, Manchester M16 8AE* Tel 0161-226 1289

BOULTON, Christopher David. b 50. Keble Coll Ox BA71 MA80. Cuddesdon Coll 71. **d** 74 **p** 75. C St Mary-at-Latton *Chelmsf* 74-77; C Shrub End 77-80; P-in-c Gt Bentley 80-83; V 83-89; V Cherry Hinton St Andr *Ely* 89-04; P-in-c Teversham 90-04; P-in-c Much Hadham *St Alb* from 04. *The Rectory, High Street, Much Hadham SG10 6DA* Tel (01279) 842609 E-mail chris@boultonc.fsnet.co.uk

BOULTON, Ms Louise Jane. b 72. Goldsmiths' Coll Lon BA93 Heythrop Coll Lon MA98. SEITE 02. **d** 05. *1A Jeffreys Road, London SW4 6QU* Tel (020) 7771 6986

BOULTON, Wallace Dawson. b 31. MCIJ86. Lon Coll of Div 65. **d** 67 **p** 68. C Bramcote *S'well* 67-71; Dioc Public Relns Officer 69-71; Hon C St Bride Fleet Street w Bridewell etc *Lon* 71-86; Guild Chapl from 86; Publicity Sec CMS 71-79; Media Sec 79-86; Ed *C of E Newspaper* 86-88; Lic to Offic *Chich* 84-94; Perm to Offic 94-96; rtd 96; Hon C St Leonards St Leon *Chich* 96-01 and from 04; P-in-c 01-03. *44 Winterbourne Close, Hastings TN34 1XQ* Tel (01424) 713743 E-mail revw.boulton@virgin.net

BOULTON-LEA, Peter John. b 46. St Jo Coll Dur BA68. Westcott Ho Cam 69. **d** 71 **p** 72. C Farlington *Portsm* 72-75; C Darlington St Jo *Dur* 75-77; R E and W Horndon w Lt Warley *Chelmsf* 77-82; V Hersham *Guildf* 82-91; R Kirk Sandall and Edenthorpe *Sheff* 91-96; RD Doncaster 95-96; V Campsall 96-97; R Burghwallis and Campsall 97-98; V Tattenham Corner and Burgh Heath *Guildf* 98-03; V Thorne *Sheff* from 03. *The Vicarage, 2 Brooke Street, Thorne, Doncaster DN8 4AZ* Tel (01405) 814055

BOULTON-REYNOLDS, Mrs Jean. b 49. Sarum Th Coll 93. **d** 96 **p** 97. C Harnham *Sarum* 96-99; C Salisbury St Mark 99-01; TV Westborough *Guildf* from 01. *St Clare's Vicarage, 242 Cabell Road, Guildford GU2 6JW* Tel (01483) 301349 E-mail revjbr@sarum26.freeserve.co.uk

BOUNDY, David. b 34. Kelham Th Coll 55. **d** 59 **p** 60. C Stirchley *Birm* 59-64; Chapl E Birm Hosp 64-74; V Bordesley St Oswald 64-70; V S Yardley St Mich 70-74; R Bideford *Ex* 74-82; RD Hartland 80-82; R Northfield *Birm* 82-88; P-in-c Penzance St Mary w St Paul *Truro* 88-90; V 90-94; rtd 94; Chapl Convent of St Mary at the Cross Edgware 94-99; Perm to Offic *Ex* 00-05. *9 Kendra Court, 167 Pampisford Road, South Croydon CR2 6LS* Tel (020) 8688 7511 E-mail retreat5@btopenworld.com

BOUNDY, Canon Gerald Neville. b 36. BA. Linc Th Coll. **d** 65 **p** 66. C Bris St Mary Redcliffe w Temple etc *Bris* 65-70; P-in-c Southmead 70-72; V 72-81; V Cotham St Sav w St Mary 81-99; Hon Can Bris Cathl 96-99; rtd 99; Perm to Offic *Bris* from 99. *10 Morley Road, Southville, Bristol BS3 1DT* Tel 0117-966 3337

BOURDEAUX, Canon Michael Alan. b 34. St Edm Hall Ox BA57 MA61 Lambeth DD96. Wycliffe Hall Ox BA59. **d** 60 **p** 61. C Enfield St Andr *Lon* 60-64; P-in-c Charlton St Luke w St Paul *S'wark* 64-65; Lic to Offic *Roch* and *Ox* 91-04; Visiting Prof St Bernard's Sem Rochester NY 69; Gen Dir Keston Inst 69-99; Hon Can Roch Cathl *Roch* 90-99; rtd 99; Perm to Offic *Ox* from 04. *101 Church Way, Iffley, Oxford OX4 4EG* Tel (01865) 777276 E-mail michael.bourdeaux@freenet.co.uk

✠**BOURKE, The Rt Revd Michael Gay.** b 41. CCC Cam BA63 MA67. Cuddesdon Coll 65. **d** 67 **p** 68 **c** 93. C Gt Grimsby St Jas *Linc* 67-71; C Digswell *St Alb* 71-73; C-in-c Panshanger CD 73-78; Course Dir St Alb Minl Tr Scheme 75-87; V Southill 78-86; Adn Bedford 86-93; Area Bp Wolverhampton *Lich* from

93. *61 Richmond Road, Wolverhampton WV3 9JH* Tel (01902) 824503 Fax 824504
E-mail bishop.wolverhampton@lichfield.anglican.org

BOURKE, Canon Ronald Samuel James. b 50. MA HDipEd. **d** 79 **p** 80. C Portadown St Mark *Arm* 79-83; I Carnteel and Crilly 83-90; I Mountmellick w Coolbanagher, Rosenallis etc *M & K* 90-97; I Kingscourt w Syddan from 97; Chan Kildare Cathl from 00; Can Meath from 00; Preb Tipper St Patr Cathl Dublin from 00. *St Ernan's Rectory, Kingscourt, Co Cavan, Irish Republic* Tel (00353) (42) 966 7255 Fax 966 7947

BOURKE, Stanley Gordon. b 48. CITC 78. **d** 78 **p** 79. C Dundonald *D & D* 78-80; C Lurgan Ch the Redeemer 81-82; I Dungiven w Bovevagh *D & R* 82-89; I Lurgan St Jo *D & D* 89-03; I Inishmacsaint *Clogh* from 03. *The Rectory, Main Street, Derrygonnelly, Enniskillen BT93 6HW* Tel (028) 6864 1638

BOURNE, Mrs Carole Sylvia. b 47. York Univ BA68 LSE MSc79 PhD85. SEITE 99. **d** 02 **p** 03. C Epsom St Martin *Guildf* from 02. *12 Worple Road, Epsom KT18 5EE* Tel (01372) 727380 Mobile 07957-295842
E-mail carolebourne@kt70rt.freeserve.co.uk

BOURNE, Colin Douglas. b 56. Culham Coll of Educn CertEd77. Oak Hill Th Coll BA04. **d** 04 **p** 05. C Wellington, All SS w Eyton *Lich* from 04. *1 Stile Rise, Telford TF5 0LR* Tel (01952) 641229 Mobile 07821-967879

BOURNE, David James. b 54. Reading Univ BA76. Trin Coll Bris 77. **d** 79 **p** 80. C W Bromwich Gd Shep w St Jo *Lich* 79-84; V Riseley w Bletsoe *St Alb* 84-05; V Hailsham *Chich* from 05. *St Mary's Vicarage, Vicarage Road, Hailsham BN27 1BL* Tel (01323) 842381 E-mail djbourne@fish.co.uk

BOURNE, Canon Dennis John. b 32. Ridley Hall Cam 58. **d** 60 **p** 61. C Gorleston St Andr *Nor* 60-64; Min Gorleston St Mary CD 64-79; V Costessey 79-86; R Hingham w Wood Rising w Scoulton 86-97; RD Hingham and Mitford 90-95; Hon Can Nor Cathl 93-97; rtd 97; Perm to Offic *Nor* from 97. *Amron, Star Lane, Long Stratton, Norwich NR15 2XH* Tel (01508) 530863
E-mail johnbourne@onetel.com

BOURNE, Mrs Diana Mary. b 46. St Jo Coll York BEd68. S Dios Minl Tr Scheme 92. **d** 95 **p** 96. C Pinner *Lon* 95-00; V Lamberhurst and Matfield *Roch* from 00. *The Vicarage, Old Town Hill, Lamberhurst, Tunbridge Wells TN3 8EL* Tel (01892) 890324

BOURNE, Henry. b 34. Spurgeon's Coll 55. **d** 64 **p** 65. C Handsworth St Mary *Birm* 64-67; Chapl RAF 67-85; Asst Chapl-in-Chief RAF 85-87; P-in-c Bourn *Ely* 87-88; V 88-89; P-in-c Kingston 87-88; R 88-89; V Caxton 88-89; R Bourn and Kingston w Caxton and Longstowe 89-91; rtd 91; Perm to Offic *Truro* 95-00 and from 01; Hon C Sampford Peverell, Uplowman, Holcombe Rogus etc *Ex* 00-01. *13 The Bowjey Hill, Newlyn, Penzance TR18 5LW* Tel (01736) 330742

BOURNE, The Ven Ian Grant. b 32. Univ of NZ BA55 Otago Univ BD75 Univ of NZ LTh61. **d** 56 **p** 57. New Zealand 56-65 and from 67; Adn Wellington 78-86 and 90-95; C Epsom St Martin *Guildf* 65-67. *26 Annan Grove, Papakowhai, Porirua, New Zealand* Tel (0064) (4) 233 0466

BOURNE, John. *See* BOURNE, Canon Dennis John

BOURNE, John Mark. b 49. Cant Sch of Min 88. **d** 91 **p** 92. C Allington and Maidstone St Pet *Cant* 91-94; V Marden 94-03; Chapl HM Pris Blantyre Ho 94-02; rtd 03. *6 Birling Close, Seaford BN25 2NY* Tel (01323) 899544
E-mail revjohnbourne@classicfm.net

BOURNE, Nigel Irvine. b 60. St Jo Coll Ox BA82 MA86. Trin Coll Bris BA92. **d** 92 **p** 93. C Bedhampton *Portsm* 92-94; C Newport St Jo 94-98; V Chalk *Roch* from 98. *The Vicarage, 2A Vicarage Lane, Gravesend DA12 4TF* Tel (01474) 567906 Fax 745147 E-mail vicarofchalk@hotmail.com

BOURNE, Canon Philip John. b 61. Sussex Univ BEd83 Aber Univ MLitt86 Ex Univ MEd96 FRSA97. Cranmer Hall Dur 85. **d** 87 **p** 88. C Gildersome *Wakef* 87-89; Chapl Ex Univ *Ex* 89-93; Assoc Chapl The Hague and Voorschoten *Eur* 94 and 95; Chapl Voorschoten from 96; Can Gib Cathl from 04. *Zwaluwweg 83, 2251 NC Voorschoten, The Netherlands* Tel (0031) (71) 561 2762 *or* 561 1528 E-mail pbourne@xs4all.nl

BOURNEMOUTH, Archdeacon of. *See* HARBIDGE, The Ven Adrian Guy

BOURNER, Paul. b 48. CA Tr Coll. **d** 90 **p** 91. CA from 79; C Ipswich St Mary at Stoke w St Pet *St E* 90-93; R Ufford w Bredfield and Hasketon 93-01; V Ipswich St Thos from 01. *St Thomas's Vicarage, 102 Cromer Road, Ipswich IP1 5EP* Tel (01473) 741215 E-mail paul.bourner@ntlworld.com

BOURNON, Dennis Harry. b 20. St Cuth Soc Dur LTh48 BA49. Oak Hill Th Coll 46. **d** 49 **p** 50. C Heworth H Trin *York* 49-51; C Bebington *Ches* 51-54; V Everton St Jo *Liv* 54-58; R Gunton St Pet *Nor* 58-65; R Eastrop *Win* 65-80; R Nursling and Rownhams 80-85; rtd 85; Perm to Offic *Win* from 96. *17 Wessex Avenue, New Milton BH25 6NG* Tel (01425) 614016

BOUSFIELD, Andrew Michael. b 70. Middx Univ BA92. Oak Hill Th Coll BA00. **d** 00 **p** 01. C Beckenham Ch Ch *Roch* 00-03; C Surbiton Hill Ch Ch *S'wark* from 03. *19 Dennan Road, Surbiton KT6 7RY* Tel (020) 8241 6472
E-mail andybous@yahoo.com

BOUSKILL, David Walter. b 72. Ox Brookes Univ HND95. Westcott Ho Cam 95. **d** 98 **p** 99. C Henley w Remenham *Ox* 98-02; TV Bicester w Bucknell, Caversfield and Launton from 02. *75 Ravencroft, Bicester OX26 6YE* Tel (01869) 321048
E-mail rev.bouskill@virgin.net

BOUTAN, Marc Robert. b 53. Univ of Iowa BA74. Fuller Th Sem California MD87 Virginia Th Sem 90. **d** 91 **p** 92. USA 91-96 and from 99; Asst Chapl Brussels *Eur* 96-99. *St James Episcopal Church, 1872 Camp Road, Charleston, SC 29412, USA*

BOUTFLOWER, David Curtis. b 45. Man Univ BSc67 Linacre Coll Ox BA69. Ripon Hall Ox 67. **d** 70 **p** 71. C Shard End *Birm* 70-73; C Mortlake w E Sheen *S'wark* 73-74; C Caldicot *Mon* from 98. *29 Wentwood View, Caldicot NP26 4QG* Tel (01291) 423229

BOUTLE, David Francis. b 44. Leeds Univ BSc67 Lon Univ DipTh72. Cuddesdon Coll 69. **d** 72 **p** 73. C Boston *Linc* 72-77; C Waltham 77-80; P-in-c Morton 80-81; V 81-94; Chapl W Lindsey NHS Trust 80-94; Local Mental Health Chapl 88-94; P-in-c Heckington *Linc* from 94. *The Vicarage, 10 Cameron Street, Heckington, Sleaford NG34 9RW* Tel (01529) 460302

BOVEY, Denis Philip. b 29. Ely Th Coll 50. **d** 53 **p** 54. C Southwick St Columba *Dur* 53-57; Perm to Offic *Ox* 57-59; Lic to Offic *Chich* 62-64; C W Hartlepool St Aid *Dur* 64-66; R Aberdeen St Jas *Ab* 66-74; R Old Deer 74-89; R Longside 74-89; R Strichen 74-89; Can St Andr Cathl 75-88; Syn Clerk 78-83; Dean Ab 83-88; I Alford 89-94; R Auchindoir 89-94; R Inverurie 89-94; P-in-c Dufftown 89-94; P-in-c Kemnay 89-94; rtd 94. *15 Loskin Drive, Glasgow G22 7QW* Tel 0141-574 3603

BOVILL, Francis William. b 34. Lon Univ DipTh58. St Aid Birkenhead 55. **d** 58 **p** 59. C Bispham *Blackb* 58-61; C Crosthwaite Keswick *Carl* 61-64; V Radcliffe St Andr *Man* 64-68; P-in-c Woodside St Steph *Glouc* 68; V 69-73; V Scotby *Carl* 73-96; P-in-c Cotehill and Cumwhinton 94-96; rtd 96; Perm to Offic *Carl* from 96. *16 Summerfields, Dalston, Carlisle CA5 7NW* Tel (01228) 710682

BOWCOTT, Jonathan Michael William. b 67. Trin Coll Bris. **d** 01 **p** 02. C Cricklewood St Gabr and St Mich *Lon* 01-04. *Address temp unknown* E-mail bowcotts@fish.co.uk

BOWDEN, Andrew. *See* BOWDEN, Canon Robert Andrew

BOWDEN, Andrew David. b 59. Newc Univ BA80 BArch83. Cranmer Hall Dur 95. **d** 97 **p** 98. C Monkseaton St Pet *Newc* 97-01; V Whorlton from 01. *St John's Vicarage, Whorlton, Westerhope, Newcastle upon Tyne NE5 1NN* Tel 0191-286 9648
E-mail abowden@tiscali.co.uk

BOWDEN, John Stephen. b 35. CCC Ox BA59 MA62 Edin Univ Hon DD81 Lambeth DD96. Linc Th Coll 59. **d** 61 **p** 62. C Nottingham St Mary *S'well* 61-64; Hon C 64-66; Lect Nottm Univ 64-66; Ed and Managing Dir SCM Press from 66; Hon C Highgate All SS *Lon* 66-00; Hon C Brentford St Faith 80-87; Perm to Offic from 87; rtd 00. *20 Southwood Avenue, London N6 5RZ* Tel and fax (020) 8340 7548 *or* tel 7359 8033

BOWDEN, John-Henry David. b 47. Magd Coll Cam BA69 MA73 MIL78. S Dios Minl Tr Scheme 81. **d** 84 **p** 85. NSM Redlynch and Morgan's Vale *Sarum* 84-88; NSM Cuckfield *Chich* 88-92; NSM St Mary le Bow w St Pancras Soper Lane etc *Lon* 92-98; NSM Chailey *Chich* 98-04; P-in-c Venice w Trieste *Eur* from 04. *Chaplain's House, Dorsoduro 253, 30123 Venezia, Italy* E-mail st.george-venice@libero.it

BOWDEN, Canon Robert Andrew. b 38. Worc Coll Ox BA62 MA67 BDQ68. Cuddesdon Coll 63. **d** 65 **p** 66. C Wolverhampton St Geo *Lich* 65-69; C Duston *Pet* 69-72; R Byfield 72-79; Chapl R Agric Coll Cirencester 79-93; R Coates, Rodmarton and Sapperton etc *Glouc* 79-04; Bp's Adv on Rural Soc 81-93; Hon Can Glouc Cathl from 90; Local Min Officer 93-04; Chapl to The Queen from 92; rtd 04; Hon C Kemble, Poole Keynes, Somerford Keynes etc *Glouc* from 04. *The Rectory, Coates, Cirencester GL7 6NR* Tel (01285) 770235
E-mail bowdencoates@care4free.net

BOWDER, Reginald William Maxwell (Bill). b 46. TCD BA68 MA81 Lon Univ DipRS80 Irish Sch of Ecum MPhil99. S'wark Ord Course 78. **d** 81 **p** 82. C Bush Hill Park St Steph *Lon* 81-84; I Fiddown w Clonegam, Guilcagh and Kilmeaden *C & O* 84-87; I Lismore w Cappoquin, Kilwatermoy, Dungarvan etc 87-89; Dean Lismore 87-89; Chapl Kent Univ and Kent Inst of Art and Design *Cant* 90-97; I Donoughmore and Donard w Dunlavin *D & G* 97-01; Reporter *Church Times* from 01; Perm to Offic *Ox* 02-04; NSM Nettlebed w Bix, Highmoor, Pishill etc from 04. *203 Greys Road, Henley-on-Thames RG9 1SP* Tel (01491) 576725 *or* (020) 7354 6258 Fax (020) 7226 3073
E-mail bill@churchtimes.co.uk

BOWEN, Canon Colin Wynford. b 48. St D Coll Lamp. **d** 71 **p** 72. C Hubberston *St D* 71-75; R Cosheston w Nash and Upton 75-77; V Carew and Cosheston w Nash and Upton 77-85; V Pembroke St Mary w St Mich 85-01; V Haverfordwest St Martin w Lambston from 01; P-in-c Camrose from 04; Can St D Cathl from 01. *St Martin's Vicarage, Barn Street, Haverfordwest SA61 1TD* Tel (01437) 762509 Mobile 07770-572464

BOWEN, Daniel Joseph George. b 51. Univ of Wales (Cardiff) Dip Past Th 98. St Mich Coll Llan CertMS98. **d** 98 **p** 99. C Gorseinon *S & B* 98-00; C Cen Swansea 00-01; TV 01-02; V Birchfield *Birm* from 02. *Holy Trinity Vicarage, 213 Birchfield Road, Birmingham B20 3DG* Tel 0121-356 4241 Mobile 07890-265429 E-mail anngbowen@lineone.net

BOWEN, David Gregory. b 47. Lanchester Poly BSc69. Cuddesdon Coll 70. **d** 74 **p** 75. C Rugby St Andr *Cov* 74-77; C Charlton St Luke w H Trin *S'wark* 78-80; TV Stantonbury *Ox* 80-82; Perm to Offic *B & W* from 89. *17 Chapel Hill, Clevedon BS21 7NL* Tel (01275) 878962

BOWEN, David John. b 46. Glouc Th Course 83. **d** 86 **p** 88. NSM Ross w Brampton Abbotts, Bridstow and Peterstow *Heref* 86-88; C Kingstone w Clehonger, Eaton Bishop etc 88-93; P-in-c Lugwardine w Bartestree and Weston Beggard 93-94; V Lugwardine w Bartestree, Weston Beggard etc from 94; P-in-c Withington w Westhide from 04; RD Heref Rural from 99. *The Vicarage, Lugwardine, Hereford HR1 4AE* Tel and fax (01432) 850244 E-mail david@djbowen.demon.co.uk

BOWEN, Ms Delyth. b 54. St D Coll Lamp BA90. St Mich Coll Llan DPS91. **d** 91 **p** 97. C Llandybie *St D* 91-95; Dn-in-c Llanllwni 95-97; V Llanybydder and Llanwenog w Llanllwni 97-02; V Betws w Ammanford from 02. *The Rectory, 78 High Street, Ammanford SA18 2NB* Tel (01269) 592084

BOWEN, Gareth James. b 60. Lon Guildhall Univ BA99 ARPS00. NTMTC 99. **d** 02 **p** 04. C Leyton St Cath and St Paul *Chelmsf* 02-05; C Upminster from 05. *6 Gaynes Park Road, Upminster RM14 2HH* Tel (01708) 226004 Mobile 07775-674504 E-mail gareth@bowen.to

BOWEN, Canon Jennifer Ethel. b 46. Liv Univ BSc68 CertEd69. N Ord Course 80. **dss** 83 **d** 87 **p** 94. Blundellsands St Nic *Liv* 83-86; W Derby St Mary 86-94; Par Dn 87-94; C from 94; AD W Derby from 01; Hon Can Liv Cathl from 03. *4 The Armoury, West Derby, Liverpool L12 5EL* Tel 0151-256 6600

BOWEN, John. b 39. **d** 68 **p** 69. C Aberavon *Llan* 68-73; Australia from 73. *3 Sculptor Street, Giralang, ACT, Australia 2617* Tel (0061) (2) 6241 5317 *or* 6234 2252 Fax 6234 2263 E-mail john.bowen@radford.com.au

BOWEN, John Roger. b 34. St Jo Coll Ox BA59 MA62. Tyndale Hall Bris 59. **d** 61 **p** 62. C Cambridge St Paul *Ely* 61-65; Tanzania 65-76; Kenya 76-80; Dir Past Studies St Jo Coll Nottm 80-85; Tutor 85-95; Gen Sec Crosslinks 96-00; rtd 99; Perm to Offic *Ely* from 01. *26 Lingholme Close, Cambridge CB4 3HW* Tel (01223) 352592 E-mail bowenrw@onetel.com

BOWEN, Lionel James. b 16. S'wark Ord Course 63. **d** 64 **p** 65. C Vauxhall St Pet *S'wark* 64-67; C Sanderstead All SS 67-74; V Pill *B & W* 74-79; Perm to Offic *Chich* from 79; rtd 81. *43 Sussex Court, Eaton Road, Hove BN3 3AS* Tel (01273) 775945

BOWEN, Roger William. b 47. Magd Coll Cam BA69 MA73 Hatf Poly Cert Counselling 91. St Jo Coll Nottm 69 Selly Oak Coll 76. **d** 72 **p** 73. C Rusholme H Trin *Man* 72-75; Rwanda Miss (CMS) Burundi 77-84; Tutor and Lect All Nations Chr Coll Ware 85-91; Hon C Ware Ch Ch *St Alb* 86-91; Gen Sec Mid-Africa Min (CMS) 91-97; V Lt Amwell *St Alb* 97-04; RD Hertford and Ware 99-04; Lect Matana Th Sem Burundi from 04. *Institut Théologique de Matana, DS 30 Bujumbura, Burundi* Tel (00257) (93) 2398

BOWEN, Stephen Allan. b 51. Leic Univ BA72. Glouc Sch of Min 88. **d** 91 **p** 92. NSM Bream *Glouc* 91-92; NSM Tidenham w Beachley and Lancaut 91-94; C Glouc St Jas and All SS 94-97; P-in-c Woodchester and Brimscombe 97-00; R from 00. *The Vicarage, Walls Quarry, Brimscombe, Stroud GL5 2PA* Tel (01453) 882204 E-mail bowen_stephen@hotmail.com

BOWEN, Stephen Guy. b 47. Qu Coll Cam BA68 MA72 Bris Univ MA72. Clifton Th Coll 69. **d** 71 **p** 72. C Chelsea St Jo *Lon* 71-73; C Chelsea St Jo w St Andr 73; C Guildf St Sav *Guildf* 73-76; C Guildf St Sav w Stoke-next-Guildford 76-77; C Wallington H Trin *S'wark* 77-79; V Felbridge from 79. *The Vicarage, The Glebe, Felbridge, East Grinstead RH19 2QT* Tel (01342) 321524 Fax (0870) 162 9334 E-mail sg@bowenfelbridge.idps.co.uk

BOWEN, Thomas Raymond. b 20. Univ of Wales (Lamp) BA42. **d** 48 **p** 49. C Monkton *St D* 48-52; C Haverfordwest St Mary w St Thos 52; Chapl RAF 53-75; Chapl Gresham's Sch Holt 75-83; rtd 83; Perm to Offic *St D* from 83. *35 Gail Rise, Llangwm, Haverfordwest SA62 4HW* Tel (01437) 891179

BOWEN, Vincent Paul. b 26. Qu Coll Cam BA50 MA55. Ely Th Coll 51. **d** 53 **p** 54. C Cowley St Jo *Ox* 53-56; C Brentwood St Thos *Chelmsf* 56-61; R Cranham 61-71; R Wanstead St Mary 71-91; rtd 91; Perm to Offic *Cant* from 92. *44 Nunnery Fields, Canterbury CT1 3JT* Tel (01227) 472036

BOWER, Brian Mark. b 60. QUB BA. **d** 85 **p** 86. C Orangefield w Moneyreagh *D & D* 85-87; I Inver w Mountcharles, Killaghtee and Killybegs *D & R* 87-93; Miss to Seafarers from 87; I Augher w Newtownsaville and Eskrahoole *Clogh* 93-03. *48 Campsie Road, Omagh BT79 0AG* Tel 07816-449399 (mobile)

BOWER, James Hugh Marsh. b 17. St Chad's Coll Dur BA39 MA43. **d** 40 **p** 41. C Shrewsbury St Mary *Lich* 40-41; C Rugeley 41-42; C Wolverhampton St Pet 42-48; V Northwood 48-54; V Caldmore 54-58; V Wolverhampton St Andr 58-74; R Cavendish *St E* 74-83; P-in-c Stansfield 78-83; RD Clare 82-83; rtd 83; Perm to Offic *St E* from 83 and *Chelmsf* 83-99. *142 Melford Road, Sudbury CO10 1JZ* Tel (01787) 372683

BOWER, Jonathan James. b 72. Bp Grosseteste Coll BA96. Ripon Coll Cuddesdon. **d** 00 **p** 01. C Spalding *Linc* 00-02; C Sanderstead St Mary *S'wark* 02-03; P-in-c from 03. *The Vicarage, 85 Purley Oaks Road, South Croydon CR2 0NY* Tel (020) 8657 1725 E-mail jontybower@ntlworld.com

BOWERING, John Anthony (Tony). b 34. SS Coll Cam BA57 MA. Wycliffe Hall Ox 57. **d** 59 **p** 60. C Hornchurch St Andr *Chelmsf* 59-62; Succ Chelmsf Cathl 62; Prec 63; V Brampton Bierlow *Sheff* 64-70; V Norton Woodseats St Paul 70-80; V Tickhill w Stainton 80-97; RD W Doncaster 87-92; rtd 97; Perm to Offic *S'well* and *Sheff* from 97. *Linthwaite Cottage, Main Street, Kirklington, Newark NG22 8ND* Tel (01636) 816995 E-mail john.bowering@which.net

BOWERING, The Ven Michael Ernest. b 35. Kelham Th Coll 55. **d** 59 **p** 60. C Middlesbrough St Oswald *York* 59-62; C Huntington 62-64; V Brayton 64-72; RD Selby 71-72; V Saltburn-by-the-Sea 72-81; Can Res York Minster 81-87; Sec for Miss and Evang 81-87; Adn Lindisfarne *Newc* 87-00; rtd 00; Perm to Offic *York* from 00. *Old Timbers, West Way, Crayke, York YO61 4TE* Tel (01347) 823682 E-mail mbwrng@aol.com

BOWERMAN, Andrew. b 67. Southn Univ BSc88 Brunel Univ MSW91. Wycliffe Hall Ox 00. **d** 02 **p** 03. C Bradf St Aug Undercliffe *Bradf* from 02. *37 Pollard Lane, Bradford BD2 4RN* Tel (01274) 638377 Mobile 07720-398659 E-mail andy.bowerman@virgin.net

BOWERS, Dale Arthur. b 69. St Steph Ho Ox BTh04. **d** 04. C St Paul's St Helena from 04. *China Lane, Jamestown STHL 122, St Helena* Tel (00290) 2960 E-mail penelope19702000@yahoo.co.uk

BOWERS, David. b 55. Man Univ BA79. Wycliffe Hall Ox 82. **d** 84 **p** 85. C Lawton Moor *Man* 84-87; C Walmsley 87-93; V Milnrow 93-98; P-in-c Deerhurst, Apperley w Forthampton and Chaceley *Glouc* 98-04; V Deerhurst and Apperley w Forthampton etc from 04; Dir of Ords 98-02. *The Vicarage, 1 The Green, Apperley, Gloucester GL19 4DQ* Tel (01452) 780880 E-mail dbowers@tinyworld.co.uk

BOWERS, Canon Francis Malcolm. b 44. Chan Sch Truro 79. **d** 82 **p** 83. NSM Penzance St Mary w St Paul *Truro* 82-83; C 86-88; NSM Madron 83-86; TV Redruth w Lanner and Treleigh 88-91; V St Blazey from 91; P-in-c Lanlivery w Luxulyan from 01; P-in-c Tywardreath w Tregaminion from 02; RD St Austell 96-05; Hon Can Truro Cathl from 01. *Church House, 2 Nursery Close, Tywardreath, Par PL24 2QW* Tel and fax (01726) 817665 Mobile 07974-818631 E-mail fathermalcolm@arktume.freeserve.co.uk

BOWERS, Canon John Edward. b 23. TD68. AKC50. **d** 51 **p** 52. C Leic St Pet *Leic* 51-55; Sacr S'wark Cathl *S'wark* 55-57; CF (TA) 56-67; V Loughborough St Pet *Leic* 57-63; V Ashby-de-la-Zouch St Helen w Coleorton 63-88; CF (R of O) 67-78; RD Akeley W *Leic* 76-88; Hon Can Leic Cathl 78-88; rtd 88; Perm to Offic *Derby* and *Leic* 88-94; *Ely* 94-00. *19 Curtis Drive, Heighington, Lincoln LN4 1GF* Tel (01522) 791330

BOWERS, Canon John Edward William. b 32. St Aid Birkenhead 60. **d** 63 **p** 64. C Bromborough *Ches* 63-68; Ind Chapl 68-74; P-in-c Crewe St Pet 69-71; V Crewe St Mich 71-74; TR Ellesmere Port 74-79; V Hattersley 79-91; Hon Can Ches Cathl 80-02; RD Mottram 88-91; V Bunbury and Tilstone Fearnall 91-98; P-in-c Leasowe 98-02; rtd 02; Perm to Offic *Ches* from 02. *2 Shalford Grove, Wirral CH48 9XY* Tel 0151-625 4831

BOWERS, Julian Michael. b 48. Middx Univ BA97 Goldsmiths' Coll Lon MA00. Edin Th Coll 69. **d** 72 **p** 73. C Chippenham St Andr w Tytherton Lucas *Bris* 72-74; C Henbury 74-77; Chapl Kandy H Trin Sri Lanka 77-82; P-in-c Evercreech w Chesterblade and Milton Clevedon *B & W* 82-83; V 83-89; V Enfield St Jas *Lon* 89-04; Chapl St Andr Hosp Northn from 04. *The Chaplaincy, St Andrew's Hospital, Billing Road, Northampton NN1 5DG* Tel (01604) 629696

BOWERS, Michael Charles. b 52. Sarum & Wells Th Coll 89. **d** 91 **p** 92. C St Peter-in-Thanet *Cant* 91-95; V Reculver and Herne Bay St Bart 95-02; P-in-c Fen Ditton *Ely* from 02; P-in-c Horningsea from 02; P-in-c Teversham from 04. *The Rectory, 29 High Street, Fen Ditton, Cambridge CB5 8ST* Tel (01223) 295927

BOWERS, Peter. b 47. Linc Th Coll 72. **d** 76 **p** 77. C Mackworth St Fran *Derby* 76-78; C Maidstone St Martin *Cant* 78-83; V Elmton *Derby* 83-89; R Swimbridge w W Buckland and Landkey *Ex* from 89; RD Shirwell from 01. *The Rectory, Barnstaple Hill, Swimbridge, Barnstaple EX32 0PH* Tel (01271) 830068 E-mail revpebo@hotmail.com

BOWERS, Peter William Albert. b 36. K Coll Lon BD61 AKC61. **d** 62 **p** 63. C Chorley St Pet *Blackb* 62-64; C New Sleaford *Linc* 64-67; C Folkestone H Trin w Ch Ch *Cant* 67-72; V Deal St Geo 72-80; Dir Galilee Community 80-85; R River 86-02; RD Dover

93-00; rtd 02; Perm to Offic *Cant* from 02. *7 River Street, River, Dover CT16 0RB* Tel (01304) 822808
E-mail pbowers4@aol.com

BOWERS, Mrs Rosemary Christine. b 49. Ripon Coll Cuddesdon 99. **d** 01 **p** 02. C Rossendale Middle Valley *Man* 01-04; P-in-c Micklehurst *Ches* from 04. *All Saints' Vicarage, Mossley, Ashton-under-Lyne OL5 9HY* Tel (01457) 837430
E-mail revrosie@fish.co.uk

BOWERS, Stanley Percival. b 20. Lon Univ BD45 AKC45. Hartley Victoria Coll 40 Wells Th Coll 66. **d** 66 **p** 66. In Methodist Ch 45-66; C Lawrence Weston *Bris* 66-69; V Two Mile Hill St Mich 69-91; rtd 91; Perm to Offic *Bris* from 91; Perm to Offic *B & W* 91-95. *1 Windsor Road, Longwell Green, Bristol BS30 9AF* Tel 0117-932 4051

BOWES, Mrs Beryl Sylvia. b 48. SRN70 RSCN71 Hull Univ BTh89. NEOC 89. **d** 91 **p** 94. NSM Kirk Ella *York* 91-99; Chapl R Hull Hosps NHS Trust 93-99; P-in-c Kexby w Wilberfoss *York* 99-04; R The Street Par from 04. *The Rectory, Church Street, Amotherby, Malton YO17 6TN* Tel (01653) 690663
E-mail rector@thestreetparishes.org.uk

BOWES, Canon John Anthony Hugh. b 39. Ch Ch Ox BA62 MA65. Westcott Ho Cam 63. **d** 65 **p** 66. C Langley All SS and Martyrs *Man* 65-68; Asst Chapl Bris Univ *Bris* 68-73; TV Cramlington *Newc* 73-76; P-in-c Oldland *Bris* 76-80; TR 80-84; V Westbury-on-Trym St Alb 84-05; Hon Can Bris Cathl from 02; rtd 05. *4 Royal Albert Road, Bristol BS6 7NY* Tel 0117-973 5844

BOWES, Peter Hugh. b 48. Hull Univ LLB69 Dur Univ MA05 Solicitor 72. Cranmer Hall Dur 02. **d** 03 **p** 04. NSM Pocklington and Owsthorpe and Kilnwick Percy etc *York* 03-04; NSM The Street Par from 04; Assoc Dir of Ords from 05. *The Rectory, Church Street, Amotherby, Malton YO17 6TN* Tel (01653) 690663 Mobile 07775-757723 E-mail phbowes@zetnet.co.uk

BOWES-SMITH, Edward Michael Crispin. b 67. K Coll Lon LLB89 AKC89 Solicitor 90 Selw Coll Cam BA96. Ridley Hall Cam 94. **d** 97 **p** 98. C Combe Down w Monkton Combe and S Stoke *B & W* 97-00; C Enfield Ch Ch Trent Park *Lon* 00-03; P-in-c Linc Minster Gp *Linc* from 03. *St Peter's Vicarage, Lee Road, Lincoln LN2 4BH* Tel (01522) 525741
E-mail bowessmith@waitrose.com

BOWETT, Canon Richard Julnes. b 45. EAMTC 86. **d** 89 **p** 90. C Hunstanton St Mary w Ringstead Parva, Holme etc *Nor* 89-93; C King's Lynn St Marg w St Nic 93-95; V Watton w Carbrooke and Ovington 95-02; RD Breckland 99-02; P-in-c Ashill w Saham Toney 00-01; Dioc Sec from 02; Hon Can Nor Cathl from 05. *110 Dereham Road, Easton, Norwich NR9 5DF* Tel (01603) 880389 E-mail richardbowett@norwich.anglican.org

BOWIE, Michael Nicholas Roderick. b 59. Sydney Univ BA78 CCC Ox DPhil90. St Steph Ho Ox MA90. **d** 91 **p** 92. C Swanley St Mary *Roch* 91-93; C Penarth w Lavernock *Llan* 93-96; Australia 96-00; R Norton *Sheff* from 00. *Norton Rectory, Norton Church Road, Norton, Sheffield S8 8JQ* Tel and fax 0114-274 5066 E-mail mnrbowie@hotmail.com

BOWIE, Sara. b 53. Open Univ BA83 Surrey Univ BA02 MSSCh MBChA. STETS 99. **d** 02 **p** 03. NSM Camberley St Mich Yorktown *Guildf* from 02. *23 Green Farm Road, Bagshot GU19 5LB* Tel (01276) 475677
E-mail sara@bowie-bagshot.fsnet.co.uk

BOWKER, Prof John Westerdale. b 35. Worc Coll Ox BA58. Ripon Hall Ox. **d** 61 **p** 62. C Endcliffe *Sheff* 61-62; Fell Lect and Dir of Studies CCC Cam 62-74; Lect Div Cam Univ 70-74; Prof RS Lanc Univ 74-86; Hon Prov Can Cant Cathl *Cant* from 85; Dean of Chpl Trin Coll Cam 86-91; rtd 91; Lic to Offic *Cant* 91-94; Perm to Offic *Ely* 94-00. *14 Bowers Croft, Cambridge CB1 8RP*

✠**BOWLBY, The Rt Revd Ronald Oliver.** b 26. Trin Coll Ox BA50 MA54. Westcott Ho Cam 50. **d** 52 **p** 53 **c** 73. C Pallion *Dur* 52-56; C Billingham St Cuth 56-57; C-in-c Billingham St Aid CD 57-60; V Billingham St Aid 60-66; V Croydon St Jo *Cant* 66-73; Hon Can Cant Cathl 70-73; Bp Newc 73-80; Bp S'wark 80-91; rtd 91; Asst Bp Lich from 91. *4 Uppington Avenue, Shrewsbury SY3 7JL* Tel (01743) 244192
E-mail rebowl@tinyworld.co.uk

BOWLER, Christopher William. *See* JAGE-BOWLER, Christopher William

BOWLER, David Henderson. b 54. Kent Univ BA75. St Jo Coll Nottm 75. **d** 78 **p** 79. C Bramcote *S'well* 78-82; TV Kirby Muxloe *Leic* 82-88; V Quorndon from 88. *Quorn Vicarage, 6 Loughborough Road, Quorn, Loughborough LE12 8DX* Tel (01509) 412593

BOWLER, Preb Kenneth Neville. b 37. K Coll Lon 57. **d** 61 **p** 62. C Buxton *Derby* 61-67; R Sandiacre 67-75; V E Bedfont *Lon* 75-87; AD Hounslow 82-87; V Fulham All SS 87-02; Preb St Paul's Cathl 85-02; rtd 02; Perm to Offic *St Alb* from 03. *62 Ickleford Road, Hitchin SG5 1TZ* Tel (01462) 454794

BOWLER, Neil. b 70. Nottm Trent Univ LLB92 Leeds Univ BA05 Solicitor 93. Coll of Resurr Mirfield 03. **d** 05. C Doncaster St Jude *Sheff* from 05. *207 Urban Road, Doncaster DN4 0HH*

BOWLES, Arthur William. b 36. Loughb Coll of Educn DLC59. LNSM course 94. **d** 96 **p** 97. OLM Gt Yarmouth *Nor* from 96. *4 Onslow Avenue, Great Yarmouth NR30 4DT* Tel (01493) 842360

BOWLES, David Anthony. b 44. Kelham Th Coll 63. **d** 68 **p** 69. C Bilborough w Strelley *S'well* 68-72; C Beeston 72-75; Ascension Is 75-77; V Wellingborough St Mark *Pet* 77-83; P-in-c Wilby 78-83; R Burton Latimer 83-90; V Sheff St Oswald *Sheff* 90-91; Perm to Offic *Derby* 93-95 and *Roch* 95-98. *Address temp unknown*

BOWLES, Preb Michael Hubert Venn. b 36. Selw Coll Cam BA59 MA63. Ridley Hall Cam 59. **d** 61 **p** 62. C Woodside Park St Barn *Lon* 61-64; C Swanage *Sarum* 64-67; Lect St Mich Coll Llan 67-72; Chapl 67-70; Lib 70-72; Lect Th Univ of Wales (Cardiff) 67-72; R Gt Stanmore *Lon* 72-01; Preb St Paul's Cathl 85-01; rtd 01; Perm to Offic *St Alb* from 02. *15 The Limes, St Albans AL1 4AT* Tel (01727) 832555

BOWLES, Peter John. b 39. Lon Univ BA60. Linc Th Coll 71. **d** 73 **p** 74. C Clay Cross *Derby* 73-76; C Boulton 76-79; R Brailsford w Shirley 79-85; P-in-c Osmaston w Edlaston 81-85; R Brailsford w Shirley and Osmaston w Edlaston 85-89; TR Old Brampton and Loundsley Green 89-98; V Hope, Castleton and Bradwell 98-04; rtd 04; Perm to Offic *Nor* from 04. *3 Blackhorse Yard, Wells-next-the-Sea NR23 1BN* Tel (01328) 711119

BOWLES, Ronald Leonard. b 24. K Coll Lon BD52 AKC52. **d** 53 **p** 54. C Berwick H Trin *Newc* 53-56; C Christchurch *Win* 56-60; R Nursling and Rownhams 60-66; V Woolston 66-75; V Moordown 75-89; rtd 89; Perm to Offic *Win* 89-99; *Portsm* from 89. *25 Cherry Tree Avenue, Cowplain, Waterlooville PO8 8BA* Tel (023) 9226 7376

BOWLEY, Canon John Richard Lyon. b 46. MRTPI76 Dur Univ BA68 QUB MSc72. CITC. **d** 79 **p** 80. C Knock *D & D* 79-81; Bp's C Knocknagoney 81-90; I Ballywalter w Inishargie from 90; Can Down Cathl from 03. *The Vicarage, 2 Whitechurch Road, Ballywalter, Newtownards BT22 2JY* Tel (028) 9175 8416

BOWMAN, Miss Alison Valentine. b 57. St Andr Univ MA79. St Steph Ho Ox 86. **d** 89 **p** 94. Par Dn Peacehaven *Chich* 89-94; C 94-95; Chapl to Bp Lewes 93-95; TV Rye 95-03; P-in-c Preston St Jo w Brighton St Aug and St Sav from 03. *33 Preston Drove, Brighton BN1 6LA* Tel (01273) 555033

BOWMAN, Clifford William. b 57. St Jo Coll Dur BA78 Nottm Univ MA96. Ridley Hall Cam 80. **d** 82 **p** 83. C Sawley *Derby* 82-85; C Hucknall Torkard *S'well* 85-89; R Warsop 89-00; Dioc Chapl amongst Deaf People from 00. *45 Clumber Avenue, Edwinstowe, Mansfield NG21 9PE* Tel (01623) 825700 Fax and minicom as telephone E-mail c.bowman@dunelm.org.uk

BOWMAN, Canon Ivelaw Alexander. b 46. LNSM course 94. **d** 97 **p** 98. OLM Stockwell Green St Andr *S'wark* 97-03; OLM Stockwell St Andr and St Mich from 03; Chapl S Lon and Maudsley NHS Trust from 03; Hon Can S'wark Cathl *S'wark* from 05. *16 Horsford Road, London SW2 5BN* Tel (020) 7733 2309 *or* 7411 6198

BOWMAN, Prof John. b 16. Glas Univ MA38 BD41 Ch Ch Ox DPhil45. **d** 50 **p** 54. Hon C Leeds St Geo *Ripon* 51-53; Hon C Kirkstall 53-54; Perm to Offic *York* 54-59; Australia from 59; rtd 73. *15 Haines Street, North Melbourne, Vic, Australia 3051* Tel (0061) (3) 9329 0794 Fax as telephone
E-mail mbowman@vicnet.net.au

BOWMAN-EADIE, Canon Russell Ian. b 45. ACP68 K Coll Lon BD71 AKC71 FCP. St Aug Coll Cant 71. **d** 72 **p** 73. C Hammersmith St Pet *Lon* 72-74; V Leic St Nic *Leic* 74-81; Chapl Leic Univ 74-81; Adult Educn Adv *Dur* 81-84; Dir of Tr *B & W* from 84; Preb Wells Cathl from 90; Can Res and Treas Wells Cathl from 02. *2 The Liberty, Wells BA5 2SU* Tel (01749) 674702 *or* 670777 Fax 674240
E-mail russell.bowman-eadie@bathwells.anglican.org

BOWN, Canon John Frederick Olney. b 13. TD50. BA36 MA70. Cuddesdon Coll 36. **d** 37 **p** 38. C Prittlewell St Mary *Chelmsf* 37-39; CF (TA) 39-44; CF 44-70; V Dover St Mary *Cant* 44-45; Hon Chapl Edin St Mary *Edin* 53-55; Can Mombasa 56-58; QHC 67-70; R Fordingbridge w Ibsley *Win* 70-79; RD Christchurch 74-78; rtd 79; Hon P-in-c Longstock w Leckford *Win* 79-87. *Dawlish House, 7 Trafalgar Way, Stockbridge SO20 6ET* Tel (01264) 810672

BOWNESS, William Gary. b 48. Warwick Univ BSc69 Chicago State Univ DMin98. Ripon Coll Cuddesdon 80. **d** 82 **p** 83. C Lancaster St Mary *Blackb* 82-86; V Lostock Hall 86-91; V Whittington w Arkholme and Gressingham 91-02; RD Tunstall 93-99; Dir Post-Ord Tr 00-02; R Alderley w Birtles *Ches* from 02. *St Mary's Rectory, Congleton Road, Nether Alderley, Macclesfield SK10 4TW* Tel (01625) 583134
E-mail gary@bowness1792.freeserve.co.uk

BOWRING, Stephen John. b 55. R Holloway Coll Lon BMus77 St Mary's Coll Twickenham PGCE78. EMMTC 89. **d** 92 **p** 93. C Thurmaston *Leic* 92-95; V Shepshed 95-02; R River *Cant* from 02; P-in-c Charlton-in-Dover from 05; AD Dover from 03; Hon Min Can Cant Cathl from 04. *The Vicarage, 23 Lewisham Road, Dover CT17 0QG* Tel (01304) 822037
E-mail bowring@fish.co.uk

BOWRON, Hugh Mark. b 52. Cant Univ (NZ) BA74 MA76 Leeds Univ DipTh78. Coll of Resurr Mirfield 76. **d** 79 **p** 80. C

Northampton St Mary *Pet* 79-82; New Zealand from 82; V Ellesmere 82-86; V Addington St Mary 86-95; V Wellington St Pet from 95. *PO Box 27 110, Wellington, New Zealand* Tel (0064) (4) 972 3250 *or* 382 8486
E-mail hugh.bowron@clear.net.nz

BOWSER, Alan. b 35. Univ of Wales (Lamp) BA60 DipTh63. **d** 63 **p** 64. C Gateshead St Chad Bensham *Dur* 63-67; C Owton Manor CD 67-72; V Horden 72-02; rtd 02. *Kengarth House, Coast Road, Blackhall Colliery, Hartlepool TS27 4HF*

BOWSHER, Andrew Peter. b 59. Reading Univ BA81. St Jo Coll Nottm 83. **d** 86 **p** 87. C Grenoside *Sheff* 86-89; C Darfield 89-91; P-in-c Haley Hill *Wakef* 91-96; V Bradf St Aug Undercliffe *Bradf* 96-99; Chapl Bradf Univ and Bradf Coll 99-04; Perm to Offic *Dur* from 04. *68 Canterbury Road, Durham DH1 5PY* Tel 07876-401339 (mobile)

BOWSKILL, Mrs Amanda. b 49. Dip Counselling 93. STETS DipTh99. **d** 99 **p** 00. NSM Winklebury *Win* 99-03; NSM Tadley S and Silchester 03-04. *St Mary's House, 10 Roman's Field, Silchester, Reading RG7 2QH* Tel 0118-970 2353
E-mail mandy.bowskill@cwcom.net

BOWSKILL, Robert Preston. b 48. S Dios Minl Tr Scheme 88. **d** 91 **p** 92. NSM Eastrop *Win* 91-94; NSM Winklebury from 94. *St Mary's House, 10 Roman's Field, Silchester, Reading RG7 2QH* Tel 0118-970 2353 E-mail bob.bowskill@cwcom.net

BOWTELL, Paul William. b 47. Lon Univ BSc68. St Jo Coll Nottm 80. **d** 82 **p** 83. C Gorleston St Andr *Nor* 82-85; TV Forest Gate St Sav w W Ham St Matt *Chelmsf* 85-91; R Spitalfields Ch Ch w All SS *Lon* 91-02; Newham Employment Project from 02; Perm to Offic *Chelmsf* from 02. *23 Gardner Road, London E13 8LN* Tel (020) 7476 2564 *or* 8548 4676 Fax 8548 4110
E-mail paul@bowtellp.freeserve.co.uk

BOWYER, Arthur Gustavus Frederick. b 36. Dioc OLM tr scheme 97. **d** 00 **p** 01. NSM Kingswood *S'wark* from 00. *41 Tattenham Grove, Epsom KT18 5QT* Tel (01737) 357913 Mobile 07939-533506 E-mail abowyer@onetel.com

BOWYER, Frank. b 28. Man Univ BA49 BD56. Oak Hill Th Coll 53. **d** 55 **p** 56. C Halliwell St Paul *Man* 55-57; C Crosthwaite Keswick *Carl* 57-59; V Thornham w Gravel Hole *Man* 59-63; R Burnage St Marg 63-81; R Gosforth w Nether Wasdale and Wasdale Head *Carl* 81-85; R Holcombe *Man* 85-93; rtd 93; Perm to Offic *Man* from 93. *43 New Church Road, Bolton BL1 5QQ* Tel (01204) 844547

BOWYER, Geoffrey Charles. b 54. ACA79 ATII82 Lanc Univ BA76. St Jo Coll Nottm 85. **d** 87 **p** 88. C Walton *St E* 87-89; C Macclesfield Team Par *Ches* 89-91; V Cinderford St Steph w Littledean *Glouc* 91-95; V Brockenhurst *Win* 95-98; Hon C Trull w Angersleigh *B & W* from 00. *36 Bakers Close, Bishops Hull, Taunton TA1 5HD* Tel (01823) 335289
E-mail us4bowyers@aol.com

BOX, David Norman. b 28. K Coll Lon BD48 AKC48. **d** 51 **p** 52. C Grays Thurrock *Chelmsf* 51-53; Hon C Aldershot St Mich *Guildf* 53-55; Asst Master St Benedict's Sch Aldershot 53-55; C Weston 55-58; C Camberley St Paul 58-61; V Blackheath and Chilworth 61-69; V Allerton *Bradf* 69-75; R Exford w Exmoor *B & W* 75-80; V Castle Cary w Ansford 80-90; P-in-c Childe Okeford, Manston, Hammoon and Hanford *Sarum* 90-91; R Childe Okeford, Okeford Fitzpaine, Manston etc 91-94; rtd 94; Perm to Offic *Carl* from 94. *Granary House, 1 Castle Street, Hilton, Appleby-in-Westmorland CA16 6LX* Tel (01768) 352689

BOX, Reginald Gilbert (Brother Reginald). b 20. Lon Univ BD41 AKC41 Em Coll Cam BA52 MA57 Lambeth STh91. Westcott Ho Cam 41. **d** 43 **p** 44. C Chingford SS Pet and Paul *Chelmsf* 43-47; Chapl Bps' Coll Cheshunt 47-50; SSF from 51; Lic to Offic *Ely* 51-55 and *Sarum* 55-61; C Cambridge St Benedict *Ely* 61-67; Chapl Coll of SS Mark and Jo Chelsea 67-69; New Zealand, Australia and Melanesia 69-84; Perm to Offic *Sarum* from 84 and *Ely* 85-97; rtd 90; Chapl Chich Th Coll 90-93. *The Friary, Hilfield, Dorchester DT2 7BE* Tel (01300) 341345 Fax 341293

BOXALL, David John. b 41. Dur Univ BA63 DipTh65. Sarum Th Coll 65. **d** 66 **p** 67. C Ipswich St Aug *St E* 66-69; C Bourne *Linc* 69-71; C Woodside Park St Barn *Lon* 71-72; C Thundersley *Chelmsf* 72-76; P-in-c Farcet *Ely* 76-77; TV Stanground and Farcet 77-85; V Guyhirn w Ring's End 85-90; V Southea w Murrow and Parson Drove 85-90; P-in-c Fletton 90-94; Perm to Offic 94-00; rtd 99. *11 Plover Drive, March PE15 9HY* Tel (01354) 659905

BOXALL, Keith Michael. b 37. Trin Coll Bris. **d** 82 **p** 83. C Staines St Pet *Lon* 82-83; C Staines St Mary and St Pet 83-85; C Lydiard Millicent w Lydiard Tregoz *Bris* 85-86; TV The Lydiards 86-93; V Mangotsfield 93-03; rtd 03; Perm to Offic *Bris* from 03. *25 Parc Plas, Blackwood NP12 1SJ* Tel (01495) 222572 Mobile 07745-016038 E-mail keith.boxall1@btinternet.com

BOXALL, Canon Martin Alleyne. b 37. Wells Th Coll 65. **d** 67 **p** 68. C Crowthorne *Ox* 67-70; C Tilehurst St Mich 70-76; V Tilehurst St Cath 76-78; V Padstow *Truro* 78-00; Miss to Seafarers from 78; RD Pydar *Truro* 93; Hon Can Truro Cathl from 93; rtd 01; Dioc Officer for Unity *Truro* from 01. *Goonhilland Farmhouse, Burnthouse, St Gluvias, Penryn TR10 9AS* Tel (01872) 863241 E-mail martinboxall@aol.com

BOXALL, Simon Roger. b 55. St Jo Coll Cam BA76 MA80. Ridley Hall Cam 77. **d** 79 **p** 80. C Eaton *Nor* 79-82; SAMS Brazil 82-04; P-in-c Belo Horizonte St Pet 84-88; P-in-c Santiago St Tim and Horizontina H Spirit 88-91; C Bagé Crucifixion 93-94; R Jaguarao Ch Ch 94-98; English Chapl Rio de Janeiro 99-04; TV Thamesmead *S'wark* from 05. *62-64 Battery Road, London SE28 0JT* Tel (020) 8836 9069

BOXLEY, Christopher. b 45. K Coll Lon BD68 AKC68 Southn Univ CertEd73 Reading Univ MA84. **d** 69 **p** 70. C Bitterne Park *Win* 69-73; Perm to Offic *Chich* 73-78; Hd RS Midhurst Gr Sch from 73; Dir Midhurst and Petworth RS Cen from 78; P-in-c Heyshott from 78. *The Rectory, Heyshott, Midhurst GU29 0DH* Tel (01730) 814405

BOYCE, Canon Brian David Michael. b 32. Fitzw Ho Cam BA55 MA62. Wells Th Coll 55. **d** 57 **p** 58. C Tavistock and Gulworthy *Ex* 57-60; C Paignton St Jo 60-62; C Germiston S Africa 62-64; R Ermelo 64-67; R Primrose 67-75; R Springs and Adn SE Transvaal 75-86; rtd 97; Perm to Offic *B & W* 98-03. *PO Box 44108, Linden, Johannesburg, 2104 South Africa*

BOYCE, Christopher Allan. b 44. Brighton Coll of Art DipArch66 ARIBA69. S Dios Minl Tr Scheme 84. **d** 87 **p** 88. NSM Eastbourne All SS *Chich* 87-93; C Upton (Overchurch) *Ches* 93-96; V New Brighton St Jas w Em 96-02; P-in-c New Brighton All SS 98-02; C Bicester w Bucknell, Caversfield and Launton *Ox* from 02. *4 Orpine Close, Bicester OX26 3ZJ* Tel (01869) 244918 Mobile 07989-269175
E-mail revcab@lineone.net

BOYCE, John Frederick. b 33. ALCD57. **d** 57 **p** 58. C Earlsfield St Andr *S'wark* 57-60; C Westerham *Roch* 60-63; C Farnborough 63-66; V Sutton at Hone 66-73; P-in-c Chiddingstone 73-74; R Chiddingstone w Chiddingstone Causeway 74-84; V Brenchley 84-98; rtd 98; Perm to Offic *Chich* from 99. *3 Orchard Rise, Groombridge, Tunbridge Wells TN3 9RU*

BOYCE, Kenneth Albert. b 51. St Edm Hall Ox BA72 MA76 Selw Coll Cam BA75 MA79. Westcott Ho Cam 73. **d** 75 **p** 76. C Evington *Leic* 75-78; P-in-c Gt Bowden w Welham 78-81; Dioc Stewardship Adv 78-81; Chapl Leic Poly 81-86; TV Leic H Spirit 82-86; Chapl to the Deaf *Worc* 86-93; P-in-c Astwood Bank 86-93; R Fladbury, Wyre Piddle and Moor 93-98; P-in-c Cropthorne w Charlton 94-98; R Fladbury w Wyre Piddle and Moor etc 98-00; RD Pershore 97-00; TR Worc SE from 00. *The Rectory, 6 St Catherine's Hill, Worcester WR5 2EA* Tel (01905) 355119 E-mail ken@kenboyce.fsnet.co.uk

BOYCE, Robert Albert Wright. b 19. BA. St Alb Minl Tr Scheme. **d** 82 **p** 83. NSM Bp's Hatfield *St Alb* 82-89; Perm to Offic from 89; rtd 90. *92 Park Meadow, Hatfield AL9 5HE* Tel (01707) 267531

BOYCE, William. **d** 03 **p** 04. C Willowfield *D & D* 03-04; C Bangor Abbey from 04. *9 Pinehill Crescent, Bangor BT19 6SF* Tel (028) 9147 7182

BOYD, Alan McLean. b 50. St Jo Coll Nottm BTh79. **d** 79 **p** 80. C Bishop's Waltham *Portsm* 79-83; Chapl Reading Univ *Ox* 83-88; Chapl E Birm Hosp 88-94; Chapl Birm Heartlands and Solihull NHS Trust from 94. *Solihull Hospital, Lode Lane, Solihull B91 2JL* Tel 0121-424 4099

BOYD, Alexander Jamieson. b 46. St Chad's Coll Dur BSc68 Nottm Univ PGCE69 MIBiol FSAScot. Coll of Resurr Mirfield 69. **d** 79 **p** 80. NSM Musselburgh *Edin* 79-83; CF 83-00; P-in-c Loddington *Leic* 00-03; Warden Launde Abbey 00-03; P-in-c Mareham-le-Fen and Revesby *Linc* from 03; P-in-c Hameringham w Scrafield and Winceby from 03; P-in-c Mareham on the Hill from 03. *The Rectory, Fieldside, Mareham-le-Fen, Boston PE22 7QU* Tel (01507) 568215
E-mail ajboyd@fish.co.uk

BOYD, Allan Gray. b 41. St Jo Coll Nottm 84. **d** 87 **p** 88. Hon Chapl Miss to Seafarers from 87; NSM Glas St Gabr *Glas* 87-93; NSM Greenock 93-96; NSM Paisley St Barn 96-00; NSM Paisley H Trin 96-00; NSM Alexandria 00-01; NSM Clydebank from 02. *47 Holms Crescent, Erskine PA8 6DJ* Tel 0141-812 2754

BOYD, Allan Newby. b 31. Ball Coll Ox BA53 MA59 MInstM73. St Alb Minl Tr Scheme 81. **d** 84 **p** 85. NSM Watford St Luke *St Alb* 84-88; C Ardsley *Sheff* 88-91; V Barrow St Jo *Carl* 91-94; rtd 94; Perm to Offic *Ripon* from 96. *Bishop Fold, Thoralby, Leyburn DL8 3SU* Tel (01969) 663474

BOYD, Canon David Anthony. b 42. Sarum & Wells Th Coll 72. **d** 75 **p** 76. C Ches H Trin *Ches* 75-79; R 85-93; V Congleton St Jas 79-85; V Farndon and Coddington from 93; RD Malpas 97-04; Hon Can Ches Cathl from 02. *The Vicarage, Church Lane, Farndon, Chester CH3 6QD* Tel and fax (01829) 270270

BOYD, David George. b 37. Cant Univ (NZ) BSc62 LTh64. St Aug Coll Cant. **d** 63 **p** 64. New Zealand 63-66; St Aug Coll Cant 66-67; Chapl RAF 67-71; New Zealand from 71; Adn Mid-Canterbury 92-96. *PO Box 178, Eltham, New Zealand* Tel (0064) (6) 764 8119 E-mail daboyd@xtra.co.nz

BOYD, Michael Victor. b 33. St Chad's Coll Dur BA57 DipAdEd69 MEd77 PhD81. Coll of Resurr Mirfield 57. **d** 59 **p** 60. C Warsop *S'well* 59-61; Chapl St Geo Coll Quilmes Argent

62-63; Chapl Wolsingham Sch 63-67; Lect St Hild Coll Dur 67-75; Lect SS Hild and Bede Dur 75-79; Lect Dur Univ 79-84; rtd 98. *4 Aykley Green, Durham DH1 4LN* Tel 0191-384 9473

BOYD, Robert Henry. b 36. **d** 66 **p** 67. C Drumcree *Arm* 66-69; I Annaghmore 69-83; Bp's C Lissan 83-90; I from 90. *The Rectory, 150 Moneymore Road, Cookstown BT80 8PY* Tel (028) 8676 6112

BOYD, Samuel Robert Thomas. b 62. **d** 90 **p** 91. NSM Derryloran *Arm* 90-95; C 95-97; I Woodschapel w Gracefield 97-05; I Killyman from 05. *St Andrew's Rectory, 85 Dungorman Road, Dungannon BT71 6SE* Tel and fax (028) 8772 2500 E-mail killyman@armagh.anglican.org

BOYD, Stephen William. b 71. Aston Tr Scheme 95 Ripon Coll Cuddesdon BTh00. **d** 00 **p** 01. C Walton-on-the-Hill *Liv* 00-04; V Westbrook St Jas from 04. *St James's Vicarage, 302 Hood Lane North, Great Sankey, Warrington WA5 1UQ* Tel (01925) 492631

BOYD, Stuart Adrian. b 51. Open Univ BA99 UWE MA02. STETS 02. **d** 05. NSM Brent Knoll, E Brent and Lympsham *B & W* from 05. *29 Stafford Road, Weston-super-Mare BS23 3BN* Tel (01934) 627897 E-mail sboyd@fish.co.uk

BOYD, Canon William John Peter. b 28. Lon Univ BA48 BD53 PhD77 Birm Univ MA60. **d** 57 **p** 58. C Aston SS Pet and Paul *Birm* 57-60; V W Smethwick 60-63; V St Breward *Truro* 63-68; Adult Educn Chapl 64-85; Dioc Ecum Officer 65-83; R St Ewe 68-73; Preb St Endellion 73-85; V St Kew 73-77; R Falmouth K Chas 77-85; RD Carnmarth S 84-85; Dir of Tr 85-93; Prin SW Minl Tr Course 85-93; Can Res and Chan Truro Cathl *Truro* 85-93; rtd 93; Perm to Offic *Truro* from 93. *7 Chapel Crescent, Zelah, Truro TR4 9HN*

BOYD-WILLIAMS, Anthony Robert. b 46. St Mich Coll Llan 86. **d** 88 **p** 89. C Tonyrefail w Gilfach Goch *Llan* 88-91; V Treharris w Bedlinog 91-96; V Ocker Hill *Lich* from 96; RD Wednesbury 03-05. *St Mark's Vicarage, Ocker Hill Road, Tipton DY4 0UT* Tel 0121-556 0678 E-mail tonybw@stmarksvicarage.fsnet.co.uk

BOYDEN, Peter Frederick. b 41. Lon Univ BSc62 AKC62 Em Coll Cam BA64 MA68 MLitt69. Ridley Hall Cam 63. **d** 66 **p** 67. C Chesterton St Andr *Ely* 66-68; C Wimbledon *S'wark* 68-72; Chapl K Sch Cant 72-89; Asst Chapl Radley Coll 89-02; rtd 02; Perm to Offic *Derby* from 02. *30 Chesterfield Road, Shirland, Alfreton DE55 6BN* Tel (01773) 830552

BOYES, Canon David Arthur Stiles. b 30. Lon Coll of Div 62. **d** 63 **p** 64. C Islington St Mary *Lon* 63-71; V Canonbury St Steph 71-75; V St Paul's Cray St Barn *Roch* 75-85; P-in-c Earl Soham w Cretingham and Ashfield *St E* 85-96; Dioc Development Officer 86-92; RD Loes 91-95; Hon Can St E Cathl 95-96; rtd 96; Perm to Offic *St E* from 96. *13 Magdalen Drive, Woodbridge IP12 4EF* Tel (01394) 383389

BOYES, Matthew John. b 70. Roehampton Inst BA91. Wycliffe Hall Ox BTh99. **d** 99 **p** 00. C Bury St Edmunds Ch Ch *St E* 99-02; P-in-c Penn Street *Ox* from 02. *The Vicarage, Penn Street, Amersham HP7 0PX* Tel (01494) 712194 E-mail mattboyz@tesco.net

BOYES, Michael Charles. b 27. Lon Univ BA53 BD58. Wells Th Coll 53. **d** 55 **p** 56. C Heavitree *Ex* 55-61; C Exwick 61-68; V Broadclyst 68-83; RD Aylesbeare 77-81; TV Sampford Peverell, Uplowman, Holcombe Rogus etc 83-85; TR 85-92; rtd 92; Perm to Offic *Ex* from 92. *Southdown, Burlescombe, Tiverton EX16 7LB* Tel (01884) 840492

BOYLAND, Alice Teresa. b 41. **d** 99 **p** 05. NSM Llangybi and Coedypaen w Llanbadoc *Mon* 99-04; NSM Chard and Distr *B & W* from 05. *62 Link Hay Orchard, South Chard, Chard TA20 2QS* Tel (01460) 221010

BOYLAND, David Henry. b 58. TCD BA79 BAI79. TCD Div Sch BTh91. **d** 91 **p** 92. C Seapatrick *D & D* 91-94; I Celbridge w Straffan and Newcastle-Lyons *D & G* 94-98; I Kilmakee *Conn* from 98. *Kilmakee Rectory, 60 Killeaton Park, Dunmurry, Belfast BT17 9HE* Tel (028) 9061 0505 *or* 9061 1024

BOYLAND, Henry Hubert. b 23. Dip Mgt. CITC. **d** 84 **p** 85. NSM Dunboyne Union *M & K* 84-87; Bp's C Carrickmacross w Magheracloone *Clogh* 87-90; I 90-93; rtd 93. *2 Spring View, Wheaton Hall, Dublin Road, Drogheda, Co Louth, Irish Republic* Tel (00353) (41) 984 4724

BOYLE, Andrew McKenzie. b 45. Down Coll Cam BA67 MA71 CEng72 MICE72. WMMTC 82. **d** 85 **p** 86. NSM Woodthorpe *S'well* 85-87; Perm to Offic *Roch* 88-90; 91-96; Hon C Sevenoaks St Luke CD 90-91; NSM Sundridge w Ide Hill and Toys Hill from 96. *Greenridge, 35 Garth Road, Sevenoaks TN13 1RU* Tel (01732) 456546 Fax 450060 E-mail andrewboyle1@compuserve.com

✠**BOYLE, The Rt Revd Christopher John.** b 51. AKC75. St Aug Coll Cant 75. **d** 76 **p** 77 **c** 01. C Wylde Green *Birm* 76-80; Bp's Dom Chapl 80-83; R Castle Bromwich SS Mary and Marg 83-01; AD Coleshill 92-99; P-in-c Shard End 96-97; Hon Can Birm Cathl 96-01; Bp N Malawi from 01. *PO Box 120, Mzuzu, Malawi* Tel (00265) 34930 Mobile 825097 Fax 333805 E-mail biggers@malawi.net

BOYLE, Paul. **d** 01 **p** 02. C Cen Cardiff *Llan* 01-03; C Barry All SS 03-05; P-in-c Pontypridd St Matt and Cilfynydd w Llanwynno from 05. *The Vicarage, 40 Heol-y-Plwyf, Ynysybwl, Pontypridd CF37 3HU* Tel (01443) 790340

BOYLE, Robert Leslie. b 52. EMMTC. **d** 00 **p** 01. NSM Derby St Anne and St Jo *Derby* from 00. *61 Rowditch Avenue, Derby DE22 3LE* Tel (01332) 349044

BOYLES, Peter John. b 59. Univ of Wales (Lamp) BA84. Sarum & Wells Th Coll 86. **d** 88 **p** 89. C Ches St Mary *Ches* 88-91; C Neston 91-95; R Lavendon w Cold Brayfield, Clifton Reynes etc *Ox* 95-99; V Dent w Cowgill *Bradf* from 99. *The Vicarage, Flintergill, Dent, Sedbergh LA10 5QR* Tel (01539) 625226

BOYLING, Canon Denis Hudson. b 16. Keble Coll Ox BA38 DipTh39 MA42. Cuddesdon Coll 39. **d** 40 **p** 41. C Sheff St Cuth *Sheff* 40-46; Chapl K Coll Hosp Lon 46-49; Chapl United Sheff Hosps 49-57; V Endcliffe *Sheff* 57-68; Hon Can Sheff Cathl 58-68; V Almondbury *Wakef* 68-75; RD Almondbury 68-75; Hon Can Wakef Cathl 72-75; Can Res Wakef Cathl 75-82; rtd 82; Perm to Offic *Heref* from 82. *7 St Mary's Close, Tenbury Wells WR15 8ES* Tel (01584) 811633

BOYLING, The Very Revd Mark Christopher. b 52. Keble Coll Ox BA74 MA78. Cuddesdon Coll 74. **d** 77 **p** 78. C Kirkby *Liv* 77-79; P-in-c 79-80; TV 80-85; Bp's Dom Chapl 85-89; V Formby St Pet 89-94; Can Res and Prec Liv Cathl 94-04; Dean Carl from 04. *The Deanery, The Abbey, Carlisle CA3 8TZ* Tel (01228) 523335 Fax 548151 E-mail dean@carlislecathedral.org.uk

BOYNS, Martin Laurence Harley. b 26. St Jo Coll Cam BA49 MA51. Ridley Hall Cam 50. **d** 52 **p** 53. C Woodmansterne *S'wark* 52-55; C Folkestone H Trin w Ch Ch *Cant* 55-58; V Duffield *Derby* 58-71; V Rawdon *Bradf* 71-76; Chapl Woodlands Hosp Rawdon 71-76; R Melton *St E* 76-85; R Gerrans w St Anthony in Roseland *Truro* 85-92; Miss to Seamen 85-92; rtd 92; Perm to Offic *Truro* from 92. *Bojunda, Boscaswell Village, Pendeen, Penzance TR19 7EP* Tel (01736) 788390

BOYNS, Timothy Martin Harley. b 58. Warwick Univ BA80 Nottm Univ BCombStuds84. Linc Th Coll 81. **d** 84 **p** 85. C Oxhey St Matt *St Alb* 84-87; TV Solihull *Birm* 87-94; V Lillington *Cov* from 94; RD Warwick and Leamington from 99. *The Vicarage, Lillington, Leamington Spa CV32 7RH* Tel (01926) 424674 *or* 470449 E-mail tim.boyns@talk21.com

BOYS, Mrs Margaret Ann. b 34. Lon Univ TCert56 Liv Univ DipPE59. Oak Hill Th Coll 91. **d** 94 **p** 95. NSM Hadleigh St Barn *Chelmsf* 94-98; NSM Thundersley 98-04; rtd 04. *10 Seymour Road, Westcliff-on-Sea SS0 8NJ* Tel (01702) 475997

BOYSE, Felix Vivian Allan. b 17. LVO78. CCC Cam BA39 MA42. Cuddesdon Coll 39. **d** 40 **p** 41. C New Mills *Derby* 40-43; P-in-c 43-45; Vice-Prin Cuddesdon Coll 46-51; V Kingswood *S'wark* 51-58; V St Mary Abchurch *Lon* 58-61; Prin St Geo Coll Jerusalem 61-64; Chapl Chpl Royal Hampton Court Palace 65-82; Preacher Lincoln's Inn 82-93; rtd 93; Perm to Offic *Chich* from 83. *Rose Cottage, Rookwood Road, West Wittering, Chichester PO20 8LT* Tel (01243) 514320

BRABIN-SMITH, Ms Lorna Daphne. b 54. Leeds Univ BSc75. Westcott Ho Cam 03. **d** 05. C Emmaus Par Team *Leic* from 05. *10 Park Hill Drive, Leicester LE2 8HR*

BRACE, Alistair Andrew. b 53. Newc Univ MB, BS76 DRCOG77. WMMTC 90. **d** 94. NSM Broseley w Benthall, Jackfield, Linley etc *Heref* 94-98. *58 Spout Lane, Benthall, Broseley TF12 1QY* Tel (01952) 884031

BRACE, Stuart. b 49. Open Univ DipMgt00 BSc01. Bp Burgess Hall Lamp DipTh74. **d** 74 **p** 75. C Llanelli Ch Ch *St D* 74-76; C Tenby w Gumfreston 76-77; V Ystradmeurig and Strata Florida 77-79; CF 79-86; CF(V) 86-93; Chapl HM Youth Cust Cen Everthorpe 86-88; Chapl HM Pris Stafford 88-93; Chapl HM Pris Long Lartin 93-95; Ecum Tr Officer HM Pris Service Chapl 95-99; Chapl HM Pris Glouc 99-03; Chapl HM Pris Leyhill from 03; Perm to Offic *Worc* from 95. *HM Prison Leyhill, 1 Tortworth Road, Wotton-under-Edge GL12 8BT* Tel (01454) 264000 E-mail brace3@chap0.freeserve.co.uk

BRACEGIRDLE, Christopher Andrew. b 56. Dur Univ BEd79 St Edm Ho Cam BA84 MA89. Ridley Hall Cam 82. **d** 85 **p** 86. C Livesey *Blackb* 85-88; TV E Farnworth and Kearsley *Man* 88-92; V Astley and Chapl Wigan and Leigh Health Services NHS Trust 92-98; P-in-c Walkden Moor w Lt Hulton *Man* 98-99; TR Walkden and Lt Hulton 99-03; V Heaton Ch Ch from 03; Tutor Dioc OLM Scheme from 97; AD Bolton from 05. *The Vicarage, 2 Towncroft Lane, Heaton, Bolton BL1 5EW* Tel and fax (01204) 840430 E-mail chris@bracegirdles.co.uk

BRACEGIRDLE, Canon Cynthia Wendy Mary. b 52. LMH Ox BA73 MA77 Liv Univ DipAE82. N Ord Course. **d** 87 **p** 94. Chapl Asst Man R Infirmary 85-88; Dir Dioc OLM Scheme *Man* 89-02; Hon Can Man Cathl 98-02; rtd 03; Perm to Offic *Carl* from 03. *The Vicarage, St George's Road, Millom LA18 4JA* Tel (01229) 772889 E-mail ignatius@globalnet.co.uk

BRACEGIRDLE, Robert Kevin Stewart. b 47. Univ Coll Ox BA69 MA73. St Steph Ho Ox 70. **d** 73 **p** 74. C Dorchester *Sarum* 73-75; C Woodchurch *Ches* 75-78; V Bidston 78-82; P-in-c Salford St Ignatius *Man* 82-86; R Salford St Ignatius and Stowell Memorial 86-02; P-in-c Salford Ordsall St Clem 99-02; P-in-c

Millom *Carl* from 02. *The Vicarage, St George's Road, Millom LA18 4JA* Tel (01229) 772889
E-mail robert.bracegirdle@btinternet.com

BRACEWELL, David John. b 44. Leeds Univ BA66 Man Univ MA82. Tyndale Hall Bris 67. **d** 69 **p** 70. C Tonbridge St Steph *Roch* 69-72; C Shipley St Pet *Bradf* 72-75; V Halliwell St Paul *Man* 75-84; R Guildf St Sav *Guildf* from 84. *St Saviour's Rectory, Wharf Road, Guildford GU1 4RP* Tel (01483) 577811 *or* 455333 Fax 456895 E-mail st.saviours@dial.pipex.com

BRACEWELL, Howard Waring. b 35. FRGS73. Tyndale Hall Bris. **d** 63 **p** 63. Canada 63-72; Travel Missr World Radio Miss Fellowship 72-77; P-in-c Ashill *Nor* 72-74; Hon C Bris St Phil and St Jacob w Em *Bris* 77-84; Perm to Offic *St Alb* 84-86; R Odell 86-88; V Pavenham 86-88; Lic to Offic *Man* 88-93; Assoc Min St Andrew's Street Bapt Ch Cambridge 94-99; Assoc Min Halliwell St Luke 99-01; rtd 01; Perm to Offic *Man* from 01. *10 Fairfields, Egerton, Bolton BL7 9EE* Tel (01204) 304028
E-mail howard@igloovut.fsnet.co.uk

BRACEY, David Harold. b 36. AKC63 Man Univ DPST83. **d** 64 **p** 65. C Westleigh St Pet *Man* 64-67; C Dunstable *St Alb* 67-70; V Benchill *Man* 70-76; V Elton St Steph 76-87; V Howe Bridge 87-00; rtd 00. *Rhiw Awel, Sarn, Pwllheli LL53 8EY* Tel (01758) 730381

BRACHER, Paul Martin. b 59. Solicitor 84 Ex Univ LLB80. Trin Coll Bris BA90. **d** 90 **p** 91. C Sparkhill St Jo *Birm* 90; C Sparkhill w Greet and Sparkbrook 90-93; Chapl Birm Women's Hosp 92-93; P-in-c Lea Hall *Birm* 93-98; V from 98. *St Richard's Vicarage, Hallmoor Road, Birmingham B33 9QY* Tel 0121-783 2319

BRACKENBURY, The Ven Michael Palmer. b 30. Linc Th Coll 64. **d** 66 **p** 67. C S Ormsby w Ketsby, Calceby and Driby *Linc* 66-69; V Scothern w Sudbrooke 69-77; RD Lawres 73-78; Bp's Personal Asst 77-88; Dioc Dir of Ords 77-87; Can and Preb Linc Cathl 79-95; Dioc Lay Min Adv 86-87; Adn Linc 88-95; rtd 95. *18 Lea View, Ryhall, Stamford PE9 4HZ* Tel (01780) 752415

✠**BRACKLEY, The Rt Revd Ian James.** b 47. Keble Coll Ox BA69 MA73. Cuddesdon Coll 69. **d** 71 **p** 72 **c** 96. C Bris Lockleaze St Mary Magd w St Fran *Bris* 71-74; Asst Chapl Bryanston Sch 74-77; Chapl 77-80; V E Preston w Kingston *Chich* 80-88; RD Arundel and Bognor 82-87; TR Haywards Heath St Wilfrid 88-96; RD Cuckfield 89-95; Suff Bp Dorking *Guildf* from 96; Hon Can Guildf Cathl from 96. *13 Pilgrim's Way, Guildford GU4 8AD* Tel (01483) 570829 Fax 567268
E-mail bishop.ian@cofeguildford.org.uk

BRACKLEY, Mark Ozanne. b 53. Boro Road Teacher Tr Coll CertEd75. S'wark Ord Course 90. **d** 93 **p** 94. C Hampstead St Steph w All Hallows *Lon* 93-97; V W Green Ch Ch w St Pet 97-04; Chapl Univ Coll Lon Hosps NHS Foundn Trust from 04. *The Department of Spiritual and Pastoral Care, The Chaplaincy, Middlesex Hospital, Mortimer Street, London W1T 8AA* Tel (020) 7636 8833 E-mail mark.brackley@uchl.org

BRADBERRY, John. b 20. Clifton Th Coll 46. **d** 47 **p** 48. C Hinckley H Trin *Leic* 47-50; C Earlham St Anne *Nor* 50-51; V Leyton Ch Ch *Chelmsf* 51-55; Argentina 55-61; V Siddal *Wakef* 61-72; R Bentham St Jo *Bradf* 72-85; rtd 85; Perm to Offic *Wakef* from 85 and *Bradf* 86-92. *18 Moor Bottom Road, Halifax HX2 9SR* Tel (01422) 244944

BRADBERRY, John Stephen. b 47. Hull Univ BSc70 Leeds Univ CertEd71 MEd86 Bradf Univ PhD91. NW Ord Course 76. **d** 79 **p** 80. NSM Warley *Wakef* from 79; Chapl H Trin Sch Holmfield from 91; Bp's Officer for NSM's from 95. *129 Paddock Lane, Halifax HX2 0NT* Tel (01422) 358282

BRADBROOK, Mrs Averyl. b 46. Girton Coll Cam BA67 MA88 Man Univ PGCE69 MA(Theol)96. N Ord Course 90. **d** 93 **p** 94. C Heaton Ch Ch *Man* 93-96; P-in-c Elton St Steph 96-02; Bp's Adv for Women's Min 01-02; V Moseley St Mary *Birm* from 02; P-in-c Moseley St Anne from 04. *St Mary's Vicarage, 18 Oxford Road, Moseley, Birmingham B13 9EH* Tel 0121-449 1459 *or* 449 2243 Mobile 07808-290817 E-mail abradbrook@onetel.com

BRADBROOK, Peter David. b 33. Kelham Th Coll 54. **d** 60 **p** 61. C Ches St Oswald St Thos *Ches* 60-63; C Fulham St Etheldreda *Lon* 64-65; V Congleton St Jas *Ches* 65-79; V Wheelock 79-92; V Crewe All SS and St Paul 92-98; rtd 98; Perm to Offic *Ches* from 00. *20 Magdelen Court, College Fields, Dane Bank Avenue, Crewe CW2 8FF* Tel (01270) 669420

BRADBURY, Cedric. *See* BRADBURY, Canon Herbert Cedric

BRADBURY, George Graham. b 35. AKC58. **d** 59 **p** 60. C Portsea St Mary *Portsm* 59-62; C Melksham *Sarum* 62-64; R Winfrith Newburgh w Chaldon Herring 64-68; CF 68-71; rtd 99. *Wayside, Brook Street, Shipton Gorge, Bridport DT6 4NA* Tel (01308) 897714

BRADBURY, Canon Herbert Cedric. b 30. FPS Man Univ PhC53. Linc Th Coll 64. **d** 66 **p** 67. C Blackpool St Steph *Blackb* 66-71; TV Hempnall *Nor* 71-75; TR 75-81; R Fritton w Morningthorpe w Shelton and Hardwick 74-77; RD Depwade 77-81; R Wroxham w Hoveton and Belaugh 81-92; RD Tunstead 83-91; Hon Can Nor Cathl 90-97; R Gt and Lt Massingham and Harpley 92-97; P-in-c South Raynham, E w W Raynham, Helhoughton, etc 94-97; rtd 97; Perm to Offic *Nor* from 97; Bp's Officer for Rtd Clergy and Widows from 99. *Morningthorpe, 66 Grove Lane, Holt NR25 6ED* Tel (01263) 712634

BRADBURY, Julian Nicholas Anstey. b 49. BNC Ox BA71 MA75 Birm Univ MA84. Cuddesdon Coll 71. **d** 73 **p** 74. C S'wark H Trin *S'wark* 73-76; In RC Ch in USA 76-79; V Tottenham H Trin *Lon* 79-85; Dir Past Th Sarum & Wells Th Coll 85-90; P-in-c Yatton Keynell *Bris* 90-97; P-in-c Biddestone w Slaughterford 90-97; P-in-c Castle Combe 90-97; P-in-c W Kington 90-97; P-in-c Nettleton 90-97; R Horfield H Trin 97-02; Fell K Fund from 02; Perm to Offic *Ox* from 02. *12 St Bernards Road, Oxford OX2 6EH* Tel (020) 7307 2610
E-mail n.bradbury@kingsfund.org.uk

BRADBURY, Kenneth James Frank. b 23. Qu Coll Birm 72. **d** 75 **p** 76. NSM Cen Telford *Lich* 75-77; C 77-80; V Chirbury *Heref* 80-88; V Marton 80-88; V Trelystan 80-88; rtd 88; Perm to Offic *Heref* 90-98 and *Lich* 98-03. *Elm Tree Cottage, Treflach, Oswestry SY10 9HG* Tel (01691) 637407

BRADBURY, Nicholas. *See* BRADBURY, Julian Nicholas Anstey

BRADBURY, Paul. b 72. St Cath Coll Cam BA93 N Lon Univ MA99. Trin Coll Bris BA04. **d** 04 **p** 05. C Bitterne Park *Win* from 04. *24 Lacon Close, Southampton SO18 1JA* Tel (023) 8058 4640
E-mail bradbreeze@surefish.co.uk

BRADBURY, Robert Douglas. b 50. Ripon Coll Cuddesdon 75. **d** 76 **p** 77. C Harlescott *Lich* 76-81; V Ruyton 81-88; P-in-c Gt w Lt Ness 84-88; V Ruyton XI Towns w Gt and Lt Ness 88-99. *Cysegr, Holyhead Road, Froncysyllte, Llangollen LL20 7PU*

BRADDICK-SOUTHGATE, Charles Anthony Michael. b 70. K Coll Lon BD92. Chich Th Coll 92. **d** 94 **p** 95. C Catford St Laur *S'wark* 94-97; V Nunhead St Antony w St Silas from 97. *St Antony with St Silas Vicarage, Athenlay Road, London SE15 3EP* Tel (020) 7639 4261 Fax 7252 8152
E-mail cambs@aol.com

BRADDOCK, Andrew Jonathan. b 71. SS Coll Cam BA92 Cam Univ MA96. Ridley Hall Cam 95. **d** 98 **p** 99. C Ranworth w Panxworth, Woodbastwick etc *Nor* 98-01; R Cringleford and Colney from 01; RD Humbleyard from 04. *The Vicarage, 7A Newmarket Road, Cringleford, Norwich NR4 6UE* Tel (01603) 458467

BRADDOCK, Arthur Derek. b 25. Bolton Inst of Educn BA90 Bolton Univ MPhil05. Lich Th Coll 56. **d** 59 **p** 60. C Droylsden St Mary *Man* 59-61; C New Bury 61-65; V Kearsley Moor 65-79; C Ellesmere Port *Ches* 79-85; rtd 85; Perm to Offic *Man* from 85. *25 Clumber House Nursing Home, 81 Dickens Lane, Poynton, Stockport SK12 1NT* Tel (01625) 850046

BRADFORD, Alan. b 57. Southn Univ BSc79 Warwick Univ PGCE80. St Jo Coll Nottm MTh04. **d** 04 **p** 05. C Countesthorpe w Foston *Leic* from 04. *7 Borrowcup Close, Countesthorpe, Leicester LE8 5XJ* Tel 0116-277 6066
E-mail abradford@hotmail.com

BRADFORD, Daphne Marcelle. b 28. Open Univ BA05. LNSM course 95. **d** 97 **p** 98. OLM Martham and Repps with Bastwick, Thurne etc *Nor* 97-01; rtd 01; Perm to Offic *Nor* from 01. *13 Pine Close, Martham, Norwich NR29 4SG* Tel (01493) 740579

BRADFORD, John. b 34. FRSA FRGS Lon Univ BA60 Birm Univ MEd81 Ox Univ AdCertEd70. Oak Hill Th Coll 55. **d** 60 **p** 61. C Walcot *B & W* 60-64; Ass Master Wendover C of E Primary Sch 64-65; Hd RE Dr Challoner's High Sch Lt Chalfont 65-69; Perm to Offic *Ox* 66-70; Lect St Pet Coll of Educn Saltley 70-77; Perm to Offic *Birm* 70-71; Lic to Offic from 71; Perm to Offic *Cov* from 77; Nat Chapl-Missr Children's Soc 77-99; Gen Perm to Offic Ch in Wales from 89; rtd 99. *27 Marsh Lane, Solihull B91 2PG* Tel 0121-704 9895 *or* (020) 7837 4299
E-mail revjohnbradford@aol.com

BRADFORD, Peter. b 38. Sarum Th Coll 69. **d** 70 **p** 71. C Holdenhurst *Win* 70-73; C Stanmore 73-77; P-in-c Eling, Testwood and Marchwood 77-78; R Marchwood 78-86; C Christchurch 86-90; C Andover w Foxcott 90-92; V E and W Worldham, Hartley Mauditt w Kingsley etc 92-04; rtd 04. *23 Drummond Road, Bournemouth BH1 4DP* Tel (01202) 396451

BRADFORD, Archdeacon of. *See* LEE, The Ven David John

BRADFORD, Bishop of. *See* JAMES, The Rt Revd David Charles

BRADFORD, Dean of. *Vacant*

BRADING, Jeremy Clive. b 74. Birm Univ BA95 MPhil98. Westcott Ho Cam 00. **d** 02 **p** 03. C Man Clayton St Cross w St Paul *Man* 02-05; TV Pendleton from 05. *The Vicarage, Moorfield Road, Salford M6 7EY* Tel 0161-736 3064 Mobile 07786-567140 E-mail jeremycbrading@yahoo.co.uk

BRADLEY, Andrew Robert. b 65. Clare Coll Cam BA88. St Jo Coll Nottm Dip Th Studies 93 MA94. **d** 94 **p** 95. C Burnage St Marg *Man* 94-98; TV Didsbury St Jas and Em 98-04; Nat Co-ord Acorn Chr Foundn from 04. *Acorn Christian Foundation, Whitehill Chase, Bordon GU35 0AP* Tel (01420) 478121 Fax 478122

BRADLEY, Anthony David. b 56. Wye Coll Lon BSc76. St Jo Coll Nottm DPS88. **d** 88 **p** 89. C Southchurch Ch Ch *Chelmsf* 88-91; C Cov H Trin *Cov* 91-97; P-in-c Budbrooke from 97; Dioc Lay Tr

Adv from 93. *The Vicarage, Budbrooke, Warwick CV35 8QL* Tel (01926) 494002 E-mail tony.bradley@dial.pipex.com

BRADLEY, Anthony Edward. b 39. Perth Bible Coll 93. **d** 89 **p** 96. Dn-in-c Ravensthorpe Australia 95-96; P-in-c 96-99; C Wotton St Mary *Glouc* 00-04; rtd 04. *58 Heacham Avenue, Hocking, W Australia 6065* Tel (0061) (8) 9405 7857 E-mail anthonybradley@onetel.com

BRADLEY, Brian Hugh Granville. b 32. Univ Coll Ox 51. Lon Coll of Div 59. **d** 62 **p** 63. C E Twickenham St Steph *Lon* 62-65; C Herne Bay Ch Ch *Cant* 65-69; Miss to Seamen Teesside 69-71; Ceylon 71-72; Sri Lanka 72-74; Chapl Amsterdam w Haarlem and Den Helder *Eur* 75-79; Chapl Lyon w Grenoble and Aix-les-Bains 79-85; TV Bucknall and Bagnall *Lich* 87-93; Assoc Chapl Dubai and Sharjah w N Emirates 93-97; rtd 97; Perm to Offic *Win* 97-03. *16 Horseguards, Exeter EX4 4UU* Tel (01392) 679282

BRADLEY, Clifford David. b 36. Lon Univ BA60. St Aid Birkenhead 60. **d** 62 **p** 63. C Stoneycroft All SS *Liv* 62-65; C Chipping Sodbury and Old Sodbury *Glouc* 65-68; Br Honduras 68-70; C Leckhampton SS Phil and Jas *Glouc* 70-71; V Badgeworth w Shurdington 71-79; Dioc Missr *S & M* 79-84; V Santan 79-84; V Braddan 79-84; Bp's Dom Chapl 81-84; V Stroud and Uplands w Slad *Glouc* 84-89; C Shepshed *Leic* 90-92; R Leire w Ashby Parva and Dunton Bassett 92-99; rtd 99; P-in-c Renhold *St Alb* from 99. *The Vicarage, 46 Church End, Renhold, Bedford MK41 0LU* Tel (01234) 771317

BRADLEY, Colin John. b 46. Edin Univ MA69 Hertf Coll Ox 71. Sarum & Wells Th Coll 72. **d** 75 **p** 76. C Easthampstead *Ox* 75-79; V Shawbury *Lich* 79-90; R Moreton Corbet 80-90; P-in-c Stanton on Hine Heath 81-90; Can Res Portsm Cathl *Portsm* 90-98; Dir of Ords 90-98; C Chich 98-00; C Chich St Paul and Westhampnett 00-01; P-in-c Cocking, Bepton and W Lavington from 01. *The Rectory, Mill Lane, Cocking, Midhurst GU29 0HJ* Tel (01730) 817340

BRADLEY, Connla John Osman. b 08. Bible Churchmen's Coll Bris. **d** 47 **p** 47. C Tunbridge Wells H Trin *Roch* 47-49; V Camberwell Ch Ch *S'wark* 49-55; V Frogmore *St Alb* 55-68; V Havering-atte-Bower *Chelmsf* 68-76; rtd 76; Perm to Offic *Chich* 76-88. *Lyndon Eventide Home, 2 High Street, Sandridge, St Albans AL4 9DH* Tel (01727) 851050

BRADLEY (née DRAPER), Mrs Elizabeth Ann. b 38. Nottm Univ BTh75. Linc Th Coll 71. **dss** 84 **d** 87 **p** 94. Ind Chapl *Linc* 84-91; Bracebridge 84-91; Hon C 87-91; GFS Ind Chapl *Lon* 91-96; Hon Chapl GFS 96-98; Riverside Chapl *S'wark* 96; C Leighton Buzzard w Eggington, Hockliffe etc *St Alb* 98-01; Perm to Offic 01-02; Chapl Luton and Dunstable Hosp NHS Trust from 02. *26 Dew Pond Road, Flitwick, Bedford MK45 1RT* Tel (01525) 712369 E-mail elizabeth.bradley@ldh-tr.anglox.nhs.uk

BRADLEY, Gary Scott. b 53. Lon Univ LLB75. Ripon Coll Cuddesdon 75. **d** 78 **p** 79. C St John's Wood *Lon* 78-83; V Paddington St Sav from 83; P-in-c Paddington St Mary from 95; P-in-c Paddington St Mary Magd from 98. *6 Park Place Villas, London W2 1SP* Tel (020) 7723 1968 Mobile 07957-140371 Fax (020) 7724 5332 E-mail bottlerot@aol.com

BRADLEY, John Owen. b 30. Jes Coll Ox BA55 MA56. St Mich Coll Llan 52. **d** 56 **p** 57. C Cardiff St Mary *Llan* 56-59; Lect St Mich Coll Llan 59-61; C Caerau w Ely *Llan* 60; C Newton Nottage 61-64; V Aberavon H Trin 65-69; Lic to Offic *Cov* 70-76; C W Kirby St Bridget *Ches* 76-79; TV Knowle *Bris* 79-80; TR 80-91; RD Brislington 83-89; Chapl St Monica Home Westbury-on-Trym 91-00; Perm to Offic *Bris* from 00. *20 Home Ground, Bristol BS9 4UB* Tel and fax 0117-907 1503 E-mail job@blueyonder.co.uk

BRADLEY, Joy Elizabeth. *See* COUSANS, Mrs Joy Elizabeth

BRADLEY, Mrs Julie Caroline. b 59. Ex Univ BSc80. WEMTC 00. **d** 03 **p** 04. NSM Stoke Gifford *Bris* from 03. *113 North Road, Stoke Gifford, Bristol BS34 8PE* Tel 0117-979 3418 E-mail cjcbradley@deltats.co.uk

BRADLEY, Michael Frederick John. b 44. Qu Coll Birm 76. **d** 77 **p** 78. C Sheff St Cuth *Sheff* 77-78; C Alford w Rigsby *Linc* 78-83; V Bracebridge 83-90; V Flitwick *St Alb* from 90. *The Vicarage, 26 Dew Pond Road, Flitwick, Bedford MK45 1RT* Tel (01525) 712369 Fax 08701-259827 E-mail mfjbradley@btopenworld.com

BRADLEY, The Ven Peter David Douglas. b 49. Nottm Univ BTh79. Ian Ramsey Coll 74 Linc Th Coll 75. **d** 79 **p** 80. C Upholland *Liv* 79-83; TR 94-01; V Dovecot 83-94; Dir CME 89-02; Hon Can Liv Cathl from 00; Adn Warrington from 01; TR Upholland from 01. *The Rectory, 1A College Road, Upholland, Skelmersdale WN8 0PY* Tel (01695) 622936 Fax 625865 E-mail archdeacon@peterbradley.fsnet.co.uk

BRADLEY, The Very Revd Peter Edward. b 64. Trin Hall Cam BA86 MA90 FRSA02. Ripon Coll Cuddesdon 86. **d** 88 **p** 89. C Northampton St Mich w St Edm *Pet* 88-91; Chapl G&C Coll Cam 91-95; TV Abingdon *Ox* 95-98; TV High Wycombe 98-03; TR 03; Dean Sheff from 03. *Sheffield Cathedral, Church Street, Sheffield S1 1HA* Tel 0114-263 6063 Fax 263 6075 E-mail dean@sheffield-cathedral.org.uk

BRADLEY, Ronald Percival. b 25. ACP51 FRSA52 TCert49. Ex & Truro NSM Scheme 80. **d** 83 **p** 84. C Honiton, Gittisham, Combe Raleigh, Monkton etc *Ex* 83-86; P-in-c Halberton 86-87; rtd 90. *Haddon House, 20 Moorland Road, Plympton, Plymouth PL7 2BH* Tel (01752) 337667

BRADLEY (née NAYLOR), Ms Vivien Frances Damaris. b 55. New Hall Cam BA78 MA82 RGN86 DTM89. Ripon Coll Cuddesdon. **d** 93 **p** 94. C Northampton St Jas *Pet* 93-95; Chapl Asst Southn Univ Hosps NHS Trust 95-98; Chapl 98-00; Chapl Addenbrooke's NHS Trust 00-03; Perm to Offic *Nor* from 03. *7 Norwich Road, Wymondham NR18 9HB* Tel (01603) 757807

BRADNUM, Canon Ella Margaret. b 41. CertEd64 St Hugh's Coll Ox MA65. **dss** 69 **d** 87 **p** 94. Illingworth *Wakef* 69-72; Batley All SS 72-73; Lay Tr Officer 77-82; Min Tr Officer 82-88; Sec Dioc Bd of Min from 88; Warden of Readers 88-02; Co-ord Lay Tr 88-02; Hon Can Wakef Cathl from 94; Prin Wakef Min Scheme from 97. *4 Hopton Hall Lane, Upper Hopton, Mirfield WF14 8EL* Tel (01924) 493569

BRADNUM, Richard James. b 39. Pemb Coll Ox BA62 MA67. Ridley Hall Cam 62. **d** 64 **p** 65. C Birm St Martin *Birm* 64-68; C Sutton St Jas *York* 68-69; Perm to Offic *Wakef* 71-72; C Batley All SS 72-74; V Gawthorpe and Chickenley Heath 74-86; V Mixenden 86-97; rtd 97; Perm to Offic *Wakef* 97-99; Hon Retirement Officer from 99. *4 Hopton Hall Lane, Mirfield WF14 8EL* Tel (01924) 493569

BRADSHAW, Charles Anthony. b 44. Qu Coll Birm MA76. **d** 75 **p** 76. C Whickham *Dur* 75-78; C Bilton *Cov* 78-81; TV Coventry Caludon 81-89; V Birstall and Wanlip *Leic* 89-99; TR Vale of Belvoir Par 00-04; TV Caterham *S'wark* from 04. *The Rectory, Station Road, Woldingham, Caterham CR3 7DD* Tel (01883) 652192 E-mail cab@paxchristi.wanadoo.co.uk

BRADSHAW, Denis Matthew. b 52. Chich Th Coll 77. **d** 80 **p** 81. C Ruislip St Martin *Lon* 80-84; C Northolt Park St Barn 84-86; V Northolt W End St Jos 86-01; P-in-c Hayes St Nic CD 94-00; V Kennington St Jo w St Jas *S'wark* from 01. *The Vicarage, 92 Vassall Road, London SW9 6JA* Tel (020) 7735 9340 Fax 7735 4548 E-mail dmb6161@compuserve.com

BRADSHAW, Graham. b 58. Edin Univ BD86. Edin Th Coll 83. **d** 86 **p** 87. C Thornton-le-Fylde *Blackb* 86-89; C Kirkby Lonsdale *Carl* 89-91; V Langford *St Alb* 91-97; Papua New Guinea 97-99; R Aspley Guise w Husborne Crawley and Ridgmont *St Alb* from 00. *The Rectory, Church Street, Aspley Guise, Milton Keynes MK17 8HN* Tel (01908) 583169 E-mail gbradshaw@tinyworld.co.uk

BRADSHAW, Miss Jennie McNeille. b 47. UEA BA69. Cranmer Hall Dur 85. **d** 90 **p** 94. Par Dn Herne *Cant* 90-94; C 94-95; P-in-c Claybrooke cum Wibtoft and Frolesworth *Leic* 95-96; R from 96. *The Vicarage, Main Road, Claybrook Parva, Lutterworth LE17 5AE* Tel (01455) 202262

BRADSHAW (née DAY), Mrs Jennifer Ann. b 67. Aber Univ BSc89. Wycliffe Hall Ox BTh95. **d** 95 **p** 96. C Whitburn *Dur* 95-98; C Monkwearmouth 98-99; TV 99-01. *St Matthew's Vicarage, Silksworth Road, Sunderland SR3 2AA* Tel 0191-521 1167

BRADSHAW, Kenneth Allan. b 23. Roch Th Coll 60. **d** 62 **p** 63. C Cheam Common St Phil *S'wark* 62-65; C Portslade St Nic *Chich* 65-67; C Preston 67-71; C Haywards Heath St Wilfrid 71-82; C Sidley 82-88; rtd 88; Perm to Offic *Llan* from 88. *The Cottage, 115A Splott Road, Cardiff CF24 2BY* Tel (029) 2046 5998

BRADSHAW, Canon Malcolm McNeille. b 45. Kelham Th Coll 65. **d** 70 **p** 71. C New Addington *Cant* 70-76; Chapl Milan w Cadenabbia, Varese and Lugano *Eur* 77-82; V Boxley w Detling *Cant* 82-99; Sen Chapl Gtr Athens *Eur* from 99; Hon Can Malta Cathl from 01. *c/o the British Embassy, Plutarchou 1, 106-75 Athens, Greece* Tel and fax (0030) (210) 721 4906

BRADSHAW, Canon Prof Paul Frederick. b 45. Clare Coll Cam BA66 MA70 K Coll Lon PhD71 FRHistS91 Ox Univ DD94. Westcott Ho Cam 67. **d** 69 **p** 70. C W Wickham St Jo *Cant* 69-71; C Cant St Martin and St Paul 71-73; Tutor Chich Th Coll 73-78; V Flamstead *St Alb* 78-82; Dir of Minl Tr Scheme 78-82; Vice-Prin Ripon Coll Cuddesdon 83-85; USA 85-95; Prof Th Notre Dame Univ from 85; Hon Can N Indiana from 90; PV Westmr Abbey from 95; Perm to Offic *Guildf* from 95. *Notre Dame London Centre, 1 Suffolk Street, London SW1Y 4HG* Tel (020) 7484 7811 Fax 7484 7853 E-mail bradshaw.1@nd.edu

BRADSHAW, Philip Hugh. b 39. Qu Coll Ox BA64 MA67 Lon Univ DipRS91. S'wark Ord Course 88. **d** 91 **p** 92. NSM Bletchingley *S'wark* 91-98; Ldr Community of Celebration 91-98; NSM Redhill St Jo from 98. *35 Cavendish Road, Redhill RH1 4AL* Tel (01737) 778760

BRADSHAW, Richard Gordon Edward. b 66. Southn Univ LLB90. Wycliffe Hall Ox BTh94. **d** 97 **p** 98. C Bishopwearmouth St Gabr *Dur* 97-00; C Silksworth 00-01; P-in-c 01-03; V from 03. *St Matthew's Vicarage, Silksworth Road, Sunderland SR3 2AA* Tel 0191-521 1167

BRADSHAW, Roy John. b 49. Sarum & Wells Th Coll 85. **d** 87 **p** 88. FSJ from 84; C Gainsborough All SS *Linc* 87-90; V New Waltham 90-94; R Killamarsh *Derby* from 94. *The Rectory,*

Sheepcote Road, Killamarsh, Sheffield S21 1DU Tel 0114-248 2769

BRADSHAW, Timothy. b 50. Keble Coll Ox BA72 MA78 PhD. St Jo Coll Nottm BA75. **d** 76 **p** 77. C Clapton Park All So *Lon* 76-79; Lect Trin Coll Bris 80-91; Hon C Sea Mills *Bris* 83-91; Tutor Regent's Park Coll Ox from 91; NSM Ox St Aldate w St Matt *Ox* 91-94; NSM Ox St Matt from 95. *54 St Giles, Oxford OX1 3LU* Tel (01865) 288147 E-mail timothy.bradshaw@regents.ox.ac.uk

BRADSHAW, Veronica. *See* CAROLAN, Mrs Veronica

BRADWELL, Area Bishop of. *See* GREEN, The Rt Revd Laurence Alexander

BRADY, Frederick Herbert James. b 33. Sydney Univ BSc55 DipEd56 Lon Univ BD65. Moore Th Coll Sydney ThL59. **d** 60 **p** 60. Australia 60-63 and from 69; Lic to Offic *Lon* 63-69; rtd 00. *18 Capel Street, West Melbourne, Vic, Australia 3003* Tel (0061) (3) 9328 8487 *or* (3) 9650 3791 Fax (3) 9650 4718 E-mail brady@ioville.net.au

BRADY, Ian. b 59. Ridley Hall Cam. **d** 01 **p** 02. C Cromer *Nor* 01-04; V Belmont *Lon* from 04. *St Anselm's Vicarage, Ventnor Avenue, Stanmore HA7 2HU* Tel (020) 8907 3186 E-mail i.bradybunch@btopenworld.com

BRADY, Mrs Madalaine Margaret. b 45. Univ of Wales (Ban) BD88 CertEd91 MA92. **d** 89 **p** 97. Asst Chapl Univ of Wales (Ban) *Ban* 89-96; Dioc Communications Officer from 94; Dioc Lay Min Officer from 95; C Arllechwedd 96-97; P-in-c Llanfaelog 97-02; R Llanfaelog and Llangwyfan from 02. *The Rectory, Station Road, Rhosneigr LL64 5JX* Tel and fax (01407) 810412 *or* tel (01248) 354999 Fax (01248) 353882 E-mail dmbrady@lineone.net

BRAGG, Mrs Rosemary Eileen. b 41. Plymouth Coll of Tech MRPharmS64. St Steph Ho Ox 99. **d** 00 **p** 01. NSM Boyne Hill *Ox* from 00. *2 Aldwick Drive, Maidenhead SL6 4JQ* Tel (01628) 629577

BRAILSFORD, Matthew Charles. b 64. Newc Univ BSc86 St Jo Coll Dur BA95. Cranmer Hall Dur 92. **d** 95 **p** 96. C Hull St Jo Newland *York* from 95. *892 Beverley High Road, Hull HU6 7DG* Tel (01482) 854526 E-mail matthew.brailsford@ukgateway.net

BRAIN, Mrs Marina. **d** 01 **p** 02. OLM Wokingham St Sebastian *Ox* 01-05; Chapl HM Pris Reading from 05; Chapl HM Pris Grendon and Spring Hill from 05. *The Chaplain's Office, HM Prison, Forbury Road, Reading RG1 3HY* Tel 0118-908 5000 E-mail suburbanday@aol.com

BRAIN, Michael Charles. b 39. Culham Coll Ox TCert61 ACP65. Lich Th Coll 68. **d** 70 **p** 71. C Stone St Mich *Lich* 70-73; C Harlescott 73-76; C Longton St Jas 76-77; P-in-c Dudley St Edm *Worc* 77-79; V 79-04; Chapl Dudley Coll of Tech 77-04; rtd 04; Perm to Offic *Worc* from 04. *33 Dibdale Road, Dudley DY1 2RX* Tel (01384) 232774

BRAITHWAITE, Albert Alfred. b 24. Clifton Th Coll. **d** 59 **p** 60. C Bestwood St Matt *S'well* 59-62; Chapl RN 62-81; QHC from 77; C Southsea St Jude *Portsm* 82-90; Perm to Offic from 90; rtd 90. *3 Lorne Road, Southsea PO5 1RR* Tel (023) 9273 8753

BRAITHWAITE, Canon Michael Royce. b 34. Linc Th Coll 71. **d** 73 **p** 74. C Barrow St Geo w St Luke *Carl* 73-77; V Kells 77-88; RD Calder 84-88; V Lorton and Loweswater w Buttermere 88-99; Ldr Rural Life and Agric Team 93-96; Member Rural Life and Agric Team 96-99; RD Derwent 94-98; Hon Can Carl Cathl 94-99; rtd 99; Perm to Offic *Carl* from 00. *High Green Farm, Bothel, Carlisle CA7 2JA* Tel (01697) 32349

BRAITHWAITE, Canon Roy. b 34. Dur Univ BA56. Ridley Hall Cam 58. **d** 60 **p** 61. C Blackb St Gabr *Blackb* 60-63; C Burnley St Pet 63-66; V Accrington St Andr 66-74; V Blackb St Jas 74-95; RD Blackb 86-91; Hon Can Blackb Cathl 93-98; V Garstang St Helen Churchtown 95-98; Dioc Ecum Officer 95-98; rtd 98; Perm to Offic *Blackb* from 98. *9 Barker Lane, Mellor, Blackburn BB2 7ED* Tel (01254) 240724

BRALESFORD, Nicholas Robert. b 53. St Jo Coll Nottm LTh79 BTh79. **d** 79 **p** 80. C Leic St Chris *Leic* 79-82; C Heeley *Sheff* 82-85; TV Kings Norton *Birm* 85-90; V Chapel-en-le-Frith *Derby* from 90. *The Vicarage, 71 Manchester Road, Chapel-en-le-Frith, High Peak SK23 9TH* Tel (01298) 812134

BRALEY, Robert James. *See* RILEY-BRALEY, Robert James

BRAMHALL, Eric. b 39. St Cath Coll Cam BA61 MA65. Tyndale Hall Bris 61. **d** 63 **p** 64. C Eccleston St Luke *Liv* 63-66; C Bolton Em *Man* 66-69; Perm to Offic *Ches* 70-74; V Aughton Ch Ch *Liv* 75-92; Chapl Ormskirk Children's Hosp 75-92; V Childwall All SS *Liv* 92-04; rtd 04. *Henfaes, Prior Street, Ruthin LL15 1LT* Tel (01824) 702757

BRAMLEY, Thomas Anthony. b 44. BSc PhD. TISEC. **d** 96 **p** 97. NSM Penicuik *Edin* from 96; NSM W Linton from 96. *44 Bavelaw Crescent, Penicuik EH26 9AT*

BRAMMER, David John. b 62. **d** 99 **p** 00. C Acton St Mary *Lon* 99-02; C Ealing All SS from 02; Chapl Twyford C of E High Sch Acton from 02. *All Saints' Vicarage, Elm Grove Road, London W5 3JH* Tel (020) 8567 8166 E-mail david.brammer@london.anglican.org

BRAMPTON, Canon Fiona Elizabeth Gordon. b 56. St Jo Coll Dur BA78 BA83. Cranmer Hall Dur 81. **dss** 84 **d** 87 **p** 94. Bris St Andr Hartcliffe *Bris* 84-90; Par Dn 87-90; C Orton Waterville *Ely* 90-96; C-in-c Orton Goldhay CD 90-96; TV The Ortons, Alwalton and Chesterton 96-00; V Haddenham from 00; V Wilburton from 00; RD Ely from 03; Hon Can Ely Cathl from 05. *The Vicarage, Church Lane, Haddenham, Ely CB6 3TB* Tel (01353) 740309 E-mail fiona.brampton@ely.anglican.org

BRANCHE, Brian Maurice. b 37. Chich Th Coll 73. **d** 75 **p** 76. C Brighton Resurr *Chich* 75-78; C Upper Norwood St Jo *Cant* 78-81; P-in-c Croydon St Martin 81-84; V Croydon St Martin *S'wark* 85-88; V St Helier 88-93; V New Eltham All SS 93-97; V Barkingside H Trin *Chelmsf* 97-02; rtd 02. *113 Tong Road, Little Lever, Bolton BL3 1PU* E-mail bbranche@aol.com

BRAND, Frank Ronald Walter. b 25. ALCD56. **d** 56 **p** 57. C Brondesbury St Anne w Kilburn H Trin *Lon* 56-58; V Port Mourant Br Guiana 58-61; V Enmore 61-67; V N Greenford All Hallows *Lon* 67-91; rtd 91; Perm to Offic *B & W* from 91. *23 Hawthorn Grove, Bath BA2 5QA* Tel (01225) 834572

BRAND, Peter John. b 32. Lon Univ BSc54. Edin Dioc NSM Course 75. **d** 83 **p** 84. NSM Edin St Jo *Edin* from 83. *24 Drum Brae Park, Edinburgh EH12 8TF* Tel 0131-339 4406

BRAND, Richard Harold Guthrie. b 65. Dur Univ BA87. Ripon Coll Cuddesdon 87. **d** 89 **p** 90. C N Lynn w St Marg and St Nic *Nor* 89-92; C King's Lynn St Marg w St Nic 92-93; C Croydon St Jo *S'wark* 93-96; New Zealand 96-98; P-in-c Hambledon *Portsm* from 98; Dir of Ords from 98. *The Vicarage, Church Lane, Hambledon, Waterlooville PO7 4RT* Tel (023) 9263 2717 Fax as telephone E-mail richard.brand@virgin.net

BRAND, Stuart William. b 30. Leeds Univ BSc53. Coll of Resurr Mirfield 53. **d** 55 **p** 56. C Stepney St Dunstan and All SS *Lon* 55-59; C Acton Green St Pet 59-60; C-in-c Godshill CD *Portsm* 60-63; Malawi 63-67; V Widley w Wymering *Portsm* 67-72; Chapl Fieldhead Hosp Wakef 72-80; Chapl Pinderfields & Stanley Royd Hosps Wakef 72-80; Chapl Brook Gen Hosp Lon 80-95; Chapl Greenwich Distr Hosp Lon 80-95; rtd 95; Perm to Offic *Ox* from 96. *17 Hayfield Road, Oxford OX2 6TX* Tel (01865) 316456

BRANDES, Simon Frank. b 62. Univ of Wales (Ban) BA83. Edin Th Coll 83. **d** 85 **p** 86. C Barton w Peel Green *Man* 85-88; C Longsight St Jo w St Cypr 88-90; R 90-94; Asst Dioc Youth Officer 88-94; V Lt Lever 94-02; P-in-c Lydgate w Friezland 02-03; TR Saddleworth from 03. *The Vicarage, Stockport Road, Lydgate, Oldham OL4 4JJ* Tel (01457) 872117 Mobile 07775-526285

BRANDIE, Canon Beaumont Lauder. b 40. K Coll Lon AKC64 BD66 SSC. **d** 65 **p** 66. C Whitton St Aug *Lon* 65-71; C Portsea St Mary *Portsm* 71-77; TR Brighton Resurr *Chich* from 77; Can and Preb Chich Cathl from 87; RD Brighton 97. *St Martin's Rectory, Upper Wellington Road, Brighton BN2 3AN* Tel (01273) 604687 Fax 621090 E-mail team.rector@resurrection-brighton.org.uk

BRANDON, Miss Vera Eileen. b 12. Univ of Wales (Abth) CertEd35 BSc40 Lon Univ DipEd42 BD53. St Mich Ho Ox 51. **dss** 60 **d** 87 **p** 98. Lect and Tutor St Mich Ho Ox 51-61; Rushden St Pet 61-63; Tutor Wilson Carlile Coll of Evang 64-74; Community of the Word of God from 75; Lower Homerton St Paul *Lon* 75-80; Clapton Park All So 75-80; Hanger Lane St Ann 80-83; rtd 83; Tunbridge Wells St Pet *Roch* 83-87; Hon Par Dn 87-89; Perm to Offic 89-98; Chapl Florence Balls Ho & Halliwell Nursing Home 98-00. *Mount Ephraim House, Mount Ephraim, Tunbridge Wells TN4 8BU* Tel (01982) 529210

BRANNAGAN, Alan McKenzie. b 34. Chich Th Coll 66. **d** 68 **p** 69. C N Hull St Mich *York* 68-70; C Dunstable *St Alb* 70-75; R E w W Rudham *Nor* 75-81; V Houghton 75-81; TV Wolverhampton *Lich* 81-87; R W Felton 87-96; Chapl Ypres *Eur* 96-97; Perm to Offic *St Alb* from 97; rtd 99. *8 Park Lane, Blunham, Bedford MK44 3NH* Tel (01767) 640868

BRANSCOMBE, Michael Peter. b 65. Cranmer Hall Dur BA95. **d** 95 **p** 96. C Ogley Hay *Lich* 95-01; Dioc Voc Officer 99-01; Asst R Palm Harbor USA 01-04; Clearwater Ascension from 04. *1010 Charles Street, Clearwater, FL 33755, USA* E-mail mikeb@churchofascension.org

BRANSON, Robert David. b 46. Linc Th Coll 74. **d** 77 **p** 78. C Kempston Transfiguration *St Alb* 77-80; C Goldington 80-82; V Marsh Farm 82-91; V Aylsham *Nor* from 91; RD Ingworth from 00; Chapl Norwich Primary Care Trust from 99. *The Vicarage, 64 Holman Road, Aylsham, Norwich NR11 6BZ* Tel (01263) 733871

BRANT, Anthony Richard. b 44. S Dios Minl Tr Scheme. **d** 82 **p** 83. NSM Felpham w Middleton *Chich* 82-84; C Clymping 84-85; NSM 85-87; Perm to Offic from 88. *Fairholme, Barnham Road, Eastergate, Chichester PO20 3RS* Tel (01243) 544735

BRANT, Anthony William. b 31. TD67. Linc Th Coll 73. **d** 75 **p** 76. C Cove St Jo *Guildf* 75-79; P-in-c Puttenham and Wanborough 79-83; V Lightwater 83-93; rtd 93; Perm to Offic *Chich* from 93. *2 Southcourt Avenue, Bexhill-on-Sea TN39 3AR* Tel (01424) 217526

BRANT, Ms Karlyn Lee. b 72. Birm Univ BA99 MA01. Ripon Coll Cuddesdon 01. **d** 03 **p** 04. C Gaywood *Nor* from 03. *The*

Church Bungalow, Gayton Road, Kings Lynn PE30 4DZ Tel (01553) 765167 E-mail lee@ciborium.fsnet.co.uk

BRANT, Leslie Harold. b 11. **d** 71 **p** 72. C Lower Sandown St Jo *Portsm* 71-74; P-in-c Newchurch 75-80; rtd 80; Perm to Offic *Portsm* from 82. *1 Dean's Court, Solent View, Ryde PO33 2AQ*

BRASIER, Ralph Henry (Jim). b 30. Cant Sch of Min 82. **d** 85 **p** 86. C S Ashford Ch Ch *Cant* 85-89; V Pembury *Roch* 89-95; rtd 95; Perm to Offic *Portsm* and *Win* from 95. *72 Jenkyns Close, Botley, Southampton SO30 2UU* Tel (01489) 788332

BRASSELL, Canon Kenneth William. b 23. Kelham Th Coll 46. **d** 50 **p** 51. C Woodbridge St Mary *St E* 50-53; C-in-c Bury St Edmunds All SS CD 53-57; V Ipswich St Thos 57-63; V Beckenham St Jas *Roch* 63-88; P-in-c Beckenham St Aug 66-77; P-in-c Beckenham St Mich w St Aug 77-78; Hon Can Roch Cathl 82-88; rtd 88; Perm to Offic *Glouc* from 88. *20 College Green, Gloucester GL1 2LR* Tel (01452) 309080

BRASSIL, Sean Adrian. b 56. Westf Coll Lon BSc79. STETS 97. **d** 00 **p** 01. NSM Westborough *Guildf* 00-04; NSM Woking St Jo 04-05; Hon C Addlestone from 05. *15 Clinton Close, Knaphill, Woking GU21 2AL* Tel (01483) 838526 Mobile 07855-810047 E-mail sean.brassil@ntlworld.com

BRATLEY, David Frederick. b 42. Linc Th Coll 80. **d** 82 **p** 83. C Holbeach *Linc* 82-85; R Fleet w Gedney from 85; RD Elloe E 01-05. *The Rectory, Church End, Fleet, Spalding PE12 8NQ* Tel (01406) 423795

BRATTON, Mark Quinn. b 62. Lon Univ BA84 Barrister-at-Law (Middle Temple) 87 K Coll Lon MA98. Wycliffe Hall Ox BA94. **d** 94 **p** 95. C W Ealing St Jo w St Jas *Lon* 94-98; Chapl Warw Univ *Cov* from 98; AD Cov S from 02. *92 De Montfort Way, Coventry CV4 7DT* Tel (024) 7669 0216 *or* 7652 3519 E-mail m.q.bratton@warwick.ac.uk *or* mark.bratton@talk21.com

BRAUN, Thom. b 53. St Jo Coll Ox BA76 MA76 Univ Coll Lon PhD80. S'wark Ord Course 89. **d** 92 **p** 93. Hon C Surbiton St Andr and St Mark *S'wark* from 92. *8 Kings Drive, Surbiton KT5 8NG* Tel (020) 8399 6898

BRAVINER, William Edward. b 66. Leic Poly BSc88 St Jo Coll Dur BA94 ACA91. Cranmer Hall Dur 92. **d** 95 **p** 96. C Royton St Anne *Man* 95-99; R Lansallos and V Talland *Truro* 99-03; P-in-c Duloe, Herodsfoot, Morval and St Pinnock 01-03; TR Jarrow *Dur* from 03; AD Jarrow from 05. *St Andrew's House, Borough Road, Jarrow NE32 5BL* Tel 0191-489 3279 E-mail bill.braviner@durham.anglican.org

BRAY, Christopher Laurence. b 53. Leeds Univ BSc74 Qu Univ Kingston Ontario MSc76. St Jo Coll Nottm 78. **d** 81 **p** 82. C Aughton Ch Ch *Liv* 81-84; Hon C Scarborough St Mary w Ch Ch and H Apostles *York* 84-88; Chapl Scarborough Coll 84-88; V St Helens St Matt Thatto Heath *Liv* 88-98; V Southport All SS and All Sö 98-02; rtd 02; Perm to Offic *Liv* from 03. *4 The Mallards, Southport PR9 8RJ* Tel (01704) 224648 E-mail chrislbray@aol.com

BRAY, Gerald Lewis. b 48. McGill Univ Montreal BA69 Sorbonne Univ Paris LittD73. Ridley Hall Cam 76. **d** 78 **p** 79. C Canning Town St Cedd *Chelmsf* 78-80; Tutor Oak Hill Th Coll 80-92; Ed *Churchman* from 83; Perm to Offic *Ely* from 92; Angl Prof Div Beeson Div Sch Samford Univ Alabama from 93. *16 Manor Court, Cambridge CB3 9BE* Tel (01223) 311804 *or* (001) (205) 726 2585 Fax (01223) 566608 *or* (001) (205) 726 2234 E-mail glbray@samford.edu

BRAY, Jason Stephen. b 69. SS Hild & Bede Coll Dur BA90 MA91 Fitzw Coll Cam PhD96 DipTh96 MSOTS97. Westcott Ho Cam 95. **d** 97 **p** 98. C Abergavenny St Mary w Llanwenarth Citra *Mon* 97-99; Min Can St Woolos Cathl 99-02; V Blaenavon w Capel Newydd from 02. *The Vicarage, Llanover Road, Blaenavon, Pontypool NP4 9HR* Tel (01495) 790292

BRAY, Jeremy Grainger. b 40. Man Univ BA62. Wells Th Coll 62. **d** 64 **p** 65. C Bris St Andr w St Bart *Bris* 64-67; C Bris H Cross Inns Court 67-71; C-in-c Stockwood CD 71-73; V Bris Ch the Servant Stockwood 73-83; RD Brislington 79-83; P-in-c Chippenham St Pet 83-88; V 88-93; V Fishponds St Jo 93-04; rtd 04. *46 Charter Road, Chippenham SN15 2RA* Tel (01249) 655661 E-mail jg.bray@btinternet.com

BRAY, Joyce. b 32. CA Tr Coll. **dss** 80 **d** 87 **p** 94. Bloxwich *Lich* 80-84; Derringham Bank *York* 84-03; Par Dn 87-94; Hon C 94-03; rtd 94; Perm to Offic *York* from 03. *413 Willerby Road, Hull HU5 5JD* Tel (01482) 502193

BRAY, Kenneth John. b 31. St Mich Coll Llan 65. **d** 67 **p** 72. C Killay *S & B* 67-68; C S Harrow St Paul *Lon* 71-73; C Hillingdon St Jo 73-76; C Chipping Sodbury and Old Sodbury *Glouc* 76-79; C Worle *B & W* 79-80; Lic to Offic *Ches* 80-83; TV Wrexham *St As* 83-85; V Llay 85-94; rtd 94. *21 Glenthorn Road, Bexhill-on-Sea TN39 3QH* Tel (01424) 213965

BRAY, Richard. b 29. Linc Th Coll 55. **d** 57 **p** 58. C Lt Ilford St Barn *Chelmsf* 57-62; R Tye Green w Netteswell 62-93; rtd 93; Perm to Offic *Chelmsf* from 93. *14 The Wayback, Saffron Walden CB10 2AX* Tel (01799) 526901

BRAYBROOKE, Marcus Christopher Rossi. b 38. Magd Coll Cam BA62 MA65 Lon Univ MPhil68. Wells Th Coll 63. **d** 64 **p** 65. C Highgate St Mich *Lon* 64-67; C Frindsbury w Upnor *Roch* 67-72; TV Frindsbury w Upnor 72-73; P-in-c Swainswick w Langridge and Woolley *B & W* 73-76; R 76-79; Dir of Tr 79-84; Hon C Bath Ch Ch Prop Chpl 84-91; Exec Dir Coun of Chrs and Jews 84-87; rtd 88; Perm to Offic *Bris* 88-93; Preb Wells Cathl *B & W* 90-93; Chapl Bath St Mary Magd Holloway 92-93; Hon C Dorchester *Ox* 93-05. *17 Courtiers Green, Clifton Hampden, Abingdon OX14 3EN* Tel (01865) 407566 E-mail marcusbray@aol.com

BRAZELL, Denis Illtyd Anthony. b 42. Trin Coll Cam BA64 MA68. Wycliffe Hall Ox 78. **d** 80 **p** 81. C Cheltenham Ch Ch *Glouc* 80-84; V Reading St Agnes w St Paul *Ox* 84-96; Perm to Offic *Guildf* 96-97; Warden and Chapl Acorn Chr Healing Trust 97-99; rtd 99; Co-Dir Word for Life Trust from 99; Perm to Offic *Glouc* from 02. *Word for Life Trust, The House of Bread, Ross Road, Christchurch, Coleford GL16 7NS* Tel (01594) 837744 Fax 837742 E-mail wflt@wflt.org

BRAZELL, Mrs Elizabeth Jane. b 44. LRAM64 ARCM65 GGSM65 AGSM65. Wycliffe Hall Ox 85. **dss** 86 **d** 87 **p** 94. Reading St Agnes w St Paul *Ox* 86-96; Par Dn 87-94; C 94-96; Dir Word for Life Trust from 96. *Word for Life Trust, The House of Bread, Ross Road, Christchurch, Coleford GL16 7NS* Tel (01594) 837744 Fax 837742 E-mail elizabeth@wflt.org

BRAZIER, Eric James Arthur. b 37. Qu Coll Birm 84. **d** 86 **p** 87. C Lighthorne *Cov* 86-89; P-in-c 89-92; P-in-c Chesterton 89-92; P-in-c Newbold Pacey w Moreton Morrell 89-92; R Astbury and Smallwood *Ches* 92-99; rtd 99; Perm to Offic *Ches* from 99; *Lich* and *Heref* from 00. *Wolf's Head Cottage, Chirbury, Montgomery SY15 6BP* Tel (01938) 561450

BRAZIER, Canon Raymond Venner. b 40. Wells Th Coll 68. **d** 71 **p** 72. C Horfield St Greg *Bris* 71-75; P-in-c Bris St Nath w St Kath 75-79; V 79-84; P-in-c Kingsdown 80-84; V Bris St Matt and St Nath from 84; RD Horfield 85-91; P-in-c Bishopston 93-97; Hon Can Bris Cathl from 94; Chapl to The Queen from 98. *The Vicarage, 11 Glentworth Road, Bristol BS6 7EG* Tel 0117-942 4186 *or* 944 1598 E-mail rbrazier@fish.co.uk

BREADEN, The Very Revd Robert William. b 37. Edin Th Coll 58. **d** 61 **p** 62. C Broughty Ferry *Bre* 61-65; R from 72; R Carnoustie 65-72; Can St Paul's Cathl Dundee from 77; Dean Bre from 84. *46 Seafield Road, Broughty Ferry, Dundee DD5 3AN* Tel (01382) 477477 Fax 477434 E-mail ateallach@aol.com

BREADMORE, Martin Christopher. b 67. Lon Univ LLB89. Wycliffe Hall Ox BTh93. **d** 93 **p** 94. C Herne Bay Ch Ch *Cant* 93-97; C Camberley St Paul *Guildf* 97-01; Chapl Elmhurst Ballet Sch 97-98; C Wallington H Trin *S'wark* from 01. *47 Park Hill Road, Wallington SM6 0RU*

BREADON, John Desmond. b 73. St Andr Univ BD96 Birm Univ PhD02. Westcott Ho Cam 99. **d** 01. C W Bromwich All SS *Lich* 01-05; Chapl St Geo Post 16 Cen *Birm* from 05. *St George's Post 16 Centre, Great Hampton Row, Birmingham B19 3JG* Tel 0121-236 9177 E-mail johnbreadon@hotmail.co.uk

BREAR, Alvin Douglas. b 43. **d** 87 **p** 96. NSM Leic H Spirit *Leic* 87-88; NSM Leic Ch Sav 88-96; NSM Leic Presentation 96-98; Finland from 98. *Sahurintie 44, 28800 Pori, Finland* Tel (00358) (2) 648 2060 E-mail douglas.brear@tukkk.fi

BREARLEY, Canon Janet Mary. b 48. Cranmer Hall Dur 88. **d** 90 **p** 94. C Prudhoe *Newc* 90-91; C Fenham St Jas and St Basil 91-95; Chapl Mothers' Union 93-95; V Warkworth and Acklington *Newc* from 95; Hon Can Newc Cathl from 04. *The Vicarage, 11 Dial Place, Warkworth, Morpeth NE65 0UR* Tel and fax (01665) 711217 E-mail jmbrearley@stlawrence-church.org.uk

BREBNER, Martin James. b 47. OBE02. ARCS68 Imp Coll Lon BSc68. St Alb Minl Tr Scheme 87. **d** 90 **p** 91. Hon C Letchworth St Paul w Willian *St Alb* 90-94; Hon C St Ippolyts 95-01; Perm to Offic *St Alb* 01-02 and *Linc* from 02. *Willowcroft, Greatford, Stamford PE9 4QA* Tel (01778) 561145 Fax 561157 E-mail martin.brebner@yahoo.com

BRECHIN, Bishop of. *See* MANTLE, The Rt Revd John Ambrose Cyril

BRECHIN, Dean of. *See* BREADEN, The Very Revd Robert William

BRECKLES, Robert Wynford. b 48. St Edm Hall Ox BA72 MA74 CertEd. Cranmer Hall Dur. **d** 79 **p** 80. C Bulwell St Mary *S'well* 79-84; V Lady Bay from 84. *The Vicarage, 121 Holme Road, Nottingham NG2 5AG* Tel 0115-981 3565

BRECKNELL, David Jackson. b 32. Keble Coll Ox BA53 MA57 SSC03. St Steph Ho Ox 56. **d** 58 **p** 59. C Streatham St Pet *S'wark* 58-62; C Sneinton St Steph w St Alb *S'well* 62-64; C Solihull *Birm* 64-68; V Streatham St Paul *S'wark* 68-75; R Rumboldswyke *Chich* 75-81; P-in-c Portfield 79-81; R Whyke w Rumboldswhyke and Portfield 81-95; rtd 95; Perm to Offic *Chich* from 95; P-in-c Boxgrove 98-99. *8 Priory Close, Boxgrove, Chichester PO18 0EA* Tel (01243) 784841 E-mail david.brecknell@tesco.net

BRECKWOLDT, Peter Hans. b 57. Man Poly BA79. Oak Hill Th Coll BA88. **d** 88 **p** 89. C Knutsford St Jo and Toft *Ches* 88-92; V

Moulton *Pet* from 92. *The Vicarage, 30 Cross Street, Moulton, Northampton NN3 1RZ* Tel (01604) 491060
E-mail peterbreckwoldt@cs.com

BRECON, Archdeacon of. *See* THOMAS, The Ven Alfred James Randolph

BRECON, Dean of. *See* DAVIES, The Very Revd John David Edward

BREED, Kenneth Wilfred. b 11. Leeds Univ BA33. Coll of Resurr Mirfield 33. **d** 35 **p** 36. C Cov H Trin *Cov* 35-37; C Parkstone St Pet w Branksea *Sarum* 37-43; Chapl RNVR 43-46; C Eastleigh *Win* 46-49; C Cheam *S'wark* 49-51; V Shirley *Birm* 51-77; rtd 77; Hon C St Andr Holborn *Lon* 77-79; Perm to Offic *Sarum* 80-03 and *B & W* 86-94. *4 Capel Court, The Burgage, Prestbury, Cheltenham GL52 3EL* Tel (01242) 582698

BREED, Mrs Verena. b 69. **d** 02 **p** 02. NSM Prestbury *Ches* 02-04; V Bosley and N Rode w Wincle and Wildboarclough from 04. *The Vicarage, Wincle, Macclesfield SK11 0QH* Tel (01260) 227234 E-mail breedy@squaremail.com

BREEDS, Christopher Roger. b 51. LGSM83 ACertCM87 Lon Univ CertEd73. Chich Th Coll 84. **d** 87 **p** 88. C E Grinstead St Swithun *Chich* 87-90; TV Aldrington 90-92; P-in-c Hove St Andr Old Ch 92-93; TV Hove 93-99; V Wivelsfield from 99. *New Vicarage, Church Lane, Wivelsfield, Haywards Heath RH17 7RD* Tel (01444) 471783
E-mail christopher.breeds@virgin.net

BREEN, Michael James. b 58. Oak Hill Th Coll BA79 MA85 LTh Cranmer Hall Dur 81. **d** 83 **p** 84. C Cambridge St Martin *Ely* 83-87; V Clapham Park All SS *S'wark* 87-92; USA 92-94; TR Crookes St Thos *Sheff* 94-04; Glendale Ch of Joy USA from 04. *3659 West Wayne Lane, Anthem, Phoenix, AZ 85086, USA* Tel (001) (623) 561 0500 Fax 561 5086

BREENE, Timothy Patrick Brownell. b 59. Kent Univ BA81 CCC Cam BA89 MA90. Ridley Hall Cam 87. **d** 90 **p** 93. C Hadleigh w Layham and Shelley *St E* 90-95; C Martlesham w Brightwell 95-03; rtd 03. *85 Cliff Road, Felixstowe IP11 9SQ* Tel (01394) 283718

BREFFITT, Geoffrey Michael. b 46. CChem MRIC72 Trent Poly CertEd77 DipPSE82. Qu Coll Birm 87. **d** 89 **p** 90. C Prenton *Ches* 89-92; V Frankby w Greasby 92-01; Dioc Ecum Officer 00-01; V German St Jo *S & M* from 01; V Foxdale from 01; V Patrick from 01; RD Castletown and Peel from 04. *The Vicarage, Patrick, Peel, Isle of Man IM5 1AW* Tel (01624) 842637 Fax 843374

BRENCHLEY, Royston Harry Peter. b 32. Lon Inst CertEd73 Lon Inst of Educn BEd77. **d** 02 **p** 03. OLM Mitcham St Olave *S'wark* 02-05; Perm to Offic from 05. *74 Manor Way, Mitcham CR4 1EE* Tel (020) 8764 3797
E-mail roy.brenchley@ukgateway.net

BRENDON-COOK, John Lyndon. b 37. FRICS. SW Minl Tr Course. **d** 81 **p** 82. NSM Bodmin *Truro* 81-82; NSM St Breoke and Egloshayle 82-90; NSM Helland 90-94; P-in-c 94-98; NSM Cardynham 90-94; rtd 98; Perm to Offic *Truro* from 98. *Treworder Byre, 119 Egloshayle Road, Wadebridge PL27 6AG* Tel (01208) 812488

BRENNAN, John Lester. b 20. MRCP51 FRCPath77 Barrister-at-Law (Middle Temple) 71 Lon Univ MB, BS44 MD52 LLM86. St Aug Coll Cant 54. **d** 55 **p** 56. India 55-65; Hon C Woodside Park St Barn *Lon* 65-69; Lic to Offic *Lich* 69-88; P-in-c Chrishall *Chelmsf* 88-89; Hon C 89-91; Hon C Heydon, Gt and Lt Chishill, Chrishall etc 91-93; Perm to Offic *St Alb* from 93. *16 Butterfield Road, Wheathampstead AL4 8PU* Tel (01582) 832230

BRENNAN, Samuel James. b 16. St Aid Birkenhead. **d** 57 **p** 58. C Magheralin *D & D* 57-60; C Down H Trin 60-63; Min Can Down Cathl 60-63; I Scarva 63-69; I Aghalee 69-84; rtd 84. *71 Bangor Road, Newtownards BT23 7BZ* Tel (028) 9181 9139

BRENNEN, Canon Colin. b 15. Lon Univ BA47 BD56 Dur Univ PhD88. Linc Th Coll 46. **d** 48 **p** 49. C Seaton Hirst *Newc* 48-50; C Bishopwearmouth Ch Ch *Dur* 50-52; V Grangetown 52-58; V Whitworth w Spennymoor 58-78; RD Auckland 74-82; Hon Can Dur Cathl 78-93; V Hamsterley 78-82; rtd 82. *1 Royton Close, Wrexham LL13 7EP* Tel (01978) 357747

BRENT, Prof Allen Leonard. b 40. Em Coll Cam BA66 Lon Univ MA72 Leeds Univ PhD78. N Queensland Coll of Min 82. **d** 84 **p** 85. Australia 84-95; Hon Can N Queensland 91-95; Sen Lect Coll of SS Mark and Jo Plymouth 95-01; Perm to Offic *Ex* 95-98; Lic to Offic 98-01; Perm to Offic *Ely* from 01. *18 St Albans Road, Cambridge CB4 2HG* Tel (01223) 362671

BRENT, Philip. b 68. K Coll Lon BD89. Cuddesdon Coll 94. **d** 96 **p** 97. C Sawbridgeworth *St Alb* 96-99; C Skegness and Winthorpe *Linc* 99-03; Chapl United Lincs Hosps NHS Trust 00-03; R Market Deeping *Linc* from 03. *The Rectory, 13 Church Street, Market Deeping, Peterborough PE6 8DA* Tel (01778) 342237 E-mail philip@candace.fsnet.co.uk

BRENTNALL, David John. b 53. UEA BA75 MPhil82. Ridley Hall Cam 84. **d** 86 **p** 87. C Eaton *Nor* 86-90; V Stevenage St Pet Broadwater *St Alb* 90-96; V St Alb St Pet from 96. *The Vicarage, 23 Hall Place Gardens, St Albans AL1 3SB* Tel (01727) 851464
E-mail david.brentnall@btinternet.com

BRERETON, Ms Catherine Louise. b 69. St Aid Coll Dur BSc90 Cranfield Univ MSc92 Fitzw Coll Cam BTh00. Ridley Hall Cam 97. **d** 00 **p** 01. C S Bank *York* 00-03; V Middlesbrough St Chad from 03. *St Chad's Vicarage, 9 Emerson Avenue, Middlesbrough TS5 7QW* Tel (01642) 819854
E-mail cathi.brereton@talk21.com

BRETEL, Keith Michael. b 51. St Mich Coll Llan 79. **d** 81 **p** 82. C Thundersley *Chelmsf* 81-84; CF from 84; Chapl Guards Chpl Lon 03-05. *c/o MOD Chaplains (Army)* Tel (01980) 615804 Fax 615800

BRETHERTON, Donald John. b 18. Lon Univ BD57. Handsworth Coll Birm 38 Headingley Coll Leeds 38 St Aug Coll Cant 59. **d** 60 **p** 61. In Methodist Ch 42-59; C Cant St Martin w St Paul *Cant* 60-62; V Thornton Heath St Jude 62-70; V Herne 70-82; RD Reculver 74-80; rtd 82; Perm to Offic *Cant* from 84. *Martin's, The Green, Chartham, Canterbury CT4 7JW* Tel (01227) 730255

BRETHERTON, Canon William Alan. b 22. St Cath Coll Cam BA43 MA47. Lon Coll of Div BD49 ALCD49. **d** 49 **p** 50. C Fazakerley Em *Liv* 49-52; V Everton St Chrys 52-65; V Ince Ch Ch 65-72; V Kirkdale St Mary 72-73; V Kirkdale St Mary and St Athanasius 73-87; RD Liv and Hon Can Liv Cathl 81-87; rtd 87; Perm to Offic *Liv* from 87. *3 Bradville Road, Liverpool L9 9BH* Tel 0151-525 0866

BRETT, Dennis Roy Anthony. b 46. Sarum & Wells Th Coll 86. **d** 88 **p** 89. C Bradford-on-Avon *Sarum* 88-92; P-in-c Bishopstrow and Boreham 92-01; R from 01; Chapl Warminster Hosp from 92. *The Rectory, 8 Rock Lane, Warminster BA12 9JZ* Tel (01985) 213000

BRETT, Canon Paul Gadsby. b 41. St Edm Hall Ox BA62 MA66. Wycliffe Hall Ox 64. **d** 65 **p** 66. C Bury St Pet *Man* 65-68; Asst Ind Chapl 68-72; Ind Chapl *Worc* 72-76; Sec Ind Cttee of Gen Syn Bd for Soc Resp 76-84; Dir Soc Resp *Chelmsf* 85-94; Can Res Chelmsf Cathl 85-94; R Shenfield from 94. *The Rectory, 41 Worrin Road, Shenfield, Brentwood CM15 8DH* Tel (01277) 220360 E-mail paul.brett@btinternet.com

BRETT, Canon Peter Graham Cecil. b 35. Em Coll Cam BA59 MA63. Cuddesdon Coll 59. **d** 61 **p** 62. C Tewkesbury w Walton Cardiff *Glouc* 61-64; C Bournemouth St Pet *Win* 64-66; Chapl Dur Univ *Dur* 66-72; R Houghton le Spring 72-83; RD Houghton 80-83; Can Res Cant Cathl *Cant* 83-01; rtd 01; Perm to Offic *Cant* from 01. *3 Appledore Road, Tenterden TN30 7AY* Tel (01580) 761794 E-mail pandgbrett@btinternet.com

BRETT YOUNG (née ROBIN), Ms Helen Mary Kathleen. b 67. St Martin's Coll Lanc BEd90. Cranmer Hall Dur BA98. **d** 98 **p** 99. C Gd Shep TM *Carl* 98-02; TV from 02. *The Rectory, Patterdale, Penrith CA11 0NL* Tel (01768) 482209
E-mail hmbrettyoung@hotmail.com

BREUILLY, Mrs Elizabeth Linda. b 48. York Univ BA70. WMMTC 02. **d** 05. NSM Bournville *Birm* from 05. *178 Bournville Lane, Birmingham B30 1LT* Tel 0121-458 2334
E-mail elizabeth.breuilly4@which.net

BREW, William Kevin Maddock. b 49. **d** 78 **p** 79. C Raheny w Coolock *D & G* 78-80; Bp's C Dublin Finglas 80-83; I Mountmellick w Coolbanagher, Rosenallis etc *M & K* 83-89; I Ahoghill w Portglenone *Conn* 89-05; I Howth *D & G* from 05. *The Rectory, Howth Road, Howth, Dublin 13, Irish Republic* Tel and fax (00353) (1) 832 3019
E-mail williamkevinbrew@aol.com

BREW, William Philip. b 43. Derby Coll of Educn CertEd64 Liv Univ Dip Special Educn 72 FCollP84. N Ord Course 84. **d** 87 **p** 88. In Independent Methodist Ch 70-83; Hd Master Birtenshaw Sch 78-90; NSM Holcombe *Man* 87-90; TV Horwich 91-93; TV Horwich and Rivington 93-97; V Lostock St Thos and St Jo from 97; P-in-c Bolton St Bede from 04; AD Deane 98-05. *Lostock Vicarage, 9 Lowside Avenue, Lostock, Bolton BL1 5XQ* Tel (01204) 848631
E-mail lostockvicar@ntlworld.com

BREWER, Barry James. b 44. Oak Hill Th Coll 72. **d** 75 **p** 76. C Hove Bp Hannington Memorial Ch *Chich* 75-78; C Church Stretton *Heref* 78-81; TV Bishopsnympton, Rose Ash, Mariansleigh etc *Ex* 81-87; R Swynnerton and Tittensor *Lich* from 87; RD Trentham from 01. *3 Rectory Gardens, Swynnerton, Stone ST15 0RT* Tel (01782) 796564
E-mail barrybrewer@btinternet.com

BREWER, Mrs Susan Comport. b 55. LMH Ox MA76. SEITE 99. **d** 02 **p** 03. C Dartford St Edm *Roch* from 02. *12 Keyes Road, Dartford DA1 5EQ* Tel (01322) 281838 Mobile 07930-492323
E-mail suec@brewer86.freeserve.co.uk

BREWERTON, Andrew Robert. b 70. Oak Hill Th Coll BA05. **d** 05. C Clacton St Jas *Chelmsf* from 05. *6 Peter Bruff Avenue, Clacton-on-Sea CO16 8UA* Tel (01255) 432600
E-mail andy@brewerton.org

BREWIN, David Frederick. b 39. Leic Poly BSc PhD. Lich Th Coll 63. **d** 66 **p** 67. C Shrewsbury H Cross *Lich* 66-69; C Birstall *Leic* 69-73; V Eyres Monsell 73-79; V E Goscote 79-82; V E Goscote w Ratcliffe and Rearsby 82-90; R Thurcaston 90-91; R Thurcaston w Cropston 92-05; rtd 05. *28 Welland Way, Oakham LE15 6SL* Tel (01572) 720073

BREWIN, Donald Stewart. b 41. Ch Coll Cam BA62 MA66. Ridley Hall Cam 68. **d** 71 **p** 72. C Ecclesall *Sheff* 71-75; V Anston 75-81; V Walton H Trin *Ox* 81-89; TR 89-94; RD Aylesbury 90-94; Nat Dir SOMA UK from 94; Perm to Offic *St Alb* from 94. *Wickham Cottage, Gaddesden Turn, Billington, Leighton Buzzard LU7 9BW* Tel (01525) 373644 *or* 237953 Fax 237954 E-mail donbrewin@compuserve.com *or* don.brewin@somauk.org

BREWIN, Canon Eric Walter. b 16. Hertf Coll Ox BA38 MA42. Ripon Hall Ox 38. **d** 40 **p** 41. C Leic St Marg *Leic* 40-42; Ind Sec SCM 42-46; C Ox St Mary V *Ox* 46-48; Sub-Chapl Nuff Coll Ox 46-48; V Coleford w Staunton *Glouc* 48-70; RD Forest S 57-70; Hon Can Glouc Cathl 65-81; R Leckhampton St Pet 70-81; rtd 81; Perm to Offic *Glouc* 82-97. *The Pleck, Llangrove, Ross-on-Wye HR9 6EU* Tel (01989) 770487

BREWIN, Karan Rosemary. b 42. Jordan Hill Coll Glas DCE68. CA Tr Coll 77 Glas NSM Course 80. **dss** 84 **d** 85. Clarkston *Glas* 84-89; Hon C 86-89 and 91-97; OHP 89 and 98-02; Perm to Offic *York* 01-02; S Africa from 02. *St Hilda's House, PO Box 1272, Manzini, Swaziland, South Africa* Tel (0026) (85) 053 323 E-mail jdean@africaonline.co.sz

BREWIN, Wilfred Michael. b 45. Nottm Univ BA69. Cuddesdon Coll 69. **d** 70 **p** 71. C Walker *Newc* 70-73; C Alnwick St Paul 73-74; C Alnwick w Edlingham and Bolton Chpl 74-77; Fell Sheff Univ 77-79; C Greenhill *Sheff* 79; P-in-c Eggleston *Dur* 79-81; V Norton St Mich 81-87; V Headington *Ox* from 87. *The Vicarage, 33 St Andrew's Road, Oxford OX3 9DL* Tel (01865) 761094 E-mail michaelbrewin@btinternet.com

BREWSTER, Miss Christine Elaine. b 45. Newc Univ BA67 CertEd68 ALCM76 LTCL78 Lon Univ DipEd82 MA84. St Alb and Ox Min Course 95. **d** 98 **p** 99. NSM Aylesbury w Bierton and Hulcott *Ox* 98-00; NSM Dacre w Hartwith and Darley w Thornthwaite *Ripon* 00-01; C Wetherby 01-04; Perm to Offic from 04. *3 Holly Villas, Dacre Banks, Harrogate HG3 4EG* Tel (01423) 780125

BREWSTER, David Pearson. b 30. Clare Coll Cam BA54 MA58 Lon Univ BA65 Oriel Coll Ox MA66 DPhil76. Ridley Hall Cam. **d** 58 **p** 59. C Southampton St Mary w H Trin *Win* 58-61; C N Audley Street St Mark *Lon* 61-62 and 63-65; Tunisia 62-63; Home Sec JEM 65-66; C Ox St Mary V w St Cross and St Pet *Ox* 66-68; Lect Lady Spencer-Churchill Coll Ox 68-71; New Zealand 71-78; V Brockenhurst *Win* 78-95; rtd 95; Perm to Offic *Win* from 95. *4 Saxonford Road, Christchurch BH23 4ES* Tel (01425) 277860

BREWSTER, David Thomas. b 68. GLCM90 ALCM89. Cranmer Hall Dur BA99. **d** 99 **p** 00. C Bidston *Ches* 99-03; TV Stockport SW from 03. *St Mark's Vicarage, 66 Berlin Road, Stockport SK3 9QF* Tel 0161-480 5896 E-mail david@chaoscity.idps.co.uk

BREWSTER, Jonathan David. b 67. Bucks Coll of Educn BA89 Bris Univ BA94 K Coll Lon MA01. Trin Coll Bris 91. **d** 94 **p** 95. C Gt Horton *Bradf* 94-98; Chapl Univ of Westmr *Lon* 98-03; V Highbury Ch Ch w St Jo and St Sav from 03. *Christ Church Vicarage, 155 Highbury Grove, London N5 1SA* Tel (020) 7226 4544 Mobile 07977-127244 E-mail vicar@dsl.pipex.com

BREWSTER (née BEATTIE), Margaret. b 43. S'wark Ord Course 90. **d** 93 **p** 94. NSM S'wark H Trin w St Matt *S'wark* 93-97; NSM Newington St Paul 97-04; NSM Dunstable *St Alb* from 04. *95 Evelyn Road, Dunstable LU5 4NQ* Tel (01582) 476334 E-mail brew95906@aol.com

BREWSTER, Mrs Susan Jacqueline. b 48. SEITE 94. **d** 97 **p** 98. NSM Goodmayes St Paul *Chelmsf* 97-01; TV Loughton St Jo from 01. *24 The Summit, Loughton IG10 1SW* Tel (020) 8508 6441 E-mail sue@brewster6441.fsnet.co.uk

BRIAN, Brother. *See* HARLEY, Brother Brian Mortimer

BRIAN, Stephen Frederick. b 54. Brighton Coll of Educn CertEd76 Sussex Univ BEd77 Birm Univ DipTh84 Open Univ MA90 Lanc Univ MPhil97 Surrey Univ PhD03. Qu Coll Birm 82. **d** 85 **p** 86. C Scotforth *Blackb* 85-88; V Freckleton 88-97; V Bagshot *Guildf* from 97. *The Vicarage, 43 Church Road, Bagshot GU19 5EQ* Tel (01276) 473348 E-mail sfb4510@aol.com

BRICE, Christopher John. b 48. St Edm Ho Cam MA80. Wycliffe Hall Ox 82. **d** 82 **p** 83. C N Hinksey *Ox* 82-86; Chapl Nuff Coll Ox 84-86; V S Hackney St Mich w Haggerston St Paul *Lon* 86-93; Dir Dioc Bd for Soc Resp 93-01; Adv for Soc Justice from 01; Hon C De Beauvoir Town St Pet from 93. *9 Beresford Road, London N5 2HS* Tel (020) 7226 3834 *or* 7932 1121 E-mail chris.brice@london.anglican.org

BRICE, Derek William Fred. b 39. Poly Cen Lon MA87 Kingston Poly DMS84 MCIM89 FCMI82. Dioc OLM tr scheme 99. **d** 02 **p** 03. OLM Cheam *S'wark* from 02. *Mallow, Parkside, Cheam, Sutton SM3 8BS* Tel (020) 8642 0241

BRICE, Jonathan Andrew William. b 61. **d** 92 **p** 93. C Buckhurst Hill *Chelmsf* 92-96; C Victoria Docks Ascension 96; P-in-c 96-98; V from 98. *The Vicarage, 10 Yarrow Crescent, London E6 5UH* Tel (020) 7476 6887

BRICE, Neil Alan. b 59. Man Univ BA81 Hughes Hall Cam CertEd87. Westcott Ho Cam 82. **d** 84 **p** 85. C Longton *Lich* 84-86; Hd of Relig Studies Coleridge Community Coll Cam 87-89; NSM Cherry Hinton St Andr *Ely* 88-89; C Fulbourn 89-92; C Gt Wilbraham 89-92; C Lt Wilbraham 89-92; V Arrington 92-00; R Orwell 92-00; R Wimpole 92-00; R Croydon w Clopton 92-00; P-in-c Barrington 98-00; R Orwell Gp from 00. *The Rectory, Fishers Lane, Orwell, Royston SG8 5QX* Tel (01223) 208653 Fax as telephone E-mail revnab@aol.com

BRICE, Paul Earl Philip. b 54. Bath Univ BSc77. Wycliffe Hall Ox 83. **d** 86 **p** 87. C Gt Baddow *Chelmsf* 86-89; Chapl Imp Coll *Lon* 89-95; St Mary's Hosp Med Sch 89-95; Chapl RCA 90-95; Sec HE/Chapl C of E Bd of Educn 95-02; Hon C S Kensington St Jude *Lon* 95-02; R Hartfield w Coleman's Hatch *Chich* from 02. *The Rectory, Church Street, Hartfield TN7 4AG* Tel (01892) 770850 E-mail anglican@pb.cix.co.uk

BRIDGE, The Very Revd Antony Cyprian. b 14. FSA. Linc Th Coll 53. **d** 55 **p** 56. C Hythe *Cant* 55-58; V Paddington Ch Ch *Lon* 58-68; Dean Guildf 68-86; rtd 86; Perm to Offic *Cant* 86-02. *34 London Road, Deal CT14 9TE* Tel (01304) 366792

BRIDGE, Miss Helen Cecily. b 25. SRN47 SCM49 Open Univ BA80 Ox Univ BTh98. Lambeth STh78 Dalton Ho Bris 70 Trin Coll Bris 70. **dss** 74 **d** 87 **p** 94. Tonbridge St Steph *Roch* 74-75; Countess of Ches Hosp 75-84; Plemstall w Guilden Sutton *Ches* 85-87; Hon Par Dn 87-88; NSM Stockport St Mary 88-98; Perm to Offic *Ches* and *Man* from 00. *25 Rectory Fields, Stockport SK1 4BX* Tel 0161-477 2154

BRIDGE, Martin. b 45. Lon Univ BA66 Linacre Coll Ox BA71 MA73. St Steph Ho Ox 69. **d** 72 **p** 73. C St Peter-in-Thanet *Cant* 72-77; New Zealand from 77. *PO Box 87-145, Meadowbank, Auckland, New Zealand* Tel (0064) (9) 521 5013 *or* 521 0636 Fax as telephone E-mail martin.bridge@xtra.co.nz

BRIDGEN, Andrew Grahame. b 57. Aston Univ BSc81 Surrey Univ BA03 FCCA95. STETS 00. **d** 03 **p** 04. NSM Portchester *Portsm* 03-04; C Portsea St Luke from 05. *9 Campbell Road, Southsea PO5 1RH* Tel (023) 9234 8617 Mobile 07753-281294 E-mail andrew.bridgen@ntlworld.com

BRIDGEN, John William. b 40. K Coll Cam BA62 MA66. Ripon Hall Ox 66. **d** 70 **p** 72. C Headstone St Geo *Lon* 70-71; C Hanwell St Mary 71-75; C Tolladine *Worc* 75; TV Worc St Barn w Ch Ch 76; R Barrow *St E* 76-83; V Denham St Mary 76-83; Perm to Offic *Ely* 84-88 and from 91; rtd 88; Perm to Offic *Glas* 89-91. *57 St Philip's Road, Cambridge CB1 3DA* Tel (01223) 571748

BRIDGEN, Mark Stephen. b 63. K Coll Lon BD85. Cranmer Hall Dur 86. **d** 88 **p** 89. C Kidderminster St Jo *Worc* 88-90; C Kidderminster St Jo and H Innocents 90-92; C Nor St Pet Mancroft w St Jo Maddermarket *Nor* 92-94; V Longbridge *Birm* 94-00; V Wednesbury St Bart *Lich* from 00. *The Vicarage, Little Hill, Wednesbury WS10 9DE* Tel 0121-556 9378

BRIDGER, Francis William. b 51. Pemb Coll Ox BA73 MA78 Bris Univ PhD80. Trin Coll Bris 74. **d** 78 **p** 79. C Islington St Jude Mildmay Park *Lon* 78-82; C Mildmay Grove St Jude and St Paul 82; Lect St Jo Coll Nottm 82-90; Dir of Courses 88-89; Dir of Studies 89-90; V Woodthorpe *S'well* 90-99; Prin Trin Coll Bris 99-05. *Address temp unknown*

BRIDGER, Canon Gordon Frederick. b 32. Selw Coll Cam BA53 MA58. Ridley Hall Cam 54. **d** 56 **p** 57. C Islington St Mary *Lon* 56-60; C Cambridge St Sepulchre *Ely* 60-62; V Fulham St Mary N End *Lon* 62-69; C Edin St Thos *Edin* 69-76; R Heigham H Trin *Nor* 76-87; RD Nor S 79-86; Hon Can Nor Cathl 84-87; Prin Oak Hill Th Coll 87-96; rtd 96; Perm to Offic *Nor* from 96. *The Elms, 4 Common Lane, Sheringham NR26 8PL* Tel (01263) 823522

✠**BRIDGES, The Rt Revd Dewi Morris.** b 33. Univ of Wales (Lamp) BA54 CCC Cam BA56 MA60. Westcott Ho Cam 57. **d** 57 **p** 58 **c** 88. C Rhymney *Mon* 57-60; C Chepstow 60-63; V Tredegar St Jas 63-65; Lect Kidderminster Coll 65-69; Lic to Offic *Worc* 65-69; V Kempsey 69-79; RD Upton 74-79; RD Narberth *St D* 80-82; R Tenby 79-88; Adn St D 82-88; Bp S & B 88-98; rtd 98. *Hafan Dawel, 4 St Mary's Hill, Heywood Lane, Tenby SA70 8BG* Tel (01834) 844087

BRIDGES, Mrs Gillian Mary. b 43. EAMTC 85. **d** 88 **p** 94. Hon C Hellesdon *Nor* 88-96; Hon C Lakenham St Jo 96-97; Assoc V Lakenham St Alb 97-99; Assoc V Sprowston w Beeston from 99. *2 Vera Road, Norwich NR6 5HU* Tel (01603) 789634

BRIDGES, John Malham. b 57. TD. Goldsmiths' Coll Lon BSc80. Ridley Hall Cam 03. **d** 05. C Cranleigh *Guildf* from 05. *22 Orchard Gardens, Cranleigh GU6 7LG* E-mail jmb2670@yahoo.co.uk

BRIDGES, The Ven Peter Sydney Godfrey. b 25. ARIBA51 Birm Univ DLA67. Linc Th Coll 56. **d** 58 **p** 59. C Hemel Hempstead *St Alb* 58-64; Warden Angl Chapl Birm Univ 64-68; Perm to Offic *Birm* 65-72; Lect Aston Univ 68-72; Adn Southend *Chelmsf* 72-77; P-in-c Southend St Jo w St Mark, All SS w St Fran etc 72-73; Dir Dioc Research and Development Unit 73-77; Adn Cov 77-83; Can Th Cov Cathl 77-90; Adn Warwick 83-90; rtd 90; Dioc Adv for Chr Spirituality 90-93; Perm to Offic *Win* from 01. *St Clare, 25 Rivermead Close, Romsey SO51 8HQ* Tel (01794) 512889

BRIDGES (née BANKS), Mrs Vivienne Philippa. b 46. Somerville Coll Ox BA69. St Alb and Ox Min Course 02. **d** 05.

NSM Wolvercote w Summertown *Ox* from 05. *6 Haslemere Gardens, Oxford OX2 8EL* Tel (01865) 558705

BRIDGEWATER, Canon Guy Stevenson. b 60. Ch Ch Ox BA83. Trin Coll Bris BA87. **d** 87 **p** 88. C Radipole and Melcombe Regis *Sarum* 87-90; Chapl Lee Abbey 90-93; V Cranbrook *Cant* 93-98; Dioc Officer for Par Resources (Miss and Lay Tr) *Glouc* from 98; Dioc Can Res Glouc Cathl from 02. *10 College Green, Gloucester GL1 2LX* Tel (01452) 410022 ext 248 Fax 308324 E-mail gbridgewater@glosdioc.org.uk

BRIDGEWOOD, Bruce William. b 41. K Coll Lon BA02. St Paul's Coll Grahamstown LTh67. **d** 67 **p** 68. C Plumstead S Africa 67-71; C Namaqualand 71-81; NSM Stanmer w Falmer *Chich* 81-86; Perm to Offic *Lon* 90-03; NSM Alexandra Park 03-04; P-in-c Friern Barnet St Pet le Poer from 04. *81 Warwick Road, London N11 2SP* Tel (020) 8368 6770 Fax 8211 9709 E-mail bridgewood@onetel.net

BRIDGMAN, Canon Gerald Bernard. b 22. St Cath Coll Cam BA50 MA55. Bible Churchmen's Coll Bris 46 Wycliffe Hall Ox 50. **d** 51 **p** 52. C Broadwater St Mary *Chich* 51-54; C Ox St Aldate *Ox* 54-56; C-in-c Southgate CD *Chich* 56-59; V Southgate 59-67; V Kingston upon Hull H Trin *York* 67-87; Chapl Hull R Infirmary 67-87; Area Dean Cen and N Hull 81-86; Can and Preb York Minster 83-87; rtd 87; Perm to Offic *Chich* from 87. *129 The Welkin, Lindfield, Haywards Heath RH16 2PL* Tel (01444) 484563

BRIDGWATER, Philip Dudley. b 31. St Alb Minl Tr Scheme 88. **d** 91 **p** 92. NSM Buxton w Burbage and King Sterndale *Derby* 91-94 and 98-01; NSM Fairfield 94-98; Perm to Offic from 01. *Millstone, 9 College Road, Buxton SK17 9DZ* Tel (01298) 72876

BRIDLE, Geoffrey Peter. b 52. CITC 87. **d** 87 **p** 88. C Lurgan Ch the Redeemer *D & D* 87-91; I Carnteel and Crilly *Arm* 91-99; I Cleenish w Mullaghdun *Clogh* from 99. *Cleenish Rectory, Bellanaleck, Enniskillen BT92 2BA* Tel (028) 6634 8259 Fax 6634 8620 E-mail geoffreypbridle@email.com

BRIDSON, Canon Raymond Stephen. b 58. Southn Univ BTh82. Chich Th Coll. **d** 82 **p** 83. C St Luke in the City *Liv* 82-86; TV Ditton St Mich 86-98; V Anfield St Columba from 98; AD Walton from 02; Hon Can Liv Cathl from 03. *St Columba's Vicarage, Pinehurst Avenue, Liverpool L4 2TZ* Tel 0151-474 7231 E-mail frray@blueyonder.co.uk

BRIDSTRUP, Juergen Walter. b 44. St Alb Minl Tr Scheme 84. **d** 87 **p** 88. C Leagrave *St Alb* 87-90; V Goff's Oak St Jas from 90. *St James's Vicarage, St James's Road, Goffs Oak, Waltham Cross EN7 6TP* Tel (01707) 872328 Fax as telephone E-mail juergen.bridstrup@ukgateway.net

BRIEN, John Richard. b 57. Kingston Poly BSc80. EAMTC 98. **d** 01 **p** 02. NSM Mistley w Manningtree and Bradfield *Chelmsf* from 01. *1 East View, Crown Street, Dedham, Colchester CO7 6AN* Tel (01206) 322706 E-mail briens@dedham.fsworld.co.uk

BRIERLEY, Charles Ian. b 46. MIMI69. S Dios Minl Tr Scheme 90. **d** 93 **p** 94. NSM Wellington and Distr *B & W* from 93. *46 Oakfield Park, Wellington TA21 8EY* Tel (01823) 666101 E-mail brierley@aol.com

BRIERLEY, Canon David James. b 53. Bris Univ BA75. Oak Hill Th Coll 75. **d** 77 **p** 78. C Balderstone *Man* 77-80; P-in-c Eccles St Andr 80-81; TV Eccles 81-85; Bp's Ecum Adv 81-88; V Harwood 85-95; V Walmsley 95-01; P-in-c Belmont 97-01; TV Turton Moorland Min 01-02; AD Walmsley 95-02; Dioc Adv in Evang *Bradf* from 02; Can Res Bradf Cathl 02-04; P-in-c Oxenhope from 04. *The Vicarage, Gledhow Drive, Oxenhope, Keighley BD22 9SA* Tel (01535) 642529 Mobile 07748-942183 E-mail david.brierley@bradford.anglican.ord

BRIERLEY, John Michael. b 32. Lon Univ BD71. Lich Th Coll 57. **d** 60 **p** 61. C Lower Mitton *Worc* 60-62; C-in-c Dines Green St Mich CD 62-68; V Worc St Mich 69-71; R Eastham w Rochford 71-79; P-in-c Knighton-on-Teme 76-79; P-in-c Reddal Hill St Luke 79-81; V 81-92; rtd 92; Perm to Offic *Worc* from 92. *10 Woodhouse Way, Cradley Heath, Warley B64 5EL* Tel (01384) 633527

BRIERLEY, Michael William. b 73. CCC Cam BA94 MA98. Ripon Coll Cuddesdon BA98. **d** 98 **p** 99. C Marnhull *Sarum* 98-01; C Okeford 98-01; Bp's Dom Chapl *Ox* from 01. *55 Marsh Lane, Marston, Oxford OX3 0NQ* Tel (01865) 767946 *or* 208221 E-mail michael.brierley@oxford.anglican.org

BRIERLEY, Philip. b 49. Salford Univ BSc74. **d** 92 **p** 93. OLM Stalybridge *Man* from 92. *Burnside, 30 Cranworth Street, Stalybridge SK15 2NW* Tel 0161-303 0809 E-mail irenephilipbrierley@yahoo.com

BRIERLEY, William David. b 64. Kent Univ BA87 New Coll Ox DPhil93. Ripon Coll Cuddesdon DipMin93. **d** 93 **p** 94. C Amersham *Ox* 93-97; TV Wheatley from 97. *The New Vicarage, Cox Lane, Stanton St John, Oxford OX33 1HW* Tel (01865) 351142 E-mail william.brierley@tesco.net

BRIGGS, Christopher Ronald. b 58. K Coll Lon BD79 AKC79 PGCE80. Sarum & Wells Th Coll 87. **d** 89 **p** 90. C Horsell *Guildf* 89-93; Hong Kong 93-97; V Norton *St Alb* 97-00; Sen Chapl Haileybury Coll from 00. *Lawrence Cottage, 2 Hailey Lane, Hertford Heath, Hertford SG13 7NX* Tel and fax (01992) 462922 *or* tel 706314 E-mail chrisbriggs@freenet.co.uk

BRIGGS, Derek. b 26. Lon Univ DipTh55. St Aid Birkenhead 52. **d** 55 **p** 56. C Brownhill *Wakef* 55-57; C Trowbridge St Jas *Sarum* 57-60; R Levenshulme St Pet *Man* 60-67; V Farsley *Bradf* 67-90; rtd 90; Perm to Offic *Bradf* 90-99. *6 College Court, Bradley, Keighley BD20 9EA* Tel (01535) 630085

BRIGGS, George William. b 76. Wadh Coll Ox BA98 Fitzw Coll Cam BA02. Ridley Hall Cam 00. **d** 03 **p** 04. C Old Trafford St Bride *Man* from 03. *38 Prestage Street, Old Trafford, Manchester M16 9JU* Tel 0161-226 4513

BRIGGS, Gordon John. b 39. CIPFA. St Alb and Ox Min Course 95. **d** 98 **p** 99. OLM Farnham Royal w Hedgerley *Ox* from 98. *52 Freemans Close, Stoke Poges, Slough SL2 4ER* Tel (01753) 662536

BRIGGS, Canon John. b 39. Edin Univ MA61. Ridley Hall Cam 61. **d** 63 **p** 64. C Jesmond Clayton Memorial *Newc* 63-66; Schs Sec Scripture Union 66-79; Tutor St Jo Coll Dur 67-74; Lic to Offic *Dur* 67-74; Lic to Offic *Edin* 74-79; V Chadkirk *Ches* 79-88; RD Chadkirk 85-88; TR Macclesfield Team Par 88-04; Hon Can Ches Cathl 96-04; Chapl W Park Hosp Macclesfield 90-99; rtd 04. *16 Lostock Hall Road, Poynton, Stockport SK12 1DP* Tel (01625) 267228 E-mail jbriggs@fish.co.uk

BRIGGS, Michael Weston. b 40. Edin Th Coll 61. **d** 64 **p** 65. C Sneinton St Steph w St Alb *S'well* 64-67; C Beeston 67-70; P-in-c Kirkby Woodhouse 70-74; V Harworth 74-81; R Harby w Thorney and N and S Clifton 81-94; R N Wheatley, W Burton, Bole, Saundby, Sturton etc from 94; P-in-c Clarborough w Hayton from 03; CF (ACF) 74-97; rtd 05. *3 Monkwood Close, Collingham, Newark NG23 7SY* Tel (01636) 893344 E-mail m_w_briggs@lineone.net

BRIGGS, The Very Revd Roger Edward. b 36. ALCD61. **d** 61 **p** 61. Canada 61-71; C Upper Armley *Ripon* 71-72; Canada 72-99; Dean Arctic 96-99; rtd 99. *Apartment 1207, 415 Greenview Avenue, Ottawa ON, Canada, K2B 8G5*

BRIGHAM, John Keith. b 48. FSAScot Man Univ CertEd70. St Steph Ho Ox 71. **d** 74 **p** 75. C Ches H Trin *Ches* 74-77; C Ealing Ch the Sav *Lon* 77-85; P-in-c Fulwell St Mich and St Geo 85-88; P-in-c Upper Teddington SS Pet and Paul 85-88; V Southport St Luke *Liv* 88-94; Dioc Chapl to the Deaf 88-94; V Lund *Blackb* 94-98. *17 South Meade, Timperley, Altrincham WA15 6QC* Tel 0161-976 2644

BRIGHOUSE, George Alexander (Alex). b 46. N Ord Course 87. **d** 90 **p** 91. NSM Ingrow cum Hainworth *Bradf* 90-91; NSM Keighley All SS 92; NSM Bradf St Wilfrid Lidget Green 92-04; NSM Bradf St Wilfrid w St Columba from 04. *38 Thirsk Grange, Clayton, Bradford BD14 6HS* Tel 07768-618562 (mobile)

BRIGHT, George Frank. b 50. Peterho Cam BA71 MA75 Leeds Univ DipTh73 LSE MSc83 SAP99. Coll of Resurr Mirfield 71. **d** 74 **p** 75. C Notting Hill *Lon* 74-77; Perm to Offic 77-84; P-in-c Kentish Town St Benet and All SS 84-89; P-in-c Kensington St Jo 89-93; V from 93. *The Vicarage, 176 Holland Road, London W14 8AH* Tel (020) 7602 4655 E-mail gfb@dircon.co.uk

BRIGHT, Reginald. b 26. Tyndale Hall Bris 57. **d** 60 **p** 61. C Toxteth Park St Philemon w St Silas *Liv* 60-63; P-in-c Everton St Polycarp 63-65; R Orton St Giles *Carl* 65-72; V Holme 72-79; P-in-c W Newton 79-81; V Bromfield w Waverton 79-81; R Bowness 81-93; rtd 93; Perm to Offic *Carl* from 93. *Spinney House, Cannonfield, Roadhead, Carlisle CA6 6NB* Tel (01697) 748645

BRIGHTMAN, Peter Arthur. b 30. Lon Coll of Div ALCD61 LTh74. **d** 64 **p** 65. C Westgate St Jas *Cant* 64-67; C Lydd 67-70; C Lt Coates *Linc* 70; C Heaton Ch Ch *Man* 71-72; V Bolton SS Simon and Jude 72-77; R Bath St Sav *B & W* 77-85; R Farmborough, Marksbury and Stanton Prior 85-90; C Coney Hill *Glouc* 90-93; C Hardwicke, Quedgeley and Elmore w Longney 93-95; rtd 95; Perm to Offic *B & W* from 95. *2 Westmead Cottages, Dean Hill Lane, Weston, Bath BA1 4DT* Tel (01225) 315076

BRIGHTON, Terrence William. b 43. SW Minl Tr Course 85. **d** 88 **p** 89. C Dawlish *Ex* 88-92; P-in-c Newton Poppleford w Harpford 92-94; V Newton Poppleford, Harpford and Colaton Raleigh 94-98; RD Ottery 96-98; P-in-c W Lavington and the Cheverells *Sarum* 98-02; Rural Officer (Ramsbury Area) 98-02; P-in-c Charleton w Buckland Tout Saints etc *Ex* 02-05; R from 05; RD Woodleigh from 03. *The Rectory, West Charleton, Kingsbridge TQ7 2AJ* Tel (01548) 531211 E-mail twb@surfaid.org

BRIGHTWELL, Ms Johanna Clare. b 64. Bris Univ BSc86 Heythrop Coll Lon MA98. Ridley Hall Cam CTM99. **d** 99 **p** 00. C Coulsdon St Jo *S'wark* 99-02; TV Morden from 02. *5 Willows Avenue, Morden SM4 5SG* Tel (020) 8646 2002 E-mail jcbrightwell@yahoo.com

BRIGNALL, Simon Francis Lyon. b 54. St Jo Coll Dur BA78. Wycliffe Hall Ox 80. **d** 83 **p** 84. C Colne St Bart *Blackb* 83-86; SAMS 86-96; Peru 86-96; P-in-c Tetsworth, Adwell w S Weston, Lewknor etc *Ox* 96-98; TV Thame from 98. *The Rectory, 46 High Street, Tetsworth, Thame OX9 7AS* Tel (01844) 281267 Mobile 07718-627674 E-mail brignall@fish.co.uk

BRIGNELL, Roger. b 39. CertEd65 ACP88 MCollP89. St Aid Birkenhead 60 St As Minl Tr Course 95. **d** 98 **p** 99. NSM Montgomery and Forden and Llandyssil *St As* from 98. *Minevia, Kerry Road, Montgomery SY15 6PD* Tel (01686) 668539 Fax as telephone

BRIMACOMBE, Keith John. b 59. Open Univ BA92 Westmr Coll Ox MTh00. SW Minl Tr Course 99. **d** 01 **p** 03. NSM Ottery St Mary, Alfington, W Hill, Tipton etc *Ex* from 01. *Banklea, Exeter Road, Newton Poppleford, Sidmouth EX10 0BJ* Tel (01395) 568404 E-mail brims@kjbrims.fsnet.co.uk

BRIMICOMBE, Mark. b 44. Nottm Univ BA66 CertEd. SW Minl Tr Course 83. **d** 85 **p** 86. NSM Plympton St Mary *Ex* from 85. *4 David Close, Stoggy Lane, Plympton, Plymouth PL7 3BQ* Tel (01752) 338454 E-mail mtbrimico@devon.gov.uk

BRIMSON, Mrs Dawn Diana. b 44. SW Minl Tr Course 02. **d** 05. NSM Quantoxhead *B & W* from 05. *Ridges, Holford, Bridgwater TA5 1DU* Tel (01278) 741413

BRINDLE, John Harold. b 21. St Jo Coll Dur LTh42 BA43 MA46. St Aid Birkenhead 39. **d** 44 **p** 44. C Ashton-on-Ribble St Mich *Blackb* 44-47; C Sandylands 47-51; V Grimsargh 51-88; rtd 88; Perm to Offic *Blackb* 88-02. *8 Sussex Drive, Garstang, Preston PR3 1ET* Tel (01995) 606588

BRINDLE, Peter John. b 47. MIStructE72. N Ord Course 78. **d** 81 **p** 82. NSM Bingley All SS *Bradf* 81-84; NSM Bingley H Trin 84-86; V Keighley All SS 86-91; V Kirkstall *Ripon* 91-96; V Beeston 96-02; TR 02-04; TR Leic Presentation *Leic* from 04; P-in-c Leic St Chad from 04. *St Barnabas' Vicarage, 32 St Barnabas Road, Leicester LE5 6BD* Tel 0116-276 6054 Mobile 07860-157363 E-mail vicbeest@aol.com

BRINDLEY, Angela Mary. *See* SPEEDY, Mrs Angela Mary

BRINDLEY, The Very Revd David Charles. b 53. K Coll Lon BD75 AKC75 MTh76 MPhil81. St Aug Coll Cant 75. **d** 76 **p** 77. C Epping St Jo *Chelmsf* 76-79; Lect Coll of SS Paul and Mary Cheltenham 79-82; Dioc Dir of Tr *Leic* 82-86; V Quorndon 82-86; Prin Glouc Sch for Min *Glouc* 87-92; Prin WEMTC 92-94; Dir of Minl Tr 87-94; Dioc Officer for NSM 88-94; Hon Can Glouc Cathl 92-94; TR Warwick *Cov* 94-02; Dean Portsm from 02. *The Deanery, 13 Pembroke Road, Portsmouth PO1 2NS* Tel (023) 9282 4400 *or* 9234 7605 Fax 9229 5480 E-mail dean@portsmouthcathedral.org.uk

BRINDLEY, Canon Stuart Geoffrey Noel. b 30. St Jo Coll Dur BA53 DipTh55. **d** 55 **p** 56. C Newc St Anne *Newc* 55-58; C Tynemouth Cullercoats St Paul 58-60; C Killingworth 60-63; V Newsham 63-69; W Germany 69-76; Asst Master Wyvern Sch Weston-super-Mare 76-80; V Stocksbridge *Sheff* 80-88; RD Tankersley 85-88; V Rotherham 88-96; Hon Can Sheff Cathl 95-96; rtd 96; Perm to Offic *Newc* from 96. *Hambury, Backcrofts, Rothbury, Morpeth NE65 7XY* Tel (01669) 621472

BRINKWORTH, Canon Christopher Michael Gibbs. b 41. Lanc Univ BA70. Kelham Th Coll 62 SSC. **d** 67 **p** 68. C Lancaster St Mary *Blackb* 67-70; C Milton *Portsm* 70-74; V Ault Hucknall *Derby* 74-84; V Derby St Anne and St Jo from 84; Hon Can Derby Cathl from 00. *The Vicarage, 25 Highfield Road, Derby DE22 1GX* Tel (01332) 332681 E-mail cbrink@ntlworld.com

BRION, Martin Philip. b 33. Ex Univ BA55. Ridley Hall Cam 57. **d** 59 **p** 60. C Balderstone *Man* 59-62; C Morden *S'wark* 62-66; V Low Elswick *Newc* 66-73; P-in-c Giggleswick *Bradf* 73-77; V 77-80; V Camerton H Trin W Seaton *Carl* 80-86; V Dearham 86-95; rtd 95; Perm to Offic *Carl* from 95. *7 Falcon Place, Moresby Parks, Whitehaven CA28 8YF* Tel (01946) 691912

BRISCOE, Allen. b 42. Liv Univ BSc64 CertEd65. Coll of Resurr Mirfield 90. **d** 92 **p** 93. C Shiremoor *Newc* 92-95; V Barnsley St Pet and St Jo *Wakef* from 95; Asst Dioc Ecum Officer 01-03; Bp's Adv for Ecum Affairs from 03; RD Barnsley from 04. *The Vicarage, 1 Osborne Mews, Barnsley S70 1UU* Tel (01226) 282220

BRISCOE, Canon Frances Amelia. b 35. Univ of Wales CertEd55 Man Univ BA71 MA74. Gilmore Course 74. **dss** 77 **d** 87 **p** 94. Gt Crosby St Luke *Liv* 77-81; Dioc Lay Min Adv 81-87; Chapl Liv Cathl 81-89; Dir Diaconal Mins 87-89; Lect St Deiniol's Minl Tr Scheme 88-00; Hon Can Liv Cathl *Liv* 88-00; AD Sefton 89-00; Dir of Reader Studies 89-00; Dn-in-c Hightown 92-94; P-in-c 94-00; rtd 00; Perm to Offic *Liv* from 01. *5 Derwent Avenue, Formby, Liverpool L37 2JT* Tel (01925) 221049

BRISCOE, Gordon Michael. b 24. Leeds Univ CertEd50. Ely Th Coll 51. **d** 53 **p** 54. C Isleworth St Fran *Lon* 53-54; Hon C 66-67; C Ealing Ch the Sav 54-57; W Germany 57-62; C Twickenham St Mary *Lon* 62-65; Chapl Fortescue Ho Sch Twickenham 62-65; Hon C Brookfield St Anne, Highgate Rise *Lon* 67-77; Hon C Paddington St Steph w St Luke 77-80; Hon C St Marylebone Annunciation Bryanston Street 80-83; Chapl Bedford Modern Sch 83-84; Hon Chapl 84-94; R Dunton w Wrestlingworth and Eyeworth *St Alb* 84-94; rtd 94. *59 Furland Road, Crewkerne TA18 8DD* Tel (01460) 78812 E-mail briskel@btinternet.com

BRISON, The Ven William Stanly. b 29. Alfred Univ NY BSc51 Connecticut Univ MDiv57 STM71. Berkeley Div Sch. **d** 57 **p** 57. USA 57-72; V Davyhulme Ch Ch *Man* 72-81; R Newton Heath All SS 81-85; AD N Man 81-85; Hon Can Man Cathl 82-85; Adn Bolton 85-92; TV E Farnworth and Kearsley 85-89; C Bolton St Thos 89-92; CMS 92-94; Nigeria 92-94; P-in-c Pendleton St Thos w Charlestown *Man* 94-95; TR Pendleton 95-98; rtd 98; Perm to Offic *Man* from 99. *2 Scott Avenue, Bury BL9 9RS* Tel 0161-764 3998

BRISTOL, Archdeacon of. *See* McCLURE, The Ven Timothy Elston

BRISTOL, Bishop of. *See* HILL, The Rt Revd Michael Arthur

BRISTOL, Dean of. *See* GRIMLEY, The Very Revd Robert William

BRISTOW, Arthur George Raymond. b 09. Lich Th Coll 32. **d** 35 **p** 36. C Longton St Mary and St Chad *Lich* 35-38; Perm to Offic *Roch* 38; Perm to Offic *Ox* 38-39 and 41; Perm to Offic *Lich* 39-40; C Sheff St Matt *Sheff* 41-43; V Saltley *Birm* 43-52; R Wednesbury St Jo *Lich* 52-57; V Willenhall St Steph 57-75; rtd 75; Perm to Offic *Lich* from 85; Hon C Emscote *Cov* 75-03. *41 Badgers Way, Heath Hayes, Cannock WS12 3XQ* Tel (01543) 275530

BRISTOW, Keith Raymond Martin. b 56. Ex Univ BA78. Chich Th Coll 87. **d** 89 **p** 90. C Kirkby *Liv* 89-93; C Portsea St Mary *Portsm* 93-03; R Ash *Guildf* from 03. *The Rectory, Ash Church Road, Ash, Aldershot GU12 6LU* Tel (01252) 321517 E-mail frkeithbristow@aol.com

BRISTOW, Peter Edmund. b 49. Pontificium Institutum Internationale Angelicum Rome JCL77 St Jos Coll Upholland 67. **d** 72 **p** 73. In RC Ch 72-87; C Poplar *Lon* 89-92; Lay Tr Officer 89-90; TV Droitwich Spa *Worc* 92-94; TR 94-00; V Boston Spa *York* from 00; P-in-c Thorp Arch w Walton from 00. *The Vicarage, 86 High Street, Boston Spa, Wetherby LS23 6EA* Tel (01937) 842454

BRISTOW, Roger. b 60. Aston Tr Scheme 81 Ridley Hall Cam 83. **d** 86 **p** 87. C Leyton St Mary w St Edw *Chelmsf* 86-90; TV Kings Norton *Birm* 90-98; V Bromley H Trin *Roch* from 98. *Holy Trinity Vicarage, Church Lane, Bromley BR2 8LB* Tel (020) 8462 1280 Mobile 07778-397224 E-mail rb3in1@lineone.co.uk *or* htc-bc@tiscali.co.uk

BRITT, Eric Stanley. b 47. St Jo Coll Nottm LTh74 BTh75. **d** 74 **p** 75. C Chorleywood Ch Ch *St Alb* 74-78; C Frimley *Guildf* 78-80; P-in-c Alresford *Chelmsf* 80-88; R Takeley w Lt Canfield 88-93; Asst Chapl R Free Hosp Lon 93-96; Chapl Mid-Essex Hosp Services NHS Trust 96-00; Chapl Algarve *Eur* from 01. *Apartado 135, Casa Sao Vicente, Boliqueime, 8100 Loule, Portugal* Tel (00351) (289) 366720 Fax 362231 E-mail britt.st.vincents@ip.pt

BRITTAIN, John. b 23. St Aug Coll Cant 59. **d** 60 **p** 61. C Heref St Martin *Heref* 60-62; V Highley 62-88; rtd 88. *26 Stuart Court, High Street, Kibworth, Leicester LE8 0LR*

BRITTLE, Miss Janice Lilian. b 50. Man Poly BA74 Open Univ BA84 Sheff Univ MMedSc00 RGN76. **d** 04 **p** 05. OLM Rugeley *Lich* from 04. *3 Norwood House, Peakes Road, Rugeley WS15 2ND* Tel (01889) 586138

BRITTON, Christine Mary. *See* BEECROFT, Mrs Christine Mary

BRITTON, John Anthony. b 39. Dur Univ BA60. Wycliffe Hall Ox 61. **d** 63 **p** 64. C Sheff St Swithun *Sheff* 63-64; C Sheff St Aid w St Luke 64-66; C Doncaster St Geo 66-68; C Grantham St Wulfram *Linc* 68-72; V Surfleet 72-76; V Bolsover *Derby* 76-86; V Harworth *S'well* 86-01; RD Bawtry 96-01; rtd 01; Perm to Offic *S'well* from 01 and *Sheff* from 02. *Beaver Lodge, 10 Weirside, Oldcotes, Worksop S81 8HW* Tel (01909) 540735 E-mail john.dorothy.britton@dunelm.org.uk

BRITTON, John Timothy Hugh. b 50. Dundee Univ BSc73. Trin Coll Bris 73. **d** 76 **p** 77. C Cromer *Nor* 76-79; P-in-c Freethorpe w Wickhampton 79-82; P-in-c Beighton and Moulton 79-82; P-in-c Halvergate w Tunstall 79-82; CMS 82-89; Uganda 83-89; R Allesley *Cov* 89-02; P-in-c Long Itchington and Marton from 02; P-in-c Wappenbury w Weston under Wetherley from 02; P-in-c Hunningham from 02; P-in-c Offchurch from 02. *The Vicarage, Leamington Road, Long Itchington, Southam CV47 9PL* Tel (01926) 812518 E-mail timbritton@myrealbox.com

BRITTON, Neil Bryan. b 35. Em Coll Cam BA59 MA63. Clifton Th Coll 61. **d** 63 **p** 64. C Eastbourne All SS *Chich* 63-67; C Ashtead *Guildf* 67-70; Chapl Scargill Ho 70-74; Asst Chapl Villars *Eur* 74-81; rtd 00. *Mercy Ships CDTS, PO Box 2020, Lindale, TX 75771, USA* Tel (001) (903) 882 0887

BRITTON, Canon Paul Anthony. b 29. SS Coll Cam BA52 MA57. Linc Th Coll 52. **d** 54 **p** 55. C Upper Norwood St Jo *Cant* 54-57; C Wantage *Ox* 57-61; V Stanmore *Win* 61-70; V Bitterne Park 70-80; Can Res Win Cathl 80-94; Lib 81-85; Treas 85-94; rtd 94; Perm to Offic *Sarum* from 94. *Pemberton, High Street, Hindon, Salisbury SP3 6DR* Tel (01747) 820406

BRITTON, Robert. b 37. Oak Hill Th Coll 78. **d** 79 **p** 80. C St Helens St Helen *Liv* 79-83; V Lowton St Mary 83-02; AD Winwick 89-01; rtd 02; Perm to Offic *Liv* and *Man* from 03. *15 Balmoral Avenue, Lowton, Warrington WA3 2ER* Tel (01942) 711135

BRITTON, Ronald George Adrian Michael (Robert). b 24. Univ of State of NY BSc78 Lambeth STh82. St D Coll Lamp 63. **d** 82 **p** 82. Arabia 82-85; Chapl Alassio *Eur* 85-90 and 92-93; Chapl San Remo 86; Hon C Southbourne St Kath *Win* 90-92; rtd 96;

Perm to Offic *Bris* from 97. *2 Cherry Tree Road, Bristol BS16 4EY* Tel 0117-965 5734
E-mail robert@britton320.fsnet.co.uk

BRITTON, Timothy. *See* BRITTON, John Timothy Hugh

BRIXTON, Miss Corinne Jayne. b 63. Ex Univ BSc84. Wycliffe Hall Ox BTh95. **d** 95. C Leytonstone St Jo *Chelmsf* 95-00; C Buckhurst Hill from 00. *63 High Road, Buckhurst Hill IG9 5SR* Tel (020) 8504 6652 E-mail cbrixton@aol.com

BRIXWORTH, Suffragan Bishop of. *See* WHITE, The Rt Revd Francis

BROAD, David Nicholas Andrew. b 59. Man Univ BA. Edin Th Coll. **d** 87 **p** 88. C Fulham All SS *Lon* 87-90; TV Clare w Poslingford, Cavendish etc *St E* 90-93; TV Totton *Win* 93-99; R Abbotts Ann and Upper and Goodworth Clatford from 99. *The Rectory, Upper Clatford, Andover SP11 7QP* Tel and fax (01264) 352906 E-mail dna.broad@virgin.net

BROAD, Canon Hugh Duncan. b 37. Lich Th Coll 64. **d** 67 **p** 68. C Heref H Trin *Heref* 67-72; Asst Master Bp's Sch Heref 72-73; C Fareham SS Pet and Paul *Portsm* 74-76; V Heref All SS *Heref* 76-90; R Matson *Glouc* 90-97; V Glouc St Geo w Whaddon 97-03; Hon Can Glouc Cathl 02-03; rtd 03; P-in-c Mojacar *Eur* from 03. *Apartado 617, Mojacar Playa, 04638 Almeria, Spain* Tel (0034) 950 478432 Mobile 617 779327
E-mail hughbroad996@hotmail.com

BROAD, Hugh Robert. b 49. St Mich Coll Llan 67. **d** 72 **p** 73. C Tenby w Gumfreston *St D* 72-75; C Caerau w Ely *Llan* 75-79; V Llanharan w Peterston-super-Montem 79-89; RD Bridgend 88-89; Ex-Paroch Officer 90; V Whatborough Gp *Leic* from 90. *The Vicarage, Oakham Road, Tilton on the Hill, Leicester LE7 9LB* Tel 0116-259 7244 E-mail hugh_broad@hotmail.com

BROAD, Canon William Ernest Lionel. b 40. Ridley Hall Cam 64. **d** 66 **p** 67. C Ecclesfield *Sheff* 66-69; Chapl HM Pris Wormwood Scrubs 69; Chapl HM Pris Albany 70-74; Chapl HM Rem Cen Risley 74-76; V Ditton St Mich *Liv* 76-81; TR 82-83; P-in-c Mayland and Steeple *Chelmsf* 83-91; V Blackhall *Dur* 91-97; TR Gt Aycliffe 97-03; P-in-c Chilton 03; TV Gt Aycliffe and Chilton 03-04; Hon Can Dur Cathl 02-04; rtd 04. *Moorcote, Thornley, Tow Law, Bishop Auckland DL13 4NU* Tel (01388) 731350
E-mail bill@deagol.fsnet.co.uk

BROADBENT, Mrs Doreen. b 36. Local Minl Tr Course 91. **d** 94 **p** 95. OLM Stalybridge *Man* 94-02; Perm to Offic from 02. *37 Ladysmith Road, Ashton-under-Lyne OL6 9DJ* Tel 0161-330 9085

BROADBENT, Hugh Patrick Colin. b 53. Selw Coll Cam BA75 MA. Wycliffe Hall Ox DipTh78. **d** 78 **p** 79. C Chatham St Steph *Roch* 78-82; C Shortlands 82-84; C Edenbridge 84-87; C Crockham Hill H Trin 84-87; V Bromley H Trin 87-97; Chapl St Olave's Gr Sch Orpington from 95; V Bromley St Jo *Roch* from 97. *St John's Vicarage, 9 Orchard Road, Bromley BR1 2PR* Tel (020) 8460 1844 E-mail hughbroadbent@hotmail.com

BROADBENT, Neil Seton. b 53. Qu Coll Birm DipTh80. **d** 81 **p** 82. C Knaresborough *Ripon* 81-84; C Leeds Gipton Epiphany 84-87; Lic to Offic 87-89; Chapl Minstead Community *Derby* 89; Perm to Offic from 89; Dir Sozein from 93. *The Old Vicarage, Church Lane, Horsley Woodhouse, Ilkeston DE7 6BB* Tel (01332) 780598

BROADBENT, Paul John. b 41. SSC02. Oak Hill Th Coll 83. **d** 85 **p** 86. C Duston *Pet* 85-88; TV Ross w Brampton Abbotts, Bridstow and Peterstow *Heref* 88-91; R Pattishall w Cold Higham and Gayton w Tiffield *Pet* from 91. *The Rectory, Church Street, Pattishall, Towcester NN12 8NB* Tel and fax (01327) 830043 Mobile 07786-865015 E-mail pjbroadbent@aol.com

✠**BROADBENT, The Rt Revd Peter Alan.** b 52. Jes Coll Cam BA74 MA78. St Jo Coll Nottm DipTh75. **d** 77 **p** 78 **c** 01. C Dur St Nic *Dur* 77-80; C Holloway Em w Hornsey Road St Barn *Lon* 80-83; Chapl N Lon Poly 83-89; Hon C Islington St Mary 83-89; V Harrow Trin St Mich 89-94; AD Harrow 94; Adn Northolt 95-01; P-in-c Southall H Trin 98-99; Area Bp Willesden from 01. *173 Willesden Lane, London NW6 7YN* Tel (020) 8451 0189 Fax 8451 4606 Mobile 07957-144674
E-mail bishop.willesden@btinternet.com

BROADBENT, Ralph Andrew. b 55. K Coll Lon BD76 AKC76 Birm Univ PhD04. Chich Th Coll 77. **d** 78 **p** 79. C Prestwich St Mary *Man* 78-82; R Man Miles Platting 82-84; CF 84-87; TV Wordsley *Lich* 88-93; Chapl Wordsley and Ridge Hill Hosps 88-93; V Wollescote *Worc* from 93. *St Andrew's Vicarage, Oakfield Road, Wollescote, Stourbridge DY9 9DG* Tel (01384) 422695

BROADBENT, Thomas William. b 45. Chu Coll Cam BA66 MA70 PhD70. Ridley Hall Cam 75. **d** 78 **p** 79. C Allington and Maidstone St Pet *Cant* 78-82; Chapl Mid Kent Coll of H&FE 80-82; C Kings Heath *Birm* 82-84; Hon C Pendleton St Thos *Man* 84-89; TV Pendleton St Thos w Charlestown 89-92; Chapl Salford Univ 84-92; Chmn Man Coun of Chr and Jews 89-92; P-in-c Claydon and Barham *St E* from 92; P-in-c Henley from 99; P-in-c Gt Blakenham from 02; Chapl Suffolk Coll 92-00. *The Rectory, 7 Back Lane, Claydon, Ipswich IP6 0EB* Tel (01473) 830362

BROADBERRY, Canon Richard St Lawrence. b 31. TCD BA53 BD59 MLitt66. **d** 54 **p** 55. C Dublin St Thos *D & G* 54-56; C Dublin Grangegorman 56-62; Min Can St Patr Cathl Dublin 58-62; Hon Clerical V Ch Ch Cathl Dublin *D & G* 62-64; C Dublin Clontarf 62-64; C Thornton Heath St Jude *Cant* 64-66; V Norwood All SS 66-82; V Upper Norwood All SS w St Marg 82-84; RD Croydon N 81-84; Hon Can Cant Cathl 82-84; V Merton St Mary *S'wark* 85-92; RD Croydon N 85; Hon Can S'wark Cathl 85-01; V Riddlesdown 92-01; rtd 01; Perm to Offic *S'wark* from 01. *73 Court Avenue, Coulsden CR5 1HG* Tel (01737) 551109

BROADHEAD, Alan John. b 38. Lon Univ MD62. Cuddesdon Coll 65. **d** 66 **p** 67. C Willenhall H Trin *Lich* 66-68; USA from 71; rtd 03. *517 3rd Avenue Southeast, Jamestown, ND 58401, USA* Tel (001) (701) 225 5026 E-mail broadheadp@aol.com

✠**BROADHURST, The Rt Revd John Charles.** b 42. AKC65. Lambeth STh82. **d** 66 **p** 67 **c** 96. C Southgate St Mich *Lon* 66-70; C Wembley Park St Aug 70-73; P-in-c 73-75; V 75-85; AD Brent 82-85; TR Wood Green St Mich w Bounds Green St Gabr etc 85-96; AD E Haringey 85-91; Suff Bp Fulham from 96. *26 Canonbury Park South, London N1 2FN* Tel (020) 7354 2334 Fax 7354 2335 E-mail bpfulham@aol.com

BROADHURST, Jonathan Robin. b 58. Univ Coll Ox BA81 MA86. Wycliffe Hall Ox 85. **d** 88 **p** 89. C Hull St Jo Newland *York* 88-91; P-in-c Burton Fleming w Fordon, Grindale etc 91-92; V 92-98; C Kingston upon Hull H Trin 98-01; P-in-c Rastrick St Jo *Wakef* from 01. *St John's Vicarage, 2 St John Street, Brighouse HD6 1HN* Tel (01484) 715889 Mobile 07790-899195 E-mail jonathan@broadhurst-jr.freeserve.co.uk

BROADLEY, Michael John. b 66. Roehampton Inst BA87. Trin Coll Bris 93. **d** 96 **p** 97. C Egham *Guildf* 96-01; TV Horsham *Chich* from 01. *St Mark's House, North Heath Lane, Horsham RH12 5PJ* Tel (01403) 254964 E-mail broadley@bigfoot.com

BROCK, Michael John. b 52. Birm Univ BSc74 Nottm Univ BA77. St Jo Coll Nottm 75. **d** 78 **p** 79. C Stapleford *S'well* 78-82; C Bestwood St Matt 82-86; TV Bestwood 86-90; R Epperstone from 90; R Gonalston from 90; V Oxton from 90; RD S'well 93-96; Dioc Adv in Rural Affairs 97-02; P-in-c Woodborough from 02. *The Rectory, Main Street, Epperstone, Nottingham NG14 6AG* Tel 0115-966 4220
E-mail mjbrock65@btinternet.com

BROCK, Preb Patrick Laurence. b 18. MBE45. Trin Coll Ox BA46 MA48. Ripon Hall Ox 55. **d** 57 **p** 58. C Gt Malvern St Mary *Worc* 57-59; C St Martin-in-the-Fields *Lon* 59-62; V Belsize Park 62-72; R Finchley St Mary 72-89; Preb St Paul's Cathl 80-89; AD Cen Barnet 80-85; rtd 89; Perm to Offic *Lon* from 89 and *Sarum* from 91. *10 Albert Street, London NW1 7NZ* Tel (020) 7383 0198

BROCKBANK, Arthur Ross. b 51. N Ord Course 87. **d** 90 **p** 91. C Haughton St Mary *Man* 90-93; V Bircle from 93; P-in-c Walmersley 04; Chapl Bury Healthcare NHS Trust 93-02; Chapl Co-ord 02-03. *The Vicarage, 33 Castle Hill Road, Bury BL9 7RW* Tel 0161-764 3853

BROCKBANK, Donald Philip. b 56. Univ of Wales (Ban) BD78. Sarum & Wells Th Coll 79. **d** 81 **p** 82. C Prenton *Ches* 81-85; TV Birkenhead Priory 85-91; V Altrincham St Jo 91-96; Urban Officer 91-96; Dioc Ecum Officer *Lich* 96-98; C Lich St Mich w St Mary and Wall 96-98; V Acton and Worleston, Church Minshull etc *Ches* from 98. *St Mary's Vicarage, Chester Road, Acton, Nantwich CW5 8LG* Tel (01270) 628864
E-mail donald@brockbankrev.freeserve.co.uk

BROCKBANK, John Keith. b 44. Dur Univ BA65. Wells Th Coll 66. **d** 68 **p** 69. C Preston St Matt *Blackb* 68-71; C Lancaster St Mary 71-73; V Habergham All SS 73-83; P-in-c Gannow 81-83; V W Burnley All SS 83-86; Dioc Stewardship Adv 86-92; P-in-c Shireshead 86-92; V Kirkham from 92. *The Vicarage, Church Street, Kirkham, Preston PR4 2SE* Tel and fax (01772) 683644 E-mail revjkb@kirkvicarage.freeserve.co.uk

BROCKBANK, John Stanley. b 41. Carl and Blackb Dioc Tr Inst 97. **d** 00 **p** 01. OLM Arnside *Carl* from 00. *Hough Close, 5 Ash Meadow Road, Arnside, Carnforth LA5 0AE* Tel (01524) 761634

BROCKHOUSE, Grant Lindley. b 47. Adelaide Univ BA71 Ex Univ MA81. St Barn Coll Adelaide 70 ACT ThL72. **d** 73 **p** 74. Australia 73-78; C Ex St Jas *Ex* 78-80; Asst Chapl Ex Univ 80-83; Dep PV Ex Cathl 81-98; V Marldon 83-98; RD Torbay 95-98; V Higham Ferrers w Chelveston *Pet* from 98; RD Higham from 03. *The Vicarage, Wood Street, Higham Ferrers, Rushden NN10 8DL* Tel (01933) 312433
E-mail grantbrockhouse@care4free.net

BROCKIE, Canon William James Thomson. b 36. Pemb Coll Ox BA58 MA62. Linc Th Coll 58. **d** 60 **p** 61. C Lin St Jo Bapt CD *Linc* 60-63; V Gt Staughton *Ely* 63-68; Chapl HM Borstal Gaynes Hall 63-68; TV Edin St Jo *Edin* 68-76; Chapl Edin Univ 71-76; USA 76; R Edin St Martin *Edin* 76-01; P-in-c Edin St Luke 79-90; Hon Can St Mary's Cathl from 98; rtd 00; Hon C Edin St Hilda and Edin St Fillan *Edin* 02-03. *31 Holly Bank Terrace, Edinburgh EH11 1SP* Tel 0131-337 6482
E-mail billjennybrockie@hotmail.com

BROCKLEBANK, John. b 32. N Ord Course 83. **d** 86 **p** 87. NSM Warrington St Barn *Liv* 86-93; NSM Orford St Marg 93-97; rtd

97; Perm to Offic *Ches* and *Liv* from 99. *53 St Mary's Road, Penketh, Warrington WA5 2DT* Tel (01925) 722063

BROCKLEHURST, John Richard. b 51. Univ Coll Ox BA72 Lon Univ CertEd74. Oak Hill Th Coll BA81. **d** 81 **p** 82. C Harwood *Man* 81-85; V Hopwood 85-97; P-in-c Friarmere 97-03; TV Saddleworth from 03. *The Vicarage, 1 Cobblers Hill, Delph, Oldham OL3 5HT* Tel (01457) 874209

BROCKLEHURST, Simon. b 63. Cranmer Hall Dur 86. **d** 89 **p** 90. C Clifton *S'well* 89-93; TV 93-96; P-in-c Mabe *Truro* 96-99; Miss to Seamen 96-99; V Ham St Andr *S'wark* from 99; Inland Hon Chapl Miss to Seafarers from 00. *St Andrew's Vicarage, Church Road, Ham, Richmond TW10 5HG* Tel (020) 8940 9017 Fax as telephone

BRODDLE, Christopher Stephen Thomas. b 57. **d** 87 **p** 88. C Lisburn St Paul *Conn* 87-90; CF from 90. *c/o MOD Chaplains (Army)* Tel (01980) 615804 Fax 615800

BRODIE, Ann. b 55. St Jo Coll Nottm. **d** 05. C Putney St Marg *S'wark* from 05. *46 Luttrell Avenue, London SW15 6PE* Tel (020) 8789 5932

BRODIE, Frederick. b 40. Leic Teacher Tr Coll TCert61. St Jo Coll Nottm DCM92. **d** 92 **p** 93. C Lutterworth w Cotesbach *Leic* 92-95; P-in-c Mountsorrel Ch Ch and St Pet 95-97; V 97-03; rtd 03. *11 Cooper Lane, Ratby, Leicester LE6 0QG* Tel 0116-238 7959 E-mail fbrodie@leicester.anglican.org

BRODRIBB, Carolyn Ann. b 48. Plymouth Univ MA CQSW. **d** 04 **p** 05. NSM Plymstock and Hooe *Ex* from 04. *Woolwell House, Woolwell Drive, Plymouth PL6 7JP* Tel (01752) 700299 E-mail carolynbrodribb@aol.com

BRODY, Paul. b 40. N Ord Course 85. **d** 88 **p** 89. C Leigh St Mary *Man* 88-90; C Peel 90-91; TR 91-97; TV Worsley from 97. *8 Landrace Drive, Worsley, Manchester M28 1UY* Tel 0161-799 1208 E-mail paul.brody@amserve.net

BROGGIO, Bernice Muriel Croager. b 35. Bedf Coll Lon BA57 K Coll Lon BD66 IDC66 Glas Univ DSS71 DASS72. **dss** 84 **d** 87 **p** 94. Bris St Paul w St Barn *Bris* 84-87; Hon Par Dn Bris St Paul's 87-88; C Charlton St Luke w H Trin *S'wark* 88-95; V Upper Tooting H Trin 95-03; Hon Can S'wark Cathl 95-03; RD Tooting 96-02; TV Bensham *Dur* from 03. *St Chad's Vicarage, Dunsmuir Grove, Gateshead NE8 4QL* Tel 0191-478 6338 Fax as telephone E-mail bernicebroggio@hotmail.com

BROMAGE, Kenneth Charles. b 51. EAMTC. **d** 90 **p** 91. NSM Woolpit w Drinkstone *St E* 90-92; Chapl RN from 92. *Royal Naval Chaplaincy Service, Room 203, Victory Building, HM Naval Base, Portsmouth PO1 3LS* Tel (023) 9272 7903 Fax 9272 7111

BROMFIELD, Michael. b 32. Kelham Th Coll 54 Lich Th Coll 59. **d** 62 **p** 63. C Sedgley All SS *Lich* 62-64; C Tunstall Ch Ch 64-67; P-in-c Grindon 67-70; R 70-80; P-in-c Butterton 67-70; V 70-80; R Hope Bowdler w Eaton-under-Heywood *Heref* 80-97; R Rushbury 80-97; V Cardington 80-97; rtd 98; Perm to Offic *Lich* from 98. *11 Walklate Avenue, Newcastle ST5 0PR* Tel (01782) 630716 E-mail bromfield@stoke54.freeserve.co.uk

BROMFIELD, Nicholas Robert. b 60. St Jo Coll Cam MA82. WEMTC 98. **d** 02 **p** 03. C Tidenham w Beachley and Lancaut *Glouc* from 02; C St Briavels w Hewelsfield from 05. *Forest Edge House, The Purples, Coalway, Coleford GL16 7JL* Tel (01594) 835533 Mobile 07905-606637 E-mail bromfields@email.msn.com

BROMFIELD, Richard Allan. b 47. LVCM85 Sussex Univ MA96. Chich Th Coll 86. **d** 88 **p** 89. C Durrington *Chich* 88-95; V Woodingdean from 95. *The Vicarage, 2 Downsway, Brighton BN2 6BD* Tel (01273) 681582

BROMILEY, Paul Nigel. b 49. Univ of Wales (Cardiff) BSc71. Oak Hill Th Coll 88. **d** 90 **p** 91. C Gee Cross *Ches* 90-94; P-in-c Millbrook 94-03; Master Wyggeston's Hosp Leic from 03. *Master's House, Wyggeston's Hospital, Hinckley Road, Leicester LE3 0UX* Tel 0116-254 8682

BROMILEY, Philip Arthur. b 73. Westmr Coll Ox BTh94 St Jo Coll Dur MA98. Cranmer Hall Dur 95. **d** 98 **p** 99. C Marton *Blackb* 98-01; Assoc P Calne and Blackland *Sarum* from 01. *7 Richmond Road, Calne SN11 9UW* Tel (01249) 818677 E-mail philbromiley@cybermail.uk.com

BROMLEY, Mrs Janet Catherine Gay. b 45. Surrey Univ BSc68 Bradf Univ MSc72 Brunel Tech Coll Bris FE TCert86. S Dios Minl Tr Scheme 91. **d** 94 **p** 96. C Westbury-on-Trym H Trin *Bris* 94-96; C Wroughton 96-00; Dean of Women's Min 98-00; R Dursley *Glouc* from 00. *The Rectory, Broadwell, Dursley GL11 4JE* Tel (01453) 542053 E-mail revjanet@dursleyparishchurch.freeserve.co.uk

BROMLEY, William James. b 44. Edin Univ BD74. Edin Th Coll 70. **d** 74 **p** 75. C Glas St Mary *Glas* 74-77; Bangladesh 77-80; R Glas H Cross *Glas* 80-89; R Stottesdon w Farlow, Cleeton St Mary etc *Heref* from 89. *The Rectory, Stottesdon, Kidderminster DY14 8UE* Tel (01746) 718297 E-mail billbromley@ukonline.co.uk

BROMLEY AND BEXLEY, Archdeacon of. *See* WRIGHT, The Ven Paul

BRONNERT, Preb David Llewellyn Edward. b 36. Ch Coll Cam BA57 MA61 PhD61 Lon Univ BD62. Tyndale Hall Bris 60. **d** 63 **p** 64. C Cheadle Hulme St Andr *Ches* 63-67; C Islington St Mary *Lon* 67-69; Chapl N Lon Poly 69-75; V Southall Green St Jo 75-01; Preb St Paul's Cathl 89-01; P-in-c Southall St Geo 92-99; AD Ealing W 84-90; rtd 01; Perm to Offic *Ox* from 04. *101 Walton Way, Aylesbury HP21 7JP* Tel (01296) 484048 E-mail david.bronnert@talk21.com

BRONNERT, John. b 33. Man Univ MA(Theol)84 Univ of Wales (Lamp) PhD98 ACA57 FCA68. Tyndale Hall Bris 65. **d** 68 **p** 69. C Hoole *Ches* 68-71; P-in-c Parr *Liv* 71-73; TV 73-85; V Runcorn St Jo Weston *Ches* 85-98; rtd 98; Perm to Offic *Liv* 85-04; *Man* from 98. *Tyndale, 15 Craig Avenue, Flixton, Urmston, Manchester M41 5RS* Tel 0161-748 7061 E-mail bronnert-revddrjohn@tyndale.freeserve.co.uk

BROOK, Kathleen Marjorie. b 23. IDC. Lightfoot Ho Dur 57. **dss** 66 **d** 87 **p** 94. Linthorpe *York* 66-75; Ormesby 75-83; rtd 83; Perm to Offic *York* from 83. *6 Station Square, Saltburn-by-the-Sea TS12 1AG* Tel (01287) 624006

BROOK, Neville. *See* BROOK, William Neville

BROOK, Peter Geoffrey (Brother Simon). b 47. N Ord Course 91. **d** 94 **p** 95. CGA from 71; NSM Heywood and Middleton Deanery 94-96; Perm to Offic *Ex* from 96. *The Priory, Lamacraft Farm, Start Point, Chivelstone, Kingsbridge TQ7 2NG* Tel (01548) 511474

BROOK, Stephen Edward. b 44. Univ of Wales (Abth) BSc65 DipEd66. Wycliffe Hall Ox 71 All Nations Chr Coll 85. **d** 74 **p** 75. C Heworth H Trin *York* 74-77; C Linthorpe 77-80; TV Deane *Man* 80-85; Crosslinks 86-96; Portugal 88-96; P-in-c Bacup St Sav *Man* 96-03; P-in-c Tunstead 99-03; V Blackpool St Mark *Blackb* from 03. *St Mark's Vicarage, 163 Kingscote Drive, Blackpool FY3 8EH* Tel (01253) 392895

BROOK, William Neville. b 31. S'wark Ord Course 66. **d** 69 **p** 70. C Maidstone St Martin *Cant* 69-75; V Hartlip w Stockbury 75-80; R Willesborough w Hinxhill 80-86; R Willesborough 87-89; V Gt Staughton *Ely* 89-96; V Hail Weston 89-96; rtd 96; Perm to Offic *Chich* from 96. *27 Middleton Drive, Eastbourne BN23 6HD* Tel (01323) 731243

BROOKE, Miss Bridget Cecilia. b 31. DBO51. Coll of Resurr Mirfield 88. **d** 89 **p** 94. Hon Par Dn Ranmoor *Sheff* 89-94; Hon C 94-04; Bp's Adv for NSMs 94-01; Perm to Offic from 04. *166 Tom Lane, Sheffield S10 3PG* Tel 0114-230 2147

BROOKE, David Fewsdale. b 43. St Paul's Coll Grahamstown 80. **d** 90 **p** 90. Asst Chapl Dioc Coll Cape Town S Africa 90-92; NSM Crawford St Jo 93-97; NSM Sea Point St Jas 98-99; Perm to Offic *Newc* 00; C Norham and Duddo 01-04; C Cornhill w Carham 01-04; C Branxton 01-04; R Dunkeld *St And* from 04; R Strathtay from 04. *St Mary's Rectory, St Mary's Road, Birnam, Dunkeld PH8 0BL* Tel (01350) 728007 E-mail david@fruitspree.freeserve.co.uk

BROOKE, David Martin. b 58. Selw Coll Cam BA80 MA83 Lon Inst of Educn PGCE81. St Alb and Ox Min Course 96. **d** 99 **p** 00. C Luton Lewsey St Hugh *St Alb* 99-00; NSM Sunnyside w Bourne End 00-02; C 02-04; V Bishopton w Gt Stainton *Dur* from 04; R Redmarshall from 04; R Grindon, Stillington and Wolviston from 04. *The Rectory, Church Lane, Redmarshall, Stockton-on-Tees TS21 1ES* Tel (01740) 630810 Mobile 07967-326085 E-mail david@revd.co.uk

BROOKE, Katherine Margaret. b 58. GRSM79 LRAM80 ARCM80. St Alb and Ox Min Course 01. **d** 04 **p** 05. C Auckland St Andr and St Anne *Dur* from 04. *The Rectory, Church Lane, Redmarshall, Stockton-on-Tees TS21 1ES* Tel (01740) 630810 Mobile 07973-539729 E-mail kate@revd.co.uk

BROOKE, Canon Robert. b 44. Birm Univ DPS77. Qu Coll Birm 70. **d** 73 **p** 74. C Man Resurr *Man* 73-76; C Bournville *Birm* 76-77; Chapl Qu Eliz Coll *Lon* 77-82; C Bramley *Ripon* 82-85; TV 85-86; V Hunslet Moor St Pet and St Cuth 86-93; Chapl People w Learning Disabilities from 86; TV Seacroft 93-03; TV Beeston from 03; Chapl Leeds Mental Health Teaching NHS Trust 94-03; Hon Can Ripon Cathl *Ripon* from 01. *St David's House, Waincliffe Drive, Leeds LS11 8ET* Tel 0113-2829 E-mail bob.brooke@another.com

BROOKE, Rosemary Jane. b 53. Cam Univ BEd75 Open Univ BA83. N Ord Course 86. **d** 89 **p** 94. NSM Poynton *Ches* 89-05; P-in-c Werneth from 05; Bp's Adv for Women in Min from 96. *The Vicarage, Compstall Brow, Compstall, Stockport SK6 5HU* Tel 0161-427 1259

BROOKE, Timothy Cyril. b 38. Jes Coll Cam BA60 MA70 Middx Poly CQSW76. Ripon Coll Cuddesdon 84. **d** 86 **p** 87. C Hillmorton *Cov* 86-90; V Earlsdon 90-98; V Cov St Fran N Radford from 98. *St Francis's Vicarage, 110 Treherne Road, Coventry CV6 3DY* Tel (024) 7659 5178 E-mail brookenet@zetnet.co.uk

BROOKE, Vernon. b 41. St Aid Birkenhead 62. **d** 65 **p** 66. C Crofton Park St Hilda w St Cypr *S'wark* 65-68; C Eccleshill *Bradf* 68-70; Ind Chapl *Linc* 70-84; Ind Chapl *Derby* 84-97; Ind Chapl *Chich* from 97. *6 Patcham Grange, Brighton BN1 8UR* Tel (01273) 564057 Fax as telephone E-mail vernonbrooke@yahoo.co.uk

BROOKE, Canon William Edward. b 13. Birm Univ BA34 MA35. Westcott Ho Cam 35. **d** 37 **p** 38. C Wylde Green *Birm*

37-40; C Sparkbrook St Agatha 40-44; P-in-c Birm St Jude 44-50; V 50-60; R Castle Bromwich SS Mary and Marg 60-78; Hon Can Birm Cathl 61-78; rtd 78; Perm to Offic *Heref* from 78. *Ivy Cottage, Tarrington, Hereford HR1 4HZ*

BROOKER, Mrs Anna Lesley. b 56. York Univ BA78 MA79 Homerton Coll Cam PGCE80. Ridley Hall Cam 01. **d** 03 **p** 04. C Brentford *Lon* from 03. *14 Heatham Park, Twickenham TW2 7SF* Tel (020) 8892 2580 *or* 8568 7442 Mobile 07960-120753 E-mail albrooker@email.com

BROOKER, Miss Ruth Muriel. b 53. Wycliffe Hall Ox 96. **d** 98 **p** 99. C Beverley Minster *York* 98-02; R Haddlesey w Hambleton and Birkin 02-03. *Bawtry Hall, South Parade, Bawtry, Doncaster DN10 6JH* Tel (01302) 710020 Fax 710027 E-mail equip@bawtryhall.co.uk

BROOKER, Mrs Wendy Ann. b 41. St Alb Minl Tr Scheme 82. **dss** 85 **d** 87 **p** 94. Pinner *Lon* 85-87; Greenhill St Jo 87; Par Dn 87-88; Ind Chapl 89-94; C Hayes St Edm 95-99; Chapl R Nat Orthopaedic Hosp NHS Trust from 99. *Royal National Orthopaedic Hospital, Brockley Hill, Stanmore HA7 4LP* Tel (020) 8954 2300 E-mail wd.brooker@ukf.net

BROOKES, Arthur George. b 21. ACIB52. Worc Ord Coll 64. **d** 66 **p** 67. C Lower Mitton *Worc* 66-67; C Fladbury w Throckmorton, Wyre Piddle and Moor 67-70; C Abberton w Bishampton 67-70; R 70-73; V Cradley 73-78; P-in-c Castle Morton 78-79; P-in-c Holly Bush w Birtsmorton 78-79; P-in-c Castlemorton, Hollybush and Birtsmorton 79-80; P-in-c Norton w Whittington 80-81; TV Worc St Martin w St Pet, St Mark etc 81-86; rtd 86; Perm to Offic *Worc* from 86. *13 Capel Court, The Burgage, Prestbury, Cheltenham GL52 3EL* Tel (01242) 580523

BROOKES, Colin Stuart. b 70. Lon Bible Coll BA93. Ridley Hall Cam 00. **d** 02 **p** 03. C Cambridge St Barn *Ely* from 02. *80 St Barnabas Road, Cambridge CB1 2DE* Tel (01223) 367578 *or* 519526 Mobile 07973-840340 Fax (01223) 536256 E-mail curate@stbs.org.uk

BROOKES, David Charles. b 45. St Mich Coll Llan 84. **d** 86 **p** 87. C Llanishen and Lisvane *Llan* 86-88; TV Brighouse St Martin *Wakef* 89-92; TV Brighouse and Clifton 92-94; V Hollingbourne and Hucking w Leeds and Broomfield *Cant* 94-03; rtd 03. *Chemin de la Garenne, Le Vivier, 16240 Longre, France* Tel (0033) (1) 15 45 31 71 88 E-mail david@dcbrookes.freeserve.co.uk

BROOKES, Derrick Meridyth. b 17. Trin Hall Cam BA38 MA42. Westcott Ho Cam 39. **d** 40 **p** 41. C Macclesfield St Mich *Ches* 40-44; Chapl RAFVR 44-47; C Wilmslow *Ches* 47-49; V Chipping Sodbury and Old Sodbury *Glouc* 49-53; Youth Chapl 51-53; Chapl RAF 53-72; Master Bris Cathl Sch 72-73; Master XIV Prep Sch Bris 73-78. *Woodpeckers, Pilcorn Street, Wedmore BS28 4AW* Tel (01934) 712988

BROOKES, Edwin William. b 39. St Mark & St Jo Coll Lon TCert63 Birm Univ BPhil(Ed)85 Open Univ BA73 BA93. OLM course 95. **d** 98 **p** 99. OLM Cen Wolverhampton *Lich* from 98. *23 Chetwynd Road, Blakenhall, Wolverhampton WV2 4NZ* Tel (01902) 654979 *or* 428491 Fax 562616 E-mail edbrookes@bleak23.freeserve.co.uk

BROOKES, Geoffrey John Denis. b 24. CMS Tr Coll Crowther Hall 78 Ridley Hall Cam 84. **d** 85 **p** 86. Bahrain 85-88; Project Officer Ch Action w the Unemployed 88-91; Hon C Hastings All So *Chich* 88-91; Asst Chapl Milan w Genoa and Varese *Eur* 91-94; Canada 94-97; Perm to Offic *Chich* 97-99 and 01-02; *Guildf* from 03. *50 Chapel Court, Church Street, Dorking RH4 1BT* Tel (01306) 884287

BROOKES, Keith Roy. b 37. JP74. MHCIMA MRSH Leeds Univ DipEd72. St Aid Birkenhead 64. **d** 80 **p** 81. Hon C Stockport St Thos *Ches* 80-86; Hon C Stockport St Thos w St Pet 86-91; C 91-98; Hon C from 99. *42 Derby Road, Stockport SK4 4NE* Tel 0161-442 0301

BROOKES, Laurence. b 33. Dioc OLM tr scheme 01. **d** 02 **p** 03. OLM Flockton cum Denby Grange *Wakef* from 02; OLM Emley from 02. *Treetops, 6 Chessington Drive, Flockton, Wakefield WF4 4TJ* Tel (01924) 848238 E-mail lauriemarybrookes@supanet.com

BROOKES, Robin Keenan. b 47. Trin Coll Bris 72. **d** 75 **p** 76. C Livesey *Blackb* 75-78; C Burnley St Pet 78-80; P-in-c Bawdeswell w Foxley *Nor* 80-83; I Donagh w Tyholland and Errigal Truagh *Clogh* 83-91; Dioc Communications Officer 90-91; I Dublin Drumcondra w N Strand *D & G* 91-99; Chapl Ayia Napa Cyprus from 99. *PO Box 33873, 5318 Paralimni, Cyprus* Tel (00357) (23) 742955 *or* 742956 Mobile 99-698049 Fax (23) 742957 E-mail angfam@spidernet.com.cy

BROOKES, Steven David. b 60. Lanc Univ BA81. Ripon Coll Cuddesdon 82. **d** 85 **p** 86. C Stanley *Liv* 85-88; C W Derby St Mary 88-90; Chapl RN 90-94; R Weybridge *Guildf* 94-03; P-in-c Liv Our Lady and St Nic w St Anne *Liv* from 03. *The Rector's Lodging, 233 South Ferry Quay, Liverpool L3 4EE* Tel 0151-709 2551 Mobile 07903-505639 E-mail rector@livpc.co.uk

BROOKFIELD, Alun John. b 50. Lon Univ BMus72 Spurgeon's Coll Lon BA82. **d** 00 **p** 01. NSM Stratton St Margaret w S Marston etc *Bris* 00-02; P-in-c Cwmtawe Uchaf *S & B* from 03. *The Vicarage, Heol Tawe, Abercrave, Swansea SA9 1TJ* Tel (01639) 730640 E-mail a.brookfield@ntlworld.com

BROOKFIELD, Patricia Anne. *See* HARDACRE, Patricia Anne

BROOKHOUSE, Leslie. b 28. Ridley Hall Cam 69 St Aid Birkenhead 68. **d** 70 **p** 71. C Tonge *Man* 70-72; C Didsbury Ch Ch 72-74; V Newall Green St Fran 74-80; V High Crompton 80-86; R Ashwater, Halwill, Beaworthy, Clawton etc *Ex* 86-98; RD Holsworthy 94-99; rtd 98; P-in-c Pyworthy, Pancrasweek and Bridgerule *Ex* 98-03. *9 St Andrew's Close, Sutcombe, Holsworthy EX22 7PL* Tel (01409) 240021 E-mail lbrookhouse@talk21.com

BROOKS, Alan Leslie. b 43. Nor City Coll TCert65. Dioc OLM tr scheme 98. **d** 01 **p** 02. OLM Waterloo Ch Ch and St Jo *Liv* from 01. *6 Kingsway, Waterloo, Liverpool L22 4RQ* Tel 0151-920 8770 E-mail alanbrooks@blueyonder.co.uk

BROOKS, Mrs Alison Margaret. b 46. EMMTC. **d** 03 **p** 04. Asst Chapl Qu Medical Cen Nottm Univ Hosp NHS Trust from 03. *12 Russell Avenue, Nottingham NG8 2BL*

BROOKS, Mrs Christine Ellen. b 43. Sheff Univ BA65 Lon Univ BD81. Lambeth STh81 EAMTC 86. **d** 88 **p** 94. NSM Palgrave w Wortham and Burgate *St E* 88-89; Par Dn Thorndon w Rishangles, Stoke Ash, Thwaite etc 89-94; P-in-c Aldringham w Thorpe, Knodishall w Buxlow etc 94-04; Asst P Sternfield w Benhall and Snape 98-03; P-in-c 03-04; P-in-c Gt and Lt Glemham, Blaxhall etc 03-04; R Aldringham w Thorpe, Knodishall w Buxlow etc from 04. *The Rectory, Aldeburgh Road, Friston, Saxmundham IP17 1NP* Tel (01728) 688972 Mobile 07752-652833 E-mail christine@brook7463.freeserve.co.uk

BROOKS, Dorothy Anne. *See* MOORE BROOKS, Dorothy Anne

BROOKS, Canon Francis Leslie. b 35. Kelham Th Coll 55. **d** 59 **p** 60. C Woodlands *Sheff* 59-61; Ind Missr S Yorkshire Coalfields 61-66; V Moorends 66-72; Chapl HM Borstal Hatfield 67-72; Chapl HM Pris Acklington 72-75; Chapl HM Borstal Wellingborough 75-79; Chapl HM Pris Wakef 79-83; Area Sec USPG *Wakef* and *Bradf* 83-88; V Carleton and E Hardwick *Wakef* 88-96; Can Mara (Tanzania) from 88; rtd 96; Perm to Offic *Wakef* 03-04; Hon C Chevington *Newc* from 04. *20 Robsons Way, Amble, Morpeth NE65 0GA* Tel (01665) 712765

BROOKS, Ian George. b 47. Selw Coll Cam BA68 MA72. Chich Th Coll 68. **d** 70 **p** 71. C Stoke Newington St Mary *Lon* 70-74; C Hoxton St Anne w St Sav and St Andr 74-75; C Hoxton St Anne w St Columba 75-80; P-in-c Croxteth St Paul CD *Liv* 80-81; V Croxteth from 81. *St Paul's Vicarage, Delabole Road, Liverpool L11 6LG* Tel 0151-548 9009 Fax as telephone

BROOKS, Jeremy Paul. b 67. Leic Univ LLB88 Clare Coll Cam BA96 MA01 K Coll Lon MA00. Ridley Hall Cam 94. **d** 97 **p** 98. C Highgate St Mich *Lon* 97-01; P-in-c Hoddesdon *St Alb* from 01. *11 Oxenden Drive, Hoddesdon EN11 8QF* Tel (01992) 464335 E-mail jpbrooks@ntlworld.com

BROOKS, Jonathan Thorburn. b 53. Solicitor 76 G&C Coll Cam BA75 DipHE. Trin Coll Bris 84. **d** 86 **p** 87. C Dagenham *Chelmsf* 86-88; Perm to Offic *Glouc* 03; NSM Thornbury and Oldbury-on-Severn w Shepperdine from 03. *12 Hyde Avenue, Thornbury, Bristol BS35 1JA* Tel (01454) 411853

BROOKS, Malcolm David. b 45. Univ of Wales (Lamp) DipTh71. **d** 71 **p** 72. C Pontlottyn w Fochriw *Llan* 71-72; C Caerphilly 72-78; V Ferndale w Maerdy 78-81; C Port Talbot St Theodore 82-84; V Ystrad Mynach 84-85; V Ystrad Mynach w Llanbradach from 85. *The Vicarage, Nelson Road, Ystrad Mynach, Hengoed CF82 7EG* Tel (01443) 813246

BROOKS, Patrick John. b 27. Man Univ BA49 DipEd. Oak Hill Th Coll 78. **d** 77 **p** 79. Burundi 77-80; Perm to Offic *Ex* 80-83; P-in-c Phillack w Gwithian and Gwinear *Truro* 83-88; R 88-93; rtd 93; Perm to Offic *Chich* from 93. *Abbots, Claigmar Road, Rustington, Littlehampton BN16 2NL*

BROOKS, Paul John. b 59. Loughb Univ BSc81 Dip Th Studies 89 DPS90. St Jo Coll Nottm 87. **d** 90 **p** 91. C Long Eaton St Jo *Derby* 90-94; Min Jersey St Paul Prop Chpl *Win* from 94. *5 Claremont Avenue, St Saviour, Jersey JE2 7SF* Tel (01534) 880393 E-mail pjbvic@aol.com

BROOKS, Peter. b 55. St Mich Coll Llan DMS99. **d** 99 **p** 00. C Morriston *S & B* 99-01; P-in-c Rhayader and Nantmel 01-02; P-in-c Cwmddauddwr w St Harmon's and Llanwrthwl from 02. *The Vicarage, Dark Lane, Rhayader LD6 5DA* Tel (01597) 810223

BROOKS, Peter Joseph. b 54. **d** 83 **p** 84. C Portslade St Nic and St Andr *Chich* 83-86; C Kingstanding St Luke *Birm* 86-91; V Nork *Guildf* from 91. *St Paul's Vicarage, Warren Road, Banstead SM7 1LG* Tel (01737) 353849 E-mail timeformass@praisethelord.co.uk

BROOKS, Philip David. b 52. MA Cam Univ MTh. St Jo Coll Nottm 80. **d** 83 **p** 84. C Ipsley *Worc* 83-87; V Fulford w Hilderstone *Lich* 87-95; Chapl Stallington Hosp 87-95; P-in-c Crich *Derby* 95-01; V Crich and S Wingfield from 01; Dioc Adv Past Care and Counselling from 03. *The Vicarage, 19 Coasthill, Crich, Matlock DE4 5DS* Tel (01773) 852449 E-mail philipdbro@aol.com

BROOKS, Roger John. b 46. Nottm Univ PhD71 Liv Univ MTh05 MRPharmS70 FFARCS81. N Ord Course 98. **d** 01 **p** 02. C Burley in Wharfedale *Bradf* 01-03; P-in-c Denholme from 03; P-in-c Harden and Wilsden from 03. *The Vicarage, Wilsden Old Road, Harden, Bingley BD16 1JD* Tel (01535) 272344 E-mail rjb@fonticulus.org.uk

BROOKS, Mrs Susan Margaret. b 50. Philippa Fawcett Coll CertEd71 Open Univ BA95. SEITE 00. **d** 03. NSM Chatham St Paul w All SS *Roch* from 03. *189 Malling Road, Snodland ME6 5EE* Tel (01634) 241350 E-mail suebrooks@talk21.com

BROOKS, Mrs Susan Vera. b 51. N Ord Course 87. **d** 90 **p** 94. Par Dn Carleton and E Hardwick *Wakef* 90-93; TV Almondbury w Farnley Tyas 93-98; Chapl Huddersfield NHS Trust 98-01; Chapl Calderdale and Huddersfield NHS Trust from 01. *Royal Infirmary, Acre Street, Huddersfield HD3 3EA* Tel (01484) 422191 *or* 323839 E-mail susan.brookes@cht.nhs.uk

BROOKS, Mrs Vivien June. b 47. Univ of Wales (Ban) BA68 Southn Univ MA70. Ridley Hall Cam 87. **d** 89 **p** 95. C Exning St Martin w Landwade *St E* 89-92; Par Dn Hermitage and Hampstead Norreys, Cold Ash etc *Ox* 92-94; C 94-95; P-in-c Cox Green 95-03; Co Ecum Officer (Berks) 00-03; P-in-c Earls Colne w White Colne and Colne Engaine *Chelmsf* 03-04; TV Halstead Area from 04. *St Andrew's Rectory, 5 Shut Lane, Earls Colne, Colchester CO6 2RE* Tel (01787) 220347 E-mail vbrooks@minnieb.com

BROOKS, Vivienne Christine. *See* ARMSTRONG-MacDONNELL, Mrs Vivienne Christine

BROOKSBANK, Alan Watson. b 43. Univ of Wales (Lamp) BA64 Edin Univ MEd76. Edin Th Coll 64. **d** 66 **p** 67. C Cleator Moor w Cleator *Carl* 66-70; V Dalston 70-80; P-in-c Greystoke, Matterdale and Mungrisdale 80-81; R 81-83; R Watermillock 81-83; R Hagley *Worc* 83-95; Bp's Officer for NSM 88-95; V Claines St Jo 95-98; rtd 98. *169 Northfields Lane, Brixham TQ5 8RD*

BROOKSHAW, Miss Janice Chitty. b 48. MIPD90. Ripon Coll Cuddesdon 96. **d** 98 **p** 99. C Beaconsfield *Ox* 98-02; P-in-c The Stodden Churches *St Alb* 02-03; R from 03. *Stodden Rectory, High Street, Upper Dean, Huntingdon PE28 0ND* Tel and fax (01234) 708531 E-mail jan@revbrookshaw.freeserve.co.uk

BROOM, Andrew Clifford. b 65. Keele Univ BSocSc86. Trin Coll Bris BA92. **d** 92 **p** 93. C Wellington, All SS w Eyton *Lich* 92-96; C Brampton St Thos *Derby* 96-00; V Walton St Jo from 00. *6 Medlock Road, Walton, Chesterfield S40 3NH* Tel (01246) 205993 E-mail a.broom@ukonline.co.uk

BROOM, Jacqueline Anne. b 52. R Holloway Coll Lon BSc73. Trin Coll Bris DipHE81. **dss** 82 **d** 95 **p** 95. Easton H Trin w St Gabr and St Lawr and St Jude *Bris* 82-86; OMF Internat 87-01; Hong Kong 87-95; Macao China 96-01; rtd 01; Perm to Offic *B & W* from 02. *25 Coralberry Drive, Weston-super-Mare BS22 6SQ* Tel (01934) 520439

BROOME, David Curtis. b 36. Leeds Univ BA63. Coll of Resurr Mirfield. **d** 65 **p** 66. C Winshill *Derby* 65-69; C Leigh-on-Sea St Marg *Chelmsf* 69-74; V Leeds St Marg *Ripon* 74-81; V Stoke H Cross w Dunston *Nor* 81-93; P-in-c Arminghall 92-93; P-in-c Caistor w Markshall 92-93; R Stoke H Cross w Dunston, Arminghall etc 93-00; rtd 00; Perm to Offic *Nor* from 00. *13 Greenacres Drive, Poringland, Norwich NR14 7JG* Tel (01508) 493201

BROOME, Mildred Dorothy. **d** 00 **p** 01. NSM Malden St Jo *S'wark* from 00. *124 The Manor Drive, Worcester Park KT4 7LW* Tel (020) 8337 1572

BROOMFIELD, David John. b 37. Reading Univ BA59. Oak Hill Th Coll 64. **d** 66 **p** 67. C Gresley *Derby* 66-71; C Rainham *Chelmsf* 71-77; R High Ongar w Norton Mandeville 77-88; RD Ongar 83-88; P-in-c Stanford Rivers 84-86; P-in-c Loughton St Mary and St Mich 88-95; P-in-c Loughton St Mary 95-97; R 97-03; rtd 03; Perm to Offic *Glouc* from 03. *15 Oriel Grove, Moreton-in-Marsh GL56 0ED* Tel (01608) 651023 E-mail david@dabroomfield.freeserve.co.uk

BROOMFIELD, Iain Jonathan. b 57. Univ Coll Ox MA87. Wycliffe Hall Ox 80. **d** 83 **p** 84. C Beckenham Ch Ch *Roch* 83-87; Sen Schs Worker Titus Trust 87-00; V Bromley Ch Ch *Roch* from 00. *Christ Church Vicarage, 18 Highland Road, Bromley BR1 4AD* Tel (020) 8313 9882

BROSNAN, Mark. b 61. St Martin's Coll Lanc BA83 RMN88 Otley Agric Coll. EAMTC 92. **d** 95 **p** 96. C Rushmere *St E* 95-98; Perm to Offic *Chelmsf* 01-05; Hon C W w E Mersea from 05; Hon C Peldon w Gt and Lt Wigborough from 05. *68 Firs Road, West Mersea, Colchester CO5 8NL* Tel (01206) 383118

BROSTER, Godfrey David. b 52. Ealing Tech Coll BA75. Ripon Coll Cuddesdon 78. **d** 81 **p** 82. C Crayford *Roch* 81-82; C Brighton Resurr *Chich* 82-86; C-in-c The Hydneye CD 86-91; R Plumpton w E Chiltington 91-93; R Plumpton w E Chiltington cum Novington from 93. *The Rectory, Station Road, Plumpton Green, Lewes BN7 3BU* Tel (01273) 890570

BROTHERSTON, Miss Isabel Mary. b 42. Cranmer Hall Dur 81. **dss** 83 **d** 87 **p** 94. Coleshill *Birm* 83-87; Par Dn Duddeston w Nechells 87-92; Par Dn Harlescott *Lich* 92-94; C 94-04; R Llanddulas and Llysfaen *St As* from 04. *The Rectory, 2 Rhodfa Wen, Llysfaen, Colwyn Bay LL29 8LE* Tel and fax (01492) 516728

BROTHERTON, The Ven John Michael. b 35. St Jo Coll Cam BA59 MA63. Cuddesdon Coll 59. **d** 61 **p** 62. C Chiswick St Nic w St Mary *Lon* 61-65; Trinidad and Tobago 65-75; V Cowley St Jo *Ox* 76-81; Chapl St Hilda's Coll Ox 76-81; RD Cowley *Ox* 78-81; V Portsea St Mary *Portsm* 81-91; Hon Can Kobe Japan from 86; Adn Chich 91-02; rtd 02; Perm to Offic *Lon* from 03. *Flat 2, 23 Gledhow Gardens, London SW5 0AZ* Tel (020) 7373 5147 E-mail jmbrotherton@amserve.com

BROTHERTON, Michael. b 56. MBE93. Univ of Wales (Abth) BD80. Wycliffe Hall Ox 80. **d** 81 **p** 82. Hon Chapl Miss to Seamen 81-84; C Pembroke Dock *St D* 81-84; Chapl RN from 84. *Royal Naval Chaplaincy Service, Room 203, Victory Building, HM Naval Base, Portsmouth PO1 3LS* Tel (023) 9272 7903 Fax 9272 7111

BROTHERWOOD, Nicholas Peter. b 50. Oak Hill Th Coll BA83. **d** 83 **p** 84. C Nottingham St Nic *S'well* 83-86; Canada from 86; Dir Quebec Lodge 86-89; Angl Chapl McGill Univ 89-91; Assoc R Westmount St Steph from 91. *3498 Harvard Avenue, Montreal PQ, Canada, H4A 2W3* Tel (001) (514) 489 4158 Fax 932 0550 E-mail st.stephens@qc.aira.com

BROTHWELL, Paul David. b 37. Lich Th Coll 62. **d** 65 **p** 66. C Honley *Wakef* 65-68; Min Can Wakef Cathl 68-71; V Whittington St Giles *Lich* 71-83; P-in-c Weeford 78-83; V Whittington w Weeford 83-92; Chapl Kidderminster Gen Hosp 92-94; Chapl Kidderminster Health Care NHS Trust 94-01; Chapl Worcs Community and Mental Health Trust 01-02; Hon Can Antananarivo 02; rtd 02; Perm to Offic *Worc* from 02. *8 Hillside Close, Stourport-on-Severn DY13 0JW* Tel (01299) 823495 *or* (01562) 823424 ext 3306

BROTHWOOD, Ian Sidney. b 56. K Coll Lon BD84. Linc Th Coll 87. **d** 89 **p** 90. C Selsdon St Jo w St Fran *S'wark* 89-93; P-in-c S Norwood St Alb 93-97; V 97-99; V Reigate St Mark 99-04; P-in-c Selsdon St Jo w St Fran from 04. *St John's Rectory, Upper Selsdon Road, South Croydon CR2 8DD* Tel (020) 8657 2343 E-mail iansb@aol.com

BROTHWOOD, John. b 31. Peterho Cam MA55 MB, BChir55. S'wark Ord Course 89. **d** 91 **p** 92. NSM Dulwich St Barn *S'wark* 91-04. *98 Woodwarde Road, London SE22 8UT* Tel (020) 8693 8273

BROUGH, Gerald William. b 32. Trin Coll Cam BA55 MA59. Ridley Hall Cam 55. **d** 57 **p** 58. C Westgate St Jas *Cant* 57-60; C New Addington 60-62; V Mancetter *Cov* 62-73; P-in-c Bourton w Frankton and Stretton on Dunsmore etc 73-74; R 74-93; rtd 93; Perm to Offic *Cov* from 93. *17 Brookhurst Court, Beverley Road, Leamington Spa CV32 6PB* Tel (01926) 430759 E-mail gwbrls@aol.com

BROUGH (née CROWLE), Mrs Sarah Ann. b 65. Ripon Coll Cuddesdon BTh99. **d** 99 **p** 00. C Godalming *Guildf* 99-03; Chapl Godalming Coll 01-03; R Chiddingfold *Guildf* from 03. *The Rectory, Coxcombe Lane, Chiddingfold, Godalming GU8 4QA* Tel (01428) 682008 Mobile 07747-031524 E-mail sarahbrough@btinternet.com

BROUGHALL, Rodney John. b 32. LNSM course 95. **d** 96 **p** 97. OLM Watton w Carbrooke and Ovington *Nor* 96-02; rtd 02; Perm to Offic *Nor* from 02. *15 Garden Close, Watton, Thetford IP25 6DP* Tel (01953) 881989

BROUGHTON, James Roger. b 48. Leeds Univ BA71 Nottm Univ CertEd72. Wycliffe Hall Ox 87. **d** 89 **p** 90. C Stoneycroft All SS *Liv* 89-92; P-in-c Carr Mill 92-94; V 94-96; Chapl Duke of York's R Mil Sch Dover from 96. *Kent House, Duke of York's Royal Military School, Guston, Dover CT15 5DR* Tel (01304) 202437 *or* 245059 E-mail roger.broughton@doyrms.com

BROUGHTON, Lynne Mary. b 46. Melbourne Univ BA67 PhD79. EAMTC 99. **d** 00 **p** 01. Hon C Wood Ditton w Saxon Street *Ely* from 00; Hon C Kirtling from 00; Hon C Cheveley from 00; Hon C Ashley w Silverley from 00. *85 Richmond Road, Cambridge CB4 3PS* Tel (01223) 322014 E-mail lmb27@hermes.cam.ac.uk

BROUGHTON, Stuart Roger. b 36. Univ of Wales DipTh65. St Mich Coll Llan 61 Wilson Carlile Coll 59. **d** 64 **p** 65. C Bromley Ch Ch *Roch* 64-67; SAMS 67-79 and 86-95; Miss Paraguayan Chaco Paraguay 67-70; R Salvador Gd Shep Brazil 70-79; V Stoke sub Hamdon *B & W* 79-83; Hon CF 82-86; V Blackb Ch Ch w St Matt *Blackb* 83-86; R Alcacer do Sal Portugal 86-91; Chapl Rio de Janeiro Brazil 91-95; rtd 96; Chapl Agia Napa Cyprus 96; Chapl Ch Ch Cathl Falkland Is 97-98; P-in-c Corfu *Eur* 98-01; Hon C Jersey St Paul Prop Chpl *Win* 01-03; Chapl to Abp Congo from 03. *c/o P Broughton Esq, Point Cottage, 29 Fir Tree Lane, Littleton, Chester CH3 7DN* E-mail kathrynbroughton@tinyworld.co.uk

BROUN, Canon Claud Michael. b 30. BNC Ox BA55. Edin Th Coll 56. **d** 58 **p** 59. Chapl St Mary's Cathl *Edin* 58-62; Can St Mary's Cathl *Glas* 84-95; Hon Can from 95; P-in-c Cambuslang 62-70; R 70-75; R Hamilton 75-88; R Gatehouse of Fleet 88-95; R Kirkcudbright 88-95; rtd 95. *Martin Lodge, Ardross Place, Alness IV17 0PX* Tel (01349) 882442

BROWN, Canon Alan. b 37. Tyndale Hall Bris 59. **d** 63 **p** 64. C Braintree *Chelmsf* 63-66; C Tooting Graveney St Nic *S'wark* 66-68; C Chesham St Mary *Ox* 68-70; V Hornsey Rise St Mary *Lon* 70-75; V Sidcup Ch Ch *Roch* 75-88; V Newport St Jo *Portsm* 88-01; P-in-c Newport St Thos 96-99; V 99-01; RD W Wight 91-96; Hon Can Portsm Cathl 95-01; rtd 01. *Beatrice Cottage, 4 Victoria Mews, Cowes PO31 7PH* Tel (01983) 281133

BROWN, Alan George. b 51. Bradf Univ BSc84 Leeds Univ CertEd81 MBA92 SRN72 RMN75 RNT81. N Ord Course 92. **d** 95 **p** 96. NSM Ilkley St Marg *Bradf* from 95; Hd of Division Applied Health Studies Leeds Univ from 98; Bp's Adv for Hosp Chapl from 03. *Waverley, Wheatley Road, Ilkley LS29 8TS* Tel and fax (01943) 601115 E-mail a.g.brown@leeds.ac.uk

BROWN, Alan Michael Ernest. b 52. St Chad's Coll Dur BA74. St Jo Coll Nottm 81. **d** 83 **p** 84. C Bridlington Priory *York* 83-86; V Morton St Luke *Bradf* 86-02; Mental Health Worker Bradf City Primary Care Trust from 02. *Bradford City Primary Care Trust, 1st Floor, Joseph Brennan House, Sunbridge Road, Bradford BD1 2SY* Tel (01274) 424780

BROWN, Albert Harry Alfred Victor. b 12. **d** 81 **p** 83. OLM Kennington Park St Agnes *S'wark* 81-92; Perm to Offic 92-00. *378 I/P Ward 23, Berth 20 Royal Hospital, London SW3 4SI* Tel (020) 7274 5982

BROWN, Alec Charles. b 33. AKC58. **d** 59 **p** 60. C S Mimms St Mary and Potters Bar *Lon* 59-63; C S Ashford Ch Ch *Cant* 63-66; Bahamas 66-71; New Zealand from 71. *151 Tasman Street, Nelson, New Zealand* Tel (0064) (3) 548 3644

BROWN, Alec George. b 53. Univ of Zimbabwe DipSW80 Univ of Wales (Cardiff) MSc(Econ)87. St Deiniol's Hawarden 88 N Ord Course 90. **d** 93 **p** 94. C Stockton Heath *Ches* 93-96; C Thelwall 96-97; V 97-01; V Gt Budworth from 01. *The Vicarage, High Street, Great Budworth, Northwich CW9 6HF* Tel (01606) 891324

BROWN, Alexander Peter-Aidan. b 48. Sarum & Wells Th Coll. **d** 82 **p** 83. C Ifield *Chich* 82-86; TV 86-91; V St Leonards SS Pet and Paul from 91. *The Vicarage, 10 Bloomfield Road, St Leonards-on-Sea TN37 6HH* Tel (01424) 445606

BROWN, Allan James. b 47. K Coll Lon BD69 AKC69 MTh70. St Aug Coll Cant 69. **d** 73 **p** 74. Jerusalem 73-75; Chapl St Geo Sch 73-74; Chapl St Marg Sch Nazareth 74-75; C Clifton *S'well* 75-77; CF 77-00; Asst Chapl Gen 99-00; V Ilkeston St Mary *Derby* from 00. *The Vicarage, 63B Manners Road, Ilkeston DE7 5HB* Tel 0115-932 4725

BROWN, Canon Andrew. b 55. St Pet Hall Ox BA80 MA82. Ridley Hall Cam 79. **d** 80 **p** 81. C Burnley St Pet *Blackb* 80-82; C Elton All SS *Man* 82-86; P-in-c Ashton St Pet 86-93; V 94-96; V Halliwell St Luke 96-03; Can Th Derby Cathl *Derby* from 03; Dioc CME Adv from 03. *149 Church Road, Quarndon, Derby DE22 5JA* Tel (01332) 553424 E-mail andie.brown@virgin.net

BROWN, Andrew. b 65. LNSM course 92. **d** 95 **p** 96. OLM Heywood *Man* from 95. *24 Honiton Close, Heywood OL10 2PF* Tel (01706) 623091

BROWN, Andrew (Bod). b 66. Man Univ BSc87. Oak Hill Th Coll BA02. **d** 03. C Hyde St Geo *Ches* from 03. *121 Dowson Road, Hyde SK14 5HJ* Tel 0161-367 9353 E-mail bod77@hotmail.com

BROWN, Anthony Frank Palmer. b 31. Fitzw Ho Cam BA56 Fitzw Coll Cam MA84. Cuddesdon Coll 56. **d** 58 **p** 59. C Aldershot St Mich *Guildf* 58-61; C Chiswick St Nic w St Mary *Lon* 61-66; Asst Chapl Lon Univ 65-70; Lic to Offic 70-72; C-in-c Hammersmith SS Mich and Geo White City Estate CD 72-74; P-in-c Upper Sunbury St Sav 74-80; V 80-01; rtd 01; Perm to Offic *Chich* from 02. *6 Church Lane, Ditchling, Hassocks BN6 8TB* Tel (01273) 843847

BROWN, Anthony Paul. b 55. Reading Univ BSc75 MRICS87. Qu Coll Birm 77. **d** 80 **p** 81. C Pelsall *Lich* 80-83; C Leighton Buzzard w Eggington, Hockliffe etc *St Alb* 83-87; TV Langley Marish *Ox* 87-93; V Pet St Mary Boongate *Pet* 93-98; TR Wombourne w Trysull and Bobbington *Lich* 98-02; TR Smestow Vale from 02. *The Vicarage, School Road, Wombourne, Wolverhampton WV5 9ED* Tel (01902) 892234 *or* 897700 E-mail revpbrown@aol.com

BROWN, Antony William Keith. b 26. RN Coll Dartmouth 43. Trin Coll Bris 86. **d** 87 **p** 88. NSM Lawrence Weston *Bris* 87-89; Chapl Casablanca *Eur* 89-93; Asst Chapl Paris St Mich 94-00; rtd 00; Perm to Offic *Bris* from 01. *13 Marklands, 37 Julian Road, Bristol BS9 1NP* Tel 0117-377 6543 Fax as telephone E-mail ansh.brown@blueyonder.co.uk

BROWN, Arthur Basil Etheredge. b 17. Reading Univ BA39. Wycliffe Hall Ox 46. **d** 47 **p** 48. C Camborne *Truro* 47-50; Org Sec (Midl) CPAS 50-53; PC Scarborough H Trin *York* 53-58; V Heworth H Trin 58-66; R Camborne *Truro* 66-82; rtd 82; Perm to Offic *Truro* from 82. *14 Tregenna Fields, Camborne TR14 7QS* Tel (01209) 716196

BROWN, Arthur William Stawell. b 26. St Jo Coll Ox BA50 MA51. Cuddesdon Coll 63. **d** 65 **p** 66. C Edin St Jo *Edin* 65-66; C Petersfield w Sheet *Portsm* 67-75; V Portsea St Alb 75-79; R Smithfield St Bart Gt *Lon* 79-91; R St Sepulchre w Ch Ch Greyfriars etc 81-91; Chapl Madeira *Eur* 90-93; rtd 91; Perm to Offic *Ex* from 93. *9 Little Silver, Exeter EX4 4HU* Tel (01392) 217630

BROWN, Barry Ronald. b 48. Ridley Coll Melbourne ThL72. **d** 73 **p** 74. Australia 73-77 and 82-95; C Richmond St Mary *S'wark* 78-79; C Richmond St Mary w St Matthias and St Jo 79; C Edin Old St Paul *Edin* 79-80; Chapl Belgrade w Zagreb *Eur* 81-82; Canada from 95. *46 Granby Street, Toronto ON, Canada, M5B 2J5* Tel (001) (416) 979 6766

BROWN, Canon Bernard Herbert Vincent. b 26. Mert Coll Ox BA50 MA52. Westcott Ho Cam 50. **d** 52 **p** 53. C Rugby St Andr *Cov* 52-56; C Stoke Bishop *Bris* 56-59; Youth Chapl 56-62; Ind Chapl *Roch* 62-73; Bp's Dom Chapl 66-73; R Crawley *Chich* 73-79; TR 79-83; Ind Chapl *Bris* 83-92; Bp's Soc and Ind Adv 84-92; Hon Can Bris Cathl 85-92; RD Bris City 85-91; rtd 92; Perm to Offic *Sarum* from 92. *33B London Road, Dorchester DT1 1NF* Tel (01305) 260806

BROWN, Bernard Maurice Newall. b 26. Oak Hill Th Coll 47. **d** 51 **p** 52. C Penn Fields *Lich* 51-53; S Area Sec BCMS 53-55; Kenya 55-62; R Hartshorne *Derby* 62-68; V Stapenhill w Cauldwell 68-72; C Weston-super-Mare Ch Ch *B & W* 72-74; R Spaxton w Charlynch 74-80; rtd 80. *12 Ewart Road, Weston-super-Mare BS22 8NU* Tel (01934) 412170

BROWN, Bill Charles Balfour. b 44. Linc Th Coll 87. **d** 89 **p** 90. C Moulsham St Luke *Chelmsf* 89-91; C Prittlewell 91-94; V Worksop St Paul *S'well* from 95. *St Paul's Vicarage, Cavendish Road, Worksop S80 2ST* Tel (01909) 473289

BROWN, Bod. *See* BROWN, Andrew

BROWN, Brian Ernest. b 36. ALA64. Oak Hill NSM Course 82. **d** 85 **p** 86. NSM Wallington H Trin *S'wark* 85-91; C 91-00; rtd 00; Perm to Offic *Nor* from 00. *6 Burnside, Necton, Swaffham PE37 8ER* Tel (01760) 721292

BROWN, Charles Henry. b 48. Tulane Univ (USA) BA70 Ch Coll Cam BA75 MA81. Westcott Ho Cam. **d** 00 **p** 01. C Boston *Linc* 00-03; Lect 03-05; Lic Preacher from 05. *The Vicarage, Church Lane, Swineshead, Boston PE20 3JA* Tel (01205) 820271

BROWN, Charles Hubert. b 21. S'wark Ord Course 82. **d** 84 **p** 85. NSM Shortlands *Roch* 84-86; P-in-c Seal St Lawr 86-90; P-in-c Underriver 86-90; rtd 90; Perm to Offic *Roch* from 90. *Barton Croft, 11 St Mary's Close, Sevenoaks TN15 8NH* Tel (01732) 882893

BROWN, Mrs Christine Lilian. b 54. Ex Univ BA75 Newc Univ MA93. NEOC 01. **d** 04 **p** 05. NSM Ponteland *Newc* from 04. *4 Woodlands, Ponteland, Newcastle upon Tyne NE20 9EU* Tel (01661) 824196

BROWN, Christopher. b 38. AKC62 CQSW68. St Boniface Warminster 62. **d** 63 **p** 64. C Crofton Park St Hilda w St Cypr *S'wark* 63-64; C S Beddington St Mich 64-67; C Herne Hill St Paul 67-68; Lic to Offic *S'wark* 68-72; *Lich* 72-74; *Birm* 74-76; *Worc* 76-79; *Ox* 79-86; Perm to Offic *Chelmsf* from 86; Dir and Chief Exec NSPCC 89-95. *7 Baronia Croft, Colchester CO4 9EE* Tel (01206) 852904 E-mail chribrow@yahoo.co.uk

BROWN, Christopher. b 43. Linc Th Coll 79. **d** 81 **p** 82. C Stafford St Jo *Lich* 81-85; C Stafford St Jo and Tixall w Ingestre 85; V Alton w Bradley-le-Moors and Oakamoor w Cotton 85-94; Chapl Asst Nottm City Hosp NHS Trust 94-05; Sen Chapl from 05. *The Chaplain's Office, Nottingham City Hospital, Hucknall Road, Nottingham NG5 1PB* Tel 0115-969 1169 *or* 962 7616

BROWN, Christopher Charles. b 58. Univ of Wales (Cardiff) LLB79 Solicitor 82. Westcott Ho Cam 87. **d** 90 **p** 91. C Taunton St Mary *B & W* 90-94; R Timsbury and Priston 94-00; P-in-c Urmston *Man* from 00; AD Stretford from 05. *St Clement's Vicarage, 24 Stretford Road, Urmston, Manchester M41 9JZ* Tel 0161-748 3972 E-mail christopher@cbrown30.fsnet.co.uk

BROWN, Christopher David. b 49. Birm Univ CertEd71 BEd72 Univ of Wales (Cardiff) Dip Practical Th 94. St Mich Coll Llan 93. **d** 94 **p** 95. C Swansea St Thos and Kilvey *S & B* 94-96; C Swansea St Jas 96-98; St Helena 99-01; Asst Chapl and Hd of RS Epsom Coll from 01. *Epsom College, Epsom KT17 4JQ* Tel (01372) 821004 E-mail kristophdavid@hotmail.com

BROWN, Christopher Edgar Newall. b 31. Oak Hill Th Coll 51. **d** 55 **p** 56. C Surbiton Hill Ch Ch *S'wark* 55-57; C Gipsy Hill Ch Ch 57-61; V Plumstead All SS 61-70; V Sissinghurst *Cant* 70-73; P-in-c Frittenden 72-73; V Sissinghurst w Frittenden 73-76; Perm to Offic *S & M* 84-91 and from 96; Bp's Dom Chapl 91-95; rtd 96. *21 College Green, Castletown, Isle of Man IM9 1BE* Tel (01624) 822364

BROWN, Canon Christopher Francis. b 44. Sarum Th Coll 68. **d** 71 **p** 72. C High Wycombe *Ox* 71-74; C Sherborne w Castleton and Lillington *Sarum* 74-77; P-in-c Wylye, Fisherton Delamere and the Langfords 77-79; R Yarnbury 79-82; R Portland All SS w St Pet 82-88; RD Weymouth 85-88; R Trowbridge St Jas from 88; Chapl Trowbridge and Distr Hosp 88-95; RD Bradford 94-01; Can and Preb Sarum Cathl from 98. *The Rectory, Union Street, Trowbridge BA14 8RU* Tel (01225) 755121 E-mail stjames@trowbridge1.fsnet.co.uk

BROWN, Christopher Howard. b 49. **d** 03 **p** 04. OLM Uttoxeter Area *Lich* from 03. *21 Carter Street, Uttoxeter ST14 8EY* Tel (01889) 567492

BROWN, Christopher James. b 50. Open Univ BA92. Trin Coll Bris DipHE93. **d** 93 **p** 94. C Skelmersdale St Paul *Liv* 93-97; Chapl Asst Salford R Hosps NHS Trust from 97. *Chaplaincy Department, Stott Lane, Salford, Manchester M6 8HD* Tel 0161-787 5167 *or* 789 7373

BROWN, Clive Lindsey. b 33. Southn Univ BA55. Oak Hill Th Coll 57. **d** 59 **p** 60. C Becontree St Mary *Chelmsf* 59-62; Australia from 62; rtd 98. *80 Bower Street, Manly, NSW, Australia 2095* Tel (0061) (2) 9977 2546

BROWN, Prof Colin. b 32. Liv Univ BA53 Lon Univ BD58 Nottm Univ MA61 DD94 Bris Univ PhD70. Tyndale Hall Bris 55. **d** 58 **p** 59. C Chilwell *S'well* 58-61; Lect Tyndale Hall Bris 61-78; Vice Prin 67-70; Dean Studies 70-71; USA from 78; Prof Systematic Th Fuller Th Sem California from 78; Assoc R Altadena St Mark from 80; Assoc Dean Adv Th Studies 88-97; rtd 00. *1024 Beverly Way, Altadena, CA 91001-2516, USA* Tel (001) (626) 798 7180 E-mail colbrn@fuller.edu

BROWN, David Andrew. b 72. York Univ BA93. Wycliffe Hall Ox BTh04. **d** 04 **p** 05. C Rugby St Matt *Cov* from 04. *14 York Street, Rugby CV21 2BL* Tel (01788) 330448 *or* 330443
E-mail david.brown@stmatthews.org.uk

BROWN, David Charles Girdlestone. b 42. Solicitor 67. S'wark Ord Course 87. **d** 90 **p** 91. NSM Milford *Guildf* 90-92; NSM Haslemere 92-00; NSM Haslemere and Grayswood 00-01; Perm to Offic *Chich* from 02. *Southdowns, Red House Court, Rogate, Petersfield GU31 5HE* Tel (01730) 821192 Fax 821937
E-mail dcgbrown@dircon.co.uk

BROWN, David Frederick. b 38. Illinois Univ BA60. Seabury-Western Th Sem MDiv67. **d** 67 **p** 67. USA 67-78; Hon C Battersea Ch Ch and St Steph *S'wark* 78-83; Sen Chapl R Marsden NHS Trust from 83; Perm to Offic *S'wark* 83-00. *The Royal Marsden NHS Trust, Fulham Road, London SW3 6JJ* Tel (020) 7352 8171 ext 2818 *or* 7351 6082 Fax 7351 2191

BROWN, David Lloyd. b 44. TCD BTh90. **d** 86 **p** 87. C Cregagh *D & D* 86-91; Bp's C Knocknagoney from 91. *The Aslan Centre, 13A Knocknagoney Road, Belfast BT4 2NR* Tel and fax (028) 9076 0420 E-mail aslan@tesco.net

BROWN, David Victor Arthur. b 44. Em Coll Cam BA66 MA70 DCG69 Em Coll Cam CertEd Bp Grosseteste Coll 74 Dip Counselling 98. Linc Th Coll 72. **d** 74 **p** 75. C Bourne *Linc* 74-77; Chapl St Steph Coll Broadstairs 77-79; Chapl Asst N Gen Hosp Sheff 81-84; C Sheff St Cuth *Sheff* 81-84; Chapl Ridge Lea Hosp Lanc 84-92; Chapl Lanc Moor Hosp 84-92; Chapl Lanc Priority Services NHS Trust 92-98; Chapl Lanc R Infirmary 87-92; Chapl Lanc Acute Hosps NHS Trust 92-98; Chapl Morecambe Bay Hosps NHS Trust from 98; Chapl Morecambe Bay Primary Care Trust from 98. *Chaplain's Office, Royal Lancaster Infirmary, Ashton Road, Lancaster LA1 4RP* Tel (01524) 583955, 762800 *or* 400308 E-mail dlgbrown@aol.com

BROWN, Canon David William. b 48. Edin Univ MA70 Oriel Coll Ox BA72 Clare Coll Cam PhD76. Westcott Ho Cam 75. **d** 76 **p** 77. Chapl, Fell and Tutor Oriel Coll Ox 76-90; Van Mildert Prof Div Dur Univ from 90; Can Res Dur Cathl *Dur* from 90. *14 The College, Durham DH1 3EQ* Tel 0191-386 4657

BROWN, Dennis Cockburn. b 27. Hatf Coll Dur BSc48 K Coll Dur PhD54. WMMTC 79. **d** 82 **p** 83. C Bilton *Cov* 82-84; V Wolford w Burmington 84-96; R Cherington w Stourton 84-96; R Barcheston 84-96; rtd 96; Perm to Offic *Cov* from 96; Dioc Rtd Clergy and Widows Officer from 98. *13 Cleveland Court, 41 Kenilworth Road, Leamington Spa CV32 6JA* Tel (01926) 423771

BROWN, Derek. *See* BROWN, Canon John Derek

BROWN, Canon Derek Frederick. b 27. St Fran Coll Brisbane ThL52. **d** 52 **p** 54. Australia 52-58; C Merstham and Gatton *S'wark* 59-61; R Deptford St Paul 61-69; Chapl RNR from 62; R Havant *Portsm* 69-00; rtd 00; Perm to Offic *Portsm* from 00. *Christ Church Bungalow, Rowan Road, Havant PO9 2XA* Tel (023) 9248 1730

BROWN, Derek Henry Pridgeon. b 46. Cam Coll of Art and Tech BA67 Leeds Univ PGCE71. St Steph Ho Ox 90. **d** 92 **p** 93. C Finchley St Mary *Lon* 92-95; C W Hampstead St Jas 95-99; V Eyres Monsell *Leic* from 99. *St Hugh's Vicarage, 51 Pasley Road, Leicester LE2 9BU* Tel 0116-278 6288
E-mail dbrown@leicester.anglican.org

BROWN, Canon Donald Fryer. b 31. St Jo Coll Dur BA56 DipTh61. Cranmer Hall Dur 60. **d** 61 **p** 62. Min Can Bradf Cathl *Bradf* 61-64; C Bingley All SS 64-66; V Low Moor H Trin 66-97; Hon Can Bradf Cathl 85-97; RD Bowling and Horton 87-95; rtd 97; Perm to Offic *Bradf* from 98. *3 Northfield Gardens, Wibsey, Bradford BD6 1LQ* Tel (01274) 671869

BROWN, Mrs Doreen Marion. b 39. Cam Univ CertEd67 Dip Counselling 85. N Ord Course 85. **d** 88 **p** 94. Par Dn Axminster, Chardstock, Combe Pyne and Rousdon *Ex* 88-92; Ind Chapl *Linc* 92-98; TV Brumby from 98. *The Vicarage, 36 Dorchester Road, Scunthorpe DN17 1YG* Tel (01724) 847671
E-mail doreen.bn@lineone.net

BROWN, Douglas Adrian Spencer. b 29. Univ of W Aus BA50 MA71 K Coll Lon MTh90. St Mich Th Coll Crafers 50. **d** 53 **p** 54. Australia 53-60, 66-88 and from 02; SSM 54-00; Chapl and Tutor St Mich Th Coll Crafers 54-60; Tutor and Chapl Kelham Th Coll 60-66; Chapl Univ of W Aus 66-71; P-in-c Canberra St Alb 71-75; Warden St Mich Th Coll Crafers 75-82; P-in-c Adelaide St Jo 78-82; Academic Dean Adelaide Coll of Div 79-81; President 88; Visiting Scholar Union Th Sem NY 82; Perm to Offic *Lon* 88-90; Chapl Bucharest w Sofia *Eur* 90-91; Dir Angl Cen Rome 91-95; Chapl Palermo w Taormina *Eur* 95-96; Lect Newton Th Coll Papua New Guinea 97; Perm to Offic *Dur* 97-00 and *S'wark* 99-00; Dir Nor Cathl Inst and Hon PV Nor Cathl *Nor* 00-02. *75/6 Manning Terrace, South Perth, W Australia 6151*

BROWN, Ms Elizabeth Ann. b 43. **d** 00 **p** 01. OLM W Bromwich All SS *Lich* from 01. *307 Beaconview Road, West Bromwich B71 3PS* Tel 0121-588 7530

BROWN, Miss Elizabeth Charlotte (Beth). b 54. Bris Univ BSc76 PGCE77. Trin Coll Bris DipHE95. **d** 95 **p** 96. C Taunton Lyngford *B & W* 95-99; TV Bath Twerton-on-Avon from 99. *20A Bellotts Road, Bath BA2 3RT* Tel (01225) 443940

BROWN, Eric. b 28. Leeds Univ BA98. NW Ord Course 73. **d** 76 **p** 77. NSM S Kirkby *Wakef* 76-83; NSM Knottingley 83-94; NSM Kellington w Whitley 89-94; Sub Chapl HM Pris Lindholme 90-94; Perm to Offic from 94. *Wynberg, Barnsley Road, South Kirby, Pontefract WF9 3BG* Tel (01977) 643683

BROWN, Canon Ernest George. b 23. Em Coll Cam BA51 MA56. Oak Hill Th Coll 52. **d** 53 **p** 54. C Darfield *Sheff* 53-56; V Ardsley 56-66; V Thurnby w Stoughton *Leic* 67-90; RD Gartree II 78-90; Hon Can Leic Cathl 82-90; rtd 90; Perm to Offic *Leic* from 90. *16 Holbeck Drive, Broughton Astley, Leicester LE9 6UR* Tel (01455) 285458
E-mail ebrown@leicester.anglican.org

BROWN, Ernest Harry. b 32. St Mich Coll Llan. **d** 59 **p** 60. C Swansea St Pet *S & B* 59-62; C Gowerton w Waunarlwydd 62-68; CF (TA) 62-68; Chapl to the Deaf *S & B* 68-98; rtd 98. *Montreaux, 30 Lon Cedwyn, Sketty, Swansea SA2 0TH* Tel (01792) 207628

BROWN, Frank Seymour. b 10. S'wark Ord Course 62 St Aug Coll Cant 65. **d** 65 **p** 66. C Bexleyheath Ch Ch *Roch* 65-70; R Cratfield w Heveningham and Ubbeston *St E* 70-76; rtd 76; Perm to Offic *St E* 76-86 and *St Alb* from 86; P-in-c Ixworth and Ixworth Thorpe *St E* 78; P-in-c Euston w Barnham and Fakenham 80. *3 Windsor Gardens, Bedford MK40 3BU* Tel (01234) 210999

BROWN, Geoffrey Alan. b 34. **d** 99 **p** 00. OLM Bury St Edmunds St Mary *St E* from 99. *Rodenkirchen, 12 Sharp Road, Bury St Edmunds IP33 2NB* Tel (01284) 769725
E-mail geoffrey@fish.co.uk

BROWN, Geoffrey Gilbert. b 38. Dur Univ BA62 DipEd63 Fitzw Coll Cam BA69 MA73 FBIS. Westcott Ho Cam 67. **d** 70 **p** 71. C Gosforth All SS *Newc* 70-73; Chapl Dauntsey's Sch Devizes 73-76; Chapl St Paul's Colleg Sch Hamilton NZ 76-78; V Barrow St Aid *Carl* 79-86; Chapl Ch Coll Canterbury NZ 86-90; C Digswell and Panshanger *St Alb* 91-93; rtd 03; Chapl E Herts Hospice Care from 94. *32 Uplands, Welwyn Garden City AL8 7EW* Tel (01707) 327565

BROWN, Canon Geoffrey Harold. b 30. Trin Hall Cam BA54 MA58. Cuddesdon Coll 54. **d** 56 **p** 57. C Plaistow St Andr *Chelmsf* 56-60; C Birm St Pet *Birm* 60-63; R Birm St Geo 63-73; TR Gt Grimsby St Mary and St Jas *Linc* 73-85; Can and Preb Linc Cathl 79-85; V St Martin-in-the-Fields *Lon* 85-95; rtd 95; Perm to Offic *Worc* from 95. *8 Worcester Close, Hagley, Stourbridge DY9 0NP* Tel (01562) 886921
E-mail browngb@surefish.co.uk

BROWN, Graeme Eric. b 37. St Jo Coll Auckland LTh61. **d** 62 **p** 63. New Zealand 62-74 and from 75; C Nor Heartsease St Fran *Nor* 74-75. *104 Masters Avenue, Hamilton 2001, New Zealand* Tel (0064) (7) 856 0074 E-mail gebrown@wave.co.nz

BROWN, Graham Stanley. b 51. Sarum & Wells Th Coll 82. **d** 84 **p** 85. C Crediton and Shobrooke *Ex* 84-87; Chapl RAF 87-93 and from 99; R Elgin w Lossiemouth *Mor* 93-98; R Castle Douglas *Glas* 98-99; Perm to Offic *Lon* from 02. *Chaplaincy Services (RAF), HQ, Personnel and Training Command, RAF Innsworth, Gloucester GL3 1EZ* Tel (01452) 712612 ext 5164 *or* (020) 8833 8535 Fax (01452) 510828

BROWN, Harold. b 53. SEN74 SRN77 RMN82 RCN CCT84. Edin Th Coll 86. **d** 88 **p** 89. C Upperby St Jo *Carl* 88-90; C Carl H Trin and St Barn 90-91; C Workington St Mich 91-93; TV 93-95; P-in-c Crosscrake and Preston Patrick 95-03. *Address temp unknown* E-mail harry@hbrown77.freeserve.co.uk

BROWN, Mrs Harriet Nina. b 37. Open Univ BA77 Lon Univ CertEd57. Gilmore Course 80 Oak Hill Th Coll 83. **dss** 83 **d** 87 **p** 94. Greenstead *Chelmsf* 83-90; Par Dn 87-90; Asst Chapl R Hosp Sch Holbrook 90-93; Perm to Offic *Chelmsf* from 93 and *St E* 93-96; P-in-c Gt and Lt Blakenham w Baylham and Nettlestead *St E* 96-01; rtd 01. *22 Gainsborough Road, Colchester CO3 4QN* Tel (01206) 523072

BROWN, Henry. b 27. Lon Univ BSc51 BSc52. NW Ord Course 72. **d** 75 **p** 76. NSM Padiham *Blackb* 75-80; V Warton St Paul 80-90; rtd 90; Perm to Offic *Blackb* from 90. *18 Windsor Gardens, Garstang, Preston PR3 1EG* Tel (01995) 606592

BROWN, Ian. b 48. N Ord Course 89. **d** 91 **p** 92. C Burnage St Marg *Man* 91-94; P-in-c Halliwell St Paul 94-98; TV Halliwell 98-01; Chapl Bolton Hosps NHS Trust 94-01; TV Melbury *Sarum* 01-03; TR from 03. *The Vicarage, Corscombe, Dorchester DT2 0NU* Tel (01935) 891247

BROWN, Ian Barry. b 53. Ruskin Coll Ox 75 St Cuth Soc Dur BA80 PGCE81. Westmr Past Foundn Cert Counselling 90 Sarum & Wells Th Coll 84. **d** 86 **p** 87. C Winchmore Hill St Paul *Lon* 86-89; Hon Chapl Chase Farm Hosp Enfield 86-88; Hon Chapl Harley Street Area Hosps 88-90; Hon Chapl RAM 89; C St Marylebone w H Trin 89-94; rtd 94; Perm to Offic *Lon* from 96; Hon Chapl Regent's Coll from 96; Gov 97-99. *Flat 4, 9 Welbeck Street, London W1G 9YB* Tel (020) 7935 6687

BROWN, Ian David. b 53. UEA BA76. Wycliffe Hall Ox BA80. **d** 81 **p** 82. C Southsea St Jude *Portsm* 81-84; Chapl Coll of SS Paul and Mary Cheltenham 84-89; V Lt Heath *St Alb* from 89. *The Vicarage, Thornton Road, Potters Bar EN6 1JJ* Tel (01707) 654414 E-mail cclh@cclh.freeserve.co.uk *or* browns@fish.co.uk

BROWN, Ivan James. b 24. Cant Sch of Min 84. **d** 86 **p** 87. NSM St Nicholas at Wade w Sarre and Chislet w Hoath *Cant* 86-94; rtd 94; Perm to Offic *Cant* 94-02. *Horseshoe Cottage, Elms Ride, West Wittering, Chichester PO20 8LP* Tel (01243) 514896

BROWN, Canon Jack Robin. b 44. Linc Th Coll 67. **d** 69 **p** 70. C Canning Town St Cedd *Chelmsf* 69-72; C Dunstable *St Alb* 72-78; V Luton St Andr 78-85; V Kempston Transfiguration 85-00; RD Bedford 92-98; Hon Can St Alb from 97; Dioc Officer for Local Min from 00. *St John's House, High Street, Markyate, St Albans AL3 8PD* Tel and fax (01582) 842150
E-mail lmo@stalbans.anglican.org

BROWN, James Douglas. b 52. S'wark Ord Course 93. **d** 96 **p** 97. NSM Shooters Hill Ch Ch *S'wark* 96-01; P-in-c E Malling *Roch* from 02; P-in-c Wateringbury and Teston from 02. *The Vicarage, 2 The Grange, East Malling, West Malling ME19 6AH* Tel (01732) 843282 Fax as telephone
E-mail jamesbrown2@tinyworld.co.uk

BROWN, Canon James Michael. b 49. Newc Univ Aus BA90. St Jo Coll Morpeth ThL78. **d** 77 **p** 78. Australia 77-81 and 83-02; C Gosford 77-79; C Cessnock 79-81; C Eyres Monsell *Leic* 81-83; C Entrance 83; P-in-c Windale 83-88; R Morpeth 88-97; Acting Registrar Wangaratta 98-00; Dom Chapl to Bp Wangaratta and Dir Min Tr 98-02; Adn The Hume 99-02; V Knowle H Nativity *Bris* from 02; P-in-c Easton All Hallows 02-03; Hon Can Wangaratta from 02. *Holy Nativity Vicarage, 41 Lilymead Avenue, Bristol BS4 2BY* Tel and fax 0117-977 4260
E-mail frjames@holynativity.org.uk

BROWN, Canon James Philip. b 30. Ex Coll Ox BA54 MA55. Westcott Ho Cam 54. **d** 56 **p** 57. C Hemel Hempstead *St Alb* 56-63; V Hellesdon *Nor* 63-71; P-in-c Kirkley w Lowestoft St Jo 71-79; TV Lowestoft St Marg 76-78; TV Lowestoft and Kirkley 79-81; P-in-c Northleach w Hampnett and Farmington *Glouc* 81-95; RD Northleach 83-92; P-in-c Cold Aston w Notgrove and Turkdean 86-95; Hon Can Glouc Cathl 91-95; rtd 95; Perm to Offic *Ex* from 95. *The Priest's House, 1 St Scholastica's Abbey, Teignmouth TQ14 8FF* Tel (01626) 773623

BROWN, Jane Madeline. *See* SHARP, Mrs Jane Madeline

BROWN, Mrs Jennifer. b 70. Geo Mason Univ Virginia BSc91. St Alb and Ox Min Course 02. **d**05. C Ox St Clem *Ox* from 05. *12A Morrell Avenue., Oxford OX4 1NE*
E-mail curate@jenbrown.org.uk

BROWN, Jenny. b 78. St Martin's Coll Lanc BA99. Oak Hill Th Coll BA03. **d** 03 **p** 04. C Hyde St Geo *Ches* from 03. *121 Dowson Road, Hyde SK14 5HJ* Tel 0161-367 9353

BROWN, Mrs Joan Leslie. b 31. SS Hild & Bede Coll Dur CertEd55. Oak Hill Th Coll BA85. **dss** 85 **d** 87 **p** 94. Fulwood *Sheff* 85-88; Par Dn 87-88; TD Netherthorpe 88-93; NSM Ellesmere St Pet 93-99; rtd 99; Perm to Offic *Sheff* from 00. *2 Kingston Street, Sheffield S4 7SU* Tel 0114-243 3534

BROWN, John. b 64. Kent Univ BA86. Westcott Ho Cam 87. **d** 90 **p** 91. C Lt Ilford St Mich *Chelmsf* 90-94; C E Ham w Upton Park St Alb 94; TV 94-01; P-in-c Gt Ilford St Luke from 01. *St Luke's Vicarage, Baxter Road, Ilford IG1 2HN* Tel (020) 8478 1248

BROWN, Canon John Bruce. b 42. Nottm Univ BA64 MA68. Cuddesdon Coll 64. **d** 66 **p** 67. C Warwick St Nic *Cov* 66-71; C Bp's Hatfield *St Alb* 71-78; V Watford St Mich from 78; RD Watford 94-99; Hon Can St Alb from 02. *St Michael's Vicarage, 5 Mildred Avenue, Watford WD18 7DY* Tel (01923) 232460
E-mail john.brown420@ntlworld.com

BROWN, Canon John Derek. b 41. Linc Th Coll 71. **d** 73 **p** 74. C Rotherham *Sheff* 73-76; P-in-c W Pinchbeck *Linc* 76-78; V Surfleet 76-82; R Boultham 83-94; RD Christianity 85-92; P-in-c Epworth and Wroot 94-97; R Epworth Gp from 97; RD Is of Axholme 96-05; Can and Preb Linc Cathl from 88. *St Andrew's Rectory, Belton Road, Epworth, Doncaster DN9 1JL* Tel (01427) 872471 E-mail derek@cbepworth.freeserve.co.uk

BROWN, John Dixon. b 28. Pemb Coll Cam BA52. Oak Hill Th Coll 52. **d** 54 **p** 55. C Worthing St Geo *Chich* 54-57; C S w N Bersted 57-63; V W Hampnett 63-91; rtd 91; Perm to Offic *Chich* from 91. *3 Manor Way, Elmer, Bognor Regis PO22 6LA* Tel (01243) 583449

BROWN, Canon John Duncan. b 43. St Pet Coll Ox BA64 BA66 MA68 Lon Univ BSc. Wycliffe Hall Ox 65. **d** 67 **p** 68. C Kingston upon Hull H Trin *York* 67-69; C St Leonards St Leon *Chich* 69-72; Hon C Norbiton *S'wark* 72-75; C Kirkcaldy *St And* 75-78; Prec and Chapl Chelmsf Cathl *Chelmsf* 78-86; P-in-c Kelvedon Hatch 86-92; P-in-c Navestock 86-92; P-in-c Fryerning w Margaretting 92-99; Bp's ACORA Officer 92-99; Hon Can Chelmsf Cathl from 93; rtd 99. *556 Galleywood Road, Chelmsford CM2 8BX* Tel (01245) 358185

✠**BROWN, The Rt Revd John Edward.** b 30. Lon Univ BD68. Kelham Th Coll 50. **d** 55 **p** 56 **c** 87. Chapl St Geo Colleg Ch Jerusalem 55-57; C Reading St Mary V *Ox* 57-60; Sudan 60-64; V Stewkley *Ox* 64-69; V Maidenhead St Luke 69-73; V Bracknell 73-77; RD Sonning 73-77; Adn Berks 78-87; Warden Ascot Priory 80-87; Bp Cyprus and the Gulf 87-95; rtd 95; Hon Asst Bp Linc from 95; RD Grimsby and Cleethorpes 03-04. *130 Oxford Street, Cleethorpes DN35 0BP* Tel (01472) 698840
E-mail bishopjohn@btinternet.com

BROWN, Canon John Roger. b 37. AKC60. **d** 61 **p** 62. C New Eltham All SS *S'wark* 61-64; C Bexhill St Pet *Chich* 64-68; V Eastbourne St Eliz 68-75; V E Grinstead St Swithun 75-97; Chapl Qu Victoria Hosp NHS Trust East Grinstead 75-97; Perm to Offic *Chich* 97-99; RD E Grinstead 82-93; Can and Preb Chich Cathl 89-98; TV Worth 00-04; rtd 05. *120 Malthouse Road, Crawley RH10 6BH* Tel (01293) 520454
E-mail jroger.brown@tesco.net

BROWN, John William Etheridge. b 13. St Pet Hall Ox BA35 MA39. Wycliffe Hall Ox 35. **d** 37 **p** 38. C Stratford New Town St Paul *Chelmsf* 37-40; C Rawtenstall St Mary *Man* 40-42; C Thame *Ox* 42-45; OCF 43-45; V St Keverne *Truro* 45-51; V Hoo All Hallows w Stoke *Roch* 51-55; V Crich *Derby* 55-61; V Leusden *Ex* 61-79; V Widecombe in the Moor 61-79; P-in-c Holne 70-74; P-in-c Princetown 74-79; RD Moreton 74-80; Asst Chapl HM Pris Dartmoor 75-82; V Widecombe, Leusden and Princetown etc *Ex* 79-82; rtd 82; Lic to Offic *Ex* from 82. *8 Emmetts Park, Ashburton, Newton Abbot TQ13 7DB* Tel (01364) 653072

BROWN, Jonathan. b 60. Univ Coll Dur BA83 MA85 Ex Univ CertEd86. Ripon Coll Cuddesdon 86 Ch Div Sch of the Pacific (USA) 88. **d** 89 **p** 90. C Esher *Guildf* 89-97; TV Crawley *Chich* 97-04; Chapl St Cath Hospice 97-04; V Earlsfield St Andr *S'wark* from 04. *St Andrew's Vicarage, St Andrew's Court, Waynflete Street, London SW18 3QE* Tel (020) 8946 4214
E-mail j.brown77@virgin.net

BROWN, Jonathan Alexander Iain. b 75. SS Hild & Bede Coll Dur BSc96 Leeds Univ BA99. Coll of Resurr Mirfield 97. **d** 00 **p** 01. C Accrington Ch the King *Blackb* 00-03; P-in-c Cynog Honddu *S & B* 03-05; Min Can Brecon Cathl 03-05. *Address temp unknown*

BROWN, Julian Keith. b 57. Magd Coll Ox BA79. St Jo Coll Nottm 82. **d** 85 **p** 86. C Kidlington w Hampton Poyle *Ox* 85-88; C Luton All SS w St Pet *St Alb* 88-91; Hon Asst Chapl Versailles *Eur* from 94. *Address temp unknown* E-mail jube@bigfoot.com

BROWN, Canon Kathleen Margaret. b 40. QUB BD BTh. **d** 88 **p** 90. C Carrickfergus *Conn* 88-92; I Belfast St Paul w St Barn from 92; Can Belf Cathl from 00. *The Rectory, 50 Sunningdale Park, Belfast BT14 6RW* Tel (028) 9071 5413

BROWN, Kenneth Arthur Charles. b 27. ACP65. LNSM course 85. **d** 84 **p** 85. OLM Ingoldsby *Linc* 84-97. *11 Ingoldsby Road, Lenton, Grantham NG33 4HB* Tel (01476) 85763

BROWN, Kenneth Roger. b 48. St Chad's Coll Dur BA69 DipTh72. Liturg Inst Trier Dip Liturg Studies 73. **d** 73 **p** 74. C Patchway *Bris* 73-77; C Fishponds St Jo 77-79; Chapl RAF 79-95; Chapl HM Pris Pentonville 95-96; Chapl HM Pris Wellingborough 96-98; Perm to Offic *B & W* 99-00; P-in-c Crook Peak from 00. *The Rectory, Sparrow Hill Way, Weare, Axbridge BS26 2LE* Tel (01934) 733140
E-mail rev_ken_brown@hotmail.com

BROWN (née BOWERS), Lady (Denise Frances). b 50. City Univ BSc72. St Alb and Ox Min Course 99. **d** 02 **p** 03. NSM Beedon and Peasemore w W Ilsley and Farnborough *Ox* from 02; NSM Brightwalton w Catmore, Leckhampstead etc from 05. *Bridleway Cottage, Stanmore, Beedon, Newbury RG20 8SR* Tel and fax (01635) 281825 Mobile 07901-914975

BROWN, Miss Louise Margaret. b 53. MBE05. Trin Coll Bris 80. **dss** 83 **d** 87 **p** 94. Woodley St Jo the Ev *Ox* 84-87; Par Dn Woodley 87-92; Asst Chapl Reading Hosps 92-94; C Shinfield 93-94; P-in-c Dedworth from 94; P-in-c Clewer St Andr from 04. *The Vicarage, 3 Pierson Road, Windsor SL4 5RJ* Tel (01753) 864591

BROWN, Malcolm Arthur. b 54. Oriel Coll Ox BA76 MA82 Man Univ PhD00. Westcott Ho Cam 77. **d** 79 **p** 80. C Riverhead w Dunton Green *Roch* 79-83; TV Southampton (City Cen) *Win* 83-91; Assoc Dir Wm Temple Foundn 91-93; Exec Sec 93-00; Hon C Heaton Moor *Man* 95-00; Prin EAMTC *Ely* from 00. *Chadkirk, School Lane, Impington, Cambridge CB4 9NS* Tel (01223) 741030 *or* 741026 E-mail mbrown@eamtc.cam.ac.uk *or* secretary@eamtc.cam.ac.uk

BROWN (née PATTERSON), Mrs Marjorie Jean. b 54. Wooster Coll USA BA76 K Coll Lon MA04. S Dios Minl Tr Scheme 92. **d** 95 **p** 96. C Poplar *Lon* 95-99; P-in-c Stamford Hill St Thos 99-02; V from 02; Dean of Women's Min Stepney Area from 02. *The Vicarage, 37 Clapton Common, London E5 9AA* Tel (020) 8806 1463 Fax 07092-189271 E-mail mjb@nworb.com

BROWN, Canon Mark Edward. b 61. Southn Univ BSc83 Cam Univ PGCE84 Brunel Univ MTh98. Trin Coll Bris BA88. **d** 88 **p** 89. C Egham *Guildf* 88-92; C Northwood Em *Lon* 92-96; Assoc V 96-02; Bp's Officer for Evang 96-02; Can Missr *S'well* from 02; Hon Can S'well Minster from 02. *5 Vicar's Court, Southwell NG25 0HP* Tel (01636) 817298 E-mail revmbrown@aol.com *or* mark.brown@southwell.anglican.org

BROWN, Michael Brian. b 56. Trin Coll Bris BA97 Coll of Resurr Mirfield 98. **d** 99 **p** 00. C Trowbridge St Jas *Sarum* 99-02; C Bruton and Distr *B & W* from 02. *The Parsonage, Gold Hill, Batcombe, Shepton Mallet BA4 6HF* Tel (01749) 850671 E-mail fr.michaelbrown@btopenworld.com

BROWN, Murray. *See* BROWN, Phillip Murray

BROWN, Nicholas Francis Palgrave. b 23. Fitzw Ho Cam BA51 MA54. **d** 53 **p** 54. C Warwick St Nic *Cov* 53-55; C Birm St Paul *Birm* 55-60; V Temple Balsall 60-66; Gen Sec Ind Chr Fellowship 66-76; V St Kath Cree *Lon* 66-71; Chapl and Dir of Studies Holland Ho Cropthorne 76-80; P-in-c Cropthorne w Charlton *Worc* 76-88; Adult Educn Officer 80-85; rtd 88; Perm to Offic *Worc* from 88. *Bredon View, Rear of 40 Bridge Street, Pershore WR10 1AT* Tel (01386) 556816

BROWN, Nina. *See* BROWN, Mrs Harriet Nina

BROWN, Canon Norman Charles Harry. b 27. Univ of Wales BSc46. St Mich Coll Llan 48. **d** 50 **p** 51. C Canton St Jo *Llan* 50-57; C Llanishen and Lisvane 58-63; V Miskin 63-97; RD Aberdare 82-97; Can Llan Cathl 86-97; rtd 97. *33 Bron y Deri, Mountain Ash CF45 4LL* Tel (01443) 476631

BROWN, Canon Norman John. b 34. Thames Poly MA90. Ripon Hall Ox 72. **d** 74 **p** 75. C High Wycombe *Ox* 74-78; V Tilehurst St Cath 78-82; V Boyne Hill 82-04; Chapl Windsor and Maidenhead Coll 87-89; Hon Can Ch Ch *Ox* 03-04; rtd 04. *Chantry House, Radley Road, Abingdon OX14 3SL* E-mail revbrown@waitrose.com

BROWN, Patricia Valerie. b 37. CertEd58. STETS BTh95. **d** 98 **p** 99. NSM Tadley St Pet *Win* 98-02; NSM Tadley S and Silchester from 02. *58 Bowmonts Road, Tadley, Basingstoke RG26 3SB* Tel 0118-981 6109

BROWN, Paul. *See* BROWN, Anthony Paul

BROWN, Paul David Christopher. b 50. Lon Univ LLB71. EMMTC 81. **d** 84 **p** 85. NSM Wollaton *S'well* from 84. *32 Benington Drive, Wollaton, Nottingham NG8 2TF* Tel 0115-928 4493

BROWN, Penelope Jane. b 57. St Steph Ho Ox DipMin94. **d** 96 **p** 97. C Croydon St Jo *S'wark* 96-99; V Croydon St Matt from 99. *The Vicarage, 7 Brownlow Road, Croydon CR0 5JT* Tel (020) 8688 5055 E-mail revpennyb@st-matthews.fsnet.co.uk

BROWN, Peter. b 38. Leeds Univ BSc62 PhD65. Nashotah Ho 85. **d** 87 **p** 88. USA 87-89; C Sprowston *Nor* 89-90; C Sprowston w Beeston 90-92; P-in-c W Winch w Setchey and N Runcton 92-98; P-in-c Middleton w E Winch 96-98; P-in-c Nor St Andr 98-99; P-in-c Nor St Geo Colegate 98-99; Chapl Norfolk and Nor Health Care NHS Trust 98-99; rtd 00; Perm to Offic *Leic* from 00. *41 Main Street, Cosby, Leicester LE9 1UW* Tel 0116-286 6184 E-mail peterbrown@tesco.net

BROWN, Canon Peter. b 47. RMN69. Kelham Th Coll 69. **d** 74 **p** 75. C Hendon *Dur* 74-80; C Byker St Ant *Newc* 80-90; C Brandon and Ushaw Moor *Dur* from 90; Hon Can Dur Cathl from 01. *The Clergy House, Sawmill Lane, Brandon, Durham DH7 8NS* Tel 0191-378 0845

BROWN, Peter. b 53. St Chad's Coll Dur BA75. Sarum & Wells Th Coll 75. **d** 77 **p** 78. C Tunstall Ch Ch *Lich* 77-79; C Tunstall 79-80; C Willenhall H Trin 80-83; V Weston Rhyn 83-88; Australia 88-90; R Hubberston *St D* 90-01; V Chilvers Coton w Astley *Cov* from 01. *Chilvers Coton Vicarage, Coventry Road, Nuneaton CV11 4NJ* Tel (024) 7638 3010

BROWN, Peter Russell. b 43. Oak Hill Th Coll. **d** 71 **p** 72. C Gt Faringdon w Lt Coxwell *Ox* 71-73; C Reading Greyfriars 73-74; V Forty Hill Jes Ch *Lon* 74-81; V Laleham from 81. *The Vicarage, The Broadway, Laleham, Staines TW18 1SB* Tel (01784) 457330 *or* 441160 E-mail office@laleham-parish-church.freeserve.co.uk

BROWN, Peter Thomas. b 43. Leic Univ BSc64. WEMTC 00. **d** 03 **p** 04. OLM Prestbury and All SS *Glouc* from 03. *32 Gallops Lane, Prestbury, Cheltenham GL52 5SD* Tel (01242) 529774 E-mail pete.brown@tinyworld.co.uk

BROWN, Philip. *See* BROWN, Canon James Philip

BROWN, Philip Anthony. b 54. Oak Hill Th Coll BA91. **d** 91 **p** 92. C Rock Ferry *Ches* 91-95; V Hattersley 95-98; V Harold Hill St Geo *Chelmsf* from 98. *St George's Vicarage, Chippenham Road, Romford RM3 8HX* Tel (01708) 343415 E-mail filb@fish.co.uk

BROWN, Canon Philip Roy. b 41. St Steph Ho Ox 78. **d** 80 **p** 81. C Highters Heath *Birm* 80-83; P-in-c Washwood Heath 83-87; V Tysoe w Oxhill and Whatcote *Cov* 87-93; R Harbury and Ladbroke from 93; RD Southam 95-97 and 99-02; Hon Can Cov Cathl from 00. *The Rectory, 2 Vicarage Lane, Harbury, Leamington Spa CV33 9HA* Tel (01926) 612377 Fax 614668 E-mail canon.roybrown@lineone.net

BROWN, Phillip Murray. b 59. Keele Univ BSc80. Trin Coll Bris DipTh86 ADPS87. **d** 87 **p** 88. C Greasbrough *Sheff* 87-91; Ind Chapl 87-93; V Thorne 91-99; V Norton Lees St Paul from 99. *St Paul's Vicarage, 6 Angerford Avenue, Sheffield S8 9BG* Tel 0114-255 1945 E-mail murray-b@fish.co.uk

BROWN, Raymond Isaac Harry. b 14. Kelham Th Coll 36. **d** 42 **p** 43. C Romford St Andr *Chelmsf* 42-48; Metrop Area Sec UMCA 48-52; V Wellingborough St Mary *Pet* 52-66; V Tintinhull *B & W* 66-74; RD Martock 70-75; Lesotho from 76; rtd 79. *Convent of the Holy Name, PO Box 43, Leribe 300, Lesotho* Tel (00266) 2240 0249

BROWN, Raymond John. b 49. Ox Univ BEd71. Wycliffe Hall Ox 72. **d** 75 **p** 76. C Barking St Marg w St Patr *Chelmsf* 75-78; C Walton H Trin *Ox* 78-82; V Enfield St Mich *Lon* 82-91; Chapl St Mich Hosp Enfield 82-91; R Springfield All SS *Chelmsf* from 91. *The Rectory, 4 Old School Field, Chelmsford CM1 7HU* Tel (01245) 356720

BROWN, Richard George. b 38. Dur Univ BSc63. Wells Th Coll 63. **d** 65 **p** 66. C Norton St Mary *Dur* 65-69; C N Gosforth *Newc* 69-71; Chapl Wells Cathl Sch 71-81; P-in-c Dulverton and Brushford *B & W* 81-83; R 83-86; Chapl Millfield Jun Sch Somerset 86-89; Chapl Brighton Coll 89-92; Chapl Benenden Sch 92-94; Perm to Offic *Chich* 94-97; P-in-c Poynings w Edburton, Newtimber and Pyecombe 97-04; rtd 04. *4 Standean Farm Cottages, Standean Farm, Brighton BN1 8ZA* Tel (01273) 501469 E-mail richardgb@ukgateway.net

BROWN, Richard Lessey. b 27. Keble Coll Ox BA51 MA55. Qu Coll Birm 51. **d** 53 **p** 54. C York St Lawr w St Nic *York* 53-55; C Fulford 55-57; V Fridaythorpe w Fimber and Thixendale 57-61; V York St Luke 61-75; V Barlby 75-92; rtd 92; Perm to Offic *York* from 92. *1 Kings Court, King Street, Cottingham HU16 5RW* Tel (01482) 845299

BROWN, Robert. b 47. Man Univ BSc72 Open Univ BA86 Dur Univ MA87. NEOC 95. **d** 98 **p** 99. C Yarm *York* 98-01; V Ormesby from 01. *The Vicarage, 54 Church Lane, Ormesby, Middlesbrough TS7 9AU* Tel (01642) 314445

BROWN, Robert Peter Cameron. b 63. K Coll Lon BSc84 Imp Coll Lon MSc87. Lon Bible Coll BA97 Cranmer Hall Dur 01. **d** 03 **p** 04. C Upper Weardale *Dur* from 03. *14 Burnfoot, St Johns Chapel, Bishop Auckland DL13 1QH* Tel (01388) 537996

BROWN, Robin. *See* BROWN, Canon Jack Robin

BROWN, Robin. b 38. Leeds Univ BA60 MPhil69. Qu Coll Birm 89. **d** 91 **p** 92. C Far Headingley St Chad *Ripon* 91-94; V Hawksworth Wood 94-00; rtd 00. *Dale Edge, 2A Harbour View, Bedale DL8 2DQ* Tel and fax (01677) 425483 E-mail robin.stel@virgin.net

BROWN, Roger. *See* BROWN, Canon John Roger

BROWN, Roger George. b 37. CA Tr Coll SEITE 92. **d** 95 **p** 96. C Maidstone St Martin *Cant* 95-97; C Oakham, Hambleton, Egleton, Braunston and Brooke *Pet* 97-04; Chapl Leics and Rutland Healthcare NHS Trust 97-04; rtd 04; Asst Chapl Kettering Gen Hosp NHS Trust from 04. *5 Valley Walk, Kettering NN16 0LY* Tel (01536) 524954

BROWN, Roger Lee. b 42. Univ of Wales (Lamp) BA63 Univ Coll Lon MA73. Wycliffe Hall Ox 66. **d** 68 **p** 69. C Dinas w Penygraig *Llan* 68-70; C Bargoed and Deri w Brithdir 70-72; TV Glyncorrwg w Afan Vale and Cymmer Afan 72-74; R 74-79; V Tongwynlais 79-93; R Welshpool w Castle Caereinion *St As* from 93; RD Pool from 01. *The Vicarage, Church Street, Welshpool SY21 7DP* Tel (01938) 553164

✠**BROWN, The Rt Revd Ronald.** b 26. St Jo Coll Dur BA50 DipTh52. **d** 52 **p** 53 **c** 74. C Chorley St Laur *Blackb* 52-56; V Whittle-le-Woods 56-61; V Halliwell St Thos *Man* 61-69; R Ashton St Mich 69-74; RD Ashton-under-Lyne 69-74; Suff Bp Birkenhead *Ches* 74-92; rtd 92; Perm to Offic *Ches* 92-00. *Hurst Cottage, Moss Lane, Burscough, Ormskirk L40 4BA* Tel (01704) 897314

BROWN, Canon Rosalind. b 53. Lon Univ BA74. Yale Div Sch MDiv97. **d** 97 **p** 97. V Canonsburg St Thos USA 97-99; Vice-Prin OLM Scheme *Sarum* 99-05; Tutor STETS 99-05; Can Res Dur Cathl *Dur* from 05. *3 The College, Durham DH1 3EQ* Tel 0191-384 2415 Fax 386 4267 E-mail rosalind.brown@durham.anglican.org

BROWN, Mrs Rosémia. b 53. Ripon Coll Cuddesdon 97. **d** 99 **p** 00. C Shoreditch St Leon and Hoxton St Jo *Lon* 99-00; C Shoreditch St Leon w St Mich 00-02; TV Hackney 02-03; V Clapton St Jas from 03. *134 Rushmore Road, London E5 0EY* Tel (020) 8985 1750

BROWN, Roy. *See* BROWN, Canon Philip Roy

BROWN, Sandra Ann. b 51. **d** 04 **p** 05. OLM Linc St Geo Swallowbeck *Linc* from 04. *10 Station Road, North Hykeham, Lincoln LN6 9AQ* Tel (01522) 870065 E-mail sandra.brown77@ntlworld.com

BROWN, Simon John. b 66. Birm Univ BSc87 PGCE88 Nottm Univ MA93. St Jo Coll Nottm 90. **d** 93 **p** 94. C Holbrooks *Cov* 93-97; C Leamington Priors All SS 97-00; C Leamington Spa H Trin and Old Milverton 97-00; P-in-c Woolavington w Cossington and Bawdrip *B & W* 00-01; V 01-05. *St Nicholas Cottage, Newtown, West Pennard, Glastonbury BA6 8NL* E-mail simon@vicar.plus.com

BROWN, Canon Simon Nicolas Danton. b 37. Clare Coll Cam BA61 MA65. S'wark Ord Course 61 Linc Th Coll 63. **d** 64 **p** 65. C Lambeth St Mary the Less *S'wark* 64-66; Chapl and Warden LMH Settlement 66-72; P-in-c Southampton St Mary w H Trin *Win* 72-73; TV Southampton (City Cen) 73-79; R Gt Brickhill w Bow Brickhill and Lt Brickhill *Ox* 79-84; TR Burnham w Dropmore, Hitcham and Taplow 84-04; RD Burnham and Slough 87-02; Hon Can Ch Ch 94-04; Dioc Consultant for Deanery Development 97-04; Sen Exec Asst to Bp Buckingham 02-04; rtd 04; Perm to Offic *St E* from 04. *Seagulls, Pin Mill Road, Chelmondiston, Ipswich IP9 1JN* Tel (01473) 780051 E-mail simon.brown1@orange.net

BROWN, Stanley George. b 19. Bps' Coll Cheshunt 66. **d** 67 **p** 68. C Shrub End *Chelmsf* 67-71; R Dengie w Asheldham 71-89; V Tillingham 71-89; RD Maldon and Dengie 82-89; rtd 89; Perm to Offic *Ely* from 90. *134 Lynn Road, Ely CB6 1DE* Tel (01353) 662888

BROWN, Stephen Charles. b 60. Leeds Univ BA83 BA89 Reading Univ PGCE89. Coll of Resurr Mirfield 87. **d** 90 **p** 91. C Whitkirk *Ripon* 90-93; Asst Youth Chapl 92-95; C Chapel Allerton 93-95; R Stanningley St Thos 95-01; V Laneside *Blackb* from 01; Hon Chapl ATC from 03. *St Peter's Vicarage, Helmshore Road, Haslingden, Rossendale BB4 4BG* Tel (01706) 213838 E-mail highlow@tesco.net

BROWN, Stephen James. b 44. Bradf Univ BSc69. Westcott Ho Cam 71. **d** 72 **p** 73. C Seaton Hirst *Newc* 72-75; C Marton-in-Cleveland *York* 75-77; Dioc Youth Adv *Dur* 77-82; V Thorner *Ripon* 82-92; Chapl Yorkshire TV from 89; Dioc Officer for Local Min 90-01; P-in-c Ripley from 92. *The Rectory, Ripley, Harrogate HG3 3AY* Tel (01423) 770147 Fax 772217 Mobile 07929-606217 E-mail stephen.brown@ppcmail.co.uk

BROWN, Susan Gertrude. b 48. Univ of Wales (Swansea) BA71 Roehampton Inst PGCE72. St Mich Coll Llan 98. **d** 02 **p** 03. NSM Gelligaer *Llan* 02-04; NSM Eglwysilan from 04. *27 Tenby Court, Hendredenny, Caerphilly CF83 2UE* Tel (029) 2086 2736 E-mail suebrown27_uk@yahoo.com

✠**BROWN, The Rt Revd Thomas John.** b 43. St Jo Coll Auckland LTh72 STh76 San Francisco Th Sem DMin84. **d** 72 **p** 73 **c** 91. New Zealand 72-74 and from 76; C Christchurch St Alban 72-74; C Leic St Jas *Leic* 74-76; V Upper Clutha 76-79; V Roslyn 79-85; V Lower Hutt St Jas 85-91; Adn Belmont 87-91; Asst Bp Wellington 91-97; Bp Wellington from 98. *20 Eccleston Hill, Wellington 6001, New Zealand* Tel (0064) (4) 473 2183 *or* 472 1057 Fax 499 1360

BROWN, Mrs Verity Joy. b 68. Qu Mary Coll Lon BA89. Ripon Coll Cuddesdon BTh93. **d** 93 **p** 94. C Barnard Castle w Whorlton *Dur* 93-95; C Bensham 95-97; Perm to Offic from 97. *75 Eamont Gardens, Hartlepool TS26 9JE* Tel (01429) 423186

BROWN, Victor Charles. b 31. S'wark Ord Course 67. **d** 71 **p** 72. C Pinhoe *Ex* 71-73; C Egg Buckland 73-74; C Oakdale St Geo *Sarum* 74-77; R Old Trafford St Hilda *Man* 77-83; R Chigwell Row *Chelmsf* 83-92; R Fenny Bentley, Kniveton, Thorpe and Tissington *Derby* 92-96; rtd 96; Perm to Offic *Sarum* from 96. *377 Sopwith Crescent, Wimborne BH21 1XJ* Tel (01202) 841274

BROWN, Wallace. b 44. Oak Hill Th Coll 77. **d** 79 **p** 80. C Oadby *Leic* 79-85; V Quinton Road W St Boniface *Birm* 85-03; Hon Can Birm Cathl 01-03; TR Ipsley *Worc* from 03. *The Rectory, Icknield Street, Ipsley, Redditch B98 0AN* Tel (01527) 516351 Fax 501215 E-mail rector_ipsley@btinternet.com

BROWN, William Martyn. b 14. Pemb Coll Cam BA36 MA47. Nor Ord Course 76. **d** 76 **p** 77. NSM Thornage w Brinton w Hunworth and Stody *Nor* 76-77; NSM Field Dalling w Saxlingham 77-84; RD Holt 84-88; NSM Gunthorpe w Bale w Field Dalling, Saxlingham etc 84-88; Perm to Offic from 88. *Lodge Cottage, Field Dalling, Holt NR25 7AS* Tel (01328) 830403

BROWNBRIDGE, Bernard Alan. b 19. NW Ord Course 74. **d** 77 **p** 78. NSM Huntington *York* 77-80; V Sand Hutton 80-86; rtd 87; Hon C Birdsall w Langton *York* 87-92; Perm to Offic from 92. *2 Duncombe Close, Malton YO17 7YY* Tel (01653) 697626

BROWNE, Arnold Samuel. b 52. St Jo Coll Ox BA73 MA77 SS Coll Cam PhD87 Surrey Univ MSc89 MBPsS92. Westcott Ho Cam 76. **d** 78 **p** 79. C Esher *Guildf* 78-81; C Worplesdon 81-86; Chapl R Holloway and Bedf New Coll 86-92; Fell and Dean of Chpl Trin Coll Cam from 92. *Trinity College, Cambridge CB2 1TQ* Tel (01223) 338563 Fax 338564 E-mail asb32@cam.ac.uk

BROWNE, Aubrey Robert Caulfeild. b 31. Moore Th Coll Sydney 54. **d** 55 **p** 56. Australia 55-71; Producer of Relig Radio Progr USPG 72-84; Hon C S Kensington St Steph *Lon* 78-88; Hd of Area Sec Dept USPG 84-87; P-in-c Nunhead St Antony *S'wark* 88-90; V Nunhead St Antony w St Silas 90-96; rtd 97; Australia from 97. *15 Caroma Avenue, Kyeemagh, NSW, Australia 2216*

BROWNE, Miss Christine Mary. b 53. Nottm Univ BEd75. EMMTC 87. **d** 90 **p** 94. C Bulwell St Mary *S'well* 90-95; TV Hucknall Torkard 95-00; Dep Chapl HM Pris Nor 00-01; Chapl HM YOI Swinfen Hall 01-03; Perm to Offic *Derby* 03-05; P-in-c Dudley St Aug Holly Hall *Worc* from 05; Chapl Merry Hill Shopping Cen from 05. *St Augustine's Vicarage, 1 Hallchurch Road, Dudley DY2 0TG* Tel (01384) 261026

BROWNE, George William. b 42. CITC 99. **d** 02 **p** 03. NSM Kildallan w Newtowngore and Corrawallen *K, E & A* from 02. *Rose Villa, Corgar, Ballinamore, Co Leitrim, Irish Republic* Tel (00353) (71) 964 4415 Mobile 86-351 7700 E-mail gwbrowne@oceanfree.net

BROWNE, Herman Beseah. b 65. Cuttington Univ Coll BTh86 K Coll Lon BD90 AKC90 Heythrop Coll Lon PhD94. **d** 87 **p** 97. C N Lambeth *S'wark* 90-91; Tutor Simon of Cyrene Th Inst 90-96; Abp's Asst Sec for Ecum and Angl Affairs *Cant* 96-01; Abp's Officer for Angl Communion 01-05; Perm to Offic *S'wark* 96-04; Hon Prov Can Cant Cathl *Cant* 01-04; Liberia from 05. *Trinity Cathedral, PO Box 10-0277, 1000 Monrovia 10, Liberia*

BROWNE, Ian Cameron. b 51. St Cath Coll Ox BA74 MA78 Fitzw Coll Cam BA76 MA80. Ridley Hall Cam 74. **d** 77 **p** 78. C Cheltenham Ch Ch *Glouc* 77-80; Hon C Shrewsbury St Chad *Lich* 80-83; Asst Chapl Shrewsbury Sch 80-83; Chapl Bedford Sch 83-96; Sen Chapl Oundle Sch from 97. *The School, Oundle, Peterborough PE8 4EN* Tel (01832) 273372 *or* 273541

BROWNE, Leonard Joseph. b 58. St Cath Coll Cam BA81 MA84. Trin Coll Bris 87. **d** 89 **p** 90. C Reading Greyfriars *Ox* 89-92; V Cambridge St Barn *Ely* 92-00; Sen Chapl and Hd Div Dean Close Sch Cheltenham 00-03; Hd Master Dean Close Prep Sch from 03. *Dean Close Preparatory School, Lansdown Road, Cheltenham GL51 6QS* Tel (01242) 512217 E-mail hmdcps@deanclose.org.uk *or* lj-browne@supanet.com

BROWNE, Peter Clifford. b 59. Bris Univ BA80 SRN82. Ripon Coll Cuddesdon 88. **d** 90 **p** 91. C Southgate Ch Ch *Lon* 90-92; NSM Kemp Town St Mary *Chich* 93-95; Chapl United Bris Healthcare NHS Trust 96-98; NSM Southmead *Bris* 98-02; Chapl HM Pris Preston from 02. *HM Prison, 2 Ribbleton Lane, Preston PR1 5AB* Tel (01772) 257734

BROWNE, Robert. *See* BROWNE, Aubrey Robert Caulfeild

BROWNING, Derek. *See* BROWNING, Robert Derek

BROWNING, Edward Barrington Lee (Barry). b 42. St Pet Coll Saltley TCert65. Ripon Coll Cuddesdon 90. **d** 92 **p** 93. C Falmouth K Chas *Truro* 92-96; R Roche and Withiel 96-01; P-in-c Manaccan w St Anthony-in-Meneage and St Martin from 01; P-in-c Cury and Gunwalloe w Mawgan from 01. *The Rectory, Mawgan, Helston TR12 6AD* Tel (01326) 221696

BROWNING, Mrs Jacqueline Ann. b 44. Sarum Th Coll 93. **d** 96 **p** 97. NSM New Alresford w Ovington and Itchen Stoke *Win* from 96; Past Asst Win Cathl from 02. *1 Paddock Way, Alresford SO24 9PN* Tel (01962) 734372 *or* 857237 E-mail jackie.browning@winchester-cathedral.org.uk

BROWNING, Canon John William. b 36. Keele Univ BA61. Ripon Hall Ox 61. **d** 63 **p** 64. C Baswich *Lich* 63-66; Chapl Monyhull Hosp Birm 67-72; Chapl Wharncliffe Hosp Sheff 72-78; Chapl Middlewood Hosp Sheff 72-94; Hon Can Sheff Cathl *Sheff* 84-97; Chapl Sheff Mental Health Unit 85-94; Chapl Community Health Sheff NHS Trust 94-97; Chapl Sheff (South) Mental Health Centres 94-97; rtd 97; Perm to Offic *Sheff* from 97. *1 Anvil Close, Sheffield S6 5JN* Tel 0114-234 3740 E-mail johnpatbrowning@hotmail.com

BROWNING, Julian. b 51. St Jo Coll Cam BA72 MA76. Ripon Coll Cuddesdon 77. **d** 80 **p** 81. C Notting Hill *Lon* 80-81; C W Brompton St Mary w St Pet 81-84; Perm to Offic 84-91; NSM Paddington St Sav from 99. *82 Ashworth Mansions, Grantully Road, London W9 1LN* Tel (020) 7286 6034

BROWNING, Kevin John. b 56. Ridley Hall Cam CTM96. **d** 98 **p** 99. C Northampton Em *Pet* 98-01; P-in-c Hardwick *Ely* from 01. *The Rectory, Main Street, Hardwick, Cambridge CB3 7QS* Tel (01954) 210695

BROWNING, Canon Richard Geoffrey Claude. b 25. Selw Coll Cam BA50 MA55. Lon Coll of Div BD53 ALCD53. **d** 53 **p** 54. C Walthamstow St Mary *Chelmsf* 53-56; V E Ham St Paul 56-65; V Old Hill H Trin *Worc* 65-91; Hon Can Worc Cathl 77-91; rtd 91; Perm to Offic *Ban* from 91. *Llwyn Rhug, Ffordd Dewi Sant, Nefyn, Pwllheli LL53 6EG* Tel (01758) 720834

BROWNING, Robert Derek. b 42. Guildf Dioc Min Course 98. **d** 01 **p** 02. OLM Lightwater *Guildf* from 01. *16 Guildford Road, Lightwater GU18 5SN* Tel (01276) 474345 E-mail derekandcarol@btinternet.com

BROWNING, Thomas Clive. b 35. Lon Univ DipTh65 BD67. Wycliffe Hall Ox 63. **d** 67 **p** 68. C Ipswich St Jo *St E* 67-69; Chapl Scargill Ho 69-70; C Downend *Bris* 70-73; C Hagley *Worc* 73-76; Asst Master Bay Ho Sch Gosport 77-00; rtd 00; Perm to Offic *Win* from 03. *30 Norfolk Road, Shirley, Southampton SO15 5AS* Tel (023) 8036 6891

BROWNING, Canon Wilfrid Robert Francis. b 18. Ch Ch Ox BA40 MA44 BD49. Cuddesdon Coll 40. **d** 41 **p** 42. C Towcester w Easton Neston *Pet* 41-44; C Woburn Square Ch Ch *Lon* 44-46; Chapl St Deiniol's Lib Hawarden 46-48; Chapl Heswall Nautical Sch 46-48; C-in-c Hove St Rich CD *Chich* 48-51; Lect Cuddesdon Coll 51-59; R Gt Haseley *Ox* 51-59; Ed *Bulletin Anglican* 55-60; Warden Whalley Abbey 59-63; Can Res Blackb Cathl *Blackb* 59-65; Dir Post-Ord Tr 62-65; Lect Cuddesdon Coll 65-70; Can Res Ch Ch *Ox* 65-87; Hon Can 87-89; Dir Post-Ord Tr 65-85; Dir of Ords 65-85; Dir Ox NSM Course 72-89; rtd 87; Tutor Westmr Coll Ox 93-99. *42 Alexandra Road, Oxford OX2 0DB* Tel (01865) 723464

BROWNLESS, Brian Paish. b 25. TD72. Keble Coll Ox BA50 MA50. Wells Th Coll 50. **d** 52 **p** 53. C Man St Aid *Man* 52-54; C Chorlton-cum-Hardy St Clem 54-56; C Swinton St Pet 56-58; V Elton St Steph 58-66; CF (TA) 60-66; Area Sec USPG *Lich* 66-77; Lic to Offic *Lich* 66-77; CF (TA - R of O) 66-72; R Yoxall *Lich* 77-82; V S Ramsey St Paul *S & M* 82-87; rtd 87; Perm to Offic *Heref* from 87. *10 Caple Avenue, Kings Caple, Hereford HR1 4UL* Tel (01432) 840246

BROWNLESS, Philip Paul Stanley. b 19. Selw Coll Cam BA41 MA45. Ridley Hall Cam 46. **d** 47 **p** 48. C Prittlewell St Mary *Chelmsf* 47-50; Min Prittlewell St Mary CD 50-54; Chapl & Hd Master Lambrook Sch Bracknell 54-71; V Heckfield cum Mattingley *Win* 71-74; V Heckfield w Mattingley and Rotherwick 74-84; RD Odiham 83-84; rtd 85; Perm to Offic *Chich* from 85. *The Hornpipe, Oak Meadow, Birdham, Chichester PO20 7BH* Tel (01243) 512177

BROWNLIE, Miss Caroline Heddon. b 47. Suffolk Poly CQSW75. St Jo Coll Nottm DPS80 Qu Coll Birm IDC81. **d** 87 **p** 94. Asst Chapl Fairfield Hosp Hitchin 87-91; NSM Ashwell w Hinxworth and Newnham *St Alb* 92-98; Chapl HM Rem Cen Low Newton 99-01. *10 Beaumonds, Upper Marlborough Road, St Albans AL1 3NL* Tel (01727) 865148

BROWNRIDGE, Canon Allan John Michael. b 32. Chan Sch Truro 80. **d** 82 **p** 83. C St Keverne *Truro* 82-86; P-in-c Werrington, St Giles in the Heath and Virginstow 86-92; R Boyton, N Tamerton, Werrington etc 92-02; RD Trigg Major 94-04; Hon Can Truro Cathl 98-04; rtd 02; Perm to Offic *Truro* from 04. *6 Cotehele View, Calstock PL18 9RJ* Tel (01822) 832006

BROWNRIDGE, David Leonard Robert. b 76. Univ of Wales (Lamp) BA97. Trin Coll Bris 98. **d** 00 **p** 01. C Henfynyw w Aberaeron and Llanddewi Aberarth *St D* 00-04; V Laugharne w Llansadwrnen and Llandawke from 04. *The Vicarage, King Street, Laugharne, Carmarthen SA33 4QE* Tel (01994) 427218 E-mail davidbecky@brownridge97.freeserve.co.uk

BROWNRIGG, Canon Ronald Allen. b 19. Em Coll Cam BA47 MA50 FRSA91. Westcott Ho Cam 47. **d** 49 **p** 50. C Beverley Minster *York* 49-51; Dean Jerusalem 51-54; C Stanmore *Win* 54-60; R Bletchingley *S'wark* 60-74; V Petersham 74-85; Hon Can S'wark Cathl 78-85; Consultant Inter-Ch Travel from 83; rtd 85. *Marlborough Lodge, 13 Marlborough Lane, Bath BA1 2NQ* Tel (01225) 334831

BROWNSELL, Preb John Kenneth. b 48. Hertf Coll Ox BA69 BA72 MA89. Cuddesdon Coll 70. **d** 73 **p** 74. C Notting Hill All SS w St Columb *Lon* 73-74; C Notting Hill 74-76; TV 76-82; V Notting Hill All SS w St Columb from 82; AD Kensington 84-92; Preb St Paul's Cathl from 92; Dir of Ords from 95. *The Vicarage, Powis Gardens, London W11 1JG* Tel (020) 7727 5919 E-mail johbrwnsll@aol.com

BROXTON, Alan. b 40. UMIST BSc72 CEng MICE79 MIStructE77. LNSM course 93. **d** 96 **p** 97. OLM Rhodes *Man* from 96. *241 Heywood Old Road, Middleton, Manchester M24 4QR* Tel 0161-643 6319 Fax as telephone

BRUCE, David Ian. b 47. Univ of Wales (Cardiff) DipTh73. St Mich Coll Llan 70. **d** 73 **p** 74. C Bordesley St Benedict *Birm* 73-74; C Llanishen and Lisvane *Llan* 74-81; V Canley *Cov* 81-90; V Longford 90-97; rtd 97; Perm to Offic *Cov* from 97. *122 Hugh Road, Coventry CV3 1AF* Tel (024) 7644 5789

BRUCE, Francis Bernard. b 30. Trin Coll Ox BA52 MA56. Westcott Ho Cam 52. **d** 54 **p** 55. C Bury St Mary *Man* 54-59; C Sherborne w Castleton and Lillington *Sarum* 59-61; R Croston *Blackb* 61-86; V Bibury w Winson and Barnsley *Glouc* 86-95; rtd 95; Perm to Offic *Glouc* from 95. *6 Gloucester Street, Cirencester GL7 2DG* Tel (01285) 641954

BRUCE, James Hamilton. b 57. Dur Univ BSc78 Newc Univ MSc79 St Andr Univ PhD99. Trin Coll Bris DipTh84. **d** 84 **p** 85. C Walmley *Birm* 84-86; Perm to Offic *Carl* 87-95; W Cumbria Sch Worker N Schs Chr Union 87-93; Nat Development Officer Wales Scripture Union 93-94; Chapl Turi St Andr Kenya 95-96; NSM St Andrews St Andr *St And* 96-99; R Penicuik *Edin* from 99; R W Linton from 99. *23 Broomhill Road, Penicuik EH26 9EE* E-mail rector@stjamespenicuik.freeserve.co.uk

BRUCE, John. b 26. **d** 50 **p** 51. Canada 50-62; V Broughton Moor *Carl* 63-66; V Carl St Herbert w St Steph 66-74; P-in-c Kendal St Geo 74-76; V 76-83; V Coundon *Dur* 83-86; rtd 86; Perm to Offic *Carl* 86-93. *9 Penton Close, Carlisle CA3 0PX*

BRUCE, John Cyril. b 41. EMMTC 95. **d** 98 **p** 99. NSM Spalding *Linc* 98-05; P-in-c Grantham, Manthorpe from 05. *The Vicarage, 114 Manthorpe Road, Grantham NG31 8DL* Tel (01476) 567047 Mobile 07947-156933 E-mail john@john-bruce.co.uk

BRUCE, Ms Kathrine Sarah. b 68. Leeds Univ BA89 St Jo Coll Dur BA01 Trin & All SS Coll Leeds PGCE91. Cranmer Hall Dur 98. **d** 01 **p** 02. C Ripon H Trin *Ripon* 01-04; Chapl Trevelyan Coll *Dur* from 04; Chapl Van Mildert Coll from 04; NSM Dur St Oswald from 04. *6 Trevelyan College Houses, Trevelyan College, Durham DH1 3LW* Tel 0191-334 7053

BRUCE, Leslie Barton. b 23. Liv Univ MB, ChB48. **d** 71 **p** 72. NSM Wavertree H Trin *Liv* from 71. *3 Childwall Park Avenue, Liverpool L16 0JE* Tel 0151-722 7664

BRUECK, Ms Jutta. b 61. LSE MSc89 Heythrop Coll Lon MA92 Fitzw Coll Cam BA96. Westcott Ho Cam 94. **d** 97 **p** 98. C Is of Dogs Ch Ch and St Jo w St Luke *Lon* 97-01; Chapl Guildhall Sch of Music and Drama from 01. *Christ Church Vicarage, Manchester Road, London E14 3BN* Tel (020) 7538 1766

BRUNDLE, Michael Roy. b 52. Qu Coll Birm. **d** 84 **p** 85. C Swindon New Town *Bris* 84-88; TV Halifax *Wakef* 88-92; Chapl HM YOI Feltham 92-94; C Notting Dale St Clem w St Mark and St Jas *Lon* 94-95; V Swanley St Mary *Roch* from 95. *St Mary's Vicarage, London Road, Swanley BR8 7AQ* Tel (01322) 662201 Fax as telephone E-mail frbrundle@ntlworld.com

BRUNN, Stephen. b 67. Ridley Hall Cam. **d** 05. C Chertsey, Lyne and Longcross *Guildf* from 05. *The Manse, 25 Abbey Road, Chertsey KT16 8AL* Tel (01932) 429937 E-mail steve.brunn@ntlworld.com

BRUNNING, Canon David George. b 32. St D Coll Lamp BA53. St Mich Coll Llan 53. **d** 55 **p** 56. C Llantwit Major and St Donat's *Llan* 55-59; C Usk and Monkswood w Glascoed Chpl and Gwehelog *Mon* 59-62; V Abercarn 62-71; V Pontnewydd 71-89; RD Pontypool 89-97; R Panteg 90-98; Can St Woolos Cathl from 94; rtd 98; Lic to Offic *Mon* from 98. *6 Spitzkop, Llantwit Major CF61 1RD* Tel (01446) 792124

BRUNNING, Neil. b 29. NW Ord Course 73. **d** 76 **p** 77. C Cheadle Hulme All SS *Ches* 76-79; V 79-88; V Glentworth *Linc* 88-93; P-in-c Hemswell w Harpswell 88-93; V Glentworth Gp 93-94; rtd 94; Perm to Offic *Linc* from 94. *11 Cavendish Drive, Lea, Gainsborough DN21 5HU* Tel and fax (01427) 617938 E-mail neilbrun@aol.com

BRUNO, Canon Allan David. b 34. AKC59. St Boniface Warminster 59. **d** 60 **p** 61. C Darlington H Trin *Dur* 60-64; S Africa 64-65 and 76-80; Rhodesia 65-70; Overseas Chapl Scottish Episc Ch 70-75; C Edin Old St Paul *Edin* 75-76; Namibia 80-86; Dean Windhoek 81-86; R Falkirk *Edin* 86-95; Hon Can Kinkizi from 95; Bp's Dom Chapl *Bradf* 96-99; Bp's Past Asst 99-01; rtd 01; Lic to Offic *Bradf* from 01. *Pump Cottage, 2 Waterside Potteries, Burton in Lonsdale, Carnforth LA6 3LL* Tel (01524) 261616 E-mail david@bruno81.freeserve.co.uk

BRUNSKILL, Mrs Sheila Kathryn. *See* BANYARD, Canon Sheila Kathryn

BRUNSWICK, Canon Robert John. b 38. TD86. St Aid Birkenhead 60. **d** 63 **p** 64. C Neston *Ches* 63-66; CF (TA - R of O) from 65; C Warrington St Paul *Liv* 66-68; V Liv St Paul Stoneycroft 68-78; V Southport St Luke 78-87; R Croston *Blackb* 87-01; R Croston and Bretherton from 01; Chapl Bp Rawstorne Sch Preston from 88; Hon Can Koforidua from 94. *St Michael's Rectory, 19 Westhead Road, Croston, Leyland PR26 9RQ* Tel (01772) 600877

BRUNT, Prof Peter William. b 36. CVO01 OBE94. Liv Univ MB59 MD67 Lon Univ FRCP74 FRCPEd. Ab Dioc Tr Course. **d** 96 **p** 97. NSM Bieldside *Ab* from 96. *17 Kingshill Road, Aberdeen AB15 5JY* Tel (01224) 314204 Fax 316899 E-mail brunt.aberdeen@btinternet.com

BRUNT, Mrs Philippa Ann. b 53. Leeds Univ BA74 Leeds and Carnegie Coll PGCE75. WEMTC 95. **d** 98 **p** 99. C Cinderford St Steph w Littledean *Glouc* 98-01; V Parkend and Viney Hill from 01. *The Vicarage, Lower Road, Yorkley, Lydney GL15 4TN* Tel (01594) 562828 E-mail pabrunt@ukonline.co.uk

BRUNYEE, Miss Hilary. b 46. Linc Th Coll 76. **dss** 81 **d** 87 **p** 94. Longsight St Jo w St Cypr *Man* 81-87; Par Dn Peel 87-94; TV 94-99; TV Walkden and Lt Hulton 99-00; rtd 00. *38 Holly Avenue, Worsley, Manchester M28 3DW* Tel 0161-790 7761

BRUSH, Canon Sally. b 47. Lon Univ BD75 Univ of Wales MPhil96. Trin Coll Bris 73. **dss** 76 **d** 80 **p** 97. Flint *St As* 76-83; C 80-83; C Cefn 83-87; C St As and Tremeirchion 83-87; Chapl St As Cathl 83-87; Dn-in-c Cerrigydrudion w Llanfihangel Glyn Myfyr etc 87-97; V from 97; RD Edeirnion 98-04; Hon Can St As Cathl from 01. *The Rectory, 1 Tyddyn Terrace, Cerrigydrudion, Corwen LL21 9NT* Tel (01490) 420313

BRUTTON, Robert Springett. b 14. Trin Coll Cam BA34 MA55. Cuddesdon Coll 54. **d** 55 **p** 56. C Wendover *Ox* 55-57; V Radley 57-65; V Sonning 65-74; rtd 74; Perm to Offic *Sarum* from 75. *7 North Street, Langton Matravers, Swanage BH19 3HL* Tel (01929) 425681

BRYAN, Canon Cecil William. b 43. TCD BA66 MA73. CITC 66. **d** 68 **p** 69. C Dublin Zion Ch *D & G* 68-72; Chapl RAF 72-75; Dioc Info Officer *D & G* 75-90; I Castleknock w Mulhuddart, Clonsilla etc 75-89; Chapl K Hosp Sch Dub 89-99; I Tullow *D & G* from 99; Can Ch Ch Cathl Dublin from 03. *Tullow Rectory, Brighton Road, Carrickmines, Dublin 18, Irish Republic* Tel (00353) (1) 289 3154 E-mail cbryan@iol.ie

BRYAN, Christopher Paul. b 75. Univ Coll Ox BA96 St Jo Coll Dur BA99. Cranmer Hall Dur 97. **d** 00 **p** 01. C Old Swinford Stourbridge *Worc* 00-04; P-in-c Lechlade *Glouc* from 04. *The Vicarage, Sherbourne Street, Lechlade GL7 3AH* Tel (01367) 252262 E-mail cpbryan@hotmail.com

BRYAN, David John. b 56. Liv Univ BSc77 Hull Univ BTh85 Qu Coll Ox DPhil89. Ox Min Course 89. **d** 90 **p** 91. C Abingdon *Ox* 90-93; Tutor Qu Coll Birm 93-01; Dean of Studies 95-01; R Haughton le Skerne *Dur* from 01. *The Rectory, Haughton Green, Darlington DL1 2DD* Tel (01325) 468142
E-mail david@portessbryan.freeserve.co.uk

BRYAN, Judith Claire. *See* STEPHENSON, Judith Claire

BRYAN, Leslie Harold. b 48. Div Hostel Dub 70. **d** 73 **p** 74. C Cork St Fin Barre's Cathl *C, C & R* 73-75; I Templebreedy w Tracton and Nohoval 75-79; CF 79-03; Chapl Guards Chpl Lon 96-01. *Address temp unknown*

BRYAN, Michael John Christopher. b 35. Wadh Coll Ox BA58 BTh59 MA63 Ex Univ PhD83. Ripon Hall Ox 59. **d** 60 **p** 61. C Reigate St Mark *S'wark* 60-64; Tutor Sarum & Wells Th Coll 64-69; Vice-Prin 69-71; USA 71-74 and from 83; Sen Officer Educn and Community Dept *Lon* 74-79; Chapl Ex Univ *Ex* 79-83; rtd 95; Perm to Offic *Ex* from 95. *148 Proctors Hall Road, Sewanee, TN 37383-1000, USA*

BRYAN, Nigel Arthur. b 39. Univ of Wales (Lamp) BA61. Burgess Hall Lamp 61. **d** 63 **p** 64. C Llanstadwel *St D* 63-69; Chapl RAF 69-94; R Gt w Lt Milton and Gt Haseley *Ox* 94-98; R Newport w Cilgwyn and Dinas w Llanllawer *St D* 98-05; rtd 05. *16 Grove Drive, Pembroke SA71 5QB* Tel (01646) 681894 Mobile 07773-456175

BRYAN, Canon Percival John Milward. b 19. St Pet Coll Ox BA40 MA46 BTh47. Wycliffe Hall Ox 46. **d** 48 **p** 49. C Belvedere All SS *Roch* 48-51; Australia 51-52; C Blindley Heath *S'wark* 53-54; R Warkton and Weekley *Pet* 54-56; R King's Cliffe 56-85; Can Pet Cathl 73-86; rtd 86; Perm to Offic *Pet* from 86; *Linc* 91-00. *3 Saxon Road, Barnack, Stamford PE9 3EQ*

BRYAN, Canon Philip Richard. b 40. Dur Univ BA61. Wycliffe Hall Ox 72. **d** 74 **p** 75. C Macclesfield St Mich *Ches* 74-77; V St Bees *Carl* from 77; Chapl St Bees Sch Cumbria from 77; RD Calder *Carl* 88-96; Hon Can Carl Cathl 91-00. *The Priory, St Bees CA27 0DR* Tel (01946) 822279

BRYAN, Canon Sherry Lee. b 49. WMMTC 88. **d** 91 **p** 94. Par Dn St Columb Minor and St Colan *Truro* 91-94; C 94-96; P-in-c St Teath from 96; RD Trigg Minor and Bodmin from 02; Hon Can Truro Cathl from 03; Chapl Cornwall Healthcare NHS Trust 99-02. *The Vicarage, Whitewell Lane, St Teath, Bodmin PL30 3LH* Tel (01208) 850292 Fax as telephone
E-mail sherry@whitewelllane.fsnet.co.uk

BRYAN, Timothy Andrew. b 56. St Edm Hall Ox MA80. S'wark Ord Course 93. **d** 96 **p** 97. NSM Morden *S'wark* 96-99; NSM Carshalton Beeches from 99; Perm to Offic *Guildf* from 99. *39 Highfield Road, Sutton SM1 4JY* Tel (020) 8642 0576 *or* 7230 1212 E-mail timbryan@tinyworld.co.uk

BRYAN, William Terence. b 38. Dudley Coll of Educn CertEd68. Chich Th Coll 73. **d** 75 **p** 76. C Shrewsbury St Giles *Lich* 75-79; V Churchstoke w Hyssington and Sarn *Heref* 79-03; rtd 04. *29 Llys Melyn, Tregynon, Newtown SY16 3EE* Tel (01686) 650899

BRYANS, Joseph. b 15. TCD BA39 MA43. CITC 40. **d** 42 **p** 43. C Kirby Moorside w Gillamoor *York* 42-45; C Thornaby on Tees St Luke 45-47; C Seapatrick *D & D* 47-54; I Gleneely w Culdaff *D & R* 54-60; I Tamlaghtard w Aghanloo 60-90; rtd 90. *23 Roe Fold, Main Street, Limavaday BT49 0EL* Tel (028) 7776 2768

BRYANT, Andrew Watts. b 57. St Jo Coll Dur BA78 Birm Univ MA81 DipTh82. Qu Coll Birm 80. **d** 83 **p** 84. C Pelsall *Lich* 83-87; NSM 91-94; Perm to Offic 87-92; NSM Streetly 94-96; NSM Beckbury, Badger, Kemberton, Ryton, Stockton etc 96-99; R Worplesdon *Guildf* from 99; Chapl Merrist Wood Coll of Agric and Horticulture from 01. *The Rectory, Perry Hill, Worplesdon, Guildford GU3 3RE* Tel and fax (01483) 234616
E-mail worplesdon.rectory@virgin.net

BRYANT, Canon Christopher. b 32. K Coll Lon AKC60. **d** 61 **p** 62. C Fareham H Trin *Portsm* 61-65; C Yatton Keynell *Bris* 65-71; C Biddestone w Slaughterford 65-71; C Castle Combe 65-71; V Chirton, Marden and Patney *Sarum* 71-76; V Chirton, Marden, Patney, Charlton and Wilsford 76-78; P-in-c Devizes St Jo w St Mary 78-79; R 79-97; RD Devizes 83-93; Can and Preb Sarum Cathl 87-04; rtd 97; Master St Nic Hosp Salisbury 97-04. *34 Mill Road, Salisbury SP2 7RZ* Tel (01722) 502336

BRYANT, David Charles. b 48. St Andr Univ BSc71. St Mich Coll Llan 71. **d** 74 **p** 75. C Llanilid w Pencoed *Llan* 74-78; C Caerphilly 78-79; V Crynant 79-84; V Llanegryn and Llanfihangel-y-Pennant etc *Ban* 84-93; V Llandwrog and Llanwnda 93-04; P-in-c Arthog w Fairbourne w Llangelynnin w Rhoslefain from 04. *The Rectory, Llwyngwril LL37 2JB* Tel (01341) 250919 E-mail davidbryant@netmatters.co.uk

BRYANT, David Henderson. b 37. K Coll Lon BD60 AKC60. **d** 61 **p** 62. C Trowbridge H Trin *Sarum* 61-63; C Ewell *Guildf* 63-67; V Leiston *St E* 67-73; Chapl RN 73; C Northam *Ex* 74-75; P-in-c Clavering w Langley *Chelmsf* 76-77; Teacher Mountview High Sch Harrow 77-85; P-in-c Boosbeck w Moorsholm *York* 85-89; V 89-90; V Sowerby 90-95; P-in-c Sessay 90-95; V Lastingham w Appleton-le-Moors, Rosedale etc 95-99; rtd 99. *35 West End, Kirkbymoorside, York YO62 6AD* Tel (01751) 430269

BRYANT, Donald Thomas. b 29. FSS59 SE Essex Coll BSc56 Birkbeck Coll Lon BSc58 Dip Counselling 99. S'wark Ord Course 85. **d** 88 **p** 89. NSM Redhill St Matt *S'wark* 88-99; Perm to Offic 99-04. *21 Windermere Way, Reigate RH2 0LW* Tel (01737) 762382

BRYANT, Canon Edward Francis Paterson. b 43. S'wark Ord Course 75. **d** 78 **p** 79. NSM Hadlow *Roch* 78-84; C Dartford St Alb 84-87; R Hollington St Leon *Chich* 87-93; V Bexhill St Aug 93-99; TR Bexhill St Pet from 99; P-in-c Sedlescombe w Whatlington 02-05; RD Battle and Bexhill 98-04; Can and Preb Chich Cathl from 00. *The Rectory, Old Town, Bexhill-on-Sea TN40 2HE* Tel (01424) 211115 Fax 07970-991268 Mobile 07710-295453 E-mail ebryant@hotpop.com

BRYANT, Graham Trevor. b 41. Keble Coll Ox BA63 DipTh64 MA67. Chich Th Coll 64. **d** 66 **p** 67. C Leeds St Wilfrid *Ripon* 66-69; C Haywards Heath St Wilfrid *Chich* 69-74; V Crawley Down All SS 74-79; V Bexhill St Aug 79-85; V Charlton Kings St Mary *Glouc* 85-02; rtd 02. *6 The Close, Cheltenham GL53 0PQ* Tel (01242) 520313

BRYANT, John. *See* BRYANT, Sidney John

BRYANT, The Ven Mark Watts. b 49. St Jo Coll Dur BA72. Cuddesdon Coll 72. **d** 75 **p** 76. C Addlestone *Guildf* 75-79; C Studley *Sarum* 79-83; V 83-88; Chapl Trowbridge Coll 79-83; Voc Development Adv *Cov* 88-96; Dioc Dir of Ords 88-96; Hon Can Cov Cathl 93-01; TR Coventry Caludon 96-01; AD Cov E 99-01; Adn Cov from 01. *9 Armorial Road, Coventry CV3 6GH* Tel (024) 7641 7750 *or* 7667 4328 Fax 7641 4640
E-mail archdeacon.mark@covdioc.org

BRYANT, Patricia Ann. b 36. Qu Mary Coll Lon BA58. St Mich Coll Llan 94. **d** 91 **p** 97. NSM Llanbadoc *Mon* 91-93; NSM Llangybi and Coedypaen w Llanbadoc 93-94; C 94-98; Asst Chapl Gwent Tertiary Coll 94-98; V Merthyr Cynog and Dyffryn Honddu etc *S & B* 98-02; rtd 03. *5 Trebarried Court, Llandefalle, Brecon LD3 0NB* Tel (01874) 754087
E-mail bryants@surfaid.org

BRYANT, Peter James. b 35. Jes Coll Cam BA58 MA64 UWIST 59 FInstM. St Deiniol's Hawarden 86 St Mich Coll Llan 96. **d** 97 **p** 98. NSM Raglan-Usk *Mon* 97-98; NSM Merthyr Cynog and Dyffryn Honddu etc *S & B* 98-02. *5 Trebarried Court, Llandefalle, Brecon LD3 0NB* Tel (01874) 754087
E-mail bryants@surfaid.org

BRYANT, Canon Richard Kirk. b 47. Ch Coll Cam BA68 MA72 Nottm Univ DipTh70. Cuddesdon Coll 70. **d** 72 **p** 73. C Newc St Gabr *Newc* 72-75; C Morpeth 75-78; C Benwell St Jas 78-82; V Earsdon and Backworth 82-93; V Wylam 93-97; Prin Local Min Scheme from 97; Prin Reader Tr from 97; Hon Can Newc Cathl from 97. *2 Burlington Court, Wallsend NE28 9YH* Tel 0191-270 4150 Fax 270 4101 *or* 263 7922
E-mail r.bryant@newcastle.anglican.org
or r.bryant@lineone.net

BRYANT, Richard Maurice. b 46. MAAIS80. WMMTC 90. **d** 93 **p** 94. NSM The Stanleys *Glouc* 93-98; NSM Glouc St Geo w Whaddon 98-04; NSM Twigworth, Down Hatherley, Norton, The Leigh etc from 04. *6 Church Street, Kings Stanley, Stonehouse GL10 3HW* Tel (01453) 823172

BRYANT, Sidney John. b 29. Linc Coll Ox BA52 MA56. St Steph Ho Ox 52. **d** 54 **p** 55. C Southgate St Andr *Lon* 54-58; C Tottenham Ch Ch W Green 58-60; V New Southgate St Paul 60-71; R Gt Leighs *Chelmsf* 71-92; P-in-c Lt Leighs 71-92; rtd 92; Perm to Offic *St E* from 92. *16 Rydal Avenue, Felixstowe IP11 9SE* Tel (01394) 275822

BRYARS, Peter John. b 54. BA MEd PhD. St Jo Coll Nottm. **d** 84 **p** 85. C Hull St Martin w Transfiguration *York* 84-87; TV Drypool 87-90; TV Glendale Gp *Newc* 90-94; P-in-c Heddon-on-the-Wall 94-01; Adult Educn Adv 94-01; V Delaval from 01; AD Bedlington from 03; Chapl Mothers' Union from 02. *The Vicarage, The Avenue, Seaton Sluice, Whitley Bay NE26 4QW* Tel 0191-237 1982 E-mail pjbryars@aol.com

BRYCE, Michael Adrian Gilpin. b 47. TCD BA71 MA95. CITC 74. **d** 77 **p** 78. C Clondalkin w Tallaght *D & G* 77-79; C Ch Ch Cathl and Chapl Univ Coll Dub 79-82; I Ardamine w Kiltennel, Glascarrig etc *C & O* 82-84; CF 84-00; I Lisbellaw *Clogh* 00-05; R Bolam w Whalton and Hartburn w Meldon *Newc* from 05; V Nether Witton from 05. *The Rectory, Whalton, Morpeth NE61 3UX* Tel (01670) 775360

BRYDON, Michael Andrew. b 73. St Chad's Coll Dur BA95 MA96 PhD00. St Steph Ho Ox BA01. **d** 02 **p** 03. C Bexhill St Pet

Chich from 02. *14 Barrack Road, Bexhill-on-Sea TN40 2AT* Tel (01424) 212453

BRYER, Anthony Colin. b 51. Qu Eliz Coll Lon BSc72. Trin Coll Bris 72. **d** 75 **p** 76. C Preston St Cuth *Blackb* 75-78; C Becontree St Mary *Chelmsf* 78-81; TV Loughton St Mary and St Mich 81-88; C Clifton St Paul *Bris* 88-91; P-in-c 91-94; R Bris St Mich and St Paul 94-96; Dir of Outreach Edin SS Andr and Geo (C of S) 96-04; Lic to Offic *Edin* 96-04; P-in-c Towcester w Easton Neston *Pet* from 04. *The Vicarage, Chantry Lane, Towcester NN12 6YY* Tel (01327) 350459 Mobile 07814-832004 E-mail tsbryer@waitrose.com

BRYER, Paul Donald. b 58. Sussex Univ BEd80 Nottm Univ MA96. St Jo Coll Nottm DipTh90. **d** 90 **p** 91. C Tonbridge St Steph *Roch* 90-94; TV Camberley St Paul *Guildf* 94-99; V Camberley St Mary 99-01; V Dorking St Paul from 01. *St Paul's Vicarage, South Terrace, Dorking RH4 2AB* Tel (01306) 881998 E-mail paulandfiona.bryer@virgin.net

BRYN-THOMAS, John. b 37. Lich Th Coll 63. **d** 66 **p** 67. C Stoke upon Trent *Lich* 66-71; R Wotton *Guildf* 71-79; P-in-c Holmbury St Mary 78-79; R Wotton and Holmbury St Mary 79-86; C Easthampstead *Ox* 86-88; TV Chambersbury *St Alb* 88-01; rtd 01; Perm to Offic *Guildf* from 02. *5 Richmond Road, Godalming GU7 2ET* Tel (01483) 429782 E-mail brynjthom@aol.com

BUBBERS, David Bramwell. b 23. Lambeth MA84 Oak Hill Th Coll 51. **d** 54 **p** 55. C Beckenham St Jo *Roch* 54-58; V Wandsworth St Mich *S'wark* 58-65; V Northwood Em *Lon* 65-74; Perm to Offic *St Alb* 74-93; Lic to Offic *Lon* 74-88; Gen Sec CPAS 74-88; rtd 88; Perm to Offic *Chich* from 88. *2 Earlsmead Court, 15 Granville Road, Eastbourne BN20 7HE* Tel (01323) 737077

BUCHAN, Geoffrey Herbert. b 38. CEng MIMechE. N Ord Course 91. **d** 94 **p** 95. NSM Barnton *Ches* 94-96; NSM Goostrey 96-99; C Stretton and Appleton Thorn from 99. *12 Hough Lane, Anderton, Northwich CW9 6AB* Tel (01606) 74512 E-mail gbuchan@tiscali.co.uk

BUCHAN, Matthew Alexander John. b 69. St Andr Univ MA92. Wycliffe Hall Ox BTh95. **d** 98 **p** 99. C Horninglow *Lich* 98-01; TV Moulsecoomb *Chich* 01-04; Bp's Chapl *Glouc* from 04. *4A Miller's Green, Gloucester GL1 2BP* Tel (01452) 410022 ext 268 E-mail mbuchan@glosdioc.org.uk

BUCHANAN, Andrew Derek. b 64. Stirling Univ BA90. Wycliffe Hall Ox 98. **d** 01 **p** 02. C Plas Newton *Ches* 01-03; C Ches Ch Ch from 03; Asst Chapl Ches Coll of HE from 03. *The Vicarage, Gloucester Street, Chester CH1 3HR* Tel (01244) 382217 E-mail rev_buchanan@hotmail.com

✠**BUCHANAN, The Rt Revd Colin Ogilvie.** b 34. Linc Coll Ox BA MA Lambeth DD93. Tyndale Hall Bris 59. **d** 61 **p** 62 **c** 85. C Cheadle *Ches* 61-64; Tutor St Jo Coll Nottm 64-85; Lib 64-69; Registrar 69-74; Dir of Studies 74-75; Vice-Prin 75-78; Prin 79-85; Hon Can S'well Minster *S'well* 81-85; Suff Bp Aston *Birm* 85-89; Asst Bp Roch 89-96; Asst Bp S'wark 90-91; V Gillingham St Mark *Roch* 91-96; Area Bp Woolwich *S'wark* 96-04; rtd 04; Hon Asst Bp Bradf from 04. *21 The Drive, Alwoodley, Leeds LS17 7QB* Tel 0113-267 7721

BUCHANAN, Eoin George. b 59. Qu Coll Birm 98. **d** 00 **p** 01. C Dovercourt and Parkeston w Harwich *Chelmsf* 00-04; C Ramsey w Lt Oakley 02-04; TR N Hinckford from 04. *The Rectory, Gages Road, Belchamp St Paul, Sudbury CO10 7BT* Tel (01787) 277210 Mobile 07947-793558 E-mail eion.buchanan@btopenworld.com

BUCHANAN, Canon Eric. b 32. Leeds Univ BA54. Coll of Resurr Mirfield 54. **d** 56 **p** 57. C Cov St Mark *Cov* 56-59; Asst Chapl Lon Univ *Lon* 59-64; C Bloomsbury St Geo w St Jo 59-64; V Duston *Pet* 64-79; RD Wootton 75-79; Can Pet Cathl 77-97; V Wellingborough All Hallows 79-90; V Higham Ferrers w Chelveston 90-97; Chapl to The Queen 92-02; rtd 97; Perm to Offic *Pet* from 97. *8 College Street, Higham Ferrers, Wellingborough NN10 8DZ* Tel (01933) 411232

BUCHANAN, George Rowland. b 15. St Aug Coll Cant. **d** 59 **p** 60. C Sherborne w Castleton and Lillington *Sarum* 59-63; V Bradford Abbas w Clifton Maybank 63-67; R Gt Wishford 67-73; R Lt Langford 67-73; RD Wylye and Wilton 69-73; Org Sec CECS *Ex* and *B & W* 73-77; rtd 77; Perm to Offic *Sarum* from 77. *6 Pageant Drive, Sherborne DT9 3LP* Tel (01935) 812263

BUCHANAN, John Fraser Walter. b 32. Em Coll Cam BA55. LNSM course 91. **d** 93 **p** 94. OLM Wainford *St E* from 93. *The Hermitage, Bridge Street, Beccles NR34 9BA* Tel (01502) 712154

BUCHANAN, Stephanie Joan. b 65. Linc Coll Ox BA88 MA02 Goldsmiths' Coll Lon PGCE93 Selw Coll Cam BA01. Ridley Hall Cam 99. **d** 02 **p** 03. C Mirfield *Wakef* from 02. *10 Greenside Road, Mirfield WF14 0AU* Tel (01924) 492684 E-mail stephanie.buchanan@btopenworld.com

BUCK, Ashley. *See* BUCK, William Ashley

BUCK, David Andrew. b 64. GRNCM88 Birm Univ DipHE97. Ripon Coll Cuddesdon DipMin99. **d** 99 **p** 00. C Poulton-le-Sands w Morecambe St Laur *Blackb* 99-03; V Hednesford *Lich* from 03. *The Vicarage, Church Hill, Cannock WS12 1BD* Tel (01543) 422635 E-mail davidbuck@care4free.net

BUCK (née JONES), Mrs Kathryn Mary. b 59. Birm Univ BA81 MEd91 Sheff Univ PGCE82. Ripon Coll Cuddesdon. **d** 99 **p** 00. C Uttoxeter Area *Lich* 99-00; C Scotforth *Blackb* 00-03; TV Cannock *Lich* from 03; C Hednesford from 05. *The Vicarage, Church Hill, Cannock WS12 1BD* Tel (01543) 426954 *or* 879814

BUCK, Nicholas John. b 57. Leic Univ BScEng79. Ridley Hall Cam 81. **d** 84 **p** 85. C Oakwood St Thos *Lon* 84-87; C Darnall and Attercliffe *Sheff* 87-90; V Kimberworth 90-96; Chapl Scargill Ho 96-01; P-in-c Bassingham Gp *Linc* from 01. *The Rectory, 11 Torgate Lane, Bassingham, Lincoln LN5 9HF* Tel (01522) 788383 E-mail the-bucks@supanet.com

BUCK, Canon Richard Peter Holdron. b 37. AKC64. Lambeth Hon MA93. **d** 65 **p** 66. C Mill Hill Jo Keble Ch *Lon* 65-68; C St Marylebone All SS 68-74; Can Res and Treas Truro Cathl *Truro* 74-76; V Primrose Hill St Mary w Avenue Road St Paul *Lon* 76-84; Bp's Ecum Adv *S'wark* 84-91; P-in-c Dulwich Common St Pet 84-86; Hon Can S'wark Cathl from 90; C Rotherhithe St Kath w St Barn 91-92; C Bermondsey St Kath w St Bart 92-94; C Greenwich St Alfege w St Pet and St Paul 94-98; rtd 98. *50 Viceroy Lodge, 143 Kingsway, Hove BN3 4RB* Tel (01273) 710155

BUCK, William Ashley. b 61. Man Univ BA82 Ox Univ BA86 MA91. Ripon Coll Cuddesdon 84. **d** 87 **p** 88. C Addington *S'wark* 87-91; C Pimlico St Pet w Westmr Ch Ch *Lon* 91-94; TV Wenlock *Heref* 94-03; RD Condover 00-03; R Cleobury Mortimer w Hopton Wafers etc from 03. *The Rectory, The Hurst, Cleobury Mortimer, Kidderminster DY14 8EG* Tel (01299) 270264

BUCKBY, Gary. b 69. Leeds Univ BA90. Coll of Resurr Mirfield 93. **d** 95 **p** 96. C Wolverhampton St Steph *Lich* 95-98; V Longford *Cov* from 98. *St Thomas's Vicarage, Hurst Road, Coventry CV6 6EL* Tel (024) 7636 4078 E-mail frgary@tesco.net

BUCKETT, Canon James Frederick. b 27. MBE97. ACP. Roch Th Coll 60. **d** 62 **p** 63. C Rowner *Portsm* 62-64; Lic to Offic 64-66; Chapl Highbury Tech Coll Portsm 64-66; V St Helens *Portsm* 66-72; CF (TA) 72-95; V Newport St Thos *Portsm* 72-95; Hon Can Portsm Cathl 81-95; rtd 95; Perm to Offic *Portsm* from 95. *The Coach House, 140A Staplers Road, Newport PO30 2DP* Tel (01983) 521847 *or* 527298 Mobile 07889-784376 E-mail jamesbuckett@cs.com

BUCKINGHAM, The Ven Hugh Fletcher. b 32. Hertf Coll Ox BA57 MA60. Westcott Ho Cam 55. **d** 57 **p** 58. C Halliwell St Thos *Man* 57-60; C Sheff Gillcar St Silas *Sheff* 60-65; V Hindolveston *Nor* 65-70; V Guestwick 65-70; R Fakenham w Alethorpe 70-88; Chmn Dioc Bd Soc Resp 81-88; RD Burnham and Walsingham 81-87; Hon Can Nor Cathl 85-88; Adn E Riding *York* 88-98; Can and Preb York Minster 88-01; rtd 98; Perm to Offic *York* from 01. *2 Rectory Corner, Brandsby, York YO61 4RJ* Tel (01347) 888202

BUCKINGHAM, Paul John. b 63. Bris Univ BVSc87. WMMTC 94. **d** 98. NSM Kington w Huntington, Old Radnor, Kinnerton etc *Heref* from 98. *The Cottage, Prospect Lane, Kington HR5 3BE* Tel (01544) 231357

BUCKINGHAM, Richard Arthur John. b 49. Univ of Wales (Cardiff) BA71 PGCE72. Chich Th Coll 73. **d** 76 **p** 77. C Llantwit Major *Llan* 76-80; C Leigh-on-Sea St Marg *Chelmsf* 80-84; C Westmr St Matt *Lon* 84-87; R Stock Harvard *Chelmsf* 87-02; Perm to Offic *Lon* from 02. *3 Priory Close, London N3 1BB* Tel (020) 8371 0178

BUCKINGHAM, Terence John. b 52. Aston Univ BSc73 MSc75 PhD78 FCOptom74. Coll of Resurr Mirfield 01. **d** 03 **p** 04. NSM Harrogate St Wilfrid *Ripon* from 03. *29 Dalesway, Guiseley, Leeds LS20 8JN* Tel (01943) 876066 Mobile 07815-994017 E-mail terry.j.buckingham@btopenworld.com

BUCKINGHAM, Archdeacon of. *See* WATSON, The Ven Sheila Anne

BUCKINGHAM, Area Bishop of. *See* WILSON, The Rt Revd Alan Thomas Lawrence

BUCKLE, Graham Martin. b 62. Southn Univ BTh89 Sheff Univ MMinTheol04. Sarum & Wells Th Coll 85. **d** 89 **p** 90. C Paddington St Jas *Lon* 89-94; P-in-c Paddington St Pet 94-00; R St Marylebone St Paul from 00; Dir of Ords Two Cities Area from 99. *St Paul's House, 9 Rossmore Road, London NW1 6NJ* Tel and fax (020) 7262 9443 Pager 07654-327687 E-mail buckle@freeuk.com

BUCKLER, Andrew Jonathan Heslington. b 68. Trin Coll Ox BA89 MA96. Wycliffe Hall Ox BTh93. **d** 96 **p** 97. C Ox St Aldate *Ox* 96-00; Crosslinks France from 00. *12 rue de Gassicourt, 78200 Mantes la Jolie, France* Tel (0033) (1) 30 33 07 95 E-mail bucklers@clara.net

BUCKLER, George Anthony (Tony). b 35. Open Univ BA74. Lich Th Coll 58. **d** 61 **p** 62. C Old Swinford *Worc* 61-65; C Droitwich St Nic w St Pet 65-67; C Droitwich St Andr w St Mary 65-67; Chapl Claybury Hosp Woodford Bridge 67-78; Chapl St Geo and Co Hosps Linc 78-87; Chapl Lawn Hosp Linc 78-81; Chapl Wexham Park Hosp Slough 87-90; Chapl Mapperley Hosp Nottm 90-94; Chapl Nottm Mental Illness and

Psychiatric Unit 90-96; Chapl Wells Rd Cen Nottm 94-96; Chapl Qu Medical Cen Nottm 94-96; Chapl Highbury Hosp Nottm 94-96; rtd 96. *73 Westfield Drive, Lincoln LN2 4RE*

BUCKLER, Guy Ernest Warr. b 46. ACA69 FCA79. Linc Th Coll 71. **d** 74 **p** 75. C Dunstable *St Alb* 74-77; C Houghton Regis 77-86; TV Willington *Newc* 86-88; TR 88-95; Chapl N Tyneside Coll of FE 88-95; R Bedford St Pet w St Cuth *St Alb* 95-05; R Bushey from 05. *The Rectory, High Street, Bushey WD23 1BD* Tel (020) 8950 1546 E-mail guybuckl@hotmail.com

BUCKLER, Kenneth Arthur. b 50. S Bank Univ MSc94. NTMTC 95. **d** 98 **p** 99. C Welwyn w Ayot St Peter *St Alb* 98-01; P-in-c Kimpton w Ayot St Lawrence from 01; Asst Chapl E Herts NHS Trust 99-00; Asst Chapl E and N Herts NHS Trust 00-04; Chapl Team Ldr 04-05; V Hounslow W Gd Shep *Lon* from 05. *The Good Shepherd House, 360 Beavers Lane, Hounslow TW4 6HJ* Tel (020) 8570 4035 Mobile 07909-970545 E-mail kenabuckler@yahoo.co.uk

BUCKLER, Canon Philip John Warr. b 49. St Pet Coll Ox BA70 MA74. Cuddesdon Coll 70. **d** 72 **p** 73. C Bushey Heath *St Alb* 72-75; Chapl Trin Coll Cam 75-81; Min Can and Sacr St Paul's Cathl *Lon* 81-87; V Hampstead St Jo 87-99; AD N Camden 93-98; Can Res St Paul's Cathl from 99; Treas from 00. *2 Amen Court, London EC4M 7BU* Tel (020) 7248 3312 Fax 7489 8579 E-mail treasurer@stpaulscathedral.org.uk

BUCKLEY, Alan. b 40. Tyndale Hall Bris. **d** 67 **p** 68. C Owlerton *Sheff* 67-70; C Mansfield SS Pet and Paul *S'well* 70-73; C Charlesworth *Derby* 73-75; P-in-c Whitfield 76-84; V Moldgreen *Wakef* 84-90; V Hadfield *Derby* 90-03; rtd 03; Perm to Offic *Derby* from 03. *6 Weavers Court, Mottram, Hyde SK14 6JY* Tel (01457) 762174

BUCKLEY, Alexander Christopher Nolan. b 67. Univ of Wales (Abth) BD89. St Mich Coll Llan. **d** 91 **p** 94. C Llandudno *Ban* 91-92; C Ynyscynhaearn w Penmorfa and Porthmadog 92-93 and 94-96; Jesuit Volunteer Community Manchester 93-94; C Caerau w Ely *Llan* 96-01; V Trowbridge Mawr *Mon* 01-03; Chapl ATC from 96. *3 Albert Avenue, Manchester M18 7JX* Tel 0161-231 4919

BUCKLEY, Anthony Graham. b 63. Keble Coll Ox BA84 MA90 PGCE85. Wycliffe Hall Ox 96. **d** 98 **p** 99. C Foord St Jo *Cant* 98-00; V from 00; AD Elham from 05. *St John's Vicarage, 4 Cornwallis Avenue, Folkestone CT19 5JA* Tel (01303) 250280 E-mail antmon64@hotmail.com

BUCKLEY, Christopher Ivor. b 48. Chich Th Coll. **d** 86 **p** 87. C Felpham w Middleton *Chich* 86-89; C Jersey St Brelade *Win* 89-93; V Jersey St Mark from 93; Chapl Jersey Airport from 00. *The Vicarage, St Mark's Road, St Helier, Jersey JE2 4LY* Tel and fax (01534) 720595 Mobile 07797-714595 E-mail christopher.buckley@jerseymail.co.uk

BUCKLEY, David Rex. b 47. Ripon Coll Cuddesdon 75. **d** 77 **p** 78. C Witton *Ches* 77-81; V Backford 81-85; Youth Chapl from 81; V Barnton 85-93; P-in-c Bickerton w Bickley 93-97; P-in-c Harthill and Burwardsley 93-97; V Bickerton, Bickley, Harthill and Burwardsley 97-01; P-in-c Sandbach 01-03; V from 03. *The Vicarage, 15 Offley Road, Sandbach CW11 1GY* Tel (01270) 762379 E-mail rex@chazandrex.freeserve.co.uk

BUCKLEY, Ernest Fairbank. b 25. Jes Coll Cam BA49 MA50 Jes Coll Ox BLitt53. Westcott Ho Cam 55. **d** 55 **p** 56. C Rochdale *Man* 55-58; V Hey 58-64; V Baguley 64-79; V Clun w Chapel Lawn, Bettws-y-Crwyn and Newcastle *Heref* 79-87; RD Clun Forest 82-87; rtd 88. *Hawthorn Bank, Clunton, Craven Arms SY7 0HP* Tel (01588) 660281

BUCKLEY, John. b 42. **d** 95 **p** 96. C Macclesfield Team Par *Ches* 95-01; P-in-c Pott Shrigley from 01; Chapl E Cheshire NHS Trust from 01. *The Vicarage, Spuley Lane, Pott Shrigley, Macclesfield SK10 5RS* Tel (01625) 573316

BUCKLEY, Michael. b 49. St Jo Coll Dur Cranmer Hall Dur 77. **d** 79 **p** 80. C Birkdale St Jo *Liv* 79-82; TV Maghull 82-88; V Earlestown 88-98; V Gt Sankey from 98. *The Parsonage, Parsonage Way, Great Sankey, Warrington WA5 1RP* Tel (01925) 723235

BUCKLEY, Rex. *See* BUCKLEY, David Rex

BUCKLEY, Richard Francis. b 44. Ripon Hall Ox 69. **d** 72 **p** 73. C Portsea St Cuth *Portsm* 72-75; C Portsea All SS w St Jo Rudmore 75-79; Chapl RN 79-00; Perm to Offic *B & W* from 00. *Ste Croix, Coryate Close, Higher Odcombe, Yeovil BA22 8UJ* Tel and fax (01935) 864039 Mobile 07810-123065 E-mail rfbuckley@onetel.com

BUCKLEY, Richard John. b 43. Hull Univ BSc(Econ)64 PhD87 Strathclyde Univ MSc69. Sarum Th Coll 64. **d** 66 **p** 67. C Huddersfield St Jo *Wakef* 66-68; C Sutton St Jas *York* 69-71; TV Sutton St Jas and Wawne 71-75; V Handsworth Woodhouse *Sheff* 75-85; R Adwick-le-Street 85-91; V Wentworth 91-97; Perm to Offic *York* from 88 and *Sheff* from 97; Area Co-ord (S and E Yorkshire) Chr Aid from 97. *2 Kirkstead Abbey Mews, Thorpe Hesley, Rotherham S61 2UZ* Tel 0114-246 5064

BUCKLEY, Richard Simon Fildes. b 63. WMMTC 97. **d** 00 **p** 01. NSM Moseley St Mary *Birm* 00-04; NSM Soho St Anne w St Thos and St Pet *Lon* from 05. *12 College Green Court, 55 Barrington Road, London SW9 7JG* Tel (020) 7095 1810 Mobile 07976-290351 E-mail puppet.buckley@virgin.net

BUCKLEY, Robert William. b 50. Grey Coll Dur BSc70 PhD73 DipEd73 CPhys75 MInstE91 FCollP92 FInstP97. N Ord Course 85. **d** 87 **p** 88. NSM N Greenford All Hallows *Lon* 87-91; P-in-c 91-94; NSM W Acton St Martin 94-95; NSM Ealing All SS 94-95; C 95-97; P-in-c Preston Ascension 97-99; TR Wembley Park 99-03; AD Brent 00-03; TR Atherton and Hindsford w Howe Bridge *Man* from 03. *St Michael's Vicarage, Leigh Road, Atherton, Manchester M46 0PH* Tel (01942) 883378 E-mail brobert@fish.co.uk

BUCKLEY, Stephen Richard. b 45. Cranmer Hall Dur 82. **d** 84 **p** 85. C Iffley *Ox* 84-88; TV Halesowen *Worc* 88-00; TR Sedgley All SS 00-05; TR Gornal and Sedgley from 05. *All Saints' Vicarage, Vicar Street, Sedgley, Dudley DY3 3SD* Tel (01902) 883255 E-mail stephen@presbyter.freeserve.co.uk

BUCKLEY, Timothy Denys. b 57. BA. St Jo Coll Nottm DipTh. **d** 83 **p** 84. C S Westoe *Dur* 83-85; C Paddington Em Harrow Road *Lon* 85-88; C Binley *Cov* 88-98; Min Binley Woods LEP 88-98; V Belton Gp *Linc* from 98. *The Vicarage, 118 High Street, Belton, Doncaster DN9 1NS* Tel (01427) 872207 E-mail timothybuckley@breathe.com

BUCKLEY, Timothy John. b 67. Jes Coll Cam BA90 MA94 ACA94. Wycliffe Hall Ox BTh99. **d** 99 **p** 00. C Langdon Hills *Chelmsf* 99-02; P-in-c Devonport St Mich and St Barn *Ex* from 02. *St Barnabas' Vicarage, 10 De la Hay Avenue, Plymouth PL3 4HU* Tel (01752) 666544 E-mail revtim@fish.co.uk

BUCKMAN, Rossly David. b 36. TCD BA64 MA67 St Pet Coll Ox BA65 MA98. Moore Th Coll Sydney. **d** 59 **p** 60. C Eastwood Australia 59-60; C Port Kembla 60-61; C Dublin Harold's Cross *D & G* 61-64; C Ox St Mich *Ox* 64-65; Lect Clifton Th Coll 65-69; CF 69-76; Tutor Canberra Coll of Min Australia 77-80; P-in-c Mid Marsh Gp *Linc* 81-82; R 82-89; P-in-c Blakehurst Australia 89-91; R 91-00; Chapl Düsseldorf *Eur* 00-05; rtd 05. *Mülheimerstrasse 15, D-40878 Ratingen NRW, Germany* Tel (0049) 172-781 3534 (mobile) E-mail buckman@t-online.de

BUCKNALL, Ms Alison Mary. b 55. Leeds Univ BA76 Trin Coll Bris MA94. Qu Coll Birm 94. **d** 96 **p** 97. C The Quinton *Birm* 96-00; C Sutton Coldfield H Trin 00-01; Asst Chapl N Bris NHS Trust from 01. *North Bristol NHS Trust, Beckspool Road, Frenchay, Bristol BS16 1LE* Tel 0117-970 1070

BUCKNALL, Allan. b 35. ALCD62. Lon Coll of Div 62. **d** 62 **p** 63. C Harlow New Town w Lt Parndon *Chelmsf* 62-69; Chapl W Somerset Miss to Deaf 69-71; Perm to Offic *Bris* 71-77; P-in-c Wisborough Green *Chich* 77-79; R Tillington 78-86; R Duncton 82-86; R Up Waltham 82-86; C Henfield w Shermanbury and Woodmancote 86-89; Asst Chapl Princess Marg Hosp Swindon 89-96; Angl Chapl Swindon and Marlborough NHS Trust 96-00; rtd 00; Perm to Offic *Bris* from 00. *5 The Willows, Highworth, Swindon SN6 7PG* Tel (01793) 762721

BUCKNALL, Miss Ann Gordon. b 32. K Coll Lon BSc53 Hughes Hall Cam DipEd54. Qu Coll Birm 80. **dss** 81 **d** 87 **p** 94. Birm St Aid Small Heath *Birm* 81-85; Balsall Heath St Paul 85-92; Par Dn 87-92; C Handsworth St Jas 92-95; rtd 95; Perm to Offic *Lich* from 95. *20 St Margaret's Road, Lichfield WS13 7RA* Tel (01543) 257382

BUDD, John Christopher. b 51. QUB BA73 DLIS77 TCD DipTh82. CITC. **d** 82 **p** 83. C Ballymena *Conn* 82-85; C Jordanstown w Monkstown 85-88; I Craigs w Dunaghy and Killagan 88-97; Dioc Info Officer 89-97; Bp's Dom Chapl from 94; I Derriaghy w Colin from 97. *Derriaghy Rectory, 20 Derriaghy Road, Magheralave, Lisburn BT28 3SH* Tel (028) 9061 0859

BUDD, John Victor. b 31. CCC Ox BA55 MA58 Open Univ BSc98. Bps' Coll Cheshunt 57. **d** 59 **p** 60. C Friern Barnet St Jas *Lon* 59-64; C Harrow Weald All SS 64-70; Lic to Offic *St Alb* 70-73; V Lt Amwell 73-96; RD Hertford 83-88; rtd 96; Perm to Offic *Worc* from 96. *37 Wykewane, Malvern WR14 2XD* Tel (01684) 566174

BUDD, Philip John. b 40. St Jo Coll Dur BA63 DipTh65 MLitt71 Bris Univ PhD78. Cranmer Hall Dur. **d** 66 **p** 67. C Attenborough w Chilwell *S'well* 66-69; Lect Clifton Th Coll 69-71; Lect Trin Coll Bris 72-80; Tutor Ripon Coll Cuddesdon 80-88; Asst Chapl and Tutor Westmr Coll Ox 80-00; Lect 88-00; Asst Chapl and Tutor Ox Brookes Univ *Ox* 00-03; Lect 00-03; Hon C N Hinksey and Wytham from 03. *4 Clover Close, Oxford OX2 9JH* Tel (01865) 863682 E-mail budds@talk21.com

BUDDEN, Alexander Mark. b 60. UEA BA84. SEITE 01. **d** 04. NSM Mitcham St Barn *S'wark* from 04. *29 Dane Road, London SW19 2NB* Tel (020) 8542 0622 Mobile 07762-020543 E-mail amarkbudden@aol.com

BUDDEN, Clive John. b 39. Liv Univ BA. Chich Th Coll. **d** 84 **p** 86. C Gaywood, Bawsey and Mintlyn *Nor* 84-87; TV Brixham w Churston Ferrers and Kingswear *Ex* 87-90; R Exton and Winsford and Cutcombe w Luxborough *B & W* 90-99; Perm to Offic *Truro* 00-02; P-in-c Veryan w Ruan Lanihorne from 02. *The Vicarage, Veryan, Truro TR2 5QA* Tel (01872) 501618

BUDGE, Leonard Percival. b 11. Dur Univ LTh40. St Aug Coll Cant 37. **d** 40 **p** 41. C Easington w Skeffling and Kilnsea *York*

40-43; C Hertford St Andr St Alb 43-45; Tanganyika 45-48; C Stourbridge St Thos Worc 48-51; V Castle Morton 51-58; V Amblecote 58-64; V Frithelstock Ex 64-76; V Monkleigh 64-76; P-in-c Littleham 64-70; R 70-76; rtd 76; Perm to Offic Ex from 76. *2 Chestnut Close, Braunton EX33 2EH* Tel (01271) 814313

BUDGELL, Peter Charles. b 50. Lon Univ BD. **d** 83 **p** 84. C Goodmayes All SS Chelmsf 83-86; C Chipping Barnet w Arkley St Alb 86-88; V Luton St Anne from 88. *St Anne's Vicarage, 7 Blaydon Road, Luton LU2 0RP* Tel and fax (01582) 720052 E-mail pcbudgell@aol.com

BUDGELL, Rosemary Anne. b 51. Lon Bible Coll BD73 CertEd76. **dss** 83 **d** 87 **p** 94. Goodmayes All SS Chelmsf 83-86; Chipping Barnet w Arkley St Alb 86-88; Hon Par Dn 87-88; Hon Par Dn Luton St Anne 88-95; Perm to Offic 95-98. *32 Hobbs Hill Road, Hemel Hempstead HP3 9QA* Tel (01442) 390556

BUDGETT, Preb Anthony Thomas. b 26. TD60. Oriel Coll Ox BA50 MA57. Wells Th Coll 57. **d** 59 **p** 60. C Hendford B & W 59-63; PC Lopen 63-68; R Seavington St Mich w St Mary 63-68; V Somerton 68-80; RD Ilchester 72-81; P-in-c Compton Dundon 76-80; R Somerton w Compton Dundon 80-81; R Somerton w Compton Dundon, the Charltons etc 81-84; Preb Wells Cathl 83-90; P-in-c Bruton w Lamyatt, Wyke and Redlynch 84-85; P-in-c Batcombe w Upton Noble 84-85; P-in-c S w N Brewham 84-85; TR Bruton and Distr 85-90; rtd 90; Perm to Offic Ex from 90; Perm to Offic B & W from 94. *Cornerways, White Ball, Wellington TA21 0LS* Tel (01823) 672321

BUFFREY, Canon Samuel John Thomas. b 28. Keble Coll Ox BA52 MA57. Cuddesdon Coll 52. **d** 54 **p** 55. C Lower Tuffley St Geo CD Glouc 54-56; C Branksome St Aldhelm Sarum 56-61; R Gussage St Michael and Gussage All Saints 61-69; V Amesbury 69-80; RD Avon 77-80; P-in-c Broadstone 80-82; V 82-93; Can and Preb Sarum Cathl 87-93; rtd 93; Perm to Offic Sarum from 93. *34 Woolslope Road, West Moors, Ferndown BH22 0PD* Tel (01202) 875522

BUFTON (née FORSHAW), Mrs Janet Elisabeth. b 41. Redland Coll of Educn CertEd61. Dioc OLM tr scheme 96. **d** 99 **p** 00. OLM Debenham w Aspall and Kenton St E 99-04; OLM Helmingham w Framsden and Pettaugh w Winston 99-04; OLM Debenham and Helmingham from 04. *Harkaway Cottage, 9 Fenn Street, Winston, Stowmarket IP14 6LD* Tel (01728) 860535

BUGBY, Timothy. b 53. AKC75. Chich Th Coll 76. **d** 77 **p** 78. C Hockerill St Alb 77-81; C Pimlico St Mary Graham-street Lon 81-87; V Highgate St Aug 87-03; Dir Educn, Min and Voc Confraternity of the Blessed Sacrament 00-03; Perm to Offic Lon and Nor from 04. *Seaview Cottage, Cromer Road, East Runton, Cromer NR27 9NH* Tel and fax (01263) 512830 Mobile 07721-022626 E-mail timbugby@aol.com

BUGDEN, Ernest William. b 16. Lich Th Coll 56. **d** 58 **p** 59. C Esher Guildf 58-68; Hon C 68-81; rtd 81; Perm to Offic Ely from 91. *32 French's Road, Cambridge CB4 3LA* Tel (01223) 311306

BUGG, Canon Peter Richard. b 33. Univ of BC BA62. Wells Th Coll 63. **d** 64 **p** 64. C Whitley Ch Ch Ox 64-67; C Ludlow Heref 67-69; Zambia 69-72; P-in-c Brill w Boarstall Ox 72-78; P-in-c Chilton w Dorton 77-78; V Brill, Boarstall, Chilton and Dorton 78-97; Hon Can Ch Ch 92-97; rtd 97; Perm to Offic Ox from 04. *66 Windmill Street, Brill, Aylesbury HP18 9TG* Tel (01844) 238204 E-mail bug.home@care4free.net

BUGLER, Canon Derek Leslie. b 25. Gen Th Sem NY LTh64. **d** 64 **p** 64. USA 64-90 and from 04; rtd 90; Lic to Offic Win 90-04. *51 Raymond Road, Brunswick, ME 04011, USA* E-mail dbugler@gwi.net

BUIK, Allan David. b 39. St Andr Univ BSc61 SSC. Coll of Resurr Mirfield 66. **d** 68 **p** 69. Perm to Offic Win 68-69; C Eastleigh 69-72; C Brighton St Bart Chich 72-74; C Lavender Hill Ascension S'wark 74-78; V Kingstanding St Mark Birm 78-86; Guyana 86-91; V Tunstall Lich from 91. *Christchurch Vicarage, 26 Stanley Street, Tunstall, Stoke-on-Trent ST6 6BW* Tel (01782) 838288 Mobile 07703-479715 E-mail allanbuik@ntlworld.com

BUIKE, Desmond Mainwaring. b 32. Ex Coll Ox BA55 MA69 Leeds Univ CertEd72. **d** 57 **p** 58. C Man St Aid Man 57-60; C Ox SS Phil and Jas Ox 60-63; V Queensbury Bradf 63-71; Perm to Offic Bradf 71-85 and York from 93; V Glaisdale York 85-93; rtd 93. *Wayside, 3 White Bridge Road, Whitby YO21 3JQ* Tel (01947) 821440

BULCOCK, Andrew Marcus. b 62. **d** 03 **p** 04. OLM Elton St Steph Man from 03. *5 Fieldhead Avenue, Bury BL8 2LX* Tel 0161-761 6347 E-mail kemamb@beeb.net

BULL, Mrs Christine. b 45. Bedf Coll Lon BA67. N Ord Course 91. **d** 94 **p** 95. NSM High Lane Ches 94-98; NSM Stockport SW 98-99; Perm to Offic Derby 98-04; Ches 99-04; Man from 00; C Hale and Ashley from 04. *8 School Road, Hale, Altrincham WA15 9HB* Tel 0161-928 1252 E-mail revchristinebull@yahoo.co.uk

BULL (née ADAMS), Mrs Christine Frances. b 53. Cam Inst of Educn CertEd74. NEOC 97. **d** 00 **p** 01. NSM St Oswald in Lee w Bingfield Newc from 00. *East Side Lodge, Bingfield, Newcastle upon Tyne NE19 2LE* Tel (01434) 672303 E-mail pc.bull@ukonline.co.uk

BULL, Christopher Bertram. b 45. Lon Bible Coll BA87. Wycliffe Hall Ox 88. **d** 90 **p** 91. C Leominster Heref 90-95; P-in-c Westbury 95-02; R from 02; P-in-c Yockleton 95-02; R from 02; P-in-c Gt Wollaston 95-02; V from 02. *The Rectory, Westbury, Shrewsbury SY5 9QX* Tel (01743) 884216 E-mail cbbull@anglican.fslife.co.uk

BULL, Christopher David. b 59. St Jo Coll Nottm 89. **d** 91 **p** 92. C Bowbrook S Worc 91-95; P-in-c Flackwell Heath Ox 95-00; V from 00; RD Wycombe 97-05. *The Vicarage, 9 Chapel Road, Flackwell Heath, High Wycombe HP10 9AA* Tel (01628) 522795 E-mail christopher.bull@virgin.net

BULL, George. *See* BULL, William George

BULL, John. *See* BULL, Michael John

BULL, Malcolm George. b 35. Portsm Dioc Tr Course 87. **d** 87 **p** 98. NSM Farlington Portsm 87-90; NSM Widley w Wymering 92-93; NSM S Hayling 93-97; NSM Hayling Is St Andr 97-00; Bp's Adv for Cults and New Relig Movements 99-00; rtd 00; Perm to Offic Portsm 00-01 and from 04; P-in-c Greatworth and Marston St Lawrence etc Pet 01-04. *20 Charleston Close, Hayling Island PO11 0JY* Tel (023) 9246 2025 E-mail bullmg@bushinternet.com

BULL, Martin Wells. b 37. Worc Coll Ox BA61 MA68. Ripon Hall Ox 61. **d** 63 **p** 64. C Blackley St Andr Man 63-67; C Horton Bradf 67-68; V Ingrow cum Hainworth 68-78; RD S Craven 74-77; V Bingley All SS 78-80; TR 80-92; P-in-c Gargrave 92-02; rtd 02; Perm to Offic Ripon from 03. *Mallard Cottage, Grewelthorpe, Ripon HG4 3BT* Tel (01765) 650473 Mobile 07870-138386

BULL, Michael John. b 35. Roch Th Coll 65. **d** 67 **p** 68. C N Wingfield Derby 67-69; C Skegness Linc 69-72; R Ingoldmells w Addlethorpe 72-79; Area Sec USPG S'wark 79-85; Area Org RNLI (Lon) 86-88; C Croydon St Jo S'wark 89-93; P-in-c Mitcham Ch Ch 93-97; V Colliers Wood Ch Ch 97-00; rtd 00; Perm to Offic Nor 00-04; Hon C Guiltcross from 04. *The Rectory, Back Street, Garboldisham, Diss IP22 2SD* Tel (01953) 688347

BULL, Robert David. b 51. Westmr Coll Ox MTh03. Ripon Coll Cuddesdon 74. **d** 77 **p** 78. C Worsley Man 77-80; C Peel 80-81; TV 81-86; P-in-c Wisbech St Aug Ely 86-88; V 88-02; RD Wisbech 92-02; RD Wisbech Lynn Marshland 02; R Lich St Chad Lich from 02. *St Chad's Rectory, The Windings, Lichfield WS13 7EX* Tel (01543) 262254 E-mail robert.chad@tiscali.co.uk

BULL, Stephen Andrew. b 58. St Jo Coll Nottm DCM93. **d** 93 **p** 94. C Wroughton Bris 93-96; P-in-c Eyemouth Edin 96-98; NSM 98; Lic to Offic from 98. *12 Craigs Court, Torphichen, Bathgate EH48 4NU* Tel (01506) 650070 E-mail steve@scotiabahn.com

BULL, Miss Susan Helen. b 58. Qu Mary Coll Lon BSc79 ACIS84. STETS BTh98. **d** 98 **p** 99. NSM Epsom St Barn Guildf from 98. *41 Stamford Green Road, Epsom KT18 7SR* Tel (01372) 742703 E-mail rev@suebull.freeserve.co.uk

BULL, Timothy Martin. b 65. Worc Coll Ox BA87 MA93 Dur Univ PhD94 Fitzw Coll Cam BA98 FRSA96. Ridley Hall Cam 96. **d** 99 **p** 00. C Bath Walcot B & W 99-03; P-in-c Langham w Boxted Chelmsf from 03; Colchester Area CME Adv from 03. *The Rectory, Wick Road, Langham, Colchester CO4 5PG* Tel (01206) 230666 E-mail tim@revbull.freeserve.co.uk

BULL, William George. b 28. Sarum Th Coll 65. **d** 66 **p** 67. C Salisbury St Mich Sarum 66-69; V Swallowcliffe w Ansty 69-75; Dioc Youth Officer 69-71; P-in-c Laverstock 75-81; V 81-93; rtd 94; Perm to Offic Sarum from 94. *Bungalow 1, Boreham Field, Warminster BA12 9EB* Tel (01985) 847830

BULLAMORE, John Richard. b 41. Linc Coll Ox BA69 MA69. Wycliffe Hall Ox 74. **d** 95 **p** 95. NSM Eorropaidh Arg 95-98; NSM Bath St Sav w Swainswick and Woolley B & W from 98. *St Mary's House, Upper Swainswick, Bath BA1 8BX* Tel (01225) 851159 E-mail john.bullamore@homecall.co.uk

BULLIMORE, Christine Elizabeth. b 46. Nottm Univ BA67 Dip Counselling 92. St Jo Coll Nottm 96. **d** 96 **p** 97. Bp's Adv Past Care and Counselling Wakef 92-99 and from 01; NSM S Ossett 96-99; P-in-c Emley from 99; P-in-c Flockton cum Denby Grange from 99. *The Rectory, 14 Grange Drive, Emley, Huddersfield HD8 9SF* Tel (01924) 849161 Mobile 07778-022163 Fax 849219 E-mail jcbullimor@aol.com

BULLIMORE, Matthew James. b 77. Em Coll Cam BA99 MA03 Man Univ MPhil02. Westcott Ho Cam 01. **d** 05. C Roberttown w Hartshead Wakef from 05. *The Vicarage, Knowler Hill, Liversedge WF15 6LJ* Tel (01924) 402414 E-mail m.j.bullimore.96@cantab.net

BULLIVANT, Ronald. b 32. CertEd Dip Counselling. St Mich Coll Llan. **d** 59 **p** 60. C Roath St German Llan 59-61; P-in-c Bradf H Trin Bradf 61-66; V Horbury Wakef 66-69; Lic to Offic Ripon 70-78; Perm to Offic Nor 78-81; Lic to Offic 81-98; Perm to Offic Man from 99. *14 St Albans Terrace, Manchester M8 8BZ* Tel 0161-832 2423

BULLOCH, William Gillespie. b 68. St Steph Ho Ox. **d** 01 **p** 02. C Bognor *Chich* 01-05; V Leigh-on-Sea St Jas *Chelmsf* from 05. *St James's Vicarage, 103 Blenheim Chase, Leigh-on-Sea SS9 3BY* Tel (01702) 471786

BULLOCK, Andrew Belfrage. b 50. Univ of Wales (Ban) BSc73 MEd81 Westmr Coll Ox PGCE79. Wycliffe Hall Ox DipMin94. **d** 97 **p** 98. C Sandhurst *Ox* 97-02; P-in-c Alfrick, Lulsley, Suckley, Leigh and Bransford *Worc* from 02. *The Rectory, Leigh, Worcester WR6 5LE* Tel (01886) 832355 Mobile 07958-654331 E-mail abullock@waitrose.com

BULLOCK, Andrew Timothy. b 56. Southn Univ BTh91. Sarum & Wells Th Coll 89. **d** 91 **p** 92. C Erdington St Barn *Birm* 91-94; TV Solihull 94-03; P-in-c Acocks Green from 03. *The Vicarage, 34 Dudley Park Road, Acocks Green, Birmingham B27 6QR* Tel and fax 0121-706 9764 E-mail andrewbullock@tinyonline.co.uk

BULLOCK, Jude Ross. b 58. Heythrop Coll Lon BD89. Allen Hall 84. **d** 89 **p** 90. In RC Ch 89-97; C Lt Ilford St Mich *Chelmsf* from 01. *The Curate's Flat, 3 Toronto Avenue, London E12 5JF* Tel (020) 8553 4627 Mobile 07976-395732 E-mail judebullock@hotmail.com

BULLOCK, Kenneth Poyser. b 27. Down Coll Cam BA50 MA55. Ridley Hall Cam 50. **d** 52 **p** 53. C Aston SS Pet and Paul *Birm* 52-56; R Openshaw *Man* 56-63; V Ainsworth 63-91; rtd 91. *26 Plas Penrhyn, Penrhyn Bay, Llandudno LL30 3EU* Tel (01492) 543343

BULLOCK, Canon Michael. b 49. Hatf Coll Dur BA71. Coll of Resurr Mirfield 72. **d** 75 **p** 76. C Pet St Jo *Pet* 75-79; Zambia 79-86; V Longthorpe *Pet* 86-91; Chapl Naples *Eur* 91-99; OGS from 93; P-in-c Liguria *Eur* 99-00; Chapl Gtr Lisbon from 00; Can Malta Cathl from 98. *rua Joao de Deus 5, Alcoitão, 2645-128 Alcabideche, Portugal* Tel (00351) (21) 469 2303 Fax as telephone E-mail gl-chaplaincy@clix.pt

BULLOCK, Miss Rosemary Joy. b 59. Portsm Poly BA81 Southn Univ BTh94. Sarum & Wells Th Coll 89. **d** 91 **p** 94. Par Dn Warblington w Emsworth *Portsm* 91-94; C 94-95; C Gt Parndon *Chelmsf* 95-98; TV Beaminster Area *Sarum* 98-03; P-in-c Ridgeway 03-04. *82 Green Lane, Shanklin PO37 7HD* Tel (01983) 863345

BULLOCK (née WHEALE), Mrs Sarah Ruth. b 64. Surrey Univ BA86 St Jo Coll Dur BA93. Cranmer Hall Dur 90. **d** 93 **p** 94. C Kersal Moor *Man* 93-98; P-in-c Whalley Range St Edm 98-04; P-in-c Moss Side St Jas w St Clem 99-04; R Whalley Range St Edm and Moss Side etc from 04. *St Edmund's Rectory, 1 Range Road, Manchester M16 8FS* Tel 0161-226 1291

BULLOCK, Stephanie Clair. b 46. St Mary's Hosp Medical Sch Lon MB, BS70. Ripon Coll Cuddesdon 90. **d** 92 **p** 94. Par Dn Cuddesdon *Ox* 92-94; Tutor Ripon Coll Cuddesdon 92-94; Asst Chapl Ox Radcliffe Hosp NHS Trust 94-97; Chapl Ox Radcliffe Hosps NHS Trust 97-03; Hon C Headington St Mary *Ox* from 03. *Church Farm, Church Lane, Old Marston, Oxford OX3 0PT* Tel (01865) 722926

BULLOCK, Victor James Allen. b 67. Southn Univ BTh90 St Mary's Coll Twickenham PGCE91. St Steph Ho Ox DipMin94. **d** 94 **p** 95. C Cowley St Jas *Ox* 94-95; C Reading St Giles 95-99; V Fenny Stratford from 99. *The Vicarage, Manor Road, Milton Keynes MK2 2HW* Tel (01908) 372825

BULLOCK-FLINT, Peter. b 22. Kelham Th Coll 39. **d** 45 **p** 46. C Deptford St Paul *S'wark* 45-48; C Streatham Ch Ch 48-50; C Boyne Hill *Ox* 50-56; C-in-c Tilehurst St Mary CD 56-72; V Hughenden 72-83; V Ivinghoe w Pitstone and Slapton 83-91; RD Mursley 86-91; rtd 91; Perm to Offic *Sarum* from 91. *1 Wellow Cottage, Salisbury Road, Pimperne, Blandford Forum DT11 8UW* Tel (01258) 450142

BULMAN, Madeline Judith. *See* STRONG, Ms Madeline Judith

BULMAN, Michael Thomas Andrew. b 34. Jes Coll Cam BA59 MA61. Ridley Hall Cam 58. **d** 60 **p** 61. C Blackpool St Mark *Blackb* 60-63; C Branksome St Clem *Sarum* 63-67; V York St Barn *York* 67-84; CMJ Israel 84-93; R Jerusalem Ch Ch 85-87; Can Jerusalem 87-93; R Maresfield and V Nutley *Chich* 94-00; rtd 00. *15 Beechcroft Road, Alverstoke, Gosport PO12 2EP* Tel (023) 9252 7353 E-mail michael.bulman@btopenworld.com

BUNCE, Michael John. b 49. St Andr Univ MTh79 PhD91 FRSA FSA. Westcott Ho Cam DipTh80. **d** 80 **p** 81. C Grantham *Linc* 80-83; TV 83-85; R Tarfside *Bre* 85-92; R Brechin 85-92; R Auchmithie 91-92; Provost St Paul's Cathl Dundee 92-97; Chapl Menorca *Eur* from 00. *Apartado de Correos 102, 07720 Es Castell, Menorca, Spain* Tel (0034) (971) 352378

BUNCE, Raymond Frederick. b 28. Lon Univ DipSocSc53. Ely Th Coll 54. **d** 57 **p** 58. C Hillingdon St Andr *Lon* 57-62; C Greenford H Cross 62-67; V Ealing All SS 67-89; Chapl Ascot Priory 89-90; rtd 90; Perm to Offic *Portsm* from 91 and *Chich* from 99. *45 Guillards Oak, Midhurst GU29 9JZ* Tel (01730) 816282

BUNCH, Andrew William Havard. b 53. Selw Coll Cam BA74 MA78 PhD79. Ox NSM Course 84. **d** 87 **p** 88. NSM Wantage *Ox* 87-91; C New Windsor 91-93; TV 93-97; V Ox St Giles and SS Phil and Jas w St Marg from 97. *The Vicarage, Church Walk, Oxford OX2 6LY* Tel (01865) 510460 E-mail awh@awhbunch.freeserve.co.uk

BUNDAY, Canon Paul. b 30. Wadh Coll Ox BA54 MA58. ALCD56. **d** 56 **p** 57. C Woking St Jo *Guildf* 56-60; Chapl Reed's Sch Cobham 60-66; R Landford w Plaitford *Sarum* 66-77; RD Alderbury 73-77; TR Radipole and Melcombe Regis 77-86; RD Weymouth 82-85; Can and Preb Sarum Cathl 83-95; TV Whitton 86-91; TR 91-95; Chapl Duchess of Somerset Hosp Froxfield 86-94; rtd 95; Perm to Offic *Sarum* from 95. *4 Springfield Park, Tisbury, Salisbury SP3 6QN* Tel (01747) 871530

BUNDAY, Richard William. b 76. Lanc Univ BA98 MA04. Cranmer Hall Dur 98. **d** 00 **p** 01. C Redcar *York* 00-01; C Marton *Blackb* 01-04; P-in-c Ashton-on-Ribble St Mich w Preston St Mark from 04. *St Michael's Vicarage, 2 Edgerton Road, Ashton-on-Ribble, Preston PR2 1AJ* Tel (01772) 726157 E-mail bundays@blueyonder.co.uk

BUNDOCK, Anthony Francis. b 49. Qu Coll Birm 81. **d** 83 **p** 84. C Stansted Mountfitchet *Chelmsf* 83-86; TV Borehamwood *St Alb* 86-94; TR Seacroft *Ripon* 94-05; AD Whitkirk 00-05; TR Leeds City from 05. *Leeds Rectory, 1 Vicarage View, Leeds LS5 3HF* Tel 0113-278 6237 E-mail tony.pat.bundock@virgin.net

BUNDOCK, Edward Leigh. b 52. Keble Coll Ox BA73 Open Univ PhD94 MAAT. St Steph Ho Ox 74. **d** 76 **p** 77. C Malvern Link w Cowleigh *Worc* 76-80; C-in-c Portslade Gd Shep CD *Chich* 80-88; V Wisborough Green 88-94; Perm to Offic *Guildf* 96-97; P-in-c E and W Rudham, Houghton-next-Harpley etc *Nor* 97-99; R E w W Rudham, Helhoughton etc from 99. *The Rectory, South Raynham Road, West Raynham, Fakenham NR21 7HH* Tel (01328) 838385

BUNDOCK, John Nicholas Edward. b 45. Wells Th Coll 66. **d** 70 **p** 71. C Chingford SS Pet and Paul *Chelmsf* 70-74; P-in-c Gt Grimsby St Matt Fairfield CD *Linc* 74-81; V Hindhead *Guildf* 81-99; RD Farnham 91-96; V Bramley and Grafham from 99; RD Cranleigh from 04; Chapl Gosden Ho Sch from 99. *The Vicarage, Birtley Rise, Bramley, Guildford GU5 0HZ* Tel (01483) 892109 E-mail johnbundock@lineone.net

BUNDOCK, Nicholas John. b 73. Sheff Univ BSc94 PhD98 Fitzw Coll Cam BA01. Ridley Hall Cam 99. **d** 02 **p** 03. C Mortomley St Sav High Green *Sheff* 02-05; TV Didsbury St Jas and Em *Man* from 05. *453 Parrs Wood Road, Manchester M20 5NE* Tel 0161-445 1310 E-mail nickbundock@stjamesandemmanuel.org

BUNDOCK, Ronald Michael. b 44. Leeds Univ BSc65. Ox NSM Course 87. **d** 90 **p** 91. NSM Buckingham *Ox* 90-98; NSM Stowe 98-03; P-in-c from 03. *1 Holton Road, Buckingham MK18 1PQ* Tel (01280) 813887 E-mail ron@bundock.com

BUNKER, Harry. b 28. Oak Hill Th Coll. **d** 59 **p** 60. C Longfleet *Sarum* 59-63; R Blisworth *Pet* 63-97; rtd 97; Perm to Offic *Pet* from 97. *14 Wardlow Close, West Hunsbury, Northampton NN4 9YQ* Tel (01604) 450230

BUNKER, John Herbert George. b 31. AKC56. **d** 57 **p** 58. C Newc St Jo *Newc* 57-60; C Cullercoats St Geo 61-65; V Byker St Mich 65-74; V Ashington 74-84; V Halifax St Aug *Wakef* 84-93; rtd 93; Perm to Offic *Wakef* 93-98. *1 Hebble Dean, Hebble Lane, Halifax HX3 5JL*

BUNKER, The Very Revd Michael. b 37. Oak Hill Th Coll 59. **d** 63 **p** 64. C Alperton *Lon* 63-66; C St Helens St Helen *Liv* 66-70; V Muswell Hill St Matt *Lon* 70-79; V Muswell Hill St Jas 78-79; V Muswell Hill St Jas w St Matt 79-92; AD W Haringey 85-90; Preb St Paul's Cathl 90-92; Dean Pet from 92. *The Deanery, Minster Precincts, Peterborough PE1 1XS* Tel (01733) 562780 Fax 897874 E-mail deanbunker@aol.com

BUNN, Mrs Rosemary Joan. b 60. EAMTC 94. **d** 97 **p** 98. NSM Sprowston w Beeston *Nor* 97-01; R Stoke H Cross w Dunston, Arminghall etc from 01. *Holy Cross Vicarage, Mill Road, Stoke Holy Cross, Norwich NR14 8PA* Tel (01508) 492305 E-mail rev.rosie@venta-group.org.uk

BUNNELL, Adrian. b 49. Univ of Wales (Abth) BSc72. St Mich Coll Llan 74. **d** 75 **p** 76. C Wrexham *St As* 75-78; C Rhyl w St Ann 78-79; CF 79-95; R Aberfoyle and Callander *St And* 95-03; P-in-c Newport-on-Tay from 03. *St Mary's Rectory, 8 High Street, Newport-on-Tay DD6 8DA* Tel (01382) 543311 E-mail adrianbunnellnewport@tiscali.co.uk

BUNTING, Edward Garth. b 70. TCD BTh99. CITC 96. **d** 99 **p** 00. C Clooney w Strathfoyle *D & R* 99-02; I Leckpatrick w Dunnalong from 02. *The Rectory, 1 Lowertown Road, Ballymagorry, Strabane BT82 0LE* Tel and fax (028) 7188 3545 Mobile 07808-206062 E-mail leckpatrick@derry.anglican.org

BUNTING, Canon Ian David. b 33. Ex Coll Ox BA58 MA61. Tyndale Hall Bris 57 Princeton Th Sem ThM60. **d** 60 **p** 61. C Bootle St Leon *Liv* 60-63; V Waterloo St Jo 64-71; Dir Past Studies St Jo Coll Dur 71-78; R Chester le Street *Dur* 78-87; RD Chester-le-Street 79-84; Kingham Hill Fellow 87-89; Dioc Dir of Ords *S'well* 90-99; C Lenton 90-97; Hon Can S'well Minster 93-99; Bp's Research Officer 97-00; rtd 00; Perm to Offic *S'well* from 00. *8 Crafts Way, Southwell NG25 0BL* Tel (01636) 813868 E-mail ibunting@waitrose.com

BUNTING, Jeremy John. b 34. St Cath Coll Cam BA56 MA60 Worc Coll Ox BA58 MA60. St Steph Ho Ox 57. **d** 59 **p** 60. C Bickley *Roch* 59-62; C Cambridge St Mary Less *Ely* 62-66; Fell and Tutor Gen Th Sem New York USA 66-68; R Stock Harvard *Chelmsf* 68-87; RD Wickford 73-79; V Hampstead Garden Suburb *Lon* 87-94; rtd 99. *Fairview, 82 New Road, Haslingfield, Cambridge CB3 7LP* Tel (01223) 871602

BUNYAN, David Richard. b 48. Edin Th Coll 93. **d** 96 **p** 97. NSM Musselburgh *Edin* 96-98; NSM Prestonpans 96-98; C Edin St Dav 98-00; R Grangemouth from 00; P-in-c Bo'ness from 00. *The Rectory, 33 Carronflats Road, Grangemouth FK3 9DG* Tel and fax (01324) 482438 E-mail drbdoe@blueyonder.co.uk

BUNYAN, Richard Charles. b 43. Oak Hill Th Coll 63 Ridley Hall Cam 69. **d** 71 **p** 72. C Luton Ch Ch *Roch* 71-74; C Bexleyheath Ch Ch 74-76; C Bexley St Jo 76-79; TV Northampton Em *Pet* 79-81; V Erith St Jo *Roch* 81-86; V S Woodham Ferrers *Chelmsf* 86-89; Chapl Scargill Ho 89-91; Sub-Chapl HM Pris Swaleside 91-94; Perm to Offic *Cant* from 91; Dep Chapl HM Pris Belmarsh 94-96; Chapl HM Pris Littlehey from 96. *HM Prison Littlehey, Perry, Huntingdon PE28 0SR* Tel (01480) 333252 Fax 812151 E-mail rcbunyan@waitrose.com

BUR, Patricia Margaret. b 59. SEITE. **d** 99 **p** 01. C Clapham Team *S'wark* 99-01; C Nunhead St Antony w St Silas 01-03; P-in-c N Woolwich w Silvertown *Chelmsf* from 03. *St John's Vicarage, Manwood Street, London E16 2JY* Tel (020) 7476 2388

BURBERY, Ian Edward. b 37. Univ of Wales (Lamp) BA59. Coll of Resurr Mirfield 59. **d** 61 **p** 62. C Penarth w Lavernock *Llan* 61-68; V Porth 68-77; V Cainscross w Selsley *Glouc* 77-89; P-in-c Cheltenham Em 89-95; V Cheltenham Em w St Steph 95-98; rtd 98. *21 Fairy Grove, Killay, Swansea SA2 7BY* Tel (01792) 204460

BURBIDGE, Barry Desmond. b 52. S Tr Scheme DipTh97. **d** 97 **p** 98. NSM Fleet *Guildf* 97-03; NSM Crondall and Ewshot from 03. *34 Ashbury Drive, Hawley, Camberley GU17 9HH* Tel (01276) 32776 E-mail b.burbidge@ntlworld.com

BURBRIDGE, The Very Revd John Paul. b 32. FSA89 K Coll Cam BA54 MA58 New Coll Ox BA54 MA58. Wells Th Coll 58. **d** 59 **p** 60. C Eastbourne St Mary *Chich* 59-62; V Choral York Minster *York* 62-66; Can Res and Prec 66-76; Adn Richmond *Ripon* 76-83; Can Res Ripon Cathl 76-83; Dean Nor 83-95; rtd 95; Perm to Offic *Ripon* from 95. *The School House, High Fremington, Richmond DL11 6AS* Tel (01748) 884440

BURBRIDGE, Richard James. b 47. Univ of Wales (Ban) BSc68. Oak Hill Th Coll 68. **d** 72 **p** 73. C Rodbourne Cheney *Bris* 72-75; C Downend 75-78; P-in-c Bris H Cross Inns Court 78-83; P-in-c Fishponds All SS 83-86; V 86-97; RD Stapleton 89-95; C Bishopston 97-98; C Bris St Andr w St Bart 97-98; TV Bishopston and St Andrews from 98. *25 Morley Square, Bristol BS7 9DW* Tel 0117-942 4359

BURCH, Christopher. *See* BURCH, Canon John Christopher

BURCH, John Anthony. b 37. Open Univ BA75. Wycliffe Hall Ox 67. **d** 69 **p** 70. C Guildf Ch Ch *Guildf* 69-72; C Cove St Jo 72-75; TV Fincham *Ely* 75-79; V Huntingdon St Barn 79-81; Perm to Offic 82-90; rtd 99. *13 Hawthorn Road, Kearsley, Bolton BL4 8SD*

BURCH, Canon John Christopher (Chris). b 50. Trin Coll Cam BA71 MA76 Leeds Univ MPhil95. St Jo Coll Nottm 73. **d** 76 **p** 77. C Sheff St Jo *Sheff* 76-79; C Holbeck *Ripon* 79-82; V Burmantofts St Steph and St Agnes 82-95; Can Res and Prec Cov Cathl *Cov* 95-02; Chapl to Clergy of UPA 99-02; C-in-c Braunstone Park CD *Leic* from 02; RD Christianity S from 04. *The Vicarage, Main Street, Leicester LE3 3AL* Tel 0116-289 3377 E-mail chris@burches.co.uk

BURCH, Paul Simon. b 75. St Jo Coll Dur MSc97 Man Metrop Univ PGCE98. St Steph Ho Ox BA03. **d** 04 **p** 05. C Carnforth *Blackb* from 04. *10 Croasdale Close, Carnforth LA5 9UN* Tel (01524) 730760 E-mail paulburch5@hotmail.com

BURCH, Canon Peter John. b 36. ACA60 FCA71. Ripon Hall Ox 62. **d** 64 **p** 65. C Brixton St Matt *S'wark* 64-67; Sierra Leone 68-72; P-in-c Chich St Pet *Chich* 72-76; V Broadwater Down 76-85; V Steyning 85-94; R Ashurst 85-94; Hon Can Bauchi from 93; V Broadway *Worc* 94-96; V Broadway w Wickhamford 96-02; rtd 02; Perm to Offic *Glouc* from 03 and *Worc* from 04. *6 Jordan's Close, Willersey, Broadway WR12 7QD* Tel (01386) 853837 E-mail canonburch@stmichaels95.freeserve.co.uk

BURCH, Stephen Roy. b 59. St Jo Coll Nottm 82. **d** 85 **p** 86. C Ipswich St Aug *St E* 85-89; Youth Chapl *Cov* 89-94; P-in-c Kinwarton w Gt Alne and Haselor 89-99; R 99-04; P-in-c Coughton 02-04; RD Alcester 99-04; V Fletchamstead from 04. *St James's Vicarage, 395 Tile Hill Lane, Coventry CV4 9DP* Tel (024) 7646 6262 E-mail stephen.burch@btinternet.com

BURCHILL, Jane. b 31. Dalhousie Univ Canada BSc54 Aber Univ PhD81. Moray Ho Edin CertEd56 St Jo Coll Nottm 85. **d** 88 **p** 94. NSM Inverurie *Ab* from 88; NSM Auchindoir from 88; NSM Alford from 88; NSM Kemnay from 88. *5 Hopetoun Avenue, Bucksburn, Aberdeen AB21 9QU* Tel (01224) 712931

BURDEN, Miss Anne Margaret. b 47. Ex Univ BSc69 CQSW72. Linc Th Coll 89. **d** 91 **p** 94. Par Dn Mill Hill Jo Keble Ch *Lon* 91-94; C 94; TV Basingstoke *Win* 94-02; Dioc Adv for Women's Min 00-02; TV Brixham w Churston Ferrers and Kingswear *Ex* from 02. *6 Durleigh Road, Brixham TQ5 9JJ* Tel and fax (01803) 954924 E-mail anne-burden@virgin.com

BURDEN, Derek. b 29. St Edm Hall Ox BA52 MA56. Wells Th Coll 56. **d** 58 **p** 59. C Mitcham St Mark *S'wark* 58-61; V Coombe Bissett w Homington *Sarum* 61-69; V N Bradley 69-79; V Steeple Ashton w Semington 79-84; V Keevil 79-84; V Steeple Ashton w Semington and Keevil 84-89; rtd 89; Perm to Offic *Sarum* from 89. *9 Farleigh Avenue, Trowbridge BA14 9DS* Tel (01225) 754759

BURDEN, Derek Ronald. b 37. Sarum Th Coll 59. **d** 62 **p** 63. C Cuddington *Guildf* 62-64; C Leamington Priors All SS *Cov* 64-66; C Stamford All SS w St Pet *Linc* 66-74; C-in-c Stamford Ch Ch CD 71-74; P-in-c Ashbury w Compton Beauchamp *Ox* 74-77; V 77-81; V Ashbury, Compton Beauchamp and Longcot w Fernham 81-84; V Wokingham St Sebastian 84-97; P-in-c Wooburn 97-02; rtd 02; Perm to Offic *Sarum* 03-05. *5 Cranford Park Drive, Yateley GU46 6JR* Tel (01276) 512343

BURDEN, Michael Henry. b 38. Selw Coll Cam BA59 MA62 Hull Univ MEd79. Ridley Hall Cam 59. **d** 61 **p** 62. C Ashton-upon-Mersey St Mary *Ches* 62-65; Chapl St Pet Sch York 65-70; Asst Master Beverley Gr Sch 70-74; R Walkington *York* 74-77; Chapl Asst Berwick R Infirmary 82-94; P-in-c Berwick H Trin *Newc* 82-87; V 87-89; P-in-c Berwick St Mary 82-87; V Berwick H Trin and St Mary 89-94; P-in-c Skirwith, Ousby and Melmerby w Kirkland *Carl* 94-98; Sec Guild of St Raphael 94-98; rtd 99; Perm to Offic *Newc* from 99. *The White House, Fenkle Street, Holy Island, Berwick-upon-Tweed TD15 2SR* Tel (01289) 389302 Fax as telephone

BURDEN, Paul. b 62. AMIMechE87 Rob Coll Cam BA84 MA88. Wycliffe Hall Ox BA91. **d** 92 **p** 93. C Clevedon St Andr and Ch Ch *B & W* 92-96; R Bathampton w Claverton from 96. *The Vicarage, Bathampton Lane, Bath BA2 6SW* Tel (01225) 463570 E-mail p.burden@talk21.com

BURDETT, John Fergusson. b 25. Pemb Coll Cam BA47 MA79. **d** 79 **p** 80. C Edin St Jo *Edin* 79-87 and 90-95; Cyprus 87-90; rtd 95. *80/1 Barnton Park View, Edinburgh EH4 6HJ* Tel 0131-339 7226 Fax 317 1179 E-mail rev@johnburdett.demon.co.uk

BURDETT, Stephen Martin. b 49. AKC72. St Aug Coll Cant 73. **d** 74 **p** 75. C Walworth St Pet *S'wark* 74-75; C Walworth 75-77; C Benhilton 77-80; P-in-c Earlsfield St Jo 80-83; V 83-89; V N Dulwich St Faith 89-99; Ldr Post Ord Tr Woolwich Area 96-99; TR Southend *Chelmsf* from 99. *144 Alexandra Road, Southend-on-Sea SS1 1HB* Tel (01702) 342687 E-mail stephenburdett@waitrose.com

BURDON, Anthony James. b 46. Ex Univ LLB67 Lon Univ BD73. Oak Hill Th Coll 71. **d** 73 **p** 74. C Ox St Ebbe w St Pet *Ox* 73-76; C Church Stretton *Heref* 76-78; Voc Sec CPAS and Hon C Bromley Ch Ch *Roch* 78-81; V Filkins w Broadwell, Broughton, Kelmscot etc *Ox* 81-84; R Broughton Poggs w Filkins, Broadwell etc 84-85; V Reading St Jo 85-96; C California 96-98; Adv for Spirituality (Berks) 96-98; Warden and P-in-c Cumbrae (or Millport) *Arg* 98-04; V Burstwick w Thorngumbald *York* from 04. *The Vicarage, Main Road, Thorngumbald, Hull HU12 9NA* Tel (01964) 601381 E-mail tony@tonyburdon.karoo.co.uk

BURDON, Christopher John. b 48. Jes Coll Cam BA70 MA74 Leeds Univ DipTh73 Glas Univ PhD95. Coll of Resurr Mirfield 71. **d** 74 **p** 75. C Chelmsf All SS *Chelmsf* 74-78; TV High Wycombe *Ox* 78-84; P-in-c Olney w Emberton 84-90; R 90-92; Lic to Offic *Glas* 92-94; Lay Tr Officer *Chelmsf* 94-99; Prin N Ord Course from 00; Lic Preacher *Man* from 00. *75 Framingham Road, Sale M33 3RH* Tel 0161-962 8900 *or* 249 2511 E-mail chris@thenoc.org.uk

BURDON, Edward Arthur. b 11. Linc Th Coll 44. **d** 46 **p** 47. C Taunton H Trin *B & W* 46-48; C Mayfield *Chich* 48-54; V Gosfield *Chelmsf* 54-72; V Coggeshall w Markshall 72-80; rtd 80; Perm to Offic *St E* 81-02. *c/o Dr C J Burdon, 75 Framingham Road, Sale M33 3RH*

BURDON, Mrs Pamela Muriel. b 46. Ex Univ BA68 Reading Univ DipEd69. Wycliffe Hall Ox 88. **d** 90 **p** 94. Par Dn Reading St Jo *Ox* 90-94; C 94-96; P-in-c California 96-98; NSM Cumbrae (or Millport) *Arg* 98-04; NSM Burstwick w Thorngumbald *York* from 04; C Preston and Sproatley in Holderness from 05. *The Vicarage, Main Road, Thorngumbald, Hull HU12 9NA* Tel (01964) 601464

BURDON, William. b 23. Leeds Univ BA51. Coll of Resurr Mirfield 51. **d** 53 **p** 54. C Derby St Anne *Derby* 53-57; C Weston-super-Mare All SS *B & W* 57-62; C Clifton All SS *Bris* 63-64; V Skirwith *Carl* 64-73; V Skirwith w Ousby and Melmerby 73-84; R Maidwell w Draughton, Scaldwell, Lamport etc *Pet* 84-88; rtd 88; Perm to Offic *Leic* 97-98. *25 Stuart Court, High Street, Kibworth, Leicester LE8 0LR* Tel 0116-279 6326

BURFITT, Edward Ronald. b 42. MIMA64 Liv Univ CSocSc67 Newc Univ DASS68. Cranmer Hall Dur 91. **d** 93 **p** 94. C Monkseaton St Mary *Newc* 93-97; rtd 97. *Eden House, 11 St Nicholas Road, Hexham NE46 2EZ* Tel (01434) 603073 Mobile 07870-762522 E-mail revburf@aol.com

BURFORD, Anthony Francis. b 55. Oak Hill Th Coll BA98. **d** 98 **p** 99. C Cov H Trin *Cov* 98-02; P-in-c Rye Park St Cuth *St Alb*

from 02. *The Vicarage, 8 Ogard Road, Hoddesdon EN11 0NU* Tel (01992) 302222 *or* 461866
E-mail revdtonyburford@ryepark.com

BURGE, Edward Charles Richard. b 70. Liv Univ BA92. Ridley Hall Cam 93. **d** 96 **p** 97. C Cayton w Eastfield *York* 96-99; P-in-c Lythe w Ugthorpe 99-03; Children's Officer (Cleveland Adnry) 99-03; Hon Chapl Miss to Seafarers 02-03; Dioc Youth and Children's Work Co-ord *Wakef* from 04. *37 Horton Street, Heckmondwike WF16 0LL* Tel (01924) 235216
E-mail richardburge@ecrb.fsnet.co.uk

BURGE-THOMAS, Mrs Ruth. b 66. **d** 04. NSM Clapham H Spirit *S'wark* from 04. *86 Englewood Road, London SW12 9NY* Tel (020) 8675 6594
E-mail ruththomas@claphamhome.freeserve.co.uk

BURGER, David Joseph Cave. b 31. Selw Coll Cam BA58 MA62 Leic Univ 68. Coll of Resurr Mirfield 58. **d** 60 **p** 61. C Chiswick St Paul Grove Park *Lon* 60-63; C Charlton St Luke w H Trin *S'wark* 63-65; Warden St Luke Tr Ho Charlton 63-65; Chapl Moor Park Coll Farnham 66; Teacher Ysgol y Gader Dolgellau 68-85; Resettlement Officer Ches Aid to the Homeless 88-93; rtd 92; Perm to Offic *Ban* from 96. *Pwllygele Mawr, Llanfachreth, Dolgellau LL40 2DP* Tel (01341) 450350

BURGESS, Alan James. b 51. Ridley Hall Cam 87. **d** 89 **p** 90. C Glenfield *Leic* 89-92; V Donisthorpe and Moira w Stretton-en-le-Field from 92; RD Akeley W from 00. *St John's Vicarage, Donisthorpe, Swadlincote DE12 7PX* Tel (01530) 271456

BURGESS, Alfred George. b 18. Univ of Wales BA39. St Mich Coll Llan 39. **d** 41 **p** 42. C Swansea Ch Ch *S & B* 41-44; C Llandrindod w Cefnllys 44-47; C Stratford-on-Avon *Cov* 47-49; V Longford 49-58; V Alveston 58-81; RD Stratford-on-Avon 69-73; R Ilmington w Stretton on Fosse and Ditchford 81-84; rtd 84; Perm to Offic *Glouc* 84-97 and *Cov* from 84. *139 Evesham Road, Stratford-upon-Avon CV37 9BP* Tel (01789) 293321

BURGESS, Clive Brian. b 63. Trin Coll Bris BA00. **d** 00 **p** 01. C Oxton *Ches* 00-03; V Brewood *Lich* from 03; V Bishopswood from 03. *The Vicarage, Sandy Lane, Brewood, Stafford ST19 9ET* Tel (01902) 850368 E-mail revdcliveburgess@btinternet.com

BURGESS, David James. b 58. Southn Univ BSc80. St Jo Coll Nottm LTh89 DPS89. **d** 89 **p** 90. C S Mimms Ch Ch *Lon* 89-93; C Hanwell St Mary w St Chris 93-97; P-in-c The Lee *Ox* from 97; P-in-c Hawridge w Cholesbury and St Leonard from 97. *The Vicarage, The Lee, Great Missenden HP16 9LZ* Tel (01494) 837315 E-mail d.burgess@clara.net

BURGESS, Preb David John. b 39. Trin Hall Cam BA62 MA66 Univ Coll Ox MA66 FRSA91. Cuddesdon Coll 62. **d** 65 **p** 66. C Maidstone All SS w St Phil *Cant* 65; Asst Chapl Univ Coll Ox 66-70; Chapl 70-78; Can and Treas Windsor 78-87; Chapl to The Queen from 87; V St Lawr Jewry *Lon* from 87; Preb St Paul's Cathl from 02. *St Lawrence Jewry Vicarage, Next Guildhall, London EC2V 5AA* Tel (020) 7600 9478

BURGESS, Mrs Denise. b 49. **d** 00 **p** 01. OLM Glascote and Stonydelph *Lich* from 00. *22 Melmerby, Wilnecote, Tamworth B77 4LP* Tel (01827) 897098

BURGESS, Edwin Michael. b 47. Ch Coll Cam BA69 MA73. Coll of Resurr Mirfield 70. **d** 72 **p** 73. C Beamish *Dur* 72-77; C Par *Truro* 77-80; P-in-c Duloe w Herodsfoot 80-83; R 83-86; Jt Dir SW Minl Tr Course 80-86; Subwarden St Deiniol's Lib Hawarden 86-91; R Oughtrington *Ches* from 91; P-in-c Warburton from 93; CME Officer 99-03; Asst Chapl (Warrington) Ches Coll of HE from 03; Dioc Chapl Mothers' Union from 02. *The Rectory, Oughtrington, Lymm WA13 9JB* Tel (01925) 752388 E-mail m.e.burgess@tesco.net

BURGESS, Canon Henry Percival. b 21. Leeds Univ BA48. Coll of Resurr Mirfield 48. **d** 50 **p** 51. C Northfield *Birm* 50-54; V Shaw Hill 54-62; V Wylde Green 62-89; Hon Can Birm Cathl 75-90; RD Sutton Coldfield 76-88; rtd 90; Perm to Offic *Birm* from 90. *39 Chestnut Drive, Birmingham B36 9BH* Tel 0121-747 9926

BURGESS, Mrs Jean Ann. b 62. Nottm Univ MA03. EMMTC 00. **d** 03 **p** 04. C Gresley *Derby* from 03. *Chapel End, Chapel Street, Church Gresley, Swadlincote DE11 9LX* Tel (01283) 551015

BURGESS, The Ven John Edward. b 30. Lon Univ BD57. ALCD56. **d** 57 **p** 58. C Bermondsey St Mary w St Olave and St Jo *S'wark* 57-60; C Southampton St Mary w H Trin *Win* 60-62; V Dunston w Coppenhall *Lich* 62-67; Chapl Stafford Coll of Tech 63-67; V Keynsham w Queen Charlton *B & W* 67-75; R Burnett 67-75; RD Keynsham 72-75; Adn Bath and Preb Wells Cathl 75-95; rtd 96; Perm to Offic *B & W* and *Sarum* from 96. *12 Berryfield Road, Bradford-on-Avon BA15 1SX* Tel (01225) 868905

BURGESS, John Henry William. b 35. Westhill Coll Birm CYCW72. Wells Th Coll 65. **d** 67 **p** 68. C Teddington St Alb *Lon* 67-72; C Northolt W End St Jos 72-74; Perm to Offic *B & W* 93-99 and from 00; rtd 95; C Bruton and Distr *B & W* 99-00; Perm to Offic *Nor* from 04. *9 Fairview Drive, Colkirk, Fakenham NR21 7NT* Tel (01328) 863410
E-mail burgess@walsingham9.wanadoo.co.uk

BURGESS, John Michael. b 36. ALCD61. **d** 61 **p** 62. C Eccleston St Luke *Liv* 61-64; S Rhodesia 64-65; Rhodesia 65-74; V Nottingham St Andr *S'well* 74-79; Bp's Adv on Community Relns 77-79; V Earlestown *Liv* 79-87; RD Warrington 82-87; TR Halewood 87-94; V Southport St Phil and St Paul 94-01; AD N Meols 95-00; rtd 01; Perm to Offic *Liv* from 03. *3 Glencoyne Drive, Southport PR9 9TS* Tel (01704) 506843

BURGESS, John Mulholland. b 32. Cranmer Hall Dur 58. **d** 61 **p** 62. C Frimley *Guildf* 61-67; C Cheltenham St Luke and St Jo *Glouc* 67-69; P-in-c Withington w Compton Abdale 69-74; R Woolstone w Gotherington and Oxenton 74-75; Chapl Rotterdam w Schiedam etc *Eur* 75-78; Chapl Sliema 78-80; C Nottingham All SS *S'well* 80; C Rolleston w Morton 80-83; C Rolleston w Fiskerton, Morton and Upton 83-84; V Mansfield St Aug 84-99; Asst RD Mansfield 88-92; RD 92-98; rtd 99; Perm to Offic *S'well* from 03. *278 Westfield Lane, Mansfield NG19 6NQ* Tel (01623) 421163

BURGESS, Kate Lamorna. b 64. Man Poly BA86 Leeds Univ MA97. NEOC 99. **d** 02 **p** 03. OHP 92-03; C Hessle *York* from 02. *167 First Lane, Hessle, Hull HU13 9EY* Tel (01482) 645745
E-mail klb6@klb6.karoo.co.uk

BURGESS (née BOND), Mrs Kim Mary. b 58. SRN79. Trin Coll Bris BA87. **d** 87 **p** 94. Par Dn Cullompton *Ex* 87-91; Asst Chapl N Staffs R Infirmary Stoke-on-Trent 91-95; NSM Audley *Lich* 95-00. *6 Quarry Cottages, Nantwich Road, Audley, Stoke-on-Trent ST7 8DW* Tel (01782) 722961

BURGESS, Miss Laura Jane. b 74. Imp Coll Lon BSc95 ARSM95. Ripon Coll Cuddesdon BTh00. **d** 00 **p** 01. C St Alb Abbey *St Alb* 00-01; C Boxmoor St Jo 01-04; Min Can and Sacr St Paul's Cathl *Lon* from 04. *7A Amen Court, London EC4M 7BU* Tel (020) 7248 6151
E-mail laura.burgess@telinco.co.uk

BURGESS, Michael. *See* BURGESS, Edwin Michael

BURGESS, Michael Anglin. b 34. St Deiniol's Hawarden 81. **d** 83 **p** 84. C Habergham Eaves St Matt *Blackb* 83-85; C Burnley St Matt w H Trin 85-86; V Preston St Matt 86-93; V Nelson St Bede 93-99; rtd 99; Perm to Offic *Blackb* from 99. *39 Reedley Road, Reedley, Burnley BB10 2LU* Tel (01282) 449727
E-mail revmab1@ntlworld.com

BURGESS, Canon Michael James. b 42. Coll of Resurr Mirfield 74. **d** 76 **p** 77. C Leigh-on-Sea St Marg *Chelmsf* 76-79; C St Peter-in-Thanet *Cant* 79-82; Canada from 82; Chapl Royal St Geo Coll Toronto 82-89; R Toronto Epiphany and St Mark 89-04; R Toronto Transfiguration from 04; Can Toronto from 01. *118 Montgomery Avenue, #318W, Toronto ON, Canada, M4R 1E3* Tel (001) (416) 482 2462
E-mail michaelburgess@sympatico.ca

BURGESS, Michael Walter. Bps' Coll Cheshunt 66. **d** 68 **p** 70. C Hammersmith St Matt *Lon* 68-70; C Boreham Wood All SS *St Alb* 70-73; V Flamstead 74-77; V St Marylebone Annunciation Bryanston Street *Lon* from 77. *4 Wyndham Place, London W1H 1AP* Tel (020) 7262 4329

BURGESS, Neil. b 53. Univ of Wales (Lamp) BA75 Nottm Univ MTh87 PhD93. St Mich Coll Llan 75. **d** 77 **p** 78. C Cheadle *Lich* 77-79; C Longton 79-82; TV Hanley H Ev 82-86; C Uttoxeter w Bramshall 86-87; Lect Linc Th Coll 87-95; Hon C Linc Minster Gp *Linc* 88-95; Dioc Dir of Clergy Tr *S'well* 95-00; C Newark 97-00; Perm to Offic *Linc* from 00. *23 Drury Lane, Lincoln LN1 3BN* Tel (01522) 539408
E-mail ann.burgess@btinternet.com

BURGESS, Sister Patricia Jean. b 16. Edin Univ BSc38. New Coll Edin 65. **dss** 69 **d** 86. NSM Roslin (Rosslyn Chpl) *Edin* 69-73; Community of the Transfiguration Midlothian from 72. *Hermitage of the Transfiguration, 70E Clerk Street, Loanhead EH20 9RG*

BURGESS, Paul Christopher James. b 41. Qu Coll Cam BA63 MA67. Lon Coll of Div 66. **d** 68 **p** 69. C Islington St Mary *Lon* 68-72; C Church Stretton *Heref* 73-74; Pakistan 74-83; Warden Carberry Tower (Ch of Scotland) 84-86; Progr Co-ord 86-88; TV Livingston LEP *Edin* 88-92. *Address temp unknown*

BURGESS, Peter Alan. b 40. St Edm Ho Cam BA86 MA89 MPhil86 St Jo Coll York MA99. Cranmer Hall Dur 02. **d** 03 **p** 04. NSM Wheldrake w Thorganby *York* from 03. *2 Derwent Drive, Wheldrake, York YO19 6AL* Tel (01904) 448309
E-mail burgesspr@btinternet.com

BURGESS, Roy. b 32. S Dios Minl Tr Scheme 80. **d** 83 **p** 84. NSM Bentworth and Shalden and Lasham *Win* 83-89; R Ingoldsby *Linc* 89-97; RD Beltisloe 93-97; rtd 97; Perm to Offic *Nor* from 98. *4 Melton Gate, Wymondham NR18 0PQ* Tel (01953) 606449

BURGESS, Roy Graham. b 47. Birm Univ CertCYW72 Bulmershe Coll of HE DMS81. Ox Min Course CBTS94. **d** 94 **p** 95. C Easthampstead *Ox* 94-99; C Wokingham St Paul 99-04; P-in-c Owlsmoor from 04. *The Vicarage, 107 Owlsmoor Road, Owlsmoor, Sandhurst GU47 0SS* Tel (01344) 780110 *or* 771286
E-mail revroy@compriest.freeserve.co.uk

BURGHALL, Kenneth Miles. b 34. Selw Coll Cam BA57 MA61. Qu Coll Birm 57. **d** 59 **p** 60. C Macclesfield St Mich *Ches* 59-63; CF 63-66; P-in-c Birkenhead Priory *Ches* 67-71; V Macclesfield

St Paul 71-87; V Lower Peover 87-04; P-in-c Over Peover 92-04; rtd 04. *45 Ullswater Road, Congleton CW12 4JE* Tel (01260) 289277

BURGON, Canon George Irvine. b 41. Edin Th Coll 62. **d** 65 **p** 66. C Dundee St Mary Magd *Bre* 65-68; C Wellingborough All Hallows *Pet* 68-71; P-in-c Norton 71-73; TV Daventry w Norton 73-75; V Northampton St Mary 75-98; R Rothwell w Orton, Rushton w Glendon and Pipewell from 98; Can Pet Cathl from 95; Hon Chapl ATC from 02. *The Vicarage, High Street, Rothwell, Kettering NN14 6BQ* Tel (01536) 710268 E-mail george@georgeburgon.demon.co.uk

BURKE, Charles Michael. b 28. Keble Coll Ox BA51 MA54 Ox Univ DipEd52. Glouc Th Course. **d** 84 **p** 85. C Colwall w Upper Colwall and Coddington *Heref* 84-88; V Canon Pyon w Kings Pyon and Birley 88-98; P-in-c Wellington 96-98; rtd 98; Perm to Offic *Heref* from 98. *Pyons, 7 Stretton Close, Fayre Oakes, Hereford HR4 0QN* Tel (01432) 270068

BURKE, Christopher Mark. b 65. Cov Poly LLB87. Ripon Coll Cuddesdon 89. **d** 92 **p** 93. C Nunthorpe *York* 92-96; V S Bank 96-02; R Stepney St Dunstan and All SS *Lon* from 02. *St Dunstan and All Saints Rectory, Rectory Square, London E1 3NQ* Tel and fax (020) 7791 3545 E-mail christopher.burke@btinternet.com

BURKE, Colin Douglas. b 41. Bp Otter Coll CertEd64. **d** 92 **p** 93. OLM Fressingfield, Mendham etc *St E* 92-99; P-in-c Oare w Culbone *B & W* from 99. *The Rectory, Oare, Lynton EX35 6NX* Tel (01598) 741270

BURKE, Elisabeth Ann. CertEd. **d** 05. OLM E Horsley and Ockham w Hatchford and Downside *Guildf* from 05. *39 Copse Road, Cobham KT11 2TW* Tel (01932) 863886

BURKE, Eric John. b 44. Llan Dioc Tr Scheme 81. **d** 85 **p** 86. NSM Cardiff St Jo *Llan* 85-95; Chapl Asst Univ Hosp of Wales and Llandough NHS Trust 95-00; Chapl Asst Cardiff and Vale NHS Trust from 00. *Chaplaincy Department, University Hospital of Wales, Heath Park, Cardiff CF4 4XW* Tel (029) 2074 3230 *or* 2079 8147

BURKE, Jonathan. b 53. Lon Univ BEd. Westcott Ho Cam 79. **d** 82 **p** 83. C Weymouth H Trin *Sarum* 82-85; R Bere Regis and Affpuddle w Turnerspuddle 85-92; NSM Talbot Village from 04. *Address temp unknown*

BURKE, Kelvin Stephen. b 56. Man Univ BA77 FCA81. Cranmer Hall Dur. **d** 99 **p** 00. C Stanley *Wakef* 99-02; P-in-c Wakef St Andr and St Mary from 02. *25 Barratts Road, Wakefield WF1 3RT* Tel (01924) 375229 Mobile 07802-677785 E-mail jburke@totalise.co.uk

BURKE, Michael Robert. b 61. Leeds Univ BA83. Trin Coll Bris BA89. **d** 89 **p** 90. C Anston *Sheff* 89-92; V Crosspool 92-00; V Hucclecote *Glouc* from 00. *128 Hucclecote Road, Gloucester GL3 3SB* Tel (01452) 610568 E-mail mikburke@aol.com

BURKE, Wayne Jackson. b 51. San Francisco State Univ BA76 MA78 Univ of Wales (Cardiff) PhD91. St Steph Ho Ox 01. **d** 02 **p** 03. NSM Gtr Athens *Eur* from 02. *Stratigou Eindou 14, 185 36 Piraeus, Greece* Tel (0030) (10) 418 2251 E-mail burke@hol.gr

BURKE, William Spencer Dwerryhouse. b 46. Ripon Coll Cuddesdon 90. **d** 92 **p** 93. C Watford St Mich *St Alb* 92-95; R Castor w Sutton and Upton w Marholm *Pet* from 95. *The Rectory, 5 Church Hill, Castor, Peterborough PE5 7AU* Tel (01733) 380244

BURKETT, Canon Christopher Paul. b 52. Warwick Univ BA75 Birm Univ DipTh77 Westmr Coll Ox DipApTh92 MTh93. Qu Coll Birm 75. **d** 78 **p** 79. C Streetly *Lich* 78-81; C Harlescott 81-83; TV Leek and Meerbrook 83-89; Chapl Leek Moorlands Hosp 83-89; Area Sec USPG *Ches* 89-92; V Whitegate w Lt Budworth *Ches* 92-00; Asst CME Officer 93-00; Can Res Ches Cathl from 00; Bp's Chapl from 00. *5 Abbey Green, Chester CH1 2JH* Tel (01244) 347500 E-mail bpchaplain@chester.anglican.org

BURKILL, Mark Edward. b 56. MA PhD. Trin Coll Bris. **d** 84 **p** 85. C Cheadle *Ches* 84-88; C Harold Wood *Chelmsf* 88-91; V Leyton Ch Ch from 91. *The Vicarage, 52 Elm Road, London E11 4DW* Tel (020) 8539 4980 E-mail mark.burkill@talk21.com

BURKITT, Paul Adrian. b 49. RMN75 SRN77 Coll of Ripon & York St Jo Cert Counselling 89. St Steph Ho Ox 84. **d** 86 **p** 87. C Whitby *York* 86-90; V Egton w Grosmont 90-93; V Newington w Dairycoates 93-96; P-in-c Kingston upon Hull St Mary from 96; P-in-c Sculcoates from 04. *223 Cottingham Road, Hull HU5 4AU* Tel (01482) 343182

BURKITT, Richard Francis. b 49. Leeds Univ BA71 CertEd72. Sarum & Wells Th Coll 82. **d** 90 **p** 90. R Fraserburgh w New Pitsligo *Ab* 90-95; R Fortrose *Mor* from 95; R Cromarty from 95; R Arpafeelie from 95. *St Andrew's Rectory, 1 Deans Road, Fortrose IV10 8TJ* Tel (01381) 620255 E-mail rfburkitt@btopenworld.com

BURKITT-GRAY, Mrs Joan Katherine. b 47. Portsm Poly BSc68 Southn Univ MPhil74. SEITE 00. **d** 04. NSM Lee St Marg *S'wark* from 04. *7 Foxes Dale, London SE3 9BD* Tel (020) 8463 0365

BURLAND, Clive Beresford. b 37. Sarum & Wells Th Coll 81. **d** 85 **p** 86. C Warblington w Emsworth *Portsm* 85-87; C Cowes St Mary 87-92; V Gurnard 92-98; R Northwood 93-98; rtd 98; Perm to Offic *Portsm* from 98. *5A Orchard Close, Freshwater PO40 9BQ* Tel (01983) 753949

BURLEIGH, David John. b 42. FCII69. St Deiniol's Hawarden 84. **d** 87 **p** 88. NSM Lache cum Saltney *Ches* 87-88; NSM Eastham 89-92; C Birkenhead Priory 92-95; P-in-c Duloe w Herodsfoot *Truro* 95-99; TV Liskeard, St Keyne, St Pinnock, Morval etc 95-99; R Duloe, Herodsfoot, Morval and St Pinnock 99-01; V Bath St Barn w Englishcombe *B & W* from 01. *The Vicarage, Mount View, Southdown, Bath BA2 1JX* Tel (01225) 478952

BURLEIGH, Walter Coleridge. b 41. WMMTC 89. **d** 89 **p** 90. NSM N Evington *Leic* 90-96; Perm to Offic from 96. *20 Border Drive, Leicester LE4 2JH* Tel 0116-235 9230

BURLES, Canon Robert John. b 54. Bris Univ BSc75. St Jo Coll Nottm LTh86. **d** 88 **p** 89. C Mansfield SS Pet and Paul *S'well* 88-91; C The Lydiards *Bris* 91-92; TV W Swindon and the Lydiards 92-97; TR Swindon St Jo and St Andr from 97; Hon Can Bris Cathl from 04. *The Vicarage, Verwood Close, Swindon SN3 2LE* Tel (01793) 611473 Fax 574924 E-mail rob@burles.waitrose.com

BURLEY, John Roland James. b 46. St Jo Coll Cam BA67 MA70 Ball Coll Ox Dip Geochemistry 68. Trin Episc Sch for Min Ambridge Penn MDiv88. **d** 81 **p** 82. SAMS Chile 81-90; TV Southgate *Chich* 90-99; R Alfold and Loxwood *Guildf* from 99. *The Rectory, Vicarage Hill, Loxwood, Billingshurst RH14 0RG* Tel and fax (01403) 752320 E-mail john@burleys.co.uk

BURLEY, Michael. b 58. Ridley Hall Cam 86. **d** 89 **p** 90. C Scarborough St Mary w Ch Ch and H Apostles *York* 89-92; C Drypool 93; TV 93-97; V Sutton St Mich 97-03; V Burley in Wharfedale *Bradf* from 03. *The Vicarage, Corn Mill Lane, Burley in Wharfedale, Ilkley LS29 7DR* Tel (01943) 863216 E-mail burley@standrews.karoo.co.uk

BURLTON, Aelred Harry. b 49. Sarum & Wells Th Coll 75. **d** 78 **p** 79. C Feltham *Lon* 78-82; Chapl Heathrow Airport 83-94; P-in-c Harmondsworth 92-94; R St Buryan, St Levan and Sennen *Truro* 94-05; rtd 05. *The Rectory, St Buryan, Penzance TR19 6BB* Tel (01736) 810216

BURLTON, William Frank. b 12. K Coll Lon. **d** 43 **p** 44. C Glouc St Mark *Glouc* 43-46; C Northleach and Hampnett w Stowell and Yanworth 46-48; C St Briavels 48-51; R Cromhall 51-78; Chapl HM Pris Leyhill 54-89; R Cromhall w Tortworth *Glouc* 78-82; rtd 82; Perm to Offic *Glouc* 82-89 and *Truro* from 89. *24 Godolphin Terrace, Marazion TR17 0EX* Tel (01736) 710699

BURMAN, Philip Harvey. b 47. Kelham Th Coll 66. **d** 70 **p** 71. C Huyton St Mich *Liv* 70-75; C Farnworth 75-77; TV Kirkby 77-83; V Hindley All SS 83-93; V Middlesbrough St Martin *York* 93-97; V Middlesbrough St Martin w St Cuth 97-99; P-in-c Eccleston St Thos *Liv* from 99. *St Thomas's Vicarage, 21 St George's Road, St Helens WA10 4LH* Tel (01744) 22295

BURMAN, Thomas George. b 41. S'wark Ord Course 86. **d** 89 **p** 90. NSM Forest Hill *S'wark* 89-03; NSM Perry Hill St Geo w Ch Ch and St Paul from 03. *131 Como Road, London SE23 2JN* Tel (020) 8699 8929

BURMAN, William Guest. b 26. St Cath Coll Cam MA55 Worc Coll Ox MA63. St Steph Ho Ox 81. **d** 83 **p** 84. C Weymouth H Trin *Sarum* 83-86; R Exton and Winsford and Cutcombe w Luxborough *B & W* 86-89; TV Langport Area Chs 89-91; rtd 91; Perm to Offic *B & W* 91-98 and from 02; Master Bath St Mary Magd Holloway from 94. *8 Stoneleigh Court, Lansdown Road, Bath BA1 5TL* Tel (01225) 312140

BURMESTER, Stephen John. b 66. Leeds Univ BSc87. Wycliffe Hall Ox 96. **d** 98 **p** 99. C Lenton *S'well* 98-02; C Bebington *Ches* from 02. *2 Wellington Road, Bebington, Wirral CH63 7NF* Tel 0151-645 9584 E-mail burmester@hotmail.com

BURN, Geoffrey Livingston. b 60. Sydney Univ BSc83 Imp Coll Lon PhD87 St Jo Coll Dur BA95. Cranmer Hall Dur DipMin96. **d** 96 **p** 97. C St Austell *Truro* 96-03; Perm to Offic *Cant* from 03. *Barramundi, Bewsbury Cross Lane, Whitfield, Dover CT16 3EZ* Tel (01304) 820314

BURN, Mrs Helen Mary. b 64. Down Coll Cam BA86 Ox Univ PGCE88 Ex Univ MA02. SW Minl Tr Course 00. **d** 03 **p** 04. C Eythorne and Elvington w Waldershare etc *Cant* from 03. *Barramundi, Bewsbury Cross Lane, Whitfield, Dover CT16 3EZ* Tel (01304) 820314

BURN, Leonard Louis. b 44. K Coll Lon BD67 AKC67. **d** 68 **p** 69. C Kingswinford St Mary *Lich* 68-70; C S Ascot *Ox* 70-72; C Caversham 72-76; Chapl Selly Oak Hosp Birm 76-81; Bris City Hosp 81-82; P-in-c Bris St Mich *Bris* 81-83; R Peopleton and White Ladies Aston w Churchill etc *Worc* 83-88; V Bengeworth 88-97; Chapl St Richard's Hospice Worc 88-97; Chapl Evesham Coll 90-97; rtd 97; Perm to Offic *Glouc* from 97 and *Worc* 97-98; Chapl Worcs Community and Mental Health Trust from 98. *Beckford Rise, Beckford, Tewkesbury GL20 7AN* Tel and fax (01386) 881160 Mobile 07734-505663

BURN, Richard James Southerden. b 34. Pemb Coll Cam BA56. Wells Th Coll 56. **d** 58 **p** 59. C Cheshunt *St Alb* 58-62; C

Leighton Buzzard 65-66; C Glastonbury St Jo *B & W* 66-68; P-in-c Prestonpans *Edin* 68-71; P-in-c Stokesay *Heref* 71-75; P-in-c Dorrington 75-81; P-in-c Stapleton 75-81; P-in-c Leebotwood w Longnor 75-81; P-in-c Smethcott w Woolstaston 81; TR Melbury *Sarum* 81-87; P-in-c Quendon w Rickling and Wicken Bonhunt *Chelmsf* 87-92; R Quendon w Rickling and Wicken Bonhunt etc 92-95; rtd 95; NSM Isleworth St Fran *Lon* 95-00. *Les Grandes Vignes, Litout, 24610 Minzac, France* Tel (0033) (5) 53 80 05 81

BURN, Robert Pemberton. b 34. Peterho Cam BA56 MA60 Lon Univ PhD68. CMS Tr Coll Chislehurst 60. **d** 63 **p** 81. India 63-71; Perm to Offic *Ely* 71-81; P-in-c Foxton 81-88; Perm to Offic *Ex* from 89. *Sunnyside, Barrack Road, Exeter EX2 6AB* Tel (01392) 430028

BURN-MURDOCH, Aidan Michael. b 35. Trin Coll Cam BA60 MA63. Ridley Hall Cam 59. **d** 61 **p** 62. C Bishopwearmouth St Gabr *Dur* 61-63; Tutor Ridley Hall Cam 63-67; CMS Miss 67-70; India 68-70; R Hawick *Edin* 70-77; Bp's Co-ord of Evang *S & B* 77-81; R Reynoldston w Penrice and Llangennith 77-83; R Port Eynon w Rhosili and Llanddewi and Knelston 83-89; R Uddingston and Cambuslang *Glas* 89-97; rtd 97; Missr Eyemouth *Edin* 98-00. *19 Blairston Avenue, Bothwell, Glasgow G71 8RZ* Tel (01698) 853377

BURNET, Norman Andrew Gray. b 32. Aber Univ BEd77 Cam Univ MLitt92. Edin Th Coll 53. **d** 55 **p** 56. C Ayr *Glas* 55-58; S Africa 58-69; C St Jo Cathl Umtata 58-63; R Mt Frere 63-69; R Leven *St And* 69-72; Perm to Offic *Ab, Bre* and *Ely* 73-81; P-in-c Brinkley, Burrough Green and Carlton *Ely* 82-83; P-in-c Westley Waterless 82-83; Australia 83-84; R Fraserburgh w New Pitsligo *Ab* 85-89; P-in-c Bicker *Linc* 89; V Bicker and Wigtoft 89-97; rtd 97; Perm to Offic *Nor* 97-99; *Linc* 97-00. *61 Westlode Street, Spalding PE11 2AE* Tel (01775) 767429 Fax as telephone

BURNETT, Canon John Capenhurst. b 19. AKC49. **d** 49 **p** 50. C Shirehampton *Bris* 49-53; C Stoke Bishop 53-56; V Wroughton 56-76; RD Cricklade 70-76; Hon Can Bris Cathl 74-85; V Bris St Andr w St Bart 76-85; rtd 85; Perm to Offic *Bris* from 85. *57 Upper Cranbrook Road, Bristol BS6 7UR* Tel 0117-924 5284

BURNETT, Mrs Patricia Kay. b 38. Newnham Coll Cam MA60. Sarum Th Coll 94. **d** 97 **p** 98. NSM Jarvis Brook *Chich* from 97. *20 St Richards Road, Crowborough TN6 3AT* Tel (01892) 655668

BURNETT, Susan Mary. b 50. Lon Univ BEd73 St Jo Coll Dur DipTh76. **dss** 78 **d** 87 **p** 94. Welling *S'wark* 78-83; E Greenwich Ch Ch w St Andr and St Mich 83-91; Par Dn 87-91; Par Dn Sydenham All SS 91-94; C 94-95; C Lower Sydenham St Mich 91-95; V from 95. *St Michael's Vicarage, Champion Crescent, London SE26 4HH* Tel (020) 8778 7196

BURNETT-HALL, Mrs Karen. b 46. Bp Grosseteste Coll CertEd68 Lon Univ BD82. Oak Hill Th Coll 86. **d** 89 **p** 94. Par Dn Norbury *Ches* 89-92; NSM York St Paul *York* 93-95; NSM York St Barn 95-99; P-in-c from 00. *5 Grosvenor Terrace, York YO30 7AG* Tel (01904) 638935 E-mail karen.bh@btinternet.com

✠**BURNHAM, The Rt Revd Andrew.** b 48. New Coll Ox BA69 BA71 MA73 Westmr Coll Ox CertEd72 ARCO(CHM). St Steph Ho Ox 81. **d** 83 **p** 84 **c** 00. Hon C Clifton *S'well* 83-85; C Beeston 85-87; V Carrington 87-94; Vice-Prin St Steph Ho Ox 95-00; Suff Bp Ebbsfleet (PEV) *Cant* from 00; Hon Asst Bp B & W, Ex, Lich and Ox from 01. *Bishop's House, Church Lane, Dry Sandford, Abingdon OX13 6JP* Tel (01865) 390746 Fax 390611 E-mail bishop.andrew@ebbsfleet.org.uk

BURNHAM, Frank Leslie. b 23. Edin Th Coll 52. **d** 55 **p** 56. C York St Mary Bishophill Senior *York* 55-58; C Marfleet 58-62; V 62-72; TR 72-74; V Acomb St Steph 74-85; C Fulford 85-88; rtd 88; Perm to Offic *York* from 88. *Dulverton Hall, Esplanade, Scarborough YO11 2AR* Tel (01723) 340101

BURNHAM, Stephen Patrick James. b 75. Ch Ch Ox BA97. Westcott Ho Cam 00. **d** 02 **p** 03. C Vale of Belvoir Par *Leic* from 02. *The Rectory, 2 Church Lane, Redmile, Nottingham NG13 0GE* Tel (01949) 844137 Mobile 07905-882805

BURNINGHAM, Frederick George. b 34. ALCD60. **d** 60 **p** 61. C New Beckenham St Paul *Roch* 60-63; Canada 63-68 and 89-95; C Wisley w Pyrford *Guildf* 68-69; P-in-c Sydenham H Trin *S'wark* 69-71; C Broadwater St Mary *Chich* 72-77; R Sotterley, Willingham, Shadingfield, Ellough etc *St E* 77-82; R Ipswich St Clem w H Trin 82-89; P-in-c Thorndon w Rishangles, Stoke Ash, Thwaite etc 95-99; rtd 99; Perm to Offic *Bradf* from 99. *8 Meadow Rise, Skipton BD23 1BT* Tel (01756) 794440

BURNINGHAM, Richard Anthony. b 47. Keele Univ BA70 Aber Univ CQSW77 Roehampton Inst PGCE85. All Nations Chr Coll 82 Oak Hill Th Coll 94. **d** 96 **p** 97. C Reigate St Mary *S'wark* 96-00; V Weston *Win* from 00. *The Vicarage, Weston Lane, Southampton SO19 9HG* Tel (023) 8044 8421 E-mail richardb@ukonline.co.uk

BURNISTON, Aubrey John. b 53. St Jo Coll Dur BA92 Leeds Univ MA03. Cranmer Hall Dur 79. **d** 83 **p** 84. C Owton Manor *Dur* 83-86; TV Rugby St Andr *Cov* 86-93; V Heaton St Martin *Bradf* from 93; Bp's Adv in Liturgy from 00. *St Martin's Vicarage, 130 Haworth Road, Bradford BD9 6LL* Tel (01274) 543004 Fax 08701-617424 E-mail john@saintmartin.demon.co.uk

BURNLEY, Suffragan Bishop of. *See* GODDARD, The Rt Revd John William

BURNS, Dane. b 51. DipTh. **d** 85 **p** 86. C Enniskillen *Clogh* 85-87; I Augher w Newtownsaville and Eskrahoole 87-92; Dioc Communications Officer 91-92; I Camus-juxta-Bann *D & R* 92-96. *86 Donneybrewer Road, Eglinton, Londonderry BT47 3PD*

BURNS, Canon Edward Joseph. b 38. Liv Univ BSc58 St Cath Soc Ox BA61 MA64. Wycliffe Hall Ox 58. **d** 61 **p** 62. C Leyland St Andr *Blackb* 61-64; C Burnley St Pet 64-67; V Chorley St Jas 67-75; V Fulwood Ch Ch 75-03; RD Preston 79-86; Chapl Sharoe Green Hosp Preston 81-94; Hon Can Blackb Cathl *Blackb* 86-03; Bp's Adv on Hosp Chapls 89-94; rtd 03. *17 Greenacres, Fulwood, Preston PR2 7DA* Tel (01772) 864741 E-mail eddieandsheila@ejburns.freeserve.co.uk

BURNS, Canon James Denis. b 43. Lich Th Coll 69. **d** 72 **p** 73. C Gt Wyrley *Lich* 72-75; C Atherton *Man* 75-76; Asst Chapl Sheff Ind Miss *Sheff* 76-79; C-in-c Masborough St Paul w St Jo 76-78; C-in-c Northfield St Mich 76-78; V Rotherham St Paul, St Mich and St Jo Ferham Park 78-79; V Lancaster Ch Ch *Blackb* 79-81; V Lancaster Ch Ch w St Jo and St Anne 81-86; V Chorley St Pet 86-96; R Rufford from 96; Warden Past Assts from 96; Hon Can Blackb Cathl from 99. *St Mary's Rectory, 17 Church Road, Rufford, Ormskirk L40 1TA* Tel (01704) 821261

BURNS, John Macdonald. *See* ODA-BURNS, John Macdonald

BURNS, Matthew. Coll of Resurr Mirfield. **d** 05. C Wrexham *St As* from 05. *6 College Street, Wrexham LL13 8LU* Tel (01978) 361724

BURNS, Michael John. b 53. AKC76. Chich Th Coll 76. **d** 77 **p** 78. C Broseley w Benthall *Heref* 77-81; C Stevenage All SS Pin Green *St Alb* 81-84; V Tattenham Corner and Burgh Heath *Guildf* 84-92; C and Chapl Younger People Milton Keynes *Ox* 92-00; P-in-c Potters Bar K Chas *St Alb* from 00. *The Vicarage, 8 Dugdale Hill Lane, Potters Bar EN6 2DW* Tel (01707) 661266

BURNS, Robert Joseph. b 34. Wycliffe Hall Ox 67. **d** 71 **p** 72. C Portswood Ch Ch *Win* 71-73; C Woking St Jo *Guildf* 73-77; C Glas St Mary *Glas* 77; Bp's Dom Chapl 77-78; R Glas Gd Shep and Ascension 78-92; rtd 92. *c/o Seaman, 25 Westfield Drive, Glasgow G52 2SG* Tel 0141-882 3363

BURNS, Stephen. b 70. Grey Coll Dur BA92 MA94 Clare Coll Cam MLitt96 Dur Univ PhD03. Ridley Hall Cam 93. **d** 96 **p** 97. C Houghton le Spring *Dur* 96-99; TV Gateshead 99-02; Dir Urban Miss Cen Cranmer Hall 99-02; Tutor Qu Coll Birm from 03. *73 Farquhar Road, Edgbaston, Birmingham B15 2QP* Tel 0121-452 2607 *or* 454 1527 E-mail sburns@queens.ac.uk

BURNS, Stuart Keith. b 66. Bp Grosseteste Coll BEd88 Lon Univ BD94 Leeds Univ MA95 PhD99. St Jo Coll Nottm. **d** 03 **p** 04. C Gt Bowden w Welham, Glooston and Cranoe etc *Leic* from 03. *The Rectory, 3 Stonton Road, Church Langton, Market Harborough LE16 7SZ* Tel (01858) 540202 E-mail s.k.burns@zetnet.co.uk

BURNS, The Rt Revd Stuart Maitland. b 46. Leeds Univ BA67. Coll of Resurr Mirfield 67. **d** 69 **p** 70. C Wyther Ven Bede *Ripon* 69-73; Asst Chapl Leeds Univ 73-77; Asst Chapl Leeds Poly 73-77; P-in-c Thornthwaite w Thruscross and Darley 77-84; V Leeds Gipton Epiphany 84-89; OSB from 89; Burford Priory from 89; Prior 96-01; Abbot from 01; Lic to Offic *Ox* from 89. *Burford Priory, Priory Lane, Burford, Oxford OX18 4SQ* Tel (01993) 823605 E-mail abbot@burfordosb.org.uk

BURNS, Stuart Sandeman. b 62. Natal Univ BA85 Ball Coll Ox BA89 MA94. St Paul's Coll Grahamstown. **d** 89 **p** 90. S Africa 89-99; C Stanger 90-91; Dir Scripture Union Ind Schs 92-94; R Drakensberg 95-97; Chapl W Prov Prep Sch 98-99; I Kinneigh Union *C, C & R* 99-02; TV Bourne Valley *Sarum* from 02. *The Vicarage, Winterbourne Earls, Salisbury SP4 6HA* Tel (01980) 611350 E-mail winterbourne@onetel.com

BURNS, Susan Janice Cronbach. b 55. Sheff Univ BA75 CertEd76. **dss** 80 **d** 83 **p** 88. Maidenhead St Andr and St Mary *Ox* 80-82; New Zealand from 82. *Reynolds Road, RD 3, Roto-o-Rangi, Cambridge, New Zealand* Tel (0064) (7) 827 8352

BURR, Mrs Ann Pamela. b 39. S Dios Minl Tr Scheme 83. **dss** 86 **d** 87 **p** 94. Fareham H Trin *Portsm* 86-87; Hon C from 87; Hon Asst Chapl Knowle Hosp Fareham 86-90; Asst Chapl Qu Alexandra Hosp Portsm 90-92; Chapl Portsm Hosps NHS Trust from 92. *3 Bruce Close, Fareham PO16 7QJ* Tel (01329) 281375

BURR, Christopher Edward. b 68. Univ of Wales (Cardiff) BTh01. St Mich Coll Llan 98. **d** 01 **p** 02. C Llantrisant *Llan* 01-04; P-in-c Pwllgwaun and Llanddewi Rhondda from 04. *The Vicarage, Lanelay Crescent, Pontypridd CF37 1JB* Tel and fax (01443) 402417 E-mail chris.burr1@ntlworld.com

BURR, Paul David. b 62. Birm Univ LLB83. St Jo Coll Nottm MA99. **d** 99 **p** 00. C Newark *S'well* 99-02; C Eaton *Nor* 02-05; P-in-c Swardeston w E Carleton, Intwood, Keswick etc from 05. *The Vicarage, The Common, Swardeston, Norwich NR14 8EB* Tel (01508) 570550 E-mail paul.burr1@ntlworld.com

BURR, Raymond Leslie. b 43. NEOC 82 Edin Th Coll 84. **d** 85 **p** 86. C Hartlepool St Paul *Dur* 85-87; C Sherburn w Pittington

87-89; R Lyons 89-95; RD Houghton 94-96; V S Shields St Hilda w St Thos from 95. *St Hilda's Vicarage, 40 Lawe Road, South Shields NE33 2EU* Tel 0191-454 1414 E-mail ray.burr@talk21.com

BURRELL, David Philip. b 56. Southn Univ BTh90. Sarum & Wells Th Coll 85. **d** 88 **p** 89. C Ixworth and Bardwell *St E* 88-91; P-in-c Haughley w Wetherden 91-96; P-in-c Culford, W Stow and Wordwell w Flempton etc 96-98; R Lark Valley from 98. *The Rectory, West Stow, Bury St Edmunds IP28 6ET* Tel (01284) 728556

BURRELL, Godfrey John. b 49. Reading Univ BSc70 Qu Coll Ox CertEd71. Wycliffe Hall Ox 84 Th Educn Coll Johannesburg DipTh00. **d** 86 **p** 87. C Didcot All SS *Ox* 86-89; S Africa 90-01; Chapl St Alb Coll Pretoria 90-95; Chapl Pretoria Cen Pris 90-94; R Lynnwood Trin Ch 96-01; Adn Pretoria E 00-01; R Lighthorne *Cov* from 01; V Chesterton from 01; V Newbold Pacey w Moreton Morrell from 01. *The Rectory, Church Lane, Lighthorne, Warwick CV35 0AR* Tel (01926) 651279 E-mail burrell@lighthorne.fsnet.co.uk

BURRELL, Martin John. b 51. ARCM71. Trin Coll Bris BA95. **d** 95 **p** 96. C Cant St Mary Bredin *Cant* 95-99; V Cranbrook from 99. *The Vicarage, Waterloo Road, Cranbrook TN17 3JQ* Tel (01580) 712150 E-mail martburr@aol.com

BURRELL, Canon Maurice Claude. b 30. Bris Univ BA54 MA63 Lanc Univ PhD78. Tyndale Hall Bris. **d** 55 **p** 56. C Wandsworth St Steph *S'wark* 55-57; C Whitehall Park St Andr Hornsey Lane *Lon* 57-59; R Kirby Cane *Nor* 59-63; R Ellingham 61-63; Chapl K Sch Gutersloh, W Germany 63-67; R Widford *Chelmsf* 67-71; Chapl and Lect St Mary's Coll Cheltenham 71-75; Dir of Educn *Nor* 75-86; Hon Can Nor Cathl 77-95; Dioc Dir of Tr 87-95; rtd 95; Perm to Offic *Nor* from 95. *37 Ireton Close, Thorpe St Andrew, Norwich NR7 0TW* Tel (01603) 702510 E-mail maurice@37iretoncl.freeserve.co.uk

BURRIDGE, Richard Alan. b 55. Univ Coll Ox BA77 MA81 Nottm Univ CertEd78 PhD89 SNTS95. St Jo Coll Nottm 82. **d** 85 **p** 86. C Bromley SS Pet and Paul *Roch* 85-87; Chapl Ex Univ *Ex* 87-94; Dean K Coll Lon from 94; Lic Preacher *Lon* from 94; Perm to Offic *S'wark* from 98 and *Chelmsf* from 05. *King's College, Strand, London WC2R 2LS* Tel (020) 7848 2333 Fax 7848 2344 E-mail richard.burridge@kcl.ac.uk

BURRIDGE-BUTLER, Paul David. *See* BUTLER, Paul David

BURROUGHS, Edward Graham. b 36. K Coll Lon BD AKC. **d** 60 **p** 61. C Walton St Mary *Liv* 60-63; Zimbabwe from 63. *Box 8045, Belmont, Bulawayo, Zimbabwe* Tel (00263) (9) 78711

BURROW, Miss Alison Sarah. b 59. Homerton Coll Cam BEd82. Westcott Ho Cam 84. **d** 87 **p** 03. Par Dn Hebden Bridge *Wakef* 87-88; Par Dn Prestwood and Gt Hampden *Ox* 88-90; Par Dn Olney w Emberton 90-92; rtd 92; Hon C Bedford St Pet w St Cuth *St Alb* from 02. *2A Waterloo Road, Bedford MK40 3PQ* Tel (01234) 315079

BURROW, Ronald. b 31. Univ Coll Dur BA55. St Steph Ho Ox 83. **d** 85 **p** 86. C Dawlish *Ex* 85-87; TV Ottery St Mary, Alfington, W Hill, Tipton etc 87-91; P-in-c Pyworthy, Pancrasweek and Bridgerule 91-95; rtd 95; Perm to Offic *Ex* from 95. *3 Riverside, Dolphin Street, Colyton EX24 6LU* Tel and fax (01297) 553882

BURROWS, Canon Brian Albert. b 34. Lon Univ DipTh59 Atlantic Sch of Th BTh83. St Aid Birkenhead 56. **d** 59 **p** 60. C Sutton St Geo *Ches* 59-62; Canada 62-69 and from 74; V Stratton St Margaret *Bris* 70-74; Hon Can Frobisher Bay 78-80; rtd 99. *334 Mary Street, Niagara on the Lake ON, Canada, L0S 1J0*

BURROWS, Prof Clifford Robert. b 37. OBE05. Univ of Wales BSc62 Lon Univ PhD69 DSc(Eng)89 Aston Univ Hon DSc01 MIMechE68 FIMechE82 FIEE98 FREng98. Chich Th Coll 75. **d** 76 **p** 77. NSM Brighton St Pet *Chich* 76-78; NSM Brighton St Pet w Chpl Royal 78-80; NSM Brighton St Pet w Chpl Royal and St Jo 80-82; Perm to Offic *Glas* 82-85 and 86-89; NSM Clarkston 85-86; NSM Bath Ch Ch Prop Chpl *B & W* from 90. *Stonecroft, Entry Hill Drive, Bath BA2 5NL* Tel (01225) 334743 Fax 429990

BURROWS, Clive Robert. b 60. Bath Coll of HE BEd82 Ches Coll of HE BA04. N Ord Course 01. **d** 04 **p** 05. C N Wingfield, Clay Cross and Pilsley *Derby* from 04. *The Vicarage, Ankerbold Road, Tupton, Chesterfield S42 6BX* Tel (01246) 864524 E-mail clive.burrows@ntlworld.com

BURROWS, David. b 62. Leeds Univ BA85 MA03. Linc Th Coll 86. **d** 88 **p** 89. C Kippax w Allerton Bywater *Ripon* 88-91; C Manston 91-95; Chapl Killingbeck Hosp 94; V Halifax St Anne Southowram *Wakef* 95-00; P-in-c Charlestown 95-00; V Southowram and Claremount 00-02; TV Elland from 02; Chapl Overgate Hospice from 02. *All Saints' Vicarage, Charles Street, Elland HX5 0JF* Tel (01422) 373184 Mobile 07932-694555 E-mail fatherdavid@micromundi.net

BURROWS, David MacPherson. b 43. N Ord Course. **d** 82 **p** 83. NSM Newburgh *Liv* 82-93; NSM Newburgh w Westhead from 93; Dioc Adv NSM from 03. *34 Woodrow Drive, Newburgh, Wigan WN8 7LB* Tel (01257) 462948

BURROWS, Diane. b 48. **d** 05. NSM Saltash *Truro* from 05. *20 Andrews Way, Hatt, Saltash PL12 6PE* Tel (01752) 842540 E-mail di.burrows@connells.co.uk

BURROWS, Graham Charles. b 47. Leeds Univ CertEd69 Open Univ BA81. N Ord Course 87. **d** 90 **p** 91. C Chorlton-cum-Hardy St Clem *Man* 90-93; TV Horwich 93; TV Horwich and Rivington 93-94. *29 Heaton Road, Lostock, Bolton BL6 4EE* Tel (01204) 494826

BURROWS, Jean. b 54. CertEd75. Trin Coll Bris 89. **d** 91 **p** 94. C Allesley *Cov* 91-95; C Thorley *St Alb* 95-99; P-in-c Harrold and Carlton w Chellington from 99. *The Rectory, 3 The Moor, Carlton, Bedford MK43 7JR* Tel and fax (01234) 720262 E-mail jeanburrows@jeanius.me.uk

BURROWS, Canon John Edward. b 36. Leeds Univ BA60 PGCE63. Coll of Resurr Mirfield. **d** 63 **p** 65. C Much Hadham *St Alb* 63-65; Hon C Haggerston St Mary w St Chad *Lon* 65-73; P-in-c Finsbury St Clem w St Barn and St Matt 73-76; Chapl Woodbridge Sch 76-83; V Ipswich St Bart *St E* 83-03; Hon Can St E Cathl 01-03; rtd 03; Perm to Offic *St E* from 03. *55 Berners Street, Ipswich IP1 3LN* Tel (01473) 216629 E-mail burrows@freenetname.co.uk

BURROWS, Joseph Atkinson. b 32. St Aid Birkenhead 58. **d** 61 **p** 62. C Hoole *Ches* 61-67; Jamaica 67-68; C Ayr *Glas* 68-74; R Prestwick 74-78; Hon Chapl RAF 74-78; Hon Chapl RN 74-78; Australia from 78; rtd 97. *3B Cowan Road, St Ives, NSW, Australia 2075* Tel (0061) (2) 9488 9393 *or* 9488 9855 Fax 9983 9352

BURROWS, The Very Revd Michael Andrew James. b 61. TCD BA82 MA85 MLitt86 DipTh87. **d** 87 **p** 88. C Douglas Union w Frankfield *C, C & R* 87-91; Dean of Res TCD 91-94; Min Can St Patr Cathl Dublin 91-94; I Bandon Union *C, C & R* 94-02; Can Cork and Cloyne Cathls 96-02; Dean Cork from 02; I Cork St Fin Barre's Union from 02. *The Deanery, 9 Dean Street, Cork, Irish Republic* Tel and fax (00353) (21) 496 4742 *or* tel 496 3387 E-mail dean@cork.anglican.org

BURROWS, Canon Paul Anthony. b 55. Nottm Univ BA77. Gen Th Sem (NY) STM88 St Steph Ho Ox 77. **d** 79 **p** 80. C Camberwell St Giles *S'wark* 79-81; C St Helier 81-83; C Fareham SS Pet and Paul *Portsm* 83-85; USA from 85; V Union St Luke and All SS New Jersey 85-90; R Temple Hills St Barn Maryland 90-95; P-in-c Des Moines St Mark Iowa 95-01; Can Des Moines Cathl 98-01; R San Francisco Advent of Ch the K California from 01. *162 Hickory Street, San Francisco, CA 94102, USA* E-mail rector@advent-sf.org

BURROWS, The Ven Peter. b 55. BTh. Sarum & Wells Th Coll 80. **d** 83 **p** 84. C Baildon *Bradf* 83-87; R Broughton Astley *Leic* 87-95; TR Broughton Astley and Croft w Stoney Stanton 95-00; RD Guthlaxton I 94-00; Dir of Ords 97-03; Par Development Officer 00-03; Dir Min, Tr and Par Development from 03; Hon Can Leic Cathl 98-05; Adn Leeds *Ripon* from 05. *Archdeacon's Lodge, 3 West Park Grove, Leeds LS8 2HQ* Tel and fax 0113-269 0594 E-mail archdeacon.leeds@riponleeds.anglican.org

BURROWS, Philip Geoffrey. b 59. Birm Univ BSc80. Oak Hill Th Coll DipHE92. **d** 92 **p** 93. C Poynton *Ches* 92-96; Min Cheadle Hulme Em CD 96-03; V Mottram in Longdendale from 03. *30A Broadbottom Road, Mottram, Hyde SK14 6JB* Tel (01457) 762268 E-mail emmanuel@domini.org

BURROWS, Samuel Reginald. b 30. AKC57. **d** 58 **p** 59. C Shildon *Dur* 58-62; C Heworth St Mary 62-67; C-in-c Leam Lane CD 67-72; C-in-c Bishopwearmouth St Mary V w St Pet CD 72-77; R Bewcastle and Stapleton *Carl* 77-82; R Harrington 82-90; P-in-c Millom 90; V 90-95; rtd 95. *40 Lindisfarne Road, Durham DH1 5YQ*

✠**BURROWS, The Rt Revd Simon Hedley.** b 28. K Coll Cam BA52 MA56. Westcott Ho Cam 52. **d** 54 **p** 55 **c** 74. C St John's Wood *Lon* 54-57; Chapl Jes Coll Cam 57-60; V Wyken *Cov* 60-67; V Fareham H Trin *Portsm* 67-71; TR 71-74; Suff Bp Buckingham *Ox* 74-87; Area Bp Buckm 87-94; rtd 94; Hon Asst Bp Win from 94. *8 Quarry Road, Winchester SO23 0JF* Tel (01962) 853332

BURROWS, Victoria Elizabeth. b 61. STETS 01. **d** 04 **p** 05. C The Bourne and Tilford *Guildf* from 04. *Heavitree, Dene Lane, Lower Bourne, Farnham GU10 3PN* Tel (01252) 733563 E-mail vicki@williamburrows.com

BURSELL, His Honour Judge Rupert David Hingston. b 42. QC86. Ex Univ LLB63 St Edm Hall Ox BA67 MA72 DPhil72. St Steph Ho Ox 67. **d** 68 **p** 69. NSM St Marylebone w H Trin *Lon* 68-69; NSM Almondsbury *Bris* 69-71; NSM Bedminster St Fran 71-75; NSM Bedminster 75-82; NSM Bris Ch Ch w St Ewen and All SS 83-88; NSM City of Bris 83-88; Lic to Offic 88-95; Lic to Offic *B & W* 72-92; Chan *Dur* from 89; Chan *B & W* 92; Chan *St Alb* from 92; NSM Cheddar *B & W* from 93; Hon Can St Alb 96-02; Hon CF from 97; Chan *Ox* from 02. *Brookside, 74 Church Road, Winscombe BS25 1BP*

BURSLEM, Christopher David Jeremy Grant. b 35. AKC85. **d** 59 **p** 60. C Bocking St Mary *Chelmsf* 59-63; C Glouc All SS *Glouc* 64-67; R Amberley 67-87; P-in-c Withington and Compton Abdale w Haselton 87-98; rtd 98; Perm to Offic *Derby* from 98. *44 Vestry Road, Oakwood, Derby DE21 2BL* Tel (01332) 830146

BURSON-THOMAS, Michael Edwin. b 52. Sarum & Wells Th Coll 84. **d** 86 **p** 87. C Bitterne Park *Win* 86-89; V Lockerley and E Dean w E and W Tytherley 89-95; P-in-c Fotherby *Linc* 95-99; Asst Local Min Officer 95-99; V Horncastle w Low Toynton from 99; R Greetham w Ashby Puerorum from 99; V High Toynton from 99; RD Horncastle from 01. *The Vicarage, 9 Langton Drive, Horncastle LN9 5AJ* Tel and fax (01507) 525564 *or* 525600 E-mail m.bursonthomas@btinternet.com

BURSTON, Richard John. b 46. MRICS70 MRTPI73. S Dios Minl Tr Scheme 89. **d** 93 **p** 94. Hon C Stratton St Margaret w S Marston etc *Bris* from 93. *17 Crawley Avenue, Swindon SN3 4LB* Tel (01793) 822403

BURSTON, Canon Robert Benjamin Stuart. b 45. St Chad's Coll Dur BA68 DipTh70. **d** 70 **p** 71. C Whorlton *Newc* 70-77; V Alwinton w Holystone and Alnham 77-83; TR Glendale Gp from 83; Hon Can Newc Cathl from 95. *The Rectory, 5 Fenton Drive, Wooler NE71 6DT* Tel and fax (01668) 281551

BURT, David Alan. b 44. K Alfred's Coll Win BTh98. STETS 95. **d** 98 **p** 99. NSM Goring-by-Sea *Chich* 98-03; C from 03. *15 Fernhurst Drive, Goring-by-Sea, Worthing BN12 5AU* Tel and fax (01903) 248671

BURT, Leslie Reginald. b 22. ACIS49. St Aug Coll Cant 65. **d** 66 **p** 67. C Petersfield w Sheet *Portsm* 66-70; Perm to Offic from 82. *44B Victoria Road South, Southsea PO5 2BT* Tel (023) 9273 0989

BURT, Paul Andrew. b 52. Leeds Univ BA74 K Coll Lon MA02. Ridley Hall Cam 82. **d** 84 **p** 85. C Edin St Thos *Edin* 84-88; CMS Bahrain 88-90; R Melrose *Edin* 91-00; Chapl Borders Gen Hosp NHS Trust 93-98; Ho Master Win Coll 00-04; Hd RS Pilgrims' Sch 00-04; Chapl and Hd RE K Coll Sch Cam from 04. *33 Pratt Street, Soham, Ely CB7 5BH* Tel (01353) 722672 E-mail pburt@kcs.cambs.sch.uk

BURT, Roger Malcolm. b 45. MBE91. St Jo Coll Auckland LTh74 SSC. **d** 73 **p** 74. V Tinui New Zealand 73-80; P-in-c Colton *Nor* 80; P-in-c Easton 80; V Easton w Colton and Marlingford 80-88; CF 88-01; P-in-c E Coker w Sutton Bingham and Closworth *B & W* from 01. *The Vicarage, East Coker, Yeovil BA22 9JG* Tel (01935) 862125

BURTON, Andrew John. b 63. St Kath Coll Liv BA84 Cert Div84. Cranmer Hall Dur 86. **d** 88 **p** 89. C Harlescott *Lich* 88-91; C Ches H Trin *Ches* 91-94; P-in-c Congleton St Jas 94-01; R Calton, Cauldon, Grindon, Waterfall etc *Lich* from 01; RD Alstonfield from 03. *The Vicarage, Waterfall Lane, Waterhouses, Stoke-on-Trent ST10 3HT* Tel (01538) 308506 E-mail ajburton@fish.co.uk

BURTON, Antony William James. b 29. Ch Coll Cam BA52 MA56. Cuddesdon Coll 52. **d** 54 **p** 55. C Linc St Nic w St Jo Newport *Linc* 54-57; C Croydon St Jo *Cant* 57-62; V Winterton *Linc* 62-82; V Roxby w Risby 70-82; RD Manlake 76-82; V Nettleham 82-94; rtd 94; Perm to Offic *Linc* 94-02. *28 Eastfield Road, Messingham, Scunthorpe DN17 3PG* Tel (01724) 763916

BURTON, Christopher Paul. b 38. FCA75 Bris Univ PhD00. Clifton Th Coll 67. **d** 69 **p** 70. C Wandsworth All SS *S'wark* 69-72; C York St Paul *York* 72-75; V Castle Vale *Birm* 75-82; R Gt Parndon *Chelmsf* 82-99; TR 99-03; rtd 03; Perm to Offic *St E* from 04. *The Hermitage, Constitution Hill, Sudbury CO10 2PT* Tel (01787) 374121

BURTON, Daniel John Ashworth. b 63. Regent's Park Coll Ox BA88 MA93 Heythrop Coll Lon MTh93. St Mich Coll Llan 93. **d** 94 **p** 95. C Mountain Ash *Llan* 94-97; R St Brides Minor w Bettws 97-02; R St Brides Minor w Bettws w Aberkenfig 02-03; P-in-c Cheetham *Man* from 03. *The Vicarage, 105 Brideoak Street, Manchester M8 0AY* Tel 0161-205 1734 E-mail daniel.burton2@virgin.net

BURTON, David Alan. b 53. St Jo Coll Dur BA. Westcott Ho Cam 81. **d** 84 **p** 85. C Bedford St Andr *St Alb* 84-87; C Leighton Buzzard w Eggington, Hockliffe etc 87-91; V Kingsbury Episcopi w E Lambrook *B & W* 91-94; V Kingsbury Episcopi w E Lambrook, Hambridge etc 94-95; R Bishops Lydeard w Bagborough and Cothelstone 95-03; rtd 04. *1 Summer Close, Hemyock, Cullompton EX15 3PA* Tel (01823) 680055 E-mail david.burton@dial.pipex.com

BURTON, Desmond Jack. b 49. Sarum & Wells Th Coll 70. **d** 73 **p** 74. C Lakenham St Jo *Nor* 73-77; C Gt Yarmouth 77-80; R Tidworth *Sarum* 80-83; Chapl HM Pris Pentonville 83-84; Chapl HM Pris Standford Hill 84-88; Chapl HM Pris Swaleside 88-93; Chapl HM Pris Roch 93-99; Chapl HM Pris Whitemoor 99-05; Chapl HM Pris Whatton from 05. *HM Prison Whatton, Nottingham NG13 9FQ* Tel (01949) 859200 Fax 859201

BURTON, Graham John. b 45. Bris Univ BA69. Tyndale Hall Bris 69. **d** 71 **p** 72. C Leic St Chris *Leic* 71-75; C Southall Green St Jo *Lon* 75-79; CMS Pakistan 80-92; P-in-c Basford w Hyson Green *S'well* 92-99; P-in-c Hyson Green and Forest Fields 99-01; Assoc P from 01; Dir Rainbow Project from 01. *All Saints' Vicarage, 16 All Saints Street, Radford NG7 4DP* Tel 0115-978 2760

BURTON, Hugh Anthony. b 56. Edin Univ BD79. Cranmer Hall Dur 81. **d** 83 **p** 84. C Coalville and Bardon Hill *Leic* 83-87; P-in-c Packington w Normanton-le-Heath 87-92; V 92-96; TV Kidderminster St Geo *Worc* from 96. *38 Comberton Avenue, Kidderminster DY10 3EG* Tel (01562) 824490 E-mail hburton@wfcsmail.com

BURTON, Leslie Samuel Bertram. b 23. **d** 91 **p** 92. NSM St Cleer *Truro* 91-93; Perm to Offic 93-00. *29 Vivian Court, Truro TR1 2TR*

BURTON, Michael John. b 55. Leeds Univ BSc76 Leeds Poly BSc80. St Jo Coll Nottm LTh88. **d** 88 **p** 89. C Charles w Plymouth St Matthias *Ex* 88-92; V Paignton St Paul Preston 92-99; TV Almondbury w Farnley Tyas *Wakef* 99-02; V Roade and Ashton w Hartwell *Pet* from 02; RD Towcester from 03. *The Vicarage, 18 Hartwell Road, Roade, Northampton NN7 2NT* Tel (01604) 862284

BURTON, Nicholas Guy. b 69. Bris Univ BSc91 ACCA00. Ridley Hall Cam 03. **d** 05. C Ore *Chich* from 05. *34 Fellows Road, Hastings TN34 3TY* Tel (01424) 440093 Mobile 07851-742049 E-mail 5.burton@tiscali.co.uk

BURTON, Nicholas John. b 52. St Steph Ho Ox 77. **d** 80 **p** 81. C Leic St Matt and St Geo *Leic* 80-82; C Leic Resurr 82-83; TV 83-88; C Narborough and Huncote 88-90; R from 90. *All Saints' Rectory, 15 Church View, Narborough, Leicester LE19 2GY* Tel 0116-275 0388

BURTON, Norman George. b 30. N Ord Course. **d** 83 **p** 84. C Rothwell w Lofthouse *Ripon* 83-86; C Rothwell 86-87; V Lofthouse 87-96; rtd 96; Perm to Offic *Ripon* from 96. *28 Temple Row Close, Leeds LS15 9HR* Tel 0113-260 1129 E-mail norman.burton3@btopenworld.com

BURTON, Mrs Virginia Ann. b 55. St As Minl Tr Course 00. **d** 03 **p** 04. C Llanrhos *St As* from 03. *The Parsonage, 12 All Saints Avenue, Deganwy, Conwy LL31 9DZ* Tel (01492) 573791 E-mail ginnyburton@llanrhosparish.wanadoo.co.uk

BURTON EVANS, David. *See* EVANS, David Burton

BURTON-JONES, Simon David. b 62. Em Coll Cam BA84 MA88. St Jo Coll Nottm BTh92 MA93. **d** 93 **p** 94. C Darwen St Pet w Hoddlesden *Blackb* 93-96; C Biggin Hill *Roch* 96-98; P-in-c Plaistow St Mary 98-00; V from 00; AD Bromley from 01. *St Mary's Vicarage, 74 London Lane, Bromley BR1 4HE* Tel and fax (020) 8460 1827 E-mail sburtonjo@aol.com

BURTT, Andrew Keith. b 50. Massey Univ (NZ) BA72 MA74 DipEd76. St Jo Coll (NZ) LTh82. **d** 81 **p** 82. New Zealand 81-83; CF 84-92; Sen Chapl Brighton Coll 93-03; Chapl Portsm Gr Sch from 03. *8 Penny Street, Portsmouth PO1 2NH*

BURTWELL, Stanley Peter. b 32. Leeds Univ BA55. Coll of Resurr Mirfield 55. **d** 57 **p** 58. C Leeds St Hilda *Ripon* 57-61; S Africa 61-72; P-in-c Gt Hanwood *Heref* 72-78; R 78-83; RD Pontesbury 80-83; V Upper Norwood St Jo *Cant* 83-84; V Upper Norwood St Jo *S'wark* 85-90; RD Croydon N 85-90; TR Bourne Valley *Sarum* 90-97; rtd 97; Perm to Offic *Sarum* from 97. *Splinters, 116 High Street, Swanage BN19 2NY* Tel (01929) 421785

BURUNDI, Archbishop of. *See* NTAHOTURI, The Most Revd Bernard

BURY, Miss Dorothy Jane. b 53. St Hild Coll Dur CertEd75 Lanc Univ BA96 MA98. Ripon Coll Cuddesdon 00. **d** 02 **p** 03. C Thornton-le-Fylde *Blackb* from 02. *2 Blackthorn Close, Thornton-Cleveleys FY5 2ZA* Tel (01253) 862451 Mobile 07715-560031 E-mail tillybury@tiscali.co.uk

BURY, The Very Revd Nicholas Ayles Stillingfleet. b 43. Qu Coll Cam BA65 MA69 Ch Ch Ox MA71. Cuddesdon Coll. **d** 68 **p** 69. C Liv Our Lady and St Nic *Liv* 68-71; Chapl Ch Ch *Ox* 71-75; V Stevenage St Mary Shephall *St Alb* 75-84; V St Peter-in-Thanet *Cant* 84-97; RD Thanet 93-97; Hon Can Cant Cathl 94-97; Dean Glouc from 97. *The Deanery, 1 Miller's Green, Gloucester GL1 2BP* Tel (01452) 524167 E-mail deanglos@uk.gateway.net

BUSBY, Ian Frederick Newman. b 32. Roch Th Coll 61. **d** 64 **p** 65. C Bedale *Ripon* 64-67; C Stevenage St Geo *St Alb* 67-71; V Stevenage St Mary Shephall 71-75; V Kildwick *Bradf* 75-92; rtd 93; Perm to Offic *Bradf* from 93. *65 Main Street, Farnhill, Keighley BD20 9BJ* Tel (01535) 633001

BUSBY, John. b 38. St Cath Coll Cam MA60 CEng. **d** 93 **p** 94. OLM Worplesdon *Guildf* 93-02; OLM Pirbright 02-04. *Iona, Fox Corner, Worplesdon, Guildford GU3 3PP* Tel (01483) 234562

BUSFIELD, Miss Lynn Maria. b 60. Trin Coll Bris ADPS97 BA99. **d** 99 **p** 00. C Scartho *Linc* 99-03; TV Marlborough *Sarum* from 03. *Preshute Vicarage, 7 Golding Avenue, Marlborough SN8 1TH* Tel (01672) 513408 E-mail lynn.busfield@virgin.net

BUSH, Mrs Ann Kathleen. b 47. MATCA65. Marlow Past Foundn Dip Counselling 90 Ox Min Course 90. **d** 93 **p** 94. NSM Warfield *Ox* 93-96; Dep Chapl HM Pris Wormwood Scrubs 96-97; Chapl HM Pris Reading 97-99; Sen Chapl HM Pris Feltham 99-01; Canada from 01. *PO Box 64, Fort Smith NT, Canada, X0E 0P0* Tel (001) (867) 872 3438 E-mail abush@auroranet.nt.ca

BUSH, David. b 25. FRIBA47 Liv Univ BArch47. S'wark Ord Course 73. **d** 77 **p** 77. C Douglas St Geo and St Barn *S & M* 77-80; Chapl Ballamona Hosp and Cronk Grianagh 80-86; V Marown 80-87; R The Rissingtons *Glouc* 87-92; rtd 92; Perm to

Offic *Glouc* from 92-98 and *Ely* from 99. *12 Kentwell Place, Burwell, Cambridge CB5 0RT* Tel (01638) 741839 E-mail dandac.bush@care4free.net

BUSH, Esther Rachma. b 66. LMH Ox BA88 St Jo Coll Dur BA04. Cranmer Hall Dur 02. **d** 04 **p** 05. C Bethnal Green St Matt w St Jas the Gt *Lon* from 04. *The Rectory Flat, Hereford Street, London E2 6EX* Tel (020) 7739 7900 Mobile 07976-922501 E-mail rachmasaid@yahoo.co.uk

BUSH, George Raymond. b 57. St Jo Coll Cam BA81 MA84 Univ of Wales LLM95. Ripon Coll Cuddesdon BA84 MA88. **d** 85 **p** 86. C Leeds St Aid *Ripon* 85-89; Chapl St Jo Coll Cam 89-94; V Hoxton St Anne w St Columba *Lon* 94-02; R St Mary le Bow w St Pancras Soper Lane etc from 02. *The Rector's Lodgings, Cheapside, London EC2V 6AU* Tel (020) 7248 5139 Fax 7248 0509 E-mail grbush@london.anglican.org

BUSH, Mrs Glenda. b 41. N Ord Course 92. **d** 95 **p** 96. NSM Bolton St Phil *Man* 95-99; C 99-02; C Bolton SS Simon and Jude 99-02; P-in-c from 02. *46 Mary Street West, Horwich, Bolton BL6 7JU* Tel (01204) 691539

BUSH, Mrs Kathryn Ann. b 60. OLM course 95. **d** 99 **p** 00. OLM Mareham-le-Fen and Revesby *Linc* from 99; OLM Mareham on the Hill from 99; OLM Hameringham w Scrafield and Winceby from 99. *Wheatsheaf Farm, Chapel Lane, New Bolingbroke, Boston PE22 7LF* Tel (01205) 480631 Mobile 07775-736344

BUSH, Rachma. *See* BUSH, Esther Rachma

BUSH, Canon Roger Charles. b 56. K Coll Lon BA78 Leeds Univ BA85. Coll of Resurr Mirfield 83. **d** 86 **p** 87. C Newbold w Dunston *Derby* 86-90; TV Leic Resurr *Leic* 90-94; TR Redruth w Lanner and Treleigh *Truro* 94-04; RD Carnmarth N 96-03; Hon Can Truro Cathl 03-04; Can Res Truro Cathl from 04. *Westwood House, Tremorvah Crescent, Truro TR1 1NL* Tel (01872) 225 630 E-mail rogerbush56@hotmail.com

BUSHAU, Reginald Francis. b 49. Shimer Coll Illinois AB71. St Steph Ho Ox BA73 MA98. **d** 74 **p** 75. C Deptford St Paul *S'wark* 74-77; C Willesden St Andr *Lon* 77; C Gladstone Park St Fran 77-82; P-in-c Brondesbury St Anne w Kilburn H Trin 83-88; V Paddington St Mary Magd 88-97; AD Westmr Paddington 92-97; P-in-c S Kensington St Steph 96-98; V from 98. *9 Eldon Road, London W8 5PU* Tel (020) 7937 5083 *or* 7370 3418 E-mail bushrf@aol.com

BUSHBY, Michael Reginald. b 42. LSE BSc70 Leeds Univ MA97. **d** 02 **p** 03. NSM S Cave and Ellerker w Broomfleet *York* 02-05; P-in-c Newbald from 05. *The Vicarage, 7 Dot Hill Close, North Newbald, York YO43 4TS* Tel (01430) 801088

BUSHELL, Anthony Colin. b 59. Pemb Coll Ox MA82 Barrister 83. S'wark Ord Course 93. **d** 96 **p** 97. NSM Felsted and Lt Dunmow *Chelmsf* 96-98; NSM Stanway from 98. *Pump Hall, Middle Green, Wakes Colne, Colchester CO6 2BJ* Tel (01787) 222487 Fax 222361

BUSHELL, Roy. b 32. NW Ord Course 75. **d** 79 **p** 80. NSM Croft w Southworth *Liv* 79-87; C Netherton 87-89; R Newton in Makerfield Em 89-97; rtd 97; Perm to Offic *Bradf* from 98. *34 Maple Avenue, Whitley Bay NE25 8JS* Tel 0191-251 9816

BUSHELL, Stephen Lionel. b 60. K Coll Lon BA84. Ripon Coll Cuddesdon 92. **d** 94 **p** 95. C Exhall *Cov* 94-97; Asst Chapl Aylesbury Vale Community Healthcare NHS Trust from 97; Asst P Shelswell *Ox* from 97. *St Fergus Cottage, Cottisford, Brackley NN13 5SW* Tel (01280) 847979 E-mail tostephenbushell@hotmail.com

BUSHYAGER, Ronald Robert. b 77. Belmont Univ Nashville BSc00. Wycliffe Hall Ox BTh04. **d** 04 **p** 05. C Gamston and Bridgford *S'well* from 04. *9 Fountains Close, West Bridgford, Nottingham NG2 6LL* Tel 0115-923 5283 E-mail ron_bushyager@yahoo.com

BUSHYAGER (née TWITCHEN), Mrs Ruth Kathleen Frances. b 77. Bris Univ MSci99. Wycliffe Hall Ox BA04. **d** 05. C Wilford *S'well* from 05. *9 Fountains Close, West Bridgford, Nottingham NG2 6LL* Tel 0115-923 5283 E-mail ruth@bushyager.net

BUSK, David Westly. b 60. Magd Coll Cam BA. Cranmer Hall Dur. **d** 89 **p** 90. C Old Swinford Stourbridge *Worc* 89-93; USPG Japan from 94; V Nagasaki H Trin from 95. *Holy Trinity Church, Oura-Machi 1-6, Nagasaki 850-90-21, Japan* Tel (0081) (958) 230455

BUSK, Horace. b 34. Clifton Th Coll 56. **d** 60 **p** 61. C Burton All SS *Lich* 60-63; Paraguay 63-66; C Silverhill St Matt *Chich* 66-67; Lic to Offic *Sarum* 67-69; C W Kilburn St Luke w St Simon and St Jude *Lon* 69-74; TV Ashwellthorpe w Wreningham *Nor* 74-81; P-in-c Meysey Hampton w Marston Meysey and Castle Eaton *Glouc* 81-82; R 82-04; rtd 04; Perm to Offic *Glouc* from 04. *23 Eastcote Road, Cirencester GL7 2DB* Tel (01285) 650884

BUSS, Gerald Vere Austen. b 36. CCC Cam PhD87. St Steph Ho Ox 59. **d** 63 **p** 64. C Petersham *S'wark* 63-66; C Brompton H Trin *Lon* 66-69; Asst Chapl Hurstpierpoint Coll 70-73; Chapl 74-90; Ho Master 90-94; History teacher 94-96; rtd 96. *Souches, The Street, Albourne, Hassocks BN6 9DJ* Tel (01273) 832465 Fax as telephone

BUSS, Philip Hodnett. b 37. Ch Coll Cam BA59 MA63. Tyndale Hall Bris 61. **d** 63 **p** 64. Tutor Lon Coll of Div 62-66; Chapl 66-69; Hon C Northwood Em *Lon* 63-70; V Handsworth Woodhouse *Sheff* 70-74; V Fulham Ch Ch *Lon* 74-82; V Woking St Pet *Guildf* 82-88; Hon C Ham St Rich *S'wark* 94-98; rtd 02. *La Barlière, 79400 St Georges-de-Noisne, France*

BUSSELL, Ian Paul. b 62. Reading Univ BA84 Kingston Poly PGCE85. Qu Coll Birm MA98. **d** 98 **p** 99. C Twickenham St Mary *Lon* 98-01; TV Godalming *Guildf* from 01. *St Mark's Vicarage, 29 Franklyn Road, Godalming GU7 2LD* Tel (01483) 424710 E-mail st-marks@supanet.com

BUSSELL, Ronald William. b 34. CA Tr Coll 57 St Deiniol's Hawarden 81. **d** 83 **p** 84. C Claughton cum Grange *Ches* 83-85; P-in-c Preston St Oswald *Blackb* 85-87; V Fleetwood St Nic 87-93; Dioc Chapl MU 91-95; R Tarleton 93-95; rtd 95; Perm to Offic *Blackb* from 95. *4 Willoughby Avenue, Thornton-Cleveleys FY5 2BW* Tel (01253) 820067 E-mail ron.bussell@talk21.com

BUSSEY, Norman. b 22. Clifton Th Coll 63. **d** 65 **p** 66. C Upton (Overchurch) *Ches* 65-69; V Bradley *Wakef* 69-88; rtd 88; Perm to Offic *Glouc* from 88. *43 Crispin Road, Winchcombe, Cheltenham GL54 5JX* Tel (01242) 602754

BUSSEY, Rachel Anne. STETS 00. **d** 03 **p** 04. NSM Durrington *Sarum* from 03. *3 Birchwood Drive, Durrington, Salisbury SP4 8ER* Tel 07899-926034 (mobile) E-mail rachel.bussey@ntlworld.com

BUSTARD, Guy Nicholas. b 51. K Coll Lon BD77 AKC77. St Steph Ho Ox 77. **d** 78 **p** 79. C Hythe *Cant* 78-81; Chapl RN 81-85; V Haddenham and Wilburton *Ely* 85-89; Chapl Qu Eliz Hosp Welwyn Garden City 89-92; Chapl E Herts NHS Trust 92-00; Chapl E and N Herts NHS Trust 00-02; Perm to Offic *St Alb* from 02. *24 Blakes Way, Welwyn AL6 9RE* Tel (01438) 716380

BUSTIN, Canon Peter Ernest. b 32. Qu Coll Cam BA56 MA60. Tyndale Hall Bris 56. **d** 57 **p** 58. C Welling *Roch* 57-60; C Farnborough *Guildf* 60-62; V Hornsey Rise St Mary *Lon* 62-70; R Barnwell *Pet* 70-78; RD Oundle 76-84; P-in-c Luddington w Hemington and Thurning 77-78; R Barnwell w Thurning and Luddington 78-84; V Southwold *St E* 84-97; RD Halesworth 90-95; Hon Can St E Cathl 91-97; rtd 97; Perm to Offic *St E* from 97. *55 College Street, Bury St Edmunds IP33 1NH* Tel (01284) 767708 E-mail bustin@saintedmunds.vispa.com

BUSTIN, Peter Laurence. b 54. St Steph Ho Ox. **d** 83 **p** 84. C Northolt St Mary *Lon* 83-86; C Pimlico St Pet w Westmr Ch Ch 86-88; C Heston 88-91; P-in-c Twickenham All SS 91-98; V from 98. *All Saints' House, Church View Road, Twickenham TW2 5BX* Tel and fax (020) 8894 3580 E-mail peter@padova.fsnet.co.uk

BUTCHER, Andrew John. b 43. Trin Coll Cam BA66 MA69. Cuddesdon Coll 66. **d** 68 **p** 69. C Sheff St Mark Broomhall *Sheff* 68-70; P-in-c Louth H Trin *Linc* 70-72; Chapl RAF 72-87; Lic to Offic *Ox* 85-87; TR Cove St Jo *Guildf* 87-91; V Egham Hythe 91-98; V Docking, the Birchams, Stanhoe and Sedgeford *Nor* from 98. *The Vicarage, Sedgeford Road, Docking, King's Lynn PE31 8PN* Tel and fax (01485) 518247 Mobile 07887-506876 E-mail andrewj.butcher@btopenworld.com

BUTCHER, Edwin William. b 39. Portsm Dioc Tr Course 91. **d** 92 **p** 05. NSM Ryde All SS *Portsm* from 92. *23 Quarry Road, Ryde PO33 2TX* Tel (01983) 616889

BUTCHER, Hubert Maxwell. b 24. Ch Coll Cam BA48 MA53. Trin Coll Toronto BD68 San Francisco Th Sem DMin78 Wycliffe Hall Ox 49. **d** 51 **p** 52. C Tunbridge Wells St Jo *Roch* 51-53; India 54-58; P-in-c Bradf St Jo *Bradf* 58-62; Canada from 63; rtd 88. *Box 129, Sorrento BC, Canada, V0E 2W0* Tel (001) (250) 675 2783

BUTCHER, Philip Warren. b 46. Trin Coll Cam BA68 MA70. Cuddesdon Coll 68. **d** 70 **p** 71. C Bris St Mary Redcliffe w Temple etc *Bris* 70-73; Hon C W Wickham St Fran *Cant* 73-78; Chapl Abingdon Sch 78-85; Chapl Nor Sch 85-98; V Horsford and Horsham w Newton St Faith *Nor* 98-04; rtd 04; Perm to Offic *Nor* from 05. *15 Delane Road, Drayton, Norwich NR8 6DL* Tel (01603) 400284

BUTCHER, Richard Peter. b 50. St Chad's Coll Dur BA71. Chich Th Coll 73. **d** 74 **p** 75. C Yeovil St Mich *B & W* 74-77; Chapl Wellingborough Sch 77-83; R Gt w Lt Billing *Pet* 83-88; Chapl Bp Stopford Sch Kettering 88-90; Perm to Offic *Pet* 90-01. *55 Field Street, Kettering NN16 8EN*

BUTCHERS, Mark Andrew. b 59. Trin Coll Cam BA81 K Coll Lon MTh90. Chich Th Coll BTh87. **d** 87 **p** 88. C Chelsea St Luke and Ch Ch *Lon* 87-90; C Mitcham SS Pet and Paul *S'wark* 90-93; R N Tawton, Bondleigh, Sampford Courtenay etc *Ex* 93-99; Chapl and Fell Keble Coll Ox 99-05; C Wolvercote w Summertown *Ox* from 05. *The Vicarage, 1 Mere Road, Oxford OX2 8AN* Tel (01865) 515640 E-mail mark.butchers@dsl.pipex.com

BUTLAND, Cameron James. b 58. BA. Ripon Coll Cuddesdon 81. **d** 84 **p** 85. C Tettenhall Regis *Lich* 84-88; V Bodicote *Ox* 88-95; TR Witney 95-04; RD Witney 97-02; R Grasmere *Carl* from 04; V Rydal from 04; Chapl Rydal Hall from 04. *The Rectory, Grasmere, Ambleside LA22 9SW* Tel (01539) 435326 E-mail cameron@butland555.fsnet.co.uk

BUTLAND, Canon Godfrey John. b 51. Grey Coll Dur BA72. Wycliffe Hall Ox 73. **d** 75 **p** 76. C Much Woolton *Liv* 75-78; Bp's

Dom Chapl 78-81; V Everton St Geo 81-94; AD Liv N 89-94; V Allerton 94-05; P-in-c Mossley Hill St Barn 04-05; TV Mossley Hill from 05; AD Liv S from 00; Hon Can Liv Cathl from 03. *Allerton Vicarage, Harthill Road, Liverpool L18 3HU* Tel 0151-724 1561

BUTLAND, William Edwin (Joe). b 09. St Andr Coll Pampisford 48 Lon Coll of Div 49. **d** 51 **p** 52. C Kentish Town *Lon* 51-54; C Chorleywood Ch Ch *St Alb* 54-58; P-in-c Colney Heath St Mark 58-59; V 59-80; rtd 80; Perm to Offic *St Alb* 80-01. *4 The Spinney, Long Lawford, Rugby CV23 9SH* Tel (01788) 578245

BUTLER, Alan. b 53. Carl Dioc Tr Inst 89. **d** 89 **p** 90. NSM Flookburgh *Carl* 89-93; C Maryport 93-96; C Flimby 93-96; P-in-c 96-98; TV Saltash *Truro* from 98. *The Vicarage, St Stephen by Saltash, Saltash PL12 4AB* Tel (01752) 842323

BUTLER, Alan. b 57. Leic Univ BA78. Coll of Resurr Mirfield 80. **d** 83 **p** 84. C Skerton St Luke *Blackb* 83-87; C Birch w Fallowfield *Man* 87-90; V Claremont H Angels 90-95; Chapl Pendleton Coll 95-99; TV Pendleton *Man* 95-99; P-in-c High Crompton from 99. *St Mary's Vicarage, 18 Rushcroft Road, Shaw, Oldham OL2 7PR* Tel and fax (01706) 847455 E-mail alanbutler@freenetname.co.uk

BUTLER, Canon Alan John. b 30. Kelham Th Coll 51. **d** 56 **p** 57. S Africa 56-65 and 79-95; Bechuanaland 65-66; Botswana 66-70; V Fletchamstead *Cov* 71-79; Adn Griqualand W 79-85; Adn Kuruman 79-85; Dir Moffat Miss, Kuruman 81-95; TV Hanley H Ev *Lich* 95; rtd 95; Perm to Offic *Sarum* and *Win* from 95. *4 Osborne Road, Wimborne BH21 1BL* Tel (01202) 848859

BUTLER, Ms Angela Elizabeth. b 31. Studley Coll Dip Horticulture 53. Gilmore Ho 60 DipTh64 Lambeth STh64. **dss** 81 **d** 87 **p** 94. Cookham *Ox* 81-86; Wheatley w Forest Hill and Stanton St John 86-97; Hon Par Dn 87-89; NSM 89-97; NSM Wheatley 97-01; Perm to Offic from 02. *10 River Gardens, Purley-on-Thames, Reading RG8 8BX* Tel 0118-942 2055

BUTLER, Angela Madeline. b 47. Oak Hill NSM Course 87. **d** 90 **p** 94. Hon Par Dn Chipperfield St Paul *St Alb* 90-93; Dn-in-c 93-94; P-in-c 94-01; Staff Oak Hill Th Coll 93-97; Springboard Missr 97-01; Dioc Springboard Missr *Glouc* from 01; P-in-c Hempsted from 01. *The Rectory, Rectory Lane, Hempsted, Gloucester GL2 5LW* Tel (01452) 523025 Fax 524592 E-mail angela.butler@talk21.com

BUTLER, Betty. b 47. **d** 96. NSM Sully *Llan* 96-97; NSM Merthyr Dyfan from 98. *10 Nurston Close, Rhoose, Barry CF62 3EF* Tel (01446) 710822

BUTLER, Christopher. b 67. St Jo Coll Nottm 99. **d** 01 **p** 02. C Retford *S'well* 01-05; P-in-c Holbeck *Ripon* from 05. *St Luke's Vicarage, Malvern View, Leeds LS11 8SG* Tel 0113-271 7996 E-mail crbutler@bigfoot.com

BUTLER, Christopher John. b 25. Leeds Univ BA50. Chich Th Coll 50. **d** 52 **p** 53. C Kensington St Mary Abbots w St Geo *Lon* 52-57; Australia 57-59; V Blackmoor *Portsm* 60-70; V Wellingborough St Andr *Pet* 70-79; P-in-c Garsington *Ox* 79-83; R Garsington and Horspath 83-95; rtd 95; Perm to Offic *Portsm, Chich, Guildf* and *Win* from 95. *33 Oak Tree Road, Whitehill, Bordon GU35 9DF* Tel (01420) 475311

BUTLER, Colin Sydney. b 59. Bradf Univ BSc81. Wycliffe Hall Ox 81. **d** 84 **p** 85. C Farsley *Bradf* 84-87; C Bradf St Aug Undercliffe 87-89; P-in-c Darlaston All SS *Lich* 89-95; Ind Missr 89-95; TR Chell 95-99; CF from 99. *c/o MOD Chaplains (Army)* Tel (01980) 615804 Fax 615800

BUTLER, The Ven Cuthbert Hilary. b 13. St Jo Coll Cam BA35 MA39. Westcott Ho Cam 37. **d** 40 **p** 41. C Preston *Chich* 40-42; Chapl RNVR 42-46; P-in-c Brighton St Matthias *Chich* 46-47; V 47-51; R Crawley 51-58; Canada 58-84; Adn Colombia 77-78; rtd 78; Perm to Offic *Ex* 85-98. *Running Waters, Winsford, Minehead TA24 7JF* Tel (01643) 851250

BUTLER, David Edwin. b 56. ACA83 Jes Coll Ox BA79 BA86. St Steph Ho Ox MA87. **d** 87 **p** 88. C Hulme Ascension *Man* 87-90; V Patricroft 90-94; Perm to Offic *Liv* 97-03 and *Man* from 03; Hon C Prestwich St Hilda 00-01. *30 Windsor Road, Prestwich, Manchester M25 0FF*

BUTLER, Derek John. b 53. Aston Univ BSc74 St Jo Coll York PGCE75. St Jo Coll Dur 79. **d** 82 **p** 83. C Bramcote *S'well* 82-86; Perm to Offic *Roch* 86-88; Perm to Offic *Portsm* 86-92; Lon and SE Co-ord CPAS 86-88; NSM Bromley Ch Ch *Roch* 88-91; NSM Chesham Bois *Ox* from 92. *121 Woodside Road, Amersham HP6 6AL* Tel (01494) 724577

BUTLER, Donald Arthur. b 31. **d** 79 **p** 80. Hon C Apsley End *St Alb* 79-80; Hon C Chambersbury from 80. *143 Belswains Lane, Hemel Hempstead HP3 9UZ*

BUTLER, George James. b 53. AKC74 Kent Univ MA95. St Aug Coll Cant 75. **d** 76 **p** 77. C Ellesmere Port *Ches* 76-79; C Eastham 79-81; Chapl RAF 81-83; C W Kirby St Bridget *Ches* 83-84; V Newton 84-86; CF 86-91; V Folkestone St Sav *Cant* 91-99; P-in-c Wool and E Stoke *Sarum* 99-04; P-in-c Mansfield St Mark *S'well* from 04. *St Mark's Vicarage, Nottingham Road, Mansfield NG18 1BP* Tel (01623) 655548 E-mail revgjb@hotmail.com

BUTLER, Canon George William. b 52. CITC DipTh. **d** 90 **p** 91. C Drung w Castleterra, Larah and Lavey etc *K, E & A* 90-93; I 93-95; I Castlemacadam w Ballinaclash, Aughrim etc *D & G* from 95; Can Ch Ch Cathl Dublin from 03. *The Rectory, Castlemacadam, Avoca, Co Wicklow, Irish Republic* Tel and fax (00353) (402) 35127 Mobile 87-679 5625

BUTLER, Mrs Helen Carole. b 66. Bath Coll of HE BA87. **d** 04 **p** 05. NSM Mirfield *Wakef* from 04. *1A Holmdene Drive, Mirfield WF14 9SZ* Tel (01924) 495189 Mobile 07764-187988 E-mail helencbutler@hotmail.com

BUTLER, Henry. b 25. Ridley Hall Cam 73. **d** 75 **p** 76. C Cambridge St Paul *Ely* 75-77; P-in-c Stilton w Denton and Caldecote 77-83; P-in-c Folksworth w Morborne 77-83; V Histon 83-90; P-in-c Impington 84-90; rtd 90; Perm to Offic *Ely* from 90. *48 Church Road, Hauxton, Cambridge CB2 5HS* Tel (01223) 874184

BUTLER, Huw. b 63. Univ of Wales (Ban) BSc84. St Mich Coll Llan DipTh94 BTh95. **d** 95 **p** 96. C Llantwit Fardre *Llan* 95-00; R Llangynhafal w Llanbedr DC and Llanychan *St As* 00-02; R Llanbedr DC w Llangynhafal, Llanychan etc from 02. *The Rectory, Llanbedr Dyffryn Clwyd, Ruthin LL15 1UP* Tel (01824) 704160 E-mail huw.butler@tesco.net

BUTLER, Ian Malcolm. b 39. Bris Univ BA67 BA69. Clifton Th Coll 67. **d** 69 **p** 70. C Clapham Common St Barn *S'wark* 69-73; C Reigate St Mary 73-78; V Sissinghurst w Frittenden *Cant* 78-91; rtd 92; Chapl Dulwich Prep Sch Cranbrook from 90; Perm to Offic *Cant* from 91. *High Cedars, Theobalds, Hawkhurst, Cranbrook TN18 4AJ* Tel (01580) 752366 Fax 754904 E-mail mail@ianbutler.net

BUTLER, Jane. *See* BUTLER, Linda Jane

BUTLER, John. b 38. Univ of Wales DipTh67 DPS68 Gwent Coll Newport CertEd77. St Mich Coll Llan. **d** 68 **p** 69. C Ebbw Vale *Mon* 68-70; TV 70-75; Perm to Offic 76-77 and 79-88; P-in-c Crumlin 77-78; R Gt and Lt Casterton w Pickworth and Tickencote *Pet* 88-91; R Woolstone w Gotherington and Oxenton etc *Glouc* 91-97; Hon C Dawlish *Ex* 98-01; P-in-c Chevington w Hargrave, Chedburgh w Depden etc *St E* 01-02; R 02-03; rtd 03; C Shaldon, Stokeinteignhead, Combeinteignhead etc *Ex* from 03. *The Rectory, Stoke in Teignhead, Newton Abbot TQ12 4QB* Tel (01626) 871013

BUTLER, John Philip. b 47. Leeds Univ BA70. Coll of Resurr Mirfield 70. **d** 72 **p** 73. C Elton All SS *Man* 72-75; C Bolton St Pet 75-78; Chapl Bolton Colls of H&FE 75-78; Hon C Clifton St Paul *Bris* 78-81; Asst Chapl Bris Univ 78-81; V Llansawel w Briton Ferry *Llan* 81-84; Warden Bp Mascall Cen *Heref* 84-88; Vice-Prin Glouc Sch for Min 85-88; Chapl Univ of Wales (Ban) from 88. *Anglican Chaplaincy Centre, Prince's Road, Bangor LL57 2BD* Tel (01248) 370566 Fax 354472 E-mail angchap@lineone.net

BUTLER, Mrs Linda. b 51. Liv Univ CertEd72. Cranmer Hall Dur 01. **d** 03 **p** 04. C Middlewich w Byley *Ches* from 03. *27 St Ann's Road, Middlewich CW10 9BN* Tel (01606) 835132 E-mail butlers@fish.co.uk

BUTLER, Linda Jane. b 56. SRN77. St Jo Coll Nottm 85. **d** 88 **p** 94. C Burbage w Aston Flamville *Leic* 88-91; Asst Chapl Leic R Infirmary 91-93; Asst Chapl Towers Hosp Humberstone 93-95; Chapl 95-97; Chapl Leics and Rutland Healthcare NHS Trust 97-03; Chapl to the Deaf *Pet* from 03. *5 Gray Lane, Sileby, Loughborough LE12 7GS* Tel (01509) 812705

BUTLER, Mrs Louise Gail. **d** 04 **p** 05. OLM Blewbury, Hagbourne and Upton *Ox* from 04. *Penridge, Church Road, Blewbury, Didcot OX11 9PY* Tel (01235) 851011

BUTLER, Malcolm. b 40. Linc Th Coll 76. **d** 78 **p** 79. C Whickham *Dur* 78-82; V Leam Lane 82-87; R Penshaw 87-90; rtd 90. *2 Lapwing Court, Barcus Close Lane, Burnopfield, Newcastle upon Tyne NE16 4DZ* Tel (01207) 271559

BUTLER, Canon Michael. b 41. Univ of Wales (Ban) DipTh62. St Mich Coll Llan 62 St Deiniol's Hawarden 63. **d** 64 **p** 65. C Welshpool *St As* 64; C Welshpool w Castle Caereinion 65-73; TV Aberystwyth *St D* 73-80; Chapl Univ of Wales (Abth) 73-80; V St Issell's and Amroth from 80; RD Narberth from 94; Can St D Cathl from 01. *St Issell's Vicarage, Saundersfoot SA69 9BD* Tel (01834) 812375

BUTLER, Canon Michael John. b 32. Keble Coll Ox BA58 MSW. Coll of Resurr Mirfield. **d** 59 **p** 60. C Poplar All SS w St Frideswide *Lon* 59-68; Hon C St Steph Walbrook and St Swithun etc 68-73; C Godalming *Guildf* 73-76; P-in-c Brighton St Anne *Chich* 77-79; Dioc Communications Officer and Dir Soc Resp 77-83; Dir Dioc Bd of Soc Resp 83-94; Soc Resp Adv 94-00; Hon C Brighton St Pet w Chpl Royal 94-00; Can and Preb Chich Cathl 85-00; rtd 00; Perm to Offic *Nor* from 00. *Railway Cottage, 2 Buxton Road, Aylsham, Norwich NR11 6JD* Tel (01263) 734820

BUTLER, Canon Michael Weeden. b 38. Clare Coll Cam BA60 MA65. Westcott Ho Cam 63. **d** 65 **p** 66. C Bermondsey St Mary w St Olave, St Jo etc *S'wark* 65-68; Ind Chapl 68-72; Sierra Leone 73-77; Ind Chapl and R Gt Chart *Cant* 77-86; RD E Charing 81-86; V Glouc St Jas and All SS *Glouc* 86-04; RD Glouc City 94-99; Hon Can Glouc Cathl from 96; rtd 04. *121 London Road, Gloucester GL2 0RR* Tel (01452) 421563 E-mail michaelbutler@michaelbutler.freeserve.co.uk

BUTLER, Ms Pamela. b 53. Nottm Univ BTh86 CertEd74. Linc Th Coll 83. **dss** 86 **d** 87 **p** 94. Rotherhithe H Trin *S'wark* 86-87;

Par Dn 87-88; Par Dn Old Trafford St Jo *Man* 88-89; Par Dn Claremont H Angels 90-94; C 94-95; C Pendleton 95-97; Chapl Asst S Man Univ Hosps NHS Trust from 96. *St Mary's Vicarage, 18 Rushcroft Road, Shaw, Oldham OL2 7PR* Tel (01706) 847455, 0161-291 2298 *or* 998 7070

BUTLER, Paul David. b 67. Sheff Univ BA88. Linc Th Coll 92. **d** 92 **p** 93. C Handsworth Woodhouse *Sheff* 92-96; V Bellingham St Dunstan *S'wark* from 96; AD E Lewisham from 99. *St Dunstan's Vicarage, 5 Gramsci Way, London SE6 3HA* Tel (020) 8698 3291 E-mail paulredbutler@compuserve.com

✠**BUTLER, The Rt Revd Paul Roger.** b 55. Nottm Univ BA77. Wycliffe Hall Ox BA82. **d** 83 **p** 84 **c** 04. C Wandsworth All SS *S'wark* 83-87; Inner Lon Ev Scripture Union 87-92; Dep Hd of Miss 92-94; NSM E Ham St Paul *Chelmsf* 87-94; P-in-c Walthamstow St Mary w St Steph 94-97; P-in-c Walthamstow St Luke 94-97; TR Walthamstow 97-04; AD Waltham Forest 00-04; Hon Can Byumba from 01; Suff Bp Southampton *Win* from 04. *Ham House, The Crescent, Romsey SO51 7NG* Tel (01794) 516005 Fax 830242
E-mail paul.butler@bpsotonoffice.clara.co.uk

BUTLER, Perry Andrew. b 49. FRHistS York Univ BA70 Lon Univ PGCE75 Jes Coll Ox DPhil78 Nottm Univ DipTh79. Linc Th Coll 78. **d** 80 **p** 81. C Chiswick St Nic w St Mary *Lon* 80-83; C S Kensington St Steph 83-87; V Bedford Park 87-95; Angl Adv Lon Weekend TV 87-99; P-in-c Bloomsbury St Geo w Woburn Square Ch Ch *Lon* 95-02; R from 02; Dioc Dir of Ords from 96. *The Rectory, 6 Gower Street, London WC1E 6DP* Tel (020) 7580 4010 *or* 7405 3044 E-mail stgeorgebloomsbury@hotmail.com *or* holmado@aol.com

BUTLER, Richard Charles Burr. b 34. St Pet Hall Ox BA59 MA62. Linc Th Coll 58. **d** 60 **p** 61. C St John's Wood *Lon* 60-63; V Kingstanding St Luke *Birm* 63-75; R Lee St Marg *S'wark* 75-00; rtd 00. *21 Defoe House, Barbican, London EC2Y 8DN* Tel (020) 7628 0527
E-mail eleanorandrichardbutler@btinternet.com

BUTLER, Robert Clifford. b 25. AKC54. **d** 55 **p** 56. C Gt Berkhamsted *St Alb* 55-59; C Dunstable 59-63; V Stanbridge w Tilsworth 63-73; R Maulden 73-80; R Oldbury *Sarum* 80-93; rtd 93; Perm to Offic *Sarum* from 93. *3 Mithras Close, Dorchester DT1 2RF* Tel (01305) 264817

BUTLER, Canon Robert Edwin. b 37. Ely Th Coll 60. **d** 62 **p** 63. C Lewisham St Jo Southend *S'wark* 62-65; C Eastbourne St Eliz *Chich* 65-69; V Langney 69-86; TR 86-96; Can and Preb Chich Cathl 94-97; rtd 96; Perm to Offic *Chich* from 97. *10 Langdale Close, Langney, Eastbourne BN23 8HS* Tel (01323) 461135

BUTLER (née McVEIGH), Mrs Sandra. b 58. Reading Univ BA80. Cranmer Hall Dur 95. **d** 95 **p** 96. C Stranton *Dur* 95-98; P-in-c Blackhall, Castle Eden and Monkhesleden 98-99; R 99-02. *Tansy Cottage, 15 Lidgett, Colne BB8 7AF* Tel (01282) 865858 E-mail revsandie@aol.com

BUTLER, Simon. b 64. UEA BSc86 RN Coll Dartmouth 86. St Jo Coll Nottm MA92. **d** 92 **p** 93. C Chandler's Ford *Win* 92-94; C Northolt W End St Jos *Lon* 94-97; V Streatham Immanuel and St Andr *S'wark* 97-04; Lambeth Adnry Ecum Officer 99-02; RD Streatham 01-04; P-in-c Sanderstead All SS from 04. *The Rectory, 1 Addington Road, South Croydon CR2 8RE* Tel (020) 8657 1366 *or* tel and fax 657 0665
E-mail rector@sanderstead-parish.org.uk

BUTLER, Stephen Ian. b 59. Edin Univ BA BSc80. Trin Coll Bris BA84. **d** 97 **p** 98. C Edin St Pet *Edin* 97-99; R Edin St Jas from 99. *71 Restalrig Road, Edinburgh EH6 8BG* Tel 0131-554 3520
E-mail stevebutler@onetel.com

✠**BUTLER, The Rt Revd Thomas Frederick.** b 40. Leeds Univ BSc61 MSc62 PhD72. Coll of Resurr Mirfield 62. **d** 64 **p** 65 **c** 85. C Wisbech St Aug *Ely* 64-66; C Folkestone St Sav *Cant* 66-67; Zambia 68-73; Chapl Kent Univ *Cant* 73-80; Six Preacher Cant Cathl 79-84; Adn Northolt *Lon* 80-85; Area Bp Willesden 85-91; Bp Leic 91-98; Bp S'wark from 98. *Bishop's House, 38 Tooting Bec Gardens, London SW16 1QZ* Tel (020) 8769 3256 Fax 8769 4126 E-mail bishop.tom@southwark.anglican.org

BUTLER, Valerie Joyce. b 58. EAMTC 99. **d** 02 **p** 03. NSM Southminster *Chelmsf* from 02. *6 Coastguard Cottages, Mill End, Bradwell-on-Sea, Southminster CM0 7HN* Tel (01621) 776513
E-mail vbutler@fish.co.uk

BUTLER-SMITH, Basil George (Bob). b 30. Bps' Coll Cheshunt 66. **d** 67 **p** 68. C Bray and Braywood *Ox* 67-71; R Norton *St E* 71-74; P-in-c Tostock 71-74; R Rotherfield Peppard *Ox* 76-02; P-in-c Rotherfield Greys 79-80; R 80-02; rtd 02. *40 Westleigh Drive, Sonning Common, Reading RG4 9LB* Tel 0118-972 1871

BUTLIN, David Francis Grenville. b 55. Bris Univ BA77 Ox Univ CertEd78. Sarum & Wells Th Coll 85. **d** 87 **p** 88. C Bedford St Andr *St Alb* 87-90; C Milton *Portsm* 90-92; V Hurst Green *S'wark* from 92; RD Godstone from 04. *The Vicarage, 14 Oast Road, Oxted RH8 9DU* Tel (01883) 712674
E-mail dfgbutlin@14oastroad.freeserve.co.uk

BUTLIN, Timothy Greer. b 53. St Jo Coll Dur BA75 Ox Univ CertEd76. Wycliffe Hall Ox 85. **d** 87 **p** 88. C Eynsham and Cassington *Ox* 87-91; V Loudwater from 91. *The Vicarage, Loudwater, High Wycombe HP10 9QL* Tel (01628) 526087 Fax 529354 E-mail vicar@loudwater.org

BUTT, Adrian. b 37. **d** 71 **p** 72. C Umtata Cathl S Africa 71-76; C Ilkeston St Mary *Derby* 76-79; R N and S Wheatley w W Burton *S'well* 79-84; P-in-c Bole w Saundby 79-84; P-in-c Sturton w Littleborough 79-84; R N Wheatley, W Burton, Bole, Saundby, Sturton etc 84-85; R Kirkby in Ashfield 85-05; rtd 05. *25 Searby Road, Sutton-in-Ashfield NG17 5JQ* Tel (01623) 555650
E-mail adrian@shopfront.freeserve.co.uk

BUTT, Mrs Catherine. b 76. St Hilda's Coll Ox BA99 MA02 St Jo Coll Dur BA02. Cranmer Hall Dur 00. **d** 03 **p** 04. C Bletchley *Ox* from 03. *1 Ashburnham Close, Bletchley, Milton Keynes MK3 7TR* Tel (01908) 631050 Mobile 07971-714223
E-mail butties01@yahoo.co.uk

BUTT, Christopher Martin. b 52. St Pet Coll Ox BA74 Fitzw Coll Cam BA77. Ridley Hall Cam 75. **d** 79 **p** 80. C Cambridge St Barn *Ely* 79-82; Hong Kong 82-89; P-in-c Windermere *Carl* 89-98; TR S Gillingham *Roch* from 98. *The Rectory, 4 Drewery Drive, Wigmore, Gillingham ME8 0NX* Tel (01634) 231071
E-mail office@parishofsgill.freeserve.co.uk

BUTT, Edward. b 46. Huddersfield Poly CQSW80. Trin Coll Bris DipHE88. **d** 88 **p** 89. C Erith St Paul *Roch* 88-92; C Shirley *Win* 92-99; V Stourbridge St Mich Norton *Worc* from 99. *St Michael's House, Westwood Avenue, Stourbridge DY8 3EN* Tel (01384) 376477

BUTT, Martin James. b 52. Sheff Univ LLB75. Trin Coll Bris 75. **d** 78 **p** 79. C Aldridge *Lich* 78-84; C Walsall 84-87; TV 87-94; P-in-c Farewell from 94; P-in-c Gentleshaw from 94; C Hammerwich 96-03; P-in-c from 03. *The Vicarage, Budds Road, Rugeley WS15 4NB* Tel (01543) 684329

BUTT, William Arthur. b 44. Kelham Th Coll 70 Linc Th Coll 71. **d** 71 **p** 72. C Mackworth St Fran *Derby* 71-75; C Aston cum Aughton *Sheff* 76-79; V Dalton 79-88; TR Staveley and Barrow Hill *Derby* from 88. *The Rectory, Staveley, Chesterfield S43 3XZ* Tel (01246) 472270

BUTTANSHAW, Graham Charles. b 59. TCD BA(Econ)80 BA85. St Jo Coll Nottm 88. **d** 91 **p** 92. C Toxteth St Cypr w Ch Ch *Liv* 91-94; CMS 94-99; Uganda 95-99; V Otley *Bradf* from 99. *The Vicarage, Burras Lane, Otley LS21 3HR* Tel (01943) 462240 E-mail buttansh@fish.co.uk

BUTTERFIELD, David John. b 52. Lon Univ BMus73. St Jo Coll Nottm DipTh75. **d** 77 **p** 78. C Southport Ch Ch *Liv* 77-81; Min Aldridge St Thos CD *Lich* 81-91; V Lilleshall, Muxton and Sheriffhales from 91; RD Edgmond 97-01; RD Shifnal 99-01; RD Edgmond and Shifnal from 01. *The Vicarage, 25 Church Road, Lilleshall, Newport TF10 9HE* Tel and fax (01952) 604281
E-mail davidbutterfield@justanote.co.uk

BUTTERFIELD, John Kenneth. b 52. Nottm Univ BCombStuds. Linc Th Coll 79. **d** 82 **p** 83. C Cantley *Sheff* 82-84; C Doncaster St Leon and St Jude 84-86; TV Ilfracombe, Lee, Woolacombe, Bittadon etc *Ex* 86-88; V Thurcroft *Sheff* 88-96; Chapl Chesterfield and N Derbyshire NHS Trust from 96. *Chesterfield and North Derbyshire Royal Hospital, Calow, Chesterfield S44 5BL* Tel (01246) 277271 ext 3398

BUTTERWORTH, Antony James. b 51. Hull Univ BSc73 Bris Univ DipTh76. Trin Coll Bris 73. **d** 76 **p** 77. C Halliwell St Pet *Man* 76-81; V Werneth 81-90; V Tonge Fold from 90. *St Chad's Vicarage, 9 Tonge Fold Road, Bolton BL2 6AW* Tel (01204) 525809 E-mail stchads@clara.net

BUTTERWORTH, David Frederick. b 48. Oak Hill Th Coll BA88. **d** 88 **p** 89. R Telegraph Creek Canada 88-92; R Barrhead and Westlock 92-94; R Yellowknife 94-98; V Hanmer, Bronington, Bettisfield, Tallarn Green *St As* 98-04. *Bettisfield Hall, Bettisfield, Whitchurch SY13 2LB* Tel (01948) 710525

BUTTERWORTH, Derek. b 27. Wells Th Coll 63. **d** 65 **p** 65. C Bottesford *Linc* 65-73; TV Bottesford w Ashby 73-83; Chapl St Hilda's Sch Whitby 83-85; V Derringham Bank *York* 85-90; rtd 90; Perm to Offic *Ripon* and *York* from 90. *26 St Mary's Gate, Ripon HG4 1LX* Tel (01765) 607827

BUTTERWORTH, Elsie. b 27. Linc Th Coll 81. **dss** 83 **d** 87 **p** 94. OHP 83-85; Derringham Bank *York* 85-87; Par Dn 87-88; Par Dn Filey 88-94; C 94-97; rtd 93; Perm to Offic *York* from 97. *3 Brooklands Close, Filey YO14 9BJ* Tel (01723) 515781

BUTTERWORTH, Frederick. *See* BUTTERWORTH, David Frederick

BUTTERWORTH, George John. b 58. Liv Univ BA85. Chich Th Coll 92. **d** 92 **p** 93. C Mayfield *Chich* 92-93; C Hastings St Clem and All SS 93-96; TV Brighton Resurr 96-02; P-in-c Saltdean from 02. *St Nicholas' Vicarage, Saltdean Vale, Saltdean, Brighton BN2 8HE* Tel (01273) 302345

BUTTERWORTH, Canon George Michael. b 41. Man Univ BSc63 Lon Univ BD67 PhD89 Nottm Univ MPhil71. Tyndale Hall Bris. **d** 67 **p** 68. C S Normanton *Derby* 67-71; India 72-79; Lect Oak Hill Th Coll 80-96; Prin St Alb and Ox Min Course *Ox* from 97; Perm to Offic *St Alb* from 80; Hon Can St Alb from 02. *9 Fulmar Court, Bicester OX26 4FG* Tel (01869) 240932 *or* (01865) 790084 E-mail mikebutterworth@waitrose.com

BUTTERWORTH, Mrs Gillian. b 49. Man Univ BA71 Dur Univ PGCE72. N Ord Course 96. **d** 99. C Barnsley St Mary *Wakef* 99-03; Min Development Officer from 03. *Outwood Vicarage, 424 Leeds Road, Wakefield WF1 2JB* Tel (01924) 823150
E-mail johnbutterworth@blueyonder.co.uk

BUTTERWORTH, Ian Eric. b 44. Aber Univ MA67 MTh79. Edin Th Coll 67. **d** 69 **p** 70. C Langley All SS and Martyrs *Man* 69-71; Prec St Andr Cathl *Ab* 71-75; V Bolton St Matt w St Barn *Man* 75-85; C-in-c Lostock CD 85-92; Laity Development Officer (Bolton Adnry) 85-92; Teacher Fairfield High Sch Droylsden 92-99; Perm to Offic *Man* 96-99; Hon C Sudden St Aidan 00-05; P-in-c Castleton Moor 00-05; V from 05. *St Martin's Vicarage, Vicarage Road North, Rochdale OL11 2TE* Tel (01706) 632353 E-mail i.butterworth@tesco.net

BUTTERWORTH, Preb James Frederick. b 49. St Chad's Coll Dur BA70 Birm Univ MA99. Cuddesdon Coll 70. **d** 72 **p** 73. C Kidderminster St Mary *Worc* 72-76; P-in-c Dudley St Barn 76-79; V 79-82; Prec and Min Can Worc Cathl 82-88; TR Bridgnorth, Tasley, Astley Abbotts, etc *Heref* 88-94; Can Res and Treas Heref Cathl 94-99; Preb Heref Cathl from 94; P-in-c Ewyas Harold w Dulas, Kenderchurch etc from 99; RD Abbeydore from 02. *The Rectory, Ewyas Harold, Hereford HR2 0EY* Tel (01981) 240079

BUTTERWORTH, James Kent. b 49. Southn Univ BTh79. Chich Th Coll 75. **d** 79 **p** 80. C Heckmondwike *Wakef* 79-83; V Wrenthorpe 83-95; V Staincross from 95. *St John's Vicarage, 48 Greenside, Staincross, Barnsley S75 6GU* Tel (01226) 382261 E-mail jim@butterworth.uk.net

BUTTERWORTH, John Walton. b 49. St Jo Coll Dur BSc70 DipTh73. **d** 74 **p** 75. C Todmorden *Wakef* 74-77; Chapl Wakef Cathl 77-78; C Wakef Cathl 77-78; V Outwood from 78. *Outwood Vicarage, 424 Leeds Road, Wakefield WF1 2JB* Tel (01924) 823150 E-mail johnbutterworth@blueyonder.co.uk

BUTTERWORTH, Canon Julia Kay. b 42. Edin Univ MA64 Bris Univ CertEd66 Nottm Univ DipTh75. Linc Th Coll 73. **dss** 77 **d** 87 **p** 94. Cov E *Cov* 77-79; Cant Cathl *Cant* 79-84; Dioc Adv in Women's Min 82-92; Faversham 84-87; Par Dn 87-92; TD Whitstable 92-94; TV 94-97; Hon Can Cant Cathl from 96; P-in-c Tenterden St Mich from 97; Dioc Adv in Spirituality from 97. *The Vicarage, Ashford Road, St Michaels, Tenterden TN30 6PY* Tel and fax (01580) 764670 E-mail jbutterworth@clara.co.uk

BUTTERWORTH, Michael. *See* BUTTERWORTH, Canon George Michael

BUTTERWORTH, Mildred Jean. b 42. Leeds Univ MB, ChB65 FRCOG84. St Jo Coll Nottm. **d** 00 **p** 01. NSM Moldgreen and Rawthorpe *Wakef* 00-03; NSM Almondbury w Farnley Tyas from 03. *1 Furnbrook Gardens, Kirkheaton, Huddersfield HD5 0DY* Tel (01484) 421375 E-mail mildred@fish.co.uk

BUTTERWORTH, Roy. b 31. Selw Coll Cam BA55 MA59. Wells Th Coll 55. **d** 57 **p** 58. C Bathwick w Woolley *B & W* 57-61; Prec St Paul's Cathl Dundee *Bre* 61-63; V Dearnley *Man* 63-81; V Tyldesley w Shakerley 81-83; V Healey 83-94; rtd 94. *102 Greenbank Road, Rochdale OL12 0EN* Tel (01706) 350808

BUTTERY, Bernard. b 36. Culham Coll Ox CertEd58 LCP75. OLM course 96. **d** 99 **p** 00. OLM Stafford *Lich* from 99. *7 Dearnsdale Close, Tillington, Stafford ST16 1SD* Tel (01785) 244771

BUTTERY, Graeme. b 62. York Univ BA84. St Steph Ho Ox 85. **d** 88 **p** 89. C Peterlee *Dur* 88-91; C Sunderland 91-92; TV 92-94; V Horsley Hill St Lawr 94-05; AD Jarrow 01-05; V Hartlepool St Oswald from 05. *St Oswald's Clergy House, Brougham Terrace, Hartlepool TS24 8EY* Tel (01429) 273201 E-mail buttery.stl@virgin.net

BUTTERY, Nathan James. b 72. Em Coll Cam BA94 MA97. Wycliffe Hall Ox BA98. **d** 00 **p** 01. C Hull St Jo Newland *York* from 00. *75 Desmond Avenue, Hull HU6 7JX* Tel (01482) 343789 E-mail nathan.debbie@ukgateway.net

BUTTIMORE, Canon John Charles. b 27. St Mich Coll Llan 55. **d** 57 **p** 58. C Treherbert *Llan* 57-60; C Aberdare St Fagan *Llan* 60-64; V Williamstown 64-71; Chapl Ely Hosp Cardiff 71-98; V Caerau w Ely *Llan* 71-97; RD Cardiff 83-89; Can Llan Cathl 87-97; rtd 97; Perm to Offic *Llan* from 97. *3 Nant y Pepra, Cardiff CF5 4UB* Tel (029) 2065 9333

BUTTLE, Leslie Albert. b 32. Open Univ BA89. Edin Th Coll 61. **d** 64 **p** 65. C Sowerby Bridge w Norland *Wakef* 64-66; C Plymstock *Ex* 66-69; C Ilfracombe H Trin 69-71; V Woolfardisworthy and Buck Mills 71-76; C Sticklepath 76-77; Asst Chapl HM Pris Leeds 77-80; Lic to Offic *Ripon* 77-80; Chapl HM Youth Cust Cen Hindley 80-84; Perm to Offic *Ex* 86-93; Hon C Braunton from 93; rtd 97. *Church House, Saunton, Braunton EX33 1LG* Tel (01271) 817022

BUTTLE, Leslie Ronald Frank. b 07. Lon Univ BA28. **d** 34 **p** 35. C Wanstead St Mary *Chelmsf* 34-36; Asst Master R Wanstead Sch 31-36; Asst Chapl 34-36; Chapl K Coll Otahuhu New Zealand 36-38; R Water Stratford *Ox* 38-39; Asst Chapl Felsted Sch 40; Chapl RNVR 41-47; R Goldhanger w Lt Totham *Chelmsf* 47-50; R Purleigh 50-55; V Gt w Lt Packington *Cov* 55-58; V Maxstoke *Birm* 55-58; R Fordham *Chelmsf* 58-63; V Hatfield Broad Oak 63-66; V Bush End 63-66; R Lowick w Sudborough and Slipton *Pet* 67-73; rtd 73; Perm to Offic *Truro* from 73. *5 Castle Street, Launceston PL15 8BA* Tel (01566) 772052

BUTTON, David Frederick. b 27. St Chad's Coll Dur BA53 DipTh54. **d** 54 **p** 55. C S Shields St Mary *Dur* 54-58; C Seacroft *Ripon* 58-60; V Holland Fen *Linc* 60-64; V Surfleet 64-71; R Belton SS Pet and Paul 71-78; V Barkston w Syston 72-78; V Honington 73-78; R Gunhouse w Burringham 78-82; P-in-c Gt w Lt Hockham w Wretham w Illington *Nor* 82-84; P-in-c Shropham w Larling and Snetterton 82-84; V Hockham w Shropham Gp of Par 84-91; rtd 91; Perm to Offic *Nor* 91-96. *6 Vallibus Close, Oulton, Lowestoft NR32 3DS*

BUTTREY, Anne Stella Ivy. b 40. Dioc OLM tr scheme 99. **d** 02 **p** 03. OLM Brandon and Santon Downham w Elveden *St E* 02-04; OLM Lakenheath 02-04; OLM Brandon and Santon Downham w Elveden etc from 04. *8 Mount Road, Brandon IP27 0DT* Tel (01842) 810172 E-mail annebuttrey@mailacc.fsnet.co.uk

BUXTON, Alyson Christina. b 65. Chelt & Glouc Coll of HE BA00 RGN86. St Jo Coll Nottm MTh01. **d** 02 **p** 03. C New Sleaford *Linc* 02-05; Lic Preacher from 05; PV Linc Cathl from 05. *West Hall, Grantham Road, Coleby, Lincoln LN5 0AP* Tel (01522) 810762 *or* 529241 Mobile 077132-490240 E-mail alybuxton@aol.uk.com

BUXTON, Canon Derek Major. b 31. Lon Univ BD63. Ripon Hall Ox 58. **d** 60 **p** 61. C Leic St Nic *Leic* 60-64; Chapl Leic Univ 60-64; Chapl Leic Coll of Art and Tech 61-65; Min Can Leic Cathl 64-69; Prec 67; R Ibstock 69-76; R Ibstock w Heather 76-87; Chapl ATC from 78; OCF and Cen and E Regional Chapl from 87; RD Akeley S *Leic* 84-87; P-in-c Woodhouse Eaves 87-91; V Woodhouse and Woodhouse Eaves 91-98; Chapl Roecliffe Manor Cheshire Home from 87; Hon Can Leic Cathl from 88; rtd 98; Perm to Offic *Leic* from 99. *Shepherd's Hill, 74 Pitsford Drive, Loughborough LE11 4NY* Tel (01509) 216663

BUXTON, Edmund Francis. b 42. Trin Coll Cam BA65 MA68 DPS74 Sheff Univ MMinTheol93. Linc Th Coll 65. **d** 67 **p** 68. C Wanstead St Mary *Chelmsf* 67-70; C Cambridge Gt St Mary w St Mich *Ely* 70-73; C Barking St Marg w St Patr *Chelmsf* 74-75; India 75-79; Chapl Bath Univ *B & W* 79-89; TR Willenhall H Trin *Lich* 89-96; Chapl Team Leader Univ Hosp Birm NHS Trust from 96. *The Chaplaincy Office, Queen Elizabeth Hospital, Edgbaston, Birmingham B15 2TH* Tel 0121-472 1311 ext 3104/3437 Fax 627 2211 E-mail francis.buxton@uhb.nhs.uk

BUXTON, Graham. b 45. York Univ BA66 Bradf Univ MSc71. St Jo Coll Nottm 83 Melbourne Coll of Div MMin97. **d** 83 **p** 84. C Ealing Dean St Jo *Lon* 83-84; C W Ealing St Jo w St Jas 84-86; C S Harrow St Paul 86-89; P-in-c 89-91; Sen Lect Tabor Coll Australia from 91. *5 Heron Place, Flagstaff Hill, S Australia 5159* Tel (0061) (8) 8370 6038 *or* 8373 8777 Fax 8373 1766 E-mail gbuxton@adelaide.tabor.edu.au

BUXTON, James Andrew Denis. b 64. Newc Univ BA86. Westcott Ho Cam 95. **d** 97 **p** 98. C Portsea St Mary *Portsm* 97-01; Succ S'wark Cathl *S'wark* from 01; Chapl Medical and Dental Students K Coll Lon from 01. *St Paul's Vicarage, 54 Kipling Street, London SE1 3RU* Tel (020) 7367 6705 *or* 7407 8290 E-mail james@buxton9.fsnet.co.uk *or* james.buxton@kcl.ac.uk

BUXTON, Richard Fowler. b 40. Lon Univ BSc62 Linacre Coll Ox BA67 MA71 Ex Univ PhD73. St Steph Ho Ox 65. **d** 68 **p** 69. C Whitley Ch Ch *Ox* 68-70; C Pinhoe *Ex* 70-71; Asst Chapl Ex Univ 71-73; Tutor Sarum & Wells Th Coll 73-77; Vice-Prin 77; Perm to Offic *Ches* 77-97; Lect Liturgy Man Univ 80-94; Subwarden St Deiniol's Lib Hawarden 94-97; Perm to Offic *Ban* from 96; *St As* from 97; rtd 00. *Golygfa'r Orsaf, 6 Rhesdai Garth, Porthmadog LL49 9BE* Tel (01766) 514782

BUXTON, Canon Trevor George. b 57. Ex Univ BEd78. Chich Th Coll 81. **d** 83 **p** 84. C Hove All SS *Chich* 83-87; C Burgess Hill St Jo 87-91; V Brighton St Aug and St Sav 91-03; P-in-c Sidley 02-04; V from 04; Can and Preb Chich Cathl from 01. *All Saints' Vicarage, All Saints Lane, Bexhill-on-Sea TN39 5HA* Tel (01424) 221071 Mobile 07885-942901 E-mail hojoe@waitrose.com

BUYERS, Stanley. b 39. Leeds Univ CertEd71 Sunderland Poly BEd78 Newc Univ MEd90. NEOC 97. **d** 00 **p** 01. NSM E Boldon *Dur* 00-03; P-in-c Boldon from 03. *37 Tarragon Way, South Shields NE34 8TB* Tel 0191-519 0370 Mobile 07979-693153 E-mail stanbuyers@btinternet.com

BYATT, John William. b 55. St Jo Coll Nottm. **d** 01 **p** 02. C Heanor *Derby* from 01. *46 Johnson Drive, Heanor DE75 7SU* Tel (01773) 716865 Mobile 07773-906919

BYE, Canon Peter John. b 39. Lon Univ BD65. Clifton Th Coll 62. **d** 67 **p** 68. C Hyson Green *S'well* 67-70; C Dur St Nic *Dur* 70-73; V Lowestoft Ch Ch *Nor* 73-80; V Carl St Jo *Carl* 80-04; Hon Can Carl Cathl from 98; RD Carl 00-04; Chapl Carl Gen Hosp 80-94; Chapl Carl Hosps NHS Trust 94-98; rtd 04. *10 The Island, Anthorn, Wigton CA7 5AN* Tel (016973) 52779

BYERS, Canon Christopher Martin. b 33. Jes Coll Ox BA59 MA62. Wycliffe Hall Ox 59. **d** 60 **p** 61. C Bermondsey St Mary w St Olave, St Jo etc *S'wark* 60-66; R Mottingham St Andr 66-86; TR Thamesmead 86-99; C 99-00; Hon Can S'wark Cathl 96-00; rtd 01; Perm to Offic *Cant* from 01. *36 Faversham Road, Whitstable CT5 4AR* Tel (01227) 272786

BYFORD, Canon David Charles. b 30. Bps' Coll Cheshunt 58. **d** 61 **p** 62. C Short Heath *Birm* 61-63; C Londonderry 63-65; Chapl Selly Oak Hosp Birm 65-70; V Rowley Regis *Birm* 70-78; V Polesworth 78-95; RD Polesworth 84-91; Hon Can Birm Cathl 87-95; rtd 95; Perm to Offic *Sarum* from 95. *Rose Cottage, Stratford sub Castle, Salisbury SP1 3LB* Tel (01722) 322569

BYFORD, The Ven Edwin Charles. b 47. Aus Nat Univ BSc70 Melbourne Coll of Div BD73 Univ of Chicago MA76 Man Univ PhD85. Trin Coll Melbourne 70. **d** 73 **p** 73. C Qeanbeyan Ch Ch Australia 73-75; Chapl Univ of Chicago USA 75-76; Hon C Chorlton-cum-Hardy St Werburgh *Man* 76-79; Australia from 79; Chapl Woden Valley Hosp 80-83; Asst P Wagga Wagga 83-84; Asst P Ainslie All SS 84-87; Chapl Aus Nat Univ 87-91; R Binda 91-95; R Broken Hill St Pet and Adn The Darling from 95. *PO Box 185, Broken Hill, NSW, Australia 2880* Tel and fax (0061) (8) 8087 3221 Mobile 409-467981 E-mail e-byford-4@alumni.uchicago.edu

BYLES, Canon Raymond Vincent. b 30. Univ of Wales (Lamp) BA52. St Mich Coll Llan 52. **d** 54 **p** 55. C Llanfairisgaer *Ban* 54-57; C Llandudno 57-59; V Carno 59-64; V Trefeglwys 63; V Newmarket and Gwaenysgor *St As* 64-72; R Llysfaen 72-80; V Bodelwyddan and St George 80-85; V Bodelywddan 85-95; Hon Can St As Cathl from 89; rtd 95. *20 Lon Dderwen, Tan-y-Goppa Parc, Abergele LL22 7DW* Tel (01745) 833604

BYLLAM-BARNES, Preb Paul William Marshall. b 38. Birm Univ BCom Lon Univ MSc. Sarum & Wells Th Coll. **d** 84 **p** 85. C Gt Bookham *Guildf* 84-87; R Cusop w Blakemere, Bredwardine w Brobury etc *Heref* 87-03; RD Abbeydore 96-00; Preb Heref Cathl 99-03; rtd 03. *Myrtle Cottage, 1 Wantz Chase, Maldon CM9 5DN* Tel (01621) 858978

BYNON, William. b 43. St Aid Birkenhead 63. **d** 66 **p** 67. C Huyton St Mich *Liv* 66-69; C Maghull 69-72; TV 72-75; V Highfield 75-82; V Southport All SS 82-88; P-in-c Southport All So 86-88; V Newton in Makerfield St Pet 88-94; V Caerhun w Llangelynin w Llanbedr-y-Cennin *Ban* from 94. *Caerhun Vicarage, Tyn-y-Groes, Conwy LL32 8UG* Tel (01492) 650250

BYRNE, Bryn. *See* BYRNE, Ronald Brendan Anthony

BYRNE, David Patrick. b 48. PGCE96. St Jo Coll Nottm 74. **d** 77 **p** 78. C Bordesley Green *Birm* 77-79; C Weoley Castle 79-82; TV Kings Norton 82-92; TV Hodge Hill 92-94; Perm to Offic 94-97; Chapl Asst Birm Heartlands and Solihull NHS Trust 96-98; Chapl NW Lon Hosp NHS Trust from 98; Chapl Harrow and Hillingdon Healthcare NHS Trust from 98. *Staff Residence, Northwick Park Hospital, Watford Road, Harrow HA1 3UJ* Tel (020) 8864 2113 *or* 8728 3319 E-mail david.byrne@nwlh.nhs.uk

BYRNE, David Rodney. b 47. St Jo Coll Cam BA70 MA73. Cranmer Hall Dur 71. **d** 73 **p** 74. C Maidstone St Luke *Cant* 73-77; C Patcham *Chich* 77-83; TV Stantonbury *Ox* 83-87; TV Stantonbury and Willen 87-92; TV Woodley 92-02; V Patchway *Bris* from 02. *St Chad's Vicarage, 1B Southsea Road, Patchway, Bristol BS34 5DP* Tel 0117-969 2935 *or* 979 3978 E-mail dbyrne@fish.co.uk

BYRNE, Miss Georgina Ann. b 72. Trin Coll Ox BA92 MA96 CCC Cam MPhil98. Westcott Ho Cam. **d** 97 **p** 98. NSM W Bromwich All SS *Lich* 97-98; C 98-01; Hon Asst Chapl CCC Cam 97-98; Chapl to Bp Kensington *Lon* 01-04; Hon C Twickenham St Mary 01-04; TV Halas *Worc* from 04. *The Rectory, St Kenelm's Road, Romsley, Halesowen B62 0PH* Tel (01562) 710050

BYRNE, Ian Barclay. b 53. Ripon Coll Cuddesdon 01. **d** 03 **p** 04. C Blyth Valley *St E* from 03. *St Ursula's House, 64 Old Station Road, Halesworth IP19 8JQ* Tel (01986) 874128 E-mail rev.ib@tesco.net

BYRNE, Canon John Victor. b 47. FCA. St Jo Coll Nottm LTh73. **d** 73 **p** 74. C Gillingham St Mark *Roch* 73-76; C Cranham Park *Chelmsf* 76-80; V Balderstone *Man* 80-87; V Southsea St Jude *Portsm* from 87; P-in-c Southsea St Pet 95-03; Hon Can Portsm Cathl from 97; RD Portsm from 01; Chapl to The Queen from 03. *St Jude's Vicarage, 7 Hereford Road, Southsea PO5 2DH* Tel and fax (023) 9282 1071 *or* tel 9275 0442 E-mail john@byrne07.freeserve.co.uk

BYRNE, The Very Revd Matthew. b 27. Man Univ MA69 TCD HDipEd81. Tyndale Hall Bris 47. **d** 51 **p** 52. C Rawtenstall St Mary *Man* 51-54; OCF 54-57; R Moss Side St Jas *Man* 57-62; R Whalley Range St Marg 62-80; P-in-c Chapelizod *D & G* 80-83; Chapl K Hosp Sch Dub 83-89; Dean Kildare *M & K* 89-93; I Kildare w Kilmeague and Curragh 89-93; Producer Relig Dept RTE 83-92; Chapl Defence Forces 89-92; rtd 92. *5 Fairfield Park, Greystones, Co Wicklow, Irish Republic* Tel and fax (00353) (1) 287 3622

BYRNE, The Very Revd Miriam Alexandra Frances. b 46. Westcott Ho Cam. **d** 87 **p** 94. Par Dn Beoley *Worc* 87-90; C Ayr *Glas* 90-92; Dn-in-c Dumbarton 92-94; P-in-c 94-98; Provost St Paul's Cathl Dundee *Bre* from 98; R Dundee St Paul from 98. *The Cathedral Rectory, 4 Richmond Terrace, Dundee DD2 1BQ* Tel and fax (01382) 646296 *or* tel 224486 Fax 202200 Mobile 07968-820665 E-mail miriambyrne@stpaulscathedral.fsnet.co.uk

BYRNE, Rodney Edmund. b 18. **d** 84 **p** 84. Hon C Leckhampton SS Phil and Jas w Cheltenham St Jas *Glouc* 84-88; rtd 88; Perm to Offic *Glouc* from 88. *39 Collum End Rise, Cheltenham GL53 0PA* Tel (01242) 526428

BYRNE, Ronald Brendan Anthony (Bryn). b 31. Reading Univ BA72. Westcott Ho Cam 86. **d** 64 **p** 65. Chapl Cov Cathl *Cov* 87-91; Chapl Lanchester Poly 87-91; Lic to Offic 91-94; Chapl Limerick Univ *L & K* 94-98; Chapl Villier's Sch Limerick 95-98; rtd 96; Chapl Lanzarote *Eur* 98-00; Perm to Offic *Lon* from 02. *28 Hendon Lane, London N3 1TR* Tel and fax (020) 8343 2526 Mobile 07960-319294 E-mail brynbyrne@aol.com

BYRNE, Roy Harold. b 71. Westmr Coll Ox BTh97 Irish Sch of Ecum MPhil00. CITC 97. **d** 99 **p** 00. C Dublin Ch Ch Cathl Gp *D & G* 99-03; I Killeshin w Cloydagh and Killabban *C & O* from 03. *The Rectory, Ballickmoyler, Carlow, Irish Republic* Tel and fax (00353) (59) 862 5321 E-mail roybyrne@eircom.net

BYROM, Alan. b 51. Magd Coll Ox BA72 Leeds Univ PGCE73 Bris Univ MA85 Man Univ MPhil99. Trin Coll Bris DipHE84 N Ord Course 97. **d** 99 **p** 00. C Leyland St Andr *Blackb* 99-03; TV Solway Plain *Carl* from 03. *The Vicarage, Wigton Road, Silloth, Wigton CA7 4NR* Tel (016973) 31413 E-mail arm@abyrom.freeserve.co.uk

BYROM, Canon John Kenneth. b 20. Selw Coll Cam BA41 MA45. Westcott Ho Cam 41. **d** 43 **p** 44. C Neston *Ches* 43-48; C Stockport St Matt 48-50; V Cheadle Hulme All SS 50-63; Warden Brasted Place Coll Westerham 64-74; V Swaffham Prior *Ely* 74-88; Dir of Ords 75-87; Dir Post-Ord Tr 75-87; Hon Can Ely Cathl 78-88; RD Fordham 78-83; rtd 88; Perm to Offic *Ely* from 88. *62 Cambridge Road, Great Shelford, Cambridge CB2 5JS* Tel (01223) 844015

BYROM, Canon Malcolm Senior. b 37. Edin Th Coll 65. **d** 67 **p** 68. C Allerton *Bradf* 67-69; C Padstow *Truro* 69-72; V Hessenford 72-77; P-in-c St Martin by Looe 72-77; V Kenwyn 77-91; R Kenwyn w St Allen 91-99; Hon Can Truro Cathl 92-00; RD Powder 88-90; Sub-Warden Community of the Epiphany Truro 85-01; Warden from 01; rtd 99; Perm to Offic *Truro* from 00. *West Haven, Dobbin Lane, Trevone, Padstow PL28 8QP* Tel (01841) 520242 E-mail malcolmbyrom@supanet.com

BYRON, Frederick. b 14. Dur Univ BA38. St Jo Coll Dur 38. **d** 39 **p** 40. C Openshaw *Man* 39-43; C Oldham St Paul 43-46; C Moston St Mary 46-50; R Old Trafford St Cuth 50-56; V Bolton St Barn 56-68; V Out Rawcliffe *Blackb* 68-78; C Standish 78-79; rtd 79. *The Acorns Care Centre, Parkside, Hindley, Wigan WN2 3LJ* Tel (01942) 259024

BYRON, Terence Sherwood. b 26. Keble Coll Ox BA50 MA54. Linc Th Coll 50. **d** 52 **p** 53. C Melton Mowbray w Burton Lazars, Freeby etc *Leic* 52-55; C Whitwick St Jo the Bapt 55-60; India 60-76; C-in-c Beaumont Leys (Extra-paroch Distr) *Leic* 76-85; V Beaumont Leys 85-86; RD Christianity N 86-92; P-in-c Leic St Phil 86-88; V 88-92; rtd 93; Perm to Offic *Leic* from 93. *84 Flax Road, Leicester LE4 6QD* Tel 0116-266 1922

BYSOUTH, Paul Graham. b 55. Oak Hill Th Coll. **d** 84 **p** 85. C Gorleston St Andr *Nor* 84-87; C Ripley *Derby* 87-91; TV N Wingfield, Clay Cross and Pilsley 91-00; V Blagreaves from 00. *St Andrew's Vicarage, 5 Greenburn Close, Littleover, Derby DE23 1FF* Tel (01332) 773877

BYTHEWAY, Phillip James. b 35. MIIExE89 BA93. **d** 97. OLM Church Stretton *Heref* 97-00; rtd 00; Perm to Offic *Heref* from 00. *Ivy Glen, 55 Watling Street South, Church Stretton SY6 7BQ* Tel (01694) 723901 Mobile 07778-391088 Fax 724440

BYWORTH, Canon Christopher Henry Briault. b 39. Oriel Coll Ox BA61 MA65 Bris Univ BA63. Lon Coll of Div 64. **d** 65 **p** 66. C Low Leyton *Chelmsf* 65-68; C Rusholme H Trin *Man* 68-70; Lic to Offic *Lon* 71-75; TR Thetford *Nor* 75-79; Warden Cranmer Hall Dur 79-83; TR Fazakerley Em *Liv* 83-90; P-in-c St Helens St Helen 90-94; TR 94-04; AD St Helens 90-00; Hon Can Liv Cathl 99-04; rtd 04. *11 Oakleigh, Skelmersdale WN8 9QU* Tel (01744) 886481

BYWORTH, Mrs Ruth Angela. b 49. Cranmer Hall Dur BA82. **dss** 83 **d** 92 **p** 94. Kirkby *Liv* 83-89; Aintree St Pet 89-97; Dn-in-c 92-94; P-in-c 94-97; P-in-c St Helens St Mark 97-98; C Sutton 98-03; TV 03-04; rtd 04. *11 Oakleigh, Skelmersdale WN8 9QU* Tel (01744) 886481

C

CABLE, Patrick John. b 50. AKC72. **d** 74 **p** 75. C Herne *Cant* 74-78; CF from 78; Lic to Offic *Cant* from 78. *c/o MOD Chaplains (Army)* Tel (01980) 615804 Fax 615800

CACKETT, Janice Susan. b 39. Goldsmiths' Coll Lon BA76 Surrey Univ MSc83. SW Minl Tr Course 99. **d** 99 **p** 00. NSM Clyst St Mary, Clyst St George etc *Ex* 99-03; P-in-c E Budleigh w

Bicton and Otterton from 03. *Manor House, Clyst St George, Exeter EX3 0NS* Tel (01392) 877468 E-mail jcackett@ukgateway.net

CADDELL, Richard Allen. b 54. Auburn Univ Alabama BIE77. Trin Coll Bris BA88. **d** 88 **p** 89. C Uphill *B & W* 88-94; Perm to Offic 94-96; TV Beaconsfield *Ox* from 96. *St Thomas's House, Mayflower Way, Beaconsfield HP9 1UF* Tel (01494) 672750

CADDEN, Brian Stuart. b 58. BSc BTh TCD. **d** 89 **p** 90. C Lecale Gp *D & D* 89-92; C Killowen *D & R* 92-95; I Muckamore *Conn* from 95. *The Rectory, 5 Ballycraigy Road, Muckamore, Antrim BT41 1QP* Tel (028) 9446 2073 E-mail muckamore@conner.anglican.org

CADDEN, Terence John. b 60. TCD BTh89. CITC 86. **d** 89 **p** 90. C Coleraine *Conn* 89-92; C Lurgan Ch the Redeemer *D & D* 92-93; Past Dir 93-01; I Gilford from 01. *The Vicarage, 18 Scarva Road, Gilford, Craigavon BT63 6BG* Tel (028) 3883 1130 Mobile 07714-386612 E-mail gilford@dromore.anglican.org

CADDICK, Jeremy Lloyd. b 60. St Jo Coll Cam BA82 MA86 K Coll Lon MA93. Ripon Coll Cuddesdon BA86 MA91. **d** 87 **p** 88. C Kennington St Jo w St Jas *S'wark* 87-90; Chapl Lon Univ *Lon* 90-94; Chapl R Free Medical Sch 90-94; Chapl R Veterinary Coll Lon 90-94; PV Westmr Abbey 92-94; Dean Em Coll Cam from 94. *Emmanuel College, Cambridge CB2 3AP* Tel (01223) 334264 *or* 330195 Fax 334426 E-mail jlc24@cam.ac.uk

CADDICK, Canon Lloyd Reginald. b 31. Bris Univ BA56 St Cath Coll Ox BA58 MA62 Nottm Univ MPhil73 K Coll Lon PhD78 Open Univ Hon MA79. St Steph Ho Ox 56. **d** 59 **p** 59. C N Lynn w St Marg and St Nic *Nor* 59-62; Chapl Oakham Sch 62-66; P-in-c Bulwick, Harringworth w Blatherwycke and Laxton *Pet* 66-67; R Bulwick, Blatherwycke w Harringworth and Laxton 67-77; V Oundle 77-96; Can Pet Cathl 94-96; rtd 96; Perm to Offic *Pet* from 96. *102 West Street, Kings Cliffe, Peterborough PE8 6XA* Tel (01780) 470332

CADDOO (née BLAKELY), Mrs Denise Irene. b 69. QUB BD91 PGCE92. CITC 93. **d** 95 **p** 96. C Holywood *D & D* 95-99; C Portadown St Columba *Arm* 99-00; I Carrowdore w Millisle *D & D* 00-04; C Holywood from 04. *51 Princess Gardens, Holywood BT18 0PN* Tel (028) 9042 4554 *or* 9042 3622

CADDY, Canon Michael George Bruce Courtenay. b 45. K Coll Lon. **d** 71 **p** 72. C Walton St Mary *Liv* 71-76; C Solihull *Birm* 76-79; TV 79-81; V Shard End 81-87; TR Shirley 87-00; P-in-c Tanworth St Patr Salter Street 97-00; TR Salter Street and Shirley from 00; AD Shirley 97-02; Hon Can Birm Cathl from 99. *The Vicarage, 2 Bishopton Close, Shirley, Solihull B90 4AH* Tel 0121-744 3123 *or* 745 8896 E-mail stjames@shirleyparishoffice.freeserve.co.uk

CADDY, Ms Susan. b 50. Westcott Ho Cam 99. **d** 01 **p** 02. C Sutton in Ashfield St Mary *S'well* from 01; P-in-c Shelton and Oxon *Lich* from 05. *Oxon Vicarage, Shelton Gardens, Bicton Heath, Shrewsbury SY3 5AG* E-mail suecee@fish.co.uk

CADE, Mrs Margaret Elizabeth. b 34. Dioc OLM tr scheme 99. **d** 00. OLM Portland All SS w St Pet *Sarum* from 00. *27 Avalanche Road, Portland DT5 2DJ* Tel (01305) 821317 Mobile 07974-696892 Fax 826453

CADE, Simon Peter Vincent. b 69. Univ of Wales BA90. Westcott Ho Cam CTM94. **d** 94 **p** 95. C Calne and Blackland *Sarum* 94-98; Chapl St Mary's Sch Calne 94-97; TV Basingstoke *Win* from 98. *45 Beaconsfield Road, Basingstoke RG21 3DG* Tel (01256) 464616 E-mail simon@cade.u-net.com

CADMAN, Kenneth Claude. b 14. St Jo Coll Dur BA40. **d** 40 **p** 41. C Harpurhey Ch Ch *Man* 40-44; C Rochdale 44-45; C Worsley 45-47; R Heaton Norris All SS 47-52; CF (TA) 49-52; CF (TA - R of O) 52-69; V Rainow w Saltersford and Forest *Ches* 52-54; R Higher Broughton *Man* 54-59; R Guernsey St Michel du Valle *Win* 59-65; V Alderney 65-69; R Guernsey St Pierre du Bois 69-81; R Guernsey St Philippe de Torteval 80-81; Vice Dean Guernsey 70-81; rtd 81; Perm to Offic *Win* 82-98. *Summerland House Nursing Home, St Peter Port, Guernsey GY1 1DX* Tel (01481) 724196

CADMAN, Robert Hugh. b 49. Nottm Univ DipTh76. St Jo Coll Nottm 77. **d** 78 **p** 79. C Ecclesall *Sheff* 78-82; C Worting *Win* 82-84; C-in-c Winklebury CD 84-87; R Widford *Chelmsf* 87-94; Chapl Anglia Poly Univ 94-95; NSM Brentwood St Thos 01-03; TV Southend from 03. *All Saints' Vicarage, 1 Sutton Road, Southend-on-Sea SS2 5PA* Tel (01702) 306999 E-mail robcadman@blueyonder.co.uk

CADMORE, Albert Thomas. b 47. Open Univ BA81 NE Lon Poly Nor City Coll DMS84 SS Mark & Jo Coll Plymouth Lon Inst of Educn CertEd68 UEA MA94. EAMTC 85. **d** 88 **p** 89. NSM Gorleston St Andr *Nor* 88-96; NSM Winterton w E and W Somerton and Horsey 94-96; NSM Flegg Coastal Benefice from 96. *10 Upper Cliff Road, Gorleston, Great Yarmouth NR31 6AL* Tel (01493) 668762

CADOGAN, Paul Anthony Cleveland. b 47. AKC74. **d** 75 **p** 76. C Fishponds St Jo *Bris* 75-79; C Swindon New Town 79-81; P-in-c Swindon All SS 81-82; V 82-90; R Lower Windrush *Ox* 90-94. *2 Malthouse Close, Ashbury SN6 8PB* Tel (01793) 710488

CADOGAN, Percil Lavine. WMMTC. **d** 01 **p** 02. NSM Bournville *Birm* 01-05; NSM Bordesley St Benedict from 05. *76 Highbury Road, Birmingham B14 7QW* Tel 0121-680 9595

CAESAR, Canon Anthony Douglass. b 24. LVO87 CVO91. Magd Coll Cam BA47 MA49 MusB47 FRCO47. St Steph Ho Ox 59. **d** 61 **p** 62. C Kensington St Mary Abbots w St Geo *Lon* 61-65; Chapl RSCM Addington 65-70; Asst Sec CACTM 65-66; ACCM 65-70; Dep P in O 67-68; P-in-O 68-70; C Bournemouth St Pet *Win* 70-73; Prec and Sacr Win Cathl 74-79; Hon Can 75-76 and 79-91; Can Res 76-79; Dom Chapl to The Queen 79-91; Extra Chapl to The Queen from 91; Sub Almoner and Dep Clerk of the Closet 79-91; Sub Dean of HM Chpls Royal 79-91; rtd 91; Chapl St Cross Hosp Win 91-93; Perm to Offic *Portsm* from 93. *Flat 2, Old Kiln, Brading, Sandown PO36 0BP* Tel (01983) 406435

CAFFYN, Douglas John Morris. b 36. ACIS77 Peterho Cam MA60 Nairobi Univ MSc69 Westmr Coll Ox DipEd61. S Dios Minl Tr Scheme 87. **d** 90 **p** 91. NSM Hampden Park *Chich* 90-94; Chapl among Deaf People 94-97; Jt Sec Cttee for Min among Deaf People 95-97; Perm to Offic from 97; rtd 01. *255 King's Drive, Eastbourne BN21 2UR* Tel (01323) 500977

CAHILL, Nigel. b 59. St Mich Coll Llan DipTh80 DPS82. **d** 82 **p** 83. C Whitchurch *Llan* 82-86; V Tonypandy w Clydach Vale 86-96; RD Rhondda 93-96; V Fairwater 96-03; V Caerau w Ely from 03. *The Vicarage, Cowbridge Road West, Ely, Cardiff CF5 5BQ3* Tel (029) 2056 3254

CAIN, Andrew David. b 63. Aber Univ BSc86. Ripon Coll Cuddesdon BA89. **d** 90 **p** 91. C Walworth St Jo *S'wark* 90-94; Bp's Dom Chapl *Ox* 94-98; P-in-c Kilburn St Mary w All So *Lon* 98-01; P-in-c W Hampstead St Jas 98-01; V Kilburn St Mary w All So and W Hampstead St Jas from 01. *St Mary's Vicarage, 134A Abbey Road, London NW6 4SN* Tel and fax (020) 7624 5434 E-mail acain@acain.screaming.net

CAIN, Frank Robert. b 56. Oak Hill Th Coll BA88. **d** 88 **p** 89. C Aughton Ch Ch *Liv* 88-91; P-in-c Toxteth Park St Clem 91-99; V Toxteth St Bede w St Clem 99-04; AD Toxteth and Wavertree 01-04; Hon Can Liv Cathl 03-04; Chapl N Mersey Community NHS Trust 96-04; V New Brighton St Jas w Em *Ches* from 04. *The Vicarage, 14 Albion Street, Wallasey CH45 9LF* Tel 0151-639 5844 E-mail frankandsuecain@ukgateway.net

CAIN, Michael Christopher. b 68. St Jo Coll Dur BA90 K Coll Lon MA92 Selw Coll Cam BA94. Ridley Hall Cam 92. **d** 95 **p** 96. C Wimbledon Em Ridgway Prop Chpl *S'wark* 95-99; Asst Chapl Leipzig *Eur* 99-02; C Clifton Ch Ch w Em *Bris* from 02. *60 Clifton Park Road, Bristol BS8 3HN* Tel 0117-973 3729

CAIN, Michael John Patrick. b 62. Chich Th Coll 88. **d** 91 **p** 92. C Cainscross w Selsley *Glouc* 91-94; C Mackworth St Fran *Derby* 94-97; V Derby St Luke 97-02; C Paignton St Jo *Ex* from 02. *St Boniface House, Belfield Road, Paignton TQ3 3UZ* Tel (01803) 556612 E-mail fathermike@stboniface.fsnet.co.uk

CAINK, Richard David Somerville. b 37. Lich Th Coll 68. **d** 71 **p** 72. C Prittlewell St Mary *Chelmsf* 71-74; C Gt Yarmouth *Nor* 74-76; P-in-c Blickling w Ingworth 76-80; P-in-c Saxthorpe and Corpusty 76-80; P-in-c Oulton SS Pet and Paul 76-80; R Cheddington w Mentmore and Marsworth *Ox* 80-87; P-in-c Wooburn 87-90; V 90-96; P-in-c Lacey Green 96-98; TV Risborough 98-02; rtd 02. *1 Whitlock Drive, Great Yeldham, Halstead CO9 4EE* Tel (01787) 236091

✠**CAIRD, The Rt Revd Prof Donald Arthur Richard.** b 25. TCD BA49 MA55 BD55 HDipEd59 Hon DD88 Hon LLD93. TCD Div Sch 49. **d** 50 **p** 51 **c** 70. C Dundela St Mark *D & D* 50-53; Chapl and Asst Master Portora R Sch Enniskillen 53-57; Lect St D Coll Lamp 57-59; I Rathmichael *D & G* 60-69; Asst Master St Columba's Coll Dub 60-62; Lect TCD 62-64; Lect in Philosophy of Relig Div Hostel Dub 64-69; Dean Ossory *C & O* 69-70; Can Leighlin Cathl 69-70; I Kilkenny 69-70; Bp Limerick, Ardfert and Aghadoe *L & K* 70-76; Bp M & K 76-85; Abp Dublin *D & G* 85-96; Preb Cualaun St Patr Cathl Dublin 85-96; rtd 96; Visiting Prof Gen Th Sem New York from 97. *3 Crofton Avenue, Dun Laoghaire, Co Dublin, Irish Republic* Tel (00353) (1) 280 7869 Fax 230 1053

CAIRNS, Henry Alfred (Jim). Melbourne Univ BA49. ACT ThL43. **d** 42 **p** 43. Australia 42-81; Can Gippsland 59-60; Perm to Offic *Cant* 81-83; Perm to Offic *St Alb* 81-83 and from 85; Hon C Radlett 83-85. *47 Westminster Court, St Stephen's Hill, St Albans AL1 2DX* Tel (01727) 850949

CALAMINUS, Peter Andrew Franz. b 14. Lon Univ BA44. Cuddesdon Coll 69. **d** 71 **p** 71. C Westbury *Sarum* 71-73; P-in-c Pitcombe w Shepton Montague and Bratton St Maur *B & W* 73-76; V 76-78; rtd 79. *Hibiscus Gardens, 2 Sigg Street, South Gladstone, Qld, Australia 4680* Tel (0061) (7) 4979 0156

CALCOTT-JAMES, Colin Wilfrid. b 25. Bris Univ BSc48. S'wark Ord Course 77. **d** 80 **p** 81. NSM Barnes H Trin *S'wark* 80-85; C Hykeham *Linc* 85-88; R Barrowby 88-92; rtd 92; Perm to Offic *Lon* 93-94 and *S'wark* from 93. *23 Gwendolen Avenue, London SW15 6ET* Tel (020) 8788 6591

CALDER, David Ainsley. b 60. NE Lon Poly BSc86 Dur Univ BA93. St Jo Coll Dur DMS95. **d** 96 **p** 97. C Ireland Wood *Ripon* 96-00; V Woodhouse and Wrangthorn from 00; Chapl Leeds Metrop Univ from 02. *2 Halcyon Hill, Leeds LS7 3PU* Tel 0113-269 0448 Mobile 07947-535044 E-mail david.calder@lineone.net

CALDER, Canon Ian Fraser. b 47. York Univ BA68 CertEd69. Glouc Sch of Min 84. **d** 87 **p** 88. NSM Lydney w Aylburton *Glouc* 87-91; C Cirencester 91-95; V Coney Hill 95-01; RD Glouc City 99-01; R Bishop's Cleeve from 01; RD Tewkesbury and Winchcombe from 02; Hon Can Glouc Cathl from 03. *The Rectory, 4 Church Approach, Bishops Cleeve, Cheltenham GL52 8NG* Tel (01242) 675103 E-mail ian.calder@cableinet.co.uk

CALDER, Roger Paul. b 53. Hatf Coll Dur BA75 SSC. Chich Th Coll 76. **d** 79 **p** 80. C Addlestone *Guildf* 79-82; C Grangetown *Dur* 82-84; TV Brighton Resurr *Chich* 84-87; CF 87-92; P-in-c Cocking, Bepton and W Lavington *Chich* 92-95; P-in-c Bognor 95-98; V 98-05; P-in-c Portsea St Sav *Portsm* from 05; P-in-c Portsea St Alb from 05. *St Saviour's Vicarage, Twyford Avenue, Portsmouth PO2 8PB* Tel (023) 9266 3664 E-mail roger.p.calder@btinternet.com

CALDERHEAD, Christopher Conrad. b 62. Princeton Univ AB84. Seabury-Western Th Sem MDiv98. **d** 98 **p** 99. C Chesterton Gd Shep *Ely* 98-02; USA from 02. *30-75 Thirty-third Street Apt A4, Astoria, NY 11102, USA* Tel (001) (718) 278 3098 E-mail cccalderhead@yahoo.com

CALDICOTT, Anthony. b 31. ARCO52 FRCO62 ADCM66 St Jo Coll Dur BA53. Ripon Hall Ox 55. **d** 57 **p** 58. C Finham *Cov* 57-61; C Bedford St Andr *St Alb* 61-64; Chapl Lindisfarne Coll 64-67; C W Bromwich All SS *Lich* 67-69; Lic to Offic *Cov* 69-75; Hon C Twickenham St Mary *Lon* 75-89; Perm to Offic from 91; rtd 96. *38 Lyndhurst Avenue, Twickenham TW2 6BX* Tel (020) 8894 6859

CALDWELL, Alan. b 29. Oak Hill Th Coll 65. **d** 67 **p** 68. C Aldershot H Trin *Guildf* 67-69; C New Malden and Coombe *S'wark* 69-73; C Edgware St Andr CD *Lon* 73-78; P-in-c Pettaugh and Winston *St E* 78; R Helmingham w Framsden and Pettaugh w Winston 78-87; R Cowden w Hammerwood *Chich* 87-94; rtd 94; Perm to Offic *Ban* from 94. *Ael-y-Bryn, Druid Road, Menai Bridge LL59 5BY* Tel (01248) 713550 E-mail alancldwll@aol.com

CALDWELL, David Denzil. b 24. TD70. Bps' Coll Cheshunt 53. **d** 55 **p** 56. C Carnmoney *Conn* 55-59; CF (TA) 57-67; C Antrim All SS w Muckamore *Conn* 59-61; I Kilwaughter w Cairncastle 61-90; CF (TAVR) 67-70; CF (R of O) 70-80; rtd 90. *30 Shandon Park, Ballymena BT42 2ED* Tel (028) 2564 2650

CALDWELL, Ian Charles Reynolds. b 43. St Mich Coll Llan 68. **d** 70 **p** 71. C Oakham w Hambleton and Egleton *Pet* 70-74; C Swindon New Town *Bris* 74-78; P-in-c Honicknowle *Ex* 78-80; V 80-88; V Norton St Mich *Dur* 88-94; rtd 03. *Address withheld by request*

CALDWELL, Mrs Jill. b 47. Lon Univ BPharm69 MRPharmS70. S Dios Minl Tr Scheme 89. **d** 92 **p** 94. NSM Yiewsley *Lon* 92-97; NSM St Marylebone w H Trin 97-02; Chapl St Marylebone Girls' Sch Lon 97-98; Chapl R Academy of Music 97-98; Chapl Lon Sch of Pharmacy 97-98; Chapl Liv Cathl *Liv* 03-04; Perm to Offic *Derby* 04-05; NSM Darley Abbey from 05. *3 Brick Row, Darley Abbey, Derby DE22 1DQ* Tel (01332) 550676 E-mail jill-caldwell@talk21.com

CALDWELL, Canon John Donaldson. b 19. TCD BA41. **d** 42 **p** 43. C Belfast St Aid *Conn* 42-47; C Magheralin *D & D* 47-50; I Drumgath 50-55; I Kilmegan w Maghera 55-89; Can Dromore Cathl 85-89; rtd 89; Lic to Offic *D & D* from 90. *66 Castlewellan Road, Newcastle BT33 0JP* Tel (028) 4472 4874

CALDWELL, Roger Fripp. b 31. Cranmer Hall Dur. **d** 64 **p** 65. C Gosforth St Nic *Newc* 64-67; C Sugley 67-74; R Helmdon w Stuchbury and Radstone *Pet* 74-91; R Greatworth 74-91; rtd 91. *Quiet Waters, Station Road, Heyford, Oxford OX5 3PD*

CALE, Canon Clifford Roy Fenton. b 38. St Mich Coll Llan 65. **d** 67 **p** 68. C Griffithstown *Mon* 67-72; V Cwm 72-73; V Abersychan 73-79; V Abersychan and Garndiffaith 79-82; R Goetre w Llanover and Llanfair Kilgeddin 82-85; R Goetre w Llanover 85-01; RD Raglan-Usk 90-01; Can St Woolos Cathl 98-01; rtd 01. *Long Mynd, 3 Fayre Oak, Raglan, Usk NP15 2HA* Tel (01291) 690544

CALE, Nicholas. b 66. St Mich Coll Llan DipTh92. **d** 92 **p** 93. C Tenby *St D* 92-95; R Begelly w Ludchurch and Crunwere 95-01; V Wiston w Walton E and Clarbeston from 01. *The Vicarage, Wiston, Haverfordwest SA62 4PL* Tel (01437) 731266 E-mail cale@tinyonline.co.uk

CALITIS, Juris. Maryland Univ BA Latvia Univ DD. Harvard Div Sch STB. **d** 98 **p** 98. Chapl Riga, Latvia *Eur* from 98; Dean Faculty of Th Univ of Latvia from 99; Assoc Prof Bibl Studies from 99; Co-ord Bible Translation (Latvian Bible Soc) from 99. *Anglikanu iela 2A, Riga, LV1050, Latvia* Tel (00371) 721 1390 Fax as telephone E-mail calitis@latnet.lv

CALLADINE, Joanne Elizabeth. b 71. Liv Inst of Educn BA93. Cranmer Hall Dur 95. **d** 97 **p** 98. NSM Blurton *Lich* 97-98; C Stoke-upon-Trent 98-01; NSM Moston St Mary *Man* from 01. *St Mary's Rectory, 47 Nuthurst Road, Moston, Manchester M40 0EW* Tel 0161-681 1201 E-mail jo.calladine@lineone.net

CALLADINE, Matthew Robert Michael. b 65. St Jo Coll Dur BSc87 Reading Univ MSc89. Cranmer Hall Dur BA93 DMS93. **d** 96 **p** 97. C Blurton *Lich* 96-01; P-in-c Moston St Mary *Man* from 01. *St Mary's Rectory, 47 Nuthurst Road, Moston, Manchester M40 0EW* Tel 0161-681 1201 E-mail matthew.calladine@lineone.net

CALLAGHAN, Canon Harry. b 34. AKC59 Open Univ BA83. **d** 60 **p** 61. C Sheff St Cecilia Parson Cross *Sheff* 60-63; Br Guiana 63-66; Guyana 66-70; Barbados 70-74; Lic to Offic *Man* 74-84; Miss to Seamen 74-76; Area Sec USPG *Blackb, Man* and *S & M* 76-84; P-in-c Wythenshawe St Martin *Man* 84-85; V 85-91; V Bolton St Jo 91-98; Hon Can Massachusetts from 92; rtd 98; Perm to Offic *Man* from 98 and *Derby* from 99. *5 Manor Park View, Glossop SK13 7TL* Tel (01457) 868886 Mobile 07778-988523 E-mail hcallaghan@compuserve.com

CALLAGHAN, Martin Peter. b 57. Edin Th Coll 91. **d** 93 **p** 94. C Ayr *Glas* 93-96; C Girvan 93-96; C Maybole 93-96; P-in-c Gretna from 96; P-in-c Eastriggs from 96; P-in-c Annan from 97; P-in-c Lockerbie from 97; P-in-c Moffat from 97. *South Annandale Rectory, 28 Northfield Park, Annan DG12 5EZ* Tel (01461) 202924 E-mail martipcal@aol.com

CALLAGHAN, Michael James. b 63. Clare Coll Cam BA85. SEITE 94. **d** 97 **p** 98. NSM Blackheath Park St Mich *S'wark* from 97. *81 St Joseph's Vale, London SE3 0XG* Tel (020) 8318 7561 *or* 7919 0928 E-mail mikecall@netcomuk.co.uk

CALLAGHAN, Robert Paul. b 59. K Coll Lon BD81 Kent Univ MA04. Linc Th Coll 81. **d** 83 **p** 85. C Winchmore Hill St Paul *Lon* 83-85; C Paddington St Jo w St Mich 85-91; V Dartford St Edm *Roch* from 91. *The Vicarage, St Edmund's Road, Temple Hill, Dartford DA1 5ND* Tel (01322) 225335 E-mail bobcallaghan@tiscali.co.uk

CALLAN, Canon Terence Frederick. b 26. CITC 55. **d** 57 **p** 58. C Monaghan *Clogh* 57-58; I Clogh 58-64; C Derriaghy *Conn* 64-66; P-in-c Ballymacash 67-70; I Belfast St Aid 70-79; I Agherton 79-94; Can Conn Cathl from 86; Treas from 90; rtd 94. *18 Central Avenue, Portstewart BT93 0DN* Tel (028) 7083 2704

CALLAN, Ms Wendy Mary. b 52. Ox Brookes Univ BA93. St Alb and Ox Min Course 96. **d** 99 **p** 00. C Bicester w Bucknell, Caversfield and Launton *Ox* 99-03; V Shipton-under-Wychwood w Milton, Fifield etc from 03. *The Vicarage, Church Street, Shipton-under-Wychwood, Chipping Norton OX7 6BP* Tel and fax (01993) 830257 Mobile 07788-442946

CALLAN-TRAVIS, Anthony. b 46. N Ord Course 90. **d** 93 **p** 94. C Tong *Bradf* 93-97; C Harrogate St Wilfrid *Ripon* 97-03; TV Knaresborough from 03. *9 Castle Yard, Knaresborough HG5 8AS* Tel (01423) 869845

CALLARD, Canon David Kingsley. b 37. St Pet Coll Ox BA61 MA65. Westcott Ho Cam 61. **d** 63 **p** 64. C Leamington Priors H Trin *Cov* 63-66; C Wyken 66-68; C Bp's Hatfield *St Alb* 68-73; R Bilton *Cov* 73-83; TR Swanage and Studland *Sarum* 83-93; TR Oakdale 93-02; Can and Preb Sarum Cathl 95-02; rtd 02. *Woodlands, 29 Folkestone Road, Salisbury SP2 8JP* Tel (01722) 501200

CALLENDER, Francis Charles. b 48. TCD BA70 DipEd71 MA73. TCD Div Sch 76. **d** 79 **p** 80. C Bandon *C, C & R* 79-82; New Zealand 82-88 and from 90; USA 88-90. *41 Bellvue Avenue, Christchurch 8005, New Zealand* Tel (0064) (3) 352 9335 Fax as telephone

CALLER, Laurence Edward Harrison. b 19. Lon Univ BMus77 MA82. Lich Th Coll 39. **d** 42 **p** 43. C Ipswich St Matt *St E* 42-45; C Walsall St Pet *Lich* 45-46; C Hednesford 46-48; R Stafford St Mary 48-55; Subchanter Lich Cathl 55-57; V Shrewsbury St Alkmund 57-63; V Harlescott 63-67; rtd 84. *103 Fronks Road, Dovercourt, Harwich CO12 4EG* Tel (01255) 504501

CALLIS, Gillian Ruth. *See* TURNER-CALLIS, Mrs Gillian Ruth

CALLON, Andrew McMillan. b 56. Chich Th Coll 77. **d** 80 **p** 81. C Wigan All SS *Liv* 80-85; V Abram 85-90; V Bickershaw 89-90; Chapl RN from 90. *Royal Naval Chaplaincy Service, Room 203, Victory Building, HM Naval Base, Portsmouth PO1 3LS* Tel (023) 9272 7903 Fax 9272 7111

CALVELEY, Mrs Susan. b 47. Dioc OLM tr scheme. **d** 02 **p** 03. OLM Birkdale St Pet *Liv* from 02. *19 Nolan Street, Southport PR8 6QQ* Tel (01704) 546746 Fax 540969 E-mail calveley@btclick.com

CALVER, Mrs Gillian Margaret. b 47. Qu Eliz Coll Lon BSc68. Cant Sch of Min 89. **d** 92 **p** 94. NSM Folkestone H Trin w Ch Ch *Cant* 92-95; P-in-c Alkham w Capel le Ferne and Hougham 95-01; V 01-02; Chapl Dover Coll 95-99; R Staplehurst *Cant* from 02. *The New Rectory, High Street, Staplehurst, Tonbridge TN12 0BJ* Tel (01580) 891258 E-mail revgc@ukonline.co.uk

CALVER, Nicholas James. b 58. Nottm Univ BTh83 Dur Univ MA90. Cranmer Hall Dur 86. **d** 88 **p** 89. C Forest Hill Ch Ch *S'wark* 88-91; C Forest Hill 91-92; P-in-c Mottingham St Edw 92-95; V 95-97; Voc Adv Lewisham Adnry 94-97; V Redhill St Jo from 97. *St John's Vicarage, Church Road, Redhill RH1 6QA* Tel (01737) 766562

CALVERT, Geoffrey Richard. b 58. Edin Univ BSc79 PhD84 Leeds Univ BA86. Coll of Resurr Mirfield 84. **d** 87 **p** 88. C Curdworth w Castle Vale *Birm* 87-90; C Barnsley St Mary *Wakef* 90-92; TV Halifax 92-94; V Halifax H Trin 95-99; V Luton St Aug Limbury *St Alb* from 99. *The Vicarage, 215 Icknield Way, Luton LU3 2JR* Tel and fax (01582) 572415 E-mail geoff.calvert@dial.pipex.com

CALVERT, Canon Jean. b 34. Lightfoot Ho Dur IDC63. **dss** 78 **d** 87 **p** 94. S Bank *York* 78-84; Chapl Asst Rampton Hosp Retford 84-88; Dn-in-c Dunham w Darlton, Ragnall, Fledborough etc *S'well* 88-94; P-in-c 94-04; Hon Can S'well Minster 93-04; rtd 04. *The Rafters, Lincoln Road, Darlton, Newark NG22 0TF* Tel (01777) 228758

CALVERT, John Raymond. b 42. Lon Coll of Div 64. **d** 67 **p** 68. C Kennington St Mark *S'wark* 67-70; C Southborough St Pet *Roch* 70-72; C Barton Seagrave *Pet* 72-75; Asst Master Shaftesbury High Sch 78-79; Dioc Children's Officer *Glouc* 79-87; P-in-c S Cerney w Cerney Wick and Down Ampney 87-89; V from 89; P-in-c Siddington w Preston from 02. *The Vicarage, Silver Street, South Cerney, Cirencester GL7 5TP* Tel (01285) 860221

CALVERT, John Stephen. b 27. Lon Univ BSc53. Wycliffe Coll Toronto BTh61. **d** 61 **p** 62. Canada 61-63; C Preston St Jo *Blackb* 63-70; rtd 92; Perm to Offic *Blackb* from 92. *17 Leyster Street, Morecambe LA4 5NF* Tel (01524) 424491

CALVERT, Canon Peter Noel. b 41. Ch Coll Cam BA63 MA67. Cuddesdon Coll 64. **d** 66 **p** 67. C Brighouse *Wakef* 66-71; V Heptonstall 71-82; V Todmorden from 82; P-in-c Cross Stone 83-93; RD Calder Valley from 84; Hon Can Wakef Cathl from 92; Chapl to The Queen from 98. *Christ Church Vicarage, Burnley Road, Todmorden OL14 7BS* Tel (01706) 813180 E-mail calverts@todvicarage.freeserve.co.uk

CALVERT, Philip. b 62. St Steph Ho Ox 00. **d** 02 **p** 03. C Holbrooks *Cov* from 02. *The Rosary, 4 Cloverdale Close, Coventry CV6 4PZ* Tel (024) 7636 0397 Mobile 07866-878278 E-mail frphilipcarlvert@aol.com

CALVIN-THOMAS, David Nigel. b 43. Univ of Wales (Cardiff) BSc64 Lon Univ BD77. St Mich Coll Llan 77. **d** 78 **p** 79. C Pontypridd St Cath *Llan* 78-80; Malawi 81-84; V Rastrick St Matt *Wakef* 84-88; V Birchencliffe 88-93; Chapl Huddersfield R Infirmary 88-93; R Aberdeen St Pet *Ab* 93-01; P-in-c Cove Bay 93-01; TV Glenrothes *St And* from 01. *141 Napier Road, Glenrothes KY6 1AU* Tel (01592) 760210 Fax 07092-113255 E-mail davidct@blueyonder.co.uk

CALWAY, Geoffrey. b 45. Bris Sch of Min. **d** 87 **p** 88. NSM Cotham St Sav w St Mary *Bris* 87-94; NSM Horfield H Trin 94-97; P-in-c Publow w Pensford, Compton Dando and Chelwood *B & W* from 97. *The Rectory, Old Road, Pensford, Bristol BS39 4BB* Tel (01761) 490221

CAM, Julian Howard. b 48. York Univ BA69 Birm Univ DipTh74 Man Univ MA99. Qu Coll Birm 73. **d** 75 **p** 76. C St Ives *Truro* 75-80; C Lelant 78-80; V Flookburgh *Carl* 80-82; V St Stephen by Saltash *Truro* 82-83; V Low Marple *Ches* from 83. *St Martin's Vicarage, 15 Brabyns Brow, Marple Bridge, Stockport SK6 5DT* Tel 0161-427 2736 E-mail julian.cam@talk21.com

CAMBRIDGE, Benedict Howard. b 73. Westmr Coll Ox BTh95. Cranmer Hall Dur 99. **d** 01 **p** 02. C Chilwell *S'well* 01-05; Sen Chapl Staffs Univ *Lich* from 05. *The Rectory, 7 Cheadle Road, Blythe Bridge, Stoke-on-Trent ST11 9PW* Tel (01782) 388900

✠**CAMERON, The Most Revd Andrew Bruce.** b 41. Edin Th Coll 61. **d** 64 **p** 65 **c** 92. C Helensburgh *Glas* 64-67; C Edin H Cross *Edin* 67-71; Prov and Dioc Youth Chapl 69-75; Chapl St Mary's Cathl 71-75; R Dalmahoy 75-82; Chapl Heriot-Watt Univ 75-82; TV Livingston LEP 82-88; R Perth St Jo *St And* 88-92; Convener Prov Miss Bd 88-92; Bp Ab from 92; Primus from 00. *Diocesan Office, 39 King's Crescent, Aberdeen AB24 3HP* Tel (01224) 636653 *or* 208142 Fax 636186 *or* 312141 E-mail bishop@aberdeen.anglican.org

CAMERON, David Alan. b 59. Glas Univ MA81 DipEd82 PGCE82. Ripon Coll Cuddesdon 88. **d** 91 **p** 92. C Farncombe *Guildf* 91-93; C Guildf H Trin w St Mary 93-96; V Fenton *Lich* from 96. *The Vicarage, 65 Glebedale Road, Stoke-on-Trent ST4 3AQ* Tel (01782) 412417 Fax as telephone

CAMERON, David Alexander. b 42. MRTPI Reading Univ BA63 Leeds Art Coll Dip Town Planning 69. St And Dioc Tr Course 80. **d** 90 **p** 93. NSM Blairgowrie *St And* from 90; NSM Coupar Angus from 90; NSM Alyth from 90. *The Rectory, Smithy Loan, Dunblane FK15 0HQ* Tel (01786) 824225 *or* (01250) 874583 E-mail dacameron@talk21.com

CAMERON, Donald Eric Nelson. b 29. St Jo Coll Dur 68. **d** 70 **p** 71. C Kingston upon Hull H Trin *York* 70-73; V Eston 73-82; R Balerno *Edin* 82-87; rtd 94. *The Granary, Crauchie, East Linton EH40 3EB* Tel (01620) 860067

✠**CAMERON, The Rt Revd Douglas MacLean.** b 35. Univ of S Tennessee 61. Edin Th Coll 59. **d** 62 **p** 63 **c** 93. C Falkirk *Edin* 62-65; Papua New Guinea 66-74; Adn New Guinea Mainland 72-74; P-in-c Edin St Fillan *Edin* 74-78; R 78-88; R Edin St Hilda 77-88; R Dalkeith 88-92; R Lasswade 88-92; Can St Mary's Cathl 90-91; Syn Clerk 90-91; Dean Edin 91-92; Bp Arg 93-03; rtd 03. *23 Craigs Way, Rumford, Falkirk FK2 0EU* Tel (01324) 714137

CAMERON, Canon Gregory Kenneth. b 59. Linc Coll Ox BA80 MA84 Down Coll Cam BA82 MA85 Univ of Wales (Cardiff) MPhil92 LLM95. St Mich Coll Llan 82. **d** 83 **p** 84. C Newport St Paul *Mon* 83-86; Tutor St Mich Coll Llan 86-89; C Llanmartin *Mon* 86-87; TV 87-88; Chapl Wycliffe Coll Glos 88-94; Dir Bloxham Project 94-00; Research Fell Cardiff Univ Cen for Law and Relig 98-00; Chapl to Abp Wales 00-03; Dir Ecum Relns ACC 03-04; Dep Sec from 04; Hon Can St Woolos Cathl *Mon* from 03. *Anglican Communion Office, 16 Tavistock Crescent, London W11 1AP* Tel (020) 7313 3900 Fax 7313 3999 E-mail gregory@cofia.fsnet.co.uk

CAMERON, Mrs Janice Irene. b 43. Reading Univ BA. TISEC 93. **d** 96 **p** 96. C Blairgowrie *St And* 96-98; C Coupar Angus 96-98; C Alyth 96-98; R Dunblane from 99. *The Rectory, Smithy Loan, Dunblane FK15 0HQ* Tel (01786) 824225 E-mail rector@stmarysdunblane.org

CAMERON, Preb Margaret Mary. b 48. Qu Mary Coll Lon BA69 Ex Univ MA95. SW Minl Tr Course 87. **d** 90 **p** 94. NSM Budleigh Salterton *Ex* 90-95; C Whipton 95-97; R Hemyock w Culm Davy, Clayhidon and Culmstock 97-03; RD Cullompton 99-03; V Plympton St Mary from 03; Preb Ex Cathl from 05. *St Mary's Vicarage, 209 Ridgeway, Plymouth PL7 2HP* Tel (01752) 336157 *or* 348525 E-mail revd.cameron@tesco.net

CAMERON, Michael John. b 41. Sheff Tech Coll HNC63. Linc Th Coll 91. **d** 92 **p** 93. C Dinnington *Sheff* 92-96; V Beighton from 96; AD Attercliffe 99-02. *The Vicarage, 27 Tynker Avenue, Beighton, Sheffield S20 1DX* Tel 0114-248 7635 E-mail mikecam@fish.co.uk

CAMERON, Peter Scott. b 45. Edin Univ LLB67 BD76 Cam Univ PhD79 LRAM64. **d** 97 **p** 97. C Perth St Jo *St And* 97-98; R Dunkeld 98-04; R Strathtay 98-04; rtd 04. *Hope Cottage, Strathtay, Pithlochry PH9 0PG* Tel and fax (01887) 840212

CAMERON, Ms Sheila. b 34. TCert54. Gilmore Ho 65. **d** 98 **p** 99. NSM Catford St Laur *S'wark* 98-02; Perm to Offic from 02. *52 Engleheart Road, London SE6 2HW* Tel (020) 8698 9282 *or* 8698 9706

CAMERON, William Hugh Macpherson. b 59. Edin Univ LLB82 BD86. Edin Th Coll 83. **d** 86 **p** 87. C Cheadle Hulme All SS *Ches* 86-89; Asst Chapl and Hd RS Wellington Coll Berks 89-93; Chapl K Sch Bruton 93-00; Perm to Offic *Chich* from 01. *Cranesden, West Street, Mayfield TN20 6DS* Tel (01435) 872991

CAMERON, William James. b 35. Brasted Th Coll 60 St Aid Birkenhead 62. **d** 64 **p** 65. C Halewood *Liv* 64-66; C-in-c Halewood St Mary CD 66-68; Asst Chapl Leeds Univ *Ripon* 68-71; Ind Chapl *Liv* 71-77; Tr Officer Gen Syn Bd of Educn 77-84; V Hickling and Waxham w Sea Palling *Nor* 89-95; P-in-c Ludham w Potter Heigham 94-95; V Ludham, Potter Heigham and Hickling 95-00; RD Waxham 93-96; rtd 00; Perm to Offic *Nor* from 00. *Forge Bungalow, The Street, Lessingham, Norwich NR12 0DG* Tel (01692) 582790

CAMMELL, William John. b 36. Glouc Sch of Min 89. **d** 92 **p** 93. OLM Ruardean *Glouc* from 92. *The Beeches, High Beech Road, The Pludds, Ruardean GL17 9UD* Tel (01594) 860603

CAMP, Brian Arthur Leslie. b 50. St Jo Coll Nottm. **d** 83 **p** 84. C Blackheath *Birm* 83-86; TV Halesowen *Worc* 86-96; P-in-c Sheldon *Birm* 96-97; R from 97. *The Rectory, 165 Church Road, Sheldon, Birmingham B26 3TT* Tel 0121-743 2033

CAMP, Frederick Walter. b 19. Sarum Th Coll 47. **d** 49 **p** 50. C Brookfield St Mary *Lon* 49-54; CF 54-58; V Brigham *Carl* 58-80; V Whittingham *Newc* 80-84; V Whittingham and Edlingham w Bolton Chapel 84-85; rtd 85; Perm to Offic *Carl* from 85. *2 Ellen Court, Church Terrace, Ellenborough, Maryport CA15 7PR* Tel (01900) 817936

CAMP, John Edward. b 44. Jes Coll Ox MA68 Brunel Univ MTech69 Univ Coll Lon Dip Forensic Psychotherapy 98 Barrister 69. Ripon Coll Cuddesdon 86. **d** 88 **p** 89. NSM High Wycombe *Ox* 88-89; Chapl Three Shires Hosp Northn 89-98; Chapl St Andr Hosp Northn 89-98; Visiting Chapl 98-01; P-in-c Turvey *St Alb* 00-01. *4 Elwes Way, Great Billing, Northampton NN3 9EA* Tel (01604) 788831 Fax 413670 E-mail john@camp.uk.net

CAMP, Michael Maurice. b 52. Southn Univ BTh83 Brentwood Coll of Educn CertEd70 K Coll Lon MA99. Sarum & Wells Th Coll 78. **d** 81 **p** 82. C Loughton St Jo *Chelmsf* 81-84; C Chingford SS Pet and Paul 84-87; V Northfleet *Roch* 87-94; V Hadlow 94-01; RD Paddock Wood 99-01; V Bromley SS Pet and Paul from 01. *The Vicarage, 9 St Paul's Square, Bromley BR2 0XH* Tel and fax (020) 8460 6275 E-mail mmcamp@zetnet.co.uk

CAMPBELL, Allan. b 14. Selw Coll Cam BA36 MA40. Westcott Ho Cam 36. **d** 38 **p** 39. C Crosthwaite Keswick *Carl* 38-39; Chapl RNVR 39-46; R Bletchley *Ox* 46-63; RD Bletchley 56-63; R Amersham 63-86; Chapl Amersham Gen Hosp 63-86; rtd 86; Perm to Offic *Carl* 86-99. *The Clerk's Lodging, Deene Park, Deene, Corby NN17 3EW* Tel (01900) 826748

CAMPBELL, Mrs Brenda. b 47. St Jo Coll Nottm DipTh94. **d** 94 **p** 95. C Rothley *Leic* 94-97; C Market Bosworth, Cadeby w Sutton Cheney etc 97-00; TV Bosworth and Sheepy Gp from 00. *4 Springfield Avenue, Market Bosworth, Nuneaton CV13 0NS* Tel (01455) 292157 E-mail campbell@leicester.anglican.org

CAMPBELL, David. b 70. St Andr Univ MTheol92 New Coll Edin MTh94. Edin Th Coll 92. **d** 94 **p** 95. C Perth St Jo *St And* 94-96; P-in-c Newport-on-Tay 96-99; P-in-c Tayport 96-99; R Dunfermline from 99; Dioc Youth Officer from 96. *The Rectory, 17 Ardeer Place, Dunfermline KY11 4YX* Tel (01383) 723901 E-mail frdavid.campbell@btinternet.com

CAMPBELL, Miss Elizabeth Hume. b 53. Glas Univ MA74 Hamilton Coll of Educn TCert75. St Jo Coll Nottm 01. **d** 02 **p** 03. NSM Alstonfield, Butterton, Ilam etc *Lich* from 02. *The Vicarage, Alstonefield, Ashbourne DE6 2FX* Tel (01335) 310216 E-mail lizzie.campbell@virgin.net

CAMPBELL, Frederick David Gordon. b 15. Ex Coll Ox BA39. Wells Th Coll 39. **d** 40 **p** 41. C Portsea St Mary *Portsm* 40-45; Chapl RNVR 45-48; C Fareham SS Pet and Paul *Portsm* 48-49; Bp's Press Sec *Lon* 49-51; V Isleworth St Mary 51-54; SSJE from 57; Superior Gen SSJE 76-91; Lic to Offic *Lon* 69-97; Perm to Offic 99-02. *St John's Home, St Mary's Road, Oxford OX4 1QE*

CAMPBELL, George St Clair. b 32. Lon Univ BSc53. Clifton Th Coll 58. **d** 60 **p** 61. C Tunbridge Wells St Pet *Roch* 60-64; C Clitheroe St Jas *Blackb* 64-70; V Tibshelf *Derby* 70-86; V W Bromwich H Trin *Lich* 86-97; Chapl Heath Lane Hosp 87-97; rtd 97; Perm to Offic *Guildf* from 98. *2 Doreen Close, Farnborough GU14 9HB* Tel (01276) 31639

CAMPBELL, Mrs Hilary Anne. b 58. UMIST BSc80. St Alb and Ox Min Course. **d** 01 **p** 02. C Goring w S Stoke *Ox* from 01. *11 Westway, Goring, Reading RG8 0BX* Tel (01491) 873890 E-mail hilary@thecampbells.demon.co.uk

CAMPBELL, Ian George. b 47. FRICS74 FBEng93. SEITE 96. **d** 99 **p** 00. NSM Chilham w Challock and Molash *Cant* 99-01; P-in-c Crundale w Godmersham from 01. *The Forge, Godmersham Park, Godmersham, Canterbury CT4 7DT* Tel (01227) 730925 E-mail campbellkent@skynow.co.uk

CAMPBELL, James Duncan. b 55. Qu Eliz Coll Lon BSc77. St Jo Coll Dur 85 Oak Hill Th Coll MA00. **d** 87 **p** 88. C Hendon St Paul Mill Hill *Lon* 87-92; V Stevenage St Hugh and St Jo *St Alb* from 92. *St Hugh's House, 4 Mobbsbury Way, Chells, Stevenage SG2 0HL* Tel (01438) 354307 E-mail shsj@nildram.co.uk

CAMPBELL, James Larry. b 46. Indiana Univ BSc69 E Kentucky Univ MA73 Hull Univ MA91. Linc Th Coll 86. **d** 88 **p** 89. C N Hull St Mich *York* 88-92; C Hessle 92-95; V Burton Pidsea and Humbleton w Elsternwick from 95. *The New Vicarage, Back Lane, Burton Pidsea, Hull HU12 9AN* Tel (01964) 671074 E-mail campbell822@aol.com

CAMPBELL, James Malcolm. b 55. MRICS81 R Agric Coll Cirencester DipREM77. Wycliffe Hall Ox 89. **d** 91 **p** 92. C Scole, Brockdish, Billingford, Thorpe Abbots etc *Nor* 91-95; R Bentley and Binsted *Win* from 95; RD Alton from 02. *Holy Cross Vicarage, Church Street, Binsted, Alton GU34 4NX* Tel (01420) 22174 E-mail campbells@fish.co.uk

CAMPBELL, James Norman Thompson. b 49. BTh MA. **d** 86 **p** 87. C Arm St Mark w Aghavilly *Arm* 86-89; I Belfast H Trin and Ardoyne *Conn* 89-95; I Dundela St Mark *D & D* 95-01; I Portadown St Mark *Arm* from 01. *The Rectory, Brownstown Road, Portadown, Craigavon BT62 3QA* Tel (028) 3833 2368 E-mail jim.campbell1@btinternet.com

CAMPBELL, Jane Judith. *See* BAKKER, Mrs Jane Judith

CAMPBELL, Kenneth Scott. b 47. BA82. Oak Hill Th Coll. **d** 82 **p** 83. C Aughton St Mich *Liv* 82-85; V Brough w Stainmore *Carl* 85-90; R Brough w Stainmore, Musgrave and Warcop 90-92; rtd 92. *4 Quarry Close, Kirkby Stephen CA17 4SS* Tel (01768) 372390

CAMPBELL, Lawrence Henry. b 41. TCD BA63 MA66. **d** 63 **p** 65. C Larne and Inver *Conn* 63-66; C Finaghy 66-67; Chapl RN 67-83; R Brancaster w Burnham Deepdale and Titchwell *Nor* 83-95; P-in-c Hunstanton St Mary w Ringstead Parva, Holme etc 94-95; R Hunstanton St Mary w Ringstead Parva etc from 95; RD Heacham and Rising from 01. *St Mary's Rectory, Church Road, Hunstanton PE36 6JS* Tel (01485) 532169 Fax 534719

CAMPBELL, Mrs Margaret Ruth. b 62. Trin Coll Bris BA02. **d** 02 **p** 03. C Yeovil w Kingston Pitney *B & W* from 02. *67 Preston Grove, Yeovil BA20 2BJ* Tel (01935) 425452

CAMPBELL, Patrick Alistair. b 36. Qu Coll Birm 64. **d** 67 **p** 68. C Paston *Pet* 67-71; C Stockton Heath *Ches* 71-73; V Egremont St Jo 73-78; V Bredbury St Mark 78-85; R Astbury and Smallwood 85-91; V Wybunbury w Doddington 91-97; rtd 97; Perm to Offic *Ches* from 97; Warden Coll of St Barn Lingfield from 01. *The Lodge, College of St Barnabas, Blackberry Lane, Lingfield RH7 6NJ* Tel (01342) 870260 Fax 870193

CAMPBELL, Robin William. b 41. TCD BA63 MA67. Ridley Hall Cam 63. **d** 65 **p** 66. C Netherton *Liv* 65-68; C Liv Our Lady and St Nic w St Anne 68-70; V Hooton *Ches* 70-99; rtd 99. *77 Seaview Parade, Lakes Entrance, Vic, Australia 3909* Tel (0061) (3) 5155 2157

CAMPBELL, Roger Stewart. b 40. Birm Univ BSc61 PhD65 St Jo Coll Dur BA71. Cranmer Hall Dur 68. **d** 71 **p** 72. C Jesmond Clayton Memorial *Newc* 71-77; V Singapore St Jo and St Marg 78-85; C Nottingham St Nic *S'well* 86-90; V Holloway St Mark w Em *Lon* 90-92; TR Tollington 92-97; Chapl Leeds Teaching Hosps NHS Trust 97-04; rtd 04; Perm to Offic *Carl* from 05. *Redesdale Cottage, Lazonby, Penrith CA10 1AJ* Tel (01768) 870695

CAMPBELL, Stephen James. b 60. TCD BTh91. CITC. **d** 91 **p** 92. C Lisburn Ch Ch *Conn* 91-95; I Kilcronaghan w Draperstown and Sixtowns *D & R* 95-00; I Dunluce *Conn* 00-03. *94A Mountsandel Road, Coleraine BT52 1TA*

CAMPBELL, Stephen Lloyd. b 46. St Andr Univ LLB67 Solicitor 72. SEITE 95. **d** 98 **p** 99. NSM Quantoxhead *B & W* from 98. *Hodderscombe Lodge, Holford, Bridgwater TA5 1SA* Tel and fax (01278) 741329 Mobile 07808-967046 E-mail stephencampbell0@tinyonline.co.uk

CAMPBELL, William George. b 31. Toronto Univ BA54 MA57 BD71. Wycliffe Coll Toronto MTh57. **d** 57 **p** 58. Canada 57-96, 01-03 and from 04; C Hamilton St Geo 57-59; R Fergus 59-64; R Hamilton St Pet 64-73; R Prince Albert 73-81; R Drumheller 81-87; R Vermilion 87-96; Bp's C Sallaghy *Clogh* 97-01; P-in-c Toronto St Dav 01-03; C Enniskillen 03-04. *Address temp unknown* E-mail bjcamp@ca.inter.net

CAMPBELL-SMITH, Robert Campbell. b 38. CCC Cam BA61 MA66 Ibadan Univ Nigeria 62. Linc Th Coll 61. **d** 63 **p** 64. C Norbury St Steph *Cant* 63-66; C W Wickham St Mary 66-71; Ind Chapl 65-76; V Croydon St Aug 71-81; Acting RD Croydon Cen 77-81; Spiritual Development Adv Nat Assn of Boys' Clubs 77-89; V Goudhurst *Cant* 81-87; Chapl Kent Assn of Boys' Clubs 81-97; RD W Charing *Cant* 82-89; P-in-c Kilndown 83-87; V Goudhurst w Kilndown 87-99; Hon Can Cant Cathl 94-99; Chapl Kent Youth Trust 97-99; TR Modbury, Bigbury, Ringmore w Kingston etc *Ex* 99-04; rtd 04. *Even Keel, Pillory Hill, Noss Mayo, Plymouth PL8 1ED* Tel (01752) 872559

CAMPBELL-TAYLOR, William Goodacre. b 65. Ox Univ BA87 Cam Univ BA93. Westcott Ho Cam 90. **d** 94 **p** 95. C Chingford SS Pet and Paul *Chelmsf* 94-97; Chapl Lon Guildhall Univ *Lon* 97-02; Chapl Lon Metrop Univ 02-04. *Address temp unknown*

CAMPBELL-WILSON, Allan. b 43. Dur Univ BEd74. NEOC 79. **d** 82 **p** 83. NSM Boosbeck w Moorsholm *York* 82-85; R Easington w Skeffling, Kilnsea and Holmpton 85-87; P-in-c Middlesbrough St Jo the Ev 89-95; V 95-99; V Cayton w Eastfield from 99. *90 Main Street, Cayton, Scarborough YO11 3RP* Tel (01723) 586569 E-mail frallancayton@aol.com

CAMPEN, William Geoffrey. b 50. Liv Univ CertEd71 Southn Univ BTh81. Sarum & Wells Th Coll 76. **d** 79 **p** 80. C Peckham St Jo w St Andr *S'wark* 79-83; P-in-c Mottingham St Edw 83-92; R Charlwood from 92; R Sidlow Bridge from 92. *The Rectory, The Street, Charlwood, Horley RH6 0EE* Tel (01293) 862343

CAMPION, Keith Donald. b 52. S Dios Minl Tr Scheme. **d** 84 **p** 87. NSM Is of Scilly *Truro* 84-96. *20 Launceston Close, St Mary's TR21 0LN* Tel (01720) 422606

CAMPION (formerly HOUSEMAN), Mrs Patricia Adele. b 39. St D Coll Lamp DipTh90 St Mich Coll Llan Dip Practical Th 93. **d** 93 **p** 97. C St Issell's and Amroth *St D* 93-95; C Llanegryn w Aberdyfi w Tywyn *Ban* 95-97; rtd 97. *3 Mariners Reach, The Strand, Saundersfoot SA69 9EX* Tel (01834) 811047

CAMPION, Peter Robert. b 64. Bp's Univ Canada BA87 TCD BTh90 MA93 MPhil97 Homerton Coll Cam PGCE94. **d** 90 **p** 91. C Belfast H Trin and Ardoyne *Conn* 90-93; C Taney *D & G* 94-00; Dean's V St Patr Cathl Dublin 96-00; Chapl Netherwood Sch Rothesday Canada 00-05; Chapl K Hosp Sch Dub from 05; Treas V St Patr Cathl Dublin from 05. *Address temp unknown*

CAMPLING, Miss Camilla Anne. b 76. St Andr Univ MA98 Jes Coll Cam MPhil04. Westcott Ho Cam 02. **d** 05. C Fountains Gp *Ripon* from 05. *1 Hazel Close, Grewelthorpe, Ripon HG4 3BL* Tel (01765) 658160 Mobile 07779-429351

CAMPLING, The Very Revd Christopher Russell. b 25. St Edm Hall Ox BA50 MA54. Cuddesdon Coll 50. **d** 51 **p** 52. C Basingstoke *Win* 51-55; Min Can Ely Cathl *Ely* 55-60; Chapl K Sch Ely 55-60; Chapl Lancing Coll 60-68; P-in-c Birlingham w Nafford *Worc* 68-75; V Pershore w Wick 68-75; RD Pershore 70-76; Hon Can Worc Cathl 74-84; V Pershore w Pinvin, Wick and Birlingham 75-76; Dioc Dir of Educn 76-84; Adn Dudley 76-84; P-in-c Dodderhill 76-84; Dean Ripon 84-95; Chmn CCC 88-94; rtd 95; Perm to Offic *Chich* from 95. *Pebble Ridge, Aglaia Road, Worthing BN11 5SW* Tel (01903) 246598

CAMPLING, Doreen Elizabeth. b 31. K Coll Lon BSc55. Dioc OLM tr scheme. **d** 01 **p** 02. OLM Bridport *Sarum* from 01. *Harbour Lights, Coneygar Park, Bridport DT6 3BA* Tel (01308) 425670

CAMPLING, Michael. b 27. Trin Coll Cam BA50 MA61. Wells Th Coll 51. **d** 53 **p** 54. C Calne *Sarum* 53-57; C Roehampton H Trin *S'wark* 57-61; V Crowthorne *Ox* 61-75; P-in-c Foleshill St Laur *Cov* 75-81; V 81-83; R Old Alresford and Bighton *Win* 83-92; rtd 92; Chapl St Marg Convent E Grinstead 92-99; Hon C Bexhill St Pet *Chich* 99-05. *9 Orchard Grove, Bloxham, Banbury OX15 4NZ* Tel (01295) 721599

CANADA, Primate of. *See* HUTCHISON, The Most Revd Andrew Sandford

CANDELAND, Thomas Blyde. b 37. **d** 99 **p** 00. OLM Lyng, Sparham, Elsing, Bylaugh, Bawdeswell etc *Nor* from 99. *2 Hammond Place, Lyng, Norwich NR9 5RQ* Tel (01603) 871674

CANDLER, David Cecil. b 24. Cape Town Univ BSc47 Keble Coll Ox BA50 MA55. St Paul's Coll Grahamstown 56. **d** 56 **p** 57. S Rhodesia 57-65; Rhodesia 65-80; Zimbabwe 80-85; R Barningham w Matlaske w Baconsthorpe etc *Nor* 85-94; rtd 94; Perm to Offic *Nor* from 94. *Millstone, Mill Lane, Aldborough, Norwich NR11 7NS* Tel (01263) 768608

CANDOW, Brian Gordon. b 58. Memorial Univ Newfoundland BComm82 BEd83. Qu Th Coll Newfoundland MDiv89. **d** 89 **p** 89. C Fogo Is Canada 89-91; R Botwood 91-95; R Summerside and St Eleanor 00-04; Hon C Skirbeck Quarter *Linc* 04-05; Assoc P Gander Canada from 05. *2 Lindberg Road, Gander NL, Canada, A1V 2E7* Tel (001) (709) 256 3700
E-mail candows@bostonengland.freeserve.co.uk

CANE, Anthony William Nicholas Strephon. b 61. Cape Town Univ BA81 Birm Univ MPhil93 PhD03. Westcott Ho Cam 87. **d** 90 **p** 91. C Kings Heath *Birm* 90-93; Chapl Brighton Univ *Chich* 93-99; P-in-c Torquay St Luke *Ex* 99-01; Dioc Adv in Adult Tr 99-01; Dioc Adv for Educn and Tr of Adults *Chich* from 01; C Ringmer from 01. *Cley House, Lewes Road, Ringmer, Lewes BN8 5QF* Tel (01273) 812967 *or* 421021
E-mail anthony_cane@lineone.net
or anthony.cane@diochi.org.uk

CANEY, Canon Robert Swinbank. b 37. St Jo Coll Cam 57. Lich Th Coll 58. **d** 61 **p** 62. C Kingswinford H Trin *Lich* 61-64; C Castle Church 64-67; V Bradwell *Derby* 67-73; V Fairfield 73-84; RD Buxton 78-84; P-in-c Peak Forest and Wormhill 79-83; R Wirksworth w Alderwasley, Carsington etc 84-92; TR Wirksworth 92-02; Hon Can Derby Cathl 93-02; rtd 02; Perm to Offic *Derby* from 02. *2 Erica Drive, South Normanton, Alfreton DE55 2ET* Tel (01773) 581106

CANHAM, Francis. *See* CANHAM, Robert Edwin Francis

CANHAM, John Graham. b 33. Univ of Wales (Lamp) BA55. Chich Th Coll 55. **d** 57 **p** 58. C Hawarden *St As* 57-64; Asst Chapl Ellesmere Coll 64-66; Chapl Ches Cathl Choir Sch 66-73; Chapl Choral Ches Cathl *Ches* 66-73; Asst Chapl Rossall Sch Fleetwood 73-76 and 83-93; Chapl 76-83; V Minera *St As* 93-05; V Bwlchgwyn and Minera from 05; RD Minera from 01. *The Vicarage, Church Road, Minera, Wrexham LL11 3DA* Tel (01978) 753133

CANHAM, Robert Edwin Francis. b 24. FRCO59 ARCM. **d** 74 **p** 75. NSM Newlyn St Pet *Truro* 74-75; C Phillack w Gwithian 75-79; P-in-c Phillack w Gwithian and Gwinear 79-83; V Greenham *Ox* 83-93; rtd 93; Perm to Offic *Chich* from 93. *Cross Way, 1A Torton Hill Road, Arundel BN18 9HF* Tel (01903) 883614

CANHAM, William Alexander. b 26. Clare Coll Cam BA47 MA56. Roch Th Coll 65. **d** 67 **p** 68. C Orpington St Andr *Roch* 67-70; C Guernsey St Steph *Win* 70-75; Chapl Eliz Coll Guernsey 72-75; R Tadley St Pet *Win* 75-83; V Bournemouth St Luke 83-91; R Guernsey St Marguerite de la Foret 91-96; rtd 96; Perm to Offic *Win* from 96; Perm to Offic *Portsm* from 96. *56 The Causeway, Petersfield GU31 4JS* Tel (01730) 269413

CANN, Christopher James. b 64. St Andr Univ BA MA. St Steph Ho Ox. **d** 91 **p** 92. C Newport St Julian *Mon* 91-93; Chapl Smallwood Manor Sch Uttoxeter from 93; Hd Master from 97. *Smallwood Manor Preparatory School, Uttoxeter ST3 3BS* Tel (01889) 563666

CANNAM, Martin Stafford John. b 68. Jes Coll Ox BA90 MA95. Wycliffe Hall Ox 93. **d** 96 **p** 97. C Childwall All SS *Liv* 96-00; V Biddulph *Lich* from 00. *The Vicarage, 7 Wrexham Close, Biddulph, Stoke-on-Trent ST8 6RZ* Tel (01782) 513247 *or* 513891 E-mail martin@cannam.fsnet.co.uk

CANNELL, Anthea Marjorie. b 45. UEA MA85. EAMTC 01. **d** 02 **p** 03. NSM Theydon Bois *Chelmsf* from 02. *118 High Street, Roydon, Harlow CM19 5EF* Tel (01279) 792543
E-mail acannell@fish.co.uk

CANNER, Canon Peter George. b 24. St Chad's Coll Dur BA49 MA55. **d** 51 **p** 52. C Stoke *Cov* 51-53; S Africa 53-63; R Piet Retief 53-56; R Eshowe 56-63; Can Eshowe 62-63; V Tynemouth Ch Ch *Newc* 63-77; V Ponteland 77-89; Hon Can Newc Cathl 80-89; rtd 89; Perm to Offic *Newc* from 89. *The Rigg, 4 Back Crofts, Rothbury, Morpeth NE65 7YB* Tel (01669) 621319

CANNING, Arthur Brian. b 12. St Jo Coll Dur BA37 MA40. **d** 37 **p** 38. C Darlington St Cuth *Dur* 37-42; V Sellack and King's Caple *Heref* 42-50; V Lugwardine w Bartestree 50-66; Bp's Dom Chapl 54-65; V New Romney w Hope and St Mary's Bay etc *Cant* 66-71; V Boughton Monchelsea 71-79; rtd 79; Perm to Offic *Heref* 81-96. *Harp Cottage, Old Radnor, Presteigne LD8 2RH* Tel (01544) 350312

CANNING, Canon Arthur James. b 45. St Jo Coll Dur BA66 Linacre Coll Ox BA70 MA74 Lambeth STh90. Ripon Hall Ox 67. **d** 71 **p** 72. C Coleshill *Birm* 71-74; C Frome St Jo *B & W* 75-76; V Frizington and Arlecdon *Carl* 76-80; P-in-c Foleshill St Paul *Cov* 80-81; V from 81; Hon Can Cov Cathl from 00. *St Paul's Vicarage, 13 St Paul's Road, Coventry CV6 5DE* Tel (024) 7668 8283 E-mail jimcanningstpcov@aol.com

CANNING, Graham Gordon Blakeman. b 33. S'wark Ord Course 73. **d** 76 **p** 77. NSM Mill Hill Jo Keble Ch *Lon* 76-78; TV Dorchester *Ox* 78-85; V Shipton-under-Wychwood w Milton, Fifield etc 85-98; RD Chipping Norton 95-00; rtd 98; Perm to Offic *Ox* from 00. *Moredays, 36 The Slade, Oxford OX7 3SJ* Tel and fax (01608) 810421 E-mail gcanning@gcanning.u-net.com

CANNING, John Graham. b 21. Edin Th Coll 47. **d** 49 **p** 50. C Penton Street St Silas w All SS *Lon* 49-54; C Poplar 54-55; N Rhodesia 55-62; V Hammersmith St Jo *Lon* 62-90; rtd 90; Perm to Offic *B & W* from 90. *11 Circus Field Road, Glastonbury BA6 9PE* Tel (01458) 833708

CANNING, Peter Christopher. b 52. Birm Poly CQSW. St Jo Coll Nottm 87. **d** 89 **p** 90. C Cov St Mary *Cov* 89-93; V Hartshill 93-96; rtd 96. *11 Thackeray Close, Galley Common, Nuneaton CV10 9RT* Tel (024) 7639 8828

CANNON, Elizabeth Mary. b 50. EAMTC 94. **d** 97 **p** 98. NSM New Catton Ch Ch *Nor* 97-00; P-in-c Cross Roads cum Lees *Bradf* from 00. *St James's Vicarage, Haworth Road, Cross Roads, Keighley BD22 9DL* Tel (01535) 642210
E-mail rev-liz@fish.co.uk

CANNON, Mark Harrison. b 60. Keble Coll Ox BA82. Cranmer Hall Dur 83. **d** 85 **p** 86. C Skipton Ch Ch *Bradf* 85-88; Dioc Youth Officer 88-92; C Baildon 88-92; P-in-c Church Coniston *Carl* 92-00; P-in-c Torver 92-00; P-in-c Brindle *Blackb* from 00; Dioc Voc Adv from 00. *The Rectory, Sandy Lane, Brindle, Chorley PR6 8NJ* Tel (01254) 854130
E-mail mhcannon@fsmail.net

CANNON, Tony Arthur. b 57. Oak Hill Th Coll 94. **d** 96 **p** 97. C Church Stretton *Heref* 96-00; P-in-c Kingham w Churchill, Daylesford and Sarsden *Ox* 00-01; TV Chipping Norton from 01. *6 The Grange, Kingham, Chipping Norton OX7 6XY* Tel (01608) 658164 Fax 08700-940150
E-mail tonycannon@tiscali.co.uk

CANSDALE, George Graham. b 38. Mert Coll Ox BA60 MA64 DipEd61. Clifton Th Coll 62. **d** 64 **p** 65. C Heatherlands St Jo *Sarum* 64-67; BCMS Kenya 68-76; P-in-c Clapham *St Alb* 76-80; V 80-89; Asst Chapl Bedford Sch 89-97; Lic to Offic *St Alb* 93-01; Perm to Offic *Wakef* from 01; rtd 03. *7 Stubbins Close, Mytholmroyd, Hebden Bridge HX7 5HP* Tel (01422) 881693
E-mail graham.cansdale@virgin.net

CANSDALE, Philip John. b 73. Keble Coll Ox BA95 MA99. Trin Coll Bris BA98 MA99. **d** 99 **p** 00. C Cant St Mary Bredin *Cant* 99-03; C Penn Fields *Lich* from 03. *100 Bellencroft Gardens, Merry Hill, Wolverhampton WV3 8DU* Tel (01902) 763603
E-mail curate@smb.org.uk

CANSDALE, Simon James Lee. b 68. Keble Coll Ox BA90. Wycliffe Hall Ox 93. **d** 95 **p** 96. C Bletchley *Ox* 95-98; C Cambridge H Trin *Ely* 98-01; R W Bridgford *S'well* from 01. *The Rectory, 86 Bridgford Road, West Bridgford, Nottingham NG2 6AX* Tel 0115-981 1112 E-mail rector@stgiles.org.uk

CANT, Anthony David. b 59. Middx Univ BA04. NTMTC 01. **d** 04 **p** 05. C Walthamstow *Chelmsf* from 04. *10 Church End, London E17 9RJ* Tel (020) 8509 8792 Mobile 07980-291940

CANT, Christopher Somerset Travers. b 51. Keble Coll Ox BA72 MA76 Ex Univ PGCE77. All Nations Chr Coll 80 Wycliffe Hall Ox 93. **d** 87 **p** 90. Pakistan 87-92; Lic to Offic *Cov* 92-93; Warden St Clem Family Cen Ox 93-95; C Gt Ilford St Andr *Chelmsf* 95-98; V Hainault from 98. *St Paul's Vicarage, 143 Arrowsmith Road, Chigwell IG7 4NZ* Tel (020) 8500 3366
E-mail chriscant@tiscali.co.uk

CANT, David Edward. b 49. Sheff Univ LLB70. Oak Hill Th Coll DipTh89. **d** 89 **p** 90. C Newburn *Newc* 89-92; C N Shields 92-93; TV 93-98; Chapl Tynemouth Coll 94-98; P-in-c Wylam *Newc* from 98. *The Vicarage, Church Road, Wylam NE41 8AT* Tel (01661) 853254 E-mail david@stoswin.totalserve.co.uk

CANTERBURY, Archbishop of. *See* WILLIAMS, The Most Revd and Rt Hon Rowan Douglas

CANTERBURY, Archdeacon of. *See* EVANS, The Ven Patrick Alexander Sidney

CANTERBURY, Dean of. *See* WILLIS, The Very Revd Robert Andrew

CANTI, Mrs Christine. b 24. St Alb Minl Tr Scheme 82. **dss** 85 **d** 87 **p** 94. Radlett *St Alb* 85-86; Hon C Pitminster w Corfe *B & W* 87-90; Perm to Offic from 90. *Brook Farm House, Corfe, Taunton TA3 7BU* Tel (01823) 421623

CANTRELL, David Grindon. b 59. Bris Univ BSc80 Nottm Univ PhD83 Pemb Coll Cam BA88. Ridley Hall Cam 86. **d** 89 **p** 90. C Low Harrogate St Mary *Ripon* 89-90; C Horsforth 90-94; Chapl Nottm Trent Univ *S'well* 94-97; V Porchester 97-00; Chapl York Univ *York* 00-04; Perm to Offic from 04. *Bede House, Heslington Lane, Heslington, York YO10 5ED* Tel (01904) 413925
E-mail david.cantrell@ukgateway.net

CANTRILL, Mark James. b 67. Lanc Univ BEd89. St Jo Coll Nottm 00. **d** 02 **p** 03. C Warsop *S'well* from 02. *Heather Villas, 23 Main Street, Blidworth, Mansfield NG21 0PX* Tel (01623) 460978 Mobile 07759-305766
E-mail revmark.cantrill@ntlworld.com

CAPE TOWN, Dean of. *See* SMITH, The Very Revd Rowan Quentin

CAPE TOWN, Archbishop of. *See* NDUNGANE, The Most Revd Winston Hugh Njongonkulu

CAPEL, Luke Thomas. *See* IRVINE-CAPEL, Luke Thomas

CAPEL-EDWARDS, Maureen. b 36. Southn Univ BSc60 Reading Univ PhD69. St Alb Minl Tr Scheme 84. **d** 87 **p** 94. NSM Ware St Mary *St Alb* 87-90; Chapl Hertf Regional Coll of FE 87-00; NSM Hertford All SS *St Alb* 90-94; NSM Aspenden and Layston w Buntingford 94-95; NSM Aspenden, Buntingford and Westmill 95-00; P-in-c Ardeley and Cottered w Broadfield and Throcking 00-05; rtd 05. *Capeland, High Street, Soberton, Southampton SO32 3PN* Tel (01489) 878192 E-mail capeland@waitrose.com

CAPELIN-JONES, Kevin Stuart. b 73. Huddersfield Univ BMus96. Oak Hill Th Coll BA02. **d** 02 **p** 03. C Croglin *Carl* from 02; C Holme Eden and Wetheral w Warwick from 02. *The Rectory, Plains Road, Wetheral, Carlisle CA4 8LA* Tel (01228) 560216 E-mail wetheral.rectory@virgin.net

CAPERON, John Philip. b 44. Bris Univ BA66 Open Univ MPhil80 Ox Univ MSc83 Kent Univ MA99. Ox NSM Course 80. **d** 83 **p** 84. NSM Hook Norton w Gt Rollright, Swerford etc *Ox* 83-86; NSM Knaresborough *Ripon* 86-92; Dep Hd St Aid Sch Harrogate 86-92; Hd and Chapl Bennett Memorial Dioc Sch Tunbridge Wells 92-04; rtd 04; Perm to Offic *Chich* 98-03; Hon C Mayfield from 03. *Sarum, 5 Twyfords, Beacon Road, Crowborough TN6 1YE* Tel (01892) 667207 E-mail jcaperon@fish.co.uk

CAPES, Arthur Geoffrey. b 33. Bps' Coll Cheshunt 58. **d** 61 **p** 62. C Seacroft *Ripon* 61-66; Guyana 66-80; V Claremont H Angels *Man* 80-85; V Blyton w Pilham *Linc* 85-90; V E Stockwith 86-90; V Laughton w Wildsworth 86-90; R Broad Town, Clyffe Pypard and Tockenham *Sarum* 90-94; R Broad Town, Clyffe Pypard, Hilmarton etc 94-99; rtd 99. *45 Leigh Road, Westbury BA13 3QW* Tel (01373) 859163

CAPES, Dennis Robert. b 34. Linc Th Coll 65 Handsworth Coll Birm DipTh58. **d** 64 **p** 65. In Methodist Ch (Sarawak) 59-63; C Lt Coates *Linc* 64-66; Malaysia 66-69; V Gosberton Clough *Linc* 69-71; V Kirton in Holland 71-80; Area Sec USPG *Cov, Heref* and *Worc* 80-87; Chapl Copenhagen w Aarhus *Eur* 87-93; TV Liv Our Lady and St Nic w St Anne *Liv* 93-99; rtd 99. *35 Hardwick Avenue, Newark NG24 4AW* Tel (01636) 672874

CAPIE, Fergus Bernard. b 47. Auckland Univ BA68 MA71. Wycliffe Hall Ox BA77. **d** 77 **p** 78. C Ox St Mich w St Martin and All SS *Ox* 77-80; Chapl Summer Fields Sch Ox 80-91; Hon C Wolvercote w Summertown *Ox* 87-91; Perm to Offic *St E* 91; TV E Ham w Upton Park St Alb *Chelmsf* 91-95; P-in-c Brondesbury St Anne w Kilburn H Trin *Lon* 95-01; V from 01; Chapl NW Lon Coll from 95. *125 Salusbury Road, London NW6 6RG* Tel (020) 7625 7470, 7372 6864 *or* 7604 3053 Fax 7604 3052 E-mail fergus.capie@london.anglican.org

CAPITANCHIK, Sophie Rebecca. *See* JELLEY, Mrs Sophie Rebecca

CAPLE, Stephen Malcolm. b 55. Chich Th Coll 86. **d** 88 **p** 89. C Newington St Mary *S'wark* 88-92; V Eltham St Sav 92-97; V Salfords from 97. *The Vicarage, Honeycrock Lane, Redhill RH1 5DF* Tel (01737) 762232 E-mail stephen@caple.fsnet.co.uk

CAPON, Canon Anthony Charles. b 26. Trin Coll Cam BA51 MA55. Wycliffe Coll Toronto BD65 DD82 Oak Hill Th Coll 51. **d** 53 **p** 54. C Portman Square St Paul *Lon* 53-56; Canada from 56; Hon Can Montreal from 78; Prin Montreal Dioc Th Coll 78-91; rtd 91. *5 Loradean Crescent, Kingston ON, Canada, K7K 6X9* Tel (001) (613) 545 9781 E-mail acapon@cgocable.net

CAPON, Gerwyn Huw. b 65. Liv Jo Moores Univ BSc92. St Steph Ho Ox 01. **d** 03. C W Derby St Mary *Liv* from 03. *St Paul's Vicarage, Carlton Lane, Stoneycroft, Liverpool L13 6QS* Tel 0151-228 0307 E-mail gerwyn@hermes7.fsnet.co.uk

CAPPER, Mrs Elizabeth Margaret. b 31. St Chris Coll Blackheath 52. **dss** 79 **d** 87 **p** 94. The Dorothy Kerin Trust Burrswood 79; Whitstable *Cant* 80-96; Hon Par Dn 87-94; Hon C 94-96; rtd 91. *11 North Road, Loughor, Swansea SA4 6QE* Tel (01792) 892834

CAPPER, Canon Richard. b 49. Leeds Univ BSc70 Fitzw Coll Cam BA72 MA79. Westcott Ho Cam 70. **d** 73 **p** 74. C Wavertree H Trin *Liv* 73-76; P-in-c Ince St Mary 76-79; V 79-83; V Gt Crosby St Faith 83-97; AD Bootle 89-97; Can Res Wakef Cathl *Wakef* 97-05; Can Res Nor Cathl *Nor* from 05; P-in-c Nor St Mary in the Marsh from 05. *52 The Close, Norwich NR1 4EG* Tel (01603) 665210

CAPPER, Robert Melville. b 52. Chu Coll Cam BA74 MA80. Wycliffe Hall Ox 74. **d** 77 **p** 78. C Maindee *Mon* 77-81; TV Aberystwyth *St D* 81-87; Chapl Univ of Wales (Abth) 81-87; V Malpas *Mon* 87-00; V Gabalfa *Llan* from 00. *St Mark's Vicarage, 208 North Road, Gabalfa, Cardiff CF14 3BL* Tel (029) 2061 3286

CAPPER, William Alan. QUB BTh. **d** 88 **p** 89. C Dundonald *D & D* 88-91; C Lisburn Ch Ch *Conn* 91-94; I Tamlaght O'Crilly Upper w Lower *D & R* 94-96; I Lack *Clogh* from 03. *The Rectory, Main Street, Lack, Enniskillen BT93 0DN* Tel (028) 6863 1360 E-mail alan_capper@onetel.com

CAPPLEMAN, Graham Robert (Sam). b 56. Chelsea Coll Lon BSc79 Sheff Univ PhD83. ADipR92 St Alb and Ox Min Course 94. **d** 97 **p** 98. NSM Bedf St Mark *St Alb* from 97. *107 Dover Crescent, Bedford MK41 8QR* Tel (01234) 266952 Fax 402624 Mobile 07836-784051 E-mail samc@tesco.net *or* nsm@thisischurch.com

CAPPLEMAN, Mrs Jennifer Margaret. b 53. Liv Univ CertEd74. St Alb and Ox Min Course 97. **d** 00 **p** 01. NSM Bedford St Pet w St Cuth *St Alb* 00-03; C Goldington from 03. *107 Dover Crescent, Bedford MK41 8QR* Tel (01234) 405253 Mobile 07714-701008 Fax (01234) 402624 E-mail jennie.cappleman@ntlworld.com

CAPRON, David Cooper. b 45. Open Univ BA80. Sarum & Wells Th Coll 71. **d** 75 **p** 76. C Cov St Mary *Cov* 75-79; V Shottery St Andr 79-86; TV Stratford-on-Avon w Bishopton 79-86; V Shottery St Andr 86; V Newton Aycliffe *Dur* 86-89; TR 89-90; P-in-c Alcester and Arrow w Oversley and Weethley *Cov* 90-95; R from 95; Chapl Warks Fire and Rescue Service from 93. *St Nicholas' Rectory, Old Rectory Garden, Alcester B49 5DB* Tel and fax (01789) 764261 Mobile 07780-707521 E-mail caprons@ntlworld.com

CAPRON, Ronald Beresford. b 35. Clifton Th Coll. **d** 62 **p** 63. Canada 62-65; C Evington *Leic* 65-67; R Gaddesby w S Croxton 67-71; R Beeby 67-71; Chapl RAF 71-83; rtd 95. *107 Coverside Road, Great Glen, Leicester LE8 9EB* Tel 0116-259 2809

CAPSTICK, John Nowell. b 30. AKC54. **d** 55 **p** 56. C Skipton Ch Ch *Bradf* 55-57; C Buxton *Derby* 57-61; V Codnor and Loscoe 61-63; C-in-c Rawthorpe CD *Wakef* 63-64; V Rawthorpe 64-70; V Netherthong 70-89; TV Upper Holme Valley 89-95; rtd 95; Perm to Offic *Wakef* from 96. *8 Town End Avenue, Holmfirth, Huddersfield HD7 1YW* Tel (01484) 688708

CAPSTICK, William Richard Dacre. b 32. Pemb Coll Ox. Chich Th Coll 61. **d** 64 **p** 65. C Hunslet St Mary and Stourton St Andr *Ripon* 64-67; C Knaresborough H Trin 67-71; V Stratfield Mortimer *Ox* 71-76; P-in-c St Marylebone Ch Ch w St Paul *Lon* 76-78; TV St Marylebone Ch Ch 78-79; TR Newbury *Ox* 79-89; TV Brighton St Pet and St Nic w Chpl Royal *Chich* 89-97; rtd 97. *28 Bloomsbury Street, Brighton BN2 1HQ* Tel (01273) 681171

CARBERRY, Derek William. b 65. SEN88 Leeds Univ BA03. Coll of Resurr Mirfield 01. **d** 03 **p** 04. C Tynemouth Cullercoats St Paul *Newc* from 03. *14 Naters Street, Whitley Bay NE26 2PG* Tel 0191-253 2781 Mobile 07814-049605 E-mail d_carberry@hotmail.com

CARBERRY, Leon Carter. b 54. Penn State Univ BSc76. St Steph Ho Ox 81. **d** 84 **p** 85. C Peterlee *Dur* 84-87; C Newton Aycliffe 87-89; V Choral York Minster *York* 89-94; Chapl St Pet Sch York 94-95; V Fylingdales and Hawsker cum Stainsacre *York* 95-01; Chapl Burrswood Chr Cen *Roch* 01-03; V Beckenham St Jas from 03. *The Vicarage, 15 St James Avenue, Beckenham BR3 4HF* Tel (020) 8650 0420 E-mail leoncarberry@hotmail.com

CARBY, Stuart Graeme. b 51. CBiol77 MIBiol77 LRSC78 Man Univ BSc73 Leeds Univ PGCE74 Open Univ MA96. St Jo Coll Nottm 92. **d** 92 **p** 93. C Magor w Redwick and Undy *Mon* 92-96; TV Cyncoed from 96. *100 Hillrise, Llanederyn, Cardiff CF23 6UL* Tel (029) 2073 3915

CARD, Terence Leslie. b 37. K Coll Lon BD68 AKC68 Heythrop Coll Lon MTh84. **d** 69 **p** 70. C Thundersley *Chelmsf* 69-72; Lic to Offic *Bradf* 72-75; V Chingford St Anne *Chelmsf* 75-81; RD Waltham Forest 78-81; R Springfield All SS 81-83; C Becontree St Jo 85-87; rtd 87; Perm to Offic *Ely* 96-00. *11 Harvey Goodwin Gardens, Cambridge CB4 3EZ* Tel (01223) 367715

CARD, Thomas Ian. b 36. RD76. Master Mariner 61. Portsm Dioc Tr Course 88. **d** 89. NSM Binstead *Portsm* 89-95; Miss to Seafarers from 89; NSM Swanmore St Mich w Havenstreet *Portsm* 89-92; NSM Havenstreet St Pet 92-95; NSM Ryde All SS from 95. *Dolphins, 49 Mayfield Road, Ryde PO33 3PR* Tel (01983) 564749

CARD-REYNOLDS, Charles Leonard. b 67. Lon Univ BD92 Hughes Hall Cam BA94 MA98. St Steph Ho Ox 96. **d** 98 **p** 99. C Reading H Trin *Ox* from 98; C Reading St Mark from 98; FSJ from 01. *St Mark's Vicarage, 88 Connaught Road, Reading RG30 2UF* Tel 0118-958 7400 Fax as telephone E-mail clcardreynolds@btinternet.com

CARDALE, Charles Anthony. b 21. St D Coll Lamp BA47 Lich Th Coll 55. **d** 56 **p** 57. C Honicknowle CD *Ex* 56-58; C Bideford 58-60; R Wembworthy w Eggesford 60-69; V Brushford 63-69; V Staverton w Landscove 69-87; R Broadhempston, Woodland, Staverton etc 88-89; Perm to Offic from 89; rtd 90. *Keyberry, 13 Woodland Close, Staverton, Totnes TQ9 6PQ* Tel (01803) 762277

CARDALE, Edward Charles. b 50. CCC Ox BA72 MA73. Cuddesdon Coll 72 Union Th Sem (NY) STM74. **d** 74 **p** 75. C E Dulwich St Jo *S'wark* 74-77; Asst P Bainbridge Is USA 77-80; V Ponders End St Matt *Lon* 80-84; V Lytchett Minster *Sarum* 84-98; Dir Past Studies Coll of the Resurr Mirfield 98-02; P-in-c

Lemsford *St Alb* from 02; Tutor St Alb and Ox Min Course from 02. *7 High Oaks Road, Welwyn Garden City AL8 7BJ* Tel (01707) 327621 E-mail edward.cardale@btopenworld.com

CARDELL-OLIVER, John Anthony. b 43. Em Coll Cam BA67 MA72 Univ of W Aus BEd75 MEd85. Westcott Ho Cam 86. **d** 86 **p** 88. C Subiaco w Leederville Australia 86-88; Perm to Offic *Ely* 88-89; C Stansted Mountfitchet *Chelmsf* 89-92; R Langham w Boxted 92-02; rtd 02. *1 Burt Street, Albany, W Australia 6330* Tel and fax (0061) (8) 9383 7381 E-mail jco@graduate.uwa.edu.au

CARDEN, Edwin William. b 54. Cranmer Hall Dur 85. **d** 87 **p** 88. C Thundersley *Chelmsf* 87-91; CUF 91-93; NSM Poplar *Lon* 91-93; Chapl Pathfinder Mental Health Services NHS Trust 93-99; Chapl SW Lon and St George's Mental Health NHS Trust 99-00; Selection Sec Min Division from 00; NSM Maldon St Mary w Mundon *Chelmsf* 00-02. *21 Plume Avenue, Maldon CM9 6LB* Tel (01621) 854908 *or* (020) 7898 1402 E-mail eddie.carden@mindiv.c-of-e.org.uk

CARDEN, John Brumfitt. b 24. Lon Coll of Div 48. **d** 52 **p** 53. Pakistan 52-55, 57-60 and 65-69; C Leeds Halton St Wilfrid *Ripon* 56-57; Lit Sec CMS 60-65; Asia Sec CMS 70-76; Hon C Croydon St Sav *Cant* 75-76; C-in-c Bath St Steph *B & W* 76-82; V 82-84; CMS 84-89; Jerusalem 84-87; Exec Asst WCC Geneva 87-89; rtd 89; Miss Partner CMS from 89; Perm to Offic *York* from 89. *81 The Village, Haxby, York YO32 2JE* Tel (01904) 750035

CARDIGAN, Archdeacon of. *See* JONES, The Ven Benjamin Jenkin Hywel

CARDINAL, Ian Ralph. b 57. Qu Coll Birm 81. **d** 84 **p** 85. C Whitkirk *Ripon* 84-87; C Knaresborough 87-89; P-in-c Wilsford *Linc* 89; P-in-c Ancaster 89; R Ancaster Wilsford Gp 89-94; P-in-c Wigginton *Lich* from 94; Warden of Readers 96-04. *The Vicarage, Main Road, Wigginton, Tamworth B79 9DN* Tel (01827) 64537 Mobile 07778-055993 E-mail ian.cardinal@lichfield.anglican.org

CARDWELL, Edward Anthony Colin. b 42. Trin Coll Cam BA63 MA68. St Jo Coll Nottm 73. **d** 75 **p** 76. C Stapenhill w Cauldwell *Derby* 75-78; C Bramcote *S'well* 78-81; V S'well H Trin 81-92; R Eastwood from 92. *The Rectory, 5A Woodland Way, Eastwood, Nottingham NG16 3BU* Tel (01773) 712395 E-mail cardwell@eastwood88.freeserve.co.uk

CARDWELL, Joseph Robin. b 47. Qu Coll Cam BA68 MA77. Trin Coll Bris 73. **d** 76 **p** 77. C Bromley Ch Ch *Roch* 76-79; C Shirley *Win* 79-82; V Somborne w Ashley 82-90; V Derry Hill *Sarum* 90-94; V Derry Hill w Bremhill and Foxham 94-00; Community Affairs Chapl 90-94; V Lyddington and Wanborough and Bishopstone etc *Bris* from 00. *The Vicarage, 19 Church Road, Wanborough, Swindon SN4 0BZ* Tel (01793) 790242 E-mail robin@cardwell99.fsnet.co.uk

CARDWELL, Pamela. b 41. **d** 02. NSM Wednesfield *Lich* from 02. *Monkswood, 100 Broad Lane South, Wednesfield WV11 3RX* Tel (01902) 635224

CARE, Canon Charles Richard. b 21. Univ of Wales (Lamp) BA42. St Mich Coll Llan 42. **d** 44 **p** 45. C Grangetown *Llan* 44-57; R St Brides Minor 57-88; RD Bridgend 75-88; Can Llan Cathl 83-88; Prec 87-88; rtd 88; Perm to Offic *Llan* from 88. *31 Laburnum Drive, Porthcawl CF36 5UA* Tel (01656) 785446

CAREW, Bryan Andrew. b 38. ACIB63. St D Coll Lamp. **d** 67 **p** 68. C Pembroke Dock *St D* 67-70; CF 70-74; P-in-c Gt and Lt Henny w Middleton *Chelmsf* 74-76; P-in-c Wickham St Paul w Twinstead 75-76; R Gt and Lt Henny w Middleton, Wickham St Paul etc 76-99; P-in-c Alphamstone w Lamarsh 99; V Alphamstone w Gt and Lt Henny, Lamarsh etc 99-03; rtd 03; Perm to Offic *Chelmsf* from 03. *The Hinckford Margin, 4 Raydon Way, Great Cornard, Sudbury CO10 0LE*

CAREW, Richard Clayton. b 72. York Univ BA94 PGCE96 St Jo Coll Dur BA04. Cranmer Hall Dur 02. **d** 05. C Beverley Minster *York* from 05. *23 Outer Trinities, Beverley HU17 0HN* Tel (01482) 888249

CAREY, Alan Lawrence. b 29. K Coll Lon AKC53. **d** 54 **p** 55. C Radford *Cov* 54-57; C Burnham *Ox* 57-65; C-in-c Cippenham CD 65-77; rtd 94. *12 Ormsby Street, Reading RG1 7YR* Tel 0118-961 2309

CAREY, Charles John. b 29. K Coll Lon BD53 AKC53. St Aug Coll Cant 71. **d** 72 **p** 73. C Spring Park *Cant* 72-74; C Ifield *Chich* 74-78; C Burgess Hill St Jo 78-80; Chapl Rush Green Hosp Romford 80-94; Chapl Oldchurch Hosp Romford 80-94; rtd 94. *Address withheld by request*

CAREY, Christopher Lawrence John. b 38. St Andr Univ BSc61 Lon Univ BD64. Clifton Th Coll 61. **d** 64 **p** 65. C Battersea Park St Sav *S'wark* 64-67; CMS Kenya 68-79; Overseas Regional Sec for E and Cen Africa CMS 79-98; NSM Chislehurst Ch Ch *Roch* 79-98; R Stickney Gp *Linc* 99-04; RD Bolingbroke 02-03; rtd 04; Perm to Offic *Mon* from 04. *83 Wentwood View, Caldicot NP26 4QH* Tel (01291) 425010 E-mail crcandkili@tiscali.co.uk

CAREY, Donald Leslie. b 50. ACII78. Carl and Blackb Dioc Tr Inst 01. **d** 04 **p** 05. OLM Ashton-on-Ribble St Mich w Preston St Mark *Blackb* from 04. *The Dell, 11 Berry Field, Penwortham, Preston PR1 9YJ* Tel (01772) 747408 Mobile 07711-328672 E-mail donald.carey@freeuk.com

CAREY, Mark Jonathan. b 65. St Jo Coll Nottm BTh94. **d** 94 **p** 95. C S Ossett *Wakef* 94-97; C Chapeltown *Sheff* 97-99; V Grenoside from 99. *St Mark's Vicarage, 19 Graven Close, Grenoside, Sheffield S35 8QT* Tel 0114-246 7513 E-mail mpjcarey@aol.com *or* church@stmarks-grenoside.org.uk

CAREY, Canon Ronald Clive Adrian. b 21. K Coll Cam BA46 MA48. Chich Th Coll 47. **d** 48 **p** 49. C Harborne St Pet *Birm* 48-50; Bp's Dom Chapl *Chich* 50-52; C Keighley *Bradf* 52-55; V Illingworth *Wakef* 55-59; Asst in Relig Broadcasting BBC 59-68; Perm to Offic *S'wark* 59-68; V Claygate *Guildf* 68-78; RD Emly 72-77; Hon Can Guildf Cathl 78-86; R Guildf H Trin w St Mary 78-86; RD Guildf 84-86; rtd 86; Perm to Offic *Roch* 86-04 and *Linc* from 04. *23 Moores Court, Jermyn Street, Sleaford NG34 7UL* Tel (01529) 303698

CAREY, Mrs Wendy Marion. b 45. Bris Univ BA66 Lon Inst of Educn CertEd67. WMMTC 90. **d** 93 **p** 94. NSM Milton Keynes *Ox* 93-96; Sub Chapl HM Pris Woodhill 93-96; Chapl HM Pris Bullingdon 96-00; Ecum Tr Officer HM Pris Service Chapl from 00; Lic to Offic *Cov* from 00; Perm to Offic *Ox* from 00. *Prison Service College, Newbold Revel, Rugby CV23 0TH* Tel (01788) 834162 E-mail wendy.carey@hmps.gsi.gov.uk

✠**CAREY OF CLIFTON, The Rt Revd and Rt Hon Lord (George Leonard).** b 35. PC91. Lon Univ BD62 MTh65 PhD71 Dur Univ Hon DD93 Open Univ Hon DD95 FRSA91 FKC93. ALCD61. **d** 62 **p** 63 **c** 87. C Islington St Mary *Lon* 62-66; Lect Oak Hill Th Coll 66-70; Lect St Jo Coll Nottm 70-75; V Dur St Nic *Dur* 75-82; Chapl HM Rem Cen Low Newton 77-81; Prin Trin Coll Bris 82-87; Hon Can Bris Cathl *Bris* 84-87; Bp B & W 87-91; Abp Cant 91-02; rtd 02; Hon Asst Bp S & B from 04. *65 Robin Hood Lane, London SW15 3PX*

CARGILL THOMPSON, Edmund Alwyn James. b 72. St Jo Coll Ox BA94. Cranmer Hall Dur 98. **d** 00 **p** 01. C St Jo on Bethnal Green *Lon* 00-03; V Barkingside H Trin *Chelmsf* from 03. *Barkingside Vicarage, 36 Mossford Green, Ilford IG6 2BJ* Tel (020) 8550 2669 E-mail father.edmund@virgin.net

CARHART, John Richards. b 29. Bris Univ BA50 Salford Univ MSc77 Liv Univ MTh99 FRSA. St Deiniol's Hawarden 63. **d** 65 **p** 66. C Ches St Oswald w Lt St Jo *Ches* 65-72; Lect Ches Coll of HE 65-72; Prin Lect from 72; Dean Academic Studies 88-94; C Ches 72; Lic to Offic 73-85; Hon C Ches St Mary 85-00; rtd 00; Perm to Offic *Ches* from 00. *29 Abbot's Grange, Chester CH2 1AJ* Tel (01244) 380923

CARLESS, Canon Frank. b 22. Lon Univ BD56. St Aid Birkenhead 53. **d** 56 **p** 57. C Normanton *Wakef* 56-59; V Rashcliffe 59-64; V Warley 64-87; RD Halifax 82-86; Hon Can Wakef Cathl 86-87; rtd 87; Perm to Offic *Wakef* from 87. *8 Crossley Almshouses, Arden Road, Halifax HX1 3AA* Tel (01422) 348379

CARLILL, Adam Jonathan. b 66. Keble Coll Ox BA88. Linc Th Coll 88. **d** 90 **p** 91. C Romford St Edw *Chelmsf* 90-94; C Uckfield *Chich* 94-98; V Tilehurst St Geo *Ox* from 98; P-in-c Tilehurst St Mary from 02. *St George's Vicarage, 98 Grovelands Road, Reading RG3 2PD* Tel 0118-958 8354

CARLILL, Richard Edward. b 38. Westcott Ho Cam 77. **d** 79 **p** 80. C Prittlewell *Chelmsf* 79-83; TV Saffron Walden w Wendens Ambo and Littlebury 83-89; V Langtoft w Foxholes, Butterwick, Cottam etc *York* 89-94; V Gt and Lt Driffield 94-03; RD Harthill 99-02; rtd 03. *31 Riverdene, Tweedmouth, Berwick-upon-Tweed TD15 2JD* Tel (01289) 303701

CARLIN, William Patrick Bruce. b 53. St Steph Ho Ox 75. **d** 78 **p** 79. C Penistone *Wakef* 78-81; C Barnsley St Mary 81-83; V Stockton St Chad *Dur* 83-93; V Hedworth 93-01; TR Kippax w Allerton Bywater *Ripon* from 01. *The Rectory, Church Lane, Kippax, Leeds LS25 7HF* Tel 0113-286 2710 Fax 286 7339 E-mail brucecarlin@freeuk.com *or* rector@stmarykippax.org.uk

CARLING, Mrs Bronwen Noël. b 43. SRN65 SCM73. Linc Th Coll 89. **d** 91 **p** 94. C Blakeney w Cley, Wiveton, Glandford etc *Nor* 91-94; C Trunch 94-96; TV 96-01; rtd 01; Perm to Offic *Nor* 01-04. *Meadowbank, Rathdermot, Bansha, Co Tipperary, Irish Republic* Tel (00353) (62) 54891 E-mail bncarling@sagainternet.co.uk

CARLISLE, Christopher John. b 39. Sheff Univ BEng62. NW Ord Course 72. **d** 75 **p** 76. C Bury St Paul *Man* 75-80; C Walkden Moor 80-82; V Lytham St Jo *Blackb* 82-02; rtd 02. *2 Reedy Acre Place, Lytham, Lytham St Annes FY8 4PR* Tel (01253) 739562

CARLISLE, John Patrick. b 66. St Andr Univ MTh89 Hughes Hall Cam PGCE90. St Steph Ho Ox 93. **d** 95 **p** 96. C Hendon St Alphage *Lon* 95-99; TV Ribbleton *Blackb* 99-03; V New Rossington *Sheff* from 03. *St Luke's Vicarage, The Circle, New Rossington, Doncaster DN11 0QP* Tel (01302) 868288 E-mail jpcarlisle@aol.com

CARLISLE, Matthew David. b 74. Man Univ BA96. Westcott Ho Cam 99. **d** 02 **p** 03. C E Crompton *Man* from 02. *9 Scarr Lane, Shaw, Oldham OL2 8HQ* Tel (01706) 291366 Mobile 07870-760746 E-mail matthew.carlisle@ntlworld.com

CARLISLE, Archdeacon of. *See* THOMSON, The Ven David

CARLISLE, Bishop of. *See* DOW, The Rt Revd Geoffrey Graham

CARLISLE, Dean of. *See* BOYLING, The Very Revd Mark Christopher

CARLOS, Francis John. b 29. Jes Coll Cam BA54 MA57. Wells Th Coll 52. **d** 55 **p** 56. C Canning Town St Matthias *Chelmsf* 55-57; C-in-c Thundersley CD *St E* 57-64; V New Thundersley *Chelmsf* 64-65; R Wentnor and Ratlinghope w Myndtown and Norbury *Heref* 65-89; P-in-c More w Lydham 82-89; P-in-c Snead 85-89; R Wentnor w Ratlinghope, Myndtown, Norbury etc 89-94; rtd 94; Perm to Offic *Heref* from 94. *16 Springfield Park, Clee Hill, Ludlow SY8 3QY* Tel (01584) 891253

CARLSON, Blair Truett. b 52. Wheaton Coll Illinois BA74. Cranmer Hall Dur 00. **d** 02 **p** 03. C Hailsham *Chich* 02-05; USA from 05. *4619 Arden Avenue, Edina, MN 55424, USA* E-mail bcarlson@onetel.com

CARLSSON, Miss Siw. b 43. **d** 92 **p** 94. Par Dn Barnes St Mary *S'wark* 92-93; C Mitcham SS Pet and Paul 93-98; Asst Chapl SW Lon and St George's Mental Health NHS Trust 99-00; Chapl Ipswich Hosp NHS Trust from 00. *Ipswich Hospital, Heath Road, Ipswich IP4 5PD* Tel (01473) 712223 *or* 704100 Fax 703400

CARLTON, Roger John. b 51. **d** 80 **p** 81. NSM Downend *Bris* 80-83; NSM Heavitree w Ex St Paul *Ex* 83-87; Chapl St Marg Sch Ex 83-87; Chapl Ex Sch 83-87; TV Bickleigh (Plymouth) *Ex* 87-91; TR 91-93; TR Bickleigh and Shaugh Prior from 94; RD Ivybridge 93-98. *The Vicarage, 2 Blackeven Close, Roborough, Plymouth PL6 7AX* Tel (01752) 702119 Fax 768882 E-mail roger.carlton@btinternet.com

CARLYON, Miss Catherine Rachel. b 67. RN89 Plymouth Univ DipN97. Ripon Coll Cuddesdon 00. **d** 02 **p** 03. C Launceston *Truro* from 02. *11 Summerhill Road, Launceston PL15 7DU* Tel (01566) 779846 E-mail catherinecarlyon@btopenworld.com

CARLYON (née ENGLAND), Mrs Jessie Marguerite Tarie. b 44. Westf Coll Lon BA66 K Coll Lon PGCE67. WMMTC 92. **d** 95 **p** 97. C Pontypool *Mon* 95-97; TV 97-00; V Bedwellty from 00. *The Rectory, Church Street, Aberbargoed, Bargoed CF81 9FF* Tel (01443) 829555

CARMAN, Jill Youde. b 37. Cartrefle Coll of Educn CertEd69 Liv Univ DipEd86. St Alb and Ox Min Course 97. **d** 99 **p** 00. NSM Markyate Street *St Alb* 99-02; NSM Quinton *Glouc* 02-05; NSM Quinton and Welford w Weston from 05. *The Vicarage, Lower Quinton, Stratford-upon-Avon CV37 8SG* Tel (01789) 720756

CARMAN, Roger Eric. b 40. Univ of Wales BSc62 MIEE. TISEC 92. **d** 97 **p** 98. C Dollar *St And* from 97. *Sule Skerry, Dollar FK14 7PG* Tel (01259) 742485 E-mail recarman@telco4u.com

CARMARTHEN, Archdeacon of. *See* EVANS, The Ven Alun Wyn

CARMICHAEL, Elizabeth Dorothea Harriet. b 46. MBE95. LMH Ox MA73 BM73 BCh73 Worc Coll Ox BA83 Ox Univ DPhil91. **d** 91 **p** 92. S Africa 91-96; Chapl and Tutor St Jo Coll Ox from 96. *St John's College, Oxford OX1 3JP* Tel (01865) 277300 Fax 277435 E-mail liz.carmichael@sjc.ox.ac.uk

CARMICHAEL, Peter Iain. b 28. Chich Th Coll 75. **d** 75 **p** 76. C Rye w Rye Harbour and Playden *Chich* 75-79; C Rye, Rye Harbour and Playden and Iden 79-80; R Earnley and E Wittering 80-94; rtd 94; Perm to Offic *Chich* from 94. *20 East Street, Selsey, Chichester PO20 0BJ* Tel (01243) 606197

CARMODY, Canon Dermot Patrick Roy. b 41. CITC 77. **d** 77 **p** 78. C Dublin Zion Ch *D & G* 77-79; I Dunganstown w Redcross 79-84; TV Dublin Ch Ch Cathl Gp 84-93; Can Ch Ch Cathl Dublin 84-92; Preb Ch Ch Cathl Dublin 92-93; I Mullingar, Portnashangan, Moyliscar, Kilbixy etc *M & K* from 93; Dir of Ords (Meath) from 97; Can Meath from 98; Can Kildare Cathl from 98; Treas from 00; P-in-c Rathmolyon w Castlerickard, Rathcore and Agher from 00. *All Saints' Rectory, Mullingar, Co Westmeath, Irish Republic* Tel and fax (00353) (44) 48376 E-mail pcarmody@iolfree.ie

CARMYLLIE, Mrs Kathryn Ruth. b 61. Cov Poly BA84 CQSW84 Univ Coll Ches BTh04. N Ord Course 01. **d** 04 **p** 05. C Leigh St Mary *Man* from 04. *St Stephen's Vicarage, 7 Holbeck, Astley, Tyldesley, Manchester M29 7DU* Tel (01942) 883313

CARMYLLIE, Robert Jonathan. b 63. Cov Poly BSc85. St Jo Coll Dur 85. **d** 88 **p** 89. C Horwich *Man* 88-92; P-in-c Edgeside 92-99; P-in-c Astley from 99. *St Stephen's Vicarage, 7 Holbeck, Astley, Tyldesley, Manchester M29 7DU* Tel (01942) 883313

CARNALL, Mrs Nicola Jane. b 66. St Jo Coll Nottm 99. **d** 01 **p** 02. C Edwinstowe *S'well* from 01. *46 Occupation Lane, Edwinstowe, Mansfield NG21 9HU* Tel (01623) 824278 E-mail njcarnall@aol.com

CARNE, Canon Brian George. b 29. FSA Liv Univ BCom50. Qu Coll Birm 53. **d** 55 **p** 56. C Swindon St Aug *Bris* 55-58; C Bris St Andr w St Bart 58-60; R Lydiard Millicent w Lydiard Tregoz 60-68; V Bris St Andr Hartcliffe 68-74; V Almondsbury 74-91; RD Westbury and Severnside 80-86; Hon Can Bris Cathl 82-91; P-in-c Littleton on Severn w Elberton 83-91; P-in-c Olveston 83-91; rtd 91; Perm to Offic *Bris* from 92; *Glouc* 92-98 and from 01. *Whitehouse Farm, English Bicknor, Coleford GL16 7PA* Tel (01594) 860200

CARNE, Norman David John. b 27. Roch Th Coll 59. **d** 62 **p** 63. C Roch St Justus *Roch* 62-66; C Strood St Mary 66-68; R Westcote Barton and Steeple Barton *Ox* 68-74; P-in-c Enstone and Heythrop 74-82; V 82-92; rtd 92; Perm to Offic *Leic* 93-98. *45 Beckingthorpe Drive, Bottesford, Nottingham NG13 0DN* Tel (01949) 843890

CARNE-ROSS, Stewart Pattison. b 24. Wycliffe Hall Ox 58. **d** 59 **p** 60. C Brockley Hill St Sav *S'wark* 59-62; C Dulwich St Barn 62-64; V Champion Hill St Sav 64-70; P-in-c Stanton Lacy *Heref* 70-72; V 72-77; V Bromfield 70-77; R Culmington w Onibury 70-77; V Hambledon *Portsm* 77-79; Chapl HM Pris Kingston (Portsm) 79-90; C Portsea St Mary *Portsm* 86-90; rtd 90; Perm to Offic *Portsm* from 90. *7 Hanover Court, Highbury Street, Portsmouth PO1 2BN* Tel (023) 9275 2698

CARNEGIE, Ms Rachel Clare. b 62. New Hall Cam BA84 Sussex Univ MA94. SEITE 01. **d** 04. NSM Richmond St Mary w St Matthias and St Jo *S'wark* from 04. *337 Petersham Road, Richmond TW10 7DB* Tel (020) 8940 7436 E-mail rcarnegie@rcmg.freeserve.co.uk

CARNELL, Canon Geoffrey Gordon. b 18. St Jo Coll Cam BA40 MA44. Cuddesdon Coll 40. **d** 42 **p** 43. C Abington *Pet* 42-49; Chapl and Lect St Gabr Coll Camberwell 49-53; R Isham *Pet* 53-71; V Gt w Lt Harrowden 53-71; Dir of Post-Ord Tr and Dir of Ords 62-85; Can Pet Cathl 65-85; R Boughton 71-85; Dioc Lib Ecton Ho 67-93; Chapl to The Queen 81-88; rtd 85; Perm to Offic *Pet* from 86. *52 Walsingham Avenue, Kettering NN15 5ER* Tel (01536) 511415

CARNELLEY, The Ven Desmond. b 29. Open Univ BA77 Leeds Univ CertEd. Ripon Hall Ox 59. **d** 60 **p** 61. C Aston cum Aughton *Sheff* 60-63; C-in-c Ecclesfield St Paul CD 63-67; V Balby w Hexthorpe 67-73; P-in-c Mosbrough 73-74; V 74-85; RD Attercliffe 79-84; Adn Doncaster 85-94; Dioc Dir of Educn 91-94; rtd 94; Perm to Offic *Sheff* and *Derby* from 94. *7 Errwood Avenue, Buxton SK17 9BD* Tel (01298) 71460

CARNELLEY, Ms Elizabeth Amy. b 64. St Aid Coll Dur BA85 Selw Coll Cam MPhil87. Ripon Coll Cuddesdon 88. **d** 90 **p** 94. Par Dn Sharrow St Andr *Sheff* 90-93; Par Dn Is of Dogs Ch Ch and St Jo w St Luke *Lon* 93-94; C 94-95; P-in-c Woolfold *Man* 95-99; TV Man Whitworth 99-02; Chapl Man Univ and Man Metrop Univ 99-02; Policy Officer Chs' Regional Commn for Yorks and the Humber from 02. *30 New Hey Road, Huddersfield HD3 4AJ* Tel (01484) 303374 E-mail liz.carnelley@yorkshirechurches.org.uk

CARNEY, David Anthony. b 42. Salford Univ BSc77. Linc Th Coll 77. **d** 79 **p** 80. C Wythenshawe St Martin *Man* 79-81; CF 81-84; Chapl Canadian Armed Forces 84-87; R Burford H Trin Ontario 87-91; P-in-c Whaplode *Linc* 91-97; V 97-02; P-in-c Holbeach Fen 91-97; V 97-02; R Colsterworth Gp 02-05; P-in-c Kirton in Holland from 05. *The Vicarage, Penny Gardens, Kirton, Boston PE20 1HN* Tel (01205) 722380

CARNEY, Mrs Mary Patricia. b 42. Univ of Wales (Ban) BSc62. Wycliffe Hall Ox. **d** 90 **p** 94. Par Dn Carterton *Ox* 90-93; Par Dn Harwell w Chilton 93-94; C 94-01; P-in-c Ray Valley from 01. *The Vicarage, Church Walk, Ambrosden, Bicester OX25 2UJ* Tel (01869) 247813 E-mail mary_carney@lineone.net *or* office@rayvalley.fsnet.co.uk

CARNEY, The Ven Richard Wayne. b 52. Lon Teachers' Coll Ontario TCert73 Toronto Univ BA79. Trin Coll Toronto MDiv84. **d** 84 **p** 85. Canada 84-95; C Scarborough St Andr 84-86; I Roche's Pt 86-91; P Asst Newmarket St Paul 91-93; Assoc P 93-95; I Clonfert Gp *L & K* 95-03; I Birr w Lorrha, Dorrha and Lockeen from 03; Adn Killaloe, Kilfenora, Clonfert etc from 02. *The Rectory, Birr, Co Offaly, Irish Republic* Tel (00353) (509) 20021 Mobile 87-677 3196 Fax (509) 25883 E-mail mapleire@eircom.net *or* archdeacon@killaloe.anglican.org

✠**CARNLEY, The Most Revd Peter Frederick.** b 37. AO98. Melbourne Univ BA66 Cam Univ PhD69 Gen Th Sem NY Hon DD84 Newc Univ Aus Hon DLitt00 Univ of W Aus Hon DLitt00. St Jo Coll Morpeth ThL62 ACT 62. **d** 62 **p** 64 **c** 81. Lic to Offic Melbourne 63-65; C Parkes 66; Lic to Offic *Ely* 66-69; Chapl Mitchell Coll Bathurst 70-71; Research Fell St Jo Coll Cam 71-72; Warden St Jo Coll Brisbane 72-81; Can Res Brisbane 75-81; Abp Perth from 81; Primate of Australia from 00. *GPO Box W2067, Perth, W Australia 6846* Tel (0061) (08) 9322 1253 *or* 9325 7455 Fax 9325 6741 E-mail abcsuite@perth.anglican.org

CAROLAN (née STUART-BLACK), Mrs Veronica. b 52. St Jo Coll Dur BA75. Cranmer Hall Dur. **dss** 82 **d** 87. Borehamwood *St Alb* 82-84; Watford Ch Ch 84-85; Stevenage St Mary Shephall 85-87; Par Dn Stevenage St Mary Shephall w Aston 87-88; Perm to Offic from 98. *18 Randalls Hill, Shephall, Stevenage SG2 9YN* Tel (01438) 235597

CARPANI, Karl Augustus. b 65. St Jo Coll Nottm 96. **d** 98 **p** 99. C Biggin Hill *Roch* 98-01; V Green Street Green and Pratts Bottom from 01. *The Vicarage, 46 World's End Lane, Orpington BR6 6AG* Tel (01689) 852905 E-mail karl@carpani.org

CARPENTER, Bruce Leonard Henry. b 32. Lon Univ BA54 St Chad's Coll Dur DipTh59. **d** 59 **p** 60. C Portsea N End St Mark *Portsm* 59-63; C Fareham SS Pet and Paul 63-67; V Locks Heath 67-74; TR Fareham H Trin 74-84; RD Alverstoke 71-76; Hon Can Portsm Cathl 79-84; V Richmond St Mary w St Matthias and St Jo *S'wark* 84-91; Chapl Ch Ch High Sch Ashford 91-93; P-in-c S Ashford Ch Ch *Cant* 94-97; rtd 97; Chapl Huggens Coll Northfleet 97-02; Perm to Offic *Portsm* from 02; Hon Chapl Mothers' Union from 03. *Pistachio, 96 Festing Grove, Southsea PO4 9QF* Tel (023) 9229 4128

CARPENTER, David James. b 52. Trin Coll Carmarthen CertEd74. St Steph Ho Ox 74. **d** 76 **p** 77. C Newport St Julian *Mon* 76-77; C Pontypool 77-79; C Ebbw Vale 79-81; TV 81-85; V Pontnewynydd 85-88; V Bedwellty 88-00; Chapl Aberbargoed Hosp 88-99; V Staincliffe and Carlinghow *Wakef* 00-05. *Address temp unknown* Tel 07702-400766 (mobile) E-mail carpenterdj@aol.com

CARPENTER, Canon Derek George Edwin. b 40. K Coll Lon BD62 AKC62. **d** 63 **p** 64. C Friern Barnet All SS *Lon* 63-66; C Chingford SS Pet and Paul *Chelmsf* 66-70; V Dartford St Alb *Roch* 70-79; R Crayford 79-90; RD Erith 82-90; R Beckenham St Geo 90-02; Hon Can Roch Cathl 97-02; rtd 02. *39 Chatfield Way, East Malling, West Malling ME19 6QD* Tel (01732) 874420

CARPENTER, Donald Arthur. b 35. Roch Th Coll 65. **d** 67 **p** 68. C Thornton Heath St Jude *Cant* 67-73; V Earby *Bradf* 73-78; V Skipton Ch Ch 78-88; V Baildon 88-91; P-in-c Perivale *Lon* 91-96; rtd 96; Perm to Offic *Lon* 96-05. *Le Moulin Verneau, 49390 Parcay-les-Pins, France* Tel (0033) (2) 41 51 42 22 Mobile 6 77 98 48 07 E-mail carpenter.sue@wanadoo.fr

CARPENTER, Mrs Judith Margaret. b 47. Bris Univ BA68 CertEd69. Trin Coll Bris BA95. **d** 95 **p** 96. C Warmley, Syston and Bitton *Bris* 95-99; V Withywood from 99. *Withywood Church House, 63 Turtlegate Avenue, Bristol BS13 8NN* Tel 0117-964 7763 E-mail revjude@fish.co.uk

CARPENTER, Leonard Richard. b 32. EMMTC 82. **d** 85 **p** 86. NSM Leic H Apostles *Leic* 85-90; P-in-c Barlestone 90-98; rtd 98; Perm to Offic *Leic* and *Derby* from 98. *10 Main Street, Albert Village, Swadlincote DE11 8EW* Tel (01283) 229335

CARPENTER, Michael John Anselm. b 77. Leeds Univ BA02. Coll of Resurr Mirfield 99. **d** 02 **p** 03. C Cudworth and Lundwood *Wakef* 02-03; C Castleford from 03. *The Vicarage, Churchfield Lane, Glasshoughton, Castleford WF10 4BP* Tel (01977) 734075

CARPENTER, William Brodie. b 35. St Alb Minl Tr Scheme 76. **d** 79 **p** 80. NSM Hemel Hempstead *St Alb* 79-85; C Bp's Hatfield 85-88; C Caversham St Pet and Mapledurham etc *Ox* 88-89; V Caversham St Andr 89-99; rtd 99; Perm to Offic *St Alb* 00-02; P-in-c Wigginton 02-05. *33 Elm Tree Walk, Tring HP23 5EB* Tel (01442) 824585 E-mail billcarp@supanet.com

CARR, Alan Cobban. b 49. Nottm Univ BTh88. Linc Th Coll 85. **d** 88 **p** 89. C Rustington *Chich* 88-92; V Highbrook and W Hoathly from 92. *The Vicarage, North Lane, West Hoathly, East Grinstead RH19 4QF* Tel (01342) 810494

CARR, Mrs Amanda Helen. b 70. Univ of Wales (Cardiff) BA91 Kent Univ MA97. SEITE 01. **d** 04 **p** 05. C Meopham w Nurstead *Roch* from 04. *38 Evenden Road, Meopham, Gravesend DA13 0HA* Tel (01474) 812569 Mobile 07866-675015 E-mail mandy@carrfamilyonline.co.uk

CARR, Anthony Howard. b 62. Ex Univ BA. **d** 92 **p** 93. C Taverham w Ringland *Nor* 92-97; P-in-c S Darley, Elton and Winster *Derby* 97-03; R E Peckham and Nettlestead *Roch* from 03. *The Rectory, Bush Road, East Peckham, Tonbridge TN12 5LL* Tel (01622) 871278

CARR, The Very Revd Arthur Wesley. b 41. Jes Coll Ox BA64 MA67 Jes Coll Cam BA66 MA70 Sheff Univ PhD75. Ridley Hall Cam 65. **d** 67 **p** 68. C Luton w E Hyde *St Alb* 67-71; Tutor Ridley Hall Cam 70-71; Chapl 71-72; Hon C Ranmoor *Sheff* 72-74; Chapl Chelmsf Cathl *Chelmsf* 74-78; Can Res Chelmsf Cathl 78-87; Dep Dir Cathl Cen for Research and Tr 74-82; Dioc Dir of Tr 76-84; Dean Bris 87-97; Dean Westmr from 97. *The Deanery, Dean's Yard, London SW1P 3PA* Tel (020) 7654 4801 *or* 7654 4802 Fax 7654 4883 E-mail wesley.carr@westminster-abbey.org

CARR, Derrick Charles. b 43. MCIPD. St Alb and Ox Min Course 99. **d** 02 **p** 03. NSM Amersham *Ox* from 02. *52 Warren Wood Drive, High Wycombe HP11 1EA* Tel and fax (01494) 452389 Mobile 07768-507391 E-mail dcarr@globalnet.co.uk

CARR, Mrs Elaine Susan. b 46. LTCL82. St Alb and Ox Min Course 99. **d** 02 **p** 03. NSM High Wycombe *Ox* from 02. *52 Warren Wood Drive, High Wycombe HP11 1EA* Tel and fax (01494) 452389 E-mail e.carr@fish.co.uk

CARR, Miss Eveline. b 45. St Jo Coll Dur 91. **d** 93 **p** 95. NSM Eighton Banks *Dur* 93-98; NSM Gateshead from 98. *10 Lanchester Avenue, Gateshead NE9 7AJ* Tel 0191-482 1157 E-mail e-carr@supnet.com

CARR, John Henry Percy. b 52. NTMTC AdDipTh98 ADPS98. **d** 98 **p** 99. C Hackney Wick St Mary of Eton w St Aug *Lon* 98-01; R Walesby *Linc* from 01. *The Rectory, Otby Lane, Walesby, Market Rasen LN8 3UT* Tel (01673) 838513 E-mail carr.ide@boltblue.com

CARR, John Robert. b 40. ACII62. Oak Hill Th Coll 63. **d** 66 **p** 67. C Tonbridge St Steph *Roch* 66-70; C Cheadle Hulme St Andr *Ches* 70-79; R Widford *Chelmsf* 79-87; TV Becontree W 87-93; V Basildon St Andr w H Cross from 93. *St Andrew's Vicarage, 3 The Fremnells, Basildon SS14 2QX* Tel (01268) 520516

CARR, Miss Joy Vera. b 32. DipEd52. Dalton Ho Bris 56. **dss** 80 **d** 87 **p** 94. Scarborough St Jas and H Trin *York* 80-82; Kingston upon Hull St Matt w St Barn 82-87; Par Dn 87-89; Par Dn Elloughton and Brough w Brantingham 89-92; rtd 92; Perm to Offic *York* from 92. *15 Sea View Gardens, Scarborough YO11 3JD* Tel (01723) 376986

CARR, Mandy. *See* CARR, Mrs Amanda Helen

CARR, Paul Anthony. b 62. Aston Tr Scheme 93 Oak Hill Th Coll 95. **d** 97 **p** 98. C Handforth *Ches* 97-01; V Chadwell Heath *Chelmsf* from 01. *7 Chadwell Heath Lane, Romford RM6 4LS* Tel (020) 8590 2054 E-mail revpaulcarr@onetel.com

CARR, Wesley. *See* CARR, The Very Revd Arthur Wesley

CARRICK, Canon Ian Ross. b 13. Clare Coll Cam BA35 MA39. Chich Th Coll 35. **d** 37 **p** 38. C Sculcoates St Paul *York* 37-39; C Staveley *Derby* 39-43; Min St Barn CD Northolt 43-54; V Northolt Park St Barn *Lon* 54-58; S Africa from 59; R Irene 59-62; P-in-c Sekhukhuniland and Prin St Fran Coll 62-66; Adn Barberton 64-66; Adn Pretoria 67-76; R Pretoria St Wilfred 68-75; R Pretoria Trin 76-80; Dir Min Tr Dioc of Pretoria 80-84; rtd 84. *65 First Crescent, Fish Hoek, 7975 South Africa* Tel (0027) (21) 782 5586 E-mail mary@carrick.dynagen.co.za

CARRINGTON, Mrs Elizabeth Ashby. b 46. EMMTC 86. **d** 90 **p** 94. NSM Nottingham St Ann w Em *S'well* 90-91; C Basford w Hyson Green 92-97; Lect Nottingham St Mary and St Cath 97-00; Assoc P W Bingham Deanery 00; Perm to Offic 00-01; Chapl Woodford Ho Sch New Zealand from 01; NSM Napier Cathl from 03. *Woodford House, Havelock North, Hastings 4201, New Zealand* Tel (0064) (6) 873 0722 Fax 873 0719 E-mail elizabeth.carrington@woodford.school.nz

CARRINGTON, Philip John. b 48. MBE03. Leeds Univ MA96 MCMI Leeds Poly CEng. Chich Th Coll 83. **d** 85 **p** 86. C W Acklam *York* 85-88; V Middlesbrough St Agnes 88-92; Chapl S Cleveland Hosp 88-92; Trust Chapl S Tees Hosps NHS Trust from 92. *The James Cook University Hospital, Marton Road, Middlesbrough TS4 3BW* Tel (01642) 850850 *or* 854802 Fax 854802 E-mail rev.carrington@stees.nhs.uk

CARRIVICK, Derek Roy. b 45. Birm Univ BSc66. Ripon Hall Ox 71. **d** 74 **p** 75. C Enfield St Jas *Lon* 74-78; C-in-c Woodgate Valley CD *Birm* 78-83; TR Chelmsley Wood 83-92; Dioc Ecum Officer 86-96; R Baxterley w Hurley and Wood End and Merevale etc 92-99; AD Polesworth 96-99; P-in-c Helland and Blisland w St Breward *Truro* 99-04; P-in-c Devoran from 04; Bp's Dom Chapl from 04. *The Vicarage, Devoran Lane, Devoran, Truro TR3 6PA* Tel (01872) 863116 E-mail pjc87@tutor.open.ac.uk

CARROLL, The Ven Charles William Desmond. b 19. TCD BA43 MA46. St Chad's Coll Dur. **d** 48 **p** 49. C Stanwix *Carl* 48-50; V 50-59; Hon Can Blackb Cathl *Blackb* 59-64; Dir RE 59-73; Can Res Blackb Cathl 64-75; Adn Blackb 73-86; V Balderstone 73-86; rtd 86; Perm to Offic *Blackb* 86-00. *11 Assheton Road, Blackburn BB2 6SF* Tel (01254) 51915

CARROLL, James Thomas. b 41. Pittsburgh Univ MA85. St Deiniol's Hawarden 89 Oblate Fathers Sem Dub 59. **d** 63 **p** 64. C Dublin St Patr Cathl Gp *D & G* 89-92; Min Can St Patr Cathl Dublin 90-96; I Raheny w Coolock *D & G* from 92; Chan V St Patr Cathl Dublin from 96. *403 Howth Road, Raheny, Dublin 5, Irish Republic* Tel (00353) (1) 831 3929 E-mail midnight@indigo.ie

CARROLL, John Hugh. b 31. Bris Univ BA57. Tyndale Hall Bris 54. **d** 58 **p** 59. C Slough *Ox* 58-61; V S Lambeth St Steph *S'wark* 61-72; V Norwood St Luke 72-81; P-in-c Purley Ch Ch 81-85; V 85-93; rtd 93; Perm to Offic *S'wark* from 93. *75 Court Avenue, Coulsdon CR5 1HJ* Tel (01737) 553471 E-mail jonthel.carroll@virgin.net

CARROLL, Laurence William. b 44. Birm Univ CertEd66 Open Univ BA73 Leic Univ BEd74 FRHS66 ACP67 LCP68. LNSM course 92. **d** 95 **p** 96. OLM Mid Marsh Gp *Linc* from 95. *Hall Farm Barn, Church Lane, Manby, Louth LN11 8HL* Tel (01507) 327630

CARROLL WALLIS, Ms Joy Ann. b 59. SS Mark & Jo Coll Plymouth BEd82. Cranmer Hall Dur 85. **d** 88 **p** 94. Par Dn Hatcham St Jas *S'wark* 88-93; Par Dn Streatham Immanuel and St Andr 93-94; C 94-97; USA from 97. *2629 13th Street NW, Washington, DC 20009, USA* Tel (001) (202) 483 0119 E-mail joycwallis@aol.com

CARRUTHERS, Arthur Christopher (Kester). b 35. Lon Coll of Div ALCD60 LTh73. **d** 60 **p** 61. C Addiscombe St Mary *Cant* 60-62; Prec Bradf Cathl *Bradf* 62-64; CF 64-92; R W Tanfield and Well w Snape and N Stainley *Ripon* 92-00; rtd 00; Perm to Offic *Guildf* from 00. *3 Park View Court, Woking GU22 7SE* Tel (01483) 721995

CARRY, Canon Edward Austin. b 18. TCD BA41 MA47. **d** 42 **p** 43. I Killiney H Trin *D & G* 56-86; Preb St Patr Cathl Dublin 83-86; rtd 86. *2 Roxboro Close, Ballinclea Road, Killiney, Co Dublin, Irish Republic* Tel (00353) (1) 285 8847

CARSON, Christopher John. b 69. QUB BA91 TCD BTh94. **d** 94 **p** 95. C Bangor St Comgall *D & D* 94-97; Bp's C Kilmegan w Maghera 97-98; I from 98. *The Rectory, 50 Main Street, Dundrum, Newcastle BT33 0LY* Tel (028) 4375 1225 Mobile 07905-660274

CARSON, Ms Claire. b 76. St Martin's Coll Lanc BA98 Birm Univ MA99. Qu Coll Birm 00. **d** 03 **p** 04. C Streetly *Lich* 03-04; C Stafford from 04. *9 Brunswick Terrace, Stafford ST16 1BB* Tel (01785) 245654 E-mail claire.c@fish.co.uk

CARSON, Ernest. b 17. S'wark Ord Course 68. **d** 71 **p** 72. C Baldock w Bygrave and Clothall *St Alb* 71-75; R Hertingfordbury 75-86; rtd 86; Perm to Offic *Worc* from 86. *16 Woodward Close, Pershore WR10 1LP* Tel (01386) 553511

CARSON, Gerald James Alexander. b 24. TCD BA49 MA52. **d** 49 **p** 50. C Belfast St Phil *Conn* 49-51; C Derry Cathl *D & R* 51-54; I Kilteevogue 54-57; I Dunfanaghy 57-68; Can Raphoe Cathl 67-81; I Urney w Sion Mills 68-85; Can Derry Cathl 81-85; I Clonallon w Warrenpoint *D & D* 85-90; rtd 90. *84 Avonbrook Gardens, Mountsandel, Coleraine BT52 1SS* Tel (028) 7035 6047

CARSON, James Irvine. b 59. TCD BA DipTh84 MTh. **d** 84 **p** 85. C Willowfield *D & D* 84-87; C Lecale Gp 87-89; I Devenish w Boho *Clogh* 89-95; Dioc Youth Adv 91-95; Dioc Communications Officer 93-95; I Belfast Upper Malone (Epiphany) *Conn* 95-99; I Lisburn St Paul from 99. *St Paul's Rectory, 3 Ballinderry Road, Lisburn BT28 1UD* Tel (028) 9266 3520 E-mail ji.carson@breathemail.net

CARSON-FEATHAM, Lawrence William. b 53. AKC. **d** 78 **p** 79. SSM from 77; C Walton St Mary *Liv* 78-82; Chapl Bolton Colls of H&FE 82-87; C Bolton St Pet *Man* 82-87; TV Oldham 87-92; V Ashton St Jas 92-95; Perm to Offic *Liv* 95-97; C Leeds Belle Is St Jo and St Barn *Ripon* 97-01; TV Accrington Ch the King *Blackb* from 01. *St Mary Magdalen's Vicarage, 5 Queen's Road, Accrington BB5 6AR* Tel (01254) 233763

CARTER, Arthur. b 32. CITC. **d** 97 **p** 98. C Clonmel w Innislounagh, Tullaghmelan etc *C & O* from 97. *Suir Villa, Barnora, Cahir, Co Tipperary, Irish Republic* Tel (00353) (52) 41524

CARTER, Barry Graham. b 54. K Coll Lon BD76 AKC76. St Steph Ho Ox 76. **d** 77 **p** 78. C Evesham *Worc* 77-81; C Amblecote 81-84; TV Ovingdean w Rottingdean and Woodingdean *Chich* 84-85; V Woodingdean 85-95; V Lancing St Mich from 95. *The Vicarage, 117 Penhill Road, Lancing BN15 8HD* Tel (01903) 753653

CARTER, Celia. b 38. JP74. Glouc Sch of Min 86. **d** 89 **p** 94. NSM Avening w Cherington *Glouc* from 89; Asst Chapl Stroud Gen Hosp 89-93; Asst Chapl Severn NHS Trust from 93. *Avening Park, West End, Avening, Tetbury GL8 8NE* Tel (01453) 836390

CARTER, Canon Charles Trevelyan Aubrey. b 14. TCD BA36 MA46. TCD Div Sch Div Test37. **d** 37 **p** 38. C Dublin Sandford *D & G* 37-43; Chapl Female Orphanage Ho Dublin 43-55; I Dublin St Steph 52-59; I Dublin Crumlin 59-67; I Dublin Sandford 67-82; I Dublin Sandford w Milltown 82-85; Can Ch Ch Cathl Dublin 71-85; rtd 85. *7 South Hill, Dartry, Dublin 6, Irish Republic* Tel (00353) (1) 497 1171

CARTER (née SMITH), Mrs Christine Lydia. b 43. Lon Hosp SRN64 Bristol Hosp SCM67 Bris Poly Dip Nursing76 Wolv Poly CertFE84. Trin Coll Bris DipHE91. **d** 91 **p** 94. Par Dn Penkridge Team *Lich* 91-94; C 94-96; Perm to Offic *Blackb* 96-97; NSM Blackb Sav 97-01; Chapl Asst St Helens and Knowsley Hosps NHS Trust 97-01; NSM Elmdon St Nic *Birm* from 01. *Elmdon Rectory, Tanhouse Farm Road, Solihull B92 9EY* Tel 0121-743 6336 E-mail vicar@tworevs.co.uk

CARTER, Christopher Franklin (Kit). b 37. Wadh Coll Ox BA59 MA63. Wycliffe Hall Ox 60. **d** 64 **p** 65. C Clifton St Jas *Sheff* 64-67; C Handsworth 67-70; C Clun w Chapel Lawn *Heref* 70-74; Lic to Offic 74-76; P-in-c Ironbridge 76-78; C Coalbrookdale, Iron-Bridge and Lt Wenlock 78-80; V Llansilin w Llangadwaladr and Llangedwyn *St As* from 80; RD Llanfyllin from 88. *The Vicarage, Llansilin, Oswestry SY10 7PX* Tel (01691) 791209

CARTER, Colin John. b 56. Fitzw Coll Cam BA77 MB, BChir80 MA81 FRCS86 FRCOphth89. Trin Coll Bris BA93. **d** 93 **p** 94. C Ripley *Derby* 93-97; TV Horsham *Chich* 97-00; St Geo Healthcare NHS Trust Lon from 00. *Address temp unknown*

CARTER, David John. b 37. Chich Th Coll 64. **d** 67 **p** 68. C Plaistow St Andr *Chelmsf* 67-70; C Wickford 70-73; Chapl Asst Runwell Hosp Wickford 71-73; Chapl Basingstoke Distr Hosp 73-80; R E Woodhay and Woolton Hill *Win* 80-02; rtd 02; Perm to Offic *Win* from 02. *24 Sandford Close, Kingsclare RG20 5QZ* Tel (01635) 299455

CARTER, Miss Derath May. b 52. N Staffs Poly LLB87. St Alb and Ox Min Course 01. **d** 02 **p** 03. C Harlington Ch Ch CD *Lon* from 02. *192 Waltham Avenue, Hayes UB3 1TF* Tel and fax (020) 8573 0112 Mobile 07962-168440 E-mail derath@fish.co.uk

CARTER, Dudley Herbert. b 25. Peterho Cam BA49 MA51. Ridley Hall Cam 49. **d** 51 **p** 52. C Longfleet *Sarum* 51-53; C Rainham *Chelmsf* 54-56; R Tollard Royal w Farnham *Sarum* 60-64; Chapl Colston's Sch Bris 65-67; Lic to Offic *B & W* 67-85; Perm to Offic from 85; rtd 90. *24 Caernarvon Way, Burnham-on-Sea TA8 2DQ* Tel (01278) 789572

CARTER, Duncan Robert Bruton. b 58. Univ of Wales (Cardiff) BA79 Cam Univ BA83 MA89. Ridley Hall Cam 81. **d** 84 **p** 85. C Harold Wood *Chelmsf* 84-88; C S Kensington St Luke *Lon* 88-90; V Henley H Trin *Ox* from 90; AD Henley from 02. *Holy Trinity Vicarage, Church Street, Henley-on-Thames RG9 1SE* Tel (01491) 574822 E-mail drbcarter@hotmail.com

CARTER, Edward John. b 67. Ex Univ BA88. Ripon Coll Cuddesdon BA96 MA01. **d** 97 **p** 98. C Thorpe St Matt *Nor* 97-00; Min Can and Dean's V Windsor 00-04; P-in-c Didcot St Pet *Ox* from 04. *St Peter's Vicarage, Glebe Road, Didcot OX11 8PN* Tel (01235) 812114 E-mail revdedward.carter@ukgateway.net

CARTER, Eric. b 17. **d** 58 **p** 59. C S Shore H Trin *Blackb* 58-62; V Preesall 62-69; RD Garstang 68-69; V Adlington 69-75; V Garstang St Thos 75-84; rtd 84; Perm to Offic *Ripon* from 84. *1 Arncliffe Road, Harrogate HG2 8NQ* Tel (01423) 884867

CARTER, Frank Howard James. b 23. Chich Th Coll 58. **d** 59 **p** 60. C Bethnal Green St Matt *Lon* 59-64; V Ipstones *Lich* 64-65; V Haggerston All SS *Lon* 65-75; V Alexandra Park St Andr 75-88; rtd 88; Perm to Offic *Lon* 91-98. *53 Naylor Road, London N20 0HE* Tel (020) 8445 0982

CARTER, Grayson Leigh. b 53. Univ of S California BSc76 Ch Ch Ox DPhil90. Fuller Th Sem California MA84 Wycliffe Hall Ox 89. **d** 90 **p** 91. C Bungay H Trin w St Mary *St E* 90-92; Chapl BNC Ox 92-96; Hon C Ox St Mary V w St Cross and St Pet *Ox* 93-96; USA from 96; Assoc Prof Methodist Coll Fayetteville 96-03; Asst R Fayetteville H Trin 96-03; Assoc Prof Fuller Th Sem from 03. *1602 Palmcroft Drive SW, Phoenix, AZ 75996, USA* Tel (001) (602) 252 5582 *or* (408) 517 1414 Fax (408) 517 1492 E-mail gcarter10@yahoo.com *or* gcarter@fuller.edu

CARTER, Hazel June. b 48. Doncaster Coll of Educn CertEd72. Carl Dioc Tr Inst 89. **d** 92 **p** 94. C Wreay *Carl* 92-98; C Dalston and Raughton Head w Gatesgill 92-98; TV Carl H Trin and St Barn 98-02; TR from 02. *Holy Trinity Rectory, 25 Wigton Road, Carlisle CA2 7BB* Tel (01228) 526284

CARTER, Heather Ruth. b 62. Trin Coll Bris 85. **d** 02 **p** 04. Dn Montevideo Cathl Uruguay 02-04; NSM Dalston w Cumdivock, Raughton Head and Wreay *Carl* from 04. *The Vicarage, Townhead Road, Dalston, Carlisle CA5 7JF* Tel and fax (01228) 710215 E-mail revhev@tiscali.co.uk

CARTER, Ian Sutherland. b 51. Trin Coll Ox BA73 MA77 DPhil77 Leeds Univ BA80. Coll of Resurr Mirfield 78. **d** 81 **p** 82. C Shildon *Dur* 81-84; C Darlington H Trin 84-87; Chapl Liv Univ *Liv* 87-93; V Hindley St Pet 93-98; Chapl Oldham NHS Trust 98-03; Chapl Salford R Hosps NHS Trust from 03. *Hope Hospital, Stott Lane, Salford M6 8HD* Tel 0161-206 5167 *or* 789 7373 E-mail ian.carter@srht.nhs.uk

CARTER (née O'NEILL), Mrs Irene. b 44. Worc Coll of Educn CertEd65. EMMTC 92. **d** 93. NSM N and S Leverton *S'well* from 93. *25 Mill Close, North Leverton, Retford DN22 0AT* Tel (01427) 880451

CARTER, Mrs Jacqueline Ann. b 50. St Mich Coll Llan 01. **d** 03 **p** 04. C Ebbw Vale *Mon* from 03. *The Vicarage, 177 Badminton Grove, Beaufort, Ebbw Vale NP23 5UN* Tel (01495) 304516 E-mail jackiecarter16@hotmail.com

CARTER, John Howard Gregory. b 55. York Univ BA76 Leeds Univ CertEd77 Nottm Univ MA96. St Jo Coll Nottm LTh87. **d** 87 **p** 88. C Nailsea H Trin *B & W* 87-91; TV Camberley St Paul *Guildf* 91-97; Chapl Elmhurst Ballet Sch 91-97; Dioc Communications Officer *Ripon* from 97; Bp's Press Officer from 00. *7 Blenheim Court, Harrogate HG2 9DT* Tel (01423) 530369 Mobile 07798-652707 Fax 08717-333778 E-mail jhgcarter@aol.com

CARTER, Leslie Alfred Arthur. b 27. K Coll Lon 50 St Boniface Warminster 53. **d** 54 **p** 55. C Northolt Park St Barn *Lon* 54-56; S Africa 57-62; C Wimbledon *S'wark* 63-68; Chapl Quainton Hall Sch Harrow 68-77; TV Brighton Resurr *Chich* 77-81; TV Southend *Chelmsf* 81-88; V Gt Waltham w Ford End 88-93; rtd 94; Perm to Offic *Sarum* from 94; and *B & W* from 00. *The Garden Flat, 11 Bathwick Street, Bath BA2 6NX*

CARTER, Ms Marian. b 40. Whitelands Coll Lon TCert61 Lon Univ BD67 Reading Univ DASE73 Nottm Univ MPhil79 Man Univ MA84. Nor Bapt Coll 81. **d** 92 **p** 94. Par Dn Kempshott *Win* 92-93; Tutor SW Minl Tr Course 92-96; Tutor Coll of SS Mark and Jo Plymouth 93-00; NSM Plymstock and Hooe *Ex* 94-98; NSM Widecombe-in-the-Moor, Leusdon, Princetown etc 98-00; Chapl St Eliz Hospice Ipswich from 00. *Shalom, 80 Woodlands, Chelmondiston, Ipswich IP9 1DU* Tel (01473) 780259

CARTER, Canon Michael John. b 32. St Alb Minl Tr Scheme 81. **d** 84 **p** 85. NSM Radlett *St Alb* 84-88; Chapl SW Herts HA 88-94; Chapl Watford Gen Hosp 88-94; Lic to Offic *St Alb* 88-99; Chapl Mt Vernon and Watford Hosps NHS Trust 94-99; Bp's

Adv for Hosp Chapl *St Alb* 95-99; Hon Can St Alb 96-99; rtd 99; Perm to Offic *St Alb* from 99; Hon Chapl Peace Hospice Watford from 99. *Greenford, 42 Oakridge Avenue, Radlett WD7 8ER* Tel (01923) 856009 E-mail mail@mjcarter.com

CARTER, Michael William. b 33. Newland Park Teacher Tr Coll TCert56. Dioc OLM tr scheme 98. **d** 01 **p** 02. OLM Lingfield and Crowhurst *S'wark* 01-04; rtd 04. *Redwood House, 76 Godstone Road, Lingfield RH7 6BT* Tel (01342) 833843

CARTER, Nicholas Adrian. b 47. Ripon Hall Ox 71. **d** 74 **p** 75. C Sowerby *Wakef* 74-79; V Hanging Heaton 79-83; CF 83-86; V Elton All SS *Man* 86-90; C Milton *Win* 90-94; P-in-c Boscombe St Andr 94-00; V from 00. *St Andrew's Vicarage, 3 Wilfred Road, Bournemouth BH5 1NB* Tel (01202) 394575

CARTER, Nigel John. b 53. Bolton Inst of Educn CertEd89. Sarum & Wells Th Coll 91. **d** 93 **p** 94. C Burntwood *Lich* 93-96; V Bentley 96-04; RD Wolverhampton 00-02; V Walsall Wood from 04. *The Vicarage, 2 St John's Close, Walsall Wood, Walsall WS9 9NH* Tel (01543) 360558 *or* 372284 E-mail nigel.carter@02.co.uk

CARTER, Noel William. b 53. Birm Univ BSc75 Bris Univ CertEd76 Nottm Univ BSc83. Linc Th Coll. **d** 83 **p** 84. C Penrith w Newton Reigny and Plumpton Wall *Carl* 83-86; C Barrow St Matt 86-87; V Netherton 87-91; TR Penrith w Newton Reigny and Plumpton Wall 91-97; P-in-c Jersey St Brelade *Win* 97-98; R 98-01; Vice-Dean Jersey 00-01; P-in-c Brymbo and Southsea *St As* from 05. *The Bryn, Bryn Road, Moss, Wrexham LL11 6EL*

CARTER, Canon Norman. b 23. Leeds Univ BSc48. Coll of Resurr Mirfield 48. **d** 50 **p** 51. C Liv Our Lady and St Nic w St Anne *Liv* 50-54; C Orford St Marg 54-56; V 56-71; PC Knotty Ash H Spirit 71-74; V Dovecot 74-83; RD W Derby 78-83; Hon Can Liv Cathl 82-88; V Formby St Pet 83-88; rtd 88; Perm to Offic *Liv* from 88. *34 Granby Close, Southport PR9 9QG* Tel (01704) 232821

CARTER, Canon Paul Brian. b 22. AKC49. **d** 50 **p** 51. C Scarborough St Columba *York* 50-53; C Pocklington w Yapham-cum-Meltonby, Owsthorpe etc 53-55; V Kingston upon Hull St Jo Newington 55-60; R Ainderby Steeple and Scruton *Ripon* 60-79; P-in-c Yafforth 76-79; R Ainderby Steeple w Yafforth and Scruton 79-87; Hon Can Ripon Cathl 86-87; rtd 87; Perm to Offic *Ripon* from 87. *Cliffe Cottage, West Tanfield, Ripon HG4 5JR* Tel (01677) 470203

CARTER, Paul Joseph. b 67. St Chad's Coll Dur BA88. St Steph Ho Ox 89. **d** 91 **p** 92. C Ipswich All Hallows *St E* 91; C Newmarket St Mary w Exning St Agnes 91-94; V Thorpe-le-Soken *Chelmsf* 94-04; V Ipswich St Bart *St E* from 04. *St Bartholomew's Vicarage, Newton Road, Ipswich IP3 8HQ* Tel (01473) 727441 E-mail frpaul@stbarts.freeserve.co.uk

CARTER, Paul Mark. b 56. BA78 MA90 Cranfield Univ MBA95. Ridley Hall Cam 79. **d** 81 **p** 82. C Kidsgrove *Lich* 81-84; CF 84-00; Asst P Vancouver St Phil Canada 00-03. *1655 West 41st Avenue, Vancouver BC, Canada, V6M 1X9* Tel (001) (604) 222 4497 E-mail paulcarter@acinw.org

CARTER, Paul Rowley. b 45. Lon Univ BD69 Lon Bible Coll ALBC69 Southn Univ PGCE70. Trin Coll Bris. **d** 91 **p** 92. C Penkridge Team *Lich* 91-96; V Blackb Sav *Blackb* 96-01; R Elmdon St Nic *Birm* from 01. *Elmdon Rectory, Tanhouse Farm Road, Solihull B92 9EY* Tel 0121-743 6336 E-mail vicar@tworevs.co.uk

CARTER, Robert Desmond. b 35. Cranmer Hall Dur 62. **d** 65 **p** 66. C Otley *Bradf* 65-69; C Keighley 69-73; V Cowling 73-00; rtd 00; Perm to Offic *Bradf* from 00. *1 Quincy Close, Eccleshill, Bradford BD2 2EP* Tel (01274) 638385

CARTER, Robert Edward. b 44. Univ of Wales (Ban) BSc66. St Jo Coll Nottm 79. **d** 81 **p** 82. C Caverswall *Lich* 81-86; V Biddulph 86-94; V Wolverhampton St Jude from 94. *St Jude's Vicarage, St Jude's Road, Wolverhampton WV6 0EB* Tel (01902) 753360 E-mail stjudes@zoom.co.uk

CARTER, Robert Thomas. b 49. Moore Th Coll Sydney 72 Ridley Coll Melbourne ThL75. **d** 75 **p** 76. Australia 75-00 and from 02; C Traralgon St Jas 75-76; P-in-c Endeavour Hills St Matt 77-79; V 80-84; Assoc Min Kew St Hilary 85-91; V Blackburn N St Alfred 92-00; C Fisherton Anger *Sarum* 00-02. *224 Maroondah Highway, Croydon, Melbourne, Vic, Australia 3136*

CARTER, Robin. b 46. Chich Th Coll 71. **d** 74 **p** 75. C Wortley de Leeds *Ripon* 74-76; C Hutton *Chelmsf* 76-78; C Wickford 78-81; TV Wickford and Runwell 81-83; Chapl HM Pris Leeds 83-85; Chapl HM Pris Reading 85-89; Chapl HM YOI Huntercombe and Finnamore 85-89; Chapl HM YOI Finnamore Wood Camp 86-89; Gov 5, Hd of Operations, HM Pris Channings Wood 89-94; Gov 4, Régime and Throughcare, HM Pris Woodhill 94-99; Gov HM Pris E Sutton Park from 99. *Prison Service Headquarters, Cleland House, Page Street, London SW1P 4LN* Tel (020) 7217 3000

CARTER, Ronald George. b 31. Leeds Univ BA58. Coll of Resurr Mirfield 58. **d** 60 **p** 61. C Wigan St Anne *Liv* 60-63; Prec Wakef Cathl *Wakef* 63-66; V Woodhall *Bradf* 66-77; Chapl Qu Marg Sch Escrick Park 77-83; Min Can, Prec and Sacr Pet Cathl *Pet* 83-88; R Upper St Leonards St Jo *Chich* 88-94; rtd 94; Perm to Offic *York* from 95. *5 Greenwich Close, York YO30 5WN* Tel (01904) 610237

CARTER, Russell James Wigney. b 29. Chich Th Coll 80. **d** 82 **p** 83. C Aldwick *Chich* 82-86; R Buxted and Hadlow Down 86-90; rtd 90; Perm to Offic *Chich* from 90. *6 Lucerne Court, Aldwick, Bognor Regis PO21 4XL* Tel (01243) 862858

CARTER, Samuel. b 49. St Jo Coll Dur BA71 DipTh72. Cranmer Hall Dur 73. **d** 74 **p** 75. C Kingswinford St Mary *Lich* 74-77; C Shrewsbury H Cross 77-84; V Normacot 84-94. *Address withheld by request*

CARTER, Sarah Helen Buchanan. *See* GORTON, Sarah Helen Buchanan

CARTER, Stanley Reginald. b 24. St Jo Coll Dur BA49 DipTh50. **d** 50 **p** 51. C Stoughton *Guildf* 50-53; C Bucknall and Bagnall *Lich* 53-56; R Salford St Matthias w St Simon *Man* 56-62; V Highbury New Park St Aug *Lon* 62-69; V Sneinton St Chris w St Phil *S'well* 69-89; rtd 89; Perm to Offic *S'well* from 89. *31 Pateley Road, Nottingham NG3 5QF* Tel 0115-953 2122 E-mail stan.carter@dunelm.org.uk

CARTER, Stephen. b 56. Univ of Wales (Lamp) BA77 Southn Univ BTh81. Sarum & Wells Th Coll 78. **d** 81 **p** 82. C Halstead St Andr w H Trin and Greenstead Green *Chelmsf* 81-84; C Loughton St Jo 84-89; V N Shoebury 89-95; R Lexden from 95; RD Colchester from 01. *The Rectory, 2 Wroxham Close, Colchester CO3 3RQ* Tel (01206) 575966

CARTER, Stephen Howard. b 47. City Univ BSc72. St Jo Coll Nottm 83. **d** 85 **p** 86. C Hellesdon *Nor* 85-88; Chapl Asst Birm Children's Hosp 88-91; Chapl Asst Birm Maternity Hosp 88-91; TV Tettenhall Wood *Lich* 91-98; Chapl Compton Hall Hospice Wolv 91-98; P-in-c Coalbrookdale, Iron-Bridge and Lt Wenlock *Heref* 98-00; R from 00; Asst Dioc Co-ord for Evang 00-01. *The Rector's House, Paradise, Coalbrookdale, Telford TF8 7NR* Tel (01952) 433309 Fax 432137 E-mail stevecarter@bigfoot.com

CARTER, Stephen Paul. b 55. Cartrefle Coll of Educn CertEd76. Trin Coll Bris BA88. **d** 98 **p** 99. Dn-in-c Montevideo H Spirit Uruguay 98-99; P-in-c 00-04; V Dalston w Cumdivock, Raughton Head and Wreay *Carl* from 04. *The Vicarage, Townhead Road, Dalston, Carlisle CA5 7JF* Tel and fax (01228) 710215 E-mail spc55@tiscali.co.uk

CARTER, Stuart Conway. b 58. Lon Bible Coll DipRS83 St Jo Coll Nottm DipMM92. **d** 92 **p** 93. C Birm St Luke *Birm* 92-96; C The Quinton from 96. *95 Oak Road, Quinton, Birmingham B68 0BH* Tel 0121-422 3621

CARTER, Terence John. b 31. K Coll Lon BD57 AKC57 Lon Univ BA68 PGCE69. **d** 58 **p** 59. C Winchmore Hill H Trin *Lon* 58-60; PV S'wark Cathl *S'wark* 60-63; Sacr S'wark Cathl 60-61; Succ S'wark Cathl 61-63; R Ockham w Hatchford *Guildf* 63-69; Lic to Offic *S'wark* 69-78; Lic to Offic *Portsm* 78-82; Perm to Offic from 82; rtd 91. *15 Balliol Road, Portsmouth PO2 7PP* Tel (023) 9269 9167 Mobile 07811-474020 E-mail terence.carter1@ntlworld.com

CARTER, Mrs Wendy Elise Grace. b 46. Battersea Coll of Educn TCert67. Qu Coll Birm 01. **d** 04 **p** 05. C Kingshurst *Birm* from 04. *125 Dunton Road, Kingshurst, Birmingham B37 6JJ* Tel 0121-604 0230 E-mail wegcarter@btinternet.com

CARTLEDGE, Margery. *See* TOLLER, Elizabeth Margery

CARTLEDGE, Mark John. b 62. Lon Bible Coll BA85 Univ of Wales PhD00. Oak Hill Th Coll MPhil89. **d** 88 **p** 89. C Formby H Trin *Liv* 88-91; Miss Partner CMS 91-93; Nigeria 91-93; Chapl Liv Univ *Liv* 93-98; Chapl and Tutor St Jo Coll Dur 98-03; Lect Univ of Wales (Lamp) from 03. *Department of Theology, University of Wales, Lampeter SA48 7ED* Tel (01570) 424954 E-mail m.cartledge@lamp.ac.uk

CARTMELL, Canon Richard Peter Watkinson. b 43. Cranmer Hall Dur 77. **d** 79 **p** 80. C Whittle-le-Woods *Blackb* 79-85; V Lower Darwen St Jas 85-03; RD Darwen 91-96; P-in-c S Shore H Trin from 03; Hon Can Blackb Cathl from 98. *92 Watson Road, Blackpool FY4 2DE* Tel (01253) 347140

CARTMILL, Canon Ralph Arthur. b 40. St Jo Coll Dur BA62 Em Coll Cam MA64. Ridley Hall Cam 63. **d** 65 **p** 66. C Dukinfield St Jo *Ches* 65-68; C Wilmslow 68-69; Warden Walton Youth Cen Liv 69-70; Asst Master Aylesbury Gr Sch 70-74; Perm to Offic *Ox* 72-74; V Terriers 74-85; P-in-c Chinnor w Emmington and Sydenham 85-86; R Chinnor w Emmington and Sydenham etc 86-98; Hon Can Ch Ch 97-98; rtd 98; Perm to Offic *Nor* from 00. *6 Longview Close, Snettisham, King's Lynn PE31 7RD* Tel (01485) 543357

CARTWRIGHT, Mrs Amanda Jane. b 58. St Jo Coll Nottm 00. **d** 02 **p** 03. C Beeston *S'well* from 02. *46 Bramcote Road, Beeston, Nottingham NG9 1DW* Tel 0115-854 3628 E-mail revdmand@hotmail.com

CARTWRIGHT, Julia Ann. b 58. Nottm Univ BA80. Linc Th Coll 84. **dss** 86 **d** 87 **p** 94. Asst Chapl HM Pris Morton Hall 85-90; Linc St Jo *Linc* 86-88; Hon C 87-88; Hon C Bardney 88-97; Chapl Linc Co Hosp 90-93; Chapl St Geo Hosp Linc 90-93; Chapl Linc Distr Health Services and Hosps NHS Trust 93-97; Chapl S Bucks NHS Trust 97-04; Lic to Offic *Ox* 97-04; Chapl S Warks Combined Care NHS Trust from 04. *St Michael's Hospital, St Michael's Road, Warwick CV34 5QW* Tel (01926) 496241 *or* 406789 Fax 406700

CARTWRIGHT, Michael. *See* CARTWRIGHT, William Michael

CARTWRIGHT, Michael John. b 42. Birm Univ DLA70. Qu Coll Birm 67. **d** 70 **p** 71. C Astwood Bank w Crabbs Cross *Worc* 70-75; P-in-c Worc St Mich 75-77; V Stockton St Paul *Dur* 77-87; V Market Rasen *Linc* from 87; R Linwood from 87; V Legsby from 87; RD W Wold 89-01; R Wickenby Gp 95-00; V Lissington from 00. *The Vicarage, 13 Lady Frances Drive, Market Rasen LN8 3JJ* Tel (01673) 843424

✠**CARTWRIGHT, The Rt Revd Richard Fox.** b 13. Pemb Coll Cam BA35 MA39 Univ of the South (USA) Hon DD69. Cuddesdon Coll 35. **d** 36 **p** 37 **c** 72. C Kennington Cross St Anselm *S'wark* 36-40; C Kingswood 40-45; V Surbiton St Andr 45-52; V Bris St Mary Redcliffe w Temple etc *Bris* 52-72; Hon Can Bris Cathl 60-72; Suff Bp Plymouth *Ex* 72-81; rtd 82; Asst Bp Truro 82-91; Asst Bp Ex from 88. *5 Old Vicarage Close, Ide, Exeter EX2 9RE* Tel (01392) 211270

CARTWRIGHT, Roy Arthur. b 29. CCC Cam BA52 MA56. Wycliffe Hall Ox. **d** 54 **p** 55. C Hornchurch St Andr *Chelmsf* 54-56; C Gt Clacton 56-60; C-in-c Prittlewell St Steph CD 60-69; V Prittlewell St Steph 69-72; rtd 72; Hon C S Shoebury *Chelmsf* 77-94; Perm to Offic *Glouc* from 94. *21 Winfield, Newent GL18 1QB* Tel (01531) 821335

CARTWRIGHT, Samuel. b 27. Cuddesdon Coll 71. **d** 72 **p** 72. C Rochdale *Man* 72-76; V Roundthorn 76-83; V Ashton Ch Ch 83-93; rtd 93; Perm to Offic *Derby* from 93. *8 Wentworth Avenue, Walton, Chesterfield S40 3JB* Tel (01246) 232252

CARTWRIGHT, Sidney Victor. b 22. Launde Abbey 73. **d** 74 **p** 75. C Braunstone *Leic* 74-78; P-in-c Arnesby w Shearsby 78-86; R Arnesby w Shearsby and Bruntingthorpe 86-87; rtd 87; Perm to Offic *Leic* and *Pet* from 87. *32 Northleigh Grove, Market Harborough LE16 9QX* Tel (01858) 463915

CARTWRIGHT, William Michael. b 44. Birm Univ CertEd67. Coll of Resurr Mirfield 83. **d** 83 **p** 84. Hd Master Chacombe Sch 83-85; Hon C Middleton Cheney w Chacombe *Pet* 83-85; Hd Master Chacombe Sch Banbury 83-85; C Kettering SS Pet and Paul *Pet* 85-86; Perm to Offic 86-88; Chapl Northaw Prep Sch Win 89-92; P-in-c Altarnon w Bolventor, Laneast and St Clether *Truro* 92-97; V Treverbyn 97-01; V Bempton w Flamborough, Reighton w Speeton *York* 01-03; V Ampleforth w Oswaldkirk, Gilling E etc from 03. *The Rectory, West End, Ampleforth, York YO62 4DU* Tel (01439) 788264

CARUANA, Mrs Rosemary Anne. b 38. St Alb Minl Tr Scheme 81. **dss** 84 **d** 87 **p** 94. Hertford St Andr *St Alb* 84-87; Par Dn Hertingfordbury 87-94; C 94-98; P-in-c from 98. *36 Holly Croft, Sele Farm Estate, Hertford SG14 2DR* Tel (01992) 306427 Mobile 07769-658756 E-mail r.caruana@ntlworld.com

CARVER, Arthur Tregarthen. b 15. Lon Univ 37. Tyndale Hall Bris 37. **d** 41 **p** 42. C Southport Ch Ch *Liv* 41-43; P-in-c 43-44; P-in-c St Helens St Matt Thatto Heath 44-48; V St Helens St Mark 48-53; V Marple All SS *Ches* 53-69; R Uphill *B & W* 69-80; rtd 80; Perm to Offic *Ches* from 80. *Copinsay, 20 Hayton Street, Knutsford WA16 0DR* Tel (01565) 651622

CARVER, Miss Elizabeth Ann. b 36. ACIB73. Bp Otter Coll BA00. **d** 99. NSM Littlehampton and Wick *Chich* from 99. *13 Hearnfield Road, Littlehampton BN17 7PR* Tel (01903) 713169

CARVOSSO, John Charles. b 45. ACA71 FCA79. Oak Hill Th Coll 75. **d** 78 **p** 79. C Chelsea St Jo w St Andr *Lon* 78-81; Chapl RAF 81-84; P-in-c Tawstock *Ex* 84-85; TV Newport, Bishops Tawton and Tawstock 85-96; TV Newton Tracey, Horwood, Alverdiscott etc from 96; RD Torrington 97-02. *The Rectory, Tawstock, Barnstaple EX31 3HZ* Tel (01271) 374963 E-mail devoncarvossos@classicfm.net

CASE, Preb Catherine Margaret. b 44. Ripon Coll Cuddesdon 86. **d** 88 **p** 94. C Blurton *Lich* 88-92; Min to Hanley Care Agencies 92-94; TD Hanley H Ev 92-94; P-in-c Wrockwardine Wood 95-98; R 98-00; V Gnosall from 00; Preb Lich Cathl from 02. *The Vicarage, Gnosall, Stafford ST20 0ER* Tel (01785) 822213

CASE, Clive Anthony. b 70. St Andr Univ MTheol93 Surrey Univ BA05 St Jo Coll Dur PGCE94. STETS 02. **d** 05. NSM Epsom St Martin *Guildf* from 05; Asst Chapl Epsom Coll from 05. *Epsom College, College Road, Epsom KT17 4JQ* Tel (01372) 821296 *or* 821206 Mobile 07801-288943 E-mail cac@epsomcollege.org.uk

CASE, Philip Thomas Charles. b 17. Lon Univ BSc(Econ)51. Sarum Th Coll 51. **d** 53 **p** 54. C Westmr St Steph w St Jo *Lon* 53-56; C Ashford St Matt 56-58; C-in-c Ashford St Hilda CD 58-61; V St Helier *S'wark* 61-66; V Witley *Guildf* 66-84; RD Godalming 79-84; rtd 84; Perm to Offic *Ex* 85-98. *15 Lawpool Court, Wells BA5 2AN* Tel (01749) 670859

CASEBOW, Ronald Philip. b 31. Roch Th Coll 59. **d** 61 **p** 62. C Southgate Ch Ch *Lon* 61-64; C Oseney Crescent St Luke w Camden Square St Paul 64-70; Warden St Paul's Ho Student Hostel 64-70; V Colchester St Steph *Chelmsf* 70-74; V Burnham 74-89; rtd 89; Perm to Offic *Nor* from 95. *The Priory, Priory Road, Palgrave, Diss IP22 1AJ* Tel (01379) 651804

CASEY, Christopher Noel. b 61. Open Univ BA95 Nottm Univ BA01. St Jo Coll Nottm 98. **d** 01 **p** 02. C Penrith w Newton Reigny and Plumpton Wall *Carl* from 01. *18 Skirsgill Close, Penrith CA11 8QF* Tel (01768) 899540 E-mail kc.family@btopenworld.com

CASH, Simon Andrew. b 62. St Jo Coll Nottm 99. **d** 01 **p** 02. C Aston cum Aughton w Swallownest and Ulley *Sheff* 01-04; P-in-c Worksop St Anne *S'well* from 04; P-in-c Norton Cuckney from 05. *The Vicarage, 11 Poplar Close, Worksop S80 3BZ* Tel (01909) 472069 E-mail s.cash@freenet.co.uk

CASHEL, Dean of. *See* KNOWLES, The Very Revd Philip John

CASHEL, WATERFORD AND LISMORE, Archdeacon of. *See* MURRAY, The Ven John Grainger

CASHEL, WATERFORD, LISMORE, OSSORY, FERNS AND LEIGHLIN, Bishop of. *See* BARRETT, The Rt Revd Peter Francis

CASIOT, David John. b 39. St Pet Coll Ox BA63 MA67. Clifton Th Coll 63. **d** 65 **p** 66. C Drypool St Columba w St Andr and St Pet *York* 65-67; C Barking St Marg *Chelmsf* 67-71; R Whalley Range St Edm *Man* 71-84; V Wandsworth St Mich *S'wark* 84-00; Perm to Offic *Roch* from 00; rtd 04. *57 Knighton Road, Otford, Sevenoaks TN14 5LE* Tel (01959) 522588 E-mail david@oakside.idps.co.uk

CASON, Preb Ronald Arthur. b 28. Kelham Th Coll 48. **d** 53 **p** 54. C Fenton *Lich* 53-56; V Brereton 56-63; V Hugglescote w Donington *Leic* 63-67; R Blakenall Heath *Lich* 67-74; R Stoke upon Trent 74-80; Preb Lich Cathl 75-93; RD Stoke 78-88; TR Stoke-upon-Trent 80-91; Lect Tettenhall Par 91-93; rtd 93; Perm to Offic *Lich* 93-00. *130 Main Road, Brereton, Rugeley WS15 1EB* Tel (01889) 582267

CASSAM, Victor Reginald. b 33. Chich Th Coll 59. **d** 62 **p** 63. C Portsea St Jo Rudmore *Portsm* 62-64; C W Leigh CD 64-66; C Torquay St Martin Barton *Ex* 66-69; C Stanmer w Falmer and Moulsecoomb *Chich* 69-73; P-in-c Catsfield 73-76; R Catsfield and Crowhurst 76-81; R Selsey 81-01; RD Chich 96-01; rtd 01; Perm to Offic *Chich* and *Portsm* from 01. *195 Oving Road, Chichester PO19 7ER* Tel and fax (01243) 783998 Mobile 07976-757451 Fax (08701) 209548 E-mail vrc@vicas.demon.co.uk

CASSELTON, John Charles. b 43. Univ of Wales (Swansea) MA95 E Lon Univ Dip Counselling 98. Oak Hill Th Coll 64. **d** 68 **p** 69. C Upton *Ex* 68-73; C Braintree *Chelmsf* 73-80; V Ipswich St Jo *St E* 80-92; RD Ipswich 86-92; Chapl St Clem Hosp Ipswich 92-98; Chapl St Eliz Hospice Ipswich 92-00; Dir Inspire Chr Counselling from 00; Perm to Offic *St E* from 00. *Rose Cottage, 41 North Hill Road, Ipswich IP4 2PN* Tel (01473) 401638 E-mail inspire.ipswich@btclick.com

CASSIDY, Brian Ross. b 31. Cape Town Univ. St Bede's Coll Umtata 88. **d** 89 **p** 91. S Africa 89-92; C Lymington *Win* 92-93; P-in-c Hyde Common 93-96; P-in-c Ellingham and Harbridge and Ibsley 95-96; V Ellingham and Harbridge and Hyde w Ibsley 96-03; rtd 03. *The Vicarage, Hyde, Fordingbridge SP6 2QJ* Tel (01425) 653216 E-mail cassidy@btinternet.com

✠**CASSIDY, The Rt Revd George Henry.** b 42. QUB BSc65 Lon Univ MPhil67. Oak Hill Th Coll 70. **d** 72 **p** 73 **c** 99. C Clifton Ch Ch w Em *Bris* 72-75; V Sea Mills 75-82; V Portman Square St Paul *Lon* 82-87; Adn Lon and Can Res St Paul's Cathl 87-99; P-in-c St Ethelburga Bishopgate 89-91; Bp S'well from 99. *Bishop's Manor, Bishop's Drive, Southwell NG25 0JP* Tel (01636) 812112 Fax 815401 E-mail bishop@southwell.anglican.org

CASSIDY, The Very Revd Herbert. b 35. TCD BA57 MA65. CITC 58. **d** 58 **p** 59. C Belfast H Trin *Conn* 58-60; C Londonderry Ch Ch *D & R* 60-62; I Aghavilly w Derrynoose *Arm* 62-65; Hon V Choral Arm Cathl 63-85; C Portadown St Columba 65-67; I 67-85; Dean Kilmore *K, E & A* 85-89; I Kilmore w Ballintemple 85-86; I Kilmore w Ballintemple, Kildallan etc 86-89; Dir of Ords 89; Dean Arm and Keeper of Public Lib *Arm* from 89; I Arm St Patr from 89; Hon Sec Gen Syn from 90. *The Library, 43 Abbey Street, Armagh BT61 7DY* Tel (028) 3752 3142 Fax 3752 4177 E-mail armroblib@aol.com *or* dean@armagh.anglican.org

CASSIDY, Ian David. b 59. N Ord Course 94. **d** 97 **p** 98. NSM Everton St Geo *Liv* from 97. *79 Gilroy Road, Liverpool L6 6BG* Tel 0151-263 9751 Mobile 0780-1933654

CASSIDY, Canon Joseph Patrick. b 54. Concordia Univ Montreal BA76 Detroit Univ MA80 Toronto Univ STB86 MDiv86 St Paul Univ Ottawa LTh89 DTh95 Ottawa Univ PhD95 FRSA. Toronto Bible Coll 82. **d** 85 **p** 86. Canada 85-96; NSM Laverstock *Sarum* 96-97; NSM Salisbury St Martin 96-97; Prin St Chad's Coll Dur from 97; Hon Can Dur Cathl *Dur* from 01. *St Chad's College, University of Durham, 18 North Bailey, Durham DH1 3RH* Tel 0191-374 3364 *or* 374 3367 Fax 374 3309 E-mail j.p.cassidy@durham.ac.uk

CASSIDY, Patrick Nigel. b 40. TCD BA63 MA66. Sarum Th Coll 64. **d** 66 **p** 67. C Heaton St Barn *Bradf* 66-68; Asst Chapl Brussels *Eur* 68-70; Chapl SW France 70-72; V Oseney Crescent St Luke w Camden Square St Paul *Lon* 72-83; Chapl Strasbourg w Stuttgart and Heidelberg *Eur* 83-84; Perm to Offic *Chich* 86-90; Chapl Marseille w Aix-en-Provence *Eur* 90-05; Hon

Chapl Miss to Seafarers 90-05; rtd 05. *73 La Canebière (Appt 83), 13001 Marseille, France* Tel (0033) (4) 91 90 18 81

CASSIDY, Canon Ronald. b 43. Lon Univ BD66 Man Univ MPhil85. Tyndale Hall Bris 63. **d** 68 **p** 69. C Kirkdale St Lawr *Liv* 68-70; C Bolton Em *Man* 70-74; V Roughtown 74-89; R Denton St Lawr from 89; AD Ashton-under-Lyne 97-03; Hon Can Man Cathl from 02. *St Lawrence's Rectory, 131 Town Lane, Denton, Manchester M34 2DJ* Tel 0161-320 4895 E-mail roncass-99@yahoo.com

CASSON, David Christopher. b 41. Qu Coll Cam BA64 MA68. Ridley Hall Cam 65. **d** 67 **p** 68. C Birm St Martin *Birm* 67-72; C Luton St Mary *St Alb* 72-77; P-in-c 77; V Luton St Fran 77-84; V Richmond H Trin and Ch Ch *S'wark* 84-97; R Acle w Fishley, N Burlingham, Beighton w Moulton *Nor* 97-04; Perm to Offic from 04. *70 The Street, Brundall, Norwich NR13 5LH* Tel (01603) 712092

CASSON, Canon James Stuart. b 32. Liv Univ BA54 Nottm Univ MPhil70. Ridley Hall Cam. **d** 61 **p** 62. C Eccleston Ch Ch *Liv* 61-64; C Littleover *Derby* 64-67; V Dearham *Carl* 67-76; V Holme Eden 76-98; RD Brampton 91-96; Hon Can Carl Cathl 93-98; P-in-c Croglin 93-98; rtd 98; Perm to Offic *Carl* from 01. *5 High Woodbank, Brisco, Carlisle CA4 0QR* Tel (01228) 525692

CASSWELL, David Oriel. b 52. Loughb Coll of Educn DipEd74 Leeds Univ CQSW79. Oak Hill Th Coll DipHE87. **d** 87 **p** 88. C Acomb St Steph *York* 87-91; Dep Chapl HM Pris Leeds 91-92; Chapl HM Pris Everthorpe 92; Chapl HM Pris Wolds 92-98; V Clifton *York* from 98. *Clifton Vicarage, Clifton, York YO30 6BH* Tel (01904) 655071 Fax 654796 E-mail davecass@fish.co.uk

CASSWELL, Canon Peter Joyce. b 22. Trin Coll Cam BA48 MA50. Ridley Hall Cam 48. **d** 50 **p** 51. C Addiscombe St Mildred *Cant* 50-53; C-in-c New Addington CD 53-55; V New Addington 55-64; Chapl Forest Gate Hosp Lon 64-78; R Buckhurst Hill *Chelmsf* 64-78; Hon Can Chelmsf Cathl 75-78; R Lutterworth w Cotesbach *Leic* 78-90; RD Guthlaxton II 89-90; rtd 90; Perm to Offic *Leic* from 90. *1 Spring Close, Lutterworth LE17 4DD* Tel (01455) 554197

CASTER, John Forristall. b 71. Texas A&M Univ BA93. St Steph Ho Ox BTh05. **d** 05. C Hendon St Alphage *Lon* from 05. *18 Montrose Avenue, Edgware HA8 0DW* Tel (020) 8952 1635

✠**CASTLE, The Rt Revd Brian Colin.** b 49. Lon Univ BA72 Ox Univ BA77 MA80 Birm Univ PhD89. Cuddesdon Coll 74. **d** 77 **p** 78 **c** 02. C Sutton St Nic *S'wark* 77; C Limpsfield and Titsey 77-81; USPG Zambia 81-84; Lect Ecum Inst WCC Geneva 84-85; V N Petherton w Northmoor Green *B & W* 85-92; Dir Past Studies and Vice-Prin Cuddesdon Coll 92-01; Suff Bp Tonbridge *Roch* from 02; Hon Can Roch Cathl from 02. *Bishop's Lodge, 48 St Botolph's Road, Sevenoaks TN13 3AG* Tel (01732) 456070 Fax 741449 E-mail bishop.tonbridge@rochester.anglican.org

CASTLE, Brian Stanley. b 47. Oak Hill Th Coll 70. **d** 73 **p** 74. C Barnsbury St Andr w St Thos and St Matthias *Lon* 73-76; C Lower Homerton St Paul 76-79; P-in-c Bethnal Green St Jas Less 79-98; V Tile Cross *Birm* from 98; P-in-c Garretts Green from 03. *The Vicarage, Haywood Road, Birmingham B33 0LH* Tel and fax 0121-779 2739 Mobile 07710-251790 E-mail revbcastle@aol.com

CASTLE, John Arthur. b 61. G&C Coll Cam BA83 St Jo Coll Dur BA95. Aston Tr Scheme 90 Cranmer Hall Dur 92. **d** 95 **p** 96. C Southborough St Pet w Ch Ch and St Matt *Roch* 95-99; Miss Partner CMS 99-04; P-in-c Sandhurst *Ox* from 04. *The Rectory, 155 High Street, Sandhurst GU47 8HR* Tel (01252) 872168

CASTLE, Michael David. b 38. Wells Th Coll 69. **d** 71 **p** 72. C Acocks Green *Birm* 71-75; C Weoley Castle 76-78; V from 78. *St Gabriel's Vicarage, 83 Marston Road, Birmingham B29 5LS* Tel 0121-475 1194

CASTLE, Phillip Stanley. b 43. LNSM course 94. **d** 97 **p** 98. OLM E Farnworth and Kearsley *Man* from 97. *73 Bradford Street, Farnworth, Bolton BL4 9JY* Tel (01204) 571439

CASTLE, Roger James. b 39. St Jo Coll Cam BA62 MA66. Clifton Th Coll 63. **d** 65 **p** 66. C Rushden w Newton Bromswold *Pet* 65-68; C Stapenhill w Cauldwell *Derby* 68-72; V Hayfield 72-89; R Coxheath, E Farleigh, Hunton, Linton etc *Roch* 89-04; Chapl Invicta Community Care NHS Trust 91-04; rtd 04. *11 Royal Close, Bristol BS10 7XF* Tel 0117-950 7028 E-mail rjcastle@fish.co.uk

CASTLE, Vincent Clifton. b 15. ALCD37 St Jo Coll Dur LTh38 BA39. **d** 39 **p** 40. C Moulsham St Jo *Chelmsf* 39-42; CF (EC) 42-47 and 54-58; C-in-c Oakdale St Geo CD *Sarum* 47-50; P-in-c Coalpit Heath *Bris* 50-54; V Avonmouth St Andr 58-63; Miss to Seamen 63-71; V Creeksea w Althorne *Chelmsf* 71-79; RD Dengie 74-82; V Creeksea w Althorne, Latchingdon and N Fambridge 80-82; rtd 82; Perm to Offic *Chelmsf* from 82. *49 Winstree Road, Burnham-on-Crouch CM0 8ET* Tel (01621) 782807

CASTLETON, David Miles. b 39. Oak Hill Th Coll 69. **d** 72 **p** 73. C Canonbury St Steph *Lon* 72-76; C Guildf St Sav w Stoke-next-Guildford *Guildf* 76-89; rtd 04. *2 Lyne Place Manor, Bridge Lane, Virginia Water GU25 4ED*

CASWELL, Roger John. b 47. St Chad's Coll Dur BA70. St Steph Ho Ox 75. **d** 77 **p** 78. C Brighton Resurr *Chich* 77-83; TV Crawley 83-90; TR Littlehampton and Wick from 90; Chapl Littlehampton Hosp 90-93; Chapl Worthing Priority Care NHS Trust from 93. *St Mary's Vicarage, 34 Fitzalan Road, Littlehampton BN17 5ET* Tel (01903) 724410 *or* 726875

CASWELL, Thomas Hubert. b 55. Aston Tr Scheme 90 Coll of Resurr Mirfield 92. **d** 94 **p** 95. C Sheff St Leon Norwood *Sheff* 94-97; P-in-c Sheff St Cecilia Parson Cross 97-04; V Masbrough from 04. *St Paul's Vicarage, 256 Kimberworth Road, Rotherham S61 1HG* Tel (01709) 557810

CATCHPOLE, Geoffrey Alan. b 53. AKC. Westcott Ho Cam 76. **d** 77 **p** 78. C Camberwell St Luke *S'wark* 77-80; C Dulwich St Barn 80-82; TV Canvey Is *Chelmsf* 82-87; Ind Chapl 83-87; P-in-c Bradwell on Sea 87-92; P-in-c St Lawrence 87-92; V Holland-on-Sea 92-00; P-in-c Witchford w Wentworth *Ely* 00-02; Adult Educn and Tr Officer 00-02; R Colchester St Mich Myland *Chelmsf* from 02. *Myland Rectory, Rectory Close, Colchester CO4 5DN* Tel (01206) 853076 E-mail ole@pole97.fsnet.co.uk

CATCHPOLE, Guy St George. b 30. **d** 82 **p** 83. Kenya 82-89; C Woodford Wells *Chelmsf* 89-95; rtd 95; Perm to Offic *Cant* from 95. *67 Trevor Drive, Allington, Maidstone ME16 0QW* Tel (01622) 761378

CATCHPOLE, Canon Keith William. b 30. MBE98. AKC56. St Boniface Warminster 54. **d** 57 **p** 58. C Woodchurch *Ches* 57-61; C W Kirby St Bridget 61-64; C-in-c Upton Priory CD 64-72; R Lavant *Chich* 72-82; RD Chich 80-96; Can and Preb Chich Cathl 82-99; V Chich St Paul and St Pet 82-95; P-in-c W Hampnett 91-95; TR Chich 95-99; rtd 99; Perm to Offic *Chich* from 01. *23 Ninevah Shipyard, Arundel BN18 9SU* Tel (01903) 885340

CATCHPOLE, Richard James Swinburne. b 65. St Steph Ho Ox 92. **d** 95 **p** 96. C Eastbourne St Andr *Chich* 95-98; C Eastbourne St Mary 98-00; C E Grinstead St Swithun from 00. *St Luke's House, Holtye Avenue, East Grinstead RH19 3EG* Tel (01342) 323800

CATCHPOLE, Roy. b 46. Sheff Univ MMinTheol95. St Jo Coll Nottm LTh74 ALCD74. **d** 74 **p** 75. C Rainham *Chelmsf* 74-76; C Hyson Green *S'well* 76-79; V Broxtowe 79-86; V Calverton 86-94; Hilfield Friary Dorchester 95-01; rtd 01. *60 Gainsborough, Milborne Port, Sherborne DT9 5BB* Tel (01963) 250040 E-mail rev.catch@virgin.net

CATER, Lois May. b 37. S Dios Minl Tr Scheme 81. **dss** 84 **d** 87 **p** 94. Calne and Blackland *Sarum* 84-89; Hon Par Dn 87-89; Hon Par Dn Devizes St Jo w St Mary 89-94; Hon C 94-96; Hon TV Alderbury Team 96-01; Hon TV Clarendon from 01. *18 St Margaret's Close, Calne SN11 0UQ* Tel (01249) 819432 E-mail 106257.17@compuserve.com

CATERER, James Albert Leslie Blower. b 44. New Coll Ox BA67 MA81. Sarum & Wells Th Coll 79. **d** 81 **p** 82. C Cheltenham St Luke and St Jo *Glouc* 81-85; V Standish w Haresfield and Moreton Valence etc 85-96; P-in-c Glouc St Steph from 96. *St Stephen's Vicarage, 84 Frampton Road, Gloucester GL1 5QB* Tel (01452) 524694 Fax as telephone E-mail jcaterer@atlas.co.uk

CATHCART, Adrian James. *See* MATTHEWS, Adrian James

CATHERALL, Mark Leslie. b 64. Chich Th Coll BTh93. **d** 93 **p** 94. C Lancing w Coombes *Chich* 93-95; C Selsey 95-98; Chapl RN 98-04; V S Thornaby *York* from 04. *St Peter's Rectory, White House Road, Thornaby, Stockton-on-Tees TS17 0AJ* Tel (01642) 888403

CATHERINE JOY, Sister. *See* MOON, Sister Catherine Joy

CATHIE, Sean Bewley. b 43. Dur Univ BA67. Cuddesdon Coll 67. **d** 69 **p** 70. C Kensal Rise St Martin *Lon* 69-73; C Paddington H Trin w St Paul 73-75; P-in-c Bridstow w Peterstow *Heref* 76-79; Hon C Westmr St Jas *Lon* 85-97; Hon C St Marylebone w H Trin from 99; Hon C St Marylebone St Cypr from 99. *23 Brookfield Mansions, Highgate West Hill, London N6 6AS* Tel (020) 8340 6603 *or* tel and and fax 8347 7050 E-mail scathie@waitrose.com

CATLEY, John Howard. b 37. AKC60. K Coll Lon 57 St Boniface Warminster 60. **d** 61 **p** 62. C Sowerby Bridge w Norland *Wakef* 61-64; C Almondbury 64-67; V Earl's Heaton 67-75; V Brownhill 75-86; V Morley St Pet w Churwell 86-92; V St Annes St Marg *Blackb* 92-98; RD Kirkham 94-98; rtd 98; Perm to Offic *Blackb* from 98. *Flat 6, Herne Hill Lodge, 598 Lytham Road, Blackpool FY4 1RB* Tel (01253) 408129

CATLING, Michael David. b 56. Goldsmiths' Coll Lon CertEd77 DipEd84 Whitelands Coll Lon DipC&S88. Cranmer Hall Dur 88. **d** 90 **p** 91. C Cullercoats St Geo *Newc* 90-94; TV Glendale Gp 94-01; V Whittingham and Edlingham w Bolton Chapel from 01. *The Vicarage, Whittingham, Alnwick NE66 4UP* Tel (01665) 574704 E-mail mike@catlingfamily.fsnet.co.uk

CATLING, Canon Robert Mason. b 19. St Jo Coll Ox BA41 MA44. St Steph Ho Ox 41. **d** 43 **p** 44. C Falmouth All SS *Truro* 43-57; Lib Pusey Ho 57-61; Asst Chapl Univ Coll Ox 57-61; C Falmouth All SS *Truro* 61-64; V Beckenham St Barn *Roch* 64-72; V Devoran *Truro* 72-87; Hon Can Truro Cathl 77-87; rtd 87;

Perm to Offic *Ex* and *Truro* from 87. *Ground Floor Flat, 31 Cranford Avenue, Exmouth EX8 2QA* Tel (01395) 267896

CATO (formerly LEGGETT), Ms Vanessa Gisela. b 51. St Osyth Coll of Educn TCert75. Westcott Ho Cam 93. **d** 93 **p** 94. C Southchurch H Trin *Chelmsf* 93-97; R Orsett and Bulphan and Horndon on the Hill 97-03; Chapl Basildon and Thurrock Gen Hosps NHS Trust 99-03; P-in-c Sandridge *St Alb* from 03; Herts Area Children's Work Adv from 03. *The Vicarage, 2 Anson Close, Sandridge, St Albans AL4 9EN* Tel (01727) 866089 E-mail vgcato@fish.co.uk

CATON, David Arthur. b 25. Trin Coll Ox BA50 MA50. St Steph Ho Ox 49. **d** 51 **p** 52. C Seaton Hirst *Newc* 51-55; S Africa 55-61; V Stapleford *Ely* 61-69; V Hurst *Man* 69-75; V Hanwell St Thos *Lon* 75-84; AD Ealing W 82-84; V Staincross *Wakef* 84-95; rtd 95; Perm to Offic *Lon* from 95. *39 Beardsley Way, London W3 7YQ* Tel (020) 8743 2126

CATON, Philip Cooper. b 47. Oak Hill Th Coll 79. **d** 81 **p** 82. C Much Woolton *Liv* 81-85; TV Parr 85-98; V Birkdale St Jo from 98. *St John's Vicarage, 17 Kirkstall Road, Southport PR8 4RA* Tel (01704) 568318 E-mail caton@dircon.co.uk

CATT, Albert Henry. b 08. St Steph Ho Ox 34. **d** 37 **p** 38. C Somers Town *Lon* 37-40; CF (EC) 40-46; Hon CF from 46; C Harrow St Pet *Lon* 46-48; V Hornsey St Geo 49-74; rtd 74; Perm to Offic *Ely* 75-88. *c/o A Catt Esq, 3 The Conifers, Oundle Road, Peterborough PE2 5WL* Tel (01733) 234329 *or* 372148 Fax 372402

CATT, Douglas Gordon. b 23. MCSP49 SRP67. Roch Th Coll 61. **d** 63 **p** 64. C Cant St Martin w St Paul *Cant* 63-66; R Croughton *Pet* 66-75; R Hinton in the Hedges w Steane 66-75; V Evenley 72-75; Chapl St Andr Hosp Northn 75-89; rtd 88; Perm to Offic *Pet* from 88. *195 Billing Road, Northampton NN1 5RS* Tel (01604) 27710

CATTELL, The Ven Jack. b 15. Univ Coll Dur BA37 DipTh38 MA40 Lon Univ BD53. Sarum & Wells Th Coll 38. **d** 39 **p** 40. C Royston *Wakef* 39-41; Perm to Offic *Sarum* 41-42; CF (EC) 42-46; Lic to Offic *Ripon* 46-49; Chapl R Wanstead Sch 49-53; Bermuda 53-82; Adn Bermuda 61-82; Perm to Offic *Mon* 82-89. *39A Risca Road, Newport NP9 4HX* Tel (01633) 54529

CATTERALL, David Arnold. b 53. Lon Univ BSc74 ARCS74. Cranmer Hall Dur DipTh78. **d** 78 **p** 79. C Swinton St Pet *Man* 78-81; C Wythenshawe St Martin 81-83; R Heaton Norris Ch w All SS 83-88; I Fanlobbus Union *C, C & R* 88-95; Can Cork and Ross Cathls 93-95; Warden Ch's Min of Healing in Ireland 95-02; I Templemichael w Clongish, Clooncumber etc *K, E & A* from 02. *Amberley, The Belfry, Abbeycartron, Co Longford, Irish Republic* E-mail djcatt@eircom.net

CATTERALL, Mrs Janet Margaret. b 53. Univ of Wales (Ban) BA74. Cranmer Hall Dur 77. **dss** 81 **d** 87 **p** 90. Wythenshawe St Martin *Man* 81-83; Heaton Norris Ch w All SS 83-87; Par Dn 87-88; C Bandon Union *C, C & R* 88-89; Dioc Youth Adv (Cork) 89-94; Dioc Youth Chapl 94-95; I Drung w Castleterra, Larah and Lavey etc *K, E & A* 95-02; P-in-c Mostrim w Granard, Clonbroney, Killoe etc from 02. *Amberley, The Belfry, Abbeycartron, Co Longford, Irish Republic* E-mail djcatt@eircom.net

CATTERICK, Matthew John. b 68. W Sussex Inst of HE BA92. St Steph Ho Ox BTh95. **d** 95 **p** 96. C Colchester St Jas, All SS, St Nic and St Runwald *Chelmsf* 95-98; C Leic Resurr *Leic* 98-99; TV 99-04; TR Wembley Park *Lon* from 04. *The Vicarage, 319 Preston Road, Harrow HA3 0QQ* Tel (020) 8904 4062 Fax 8908 2207 E-mail matthew.catterick@ntlworld.com

CATTLE, Canon Richard John. b 40. WMMTC 88. **d** 90 **p** 91. NSM Brixworth Deanery *Pet* 90-91; NSM Welford w Sibbertoft and Marston Trussell 91-92; V 92-97; Bp's Dioc Chapl 97-00; Dioc Sec 98-00; Can Pet Cathl 98-02; rtd 01; Perm to Offic *Pet* from 02. *PO Box 1617, Newport Pagnell MK16 0ZU* Tel (01908) 830250

CATTLEY, Richard Melville. b 49. Trin Coll Bris. **d** 73 **p** 74. C Kendal St Thos *Carl* 73-77; Nat Sec Pathfinders CPAS 77-82; Exec Sec 82-85; V Dalton-in-Furness *Carl* 85-90; V Dulwich St Barn *S'wark* 90-99; Chapl Alleyn's Foundn Dulwich 90-99; V Milton Keynes *Ox* 99-05; AD Milton Keynes 01-05; V Dorking w Ranmore *Guildf* from 05. *St Martin's Vicarage, Westcott Road, Dorking RH4 3DN* Tel (01306) 882875 *or* 884229 E-mail richardmcattley@aol.com

CATTON, Canon Cedric Trevor. b 36. JP. Lambeth STh94 Wells Th Coll 70. **d** 72 **p** 73. C Solihull *Birm* 72-74; R Whepstead w Brockley *St E* 74-75; R Hawstead and Nowton w Stanningfield etc 74-79; Dioc Stewardship Adv 77-83; R Cockfield 79-83; V Exning St Martin w Landwade 83-99; Chapl Newmarket Gen Hosp 85-93; Chapl Mid Anglia Community Health NHS Trust 93-99; Hon Can St E Cathl *St E* 90-02; Chapl Dioc MU from 94; Dioc Par Resources and Stewardship Officer 99-02; Asst Can Past St E Cathl 02; rtd 02. *60 Sextons Meadows, Bury St Edmunds IP33 2SB* Tel and fax (01284) 749429 E-mail moretee@vicar1.freeserve.co.uk

CATTON, Stanley Charles. b 44. OLM course 96. **d** 99 **p** 00. OLM Bermondsey St Jas w Ch Ch and St Crispin *S'wark* from 99. *4 Reverdy Road, London SE1 5QE* Tel (020) 7237 7703

CAUDWELL, Juliet Lesley. *See* STRAW, Mrs Juliet Lesley

CAUNT, Mrs Margaret. b 55. Coll of Ripon & York St Jo MA97. N Ord Course 93. **d** 97 **p** 98. NSM Brightside w Wincobank *Sheff* 97-00; C Ecclesfield 00-02; TV Gleadless from 02. *St Peter's Vicarage, 51 White Lane, Sheffield S12 3ED* Tel 0114-239 6132

CAVAGAN, Raymond. b 35. Hull Univ MA86 PhD87. **d** 63 **p** 64. C Upper Holloway St Pet *Lon* 63-66; C Hurworth *Dur* 66-68; V New Shildon 68-76; V Toxteth Park St Mich *Liv* 76-77; P-in-c Toxteth Park St Andr Aigburth Road 76-77; V Toxteth Park St Mich w St Andr 78-88; V Stamfordham w Matfen *Newc* 88-05; Hon CF from 90; rtd 05. *1 Leys Road, Timperley, Altrincham WA14 5AT* Tel 0161-969 5603

CAVAGHAN, Dennis Edgar. b 45. Ex Univ MA99. St Jo Coll Nottm BTh74. **d** 74 **p** 75. C Hartford *Ches* 74-77; C Plymouth St Andr w St Paul and St Geo *Ex* 77-80; V Cofton w Starcross 80-88; P-in-c W Exe 88-93; Perm to Offic *B & W* 93-02; Hon C Taunton St Mary from 02. *Combe House, Corfe, Taunton TA3 7BU* Tel (01823) 421013

CAVALCANTI, Joabe Gomes. b 69. Federal Univ of Pernambuco BA97 Trin Coll Bris MA00. Nordeste Th Sem BA91. **d** 98 **p** 98. Perm to Offic *Bris* 99 and *S'wark* 01-05; Chapl St Sav and St Olave's Sch Newington *S'wark* from 05; C Bermondsey St Hugh CD from 05. *54 Balin House, Long Lane, London SE1 1YH* Tel (020) 7207 9767 Mobile 07960-157468 E-mail joabegcavalcanti@yahoo.co.uk

CAVALIER, Mrs Sandra Jane. b 48. Guildf Dioc Min Course 98. **d** 00 **p** 01. OLM Guildf Ch Ch w St Martha-on-the-Hill *Guildf* 00-04; NSM Westborough from 04. *10 The Greenwood, Guildford GU1 2ND* Tel (01483) 822496 Mobile 07990-658445 E-mail sandy.cavalier@ntlworld.com

CAVAN, Lawrence Noel. b 38. Trin Coll Bris 72. **d** 75 **p** 76. C Lurgan Ch the Redeemer *D & D* 75-78; C Chorleywood Ch Ch *St Alb* 78-82; I Durrus *C, C & R* 82-85; I Portarlington w Cloneyhurke and Lea *M & K* 85-90; TV Eston w Normanby *York* 90-03; rtd 03. *22 Wentworth Road, Dronfield Woodhouse, Dronfield S18 8ZU* Tel (01246) 418814

CAVANAGH, Anthony James. b 49. Ushaw Coll Dur 72. **d** 79 **p** 80. In RC Ch 79-95; C Goole *Sheff* 99-01; TV Cullercoats St Geo *Newc* from 01. *St Hilda's Vicarage, Preston Gate, North Shields NE29 9QB* Tel 0191-257 6595

CAVANAGH, Capt Kenneth Joseph. b 41. CA Tr Coll 60. **d** 77 **p** 77. CA from 64; Paraguay 70-83; P-in-c Gt w Lt Snoring *Nor* 83-85; R Gt w Lt Snoring w Kettlestone and Pensthorpe 85-88; R Glencarse *Bre* 88-94; CA Co-ord (Scotland/Ireland) & Regional Voc Adv 90-95; R Dundee St Luke from 95. *The Rectory, 4 St Luke's Road, Downfield, Dundee DD3 0LD* Tel and fax (01382) 825165 E-mail cavanagh@tinyworld.co.uk

CAVANAGH, Lorraine Marie. b 46. Lucy Cavendish Coll Cam BA97 MA01 PhD03. Ridley Hall Cam 00. **d** 01 **p** 02. Perm to Offic *Ely* 01-03; Chapl Fitzw Coll Cam 03; Chapl Univ of Wales (Cardiff) *Llan* from 04. *The Anglican Chaplaincy, 61 Park Place, Cardiff CF10 3AT* Tel and fax (029) 2023 2550 E-mail lorraine@lmcav.net

CAVANAGH, Michael Richard. b 49. Salford Univ MSc00. N Ord Course 89. **d** 92 **p** 93. NSM Stalybridge H Trin and Ch Ch *Ches* 92-98; P-in-c Over Tabley and High Legh 98-03; V from 03. *The Vicarage, The Avenue, High Legh, Knutsford WA16 6ND* Tel (01925) 753612 Fax 753216 Mobile 07767-771599 E-mail michael@balmoralconsulting.co.uk

CAVANAGH, Canon Peter Bernard. b 49. Sarum & Wells Th Coll 71. **d** 73 **p** 74. C Gt Crosby St Faith *Liv* 73-76; C Stanley 76-79; V Anfield St Columba 79-97; V Lancaster St Mary w St John and St Anne *Blackb* from 97; Hon Can Blackb Cathl from 00. *The Vicarage, Priory Close, Lancaster LA1 1YZ* Tel and fax (01524) 63200 E-mail manderley@ic24.net

CAVE, Anthony Sidney. b 32. EMMTC. **d** 84 **p** 85. C Immingham *Linc* 84-88; V Keelby 88-89; V Riby 88-89; V Keelby w Riby and Aylesby 89-98; rtd 99; Perm to Offic *Linc* from 00. *Polruan, The Bungalow, Cherry Lane, Barrow-upon-Humber DN19 7AX* Tel (01469) 532350

CAVE, Bill. *See* CAVE-BROWNE-CAVE, Bernard James William

CAVE, Brian Malcolm. b 37. St Cath Soc Ox BA60 MA64. Oak Hill Th Coll. **d** 63 **p** 64. C Streatham Park St Alb *S'wark* 63-66; C Ruskin Park St Sav and St Matt 66-68; C Tunbridge Wells St Jas *Roch* 68-71; V Bootle St Leon *Liv* 71-75; Min St Mary w St John Bootle 73-75; Area Sec Leprosy Miss 75-81; V Hurst Green *Bradf* 81-82; P-in-c Mitton 81-82; V Hurst Green and Mitton 82-91; rtd 91; Perm to Offic *B & W* from 97. *63 Westway, Nailsea, Bristol BS48 2NB* Tel (01275) 654892

CAVE, Cyril Hayward. b 20. Nottm Univ MA60 BD63. AKC49. **d** 50 **p** 51. C Upholland *Liv* 50-53; P-in-c Darley w S Darley *Derby* 53-56; V Ticknall 56-65; Lic to Offic *Ex* 65-95; Lect Th Ex Univ 65-80; Sen Lect 80-85; rtd 85; Perm to Offic *Ex* from 95. *Berry House, Cheriton Fitzpaine, Crediton EX17 4HZ* Tel (01363) 866548

CAVE, Douglas Lionel. b 26. Lon Bible Coll 50 Lon Coll of Div 64. **d** 66 **p** 67. C Upper Holloway St Jo *Lon* 66-69; C Barking

St Marg *Chelmsf* 69-73; V Blackb St Barn *Blackb* 73-81; Ind Chapl *Lon* 81-91; rtd 91; Perm to Offic *Lon* from 93. *8 Wood Rise, Pinner HA5 2JD* Tel (01895) 677426

CAVE, The Ven Guy Newell. b 19. TCD BA41 MA58. CITC 41. **d** 42 **p** 43. C Knockbreda *D & D* 42-45; P-in-c Kildrumferton w Ballymachugh *K, E & A* 45-73; Preb St Patr Cathl Dublin 65-72; Adn Kilmore *K, E & A* 72-87; P-in-c Ballymachugh w Kildrumferton and Ballyjamesduff 73-87; rtd 87. *5 Yew Point, Hodson's Bay, Athlone, Co Westmeath, Irish Republic* Tel (00353) (90) 649 2718

CAVE, John Edwin Dawson. b 43. Cranmer Hall Dur 71. **d** 74 **p** 75. C Gt Ayton w Easby and Newton in Cleveland *York* 74-77; C Redcar w Kirkleatham 77-78; C Redcar 78-80; P-in-c Aislaby and Ruswarp 80-81; V 81-87; V Dormanstown 87-97; V Marton-in-Cleveland 97-00; P-in-c Bilborough St Jo *S'well* from 01; P-in-c Bilborough w Strelley from 01. *St John's Vicarage, Graylands Road, Nottingham NG8 4FD* Tel 0115-929 3320 E-mail revjohncave@bilborough.fsnet.co.uk

CAVE, Mrs Rachel Mary. b 53. Warwick Univ BA75. N Ord Course 98. **d** 01 **p** 02. NSM Gomersal *Wakef* 01-04; NSM Scholes from 04; NSM Cleckheaton St Luke and Whitechapel from 04. *Yew Tree Hall, 13 Leeds Road, Mirfield WF14 0BY* Tel (01924) 480666 E-mail robertcave@msn.com

CAVE, Robert Philip. b 23. Roch Th Coll 64. **d** 67 **p** 68. C York Town St Mich *Guildf* 67-71; C Yaxley *Ely* 71-75; R Cottenham 75-88; rtd 88; Perm to Offic *Pet* from 89. *14 St Mary's Way, Roade, Northampton NN7 2PQ* Tel (01604) 864420

CAVE BERGQUIST, Julie Anastasia. b 59. St Jo Coll Dur BA80 Franciscan Univ Rome STL87. St Steph Ho Ox 85. **d** 87 **p** 98. Par Dn Kennington *Cant* 87-89; Chapl Trin Coll Cam 89-94; Chapl Westcott Ho Cam 94-97; C St Alb St Steph *St Alb* 98-02; P-in-c S Kensington H Trin w All SS *Lon* from 02; Dir of Ords Two Cities Area from 02. *St John's House, St John's Wood High Street, London NW8 7NE* Tel (020) 7722 4378 *or* 7449 9681 E-mail julescb@london.anglican.org

CAVE-BROWNE-CAVE, Bernard James William (Bill). b 54. Trin Hall Cam BA76 MA80 Bradf Univ MA90. Westcott Ho Cam 77. **d** 79 **p** 80. C Chesterton Gd Shep *Ely* 79-83; Chapl Lanc Univ *Blackb* 83-95; Chapl HM Pris Service from 95. *HM Prison Service Chaplaincy, Abell House, John Islip Street, London SW1P 4LH* Tel (020) 7217 5685 Fax 7217 5090 E-mail bill@cave_browne_cave.freeserve.co.uk

CAVEEN, David Francis. b 44. Univ of Wales (Cardiff) BSc66 DipEd67. STETS DipTh95. **d** 98 **p** 99. C Swaythling *Win* 98-02; V Lord's Hill from 02. *The Vicarage, 1 Tangmere Drive, Southampton SO16 8GY* Tel (023) 8073 1182 E-mail davidcaveen@tinyworld.co.uk

✠**CAVELL, The Rt Revd John Kingsmill.** b 16. Qu Coll Cam BA39 MA44. Wycliffe Hall Ox 39. **d** 40 **p** 41 **c** 72. C Folkestone H Trin *Cant* 40; C Addington 40-44; Lic to Offic *Ox* 45-52; Area Sec (Dio Ox) CMS 44-52; Dio Pet 44-49; Tr Officer 49-52; V Cheltenham Ch Ch *Glouc* 52-62; V Plymouth St Andr *Ex* 62-72; RD Plymouth 67-72; Preb Ex Cathl 67-72; V E Stonehouse 68-72; Suff Bp Southampton *Win* 72-84; Hon Can Win Cathl 72-84; rtd 84; Perm to Offic *Win* from 84; Hon Asst Bp Sarum from 88; Can and Preb Sarum Cathl from 88. *143 The Close, Salisbury SP1 2EY* Tel (01722) 334782 Fax 413112

CAVELL-NORTHAM, Canon Cavell Herbert James. b 32. St Steph Ho Ox 53. **d** 56 **p** 57. C W Wycombe *Ox* 56-61; CF (TA) 60-63; V Lane End *Ox* 61-68; V Stony Stratford 68-97; P-in-c Calverton 69-72; R 72-97; Hon Can Ch Ch 91-97; rtd 97; Lic to Offic *Ox* 97-04; Perm to Offic from 04. *The Glebe House, Finings Road, Lane End, High Wycombe HP14 3EU* Tel (01494) 881552

CAW (née FINLAY), Alison Mary. b 40. Natal Univ BA62 Ox Univ PGCE64. Ox Min Course CBTS93. **d** 93 **p** 94. NSM Beaconsfield *Ox* 93-04; NSM Penn and Tylers Green from 04. *1 Westway, Beaconsfield HP9 1DQ* Tel (01494) 674524

CAW, Hannah Mary. *See* JEFFERY, Mrs Hannah Mary

CAWDELL, Mrs Sarah Helen Louise. b 65. St Hugh's Coll Ox BA88 St Hugh's Coll Ox MA91 Trin Coll Cam BA94 MA99 K Coll Lon MA99. Ridley Hall Cam CTM95. **d** 95 **p** 96. C Belmont *S'wark* 95-98; Perm to Offic *Heref* 98-00; NSM Claverley w Tuckhill from 00. *The Vicarage, Lodge Park, Claverley, Wolverhampton WV5 7DP* Tel (01746) 710268 E-mail s.h.cawdell@btinternet.com

CAWDELL, Simon Howard. b 65. Univ Coll Dur BA86 K Coll Lon MA99. Ridley Hall Cam CTM94. **d** 94 **p** 95. C Cheam Common St Phil *S'wark* 94-98; V Claverley w Tuckhill *Heref* from 98. *The Vicarage, Lodge Park, Claverley, Wolverhampton WV5 7DP* Tel (01746) 710268 E-mail s.h.cawdell@btinternet.com

CAWLEY, David Lewis. b 44. FSA81. AKC71 St Aug Coll Cant 71. **d** 72 **p** 73. C Sprowston *Nor* 72-75; Chapl HM Pris Nor 74-75; C Wymondham *Nor* 75-77; C Buckland in Dover w Buckland Valley *Cant* 77-83; V Eastville St Anne w St Mark and St Thos *Bris* 83-95; V Leic St Mary *Leic* from 95; TV Leic H Spirit from 97; Chapl Trin Hosp Leic from 96. *The Vicarage, 15 Castle Street, Leicester LE1 5WN* Tel 0116-262 8727 E-mail dave@dcawley.worldonline.co.uk

CAWLEY, Stephen. b 42. GRSM63 ARMCM63. St Deiniol's Hawarden 81. **d** 84 **p** 85. C Tranmere St Paul w St Luke *Ches* 84-88; TV Hawarden *St As* 88-93; V Gwernaffield and Llanferres 93-02; V Gorsedd w Brynford, Ysgeifiog and Whitford from 02. *The Vicarage, Babell Road, Gorsedd, Holywell CH8 8RB* Tel (01352) 711675

CAWRSE, Christopher William. b 60. Birkbeck Coll Lon BA97 Qu Mary and Westf Coll Lon MA00. Westcott Ho Cam 82. **d** 84 **p** 85. C Stoke Newington St Mary *Lon* 84-86; Chapl St Mark's Hosp Lon 86-90; C Islington St Jas w St Pet *Lon* 86-90; Chapl Asst Charing Cross Hosp Lon 90-93; Perm to Offic *Lon* from 93. *34 Spring Way, Sible Hedingham, Halstead CO9 3SB* Tel (01787) 463645 E-mail chris@cawrse.freeserve.co.uk

CAWTE, Canon David John. b 30. St Mich Coll Llan. **d** 65 **p** 66. C Chorley St Laur *Blackb* 65-67; C Boyne Hill *Ox* 67-74; C-in-c Cox Green CD 75-78; V Cox Green 78-94; Hon Can Ch Ch 88-94; rtd 94; Perm to Offic *Win* from 94. *6 Broadfields Close, Milford on Sea, Lymington SO41 0SE* Tel (01590) 642793 E-mail david.cawte@tinyworld.co.uk

CAWTE, Martin Charles. b 51. Jes Coll Ox BA73 MA77 Lanchester Poly IPFA77. SEITE 97. **d** 00 **p** 01. NSM Sanderstead All SS *S'wark* 00-03; Perm to Offic *Ox* from 03. *9 Night Owls, Pinchington Lane, Greenham, Newbury RG19 8FB* Tel (01635) 32636 Mobile 07808-143809 E-mail martin_cawte@hotmail.com

CAWTHORNE, Jack. b 22. ATD50 Lon Univ DipTh71. Cuddesdon Coll 69. **d** 71 **p** 72. NSM Newchurch *Man* 71-86; NSM Garforth *Ripon* 87-88; Perm to Offic from 88. *15 Arran Drive, Garforth, Leeds LS25 2BU* Tel 0113-286 9527 Mobile 077451-325559

CAWTHORNE, Paul Howarth. b 66. St Hild Coll Dur BA88. Cuddesdon Coll 98. **d** 98 **p** 99. C Cen Telford *Lich* 98-01; TV Wrockwardine Deanery from 01. *The Vicarage, Eaton Constantine, Shrewsbury SY5 6RF* Tel (01952) 510333 E-mail paul@cawthorne52.fsnet.co.uk

CAYTON, John. b 32. Bps' Coll Cheshunt 54. **d** 57 **p** 58. C Hindley All SS *Liv* 57-59; C Littleham w Exmouth *Ex* 59-63; V Burnley St Cath *Blackb* 63-72; V Marton 72-87; V Fleetwood St Pet 87-97; Miss to Seamen 87-97; rtd 97; Perm to Offic *Blackb* from 97. *19 Parkstone Avenue, Thornton-Cleveleys FY5 5AE* Tel (01253) 854088

CECIL, Kevin Vincent. b 54. BA PGCE. St Mich Coll Llan. **d** 82 **p** 83. C Llanilid w Pencoed *Llan* 82-85; C Coity w Nolton 85-88; Area Co-ord CMS *St D, Llan, Mon* and *S & B* 88-05; P-in-c Dixton *Heref* from 05. *The Vicarage, 38 Hillcrest Road, Wyesham, Monmouth NP25 3LH* Tel (01600) 712565

CECILE, Sister. *See* HARRISON, Sister Cécile

CEELY, Ms Sandra Elizabeth. b 44. N Ord Course 94. **d** 97 **p** 98. C Gt and Lt Driffield *York* 97-98; C S Cave and Ellerker w Broomfleet 98-01; Chapl Hull and E Yorks Hosps NHS Trust from 02. *The Chaplaincy, Castle Hill Hospital, Castle Road, Cottingham HU16 5JQ* Tel (01482) 875875 *or* 624154 E-mail sandra@sandra-ceely.fsnet.co.uk *or* sandra.ceely@hey.nhs.uk

CENTRAL AFRICA, Archbishop of. *See* MALANGO, The Most Revd Bernard Amos

CENTRAL MELANESIA, Bishop of. *See* POGO, The Most Revd Sir Ellison Leslie

CERMAKOVA, Helena Maria Alija. b 43. **d** 88 **p** 95. NSM Roath *Llan* 88-91; Westcott Ho Cam 91-92; Asst Chapl Univ Hosp of Wales Cardiff 92-95; Chapl United Bris Healthcare NHS Trust 95-99; Chapl Jersey Gp of Hosps from 99. *Chaplain's Office, General Hospital, Gloucester Street, St Helier, Jersey JE1 3QS* E-mail hss34@psilink.co.uk

CERRATTI, Christa Elisabeth. b 54. Ox Coll FE NNEB93. Wycliffe Hall Ox DipMin94. **d** 97 **p** 98. C Chipping Norton *Ox* 97-00; P-in-c Lavendon w Cold Brayfield, Clifton Reynes etc from 00; Deanery Youth Co-ord from 00. *The New Rectory, 7A Northampton Road, Lavendon, Olney MK46 4EY* Tel (01234) 240013

CHADD, Jeremy Denis. b 55. Jes Coll Cam BA77 MA81. Coll of Resurr Mirfield 78. **d** 81 **p** 82. C Seaton Hirst *Newc* 81-84; C N Gosforth 84-88; V Sunderland St Chad *Dur* from 88. *St Chad's Vicarage, Charter Drive, Sunderland SR3 3PG* Tel 0191-528 2397

CHADD, Canon Leslie Frank. b 19. Leeds Univ BSc41. Coll of Resurr Mirfield 41. **d** 43 **p** 44. C Portsea All SS w St Jo Rudmore *Portsm* 43-46; Chapl RNVR 46-48; C Greenford H Cross *Lon* 48-54; C Littlehampton St Mary *Chich* 54-58; V Hanworth All SS *Lon* 58-65; V Fareham SS Pet and Paul *Portsm* 65-92; Relig Adv STV 72-81; Hon Can Portsm Cathl 81-92; rtd 92; Perm to Offic *Portsm* from 92. *Tree Tops, Hoads Hill, Wickham, Fareham PO17 5BX* Tel (01329) 834397

CHADDER, Philip Thomas James. b 66. Ex Univ BA88. Oak Hill Th Coll 01. **d** 03 **p** 04. C Gt Chesham *Ox* from 03. *7 Whitelands Avenue, Chorleywood, Rickmansworth WD3 5RE* Tel (01923) 285357 Mobile 07796-815285 E-mail philchadder@yahoo.co.uk

CHADWICK, Alan Michael. b 61. St Cath Coll Cam BA83 MA87. Wycliffe Hall Ox DipMin98. **d** 98 **p** 99. C Hubberston

St D 98-01; R from 01. *Hubberston Rectory, 35 Westaway Drive, Hubberston, Milford Haven SA73 3EQ* Tel (01646) 692251

CHADWICK, Arnold. *See* CHADWICK, Francis Arnold Edwin

CHADWICK, Charles John Peter. b 59. Birm Univ BA81 Slough Coll DMS84 Southn Univ BTh90. Sarum & Wells Th Coll 85. **d** 88 **p** 89. C Chalfont St Peter *Ox* 88-91; C Gt Marlow 91-93; TV Gt Marlow w Marlow Bottom, Lt Marlow and Bisham 93-95; P-in-c Stokenchurch and Ibstone 95-01; Asst Dir Chiltern Ch Tr Course 95-01; V Bridgwater St Mary, Chilton Trinity and Durleigh *B & W* from 01. *The Vicarage, 7 Durleigh Road, Bridgwater TA6 7HU* Tel (01278) 422437 *or* 424972 E-mail charles@chad0205.fsnet.co.uk

CHADWICK, David Emmerson. b 73. Lincs & Humberside Univ BA96. Ridley Hall Cam BTh00. **d** 00 **p** 01. C Whickham *Dur* from 00. *7A Coalway Drive, Whickham, Newcastle upon Tyne NE16 4BT* Tel 0191-488 3015

CHADWICK, David Guy Evelyn St Just. b 36. Bps' Coll Cheshunt 61. **d** 68 **p** 69. C Edmonton All SS *Lon* 68-71; C Edmonton St Mary w St Jo 71-72; C Greenhill St Jo 72-74; Bp's Dom Chapl *Truro* 74-79; Chapl Community of the Epiphany Truro 77-78; P-in-c Crantock *Truro* 79-83; R Clydebank *Glas* 83-87; R Renfrew 87-94; rtd 94. *Alverna, 1 Nithsdale Crescent, Bearsden, Glasgow G61 4DF*

CHADWICK, Francis Arnold Edwin. b 30. AKC54. **d** 55 **p** 56. C Chapel Allerton *Ripon* 55-58; C Hayes *Roch* 58-61; V Arreton *Portsm* 61-67; V Newchurch 61-67; V Kingshurst *Birm* 67-73; V York Town St Mich *Guildf* 73-83; P-in-c Long Sutton w Long Load *B & W* 83-87; R Stockbridge and Longstock and Leckford *Win* 87-93; rtd 93; Chapl Helsinki w Tallinn *Eur* 95-98; Perm to Offic *B & W* from 98 and *Sarum* from 02. *Hillway, Wickfield, Devizes SN10 5DU* Tel (01380) 721489

✠**CHADWICK, The Rt Revd Graham Charles.** b 23. Keble Coll Ox BA49 MA53. St Mich Coll Llan 49. **d** 50 **p** 51 **c** 76. C Oystermouth *S & B* 50-53; Basutoland 53-63; C Masite St Barn 53-54; R Qacha's Nek 54-59; R Mohales Hoek 59-63; Chapl Univ of Wales (Swansea) *S & B* 63-68; Sen Bursar Qu Coll Birm 68-69; Lic to Offic *S'wark* 69-70; Warden Dioc Tr Cen Lesotho 70-76; Bp Kimberley and Kuruman 76-82; Dioc Adv on Spirituality *St As* 83-90; Chapl St As Cathl 83-90; rtd 90; Asst Bp Liv 90-95; Dir Inst for Chr Spirituality Sarum Coll 95-98. *66 Hulse Road, Salisbury SP1 3LY* Tel (01722) 505801 Fax 505802 E-mail gcchadwick@aol.com

CHADWICK, Helen Jane. *See* MARSHALL, Mrs Helen Jane

CHADWICK, Prof Henry. b 20. KBE89 OM(Ger)93. Magd Coll Cam BA41 MA45 MusBac41 DD57 Glas Univ Hon DD57 Uppsala Univ Hon DD67 Yale Univ Hon DD70 Man Univ Hon DD75 Leeds Univ Hon DD80 Surrey Univ Hon DD96 Harvard Univ Hon DD97 Nashotah Ho Wisconsin Hon DD98 MRIA FBA60. Ridley Hall Cam 42. **d** 43 **p** 44. C S Croydon Em *Cant* 43-45; Asst Chapl Wellington Coll Berks 45-46; Chapl Qu Coll Cam 46-50; Dean 50-55; Regius Prof Div Ox Univ 59-69; Can Ch Ch *Ox* 59-69; Dean Ch Ch 69-79; Vice-Pres Br Academy 68-69; Regius Prof Div Cam Univ 79-82; Hon Can Ely Cathl *Ely* 79-83; Lic to Offic 83-93; Master Peterho Cam 87-93. *46 St John Street, Oxford OX1 2LH* Tel (01865) 512814

CHADWICK, Mark William Armstrong. Coll of Resurr Mirfield. **d** 05. C Colwyn Bay w Brynymaen *St As* from 05. *11 Rhiw Road, Colwyn Bay LL29 7TE*

CHADWICK, Peter MacKenzie. b 21. Lich Th Coll 63. **d** 65 **p** 66. C Buckhurst Hill *Chelmsf* 65-66; Jt Hd Master Forres Sch Swanage 56-81; Chapl 66-85; NSM Kingston, Langton Matravers and Worth Matravers *Sarum* 85-92; rtd 89; Perm to Offic *Sarum* from 92. *Cull's, Garfield Lane, Langton Matravers, Swanage BH19 3HJ* Tel (01929) 422258

CHADWICK, Prof William Owen. b 16. OM83 KBE82. St Jo Coll Cam BA39 MA42 BD51 DD55 St Andr Univ Hon DD60 Ox Univ Hon DD73 Univ of Wales Hon DD93 FBA62. Cuddesdon Coll 39. **d** 40 **p** 41. C Huddersfield St Jo *Wakef* 40-42; Chapl Wellington Coll Berks 42-46; Fell Trin Hall Cam 47-56; Dean 49-56; Master Selw Coll Cam 56-83; Fell from 83; Dixie Prof Ecclesiastical Hist Cam 58-68; Regius Prof Modern Hist Cam 68-83; Pres Br Academy 81-85; Chan UEA 85-94; Perm to Offic *Ely* from 94. *67 Grantchester Street, Cambridge CB7 9HZ* Tel (01223) 314000

CHAFFEY, Jane Frances. b 59. Somerville Coll Ox BA80 MA84 St Jo Coll Dur BA86. Cranmer Hall Dur 84. **d** 88 **p** 94. Par Dn Roby *Liv* 88-90; NSM Finningley w Auckley *S'well* 95-96; Perm to Offic *Pet* 96-99 and *Linc* 98-01; Perm to Offic RAF from 98. *Address temp unknown*

CHAFFEY, Jonathan Paul Michael. b 62. St Chad's Coll Dur BA83. Cranmer Hall Dur 84. **d** 87 **p** 88. C Gateacre *Liv* 87-90; Chapl RAF from 90. *Chaplaincy Services (RAF), HQ, Personnel and Training Command, RAF Innsworth, Gloucester GL3 1EZ* Tel (01452) 712612 Ext 5164 Fax 510828

CHAFFEY, Michael Prosser. b 30. Lon Univ BA51. St Steph Ho Ox 53. **d** 55 **p** 56. C Victoria Docks Ascension *Chelmsf* 55-59; C Leytonstone H Trin Harrow Green 59-62; V Walthamstow St Mich 62-69; R Cov St Jo *Cov* 69-85; P-in-c Cov St Thos 69-75; Hon C Bideford *Ex* 85; P-in-c Charlestown *Man* 85-88; V Sutton St Mich *York* 88-96; rtd 96; Perm to Offic *York* from 96. *1 School Lane, Burton Fleming, Driffield YO25 3PX* Tel (01262) 470439

CHALCRAFT, Christopher Warine Terrell (Kit). b 37. Oak Hill Th Coll. **d** 67 **p** 68. C Egham *Guildf* 67-70; P-in-c Slough *Ox* 70-73; TV Bramerton w Surlingham *Nor* 73-87; P-in-c Cockley Cley w Gooderstone 87-95; P-in-c Gt and Lt Cressingham w Threxton 87-95; P-in-c Didlington 87-95; P-in-c Hilborough w Bodney 87-95; P-in-c Oxborough w Foulden and Caldecote 87-95; Perm to Offic from 02. *The Malthouse, London Street, Swaffham PE37 7DD* Tel (01760) 724805 E-mail k.chalcraft@btinternet.com

CHALK, Francis Harold. b 25. Lich Th Coll 61. **d** 62 **p** 63. C Linc St Nic w St Jo Newport *Linc* 62-64; R Kirkby Laythorpe w Asgarby 64-69; V Ewerby w Evedon 65-69; R Gt Gonerby 69-89; rtd 89; Perm to Offic *Truro* from 90. *Chalkleigh, 3 Church Street, St Just, Penzance TR19 7HA* Tel (01736) 787925

CHALK, John Edward. b 33. St D Coll Lamp BA57. **d** 58 **p** 59. C Connah's Quay *St As* 58-61; C Abergele 61-65; V Cyfarthfa *Llan* 65-72; V Pyle w Kenfig 72-77; Lect in FE 84-92; NSM Mansfield Woodhouse *S'well* 92; Perm to Offic *Lich* 92-94; NSM Salt and Sandon w Burston 94-96; rtd 96. *Hendre Penprys, Pentre Uchaf, Pwllheli LL53 8EZ* Tel (01758) 750306

CHALK, Miss Susan Christine. b 50. Warwick Univ BSc71 Man Univ CETD72. S Dios Minl Tr Scheme 90. **d** 93 **p** 94. NSM Bradford Peverell, Stratton, Frampton etc *Sarum* 93-03. *Address temp unknown*

CHALKLEY, Andrew William Guy. b 64. Aston Tr Scheme 90 St Jo Coll Nottm BTh92. **d** 95 **p** 96. C Liskeard, St Keyne, St Pinnock, Morval etc *Truro* 95-99; C Liskeard and St Keyne 99; TV Uphill *B & W* from 99. *St Barnabas' Vicarage, 2 Westbury Crescent, Weston-super-Mare BS23 4RB* Tel (01934) 623195 E-mail stbarnabas@uphillteam.fsnet.co.uk

CHALKLEY, Henry Roy. b 23. Brasted Th Coll 57 St Aid Birkenhead 58. **d** 59 **p** 60. C Bromborough *Ches* 59-63; Miss to Seamen 63-88; Asst Chapl Hong Kong 63-64; Chapl Beira Mozambique 64-65; Chapl Port of Spain Trinidad 65-68; Chapl Suva Fiji 69-73; Chapl HMS Conway 73-74; Sen Chapl Port of Lon 74-75; Sen Chapl Fremantle Australia 75-79; Chapl Cornish Ports 79-82; Chapl Dar es Salaam Tanzania 82-83; Chapl Nat Sea Tr Coll Gravesend 83-85; Chapl Felixstowe Seafarers' Cen 85-88; rtd 88; Perm to Offic *St E* 93-05. *58 Derrycoose Road, Portadown, Craigavon BT62 1LY* Tel (028) 3885 1887

CHALLEN, Canon Peter Bernard. b 31. Clare Coll Cam BA56 MA60 FRSA94. Westcott Ho Cam 56. **d** 58 **p** 59. C Goole *Sheff* 58-61; V Dalton 61-67; Sen Ind Chapl *S'wark* 67-96; R S'wark Ch Ch 67-96; Hon Can S'wark Cathl 74-96; rtd 96; Perm to Offic *S'wark* from 96. *21 Bousfield Road, London SE14 5TP* Tel and fax (020) 7207 0509 E-mail peter@southwark.org.uk *or* 101665.1247@compuserve.com

CHALLENDER, John Clifford. b 32. CITC 67. **d** 67 **p** 68. C Belfast St Luke *Conn* 67-70; C Kilkenny w Aghour and Odagh *C & O* 70-71; Bp's V and Lib Kilkenny Cathl 70-71; Dioc Registrar (Ossory, Ferns and Leighlin) 70-71; I Fenagh w Myshall and Kiltennel 71-76; I Fenagh w Myshall, Aghade and Ardoyne 76-79; I Crosspatrick Gp 79-95; Preb Ferns Cathl 85-88; Dioc Glebes Sec (Ferns) 86-91; Treas Ferns Cathl 88-91; Chan 91-95; I Killeshin w Cloydagh and Killabban 95-02; Can Ossory and Leighlin Cathls 00-02; rtd 02. *3 Adare Close, Killincarrig, Greystones, Co Wicklow, Irish Republic* Tel (00353) (1) 201 7268 *or* 287 6359 Mobile 86-243 3678 E-mail challen1@gofree.indigo.ie

CHALLENGER, Peter Nelson. b 33. St Jo Coll Cam BA57 MA61. Ripon Hall Ox 57. **d** 59 **p** 60. C Bushbury *Lich* 59-62; V Horsley Woodhouse *Derby* 62-67; V Derby St Barn 67-75; Brazil 75-80; TV New Windsor *Ox* 80-89; V Wootton (Boars Hill) 89-98; rtd 99. *39 Moorland Road, Witney OX28 6LS* Tel (01993) 774630

CHALLICE, John Richard. b 34. ACP65. Sarum & Wells Th Coll 73. **d** 75 **p** 76. C Warminster St Denys *Sarum* 75-78; R Longfield *Roch* 78-00; rtd 00; Perm to Offic *Roch* from 00. *Magnolia, Allhallows Road, Lower Stoke, Rochester ME3 9SL* Tel (01634) 272468

CHALLIS, Douglas James. b 21. Selw Coll Cam BA48 MA55. Cuddesdon Coll 49. **d** 51 **p** 58. Kimbolton Sch Cambs 53-58; Chapl Summer Fields Sch Ox 58-60; Asst Chapl Stowe Sch 60-64; Chapl St Bees Sch Cumbria 64-67; Chapl Reed's Sch Cobham 67-80; rtd 80; Perm to Offic *Cant* from 89. *20 Ryders Avenue, Westgate-on-Sea CT8 8LW* Tel (01843) 831052

CHALLIS, Ian. b 46. St Jo Coll Nottm 82. **d** 84 **p** 85. C Heatherlands St Jo *Sarum* 84-86; C Lytchett Minster 86-88; Perm to Offic from 88; NSM Canford Magna 95-00. *50 Constitution Hill Road, Poole BH14 0QD* Tel (01202) 691300

CHALLIS, John William Anthony. b 68. St Steph Ho Ox 98. **d** 00 **p** 01. C Ifield *Chich* 00-04; P-in-c Buxted and Hadlow Down from 04. *The Rectory, Church Road, Buxted, Uckfield TN22 4LP* Tel (01825) 733103

CHALLIS, Terence Peter. b 40. St Aid Birkenhead 65. **d** 68 **p** 69. C Billericay St Mary *Chelmsf* 68-71; Admin Sec Dio Maseno S Kenya 72-75; Bp's Chapl 72-74; P-in-c Sparkbrook Ch Ch *Birm*

76-80; V Enfield St Jas *Lon* 80-89; V Astley Bridge *Man* 89-98; P-in-c Leigh St Mary and Leigh St Jo 99-02; rtd 02; Perm to Offic *Blackb* from 03. *48 Wilson Square, Thornton-Cleveleys FY5 1RF* Tel (01253) 864534

CHALLIS, William George. b 52. Keble Coll Ox BA73 K Coll Lon MTh75. Oak Hill Th Coll 73. **d** 75 **p** 76. C Islington St Mary *Lon* 75-79; Lect Trin Coll Bris 79-81; C Stoke Bishop *Bris* 79-81; Lect Oak Hill Th Coll 82; Burundi 82-85; P-in-c Bishopston *Bris* 86-89; TR 89-92; Vice-Prin Wycliffe Hall Ox 93-98; V Bitterne *Win* 98-03; Dir of Ords *Guildf* from 03. *80 York Road, Woking GU22 7XR* Tel (01483) 769759 *or* 790322 E-mail ddo@cofeguildford.org.uk

CHALMERS, Canon Brian. b 42. Oriel Coll Ox BA64 MA68 DPhil70 BA71. Wycliffe Hall Ox 71. **d** 72 **p** 73. C Luton St Mary *St Alb* 72-76; Chapl Cranfield Inst of Tech 76-81; Chapl Kent Univ *Cant* 81-89; Six Preacher Cant Cathl 85-96; V Charing w Charing Heath and Lt Chart from 89; AD Ashford 98-03; Hon Can Cant Cathl from 97. *The Vicarage, Pett Lane, Charing, Ashford TN27 0DL* Tel (01233) 712598 E-mail brian.chalmers@tesco.net

CHAMBERLAIN, Allen Charles William. b 29. Lon Univ CertEd52 Birkbeck Coll Lon BSc56. LNSM course 95. **d** 96 **p** 97. OLM Gunton St Pet *Nor* 96-99; rtd 99; Perm to Offic *Nor* from 99. *28 Yarmouth Road, Lowestoft NR32 4AG* Tel (01502) 573637

CHAMBERLAIN, David (Bernard). b 28. Fitzw Ho Cam BA51. Linc Th Coll 52. **d** 54 **p** 55. C Brighouse *Wakef* 54-57; C Sheff St Cecilia Parson Cross *Sheff* 57-61; CR 63-85; S Africa 68-70; Bp's Adv on Community Relns *Wakef* 71-85; Bp's Adv Community Relns & Inter-Faith Dialogue *Bris* 86-93; V Easton All Hallows 86-93; rtd 93; Perm to Offic *B & W* from 94. *43 Bath Road, Wells BA5 3HR* Tel (01749) 679369

CHAMBERLAIN, David Murray. b 22. Cuddesdon Coll 55. **d** 57 **p** 58. C Barkingside H Trin *Chelmsf* 57-60; Japan 60-71 and 76-81; V Edgbaston St Germain *Birm* 71-76; Miss to Seamen N Australia 81-88; rtd 88; Perm to Offic *Truro* from 88. *42 Tresawls Road, Truro TR1 3LE* Tel (01872) 272270

CHAMBERLAIN, Eric Edward. b 34. Lon Univ DipTh64. Tyndale Hall Bris 62. **d** 65 **p** 66. C Chell *Lich* 65-73; P-in-c Preston St Mary *Blackb* 73-76; V 76-89; P-in-c Preston St Luke 81-83; R S Normanton *Derby* 89-99; rtd 99; Perm to Offic *Ox* from 00. *1 The Closes, Haddenham, Aylesbury HP17 8JN* Tel (01844) 299303

CHAMBERLAIN, Frederick George. b 19. Univ of Wales (Lamp) BA50. Chich Th Coll 50. **d** 52 **p** 53. C Weybridge *Guildf* 52-54; C Bourne 54-57; V Blindley Heath *S'wark* 57-63; V Tilshead *Sarum* 63-71; R The Orchestons 66-71; V Chitterne 69-71; R Tilshead, Orcheston and Chitterne 71-80; P-in-c Handley w Pentridge 80-82; R 82-84; rtd 84; Perm to Offic *Sarum* 84-04. *22 Gracey Court, Woodland Road, Broadclyst, Exeter EX5 3GA* Tel (01392) 462633

CHAMBERLAIN, Malcolm Leslie. b 69. York Univ BA92. Wycliffe Hall Ox 93. **d** 96 **p** 97. C Walsall Pleck and Bescot *Lich* 96-99; C Mossley Hill St Matt and St Jas *Liv* 99-02; Asst Chapl Liv Univ 99-02; Chapl from 02; Dioc 18-30s Officer from 02. *71 Woodlands Road, Aigburth, Liverpool L17 0AL*

✠**CHAMBERLAIN, The Rt Revd Neville.** b 39. Nottm Univ BA61 MA73 CQSW73. Ripon Hall Ox 61. **d** 63 **p** 64 **c** 97. C Balsall Heath St Paul *Birm* 63-64; C Hall Green Ascension 64-66; C-in-c Gospel Lane CD 66-69; V Gospel Lane St Mich 69-72; Lic to Offic *Linc* 73-74; Soc Resp Sec 74-82; Can and Preb Linc Cathl 79-98; R Edin St Jo *Edin* 82-97; Bp Bre 97-05; rtd 04; Master Hugh Sexey's Hosp Bruton from 05. *The Master's House, Hugh Sexey's Hospital, Bruton BA10 0AS* Tel (01749) 813369

CHAMBERLAIN, Nicholas Alan. b 63. St Chad's Coll Dur BA85 PhD91 New Coll Edin BD91. **d** 91 **p** 92. C Cockerton *Dur* 91-94; C Newton Aycliffe 94-95; TV 95-96; TV Gt Aycliffe 96-98; P-in-c Burnmoor from 98; Bp's Adv for CME from 98. *The Rectory, Burnmoor, Houghton le Spring DH4 6EX* Tel 0191-385 2695 *or* 374 6016 Fax 384 7529 E-mail nick.chamberlain@durham.anglican.org

CHAMBERLAIN, Roger Edward. b 53. BEd76 BA87. Trin Coll Bris 84. **d** 87 **p** 88. C Plymouth Em w Efford *Ex* 87-90; C Selly Park St Steph and St Wulstan *Birm* 90-94; V Yardley St Cypr Hay Mill 94-96; Perm to Offic from 96. *22 Hanbury Croft, Acocks Green, Birmingham B27 6RX* Tel 0121-708 0998

CHAMBERLAIN, Roy Herbert. b 44. Oak Hill Th Coll 91 N Ord Course 95. **d** 96 **p** 97. C Gee Cross *Ches* 96-98; Perm to Offic *Blackb* from 01. *125 Lancaster Road, Morecambe LA4 5QJ* Tel (01524) 409070

CHAMBERLAIN, Russell Charles. b 51. Univ of Wales (Cardiff) LLM00. Oak Hill Th Coll DipHE78. **d** 78 **p** 79. C Harold Hill St Geo *Chelmsf* 78-80; C Uckfield *Chich* 80-83; R Balcombe 83-90; V Okehampton w Inwardleigh *Ex* 90-94; TR Okehampton w Inwardleigh, Bratton Clovelly etc 94-01; RD Okehampton 93-98; R Wolborough and Ogwell from 01. *The Rectory, 5 Coach Place, Newton Abbot TQ12 1ES* Tel (01626) 368889 E-mail russell@chamberlain70.fsnet.co.uk

CHAMBERLIN, David John. b 56. St Jo Coll Nottm. **d** 94 **p** 95. C Chatham St Phil and St Jas *Roch* 94-97; R Swardeston w E Carleton, Intwood, Keswick etc *Nor* 97-04; RD Humbleyard 03-04; R Milton *Ely* from 04. *The Rectory, Church Lane, Milton, Cambridge CB4 6AB* Tel (01223) 861511 E-mail david@chamberlin.org.uk

CHAMBERLIN, John Malcolm. b 38. Carl Dioc Tr Course 84. **d** 87 **p** 88. NSM Cockermouth w Embleton and Wythop *Carl* 87-97; Master St Mary Magd and H Jes Trust Newc 97-05; Hon C Newc St Jo *Newc* 98-05; rtd 05. *45 Wansbeck Avenue, North Shields NE30 3DU* Tel 0191-253 0022 Fax 08701-331974 E-mail jmandmic@surfaid.org

CHAMBERS, Canon Anthony Frederick John. b 40. Sarum Th Coll 69. **d** 71 **p** 72. C Hall Green St Pet *Birm* 71-74; C Holdenhurst *Win* 74-77; P-in-c Ropley w W Tisted 77-79; R Bishop's Sutton and Ropley and W Tisted 79-83; V Pokesdown St Jas 83-99; RD Bournemouth 95-99; P-in-c Heckfield w Mattingley and Rotherwick 99-02; V 02-04; Chapl N Foreland Lodge Sch Basingstoke 99-04; Hon Can Win Cathl *Win* 03-04; rtd 05. *1 The Stables, Golf Links Road, Westward Ho!, Bideford EX39 1HH* Tel (01237) 421306 E-mail anthony.chambers1@virgin.net

CHAMBERS, Miss Barbara Ada. b 51. LNSM course 95. **d** 98 **p** 99. OLM Gt Crosby St Luke *Liv* from 98. *12 Vale Road, Crosby, Liverpool LS23 5RZ* Tel 0151-924 5851

CHAMBERS, Mrs Barbara Mary Sinnott. b 43. SRN65 RM67 Birm Poly HVCert75 TCert77. WMMTC 87. **d** 93 **p** 94. Par Dn Blurton *Lich* 93-94; C 94-96; Chapl Asst Qu Medical Cen Nottm Univ Hosp NHS Trust 96-03; Chapl from 03. *Queen's Medical Centre University Hospital, Derby Road, Nottingham NG7 2UH* Tel 0115-942 9924 ext 43799

CHAMBERS, Carl Michael. b 68. Pemb Coll Cam BA90 Oak Hill Th Coll BA00. **d** 01 **p** 02. C Hove Bp Hannington Memorial Ch *Chich* 01-05; C Preston St Jo w Brighton St Aug and St Sav from 05. *24 Stanford Avenue, Brighton BN1 6EA* Tel (01273) 553207

CHAMBERS, George William. b 24. TCD BA46 MA57. CITC 47. **d** 47 **p** 48. C Conwall *D & R* 47-50; Chapl Portora R Sch Enniskillen 50-51; I Tullyaughnish w Milford *D & R* 51-61; I Adare *L & K* 61-81; Dioc Registrar (Limerick etc) 62-81; Adn Limerick 69-81; Dean Limerick 81-86; I Limerick City 81-86; I Killeshin w Cloydagh and Killabban *C & O* 86-95; Can Ossory and Leighlin Cathls 90-92; Treas Ossory and Leighlin Cathls 92-95; rtd 95. *12 Rathdown Court, Greystones, Co Wicklow, Irish Republic* Tel (00353) (1) 287 1140

CHAMBERS, John Richard. b 50. EMMTC 01. **d** 04 **p** 05. C Farnsfield *S'well* from 04; C Kirklington w Hockerton from 04; C Bilsthorpe from 04; C Eakring from 04; C Maplebeck from 04; C Winkburn from 04. *The Rectory, Church Hill, Bilsthorpe, Newark NG22 8RU* Tel (01623) 870256 Mobile 07900-238946 E-mail j_echambers@tiscali.co.uk

CHAMBERS, Mrs Lynn. b 53. Northd Coll of Educn TCert74 Greenwich Univ MA96. St Mich Coll Llan 03. **d** 05. Dioc Children's Officer *St D* from 01; NSM Carmarthen St Pet from 05. *Bromihangel, Gwernogle, Carmarthen SA32 7RP* Tel (01267) 223052 E-mail chambers@bromihangel.freserve.co.uk

CHAMBERS, Canon Peter Lewis. b 43. Imp Coll Lon BScEng64. St Steph Ho Ox 64. **d** 66 **p** 67. C Llandaff w Capel Llanilltern *Llan* 66-70; Chapl Ch in Wales Youth Coun 70-73; Youth Chapl *Bris* 73-78; V Bedminster St Mich 78-84; RD Bedminster 81-84; Adv Ho of Bps Marriage Educn Panel Gen Syn 84-88; Dir Dioc Coun for Soc Resp *Guildf* 88-94; Hon Can Guildf Cathl 89-94; Dir Tr *Sheff* 95-00; P-in-c Harthill and Thorpe Salvin from 00; Dioc Min Teams Officer 00-04; Hon Can Sheff Cathl from 96. *27 Common Road, Thorpe Salvin, Worksop S80 3JJ* Tel (01909) 770279

CHAMBERS, Simon Paul. b 65. Liv Univ BEng87 PhD91. Ripon Coll Cuddesdon 00. **d** 02 **p** 03. C Parkstone St Pet and St Osmund w Branksea *Sarum* from 02. *79 Church Road, Parkstone, Poole BH14 0NS* Tel (01202) 743016 Fax 710591 E-mail simon@simonchambers.com

CHAMP, Darren David. b 60. Kent Univ BA93. Linc Th Coll MA95. **d** 95 **p** 96. C Ashford *Cant* 95-97; Perm to Offic 02-03. *154 Beaver Road, Ashford TN23 7SS* Tel (01233) 663090 E-mail daz@dazchamp.co.uk

CHAMPION, Canon John Oswald Cecil. b 27. St Chad's Coll Dur BA49 DipTh51. **d** 51 **p** 52. C Worc St Martin *Worc* 51-53; Chapl RN 53-57; C Cant St Martin w St Paul *Cant* 57-60; C-in-c Stourbridge St Mich Norton CD *Worc* 60-64; V Astwood Bank w Crabbs Cross 64-68; V Redditch St Steph 68-75; R Fladbury, Wyre Piddle and Moor 75-93; RD Pershore 79-85; Hon Can Worc Cathl 81-93; rtd 93; Perm to Offic *Worc* from 93. *Black Horse Cottage, 3 Church Row, Pershore WR10 1BL* Tel (01386) 552403

CHAMPNEYS, Michael Harold. b 46. LRAM66 GRSM67 ARCO67. Linc Th Coll 69. **d** 72 **p** 73. C Poplar *Lon* 72-73; C Bow w Bromley St Leon 73-75; P-in-c Bethnal Green St Barn 75-76; C Tewkesbury w Walton Cardiff *Glouc* 76-78; V Bedford

Park *Lon* 78-83; V Shepshed *Leic* 84-87; Community Educn Tutor Bolsover 88-93; Perm to Offic *Derby* 90-92; NSM Bolsover 92-93; V Potterspury, Furtho, Yardley Gobion and Cosgrove *Pet* 93-98; RD Towcester 94-98; V Shap w Swindale and Bampton w Mardale *Carl* 98-01; R Calow and Sutton cum Duckmanton *Derby* from 01. *The Rectory, Top Road, Calow, Chesterfield S44 5AF* Tel (01246) 273486
E-mail michaelchampneys@yahoo.co.uk

CHANCE, David Newton. b 44. Univ of Wales (Lamp) BA68. St Steph Ho Ox 68. **d** 70 **p** 71. C Selsdon St Jo w St Fran *Cant* 70-73; C Plymstock *Ex* 73-77; P-in-c Northam 77-79; TR Northam w Westward Ho! and Appledore 79-93; V Banstead *Guildf* from 93. *The Vicarage, 21 Court Road, Banstead SM7 2NQ* Tel (01737) 351134

CHAND, Richard. b 62. St Alb and Ox Min Course 02. **d** 05. NSM Westcote Barton w Steeple Barton, Duns Tew etc *Ox* from 05. *100 Bayswater Road, Headington, Oxford OX3 9NZ* Tel (01865) 741311 Mobile 07966-659270
E-mail richardchandrw@ministry.fsbusiness.co.uk

CHAND, Wazir. b 29. Punjab Univ BA56 BT59. Ox NSM Course. **d** 90 **p** 91. NSM Cowley St Jas *Ox* 90-04; Perm to Offic from 04. *38 Garsington Road, Oxford OX4 2LG* Tel (01865) 714160 *or* 433015

CHANDA, Daniel Khazan. b 28. Punjab Univ BA57 MA62 Saharanputh Coll. **d** 70 **p** 70. Hon C Handsworth St Jas *Birm* 70-83; Hon C Perry Barr 83-89; C Small Heath 89-98; rtd 98; Perm to Offic *Birm* 98-99 and from 00. *173 Wood Lane, Handsworth, Birmingham B20 2AG* Tel 0121-554 1093

CHANDLER, Anthony. b 43. Lon Inst of Educn CertEd65. EAMTC 94. **d** 97 **p** 98. Dioc Youth Officer *Ely* 96-00; NSM March St Mary 97-00; R from 00; NSM March St Pet 97-00; R from 00. *17 St Peter's Road, March PE15 9NA* Tel and fax (01354) 652894 E-mail anthony.chandler@ely.anglican.org

CHANDLER, Derek Edward. b 67. Southn Univ BTh91 Nottm Univ MDiv93. Linc Th Coll 91. **d** 93 **p** 94. C Bitterne Park *Win* 93-97; C Sholing 97-00; R Emmer Green w Caversham Park *Ox* from 00. *20 St Barnabas Road, Emmer Green, Reading RG4 8RA* Tel 0118-947 8239 E-mail rev.derek.chandler@virgin.net

CHANDLER, Ian Nigel. b 65. K Coll Lon BD89 AKC89. Chich Th Coll 92. **d** 92 **p** 93. C Hove *Chich* 92-96; Bp's Dom Chapl 96-00; V Haywards Heath St Rich from 00; RD Cuckfield from 04. *St Richard's Vicarage, Queen's Road, Haywards Heath RH16 1EB* Tel (01444) 413621
E-mail ianchandler@hotmail.com

CHANDLER, John Charles. b 46. Solicitor. Oak Hill Th Coll 91. **d** 94 **p** 95. C Tonbridge St Steph *Roch* 94-98; V Felsted and Lt Dunmow *Chelmsf* 98-05; V Hildenborough *Roch* from 05. *The Vicarage, 194 Tonbridge Road, Hildenborough, Tonbridge TN11 9HR* Tel (01732) 833569
E-mail jm@chandler464.freeserve.co.uk

CHANDLER, John Edmond Owen. b 18. St Cath Soc Ox BA48 MA48. Cuddesdon Coll 68. **d** 68 **p** 69. Hon C Quarndon *Derby* 68-72; Lic to Offic *S'well* 73-78; P-in-c Oxton 79-85; R Epperstone 79-85; R Gonalston 79-85; rtd 85; Perm to Offic *S'well* from 85. *18 Thoresby Dale, Hucknall, Nottingham NG15 7UG* Tel 0115-963 5945

CHANDLER, The Very Revd Michael John. b 45. Lambeth STh80 K Coll Lon PhD87. Linc Th Coll 70. **d** 72 **p** 73. C Cant St Dunstan w H Cross *Cant* 72-75; C Margate St Jo 75-78; V Newington w Bobbing and Iwade 78-83; P-in-c Hartlip w Stockbury 80-83; V Newington w Hartlip and Stockbury 83-88; RD Sittingbourne 84-88; R Hackington 88-95; RD Cant 94-95; Can Res Cant Cathl 95-03; Dean Ely from 03. *The Deanery, The College, Ely CB7 4DN* Tel (01353) 667735 Fax 665668
E-mail dean@cathedral.ely.anglican.org

CHANDLER, Quentin David. b 62. Aston Tr Scheme 87 Trin Coll Bris BA92. **d** 92 **p** 93. C Goldington *St Alb* 92-96; TV Rushden w Newton Bromswold *Pet* 96-00; V Rushden St Pet 00-03; Dir Tr for Past Assts from 03; R Burton Latimer from 03. *The Rectory, Preston Court, Burton Latimer, Kettering NN15 5LR* Tel (01536) 722959 E-mail q.chandler@btopenworld.com

CHANDRA, Kevin Douglas Naresh. b 65. Lon Bible Coll BA91. Qu Coll Birm 94. **d** 96 **p** 97. C Walmley *Birm* 96-00; P-in-c Erdington St Chad 00-02; TV Erdington 02-05. *Address temp unknown* E-mail kc@chandra.plus.com

CHANDRAN, Nirmalan (Alain). b 68. Trin Coll Bris. **d** 03 **p** 04. C Southborough St Pet w Ch Ch and St Matt etc *Roch* from 03. *54 Holden Park Road, Southborough, Tunbridge Wells TN4 0EP* Tel (01892) 529153 E-mail alainchandran@yahoo.com

CHANDY, Sugu John Mathai. b 40. Kerala Univ BSc61 Serampore Univ BD66. Wycliffe Coll Toronto 67. **d** 66 **p** 68. India 66-74 and from 80; C Ormesby *York* 74-77; C Sutton St Jas and Wawne 78-80; rtd 99. *Matteethra, Muttambalam, Kottayam, Kerala, 686004, India* Tel (0091) (481) 572438 *or* 572590

✠**CHANG-HIM, The Rt Revd French Kitchener.** b 38. Lich Th Coll. **d** 62 **p** 63 **c** 79. C Goole *Sheff* 62-63; R Praslin Seychelles 63-67; C Sheff St Leon Norwood *Sheff* 67-68; C Mahé Cathl Mauritius 68-70; Missr Praslin 70-73; R Anse Royale St Sav and Adn Seychelles 73-79; Bp Seychelles 79-04; rtd 04. *PO Box 44, Victoria, Seychelles* Tel (00248) 224242 Fax 224296
E-mail angdio@seychelles.net

CHANNER, Christopher Kendall. b 42. K Coll Lon BD64 AKC64. St Boniface Warminster 64. **d** 65 **p** 66. C Norbury St Steph *Cant* 65-68; C S Elmsall *Wakef* 68-70; V Dartford St Edm *Roch* 70-75; Chapl Joyce Green Hosp Dartford 73-75; V Bromley St Andr *Roch* 75-81; V Langton Green 81-94; Chapl Holmewood Ho Sch Tunbridge Wells 94-98; P-in-c Lewes All SS, St Anne, St Mich and St Thos *Chich* 98-00; R Lewes St Mich and St Thos at Cliffe w All SS from 00. *St Michael's Rectory, St Andrew's Lane, Lewes BN7 1UW* Tel (01273) 474723

CHANT, Edwin John. b 14. Lon Univ BA62. K Coll Lon 39 Clifton Th Coll 46. **d** 47 **p** 48. C Erith St Paul *Roch* 47-49; C Darfield *Sheff* 49-51; C Conisbrough 51-53; C Cliftonville *Cant* 53-56; V Gentleshaw *Lich* 56-80; V Farewell 56-80; rtd 80; Perm to Offic *Lich* from 80. *31 Huntsmans Gate, Burntwood WS7 9LL*

CHANT, Harry. b 40. Oak Hill Th Coll. **d** 78 **p** 79. C Heatherlands St Jo *Sarum* 78-81; P-in-c Bramshaw 81-83; P-in-c Landford w Plaitford 81-83; R Bramshaw and Landford w Plaitford 83-87; V Fareham St Jo *Portsm* 87-00; rtd 00; Perm to Offic *Truro* from 00. *Paradise Cottage, 34 Nanscober Place, Helston TR13 0SP* Tel and fax (01326) 561916 E-mail handrchant@aol.com

CHANT, Kenneth William. b 37. St Deiniol's Hawarden 67. **d** 70 **p** 71. C Ynyshir *Llan* 70-74; C Bargoed and Deri w Brithdir 74; P-in-c Aberpergwm and Blaengwrach 74-77; V 77-81; V Cwmavon 81-02; rtd 02. *22 Chalice Court, Port Talbot SA12 7DA* Tel (01639) 813456

CHANT, Maurice Ronald. b 26. Chich Th Coll 51. **d** 54 **p** 55. C Mitcham St Mark *S'wark* 54-57; C Surbiton St Matt 57-60; P-in-c Cookridge CD Ripon 60-64; V Cookridge H Trin 64-67; Chapl Miss to Seamen Tilbury 67-71; Gt Yarmouth 71-77; Australia 77-84 and from 85; Singapore 84-85; rtd 91. *Unit 2, 95 Charlotte Street, Wynnum, Qld, Australia 4178* Tel (0061) (7) 3893 1251

CHANTER, Canon Anthony Roy. b 37. ACP60 Open Univ BA72 Lon Univ MA75. Sarum Th Coll 64. **d** 66 **p** 67. C W Tarring *Chich* 66-69; Chapl St Andr Sch Worthing 69-70; Hd Master Bp King Sch Linc 70-73; Hon PV Linc Cathl *Linc* 70-73; Hd Master Grey Court Comp Sch Richmond 73-76; Hon C Kingston All SS *S'wark* 73-76; Hd Master Bp Reindorp Sch Guildf 77-84; Dir of Educn *Guildf* 84-01; Hon Can Guildf Cathl 84-01; rtd 02; Perm to Offic *Chich* from 02. *Thalassa, 62 Sea Avenue, Rustington, Littlehampton BN16 2DJ* Tel (01903) 774288
E-mail tonychanter@hotmail.com

CHANTREY, Preb David Frank. b 48. K Coll Cam BA70 PhD73 MA74. Westcott Ho Cam 83. **d** 86 **p** 87. C Wordsley *Lich* 86-89; C Beckbury 89-90; P-in-c 90-93; C Badger 89-90; P-in-c 90-93; C Kemberton, Sutton Maddock and Stockton 89-90; P-in-c 90-93; C Ryton 89-90; P-in-c 90-93; R Beckbury, Badger, Kemberton, Ryton, Stockton etc from 93; Preb Lich Cathl from 99. *The Rectory, Beckbury, Shifnal TF11 9DG* Tel and fax (01952) 750474 Mobile 07785-524495 E-mail chantrey@fish.co.uk

CHANTRY, Ms Helen Fiona. b 59. Bradf Univ BSc82 Leeds Univ CertEd83. Trin Coll Bris BA89. **d** 89 **p** 94. NSM Hyde St Geo *Ches* 89-92; Dioc Youth Officer 92-00; NSM Barrow 94-99; C Acton and Worleston, Church Minshull etc 00-04; P-in-c Audlem from 04. *The Rectory, Church Lane, Nantwich CW5 5RQ* Tel (01270) 625268 *or* 811543
E-mail helenchantry@btopenworld.com

CHANTRY, Peter Thomas. b 62. Bradf Univ BSc83. Trin Coll Bris BA89. **d** 89 **p** 90. C Hyde St Geo *Ches* 89-92; Dioc Youth Officer 91-99; P-in-c Barrow 94-99; R Nantwich from 99. *The Rectory, Church Lane, Nantwich CW5 5RQ* Tel (01270) 625268
E-mail peterchantry@hotmail.com

CHANTRY, Mrs Sandra Mary. b 41. Cam Inst of Educn CertEd63. EMMTC 83. **dss** 86 **d** 87 **p** 94. Loughb Gd Shep *Leic* 86-87; Par Dn 87-89; Par Dn Belton and Osgathorpe 89-90; Par Dn Hathern, Long Whatton and Diseworth w Belton etc 90-94; C 94-97; P-in-c 97-01; rtd 01. *4 The Toft, Mill Lane, Belton, Loughborough LE12 9UL* Tel (01530) 222678
E-mail sandrachantry@aol.com

CHAPLIN, Ann. b 39. LRAM59 FE TCert75 Em Coll Boston (US) MA93 Cheltenham & Glouc Coll of HE DipHE98. WEMTC 95. **d** 98 **p** 99. NSM Heref S Wye *Heref* 98-02; NSM St Weonards w Orcop, Garway, Tretire etc from 02. *45 Fonteine Court, Grey Tree Road, Ross-on-Wye HR9 7JU* Tel (01989) 576119

CHAPLIN, Colin. b 33. Edin Dioc NSM Course 74. **d** 76 **p** 77. NSM Penicuik *Edin* 76-91; P-in-c Peebles 89-90; NSM Bathgate 91-95; rtd 95; Asst P Edin St Mark *Edin* 97-00; Asst P Innerleithen from 00; Asst P Peebles from 00. *26 Broomhill Road, Penicuik, Edinburgh EH26 9EE* Tel (01968) 672050

CHAPLIN, Douglas Archibald. b 59. Em Coll Cam BA81. St Jo Coll Nottm DipTh84. **d** 86 **p** 87. C Glouc St Geo w Whaddon *Glouc* 86-89; C Lydney w Aylburton 89-93; R Worc St Clem *Worc* 93-01; TV Droitwich Spa from 01. *The Vicarage, 29 Old Coach Road, Droitwich WR9 8BB* Tel (01905) 798929 Mobile 07905-842565 E-mail fatherdoug@actually.me.uk

CHAPLIN, Paul. b 57. Hull Univ BA80 CertEd81 K Coll Lon MA89. St Steph Ho Ox 85. **d** 87 **p** 88. C Ex St Jas *Ex* 87-90; C Wokingham St Paul *Ox* 90-98; V Stratfield Mortimer 98-99; V Stratfield Mortimer and Mortimer W End etc from 99. *The Vicarage, 10 The Avenue, Mortimer, Reading RG7 3QY* Tel 0118-933 2404 *or* 933 3704

CHAPMAN, Ms Ann Beatrice. b 53. Hull Coll of Educn BEd77 Leeds Univ BA87. St Jo Coll Nottm MA95. **d** 95 **p** 96. C Burley *Ripon* 95-98; TV Sheff Manor *Sheff* 98-01; P-in-c Askrigg w Stallingbusk *Ripon* from 01; Dir Practical Th NEOC from 04. *The Vicarage, Askrigg, Leyburn DL8 3HZ* Tel (01969) 650301 E-mail beaty@fish.co.uk

CHAPMAN, Barry Frank. b 48. Trin Coll Bris 83. **d** 82 **p** 83. NSM Bradford-on-Avon Ch Ch *Sarum* from 82; Assoc Chapl Bath Univ *B & W* from 83. *16 Church Acre, Bradford-on-Avon BA15 1RL* Tel (01225) 866861 *or* 461244 E-mail b.f.chapman@bath.ac.uk

CHAPMAN, Mrs Celia. b 32. Whitelands Coll Lon TCert53 Open Univ BA82. WMMTC 84. **d** 87 **p** 94. NSM Bilston St Leon *Lich* 87-93; Ind Chapl Black Country Urban Ind Miss 93-98; Chapl St Pet Colleg Sch Wolv 93-98; rtd 99; Perm to Offic *Glouc* and *Worc* from 99. *5 Tyne Drive, Evesham WR11 7FG* Tel (01386) 765878

CHAPMAN, Canon Christopher Robin. b 37. Nottm Univ DipAdEd71 Cam Univ DipRK74. Ripon Hall Ox 72. **d** 73 **p** 74. C Kidbrooke St Jas *S'wark* 73-77; V Corton *Nor* 77-80; V Hopton 77-80; RD Lothingland 80-86; V Hopton w Corton 80-92; P-in-c Loddon w Sisland 92-93; P-in-c Loddon, Sisland w Hales and Heckingham 93-98; P-in-c Chedgrave w Hardley and Langley 97-98; V Loddon, Sisland, Chedgrave, Hardley and Langley 98-03; RD Loddon 95-98; Hon Can Nor Cathl 96-03; Chapl Langley Sch Nor 00-03; rtd 04; Perm to Offic *Chelmsf* from 04. *St Luke's House, 26 Lewis Drive, Chelmsford CM2 9EF* Tel (01245) 354479

CHAPMAN, Colin Gilbert. b 38. St Andr Univ MA60 Lon Univ BD62 Birm Univ MPhil94. Ridley Hall Cam 62. **d** 64 **p** 65. C Edin St Jas *Edin* 64-67; Egypt 68-73; Tutor Crowther Hall CMS Tr Coll Selly Oak 73-75; Prin 90-97; Lebanon 75-82; Chapl Limassol St Barn 82-83; Lect Trin Coll Bris 83-90; Dir Faith to Faith Consultancy 97-99; Lect Near E Sch of Th Lebanon 99-03; rtd 04. *Rose Cottage, 2 Quest Hills Road, Malvern WR14 1RW* Tel (01684) 563180

CHAPMAN, Mrs Deborah Herath. b 55. Fort Lewis Coll (USA) BA76 Lon Bible Coll MA94. NTMTC 04. **d** 05. C Hanwell St Mellitus w St Mark *Lon* from 05. *St Hugh's House, 22 Gosling Close, Greenford UB6 9UE* Tel (020) 8813 0162 E-mail bee@rechord.com

CHAPMAN, Canon Derek. b 22. Westcott Ho Cam 52. **d** 53 **p** 54. C Earlsdon *Cov* 53-56; C Rugby St Andr 56-58; V E Malling *Roch* 58-79; CF (TA) 60-67; R Hever w Mark Beech *Roch* 79-89; P-in-c Four Elms 80-89; Hon Can Roch Cathl 84-89; rtd 89; Perm to Offic *Roch* 89-98; Perm to Offic *Chich* from 89. *1 Moat Lane, Sedlescombe, Battle TN33 0RZ* Tel (01424) 754455

CHAPMAN, Mrs Dorothy. b 38. Nottm Univ Cert Th & Past Studies. EMMTC. **d** 89 **p** 94. Par Dn Bingham *S'well* 89-92; Sub-Chapl HM Pris Whatton 89-92; C Lenton 92-98; rtd 98; Perm to Offic *S'well* from 04. *86 Kenrick Road, Nottingham NG3 6FB* Tel 0115-950 3088

CHAPMAN, Drummond John. b 36. NDD. Cant Sch of Min 80. **d** 83 **p** 86. C Kington w Huntington, Old Radnor, Kinnerton etc *Heref* 83-84; C Llanidloes w Llangurig *Ban* 86-90; V Llanwnnog and Caersws w Carno from 90. *The Vicarage, Llanwnnog, Caersws SY17 5JG* Tel (01686) 688318

CHAPMAN, Edwin Thomas. b 32. Man Univ BA60. St Mich Coll Llan 62. **d** 63 **p** 64. C Cleveleys *Blackb* 63-65; C Ox St Mary V w St Cross and St Pet *Ox* 65-67; Chapl LMH Ox 67-68; Asst Dir of Educn *York* 68-75; R E Gilling 68-76; P-in-c Hockley *Chelmsf* 76-77; V 77-82; P-in-c Gosberton Clough and Quadring *Linc* 82-83; Chapl St Cath Sch Bramley 83-86; R Bulmer w Dalby, Terrington and Welburn *York* 86-97; RD Bulmer and Malton 91-97; rtd 97; Perm to Offic *York* from 97. *6 Undercroft, Dunnington, York YO19 5RP* Tel (01904) 488637

CHAPMAN, Canon Eric Ronald. b 19. Man Univ BA41 BD59. Bps' Coll Cheshunt 41. **d** 43 **p** 44. C Chorley St Pet *Blackb* 43-46; C Skerton St Luke 46-51; V Bolton St Mark *Man* 51-58; V Kells *Carl* 58-66; RD Whitehaven 66-70; R Egremont 66-81; Hon Can Carl Cathl 79-85; TR Egremont and Haile 81-85; rtd 85; Perm to Offic *Carl* from 86. *Bernaville, Highfield Road, Grange-over-Sands LA11 7JA* Tel (01539) 534351

CHAPMAN, Gorran. b 55. Dur Univ BA. Westcott Ho Cam 78. **d** 80 **p** 81. C Par *Truro* 80-82; C Kenwyn 82-84; P-in-c Penwerris 84-89; V 89-92; V Torquay St Martin Barton *Ex* from 92; Perm to Offic *Truro* from 92. *St Martin's Vicarage, Beechfield Avenue, Barton, Torquay TQ2 8HU* Tel (01803) 327223

CHAPMAN, Guy Godfrey. b 33. Southn Univ BSc57. Clifton Th Coll 60. **d** 62 **p** 63. C Chadderton Ch Ch *Man* 62-67; V Edgeside 67-70; P-in-c Shipton Bellinger *Win* 70-72; V 72-83; RD Andover 75-85; Hon Can Win Cathl 79-91; R Over Wallop w Nether Wallop 83-91; V Ambrosden w Merton and Piddington *Ox* 91-00; RD Bicester and Islip 95-00; rtd 00; Perm to Offic *Sarum* and *Win* from 01. *65 St Ann Place, Salisbury SP1 2SU* Tel (01722) 335339 E-mail gandachapman@fish.co.uk

CHAPMAN, Henry Davison. b 31. Bris Univ BA55. Tyndale Hall Bris 52. **d** 56 **p** 57. C St Helens St Mark *Liv* 56-60; R Clitheroe St Jas *Blackb* 60-67; V Tipton St Martin *Lich* 67-68; SW Area Sec CPAS 68-72; V Eccleston St Luke *Liv* 72-78; P-in-c Ringshall w Battisford, Barking w Darmsden etc *St E* 78-80; R 80-93; RD Bosmere 87-91; rtd 93; Perm to Offic *Sarum* from 93. *Daracombe, 4 The Clays, Market Lavington, Devizes SN10 4AY* Tel (01380) 813774

CHAPMAN, Ian Martin. b 47. Oak Hill Th Coll BA94. **d** 94 **p** 95. C S Mimms Ch Ch *Lon* 94-99; Perm to Offic from 02. *24 Vicars Close, Enfield EN1 3DN*

CHAPMAN (née CRAVEN), Mrs Janet Elizabeth. b 58. St Jo Coll Dur BSc80 MA92. Cranmer Hall Dur 84. **d** 87 **p** 95. Par Dn Darlington St Cuth *Dur* 87-92; NSM Edin Gd Shep *Edin* 93-95; NSM Long Marston and Rufforth w Moor Monkton and Hessay *York* 95-98; Chapl Qu Ethelburga's Coll York 97-99; Chapl Harrogate Ladies' Coll 00; P-in-c Banbury *Ox* from 01. *The Vicarage, 89 Oxford Road, Banbury OX16 9AJ* Tel (01295) 262370 E-mail janet.chapman@care4free.net

CHAPMAN, John. b 24. St Cuth Soc Dur BA51. St Chad's Coll Dur. **d** 53 **p** 54. C Billingham St Cuth *Dur* 53-55; C Harton 55-57; PC Hedgefield 57-63; PC Annfield Plain 63-78; V Bolton All So w St Jas *Man* 78-85; V Baddesley Ensor w Grendon *Birm* 85-91; rtd 91; Perm to Offic *Birm* 91-97; *Cov* from 91; *Man* from 01. *The Angelus, 49 Alfriston Road, Coventry CV3 6FG* Tel (024) 7641 3758

CHAPMAN, John Brown. b 54. Strathclyde Univ BSc76 Lon Bible Coll BA80. NTMTC 00. **d** 02 **p** 03. C W Ealing St Jo w St Jas *Lon* 02-05; C Northolt St Mary from 05. *St Hugh's House, 22 Gosling Close, Greenford UB6 9UE* Tel (020) 8813 0162

CHAPMAN (née WHITFIELD), Mrs Joy Verity. b 46. SRN67 SCM71 Midwife Teacher's Dip 80. Trin Coll Bris BA88. **d** 88 **p** 94. C Littleover *Derby* 88-92; Par Dn Bucknall and Bagnall *Lich* 92-94; C 94; TV 94-97; Chapl LOROS Hospice 97-03; rtd 03; Perm to Offic *Leic* from 03. *15 Templar Way, Rothley, Leicester LE7 7RB* Tel 0116-230 1994 E-mail chapman@leicester.anglican.org

CHAPMAN, Mrs Lesley. b 61. NEOC 02. **d** 05. C Fenham St Jas and St Basil *Newc* from 05. *32 Auburn Gardens, Newcastle upon Tyne NE4 9XP* E-mail lesley.chapman414@btopenworld.com

CHAPMAN, Mrs Linda. b 46. Lon Univ BSc67 Lon Inst of Educn PGCE68. Guildf Dioc Min Course 98. **d** 00 **p** 01. NSM Ewell St Fran *Guildf* 00-04; NSM Cheswardine, Childs Ercall, Hales, Hinstock etc *Lich* from 04. *The Vicarage, High Street, Cheswardine, Market Drayton TF9 2RS* Tel (01630) 661204 E-mail rev.linda.chapman@dsl.pipex.com

CHAPMAN, Margaret. *See* FLINTOFT-CHAPMAN, Mrs Margaret

CHAPMAN, Mrs Margaret. b 34. Univ Coll Lon BA72 Qu Mary Coll Lon MA74. EAMTC 94. **d** 95 **p** 96. NSM Theydon Bois *Chelmsf* 95-01; P-in-c Gt Hallingbury and Lt Hallingbury from 01. *The Rectory, Wright's Green Lane, Little Hallingbury, Bishop's Stortford CM22 7RE* Tel (01279) 723341 E-mail revdmchapman@xalt.co.uk

CHAPMAN, Mark David. b 60. Trin Coll Ox MA83 DipTh84 DPhil89. Ox Min Course 93. **d** 94 **p** 95. Lect Ripon Coll Cuddesdon from 92; NSM Dorchester *Ox* 94-99; NSM Wheatley from 99. *Ripon College, Cuddesdon, Oxford OX44 9EX* Tel (01865) 874310 E-mail markchapman@ripon-cuddesdon.ac.uk

CHAPMAN, The Ven Michael Robin. b 39. Leeds Univ BA61. Coll of Resurr Mirfield 61. **d** 63 **p** 64. C Southwick St Columba *Dur* 63-68; Chapl RN 68-84; V Hale *Guildf* 84-91; RD Farnham 88-91; Adn Northn *Pet* 91-04; Can Pet Cathl 91-04; rtd 04. *Asher House, 4 Chapel Lane, Thurlby, Bourne PE10 0EW* Tel (01778) 424072 E-mail michaelrchapman@compuserve.com

CHAPMAN, Nigel Leonard. b 58. York St Jo Coll MA02. Cranmer Hall Dur 04. **d** 05. Dioc Youth Officer *York* from 00; NSM Coxwold and Husthwaite from 05. *The Vicarage, Coxwold, York YO61 4AD*

CHAPMAN, Miss Patricia Ann. b 42. **dss** 84 **d** 87 **p** 94. Rainworth *S'well* 84-96; Par Dn 87-94; C 94-96; P-in-c Mansfield Oak Tree Lane from 96. *8 Hartington Court, Mansfield NG18 3QJ* Tel (01623) 645030

CHAPMAN, Peter Harold White. b 40. AKC64. **d** 65 **p** 66. C Havant *Portsm* 65-69; C Stanmer w Falmer and Moulsecoomb *Chich* 69-73; Chapl RN 73-86; Chapl Chigwell Sch Essex 86-90; P-in-c Stapleford Tawney w Theydon Mt *Chelmsf* 87-01; rtd 02. *The Old Rectory, Theydon Mount, Epping CM16 7PW* Tel (01992) 578723 E-mail phwchapman@aol.com

CHAPMAN, Peter John. b 33. Dur Univ BA56. Cranmer Hall Dur DipTh59. **d** 59 **p** 60. C Boulton *Derby* 59-62; Uganda 63-70; P-in-c Southampton St Matt *Win* 71-73; TV Southampton (City Cen) 73-78; V Bilston St Leon *Lich* 78-79; P-in-c Bilston St Mary 78-79; TR Bilston 80-98; RD Wolverhampton 89-98; rtd 99;

Perm to Offic *Glouc* and *Worc* from 99. *5 Tyne Drive, Evesham WR11 6FG* Tel (01386) 765878

CHAPMAN, Prof Raymond. b 24. Jes Coll Ox BA45 MA59 Lon Univ MA47 BD75 PhD78. S'wark Ord Course 72. **d** 74 **p** 75. NSM St Mary le Strand w St Clem Danes *Lon* 74-82; NSM Barnes St Mary *S'wark* 82-94; Perm to Offic *Lon* 82-91 and *S'wark* from 94. *6 Kitson Road, London SW13 9HJ* Tel (020) 8748 9901

CHAPMAN, Raymond. b 41. Linc Th Coll 68. **d** 71 **p** 72. C Dronfield *Derby* 71-74; C Delaval *Newc* 75-76; TV Whorlton 76-79; V Newc St Hilda 79-83; V Blyth St Cuth 83-89; Hon C Fareham SS Pet and Paul *Portsm* 95-98; Perm to Offic 98-00 and from 05; C Purbrook 00-05. *170 White Hart Lane, Fareham PO16 9AX* Tel (023) 9232 4537 Mobile 07944-1245467 Fax (023) 9264 4237

CHAPMAN, Canon Rex Anthony. b 38. Univ Coll Lon BA62 St Edm Hall Ox BA64 MA68. Wells Th Coll 64. **d** 65 **p** 66. C Stourbridge St Thos *Worc* 65-68; Chapl Aber Univ *Ab* 68-78; Can St Andr Cathl 76-78; Bp's Adv for Educn *Carl* 78-85; Dir of Educn 85-04; Can Res Carl Cathl 78-04; rtd 04; Chapl to The Queen from 97. *The Cottage, Myreside, Finzean, Banchory AB31 6NB* Tel (01330) 850645
E-mail rex.chapman@ukgateway.net

CHAPMAN, Robert Bertram. b 68. St Jo Coll Nottm BA00. **d** 00 **p** 01. C Daybrook *S'well* 00-03; P-in-c Colwick from 03; P-in-c Netherfield from 03. *St George's Rectory, 93 Victoria Road, Netherfield, Nottingham NG4 2GY* Tel 0115-961 5566
E-mail robertsarah@chapm64.freeserve.co.uk

CHAPMAN, Rodney Andrew. b 53. AKC75. St Aug Coll Cant 75. **d** 76 **p** 77. C Hartlepool St Aid *Dur* 76-81; Lic to Offic 81-83; C Owton Manor 83-87; P-in-c Kelloe 87-92; V Sharlston *Wakef* 92-01; V Stainland w Outlane from 01. *The Vicarage, 345 Stainland Road, Stainland, Halifax HX4 9HF* Tel (01422) 311848

CHAPMAN, Roger John. b 34. AKC58. **d** 59 **p** 60. C Guildf Ch Ch *Guildf* 59-61; Kenya 61-67; R S Milford *York* 68-77; RD Selby 72-77; V Beverley St Mary 77-88; RD Beverley 85-88; V Desborough *Pet* 88-95; R Brampton Ash w Dingley and Braybrooke 88-95; rtd 95; Perm to Offic *York* from 95. *14 Scrubwood Lane, Beverley HU17 7BE* Tel (01482) 881267

CHAPMAN, Preb Sally Anne. b 55. Lanchester Poly BSc76 Univ of Wales (Swansea) PGCE77. WMMTC 87. **d** 90 **p** 94. Par Dn Stoneydelph St Martin CD *Lich* 90; Par Dn Glascote and Stonydelph 90-93; Par Dn Willenhall H Trin 93-94; C 94-96; TV 96-99; V Streetly from 99; Dioc Adv for Women in Min 99-04; RD Walsall 04-05; Preb Lich Cathl from 04. *All Saints' Vicarage, 2 Foley Church Close, Sutton Coldfield B74 3JX* Tel 0121-353 2292 *or* 353 3582 E-mail robert@furzebank.freeserve.co.uk

CHAPMAN, Mrs Sarah Jean. b 55. Lon Univ DipCOT77. Sarum & Wells Th Coll 86. **d** 89 **p** 94. NSM Rogate w Terwick and Trotton w Chithurst *Chich* 89-94; NSM Easebourne 94-96; Perm to Offic *Portsm* 96-97; V Sheet 97-02; V Bitterne Park *Win* from 02. *Bitterne Park Vicarage, 7 Thorold Road, Southampton SO18 1HZ* Tel (023) 8055 1560 E-mail revsarah@sargil.co.uk

CHAPMAN (formerly WOOD), Canon Sylvia Marian. b 40. Gilmore Ho 77. **dss** 80 **d** 87 **p** 94. Tolleshunt Knights w Tiptree *Chelmsf* 80-83; Leigh-on-Sea St Jas 83-86; Canvey Is 86-87; Par Dn 87-92; Miss to Seamen 87-92; Warden of Ords *Chelmsf* 89-92; Par Dn Hutton 92-94; CME Officer 92-94; C Hutton 94-97; Ind Chapl 97-99; V Moulsham St Luke from 99; Hon Can Chelmsf Cathl from 01; Perm to Offic *Nor* from 00. *St Luke's House, 26 Lewis Drive, Chelmsford CM2 9EF* Tel and fax (01245) 354479 E-mail chapman@fish.co.uk

CHAPMAN, Thomas Graham. b 33. Trin Coll Bris 73. **d** 75 **p** 76. C Branksome St Clem *Sarum* 75-81; V Quarry Bank *Lich* 81-93; V Quarry Bank *Worc* 93-99; rtd 99; Perm to Offic *Worc* from 99. *8 Somerset Drive, Wollaston, Stourbridge DY8 4RH* Tel (01384) 373921 E-mail thomas.chapman1@btinternet.com

CHAPMAN, Timothy Mark. b 69. Clare Coll Cam BA91. Oak Hill Th Coll BA02. **d** 02 **p** 03. C Lt Shelford *Ely* from 02. *5 Garden Fields, Little Shelford, Cambridge CB2 5HH* Tel (01223) 844963 *or* 843710 Mobile 07815-686072
E-mail timandlucychapman@btopenworld.com

CHAPMAN, Miss Yvonne Hazel. b 35. Serampore Th Coll BRE63 Brighton Coll of Educn CertEd55. Coll of Ascension 60 EAMTC 95. **d** 96 **p** 97. NSM Duston Team *Pet* 96-02; NSM Officer 99-02; rtd 02. *18 Sundew Court, Northampton NN4 9XH* Tel (01604) 762091 E-mail rev.ychapman@virgin.net

CHAPPELL, Allan. b 27. Selw Coll Cam BA51 MA56. Coll of Resurr Mirfield 51. **d** 53 **p** 54. C Knowle *Bris* 53-57; Zanzibar 57-63; C Long Eaton St Laur *Derby* 64-67; C-in-c Broxtowe CD *S'well* 67-73; P-in-c Flintham 73-82; R Car Colston w Screveton 73-82; V Mansfield St Lawr 82-92; rtd 93; Perm to Offic *S'well* from '93 and *Derby* from 00. *43 Hillsway Crescent, Mansfield NG18 5DR* Tel (01623) 654155

CHAPPELL, Edward Michael. b 32. Glouc Sch of Min 84. **d** 87 **p** 88. NSM Wotton-under-Edge w Ozleworth and N Nibley *Glouc* 87-01; Perm to Offic from 01. *5 Parklands, Wotton-under-Edge GL12 7LT* Tel (01453) 844250

CHAPPELL, Frank Arnold. b 37. Dur Univ BA58. Bps' Coll Cheshunt. **d** 60 **p** 61. C Headingley *Ripon* 60-65; V Beeston Hill St Luke 65-73; R Garforth 73-91; V Dacre w Hartwith and Darley w Thornthwaite 91-02; rtd 02; Perm to Offic *York* and *Ripon* from 02. *14 Nelsons Lane, York YO24 1HD* Tel (01904) 709566

CHAPPELL, Preb George Thomas. b 04. St Jo Coll Dur LTh28 BA29 MA32. Lon Coll of Div 24. **d** 28 **p** 29. C Birkenhead St Mary w St Paul *Ches* 28-31; C Cliftonville *Cant* 31-34; Org Sec (Dios Ox and Cov) CMS 34-41; (Dio Pet) 35-41; P-in-c Paddington St Jas *Lon* 41-43; V 43-71; Chapl St Mary's Hosp Paddington 44-54; RD Paddington 56-67; RD Westmr Paddington 67-69; Preb St Paul's Cathl 63-71; rtd 71; C S Kensington H Trin w All SS *Lon* 71-74; P-in-c 74-75; Perm to Offic 75-85. *Flat 3, 19 Burton Road, Poole BH13 6DT* Tel (01202) 764665

CHAPPELL, Michael. *See* CHAPPELL, Edward Michael

CHAPPELL, Michael Paul. b 35. Selw Coll Cam BA57 MA61 ACertCM65. Cuddesdon Coll 60. **d** 62 **p** 63. C Pershore w Pinvin, Wick and Birlingham *Worc* 62-65; Malaysia 65-67; V Choral and Chapl Heref Cathl *Heref* 67-71; Min Can Dur Cathl *Dur* 71-76; Prec 72-76; Chapl H Trin Sch Stockton 76-87; C-in-c Stockton Green Vale H Trin CD *Dur* 82-87; V Scarborough St Luke *York* 87-01; Chapl Scarborough Gen Hosp 87-97; rtd 01; Perm to Offic *York* from 01. *26 Dulverton Hall, Esplanade, Scarborough YO11 2AR* Tel (01723) 340126

CHARD, Canon Francis Eric. b 24. Dur Univ BA53 MLitt81. St Jo Coll Dur. **d** 55 **p** 56. C Cleveleys *Blackb* 55-57; C Preston St Jo 57-60; V Ewood 60-72; V Downham 72-88; RD Whalley 83-89; Hon Can Blackb Cathl 86-93; Co Ecum Officer 88-93; rtd 93; Perm to Offic *Blackb* from 93. *21 Moorland Crescent, Clitheroe BB7 4PY* Tel (01200) 427480

CHARD, Reginald Jeffrey. b 40. Univ of Wales (Lamp) BA62 Birm Poly CQSW75. Coll of Resurr Mirfield 62. **d** 64 **p** 65. C Ystrad Mynach *Llan* 64-67; C Aberdare St Fagan 67-71; V Hirwaun 71-74; Hon C Stechford *Birm* 74-78; TV Banbury *Ox* 78-86; Ind Chapl from 86; P-in-c Claydon w Mollington 86-96; R Ironstone from 96. *The Rectory, Church Street, Wroxton, Banbury OX15 6QE* Tel and fax (01295) 730344
E-mail jeffreychard@aol.com

CHARING CROSS, Archdeacon of. *See* JACOB, The Ven William Mungo

CHARKHAM, Rupert Anthony. b 59. Ex Univ BA81. Wycliffe Hall Ox 83. **d** 89 **p** 89. C Ox St Aldate w St Matt *Ox* 89-92; P-in-c Fisherton Anger *Sarum* 92-99; R 99-03; V Cambridge H Trin *Ely* from 03. *Holy Trinity Vicarage, 1 Selwyn Gardens, Cambridge CB3 9AX* Tel (01223) 354774 *or* 355397
E-mail rupert.charkham@htcambridge.org.uk

CHARLES, George Edward. b 41. St Jo Coll Morpeth ThL63. **d** 66 **p** 67. Australia 66-01; C Bentleigh St Jo 66-67; C Broadmeadows 67-70; I Montmorency 70-74; I Mooroolbark 74-81; I Bacchus Marsh 81-86; I Sorrento 86-93; I Altona 93-98; I Inverleigh, Bannockburn and Meredith 98-01; TV Hanley H Ev *Lich* from 02. *19 Widecombe Road, Stoke-on-Trent ST1 6SL* Tel (01782) 267243 E-mail gpsecharles@aol.com

CHARLES, James Richard. b 67. St Edm Hall Ox BA90 CertEd91. Oak Hill Th Coll BA03. **d** 03 **p** 04. C Throop *Win* from 03. *51 Landford Way, Bournemouth BH8 0NY* Tel (01202) 526731 E-mail jimrcharles@yahoo.co.uk

CHARLES, Canon Jonathan. b 42. St Luke's Coll Ex CertEd64. Ripon Hall Ox 72 Ripon Coll Cuddesdon 78. **d** 79 **p** 80. C Leagrave *St Alb* 79-82; Chapl Denstone Coll Uttoxeter 82-86; Chapl Malvern Girls' Coll 86-89; Chapl K Sch Worc 89-95; Min Can Worc Cathl *Worc* 89-95; R Burnham Gp of Par *Nor* from 95; RD Burnham and Walsingham from 00; Hon Can Nor Cathl from 05. *The Rectory, The Pound, Burnham Market, King's Lynn PE31 8UL* Tel (01328) 738317 E-mail revj.charles@virgin.net

CHARLES, Martin. *See* CHARLES, William Martin Darrell

CHARLES, Mary Cecilia. b 49. Univ of Wales BEd. Trin Coll Carmarthen. **d** 96 **p** 97. NSM Letterston w Llanfair Nant-y-Gof etc *St D* from 96. *Heneglwys Farm, St David's Road, Letterston, Haverfordwest SA62 5SR* Tel (01348) 840452

CHARLES, Meedperdas Edward. b 28. Fitzw Ho Cam BA60 MA64. Bangalore Th Coll BD54. **d** 54 **p** 55. C Malacca Malaya 54-55; P-in-c Singapore St Paul and St Pet 55-58; Perm to Offic *Ely* 58-60; V Sheff St Bart Langsett Road *Sheff* 60-64; Chapl Univ of Singapore 64-66; V Gravelly Hill *Birm* 66-78; V Endcliffe *Sheff* 79-90; rtd 91; Perm to Offic *Sheff* from 91. *60 Ringinglow Road, Sheffield S11 7PQ* Tel 0114-266 4980

CHARLES, Robert Sidney James. b 40. Lon Univ CertEd77 Open Univ BA79 Univ of Wales LLM97. St Mich Coll Llan DipTh65. **d** 65 **p** 66. C Merthyr Tydfil *Llan* 65-68; C Shotton *St As* 68-70; R Stock and Lydlinch *Sarum* 70-74; R Hubberston *St D* 74-76; Perm to Offic *Chelmsf* 81-83; V Crossens *Liv* 83-97; V Budleigh Salterton *Ex* from 97. *St Peter's Vicarage, 4A West Hill Lane, Budleigh Salterton EX9 6AA* Tel (01395) 443195

CHARLES, Robin. b 50. Sarum & Wells Th Coll. **d** 86 **p** 87. C Chesterton *Lich* 86-89; C Rugeley 89-90; TV 90-97; TV E Scarsdale *Derby* 97-01; C Chesterfield St Mary and All SS 01-04;

V Worc Dines Green St Mich and Crown E, Rushwick *Worc* from 04. *3 Grove Farm, Farmbrook Close, Worcester WR2 5UG* Tel and fax (01905) 749995 Mobile 07788-724581 E-mail robin@maize45.freeserve.co.uk

CHARLES, William Martin Darrell. b 40. **d** 90 **p** 91. C Market Harborough *Leic* 90-91; P-in-c Higham-on-the-Hill w Fenny Drayton and Witherley 91-99; P-in-c Breedon cum Isley Walton and Worthington 99-02; rtd 02. *37 Whatton Road, Kegworth, Derby DE74 2EZ* Tel (01509) 672040

CHARLES-EDWARDS, David Mervyn. b 38. Trin Coll Cam BA61. Linc Th Coll 62. **d** 64 **p** 89. C Putney St Mary *S'wark* 64-65; Chief Exec Officer Br Assn for Counselling 82-87; Gen Manager Lon Lighthouse AIDS Project 87-88; Consultant in leadership and team building from 88; NSM Rugby St Andr *Cov* 89-99; P-in-c Clifton upon Dunsmore and Newton 99-03; Perm to Offic from 03. *236 Hillmorton Road, Rugby CV22 5BG* Tel (01788) 569212 E-mail cwa.david@btinternet.com

CHARLESWORTH, Eric Charlesworth. b 29. Kelham Th Coll 49. **d** 54 **p** 56. C Woodbridge St Mary *St E* 54-57; Asst Chapl Oslo St Edm *Eur* 57-59; Canada 60-66; R Huntingfield w Cookley *St E* 66-70; R Slimbridge *Glouc* 70-96; rtd 96; Perm to Offic *Glouc* from 96 and *Ox* from 04. *Gardener's Cottage, Fairford Park, Fairford GL7 4JQ* Tel (01285) 712411

CHARLESWORTH, Ian Peter. b 65. Lanc Univ BA87. St Mich Coll Llan DipTh93. **d** 93 **p** 94. C Caereithin *S & B* 93-95; C Oystermouth 95-97; R Llandefalle and Llyswen w Boughrood etc from 97. *The Rectory, Church Lane, Llyswen, Brecon LD3 0UU* Tel (01874) 754255 E-mail ianpcharl@aol.com

CHARLEY, Canon Julian Whittard. b 30. New Coll Ox BA55 MA58. Ridley Hall Cam 55. **d** 57 **p** 58. C St Marylebone All So w SS Pet and Jo *Lon* 57-64; Lect Lon Coll of Div 64-70; Vice-Prin St Jo Coll Nottm 70-74; TR Everton St Pet *Liv* 74-87; Warden Shrewsbury Ho 74-87; P-in-c Gt Malvern St Mary *Worc* 87-97; Hon Can Worc Cathl 91-97; rtd 97; Perm to Offic *Heref* and *Worc* from 97. *155A Old Hollow, Malvern WR14 4NN* Tel (01684) 569801

CHARLTON, Canon Arthur David. b 23. Open Univ BA73 BPhil83. Chich Th Coll. **d** 66 **p** 67. C Rotherfield *Chich* 66-70; C Uckfield 70-72; C Isfield 70-72; C Lt Horsted 70-72; R Cocking w Bepton 72-79; P-in-c W Lavington 78-79; R Cocking, Bepton and W Lavington 79-90; Can and Preb Chich Cathl 88-90; rtd 90; Perm to Offic *Chich* from 91; Perm to Offic *Roch* 91-98. *33 High Cross Fields, Crowborough TN6 2SN* Tel (01892) 661351

CHARMAN, Ms Jane Ellen Elizabeth. b 60. St Jo Coll Dur BA81 Selw Coll Cam BA84 MA88. Westcott Ho Cam 82. **d** 87 **p** 94. C Glouc St Geo w Whaddon *Glouc* 87-90; Chapl and Fell Clare Coll Cam 90-95; R Duxford *Ely* 95-04; V Hinxton 95-04; V Ickleton 95-04; RD Shelford 03-04; Dir of Min *Sarum* from 04. *4 The Sidings, Downton, Salisbury SP5 3QZ* Tel (01722) 411944 Mobile 07867-146524 E-mail jane.charman@salisbury.anglican.org

CHARMLEY, Mark Richard. b 71. Ex Univ BA93. Qu Coll Birm MA01. **d** 01 **p** 02. C Blurton *Lich* 01-04; P-in-c Banbury St Leon *Ox* from 04. *St Leonard's Vicarage, Middleton Road, Banbury OX16 4RG* Tel (01295) 262120 E-mail charmley@totalise.co.uk

CHARNOCK, Deryck Ian. b 47. Oak Hill Th Coll 78. **d** 80 **p** 81. C Rowner *Portsm* 80-84; TV Southgate *Chich* 84-90; V Penge St Paul *Roch* 90-98; V Whitwick St Jo the Bapt *Leic* from 98. *The Vicarage, 37 North Street, Whitwick, Coalville LE67 5HB* Tel (01530) 836904 E-mail dc.whit1@ntlworld.com

CHARRETT, Geoffrey Barton. b 36. ALCM Nottm Univ BSc57. Ridley Hall Cam 65. **d** 67 **p** 68. C Clifton *York* 67-68; Lic to Offic *Blackb* 69-80; C Walthamstow St Mary w St Steph *Chelmsf* 81-82; TV 82-87; Chapl Gordon's Sch Woking 87-94; P-in-c Hambledon *Guildf* 94-97; rtd 97; Perm to Offic *Linc* from 00. *2 Station Road, Sutton-on-Sea, Mablethorpe LN12 2HN* Tel (01507) 443525

CHARRINGTON, Nicholas John. b 36. MA. Cuddesdon Coll 60. **d** 62 **p** 63. C Shrewsbury St Chad *Lich* 62-65; C Gt Grimsby St Mary and St Jas *Linc* 65-72; P-in-c Wellington Ch Ch *Lich* 72-78; R Edgmond 78-89; R Edgmond w Kynnersley and Preston Wealdmoors 89-91; C Plymstock *Ex* 91-94; Chapl St Luke's Hospice Plymouth 91-94; P-in-c Longden and Annscroft w Pulverbatch *Heref* 94-00; rtd 00; Perm to Offic *Heref* from 00. *Domas Cottage, Harley, Shrewsbury SY5 6LX* Tel (01952) 510721 E-mail nick@charrington.enta.net

CHARTERIS, Hugo Arundale. b 64. Witwatersrand Univ BA88. Cranmer Hall Dur 90. **d** 93 **p** 94. C Byker St Mark and Walkergate St Oswald *Newc* 93-97; P-in-c New Ferry *Ches* 97-02; V 02-05. *18 Kimberley Gardens, Newcastle upon Tyne NE2 1HJ* Tel 0191-281 1144 E-mail hugo@charteris.org.uk

CHARTERS, Alan Charles. b 35. Trin Hall Cam BA60 MA63 FCollP88. Linc Th Coll 60. **d** 62 **p** 63. C Gt Grimsby St Mary and St Jas *Linc* 62-65; Chapl and Hd RE Eliz Coll Guernsey 65-70; P-in-c Guernsey St Jas the Less 65-70; Dep Hd Master Park Sen High Sch Swindon 70-73; Chapl St Jo Sch Leatherhead 73-83; Dep Hd Master 76; Visiting Lect and Tutor Lon Univ Inst of Ed 76-80; Headmaster The K Sch Glouc 83-92; V Aberedw w Llandeilo Graban and Llanbadarn etc *S & B* 92-00; Bp's Visitor to Schs 92-00; rtd 00; Perm to Offic *Eur* 00-03; P-in-c Dinard from 03. *Crescent House, Church Street, Talgarth, Brecon LD3 0BL* Tel (01874) 711135 E-mail alan@ccharterss.net.uk

✠**CHARTRES, The Rt Revd and Rt Hon Richard John Carew.** b 47. PC96. Trin Coll Cam BA68 MA73 BD83 Hon DLitt98 Hon DD99 FSA99 Hon FGCM97. Cuddesdon Coll 69 Linc Th Coll 72. **d** 73 **p** 74 **c** 92. C Bedford St Andr *St Alb* 73-75; Bp's Dom Chapl 75-80; Abp's Chapl *Cant* 80-84; P-in-c Westmr St Steph w St Jo *Lon* 84-85; V 86-92; Dir of Ords 85-92; Prof Div Gresham Coll 86-92; Six Preacher Cant Cathl *Cant* 91-97; Area Bp Stepney *Lon* 92-95; Bp Lon from 95; Dean of HM Chpls Royal and Prelate of OBE from 95. *The Old Deanery, Dean's Court, London EC4V 5AA* Tel (020) 7248 6233 Fax 7248 9721 E-mail bishop@londin.clara.co.uk

CHATER, John Augustus. b 43. SEITE 99. **d** 04 **p** 05. NSM St Peter-in-Thanet *Cant* from 04. *125 High Street, Ramsgate CT11 9UA* Tel (01843) 596175 E-mail johnchater@rya-online.net

CHATER, John Leathley. b 29. Qu Coll Cam BA54 MA58. Ridley Hall Cam 54. **d** 56 **p** 57. C Bath Abbey w St Jas *B & W* 56-60; V Bermondsey St Anne *S'wark* 60-64; Ind Chapl 60-64; V Heslington *York* 64-69; Chapl York Univ 64-69; V Lawrence Weston *Bris* 69-73; Perm to Offic 74-80; P-in-c Wraxall *B & W* 80-82; R 82-84; V Battle *Chich* 84-90; Dean Battle 84-90; RD Battle and Bexhill 86-90; R St Marylebone w H Trin *Lon* 90-96; rtd 96; Perm to Offic *Chich* from 96. *75 Braemore Road, Hove BN3 4HA* Tel (01273) 748402

CHATFIELD, Adrian Francis. b 49. Leeds Univ BA71 MA72 MPhil89 PhD97. Coll of Resurr Mirfield 71. **d** 72 **p** 73. Trinidad and Tobago 72-83; TV Barnstaple, Goodleigh and Landkey *Ex* 83-85; TR Barnstaple 85-88; Lect St Jo Coll Nottm 88-98; S Africa 99-05; Tutor Wycliffe Hall Ox from 05; Hon C Wallingford *Ox* from 05. *The Vicarage, 34 Thames Mead, Crowmarsh Gifford, Wallingford OX10 8EY* Tel (01491) 837626

CHATFIELD, Mrs Gillian. b 50. Leeds Univ BA71 PGCE72. St Jo Coll Nottm MA94. **d** 94 **p** 95. C Greasley *S'well* 94-98; S Africa 99-05; TV Wallingford *Ox* from 05. *The Vicarage, 34 Thames Mead, Crowmarsh Gifford, Wallingford OX10 8EY* Tel (01491) 837626

CHATFIELD, Michael Francis. b 75. York Univ BSc96 Fitzw Coll Cam BA99 MA03. Ridley Hall Cam. **d** 00 **p** 01. C Attenborough *S'well* 00-03; P-in-c Chaguanas St Thos Trinidad and Tobago from 04. *Light Pole #65, #29 Serene Gardens, Longdenville, Trinidad, West Indies* Tel (001) (868) 754 4209 (mobile) E-mail thechatalots@hotmail.com

CHATFIELD, Neil Patrick. b 66. Nottm Univ BTh95. Linc Th Coll 93 Westcott Ho Cam 95. **d** 96 **p** 97. C Bexhill St Pet *Chich* 96-00; V Eastbourne Ch Ch from 00; Chapl Eastbourne Hosps NHS Trust from 01. *Christ Church Vicarage, 18 Addingham Road, Eastbourne BN22 7DY* Tel (01323) 721952

CHATFIELD, Canon Norman. b 37. Fitzw Ho Cam BA59 MA68. Ripon Hall Ox 60. **d** 62 **p** 63. C Burgess Hill St Jo *Chich* 62-65; C Uckfield 65-69; V Lower Sandown St Jo *Portsm* 69-76; V Locks Heath 76-83; Bp's Chapl for Post-Ord Tr 78-85; R Alverstoke 83-91; Chapl HM Pris Haslar 83-90; Chapl Gosport War Memorial Hosp 83-91; Hon Can Portsm Cathl *Portsm* 85-91; Can Res Glouc Cathl *Glouc* 91-02; rtd 02; Perm to Offic *Portsm* from 03. *16 Meadow Gardens, Waltham Chase, Southampton SO32 2NJ* Tel (01489) 891995 E-mail chat.field@virgin.net

CHATFIELD, Thomas William. b 19. Lon Univ. Chich Th Coll 44. **d** 46 **p** 47. C Hanworth All SS *Lon* 46-49; C Woolwich St Mich *S'wark* 49-51; C Eastbourne St Andr *Chich* 51-55; V Halton in Hastings St Clem 55-68; P-in-c Hastings St Mary Magd 68-71; R 71-78; P-in-c Bishopstone 78-84; rtd 84; Perm to Offic *Chich* from 84. *5 Leeds Close, Victoria Avenue, Ore Village, Hastings TN35 5BX* Tel (01424) 437413

CHATHAM, Richard Henry. b 28. Launde Abbey 71. **d** 71 **p** 72. C Aylestone *Leic* 71-76; R Hoby cum Rotherby 76-77; P-in-c Brooksby 76-77; R Hoby cum Rotherby w Brooksby, Ragdale & Thru'ton 77-85; R Overstrand *Nor* 85-93; rtd 93; Perm to Offic *Nor* from 93. *Sandyside, Sandy Lane, Cromer NR27 9JT* Tel (01263) 513456

CHATTELL, David Malcolm. b 63. St Luke's Coll Ex BEd93. Wycliffe Hall Ox 03. **d** 05. C Bucklebury w Marlston *Ox* from 05. *The Rectory, Southend Road, Southend, Reading RG7 6EU* E-mail dchattell@tinyonline.co.uk

CHATTERJI DE MASSEY, Robert Arthur Sovan Lal. b 15. Chich Th Coll 54. **d** 56 **p** 57. C Romford St Edw *Chelmsf* 56-60; R Abberton w Langenhoe 60-90; rtd 90; Perm to Offic *Ely* 96-98. *Clare House, 82 Main Street, Witchford, Ely CB6 2HQ*

CHATTERLEY, Mrs Marion Frances. b 55. Open Univ DipHSW95. Edin Th Coll 95. **d** 98 **p** 99. C Edin Gd Shep *Edin* 98-00; Chapl Napier Coll from 00; C Edin Ch Ch from 00. *102 Relugas Road, Edinburgh EH9 2LZ* Tel 0131-667 6847 Mobile 07771-982163 E-mail marion.chatterley@blueyonder.co.uk *or* marion@6a.org.uk

CHATTERTON, Thomas William. b 50. SEITE. **d** 99 **p** 00. OLM Blackheath All SS *S'wark* from 99. *44 Harland Road, London SE12 0JA* Tel (020) 8851 6813 *or* 7525 7912 ext 4482

CHATWIN, Ronald Ernest. b 34. St Aid Birkenhead 58. **d** 60 **p** 61. C Selsdon *Cant* 60-64; C Crawley *Chich* 64-68; V Coldwaltham 68-74; TV Ovingdean w Rottingdean and Woodingdean 74-83; V Saltdean 83-91; V Hellingly and Upper Dicker 91-02; rtd 02. *Cold Waltham, 29A New Road, Hellingly, Hailsham BN27 4EW* Tel (01323) 843346

CHAVE, Preb Brian Philip. b 51. Open Univ BA. Trin Coll Bris. **d** 84 **p** 85. C Cullompton *Ex* 84-87; TV Bishopsnympton, Rose Ash, Mariansleigh etc 87-93; Chapl for Agric *Heref* 93-96; Communications Adv and Bp's Staff Officer 97-01; Bp's Dom Chapl 97-01; TV W Heref from 01; Preb Heref Cathl from 97; Can 97-01; RD Heref City from 04. *The Vicarage, Vowles Close, Hereford HR4 0DF* Tel (01432) 273086 E-mail chave@hfddiocesan.freeserve.co.uk

CHAVE-COX, Guy. b 56. St Andr Univ BSc79. Wycliffe Hall Ox 83. **d** 86 **p** 87. C Wigmore Abbey *Heref* 86-88; C Bideford *Ex* 88-91; TV Barnstaple from 91. *St Paul's Vicarage, Old Sticklepath Hill, Barnstaple EX31 2BG* Tel (01271) 344400 E-mail vicar@barnstaple-st-paul.org.uk

CHAVNER, Robert. b 59. ALCM82 AGSM85 FGMS00 FRSA05. Linc Th Coll 90. **d** 92 **p** 93. C Beckenham St Geo *Roch* 92-96; Min Sevenoaks St Luke CD 96; V Sevenoaks St Luke from 96. *St Luke's House, 30 Eardley Road, Sevenoaks TN13 1XT* Tel and fax (01732) 452462

CHEADLE, Preb Robert. b 24. MBE71 TD66. Leeds Univ BA49. Coll of Resurr Mirfield 49. **d** 51 **p** 52. C Newbury St Jo *Ox* 51-55; C Tunstall Ch Ch *Lich* 55-57; TR Hanley H Ev 57-60; V Bloxwich 60-72; V Penkridge w Stretton 72-89; Preb Lich Cathl 79-89; P-in-c Dunston w Coppenhall 79-82; V 82-89; P-in-c Acton Trussell w Bednall 80-82; V 82-89; rtd 89; Perm to Offic *Lich* from 89. *26 Audley Place, Newcastle ST5 3RS* Tel (01782) 618685

CHEATLE, Adèle Patricia. b 46. York Univ BA73. Trin Coll Bris 76. **d** 87 **p** 98. Par Dn Harborne Heath *Birm* 87; NSM 92-93; Perm to Offic *Heref* 96-97; NSM Burghill 97-99; NSM Stretton Sugwas 97-99; NSM Heref St Pet w St Owen and St Jas 99-04; NSM Ches Square St Mich w St Phil *Lon* from 04. *142 Cambridge Street, London SW1V 4QF* Tel (020) 7730 1673 E-mail adele@cheatle.fslife.co.uk

CHEDZEY, Derek Christopher. b 67. Trin Coll Bris BA93. **d** 93 **p** 94. C Bedgrove *Ox* 93-95; C Haddenham w Cuddington, Kingsey etc 95-98; TV High Wycombe 98-01; C Washfield, Stoodleigh, Withleigh etc *Ex* 01-04; Deanery Tr Officer 01-04; P-in-c Frenchay and Winterbourne Down *Bris* from 04; Dir Lay Min from 04. *The Rectory, Frenchay Common, Frenchay, Bristol BS16 1LJ* Tel 0117-957 1170 Mobile 07811-878774 E-mail chedzey1@aol.com

CHEEK, Richard Alexander. b 35. Lon Univ LDS60 RCS 60. Ox NSM Course 72. **d** 75 **p** 76. NSM Maidenhead St Luke *Ox* 75-94; Asst Chapl Heatherwood and Wexham Park Hosp NHS Trust from 94. *Windrush, 26 Sheephouse Road, Maidenhead SL6 8EX* Tel (01628) 628484 E-mail r.a.cheek@dialpipex.com

CHEESEMAN, Mrs Angela Mary. b 40. **d** 05. OLM Eastling w Ospringe and Stalisfield w Otterden *Cant* from 05. *New House Farm, Otterden Road, Eastling, Faversham ME13 0BN* Tel (01795) 890629 E-mail angiecheeseman45@hotmail.com

CHEESEMAN, Colin Henry. b 47. Reading Univ BA69 Kent Univ PhD00. Sarum & Wells Th Coll 82. **d** 84 **p** 85. C Cranleigh *Guildf* 84-87; C Godalming 87-89; V Cuddington 89-96; Chapl HM Pris Wealstun 96-97; P-in-c Tockwith and Bilton w Bickerton *York* 97-01; RD New Ainsty 99-01; P-in-c Roundhay St Jo *Ripon* from 01. *The Vicarage, 2A Ryder Gardens, Leeds LS8 1JS* Tel 0113-266 9747 E-mail colin@stjohnsroundhay.co.uk

CHEESEMAN (née GOODAIR), Ms Janet. b 59. K Coll Lon BA81 Roehampton Inst PGCE82. NEOC 97. **d** 00 **p** 01. NSM Tockwith and Bilton w Bickerton *York* 00-01; NSM York St Olave w St Giles 00-01; Chapl Harrogate Ladies' Coll from 01. *Harrogate Ladies' College, Clarence Drive, Harrogate HG1 2QG* Tel (01423) 504543 Mobile 07866-186471 Fax (01423) 568893 E-mail revd.cheeseman@mail.hlc.org.uk

CHEESEMAN, John Anthony. b 50. Oriel Coll Ox BA73 MA75. Trin Coll Bris DipTh76. **d** 76 **p** 77. C Sevenoaks St Nic *Roch* 76-79; C Egham *Guildf* 79-82; V Leyton Ch Ch *Chelmsf* 82-90; V Westgate St Jas *Cant* 90-01; V Eastbourne H Trin *Chich* from 01. *Holy Trinity Vicarage, Trinity Trees, Eastbourne BN21 3BE* Tel (01323) 729046

CHEESEMAN, Kenneth Raymond. b 29. Roch Th Coll 63. **d** 66 **p** 67. C Crayford *Roch* 66-69; C Beckenham St Jas 69-75; V Belvedere St Aug 75-83; V Thorley *Portsm* 83-94; R Yarmouth 83-94; rtd 94; Perm to Offic *Portsm* from 94. *10 St Catherine's View, Godshill, Ventnor PO38 3JJ* Tel (01983) 840700

CHEESEMAN, Nicholas James. b 72. Qu Mary and Westf Coll Lon BA94 Leeds Univ BA02. Coll of Resurr Mirfield 00. **d** 03 **p** 04. C Wantage *Ox* from 03. *5 Barnard's Way, Wantage OX12 7EA* Tel (01235) 763309 Mobile 07732-252709 E-mail nicholascheeseman@fish.co.uk

CHEESEMAN, Trevor Percival. b 38. Auckland Univ PhD64 Lon Univ BD67. K Coll Lon and St Boniface Warminster AKC67. **d** 68 **p** 69. C Warmsworth *Sheff* 68-71; New Zealand from 71. *49 Birdwood Avenue, Papatoetoe, New Zealand* Tel (0064) (9) 277 6145 E-mail tpandhmc@internet.co.nz

CHEESMAN, Canon Andrew Walford. b 36. St Mark's Coll Adelaide BA58. Cuddesdon Coll 59. **d** 61 **p** 62. C Man St Aid *Man* 61-63; Australia from 63; P-in-c Keith 64-68; Prec St Pet Cathl Adelaide 68-70; Chapl Flinders Univ 68-70; Asst Chapl St Pet Coll Adelaide 70-73; P-in-c Tea Tree Gully 73-76; R Mitcham Adelaide 76-01; Adn Torrens 85-93; Can Adelaide from 85. *1/4 Torrens Street, Mitcham, S Australia 5062* Tel and fax (0061) (8) 8272 1864 E-mail mousal@bigbutton.com.au

CHEESMAN, Ashley Frederick Bruce. b 53. Oak Hill Th Coll. **d** 83 **p** 84. C Tranmere St Cath *Ches* 83-88; R Gaulby *Leic* 88-99; V from 99. *The Rectory, Gaulby Road, Gaulby, Leicester LE7 9BB* Tel 0116-259 6228

CHEESMAN, Peter. b 43. ACA65 FCA76 MCMI. Ridley Hall Cam 66. **d** 69 **p** 70. C Herne Bay Ch Ch *Cant* 69-74; TV Lowestoft St Marg *Nor* 75-78; TV Lowestoft and Kirkley 79-81; Ind Chapl *Glouc* 81-84; P-in-c Saul w Fretherne and Framilode 84-85; V Frampton on Severn, Arlingham, Saul etc from 85. *The Vicarage, The Street, Frampton on Severn, Gloucester GL2 7ED* Tel and fax (01452) 740966 E-mail peter@the-cheesman.net

CHEETHAM (née MUMFORD), Mrs Lesley Anne. b 51. Man Univ BA73. N Ord Course 01. **d** 04 **p** 05. C Halifax *Wakef* from 04. *27 Central Park, Halifax HX1 2BT* Tel (01422) 361942

✠**CHEETHAM, The Rt Revd Richard Ian.** b 55. CCC Ox BA77 CertEd78 MA82 Lon Univ PhD99. Ripon Coll Cuddesdon 85. **d** 87 **p** 88 **c** 02. C Newc H Cross *Newc* 87-90; V Luton St Aug Limbury *St Alb* 90-99; RD Luton 95-98; Adn St Alb 99-02; Area Bp Kingston *S'wark* from 02. *24 Albert Drive, London SW19 6LS* Tel (020) 8789 3218 *or* 8785 1983 Fax 7835 1981 E-mail bishop.richard@southwark.anglican.org

CHEEVERS, George Alexander. b 42. CITC 70. **d** 73 **p** 74. C Carrickfergus *Conn* 73-81; C Kilroot 78-81; I Kilmakee 82-91; I Magheragall 91-04; Can Belf Cathl 01-04; rtd 04. *1 Hampton Court, Dromore BT25 1SB* Tel (028) 9269 0701

CHELMSFORD, Bishop of. *See* GLADWIN, The Rt Revd John Warren

CHELMSFORD, Dean of. *See* JUDD, The Very Revd Peter Somerset Margesson

CHELTENHAM, Archdeacon of. *See* RINGROSE, The Ven Hedley Sidney

CHENNELL, Capt Arthur John. b 28. St Deiniol's Hawarden 77. **d** 77 **p** 78. CA from 58; C Prenton *Ches* 77-79; V Liscard St Thos 79-82; V Lt Thornton *Blackb* 82-94; rtd 94; Perm to Offic *Ches* from 94. *79 Cobham Road, Moreton, Wirral CH46 0RA* Tel 0151-678 5708

CHERRILL, John Oliver. b 33. Bath Univ MArch75 DipArch61. Sarum & Wells Th Coll 76. **d** 79 **p** 80. NSM Blackmoor *Portsm* 79-83; NSM Headley All SS *Guildf* 83-85; C 86-90; Perm to Offic *Portsm* from 95; rtd 98. *8 Londlandes, Church Crookham, Fleet GU52 6ZB* Tel (01252) 624508

CHERRIMAN, Colin Wilfred (Brother Colin Wilfred). b 37. Leeds Univ BA63. Coll of Resurr Mirfield 63. **d** 65 **p** 66. C Bournemouth St Fran *Win* 65-69; SSF from 69; Prov Min from 97; Lic to Offic *Chelmsf* 73-75; *Cant* 75-77; *Edin* 77-79; *Sarum* 79-82; *Newc* 82-88; Perm to Offic *Lon* 88-91; Adv HIV/AIDS Unit 91-92; HIV Support Worker St Botolph Aldgate *Lon* 92-96; New Zealand 96-02; rtd 02; Perm to Offic *Cant* from 03. *The Friary, 6A Stour Street, Canterbury CT1 2NR*

CHERRY, David. b 30. Roch Th Coll 59. **d** 61 **p** 62. C Seacroft *Ripon* 61-67; R Bamford *Derby* 67-75; Chapl Malaga w Almunecar and Nerja *Eur* 83-91; rtd 91; NSM Waltham St Lawrence *Ox* 97-01; Perm to Offic *Leic* from 01. *2 Church Lane, Rearsby, Leicester LE7 4YE* Tel (01664) 424099

CHERRY, David Warwick. b 61. Cape Town Univ BMus86 Leeds Univ BA91. Coll of Resurr Mirfield 92. **d** 92 **p** 93. C Hammersmith SS Mich and Geo White City Estate CD *Lon* 92-01; C Hammersmith St Luke 94-01; Chapl Univ of Greenwich *S'wark* 01-03; Chapl Univ of Westmr *Lon* from 03. *4A Luxborough Street, London W1U 5BF* Tel (020) 7911 5822 Mobile 07939-553547

CHERRY, Malcolm Stephen. b 28. Open Univ BA81. Sarum Th Coll 51. **d** 54 **p** 55. C Mill Hill Jo Keble Ch *Lon* 54-57; C Hendon All SS Childs Hill 57-59; Min Colchester St Anne CD *Chelmsf* 59-68; V Horndon on the Hill 68-79; Ind Chapl 69-79; Voc Officer Southend Adnry 74-79; R Lochgilphead *Arg* 79-82; V Mill End and Heronsgate w W Hyde *St Alb* 82-90; TV Chipping Barnet w Arkley 90-94; rtd 94; Perm to Offic *St E* from 94. *Nether Hankleys, Barrow Road, Higham, Bury St Edmunds IP28 6NN* Tel (01284) 810269

CHERRY, Canon Stephen Arthur. b 58. St Chad's Coll Dur BSc79 Fitzw Coll Cam BA85 MA90 K Coll Lon PhD95. Westcott Ho Cam 83. **d** 86 **p** 87. C Baguley and Asst Chapl Wythenshawe

Hosp Man 86-89; Chapl K Coll Cam 89-94; R Loughborough All SS w H Trin *Leic* from 94; RD Akeley E 96-99; Hon Can Leic Cathl from 04. *The Rectory, 60 Westfield Drive, Loughborough LE11 3QL* Tel (01509) 212780 E-mail sacherry@btinternet.com

CHESHAM, William Gerald. b 23. MIMechE55 Birm Univ DPS66. Wells Th Coll 61. **d** 63 **p** 64. C Ashford *Cant* 63-66; C Edgbaston St Bart *Birm* 66-68; V Smethwick 68-72; Lic to Offic *Heref* 72-78; TV Glendale Gp *Newc* 78-84; rtd 84; Hon Asst Chapl Algarve *Eur* 84-97; Perm to Offic *Sarum* from 97. *1 St George's Close, Lower Street, Salisbury SP2 8HA* Tel (01722) 323484

CHESHER, Michael. b 52. Open Univ BA84. EAMTC. **d** 00 **p** 01. C Littleport *Ely* 00-03; V Chelmsf All SS *Chelmsf* 03-04; P-in-c Walpole St Peter w Walpole St Andrew *Ely* from 04; P-in-c W Walton from 04. *The Rectory, Church Road, Walpole St Peter, Wisbech PE14 7NS* Tel (01945) 780252 E-mail mchesher@fsmail.net

✠**CHESSUN, The Rt Revd Christopher Thomas James.** b 56. Univ Coll Ox BA78 MA82 Trin Hall Cam BA82. Westcott Ho Cam. **d** 83 **p** 84 **c** 05. C Sandhurst *Ox* 83-87; C Portsea St Mary *Portsm* 87-89; Min Can and Chapl St Paul's Cathl *Lon* 89-93; Voc Adv 90-05; R Stepney St Dunstan and All SS 93-01; AD Tower Hamlets 97-01; Adn Northolt 01-05; Area Bp Woolwich *S'wark* from 05. *Trinity House, 4 Chapel Court, London SE1 1HW* Tel (020) 7939 9407 Fax 7939 9465 E-mail bishop.christopher@southwark.anglican.org

CHESTER, David Kenneth. b 50. Dur Univ BA73 Aber Univ PhD78 CGeol92 FGS88. N Ord Course 93. **d** 96 **p** 97. Hon C Hoylake *Ches* from 96. *Yenda, Grange Old Road, West Kirby, Wirral CH48 4ET* Tel 0151-625 8004 E-mail jg54@liverpool.ac.uk

CHESTER, Mark. b 55. Lanc Univ BA79. Wycliffe Hall Ox 86. **d** 88 **p** 89. C Plymouth St Andr w St Paul and St Geo *Ex* 88-94; V Burney Lane *Birm* 94-99; V Camberley St Paul *Guildf* from 99. *The Vicarage, Sandy Lane, Camberley GU15 2AG* Tel (01276) 21100 *or* 700211 E-mail mzbg@mzchester.freeserve.co.uk

CHESTER, Maureen Olga. b 47. Univ of Wales (Swansea) BA70. NEOC DipHE94. **d** 97 **p** 98. NSM Morpeth *Newc* from 97. *10 Leland Place, Morpeth NE61 2AN* Tel (01670) 514569 E-mail mochester@classicfm.net

CHESTER, Philip Anthony Edwin. b 55. Birm Univ LLB76. Cranmer Hall Dur 77. **d** 80 **p** 81. C Shrewsbury St Chad *Lich* 80-85; C St Martin-in-the-Fields *Lon* 85-88; Chapl K Coll Lon 88-95; PV Westmr Abbey from 90; P-in-c Westmr St Matt *Lon* 95-03; V from 03. *St Matthew's Clergy House, 20 Great Peter Street, London SW1P 2BU* Tel (020) 7222 3704 Fax 7233 0255 E-mail office@stmw.org

CHESTER, Mrs Violet Grace. b 50. WEMTC 97. **d** 00 **p** 01. OLM Dymock w Donnington and Kempley *Glouc* 00; OLM Redmarley D'Abitot, Bromesberrow, Pauntley etc from 00. *1 Longbridge, Dymock GL18 2DA* Tel (01531) 890633 Fax 635919 E-mail vialanrev@netscapeonline.co.uk

CHESTER, Archdeacon of. *See* ALLISTER, The Ven Donald Spargo

CHESTER, Bishop of. *See* FORSTER, The Rt Revd Peter Robert

CHESTER, Dean of. *See* McPHATE, The Very Revd Gordon Ferguson

CHESTERFIELD, Archdeacon of. *See* GARNETT, The Ven David Christopher

CHESTERMAN, Canon George Anthony (Tony). b 38. Man Univ BSc62 DipAdEd Nottm Univ PhD89. Coll of Resurr Mirfield 62. **d** 64 **p** 65. C Newbold w Dunston *Derby* 64-68; C Derby St Thos 68-70; Adult Educn Officer 70-79; R Mugginton and Kedleston 70-89; Vice-Prin EMMTC 79-86; Can Res Derby Cathl and Dioc Clergy In-Service Tr Adv *Derby* 89-03; Chapl to The Queen from 98; rtd 03. *7 Hillside, Lesbury, Alnwick NE66 3NR* Tel (01665) 833124

✠**CHESTERS, The Rt Revd Alan David.** b 37. St Chad's Coll Dur BA59 St Cath Soc Ox BA61 MA65. St Steph Ho Ox 59. **d** 62 **p** 63 **c** 89. C Wandsworth St Anne *S'wark* 62-66; Hon C 66-68; Chapl Tiffin Sch Kingston 66-72; Hon C Ham St Rich *S'wark* 68-72; Dioc Dir of Educn *Dur* 72-85; R Brancepeth 72-85; Hon Can Dur Cathl 75-85; Adn Halifax *Wakef* 85-89; Bp Blackb 89-03; rtd 03; Hon Asst Bp Ches from 03. *64 Hallfields Road, Tarvin, Chester CH3 8ET* Tel (01829) 740825

CHESTERS, David. b 45. **d** 04 **p** 05. NSM Wallasey St Hilary *Ches* from 04. *The Gables, 26 Warren Drive, Wallasey CH45 0JR* Tel 0151-639 9562

CHESTERS, Simon. b 66. Rob Coll Cam BA87 MA91. Wycliffe Hall Ox BA94 DipMin95. **d** 95 **p** 96. C Bidston *Ches* 95-99; P-in-c Runcorn St Jo Weston 99-03; Dioc Min Development Officer from 03; Hon C Lache cum Saltney from 03; Dir Reader Tr from 99. *7 Earlsway, Chester CH4 8AX,* or *Church House, Lower Lane, Aldford, Chester CH4 8AX* Tel (01244) 679311 *or* 620444 E-mail simon@schesters.freeserve.co.uk

CHESTERTON, Robert Eric. b 31. St Aid Birkenhead 63. **d** 65 **p** 66. C Kirby Muxloe *Leic* 65-67; Canada 67-68 and 75-78; C St Annes St Thos *Blackb* 68-69; V Southminster *Chelmsf* 69-75; V Wythenshawe Wm Temple Ch *Man* 78-82; TV Marfleet *York* 82-85; V Marshchapel *Linc* 85-88; R N Coates 85-88; V Grainthorpe w Conisholme 85-88; V Langtoft Gp 88-91; V Kingsbury *Birm* 91-94; rtd 94; Perm to Offic *Pet* from 95; *Leic* 96-99. *46 Tyne Road, Oakham LE15 6SJ* Tel (01572) 757262

CHESWORTH (née NAYLOR), Mrs Alison Louise. b 68. St Andr Univ MTheol97 Edin Univ MTh99. TISEC 98. **d** 00 **p** 01. C Ayr, Girvan and Maybole *Glas* 00-03; R Glas All SS from 03; P-in-c Glas H Cross from 03. *2 Skaterigg Drive, Glasgow G13 1SR* Tel 0141-959 3730 E-mail alichesworth@tiscali.co.uk

CHESWORTH, John Martin. b 44. Leeds Univ BSc67 PhD71 FRSC80. S Dios Minl Tr Scheme 90. **d** 92 **p** 93. Oman 92-95; Perm to Offic *Ab* 96-98 and *Ches* 98-03; C Egremont St Jo *Ches* 03-04; V Tranmere St Paul w St Luke from 04. *St Paul's Vicarage, 306 Old Chester Road, Birkenhead CH42 3XD* Tel 0151-645 3547 E-mail johnchesworth@compuserve.com

CHETWYND, Edward Ivor. b 45. Leeds Univ DipTh68. Coll of Resurr Mirfield 68. **d** 70 **p** 71. C Westgate Common *Wakef* 70-74; C Penistone w Midhope 74-75; V Smawthorpe St Mich from 75. *St Michael's Vicarage, St Michael's Close, Castleford WF10 4ER* Tel (01977) 557079

CHEUNG, Anita Yen. b 40. LNSM course 95. **d** 98 **p** 99. OLM St Luke in the City *Liv* from 98. *10 Pine Walks, Prenton, Birkenhead CH42 8LQ* Tel 0151-609 1459 Fax as telephone

CHEVERTON, Miss Jill. b 48. RGN71 RHV77 Leeds Poly DSS73. Cranmer Hall Dur 93. **d** 93 **p** 94. Par Dn Bilton *Ripon* 93-94; C 94-96; V Burmantofts St Steph and St Agnes 96-03; Min Binley Woods LEP *Cov* from 03. *20 Daneswood Road, Binley Woods, Coventry CV3 2BJ* Tel (024) 7654 3003 E-mail revchev@email.com

CHEW, Philip Vivian Frederick. b 62. St Martin's Coll Lanc BA96. Qu Coll Birm 96. **d** 98 **p** 99. C Chorley St Laur *Blackb* 98-02; V Burnley St Steph from 02. *St Stephen's Vicarage, 154 Todmorden Road, Burnley BB11 3ER* Tel (01282) 424733 E-mail revchew@fsmail.net

CHICHESTER, Archdeacon of. *See* McKITTRICK, The Ven Douglas Henry

CHICHESTER, Bishop of. *See* HIND, The Rt Revd John William

CHICHESTER, Dean of. *See* FRAYLING, The Very Revd Nicholas Arthur

CHICKEN, Canon Peter Lindsay. b 46. St Andr Univ BSc71. Chich Th Coll 77. **d** 79 **p** 80. C High Wycombe *Ox* 79-83; V The Stanleys *Glouc* 83-96; V Leckhampton SS Phil and Jas w Cheltenham St Jas from 96; Bp's Adv for CME from 92; Hon Can Glouc Cathl from 03. *St Philip and St James Vicarage, 80 Painswick Road, Cheltenham GL50 2EU* Tel (01242) 525460 E-mail rev.peterchicken@btopenworld.com

CHIDLAW, Richard Paul. b 49. St Cath Coll Cam BA71 MA. Ripon Hall Ox 72. **d** 74 **p** 81. C Ribbesford w Bewdley and Dowles *Worc* 74-76; NSM Coaley *Glouc* 81-83; NSM Frampton on Severn 81-83; NSM Arlingham 81-83; NSM Saul w Fretherne and Framilode 83-84; NSM Cam w Stinchcombe 85-90; Perm to Offic 90-91; NSM Berkeley w Wick, Breadstone and Newport 91-02; NSM Berkeley w Wick, Breadstone, Newport, Stone etc from 02. *38 May Lane, Dursley GL11 4HU* Tel (01453) 547838

CHIDWICK, Alan Robert. b 49. MA MIL. Oak Hill NSM Course. **d** 84 **p** 85. NSM Pimlico St Pet w Westmr Ch Ch *Lon* from 84. *119 Eaton Square, London SW1W 9AL* Tel (020) 7235 4242 E-mail monsieur@btopenworld.com *or* nsm@stpetereatonsquare.co.uk

CHILCOTT, Mark David. b 62. Ch Coll Cam BA83 MA87 PhD88. Ripon Coll Cuddesdon BA92. **d** 93 **p** 94. C Warrington St Elphin *Liv* 93-99; P-in-c Westbrook St Jas 99-01; V 01-02. *Estates Branch, Sedgley Park Centre, Sedgley Park Road, Prestwich, Manchester M25 0JT* Tel 0161-856 0505 Fax 856 0506

CHILD, Corin James. b 73. Man Univ BA95. Trin Coll Bris BA02 MA03. **d** 03 **p** 04. C Sanderstead All SS *S'wark* from 03. *285 Limpsfield Road, Sanderstead CR2 9DG* Tel (020) 8657 0613 E-mail corin.child@ntlworld.com

CHILD, David Francis. b 44. Birm Univ MB, ChB67 FRCP88. St As Minl Tr Course 02. **d** 04 **p** 05. NSM Gresford *St As* from 04. *Whitegate Farm, Gyfelia, Wrexham LL13 0YH* Tel (01978) 823396 E-mail d_f_child@yahoo.co.uk

CHILD, Margaret Mary. *See* MASLEN, Mrs Margaret Mary

CHILD, Canon Rupert Henry. b 29. St Jo Coll Dur 50 K Coll Lon 56 St Boniface Warminster 57. **d** 58 **p** 59. C Tavistock and Gulworthy *Ex* 58-61; C Dunstable *St Alb* 61-65; V Luton St Chris Round Green 65-74; V Sawbridgeworth 74-95; Hon Can St Alb 86-95; rtd 95; Perm to Offic *St Alb* from 00. *6 Lakes Close, Langford, Biggleswade SG18 9SJ* Tel (01462) 700303

CHILDS, David Robert. b 64. Univ Coll Lon BSc86 Regent's Park Coll Ox MA95. Ripon Coll Cuddesdon 99. **d** 99 **p** 00. C Bloxham w Milcombe and S Newington *Ox* 99-02; TV Witney from 02. *The Vicarage, 292 Thorney Leys, Witney OX28 5PB* Tel (01993) 703507

CHILDS, Emma Jane. *See* WESTERMANN-CHILDS, Miss Emma Jane

CHILDS, Ernest Edmund. b 23. Lich Th Coll 63. **d** 65 **p** 66. C Billesley Common *Birm* 65-68; C Elland *Wakef* 68-69; Clerical Org Sec CECS *Pet, Leic* and *Ely* 69-72; V Staverton w Helidon and Catesby *Pet* 72-76; rtd 77; Perm to Offic *Nor* 77-91; Hon C W Lynn *Ely* 92-94; P-in-c 94-95; Perm to Offic *Ely* from 95; *Nor* from 96. *4 Fieldview Court, Fakenham NR21 8PB* Tel (01328) 856595

CHILDS, Martin James. b 63. Univ of Wales (Lamp) BA Plymouth Univ PGCE. St Mich Coll Llan BD99. **d** 99 **p** 00. C Mountain Ash and Miskin *Llan* 99-04. *Address temp unknown*

CHILLINGTON, Barbara Anne. b 42. Staffs Poly RGN84. WEMTC. **d** 00 **p** 01. NSM Madley w Tyberton, Peterchurch, Vowchurch etc *Heref* from 00. *Cephas House, 2 Princes Orchard, Peterchurch, Hereford HR2 0RW* Tel and fax (01981) 550979 Mobile 07891-248723 E-mail barbarathrv@aol.com

✠**CHILLINGWORTH, The Rt Revd David Robert.** b 51. TCD BA73 Oriel Coll Ox BA75 MA81. Ripon Coll Cuddesdon 75. **d** 76 **p** 77 **c** 05. C Belfast H Trin *Conn* 76-79; Ch of Ireland Youth Officer 79-83; C Bangor Abbey *D & D* 83-86; I Seagoe 86-05; Dean Dromore 95-02; Adn Dromore 02-05; Bp St And from 05. *Perth Diocesan Centre, 28A Balhousie Street, Perth PH1 5HJ* Tel (01738) 443173 *or* 564432 Fax 443174 Mobile 07921-168666 E-mail bishop@standrews.anglican.org

CHILLMAN, David James. b 59. Southn Univ BA82. Trin Coll Bris ADMT95. **d** 95 **p** 96. C Yateley *Win* 95-99; V Halifax All So and St Aug *Wakef* from 99. *The Vicarage, 13 Boothtown Road, Halifax HX3 6EU* E-mail david.chillman@tesco.net

CHIN, Michael Shoon Chion. b 41. Lon Univ BD71 Melbourne Univ BA76 DipEd79. Trin Th Coll Singapore BTh64 Melbourne Coll of Div. **d** 64 **p** 65. Malaysia 64-68; Australia 69-80, 87-91 and from 97; Miss to Seamen 72-81 and 83-89; USA 81-82; Gen Sec Internat Chr Maritime Assn 91-96. *21/110 Hull Road, Croydon, Australia 3136* Tel (0061) (3) 9723 8287 Mobile 41-859 7966 E-mail mschin22@goldenit.net.au

CHING, Derek. b 37. St Cath Coll Cam BA58 MA Cam Inst of Educn CertEd59. Qu Coll Birm 81. **d** 83 **p** 84. C Finham *Cov* 83-87; V Butlers Marston and the Pillertons w Ettington 87-96; rtd 96; Perm to Offic *Ripon* from 96. *25 Kirkby Road, Ripon HG4 2EY* Tel (01765) 609419

CHIPLIN, Christopher Gerald. b 53. Lon Univ BSc75. St Steph Ho Ox BA77 MA81. **d** 78 **p** 79. C Chesterfield St Mary and All SS *Derby* 78-80; C Thorpe *Nor* 80-84; V Highbridge *B & W* 84-94; V Midsomer Norton w Clandown from 94. *The Vicarage, 42 Priory Close, Midsomer Norton, Radstock BA3 2HZ* Tel (01761) 412118 E-mail cchi759070@aol.com

CHIPLIN, Gareth Huw. b 50. Worc Coll Ox BA71 MA. Edin Th Coll 71. **d** 73 **p** 74. C Friern Barnet St Jas *Lon* 73-75; C Eastcote St Lawr 76-79; C Notting Hill St Mich and Ch Ch 79-84; V Hammersmith St Matt from 84. *St Matthew's Vicarage, 1 Fielding Road, London W14 0LL* Tel (020) 7603 9769

CHIPLIN, Howard Alan. b 43. Sarum & Wells Th Coll 84. **d** 86 **p** 87. C Caerleon *Mon* 86-89; V Ferndale w Maerdy *Llan* 89-91; V Ysbyty Cynfyn w Llantrisant and Eglwys Newydd *St D* 91-95; R Narberth w Mounton w Robeston Wathen and Crinow 95-02; V Llanfihangel w Llanafan and Llanwnnws etc from 02. *The Vicarage, Llanafon, Aberystwyth SY23 4AZ* Tel (01974) 261101

CHIPLIN, Malcolm Leonard. b 42. Univ of Wales (Cardiff) DPS88. St Mich Coll Llan 86. **d** 88 **p** 89. C Newton Nottage *Llan* 88-91; V Pwllgwaun w Llanddewi Rhondda 91-03; V Mountain Ash and Miskin from 03. *The Vicarage, Ty Tournai, Duffryn Road, Caegarw, Mountain Ash CF45 4DA* Tel (01443) 473700

CHIPPENDALE, Peter David. b 34. Dur Univ BA55. Linc Th Coll 57. **d** 59 **p** 60. C Claines St Jo *Worc* 59-63; V Defford w Besford 63-73; P-in-c Eckington 66-69; V 69-73; V Kidderminster St Geo 73-76; V The Lickey *Birm* 76-96; rtd 96. *1 Fairways, Pershore WR10 1HA* Tel (01386) 553478

CHIPPENDALE, Robert William. b 42. DipTh68 Ox Univ BA79 Dip Teaching84. **d** 67 **p** 68. Australia 67-72 and from 79; V Shaw *Man* 72-78. *4 Violet Way, Gaven, Qld, Australia 4211* Tel (0061) (7) 5596 2247 *or* 5532 4922

CHISHOLM, Canon Ian Keith. b 36. AKC62. **d** 63 **p** 64. C Lich St Chad *Lich* 63-66; C Sedgley All SS 66-69; V Rough Hills 69-77; V Harrow Weald All SS *Lon* 77-88; V W Moors *Sarum* 88-01; Can and Preb Sarum Cathl 00-01; rtd 01; Perm to Offic *Sarum* from 02. *33 Meadoway, Shrewton, Salisbury SP3 4HE* Tel (01980) 620579

CHISHOLM, Ian Stuart. b 37. ALCD63. **d** 63 **p** 64. C Worksop St Jo *S'well* 63-66; Succ Sheff Cathl *Sheff* 66-68; Bp's Chapl for Soc Resp 68-72; C Ox St Andr *Ox* 72-76; Tutor Wycliffe Hall Ox 72-76; V Conisbrough *Sheff* 76-94; Chapl Conisbrough Hosp 76-94; RD W Doncaster 82-87 and 93-94; V Chilwell *S'well* 94-99; rtd 99; Perm to Offic *Sheff* from 94; *Linc* from 00; *S'well* from 03. *72 Broadbank, Louth LN11 0EW* Tel (01605) 605970 E-mail ichisholm@waitrose.com

CHISHOLM, Canon Reginald Joseph. b 13. TCD BA40 MA51. TCD Div Sch 42. **d** 42 **p** 43. C Belfast St Donard *D & D* 42-45; C Bangor St Comgall 45-48; I Ardglass w Dunsford 48-51; I Newtownards 51-82; Min Can Belf Cathl 52-62; Treas Down Cathl *D & D* 80-82; rtd 82. *20 Glendun Park, Bangor BT20 4UX* Tel (028) 9145 0100

CHISHOLM, Samuel James. b 20. Edin Th Coll 74 St Jo Coll Nottm 86. **d** 86 **p** 87. NSM Eastriggs *Glas* 87-92; NSM Gretna 90-91; rtd 92; Perm to Offic *Chich* from 95. *36 Peterhouse, Church Street, Bexhill-on-Sea TN40 2HF* Tel (01424) 219294

CHISLETT, David Norman Hilton. b 61. Kingston Poly BSc83 UEA PGCE84. Ridley Hall Cam 00. **d** 02 **p** 03. C Highley w Billingsley, Glazeley etc *Heref* 02-05; TV Eston w Normanby *York* from 05. *Christ Church Vicarage, 73A High Street, Eston, Middlesbrough TS6 9EH* E-mail davenhchislett@aol.com

CHITHAM, Ernest John. b 57. LSE BSc79 Leeds Univ PGCE80 Dur Univ MA84. NEOC 88. **d** 91 **p** 92. C Swanborough *Sarum* 91-94; CMS Lebanon 95-98; TV Worthing Ch the King *Chich* from 99. *85 Heene Road, Worthing BN11 4PP* Tel (01903) 218026 E-mail chitham@iname.com

CHITTENDEN, John Bertram d'Encer. b 24. ASCA. Lon Coll of Div 56. **d** 58 **p** 59. C St Mary-at-Lambeth *S'wark* 58-64; R Acrise *Cant* 64-82; R Hawkinge 64-82; R Hawkinge w Acrise and Swingfield 82-90; rtd 91; Perm to Offic *Cant* from 91. *19 Hasborough Road, Folkestone CT19 6BQ* Tel (01303) 241773

CHITTENDEN, Nils Philip d'Encer. b 69. St Chad's Coll Dur BA91 Univ of Northumbria at Newc MA99. Westcott Ho Cam 93. **d** 95. C Benfieldside *Dur* 95-97; Chapl Community Health Care N Dur NHS Trust 96-97; Urban Regeneration Chapl Gateshead *Dur* 97-01; Perm to Offic from 01; UK Co-ord Chs Community Work Alliance from 01; Dir Transferable Skills Progr St Chad's Coll Dur from 01; Hon Min Can Dur Cathl *Dur* from 03; Chapl St Mary's Coll Dur from 04. *St Chad's College, North Bailey, Durham DH1 3RH* Tel 0191-334 3346 Fax 334 3371 Mobile 07866-804460 E-mail nilsc@ccwa.org.uk *or* n.p.d.chittenden@durham.ac.uk

CHITTY, Philip Crofts. b 27. Roch Th Coll 61. **d** 63 **p** 64. C Holbrooks *Cov* 63-68; V Long Itchington 68-77; R Ufton 69-77; P-in-c Cov St Marg 77-84; rtd 84. *17 Rotherham Road, Coventry CV6 4FF* Tel (024) 7668 5398

✠**CHIU, The Rt Revd Joshua Ban It.** b 18. K Coll Lon LLB41 AKC41 Barrister-at-Law (Inner Temple) 41. Westcott Ho Cam 43. **d** 45 **p** 46 **c** 66. C Bournville *Birm* 45-47; Malaya 47-50; Singapore 50-59 and 66-82; Hon Can St Andr Cathl Singapore 56-59; Australia 59-62; Service Laymen Abroad WCC Geneva 62-65; Fell St Aug Coll Cant 65-66; Bp Singapore and Malaya 66-70; Bp Singapore 70-82; Member Cen Cttee WCC 68-75; Member ACC 75-79; rtd 82; Perm to Offic *Sarum* 82-00 and *Chelmsf* from 02. *40 Beverley Crescent, Woodford Green IG8 9DD* Tel (020) 8924 6490

CHIUMBU, Esther Tamisa. *See* PRIOR, Esther Tamisa

CHIVERS, Canon Christopher Mark. b 67. Magd Coll Ox BA88 MA92 Selw Coll Cam BA96 MA00. Westcott Ho Cam 94. **d** 97 **p** 98. C Friern Barnet St Jas *Lon* 97-99; Can Prec St Geo Cathl Cape Town 99-01; Min Can and Prec Westmr Abbey 01-05; Can Res and Chan Blackb Cathl *Blackb* from 05; Select Preacher Ox Univ 05. *1 St Francis Road, Blackburn BB2 2TZ* Tel (01254) 200720 *or* 51491 Mobile 07706-632508 E-mail chris.chivers@blackburn.anglican.org

CHIVERS, Ernest Alfred John. b 34. Bris & Glouc Tr Course. **d** 83 **p** 84. NSM Bedminster *Bris* 83-87; NSM Whitchurch 87-98; NSM Knowle St Martin 98-00; Sen Asst P Chard and Distr *B & W* 00-04; P-in-c 04-05; rtd 05. *40 Calcott Road, Bristol BS4 2HD* Tel 0117-977 7867

CHIVERS, Royston George. b 34. Glouc Th Course. **d** 83 **p** 84. NSM Gorsley w Cliffords Mesne *Glouc* 83-85; NSM Newent and Gorsley w Cliffords Mesne from 85. *Mayfield, Gorsley, Ross-on-Wye HR9 7SJ* Tel (01989) 720492

CHIVERTON, Dennis Lionel Dunbar. b 26. St D Coll Lamp BA51. **d** 53 **p** 54. C Cardiff St Mary *Llan* 53-54; C Dowlais 54-57; C Bargoed w Brithdir 57-61; P-in-c Cymmer and Abercregan 61-67; R Llanfabon 67-91; rtd 91; Perm to Offic *Llan* from 91. *3 Park Terrace, Trelewis, Treharris CF46 6BT* Tel (01443) 411237

CHO, Paul Hang-Sik. b 61. Kent Univ MA96 PhD04. Chr Th Sem & Div Sch of Korea BTh93. **d** 00 **p** 01. C Munster Square Ch Ch and St Mary Magd *Lon* from 00; Chapl Angl Korean Community from 00. *4 Silsoe House, 50 Park Village East, London NW1 7QH* Tel (020) 7388 2166 Mobile 07960-567585 Fax (020) 7387 9922 *or* 0870-131 7923 E-mail frpaulcho@hotmail.com

CHORLTON, John Samuel Woodard. b 45. Newc Univ BSc67. Wycliffe Hall Ox 89. **d** 89 **p** 91. Jerusalem 79-92; C Ox St Aldate w St Matt *Ox* 92-94; C Ox St Aldate 95-04; Voc Adv from 98; AD Ox 99-04; TV W Slough from 04. *St George's House, Long Furlong Drive, Slough SL2 2LX* Tel (01753) 525935 Mobile 07709-873831 E-mail chorltonfamily@email.com

CHOTANAGPUR, Bishop of. *See* TEROM, The Rt Revd Zechariah James

CHOUFAR, Joseph Oriho Abulemoi. b 63. Nile Th Coll Khartoum BA95 ICI Univ Amman BA98. **d** 87 **p** 88. Sudan

87-96; All SS Cathl Khartoum 87-88 and 91-96; Torit Congregation Lologo Displaced Camp 88-90; NSM Ealing St Pet Mt Park *Lon* from 00. *8 Wesley Avenue, London NW10 7BN* Tel (020) 8453 1624
E-mail abulemoi@hotmail.com

CHOW, Ting Suie Roy. b 46. Brasted Th Coll 68 Sarum & Wells Th Coll 70. **d** 72 **p** 73. C Weaste *Man* 72-74; C Swinton St Pet 74-78; R Blackley St Paul 78-85; Sec SPCK (Dio Man) from 80; R Burnage St Nic *Man* 85-95; P-in-c Man Gd Shep 95-97; P-in-c Openshaw 95-97; R Manchester Gd Shep and St Barn from 97. *All Soul's Rectory, Every Street, Ancoats, Manchester M4 7DQ* Tel 0161-273 6582

CHOW, Wai Meng. b 65. Bris Univ BSc89 ACA93. Trin Coll Bris BA97 MA02. **d** 02 **p** 03. NSM Westminster St Jas the Less *Lon* from 02. *29 Carillon Court, Oxford Road, London W5 3SX* Tel (020) 8810 1651 *or* 7630 6282 Mobile 07968-776557
E-mail waimeng.chow@sjtl.org

CHOWN, William Richard Bartlett. b 27. AKC54. **d** 55 **p** 56. C Egremont *Carl* 55-58; C Upminster *Chelmsf* 58-61; R Romford St Andr 61-78; R Newton Longville w Stoke Hammond, Whaddon etc *Ox* 78-83; P-in-c Kidmore End 83-85; V 85-90; rtd 90; NSM Harpsden *Ox* 93-94; Perm to Offic 94-03; Hon C Shiplake w Dunsden and Harpsden 03-05. *3 Coniston Court, Weybridge KT13 9YR*

CHRICH, Andrew James. b 70. Girton Coll Cam BA92 MA96. Cranmer Hall Dur BA96. **d** 96 **p** 97. C Gerrards Cross and Fulmer *Ox* 96-99; Chapl Trin Coll Cam 99-04; R Linton in Craven *Bradf* from 04; P-in-c Burnsall w Rylstone from 04. *The Rectory, Hebden Road, Grassington, Skipton BD23 5LA* Tel (01756) 752575 E-mail andychrich@surefish.co.uk

CHRICH-SMITH, Joanne Elizabeth. b 71. Qu Coll Cam BA93 MA97. Cranmer Hall Dur BA96 Ripon Coll Cuddesdon 96. **d** 97 **p** 98. C Amersham on the Hill *Ox* 97-99; Perm to Offic *Ely* 99-04; Chapl Girton Coll Cam 00-02; Perm to Offic *Bradf* from 04. *The Rectory, Hebden Road, Grassington, Skipton BD23 5LA* Tel (01756) 752575

CHRISMAN, John Aubrey. b 33. US Naval Academy BS58. Westcott Ho Cam 86. **d** 88 **p** 89. NSM Orwell *Ely* 88-89; NSM Wimpole 88-89; NSM Arrington 88-89; NSM Croydon w Clopton 88-89; Asst Chapl Oslo St Edm *Eur* 89-91; USA from 91. *7118 Treymore Court, Sarasota, FL 34243, USA* Tel (001) (941) 351 3177 E-mail fatherjack@comcast.net

CHRIST THE KING, Bishop of. *See* LEE, The Rt Revd Peter John

CHRISTCHURCH, Bishop of. *See* COLES, The Rt Revd David John

CHRISTENSEN, Canon Norman Peter. b 37. St D Coll Lamp BA63. Ridley Hall Cam 63. **d** 65 **p** 66. C Barnston *Ches* 65-70; V Over St Jo 70-77; R Bromborough 77-92; RD Wirral S 86-92; Hon Can Ches Cathl 90-02; Chapl Arrowe Park Hosp Wirral 92-96; V Higher Bebington *Ches* 96-02; rtd 02; Perm to Offic *Ches* from 02. *13 Howbeck Close, Prenton CH43 6TH* Tel 0151-652 9869 E-mail canonpc@aol.com

CHRISTIAN, Mrs Alison Jean. b 51. Cen Sch Speech & Drama Dip Acting72. S Dios Minl Tr Scheme 88. **d** 91 **p** 94. Par Dn Uxbridge *Lon* 91-94; C 94-95; Chapl Uxbridge Coll 91-95; V Sudbury St Andr *Lon* 95-02; R Gt Stanmore from 02. *St John's Rectory, Rectory Lane, Stanmore HA7 4AQ* Tel (020) 8954 0276
E-mail alison.christian1@btopenworld.com

CHRISTIAN, Anthony Clive Hammond. b 46. Kent Univ BA74 Sussex Univ MA95 DPhil99 FRSA01. K Coll Lon 74 St Aug Coll Cant 74. **d** 76 **p** 77. C Faversham *Cant* 76-79; C St Laur in Thanet 79-81; P-in-c 81-84; R Gt Mongeham w Ripple and Sutton by Dover 84-88; V Pevensey *Chich* 88-94; P-in-c 94-01; V from 01. *Marsh Hall, Church Lane, Pevensey BN24 5LD* Tel and fax (01323) 762247 Mobile 07711-170350

CHRISTIAN, Brother. *See* PEARSON, Christian David John

CHRISTIAN, Mark Robert. b 58. Linc Th Coll 95. **d** 95 **p** 96. C Stockport SW *Ches* 95-98; CF from 98. *c/o MOD Chaplains (Army)* Tel (01980) 615802 Fax 615800
E-mail mark@padre.me.uk

CHRISTIAN, Paul. b 49. Cant Sch of Min 84. **d** 87 **p** 88. C Folkestone St Sav *Cant* 87-91; R Temple Ewell w Lydden from 91. *The Rectory, Green Lane, Temple Ewell, Dover CT16 3AS* Tel (01304) 822865

CHRISTIAN, Richard. b 37. Nottm Univ DipEd74 Ox Univ MA81. AKC62. **d** 63 **p** 65. C Camberwell St Mich w All So w Em *S'wark* 63-66; C Woolwich St Mary w H Trin 66-70; Chapl and Lect Bp Lonsdale Coll Derby 70-74; P-in-c Hurley *Ox* 76-79; Chapl Lancing Coll 79-81; Chapl Harrow Sch 82-89; Chapl R W Sussex Hosp Chich 89-91; P-in-c Cowley *Lon* 91-95; Chapl Hillingdon Hosp NHS Trust from 91. *St John's Rectory, Rectory Lane, Stanmore HA7 4AQ* Tel (020) 8954 0276 *or* (01895) 279433 E-mail richard.christian@thh.nhs.uk

CHRISTIAN-EDWARDS, Canon Michael Thomas. b 36. Down Coll Cam BA60 MA64. Clifton Th Coll 60. **d** 62 **p** 63. C Ex St Leon w H Trin *Ex* 62-67; V Trowbridge St Thos *Sarum* 67-75; R Wingfield w Rowley 67-75; P-in-c Fisherton Anger 75-81; R 81-92; Ind Chapl 85-92; RD Salisbury 85-90; Can and Preb Sarum Cathl 87-92; V Crofton *Portsm* 92-00; rtd 00; Perm to Offic *Win* from 02. *Rivendell, Westbeams Road, Sway, Lymington SO41 6AE* Tel (01590) 682353
E-mail mmce@cerivendell.freeserve.co.uk

CHRISTIAN-IWUAGWU, Canon Amatu Onundu. b 73. Port Harcourt Univ Nigeria BEng93. **d** 00 **p** 01. NSM Stonebridge St Mich *Lon* 00-03; NSM Welwyn *St Alb* from 04; Can Ideato from 03. *22 Nursery Hill, Welwyn Garden City AL7 1UF* Tel (01707) 334183 Mobile 07961-593880
E-mail iwuagwuoa@yahoo.co.uk

CHRISTIANSON, Canon Rodney John (Bill). b 47. St Paul's Coll Grahamstown DipTh72. **d** 72 **p** 73. S Africa 72-76 and 82-91; C St Sav Cathl Pietermaritzburg 72-76; Miss to Seafarers from 76; Min Sec 93-00; Sec Gen from 00; Hon C Milton next Gravesend Ch Ch *Roch* 78-82; Chapl Miss to Seamen and R St Andr Richard's Bay 82-91; Chapl Hull Miss to Seamen 91-93; Hon Can Bloemfontein Cathl from 93; Lic to Offic *Lon* 94-97; V St Mich Paternoster Royal from 00. *The Mission to Seafarers, St Michael Paternoster Royal, College Hill, London EC4R 2RL* Tel (020) 7248 5202 Fax 7248 4761
E-mail secgen@missiontoseafarers.org

CHRISTIE, Alexander Robert. b 58. Qu Coll Cam BA79 LLM80. Oak Hill Th Coll DipHE94. **d** 94 **p** 95. C W Norwood St Luke *S'wark* 94-98; C Wandsworth All SS 98-03; V Blackheath Park St Mich from 03. *St Michael's Vicarage, 2 Pond Road, London SE3 9JL* Tel (020) 8852 5287
E-mail ar.christie@virgin.net

CHRISTIE, David James. b 58. York Univ BA80 MA83 PGCE81 Leeds Univ MPhil88. Cranmer Hall Dur 89. **d** 91 **p** 92. C Drypool *York* 91-95; V Patrick Brompton and Hunton *Ripon* from 95; V Hornby from 95; V Crakehall from 95. *The Vicarage, Patrick Brompton, Bedale DL8 1JN* Tel (01677) 450439
E-mail dc@christiepb.fsnet.co.uk

CHRISTIE, Canon Thomas Richard. b 31. CCC Cam BA53 MA57. Linc Th Coll 55. **d** 57 **p** 58. C Portsea N End St Mark *Portsm* 57-60; C Cherry Hinton St Andr *Ely* 60-62; C-in-c Cherry Hinton St Jas CD 62-66; V Wisbech St Aug 66-73; V Whitstable All SS *Cant* 73-75; V Whitstable All SS w St Pet 75-80; Can Res and Treas Pet Cathl *Pet* 80-01; Perm to Offic *Ely* from 80; RD Pet 87-96; Chapl to Rtd Clergy from 00; rtd 01; P-in-c Wittering w Thornhaugh and Wansford *Pet* 01-02; P-in-c Thornhaugh and Wansford from 03. *16 College Park, Peterborough PE1 4AW* Tel (01733) 344228

CHRISTOPHER, Richard. b 53. NTMTC 94. **d** 97 **p** 98. C Southall Green St Jo *Lon* 97-04; C Reading St Luke w St Bart *Ox* from 04. *107 Anderson Avenue, Earley, Reading RG6 1HA* Tel 0118-987 1495 E-mail rev.r.christopher@yahoo.com

CHRISTOU, Sotirios. b 51. Avery Hill Coll DipHE80. St Jo Coll Nottm 84. **d** 88 **p** 92. C Berechurch St Marg w St Mich *Chelmsf* 88-89; C Goodmayes All SS 89-90; NSM Harston w Hauxton *Ely* 92-94; Lic to Offic 94-95; C Burgess Hill St Andr *Chich* 95-98; Perm to Offic *Ely* from 98. *18 Bullen Close, Cambridge CB1 8YU* Tel (01223) 514593

CHUBB, John Nicholas. b 33. St Cath Soc Ox BA55 MA58. Qu Coll Birm 57. **d** 59 **p** 60. C Kirby Moorside w Gillamoor *York* 59-62; C Scarborough St Mary 62-64; V Potterspury w Furtho and Yardley Gobion *Pet* 64-69; V Brixworth 69-74; P-in-c Holcot 73-74; V Brixworth w Holcot 74-81; V Hampton Hill *Lon* 81-88; Chapl Pet Distr Hosp 88-97; Chapl Edith Cavell Hosp 88-97; rtd 97. *12 Alness Drive, York YO24 2XZ*

CHUBB, Richard Henry. b 45. Univ of Wales (Cardiff) BMus67 Bris Univ PGCE76. Linc Th Coll 67. **d** 70 **p** 71. C Chippenham St Andr w Tytherton Lucas *Bris* 71-72; C-in-c Stockwood CD 72-73; C Bris Ch the Servant Stockwood 73-76; Perm to Offic 76-79; Min Can and Succ Bris Cathl 79-88; Chapl w Deaf People 83-02; Chapl Qu Eliz Hosp Sch Bris 87-92; rtd 02. *17 Southmead Road, Westbury-on-Trym, Bristol BS10 5DL* Tel 0117-962 9508 Fax as telephone E-mail richard.chubb@lineone.net

CHUDLEY, Cyril Raymond. b 29. Lon Univ BA53 DipEd. Wells Th Coll 70. **d** 72 **p** 73. C Newark St Mary *S'well* 72-75; C Egg Buckland *Ex* 75-77; P-in-c Plymouth St Aug 77-80; V 80-83; V Milton Abbot, Dunterton, Lamerton etc 83-91; TV Wickford and Runwell *Chelmsf* 91-95; rtd 95; Perm to Offic *Truro* from 95. *Ten Acres, Coxpark, Gunnislake PL18 9BB* Tel (01822) 832345

CHUMU MUTUKU, Norbert. b 68. Urbanian Univ Rome BA89 St Jo Fisher Coll USA MSc00. St Mathias Mulumba Sem Kenya 89. **d** 93 **p** 94. Ngong Kenya 93-98; Rochester USA 98-02; C Milton *Portsm* from 03. *51 Goldsmith Avenue, Southsea PO4 8DU* Tel (023) 9275 1811 E-mail nchumu@yahoo.com

✠**CHUNG, The Most Revd Matthew Chul Bum. c** 95. Bp Seoul from 95; Presiding Bp Korea from 02. *3 Chong Dong, Chung Ku, Seoul 100-120, Republic of Korea* Tel (0082) (2) 735 6157 *or* 738 6597 Fax 723 2640 E-mail mcbchung@hotmail.com *or* mcbchung@chollian.net

CHURCH, Mrs Linda Ann. b 51. MCSP73 Open Univ 93. EMMTC 88. **d** 91 **p** 94. NSM Kirkby in Ashfield St Thos *S'well* 91-95; NSM Skegby and Teversal 95-98; P-in-c Annesley w Newstead 98-03; TR Hucknall Torkard from 03. *The Rectory,*

Annesley Road, Hucknall, Nottingham NG15 7DE Tel 0115-963 2033 E-mail lawrence@annesleycutting.freeserve.co.uk

CHURCH, William John. b 41. Qu Coll Cam MA62 Solicitor. St Alb and Ox Min Course 96. **d** 99 **p** 00. NSM Bengeo *St Alb* 99-01; NSM Gt Amwell w St Margaret's and Stanstead Abbots 01-05; NSM Hertford St Andr from 05. *115 Queen's Road, Hertford SG13 8BJ* Tel (01992) 410469 Fax 583079 E-mail bill.church@hertscc.gov.uk *or* churchwj@hotmail.com

CHURCHER, Ms Mandy. b 54. RN75 RM77 Surrey Univ PGCE87 Brunel Univ MEd92. NTMTC 96. **d** 99 **p** 00. C Wolverhampton St Matt *Lich* 99-02; Assoc Chapl Plymouth Hosps NHS Trust from 02. *The Chaplaincy, Derriford Hospital, Derriford Road, Plymouth PL6 8DH* Tel (01752) 792022 E-mail mandy.churcher@phntswest.nhs.uk

CHURCHMAN, David Ernest Donald (Don). b 21. Clifton Th Coll 45. **d** 48 **p** 49. C Preston All SS *Blackb* 48-49; C Braintree *Chelmsf* 50-52; V Harold Wood 52-59; V Southsea St Jude *Portsm* 59-74; V Enfield Ch Ch Trent Park *Lon* 74-86; RD Enfield 75-82; rtd 86; Perm to Offic *Portsm* from 87. *Heronsbrook, 158 Havant Road, Hayling Island PO11 0LJ* Tel (023) 9246 3216

CHURCHUS, Eric Richard Ivor. b 28. Lon Univ BSc MSc56. **d** 78 **p** 79. Hon C Withington w Westhide *Heref* 78-82; C Heref St Martin 82-85; P-in-c Woolhope 85-93; rtd 93; Perm to Offic *Heref* from 93. *27 Aconbury Avenue, Hereford HR2 6HR* Tel (01432) 267022

CHYNCHEN, John Howard. b 38. FRICS72. Sarum & Wells Th Coll 88. **d** 89 **p** 90. Bp's Dom Chapl *Sarum* from 89; Hon Chapl Hong Kong Cathl from 90. *64 Courtenay Street, London SE11 5PQ,* or *2004 Fairmont House, 8 Cotton Tree Drive, Hong Kong* Tel (020) 7582 3541 *or* (00852) 2541 4155 Fax (00852) 2544 2638 E-mail chynchen@btinternet.com

CIANCHI, Dalbert Peter. b 28. Lon Univ BSc57. Westcott Ho Cam 69. **d** 70 **p** 71. C Harpenden St Nic *St Alb* 70-74; TV Woughton *Ox* 74-80; P-in-c Wavendon w Walton 74-80; P-in-c Lavendon w Cold Brayfield 80-84; R Lavendon w Cold Brayfield, Clifton Reynes etc 84-94; rtd 94. *20 Fisken Crescent, Kambah, ACT, Australia 2902* Tel (0061) (2) 6231 8556 E-mail pcianchi@cyberone.com.au

CIECHANOWICZ, Edward Leigh Bundock. *See* BUNDOCK, Edward Leigh

CINNAMOND, Andrew Victor. b 71. St Andr Univ MA94. Wycliffe Hall Ox BA00. **d** 01 **p** 02. C Clapham H Trin and St Pet *S'wark* 01-05; C Wandsworth All SS from 05. *74 Haldon Road, London SW18 1QG* Tel (020) 8870 2475 *or* 8788 4606 E-mail andrew_cinnamond@hotmail.com

CIRCUS, Robert William. b 19. Lon Univ BSc(Econ)90. Wycliffe Hall Ox 52. **d** 54 **p** 55. C Rayleigh *Chelmsf* 54-56; V Northampton St Andr *Pet* 56-60; V Werrington 60-70; R The Quinton *Birm* 70-76; P-in-c Wolverley *Worc* 76-82; V Wolverley and Cookley 82-84; rtd 84; Perm to Offic *Worc* 84-01. *90 Audley Drive, Kidderminster DY11 5NF* Tel (01562) 750286

CLABON, Ronald Oliver Edwin. b 30. **d** 97. NSM Pontnewydd *Mon* 97-03. *72 Anthony Drive, Caerleon, Newport NP18 3DX* Tel (01633) 420790

CLACEY, Derek Phillip. b 48. St Jo Coll Nottm 76. **d** 79 **p** 80. C Gt Parndon *Chelmsf* 79-82; C Walton H Trin *Ox* 82-88; R Bramshaw and Landford w Plaitford *Sarum* 88-04; P-in-c Redlynch and Morgan's Vale 03-04; TV E Greenwich *S'wark* from 04. *The Vicarage, 52 Earlswood Street, London SE10 9ES* E-mail derekclacey@aol.com

CLACK, Robert John Edmund. b 63. Lanc Univ BA85. Coll of Resurr Mirfield 89. **d** 92 **p** 93. C Bury St Pet *Man* 92-95; Chapl Bury Colls of FE 93-95; TV New Bury 95-97; R Ashton-upon-Mersey St Martin *Ches* from 97. *St Martin's Rectory, 367 Glebelands Road, Sale M33 5GG* Tel 0161-973 4204 E-mail robert@rclack.fsbusiness.co.uk

CLACKER, Martin Alexander. b 56. Trin Coll Bris DipHE95. **d** 95 **p** 96. C Yate New Town *Bris* 95-98; V Southmead 98-00; C Portishead *B & W* 00-02; TV 02-03; rtd 03. *55 Glenfall, Yate, Bristol BS37 4LY* Tel (01454) 329849

CLAMMER, Thomas Edward. b 80. Sussex Univ BA01 CCC Cam BA04. Westcott Ho Cam 02. **d** 05. C Wotton St Mary *Glouc* from 05. *30 Simon Road, Longlevens, Gloucester GL2 0TP* Tel (01452) 523803 E-mail tomclammer@hotmail.com

CLANCEY, Ms Blanche Elizabeth Fisher. b 28. SRN50 Lon Univ CertEd71. Gilmore Ho 64. **dss** 78 **d** 87 **p** 94. Bromley Common St Aug *Roch* 78-83; Hanley H Ev *Lich* 83-89; Dn-in-c 87-89; rtd 89; NSM Wilford Hill *S'well* 89-91; NSM Gamston and Bridgford 91-97; NSM Cropwell Bishop w Colston Bassett, Granby etc 97-99; Perm to Offic *S'wark* 00-02. *83 Church Way, South Croydon CR2 0JU* Tel (020) 8657 6376

CLANCY, Michael. b 24. Kensington Univ (USA) BA82. Glas NSM Course 76. **d** 79 **p** 80. Hon C Glas St Silas *Glas* 79-96; Perm to Offic from 96. *33 Highfield Drive, Clarkston, Glasgow G76 7SW* Tel 0141-638 4469

CLAPHAM, Christopher Charles. b 69. Man Univ BA91 St Jo Coll Dur BA96. Cranmer Hall Dur 94 Union Th Sem (NY) STM98. **d** 99 **p** 00. NSM Withington St Chris *Man* 99-01; C Didsbury Ch Ch 01-03; P-in-c Swinton H Rood from 03. *Holy Rood Vicarage, 33 Moorside Road, Swinton, Manchester M27 3EL* Tel 0161-794 2464 E-mail charlesclapham@lineone.net

CLAPHAM, John. b 47. Open Univ BA76. Sarum & Wells Th Coll 77. **d** 80 **p** 81. Dep PV Ex Cathl *Ex* from 80; C Lympstone 85-87; P-in-c 87-99; P-in-c Woodbury 97-99; RD Aylesbeare 96-01; R Lympstone and Woodbury w Exton from 99. *The Rectory, Lympstone, Exmouth EX8 5HP* Tel (01395) 273343

CLAPHAM, Kenneth. b 47. Trin Coll Bris 76. **d** 78 **p** 79. C Pemberton St Mark Newtown *Liv* 78-81; C Darfield *Sheff* 81-83; P-in-c Over Kellet *Blackb* 83-88; V from 88. *The Vicarage, 3 Kirklands Road, Over Kellet, Carnforth LA6 1DJ* Tel and fax (01524) 734189 E-mail ukvicar@aol.com

CLAPHAM, Stephen James. b 61. Portsm Poly BSc84 Ches Coll of HE BTh04. N Ord Course 01. **d** 04 **p** 05. C Nantwich *Ches* from 04. *22 Beatty Road, Nantwich CW5 5JP* Tel (01270) 623620 E-mail steve.clapham@ntlworld.com

CLAPP, Nicholas Michel Edward. b 48. Univ of Wales (Cardiff). St Mich Coll Llan 71. **d** 74 **p** 75. C Walsall St Gabr Fulbrook *Lich* 74-77; C Burnley St Cath *Blackb* 77-80; R Blackley H Trin *Man* 80-87; V Carl St Aid and Ch Ch *Carl* 87-98; Perm to Offic *Blackb* from 00. *3 Arnold Close, Ribbleton, Preston PR2 6DX* Tel (01772) 798613

CLAPPERTON, Mrs Carolin Beryl. b 43. Westcott Ho Cam 04. **d** 05. NSM Faversham *Cant* from 05. *78 Cyprus Road, Faversham ME13 8DH* Tel (01795) 538334 Mobile 07946-420745 E-mail carolin@fish.co.uk

CLAPSON, Clive Henry. b 55. Leeds Univ BA76. Trin Coll Toronto MDiv79. **d** 79 **p** 80. C Belleville St Thos Canada 79-80; R Loughborough 80-83; V Alpine Ch the K USA 83-88; C Hawley H Trin *Guildf* 88-90; R Invergordon St Ninian *Mor* 90-00; Prin Moray Ord and Lay Tr Course 90-94; Can St Andr Cathl Inverness 97-00; R Aberdeen St Mary *Ab* 00-05; P-in-c Dundee St Salvador *Bre* from 05. *9 Minard Crescent, Dundee DD3 6LH* Tel (01382) 221785 E-mail father.clive@virgin.net

CLAPTON, Timothy. b 59. Westmr Coll Ox MTh92. CA Tr Coll 82 Westcott Ho Cam 96. **d** 98 **p** 99. C Wimborne Minster *Sarum* 98-02; Ecum Chapl Milton Keynes Gen NHS Trust from 02. *Milton Keynes General Hospital, Standing Way, Milton Keynes MK6 5LD* Tel (01908) 243700 E-mail clapton@clapton.force9.co.uk

CLARE, Christopher. b 52. Sheff Univ BSc73 Nottm Univ PGCE74. Ox Min Course 89. **d** 92 **p** 93. NSM Chesham Bois *Ox* from 92. *5 Lime Tree Walk, Amersham HP7 9HY* Tel (01494) 766513

CLARE, Lionel Philip. b 19. St Aid Birkenhead 46. **d** 49 **p** 50. C Far Headingley St Chad *Ripon* 49-52; C Low Harrogate St Mary 52-54; R Addingham *Bradf* 54-66; V Sunnyside w Bourne End *St Alb* 66-74; V Kirkbymoorside w Gillamoor, Farndale etc *York* 74-84; rtd 84; Perm to Offic *Bradf* from 84. *4 Abbeyfield Grove House, 12 Riddings Road, Ilkley LS29 9BF*

CLARE, Sister. *See* LOCKHART, Clare Patricia Anne

CLARIDGE, Antony Arthur John. b 37. Hull Univ MA LRAM. Bris & Glouc Tr Course. **d** 84 **p** 85. NSM Keynsham *B & W* 84-97; Bp's Officer for NSMs from 90; Min Bath Ch Ch Prop Chpl from 97. *62 Cranwells Park, Bath BA1 2YE* Tel (01225) 427462 E-mail chantrybath@breathemail.net

CLARIDGE, Michael John. b 61. MIEH Matt Bourton Tech Coll Birm DipEH82. Qu Coll Birm 89 Bossey Ecum Inst Geneva Cert Ecum Studies 92. **d** 92 **p** 93. C Harlescott *Lich* 92-95; P-in-c Wellington Ch Ch 95-97; V 97-03; V W Bromwich St Andr w Ch Ch from 03. *St Andrew's Vicarage, Oakwood Street, West Bromwich B70 9SN* Tel 0121-553 1871 E-mail mjc@fish.co.uk

CLARINGBULL, Canon Denis Leslie. b 33. K Coll Lon BD57 AKC57 Univ of Cen England in Birm DUniv98 MCIPD85 FCIPD01. **d** 58 **p** 59. C Croydon St Aug *Cant* 58-62; Ind Chapl to Bp Croydon 62-71; Ind Chapl *Cov* 71-75; Chapl Cov Cathl 71-75; Succ 72-75; V Norbury St Phil *Cant* 75-80; Sen Ind Chapl *Birm* 80-98; P-in-c Birm St Paul 85-88; V 88-98; Hon Can Birm Cathl 87-98; rtd 98; Perm to Offic *Birm* and *Heref* from 98. *17 Merrivale Crescent, Ross-on-Wye HR9 5JU* Tel (01989) 567771 E-mail gms58@dial.pipex.com

CLARINGBULL (née DAVID), Mrs Faith Caroline. b 55. St Aid Coll Dur BA77 Univ of Wales (Abth) Dip Librarianship 80. Ripon Coll Cuddesdon 87. **d** 89 **p** 94. Par Dn Is of Dogs Ch Ch and St Jo w St Luke *Lon* 89-93; Asst Chapl R Lon Hosps NHS Trust 93-98; NSM Wheatley *Ox* 98-00; Asst Dioc Dir of Ords *Worc* 00-04; Dioc CME Officer 02-04; Dioc Dir of Ords *Birm* from 04; Dean of Women's Min from 04. *175 Harborne Park Road, Birmingham B17 0BH* Tel 0121-426 0445 E-mail f.claringbull@birmingham.anglican.org

CLARINGBULL, Keith. b 49. Ripon Coll Cuddesdon 98. **d** 00 **p** 01. SSF 69-89; C Droitwich Spa *Worc* 00-04; P-in-c Hampton in Arden *Birm* from 04; P-in-c Bickenhill from 04. *The Vicarage, 1 High Street, Hampton-in-Arden, Solihull B92 0AE* Tel (01675) 442604 E-mail claring.bull@virgin.net

CLARK, Albert Percival (Peter). b 17. Hatf Coll Dur BA39. St Boniface Warminster 36. **d** 40 **p** 41. C Wildmore *Linc* 40-42; C

New Cleethorpes 42-44; C Linc St Botolph 44-46; R Strubby w Woodthorpe and Maltby-le-Marsh 46-50; S Africa 50-61 and 77-80; R The Quinton *Birm* 61-70; V Werrington *Pet* 70-77; R Chipping Warden w Edgcote and Aston le Walls 80-83; rtd 83; Perm to Offic *S'wark* from 83 and *Guildf* from 86. *3 Falconhurst, The Crescent, Surbiton KT6 4BP* Tel (020) 8399 2032

CLARK, Andrew James. b 50. ACIB72 ACIS76. EMMTC 91. **d** 94 **p** 95. NSM Allestree *Derby* 94-97; NSM Allenton and Shelton Lock 97-03; NSM Walbrook Epiphany from 03. *44 Crabtree Close, Allestree, Derby DE22 2SW* Tel (01332) 552492

CLARK, Antony. b 61. York Univ BA83. Wycliffe Hall Ox 84. **d** 88 **p** 89. C Ashton-upon-Mersey St Mary *Ches* 88-92; Chapl Lee Abbey 92-95; Lic to Offic *Ex* 92-95; Chapl Univ of Westmr *Lon* 95-98; C Bletchley *Ox* 98-00. *Divinity School, St Mary's College, St Andrews KY16 9JU* or *Westerlea, Pittenweem Road, Anstruther KY10 3DT* Tel (01333) 313124

CLARK, Arthur. b 30. MIBiol FRSC Sheff Univ BSc MCB. St D Dioc Tr Course. **d** 88 **p** 89. NSM Haverfordwest St Mary and St Thos w Haroldston *St D* 88-91; C 91-92; V Llawhaden w Bletherston and Llanycefn 92-96; rtd 96. *84 Portfield, Haverfordwest SA61 1BT* Tel (01437) 762694

CLARK, Bernard Charles. b 34. Open Univ BA81. S'wark Ord Course 65. **d** 68 **p** 69. C Pemberton St Jo *Liv* 68-71; C Winwick 71-73; P-in-c Warrington St Barn 74-76; V 76-78; V Hindley All SS 78-83; Perm to Offic 86-94; R Glazebury w Hollinfare 94-99; rtd 99; Perm to Offic *Man* from 00. *31 Linkfield Drive, Worsley, Manchester M28 1JU* Tel 0161-799 7998
E-mail bckathcain31@aol.com

CLARK, Brian John. b 48. Portsm Poly CQSW89 Portsm Univ MA94. STETS 97. **d** 00 **p** 01. NSM Titchfield *Portsm* 00-01; NSM Helston and Wendron *Truro* 01-02; Perm to Offic *Portsm* from 02. *30 Selhurst Way, Fair Oak, Eastleigh SO50 7JX* Tel (023) 8060 0484

CLARK, Cecil. b 44. Sarum Th Coll. **d** 98 **p** 99. OLM Canford Magna *Sarum* from 98. *Fermain Cottage, 133 Magna Road, Bearwood, Bournemouth BH11 9NE* Tel (01202) 577898 *or* 663275 E-mail cclark@rnli.org.uk

CLARK, Mrs Christine Margaret. b 44. St Alb and Ox Min Course 01. **d** 01 **p** 02. NSM Croxley Green St Oswald *St Alb* from 01. *2 Clutterbucks, Church Lane, Sarratt, Rickmansworth WD3 6HL* Tel (01923) 261861 Mobile 07812-524992
E-mail cmclark@fish.co.uk

CLARK, Daniel Alastair. b 74. St Jo Coll Dur BA96. Wycliffe Hall Ox BA99. **d** 00 **p** 01. C Rusholme H Trin *Man* 00-04; NSM from 04. *Holy Trinity Church, Platt Lane, Manchester M14 5NF* Tel 0161-224 1123 *or* 256 3718 E-mail daniel@plattchurch.org

CLARK, David. b 30. Nottm Univ BSc51 Lon Univ DipTh57. St Aid Birkenhead 55. **d** 57 **p** 58. C Tyldesley w Shakerley *Man* 57-60; V Ashton St Jas 60-64; rtd 93. *Roz an Avalou, 22340 Mael-Carhaix, France* Tel (0033) 96 24 65 04

CLARK, Canon David George Neville. b 25. Linc Coll Ox BA49 MA59. Wells Th Coll 49. **d** 51 **p** 52. C Sanderstead All SS *S'wark* 51-54; C Lewisham St Jo Southend 54-59; V Sutton New Town St Barn 59-72; R Charlwood 72-90; P-in-c Sidlow Bridge 76-77; R 77-90; P-in-c Buckland 85-87; P-in-c Leigh 87-90; Hon Can S'wark Cathl 88-90; rtd 90; Perm to Offic *Cov* from 90. *12 Marlborough Road, Coventry CV2 4EP* Tel (024) 7644 2400

CLARK, David Gordon. b 29. Clare Coll Cam BA52 MA57. Ridley Hall Cam 52. **d** 54 **p** 55. C Walthamstow St Jo *Chelmsf* 54-57; V 60-69; C Gt Ilford St Andr 57-60; R Stansted *Roch* 69-82; R Stansted w Fairseat and Vigo 82-94; rtd 94; Perm to Offic *Sarum* from 94. *1 Coastguard Cottages, Wareham BH20 5PE* Tel (01929) 480753

CLARK, David Humphrey. b 39. G&C Coll Cam BA60. Wells Th Coll 62. **d** 64 **p** 65. C Leigh St Mary *Man* 64-68; Min Can and Prec Man Cathl 68-70; Ind Chapl *Nor* 70-85; P-in-c Nor St Clem and St Geo 70-76; P-in-c Nor St Sav w St Paul 70-76; V Norwich-over-the-Water Colegate St Geo 76-79; Hon Asst P Nor St Pet Mancroft 79-85; TR Oadby *Leic* 85-98; C Leic St Jas 98-04; rtd 04. *46 St James Road, Leicester LE2 1HQ*
E-mail dhclark@leicester.anglican.org

CLARK, David John. b 40. Surrey Univ MPhil75 CEng MIStructE. Ridley Hall Cam 81. **d** 83 **p** 84. C Combe Down w Monkton Combe and S Stoke *B & W* 83-89; Voc Adv Bath Adnry 89-96; R Freshford, Limpley Stoke and Hinton Charterhouse 89-05; rtd 05. *14 Barn Close, Frome BA11 4ER* Tel (01373) 461073 E-mail david@freshford313.freeserve.co.uk

CLARK, Dennis Henry Graham. b 26. St Steph Ho Ox 52. **d** 55 **p** 56. C Southall St Geo *Lon* 55-58; C Barbourne *Worc* 58-61; Chapl RAF 61-78; Asst Chapl-in-Chief RAF 78-82; Chapl St Clem Danes (RAF Ch) 79-82; V Godmanchester *Ely* 82-91; rtd 91; Perm to Offic *Ely* from 91. *8 Arran Way, St Ives PE27 3DT* Tel (01480) 301951

CLARK, Diane Catherine. *See* FITZGERALD CLARK, Mrs Diane Catherine

CLARK, Edward Robert. b 39. Ex Coll Ox BA61 MA65 Bris Univ CASS69. St Steph Ho Ox 61. **d** 63 **p** 64. C Solihull *Birm* 63-67; Perm to Offic *Bris* 67-69; *Leic* 69-71; *Ox* 71-80; *St Alb* 80-84; *Cant* from 84; rtd 04. *3 Hunters Bank, Old Road, Elham, Canterbury CT4 6SS* Tel (01303) 840134
E-mail edward.clark@virgin.net

CLARK, Ellen Jane. *See* CLARK-KING, Ellen Jane

CLARK, Frederick Albert George. b 15. MBE68. ACP66. **d** 67 **p** 68. Hon C Stroud *Glouc* 67-84; Hon C Stroud and Uplands w Slad 84-85; Perm to Offic 85-97. *2 Terrace Cottages, Thrupp, Stroud GL5 2BN* Tel (01453) 882060

CLARK, Harold Clive. b 28. Witwatersrand Univ LTh53. St Paul's Coll Grahamstown. **d** 54 **p** 55. S Africa 54-60 and 62-77; C Orange Grove 54-56; R Mayfair 56-60; P-in-c Morden *S'wark* 60-62; R Verulam 62-68; Chapl Michaelhouse 68-77; New Zealand from 77; V Green Island 77-85; V Kaitaia 85-92; Chapl Kristin Sch Albany from 92. *351 East Coast Road, Mairangi Bay 1310, New Zealand* Tel (0064) (9) 479 3434

CLARK, Ian Duncan Lindsay. b 35. K Coll Cam BA59 MA63 PhD64 Linacre Ho Ox DipTh63. Ripon Hall Ox 62. **d** 64 **p** 65. C Willington *Newc* 64-66; India 66-76; Lect Bp's Coll Calcutta 66; Vice-Prin 69-74; Chapl St Cath Coll Cam 76; Fell 77-85; Tutor 78-85; Dean of Chpl and Lect 80-85; Select Preacher Cam Univ 82; Hon Asst P Kelso *Edin* from 85. *4 Yewtree Lane, Yetholm, Kelso TD5 8RZ* Tel (01573) 420323

CLARK, Miss Janet Elizabeth. b 44. Derby Coll of Educn CertEd65 Open Univ BA75. All Nations Chr Coll CertRS84 Oak Hill Th Coll DipHE91 BA92. **d** 92 **p** 94. Par Dn Edmonton All SS w St Mich *Lon* 92-94; C 94-96; V Ealing St Steph Castle Hill from 96. *St Stephen's Vicarage, Sherbourne Gardens, London W13 8AQ* Tel (020) 8810 4929 *or* 8991 0164
E-mail jan@fortaguada.freeserve.co.uk

CLARK, Mrs Jean Robinson. b 32. K Coll Lon AKC BD79. St Chris Coll Blackheath CertRK53. **dss** 85 **d** 87 **p** 94. Cov E *Cov* 85-87; C 87-88; NSM Upper Mole Valley Gp *S'wark* 89-90; Hon Par Dn Charlwood 89-90; Lic to Offic *Cov* 90-92; rtd 92; Perm to Offic *Cov* from 92. *12 Marlborough Road, Coventry CV2 4EP* Tel (024) 7644 2400

CLARK, Jeremy James. b 66. Cant Univ (NZ) BA88. St Jo Coll Auckland BTh97. **d** 94 **p** 95. C Shirley St Steph New Zealand 94-97; C Upton (Overchurch) *Ches* 97-01; P-in-c Ilfracombe SS Phil and Jas w W Down *Ex* from 01. *St James's Vicarage, Kingsley Avenue, Ilfracombe EX34 8ET* Tel (01271) 863519
E-mail pipjimcalix@aol.com *or* jemkiwi@aol.com

CLARK, John David Stanley. b 36. Dur Univ BA64. Ridley Hall Cam 64. **d** 66 **p** 67. C Benchill *Man* 66-69; C Beverley Minster *York* 69-74; Perm to Offic *S'well* 74-76; Lic to Offic 76-77; Miss to Seamen 77-80; Perm to Offic *York* 80-83; V Egton w Grosmont 83-89; R Thornton Dale w Ellerburne and Wilton 89-01; R Thornton Dale w Allerston, Ebberston etc 01-05; rtd 05; Perm to Offic *York* from 05. *22 Swainsea Lane, Pickering YO18 8AP* Tel (01751) 476118

CLARK, John Edward Goodband. b 49. Leeds Univ MA01. Chich Th Coll 70. **d** 73 **p** 74. C Thorpe *Nor* 73-76; C Earlham St Anne 76-78; Chapl RN 78-82; P-in-c Tittleshall w Godwick, Wellingham and Weasenham *Nor* 82-85; P-in-c Helhoughton w Raynham 82-85; R South Raynham, E w W Raynham, Helhoughton, etc 85-90; R Taverham w Ringland 90-96; V Eggleston and R Middleton-in-Teesdale w Forest and Frith *Dur* 96-03; AD Barnard Castle 00-03; R Caston, Griston, Merton, Thompson etc *Nor* 03-05. *5 Foundry Square, Dereham NR19 1AL* Tel (01362) 698948
E-mail hudeshope@rapidial.co.uk

CLARK, John Michael. b 35. Dip Sales Mgt Studies 63 Dip Youth Work 65 Leic Poly Dip Community Educn 80. EMMTC 87. **d** 90 **p** 91. Chapl to the Deaf *Linc* 86-00; NSM Bracebridge Heath 90-00; rtd 00; Perm to Offic *Linc* from 00. *3 Hawthorn Road, Cherry Willingham, Lincoln LN3 4JU* Tel (01522) 751759

CLARK, John Patrick Hedley. b 37. St Cath Coll Cam BA61 MA65 Worc Coll Ox BA63 MA72 BD74 Lambeth Hon DD89. St Steph Ho Ox 61. **d** 64 **p** 65. C Highters Heath *Birm* 64-67; C Eglingham *Newc* 67-72; P-in-c Newc St Anne 72-77; V Longframlington w Brinkburn 77-95; V Chevington 95-02; rtd 02; Perm to Offic *Dur* from 02. *6 The Cottage, West Row, Greatham, Hartlepool TS25 2HW* Tel (01429) 870203

CLARK, John <u>Ronald</u> Lyons. b 47. TCD BA69 MA72. Div Hostel Dub 67. **d** 70 **p** 71. C Dundela St Mark *D & D* 70-72; CF 72-75; C Belfast St Aid *Conn* 75-76; I Stranorlar w Meenglas and Kilteevogue *D & R* 76-81; Chapl Wythenshawe Hosp Man 81-95; I Kilgariffe Union *C, C & R* 95-96; Chapl Blackb, Hyndburn and Ribble Valley NHS Trust 96-04; Chapl Co-ord E Lancs Hosps NHS Trust from 03; Chapl E Lancs Hospice from 96. *Queen's Park Hospital, Haslingden Road, Blackburn BB2 3HH* Tel (01254) 263555 *or* 294807 Mobile 07774-274410

CLARK, Jonathan Dunnett. b 61. Ex Univ BA83 Bris Univ MLitt90 Southn Univ MA96. Trin Coll Bris 84. **d** 88 **p** 89. C Stanwix *Carl* 88-92; Chapl Bris Univ *Bris* 92-93; Dir of Studies S Dios Minl Tr Scheme 94-97; Chapl Univ of N Lon 97-02; Chapl Lon Metrop Univ 02-03; AD Islington 99-03; R Stoke Newington St Mary from 03; P-in-c Brownswood Park from 04. *St Mary's Rectory, Stoke Newington Church Street, London N16 9ES* Tel (020) 7254 6072 Fax 7923 4135 Mobile 07968-845698 E-mail rector@stmaryn16.org.uk

CLARK, Jonathan Jackson. b 57. Linc Coll Ox 79 Down Coll Cam 83. Ridley Hall Cam 81. **d** 84 **p** 85. C W Derby St Luke *Liv* 84-87; C Gt Clacton *Chelmsf* 87-93; V Hammersmith St Simon *Lon* 93-03; AD Hammersmith and Fulham 96-01; TR Leeds St Geo *Ripon* from 03. *St George's Vicarage, 208 Kirkstall Lane, Leeds LS5 2AB* Tel 0113-243 8498 Fax 383 2145 E-mail jonathan.clark@stgeorgesleeds.org.uk

CLARK, The Ven Kenneth James. b 22. DSC44. St Cath Soc Ox BA48 MA52. Cuddesdon Coll 52. **d** 52 **p** 53. C Brinkworth *Bris* 52-53; C Cricklade w Latton 53-56; C-in-c Filwood Park CD 56-59; V Bris H Cross Inns Court 59-61; V Westbury-on-Trym H Trin 61-72; V Bris St Mary Redcliffe w Temple etc 72-82; P-in-c Bedminster St Mich 73-78; RD Bedminster 73-79; Hon Can Bris Cathl 74-92; Adn Swindon 82-92; rtd 92; Perm to Offic *Sarum* 92-04. *25 Emmanuel Court, Guthrie Road, Bristol BS8 3EP* Tel 0117-923 9083

CLARK, Kenneth William. b 69. R Holloway Coll Lon BA92 Trin Coll Cam BA99 MA04. Westcott Ho Cam 97. **d** 00 **p** 01. C Bromley St Mark *Roch* 00-04; R Stone from 04. *The Rectory, Church Road, Greenhithe DA9 9BE* Tel (01322) 382076 E-mail kenofkent@amserve.net

CLARK, Lance Edgar Dennis. b 52. MBE93. Linc Th Coll 74. **d** 77 **p** 78. C Arnold *S'well* 77-82; V Brinsley w Underwood 82-87; Chapl RAF 87-02; Chapl Cardiff and Vale NHS Trust from 02. *Chaplaincy Department, University Hospital of Wales, Heath Park, Cardiff CF14 4XW* Tel (029) 2074 3230

CLARK, Lynn. *See* PURVIS, Lynn

CLARK, Canon Martin Hudson. b 46. K Coll Lon BD68 AKC68 MTh91 Birm Univ PGCE89. **d** 71 **p** 72. C S'wark H Trin *S'wark* 71-74; C Parkstone St Pet w Branksea and St Osmund *Sarum* 74-77; V E Wickham *S'wark* 77-86; V Wandsworth St Anne 86-98; RD Wandsworth 90-95; V Angell Town St Jo from 98; RD Brixton from 01; Hon Can S'wark Cathl from 05. *St John's Vicarage, 49 Wiltshire Road, London SW9 7NE* Tel and fax (020) 7733 0585 E-mail martin@jemima.globalnet.co.uk

CLARK, Michael Arthur. b 46. S Dios Minl Tr Scheme. **d** 83 **p** 84. NSM Monkton Farleigh, S Wraxall and Winsley *Sarum* from 83. *62 Tyning Road, Winsley, Bradford-on-Avon BA15 2JW* Tel (01225) 866652

CLARK, Michael David. b 45. Ox Univ MA68. Trin Coll Bris DipTh72. **d** 72 **p** 73. C Cheadle *Ches* 72-76; Brazil 77-86; Bolivia 86-88; C Wilton *B & W* 89-90; TV 90-99; C Tollington *Lon* 99-01; TR Edgware from 01. *The Rectory, Rectory Lane, Edgware HA8 7LG* Tel (020) 8952 1081 *or* tel and fax 8952 4066 E-mail mikeclark@wayfarer99.freeserve.co.uk

CLARK, Michael James. b 71. Univ of Wales (Cardiff) BSc92. Trin Coll Bris BA02. **d** 02 **p** 03. C Tiverton St Geo and St Paul *Ex* from 02. *St George's Vicarage, St Andrew Street, Tiverton EX16 6PH* Tel (01884) 252184 E-mail mjclark@lycos.co.uk *or* mandhclark@hot6mail.com

CLARK, Pamela Ann. b 45. Garnett Coll Lon CertEd72 DipFE75 Ch Ch Coll Cant PGCE93. SEITE 00 St Jo Coll Nottm 03. **d** 04 **p** 05. NSM Orlestone w Snave and Ruckinge w Warehorne etc *Cant* from 04. *20 Wakefield Way, Hythe CT21 6HT* Tel (01303) 267564

CLARK, Miss Patricia Mary. b 36. Liv Univ BSc. **d** 88 **p** 94. Par Dn Leasowe *Ches* 88-92; Bp's Officer for Women in Min 89-97; Par Dn Davenham 92-94; C 94-97; rtd 97; Perm to Offic *Ches* from 97. *18 Farmstead Way, Great Sutton, Ellesmere Port CH66 2RU* Tel 0151-339 1450

CLARK, Peter. *See* CLARK, Albert Percival

CLARK, Canon Peter. b 39. Ch Coll Cam BA61 MA65. Chich Th Coll 61. **d** 63 **p** 64. C Huddersfield SS Pet and Paul *Wakef* 63-67; C Notting Hill St Jo *Lon* 67-74; Grenada 75-79; C Hove All SS *Chich* 79; P-in-c Hove St Patr 79-82; V Hove St Patr w Ch Ch and St Andr 82-83; V Battersea Ch Ch and St Steph *S'wark* from 83; RD Battersea 90-01; Hon Can S'wark Cathl from 96. *Christ Church Vicarage, Candahar Road, London SW11 2PU* Tel (020) 7228 1225

CLARK, Peter. b 45. Sarum & Wells Th Coll 87. **d** 89 **p** 90. C Portsea St Cuth *Portsm* 89-92; TV Rye *Chich* 92-96; TV from 04; P-in-c Chiddingly w E Hoathly 96-98; R 98-04. *The Vicarage, 21 Fair Meadow, Rye TN31 7NL* Tel (01797) 225769 E-mail clucksville1@onetel.com

CLARK, Peter Norman. b 53. Qu Coll Cam BA79. Westcott Ho Cam 78. **d** 80 **p** 81. C Bris St Mary Redcliffe w Temple etc *Bris* 80-83; C Potternewton *Ripon* 83-86; R Longsight St Luke *Man* from 86; AD Ardwick 00-03. *St Luke's Rectory, Stockport Road, Longsight, Manchester M13 9AB* Tel 0161-273 6662

CLARK, Peter Rodney. b 58. Oriel Coll Ox BA81 MCIH93. N Ord Course 97. **d** 00 **p** 01. C Stone St Mich and St Wulfad w Aston St Sav *Lich* 00-03; TV Hanley H Ev from 03. *Christ Church Vicarage, 10 Emery Street, Stoke-on-Trent ST6 2JJ* Tel (01782) 212639 E-mail rod@prclark.freeserve.co.uk

CLARK, Mrs Prudence Anne. b 44. Man Coll of Educn CertEd78. N Ord Course 89. **d** 92 **p** 94. NSM Royton St Anne *Man* 92-94; Hon C 94-95; NSM Haughton St Anne from 95. *1 Hereford Way, Stalybridge SK15 2TD* Tel 0161-338 5275

CLARK, Reginald Isaac. b 16. AKC47. **d** 47 **p** 48. C Somersham w Pidley and Oldhurst *Ely* 47-49; C Luton St Mary *St Alb* 49-53; C-in-c Luton St Chris Round Green CD 53-59; V Luton St Chris Round Green 59-65; Chapl Shenley Hosp Radlett Herts 65-84; rtd 84; Perm to Offic *Linc* from 84. *1 Monks Walk, Spalding PE11 3LG* Tel (01775) 768304

CLARK, Richard Martin. b 60. Ch Coll Cam MA81 Nottm Univ MA99. Trin Coll Bris BA86. **d** 86 **p** 87. C Orpington Ch Ch *Roch* 86-89; C Marple All SS *Ches* 89-92; V Nottingham St Andr *S'well* from 92. *St Andrew's Vicarage, Chestnut Grove, Nottingham NG3 5AD* Tel 0115-912 0098 Mobile 07970-823462 E-mail stan.vic@virgin.net

CLARK, Robert Henry. b 32. Oak Hill Th Coll 61. **d** 64 **p** 65. C Haydock St Mark *Liv* 64-67; C Tranmere St Cath *Ches* 67-75; V Platt Bridge *Liv* 75-84; V Litherland St Paul Hatton Hill 84-94; rtd 94; Perm to Offic *Liv* from 94. *9 Lime Vale, Ince, Wigan WN3 4PE* Tel (01942) 861751

CLARK, Canon Robin. b 27. Lon Univ BA49 BD69 MPhil77 St Jo Coll Dur DipTh54 Sheff Univ MA00. **d** 54 **p** 55. C Newton Heath All SS *Man* 54-58; Asst Master Woodhouse Gr Sch Sheff 58-61; R Brant Broughton w Stragglethorpe *Linc* 61-90; P-in-c Welbourn 65-66; RD Loveden 72-93; Can and Preb Linc Cathl from 84; R Brant Broughton and Beckingham 90-93; rtd 93; Perm to Offic *Linc* 93-01. *Ravenshurst Cottage, 23 The Green, Ingham, Lincoln LN1 2XT*

CLARK, Rodney. *See* CLARK, Peter Rodney

CLARK, Preb Roland Mark Allison. b 21. St Cath Coll Cam BA48 MA53. Wells Th Coll 48. **d** 50 **p** 51. C Battersea St Paul *S'wark* 50-52; C Greenwich St Alfege w St Pet 52-56; Chapl RNVR 53-56; V Wilton *B & W* 56-79; RD Taunton S 60-65; Preb Wells Cathl from 63; R Backwell 79-88; RD Portishead 82-86; rtd 88; Perm to Offic *B & W* and *Chich from 88; Bris* from 95. *21 The Chimes, Nailsea, Bristol BS48 4NH* Tel (01275) 852670

CLARK, Ronald. *See* CLARK, John Ronald Lyons

CLARK, Sarah Elizabeth. b 65. Loughb Univ BA86 Keele Univ MBA94. St Jo Coll Nottm MA97 DipMM98. **d** 98 **p** 99. C Porchester *S'well* 98-02; R Carlton-in-Lindrick and Langold w Oldcotes from 02. *21 Grange Close, Carlton-in-Lindrick, Worksop S81 9DX* Tel (01909) 730398 E-mail sec1@tinyworld.co.uk

CLARK, Simon Peter John. b 68. Westcott Ho Cam 95. **d** 98 **p** 99. C Bocking St Mary *Chelmsf* 98-02; C Edmonton St Alphege *Lon* from 02; C Ponders End St Matt from 02. *St Matthew's Vicarage, Church Road, Enfield EN3 4NT* Tel (020) 8443 2255 E-mail Fr.Simon@btopenworld.com

CLARK, Stephen Kenneth. b 52. Bris Univ BEd74. Wycliffe Hall Ox 80. **d** 83 **p** 84. C Pitsea *Chelmsf* 83-86; Chapl Scargill Ho 86-89; R Elmley Castle w Bricklehampton and Combertons *Worc* 89-96; Chapl Burrswood Chr Cen *Roch* 96-01; Chapl Team Ldr from 01. *Swedish Log House, Burrswood, Groombridge, Tunbridge Wells TN3 9PU* Tel (01892) 863637 Fax 863623 E-mail admin@burrswood.org.uk

CLARK, Terence Paul. b 62. Leeds Univ BSc85 PGCE94 St Jo Coll Ox DPhil91 FLS. Wycliffe Hall Ox 98. **d** 00 **p** 01. C Whitfield *Derby* from 00. *1 Cedar Close, Glossop SK13 7BP* Tel and fax (01457) 860412 E-mail terry@glossop.org

CLARK, Trevor Bartholomew. b 44. Qu Coll Birm 68. **d** 71 **p** 72. C Maltby *Sheff* 71-75; V New Rossington 75-80; V Campsall 80-95; rtd 96; Perm to Offic *Sheff* from 96. *44 Elmdale Drive, Edenthorpe, Doncaster DN3 2LE*

CLARK-KING (née CLARK), Ellen Jane. b 62. Newnham Coll Cam BA85 MA89 Reading Univ PCVG86 Lon Univ MA99 Lanc Univ PhD03. Ripon Coll Cuddesdon 89. **d** 92 **p** 94. C Colwall w Upper Colwall and Coddington *Heref* 92-95; Chapl SS Coll Cam 95-00; NSM N Shields *Newc* 00-05; Asst Dioc Dir of Ords 01-05; Canada from 05. *3166 St George's Avenue, North Vancouver BC, Canada, V7N 1V2* E-mail ejck@lineone.net

CLARK-KING (formerly KING), Jeremy Norman. b 66. K Coll Lon BD88 AKC88 Lon Univ MA99. Ripon Coll Cuddesdon 88. **d** 90 **p** 91. C Ashby-de-la-Zouch St Helen w Coleorton *Leic* 90-93; C Ledbury w Eastnor *Heref* 93-96; C Cambridge Gt St Mary w St Mich *Ely* 96-00; Chapl Girton Coll Cam 96-99; Chapl Cam Univ 96-99; V Byker St Ant *Newc* 00-05; R N Vancouver St Martin Canada from 05. *3166 St George's Avenue, North Vancouver BC, Canada, V7N 1V2* E-mail jncknv@tiscali.co.uk

CLARKE, Alan John. b 55. St Jo Coll Dur BA77 MA85 PGCE. Westcott Ho Cam 78. **d** 80 **p** 81. C Heworth St Mary *Dur* 80-83; C Darlington St Jo 83-87; Asst Chapl Bryanston Sch 87-91; Chapl St Pet High Sch Ex 93-99; Lic to Offic *Ex* 93-99; Chapl and Hd RS Reed's Sch Cobham from 99. *Clover, Reed's School, Sandy Lane, Cobham KT11 2BL* Tel (01932) 869006

CLARKE, Alexandra Naomi Mary. b 75. Trin Coll Cam BA96 MA99 MPhil97 SS Hild & Bede Coll Dur PhD02 Anglia Poly Univ BA04. Westcott Ho Cam 02. **d** 05. C Papworth *Ely* from 05. *The Rectory, The Green, Eltisley, St Neots PE19 6TG* E-mail alexandra.clarke@ely.anglican.org

CLARKE, Miss Alison Clare. b 33. MCST54 Open Univ BA85. EAMTC 90. **d** 93 **p** 94. NSM Lt Ilford St Mich *Chelmsf* 93-98; Asst Chapl Newham Healthcare NHS Trust Lon 93-98; Perm to

Offic *Lon* 94-98; NSM Woodford St Mary w St Phil and St Jas *Chelmsf* 98-03; rtd 03; Perm to Offic *Chelmsf* from 03. *29 Glengall Road, Woodford Green IG8 0DN* Tel (020) 8504 5106

CLARKE, Andrew John. b 58. New Coll Edin BD82 Graduate Soc Dur PGCE89. Linc Th Coll 84. **d** 86 **p** 87. C High Harrogate Ch Ch *Ripon* 86-88; RE Teacher Royds Hall High Sch Huddersfield 89-91; C Thornbury *Bradf* 91-93; P-in-c Bingley H Trin 93-99; V from 99; RD Airedale 00-05. *Holy Trinity Vicarage, Oak Avenue, Bingley BD16 1ES* Tel (01274) 563909 E-mail andrewclarkebd@aol.com

CLARKE, Ann. *See* CLARKE, Geraldine Ann

CLARKE, Anne. b 51. **d** 04. OLM E Dulwich St Jo *S'wark* from 04. *62 Oakhurst Grove, London SE22 9AQ* Tel (020) 8693 1276 E-mail apsy73@dsl.pipex.com

CLARKE, Arthur. b 34. Lon Univ BD66 Nottm Univ MPhil75 DipEd. Sarum & Wells Th Coll 75. **d** 76 **p** 77. C Wollaton *S'well* 76-79; R Sutton Bonington 79-91; P-in-c Normanton on Soar 79-91; R Sutton Bonington w Normanton-on-Soar 91-93; P-in-c Arnold 93-94; V 94-02; rtd 02; Perm to Offic *S'well* from 02. *16 Kegworth Road, Kingston-on-Soar, Nottingham NG11 0DB* Tel (01509) 674545 E-mail aclarke@kos16.fsnet.co.uk

CLARKE, Miss Audrey May. b 35. Gilmore Ho 65. **dss** 75 **d** 87 **p** 94. Crofton Park St Hilda w St Cypr *S'wark* 75-79; Chapl Asst Middx Hosp Lon 80-84; Mottingham St Andr *S'wark* 84-87; Par Dn 87-89; C Westborough *Guildf* 89-95; rtd 95; Hon C St Mary's Bay w St Mary-in-the-Marsh etc *Cant* 95-98; Hon C New Romney w Old Romney and Midley 95-98; Perm to Offic *Pet* from 98. *47 Lindsay Street, Kettering NN16 8RG* Tel (01536) 410586

CLARKE, Bernard Ronald. b 53. FRGS. Ridley Hall Cam 74. **d** 77 **p** 78. C Leigh Park *Portsm* 77-78; C Petersfield w Sheet 78-81; Chapl RN from 81; Dir of Ords RN 93-03. *Royal Naval Chaplaincy Service, Room 205, Victory Building, HM Naval Base, Portsmouth PO1 3LS* Tel (023) 9272 7900 Fax 9272 7111

CLARKE, Mrs Caroline Anne. b 49. Girton Coll Cam BA75 MA79 K Coll Lon PGCE76. SEITE 97. **d** 00 **p** 01. NSM Clapham H Trin and St Pet *S'wark* from 00; Chapl Trin Hospice Lon from 03. *42 The Chase, London SW4 0NH* Tel (020) 7622 0765 Fax 7652 4555 Mobile 07808-858674 E-mail carolineclarke@lineone.net

CLARKE, Charles David. b 37. Univ of Wales BA76 MA93 PhD98 Cam Univ DipEd77 MEd Lambeth MA95 LCP77. St Mich Coll Llan 88. **d** 90 **p** 91. C Whitchurch *Llan* 90-93; V Graig 93-96; P-in-c Cilfynydd 93-96; TV Cyncoed *Mon* 96-98; R Neath w Llantwit *Llan* 98-01; TR Neath 01-02; rtd 02. *Lough Cutra, 11 Davies Andrews Road, Tonna, Neath SA11 1EU* Tel (01639) 638049

CLARKE, Miss Christine Vera. b 45. Lon Univ CertEd66 Bris Univ MSc00. Qu Coll Birm 79. **dss** 81 **d** 87 **p** 94. Bris St Mary Redcliffe w Temple etc *Bris* 81-86; Ind Chapl 86-95; NSM Westbury-on-Trym St Alb 94-95; P-in-c Wraxall *B & W* 95-97; R 97-03; rtd 03; Perm to Offic *B & W* from 03. *32 St Andrew's Mews, Wells BA5 2LB* Tel (01749) 673675

CLARKE, Canon Christopher George. b 43. Sarum Th Coll 67. **d** 68 **p** 69. C Sprowston *Nor* 68-72; V Hemsby 72-77; V Sutton Courtenay w Appleford *Ox* 77-84; TR Bracknell 84-97; RD Bracknell 90-96; Hon Can Ch Ch from 95; P-in-c Sonning 97-98; V from 98. *The Vicarage, Thames Street, Sonning, Reading RG4 6UR* Tel 0118-969 3298 E-mail chris@cgc.fsnet.co.uk

CLARKE, Daniel. b 17. TCD BA39 MA44 BD66. TCD Div Sch 39. **d** 41 **p** 42. C Dublin St Bart *D & G* 41-44; Dioc C Killaloe *L & K* 44-46; Chapl Roscrea Hosp Inst 46-48; C-in-c Corbally 46-48; I Borrisokane 48-59; Asst Master Robert Bloomfield Sch Shefford 59-62; Hd Relig Studies Reigate Gr Sch 62-82; Chapl 75-84; Chapl Reigate St Mary's Sch 85-92; Hon Chapl 92-97; rtd 97; Perm to Offic *S'wark* 66-80 and 85-02. *Address temp unknown*

CLARKE, David James. b 55. Univ of Wales (Abth) BSc(Econ)77 Keele Univ MA78 PhD83. Trin Coll Bris DipTh84. **d** 84 **p** 85. C Cardigan w Mwnt and Y Ferwig *St D* 84-87; P-in-c Llansantffraed and Llanbadarn Trefeglwys etc 87-88; V 88-91; Chapl Coll of SS Mark and Jo Plymouth 91-96; V Lindfield *Chich* from 96. *The Vicarage, High Street, Lindfield, Haywards Heath RH16 2HR* Tel (01444) 482386

CLARKE, Denis John. b 23. LNSM course. **d** 87 **p** 88. OLM Brothertoft Gp *Linc* 87-98; rtd 98; Perm to Offic *Linc* 98-01. *Address temp unknown*

CLARKE, Douglas Charles. b 33. Bps' Coll Cheshunt 65. **d** 66 **p** 67. C Chingford SS Pet and Paul *Chelmsf* 66-72; V Romford Ascension Collier Row 72-79; V Bembridge *Portsm* 79-83; V Bournemouth St Mary *Win* 83-87; R High Wych and Gilston w Eastwick *St Alb* 87-00; rtd 00; Perm to Offic *Linc* and *St Alb* from 00. *36 Tennyson Drive, Bourne PE10 9WD* Tel (01778) 394840

CLARKE, Dudley Barrington. b 22. OBE. Em Coll Cam BA46 MA48 PhD. Ridley Hall Cam 46. **d** 48 **p** 49. C Aldershot H Trin *Guildf* 48-50; Chapl Monkton Combe Sch Bath 50-58; Australia from 59; rtd 87. *60 Duke Street, Sandy Bay, Tas, Australia 7005* Tel (0061) (02) 6224 0784 *or* 6220 2385

CLARKE, Duncan James Edward. b 54. Wycliffe Hall Ox 75. **d** 78 **p** 79. C Newport St Andr *Mon* 78-80; C Griffithstown 80-82; Trinidad and Tobago 82-84 and 95-99; NSM Fleckney and Kilby *Leic* 92-95; USPG 95-99; C Wednesfield *Lich* 99; TV 99-01; Asst Chapl HM Pris Wormwood Scrubs 01-03; Chapl HM Pris Haverigg from 03. *HM Prison, North Lane, Haverigg, Millom LA18 4NA* Tel (01229) 713000 Mobile 07931-111276

CLARKE, Mrs Elizabeth Hazel. b 55. Ridley Hall Cam 02. **d** 04 **p** 05. C Frankby w Greasby *Ches* from 04. *5 Flail Close, Wirral CH49 2RN* Tel 0151-605 0735

CLARKE, Eric Samuel. b 26. Nottm Univ BSc51 St Cath Coll Ox BA69 MA69. Wycliffe Hall Ox 51. **d** 54 **p** 55. C Gedling *S'well* 54-57; C Nottingham St Pet and St Jas 57-69; Perm to Offic *Derby* 63-02; rtd 02. *Hillcrest, Cottington Mead, Sidmouth EX10 8HB*

CLARKE, Frank. b 21. St Jo Coll Nottm. **d** 85 **p** 87. NSM Farnsfield *S'well* 85-97; rtd 98; Perm to Offic *S'well* from 03. *Belvedere, Tippings Lane, Farnsfield, Newark NG22 8EP* Tel (01623) 882528 E-mail doreen@onetel.com

CLARKE, Capt Geoffrey. b 53. CA Tr Coll 84 Trin Coll Bris 94. **d** 97 **p** 98. C Belmont *Lon* 97-00; C Tonbridge SS Pet and Paul *Roch* from 00. *14 Salisbury Road, Tonbridge TN10 4PB* Tel and fax (01732) 355200 E-mail geoff.clarke@diocese-rochester.org

CLARKE, Geraldine Ann. b 46. Hockerill Coll of Educn CertEd68 ACP81. NTMTC 93. **d** 96 **p** 97. NSM Aldersbrook *Chelmsf* 96-01; TR Becontree S from 01. *St Martin's Vicarage, Goresbrook Road, Dagenham RM9 6UX* Tel and fax (020) 8592 0967 E-mail ann.clarke@virgin.net

CLARKE, Canon Harold George. b 29. St D Coll Lamp 58. **d** 61 **p** 62. C Ebbw Vale Ch Ch *Mon* 61-64; C Roath St German *Llan* 64-73; Chapl Wales Poly 73-74; V Glyntaff 73-84; V Roath St Martin 84-00; RD Cardiff 89-99; Can Res Llan Cathl 91-99; rtd 00. *12 St Margaret's Crescent, Cardiff CF23 5AU* Tel (029) 2046 2280

CLARKE, Harold Godfrey Codrington. *See* CODRINGTON CLARKE, Harold Godfrey

CLARKE, Hazel. *See* CLARKE, Mrs Elizabeth Hazel

CLARKE, Hilary James. b 41. JP. Univ of Wales (Lamp) BA64 Ox Univ DipEd65. St Steph Ho Ox 64. **d** 66 **p** 67. C Kibworth Beauchamp *Leic* 66-68; Chapl to the Deaf 68-71; Prin Officer Ch Miss for Deaf Walsall 71-73; Prin Officer & Sec Leic and Co Miss for the Deaf 73-89; Hon C Leic St Anne *Leic* 73-98; TV Leic H Spirit 82-89; Hon Can Leic Cathl 88-96; Bp's Press Relns and Dio Communications Officer 95-96; Sec Gen Syn Coun for the Deaf 88-02; rtd 02. *The Gate House, Brough, Kirkby Stephen CA17 4DS* Tel 07730-002570 (mobile)

CLARKE, James. *See* CLARKE, David James

CLARKE, Jason Philip. b 66. Lon Hosp BDS. Oak Hill Th Coll. **d** 01 **p** 02. C Fulwood *Sheff* from 01. *50 Brooklands Crescent, Sheffield S10 4GG* Tel 0114-229 5567, 230 1588 *or* 230 1911 E-mail jason@fulwoodchurch.co.uk

CLARKE, Jason Scott. b 65. Leeds Univ BA87. Coll of Resurr Mirfield 89. **d** 91 **p** 92. C Hendon St Mary *Lon* 91-95; V Enfield St Geo 95-01; V Ditchling *Chich* from 01. *St Margaret's Vicarage, 2 Charlton Gardens, Lewes Road, Ditchling, Hassocks BN6 8WA* Tel (01273) 843165

CLARKE, John Charles. b 31. St Jo Coll Nottm 91. **d** 92 **p** 93. NSM Winshill *Derby* 92-95; P-in-c Stanley 95-98; rtd 98; Perm to Offic *Win* from 98. *5 The Tyleshades, Tadburn, Romsey SO51 5RJ* Tel (01794) 523945

CLARKE, Canon John David Maurice. b 60. **d** 89 **p** 90. C Dublin Whitechurch *D & G* 89-92; Asst Chapl St Vin Hosp Donnybrook 89-92; I Navan w Kentstown, Tara, Slane, Painestown etc *M & K* from 92; Can Meath from 00; Can Kildare Cathl from 00. *The Rectory, Boyne Road, Navan, Co Meath, Irish Republic* Tel and fax (00353) (46) 902 1172 E-mail johndmclarke@eircom.net

CLARKE, The Very Revd John Martin. b 52. Edin Univ BD76 Hertf Coll Ox BA89 MA89. Edin Th Coll 73. **d** 76 **p** 77. C Kenton Ascension *Newc* 76-79; Prec St Ninian's Cathl Perth *St And* 79-82; Info Officer to Gen Syn of Scottish Episc Ch 82-87; Greece 87-88; V Battersea St Mary *S'wark* 89-96; Prin Ripon Coll Cuddesdon 97-04; Can and Preb Linc Cathl *Linc* 00-04; Dean Wells *B & W* from 04. *The Dean's Lodging, 25 The Liberty, Wells BA5 2SZ* Tel and fax (01749) 670278 E-mail dean@wellscathedral.uk.net

CLARKE, John Patrick Hatherley. b 46. Pemb Coll Ox BA68 Man Univ MBA73. St Jo Coll Nottm DipTh83. **d** 83 **p** 84. C Leic H Trin w St Jo *Leic* 83-87; C Selly Park St Steph and St Wulstan *Birm* 87-92; Hon C Woking St Mary *Guildf* 92-94; V Greenham *Ox* from 94. *Greenham Vicarage, New Road, Greenham, Newbury RG19 8RZ* Tel (01635) 41075

CLARKE, Canon John Percival. b 44. TCD BA67 MA98. **d** 69 **p** 70. C Belfast St Simon *Conn* 69-72; C Monkstown *D & G* 72-76; Asst Chapl TCD 76-78; I Durrus *C, C & R* 79-82; I Carrigrohane Union 82-89; Tanzania 89-92; I Wicklow w Killiskey *D & G* from 92; Abp's Dom Chapl 95-97; Can Ch Ch Cathl Dublin from 97. *The Rectory, Wicklow, Irish Republic* Tel (00353) (404) 67132

CLARKE, John Philip. b 31. Trin Hall Cam BA54 MA62. Linc Th Coll. **d** 57 **p** 58. C Walworth Lady Marg w St Mary *S'wark* 57-59; C Warlingham w Chelsham and Farleigh 59-62; C

Mottingham St Andr 62-67; C Eltham Park St Luke 67-72; Chapl Leeds Gen Infirmary 72-91; C Far Headingley St Chad *Ripon* 91-96; Bp's Adv on Chr Healing 91-96; rtd 96; Perm to Offic *Ripon* from 96. *2 Raikes View, Wilsill, Harrogate HG3 5EG* Tel (01423) 711646

CLARKE, Mrs Joy Irene. b 44. LNSM course 95. **d** 98 **p** 02. OLM Ditton St Mich w St Thos *Liv* from 98. *55 Spinney Avenue, Widnes WA8 8LB* Tel 0151-424 8747

CLARKE, Judith Irene. b 46. SRN67 SCM69. EAMTC 97. **d** 00 **p** 01. NSM Shingay Gp *Ely* 00-02; P-in-c Gt Staughton 02-05; P-in-c Hail Weston and Southoe 04-05; R Gt Staughton w Hail Weston w Southoe from 05. *The Vicarage, Causeway, Great Staughton, St Neots PE19 5BF* Tel (01480) 861215 E-mail revjudi@fish.co.uk

✠**CLARKE, The Rt Revd Kenneth Herbert.** b 49. TCD BA71. **d** 72 **p** 73 **c** 01. C Magheralin *D & D* 72-75; C Dundonald 75-78; Chile 78-81; I Crinken *D & G* 82-86; I Coleraine *Conn* 86-01; Chmn SAMS (Ireland) from 94; Can Conn Cathl 96-98; Adn Dalriada 98-01; Bp K, E & A from 01. *48 Carrickfern, Co Cavan, Irish Republic* Tel (00353) (49) 437 2759 Fax 436 2829 E-mail ken@atnaf.freeserve.co.uk *or* bishop@kilmore.anglican.org

CLARKE, Canon Margaret Geraldine. b 33. Dalton Ho Bris 62. **dss** 68 **d** 87 **p** 94. Wells St Thos w Horrington *B & W* 68-74; Easthampstead *Ox* 74-94; Par Dn 87-94; C 94; Hon Can Ch Ch 90-94; rtd 94; Hon C Bracknell *Ox* from 97. *Hermon, London Road, Bracknell RG12 2XH* Tel (01344) 427451

CLARKE, Martin Howard. b 47. AKC70. St Aug Coll Cant 70. **d** 71 **p** 72. C Saffron Walden w Wendens Ambo *Chelmsf* 71-74; C Ely 74-78; V Messing w Inworth *Chelmsf* 78-90; V Layer de la Haye 90-02; R Layer de la Haye and Layer Breton w Birch etc from 03. *The Vicarage, 45 Malting Green Road, Layer-de-la-Haye, Colchester CO2 0JJ* Tel (01206) 734243

CLARKE, Ms Mary Margaret. b 65. K Coll Lon BD86 AKC86. Linc Th Coll 89. **d** 89 **p** 94. Par Dn Northampton St Jas *Pet* 89-93; Chapl Nene Coll of HE Northn 92-93; TD Coventry Caludon *Cov* 93-94; TV 94-01; Perm to Offic *Lon* from 01. *1 Porchester Gardens, London W2 3LA* Tel (020) 7229 6359 E-mail mary-andrew@clarkewillson.fsnet.co.uk

CLARKE, Maurice Fulford Lovell. b 12. Clare Coll Cam BA34 MA38. Wells Th Coll 35. **d** 36 **p** 37. C Benwell St Jas *Newc* 36-46; CF (EC) 40-46; CF (TA) 48-54; Vice-Prin Sarum Th Coll 46-53; V Lewisham St Swithun *S'wark* 54-65; Chapl Hither Green Hosp 54-65; R Ashley *Lich* 65-77; P-in-c Hales 65-73; rtd 77; Perm to Offic *Heref* 77-99. *25 Ramsay Hall, 11-13 Byron Road, Worthing BN11 3HN* Tel (01903) 201830

CLARKE, Maurice Harold. b 30. K Alfred's Coll Win CertEd56 Sussex Univ MA79 LCP69. Cuddesdon Coll 65. **d** 67 **p** 68. Hd Master Co Sec Sch Cowplain (Lower Sch) 67-72; Hon C Waterlooville *Portsm* 67-70; Hon C Fareham SS Pet and Paul 70-72; Hon C Higham and Merston *Roch* 72-83; Dep Hd Master Thamesview High Sch 72-80; Hd Master Eltham Green Comp Sch 80-83; V Hamble le Rice *Win* 83-90; rtd 91; Perm to Offic *Win* from 91 and *Chich* from 92. *10 Worcester Road, Chichester PO19 8DJ* Tel (01243) 775646

CLARKE, Michael. b 39. Ely Th Coll 60. **d** 62 **p** 63. C S Stoneham *Win* 62-64; C N Greenford All Hallows *Lon* 64-69; Hon C Milton *Portsm* 69-74; Chapl St Jas Hosp Portsm 69-91; Chapl Hurstpierpoint Coll 91-92; R Highnam, Lassington, Rudford, Tibberton etc *Glouc* 92-98; rtd 99; Perm to Offic *Glouc* 99-01 and *Portsm* from 02. *Little Barns, 77 Fishbourne Lane, Ryde PO33 4EX* Tel (01983) 883858

CLARKE, Canon Neil Malcolm. b 53. OBE05. Solicitor 79. WMMTC 89. **d** 92 **p** 93. NSM Desborough, Brampton Ash, Dingley and Braybrooke *Pet* from 92; Can Pet Cathl from 04. *53 Breakleys Road, Desborough, Kettering NN14 2PT* Tel (01536) 760667

CLARKE, Nicholas John. b 57. Lon Univ BA78 Lon Inst of Educn PGCE80. Ridley Hall Cam 95. **d** 97 **p** 98. C Attleborough *Cov* 97-00; V Fillongley and Corley from 00. *The Vicarage, Holbeche Crescent, Fillongley, Coventry CV7 8ES* Tel (01676) 540320 E-mail cool.clarkes@virgin.net

CLARKE, Norman. b 28. Keble Coll Ox BA52 MA58. St Steph Ho Ox 52. **d** 54 **p** 55. C Ellesmere Port *Ches* 54-57; C Kettering St Mary *Pet* 57-60; Ghana 60-62; C Friern Barnet All SS *Lon* 62-63; Lic to Offic *Leic* 63-74; C Knighton St Mary Magd 74-81; Dioc Communications Officer 81-88; P-in-c Sproughton w Burstall *St E* 81-88; P-in-c Dunsford and Doddiscombsleigh *Ex* 88-95; P-in-c Cheriton Bishop 88-95; rtd 95; Perm to Offic *Ex* from 95; RD Ottery 02-03. *78 Malden Road, Sidmouth EX10 9NA* Tel (01395) 515849

CLARKE, Oswald Reeman. b 12. Liv Univ BA35 St Cath Soc Ox BA37 MA40. Ripon Hall Ox 34. **d** 36 **p** 37. C Whitehaven Ch Ch w H Trin *Carl* 36-37; C Addingham 37-38; Hon C Carl H Trin 38-39; C Wavertree St Mary *Liv* 39-43; P-in-c Widnes St Mary 43-44; V Liv St Sav 44-53; V Tulse Hill H Trin *S'wark* 53-58; V Upper Chelsea St Simon *Lon* 58-85; rtd 85; Perm to Offic *Lon* 85-90; P-in-c St Mary Abchurch 90-04. *14 Down, Morden College, 19 St Germans Place, London SE3 0PW* Tel (020) 8293 1181 E-mail robinthomas@dixonwilson.co.uk

CLARKE, Canon Peter. b 25. Lon Univ BSc49 St Chad's Coll Dur DipTh51. **d** 51 **p** 52. C Linc St Giles *Linc* 51-53; C Gt Grimsby St Mary and St Jas 53-60; V Linc All SS 60-68; V Bardney 68-75; V Apley w Stainfield 68-75; V Linc St Nic w St Jo Newport 75-88; RD Christianity 78-85; Can and Preb Linc Cathl 79-99; rtd 88; Perm to Offic *Linc* 88-00. *1 North Croft, Saxilby, Lincoln LN1 2PU* Tel (01522) 702795

CLARKE, Preb Peter Gerald. b 38. Cuddesdon Coll 74. **d** 76 **p** 77. Hon C Marston Magna w Rimpton *B & W* 76-79; Hon C Queen Camel, Marston Magna, W Camel, Rimpton etc 79-87; Hon C Chilton Cantelo, Ashington, Mudford, Rimpton etc 87-88; R Tintinhull w Chilthorne Domer, Yeovil Marsh etc 88-94; TV Weston-super-Mare Cen Par 94-95; V Weston super Mare All SS and St Sav from 96; Preb Wells Cathl from 02. *All Saints' Vicarage, 46 Manor Road, Weston-super-Mare BS23 2SU* Tel (01934) 623230 E-mail peter_g_clarke@ntlworld.com

CLARKE, Peter John. b 36. Qu Coll Ox BA60 MA64 Lon Univ BD79. Clifton Th Coll 62. **d** 62 **p** 63. C Upper Tulse Hill St Matthias *S'wark* 62-64; CMJ 64-96; Dir for S America 88-96; rtd 97. *Pedro Moran 4414, C 1419 HLH Buenos Aires, Argentina* Tel (0054) (11) 4501 4629 Fax as telephone

CLARKE, Philip John. b 44. Bris Univ BA65 Univ of Wales (Abth) DipEd66. N Ord Course 84. **d** 87 **p** 88. NSM Crewe Ch Ch and St Pet *Ches* 87-88; NSM Coppenhall 88-90; Lic to Offic 90-91; C Altrincham St Geo 91-95; C Odd Rode 95-97; P-in-c Peterchurch w Vowchurch, Turnastone and Dorstone *Heref* 97-98; V Llansantffraid Glyn Ceirog and Llanarmon etc *St As* from 98. *The Vicarage, High Street, Glyn Ceiriog, Llangollen LL20 7EH* Tel (01691) 718245 E-mail pjclarke@barclays.net

CLARKE, Richard Leon. b 37. Sarum Th Coll 62. **d** 65 **p** 66. C Fordington *Sarum* 65-68; C Haywards Heath St Rich *Chich* 68-72; C Goring-by-Sea 72-76; P-in-c Portslade St Andr 76-77; P-in-c Southwick St Pet 76-77; V Portslade St Pet and St Andr 77-79; R Clayton w Keymer 79-02; RD Hurst 90-98; rtd 03. *107 Freshfield Road, Brighton BN2 0BL* Tel (01273) 628006

✠**CLARKE, The Most Revd Richard Lionel.** b 49. TCD BA71 MA79 PhD90 K Coll Lon BD75 AKC75. **d** 75 **p** 76 **c** 96. C Holywood *D & D* 75-77; C Dublin St Bart w Leeson Park *D & G* 77-79; Dean of Residence TCD 79-84; I Bandon Union *C, C & R* 84-93; Dir of Ords 85-93; Cen Dir of Ords 82-97; Can Cork and Ross Cathls 91-93; Dean Cork 93-96; I Cork St Fin Barre's Union 93-96; Chapl Univ Coll Cork 93-96; Bp M & K from 96; Hon Can St Ninian's Cathl Perth *St And* from 04. *Bishop's House, Moyglare, Maynooth, Co Kildare, Irish Republic* Tel (00353) (1) 628 9354 Fax 628 9696 E-mail bishop@meath.anglican.org

CLARKE, Canon Robert George. b 36. St Jo Coll Dur BA65 Natal Univ PhD83. Cranmer Hall Dur 65. **d** 67 **p** 68. C Basingstoke *Win* 67-70; R Ixopo 71-74; C Pietermaritzburg Cathl 75-80; Dir Pietermaritzburg Urban Min Project 77-83; R Grahamstown St Bart 84-87; Lect St Paul's Coll 84-87; Ecum Officer Albany Regional Coun of Chs 88-95; Hon Can Grahamstown from 05. *26 Somerset Street, Grahamstown, 6139 South Africa* Tel (0027) (046) 622 7803 E-mail bobandmaggy@imaginet.co.za

CLARKE, Robert Graham. b 28. S Dios Minl Tr Scheme 78. **d** 81 **p** 82. NSM Woolston *Win* 81-89; NSM Portswood St Denys 89-93; Chapl Torrevieja *Eur* 93-95; Perm to Offic *Win* and *Eur* from 95. *10 River Green, Hamble, Southampton SO31 4JA* Tel (023) 8045 4230

CLARKE, Robert Michael. b 45. Oak Hill Th Coll BD71 Sarum & Wells Th Coll 78. **d** 78 **p** 79. Hon C Glastonbury St Jo w Godney *B & W* 78-81; Asst Hd Master Edington Sch 78-81; Chapl Felsted Sch 81-84; Asst Chapl and Ho Master 85-92; Hd Master Brocksford Hall 92-94; Hd Master The Park Sch Bath 94-96; Chapl Seaford Coll Petworth 96-99; Hd Master Bredon Sch 99-00; Perm to Offic *Lich* from 01. *17 Top Street, Whittington, Oswestry SY11 4DR* Tel (01691) 662548

CLARKE, Robert Sydney. b 35. OBE00. K Coll Lon AKC64 MA65. **d** 65 **p** 66. C Hendon St Mary *Lon* 65-69; C Langley Marish *Ox* 69-70; Chapl New Cross Hosp Wolv 70-74; Chapl Dorchester Hosps 74-79; Sen Chapl Westmr Hosp Lon 80-85; Sen Chapl Win Hosps 88-94; Sen Chapl Win and Eastleigh Healthcare NHS Trust 94-00; Chapl to The Queen 87-05; Sec and Dir Tr Gen Syn Hosp Chapl Coun 94-00; rtd 00; Perm to Offic *Lon* and *S'wark* from 95; *Eur* from 00. *3 Brook Court, Middlebridge Street, Romsey SO51 8HR* Tel (01794) 524215

CLARKE, Canon Robert William. b 56. CITC. **d** 83 **p** 84. C Cloughfern *Conn* 83-85; C Drumragh w Mountfield *D & R* 85-87; I Edenderry w Clanabogan from 87; Can Derry Cathl from 05. *Edenderry Rectory, 91 Crevenagh Road, Omagh BT79 0EZ* Tel (028) 8224 5525

CLARKE, Roger David. b 58. Man Univ BA Ox Univ MA. Ripon Coll Cuddesdon 80. **d** 83 **p** 84. C Frodsham *Ches* 83-86; C Wilmslow 86-88; V High Lane 88-93; V Heald Green St Cath 93-99; R W Kirby St Bridget from 99. *St Bridget's Rectory, Rectory Road, Wirral CH48 7HL* Tel 0151-625 5229

CLARKE, Ronald George. b 31. Oak Hill Th Coll. **d** 64 **p** 65. C Carlton-in-the-Willows *S'well* 64-68; V Bestwood St Matt 68-76; V Barnsbury St Andr w St Thos and St Matthias *Lon* 76-77; V Barnsbury St Andr 77-78; V Barnsbury St Andr w H Trin 79-80; P-in-c Battle Bridge All SS w Pentonville St Jas 79-80; V Barnsbury St Andr and H Trin w All SS 81-86; TR Bath Twerton-on-Avon *B & W* 86-94; rtd 94; P-in-c Churchstanton, Buckland St Mary and Otterford *B & W* 94-97; Perm to Offic from 97. *Myrtle Cottage, 35 High Street, Chard TA20 1QL* Tel (01460) 65495

CLARKE, Steven Peter. b 61. Oak Hill Th Coll DipHE95. **d** 97 **p** 98. C Frinton *Chelmsf* 97-01; C Woodford Wells from 01. *80 Montalt Road, Woodford Green IG8 9SS* Tel (020) 8505 1431 E-mail revsclarke@aol.com

CLARKE, Thomas Percival. b 15. Univ of Wales BA39. Lich Th Coll 39. **d** 41 **p** 42. C Cardiff St Mary *Llan* 41-45; C Walcot *B & W* 45-48; C Bathwick w Woolley 48-49; V Hendford 49-52; Area Sec (E Counties) UMCA 52-56; Metrop Area Sec UMCA 56-59; C S Kensington St Steph *Lon* 56-59; V Blackheath All SS *S'wark* 59-72; Chapl Leighton Hosp Crewe 72-73; Chapl Charing Cross Hosp Lon 73-82; rtd 82. *Flat 1, 29 Westbourne Road, Penarth, Cardiff CF64 3HA* Tel (029) 2030 8864

CLARKE, Timothy John. b 69. Jes Coll Cam BA91 MA95 Barrister 92. WMMTC 00. **d** 03 **p** 04. NSM Birm Cathl *Birm* from 03. *The Rectory, St Kenelm's Road, Romsley, Halesowen B62 0PH* Tel (01562) 710057 E-mail timclarke@waitrose.com

CLARKE, Ms Valerie Diane. b 45. St Jo Coll Nottm BA00. N Ord Course 91. **d** 95 **p** 96. C Sherburn in Elmet w Saxton *York* 95-97; C Brayton 97-99; Chapl Scargill Ho 00-03; P-in-c Barnburgh w Melton on the Hill etc *Sheff* from 03. *The Rectory, Fox Lane, Barnburgh, Doncaster DN5 7ET* Tel (01709) 892598 Mobile 07974-698468 E-mail valerie@clarke3116.freeserve.co.uk

CLARKE, Vernon Douglas. b 18. Jes Coll Cam BA48 MA50. Bps' Coll Cheshunt 47. **d** 49 **p** 50. C Bulwell St Mary *S'well* 49-51; C Ambleside w Rydal *Carl* 51-54; V Aspatria 54-63; V Millom H Trin 63-71; V Cockermouth All SS w Ch Ch 71-74; P-in-c Kirkland 75-83; P-in-c Gt Salkeld 79-80; C Gt Salkeld w Lazonby 80-83; rtd 83; Perm to Offic *Carl* 84-93. *Birchfield, Great Salkeld, Penrith CA11 9LW* Tel (01768) 898380

CLARKE, Mrs Yvonne Veronica. b 58. CA Tr Coll. **dss** 86 **d** 87 **p** 94. Nunhead St Silas *S'wark* 86-90; Par Dn 87-90; Par Dn Nunhead St Antony w St Silas 90-91; Par Dn Mottingham St Andr 91-94; C 94-98; V Spring Park All SS from 98. *All Saints' Vicarage, 1 Farm Drive, Croydon CR0 8HX* Tel (020) 8777 2775

CLARKSON, The Ven Alan Geoffrey. b 34. Ch Coll Cam BA57 MA61. Wycliffe Hall Ox 57. **d** 59 **p** 60. C Penn *Lich* 59-60; C Oswestry St Oswald 60-63; C Wrington *B & W* 63-65; V Chewton Mendip w Emborough 65-74; Dioc Ecum Officer 65-75; V Glastonbury St Jo w Godney 74-84; P-in-c W Pennard 80-84; P-in-c Meare 81-84; P-in-c Glastonbury St Benedict 82-84; V Glastonbury w Meare, W Pennard and Godney 84; Hon Can Win Cathl *Win* 84-99; Adn Win 84-99; V Burley Ville 84-99; rtd 99; Perm to Offic *Chelmsf* and *Ely* from 99. *Cantilena, 4 Harefield Rise, Linton, Cambridge CB1 6LS* Tel (01223) 892988 Mobile 07817-392745 E-mail aclarkso@fish.co.uk

CLARKSON, David James. b 42. St Andr Univ BSc66. N Ord Course 85. **d** 88 **p** 89. NSM Slaithwaite w E Scammonden *Wakef* 88-89; C Morley St Pet w Churwell 89-91; R Cumberworth w Denby Dale 91-93; P-in-c Denby 91-93; R Cumberworth, Denby and Denby Dale 93-02; rtd 03. *Waulkmill Cottage, Westerkirk, Langholm DG13 0NJ* Tel (01387) 370279

CLARKSON, Eric George. b 22. St Jo Coll Dur BA48. **d** 50 **p** 51. C Birkdale St Jo *Liv* 50-52; C Grassendale 52-54; PC W Derby St Luke 54-66; V Blackb St Mich *Blackb* 66-75; V Blackb St Mich w St Jo 75; V Chapeltown *Sheff* 75-86; C Ranmoor 86-87; V Crosspool 87-92; rtd 92; Perm to Offic *York* from 92. *2 Harewood Drive, Filey YO14 0DE* Tel and fax (01723) 513957

CLARKSON, Geoffrey. b 35. AKC61. **d** 62 **p** 63. C Shildon *Dur* 62-65; Asst Chapl HM Pris Liv 65-66; Chapl HM Borstal Feltham 66-71; Hon C Hampton St Mary *Lon* from 71; Development Officer Br Assn of Settlements 71-74; Chapl HM Rem Cen Ashford 88-90; Chapl HM Pris Coldingley 90-99; Chapl HM Pris Send 92-94; rtd 00. *109 Cambridge Road, Teddington TW11 8DF* Tel (020) 8977 1434 *or* 8979 2377 E-mail gfclarkson@aol.com

CLARKSON, Canon John Thomas. b 30. AKC53. St Boniface Warminster 54. **d** 54 **p** 55. C Luton St Sav *St Alb* 54-59; Australia 59-73 and from 77; Brotherhood of St Barn 59-64; R Mundingburra 64-72; V Dallington *Pet* 73-77; R W Wyalong St Barn 77-82; R Blayney Ch Ch 82-95; Hon Can Bathurst 95-96; rtd 96. *134 Mitre Street, Bathurst, NSW, Australia 2795* Tel (0061) (2) 6332 6032 E-mail clarkson@netwit.net.au

CLARKSON, Michael. *See* CLARKSON, Richard Michael

CLARKSON, Michael Livingston. b 48. California Univ BA70 Loyola Univ JD73. Wycliffe Hall Ox 87. **d** 89 **p** 90. C Kensington St Barn *Lon* 89-93; Min Oak Tree Angl Fellowship 93-04; Oman from 04. *The Protestant Church in Oman, PO Box 1982, Ruwi 112, Oman* Tel (00968) 799475 E-mail mikec@gulf-net.org

CLARKSON, Canon Richard. b 33. Man Univ BSc54 Ball Coll Ox DPhil57. Oak Hill Th Coll 89. **d** 91 **p** 92. NSM Sunnyside w Bourne End *St Alb* from 91; RD Berkhamsted 97-02; Hon Can St Alb from 02. *Kingsmead, Gravel Path, Berkhamsted HP4 2PH* Tel (01442) 873014 E-mail r.sclarkson@btopenworld.com

CLARKSON, Richard Michael. b 38. St Jo Coll Dur BA60 DipTh62 Lanc Univ PGCE68. Cranmer Hall Dur 60. **d** 62 **p** 63. C St Annes St Thos *Blackb* 62-66; C Lancaster St Mary 66-68; Asst Master Kirkham Gr Sch 68-90; Asst Master Hurstpierpoint Coll 90-91; Asst Master St Mary's Hall Brighton 92-98; Chapl 96-98; rtd 93; Perm to Offic *Chich* 93-00. *121 College Lane, Hurstpierpoint, Hassocks BN6 9AF* Tel (01273) 834117

CLARKSON, Robert Christopher. b 32. Dur Univ BA53 DipEd54. S Dios Minl Tr Scheme 85. **d** 87 **p** 88. NSM Lower Dever Valley *Win* 87-03; Perm to Offic from 03. *27 Wrights Way, South Wonston, Winchester SO21 3HE* Tel (01962) 881692

CLARRIDGE, Mrs Ann. b 44. Bournemouth Univ BSc89 S Bank Univ MSc94. SEITE 01. **d** 04 **p** 05. NSM Shepherd's Bush St Steph w St Thos *Lon* from 04. *80 Greenford Gardens, Greenford UB6 9NA* Tel (020) 8578 7025 E-mail clarria@lsbu.ac.uk

CLARRIDGE, Donald Michael. b 41. DipOT86. Oak Hill Th Coll 63. **d** 66 **p** 67. C Newc St Barn and St Jude *Newc* 66-70; C Pennycross *Ex* 70-76; R Clayhanger 76-83; R Petton 76-83; R Huntsham 76-83; V Bampton 76-83. *5 Surrey Close, Tunbridge Wells TN2 5RF* Tel (01892) 533796

CLASBY, Michael Francis Theodore. b 37. Univ Coll Lon BA59. Chich Th Coll 59. **d** 61 **p** 62. C Leigh-on-Sea St Marg *Chelmsf* 61-64; C Forest Gate St Edm 64-69; V Walthamstow St Mich 69-70; Chapl Community of Sisters of the Love of God 87-89; Perm to Offic *St Alb* 87-89; NSM Hemel Hempstead 90-93; Perm to Offic 93-98; rtd 02. *14 Richmond Walk, St Albans AL4 9BA* Tel (01727) 853913

CLASPER, John. b 42. AKC67. **d** 68 **p** 69. C Leeds All Hallows w St Simon *Ripon* 68-71; C Hawksworth Wood 72-74; Ind Chapl *Dur* 74-97; TV Jarrow St Paul 75-77; TV Jarrow 77-91; Dioc Urban Development Officer 90-91; TR E Darlington 91-97; V Fenham St Jas and St Basil *Newc* 97-02; RD Newc W 98-02; rtd 03; Perm to Offic *Newc* from 03. *103 Warkworth Woods, Newcastle upon Tyne NE3 5RB* Tel 0191-217 1325 Mobile 07710-078945 E-mail john.clasper@virgin.net

CLASSON, Michael Campbell. b 32. TCD BA52 HDipEd54 MA55. CITC 87. **d** 89 **p** 91. NSM Conwal Union w Gartan *D & R* 89-90; NSM Ardara w Glencolumbkille, Inniskeel etc from 90. *Summy, Portnoo, Co Donegal, Irish Republic* Tel (00353) (74) 954 5242

CLATWORTHY, Jonathan Richard. b 48. Univ of Wales BA70. Sarum & Wells Th Coll 71. **d** 76 **p** 77. C Man Resurr *Man* 76-78; C Bolton St Pet 78-81; V Ashton St Pet 81-85; Chapl Sheff Univ *Sheff* 85-91; V Denstone w Ellastone and Stanton *Lich* 91-98; Chapl Liv Univ *Liv* 98-02; rtd 02; Perm to Offic *Liv* from 04. *9 Westward View, Aigburth, Liverpool L17 7EE* Tel 0151-727 6291 E-mail jonathan@clatworthy.org

CLAUSEN, John Frederick. b 37. Sarum Th Coll 65. **d** 68 **p** 69. C Kentish Town St Jo *Lon* 68-71; C Rainham *Roch* 71-77; R Stone 77-89; Lic to Dartford RD 89-02; rtd 02. *24 Spring Vale North, Dartford DA1 2LL*

CLAWSON, Derek George. b 35. AMCST62. Qu Coll Birm 63. **d** 66 **p** 67. C Ditton St Mich *Liv* 66-70; C Speke All SS 70-72; V Hindley Green 72-85; V Wigan St Mich 85-00; rtd 00; Perm to Offic *Liv* from 01. *20 Parklands Drive, Aspull, Wigan WN2 1ZA* Tel (01942) 830769

CLAY, Canon Colin Peter. b 32. Ch Coll Cam BA55 MA59. Em Coll Saskatoon Hon DD91 Wells Th Coll 55. **d** 57 **p** 58. C Malden St Jas *S'wark* 57-59; Canada from 59; C Sudbury Epiphany 59-60; R Sudbury St Jas 60-69; R Sudbury St Geo 60-64; R French River St Thos 64-69; Asst Prof RS Laurentian Univ 69-72; R Capreol St Alb 70-77; Chapl Saskatchewan Univ 77-00; Hon Can Saskatoon from 97; Interim I St Jo Cathl 00-01; Hon Asst from 01. *812 Colony Street, Saskatoon SK, Canada, S7N 0S1* Tel (001) (306) 664 4628 E-mail clay@sask.usask.ca

CLAY, Canon Elizabeth Jane. b 50. Ridley Hall Cam. **dss** 86 **d** 87 **p** 94. Birstall *Wakef* 86-87; Hon Par Dn Lupset 87-90; Par Dn 90-94; C 94-96; Chapl HM Pris and YOI New Hall from 96; Hon Can Wakef Cathl *Wakef* from 00. *The Vicarage, 20A Station Road, Marsden, Huddersfield HD7 6DG* Tel and fax (01484) 847864

CLAY, Geoffrey. b 51. CertEd. Ridley Hall Cam. **d** 86 **p** 87. C Birstall *Wakef* 86-90; V Lupset 90-03; P-in-c Marsden from 03; Min Development Officer from 03. *The Vicarage, 20A Station Road, Marsden, Huddersfield HD7 6DG* Tel (01484) 847864 Fax as telephone E-mail gjrstg@aol.com

CLAY, Peter Herbert. b 31. Lich Th Coll 62. **d** 64 **p** 65. C Ross *Heref* 64-67; C Leamington Priors All SS *Cov* 67-70; P-in-c Temple Grafton w Binton 70-73; V 73-75; P-in-c Exhall w Wixford 70-73; R 73-75; TV Cen Telford *Lich* 75-86; USPG

86-90; V Loughb Gd Shep *Leic* 90-96; rtd 96; Perm to Offic *Cov* and *Leic* from 96. *78 Eastlands Road, Rugby CV21 3RR* Tel (01788) 569138

CLAY, Timothy Francis. b 61. St Mark & St Jo Coll Lon BA85 Ealing Coll of Educn 89. Linc Th Coll 95. **d** 95 **p** 96. C Wickford and Runwell *Chelmsf* 95-98; C S Ockendon 98-01; C S Ockendon and Belhus Park 01-02; P-in-c Ashingdon w S Fambridge from 02; P-in-c Canewdon w Paglesham from 03. *The Rectory, Church Road, Rochford SS4 3HY* Tel (01702) 549318 E-mail tim@tclay.fslife.co.uk

CLAYDEN, David Edward. b 42. Oak Hill Th Coll 74. **d** 76 **p** 77. C Worksop St Jo *S'well* 76-79; V Clarborough w Hayton 79-84; C Bloxwich *Lich* 87-90; TV 90-93; TV Tollington *Lon* 93-99; P-in-c Thorndon w Rishangles, Stoke Ash, Thwaite etc *St E* 99-00; P-in-c Thornhams Magna and Parva, Gislingham and Mellis 99-00; R S Hartismere from 00. *The Rectory, Standwell Green, Thorndon, Eye IP23 7JL* Tel (01379) 678603 E-mail davidclayden@cwcom.net

CLAYDON, Preb Graham Leonard. b 43. K Coll Lon BA65. Clifton Th Coll 66. **d** 68 **p** 69. C Walthamstow St Mary w St Steph *Chelmsf* 68-71; C St Marylebone All So w SS Pet and Jo *Lon* 71-73; Hon C 73-81; Warden All So Clubhouse 71-81; V Islington St Mary 81-99; Dioc Ev (Stepney) and C Highbury Ch Ch w St Jo and St Sav 99-03; TV Hackney Marsh from 03; Preb St Paul's Cathl from 92. *All Souls' Vicarage, 44 Overbury Street, London E5 0AJ* Tel (020) 8525 2863 E-mail graham@lclaydon.fsnet.co.uk

CLAYDON, John Richard. b 38. St Jo Coll Cam BA61 MA65. Trin Coll Bris 71. **d** 73 **p** 74. C Finchley Ch Ch *Lon* 73-76; Asst Chapl K Edw Sch Witley 76-77; C Macclesfield St Mich *Ches* 77-81; V Marple All SS 81-91; CMJ Israel 91-99; V Blackb Redeemer *Blackb* 99-02; rtd 02; Perm to Offic *Chelmsf* from 03. *54 Old Forge Road, Layer-de-la-Haye, Colchester CO2 0LH* Tel (01206) 734056 E-mail john@claydon4295.freeserve.co.uk

CLAYTON, Adam. b 78. Keble Coll Ox BA99. Westcott Ho Cam 00. **d** 02 **p** 03. C Far Headingley St Chad *Ripon* from 02. *64 Becketts Park Crescent, Leeds LS6 3PF* Tel 0113-274 0946 E-mail revdaclayton@aol.com

CLAYTON, Canon Anthony Edwin Hay. b 36. Sarum Th Coll 61. **d** 63 **p** 64. C Tooting All SS *S'wark* 63-68; Perm to Offic *Leic* 69-74; Perm to Offic *S'well* 73-80; Hon C Lockington w Hemington *Leic* 74-80; P-in-c Eastwell 80-83; P-in-c Eaton 80-83; P-in-c Croxton Kerrial, Knipton, Harston, Branston etc 83-84; R 84-93; R High Framland Par 93-96; RD Framland 90-94; Hon Can Leic Cathl 92-96; rtd 97; Perm to Offic *Leic* 97-00. *18 Commerce Square, Nottingham NG1 1HS* Tel 0115-988 1920 Fax as telephone

CLAYTON, Geoffrey Buckroyd. b 26. Newc Univ BA67. Roch Th Coll 62. **d** 64 **p** 65. C Newc St Geo *Newc* 64-67; C Byker St Ant 67-68; Chapl Salonika *Eur* 68-69; C Cheddleton *Lich* 69-72; V Arbory *S & M* 72-97; RD Castletown 82-97; V Santan 88-97; rtd 97; Perm to Offic *St D* from 97. *Y Rheithordy, Llangeitho, Tregaron SY25 6TR* Tel (01974) 821388

CLAYTON, George Hamilton. b 42. Strathclyde Univ BSc65. S'wark Ord Course 90. **d** 93 **p** 94. NSM Send *Guildf* 93-99. *Address temp unknown*

CLAYTON, Canon John. b 11. Leeds Univ BA33 MA43. Wells Th Coll 34. **d** 35 **p** 36. C Dewsbury Moor *Wakef* 35-38; C Halifax St Jo Bapt 38-41; Lect 40-41; V Lupset 41-51; Chapl Snapethorpe Hosp 49-51; V Bolton St Jas *Bradf* 51-65; RD Calverley 56-65; V Otley 65-76; RD Otley 68-73; Hon Can Bradf Cathl 63-76; rtd 76; Perm to Offic *Bradf* and *Ripon* from 76. *10 Sandy Walk, Bramhope, Leeds LS16 9DW* Tel 0113-261 1388

CLAYTON, Melanie Yvonne. b 62. St Aid Coll Dur BA84 Victoria Univ (BC) MA85 Hertf Coll Ox DPhil89. WMMTC 91. **d** 94 **p** 95. C Penn *Lich* 94-97; TV Wolverhampton 97-98; TV Cen Wolverhampton from 98. *St Chad's Vicarage, Manlove Street, Wolverhampton WV3 0HG* Tel (01902) 426580 E-mail snap1@tinyworld.co.uk

CLAYTON, Norman James. b 24. AKC52. **d** 53 **p** 54. C Long Benton St Mary *Newc* 53-55; R Lomagundi S Rhodesia 55-60; Chapl St Geo Home Johannesburg 60-78; Dioc Communications Officer *Derby* 78-88; P-in-c Risley 78-87; R 87-89; rtd 89; Perm to Offic *Derby* and *S'well* from 89. *6 Allendale Avenue, Beeston, Nottingham NG9 6AN* Tel 0115-925 0060

CLAYTON, Paul. b 47. Cranmer Hall Dur 03. **d** 04 **p** 05. NSM Preston-on-Tees and Longnewton *Dur* from 04; NSM Elton from 04. *144 Darlington Lane, Stockton-on-Tees TS19 0NG* Tel (01642) 607233 E-mail pclayton@tinyonline.co.uk

CLAYTON, Sydney Cecil Leigh. b 38. Pemb Coll Ox BA62 MA65 Lon Univ BD65. Linc Th Coll. **d** 65 **p** 66. C Birch St Jas *Man* 65-68; Lect Bolton Par Ch 68-77; V Denshaw from 77. *The Vicarage, Huddersfield Road, Denshaw, Oldham OL3 5SB* Tel (01457) 874575

CLAYTON, William Alan. b 32. Liv Univ BSc54 Lon Univ BD60. **d** 63 **p** 64. C Wallasey St Hilary *Ches* 63-67; R Burton Agnes w Harpham *York* 67-69; V Batley St Thos *Wakef* 69-72; Lic to Offic *Ripon* 73-85; Hon C Grinton 75-85; R Barningham w Hutton Magna and Wycliffe 85-97; rtd 97; Perm to Offic *Newc* from 00. *Halidon View, 1 The Pastures, Tweedmouth, Berwick-upon-Tweed TD15 2NT*

CLEALL-HILL, Malcolm John. b 51. Salford Univ Man Metrop Univ. Dioc OLM tr scheme. **d** 01 **p** 02. OLM Chorlton-cum-Hardy St Werburgh *Man* from 01. *62 Buckingham Road, Chorlton cum Hardy, Manchester M21 0RP* Tel 0161-881 7024 *or* 247 2288 E-mail m.cleall-hill@mmu.ac.uk

CLEASBY, The Very Revd Thomas Wood Ingram. b 20. Magd Coll Ox BA47 MA47. Cuddesdon Coll 47. **d** 49 **p** 50. C Huddersfield St Pet *Wakef* 49-52; Abp's Dom Chapl *York* 52-56; C Nottingham St Mary *S'well* 56-63; Chapl Nottm Univ 56-63; V Chesterfield St Mary and All SS *Derby* 63-70; Hon Can Derby Cathl 63-78; Adn Chesterfield 63-78; R Morton 70-78; Dean Ches 78-86; rtd 86; Perm to Offic *Carl* from 86; *Bradf* from 87. *Low Barth, Dent, Sedbergh LA10 5SZ* Tel (01539) 625476

CLEATON, John. b 39. Open Univ BA86. S Dios Minl Tr Scheme 89. **d** 92 **p** 93. NSM Wareham *Sarum* 92-02. *1 Avon Drive, Wareham BH20 4EL* Tel (01929) 553149

CLEAVER, Gerald. b 20. Lon Univ BSc52. St Jo Coll Nottm 85. **d** 86 **p** 87. NSM W Bridgford *S'well* 86-96; NSM Clifton 96-02; rtd 02; Perm to Offic *S'well* from 02. *62 South Road, West Bridgford, Nottingham NG2 7AH* Tel 0115-914 3558 E-mail gerald.cleaver@ntlworld.com

CLEAVER, Gordon Philip. b 29. SW Minl Tr Course. **d** 78 **p** 79. NSM St Ruan w St Grade *Truro* 78-86; Perm to Offic from 86. *Bryn-Mor, Cadgwith, Ruan Minor, Helston TR12 7JZ* Tel (01326) 290328

CLEAVER, John Martin. b 42. K Coll Lon BD64 AKC64. St Boniface Warminster 61. **d** 65 **p** 66. C Bexley St Mary *Roch* 65-69; C Ealing St Steph Castle Hill *Lon* 69-71; P-in-c Bostall Heath *Roch* 71-76; V Green Street Green 76-85; Primary Adv Lon Dioc Bd for Schs *Lon* 85-92; V Teddington St Mary w St Alb from 92. *The Vicarage, 11 Twickenham Road, Teddington TW11 8AQ* Tel (020) 8977 2767 E-mail jm.cleaver@amserve.net

CLEAVER, Stuart Douglas. b 46. ACIS. Oak Hill Th Coll. **d** 83 **p** 84. C Portsdown *Portsm* 83-86; C Blendworth w Chalton w Idsworth etc 86-88; P-in-c Whippingham w E Cowes 88-98; R 98-01; rtd 01. *The Crest, Soake Road, Waterlooville PO7 6HY* Tel (023) 9226 2277

CLEEVE, Admire William. b 43. Ox Univ MTh96 ACIS78 MBIM81 CPPS83. Sierra Leone Th Hall 78. **d** 82 **p** 83. Sierra Leone 82-86; NSM Douglas St Geo and St Barn *S & M* 87-91; TV Langley Marish *Ox* 91-97; P-in-c Tilehurst St Mary 97-02; rtd 02. *St Paul's Episcopal Church, 61 Wood Street, PO Box 165, Hopkinton, MA 01748, USA* Tel (001) (508) 497 6388 E-mail admirecleeve@pastors.com

CLEEVE, Martin. b 43. Bp Otter Coll TCert65 ACP67 Open Univ BA80. Oak Hill Th Coll 69. **d** 72 **p** 73. C Margate H Trin *Cant* 72-76; V Southminster *Chelmsf* 76-86; Teacher Castle View Sch Canvey Is 86-91; Hd RE Bromfords Sch Wickford 91-94; Hd RE Deanes Sch Thundersley 94-98; P-in-c Gt Mongeham w Ripple and Sutton by Dover *Cant* 99-04; rtd 04; Perm to Offic *Cant* from 04. *Euphony, Waldershare Road, Ashley, Dover CT15 5JA* E-mail martindot@mcleeve.freeserve.co.uk

CLEEVES, David John. b 56. Univ of Wales (Lamp) BA Fitzw Coll Cam MA85. Westcott Ho Cam. **d** 82 **p** 83. C Cuddington *Guildf* 82-85; C Dorking w Ranmore 85-87; V Ewell St Fran 87-94; P-in-c Rotherfield w Mark Cross *Chich* 94-01; V Masham and Healey *Ripon* from 01; Jt AD Ripon 04-05; AD from 05. *The Vicarage, Rodney Terrace, Masham, Ripon HG4 4JA* Tel (01765) 689255

CLEGG, Anthony. *See* CLEGG, Canon John Anthony Holroyd

CLEGG, David Kneeshaw. b 46. N Ord Course 77. **d** 80 **p** 81. C Briercliffe *Blackb* 80-83; Chapl Lancs (Preston) Poly 83-89; rtd 89; Perm to Offic *Dur* from 89. *126 York Crescent, Newton Hall, Durham DH1 5QS*

CLEGG, Herbert. b 24. Fitzw Ho Cam BA59 MA63 Bris Univ MA65. Sarum Th Coll 52. **d** 54 **p** 55. C Street *B & W* 54-56; Perm to Offic *Ely* 56-59; Tutor St Pet Th Coll Jamaica 59-61; R Newington Bagpath w Kingscote and Ozleworth *Glouc* 61-65; Prin Bp Willis Coll Uganda 65-69; P-in-c Aldsworth *Glouc* 70-75; P-in-c Sherborne w Windrush 70-75; V Marcham w Garford *Ox* 75-83; R Chipping Warden w Edgcote and Aston le Walls *Pet* 83-89; rtd 89; C Ox St Giles and SS Phil and Jas w St Marg *Ox* 90-94. *3 Case Gardens, Seaton EX12 2AP* Tel (01297) 23103

CLEGG, Jeffrey Thomas. *See* MIDDLEMISS, Jeffrey Thomas

CLEGG, Canon John Anthony Holroyd. b 44. Kelham Th Coll 65. **d** 70 **p** 71. C St Annes St Thos *Blackb* 70-74; C Lancaster St Mary 74-76; V Lower Darwen St Jas 76-80; TV Shaston *Sarum* 80-86; Chapl HM Youth Cust Cen Guys Marsh 80-86; R Poulton-le-Sands w Morecambe St Laur *Blackb* 86-97; RD Lancaster 89-94; TR Cartmel Peninsula *Carl* 97-04; RD Windermere 01-04; P-in-c Appleby from 04; P-in-c Ormside from 04; RD Appleby from 04; Hon Can Carl Cathl from 01. *The Vicarage, Appleby-in-Westmorland CA16 6QW* Tel (017683) 51461 E-mail anthonyclegg@care4free.net

CLEGG, John Lovell. b 48. Qu Coll Ox BA70 MA74. Trin Coll Bris DipTh75. **d** 75 **p** 76. C Barrow St Mark *Carl* 75-79; R S Levenshulme *Man* 79-98; P-in-c Blackley St Paul from 98. *St Paul's Rectory, Erskine Road, Manchester M9 6RB* Tel 0161-740 1518

CLEGG, Patricia Ann. b 45. STETS 96. **d** 99 **p** 00. NSM Harnham *Sarum* 99-03; Perm to Offic 03-05; NSM Bemerton from 05. *28 Bishops Drive, East Harnham, Salisbury SP2 8NZ* E-mail pat@newsarum.fsnet.co.uk

CLEGG, Peter Douglas. b 49. Sarum & Wells Th Coll 83. **d** 85 **p** 86. C Hangleton *Chich* 85-88; C-in-c Portslade Gd Shep CD 88-94; V Portslade Gd Shep from 94. *The Vicarage, 35 Stanley Avenue, Portslade, Brighton BN41 2WH* Tel (01273) 419518

CLEGG, Roger Alan. b 46. St Jo Coll Dur BA68 Nottm Univ CertEd69. St Jo Coll Nottm 75. **d** 78 **p** 79. C Harwood *Man* 78-81; TV Sutton St Jas and Wawne *York* 81-87; V Kirk Fenton w Kirkby Wharfe and Ulleskelfe from 87; OCF from 87; Chapl HM Pris Askham Grange from 95. *The Vicarage, Church Street, Church Fenton, Tadcaster LS24 9RD* Tel (01937) 557387 E-mail rogclegg@ntlworld.com

CLELAND, Miss Lucy Eleanor. b 74. Aston Univ BSc97 Anglia Poly Univ BTh05. Ridley Hall Cam 02. **d** 05. C Yaxley and Holme w Conington *Ely* from 05. *26 Daimler Avenue, Yaxley, Peterborough PE7 3AU* Tel 07986-685792 (mobile) E-mail lecleland@hotmail.com

CLELAND, Richard. b 26. Belf Coll of Tech MPS47. St Aid Birkenhead 58. **d** 60 **p** 61. C Lisburn Ch Ch *Conn* 60-63; C Ballynafeigh St Jude *D & D* 63-66; C Portman Square St Paul *Lon* 66-67; V Ilkley All SS *Bradf* 67-83; Master Wyggeston's Hosp Leic 83-97; rtd 97; Perm to Offic *S'well* 97-02. *23 Stuart Court, High Street, Kibworth, Leicester LE8 0LR* Tel 0116-279 6245

CLELAND, Trevor. b 66. QUB BTh94 TCD MPhil97. CITC 94. **d** 96 **p** 97. C Lisburn Ch Ch *Conn* 96-99; C Carrickfergus 99-03; I Belfast Upper Falls from 03. *31 Dunmurry Lane, Belfast BT17 9RP* Tel (028) 9062 2400

CLEMAS, Nigel Antony. b 53. Wycliffe Hall Ox. **d** 83 **p** 84. C Bootle St Mary w St Paul *Liv* 83-87; V Kirkdale St Mary and St Athanasius 87-91; TV Netherthorpe *Sheff* 91-93; V Netherthorpe St Steph 93-98; R Chapel Chorlton, Maer and Whitmore *Lich* from 98; RD Eccleshall from 00. *The Rectory, Snape Hall Road, Whitmore, Newcastle ST5 5HS* Tel (01782) 680258

CLEMENCE, Paul Robert Fraser. b 50. MRTPI82 Man Univ Dip Town Planning 74 St Edm Hall Ox MA90. Wycliffe Hall Ox 88. **d** 90 **p** 91. C Lancaster St Mary *Blackb* 90-94; Chapl HM Pris Lanc Castle 90-94; V Lt Thornton *Blackb* from 94; AD Poulton from 00. *St John's Vicarage, 35 Station Road, Thornton-Cleveleys FY5 5HY* Tel and fax (01253) 825107 E-mail p.clemence@ukonline.co.uk

CLEMENT, Miss Barbara Winifred. b 20. Gilmore Ho 49. **dss** 56 **d** 87. Frimley Green *Guildf* 53-66; Hd Dss 66-74; Dioc Adv Lay Min 74-82; Frimley 74-82; Frimley Hosp 74-87; rtd 82; Perm to Offic *Guildf* 82-99 and from 01. *9 Merlin Court, The Cloisters, Frimley, Camberley GU16 5JN* Tel (01276) 22527

CLEMENT, Geoffrey Paul. b 69. **d** 94 **p** 96. Uruguay 94-01; Hipodrome Gardens St Aug 94-95; Miss of St Jas the Apostle Coln 95-97; Barruo Fatima Salto St Luke w the H Spirit 97-01; TV Wilford Peninsula *St E* from 01. *The Rectory, Church Lane, Shottisham, Woodbridge IP12 3HG* Tel (01394) 411748 Mobile 07766-601011 E-mail gclement@onetel.com

CLEMENT, Paskal. b 63. Punjab Univ BA97. Nat Catholic Inst of Th Karachi 82. **d** 88 **p** 88. NSM Hounslow H Trin w St Paul *Lon* from 04. *57 Montague Road, Hounslow TW3 1LG* Tel and fax (020) 8814 1488 Mobile 07789-813082

CLEMENT, Peter James. b 64. UMIST BSc88 Man Univ MA98. Qu Coll Birm 89. **d** 92 **p** 93. C Grange St Andr *Ches* 92-95; C Man Apostles w Miles Platting *Man* 95-97; TV Uggeshall w Sotherton, Wangford and Henham *St E* 97-99; TV Sole Bay 99-00; Dioc Youth Officer 01-02; V Fairweather Green *Bradf* from 02; Assoc Dioc Dir of Ords from 04. *St Saviour's Vicarage, 25 Ings Way, Bradford BD8 0LU* Tel (01274) 544807 E-mail peter.clement@bradford.anglican.org

CLEMENT, Thomas Gwyn. b 51. Lon Univ BMus73 Goldsmiths' Coll Lon PGCE74. St Steph Ho Ox. **d** 93 **p** 94. C Friern Barnet St Jas *Lon* 93-96; V Edmonton St Alphege 96-04; P-in-c Ponders End St Matt 02-04; AD Enfield 01-04; V Hendon St Mary and Ch Ch from 04. *The Vicarage, 34 Parson Street, London NW4 1QR* Tel (020) 8203 2884 E-mail frgwyn@gclement.freeserve.co.uk

CLEMENT, Timothy Gordon. b 54. Usk Coll of Agric NCA75. Trin Coll Bris 92. **d** 94 **p** 95. C Chepstow *Mon* 94-97; R Bettws Newydd w Trostrey etc from 97; Rural Min Adv from 02; AD Raglan-Usk from 05. *The Rectory, Bettws Newydd, Usk NP15 1JN* Tel (01873) 880258

CLEMENTS, Alan Austin. b 39. Newc Univ MA93 ACIB66. Linc Th Coll 74. **d** 76 **p** 77. C Woodley St Jo the Ev *Ox* 76-79; C Wokingham All SS 79-83; V Felton *Newc* 83-95; P-in-c Wallsend St Pet 95-01; rtd 01; Perm to Offic *Newc* from 01. *3 Woodkirk Close, Seghill, Cramlington NE23 7TZ* Tel 0191-237 7366 Fax as telephone E-mail alanaclements@aol.com

CLEMENTS, Andrew. b 48. K Coll Lon BD72 AKC72 Leeds Univ MA02. St Aug Coll Cant 72. **d** 73 **p** 74. C Langley All SS and Martyrs *Man* 73-76; C Westhoughton 76-81; R Thornton Dale w Ellerburne and Wilton *York* 81-89; Prec Leic Cathl *Leic* 89-91; V Market Weighton *York* 91-97; R Goodmanham 91-97; V Osbaldwick w Murton from 97. *The Vicarage, 80 Osbaldwick Lane, York YO10 3AX* Tel (01904) 416763 E-mail andrew@ozmurt.freeserve.co.uk

CLEMENTS, Miss Christine Hilda. b 49. Ex Univ BTh04. SW Minl Tr Course 99. **d** 02 **p** 03. C Halsetown *Truro* from 02. *St John's-in-the-Fields Vicarage, Hellesvean, St Ives TR26 2HG* Tel (01736) 796035 Mobile 07890-708773 E-mail lamorna21@eurobell.co.uk

CLEMENTS, Canon Doris Thomasina Sara. b 46. TCD BA68 MA90. CITC 92. **d** 95 **p** 96. NSM Killala w Dunfeeny, Crossmolina, Kilmoremoy etc *T, K & A* from 95; Can Achonry Cathl from 05. *Doobeg House, Bunninadden, Ballymote, Co Sligo, Irish Republic* Tel (00353) (71) 918 5425 Fax 918 5255 Mobile 86-249 7806 E-mail dorisc.ias@eircom.net *or* dcolhoun@gofree.indigo.ie

CLEMENTS, Edwin George. b 41. Chich Th Coll 77. **d** 79 **p** 80. C Didcot St Pet *Ox* 79-83; C Brixham w Churston Ferrers *Ex* 83; TV 84-86; TV Brixham w Churston Ferrers and Kingswear 86-88; P-in-c Hagbourne *Ox* 88; V 88-90; P-in-c Blewbury 89-90; P-in-c Upton 89-90; R Blewbury, Hagbourne and Upton from 90; AD Wallingford from 99. *The Rectory, Blewbury, Didcot OX11 9QH* Tel (01235) 850267 Mobile 07703-342950 Fax 851736 E-mail revedwin@aol.com

CLEMENTS, Miss Mary Holmes. b 43. Bedf Coll Lon BA64 Lon Bible Coll DipTh66 Lon Inst of Educn PGCE69. Ox Min Course 92. **d** 94 **p** 95. NSM High Wycombe *Ox* 94-01; C N Petherton w Northmoor Green *B & W* 01-03; C N Newton w St Michaelchurch, Thurloxton etc 01-03; C Alfred Jewel from 03. *8 Alder Close, North Petherton, Bridgwater TA6 6TT* Tel (01278) 662905 E-mail mary@holmesclements.freeserve.co.uk

CLEMENTS, Philip Christian. b 38. K Coll Lon BD64 AKC64. **d** 65 **p** 66. C S Norwood St Mark *Cant* 65-68; Chapl R Russell Sch Croydon 68-75; Asst Chapl Denstone Coll Uttoxeter 75-76; Chapl 76-81; Chapl Lancing Coll 82-90; R Ninfield *Chich* 90-99; V Hooe 90-99; rtd 99; Perm to Offic *Cant* from 95; Chapl St Bart Hosp Sandwich from 04. *21 Swaynes Way, Eastry, Sandwich CT13 0JP* Tel (01304) 617413 *or* 613982 E-mail philip@clements3739.freeserve.co.uk

CLEMENTS, Philip John Charles. b 42. Nottm Univ CertEd64 Loughb Univ DLC64. Ridley Hall Cam. **d** 85 **p** 86. C Aylestone St Andr w St Jas *Leic* 85-87; P-in-c Swinford w Catthorpe, Shawell and Stanford 87-91; V 91-99; Rural Officer (Leic Adnry) 91-96; RD Guthlaxton II 94-99; P-in-c N w S Kilworth and Misterton 96-99; P-in-c Barrowden and Wakerley w S Luffenham *Pet* 99-02; R Barrowden and Wakerley w S Luffenham etc from 03; RD Barnack from 00. *The Rectory, 11 Church Lane, Barrowden, Oakham LE15 8ED* Tel (01572) 747192 Fax as telephone E-mail pipclements@lineone.net

CLEMENTS, Canon Roy Adrian. b 44. Dur Univ BA68 DipTh69 MA74. St Chad's Coll Dur 65. **d** 69 **p** 70. C Royston *Wakef* 69-73; V Clifton 73-77; V Rastrick St Matt 77-84; V Horbury Junction 84-92; Dioc Communications Officer 84-98; Bp's Chapl 92-00; Hon Can Wakef Cathl from 94; V Battyeford from 00. *Battyeford Vicarage, 107A Stocksbank Road, Mirfield WF14 9QT* Tel (01924) 493277 E-mail roy@christ-the-king.co.uk

CLEMETT, Peter Thomas. b 33. Univ of Wales (Lamp) BA60. Sarum Th Coll 59. **d** 61 **p** 62. C Tredegar St Geo *Mon* 61-63; Chapl St Woolos Cathl 63-66; CF 66-99; Chapl R Memorial Chpl Sandhurst 84-88; rtd 88; OCF from 99; Perm to Offic *Win* from 01. *Silver Birches, Gardeners Lane, East Wellow, Romsey SO51 6AD* Tel (023) 8081 4261

CLEMOW (née WINDER), Cynthia Frances. b 48. SW Minl Tr Course 02. **d** 05. NSM Bodmin w Lanhydrock and Lanivet *Truro* from 05. *Denton, 2 Boxwell Park, Bodmin PL31 2BB* Tel (01208) 73306

CLENCH, Brian Henry Ross. b 31. Ripon Coll Cuddesdon. **d** 82 **p** 83. C Fulham All SS *Lon* 82-85; Ind Chapl *Truro* 85-92; P-in-c St Mewan 85-92; rtd 92; Perm to Offic *Sarum* from 96. *Tamworth Barn, Hampton Lane, Whitford, Axminster EX13 7NJ*

CLEPHANE, Alexander Honeyman. b 48. LNSM course 94. **d** 97 **p** 98. OLM Flixton St Mich *Man* from 97. *306 Church Road, Urmston, Manchester M41 6JJ* Tel 0161-747 8816 Mobile 07798-613291

CLEVELAND, Mrs Lorna Christina (Dickie). b 39. State Univ NY BSc60. SEITE 99. **d** 02 **p** 03. NSM Wye w Brook *Cant* from 02. *2 Church Street, Wye, Ashford TN25 5BJ* Tel (01233) 813051 E-mail dickie@clevelp.freeserve.co.uk

CLEVELAND, Michael Robin. b 52. Warwick Univ BA73. St Jo Coll Nottm 86 Serampore Th Coll BD88. **d** 88 **p** 89. C Bushbury *Lich* 88-92; V Foleshill St Laur *Cov* from 92. *St Laurence's*

Vicarage, 142 Old Church Road, Coventry CV6 7ED Tel (024) 7668 8271

CLEVELAND, Archdeacon of. *See* FERGUSON, The Ven Paul John

CLEVERLEY, Michael Frank. b 36. Man Univ BScTech57. Wells Th Coll 61. **d** 63 **p** 64. C Halifax St Aug *Wakef* 63; C Huddersfield St Jo 63-66; C Brighouse 66-69; V Gomersal 69-83; P-in-c Clayton W w High Hoyland 83-89; P-in-c Scissett St Aug 83-89; R High Hoyland, Scissett and Clayton W 89-96; rtd 96; NSM Leathley w Farnley, Fewston and Blubberhouses *Bradf* from 96. *86 Riverside Park, Otley LS21 2RW*
E-mail mclef@argonet.co.uk

CLEVERLY, Charles St George. b 51. St Jo Coll Ox MA75 Goldsmiths' Coll Lon PGCE76. Trin Coll Bris 79. **d** 82 **p** 83. C Cranham Park *Chelmsf* 82-89; V 89-92; Crosslinks Paris 92-02; R Ox St Aldate *Ox* from 02. *Holy Trinity House, 19 Turn Again Lane, Oxford OX1 1QL* Tel (01865) 244713 Fax 201543
E-mail charlie.cleverly@staldates.org.uk

CLEWS, Nicholas. b 57. SS Coll Cam BA80 MA84 Leeds Univ BA87 CIPFA85. Coll of Resurr Mirfield 85. **d** 88 **p** 89. C S Elmsall *Wakef* 88-91; V Featherstone from 91; P-in-c Purston cum S Featherstone from 04. *All Saints' Vicarage, Ackton Lane, Featherstone, Pontefract WF7 6AP* Tel (01977) 792280
E-mail clewsclan@btopenworld.com

CLIFF, Frank Graham. b 38. St Paul's Cheltenham TCert60 Lon Univ DipTh66. Clifton Th Coll 63. **d** 66 **p** 67. C Leic St Chris *Leic* 66-69; C Whitton and Thurleston w Akenham *St E* 69-71; USA from 71; Asst R Houston St Thos 71-72; Asst R Waco St Alb 72-74; Asst R Potomac St Jas 74-78; R Denton Ch Ch 78-85; V Pittsburgh St Phil 86-87; R Pittsburgh Advent Ch 87-94; R Honesdale Grace Ch from 94. *15 Bede Circle, Honesdale, PA 18431, USA* E-mail cliffam@ptd.net

CLIFF, Julian Arnold. b 41. Cranmer Hall Dur 63. **d** 66 **p** 67. C Bowdon *Ches* 66-69; C Poynton 69-73; P-in-c Crewe St Barn 73-75; V 75-79. *24 Exmoor Close, Wirral L61 9QN* Tel 0151-648 1408

CLIFF, Philip Basil. b 15. Lon Univ BSc61 Birm Univ PhD. Independent Coll Bradf 36. **d** 77 **p** 77. Hon C Northfield *Birm* 77-91; Perm to Offic from 91. *4 Fox Hill Close, Birmingham B29 4AH* Tel 0121-472 1556

CLIFFE, Christopher George. b 47. CITC 94. **d** 97 **p** 98. Bp's Dom Chapl *C & O* from 97; C Fiddown w Clonegam, Guilcagh and Kilmeaden 97-00; I from 00. *The Rectory, Piltown, Co Kilkenny, Irish Republic* Tel (00353) (51) 643275 Mobile 87-236 8682 E-mail fiddown@lismore.anglican.org *or* cgc2@eircom.net

CLIFFORD, Raymond Augustine. b 45. Birkbeck Coll Lon CertRS91. Coll of Resurr Mirfield 91. **d** 93 **p** 94. C Saltdean *Chich* 93-96. *124 Arnold Estate, Druid Street, London SE1 2DT* Tel (020) 7232 2439

CLIFFORD, Miss Susan Frances. b 58. Qu Univ Kingston Ontario BA87. Westcott Ho Cam 02. **d** 04 **p** 05. C Winchmore Hill St Paul *Lon* from 04. *St Paul's Lodge, 58 Church Hill, London N21 1JA* Tel (020) 8882 3298
E-mail susanclif@hotmail.com

CLIFTON, Canon Robert Walter. b 39. Solicitor. Westcott Ho Cam 82. **d** 84 **p** 85. C Bury St Edmunds St Geo *St E* 84-87; P-in-c Culford, W Stow and Wordwell 87-88; R Culford, W Stow and Wordwell w Flempton etc 88-95; P-in-c Fornham All SS and Fornham St Martin w Timworth 93-95; RD Thingoe 93-95; P-in-c Orford w Sudbourne, Chillesford, Butley and Iken 95-00; P-in-c Eyke w Bromeswell, Rendlesham, Tunstall etc 98-99; TR Wilford Peninsula 00-05; RD Woodbridge 96-04; Hon Can St E Cathl 00-05; rtd 05; Perm to Offic *Nor* and *St E* from 05. *12 Stan Petersen Close, Norwich NR1 4QJ* Tel (01603) 631758 Mobile 07713-237754

CLIFTON, Canon Roger Gerald. b 45. ACA70 FCA. Sarum & Wells Th Coll 70. **d** 73 **p** 74. C Winterbourne *Bris* 73-76; P-in-c Brislington St Cuth 76-83; P-in-c Colerne w N Wraxall 83-95; RD Chippenham 88-94; Hon Can Bris Cathl from 94; TR Gtr Corsham 95-01; TR Gtr Corsham and Lacock from 01. *The Rectory, Newlands Road, Corsham SN13 0BS* Tel and fax (01249) 713232 E-mail rogerclifton@btopenworld.com

CLIFTON-SMITH, Gregory James. b 52. GGSM73 Lon Univ TCert74 Goldsmiths' Coll Lon BMus82. Sarum & Wells Th Coll 87. **d** 89 **p** 90. C Welling *S'wark* 89-93; V Tattenham Corner and Burgh Heath *Guildf* 93-97; Asst Chapl R Berks and Battle Hosps NHS Trust 97-99; Chapl Isle of Wight Healthcare NHS Trust from 99. *The Chaplaincy, St Mary's Hospital, Parkhurst Road, Newport PO30 5TG* Tel (01983) 534639 *or* 856781 Mobile 07790-089981
E-mail gregory.clifton-smith@lowht.swest.nhs.uk

CLINCH, Christopher James. b 60. Nottm Univ BEd82 BTh89. Linc Th Coll 86. **d** 89 **p** 90. C Newc St Geo *Newc* 89-92; C Seaton Hirst 92-94; TV Ch the King 94-00; V Newc St Fran from 00. *St Francis's Vicarage, 66 Cleveland Gardens, Newcastle upon Tyne NE7 7QH* Tel 0191-266 1071
E-mail ccne12747@blueyonder.co.uk

CLINCH, Kenneth Wilfred. b 22. Bps' Coll Cheshunt 62. **d** 64 **p** 65. C Old Shoreham *Chich* 64-67; C Lancing St Mich 67-73; R Upper St Leonards St Jo 73-88; rtd 88; Perm to Offic *Chich* from 88. *7 The Leas, Essenden Road, St Leonards-on-Sea TN38 0PU* Tel (01424) 438286 Fax as telephone
E-mail ken22@globalnet.co.uk

CLINES, Emma Christine. *See* LOUIS, Ms Emma Christine

CLINES, Jeremy Mark Sebastian. b 68. Cranmer Hall Dur. **d** 97 **p** 98. C Birm St Martin w Bordesley St Andr *Birm* 97-99; Chapl York St Jo Coll from 99. *York St John College, Lord Mayor's Walk, York YO31 7EX* Tel (01904) 716606 Fax 612512
E-mail j.clines@yorksj.ac.uk

CLITHEROW, Canon Andrew. b 50. St Chad's Coll Dur BA72 Ex Univ MPhil87. Sarum & Wells Th Coll 78. **d** 79 **p** 80. Hon C Bedford Ch Ch *St Alb* 79-84; Asst Chapl Bedford Sch 79-84; Chapl Caldicott Sch Farnham Royal 84-85; C Penkridge w Stretton *Lich* 85-88; Min Acton Trussell w Bednall 85-88; Chapl Rossall Sch Fleetwood 89-94; V Scotforth *Blackb* 94-00; Can Res Blackb Cathl from 00; Dioc Dir of Tr from 00. *St Leonard's House, Potters Lane, Samlesbury, Preston PR5 0UE* Tel and fax (01772) 877229 E-mail andrew@clithcan.freeserve.co.uk

CLOCKSIN (née HOYLE), Mrs Pamela Margaret. b 61. Nottm Univ BA82. St Jo Coll Nottm 84. **d** 87 **p** 94. Par Dn Bulwell St Jo *S'well* 87-91; Cam Pastorate Chapl 91-95; C Cambridge H Trin *Ely* 91-95; Perm to Offic 95-01. *5 Stansfield Close, Oxford OX3 8TH* Tel (01865) 426022

CLOCKSIN, Prof William Frederick. b 55. BA76 St Cross Coll Ox MA81 Trin Hall Cam MA87 PhD93. EAMTC 91. **d** 94 **p** 95. Asst Chapl Trin Hall Cam 94-01; Acting Dean 00-01. *5 Stansfield Close, Oxford OX3 8TH* Tel (01865) 426022
E-mail wfc@brookes.ac.uk

CLODE, Arthur Raymond Thomas. b 35. Roch Th Coll 67. **d** 69 **p** 70. C Blackheath *Birm* 69-72; V Londonderry 73-75; R Kirkbride *S & M* 75-79; UAE 80-83; Min Stewartly LEP 86-90; C Wootton *St Alb* 86-90; C St Alb St Paul 90-94; rtd 94; Perm to Offic *Glouc* from 01. *60 Albemarle Gate, Cheltenham GL50 4PJ* Tel (01242) 577521

CLOETE, Richard James. b 47. AKC71. St Aug Coll Cant 72. **d** 72 **p** 73. C Redhill St Matt *S'wark* 72-76; V Streatham St Paul 76-84; P-in-c W Coker *B & W* 84-88; P-in-c Hardington Mandeville w E Chinnock and Pendomer 84-88; R W Coker w Hardington Mandeville, E Chinnock etc 88; R Wincanton and Pen Selwood 88-97; Sec and Treas Dioc Hosp Chapl Fellowship 91-97; Perm to Offic *Lon* 97-98 and *Ex* 99-02; C Sampford Peverell, Uplowman, Holcombe Rogus etc *Ex* from 02. *The Retreat, Gravel Walk, Cullompton EX15 1DA* Tel (01884) 38788 Mobile 07855-493868

CLOGHER, Archdeacon of. *See* PRINGLE, The Ven Cecil Thomas

CLOGHER, Bishop of. *See* JACKSON, The Rt Revd Michael Geoffrey St Aubyn

CLOGHER, Dean of. *See* THOMPSON, The Very Revd Raymond Craigmile

CLONMACNOISE, Dean of. *See* JONES, The Very Revd Robert William

CLOSE, Brian Eric. b 49. St Chad's Coll Dur BA74 MA76. Ridley Hall Cam 74. **d** 76 **p** 77. C Far Headingley St Chad *Ripon* 76-79; C Harrogate St Wilfrid 79-80; C Harrogate St Wilfrid and St Luke 80-82; P-in-c Alconbury w Alconbury Weston *Ely* 82-83; V 83-86; P-in-c Buckworth 82-83; R 83-86; P-in-c Upton and Copmanford 82-83; Chapl Reed's Sch Cobham 86-96; Chapl Malvern Coll 96-01; Chapl Uppingham Sch 01-04; R Easington, Easington Colliery and S Hetton *Dur* from 04. *The Rectory, 5 Tudor Grange, Easington Village, Peterlee SR8 3DF* Tel 0191-527 0287

CLOSE (née HITCHEN), Mrs Carol Ann. b 47. St Mary's Coll Ban CertEd69 St Martin's Coll Lanc DipEd91 Chester Coll of HE BTh02. N Ord Course 99. **d** 02 **p** 03. NSM Hindley St Pet *Liv* from 02. *271 Warrington Road, Abram, Wigan WN2 5RQ* Tel (01942) 861670

CLOSE, Mrs Jane. b 48. Warwick Univ Dip Counselling 00. WMMTC 00. **d** 03 **p** 04. NSM Fillongley and Corley *Cov* from 03. *316 Allesley Old Road, Coventry CV5 8GH* Tel and fax (024) 7672 2160 Mobile 07957-233502 E-mail j-b.close@ntlworld.com

CLOSE, Timothy John. b 68. QUB BA91 Leic Univ MSc95 TCD BTh00. CITC 97. **d** 00 **p** 01. C Glenageary *D & G* 00-03; Dean's V Belf Cathl from 03. *The Vicarage, 11 Woodfield, Newtownabbey BT37 0ZH* Tel (028) 9086 0023

CLOSS-PARRY, The Ven Selwyn. b 25. Univ of Wales (Lamp) BA50. St Mich Coll Llan 50. **d** 52 **p** 53. C Dwygyfylchi *Ban* 52-58; V Treuddyn *St As* 58-66; R Llangystennin 66-71; V Holywell 71-77; Can St As Cathl 76-82; Prec 82-84; Preb 82-90; V Colwyn 77-84; Adn St As 84-90; R Trefnant 84-90; rtd 91. *3 Llys Brompton, Brompton Avenue, Rhos-on-Sea LL28 4TB* Tel (01492) 545801

CLOTHIER, Gerald Harry. b 34. Oak Hill Th Coll 75. **d** 78 **p** 79. Hon C Highwood *Chelmsf* 78-79; Hon C Writtle w Highwood 79-83; P-in-c Westhall w Brampton and Stoven *St E* 83-86; TV

Beccles St Mich 86-93; R Rougham, Beyton w Hessett and Rushbrooke 93-97; rtd 97; Perm to Offic *Nor* from 97; P-in-c Tenerife Sur *Eur* 01-02. *4 Wiggs Way, Corton, Lowestoft NR32 5JJ* Tel (01502) 733231

CLOUSTON, Eric Nicol. b 63. G&C Coll Cam BA85 MA88 PhD89. Ridley Hall Cam 03. **d** 05. C Chatham St Phil and St Jas *Roch* from 05. *3A Kit Hill Avenue, Chatham ME5 9ET* Tel 07743-601219 (mobile) E-mail clouston@ntlworld.com

CLOVER, Canon Brendan David. b 58. LTCL74 G&C Coll Cam BA79 MA83. Ripon Coll Cuddesdon 79. **d** 82 **p** 83. C Friern Barnet St Jas *Lon* 82-85; C W Hampstead St Jas 85-87; Chapl Em Coll Cam 87-92; Dean Em Coll Cam 92-94; P-in-c St Pancras w St Jas and Ch Ch *Lon* 94-99; P-in-c St Pancras H Cross w St Jude and St Pet 96-99; Can Res Bris Cathl *Bris* from 99. *55 Salisbury Road, Redland, Bristol BS6 7AS* Tel 0117-942 1452 Fax 925 3678

CLOW, Laurie Stephen. b 65. Man Univ BA86 MA88. Wycliffe Hall Ox DipMin98. **d** 98 **p** 99. C Trentham *Lich* 98-01; TV Hampreston *Sarum* from 01. *19 Canford Bottom, Wimborne Minster BH21 2HA* Tel (01202) 884796
E-mail w.m.clow@uclan.ac.uk *or* isclow@ccssite.freeserve.co.uk

CLOWES, John. b 45. AKC67. **d** 68 **p** 69. C Corby St Columba *Pet* 68-71; R Itchenstoke w Ovington and Abbotstone *Win* 71-74; V Acton w Gt and Lt Waldingfield *St E* 74-80; Asst Dioc Chr Stewardship Adv 75-80; TV Southend St Jo w St Mark, All SS w St Fran etc *Chelmsf* 80-82; TV Southend 82-85; Ind Chapl 80-85; R Ashwick w Oakhill and Binegar *B & W* 85-91; P-in-c Brompton Regis w Upton and Skilgate 91-97; rtd 98. *The Tythings, Tythings Court, Minehead TA24 5NT* Tel 07808-200619 (mobile)

CLOYNE, Dean of. *See* MARLEY, The Very Revd Alan Gordon

CLUCAS, Anthony John. b 56. WMMTC 96. **d** 99 **p** 00. NSM Erdington *Birm* 99-04; NSM Nechells 04-05; P-in-c Shard End from 05. *7 Arden Drive, Henley Close, Sutton Coldfield B73 5ND* Tel 0121-382 4461 E-mail clucas@btinternet.com

CLUCAS, Robert David. b 55. Cranmer Hall Dur. **d** 82 **p** 83. C Gateacre *Liv* 82-86; P-in-c Bishop's Itchington *Cov* 86-93; CPAS Staff 93-98; Freelance Tr GodStuff from 99; Perm to Offic *Cov* from 93. *1 Church Hill, Leamington Spa CV32 5AZ* Tel (01926) 887792 E-mail bob@godstuff.org.uk

CLUER, Donald Gordon. b 21. S'wark Ord Course 61. **d** 64 **p** 65. C Malden St Jas *S'wark* 64-68; C Bexhill St Pet *Chich* 68-73; V Shoreham Beach 73-77; V Heathfield St Rich 77-86; C Eastbourne St Mary 86-90; rtd 90; Perm to Offic *Ox* from 90. *10 Windsor Street, Oxford OX3 7AP* Tel (01865) 767270

CLUES, David Charles. b 66. K Coll Lon BD87 Lon Univ PGCE95. St Steph Ho Ox 88. **d** 90 **p** 91. C Notting Hill All SS w St Columb *Lon* 90-94; NSM 94-96; NSM Notting Hill St Mich and Ch Ch 96-98; Asst Chapl HM Pris Wormwood Scrubs 97-98; C Paddington St Mary Magd *Lon* 98-03; C Paddington St Mary 98-03; C Paddington St Sav 98-03; V Willesden St Mary from 03. *St Mary's Vicarage, 18 Neasden Lane, London NW10 2TT* Tel (020) 8459 2167 E-mail transpontem@aol.com *or* stmarywillesden@aol.com

CLUETT, Michael Charles. b 53. Kingston Poly BSc78. St Steph Ho Ox 84. **d** 86 **p** 87. C Pontesbury I and II *Heref* 86-90; TV Wenlock 90-99; P-in-c Canon Pyon w Kings Pyon and Birley 99-04; V Canon Pyon w King's Pyon, Birley and Wellington from 04. *The Vicarage, Brookside, Canon Pyon, Hereford HR4 8NY* Tel (01432) 830802 E-mail mccluett@aol.com

CLUNIE, Grace. b 60. Ulster Univ BA82 MA91 QUB Dip Librarianship 85. CITC BTh95. **d** 95 **p** 96. C Newtownards *D & D* 95-99; C Seagoe 99-01; I Belfast St Nic *Conn* from 01. *St Nicholas' Rectory, 15 Harberton Park, Belfast BT9 6TW* Tel (028) 9066 7753 *or* tel and fax 9068 2924
E-mail belfast.stnicholas@connor.anglican.org

CLUTTERBUCK, Herbert Ivan. b 16. Ch Coll Cam BA38 MA42. Chich Th Coll 38. **d** 39 **p** 40. C Lamorbey H Trin *Roch* 39-41; Hon CF 41-44; Chapl and Sen Classics Master Wellingborough Sch 44-47; Chapl RN 47-62; V Lanteglos by Fowey *Truro* 62-66; Org Sec Ch Union 66-74; Chapl Qu Marg Sch Escrick Park 74-76; Chapl and Dir Relig Studies Roedean Sch Brighton 76-81; rtd 82; Master St Jo Hosp Lich 82-91; Perm to Offic *Truro* 99-05 and *Roch* 00-05. *The College of St Barnabas, Blackberry Lane, Lingfield RH7 6NJ* Tel (01342) 870184

CLUTTERBUCK, Miss Marion Isobel. b 56. Oak Hill Th Coll BA91. **d** 92 **p** 94. C Lindfield *Chich* 92-96; TV Alderbury Team *Sarum* 96-01; TV Clarendon 01-05. *3 Hillside Close, West Dean, Salisbury SP5 1EX* Tel (01794) 342377
E-mail marion@mclutterbuck.fsnet.co.uk

CLUTTON, Mrs Barbara Carol. b 47. WMMTC 00. **d** 04 **p** 05. NSM Bourton w Frankton and Stretton on Dunsmore etc *Cov* from 04. *Grange Farm, Sawbridge Road, Grandborough, Rugby CV23 8DN* Tel (01788) 810372 Fax 521239 Mobile 07808-137550 E-mail r.and.b.clutton@farmline.com

CLYDE, John. b 39. Univ of Wales (Lamp) MA99 Greenwich Univ PhD. CITC. **d** 71 **p** 72. C Belfast St Aid *Conn* 71-74; I Belfast St Barn 74-80; I Belfast H Trin 80-89; Bp's C Acton and Drumbanagher *Arm* 89-94; I Desertlyn w Ballyeglish 94-02; rtd 02. *25 Castleoak, Castledawson, Magherafelt BT45 8RX* Tel (028) 7946 9153 E-mail jc@rclyde.freeserve.co.uk

CLYNES, William. b 33. Sarum & Wells Th Coll 78. **d** 79 **p** 80. C Winterbourne *Bris* 79-83; TV Swindon St Jo and St Andr 83-91; rtd 91. *185A Claverham Road, Claverham, Bristol BS49 4LE*

COAKLEY (née FURBER), Prof Sarah Anne. b 51. New Hall Cam BA73 PhD82. Harvard Div Sch ThM75. **d** 00. Edw Mallinckrodt Jun Prof of Div Harvard Div Sch from 95; Hon C Waban The Gd Shep from 00; Hon C Littlemore *Ox* from 00. *Harvard Divinity School, 45 Francis Avenue, Cambridge, MA 02138, USA* Tel (001) (617) 495 4518 *or* (01865) 552549

COATES, Alan Thomas. b 55. St Jo Coll Nottm 87. **d** 89 **p** 90. C Heeley *Sheff* 89-90; C Bramley and Ravenfield 90-92; V Askern 92-96; Chapl RAF from 96; Perm to Offic *Ripon* from 96. *Chaplaincy Services (RAF), HQ, Personnel and Training Command, RAF Innsworth, Gloucester GL3 1EZ* Tel (01452) 712612 ext 5164 Fax 510828

COATES, Archie. *See* COATES, Richard Michael

COATES, Christopher Ian. b 59. Qu Coll Birm 81. **d** 84 **p** 85. C Cottingham *York* 84-87; TV Howden 87-91; V Sherburn in Elmet 91-94; V Sherburn in Elmet w Saxton 94-02; V Bishopthorpe from 02; V Acaster Malbis from 02. *The Vicarage, 48 Church Lane, Bishopthorpe, York YO23 2QG* Tel (01904) 707840

COATES, Jean Margaret. b 47. Sussex Univ BSc68 Reading Univ PhD77 MIBiol CBiol. St Alb and Ox Min Course 93. **d** 96 **p** 97. C Wallingford *Ox* 96-99; P-in-c Watercombe *Sarum* 99-02; R from 02; Rural Officer (Dorset) from 99. *The Rectory, Main Street, Broadmayne, Dorchester DT2 8EB* Tel (01305) 852435
E-mail jeancoates@macunlimited.net

COATES, John David Spencer. b 41. Dur Univ BA64 DipTh66. Cranmer Hall Dur 64. **d** 66 **p** 67. C Chipping Campden w Ebrington *Glouc* 66-69; CF 69-96; rtd 96; Perm to Offic *B & W* from 96; CF(V) from 97. *c/o Lloyds TSB PLC, 19 The Parade, Minehead TA24 5LU* Tel (01643) 862772

COATES, Canon Kenneth Will. b 17. St Jo Coll Dur LTh45 BA46. Bible Churchmen's Coll Bris 39. **d** 42 **p** 43. C Daubhill *Man* 42-44; Perm to Offic *Bris* 44-47; C Cheadle *Ches* 47-49; V Preston All SS *Blackb* 49-60; V St Helens St Helen *Liv* 60-88; Hon Can Liv Cathl 71-88; rtd 88; Perm to Offic *Liv* from 88. *122 Broadway, Eccleston, St Helens WA10 5DH* Tel (01744) 29629

COATES, Maxwell Gordon. b 49. Lon Univ CertEd70 Open Univ BA83 AdDipEd87 UEA MA86. Trin Coll Bris DipTh77. **d** 77 **p** 78. C Blackheath Park St Mich *S'wark* 77-79; Chapl Greenwich Distr Hosp Lon 77-79; Asst Teacher Saintbridge Sch Glouc 79-81; Teacher Gaywood Park High Sch King's Lynn 81-85; NSM Lynn St Jo *Nor* 81-85; Dep Hd Teacher Winton Comp Sch Bournemouth 85-90; Hd Teacher St Mark's Comp Sch Bath 90-97; NSM Canford Magna *Sarum* 85-90 and from 99; NSM Stoke Gifford *Bris* 93-96; rtd 97; Perm to Offic *B & W* 91-96. *3 Oakley Road, Wimborne BH21 1QJ* Tel (01202) 883162

COATES, Michael David. b 60. Chester Coll of HE BTh01. N Ord Course 98. **d** 01 **p** 02. C Orrell Hey St Jo and St Jas *Liv* from 01. *20 Mount Avenue, Bootle L20 6DT* Tel (01695) 570307

COATES, Canon Nigel John. b 51. Reading Univ BSc MA. Trin Coll Bris. **d** 83 **p** 84. C Epsom St Martin *Guildf* 83-86; C Portswood Ch Ch *Win* 86-88; Chapl Southn Univ 89-97; Chapl Southn Inst of HE 89-95; P-in-c Freemantle 97-00; R 00-05; Can Res S'well Minster *S'well* from 05. *3 Vicars Court, Southwell NG25 0HP* Tel (01636) 817296 E-mail coates@btinternet.com

COATES, Canon Peter Frederick. b 50. K Coll Lon BD79 AKC79. St Steph Ho Ox 79. **d** 80 **p** 81. C Woodford St Barn *Chelmsf* 80-83; C E and W Keal *Linc* 83-86; R The Wainfleets and Croft 86-94; R The Wainfleet Gp 94-03; RD Calcewaithe and Candleshoe 92-03; P-in-c Spilsby Gp from 03; RD Bolingbroke from 03; Can and Preb Linc Cathl from 02. *The Vicarage, Church Street, Spilsby PE23 5DU* Tel (01790) 752526
E-mail peter.coates@onetel.net

COATES, Richard Michael (Archie). b 70. Birm Univ BA92. Wycliffe Hall Ox BA99. **d** 00 **p** 01. C Ashtead *Guildf* 00-03; C Brompton H Trin w Onslow Square St Paul *Lon* from 03. *3 Holy Trinity Church House, Brompton Road, London SW7 2RW* Tel 08456-447533 E-mail coates@archieandson.co.uk *or* archie.coates@htb.org.uk

COATES, Robert. b 63. Aston Tr Scheme 87 St Steph Ho Ox 89. **d** 92 **p** 93. C Heavitree w Ex St Paul *Ex* 92-95; Chapl RN 95-00; V Bexhill St Aug *Chich* from 00. *St Augustine's Vicarage, St Augustine's Close, Bexhill-on-Sea TN39 3AZ* Tel (01424) 210785 Fax as telephone E-mail ert@rcoates42.freeserve.co.uk

COATES, Robert Charles. b 44. Open Univ BA76. Cant Sch of Min 83. **d** 86 **p** 87. C Deal St Leon and St Rich and Sholden *Cant* 86-89; V Loose 89-00; V Barnwood *Glouc* from 00. *Barnwood Vicarage, 62 Newstead Road, Gloucester GL4 3TQ* Tel (01452) 613760 E-mail robert.coates1@virgin.net

COATES, Stuart Murray. b 49. Lon Univ BA70 Edin Univ MTh91. Wycliffe Hall Ox 72. **d** 75 **p** 76. C Rainford *Liv* 75-78; C Orrell 78-79; V 79-86; Chapl Strathcarron Hospice Denny from 86; Hon C Stirling *Edin* 86-90; NSM Doune *St And* from 89;

NSM Aberfoyle 89-94. *Westwood Smithy, Chalmerston Road, Stirling FK9 4AG* Tel (01786) 860531 *or* (01324) 826222

COATSWORTH, Nigel George. b 39. Trin Hall Cam BA61 MA. Cuddesdon Coll 61. **d** 63 **p** 64. C Hellesdon *Nor* 63-66; Ewell Monastery 66-80; TV Folkestone H Trin and St Geo w Ch Ch *Cant* 83-85; C Milton next Sittingbourne 85-86; P-in-c Selattyn *Lich* 86-91; P-in-c Weston Rhyn 88-91; R Weston Rhyn and Selattyn 91-05; rtd 05; Perm to Offic *Lich* from 05. *Oakmere House, 69 Hill Park, Dudleston Heath, Ellesmere SY12 9LB* Tel (01691) 690261 E-mail rev.coatsworth@micro-plus-web.net

COBB, Douglas Arthur. b 25. Kelham Th Coll 49. **d** 54 **p** 55. C Notting Hill St Mich and Ch Ch *Lon* 54-57; C Ruislip St Mary 57-63; V Kentish Town St Silas 63-87; P-in-c Kentish Town St Martin w St Andr 81-85; Chapl Convent of St Mary at the Cross Edgware 87-92; rtd 92; Perm to Offic *Lon* from 97. *Padre Pio House, 10 Buckingham Gardens, Edgware HA8 6NB* Tel (020) 8933 1789 E-mail ddacobb@aol.com

COBB, George Reginald. b 50. Oak Hill Th Coll BA81. **d** 81 **p** 82. C Ware Ch Ch *St Alb* 81-84; C Uphill *B & W* 84-89; R Alresford *Chelmsf* 89-99; Chapl Mt Vernon and Watford Hosps NHS Trust 99-00; Chapl W Herts Hosps NHS Trust from 00. *Mount Vernon Hospital, Rickmansworth Road, Northwood HA6 2RN* Tel (01923) 844487 *or* (020) 8861 2720
E-mail gcobb83618@aol.com *or* george.cobb@whht.nhs.uk

COBB, John Philip Andrew. b 43. Man Univ BSc65 New Coll Ox BA67 MA71. Wycliffe Hall Ox 66. **d** 68 **p** 69. Par Dn Reading St Jo *Ox* 68-71; Par Dn Romford Gd Shep Collier Row *Chelmsf* 71-73; SAMS from 74; Chile from 74. *Iglesia Anglicana del Chile, Casilla 50675, Correo Central, Santiago, Chile* Tel (0056) (2) 696 7107 Fax 639 4581 E-mail jcobb@evangel.cl

COBB, Miss Marjorie Alice. b 24. St Chris Coll Blackheath IDC52. **dss** 61 **d** 87. CSA 56-85; rtd 85; Perm to Offic *Cant* from 87; Chapl Jes Hosp Cant from 90. *2 John Boys Wing, Jesus Hospital, Sturry Road, Canterbury CT1 1BS* Tel (01227) 472615

COBB, Mark Robert. b 64. Lanc Univ BSc86 Derby Univ 96 Keele Univ CertMan99. Ripon Coll Cuddesdon 88. **d** 91 **p** 92. C Hampstead St Jo *Lon* 91-94; Asst Chapl Derbyshire R Infirmary NHS Trust 94-96; Palliative & Health Care Chapl Derbyshire R Infirmary NHS Trust 96-98; Chapl Manager Cen Sheff Univ Hosps NHS Trust 98-02; Sen Chapl from 98. *Chaplaincy Services, Royal Hallamshire Hospital, Glossop Road, Sheffield S10 2JF* Tel 0114-271 2718 *or* 271 1900
E-mail mark.cobb@sth.nhs.uk

COBB, Canon Peter George. b 37. Ch Ch Ox BA59 MA63. St Steph Ho Ox 64. **d** 65 **p** 66. C Solihull *Birm* 65-69; Lib Pusey Ho 69-71; Sen Tutor St Steph Ho Ox 71-76; Cust Lib Pusey Ho 76-78; V Midsomer Norton *B & W* 78-83; V Clandown 78-83; V Midsomer Norton w Clandown 83-84; RD Midsomer Norton 83-84; V Clifton All SS w St Jo *Bris* 84-02; Hon Can Bris Cathl 92-02; rtd 02. *13 Knoll Court, Knoll Hill, Bristol BS9 1QX* Tel 0117-968 7460

COBB, Peter Graham. b 27. St Jo Coll Cam BA48 MA52. Ridley Hall Cam 66. **d** 68 **p** 69. C Porthkerry *Llan* 68-71; P-in-c Penmark 71-72; V Penmark w Porthkerry 72-81; V Magor w Redwick and Undy *Mon* 82-95; rtd 95. *2 Talycoed Court, Talycoed, Monmouth NP25 5HR* Tel (01600) 780309

COCHLIN, Maurice Reginald. b 19. TCert57 FVCM57 ACP60 FFChM Sussex Univ CertEd70 Lambeth STh74. Chich Th Coll 70. **d** 70 **p** 71. C Rowlands Castle *Portsm* 70-72; Chapl Paulsgrove Sch Cosham 71; C Warblington w Emsworth *Portsm* 72-75; C S w N Bersted *Chich* 76-78; Hd Littlemead Upper Sch Chich 78-79; C Saltdean *Chich* 79-83; V Kirdford 83-88; rtd 88; Perm to Offic *Chich* from 88. *56 Farnhurst Road, Barnham, Bognor Regis PO22 0JW* Tel (01243) 553584

COCHRANE, Alan George. b 28. S'wark Ord Course. **d** 82 **p** 83. NSM Clapham Old Town *S'wark* 82-85; C Spalding St Jo w Deeping St Nicholas *Linc* 85-87; R Southery and Hilgay *Ely* 87-98; V Fordham St Mary 87-91; rtd 98; Perm to Offic *Nor* from 99. *34 Pightle Way, Lyng, Norwich NR9 5RL* Tel (01603) 872795

COCHRANE, Mrs Anthea Mary. b 38. **d** 02 **p** 03. OLM Clarendon *Sarum* from 02. *Old Timbers, Silver Street, Alderbury, Salisbury SP5 3AN* Tel (01722) 710503

COCHRANE, Canon Kenneth Wilbur. b 27. TCD BA58 MA61 Trin Coll Newburgh PhD88. **d** 58 **p** 59. C Belfast St Aid *Conn* 58-61; C Belfast St Nic 61-62; C Lisburn Ch Ch 62-63; P-in-c Lisburn St Paul 63-65; I 65-98; Can Belf Cathl 86-90; Preb Clonmethan St Patr Cathl Dublin 90-98; rtd 98. *3 Knockmore Park, Ballinderry Road, Lisburn BT28 2SJ* Tel (028) 9262 7934

COCHRANE, Canon Roy Alan. b 25. AKC53. **d** 54 **p** 55. C Linc St Faith *Linc* 54-56; C Skegness 56-59; R Thurlby w Norton Disney 59-65; V Swinderby 59-65; Chapl HM Borstal Morton Hall 59-65; R N Coates *Linc* 65-69; Chapl RAF 65-69; V Marshchapel *Linc* 65-69; V Grainthorpe w Conisholme 65-69; V Glanford Bridge 69-89; Chapl Glanford Hosp 69-89; RD Yarborough 76-81; Can and Preb Linc Cathl 77-97; Chapl and Warden St Anne's Bedehouses 89-93; rtd 90. *5 Chippendale Close, Doddington Park, Lincoln LN6 3PR* Tel (01522) 689221

COCKAYNE, Gordon. b 34. RMN73. **d** 92 **p** 93. NSM Owlerton *Sheff* 92-94; Ind Chapl 92-94; NSM Brightside w Wincobank 94-99; Perm to Offic from 99. *6 Austin Close, Loxley, Sheffield S6 6QD* Tel 0114-220 6626

COCKAYNE, Mark Gary. b 61. UEA LLB82. St Jo Coll Nottm BTh92 MA93. **d** 93 **p** 94. C Armthorpe *Sheff* 93-96; V Malin Bridge 96-05; AD Hallam 02-05; C Haydock St Mark *Liv* from 05. *99 Springfield Park, Haydock, Warrington WA11 6XP*

COCKBILL, Douglas John. b 53. Chicago Univ BA75. Gen Th Sem (NY) MDiv78. **d** 78 **p** 79. Virgin Is 79-80; Bahamas 80-83; USA 84-90 and from 05; P-in-c Roxbourne St Andr *Lon* 90-92; V 92-04. *Address temp unknown*
E-mail dcockbill22@yahoo.com

COCKBURN, Sidney. b 14. Leeds Univ BA36. Coll of Resurr Mirfield 36. **d** 38 **p** 40. C Hartlepool St Jas *Dur* 38-39; Hon C Roath St German *Llan* 39-40; C Gateshead St Cuth w St Paul *Dur* 40-42; C Newc St Mary *Newc* 42-43; RAFVR 43-47; C Heanor *Derby* 47-51; C-in-c Marlpool 47-51; V Long Eaton St Jo 51-85; rtd 85; Perm to Offic *Derby* from 85. *10 Poplar Road, Breaston, Derby DE7 3BH* Tel (01332) 872363

COCKCROFT, Basil Stanley. b 26. CEng MICE Leeds Univ BSc49. Wells Th Coll 64. **d** 66 **p** 67. C Featherstone *Wakef* 66-69; C Norton St Mary *Dur* 69-71; P-in-c Eldon 71-75; NSM Elland *Wakef* 75-92; rtd 91; Perm to Offic *Wakef* from 92. *9 Dene Close, South Parade, Elland HX5 0NS* Tel (01422) 374465

COCKE, James Edmund. b 26. Wadh Coll Ox BA50 MA55. Wells Th Coll 50. **d** 52 **p** 53. C Christchurch *Win* 52-57; V Highfield *Ox* from 57; Chapl Wingfield-Morris Hosp Ox 57-90; Chapl Nuffield Orthopaedic Centre NHS Trust from 90. *All Saints' Vicarage, 85 Old Road, Oxford OX3 7LB* Tel (01865) 62536

COCKELL, Ms Helen Frances. b 69. Trin Hall Cam BA90 MA94. Qu Coll Birm BD94. **d** 95. C Bracknell *Ox* 95-98; NSM Rugby St Andr *Cov* from 00. *The New Rectory, Pool Close, Rugby CV22 7RN* Tel (01788) 812613

COCKELL, Timothy David. b 66. Qu Coll Birm BTheol95. **d** 95 **p** 96. C Bracknell *Ox* 95-98; C Rugby St Andr *Cov* 98-99; TV 99-04; P-in-c Bilton from 04. *The New Rectory, Pool Close, Rugby CV22 7RN* Tel (01788) 812613
E-mail tim.cockell@btopenworld.com

COCKER (née BENTLEY), Mrs Frances Rymer (Sister Frances Anne). b 22. Man Univ BSc48 TDip49 PGCE49. **d** 95 **p** 95. Mother Superior CSD 87-00; Perm to Offic *Sarum* from 95. *Sarum College, 19 The Close, Salisbury SP1 2EE* Tel (01722) 339761 Mobile 07702-659609

COCKERELL, David John. b 47. Univ of Wales (Cardiff) BA71 Univ of Wales (Swansea) MA74 Qu Coll Cam BA75. Westcott Ho Cam 73. **d** 76 **p** 77. C Chapel Allerton *Ripon* 76-79; C Farnley 79-81; TV Hitchin *St Alb* 81-89; TV Dorchester *Ox* 89-92; Adult Educn and Tr Officer *Ely* 92-00; R Raddesley Gp from 00. *The Rectory, Stetchworth Road, Dullingham, Newmarket CB8 9UJ* Tel (01638) 507263
E-mail david@cockerell.co.uk

COCKERTON, Canon John Clifford Penn. b 27. Liv Univ BA48 St Cath Soc Ox BA54 MA58. Wycliffe Hall Ox 51. **d** 54 **p** 55. C St Helens St Helen *Liv* 54-58; Tutor Cranmer Hall Dur 58-60; Chapl 60-63; Warden 68-70; Vice-Prin St Jo Coll Dur 63-70; Prin 70-78; R Wheldrake *York* 78-84; R Wheldrake w Thorganby 84-92; Can and Preb York Minster 87-92; rtd 92; Perm to Offic *York* from 98. *42 Lucombe Way, New Earswick, York YO32 4DS* Tel (01904) 765505

COCKERTON, Thomas Charles. b 24. **d** 88 **p** 90. NSM Bermondsey St Mary w St Olave, St Jo etc *S'wark* 88-94; Perm to Offic from 94. *30 Carrick Court, Kennington Park Road, London SE11 4EE* Tel (020) 7735 6966

COCKETT, Elwin Wesley. b 59. Aston Tr Scheme 86 Oak Hill Th Coll DipHE90 BA91. **d** 91 **p** 92. C Chadwell Heath *Chelmsf* 91-94; Chapl W Ham United Football Club from 92; C Harold Hill St Paul 94-95; P-in-c 95-97; V 97-00; TR Billericay and Lt Burstead from 00; RD Basildon from 04. *The Rectory, 40 Laindon Road, Billericay CM12 9LD* Tel (01277) 658055 Fax 658056 E-mail elwin@billericaychurches.org

COCKING, Ann Louisa. b 44. **d** 03 **p** 04. OLM The Lavingtons, Cheverells, and Easterton *Sarum* from 03. *High Acre, Eastcott, Devizes SN10 4PH* Tel (01980) 812763
E-mail highacre@fish.co.uk

COCKING, Martyn Royston. b 53. Trin Coll Bris 83. **d** 85 **p** 86. C Weston-super-Mare Cen Par *B & W* 85-88; C Kingswood *Bris* 88-89; TV 89-93; V Pill w Easton in Gordano and Portbury *B & W* 93-96. *68 Friary Grange Park, Winterbourne, Bristol BS36 1NB* Tel (01454) 886771

COCKMAN, David Willie. b 32. Ex & Truro NSM Scheme 89. **d** 82 **p** 83. C Christow, Ashton, Trusham and Bridford *Ex* 82; NSM Exwick 83-84; Warden Mercer Ho 83-97; Lic to Offic from 83; rtd 97. *4 The Fairway, Pennsylvania, Exeter EX4 5DW* Tel (01392) 278590

COCKRAM, Anthony John. b 44. Leeds Univ BSc65 Birm Univ MEd83 Ex Univ BA04. SW Minl Tr Course 98. **d** 01 **p** 02. NSM Seaton *Ex* 01-03; NSM Seaton and Beer 03-04; Asst Chapl R Devon and Ex Healthcare NHS Trust from 04. *1 Hillymead, Seaton EX12 2LF* Tel (01297) 20426 E-mail suton@ic24.net

COCKS, Howard Alan Stewart. b 46. St Barn Coll Adelaide 78. **d** 80 **p** 81. Australia 80-82; C Prestbury *Glouc* 82-87; P-in-c Stratton w Baunton 87-94; P-in-c N Cerney w Bagendon 91-94; R Stratton, N Cerney, Baunton and Bagendon 95-98; V Leic St Aid *Leic* 98-04; RD Christianity S 01-04; R Winchelsea and Icklesham *Chich* from 04. *The Rectory, St Thomas Street, Winchelsea TN36 4EB* Tel (01797) 226254

COCKS, Michael Dearden Somers. b 28. Univ of NZ MA50 St Cath Coll Ox BA53 MA57. Ripon Hall Ox. **d** 53 **p** 54. New Zealand 53-93 and from 98; Chapl Gothenburg w Halmstad, Jönköping etc *Eur* 93-98; rtd 98. *23 Fairfield Avenue, Addington, Christchurch, New Zealand 8020* Tel (0064) (3) 377 7053 Fax as telephone E-mail cocks@ihug.co.nz

COCKSEDGE, Hugh Francis. b 26. Magd Coll Cam BA50 MA52. **d** 88 **p** 89. NSM Alton All SS *Win* 88-89; Lic to Offic 89-91; Chapl Ankara *Eur* 91-96; rtd 96; Perm to Offic *Win* from 96; *Eur* from 97; *Portsm* from 01. *Stancomb, Stancomb Lane, Medstead, Alton GU34 5QB* Tel (01420) 563624 E-mail hughcocksedge@onetel.com

COCKSHAW, Evan David. b 74. Sussex Univ BSc95 Nottm Univ MA99. St Jo Coll Nottm 97. **d** 00 **p** 01. C Horncastle w Low Toynton *Linc* 00-02; C Pennington *Man* from 02. *11 Ruby Grove, Leigh WN7 4JW* Tel (01942) 675832 Mobile 07958-050009 E-mail evan@penningtonchurch.com

COCKSWORTH, Canon Christopher John. b 59. Man Univ BA80 PhD89 PGCE81. St Jo Coll Nottm 84. **d** 88 **p** 89. C Epsom Common Ch Ch *Guildf* 88-92; Chapl R Holloway and Bedf New Coll 92-97; Dir STETS 97-01; Hon Can Guildf Cathl *Guildf* 99-01; Prin Ridley Hall Cam from 01. *The Principal's Lodge, Ridley Hall, Cambridge CB3 9HG* Tel (01223) 741060 *or* 353040 Fax 741081 E-mail cjc70@cam.ac.uk

CODLING, Timothy Michael. b 62. Trin Coll Ox BA84 MA91. St Steph Ho Ox 89. **d** 91 **p** 92. C N Shoebury *Chelmsf* 91-97; V Tilbury Docks from 97; Hon Chapl Miss to Seafarers from 97. *St John's Vicarage, Dock Road, Tilbury RM18 7PP* Tel (01375) 842417 E-mail tim@frcodling.fsnet.co.uk

CODRINGTON CLARKE, Harold Godfrey. b 26. S'wark Ord Course 71. **d** 74 **p** 75. C Redhill St Jo *S'wark* 74-79; P-in-c Blindley Heath 79-96; rtd 96. *77 Oaklands, South Godstone, Godstone RH9 8HX* Tel (01342) 892905

COE, Andrew Derek John. b 58. Nottm Univ BTh86. St Jo Coll Nottm 83. **d** 86 **p** 87. C Pype Hayes *Birm* 86-88; C Erdington St Barn 88-91; C Birm St Martin w Bordesley St Andr 91-96; P-in-c Hamstead St Bernard 96; V 96-02; P-in-c Newdigate *Guildf* 02-03; TR Surrey Weald from 03; RD Dorking from 04. *The Rectory, Church Road, Newdigate, Dorking RH5 5DL* Tel (01306) 631469 E-mail revdandrewdj.coe@btinternet.com

COE, David. b 45. **d** 69 **p** 70. C Belfast St Matt *Conn* 69-72; C Belfast St Donard *D & D* 72-75; I Tullylish 75-81; I Lurgan St Jo 81-89; I Ballymacarrett St Patr 89-02; I Richhill *Arm* from 02. *The Rectory, 15 Annareagh Road, Richhill BT61 9JT* Tel (028) 3887 1232 E-mail davidcoe144@aol.com

COE, John Norris. b 31. Oak Hill Th Coll 57. **d** 59 **p** 60. C Stoughton *Guildf* 59-61; C Guernsey St Michel du Valle *Win* 61-63; C Norbiton *S'wark* 63-67; V Bath Widcombe *B & W* 67-84; R Publow w Pensford, Compton Dando and Chelwood 84-96; rtd 96; Perm to Offic *B & W* from 96. *12 Stirtingale Road, Bath BA2 2NF* Tel (01225) 789752

COE, Michael Stephen. b 63. Bath Univ BSc85. Wycliffe Hall Ox. **d** 00 **p** 01. C Moulton *Pet* 00-03; P-in-c Silverhill St Matt *Chich* 03-05; R from 05. *The Rectory, 9 St Matthew's Road, St Leonards-on-Sea TN38 0TN* Tel (01424) 430262 E-mail mikelisac@aol.com

COE, Stephen David. b 49. Ch Coll Cam MA72. Ox Min Course 90. **d** 93 **p** 94. NSM Abingdon *Ox* 93-97; Assoc Min Ox St Andr 97-05; V Wallington H Trin *S'wark* from 05. *Holy Trinity Vicarage, Maldon Road, Wallington SM6 8BL* Tel (020) 8647 7605

COEKIN, Philip James. b 64. Wye Coll Lon BScAgr87. Oak Hill Th Coll BA93. **d** 96 **p** 97. C Eastbourne All SS *Chich* 96-00; V Hastings Em and St Mary in the Castle from 00. *The Vicarage, Vicarage Road, Hastings TN34 3NA* Tel (01424) 421543 E-mail phil@p.coekin.freeserve.co.uk

COEKIN, Richard John. b 61. Solicitor 86 Jes Coll Cam BA83 MA87. Wycliffe Hall Ox 89. **d** 91 **p** 92. C Cheadle *Ches* 91-95; NSM Wimbledon Em Ridgway Prop Chpl *S'wark* from 95; Perm to Offic *Lon* from 02. *264 Worple Road, London SW20 8RG* Tel (020) 8545 2734

COFFEY, Hubert William (Bill). b 15. MBE46. TCD BA37 MA40. TCD Div Sch Div Test38. **d** 38 **p** 39. C Errigle Keerogue w Ballygawley and Killeshil *Arm* 38-41; Chapl RN 41-47; I Milltown *Arm* 47-52; Chapl Miss to Seamen 52-64; Australia from 53; V Melbourne S 64-80; rtd 80; Perm to Offic *Melbourne* from 80. *23 Hawthorn Avenue, Caulfield North, Vic, Australia 3161* Tel (0061) (3) 9527 7875

COFFEY, Wesley Samuel. b 70. QUB BSc92. **d** 03. C Shellharbour Australia 03-04; C Carrickfergus *Conn* from 04. *12 Albany Drive, Carrickfergus BT38 8BF* Tel (028) 9336 7739

COFFIN, Pamela. *See* PENNELL, Ms Pamela

COFFIN, Stephen. b 52. Pemb Coll Ox BA74 MA79. Trin Coll Bris 74. **d** 77 **p** 78. C Illogan *Truro* 77-80; C Liskeard w St Keyne and St Pinnock 80-82; CMS Burundi 82-86; V St Germans *Truro* 86-00; Chapl Grenoble *Eur* from 00. *14 rue Gérard Philippe, 38100 Grenoble, France* Tel (0033) (4) 76 25 33 79 E-mail chaplain@grenoble-church.org *or* coffin@onetelnet.fr

COGGINS, Glenn. b 60. Warwick Univ BA81. St Jo Coll Dur CTM95. **d** 95 **p** 96. C Cley Hill Warminster *Sarum* 95-99; R Doddington w Benwick and Wimblington *Ely* from 99. *The Rectory, Ingle's Lane, Doddington, March PE15 0TE* Tel (01354) 740692 E-mail glenn.coggins@ely.anglican.org

COGHLAN, Patrick John. b 47. Down Coll Cam BA(Econ)69 Nottm Univ MA73. St Jo Coll Nottm LTh72. **d** 73 **p** 74. C Crookes St Thos *Sheff* 73-78; Brazil 78-92; V Anston *Sheff* from 92. *The Vicarage, 17 Rackford Road, Anston, Sheffield S25 4DE* Tel (01909) 563447

COHEN, The Ven Clive Ronald Franklin. b 46. ACIB71. Sarum & Wells Th Coll 79. **d** 81 **p** 82. C Esher *Guildf* 81-85; R Winterslow *Sarum* 85-00; RD Alderbury 89-93; Can and Preb Sarum Cathl 92-00; Adn Bodmin *Truro* from 00; Hon Can Truro Cathl from 00. *Archdeacon's House, Cardinham, Bodmin PL30 4BL* Tel (01208) 821614 Fax 821602 E-mail clive@truro.anglican.org

COHEN, David Mervyn Stuart. b 42. Sydney Univ BA63 MA78. **d** 67 **p** 68. Mauritius 67-69; New Zealand 70-72; Regional Sec (Africa) Bible Soc 73-75; Australia 75-85 and from 94; Gen Dir Scripture Union (England and Wales) 86-93; Perm to Offic *Lon* 92-94; Tear Fund UK 93-96. *PO Box 67, Croydon Park, NSW, Australia 2133* Tel (0061) (2) 9745 2840 Fax 9744 3496 E-mail dcohen1@compuserve.com

COHEN, Ian Geoffrey Holland. b 51. Nottm Univ BA74. Ripon Coll Cuddesdon 77. **d** 79 **p** 80. C Sprowston *Nor* 79-83; TV Wallingford w Crowmarsh Gifford etc *Ox* 83-88; V Chalgrove w Berrick Salome from 88. *The Vicarage, 58 Brinkinfield Road, Chalgrove, Oxford OX44 7QX* Tel (01865) 890392 E-mail ianghcohen@hotmail.com

COHEN, Malcolm Arthur. b 38. Canberra Coll of Min DipTh79. **d** 78 **p** 79. Australia 79-84; C Moruya, Bega and Cootamundra 79-80; R Braidwood 82-83; R Stifford *Chelmsf* 84-92; Chapl Asst Thurrock Community Hosp Grays 84-86; Hon Chapl ATC from 86; P-in-c Mayland and Steeple *Chelmsf* 92-95; C Prittlewell 95-99; C Greenstead 99-00; TV Greenstead w Colchester St Anne 00-03; rtd 03. *177 Straight Road, Colchester CO3 5DG* Tel (01206) 573231

COHEN, Michael Neil. b 45. Ripon Coll Cuddesdon 79. **d** 81 **p** 82. C Gt Bookham *Guildf* 81-84; C York Town St Mich 84-93; V Camberley St Martin Old Dean 93-95; Regional Adv (SE) CMJ 96-99; R Jerusalem Ch Ch 99-03. *12/31 Israel Eldad, Narnonah, Jerusalem 93399, Israel*

COKE, William Robert Francis. b 46. St Edm Hall Ox BA68 MA79 Lon Univ BD78. Trin Coll Bris 75. **d** 79 **p** 80. C Blackb Sav *Blackb* 79-83; V Fence in Pendle 83-84; P-in-c Newchurch-in-Pendle 83-84; V Fence and Newchurch-in-Pendle 84-89; Switzerland 89-95; Chapl Ardingly Coll 95-96; V Ambleside w Brathay *Carl* from 96; P-in-c Langdale from 97; RD Windermere from 04. *The Vicarage, Millans Park, Ambleside LA22 9AD* Tel (01539) 433205 E-mail randpcoke@cwcom.net

COKE-WOODS, Sylvia Jessie. b 47. Sheff Univ BA69. Qu Coll Birm 81 N Ord Course 98. **d** 99 **p** 00. C Widnes St Mary *Liv* 99-03. *29 Southwoods, Yeovil BA20 2QQ* Tel (01935) 474542

COKER, Alexander Bryan. b 48. Fourah Bay Coll (Sierra Leone) LDiv73 K Coll Lon BD75 MTh76 Brunel Univ MA84 MEd89 AKC76 MCollP84. St Aug Coll Cant 75. **d** 86 **p** 87. NSM Belsize Park *Lon* 86-90; C Croydon Woodside *S'wark* 90-93; C Cheam Common St Phil 93-94; Perm to Offic *Lon* from 02. *The Mission House, 19 Rosehill Park West, Sutton SM1 3LA* Tel (020) 8641 8690

COKER, Canon Barry Charles Ellis. b 46. K Coll Lon BD69 AKC69. **d** 70 **p** 71. C Newton Aycliffe *Dur* 70-74; Trinidad and Tobago 74-78; R Matson *Glouc* 78-90; V Stroud and Uplands w Slad from 90; RD Bisley from 94; Hon Can Glouc Cathl from 98; P-in-c The Edge, Pitchcombe, Harescombe and Brookthorpe 00-01. *The Vicarage, Church Street, Stroud GL5 1JL* Tel (01453) 764555 Fax 751494 E-mail barrycoker@thevicarage.fsnet.co.uk

COLBOURN, John Martin Claris. b 30. Selw Coll Cam BA52 MA56. Ridley Hall Cam 52. **d** 54 **p** 55. C Cheadle *Ches* 54-58; V Trowbridge St Thos *Sarum* 59-65; V Fareham St Jo *Portsm* 65-87; V Crich *Derby* 87-95; RD Alfreton 88-95; rtd 95; Perm to Offic *Derby* from 95. *Stanton View Cottage, Dale Road North, Darley Dale, Matlock DE4 2HX* Tel (01629) 733284

COLBY, David Allan. b 33. Ox NSM Course 78. **d** 81 **p** 82. NSM Gt Faringdon w Lt Coxwell *Ox* 81-83; TV Ewyas Harold w Dulas, Kenderchurch etc *Heref* 83-91; V Westbury-on-Severn w Flaxley and Blaisdon *Glouc* 91-99; rtd 99; Perm to Offic *Ox* from 01. *Solway House, Faringdon Road, Kingston Bagpuize, Abingdon OX13 5AQ* Tel (01865) 820360

COLCHESTER, Archdeacon of. *See* COOPER, The Ven Annette Joy

COLCHESTER, Area Bishop of. *See* MORGAN, The Rt Revd Christopher Heudebourck

✠**COLCLOUGH, The Rt Revd Michael John.** b 44. Leeds Univ BA69. Cuddesdon Coll 69. **d** 71 **p** 72. C Burslem St Werburgh *Lich* 71-75; C Ruislip St Mary *Lon* 75-79; P-in-c Hayes St Anselm 79-85; V 85-86; AD Hillingdon 85-92; P-in-c Uxbridge St Marg 86-88; P-in-c Uxbridge St Andr w St Jo 86-88; TR Uxbridge 88-92; Adn Northolt 92-94; P-in-c St Vedast w St Mich-le-Querne etc 94-96; Bp's Sen Chapl 94-96; Dean of Univ Chapls from 94; Dep P in O 95-96; Area Bp Kensington *Lon* from 96. *Dial House, Riverside, Twickenham TW1 3DT* Tel (020) 8892 7781 Fax 8891 3969
E-mail bishop.kensington@london.anglican.org

COLDERWOOD, Alfred Victor. b 26. Bps' Coll Cheshunt 58. **d** 60 **p** 61. C Oakwood St Thos *Lon* 60-63; C Enfield St Jas 63-66; V Edmonton St Aldhelm 66-91; rtd 91; Perm to Offic *Cant* from 91. *11 Mill Row, Birchington CT7 9TT* Tel (01843) 841544

COLDHAM, Miss Geraldine Elizabeth. b 35. FLA66 Trevelyan Coll Dur BA80. Cranmer Hall Dur 82. **dss** 83 **d** 87 **p** 94. S Normanton *Derby* 83-87; Par Dn 87; Par Dn Barking St Marg w St Patr *Chelmsf* 87-90; Par Dn Stifford 90-94; C 94-95; rtd 95; Perm to Offic *Glouc* from 01. *27 Capel Court, The Burgage, Prestbury, Cheltenham GL52 3EL* Tel (01242) 576425

COLE, Adrian Peter. *See* ROBBINS-COLE, Adrian Peter

COLE, Canon Alan John. b 35. Cam Univ Cert Counselling 90. Bps' Coll Cheshunt 63. **d** 66 **p** 67. C Boreham Wood All SS *St Alb* 66-69; C St Alb St Mich 69-72; V Redbourn 72-80; R Thorley w Bishop's Stortford H Trin 80-87; Chapl St Edw K and Martyr Cam *Ely* 87-94; Chapl Arthur Rank Hospice Cam 87-94; P-in-c Gamlingay w Hatley St Geo and E Hatley *Ely* 94-99; Hon Can Ely Cathl 96-00; P-in-c Everton w Tetworth 98-99; R Gamlingay and Everton 99-00; rtd 01; Perm to Office *St E* and *Ely* from 01. *73 Finchams Close, Linton, Cambridge CB1 6ND* Tel (01223) 892286 E-mail ajc-73@tiscali.co.uk

COLE, Alan Michael. b 40. Melbourne Univ DipEd74 BA74 SSC. ACT DipTh67. **d** 66 **p** 67. Australia 66-75 and 90-97; Chapl Bp Otter Coll Chich 76-77; Chapl Ardingly Coll 77-82; Chapl Bonn w Cologne *Eur* 82-86; Chapl Helsinki w Moscow 86-90; P-in-c Ilkeston H Trin *Derby* 97-01; V from 02. *Holy Trinity Vicarage, 1 Cotmanhay Road, Ilkeston DE7 8HR* Tel 0115-932 0833

COLE, Canon Brian Robert Arthur. b 35. Nottm Univ BA57. Ridley Hall Cam 59. **d** 61 **p** 62. C Tye Green w Netteswell *Chelmsf* 61-64; C Keighley *Bradf* 64-67; Chapl Halifax Gen Hosp 67-73; V Copley *Wakef* 67-73; R Gt w Lt Dunham *Nor* 73-82; R Gt w Lt Fransham 74-82; P-in-c Sporle w Gt and Lt Palgrave 81-82; R Gt and Lt Dunham w Gt and Lt Fransham and Sporle 83-03; P-in-c from 03; RD Brisley and Elmham from 93; Hon Can Nor Cathl from 98. *The Rectory, Pound Lane, Litcham, King's Lynn PE32 2QR* Tel (01328) 701466 Fax 701338

COLE, Charles Vincent. b 26. Kelham Th Coll 47. **d** 51 **p** 52. C Harton *Dur* 51-54; C Gateshead St Jas 54-56; V Blackhall 56-91; rtd 91; Perm to Offic *Wakef* from 91. *66 Scott Green Crescent, Gildersome, Morley, Leeds LS27 7DF* Tel 0113-253 0021

COLE, David. b 40. Hon FGCM95. Qu Coll Birm 66. **d** 66 **p** 67. C Kensington St Helen w H Trin *Lon* 66-69; C Altham w Clayton le Moors *Blackb* 69-72; P-in-c Preston St Luke 72-75; V Inskip 75-80; C-in-c Chelmsley Wood St Aug CD *Birm* 80-87; C Cannock *Lich* 87-93; I Kinneigh Union *C, C & R* 93-98; Can Cork Cathl 96-98; Can Ross Cathl 96-98; Bp's C Gweedore, Carrickfin and Templecrone *D & R* 98-01; I Carrickmacross w Magheracloone *Clogh* from 01. *The Rectory, Drumconrath Road, Carrickmacross, Co Monaghan, Irish Republic* Tel (00353) (42) 966 1931

COLE, David Henry. *See* GIFFORD-COLE, David Henry

COLE, Denise Helen. b 42. WEMTC 98. **d** 00 **p** 01. OLM Whiteshill and Randwick *Glouc* from 00. *Bethany, The Plain, Whiteshill, Stroud GL6 6AB* Tel (01453) 764504

COLE, Canon Donald Robertson. b 24. Edin Th Coll 57. **d** 59 **p** 60. C Edin Ch Ch *Edin* 59-62; R Lasswade 62-69; R Edin St Cuth 69-94; Hon Can St Mary's Cathl from 91; rtd 94. *9 Outlooks Jubilee House, 48 Polwarth Terrace, Edinburgh EH11 1NJ* Tel 0131-337 3403

COLE, Mrs Elizabeth Marie. b 42. **d** 04. OLM Westleton w Dunwich *St E* from 04; OLM Darsham from 04; OLM Middleton cum Fordley and Theberton w Eastbridge from 04; OLM Yoxford, Peasenhall and Sibton from 04. *Middlegate Barn, High Street, Dunwich, Saxmundham IP17 3DP* Tel (01728) 648244 E-mail ecoledun@aol.com

COLE, Guy Spenser. b 63. Univ of Wales (Ban) BA84 Jes Coll Cam BA88 MA91. Westcott Ho Cam 85. **d** 88 **p** 89. C Eastville St Anne w St Mark and St Thos *Bris* 88-92; P-in-c Penhill 92-95; V 95-01; R Easthampstead *Ox* from 01. *The Rectory, Crowthorne Road, Easthampstead, Bracknell RG12 7ER* Tel (01344) 423253 *or* 425205 E-mail guycole@guycole.freeserve.co.uk

COLE, Henry Frederick Charles. b 23. ALCD52. **d** 52 **p** 53. C Bexleyheath Ch Ch *Roch* 52-55; C-in-c Wigmore w Hempstead CD 55-59; V Lawkholme *Bradf* 59-67; Ind Chapl *Sheff* 67-72; V Wadsley 72-88; RD Hallam 83-87; rtd 88; Perm to Offic *Sheff* from 88. *Julians, 217 Tullibardine Road, Sheffield S11 7GQ* Tel 0114-268 4719

COLE, John Gordon. b 43. Magd Coll Cam BA65 MA69. Cuddesdon Coll 66. **d** 68 **p** 69. C Leeds St Pet *Ripon* 68-71; C Moor Allerton 71-75; P-in-c Pendleton *Blackb* 75-86; Dioc Communications Officer 75-86; Dioc Missr *Linc* 86-98; Ecum Development Officer 98-02; Nat Adv for Unity in Miss from 03. *Pelham House, Little Lane, Wrawby, Brigg DN20 8RW* Tel and fax (01652) 657484 E-mail johngcole@lineone.net

COLE, John Spensley. b 39. Clare Coll Cam BA62 MA66 FCA65. Linc Th Coll 78. **d** 80 **p** 81. C Cowes St Mary *Portsm* 80-83; C Portchester 83-87; V Modbury *Ex* 87-95; R Aveton Gifford 87-95; TR Modbury, Bigbury, Ringmore w Kingston etc 95-98; P-in-c Alne and Brafferton w Pilmoor, Myton-on-Swale etc *York* 98-05; rtd 05. *16 Tannery Wharf, Newark NG24 4US* Tel (01636) 611926 E-mail johnlizcole@firenet.uk.net

COLE, Michael Berkeley. b 44. Cuddesdon Coll. **d** 72 **p** 73. C Shepshed *Leic* 72-76; V Leic St Chad 76-79; Hon C Painswick w Sheepscombe *Glouc* 94-97; Hon C Painswick w Sheepscombe and Cranham 97-98; Hon C Fairford and Kempsford w Whelford 98-04; TR Redhorn *Sarum* from 04. *The Rectory, High Street, Urchfont, Devizes SN10 4QP* Tel (01380) 840672
E-mail mbcole@btinternet.com

COLE, Michael George. b 35. CD75. Wesley Th Sem Washington DMin88 Kelham Th Coll 56 Lich Th Coll 57. **d** 60 **p** 61. C Doncaster Ch Ch *Sheff* 60-63; Chapl RAF 63-68; Canada 68-82; USA from 82; rtd 98. *48 Pierpont Court, Pawleys Island, SC 29585, USA* Tel (001) (843) 237 9962
E-mail mcole@sc.rr.com

COLE, Canon Michael John. b 34. St Pet Hall Ox BA56 MA60. Ridley Hall Cam 56. **d** 58 **p** 59. C Finchley Ch Ch *Lon* 58; C Leeds St Geo *Ripon* 58-61; Travelling Sec IVF 61-64; V Crookes St Thos *Sheff* 64-71; R Rusholme H Trin *Man* 71-75; V Woodford Wells *Chelmsf* 75-00; Chapl Leytonstone Ho Hosp 85-00; Hon Can Chelmsf Cathl *Chelmsf* 89-00; RD Redbridge 95-00; rtd 00; Perm to Offic *Chelmsf* from 00. *67 Princes Road, Buckhurst Hill IG9 5DZ* Tel (020) 8506 0702

COLE, Mrs Norma Joan. b 46. EAMTC 93. **d** 96 **p** 97. C Ipswich St Mary at Stoke w St Pet *St E* 96-97; C Ipswich St Mary at Stoke w St Pet and St Fran 97-99; V Gt Cornard 99-04; V Rushen *S & M* from 04. *Rushen Vicarage, Barracks Road, Port St Mary, Isle of Man IM9 5LP* Tel (01624) 832275

COLE, Canon Peter George Lamont. b 27. Pemb Coll Cam BA49 MA52. Cuddesdon Coll 50. **d** 52 **p** 53. C Aldershot St Mich *Guildf* 52-55; S Rhodesia 55-65; V Bromley St Andr *Roch* 65-72; V Folkestone St Mary and St Eanswythe *Cant* 72-87; Hon Can Cant Cathl 80-87; V E and W Worldham, Hartley Mauditt w Kingsley etc *Win* 87-92; RD Alton 89-92; rtd 92; RD Petworth *Chich* 94-95; Perm to Offic from 95. *Marula Cottage, Lower Street, Fittleworth, Pulborough RH20 1JE* Tel (01798) 865540

COLE, Stanley Westley Tom. b 28. **d** 97 **p** 98. NSM Chalke Valley *Sarum* from 97. *Cranborne Farm, Old Blandford Road, Coombe Bissett, Salisbury SP5 4LF* Tel and fax (01722) 718240
E-mail wescol@cfcb.freeserve.co.uk

COLE, Timothy Alexander Robertson. b 60. Aber Univ MA83 Edin Univ BD86. Edin Th Coll 83. **d** 86 **p** 87. C Dunfermline *St And* 86-89; Vice-Provost St Andr Cathl Inverness *Mor* 89-90; R Inverness St Andr 89-90; R Edin St Mich and All SS *Edin* 90-95; CF from 95. *c/o MOD Chaplains (Army)* Tel (01980) 615804 Fax 615800

COLE, Mrs Vanessa Anne. b 73. K Alfred's Coll Win BA94. Trin Coll Bris BA03. **d** 04 **p** 05. C Congresbury w Puxton and Hewish St Ann *B & W* from 04. *7 Weetwood Road, Congresbury, Bristol BS49 5BN* Tel (01934) 876535 Mobile 07813-519092
E-mail vanessa@cole.org.uk

COLE, William. b 45. Oak Hill Th Coll BA96. **d** 96 **p** 97. NSM St Keverne *Truro* 96-99; P-in-c St Ruan w St Grade and Landewednack from 99 *The Rectory, Church Cove, The Lizard, Helston TR12 7PQ* Tel (01326) 291011

COLE-BAKER, Peter Massey. b 58. New Univ of Ulster BSc80 TCD BTh98. CITC 95. **d** 98 **p** 99. C Ballywillan *Conn* 98-01; I Templemore w Thurles and Kilfithmone *C & O* from 01. *The Rectory, Roscrea Road, Templemore, Co Tipperary, Irish Republic* Tel and fax (00353) (504) 31175 E-mail pcolebaker@eircom.net

COLEBROOK, Canon Christopher John. b 36. Qu Mary Coll Lon BA60 BD69. St D Coll Lamp DipTh62. **d** 62 **p** 63. C Llandeilo Tal-y-bont *S & B* 62-66; C Llansamlet 66-71; V Nantmel w St Harmon's and Llanwrthwl 71-76; V Glantawe 76-85; V Gowerton 85-01; RD Llwchwr 93-00; Hon Can Brecon Cathl 97-01; Prec´ 00-01; rtd 01. *65 Pentregethin Road, Cwmbwrla, Swansea SA5 8BA*

COLEBROOK, Peter Acland. b 29. Coates Hall Edin 52. **d** 55 **p** 56. C Northfield *Birm* 58-62; C Bideford *Ex* 62-66; rtd 89; Perm to Offic *Sarum* from 01. *Vale Cottage, Ham Lane, Marnhull, Sturminster Newton DT10 1JN* Tel (01258) 820246

COLEBROOKE, Andrew. b 50. Imp Coll Lon BSc71 MSc72 PhD75. Ridley Hall Cam 92. **d** 94 **p** 95. C Shrub End *Chelmsf* 94-98; R Mistley w Manningtree and Bradfield from 98; RD Harwich from 04. *The Rectory, 21 Malthouse Road, Mistley, Manningtree CO11 1BY* Tel (01206) 392200
E-mail a.colebrooke@btinternet.com

COLEBY, Andrew Mark. b 59. Linc Coll Ox MA85 DPhil85 Dur Univ BA90 FRHistS88. Cranmer Hall Dur 88. **d** 91 **p** 92. C Heeley *Sheff* 91-93; TV Gleadless 94-97; Chapl Ox Brookes Univ *Ox* 97-01; P-in-c Didcot All SS from 01. *The Rectory, 140 Lydalls Road, Didcot OX11 7EA* Tel and fax (01235) 813244 E-mail am.coleby@btopenworld.com

COLEMAN, Aidan William. b 56. St Jo Coll Nottm 97. **d** 99 **p** 00. C Llandudno *Ban* 99-02; TV Bangor from 02; P-in-c Llandygai and Maes y Groes from 02. *The Vicarage, 18 Coed y Castell, Bangor LL57 1PH* Tel (01248) 372417

COLEMAN, Mrs Ann Valerie. b 51. K Coll Lon BD72 Heythrop Coll Lon MA03. St Aug Coll Cant. **dss** 80 **d** 87 **p** 94. Hampstead Garden Suburb *Lon* 80-84; Golders Green 85-87; Selection Sec and Voc Adv ACCM 87-91; Teacher Bp Ramsey Sch 92-93; Chapl 93-04; Hon C Eastcote St Lawr *Lon* 93-04; Course Leader NTMTC 99-04; Dir Wydale Hall *York* from 04; Dioc Moderator Reader Tr from 05. *Dove Cottage, Wydale Hall, Brompton-by-Sawdon, Scarborough YO13 9DG* Tel (01723) 859270 Fax 859702 E-mail retreat@wydale.co.uk

COLEMAN, Beverley Warren. b 20. Leeds Univ BA41. Coll of Resurr Mirfield 41. **d** 43 **p** 44. C Greenford H Cross *Lon* 43-46; C Stepney St Dunstan and All SS 46-47; CF 47-52; CF (TA) 52-87; PC Barrow Gurney *B & W* 52-54; Malaya 54-56; Indonesia 56-63; P-in-c Albrighton *Lich* 63-64; V 64-71; R Jersey St Sav *Win* 71-84; rtd 87; Perm to Offic *Worc* 87-99. *44 Walnut Crescent, Malvern WR14 4AX* Tel (01684) 563535

COLEMAN, Brian James. b 36. K Coll Cam BA58 MA61. Ripon Hall Ox 58. **d** 60 **p** 61. C Allestree *Derby* 60-65; V Allestree St Nic 65-69; Chapl and Lect St Mich Coll Salisbury 69-77; P-in-c Matlock Bank *Derby* 77-86; R Frimley *Guildf* 86-92; V Guildf All SS 92-02; rtd 02; Perm to Offic *Sarum* from 03. *6 Kingfisher Close, Salisbury SP2 8JE* Tel (01722) 410034

COLEMAN, Brian Ray. b 71. California State Univ Fullerton BPhil94. Seabury-Western Th Sem MDiv98. **d** 98 **p** 99. Assoc R Los Angeles St Jas USA 98-01; C Sheff St Leon Norwood *Sheff* 01-03; Chapl N Gen Hosp NHS Trust Sheff 01-03; P-in-c Sheff St Pet Abbeydale *Sheff* from 03; P-in-c Sheff St Oswald from 03. *St Peter's Vicarage, 17 Ashland Road, Sheffield S7 1RH* Tel 0114-250 9716 E-mail frbrian@btopenworld.com

COLEMAN, Charles Romaine Boldero. b 10. Clifton Th Coll 46. **d** 39 **p** 40. C Downend *Bris* 39-41; C Keynsham *B & W* 41-43; R Felthorpe w Haveringland *Nor* 43-49; V Waxham w Sea Palling 49-55; R Horsey 52-55; R Buckenham w Hassingham and Strumpshaw 55-61; R Sampford Brett *B & W* 61-77; rtd 78; Perm to Offic *Nor* 81-05. *1 The Firs, Redgate Hill, Hunstanton PE36 6LQ* Tel (01485) 532946

COLEMAN, David. b 49. K Coll Lon BD72 AKC72. St Aug Coll Cant 72. **d** 73 **p** 74. C Is of Dogs Ch Ch and St Jo w St Luke *Lon* 73-77; C Greenford H Cross 77-80; V Cricklewood St Pet 80-85; V Golders Green 85-90; V Eastcote St Lawr 90-04; P-in-c Upper Ryedale *York* from 04; CME Officer Cleveland Adnry from 04. *The Rectory, Old Byland, York YO62 5LG* Tel (01439) 798355

COLEMAN, Frank. b 58. Hull Univ BA79. St Steph Ho Ox BA83 MA87. **d** 83 **p** 84. C Brandon *Dur* 83-85; C Newton Aycliffe 85-88; V Denford w Ringstead *Pet* 88-00; P-in-c Islip 95-00; V Caldecote, Northill and Old Warden *St Alb* from 00. *The Vicarage, 2A Biggleswade Road, Upper Caldecote, Biggleswade SG18 9BL* Tel (01767) 315578 Fax 317988 Mobile 07759-454252 E-mail frankcoleman@ntlworld.com

COLEMAN, John Harold. b 38. Cant Sch of Min 83. **d** 86 **p** 87. NSM Dover St Martin *Cant* 86-92; V St Mary's Bay w St Mary-in-the-Marsh etc 92-03; P-in-c New Romney w Old Romney and Midley 95-03; rtd 03; Perm to Offic *Cant* from 03. *119 Canterbury Road, Hawkinge, Folkestone CT18 7BS* Tel (01303) 893952

COLEMAN, Jonathan Mark. b 59. Kent Univ BA81 Man Poly DMS91. Qu Coll Birm MA99. **d** 99 **p** 00. C Warrington St Elphin *Liv* 99-02; P-in-c Liv St Chris Norris Green from 02. *St Christopher's Vicarage, Lorenzo Drive, Norris Green, Liverpool L11 1BQ* Tel 0151-226 1637 Fax 07092-176537 E-mail markcoleman@bigfoot.com

COLEMAN, Michael. b 28. Glas Bible Coll DipTh85 Nat Coll Div LTh90. **d** 95. NSM E Kilbride *Glas* 95-99; NSM Motherwell 99-01; NSM Wishaw 99-01; rtd 01; Perm to Offic *Glas* from 01. *51 Lammermoor, Calderwood, East Kilbride, Glasgow G74 3SE* Tel (01355) 902523

COLEMAN, Ms Nicola Jane. b 63. Goldsmiths' Coll Lon BA86. Ripon Coll Cuddesdon 99. **d** 01 **p** 02. C Croydon St Jo *S'wark* 01-05; P-in-c S Norwood H Innocents from 05. *Holy Innocents' Vicarage, 192A Selhurst Road, London SE25 6XX*

COLEMAN, Patrick Francis. b 58. Reading Univ Pontifical Univ Rome STL STB PhB. Ven English Coll Rome 77. **d** 82 **p** 83. In RC Ch 82-91; NSM Abergavenny St Mary w Llanwenarth Citra *Mon* 96-99; Asst Chapl Milan w Genoa and Varese *Eur* 99-01; R Goetre w Llanover *Mon* from 01; Dir CME from 02. *The Rectory, Nantyderry, Abergavenny NP7 9DW* Tel (01873) 880378

COLEMAN, Canon Peter Nicholas. b 42. St Mich Coll Llan 83. **d** 85 **p** 86. C Skewen *Llan* 85-88; R Ystradyfodwg from 88; P-in-c Treorchy and Treherbert from 04; RD Rhondda 96-04; Can Llan Cathl from 04. *The Vicarage, St David's Close, Pentre CF41 7AX* Tel (01443) 434201

COLEMAN, Canon Sybil Jean. b 30. St Deiniol's Hawarden 83. **d** 85 **p** 97. NSM Manselton *S & B* 85-90; C Swansea St Mark and St Jo 90-94; P-in-c 94-98; V 98-00; Hon Can Brecon Cathl 98-00; rtd 00. *Beckley, 25 Beverley Gardens, Fforestfach, Swansea SA5 5DR* Tel (01792) 584280

COLEMAN, Terence Norman. b 37. St Mich Coll Llan 83. **d** 85 **p** 86. C Machen *Mon* 85-87; C Penmaen and Crumlin 87-89; V 89-93; V Newbridge 93-02; rtd 02. *2 Fox Avenue, Newbridge, Newport NP11 4HP*

COLEMAN, Timothy. b 57. Southn Univ BSc79 CEng86 MIChemE86. Ridley Hall Cam 87. **d** 89 **p** 90. C Bisley and W End *Guildf* 89-93; C Hollington St Jo *Chich* 93-97; V Aldborough Hatch *Chelmsf* 97-02; Chapl Princess Alexandra Hosp NHS Trust 02-05; Chapl Barking Havering and Redbridge Hosps NHS Trust from 05. *Oldchurch Hospital, Waterloo Road, Romford RM7 0BE* Tel (01708) 746090 E-mail tim.coleman@tesco.net

COLES, Alasdair Charles. b 67. St Andr Univ BSc90 Homerton Coll Cam PGCE91 Ox Univ BTh96 Heythrop Coll Lon PhD03. Ripon Coll Cuddesdon 93. **d** 96 **p** 97. C Wymondham *Nor* 96-99; Min Can and Sacr St Paul's Cathl *Lon* 99-04; P-in-c Pimlico St Mary Bourne Street from 04; P-in-c Pimlico St Barn from 04; PV Westmr Abbey from 04. *26 Graham Terrace, London SW1W 8JH* Tel (020) 7259 9425 E-mail alasdaircoles@btinternet.com

COLES, Miss Alison Elizabeth. b 60. St Mary's Coll Dur BA81. Ripon Coll Cuddesdon 95. **d** 97 **p** 98. C Leckhampton SS Phil and Jas w Cheltenham St Jas *Glouc* 97-00; Asst Chapl Dudley Gp of Hosps NHS Trust 00-04; Chapl Walsall Hosps NHS Trust from 04. *Walsall Hospitals NHS Trust, Manor Hospital, Moat Road, Walsall WS2 9PS* Tel (01922) 656216

COLES, Christopher Wayne. b 58. St Mich Coll Llan 97. **d** 99 **p** 00. C Coity w Nolton *Llan* 99-02; C Canton Cardiff from 02. *8 Berthwin Street, Pontcanna, Cardiff CF11 9JH*

✠**COLES, The Rt Revd David John.** b 43. Auckland Univ MA67 Otago Univ BD69 MTh71 Man Univ PhD74. St Jo Coll Auckland 66 Melbourne Coll of Div DipRE71. **d** 68 **p** 69 **c** 90. New Zealand 68-71 and from 74; C Remuera 68-70; Chapl Selwyn Coll Dunedin 70-71; Hon C Fallowfield *Man* 72-74; Chapl Hulme Hall 73-74; V Glenfield 74-76; V Takapuna 76-80; Dean Napier 80-84; Dean Christchurch 84-90; Bp Christchurch from 90. *Bishop's Lodge, 12 Idris Road, Christchurch 8005, New Zealand* Tel (0064) (3) 351 7711 *or* 363 0913 Fax 372 3357 E-mail bishop@chch.ang.org.nz

COLES, Preb Francis Herbert. b 35. Selw Coll Cam BA59 MA63. Coll of Resurr Mirfield 59. **d** 61 **p** 62. C Wolvercote *Ox* 61-65; C Farnham Royal 65-69; V Lynton and Brendon *Ex* 69-73; V Countisbury 70-73; TR Lynton, Brendon, Countisbury, Lynmouth etc 73-76; P-in-c Iffley *Ox* 76-88; V Ivybridge w Harford *Ex* 88-00; Preb Ex Cathl from 98; rtd 00; Perm to Offic *Ex* from 00. *8 Glenthorne Road, Exeter EX4 4QU* Tel (01392) 420238

COLES, Geoffrey Herbert. b 38. Nottm Univ CertEd59 TCert60 Loughb Coll of Educn DLC60. N Ord Course 77. **d** 80 **p** 81. NSM Shelf *Bradf* 80-85; C Manningham 85-86; TV 86-92; P-in-c Wyke 92-97; P-in-c Riddlesden 97-04; rtd 04. *4 Ferndale Avenue, Clayton, Bradford BD14 6PG*

COLES, John Spencer Halstaff. b 50. Hertf Coll Ox BA72 MA76. Wycliffe Hall Ox 72. **d** 75 **p** 76. C Reading Greyfriars *Ox* 75-79; C Clifton Ch Ch w Em *Bris* 79-82; V Woodside Park St Barn *Lon* from 82. *St Barnabas' Vicarage, 68 Westbury Road, London N12 7PD* Tel (020) 8445 3598 *or* 8446 7506 Fax 8343 9406 E-mail johncoles@stbarnabas.co.uk

COLES, Mrs Pamela. b 39. Nottm Univ CertEd59. N Ord Course 04. **d** 05. NSM Clayton *Bradf* from 05. *4 Ferndale Avenue, Clayton, Bradford BD14 6PG* Tel (01274) 427956 E-mail geoffandpamcoles@yahoo.com

COLES, Richard Keith Robert. b 62. K Coll Lon BA94 AKC94 Leeds Univ MA05. Coll of Resurr Mirfield 03. **d** 05. C Boston *Linc* from 05. *5 Irby Street, Boston PE21 8SA* Tel (01205) 369266 E-mail revdrichardcoles@yahoo.co.uk

COLES, Robert Reginald. b 47. Surrey Univ BSc69. Cant Sch of Min 82. **d** 85 **p** 86. NSM Sittingbourne St Mich *Cant* 85-87; C St Laur in Thanet 87-93; P-in-c St Nicholas at Wade w Sarre and Chislet w Hoath from 93; P-in-c Minster w Monkton from 96. *The Vicarage, St Mildred's Road, Minster, Ramsgate CT12 4DE* Tel (01843) 821250 E-mail bobcoles@fish.co.uk

COLES, Stephen Richard. b 49. Univ Coll Ox BA70 MA74 Leeds Univ BA80. Coll of Resurr Mirfield 78. **d** 81 **p** 82. C Stoke Newington St Mary *Lon* 81-84; Chapl K Coll Cam 84-89; V Finsbury Park St Thos *Lon* from 89. *25 Romilly Road, London N4 2QY* Tel (020) 7359 5741 E-mail cardinal.jeoffry@btconnect.com

COLEY (née JOHNSON), Mrs Emma Louise. b 76. Ex Univ BA97 PGCE98. Wycliffe Hall Ox BTh04. **d** 04 **p** 05. C Wendover and Halton *Ox* from 04. *1 Icknield Close, Wendover, Aylesbury HP22 6HG*

COLEY, Peter Leonard. b 45. CEng MIMechE Bath Univ BSc67 City Univ MSc84. Oak Hill Th Coll 85. **d** 87 **p** 88. C Mile Cross *Nor* 87-92; R Stratton St Mary w Stratton St Michael etc 92-01; R Kirby-le-Soken w Gt Holland *Chelmsf* from 01. *The Rectory, 18 Thorpe Road, Kirby Cross, Frinton-on-Sea CO13 0LT* Tel and fax (01255) 675997 E-mail rev.petercoley@lineone.net

COLIN WILFRED, Brother. *See* CHERRIMAN, Colin Wilfred

COLLARD, Canon Harold. b 27. Wycliffe Hall Ox 51. **d** 53 **p** 54. C Rainham *Chelmsf* 53-56; C Kingston upon Hull H Trin *York* 56-59; V Upper Armley *Ripon* 59-68; R Chesterfield H Trin *Derby* 68-77; P-in-c Matlock Bath 77-83; V 83-92; Hon Can Derby Cathl 87-92; RD Wirksworth 88-92; rtd 92; Perm to Offic *Ripon* from 92. *10 Kirkby Avenue, Ripon HG4 2DR* Tel (01765) 606306

COLLARD, John Cedric. b 30. Pemb Coll Cam BA53 MA76. St Alb Minl Tr Scheme 77. **d** 80 **p** 81. NSM Roxton w Gt Barford *St Alb* 80-84; C Liskeard w St Keyne, St Pinnock and Morval *Truro* 84-87; TV Liskeard, St Keyne, St Pinnock, Morval etc 87-93; rtd 93; Perm to Offic *Truro* from 93. *Curlew Cottage, Bohetherick, Saltash PL12 6SZ* Tel (01579) 350560

COLLARD, Norton Harvey. b 22. Open Univ BA80. Roch Th Coll 63. **d** 65 **p** 66. C Swanley St Mary *Roch* 65-67; C Dartford H Trin 67-70; V Grantham St Anne *Linc* 70-87; rtd 87; Perm to Offic *Linc* 87-02. *1 Kenwick Drive, Grantham NG31 9DP* Tel (01476) 577345

COLLAS, Canon Victor John. b 23. Pemb Coll Ox BA44 MA48. Wycliffe Hall Ox 49. **d** 51 **p** 52. C Milton *Win* 51-58; R Guernsey St Andr 58-81; Hon Can Win Cathl 78-81; Perm to Offic from 81; rtd 88. *Paradis, La Rue du Paradis, Vale, Guernsey GY3 5BL* Tel (01481) 44450

COLLEDGE, Christopher Richard. b 58. Chich Th Coll. **d** 82 **p** 83. C Deal St Leon *Cant* 82-83; C Deal St Leon and St Rich and Sholden 83-85; Bermuda 85-88; TV Wickford and Runwell *Chelmsf* 88-90; Chapl Runwell Hosp Wickford 88-90; Chapl RAD 90-03; rtd 04. *82 Estcourt Road, London SE25 4SB* Tel 07721-864517 (mobile)

COLLESS, Mrs Salma. b 55. SRN77 RM80. EAMTC 89. **d** 92 **p** 94. NSM Chesterton St Andr *Ely* 92-93; Australia from 93; Hon Dn Chapman 93; C Curtin 94-96; Chapl Brindabella Gardens 96; P Worker Bernie Court 97; Asst P Woden 97-98. *12 Sollya Place, Rivett, ACT, Australia 2611* Tel (0061) (2) 6288 7835 Mobile 414-755756

COLLETT, George Ernest. **d** 04 **p** 05. NSM Bromley H Trin *Roch* from 04. *Holy Trinity Cottage, 1 Church Lane, Bromley BR2 8LB* Tel (020) 462 7561

COLLETT-WHITE, Thomas Charles. b 36. Trin Coll Cam BA61 MA86. Ridley Hall Cam 60. **d** 62 **p** 63. C Gillingham St Mark *Roch* 62-66; V 79-90; C Normanton *Wakef* 66-69; V Highbury New Park St Aug *Lon* 69-76; Canada 76-79; Chapl Medway Hosp Gillingham 79-85; P-in-c Clerkenwell St Jas and St Jo w St Pet *Lon* 90-96; rtd 01. *77 The Street, Boughton under Blean, Faversham ME13 9BE* Tel (01227) 750770

COLLIE, Canon Bertie Harold Guy. b 28. Glas Univ MB, ChB56. Glas NSM Course 75. **d** 76 **p** 77. NSM Ayr *Glas* 76-84; NSM Maybole from 76; NSM Girvan from 76; NSM Pinmore from 76; Dioc Supernumerary 91-99; Can St Mary's Cathl 96-99; Hon Can from 99. *52 Bellevue Crescent, Ayr KA7 2DR* Tel (01292) 285889 Pager 07625-138817 E-mail bertiecollie@tiscali.co.uk

COLLIE, Canon John Norman. b 25. Em Coll Cam BA51 MA56. Ridley Hall Cam 52. **d** 54 **p** 55. C Leic H Apostles *Leic* 54-57; C Melton Mowbray w Thorpe Arnold 57-59; Chapl Lee Abbey 59-62; V Streatham Immanuel w St Anselm *S'wark* 62-68; V Ecclesall *Sheff* 68-90; Hon Can Sheff Cathl 83-90; RD Ecclesall 85-89; rtd 90; Perm to Offic *Sheff* from 90. *46 Sunnyvale Road, Sheffield S17 4FB* Tel 0114-235 2249

COLLIER, Anthony Charles. b 45. Peterho Cam BA68 MA72 Whitelands Coll Lon PGCE76. Cuddesdon Coll 68. **d** 71 **p** 72. C N Holmwood *Guildf* 71-75; Perm to Offic *S'wark* 75-79; Chapl Colfe's Sch Lon from 80; Hon C Shirley St Jo *Cant* 80-84; Hon C Shirley St Jo *S'wark* from 85. *56 Bennetts Way, Croydon CR0 8AB* Tel (020) 8777 6456 E-mail anthony.collier@lineone.net

COLLIER, Clive. *See* COLLIER, Paul Clive

COLLIER, Mrs Janice Margaret. b 57. MCSP79. Cam Th Federation 99. **d** 01 **p** 02. C Formby H Trin *Liv* 01-05; P-in-c Hale from 05. *The Vicarage, 2 Vicarage Close, Hale Village, Liverpool L24 4BH* Tel 0151-425 3195

COLLIER, Michael Francis. b 29. Wycliffe Hall Ox 71. **d** 73 **p** 74. C Hamstead St Paul *Birm* 73-75; P-in-c Castleton *Derby* 75-80; P-in-c Hope 78-80; V Hope and Castleton 80-97; RD Bakewell and Eyam 90-95; rtd 97; Perm to Offic *Derby* from 97. *Buffers Cottage, Station Road, Hope, Hope Valley S33 6RR* Tel (01433) 620915

COLLIER, Paul Clive. b 53. Trin Coll Bris 80. **d** 82 **p** 83. C Hazlemere *Ox* 82-90; V from 90. *The New Vicarage, 260 Amersham Road, High Wycombe HP15 7PZ* Tel (01494) 439404

COLLIER, Paul Edward. b 63. Mert Coll Ox BA85 Lon Univ PGCE87 Solicitor 93. S'wark Ord Course 91. **d** 94 **p** 95. C E Dulwich St Jo *S'wark* 94-97; C-in-c Bermondsey St Hugh CD 97-02; Chapl Goldsmiths' Coll Lon from 03. *7 Morval Road, London SW2 1DG* Tel (020) 7733 0278 E-mail pcollier@fish.co.uk

COLLIER, Richard John Millard. b 45. FRSA92. EAMTC 78. **d** 81 **p** 82. NSM Nor St Pet Mancroft w St Jo Maddermarket *Nor* 81-99; NSM Thurton from 99. *Old Manor Farm, Fox Road, Framingham Pigot, Norwich NR14 7PZ* Tel (01508) 492916

COLLIER, Stephen John. b 46. St Pet Coll Ox MA68 Univ of Wales (Cardiff) DipSW74. Qu Coll Birm 92. **d** 94 **p** 95. C Thorpe *Nor* 94-98; C Nor St Pet Mancroft w St Jo Maddermarket 98-01; R Kessingland, Gisleham and Rushmere from 01. *The Rectory, 1 Wash Lane, Kessingland, Lowestoft NR33 7QZ* Tel (01502) 740256

COLLIER, Susan Margaret. b 47. Cam Univ MB, BChir73. N Ord Course 95. **d** 98 **p** 99. NSM Dringhouses *York* from 98. *12 St Helen's Road, York YO24 1HP* Tel (01904) 706064 Fax 708052

COLLIN, Terry. b 39. St Aid Birkenhead 65. **d** 67 **p** 68. C Bolton St Jas w St Chrys *Bradf* 67-71; C Keighley 71-74; V Greengates 74-04; rtd 04. *275 Leeds Road, Eccleshill, Bradford BD2 3LD*

COLLING, Canon James Oliver (Joc). b 30. MBE95. Man Univ BA50. Cuddesdon Coll 52. **d** 54 **p** 55. C Wigan All SS *Liv* 54-59; V Padgate Ch Ch 59-71; R Padgate 71-73; RD Warrington 70-82 and 87-89; AD 89-95; R Warrington St Elphin 73-97; Hon Can Liv Cathl 76-97; Chapl to The Queen 90-00; rtd 97; Perm to Offic *Ches* from 99. *19 King Street, Chester CH1 2AH* Tel (01244) 317557

COLLING, Terence John. b 47. Linc Th Coll 84. **d** 86 **p** 87. C Wood End *Cov* 86-90; V Willenhall 90-02; V Wolvey w Burton Hastings, Copston Magna etc from 02. *St John's Vicarage, School Lane, Wolvey, Hinckley LE10 3LH* Tel (01455) 220385 Fax 221590 E-mail tc@vicwolvey.fsnet.co.uk

COLLINGBOURNE, David Edward. b 42. St D Coll Lamp. **d** 01. Treas Dioc Coun of Educn *Mon* from 94; NSM Bishton from 01. *The Gables, Llanwern, Newport NP18 2DS* Tel (01633) 412742 Fax as telephone E-mail susan.collingbourne@tinyworld.co.uk

COLLINGE, Mrs Christine Elizabeth. b 47. Doncaster Coll of Educn CertEd68. St Alb and Ox Min Course 95. **d** 98 **p** 99. NSM W Slough *Ox* 98-04; TV Stantonbury and Willen from 04. *29 Bradwell Road, Bradville, Milton Keynes MK13 7AX* Tel (01908) 314224 E-mail chriscollinge@hotmail.com

COLLINGS, Canon Neil. b 46. K Coll Lon BD69 AKC69. **d** 70 **p** 71. C Littleham w Exmouth *Ex* 70-72; TV 72-74; Chapl Westmr Abbey 74-79; Preb Heref Cathl *Heref* 79-86; Dir of Ords and Post-Ord Tr 79-86; R Heref St Nic 79-86; Bp's Dom Chapl 82-86; R Harpenden St Nic *St Alb* 86-99; Hon Can St Alb 96-99; Can Res and Treas Ex Cathl *Ex* from 99; Chapl Devon and Cornwall Constabulary from 99. *9 Cathedral Close, Exeter EX1 1EZ* Tel (01392) 279367 Fax 498769 E-mail collings@exeter-cathedral.org.uk

COLLINGS, Robert Frank. b 26. Lon Univ BD53. ALCD52. **d** 52 **p** 53. C Bayswater *Lon* 52-55; Australia from 55; rtd 87. *Unit 5, 2 Wattle Street, Bunbury, W Australia 6230* Tel (0061) (8) 9721 4520

COLLINGTON, Cameron James. b 68. Wycliffe Hall Ox BTh01. **d** 01 **p** 02. C Ealing St Paul *Lon* 01-05; V Hammersmith St Simon from 05. *153 Blythe Road, London W14 0HL* Tel (020) 7602 1043 E-mail bagpipes.collington@xalt.co.uk

COLLINGWOOD, Christopher Paul. b 54. Birm Univ BMus76 Ox Univ BA82 MA87 K Coll Lon MA01. Ripon Coll Cuddesdon 80. **d** 83 **p** 84. C Tupsley *Heref* 83-86; Prec St Alb Abbey *St Alb* 86-90; V Bedford St Paul 90-97; Can Res and Prec Guildf Cathl *Guildf* 97-99; Chapl Chigwell Sch Essex from 99; Sen Tutor from 01; Hon C Loughton St Jo *Chelmsf* from 99. *Address temp unknown* E-mail ccollingwood@chigwell-school.org

COLLINGWOOD, Deryck Laurence. b 50. St Jo Coll Cam BA72. Edin Th Coll BD85. **d** 85 **p** 85. Chapl Napier Poly *Edin* 85-88; C Edin Ch Ch 85-88; TV 88-89; Tutor Edin Th Coll 89-94; Asst P Edin St Hilda and Edin St Fillan *Edin* 94-03; Chapl Napier Univ 95-03; P-in-c Dalmahoy from 03. *St Mary's Rectory, Dalmahoy, Kirknewton EH27 8EB* Tel 0131-333 1312 E-mail collingwoods@supanet.com

COLLINGWOOD, Graham Lewis. b 63. Open Univ BA92 Ex Univ MA98. St Steph Ho Ox DipMin95. **d** 95 **p** 96. C Heavitree w Ex St Paul *Ex* 95-97; CF 97-99; C St Marychurch *Ex* 99-00; C Cottingham *York* 00-02; Chapl RAF from 02. *Chaplaincy Services (RAF), HQ, Personnel and Training Command, RAF Innsworth, Gloucester GL3 1EZ* Tel (01452) 712612 ext 5164 Fax 510828

COLLINGWOOD, John Jeremy Raynham. b 37. Barrister 64 CCC Cam BA60 MA68 Lon Univ BD78. Trin Coll Bris 75. **d** 78 **p** 79. C Henleaze *Bris* 78-80; P-in-c Clifton H Trin, St Andr and St Pet 80-81; V 81-91; RD Clifton 84-87; Bp's Officer for Miss and Evang 87-91; V Guildf Ch Ch *Guildf* 91-98; V Guildf Ch Ch w St Martha-on-the-Hill 98-02; RD Guildf 95-00; rtd 02. *The*

Old Manse, 55 Audley Road, Saffron Walden CB11 3HD Tel (01799) 529055 E-mail mporokoso@aol.com

COLLINS, Adelbert Andrew. b 15. Lich Th Coll. **d** 61 **p** 62. C Sedgley All SS *Lich* 61-77; P-in-c Enville 77-81 and 86-88; R 81-86; C Kinver and Enville 88-90; rtd 90; Perm to Offic *Lich* and *Worc* from 90. *West Cottage, Bridgnorth Road, Enville, Stourbridge DY7 5JA* Tel (01384) 873733

COLLINS, Barry Douglas. b 47. Kelham Th Coll 66. **d** 70 **p** 71. C Peel Green *Man* 70-73; C Salford St Phil w St Steph 73-75; R Blackley H Trin 75-79; Perm to Offic *Ripon* 80-82; *Pet* 83-93; *Cov* 85-93; *Ox* 93-97; P-in-c Bengeworth *Worc* 98-99; V from 99. *The Vicarage, 1 Broadway Road, Evesham WR11 3NB* Tel and fax (01386) 446164 E-mail barry.collins@tesco.net

COLLINS, Bruce Churton. b 47. BSc. Oak Hill Th Coll. **d** 83 **p** 84. C Notting Hill St Jo *Lon* 83-87; C Notting Hill St Jo and St Pet 87-90; V Roxeth Ch Ch and Harrow St Pet 90-93; P-in-c S Harrow St Paul 91-93; TR Roxeth 93-03; NSM from 03; Overseer New Wine Internat Min from 03. *48 Whitmore Road, Harrow HA1 4AD* Tel (020) 8423 6261 *or* 8422 3241 E-mail brucepriv@aol.com *or* brucertm@aol.com

COLLINS, Ms Cheryl Anne. b 62. Rob Coll Cam BA85 MA89 MCA90. Ripon Coll Cuddesdon 91. **d** 93 **p** 94. C Sharrow St Andr *Sheff* 93-95; Chapl Sheff Univ 95-01; Hon C Endcliffe 96-01; P-in-c Barton *Ely* from 01; P-in-c Coton from 01; P-in-c Dry Drayton from 01; RD Bourn from 03. *St Peter's Parsonage, 70 High Street, Coton, Cambridge CB3 7PL* Tel (01954) 210287 E-mail revcherylc@aol.com

COLLINS, Christopher. b 46. K Coll Lon BSc67 AKC67 Pemb Coll Ox BA70. St Steph Ho Ox 68. **d** 71 **p** 72. C Pennywell St Thos and Grindon St Oswald CD *Dur* 71-74; C Pallion 74-76; C Millfield St Mary 74-76; C Bishopwearmouth Gd Shep 74-76; C Harton Colliery 76-78; TV Winlaton 78-85; V Grangetown from 85. *St Aidan's Vicarage, Ryhope Road, Sunderland SR2 9RS* Tel 0191-514 3485

COLLINS, Canon Christopher David. b 43. Sheff Univ BA(Econ)64. Tyndale Hall Bris 65. **d** 68 **p** 69. C Rusholme H Trin *Man* 68-71; C Bushbury *Lich* 71-74; V Fairfield *Liv* 74-81; V Tunbridge Wells St Jo *Roch* 81-92; R Luton Ch Ch and Chapl Thames Gateway NHS Trust 92-05; Chapl Medway NHS Trust 92-99; RD Roch 94-00; P-in-c Cobham w Luddesdowne and Dode from 05; Hon Can Roch Cathl from 98. *The Vicarage, Battle Street, Cobham, Gravesend DA12 3DB* Tel (01474) 814332 E-mail cdcollins@tiscali.co.uk

COLLINS, Darren Victor. b 69. NTMTC. **d** 05. C Chingford SS Pet and Paul *Chelmsf* from 05. *2 Sunnyside Drive, London E4 7DZ* Tel (020) 8529 0368 E-mail collins@brodessa.freeserve.co.uk

COLLINS, Donard Michael. b 55. TCD. Oak Hill Th Coll BA83. **d** 83 **p** 84. C Lurgan Ch the Redeemer *D & D* 83-87; I Ardmore w Craigavon 87-98; I Killowen *D & R* from 98. *St John's Rectory, 4 Laurel Hill, Coleraine BT51 3AT* Tel (028) 7034 2629

COLLINS, Canon Frederick Spencer. b 36. FACCA Birm Univ DipTh67. Ripon Hall Ox. **d** 67 **p** 68. C Evington *Leic* 67-71; C Hall Green Ascension *Birm* 71-73; V Burney Lane 73-79; Dioc Stewardship Adv 79-84; V Yardley St Edburgha 84-96; RD Yardley 86-92; Hon Can Birm Cathl 89-97; rtd 96; Perm to Offic *Birm* from 96 and *Worc* from 03. *237 Old Birmingham Road, Marlbrook, Bromsgrove B60 1HQ* Tel 0121-447 7687 E-mail fy.collins@virgin.net

COLLINS, Gavin Andrew. b 66. Trin Hall Cam BA89 MA93. Trin Coll Bris BA96 MA97. **d** 97 **p** 98. C Cambridge St Barn *Ely* 97-02; V Chorleywood Ch Ch *St Alb* from 02. *Christ Church Vicarage, Chorleywood Common, Rickmansworth WD3 5SG* Tel (01923) 284224 *or* 282149 E-mail gavin.collins@cccw.org.uk *or* gavin-collins@supanet.com

COLLINS, Guy James Douglas. b 74. St Andr Univ MTheol96 Peterho Cam PhD00. Westcott Ho Cam 96. **d** 00 **p** 01. C Barnes *S'wark* 00-03; R Huntington Valley USA from 03. *The Rectory, 2122 Washington Lane, Huntington Valley, Philly, PA 19006, USA*

COLLINS, Canon Ian Geoffrey. b 37. Hull Univ BA60 CertEd. Sarum Th Coll 60. **d** 62 **p** 63. C Gainsborough All SS *Linc* 62-65; Min Can Windsor 65-81; Succ Windsor 67-81; R Kirkby in Ashfield *S'well* 81-85; Can Res S'well Minster 85-02; P-in-c Edingley w Halam 91-00; rtd 02. *2 Marston Moor Road, Newark NG24 2GN* Tel (01636) 702866

COLLINS, Miss Janet May. b 55. Qu Mary Coll Lon BA78 St Jo Coll Dur BA84. Cranmer Hall Dur 82. **dss** 85 **d** 87 **p** 94. Willington *Newc* 85-88; C 87-88; Par Dn Stevenage St Hugh Chells *St Alb* 88-90; Par Dn Goldington 90-93; TD Witney *Ox* 93-94; TV 94-96; Tutor St Alb and Ox Min Course 96-01; TV Langtree 99-01; P-in-c Weldon w Deene *Pet* from 01; RD Corby from 02. *24 Garston Road, Corby NN18 8NH* Tel (01536) 746560 E-mail revd.jan@btopenworld.com

COLLINS, John Gilbert. b 32. S'wark Ord Course 67. **d** 71 **p** 72. C Coulsdon St Jo *S'wark* 71-75; Chapl St Fran Hosp Haywards Heath 75-84; Chapl Hurstwood Park Hosp Haywards Heath 75-84; R Stedham w Iping, Elsted and Treyford-cum-Didling *Chich* 84-92; rtd 92; Perm to Offic *Chich* 94-00. *12 Exeter Road, Broyle, Chichester PO19 5EF* Tel (01243) 536861

COLLINS, Preb John Theodore Cameron Bucke. b 25. Clare Coll Cam BA49 MA52. Ridley Hall Cam 49. **d** 51 **p** 52. C St Marylebone All So w SS Pet and Jo *Lon* 51-57; V Gillingham St Mark *Roch* 57-71; Chapl Medway Hosp Gillingham 70-71; V Canford Magna *Sarum* 71-80; RD Wimborne 79-80; V Brompton H Trin w Onslow Square St Paul *Lon* 80-85; C 85-89; AD Chelsea 84-88; Preb St Paul's Cathl 85-89; rtd 89; Perm to Offic *Lon* 89-90; Perm to Offic *Win* 89-97. *27 Woodstock Close, Oxford OX2 8DB* Tel (01865) 556228

COLLINS, John William Michael. b 54. Univ Coll Chich Dip Th & Min 99. Bp Otter Coll 95. **d** 98. NSM S Patcham *Chich* from 98. *2 Buxted Rise, Brighton BN1 8FG* Tel (01273) 509388

COLLINS, Ms Kathryne Broncy. b 51. Portland State Univ BSc75 Lon Univ MSc76. Linc Th Coll 92. **d** 94 **p** 95. C Bishop's Castle w Mainstone *Heref* 94-98; P-in-c 98-01; V Bishop's Castle w Mainstone, Lydbury N etc 01-03; TV Wrexham *St As* from 03; Chapl NE Wales NHS Trust from 03. *All Saints' Vicarage, 55 Princess Street, Wrexham LL13 7US* Tel (01978) 266145 E-mail kathy.collins@virgin.net

COLLINS, Ms Linda Kathleen. b 56. Girton Coll Cam BA77 MA80 Bris Univ PGCE78. WMMTC 99. **d** 02 **p** 03. C Harborne St Pet *Birm* 02-05; C Cen Wolverhampton *Lich* from 05. *9 Sanstone Road, Walsall WS3 3SJ* Tel (01922) 711225 Mobile 07985-033476 E-mail tobycol@aol.com

COLLINS, Mrs Lindsay Rosemary Faith. b 70. K Coll Lon BD91 AKC91 PGCE92. Ripon Coll Cuddesdon MTh95. **d** 97 **p** 98. C Witney *Ox* 97-99; NSM 00-01; Chapl Cokethorpe Sch Witney 00-01; Chapl and Hd RE St Paul's Girls' Sch Hammersmith 01-04; Hon C Barnes *S'wark* from 04; Chapl K Coll Sch Wimbledon from 04. *25 Glebe Road, London SW13 0DZ* Tel (020) 8878 6982

COLLINS, Martin. *See* COLLINS, Canon William Francis Martin

COLLINS, Canon Norman Hilary. b 33. Mert Coll Ox BA55 MA58. Wells Th Coll 58. **d** 60 **p** 61. C Ystrad Mynach *Llan* 60-62; C Gelligaer 62-67; V Maerdy 67-77; R Penarth w Lavernock 77-98; RD Penarth and Barry 87-98; Can Llan Cathl 92-98; rtd 98. *4 Llys Steffan, Llantwit Major CF61 2UF* Tel (01446) 794976

COLLINS, Paul David Arthur. b 50. Lanc Univ MSc91. K Coll Lon BD72 AKC72 St Aug Coll Cant 73. **d** 73 **p** 74. C Rotherhithe St Mary w All SS *S'wark* 73-76; C Stocking Farm *Leic* 76-78; V 78-83; R Husbands Bosworth w Mowsley and Knaptoft etc 83-87; Soc Resp Officer *Blackb* 87-94; R Worc City St Paul and Old St Martin etc *Worc* 94-03; Min Can Worc Cathl 95-03; P-in-c Bishop's Castle w Mainstone, Lydbury N etc *Heref* from 03. *The Vicarage, Church Lane, Bishops Castle SY9 5AF* Tel (01588) 638095

COLLINS, Paul Myring. b 53. St Jo Coll Dur BA75 Ox Univ BA78 MA83 K Coll Lon PhD95. St Steph Ho Ox 76. **d** 79 **p** 80. C Meir *Lich* 79-82; C Fenton 82-83; TV Leek and Meerbrook 83-87; Tutor in Th and Liturgy Chich Th Coll 87-94; Dir of Studies 90-94; V Brighton Gd Shep Preston *Chich* 94-96; Tutor Qu Coll Birm 96-01; V Bournville *Birm* 01-02; Reader Chr Th Univ Coll Chich from 02. *University College, College Lane, Chichester PO19 6PE* Tel (01243) 816000 E-mail p.collins@ucc.ac.uk

COLLINS, Peter John. b 33. Open Univ BA. Oak Hill Th Coll 64. **d** 66 **p** 67. C Low Leyton *Chelmsf* 66-69; C Portsdown *Portsm* 69-72; V Gatten St Paul 72-79; C-in-c Ingrave St Steph CD *Chelmsf* 79-85; V Roydon 85-98; rtd 98; Perm to Offic *S'wark* from 00. *14 Glyndale Grange, Mulgrave Road, Sutton SM2 6LP* Tel (020) 8770 7683

COLLINS, Philip Howard Norton. b 50. AKC73. St Aug Coll Cant 73. **d** 74 **p** 75. C Stamford Hill St Thos *Lon* 74-78; C Upwood w Gt and Lt Raveley *Ely* 78-81; C Ramsey 78-81; R Leverington 81-92; P-in-c Wisbech St Mary 89-92; RD Wisbech 90-92; TR Whittlesey and Pondersbridge 92-95; TR Whittlesey, Pondersbridge and Coates 95-02; R New Alresford w Ovington and Itchen Stoke *Win* from 02. *The Rectory, 37 Jacklyns Lane, Alresford SO24 9LF* Tel (01962) 732105 E-mail philip_nortoncollins@hotmail.com

COLLINS (née SHIRRAS), Rachel Joan. b 66. Univ of Wales (Abth) BSc88. St Jo Coll Nottm 88. **d** 91 **p** 94. Par Dn Ockbrook *Derby* 91-94; C Bris St Matt and St Nath *Bris* 94-97; V Beckton St Mark *Chelmsf* 97-02; NSM Wandsworth St Steph *S'wark* from 02; NSM Wandsworth St Mich from 02. *87 Lambton Road, London SW20 0LW* Tel (020) 8947 7440 E-mail rshirras@aol.com

COLLINS, Richard Andrew. b 65. K Coll Lon BD92 AKC92 Dur Univ MA00. St Steph Ho Ox 92. **d** 94 **p** 95. C Whickham *Dur* 94-97; C Bensham 97-98; TV 98-03; P-in-c Greatham from 03; Local Min Officer from 03; Chapl Greatham Hosp from 03. *Greatham House, 6 Front Street, Greatham, Hartlepool TS25 2ER* Tel (01429) 872626 E-mail richard.collins@durham.anglican.org

COLLINS, Roger Richardson. b 48. Birm Univ BPhil88. WMMTC 78. **d** 81 **p** 82. NSM Cotteridge *Birm* from 81. *6 Chesterfield Court, Middleton Hall Road, Birmingham B30 1AF* Tel 0121-459 4009 E-mail roger@rrcollins.freeserve.co.uk

COLLINS, Ross Nicoll Ferguson. b 64. Edin Univ MA87 Ven English Coll Rome 91 Pontifical Univ Rome 91. Ripon Coll Cuddesdon BA91. **d** 92 **p** 93. C Goring w S Stoke *Ox* 92-96; P-in-c N Leigh 96-01; TR Barnes *S'wark* from 01. *The Rectory, 25 Glebe Road, London SW13 0DZ* Tel and fax (020) 8404 3177 *or* 8741 5422 E-mail ross@stmarybarnes.org

COLLINS, Canon Stella Vivian. b 32. S Dios Minl Tr Scheme 74. **dss** 77 **d** 87 **p** 94. Harnham *Sarum* 77-88; Hon Par Dn 87-88; Dioc Lay Min Adv 82-97; Adv for Women's Min 82-97; Hon Par Dn Wilton w Netherhampton and Fugglestone 88-94; Hon C 94-97; RD Wylye and Wilton 89-94; Can and Preb Sarum Cathl 93-97; rtd 97; Perm to Offic *Sarum* from 97. *1 Meadowside, Hanging Langford, Salisbury SP3 4NW* Tel (01722) 790743

COLLINS, William Arthur Donovan. b 21. AKC49. **d** 50 **p** 51. C Huddersfield St Jo *Wakef* 50-52; R Rustenburg S Africa 52-57; Nelspruit and White River w Plaston 57-61; C Friern Barnet All SS *Lon* 61-62; V Kellington w Whitley *Wakef* 62-66; R Claremont Ch the King S Africa 66-75; Adn Cape Town 75-80; V Birchington w Acol and Minnis Bay *Cant* 80-85; Warden Coll of St Barn Lingfield 85-88; rtd 88; Perm to Offic *St E* 88-02. *The College of St Barnabas, Blackberry Lane, Lingfield RH7 6NJ* Tel (01342) 870350

COLLINS, Canon William Francis Martin. b 43. St Cath Coll Cam BA66 MA70. Cuddesdon Coll 68. **d** 70 **p** 71. C Man Victoria Park *Man* 70-73; P-in-c Ancoats 73-78; Chapl Abraham Moss Cen 78-91; Hon C Cheetham Hill 81-84; Chs' FE Officer for Gtr Man 84-91; V Norbury *Ches* from 91; Hon Can Ches Cathl from 05. *Norbury Vicarage, 75 Chester Road, Hazel Grove, Stockport SK7 5PE* Tel 0161-483 8640 E-mail martin@norbury75.freeserve.co.uk

COLLINS, Winfield St Clair. b 41. Univ of W Indies BA83 Man Univ BA88 MEd91. Codrington Coll Barbados LTh77. **d** 76 **p** 76. Asst Chapl HM Pris Wakef 76; Barbados 76-84; C St Jo 76; P-in-c St Mark and St Cath 77-84; Asst Chapl HM Pris Wandsworth 85; Chapl HM YOI Thorn Cross 85-91; Chapl HM Pris Pentonville 91-01; Can Res Barbados 01-02; rtd 02. *92 Barclay Road, London N18 1EQ* Tel (020) 8245 4145

COLLINSON, Ernest John. b 12. ALCD36. **d** 36 **p** 37. C Southall Green St Jo *Lon* 36-38; Sudan 38-46; R Graveley w Chivesfield *St Alb* 46-48; V Laleham *Lon* 48-52; Africa Inland Miss 52-54; V Penge St Jo *Roch* 54-63; Rwanda Miss 63-66; V Tiverton St Geo *Ex* 66-73; Perm to Offic from 74; rtd 77. *2 St Helens Court, Cotmaton Road, Sidmouth EX10 8SS* Tel (01395) 513878

COLLINSON, Leslie Roland. b 47. St Jo Coll Nottm 90. **d** 92 **p** 93. C Gorleston St Andr *Nor* 92-96; TV Banbury *Ox* 96-98; V Banbury St Fran 98-00; V Darwen St Barn *Blackb* from 00. *St Barnabas' Vicarage, 68 Park Road, Darwen BB3 2LD* Tel (01254) 702732 E-mail revles@ntlworld.com

COLLINSON, Mark Peter Charles. b 68. City Univ BSc90 Fitzw Coll Cam BA97 MA01. Ridley Hall Cam 95. **d** 98 **p** 99. C Ashton-upon-Mersey St Mary *Ches* 98-01; Chapl Amsterdam w Den Helder and Heiloo *Eur* from 01. *Bouwmeester 2, 1188 DT Amstelveen, The Netherlands* Tel (0031) (20) 441 0355 E-mail mark@christchurch.nl

COLLINSON, Roger Alfred. b 36. St Jo Coll Dur BA58 Cranmer Hall Dur 60. **d** 63 **p** 97. C Liv St Mich *Liv* 63-64; NSM Ormside *Carl* from 97; NSM Appleby from 97. *1 Caesar's View, Appleby-in-Westmorland CA16 6SH* Tel (01768) 352886

COLLIS, Jonathan. b 69. Selw Coll Cam BA91 MA94. Aston Tr Scheme 96 Westcott Ho Cam 97. **d** 99 **p** 00. C St Neots *Ely* 99-02; Chapl Jes Coll Cam from 02. *Jesus College, Cambridge CB5 8BL* Tel (01223) 339438 *or* 359196 E-mail j.collis@jesus.cam.ac.uk

COLLIS, Michael Alan. b 35. K Coll Lon BD60 AKC60. **d** 61 **p** 62. C Worc St Martin *Worc* 61-63; C Dudley St Thos 63-66; C St Peter-in-Thanet *Cant* 66-70; V Croydon H Trin 70-77; P-in-c Norbury St Steph 77-81; V 81-82; V Sutton Valence w E Sutton and Chart Sutton 82-89; R New Fishbourne *Chich* 89-00; P-in-c Appledram 89-00; rtd 00; Perm to Offic *Chich* from 00. *66 Orchard Way, Barnham, Bognor Regis PO22 0HY* Tel (01243) 552429

COLLIS, The Very Revd Stephen Thomas. b 47. MHCIMA94. Cranmer Hall Dur 80. **d** 82 **p** 83. C Crewe All SS and St Paul *Ches* 82-84; C Wilmslow 84-86 and 95-98; Chapl RAF 86-95; P-in-c Barthomley *Ches* 98-00; S Cheshire Ind Chapl 98-00; Chapl Abu Dhabi UAE 00-02; Dean St Paul's Cathl and Chapl Nicosia from 02. *2 Grigori Afxentiou Street, PO Box 22014, 1516 Nicosia, Cyprus* Tel (00357) (22) 677897 Mobile 99-809257 Fax (22) 672241 E-mail stpauls@spidernet.com.cy

COLLISON, Christopher John. b 48. Oak Hill Th Coll 68. **d** 72 **p** 73. C Cromer *Nor* 72-75; C Costessey 76-78; V 87-95; C Heckmondwike *Wakef* 78-79; P-in-c Shepley 79-83; Dioc Communications Officer 79-83; Chapl Flushing Miss to Seamen *Eur* 83-85; Asst Min Sec Miss to Seamen 85-87; C St Mich Paternoster Royal *Lon* 85-87; P-in-c Swainsthorpe w Newton Flotman *Nor* 95-97; TV Newton Flotman, Swainsthorpe, Tasburgh, etc 98-02; Dioc Evang Officer 95-01; V Henfield w Shermanbury and Woodmancote *Chich* from 02; RD Hurst from 04. *The Vicarage, Church Lane, Henfield BN5 9NY* Tel and fax (01273) 492017 E-mail stpeters.henfield@virgin.net

COLLISON, Ms Elizabeth. b 38. Man Univ CertEd58. N Ord Course 85. **d** 88 **p** 94. C Huyton St Mich *Liv* 88-94; C Rainhill 94-05; rtd 05. *25 Lowther Drive, Rainhill, Prescot L35 0NG* Tel 0151-426 3853 E-mail liz-collison@yahoo.co.uk

COLLYER, Canon David John. b 38. JP. Keble Coll Ox BA61 Ox Univ MA86. Westcott Ho Cam 61. **d** 63 **p** 64. C Perry Beeches *Birm* 63-65; Bp's Chapl for Special Youth Work 65-70; P-in-c Deritend 66-70; Bp's Youth Chapl and Dioc Youth Officer 70-73; R Northfield 73-78; Hon Chapl Birm Cathl 78-81; Hon C Birm St Geo 81-86; V Handsworth St Andr 86-97; Hon Can Birm Cathl from 95; Dioc Development Officer 97-01; Perm to Offic from 01. *24 Sundbury Rise, Northfield, Birmingham B31 2EZ* Tel 0121-477 0429 *or* 426 0400 Fax 428 1114 E-mail d.collyer@birmingham.anglican.org

COLLYER, Leon John. b 72. SS Hild & Bede Coll Dur BSc95 Leeds Univ BA00. Coll of Resurr Mirfield 98. **d** 01 **p** 02. C Airedale w Fryston *Wakef* 01-04; P-in-c Crofton from 04; P-in-c Warmfield from 04. *The Vicarage, Kirkthorpe Lane, Kirkthorpe, Wakefield WF1 5SZ* Tel 07714-986462 (mobile) E-mail frleon@o2.co.uk

COLMAN, Geoffrey Hugh. b 29. Univ Coll Ox BA53 MA68. Wells Th Coll 67. **d** 68 **p** 69. C Wanstead St Mary *Chelmsf* 68-72; V Barking St Erkenwald 72-77; Youth Chapl 78-81; C Maidstone All SS and St Phil w Tovil *Cant* 85-88; P-in-c Norton 88-93; R 93-96; P-in-c Teynham 88-93; P-in-c Lynsted w Kingsdown 88-93; V Teynham w Lynsted and Kingsdown 93-96; rtd 96; Perm to Offic *Cant* 98-99. *c/o Georgina Fulcher, Bramble Barn, Binsted Lane, Binsted, Arundel BN18 0LQ*

COLMER, Andrew John. b 68. De Montfort Univ Leic BSc90. St Jo Coll Nottm MA96 LTh97. **d** 97 **p** 98. C Roby *Liv* 97-01; C Litherland St Andr 01-02; P-in-c Liv All So Springwood from 02. *Springwood Vicarage, 499 Mather Avenue, Liverpool L19 4TF* Tel and fax 0151-427 5699 E-mail andrew.colmer@virgin.net

COLMER, The Ven Malcolm John. b 45. Sussex Univ MSc67. St Jo Coll Nottm BA73. **d** 73 **p** 74. C Egham *Guildf* 73-76; C Chadwell *Chelmsf* 76-79; V S Malling *Chich* 79-85; V Hornsey Rise St Mary w St Steph *Lon* 85-87; TR Hornsey Rise Whitehall Park Team 87-96; AD Islington 90-94; Adn Middx 96-05; Adn Heref from 05; Can Res Heref Cathl from 05. *The Palace, Palace Yard, Hereford HR4 9BL* Tel (01432) 373324 E-mail archdeacon@hereford.anglican.org

COLPUS (née EDWARDS), Mrs Anita Carolyn. b 71. Trin Coll Bris 01. **d** 03 **p** 04. C Notting Hill St Pet *Lon* from 03. *7 The Lodge, Kensington Park Gardens, London W11 3HA* Tel (020) 7792 8527 *or* 792 8227 E-mail anitacolpus@tesco.net

COLSON, Major Alexander Francis Lionel. b 21. MBE45. St Jo Coll Cam BA43 MA61. Tyndale Hall Bris 60. **d** 62 **p** 63. C Slough *Ox* 62-65; R Elmswell *St E* 65-73; V W Kilburn St Luke w St Simon and St Jude *Lon* 73-82; R Thrandeston, Stuston and Brome w Oakley *St E* 82-86; rtd 86; Perm to Offic *Nor* from 86. *10 Soanes Court, Lyng, Norwich NR9 5RE* Tel (01603) 872812

COLSON, Ian Richard. b 65. Wolv Poly BSc86 Nottm Univ BTh89 Westmr Coll Ox DipRE98. Linc Th Coll 86. **d** 89 **p** 90. C Nunthorpe *York* 89-92; C Thornaby on Tees 92-93; Chapl RAF 93-00; V Sunbury *Lon* 00-02; Chapl Ardingly Coll from 02. *Ardingly College, College Road, Haywards Heath RH17 6SQ* Tel (01444) 892577 E-mail ianrcolson@aol.com

COLSTON, John Edward. b 43. Open Univ BA91 Leeds Univ MA94. Lich Th Coll 65. **d** 68 **p** 69. C Bromsgrove All SS *Worc* 68-71; C Tettenhall Wood *Lich* 71-74; V Alrewas and Wychnor 74-88; R Ainderby Steeple w Yafforth and Kirby Wiske etc *Ripon* 88-95; V High Harrogate Ch Ch from 95; Warden of Readers 90-96; AD Harrogate 01-05. *Christ Church Vicarage, 11 St Hilda's Road, Harrogate HG2 8JX* Tel (01423) 883390 *or* 530750 Mobile 07958-112312 E-mail jecolston@yahoo.com

COLTHURST, The Ven Reginald William Richard. b 22. TCD BA44. CITC 45. **d** 45 **p** 46. C Portadown St Mark *Arm* 45-48; C Belfast All SS *Conn* 48-55; I Ardtrea w Desertcreat *Arm* 55-66; I Richhill 66-94; Adn Arm 85-92; rtd 94. *14 Cabin Hill Gardens, Belfast BT75 7AP* Tel (028) 9047 2288

COLTON, Martin Philip. b 67. Sheff Univ BMus89 MMus92 FRCO92 Open Univ PGCE97. St Mich Coll Llan BA03. **d** 03 **p** 04. C Whitchurch *Llan* from 03. *16 St John's Crescent, Whitchurch, Cardiff CF14 7AF* Tel (029) 2062 5947 E-mail martin.colton@which.net

✠**COLTON, The Rt Revd William Paul.** b 60. NUI BCL81 TCD DipTh84 MPhil87. **d** 84 **p** 85 **c** 99. C Lisburn St Paul *Conn* 84-87; Bp's Dom Chapl 85-90; V Choral Belf Cathl 87-90; Min Can Belf Cathl 89-90; PV, Registrar and Chapter Clerk Ch Ch Cathl Dub *D & G* 90-95; I Castleknock and Mulhuddart, w Clonsilla 90-99; Co-ord Protestant Relig Progr RTE 93-99; Hon Chapl Actors' Ch Union 94-96; Area Chapl (Ireland) Actors' Ch Union 96-97; Can Ch Ch Cathl Dublin 97-99; Bp C, C & R from

99. *The Palace, Bishop Street, Cork, Irish Republic* Tel (00353) (21) 431 6114 Fax 427 3437 E-mail bishop@cork.anglican.org *or* pcolton@iol.ie

COLVILLE, Gary Stanley. b 59. Sarum & Wells Th Coll 90. **d** 92 **p** 94. C Plaistow St Mary *Roch* 92-94; P-in-c Foots Cray 94-96; R 96-00; P-in-c N Cray 97-00; R Footscray w N Cray 00; R Pembroke Bermuda 01-04; V Roch from 04. *The Vicarage, 138 Delce Road, Rochester ME1 2EH* Tel (01634) 845122 E-mail moiracolville@hotmail.com

COLWILL, James Patrick (Jay). b 68. Man Poly BA91. St Jo Coll Nottm BTh93 MA94. **d** 94 **p** 95. C Reading St Agnes w St Paul *Ox* 94-97; C Easthampstead 97-03; V Orpington Ch Ch *Roch* from 03. *The Vicarage, 165 Charterhouse Road, Orpington BR6 9EP* Tel (01689) 870923 E-mail j.colwill@ntlworld.com

COMBE, Edward Charles. b 40. Man Univ MSc PhD QUB DSc. N Ord Course. **d** 89 **p** 90. NSM Broadheath *Ches* 89-94; USA from 94. *1760 Southwind Lane, Maplewood, MN 55109, USA* Tel (001) (651) 773 3066 E-mail combe001@gold.tc.umn.edu

COMBE, The Very Revd John Charles. b 33. TCD BA53 MA56 BD57 MLitt65 PhD70. **d** 56 **p** 57. C Cork St Luke w St Ann *C, C & R* 56-58; C Ballynafeigh St Jude *D & D* 58-61; I Crinken *D & G* 61-66; Hon Clerical V Ch Ch Cathl Dublin 63-66; C Belfast St Bart *Conn* 66-70; I Belfast St Barn 70-74; I Portadown St Mark *Arm* 74-84; I Arm St Mark w Aghavilly 84-90; Can Arm Cathl 85-90; Dean Kilmore *K, E & A* 90-96; I Kilmore w Ballintemple, Kildallan etc 90-96; rtd 96. *24 Kensington Park, Maxwell Road, Bangor BT20 3RF* Tel (028) 9146 6123

COMBER, Mrs Alison. LNSM course. **d** 94 **p** 95. OLM New Bury *Man* from 94. *12 Seymour Grove, Farnworth, Bolton BL4 0HF* Tel (01204) 397745

COMBER, The Ven Anthony James. b 27. Leeds Univ BSc49 MSc52. St Chad's Coll Dur 53. **d** 56 **p** 57. C Manston *Ripon* 56-60; V Oulton 60-69; V Hunslet St Mary 69-77; RD Armley 72-75 and 79-81; R Farnley 77-82; Hon Can Ripon Cathl 80-92; Adn Leeds 82-92; rtd 92; Perm to Offic *Ripon* from 92 and *Bradf* 93-99. *10 Tavistock Park, Leeds LS12 4DD* Tel 0113-263 0311

COMBER, Keith Charles. b 15. Wycliffe Hall Ox 71. **d** 73 **p** 74. C Walmley *Birm* 73-76; V Barston 76-79; rtd 80; Perm to Offic *Ely* and *Nor* 80-86; Lic to Offic *Chich* 86-88; Perm to Offic *Chich* from 88. *The Derwent Hotel, 38 Sedlescombe Road South, St Leonards-on-Sea TN38 0TB* Tel (01424) 720334

COMBER, Michael. b 35. Carl Dioc Tr Inst. **d** 72 **p** 72. CA 59-72; C Carl H Trin and St Barn *Carl* 72-73; C Upperby St Jo 73-76; V Dearham 76-81; V Harraby 81-84; R Orton and Tebay w Ravenstonedale etc 84-90; I Clonfert Gp *L & K* 90-94; I Convoy w Monellan and Donaghmore *D & R* 94-97; I Tamlaght O'Crilly Upper w Lower 97-02; rtd 02; Perm to Offic *Carl* from 03. *87 Pinecroft, Kingstown, Carlisle CA3 0DB* Tel (01228) 401428 Mobile 07742-392124 E-mail m.comber@talk21.com

COMBES, The Ven Roger Matthew. b 47. K Coll Lon LLB69. Ridley Hall Cam 72. **d** 74 **p** 75. C Onslow Square St Paul *Lon* 74-77; C Brompton H Trin 76-77; C Cambridge H Sepulchre w All SS *Ely* 77-86; R Silverhill St Matt *Chich* 86-03; RD Hastings 98-02; Adn Horsham from 03. *3 Danehurst Crescent, Horsham RH13 5HS* Tel (01403) 262710 Fax 210778 E-mail archhorsham@diochi.org.uk *or* combes@fish.co.uk

COMER, Michael John. b 30. St Mich Coll Llan 79. **d** 81 **p** 82. C Bistre *St As* 81-84; R Llanfyllin and Bwlchycibau 84-91; C Hattersley *Ches* 91; V 91-94; rtd 94. *134 Sycamore Drive, Newtown SY16 2QE* Tel (01686) 624557

COMERFORD, Patrick. b 52. Pontifical Univ Maynooth BD87 FRSAI87. CITC 99. **d** 00 **p** 01. NSM Dublin Whitechurch *D & G* from 00. *75 Glenvara Park, Knocklyon, Dublin 16, Irish Republic* Tel (00353) (1) 495 0934 Mobile 87-663 5116 E-mail theology@ireland.com

COMERFORD, Mrs Suzanne Lyn. b 46. St Alb and Ox Min Course 97. **d** 00 **p** 01. OLM Woodley *Ox* from 00. *35 Southlake Crescent, Woodley, Reading RG5 3QJ* Tel 0118-376 9646 E-mail minister@emmanuel-woodley.org

COMFORT, Alan. b 64. Ridley Hall Cam CTM94. **d** 94 **p** 95. C Chadwell Heath *Chelmsf* 94-97; C Buckhurst Hill 97-98; TV 98-03; R Loughton St Mary from 03. *The Rectory, 203 High Road, Loughton IG10 1BB* Tel (020) 8508 7892 E-mail alan@comfort11.freeserve.co.uk

COMLEY, Thomas Hedges. b 36. Leeds Univ BA62. Coll of Resurr Mirfield 62. **d** 64 **p** 65. C Leadgate *Dur* 64-67; C Shirley *Birm* 67-71; V Smethwick St Alb 71-76; Perm to Offic 76-82; V N Wembley St Cuth *Lon* 82-92; V Taddington, Chelmorton and Flagg, and Monyash *Derby* 92-01; rtd 01; Perm to Offic *Derby* from 01. *19 Wentworth Avenue, Walton, Chesterfield S40 3JB* Tel (01246) 270911 E-mail tom_comley@lineone.net

COMMANDER, Reginald Arthur. b 20. RGN Aston Univ DHSA BA. Qu Coll Birm 75. **d** 78 **p** 79. NSM Wolverhampton *Lich* 78-92; Perm to Offic from 92; Perm to Offic *Heref* from 95. *15 Coulter Grove, Perton, Wolverhampton WV6 7UA* Tel (01902) 744276

COMMIN, Robert William. b 47. Cape Town Univ BA79. St Paul's Coll Grahamstown. **d** 70 **p** 71. S Africa 70-80 and from 89; Chapl Loretto Sch Musselburgh 80-84; TV Thetford *Nor* 84-89. *42 Earl Street, Woodstock, 7925 South Africa* Tel (0027) 82-202 5303 (mobile) E-mail bcommin@netactive.co.za

COMPTON, Barry Charles Chittenden. b 33. Linc Th Coll 60. **d** 62 **p** 63. C Beddington *S'wark* 62-65; C Limpsfield and Titsey 66-68; Hon C 71-94; R Ridley *Roch* 69-70; R Ash 69-70; Perm to Offic *S'wark* from 70; rtd 94. *14 Hallsland Way, Oxted RH8 9AL* Tel (01883) 714896 Fax 722842

COMPTON, Penelope. b 55. Bulmershe Coll of HE BEd87. NTMTC 98. **d** 01 **p** 02. C Northolt Park St Barn *Lon* 01-04; TV Hucknall Torkard *S'well* from 04. *The Parsonage, 1 Nottingham Road, Hucknall, Nottingham NG15 7QN* Tel 0115-963 3490 E-mail pgcompton@aol.com

COMYNS, Clifford John. b 28. TCD BA50 HDipEd53 MA53 BD67. **d** 51 **p** 52. C Chapelizod *D & G* 51-55; CF 55-75; Asst Master Eastbourne Coll from 75; Asst Chapl from 85; Perm to Offic *Chich* from 75. *Eastbourne College, Old Wish Road, Eastbourne BN21 4JY* Tel (01323) 737411

CONALTY, Julie Anne. b 63. SEITE. **d** 99 **p** 00. NSM E Wickham *S'wark* 99-04; Hon C Charlton from 04. *12 Littleheath, London SE7 8HU* Tel (020) 8855 6203 *or* 7740 8500

CONANT, Fane Charles. b 44. Oak Hill Th Coll 83. **d** 85 **p** 86. C Hoole *Ches* 85-89; V Kelsall 89-01; P-in-c Seer Green and Jordans *Ox* from 01. *The Vicarage, 43 Long Grove, Seer Green, Beaconsfield HP9 2YN* Tel (01494) 675013 E-mail fanesue@aol.com

CONAWAY, Barry Raymond. b 41. CertEd69 Nottm Univ BEd70. Sarum & Wells Th Coll 86. **d** 88 **p** 89. C Ross w Brampton Abbotts, Bridstow and Peterstow *Heref* 88-91; R Bishop's Frome w Castle Frome and Fromes Hill 91-96; P-in-c Acton Beauchamp and Evesbatch 91-96; P-in-c Charminster and Stinsford *Sarum* 96-01; rtd 01; Perm to Offic *Glouc* 01-02 and *Sarum* from 03. *9 Constable Way, West Harnham, Salisbury SP2 8LN* Tel (01722) 334870

CONDELL, Canon Joseph Alfred Ambrose. b 48. CITC 70. **d** 73 **p** 74. C Donaghcloney *D & D* 73-76; I Achonry w Tubbercurry and Killoran *T, K & A* 76-79; I Roscrea w Kyle, Bourney and Corbally *L & K* from 79; Can Killaloe Cathl 83-89; Prec Limerick and Killaloe Cathls from 89; Dioc Sec from 91. *St Conan's Rectory, Roscrea, Co Tipperary, Irish Republic* Tel (00353) (505) 21725 Mobile 87-243 5737 Fax (505) 21993 E-mail secretary@limerick.anglican.org *or* condell@iol.ie

CONDER, Paul Collingwood Nelson. b 33. St Jo Coll Cam BA56 MA60. Ridley Hall Cam 56. **d** 58 **p** 59. C Grassendale *Liv* 58-61; Tutor St Jo Coll Dur 61-67; R Sutton *Liv* 67-74; TR 74-75; V Thames Ditton *Guildf* 75-86; RD Emly 82-86; V Blundellsands St Mich *Liv* 86-99; rtd 99; Perm to Offic *York* from 00. *112 Strensall Road, Earswick, York YO32 9SJ* Tel (01904) 763071

CONDRY, Canon Edward Francis. b 53. UEA BA74 Ex Coll Ox Dip Soc Anthropology 75 BLitt77 DPhil80 Nottm Univ DipTh81 Open Univ MBA02. Linc Th Coll 80. **d** 82 **p** 83. C Weston Favell *Pet* 82-85; V Bloxham w Milcombe and S Newington *Ox* 85-93; TR Rugby St Andr *Cov* 93-02; Dir Post-Ord Tr *Cant* from 02; Can Res Cant Cathl from 02. *22 The Precincts, Canterbury CT1 2EP* Tel (01227) 865228 E-mail edwardc@canterbury-cathedral.org

CONEY, Christopher Thomas. b 32. Magd Coll Cam BA56 MA60. Cuddesdon Coll 68. **d** 69 **p** 70. C Farnham *Guildf* 69-72; Chapl Pangbourne Coll 72-86; R W Woodhay w Enborne, Hampstead Marshall etc *Ox* 86-90; rtd 97; Lic to Offic *St D* from 02. *Jubilee House, Pen-y-Bryn, Begelly, Kilgetty SA68 0XE* Tel (01834) 814652

CONEY, Joanna Margery. b 39. Culham Coll of Educn CertEd75 Open Univ BA83. Ox Min Course 90. **d** 93 **p** 94. Par Dn Wolvercote w Summertown *Ox* 93-94; C 94-97; OLM Tr Officer (Ox Adnry) 97-00; Dioc Portfolio Officer 00-04; rtd 04; Dioc Adv to Lic Lay Min *Ox* from 02. *4 Rowland Close, Wolvercote, Oxford OX2 8PW* Tel and fax (01865) 556456 E-mail portox@oxford.anglican.org

CONEY, Preb Peter Norman Harvey. b 28. Keble Coll Ox BA51 MA55. Cuddesdon Coll 51. **d** 53 **p** 54. C Northallerton w Deighton and Romanby *York* 53-56; C Wakef Cathl *Wakef* 56-59; V Milverton *B & W* 59-65; Chapl K Coll Taunton 65-70; V Martock *B & W* 70-72; V Martock w Ash 72-92; RD Martock 80-90; Dioc Press Officer 83-88; Preb Wells Cathl 85-92; rtd 93; Perm to Offic *Eur* from 92. *Les Aubépines, Le Causse, 46500 Mayrinhac-Lentour, France* Tel (0033) (5) 65 38 22 19

CONEYS, Stephen John. b 61. Sheff Univ LLB82. St Jo Coll Nottm 87. **d** 90 **p** 91. C Plymouth Em w Efford *Ex* 90-92; C Plymouth Em, Efford and Laira 93-94; TV Whitstable *Cant* 94-02; TR from 02. *The Vicarage, 11 Kimberley Grove, Seasalter, Whitstable CT5 4AY* Tel (01227) 276795 E-mail steve@sconeys.freeserve.co.uk

CONGDON, John Jameson. b 30. St Edm Hall Ox BA53 MA57. Wycliffe Hall Ox 53. **d** 55 **p** 56. C Aspley *S'well* 55-58; C-in-c Woodthorpe CD 58-63; V Woodthorpe 63-69; V Spring Grove St Mary *Lon* 70-84; V Woodley St Jo the Ev *Ox* 84-89; Chapl W Middx Univ Hosp Isleworth 89-95; rtd 95; Perm to Offic *Lon* from 95. *23 Pates Manor Drive, Feltham TW14 8JJ* Tel (020) 8893 1823

CONLEY, James Alan. b 29. Dur Univ BSc51. St Jo Coll Nottm. **d** 87 **p** 88. NSM Cropwell Bishop w Colston Bassett, Granby etc *S'well* 87-97; Perm to Offic *Sarum* from 97. *30 The Waldrons, Thornford, Sherborne DT9 6PX* Tel (01935) 872672

CONLIN, Tiffany Jane Kate. b 71. K Coll Lon BA93 MA94 PhD00 AKC93. Westcott Ho Cam 03. **d** 05. C Wisbech St Aug *Ely* from 05; C Wisbech SS Pet and Paul from 05. *St Peter's Lodge, Love Lane, Wisbech PE13 1HP* E-mail tiffanyjkconlin@yahoo.com

CONLON, Shaun. b 69. Birm Univ BA90. Ripon Coll Cuddesdon DipMin93. **d** 93 **p** 94. C Castle Bromwich SS Mary and Marg *Birm* 93-97; C Hockerill *St Alb* 97-00; V St Mary-at-Latton *Chelmsf* from 00. *St Mary-at-Latton Vicarage, The Gowers, Harlow CM20 2JP* Tel (01279) 424005

CONN, Alistair Aberdein. b 37. Down Coll Cam BA60 MA64. Linc Th Coll 60. **d** 62 **p** 63. C W Hartlepool St Paul *Dur* 62-65; Uganda 65-66; Chapl Shrewsbury Sch 66-73; R Coupar Angus *St And* 73-78; V Ravenshead *S'well* 78-93; RD Newstead 90-93; R Collingham w S Scarle and Besthorpe and Girton 93-02; RD Newark 95-02; rtd 02; Perm to Offic *S'well* from 02. *17 Beacon Heights, Newark NG24 2JS* Tel (01636) 706291

CONNELL, Clare. *See* CONNELL, Mrs Penelope Clare

CONNELL, Frederick Philip Richard John. b 45. St Jo Coll Nottm MA98. **d** 99 **p** 00. Deacon Jos St Piran Nigeria 99-00; V 00-01; NSM Nottingham St Pet and All SS *S'well* 01-03; Perm to Offic 03-04; NSM Nottingham St Nic from 04. *Colston Basset House, Church Gate, Colston Basset, Nottingham NG12 3FE* Tel (01949) 81424 Mobile 07801-140630 Fax (01949) 81118 E-mail frederickconnell@octeam.com

CONNELL, Miss Heather Josephine. b 38. SRN60 SCM61 HVCert69 Open Univ BA93. S'wark Ord Course DipRS79. **dss** 79 **d** 87 **p** 94. Heston *Lon* 79-84; Gillingham St Barn *Roch* 84-90; Par Dn 87-90; Distr Chapl Medway NHS Trust 91-96; NSM Gillingham H Trin *Roch* from 94; rtd 98. *31 Brenchley Road, Gillingham ME8 6HD* Tel (01634) 230289

CONNELL, John Richard. b 63. K Coll Lon BD84. St Mich Coll Llan 92. **d** 94 **p** 96. C Caldicot *Mon* 94-97; C Risca 97-00; V Llantilio Pertholey w Bettws Chpl etc 00-05; P-in-c Wokingham St Paul *Ox* from 05. *St Paul's Rectory, Holt Lane, Wokingham RG41 1ED* Tel 0118-978 0629 E-mail revjoncon@tesco.net

CONNELL, Mrs Penelope Clare. b 44. EMMTC. **d** 03 **p** 04. NSM Whatton w Aslockton, Hawksworth, Scarrington etc *S'well* from 03. *Colston Basset House, Church Gate, Colston Basset, Nottingham NG12 3FE*

CONNELL, Ms Sharon Margaret. b 65. St Jo Coll Nottm BA03. **d** 03 **p** 04. C S Hackney St Jo w Ch Ch *Lon* from 03. *19 Valentine Road, London E9 7AD* Tel (020) 8533 0688 E-mail sharon.connell@virgin.net

CONNER, Mrs Cathryn. b 42. Birm Univ BSc64. NEOC 91. **d** 94 **p** 95. NSM Bainton w N Dalton, Middleton-on-the-Wolds etc *York* 94-98; NSM Woldsburn 98-04; rtd 04. *Centre House, North Dalton, Driffield YO25 9XA* Tel (01377) 217265

CONNER, Charles Borthwick. b 20. Keble Coll Ox BA43 MA49. St Steph Ho Ox 48. **d** 50 **p** 51. C Saltburn-by-the-Sea *York* 50-52; Chapl Ely Th Coll 52-53; CF 53-70; Perm to Offic *Sarum* from 80. *Angel Cottage, West Knighton, Dorchester DT2 8PE* Tel (01305) 852465

✠**CONNER, The Rt Revd David John.** b 47. Ex Coll Ox BA69 MA77. St Steph Ho Ox 69. **d** 71 **p** 72 **c** 94. Asst Chapl St Edw Sch Ox 71-73; Chapl 73-80; Hon C Summertown *Ox* 71-76; TV Wolvercote w Summertown 76-80; Chapl Win Coll 80-87; V Cambridge Gt St Mary w St Mich *Ely* 87-94; RD Cambridge 89-94; Suff Bp Lynn *Nor* 94-98; Dean Windsor and Dom Chapl to The Queen from 98; Bp HM Forces from 01. *The Deanery, Windsor Castle, Windsor SL4 1NJ* Tel (01753) 865561 Fax 819002 E-mail david.conner@stgeorges-windsor.org

CONNING, Dowell Paul. b 64. Ripon Coll Cuddesdon BTh00. **d** 00 **p** 01. C Leckhampton St Pet *Glouc* 00-03; CF from 03. *c/o MOD Chaplains (Army)* Tel (01980) 615804 Fax 615800 E-mail dowell@freenet.co.uk

CONNOLL, Miss Helen Dorothy. b 45. Oak Hill Th Coll BA86. **dss** 86 **d** 87 **p** 94. Leytonstone St Jo *Chelmsf* 86-87; Par Dn 87-90; Asst Chapl Grimsby Distr Gen Hosp 90-93; Chapl Kent and Cant Hosp 93-94; Chapl Kent and Cant Hosps NHS Trust 94-99; Chapl E Kent Hosps NHS Trust 99-01; Hon C Aylesham w Adisham *Cant* from 01; Hon C Nonington w Wymynswold and Goodnestone etc from 01. *The Vicarage, Vicarage Lane, Nonington, Dover CT15 4JT* Tel (01304) 840271 E-mail helen.therev@virgin.net

CONNOLLY, Daniel. b 51. BEng. St Jo Coll Nottm 82. **d** 84 **p** 85. C Bedgrove *Ox* 84-87; C-in-c Crookhorn Ch Cen CD *Portsm* 87-88; V Crookhorn 88-97; R Sutton Coldfield H Trin *Birm* 97-98; V Reigate St Mary *S'wark* 98-05; RD Reigate 03-05; P-in-c Kenilworth St Jo *Cov* from 05. *St John's Vicarage, Clarke's Avenue, Kenilworth CV8 1HX* Tel (01926) 779297 *or* 853203 E-mail dan@famcon.co.uk

CONNOLLY, Miss Lynne. b 53. Aston Tr Scheme 88 Linc Th Coll 92. **d** 92 **p** 94. Par Dn Hurst *Man* 92-94; C 94-96; R Burnage St Nic 96-02; V Spotland from 02. *10 Little Flatt, Rochdale OL12 7AU* Tel (01706) 648972

CONNOLLY, Canon Sydney Herbert. b 40. Leeds Univ BA66. Coll of Resurr Mirfield 66. **d** 68 **p** 69. C W Derby St Mary *Liv* 68-71; C Prescot 71-74; V Burtonwood 74-80; V Walker *Newc* 80-89; TR Whorlton 89-96; V Chapel House 96-99; TR N Shields from 99; Hon Can Newc Cathl from 04. *Christ Church Vicarage, 26 Cleveland Road, North Shields NE29 0NG* Tel 0191-257 1721 E-mail sydandpat@blueyonder.co.uk

CONNOR, Ellis Jones. b 16. Univ of Wales BA38. St Mich Coll Llan 38. **d** 39 **p** 41. C Broughton *St As* 39-43; C Llandegfan and Beaumaris *Ban* 43-48; V Liv St Chris Norris Green *Liv* 48-55; R Desford *Leic* 55-73; R N Hill *Truro* 73-75; V Lewannick 73-75; R Llanddewi Skirrid w Llanvetherine etc *Mon* 75-78; C Spalding St Jo *Linc* 79-82; rtd 82; Perm to Offic *Leic* from 82. *35 Sycamore Street, Blaby, Leicester LE8 4FL* Tel 0116-277 7725

CONNOR, Geoffrey. b 46. K Coll Lon BD73 AKC73. St Aug Coll Cant. **d** 74 **p** 75. C Cockerton *Dur* 74-79; Dioc Recruitment Officer 79-87; Chapl St Chad's Coll 84-87; R Edin St Mary and Vice-Provost St Mary's Cathl *Edin* 87-90; Dioc Dir of Ords *Edin* and *Arg* 87-90; V Whitechapel w Admarsh-in-Bleasdale *Blackb* 90-00; Dir of Ords 90-00; TR Epping Distr *Chelmsf* from 00; RD Epping Forest from 04. *The Rectory, Hartland Road, Epping CM16 4PD* Tel and fax (01992) 572906 E-mail geoffrey_connor@priest.com

CONNOR, Patrick Francis Latham. b 25. Ex Coll Ox BA47 MA52. Gen Th Sem (NY) STB53. **d** 53 **p** 53. USA 53-55 and 59-62; R N Tamerton *Truro* 55-59; R St Ive 62-64; R Sparkford w Weston Bampfylde *B & W* 64-85; P-in-c Sutton Montis 70-85; R Mawnan *Truro* 85-89; rtd 89; Perm to Offic *Truro* from 89. *Trelatham, Boyton, Launceston PL15 9RJ* Tel (01566) 776078

CONNOR, Archdeacon of. *See* McBRIDE, The Ven Stephen Richard

CONNOR, Bishop of. *See* HARPER, The Rt Revd Alan Edwin Thomas

CONNOR, Dean of. *See* BOND, The Very Revd John Frederick Augustus

CONRAD, Paul Derick. b 54. Worc Coll Ox BA76 MA82. St Steph Ho Ox 78. **d** 80 **p** 81. C Wanstead St Mary *Chelmsf* 80-83; C Somers Town *Lon* 83-85; P-in-c Kentish Town St Martin w St Andr 85-91; V 91-95; P-in-c Hampstead Ch Ch 95-97; V from 97; Chapl R Free Hampstead NHS Trust from 95. *Christ Church Vicarage, 10 Cannon Place, London NW3 1EJ* Tel and fax (020) 7435 6784

CONSTABLE, Douglas Brian. b 40. Lon Univ BA62. Linc Th Coll 63. **d** 65 **p** 66. C Stockwood CD *Bris* 65-70; Asst Chapl Bris Univ 70-72; Hon C Clifton St Paul 70-72; Chapl Lee Abbey 72-77; V Derby St Thos *Derby* 77-85; TV Southampton (City Cen) *Win* 85-92; rtd 92; Perm to Offic *Win* 92-05. *Y Bwthyn, 9 Church Street, Llandeilo SA19 6BH* Tel (01558) 823518 E-mail cdouglas@fish.co.uk

CONSTABLE, Mrs Sharon Joanne. b 57. STETS 95. **d** 98 **p** 99. NSM Hutton *B & W* 98-01; Bp's Officer for NSMs 01-04; C E Clevedon w Clapton in Gordano etc 01-04; Hong Kong from 04. *Address temp unknown* E-mail sharon.constable@ntlworld.com

CONSTABLE, Mrs Sybil Margaret. b 43. **d** 00 **p** 01. NSM Montgomery and Forden and Llandyssil *St As* 00-04; P-in-c Slindon, Eartham and Madehurst *Chich* from 04. *The Rectory, Dyers Lane, Slindon, Arundel BN18 0RE* Tel (01243) 814275

CONSTANTINE, Miss Elaine Muriel. b 50. Univ of Wales (Swansea) BSc72 CertEd73 DipEd75 Lon Univ MEd78. St Alb Minl Tr Scheme. **dss** 86 **d** 87 **p** 94. Bedford St Martin *St Alb* 86-88; Par Dn 87-88; Par Dn Leighton Buzzard w Eggington, Hockliffe etc 88-94; C 94-98; TV Dunstable 98-04; P-in-c Earlham St Eliz *Nor* from 04. *St Elizabeth's Vicarage, 75 Cadge Road, Norwich NR5 8DG* Tel (01603) 250764 E-mail revd.elaine@virgin.net

CONSTANTINE, Leonard. b 30. AKC57. **d** 58 **p** 59. C W Hartlepool St Aid *Dur* 58-61; C Sheff St Geo and St Steph *Sheff* 61-62; Nyasaland 62-64; Malawi 64-69; V W Pelton *Dur* 69-73; V Shotton 73-78; V Stillington 78-80; V Grindon and Stillington 80-82; V Corbridge w Halton and Newton Hall *Newc* 82-95; Chapl Charlotte Straker Hosp 82-95; rtd 95; Perm to Offic *Wakef* from 95. *28 Tenterfield Road, Ossett WF5 0RU* Tel (01924) 276180

CONVERY, Canon Arthur Malcolm. b 42. Sheff Univ BSc63 DipEd64. N Ord Course 79. **d** 82 **p** 83. NSM Parr *Liv* 82-87; V Marown *S & M* 87-04; V Onchan from 04; Can St German's Cathl from 99. *The Vicarage, Church Road, Onchan, Isle of Man IM3 1BF* Tel (01624) 675797

CONWAY, Alfred Sydney. b 22. Kelham Th Coll 40. **d** 45 **p** 46. C Fulham St Oswald w St Aug *Lon* 45-49; V Allenton and Shelton Lock *Derby* 49-55; P-in-c Chaddesden St Phil 55-63; V Croxley Green All SS *St Alb* 63-81; V Walton St Jo *Liv* 81-89; rtd 89; Perm to Offic *Ex* from 89. *58 Millhead Road, Honiton EX14 1RA* Tel (01404) 46052

CONWAY, Canon Glyn Haydn. b 38. St Mich Coll Llan DipTh65. **d** 65 **p** 66. C Wrexham *St As* 65-71; TV 71-77; V Holywell 77-83; V Upton Ascension *Ches* from 83; Hon Can Accra from 03. *The Vicarage, Demage Lane, Chester CH2 1EL* Tel (01244) 383518

CONWAY, John Arthur. b 67. Leeds Univ BEng90 Edin Univ BD97. Linc Th Coll 94 TISEC 95. **d** 97 **p** 98. C Edin St Mary *Edin* 97-01; R Edin St Martin from 01; Chapl Edin Sick Children's NHS Trust 98-01. *15 Ardmillan Terrace, Edinburgh EH11 2JW* Tel 0131-337 5471 E-mail jconway@fish.co.uk

CONWAY, Philip James. b 66. Liv Inst of Educn BA91. St Steph Ho Ox DipMin95. **d** 95 **p** 96. C High Harrogate Ch Ch *Ripon* 95-99; P-in-c Menheniot *Truro* from 99; C St Ive and Pensilva w Quethiock from 02. *The Vicarage, Menheniot, Liskeard PL14 3SU* Tel (01579) 342195
E-mail fatherphilip@menheniotvicarage.fsnet.co.uk

CONWAY, Mrs Sandra Coralie. b 45. Bris Univ BA66. S'wark Ord Course DipRS92. **d** 92 **p** 00. NSM Kenley *S'wark* from 92. *28 Russell Hill, Purley CR8 2JA* Tel (020) 8668 2890

CONWAY, The Ven Stephen David. b 57. Keble Coll Ox BA80 MA84 CertEd81 Selw Coll Cam BA85. Westcott Ho Cam 83. **d** 86 **p** 87. C Heworth St Mary *Dur* 86-89; C Bishopwearmouth St Mich w St Hilda 89-90; Hon C Dur St Marg 90-94; Dir of Ords 90-94; P-in-c Cockerton 94-96; V 96-98; Bp's Sen Chapl 98-02; Communications Officer 98-02; Adn Dur and Can Res Dur Cathl from 02. *15 The College, Durham DH1 3EQ* Tel 0191-384 7534
E-mail archdeacon.of.durham@durham.anglican.org

CONWAY, Thomas Robertson. b 36. DipTh. **d** 86 **p** 87. C Bangor Abbey *D & D* 86-95; I Dungiven w Bovevagh *D & R* 89-95; I Carrowdore w Millisle *D & D* 95-00; rtd 00. *6 Rosstulla Drive, Newtownabbey BT37 0QJ* Tel (028) 9086 0523

CONWAY-LEE, Stanley. b 17. Linc Th Coll 68. **d** 70 **p** 71. C Dedham *Chelmsf* 70-72; C Lt Ilford St Mich 72-74; V Tollesbury 74-75; V Tollesbury w Salcot Virley 75-79; V Bocking St Pet 79-85; rtd 85; Perm to Offic *Chelmsf* from 85. *10 Northumberland Close, Braintree CM7 9NL* Tel and fax (01376) 550117

COOGAN, The Ven Robert Arthur William. b 29. Univ of Tasmania BA51. Cranmer Hall Dur. **d** 53 **p** 54. C Plaistow St Andr *Chelmsf* 53-56; Australia 56-62; V N Woolwich *Chelmsf* 62-73; P-in-c W Silvertown St Barn 62-73; V Hampstead St Steph *Lon* 73-77; P-in-c N St Pancras All Hallows 74-77; RD S Camden 75-81; P-in-c Old St Pancras w Bedford New Town St Matt 76-80; V Hampstead St Steph w All Hallows 77-85; P-in-c Kentish Town St Martin w St Andr 78-81; AD N Camden 78-83; Preb St Paul's Cathl 82-85; Adn Hampstead 85-94; rtd 94; Perm to Offic *Chich* 94-00 and *St E* from 03. *Salters Hall West, Stour Street, Sudbury CO10 2AX* Tel (01787) 370026

COOK, Alan. b 27. St Deiniol's Hawarden 79. **d** 80 **p** 81. Hon C Gatley *Ches* 80-83; Chapl Man R Eye Hosp 83-86; Chapl Asst Man R Infirmary 80-83 and 86-88; V Congleton St Jas *Ches* 89-93; rtd 93; Perm to Offic *Ches* from 93. *15 Buttermere Road, Gatley, Cheadle SK8 4RQ* Tel 0161-428 4350

COOK, Canon Brian Edwin. b 36. Sarum & Wells Th Coll 78. **d** 80 **p** 81. C E Wickham *S'wark* 80-83; C Petersfield w Sheet *Portsm* 83-86; R Liss 86-01; RD Petersfield 91-96 and 99; Hon Can Portsm Cathl 96-01; rtd 01; Perm to Offic *Chich* from 01. *Daubeney Cottage, Bersted Street, South Bersted, Bognor Regis PO22 9QE* Tel (01243) 828379 E-mail daubeney@tesco.net

COOK, Brian Robert. b 43. Chich Th Coll 83. **d** 85 **p** 86. C Whyke w Rumboldswhyke and Portfield *Chich* 85-87; C Worth 87-90; TV 90-94; P-in-c Chidham 94-99; V 99-04; RD Westbourne 99-04; P-in-c E Blatchington from 04. *The Rectory, 86 Belgrave Road, Seaford BN25 2HE* Tel (01323) 892964

COOK, Canon Charles Peter. b 32. St Jo Coll Dur BA54. Cranmer Hall Dur. **d** 58 **p** 59. C Kingston upon Hull H Trin *York* 58-64; V High Elswick St Paul *Newc* 64-74; V Cheadle Hulme St Andr *Ches* 74-98; Hon Can Ches Cathl 91-98; rtd 98; Perm to Offic *Newc* 00-05 and *Carl* from 01. *4 Moseley Grange, Cheadle Hulme, Cheadle SK8 5EZ* Tel 0161-485 1702

COOK, Christopher. *See* COOK, James Christopher Donald

COOK, Christopher. b 44. Qu Coll Birm 68. **d** 69 **p** 70. C Gt Ilford St Mary *Chelmsf* 69-72; C Corringham 72-77; R E Donyland 77-84; R Pentlow, Foxearth, Liston and Borley 84-88; Chapl RAD Essex Area 88-89; rtd 89; Perm to Offic *Chelmsf* from 89. *Oak Mill, Field View Drive, Little Totham, Maldon CM9 8ND* Tel (01621) 893280

COOK, Canon Christopher Arthur. Edin Th Coll 53. **d** 56 **p** 58. C Motherwell *Glas* 56-59; S Africa 59-64 and from 70; Clydesdale Miss 59-60; Matatiele St Steph 60-61; Idutywa St Barn 61-64; Area Sec USPG *Wakef* and *Sheff* 65-70; R Grahamstown St Matt Miss 70-95; Adn Grahamstown 80-95; Hon Can Grahamstown from 96; rtd 96. *PO Box 7641, East London, 5200 South Africa* Tel (0027) (431) 385357

COOK, Christopher Charles Holland. b 56. K Coll Lon BSc77 MB, BS81 MD95 MRCPsych87. SEITE 97. **d** 00 **p** 01. Prof Psychiatry Alcohol Misuse Kent Inst of Medicine and Health Science 97-03; NSM Otham w Langley *Cant* 00-03; Chapl and Prof Fell St Chad's Coll Dur from 03. *Department of Theology and Religion, Abbey House, Palace Green, Durham DH1 3RS* Tel 0191-334 3362 E-mail c.c.h.cook@durham.ac.uk

COOK, David. b 46. Hertf Coll Ox BA MA72. Wycliffe Hall Ox 69. **d** 73 **p** 74. C Hartlepool All SS Stranton *Dur* 74-75; Lect Qu Coll Birm 75-81; Chapl Cranbrook Sch Kent from 81. *33 Oatfield Drive, Cranbrook TN17 3LA* Tel (01580) 713310

COOK, David Arthur. b 50. St Jo Coll Dur BA74. St Steph Ho Ox 86. **d** 88 **p** 89. C S Bank *York* 88-91; C Up Hatherley *Glouc* 91-93; P-in-c Cumbernauld *Glas* 93-04; P-in-c Helensburgh from 04. *The Rectory, 16 William Street, Helensburgh G84 8BD* Tel (01436) 672500

COOK, Canon David Charles Murray. b 41. MA. Wycliffe Hall Ox 65. **d** 67 **p** 68. C Chatham St Phil and St Jas *Roch* 67-71; S Africa 71-89; TR Newbury *Ox* 89-02; RD Newbury 98-02; Hon Can Ch Ch 02; P-in-c Chipping Campden w Ebrington *Glouc* from 02. *The Vicarage, Church Street, Chipping Campden GL55 6JG* Tel (01386) 840671

COOK, David Smith. b 47. Hull Univ BTh88 MA93. Lich Th Coll 68. **d** 71 **p** 72. C Tudhoe Grange *Dur* 71-75; C Bishopwearmouth St Mary V w St Pet CD 75-77; V Copley *Wakef* 77-80; V Birstall 80-83; V Holme upon Spalding Moor *York* 83-98; R Holme and Seaton Ross Gp 98-01; RD S Wold 96-01; V Copmanthorpe from 01; P-in-c Askham Bryan from 01; Chapl Askham Bryan Coll 01-04. *The Vicarage, 17 Sutor Close, Copmanthorpe, York YO23 3TX* Tel (01904) 778701
E-mail revcook@btinternet.com

COOK, Canon Edward Rouse. b 28. Linc Coll Ox BA51 MA55. Linc Th Coll 51. **d** 53 **p** 54. C Louth w Welton-le-Wold *Linc* 53-56; C Crosby 56-57; Lect Boston 58-60; R Lt Coates 60-67; V Saxilby 67-90; R Broxholme 69-90; P-in-c Burton by Linc 78-94; Can and Preb Linc Cathl 79-03; Chmn Dioc Readers 86-94; RD Corringham 87-93; R Saxilby w Ingleby and Broxholme 90-94; rtd 94; Perm to Offic *Linc* 94-97. *80 Lincoln Road, Dunholme, Lincoln LN2 3QY* Tel (01673) 861534

COOK, Elspeth Jean. b 34. Edin Univ BSc56 PhD66. S Dios Minl Tr Scheme 85. **d** 88 **p** 94. C Yateley *Win* 88-91; Assoc Chapl Ld Mayor Treloar Hosp Alton 91-93; NSM Dunfermline *St And* 93-99; P-in-c Aberdour 96-01; rtd 01. *12 River View, Dalgety Bay, Dunfermline KY11 9YE* Tel (01383) 825222
E-mail tacook@surfaid.org

COOK, Geoffrey John Anderson. b 64. St Steph Ho Ox. **d** 97 **p** 98. C St Leonards Ch Ch and St Mary *Chich* 97-99; Hon Asst P Brighton St Mich 00-02; Hon C Southwick St Mich 02-03; Asst Chapl Univ Coll Lon Hosps NHS Foundn Trust 03-05; Chapl W Herts Hosps NHS Trust from 05. *Hemel Hempstead General Hospital, Hillfield Road, Hemel Hempstead HP2 4AD* Tel (01442) 287600 E-mail geofrey.cook@whht.nhs.uk

COOK, Helen. b 50. New Coll Edin BD74 Glas Univ MA92. **d** 96. C Rothiemurchus *Mor* from 96. *Address temp unknown*
E-mail helen.cook@highland.gov.uk

COOK, Ian Bell. b 38. NW Ord Course 70. **d** 73 **p** 74. C Oldham St Paul *Man* 73-75; Ind Chapl 76-79; P-in-c Newton Heath St Wilfrid and St Anne 76-79; V Middleton Junction from 79. *The Vicarage, Greenhill Road, Middleton Junction, Manchester M24 2BD* Tel 0161-643 5064

COOK, Preb Ian Brian. b 38. MBIM73 Aston Univ MSc72 Birm Univ MA76. Kelham Th Coll 58. **d** 63 **p** 64. C Langley Marish *Ox* 63-66; C Stokenchurch and Cadmore End 66-68; V Lane End 68-72; P-in-c Ibstone w Fingest 68-72; Tutor W Bromwich Coll of Comm and Tech 72-74; Sen Tutor 74-80; NSM W Bromwich St Pet *Lich* 77-80; R Wednesbury St Jas and St Jo 80-03; Dir St Jas Tr Inst 81-03; RD Wednesbury 88-03; Preb Lich Cathl from 94; rtd 03; Perm to Offic *Lich* from 03. *4 Orams Lane, Brewood, Stafford ST19 9EA* Tel (01902) 850960

COOK, James Christopher Donald. b 49. Ch Ch Ox BA70 MA74. St Steph Ho Ox 79. **d** 80 **p** 81. C Witney *Ox* 80-83; CF 83-04; P-in-c Toxteth Park St Agnes and St Pancras *Liv* from 04. *St Agnes's Presbytery, 1 Buckingham Avenue, Liverpool L17 3BA* Tel 0151-733 1742 E-mail leoclericus@aol.com

COOK, Jean. *See* COOK, Elspeth Jean

COOK, Mrs Joan Lindsay. b 46. SRN70. St Jo Coll Dur 86. **d** 88 **p** 94. Par Dn Hartlepool St Hilda *Dur* 88-93; Dn-in-c 93-94; P-in-c 94-96; rtd 96. *10 Peakston Close, Hartlepool TS26 0PN* Tel (01429) 231778

COOK, John. b 32. Linc Th Coll 87. **d** 89 **p** 90. C Bourne *Linc* 89-92; R Colsterworth Gp 92-02; rtd 02. *24 Portrush Drive, Grantham NG31 9GD* Tel (01476) 569063

COOK, John Edward. b 35. AKC61. **d** 62 **p** 63. C York Town St Mich *Guildf* 62-67; Singapore 67-77; P-in-c Beoley *Worc* 78-83; V 83-89; V Bromsgrove All SS 89-01; rtd 01; Perm to Offic *Cov* from 02. *61 Newport Drive, Alcester B49 5BJ* Tel (01789) 762553 Fax 400040 E-mail johnedwardcook@aol.com

COOK, John Henry. b 11. Mert Coll Ox BA34 BSc35 MA39 MSc81. Clifton Th Coll 36. **d** 38 **p** 39. C Gt Faringdon w Lt Coxwell *Ox* 38-42; C Newbury St Nic 42-45; V Winkfield 45-52; V Furze Platt 52-68; R Witney 68-78; rtd 79; Hon C Witney *Ox* from 79. *9 Church View Road, Witney OX28 5HT* Tel (01993) 704609

COOK, John Michael. b 48. Coll of Resurr Mirfield 72. **d** 74 **p** 75. C Weymouth H Trin *Sarum* 74-76; C Felixstowe St Jo *St E*

76-79; P-in-c Gt and Lt Whelnetham 79-84; P-in-c Cockfield 84-85; P-in-c Bradfield St George w Bradfield St Clare etc 84-85; R Cockfield w Bradfield St Clare, Felsham etc 85-87; V Workington St Jo *Carl* from 87. *St John's Vicarage, 59 Thorncroft Gardens, Workington CA14 4DP* Tel (01900) 602383

COOK, John Richard Millward. b 61. St Jo Coll Dur BA. Wycliffe Hall Ox 83. **d** 85 **p** 86. C Brampton St Thos *Derby* 85-89; C Farnborough *Guildf* 89-92; C Langham Place All So *Lon* 92-98; V Chelsea St Jo w St Andr from 98. *The Vicarage, 43 Park Walk, London SW10 0AU* Tel (020) 7352 1675 Fax as telephone E-mail johnrmcook@ukgateway.net

COOK, Kenneth George Thomas. b 36. ACA59 AHA69 FCA70. Coll of Resurr Mirfield 86. **d** 88 **p** 89. C Stocking Farm *Leic* 88-91; Chapl Leics Hospice 91-96; Chapl Hinchingbrooke Health Care NHS Trust 96-01; rtd 01; Perm to Offic *Ely* from 01. *1 Peregrine Close, Hartford, Huntingdon PE29 1UZ* Tel (01480) 451790

COOK, Kenneth Hugh. b 30. ALAM. AKC55. **d** 56 **p** 57. C Netherfield *S'well* 56-59; C Newark w Coddington 59-61; V Basford St Aid 61-67; V Gargrave *Bradf* 67-77; Dir of Ords 77-89; Can Res Bradf Cathl 77-95; rtd 95; Perm to Offic *Ripon* from 95. *25 Hollins Close, Hampsthwaite, Harrogate HG3 2EH* Tel (01423) 772521

COOK, Kenneth Robert. b 42. Huddersfield Poly BA86. Chich Th Coll 66. **d** 68 **p** 69. C Upton *Ox* 68-72; C Duston *Pet* 72-76; V Halifax St Hilda *Wakef* 76-79; Chapl Huddersfield Poly 79-90; V Linc St Mary-le-Wigford w St Benedict etc *Linc* 90-02; P-in-c Skirbeck Quarter 02-03; rtd 03; Perm to Offic *Linc* from 03. *25 Western Crescent, Lincoln LN6 7TD*

COOK (née McCLEAN), Mrs Lydia Margaret Sheelagh. b 72. Ball Coll Ox BA94 MA98. Cuddesdon Coll 94. **d** 96 **p** 97. C Brackley St Pet w St Jas *Pet* 96-99; NSM Wallingford *Ox* 99-01; Chapl Cranford Ho Sch Ox 99-01; NSM Wallingford Deanery 01-04; NSM Sandford-on-Thames *Ox* from 04. *Chestnut Cottage, The Street, Brightwell-cum-Sotwell, Wallingford OX10 0RR* Tel (01491) 833242 E-mail revrock@brightwell99.freeserve.co.uk

COOK, Marcus John Wyeth. b 41. Chich Th Coll 67. **d** 70 **p** 71. C Friern Barnet St Jas *Lon* 70-73; Hon C St Geo-in-the-East w St Paul 73-00; Perm to Offic 73-00. *St George-in-the-East Church, Cannon Street Road, London E1 0BH* Tel (020) 7481 1345

COOK, Mrs Myrtle Bridget Weigela. b 47. BA LLM. EMMTC. **d** 04 **p** 05. NSM Kibworth and Smeeton Westerby and Saddington *Leic* from 04. *1 Highcroft, Husbands Bosworth, Lutterworth LE17 6LF* Tel (01858) 880935 E-mail mchighcroft@aol.com

COOK, Nicholas Leonard. b 59. Nottm Univ BCombStuds84. Linc Th Coll 81. **d** 84 **p** 85. C Leic St Pet *Leic* 84-85; C Knighton St Mich 85-86; Chapl Asst Towers Hosp Humberstone 86-89; Chapl Leics Mental Health Service Unit 89-91; Chapl Quainton Hall Sch Harrow 91-94; CF(V) 88-94; CF from 94. *c/o MOD Chaplains (Army)* Tel (01980) 615804 Fax 615800

COOK, Paul Raymond. *See* McLAREN-COOK, Paul Raymond

COOK, Peter John. b 57. Ridley Hall Cam CTM95. **d** 95 **p** 96. C Romford Gd Shep Collier Row *Chelmsf* 95-98; C Colchester St Jo from 98. *3 Northfield Gardens, Highwoods, Colchester CO4 4TL* Tel (01206) 532550 E-mail peter_cook@ntlworld.com

COOK, Peter John Arthur. b 42. Reading Univ BA64 Brandeis Univ (USA) MA65 QUB PhD81. Tyndale Hall Bris 68. **d** 71 **p** 72. C Everton St Chrys *Liv* 71-74; Chapl Stranmillis Coll of Educn Belf 74-87; Hon C Belfast All SS *Conn* 81-87; USA from 87. *123 West Sale Road, Lake Charles, LA 70605, USA*

COOK, Richard John Noel. b 49. Univ Coll Ox BA70 MA74 PGCE72. Wycliffe Hall Ox MA77. **d** 78 **p** 79. C Fulwood *Sheff* 78-80; C Bolton St Paul w Em *Man* 81-86; TV 86-93; V Goldsworth Park *Guildf* from 93; RD Woking 99-03. *St Andrew's Vicarage, 8 Cardingham, Woking GU21 3LN* Tel (01483) 764523 E-mail cookingwok@tiscali.co.uk

COOK, Canon Robert Bond. b 28. Dur Univ BSc54. Ripon Hall Ox 54. **d** 56 **p** 57. C Benwell St Jas *Newc* 56-60; C Sugley 60-64; V Denton 64-75; V Haltwhistle 75-88; P-in-c Greenhead 84-88; V Haltwhistle and Greenhead 88-93; RD Hexham 88-93; Hon Can Newc Cathl 92-93; rtd 93; Perm to Offic *St E* from 94; RD Lavenham 03-05. *Ashcroft, Heath Road, Woolpit, Bury St Edmunds IP30 9RN* Tel (01359) 240670

COOK, Ronald Thomas. b 50. St Steph Ho Ox BA79 MA83. **d** 80 **p** 81. C Willesden St Andr *Lon* 80-83; USA 83-87; C Northolt Park St Barn *Lon* 87-90; Chapl HM Pris Blundeston 90-96; V Kettering All SS *Pet* from 96; RD Kettering from 02. *All Saints' Vicarage, 80 Pollard Street, Kettering NN16 9RP* Tel (01536) 513376 E-mail ronaldcook@btinternet.com

COOK, Stephen. b 62. Brunel Univ BSc(Econ)84 Birkbeck Coll Lon DipRS92. S'wark Ord Course 89. **d** 92 **p** 93. Hon C Forest Hill St Aug *S'wark* 92-98; P-in-c Eltham St Barn from 98; CF (TA) from 00. *St Barnabas' Vicarage, 449 Rochester Way, London SE9 6PH* Tel (020) 8856 8294 E-mail cooksca@aol.com

COOK, Stephen William. b 57. BA DipHE Lambeth STh87. Trin Coll Bris. **d** 85 **p** 86. C Heref St Pet w St Owen and St Jas *Heref* 85-89; TV Keynsham *B & W* 89-95; V Hanham *Bris* 95-02; RD Bitton 98-99; AD Kingswood and S Glos 99-02; TR Okehampton w Inwardleigh, Bratton Clovelly etc *Ex* from 02. *The Vicarage, 1 Church Path, Okehampton EX20 1LW* Tel (01837) 659297

COOK, Timothy John. b 62. Cranmer Hall Dur 95. **d** 95 **p** 96. C Dorchester *Sarum* 95-99; TV Ilminster and Distr *B & W* 99-03; R Yeovil H Trin w Barwick from 03. *Holy Trinity Vicarage, 24 Turners Barn Lane, Yeovil BA20 2LM* Tel (01935) 423774 E-mail timcook@tesco.net

COOK, Trevor Vivian. b 43. Sarum Th Coll 67. **d** 69 **p** 70. C Lambeth St Phil *S'wark* 69-73; C St Buryan, St Levan and Sennen *Truro* 73-75; V The Ilketshalls *St E* 75-79; P-in-c Rumburgh w S Elmham 75-79; R Rumburgh w S Elmham w the Ilketshalls 79-84; TR Langport Area Chs *B & W* 84-96; P-in-c Rode Major 96-02; C Hardington Vale 02-04; rtd 04. *Hedge End, 5 Queen Street, Keinton Mandeville, Somerton TA11 6EH* Tel (01458) 224448

COOKE, Alan. b 50. Nottm Univ BTh74 Lanc Univ PGCE75. Kelham Th Coll 69. **d** 75 **p** 76. C Tyldesley w Shakerley *Man* 75-78; C Langley All SS and Martyrs 80-82; TV Langley and Parkfield 82-83; P-in-c Chadderton St Mark 83-85; V from 85. *St Mark's Vicarage, Milne Street, Chadderton, Oldham OL9 0HR* Tel 0161-624 2005

COOKE, Angela Elizabeth. b 42. SRN65 SCM67 Midwife Teacher's Dip 72. St Jo Coll Nottm 85. **d** 87 **p** 94. Par Dn Walton H Trin *Ox* 87-92; Par Dn Bexleyheath Ch Ch *Roch* 92-94; C 94-97; V St Mary Cray and St Paul's Cray 97-05; rtd 05. *7 Maytree Gardens, Bexhill-on-Sea TN40 2PE* Tel (01424) 213268 E-mail angelacooke@hotmail.com

COOKE (née LEA), Mrs Carolyn Jane. b 65. Nottm Univ BA88 PGCE90. St Jo Coll Nottm MTh02. **d** 02 **p** 03. C Hyson Green and Forest Fields *S'well* from 02. *8 Austen Avenue, Nottingham NG7 6PE* Tel 0115-961 7555 E-mail d.cooke3@ntlworld.com

COOKE, Christopher Stephen. b 54. Lon Univ BA76 MA77 Ox Univ BA81 MA88. Ripon Coll Cuddesdon 79. **d** 82 **p** 83. C Cen Telford *Lich* 82-86; R Uffington, Upton Magna and Withington 86-95; RD Wrockwardine 92-01; TR Wrockwardine Deanery 95-01; P-in-c Wem from 01; P-in-c Lee Brockhurst from 01; P-in-c Loppington w Newtown 01-02. *The Rectory, Ellesmere Road, Wem, Shrewsbury SY4 5TU* Tel (01939) 232550 E-mail christopher@csc2000.f9.co.uk

COOKE, David John. b 31. Linc Th Coll 60. **d** 62 **p** 63. C Brighton Gd Shep Preston *Chich* 62-65; C Clayton w Keymer 65-70; R Stone w Hartwell w Bishopstone *Ox* 70-77; R Stone w Dinton and Hartwell from 77. *The Rectory, Stone, Aylesbury HP17 8RZ* Tel (01296) 748215

COOKE, Francis Theodore. b 34. Tyndale Hall Bris 53 Clifton Th Coll 58. **d** 02 **p** 03. Ind Missr Bentley Motors *Ches* from 02; NSM Poynton from 02. *13 Maple Avenue, Poynton, Stockport SK12 1PR* Tel (01625) 859246

COOKE, Frederic Ronald. b 35. Selw Coll Cam BA58 MA61. Ridley Hall Cam 59. **d** 61 **p** 62. C Flixton St Mich *Man* 61-64; C-in-c Flixton St Jo CD 64-67; V Flixton St Jo 68-74; R Ashton St Mich 74-77; Jerusalem 77-80; V Walmsley *Man* 80-85; AD Walmsley 81-85; Malaysia 85-90; Prin Ho of Epiphany Th Coll Borneo 85-90; P-in-c Accrington *Blackb* 90-91; TR 91-96; P-in-c Ringley w Prestolee *Man* 96-01; rtd 01. *41 Knights Court, Canterbury Gardens, Salford M5 5AB* Tel 0161-788 7713

COOKE, Geoffrey. b 38. Sarum Th Coll 61. **d** 64 **p** 65. C Eastover *B & W* 64-67; Chapl RAF 67-71; C Bridgwater St Jo *B & W* 71-76; R N Newton w St Michaelchurch and Thurloxton 76-78; R N Newton w St Michaelchurch, Thurloxton etc 78-83; TV Yeovil 83-88; V Yeovil H Trin 88-89; R Staple Fitzpaine, Orchard Portman, Thurlbear etc 89-96; rtd 96; Perm to Offic *B & W* from 96. *34 Bluebell Close, Taunton TA1 3XQ* Tel (01823) 324235 E-mail endymion.99@virgin.net

COOKE (married name SHEARD), Ms Gillian Freda. b 39. Lon Univ BD73 Leeds Univ MA87. Linc Th Coll 74. **dss** 78 **d** 87 **p** 94. Cricklewood St Pet CD *Lon* 78-80; Chapl Middx Poly 78-80; Chapl Leeds Poly *Ripon* 80-87; N Humberside Ind Chapl *York* 87-90; Asst Chapl HM Pris Hull 90-94; Chapl Keele Univ *Lich* 94-97; Assoc Min Betley and Keele 94-97; Chapl Rampton Hosp Retford 97-99; rtd 99; Perm to Offic *York* from 00; Chapl HM Pris Wolds from 05. *The Chaplain's Office, HM Prison Wolds, Everthorpe, Brough HU15 2JZ* Tel (01430) 421588 E-mail gilalsrd@fish.co.uk

COOKE (née MORRALL), Mrs Heather Lynne. b 55. LMH Ox BA76 MA80 MIPR88. Open Th Coll 94 Dioc OLM tr scheme 96. **d** 99 **p** 00. OLM Martlesham w Brightwell *St E* from 99. *9 Swan Close, Martlesham Heath, Ipswich IP5 3SD* Tel (01473) 623770 Mobile 07703-568051 E-mail hcookema@aol.com

COOKE, Canon Hereward Roger Gresham. b 39. FCA64. K Coll Lon BD69 AKC70. **d** 70 **p** 71. C Rugby St Andr *Cov* 70-76; P-in-c St Kath Cree *Lon* 76-82; P-in-c St Botolph without Aldersgate 82-89; AD The City 82-85; P-in-c St Edm the King and St Mary Woolnoth etc 82-89; TV Nor St Pet Parmentergate w St Jo *Nor* 89-93; Ind Miss 89-05; Sen Ind Chapl 93-05; Hon C Nor St Pet Mancroft w St Jo Maddermarket from 93; P-in-c Nor St Steph from 03; RD Nor E 93-02; Hon Can Nor Cathl 97-05; rtd 05. *31 Bracondale, Norwich NR1 2AT* Tel (01603) 624827 Fax 477323 E-mail cookehd@paston.co.uk

COOKE, James Percy. b 13. St D Coll Lamp BA51. **d** 52 **p** 54. C Prestatyn *St As* 52-57; R Derwen and Llanelidan 57-83; rtd 83. *c/o C J Davies, Maesmor, Wrexham Road, Ruthin LL15 1BY*

COOKE, John Stephen. b 35. K Coll Lon BD58 AKC58. **d** 59 **p** 60. C W Bromwich St Fran *Lich* 59-62; C Chalfont St Peter *Ox* 62-66; V Cross Heath *Lich* 66-72; R Haughton 72-86; P-in-c Ellenhall w Ranton 72-80; V Eccleshall 86-00; Sub Chapl HM Pris Drake Hall 89-95; rtd 00; Perm to Offic *Lich* from 00. *50 High Street, Eccleshall, Stafford ST21 6BZ* Tel (01785) 850570

COOKE, Canon Kenneth John. b 29. Linc Coll Ox BA53 MA57. Ely Th Coll 53. **d** 55 **p** 56. C Nuneaton St Mary *Cov* 55-58; C Cov St Thos 58-61; V Willenhall 61-66; V Meriden 66-76; V Cov St Geo 76-84; V Leamington Spa H Trin and Old Milverton 84-94; Hon Can Cov Cathl 92-94; rtd 94; Perm to Offic *Cov* from 94. *2 Chantry Crescent, Alcester B49 5BT* Tel (01789) 763460

COOKE, Michael David. b 46. New Coll Ox BA68 MA71 DPhil71. Ox NSM Course 75. **d** 78 **p** 79. NSM Newport Pagnell *Ox* 78-85; NSM Newport Pagnell w Lathbury and Moulsoe 85-88; NSM Beckenham Ch Ch *Roch* 90-96; P-in-c Seal St Lawr from 96; P-in-c Underriver from 96; Perm to Offic *Cant* from 98. *St Lawrence Vicarage, Stone Street, Sevenoaks TN15 0LQ* Tel (01732) 761766 Fax as telephone
E-mail mcooke7oaks@btopenworld.com

COOKE, Michael John. b 39. Ab Dioc Tr Course 78. **d** 80 **p** 81. NSM St Andr Cathl *Ab* 80-81; Chapl Miss to Seamen 81-88; Miss to Seamen Tilbury 88-91; Hon C Immingham *Linc* 81-88; Ind Chapl Teesside *Dur* 91-97; V Kelloe and Coxhoe from 97. *8 Mulberry, Coxhoe, Durham DH6 4SN* Tel 0191-377 3722

COOKE, Miss Priscilla Garland Hamel. b 24. Gilmore Ho 69. **dss** 80 **d** 87 **p** 94. Bromsgrove St Jo *Worc* 80-82; Lee Abbey 82-85; Torquay St Matthias, St Mark and H Trin *Ex* 86-87; NSM 87-92 and 94-98; Perm to Offic 92-94 and from 98. *St Nicolas, Woodend Road, Torquay TQ1 2PZ* Tel (01803) 297366

COOKE, Raymond. b 34. Liv Univ BSc56. Wells Th Coll 58. **d** 60 **p** 61. C Newton Heath All SS *Man* 60-64; C-in-c Failsworth H Family CD 64-75; R Failsworth H Family 75-83; P-in-c Man Gd Shep 83-88; V Westleigh St Pet 88-99; rtd 99. *136 Victoria Avenue East, Manchester M9 6HF* Tel 0161-740 0664

COOKE, Richard James. b 60. Pemb Coll Ox BA82 MA88 Bris Univ PhD96. Trin Coll Bris 85. **d** 88 **p** 89. C Rugby St Matt *Cov* 88-92; V Fletchamstead 92-04; Dir Initial Tr for Readers 97-04; CME Adv from 04. *Diocesan Office, 1 Hill Top, Coventry CV1 5AB* Tel (024) 7652 1200 Fax 7652 1330
E-mail richard.cooke@covcofe.org

COOKE, Roger. b 68. Heriot-Watt Univ BA90 BArch91 DipArch92 Edin Univ MTh02. TISEC 98. **d** 99 **p** 00. C Prestonpans *Edin* 99-02; R from 02; C Musselburgh 99-02; R from 02. *12 Windsor Gardens, Musselburgh EH21 7LP* Tel 0131-665 2925 E-mail carrington20@aol.com

COOKE, Stephen. *See* COOKE, John Stephen

COOKSON, Canon Diane Veronica. b 51. N Ord Course 81. **dss** 84 **d** 87 **p** 94. Gt Sutton *Ches* 84-86; Neston 86-87; Par Dn 87-94; C 94-96; V Stockport St Sav from 96; Ecum Adv (Gtr Man) 00-02; Hon Can Ches Cathl from 04. *St Saviour's Vicarage, 22 St Saviour's Road, Great Moor, Stockport SK2 7QE* Tel 0161-483 2633 E-mail st.saviours@virgin.net

COOKSON, Canon Graham Leslie. b 37. Sarum Th Coll 64. **d** 67 **p** 68. C Upton Ascension *Ches* 67-69; C Timperley 69-75; V Godley cum Newton Green 75-83; R Tarporley from 83; Hon Can Ches Cathl from 04. *The Rectory, High Street, Tarporley CW6 0AG* Tel (01829) 732491

COOKSON, William. b 61. **d** 98 **p** 99. C Haydock St Mark *Liv* 98-02; Min Wallington Springfield Ch *S'wark* from 02. *49 Stanley Park Road, Carshalton SM5 3HT* Tel (020) 8404 6064 E-mail willcookson@blueyonder.co.uk

COOLING, Derrick William. b 35. AKC58 Heref Coll of Educn TCert68 Lon Univ BD69 DipEd71 Univ of Wales (Cardiff) MEd81. St Boniface Warminster 58. **d** 59 **p** 60. C Haydock St Jas *Liv* 59-61; C Hove St Barn *Chich* 61-63; V Llangattock w St Maughan's etc *Mon* 63-68; R Blaina 68-70; Perm to Offic *Sarum* 70-74; Chapl Windsor Girls' Sch Hamm 74-75; Asst Master Croesyceiliog Sch Cwmbran 75-81; Chapl Epsom Coll 81-84; V Bettws *Mon* 84-95; P-in-c Purleigh, Cold Norton and Stow Maries *Chelmsf* 95-98; rtd 98; Perm to Offic *Mon* from 98 and *Glouc* from 05. *St Thomas Cottage, The Fence, St Briavels, Lydney GL15 6QG* Tel and fax (01594) 530926
E-mail clericderrick@aol.com

COOLING (née YOUNG), Mrs Margaret Dorothy. b 37. K Coll Lon BA59 AKC Lon Univ BD69 DipEd71 Univ of Wales (Cardiff) MEd81. Mon Dioc Tr Scheme 89. **d** 90 **p** 95. NSM Bettws *Mon* 90-95; NSM Purleigh, Cold Norton and Stow Maries *Chelmsf* 95-98; rtd 98; Perm to Offic *Mon* from 98 and *Glouc* from 01; Warden, Lect and Preacher Newland Almshouses from 04. *St Thomas Cottage, The Fence, St Briavels, Lydney GL15 6QG* Tel and fax (01594) 530926
E-mail clericderrick@aol.com

COOMBE, James Anthony. b 31. Em Coll Cam BA53 MA57 Lon Univ BD60. Tyndale Hall Bris 57. **d** 60 **p** 61. C Chadderton Ch Ch *Man* 60-63; C Worthing St Geo *Chich* 63-65; V Wandsworth St Mich *S'wark* 65-74; P-in-c Warboys *Ely* 74-76; R 76-87; RD St Ives 83-87; P-in-c Broughton 84-87; P-in-c Wistow 84-87; V Alconbury w Alconbury Weston 87-96; R Buckworth 87-96; rtd 96. *12 Nursery Fields, Hythe CT21 4DL* Tel (01303) 262151

COOMBE, John Morrell (Brother Martin). b 25. Chich Th Coll 56. **d** 57 **p** 58. SSF from 49; Lic to Offic *Sarum* 57-59; C-in-c Hillfield and Hermitage 59-66; Asst Chapl Ellesmere Coll 66-69; Chapl Ranby Ho Sch Retford 69-71; V Cambridge St Benedict *Ely* 71-85; Perm to Offic *Jerusalem* 85-86; Prov Sec SSF 86-94; Lic to Offic *Linc* 86-95; Perm to Offic *Ely* from 97; Sec for Miss SSF from 99. *St Francis's House, 14/15 Botolph Lane, Cambridge CB2 3RD* Tel (01223) 321576
E-mail martinssf@franciscans.org.uk

COOMBE, Kenneth Harry Southcott. b 24. Clifton Th Coll 61. **d** 63 **p** 64. C Cullompton *Ex* 63-66; C-in-c Elburton CD 66-73; V Elburton 73-97; rtd 97; Perm to Offic *Ex* from 97. *80 Mewstone Avenue, Wembury, Plymouth PL9 0HT* Tel (01752) 863297
E-mail mewstone@aol.com

COOMBE, Canon Michael Thomas. b 31. Lon Univ BA64. Ox NSM Course 73. **d** 75 **p** 76. Chapl St Piran's Sch Maidenhead 75-81; NSM Furze Platt *Ox* 75-81; C 86-88; Asst Chapl Oslo St Edm *Eur* 81-84; Chapl Belgrade w Zagreb 84-86; Chapl Marseille w St Raphaël, Aix-en-Provence etc 88-89; Chapl Reading Gp of Hosps 89-91; P-in-c Clewer St Andr *Ox* 91-92; C New Windsor 92-93; C Reading St Mark 93-95; C Reading H Trin 93-95; Prec Gib Cathl and Port Chapl *Eur* 95-03; Can Gib Cathl 00-03; rtd 03. *28 Gipsy Lane, Exmouth EX8 3HN* Tel (01395) 272923

COOMBER, Ian Gladstone. b 47. Ch Ch Coll Cant CertEd68 Southn Univ BTh79. Sarum & Wells Th Coll 73. **d** 76 **p** 77. C Weeke *Win* 76-79; TV Saffron Walden w Wendens Ambo and Littlebury *Chelmsf* 79-82; V Weston *Win* 82-90; R Bedhampton *Portsm* 90-96; R Botley and Durley 96-05; V Curdridge 96-05; RD Bishop's Waltham 98-03; TR Cartmel Peninsula *Carl* from 05. *The Rectory, Hampsfell Road, Grange-over-Sands LA11 6BE* Tel (01539) 532757

COOMBES, Derek Fennessey. b 42. Nottm Univ Cert Counselling 95 Dip Counselling & Psychotherapy 00. Edin Th Coll LTh61. **d** 65 **p** 66. Prec St Andr Cathl Inverness *Mor* 65-68; Bp's Chapl 65-68; Perm to Offic *Nor* 76-79; V Happisburgh w Walcot 79-83; C Tewkesbury Abbey 84-85; Ind Chapl *S'wark* 85-89; R Asterby Gp *Linc* 89-95; Mental Health Chapl Louth 91-95; Perm to Offic *Lich* 95-97; TV Haywards Heath St Wilfrid *Chich* from 97. *The Vicarage, 1 Marylands, New England Road, Haywards Heath RH16 3JZ* Tel (01444) 443450 Fax as telephone

COOMBES, Edward David. b 39. Dur Univ BA61. Qu Coll Birm. **d** 63 **p** 64. C Claines St Jo *Worc* 63-65; C Halesowen 65-69; V Beoley 69-77; V Edgbaston St Bart *Birm* 77-05; Chapl Birm Univ 77-05; rtd 05; Perm to Offic *Birm* from 05. *Hazelmere House, 3 Jackfield Close, Redditch B98 0BF* Tel (01527) 522693
E-mail edcoombes@bigfoot.com

COOMBES, Frederick Brian John. b 34. Nottm Univ BA56 Plymouth Poly MPhil73 Univ Coll Lon Dip Town Planning 63 FRGS. SW Minl Tr Course 85. **d** 88 **p** 89. NSM Bodmin w Lanhydrock and Lanivet *Truro* from 88. *5 Valley View, Bodmin PL31 1BE* Tel (01208) 73036

COOMBS, Edward Neve. b 66. Bris Univ BSc88. Cranmer Hall Dur BA93. **d** 94 **p** 95. C Edin St Thos *Edin* 94-96; C Dagenham *Chelmsf* 97-01; P-in-c Banbury St Paul *Ox* from 01. *St Paul's House, Bretch Hill, Banbury OX16 0LR* Tel (01295) 264003
E-mail encoombs@tesco.net

COOMBS, John Allen. b 46. Portsm Poly BSc70. Oak Hill Th Coll DipHE88 Sarum & Wells Th Coll 89. **d** 89 **p** 90. C Leverington *Ely* 89-93; C Wisbech St Mary 89-93; P-in-c Emneth 93-96; V Emneth and Marshland St James 96-99; P-in-c Papworth Everard 99-00; TV Papworth 00-02; Chapl Papworth Hosp NHS Trust from 99. *Papworth Hospital, Papworth Everard, Cambridge CB3 8RE* Tel (01480) 830541 Fax 831315
E-mail john.coombs@papworth.nhs.uk

COOMBS, John Kendall. b 47. Culham Coll Ox BEd73. Sarum & Wells Th Coll 75. **d** 77 **p** 78. C Fareham H Trin *Portsm* 77-80; C Petersfield w Sheet 80-83; TV Beaminster Area *Sarum* 83-87; TR Preston w Sutton Poyntz and Osmington w Poxwell 87-97; TR Hermitage *Ox* from 97. *The Rectory, High Street, Hermitage, Thatcham RG18 9ST* Tel (01635) 202967

COOMBS, Martin. *See* COOMBS, Canon Walter James Martin

COOMBS, The Ven Peter Bertram. b 28. Bris Univ BA58 MA61. Clifton Th Coll 55. **d** 60 **p** 61. C Beckenham Ch Ch *Roch* 60-63; R Nottingham St Nic *S'well* 63-68; V New Malden and Coombe *S'wark* 68-75; RD Kingston 71-75; Adn Wandsworth 75-88; Adn Reigate 88-95; rtd 95; Perm to Offic *Portsm* from 97. *92 Locks*

Heath Park Road, Locks Heath, Southampton SO31 6LZ Tel (01489) 577288

COOMBS, Richard Murray. b 63. St Chad's Coll Dur BSc85 Rob Coll Cam BA89 MA90. Ridley Hall Cam 87. **d** 90 **p** 91. C Enfield Ch Ch Trent Park *Lon* 90-94; C St Helen Bishopsgate w St Andr Undershaft etc 94-98; P-in-c St Pet Cornhill 95-98; V Burford w Fulbrook, Taynton, Asthall etc *Ox* from 98. *The Vicarage, Church Lane, Burford OX18 4SD* Tel (01993) 822275 Fax 824699 E-mail rmcoombs@lineone.net

COOMBS, Stephen John. b 54. Open Univ BA86. Trin Coll Bris 85. **d** 87 **p** 88. C Norton Canes *Lich* 87-90; Chapl Trowbridge Coll *Sarum* 90-94; C Studley 90-94. *48 Whitstone Rise, Shepton Mallet BA4 5QB* Tel (01749) 343750

COOMBS, Canon Walter James Martin. b 33. Keble Coll Ox BA57 MA61. Cuddesdon Coll 59. **d** 61 **p** 62. C Kennington St Jo *S'wark* 61-64; Chapl Em Coll Cam 64-68; Bp's Dom Chapl *S'wark* 68-70; V E Dulwich St Jo 70-77; V Pershore w Pinvin, Wick and Birlingham *Worc* 77-92; Hon Can Worc Cathl 84-92; RD Pershore 85-91; TV Dorchester *Ox* 92-98; rtd 98; Perm to Offic *Ox* from 01. *54 Divinity Road, Oxford OX4 1LJ* Tel (01865) 243865

COONEY, Canon Michael Patrick. b 55. City of Lon Poly BA77. Ripon Coll Cuddesdon 77. **d** 80 **p** 81. C Cov E *Cov* 80-83; C Old Brumby *Linc* 83-85; V Linc St Jo 85-90; V Frodingham from 90; RD Manlake from 99; RD Is of Axholme from 05; Can and Preb Linc Cathl from 04. *The Vicarage, Vicarage Gardens, Scunthorpe DN15 7AZ* Tel (01724) 842726 E-mail michael.cooney@ntlworld.com

COONEY, William Barry. b 47. K Coll Lon 69. **d** 70 **p** 71. C W Bromwich All SS *Lich* 70-73; C Wolverhampton St Pet 73-75; C Rugeley 75-78; V Sneyd Green 78-87; R Sandiacre *Derby* from 87. *St Giles's Rectory, Church Drive, Sandiacre, Nottingham NG10 5EE* Tel 0115-939 7163

COOPER, Alfred Philip. b 50. Bris Univ BA71. All Nations Chr Coll 72. **d** 77 **p** 78. Chile from 75; SAMS from 77. *Inglesia Anglicana del Chile, Casilla 50675, Correo Central, Santiago, Chile* Tel (0056) (2) 226 8794

COOPER, Mrs Alison. b 51. Ripon Coll Cuddesdon 03. **d** 04 **p** 05. NSM Ascot Heath *Ox* from 04. *2 Beaufort Gardens, Ascot SL5 8PG* Tel (01344) 624027 Mobile 07747-682139 E-mail alison8@fish.co.uk

COOPER, Andrew John. b 62. W Sussex Inst of HE BA87 Greenwich Univ PGCE03. St Steph Ho Ox 88. **d** 91 **p** 92. C Rawmarsh w Parkgate *Sheff* 91-93; C Mosbrough 93-95; P-in-c Donnington Wood *Lich* 95-96; CF from 96. *c/o MOD Chaplains (Army)* Tel (01980) 615804 Fax 615800

COOPER, Andrew John Gearing. b 48. Sir John Cass Coll Lon BSc70. Ripon Coll Cuddesdon 73. **d** 76 **p** 77. C Potternewton *Ripon* 76-79; Antigua 79-81; Anguilla 81-87; V W Bromwich St Andr w Ch Ch *Lich* 88-92. *45 Dimbles Lane, Burntwood WS13 7HW* Tel (01543) 416020 E-mail andrew.cooper@lichfield.anglican.org

COOPER, The Ven Annette Joy. b 53. Open Univ BA80 CQSW84. S'wark Ord Course 85. **d** 88 **p** 94. NSM Pembury *Roch* 88; Chapl Asst Kent and Sussex Hosp Tunbridge Wells 88-91; Chapl Asst Leybourne Grange Hosp W Malling 88-91; Chapl Bassetlaw Hosp and Community Services NHS Trust 91-96; P-in-c Edwinstowe *S'well* 96-04; Chapl Center Parcs Holiday Village 96-01; AD Worksop 99-04; Hon Can S'well Minster 02-04; Adn Colchester *Chelmsf* from 04. *63 Powers Hall End, Witham CM8 1NH* Tel (01376) 513130 Fax 500789 E-mail a.colchester@chelmsford.anglican.org

COOPER, Barrie Keith. b 56. Oak Hill Th Coll. **d** 85 **p** 86. C Partington and Carrington *Ches* 85-89; V Stockport St Mark 89-93; Chapl HM YOI Stoke Heath 93-01; Chapl HM Pris Acklington from 01. *HM Prison Acklington, Morpeth NE65 9XF* Tel (01670) 762300

COOPER, Barry Jack. Sarum Th Coll 59. **d** 61 **p** 62. C Norbury St Oswald *Cant* 61-64; C Crook *Dur* 64-68; R Cheriton *Cant* 68-84; V Cant All SS 84-00; rtd 00; Perm to Offic *Cant* from 01. *11 Wind Hill Lane, Charing Heath, Ashford TN27 0BG* Tel (01233) 714787

COOPER, Canon Bede Robert. b 42. Ex Univ BA69. Coll of Resurr Mirfield 69. **d** 71 **p** 72. C Weymouth H Trin *Sarum* 71-74; P-in-c Broad Town 74-79; V Wootton Bassett 74-86; R Wilton w Netherhampton and Fugglestone from 86; Can and Preb Sarum Cathl from 88. *The Rectory, 27A West Street, Wilton, Salisbury SP2 0DL* Tel (01722) 743159

COOPER, Benedict Christopher. b 68. K Coll Cam BA90 Wolfs Coll Ox MPhil94 DPhil97. Oak Hill Th Coll BA03. **d** 03 **p** 04. C St Helen Bishopsgate w St Andr Undershaft etc *Lon* from 03. *5 Louisa Gardens, London E1 4NG* Tel (020) 7790 6045 *or* 7283 2231 E-mail bc_cooper@hotmail.com

COOPER, Bert. *See* COOPER, Herbert William

COOPER, Brian Hamilton. b 35. Keble Coll Ox BA58 MA67. Ripon Hall Ox 58. **d** 60 **p** 61. C Woolwich St Mary w H Trin *S'wark* 60-64; Canada 64-66; Vice-Prin Westcott Ho Cam 66-71; R Downham Market w Bexwell *Ely* 71-82; RD Fincham 80-82; V Chesterfield St Mary and All SS *Derby* 82-91; V Herringthorpe *Sheff* 91-00; RD Rotherham 93-98; rtd 00; Perm to Offic *Sheff* from 00. *51 Anston Avenue, Worksop S81 7HU* Tel (01909) 479306 E-mail m.y.cooper1723@aol.com

✠**COOPER, The Rt Revd Carl Norman.** b 60. Univ of Wales (Lamp) BA82 Trin Coll Carmarthen MPhil99. Wycliffe Hall Ox 82. **d** 85 **p** 86 **c** 02. C Llanelli *St D* 85-87; P-in-c Llanerch Aeron w Ciliau Aeron and Dihewyd etc 87-88; R 88-93; R Dolgellau w Llanfachreth and Brithdir etc *Ban* 93-02; Warden of Readers 88-02; Adn Meirionnydd 00-02; Bp St D from 02. *Llys Esgob, Abergwili, Carmarthen SA31 2JG* Tel (01267) 236597 E-mail bishop.stdavids@churchinwales.org.uk

COOPER, Cecil Clive. b 26. TD75. AKC52. **d** 53 **p** 54. C Chipping Campden *Glouc* 53-55; C Cheltenham St Mary 55-60; V Stroud 60-65; CF (TA) 63-75; R Woodmansterne *S'wark* 65-91; RD Sutton 80-90; rtd 91; Perm to Offic *Cov* and *Pet* from 91. *10 Mill Close, Braunston, Daventry NN11 7HY* Tel (01788) 890596

COOPER, Canon Cecil William Marcus. b 32. TCD BA58 MA66. CITC 57. **d** 59 **p** 60. C Cork St Fin Barre and St Nic *C, C & R* 59-62; Bp's V, Lib and Registrar Kilkenny Cathl *C & O* 62-64; C Knockbreda *D & D* 65-67; Asst Ed *Church of Ireland Gazette* 66-82; Ed 82-00; I Magheradroll 67-82; Dioc Registrar 81-90; I Drumbeg 82-00; Can Down Cathl 86-00; Prec 90-91; Chan 91-00; rtd 00. *35 Manor Drive, Lisburn BT28 1JH* Tel (028) 9263 4425

COOPER, Clive Anthony Charles. b 38. Lon Univ BEd74. ALCD62. **d** 62 **p** 63. C Morden *S'wark* 62-65; SAMS Argentina 65-71; Asst Master St Nic Sch Cranleigh 74-82; Hon C Cranleigh *Guildf* 78-79; Hon C Ewhurst 80-82; Hon Chapl Duke of Kent Sch 83-92; Chapl Felixstowe Coll 92-93; Perm to Offic *Ex* 94-95; Chapl Puerto Pollensa *Eur* 95-02; P-in-c Instow *Ex* from 03; P-in-c Westleigh from 03. *1 Stanbridge Park, Bideford EX39 3RS* Tel (01237) 473839 E-mail pinc.instow@btopenworld.com

COOPER, Colin. b 55. Open Univ BA. St Jo Coll Nottm 83. **d** 86 **p** 87. C Cheadle Hulme St Andr *Ches* 86-89; C Tunbridge Wells St Jo *Roch* 89-93; V Whitfield *Derby* from 93. *The Vicarage, 116 Charlestown Road, Glossop SK13 8LB* Tel (01457) 864938 E-mail colin@glossop.org

COOPER, Colin Charles. b 40. Middx Univ BA94. Oak Hill Th Coll 62. **d** 66 **p** 67. C Islington St Andr w St Thos and St Matthias *Lon* 66-69; Bermuda 69-76; V Gorleston St Andr *Nor* 77-94; USA from 94; R Emporia Ch Ch w Purdy Grace Virginia from 94. *111 Battery Avenue, Emporia, VA 23847, USA* E-mail cooperc@3rddoor.com

COOPER, Mrs Corynne Elizabeth. b 54. Kent Univ BA76 PGCE77 Nottm Univ MA98. EMMTC 95. **d** 98 **p** 99. NSM Kneesall w Laxton and Wellow *S'well* 98-01; C Widecombe-in-the-Moor, Leusdon, Princetown etc *Ex* from 01. *The Vicarage, Holne, Newton Abbot TQ13 7RT* Tel (01364) 631522 E-mail corynne.cooper@virgin.net

COOPER, David. b 44. AKC69. **d** 69 **p** 70. C Wortley de Leeds *Ripon* 69-73; CF 73-83; Lic to Offic *Ox* from 84; Chapl Eton Coll from 85. *Eton College, Windsor SL4 6DW* Tel (01753) 864587

COOPER, David Jonathan. b 44. Sarum & Wells Th Coll 70. **d** 74 **p** 75. C Charlton-in-Dover *Cant* 74-79; TV Wednesfield *Lich* 79-83; SSF 83-85; V Grimsby St Aug *Linc* 85-89; TV Trowbridge H Trin *Sarum* 89-98; TV Manningham *Bradf* 98-04; P-in-c Fairfield *Derby* from 04. *The Vicarage, St Peter's Road, Fairfield, Buxton SK17 7EB* Tel (01298) 23629

COOPER, David Philip. b 65. York Univ BA86. Qu Coll Birm BTheol94. **d** 94 **p** 95. C Burslem *Lich* 94-98; TV Cen Wolverhampton and Dioc Inter-Faith Officer 98-05; V Arnside *Carl* from 05. *The Vicarage, 45 Church Hill, Arnside, Carnforth LA5 0DW* Tel (01524) 761319

COOPER, Derek Edward. b 30. Bps' Coll Cheshunt 61. **d** 62 **p** 63. C Bishop's Stortford St Mich *St Alb* 62-66; V Westcliff St Cedd *Chelmsf* 66-89; R Camerton w Dunkerton, Foxcote and Shoscombe *B & W* 89-95; rtd 95; Perm to Offic *Win* from 95. *6 Caerleon Drive, Andover SP10 4DE* Tel (01264) 362807

COOPER, Eric John. b 22. Cam Univ MA47. Chich Th Coll 52. **d** 53 **p** 54. V Bedminster Down *Bris* 66-72; rtd 87. *6 Deveron Grove, Keynsham, Bristol BS31 1UJ* Tel 0117-986 7339

COOPER, Frederick. b 30. Cranmer Hall Dur 68. **d** 70 **p** 71. C Preston All SS *Blackb* 70-72; C Preston St Jo 72-76; TV 76-78; V Higher Walton 78-91; P-in-c Preston All SS 91-95; rtd 95; Perm to Offic *Blackb* from 95. *10 Guardian Close, Fulwood, Preston PR2 8EX* Tel (01772) 713808

COOPER, Ms Gillian Anne. b 55. LMH Ox BA76 CertEd77 MA80 Nottm Univ MEd94. St Jo Coll Nottm 84. **dss** 86 **d** 87 **p** 94. Tutor EMMTC 86-01; Beeston *S'well* 86-91; Hon C 87-91; Hon C Bilborough w Strelley 91-01; Lect St Jo Coll Nottm 87-01; New Zealand from 01. *Address temp unknown*

COOPER, Gordon William. b 54. Aston Tr Scheme 93 Ripon Coll Cuddesdon DipMin95. **d** 97 **p** 98. C Kippax w Allerton Bywater *Ripon* 97-01; V Wyther Ven Bede from 01. *Wyther Vicarage, Houghley Lane, Leeds LS13 4AU* Tel 0113-279 8014 E-mail gordon@williamcooper.freeserve.co.uk

COOPER, Graham Denbigh. b 48. Nottm Univ BTh75. St Jo Coll Nottm LTh75. **d** 75 **p** 76. C Collyhurst *Man* 75-78; C Stambermill *Worc* 78-80; V The Lye and Stambermill 80-90; P-in-c Frome H Trin *B & W* 90; V 91-95; Appeals Organiser Children's Soc 95-97; Area Manager Save the Children Fund from 97. *2 Coombe View, Shepton Mallet BA4 5YF* Tel (01749) 343157

COOPER, Herbert William. b 29. Chich Th Coll 77. **d** 79 **p** 80. C Leigh Park *Portsm* 79-82; C-in-c Hayling St Pet CD 82-85; V Whitwell and R St Lawrence 85-94; P-in-c Niton 89-94; rtd 94. *10 Andrew Avenue, Felpham, Bognor Regis PO22 7QS* Tel (01243) 584212

COOPER, Ian. b 57. St Jo Coll Nottm 00. **d** 02 **p** 03. C Mildenhall *St E* 02-05; TV from 05. *The Vicarage, 1 The Street, Barton Mills, Bury St Edmunds IP28 6AP* Tel (01638) 715112 E-mail ian@rpmo.co.uk

COOPER, Ian Clive. b 48. Ex Univ BA76 K Coll Lon MTh94 FCA. Linc Th Coll 76. **d** 78 **p** 79. C Sunbury *Lon* 78-81; P-in-c Astwood Bank *Worc* 81-85; P-in-c Feckenham w Bradley 82-85; TV Hemel Hempstead *St Alb* 85-95; R Bushey 95-04; TR Witney *Ox* from 04. *The Rectory, 13 Station Lane, Witney OX28 4BB* Tel (01993) 200323 E-mail iancooperwitney@aol.com

COOPER, Jack. b 44. St Jo Coll Nottm 76. **d** 78 **p** 79. C Roundhay St Edm *Ripon* 78-80; C Ripley *Derby* 81-82; V Willington 82-88; V Findern 82-88; P-in-c Parwich w Alsop-en-le-Dale 88-94; Perm to Offic *York* from 95; rtd 04. *Park View, 14 Chubb Hill Road, Whitby YO21 1JU* Tel (01947) 604213 E-mail jackanann@btopenworld.com

COOPER, James Peter. b 61. Westf Coll Lon BSc82. Sarum & Wells Th Coll 82. **d** 85 **p** 86. C Durrington *Chich* 85-88; C Clayton w Keymer 88-95; TV Chich 95-00; Chapl Chich Coll of Tech from 95; C Chich St Paul and Westhampnett *Chich* 00-01; Chapl R W Sussex Trust from 01. *St Richard's Hospital, Spitalfield Lane, Chichester PO19 6SE* Tel (01243) 788122 Mobile 07989-741004 Fax 531269

COOPER, Mrs Jennifer Ann Lisbeth. b 45. MCSP67. **d** 04 **p** 05. OLM Newton Flotman, Swainsthorpe, Tasburgh, etc *Nor* from 04. *10 Boileau Avenue, Tacolneston, Norwich NR16 1DQ* Tel (01953) 789702

COOPER, Jeremy John. b 45. Kelham Th Coll 65 Linc Th Coll 71. **d** 71 **p** 72. C Derby St Luke *Derby* 71-76; TV Malvern Link w Cowleigh *Worc* 76-79; P-in-c Claypole *Linc* 79-80; P-in-c Westborough w Dry Doddington and Stubton 79-80; C Eye w Braiseworth and Yaxley *St E* 80-82; P-in-c Hundon w Barnardiston 82-83; R 83-97; V Hundon 97-99; Chapl St Marg Convent E Grinstead 99-03; Warden, Lect and Preacher Newland Almshouses 03-04. *52 Wilson Street, Lincoln LN1 3HY*

COOPER, John. b 34. BEd. N Ord Course. **d** 83 **p** 84. C Tong *Bradf* 83-87; V Bingley H Trin 87-92; V Silsden 92-99; rtd 99; Perm to Offic *Bradf* from 01. *58 Cambridge Drive, Otley LS21 1DD* Tel (01943) 463915

COOPER, John. b 47. Sarum & Wells Th Coll 71. **d** 74 **p** 75. C Spring Grove St Mary *Lon* 74-77; C Shepherd's Bush St Steph w St Thos 77-82; V Paddington St Pet 82-89; V Darwen St Cuth w Tockholes St Steph *Blackb* 89-96; V Northampton St Mich w St Edm *Pet* 96-99; Perm to Offic *Lon* from 02. *29 Turner Way, Bedford MK41 7ND* Tel (01234) 315194 E-mail jco4328743@aol.com

COOPER, John Edward. b 40. K Coll Lon BD63 AKC63. **d** 64 **p** 65. C Prittlewell St Mary *Chelmsf* 64-67; C Up Hatherley *Glouc* 67-69; C-in-c Dorridge CD *Birm* 69-71; P-in-c Alkmonton w Yeaveley *Derby* 71-76; V Longford 71-76; TV Canvey Is *Chelmsf* 76-82; R Spixworth w Crostwick *Nor* 82-91; R Frettenham w Stanninghall 82-91; V Gt w Lt Harrowden and Orlingbury *Pet* 91-01; rtd 01; Perm to Offic *Leic* from 01. *Staveley House, 30 Brooke Road, Braunston, Oakham LE15 8QR* Tel (01572) 770984

COOPER, Canon John Leslie. b 33. Lon Univ BD65 MPhil78. Chich Th Coll 59. **d** 62 **p** 63. C Kings Heath *Birm* 62-65; Asst Chapl HM Pris Wandsworth 65-66; Chapl HM Borstal Portland 66-68; Chapl HM Pris Bris 68-72; P-in-c Balsall Heath St Paul *Birm* 73-81; V 81-82; Adn Aston and Can Res Birm Cathl 82-90; Adn Coleshill 90-93; C Sutton Coldfield H Trin 93-97; Hon Can Birm Cathl 93-97; rtd 97; Perm to Offic *Derby* from 98. *4 Ireton Court, Kirk Ireton, Ashbourne, Derby DE6 3JP* Tel (01335) 370459

COOPER, John Northcott. b 44. Ox Min Course 89. **d** 92 **p** 93. NSM Burghfield *Ox* 92-99; P-in-c Wootton (Boars Hill) 99-00; V Wootton and Dry Sandford from 00; AD Abingdon from 02. *The Vicarage, Wootton Village, Boars Hill, Oxford OX1 5JL* Tel (01865) 735661 E-mail cooper@woottonvic.freeserve.co.uk

COOPER, Jonathan. *See* COOPER, David Jonathan

COOPER, Jonathan Mark Eric. b 62. Man Univ BSc83 Edin Univ BD88. Edin Th Coll 85. **d** 88 **p** 89. C Stainton-in-Cleveland *York* 88-91; C W Bromwich All SS *Lich* 91-93; C-in-c Ingleby Barwick CD *York* 93-98; P-in-c Hinderwell w Roxby 98-03; R Kirby Misperton w Normanby, Edston and Salton from 03. *The Rectory, Normanby, Sinnington, York YO62 6RH* Tel (01751) 431288 E-mail jonathan@jmec.freeserve.co.uk

COOPER, Joseph Trevor. b 32. Linc Th Coll 65. **d** 67 **p** 68. C Fletchamstead *Cov* 67-69; Ind Chapl 69-90; rtd 92; Perm to Offic *Cov* 92-00. *16 Trevor Close, Tile Hill, Coventry CV4 9HP* Tel (024) 7646 2341

COOPER, Kenneth Cantlay. b 17. Qu Coll Cam BA39 MA43. Ridley Hall Cam 39. **d** 41 **p** 42. C Radipole and Melcombe Regis *Sarum* 41-46; C Broadwater St Mary *Chich* 46-50; V Cumnor *Ox* 50-65; R Fisherton Anger *Sarum* 65-74; P-in-c Fovant w Compton Chamberlayne etc 74-79; R Fovant, Sutton Mandeville and Teffont Evias etc 79-82; rtd 82; Perm to Offic *B & W* from 83. *8 Helena Road, East Coker, Yeovil BA20 2HQ* Tel (01935) 862291

COOPER, Ms Louise Helena. b 68. Leeds Univ BA90. Qu Coll Birm. **d** 93 **p** 94. Par Dn Dovecot *Liv* 93-94; C 94-96; Dep Chapl HM YOI Glen Parva 96-01; Chapl HM Pris Styal 01-02; Chapl HM Pris Man from 02. *The Chaplain's Office, HM Prison, Southall Street, Manchester M60 9AH* Tel 0161-817 5840 Fax 817 5601

COOPER, Malcolm Tydeman. b 37. Pemb Coll Ox BA61 MA64. Linc Th Coll 63. **d** 63 **p** 64. C Spennithorne *Ripon* 63-66; C Caversham *Ox* 66-71; Hon C Blackbird Leys CD 71-75; Lic to Offic *Sarum* 75-78; Lic to Offic *B & W* 78-82; NSM Sutton *Ely* 82-97; NSM Witcham w Mepal 82-97; rtd 97; P-in-c Coveney *Ely* from 97. *91 The Row, Sutton, Ely CB6 2PB* Tel (01353) 777310 Fax 777422 E-mail mtcm4@waitrose.com

COOPER, Marc Ashley Rex. b 62. Leeds Univ BA85 MA95. Linc Th Coll 92. **d** 92 **p** 93. C Bolton St Jas w St Chrys *Bradf* 92-96; P-in-c Fishtoft *Linc* 96-97; R from 97; RD Holland E from 03. *The Rectory, Rectory Close, Fishtoft, Boston PE21 0RZ* Tel (01205) 363216 Fax as telephone E-mail revmarccooper@lineone.net

COOPER, Sister Margery. b 26. Cam Inst of Educn CertRK52 CA52. CA Tr Coll 49. **dss** 79 **d** 87 **p** 94. Evang Family Miss *Dur, Newc* and *York* 79-86; Perm to Offic *York* 86-91 and from 00; NSM Fulford 91-00; rtd 00. *7 Grange Street, Fulford Road, York YO10 4BH* Tel (01904) 633990

COOPER, Mark Richard. b 69. Kent Univ BA98. St Jo Coll Morpeth DipTh95. **d** 95 **p** 95. Australia 95-96 and from 98; C Hamilton 95-96; C Rainham *Roch* 96-98; Assoc P Kincumber from 98. *167 Avoca Drive, PO Box 1065, Kincumber, NSW, Australia 2251* Tel (0061) (2) 4369 2018 Fax 4369 1204 E-mail markcooper1969@hotmail.com

COOPER, Canon Michael Leonard. b 30. St Jo Coll Cam BA53 MA58. Cuddesdon Coll 53. **d** 55 **p** 56. C Croydon St Jo *Cant* 55-61; V Spring Park 61-71; V Boxley 71-82; RD Sutton 74-80; Hon Can Cant Cathl 76-97; V Cranbrook 82-92; Hon Chapl to Bp Dover 93-97; Asst Chapl Kent and Cant Hosps NHS Trust 94-97; Perm to Offic *Roch* from 97; rtd 00. *The Rectory, The Street, Plaxtol, Sevenoaks TN15 0QG* Tel (01732) 810319

COOPER, Canon Michael Sydney. b 41. Univ of Wales (Lamp) BA63. Westcott Ho Cam 63. **d** 65 **p** 66. C Farlington *Portsm* 65-69; Pakistan 70-71; Mauritius 71-73; C-in-c Hayling St Pet CD *Portsm* 74-81; V Carisbrooke St Mary 81-92; V Carisbrooke St Nic 81-92; V Hartplain 92-98; V Portchester from 98; RD Fareham 99-04; Hon Can Portsm Cathl from 02. *The Vicarage, 164 Castle Street, Portchester, Fareham PO16 9QH* Tel and fax (023) 9237 6289 *or* tel 9232 1380 E-mail stmary@lineone.net

COOPER, Nigel Scott. b 53. Qu Coll Cam BA75 MA79 PGCE76 MIEEM CBiol FIBiol FLS. Ripon Coll Cuddesdon BA83 MA88. **d** 83 **p** 84. C Moulsham St Jo *Chelmsf* 83-88; R Rivenhall 88-05; Chapl Anglia Poly Univ *Ely* from 05. *The Chaplaincy Office, Anglia Polytechnic University, East Road, Cambridge CB1 1PT* Tel (01223) 363271 ext 2398 E-mail n.cooper@apu.ac.uk

COOPER, Noel. b 49. Oak Hill Th Coll. **d** 88 **p** 89. C Plymouth St Jude *Ex* 88-92; V Clapham Park All SS *S'wark* 92-99; R Bedford St Jo and St Leon *St Alb* from 99. *St John's Rectory, 36 St John's Street, Bedford MK42 0DH* Tel (01234) 354818 E-mail stjohns@nascr.net

COOPER, Peter. *See* COOPER, Wallace Peter

COOPER, Canon Peter David. b 48. Sarum & Wells Th Coll 70. **d** 73 **p** 74. C Yateley *Win* 73-78; C Christchurch 78-81; P-in-c Southampton St Mark 81-83; V 83-98; P-in-c Tadley St Pet 98-02; Hon Can Ife Nigeria from 00; R Tadley S and Silchester *Win* from 02. *The Rectory, The Green, Tadley RG26 3PB* Tel 0118-981 4860 E-mail peter.cooper@xaltmail.com

COOPER, Peter Timothy. b 65. Brunel Univ BSc95. Ridley Hall Cam 01. **d** 03 **p** 04. C Edgware *Lon* from 03. *St Peter's Parsonage, Stonegrove, Edgware HA8 8AB* Tel (020) 8958 8142 Mobile 07900-462505 E-mail rev.cooper@btinternet.com

COOPER, Canon Richard Thomas. b 46. Leeds Univ BA69. Coll of Resurr Mirfield 69. **d** 71 **p** 72. C Rothwell *Ripon* 71-75; C Adel 75-78; C Knaresborough 78-81; P-in-c Croft 81-90; P-in-c Eryholme 81-90; P-in-c Middleton Tyas and Melsonby 81-90; RD Richmond 86-90; V Aldborough w Boroughbridge and Roecliffe 90-98; RD Ripon 93-96; R Richmond w Hudswell 98-05; R Richmond w Hudswell and Downholme and Marske from 05; Hon Can Ripon Cathl from 97; Chapl to The Queen from 03. *The Rectory, Church Wynd, Richmond DL10 7AQ* Tel (01748) 823398 E-mail richard@churchwynd.freeserve.co.uk

COOPER, Robert Gerard. b 68. Univ of Wales (Abth) BD91. Linc Th Coll 93. **d** 93 **p** 94. C Whitkirk *Ripon* 93-96; C Leeds Richmond Hill 96-97; Chapl Agnes Stewart C of E High Sch Leeds 96-97; Chapl Chigwell Sch Essex 97-98; V Lightcliffe *Wakef* 98-05; V Pontefract St Giles from 05. *The Vicarage, 9 The Mount, Pontefract WF8 1NE* Tel (01977) 706803 Mobile 07931-565516 E-mail robert_cooper@msn.com

COOPER, Robert James. b 52. Bris Univ BA75. Ridley Hall Cam 76. **d** 78 **p** 79. C Street w Walton *B & W* 78-82; C Batheaston w St Cath 82-86; Asst Chapl to Arts and Recreation *York* and *Dur* 86-03; P-in-c Sadberge 86-03; Chapl Arts and Recreation from 03. *24 North Close, Thorpe Thewles, Stockton-on-Tees TS21 3JY* Tel (01740) 630549 E-mail robertj.cooper@ntlworld.com

COOPER, Roger Charles. b 48. GRSM ARMCM69 PGCE70. Coll of Resurr Mirfield 79. **d** 81 **p** 82. C Monkseaton St Mary *Newc* 81-83; C Morpeth 83-87; Min Can and Prec Man Cathl *Man* 87-90; V Blackrod from 90; AD Deane from 05. *St Katharine's Vicarage, Blackhorse Street, Blackrod, Bolton BL6 5EN* Tel (01204) 468150

COOPER, Seth William. b 62. Westcott Ho Cam 94. **d** 96 **p** 97. C Golders Green *Lon* 96-00; TV Uxbridge from 00. *The Rectory, Nursery Waye, Uxbridge UB8 2BJ* Tel (01895) 239055 E-mail sethandjen@tinyworld.co.uk

COOPER, Mrs Shirley Ann. b 58. St Steph Ho Ox 96. **d** 98 **p** 99. C Gt Bookham *Guildf* 98-03; R Long Ditton from 03. *5 Church Meadow, Surbiton KT6 5EP* Tel (020) 8398 1583 Mobile 07736-680737 E-mail mailtherector@aol.com

COOPER, Stephen. b 54. Bernard Gilpin Soc Dur 73 Chich Th Coll 74. **d** 77 **p** 78. C Horbury *Wakef* 77-78; C Horbury w Horbury Bridge 78-81; C Barnsley St Mary 81-84; TV Elland 84-91; Hon C Huddersfield St Thos 93-94; P-in-c Middlesbrough St Columba w St Paul *York* from 94; Chapl S Tees Hosps NHS Trust 94-05; P-in-c Middlesbrough St Jo the Ev *York* from 05. *St Columba's Vicarage, 115 Cambridge Road, Middlesbrough TS5 5HF* Tel (01642) 824779 E-mail fr_s_cooper@hotmail.com

COOPER, Stephen Paul Crossley. b 58. Aston Tr Scheme 89 Trin Coll Bris 91. **d** 93 **p** 94. C Blackb Redeemer *Blackb* 93-95; C Altham w Clayton le Moors 95-98; V Langho Billington 98-03; Chapl Rossall Sch Fleetwood from 03. *2 Sandy Lane Cottages, Broadway, Fleetwood FY7 8SW* Tel (01253) 777440 *or* 774201 E-mail chaplain@rossall-school.lancs.sch.uk

COOPER, Mrs Susan Mary. b 45. Westcott Ho Cam 01. **d** 03 **p** 04. C Syston *Leic* from 03. *1121 Melton Road, Syston, Leicester LE7 2JS* Tel 0116-260 1670 E-mail scoople@yahoo.com

COOPER, Susan Mira. *See* RAMSARAN, Susan Mira

COOPER, Thomas Joseph Gerard Strickland. b 46. Lanc Univ PhD85. Ven English Coll & Pontifical Gregorian Univ Rome PhB66 PhL67 STB69 STL71. **d** 70 **p** 70. In RC Ch 70-92; Chapl St Woolos Cathl *Mon* 93-95; V Llandaff N *Llan* from 95. *All Saints' Vicarage, 59 Station Road, Llandaff, Cardiff CF14 2FB* Tel (029) 2056 4096 E-mail teilo@woolos.supanet.com

COOPER, Trevor. *See* COOPER, Joseph Trevor

COOPER, Trevor John. b 51. Ex Univ MA95. Wycliffe Hall Ox 75. **d** 79 **p** 95. C Southsea St Pet *Portsm* 79-80; NSM Heavitree w Ex St Paul *Ex* 93-96; C Standish *Blackb* 96-99; V Burnley St Cuth 99-03; P-in-c Lytham St Jo from 03. *The Vicarage, East Beach, Lytham, Lytham St Annes FY8 5EX* Tel (01253) 734396

COOPER, Wallace Peter. b 24. Kelham Th Coll 47. **d** 51 **p** 52. C Watford St Mich *St Alb* 51-52; C Ealing St Barn *Lon* 52-54; C New Brompton St Luke *Roch* 54-56; Perm to Offic *Ox* 62-81; Hon C Earley St Pet 81-83; Hon C Earley St Nic 83-92; rtd 90; Hon C Reading St Mark *Ox* 92-99; Perm to Offic *Ex* from 99. *7 Gracey Court, Woodland Road, Broadclyst, Exeter EX5 3GA* Tel (01392) 460612

COOPER, William Douglas. b 42. Open Univ BA83 Dur Univ CertEd69 ARCST65. St Jo Coll Nottm 88. **d** 94 **p** 95. NSM Melbourne *Derby* 94-97; C Penwortham St Mary *Blackb* 97-00; P-in-c Smeeth w Monks Horton and Stowting and Brabourne *Cant* 00-04; rtd 04. *18A Market Street, St Andrews KY16 9NS* Tel (01334) 460678

COOTE, Anthony John. b 54. Qu Coll Birm 95. **d** 97 **p** 98. C Malvern H Trin and St Jas *Worc* 97-01; TV Heref S Wye *Heref* 01-02; P-in-c Cradley *Worc* 02-04; rtd 04. *43 The Poplars, Stourbridge DY8 5SN* Tel (01384) 482446

COOTE, Bernard Albert Ernest. b 28. Lon Univ BD53. Chich Th Coll 54. **d** 55 **p** 56. C Addiscombe St Mary *Cant* 55-57; C Hawkhurst 57-59; C Sanderstead All SS *S'wark* 59-63; Chapl HM Borstal E Sutton Park 63-74; V Sutton Valence w E Sutton *Cant* 63-76; P-in-c Chart next Sutton Valence 71-76; Chapl and Dir R Sch for the Blind Leatherhead 76-91; rtd 91; Perm to Offic *Chich* and *Guildf* from 91. *6 Coxham Lane, Steyning BN44 3JG* Tel (01903) 813762

COPE, James Brian Andrew. b 58. SSC. Chich Th Coll 80. **d** 83 **p** 84. C Poulton-le-Fylde *Blackb* 83-86; C Fleetwood St Pet 86-87; V Fleetwood St Dav 87-94; P-in-c Somercotes *Derby* 94-99; V Watford St Jo *St Alb* from 99. *St John's Vicarage, 9 Monmouth Road, Watford WD17 1QW* Tel (01923) 236174 E-mail frjames-copessc@lineone.net

COPE, Judith Diane. b 50. St Hilda's Coll Ox BA72 Lon Univ MB, BS75 MRCGP80. St Alb and Ox Min Course 00. **d** 03 **p** 04. NSM Lt Berkhamsted and Bayford, Essendon etc *St Alb* from 03. *18 Hatherleigh Gardens, Potters Bar EN6 5HZ* Tel (01707) 644391 E-mail m_cope@btinternet.com

COPE, Mrs Melia Lambrianos. b 53. Cape Town Univ BSocSc73 Worc Coll of Tech CertMS84. St Jo Coll Nottm 80 WMMTC 83. **dss** 86 **d** 93 **p** 94. W Bromwich All SS *Lich* 86-93; NSM 93-94; NSM W Bromwich St Mary Magd CD 93-94; TV Cen Telford 94-02; Chapl HM Pris Shrewsbury 95-98; P-in-c Stokesay *Heref* from 02; P-in-c Sibdon Carwood w Halford from 02; P-in-c Acton Scott from 02. *Stokesay Vicarage, Clun Road, Craven Arms SY7 9QW* Tel (01588) 673463 E-mail meliacope@fish.co.uk

COPE, Miss Olive Rosemary. b 29. Birm Univ DPS73. Gilmore Ho 63. **dss** 69 **d** 87 **p** 94. Kentish Town St Martin w St Andr *Lon* 69-72; Enfield St Andr 73-87; Par Dn 87-89; Hon Par Dn 89-94; Hon C from 94; rtd 89. *7 Calder Close, Enfield EN1 3TS* Tel (020) 8363 8221 E-mail oliveclose2003@yahoo.co.uk

COPE, Peter John. b 42. Mert Coll Ox BA64 MA68 Lon Univ MSc74 Man Univ PhD91. Cuddesdon Coll 64. **d** 66 **p** 67. C Chapel Allerton *Ripon* 66-69; Ind Chapl *Lon* 69-76; Ind Chapl *Worc* 76-85; Min Can Worc Cathl 76-85; P-in-c Worc St Mark 76-81; Min W Bromwich St Mary Magd CD *Lich* 85-94; Ind Chapl 85-94; Telford Town Cen Chapl from 94; W Midl FE Field Officer from 94; Churches Ind Officer from 97; Perm to Offic *Heref* from 96. *Stokesay Vicarage, Clun Road, Craven Arms SY7 9QW* Tel (01588) 673463 E-mail petercope@telfordchristiancouncil.co.uk

COPE, Ralph Bruce. Sir Geo Williams Univ Montreal BA60 McGill Univ Montreal BD62. **d** 60 **p** 61. Canada 60-99 and from 00; P-in-c Sophia Antipolis *Eur* 99-00. *Unit 407, 4701 Uplands Drive, Nanaimo BC, Canada, V9T 5Y2* Tel (001) (250) 758 3296 E-mail ralglo@compuserve.com

COPE, Stephen Victor. b 60. St Jo Coll Ox BA81 DipTh84 MA87. Chich Th Coll 86. **d** 89 **p** 90. C Newmarket St Mary w Exning St Agnes *St E* 89-92; C Northampton St Matt *Pet* 92-94; V Rudston w Boynton and Kilham *York* 94-98; V Rudston w Boynton, Carnaby and Kilham from 98; P-in-c Burton Fleming w Fordon, Grindale etc from 00; RD Bridlington 98-03. *The Vicarage, Rudston, Driffield YO25 4XA* Tel (01262) 420313 E-mail stephen.cope@dial.pipex.com

COPELAND, Annabel. b 64. Roehampton Inst BEd87. Wycliffe Hall Ox 03. **d** 05. C Billericay and Lt Burstead *Chelmsf* from 05. *9 Arundel Close, Billericay CM12 0FN* Tel (01277) 632822 E-mail annabel@billericaychurches.org

COPELAND, Christopher Paul. b 38. AKC64. **d** 65 **p** 66. C Luton St Andr *St Alb* 65-67; C Droitwich St Nic w St Pet *Worc* 67-71; C Kings Norton *Birm* 71-72; TV 73-78; V Tyseley 78-88; P-in-c Grimley w Holt *Worc* 88-96; Dioc Stewardship Missr 88-96; P-in-c Forest of Dean Ch Ch w English Bicknor *Glouc* 96-03; rtd 03; Perm to Offic *Worc* from 03. *24 Players Avenue, Malvern WR14 1DU* Tel (01684) 563323

COPELAND, Derek Norman. b 38. Worc Coll Ox BA62 MA68. Westcott Ho Cam 63. **d** 64 **p** 65. C Portsea St Mary *Portsm* 64-71; P-in-c Avonmouth St Andr *Bris* 71-77; P-in-c Chippenham St Paul w Langley Burrell 78-79; Ind Chapl from 78; TR Chippenham St Paul w Hardenhuish etc 79-89; V Kington St Michael 79-89; Perm to Offic *Bris*; *B & W* and *Sarum* from 89; rtd 03. *51B Lowden, Chippenham SN15 2BG* Tel (01249) 443879

COPELAND, Ian Trevor. b 51. FCA83. OLM course 98. **d** 99 **p** 00. NSM Werrington *Lich* from 99. *4 Heather Close, Werrington, Stoke-on-Trent ST9 0LB* Tel (01782) 303525

COPLAND, Miss Carole Jean. b 37. Man Univ BA60. Wm Temple Coll Rugby DipRK67. **d** 87 **p** 94. NSM Northallerton w Kirby Sigston *York* 87-90; Dioc Adv in Children's Work 81-90; Par Dn Dunnington 90-94; Faith in the City Link Officer 90-96; C Dunnington 94-96; V Ledsham w Fairburn 96-99; rtd 99; Perm to Offic *York* from 99. *4 Jedwell Close, New Earswick, York YO32 4DQ* Tel (01904) 767110 E-mail carolecopland@hotmail.com

COPLAND, Canon Charles McAlester. b 10. CCC Cam BA33 MA36. Cuddesdon Coll 33. **d** 34 **p** 35. C Pet St Jo *Pet* 34-38; India 38-52; Can All SS Cathl Nagpur from 52; R Arbroath *Bre* 53-59; Can St Paul's Cathl Dundee 53-59; R Oban St Jo *Arg* 59-79; Provost St Jo Cathl Oban 59-79; Dean Arg 77-79; rtd 79; Hon Can St Jo Cathl Oban *Arg* from 79. *3 West Hill Road, Kirriemuir DD8 4PR* Tel (01575) 575415

COPLETON, Roger Boyd. b 62. Edin Univ BD87. TISEC 97. **d** 97 **p** 98. NSM Haddington *Edin* from 97; NSM Dunbar from 97. *6 Traprain Terrace, Haddington EH41 3QD* Tel (01620) 822994 *or* 0131-661 7704 Mobile 07759-952618 E-mail roger@copleton.fslife.co.uk

COPLEY, Colin. b 30. FRSA85. Kelham Th Coll 51. **d** 55 **p** 56. C Linc St Swithin *Linc* 55-58; C Bottesford 58-60; Chapl HM Borstal Hollesley Bay 60-66; Chapl HM Pris Liv 66-70; Chapl HM Pris Styal 70-73; N Regional Chapl HM Pris and Borstals 70-73; Midl Region 73-75; Chapl HM Pris Drake Hall 73-75; Asst Chapl Gen of Pris (Midl) 75-90; Chapl HM Pris Sudbury and Foston Hall 90-95; rtd 95; Perm to Offic *Lich* from 90. *67 Porlock Avenue, Stafford ST17 0HT* Tel (01785) 663162

COPLEY, David Judd. b 15. Linc Coll Ox BA48 MA53. Wycliffe Hall Ox 48. **d** 50 **p** 51. C Old Swinford *Worc* 50-53; Chapl to Bp Worc 52-55; Min Stourbridge St Mich Norton CD 53-56; R Romsley 56-67; Chapl Romsley Hosp 56-67; V Tardebigge 67-81; rtd 81; Perm to Offic *Worc* from 82. *212 Bromsgrove Road, Hunnington, Halesowen B62 0JU* Tel (01562) 710247

COPLEY, Paul. b 58. NEOC DipHE99. **d** 99 **p** 00. C Hessle *York* 99-02; TV Sutton St Jas and Wawne from 02. *The Vicarage, 11 Sovereign Way, Kingswood, Hull HU7 3JG*

COPPEN, Colin William. b 53. BCombStuds85. Linc Th Coll. **d** 85 **p** 86. C Tokyngton St Mich *Lon* 85-88; C Somers Town 88-90; P-in-c Edmonton St Alphege 90-92; V 92-95; P-in-c W Hampstead St Jas 95-97; P-in-c Kilburn St Mary w All So 95-97; TR Wood Green St Mich w Bounds Green St Gabr etc from 97. *St Michael's Rectory, 1A Selborne Road, London N22 7TL* Tel (020) 8888 1968 E-mail rector@woodgreenparish.com

COPPEN, George. *See* COPPEN, Robert George

COPPEN, Canon Martin Alan. b 48. Ex Univ BA69 Nottm Univ DipTh84. St Jo Coll Nottm 83. **d** 85 **p** 86. C Bitterne *Win* 85-88; V St Mary Bourne and Woodcott 88-99; V Hurstbourne Priors, Longparish etc from 00; RD Whitchurch 98-03; Hon Can Win Cathl from 04. *The Vicarage, St Mary Bourne, Andover SP11 6AY* Tel (01264) 738308 E-mail martin.coppen@ukgateway.net

COPPEN, Peter Euan. b 39. Ripon Coll Cuddesdon 79. **d** 81 **p** 82. C New Sleaford *Linc* 81-86; V Scawby and Redbourne 86-89; V Scawby, Redbourne and Hibaldstow 89-95; rtd 95; Perm to Offic *Pet* from 95. *Bay Cottage, The Close, Greatworth, Banbury OX17 2EB* Tel (01295) 711537

COPPEN, Robert George. b 39. Cape Town Univ BA66. St Jo Coll Dur 79. **d** 81 **p** 82. C Douglas St Geo and St Barn *S & M* 81-84; TV Kidlington w Hampton Poyle *Ox* 84-05; Chapl HM YOI Campsfield Ho 84-91; rtd 05. *Taobh Mol, Kildary, Invergordon IV18 0NJ* Tel (01862) 842381 E-mail coppen@dunelm.org.uk

COPPIN, Canon Ronald Leonard. b 30. Birm Univ BA52. Ridley Hall Cam 54. **d** 56 **p** 57. C Harrow Weald All SS *Lon* 56-59; Bp's Dom Chapl *Man* 59-63; Chapl St Aid Birkenhead 63-65; Vice-Prin 65-68; Selection Sec ACCM 68-74; Sec Cttee for Th Educn 71-74; Can Res and Lib Dur Cathl *Dur* 74-97; Dir of Clergy Tr 74-96; Warden NEOC 76-84; Dir Post-Ord Tr 86-97; rtd 97; Perm to Offic *Lon* from 02. *157 Defoe House, London EC2Y 8ND* Tel (020) 7588 9228 E-mail ronald.coppin@virgin.net

COPPING, Adrian Walter Alexander. b 52. Ridley Hall Cam. **d** 00 **p** 01. C Royston *St Alb* 00-04; R Bangor Monachorum, Worthenbury and Marchwiel *St As* from 04; AD Bangor Isycoed from 05. *The Rectory, 8 Ludlow Road, Bangor Isycoed, Wrexham LL13 0JG* Tel (01978) 780608 E-mail adriancopping@hotmail.com

COPPING, John Frank Walter Victor. b 34. K Coll Lon BD58 AKC58. **d** 59 **p** 60. C Hampstead St Jo *Lon* 59-62; C Bray and Braywood *Ox* 62-65; V Langley Mill *Derby* 65-71; V Cookham Dean *Ox* 71-03; RD Maidenhead 87-94; rtd 03; Perm to Offic *Ox* from 03. *41 Golden Ball Lane, Pinkneys Green, Maidenhead SL6 6NW* Tel (01628) 674433 E-mail john.copping@zoom.co.uk

COPPING, Raymond. b 36. St Mark & St Jo Coll Lon TCert59 St Paul's Cheltenham DivCert60. Wycliffe Hall Ox 72. **d** 74 **p** 75. C High Wycombe *Ox* 74-77; TV 77-87; TV Digswell and Panshanger *St Alb* 87-95; P-in-c Charlton Kings H Apostles *Glouc* 95-00; rtd 00; Hon C Thame *Ox* from 04. *20 Friars Furlong, Long Crendon, Aylesbury HP18 9DQ* Tel (01844) 208509

COPSEY, Nigel John. b 52. K Coll Lon BD75 AKC75 Surrey Univ MSc88 Middx Univ DProf01. St Aug Coll Cant 72. **d** 76 **p** 77. C Barkingside St Fran *Chelmsf* 76-78; C Canning Town St Cedd 78-80; P-in-c Victoria Docks Ascension 80-87; Chapl E Surrey Mental Health Unit 87-90; Hd Past & Spiritual Care E Surrey Priority Care NHS Trust from 90; Co-ord Past Care Surrey Oaklands NHS Trust from 99; Co-ord Relig Care Newham Community Health Services NHS Trust 99-01; Co-ord Relig Care Newham Primary Care Trust from 01. *Newham Centre for Mental Health, Glen Road, London E13 8SP* Tel (020) 7540 4380 Fax 7540 2970 E-mail n.copsey@btopenworld.com

COPUS, Brian George. b 36. AKC59. **d** 60 **p** 61. C Croydon St Mich *Cant* 60-63; C Swindon New Town *Bris* 63-69; V Colebrooke *Ex* 69-73; P-in-c Hittisleigh 69-73; R Perivale *Lon* 73-82; V Ruislip St Mary 82-01; rtd 01; Perm to Offic *Win* from 02. *2 Casterbridge Court, 1 Grosvenor Road, Bournemouth BH4 8BQ* Tel (01202) 752840

COPUS, John Cecil. b 38. TCert64 Maria Grey Coll Lon DipEd71 Open Univ BA78. Cant Sch of Min. **d** 83 **p** 84. Hon C Folkestone H Trin and St Geo w Ch Ch *Cant* 83-85; Hon C Midsomer Norton w Clandown *B & W* 85-91; Dioc Adv for Children's Work *Ex* 91-98; Hon C Aylesbeare, Rockbeare, Farringdon etc 95-98; P-in-c 98-01; rtd 01; Perm to Offic *Ex* from 01; Clergy Widow(er)s Officer from 02. *The Sidings, Park Road, Lapford, Crediton EX17 6QJ* Tel (01363) 83408

COPUS, Jonathan Hugh Lambert. b 44. BNC Ox BA66 MA71 LGSM66 MInstPI94. S'wark Ord Course 68. **d** 71 **p** 72. C Horsell *Guildf* 71-73; Producer Relig Progr BBC Radio Solent 73-87; Lic to Offic *Win* from 73. *Llys Myrddin, Efailwen, Clynderwen SA66 7XG* Tel (01994) 419792 Mobile 07971-545910 Fax (01994) 419796

CORBAN-BANKS, Edrick Hale. b 53. Victoria Univ Wellington BMus74 LTCL79 FTCL81. St Jo Coll Auckland BTh91. **d** 91 **p** 92. New Zealand 91-99; P Asst Johnsonville St Jo 92-94; Ch Planter Churton Park 93-94; V Katikati 94-99; P Missr Alicante Spain 99; R Alicante St Paul 99-00; Chapl Ibiza *Eur* 00-03; V Stoke New Zealand from 04. *523 Main Road, Stoke, Nelson, New Zealand 7001* Tel (0064) (3) 547 3478 E-mail vicar.stbarnabas@paradise.net.nz

CORBETT, George. b 18. Bible Churchmen's Coll Bris 47. **d** 50 **p** 51. C Wednesfield Heath *Lich* 50-52; R Salford St Matthias w St Simon *Man* 52-55; N Area Sec BCMS 55-58; V S Lambeth St Steph *S'wark* 58-61; Assoc Home Sec BCMS 61-63; V Hatherleigh *Ex* 63-78; P-in-c Ringmore and Kingston 78-84; R Bigbury, Ringmore and Kingston 84-86; rtd 86; Perm to Offic *Heref* from 87. *2 Quantock Close, Hereford HR4 0TD* Tel (01432) 269211

CORBETT, Canon Henry. b 53. CCC Cam BA75. Wycliffe Hall Ox. **d** 78 **p** 79. C Everton St Pet *Liv* 78-84; TV 84-87; TR 87-02; R Everton St Pet w St Chrys from 02; AD Liv N from 03; Hon Can Liv Cathl from 03. *Shrewsbury House, Langrove Street, Liverpool L5 3LT* Tel 0151-207 1948 E-mail hjcorbett@shewsy.freeserve.co.uk

CORBETT, Ian Deighton. b 42. St Cath Coll Cam BA64 MA68 Salford Univ MSc83. Westcott Ho Cam 67. **d** 69 **p** 70. C New Bury *Man* 69-72; C Bolton St Pet 72-75; Chapl Bolton Colls of H&FE 72-75; Dioc FE Officer 74-83; R Man Victoria Park *Man* 75-80; Chapl Salford Univ 80-83; Hon Can Man Cathl 83-87; P-in-c Salford Sacred Trin 83-87; Dir of In-Service Tr 83-87; Lesotho 87-91; Zimbabwe 91-92; Botswana 92-94; S Africa 94-95; Dean Tuam *T, K & A* 97-99; I Tuam w Cong and Aasleagh 97-99; R Whitesands Canada 99-01; V Navajoland Area Miss USA from 01. *PO Box 28, Bluff, UT 84512, USA* Tel (001) (505) 325 5832 Fax 327 7933 E-mail iancorbett@hubwest.com

CORBETT, Jocelyn Rory. **d** 05. Aux Min Aghalee *D & D* from 05. *Badger Hill, 23 Magherabeg Road, Dromore BT25 1RS* Tel (028) 9269 2067 E-mail rory.corbett@ukonline.co.uk

CORBETT, John David. b 32. Oriel Coll Ox BA55 MA59. St Steph Ho Ox 55. **d** 57 **p** 58. C Plymouth St Pet *Ex* 57-64; V Marldon 64-74; TV Bournemouth St Pet w St Swithun, H Trin etc *Win* 74-83; V Beckenham St Barn *Roch* 83-88; V King's Sutton and Newbottle and Charlton *Pet* 88-97; rtd 97; Perm to Offic *Portsm* and *Win* from 98. *119 St Augustine Road, Southsea PO4 9AA* Tel (023) 9275 3212 E-mail jdc.augustine@virgin.net

CORBETT, Miss Phyllis. b 34. Cranmer Hall Dur 76. **dss** 80 **d** 87 **p** 94. Walsall Wood *Lich* 80-87; Par Dn Baswich 87-94; C 94-95; rtd 95; Perm to Offic *Lich* from 95. *9 Redhill Gorse, Crab Lane, Trinity Fields, Stafford ST16 1SW*

CORBETT, Rory. *See* CORBETT, Jocelyn Rory

CORBETT, Stephen Paul. b 57. BA80. St Jo Coll Nottm 83. **d** 85 **p** 86. C Tollington Park St Mark w St Anne *Lon* 85-86; C Holloway St Mark w Em 86-91; V Chitts Hill St Cuth 91-93; V Springfield *Birm* 93-04; AD Moseley 02-04; V Walmley from 04. *The Vicarage, 2 Walmley Road, Sutton Coldfield B76 1QN* Tel 0121-351 1030 E-mail stephencorbett@stchrist.freeserve.co.uk

CORBIN, Frederick Athelston. b 42. S Dios Minl Tr Scheme 80. **d** 83 **p** 85. NSM Basingstoke *Win* 83-84; C Hulme Ascension *Man* 84-86; Lic to Hulme Deanery 86-87; C E Crompton 87-89; V Oldham St Barn 89-00; rtd 00; Grenada 00-01; Perm to Offic *Man* from 01. *11 Westminster Close, Shaw, Oldham OL2 7XZ* Tel (01706) 847405

CORBYN, John. b 58. Man Univ BA79 Ven English Coll & Pontifical Gregorian Univ Rome 83. Wycliffe Hall Ox BA83 MA87. **d** 84 **p** 85. C Deane *Man* 84-87; C Lancaster St Mary *Blackb* 87-90; Chapl HM Pris Lanc 89-90; V Blackb St Gabr *Blackb* 90-01; V Bearsted w Thurnham *Cant* from 01. *The Vicarage, Church Lane, Bearsted, Maidstone ME14 4EF* Tel (01622) 737135 E-mail johncorbyn@garlick.net

CORBYN, John Robert. b 54. Qu Coll Birm. **d** 82 **p** 83. C Northolt W End St Jos *Lon* 82-86; Urban Miss P *York* 86-88; C Sutton St Mich 86-88; V Dalton *Sheff* 88-96; R Cressing *Chelmsf* 96-99; R Cressing w Stisted and Bradwell etc from 99. *The House, The Street, Bradwell, Braintree CM77 8EL* Tel (01376) 562398 E-mail frjohn@crestibrad.freeserve.co.uk

CORCORAN, Mrs Valerie A'Court. b 46. UEA BA68 Lon Inst of Educn PGCE69. STETS 99. **d** 02 **p** 03. NSM Boyatt Wood *Win* from 02. *Ashley, Finches Lane, Twyford, Winchester SO21 1QB* Tel (01962) 712951 Mobile 07736-459500 Fax (01962) 715770 E-mail v.corcoran@btinternet.com

CORDELL, Derek Harold. b 34. Chich Th Coll 57. **d** 60 **p** 61. C Whitstable All SS *Cant* 60-63; C Moulsecoomb *Chich* 63-69; Chapl Bucharest *Eur* 69-71; V Brighton St Wilfrid *Chich* 71-74; Chapl HM Borstal Roch 74-80; Asst Chapl HM Pris Man 80-81; Chapl HM Pris The Verne 81-89; Chapl HM Pris Channings Wood 89-90; Chapl Milan w Genoa and Varese *Eur* 90-91; Chapl Mojacar 91-94; Perm to Offic from 95; rtd 97. *49 Tower Way, Dunkeswell, Honiton EX14 4XH* Tel (01404) 891859

CORDINER, Alan Dobson. b 61. Westmr Coll Ox BA87. **d** 92 **p** 93. C Upperby St Jo *Carl* 92-98; P-in-c Bootle, Corney, Whicham and Whitbeck 98-05; Asst Chapl HM Pris Haverigg 98-03. *Address temp unknown*

CORDINGLEY, Canon Brian Lambert. b 30. St Aid Birkenhead 55. **d** 57 **p** 58. Ind Chapl *Sheff* 57-63; C Clifton St Jas 57-61; C Rotherham 61-63; Ind Chapl *Man* 63-92; R Old Trafford St Cuth 63-81; V Hamer 81-92; Hon Can Man Cathl 87-92; rtd 92; Perm to Offic *Man* from 99. *Wellsprings, 27 Fernthorpe Avenue, Uppermill, Oldham OL3 6EA* Tel (01457) 820130

CORE, Edward. b 54. BTh. Sarum & Wells Th Coll. **d** 82 **p** 83. C Newbold w Dunston *Derby* 82-86; Chapl RAF 86-01; Command Chapl RAF from 01. *Chaplaincy Services (RAF), HQ, Personnel and Training Command, RAF Innsworth, Gloucester GL3 1EZ* Tel (01452) 712612 ext 5164 Fax 510828

CORFE, David Robert. b 35. Pemb Coll Cam BA58 MA60 Lambeth STh70. Cuddesdon Coll 58. **d** 60 **p** 61. C Wigan All SS *Liv* 60-63; SPG Miss India 63-68; V Lucknow Ch Ch w All SS and St Pet 70-75; C Northwood Em *Lon* 75; V Westwell and Eastwell w Boughton Aluph *Cant* 75-80; V Hildenborough *Roch* 80-91; Lic Preacher Stretford St Bride *Man* 91-98; Team Ldr Interserve 98-00; rtd 00; Perm to Offic *Win* from 03. *1 Hartley Court, 12 Winn Road, Southampton SO17 1EN* Tel (023) 8058 5557 E-mail drcorfe@freedomland.co.uk

CORK, Ronald Edward. b 43. Plymouth Poly CQSW72. N Ord Course 89. **d** 92 **p** 93. Hon C Altrincham St Geo *Ches* 92-96; P-in-c Altrincham St Jo 96-01; rtd 01. *9 Dodgson Close, Llandudno LL30 1AJ* Tel (01492) 873889 E-mail roncork@aol.com

CORK, CLOYNE AND ROSS, Archdeacon of. *See* WHITE, The Ven Robin Edward Bantry

CORK, CLOYNE AND ROSS, Bishop of. *See* COLTON, The Rt Revd William Paul

CORK, Dean of. *See* BURROWS, The Very Revd Michael Andrew James

CORKE, Andrew John. b 55. Bris Univ LLB77. **d** 98 **p** 00. OLM Canford Magna *Sarum* from 98. *2 Silverwood Close, Wimborne Minster BH21 1QZ* Tel (01202) 882449 Mobile 07711-898723 Fax 786140 E-mail a.corke@talk21.com

CORKE, Bryan Raymond. b 49. Westmr Coll Lon 81. LNSM course 92. **d** 95 **p** 96. OLM Flixton St Jo *Man* from 95. *40 Daresbury Avenue, Manchester M41 8GL* Tel 0161-748 1827

CORKE, Colin John. b 59. St Pet Coll Ox BA81. Cranmer Hall Dur 83. **d** 85 **p** 86. C Chapel Allerton *Ripon* 85-88; C Burmantofts St Steph and St Agnes 88-91; P-in-c Tatsfield *S'wark* 91-01; Reigate Adnry Ecum Officer 92-01; V Longbridge *Birm* from 01; Dioc Ecum Officer from 02. *St John's Vicarage, 220 Longbridge Lane, Birmingham B31 4JT* Tel 0121-475 3484 E-mail ado67@btinternet.com

CORKE, Francis Bonny. *See* RODRIGUEZ-VEGLIO, Francis Bonny

CORKE, John Harry. b 29. AKC55. **d** 56 **p** 57. C Stockingford *Cov* 56-58; C Nuneaton St Nic 58-60; V Hartshill 60-80; R Hampton Lucy w Charlecote and Loxley 80-94; rtd 94; Perm to Offic *Linc* from 95. *18 Haven Close, Fleet, Spalding PE12 8NS* Tel (01406) 426038

CORKE, Louise Dorothy. b 59. Southn Univ BSc80 PGCE81. Trin Coll Bris BA94. **d** 97 **p** 98. C Ipsley *Worc* 97-01; TV Bradgate Team *Leic* from 01. *The Rectory, 58 Pymm Ley Lane, Groby, Leicester LE6 0GZ* Tel 0116-231 3090 E-mail standstill@btopenworld.com

CORKE, Roderick Geoffrey. b 58. UEA BEd79 Open Univ MA96. St Jo Coll Nottm 90. **d** 92 **p** 93. C Trimley *St E* 92-95; C Walton 95-00; TR Walton and Trimley from 00; P-in-c Taunton St Mary *B & W* from 05. *The Vicarage, Church Square, Taunton TA1 1TA* Tel (01823) 272441 E-mail rodcorke@tiscali.co.uk

CORKER, Mrs Elizabeth Jane. b 42. **d** 99 **p** 00. OLM Martlesham w Brightwell *St E* from 99. *12 Fairfield Avenue, Felixstowe IP11 9JN* Tel (01394) 210793 E-mail e.corker@ntlworld.com

CORKER, John Anthony. b 37. TD93. ACIB75 AKC63. **d** 64 **p** 65. C Lindley *Wakef* 64-68; V Brotherton 68-72; Perm to Offic 72-82; CF (TA) 80-93; Hon C Askham Bryan *York* 82-91; TV York All SS Pavement w St Crux and St Martin etc 91-96; Asst P Amblecote *Worc* 96-01; C Dudley St Barn 01-02; rtd 02; Perm to Offic *Worc* from 02. *69 Lakeside Court, Brierley Hill DY5 3RQ* Tel (01384) 897378

CORKER, Canon Ronald. b 30. Ely Th Coll 51. **d** 54 **p** 55. C Whitworth w Spennymoor *Dur* 54-58; Min Dunstan St Nic ED 58-65; Chapl Dunston Hill Hosp Gateshead 58-68; V Dunston St Nic *Dur* 65-68; R Willington 68-75; P-in-c Sunnybrow 73-75; R Willington and Sunnybrow 75-80; V Billingham St Cuth 80-85; RD Stockton 83-85; TR Jarrow 85-95; Hon Can Dur Cathl 90-00; rtd 95. *195 Beaconsides, Cleadon Manor, South Shields NE34 7PT* Tel 0191-454 2987

CORLESS, Canon Keith Ronald. b 37. Edin Th Coll 58. **d** 61 **p** 62. C Pittville All SS *Glouc* 61-64; C Leckhampton SS Phil and Jas 66-69; R Ashchurch 69-96; Hon Can Glouc Cathl 95-00; V Staverton w Boddington and Tredington etc 96-00; rtd 00; Perm to Offic *Glouc* from 00. *1 Tanners Close, Brockworth, Gloucester GL3 4QN* Tel (01452) 863766

CORLEY, Samuel Jon Clint. b 76. St Aid Coll Dur BA97 MA98 Hughes Hall Cam PGCE99. St Jo Coll Nottm MA04. **d** 04 **p** 05. C Lancaster St Thos *Blackb* from 04. *6 Jackson Close, Lancaster LA1 5EY* Tel (01524) 33741 *or* 590417 Mobile 07966-524683 E-mail sam@st.tees.org.uk

CORNE, Ronald Andrew. b 51. Sarum & Wells Th Coll 87. **d** 89 **p** 90. C Bitterne Park *Win* 89-93; R Headbourne Worthy and King's Worthy 93-01; P-in-c Broughton, Bossington, Houghton and Mottisfont 01-03; R from 03. *The Rectory, Rectory Lane, Broughton, Stockbridge SO20 8AB* Tel (01794) 301287 E-mail cronandrew@aol.com

CORNECK, Canon Warrington Graham. b 35. MBE05. ACA60 FCA62. Clifton Th Coll. **d** 65 **p** 66. C Islington St Jude Mildmay Park *Lon* 65-67; C Southgate *Chich* 67-73; P-in-c Deptford St Nic w Ch Ch *S'wark* 73-76; P-in-c Deptford St Luke 73-76; V Deptford St Nic and St Luke from 76; RD Deptford from 85; Hon Can S'wark Cathl from 91. *St Nicholas' Vicarage, 41 Creek Road, London SE8 3BU* Tel and fax (020) 8692 2749 E-mail corneck@corneck.freeserve.co.uk

CORNELIUS, Donald Eric. b 31. K Coll Lon BD52 AKC. Linc Th Coll 84. **d** 84 **p** 85. NSM Crowle *Linc* 84-97; NSM Crowle Gp 97-02; NSM Flixborough w Burton upon Stather 91-02; P-in-c Gunhouse w Burringham 91-02; Perm to Offic from 02. *4 Mulberry Drive, Crowle, Scunthorpe DN17 4JF* Tel (01724) 710279

CORNELL, Miss Jean Cranston. b 36. Man Univ CertEd59 BA64 York Univ BPhil71. Ripon Coll Cuddesdon 87 MTh00. **d** 89 **p** 94. C Matson *Glouc* 89-92; C Bishop's Cleeve 92-96; rtd 96; NSM Winchcombe, Gretton, Sudeley Manor etc *Glouc* 96-01; Perm to Offic 01-02. *20 Darent Close, Stone Cross, Pevensey BN24 5PW* Tel (01323) 763171 E-mail naej@chris47.freeserve.co.uk

CORNELL, Michael Neil. *See* COHEN, Michael Neil

CORNES, Alan Stuart. b 70. Open Univ BA98 Nottm Univ MA00. St Jo Coll Nottm 98. **d** 01 **p** 02. C Meole Brace *Lich* 01-04; P-in-c Halliwell St Luke *Man* from 04. *St Luke's Vicarage, Chorley Old Road, Bolton BL1 3BE* Tel (01204) 843060 Fax 848987 E-mail stuart.cornes@new-wine.net

CORNES, Andrew Charles Julian. b 49. CCC Ox BA70 MA73 St Jo Coll Dur DipTh73. Wycliffe Hall Ox 70 Cranmer Hall Dur 72. **d** 73 **p** 74. C York St Mich-le-Belfrey *York* 73-76; C St Marylebone All So w SS Pet and Jo *Lon* 76-85; USA 85-88; V Crowborough *Chich* from 89; RD Rotherfield 97-03; Chapl Eastbourne and Co Healthcare NHS Trust from 89. *All Saints' Vicarage, Chapel Green, Crowborough TN6 1ED* Tel (01892) 667384 *or* 652081

CORNESS, Andrew Stuart. b 69. Bp Otter Coll Chich BA91 Westmr Coll Ox PGCE93. Wycliffe Hall Ox BA00. **d** 01 **p** 02. C Ewood *Blackb* 01-04; Chapl RN from 04. *Royal Naval Chaplaincy Service, Room 203, Victory Building, HM Naval Base, Portsmouth PO1 3LS* Tel (01705) 727903 Fax 727112 E-mail andrewcorness@hotmail.com

CORNFIELD, Richard James. b 67. St Jo Coll Nottm BA96. **d** 96 **p** 97. C Cheltenham Ch Ch *Glouc* 96-00; C Aldridge *Lich* 00-03; R from 03. *The Rectory, 14 The Green, Aldridge, Walsall WS9 8NH* Tel (01922) 452414 E-mail richard.cornfield@virgin.net

CORNISH, Anthony. b 30. Roch Th Coll 64. **d** 67 **p** 68. C Goodmayes All SS *Chelmsf* 67-71; C Buckhurst Hill 71-73; V Westcliff St Andr 73-83; R Rawreth w Rettendon 83-96; rtd 96; Perm to Offic *Chelmsf* from 99. *12 Fleetwood Avenue, Clacton-on-Sea CO15 5SE* Tel (01255) 813826

CORNISH, Dennis Henry Ronald. b 31. FCIB72 FCIS81. S'wark Ord Course 83. **d** 86 **p** 87. NSM Uxbridge *Lon* 86-89; R Lurgashall, Lodsworth and Selham *Chich* 89-96; rtd 96; Perm to Offic *Chich* from 96. *Peerley Lodge, 1 Peerley Road, East Wittering, Chichester PO20 8DW* Tel (01243) 672481

CORNISH, Gillian Lesley. b 45. ACIB77. St Jo Coll Nottm 90 LNSM course 93. **d** 96 **p** 97. OLM Moston St Mary *Man* from 96. *11 Rishworth Drive, New Moston, Manchester M40 3PS* Tel 0161-681 2839

CORNISH, Graham Peter. b 42. Dur Univ BA67 FLA. NEOC 82. **d** 84 **p** 85. NSM Harrogate St Wilfrid and St Luke *Ripon*

84-96; Perm to Offic *York* from 84; NSM Bilton *Ripon* from 96. *33 Mayfield Grove, Harrogate HG1 5HD* Tel (01423) 562747 Fax 529928 E-mail gp-jm.cornish@virgin.net

CORNISH, Ivor. b 40. Reading Univ BSc61 DipEd62 ADipR79. Ox Min Course 86. **d** 89 **p** 90. NSM Aston Clinton w Buckland and Drayton Beauchamp *Ox* 89-97; NSM The Lee from 97; NSM Hawridge w Cholesbury and St Leonard from 97. *79 Weston Road, Aston Clinton, Aylesbury HP22 5EP* Tel (01296) 630345

CORNISH, John Douglas. b 42. Lich Th Coll 67. **d** 70 **p** 71. C Lt Stanmore St Lawr *Lon* 70-73; C Harefield 73-96; Perm to Offic 96-02; rtd 02; Hon C Winchmore Hill H Trin *Lon* from 02. *46 Arnos Grove, London N14 7AR*

CORNISH, Peter Andrew. b 55. Ch Ch Ox BA77 MA80 Ex Univ CertEd78. St Jo Coll Nottm 84. **d** 87 **p** 88. C Sanderstead All SS *S'wark* 87-92; TV Cen Telford *Lich* 92-98; R Sturry w Fordwich and Westbere w Hersden *Cant* from 98. *The Rectory, 2 The Hamels, Sturry, Canterbury CT2 0BL* Tel (01227) 710320 E-mail peter.cornish@amserve.net

CORNWALL, Archdeacon of. *See* WHITEMAN, The Ven Rodney David Carter

CORNWELL, Christopher Richard. b 43. Dur Univ BA67. Cuddesdon Coll 67. **d** 69 **p** 70. C Cannock *Lich* 69-75; P-in-c Hadley 75-80; V 80-81; Bp's Dom Chapl 81-86; Subchanter Lich Cathl 81-86; V Ellesmere 86-89; V Welsh Frankton 86-89; V Ellesmere and Welsh Frankton 89-92; TV Leeds City *Ripon* 92-00; AD Allerton 94-97; V Ireland Wood from 00; AD Headingley from 01. *St Paul's Vicarage, Raynel Drive, Leeds LS16 6BS* Tel 0113-267 2907 E-mail vicar.roundchurch@virgin.net

CORNWELL, Gertrude Florence. b 21. CertEd48 Nottm Univ DipEd72. Gilmore Ho 56 Lambeth STh60. **dss** 62 **d** 87. Sen Lect Bp Grosseteste Coll Linc 64-81; rtd 81; Perm to Offic *Linc* from 91. *Flat 2A, 14 Minster Yard, Lincoln LN2 1PW* Tel (01522) 527249

CORNWELL, Lisa Michele. b 70. Lon Bible Coll BA94 Westmr Coll Ox PGCE95 K Coll Lon MA99. Ridley Hall Cam 00. **d** 02 **p** 03. C Newport Pagnell w Lathbury and Moulsoe *Ox* from 02. *3 Castle Meadow Close, Newport Pagnell MK16 9EJ* Tel (01908) 613161 Mobile 07789-778885

CORP, Ronald Geoffrey. b 51. Ch Ch Ox MA77. STETS DipTh98. **d** 98 **p** 99. NSM Kilburn St Mary w All So and W Hampstead St Jas *Lon* 98-02; NSM Hendon St Mary and Ch Ch from 02. *76 Brent Street, London NW4 2ES* Tel (020) 8202 8123 E-mail reynaldo@angkor.demon.co.uk

CORRAN, Henry Stanley. b 15. Trin Coll Cam BA36 PhD41. CITC 76. **d** 77 **p** 78. NSM Bray Ch Ch *D & G* 77-85; rtd 85. *71 Alderley Road, Hoylake, Wirral CH47 2AU* Tel 0151-632 2750

CORRIE, Jennifer Sylvia. b 46. RMN68 SRN76 DN77. OLM course 96. **d** 99 **p** 00. OLM Broughton *Man* from 99. *6 Briardene, Back Hilton Street, Salford M7 2GQ*

CORRIE, John. b 48. Imp Coll Lon BScEng69 MSc70 PhD73 Nottm Univ MTh86. Trin Coll Bris 74. **d** 77 **p** 78. C Kendal St Thos *Carl* 77-80; C Attenborough *S'well* 80-86; ICS Peru 86-91; Tutor and Lect All Nations Chr Coll Ware 91-02; Lect/Development Officer Cen for Angl Communion Studies Selly Oak 02-05; Abp's Internat Project Officer *Cant* from 05. *15 Woodfield Road, Kings Heath, Birmingham B13 9UL* Tel 0121-444 2767

CORRIE, Paul Allen. b 43. St Jo Coll Nottm 77. **d** 79 **p** 80. C Beverley Minster *York* 79-82; V Derby St Werburgh *Derby* 82-84; V Derby St Alkmund and St Werburgh 84-95; Singapore 95-99; R Hawkwell *Chelmsf* from 00. *The Rectory, Ironwell Lane, Hawkwell, Hockley SS5 4JY* Tel (01702) 200620 E-mail plcorrie@waitrose.com

CORRIGAN, The Ven Thomas George. b 28. TCD Dip Bibl Studies 56 BTh91. CITC 56. **d** 58 **p** 59. C Cavan and Drung *K, E & A* 58-60; I Drung 60-67; I Belfast St Mich *Conn* 67-70; I Kingscourt w Syddan *M & K* 70-96; Adn Meath 81-96; Dioc Registrar (Meath) 87-90; rtd 96. *The Beeches, Turner's Hill, Kingscourt, Co Cavan, Irish Republic* Tel (00353) (42) 966 8348 Fax 966 8388 E-mail adngcorrigan@eircom.net

CORRY, Caroline Anne. b 58. St Hilda's Coll Ox BA79 Ox Univ MA97. S Tr Scheme 94. **d** 97 **p** 98. C Weston *Guildf* 97-01; P-in-c N Holmwood from 01. *The Vicarage, Willow Green, North Holmwood, Dorking RH5 4JB* Tel (01306) 882135 E-mail caroline_corry@hotmail.com

CORSIE, Andrew Russell. b 57. Middx Univ BA97. Trin Coll Bris DipHE93. **d** 93 **p** 94. C Northolt Park St Barn *Lon* 93-97; C Perivale 97-01; P-in-c from 01; AD Ealing from 03. *Perivale Rectory, Federal Road, Greenford UB6 7AP* Tel (020) 8997 1948 E-mail acorsie@aol.com

CORSTORPHINE, Miss Margaret. b 34. SRN57 SCM59. Cranmer Hall Dur 70. **dss** 84 **d** 87 **p** 94. Colchester St Jo *Chelmsf* 84-87; Par Dn 87-94; C 94; rtd 94; Perm to Offic *Portsm* from 94. *12 Oakmeadow Close, Emsworth PO10 7RL*

CORWIN, Nigel Trevor. b 47. EAMTC 95. **d** 97 **p** 98. NSM Bury St Edmunds Ch Ch *St E* from 97. *121 Raedwald Drive, Bury St Edmunds IP32 7DG* Tel (01284) 725284 Fax 725391 Mobile 07713-769816 E-mail nigel@corwin.fsnet.co.uk

CORY, Ms Valerie Ann. b 44. CertEd65 Nottm Univ BEd85. EMMTC 85. **d** 88 **p** 94. Area Sec CMS *Linc* and *Pet* 87-91; NSM Grantham *Linc* 88-91; Par Dn Ealing St Mary *Lon* 91-94; Chapl NW Lon Poly 91-92; Chapl Thames Valley Univ 92-96; C Ealing St Mary 94-96; Chapl Birm Cathl *Birm* 96-99; C Surbiton St Andr and St Mark *S'wark* from 99. *The Vicarage, 1 The Mall, Surbiton KT6 4EH* Tel (020) 8399 6806 E-mail valcory@ukgateway.net

COSBY, Ingrid St Clair. b 34. ALCM LLCM DipEd Lon Univ DipTh. **dss** 71 **d** 86 **p** 96. Cumbernauld *Glas* 71-73; Asst CF 73-78; Stromness *Ab* 83-86; NSM from 86. *Quarrybrae, Hillside Road, Stromness KW16 3HR* Tel (01856) 850832 Fax as telephone

COSENS, William Edward Hyde (Ted). b 38. Lich Th Coll 61. **d** 64 **p** 65. C W Drayton *Lon* 64-68; C Roehampton H Trin *S'wark* 68-70; ILEA Youth Ldr 69-70; Miss to Seamen 70-94; Rotterdam 70-72; Tilbury 72-76; Australia 76-81 and 99-03; Dampier 76-81; Auckland New Zealand 81-89; Chapl Immingham Seafarers' Cen 89-94; Hon C Immingham *Linc* 89-94; Chapl Felixstowe Seafarers' Cen 94-97; Chapl Avonmouth Miss to Seamen 97-99; Sen Chapl Melbourne Miss to Seafarers 99-03; Chapl State of Vic 99-03; rtd 03; Perm to Offic *Sarum* from 04. *c/o Mrs C E H Gilbert, 44 Church Avenue, Beckenham BR3 1DT* Tel 07963-093816 (mobile) E-mail ted.caroline.cosens@virgin.net

COSGRAVE-HANLEY, Mirt Joseph. *See* HANLEY, Mirt Joseph

COSH, Roderick John. b 56. Lon Univ BSc78 Heythrop Coll Lon MA03. St Steph Ho Ox 78. **d** 81 **p** 82. C Swindon New Town *Bris* 81-86; Chapl Asst R Marsden Hosp Lon and Surrey 86-91; V Whitton St Aug *Lon* 91-00; P-in-c Staines St Mary and St Pet from 00; P-in-c Staines Ch Ch from 04; AD Spelthorne from 04. *St Peter's Vicarage, 14 Thames Side, Staines TW18 2HA* Tel (01784) 453039 *or* 469155 E-mail rod@stainesparish.fsnet.co.uk

COSLETT, Anthony Allan. b 49. Cuddesdon Coll. **d** 84 **p** 85. C Notting Hill St Clem and St Mark *Lon* 84-85; C Brentford 85-87; C-in-c Hounslow Gd Shep Beavers Lane CD 87-90; V Hounslow W Gd Shep 90-92; CF from 92. *c/o MOD Chaplains (Army)* Tel (01980) 615804 Fax 615800

COSLETT (née SLATER), Mrs Carol Ann. b 63. Univ of Wales (Ban) BD85 Jes Coll Cam PGCE86 Lon Inst of Educn MA92. Ripon Coll Cuddesdon 01. **d** 03 **p** 04. C Horsell *Guildf* from 03. *6 Waldens Park Road, Horsell, Woking GU21 4RN* Tel (01483) 764094 Mobile 07803-671256 E-mail carolcoslett@tiscali.co.uk

COSSAR, David Vyvyan. b 34. Lon Univ BA63. Chich Th Coll 63. **d** 65 **p** 66. C Upper Clapton St Matt *Lon* 65-68; C Withycombe Raleigh *Ex* 68-72; V Honicknowle 72-78; V Brixham w Churston Ferrers 78-86; P-in-c Kingswear 85-86; TR Brixham w Churston Ferrers and Kingswear 86-90; V Lamorbey H Trin *Roch* 90-03; rtd 03. *31 Bromley College, London Road, Bromley BR1 1PE* Tel (020) 8464 6911 E-mail diane.cossar@tinyonline.uk

COSSAR, Canon Heather Jillian Mackenzie. b 27. **dss** 83 **d** 91 **p** 94. CMS Kenya 83-90; NSM Slindon, Eartham and Madehurst *Chich* 90-99; Perm to Offic from 99; Can Nyahururu from 03. *Gwitu, 38 Spinney Walk, Barnham, Bognor Regis PO22 0HT* Tel (01243) 552718

COSSINS, John Charles. b 43. Hull Univ BSc65. Oak Hill Th Coll 65. **d** 67 **p** 68. C Kenilworth St Jo *Cov* 67-70; C Huyton St Geo *Liv* 70-73; TV Maghull 73-79; Chapl Oakwood Hosp Maidstone 79-85; Maidstone Hosp 85-88; Chapl Park Lane Hosp Maghull 88-03; Chapl Moss Side Hosp Liv 88-03; Chapl Ashworth Hosp Maghull 88-03; rtd 03; Perm to Offic *Liv* from 03. *9 Longton Drive, Liverpool L37 7ET* Tel (01704) 833136 Fax 08700-553669 E-mail jcossins@jcossins.demon.co.uk

COSSINS, Roger Stanton. b 40. K Coll Lon BD67 AKC67. **d** 68 **p** 69. C Bramley *Ripon* 68-71; C W End *Win* 71-76; V Bramley 76-91; P-in-c Bournemouth H Epiphany 91-94; V 94-00; rtd 00. *5 Allen Court, Trumpington, Cambridge CB2 2LU* Tel (01223) 841726

COSSLETT, Dominic Simon. b 72. Univ of Wales (Lamp) BA94 Leeds Univ MA96. Coll of Resurr Mirfield 94. **d** 96 **p** 97. C Newton St Pet *S & B* 96-99; C Abergavenny St Mary w Llanwenarth Citra *Mon* 99-02; V Kingstanding St Mark *Birm* from 02. *St Mark's Clergy House, Bandywood Crescent, Birmingham B44 9JX* Tel 0121-360 7288

COSTER, Mrs Catherine Anne. b 47. Bris Poly BEd85. WEMTC 97. **d** 00 **p** 01. NSM Yate New Town *Bris* 00-04; NSM Warmley, Syston and Bitton from 04; Hon Min Can Bris Cathl from 04. *31 Vayre Close, Chipping Sodbury, Bristol BS37 6NT* Tel (01454) 314858 Fax 0117-927 7454 E-mail catherine.coster@bristoldiocese.org

COSTERTON, Alan Stewart. b 40. Bris Univ BA67. Clifton Th Coll 67. **d** 69 **p** 70. C Peckham St Mary Magd *S'wark* 69-73; C Forest Gate St Sav w W Ham St Matt *Chelmsf* 73-76; TV 76-79; V Thornton cum Bagworth *Leic* 79-85; V Thornton, Bagworth and Stanton 85-95; TR Sileby, Cossington and Seagrave 95-04; R 04-05; rtd 05. *59 Station Road, Cropston, Leicester LE7 7HG* Tel 0116-234 1026 E-mail alan@costerton.freeserve.co.uk

COSTIGAN, Esther Rose. b 79. Regent's Park Coll Ox BA00 MA04 Clare Hall Cam MPhil04. Westcott Ho Cam 03. **d** 05. C Altrincham St Geo *Ches* from 05. *18 Hawarden Road, Altrincham WA14 1NG* E-mail esthercostigan@yahoo.co.uk

COSTIN, Richard George Charles. b 38. Liv Univ CertEd59 Anglia Poly BEd85 ACP67 FCollP82. Coll of Resurr Mirfield 04. **d** 05. NSM Scarborough St Martin *York* from 05. *12 Lightfoots Close, Scarborough YO12 5NR* Tel (01723) 376141 Mobile 07768-856175 E-mail rcos38@hotmail.com

COTGROVE, Canon Edwin John. b 23. Kelham Th Coll 42. **d** 47 **p** 48. C Bris St Jude w St Matthias *Bris* 47-50; C Southall St Geo *Lon* 50-52; S Africa 52-56; Swaziland 56-57; V Bromley St Mich *Lon* 57-64; V Hampton All SS 64-82; RD Hampton 72-82; R Bartlow *Ely* 82-91; V Linton 82-91; P-in-c Shudy Camps 85-91; P-in-c Castle Camps 85-91; RD Linton 88-93; Hon Can Ely Cathl 89-91; rtd 91; Perm to Offic *Ely* from 91. *96 The High Street, Great Abington, Cambridge CB1 6AE* Tel (01223) 893735

COTMAN, John Sell Granville (Jan). b 44. St Jo Coll Dur BA69. Wells Th Coll 70. **d** 73 **p** 74. C Leigh St Mary *Man* 73-76; P-in-c Coldhurst 76-78; TV Oldham 78-82; TV E Ham w Upton Park St Alb *Chelmsf* 82-85; C Hove All SS *Chich* 88-93; TV Hove 93-00; TV W Slough *Ox* from 01. *298 Stoke Poges Lane, Slough SL1 3LL* Tel (01753) 578503

COTSON, Tony Arthur. b 53. NEOC 00. **d** 03 **p** 04. C Kingston upon Hull St Nic *York* from 03. *11 Kipling Walk, Summergroves Way, Hull HU4 6SX* Tel (01482) 504189 Mobile 07718-567675 E-mail tony@cotson.karoo.co.uk

COTTAM, Kenneth Michael David. b 46. FTC70 Leic Univ NDA70 Brooksby Agric Coll NDFOM70. St Mich Coll Llan 93. **d** 93 **p** 94. Lic to Offic Llangadog and Llandeilo Deanery *St D* 93-96; V Llangadog and Gwynfe w Llanddeusant from 96. *The Vicarage, Walters Road, Llangadog SA19 9AE* Tel (01550) 777604

COTTEE, Christopher Paul. b 54. Newc Univ BSc75. Wycliffe Hall Ox 77. **d** 80 **p** 81. C Much Woolton *Liv* 80-84; C Prescot 84-88; NSM Parr 89-91; V Watford St Pet *St Alb* from 91. *St Peter's Vicarage, 61 Westfield Avenue, Watford WD24 7HF* Tel (01923) 226717 E-mail c.p.cottee@cwcom.net

COTTEE, Mary Jane. b 43. CertEd64 Open Univ BA81. Oak Hill Th Coll 87. **d** 90 **p** 94. NSM Gt Baddow *Chelmsf* 90-95; P-in-c Woodham Ferrers and Bicknacre from 95. *Church House, Main Road, Bicknacre, Chelmsford CM3 4HA* Tel (01245) 224895

COTTELL, Avril Jane. *See* GAUNT, Mrs Avril Jane

COTTER, Graham Michael. b 50. Univ of Wales (Ban) BA72. Ridley Hall Cam 75. **d** 78 **p** 79. C Headley All SS *Guildf* 78-81; C Plymouth St Andr w St Paul and St Geo *Ex* 81-84; V Buckland Monachorum from 84; RD Tavistock 93-98. *The Vicarage, Buckland Monachorum, Yelverton PL20 7LQ* Tel (01822) 852227 E-mail cotters@onetel.com

COTTER, James England. b 42. G&C Coll Cam BA64 MA67. Linc Th Coll 65. **d** 67 **p** 68. C Stretford St Matt *Man* 67-70; Lect Linc Th Coll 70-73; Lic to Offic *Lon* 73-74; Chapl G&C Coll Cam 74-77; C Leavesden All SS *St Alb* 77-83; Asst Prin St Alb Minl Tr Scheme 77-83; Course Dir 83-86; Perm to Offic *Ex* 86-88 and *Sheff* 88-89; Lic to Offic *Sheff* 89-01; Perm to Offic *Ban* from 99. *Dwylan, Stryd Fawr, Harlech LL46 2YA* Tel (01766) 781368 E-mail jim@cottercairns.co.uk

COTTER, Canon John Beresford Dolmage. b 20. TCD BA47 BD55. **d** 47 **p** 48. C Glencraig *D & D* 47-49; Chile and Bolivia 49-53; Peru 53; I Tempo *Clogh* 54-55; I Garrison 55-60; I Donagh 60-67; Dir of Ords 62-69; Can Clogh Cathl 62-69; I Dromore 67-69; Preb Donaghmore St Patr Cathl Dublin 69; Bahrain 69-75; V Towednack *Truro* 76-89; V Zennor 76-89; Past Tr Chapl 82-89; rtd 89; Perm to Offic *B & W* 89-03. *20 Gracey Court, Broadclyst, Exeter EX5 3GA* Tel (01392) 460319

COTTER, Robert Edmund. **d** 05. Aux Min Mossley *Conn* from 05. *12 Clonaslea, Newtownabbey BT37 0UL* Tel (028) 9085 3888 E-mail recotter@supanet.com

COTTERELL, Michael Clifford. b 54. Oak Hill Th Coll 81. **d** 84 **p** 85. C Lutterworth w Cotesbach *Leic* 84-87; C Belper *Derby* 87-91; V Locking *B & W* 91-98; V Slough *Ox* from 98. *St Paul's Vicarage, 196 Stoke Road, Slough SL2 5AY* Tel (01753) 521497 E-mail mikeccotterell@aol.com

COTTERILL, Joseph Charles. b 17. AMCT38 Lon Univ DipTh BD California Coll Peking MA46. Ox Min Course 92. **d** 93 **p** 94. NSM Marcham w Garford *Ox* 93-98; Perm to Offic from 98. *8 Draycott Road, Southmoor, Abingdon OX13 5BY* Tel (01865) 820436

COTTINGHAM, Peter John Garnet. b 24. Wadh Coll Ox BA48 MA50. Ridley Hall Cam 48. **d** 50 **p** 51. C Cheadle *Ches* 50-55; R Ox St Clem *Ox* 55-68; V S Mimms Ch Ch *Lon* 68-81; V Derby St Pet and Ch Ch w H Trin *Derby* 81-89; rtd 89; Perm to Offic *Ban* from 89. *5 Broadway, Rhos-on-Sea, Colwyn Bay LL28 4AR* Tel (01492) 548840

COTTON, Charles Anthony. b 50. Linc Coll Ox BA72 MA77 PGCE73. Ridley Hall Cam 89. **d** 91 **p** 92. C Hendon St Paul Mill Hill *Lon* 91-96; C Wandsworth All SS *S'wark* 96-97; V Clapham St Jas from 97. *St James's Vicarage, 1 Rodenhurst Road, London SW4 8AE* Tel (020) 8674 3973 E-mail revcharlie@onetel.com

COTTON, Canon John Alan. b 24. Qu Coll Ox BA48 MA52. Chich Th Coll 50. **d** 51 **p** 52. C Doncaster St Geo *Sheff* 51-54; C Ifield *Chich* 54-56; P-in-c Jevington 56-57; R 57-60; Chief Org Sec SPCK 60-63; Chapl Sussex Univ 63-69; V Fairwarp 69-82; Dir of Educn 72-78; Can and Preb Chich Cathl 72-89; Bp's Adv on Min 79-89; Dir of Ords 79-89; rtd 89; Perm to Offic *Carl* 91-99. *1 Westhaven, Thursby, Carlisle CA7 6PH* Tel (01228) 711506

COTTON, John Horace Brazel. b 28. MIMechE St Jo Coll Cam BA50 MA76. St Alb Minl Tr Scheme 78. **d** 81 **p** 82. NSM Lt Berkhamsted and Bayford, Essendon etc *St Alb* 81-87; P-in-c 87-96; rtd 96; Perm to Offic *St Alb* from 96. *49 Sherrardspark Road, Welwyn Garden City AL8 7LD* Tel (01707) 321815

COTTON, John Kenneth. b 25. Westcott Ho Cam 57. **d** 58 **p** 59. C S Ormsby w Ketsby, Calceby and Driby *Linc* 58-61; R Wrentham w Benacre, Covehithe and Henstead *St E* 61-68; R Sotterley w Willingham 63-68; R Shadingfield 63-68; Canada 68-71; TV Sandringham w W Newton *Nor* 71-76; P-in-c Assington *St E* 80-86; P-in-c Lt Cornard 80-86; P-in-c Newton 80-86; P-in-c Eyke w Bromeswell, Rendlesham, Tunstall etc 87-92; P-in-c Alderton w Ramsholt and Bawdsey 89-92; rtd 92; Perm to Offic *St E* from 92. *8 Chillesford Lodge Bungalows, Sudbourne, Woodbridge IP12 2AN* Tel (01394) 450740 E-mail john.cotton@btinternet.com

COTTON, Canon John Wallis. b 31. Wells Th Coll 57. **d** 59 **p** 60. C Stepney St Dunstan and All SS *Lon* 59-64; C Hanworth All SS 64-67; V Hammersmith St Sav 67-74; R Lancing w Coombes *Chich* 75-86; RD Worthing 83-85; R Bexhill St Pet 86-90; TR 90-99; RD Battle and Bexhill 92-98; Can and Preb Chich Cathl 96-02; P-in-c Arlington, Folkington and Wilmington 99-02; rtd 02. *7 Jevington Close, Bexhill-on-Sea TN39 3BB* Tel (01424) 845273

COTTON, John William. b 53. Basford Coll Nottm DipInstBM74. Oak Hill Th Coll DipHE86. **d** 86 **p** 87. C New Clee *Linc* 86-89; Chapl St Andr Hospice Grimsby 88-89; R Middle Rasen Gp 89-95; P-in-c Broughton 95-97; R from 97; Chapl Humberside Airport 99-00. *The Rectory, 22 Scawby Road, Broughton, Brigg DN20 0AF* Tel (01652) 652506

COTTON, Mrs Margaret Elizabeth. b 30. JP79. Newnham Coll Cam BA53 MA66. St Alb Minl Tr Scheme 78. **dss** 82 **d** 87 **p** 94. Lt Berkhamsted and Bayford, Essendon etc *St Alb* 82-87; Hon Par Dn 87-94; Hon C 94-96; rtd 96; Perm to Offic *St Alb* from 96. *49 Sherrardspark Road, Welwyn Garden City AL8 7LD* Tel (01707) 321815

COTTON, Norman Joseph. b 39. Kelham Th Coll 59. **d** 64 **p** 65. C Auckland St Helen *Dur* 64-67; C Withington St Chris *Man* 67-68; C Hucknall Torkard *S'well* 69-71; TV 71-73; TV Fenny Stratford *Ox* 73-75; TV Fenny Stratford and Water Eaton 75-82; R Walton 82-90; TR Walton Milton Keynes 90-92; V Stewkley w Soulbury and Drayton Parslow 92-04; RD Mursley 94-01; rtd 04. *5 Whites Close, Steeple Claydon, Buckingham MK18 2HN* Tel (01296) 738602 E-mail nomo_uk@yahoo.co.uk

COTTON, Miss Patricia Constance. b 32. Gilmore Ho 54. **dss** 60 **d** 87 **p** 94. Forest Gate St Edm *Chelmsf* 60-64; Reading St Giles *Ox* 64-65; Basildon St Martin w H Cross and Laindon *Chelmsf* 65-79; Gt Burstead 79-87; Par Dn Maldon All SS w St Pet 87-91; rtd 92; NSM Holland-on-Sea *Chelmsf* 94-96; Perm to Offic from 96. *67 Copperfield Gardens, Brentwood CM14 4UD* Tel (01255) 672711

COTTON, Patrick Arthur William. b 46. Essex Univ BA67 Cam Univ MA73. Linc Th Coll 68. **d** 71 **p** 72. C Earlham St Anne *Nor* 71-73; Chapl Down Coll Cam 73-78; V Eaton Socon *St Alb* 78-84; TR Newc Epiphany *Newc* 84-90; V Tunstall w Melling and Leck *Blackb* 90-95; Chapl Pet High Sch from 01. *Peterborough High School, Westwood House, Thorpe Road, Peterborough PE3 6JF* Tel (01733) 343357

COTTON, Peter John. b 45. BNC Ox BA66 Bris Univ CQSW76. Cuddesdon Coll 67. **d** 69 **p** 70. C Salford St Phil w St Steph *Man* 69-73; Asst Educn Officer *St Alb* 73-75; C Bris St Geo *Bris* 75-76; C-in-c Portsea St Geo CD *Portsm* 76-80; Soc Resp Adv 78-88; Can Res Portsm Cathl 84-88; V St Laur in Thanet *Cant* 88-93; TR 93-97; Hon Min Can Cant Cathl 93-97; TR Hemel Hempstead *St Alb* from 97; RD Hemel Hempstead from 03. *The Rectory, High Street, Hemel Hempstead HP1 3AE* Tel and fax (01442) 213838 *or* 253977 E-mail petercotton2@compuserve.com

COTTON, Canon Richard William. b 35. Hertf Coll Ox BA58 MA62. Clifton Th Coll 58. **d** 60 **p** 61. C Harold Wood *Chelmsf* 60-64; C Higher Openshaw *Man* 64-67; Lic to Offic 67-71; Ch Youth Fellowships Assn and Pathfinders 67-71; Nat Sec Pathfinders CPAS 71-76; Lic to Offic *St Alb* 73-76; V Chislehurst Ch Ch *Roch* 76-92; V Herne Bay Ch Ch *Cant* 92-01; RD Reculver 93-01; Hon Can Cant Cathl 99-01; rtd 01; Perm to Offic

Cant from 01. *16 Crundale Way, Cliftonville, Margate CT9 3YH* Tel (01843) 221970 E-mail rwcotton67@hotmail.com

COTTON, Robert Lloyd. b 58. Mert Coll Ox MA79 Louvain Univ Belgium DipTh81. Westcott Ho Cam 81. **d** 83 **p** 84. C Plaistow St Mary *Roch* 83-86; C Bisley and W End *Guildf* 87-89; P-in-c E Molesey St Paul 89-96; Dir of Reader Tr from 90; R Guildf H Trin w St Mary from 96. *Holy Trinity Rectory, 9 Eastgate Gardens, Guildford GU1 4AZ* Tel (01483) 575489 E-mail rector@holytrinityguildford.org.uk

COTTON, Roy William. b 29. Jes Coll Ox BA53 MA61. Chich Th Coll 66. **d** 66 **p** 67. C Eastney *Portsm* 66-71; R Harting *Chich* 71-74; P-in-c Eastbourne St Andr 74-76; V 76-84; R Brede w Udimore 84-99; rtd 99; Perm to Offic *Chich* from 99. *c/o Fynmores, 10-12 Parkhurst Road, Bexhill-on-Sea TN40 1DF* Tel (01424) 732333 Fax 739832

COTTON, Timothy. b 61. Ripon Coll Cuddesdon 97. **d** 99 **p** 00. C Godrevy *Truro* 99-02; P-in-c St Breoke and Egloshayle from 02. *The Rectory, 31 Trevanion Road, Wadebridge PL27 7NZ* Tel (01208) 812460 E-mail tim@cottonh.fsnet.co.uk

COTTON-BETTRIDGE, Mrs Fiona Jane Marson. b 56. EMMTC 02. **d** 05. NSM Burton Joyce w Bulcote and Stoke Bardolph *S'well* from 05. *Heronby House, 1 Riverside, Whatton, Nottingham NG13 9EJ* Tel (01949) 851065 E-mail fionacb@aol.com

✠**COTTRELL, The Rt Revd Stephen Geoffrey.** b 58. Poly Cen Lon BA79. St Steph Ho Ox 81. **d** 84 **p** 85 **c** 04. C Forest Hill Ch Ch *S'wark* 84-88; C-in-c Parklands St Wilfrid CD *Chich* 88-93; Asst Dir Past Studies Chich Th Coll 88-93; Dioc Missr *Wakef* 93-98; Bp's Chapl for Evang 93-98; Springboard Missr and Consultant in Evang 98-01; Can Res Pet Cathl *Pet* 01-04; Area Bp Reading *Ox* from 04. *Bishop's House, Tidmarsh Lane, Tidmarsh, Reading RG8 8HA* Tel 0118-984 1216 Fax 984 1218 E-mail bishopreading@oxford.anglican.org

COTTRILL, Derek John. b 43. MA. Qu Coll Birm. **d** 82 **p** 83. C Southampton Maybush St Pet *Win* 82-85; V Barton Stacey and Bullington etc 85-92; R Bishopstoke from 92; Asst Chapl Win and Eastleigh Healthcare NHS Trust from 92. *The Rectory, 10 Stoke Park Road, Eastleigh SO50 6DA* Tel (023) 8061 2192

COUCH, Andrew Nigel. b 48. K Coll Lon BD70 AKC70 Ex Coll Ox PGCE72. St Aug Coll Cant 70. **d** 71 **p** 72. C St Ives *Truro* 71-74; C St Martin-in-the-Fields *Lon* 74-78; USPG 78-91; Uruguay 79-84; Argentina 85-91; Chapl Qu Mary Coll *Lon* 91-94; V St Ives *Truro* from 94; P-in-c Halsetown from 98; RD Penwith 98-03; Chapl W of Cornwall Primary Care Trust from 98. *The Vicarage, St Andrew's Street, St Ives TR26 1AH* Tel (01736) 796404 E-mail andycouch@bigfoot.com

COUCH, Ms Felicity Anne. b 59. CQSW85. SEITE 00. **d** 03 **p** 04. NSM Stockwell St Andr and St Mich *S'wark* from 03. *20 Camsey House, St Matthew's Road, London SW2 1SX* Tel (020) 7501 9449 Mobile 07745-905417 E-mail fcouch@supanet.com

COUCHMAN, Anthony Denis. b 37. Sarum Th Coll 66. **d** 69 **p** 70. C Barkingside St Fran *Chelmsf* 69-71; C Chingford SS Pet and Paul 71-76; P-in-c Walthamstow St Barn and St Jas Gt 76-80; V from 80. *St Barnabas' Vicarage, St Barnabas Road, London E17 8JZ* Tel (020) 8520 5323

COUGHLIN, Wayne Michael Timothy Vianney. b 77. Writtle Agric Coll BSc99 Leeds Univ BA03. Coll of Resurr Mirfield 00. **d** 03 **p** 04. C Neath *Llan* from 03. *The Presbytery, 18 Woodland Road, Neath SA11 3AL* Tel (01639) 635738

COUGHTREY, Miss Sheila Frances. b 48. RSCN73 SRN73 S Bank Poly BSc79. Qu Coll Birm 79. **dss** 81 **d** 87 **p** 94. Sydenham St Bart *S'wark* 81-85; Roehampton H Trin 85-91; Par Dn 87-91; Par Dn Brixton Hill St Sav 91-94; P-in-c 94-01; Min King's Acre LEP 91-01; RD Brixton 99-01; P-in-c Pleshey *Chelmsf* from 01; Warden Dioc Retreat Ho from 01. *The Vicarage, The Street, Pleshey, Chelmsford CM3 1HA* Tel (01245) 237576 E-mail sheila@scoughtrey.fsnet.co.uk

COULDRIDGE, Janice Evelyn. *See* FOX, Mrs Janice Evelyn

COULING, Canon David Charles. b 36. Open Univ BA89. Qu Coll Birm 61. **d** 63 **p** 64. C Harborne St Faith and St Laur *Birm* 63-66; C E Grinstead St Mary *Chich* 66-70; V Copthorne 70-75; V Eastbourne St Mich 75-82; V Brighton St Matthias 82-83; C-in-c Harton St Lawr CD *Dur* 84-90; V Horsley Hill St Lawr 91-94; P-in-c Greatham 94-97; V 97-01; AD Hartlepool 95-01; Master Greatham Hosp 94-00; Hon Can Dur Cathl *Dur* 99-01; rtd 01; P-in-c Brancepeth *Dur* 01-04; Chapl Dur Cathl from 04. *11 Shropshire Drive, Durham DH1 2LT* Tel 0191-375 7367

COULSON, Renée. b 45. **d** 03 **p** 04. OLM Potterne w Worton and Marston *Sarum* from 03. *40 Highlands, Potterne, Devizes SN10 5NS* Tel (01380) 726609 E-mail rcoulson@totalise.co.uk

COULSON, Canon Stephen Hugh. b 60. St Edm Hall Ox BA82 MA88 Lon Univ CertEd83. Wycliffe Hall Ox 85. **d** 88 **p** 89. C Summerfield *Birm* 88-91; Perm to Offic 91-92; CMS Uganda 92-01; Asst V Namirembe 92-96; Can from 99; Prin Uganda Martyrs Sem Namugongo 96-01; V Mitcham St Mark *S'wark* from 01. *St Mark's Vicarage, Locks Lane, Mitcham CR4 2JX* Tel (020) 8648 2397 E-mail steve@scoulson.freeserve.co.uk

COULSON, Thomas Stanley. b 32. TCD BA54 MA68. TCD Div Sch 55. **d** 55 **p** 56. C Maghera *D & R* 55-62; I Aghalurcher and Tattykeeran *Clogh* 62-63; I Woodschapel w Gracefield *Arm* 63-97; Preb Arm Cathl 88-97; Treas Arm Cathl 94-96; Chan Arm Cathl 96-97; rtd 97. *Lisadian, 84 Coleraine Road, Portrush BT56 8HN* Tel (028) 7082 4202

COULSON, Tony Erik Frank. b 32. St Edm Hall Ox BA55 DipTh56 MA59. Wycliffe Hall Ox 55. **d** 57 **p** 58. C Walthamstow St Mary *Chelmsf* 57-60; C Reading St Jo *Ox* 60-63; V Iver 63-86; R White Waltham w Shottesbrooke 86-97; rtd 97; Perm to Offic *Ox* from 98. *30 Ravensbourne Drive, Reading RG5 4LH* Tel 0118-969 3556

COULTER, Edmond James. b 60. QUB BSc82 BD96 TCD DipTh87. **d** 87 **p** 88. C Ballymena w Ballyclug *Conn* 87-90; C Knockbreda *D & D* 90-92; I Belfast Upper Falls *Conn* 92-97; I Milltown *Arm* 97-03; Superintendent Dublin Irish Ch Miss *D & G* from 03. *38 Woodpark, Castleknock, Dublin 15, Irish Republic* Tel (00353) (1) 821 2336 *or* 873 0829 Fax 878 4049 E-mail ecoulter@eircom.net *or* icm@iol.ie

COULTER, Ian Herbert Young. b 54. TCD BA77 HDipEd78. **d** 99 **p** 00. Lic to Offic (Cashel, Waterford and Lismore) *C & O* from 99. *22 Rose Hill Court, Kilkenny, Co Kilkenny, Irish Republic* Tel and fax (00353) (56) 776 2675 E-mail coulters@gofree.indigo.ie

COULTER, Mrs Kirsten Ruth. b 43. Univ of Wales (Abth) BSc64 Homerton Coll Cam CertEd65 Lon Univ BD89 Newc Univ MA93. Dioc OLM tr scheme 98. **d** 01 **p** 02. OLM Tweedmouth *Newc* from 01. *90 Shielfield Terrace, Tweedmouth, Berwick-upon-Tweed TD15 2EE* Tel (01289) 308485 E-mail timothy.coulter@btinternet.com

COULTER (née REEVES), Mrs Maria Elizabeth Ann. b 72. Leeds Univ BA95 Heythrop Coll Lon MTh03. St Steph Ho Ox 96. **d** 98 **p** 99. C Newington St Mary *S'wark* 98-02; V Dulwich St Clem w St Pet from 02. *St Clement's Vicarage, 140 Friern Road, London SE22 0AY* Tel (020) 8693 1890

COULTER, Miss Marilyn Judith. b 48. City of Birm Coll BEd70 Qu Coll Birm BA05. WMMTC 02. **d** 05. NSM Brewood *Lich* from 05; NSM Bishopswood from 05. *14 St Chad's Close, Brewood, Stafford ST19 9DA* Tel (01902) 851168 E-mail coulter14@aol.com

COULTER, Richard Samuel Scott. b 09. Dur Univ LTh39. Clifton Th Coll 35. **d** 38 **p** 39. C Parr Mt *Liv* 38-40; CF 40-46; Hon CF from 46; C Huyton St Mich *Liv* 46-50; Chapl Whiston Hosp 47-50; V Wavertree St Bridget *Liv* 50-61; V Upton Snodsbury w Broughton Hackett etc *Worc* 61-77; rtd 77. *29 Greenheart Way, Southmoor, Abingdon OX13 5DF* Tel (01865) 820912

COULTHARD, Miss Nina Marion. b 50. CertEd71 Bp Lonsdale Coll BEd72. Trin Coll Bris DipHE91. **d** 91 **p** 94. Par Dn Cant St Mary Bredin *Cant* 91-94; C 94-95; C Bath Abbey w St Jas *B & W* 95-99; Chapl R Nat Hosp for Rheumatic Diseases NHS Trust 95-99; C Northwood Em *Lon* from 99. *64 Chester Road, Northwood HA6 1AG* Tel (01923) 825019 *or* 845200 E-mail office@ecn.org.uk

COULTHURST, Jeffrey Evans. b 38. Man Univ BA61 Leeds Univ PGCE62. **d** 84 **p** 85. OLM Ancaster *Linc* 84-89; OLM Ancaster Wilsford Gp 89-05. *5 North Drive, Ancaster, Grantham NG32 3RB* Tel (01400) 230280 E-mail jeff@jcoulthurst.fsnet.co.uk

COULTON, David Stephen. b 41. Sarum Th Coll 64. **d** 67 **p** 68. C Guildf H Trin w St Mary *Guildf* 67-70; Asst Chapl St Luke's Hosp Guildf 67-70; Sen Chapl Radley Coll 70-83; Chapl 83-01; Chapl Eton Coll 01-04. *3 Wollescote House, 37 Spring Hill, Ventnor PO38 1PF*

COULTON, The Very Revd Nicholas Guy. b 40. Lon Univ BD72. Cuddesdon Coll 65. **d** 67 **p** 68. C Pershore w Wick *Worc* 67-70; Bp's Dom Chapl *St Alb* 71-75; P-in-c Bedford St Paul 75-79; V 79-90; Hon Can St Alb 89-90; Provost Newc 90-01; Dean Newc 01-03; Can Res and Sub-Dean Ch Ch *Ox* from 03. *Christ Church, Oxford OX1 1DP* Tel (01865) 276278 *or* 276155 E-mail nicholas.coulton@chch.ox.ac.uk

COULTON, Philip Ernest. b 31. St Cath Coll Cam BA54 MA58 TCD BD68 Open Univ BA84. Ely Th Coll 55. **d** 57 **p** 58. Asst Master Perse Sch Cam 54-55; Asst Master Bradf Gr Sch 57; C Newark w Coddington *S'well* 57-61; Min Can and Sacr Cant Cathl *Cant* 61-63; Min Can Ripon Cathl *Ripon* 63-68; Hd of RE Ashton-under-Lyne Gr Sch 69-84; V Ulceby Gp *Linc* 85-89; P-in-c Ingatestone w Buttsbury *Chelmsf* 89-99; P-in-c Fryerning w Margaretting 89-92; rtd 99; Perm to Offic *Sarum* from 01 and *B & W* from 02. *90 Boreham Road, Warminster BA12 9JW* Tel (01985) 219353 Fax 847719 E-mail pecoulton@onetel.com

COUNSELL, Edwin Charles Robert. b 63. Univ of Wales (Cardiff) BA84 MTh97. St Steph Ho Ox 85. **d** 88 **p** 89. C Cardiff St Mary and St Steph w St Dyfrig etc *Llan* 88-94; Sub-Chapl HM Pris Cardiff from 90; V Pendoylan w Welsh St Donats from 94; Dioc Dir Statutory Educn from 00. *The Vicarage, 9 Heol St Cattwg, Pendoylan, Cowbridge CF71 7UG* Tel (01446) 760195 *or* tel and fax 760210 E-mail post@llandaffschools.fs.net.co.uk

COUNSELL, Michael John Radford. b 35. Pemb Coll Cam BA59 MA63. Ripon Hall Ox 59. **d** 61 **p** 62. C Handsworth St Mary *Birm* 61-63; Singapore 64-68; Vietnam and Cambodia 68-71; Seychelles 72-76; Dean Mahe 73-76; V Harborne St Pet *Birm* 76-89; Relig Consultant Inter-Ch Travel Ltd 89-90; V Forest Hill St Aug *S'wark* 90-00; Perm to Offic *Cant* 91-00; rtd 00; Perm to Offic *Birm* and *Eur* from 05. *Flat 2, 340 Tessall Lane, Birmingham B31 5EN* Tel and fax 0121-628 2028 Mobile 07891-860473 E-mail mjrcounsell@hotmail.com

COUPAR, Thomas. b 50. BA71 ACE80. Edin Dioc NSM Course 77. **d** 80 **p** 81. NSM Dunbar *Edin* 80-86; NSM Haddington 80-86; Hd Master Pencaitland Primary Sch E Lothian 80-81; Hd Master K Meadow Sch E Lothian 81-87; Asst Dioc Supernumerary *Edin* 87-89; Primary Educn Adv Fife from 88; Dioc Supernumerary 90-96. *Earlshall Cottage, Carberry, Musselburgh EH21 8PZ* Tel 0131-665 1780 E-mail tcoupar@hotmail.com

COUPER, Jeanette Emily (Jean). b 40. S'wark Ord Course 85. **d** 88. Par Dn Mitcham SS Pet and Paul *S'wark* 88-93; Chapl Asst Guy's Hosp Lon 93-94; Perm to Offic *S'wark* 93-04; rtd 00. *Rose Cottage, Wentnor, Bishops Castle SY9 5EE* Tel (01588) 650590

COUPER, Jonathan George. b 51. St Jo Coll Dur BA73. Wycliffe Hall Ox 73. **d** 75 **p** 76. C Clifton *York* 75-78; C Darfield *Sheff* 78-81; V Bridlington Quay Ch Ch *York* from 81. *21 Kingston Road, Bridlington YO15 3NF* Tel (01262) 673538

COUPLAND, Simon Charles. b 59. St Jo Coll Cam BA82 PGCE83 MA85 PhD87. Ridley Hall Cam 88. **d** 91 **p** 92. C Bath St Luke *B & W* 91-95; TV Broadwater St Mary *Chich* 95-04; V Kingston Hill St Paul *S'wark* from 04. *The Vicarage, 33 Queen's Road, Kingston upon Thames KT2 7SF* Tel (020) 8549 8597 *or* 8549 5444 E-mail simon.coupland@stpaulskingston.org.uk

COURT, David Eric. b 58. Southn Univ BSc80 PhD83 PGCE84. Oak Hill Th Coll BA91. **d** 91 **p** 92. C Barton Seagrave w Warkton *Pet* 91-94; C Kinson *Sarum* 94-97; P-in-c Mile Cross *Nor* 97-99; V 99-03; V Cromer from 03. *The Vicarage, 30 Cromwell Road, Cromer NR27 0BE* Tel (01263) 512000 E-mail david@cromervicarage.fsnet.co.uk

COURT, Canon Kenneth Reginald. b 36. AKC60. **d** 61 **p** 62. C Garforth *Ripon* 61-63; C Harrogate St Wilfrid 63-65; V Thornbury *Bradf* 65-73; Prec Leic Cathl *Leic* 73-76; V Douglas St Matt *S & M* 76-84; V Syston *Leic* 84-93; TR Syston 93-98; RD Goscote 90-95; Hon Can Leic Cathl 92-98; rtd 98; Perm to Offic *Pet* from 99 and *Linc* from 01. *12 Lord Burghley's Hospital, Station Road, Stamford PE9 2LD* E-mail kcourt@webbleicester.co.uk

COURT, Martin. b 64. Ridley Hall Cam 03. **d** 05. C Blandford Forum and Langton Long *Sarum* from 05. *17 Bayfran Way, Blandford Forum DT11 7RZ* Tel (01258) 489321 Mobile 07905-612542 E-mail martin@bfpc.org.uk

COURT, Martin Jeremy. b 61. GRNCM84 Nottm Univ BTh89. Linc Th Coll 86. **d** 89 **p** 90. C Thurmaston *Leic* 89-92; C Leic St Jas 92-93; TV Leic Resurr 93-98; V Scraptoft from 98; Dioc Info Tech Co-ord from 96. *331 Scraptoft Lane, Scraptoft, Leicester LE5 2HU* Tel 0116-241 3205 Mobile 07798-876837 E-mail mcourt@leicester.anglican.org

COURT, Nicholas James Keble. b 56. SSC. Chich Th Coll 86. **d** 88 **p** 89. C Golders Green *Lon* 88-91; C Westbury-on-Trym H Trin *Bris* 91-94; PV Llan Cathl *Llan* 94-96; V Graig 96-02; P-in-c Cilfynydd 96-01. *Cair Paravel, Ardmuir, Ullapool IV26 2TN*

COURT, Richard Leonard. b 54. Univ of Wales (Ban) MTh04. EAMTC 94. **d** 97 **p** 98. NSM Framlingham w Saxtead *St E* 97-05; V Badsey w Aldington and Offenham and Bretforton *Worc* from 05. *The Vicarage, High Street, Badsey, Evesham WR11 7EW* Tel (01386) 834550 Mobile 07751-775917 E-mail richard.court@btinternet.com

COURTAULD, Augustine Christopher Caradoc. b 34. Trin Coll Cam BA58 MA61. Westcott Ho Cam 58. **d** 60 **p** 61. C Oldham St Mary *Man* 60-63; Chapl Trin Coll Cam 63-68; Chapl The Lon Hosp (Whitechapel) 68-78; V Wilton Place St Paul *Lon* 78-99; AD Westmr St Marg 92-97; rtd 99; Perm to Offic *St E* from 00. *Broke House, The Drift, Levington, Ipswich IP10 0LF* Tel (01473) 659773

COURTIE, John Malcolm. b 42. BNC Ox BA65 DPhil72 St Jo Coll Dur BA76. Cranmer Hall Dur 74. **d** 77 **p** 78. C Mossley Hill St Matt and St Jas *Liv* 77-80; V Litherland St Paul Hatton Hill 80-84; Wellingborough Sch 84-89; Hon C Wollaston and Strixton *Pet* 84-89; V Woodford Halse w Eydon 89-99; R Blisworth and Stoke Bruerne w Grafton Regis etc 99-02; rtd 02. *The Baptist Manse, Stoke St Gregory, Taunton TA3 6JG* Tel (01823) 490388 E-mail john@courtie.fsnet.co.uk

COURTNEY (née JORDAN), Mrs Avril Marilyn. b 35. Lon Univ DipEd56. SW Minl Tr Course 79. **dss** 82 **d** 87 **p** 94. Highweek and Teigngrace *Ex* 82-88; Par Dn 87-88; Par Dn Ottery St Mary, Alfington, W Hill, Tipton etc 88-94; C 94-99; rtd 99; Perm to Offic *Ex* from 00. *Fairholme, Exeter Road, Newton Poppleford, Sidmouth EX10 0BJ* Tel (01395) 568691

COURTNEY, Canon Brian Joseph. b 44. BD92 MA97. CITC 70. **d** 73 **p** 74. C Willowfield *D & D* 73-75; P-in-c Knocknagoney 75-78; I Aghavea *Clogh* 78-83; I Carrickfergus *Conn* 83-95; I Enniskillen *Clogh* from 95; Prec Clogh Cathl from 95. *St Macartin's Rectory, 13 Church Street, Enniskillen BT74 7DW* Tel (028) 6632 2465 *or* 6632 2917 E-mail briancourtney@nireland.com

COURTNEY, Miss Louise Anita Hodd. b 48. Ex Univ BTh04. SW Minl Tr Course 99. **d** 02 **p** 03. C St Keverne *Truro* from 02; P-in-c Lansallos from 05; P-in-c Lanteglos by Fowey from 05. *The Vicarage, 4 Ocean View, Polruan, Fowey PL23 1QJ* E-mail louiseah@eurobell.co.uk

COURTNEY, Martin Horace. b 34. St Alb and Ox Min Course 95. **d** 98 **p** 99. OLM Flackwell Heath *Ox* from 98. *1 Green Crescent, Flackwell Heath, High Wycombe HP10 9JQ* Tel (01628) 526354

COURTNEY, Michael Monlas. b 19. Coll of Resurr Mirfield 58. **d** 60 **p** 61. C Shrewsbury St Chad *Lich* 60-63; P-in-c N Keyham *Ex* 63-68; V 68-73; TV Sidmouth, Woolbrook, Salcombe Regis etc 73-84; rtd 84; Perm to Offic *Ex* from 86. *Fairholme, Exeter Road, Newton Poppleford, Sidmouth EX10 0BJ* Tel (01395) 568691

COUSANS (née BRADLEY), Mrs Joy Elizabeth. b 63. Sheff Univ BA85 Fitzw Coll Cam BA91 MA95. Ridley Hall Cam 89. **d** 92 **p** 94. Par Dn Wadsley *Sheff* 92-94; C 94-96; C Mosbrough 96-97; V Hillsborough and Wadsley Bridge from 97. *Christ Church Vicarage, 218 Fox Hill Road, Sheffield S6 1HJ* Tel 0114-231 1576

COUSINS, Christopher William. b 44. Ox Univ MTh95. **d** 87 **p** 88. C Wallasey St Hilary *Ches* 87-90; R Rollesby w Burgh w Billockby w Ashby w Oby etc *Nor* 90-94; P-in-c Ormesby w Scratby 92-94; V Ormesby St Marg w Scratby, Ormesby St Mich etc 94-98; RD Gt Yarmouth 94-98; V Altham w Clayton le Moors *Blackb* 98-03; P-in-c Rochford *Chelmsf* from 03; P-in-c Stambridge from 03; P-in-c Sutton w Shopland from 03; RD Rochford from 04. *The Rectory, 36 Millview Meadows, Rochford SS4 1EF* Tel (01702) 530621 E-mail c4cousins@yahoo.com

COUSINS, Graham John. b 55. Oak Hill Th Coll BA91. **d** 91 **p** 92. C Birkenhead St Jas w St Bede *Ches* 91-95; C Bebington 95-01; R Moreton from 01. *The Rectory, Dawpool Drive, Moreton, Wirral CH46 0PH* Tel 0151-641 0303 E-mail graham-c@fish.co.uk

COUSINS, Peter Gareth. b 37. **d** 95 **p** 96. NSM Cwmparc *Llan* 95-02. *15 Conway Road, Cwmparc, Treorchy CF42 6UW* Tel (01443) 773669

COUSINS, Canon Philip John. b 35. K Coll Cam BA58 MA62. Cuddesdon Coll 59. **d** 61 **p** 62. C Marton *Blackb* 61-63; PV Truro Cathl *Truro* 63-67; USPG Ethiopia 67-75; V Henleaze *Bris* 75-84; RD Clifton 79-84; Provost All SS Cathl Cairo 84-89; Chan Malta Cathl *Eur* 89-95; Chapl Valletta w Gozo 89-95; R Llandudno *Ban* 95-04; rtd 04; Perm to Offic *York* from 04 and *Eur* from 05. *17 Chalfonts, York YO24 1EX* Tel (01904) 700316

COUSINS, Stephen Michael. b 53. St Alb and Ox Min Course 98. **d** 01 **p** 02. OLM Caversham St Jo *Ox* 01-03; Perm to Offic 03-04; NSM Shiplake w Dunsden and Harpsden from 04. *15 Champion Road, Caversham, Reading RG4 8EL* Tel 0118-948 1679 Mobile 07753-166687 E-mail stephen.cousins@btinternet.com

COUSLAND, Andrew Oliver. b 41. Goldsmiths' Coll Lon MA92. Edin Th Coll 62. **d** 65 **p** 66. C Broughty Ferry *Bre* 65-68; C Ayr *Glas* 68-70; R Renfrew 70-75; Perm to Offic *St E* 75-79; CF (TAVR) 76-82; Perm to Offic *Bre* 79-84 and *S'wark* 89-94; R Fraserburgh w New Pitsligo *Ab* 94-99; R Clogherny w Seskinore and Drumnakilly *Arm* 99-03; rtd 03; Perm to Offic *Carl* from 03. *145 The Parklands, Cockermouth CA13 0XJ* Tel (01900) 821959 E-mail ao@land24.freeserve.co.uk

COUSSENS, Mervyn Haigh Wingfield. b 47. St Jo Coll Nottm BTh74. **d** 74 **p** 75. C Clifton Ch Ch w Em *Bris* 74-77; C Morden *S'wark* 77-83; V Patchway *Bris* 83-91; R Lutterworth w Cotesbach *Leic* 91-98; P-in-c Bitteswell 95-98; R Lutterworth w Cotesbach and Bitteswell from 99; RD Guthlaxton II from 01. *The Rectory, Coventry Road, Lutterworth LE17 4SH* Tel (01455) 552669 E-mail rector.stmary.lutterworth@care4free.net

COUSSMAKER, Canon Colin Richard Chad. b 34. OBE99. Worc Coll Ox BA57 BSc58 MA63 MSc85. Chich Th Coll 59. **d** 60 **p** 61. C Newtown St Luke *Win* 60-64; C Whitley Ch Ch *Ox* 64-67; Chapl Istanbul *Eur* 67-72; Chapl Sliema 72-77; Chapl Antwerp St Boniface 77-93; Can Brussels Cathl 81-00; Chapl Moscow 93-99; rtd 99; Hon Asst Chapl Nice w Vence *Eur* 99-00; Perm to Offic from 00. *533 Route des Vallettes Sud, 06140 Tourrettes-sur-Loup, France* Tel (0033) (4) 93 59 28 74

COUTTS, Ian Alexander. b 56. Warwick Univ BA77 Jes Coll Ox MSc80 CQSW80. St Jo Coll Nottm 87. **d** 89 **p** 90. C Hamstead St Bernard *Birm* 89-92; C Warlingham w Chelsham and Farleigh *S'wark* 92-97; TV 97-00; Perm to Offic *S'wark* 00-03 and *Ox* from 03. *220 Headley Way, Headington, Oxford OX3 7TB* Tel (01865) 742655

COUTTS, James Allan. b 58. Fitzw Coll Cam MA. St Jo Coll Nottm MTh84. **d** 84 **p** 85. C Thorpe Acre w Dishley *Leic* 84-88; TV Kirby Muxloe 88-99; P-in-c Trowbridge St Thos and W Ashton *Sarum* from 99; Chapl Wilts and Swindon Healthcare

NHS Trust from 99. *St Thomas's Vicarage, York Buildings, Trowbridge BA14 8PT* Tel (01225) 754826

COUTTS, Canon James Walter Cargill. b 35. Univ of Wales (Lamp) BA57 CCC Cam BA59. St Mich Coll Llan 59. **d** 60 **p** 61. C Cardiff St Mary *Llan* 60-63; C Greenford H Cross *Lon* 63-67; C Swansea St Gabr *S & B* 67-71; V Llanwrtyd w Llanddulas in Tir Abad etc 71-78; V Brecon St Dav 78-80; V Brecon St David w Llanspyddid and Llanilltyd 80-84; V Monmouth *Mon* 84-02; Can St Woolos Cathl 94-02; RD Monmouth 99-01; rtd 02. *The Reynolds, Penallt, Monmouth NP25 4RX*

COUTTS, Robin Iain Philip. b 52. Portsm Univ MA00. Sarum & Wells Th Coll 80. **d** 83 **p** 84. C Alverstoke *Portsm* 83-86; Min Leigh Park St Clare CD 86-89; V Warren Park 89-91; V Purbrook 91-04; RD Havant 00-04; P-in-c Blendworth w Chalton w Idsworth from 04; Dioc Dir NSM from 04. *The Rectory, 6 Idsworth Close, Horndean, Waterlooville PO8 0DW* Tel (023) 9295 8748 E-mail robin.rocket@virgin.net

COUVELA, Ms Stephanie Joy. b 68. Sheff City Poly BA89. Ridley Hall Cam 95. **d** 98 **p** 99. C Upper Holloway *Lon* 98-01; TV 01-04; C Busbridge and Hambledon *Guildf* from 04. *Mervil Bottom, Malthouse Lane, Hambledon, Godalming GU8 4HG* Tel (01428) 682753 E-mail stephanie.couvela@btinternet.com

COVE, Kenneth John. b 34. Lich Th Coll 58. **d** 60 **p** 61. C Crosland Moor *Wakef* 60-63; C Halifax St Jo Bapt 63-65; V Wakef St Jo 65-73; V Appleby *Carl* 73-78; RD Appleby 74-78; V Ambleside w Brathay 78-87; V Thames Ditton *Guildf* 87-94; P-in-c Morland, Thrimby and Gt Strickland *Carl* 94-96; V Morland, Thrimby, Gt Strickland and Cliburn 96-99; rtd 99; Perm to Offic *Carl* from 01. *The Barn, Maulds Meaburn, Penrith CA10 3HN* Tel (01931) 715067 E-mail kencove@care4free.net

COVENTRY, Archdeacon of. *See* BRYANT, The Ven Mark Watts

COVENTRY, Bishop of. *See* BENNETTS, The Rt Revd Colin James

COVENTRY, Dean of. *See* IRVINE, The Very Revd John Dudley

COVERLEY, Mrs Cheryl Joy. b 62. SS Hild & Bede Coll Dur BA83 PGCE84. St Jo Coll Nottm 03. **d** 05. C Birkenhead St Jas w St Bede *Ches* from 05. *3 Buckingham Avenue, Prenton CH43 8TD* Tel and fax 0151-652 1300

COVINGTON, Canon Michael William Rock. b 38. Open Univ BA78. Sarum Th Coll 60. **d** 63 **p** 64. C Daventry *Pet* 63-66; C Woolwich St Mary w H Trin *S'wark* 66-68; C Northampton All SS w St Kath *Pet* 68-71; V Longthorpe 71-86; Hon Min Can Pet Cathl 75-86; Can Pet Cathl 86-03; V Warmington, Tansor, Cotterstock and Fotheringhay 86-95; Warden of Readers 87-95; RD Oundle 89-95; V Oakham, Hambleton, Egleton, Braunston and Brooke 95-03; P-in-c Langham 97-03; RD Rutland 02-03; rtd 03. *Hall Farm House, Burrough Road, Little Dalby, Melton Mowbray LE14 2UG* Tel (01664) 454015

COWAN, Helen Jane. b 42. Dioc OLM tr scheme 97. **d** 00 **p** 01. NSM Redhill H Trin *S'wark* from 00. *15 Westway Gardens, Redhill RH1 2JA* Tel (01737) 762543

COWAN, John Conway. b 71. Trin Coll Bris. **d** 03 **p** 04. C Redcar *York* from 03. *34 Ings Road, Redcar TS10 2DL* Tel (01642) 498241

COWAN, Mrs Lynda Barbette. b 55. ALAM77. Ban Ord Course 02. **d** 05. Lic to Offic *Ban* from 05; C Arwystli Deanery *Ban* from 05. *The Coach House, Old Hall Road, Llanidloes SY18 6PQ*

COWAN, Malcolm. b 45. Carl and Blackb Dioc Tr Inst. **d** 00 **p** 01. NSM Keswick St Jo *Carl* 00-05; TV Whitehaven from 05. *The Vicarage, Oakfield Court, Whitehaven CA28 6TG* Tel (01946) 692630

COWAN, Malcolm. b 60. Ches Coll of HE BTh04. N Ord Course 01. **d** 04 **p** 05. C W Kirby St Bridget *Ches* from 04. *13 Caldy Road, Wirral CH48 2HE* Tel 0151-625 4948 E-mail jandmcowan@ukonline.co.uk

COWAN, Paul Hudson. b 69. Ripon Coll Cuddesdon 00. **d** 02 **p** 03. C Wokingham All SS *Ox* from 02. *7 Tamarisk Rise, Wokingham RG40 1WG* Tel 0118-989 2772 E-mail cowans@ukonline.co.uk

COWARD, Colin Charles Malcolm. b 45. Kingston Poly DArch72. Westcott Ho Cam 75. **d** 78 **p** 79. C Camberwell St Geo *S'wark* 78-82; P-in-c Wandsworth St Faith 82-90; V 90-96; Chapl Richmond, Twickenham and Roehampton NHS Trust 96-97; Co-ord Changing Attitude 97-03; Dir from 03; Perm to Offic *S'wark* 99-03. *6 Norney Bridge, Mill Road, Worton, Devizes SN10 5SF* Tel (01380) 724908 E-mail colin@changingattitude.org

COWARD, Raymond. b 41. NW Ord Course 79. **d** 82 **p** 83. C Turton *Man* 82-84; C Heaton Ch Ch 84-86; V Rochdale St Geo w St Alb 86-92; V Daisy Hill from 92. *46 Parkway, Westhoughton, Bolton BL5 2RY*

COWBURN, John Charles. b 48. Sarum & Wells Th Coll 88. **d** 90 **p** 91. C Andover w Foxcott *Win* 90-94; C Christchurch 94-96; Chapl to the Deaf *Lich* from 96; P-in-c Church Aston from 01. *St Andrew's Rectory, 7 Wallshead Way, Church Aston, Newport TF10 9JG* Tel (01952) 810942 *or* 493282 E-mail john.cowburn@lichfield.anglican.org

COWDREY, Herbert Edward John. b 26. Trin Coll Ox BA49 MA51. St Steph Ho Ox 50. **d** 52 **p** 53. Tutor St Steph Ho Ox 52-56; Chapl 54-56; Asst Chapl Ex Coll Ox 52-56; Fell St Edm Hall Ox from 56; Chapl 56-78; rtd 91; Perm to Offic *Ox* from 04. *19 Church Lane, Old Marston, Oxford OX3 0NZ* Tel (01865) 794486 Fax 279090

COWELL, Anthony. *See* COWELL, Neil Anthony

COWELL, Irene Christine. b 58. RGN80. Ridley Hall Cam CTM94. **d** 94 **p** 95. C Litherland St Phil *Liv* 94-98; R Sefton and Thornton from 98; Dioc Adv on HIV/AIDS and Sexual Health from 97; Dioc Dir CME from 02. *The Vicarage, Water Street, Liverpool L23 1TB* Tel 0151-931 4676 E-mail irene@rectory.fsnet.co.uk

COWELL, Neil Anthony. b 61. LNSM course 95. **d** 98 **p** 99. OLM New Bury *Man* from 98. *166 Harrowby Street, Farnworth, Bolton BL4 7DE* Tel (01204) 706957

COWELL, Peter James. b 58. Peterho Cam BA80 MA84. Coll of Resurr Mirfield 80. **d** 82 **p** 83. C Folkestone St Sav *Cant* 82-86; Chapl Asst St Thos Hosp Lon 86-90; Co-ord Chapl R Lon Hosp 90-94; Lead Trust Chapl Barts and The Lon NHS Trust from 94; Hospitaller from 05; V St Bart Less *Lon* from 05; PV Westmr Abbey from 94. *The Hospitaller, St Bartholomews Hospital, West Smithfield, London EC1A 7BE* Tel (020) 7601 8066 E-mail peter.cowell@bartsandthelondon.nhs.uk

COWEN, Canon Brian. b 45. Nottm Univ BTh77. Linc Th Coll 73. **d** 77 **p** 78. C Hexham *Newc* 77-80; C Eastnor *Heref* 80-81; C Ledbury 80-81; TV Glendale Gp *Newc* 81-90; V Lesbury w Alnmouth from 90; V Longhoughton w Howick from 98; AD Alnwick from 93; Hon Can Newc Cathl from 01. *The Vicarage, Lesbury, Alnwick NE66 3AU* Tel (01665) 830281 E-mail rev.cowen@btopenworld.com

COWGILL, Michael. b 48. Linc Th Coll 84. **d** 86 **p** 87. C Bolton St Jas w St Chrys *Bradf* 86-89; V Buttershaw St Paul 89-93; P-in-c Cullingworth 93-97; Dir Dioc Foundn Course 93-97; V Sutton from 97. *The Vicarage, Main Street, Sutton-in-Craven, Keighley BD20 7JS* Tel (01535) 633372

COWIE, Derek Edward. b 33. S'wark Ord Course 70. **d** 73 **p** 74. C Maldon All SS w St Pet *Chelmsf* 73-76; R Bowers Gifford w N Benfleet 76-79; V Chelmsf Ascension 79-84; V Shrub End 84-95; P-in-c Gosfield 95-03; RD Hinckford 01-03; rtd 03; Perm to Offic *Nor* from 03. *Bruar Cottage, 68 Wash Lane, Kessingland, Lowestoft NR33 7QY* Tel (01502) 740989 Mobile 07788-662211 E-mail decow@lineone.net *or* derekecowie@tiscali.co.uk

COWIE, John William Stephen. b 64. Wycliffe Hall Ox BTh97. **d** 97 **p** 98. C Shoreditch St Leon and Hoxton St Jo *Lon* 97-00. *Address withheld by request* E-mail williamcowie@onetel.com

COWLES, Richard Martin. b 53. Birm Univ BSc74 DipTh76. Ripon Coll Cuddesdon DipMin93. **d** 93 **p** 94. C Iffley *Ox* 93-96; TV Wheatley w Forest Hill and Stanton St John 96-97; TV Wheatley from 97. *The Rectory, 17 South End, Garsington, Oxford OX44 9DH* Tel (01865) 361381 E-mail vicar@cowles.globalnet.co.uk

COWLEY, Charles Frederick. *See* HOWARD-COWLEY, Joseph Charles

COWLEY, Mrs Elizabeth Mary. b 47. Bris Univ PQCSW84. WMMTC 89. **d** 92 **p** 94. NSM Wolston and Church Lawford *Cov* 92-97; Soc Resp Officer 97-02; P-in-c Churchover w Willey 97-02; TV Daventry, Ashby St Ledgers, Braunston etc *Pet* from 02. *The Vicarage, 19 Church Street, Staverton, Daventry NN11 6JJ* Tel (01327) 702466 E-mail liz.cowley@btinternet.com

COWLEY, Herbert Kenneth. b 20. Glouc Sch of Min 75. **d** 79 **p** 80. Hon C Lydney w Aylburton *Glouc* 79-89; rtd 89; Perm to Offic *B & W* 89-98. *19 Beechwood Road, Nailsea, Bristol BS48 2AF* Tel (01275) 856198

COWLEY, Ian Michael. b 51. Natal Univ BCom72 BA75 Sheff Univ MA83. Wycliffe Hall Ox 75. **d** 78 **p** 79. C Scottsville S Africa 78-81; C Norton Woodseats St Chad *Sheff* 81-83; R Hilton S Africa 83-94; R Milton *Ely* 94-03; RD Quy 00-02; V Yaxley and Holme w Conington from 03. *The Vicarage, Church Street, Yaxley, Peterborough PE7 3LH* Tel (01733) 240339 E-mail iancowley@ukonline.co.uk

COWLEY, Kenneth. *See* COWLEY, Herbert Kenneth

COWLEY, Mrs Jean Louie Cameron. *See* HERRICK, Mrs Jean Louie Cameron

COWLEY, Paul William. b 55. Middx Univ BA02. NTMTC 99. **d** 02 **p** 03. C Brompton H Trin w Onslow Square St Paul *Lon* from 02. *72 Archel Road, London W14 9QP* Tel (020) 7386 5140 *or* 08456-447544 Mobile 07860-146552 E-mail amanda.wilkie@htb.org.uk

COWLEY, Samuel Henry. b 44. St Jo Coll Nottm 85. **d** 87 **p** 88. C Hadleigh w Layham and Shelley *St E* 87-91; P-in-c Ipswich St Mich 91-99; P-in-c Westerfield and Tuddenham w Witnesham from 99. *The Rectory, Westerfield Road, Westerfield, Ipswich IP6 9AG* Tel (01473) 254483 Fax 236407 E-mail sam.cowley@stedmundsbury.anglican.org

COWLING, Canon Douglas Anderson. b 19. Leeds Univ BA40. Coll of Resurr Mirfield 40. **d** 42 **p** 43. C Linc St Andr *Linc* 42-45; R Candlesby w Scremby 47-53; R Carlton Scroop w Normanton 53-61; V Spalding St Paul 61-84; Can and Preb Linc Cathl 77-93;

rtd 84; Perm to Offic *Linc* from 84. *24 Campbell's Close, Spalding PE11 2UH* Tel (01775) 767044

COWLING, John Francis. b 32. K Coll Cam BA56. Linc Th Coll 56. **d** 58 **p** 59. C Leigh St Mary *Man* 58-61; Sec SCM in Schs Liv and Ches 61-65; V Bolton St Matt 65-71; V Bolton St Matt w St Barn 71-75; V Southport H Trin *Liv* 75-91; R St Olave Hart Street w All Hallows Staining etc *Lon* 91-05; P-in-c St Kath Cree 02-05; Dir of Ords 92-02; rtd 05. *St Olave's Rectory, 8 Hart Street, London EC3R 7NB* Tel (020) 7488 4318 *or* 7702 0244 Fax 7702 0811

COWLING, Simon Charles. b 59. G&C Coll Cam BA80 MA88 K Coll Lon PGCE82. Linc Th Coll BTh91. **d** 91 **p** 92. C Potternewton *Ripon* 91-94; C Far Headingley St Chad 94-96; V Roundhay St Edm from 96; AD Allerton from 04. *St Edmund's Vicarage, 5A North Park Avenue, Leeds LS8 1DN* Tel 0113-266 2550 E-mail simoncowling@ntlworld.com

COWMEADOW, Derek Lowe. b 28. Wells Th Coll 68. **d** 70 **p** 71. C Ledbury *Heref* 70-72; C Llanrhos *St As* 72-74; V Bringhurst w Gt Easton *Leic* 74-77; P-in-c Coln St Aldwyn w Hatherop and Quenington *Glouc* 77-82; V Coln St Aldwyns, Hatherop, Quenington etc 82-93; rtd 93; Perm to Offic *Glouc* from 93. *2 Hampton Grove, Meysey Hampton, Cirencester GL7 5JN* Tel (01285) 851645

COWPER, Christopher Herbert. b 44. AKC67 Open Univ BA76. **d** 68 **p** 69. C Pitsmoor *Sheff* 68-71; C Ulverston St Mary w H Trin *Carl* 71-74; R Kirklinton w Hethersgill and Scaleby 74-83; V Bridekirk 83-94; Chapl Dovenby Hall Hosp Cockermouth 83-94; P-in-c Wetheral w Warwick *Carl* 94-98; R Barningham w Hutton Magna and Wycliffe *Ripon* from 98. *The Rectory, Barningham, Richmond DL11 7DW* Tel (01833) 621217

COWPER, Peter James. *See* SELLICK, Peter James

COX, Alan John. b 34. Lon Coll of Div ALCD65 LTh. **d** 65 **p** 66. C Kirkheaton *Wakef* 65-67; C Keynsham w Queen Charlton *B & W* 67-71; R Chipstable w Huish Champflower and Clatworthy 71-76; TV Strood *Roch* 76-80; V Strood St Fran 80-83; R Keston 83-95; rtd 95; Perm to Offic *Roch* from 00. *12 Beech Court, 46 Copers Cope Road, Beckenham BR3 1LD* Tel (020) 8639 0082

COX, Albert Horace Montague. b 26. **d** 86 **p** 87. Zimbabwe 86-03; Hon C Winchelsea and Icklesham *Chich* from 03. *Parsonage Residence, Pilgrim's End, Manor Close, Icklesham, Winchelsea TN36 4BT* Tel (01424) 815295

COX, Ms Alison Clare. b 63. MHort(RHS)89. Ripon Coll Cuddesdon 01. **d** 03 **p** 04. C Spalding *Linc* from 03. *18 Maple Grove, Spalding PE11 2LE* Tel (01775) 725637 E-mail alisoncox19@hotmail.com

COX, Mrs Alison Hilda. b 57. Coll of Ripon & York St Jo BEd79 Nottm Univ MA02. EMMTC 99. **d** 02 **p** 03. NSM Bakewell *Derby* 02-05; TV Buxton w Burbage and King Sterndale from 05. *St Mary's Vicarage, 2A New Market Street, Buxton SK17 6LP* E-mail alison.cox@totalise.co.uk

COX, Canon Anthony James Stuart. b 46. BNC Ox BA68 MA74. Qu Coll Birm DipTh70 DPS71. **d** 71 **p** 72. C Smethwick St Matt w St Chad *Birm* 71-74; Chapl Liv Univ *Liv* 74; Malawi 75-87; Chapl Malosa Secondary Sch 75-79; Hd Master 80-87; Hon Can S Malawi from 80; Chapl Loughborough Gr Sch from 87; Perm to Offic *S'well* from 98. *Orchard House, 169 Main Street, Willoughby on the Wolds, Loughborough LE12 6SY* Tel (01509) 880861 E-mail cox@argonet.co.uk

COX, Brian Leslie. b 49. S Dios Minl Tr Scheme 91. **d** 94 **p** 95. C Southampton Maybush St Pet *Win* 94-98; P-in-c Knights Enham 98-05; R Knight's Enham and Smannell w Enham Alamein from 05. *The Rectory, 1 Ryon Close, Andover SP10 4DG* Tel (01264) 357032

COX, David John. b 51. S Bank Poly HNC76 Lon Univ BD97. Qu Coll Birm 76. **d** 79 **p** 80. C Brampton Bierlow *Sheff* 79-82; Miss Partner CMS 82-88; V N Perak W Malaysia 83-88; V Friarmere *Man* 88-96; P-in-c Denton Ch Ch from 96. *Christ Church Rectory, 1 Windmill Lane, Denton, Manchester M34 3RN* Tel 0161-336 2126 Fax as telephone E-mail djcox1779@aol.com

COX, Edward. *See* COX, James Edward Thomas

COX, Elizabeth Anne. b 55. SEITE 01. **d** 04 **p** 05. NSM Newington w Hartlip and Stockbury *Cant* from 04. *Appleden, 20 Pear Tree Walk, Newington, Sittingbourne ME9 7NG* Tel (01795) 844241 Mobile 07789-510499 E-mail lizapple@btopenworld.com

COX, Canon Eric William. b 30. Dur Univ BA54. Wells Th Coll 54. **d** 56 **p** 57. C Sutton in Ashfield St Mary *S'well* 56-59; Asst Chapl Brussels *Eur* 59-62; V Winnington *Ches* 62-71; V Middlewich 71-76; Chapl Mid Cheshire Hosps Trust 73-95; P-in-c Biley *Ches* 73-76; V Middlewich w Byley 76-95; RD Middlewich 80-94; Hon Can Ches Cathl 84-95; rtd 95; Perm to Offic *Ches* from 95 and *Lich* from 96. *Lovel Hollow, Church Road, Baschurch, Shrewsbury SY4 2EE* Tel (01939) 261258 E-mail canoneric@lovelhollow.fsnet.co.uk

COX, Geoffrey Sidney Randel. b 33. Mert Coll Ox BA56 MA60. Tyndale Hall Bris. **d** 58 **p** 59. C St Paul's Cray St Barn CD *Roch* 58-61; C Bromley Ch Ch 61-64; V Gorsley w Cliffords Mesne *Glouc* 64-79; V Hucclecote 79-89; V Wollaston and Strixton *Pet* 89-96; rtd 96; Perm to Offic *Glouc* from 96; Clergy Widows Officer (Cheltenham Adnry) from 99. *32 Murvagh Close, Cheltenham GL53 7QY* Tel (01242) 251604 E-mail geoffandjunecox@amserve.net

COX, George William. b 25. St Steph Ho Ox 83. **d** 86 **p** 87. NSM Abingdon *Ox* 86-95; rtd 92. *103 Bath Street, Abingdon OX14 1EG* Tel (01235) 521375

COX, Hugh Teversham. b 42. Moore Th Coll Sydney ThL68 ThSchol71 Keble Coll Ox BA76 MA82 Trin Evang Div Sch IL DMin99 Chas Sturt Univ NSW DipAgr63 Melbourne Coll of Div DipRE72. **d** 69 **p** 70. Australia 69-74 and 76-01; C Manuka St Paul 70-71; P-in-c Kameruka 71-74; Perm to Offic *Ox* 75-76; Chapl Commonwealth and Continental Ch Soc 76; P-in-c Canberra Ch Ch 76-82; Tutor and Lect St Mark's Nat Th Cen 77-82; R Lane Cove 82-87; R Castle Hill St Paul 87-01; Chapl Tervuren *Eur* from 01. *St Paul's Church Centre, Hoornzeelstraat 24, 3080 Tervuren, Belgium* Tel (0032) (2) 767 3435 Fax 688 0989 E-mail chaplain@stpaulstervuren.com *or* info@stpaulstervuren.com

COX, James David Robert. b 65. Lanc Univ BA88. Qu Coll Birm BD92. **d** 93 **p** 94. C Harborne St Pet *Birm* 93-96; C Chelmsley Wood 96-97; TV 97-00; V Smethwick Resurr from 00. *The Vicarage, 69 South Road, Smethwick, Warley B67 7BP* Tel 0121-558 0373

COX, James Edward Thomas. b 20. Sheff Univ BA47. Cuddesdon Coll 47. **d** 49 **p** 50. C Boxley *Cant* 49-52; C-in-c Buckland Valley CD 52-59; R Hawkinge 59-64; R Acrise 59-64; Chapl RAF 59-62; Chapl Abbey Sch Malvern 64-79; V Lt Malvern *Worc* 65-85; P-in-c 85-90; rtd 85; Perm to Offic *Heref* and *Worc* from 93. *4 Lucerne Avenue, Malvern WR14 3QA* Tel (01684) 564392

COX, Janet. b 48. Carl and Blackb Dioc Tr Inst 04. **d** 05. NSM Long Marton w Dufton and w Milburn *Carl* from 05. *Broom Cottage, Long Marton, Appleby-in-Westmorland CA16 6JP* Tel (017683) 62896 E-mail peter_janet_cox@hotmail.com

COX, John Anthony. b 45. Hull Univ BA67. Qu Coll Birm 71. **d** 73 **p** 74. C Buckingham *Ox* 73-76; C Whitley Ch Ch 76-81; V Reading St Agnes w St Paul 81-83; V Chaddesley Corbett and Stone *Worc* from 83. *The Vicarage, Butts Lane, Stone, Kidderminster DY10 4BH* Tel (01562) 69438

COX, John Edgar. b 26. CEng MIEE56 Lon Univ BSc50 MSc69. Bps' Coll Cheshunt 67. **d** 68 **p** 69. NSM Harlow St Mary Magd *Chelmsf* 68-76; C S Petherwin w Trewen *Truro* 77-79; P-in-c 79-82; P-in-c Lawhitton 81-82; P-in-c Lezant 81-82; R Lezant w Lawhitton and S Petherwin w Trewen 82-83; V Breage w Germoe 83-91; rtd 91; Perm to Offic *Truro* from 91. *Manderley, 8 Trewartha Road, Praa Sands, Penzance TR20 9ST* Tel (01736) 762582

COX, The Ven John Stuart. b 40. Fitzw Ho Cam BA62 MA66 Linacre Coll Ox BA67 Birm Univ DPS68. Wycliffe Hall Ox 64. **d** 68 **p** 69. C Prescot *Liv* 68-71; C Birm St Geo *Birm* 71-73; R 73-78; Selection Sec ACCM 78-83; Hon C Orpington All SS *Roch* 78-83; Dioc Dir of Ords *S'wark* 83-91; Can Res and Treas S'wark Cathl 83-91; V Roehampton H Trin 91-95; Adn Sudbury *St E* from 95. *2 Bullen Close, Bury St Edmunds IP33 3JP* Tel and fax (01284) 766796 E-mail archdeacon.john@stedmundsbury.anglican.org

COX, Jonathan James. b 63. Wollongong Univ BA85 Univ of NSW DipEd86. Ridley Hall Cam. **d** 00 **p** 01. C Tonbridge SS Pet and Paul *Roch* 00-03; R Oxley Vale Australia from 03. *95 Glengarvin Drive, Tamworth, NSW, Australia 2340* Tel (0061) (2) 6761 7271 E-mail seven@fish.co.uk

COX, Julie Margaret. b 55. St Alb and Ox Min Course. **d** 00 **p** 01. NSM Luton St Chris Round Green *St Alb* from 00. *29 Maple Close, Pulloxhill, Bedford MK45 5EF* Tel (01525) 717002 E-mail revjuliecox@hotmail.com

COX, Leonard James William. b 27. Sarum & Wells Th Coll 79. **d** 81 **p** 82. C Hythe *Cant* 81-84; V Thanington 84-92; rtd 92; Perm to Offic *Cant* 92-01. *31 Wheatfield Crescent, Mansfield Woodhouse, Mansfield NG19 9HH*

COX, Martin Brian. b 64. Keele Univ BA91 CQSW91. St Jo Coll Nottm 01. **d** 03. C Sale St Anne *Ches* from 03. *3 Windermere Avenue, Sale M33 3FP* Tel 0161-962 0951 E-mail martin_b_cox@btopenworld.com

COX, Martin Lloyd. b 57. Wilson Carlile Coll and Sarum & Wells Th Coll. **d** 88 **p** 89. C Risca *Mon* 88-91; TV Pontypool 91-96; V Monkton *St D* 96-04; TR from 04. *The Vicarage, Church Terrace, Monkton, Pembroke SA71 4LW* Tel (01646) 682723

COX, Ms Patricia Jean. b 44. WEMTC. **d** 00 **p** 01. Hon C Coleford w Staunton *Glouc* from 00. *67 Primrose Hill, Lydney GL15 5SW* Tel (01594) 843852 E-mail revpat_cox@tinyworld.co.uk

COX, Canon Paul Graham. b 40. Keele Univ BA62 DipEd62 Ibadan Univ Nigeria 63. Westcott Ho Cam 77. **d** 78 **p** 79. NSM Kemsing w Woodlands *Roch* 78-80; Hd Master and Chapl St Mich Sch Otford 81-90; C Petham and Waltham w Lower Hardres etc *Cant* 90-95; P-in-c 95-97; C Elmsted w Hastingleigh 90-95; P-in-c 95-97; Bp's Officer for NSM 91-98; R Biddenden and Smarden from 97; Dioc Dir of Reader Selection and Tr 98-00; Bp's Officer for OLM from 00; Hon Can Cant Cathl from 01. *The Rectory, High Street, Biddenden, Ashford TN27 8AH* Tel and fax (01580) 291454 Mobile 07799-300589 E-mail pcox@fish.co.uk

COX, Peter Allard. b 55. Univ of Wales (Lamp) BA76. Wycliffe Hall Ox 77. **d** 79 **p** 80. C Penarth All SS *Llan* 79-82; V Aberpergwm and Blaengwrach 82-86; V Bargoed and Deri w Brithdir 86-97; V Penarth All SS from 97. *All Saints' Vicarage, 2 Lower Cwrt-y-Vil Road, Penarth CF64 3HQ* Tel (029) 2070 8952 E-mail petercox6@virgin.net

COX, Philip Gordon. b 36. St Jo Coll Cam MA62 Lon Univ PGCE71. Dioc OLM tr scheme 99. **d** 02 **p** 03. OLM Charing w Charing Heath and Lt Chart *Cant* from 02. *Home Meadow, Little Chart Forstal, Little Chart, Ashford TN27 0PU* Tel (01233) 840274 E-mail philip@homemeadow.plus.com

COX, Miss Rosemary Jennifer. b 54. St Aid Coll Dur BA75 Lon Bible Coll BTh97 Trin Coll Bris MA99. Cranmer Hall Dur 01. **d** 03 **p** 04. C Leeds All SS w Osmondthorpe *Ripon* 03-05; C Ireland Wood from 05. *6 Holt Park Gardens, Leeds LS16 7RB* Tel 0113-281 7854 E-mail rosemaryjcox@aol.com

COX, Mrs Sheila Margaret. b 54. Nottm Univ BA76 Reading Univ PGCE77. SEITE 00. **d** 03 **p** 04. NSM Cranbrook *Cant* from 03. *12 Westwell Court, Tenterden TN30 6TS* Tel (01580) 764556 Mobile 07985-003095 Fax (01580) 765981 E-mail sheila.cox@medix-uk.com

COX, Mrs Sheila Stuart. b 41. Aber Coll of Educn CertEd63. Edin Dioc NSM Course 85. **d** 88 **p** 94. NSM Livingston LEP *Edin* 88-93; Asst Chapl St Jo and Bangour Hosps W Lothian 89-93; Chapl 96-98; Hon C Edin St Mark 93-96; Missr Edin St Andr and St Aid 95-96; NSM Eyemouth from 98. *The Parsonage, Beach Avenue, Eyemouth TD14 5AB* Tel (01890) 771764 *or* 750000

COX, Simon John. b 53. MIBiol79 CBiol79 Qu Mary Coll Lon BSc74 Liv Univ PhD81 Selw Coll Cam BA81 MA85 Lanc Univ MA87. Ridley Hall Cam 79. **d** 82 **p** 83. C Livesey *Blackb* 82-85; C Cheadle Hulme St Andr *Ches* 85-89; V Disley 89-94; R Bispham *Blackb* from 94; AD Blackpool from 04. *All Hallows Rectory, 86 All Hallows Road, Blackpool FY2 0AY* Tel (01253) 351886 E-mail drsjcox@yahoo.co.uk

COX, Stephen. b 38. Open Univ BA80. Bps' Coll Cheshunt 65. **d** 68 **p** 69. C Gaywood, Bawsey and Mintlyn *Nor* 68-72; Youth Chapl 72-82; C N Lynn w St Marg and St Nic 73-82; Chapl Guildf Coll of Tech 82-87; Chapl Surrey Univ *Guildf* 82-91; Tr and Devlpt Manager Jas Paget Hosp Gorleston 91-93; Manager Medical Records 93-96; Consumer Relns and Litigation Manager 96-99; rtd 99. *56 Bately Avenue, Gorleston, Great Yarmouth NR31 6HN* Tel (01493) 662061

COX, Stephen John Wormleighton. b 54. New Coll Ox MA79 Fitzw Coll Cam BA79. Ridley Hall Cam 77. **d** 80 **p** 81. C Clapton Park All So *Lon* 80-85; TV Hackney Marsh 85-87; V Holloway St Mary w St Jas 87-88; P-in-c Barnsbury St Dav w St Clem 87-88; V Holloway St Mary Magd 88-97; AD Islington 95-99; TR Upper Holloway from 97. *St Mary's Vicarage, 3 Highcroft Road, London N19 3AQ* Tel (020) 7272 9084 *or* 7272 1783 Fax 7272 9934 E-mail stephenj.cox@virgin.net

COX, William John Francis. b 24. SW Minl Tr Course. **d** 77 **p** 78. NSM Liskeard w St Keyne and St Pinnock *Truro* 77-82; NSM Liskeard w St Keyne, St Pinnock and Morval 82-86; NSM N Hill w Altarnon, Bolventor and Lewannick 86-87; TV Bolventor 87-92; P-in-c North Hill and Lewannick 92-94; rtd 94; Perm to Offic *Truro* from 94. *9 Trelawney Rise, Callington PL17 7PT* Tel (01579) 384347

COXHEAD, Mrs Margaret. b 40. S Dios Minl Tr Scheme 91. **d** 94 **p** 95. NSM High Hurstwood *Chich* 94-00; P-in-c from 00; P-in-c Fairwarp from 00. *Rock Hall, Chillies Lane, High Hurstwood, Uckfield TN22 4AD* Tel (01825) 733833

COYNE, John Edward. b 55. Sheff Univ MA98. Oak Hill Th Coll BA79. **d** 79 **p** 80. C Cheadle Hulme St Andr *Ches* 79-81; C Macclesfield St Mich 81-83; V Stalybridge H Trin and Ch Ch 83-88; Chapl RAF 88-03; Command Chapl RAF 03-05; RAF Adv in Evangelism 93-98; Hon C Hemingford Grey *Ely* 96-98; Dean of Coll St Jo Coll Nottm from 05. *St John's College, Chilwell Lane, Bramcote, Nottingham NG9 3DS* Tel 0115-925 1114 E-mail j2scoyne@hotmail.com

COYNE, Terence Roland Harry. b 37. Chich Th Coll 64. **d** 66 **p** 67. C Meir *Lich* 66-69; C Horninglow 69-72; V Walsall St Gabr Fulbrook from 72; C Walsall St Mary and All SS Palfrey 97-02; C Caldmore w Palfrey from 02. *St Gabriel's Vicarage, Walstead Road, Walsall WS5 4LZ* Tel (01922) 622583

COZENS, Mrs Audrey Lilian. b 35. St Hugh's Coll Ox BA56 MA84. Gilmore Course 79. **dss** 82 **d** 87 **p** 94. Shenfield *Chelmsf* 82-87; Par Dn 87-89; Par Dn Westcliff St Andr 89-94; C 94-95; P-in-c Chelmsf St Andr 95-02; P-in-c The Chignals w Mashbury 95-02; rtd 02; Perm to Offic *Chelmsf* from 02. *56 Victoria Road, Writtle, Chelmsford CM1 3PA* Tel (01245) 420165 E-mail revacozens@supanet.com

COZENS, Daniel Harry. b 44. Oak Hill Th Coll DipTh70. **d** 71 **p** 72. C St Paul's Cray St Barn *Roch* 71-74; C Deptford St Nic w Ch Ch *S'wark* 74-76; C Deptford St Nic and St Luke 76-78; Rees Missr *Ely* from 78; Six Preacher Cant Cathl *Cant* from 94. *The Rectory, 73 High Street, Coton, Cambridge CB3 7PL* Tel (01954) 210239 *or* 211184 Fax 211983 E-mail walk1000@btinternet.com

COZENS, Michael Graeme. b 59. Chich Th Coll 91. **d** 93 **p** 94. C Emscote *Cov* 93-96; C Prestbury *Glouc* 96-03; TV Prestbury and All SS from 03. *The Vicarage, 66 All Saints Road, Cheltenham GL52 2HA* Tel (01242) 523177 E-mail mg.cozens@8prestbury.fsnet.co.uk

✠**CRABB, The Most Revd Frederick Hugh Wright.** b 15. Lon Univ BD39. Wycliffe Coll Toronto Hon DD60 St Andr Coll Saskatoon Hon DD67 Coll of Em and St Chad Hon DD77 ALCD39. **d** 39 **p** 40 **c** 75. C W Teignmouth *Ex* 39-41; C Plymouth St Andr 41-42; CMS Sudan 42-51; Prin Bp Gwynne Coll 42-51; Vice-Prin Lon Coll of Div 51-57; Canada from 57; Prin Em Coll Saskatoon 57-67; Bp Athabasca 75-83; Abp Rupertsland 77-83. *324-6700 Hunterview Drive NW, Calgary AB, Canada, T2K 6K4*

CRABB, Paul Anthony. b 58. St Chad's Coll Dur BSc79 Leeds Univ PGCE80. Qu Coll Birm 90. **d** 91 **p** 92. C Gomersal *Wakef* 91-95; V Drighlington 95-01; TV Dewsbury from 01. *96 Old Bank Road, Dewsbury WF12 7AJ* Tel (01924) 438577 Mobile 07946-530415 E-mail pauldewsteamvic@aol.com

CRABTREE, Derek. b 32. Leic Univ BSc(Econ)53. Cant Sch of Min 91. **d** 94 **p** 95. NSM Hackington *Cant* 94-02; Asst Chapl Kent Univ 94-02; rtd 02; Perm to Offic *Cant* from 02. *19 Monastery Street, Canterbury CT1 1NJ* Tel (01227) 471503

CRABTREE, Eric. b 30. Chelt & Glouc Coll of HE BA99 ACA55 FCA68. Premontre Community (RC) 58. **d** 64 **p** 64. In RC Ch 64-90; Perm to Offic *Glouc* 00-04 and *Ox* from 04. *St Katharine's House, Ormond Road, Wantage OX12 8EA* Tel (01235) 769279

CRABTREE, Martine Charmaine. b 74. Glas Bible Coll BA96 St Jo Coll Nottm MTh02. **d** 02 **p** 03. C Kippax w Allerton Bywater *Ripon* from 02. *55 Goodwood Avenue, Kippax, Leeds LS25 7HS* Tel 0113-286 1442 E-mail martinecrabtree@aol.com *or* curate@stmarykippax.org.uk

CRABTREE, Stephen. *See* JONES-CRABTREE, Stephen

CRABTREE, Stephen John. b 62. Roehampton Inst BEd85 Surrey Univ MA93. SEITE 93. **d** 96 **p** 97. NSM N Farnborough *Guildf* from 96. *42 Avenue Road, Farnborough GU14 7BL* Tel (01252) 541873 E-mail stephecrab@aol.com

CRADDOCK, Brian Arthur. b 40. Chich Th Coll 67. **d** 70 **p** 71. C Stoke-upon-Trent *Lich* 70-74; Bermuda 75-89; P-in-c Bury and Houghton *Chich* 89-95; Chapl St Mich Sch Burton Park 89-94; Chapl Mojacar *Eur* 95-99; rtd 99; Perm to Offic *Lich* from 04. *72 Pacific Road, Trentham, Stoke-on-Trent ST4 8UD* Tel (01782) 643602

CRADDOCK, Jeremy Graham. b 37. Lon Univ BSc64 Nottm Univ MPhil72. EAMTC 93. **d** 94 **p** 95. NSM Godmanchester *Ely* 94-99; Perm to Offic from 99. *8 Hall Close, Hartford, Huntingdon PE29 1XJ* Tel (01480) 458011

CRADDUCK, Martin Charles. b 50. Hull Univ BSc71. St Jo Coll Nottm DipTh77. **d** 79 **p** 80. C W Kilburn St Luke w St Simon and St Jude *Lon* 79-83; C Oxhey All SS *St Alb* 83-86; Asst Chapl HM Pris Man 86-87; Dep Chapl HM Young Offender Inst Glen Parva 87-89; Chapl HM Pris Stocken 89-95. *35 Worcester Road, Grantham NG31 8SF* Tel (01476) 571351

CRADDUCK, Stuart William. b 74. Bp Otter Coll Chich BA97. Ripon Coll Cuddesdon BTh00. **d** 00 **p** 01. C W Leigh *Portsm* 00-03; Chapl and Min Can St Alb Abbey *St Alb* from 03. *The Deanery Barn, Sumpter Yard, St Albans AL1 1BY* Tel (01727) 890206 E-mail stuart@cradduckmail.freeserve.co.uk

CRAFER, Mrs Jeanette Angela. b 48. Keswick Hall Coll CertEd78. EAMTC 99. **d** 01 **p** 02. C Ashmanhaugh, Barton Turf etc *Nor* 01-05; P-in-c Martham and Repps with Bastwick, Thurne etc from 05. *The Rectory, 68 Black Street, Martham, Great Yarmouth NR29 4PR* Tel (01493) 740240 E-mail jeanette.crafer@tesco.net

CRAFT, William Newham. b 46. MCIPD70 Lon Univ BSc68. Oak Hill Th Coll 87. **d** 89 **p** 90. C Werrington *Pet* 90-93; C-in-c Norfolk Park St Leonard CD *Sheff* 93-02; P-in-c Sheff St Jo 99-02; V 02-03; V Stapleford *S'well* from 03. *The Vicarage, 61 Church Street, Stapleford, Nottingham NG9 8GA* Tel 0115-875 3462 *or* 917 6202 E-mail w.craft@ntlworld.com

✠**CRAGG, The Rt Revd Albert Kenneth.** b 13. Jes Coll Ox BA34 MA38 DPhil50 Huron Coll Hon DD63 Virginia Th Sem Hon DD85 Leeds Univ Hon DD93 Lambeth DD02. Tyndale Hall Bris 34. **d** 36 **p** 37 **c** 70. C Tranmere St Cath *Ches* 36-39; Lebanon 39-47; R Longworth *Ox* 47-51; USA 51-56; Can Res Jerusalem 56-59; St Aug Coll Cant 59-60; Sub-Warden 60-61; Warden 61-67; Hon Can Cant Cathl *Cant* 61-80; Hon Can Jerusalem 65-73; Asst Bp Jerusalem 70-73; Bye-Fellow G&C Coll Cam 69-70; Asst Bp Chich 73-78; Asst Bp Wakef 78-81; V Helme 78-81; rtd 81; Asst Bp Ox from 82. *3 Goring Lodge, White House Road, Oxford OX1 4QE* Tel (01865) 249895

CRAGG, Edward William Adrian. b 55. St Cath Coll Cam BA77 MA81. Cranmer Hall Dur 97. **d** 99 **p** 00. C Clifton *York* 99-02; R Skelton w Shipton and Newton on Ouse from 02; Chapl York Health Services NHS Trust from 02. *The Rectory, Church Lane, Skelton, York YO30 1XT* Tel (01904) 470045 E-mail acragg@fish.co.uk

CRAGG, Mrs Sandra Anne. b 45. St Hugh's Coll Ox BA67. SEITE 94. **d** 97 **p** 98. NSM Kingston All SS w St Jo *S'wark* from 97. *10 Lingfield Avenue, Kingston upon Thames KT1 2TN* Tel (020) 8546 1997 Fax 8541 5281 E-mail sandy.cragg@cableinet.co.uk

CRAGGS, Colin Frederick. b 41. Open Univ BA80. Sarum & Wells Th Coll 85. **d** 88 **p** 89. NSM Wilton *B & W* 88-90 and from 93; NSM Taunton St Andr 90-93; Chapl Taunton and Somerset NHS Trust from 90. *89 Galmington Road, Taunton TA1 5NW* Tel (01823) 271989 Fax as telephone

CRAGGS, Michael Alfred. b 43. Open Univ BA79. St Mich Coll Llan 66. **d** 69 **p** 70. C Clee *Linc* 69-72; C Old Brumby 72-76; TV Kingsthorpe w Northampton St Dav *Pet* 76-83; P-in-c Gt w Lt Addington 83-89; RD Higham 88-89; TR Corby SS Pet and Andr w Gt and Lt Oakley 89-02; V Corby SS Pet and Andr from 02; RD Corby 90-95. *The Rectory, 40 Beanfield Avenue, Corby NN18 0EH* Tel (01536) 267620 *or* 402442 E-mail mikeccorb@aol.com

CRAGO, Geoffrey Norman. b 44. Linc Th Coll 67. **d** 70 **p** 71. C Matson *Glouc* 70-75; V Dean Forest H Trin 75-80; Relig Progr Producer Radio Severn Sound 80-85; P-in-c Huntley 80-82; Perm to Offic 82-90; Dioc Communications Officer 84; Gen Syn Broadcasting Dept 85-88; Hon C Highnam, Lassington, Rudford, Tibberton etc from 90; Relig Progr Producer BBC Radio Gloucestershire from 94; Bp's Press Officer and Dioc Communications Officer from 97. *Milestones, 2 Two Mile Lane, Highnam, Gloucester GL2 8DW* Tel (01452) 750575 Fax 750105 E-mail glosdco@star.co.uk

CRAIG, Canon Alan Stuart. b 38. Leeds Univ BA59. Cranmer Hall Dur DipTh61. **d** 61 **p** 62. C Newcastle w Butterton *Lich* 61-65; C Scarborough St Mary w Ch Ch, St Paul and St Thos *York* 65-67; V Werrington *Lich* 67-72; Asst Chapl HM Pris Man 72-73; Chapl HM Borstal Hindley 73-78; Chapl HM Pris Acklington 78-84; V Longhirst *Newc* 84-90; R Morpeth 90-99; RD Morpeth 84-95; Hon Can Newc Cathl 90-02; Chapl St Geo and Cottage Hosp Morpeth 90-93; Chapl Northd Mental Health NHS Trust 93-99; Chapl to The Queen from 95; Dir of Ords and Bp's Chapl *Newc* 99-02; rtd 02; Perm to Offic *Newc* from 02. *5 Springfield Meadows, Alnwick NE66 2NY* Tel (01665) 602806 Mobile 07779-519040 E-mail acraig@fish.co.uk

CRAIG, Andrew John. b 54. Selw Coll Cam BA76 MA80 PhD80 Dur Univ MBA92. NEOC 00. **d** 03 **p** 04. NSM Stranton *Dur* from 03. *25 Egerton Road, Hartlepool TS26 0BW* Tel (01429) 422461 E-mail andrewj.craig@ntlworld.com

CRAIG, David Paul. b 46. Univ of K Coll Halifax NS Hon DD94. ACT ThDip. **d** 84 **p** 85. Australia 84-89; Canada 89-94; Miss to Seamen 89-94; Chapl Immingham Seafarers' Cen from 94; Gen Preacher *Linc* from 97. *The Seafarers' Centre, Lockside Road, Immingham DN40 2NN* Tel (01469) 574195 Fax 574740

CRAIG, Eric. b 39. Birm Univ BA62. Qu Coll Birm 62. **d** 64 **p** 65. C Todmorden *Wakef* 64-68; C Hurstpierpoint *Chich* 68-70; C Cobham *Guildf* 70-73; V Dawley St Jerome *Lon* 73-76; V Stainland *Wakef* 76-87; R Yarnton w Begbroke and Shipton on Cherwell *Ox* 87-04; rtd 04. *17 Farmers Close, Witney OX28 1NN* Tel (01993) 704892

CRAIG, Gillean Weston. b 49. York Univ BA72 Qu Coll Cam BA76 MA80. Westcott Ho Cam 76. **d** 77 **p** 78. C St Marylebone Ch Ch *Lon* 77-82; C Ealing St Barn 82-88; P-in-c St Geo-in-the-East w St Paul 88-89; R 89-02; V Kensington St Mary Abbots w St Geo from 02. *St Mary Abbots Vicarage, Vicarage Gate, London W8 4HN* Tel (020) 7937 6032 E-mail gillean.craig@stmaryabbotschurch.org

CRAIG, James Owen Maxwell. b 72. Open Univ BA98. Cranmer Hall Dur 99. **d** 02 **p** 03. C Ch the K *Dur* 02-05; Gateshead and Bensham Community Chapl to Arts from 05. *St Columba House, Peterborough Close, Gateshead NE8 1NL* E-mail james.craig@durham.ac.uk

CRAIG, Canon John Newcome. b 39. Selw Coll Cam BA63 MA67. Linc Th Coll 63. **d** 65 **p** 66. C Cannock *Lich* 65-71; V Gt Wyrley 71-79; TR Wednesfield 79-91; Prec Leic Cathl *Leic* 91-03; Hon Can 93-03; Can Res Leic Cathl 03-04; rtd 04; Perm to Offic *Birm* from 04. *109 Kingsbury Road, Erdington, Birmingham B24 8QH* Tel 0121-373 2809 E-mail john.olivia.craig@lineone.net

CRAIG, Judy Howard. *See* CRAIG PECK, Judy Howard

CRAIG, Julie Elizabeth. *See* LEAVES, Julie Elizabeth

CRAIG, Julie Elizabeth. *See* EATON, Mrs Julie Elizabeth

CRAIG, Patrick Thomas. b 36. BA. St D Coll Lamp 59 Bps' Coll Cheshunt 59. **d** 61 **p** 62. C Belfast St Mary *Conn* 61-65; C Belfast St Pet 65-69; CF 69-88; R Hartfield w Coleman's Hatch *Chich* 88-01; rtd 01; P-in-c Six Pilgrims *B & W* from 03. *Briars, Broadclose Way, Barton St David, Somerton TA11 6BS* Tel (01458) 850825

CRAIG, Richard Harvey. b 31. Em Coll Cam BA58. Linc Th Coll. **d** 60 **p** 61. C Bottesford *Linc* 60-65; Bp's Ind Chapl 65-69; Dioc Adv on Laity Tr *Bris* 69-74; V Whitchurch 74-86; TV N Lambeth *S'wark* 86-96; Bp's Ecum Adv 88-96; Ecum Officer 90-96; rtd 96; Perm to Offic *St Alb* 96-99 and *S'wark* from 01. *18 Holst Court, Westminster Bridge Road, London SE1 7JQ* Tel (020) 7928 0495

CRAIG, Robin Joseph. b 43. TCD BA65 Div Test66 Birm Univ CertEd70. **d** 66 **p** 67. C Carrickfergus *Conn* 66-69; Chapl Ld Wandsworth Coll Hants 75-85; Chapl K Sch Macclesfield 85-01; Lic to Offic *Ches* 85-01; rtd 01. *5 Winston Court, Lavant Road, Chichester PO19 5RG*

CRAIG PECK, Judy Howard. b 57. Lon Univ MB, BS81 DRCOG83 MRCGP86. WMMTC 97. **d** 00 **p** 01. NSM Billing *Pet* from 00; NSM Officer from 03. *Dreamstead, 10 Sharplands, Grendon, Northampton NN7 1JL* Tel (01933) 665965 E-mail judy@peckc.fsnet.co.uk

CRAIG-WILD, Ms Dorothy Elsie (Dhoe). b 54. Birm Univ BA77. Qu Coll Birm 79. **dss** 81 **d** 87 **p** 94. Middleton St Mary *Ripon* 81-87; Par Dn Chapeltown *Sheff* 88-94; C 94-96; P-in-c Bruntcliffe *Wakef* 96-02; RD Birstall from 98; Jt P-in-c Morley St Paul 00-02; P-in-c Roberttown w Hartshead from 02; C Heckmondwike from 05; C Liversedge w Hightown from 05. *The Vicarage, 3 Vicarage Meadow, Mirfield WF14 9JL* Tel and fax (01924) 505791 E-mail dhoecraigwild@hotmail.com

CRAIG-WILD, Canon Peter John. b 55. Leeds Univ BA77. Qu Coll Birm 77. **d** 80 **p** 81. C Rothwell w Lofthouse *Ripon* 80-83; C Beeston 83-87; V Chapeltown *Sheff* 87-96; RD Tankersley 93-96; V Mirfield *Wakef* from 96; P-in-c Eastthorpe and Upper Hopton from 03; Hon Can Wakef Cathl from 03. *The Vicarage, 3 Vicarage Meadow, Mirfield WF14 9JL* Tel (01924) 505790 Fax 505791 E-mail peter.craig-wild@ntlworld.com

CRAM, Mrs Ruth Frances Isobel. b 52. Kingston Poly BA87 Poly Cen Lon MA92. N Ord Course 94. **d** 97 **p** 98. C E Crompton *Man* 97-99; C Cirencester *Glouc* 99-02; C Broad Blunsdon *Bris* 02; V N Swindon St Andr from 02. *8 Figsbury Close, Swindon SN25 1UA* Tel (01793) 701353 E-mail rc.cram@btinternet.com

CRAMERI, Mrs Mary Barbara. b 44. K Coll Lon BD65 AKC91 Lon Inst of Educn PGCE66. S Dios Minl Tr Scheme 86. **d** 88 **p** 94. C Whitton SS Phil and Jas *Lon* 88-91; Staff Member S Dios Minl Tr Scheme 91-97; Minl Development Officer STETS 97-98; Vice-Prin Sarum & Wells Th Coll 93-98; Par Dn Bemerton *Sarum* 91-92; TV Pewsey and Swanborough 98-00; TR Whitton 00-01; rtd 01; Perm to Offic *Sarum* 02-05; Hon C Chase and Ascott under Wychwood *Ox* from 05 *The Vicarage, Church Enstone, Chipping Norton OX7 4NL* Tel (01608) 678424

CRAMP, Barry Leonard. b 46. St Luke's Coll Ex CertEd67 CChem76 MRSC76. **d** 04 **p** 05. OLM Earsham w Alburgh and Denton *Nor* from 04. *Wyvern, The Street, Earsham, Bungay NR35 2TY* Tel (01986) 895535 E-mail barry@pacific.org.uk

CRAMP, Susan Louise. b 53. Univ of Wales (Abth) BSc74 Leic Univ PGCE75. **d** 04 **p** 05. OLM Earsham w Alburgh and Denton *Nor* from 04. *Wyvern, The Street, Earsham, Bungay NR35 2TY* Tel (01986) 895535 E-mail sue@pacific.org.uk

CRAMPTON, John Leslie. b 41. CITC 64. **d** 67 **p** 68. C Lurgan Ch the Redeemer *D & D* 67-71; C Dundela St Mark 71-73; Rhodesia 73-80; Zimbabwe 80-82; I Killanne w Killegney, Rossdroit and Templeshanbo *C & O* 82-88; Preb Ferns Cathl 85-88; Chapl Wilson's Hosp Sch Multyfarnham *M & K* 88-91; C Mullingar, Portnashangan, Moyliscar, Kilbixy etc 89-91; I Athy w Kilberry, Fontstown and Kilkea *D & G* 91-01; Can Ch Ch Cathl Dublin 95-01; I Geashill w Killeigh and Ballycommon *M & K* from 01. *The Rectory, Geashill, Tullamore, Co Offaly, Irish Republic* Tel and fax (00353) (506) 43242 Mobile 87-907 7981 E-mail geashill@kildare.anglican.org

CRANE, John Walter. b 32. Chich Th Coll. **d** 58 **p** 59. C Forest Town *S'well* 58-60; C Primrose Hill St Mary w Avenue Road St Paul *Lon* 60-64; R Greenford H Cross 64-67; Min Can and Chapl Windsor 67-79; Chapl St Geo Sch Ascot 67-79; Warden Dioc Retreat Ho (Holland Ho) Cropthorne *Worc* 79-83; P-in-c Harvington and Norton and Lenchwick 84-87; rtd 87. *16 Allesborough Drive, Pershore WR10 1JH* Tel (01386) 556444

CRANE, Mrs Judith. b 53. Matlock Coll of Educn BCombStuds81. Cranmer Hall Dur 94. **d** 96 **p** 97. C Tadcaster w Newton Kyme *York* 96-99; TV Brayton 99-02; V Blackwell w Tibshelf *Derby* from 02. *The Vicarage, 67 High Street, Tibshelf, Alfreton DE55 5NU* Tel (01773) 873305

CRANE, Ronald Edward. b 48. SSC. Wilson Carlile Coll 73 St Steph Ho Ox 83. **d** 85 **p** 86. C Bicester w Bucknell, Caversfield and Launton *Ox* 85-88; P-in-c Washwood Heath *Birm* 88-92; V 92-01; V Wylde Green from 01. *Emmanuel Vicarage, 17 Greenhill Road, Sutton Coldfield B72 1DS* Tel 0121-373 8348 Fax as telephone E-mail whr@rcrane9.fsnet.co.uk

CRANE, Vincent James. b 10. St Aid Birkenhead 62. **d** 64 **p** 65. C Penn *Lich* 64-70; R Himley 70-78; V Swindon 70-78; rtd 78;

Perm to Offic *Worc* 78-01 and *Lich* from 01. *14 Holcroft Road, Wall Heath, Kingswinford DY6 0HP* Tel (01384) 292208

CRANFIELD, Nicholas William Stewart. b 56. Mert Coll Ox BA77 MA81 DPhil88 Leeds Univ BA81 Selw Coll Cam PhD95. Coll of Resurr Mirfield 79 Union Th Sem (NY) STM84. **d** 86 **p** 87. C Ascot Heath *Ox* 86-89; Prin Berks Chr Tr Scheme 89-92; Hon C Reading St Mary w St Laur 89-92; Chapl and Fell Selw Coll Cam 92-99; Dean of Chpl 94-99; Chapl Newnham Coll Cam 92-99; V Blackheath All SS *S'wark* from 99; Chapl St Dunstan's Coll Catford from 00. *All Saints' Vicarage, 10 Duke Humphrey Road, London SE3 0TY* Tel (020) 8852 4280 E-mail vicar_blackheath@hotmail.com

CRANIDGE, Mrs Wendy Ann. b 31. Sheff Univ CertEd52. Cant Sch of Min 81. **dss** 84 **d** 87 **p** 94. Roch 84-88; Hon Par Dn 87-88; Soc Resp Adv *Cant* and *Roch* 86-88; Hon C Washingborough w Heighington and Canwick *Linc* 88-92; Perm to Offic *Linc* 92-93; *Roch* 93-94; C Farnborough *Roch* 94-96; rtd 96; Perm to Offic *Roch* 96-02. *Ashburton House, 948 Rochdale Road, Walsden, Todmorden OL14 6TY* Tel (01706) 815062

CRANKSHAW, Ronald. b 41. Coll of Resurr Mirfield 74. **d** 76 **p** 77. C Orford St Andr *Liv* 76; C N Meols 76-79; V Abram 79-85; V Wigan St Anne 85-99; AD Wigan W 94-99; V Heston *Lon* from 99. *The Vicarage, 147 Heston Road, Hounslow TW5 0RD* Tel (020) 8570 2288 Fax 8570 8785 E-mail crankshaw@freeuk.co.uk

CRANMER, Ms Elaine. b 56. Hockerill Coll Cam CertEd77. SEITE 97. **d** 00 **p** 01. C Charlton *S'wark* 00-03; P-in-c Eltham Park St Luke from 03. *St Luke's Vicarage, 107 Westmount Road, London SE9 1XX* Tel (020) 8850 3030 E-mail rev.elaine@virgin.net

CRANMER, John Abery. b 33. K Alfred's Coll Win CertEd56 Southn Univ MPhil69. **d** 94 **p** 00. NSM Crawley and Littleton and Sparsholt w Lainston *Win* 94-02; rtd 02; Perm to Offic *Win* from 02. *The Coach House, Crawley, Winchester SO21 2PU* Tel (01962) 776214

CRANSHAW, Trevor Raymond. b 58. Trin Coll Bris 00. **d** 03 **p** 04. C Westbury-on-Trym H Trin *Bris* from 03. *16 Southfield Road, Westbury-on-Trym, Bristol BS9 3BH* Tel 0117-962 5693 Mobile 07734-304116

CRANSWICK, James Harvard. b 22. Melbourne Univ BA47 St Cath Coll Ox BA50 MA54 Birm Univ MA76. Wycliffe Hall Ox 49. **d** 50 **p** 51. C Werneth *Man* 50-51; C St Pancras H Cross w St Jude and St Pet *Lon* 52-54; P-in-c Dartford St Alb *Roch* 54-56; Australia 56-66 and from 70; C Raynes Park St Sav *S'wark* 68-70; rtd 88. *Rhodoglade Retirement Village, 3/1502 Mount Dandenong Tourist Road, Olinda, Vic, Australia 3788* Tel (0061) (3) 9751 0021 Fax 9754 3518 E-mail jimcranswick@hotmail.com

CRANWELL, Brian Robert. b 32. Sheff Poly MSc. Cranmer Hall Dur. **d** 84 **p** 85. C Ecclesfield *Sheff* 84-86; V Handsworth Woodhouse 86-99; rtd 99; Perm to Offic *Sheff* from 99 and *Derby* from 00. *9 Westview Close, Totley, Sheffield S17 3LT* Tel 0114-262 1499 E-mail brian_cranwell@lineone.net

CRASKE, Leslie Gordon Hamilton. b 29. AKC54 Lambeth STh80. **d** 55 **p** 56. C Malden St Jo *S'wark* 55-58; C Streatham St Leon 58-60; S Rhodesia 60-65; Rhodesia 65-66; V Upper Norwood St Jo *Cant* 67-83; R Guernsey St Sav *Win* 83-97; rtd 97; Perm to Offic *Win* from 97. *La Gruterie, 3 Mount Row, St Peter Port, Guernsey GY1 1NS* Tel (01481) 716027

CRASTON (née FULLALOVE), Mrs Brenda Hurst. b 33. Open Univ BA75 Man Univ MPhil86. St Mich Ho Ox 58. **dss** 80 **d** 87 **p** 94. Bolton St Paul w Em *Man* 80-87; Par Dn 87-93; rtd 93; Perm to Offic *Man* from 94. *12 Lever Park Avenue, Horwich, Bolton BL6 7LE* Tel (01204) 699972

CRASTON, Canon Richard Colin. b 22. Bris Univ BA49 Lon Univ BD51 Lambeth DD92. Tyndale Hall Bris 46. **d** 51 **p** 52. C Dur St Nic *Dur* 51-54; V Bolton St Paul *Man* 54-76; P-in-c Bolton Em 64-66; V 66-76; Hon Can Man Cathl 68-95; RD Bolton 72-92; V Bolton St Paul w Em 77-86; TR 86-93; Chapl to The Queen 85-92; rtd 93; Perm to Offic *Man* from 93. *12 Lever Park Avenue, Horwich, Bolton BL6 7LE* Tel (01204) 699972

CRATE, Canon George Frederick Jackson. b 28. Lon Univ BD56. ALCD55. **d** 56 **p** 57. C Penge St Jo *Roch* 56-58; C Tonbridge St Steph 58-60; R Knossington and Cold Overton *Leic* 60-64; V Owston and Withcote 60-64; V Mountsorrel Ch Ch 64-83; RD Akeley E 75-92; Hon Can Leic Cathl 80-94; V Mountsorrel Ch Ch and St Pet 83-94; rtd 94; Perm to Offic *Leic* from 94. *115 Nanpantan Road, Loughborough LE11 3YB* Tel (01509) 269505

CRAVEN, Canon Allan. b 35. LTCL77 Univ of Wales (Lamp) BA57 Lon Univ BD72. Chich Th Coll 57. **d** 59 **p** 60. C Blaenau Ffestiniog *Ban* 59-61; C Milford Haven *St D* 61-65; V Llwynhendy 65-68; R Nolton w Roch 68-00; RD Roose 85-99; Can St D Cathl from 91; rtd 00. *25 West Lane Close, Keeston, Haverfordwest SA62 6EW* Tel (01437) 710709

CRAVEN, Colin Peter. b 48. Dartmouth RN Coll. St Steph Ho Ox 83. **d** 85 **p** 86. C Holbeach *Linc* 85-88; Chapl Fleet Hosp 86-97; TV Grantham *Linc* 88-97; P-in-c Fairfield *Derby* 97-03; OCF 88-03; CF from 03. *c/o MOD Chaplains (Army)* Tel (01980) 615804 Fax 615800

CRAVEN, Gordon Forster. b 26. Qu Coll Cam BA50 MA55. Wells Th Coll 51. **d** 53 **p** 54. C Castleford All SS *Wakef* 53-57; V King Sterndale *Derby* 57-72; V Fairfield 57-72; Perm to Offic *B & W* from 81; rtd 91. *Kingfisher Cottage, 41 Southover, Wells BA5 1UH* Tel (01749) 672282

CRAVEN, Janet Elizabeth. *See* CHAPMAN, Mrs Janet Elizabeth

CRAVEN, Rebecca Clare. b 58. Bris Univ BDS80 Glas Univ MPH90 Man Univ PhD97 RCS DDPH90 RCPS FDS97. Dioc OLM tr scheme 98. **d** 01 **p** 02. OLM Reddish *Man* from 01. *35 Middleton Road, Reddish, Stockport SK5 6SH* Tel 0161-443 2701

CRAVEN, Archdeacon of. *See* SLATER, The Ven Paul John

CRAWFORD, Mrs Anne Elizabeth. b 59. St Alb and Ox Min Course 01. **d** 04. C Leighton Buzzard w Eggington, Hockliffe etc *St Alb* from 04. *138 Brooklands Drive, Leighton Buzzard LU7 3PG* Tel (01525) 850204 E-mail annie.anselm@btinternet.com

CRAWFORD, Duncan Alexander. b 59. Newc Univ BA81 MA83 K Coll Lon CertEd83. St Jo Coll Nottm 86. **d** 89 **p** 90. C Hatcham St Jas *S'wark* 89-92; Perm to Offic 93-02. *42 Furzefield Road, London SE3 8TX*

CRAWFORD, Canon Ivy Elizabeth. b 50. Trin Coll Bris DipTh85. **dss** 85 **d** 87 **p** 94. Collier Row St Jas *Chelmsf* 85; Collier Row St Jas and Havering-atte-Bower 86-87; Par Dn 87-89; Par Dn Harlow New Town w Lt Parndon 89-94; C Harlow Town Cen w Lt Parndon 94-95; V Blackmore and Stondon Massey from 95; Hon Can Chelmsf Cathl from 98. *The Vicarage, Church Street, Blackmore, Ingatestone CM4 0RN* Tel (01277) 821464 E-mail ivy@vicarage50.fsnet.co.uk

CRAWFORD, James Robert Harry. b 55. Carl and Blackb Dioc Tr Inst 00. **d** 03 **p** 04. OLM Lower Darwen St Jas *Blackb* from 03. *31 Tynwald Road, Blackburn BB2 3NS* Tel (01254) 693822

CRAWFORD, Canon John William Rowland. b 53. AKC75 Open Univ BA81 NUI MA95 PhD03. CITC 75. **d** 76 **p** 77. C Dundela St Mark *D & D* 76-79; C Taney Ch Ch *D & G* 79-84; V Dublin St Patr Cathl Gp from 84; Preb Tipperkevin St Patr Cathl Dublin from 84. *248 South Circular Road, Dolphin's Barn, Dublin 8, Irish Republic* Tel (00353) (1) 454 2274 E-mail jwrcrawf@iol.ie

CRAWFORD, Kenneth Ian. b 48. Melbourne Univ BMus77 Columbia Univ MA79 MEd80 MACE84. Trin Coll Melbourne BD86. **d** 87 **p** 87. Australia 87-97; C Ringwood St Paul 87-89; C Cheltenham St Matt 89-90; P-in-c Vermont S H Name 90-93; Can Prec Melbourne Cathl 93-97; P-in-c Warndon St Nic *Worc* 97-03; V Pershore w Pinvin, Wick and Birlingham from 03. *The Abbey Vicarage, Church Street, Pershore WR10 1DT* Tel (01386) 552071 E-mail vicar@pershoreabbey.fsnet.co.uk

CRAWFORD, Louise Dorothy Anita. b 60. Oak Hill Th Coll BA91 Princeton Th Sem MDiv00. Irish Sch of Ecum MPhil02. **d** 02 **p** 03. C Drumragh w Mountfield *D & R* from 02. *12 Crevenagh Way, Omagh BT79 0JE* Tel (028) 8224 7862 Mobile 07881-826499 E-mail anamchara00@yahoo.com

CRAWFORD, Michael Davis. b 45. Oak Hill Th Coll BA97 K Coll Lon PGCE98. **d** 00 **p** 01. NSM New Barnet St Jas *St Alb* 00-04; C Limassol St Barn Cyprus from 04. *Apartment 1, Kavouri Court, 16 Panayiosi, Symeon Street, Neapolis, Limassol, Cyprus* E-mail michaelrev@hotmail.com

CRAWFORD, Peter. b 22. Trin Coll Cam BA49 MA54. Wycliffe Hall Ox 49. **d** 51 **p** 52. C Ashton St Mich *Man* 51-54; V Pendlebury St Jo 54-60; Chapl R Man Children's Hosp 54-60; V Masham *Ripon* 60-75; RD Ripon 70-75; V Masham and Healey 75-79; R E Bergholt *St E* 79-87; RD Samford 82-86; rtd 87; Perm to Offic *St E* 87-02. *3 Burl's Yard, Crown Street, Needham Market, Ipswich IP6 8AJ* Tel (01449) 722343

CRAWFORD, Canon Robin. b 33. Pemb Coll Cam BA57 MA61. Roch Th Coll 66. **d** 67 **p** 80. Ghana 67-69; Dep Sec Chrs Abroad 69-73; Dep Hd Priory Sch Lewes 74-76; Nigeria 77-79; Dep Sec Buttle Trust 79-86; Sec 86-90; Dir 90-92; Hon C Win H Trin *Win* 80-82; Hon C Notting Hill All SS w St Columb *Lon* 82-87; Hon C Westmr St Matt from 87; Hon Can Tamale from 01. *52 Dean Abbott House, 70 Vincent Street, London SW1P 4BS* Tel and fax (020) 7931 8013

CRAWLEY, David. b 47. TD. St Steph Ho Ox 75. **d** 78 **p** 79. C Solihull *Birm* 78-81; TV Newbury *Ox* 81-84; Lic to Offic 84-95; Chapl Stoke Mandeville Hosp Aylesbury 84-95; Distr Chapl 88-95; Hd Chapl Services W Suffolk Hosps NHS Trust from 95; Bp's Adv on Hosp Chapl *St E* from 00. *22 Westbury Avenue, Bury St Edmunds IP33 3QE* Tel (01284) 750526 *or* 713486 Fax 701993 E-mail david.crawley@wsh.nhs.uk

CRAWLEY, John Lloyd Rochfort. b 22. Selw Coll Cam BA47 MA52. Cuddesdon Coll 47. **d** 49 **p** 50. C Newc H Cross *Newc* 49-52; V Byker St Ant 52-59; V Longhoughton w Howick 59-69; Chapl Newc Univ 69-74; Master Newc St Thos Prop Chpl 69-74; P-in-c Cockermouth All SS w Ch Ch *Carl* 74-77; TR Cockermouth w Embleton and Wythop 77-86; Perm to Offic *Arg* from 86; rtd 87. *Croft House, Cove Road, Tarbert, Argyll PA29 6TX* Tel (01880) 820842

CRAWLEY, Nicholas Simon. b 58. Southn Univ BSc79 ACIB82 AIIM85. Wycliffe Hall Ox 85. **d** 88 **p** 89. C E Twickenham St Steph *Lon* 88-93; R Avondale Zimbabwe 93-99; P-in-c Netherthorpe St Steph *Sheff* 99-04; Network Miss P (Bris Adnry) *Bris* from 04. *27 Carnarvon Road, Bristol BS6 7DU* Tel 0117-944 1980 E-mail nick.crawley@btopenworld.com

CRAWLEY, Simon Ewen. b 31. Em Coll Cam BA57 MA60. Ridley Hall Cam 56. **d** 58 **p** 59. C Denton Holme *Carl* 58-61; P-in-c Cinderford St Steph w Littledean *Glouc* 61-67; V Margate H Trin *Cant* 67-74; V Folkestone H Trin w Ch Ch 74-81; R Patterdale *Carl* 81-87; RD Penrith 83-86; R Culworth w Sulgrave and Thorpe Mandeville etc *Pet* 87-95; RD Brackley 89-95; rtd 95; Perm to Offic *Ex* from 96 and *York* from 03. *The Old Vicarage, Main Street, Healaugh, Tadcaster LS24 8DB* Tel (01937) 830160

CRAWLEY-BOEVEY, Robert Arthur. b 12. Hertf Coll Ox BA34 MA38. Cuddesdon Coll 35. **d** 37 **p** 38. C Farnham Royal *Ox* 37-43; Chapl RNVR 43-46; R Waltham on the Wolds and Stonesby *Leic* 47-51; V Cuddington w Dinton *Ox* 51-59; V Seer Green 59-78; rtd 78; Perm to Offic *Sarum* 78-05. *c/o D A Crawley-Boevey Esq, Lewins, The Street, Shurlock Row, Reading RG10 0PR* Tel 0118-934 3225

CRAWSHAW, Clinton. b 70. St Steph Ho Ox. **d** 02 **p** 03. C Hendon St Alphage *Lon* 02-04; rtd 04. *57 Dixon Clark Court, Canonbury Road, London N1 2UR* Tel (020) 7688 0978 E-mail fathercrawshaw@email.com

CRAWTE, William Richard. b 30. TCD BA54. **d** 55 **p** 56. C Belfast St Aid *Conn* 55-57; C Newcastle *D & D* 57-59; CF 59-79. *23 Gotsfield Close, Acton, Sudbury CO10 0AS* Tel (01787) 377356

✠**CRAY, The Rt Revd Graham Alan.** b 47. Leeds Univ BA68. St Jo Coll Nottm 69. **d** 71 **p** 72 **c** 01. C Gillingham St Mark *Roch* 71-75; N Area Co-ord CPAS Youth Dept 75-78; C York St Mich-le-Belfrey *York* 78-82; V 82-92; Prin Ridley Hall Cam 92-01; Six Preacher Cant Cathl *Cant* 97-01; Suff Bp Maidstone from 01. *Bishop's House, Pett Lane, Charing, Ashford TN27 0DL* Tel (01233) 712950 Fax 713543 E-mail bishop@bishmaid.org

CRAY, Mrs Jacqueline. b 49. Glos Coll of Educn CertEd70. SEITE 01. **d** 04 **p** 05. NSM Gt Chart *Cant* from 04. *Bishop's House, Pett Lane, Charing, Ashford TN27 0DL* Tel (01233) 713687 Fax 713543 Mobile 07889-742973 E-mail jackiecray@hotmail.com

CREAN, Patrick John Eugene. b 38. TCD BA81 MA84. Edin Th Coll 82. **d** 84 **p** 85. C Perth St Jo *St And* 84-86; P-in-c Liv St Phil w St Dav *Liv* 86-87; V 87-90; R Cupar and Ladybank *St And* 90-92; P-in-c Sefton *Liv* 92-97; Dioc Children's Officer 92-03; V Aintree St Giles 97-98; V Aintree St Giles w St Pet 98-03; rtd 03; Perm to Offic *Liv* from 03. *36 Lingfield Close, Netherton, Bootle L30 1BB* Tel 0151-525 8838

CREASER, Canon David Edward. b 35. St Cath Coll Cam BA58 MA62. Clifton Th Coll 59. **d** 61 **p** 62. C Cheadle *Ches* 61-67; V Weston *Bradf* 67-69; P-in-c Denton 67-69; V Weston w Denton 69-74 and 82-02; Dir Educn 73-96; V Frizinghall 74-82; V Weston w Denton 82-02; Hon Can Bradf Cathl 80-02; P-in-c Leathley w Farnley, Fewston and Blubberhouses 96-02; rtd 02; Perm to Offic *Bradf* from 03. *Rose Cottage, Pant Lane, Austwick, Lancaster LA2 8BH* Tel (01542) 51536

CREASEY, Graham. *See* GOLDSTONE-CREASEY, Graham

CREBER, Preb Arthur Frederick. b 45. Lon Univ DipTh67. N Ord Course 84. **d** 87 **p** 88. C Rickerscote *Lich* 87-91; V Gt Wyrley 91-99; RD Rugeley 94-98; P-in-c Newcastle w Butterton from 99; Preb Lich Cathl from 04. *The Rectory, Seabridge Road, Newcastle ST5 2HS* Tel (01782) 616397 E-mail afcreber10@hotmail.com

CREDITON, Suffragan Bishop of. *See* EVENS, The Rt Revd Robert John Scott

CREE, John Richard. b 44. Open Univ BA74 Lanc Univ MA92. Coll of Resurr Mirfield. **d** 83 **p** 84. C Blackb St Jas *Blackb* 83-86; V Feniscowles 86-01; Chapl Blackb Coll 86-01; R Chorley St Laur *Blackb* from 01; Perm to Offic *Bre* from 86. *The Rectory, Rectory Close, Chorley PR7 1QW* Tel (01257) 263114 E-mail johnrcree@hotmail.com

CREER, Irene. *See* SHAW, Mrs Irene

CREERY-HILL, Anthony Thomas. b 23. BNC Ox BA49 MA54. Ridley Hall Cam 49. **d** 51 **p** 52. C Highbury Ch Ch *Lon* 51-53; Travelling Sec CSSM 53-58; Chapl Dean Close Sch Cheltenham 59-74; Dep Hd Master Larchfield Sch Helensburgh 75-77; Kenya 77-83; Chapl Chantilly *Eur* 83-86; rtd 87; Perm to Offic *Heref* from 87. *c/o D G Standish Hayes Esq, Little Short Close, Shaw Green Lane, Prestbury, Cheltenham GL52 3BP* Tel (01242) 574100

CREES, David Paul. b 68. Southn Univ BSc89. Trin Coll Bris BA99 MA00. **d** 00 **p** 01. C Patcham *Chich* 00-04; CF from 04. *c/o MOD Chaplains (Army)* Tel (01980) 615804 Fax 615800

CREES, Geoffrey William. b 35. Open Univ BA85. Cranmer Hall Dur 65. **d** 67 **p** 68. C Hoddesdon *St Alb* 67-70; C Harwell and Chilton All SS *Ox* 70-73; V Greenham 73-82; TR Marfleet and AD E Hull *York* 82-88; TR Rodbourne Cheney *Bris* 88-99; rtd 99; Perm to Offic *Glouc* from 99. *The Thatch, New Road, Popes Hill, Newnham GL14 1JT* Tel (01452) 760843

CREGAN, Mark. b 59. Lon Bible Coll BA91. Wycliffe Hall Ox 95. **d** 97 **p** 98. C Chippenham St Pet *Bris* 97-01; P-in-c Stapleton 01-05; Asst Chapl Colston's Sch Bris 01-05; USPG from 05. *USPG, Partnership House, 157 Waterloo Road, London SE1 8XA* Tel (020) 7928 8681 E-mail cregans1@surefish.co.uk

CREGEEN, Gary Marshall. b 62. Oak Hill Th Coll BA00. **d** 00 **p** 01. C Carl St Jo *Carl* 00-03; P-in-c Scotby and Cotehill w Cumwhinton from 03. *The Vicarage, Lambley Bank, Scotby, Carlisle CA4 8BX* Tel (01228) 513205 E-mail gary@gandjcregeen.co.uk

CREIGHTON, Frederick David. b 50. TCD BTh88 ACII74. **d** 88 **p** 89. C Lisburn Ch Ch *Conn* 88-91; I Drumclamph w Lower and Upper Langfield *D & R* 91-00; I Glendermott from 00. *Glendermott Rectory, Church Brae, Altnagelvin BT47 2LS* Tel (028) 7134 3001

CREIGHTON, Mrs Judith. b 36. Reading Univ BSc57. Trin Coll Bris 80 Edin Th Coll 81. **dss** 83 **d** 87 **p** 94. Greenock *Glas* 83-85; Lawrence Weston *Bris* 85-87; Par Dn Kingswood 87-90; Chapl Stoke Park and Purdown Hosps Stapleton 90-93; Hon C Marshfield w Cold Ashton and Tormarton etc *Bris* 93-97; rtd 96; Perm to Offic *Bris* from 97. *Rose Cottage, West Littleton, Marshfield, Chippenham SN14 8JE* Tel (01225) 891021

CREIGHTON, Ms Rachel Margaret Maxwell. b 64. Br Is Nazarene Coll BTh86 BD87. Cranmer Hall Dur 94 Lon Bible Coll MA89. **d** 94 **p** 95. C Basford w Hyson Green *S'well* 94-96; C Nottingham All SS 96-98; P-in-c Broxtowe 98-02; Chapl HM Pris Bedf 02-04; Chapl HM Pris Wellingborough from 04. *Chaplaincy, HM Prison, Millers Park, Wellingborough NN8 2NH* Tel (01933) 232700 ext 487 Fax 232701

CRELLIN, Howard Joseph. b 30. Magd Coll Cam BA52 MA56 Magd Coll Ox BA54 MA56. Wycliffe Hall Ox 53. **d** 55 **p** 56. C Dovercourt *Chelmsf* 55-58; R Theydon Garnon 58-70; Select Preacher Ox Univ 68; Perm to Offic *Ox* 70-82; Hon C High Wycombe 72-77; Asst Master K Chas I Sch Kidderminster 74-80; Caldicott Sch Farnham 80-82; Perm to Offic *Chelmsf* 82-91; Asst Master Fryerns Sch Basildon 82-88; St Anselm's Sch Basildon 88-91; P-in-c Whatfield w Semer, Nedging and Naughton *St E* 91-98; rtd 98; Perm to Offic *St E* from 98 and *Eur* from 02. *10 Green Willows, Lavenham, Sudbury CO10 9SP* Tel (01787) 247588

CREMIN (née LAKE), Mrs Eileen Veronica. b 58. Lon Univ Cert Counselling 93. Aston Tr Scheme 83 Sarum & Wells Th Coll 85. **d** 88 **p** 94. Par Dn Islington St Mary *Lon* 88-92; Asst Chapl Homerton Hosp Lon 92-94; Asst Chapl Hackney Hosp Gp 92-94; P-in-c Brondesbury Ch Ch and St Laur *Lon* 94-01; C Douglas Union w Frankfield *C, C & R* from 01. *64 Willowbank, Church Road, Blackrock, Co Cork, Irish Republic* Tel (00353) (21) 435 8226 E-mail evcremin@eircom.net *or* ecremin@hotmail.com

CRESSALL, Paul Richard. b 51. UEA BA74. Ripon Coll Cuddesdon 86. **d** 88 **p** 89. C Stevenage H Trin *St Alb* 88-91; V Caldecote All SS 91-95; V Old Warden 91-95; V Rothwell *Ripon* from 95. *The Vicarage, Beech Grove, Rothwell, Leeds LS26 0EF* Tel 0113-282 2369 Mobile 07801-582503 E-mail paul@cressall.fsnet.co.uk

CRESSEY, Canon Roger Wilson. b 35. Chich Th Coll 72. **d** 74 **p** 75. C Pontefract St Giles *Wakef* 74-77; Hon C Dewsbury All SS 77-80; Chapl Pinderfields Gen Hosp Wakef 80-94; Chapl Carr Gate Hosp Wakef 80-94; Chapl Fieldhead Hosp Wakef 80-94; Chapl Pinderfields and Pontefract Hosps NHS Trust 94-00; Hon Can Wakef Cathl *Wakef* 98-00; rtd 00. *1 Wellhead Mews, Chapelthorpe, Wakefield WF4 3JG* Tel (01924) 258972 E-mail roger-cressey@supanet.com

CRESSWELL, Howard Rex. b 31. Ely Th Coll 56. **d** 59 **p** 60. C Dovercourt *Chelmsf* 59-61; C Victoria Docks Ascension 61-64; V 64-71; R E w W Harling *Nor* 71-72; TV Quidenham w Eccles and Snetterton 72-75; V Arminghall 75-82; R Caistor w Markshall 75-82; V Trowse 75-82; V Heigham St Barn w St Bart 82-91; rtd 91; Perm to Offic *Nor* from 91. *28 Penryn Close, Norwich NR4 7LY* Tel (01603) 458591

CRESSWELL, Canon Jeremy Peter. b 49. St Jo Coll Ox BA72 MA78 K Coll Lon MA83. Ridley Hall Cam 73. **d** 75 **p** 76. C Wisley w Pyrford *Guildf* 75-78; C Weybridge 78-82; P-in-c E Clandon 82-83; P-in-c W Clandon 82-83; R E and W Clandon 83-90; V Oxshott from 90; RD Leatherhead from 03; Hon Can Owerri from 01. *The Vicarage, Steel's Lane, Oxshott, Leatherhead KT22 0QH* Tel (01372) 842071 E-mail vicar@oxshott.co.uk

CRETNEY, Mrs Antonia Lois. b 48. York Univ BA69 Bris Univ BA87 PGCE89. S Dios Minl Tr Scheme 92. **d** 94 **p** 95. NSM Bedminster *Bris* 94-96; C 96-97; P-in-c Beedon and Peasemore w W Ilsley and Farnborough *Ox* 97-99; R 99-04; Adv for Voc, Prayer and Spirituality from 04. *8 Elm Farm Close, Grove, Wantage OX12 9FD* Tel (01235) 763192 E-mail antcret@aol.com

CRIBB, Robert John. b 22. Spurgeon's Coll 45. **d** 85 **p** 86. NSM Curry Rivel w Fivehead and Swell *B & W* 85-89; rtd 89; Perm to

Offic *B & W* 89-94. *4 Heale Lane, Curry Rivel, Langport TA10 0PG* Tel (01458) 252333

CRICHTON, James Kenneth. b 35. Glouc Sch of Min 78. **d** 80 **p** 80. NSM Minchinhampton *Glouc* 80-83; NSM Nailsworth 83-86; Dep Chapl HM Pris Pentonville 86-87; Chapl HM Pris The Mount 87-97; rtd 97. *Pennant, Horeb, Llandysul SA44 4JG* Tel (01559) 362448

CRICK, Peter. b 39. Lon Univ BD68 NY Univ DMin84. Wells Th Coll 66. **d** 67 **p** 68. C Horsham *Chich* 67-71; Asst Dioc Youth Officer *Ox* 71-75; R Denham 75-88; Bp's Adv for CME *Dur* 88-97; P-in-c Coniscliffe 88-97; Hon Can Dur Cathl 93-97; R City of Bris 97-04; rtd 04. *7 Westfield Common, Hamble, Southampton SO31 4LB* E-mail crick@cix.co.uk

CRICK, Philip Benjamin Denton (Ben). b 33. Bris Univ BA63. Clifton Th Coll 60. **d** 64 **p** 65. C Clerkenwell St Jas and St Jo w St Pet *Lon* 64-67; CF 67-72; C Southall Green St Jo *Lon* 72-75; P-in-c Southall H Trin 75-83; P-in-c Kidbrooke St Jas *S'wark* 83-85; TV 85-92; C E Acton St Dunstan w St Thos *Lon* 92-95; Sub-Chapl HM Pris Wormwood Scrubs 92-95; rtd 95; Perm to Offic *Cant* from 95; Sub-Chapl HM Pris Cant from 97. *232 Canterbury Road, Birchington CT7 9TD* Tel (01843) 846049 Mobile 07818-040651 E-mail ben.crick@argonet.co.uk

CRINKS, Kevin David. b 63. Aston Tr Scheme 86 Sarum & Wells Th Coll BTh91. **d** 93 **p** 94. C Aylesford *Roch* 93-96; C Hessle *York* 96-97; TV Upholland *Liv* 97-00; V Platt Bridge from 00. *The Vicarage, 9 Lee Lane, Abram, Wigan WN2 5QU* Tel (01942) 866269 Fax 866396 E-mail fatherkev@btopenworld.com

CRIPPS, Keith Richard John. b 21. Trin Coll Cam BA43 MA47 Newc Univ PhD80. Ridley Hall Cam 43. **d** 45 **p** 47. Inter-Colleg Sec SCM (Man) 45-47; C Man Victoria Park *Man* 45-47; C Aston SS Pet and Paul *Birm* 47-50; R Chorlton upon Medlock *Man* 50-60; Chapl Man Univ 51-60; Lect 52-60; Chapl and Lect Ripon Coll of Educn 60-65; Sen Lect Kenton Lodge Coll of Educn 65-71; Sen Lect City of Newc Coll of Educn 71-84; Lect Newc Poly 74-79; Chapl Jes Coll Cam 84-88; rtd 88; Perm to Offic *Ely* 88-02. *24 Mowbray Court, Butts Road, Exeter EX2 5TQ*

CRIPPS, Martyn Cyril Rowland. b 46. Birm Univ LLB68 Solicitor 71. Wycliffe Hall Ox 80. **d** 82 **p** 83. C Canford Magna *Sarum* 82-86; V Preston St Cuth *Blackb* 87-94; Warden Les Cotils *Win* 94-96; V Gipsy Hill Ch Ch *S'wark* 96-00; R Ashmanhaugh, Barton Turf etc *Nor* 00-04; P-in-c Davenham *Ches* from 04. *The Rectory, Church Street, Davenham, Northwich CW9 8NF* Tel (01606) 42450 E-mail mandmc@btopenworld.com

CRIPPS, Michael Frank Douglas. b 28. Ch Ch Ox BA50 MA53. Ridley Hall Cam 58. **d** 59 **p** 60. C Cambridge Gt St Mary w St Mich *Ely* 59-62; Ceylon 62-66; C-in-c Swindon Covingham CD *Bris* 66-72; V Swindon St Paul 72-73; P-in-c Aldbourne and Baydon *Sarum* 73; TV Whitton 73-81; C Marlborough 81-94; rtd 94; Chapl Pau *Eur* 94-96; Perm to Offic *Sarum* from 96. *9 Silverless Street, Marlborough SN8 1JQ* Tel (01672) 512748

CRITCHELL, Denise Eileen. b 49. St Alb and Ox Min Course 96. **d** 99 **p** 00. C Flackwell Heath *Ox* 99-03; TV Risborough from 03. *The Vicarage, Church Lane, Lacey Green, Princes Risborough HP27 0QX* Tel (01844) 347741 E-mail denise@dncritchell.fsnet.co.uk

CRITCHLEY, Colin. b 41. Dur Univ BA63 Liv Univ MA69 AFBPsS94. NW Ord Course 75. **d** 78 **p** 79. NSM Halewood *Liv* from 78; Dioc Child Protection Adv from 96. *53 Elwyn Drive, Halewood, Liverpool L26 0UX* Tel 0151-487 5710 Fax 280 4937

CRITCHLOW, Mrs Anne-Louise. b 51. Westf Coll Lon BA73 Qu Mary Coll Lon MA75 Leeds Univ MA05 Grenoble Univ MèsL74 Cam Univ PGCE76. N Ord Course 03. **d** 05. C Eccles *Man* from 05. *36 Trafalgar Road, Salford M6 8JD* E-mail mmcritchlow@btinternet.com

CRITCHLOW, Trevor Francis. b 61. Lanc Univ BA83 K Coll Lon MA96. Westcott Ho Cam 88. **d** 90 **p** 91. C Croydon St Jo *S'wark* 90-92; C Lewisham St Mary 92-94; Perm to Offic *Ely* 94-05; Development Dir Westmr St Matt *Lon* 95-99; TV Wembley Park *Lon* from 05. *The Vicarage, 13 Forty Avenue, Wembley HA9 8JL* Tel (020) 8908 5995 E-mail trevor.critchlow@btinternet.com

CRITTALL, Richard Simon. b 47. Sussex Univ BA69 Linacre Coll Ox BA71. St Steph Ho Ox 69. **d** 72 **p** 73. C Oswestry H Trin *Lich* 72-75; C E Grinstead St Mary *Chich* 75-78; TV Brighton Resurr 78-83; R E Blatchington 83-95; V Heathfield St Rich from 95. *St Richard's Vicarage, Hailsham Road, Heathfield TN21 8AF* Tel (01435) 862744 E-mail simon.crittall@breathemail.net

CROAD, Arthur Robert. b 35. Down Coll Cam BA58 MA61. Clifton Th Coll 58. **d** 61 **p** 62. C Sneinton St Chris w St Phil *S'well* 61-64; C Kinson *Sarum* 64-72; R Sherfield English *Win* 72-74; R Awbridge w Sherfield English 74-92; P-in-c Hinton Ampner w Bramdean and Kilmeston 92-01; rtd 01. *48 Woodfield Drive, Winchester SO22 5PU* Tel (01962) 851978

CROAD, David Richard. b 31. Reading Univ BSc55. Clifton Th Coll. **d** 57 **p** 58. C Iver *Ox* 57-60; C Rushden *Pet* 60-63; V Loudwater *Ox* 63-72; SW Area Sec CPAS 72-78; V Bovingdon *St Alb* 78-91; Min Hampstead St Jo Downshire Hill Prop Chpl *Lon* 91-94; rtd 94; Perm to Offic *Guildf* and *Win* from 97. *5 Berryfield Road, Hordle, Lymington SO41 0HQ* Tel (01425) 614613

CROCKER, Jeremy Robert. b 67. S Bank Univ MA94 Heythrop Coll Lon MA98 MCIM92. Westcott Ho Cam 94 CITC 96. **d** 97 **p** 98. C Stevenage H Trin *St Alb* 97-00; TV Bp's Hatfield 00-04; TR Elstow from 04. *The Abbey Vicarage, Church End, Elstow, Bedford MK42 9XT* Tel (01234) 261477 E-mail jeremy.crocker@tesco.net

CROCKER, Keith Gwillam. b 49. Lanchester Poly BSc70 DipTh78. Oak Hill Th Coll 74. **d** 77 **p** 78. C Whitnash *Cov* 77-80; C Gt Horton *Bradf* 80-83; C Grays SS Pet and Paul, S Stifford and W Thurrock *Chelmsf* 83-84; TV Grays Thurrock 84-88; TR Wreningham *Nor* 88-95; P-in-c New Catton Ch Ch 95-99; V from 99. *Christ Church Vicarage, 65 Elm Grove Lane, Norwich NR3 3LF* Tel (01603) 408332 E-mail keith.crocker@which.net

CROCKER, Peter David. b 56. Lon Univ MB, BS80 MRCGP. Mon Dioc Tr Scheme 93. **d** 96 **p** 97. NSM Bassaleg *Mon* 96-02; TV from 02. *St John's Vicarage, Wern Terrace, Rogerstone, Newport NP10 9FG* Tel (01633) 893357

CROCKER, Richard Campbell. b 54. Nottm Univ BSc76. Wycliffe Hall Ox BA81 MA85. **d** 82 **p** 83. C Summerfield *Birm* 82-84; Chapl K Edw Sch Birm 84-91; R Council Bluffs USA 91-99; Assoc R Truro Episc Ch from 99. *10520 Main Street, Fairfax, VA 22030, USA* Tel (001) (703) 273 1300 E-mail rccrocker@trurochurch.org

CROCKETT, Peter James Sinclair. b 44. Sarum & Wells Th Coll 74. **d** 77 **p** 78. C Heavitree *Ex* 77; C Heavitree w Ex St Paul 78-80; TV Ex St Thos and Em 80-87; V Countess Wear from 87; Chapl St Loyes Tr Coll for the Disabled from 87; Chapl W of England Sch for those w little or no sight from 87; CF (TA) from 88. *The Vicarage, 375 Topsham Road, Exeter EX2 6HB* Tel (01392) 873263

✠**CROCKETT, The Rt Revd Phillip Anthony.** b 45. K Coll Lon BA67 BD70 AKC70 Univ of Wales MA91. St Mich Coll Llan 70. **d** 71 **p** 72 **c** 04. C Aberdare *Llan* 71-74; C Whitchurch 74-78; V Llanfihangel-y-Creuddyn, Llanafan w Llanwnnws *St D* 78-86; Sec Prov Selection Panel 83-87; V Ysbyty Ystwyth 84-86; R Dowlais *Llan* 86-91; Sec Bd of Min 91-99; V Cynwil Elfed and Newchurch *St D* 99-04; Adn Carmarthen 99-04; Warden of Readers 00-04; Bp Ban from 04. *Ty'r Esgob, Upper Garth Road, Bangor LL57 2SS* Tel (01248) 362895 Fax 372454 E-mail bishop.bangor@churchinwales.org.uk

CROFT, James Stuart. b 57. K Coll Lon BD80 Leeds Univ MA95. Ripon Coll Cuddesdon 83. **d** 85 **p** 86. C Friern Barnet St Jas *Lon* 85-88; R Lea *Linc* 88-93; V Knaith 88-93; V Upton 88-93; R Gate Burton 88-93; R Lea Gp 93-97; Chapl N Lincs Coll 90-93; V Froyle and Holybourne *Win* from 97. *The Vicarage, 7 Church Lane, Holybourne, Alton GU34 4HD* Tel (01420) 83240 E-mail revjcroft@cro45.fsnet.co.uk

CROFT, John Armentieres. b 15. MC44. Sarum Th Coll 56. **d** 57 **p** 58. C Madron w Morvah *Truro* 57-60; V Gwinear 60-70; rtd 70; Perm to Offic *Sarum* and *Truro* from 70; *B & W* 70-98. *Winnards Perch, Coles Cross, East Allington, Totnes TQ9 7RH*

CROFT, Michael Peter. b 60. GradIPM. Trin Coll Bris BA88. **d** 88 **p** 89. C Drypool *York* 88-91; P-in-c Sandal St Cath *Wakef* 91-95; V from 95; Chapl Manygates Maternity Hosp Wakef from 91. *9 Sandal Cliff, Wakefield WF2 6AU* Tel and fax (01924) 256108 Mobile 07866-367182 E-mail mike@croftie.fsnet.co.uk

CROFT, Ronald. b 30. St Aid Birkenhead 61. **d** 63 **p** 64. C Lawton Moor *Man* 63-65; C Withington St Crispin 65-66; R 74-86; C Prestwich St Marg 66-67; V Oldham St Ambrose 67-71; P-in-c Oldham St Jas 67-68; V 68-71; V Prestwich St Hilda 71-74; P-in-c 96-00; R Heaton Norris St Thos 86-96; rtd 00. *St Hilda's Vicarage, 55 Whittaker Lane, Prestwich, Manchester M25 5ET* Tel 0161-773 1642

CROFT, Simon Edward Owen. b 51. Ch Ch Coll Cant CertEd73. St Steph Ho Ox 75. **d** 78 **p** 79. C Heavitree w Ex St Paul *Ex* 78-83; V Seaton 83-93; P-in-c Ex St Mark 93-96; P-in-c Ex St Sidwell and St Matt 96; R Ex St Mark, St Sidwell and St Matt from 96. *St Mark's Rectory, 8 Lamacraft Drive, Exeter EX4 8QS* Tel (01392) 421050 E-mail simoncdevon@yahoo.co.uk

CROFT, Steven John Lindsey. b 57. Worc Coll Ox BA80 MA83 St Jo Coll Dur PhD84. Cranmer Hall Dur 80. **d** 83 **p** 84. C Enfield St Andr *Lon* 83-87; V Ovenden *Wakef* 87-96; Dioc Miss Consultant 94-96; Warden Cranmer Hall Dur 96-04; Abps' Missr and Team Ldr Fresh Expressions from 04. *15 Fyfield Road, Oxford OX2 6QE* Tel (01865) 311838 Mobile 07792-975855 E-mail steven.croft@freshexpressions.org.uk

CROFT, Canon Warren David. b 36. ACT ThL62. **d** 61 **p** 62. Australia 61-69 and from 79; Papua New Guinea 69-77; C Mottingham St Andr *S'wark* 77-78; Hon Can Dogura 86; C Hunters Hill 87; R Kogarah 87-01; rtd 01. *43 Sierra Avenue, PO Box 3078, Bateau Bay, NSW, Australia 2261* Tel (0061) (2) 4333 3967 Mobile 425-206621 Fax 9553 8594 E-mail isandwas@bigpond.com

CROFT, Canon William Stuart. b 53. Trin Hall Cam BA76 MA79 K Coll Lon MTh88. Ripon Coll Cuddesdon BA80. **d** 80 **p** 81. C

Friern Barnet St Jas *Lon* 80-83; Tutor Chich Th Coll 83-92; Vice-Prin 88-92; V Fernhurst *Chich* 92-98; Dir of Ords *Pet* 98-03; Prec and Min Can Pet Cathl 98-01; Can Res and Prec 01-04; Non-res Can from 04; P-in-c Longthorpe from 04; Liturg Officer 03-04. *The Vicarage, 315 Thorpe Road, Longthorpe, Peterborough PE3 6LU* Tel (01733) 263016
E-mail williamsbill_croft@hotmail.com

CROFTON, Edwin Alan. b 46. Univ Coll Ox BA68 MA72. Cranmer Hall Dur DipTh72. **d** 73 **p** 74. C Hull St Jo Newland *York* 73-77; C Worksop St Jo *S'well* 77-81; Chapl Kilton Hosp Worksop 80-81; V Scarborough St Mary w Ch Ch and H Apostles *York* 81-91; Miss to Seamen 81-91; Chapl St Mary's Hosp Scarborough 82-91; V Cheltenham Ch Ch *Glouc* 91-02; RD Cheltenham 95-00; Hon Can Glouc Cathl 01-02; TR Eccles *Man* from 02. *The Rectory, 12B Westminster Road, Eccles, Manchester M30 9EB* Tel 0161-281 5739
E-mail ea_crofton@msn.com

CROFTS, Charles Arthur. b 14. Ball Coll Ox BA38 MA48. Lich Th Coll 38. **d** 39 **p** 40. C Shrewsbury St Chad *Lich* 39-41; C Tettenhall Regis 42-48; Min Can Worc Cathl *Worc* 48-50; Asst Master K Sch Worc 48-50; V Ox St Cross *Ox* 51-62; CF (TA) 54-64; V Crowhurst *S'wark* 62-68; Sen Insp of Schools 62-68; V Hexton *St Alb* 69-77; Hon Can St Alb 69-76; Dir RE 69-71; Teacher Herts and Beds Secondary Schools 71-76; N Herts FE Coll 76; Chapl St Bede's Ecum Sch Reigate 77-80; C Merstham and Gatton *S'wark* 77-80; rtd 80; Perm to Offic *Chich* from 80. *7 Ramsay Hall, 11-13 Byron Road, Worthing BN11 3HN* Tel (01903) 206599

CROFTS, David Thomas. b 47. Cheshire Coll of Educn CertEd68 Open Univ BA76. Dioc OLM tr scheme. **d** 99 **p** 00. OLM Bury St Edmunds St Mary *St E* from 99. *8 Linton Gardens, Bury St Edmunds IP33 2DZ* Tel (01284) 761801 Fax 765501
E-mail david@pandda.co.uk

CROFTS, Ian Hamilton. b 55. BSc. St Jo Coll Nottm 79. **d** 82 **p** 83. C Leamington Priors St Paul *Cov* 82-86; C Oadby *Leic* 86; TV 86-91; V Maidstone St Faith *Cant* from 91. *St Faith's Vicarage, Moncktons Lane, Maidstone ME14 2PY* Tel (01622) 201164 E-mail ian_crofts@msn.com

CROISDALE-APPLEBY, Mrs Carolynn Elizabeth. b 46. Ch Ch Coll Cant CertEd68. St Alb and Ox Min Course 01. **d** 04 **p** 05. NSM Amersham *Ox* from 04; NSM Gt Coxwell w Buscot, Coleshill etc from 04. *Abbotsholme, Hervines Road, Amersham HP6 5HS* Tel (01494) 725194 Fax 725474
E-mail croisdaleappleby@aol.com

CROMPTON, Holly Jo. b 74. Bath Coll of HE BA95. Wycliffe Hall Ox BTh01. **d** 01 **p** 02. C Luton Lewsey St Hugh *St Alb* 01-04; Chapl Bennett Memorial Dioc Sch Tunbridge Wells 04-05; Chapl Bedgebury Sch Kent from 05. *Bedgebury School, Cranbrook TN17 2SH* Tel (01580) 878143 Mobile 07761-628335 E-mail hollycrompton@hotmail.com

CROMPTON, Roger Martyn Francis. b 47. Sheff Univ BA69 PGCE73. St Jo Coll Dur Cranmer Hall Dur BA84. **d** 85 **p** 86. C Woodford Wells *Chelmsf* 85-89; V Golcar *Wakef* from 89; RD Huddersfield from 99. *The Vicarage, Church Street, Golcar, Huddersfield HD7 4PX* Tel (01484) 654647
E-mail martyncrompton@stjohnsgolcar.freeserve.co.uk

CRONK, Simon Nicholas. b 59. CQSW85 Poly of Wales BA82. Wycliffe Hall Ox 89. **d** 92 **p** 93. C Cheltenham Ch Ch *Glouc* 92-96; V Cinderford St Steph w Littledean 96-02; V Hughenden *Ox* from 02. *The Vicarage, Valley Road, Hughenden Valley, High Wycombe HP14 4PF* Tel (01494) 563439

CROOK, Colin. b 44. JP78. Lon Univ BSc(Econ)74 Brighton Poly ALA67 FLA93. S'wark Ord Course 87. **d** 90 **p** 91. NSM Dartford Ch Ch *Roch* 90-97; P-in-c Crockenhill All So from 97; Dioc Ecum Officer 96-04. *The Vicarage, Eynsford Road, Crockenhill, Swanley BR8 8JS* Tel and fax (01322) 662157

CROOK, David Creighton. b 37. Trin Coll Cam BA61 MA68. Cuddesdon Coll 61. **d** 63 **p** 64. C Workington St Mich *Carl* 63-66; C Penrith St Andr 66-70; V Barrow St Jas 70-78; V Maryport 78-81; TV Greystoke, Matterdale and Mungrisdale 81-87; TV Watermillock 84-87; V Hesket-in-the-Forest and Armathwaite 87-98; rtd 98; Perm to Offic *Carl* from 01. *11 Lowther Street, Penrith CA11 7UW* Tel (01768) 866773

CROOK, Mrs Diana Elizabeth. b 47. Hull Univ BA73 Open Univ BSc93 City Univ MSc97 Middx Univ BA03 RGN70 MBPsS. NTMTC 00. **d** 03 **p** 04. NSM Waltham H Cross *Chelmsf* from 03. *Great Chalks, High Street, Hatfield Broad Oak, Bishop's Stortford CM22 7HQ* Tel (01279) 718201 Fax 718109
E-mail diana@famille.demon.co.uk

CROOK, Graham Leslie. b 49. Chich Th Coll 74. **d** 76 **p** 77. C Withington St Crispin *Man* 76-79; C Prestwich St Marg 79-82; V Nelson St Bede *Blackb* 82-92; Chapl Southend Health Care NHS Trust from 92; Bp's Adv for Hosp Chapl *Chelmsf* from 98. *Southend Hospital, Prittlewell Chase, Westcliff-on-Sea SS0 0RY* Tel (01702) 435555 ext 2423

✠**CROOK, The Rt Revd John Michael.** b 40. Univ of Wales (Lamp) BA62. Coll of Resurr Mirfield 62. **d** 64 **p** 65 **c** 99. C Horninglow *Lich* 64-66; C Bloxwich 66-70; R Inverness St Mich *Mor* 70-78; R Inverness St Jo 74-78; Dioc Youth Chapl *St And* 78-86; R Aberfoyle 78-87; R Doune 78-87; R Callander 78-87; Can St Ninian's Cathl Perth 85-99; R Bridge of Allan 87-99; Syn Clerk 97-99; Bp Mor from 99. *Diocesan Office, 11 Kenneth Street, Inverness IV3 5NR* Tel and fax (01463) 226255 *or* 231059
E-mail bishop@morayrossandcaithness.co.uk

CROOK, Malcolm Geoffrey. b 53. St Steph Ho Ox 88. **d** 90 **p** 91. C Pet St Jude *Pet* 90-93; C Barrow St Matt *Carl* 93-96; TV Langley and Parkfield *Man* 96-97; R Man Apostles w Miles Platting 97-03; P-in-c Sneinton St Steph w St Alb *S'well* 03-04; P-in-c Sneinton St Matthias 03-04; V Sneinton St Steph w St Matthias from 04. *The Vicarage, 4 Barnston Road, Nottingham NG2 4HW* Tel 0115-924 1917

CROOK, Marie Elizabeth. b 46. Carl and Blackb Dioc Tr Inst 02. **d** 05. OLM Over Darwen St Jas *Blackb* from 05. *56 Roman Road, Darwen BB3 3BN* Tel (01254) 775820 Mobile 07742-029757 E-mail mariecrook500@hotmail.com

CROOK, Rowland William. b 39. Lon Univ DipTh63. Tyndale Hall Bris 61. **d** 64 **p** 65. C Penn Fields *Lich* 64-68; C Lower Broughton St Clem w St Matthias *Man* 68-70; C Bucknall and Bagnall *Lich* 70-76; V New Shildon *Dur* 76-86; V Northwich St Luke and H Trin *Ches* 86-99; P-in-c Helsby and Dunham-on-the-Hill 99-04; rtd 04. *14 Bollington Avenue, Northwich CW9 8SB* Tel (01606) 45177 E-mail rowland@rpwland.co.uk

CROOK, Timothy Mark. b 68. Oak Hill Th Coll BA00. **d** 00 **p** 01. C Charles w Plymouth St Matthias *Ex* 00-03; C Harold Wood *Chelmsf* from 03. *8 Archibald Road, Harold Wood RM3 0RH* Tel (01708) 348406 E-mail tim.crook@stpetersharoldwood.org

CROOKES, Keith John. **d** 05. NSM Deepcar *Sheff* from 05. *219 High Greave, Sheffield S5 9GS* Tel 0114-240 3790

CROOKS, Christopher John (Kip). b 53. St Bede's Coll Dur CertEd75. Trin Coll Bris BA90. **d** 90 **p** 91. C The Quinton *Birm* 90-93; V Ince Ch Ch *Liv* 93-03; R Much Woolton from 03. *The Rectory, 67 Church Road, Woolton, Liverpool L25 6DA* Tel 0151-428 1853

CROOKS, Canon David William Talbot. b 52. TCD BA75 MA78 BD83. **d** 77 **p** 78. C Glendermott *D & R* 77-81; C Edin Old St Paul *Edin* 81-84; I Taughboyne, Craigadooish, Newtowncunningham etc *D & R* from 84; Bp's Dom Chapl from 88; Can Raphoe Cathl from 91. *Taughboyne Rectory, Churchtown, Carrigans, Lifford, Co Donegal, Irish Republic* Tel (00353) (74) 914 0135 E-mail dcrooks@eircom.net

CROOKS, Eric. b 34. Oak Hill Th Coll 68. **d** 70 **p** 71. C Chadderton Ch Ch *Man* 70-73; C Bolton St Paul 73-75; C Lurgan Ch the Redeemer *D & D* 75-77; I Aghaderg w Donaghmore 77-80; I Dundonald 80-01; rtd 01. *17 Cumberland Court, Dundonald, Belfast BT16 2AW* Tel (028) 9048 0540

CROOKS, Henry Cecil. b 15. Edin Th Coll 71. **d** 72 **p** 72. P-in-c Kinross *St And* 72-75; R 75-81; P-in-c Dollar 76-81; rtd 81; Perm to Offic *Bris* 81-86 and *Chich* from 87. *Terry's Cross, Bungalow 8, Brighton Road, Woodmancote, Henfield BN5 9SX* Tel (01273) 493802

CROOKS, Mrs Jayne Barbara. b 52. Birm Univ BSc73 Avery Hill Coll PGCE74. WMMTC 01. **d** 04 **p** 05. NSM Kings Norton *Birm* from 04. *15 Chalgrove Avenue, Birmingham B38 8YP* Tel 0121-459 3733 E-mail jayne.crooks@blueyonder.co.uk

CROOKS, Kenneth Robert. b 36. CEng FIEE FCMI. S'wark Ord Course 80. **d** 83 **p** 84. NSM Wisley w Pyrford *Guildf* 83-92; Perm to Offic *Ex* from 98. *Foxes Corner, Peak Hill Road, Sidmouth EX10 0NW* Tel (01395) 577578

CROOKS, Kip. *See* CROOKS, Christopher John

CROOKS, Peter James. b 50. St Jo Coll Cam BA72. Cranmer Hall Dur. **d** 76 **p** 77. C Onslow Square St Paul *Lon* 76-77; C Brompton H Trin w Onslow Square St Paul 77-79; C Wembley St Jo 79-82; CMS 82-92; Lebanon 83-89; Syria 85-89; Dean Jerusalem 89-92; P-in-c Hunningham and Wappenbury w Weston under Wetherley *Cov* 92-01; P-in-c Offchurch 96-01; V Long Itchington and Marton 96-01; CMS 01-02; TV Dolgellau w Llanfachreth and Brithdir etc *Ban* 02-04; Yemen from 04. *Christ Church Centre, PO Box 1319, Tawani, Aden, Yemen*
E-mail pncrooks@ukonline.com.uk

CROOS, John Princely. b 59. Madurai Univ BA82. Oak Hill Th Coll BA04. **d** 04 **p** 05. C Becontree St Mary *Chelmsf* from 04. *104 Temple Avenue, Dagenham RM8 1LS* Tel (020) 8595 8625
E-mail sprincecroos@hotmail.com

CROSBIE, Andrew. b 62. St Steph Ho Ox 96. **d** 98 **p** 99. C St Paul's Cathl St Helena 98-00; CF 00-03; Perm to Offic *Blackb* from 03 and *Lon* from 04. *Flat 4, 56 Millbank, London SW1P 4RL* Tel (020) 7233 5986 Mobile 07769-973129
E-mail fathercrosbie@aol.com

CROSBIE, Timothy John. b 44. ACMA72. **d** 00 **p** 01. OLM Shotley *St E* from 00. *27 Kitchener Way, Shotley Gate, Ipswich IP9 1RN* Tel (01473) 787316
E-mail tim@timcrosbie.fsnet.co.uk

CROSBY, Bernard Edward. b 47. Oak Hill Th Coll 86. **d** 88 **p** 89. C Springfield H Trin *Chelmsf* 88-91; C Penn Fields *Lich* 91-94; V St Leonards St Ethelburga *Chich* 94-02; R Fairlight, Guestling and Pett from 02. *The Rectory, Battery Hill, Fairlight, Hastings TN35 4AP* Tel (01424) 812799
E-mail bernardcrosby@supanet.com

CROSBY, David Edward. b 48. St Alb and Ox Min Course 96. **d** 99 **p** 00. NSM Newbury *Ox* 99-01; C The Bourne and Tilford *Guildf* 01-04; P-in-c Hurst Green and Mitton *Bradf* 04. *c/o Crockford, Church House, Great Smith Street, London SW1P 3NZ*

CROSFIELD, Canon George Philip Chorley. b 24. OBE90. Selw Coll Cam BA50 MA55. Edin Th Coll 46. **d** 51 **p** 52. C Edin St Dav *Edin* 51-53; C St Andrews St Andr *St And* 53-55; R Hawick *Edin* 55-60; Chapl Gordonstoun Sch 60-67; Can St Mary's Cathl 68-91; Vice-Provost 68-70; Provost 70-90; R Edin St Mary 70-90; rtd 90; Hon Can St Mary's Cathl *Edin* from 91; Hon C Penicuik from 91; Hon C W Linton from 91. *21 Biggar Road, Silverburn, Penicuik EH26 9LQ* Tel (01968) 676607

CROSS, Alan. *See* CROSS, Thomas Alan

CROSS, Canon Alan. b 43. Chich Th Coll 68. **d** 70 **p** 71. C Bordesley St Oswald *Birm* 70; C S Yardley St Mich 70-73; C Colchester St Jas, All SS, St Nic and St Runwald *Chelmsf* 73-77; V Leigh-on-Sea St Jas 77-89; V Woodford St Barn from 89; Hon Can Chelmsf Cathl from 97. *127 Snakes Lane East, Woodford Green IG8 7HX* Tel (020) 8504 4687

CROSS, Preb Elizabeth Mary. b 46. Leeds Univ BA69 CertEd70. Sarum Th Coll 80. **dss** 83 **d** 87 **p** 94. Wootton Bassett *Sarum* 83-86; Westbury 86-87; Par Dn 87-89; C Glastonbury w Meare, W Pennard and Godney *B & W* 89-95; Asst Dir of Ords 89-95; Preb Wells Cathl from 93; V Wedmore w Theale and Blackford from 95. *The Vicarage, Manor Lane, Wedmore BS28 4EL* Tel (01934) 713566 Fax 713437

CROSS, Canon Greville Shelly. b 49. Sarum & Wells Th Coll 73. **d** 76 **p** 77. C Kidderminster St Mary *Worc* 76-80; P-in-c Worc St Mark 80-81; TV Worc St Martin w St Pet, St Mark etc 81-85; R Inkberrow w Cookhill and Kington w Dormston 85-98; RD Evesham 93-97; R Old Swinford Stourbridge from 98; RD Stourbridge 01-04; Hon Can Worc Cathl from 05. *The Rectory, Rectory Road, Stourbridge DY8 2HA* Tel (01384) 395410 *or* 441003 E-mail stmaryos@fish.co.uk

CROSS, James Stuart. b 36. Magd Coll Ox BA65 MA71. Ripon Hall Ox 62. **d** 65 **p** 66. C Leckhampton SS Phil and Jas *Glouc* 65-66; CF 66-92; QHC 89-92; R Stretford St Pet *Man* 92-00; rtd 00. *St Davids, Redbrook Road, Monmouth NP25 3LY* Tel (01600) 715977 Fax as telephone E-mail jimcross1@aol.com

CROSS, Jeremy Burkitt. b 45. St Pet Coll Ox BA68 MA71. Wycliffe Hall Ox 67. **d** 69 **p** 70. C Mildenhall *St E* 69-72; C Lindfield *Chich* 72-77; V Framfield 77-89; R St Leonards St Leon 89-01; R Birling, Addington, Ryarsh and Trottiscliffe *Roch* from 01. *The Vicarage, Birling Road, Ryarsh, West Malling ME19 5AW* Tel (01732) 842249 E-mail j-scross@81afilsham.freeserve.co.uk

CROSS, John Henry Laidlaw. b 30. Peterho Cam BA53 MA57. Ridley Hall Cam 53. **d** 55 **p** 56. C Ealing Dean St Jo *Lon* 55-58; C Gt Baddow *Chelmsf* 58-60; V Maidenhead St Andr and St Mary *Ox* 60-68; News Ed *C of E Newspaper* 68-71; Assoc Ed 71-72; Ed 72-75; Hon C St Pet Cornhill *Lon* 68-87; P-in-c 87-95; Hon C Chelsea All SS 76-93; rtd 95. *8 Pinetum Close, Devizes SN10 5EW* Tel (01380) 722997 E-mail revjhlcross@aol.com

CROSS, Michael Anthony. b 45. Leeds Univ BA67 BA69. Coll of Resurr Mirfield 68. **d** 70 **p** 71. S Africa 70-73; C Adel *Ripon* 74-76; Chapl Birm Univ *Birm* 76-81; V Chapel Allerton *Ripon* 81-92; V Headingley 92-04; AD Headingley 96-01; P-in-c Wetherby from 04. *3 Lazenby Drive, Wetherby LS22 6WL* Tel (01937) 582423 E-mail mandacross@yahoo.co.uk

CROSS, Canon Michael Harry. b 28. Liv Univ BVSc50. Cuddesdon Coll 74. **d** 76 **p** 77. C Ledbury *Heref* 76-79; P-in-c Bosbury 79-82; P-in-c Coddington 79-82; P-in-c Wellington Heath 79-82; V Bosbury w Wellington Heath etc 82-83; V Bishop's Castle w Mainstone 83-84; P-in-c Snead 83-84; V Morland, Thrimby and Gt Strickland *Carl* 84-93; RD Appleby 91-93; Hon Can Carl Cathl 92-93; rtd 93; Perm to Offic *Carl* from 93. *Hollin Knowle, Kilmidyke Road, Grange-over-Sands LA11 7AQ* Tel (01539) 535908

CROSS, Stephanie. b 53. Essex Univ BSc74 Loughb Univ MSc76 Bris Univ BA01 Reading Univ PGCE93. Trin Coll Bris 99. **d** 01 **p** 02. C Lytchett Minster *Sarum* from 01. *15 Guest Road, Upton, Poole BH16 5LQ* Tel (01202) 623637 E-mail crossstevie@hotmail.com

CROSS, Thomas Alan. b 58. CITC BTh05. **d** 05. C Drumglass w Moygashel *Arm* from 05. *Kinore, 84 Killyman Road, Dungannon BT71 6DQ* Tel (028) 8772 7131 E-mail curate.drumglass@armagh.anglican.org

CROSSE, Anne-Marie. **d** 99. NSM W Worthing St Jo *Chich* 99-02; NSM Arundel w Tortington and S Stoke from 02. *25 Strathmore CLose, Worthing BN13 1PQ* Tel (01903) 247706 E-mail topaz@across.freeserve.co.uk

CROSSEY, Nigel Nicholas. b 59. Cam Univ BA TCD DipTh84. **d** 84 **p** 85. C Drumglass w Moygashel *Arm* 84-87; I Magheraculmoney *Clogh* 87-93; CF from 93. *c/o MOD Chaplains (Army)* Tel (01980) 615804 Fax 615800

CROSSLAND, Felix Parnell. b 20. CEng MIMechE57 Univ of Wales (Swansea) BSc49. St Deiniol's Hawarden 73. **d** 75 **p** 76. Hon C Skewen *Llan* 75-78; Hon C Neath w Llantwit 78-85; rtd 85; Perm to Offic *Llan* from 85. *21 Cimla Road, Neath SA11 3PR* Tel (01639) 643560

CROSSLAND, Sister Joyce. b 19. Gilmore Ho IDC48. **dss** 54 **d** 87. CSA 49-78; St Etheldreda's Children's Home Bedf 62-90; Hon Par Dn Bedford St Paul *St Alb* 87-91; rtd 91; Perm to Offic *St Alb* from 91 and *Ox* from 94; Assoc Sister CSA from 03. *Paddock House, 6 Linford Lane, Willen, Milton Keynes MK15 9DL* Tel (01908) 661554

CROSSLAND, June Marcia. b 44. **d** 01. OLM Monk Bretton *Wakef* from 01; OLM Athersley from 04. *16 Deacons Way, Barnsley S71 2HU* Tel (01226) 203895

CROSSLAND, Richard Henry. b 49. Ex Univ BA72. S'wark Ord Course 91. **d** 94 **p** 96. NSM Surbiton St Andr and St Mark *S'wark* 94-95; NSM Linc Cathl *Linc* 95-98. *3 Vicars' Court, Minster Yard, Lincoln LN2 1PT* Tel (01522) 535225

CROSSLEY, Dennis Thomas. b 23. AKC52 St Boniface Warminster. **d** 53 **p** 54. C Crofton Park St Hilda *S'wark* 53-56; C Beddington 56-59; C Talbot Village *Sarum* 59-62; R Finchampstead *Ox* 62-97; rtd 97; Perm to Offic *Ox* from 97. *1 Larkswood Close, Sandhurst, Camberley GU47 8QJ*

CROSSLEY, George Alan. b 34. St Jo Coll Dur BA56. Cranmer Hall Dur DipTh60. **d** 60 **p** 61. C Blackb St Steph *Blackb* 60-63; C Ashton-on-Ribble St Andr 63-65; V Oswaldtwistle St Paul 65-72; R Dufton *Carl* 72-73; P-in-c Milburn w Newbiggin 72-73; R Long Marton w Dufton and w Milburn 73-76; P-in-c Beckermet St Jo 76-78; V Beckermet St Jo and St Bridget w Ponsonby 78-84; Chapl Furness Gen Hosp 84-89; TV Newbarns w Hawcoat *Carl* 84-89; Chapl Princess R Hosp Telford 89-97; rtd 95; P-in-c Bilsborrow *Blackb* 97-99; Perm to Offic from 00. *6 Eden Mount Way, Carnforth LA5 9XN* Tel (01524) 734568

CROSSLEY, George John. b 57. Bradf Univ BA81 PhD84. N Ord Course 91. **d** 94 **p** 95. C Balderstone *Man* 94-98; V Branston w Tatenhill *Lich* 98-02; RD Tutbury 00-02; Chapl S Staffs Healthcare NHS Trust from 04. *81 Ash Street, Burton-on-Trent DE14 3PX* Tel (01283) 516804 E-mail georgecrossley@fish.co.uk

CROSSLEY, Hugh Vaughan. b 20. AKC42. Bps' Coll Cheshunt. **d** 47 **p** 48. C Loughton St Jo *Chelmsf* 47-49; S Africa 49-52; Portuguese E Africa 52-57; Org Sec Miss to Seamen E Distr 57-58; V Shalford *Chelmsf* 58-60; S Africa 60-73; Adn Mafeking 66-70; R Orsett *Chelmsf* 73-85; P-in-c Bulphan 77-85; rtd 85; Perm to Offic *Nor* 86-96; *Chich* from 99. *Flat 4, 7 Chatsworth Gardens, Eastbourne BN20 7JP* Tel (01323) 412966

CROSSLEY, James Salter Baron. b 39. Linc Th Coll 70. **d** 72 **p** 74. C Chesterfield St Mary and All SS *Derby* 72-75; Chapl Doncaster R Infirmary 75-92; Chapl Doncaster R Infirmary and Montagu Hosp NHS Trust 92-95; Chapl Asst Tickhill Road and St Cath Hosps 75-92; Hon C Doncaster Intake *Sheff* 78-95; rtd 95; Perm to Offic *Sheff* 95-99. *The Gables, Low Row, Richmond DL11 6NH* Tel (01748) 886429 E-mail melbecks45491243@aol.com

CROSSLEY, Jeremy. *See* CROSSLEY, William Jeremy Hugh

CROSSLEY, Joan Winifred. b 57. Sussex Univ BA78 Leic Univ MA80 Univ Coll Lon PhD85. St Alb and Ox Min Course 97. **d** 00 **p** 01. C Goldington *St Alb* 00-02; C Bedf St Mark from 02; Asst Chapl Gt Ormond Street Hosp for Children NHS Trust from 03. *30 Cutcliffe Grove, Bedford MK40 4DD* Tel (01234) 346820 *or* tel and fax 344536 E-mail crossley@thisischurch.com *or* jwcrossley@aol.com

CROSSLEY, John Eric. b 51. St Martin's Coll Lanc BA92. Carl Dioc Tr Inst 92. **d** 94 **p** 95. C Westfield St Mary *Carl* 94-97; P-in-c Penrith w Newton Reigny and Plumpton Wall 97-02; Chapl Newton Rigg Coll of H&FE 97-02; TV Cartmel Peninsula *Carl* from 02. *The Vicarage, Station Road, Flookburgh, Grange-over-Sands LA11 7JY* Tel (01539) 558245 E-mail rjoncros@aol.com

CROSSLEY, Kenneth Ernest. b 38. NEOC 01. **d** 03 **p** 04. NSM Ripon Cathl *Ripon* from 03. *11 Station Drive, Ripon HG4 1JA* Tel (01765) 692499

CROSSLEY, Canon Robert Scott. b 36. Lon Univ BSc61 BD68 PhD75. ALCD64. **d** 64 **p** 65. C Beckenham St Jo *Roch* 64-68; C Morden *S'wark* 68-72; Chapl Ridley Hall Cam 72-75; V Camberley St Paul *Guildf* 75-83; TR 83-98; RD Surrey Heath 81-84; Hon Can Guildf Cathl 89-98; rtd 98; Perm to Offic *Guildf* 98-01; Hon C Camberley St Mich Yorktown from 01. *20 Highbury Crescent, Camberley GU15 1JZ* Tel (01276) 500036

CROSSLEY, Mrs Ruth Joy. b 54. Cranmer Hall Dur 00. **d** 02 **p** 03. C Cartmel Peninsula *Carl* from 02. *The Vicarage, Station Road, Flookburgh, Grange-over-Sands LA11 7JY* Tel (01539) 558245 E-mail rcross3357@aol.com

CROSSLEY, William Jeremy Hugh. b 55. St Jo Coll Dur BA76. Cranmer Hall Dur 81. **d** 84 **p** 85. C Gillingham St Mark *Roch* 84-87; C Ches Square St Mich w St Phil *Lon* 87-94; V Westminster St Jas the Less 94-00; R St Marg Lothbury and St Steph Coleman Street etc from 00. *The Rectory, 1 St Olave's Court, London EC2V 8EX* Tel (020) 7600 2379 Fax 7606 1204 E-mail the.rector@stml.org.uk

CROSSMAN, Mrs Charmian Jeanette. b 27. Lon Univ BA48 Lanc Univ MA81. **d** 91 **p** 94. NSM Carl St Jo *Carl* 91-94; P-in-c

Thursby 95-97; Perm to Offic *Sheff* from 97. *12 Ashfurlong Road, Sheffield S17 3NL* Tel 0114-236 0731

CROSSMAN, Ms Sharon Margaret Joan. b 65. DipCOT87. Linc Th Coll BTh93. **d** 93 **p** 94. Par Dn Chippenham St Andr w Tytherton Lucas *Bris* 93-94; C 94-96; Chapl UWE 96-02; Hon C Almondsbury 97-98; Hon C Almondsbury and Olveston 98-02; Chapl Würzburg Univ Germany 02-03; TV Portishead *B & W* from 03; Chapl Mothers' Union from 05. *25 Lambourne Way, Portishead, Bristol BS20 7LQ* Tel (01275) 840526 E-mail sharon.crossman@btopenworld.com

CROSTHWAITE, George Roger. b 38. Dur Univ BSc62. Ridley Hall Cam 62 Fuller Th Sem California DMin83. **d** 65 **p** 66. C Bradf Cathl Par *Bradf* 65-67; C Ox St Aldate w H Trin *Ox* 67-70; Youth Adv CMS 70-73; P-in-c Derby St Werburgh *Derby* 73-78; V 78-82; C La Crescenta St Luke USA 77-78; V Anston *Sheff* 82-83; Regisrar St Giles-in-the-Fields *Lon* 83-86; V Barnes St Mich *S'wark* 86-88; Perm to Offic *Guildf* 88-93; Dir Cen Essential Psychology from 92; Perm to Offic *Derby* from 01 and *Chich* from 04. *8 Sussex Road, Worthing BN11 1DS* Tel (01903) 609716

CROSTHWAITE, Howard Wellesley. b 37. St Cuth Soc Dur BA59. St Steph Ho Ox 59. **d** 61 **p** 62. C Workington St Mich *Carl* 61-63; Grenada 63-64; C Barnsley St Mary *Wakef* 64-68; V Milnsbridge 68-70; V Thurgoland 70-79; rtd 99. *50 Low Road West, Warmsworth, Doncaster DN4 9LE* Tel (01302) 859213 Mobile 07370-966629

CROUCH, Prof David Bruce. b 53. Univ of Wales (Cardiff) BA75 PhD84 FRHistS86. NEOC DipTh98. **d** 98 **p** 99. NSM Scarborough St Martin *York* 98-01; NSM Scarborough St Columba from 01. *29 Royal Avenue, Scarborough YO11 2LS* Tel (01723) 374867 Fax 378015 E-mail david@ucscarb.ac.uk

CROUCH, Keith Matheson. b 45. Whitelands Coll Lon CertEd71 Westhill Coll Birm BPhil00. K Coll Lon AKC70. **d** 72 **p** 73. C Hill *Birm* 72-75; C-in-c Woodgate Valley CD 75-77; V Bishop's Castle w Mainstone *Heref* 91-98; Vice-Prin WEMTC 98-04; TV Tenbury 98-02; Public Preacher 02-04; Chapl Dorothy House Hospice Winsley from 05. *Dorothy House, Winsley, Bradford-on-Avon BA15 2LE* Tel (01225) 722988

CROUCHER, Jonathan Edward. b 68. Trin Coll Cam BA90 MA93. SEITE 01. **d** 04. NSM Lee Gd Shep w St Pet *S'wark* from 04. *14 Southbrook Road, London SE12 8LQ* Tel (020) 8852 6913 Mobile 07956-649902 Fax 7300 7100 E-mail j.croucher@taylorwessing.com

CROUCHMAN, Eric Richard. b 30. Bps' Coll Cheshunt 64. **d** 66 **p** 67. C Ipswich H Trin *St E* 66-69; C Ipswich All Hallows 69-72; R Crowfield w Stonham Aspal and Mickfield 72-81; R Combs 81-90; RD Stowmarket 84-90; P-in-c Lydgate w Ousden and Cowlinge 90-95; R Wickhambrook w Lydgate, Ousden and Cowlinge 95-96; rtd 96; Perm to Offic *St E* from 97. *6 Mitre Close, Woolpit, Bury St Edmunds IP30 9SJ* Tel and fax (01359) 240070 E-mail ericthecleric@lineone.net

CROW, Arthur. b 26. St Chad's Coll Dur BA51 DipTh52. **d** 52 **p** 53. C Thornhill *Wakef* 52-54; C Holmfirth 54-57; V Shelley 57-63; V Flockton cum Denby Grange 63-91; rtd 91; Perm to Offic *York* from 91. *2 Thatchers Croft, Copmanthorpe, York YO23 3YD* Tel (01904) 709861

CROW, Michael John. b 35. AKC63. **d** 64 **p** 65. C Welwyn Garden City *St Alb* 64-67; C Sawbridgeworth 67-69; C Biscot 69-71; V Luton St Aug Limbury 71-79; TR Borehamwood 79-87; V Markyate Street 87-00; P-in-c Flamstead 98-00; rtd 00; Perm to Offic *Ex* from 00. *216 Pinhoe Road, Exeter EX4 7HH* Tel (01392) 424804

CROWDER, The Ven Norman Harry. b 26. St Jo Coll Cam BA48 MA52. Westcott Ho Cam 50. **d** 52 **p** 53. C Radcliffe-on-Trent *S'well* 52-55; Bp's Res Chapl *Portsm* 55-59; Asst Chapl Canford Sch Wimborne 59-64; Chapl 64-72; V Oakfield St Jo *Portsm* 72-75; Can Res Portsm Cathl 75-85; Dir RE 75-85; Adn Portsm 85-93; rtd 93; Perm to Offic *Portsm* and *Sarum* from 94. *37 Rectory Road, Salisbury SP2 7SD* Tel (01722) 320052 E-mail pauleen@pcrowder.freeserve.co.uk

CROWE, Anthony Murray. b 34. St Edm Hall Ox BA58 MA61. Westcott Ho Cam 57. **d** 59 **p** 60. C Stockingford *Cov* 59-62; C New Eltham All SS *S'wark* 62-66; V Clapham St Jo 66-73; R Charlton St Luke w H Trin 73-94; rtd 94; Sub-Chapl HM Pris Elmley 94-97; Sub-Chapl HM Pris Swaleside 94-99; Perm to Offic *Cant* from 94. *9 Park Avenue, Whitstable CT5 2DD* Tel (01227) 273046 E-mail ailsaandtonyc@aol.com

CROWE, Brian David. QUB BA92 PhD95 TCD BA98. **d** 98 **p** 99. C Ballynure and Ballyeaston *Conn* 98-01; I Galloon w Drummully *Clogh* 01-02. *17 Causeway End Road, Lisburn BT28 1UB*

CROWE, Eric Anthony. b 29. St Jo Coll Dur BA53 MA98. Cuddesdon Coll 53. **d** 55 **p** 56. C Huddersfield St Jo *Wakef* 55-58; C Barnsley St Pet 58-60; R High Hoyland w Clayton W 60-68; V Battyeford 68-74; P-in-c Pitminster w Corfe *B & W* 75-76; V 76-90; rtd 90; Perm to Offic *Ex* 95-01 and *B & W* from 02. *5 Minster Close, Galmington, Taunton TA1 4LB* Tel (01823) 257197

CROWE, Grant Norman. b 74. Keele Univ LLB96. Cranmer Hall Dur 00. **d** 03 **p** 04. C Burton All SS w Ch Ch *Lich* from 03. *1A Moor Street, Burton-on-Trent DE14 3AU* Tel (01283) 538149

CROWE, Canon John Yeomans. b 39. Keble Coll Ox BA62 MA66. Linc Th Coll 62. **d** 64 **p** 65. C Tettenhall Regis *Lich* 64-67; C Caversham *Ox* 67-71; V Hampton *Worc* 72-76; P-in-c Leek St Edw *Lich* 76-79; TR Leek 79-83; TR Leek and Meerbrook 83-87; RD Leek 82-87; TR Dorchester and V Warborough *Ox* 87-04; RD Aston and Cuddesdon 93-02; Hon Can Ch Ch 94-04; rtd 04. *9 Pierrepont Road, Leominster HR6 8RB* Tel (01568) 611081 E-mail john.crowe90@ntlworld.com

CROWE, Leonard Charles. b 25. S Dios Minl Tr Scheme 80. **d** 82 **p** 83. NSM Buxted and Hadlow Down *Chich* 82-84; NSM Fairlight 84-86; P-in-c 86-89; V 89-92; RD Rye 93-95; Perm to Offic 95-98; P-in-c Ashburnham w Penhurst 98-99; rtd 99; Perm to Offic *Chich* from 99. *3 St Kitts, West Parade, Bexhill-on-Sea TN39 3DR* Tel (01424) 218676

CROWE, Canon Norman Charles. b 23. ADipR62. Launde Abbey. **d** 63 **p** 64. C Leic Martyrs *Leic* 63-66; C-in-c Leic St Chad CD 66-68; V Leic St Chad 68-73; V Market Harborough 73-88; RD Gartree I 76-81; Hon Can Leic Cathl 80-88; rtd 88; Perm to Offic *Leic* 88-98 and *Pet* from 88. *8 Wilton Close, Desborough, Kettering NN14 2QJ* Tel (01536) 760820

CROWE, Canon Philip Anthony. b 36. Selw Coll Cam BA60 MA64. Ridley Hall Cam 60. **d** 62 **p** 63. Tutor Oak Hill Th Coll 62-67; C Enfield Ch Ch Trent Park *Lon* 62-65; Ed *C of E Newspaper* 67-71; Lect Birm St Martin 71-76; R Breadsall *Derby* 77-88; Prin and Tutor Sarum & Wells Th Coll 88-95; Can and Preb Sarum Cathl *Sarum* 91-95; R Overton and Erbistock and Penley *St As* 95-97; Dir St As and Ban Minl Tr from 96; rtd 97; Perm to Offic *Lich* from 01. *Alder Lea, Babbinswood, Whittington, Oswestry SY11 4PQ* Tel (01691) 671698

CROWE, Canon Sydney Ralph. b 32. Edin Th Coll 61. **d** 63 **p** 64. C Bingley H Trin *Bradf* 63-66; C Bierley 66-69; V Toller Lane St Chad from 69; Hon Can Bradf Cathl from 85; RD Airedale 95-99. *The Vicarage, St Chad's Road, Toller Lane, Bradford BD8 9DE* Tel (01274) 543957

CROWHURST, Preb David Brian. b 40. Qu Coll Birm 77. **d** 80 **p** 81. NSM Ribbesford w Bewdley and Dowles *Worc* 80-82; Hon Chapl Birm Cathl *Birm* 81-82; C Kidderminster St Jo *Worc* 82-83; C-in-c Wribbenhall 83-84; P-in-c 84-87; V Oswestry St Oswald *Lich* 87-94; P-in-c Oswestry H Trin 93-94; V Oswestry from 94; P-in-c Rhydycroesau 90-91; R from 91; RD Oswestry 95-01; Preb Lich Cathl from 00. *The Vicarage, Penylan Lane, Oswestry SY11 2AJ* Tel (01691) 653467 *or* 652861 Fax 655235 E-mail d.crowhurst@btinternet.com

CROWIE, Hermon John. b 41. Kelham Th Coll 61. **d** 69 **p** 73. C Sneinton St Cypr *S'well* 69; C Balderton 72-75; V Basford St Aid 75-78; R Everton and Mattersey w Clayworth 78-84; St Helena 84-89; Chapl HM Pris Nor 89-91; Chapl HM Pris Cant 91-02; Bulgaria from 02. *Zora 23, Nickolaevo, Stara Zagora, Bulgaria*

CROWLE, Sarah Ann. *See* BROUGH, Mrs Sarah Ann

CROWLEY, Mrs Jennifer Eileen. b 55. CITC 00. **d** 03 **p** 04. Aux Min Waterford w Killea, Drumcannon and Dunhill *C & O* from 03. *Glen, Stradbally, Kilmacthomas, Co Waterford, Irish Republic* Tel (00353) (51) 293143

✠**CROWTHER, The Rt Revd Clarence Edward.** b 29. Leeds Univ BA50 LLB52 LLM53 California Univ PhD75. Cuddesdon Coll 55. **d** 56 **p** 57 **c** 65. C Ox SS Phil and Jas *Ox* 56-59; USA 59-64 and from 67; Episc Chapl California Univ 59-64; Dean Kimberley S Africa 64-65; Bp Kimberley and Kuruman 65-67; Asst Bp California 70-84; Asst Bp Los Angeles from 84. *PO Box 1559, Summerland, CA 93067, USA* E-mail cctravel@west.net

CROWTHER, Donald James. b 23. Oak Hill NSM Course 80. **d** 82 **p** 83. NSM Seal St Lawr *Roch* 82-85; NSM Sevenoaks St Nic 85-87; P-in-c Sevenoaks Weald 87-90; Perm to Offic from 90. *Midhope, Pilgrims Way, Kemsing, Sevenoaks TN15 6LS* Tel (01732) 761035

CROWTHER, Frank. b 28. Qu Coll Birm 68. **d** 69 **p** 70. C Bulwell St Mary *S'well* 69-72; TV Clifton 72-77; V Kirkby in Ashfield St Thos 77-85; rtd 86; Perm to Offic *S'well* from 86; Perm to Offic *Derby* 86-00. *30 Bramley Court, Sutton-in-Ashfield NG17 4AT* Tel (01623) 443251

CROWTHER, Gordon Allan. b 63. Rhodes Univ BA85 LLB87. Spurgeon's Coll BD94 St Jo Coll Dur MA98. **d** 00 **p** 01. C Lancaster St Thos *Blackb* 00-03; Miss P Newcastle and Stoke *Lich* from 03. *12 Tansey Close, Stoke-on-Trent ST2 9QX* Tel (01782) 285635 Mobile 07966-973162 E-mail gordon.crowther@btinternet.com

CROWTHER, Stephen Alfred. b 59. TCD DipTh87. **d** 87 **p** 88. C Willowfield *D & D* 87-89; I Belfast St Chris 89-92; I Kiltegan w Hacketstown, Clonmore and Moyne *C & O* 93-99; Philippines 99-00; C Kill *D & G* 00-01; I Lisnaskea *Clogh* from 01. *The Rectory, Castlebalfour, Lisnaskea BT92 0LT* Tel and fax (028) 6772 1237 E-mail crowther@oceanfree.net *or* lisnaskea@clogher.anglican.org

CROWTHER-ALWYN, Benedict Mark. b 53. Kent Univ BA74. Qu Coll Birm 74. **d** 77 **p** 78. C Fenny Stratford and Water Eaton *Ox* 77-80; C Moulsecoomb *Chich* 80-81; TV 81-83; R Glas

St Serf and Baillieston *Glas* 83-87; R Bassingham *Linc* 87-90; V Aubourn w Haddington 87-90; V Carlton-le-Moorland w Stapleford 87-90; R Thurlby w Norton Disney 87-90; V Elmton *Derby* 90-03; P-in-c Matlock from 03; P-in-c Dethick, Lea and Holloway from 04. *The Rectory, Church Street, Matlock DE4 3BZ* Tel (01629) 582199

CROWTHER-GREEN, Canon John Patrick Victor. b 18. Hatf Coll Dur LTh41 BA42. St Boniface Warminster 39. **d** 42 **p** 44. C Croydon H Trin *Cant* 42-44; C New Windsor H Trin *Ox* 44-49; V Shackerstone and Congerstone *Leic* 49-53; R Willoughby Waterleys, Peatling Magna etc 53-58; V Leic St Sav 58-73; V Blaby 73-87; RD Guthlaxton I 81-87; Hon Can Leic Cathl 82-87; rtd 87; Perm to Offic *Leic* from 87. *40 Craighill Road, Knighton, Leicester LE2 3FB* Tel 0116-270 7615

CROWTHER-GREEN, Michael Leonard. b 36. K Coll Lon 56. **d** 60 **p** 61. C Caterham *S'wark* 60-64; C Lewisham St Jo Southend 64-69; Chr Aid Area Sec (Berks, Oxon and Bucks) 69-78; Lic to Offic *Ox* 78-83; Dioc Stewardship Adv 83-92; rtd 92; Perm to Offic *Ox* from 92. *8 Egerton Road, Reading RG2 8HQ* Tel 0118-987 2502

CROYDON, Archdeacon of. *See* DAVIES, The Ven Vincent Anthony

CROYDON, Area Bishop of. *See* BAINES, The Rt Revd Nicholas

CRUICKSHANK, Ian Morison. QUB BTh. **d** 04. C Bray *D & G* from 04. *14 Rosslyn Court, Bray, Co Wicklow, Irish Republic* Tel (00353) (1) 282 9044 Mobile 87-948 4408
E-mail ian.mcruickshank@btopenworld.com

CRUICKSHANK, Jonathan Graham. b 52. K Coll Lon BD74 AKC74 Keble Coll Ox PGCE75. St Aug Coll Cant 75. **d** 76 **p** 77. C Stantonbury *Ox* 76-79; C Burnham 79-82; Chapl RNR 80-83; C Burnham w Dropmore, Hitcham and Taplow *Ox* 82-83; Chapl RN 83-89; TV New Windsor *Ox* 89-01; R Itchen Valley *Win* from 01; RD Alresford from 01; Corps Chapl Sea Cadet Corps from 95. *Itchen Valley Rectory, Chillandham Lane, Itchen Abbas, Winchester SO21 1AS* Tel and fax (01962) 779832
E-mail jcruickshank@btclick.com

CRUISE, Brian John Alexander. Bris Univ BA86 TCD BTh88. **d** 88 **p** 89. C Lurgan Ch the Redeemer *D & D* 88-92; I Kildress w Altedesert *Arm* from 92. *Kildress Rectory, 6 Rectory Road, Cookstown BT80 9RX* Tel (028) 7965 1215
E-mail brian@aonet.org.uk

CRUMPTON, Colin. b 38. AKC61 Sheff Univ Dip Leadership, Renewal & Miss Studies 97. **d** 64 **p** 65. C Billingham St Cuth *Dur* 64-66; C Shirley *Birm* 66-69; V Mossley *Ches* 69-75; Miss to Seamen 75-77; V Burslem St Paul *Lich* 77-82; V Edensor 82-97; V Llanrhaeadr-ym-Mochnant etc *St As* 97-00; Dir Accra Retreat Cen Ghana 00-01; rtd 02; Hon C Redmarley D'Abitot, Bromesberrow, Pauntley etc *Glouc* 02-03; Perm to Offic *Lich* from 03. *60 Craig Walk, Alsager ST7 2RJ* Tel (01270) 882666 Mobile 07799-183971

CRUSE, Jack. b 35. ARIBA67. Sarum & Wells Th Coll 76. **d** 79 **p** 80. NSM W Teignmouth *Ex* 79-85; C Ideford, Luton and Ashcombe 85-89; C Bishopsteignton 85-89; R Broadhempston, Woodland, Staverton etc 90-98; RD Totnes 94-98; rtd 98; Perm to Offic *Ex* from 98. *41 Butts Close, Honiton EX14 2FS* Tel (01404) 46567 E-mail jack@jcruse.freeserve.co.uk

CRUSE, John Jeremy. b 58. Univ of Wales (Lamp) BA79 Hughes Hall Cam CertEd87. Sarum & Wells Th Coll 81. **d** 82 **p** 83. C Newton St Pet *S & B* 82-84; P-in-c Newbridge-on-Wye and Llanfihangel Brynpabuan 84-86; Perm to Offic *Heref* 88-89; C Waltham H Cross *Chelmsf* 89-91; TV Yatton Moor *B & W* 91-00; V Shalford *Guildf* from 00. *The Vicarage, East Shalford Lane, Shalford, Guildford GU4 8AE* Tel and fax (01483) 562396 Mobile 07889-919928 E-mail john@cruse60.freeserve.co.uk

CRUSE, Mrs Susan Elizabeth. b 51. RGN72 Middx Univ BA04. NTMTC 01. **d** 04 **p** 05. NSM Ingatestone w Fryerning *Chelmsf* from 04. *Silverstone, Butts Way, Chelmsford CM2 8TJ* Tel (01245) 258083 Mobile 07885-909837
E-mail cruse@classicfm.net

CRUTCHLEY, John Hamilton. b 62. Kingston Poly LLB85. Trin Coll Bris 99. **d** 01 **p** 02. C Barnstaple *Ex* from 01. *28 Old School Road, Barnstaple EX32 9DP* Tel (01271) 325553
E-mail crutchleyfam@tesco.net

CRUTTENDEN, Leslie Roy. b 39. Cant Sch of Min. **d** 84 **p** 85. NSM Maidstone St Luke *Cant* 84-86; NSM Charlton-in-Dover 86-90; NSM River 90-01. *Address temp unknown*

CRYER, Gordon David. b 34. St D Coll Lamp BA63 DipTh64. **d** 64 **p** 65. C Mortlake w E Sheen *S'wark* 64-67; C Godstone 67-70; Chapl St Dunstan's Abbey Sch Plymouth 71-02; R Stoke Damerel *Ex* 71-02; P-in-c Devonport St Aubyn 88-02; rtd 02; Perm to Offic *Truro* from 02. *9 St Stephens Road, Saltash PL12 4BG* Tel (01752) 510436

CRYER, Neville Barker. b 24. Hertf Coll Ox BA48 MA52. Ridley Hall Cam. **d** 50 **p** 51. C Derby St Werburgh *Derby* 50-53; C Ilkeston St Mary 53-54; R Blackley St Pet *Man* 55-59; V Addiscombe St Mary *Cant* 59-67; Sec Conf Br Miss Socs 67-70; Gen Sec BFBS 70-86; rtd 86; Perm to Offic *York* from 90. *14 Carmires Road, Haxby, York YO32 3NN* Tel (01904) 763371

CUBA, Bishop of. *See* HURTADO, The Rt Revd Jorge A Perera

CUBITT, Paul. b 64. Sheff Univ BA86. Cranmer Hall Dur 95. **d** 97 **p** 98. C Bromyard *Heref* 97-01; V Elloughton and Brough w Brantingham *York* from 01. *The Vicarage, Church Street, Elloughton, Brough HU15 1HN* Tel (01482) 667431

CUDBY, Paul Edward Frank. b 66. Hatf Poly BSc88. Ridley Hall Cam 99. **d** 02 **p** 03. C Bedford St Andr *St Alb* from 02. *5 St Minver Road, Bedford MK40 3DQ* Tel (01234) 217330

CUERNAVACA, Bishop of. *See* GARCIA-MONTEIL, The Rt Revd Martiniano

CUFF, Gregor John. b 61. Keele Univ BSc82. Ridley Hall Cam Cert Th & Min 95. **d** 95 **p** 96. C Stanley *Liv* 95-99; V Waterloo Ch Ch and St Jo from 99. *The Vicarage, 22 Crosby Road South, Liverpool L22 1RQ* Tel and fax 0151-920 7791
E-mail g.cuff@virgin.net

CUFF, Mrs Pamela. b 47. MCSP68. S Dios Minl Tr Scheme 89. **d** 92 **p** 94. NSM Nether Stowey w Over Stowey *B & W* 92-93; NSM Quantoxhead from 93; Asst Chapl Taunton Hosps 93-94; Asst Chapl Taunton and Somerset NHS Trust from 94. *Millands, Kilve, Bridgwater TA5 1EA* Tel (01278) 741229

CULBERTSON, Eric Malcolm. b 54. Ch Ch Ox BA76 MA80 K Coll Lon PhD91. Edin Th Coll 78. **d** 80 **p** 81. C Edin St Thos *Edin* 80-83; C Ealing St Mary *Lon* 83-87; R Clarkston *Glas* 87-89; Area Sec Crosslinks 89-94; I Tullaniskin w Clonoe *Arm* from 94. *215 Brackaville Road, Newmills, Dungannon BT71 4EJ* Tel (028) 8774 7154 E-mail ericmculbertson@yahoo.co.uk

CULL, John. b 31. Oak Hill Th Coll 56. **d** 59 **p** 60. C Radipole *Sarum* 59-66; Chapl Mariners' Ch Glouc 66-70; R Woodchester *Glouc* 70-90; RD Stonehouse 85-89; V Walton *St E* 90-94; rtd 94; Perm to Offic *Glouc* from 94. *Hillgrove Stables, Bear Hill, Woodchester, Stroud GL5 5DH* Tel (01453) 872145

CULLEN, Canon John Austin. b 43. Auckland Univ BA67 Otago Univ BD76 Keble Coll Ox DPhil86 FRSA89. St Jo Coll Auckland 66. **d** 69 **p** 70. C Papatoetoe New Zealand 69-73; Assoc P Mt Albert St Luke 73-75; P-in-c 74; Hon C Remuera St Aidan 75-78; Asst Chapl Keble Coll Ox 79-82; Perm to Offic *Lon* 82-84; Chapl and Lect Worc Coll Ox 84-86; C St Botolph Aldgate w H Trin Minories *Lon* 86-87; Dir Inst of Chr Studies 87-91; Hon C St Marylebone All SS 87-91; Dir of Tr *Win* 91-97; Dir of Min Development 97-01; Hon Can Win Cathl 96-02; Sen Asst to Bp Lon 02-04; P-in-c St Geo-in-the-East w St Paul 03-04; Perm to Offic from 05. *60 Cephas Avenue, London E1 4AR* Tel (020) 7265 9028 *or* 7481 1345
E-mail john.cullen@ukgateway.net

CULLIFORD, Michael. b 26. Qu Coll Birm 56. **d** 58 **p** 59. C Birkenhead St Jas *Ches* 58-60; C Bollington St Jo 60-62; V Heald Green St Cath 62-80; Perm to Offic *Man* from 89; rtd 91. *c/o Mrs A Carroll, 35 Hivings Hill, Chesham HP5 2PG*

CULLING, Elizabeth Ann. *See* HOARE, Elizabeth Ann

CULLINGWORTH, Anthony Robert. b 42. BSc. Ox NSM Course. **d** 83 **p** 84. NSM Slough *Ox* 83-99; NSM Denham 99-02; NSM Morton St Luke *Bradf* 02-04. *2 Thurleston Court, East Morton, Keighley BD20 5RG* Tel (01535) 601187
E-mail theculties@aol.com

CULLIS, Andrew Stanley Weldon. b 48. Hertf Coll Ox BA69 LTh. St Jo Coll Nottm 70. **d** 73 **p** 74. C Reigate St Mary *S'wark* 73-78; C Yateley *Win* 78-82; V Dorking St Paul *Guildf* 82-00; RD Dorking 94-99; P-in-c Chilwell *S'well* 00-04; R Fisherton Anger *Sarum* from 04. *St Paul's Rectory, Fisherton Street, Salisbury SP2 7QW* Tel (01722) 334005

CULLWICK, Christopher John. b 53. Hull Univ BA75 Reading Univ Ox Univ BA80 MA85. Wycliffe Hall Ox 78. **d** 81 **p** 82. C Nottingham St Jude *S'well* 81-84; C York St Mich-le-Belfrey *York* 84-87; TV Huntington 87-03; Ind Chapl from 02. *The Vicarage, 64 Strensall Road, Huntington, York YO32 9SH* Tel (01904) 764608

CULLY, Miss Elizabeth Faith. b 46. SRN67 SCM69 RGN72. Trin Coll Bris BA88. **d** 88 **p** 94. Par Dn Filton *Bris* 88-92; Par Dn Fishponds St Jo 92-94; C 94-95; P-in-c Brinsley w Underwood *S'well* 95-98; V 98-02; P-in-c Farnsfield from 02; P-in-c Kirklington w Hockerton from 02; P-in-c Bilsthorpe from 02; P-in-c Eakring from 02; P-in-c Maplebeck from 02; P-in-c Winkburn from 02. *The Vicarage, Beck Lane, Farnsfield, Newark NG22 8ER* Tel (01623) 882247
E-mail faith.cully@btopenworld.com

CULROSS, James Fred. b 17. Lon Univ BD51. Bps' Coll Cheshunt 47. **d** 50 **p** 51. C Pateley Bridge *Ripon* 50-54; C Romaldkirk 54-55; V Middleton St Cross 55-62; R Glas St Jas *Glas* 62-65; C Bramley and Grafham *Guildf* 65-67; Chapl R Wanstead Sch 67-71; Chapl Sir Roger Manwood's Sch Sandwich 71-79; R Barrowden and Wakerley w S Luffenham *Pet* 79-82; rtd 82; Perm to Offic *B & W* 82-97; Perm to Offic *Pet* from 77. *1 St Christopher's Walk, Abington Park Crescent, Northampton NN3 3AD* Tel (01604) 234388

CULVERWELL, Martin Phillip. b 48. Sarum & Wells Th Coll 72. **d** 75 **p** 76. C Ashford St Hilda *Lon* 75-78; C Chelsea St Luke 78-80; Chapl RN 80-83; TV Yeovil *B & W* 83-87; P-in-c Sarratt *St Alb* 87-90; NSM Bradford w Oake, Hillfarrance and Heathfield *B & W* 90-92; R Rode Major 92-96. *The Old Ebenezer, High Street, Rode, Frome BA11 6NZ* Tel (01373) 830476 E-mail mpcul@aol.com

CUMBERLAND, The Very Revd Barry John. b 44. Birm Univ BA67 Worc Coll Ox DipEd68 Trin Coll Singapore MDiv88. **d** 88 **p** 89. NSM Westmr St Matt *Lon* 88-90; Perm to Offic 90-96; Philippines 90-96, 98-01 and from 03; Dean Manila 92-96; Chapl Stockholm w Gävle and Västerås *Eur* 96-98; P-in-c Las Palmas 01-03. *19 E Padua Street, BF Resort Village, Las Pinas City 1740, Metro Manila, Philippines* Tel and fax (0063) (2) 875 3528 E-mail bclaspalmas44@hotmail.com

CUMBERLEGE, Francis Richard. b 41. AKC65. **d** 66 **p** 67. C Leigh Park St Fran CD *Portsm* 66-71; Papua New Guinea 71-81; Adn N Papua 74-81; C Portsea St Mary *Portsm* 81; R Hastings St Clem and All SS *Chich* 81-86; V Broadwater Down 86-91; V Tunbridge Wells St Mark *Roch* 91-99; RD Tunbridge Wells 96-99; P-in-c Brockenhurst *Win* 99-03; V from 03. *The Vicarage, Meerut Road, Brockenhurst SO42 7TD* Tel (01590) 623309 E-mail cum.cum@littleoaks.net

CUMBERLIDGE, Anthony Wynne. b 49. ACIB75. Sarum & Wells Th Coll 79. **d** 82 **p** 83. C Llanrhos *St As* 82-85; R Llanfair Talhaearn and Llansannan etc 85-87; CF 87-04; P-in-c Lambourn *Ox* from 04; P-in-c Eastbury and E Garston from 04. *The Vicarage, Newbury Street, Lambourn, Hungerford RG17 8PD* Tel (01488) 71546 E-mail vicaratlambourn@aol.com

CUMBRAE, Provost of. *Vacant*

CUMINGS, Llewellyn Frank Beadnell. b 29. Natal Univ BA50 St Cath Coll Cam CertEd53. Ridley Hall Cam 65. **d** 67 **p** 68. C Leamington Priors St Mary *Cov* 67-70; V Lobley Hill *Dur* 70-74; R Denver *Ely* 74-82; V Ryston w Roxham 74-82; R St Leonards St Leon *Chich* 82-88; V Billinghay *Linc* 88-93; rtd 93. *Y Bwthyn, Coedllan, Llanfyllin SY22 5BP* Tel (01691) 648013

CUMMING, Canon Nigel Patrick. b 42. St Jo Coll Nottm 73. **d** 75 **p** 76. C Castle Hall *Ches* 75-77; C Stalybridge H Trin and Ch Ch 77-78; C Tadley St Pet *Win* 78-82; R Overton w Laverstoke and Freefolk from 82; RD Whitchurch 89-98; Hon Can Win Cathl from 99. *The Rectory, 54 Lordsfield Gardens, Overton, Basingstoke RG25 3EW* Tel and fax (01256) 770207 E-mail nigel.cumming@ukgateway.net

CUMMING, Ms Susan Margaret. b 47. Man Univ BSc68 Makerere Univ Kampala DipEd69. EMMTC 82. **dss** 82 **d** 87 **p** 95. Cinderhill *S'well* 82-85; Dioc Adv in Adult Educn 85-92; Par Dn Nottingham St Mary and St Cath 93-95; Lect 95-97; Asst Chapl Qu Medical Cen Nottm Univ Hosp NHS Trust 97-03; Sen Chapl from 03. *33 Upton Close, Millers Reach, Castle Donington, Derby DE74 2GN* Tel (01332) 858267

CUMMING-LATTEY, Mrs Susan Mary Ruth. b 47. Open Univ BA77 SRN69. STETS 00. **d** 03 **p** 04. NSM Ash Vale *Guildf* from 03. *38A Elms Road, Fleet GU51 3EQ* Tel and fax (01252) 621295 Mobile 07761-126354 Fax (01252) 815882 E-mail erinboy@totalise.co.uk

CUMMINGS, Mrs Elizabeth. b 45. St Jo Coll Dur BA84. NEOC 85. **d** 87 **p** 94. NSM Dur St Giles *Dur* 87-89; Chapl HM Pris Dur 89-90; Chapl HM Rem Cen Low Newton 90-95; Chapl HM Pris Stocken 95-96; Chapl HM Pris Frankland 96-05; rtd 05. *8 Bridgemere Drive, Framwellgate Moor, Durham DH1 5FG* Tel 0191-383 0832

CUMMINGS, Michael. b 53. Solicitor 87. SW Minl Tr Course 02. **d** 05. NSM Langport Area Chs *B & W* from 05. *32 Bishops Drive, Langport TA10 9HW* Tel (01458) 250449 Mobile 07966-416675 E-mail m.cummings2@btopenworld.com

CUMMINGS, Richard Vivian Payn. b 21. Lon Univ BSc41. Chich Th Coll 51. **d** 53 **p** 54. C Pet All SS *Pet* 53-55; C Wellingborough All SS 55-60; V Wollaston and Strixton 60-69; V Wellingborough St Barn 69-73; RD Wellingborough 70-73; R Collingtree w Courteenhall 73-80; P-in-c Milton Malsor 73-80; R Collingtree w Courteenhall and Milton Malsor 80-90; rtd 90; Perm to Offic *Pet* from 90. *55 Watersmeet, Northampton NN1 5SQ* Tel (01604) 37027

CUMMINGS, Canon William Alexander Vickery. b 38. Ch Ch Ox BA62 MA64. Wycliffe Hall Ox 61. **d** 64 **p** 65. C Leytonstone St Jo *Chelmsf* 64-67; C Writtle 67-71; R Stratton St Mary w Stratton St Michael *Nor* 71-73; R Wacton Magna w Parva 71-73; R Stratton St Mary w Stratton St Michael etc 73-91; RD Depwade 81-91; Hon Can Nor Cathl 90-91; V Battle *Chich* 91-04; Dean Battle 91-04; rtd 04. *80 Samber Close, Lymington SO41 9LF* Tel (01590) 610426

CUMMINS, Ashley Wighton. b 56. St Andr Univ BD83. Coates Hall Edin DipMin84. **d** 84 **p** 85. C Broughty Ferry *Bre* 84-87; P-in-c Dundee St Ninian 87-92; P-in-c Invergowrie from 92; Chapl Angl Students Dundee Univ from 92. *27 Errol Road, Invergowrie, Dundee DD2 5AG* Tel (01382) 562525 E-mail acummins@fish.co.uk

CUMMINS, Daphne Mary. *See* GREEN, Daphne Mary

CUMMINS, James Ernest. b 32. Brasted Th Coll 56 Westcott Ho Cam 57. **d** 60 **p** 61. C Baswich *Lich* 60-64; V Hales w Heckingham *Nor* 64-70; V Raveningham 70-76; Perm to Offic *Heref* and *S & B* from 76; rtd 97. *Skyborry, Knighton LD7 1TW* Tel (01547) 528369 Fax 640677

CUMMINS, Julian Peter Francis. b 55. TD91. K Coll Cam BA77 MA80 Bradf Univ MBA91 Leeds Univ PhD99 MCIM84 FCIM99. N Ord Course 94. **d** 97 **p** 98. NSM Lower Wharfedale *Ripon* 97-01; C Bramley 01-02; Perm to Offic from 03. *50 Lane End, Pudsey LS28 9AD* Tel 0113-255 0909 Mobile 07957-357634 Fax 0113-255 0910 E-mail julian@avista.co.uk

CUMMINS, The Very Revd Nicholas Marshall. b 36. CITC 65. **d** 67 **p** 68. C Ballymena *Conn* 67-70; C Belfast St Nic 70-73; I Buttevant Union *C, C & R* 73-78; I Mallow Union 78-83; I Kilmoe Union 83-96; Can Cork Cathl 90-96; Treas Cork Cathl 95-96; Preb Tymothan St Patr Cathl Dublin 95-01; Dean Killaloe and Clonfert *L & K* 96-01; Dean Kilfenora and Provost Kilmacduagh 96-01; I Killaloe w Stradbally 96-01; rtd 01. *Ard Mhuire, Annabella, Mallow, Co Cork, Irish Republic* Tel (00353) (22) 20329

CUMPSTY, Prof John Sutherland. b 31. K Coll Dur BSc54 PhD56 Barrister-at-Law (Middle Temple) 56 Carnegie-Mellon Univ MS58 St Jo Coll Dur DipTh60. Cranmer Hall Dur 58. **d** 60 **p** 61. C Normanton *Wakef* 60-62; Tutor St Jo Coll Dur 62-66; Lect Glas Univ 66-69; S Africa from 70; Prof RS Cape Town Univ from 70; rtd 96. *University of Cape Town, Dept of Religious Studies, Rondebosch, 7700 South Africa* Tel (0027) (21) 650 3454 Fax 650 3761

CUNDIFF, Mrs Margaret Joan. b 32. Man Univ DMS60. St Mich Ho Ox 51. **dss** 77 **d** 87 **p** 94. Broadcasting Officer *York* 75-99; Angl Adv Yorkshire TV 79-90; Selby St Jas *York* 77-01; Par Dn 87-94; Assoc Min 94-01; rtd 01; Perm to Offic *York* from 01. *37 Oaklands, Camblesforth, Selby YO8 8HH* Tel (01757) 618148

CUNDILL, David James. b 65. BEng. St Jo Coll Nottm. **d** 05. C Leic Martyrs *Leic* from 05. *Address temp unknown*

✠**CUNDY, The Rt Revd Ian Patrick Martyn.** b 45. Trin Coll Cam BA67 MA71. Tyndale Hall Bris 67. **d** 69 **p** 70 **c** 92. C New Malden and Coombe *S'wark* 69-73; Lect Oak Hill Th Coll 73-77; TR Mortlake w E Sheen *S'wark* 78-83; Warden Cranmer Hall Dur 83-92; Area Bp Lewes *Chich* 92-96; Bp Pet from 96; Asst Bp Ely from 04. *The Palace, Peterborough PE1 1YA* Tel (01733) 562492 Fax 890077 E-mail bishop@peterborough-diocese.org.uk

CUNLIFFE, Anne. b 48. Carl and Blackb Dioc Tr Inst 01. **d** 04 **p** 05. OLM Poulton-le-Sands w Morecambe St Laur *Blackb* from 04. *14 Coniston Road, Morecambe LA4 5PS* Tel (01524) 422509

CUNLIFFE, Christopher John. b 55. Ch Ch Ox BA77 MA81 DPhil81 Trin Coll Cam BA82 MA86 ARHistS94. Westcott Ho Cam 80. **d** 83 **p** 84. C Chesterfield St Mary and All SS *Derby* 83-85; Chapl Linc Coll Ox 85-89; Chapl City Univ and Guildhall Sch of Music and Drama *Lon* 89-91; Voc Officer and Selection Sec ABM 91-97; Dir Professional Min *Lon* 97-03; Chapl to Bp Bradwell *Chelmsf* from 04. *The Glebe House, High Road, Fobbing, Stanford-le-Hope SS17 9JH*

CUNLIFFE, Harold. b 28. St Aid Birkenhead 57. **d** 60 **p** 61. C Hindley All SS *Liv* 60-64; V Everton St Chad w Ch Ch 64-69; R Golborne 70-93; rtd 93; Perm to Offic *Liv* from 93. *51 Greenfields Crescent, Ashton-in-Makerfield, Wigan WN4 8QY* Tel (01942) 202956 E-mail cunliffe@cableinet.co.uk

CUNLIFFE, The Ven Helen Margaret. b 54. St Hilda's Coll Ox BA77 MA78. Westcott Ho Cam 81. **dss** 83 **d** 87 **p** 94. Chesterfield St Mary and All SS *Derby* 83-85; Ox St Mary V w St Cross and St Pet *Ox* 86-89; Par Dn 87-89; Chapl Nuff Coll Ox 86-89; TD Clapham Team *S'wark* 89-94; TV 94-96; Can Res S'wark Cathl 96-03; Chapl Welcare 96-03; Adn St Alb from 03. *6 Sopwell Lane, St Albans AL1 1RR* Tel (01727) 847212 Fax 848311 E-mail archdstalbans@stalbans.anglican.org

CUNLIFFE, Peter Henry. b 54. SRN77 RSCN79 RCNT83 Univ of Wales MA93 Lon Univ DN84. Trin Coll Bris 92. **d** 94 **p** 95. C Carshalton Beeches *S'wark* 94-95; C Reigate St Mary 95-02; P-in-c Hemingford Grey *Ely* 02-04; V from 04; P-in-c Hemingford Abbots from 04. *The Vicarage, 6 Braggs Lane, Hemingford Grey, Huntingdon PE28 9BW* Tel (01480) 394378 E-mail peter.cunliffe@ukonline.co.uk

CUNNINGHAM, Arthur. b 48. Man Univ PhD95. Inst of Chr Tr Dallas DipMin79 Oak Hill Th Coll DipHE87 BA88 Lon Bible Coll MA89 N Ord Course 92. **d** 93 **p** 94. C Walkden Moor *Man* 93; C Walkden Moor w Lt Hulton 93-96; Chapl Salford Coll 93-96; C Camelot Par *B & W* 96-98; Chapl Yeovil Coll 96-97; R Berrow w Pendock, Eldersfield, Hollybush etc *Worc* 98-03; Dioc Warden of Readers and Moderator of Reader Tr 98-03; P-in-c Leigh St Mary *Man* from 03. *The Vicarage, 34 Vicarage Square, Leigh WN7 1YD* Tel (01942) 673546 E-mail artcunningham@compuserve.com

CUNNINGHAM, Brian James. b 65. York Univ BA88. Ripon Coll Cuddesdon BA91. **d** 92 **p** 93. C Merrow *Guildf* 92-96; C Kennington St Jo w St Jas *S'wark* 96-99; Chapl Pangbourne Coll from 99. *Sunbeam, Pangbourne College, Pangbourne, Reading RG8 8LA* Tel 0118-984 2101

CUNNINGHAM, John James. b 50. Belf Coll of Tech ONC70. TCD Div Sch BTh98. **d** 98 **p** 99. C Drumachose *D & R* 98-01; I Camus-juxta-Bann from 01. *19 Dunderg Road, Macosquin, Coleraine BT51 4PN* Tel (028) 7034 3918 E-mail revon50@aol.com

CUNNINGHAM, Philip John. b 52. St Jo Coll Dur BA74 PGCE75 MA85. N Ord Course 93. **d** 95 **p** 96. NSM York St Luke *York* 95-97; NSM York St Olave w St Giles 97-99; TV Haxby w Wigginton 99-02; V Gosforth St Nic *Newc* from 02. *The Vicarage, 17 Rectory Road, Gosforth, Newcastle upon Tyne NE3 1XR* Tel 0191-285 1326
E-mail philipcunningham@hotmail.com

CUNNINGHAM, Richard Martin. b 61. Goldsmiths' Coll Lon BEd84. St Alb and Ox Min Course 95. **d** 98 **p** 99. NSM Kingham w Churchill, Daylesford and Sarsden *Ox* 98-01; NSM Chipping Norton 01-02; NSM Ox St Andr from 01. *Churchill Mill, Sarsden Halt, Churchill, Chipping Norton OX7 6NT* Tel (01608) 659426 Fax 659134
E-mail richard.cunningham@standrewsoxford.org.uk

CUNNINGHAM, Robert Stewart. b 16. **d** 59 **p** 60. C Belfast St Mary *Conn* 59-62; C Belfast All SS 62-63; I Portglenone 63-74; I Belfast Whiterock 74-83; I Sallaghy *Clogh* 83-86; I Monaghan w Tydavnet and Kilmore 86-91; Can Clogh Cathl 88-89; Preb Clogh Cathl 89-91; rtd 91. *19 Edenaveys Crescent, Newry Road, Armagh BT60 1NT* Tel (028) 3752 7868

CUNNINGHAM, Wendy. b 42. St Alb and Ox Min Course 01. **d** 04 **p** 05. NSM Hook Norton w Gt Rollright, Swerford etc *Ox* from 04. *Dewlands, Church End, Great Rollright, Chipping Norton OX7 5RX* Tel (01608) 737135

CUNNINGTON, Andrew Thomas. b 56. Southn Univ BTh86. Sarum & Wells Th Coll 82. **d** 85 **p** 86. C Ifield *Chich* 85-89; TV Haywards Heath St Wilfrid 89-94; V Midhurst from 94; R Woolbeding from 94; RD Midhurst from 03. *The Vicarage, June Lane, Midhurst GU29 9EW* Tel (01730) 813339

CUNNINGTON, Miss Averil. b 41. St Mary's Coll Chelt CertEd61 Man Univ BA68 MEd73. N Ord Course 93. **d** 95 **p** 96. Hd Mistress Counthill Sch Oldham 84-96; NSM Milnrow *Man* 95-98; NSM Hey 98-02; Lic Preacher from 02. *Alston Londes, 629 Huddersfield Road, Lees, Oldham OL4 3PY* Tel 0161-624 9614

CUNNINGTON, Howard James. b 56. Southn Univ BA77 St Jo Coll Dur PGCE78. Trin Coll Bris 90. **d** 92 **p** 93. C Ex St Leon w H Trin *Ex* 92-96; V Sandown Ch Ch and Lower Sandown St Jo *Portsm* 96-04; Perm to Offic from 04. *5 The Mall, Lake Hill, Sandown, Isle of Wight PO36 9ED*
E-mail howard@jcunnington2.freeserve.co.uk

CUPITT, Don. b 34. Trin Hall Cam BA55 MA58 Bris Univ Hon DLitt84. Westcott Ho Cam 57. **d** 59 **p** 60. C Salford St Phil w St Steph *Man* 59-62; Vice-Prin Westcott Ho Cam 62-66; Dean Em Coll Cam 66-91; Asst Lect Div Cam Univ 68-73; Lect 73-96; Lic to Offic *Ely* 63-94; rtd 96; Life Fell Em Coll Cam from 96. *Emmanuel College, Cambridge CB2 3AP* Tel (01223) 334200

CURD, Preb Christine Veronica. b 51. Bris Univ BA. Oak Hill Th Coll 84 WMMTC 88. **d** 89 **p** 94. NSM Widecombe-in-the-Moor, Leusdon, Princetown etc *Ex* 89-93; NSM Bovey Tracey SS Pet, Paul and Thos w Hennock 94-97; Asst Chapl HM Pris Channings Wood 92-02; Chapl HM Pris Ex from 02; Preb Ex Cathl *Ex* from 05. *HM Prison Exeter, New North Road, Exeter EX4 4EX* Tel (01392) 415700 Fax 422647
E-mail christine.curd@hmps.gsi.gov.uk

CURD, Clifford John Letsom. b 45. SRN RNT. Oak Hill Th Coll 84. **d** 86 **p** 87. C Stone Ch Ch *Lich* 86-89; TV Widecombe-in-the-Moor, Leusdon, Princetown etc *Ex* 89-93; P-in-c Ilsington 93-04; rtd 05. *Marsh View, 2 Middlewood, Starcross, Exeter EX6 8RN* Tel (01626) 899188 E-mail cliff-chris@ccurd.freeserve.co.uk

CURL, Roger William. b 50. BA BD DPhil. Oak Hill Th Coll. **d** 82 **p** 83. C Cromer *Nor* 82-86; C Sevenoaks St Nic *Roch* 86-88; V Fulham St Mary N End *Lon* from 88. *St Mary's Vicarage, 2 Edith Road, London W14 9BA* Tel (020) 7602 1996
E-mail stmarys.westken@london.anglican.org

CURNEW, Preb Brian Leslie. b 48. Qu Coll Ox BA69 DPhil77 MA77 DipTh78. Ripon Coll Cuddesdon 77. **d** 79 **p** 80. C Sandhurst *Ox* 79-82; Tutor St Steph Ho Ox 82-87; V Fishponds St Mary *Bris* 87-94; TR Ludlow, Ludford, Ashford Carbonell etc *Heref* from 94; Preb Heref Cathl from 02. *The Rectory, 4 College Street, Ludlow SY8 1AN* Tel (01584) 874988 *or* 872073 Fax 875138 E-mail rector@stlaurences.org.uk

CURNOCK, Canon Karen Susan. b 50. Nottm Univ BTh78. Linc Th Coll 74. **d** 95 **p** 97. NSM Graffoe Gp *Linc* 95-96; Dioc Sec *Sarum* 96-03; NSM Chalke Valley 96-03; V Buckland Newton, Cerne Abbas, Godmanstone etc from 03; Can and Preb Sarum Cathl from 02. *The Vicarage, 4 Back Lane, Cerne Abbas, Dorchester DT2 7LW* Tel (01300) 341251
E-mail curnock@screaming.net

CURNOW, Terence Peter. b 37. Univ of Wales (Lamp) BA62 DipTh63. **d** 63 **p** 64. C Llanishen and Lisvane *Llan* 63-71; Youth Chapl 67-71; Asst Chapl K Coll Taunton 71-74; Chapl Taunton Sch 74-84; Ho Master 84-98; Perm to Offic *B & W* from 84; rtd 02. *19 Stonegallows, Taunton TA1 5JW* Tel (01823) 330003

CURRAH, Michael Ewart. b 31. Down Coll Cam BA54 MA58. Sarum Th Coll 54. **d** 56 **p** 57. C Calne *Sarum* 56-60; V Southbroom 60-69; Perm to Offic 70-88; Asst Master Woodroffe Sch Lyme Regis 71-85; Hon C Taunton H Trin *B & W* 88-96; rtd 96; Perm to Offic *B & W* from 96. *123 South Road, Taunton TA1 3ED* Tel (01823) 284057

CURRAN, John Henry. b 77. Nottm Univ BA00. Wycliffe Hall Ox 00. **d** 02 **p** 03. C W Bridgford *S'well* from 02. *9 Church Drive, West Bridgford, Nottingham NG2 6AY* Tel 0115-878 0434
E-mail curate@stgiles.org.uk

CURRAN, The Ven Patrick Martin Stanley. b 56. K Coll (NS) BA80 Southn Univ BTh84. Chich Th Coll 80. **d** 84 **p** 85. C Heavitree w Ex St Paul *Ex* 84-87; Bp's Chapl to Students *Bradf* 87-93; Chapl Bonn w Cologne *Eur* 93-00; Chapl Vienna from 00; Can Malta Cathl from 00; Adn E Adnry from 02. *The British Embassy, Jauresgasse 12, A-1010 Vienna, Austria* Tel and fax (0043) (1) 714 8900 *or* 718 5902
E-mail office@christchurchvienna.org

CURRAN, Thomas Heinrich. b 49. Toronto Univ BA72 Dalhousie Univ Canada MA75 Hatf Coll Dur PhD91. Atlantic Sch of Th MTS80. **d** 78 **p** 79. Canada 77-81 and from 92; Chapl Hatf Coll Dur 88-92. *Tacoma RPO, Box 28010, Dartmouth NS, Canada, B2W 6E2*

CURRELL, Linda Anne. *See* SCOTT, Mrs Linda Anne

CURRER, Caroline Mary. b 49. Keele Univ BA71 CQSW71 Warwick Univ PhD86. EAMTC 02. **d** 04 **p** 05. NSM Stansted Mountfitchet w Birchanger and Farnham *Chelmsf* from 04. *28 West Road, Saffron Walden CB11 3DS* Tel (01799) 500515
E-mail c.currer@ntlworld.com

CURRIE, Alan Richard. b 58. St Andr Univ MA82 Aber Univ DipEd83. NEOC 97. **d** 00 **p** 01. NSM Haydon Bridge and Beltingham w Henshaw *Newc* 00-05; NSM Warden w Newbrough from 05; NSM St John Lee from 05. *35 Dotland Close, Eastwood Grange, Hexham NE46 1UF* Tel (01434) 607614

CURRIE, John Stuart. b 47. SEITE 94. **d** 97 **p** 98. C S Chatham H Trin *Roch* 97-01; TV from 01. *The Team Vicarage, 18 Marion Close, Walderslade, Chatham ME5 9QA* Tel and fax (01634) 684888 Mobile 07803-283917
E-mail john.currie@blueyonder.co.uk

CURRIE, Stuart William. b 53. Hertf Coll Ox MA79 Fitzw Coll Cam BA85 CertEd. Westcott Ho Cam 82. **d** 85 **p** 86. C Whitley Ch Ch *Ox* 85-89; TV Banbury 89-94; V Barbourne *Worc* from 94. *St Stephen's Vicarage, 1 Beech Avenue, Worcester WR3 8PZ* Tel (01905) 452169 E-mail stuartcurrie@macunlimited.net

CURRIE, Walter. b 39. Tyndale Hall Bris 64. **d** 67 **p** 68. C Cromer *Nor* 67-70; C Macclesfield St Mich *Ches* 70-74; R Postwick *Nor* 74-87; Chapl Jas Paget Hosp Gorleston 87-94; Chapl Jas Paget Hosp NHS Trust Gorleston 94-01; rtd 01; Perm to Offic *Nor* from 01. *11 Langham Green, Blofield, Norwich NR13 4LD* Tel (01603) 713484 E-mail w.and.m.currie@barclays.net

CURRIN, John. b 56. Keele Univ CertEd78 Birm Poly Dip Maths Educn 87. St Jo Coll Nottm Dip Th Studies 92 MA93. **d** 93 **p** 94. C Eastwood *S'well* 93-97; P-in-c Matlock Bath and Cromford *Derby* 97-02; V from 02. *Holy Trinity Vicarage, 8 Derby Road, Matlock DE4 3PU* Tel (01629) 582947

CURRY, Anthony Bruce. b 31. ARCO49 St Edm Hall Ox BA53 MA56. Wells Th Coll 53. **d** 55 **p** 56. C Northfleet *Roch* 55-56; Chapl K Sch Cant 56-61; R Penshurst *Roch* 61-75; Dir Music Kelly Coll Tavistock 75-85; Hon C Calstock *Truro* 75-85; R Brasted *Roch* 85-93; rtd 93. *Monta Rosa, King Street, Gunnislake PL18 9JU* Tel (01822) 834133 Fax as telephone

CURRY, Canon Bruce. b 39. Dur Univ BA61. Wells Th Coll 61. **d** 63 **p** 64. C Shepton Mallet *B & W* 63-67; C Cheam *S'wark* 67-71; R W Walton *Ely* 71-78; V St Neots 78-94; P-in-c Everton w Tetworth 94-98; P-in-c Abbotsley 94-99; P-in-c Waresley 94-99; P-in-c Gt w Lt Gransden 98-99; R Gt Gransden and Abbotsley and Lt Gransden etc 99-04; RD St Neots 90-02; Hon Can Ely Cathl from 98; rtd 04. *10 Ravens Court, Ely CB6 3ED* Tel (01353) 661494 E-mail bruce@jcurry.fsnet.co.uk

CURRY, David John. b 24. St Cath Coll Cam BA48 MA58 DipTh. Oak Hill Th Coll 73. **d** 74 **p** 75. C Watford *St Alb* 74-77; V Whitehall Park St Andr Hornsey Lane *Lon* 77-82; P-in-c Heydon w Lt Chishall *Chelmsf* 82; R Heydon w Gt and Lt Chishill 82-88; rtd 89; Perm to Offic *Chich* from 89. *40 Finches Gardens, Haywards Heath RH16 2PB* Tel (01444) 483670

CURRY, Canon George Christopher. b 14. TCD BA42 MA55 Div Test. **d** 44 **p** 45. I Edenderry *D & R* 57-64; I Edenderry w Clanabogan 64-86; Can Derry Cathl 79-86; rtd 86. *8 Rutherglen Park, Bangor BT19 1DX* Tel (028) 9145 5970

CURRY, George Robert. b 51. JP90. Bede Coll Dur BA72 Newc Univ MA97. Cranmer Hall Dur DipTh74 Oak Hill Th Coll 75. **d** 76 **p** 77. C Denton Holme *Carl* 76-81; V Low Elswick *Newc* from 81; P-in-c High Elswick St Paul from 97. *St Stephen's Vicarage, Clumber Street, Newcastle upon Tyne NE4 7ST* Tel 0191-273 4680 E-mail g.r.curry@btinternet.com

CURRY, James Sebastian. b 63. Hatf Coll Dur BA84. Ripon Coll Cuddesdon BTh93. **d** 93 **p** 94. C Four Oaks *Birm* 93-96; C Erdington St Barn 96-99; TV Jarrow *Dur* from 99. *St Peter's House, York Avenue, Jarrow NE32 5LP* Tel 0191-489 0946

CURRY, Thomas Christopher. b 47. Sarum & Wells Th Coll 71. **d** 74 **p** 75. C Bradford-on-Avon *Sarum* 74-78; Asst Chapl Hurstpierpoint Coll 78-82; P-in-c The Donheads *Sarum* from 82; RD Chalke 87-92. *The Rectory, Donhead St Andrew, Shaftesbury SP7 9DZ* Tel (01747) 828370

CURTIS, Bert. b 20. Lon Univ BCom42 BA46. Ripon Hall Ox. **d** 46 **p** 47. Perm to Offic *Carl* from 74. *Greystones, Embleton, Cockermouth CA13 9YP* Tel (01768) 776503

CURTIS, Colin. b 47. Open Univ BA80 ALA69. St Jo Coll Nottm 83. **d** 93 **p** 94. NSM Clarkston *Glas* from 93. *78 Auldhouse Road, Glasgow G43 1UR* Tel 0141-569 4206 E-mail colinrosemary@curtis83.fsnet.co.uk

CURTIS, Frederick John. b 36. SS Coll Cam MA64. Ridley Hall Cam 77. **d** 79 **p** 80. C Chilvers Coton w Astley *Cov* 79-82; V Claverdon w Preston Bagot 82-87; V Allesley Park and Whoberley 87-98; rtd 98; Perm to Offic *York* from 98. *29A Undercliffe, Pickering YO18 7BB*

CURTIS, Canon Geoffrey John. b 35. Dur Univ BA57. Ripon Hall Ox 59. **d** 61 **p** 62. C Gosport Ch Ch *Portsm* 61-65; C Bedhampton 65-68; Producer Schs Broadcasting Dept BBC Lon 68-75; Dioc Communications Adv *Guildf* 75-00; P-in-c Grayswood 75-91; Dir Grayswood Studio 84-00; Hon Can Guildf Cathl 87-00; rtd 00; Perm to Offic *Guildf* from 00. *1 Clairville, Woodside Road, Chiddingfold, Godalming GU8 4QY* Tel (01428) 685943

CURTIS, Gerald Arthur. b 46. Lon Univ BA69. Sarum & Wells Th Coll 85. **d** 87 **p** 88. C Allington and Maidstone St Pet *Cant* 87-90; TV Gt Grimsby St Mary and St Jas *Linc* 90-95; P-in-c Morton w Hacconby 95-96; R Ringstone in Aveland Gp 96-02; rtd 03. *Le Val, 61560 St Germain de Martigny, France* E-mail gacurt@btinternet.com

CURTIS, Mrs Jacqueline Elaine. b 60. Sarum & Wells Th Coll 87. **d** 90 **p** 94. Par Dn Bridport *Sarum* 90-94; C 94-95; TV Melbury 95-00; TV Maltby *Sheff* 00-02; TR from 02. *The Rectory, 69 Blyth Road, Maltby, Rotherham S66 7LF* Tel (01709) 812684 E-mail j.curtis@dogcollar.org.uk

CURTIS, Mrs Jane Darwent. b 64. Leic Univ BA86. Linc Th Coll BTh93. **d** 93 **p** 94. Par Dn Oadby *Leic* 93-94; C 94-96; Chapl De Montfort Univ 96-03; C Leic H Spirit 96-97; TV 97-03; TV Gilmorton, Peatling Parva, Kimcote etc from 03; Bp's Adv for Women's Min from 04. *The Rectory, Church Lane, Gilmorton, Lutterworth LE17 5LU* Tel (01455) 552119 E-mail jcurtis@leicester.anglican.org

CURTIS, John. See CURTIS, Frederick John

CURTIS, John Durston. b 43. Lich Th Coll 65. **d** 68 **p** 69. C Coseley Ch Ch *Lich* 68-71; C Sedgley All SS 71-74; CF 74-79; P-in-c Newton Valence *Win* 79-82; P-in-c Selborne 79-82; R Newton Valence, Selborne and E Tisted w Colemore 82-87; R Marchwood from 87; AD Lyndhurst from 05. *St John's Vicarage, Vicarage Road, Marchwood, Southampton SO40 4SX* Tel and fax (023) 8086 1496 E-mail john.curtis@care4free.net

CURTIS, Layton Richard. b 61. Leic Univ BSc84 PGCE85. Linc Th Coll BTh93. **d** 93 **p** 94. C Knighton St Mary Magd *Leic* 93-96; C Leic St Phil 96-01; P-in-c Wigston Magna from 01. *The Rectory, Church Lane, Gilmorton, Lutterworth LE17 5LU* Tel (01455) 552119 E-mail rcurtis@leicester.anglican.org

CURTIS, Mrs Marian Ruth. b 54. Nottm Univ BA75 CQSW80. Trin Coll Bris 03. **d** 05. C Blackheath Park St Mich *S'wark* from 05. *St Michael's Church, 1 Pond Road, London SE3 9JL* Tel (020) 8852 1205 Mobile 07761-853000

CURTIS, Peter Bernard. b 35. St Pet Hall Ox BA60 MA64. Westcott Ho Cam 60. **d** 62 **p** 63. C Warsop *S'well* 62-65; Chapl Dur Univ *Dur* 65-69; V Worle *B & W* 69-78; R Crewkerne w Wayford 78-00; rtd 00; Perm to Offic *B & W* from 01. *The Old Farmhouse, 28 Millstream Gardens, Wellington TA21 0AA* Tel (01823) 662638

CURTIS, Ronald Victor. b 47. St Alb and Ox Min Course 98. **d** 01 **p** 02. NSM Shipton-under-Wychwood w Milton, Fifield etc *Ox* 01-05; P-in-c Stourbridge St Thos *Worc* from 05. *St Thomas's Vicarage, 34 South Road, Stourbridge DY8 3YB* Tel (01384) 392401

CURTIS, Thomas John. b 32. Pemb Coll Ox BA55 MA59 Lon Univ BD58. Clifton Th Coll 55. **d** 58 **p** 59. C Wandsworth All SS *S'wark* 58-61; Chile 61-71; R Saxmundham *St E* 71-77; V Cheltenham St Mark *Glouc* 77-84; TR 84-86; V Chipping Norton *Ox* 86-95; rtd 95; Hon Dioc Rep SAMS *St E* 95-01; Perm to Offic *Glouc* and *Worc* from 01. *60 Courtney Close, Tewkesbury GL20 5FB* Tel (01684) 295298 E-mail curtistomjon@aol.com

CURWEN, Canon David. b 38. St Cath Coll Cam BA62. Cuddesdon Coll 62. **d** 64 **p** 65. C Orford St Andr *Liv* 64-67; Ind Chapl *Cant* 67-77 and 83-84; C S'wark Ch Ch *S'wark* 78-83; Ind Chapl *S'wark* 78-83 and 85-88; Dioc Soc Resp Adv *St E* 88-93; Dioc Adv for CME 93-97; R Capel St Mary w Lt and Gt Wenham 97-03; Hon Can St E Cathl 97-03; rtd 03; Perm to Offic *St E* from 03. *41 Cuckfield Avenue, Ipswich IP3 8SA* Tel (01473) 272706

CURZEN, Prof Peter. b 31. MRCOG62 FRCOG70 Lon Univ BSc52 MB, BS55 MD66. Sarum & Wells Th Coll 93. **d** 94 **p** 95. NSM Bemerton *Sarum* 94-98; NSM Wylye and Till Valley 98-00; rtd 01; Perm to Offic *Sarum* from 01. *2 Bishop's Drive, Harnham Wood, Salisbury SP2 8NZ* Tel (01722) 412713

CUTCLIFFE, Neil Robert. b 50. NUU BA72 TCD BA72. **d** 75 **p** 76. C Belfast St Mary *Conn* 75-78; C Lurgan Ch the Redeemer *D & D* 78-80; I Garrison w Slavin and Belleek *Clogh* 80-86; I Mossley *Conn* from 86. *558 Doagh Road, Mossley, Newtownabbey BT36 6TA* Tel (028) 9083 2726 E-mail cutcliffe@rathdune.freeserve.co.uk

CUTHBERT, John. b 52. Edin Univ BSc76 PhD80. Coates Hall Edin BD92. **d** 92 **p** 93. Chapl St Mary's Cathl *Edin* 92-98; C Edin St Mary 92-98; P-in-c Forres *Mor* 98-03; R Arbroath *Bre* from 04; R Auchmithie from 04. *St Mary's Rectory, 2 Springfield Terrace, Arbroath DD11 1EL* Tel (01241) 873392 E-mail john@cuth100.freeserve.co.uk

CUTHBERT, John Hamilton. b 34. Univ of Wales (Lamp) BA59. Coll of Resurr Mirfield 59. **d** 61 **p** 62. C Cov St Pet *Cov* 61-64; Australia 64-69; C Willesden St Andr *Lon* 69-72; C Sheff St Cecilia Parson Cross *Sheff* 72-74; V Lavender Hill Ascension *S'wark* 74-97; rtd 97; Perm to Offic *St Alb* from 97 and *Lon* from 99. *29 The Cloisters, Welwyn Garden City AL8 6DU* Tel (01707) 376748

CUTHBERT, Vernon John. b 66. Trin Coll Bris 02. **d** 04 **p** 05. C Alvaston *Derby* from 04. *The Beehive, 1B Grange Road, Alvaston, Derby DE24 0JW* Tel (01332) 571254

CUTHBERT, Victor. b 46. Dioc OLM tr scheme 98. **d** 01 **p** 02. OLM Surbiton St Matt *S'wark* from 01. *4 St Thomas Close, Surbiton KT6 7TU* Tel (020) 8399 8722

CUTHBERTSON, Mrs Amanda. b 54. ALCM85 LLCM87 K Coll Lon BD92 AKC92 Open Univ PGCE98 Loughb Univ MA00. EAMTC 98. **d** 00 **p** 01. C Northampton St Benedict *Pet* 00-03; V Wellingborough St Mark from 03. *St Mark's Vicarage, Queensway, Wellingborough NN8 3SD* Tel (01933) 673893 E-mail revacuthbertson@talk21.com

CUTHBERTSON, Christopher Martin. b 48. K Coll Lon BD74 AKC74 CertEd75 MTh80. St Aug Coll Cant 75. **d** 76 **p** 77. C Whitstable All SS w St Pet *Cant* 76-79; Chapl Princess Marg R Free Sch Windsor 79-84; Chapl Bp Wordsworth Sch Salisbury 84-01; Perm to Offic *Win* from 84 and *Sarum* from 02. *14 Stephen Martin Gardens, Parsonage Park, Fordingbridge SP6 1RF* Tel (01425) 655865

CUTHBERTSON, Raymond. b 52. AKC75. Coll of Resurr Mirfield 76. **d** 77 **p** 78. C Darlington St Mark w St Paul *Dur* 77-81; C Usworth 81-83; C Darlington St Cuth 83-86; V Shildon w Eldon 86-00; V Shildon 00-04; RD Auckland 94-96; Chapl N Tees and Hartlepool NHS Trust from 04. *Hartlepool General Hospital, Holdforth Road, Hartlepool TS24 9AH* Tel (01429) 266654

CUTLER, Robert Francis. b 37. Lon Univ BSc57. Clifton Th Coll 62. **d** 64 **p** 65. C Peckham St Mary Magd *S'wark* 64-68; C Redhill H Trin 68-70; Travel Sec Inter-Coll Chr Fellowship of IVF 70-74; Hon C Selly Hill St Steph *Birm* 70-74; Interserve Internat Bangladesh 74-93; Internat Fellowship Evang Students 74-85; Bible Students Fellowship of Bangladesh 85-93; V Rochdale Deeplish St Luke *Man* 94-99; TV S Rochdale 00-02; rtd 02; Perm to Offic *St Alb* from 03. *17 Woodlands, Park Street, St Albans AL2 2AD* Tel (01727) 872248 E-mail rfcutler@zetnet.co.uk

CUTLER, Roger Charles. b 49. MInstPkg76. Coll of Resurr Mirfield 86. **d** 88 **p** 89. C Walney Is *Carl* 88-91; Chapl RN 91-98; Perm to Offic *Glas* 91-95; Hon C Challoch w Newton Stewart 95-98; V Gosforth St Nic *Newc* 98-01; P-in-c St John Lee 01-04; R from 05; P-in-c Warden w Newbrough 01-04; V from 05. *St John Lee Rectory, Acomb, Hexham NE46 4PE* Tel (01434) 601024 E-mail cogito@ergo-sum.freeserve.co.uk

CUTMORE, Simon Giles. b 72. Trin Coll Bris BA95 St Jo Coll Dur MA00. Cranmer Hall Dur 97. **d** 99 **p** 00. C Biggleswade *St Alb* 99-03; TV Chambersbury from 03. *The Rectory, 14 Pancake Lane, Laverstock Green, Hemel Hempstead HP2 4NB* Tel and fax (01442) 264860 E-mail simonandalexc@aol.com

CUTT, Canon Samuel Robert. b 25. Selw Coll Cam BA50 MA54. Cuddesdon Coll 51. **d** 53 **p** 54. C W Hartlepool St Aid *Dur* 53-56; Tutor St Boniface Coll Warminster 56-59; Sub Warden 59-65; Tutor Chich Th Coll 65-71; PV Chich Cathl *Chich* 66-71; Min Can St Paul's Cathl *Lon* 71-79; Lect K Coll Lon 73-79; P in O 75-79; Can Res Wells Cathl *B & W* 79-93; Chan 79-85; Treas 85-93; Dir of Ords 79-86; Warden CSD 87-93; rtd 93; Perm to Offic *Pet* from 94. *c/o J C Cutt Esq, 37 Sallows Road, Peterborough PE1 4EX* Tel (01733) 562796

CUTTELL, Jeffrey Charles. b 59. Birm Univ BSc80 PhD83 Sheff Univ MA91. Trin Coll Bris DipHE86. **d** 87 **p** 88. C Normanton *Wakef* 87-91; V 91-95; Producer Relig Progr BBC Radio Stoke 95-97; Presenter Relig Progr BBC 97-99; CF (TA) from 97; R Astbury and Smallwood *Ches* from 99; RD Congleton from 04; Assoc Lect Th Univ of Wales (Cardiff) from 01; Tutor St Mich Coll Llan from 01. *The Rectory, Astbury, Congleton CW12 4RQ* Tel (01260) 272625 Mobile 07941-373578 E-mail rector@astburychurch.org.uk

CUTTER, John Douglas. b 31. Lon Univ BD61. Chich Th Coll 56. **d** 59 **p** 60. C Blyth St Mary *Newc* 59-62; C Rugeley *Lich* 62-65; V Rocester 65-73; V Shrewsbury St Giles 73-83; R Yoxall and Dean's V Lich Cathl 83-91; rtd 91; Perm to Offic *Win* from 91; Hon Chapl Win Cathl from 98. *Little Wykeham, 111 Teg Down Meads, Winchester SO22 5NN* Tel (01962) 852203

CUTTING, Alastair Murray. b 60. Westhill Coll Birm BEd83 Heythrop Coll Lon MA03. St Jo Coll Nottm LTh86 DPS87. **d** 87 **p** 88. C Woodlands *Sheff* 87-88; C Wadsley 89-91; C Uxbridge *Lon* 91-96; Chapl to the Nave and Uxbridge Town Cen 91-96; V Copthorne *Chich* from 96. *St John's Vicarage, Copthorne, Crawley RH10 3RD* Tel (01342) 712063 E-mail acutting@mac.com

CUTTS, Canon David. b 52. Van Mildert Coll Dur BSc73. St Jo Coll Nottm BA79. **d** 80 **p** 81. C Ipswich St Matt *St E* 80-82; Bp's Dom Chapl 82-85; R Coddenham w Gosbeck and Hemingstone w Henley 85-94; RD Bosmere 92-94; V Ipswich St Marg from 94; RD Ipswich 96-01; Hon Can St E Cathl from 00. *St Margaret's Vicarage, 32 Constable Road, Ipswich IP4 2UW* Tel (01473) 253906 Fax 413348 Mobile 07711-370702 E-mail cutts.family@tesco.net

CUTTS, Elizabeth Joan Gabrielle. *See* STRICKLAND, Mrs Elizabeth Joan Gabrielle

CUTTS, Nigel Leonard. b 57. Sheff Univ BA86 BTh. Linc Th Coll 83. **d** 87 **p** 88. C Old Brampton and Loundsley Green *Derby* 87-89; C Chesterfield St Mary and All SS 89-91; V Morecambe St Barn *Blackb* 91-99; V Colwyn *St As* 99-03; rtd 03. *2 Cwm Road, Dyserth, Rhyl LL18 6BB* Tel (01745) 571496

CYPRUS AND THE GULF, Bishop of. *See* HANDFORD, The Most Revd George Clive

CYSTER, Canon Raymond Frederick. b 13. CCC Ox BA35 MA40. Wycliffe Hall Ox 40. **d** 42 **p** 43. C Ipswich St Jo *St E* 42-45; Chapl Norwich Tr Coll 45-64; R Fenny Compton and Wormleighton *Cov* 64-76; Hon Can Cov Cathl 74-80; P-in-c Hampton Lucy w Charlecote 76-79; R Hampton Lucy w Charlecote and Loxley 79-80; rtd 80; Perm to Offic *Cov* from 80. *47 Cherry Orchard, Stratford-upon-Avon CV37 9AP* Tel (01789) 295012

CZERNIAWSKA EDGCUMBE, Mrs Irena Christine. b 59. Trin Coll Ox BA82. Oak Hill Th Coll 93. **d** 95 **p** 96. NSM De Beauvoir Town St Pet *Lon* 95-99; Chapl Raines Foundn Sch Tower Hamlets 99-04; NSM Bow Common 00-04; P-in-c Hoxton St Anne w St Columba from 04; Min Development Adv (Stepney Area) from 04. *St Anne's Vicarage, 37 Hemsworth Street, London N1 5LF* Tel (020) 7729 1243 E-mail irenaczerniawskaedgcumbe@hotmail.com

D

DABORN, Mark. **d** 05. NSM Cleobury Mortimer w Hopton Wafers etc *Heref* from 05. *Moffats School, Kinlet Hall, Kinlet, Bewdley DY12 3AY* Tel (01299) 841230 Fax 841444 E-mail mhd@moffats.co.uk

DABORN, Robert Francis. b 53. Keble Coll Ox BA74 MA78 Fitzw Coll Cam BA77. Ridley Hall Cam 75. **d** 78 **p** 79. C Mortlake w E Sheen *S'wark* 78-81; Chapl Collingwood and Grey Coll *Dur* 82-86; V Lapley w Wheaton Aston *Lich* 86-91; P-in-c Blymhill w Weston-under-Lizard 89-91; P-in-c Tibberton w Bolas Magna and Waters Upton 91-99; Shropshire Local Min Adv 91-99; P-in-c Childs Ercall and Stoke upon Tern 92-95; Dir Local Min Development 99-05; Dir Past Studies WEMTC *Heref* from 05. *The Vicarage, Orleton, Ludlow SY8 4HN* Tel (01568) 780881 E-mail harbinger@cix.co.uk *or* rob.daborn@lichfield.anglican.org

DACK, Miss Margaret Patricia. b 39. Offley Teacher Tr Coll TCert61. Oak Hill NSM Course 91. **d** 93 **p** 94. NSM Letchworth St Paul w Willian *St Alb* from 93. *91 Penn Way, Letchworth Garden City SG6 2SH* Tel (01462) 634956 E-mail mdack@fish.co.uk

DACK, Paul Marven. K Coll Lon AKC51 BD51. St Boniface Warminster. **d** 52 **p** 53. C Leckhampton St Pet *Glouc* 52-55; R Bourton on the Hill 55-61; R Quedgeley 61-82; P-in-c Hasfield w Tirley and Ashleworth 82-90; rtd 90; Perm to Offic *Glouc* 90-96; and from 01. *19 Arle Gardens, Cheltenham GL51 8HP* Tel (01242) 261627

DADD, Alan Edward. b 50. St Jo Coll Nottm 77. **d** 78 **p** 79. C Bishopsworth *Bris* 78-81; V Springfield *Birm* 81-85; Chapl Poly Cen Lon 85-86; V Hanger Lane St Ann 86-93; rtd 93. *124 Chelsfield Lane, Orpington BR5 4PZ* Tel (01689) 570558

DADD, Canon Peter Wallace. b 38. Sheff Univ BA59. Qu Coll Birm 59. **d** 61 **p** 62. C Grays Thurrock *Chelmsf* 61-65; C Grantham St Wulfram *Linc* 65-70; C Grantham w Manthorpe 70-72; TV 72-73; V Haxey 73-90; RD Is of Axholme 82-90; V Gainsborough All SS 90-98; Can and Preb Linc Cathl from 91; P-in-c Flixborough w Burton upon Stather 98-00; V from 00. *The Vicarage, 12 Darby Road, Burton-upon-Stather, Scunthorpe DN15 9DZ* Tel (01724) 720276 E-mail peterdadd@tiscali.co.uk

DADSON, Lawrence Michael (Mike). b 29. G&C Coll Cam MA56 Lon Univ BSc(Econ)64. St Deiniol's Hawarden 80. **d** 92 **p** 92. NSM Bramhall *Ches* 92-95; Perm to Offic from 97. *14 Yew Tree Park Road, Cheadle Hulme, Cheadle SK8 7EP* Tel 0161-485 2482

DADSWELL, David Ian. b 58. New Coll Ox BA80 MA83 Brunel Univ MPhil97. Westcott Ho Cam 80. **d** 83 **p** 84. C W Derby St Mary *Liv* 83-87; Chapl Brunel Univ *Lon* 87-96; Perm to Offic *Lon* from 96 and *Ox* 98-04; Hon C New Windsor *Ox* from 04. *243 St Leonards Road, Windsor SL4 3DR* Tel (01753) 864827 Fax (01895) 2707701 E-mail david.dadswell@dial.pipex.com

DADSWELL, The Ven Richard Edward. b 46. CITC BTh98. **d** 98 **p** 99. C Cork St Fin Barre's Union *C, C & R* 98-01; Min Can Cork Cathl 00-01; I Ballisodare w Collooney and Emlaghfad *T, K & A* from 01; Dioc Dir of Ords from 03; Adn Killala and Achonry from 05. *The Rectory, Ballisodare, Co Sligo, Irish Republic* Tel (00353) (71) 913 0865 E-mail archdeacon@killala.anglican.org

DAFFERN, Canon Adrian Mark. b 68. St Jo Coll Dur BA89 FRCO98 FRSA99. St Steph Ho Ox 90. **d** 92 **p** 93. C Lich St Chad *Lich* 92-95; TV Stafford 95-00; V Walsall Wood 00-03; Treas V Lich Cathl 97-03; Can Res and Prec Cov Cathl *Cov* from 03. *22 Radcliffe Road, Coventry CV5 6AA* Tel (024) 7622 7597 E-mail precentor@coventrycathedral.org.uk

DAFFURN, Lionel William. b 19. DFC43. AKC49. **d** 50 **p** 51. C Rugby St Andr *Cov* 50-53; V Cov St Thos 53-57; R Brampton St Thos *Derby* 57-74; P-in-c Hindon w Chicklade w Pertwood *Sarum* 74-76; R E Knoyle, Hindon w Chicklade and Pertwood 76-84; rtd 84; Perm to Offic *Cov* from 84. *Bankside, 9 Quineys Road, Stratford-upon-Avon CV37 9BW* Tel (01789) 292703

DAGGETT, Michael Wayne. b 47. Portland State Univ BSc72. Ridley Hall Cam 84. **d** 86 **p** 87. C Tyldesley w Shakerley *Man* 86-90; V Swinton H Rood 90-02; Chapl Eccles Sixth Form Coll 90-02; rtd 02. *138 Elliott Street, Tyldesley, Manchester M29 8FJ* Tel (01942) 883437

DAGLEISH, John. b 38. Goldsmiths' Coll Lon MA01 ACIB74. S'wark Ord Course 75. **d** 78 **p** 79. NSM Riddlesdown *S'wark* 78-99; NSM All Hallows by the Tower etc *Lon* 79-89; Chapl Asst Guy's Hosp Lon 87-89. *42 Brancaster Lane, Purley CR8 1HF* Tel and fax (020) 8660 6060

DAGLISH, John David. b 44. RMCS BSc70. Cranmer Hall Dur 74. **d** 77 **p** 78. C Ormesby *York* 77-79; C Kirk Ella 79-82; V Hull St Cuth 82-97; NSM Beverley St Mary 00-01; P-in-c Thorpe Edge *Bradf* 01-05; V Gt Marsden w Nelson St Phil *Blackb* from 05. *St Philip's Vicarage, 1 Victory Close, Nelson BB9 9ED* Tel (01282) 697011 E-mail john@jdaglish.fsnet.co.uk

DAGNALL, Canon Bernard. b 44. K Coll Lon BSc65 AKC65 Ox Univ BA75 MA78 CChem MRSC MSOSc88. St Steph Ho Ox 72. **d** 75 **p** 76. C Stanningley St Thos *Ripon* 75-76; C Lightbowne *Man* 76-78; C-in-c Grahame Park St Aug CD *Lon* 78-84; V Earley St Nic *Ox* 84-91; Ind Chapl 85-91; TR N Huddersfield *Wakef* 91-93; TV Newbury *Ox* from 93; Chapl W Berks Priority Care Services NHS Trust 93-01; Chapl Newbury and Community Primary Care Trust from 01; Hon Can Ho Ghana from 04. *The Vicarage, 1 Chesterfield Road, Newbury RG14 7QB* Tel (01635) 230216 Fax 230215 E-mail dagnall@boltblue.com *or* frbernard@saintjohn.co.uk

DAILEY, Arthur John Hugh. b 25. Lon Univ BScEng45. Clifton Th Coll 63. **d** 65 **p** 66. C Wandsworth All SS *S'wark* 65-70; V Frogmore *St Alb* 70-81; RD Aldenham 75-79; C St Alb St Paul 82-90; rtd 90; Perm to Offic *St Alb* from 90. *24 Clifton Street, St Albans AL1 3RY* Tel (01727) 850639

DAILEY, Douglas Grant. b 56. Nottm Univ BTh88. Linc Th Coll 85. **d** 88 **p** 89. C Leominster *Heref* 88-91; USA from 91. *PO Box 1103, Statesville, NC 28677, USA* E-mail trinity@vnet.net

DAIMOND, John Ellerbeck. b 39. St Cuth Soc Dur BA61. Ripon Hall Ox 61. **d** 63 **p** 64. C Caverswall *Lich* 63-66; Chapl RAF 66-85; Asst Chapl-in-Chief RAF 85-91; QHC 89-91; V Shawbury *Lich* 91-95; R Moreton Corbet 91-95; V Stanton on Hine Heath 91-95; rtd 99; P-in-c Pattingham w Patshull *Lich* from 02. *The Vicarage, 20 Dartmouth Avenue, Pattingham, Wolverhampton WV6 7DP* Tel (01902) 700257 Fax as telephone

DAINTREE, Canon Geoffrey Thomas. b 54. Bris Univ BSc77. Trin Coll Bris 78. **d** 81 **p** 82. C Old Hill H Trin *Worc* 81-85; C Tunbridge Wells St Jo *Roch* 85-89; V Framfield *Chich* 89-00; RD Uckfield 96-00; Hon Can Cyangugu (Rwanda) from 97; V Eastbourne St Jo *Chich* from 00. *St John's Vicarage, 9 Buxton Road, Eastbourne BN20 7LL* Tel (01323) 721105 Fax as telephone E-mail gdaintree@aol.com

DAINTY, James Ernest. b 46. Open Univ BA86 Liv Univ MA01 Lon Univ DipTh68 Lon Bible Coll ALBC68. Cranmer Hall Dur 71. **d** 73 **p** 74. C Normanton *Wakef* 73-76; C Gillingham St Mark *Roch* 76-78; V Barnsley St Geo *Wakef* 78-88; Chapl Barnsley Distr Gen Hosp 78-88; Chapl Seacroft Hosp Leeds 88-94; Chapl Killingbeck and Meanwood Park Hosps Leeds

88-94; P-in-c Turnham Green Ch Ch *Lon* 94-97; V from 97. *The Vicarage, 2 Wellesley Road, London W4 4BL* Tel (020) 8994 1617 Fax 0870-168 0680 E-mail jimdainty@dunelm.org.uk

DAKIN (née HOLLETT), Mrs Catherine Elaine. b 53. Qu Eliz Coll Lon BSc74. St Jo Coll Nottm DipTh90. **d** 90. Par Dn Horley *S'wark* 90-93; NSM Heydon, Gt and Lt Chishill, Chrishall etc *Chelmsf* 93-97; NSM Gt and Lt Maplestead w Gestingthorpe 97-99; NSM Knights and Hospitallers Par 99-01; NSM Fulford w Hilderstone *Lich* from 01. *20 Tudor Hollow, Fulford, Stoke-on-Trent ST11 9NP* Tel (01782) 397073

DAKIN, Peter David. b 57. Wye Coll Lon BSc79. St Jo Coll Nottm 91. **d** 91 **p** 92. NSM Southgate *Chich* 91-93; C Heydon, Gt and Lt Chishill, Chrishall etc *Chelmsf* 93-97; P-in-c Gt and Lt Maplestead w Gestingthorpe 97-99; P-in-c Pebmarsh 99; V Knights and Hospitallers Par 99-01; P-in-c Fulford w Hilderstone *Lich* from 01; Rural Officer for Staffs from 01. *20 Tudor Hollow, Fulford, Stoke-on-Trent ST11 9NP* Tel (01782) 397073 Fax (01780) 761764 E-mail pdakin@waitrose.com

DAKIN, Reginald James Blanchard. b 25. S'wark Ord Course 66. **d** 70 **p** 71. C Preston Ascension *Lon* 70-74; C Greenhill St Jo 74-76; P-in-c Littleton 76-80; R 80-95; CF (ACF) 78-95; Warden for Readers (Kensington Episc Area) 88-95; rtd 95; Perm to Offic *Nor* 95-00 and from 01; Chapl Malta 97-99. *22 Heywood Avenue, Diss IP22 4DN* Tel (01379) 641167

DAKIN, Mrs Sally. b 58. SRN79 SCM82 RHV85 K Coll Lon MSc89 TCert92. St Alb and Ox Min Course 02. **d** 04 **p** 05. NSM Ruscombe and Twyford *Ox* from 04. *3 Highgrove Place, Ruscombe, Reading RG10 9LF* Tel 0118-934 3909 E-mail timsal@tinyworld.co.uk

DAKIN, Canon Stanley Frederick. b 30. CA52. Roch Th Coll 63. **d** 65 **p** 66. C Meole Brace *Lich* 65-68; V 68-72; R Sutton 68-72; Hosp Chapl Nairobi Kenya 72-75; P-in-c Nettlebed *Ox* 75-81; P-in-c Bix w Pishill 77-81; P-in-c Highmore 78-81; R Nettlebed w Bix and Highmore 81; V Ealing Dean St Jo *Lon* 81-84; V W Ealing St Jo w St Jas 84-92; Hon Can Mombasa from 89; Gen Sec CA Africa from 92; rtd 99; Perm to Offic *Lich* 99-02; *Ox* from 02. *71 Rectory Crescent, Middle Barton, Chipping Norton OX7 7BP* Tel (01869) 349983

DAKIN, Canon Timothy John. b 58. SS Mark & Jo Coll Plymouth BA86 K Coll Lon MTh87. **d** 93 **p** 94. Prin Carlile Coll Kenya 93-00; C Nairobi Cathl 94-00; Gen Sec CMS from 00; Hon C Ruscombe and Twyford *Ox* from 00; Can Th Cov Cathl *Cov* from 01. *3 Highgrove Place, Ruscombe, Reading RG10 9LF* Tel and fax 0118-934 3909 E-mail timsal@tinyworld.co.uk

DALAIS, Duncan John. b 56. St Paul's Coll Grahamstown. **d** 83 **p** 84. C Pinetown St Jo B S Africa 83-87; C Chingford SS Pet and Paul *Chelmsf* 87-92; V Aldersbrook 92-02; P-in-c Leytonstone St Andr from 02; Asst Chapl Forest Healthcare NHS Trust Lon from 02. *St Andrew's Vicarage, 7 Forest Glade, London E11 1LU* Tel (020) 8989 0942 *or* 8520 6328 Mobile 07714-760068 E-mail duncan.dalais@virgin.net

DALBY, The Ven John Mark Meredith. b 38. Ex Coll Ox BA61 MA65 Nottm Univ PhD77. Ripon Hall Ox 61. **d** 63 **p** 64. C Hambleden *Ox* 63-68; C Medmenham 66-68; V Birm St Pet *Birm* 68-75; RD Birm City 73-75; Hon C Tottenham All Hallows *Lon* 75-80; Selection Sec and Sec Cttee for Th Educn ACCM 75-80; V Worsley *Man* 80-84; TR 84-91; AD Eccles 87-91; Adn Rochdale 91-00; rtd 00; Chapl Beauchamp Community from 00. *The Chaplain's House, The Beauchamp Community, Newland, Malvern WR13 5AX* Tel and fax (01684) 899198 E-mail markdalby@dalbyj.fsnet.co.uk

DALE, Miss Barbara. b 48. Cranmer Hall Dur 78. **dss** 81 **d** 87 **p** 94. N Wingfield, Pilsley and Tupton *Derby* 81-90; Par Dn 87-90; Par Dn N Wingfield, Clay Cross and Pilsley 90-94; TV 94-00; C Eckington and Ridgeway 00-04; TV E Scarsdale from 04. *The Vicarage, Main Street, Shirebrook, Mansfield NG20 8DN* Tel (01623) 740479

DALE, Charles William. b 49. **d** 02 **p** 03. OLM Uttoxeter Area *Lich* from 02. *Manor Court, Kingstone, Uttoxeter ST14 8QH* Tel (01889) 500428 E-mail charles.dale@tesco.net

DALE, Ms Christine. b 62. Ox Poly DipCart82. Trin Coll Bris BA94. **d** 94 **p** 95. C Thatcham *Ox* 94-98; TV Bracknell 98-02; R E Woodhay and Woolton Hill *Win* from 02. *The Rectory, The Mount, Highclere, Newbury RG20 9QZ* Tel (01635) 253323

DALE, Eric Stephen. b 24. Roch Th Coll 63. **d** 65 **p** 66. C Kippax *Ripon* 65-67; C Fulford *York* 67-69; V Askham Bryan 69-70; V Askham Richard 69-70; V Askham Bryan w Askham Richard 70-78; Chapl HM Pris Askham Grange 69-78; Chapl HM Pris Wakef 78-79; Chapl HM Pris Gartree 79-82; Chapl HM Pris Leeds 82-89; rtd 89; Perm to Offic *Ripon* from 03. *31 Kirkwood Lane, Leeds LS16 7EN* Tel 0113-230 0766

DALE, John Anthony. b 42. Open Univ BSc00. Qu Coll Birm 72. **d** 75 **p** 76. C Elmley Castle w Bricklehampton and Combertons *Worc* 75-81; P-in-c 81-83; R 83-88; Hon Can Worc Cathl 87-92; V Hallow 88-92; Dioc Registrar 92; P-in-c Michaelston-y-Fedw *Mon* from 03. *The Rectory, Michaelston-y-Fedw, Cardiff CF3 9XS* Tel (01633) 680414

DALE, Martin Nicholas. b 55. Chelsea Coll Lon BSc76 CPA83. Wycliffe Hall Ox 99. **d** 01 **p** 02. C Stiffkey and Cockthorpe w Morston, Langham etc *Nor* 01-03; C Stiffkey and Bale 03-04; P-in-c New Romney w Old Romney and Midley *Cant* from 04; P-in-c St Mary's Bay w St Mary-in-the-Marsh etc from 04; P-in-c Dymchurch w Burmarsh and Newchurch from 05. *The Vicarage, North Street, New Romney TN28 8DR* Tel (01797) 362308 E-mail mndale@aol.com

DALE, Miss Olive Sylvia. b 44. Stockwell Coll of Educn TCert66. Faculté de Théologie Évangélique Vaux-sur-Seine France MScRel76 WMMTC 91. **d** 94 **p** 97. C Highley *Heref* 94-96; C Leominster 96-98; Chapl Asst Linc and Louth NHS Trust 98-00; rtd 00; Perm to Offic *Heref* from 00. *c/o Miss V M Dale, 228 Whittern Way, Hereford HR1 1QP* Tel (01432) 352406

DALES, Douglas John. b 52. FRHistS90 Ch Ch Ox BA74 MA78 BD89. Cuddesdon Coll 74. **d** 77 **p** 78. C Shepperton *Lon* 77-81; C Ely 81-83; Chapl Marlborough Coll from 84; Hd of RE from 84. *Hillside, Bath Road, Marlborough SN8 1NN* Tel (01672) 514557

DALEY, David Michael. b 50. Oak Hill Th Coll BA90. **d** 92 **p** 92. C Enfield Ch Ch Trent Park *Lon* 92-94; V Chitts Hill St Cuth from 94. *St Cuthbert's Vicarage, 85 Wolves Lane, London N22 5JD* Tel (020) 8888 6178 E-mail ddaley@ukonline.co.uk *or* st.cuthbert@ukonline.co.uk

DALEY, Judith. b 54. Sheff Univ BA94 Leeds Univ PhD03. N Ord Course 03. **d** 04 **p** 05. NSM Sheff St Leon Norwood *Sheff* from 04; Chapl Sheff Teaching Hosps NHS Trust from 02. *112 Broad Inge Crescent, Chapeltown, Sheffield S35 1RU* Tel 0114-246 8824 E-mail judith.daley@sth.nhs.uk

DALEY, Preb Victor Leonard. b 38. Chich Th Coll 76. **d** 78 **p** 79. C Durrington *Chich* 78-81; C Somerton w Compton Dundon, the Charltons etc *B & W* 81-87; P-in-c Cheddar 87-88; V from 88; P-in-c Rodney Stoke w Draycott 02-03; RD Axbridge 91-03; Preb Wells Cathl from 97. *The Vicarage, Church Street, Cheddar BS27 3RF* Tel (01934) 742535 Fax as telephone E-mail victor@daley4395.freeserve.co.uk

DALLAWAY, Philip Alan. b 48. Chich Th Coll 80. **d** 81 **p** 82. C Newbury *Ox* 81-83; C Newport Pagnell w Lathbury 83-85; V Stewkley w Soulbury and Drayton Parslow 85-92; P-in-c Didcot All SS 92-97; R 97-00; V Caversham St Jo from 00. *The Vicarage, St John's Road, Caversham, Reading RG4 5AN* Tel 0118-947 1814

DALLING, Roger Charles. b 26. Lon Univ BSc53 DChemEng55. S Dios Minl Tr Scheme 79. **d** 83 **p** 84. NSM Lewes St Jo sub Castro *Chich* 83-84; NSM Uckfield 84-98; NSM Isfield 84-98; NSM Lt Horsted 84-98; rtd 98; Perm to Offic *Chich* from 98. *1 Avis Close, Denton, Newhaven BN9 0DN* Tel (01273) 515970

DALLISTON, The Very Revd Christopher Charles. b 56. Ox Univ BA Cam Univ MA. St Steph Ho Ox 81. **d** 84 **p** 85. C Halstead St Andr w H Trin and Greenstead Green *Chelmsf* 84-87; Bp's Dom Chapl 87-91; V Forest Gate St Edm 91-95; P-in-c Boston *Linc* 95-97; V 97-03; RD Holland E 97-03; Dean Newc from 03. *The Cathedral Vicarage, 26 Mitchell Avenue, Jesmond, Newcastle upon Tyne NE2 3LA* Tel 0191-281 6554 *or* 232 1939 Fax 230 0735 E-mail ccd@fish.co.uk *or* stnicholas@aol.com

DALLOW, Gillian Margaret. b 45. Univ of Wales (Ban) BA66 DipEd67 Bris Univ MEd87 Univ Coll of SW CertMS88. Oak Hill Th Coll 93. **d** 96 **p** 97. NSM W Ealing St Jo w St Jas *Lon* 96-99; P-in-c Barlestone *Leic* from 99; Dioc Children's Min Adv from 99. *The New Vicarage, 22 Bosworth Road, Barlestone, Nuneaton CV13 0EL* Tel (01455) 290249 Mobile 07801-650187 Fax 242450 E-mail gdallow@leicester.anglican.org

DALLY, Keith Richard. b 47. FCCA77. St Jo Coll Nottm 80. **d** 82 **p** 83. C Southend St Sav Westcliff *Chelmsf* 82-85; Ind Chapl 85-93; C Southend 85-86; TV 86-92; C Harold Hill St Geo 92-93; Cen Co-ord Langham Place All So Clubhouse *Lon* 97-02; Perm to Offic *Ox* from 02. *172 Grasmere Way, Leighton Buzzard LU7 2QJ* Tel (01525) 378668

DALRIADA, Archdeacon of. *See* ROOKE, The Ven Patrick William

DALTON, Anthony Isaac. b 57. Em Coll Cam BA78 MA82 Leeds Univ BA82. Coll of Resurr Mirfield. **d** 82 **p** 83. C Carl St Aid and Ch Ch *Carl* 82-86; C Caversham St Pet and Mapledurham etc *Ox* 86-88; P-in-c Accrington St Mary *Blackb* 88-91; V 91-92; Chapl Victoria Hosp Accrington 88-92; V Sheff St Cecilia Parson Cross *Sheff* 92-96; P-in-c Burnley St Cath w St Alb and St Paul *Blackb* 96-98; V 98-01; R Orton and Tebay w Ravenstonedale etc *Carl* from 01. *The Vicarage, Orton, Penrith CA10 3RQ* Tel (01539) 624532 E-mail tony@dalton01.globalnet.co.uk

DALTON, Bertram Jeremy (Tod). b 32. ACIB64. Sarum & Wells Th Coll 81. **d** 83 **p** 84. C Ringwood *Win* 83-86; R Norton sub Hamdon, W Chinnock, Chiselborough etc *B & W* 86-97; rtd 97; Perm to Offic *B & W* from 97. *Meadow Cottage, 8 Woodbarton, Milverton, Taunton TA4 1LU* Tel (01823) 400302

DALTON, Derek. b 40. N Ord Course. **d** 84 **p** 85. NSM Pool w Arthington *Ripon* 84-87; P-in-c Thornton Watlass w Thornton Steward 87-90; C Bedale 87-90; R Wensley 90-95; V W Witton 90-95; R Romaldkirk w Laithkirk 95-97; rtd 97; Perm to Offic *Ripon* from 98. *North Wing, Thornton Watlass Hall, Ripon HG4 4AS* Tel (01677) 425302

DALTON, Kevin. b 32. TCD BA65. Ch Div Sch of the Pacific (USA) BD67 CITC 66. **d** 66 **p** 67. C Stillorgan *D & G* 66-72; I Dublin Drumcondra w N Strand 72-79; I Monkstown from 79. *62 Monkstown Road, Monkstown, Blackrock, Co Dublin, Irish Republic* Tel and fax (00353) (1) 280 6596 Mobile 87-663 3232 E-mail monkstown@dublin.anglican.org

DALTON, Tod. *See* DALTON, Bertram Jeremy

DALTRY, Paul Richard. b 56. St Jo Coll Nottm 90. **d** 92 **p** 93. C Ipswich St Matt *St E* 92-96; P-in-c Needham Market w Badley 96-05; RD Bosmere 01-05; R Ipswich St Helen, H Trin, and St Luke from 05. *The Rectory, 42 Clapgate Lane, Ipswich IP3 0RD* Tel (01473) 723467 E-mail paul@daltrys.freeserve.co.uk

DALY, Ms Bernadette Theresa. b 45. TCD BTh94. **d** 97 **p** 98. C Taney *D & G* 97-00 and from 05; Dir Past Studies CITC 00-04. *Church Lodge, 21 Taney Road, Dundrum, Dublin 14, Irish Republic* Tel (00353) (1) 295 1895 *or* 298 5491

DALY, Jeffrey. b 50. Bris Univ BA73 Jes Coll Cam PGCE74 Fitzw Coll Cam BA82 MA86 Westmr Coll Ox MTh03. Ridley Hall Cam 80. **d** 83 **p** 84. C Tilehurst St Mich *Ox* 83-89; P-in-c Steventon w Milton 89-92; Asst Chapl Sherborne Sch 92-96; Chapl St Pet Sch York from 96. *St Peter's School, Clifton, York YO30 6AB* Tel (01904) 623213 ext 412 E-mail j.daly@st-peters.york.sch.uk

DALY, Martin Jonathan. b 48. Woolwich Poly BSc69. **d** 05. NSM Upton (Overchurch) *Ches* from 05. *1 Columbia Road, Prenton CH43 6TU* Tel 0151-670 1461 Mobile 07710-242241 E-mail m.daly3@ntlworld.com

DAMIAN, Brother. *See* KIRKPATRICK, Roger James

DANCE, Peter Patrick. b 31. Em Coll Saskatoon 66. **d** 69 **p** 69. Canada 69-71; C Hednesford *Lich* 71-75; P-in-c Westcote Barton and Steeple Barton *Ox* 76-77; P-in-c Sandford St Martin 76-77; R Westcote Barton w Steeple Barton, Duns Tew etc 77-89; R Castle Douglas *Glas* 89-97; rtd 97. *Mannville, High Street, Adderbury, Banbury OX17 3NA* Tel (01295) 811989

DAND, Mrs Angela Jane. b 49. St Andr Univ BSc70 Newc Univ PGCE71. LNSM course 95. **d** 98 **p** 99. OLM Astley *Man* from 98. *20 Acresfield, Astley, Tyldesley, Manchester M29 7NL* Tel (01942) 879608

DANDO, Ms Elaine Vera. b 53. Coll of Resurr Mirfield 94 N Ord Course 98. **d** 00 **p** 01. C Luddenden w Luddenden Foot *Wakef* 00-03; C Halifax 03-04; Lic to Offic 04-05; Chapl Univ Coll *Lon* from 05; C St Pancras w St Jas and Ch Ch from 05. *St Lawrence's Vicarage, 2 Bridle Road, Pinner HA5 2SJ* Tel (020) 8866 1263 E-mail evd.macrina@btinternet.com

DANDO, Stephen. b 49. Goldsmiths' Coll Lon TCert70. Coll of Resurr Mirfield 81. **d** 83 **p** 84. C Wandsworth St Anne *S'wark* 83-87; V Stainland *Wakef* 87-99; V Illingworth 99-05; V Eastcote St Lawr *Lon* from 05. *St Lawrence's Vicarage, 2 Bridle Road, Pinner HA5 2SJ* Tel (020) 8866 1263 E-mail dandostephen@hotmail.com

DANES, Charles William. b 28. Chich Th Coll 54. **d** 56 **p** 57. C N Greenford All Hallows *Lon* 56-59; C Caversham *Ox* 59-63; V Walsgrave on Sowe *Cov* 63-65; P-in-c Hanworth All SS *Lon* 65-67; V 68-76; P-in-c Wick *Chich* 76-78; V Littlehampton St Jas 76-78; P-in-c Littlehampton St Mary 76-78; V W Worthing St Jo 78-87; Chapl Monte Carlo *Eur* 87-93; rtd 93; Perm to Offic *Chelmsf* and *Eur* from 93. *31 Oakley Road, Braintree CM7 5QS* Tel (01376) 324586

DANGERFIELD, Andrew Keith. b 63. Univ of Wales (Ban) BD87. St Steph Ho Ox 87. **d** 89 **p** 90. C St Marychurch *Ex* 89-93; C-in-c Grahame Park St Aug CD *Lon* 93-96; V Tottenham St Paul from 96; P-in-c Edmonton St Mary w St Jo 98-04; AD E Haringey 00-05. *St Paul's Vicarage, 60 Park Lane, London N17 0JR* Tel (020) 8808 7297 Fax 8376 0446 Mobile 07767-687954 E-mail danger@stpaulstottenham.org.uk

DANIEL, Arthur Guy St John. b 12. K Coll Cam BA33 MA37. Cuddesdon Coll 34. **d** 35 **p** 36. C Blandford Forum *Sarum* 35-38; C Reading St Giles *Ox* 38-40; C Gt Marlow 40-46; V Colnbrook 46-78; TV Riverside 78-80; rtd 80; Perm to Offic *Ox* 80-87. *2 Gervis Court, Penwerris Avenue, Osterley TW7 4QU* Tel (020) 8572 1848

DANIEL, Mrs Gaynor Elizabeth. b 46. NNEB65. Llan Ord Course 98. **d** 98 **p** 99. NSM St Brides Minor w Bettws *Llan* 98-01; C 01-02; C St Brides Minor w Bettws w Aberkenfig 02-04; C Llansantffraid, Bettws and Aberkenfig from 04. *5 Coronation Street, Bryn, Port Talbot SA13 2SE* Tel (01639) 891871

DANIEL, Canon Herrick Haynes. b 38. Open Univ BA81. Trin Coll Bris 73. **d** 75 **p** 76. C Harlesden St Mark *Lon* 75-78; C Livesey *Blackb* 78-81; V Blackb St Barn from 81; Hon Can Blackb Cathl from 98. *St Barnabas' Vicarage, 20 Buncer Lane, Blackburn BB2 6SE* Tel (01254) 56587 *or* 681594

DANIEL, Mrs Joy. b 44. Gilmore Course 81 Oak Hill Th Coll 82. **dss** 84 **d** 87 **p** 94. Luton St Fran *St Alb* 84-02; Par Dn 87-94; C 94-02; P-in-c Woodside w E Hyde from 02. *St Andrew's Vicarage, Church Road, Slip End, Luton LU1 4BJ* Tel (01582) 424363 E-mail joy@daniel67.freeserve.co.uk

DANIEL, Philip Sharman. b 62. Man Univ BA83 Rob Coll Cam CertEd84. Wycliffe Hall Ox 84. **d** 86 **p** 87. C Macclesfield Team Par *Ches* 86-89; C Cheadle 89-94; V Disley from 94. *Disley Vicarage, Red Lane, Disley, Stockport SK12 2NP* Tel (01663) 762068 E-mail revpsdan@daniel192.freeserve.co.uk

DANIEL, Rajinder Kumar. b 34. St Steph Coll Delhi 55 Westcott Ho Cam 61. **d** 63 **p** 64. C Purley St Barn *S'wark* 63-66; C Battersea St Pet 66-67; C N Harrow St Alb *Lon* 67-72; TV Beaconsfield *Ox* 72-75; V Smethwick St Matt w St Chad *Birm* 75-87; Dioc Adv on Black Min 87-92; Chapl Birm Gen Hosp 91-92; TR Braunstone *Leic* 92-01; rtd 01; USPG and R Arima St Jude Trinidad and Tobago 03-04; Perm to Offic *Birm* from 04. *508 Chester Road, Kingshurst, Birmingham B36 0LG* Tel 0121-770 1066

DANIELL, Robert. b 37. **d** 87 **p** 88. C Camberwell St Giles w St Matt *S'wark* 90-92; V Lewisham St Swithun from 92. *St Swithun's Vicarage, 191 Hither Green Lane, London SE13 6QE* Tel (020) 8852 5088

DANIELS, Geoffrey Gregory. b 23. St Pet Coll Ox BA48 MA53. Lambeth STh60 Linc Th Coll 73. **d** 73 **p** 75. NSM Diss *Nor* 73-74; NSM Bexhill St Pet *Chich* 74-83; C Eastbourne St Andr 83-84; V Horam 84-88; rtd 88; Chapl Convent of Dudwell St Mary from 88; NSM Bexhill St Andr CD *Chich* 90-95; Perm to Offic from 95. *20 Richmond Grove, Bexhill-on-Sea TN39 3EQ* Tel (01424) 211719

DANIELS, John Wyn. b 60. Southn Univ BSc82 PhD87. Trin Coll Bris MA92. **d** 92 **p** 93. C Roundhay St Edm *Ripon* 92-95; India 96; C Ambleside w Brathay *Carl* 97-01; Chapl St Martin's Coll Lanc 97-01; Res Can Ban Cathl *Ban* 01-05; Min Development Officer *Bradf* from 05; C Embsay w Eastby from 05. *The Vicarage, 21 Shires Lane, Embsay, Skipton BD23 6SB* Tel (01756) 798057 E-mail jd001@supanet.com

DANIELS, Lee Martin. b 61. Coll of Resurr Mirfield 99. **d** 01 **p** 02. C Toxteth Park St Agnes and St Pancras *Liv* from 01. *St Agnes Flat, 51 Heysmoor Heights, Liverpool L8 3SW* Tel 0151-727 2458 E-mail lmartindaniels@aol.com

DANKS, Alan Adam. b 41. Edin Th Coll 61. **d** 64 **p** 65. C Dumfries *Glas* 64-67; C Earl's Court St Cuth w St Matthias *Lon* 68-71; C St Steph Walbrook and St Swithun etc 71-74; C Brookfield St Mary 75-76; C Hendon St Mary 76-85. *33 Park Road, London W4 3EY* Tel (020) 8994 3131

DANSIE, Bruce John. b 40. Woolwich Poly BSc67 Univ Coll Lon MSc71 CEng72. Linc Th Coll 92. **d** 92 **p** 93. C Ivybridge w Harford *Ex* 92-96; P-in-c Charleton w Buckland Tout Saints etc 96-01; rtd 01. *566 Ostrea Lake Road, Musquodoboit Harbour NS, Canada, B0J 2L0*

DANSON, Mrs Mary Agatha. MPS48 Strathclyde Univ PhC48. St Jo Coll Nottm 82. **d** 88 **p** 94. NSM Uddingston *Glas* from 88; NSM Cambuslang from 88. *3 Golf Road, Rutherglen, Glasgow G73 4JW* Tel 0141-634 4330

DAPLYN, Timothy James. b 52. Ripon Coll Cuddesdon DipMin94. **d** 94 **p** 95. C Southmead *Bris* 94-97; P-in-c Abbots Leigh w Leigh Woods 97-99; Dioc Communications Officer 97-99; R Clutton w Cameley *B & W* 99-04; RD Chew Magna 03-04; P-in-c E w W Harptree and Hinton Blewett from 04. *The Rectory, Bath Road, West Harptree, Bristol BS40 6HB* Tel (01761) 221239 E-mail tim@tdaplyn.freeserve.co.uk

DARBY, Canon Anthony Ernest. b 26. Linc Th Coll 74. **d** 76 **p** 77. C Chilvers Coton w Astley *Cov* 76-79; P-in-c Longford 79-81; V 81-84; V Cov St Mary 84-91; RD Cov S 88-91; rtd 91; Chapl Cov Cathl from 91; Hon Can Th 00. *53 Ivybridge Road, Coventry CV3 5PF* Tel (024) 7641 4174 E-mail darby@bushinternet.com

DARBY, Michael Barwick. b 34. St D Coll Lamp BA61 Tyndale Hall Bris 61. **d** 63 **p** 64. C Islington St Andr w St Thos and St Matthias *Lon* 63-66; C Ealing Dean St Jo 66-68; V Broomfleet *York* 68-73; Area Sec CCCS *York* and *Sheff* 68-73; V Paddington Em Harrow Road *Lon* 73-78; Iran 78-79; Brazil 80-83; Perm to Offic *Cant* 80-84; from 01; V Maidstone St Faith 84-90; UAE 90-92; V Platt Bridge *Liv* 93-99; rtd 99. *Paqueta, 79 Sandwich Road, Cliffsend, Ramsgate CT12 5JA* Tel (01843) 597228 Mobile 07947-582469

DARBY, The Very Revd Nicholas Peter. b 50. Kent Univ BA82 Surrey Univ MSc02. Sarum & Wells Th Coll 71. **d** 74 **p** 75. C Walton-on-Thames *Guildf* 74-78; C Horsell 78-80; USA 82-84; Chapl Lon Univ *Lon* 84-89; Chapl R Lon Hosp (Whitechapel) 90-91; V Kew St Phil and All SS w St Luke *S'wark* 91-04; Dean Gaborone Botswana from 04. *Cathedral of the Holy Cross, PO Box 1315, Gaborone, Botswana* Tel (00267) 395 3280 *or* 390 1527 E-mail holycross@it.bw

DARBY, Preb Philip William. b 44. Bede Coll Dur TCert66. Qu Coll Birm DipTh70. **d** 70 **p** 71. C Kidderminster St Geo *Worc* 70-74; P-in-c Dudley St Jo 74-79; V 79-80; P-in-c Catshill 80-82; V Catshill and Dodford 82-88; V Ipplepen w Torbryan *Ex* 88-00; V Ipplepen, Torbryan and Denbury 01-02; RD Newton Abbot and Ipplepen 93-01; V Ashburton w Buckland in the Moor and Bickington from 02; P-in-c Widecombe-in-the-Moor, Leusdon, Princetown etc from 04; Preb Ex Cathl from 02. *The Vicarage, Copperwood Close, Ashburton, Newton Abbot TQ13 7JQ* Tel (01364) 652506 E-mail pwdarby@supanet.com

DARBYSHIRE, Brian. b 48. TD04. Kent Univ DipTh81 BA83. Oak Hill Th Coll. **d** 83 **p** 84. C Enfield St Jas *Lon* 83-86; R

Slaidburn *Bradf* 86-92; V Gt Harwood St Jo *Blackb* 92-02; V Douglas St Ninian *S & M* from 02; CF (TA) 90-04. *58 Ballanard Road, Douglas, Isle of Man IM2 5HE* Tel (01624) 621694 E-mail darbyshirebrian@hotmail.com

DARCH, John Henry. b 52. Univ of Wales (Lamp) BA73 PhD97 Lon Univ PGCE74 MA77. Trin Coll Bris 80. **d** 82 **p** 83. C Meole Brace *Lich* 82-85; C Hoole *Ches* 85-88; V Hyde St Geo 88-99; P-in-c Godley cum Newton Green 89-93; RD Mottram 91-99; Lect St Jo Coll Nottm from 99; Chapl from 03; Public Preacher *S'well* from 99; Perm to Offic *Derby* from 03. *St John's College, Chilwell Lane, Bramcote, Nottingham NG9 3DS* Tel 0115-925 1114 Fax 943 6438 E-mail j.darch@stjohns-nottm.ac.uk

DARK, Nicholas John. b 62. Leic Univ BA83 ACIB92. CITC BTh98. **d** 98 **p** 99. C Ballyholme *D & D* 98-05; I Magheragall *Conn* from 05. *Magheragall Rectory, 70 Ballinderry Road, Lisburn BT28 2QS* Tel (028) 9262 1273 E-mail magheragall@aol.com

DARLEY, Canon Shaun Arthur Neilson. b 36. Dur Univ BA61 DipTh63 Reading Univ MSc75. Cranmer Hall Dur 61. **d** 63 **p** 64. C Luton w E Hyde *St Alb* 63-67; Chapl Bris Tech Coll 67-69; Chapl Bris Poly *Bris* 69-92; Sen Chapl UWE 92-01; Lect 69-75; Sen Lect 75-01; Dir Cen for Performing Arts 85-02; Bp's Cathl Chapl 69-76; Hon Can Bris Cathl 89-01; rtd 01; Perm to Offic *B & W* from 98 and *Bris* from 02. *Church Paddock, Winscombe Hill, Bristol BS25 1DE* Tel (01934) 843633

DARLING, David Francis. b 55. TISEC 93. **d** 96 **p** 97. SSF 88-05; Novice Guardian 99-05; NSM Edin St Ninian *Edin* 96-98; Chapl W Gen Hosps NHS 96-98; Chapl Edin Sick Children's NHS Trust 96-98; Lic Preacher *Lon* 03-05. *8 Church Mead, 234 Camberwell Road, London SE5 0ET* Tel (020) 7703 9794

✠**DARLING, The Rt Revd Edward Flewett.** b 33. TCD BA55 MA58. CITC. **d** 56 **p** 57 **c** 85. C Belfast St Luke *Conn* 56-59; C Orangefield *D & D* 59-62; C-in-c Carnalea 62-72; Chapl Ban Hosp 63-72; I Belfast Malone St Jo *Conn* 72-85; Min Can Belf Cathl 78-85; Chapl Ulster Independent Clinic 81-85; Bp L & K 85-00. *15 Beechwood Park, Moira, Craigavon BT67 0LL* Tel (028) 9261 2982 E-mail darling-moira@utvinternet.com

DARLING, John. b 47. CMBHI. Sarum & Wells Th Coll 76. **d** 79 **p** 80. NSM Trowbridge St Thos *Sarum* 79-82; NSM Trowbridge St Thos and W Ashton 82-92; NSM Melksham from 01. *43 Horse Road, Hilperton Marsh, Trowbridge BA14 7PF*

DARLINGTON, Paul Trevor. b 71. Imp Coll Lon BSc92 K Coll Lon PGCE93. Oak Hill Th Coll BA99 MPhil00. **d** 00 **p** 01. C Bispham *Blackb* 00-05; P-in-c Oswestry H Trin *Lich* from 05. *Holy Trinity Vicarage, 29 Balmoral Crescent, Oswestry SY11 2XQ* Tel (01691) 652184 E-mail paul.t.darlington@ntlworld.com

DARLISON, Geoffrey Stuart. b 49. Liv Poly DipTP74 MRTPI80. St Jo Coll Nottm DCM91. **d** 91 **p** 92. C Horncastle w Low Toynton *Linc* 91-95; P-in-c Welton and Dunholme w Scothern 95-97; V from 97. *The New Vicarage, Holmes Lane, Dunholme, Lincoln LN2 3QT* Tel (01673) 862820 E-mail stuart@darlisons.freeserve.co.uk

DARMODY, Richard Arthur. b 52. Lon Univ DipTh77 BD90. Linc Th Coll MDiv94. **d** 94 **p** 95. C Cherry Hinton St Jo *Ely* 94-97; I Belfast St Aid *Conn* 97-99; TR The Ramseys and Upwood *Ely* from 99; RD St Ives from 02. *The Rectory, Hollow Lane, Ramsey, Huntingdon PE26 1DE* Tel (01487) 813271 E-mail darmodyrichard@hotmail.com

DARRALL, Charles Geoffrey. b 32. Nottm Univ BA55 MA57. Qu Coll Birm 56. **d** 57 **p** 58. C Cockermouth All SS w Ch Ch *Carl* 57-63; Chapl Dioc Youth Cen 63-95; V St John's in the Vale w Wythburn 63-95; P-in-c Threlkeld 85-95; rtd 96; Perm to Offic *Carl* from 98. *Piper House, Naddle, Keswick CA12 4TF* Tel (01768) 774500

DARRALL, John Norman. b 34. Nottm Univ BA57. Ripon Hall Ox 57. **d** 60 **p** 61. C Nottingham St Mary *S'well* 60-65; Chapl Nottm Children's Hosp 64-65; V Bole w Saundby *S'well* 65-66; V Sturton w Littleborough 65-66; Chapl Oakham Sch 84-99; rtd 99. *Grange Cottage, 69 Main Street, Cottesmore, Oakham LE15 7DH* Tel (01572) 812443

DARRANT, Louis Peter. b 77. Aber Univ BD00 Leeds Univ MA03. Coll of Resurr Mirfield 01. **d** 03 **p** 04. C Kennington St Jo w St Jas *S'wark* from 03. *96 Vassall Road, London SW9 6JA* Tel (020) 7582 2162 Mobile 07949-765523

DARROCH, Ronald Humphrey. b 45. Trin Coll Cam BA67 MA71 Ch Ch Ox BA67 MA71. Ripon Hall Ox 67. **d** 70 **p** 71. C Kingston upon Hull St Nic *York* 70-73; Hon C 73-74; Hon C Perth St Jo *St And* from 74; Chapl Stancliffe Hall Derby 84-87; Perm to Offic *Worc* 87-98; Chapl Old Swinford Hosp Sch Worc 89-98. *17 Viewlands Terrace, Perth PH1 1BN* Tel (01738) 628880

DART, John Peter. b 40. St Jo Coll Ox BA62. Cuddesdon Coll 62. **d** 64 **p** 65. C W Hartlepool St Aid *Dur* 64-67; C Alverthorpe *Wakef* 67-70; Lic to Offic 70-79; rtd 05. *3 Springhill Avenue, Crofton, Wakefield WF4 1HA* Tel (01924) 860374 E-mail mail@dart.eclipse.co.uk

DARVILL, Christopher Mark. b 61. Ox Univ BA83. St Steph Ho Ox 84. **d** 86 **p** 87. C Tottenham St Paul *Lon* 86-88; C Oystermouth *S & B* 88-90; Chapl Univ of Wales (Swansea) 90-94; Asst Dioc Warden of Ords from 92; V Llansamlet from 94. *The Vicarage, 61 Church Road, Llansamlet, Swansea SA7 9RL* Tel (01792) 771420

DARVILL, Geoffrey. b 43. Oak Hill Th Coll 79. **d** 81 **p** 82. C Barking St Marg w St Patr *Chelmsf* 81-84; C Widford 84-86; P-in-c Ramsden Crays w Ramsden Bellhouse 86-90; Dep Chapl HM Pris Pentonville 90-91; Chapl HM YOI Onley 91-97; Chapl HM Pris Nor 97-01; Chapl HM Pris Man 01-02; P-in-c Chadderton Em *Man* 02-03; V 03-04; P-in-c Chevington w Hargrave, Chedburgh w Depden etc *St E* from 04. *The Rectory, New Road, Chevington, Bury St Edmunds IP29 5QL* Tel (01284) 850512 E-mail geoffdarvill@hotmail.com

DARVILL, Canon George Collins. b 36. Kelham Th Coll 56. **d** 61 **p** 62. C Middlesbrough St Chad *York* 61-64; C Manston *Ripon* 64-66; V Kippax 66-79; V Catterick 79-88; RD Richmond 80-86; P-in-c Adel 88-89; R 89-01; RD Headingley 91-96; Hon Can Ripon Cathl 91-01; rtd 01; Perm to Offic *Ripon* from 01. *39 Woodlea Lane, Meanwood, Leeds LS6 4SX* Tel 0113-275 7973

✠**DARWENT, The Rt Revd Frederick Charles.** b 27. JP87. ACIB. Wells Th Coll 61. **d** 63 **p** 64 **c** 78. C Pemberton St Jo *Liv* 63-65; R Strichen *Ab* 65-71; R New Pitsligo 65-71; R Fraserburgh w New Pitsligo 71-78; Can St Andr Cathl 71-78; Dean Ab 73-78; Bp Ab 78-92; rtd 92; Lic to Offic *Ab* from 92. *107 Osborne Place, Aberdeen AB25 2DD* Tel (01224) 646497

DASH, Mrs Janet Eleanor Gillian. b 47. SRN69. Cant Sch of Min 89. **d** 93 **p** 94. C Morden *S'wark* 93-96; C S Croydon Em 96-98; P-in-c Borstal *Roch* from 98; Chapl HM Pris Cookham Wood from 98. *The Vicarage, 76 Borstal Street, Rochester ME1 3HL* Tel and fax (01634) 845948 Mobile 07770-741291 E-mail jandash@talktalk.net

DASHFIELD, Edward Maurice. b 26. LTh65. **d** 51 **p** 52. New Zealand 51-55 and from 57; C Masterton 51-55; C Cannock *Lich* 55-57; V Tinui 57-64; P-in-c 83-88; V Carterton 64-69; Hd Master St Matt Sch Masterton 69-80; rtd 88. *53 Miro Street, Masterton, New Zealand* Tel (0064) (6) 377 0418

DATE, Stephen James. b 69. LSE BA90 Dur Univ MA92. SEITE 99. **d** 02 **p** 03. NSM Brighton Gd Shep Preston *Chich* from 02. *67 Stanford Road, Brighton BN1 5PR* Tel (01273) 565927 Mobile 07747-895213 E-mail stephend@yahoo.co.uk

DATSON, Mrs Sheila Mary. b 24. CertEd67. S'wark Ord Course 76. **dss** 78 **d** 87 **p** 94. Bexleyheath Ch Ch *Roch* 78-91; Hon Par Dn 87-91; rtd 91; Perm to Offic *Worc* 91-94 and from 95; NSM Stourport and Wilden 94-95. *17 Moorhall Lane, Stourport-on-Severn DY13 8RB* Tel (01299) 823044 E-mail datson@fish.co.uk

DAUBNEY, Howard. b 49. Woolwich Poly BA70. S'wark Ord Course 86. **d** 89 **p** 90. NSM Roch 89-02; C 02-04; V Strood St Fran from 04. *St Francis's Vicarage, Galahad Avenue, Rochester ME2 2YS* Tel and fax (01634) 717162 Mobile 07932-384823 E-mail howarddaubney@yahoo.co.uk

DAUGHTERY, Stephen John. b 61. Kent Univ BSc82. Trin Coll Bris BA94. **d** 96 **p** 97. C Guildf Ch Ch *Guildf* 96-98; C Guildf Ch Ch w St Martha-on-the-Hill 98-03; R Southover *Chich* from 03. *The Rectory, Southover High Street, Lewes BN7 1HT* Tel (01273) 472018 E-mail steve@daughtery.freeserve.co.uk

DAULMAN, John Henry. b 33. Lich Th Coll 60. **d** 62 **p** 63. C Monkseaton St Mary *Newc* 62-65; Min Can Newc Cathl 65-67; Chapl Crumpsall and Springfield Hosp 67-73; V Tyldesley w Shakerley *Man* 73-81; V Turton 81-00; rtd 00; Perm to Offic *Blackb* from 01. *17 Higher Bank Street, Withnell, Chorley PR6 8SF* Tel (01254) 832597

DAUNTON-FEAR, Andrew. b 45. Univ of Tasmania BSc64 Qu Coll Cam BA67 MA72 ACT ThL68 St Andr Univ BPhil76 K Coll Lon PhD00 Dip Librarianship 74. Ridley Hall Cam 67. **d** 68 **p** 70. C Thomastown Australia 68-71; P-in-c Islington H Trin Cloudesley Square *Lon* 71-75; Hon C Islington St Mary 71-75; C Stoke Bishop *Bris* 76-79; R Thrapston *Pet* 79-89; R Barming *Roch* 89-03; Lect St Andr Th Sem Philippines from 03. *PO Box 3167, 1099 Manila, Philippines* Tel (0063) (2) 722 2571 E-mail nothingdaunted@hotmail.com

DAVAGE, William Ernest Peter. b 50. MA94. St Steph Ho Ox 89. **d** 91 **p** 92. C Eyres Monsell *Leic* 91-94; P Lib Pusey Ho Ox from 94. *Pusey House, St Giles, Oxford OX1 3LZ* Tel (01865) 278415 Fax 278416

DAVENPORT (née HILL), Elizabeth Jayne Louise. b 55. St Hugh's Coll Ox BA77 MA81 Univ of S California PhD03. Fuller Th Sem California ThM89 N Ord Course 79. **dss** 82 **d** 87 **p** 91. Halliwell St Pet *Man* 82-83; Paris St Mich *Eur* 83-85; Lic to Offic *St Alb* 85-87; Hon Par Dn Chorleywood St Andr 87-89; USA from 89. *University of Southern California, Univ Religious Center, Los Angeles, CA 90089-0751, USA* Tel (001) (213) 740 1366 E-mail ejld@usc.edu

DAVENPORT, Ian Arthan. b 54. Linc Th Coll 85. **d** 87 **p** 88. C Ches H Trin *Ches* 87-91; V Newton 91-97; V Oxton from 97. *Oxton Vicarage, 8 Wexford Road, Prenton CH43 9TB* Tel 0151-652 1194 Fax 653 9211

DAVENPORT, Mrs Joy Gwyneth. b 46. Glam Coll of Educn TCert68. SEITE 01. **d** 04. NSM Rye *Chich* from 04; Asst Chapl

E Sussex Hosps NHS Trust from 04. *2 The Oakfield, Houghton Lane, Playden, Rye TN31 7UA* Tel (01797) 224209

DAVENPORT, Michael Arthur. b 38. Kelham Th Coll 58 Lich Th Coll 60. **d** 62 **p** 63. C Bilborough w Strelley *S'well* 62-66; C Kettering St Mary *Pet* 66-69; V Tottenham St Benet Fink *Lon* from 69; Chapl ATC from 79; Wing Chapl Middx 83-96; Regional Chapl Lon and SE 86-96. *St Benet's Vicarage, Walpole Road, London N17 6BH* Tel (020) 8888 4541 Fax 8829 9593

DAVENPORT, Ms Sally Elizabeth. b 59. Lon Bible Coll BA99. Ripon Coll Cuddesdon 99. **d** 01 **p** 02. C Bishop's Stortford St Mich *St Alb* 01-05; P-in-c N Mymms from 05. *The Vicarage, North Mymms Park, North Mymms, Hatfield AL9 7TN* Tel (01727) 822062 E-mail sally.d@fish.co.uk

DAVENPORT, Miss Sybil Ann. b 36. Nottm Univ CertEd57 DipTh88. EMMTC 85. **d** 89 **p** 94. NSM Thurgarton w Hoveringham and Bleasby etc *S'well* 89-94; NSM Collingham w S Scarle and Besthorpe and Girton 94-02; rtd 02; Perm to Offic *S'well* from 02. *Holmedale, North Muskham, Newark NG23 6HQ* Tel (01636) 701552

DAVEY, Andrew John. b 53. Univ of Wales (Cardiff) DPS77. St Mich Coll Llan DipTh76. **d** 77 **p** 78. C Gt Stanmore *Lon* 77-79; NSM Watford St Jo *St Alb* 87-92; C Potters Bar 92-95; P-in-c Clenchwarton *Ely* 95-96; P-in-c W Lynn 95-96; R Clenchwarton and W Lynn from 96. *The Rectory, Clenchwarton, King's Lynn PE34 4DT* Tel (01553) 772089 Fax as telephone E-mail andrewdavey@route56.co.uk

DAVEY, Andrew John. b 57. Magd Coll Ox BA78 MA83. Wycliffe Hall Ox 80. **d** 83 **p** 84. C Bermondsey St Jas w Ch Ch *S'wark* 83-87; Chapl Trin Coll Cam 87-92; Pilsdon Community 94-04. *Address temp unknown*

DAVEY, Andrew Paul. b 61. Southn Univ BA82 Sheff Univ DMinTh99. Westcott Ho Cam 85. **d** 87 **p** 88. C S'wark H Trin w St Matt *S'wark* 87-91; V Camberwell St Luke 91-96; Min Development Officer Woolwich Area Miss Team 96-98; Ho of Bps' Officer for UPAs 96-98; Asst Sec Abps' Coun Bd for Soc Resp from 98; Chapl S'wark Cathl *S'wark* from 01. *7 Bousfield Road, London SE14 5TP* Tel (020) 7277 9688 *or* 7898 1446 E-mail andrew.davey@c-of-e.org.uk

DAVEY, Christopher Mark. b 64. EN(G)84 RGN89. St Steph Ho Ox DipMin95. **d** 95 **p** 96. C Leeds Belle Is St Jo and St Barn *Ripon* 95-97; C-in-c Grahame Park St Aug CD *Lon* 97-01; V St Alb St Mary Marshalswick *St Alb* from 01. *The Vicarage, 1 Sherwood Avenue, St Albans AL4 9QA* Tel (01727) 851544 E-mail cdavey2776@aol.com

DAVEY, Colin Hugh Lancaster. b 34. Em Coll Cam BA56 MA60 PhD89. Cuddesdon Coll 59. **d** 61 **p** 62. C Moseley St Agnes *Birm* 61-64; Lic to Offic *Eur* 64-65; Sub Warden St Boniface Coll Warminster 66-69; C Bath Weston St Jo *B & W* 69-70; Asst Chapl Abp Cant's Cllrs on Foreign Relns 70-74; Angl Sec ARCIC 70-74; Hon C St Dunstan in the West *Lon* 71-73; Hon C Kennington St Jo *S'wark* 73-74; V S Harrow St Paul *Lon* 74-80; V Paddington St Jas 80-83; Sec Ecum Affairs BCC 83-90; Ch Life Sec CCBI 90-99; Perm to Offic *St Alb* from 97; rtd 00. *20 Honeysuckle Way, Bedford MK41 0TF* Tel (01234) 360851 E-mail colinandjane@davey8.freeserve.co.uk

DAVEY, Canon Frederick Hutley David. b 14. Cranmer Hall Dur 58. **d** 60 **p** 62. C Bishopwearmouth St Nic *Dur* 60-62; C Dur St Giles 62-64; India 64-69; E Pakistan 69-71; Bangladesh 71-76; Chapl De Beer Miss to Seamen *Eur* 77-82; rtd 82; Perm to Offic *B & W* 82-95. *126 Ashtree Road, Frome BA11 2SF* Tel (01373) 467545

DAVEY, Mrs Hilary Margaret. b 49. Bris Univ BSc70. EAMTC 98. **d** 01 **p** 02. NSM Saffron Walden w Wendens Ambo, Littlebury etc *Chelmsf* from 01. *3 Springhill Road, Saffron Walden CB11 4AH* Tel (01799) 522616 E-mail st.mary's@virgin.net

DAVEY, James Garland. b 21. **d** 75 **p** 76. C Liskeard w St Keyne and St Pinnock *Truro* 75-77; Perm to Offic *B & W* 77-80; TV S Molton w Nymet St George, High Bray etc *Ex* 80-86; rtd 86; Perm to Offic *B & W* from 86. *43 Tree Field Road, Clevedon BS21 6JD* Tel (01275) 540648

DAVEY, John. b 35. FRSH89 CPsychol92 AFBPsS92 Birkbeck Coll Lon BSc84 MPhil87 PhD91. Chich Th Coll 67. **d** 69 **p** 70. C Eastbourne St Eliz *Chich* 69-72; C Eastbourne St Mary 72-74; V W Wittering 74-77; Min Can and Chapl Windsor 77-81; R The Rissingtons *Glouc* 81-85; R Alfriston w Lullington, Litlington and W Dean *Chich* 85-92; Chapl Bramshill Police Coll *Win* 92-96; rtd 97; P-in-c Amberley w N Stoke and Parham, Wiggonholt etc *Chich* 97-98; Perm to Offic from 98. *Bewick, 13 Fairfield Close, Bosham, Chichester PO18 8JQ*

DAVEY, John Michael. b 31. St Chad's Coll Dur BA54 Sunderland Poly DMS76. St Chad's Coll Dur DipTh56. **d** 56 **p** 61. C Southwick H Trin *Dur* 56-57; C Harton 60-64; C Bawtry w Austerfield *S'well* 64-67; V Stillington *Dur* 67-70; Lic to Offic 70-78; Perm to Offic *Sheff* 78-93; rtd 96. *11 Darfield Close, Owlthorpe, Sheffield S20 6SW* Tel 0114-248 0917

DAVEY, Julian Metherall. b 40. Jes Coll Ox BA62 MA65. Wells Th Coll 62. **d** 64 **p** 65. C Weston-super-Mare St Jo *B & W* 64-66; Perm to Offic *St Alb* 66-68; Chapl St Alb Sch 68-73; Chapl Merchant Taylors' Sch Crosby 73-82; Perm to Offic *Truro* 82-83; P-in-c Meavy w Sheepstor *Ex* 83-85; P-in-c Walkhampton 83-85; R Meavy, Sheepstor and Walkhampton 85; Chapl Warw Sch 86-89; P-in-c The Winterbournes and Compton Valence *Sarum* 89-94; TV Marshwood Vale 96-98; P-in-c St Gennys, Jacobstow w Warbstow and Treneglos *Truro* 98-02; rtd 02; Perm to Offic *Truro* from 02. *18 Pondfield Road, Latchbrook, Saltash PL12 4UA* Tel (01752) 840086

DAVEY, Julian Warwick. b 45. LRCPI DCH DRCOG. Qu Coll Birm 78. **d** 81 **p** 82. NSM Ipsley *Worc* from 81. *The Field House, Allimore Lane, Alcester B49 5PR* Tel (01789) 764640

DAVEY, Kenneth William. b 41. Lanc Coll HNC. Qu Coll Birm 84. **d** 86 **p** 87. C Baswich *Lich* 86-90; V Lostock Gralam *Ches* 90-96; P-in-c Thornton-le-Moors w Ince and Elton from 96. *The Vicarage, Ince Lane, Elton, Chester CH2 4QB* Tel (01928) 724028 E-mail kenzor@daveyk1.fsnet.co.uk

DAVEY, Nathan Paul. *See* PAINE DAVEY, Nathan Paul

DAVEY, Peter James. b 59. Bris Univ BSc81 Loughb Univ MBA91. Trin Coll Bris BA00. **d** 00 **p** 01. C Long Eaton St Jo *Derby* 00-04; V Cotmanhay from 04. *The Vicarage, 197 Heanor Road, Ilkeston DE7 8TA* Tel 0115-932 5670 E-mail petedavey@aol.com

DAVEY, Peter William. b 44. Culham Coll of Educn TCert65. Linc Th Coll 93. **d** 93 **p** 94. C Cheadle w Freehay *Lich* 93-96; P-in-c Calton, Cauldon, Grindon and Waterfall 96-99; R Calton, Cauldon, Grindon, Waterfall etc 99-00; R Norton in the Moors from 04. *The New Rectory, Norton Lane, Stoke-on-Trent ST6 8BY* Tel (01782) 534622

DAVEY, Piers Damer. b 57. Dur Univ BSc. Coll of Resurr Mirfield 80. **d** 83 **p** 84. C Heworth St Mary *Dur* 83-86; C Barnard Castle w Whorlton 86-89; V Aycliffe 89-95; V Chilton Moor from 95. *St Andrew's Vicarage, Chilton Moor, Houghton le Spring DH4 6LU* Tel 0191-385 8747

DAVEY, Canon Richard Henry. b 66. Man Univ BA88. Linc Th Coll BTh93. **d** 93 **p** 94. C Parkstone St Pet w Branksea and St Osmund *Sarum* 93-96; Chapl and Min Can St E Cathl *St E* 96-99; Can Res S'well Minster *S'well* 99-04; Chapl Nottm Trent Univ from 04; C Clifton from 04. *St Mary's Vicarage, 58 Village Road, Clifton, Nottingham NG11 8NE* Tel 0115-921 1856 E-mail rdavey1175@aol.com

DAVID, Brother. *See* JARDINE, David John

DAVID, Faith Caroline. *See* CLARINGBULL, Mrs Faith Caroline

DAVID, Canon Kenith Andrew. b 39. Natal Univ BA(Theol)64. Coll of Resurr Mirfield 64. **d** 66 **p** 67. C Harpenden St Nic *St Alb* 66-69; R Chatsworth Epiphany S Africa 69-71; P-in-c Southwick St Mich *Chich* 71-72; Th Educn Sec Chr Aid 72-75; Project Officer India and Bangladesh 76-81; Hon C Kingston All SS *S'wark* 72-76; Hon C Kingston All SS w St Jo 76-81; Lic to Offic Botswana 81-83; Hon C Geneva *Eur* 83-95; Co-ord Urban Rural Miss WCC 83-94; Can Lundi Zimbabwe from 93; V Hessle *York* 95-05; rtd 05. *5 Randolph Close, Canterbury CT1 3AZ*

DAVID, Michael Anthony Louis. b 29. AKC58. **d** 59 **p** 60. C Greenhill St Jo *Lon* 59-63; V Gravesend St Mary *Roch* 63-78; V Foremark *Derby* 78-81; V Repton 78-81; TV Buxton w Burbage and King Sterndale 81-85; R Warlingham w Chelsham and Farleigh *S'wark* 85-90; rtd 91; Perm to Offic *Sarum* from 91. *95 Lulworth Avenue, Hamworthy, Poole BH15 4DH* Tel (01202) 684475

DAVID, Philip Evan Nicholl. b 31. Jes Coll Ox BA53 MA57 Univ of Wales BA61 Nottm Univ MPhil86 Leic Univ MEd88. St Mich Coll Llan 56. **d** 57 **p** 58. C Llanblethian w Cowbridge *Llan* 57-60; C Cardiff St Jo 60-64; Chapl Ch Coll Brecon 64-75; P-in-c Aberyscir and Llanfihangel Nantbran *S & B* 70-75; Chapl Loretto Sch Musselburgh 75-82; Chapl Trent Coll Nottm 83-91; R Llanfyllin and Bwlchycibau *St As* 91-96; P-in-c Llangynog 95-96; rtd 96; P-in-c Newbridge-on-Wye and Llanfihangel Brynpabuan etc *S & B* 98-00; P-in-c Llanwrtyd w Llanddulas in Tir Abad etc from 05. *Woodside Cottage, The Bron, Cross Gates, Llandrindod Wells LD1 6RS* Tel (01597) 851401

DAVID, William John. b 57. **d** 04. OLM Eltham St Barn *S'wark* from 04. *10 Allenswood Road, London SE9 6RP* Tel (020) 8319 0189 Mobile 07929-644503

DAVID FRANCIS, Brother. *See* DARLING, David Francis

DAVIDGE-SMITH, Mrs Margaret Kathleen. b 53. Trent Poly CQSW77. STETS 99. **d** 02 **p** 03. NSM E Acton St Dunstan w St Thos *Lon* 02-04; Asst Chapl Ealing Hosp NHS Trust from 04. *36 Newburgh Road, London W3 6DQ* Tel and fax (020) 8993 0868 E-mail mdavidge_s@hotmail.com

DAVIDSON, Canon Charles Hilary. b 29. St Edm Hall Ox BA52 MA56 Leic Univ MPhil89. Lich Th Coll 52. **d** 54 **p** 55. C Abington *Pet* 54-59; C Pet St Jo 59-60; R Sywell w Overstone 60-66; P-in-c Lamport w Faxton 66-76; R Maidwell w Draughton and Scaldwell 67-76; R Maidwell w Draughton, Scaldwell, Lamport etc 77-80; RD Brixworth 77-79; Can Pet Cathl 79-94; V Roade 80-87; V Roade and Ashton w Hartwell 87-94; RD Towcester 91-94; rtd 94; Perm to Offic *Pet* from 94.

Croftside, Butlins Lane, Roade, Northampton NN7 2PU Tel (01604) 863016

DAVIDSON, Christopher John. b 45. St Luke's Coll Ex CertEd67 CertRE67 St Martin's Coll Lanc BEd74. EAMTC. **d** 91 **p** 92. NSM Taverham w Ringland *Nor* 91-93; Dir of Educn 87-93; P-in-c Whixley w Green Hammerton *Ripon* 93-96; RE Adv 93-96; Dioc Dir of Educn *Ex* 97-01; Assoc P Exminster and Kenn 97-01; R Quidenham Gp *Nor* from 01; P-in-c Guiltcross from 04. *The Rectory, Church Hill, Banham, Norwich NR16 2HN* Tel (01953) 887562 E-mail chris.davidson@virgin.net

DAVIDSON, Donald. b 52. TISEC 00. **d** 05. C W Highland Region *Arg* from 05. *4 Kearan Road, Kinlochleven, Argyll PH50 4QU* Tel (01855) 831444 E-mail donaldd@btinternet.com

DAVIDSON, Graeme John. b 42. Victoria Univ Wellington BA64 BA66 Ox Univ MA70. St Steph Ho Ox 67. **d** 70 **p** 71. C Maidenhead St Luke *Ox* 70-73; New Zealand 73-77 and from 93; USA 77-88. *103 Upland Road, Kelburn, Wellington, New Zealand* Tel (0064) (4) 475 8228 Fax 475 8219 E-mail davidson@betterlearn.co.nz

DAVIDSON, Hilary. *See* DAVIDSON, Canon Charles Hilary

DAVIDSON, Ian George. b 32. LSE BSc(Econ)54. Linc Th Coll 55. **d** 58 **p** 59. C Waltham Cross *St Alb* 58-60; C St Alb Abbey 61-63; Hon PV S'wark Cathl *S'wark* 63-67; V Gt Cornard *St E* 67-72; R Lt Cornard 67-70; Lic to Offic 72-79; Student Counsellor Suffolk Coll 72-79; P-in-c Witnesham w Swilland and Ashbocking 79-83; Warden Scargill Ho 83-88; Chapl Chr Fellowship of Healing *Edin* 88-97; rtd 97. *28 Fox Spring Crescent, Edinburgh EH10 6NQ* Tel 0131-445 3381 E-mail iangill@foxspring.freeserve.co.uk

DAVIDSON, John Lindsay. b 27. LRCP51 St Cath Soc Ox DipTh57. St Steph Ho Ox. **d** 58 **p** 59. C Croydon St Mich *Cant* 58-61; P-in-c H Cross Miss 62-66; V Lewisham St Steph *S'wark* 67-70; V Croydon St Mich *Cant* 70-80; V Croydon St Mich w St Jas 80-81; TR N Creedy *Ex* 81-92; RD Cadbury 86-90; rtd 92; Perm to Offic *Ex* from 92. *12 Highfield, Lapford, Crediton EX17 6PY* Tel (01363) 83764

DAVIDSON, Ralph. b 38. Dioc OLM tr scheme 98. **d** 01 **p** 02. OLM Birkenshaw w Hunsworth *Wakef* from 01. *Bedale, Moorhouse Lane, Birkenshaw, Bradford BD11 2BA* Tel (01274) 681955

DAVIDSON, Trevor John. b 49. CertEd DipHE. Oak Hill Th Coll 80. **d** 85 **p** 86. C Drypool *York* 85-88; V Bessingby 88-97; V Carnaby 88-97; Chapl Bridlington and Distr Gen Hosp 88-94; Chapl E Yorks Community Healthcare NHS Trust 94-97; V Felling *Dur* from 97; CUF Projects Officer from 97. *The Vicarage, Carlisle Street, Felling, Gateshead NE10 0HQ* Tel 0191-420 3434 E-mail trevor@christchurch5.freeserve.co.uk

DAVIDSON, William Watkins. b 20. Wadh Coll Ox BA48 MA53. Westcott Ho Cam 49. **d** 50 **p** 51. C Radcliffe-on-Trent *S'well* 50-53; Chapl RN 53-57; R Esher *Guildf* 57-65; V Westmr St Steph w St Jo *Lon* 65-83; rtd 85. *61/62 Calmsden, Cirencester GL7 5ET* Tel (01825) 831823

DAVIE (née JONES), Mrs Alyson Elizabeth. b 58. Ex Univ BA86. Wycliffe Hall Ox 86. **d** 88 **p** 94. Par Dn Ipswich St Fran *St E* 88-92; Perm to Offic *Ox* 92-93 and *St Alb* 93-94; NSM E Barnet *St Alb* 94-97; Asst Chapl Oak Hill Th Coll 94-96; P-in-c The Mundens w Sacombe *St Alb* from 97. *2 Forge Cottages, Munden Road, Dane End, Ware SG12 0LP* Tel (01920) 438736 E-mail alyson.davie@btopenworld.com

DAVIE, Peter Edward Sidney. b 36. LSE BSc57 Birm Univ MA73 K Coll Lon MPhil78 Kent Univ PhD90. Coll of Resurr Mirfield 57. **d** 60 **p** 61. C De Beauvoir Town St Pet *Lon* 60-63; C-in-c Godshill CD *Portsm* 63-67; R Upton St Leonards *Glouc* 67-73; Sen Lect Ch Ch Coll of HE Cant 73-98; Prin Lect Cant Ch Ch Univ Coll 98-01; Lic to Offic *Cant* from 73; Hon C Cant St Pet w St Alphege and St Marg etc from 79. *8 Brockenhurst Close, Canterbury CT2 7RX* Tel (01227) 451572 E-mail pedavie@dircon.co.uk

DAVIE, Stephen Peter. b 52. S Bank Poly BA75 MRTPI77 Cam Univ DipRS90. Oak Hill Th Coll BA93. **d** 93 **p** 94. C Luton Ch Ch *Roch* 93-97; R Cobham w Luddesdowne and Dode 97-04; P-in-c Horley *S'wark* from 04. *4 Russells Crescent, Horley RH6 7DN* Tel (01293) 783509 E-mail steve.davie@btinternet.com

DAVIES, Adrian Paul. b 43. K Coll Lon. **d** 69 **p** 70. C Nottingham St Mary *S'well* 69-74; C Gt w Lt Billing *Pet* 74-75; P-in-c Marholm 75-82; R Castor 75; R Castor w Sutton and Upton 76-82; V Byker St Mich w St Lawr *Newc* 82-94; rtd 95. *9 Arrow Lane, Halton, Lancaster LA2 6QW* Tel (01524) 811141

DAVIES, Alan. *See* DAVIES, James Alan

DAVIES, Alan Arthur. b 35. Sarum & Wells Th Coll 83. **d** 85 **p** 86. C Eastleigh *Win* 85-88; C Portsea N End St Mark *Portsm* 88-90; V Lydiate *Liv* 90-00; rtd 00; Perm to Offic *Sarum* from 01. *25 St Catherine's, Wimborne BH21 1BE* Tel (01202) 848233

DAVIES, Alastair John. b 56. Nottm Univ BA MTh. Westcott Ho Cam. **d** 84 **p** 85. C Eltham St Jo *S'wark* 84-87; C Dulwich St Barn 87-89; Chapl RAF from 89; P-in-c Lyneham w Bradenstoke *Sarum* 01-03. *Chaplaincy Services (RAF), HQ, Personnel and Training Command, RAF Innsworth, Gloucester GL3 1EZ* Tel (01452) 712612 ext 5032 Fax 510828

DAVIES, Albert Brian. b 37. Worc Coll of Educn CertEd60. Wycliffe Hall Ox 03. **d** 04 **p** 05. C Poitou-Charentes *Eur* from 04. *La Basse Coussaie, 85140 Les Essarts, France* Tel (0033) (2) 51 62 96 32 E-mail briandpam@free.fr

DAVIES, Canon Alfred Joseph. b 23. St D Coll Lamp BA49. **d** 50 **p** 51. C Llanegwad *St D* 50-53; C Llanelli Ch Ch 53-54; V Llangeler 54-74; RD Emlyn 70-73; Chapl Cardigan Hosp 74-88; V Cardigan w Mwnt and Y Ferwig *St D* 74-88; Can St D Cathl 79-88; rtd 88; Hon Can St D Cathl *St D* from 88. *Isfoel, Heol Llynyfran, Llandysul SA44 4JW* Tel (01559) 362040

DAVIES, Mrs Alison Margaret. b 57. Nottm Univ BA78. STETS Dip Th & Min 99. **d** 99 **p** 00. NSM Win St Barn *Win* from 99. *13 Silwood Close, Winchester SO22 6EN* Tel (01962) 856432 Fax 862642

DAVIES, Alun Edwards. b 13. Univ of Wales BA40. St D Coll Lamp 45. **d** 46 **p** 47. C Treharris *Llan* 46-48; C Cardigan *St D* 48-50; CF 50-56; Hon CF 56; R Byford w Mansel Gamage *Heref* 56-58; P-in-c Preston-on-Wye w Blakemere 56-58; V Birch St Mary *Man* 58-62; R Lower Crumpsall 62-84; rtd 84; Perm to Offic *Man* from 84. *48 Ashtree Road, Crumpsall, Manchester M8 5AT* Tel 0161-720 8345

DAVIES, Andrew James. b 53. Univ of Wales (Cardiff) BD00. St Mich Coll Llan 01. **d** 03 **p** 04. C Caerphilly *Llan* from 03. *St Andrew's House, 26 Troed y Bryn, Penyrheol, Caerphilly CF83 2PX* Tel (029) 2088 4103 Mobile 07931-370054 E-mail daviesaj8@hotmail.com

DAVIES, Andrew John. b 54. FRCO75 FTCL76 LRAM75 Univ of Wales (Abth) BMus76 St Martin's Coll Lanc PGCE78. Sarum & Wells Th Coll 79. **d** 81 **p** 82. C Tenby w Gumfreston *St D* 81-84; C Llanelli 84-86; V Monkton 86-91; V Fairfield *Derby* 91-96; P-in-c Barlborough 96-01; R Barlborough and Renishaw 01-03; V Pembroke Dock *St D* 03-04; TR Carew from 04. *The Vicarage, Church Street, Pembroke Dock SA72 6AR* Tel (01646) 682943 E-mail andrewdavies19@aol.com

DAVIES, Anthony. *See* DAVIES, The Ven Vincent Anthony

DAVIES, Anthony. *See* DAVIES, David Anthony

DAVIES, Arthur Gerald Miles. b 29. Univ of Wales (Ban) BA51. St Mich Coll Llan 51. **d** 53 **p** 54. C Shotton *St As* 53-60; R Nannerch 60-63; V Llansilin and Llangadwaladr 63-68; V Llansilin w Llangadwaladr and Llangedwyn 68-71; V Llanfair Caereinion w Llanllugan 71-75; TV Wrexham 75-83; V Hanmer, Bronington, Bettisfield, Tallarn Green 83-94; rtd 94. *Elland, School Lane, Bronington, Whitchurch SY13 3HN* Tel (01948) 780296

DAVIES, Arthur Lloyd. *See* LLOYD-DAVIES, Arthur

DAVIES, Barry Lewis. **d** 05. NSM Hardington Vale *B & W* from 05. *3 The Lays, Goose Street, Beckington, Frome BA11 6RS*

DAVIES, Benjamin John. b 27. Glouc Sch of Min 80 Trin Coll Bris 87. **d** 88 **p** 89. NSM Cinderford St Steph w Littledean *Glouc* 88-98; Perm to Offic 98-00. *22 Withy Park, Bishopston, Swansea SA3 3EY* Tel (01792) 232352

DAVIES, Bernard. b 24. St D Coll Lamp BA49. **d** 51 **p** 52. C New Tredegar *Mon* 51-53; C Gelligaer *Llan* 53-54; V Deeping Fen *Linc* 56-58; R Beswick *Man* 58-63; V Stand Lane St Jo 63-66; rtd 84. *26 Cwrt Bryn Coed, Coed Pella Road, Bron y Nant, Colwyn Bay LL29 7BJ*

DAVIES, Canon Bernard. b 34. Lon Univ BD63. Oak Hill Th Coll 59. **d** 63 **p** 64. C Rawtenstall St Mary *Man* 63-69; Sec Rwanda Miss 69-71; R Widford *Chelmsf* 71-78; V Braintree 78-00; RD Braintree 87-95; Hon Can Chelmsf Cathl 92-00; rtd 00; Perm to Offic *Nor* from 00 and *St E* from 01. *3 Brookwood Close, Worlingham, Beccles NR34 7RJ* Tel (01502) 719739

DAVIES, Brian. *See* DAVIES, Albert Brian

DAVIES, Carol Ann. b 52. Bp Otter Coll 94. **d** 96 **p** 98. NSM Oakfield St Jo *Portsm* 96-00; NSM Bonchurch 00-04; NSM Ventnor St Cath 00-04; NSM Ventnor H Trin 00-04; TR Upper Kennet *Sarum* 04; R from 04. *The Rectory, 27 High Street, Avebury, Marlborough SN8 1RF* Tel (01672) 539643 E-mail upkennet@fish.co.uk

DAVIES, Catharine Mary. *See* FURLONG, Mrs Catharine Mary

DAVIES, Ceri John. b 61. Univ of Wales (Lamp) BA91 Univ of Wales (Abth) PGCE92 Univ of Wales (Cardiff) BTh00. St Mich Coll Llan 97. **d** 00 **p** 01. C Carmarthen St Dav *St D* 00-03; TV Llanelli from 03. *St Peter's Vicarage, St Peter's Terrace, Llanelli SA15 2RT* Tel (01554) 752378 E-mail ruth_ceri2000@coleg88.freeserve.co.uk

DAVIES, Chris. *See* DAVIES, Canon David Christopher

DAVIES, Christopher. b 51. NE Lon Poly BA72. SEITE 99. **d** 02 **p** 03. NSM Peckham St Sav *S'wark* from 02. *5 Wyleu Street, London SE23 1DU* Tel and fax (020) 8291 3831 Mobile 07941-392682 E-mail christopherscott@tinyworld.co.uk

DAVIES, Christopher Edward. b 72. **d** 03 **p** 04. OLM Bilston *Lich* from 03. *10 Wroxham Glen, Willenhall WV13 3HU* Tel (01902) 655305 Mobile 07952-196204

DAVIES, Christopher John. b 55. St Alb Minl Tr Scheme 83. **d** 86 **p** 87. C Tooting All SS *S'wark* 86-90; V Malden St Jas 90-96; RD Kingston 92-96; TR Wimbledon from 96. *St Mary's Rectory, 14 Arthur Road, London SW19 7DZ* Tel (020) 8946 2830 *or* 8946 2605 Fax 8946 6293
E-mail church@stmaryswimbledon.fsnet.co.uk

DAVIES, Canon Clifford Thomas. b 41. Glouc Th Course. **d** 83 **p** 84. NSM Dean Forest H Trin *Glouc* 83-87; C Huntley and Longhope 87; R Ruardean from 87; Hon Can Glouc Cathl from 02. *The Rectory, High Street, Ruardean GL17 9US* Tel (01594) 542214

DAVIES, David Anthony (Tony). b 57. Thames Poly BSc81 MRICS84. Coll of Resurr Mirfield 85. **d** 88 **p** 89. C Stalybridge *Man* 88-91; C Swinton and Pendlebury 91-92 and 01-02; TV 92-01; V Tonge Moor from 02. *St Augustine's Vicarage, Redthorpe Close, Bolton BL2 2PQ* Tel and fax (01204) 523899 Mobile 07866-359864 E-mail tony@davieses.co.uk

DAVIES, David Arthur Guy Hampton. b 27. St Jo Coll Ox BA50 DipTh51 MA55. Ely Th Coll 51. **d** 53 **p** 54. C Somers Town *Lon* 53-55; C Cranford 55-60; C Shrewsbury H Cross *Lich* 60-62; R Stamford St Mary and St Mich *Linc* 62-90; rtd 90; Perm to Offic *Lich* from 97. *8 Holywell Terrace, Shrewsbury SY2 5DF* Tel (01743) 245086

DAVIES, David Barry Grenville. b 38. St Jo Coll Dur BA60 MA77. Sarum Th Coll 61. **d** 63 **p** 64. C Aberystwyth St Mich *St D* 63-66; Min Can St D Cathl 66-72; R Stackpole Elidor w St Petrox 72-83; V Laugharne w Llansadwrnen and Llandawke 83-03; rtd 03. *3 Clos y Drindod, Buarth Road, Aberystwyth SY23 1LR* Tel (01970) 626289

DAVIES, David Berwyn. b 42. SSC Univ of Wales Dip Past Th 66. St Mich Coll Llan 95. **d** 96 **p** 97. C Llanelli *St D* 96-98; R Llanerch Aeron w Ciliau Aeron and Dihewyd etc from 98. *The Rectory, Ciliau Aeron, Lampeter SA48 7SG* Tel (01570) 471283
E-mail taddavid@aol.com

DAVIES, Canon David Christopher (Chris). b 52. Lon Univ BSc73 Leeds Univ DipTh75. Coll of Resurr Mirfield 73. **d** 76 **p** 77. C Bethnal Green St Jo w St Simon *Lon* 76-78; C Bethnal Green St Jo w St Bart 78-80; C-in-c Portsea St Geo CD *Portsm* 80-81; Relig Affairs Producer Radio Victory 81-86; V Portsea St Geo 81-87; Chapl Ham Green Hosp Bris 87-94; Chapl Southmead Hosp Bris 87-94; Chapl Southmead Health Services NHS Trust 94-99; Chapl N Bris NHS Trust from 99; Perm to Offic *B & W* from 94; Hon Can Bris Cathl *Bris* from 99. *Southmead Hospital, Westbury-on-Trym, Bristol BS10 5NB,* or *28 Hortham Lane, Almondsbury, Bristol BS32 4JL* Tel 0117-950 5050 *or* 959 5447 E-mail davies_c@southmead.swest.nhs.uk

DAVIES, David Geoffrey George. b 24. Univ of Wales (Ban) BA49 Lon Univ BD55 Chorley Coll of Educn PGCE75. St Mich Coll Llan 49. **d** 51 **p** 52. C Brecon St Mary w Battle and Llanhamlach *S & B* 51-55; Min Can Brecon Cathl 53-55; C Oystermouth 55-59; V Cwm *St As* 59-63; Warden of Ords 62-70; V Ruabon 63-70; Hon Can St As Cathl 66-69; Cursal Can 69-70; Hon C W Derby St Jo *Liv* 70-81; Chapl to Welsh Speaking Angl in Liv 74-81 and from 96; TV Bourne Valley *Sarum* 81-87; TR 87-89; Bp's Chapl to Schs 83-89; RD Alderbury 86-89; rtd 89; Hon Chapl Liv Cathl *Liv* 89-04; Sub-Chapl HM Pris Risley 90-96. *55 Hattons Lane, Liverpool L16 7QR* Tel 0151-722 1415

DAVIES, David Islwyn. b 42. St Deiniol's Hawarden 83. **d** 85 **p** 86. C Llangiwg *S & B* 85-87; C Swansea St Pet 87-89; Miss to Seamen 89-94; The Netherlands *Eur* 89-92; Chapl Schiedam Miss to Seamen 89-92; Chapl Milford Haven Miss to Seamen 92-94; V Pontyates and Llangyndeyrn *St D* 94-99; R Ystradgynlais *S & B* from 99. *The Rectory, 2 Heol Eglwys, Ystradgynlais, Swansea SA9 1EY* Tel (01639) 843200

DAVIES, Canon David Jeremy Christopher. b 46. CCC Cam BA68 MA72. Westcott Ho Cam 68. **d** 71 **p** 72. C Stepney St Dunstan and All SS *Lon* 71-74; Chapl Qu Mary Coll 74-78; Chapl Univ of Wales (Cardiff) *Llan* 78-85; Can Res Sarum Cathl *Sarum* from 85. *Hungerford Chantry, 54 The Close, Salisbury SP1 2EL* Tel (01722) 555179 E-mail djcdavies@aol.com *or* precentor@salcath.co.uk

DAVIES, David Leslie Augustus. b 25. St D Coll Lamp BA50. **d** 51 **p** 52. C Aberystwyth *St D* 51-55; C Llanelli St Paul 55-56; V Castlemartin and Warren 56-61; R Eglwysilan *Llan* 61-65; Chapl Mayday, Qu and St Mary's Hosps Croydon 65-71; V Penrhyncoch and Elerch *St D* 71-74; Chapl R Berks and Reading Distr Hosps 74-89; rtd 90; Perm to Offic *Win* from 90. *Basset Down, 31 Three Acre Drive, New Milton BH25 7LG* Tel (01425) 610376

DAVIES, Canon David Michael Cole. b 44. St D Coll Lamp DipTh69. **d** 68 **p** 69. C Carmarthen St Pet *St D* 68-72; R Dinas 72-77; V Ty-Croes w Saron 77-80; V Llanedi w Tycroes and Saron 80-90; RD Dyffryn Aman 85-90; V Dafen and Llwynhendy 90-94; V Dafen from 94; Hon Can St D Cathl from 00. *The Vicarage, Bryngwyn Road, Dafen, Llanelli SA14 8LW* Tel (01554) 774730 E-mail dcmcd@aol.com

DAVIES, Prof David Protheroe. b 39. CCC Cam BA62 MA66 CCC Ox MA69 BD69. Ripon Hall Ox 62. **d** 64 **p** 65. C Swansea St Mary w H Trin *S & B* 64-67; Lect Th Univ of Wales (Lamp) 67-75; Sen Lect 75-86; Dean Faculty of Th 75-77 and from 81; Hd Th and Relig Studies from 84; Prof Th Univ of Wales (Lamp) from 86; Pro Vice-Chan from 88; Bp's Chapl for Th Educn *S & B* from 79. *University of Wales, Lampeter SA48 7ED* Tel (01570) 422351

DAVIES, David Vernon. b 14. AFBPsS68 Univ of Wales (Swansea) BA35 BD38 St Cath Coll Ox MA40 K Coll Lon PhD56. St D Coll Lamp 41. **d** 41 **p** 42. C Llanelli Ch Ch *St D* 41-46; Chapl St John's Coll Nassau Bahamas 46-50; Chapl Cane Hill Hosp Coulsdon 50-61; Lect St Luke's Coll Ex 61-65; Lic to Offic *Ex* 61-68; Sen Lect St Luke's Coll Ex 65-68; Lic to Offic *Llan* from 68; Prin Lect Llan Coll of Educn 68-77; Sen Lect Univ of Wales (Cardiff) 77-79; rtd 79. *41 Cefn Coed Avenue, Cyncoed, Cardiff CF23 6HF* Tel (029) 2075 7635

DAVIES, David William. b 64. **d** 90 **p** 91. C Newton St Pet *S & B* 90-93; V Llywel and Traean-glas w Llanulid 93-97; CF from 97. *c/o MOD Chaplains (Army)* Tel (01980) 615804 Fax 615800

DAVIES, Dennis William. b 24. Leeds Univ BA46 K Coll Lon AKC54 BD65 Open Univ BA92. **d** 54 **p** 55. C Aylesbury *Ox* 54-58; Lic to Offic from 60; rtd 90. *45 Green End Street, Aston Clinton, Aylesbury HP22 5JE* Tel (01296) 630989

DAVIES, Derek George. b 47. UWIST BEng74 Univ of Wales (Lamp) BD03. St Mich Coll Llan 03. **d** 05. NSM Steynton *St D* from 05. *Ty Llosg, Clarbeston Road, Pembroke SA63 4SG* Tel (01437) 563560 E-mail derekgeorgedavies@hotmail.com

DAVIES, Derwent. *See* DAVIES, Preb Thomas Derwent

DAVIES, Dewi Gwynfor. b 56. Thames Poly DipArch80 RIBA81 Univ of Wales (Abth) BD92 MTh98. **d** 98 **p** 99. C Llangunnor w Cwmffrwd *St D* 98-99; P-in-c Elerch w Penrhyncoch w Capel Bangor and Goginan 99-00; P-in-c Cil-y-Cwm and Ystrad-ffin w Rhandir-mwyn etc 00-01; V 01-03; V Llanedi w Tycroes and Saron from 03. *The Vicarage, 37 Hendre Road, Tycroes SA18 3LA* Tel (01269) 592384

DAVIES, Dillwyn. b 30. St Mich Coll Llan 52. **d** 54 **p** 55. C Laugharne w Llansadwrnen and Llandawke *St D* 54-57; Lic to Offic *Dur* 57-58; Miss to Seamen 57-58; Ceylon 58-62; R Winthorpe *S'well* 62-71; V Langford w Holme 62-71; V Mansfield Woodhouse 71-85; R Gedling 85-92; RD Gedling 85-90; Hon Can S'well Minster 90-92; rtd 92. *7 Norbury Drive, Mansfield NG18 4HT* Tel (01623) 458594

DAVIES, Dorrien Paul. b 64. Univ of Wales (Ban) DipTh86 Univ of Wales (Lamp) BA95. Llan Dioc Tr Scheme 86 St Mich Coll Llan DPS88. **d** 88 **p** 89. C Llanelli *St D* 88-91; V Llanfihangel Ystrad and Cilcennin w Trefilan etc 91-99; V St Dogmael's w Moylgrove and Monington from 99. *The Vicarage, St Dogmael's, Cardigan SA43 3DX* Tel (01239) 612030

DAVIES, Prof Douglas James. b 47. St Jo Coll Dur BA69 St Pet Coll Ox MLitt72 Nottm Univ PhD80 Uppsala Univ DTh98. Cranmer Hall Dur 71. **d** 75 **p** 76. Lect Nottm Univ 75-97; Sen Lect 90-97; Hon C Wollaton *S'well* 75-83; Hon C Attenborough 83-85; Hon C E Leake 85-91; Hon C Daybrook 91-97; Prof RS Nottm Univ 93-97; Prin SS Hild and Bede Coll Dur 97-00; Prof Th Dur Univ from 97; Prof Study of Relig Dur Univ from 00; Perm to Offic *Dur* from 97. *Department of Theology, Abbey House, Palace Green, Durham DH1 3RS* Tel 0191-375 7697
E-mail douglas.davies@durham.ac.uk

DAVIES, Canon Douglas Tudor. b 20. Univ of Wales (Ban) BA44. Coll of Resurr Mirfield 44. **d** 46 **p** 47. C Swansea Ch Ch *S & B* 46-52; C Oystermouth 52-57; R Llangynllo and Bleddfa 57-63; C-in-c Treboeth CD 63-65; V Treboeth 65-90; RD Penderi 78-90; Hon Can Brecon Cathl 82-83; Can 83-90; rtd 90. *245A Swansea Road, Waunarlwydd, Swansea SA5 4SN* Tel (01792) 879587

DAVIES, Edward Earl. b 40. Llan Dioc Tr Scheme 88. **d** 90 **p** 91. C Pontypridd St Cath w St Matt *Llan* 90-93; V Ferndale w Maerdy 93-00; V Cardiff Ch Ch Roath Park from 00. *154 Lake Road East, Cardiff CF23 5NQ* Tel (029) 2075 7190

DAVIES, Edward Trevor. b 37. MRSC62 MInstE74 CEng78. N Ord Course 92. **d** 95 **p** 96. NSM Waverton *Ches* 95-99; NSM Hargrave 99-00; C Bunbury and Tilstone Fearnall 00-02; NSM 02-03; Hon Asst Chapl Countess of Chester Hosp NHS Trust 95-02; Chapl from 02. *Athergreen, 5 Allansford Avenue, Waverton, Chester CH3 7QH* Tel and fax (01244) 332106 *or* 365000 E-mail e.trevordavies@virgin.net

DAVIES, Edward William Llewellyn. b 51. St Jo Coll Nottm BTh77. **d** 78 **p** 79. C Southsea St Jude *Portsm* 78-81; C Alverstoke 81-84; R Abbas and Templecombe w Horsington *B & W* 84-89; Perm to Offic *Ches* 89-99; V Sutton St Jas from 99; Asst Warden of Readers from 02; RD Macclesfield from 05. *St James's Vicarage, Church Lane, Sutton, Macclesfield SK11 0DS* Tel (01260) 252228 E-mail taffy@parishpump.co.uk

DAVIES, Eileen. *See* DAVIES, Mrs Rachel Hannah Eileen

DAVIES, Ms Elizabeth Jane. b 58. Man Univ BA97 Birm Univ MA02 RGN82 RSCN88. Qu Coll Birm 99. **d** 01 **p** 02. C Spotland *Man* 01-04; Chapl Pennine Acute Hosps NHS Trust from 04; Chapl Springhill Hospice from 04. *Rochdale Infirmary, Whitehall Street, Rochdale OL12 0NB* Tel (01706) 517044
E-mail elizabeth.davies@pat.nhs.uk

DAVIES, Mrs Elizabeth Jean. b 39. Lon Univ MB, BS63 MRCS63 LRCP63. Chich Th Coll 86. **d** 89 **p** 95. Par Dn Southwick St Mich *Chich* 89-91; Par Dn Littlehampton and Wick 91-95; C Seaford w Sutton 95-97; NSM E Preston w Kingston 97-04; rtd 99; P-in-c Everton and Mattersey w Clayworth *S'well* 04-05. *Mayfield, Bone Mill Lane, Welham, Retford DN22 9NL* Tel (01777) 703727

DAVIES, Eric Brian. b 36. St Jo Coll Nottm. **d** 87 **p** 89. NSM Castle Donington and Lockington cum Hemington *Leic* 87-88; Hon C Hathern, Long Whatton and Diseworth 89-90; Hon C Hathern, Long Whatton and Diseworth w Belton etc 90-93; C Minster-in-Sheppey *Cant* 93-00; rtd 00; NSM Walsall St Gabr Fulbrook *Lich* 00-03; NSM Caldmore 00-02; NSM Caldmore w Palfrey 02-03; NSM Kinver and Enville from 03. *The Vicarage, The Close, Enville, Stourbridge DY7 5HX* Tel (01384) 878228

DAVIES, Evelyn Dorothy. MBE99. BEd72 Liv Univ CertEd56 Dip Psychology 58. **d** 96 **p** 97. NSM Llangynog *St As* 96-00; P-in-c Aberdaron w Rhiw and Llanfaelrhys etc *Ban* 00-04; R from 04. *Dyffryn, Aberdaron, Pwllheli LL53 8BG* Tel and fax (01758) 760229 E-mail melangell@pennant1.demon.co.uk

DAVIES, Frances Elizabeth. b 38. BA CertEd. Moray Ord Course. **d** 95. Hon C Thurso *Mor* from 95; Hon C Wick from 95. *22 Granville Crescent, Thurso, Caithness KW14 7NP* Tel (01847) 892386 E-mail reallyfed@yahoo.co.uk

✠**DAVIES, The Rt Revd Francis James Saunders.** b 37. Univ of Wales (Ban) BA60 Selw Coll Cam BA62 MA66 Bonn Univ 63. St Mich Coll Llan 62. **d** 63 **p** 64 **c** 00. C Holyhead w Rhoscolyn *Ban* 63-67; Chapl Ban Cathl 67-69; R Llanllyfni 69-75; Can Missr Ban Cathl 75-78; V Gorseinon *S & B* 78-86; RD Llwchwr 83-86; V Cardiff Dewi Sant *Llan* 86-93; R Criccieth w Treflys *Ban* 93-99; Adn Meirionnydd 93-99; Bp Ban 99-04; rtd 04. *Ger-y-Nant, 5 Maes-y-Coed, Cardigan SA43 1AP*

DAVIES, Gareth Rhys. b 51. DipHE. Oak Hill Th Coll. **d** 83 **p** 84. C Gt Warley Ch Ch *Chelmsf* 83-86; C Oxhey All SS *St Alb* 86-90; C Aldridge *Lich* 90-99; V Colney Heath St Mark *St Alb* 99-00; V Sneyd Green *Lich* from 00. *St Andrew's Vicarage, 42 Granville Avenue, Sneyd Green, Stoke-on-Trent ST1 6BH* Tel (01782) 215139

DAVIES, Geoffrey. *See* DAVIES, David Geoffrey George

✠**DAVIES, The Rt Revd Geoffrey Francis.** b 41. Cape Town Univ BA62 Em Coll Cam BA67 MA71. Cuddesdon Coll 67. **d** 69 **p** 70 **c** 87. C W Brompton St Mary *Lon* 69-72; Serowe St Aug Botswana 72-76; S Africa from 77; R Kalk Bay H Trin Cape Town 77-80; Dir Dept of Miss 81-87; Suff Bp St John 88-91; Bp Umzimvubu from 91. *PO Box 644, Kokstad, 4700 South Africa* Tel (0027) (39) 727 3351 Fax 727 4117 E-mail umzimvubu@cosa.org.za

DAVIES, Canon Geoffrey Lovat. b 30. St Aid Birkenhead. **d** 62 **p** 63. C Davenham *Ches* 62-65; C Higher Bebington 65-67; V Witton 67-80; R Lymm 80-96; Dioc Clergy Widows and Retirement Officer 87-91; Hon Can Ches Cathl 88-96; RD Gt Budworth 91-96; P-in-c Weaverham 96; rtd 96; Perm to Offic *Liv* and *Ches* from 96. *21 Howbeck Close, Prenton CH43 6TH* Tel 0151-653 2441

DAVIES, Geoffrey Michael. b 43. St D Coll Lamp. **d** 70 **p** 71. C Brynmawr *S & B* 70-73; Coll of Ascension Selly Oak 73-74; S Africa 74-91 and from 99; C Claremont St Sav 74-76; R Strand 76-82; R E London St Sav 82-84; Assoc R Constantia Ch Ch 90-91; C Roath *Llan* 91-95; V Llanishen w Trellech Grange and Llanfihangel etc *Mon* 95-99; R Graaff-Reinet St Jas from 03. *PO Box 473, Graaff-Reinet, 6280 South Africa* Tel (0027) (498) 922458

DAVIES, George Vivian. b 21. CCC Cam BA47 MA49. Ely Th Coll. **d** 49 **p** 50. C Maidstone St Martin *Cant* 49-51; C Folkestone St Mary and St Eanswythe 51-56; V Leysdown w Harty 56-59; R Warehorne w Kenardington 59-74; R Rounton w Welbury *York* 74-86; rtd 86; Perm to Offic *Derby* 86-99. *12 Rectory Drive, Wingerworth, Chesterfield S42 6RT* Tel (01246) 279222

DAVIES, George William. b 51. Open Univ BA74 MPhil89 MIPD. Sarum & Wells Th Coll 83. **d** 85 **p** 86. C Mansfield SS Pet and Paul *S'well* 85-89; Chapl Cen Notts HA 86-89; P-in-c Fobbing and Ind Chapl *Chelmsf* 89-96; Chapl Thurrock Lakeside Shopping Cen 93-96; R Mottingham St Andr *S'wark* 96-04; V Lamorbey H Trin *Roch* from 04; Chapl Rose Bruford Coll from 04. *Holy Trinity Vicarage, 1 Hurst Road, Sidcup DA15 9AE* Tel (020) 8309 7886 *or* 8300 8231 E-mail george@daviesgeorge.wanadoo.co.uk

DAVIES, Glanmor Adrian. b 51. St D Coll Lamp DipTh73. **d** 73 **p** 75. C Llanstadwel *St D* 73-78; R Dinas w Llanllawer and Pontfaen w Morfil etc 78-84; V Lamphey w Hodgeston 84-85; V Lamphey w Hodgeston and Carew 85-03; V Borth and Eglwys-fach w Llangynfelyn from 03. *The Vicarage, Swn y Mor, The Cliff, Borth SY24 5NG* Tel (01970) 871594

✠**DAVIES, The Rt Revd Glenn Naunton.** b 50. Sydney Univ BSc72 Sheff Univ PhD88. Westmr Th Sem (USA) BD78 ThM79. **d** 81 **p** 81 **c** 01. Australia 81-85; Hon C Fulwood *Sheff* 85-87; Hon C Lodge Moor St Luke 86-87; Australia from 87; Lect Moore Th Coll 83-95; R Miranda 95-01; Bp N Sydney from 01. *PO Box Q190, Queen Victoria Buildings, Sydney, NSW, Australia 1230* Tel (0061) (2) 9265 1527 *or* 9419 6761 Fax 9265 1543

DAVIES, Glyn Richards. b 28. Solicitor 52. Mon Dioc Tr Scheme 76. **d** 79 **p** 80. NSM Michaelston-y-Fedw and Rudry *Mon* 79-88; NSM St Mellons and Michaelston-y-Fedw 88-96; NSM St Mellons from 96. *Ty Golau, 8 Tyr Winch Road, St Mellons, Cardiff CF3 5UX* Tel (029) 2041 3426

DAVIES, Glyndwr George. b 36. Glouc Sch of Min 88. **d** 91 **p** 92. NSM Clodock and Longtown w Craswall, Llanveynoe etc *Heref* 91-02; rtd 02; Perm to Offic *Heref* from 02. *White House Farm, Llanfihangel Crucorney, Abergavenny NP7 8HW* Tel (01873) 890251

DAVIES, The Ven Graham James. b 35. Univ of Wales BD72 St D Coll Lamp BA56. St Mich Coll Llan 56 Episc Th Sch Cam Mass 58. **d** 59 **p** 60. C Johnston w Steynton *St D* 59-62; C Llangathen w Llanfihangel Cilfargen 62-64; Min Can St D Cathl 64-66; R Burton 66-71; R Hubberston 71-74; Hon C Lenham w Boughton Malherbe *Cant* 74-80; V Cwmddauddwr w St Harmon's and Llanwrthwl *S & B* 80-86; V Cydweli and Llandyfaelog *St D* 86-97; Can St D Cathl 92-02; Adn St D 96-02; V Steynton 97-02; rtd 02. *Mistral, 4 Lloyd George Lane, Pembroke SA71 4EZ*

DAVIES, Canon Henry Joseph. b 38. Univ of Wales (Cardiff) BSc61. St Mich Coll Llan 75. **d** 76 **p** 77. C Griffithstown *Mon* 76-79; TV Cwmbran 79-85; V Newport St Andr 85-03; Can St Woolos Cathl 98-03; rtd 03. *14 Morden Road, Newport NP19 7EU*

DAVIES, Canon Henry Lewis. b 20. St Jo Coll Dur BA42 DipTh43 MA45. **d** 43 **p** 44. C Upton on Severn *Worc* 43-47; C Dudley St Jo 47-49; C Halesowen 49-52; V Cradley 52-65; R Old Swinford 65-78; R Old Swinford Stourbridge 78-85; rtd 85; Perm to Offic *Worc* from 87. *15 Bramley Way, Bewdley DY12 2PU* Tel (01299) 402713

DAVIES, Herbert John. b 30. Cheltenham & Glouc Coll of HE BA97. Glouc Sch of Min 84. **d** 87 **p** 88. NSM Cheltenham St Mark *Glouc* 87-01; Perm to Offic from 01. *45 Farmington Road, Benhall, Cheltenham GL51 6AG* Tel (01242) 515996

✠**DAVIES, The Rt Revd Howell Haydn.** b 27. ARIBA55 DipArch54. Tyndale Hall Bris 56. **d** 59 **p** 60 **c** 81. C Heref St Pet w St Owen *Heref* 59-61; Kenya 61-79; Adn N Maseno 71-74; Provost Nairobi 74-79; V Woking St Pet *Guildf* 79-81; Bp Karamoja Uganda 81-87; V Wolverhampton St Jude *Lich* 87-93; rtd 93; Perm to Offic *Heref* 93-99. *3 Gilberts Wood, Ewyas Harold, Hereford HR2 0JL* Tel (01981) 240984

DAVIES, Huw. *See* DAVIES, Philip Huw

DAVIES, Huw. *See* DAVIES, Peter Huw

DAVIES, Hywel John. b 45. Univ of Wales (Abth) BA67 Univ of Wales (Ban) DipEd68 Univ of Wales (Cardiff) MA90 Univ of Wales (Ban) BTh99. St Mich Coll Llan Qu Coll Birm. **d** 97 **p** 98. Min Can Ban Cathl *Ban* 97-98; C Llandudno 98-99; Lic to Offic *Llan* 99-03; NSM Canton Cardiff 03-04; P-in-c Llanarthne and Llanddarog *St D* from 04; Chapl Coleg Sir Gâr from 04. *The Vicarage, Llanddarog, Carmarthen SA32 8PA* Tel (01267) 275268

DAVIES, Ian. b 45. Man Coll of Educn TCert74 Open Univ BA79. Carl Dioc Tr Inst 88. **d** 91 **p** 92. NSM Harraby *Carl* 91-95; C Barrow St Jo 95-96; P-in-c 96-00; P-in-c Beetham and Youth and Sch Support Officer 00-05; V Marown *S & M* from 05. *Marown Vicarage, Main Road, Crosby, Isle of Man IM4 4BH* Tel (01624) 851378 E-mail reviand@manx.net

DAVIES, Ian. b 54. Sheff Hallam Univ BA80 Univ of Wales (Cardiff) MSc(Econ)86 MBA92 Bris Univ PhD01 CQSW80. Wycliffe Hall Ox 02. **d** 04 **p** 05. C Swansea St Pet *S & B* from 04. *The Parsonage, 18 Ystrad Road, Fforestfach, Swansea SA5 4BT* Tel (01792) 541244 Mobile 07779-145267 E-mail iandavies12@hotmail.com

DAVIES, Ian Charles. b 51. Sarum & Wells Th Coll 78. **d** 81 **p** 82. C E Bedfont *Lon* 81-84; C Cheam *S'wark* 84-87; V Merton St Jas 87-96; RD Merton 91-96; Chapl Tiffin Sch Kingston 96-97; P-in-c Kingston St Luke *S'wark* 96-98; V S Beddington St Mich 98-99. *111 Milton Road, London W7 1LG* Tel (020) 8621 4450

DAVIES, Ian Elliott. b 64. Univ of Wales (Ban) BD85. Ridley Hall Cam 86. **d** 88 **p** 89. C Baglan *Llan* 88-90; C Skewen 90-96; C St Marylebone All SS *Lon* 96-01; R Hollywood St Thos USA from 02. *St Thomas's Church, 7501 Hollywood Boulevard, Hollywood, CA 90046, USA* Tel (001) (323) 876 2102 Fax 876 7738 E-mail frdavies@saintthomashollywood.org

DAVIES, Ion. *See* DAVIES, Johnston ap Llynfi

DAVIES, Islwyn. *See* DAVIES, David Islwyn

DAVIES, Canon Ivor Llewellyn. b 35. Univ of Wales BA56 St Cath Soc Ox BA58 MA63. Wycliffe Hall Ox 56. **d** 62 **p** 63. C Wrexham *St As* 62-64; India 65-71; V Connah's Quay *St As* 71-79; P-in-c Gorsley w Cliffords Mesne *Glouc* 79-84; P-in-c Hempsted 84-90; Dir of Ords 84-90; Hon Can Glouc Cathl 89-01; V Parkend 90-01; P-in-c Viney Hill 97-01; rtd 01; Perm to Offic *Glouc* from 01. *Rose Cottage, Church Walk, Parkend, Lydney GL15 4HQ* Tel (01594) 564512

DAVIES, James Alan. b 38. Lambeth STh95. St Jo Coll Nottm. **d** 83 **p** 84. C Fletchamstead *Cov* 83-87; P-in-c Hartshill 87-89; V 89-93; V E Green 93-03; rtd 03; Hon C Mickleton, Willersey, Saintbury etc *Glouc* from 04. *50 Ballards Close, Mickleton, Chipping Campden GL55 6TN* Tel (01386) 430210 E-mail alan.davies@ukonline.co.uk

DAVIES, Canon James Trevor Eiddig. b 17. St D Coll Lamp BA39 AKC41. **d** 41 **p** 42. C Rhymney *Mon* 41-44; C Newport St Andr 44-47; P-in-c 47-51; P-in-c Nash 50-51; R Bettws Newydd w Trostrey and Kemeys Commander 51-58; V Blaenavon w Capel Newydd 58-68; V Llantarnam 68-71; TR Cwmbran 71-86; Hon Can St Woolos Cathl 83-86; rtd 86; Lic to Offic *Mon* from 86. *34 Rockfield Road, Monmouth NP25 5BA* Tel (01600) 716649

DAVIES, James William. b 51. Trin Hall Cam BA72 MA76 St Jo Coll Dur BA79. **d** 80 **p** 81. C Croydon Ch Ch Broad Green *Cant* 80-83; CMS 83-86; Chapl Bethany Sch Goudhurst 86-90; P-in-c Parkstone St Luke *Sarum* 90-00. *Address temp unknown*

DAVIES, Mrs Jane Ann. b 58. Heref Coll of FE ONC77 Coll of Ripon & York St Jo MA97. N Ord Course 94 Aston Tr Scheme 91 WMMTC 93. **d** 96 **p** 97. NSM Heref S Wye *Heref* 96-97; C 97-00; P-in-c Bishop's Frome w Castle Frome and Fromes Hill from 00; P-in-c Acton Beauchamp and Evesbatch w Stanford Bishop from 00; P-in-c Stoke Lacy, Moreton Jeffries w Much Cowarne etc from 00. *The Vicarage, Bishop's Frome, Worcester WR6 5AP* Tel (01885) 490204 E-mail jane@davies4771.fsnet.co.uk

DAVIES, Mrs Jaqueline Ann. b 42. Bris Univ BA64 CertEd65 Univ of Wales (Lamp) MA99. EMMTC 84 St As Minl Tr Course 97. **d** 98 **p** 99. NSM Llanfair DC, Derwen, Llanelidan and Efenechtyd *St As* 98-00; Perm to Offic from 00. *The Vicarage, Llanrhaeadr-ym-Mochnant, Oswestry SY10 0JZ* Tel (01691) 780247

DAVIES, Jeffrey William. b 45. St Cath Coll Cam MA63 LLM64 Solicitor 69. N Ord Course 01. **d** 04 **p** 05. NSM Ramsbottom St Andr *Man* from 04. *44 Higher Dunscar, Egerton, Bolton BL7 9TF* Tel and fax (01204) 412503 E-mail jeffdavies@higherdunscar.fsnet.co.uk

DAVIES, Jeremy. *See* DAVIES, Canon David Jeremy Christopher

DAVIES, Sister Joan Margaret. b 06. Bedf Coll Lon BA28 Maria Grey Coll Lon DipEd29. St Andr Ho Ox 31. **dss** 37 **d** 87. CSA from 34; Notting Hill St Clem *Lon* 37-43; Paddington St Steph w St Luke 48-69; Shadwell St Paul w Ratcliffe St Jas 69-73; R Foundn of St Kath in Ratcliffe 69-73; Abbey Ho Malmesbury 76-79; Lic to Offic *Bris* 76-79. *St Andrew's House, 2 Tavistock Road, London W11 1BA* Tel (020) 7229 2662

DAVIES, John. *See* DAVIES, Herbert John

DAVIES, John. *See* DAVIES, Benjamin John

DAVIES, John. *See* PAGE DAVIES, David John

DAVIES, John. *See* DAVIES, Kenneth John

DAVIES, John. b 62. Univ of Wales (Cardiff) BA88. Ridley Hall Cam 98. **d** 00 **p** 01. C Wavertree H Trin *Liv* 00-04; P-in-c W Derby Gd Shep from 04. *345 Utting Avenue East, Liverpool L11 1DF* Tel 0151-256 0510 E-mail johndavies.liverpool@blueyonder.co.uk

DAVIES, John Barden. b 47. Univ of Wales (Ban) DipTh70. St D Coll Lamp 70. **d** 71 **p** 72. C Rhosllannerchrugog *St As* 71-75; R Llanbedr-y-Cennin *Ban* 75-86; Adult Educn Officer 86-93; V Betws-y-Coed and Capel Curig w Penmachno etc 86-93; R Llanfwrog and Clocaenog and Gyffylliog *St As* from 93; RD Dyffryn Clwyd from 95. *The Rectory, Mwrog Street, Ruthin LL15 1LE* Tel (01824) 704866 Mobile 07050-152824 Fax 702724 E-mail jbarden@btinternet.com

DAVIES, John Daniel Lee. b 55. Trin Coll Carmarthen BEd79 CertRE91. **d** 00 **p** 00. C Leverburgh *Arg* 00-01; P-in-c Harris Ch Ch from 01. *3A Cluer, Isle of Harris HS3 3EP* Tel (01859) 530344

DAVIES, The Very Revd John David Edward. b 53. Southn Univ LLB74 Univ of Wales (Cardiff) LLM95. St Mich Coll Llan 82. **d** 84 **p** 85. C Chepstow *Mon* 84-86; C-in-c Michaelston-y-Fedw and Rudry 86-89; R Bedwas and Rudry 89-95; V Maindee 95-00; Dean Brecon *S & B* from 00; V Brecon St Mary w Llanddew from 00; P-in-c Cynog Honddu from 05. *The Deanery, Cathedral Close, Brecon LD3 9DP* Tel (01874) 623344

✠**DAVIES, The Rt Revd John Dudley.** b 27. Trin Coll Cam BA51 MA63. Linc Th Coll 52. **d** 53 **p** 54 **c** 87. C Leeds Halton St Wilfrid *Ripon* 53-56; C Yeoville S Africa 57; R Evander 57-61; R Empangeni 61-63; Chapl Witwatersrand Univ 63-71; Sec Chapls in HE Gen Syn Bd of Educn 71-74; P-in-c Keele *Lich* 74-76; Chapl Keele Univ 74-76; Prin USPG Coll of the Ascension Selly Oak 76-81; Preb Lich Cathl *Lich* 76-87; Can Res, Preb and Sacr St As Cathl *St As* 82-85; Dioc Missr 82-87; V Llanrhaeadr-ym-Mochnant, Llanarmon, Pennant etc 85-87; Suff Bp Shrewsbury *Lich* 87-92; Area Bp 92-94; rtd 94; Perm to Offic *Lich* from 05. *Nyddfa, By-Pass Road, Gobowen, Oswestry SY11 3NG* Tel and fax (01691) 653434 E-mail sddjdd@sddjdd.free-online.co.uk

DAVIES, John Edwards Gurnos. b 18. Ch Coll Cam BA41 MA45. Westcott Ho Cam 40. **d** 42 **p** 43. C Portwood St Paul *Ches* 42-44; CF (EC) 44-46; CF 46-73; Asst Chapl Gen 70; QHC 72; R Monk Sherborne and Pamber *Win* 73-76; P-in-c Sherborne 76; R The Sherbornes w Pamber 76-83; rtd 83. *3 Parsonage Lane, Edington, Westbury BA13 4QS* Tel (01380) 830479

DAVIES, John Gwylim. b 27. Ripon Hall Ox 67. **d** 70 **p** 71. C Ox St Mich *Ox* 70-71; C Ox St Mich w St Martin and All SS 71-72; TV New Windsor 73-77; R Hagley *Worc* 77-83; TV Littleham w Exmouth *Ex* 83-92; Asst Dioc Stewardship Adv 83-92; rtd 92; Perm to Offic *Ex* from 92. *5 The Retreat, The Retreat Drive, Topsham, Exeter EX3 0LS* Tel (01392) 876995

DAVIES, John Harverd. b 57. Keble Coll Ox BA80 MA84 CCC Cam MPhil82 Lanc Univ PhD. Westcott Ho Cam 82. **d** 84 **p** 85. C Liv Our Lady and St Nic w St Anne *Liv* 84-87; C Pet St Jo *Pet* 87-90; Min Can Pet Cathl 88-90; V Anfield St Marg *Liv* 90-94; Chapl, Fell and Lect Keble Coll Ox 94-99; V Melbourne *Derby* from 99; Dioc Dir of Ords from 00. *The Vicarage, Church Square, Melbourne, Derby DE73 8JH* Tel (01332) 862347 E-mail jhd@rdplus.net

DAVIES, Canon John Howard. b 29. St Jo Coll Cam BA50 MA54 Nottm Univ BD62. Westcott Ho Cam 54. **d** 55 **p** 56. Succ Derby Cathl *Derby* 55-58; Chapl Westcott Ho Cam 58-63; Lect Th Southn Univ 63-81; Lic to Offic *Win* 63-81; Sen Lect 74-81; Dir Th and RS Southn Univ 81-94; Can Th Win Cathl *Win* 81-91; Hon C Southampton St Alb 88-91; Hon C Swaythling 91-94; rtd 94. *13 Glen Eyre Road, Southampton SO16 3GA* Tel (023) 8067 9359

DAVIES, Canon John Howard. b 35. Brasted Th Coll 60 Ely Th Coll 62. **d** 64 **p** 65. C Bromsgrove All SS *Worc* 64-67; C Astwood Bank w Crabbs Cross 67-70; R Worc St Martin 70-74; P-in-c Worc St Pet 72-74; R Worc St Martin w St Pet 74-79; RD Worc E 77-79; TR Malvern Link w Cowleigh 79-93; Hon Can Worc Cathl 81-00; RD Malvern 83-92; V Bromsgrove St Jo 93-00; rtd 00; Perm to Offic *Worc* from 00. *10 Baveney Road, Worcester WR2 6DS* Tel (01905) 428086 E-mail jjhd39@aol.com

DAVIES, John Howard. b 51. EAMTC 98. **d** 01 **p** 02. NSM Walsingham, Houghton and Barsham *Nor* 01-04; NSM Holt w High Kelling from 04. *The Anchorage, Whissonsett Road, Colkirk, Fakenham NR21 7NL* Tel (01328) 863385 Mobile 07870-509439 E-mail john@apostle.co.uk

DAVIES, John Hugh Conwy. b 42. Bris Univ BSc64 PhD67 CEng72 MICE72. Linc Th Coll 84. **d** 86 **p** 87. C Limber Magna w Brocklesby *Linc* 86-89; R Wickenby Gp 89-94; R Denbigh and Nantglyn *St As* 94-99; R Denbigh 99-00; V Llanrhaeadr-ym-Mochnant etc from 01. *The Vicarage, Llanrhaeadr ym Mochnant, Oswestry SY10 0JZ* Tel (01691) 780247

DAVIES, Canon John Hywel Morgan. b 45. St D Coll Lamp BA71 LTh73. **d** 73 **p** 74. C Milford Haven *St D* 73-77; V from 89; R Castlemartin w Warren and Angle etc 77-82; R Walton W w Talbenny and Haroldston W 82-89; Can St D Cathl from 03. *St Katharine's Vicarage, 1 Sandhurst Road, Milford Haven SA73 3JU* Tel (01646) 693314 E-mail johnmorgandavies@talk21.com

DAVIES, John Ifor. b 20. ACP DipEd. **d** 80 **p** 81. Hon C Allerton *Liv* 80-84; Hon C Ffynnongroew *St As* 84-87; Hon C Whitford 87-88. *Hafan Deg, Ffordd-y-Graig, Lixwm, Holywell CH8 8LY* Tel (01352) 781151

DAVIES, John Keith. b 33. St Mich Coll Llan 80. **d** 82 **p** 83. C Llanbadarn Fawr w Capel Bangor and Goginan *St D* 82-84; V Llandygwydd and Cenarth w Cilrhedyn etc 84-89; V Abergwili w Llanfihangel-uwch-Gwili etc 89-98; RD Carmarthen 93-98; rtd 98. *Tanyfron, 81 Hafod Cwnin, Carmarthen SA31 2AS* Tel (01267) 223931

DAVIES, John Melvyn George. b 37. Wycliffe Hall Ox 68. **d** 71 **p** 72. C Norbury *Ches* 71-75; C Heswall 76-78; V Claughton cum Grange 78-83; R Waverton 83-02; RD Malpas 90-97; rtd 02. *15 Tattenhall Road, Tattenhall, Chester CH3 9QQ* Tel (01829) 770184

DAVIES, Canon John Oswell. b 27. St D Coll Lamp 74. **d** 75 **p** 76. C Henfynyw w Aberaeron and Llanddewi Aberarth *St D* 75-76; P-in-c Eglwysnewydd w Ysbyty Ystwyth 76-77; V 77-83; R Maenordeifi and Capel Colman w Llanfihangel etc 83-93; RD Cemais and Sub-Aeron 87-93; Hon Can St D Cathl 92-93; rtd 93. *Hafod, Carregwen, Llechryd, Cardigan SA43 2PJ* Tel (01239) 682568

✠**DAVIES, The Rt Revd John Stewart.** b 43. Univ of Wales BA72 Qu Coll Cam MLitt74. Westcott Ho Cam 72. **d** 74 **p** 75 **c** 99. C Hawarden *St As* 74-78; Tutor St Deiniol's Lib Hawarden 76-83; V Rhosymedre *St As* 78-87; Dir Dioc Minl Tr Course 83-93; Warden of Ords 83-91; Hon Can St As Cathl 86-91; V Mold 87-92; Adn St As 91-99; R Llandyrnog and Llangwyfan 92-99; Bp St As from 99. *Esgobty, St Asaph LL17 0TW* Tel (01745) 583503 Fax 584301 E-mail bishop.stasaph@churchinwales.org.uk

DAVIES, Johnston ap Llynfi (Ion). b 28. St D Coll Lamp BA51 St Mich Coll Llan 51. **d** 53 **p** 54. C Swansea Ch Ch *S & B* 53-55; C Sketty 55-57; Nigeria 57-61; R Whittington *Derby* 61-64; Chapl Broadmoor Hosp Crowthorne 64-66; Perm to Offic *Ox* 67-72; Perm to Offic *York* 72-86; V Creeksea w Althorne, Latchingdon and N Fambridge *Chelmsf* 86-88; rtd 88; Asst Chapl Costa Blanca *Eur* 89-92; Chapl 92-93; Lic to Offic 93-95.

Apartmentos Esmeralda 41A, Playa de Levante, 03710 Calpe, Alicante, Spain Tel (0034) (96) 583 8063

DAVIES, Jonathan Byron. b 69. Univ of Wales (Cardiff) BTh95. St Mich Coll Llan 94. **d** 96 **p** 97. C Betws w Ammanford *St D* 96-99; C Newton St Pet *S & B* 99-00; P-in-c Swansea St Luke from 03. *The Vicarage, 8 Vicarage Lane, Cwmdu, Swansea SA5 8EU* Tel (01792) 587717 Mobile 07760-210975 E-mail revdjbd@aol.com

DAVIES, Judith. b 54. Man Univ BA75. WEMTC 97. **d** 00 **p** 01. C Harlescott *Lich* 00-04; Chapl Shrewsbury and Telford NHS Trust from 04. *The Royal Shrewsbury Hospital, Mytton Oak Road, Shrewsbury SY3 8XQ* Tel (01743) 261000 E-mail judyd@fish.co.uk

DAVIES, Prof Julia Mary. b 44. Ex Univ BA65 FCIPD00. **d** 04 **p** 05. OLM Deane *Man* from 04. *15 Newland Drive, Bolton BL5 1DS* Tel (01204) 660260 Mobile 07966-528877

DAVIES, Julian Edward. b 60. Jes Coll Ox BA82 MA86 DPhil87 Selw Coll Cam BA92 MA96. Ridley Hall Cam 90. **d** 94 **p** 95. C Hucknall Torkard *S'well* 94-96; C Eglwysilan *Llan* 96-99; Assoc R St Marylebone w H Trin *Lon* 99-03; Assoc R St Giles-in-the-Fields from 03. *Flat 2, 26 West Street, London WC2H 9NA* Tel (020) 7240 1579 E-mail jed.ihs@btinternet.com

DAVIES, Keith. *See* DAVIES, John Keith

DAVIES, Keith. *See* BERRY-DAVIES, Charles William Keith

DAVIES, Kenneth John. b 42. Ripon Coll Cuddesdon 79. **d** 80 **p** 81. C Buckingham *Ox* 80-83; V Birstall *Wakef* 83-91; TV Crookes St Thos *Sheff* 91-94; TR Huntington *York* from 94. *The Rectory, New Lane, Huntington, York YO32 9NU* Tel (01904) 768160 E-mail johnsuedavies@aol.com

DAVIES, The Ven Lorys Martin. b 36. JP78. Univ of Wales (Lamp) BA57 ALCM52. Wells Th Coll 57. **d** 59 **p** 60. C Tenby w Gumfreston *St D* 59-62; Asst Chapl Brentwood Sch Essex 62-66; Chapl Solihull Sch 66-68; V Moseley St Mary *Birm* 68-81; Can Res Birm Cathl 81-92; Dioc Dir of Ords 82-90; Adn Bolton *Man* 92-01; Bp's Adv Hosp Chapl 92-01; Warden of Readers 94-01; rtd 02; Perm to Offic *Birm* and *Worc* from 04. *Heol Cerrig, 28 Penshurst Road, Bromsgrove B60 2SN* Tel (01527) 577337

DAVIES (née ROACH), Mrs Lynne Elisabeth. b 44. WMMTC 95. **d** 98 **p** 99. NSM Snitterfield w Bearley *Cov* 98-01; NSM Salford Priors from 01; NSM Exhall w Wixford from 01; NSM Temple Grafton w Binton from 01. *19 Garrard Close, Salford Priors, Evesham WR11 8XG* Tel (01789) 773711 Fax 490231

DAVIES, Malcolm. b 35. St Mich Coll Llan 82. **d** 84 **p** 85. C Roath *Llan* 84-88; C Pentre 88-94; V Llancarfan w Llantrithyd 94-02; rtd 02. *141 Fontygary Road, Rhoose, Barry CF62 3DU* Tel (01446) 710509

DAVIES, Malcolm Thomas. b 36. Open Univ BA81. St Mich Coll Llan 71. **d** 73 **p** 74. C Betws w Ammanford *St D* 73-76; V Cil-y-Cwm and Ystrad-ffin w Rhandir-mwyn etc 76-80; V Llangyfelach *S & B* 80-85; V Loughor 85-94; V Llanelli St Paul *St D* 94-95; V Llanelli St Pet 95-01; rtd 01. *25 Walters Road, Llanelli SA15 1LR* Tel (01554) 770295

DAVIES, Mrs Margaret Adelaide. b 45. Weymouth Coll of Educn CertEd67 DipTh96. S Dios Minl Tr Scheme 92. **d** 95 **p** 96. NSM Westbury *Sarum* 95-02; NSM White Horse from 02. *60 Newtown, Westbury BA13 3EF* Tel (01373) 823735

DAVIES, Mrs Margot Alison Jane. b 55. SW Minl Tr Course 02. **d** 05. C St Ives *Truro* from 05. *The Vicarage, Hellesvean, St Ives TR26 2HG* Tel (01736) 797749

DAVIES, Canon Mark. b 62. Leeds Univ BA85. Coll of Resurr Mirfield 86. **d** 89 **p** 90. C Barnsley St Mary *Wakef* 89-95; R Hemsworth from 95; Dioc Vocations Adv and Asst Dir of Ords from 98; RD Pontefract from 00; Hon Can Wakef Cathl from 02. *The Rectory, 3 Church Close, Hemsworth, Pontefract WF9 4SJ* Tel (01977) 610507 E-mail markdavies62@bigfoot.com

DAVIES, Martin. *See* DAVIES, William Martin

DAVIES, Martyn John. b 60. Chich Th Coll 82. **d** 85 **p** 86. C Llantrisant *Llan* 85-87; C Whitchurch 87-90; V Porth w Trealaw 90-01; R Merthyr Tydfil St Dav from 01; AD Merthyr Tydfil from 04. *The Rectory, Bryntirion Road, Merthyr Tydfil CF47 0ER* Tel (01685) 722992 E-mail msd@learnfree.co.uk

DAVIES, Melvyn. *See* DAVIES, John Melvyn George

DAVIES, Canon Mervyn Morgan. b 25. Univ of Wales BA49. Coll of Resurr Mirfield 49. **d** 51 **p** 52. C Penarth w Lavernock *Llan* 51-58; Lic to Offic *Wakef* 58-60; C Port Talbot St Theodore *Llan* 60-63; V Pontycymer and Blaengarw 63-69; V Fairwater 69-95; RD Llan 81-95; Jt Ed *Welsh Churchman* 82-95; Can Llan Cathl 84-89; Prec 89-95; rtd 95; Perm to Offic *Llan* from 95. *20 Palace Avenue, Llandaff, Cardiff CF5 2DW* Tel (029) 2057 5327

DAVIES, Miss Moira Kathleen. b 41. Cant Sch of Min. **d** 88 **p** 94. Par Dn Walmer *Cant* 88-94; C 94-96; P-in-c Somercotes and Grainthorpe w Conisholme *Linc* 96-99; R from 99. *The Rectory, Keeling Street, North Somercotes, Louth LN11 7QU* Tel (01507) 358829

DAVIES, Canon Mostyn David. b 37. AKC64. **d** 65 **p** 66. C Corby St Columba *Pet* 65-69; Ind Chapl 69-03; P-in-c Pet St Barn 80-03; Can Pet Cathl from 95; rtd 03; Perm to Offic *Pet* from 03. *92 West End, Langtoft, Peterborough PE6 9LU* Tel (01778) 342838 E-mail mostyn@zetnet.co.uk

DAVIES, Canon Myles Cooper. b 50. Sarum & Wells Th Coll 71. **d** 74 **p** 75. C W Derby St Mary *Liv* 74-77; C Seaforth 77-80; V 80-84; V Stanley from 84; P-in-c Liv St Paul Stoneycroft from 05; Chapl Rathbone Hosp Liv 84-92; Chapl N Mersey Community NHS Trust from 92; Hon Can Liv Cathl *Liv* from 01. *St Anne's Vicarage, 8 Derwent Square, Liverpool L13 6QT* Tel and fax 0151-228 5252 E-mail frmyles@saint-anne.freeserve.co.uk

DAVIES, Neil Anthony Bowen. b 52. Ex Univ BSc74. Westcott Ho Cam 75. **d** 78 **p** 79. C Llanblethian w Cowbridge and Llandough etc *Llan* 78-80; C Aberdare 80-82; V Troedyrhiw w Merthyr Vale 82-88; Min Lower Earley LEP *Ox* 88-92; V Earley Trinity 92-95; P-in-c Reading St Luke w St Bart 95-99; Perm to Offic from 99. *14 Measham Way, Lower Earley, Reading RG6 4ES* Tel 0118-931 4847 E-mail neil@daviesuk30.freeserve.co.uk

DAVIES, Mrs Nicola Louise. b 55. Birm Univ BA77 Lon Inst of Educn PGCE78. STETS 02. **d** 05. NSM Rowledge and Frensham *Guildf* from 05. *1 Little Austins, Farnham GU9 8JR* Tel (01252) 714640 E-mail nicoladavies27@hotmail.com

DAVIES, Nigel Lawrence. b 55. Lanc Univ BEd77. Sarum & Wells Th Coll 84. **d** 87 **p** 88. C Heywood St Luke w All So *Man* 87-91; V Burneside *Carl* from 91; RD Kendal from 03; P-in-c Crosscrake from 04. *St Oswald's Vicarage, Burneside, Kendal LA9 6QX* Tel (01539) 722015 Fax 07974-448370 E-mail vicar_stoswald@hotmail.com *or* ruraldean_kendal@hotmail.com

DAVIES, Noel Paul. b 47. Chich Th Coll 83. **d** 85 **p** 86. C Milford Haven *St D* 85-89; R Jeffreyston w Reynoldston and E Williamston etc from 89. *The Rectory, Jeffreyston, Kilgetty SA68 0SG* Tel (01646) 651269

DAVIES, Canon Patricia Elizabeth. b 36. Westf Coll Lon BA58 Hughes Hall Cam CertEd59 Leeds Univ MA74. NEOC 83. **dss** 86 **d** 87 **p** 94. Killingworth *Newc* 86-90; Hon C 87-90; Hon C Newc H Cross 91-96; NSM Newc Epiphany 96-99; NSM Gosforth St Hugh 99-00; P-in-c 00-01; Hon Can Newc Cathl 00-01; rtd 01; Perm to Offic *York* from 01. *Applegarth, Middlewood Lane, Fylingthorp, Whitby YO22 4TT* Tel (01947) 881175

DAVIES, Patrick Charles Steven. b 59. RGN86 RMN92 RHV94 Man Poly DN92 Man Metrop Univ DipHE94 Man Univ DipTh97 Leeds Univ BA99. Coll of Resurr Mirfield 97. **d** 99 **p** 00. C Reddish *Man* 99-04; P-in-c Withington St Crispin from 04. *St Crispin's Rectory, 2 Hart Road, Manchester M14 7LE* Tel 0161-224 3452 E-mail fatherpat@btinternet.com

DAVIES, Paul. *See* DAVIES, Richard Paul

DAVIES, Paul Lloyd. b 46. Solicitor 71 Bris Univ LLB68 Trin Coll Carmarthen 84. **d** 87 **p** 88. NSM Newport w Cilgwyn and Dinas w Llanllawer *St D* 87-97; P-in-c Mathry w St Edren's and Grandston etc 97-01; V from 01. *The Rectory, St Nicholas, Goodwick SA64 0LG* Tel (01348) 891230

DAVIES, Paul Martin. b 35. Lon Univ BD75. Sarum & Wells Th Coll 75. **d** 75 **p** 76. C Walthamstow St Mary w St Steph *Chelmsf* 75-79; Kenya 79-86; R Leven w Catwick *York* 86-95; RD N Holderness 90-95; rtd 95; Perm to Offic *York* from 95. *54 The Meadows, Cherry Burton, Beverley HU17 7SD* Tel (01964) 551739

DAVIES, Paul Scott. b 59. Cranmer Hall Dur 85. **d** 88 **p** 89. C New Addington *S'wark* 88-91; C Croydon H Sav 91-94; P-in-c Norton in the Moors *Lich* 94-99; R 99-03; V Sunbury *Lon* from 03. *The Vicarage, Thames Street, Sunbury-on-Thames TW16 6AA* Tel (01932) 779431 E-mail paul@zippor.com

DAVIES, Peter Huw. b 57. Crewe & Alsager Coll BEd79. Wycliffe Hall Ox 87. **d** 89 **p** 90. C Moreton *Ches* 89-93; V Weston-super-Mare St Paul *B & W* from 93; P-in-c Chesham Bois *Ox* from 05. *The New Rectory, Glebe Way, Amersham HP6 5ND* Tel (01494) 726139

DAVIES, Peter Richard. b 32. St Jo Coll Ox BA55 MA58. Westcott Ho Cam 56. **d** 58 **p** 59. C Cannock *Lich* 58-62; Kenya 63-76; Chapl Bedford Sch 76-85; V Dale and St Brides w Marloes *St D* 85-92; rtd 92. *Canthill Cottage, Dale, Haverfordwest SA62 3QZ* Tel (01646) 636535

DAVIES, Peter Timothy William. b 50. Leeds Univ BSc74. Oak Hill Th Coll 75. **d** 78 **p** 79. C Kingston Hill St Paul *S'wark* 78-81; C Hove Bp Hannington Memorial Ch *Chich* 81-88; V Audley *Lich* from 88. *The Vicarage, 1 Wilbrahams Walk, Audley, Stoke-on-Trent ST7 8HL* Tel (01782) 720392

DAVIES, Philip Huw. b 64. Aston Univ BSc86 MRPharmS87. St Mich Coll Llan 00. **d** 02 **p** 03. C Llangynwyd w Maesteg *Llan* 02-03; C Betws w Ammanford *St D* from 03. *19 Llwyn-y-Bryn, Bonllwyn, Ammanford SA18 2ES* Tel (01269) 595753

DAVIES, Philip James. b 58. UEA BA79 Keswick Hall Coll PGCE80 K Coll Lon MA92. Ridley Hall Cam 86. **d** 89 **p** 90. C Rainham *Roch* 89-90; C Gravesend St Geo and Rosherville 90-95; V Rosherville 95-98; P-in-c King's Cliffe *Pet* from 98; Dioc Schs Development Officer from 98. *The Rectory, 3 Hall Yard, King's Cliffe, Peterborough PE8 6XQ* Tel (01780) 470314 E-mail p.j.davies@tesco.net

DAVIES, Philip Simon. b 65. Trin Coll Ox BA87 MA91. Aston Tr Scheme 93 Ridley Hall Cam 95. **d** 97 **p** 98. C Burntwood *Lich* 97-00; TV Cheswardine, Childs Ercall, Hales, Hinstock etc 00-03; TR 03-04; P-in-c Olney *Ox* from 04. *Olney Rectory, 9 Orchard Rise, Olney MK46 5HB* Tel (01234) 713308 E-mail davies1@ukonline.co.uk

DAVIES, Philip Wyn. b 50. Univ of Wales BA72 MA82 DAA82. St D Dioc Tr Course 93 St Mich Coll Llan BD96. **d** 96 **p** 97. C Llandysul *St D* 96-98; V Tregaron w Ystrad Meurig and Strata Florida from 98; Dioc Archivist from 04. *The Vicarage, Tregaron SY25 6HL* Tel (01974) 299010

DAVIES, Mrs Rachel Hannah Eileen. b 64. St Mich Coll Llan 01. **d** 04 **p** 05. NSM Lamp and Ultra-Aeron Deanery *St D* from 04. *Gwndwn, New Inn, Pencader SA39 9BE* Tel and fax (01559) 384248 Mobile 07814-272998

DAVIES, Raymond Emlyn Peter. b 25. St Mich Coll Llan 51. **d** 53 **p** 54. C Llangeinor *Llan* 53-58; C Llanishen and Lisvane 58-62 and 65-68; R Glyncorrwg w Afan Vale and Cymmer Afan 62-65; V Penrhiwceiber w Matthewstown and Ynysboeth 68-72; C Whitchurch 72-73; V Childs Ercall *Lich* 73-81; R Stoke upon Tern 73-81; P-in-c Hamstall Ridware w Pipe Ridware 81-82; P-in-c Kings Bromley 81-82; P-in-c Mavesyn Ridware 81-82; R The Ridwares and Kings Bromley 83-90; rtd 90; Perm to Offic *B & W* from 95. *51 Vereland Road, Hutton, Weston-super-Mare BS24 9TH* Tel (01934) 814680

DAVIES, Rebecca Jane. b 75. Clare Coll Cam MA96. St Mich Coll Llan 01. **d** 03 **p** 04. C Llandeilo Fawr and Taliaris *St D* from 03. *19 Llwyn-y-Bryn, Ammanford SA18 2ES* Tel (01269) 595753

DAVIES, Reginald Charles. b 33. Tyndale Hall Bris 58. **d** 64 **p** 65. C Heywood St Jas *Man* 64-66; C Drypool St Columba w St Andr and St Pet *York* 66-69; V Denaby Main *Sheff* from 69. *The Vicarage, Church Road, Denaby Main, Doncaster DN12 4AD* Tel (01709) 862297

DAVIES, Rendle Leslie. b 29. St Chad's Coll Dur BA52 DipTh54 CertFE DipSS. **d** 54 **p** 55. C Monmouth *Mon* 54-58; V Llangwm Uchaf w Llangwm Isaf w Gwernesney etc 58-63; V Usk and Monkswood w Glascoed Chpl and Gwehelog 63-99; Chapl HM YOI Usk and Prescoed 63-94; rtd 99. *12 Ridgeway, Wyesham, Monmouth NP25 3JX*

DAVIES, Rhiannon Mary Morgan. *See* JOHNSON, Rhiannon Mary Morgan

DAVIES, Richard Paul. b 48. Wycliffe Hall Ox 72. **d** 75 **p** 76. C Everton St Sav w St Cuth *Liv* 75-78; Chapl Asst Basingstoke Distr Hosp 78-80; TV Basingstoke *Win* 80-85; V Southampton Thornhill St Chris 85-94; V Eastleigh from 94. *The Vicarage, 1 Cedar Road, Eastleigh SO50 9NR* Tel (023) 8061 2073

DAVIES, Richard Paul. b 73. Univ of Wales (Lamp) BA94 Ox Univ MTh98. Ripon Coll Cuddesdon 94. **d** 97 **p** 98. Min Can St D Cathl *St D* from 97; TV Dewisland from 01. *The Vicarage, Whitchurch, Solva, Haverfordwest SA62 6UD* Tel (01437) 721281 E-mail rpledavies@aol.com

DAVIES, Robert Emlyn. b 56. N Staffs Poly BA79. Coll of Resurr Mirfield 83. **d** 86 **p** 87. C Cardiff St Jo *Llan* 86-90; V Cwmparc 90-97; V Aberdare from 97; AD Cynon Valley from 02. *The Vicarage, 26 Abernant Road, Aberdare CF44 0PY* Tel (01685) 884769

DAVIES, Roger Charles. b 46. Univ of Wales BD72. St Mich Coll Llan 67. **d** 73 **p** 74. C Llanfabon *Llan* 73-75; C Llanblethian w Cowbridge and Llandough etc 75-78; CF 78-84; TV Halesworth w Linstead, Chediston, Holton etc *St E* 84-87; R Claydon and Barham 87-91; R Lavant and Chapl Lavant Ho Sch 91-94; TV Gt Aycliffe and Chilton *Dur* from 04. *St Francis Vicarage, Burnhope, Newton Aycliffe DL5 7ER* Tel (01325) 321533 Mobile 07866-649300 E-mail roger@daviesrl.fsnet.co.uk

✠**DAVIES, The Rt Revd Ross Owen.** b 55. Melbourne Univ BA77 LLB79. ACT ThL81. **d** 81 **p** 82 **c** 02. Australia 81-91 and from 97; P-in-c Mundford w Lynford *Nor* 91-94; P-in-c Ickburgh w Langford 91-94; P-in-c Cranwich 91-94; C Somerton w Compton Dundon, the Charltons etc *B & W* 94-97; R Hindmarsh 97-00; Vic Gen and Adn The Murray 00-02; Bp from 02. *23 Ellendale Avenue, PO Box 269, Murray Bridge, S Australia 5253* Tel (0061) (8) 8532 2270 Mobile 428-891850 Fax (8) 8532 5760 E-mail r.davies@murray.anglican.org

DAVIES, Miss Rowan. b 55. Univ of Wales (Swansea) BA78 PGCE79. WMMTC 00. **d** 03 **p** 04. NSM Wigginton *Lich* from 03. *16 Queen's Way, Tamworth B79 8QD* Tel (01827) 69651 E-mail hedgerow@tinyworld.co.uk

DAVIES, Preb Roy Basil. b 34. Bris Univ BA55. Westcott Ho Cam 57. **d** 59 **p** 60. C Ipswich St Mary le Tower *St E* 59-63; C Clun w Chapel Lawn *Heref* 63-70; V Bishop's Castle w Mainstone 70-83; RD Clun Forest 72-83; Preb Heref Cathl 82-99; P-in-c Billingsley w Sidbury 83-86; P-in-c Chelmarsh 83-86; P-in-c Chetton w Deuxhill and Glazeley 83-86; P-in-c Middleton Scriven 83-86; R Billingsley w Sidbury, Middleton Scriven etc 86-89; RD Bridgnorth 87-89; TR Wenlock 89-99; rtd 99; Perm to Offic *Heref* from 00. *13 Courtnay Rise, Hereford HR1 1BP* Tel (01432) 341154

✠**DAVIES, The Rt Revd Roy Thomas.** b 34. St D Coll Lamp BA55 Jes Coll Ox DipTh58 BLitt59. St Steph Ho Ox 57. **d** 59 **p** 60 **c** 85. C Llanelli St Paul *St D* 59-64; V Llanafan y Trawscoed and Llanwnnws 64-67; Chapl Univ of Wales (Abth) 67-73; C Aberystwyth 67-69; TV 70-73; Sec Ch in Wales Prov Coun for Miss and Unity 73-79; V Carmarthen St Dav *St D* 79-83; Adn Carmarthen 82-85; V Llanegwad w Llanfynydd 83-85; Bp Llan 85-99; rtd 99. *25 Awel Tywi, Llangunnor, Carmarthen SA31 2NL*

DAVIES, Miss Sally Jane. b 63. Linc Coll Ox BA86. Trin Coll Bris BA92. **d** 92 **p** 94. C E Molesey St Paul *Guildf* 92-96; C Chalfont St Peter *Ox* 96-99; Chapl RN Coll Greenwich from 99; Hon C Greenwich St Alfege *S'wark* from 99. *The Chaplain's Lodging, The Old Royal Naval College, London SE10 9LW* Tel (020) 8858 2154 *or* 8269 4766 E-mail sallyd@ftech.co.uk

DAVIES, Sarah Isabella. b 39. Llan Dioc Tr Scheme 87. **d** 91 **p** 97. NSM Pontypridd St Cath w St Matt *Llan* 91-93; NSM Ferndale w Maerdy 93-97; C 97-00; Chapl Univ Hosp of Wales and Llandough NHS Trust 98-00; Chapl Pontypridd and Rhondda NHS Trust 98-00; C Cardiff Ch Ch Roath Park *Llan* 00-02; Dioc Child Protection Officer from 02. *154 Lake Road East, Cardiff CF23 5NQ* Tel (029) 2075 7190

DAVIES, Saunders. *See* DAVIES, The Rt Revd Francis James Saunders

DAVIES, Sidney. b 16. St D Coll Lamp BA40. **d** 41 **p** 42. C Llandysul *St D* 41-44; C Llanfihangel-ar-arth 44-53; V Llanerch Aeron w Ciliau Aeron 53-69; R Llanerch Aeron w Ciliau Aeron and Dihewyd 69-82; rtd 82. *12 Pontfaen, Porthyrhyd, Carmarthen SA32 8PE* Tel (01267) 275525

DAVIES, Simon Stanley Miles. b 65. Cranfield Univ BEng88 MSc95. Seabury-Western Th Sem 97 Westcott Ho Cam 98. **d** 00 **p** 01. C Llanrhos *St As* 00-03; R Alberton Canada from 03. *535 Church Street, PO Box 152, Alberton PE, Canada, C0B 1B0* Tel (001) (902) 853 2524 Fax 853 3098 E-mail rev.simondavies@pei.sympatico.ca

DAVIES, Stanley James. b 18. MBE54. St Chad's Coll Dur BA40 MA44. **d** 41 **p** 42. C Walton St Marg Belmont Road *Liv* 41-42; C Wigan All SS 42-45; CF 45-66; Dep Asst Chapl Gen 66-68; Chapl Guards Chpl Lon 68-70; Asst Chapl Gen (BOAR) 70-73; R Uley w Owlpen and Nympsfield *Glouc* 73-84; rtd 84; QHC from 72; Perm to Offic *Ex* from 86. *Peverell Cottage, Doddiscombsleigh, Exeter EX6 7PR* Tel (01647) 252616

DAVIES, Stephen. b 56. Nottm Univ BSc77. Wycliffe Hall Ox 01. **d** 03 **p** 04. C Crawley and Littleton and Sparsholt w Lainston *Win* from 03. *13 Silwood Close, Winchester SO22 6EN* Tel (01962) 856432 E-mail sd@fish.co.uk

DAVIES, Stephen John. b 55. Bp Otter Coll Chich BA01 IEng77. St Steph Ho Ox 96. **d** 98 **p** 99. C Leigh Park and Warren Park *Portsm* 98-02; C Durrington *Chich* 02-05; P-in-c Earnley and E Wittering from 05; Chapl Chich Cathl from 02. *The Rectory, Church Road, East Wittering, Chichester PO20 8PS* Tel (01243) 672260

DAVIES, Stephen John. b 65. Nottm Univ BA86 Reading Univ MPhil88 MRICS90. Wycliffe Hall Ox BTh97. **d** 97 **p** 98. C Barton Seagrave w Warkton *Pet* 97-01; P-in-c Enderby w Lubbesthorpe and Thurlaston *Leic* from 01. *The Rectory, 16A Desford Road, Leicester LE9 7TE* Tel (01455) 888488 E-mail alisonrosedavies@lineone.net

DAVIES, Stephen Walter. b 26. AKC54. **d** 55 **p** 56. C Plympton St Mary *Ex* 55-58; C Ex St Mark 58-61; Chapl RAF 61-77; R Feltwell *Ely* 78-84; R N Newton w St Michaelchurch, Thurloxton etc *B & W* 84-91; rtd 91. *5 Manchester Road, Exmouth EX8 1DE*

DAVIES, Mrs Susan Anne. b 48. N Co Coll Newc CertEd69. St Mich Coll Llan 98. **d** 01 **p** 02. NSM Overmonnow w Wonastow and Michel Troy *Mon* 01-03; NSM Monmouth w Overmonnow etc 03-05; NSM Goetre w Llanover 05; TV Rossendale Middle Valley *Man* from 05. *The Rectory, 529 Newchurch Road, Rossendale BB4 9HH* E-mail susananneddavies@aol.com

DAVIES, Taffy. *See* DAVIES, Edward William Llewellyn

DAVIES, Mrs Teresa Ann. b 71. St Steph Ho Ox BTh02. **d** 02 **p** 03. C Barbourne *Worc* from 02. *5 Keats Avenue, Worcester WR3 8DU* Tel (01905) 455486 Mobile 07887-550770 E-mail teresa_a_davies@hotmail.com

DAVIES, Preb Thomas Derwent. b 16. St D Coll Lamp BA38. St Mich Coll Llan 39. **d** 39 **p** 41. C Pontypridd St Cath *Llan* 39-45; C Bideford *Ex* 45-48; Lic to Offic 48-51; Asst Sec DBF 48-51; V Devonport St Mark Ford 51-58; R Bideford 58-74; Preb Ex Cathl 69-97; V Cadbury 74-81; V Thorverton 74-81; rtd 82; Perm to Offic *Ex* from 82. *17 Lennard Road, Crediton EX17 2AP* Tel (01363) 773765

DAVIES, Canon Thomas Philip. b 27. Univ of Wales (Ban) BEd73. St Mich Coll Llan 55. **d** 56 **p** 57. C Ruabon *St As* 56-59; C Prestatyn 59-62; V Penley 62-69; V Bettisfield 66-69; V Holt and Isycoed 69-77; Dioc Dir of Educn 76-92; Dioc RE Adv 76-92; RD Wrexham 76-77; TR Hawarden 77-92; Can St As Cathl 79-92; rtd 93. *53 Muirfield Road, Buckley CH7 2NN* Tel (01244) 547099

DAVIES, Timothy Robert. b 64. Bradf Univ BSc87. Wycliffe Hall Ox BTh93. **d** 93 **p** 94. C Eynsham and Cassington *Ox* 93-97; C Fulwood *Sheff* 97-03; Crosslinks Assoc Ch Ch Cen from 03;

Perm to Offic from 04. *Egerton Hall, Fitzwilliam Street, Sheffield S1 4JR* E-mail tim@christchurchcentral.co.uk

DAVIES, Trevor. *See* DAVIES, Edward Trevor

DAVIES, Canon Trevor Gwesyn. b 28. Univ of Wales (Ban) BEd73. St Mich Coll Llan 55. **d** 56 **p** 57. C Holywell *St As* 56-63; V Cwm 63-74; V Colwyn Bay 74-95; Can St As Cathl from 79; rtd 95. *Dalkeith, 37 Brompton Avenue, Rhos on Sea, Colwyn Bay LL28 4TF* Tel (01492) 548044

DAVIES, The Ven Vincent Anthony (Tony). b 46. Brasted Th Coll 69 St Mich Coll Llan 71. **d** 73 **p** 74. C Owton Manor CD *Dur* 73-76; C Wandsworth St Faith *S'wark* 76-78; P-in-c 78-81; V Walworth St Jo 81-94; RD S'wark and Newington 88-93; Adn Croydon from 94; Bp's Adv for Hosp Chapl from 00; P-in-c Sutton New Town St Barn from 04. *246 Pampisford Road, South Croydon CR2 6DD* Tel (020) 8688 2943 *or* 8681 5496 Fax 8686 2074 E-mail tony.davies@southwark.anglican.org

DAVIES, Canon William David. b 19. Bris Univ BA41. St Mich Coll Llan 48. **d** 43 **p** 44. C Ebbw Vale Ch Ch *Mon* 43-46; C Buckley *St As* 46-48; Chapl Llan Cathl *Llan* 48-50; C-in-c Fairwater CD 50-67; V Fairwater 67-68; R Porthkerry 68-72; R Barry All SS 72-85; RD Penarth and Barry 75-85; Can Llan Cathl 82-85; rtd 85; Perm to Offic *Llan* from 85. *3 Brookfield Park Road, Cowbridge CF71 7HJ* Tel (01446) 775259

DAVIES, William Martin. b 56. Univ of Wales (Cardiff) BSc78. Wycliffe Hall Ox 78. **d** 81 **p** 82. C Gabalfa *Llan* 81-84; P-in-c Beguildy and Heyope *S & B* 84-85; V 85-87; V Swansea St Thos and Kilvey 87-93; V Belmont *Lon* 93-03; Asst Chapl Miss to Seafarers 89-03; Area Co-ord Leprosy Miss for Wales from 04. *25 Earls Court Road, Penylan, Cardiff CF23 9DE* Tel (029) 2019 8720 E-mail martind@tlmew.org.uk

DAVIES, William Morris. b 19. Univ of Wales (Lamp) BA41 Jes Coll Ox BA43 MA47 Man Univ DipEd61 Liv Univ MEd68 LCP56. St Mich Coll Llan 43. **d** 44 **p** 45. C Ysbyty Ystwyth w Ystradmeurig *St D* 44-49; V 49-57; Asst Master Ystrad Meurig Gr Sch 44-49; Hd Master 49-57; Chapl and Hd Div Sandbach Sch 57-65; Lect Div Crewe Coll Educn 65-68; Sen Lect 68-71; Hd Div Dept 71-75; Tutor Th and Educn Crewe and Alsager Coll of HE 75-79; Tutor Open Univ 78-81; V Norley *Ches* 79-85; Tutor St Deiniol's Lib Hawarden 83-85; rtd 85; Sub-Chapl HM Young Offender Inst Thorn Cross 85-89; Perm to Offic *Ches* from 90. *Eastwood, Willington, Tarporley CW6 0NE* Tel (01829) 752181

DAVIES-COLE, Charles Sylester. b 38. New Coll Dur BA BD. Edin Th Coll 66. **d** 66. Hon C Edin Old St Paul *Edin* from 66; Prin Teacher Jas Gillespie's High Sch from 82. *121 Mayburn Avenue, Loanhead EH20 9ER* Tel 0131-440 4190

DAVIES-HANNEN, Robert John. b 65. W Glam Inst of HE DipHE87 BEd89. St Mich Coll Llan DipTh91 BTh92. **d** 92 **p** 93. C Gorseinon *S & B* 92-95; P-in-c Swansea St Luke 95-02; V Llangyfelach from 02. *The Vicarage, 64 Heol Pentrefelin, Morriston, Swansea SA6 6BY* Tel (01792) 774120

DAVIES-JAMES, Rana. **d** 05. OLM Cusop w Blakemere, Bredwardine w Brobury etc *Heref* from 05. *Brickleys, Dorstone, Hereford HR3 6BA* Tel (01497) 831567

DAVILL, Robin William. b 51. SS Paul & Mary Coll Cheltenham CertEd73 BEd74 Leic Univ MA79. Westcott Ho Cam 86. **d** 88 **p** 89. C Broughton *Blackb* 88-91; C Howden *York* 91-93; NSM Crayke w Brandsby and Yearsley 93-97; P-in-c 97-03; P-in-c Thirkleby w Kilburn and Bagby from 03. *Leyland House, 44 Uppleby, Easingwold, York YO61 3BB* Tel (01347) 823472

DAVINA, Sister. *See* WILBY, Mrs Jean

DAVIS, Alan. b 34. Birm Univ BSc56. Ox NSM Course. **d** 75 **p** 76. NSM Chesham St Mary *Ox* 75-80; NSM Gt Chesham 80-00; rtd 00; Perm to Offic *Ox* from 00. *18 Cheyne Walk, Chesham HP5 1AY* Tel (01494) 782124

DAVIS, Alan John. b 33. St Alb Minl Tr Scheme 77. **d** 80 **p** 81. NSM Goldington *St Alb* 80-84; C Benchill *Man* 84-86; R Gt Chart *Cant* 86-02; rtd 02; Perm to Offic *Cant* from 02. *8 Roberts Road, Greatstone, New Romney TN28 8RL* Tel (01797) 361917

DAVIS, The Ven Alan Norman. b 38. Open Univ BA75. Lich Th Coll 63. **d** 65 **p** 66. C Kingstanding St Luke *Birm* 65-68; C-in-c Ecclesfield St Paul CD *Sheff* 68-73; V Sheff St Paul 73-75; V Shiregreen St Jas and St Chris 75-80; R Maltby 80-81; TR 81-89; Abp's Officer for UPA 90-92; P-in-c Carl St Cuth w St Mary *Carl* 92-96; Dioc Communications Officer 92-96; Adn W Cumberland and Hon Can Carl Cathl 96-04; RD Solway 98-99; rtd 04. *71 North Street, Atherstone CV9 1JW* Tel (01827) 718210

DAVIS, Andrew Fisher. b 46. St Chad's Coll Dur BA67 K Coll Lon MA99. St Steph Ho Ox 68. **d** 70 **p** 71. C Beckenham St Jas *Roch* 70-74; C Kensington St Mary Abbots w St Geo *Lon* 74-80; V Sudbury St Andr 80-90; AD Brent 85-90; V Ealing Ch the Sav from 90. *The Clergy House, The Grove, London W5 5DX* Tel and fax (020) 8567 1288 E-mail christ.the.saviour@mcmail.com *or* fr.a@btopenworld.com

DAVIS, Andrew George. b 63. Bath Univ BSc Edin Univ BD. Edin Th Coll. **d** 89 **p** 90. C Alverstoke *Portsm* 89-92; C Portsea N End St Mark 92-96; Bp's Dom Chapl 96-98; R Bishop's Waltham from 98; R Upham from 98. *The Rectory, Free Street, Bishops Waltham, Southampton SO32 1EE* Tel (01489) 892618

DAVIS, Anne. *See* DAVIS, Mrs Maureen Anne

DAVIS, Arthur Vivian. b 24. Clifton Th Coll 60. **d** 62 **p** 63. C Derby St Chad *Derby* 62-65; C Cambridge St Andr Less *Ely* 65-68; V 68-75; V Kirtling 75-86; V Wood Ditton w Saxon Street 75-86; P-in-c Cheveley 83-86; P-in-c Ashley w Silverley 83-86; rtd 86; Perm to Offic *St E* from 93. *408 Studland Park, Newmarket CB8 7BB* Tel (01638) 661709

DAVIS, Canon Bernard Rex. b 33. Sydney Univ BA55 Gen Th Sem (NY) MDiv60 Newc Univ MA67 FRSA87. Coll of Resurr Mirfield 55. **d** 57 **p** 58. C Guildf St Nic *Guildf* 57-59; USA 59-61; Australia 62-68; Exec Sec Unit 3 WCC Geneva 68-77; Warden Edw K Ho 77-03; Can Res and Subdean Linc Cathl *Linc* 77-03; Perm to Offic *S'well* 01-03; rtd 03. *51 Parma Crescent, London SW11 1LT* Tel (020) 7223 4342

DAVIS, Canon Brian. b 40. AKC69 BD69. St Aug Coll Cant 69. **d** 70 **p** 71. C Humberstone *Leic* 70-73; C Kirby Muxloe 73-74; V Countesthorpe w Foston 74-91; RD Guthlaxton I 90-91; V Hinckley St Mary from 91; RD Sparkenhoe W 92-02; Hon Can Leic Cathl from 94; Bp's Adv for Wholeness and Healing from 04. *St Mary's Vicarage, St Mary's Road, Hinckley LE10 1EQ* Tel (01455) 234241 E-mail bdavis@leicester.anglican.org

DAVIS, Mrs Bryony Elizabeth. b 64. DipCOT86. EAMTC 99. **d** 02 **p** 03. C Beccles St Mich *St E* from 02. *The New House, Queen's Road, Beccles NR34 9DU* Tel (01502) 715258 E-mail bryony.davis@tiscali.co.uk

DAVIS, Christopher Eliot. b 28. Pemb Coll Cam BA50 MA55. Wells Th Coll 52. **d** 54 **p** 55. C Dudley St Aug Holly Hall *Worc* 54-56; C Bromyard *Heref* 57; Min Can Carl Cathl *Carl* 57-59; Prec Worc Cathl *Worc* 60-62; Perm to Offic *Lich* 62-95; P-in-c Lich St Mary 65-66; PV Lich Cathl 65-67; Chapl Magd Coll Ox 71-74; rtd 93. *28 Newbridge Crescent, Wolverhampton WV6 0LH* Tel (01902) 759220

DAVIS, Christopher James. b 63. Worc Coll Ox BA85. Cranmer Hall Dur 88. **d** 91 **p** 92. C Margate H Trin *Cant* 91-94; C Cambridge H Sepulchre *Ely* 94-00; C Wimbledon Em Ridgway Prop Chpl *S'wark* 00-04; R Tooting Graveney St Nic from 04. *The Rectory, 20A Rectory Lane, London SW17 9QJ* Tel (020) 8672 7691 E-mail cjd-stnicholas@ukonline.co.uk

DAVIS, Clinton Ernest Newman. b 46. Solicitor 71. Wycliffe Hall Ox 78. **d** 80 **p** 81. C Margate H Trin *Cant* 80-84; C St Laur in Thanet 84-87; V Sandgate St Paul 87-92; P-in-c Folkestone St Geo 92; V Sandgate St Paul w Folkestone St Geo 92-97; Chapl HM Pris Standford Hill from 97. *HM Prison Standford Hill, Church Road, Eastchurch, Sheerness ME12 4AA* Tel (01795) 884559 Fax 884638 E-mail clinton.davis@hmps.gsi.gov.uk

DAVIS, Colin Anthony John. b 65. St Jo Coll Nottm. **d** 99 **p** 00. C Bletchley *Ox* 99-02; C S Molton w Nymet St George, High Bray etc *Ex* 02-03; TV from 03. *The Vicarage, Chittlehampton, Umberleigh EX37 9QL* Tel (01769) 540654 Mobile 07768-781357 E-mail revcol@chelseafc.net

DAVIS, David John. b 35. St Steph Ho Ox 79. **d** 81 **p** 82. C Reading St Mark *Ox* 81-84; C Gt Grimsby St Mary and St Jas *Linc* 84-85; TV 85-89; V Caistor w Clixby 89-94; TV Louth 98-01; rtd 01; Perm to Offic *Linc* from 03 and *Nor* from 04. *34 Park Road, Hunstanton PE36 5BY* Tel (01485) 534700

DAVIS, Donald Cyril. b 26. Open Univ BA79. NTMTC 94. **d** 96 **p** 97. NSM N Greenford All Hallows *Lon* from 96. *33 Sherwood Avenue, Greenford UB6 0PG* Tel (020) 8864 1060 E-mail dnlddavis7@aol.com

DAVIS, Donald Richard. b 59. Oak Hill Th Coll 92. **d** 94 **p** 95. C Plymouth St Jude *Ex* 94-99; C Devonport St Boniface and St Phil from 99. *St Philip's Vicarage, Bridewell Lane North, Plymouth PL5 1AN* Tel (01752) 212091 E-mail dondavis@blueyonder.co.uk

DAVIS, Edward Gabriel Anastasius. b 75. R Holloway Coll Lon BA97. Trin Coll Bris BA02 MA03. **d** 03 **p** 04. C Boldmere *Birm* from 03. *19 Southam Drive, Sutton Coldfield B73 5PD* Tel 0121-354 8432

DAVIS, Edwin John Charles. b 36. Dur Univ BA60 St Cath Soc Ox BA62 MA66. Ripon Hall Ox 60. **d** 62 **p** 63. C Kington w Huntington *Heref* 62-65; Lect Lich Th Coll 65-66; Chapl Edin Th Coll 66-70; Hon Chapl St Mary's Cathl *Edin* 66-70; P-in-c Hope w Shelve *Heref* 70-78; R 78-81; P-in-c Middleton 70-78; V 78-81; P-in-c Worthen 75-78; R 78-81; V S Hinksey *Ox* 81-01; Dep Dir Tr Scheme for NSM 84-01; rtd 01. *13 Kennett Road, Headington, Oxford OX3 7BH* Tel (01865) 763383 E-mail ejcdavis@uk.packardbell.org

DAVIS, Mrs Elizabeth Jane. b 42. S'wark Ord Course 91. **d** 94 **p** 95. NSM Plaistow St Mary *Roch* 94-99; NSM Bromley St Andr from 99. *3 Kinnaird Avenue, Bromley BR1 4HG* Tel (020) 8460 4672

DAVIS, Felicity Ann. *See* SMITH, Felicity Ann

DAVIS, Geoffrey. *See* DAVIS, Ronald Geoffrey

DAVIS, Canon Herbert Roger. b 36. Kelham Th Coll 60. **d** 65 **p** 66. C Barkingside St Fran *Chelmsf* 65-69; C Harpenden St Nic *St Alb* 69-73; P-in-c Eaton Bray 73-75; V Eaton Bray w Edlesborough 75-81; RD Dunstable 77-81; R Gt Berkhamsted 81-95; Hon Can St Alb 93-95; rtd 99. *6 St Thomas Terrace, St Thomas Street, Wells BA5 2XG* Tel (01749) 677195

DAVIS, Ian Andrew. b 58. Sheff Univ BSc79 PGCE80 MIBiol85 CBiol85. St Jo Coll Nottm 87. **d** 90 **p** 91. C Hatfield *Sheff* 90-92; C Beighton 92-95; R Thurnscoe St Helen 95-99; P-in-c Chesterfield St Aug *Derby* 99-01; V 01-05; P-in-c Hope, Castleton and Bradwell from 05. *The Vicarage, Church Street, Bradwell, Hope Valley S33 9HJ* Tel (01433) 620485 E-mail reviandavis@compuserve.com

DAVIS, Jack. b 35. LRSC63 CChem80 MRSC80 Sheff Univ MSc88. Oak Hill Th Coll 86. **d** 88 **p** 89. C Owlerton *Sheff* 88-91; V Manea *Ely* 91-93; R Wimblington 91-93; P-in-c Walsoken 93-94; R 94-00; rtd 00; Perm to Offic *Sheff* from 00. *5 Pinfold Court, Barnby Dun, Doncaster DN3 1RQ* Tel and fax (01302) 888065 E-mail revjackdavis@aol.com

DAVIS, Mrs Jacqueline. b 47. Cant Ch Ch Univ Coll BA01. **d** 05. OLM Upchurch w Lower Halstow *Cant* from 05. *Mill House, The Street, Lower Halstow, Sittingbourne ME9 7DY* Tel (01795) 842557 E-mail jackytd@dsl.pipex.com

DAVIS, John. *See* DAVIS, Edwin John Charles

DAVIS, John Basil. b 20. Lon Univ BA69. Bps' Coll Cheshunt 46. **d** 49 **p** 50. V Bacton w Edingthorpe *Nor* 61-66; Perm to Offic *S'well* 71-86; rtd 85; Hon C Bingham *S'well* 86-90. *1 Banks Crescent, Bingham, Nottingham NG13 8BP* Tel (01949) 837721

DAVIS, John Brian. b 33. Linc Th Coll 72. **d** 75 **p** 76. Hon C Bungay H Trin w St Mary *St E* 75-84; P-in-c Barrow 84-85; P-in-c Denham St Mary 84-85; R Barrow w Denham St Mary and Higham Green 85-98; rtd 98; Perm to Offic *Nor* and *St E* from 98. *Cherry Tree House, 4 Outney Road, Bungay NR35 1DY* Tel (01986) 895574

DAVIS, John George. b 65. Roehampton Inst BSc87 S Glam Inst HE PGCE88. St Steph Ho Ox BTh96. **d** 96 **p** 97. C Newton Nottage *Llan* 96-00; V Tredegar *Mon* from 00. *St George's Vicarage, Church Street, Tredegar NP22 3DU* Tel (01495) 722672

DAVIS, John Harold. b 54. St Jo Coll Dur BSc76 MA86. Cranmer Hall Dur 76. **d** 79 **p** 80. C Marske in Cleveland *York* 79-82; C Pocklington w Yapham-cum-Meltonby, Owsthorpe etc 82-83; TV Pocklington Team 84-86; V Carlton and Drax 86-95; P-in-c Sessay 95-98; R 98-03; V Sowerby 95-03; Ind Chapl 88-97; Sen Chapl Selby Coalfield Ind Chapl from 03; Chapl Askham Bryan Coll from 04. *The Vicarage, 25 Fox Lane, Thorpe Willoughby, Selby YO8 9NA* Tel (01757) 290840 *or* 704385 E-mail john@davishome.plus.com

DAVIS, John James. b 48. Keele Univ MA93 Staffs Univ PGCE98. Qu Coll Birm BA05. **d** 05. NSM Baswich *Lich* from 05. *Stockton Croft, 87 Weeping Cross, Stafford ST17 0DQ* Tel (01785) 661382 E-mail john@davis8943.freeserve.co.uk

DAVIS, John Stephen. b 51. N Staffs Poly BSc75. Wycliffe Hall Ox 75. **d** 78 **p** 79. C Meole Brace *Lich* 78-81; C Bloxwich 81-85; V Walsall St Paul 85-96; Development Officer Prince's Trust from 96. *15 Heygate Way, Aldridge, Walsall WS9 8SD* Tel (01922) 58510

DAVIS, Preb Kenneth William. b 25. Ripon Hall Ox 60. **d** 62 **p** 63. C Lyngford *B & W* 62-65; R Axbridge 65-72; V Wells St Cuth 72-73; V Wells St Cuth w Wookey Hole 73-92; RD Shepton Mallet 79-86; Preb Wells Cathl from 83; rtd 92; Perm to Offic *B & W* from 92. *Beach Lawns, 67 Beach Road, Weston-super-Mare BS23 4BG* Tel (01934) 629130

DAVIS, Matthias. *See* DAVIS, Peter Langdon

DAVIS, Mrs Maureen Anne. b 59. St Hilda's Coll Ox BA80 MA84. N Ord Course 96. **d** 99 **p** 00. NSM Plemstall w Guilden Sutton *Ches* 99-01; C Ches St Mary 01-03; R Woodchurch from 03. *The Rectory, Church Lane, Upton, Wirral CH49 7LS* Tel 0151-677 5352 Mobile 07974-816390 E-mail revannedavis@yahoo.co.uk

DAVIS, Michael James Burrows. b 36. ED JP87. St Deiniol's Hawarden Ridley Hall Cam. **d** 72 **p** 72. Bermuda from 72. *PO Box SN 74, Southampton SN BX, Bermuda* Tel (001441) 238 0236 Fax 238 3767

DAVIS, Nicholas Anthony Wylie. b 56. Univ of Wales (Lamp) BA80. Chich Th Coll 82. **d** 84 **p** 85. C N Lambeth *S'wark* 84-88; TV Catford (Southend) and Downham 88-94; V Camberwell St Phil and St Mark 94-04; V Shrub End *Chelmsf* from 04. *All Saints' Vicarage, 270 Shrub End Road, Colchester CO3 4RL* Tel (01206) 503131 E-mail nicholas_a.davis@virgin.net

DAVIS, Nicholas Edward. b 75. Univ of Wales (Ban) BD96. Coll of Resurr Mirfield 98. **d** 00 **p** 01. C Darwen St Cuth w Tockholes St Steph *Blackb* 00-05; P-in-c Tarleton from 05. *The Rectory, 92 Blackgate Lane, Tarleton, Preston PR4 6UT* Tel and fax (01772) 812614

DAVIS, Canon Norman. b 38. FCII66. Oak Hill Th Coll 77. **d** 79 **p** 80. C Walton *St E* 79-82; P-in-c Grundisburgh w Burgh 82-91; P-in-c Bredfield w Boulge 86-91; R Boulge w Burgh and Grundisburgh 91-03; P-in-c Hasketon 01-03; R Boulge w Burgh, Grundisburgh and Hasketon 03-04; RD Woodbridge 90-96; Hon Can St E Cathl 01-04; rtd 04; Perm to Offic *St E* from 04. *The Randalls, Front Street, Orford, Woodbridge IP12 2LN* Tel (01394) 450509

DAVIS, Norman John. b 41. Oak Hill Th Coll 63. **d** 66 **p** 67. C Wellington w Eyton *Lich* 66-70; C Higher Openshaw *Man* 70-72; R S Levenshulme 72-79; P-in-c Berrow w Pendock and Eldersfield *Worc* 79-81; V 81-87; R Churchill-in-Halfshire w Blakedown and Broome from 87. *The Rectory, 5 Mill Lane, Blakedown, Kidderminster DY10 3ND* Tel (01562) 700293 E-mail norsuedavis@onetel.com

DAVIS, Peter Langdon (Matthias). b 51. Univ of Wales (Cardiff) BD99 PGCE00. Westcott Ho Cam 03. **d** 05. C Daventry, Ashby St Ledgers, Braunston etc *Pet* from 05. *The Rectory, Golding Close, Daventry NN11 5PE* Tel (01327) 876893

DAVIS, Peter Thomas. b 61. Flinders Univ Aus BTh87. Adelaide Coll of Div DPS88 St Barn Coll Adelaide 83. **d** 87 **p** 87. Australia 87-91 and 92-01; TV Gt and Lt Coates w Bradley *Linc* 91-92; Dioc Youth Officer Adelaide 92-94; P-in-c Parafield Gardens St Barbara 94-98; R Elizabeth H Cross 98-01; Chapl Anglicare S Australia 98-01; V Satley, Stanley and Tow Law *Dur* 01-04. *SSM Priory, 90 Vassall Road, London SW9 6JA* Tel (020) 7582 2040 Fax 7582 6640 E-mail peter.davis@flinders.edu.au

DAVIS, Rex. *See* DAVIS, Canon Bernard Rex

DAVIS, Roger. *See* DAVIS, Canon Herbert Roger

DAVIS, Ronald Frank. b 26. Oak Hill Th Coll 62. **d** 64 **p** 65. C Bilton *Ripon* 64-67; V N and S Otterington *York* 67-77; C Rainham *Chelmsf* 77-82; V Hainault 82-88; rtd 88; Perm to Offic *Bradf* from 90. *Home View, Westview Grove, Keighley BD20 6JJ* Tel (01535) 681294

DAVIS, Ronald Geoffrey (Geoff). b 47. St Jo Coll Nottm 79. **d** 81 **p** 81. C Maidstone St Luke *Cant* 81-84; P-in-c Lostwithiel *Truro* 84-86; P-in-c Lanhydrock 84-86; Asst Dioc Youth Officer 84-86; P-in-c Boughton Monchelsea *Cant* 86-88; V from 88; Six Preacher Cant Cathl 94-99; C-in-c Parkwood CD 95-98; AD N Downs 99-02. *The Vicarage, Church Hill, Boughton Monchelsea, Maidstone ME17 4BU* Tel and fax (01622) 743321 E-mail stpeters.church@btinternet.com

DAVIS, Russell Earls. b 14. Sydney Univ LLB50. Moore Th Coll Sydney ThL52. **d** 52 **p** 53. Australia 52-88; C Launceston Holy Trin 54-60; Prec St Geo Cathl 60-66; Chapl Hale Sch 66-88; P-in-c Brislington St Luke *Bris* 76-77; rtd 88. *66B Dover Road, Scarborough, W Australia 6019* Tel (0061) (8) 9205 1684

DAVIS, Ruth Elizabeth. *See* TAIT, Canon Ruth Elizabeth

DAVIS, Simon Charles. b 63. Plymouth Poly BSc86. Trin Coll Bris BA92. **d** 92 **p** 93. C Bollington St Jo *Ches* 92-96; P-in-c Abbots Bromley w Blithfield *Lich* from 96; P-in-c Colton, Colwich and Gt Haywood from 05. *The Vicarage, Market Place, Abbots Bromley, Rugeley WS15 3BP* Tel (01283) 840242 E-mail simon.davis@freeuk.com

DAVIS, Stephen Charles. b 19. AKC48 St Cath Soc Ox BA50 MA54. Wycliffe Hall Ox 48. **d** 50 **p** 51. C Slough *Ox* 50-52; S Africa 52-57; V Leic H Trin *Leic* 58-64; Chapl HM Pris Leic 58-64; R Dur St Marg *Dur* 64-87; rtd 87; Perm to Offic *Worc* from 87. *10 Spencer Avenue, Bewdley DY12 1BD* Tel (01299) 409014

DAVIS, Thomas Edward. b 20. **d** 83 **p** 84. NSM Cen Telford *Lich* 83-91; Perm to Offic 91-00. *14 Bembridge, Telford TF3 1NA* Tel (01952) 592352

DAVIS, Thomas Henry. b 60. SSC01. Dioc OLM tr scheme 97 Coll of Resurr Mirfield 05. **d** 99 **p** 00. OLM Sudbury and Chilton *St E* 99-03; NSM Preston St Jo and St Geo *Blackb* 03-05; C Torrisholme from 05. *St Martin's House, Braddon Close, Morecambe LA4 4UZ* Tel and fax (01524) 422249 Mobile 07854-770360 E-mail father-davis@tinyworld.co.uk

DAVIS, Timothy Alwyn. b 74. Trin Coll Bris BTh. **d** 01 **p** 02. C Crich and S Wingfield *Derby* from 01. *6 Dowie Way, Crich, Matlock DE4 5NJ* Tel (01773) 853923

DAVIS, Timothy Charles. b 59. Reading Univ BA81 Homerton Coll Cam PGCE82. Trin Coll Bris DipHE91. **d** 91 **p** 92. C Normanton *Wakef* 91-95; C Fisherton Anger *Sarum* 95-99; TV Abingdon *Ox* from 99. *69 Northcourt Road, Abingdon OX14 1NR* Tel (01235) 520115 *or* 539172 Fax 522549 E-mail chch@clara.net

DAVIS, Trevor Lorenzo. b 45. Simon of Cyrene Th Inst 92. **d** 94 **p** 95. NSM Upper Norwood St Jo *S'wark* 94-00. *31B Thornlaw Road, London SE27 0SH* Tel (020) 8766 6238

DAVIS, William Henry. b 17. Open Univ BA84. Bps' Coll Cheshunt. **d** 67 **p** 68. C Sudbury St Andr *Lon* 67-70; V Wickhambrook *St E* 70-72; V Wickhambrook w Stradishall and Denston 72-91; V Wickhambrook 91-95; P-in-c Stansfield 76-78; rtd 95. *Folly Barn, 10 Bellevue Road, Weymouth DT4 8RX* Tel (01305) 784853

DAVIS, Mrs Yvonne Annie. b 30. CQSW75. LNSM course 93. **d** 96 **p** 97. OLM Purley St Barn *S'wark* 96-00; Perm to Offic from 00. *1 Hurnford Close, South Croydon CR2 0AN* Tel (020) 8657 2097

DAVISON, Andrew Paul. b 74. Mert Coll Ox BA96 MA99 DPhil00 CCC Cam BA02. Westcott Ho Cam 00 Ven English Coll Rome 02. **d** 03 **p** 04. C Bellingham St Dunstan *S'wark* from 03. *38 Playgreen Way, London SE6 3HU* Tel (020) 8697 3878 E-mail email@apdavison.co.uk

DAVISON, Miss Beryl. b 37. Lightfoot Ho Dur 62. **d** 87 **p** 94. Par Dn Consett *Dur* 87-92; Dn-in-c Holmside 92-94; P-in-c 94-97;

rtd 97. *48 Deanery View, Lanchester, Durham DH7 0NJ* Tel (01207) 520137

DAVISON, The Ven George Thomas William. b 65. St Andr Univ BD88. Oak Hill Th Coll 88 CITC BTh92. **d** 92 **p** 93. C Portadown St Mark *Arm* 92-95; I Kinawley w H Trin *K, E & A* from 95; Dir of Ords from 97; Preb Kilmore Cathl from 02; Adn Kilmore from 04. *The Rectory, Cloghan, Derrylin, Enniskillen BT92 9LD* Tel and fax (028) 6674 8994 E-mail kinawley@kilmore.anglican.org

DAVISON, Philip Anthony. b 66. Magd Coll Cam BA88 MA93. Cuddesdon Coll BA98. **d** 98 **p** 99. C Lancaster St Mary w St John and St Anne *Blackb* 98-02; P-in-c Feniscowles from 02. *The Vicarage, 732 Preston Old Road, Feniscowles, Blackburn BB2 5EN* Tel (01254) 201236

DAVISON, Canon Richard Ireland. b 42. St Chad's Coll Dur BSc63. Linc Th Coll 64. **d** 66 **p** 67. C Cockerton *Dur* 66-70; C Houghton le Spring 70-73; V Heworth St Alb 73-80; Ascension Is 80-82; V Dunston *Dur* 82-85; V Bishopwearmouth Ch Ch 85-98; AD Wearmouth 94-99; Hon Can Dur Cathl from 97; P-in-c Dur St Giles 99-00; V from 00; P-in-c Pittington, Shadforth and Sherburn from 03. *St Giles's Vicarage, Gilesgate, Durham DH1 1QH* Tel 0191-384 2452 E-mail atthevicarage@hotmail.com

DAVISON, Richard John. b 32. St Andr Univ MA56. Linc Th Coll 56. **d** 58 **p** 59. C S Shields St Hilda *Dur* 58-61; C Dur St Cuth 61-63; R Wyberton *Linc* 63-86; RD Holland W 84-86; TR Swan *Ox* 86-91; V Streatley w Moulsford 91-96; rtd 97; Perm to Offic *Linc* from 00. *37 Stirling Road, Stamford PE9 2XF* Tel (01780) 766794

DAVISON, Canon Roger William. b 20. Kelham Th Coll 46. **d** 51 **p** 52. C Tonge Moor *Man* 51-55; V 55-65; Hon Can Man Cathl 63-65; V Higham Ferrers w Chelveston *Pet* 65-88; rtd 88; Perm to Offic *Roch* 88-05. *The College of St Barnabas, Blackberry Lane, Lingfield RH7 6NJ* Tel (01342) 870710

DAVISON, Thomas Alfred. b 28. St Aug Coll Cant 48 St Chad's Coll Dur 52. **d** 60 **p** 61. C Tetbury w Beverston *Glouc* 60-62; C Malvern Link St Matthias *Worc* 62-65; R Coates *Glouc* 65-76; R Coates, Rodmarton and Sapperton etc 76-78; Chapl R Agric Coll Cirencester 67-78; P-in-c Bleadon *B & W* 78-81; Chapl HM Pris Leeds 81-84; Chapl HM Pris Channings Wood 84-89; P-in-c Pyworthy, Pancrasweek and Bridgerule *Ex* 89-91; P-in-c Otterton and Colaton Raleigh 91-94; rtd 94; Perm to Offic *Ex* from 94. *6 Grosvenor Terrace, Ferndale Road, Teignmouth TQ14 8NE* Tel (01626) 779202

DAVOLL, Ivan John (Snowy). b 33. Dip Youth Work 67. LNSM course 87. **d** 88 **p** 90. NSM Bermondsey St Jas w Ch Ch *S'wark* 88-93; C 93-98; rtd 98; Perm to Offic *S'wark* 98-03 and *Heref* from 03. *42 Ecroyd Park, Credenhill, Hereford HR4 7EL*

DAVY, Mrs Judith Ann. b 60. SRN82. STETS 01. **d** 04 **p** 05. Hon Par Dn Jersey St Brelade *Win* from 04. *25 Le Bernage, Rue St Thomas, St Saviour, Jersey JE2 7GZ* Tel (01534) 507800 Mobile 07797-730983 E-mail judith@davyclan.com

DAVY, Peter Geoffrey. b 31. St Pet Coll Saltley TCert54 DipPE56. SW Minl Tr Course 93. **d** 94 **p** 94. NSM St Columb Minor and St Colan *Truro* 94-99; rtd 99; Perm to Offic *Truro* from 00. *9 Tredour Road, Newquay TR7 2EY* Tel (01637) 872241

DAVYS, Mark Andrew. b 66. St Cath Coll Ox BA87 MA97 Keele Univ MA01 Qu Coll Birm BA04 Solicitor 00. WMMTC 01. **d** 04 **p** 05. NSM Colton, Colwich and Gt Haywood *Lich* from 04. *Deers Leap, Meadow Lane, Little Haywood, Stafford ST18 0TT* Tel (01889) 882855 E-mail madavys@fish.co.uk

DAW, Geoffrey Martin. b 57. Oak Hill Th Coll 81. **d** 84 **p** 85. C Hollington St Leon *Chich* 84-87; C Seaford w Sutton 87-90; V Iford w Kingston and Rodmell from 90. *The Rectory, 14 Lockitt Way, Kingston, Lewes BN7 3LG* Tel (01273) 473665

DAWE, David Fife Purchas. b 20. Keble Coll Ox BA41 MA45. Wells Th Coll 41. **d** 43 **p** 44. C Wolstanton *Lich* 43-46; C Meole Brace 46-47; C Leek All SS 47-50; C Tardebigge *Worc* 50-52; R Stoke Bliss w Kyre Wyard 52-54; R Jackfield *Heref* 54-61; V Criftins *Lich* 61-77; V Dudleston 63-77; P-in-c Alkmonton w Yeaveley *Derby* 77-81; P-in-c Cubley w Marston Montgomery 77-81; R Alkmonton, Cubley, Marston, Montgomery etc 81-85; rtd 85; Perm to Offic *Derby* 85-94; Perm to Offic *Lich* 85-94; Perm to Offic *Pet* from 94. *11 Coaching Walk, Northampton NN3 3EU* Tel (01604) 414083

DAWES, Dori Katherine. b 37. ARCM. Oak Hill Th Coll 85. **d** 88 **p** 94. Par Dn Watford St Luke *St Alb* 88-90; Par Dn Watford 90-94; C 94-96; P-in-c Dunton w Wrestlingworth and Eyeworth 96-01; rtd 01. *Orchard House, Upway, Porlock, Minehead TA24 8QE* Tel (01643) 862474

DAWES, Mrs Helen Elizabeth. b 74. Trin Coll Cam BA96 MA00. Westcott Ho Cam 99. **d** 02 **p** 03. C Chesterton St Andr *Ely* from 02. *258 Milton Road, Cambridge CB4 1LQ* Tel (01223) 740110 E-mail helen.dawes@ely.anglican.org

DAWES, Hugh William. b 48. Univ Coll Ox BA71 MA76. Cuddesdon Coll 71. **d** 74 **p** 75. C Purley St Mark *S'wark* 74-77; Chapl G&C Coll Cam 77-82; Chapl Em Coll Cam 82-87; V Cambridge St Jas *Ely* 87-00; V N Dulwich St Faith *S'wark* from 00. *St Faith's Vicarage, 62 Red Post Hill, London SE24 9JQ* Tel (020) 7274 1338 E-mail hugh@tcpost.fsnet.co.uk

DAWES, Julian Edward. b 27. RAF Coll Cranwell 49. Bps' Coll Cheshunt 58. **d** 59 **p** 60. C Whitton St Aug *Lon* 59-62; Chapl RAF 62-65; V Overbury w Alstone, Teddington and Lt Washbourne *Worc* 65-70; V Cropthorne w Charlton 70-76; Chapl Dioc Conf Cen 70-76; Chapl Exe Vale Hosp Gp 76-84; Chapl Bromsgrove and Redditch Distr Gen Hosp 84-86; rtd 91; Perm to Offic *Ex* from 91. *Maranatha, Exeter Road, Rewe, Exeter EX5 4EU* Tel (01392) 841877 Fax 841577

DAWES, Peter Martin. b 24. Westmr Coll Cam 52. **d** 81 **p** 81. C Dunscroft Ch Ch *Sheff* 81-83; V 83-89; rtd 89; Perm to Offic *Bris* from 89. *2 Holway Cottages, 71B The Mall, Swindon SN1 4JB* Tel (01793) 615878

✠**DAWES, The Rt Revd Peter Spencer.** b 28. Hatf Coll Dur BA52. Tyndale Hall Bris 53. **d** 54 **p** 55 **c** 88. C Whitehall Park St Andr Hornsey Lane *Lon* 54-57; C Ox St Ebbe *Ox* 57-60; Tutor Clifton Th Coll 60-65; V Romford Gd Shep Collier Row *Chelmsf* 65-80; Hon Can Chelmsf Cathl 78-80; Adn W Ham 80-88; Dioc Dir of Ords 80-86; Bp Derby 88-95; rtd 95; Hon Asst Bp Ely from 95. *45 Arundell, Ely CB6 1BQ* Tel (01353) 661241

DAWKES, Peter. b 31. Roch Th Coll 64. **d** 66 **p** 67. C Newbold w Dunston *Derby* 66-69; C Buxton 69-72; V Somercotes 72-93; rtd 93; Hon C Kenton, Mamhead, Powderham, Cofton and Starcross *Ex* from 93. *115 Exeter Road, Dawlish EX7 0AN* Tel (01626) 862593

DAWKIN, Peter William. b 60. Nottm Univ BTh88 Open Univ BA91. St Jo Coll Nottm 85. **d** 88 **p** 89. C Birkdale St Jo *Liv* 88-91; C Netherton 91-93; V Liv Ch Ch Norris Green 93-03; C Ince St Mary 03-04; Assoc Min Wigan Deaneries from 05. *The Vicarage, 70 Belle Green Lane, Ince, Wigan WN2 2EP* Tel (01942) 495831 Mobile 07947-164207

DAWKINS, Canon Alan Arthur Windsor. b 26. Lon Univ DipTh54. St Aid Birkenhead 53. **d** 55 **p** 56. C Preston Em *Blackb* 55-57; C S Shore H Trin 57-59; V Slade Green *Roch* 59-61; V St Mary Cray and St Paul's Cray 61-63; V White Colne *Chelmsf* 63-66; R Pebmarsh 63-66; P-in-c Mt Bures 65-66; V Westgate St Jas *Cant* 66-74; V Herne Bay Ch Ch 74-83; Hon Can Cant Cathl 79-91; P-in-c Chilham 83-85; Adv for Miss and Unity 85-91; rtd 91; Perm to Offic *Cant* from 96; Chapl St Jo Hosp Cant from 96. *St John's House, 40 Northgate, Canterbury CT1 1BE* Tel (01227) 764935

DAWKINS, John Haswell. b 47. Lon Univ DipTh70. NEOC 98. **d** 01 **p** 02. NSM Barmby Moor Gp *York* from 01. *9 Fossbeck Close, Wilberfoss, York YO41 5PR* Tel (01759) 388144

DAWKINS, Michael Howard. b 44. Bris Univ BTh68 Man Univ MA96. Tyndale Hall Bris 67. **d** 69 **p** 69. C Drypool St Columba w St Andr and St Pet *York* 69-73; CF 74-80; P-in-c Bulford *Sarum* 80-81; P-in-c Figheldean w Milston 80-81; R Meriden *Cov* from 85. *The Rectory, The Green, Meriden, Coventry CV7 7LN* Tel (01676) 522719 E-mail mhdawkins@aol.com

DAWN, Maggi Eleanor. b 59. Fitzw Coll Cam MA96 Selw Coll Cam PhD02. Ridley Hall Cam CTM96. **d** 99 **p** 00. C Ely 99-01; Chapl K Coll Cam 01-03; Chapl Rob Coll Cam from 03. *Robinson College, Cambridge CB3 9AN* Tel (01223) 339140 Mobile 07743-351467 E-mail med1000@cam.ac.uk

DAWSON, Alan. b 28. St Jo Coll Dur BA54 Liv Univ MA67. Clifton Th Coll 54. **d** 56 **p** 57. C Bowling St Steph *Bradf* 56-59; C Attenborough w Bramcote *S'well* 59-62; V Everton St Jo *Liv* 62-69; V Birkdale St Pet 69-91; rtd 91; NSM Kirkcudbright *Glas* from 98; NSM Gatehouse of Fleet from 98. *8 Dunbar Avenue, Kirkcudbright DG6 4HD* Tel (01557) 330017

DAWSON, Andrew. *See* DAWSON, Canon William James Andrew

DAWSON, Andrew. *See* DAWSON, Francis Andrew Oliver Duff

DAWSON, Barry. b 38. Lon Univ DipTh65. Oak Hill Th Coll 63. **d** 66 **p** 67. C Fulham St Mary N End *Lon* 66-69; C St Marylebone All So w SS Pet and Jo 69-73; Bp's Chapl *Nor* 73-76; Gen Sec CEMS 76-81; V Rye Park St Cuth *St Alb* 81-89; V Attenborough *S'well* 89-98; rtd 98; Perm to Offic *S'well* from 98. *88 Conway Crescent, Carlton, Nottingham NG4 2PZ*

DAWSON, Brian. b 33. Leeds Univ BA54 Lon Univ DipTh57 Man Univ MA84 Newc Univ MPhil01. Coll of Resurr Mirfield 56. **d** 58 **p** 59. C Hollinwood *Man* 58-62; C Rawmarsh w Parkgate *Sheff* 62-63; V Royton St Anne *Man* 63-75; V Urswick *Carl* 75-86; V Bardsea 75-86; R Skelton and Hutton-in-the-Forest w Ivegill 86-98; RD Penrith 91-96; Hon Can Carl Cathl 94-98; rtd 98; Perm to Offic *Carl* from 98. *Apple Croft, High Hesket, Carlisle CA4 0HS* Tel (01697) 473069

DAWSON, Christopher John Rowland. b 26. OBE QPM. Lon Univ DipTh86. S'wark Ord Course 82. **d** 86 **p** 87. NSM Sevenoaks St Jo *Roch* 86-98; Perm to Offic 98-99. *Craggan House, 58 Oak Hill Road, Sevenoaks TN13 1NT* Tel (01732) 458037

DAWSON, Miss Claire Louise. b 68. Nottm Poly BA92 CQSW92 Nottm Univ MA04. EMMTC 01. **d** 04 **p** 05. C Mansfield Woodhouse *S'well* from 04. *68 Ley Lane, Mansfield Woodhouse NG19 8JX* Tel (01623) 464603 E-mail claire.dawson1@virgin.net

DAWSON, Canon Cyril. b 34. St Chad's Coll Dur BA58 DipTh59. **d** 59 **p** 60. C Honicknowle *Ex* 59-63; C Paignton St Jo 63-66; V Heptonstall *Wakef* 66-71; V Todmorden 71-82; RD Calder Valley 75-82; Can Res Wakef Cathl 82-92; Vice-Provost 86-92; Hon Can 92-99; V Darrington 92-99; rtd 99; Perm to Offic *York* and *Linc* from 00. *24 Beacon Road, Bridlington YO16 6UX* Tel (01262) 672911

DAWSON, David. b 57. TISEC 99. **d** 99 **p** 00. NSM Kirkwall *Ab* from 99. *Cottage of Ronaldsvoe, School Road, St Margaret's Hope, Orkney KW17 2TN* Tel (01856) 831596 Fax 831451 Mobile 07881-932657 E-mail frdave_473@hotmail.com

DAWSON, Edward. **d** 81 **p** 83. NSM Newington St Paul *S'wark* 81-85; NSM Walworth St Jo 85-00; Chapl Asst Maudsley Hosp Lon from 87. *3 Ethel Street, London SE17 1NH* Tel (020) 7701 8923

DAWSON, Francis Andrew Oliver Duff. b 48. Keble Coll Ox BA70 MA74. St Jo Coll Nottm 74. **d** 76 **p** 77. C Billericay St Mary *Chelmsf* 76-77; C Billericay and Lt Burstead 77-80; C Childwall All SS *Liv* 80-84; Chapl St Kath Coll 80-84; V Shevington *Blackb* 84-97; Internat Officer and Team Ldr for Evang Affairs *Man* 97-03; P-in-c Werneth from 03. *St Thomas's Vicarage, 3 Regency Close, Oldham OL8 1SS* Tel 0161-678 8926 Fax 832 2869 E-mail andrewdawson51@hotmail.com

DAWSON, Frederick William. b 44. St Chad's Coll Dur BA66 Nottm Univ MTh74. Linc Th Coll 67. **d** 69 **p** 70. C Caversham *Ox* 69-72; C Ranmoor *Sheff* 72-79; R Kibworth Beauchamp *Leic* 79-82; R Kibworth and Smeeton Westerby and Saddington 82-94; R Tilehurst St Mich *Ox* from 94. *Tilehurst Rectory, Routh Lane, Reading RG30 4JY* Tel 0118-941 1127 Fax as telephone E-mail freddawson@ukonline.co.uk

DAWSON, Ian Douglas. b 52. Liv Univ BSc73. N Ord Course 83. **d** 86 **p** 87. NSM Southport SS Simon and Jude *Liv* 86-93; NSM Birkdale St Jas 93-95; NSM Southport St Phil and St Paul 96-01; Perm to Offic *Linc* from 01. *18 Park View, Barton-upon-Humber DN18 6AX* Tel (01652) 637554

DAWSON, John William Arthur. b 43. EMMTC DipTh95. **d** 95 **p** 96. NSM Breedon cum Isley Walton and Worthington *Leic* 95-05; NSM Ashby-de-la-Zouch and Breedon on the Hill from 05. *Orchard House, 2 Manor Drive, Worthington, Ashby-de-la-Zouch LE65 1RN* Tel (01530) 222673 E-mail johndawson@benefice.org.uk

DAWSON, Miss Mary. b 51. Loughb Coll ALA73. EMMTC 85. **d** 90 **p** 94. Par Dn Braunstone *Leic* 90-92; Par Dn Shrewsbury H Cross *Lich* 92-94; C 94-95; P-in-c Glentworth Gp *Linc* 95-97; V from 97. *The Vicarage, 1 Stoney Lane, Glentworth, Gainsborough DN21 5DF* Tel (01427) 668203 Fax as telephone E-mail mrydaw@aol.com

DAWSON, Neil. b 49. Ripon Hall Ox 71. **d** 74 **p** 75. C Putney St Mary *S'wark* 74-78; C Camberwell St Giles 78-80; TV N Lambeth 84-86; V E Dulwich St Clem 86; V Dulwich St Clem w St Pet 86-89; NSM Wilton Place St Paul *Lon* from 92. *8 Broxholm Road, London SE27 0LZ* Tel (020) 8265 0647 E-mail neil.dawson13@ntlworld.com

DAWSON, Nicholas Anthony. b 52. St Jo Coll Nottm 88. **d** 90 **p** 91. C Mortomley St Sav High Green *Sheff* 90-95; V Owlerton from 95. *Owlerton Vicarage, Forbes Road, Sheffield S6 2NW* Tel 0114-234 3560

DAWSON, Canon Norman William. b 41. MBE99. K Coll Lon BD63 AKC63. **d** 65 **p** 66. C Salford St Phil w St Steph *Man* 65-68; C Heaton Ch Ch 68-70; R Longsight St Jo 70-75; R Longsight St Jo w St Cypr 75-82; R Withington St Paul 82-99; AD Withington 91-99; P-in-c Davyhulme St Mary 99-04; Hon Can Man Cathl 98-04; rtd 04; Perm to Offic *Blackb* from 04. *Well House, Lowgill, Lancaster LA2 8RA* Tel (01524) 262936

DAWSON, Paul Christopher Owen. b 61. Leeds Univ BA82. Ripon Coll Cuddesdon 83. **d** 85 **p** 86. C Dovecot *Liv* 85-89; V Westbrook St Phil 89-94; Bp's Dom Chapl 94-98; V Witton *Ches* from 98. *The Vicarage, 61 Church Road, Northwich CW9 5PB* Tel (01606) 42943 E-mail pauldawson@pcod.fsnet.co.uk

DAWSON, Paul Richard. b 67. Bris Univ BSc89. Oak Hill Th Coll 99. **d** 01 **p** 02. C Wimbledon Em Ridgway Prop Chpl *S'wark* from 01. *41 Circle Gardens, London SW19 3JX* Tel (020) 8404 3894 E-mail paul.dawson@dundonald.org

DAWSON, The Ven Peter. b 29. Keble Coll Ox BA52 MA56. Ridley Hall Cam 52. **d** 54 **p** 55. C Morden *S'wark* 54-59; R 68-77; V Barston *Birm* 59-63; R Higher Openshaw *Man* 63-68; RD Merton *S'wark* 75-77; Adn Norfolk *Nor* 77-93; rtd 93; Perm to Offic *Nor* from 93 and *Carl* from 98. *The Coach House, Harmony Hill, Milnthorpe LA7 7QA* Tel (01539) 562020

DAWSON, Peter Rodney. b 44. Guildf Dioc Min Course 95. **d** 98 **p** 99. OLM Ashtead *Guildf* from 98. *28 Sunny Bank, Epsom KT18 7DX* Tel (01372) 727761 E-mail chateau.noswad@virgin.net

DAWSON, Ronald Eric John. b 27. St Mark & St Jo Coll Lon TCert54 Lon Univ BD64. Bps' Coll Cheshunt 62. **d** 62 **p** 63. C Dartford H Trin *Roch* 62-66; C Fulham St Etheldreda *Lon* 66-74; V Brentford St Faith 74-80; rtd 92. *13 Birkbeck Road, London W5 4ES* Tel (020) 8560 3564

DAWSON, Thomas Douglas. b 52. Newc Univ BA. St Steph Ho Ox. **d** 80 **p** 82. C N Gosforth *Newc* 80-81; C Leic St Chad *Leic* 82-85; TV Catford (Southend) and Downham *S'wark* 85-88; V Chevington *Newc* 88-94; V Cowgate 94-96; P-in-c Cresswell and Lynemouth 96-98; C Blyth St Mary 98-01; rtd 01; Perm to Offic *Newc* from 02. *Iona, 2 Hillside, Lesbury, Alnwick NE66 3NR* Tel (01665) 830412 Mobile 07763-122259 E-mail fr_tom_dawson@hotmail.com

DAWSON, Canon William James Andrew. b 48. TCD MA72. CITC 88. **d** 88 **p** 89. NSM Killyman *Arm* 88-91; NSM Pomeroy from 91; Can Arm Cathl from 98; Preb 98-01. *Tamlaght, Coagh, Cookstown BT80 0AB* Tel (028) 8673 7151 *or* tel and fax 8676 2227

DAWSON-CAMPBELL, Olive Sheila. b 37. ACIB70. WEMTC 99. **d** 00 **p** 01. OLM Longden and Annscroft w Pulverbatch *Heref* from 00. *Sheaves, Lyth Bank, Lyth Hill, Shrewsbury SY3 0BE* Tel (01743) 872071

DAWSWELL, Jonathan Andrew. b 65. Jes Coll Cam BA86. Wycliffe Hall Ox BA91. **d** 92 **p** 93. C Childwall All SS *Liv* 92-96; C Leyland St Andr *Blackb* 96-99; V Knypersley *Lich* from 99; P-in-c Biddulph Moor from 05. *St John's Vicarage, 62 Park Lane, Knypersley, Stoke-on-Trent ST8 7AU* Tel (01782) 512240 E-mail andrew@dawswell.freeserve.co.uk

DAWTRY, Anne Frances. b 57. Westf Coll Lon BA79 PhD85. Ripon Coll Cuddesdon 91. **d** 93 **p** 94. C Corfe Mullen *Sarum* 93-96; C Parkstone St Pet w Branksea and St Osmund 96-97; Chapl Bournemouth Univ *Win* 97-99; Prin OLM and Integrated Tr *Sarum* 99-03; Prin Dioc OLM Scheme *Man* from 03. *34 Waterslea, Eccles, Manchester M30 0BR* Tel 0161-789 5949 E-mail annedawtry@manchester.anglican.org

DAXTER, Preb Gregory. b 42. Chelmer Inst of HE PGCE76. Oak Hill Th Coll 64. **d** 68 **p** 69. C Paignton St Paul Preston *Ex* 68-72; C Woodford Wells *Chelmsf* 72-75; Hon C Harold Hill St Paul 75-77; Hon C Wilmington *Roch* 77-87; PV Ex Cathl and Chapl Ex Cathl Sch 87-03; Preb Ex Cathl *Ex* from 02; rtd 03. *36 Lyncombe Crescent, Higher Lincombe Road, Torquay TQ1 2HP*

DAY, Audrey. b 30. CA Tr Coll IDC57. **d** 88 **p** 94. Par Dn Mildenhall *St E* 88-91; Dioc Officer for the Care of the Elderly 91-95; NSM Blackbourne 94-95; rtd 95; Perm to Offic *St E* 95-04 and *Glouc* from 04. *25 Capel Court, The Burgage, Prestbury, Cheltenham GL52 3EL* Tel (01242) 576494

DAY, Charles George. b 28. Keble Coll Ox BA51 MA63. Cuddesdon Coll 51. **d** 53 **p** 54. C Hythe *Cant* 53-56; C S Norwood St Alb 56-59; R Stisted *Chelmsf* 59-65; V Brenchley *Roch* 65-75; rtd 93. *Sparks Hall, Forsham Lane, Sutton Valence, Maidstone ME17 3EW* Tel (01622) 843248 Fax 844298

DAY, Charles Ian. b 48. Univ of Wales (Ban) BA72. St Mich Coll Llan 73. **d** 75 **p** 76. C Llanrhos *St As* 75-79; V Mochdre 79-83; CF 80-91; V Minera *St As* 83-92; Dioc Soc Resp Officer 89-94; V Mold from 92; AD Mold from 03. *The Vicarage, Church Lane, Mold CH7 1BW* Tel and fax (01352) 752960 Mobile 07977-001692 E-mail friday@cwcom.net

DAY, Christine Audrey. b 63. K Alfred's Coll Win BTh01. STETS 02. **d** 04 **p** 05. NSM N Stoneham *Win* from 04. *86 Copperfield Road, Southampton SO16 3NY* Tel (023) 8058 2042 E-mail chrisday@fish.co.uk

DAY, Canon Colin Michael. b 40. Lon Univ BSc62 AKC62 Em Coll Cam BA66 MA71. Ridley Hall Cam 65. **d** 67 **p** 68. C Heworth w Peasholme St Cuth *York* 67-70; C Ox St Clem *Ox* 70-76; V Kidsgrove *Lich* 76-86; Exec Officer Angl Evang Assembly and C of E Coun 86-90; Adv on Miss and Evang *Sarum* 90-95; Can and Preb Sarum Cathl from 94; P-in-c Branksome Park All SS 95-01; V from 01; Dioc Tr in Evang from 95. *The Vicarage, 28 Western Road, Poole BH13 7BP* Tel (01202) 708202 E-mail colin.m.day@tesco.net

DAY, David John. b 44. CEng72 MICE72. Trin Coll Bris DipHE. **d** 90 **p** 91. C Stratton St Margaret w S Marston etc *Bris* 90-94; Perm to Offic from 94; Manager SA Alcohol Rehabilitation Cen Highworth from 98. *56 Beechcroft Road, Swindon SN2 7PX* Tel (01793) 725721

DAY, David Vivian. b 36. Lon Univ BA57 Nottm Univ MEd73 MTh77. **d** 99 **p** 00. NSM Dur St Nic *Dur* from 99. *35 Orchard Drive, Durham DH1 1LA* Tel 0191-386 6909 E-mail dv.day@virgin.net

DAY, David William. b 37. St Andr Univ MA58 BD61 CertEd73. St And Dioc Tr Course 74. **d** 76 **p** 77. C St Andrews All SS *St And* 76-77; P-in-c Dundee St Ninian *Bre* 77-84; Itinerant Priest *Arg* 84-02; R Duror 84-02; P-in-c Gruline 84-02; P-in-c Kentallen 84-02; P-in-c Kinlochleven 84-02; P-in-c Kinlochmoidart 84-96; P-in-c Lochbuie 84-96; P-in-c Portnacrois 84-02; P-in-c Strontian 84-96; Can St Jo Cathl Oban 99-02; rtd 02. *10 Doocot Road, St Andrews KY16 8QP* Tel (01334) 476991 E-mail david@arkville.freeserve.co.uk

DAY, George Chester. b 45. Ex Univ BA66 Lon Univ BD70. Clifton Th Coll 67. **d** 71 **p** 72. C Reading St Jo *Ox* 71-75; C Morden *S'wark* 75-81; Sec for Voc and Min CPAS 81-86; Hon C Bromley Ch Ch *Roch* 83-86; V St Paul's Cray St Barn 86-05; RD Orpington 01-05; V Joydens Wood St Barn from 05. *The*

Vicarage, 6 Tile Kiln Lane, Bexley DA5 2BB Tel (01322) 528923 E-mail georgeday@telco4u.net

DAY, Canon James Alfred. b 23. DFC44. AKC49. **d** 50 **p** 51. C Wembley Park St Aug *Lon* 50-52; Mauritius 52-57; V E and W Ravendale w Hatcliffe *Linc* 57-60; R Beelsby 57-60; PC Gt Grimsby St Paul 60-66; V Tattershall 66-80; R Coningsby 66-80; RD Horncastle 73-80; Can and Preb Linc Cathl from 77; V Heckington 80-89; rtd 89. *22 Ancaster Drive, Sleaford NG34 7LY* Tel (01529) 305318

DAY, Prof James Meredith. b 55. Oberlin Coll (USA) AB77 Harvard Univ EdM81 Univ of Penn PhD87. Westcott Ho Cam 01. **d** 03 **p** 04. C Antwerp St Boniface *Eur* from 03; C Ostend from 03. *Mozartstraat 20 bus 6, 2018 Antwerp, Belgium* Tel (0032) 486-141323 (mobile) E-mail james.day@psp.ucl.ac.be

DAY, Jennifer Ann. *See* BRADSHAW, Mrs Jennifer Ann

DAY, John. b 44. Oak Hill NSM Course 87. **d** 90 **p** 91. NSM Bexleyheath St Pet *Roch* 90-93; C Erith Ch Ch and Erith St Jo 93-95; P-in-c Erith St Jo 95-97; V 97-03; rtd 03. *56 Barrington Road, Bexleyheath DA7 4UW* Tel (020) 8331 5177

DAY, Canon John Alfred. b 25. TCD BA51. **d** 51 **p** 52. C Enniskillen and Trory *Clogh* 51-54; I Clontibret w Tullycorbet 54-58; I Drumkeeran 58-67; I Maguiresbridge w Derrybrusk 67-91; Can Clogh Cathl from 78; rtd 91. *Killeenifinane Cottage, 40 Ballylucas Road, Tamlaght, Enniskillen BT74 4HD* Tel (028) 6638 7835

DAY, John Cuthbert. b 36. Sarum Th Coll 66. **d** 68 **p** 69. C Bedhampton *Portsm* 68-72; V Froxfield 72-73; V Froxfield w Privett 73-77; V Warminster Ch Ch *Sarum* 77-81; R Pewsey 81-90; Chapl Pewsey Hosp 81-90; P-in-c Sturminster Newton and Hinton St Mary *Sarum* 90-01; P-in-c Stock and Lydlinch 90-01; rtd 01; Perm to Offic *B & W* and *Sarum* from 01. *Kingfisher Cottage, Clements Lane, Mere, Warminster BA12 6DF* Tel (01347) 860984

DAY, John Kenneth. b 58. Hull Univ BA85. Cranmer Hall Dur 85. **d** 87 **p** 88. C Thornbury *Bradf* 87-90; V 90-96; V Whitkirk *Ripon* 96-01; New Zealand from 01. *7 Makora Street, Fendalton, Christchurch 8004, New Zealand* Tel (0064) (3) 351 7392 E-mail johnkday@btinternet.com

DAY, Miss Mary Elizabeth. b 57. Leic Poly BEd79. St Jo Coll Nottm 93. **d** 93 **p** 94. C Newbarns w Hawcoat *Carl* 93-98; P-in-c Allonby 98-03; P-in-c Cross Canonby 98-03; P-in-c Dearham 02-03; V Allonby, Cross Canonby and Dearham from 03. *The Vicarage, Crosscanonby, Maryport CA15 6SJ* Tel (01900) 812146 E-mail mary.day1@tesco.net

DAY, Michael. b 37. AKC61 RCA(Lon) MA75. **d** 62 **p** 63. C Hulme St Phil *Man* 62-65; Asst Chapl Newc Univ *Newc* 65-70; Chapl Chelsea Coll *Lon* 70-85; Chapl R Coll of Art 70-90; Chapl Cen, Chelsea and St Martin's Schs of Art *Lon* 85-90; P-in-c Bloomsbury St Geo w Woburn Square Ch Ch 91-95; C St Pancras w St Jas and Ch Ch 95-02; Chapl Lon Art Colls 95-02; rtd 02. *40 Thistlewaite Road, London E5 0QQ* Tel (020) 8985 8568

DAY, Paul Geoffrey. b 51. Dur Univ BEd75. Trin Coll Bris 76. **d** 78 **p** 79. C Roxeth Ch Ch *Lon* 78-82; TV Barking St Marg w St Patr *Chelmsf* 82-87; V Barrow St Mark *Carl* 87-00; V Eccleston St Luke *Liv* from 00. *St Luke's Vicarage, Mulberry Avenue, St Helens WA10 4DE* Tel (01744) 21173 E-mail paulgday@btinternet.com

DAY, Paul Geoffrey. b 56. St Pet Coll Ox BA77. St Jo Coll Nottm 87. **d** 89 **p** 90. C Mildmay Grove St Jude and St Paul *Lon* 89-92; C Loughborough Em *Leic* 92-95; TV Loughborough Em and St Mary in Charnwood 95-98; Lic to Adn Loughb 98. *Address temp unknown*

DAY, Peter. b 50. BPharm71. Coll of Resurr Mirfield 85. **d** 87 **p** 88. C Eastcote St Lawr *Lon* 87-91; C Wembley Park St Aug 91-94; V Glen Parva and S Wigston *Leic* from 94. *The Vicarage, 1 St Thomas's Road, Wigston LE18 4TA* Tel 0116-278 2830 E-mail peterday@leicester.anglican.org

DAY, Peter Maurice. b 43. **d** 04 **p** 05. OLM Dover St Martin *Cant* from 04. *42 Elms Vale Road, Dover CT17 9NT* Tel (01304) 201966 E-mail peterm.day@ntlworld.com

DAY, Roy Frederick. b 24. S'wark Ord Course 63. **d** 67 **p** 68. C Newington St Paul *S'wark* 67-70; C Radlett *St Alb* 70-72; P-in-c Ponsbourne 72-76; R Campton 76-82; V Shefford 76-82; R Shenley 82-89; rtd 89; Perm to Offic *St Alb* from 89. *11 Hill End Lane, St Albans AL4 0TX* Tel (01727) 845782

DAY, Canon Samuel Richard. b 14. Reading Univ BSc36 Ch Ch Ox BA48 MA52 DPhil56. St D Coll Lamp 37. **d** 38 **p** 39. C Birkdale St Jo *Liv* 38-40; CF (EC) 40-46; C Ox St Mich *Ox* 46-49; R Chinnor 49-66; R Emmington 50-66; P-in-c Sydenham 51-66; Lect Ripon Hall Ox 57-62; V Gt Marlow 66-89; RD Wycombe 68-74; Hon Can Ch Ch 70-89; rtd 89. *3 Leighton House, Glade Road, Marlow SL7 1EA* Tel (01628) 484922

DAY, Stephen Michael. b 60. Down Coll Cam BA82 MA85 Open Univ BA00. Ridley Hall Cam 02. **d** 05. C Waltham H Cross *Chelmsf* from 05. *35 Marle Gardens, Waltham Abbey EN9 2DZ* Tel (01992) 786083 E-mail thedays@tesco.net

DAY, William Charles. b 47. Portsm Poly BEd86. Ripon Coll Cuddesdon 88. **d** 90 **p** 91. C Bishop's Waltham *Portsm* 90-93; P-in-c Greatham w Empshott and Hawkley w Prior's Dean 93-95; R 95-98; V Titchfield from 98; RD Fareham from 04. *The Vicarage, 24 Frog Lane, Titchfield, Fareham PO14 4DU* Tel (01329) 842324 *or* tel and fax 847003 E-mail bill@stptitchfield.freeserve.co.uk

DAYKIN, Mrs Jean Elizabeth. b 43. **d** 04 **p** 05. NSM Cawthorne *Wakef* from 04. *13 Maltkiln Road, Cawthorne, Barnsley S75 4HH* Tel (01226) 793804 Mobile 07967-767839 E-mail daykin.jeantom@tiscali.co.uk

DAYKIN, Timothy Elwin. b 54. R Holloway Coll Lon BSc75 St Jo Coll Dur MA81 K Coll Lon MPhil93 MEHS89. Cranmer Hall Dur 75. **d** 78 **p** 79. C Bourne *Guildf* 78-81; Chapl K Alfred Coll *Win* 82-87; C-in-c Valley Park CD 87-91; V Valley Park 91-92; P-in-c Fordingbridge 92-98; V 98-01; P-in-c Hale w S Charford 94-01; P-in-c Breamore 99-01; TR Fordingbridge and Breamore and Hale etc 01-05; TV Southampton (City Cen) from 05. *St Michael's Vicarage, 55 Bugle Street, Southampton SO14 2AG* Tel (023) 8022 4242

DAYNES, Andrew John. b 47. Jes Coll Cam BA69 MA73. Westcott Ho Cam 69. **d** 72 **p** 73. C Radlett *St Alb* 72-76; Chapl St Alb Abbey 76-80; Chapl Bryanston Sch from 80. *Bryanston School, Blandford Forum DT11 0PX* Tel (01258) 484655 *or* 452411 E-mail post@bryanston.co.uk

DAZELEY, Mrs Lorna. b 31. CertEd53 New Hall Cam BA82 MA86. EAMTC 82. **dss** 84 **d** 87 **p** 94. Chesterton St Andr *Ely* 84-87; C 87-97; rtd 97; Perm to Offic *Ely* from 01. *Chesterton House, Church Street, Chesterton, Cambridge CB4 1DT* Tel (01223) 356243

DE ALWIS, Anthony Clarence. b 39. Nottm Univ MA99. EAMTC 96. **d** 99 **p** 00. NSM Carrington *S'well* 99-04; NSM Basford St Leodegarius from 04. *85 Marlborough Road, Beeston, Nottingham NG9 2HL* Tel 0115-922 0443 Mobile 07974-084514 E-mail tonydealwis270@hotmail.com

de BERRY, Andrew Piers. b 44. St Jo Coll Dur BA66. Ripon Hall Ox 70. **d** 74 **p** 75. C Aylesbury *Ox* 74-77; USA 78; TV Clyst St George, Aylesbeare, Clyst Honiton etc *Ex* 78-80; Asst Chapl HM Pris Wormwood Scrubs 80-82; Chapl HM Pris Sudbury 82-84; V Blackwell *Derby* 84-91; V Thurgarton w Hoveringham and Bleasby etc *S'well* from 91. *The Vicarage, Southwell Road, Thurgarton, Nottingham NG14 7GP* Tel (01636) 830234 E-mail de_berry@totalise.co.uk

de BERRY, Barnabas John de la Tour. b 75. Heythrop Coll Lon BA99. Wycliffe Hall Ox 99. **d** 01 **p** 02. C Derby St Alkmund and St Werburgh *Derby* 01-04; C Cambridge H Trin *Ely* from 04. *42 Pretoria Road, Cambridge CB4 1HE* Tel (01223) 479473 Mobile 07968-728840 E-mail barneydeb@hotmail.com

DE BERRY, Robert Delatour. b 42. Qu Coll Cam BA64 MA68. Ridley Hall Cam 65. **d** 67 **p** 68. C Bradf Cathl *Bradf* 67-70; Uganda 71-75; V Attercliffe *Sheff* 75-83; V W Kilburn St Luke w St Simon and St Jude *Lon* 83-97; Gen Sec Mid-Africa Min (CMS) 97-99; P-in-c Kennington St Mark *S'wark* 99-01; V from 01. *St Mark's Vicarage, 56 Kennington Oval, London SE11 5SW* Tel (020) 7735 1801 Fax as telephone E-mail 100646@compuserve.com

de BOWEN, Alfred William. b 24. Leeds Univ Dip Horticulture. St Paul's Coll Grahamstown 76. **d** 78 **p** 86. NSM Port Alfred S Africa 78-86; NSM Cil-y-Cwm and Ystrad-ffin w Rhandir-mwyn etc *St D* 86-88; Lic to Offic *Linc* 88-92; rtd 90. *Elmham House, Bay Hill, Ilminster TA19 0AT* Tel (01460) 52694

de BURGH-THOMAS, George Albert. b 30. Univ of Wales (Ban) BA50. St Mich Coll Llan 51. **d** 53 **p** 54. C Hawarden *St As* 53-56 and 60-63; C Roath St Martin *Llan* 56-58; C Llangeinor 58-60; V Bampton and Mardale *Carl* 63-70; V Fritwell *Ox* 70-83; R Souldern 70-83; R Fritwell w Souldern and Ardley w Fewcott 83-87; R Hawridge w Cholesbury and St Leonard 87-96; V The Lee 87-96; rtd 96; Perm to Offic *Ox* from 01. *6 Priory Orchard, Wantage OX12 9EL* Tel (01235) 767780

de CHAZAL, John Robert. b 16. Bris Univ. Wycliffe Hall Ox 53. **d** 55 **p** 56. C Redland *Bris* 55-57; C Brislington St Anne 57; C Boxwell w Leighterton *Glouc* 58-60; C Newington Bagpath w Kingscote and Ozleworth 58-60; P-in-c 60; Iraq 61-64; R Caldecote *Cov* 64-71; R Bradford Peverell w Stratton *Sarum* 72-77; P-in-c Sydling St Nic 77; P-in-c Frampton 77; R Bradford Peverell, Stratton, Frampton etc 77-80; rtd 81; Perm to Offic *Sarum* from 81. *Lavender Cottage, East Street, Sydling, Dorchester DT2 9NX* Tel (01300) 341693

de CHAZAL, Mrs Nancy Elizabeth. b 28. Bedf Coll Lon BA52 Lambeth STh90. Sarum & Wells Th Coll 81. **dss** 84 **d** 87 **p** 94. NSM Melbury *Sarum* 84-98; Perm to Offic from 98. *Lavender Cottage, East Street, Sydling St Nicholas, Dorchester DT2 9NX* Tel (01300) 341693

de COSTOBADIE, James Palliser. b 72. G&C Coll Cam BA94 MA98. Oak Hill Th Coll BA01. **d** 02. C St Helen Bishopsgate w St Andr Undershaft etc *Lon* from 02; C Mayfair Ch Ch from 02. *49A Chester Way, London SE11 4UR* Tel (020) 7629 5885 E-mail jdecostobadie@hotmail.com

de GARIS, Jean Helier Thomson. b 60. K Alfred's Coll Win BA82 PGCE83. Sarum & Wells Th Coll BTh93. **d** 93 **p** 94. C Chandler's Ford *Win* 93-98; P-in-c Lytchett Minster *Sarum* from

98. *The Vicarage, New Road, Lytchett Minster, Poole BH16 6JQ* Tel (01202) 622253 E-mail jdg@fish.co.uk

de GREY-WARTER, Philip. b 67. Leeds Univ BEng89. Ridley Hall Cam BA94. **d** 94 **p** 95. C Bromley Ch Ch *Roch* 94-97; C Sevenoaks St Nic 97-02; P-in-c Fowey *Truro* from 02; P-in-c St Sampson from 02; Chapl Cen Cornwall Primary Care Trust from 02; Hon Chapl Miss to Seafarers from 04. *The Vicarage, Church Avenue, Fowey PL23 1BU* Tel (01726) 833535 E-mail pdgw@btinternet.com

DE KEYSER, Nicholas David Llewellyn. b 49. Nottm Univ BTh75 MTh86. St Jo Coll Nottm 71. **d** 75 **p** 76. C Portswood Ch Ch *Win* 75-77; C Yateley 77-81; TV Grantham *Linc* 81-86; V Heyside *Man* 86-91; R Charlton-in-Dover *Cant* 91-03; R Stock Harvard *Chelmsf* from 03. *The Rectory, 61 High Street, Stock, Ingatestone CM4 9BN* Tel (01277) 840453 Mobile 07050-155481 Fax 08701-249842 E-mail nickdekeyser@btopenworld.com

de la BAT SMIT, Reynaud. b 50. St Edm Hall Ox BA80 MA86 Dur Univ PhD94 FRSA94. Ripon Coll Cuddesdon. **d** 82 **p** 83. C Headington *Ox* 82-85; Chapl St Hild and St Bede Coll *Dur* 85-96; Chapl Cheltenham Coll from 96; Sec Chs' Peace Forum CTBI from 97. *Cheltenham College, Bath Road, Cheltenham GL53 7LD* Tel (01242) 513540 *or* 230800 E-mail reynaud@ukonline.co.uk

de la HOYDE, Canon Denys Ralph Hart. b 33. G&C Coll Cam BA57 MA61. Westcott Ho Cam 57. **d** 59 **p** 60. C Moss Side Ch Ch *Man* 59-60; Chapl G&C Coll Cam 60-64; P-in-c Naini Tal etc India 64-68; C Eltham H Trin *S'wark* 68-69; Chapl Bromsgrove Sch 69-71; Asst Master Harrogate High Sch 71-78; Lic to Offic *Ripon* 71-78; V Pool w Arthington 86-98; Dioc Dir of Ords 86-98; Hon Can Ripon Cathl 92-98; rtd 98. *36 Hookstone Chase, Harrogate HG2 7HS* Tel (01423) 548146 E-mail delahoyde@onetel.com

de la MARE, Benedick James Hobart. b 38. Trin Coll Ox BA63 MA67. Cuddesdon Coll 63. **d** 65 **p** 66. C Gosforth All SS *Newc* 65-68; Chapl Trin Coll Cam 68-73; V Newc St Gabr *Newc* 73-81; V Dur St Oswald *Dur* 81-02; rtd 02; Chapl Collingwood Coll Dur 95-04; Hon Chapl from 04. *216 Gilesgate, Durham DH1 1QN* Tel 0191-383 2634

de la MOUETTE, Norman Harry. b 39. Southn Univ BEd73 MA98. Sarum & Wells Th Coll 76. **d** 79 **p** 80. NSM Win St Lawr and St Maurice w St Swithun *Win* 79-99; Deputation Appeals Org CECS *Win* and *Portsm* 83-96; Chapl St Jo Win Charity 96-99; NSM Win St Lawr and St Maurice w St Swithun *Win* 99-04; rtd 04. *146 Greenhill Road, Winchester SO22 5DR* Tel (01962) 853191

DE LACEY, Thomas. b 46. HNC68. Carl Dioc Tr Inst 88. **d** 91 **p** 92. NSM Ingol *Blackb* 91-93; NSM Ribbleton 93-94. *5 Fulwood Hall Lane, Fulwood, Preston PR2 8DA* Tel (01772) 700923

de MELLO, Gualter Rose. b 34. MBE96. Ridley Hall Cam 63. **d** 64 **p** 65. C S Hackney St Jo w Ch Ch *Lon* 64-66; Toc H Chapl (Hackney) 66-72; Hon C All Hallows by the Tower etc *Lon* from 73; Dir Friends Anonymous Service from 73; Dir Community of Reconciliation and Fellowship from 88; rtd 99. *Prideaux House, 10 Church Crescent, London E9 7DL*

DE MURALT, Robert Willem Gaston. b 25. Utrecht Univ LLM48 DLSc54. Chich Th Coll 90. **d** 90 **p** 91. Hon Asst Chapl The Hague *Eur* 90-02; rtd 02. *Burgemeester de Monchyplein 173, 2585 DH The Hague, The Netherlands* Tel (0031) (70) 383 8520

✠**de PINA CABRAL, The Rt Revd Daniel Pereira dos Santos.** b 24. Lisbon Univ LLB47. Lon Coll of Div. **d** 47 **p** 49 **c** 67. Portugal 47-67; Portuguese E Africa 67-75; Mozambique 75-76; Asst Bp Lebombo 67-68; Bp Lebombo 68-76; Asst Bp Eur from 76; Hon Can Gib Cathl 79-87; Adn Gib 87-93; rtd 89. *Rua Henrique Lopes de Mendonça, 253-42 Dto hab 42, 4150-396 Porto, Portugal* Tel (00351) (22) 617 7772

DE POE SILK, Ronald Charles. b 32. Lich Th Coll 65. **d** 67 **p** 68. C Tottenham St Phil *Lon* 67-68; C Edmonton St Mary w St Jo 68-70; V Stamford Hill St Bart 70-74; rtd 97. *Montana, East Barton Road, Great Barton, Bury St Edmunds IP31 2RF*

de POMERAI, David Ian Morcamp. b 50. Edin Univ BSc72 Univ Coll Lon PhD75. EMMTC 90. **d** 93 **p** 94. NSM Sutton in Ashfield St Mary *S'well* 93-96; NSM Clifton 96-02; NSM Walton-on-Trent w Croxall, Rosliston etc *Derby* from 02. *The Rectory, 2 Station Lane, Walton-on-Trent, Swadlincote DE12 8NA* Tel (01283) 711350 E-mail david.depomerai@nottingham.ac.uk

de POMERAI, Mrs Lesley Anne. b 60. ACIPD82. St Jo Coll Nottm BTh90. **d** 92 **p** 94. Par Dn Sutton in Ashfield St Mary *S'well* 92-94; C 94-96; TV Clifton 96-02; R Walton-on-Trent w Croxall, Rosliston etc *Derby* from 02. *The Rectory, 2 Station Lane, Walton-on-Trent, Swadlincote DE12 8NA* Tel (01283) 712442 E-mail ddepomerai@aol.com

DE PURY, Andrew Robert. b 28. K Coll Lon BD57 AKC57. **d** 58 **p** 59. C Epping St Jo *Chelmsf* 58-60; C Loughton St Jo 60-65; V Harold Hill St Geo 65-72; Missr Swan Par Gp *Ox* 72-76; TR Swan 76-85; R Worminghall w Ickford, Oakley and Shabbington 85-95; rtd 95; Perm to Offic *B & W* from 95. *8 Russell Pope Avenue, Chard TA20 2JN* Tel (01460) 66714

de QUIDT, Mrs Fiona Margaret Munro. b 53. St Andr Univ MTheol76. NTMTC 97. **d** 00 **p** 01. NSM Kingston Hill St Paul *S'wark* from 00. *10 Norbiton Avenue, Kingston-upon-Thames KT1 3QS* Tel (020) 8549 4175

DE ROBECK, Fiona Caroline. *See* GIBBS, Mrs Fiona Caroline

DE SAUSMAREZ, Canon John Havilland Russell. b 26. Lambeth MA81 Wells Th Coll 54. **d** 56 **p** 57. C N Lynn w St Marg and St Nic *Nor* 56-58; C Hythe *Cant* 58-61; V Maidstone St Martin 61-68; V St Peter-in-Thanet 68-81; RD Thanet 74-81; Hon Can Cant Cathl 78-81; Can Res Cant Cathl 81-94; rtd 94; Perm to Offic *Cant* from 94. *9 St Peter's Court, Broadstairs CT10 2UU* Tel (01843) 867050

DE SILVA, David Ebenezer Sunil. b 48. **d** 72 **p** 73. Sri Lanka 72-84; C Elm Park St Nic Hornchurch *Chelmsf* 84-87; R Mistley w Manningtree and Bradfield 87-90; TR Stanground and Farcet *Ely* 90-01; V Stanground 01-05; rtd 05. *20 Freston, Peterborough PE4 7EN* Tel (01733) 890552

DE SMET, Andrew Charles. b 58. Ex Univ BSc79 Southn Univ BTh88. Sarum & Wells Th Coll 85. **d** 88 **p** 89. C Portsea St Mary *Portsm* 88-93; R Shipston-on-Stour w Honington and Idlicote *Cov* 93-00; Warden Offa Retreat Ho and Dioc Spirituality Adv from 00. *The Vicarage, School Hill, Offchurch, Leamington Spa CV33 9AL* Tel (01926) 424401 *or* 423309 E-mail offahouse@btconnect.com

DE VERNY, David Dietrich. b 55. Trier Univ MTh81 DTh89. **d** 83 **p** 83. Asst Chapl Bonn *Eur* 83; C Henfield w Shermanbury and Woodmancote *Chich* 84-86; C Westmr St Sav and St Jas Less *Lon* 86-88; P-in-c Cheddington w Mentmore and Marsworth *Ox* 88-90; Gen Sec Fellowship of St Alb and St Sergius 90-92. *Address temp unknown*

de VIAL, Raymond Michael. b 39. Oak Hill Th Coll 77. **d** 80 **p** 81. NSM Beckenham St Jo *Roch* 80-84; C Morden *S'wark* 84-88; TV 88-94; V Kingston Hill St Paul 94-04; rtd 04; Perm to Offic *S'wark* from 04. *39 Helme Drive, Kendal LA9 7JB* Tel (01539) 729396 E-mail revray@btinternet.com

✠**de WAAL, The Rt Revd Hugo Ferdinand.** b 35. Pemb Coll Cam BA58 MA63. Ridley Hall Cam 59. **d** 60 **p** 61 **c** 92. C Birm St Martin *Birm* 60-64; Chapl Pemb Coll Cam 64-68; P-in-c Dry Drayton *Ely* 64-68; R 68-74; Min Bar Hill LEP 68-74; V Blackpool St Jo *Blackb* 74-78; Prin Ridley Hall Cam 78-92; Hon Can Ely Cathl *Ely* 86-92; Suff Bp Thetford *Nor* 92-00; rtd 01; Perm to Offic *St E* from 01; Hon Asst Bp Eur from 02. *Folly House, The Folly, Haughley, Stowmarket IP14 3NS* Tel (01449) 774915 E-mail dewaal@btinternet.com

de WAAL, Victor Alexander. b 29. Pemb Coll Cam BA49 MA53 Nottm Univ Hon DD83. Ely Th Coll 50. **d** 52 **p** 53. C Isleworth St Mary *Lon* 52-56; Chapl Ely Th Coll 56-59; Chapl K Coll Cam 59-63; Hon C Nottingham St Mary *S'well* 63-69; Chapl Nottm Univ 63-69; Can Res and Chan Linc Cathl *Linc* 69-76; Dean Cant 76-86; Perm to Offic *Heref* 88-99; rtd 90; Chapl Soc of Sacred Cross Tymawr 90-00; Lic to Offic *Mon* 90-02; Perm to Offic from 02. *6 St James Close, Bishop Street, London N1 8PH* Tel (020) 7354 2741 E-mail victordewaal@aol.com

DE WIT, John. b 47. Oriel Coll Ox BA69 MA73 Clare Coll Cam BA78 MA84. Westcott Ho Cam 75. **d** 78 **p** 79. C The Quinton *Birm* 78-81; TV Solihull 81-85; V Kings Heath 85-94; RD Moseley 91-94; P-in-c Hampton in Arden 94-04; Chapl Utrecht w Amersfoort, Harderwijk and Zwolle *Eur* from 04. *Van Hogendorpstraat 26, 3581KE Utrecht, The Netherlands* Tel (0031) (30) 251 3424 E-mail chaplain@holytrinityutrecht.nl

DE WOLF, Mark Anthony. b 32. BA55. Ely Th Coll 56. **d** 59 **p** 60. C Hackney Wick St Mary of Eton w St Aug *Lon* 59-64; USA from 64; rtd 97. *9 Weetamoe Farm Drive, Bristol, RI 02809, USA*

DEACON, Charles Edward. b 57. Westf Coll Lon BSc78. Ridley Hall Cam CTM94. **d** 94 **p** 95. C Ex St Jas *Ex* 94-98; V Shiphay Collaton from 98. *St John's Vicarage, 83 Cadewell Lane, Torquay TQ2 7HP* Tel (01803) 401316

DEACON, Donald (Brother Angelo). Chich Th Coll 66. **d** 68 **p** 69. SSF from 63; Lic to Offic *Man* 69-70; USA 70-72; C Kennington St Jo *S'wark* 72-74; C Wilton Place St Paul *Lon* 74-75; Angl-Franciscan Rep Ecum Cen Assisi *Eur* 75; Franciscanum Sem 76-78; Perm to Offic *Sarum* 78-82; Lic to Offic *Chelmsf* 82-90; *Birm* 90-93; *Linc* 94-97; rtd 98; Lic to Offic *Lon* from 98. *Society of St Francis, Alverna, 110 Ellesmere Road, London NW10 1JS* Tel (020) 8452 7285 Fax as telephone

DEACON, Frederick George Raymond. b 15. Tyndale Hall Bris 63. **d** 65 **p** 66. C Kingswood *Bris* 65-69; C Leckhampton SS Phil and Jas *Glouc* 69-71; V Longcot *Ox* 71-72; V Longcot w Fernham and Bourton 72-77; Zambia 77-80; P-in-c Cressage w Sheinton *Heref* 80-81; P-in-c Harley w Kenley 80-81; TV Wenlock 81-85; rtd 85; Perm to Offic *Heref* 85-90; *Glouc* from 1986 and *Worc* from 90. *29 Robinson Meadow, Ledbury HR8 1SU* Tel (01531) 634500

DEACON, John. b 37. Arm Aux Min Course 87. **d** 90 **p** 91. NSM Enniscorthy w Clone, Clonmore, Monart etc *C & O* from 90. *The Rectory, Creagh, Gorey, Co Wexford, Irish Republic* Tel (00353) (55) 20354

DEACON, Mrs Selina Frances. b 52. SRN74. Ripon Coll Cuddesdon 01. **d** 03 **p** 04. C White Horse *Sarum* from 03. *37 Timor Road, Westbury BA13 2GA* Tel (01373) 826509 Mobile 07867-521909 E-mail selinadeacon@hotmail.com

DEACON, Timothy Randall. b 55. Ex Univ BA78. Chich Th Coll 79. **d** 80 **p** 81. C Whitleigh *Ex* 80-83; P-in-c Devonport St Aubyn 83-88; P-in-c Newton Ferrers w Revelstoke 88-94; R from 94; P-in-c Holbeton from 93; RD Ivybridge 98-03. *The Rectory, Court Road, Newton Ferrers, Plymouth PL8 1DL* Tel and fax (01752) 872530 E-mail timdeacon@bigfoot.com

DEADMAN, Richard George Spencer. b 63. Ex Univ BA85. Coll of Resurr Mirfield 86. **d** 88 **p** 89. C Grangetown *York* 88-91; P-in-c 91-93; V 93-96; V Wallsend St Luke *Newc* 96-01; V Newc St Phil and St Aug and St Matt w St Mary from 01. *St Matthew's Vicarage, 10 Winchester Terrace, Newcastle upon Tyne NE4 6EY* Tel 0191-232 9039 E-mail richardgsd@aol.com

DEAKIN, Christopher Harold. b 49. ARMCM72. Qu Coll Birm 02. **d** 04 **p** 05. C Wrockwardine Deanery *Lich* from 04. *The Parsonage, Upton Magna, Shrewsbury SY4 4TZ* E-mail deaks@fsmail.net

DEAKIN, John David. b 58. Qu Coll Birm BA03. **d** 03 **p** 04. C Blakenall Heath *Lich* from 03. *St Aidan's Vicarage, 78A Chestnut Road, Walsall WS3 1AP* Tel (01922) 494655

DEAKIN, Preb John Hartley. b 27. K Coll Cam BA50 MA63. Cranmer Hall Dur DipTh65. **d** 65 **p** 66. C Newcastle St Geo *Lich* 65-70; V Cotes Heath 70-84; RD Eccleshall 82-92; R Standon and Cotes Heath 84-95; Preb Lich Cathl 88-02; Sub-Chapl HM Pris Drake Hall 89-95; rtd 95; Hon C Kinver and Enville *Lich* 95-02. *8C Cliff Road, Bridgnorth WV16 4EY* Tel (01746) 762574

DEAMER, Mrs Carylle. b 40. St Alb and Ox Min Course 96. **d** 99 **p** 00. OLM Riverside *Ox* from 99. *6 Parkland Avenue, Slough SL3 7LQ* Tel (01753) 543818 Mobile 07711-611318

DEAN, The Ven Alan. b 38. Hull Univ BA61. Qu Coll Birm DipTh63. **d** 63 **p** 64. C Clitheroe St Mary *Blackb* 63-67; C Burnley St Pet 67-68; CF 68-93; Dep Chapl Gen and Adn for the Army 93-95; rtd 96; QHC from 93; Perm to Offic *York* from 95. *1 Midway Avenue, Nether Poppleton, York YO26 6NT* Tel (01904) 785305

DEAN, Andrew James. b 40. FCII ACIArb. WEMTC 92. **d** 95 **p** 96. NSM Rodbourne Cheney *Bris* 95-05; rtd 05; Perm to Offic *Bris* from 05. *Koinonia, 2 Wicks Close, Haydon Wick, Swindon SN25 1QH* Tel (01793) 725526

DEAN, Archibald Charles. b 13. Wycliffe Hall Ox 52. **d** 54 **p** 55. C Yeovil St Jo w Preston Plucknett *B & W* 54-61; R Odcombe 61-91; R Brympton 61-91; R Lufton 61-91; P-in-c Montacute 78-86; rtd 91; Perm to Offic *B & W* from 91. *3 Chur Lane, West Coker, Yeovil BA22 9BH* Tel (01935) 862224

DEAN, Canon Arthur. b 32. Southn Univ CQSW80. Wesley Coll Leeds 55 S Dios Minl Tr Scheme 89. **d** 90 **p** 90. NSM Eastney *Portsm* 90-96; P-in-c Portsea St Alb 96-02; Hon Can Portsm Cathl from 02; rtd 02; Perm to Offic *Portsm* from 02. *9 Kingsley Road, Southsea PO4 8HJ* Tel (023) 9273 5773 Mobile 07855-146929 Fax (023) 9222 1910 E-mail annenarthur.dean@btopenworld.com

DEAN, John Milner. b 27. S'wark Ord Course 69. **d** 72 **p** 73. C Lewisham St Mary *S'wark* 72-75; C Merton St Mary 75-77; V S Beddington St Mich 77-97; rtd 97. *69 Groveside Close, Carshalton SM5 2ER* Tel (020) 8669 9369

DEAN, Mrs Linda Louise. b 39. **d** 04. NSM Primrose Hill St Mary w Avenue Road St Paul *Lon* from 04. *52 Lancaster Road, London N6 4TA* Tel (020) 8883 5417 E-mail linda@lindadean.wanadoo.co.uk

DEAN, Malcolm. b 34. Tyndale Hall Bris 67. **d** 69 **p** 70. C Daubhill *Man* 69-73; P-in-c Constable Lee 73-74; V 74-79; P-in-c Everton St Sav w St Cuth *Liv* 79-86; P-in-c Anfield SS Simon and Jude 81-86; V Walton Breck Ch Ch 86-89; rtd 89; Perm to Offic *Man* from 89. *40 Grasmere Road, Haslingden, Rossendale BB4 4EB* Tel (01706) 215953

DEAN, Preb Raymond Charles. b 27. Bris Univ BA51. Wycliffe Hall Ox 51. **d** 53 **p** 54. C Weston-super-Mare St Jo *B & W* 53-59; V Lyngford 59-70; V Burnham 70-93; Preb Wells Cathl from 73; RD Burnham 82-91; RD Axbridge 87-91; rtd 93; Perm to Offic *B & W* from 93. *258 Berrow Road, Berrow, Burnham-on-Sea TA8 2JH* Tel (01278) 780979

DEAN, Simon Timothy Michael Rex. b 62. Liv Univ BEng83. Ridley Hall Cam 86. **d** 89 **p** 90. C St German's Cathl *S & M* 89-92; V Castletown 92-05. *9 rue de la Fraternelle, 10500 Radonvilliers, France*

DEANE, Mrs Angela Christine. b 52. WEMTC 00. **d** 04. NSM Credenhill w Brinsop and Wormsley etc *Heref* from 04. *The Oak, Mansel Lacy, Hereford HR4 7HQ* Tel (01981) 590615 E-mail angiestutheoak@lineone.net

DEANE, John. **d** 02 **p** 03. C Stranorlar w Meenglas and Kilteevogue *D & R* from 02. *Copany, Donegal PO, Donegal, Irish Republic* Tel (00353) (74) 972 2101

DEANE, Nicholas Talbot Bryan. b 46. Bris Univ BA69. Clifton Th Coll 70. **d** 72 **p** 73. C Accrington Ch Ch *Blackb* 72-75; OMF 75-89; Korea 75-89; P-in-c Newburgh *Liv* 90-93; P-in-c Westhead 90-93; V Newburgh w Westhead 93-97; R Chadwell *Chelmsf* from 97. *The Rectory, 10 Rigby Gardens, Grays RM16 4JJ* Tel (01375) 842176 E-mail nic.deane@virgin.net

DEANE, Robert William. b 52. DipTh85. CITC 85. **d** 85 **p** 86. C Raheny w Coolock *D & G* 85-88; I Clonsast w Rathangan, Thomastown etc *M & K* 88-00; Can Kildare Cathl 97-00; Can Meath Cathl 98-00; I Swords w Donabate and Kilsallaghan *D & G* from 00. *The Rectory, Church Road, Swords, Co Dublin, Irish Republic* Tel (00353) (1) 840 2308

DEANE, Stuart William. b 45. Sarum & Wells Th Coll 86. **d** 88 **p** 89. C Bromyard *Heref* 88-92; V Astley, Clive, Grinshill and Hadnall *Lich* 92-98; TV Cen Telford 98-00; TR 00-05; rtd 05. *38 Crest Court, Hereford HR4 9QD*

DEANE-HALL, Henry Michael. b 21. Leeds Univ BA46. Coll of Resurr Mirfield 47. **d** 49 **p** 50. C Poplar St Sav w St Gabr and St Steph *Lon* 49-51; C Kirkley *Nor* 51-53; C Reading St Mary V *Ox* 53-56; Chapl St Gabr Convent Sch Newbury 56-62; V Hermitage *Ox* 58-65; V Patrick *S & M* 65-67; R Boughton *Pet* 67-71; R Duloe w Herodsfoot *Truro* 71-79; V Morval 71-79; P-in-c Donhead St Mary *Sarum* 79-80; R The Donheads 80-82; rtd 82; Perm to Offic *Ex* 82-95; Warden CJGS 82-95. *33 Dulverton Hall, Esplanade, Scarborough YO11 2AR* Tel (01723) 340133

DEANS, Bruce Gibson. b 64. MCIBS86. Wycliffe Hall Ox 02. **d** 04 **p** 05. C Hartley Wintney, Elvetham, Winchfield etc *Win* from 04. *40 Pool Road, Hartley Wintney, Basingstoke RG27 8RD* Tel (01252) 843389

DEAR, Graham Frederick. b 44. St Luke's Coll Ex CertEd66. Wycliffe Hall Ox 67. **d** 70 **p** 71. C Chigwell *Chelmsf* 70-73; C Chingford SS Pet and Paul 73-75; V Southchurch Ch Ch 75-82; CF 82-89; P-in-c The Cowtons *Ripon* 89-94; RE Adv 89-94; V Startforth and Bowes and Rokeby w Brignall 94-97; Chapl HM Pris Garth 97-01; Perm to Offic *Ripon* from 01. *1 The Old Wynd, Bellerby, Leyburn DL8 5QJ* Tel (01969) 623960

DEAR, Neil Douglas Gauntlett. b 35. Linc Th Coll 87. **d** 89 **p** 90. C Framlingham w Saxtead *St E* 89-92; P-in-c Eyke w Bromeswell, Rendlesham, Tunstall etc 92-98; Chapl Local Health Partnerships NHS Trust 98-02; Chapl Cen Suffolk Primary Care Trust 02-05; P-in-c Worlingworth, Southolt, Tannington, Bedfield etc *St E* 02-05; rtd 05. *Peacehaven, Duke Street, Stanton, Bury St Edmunds IP31 2AB*

DEARDEN, James Varley. b 22. Wycliffe Hall Ox 61. **d** 62 **p** 63. C Drypool St Columba w St Andr and St Pet *York* 62-66; V Newington Transfiguration 66-75; V Huddersfield H Trin *Wakef* 75-87; rtd 87; Perm to Offic *Wakef* from 87. *26 Sycamore Avenue, Meltham, Holmfirth HD9 4EE* Tel (01484) 852519

DEARDEN, Canon Philip Harold. b 43. AKC65. **d** 66 **p** 67. C Haslingden w Haslingden Grane *Blackb* 66-69; C Burnley St Pet 69-71; V Langho Billington 71-78; TR Darwen St Pet w Hoddlesden 78-91; RD Darwen 86-91; V Altham w Clayton le Moors 91-97; RD Accrington 95-97; V Clitheroe St Mary from 97; Hon Can Blackb Cathl from 96. *St Mary's Vicarage, Church Street, Clitheroe BB7 2DD* Tel and fax (01200) 423317 *or* 22828 E-mail philipdearden@aol.com

DEARING, Henry Ernest. b 26. Lon Univ BD53. St Deiniol's Hawarden 55. **d** 55 **p** 56. C Skerton St Chad *Blackb* 55-57; V Huncoat 57-60; rtd 95. *7 Troon Way, Abergele LL22 7TT* Tel (01745) 826714

DEARING, Trevor. b 33. Lon Univ BD58. Qu Coll Birm MA63. **d** 61 **p** 62. C Todmorden *Wakef* 61-63; V Silkstone 63-66; V Northowram 66-68; C Harlow New Town w Lt Parndon *Chelmsf* 68-70; V Hainault 70-75; Dir Healing Miss 75-79; Hon C Gt Ilford St Andr 75-79; Perm to Offic *Linc* 80-81; 99-02; USA 81-83; rtd 83. *4 Rock House Gardens, Radcliffe Road, Stamford PE9 1AS* Tel (01780) 751680

DEARNLEY, Miss Helen Elizabeth. b 77. De Montfort Univ LLB98 Cam Univ BTh02. Westcott Ho Cam 99. **d** 02 **p** 03. C Knighton St Mary Magd *Leic* from 02. *39 Woodcroft Avenue, Leicester LE2 6HU* Tel 0116-288 6443 E-mail helen.dearnley@ukgateway.net

DEARNLEY, John Wright. b 37. Open Univ BA81 Bris Univ CASS65 Univ of Wales (Lamp) DipTh91. **d** 99. NSM Llandogo w Whitebrook Chpl and Tintern Parva *Mon* from 99. *2 Greenbanks, Llandogo, Monmouth NP25 4TG* Tel (01594) 530080

DEARNLEY, Mark Christopher. b 59. Cranmer Hall Dur 84. **d** 87 **p** 88. C Purley Ch Ch *S'wark* 87-91; C Addiscombe St Mary 91-93; C Addiscombe St Mary Magd w St Martin 93-94; V Hook 94-02; R Wendover and Halton *Ox* from 02; AD Wendover from 04. *The Vicarage, 34 Dobbins Lane, Wendover, Aylesbury HP22 6DH* Tel (01296) 622230 E-mail dearnley@ukgateway.net

DEARNLEY, Preb Patrick Walter. b 34. Nottm Univ BA55 LTh75. ALCD64. **d** 64 **p** 65. C New Malden and Coombe *S'wark* 64-68; C Portswood Ch Ch *Win* 68-71; C Leeds St Geo *Ripon* 71-74; Hon C Nottingham St Nic *S'well* 74-77; P-in-c Holloway Em w Hornsey Road St Barn *Lon* 77-85; AD Islington 80-85; Abp's Officer for UPA 85-90; Preb St Paul's Cathl *Lon* 86-91; P-in-c Waterloo St Jo *Liv* 91-99; rtd 99; Perm to Offic

Bradf from 00. *14 Beanlands Parade, Ilkley LS29 8EW* Tel (01943) 603927

DEAS, Leonard Stephen. b 52. New Coll Ox BA75 CertEd76 MA78. St Mich Coll Llan 81. **d** 82 **p** 83. C Dowlais *Llan* 82-84; Chapl St Mich Coll Llan 84-85; Chapl Univ of Wales (Cardiff) *Llan* 85-86; V Newbridge *Mon* 86-93; Can Res St Woolos Cathl 92-96; Master of the Charterhouse Kingston upon Hull from 96. *The Charterhouse, Charterhouse Lane, Hull HU2 8AF* Tel (01482) 329307

DEAVE, Mrs Gillian Mary. b 31. EMMTC 79. **dss** 82 **d** 87 **p** 94. Nottingham St Pet and St Jas *S'well* 82-87; Par Dn 87-91; rtd 91; Perm to Offic *Pet* and *S'well* from 91. *Greensmith Cottage, 8 City Road, Stathern, Melton Mowbray LE14 4HE* Tel (01949) 860340 E-mail g.deave@leicester.anglican.org

DEBENHAM, Peter Mark. b 68. Nottm Univ BSc89 PhD94. EAMTC 98. **d** 01 **p** 03. NSM Burwell *Ely* 01-02; NSM Swaffham Bulbeck and Swaffham Prior w Reach 01-02; Perm to Offic 02-03; NSM Fordham St Pet from 03; NSM Kennett from 03. *23 Burleigh Rise, Burwell, Cambridge CB5 0RS* Tel (01638) 603142 *or* (07941) 258253
E-mail peter.debenham@ely.anglican.org

DEBNEY, Canon Wilfred Murray. b 26. ACA48 FCA60. Wycliffe Hall Ox 58. **d** 60 **p** 61. C Leic H Apostles *Leic* 60-65; V Thorpe Edge *Bradf* 65-69; TV Wendy w Shingay *Ely* 69-75; R Brampton 75-94; Offg Chapl RAF 75-94; RD Huntingdon *Ely* 81-94; Hon Can Ely Cathl 85-94; rtd 94; Lic to Offic *Eur* 94-01; Chapl Lugano 98-02; Perm to Offic *Ely* from 02. *3 Hoo Close, Buckden, St Neots PE19 5TX* Tel (01480) 810652

DEBOO, Alan John. b 45. Qu Coll Cam BA73 MA77. Westcott Ho Cam 72. **d** 74 **p** 75. C Brackley St Pet w St Jas *Pet* 74-77; Perm to Offic *Sarum* 85-94; NSM Wexcombe 94-02; NSM Savernake from 02; Bp's Officer for NSMs from 03. *Mayzells Cottage, Collingbourne Kingston, Marlborough SN8 3SD* Tel (01264) 850683 E-mail alandeboo@aol.com

DEBOYS, David Gordon. b 54. QUB BD76 Wolfs Coll Ox MLitt. Ridley Hall Cam 90. **d** 92 **p** 93. C Ipswich St Aug *St E* 92-93; C Whitton and Thurleston w Akenham 93-95; R Hardwick *Ely* 95-00; R Toft w Caldecote and Childerley 95-00; V Cambridge St Jas from 00; Dir Focus Chr Inst Cambridge from 00. *St James's Vicarage, 110 Wulfstan Way, Cambridge CB1 8QJ* Tel (01223) 246419 E-mail daviddeboys@btinternet.com

DEDMAN, Canon Roger James. b 45. Oak Hill Th Coll 68. **d** 71 **p** 72. C Gresley *Derby* 71-74; C Ipswich St Fran *St E* 74-79; P-in-c Bildeston w Wattisham 79-92; P-in-c Bramford from 92; P-in-c Somersham w Flowton 94-02; RD Bosmere 96-01; Hon Can St E Cathl from 01; P-in-c Lt Blakenham, Baylham and Nettlestead from 02. *The Vicarage, Vicarage Lane, Bramford, Ipswich IP8 4AE* Tel (01473) 741105
E-mail roger.dedman@virgin.net

DEE, Clive Hayden. b 61. Ripon Coll Cuddesdon 86. **d** 89 **p** 90. C Bridgnorth, Tasley, Astley Abbotts, etc *Heref* 89-93; P-in-c Wellington w Pipe-cum-Lyde and Moreton-on-Lugg 93-96. *Ross Cottage, Crumpton Hill Road, Storridge, Malvern WR13 5HE* Tel (01886) 832639

DEED, Michael James. b 77. **d** 04 **p** 05. C Notting Dale St Clem w St Mark and St Jas *Lon* from 04. *95 Sidar Road, London W11 4EQ* Tel (020) 7313 4674 E-mail m_deed@hotmail.com

DEEDES, Canon Arthur Colin Bouverie. b 27. Bede Coll Dur BA51. Wells Th Coll 51. **d** 53 **p** 54. C Milton *Portsm* 53-58; C Worplesdon *Guildf* 58-60; V Weston 60-66; V Fleet 66-73; RD Aldershot 69-73; TR Bournemouth St Pet w St Swithun, H Trin etc *Win* 73-80; RD Bournemouth 74-80; Hon Can Win Cathl 78-92; Master Win St Cross w St Faith 80-92; rtd 92; Perm to Offic *Win* from 92; Hon Chapl Win Cathl from 97. *Dolphins, 17 Chesil Street, Winchester SO23 0HU* Tel (01962) 861617

DEEDES, Ms Rosie Anne. b 66. Birm Univ BA87 City Univ 90. Westcott Ho Cam 94. **d** 96 **p** 97. C St Botolph Aldgate w H Trin Minories *Lon* 96-99; Asst Chapl HM Pris Holloway 99-02; Chapl HM Pris Downview from 02. *HM Prison Downview, Sutton Lane, Sutton SM2 5PD* Tel (020) 8929 3300

DEEGAN, Arthur Charles. b 49. CertEd71 Birm Univ BEd86. Qu Coll Birm 86. **d** 88 **p** 89. C Leic St Jas *Leic* 88-91; C Melton Gt Framland 91-92; TV 92-93; TV Melton Mowbray 93-96; CF (TA) from 95; Chapl ACF Leics, Northants, and Rutland from 95; R Barwell w Potters Marston and Stapleton *Leic* from 96. *The Rectory, 14 Church Lane, Barwell, Leicester LE9 8DG* Tel (01455) 444927 Fax 444928 E-mail ac.deegan@ntlworld.com

DEELEY, Mrs Elke Christiane. b 58. Birm Univ BA81. SW Minl Tr Course 99. **d** 02 **p** 03. NSM Roche and Withiel *Truro* from 02. *44 Duporth Bay, St Austell PL26 6AQ* Tel (01726) 63083
E-mail elke1@tinyonline.co.uk

DEEMING, Paul Leyland. b 44. CA Tr Coll 65 CMS Tr Coll Selly Oak 70. **d** 80 **p** 80. CMS 71-82; Pakistan 71-82; R E and W Horndon w Lt Warley *Chelmsf* 83-89; V Gt Ilford St Andr 89-01; Co-ord Chapl Heatherwood and Wexham Park Hosp NHS Trust from 01. *Wexham Park Hospital, Wexham, Slough SL2 4HL* Tel (01753) 633000

DEER, Diane Antonia. b 45. SEITE. **d** 00 **p** 01. C Hackington *Cant* 00-04; P-in-c Pitsea w Nevendon *Chelmsf* from 04. *The Rectory, Rectory Road, Pitsea, Basildon SS13 2AA* Tel (01268) 556874 Mobile 07957-758721
E-mail diane@revdiane.freeserve.co.uk

DEERING, Alan George. b 36. **d** 99 **p** 00. OLM Blyth Valley *St E* from 99. *11 Walpole Road, Halesworth IP19 8DL* Tel (01986) 873388 E-mail alan.deering@ukonline.co.uk

DEES, Miss Marilyn Monica (Mandy). b 34. Nottm Univ BSc55 PGCE56. WEMTC 94. **d** 96 **p** 97. NSM Fownhope w Mordiford, Brockhampton etc *Heref* from 96. *Hazelbank, 24 Nover Wood Drive, Fownhope, Hereford HR1 4PN* Tel (01432) 860369

DEETH, William Stanley. b 38. St Pet Coll Ox BA59 MA67. St Steph Ho Ox 66. **d** 68 **p** 69. C Eastbourne St Mary *Chich* 68-71; C Benwell St Jas *Newc* 71-75; C-in-c Byker St Martin CD 75-76; P-in-c Byker St Martin 76; V 76-89; P-in-c Bothal 89-91; R Bothal and Pegswood w Longhirst 91-94; rtd 94; Perm to Offic *Newc* from 94. *17 Osborne Gardens, North Sunderland, Seahouses NE68 7UF* Tel (01665) 720067

DeGROOSE, Leslie John. b 28. Oak Hill Th Coll 62. **d** 64 **p** 65. C Gunton St Pet *Nor* 64-67; Chapl RN 67-83; P-in-c Gt Oakley *Chelmsf* 83-85; R Gt Oakley w Wix 85-92; rtd 92; Perm to Offic *St E* from 92. *1 Queensberry Mews, Newmarket CB8 9AE* Tel (01638) 660599

DEHOOP, Brother Thomas Anthony. b 38. Bp's Univ Lennox BA63 LTh63. **d** 68 **p** 69. Canada 68-79; C Fort George w Painthills 68-70; I Mistassini 70-72; R La Tuque 72-75; Assoc P Pierrefonds 75-79; SSF from 79; Perm to Offic *Sarum* 79-80; Hon C Toxteth St Marg *Liv* 80-85; Chapl Newsham Gen Hosp Liv 82-85; P-in-c Cambridge St Benedict *Ely* 85-88; V 88-92; Perm to Offic *Liv* 92-94 and *Eur* from 94. *Glasshampton Monastery, Shrawley, Worcester WR6 6TQ* Tel (01299) 896345
E-mail glasshamptonssf@franciscans.org.uk

✠DEHQANI-TAFTI, The Rt Revd Hassan Barnaba. b 20. Tehran Univ BA43. Virginia Th Sem DD81 Ridley Hall Cam 47. **d** 49 **p** 50 **c** 61. Iran 49-61; Bp Iran 61-90; Pres Bp Episc Ch Jerusalem and Middle E 76-86; Asst Bp Win from 82; rtd 90. *Sohrab House, 1 Camberry Close, Basingstoke RG21 3AG* Tel (01256) 327457

DEIGHTON, Ian Armstrong. b 19. Glas Univ MA40. Edin Th Coll 40. **d** 43 **p** 44. C Paisley H Trin *Glas* 43-45; Bp's Dom Chapl *Arg* 45-47; P-in-c Nether Lochaber 45-47; P-in-c Kinlochleven 45-47; P-in-c Glas St Mark 47-52; R Clydebank *Glas* 52-57; R Musselburgh *Edin* 57-84; P-in-c Prestonpans 76-84; rtd 84. *6 Duddingston Park South, Edinburgh EH15 3PA* Tel 0131-669 5108

DEIGHTON, William John. b 44. K Coll Lon AKC68 Plymouth Poly CQSW74. St Boniface Warminster 68. **d** 69 **p** 70. C Kenwyn *Truro* 69-72; Hon C Winterbourne *Bris* from 90. *22 Salem Road, Winterbourne, Bristol BS36 1QF* Tel (01454) 778847

DEIMEL, Margaret Mary. b 49. CertEd71. WMMTC 91. **d** 94 **p** 95. NSM Bidford-on-Avon *Cov* 94-97; NSM Studley from 97; Dioc Adv on New Relig Movements from 02. *The Vicarage, 3 Manor Mews, Manor Road, Studley B80 7NA* Tel (01527) 852830 E-mail studley.vic@virgin.net

DEIMEL, Richard Witold. b 49. Lon Univ BA84. Cranmer Hall Dur 86. **d** 88 **p** 89. C Bilton *Cov* 88-93; P-in-c Studley 93-97; V from 97; Dioc Adv on New Relig Movements from 02. *The Vicarage, Manor Mews, Manor Road, Studley B80 7NA* Tel (01527) 852830 E-mail studley.vic@virgin.net

del RIO, Michael Paul Juan. b 73. Univ of Wales (Cardiff) BScEcon94 PGCE00. Oak Hill Th Coll MTh05. **d** 05. NSM Ealing St Mary *Lon* from 05. *25 Cambridge Road North, London W4 4AA* Tel (020) 8747 0424 E-mail michael@didasko.org.uk

DELAMERE, Allen Stephen. BTh. **d** 90 **p** 91. C Bangor Abbey *D & D* 90-93; I Saintfield 93-03; P-in-c Cumbernauld *Glas* from 05. *1R Blake Road, Cumbernauld, Glasgow G67 1AG* Tel (01236) 722554 E-mail allen@sonow.com

DELAMERE, Isaac George. b 71. CITC BTh02. **d** 02 **p** 03. C Newtownards *D & D* from 02. *10 Londonderry Road, Newtownards BT23 3AY* Tel (028) 9181 4750

DELANEY, Anthony. b 65. St Jo Coll Nottm BTh95. **d** 95 **p** 96. C Cullompton *Ex* 95-98; C Maidstone St Luke *Cant* 98-01; P-in-c W Horsley *Guildf* 01-03; R from 03. *The Rectory, 80 East Lane, West Horsley, Leatherhead KT24 6LQ* Tel (01483) 283783
E-mail antdel@tiscali.co.uk

DELANEY, The Ven Peter Anthony. b 39. MBE01. AKC65. **d** 66 **p** 67. C St Marylebone w H Trin *Lon* 66-70; Chapl Nat Heart Hosp Lon 66-70; Res Chapl Univ Ch Ch the K 70-73; Can Res and Prec S'wark Cathl *S'wark* 73-77; V All Hallows by the Tower etc *Lon* 77-04; P-in-c St Kath Cree 98-02; Can Cyprus and the Gulf from 88; Preb St Paul's Cathl *Lon* 95-99; Adn Lon from 99; P-in-c St Steph Walbrook and St Swithun etc from 04. *29 Portland Square, London E1W 2QR* Tel (020) 7481 1786
E-mail archdeacon.london@london.anglican.org

DELANY, Michael Edward. b 34. Lon Univ BSc55 PhD58. S'wark Ord Course 80. **d** 83 **p** 84. NSM Hampton St Mary *Lon* 83-87; R Copythorne and Minstead *Win* 87-94; rtd 94; Perm to

Offic *Win* 94-00. *Littlecott, Tytherley Road, Winterslow, Salisbury SP5 1PZ* Tel (01980) 862183

DELFGOU, John. b 35. Oak Hill Th Coll 81. **d** 84 **p** 85. NSM Loughton St Mary and St Mich *Chelmsf* 84-90; NSM Loughton St Jo 90-93; C 93-94; TV 94-00; rtd 01; Perm to Offic *Chelmsf* from 01. *20 Carroll Hill, Loughton IG10 1NN* Tel (020) 8508 6333 E-mail john@delfgou.freeserve.co.uk

DELFGOU, Jonathan Hawke. b 63. Aston Tr Scheme 89 Linc Th Coll BTh94. **d** 94 **p** 95. C Greenstead *Chelmsf* 94-98; TV Wickford and Runwell from 98; Chapl Southend Community Care Services NHS Trust 98-99; Chapl S Essex Mental Health & Community Care NHS Trust from 00. *St Mary's Vicarage, Church End Lane, Runwell, Wickford SS11 7JQ* Tel (01268) 732068 E-mail delfgou@fish.co.uk

DELIGHT, The Ven John David. b 25. Liv Univ CSocSc48 Open Univ BA75. Oak Hill Th Coll 49. **d** 52 **p** 53. C Tooting Graveney St Nic *S'wark* 52-55; C Wallington H Trin 55-58; Lic to Offic *Man* 58-61; Travelling Sec IVF 58-61; C-in-c Leic St Chris CD *Leic* 61-68; Chapl HM Pris Leic 64-67; V Leic St Chris *Leic* 68-69; R Aldridge *Lich* 69-82; Preb Lich Cathl 80-90; RD Walsall 81-82; Adn Stoke 82-90; Dir Th Educn Machakos Kenya 90-94; Hon Can Machakos 90-94; Perm to Offic *Lich* 99-04 and *Ches* from 99. *Karibuni, 17 Hillside Drive, Macclesfield SK10 2PL* Tel (01625) 428117 E-mail delight@fish.co.uk

DELINGER, Ian Michael. b 70. Truman State Univ (USA) BS92 SS Coll Cam BTh04. Westcott Ho Cam 01. **d** 04 **p** 05. C Chorlton-cum-Hardy St Clem *Man* from 04. *94 Hardy Lane, Manchester M21 8DN* Tel 0161-881 9458 E-mail revimd@aol.com

DELL, Murray John. b 31. Cape Town Univ BA51 BSc54 Edin Univ MB, ChB59. Westcott Ho Cam 63. **d** 65 **p** 65. S Africa 65-70; Dean Windhoek 71-80; V Lyme Regis *Sarum* 80-96; Chapl Lyme Regis Hosp 80-96; rtd 96. *3 Empsons Close, Dawlish EX7 9BG* Tel (01626) 866193

DELL, The Ven Robert Sydney. b 22. Em Coll Cam BA46 MA50. Ridley Hall Cam 46. **d** 48 **p** 49. C Islington St Mary *Lon* 48-50; C Cambridge H Trin *Ely* 50-53; Lic to Offic *Lich* 53-55; Asst Chapl Wrekin Coll Telford 53-55; R Mildenhall *St E* 55-57; Vice-Prin Ridley Hall Cam 57-65; V Chesterton St Andr *Ely* 66-73; Adn Derby 73-92; Hon Can Derby Cathl 73-81; Can Res 81-92; rtd 92; Perm to Offic *Ely* 92-00 and *Derby* from 92. *Pinehurst Lodge, 35 Grange Road, Cambridge CB3 9AU* Tel (01223) 365466

DELMEGE, Andrew Mark. b 68. Essex Univ BA91 Southn Univ MTh98. SW Minl Tr Course 94. **d** 97 **p** 98. C Kings Heath *Birm* 97-01; V Brandwood from 01; Chapl to Deaf People from 01. *The Vicarage, 77 Doversley Road, Birmingham B14 6NN* Tel 0121-693 0217, 246 6100 *or* 456 1535 Fax 246 6101 E-mail adelmege@compuserve.com

DELVE, Eric David. b 42. Trin Coll Bris. **d** 89 **p** 90. NSM Bris St Matt and St Nath *Bris* 89-92; P-in-c Kirkdale St Lawr *Liv* 93-96; V Maidstone St Luke *Cant* from 96; AD Maidstone 99-03; Six Preacher Cant Cathl from 99. *The Vicarage, 24 Park Avenue, Maidstone ME14 5HN* Tel (01622) 754856 E-mail ericdelve@stlukes.org.uk

DELVES, Canon Anthony James. b 47. Birm Univ BSocSc70 Hull Univ PhD94. St Steph Ho Ox 83. **d** 85 **p** 86. C Cantley *Sheff* 85-90; V Goldthorpe w Hickleton from 90; Hon Can Sheff Cathl from 98; AD Wath from 00. *Goldthorpe Presbytery, Lockwood Road, Goldthorpe, Rotherham S63 9JY* Tel (01709) 898426

DELVES (formerly MANHOOD), Canon Phyllis. b 32. Aston Tr Scheme 78 Qu Coll Birm 79. **dss** 82 **d** 87 **p** 94. Harwich *Chelmsf* 82-83; Dovercourt and Parkeston 83-85; Fawley *Win* 85-87; Par Dn 87-92; P-in-c Bournemouth St Aug 92-99; Hon Can Win Cathl 96-99; rtd 99; Perm to Offic *Win* from 01. *11 Rhyme Hall Mews, Fawley, Southampton SO45 1FX* Tel (023) 8089 4450

DELVES BROUGHTON, Simon Brian Hugo. b 33. Ex Coll Ox BA56 MA64. Kelham Th Coll 56. **d** 59 **p** 60. Ox Miss to Calcutta 60-64; C Skirbeck St Nic *Linc* 64-67; E Pakistan/Bangladesh 67-74; Chapl Chittagong 67-69; V St Thos Cathl Dhaka 69-74; V Northampton Ch Ch *Pet* 74-95; Chapl Northn Gen Hosp 77-87; rtd 95; Perm to Offic *Ox* 95-00. *71A Observatory Street, Oxford OX2 6EP* Tel (01865) 515463

DEMERY, Rupert Edward Rodier. b 72. Trin Hall Cam BA94 MA01 BTh01. Ridley Hall Cam 98. **d** 01 **p** 02. C New Borough and Leigh *Sarum* from 01. *7 Ethelbert Road, Wimborne BH21 1BH* Tel (01202) 889405 Mobile 07801-825671 E-mail rdemery@clara.net

DENBY, Canon Paul. b 47. NW Ord Course 73. **d** 76 **p** 77. C Stretford All SS *Man* 76-80; V Stalybridge 80-87; Chapl Tameside Distr Gen Hosp Ashton-under-Lyne 82-87; Dir of Ords *Man* 87-95; LNSM Officer 91-95; Hon Can Man Cathl 92-95; Bp's Dom Chapl 94-95; Can Admin and Prec Man Cathl from 95. *2 Booth Clibborn Court, Salford M7 4PJ* Tel 0161-792 0979 *or* 833 2220 Fax 839 6226 E-mail paul.denby@manchestercathedral.com

DENCH, Christopher David. b 62. RGN83. Aston Tr Scheme 86 Sarum & Wells Th Coll 88. **d** 91 **p** 92. C Crayford *Roch* 91-94; P-in-c Leybourne 94-98; R from 98; Dioc Lay Tr Adv from 01; Tr Officer for CME from 03. *The Rectory, 73 Rectory Lane North, Leybourne, West Malling ME19 5HD* Tel (01732) 842187 E-mail chrisdench@tiscali.co.uk

DENERLEY, John Keith Christopher. b 34. Qu Coll Ox BA58 MA61. St Steph Ho Ox 58. **d** 61 **p** 62. C Airedale w Fryston *Wakef* 61-64; Chapl Sarum Th Coll 64-68; Min Can Cov Cathl *Cov* 68-76; Chapl Lanchester Poly 70-76; Chapl The Dorothy Kerin Trust Burrswood 76-85; V Trellech and Cwmcarvan *Mon* 85-87; V Penallt 85-87; V Penallt and Trellech 87-99; Chapl Ty Mawr Convent (Wales) 85-90; RD Monmouth *Mon* 93-99; rtd 99; Perm to Offic *Glouc* from 00. *1 The Pales, English Bicknor, Coleford GL16 7PQ* Tel (01594) 860028

DENFORD, Keith Wilkie. b 35. AKC62. **d** 63 **p** 64. C Gunnersbury St Jas *Lon* 63-66; C Brighton St Pet *Chich* 66-71; Min Can Cant Cathl *Cant* 71-75; R W Tarring *Chich* 75-85; V Burgess Hill St Jo 85-90; R Pulborough 90-96; rtd 96; Perm to Offic *Chich* from 96. *31 John Street, Shoreham-by-Sea BN43 5DL* Tel (01273) 464251

DENGATE, Richard Henry. b 39. Cant Sch of Min 82. **d** 85 **p** 86. NSM Wittersham w Stone-in-Oxney and Ebony *Cant* 85; R Sandhurst w Newenden 90-01; rtd 01; Perm to Offic *Cant* from 01. *Apuldrum, Main Street, Peasemarsh, Rye TN31 6UL* Tel (01797) 230980

DENHAM, Anthony Christopher (Chris). b 43. Keble Coll Ox BA65 MA70. Oak Hill Th Coll DipHE93. **d** 93 **p** 94. C Hythe *Cant* 93-97; V Haddenham w Cuddington, Kingsey etc *Ox* from 97. *The Vicarage, 27A The Gables, Haddenham, Aylesbury HP17 8AD* Tel (01844) 291244 E-mail chris@revdenham.freeserve.co.uk

DENHAM, Nicholas Philip. b 50. Salford Univ BSc72 Birm Univ CertEd74. Wycliffe Hall Ox 87. **d** 89 **p** 90. C Bishopwearmouth St Gabr *Dur* 89-90; C Chester le Street 90-92; TV Rushden w Newton Bromswold *Pet* 92-95; R Teigh w Whissendine and Market Overton 95-02; P-in-c Thistleton 01-02; RD Rutland 01-02; TR Bedworth *Cov* 02-05; V Escomb *Dur* from 05; R Etherley from 05; V Witton Park from 05; V Hamsterley and Witton-le-Wear from 05. *The Vicarage, Escomb, Bishop Auckland DL14 7ST* Tel (01388) 602861 E-mail nickden@fish.co.uk

DENHOLM, Robert Jack. b 31. Edin Th Coll 53. **d** 56 **p** 57. C Dundee St Mary Magd *Bre* 56-59; C Edin St Pet *Edin* 59-61; R Bridge of Allan *St And* 61-69; Chapl Stirling Univ 67-69; R N Berwick *Edin* 69-80; R Gullane 76-80; R Edin St Mark 80-90; Can St Mary's Cathl 88-90; rtd 90. *15 Silverknowes, Midway, Edinburgh EH4 5PP* Tel 0131-312 6462 E-mail jackdenholm@blueyonder.co.uk

DENING, John Cranmer. b 21. Clare Coll Cam BA48 MA52. Qu Coll Birm 50. **d** 52 **p** 53. C Allerton *Liv* 52-55; C Bournemouth St Andr *Win* 55-58; C Lillington *Cov* 59-60; C Yeovil St Jo w Preston Plucknett *B & W* 61-67; C Moulsham St Jo *Chelmsf* 69-70; C W Teignmouth *Ex* 70-73; C N Stoneham *Win* 73-80; C Sholing 80-85; rtd 86. *27 The Paddocks, Brandon IP27 0DX*

DENIS LE SEVE, Hilary. *See* LE SEVE, Mrs Jane Hilary

DENISON, Canon Keith Malcolm. b 45. Down Coll Cam BA67 MA71 PhD70. Westcott Ho Cam 70. **d** 71 **p** 72. C Chepstow *Mon* 71-72; C Bassaleg 72-75; Post-Ord Tr Officer 75-85; V Mathern and Mounton 75-80; V Mathern and Mounton w St Pierre 80-85; RD Chepstow 82-85; V Risca 85-91; V Goldcliffe and Whitson and Nash 91-96; Dioc Dir of Educn from 91; Hon Can St Woolos Cathl 91-94; Can from 94; Can Res from 96. *Canon's House, Stow Hill, Newport NP20 4EA* Tel (01633) 264919

DENISON, Philip. b 55. York Univ BA77 CertEd. St Jo Coll Nottm 83. **d** 86 **p** 87. C Barnoldswick w Bracewell *Bradf* 86-88; P-in-c Basford St Leodegarius *S'well* 88-91; C Basford w Hyson Green 91-94; V Nether Stowey w Over Stowey *B & W* 94-04; R Aisholt, Enmore, Goathurst, Nether Stowey etc from 05; RD Quantock from 01. *New Vicarage, St Mary Street, Nether Stowey, Bridgwater TA5 1LJ* Tel (01278) 732247 E-mail denisonphil@hotmail.com

DENMAN, Frederick George. b 46. Chich Th Coll 67. **d** 70 **p** 71. C Stafford St Mary *Lich* 70-72; C Ascot Heath *Ox* 72-75; P-in-c Culham 75-77; P-in-c Sutton Courtenay w Appleford 75-77; TV Dorchester 78-81; Chapl Henley Memorial Hosp 81-82; P-in-c W Hill *Ex* 82; TV Ottery St Mary, Alfington and W Hill 82-87; V Sparkwell from 87; V Shaugh Prior 87-93; P-in-c Cornwood from 98. *The Vicarage, Sparkwell, Plymouth PL7 5DB* Tel (01752) 837218 E-mail freddie@sparkwell.fsnet.com

DENNEN, The Ven Lyle. b 42. Harvard Univ LLB67 Trin Coll Cam BA70 MA75. Cuddesdon Coll 70. **d** 72 **p** 73. C S Lambeth St Ann *S'wark* 72-75; C Richmond St Mary 75-78; P-in-c Kennington St Jo 78-79; V Kennington St Jo w St Jas 79-99; P-in-c Brixton Road Ch Ch 81-89; RD Brixton 90-99; Hon Can S'wark Cathl 99; Adn Hackney *Lon* from 99; V St Andr Holborn from 99. *St Andrew's Vicarage, 5 St Andrew's Street, London EC4A 3AB* Tel (020) 7353 3544 Fax 7583 2750 E-mail archdeacon.hackney@london.anglican.org

DENNESS, Mrs Linda Christine. b 51. Portsm Dioc Tr Course. **d** 89 **p** 01. NSM Milton *Portsm* 89-93; NSM Portsea St Mary 93-96; Lic to Offic 96-98; NSM Widley w Wymering from 98.

19 Fourth Avenue, Cosham, Portsmouth PO6 3HX Tel (023) 9278 1381

DENNETT, John Edward. b 36. Tyndale Hall Bris 66. **d** 68 **p** 69. C Chell *Lich* 68-71; C Bispham *Blackb* 71-73; C Cheltenham Ch Ch *Glouc* 73-75; V Coppull *Blackb* 75-79; P-in-c Parkham, Alwington and Buckland Brewer *Ex* 79-80; R 80-84; V Blackpool St Thos *Blackb* 84-92; rtd 92; Chapl Trin Hospice in the Fylde from 88; Perm to Offic *Blackb* from 92. *37 Village Way, Bispham, Blackpool FY2 0AH* Tel (01253) 358039 E-mail johned.dennett@virgin.net

DENNIS, Mrs Barbara Christine. b 56. NTMTC 94. **d** 97 **p** 98. NSM Romford St Edw *Chelmsf* 97-01; C from 01. *4 Oaklands Avenue, Romford RM1 4DB* Tel (01708) 739676

DENNIS, Miss Drucilla Lyn. b 49. Culham Coll of Educn BEd71 Southn Univ MA82. S Dios Minl Tr Scheme 92. **d** 95 **p** 96. NSM Cowes H Trin and St Mary *Portsm* 95-01; TV Dorchester *Sarum* from 01. *The Vicarage, 2 Longmoor Street, Poundbury, Dorchester DT1 3GN* Tel (01305) 259355

✠**DENNIS, The Rt Revd John.** b 31. St Cath Coll Cam BA54 MA59. Cuddesdon Coll 54. **d** 56 **p** 57 **c** 79. C Armley St Bart *Ripon* 56-60; C Kettering SS Pet and Paul *Pet* 60-62; V Is of Dogs Ch Ch and St Jo w St Luke *Lon* 62-71; V Mill Hill Jo Keble Ch 71-79; RD W Barnet 73-79; Preb St Paul's Cathl 77-79; Suff Bp Knaresborough *Ripon* 79-86; Dioc Dir of Ords 80-86; Bp St E 86-96; rtd 96; Perm to Offic *St E* from 96; Hon Asst Bp Win from 99. *7 Conifer Close, Winchester SO22 6SH* Tel (01962) 868881 E-mail johndor_dennis@onetel.com

DENNIS, Canon John Daniel. b 20. LLCM. St D Coll Lamp BA41 LTh43. **d** 43 **p** 44. C Haverfordwest St Mary w St Thos *St D* 43-48; C Newport St Mark *Mon* 48-54; V New Tredegar 54-62; R Worthenbury w Tallarn Green *St As* 62-71; V Chirk 71-86; RD Llangollen 74-86; Hon Can St As Cathl 83-86; rtd 86; Perm to Offic *St As* from 86. *Mount Cottage, Chirk, Wrexham LL14 5HD* Tel (01691) 773382

DENNIS, Keith Aubrey Lawrence. b 55. City of Lon Poly BA79. Cranmer Hall Dur 88. **d** 90 **p** 91. C Bushbury *Lich* 90-94; P-in-c Newcastle St Geo 94-99; TV Kirby Muxloe *Leic* 99-03; C Ashby-de-la-Zouch St Helen w Coleorton 03; C Breedon cum Isley Walton and Worthington 03; Chapl HM Pris Glouc from 04. *The Chaplaincy, HM Prison Gloucester, Barrack Square, Gloucester GL1 2JN* Tel (01452) 529551

DENNIS, Patrick John. b 44. Linc Th Coll 67. **d** 70 **p** 71. C Eccleshill *Bradf* 70-72; C Ponteland *Newc* 73-75; Chr Aid Org Leic and Linc 75-78; TV Cullercoats St Geo *Newc* 78-82; Dioc Ecum Officer 79-82; R Bradfield *Sheff* 82-91; Dioc Ecum Adv 82-93; Sec & Ecum Officer S Yorkshire Ecum Coun 91-93; R Braithwell w Bramley 91-93. *Address withheld by request*

DENNIS, Canon Trevor John. b 45. St Jo Coll Cam BA68 MA71 PhD74. Westcott Ho Cam 71. **d** 72 **p** 73. C Newport Pagnell *Ox* 72-74; Chapl Eton Coll 75-82; Tutor Sarum & Wells Th Coll 82-94; Vice-Prin 89-94; Can Res Ches Cathl *Ches* from 94. *13 Abbey Street, Chester CH1 2JF* Tel (01244) 314408 E-mail dennis@chestercathedral.com

DENNISON, Philip Ian. b 52. Nottm Univ BTh81. St Jo Coll Nottm 77. **d** 81 **p** 82. C Stalybridge H Trin and Ch Ch *Ches* 81-84; C Heswall 84-91; TV Bushbury *Lich* 91-04; V Shevington *Blackb* from 04. *St Anne's Vicarage, Gathurst Lane, Shevington, Wigan WN6 8HW* Tel (01257) 252136 E-mail revd.pidennison@tinyworld.co.uk

DENNISS, Mrs Amanda Jane. b 57. Univ Coll Lon LLB78. Oak Hill Th Coll 98 NTMTC 00. **d** 03 **p** 04. C Turnham Green Ch Ch *Lon* from 03. *27 Stratford Road, London W8 6RA* Tel (020) 7937 6761 E-mail amandadenniss@aol.com

DENNISTON, James Keith Stuart. b 49. Barrister-at-Law 70 Down Coll Cam MA70. Oak Hill Th Coll DipEd92. **d** 93 **p** 94. C Harborne Heath *Birm* 93-97; Chapl Lee Abbey 97-02; Perm to Offic *Ex* 02-03; TV Chippenham St Paul w Hardenhuish etc *Bris* from 03. *11 Lanhill View, Chippenham SN14 6XS* Tel (01249) 462378 E-mail james@thedennistons.freeserve.co.uk

DENNISTON, Robin Alastair. b 26. Ch Ch Ox MA48 Edin Univ MSc92 Univ Coll Lon PhD96. **d** 78 **p** 79. NSM Clifton upon Teme *Worc* 78-81; NSM Clifton-on-Teme, Lower Sapey and the Shelsleys 81-85; NSM S Hinksey *Ox* 85-87; NSM Gt w Lt Tew 87-90; NSM Aberdour *St And* 90-94; NSM W Fife Team Min 90-94; NSM St Marylebone St Mark Hamilton Terrace *Lon* 94-95; P-in-c Gt w Lt Tew and Over w Nether Worton *Ox* 95-02; rtd 02. *112 Randolph Avenue, London W9 1PQ* Tel (020) 7286 0880

DENNO, Basil. b 52. Dundee Univ BSc74. Oak Hill Th Coll BA81. **d** 81 **p** 83. C Chaddesden St Mary *Derby* 81-83; Hon C 83-84. *21 Parkside Road, Chaddesden, Derby DE21 6QR* Tel (01332) 672687

DENNY, John Peter Sekeford. b 43. DipArch67 RIBA69. Chich Th Coll 90. **d** 91 **p** 92. C Aylmerton w Runton *Nor* 91-95; P-in-c Barney, Fulmodeston w Croxton, Hindringham etc 95-96; R 96-98; rtd 98; Perm to Offic *Truro* 98-04 and *Nor* from 04. *1-3 The High Street, Walsingham NR22 6BY* Tel (01328) 821710

DENNY, Lorne Robert. b 58. Pemb Coll Ox MA84. St Alb and Ox Min Course 98. **d** 01 **p** 02. NSM Ox St Barn and St Paul *Ox* 01-04; NSM Cowley St Jo from 04. *35 Stapleton Road, Oxford OX3 7LX* Tel (01865) 768009

DENNY, Michael Thomas. b 47. Kelham Th Coll 68 St Jo Coll Nottm 71. **d** 73 **p** 74. C Gospel Lane St Mich *Birm* 73-77; P-in-c Frankley 77-82; R from 82. *The Rectory, Frankley Green, Birmingham B32 4AS* Tel 0121-475 3724 E-mail michael@revdenny1.freeserve.co.uk

DENNY, Peter Bond. b 17. Lon Univ BA41. Bps' Coll Cheshunt 41. **d** 43 **p** 44. C Bushey Heath *St Alb* 43-45; C Calstock *Truro* 52-56; V Newlyn St Newlyn 56-83; RD Pydar 61-64 and 74-81; rtd 83; Perm to Offic *Truro* from 83. *Tralee, The Crescent, Truro TR1 3ES* Tel (01872) 274492

DENT, Canon Christopher Mattinson. b 46. K Coll Lon BA68 AKC68 MTh69 Jes Coll Cam BA72 MA76 New Coll Ox MA76 DPhil80. Westcott Ho Cam 70. **d** 72 **p** 73. C Chelsea St Luke *Lon* 72-76; Asst Chapl New Coll Ox 76-79; Fell Chapl and Dean Div 79-84; V Hollingbourne and Hucking w Leeds and Broomfield *Cant* 84-93; V Bedford St Andr *St Alb* from 93; Hon Can St Alb from 01; RD Bedford from 05. *St Andrew's Vicarage, 1 St Edmond Road, Bedford MK40 2NQ* Tel (01234) 354234 *or* 216881 E-mail dent@tinyworld.co.uk

DENT, Joseph Michael. b 73. Jes Coll Cam BA94. Wycliffe Hall Ox 96. **d** 99 **p** 00. C Plymouth St Andr and St Paul Stonehouse *Ex* 99-03; C Sevenoaks St Nic *Roch* from 03. *6 Sackville Close, Sevenoaks TN13 3QD* Tel (01732) 779140

DENT, Marie Penelope. b 46. K Coll Lon BA88. Westcott Ho Cam 02. **d** 04 **p** 05. C N Walsham w Antingham *Nor* from 04. *8 Plumbly Close, North Walsham NR28 9YB* Tel (01692) 409783 Mobile 07799-220357 E-mail aviationresearch@tiscali.com

DENT, Michael Leslie. b 54. Leeds Univ BEd76. St Steph Ho Ox DipMin95. **d** 95 **p** 96. C Cockerton *Dur* 95-98; V Escomb 98-03; R Etherley 98-03; V Witton Park 98-03; Chapl Dur Constabulary 02-03; TR E Darlington from 03. *30 Smithfield Road, Darlington DL1 4DD* Tel (01325) 244430

DENT, Raymond William. b 47. TD03. Open Univ BA84 Birm Coll of Educn CertEd68. Ridley Hall Cam 70. **d** 73 **p** 74. C Hyde St Geo *Ches* 73-76; C Eastham 76-79; TV E Runcorn w Halton 79-80; V Hallwood 80-83; V New Brighton Em 83-94; V Willaston from 94. *The Vicarage, 13 Hooton Road, Willaston, Neston CH64 1SE* Tel 0151-327 4737 E-mail raymond@raydent.freeserve.co.uk

DENT, Richard William. b 32. Down Coll Cam BA56 MA LLB59. Bris Sch of Min 73. **d** 77 **p** 78. NSM Southmead *Bris* 77-81; NSM Henleaze 81-85; V Highworth w Sevenhampton and Inglesham etc 85-88; TV Oldland 88-91; V Longwell Green 91-93; C Bedminster St Mich 93-94; C 94-97; Chapl Asst Frenchay Healthcare NHS Trust Bris 94-97; rtd 97; Perm to Offic *Bris* from 99. *1 Bakers Buildings, Wrington, Bristol BS40 5LQ* Tel (01934) 861070

DENTON, Kenneth Percival. b 14. Clifton Th Coll 54. **d** 55 **p** 56. C Buttershaw St Paul *Bradf* 55-57; C Otley 57-59; C Morpeth *Newc* 59-62; R Winteringham *Linc* 62-69; V Middlesbrough St Thos *York* 69-73; C Rufforth w Moor Monkton and Hessay 73-76; P-in-c Escrick 76-80; rtd 80; Perm to Offic *B & W* from 81. *c/o Mrs B C Coxon, 2 New Barn, Kirdford, Billingshurst RH14 0LS* Tel (01403) 820040

DENTON, Peter Brian. b 37. Kelham Th Coll 57. **d** 62 **p** 63. C Ellesmere Port *Ches* 62-66; Chapl HM Borstal Hollesley Bay 66-69; CF 69-90; Warden Bridge Cen from 90; C Hounslow H Trin w St Paul *Lon* 90-92; V Northolt Park St Barn 92-04; P-in-c Southall Green St Jo 97-03; P-in-c N Greenford All Hallows 00-04; rtd 04. *52 Lornas Field, Hampton Hargate, Peterborough PE7 8AY* Tel (01733) 552353 E-mail revddenton@aol.com

DENTON, Peter Charles. St Jo Coll Dur BA52. Oak Hill Th Coll 49. **d** 52 **p** 53. C Ushaw Moor *Dur* 52-54; C-in-c Throckley St Mary CD *Newc* 54-58; V Long Horsley 58-67; Lect City of Newc Coll of Educn 67-75; Sen Lect Newc Poly 75-90; rtd 90. *11 Cornwall Walk, Belmont, Durham DH1 2DD* Tel 0191-384 3247

DENYER, Alan Frederick. b 31. Wycliffe Hall Ox 80. **d** 82 **p** 83. C Rodbourne Cheney *Bris* 82-84; P-in-c Garsdon w Lea and Cleverton 84-87; R Garsdon, Lea and Cleverton and Charlton 87-91; R Lydbury N w Hopesay and Edgton *Heref* 91-97; Asst Dioc Soc Resp Officer 91-97; rtd 97; Hon C Long Preston w Tosside *Bradf* 97-02. *25 Lupton Close, Glasshouses, Harrogate HG3 5QX* Tel (01423) 711667

DENYER, Canon Paul Hugh. b 46. Lon Univ BA68. Ripon Coll Cuddesdon 74. **d** 77 **p** 78. C Horfield H Trin *Bris* 77-82; TV Yate New Town 82-88; V Bris Lockleaze St Mary Magd w St Fran 88-95; Dioc Dir of Ords 95-02; Hon Can Bris Cathl from 99; R Warmley, Syston and Bitton from 02. *The Rectory, Church Avenue, Warmley, Bristol BS30 5JJ* Tel 0117-967 3965 E-mail paul@denyer03.freeserve.co.uk

DENZIL, Sister. *See* ONSLOW, Sister Denzil Octavia

DEO, Paul. b 60. Coll of Ripon & York St Jo CertEd81. St Jo Coll Nottm 95. **d** 97 **p** 98. C Tong *Bradf* 97-00; P-in-c Laisterdyke 00-02; V from 02. *The Vicarage, Parsonage Road, Laisterdyke, Bradford BD4 8PY* Tel (01274) 661449 E-mail pauldeo@blueyonder.co.uk

DERBY, Archdeacon of. *See* GATFORD, The Ven Ian
DERBY, Bishop of. *See* REDFERN, The Rt Revd Alastair Llewellyn John
DERBY, Dean of. *See* KITCHEN, The Very Revd Martin
DERBYSHIRE, Mrs Anne Margaret. b 31. Open Univ BA87 Lon Univ CertEd75. SW Minl Tr Course. **dss** 84 **d** 87 **p** 01. NSM Tiverton St Pet *Ex* 87-90; Perm to Offic 90-01 and 02-04; NSM Washfield, Stoodleigh, Withleigh etc 01-02. *6 Devenish Close, Weymouth DT4 8RU* Tel (01305) 750909
DERBYSHIRE, Douglas James. b 26. **d** 81 **p** 82. Hon C Heald Green St Cath *Ches* 81-86; Hon C Stockport St Geo 86-89; C 89-91; rtd 91; Perm to Offic *Man* 92-95 and from 00; *Ches* from 92. *91 East Avenue, Heald Green, Cheadle SK8 3BR* Tel 0161-437 3748
DERBYSHIRE, Philip Damien. b 50. Sarum & Wells Th Coll 80. **d** 82 **p** 83. C Chatham St Wm *Roch* 82-86; Zimbabwe 86-88; TV Burnham w Dropmore, Hitcham and Taplow *Ox* 88-92; Chapl HM Pris Reading 92-97; Chapl HM Pris Holloway 97-00; Chapl HM Pris Bullingdon 00-04; NSM Buckingham *Ox* from 04. *The Rectory, Chapel Lane, Thornborough, Buckingham MK18 2DJ* Tel (01280) 812515 Mobile 07894-227316 E-mail joydotphil@aol.com
DERHAM, Miss Hilary Kathlyn. b 50. Nottm Univ BPharm71 MRPharmS71. Chich Th Coll 89. **d** 91 **p** 95. Par Dn Stevenage H Trin *St Alb* 91-94; C 94-98; P-in-c London Colney St Pet 98-03; rtd 03; Perm to Offic *St Alb* from 03. *39 Brecken Close, St Albans AL4 9LF* Tel (01727) 842089 E-mail h.derham@btopenworld.com
DERISLEY, Canon Albert Donald. b 20. Ely Th Coll 60. **d** 62 **p** 63. C Gt Yarmouth *Nor* 62-66; V Gt w Lt Plumstead 66-72; V N Elmham w Billingford 72-85; RD Brisley and Elmham 77-85; Hon Can Nor Cathl 78-85; rtd 85; Perm to Offic *Nor* from 85. *22 Stuart Road, Aylsham, Norwich NR11 6HN* Tel (01263) 734579
DEROSAIRE, Leslie John. b 50. Univ of Wales BA85 Univ of Wales Coll Newport MA03. St Mich Coll Llan 01. **d** 04 **p** 05. NSM Govilon w Llanfoist w Llanelen *Mon* from 04. *Elmgrove, Hereford Road, Mardy, Abergavenny NP7 6HU* Tel (01873) 857256 E-mail derosaire@tiscali.co.uk
DEROY-JONES, Philip Antony (Tony). b 49. St Mich Coll Llan 92. **d** 92 **p** 93. C Neath w Llantwit *Llan* 92-95; V Caerau St Cynfelin 95-98; V Pontlottyn w Fochriw from 98. *The Vicarage, Picton Street, Pontlottyn, Bargoed CF81 9PS* Tel (01685) 841322 Fax as telephone E-mail tony@deroy-jones.freeserve.co.uk
DERRICK, David John. b 46. S'wark Ord Course. **d** 84 **p** 85. NSM Angell Town St Jo *S'wark* 84-98; NSM St Mary le Strand w St Clem Danes *Lon* 86-93. *Weavers Cottage, 8 Bellvue Place, London E1 4UG* Tel (020) 7791 2943
DERRICK, Mrs Dorothy Margaret. b 41. St Mary's Coll Chelt CertEd63. Ox Min Course 89. **d** 92 **p** 94. NSM Gt Missenden w Ballinger and Lt Hampden *Ox* 92-98; P-in-c Drayton St Pet (Berks) 98-04; rtd 04. *33 Parkland Avenue, Carlisle CA1 3GN* E-mail dorothyderrick@aol.com
DERRIMAN, Canon Graham Scott. b 39. Bps' Coll Cheshunt 63. **d** 66 **p** 67. C Wandsworth St Mich *S'wark* 66-70; C Merton St Mary 70-74; P-in-c Earlsfield St Andr 74-79; V 79-81; V Camberwell St Luke 81-90; V Croydon St Aug 90-04; Voc Adv Croydon Adnry 93-04; RD Croydon Cen 95-04; Hon Can S'wark Cathl from 01; rtd 04; Perm to Offic *S'wark* from 05. *15 Goodwood Close, Morden SM4 5AW* Tel (020) 8648 1550 E-mail g.derriman@btinternet.com
DERRY AND RAPHOE, Bishop of. *See* GOOD, The Rt Revd Kenneth Raymond
DERRY, Archdeacon of. *See* McLEAN, The Ven Donald Stewart
DERRY, Dean of. *See* MORTON, The Very Revd William Wright
DESBRULAIS, Mrs Patricia Mary. b 27. Qu Coll Birm 77. **dss** 79 **d** 87. Gt Bowden w Welham *Leic* 79-83; Market Harborough 83-87; Hon Par Dn 87-89; rtd 89; Perm to Offic *Leic* 89-00. *78 Rainsborough Gardens, Market Harborough LE16 9LW* Tel (01858) 466766
DESERT, Thomas Denis. b 31. Bps' Coll Cheshunt 54. **d** 56 **p** 57. C Goldington *St Alb* 56-60; C-in-c Luton St Hugh Lewsey CD 60-63; C St Alb St Sav 63-65; C Cheshunt 65-68; V Bedford All SS 68-89; R Northill w Moggerhanger 89-96; rtd 96; Perm to Offic *St Alb* from 96. *2 Phillpotts Avenue, Bedford MK40 3UJ* Tel (01234) 211413
DESHPANDE, Lakshmi Anant. *See* JEFFREYS, Mrs Lakshmi Anant
DESICS, Robert Anthony. b 77. Bp Grosseteste Coll BA99 Open Univ MA00. St Jo Coll Nottm 99. **d** 01 **p** 02. C Potters Bar *St Alb* 01-04; C Rainham w Wennington *Chelmsf* from 04. *Address withheld by request*
DESMOND, Mrs Margaret Elspeth. b 49. Trin Coll Bris CPS90 S Dios Minl Tr Scheme 90. **d** 93 **p** 95. NSM Filton *Bris* from 93; Asst Chapl HM Pris Bris from 98. *The Chaplain's Office, HM Prison, Cambridge Road, Bristol BS7 8PS* Tel 0117-372 3246 *or* 372 3100 Fax 372 3153
DESON, Rolston Claudius. b 39. Qu Coll Birm 85. **d** 84 **p** 85. NSM Saltley *Birm* 84-86; C Edgbaston SS Mary and Ambrose 86-90; V W Bromwich St Phil *Lich* from 90. *The Vicarage, 33 Reform Street, West Bromwich B70 7PF* Tel 0121-525 1985
DESPARD, Canon Eric Herbert. b 17. TCD BA40 BD48. CITC 41. **d** 41 **p** 42. C Roscommon *K, E & A* 41-43; C Dublin St Pet *D & G* 43-51; I Blessington w Kilbride 51-65; I Lucan w Leixlip 65-92; Can Ch Ch Cathl Dublin 73-92; rtd 92. *59 Sweetmount Park, Dundrum, Dublin 14, Irish Republic* Tel (00353) (1) 298 2489
DESROSIERS, Jacques Thomas Maurice. b 55. Qu Univ Kingston Ontario BCom77. S'wark Ord Course 91. **d** 94 **p** 95. NSM Benenden *Cant* 94-97; C Maidstone All SS and St Phil w Tovil 97-01; TV Pewsey and Swanborough *Sarum* 01-04; P-in-c Rolvenden *Cant* from 04. *The Vicarage, Rolvenden, Cranbrook TN17 4ND* Tel (01580) 241235 E-mail stowdesrosiers@btinternet.com
d'ESTERRE, Mrs Jennifer Ann. b 48. Coll of St Matthias Bris BEd77. WEMTC 01. **d** 04 **p** 05. NSM Sharpness, Purton, Brookend and Slimbridge *Glouc* from 04. *Gossington Cottage, Gossington, Slimbridge GL2 7DN* Tel (01453) 890384 Mobile 07855-243264 E-mail jenny.desterre@btinternet.com
DETTMER, Douglas James. b 64. Univ of Kansas BA86 Yale Univ MDiv90. Berkeley Div Sch 90. **d** 90 **p** 91. C Ilfracombe, Lee, Woolacombe, Bittadon etc *Ex* 90-94; Bp's Dom Chapl 94-98; P-in-c Thorverton, Cadbury, Upton Pyne etc from 98. *The Rectory, School Lane, Thorverton, Exeter EX5 5NR* Tel (01392) 860332
DEUCHAR, Canon Andrew Gilchrist. b 55. Southn Univ BTh86. Sarum & Wells Th Coll 81. **d** 84 **p** 85. C Alnwick *Newc* 84-88; TV Heref St Martin w St Fran *Heref* 88-90; Adv to Coun for Soc Resp *Roch* and *Cant* 90-94; Sec for Angl Communion Affairs 94-00; Hon Prov Can Cant Cathl from 95; R Nottingham St Pet and St Jas *S'well* 00-02; R Nottingham St Pet and All SS from 02; P-in-c Nottingham St Mary and St Cath from 04; Chapl to The Queen from 03. *St Peter's Rectory, 3 King Charles Street, Nottingham NG1 6GB* Tel 0115-947 4891 E-mail office@stpetersnottingham.org
DEVAL, Mrs Joan Margaret. b 38. Southlands Coll Lon TDip58 Lon Univ CertRK59 Lon Bible Coll DipTh71. St Alb and Ox Min Course 95. **d** 98 **p** 99. OLM Chinnor, Sydenham, Aston Rowant and Crowell *Ox* from 98. *3 Orchard Way, Chinnor OX9 4UD* Tel (01844) 353404
DEVENISH, Nicholas Edward. b 64. Ridley Hall Cam 02. **d** 04 **p** 05. C Huntingdon *Ely* from 04. *The Rectory, 29 Church Road, Great Stukeley, Huntingdon PE28 4AL* Tel (01480) 453016 E-mail nickdevenish@aol.com
DEVENNEY, Raymond Robert Wilmont. b 47. TCD BA69 MA73. CITC 70. **d** 70 **p** 71. C Ballymena *Conn* 70-75; C Ballyholme *D & D* 75-81; I Killinchy w Kilmood and Tullynakill 81-00; I Drumbeg from 00. *The Rectory, 64 Drumbeg Road, Dunmurry, Belfast BT17 9LE* Tel (028) 9061 0255 E-mail raydev@hotmail.com
✠**DEVENPORT, The Rt Revd Eric Nash.** b 26. Open Univ BA74. Kelham Th Coll 46. **d** 51 **p** 52 **c** 80. C Leic St Mark *Leic* 51-54; C Barrow St Matt *Carl* 54-56; Succ Leic Cathl *Leic* 56-59; V Shepshed 59-64; R Oadby 64-73; Hon Can Leic Cathl 73-80; Dioc Missr 73-80; Suff Bp Dunwich *St E* 80-92; rtd 92; Chapl Adn Italy and Malta *Eur* 92-97; Florence w Siena 92-97; Asst Bp Eur 93-97; Perm to Offic *Nor* from 97; Hon PV Nor Cathl from 98; Hon Asst Bp Nor from 00. *32 Bishopgate, Norwich NR1 4AA* Tel (01603) 664121
DEVERELL, William Robert Henry. b 61. CITC 88 St Jo Coll Nottm CertCS92. **d** 92 **p** 93. C Agherton *Conn* 92-95; I Sixmilecross w Termonmaguirke *Arm* 95-99; I Tallaght *D & G* from 99. *St Maelruain's Rectory, 6 Sally Park, Firhouse Road, Tallaght, Dublin 24, Irish Republic* Tel (00353) (1) 462 1044 *or* 462 6006 Mobile 86-803 0239 Fax (1) 462 1044 E-mail tallaght@dublin.anglican.org
DEVEREUX, Canon John Swinnerton. b 32. Lon Univ BSc53. Wells Th Coll. **d** 58 **p** 59. C Wigan St Mich *Liv* 58-60; C Goring-by-Sea *Chich* 60-69; Ind Chapl 69-97; Can and Preb Chich Cathl 90-97; rtd 97; Perm to Offic *Chich* from 97. *40 Hillside Avenue, Worthing BN14 9QT* Tel (01903) 234044
DEVERILL, Jennifer. b 40. Auckland Medical Sch MSR62. LNSM course 93. **d** 96 **p** 97. OLM Battersea St Luke *S'wark* from 96; Chapl St Geo Healthcare NHS Trust Lon from 96. *60 Badminton Road, London SW12 8BL* Tel (020) 8675 0503 *or* 8725 3285 E-mail jenny@deverill.fsnet.co.uk
DEVINE, Margaret Rose. b 50. Sunderland Poly BEd76. NEOC 00. **d** 03 **p** 04. NSM E Boldon *Dur* from 03. *22 Dunelm Street, South Shields NE33 3JT* Tel 0191-455 6125
DEVINE, Maureen Mary. b 37. Cheltenham & Glouc Coll of HE TCert74. St Alb and Ox Min Course 95. **d** 98 **p** 99. NSM Reading St Jo *Ox* 98-01; NSM Beech Hill, Grazeley and Spencers Wood 01-05; NSM Loddon Reach from 05. *33 Radstock Lane, Earley, Reading RG6 5RX* Tel 0118-921 2767 E-mail julmar99@aol.com

DEVONISH, Clive Wayne. b 51. Ridley Hall Cam. **d** 96 **p** 97. C Meole Brace *Lich* 96-05; V Greenside *Dur* from 05. *The Vicarage, Greenside, Ryton NE40 4AA* Tel 0191-413 8281 E-mail rev.cw.devo@cwcom.net

DEVONSHIRE, Canon Roger George. b 40. AKC62. **d** 63 **p** 64. C Rotherhithe St Mary w All SS *S'wark* 63-67; C Kingston Hill St Paul 67-71; Chapl RN 71-95; QHC 92-95; R Pitlochry and Kilmaveonaig *St And* 95-05; Syn Clerk and Can St Ninian's Cathl Perth 00-05; rtd 05. *4 Chiltern Court, 27 Florence Road, Southsea PO5 2NX* Tel (023) 9287 3397 Mobile 07769-680922 E-mail rdevonshire@btinternet.com

DEVONSHIRE JONES, Thomas Percy Norman. *See* JONES, Thomas Percy Norman Devonshire

DEW, Glyn. b 55. Worc Coll of Educn BEd90. St Jo Coll Nottm MA97. **d** 97 **p** 98. C Beoley *Worc* 97-01; TV Redditch, The Ridge 01-05; P-in-c Tardebigge 04-05; TV Redditch H Trin from 05. *The Vicarage, Church Road, Webheath, Redditch B97 5PD* Tel (01527) 403939 E-mail gdew@cofe-worcester.org.uk

DEW, Canon Lindsay Charles. b 52. Cranmer Hall Dur 85. **d** 86 **p** 86. C Knottingley *Wakef* 86-89; V Batley St Thos 89-97; RD Dewsbury from 96; R Thornhill and Whitley Lower from 97; Hon Can Wakef Cathl from 05. *The Rectory, 51 Frank Lane, Dewsbury WF12 0JW* Tel (01924) 465064 Mobile 07767-367483 E-mail lindsayallangels@aol.com

DEW, Martin John. b 49. Carl and Blackb Dioc Tr Inst 00. **d** 04 **p** 05. NSM Natland *Carl* from 04. *9 Burton Park, Burton, Carnforth LA6 1JB* Tel (01524) 781645

DEW, Maureen. b 51. Univ of Wales MA98. Qu Coll Birm BA99. **d** 99 **p** 00. C Inkberrow w Cookhill and Kington w Dormston *Worc* 99-02; C Redditch, The Ridge 02-05; TV Redditch Ch the K from 05. *The Vicarage, Church Road, Webheath, Redditch B97 5PD* Tel (01527) 402404 E-mail modew@thesharpend33.freeserve.co.uk

DEW, Robert David John. b 42. St Pet Coll Ox BA63. St Steph Ho Ox 63. **d** 65 **p** 66. C Abington *Pet* 65-69; Chapl Tiffield Sch Northants 69-71; Ind Chapl *Pet* 71-79; Ind Chapl *Liv* 79-87; Sen Ind Missr 88-91; V Skelsmergh w Selside and Longsleddale *Carl* from 91; Bp's Research Officer 91-95; CME Adv from 95. *The Vicarage, Skelsmergh, Kendal LA9 6NU* Tel (01539) 724498 Fax 734655 E-mail carlisle.cme@virgin.net

DEWAR, Francis John Lindsay. b 33. Keble Coll Ox BA56 MA59. Cuddesdon Coll 58. **d** 60 **p** 61. C Hessle *York* 60-63; C Stockton St Chad *Dur* 63-66; V Sunderland St Chad 66-81; Org Journey Inward, Journey Outward Project from 82; Perm to Offic *B & W* from 01. *Wellspring, Church Road, Wookey, Wells BA5 1JX* Tel (01749) 675365 E-mail dewar@fish.co.uk

DEWAR, Ian John James. b 61. Kingston Poly BA83. Cranmer Hall Dur 89. **d** 92 **p** 93. C Blackb St Gabr *Blackb* 92-95; C Darwen St Cuth w Tockholes St Steph 95-97; V Appley Bridge from 97. *The Vicarage, Finch Lane, Appley Bridge, Wigan WN6 9DT* Tel (01257) 252875 E-mail ijjdewar@hotmail.com

DEWAR, John. b 32. Chich Th Coll 58. **d** 61 **p** 62. C Leeds St Hilda *Ripon* 61-65; C Cullercoats St Geo *Newc* 65-69; V Newsham 69-76; V Kenton Ascension 76-86; R Wallsend St Pet 86-92; V Longhorsley and Hebron 92-96; rtd 96; Perm to Offic *S'well* from 04. *51 Bonner Lane, Calverton, Nottingham NG14 6FU* Tel 0115-965 2599 E-mail j.dewar2@ntlworld.com

DEWES, Ms Deborah Mary. b 59. Homerton Coll Cam BEd81 St Jo Coll Dur BA90 MA93. Cranmer Hall Dur 88. **d** 92 **p** 94. C Stockton St Pet *Dur* 92-96; C Knowle *Birm* 96-03; C Bath Abbey w St Jas *B & W* from 03. *7 Holloway, Bath BA2 4PS* Tel (01225) 484469 E-mail dd@bathabbey.org

DEWEY, David Malcolm. b 43. Lon Univ BA72 LSE MSc(Econ)87 Fitzw Coll Cam MPhil94. Westcott Ho Cam 76. **d** 78 **p** 79. Sen Lect Middx Poly 72-92; Sen Lect Middx Univ 92-01; Hon C Enfield St Mich *Lon* 78-79; Hon C Bush Hill Park St Steph 79-84; Hon C Palmers Green St Jo 84-90; Perm to Offic *Lon* 90-95 and *St Alb* 95-98; Hon C Hertford All SS *St Alb* 98-01; P-in-c St Paul's Walden from 01. *The Vicarage, Bendish Lane, Whitwell, Hitchin SG4 8HX* Tel (01438) 871658 Mobile 07713-328780 E-mail daviddewey8566@fsmail.net

DEWEY, Peter Lewis. b 38. Wycliffe Hall Ox 69. **d** 71 **p** 72. C Hammersmith St Sav *Lon* 71-73; Chapl to Bp Kensington 73-75; C Isleworth All SS 75-81; TV Dorchester *Ox* 81-91; CF (TA) 86-91; Chapl Gordonstoun Sch 92-97; TR St Laur in Thanet *Cant* 97-03; rtd 03; P-in-c Sulhamstead Abbots and Bannister w Ufton Nervet *Ox* from 03. *The Rectory, Sulhamstead Road, Ufton Nervet, Reading RG7 4DH* Tel 0118-983 2328

DEWEY, Sanford Dayton. b 44. Syracuse Univ AB67 MA72. Gen Th Sem (NY) MDiv79. **d** 79 **p** 80. USA 79-87; C St Mary le Bow w St Pancras Soper Lane etc *Lon* 87-92; C Hampstead St Steph w All Hallows 92-94; Co-Dir Hampstead Counselling Service 94-00; Dir from 00; NSM Hampstead Ch Ch 94-96; Hon C Grosvenor Chpl from 96; Prov Past Consultant URC from 96; Perm to Offic from 97. *43 Shirlock Road, London NW3 2HR* Tel (020) 7482 1527 E-mail daytondewey@aol.com

DEWHIRST, Janice. b 50. EMMTC 99. **d** 02 **p** 03. NSM Forest Town *S'well* 02-04; NSM Mansfield SS Pet and Paul from 04. *26 King Street, Mansfield Woodhouse, Mansfield NG19 9AU* Tel (01623) 454471 E-mail revd.jan.d@ntlworld.com

DEWHURST, Gabriel George. b 30. **d** 59 **p** 60. In RC Ch 60-69; C Darlington St Jo *Dur* 70; C Bishopwearmouth St Nic 71-73; C-in-c Stockton St Mark CD 73-81; V Harton 81-86; R Castle Eden w Monkhesleden 86-97; rtd 97; Perm to Offic *York* from 98. *9 Knott Lane, Easingwold, York YO61 3LX* Tel (01347) 823526

DEWHURST, George. b 34. TD76. AKC58. **d** 59 **p** 60. C Chorley St Pet *Blackb* 59-61; C-in-c Oswaldtwistle All SS CD 61-65; V Shevington 65-83; V Horsley and Newington Bagpath w Kingscote *Glouc* 83-96; CF (TA) 63-67; CF (TAVR) 67-83; CF (TA - R of O) 83-88; rtd 96; Perm to Offic *Glouc* from 96. *St Nicholas House, Cherington, Tetbury GL8 8SN* Tel (01285) 841367 E-mail gdewhurst@hotmail.com

DEWHURST, Russell James Edward. b 77. Magd Coll Ox MPhys99 Selw Coll Cam BTh03. Westcott Ho Cam 00. **d** 03. C Blewbury, Hagbourne and Upton *Ox* from 03. *St Andrew's House, 1 Saxons Way, Didcot OX11 9RA* Tel (01235) 814729 E-mail russell_dewhurst@yahoo.co.uk

DEWICK, David Richard. b 36. St Alb and Ox Min Course 96. **d** 99 **p** 00. NSM Risborough *Ox* from 99. *The Rectory, Church End, Bledlow, Princes Risborough HP27 9PD* Tel (01844) 344762

DEWING, Robert Mark Eastwood. b 68. Bris Univ BA90 PGCE91. Ridley Hall Cam BA98. **d** 99 **p** 00. C Alverstoke *Portsm* 99-03; V Sheet from 03. *Sheet Vicarage, 2 Pulens Lane, Petersfield GU31 4DB* Tel (01730) 263673 E-mail robdewing@hotmail.com

DEWING, William Arthur. b 52. NEOC 99. **d** 02 **p** 03. NSM Middlesbrough St Oswald *York* from 02. *19 Monarch Grove, Marton, Middlesbrough TS7 8QQ* Tel (01642) 321074 Mobile 07966-191640 Fax (01642) 500661 E-mail w.dewing@ntlworld.com

DEWIS, Harry Kenneth. b 19. NW Ord Course 75. **d** 78 **p** 79. NSM Bedale *Ripon* 78-89; Perm to Offic from 89. *11 Masham Road, Bedale DL8 2AF* Tel (01677) 423588

DEWSBURY, Michael Owen. b 31. St Aid Birkenhead 54 St Jo Coll Dur 53. **d** 57 **p** 58. C Hellesdon *Nor* 57-60; C Speke All SS *Liv* 60-62; R Gt and Lt Glemham *St E* 62-67; R W Lynn *Nor* 67-68; Australia from 68; rtd 99. *6B Livingstone Street, Beaconsfield, W Australia 6162* Tel (0061) (8) 9335 6852 *or* (8) 9386 3675 E-mail dewsbury@iinet.net.au

DEXTER, Canon Frank Robert. b 40. Cuddesdon Coll 66. **d** 68 **p** 69. C Newc H Cross *Newc* 68-71; C Whorlton 71-73; V Pet Ch Carpenter *Pet* 73-80; V High Elswick St Phil *Newc* 80-85; RD Newc W 81-85; V Newc St Geo from 85; Hon Can Newc Cathl from 94; P-in-c Newc St Hilda 95-98. *St George's Vicarage, St George's Close, Jesmond, Newcastle upon Tyne NE2 2TF* Tel and fax 0191-281 1628 *or* tel 281 1659 Mobile 07885-524138 E-mail frank.dexter@talk21.com

DEY, Canon Charles Gordon Norman. b 46. Lon Coll of Div DipTh70. **d** 71 **p** 72. C Almondbury *Wakef* 71-76; V Mixenden 76-85; TR Tong *Bradf* from 85; Hon Can Bradf Cathl from 00. *The Rectory, Holmewood Road, Tong, Bradford BD4 9EJ* Tel (01274) 682100 E-mail gordon@thedeyteam.freeserve.co.uk

DEY, John Alfred. b 33. ALCD57 ALCM57. **d** 57 **p** 58. C Man Albert Memorial Ch *Man* 57-60; C Pennington 60-62; V Mosley Common 62-69; V Chadderton Em 69-79; V Flixton St Jo 79-96; rtd 96; Perm to Offic *Man* from 96. *8 Woodlands Avenue, Urmston, Manchester M41 6NE*

DHAKA, Bishop of. *See* BAROI, The Rt Revd Michael

DI CASTIGLIONE, Nigel Austin. b 57. St Jo Coll Dur BA78. St Jo Coll Nottm MA94. **d** 94 **p** 95. C Tamworth *Lich* 94-97; P-in-c Trentham 97-01; V from 02; V Hanford from 02. *The Vicarage, Trentham Park, Stoke-on-Trent ST4 8AE* Tel (01782) 658194 E-mail nigel@dicastiglione.fsnet.co.uk

DI CHIARA, Miss Alessandra Maddalena. b 59. Univ of Wales (Swansea) BA80. Wycliffe Hall Ox 00. **d** 02 **p** 03. C Hooton *Ches* 02-05; P-in-c Millbrook from 05. *11 Standrick Hill Rise, Stalybridge SK15 3RT* E-mail alessandra@di-chiara.freeserve.co.uk

DIALI, The Ven Daniel Chukwuma. b 47. Portsm Univ BA80. Immanuel Coll Ibadan 88. **d** 84 **p** 86. Nigeria 84-01; V Lagos St Bart 86-92; V Bp Tugwell Ch 92-96; Can Lagos W 96-99; Adn St Paul's 00-01; Perm to Offic *S'wark* from 02. *6 Townsend House, Strathnairn Street, London SE1 5BU* Tel (020) 7394 0540 E-mail dcdvnd@yahoo.com

DIAMOND, Canon Michael Lawrence. b 37. St Jo Coll Dur BA60 MA74 Sussex Univ DPhil84. ALCD62. **d** 62 **p** 63. C Wandsworth St Mich *S'wark* 62-64; C Patcham *Chich* 64-69; R Hamsey 70-75; P-in-c Cambridge St Andr Less *Ely* 75-86; V 86-04; Hon Can Ely Cathl 94-04; RD Cambridge 96-04; rtd 04; Perm to Offic *S'well* from 04. *16 St Michael's Square, Beeston, Nottingham NG9 3HG* Tel 0115-925 4452

DIAMOND, Capt Richard Geoffrey Colin. b 49. MBE00. CA Tr Coll Dip Evang89. **d** 93 **p** 93. Miss to Seafarers Kenya 90-01; rtd 01; Perm to Offic *Win* from 02. *209A Priory Road, Southampton SO17 2LR* Tel (02380) 678558 E-mail rgcdiamond@ic24.net

DIANA, Sister. *See* MORRISON, Diana Mary

DIAPER, James Robert (Bob). b 30. Portsm Dioc Tr Course 84. **d** 85. NSM Portsea St Sav *Portsm* 85-89 and 91-95; NSM Milton 89-91; rtd 95; Perm to Offic *Portsm* from 95. *48 Wallington Road, Portsmouth PO2 0HB* Tel (023) 9269 1372

DIAPER, Trevor Charles. b 51. ALA79. Coll of Resurr Mirfield 88. **d** 90 **p** 91. C N Walsham w Antingham *Nor* 90-94; P-in-c Ardleigh *Chelmsf* 94-95; P-in-c The Bromleys 94-95; R Ardleigh and The Bromleys 95-97; V Bocking St Pet from 97. *The Vicarage, 6 St Peter's in the Fields, Bocking, Braintree CM7 9AR* Tel (01376) 322698 E-mail father.trevor@btinternet.com

DIBB SMITH, John. b 29. Ex & Truro NSM Scheme 78. **d** 81 **p** 82. NSM Carbis Bay *Truro* 81-82; NSM Carbis Bay w Lelant 82-84; Warden Trelowarren Fellowship Helston 84-89; Chapl 89-91; NSM Halsetown *Truro* 91-97; rtd 98; Perm to Offic *Truro* from 00. *Cargease Cottage, Cockwells, Penzance TR20 8DG* Tel (01736) 740707

DIBBENS, Canon Hugh Richard. b 39. Lon Univ BA63 MTh67 St Pet Coll Ox BA65 MA74. Oak Hill Th Coll 60. **d** 67 **p** 68. C Holborn St Geo w H Trin and St Bart *Lon* 67-72; CMS 73-74; Japan 74-77; TR Chigwell *Chelmsf* 78-92; V Hornchurch St Andr from 92; RD Havering 98-04; Hon Can Chelmsf Cathl from 01. *222 High Street, Hornchurch RM12 6QP* Tel (01708) 454594 *or* 441571
E-mail hughandruth@dibbens10.freeserve.co.uk

DIBBS, Canon Geoffrey. b 24. Man Univ BA51 ThD69. Wycliffe Hall Ox 51. **d** 53 **p** 54. C Droylsden St Mary *Man* 53-56; V Chadderton St Luke 56-59; R Burton Agnes w Harpham *York* 59-66; Canada 66-88; rtd 88. *13414 Desert Glen Drive, Sun City West, AZ 85375, USA* Tel (001) (623) 546 1920

DIBDEN, Alan Cyril. b 49. Hull Univ LLB70 Fitzw Coll Cam BA72 MA76. Westcott Ho Cam 70. **d** 73 **p** 74. C Camberwell St Luke *S'wark* 73-77; TV Walworth 77-79; TV Langley Marish *Ox* 79-84; C Chalfont St Peter 84-90; TV Burnham w Dropmore, Hitcham and Taplow from 90. *The Rectory, Rectory Road, Taplow, Maidenhead SL6 0ET* Tel (01628) 661182

DICK, Alexander Walter Henry. b 20. Lon Univ BSc49 BSc(Econ)56. Sarum & Wells Th Coll 73. **d** 74 **p** 75. C Totnes *Ex* 74-77; Min Estover LEP 77-80; V Estover 80-81; P-in-c Broadwoodwidger 81-83; V 83-86; P-in-c Kelly w Bradstone 81-83; R 83-86; P-in-c Lifton 81-83; R 83-86; rtd 86; Perm to Offic *Ex* from 86 and *Lon* 86-94. *1 Fairfield, Huxtable Hill, Torquay TQ2 6RN* Tel (01803) 605126
E-mail alex.w.h.dick@btinternet.com

DICK, Miss Angela. b 62. Sheff Univ BA92. St Jo Coll Nottm MA94. **d** 96 **p** 97. C Mixenden *Wakef* 96-97; C Mount Pellon 97-99; P-in-c Bradshaw 99-00; P-in-c Holmfield 99-00; V Bradshaw and Holmfield from 00. *The Vicarage, Pavement Lane, Bradshaw, Halifax HX2 9JJ* Tel (01422) 244330
E-mail ange@dix110.freeserve.co.uk

DICK, Canon Caroline Ann. b 61. Nottm Univ BTh88. Linc Th Coll 85. **d** 88 **p** 94. Par Dn Houghton le Spring *Dur* 88-93; Par Dn Hetton le Hole 93-94; C 94-96; Asst Chapl Sunderland Univ 94-98; C Harton from 96; Development Officer Dioc Bd of Soc Resp from 98; Adv for Women's Min from 02; Hon Can Dur Cathl from 03. *Harton Vicarage, 182 Sunderland Road, South Shields NE34 6AH* Tel and fax 0191-427 5538
E-mail bsr.development.officer@durham.anglican.org

DICK, Cecil Bates. b 42. TD97. Selw Coll Cam BA68 MA72. EMMTC 73. **d** 76 **p** 78. NSM Cinderhill *S'well* 76-79; Chapl Dame Allan's Schs Newc 79-85; CF (TA) 84-99; C Gosforth All SS *Newc* 85-87; Chapl HM Pris Dur 88-89; Chapl HM Pris Hull 89-04; rtd 04; Perm to Offic *Newc* from 01 and *York* from 04. *11 Juniper Chase, Beverley HU17 8GD* Tel (01482) 862985

DICK, Norman MacDonald. b 32. ACIB. Ox NSM Course 87. **d** 90 **p** 91. NSM Bedgrove *Ox* 90-95; NSM Ellesborough, The Kimbles and Stoke Mandeville 95-01; Perm to Offic from 01. *21 Camborne Avenue, Aylesbury HP21 7UH* Tel (01296) 85530

DICK, Raymond Owen. b 53. Edin Univ BD77. Edin Th Coll 73. **d** 77 **p** 78. C Glas St Mary *Glas* 77-84; Perm to Offic *St Alb* 84-85; P-in-c Edin St Paul and St Geo *Edin* 85; Edin St Phil 85-86; P-in-c Edin St Marg 85-87; TV Edin Old St Paul 87-88; R Hetton le Hole *Dur* 88-96; V Harton from 96. *Harton Vicarage, 182 Sunderland Road, South Shields NE34 6AH* Tel and fax 0191-427 5538 E-mail rodick182@aol.com *or* raymond.dick@durham.anglican.org

DICKENS, Adam Paul. b 65. Man Univ BA89 Nottm Univ MDiv93. Linc Th Coll 91. **d** 93 **p** 94. C Pershore w Pinvin, Wick and Birlingham *Worc* 93-98; C Portsea St Mary *Portsm* 98-04; Pilsdon Community from 04. *Pilsdon Manor, Pilsdon, Bridport DT6 5NZ* Tel (01308) 868308

DICKENS, Timothy Richard John. b 45. Leeds Univ BSc68. Westcott Ho Cam 68. **d** 71 **p** 72. C Meole Brace *Lich* 71-74; C-in-c Stamford Ch Ch CD *Linc* 74-80; V Anlaby St Pet *York* 80-91; V Egg Buckland *Ex* from 91; P-in-c Estover from 04; RD Plymouth Moorside from 03. *The Vicarage, 100 Church Hill, Eggbuckland, Plymouth PL6 5RD* Tel (01752) 701399
E-mail tim.dickens@lineone.net

DICKENSON, Charles Gordon. b 29. Bps' Coll Cheshunt 53. **d** 56 **p** 57. C Ellesmere Port *Ches* 56-61; R Egremont St Columba 61-68; V Latchford Ch Ch 68-74; P-in-c Hargrave 74-79; Bp's Chapl 75-79; V Birkenhead St Jas w St Bede 79-83; R Tilston and Shocklach 83-94; rtd 94; Perm to Offic *Ches* from 94. *58 Kingsway, Crewe CW2 7ND* Tel (01270) 560722
E-mail charles.dickenson@tesco.net

DICKENSON, Robin Christopher Wildish. b 44. Lon Univ CertEd67 Ex Univ BPhil81 MA98. SW Minl Tr Course 94. **d** 97 **p** 98. NSM Week St Mary w Poundstock and Whitstone *Truro* 97-98; P-in-c from 98; P-in-c St Gennys, Jacobstow w Warbstow and Treneglos from 02. *The Rectory, The Glebe, Week St Mary, Holsworthy EX22 6UY* Tel (01288) 341134 Fax as telephone
E-mail parsonrob@aol.com

DICKER, Canon David. b 31. St Pet Hall Ox BA57 MA58. Linc Th Coll 55. **d** 57 **p** 58. C Wootton Bassett *Sarum* 57-60; C Broad Town 57-60; C Weymouth H Trin 60-63; Antigua 63-64; R Tisbury *Sarum* 64-71; Argentina 71-77; Miss to Seamen 77-81; Chapl Dunkerque w Lille Arras etc Miss to Seamen *Eur* 81-86; TR Shaston *Sarum* 86-96; RD Blackmore Vale 90-95; Can and Preb Sarum Cathl 95-96; rtd 96; Perm to Offic *Linc* from 00. *25 Dunholme Road, Welton, Lincoln LN2 3RS* Tel (01673) 863233

DICKER, Ms Jane Elizabeth. b 64. Whitelands Coll Lon BA87. Linc Th Coll 87. **d** 89 **p** 94. Par Dn Merton St Jas *S'wark* 89-93; C Littleham w Exmouth *Ex* 93-97; Chapl Plymouth Univ 93-97; Ecum Chapl for F&HE Grimsby *Linc* 97-02; Chapl Univ of Greenwich *Roch* from 02; Chapl Kent Inst of Art and Design from 02. *15 Oaks Dene, Chatham ME5 9HN* Tel (01634) 684155 Mobile 07932-166426

DICKER, Miss Mary Elizabeth. b 45. Girton Coll Cam BA66 MA70 Sheff Univ MSc78. Cranmer Hall Dur 83. **dss** 85 **d** 87 **p** 94. Mortlake w E Sheen *S'wark* 85-88; Par Dn 87-88; Par Dn Irlam *Man* 88-92; Par Dn Ashton Ch Ch 92-94; C 94-97; P-in-c Hopwood 97-98; TV Heywood 98-05; rtd 05. *32 Souchay Court, 1 Clothorn Road, Manchester M20 6BR* Tel 0161-434 7634

DICKERSON, Richard Keith. b 31. Sir Geo Williams Univ Montreal BA60 McGill Univ Montreal BD60. Montreal Dioc Th Coll. **d** 60 **p** 60. Canada 60-69 and from 78; C Hampstead St Matt 60-63; R Waterloo St Luke 63-69; Perm to Offic *Cant* 72; C Canvey Is *Chelmsf* 73-75; Perm to Offic Montreal 75-78; C Georgeville St Geo 78-82; P-in-c 82-91; R Lennoxville St Geo 91-01; rtd 96. *172 McGowan Road, Georgeville PQ, Canada, J0B 1T0* E-mail stgeorgeslennox@qc.aibn.com

DICKIE, James Graham Wallace. b 50. Worc Coll Ox BA72 MA BLitt77. Westcott Ho Cam 78. **d** 81 **p** 82. C Bracknell *Ox* 81-84; Lic to Offic *Ely* 84-89; Chapl Trin Coll Cam 84-89; Chapl Clifton Coll Bris 89-96; Sen Chapl Marlborough Coll from 96. *The Old Rectory, High Street, Marlborough SN8 1HQ* Tel (01672) 892204 E-mail chaplain@marlboroughcollege.wilts.sch.uk

DICKINSON, Albert Hugh. b 34. Trin Coll Connecticut AB55. Episc Th Sch Harvard STB58. **d** 58 **p** 59. USA 58-97 and from 99; C Portarlington w Cloneyhurke and Lea *M & K* 97-99. *807 Seashore Road, Cold Spring, NJ 08204, USA*
E-mail husan@avaloninternet.net

DICKINSON, Canon Anthony William. b 48. New Coll Ox BA71 MA74 Nottm Univ DipHE82. Linc Th Coll 80. **d** 82 **p** 83. C Leavesden All SS *St Alb* 82-86; TV Upton cum Chalvey *Ox* 86-94; P-in-c Terriers 94-99; V from 99; Chapl Bucks Chilterns Univ Coll from 03; Hon Can Ch Ch *Ox* from 05. *St Francis's Vicarage, Amersham Road, High Wycombe HP13 5AB* Tel (01494) 520676 E-mail tony.dickinson@ukonline.co.uk *or* sainsw01@bcuc.ac.uk

DICKINSON, David Charles. b 58. BA79 Lanc Univ MA97. Carl and Blackb Dioc Tr Inst. **d** 99 **p** 00. NSM Ewood *Blackb* 99-04; NSM Blackb Redeemer 04-05; P-in-c Hoghton from 05. *The Vicarage, Chapel Lane, Hoghton, Preston PR5 0RY* Tel (01254) 852529

DICKINSON, Dyllis Annie. b 52. **d** 01 **p** 02. OLM Stalmine w Pilling *Blackb* from 01. *Springfield, Moss Side Lane, Stalmine, Poulton-le-Fylde FY6 0JP* Tel (01253) 700011
E-mail dyljohn@lineone.net

DICKINSON, Henry. b 29. St Deiniol's Hawarden 84. **d** 86 **p** 87. NSM Blackb St Mich w St Jo and H Trin *Blackb* 86-89; NSM Burnley St Cath w St Alb and St Paul 89-95; Perm to Offic from 98. *22 Notre Dame Gardens, Blackburn BB1 5EF* Tel (01254) 693414

DICKINSON, The Very Revd the Hon Hugh Geoffrey. b 29. Trin Coll Ox BA53 DipTh54 MA56. Cuddesdon Coll 54. **d** 56 **p** 57. C Melksham *Sarum* 56-58; Chapl Trin Coll Cam 58-63; Chapl Win Coll 63-69; P-in-c Milverton *Cov* 69-77; V St Alb St Mich *St Alb* 77-86; Dean Sarum 86-96; rtd 96; Perm to Offic *Glouc* from 96. *5 St Peter's Road, Cirencester GL7 1RE* Tel (01285) 657710
E-mail hughanjean@aol.com

DICKINSON, Canon Robert Edward. b 47. Nottm Univ BTh74. St Jo Coll Nottm 70. **d** 74 **p** 75. C Birm St Martin *Birm* 74-78; P-in-c Liv St Bride w St Sav *Liv* 78-81; TV St Luke in the City 81-86; Chapl Liv Poly 86-92; Chapl Liv Jo Moores Univ from 92; Hon Can Liv Cathl from 03. *45 Queen's Drive, Liverpool L18 2DT* Tel 0151-722 1625 *or* 231 2121

DICKINSON, Simon Braithwaite Vincent. b 34. St Alb and Ox Min Course 94. **d** 97 **p** 98. OLM Waddesdon w Over Winchendon and Fleet Marston *Ox* 97-02; OLM Schorne 02-04; Perm to Offic from 04. *The White House, Waddesdon, Aylesbury HP18 0JA* Tel (01296) 651693 *or* 658038

DICKINSON, Stephen Paul. b 54. SRN75. N Ord Course 85. **d** 88 **p** 89. Hon C Purston cum S Featherstone *Wakef* 88-91; C Goldthorpe w Hickleton *Sheff* 91-94; V New Bentley from 94; P-in-c Arksey from 04. *The Vicarage, Victoria Road, Bentley, Doncaster DN5 0EZ* Tel (01302) 875266

DICKINSON, Victor Tester. b 48. Univ of Wales (Cardiff) BSc70. St Steph Ho Ox 70. **d** 73 **p** 74. C Neath w Llantwit *Llan* 73-76; Asst Chapl Univ of Wales (Cardiff) 76-79; TV Willington *Newc* 79-86; V Kenton Ascension 86-97; V Lowick and Kyloe w Ancroft from 97; R Ford and Etal from 97. *The Vicarage, 1 Main Street, Lowick, Berwick-upon-Tweed TD15 2UD* Tel (01289) 388229

DICKSON, Anthony Edward. b 59. Nottm Univ BTh88. Linc Th Coll 85. **d** 88 **p** 89. C Portsea St Alb *Portsm* 88-91; C Cleobury Mortimer w Hopton Wafers *Heref* 91-94; R Fownhope w Mordiford, Brockhampton etc 94-99. *Address temp unknown* E-mail anthony@fownhope.kc3ltd.co.uk

DICKSON, Brian John. b 19. Reading Univ BSc41 Birm Univ DipTh51. Qu Coll Birm 49. **d** 51 **p** 52. C S Wimbledon H Trin *S'wark* 51-53; C Golders Green St Alb *Lon* 53-55; Sec SCM Th Colls Dept 53-55; Chapl Hulme Gr Sch Oldham 55-59; Chapl K Sch Worc 60-67; Min Can Worc Cathl *Worc* 60-67; Chapl Colston's Sch Bris 67-74; V Bishopston *Bris* 74-85; RD Horfield 80-85; rtd 85; Perm to Offic *Worc* from 85. *One Acre Cottage, Abberley, Worcester WR6 6BS* Tel (01299) 896442

DICKSON, Colin James. b 74. St Andr Univ MA96 MPhil00 Leeds Univ BA01. Coll of Resurr Mirfield 99. **d** 02 **p** 03. C Tottenham St Paul *Lon* from 02. *The Curate's Flat, St Paul's Vicarage, 60 Park Lane, London N17 0JR* Tel (020) 8885 1395 E-mail frcolin@stpaulstottenham.org.uk

DICKSON, Colin Patrick Gavin. b 56. **d** 96 **p** 97. C Grays Thurrock *Chelmsf* 96-00; V Glantawe *S & B* from 00. *The Vicarage, 122 Mansel Road, Bonymaen, Swansea SA1 7JR* Tel (01792) 652839

DICKSON, Richard Arthur. b 67. LSE BSc(Econ)88. Ripon Coll Cuddesdon BA92. **d** 93 **p** 94. C Sale St Anne *Ches* 93-96; Sweden from 96. *Address temp unknown* E-mail dickson@swipnet.se

DICKSON, Canon Samuel Mervyn James. b 41. CITC. **d** 66 **p** 67. C Ballyholme *D & D* 66-70; C Knockbreda 70-75; I Clonallon w Warrenpoint 75-84; I Down H Trin w Hollymount from 84; Bp's C Rathmullan w Tyrella from 00; Bp's C Lecale Gp from 01; Bp's C Loughinisland from 01; Can Down Cathl from 91; Treas 98-00; Prec 00-01; Chan from 01. *12 The Meadows, Strangford Road, Downpatrick BT30 6LN* Tel (028) 4461 2286

DIFFEY, Margaret Elsie. b 39. MCSP. **d** 02 **p** 03. OLM Nor St Geo Tombland *Nor* from 02. *45 Welsford Road, Norwich NR4 6QB* Tel and fax (01603) 457248 E-mail ericandmaggie@ediffey.freeserve.co.uk

DIGGLE, Richard James. b 47. Lon Inst BA69 Man Poly CertEd74. **d** 01 **p** 02. OLM Chorlton-cum-Hardy St Werburgh *Man* 01-05; NSM Bickerton, Bickley, Harthill and Burwardsley *Ches* from 05. *Swanwick Green Cottage, Swanwick Green, Norbury, Whitchurch SY13 4HL* Tel (01948) 666317 E-mail diggles@ntlworld.com

DILL, Nicholas Bayard Botolf. b 63. Toronto Univ BA86 Lon Univ LLB89 Barrister 91. Wycliffe Hall Ox 96. **d** 98 **p** 99. C Lindfield *Chich* 98-05; R Pembroke St Jo Bermuda from 05. *Marias Hill, Langton Hill, Pembroke, Bermuda* Tel (001) (441) 292 5308 Fax 296 9173

DILL, Peter Winston. b 41. ACP66 K Coll Lon BD72 AKC72. St Aug Coll Cant 72. **d** 73 **p** 74. C Warsop *S'well* 73-75; C Rhyl w St Ann *St As* 75-77; C Oxton *Ches* 77-78; V Newton in Mottram 78-82; P-in-c Shelton and Oxon *Lich* 82-84; V 84-87; Chapl Clifton Coll Bris 87-00; C Thorverton, Cadbury, Upton Pyne etc *Ex* 00-01; Perm to Offic *Bris* 02-03; Past Co-ord St Monica Home Westbury-on-Trym from 03. *85B Pembroke Road, Clifton, Bristol BS8 3EB* Tel 0117-973 9769

DILNOT, Canon John William. b 36. Selw Coll Cam BA60 MA64. Cuddesdon Coll 60. **d** 62 **p** 63. C Stafford St Mary *Lich* 62-66; C Stoke upon Trent 66-67; V Leek All SS 67-74; V Leeds w Broomfield *Cant* 74-79; P-in-c Aldington 79-81; P-in-c Bonnington w Bilsington 79-81; P-in-c Fawkenhurst 79-81; R Aldington w Bonnington and Bilsington 81-87; RD N Lympne 82-87; Hon Can Cant Cathl 85-99; V Folkestone St Mary and St Eanswythe 87-99; rtd 99; Perm to Offic *Cant* from 99. *Underhill Cottage, The Undercliff, Sandgate, Folkestone CT20 3AT* Tel (01303) 248000

DILWORTH, Anthony. b 41. St Deiniol's Hawarden 87. **d** 90 **p** 91. NSM Gt Saughall *Ches* 90-93; P-in-c Cwmcarn *Mon* 93-95; V 95-99; V Abercarn and Cwmcarn 99-01; TV Upholland *Liv* from 01. *158 Back Lane, Skelmersdale WN8 9BX* Tel (01695) 728091 Mobile 07773-389179

DIMERY, Richard James. b 76. CCC Cam MA98 Leeds Univ MA99. Wycliffe Hall Ox MA03. **d** 04 **p** 05. C Upper Armley *Ripon* from 04. *7 Stephenson Drive, Leeds LS12 5TN* Tel 0113-219 0867 E-mail richard@dimery.com

DIMES, Stuart Christopher Laurence. b 60. Warwick Univ BSc81. St Jo Coll Nottm 99. **d** 01 **p** 02. C Branksome St Clem *Sarum* from 01. *29 Croft Road, Parkstone, Poole BH12 3LB* Tel (01202) 721056 E-mail sdimes@fish.co.uk

DIMMICK, Mrs Margaret Louisa. b 44. Keswick Hall Coll TCert66 Open Univ BA75. St Alb and Ox Min Course 97. **d** 00 **p** 02. Oxfam from 95; OLM Caversham St Pet and Mapledurham etc *Ox* 00-03; OLM Emmer Green w Caversham Park from 03. *12 Lowfield Road, Caversham, Reading RG4 6PA* Tel 0118-947 0258 E-mail margaret@dimmick33.freeserve.co.uk

DIMOLINE, Keith Frederick. b 22. Clifton Th Coll 48. **d** 51 **p** 52. C Watford Ch Ch *St Alb* 51-54; C Corsham *Bris* 54-59; C-in-c Swindon St Jo Park CD 59-62; V Swindon St Jo 62-65; V Coalpit Heath 65-74; V Hanham 74-83; C Cudworth w Chillington *B & W* 83-84; P-in-c Dowlishwake w Chaffcombe, Knowle St Giles etc 83-84; R Dowlishwake w Chaffcombe, Knowle St Giles etc 84-88; rtd 88; Perm to Offic *B & W* from 88. *16 Exeter Road, Weston-super-Mare BS23 4DB* Tel (01934) 635006

DINES, The Very Revd Philip Joseph (Griff). b 59. Univ Coll Lon BScEng80 Clare Coll Cam PhD84 Man Univ MA(Theol)93. Westcott Ho Cam 83. **d** 86 **p** 87. C Northolt St Mary *Lon* 86-89; C Withington St Paul *Man* 89-91; V Wythenshawe St Martin 91-98; P-in-c Newall Green St Fran 95-98; Provost St Mary's Cathl *Glas* from 98; R Glas St Mary from 98. *45 Rowallan Gardens, Glasgow G11 7LH* Tel 0141-339 4956 *or* 339 6691 Fax 0141-334 5669 Mobile 07974-611438 E-mail griff@dines.org *or* provost@glasgow.anglican.org

DINNEN, The Very Revd John Frederick. b 42. TCD BA65 BD72 QUB MTh91. CITC. **d** 66 **p** 67. C Belfast All SS *Conn* 66-68; ICM Dub 69-71; C Carnmoney 71-73; Asst Dean of Residences QUB 73-74; Dean 74-84; I Hillsborough *D & D* from 84; Preb Down Cathl 93-96; Dir of Ords 96-98; Dean Down from 96. *17 Dromore Road, Hillsborough BT26 6HS* Tel and fax (028) 9268 2366

DINNEN, Mrs Judith Margaret. b 48. Open Univ BA87 Univ of Wales (Cardiff) MA00 Goldsmiths' Coll Lon TCert71. WEMTC 01. **d** 05. NSM Madley w Tyberton, Peterchurch, Vowchurch etc *Heref* from 05. *Minstercote, Much Birch, Hereford HR2 8HT* Tel (01981) 540730 E-mail judy@dinnen5.fsnet.co.uk

DINSMORE, Ivan Ernest. b 71. TCD BTh01. CITC 98. **d** 01 **p** 02. C Glendermott *D & R* 01-04; I Balteagh w Carrick from 04; I Tamlaghtard w Aghanloo from 04. *Balteagh Rectory, 115 Drumsurn Road, Limavady BT49 0PD* Tel (028) 7776 3069 E-mail ivandinsmore@hotmail.com

DINSMORE, Stephen Ralph. b 56. Wye Coll Lon BSc78. Cranmer Hall Dur 82. **d** 85 **p** 86. C Haughton le Skerne *Dur* 85-88; C Edgware *Lon* 88-93; V Plymouth St Jude *Ex* 93-05; RD Plymouth Sutton 96-01; Adv for Miss and Par Development *Chelmsf* from 05. *4 Gridiron Place, Upminster RM14 2BE* E-mail judeplym@aol.com

DISLEY, Mrs Edith Jennifer. b 51. Sheff Univ BSc72 Man Univ BD79. N Ord Course 99. **d** 01 **p** 02. NSM Man Victoria Park *Man* from 01. *49 Broadstone Hall Road North, Heaton Chapel, Stockport SK4 5LA* Tel 0161-432 5114 E-mail sisteredith@priest.com

DISS, Canon Ronald George. b 31. Sarum Th Coll 58. **d** 61 **p** 62. C Greenwich St Alfege w St Pet *S'wark* 61-65; Lic to Offic 65-80; Lic to Offic *Lon* 68-77; Chapl Lon Univ 68-71; Bp's Dom Chapl *Win* 78-80; V Southampton Maybush St Pet 80-91; Hon Can Win Cathl 85-96; R Freemantle 91-96; rtd 96; Hon Chapl to Bp Dover *Cant* from 97. *35 Castle Row, Canterbury CT1 2QY* Tel (01227) 462410

DITCH, David John. b 45. St Cath Coll Cam BA67 MA70 Leeds Univ PGCE68. WMMTC 88. **d** 91 **p** 92. C Biddulph *Lich* 91-94; V Hednesford 94-02; V Chasetown from 02. *The Vicarage, 158A High Street, Chasetown, Burntwood WS7 3XG* Tel (01543) 686276 *or* 686111

DITCHBURN, Canon Hazel. b 44. NEOC 82. **dss** 84 **d** 87 **p** 94. Scotswood *Newc* 84-86; Ind Chapl *Dur* 86-95; TV Gateshead 95-98; AD Gateshead 92-98; P-in-c Stella 98-04; P-in-c Swalwell 01-04; R Blaydon and Swalwell from 04; AD Gateshead W 98-00; Hon Can Dur Cathl from 94. *St Cuthbert's Rectory, Shibdon Road, Blaydon-on-Tyne NE21 5AE* Tel and fax 0191-414 2720 E-mail hazel.ditchburn@durham.anglican.org

DITCHFIELD, Timothy Frederick. b 61. CCC Cam BA83. Cranmer Hall Dur 85. **d** 88 **p** 89. C Accrington St Jo *Blackb* 88-89; C Accrington St Jo w Huncoat 89-91; C Whittle-le-Woods 91-95; Chapl K Coll Lon from 95; Perm to Offic *S'wark* from 98. *19 Maunsel Street, London SW1P 2QN,* or *King's College, Strand, London WC2R 2LS* Tel (020) 7828 1772 *or* 7848 2373 Fax 7848 2344 E-mail tim.ditchfield@kcl.ac.uk

DITTMER, Canon Michael William. b 17. St Edm Hall Ox BA39 MA43. Sarum Th Coll 40. **d** 41 **p** 42. C Bromley St Andr *Roch* 41-43; C Horfield H Trin *Bris* 43-49; C-in-c Lockleaze St Fran CD 49-52; V Yatton Keynell 52-88; R Biddestone w

Slaughterford 53-88; R Castle Combe 53-88; RD Chippenham 66-76; R W Kington 75-88; Hon Can Bris Cathl 84-88; P-in-c Nettleton w Littleton Drew 85-88; rtd 88; Perm to Offic *B & W* from 88. *Greenacres, Summerhedge Lane, Othery, Bridgwater TA7 0JD* Tel (01823) 698288

DIVALL, David Robert. b 40. New Coll Ox BA64 Sussex Univ DPhil74. Sarum & Wells Th Coll 75. **d** 77 **p** 78. Hon C Catherington and Clanfield *Portsm* 77-92; Hon C Rowlands Castle 92-93; Perm to Offic from 01. *17 Pipers Mead, Clanfield, Waterlooville PO8 0ST* Tel (023) 9259 4845

DIVALL, Stephen Robert. b 70. Pemb Coll Ox MA92. Ridley Hall Cam BA97. **d** 98 **p** 99. C Cheadle *Ches* 98-01; UCCF from 01. *UCCF, 38 De Montfort Street, Leicester LE1 7GP* Tel 0116-255 1700 Fax 255 5672

DIXON, Ms Anne Elizabeth. b 56. Leeds Univ LLB77 Solicitor 80. Westcott Ho Cam. **d** 01 **p** 02. C Guildf H Trin w St Mary *Guildf* from 01. *27 Pewley Way, Guildford GU1 3PX* Tel (01483) 568477 E-mail annied@fish.co.uk *or* curate@holytrinityguildford.org.uk

DIXON, Bruce Richard. b 42. Lon Univ BScEng63. Sarum Th Coll 66. **d** 68 **p** 69. C Walton St Mary *Liv* 68-70; C Harnham *Sarum* 70-73; C Streatham St Leon *S'wark* 73-77; R Thurcaston *Leic* 77-83; R Cranborne w Boveridge, Edmondsham etc *Sarum* 83-02. *East Heddon, Filleigh, Barnstaple EX32 0RY* Tel (01598) 760513

DIXON, Bryan Stanley. b 61. St Jo Coll Nottm BTh93. **d** 93 **p** 94. C Beverley Minster *York* 93-96; C Kingston upon Hull St Aid Southcoates 96-97; Asst Chapl HM Pris Dur 97-98; R Mid Marsh Gp *Linc* 98-03; R Brandesburton and Leven w Catwick *York* from 03. *The Rectory, West Street, Leven, Beverley HU17 5LR* Tel (01964) 543793

DIXON, Charles William. b 41. NW Ord Course 78. **d** 81 **p** 82. C Almondbury *Wakef* 81-82; C Almondbury w Farnley Tyas 82-84; P-in-c Shepley 84-88; P-in-c Shelley 84-88; V Shelley and Shepley 88-89; V Ripponden 89-94; V Barkisland w W Scammonden 89-94; P-in-c Thornes St Jas w Ch Ch 94-98; Chapl among Deaf People *Chelmsf* from 98. *156C Rayleigh Road, Hutton, Brentwood CM13 1PH* Tel (01277) 216544 Fax 215154 E-mail dchas58@aol.com

DIXON, Clive Raylton. b 58. Man Univ BSc81. EMMTC 94. **d** 05. C Stamford All SS w St Jo *Linc* from 05. *Church House, 26 Hazel Grove, Stamford PE9 2HJ* Tel (01780) 767759 Mobile 07836-732590 E-mail revcdixon@yahoo.co.uk

DIXON, Canon David. b 19. Lich Th Coll 57. **d** 58 **p** 59. C Barrow St Luke *Carl* 58-61; V Westfield St Mary 61-68; Warden Rydal Hall 68-84; P-in-c Rydal 78-84; rtd 84; Perm to Offic *Carl* from 84; Hon Can Carl Cathl 84-85. *Rheda, The Green, Millom LA18 5JA* Tel (01229) 774300

DIXON, David Hugh. b 40. Chich Th Coll 90. **d** 92 **p** 93. C Launceston *Truro* 92-95; TV Probus, Ladock and Grampound w Creed and St Erme from 95. *The Rectory, Ladock, Truro TR2 4PL* Tel (01726) 882554 E-mail ddixon@fish.co.uk

DIXON, David Michael. b 58. Preston Poly BA82 Barrister 83. Coll of Resurr Mirfield BA98. **d** 98 **p** 99. C Goldthorpe w Hickleton *Sheff* 98-01; P-in-c W Kirby St Andr *Ches* from 01. *St Andrew's Vicarage, 2 Lingdale Road, West Kirby, Wirral CH48 5DQ* Tel 0151-632 4728

DIXON, Edward Michael (Mike). b 42. St Chad's Coll Dur BA64 DipTh66 Newc Univ MA93. **d** 66 **p** 67. C Hartlepool H Trin *Dur* 66-70; C Howden *York* 70-73; Chapl HM Pris Liv 73; Chapl HM Pris Onley 74-82; Chapl HM Pris Frankland 82-87; Chapl HM Pris Dur 87-97; Chapl HM Pris Acklington 97-98; Asst Chapl 98-02; P-in-c Shilbottle *Newc* from 98; P-in-c Chevington from 03. *The Vicarage, Shilbottle, Alnwick NE66 2XR* Tel and fax (01665) 575800 E-mail mdixon@fish.co.uk

DIXON, Eric. b 31. MPS. EMMTC 78. **d** 81 **p** 82. NSM Kirk Langley *Derby* 81-96; NSM Mackworth All SS 81-96; Perm to Offic from 96. *5 Wentworth Close, Mickleover, Derby DE3 9YE* Tel (01332) 516546

DIXON, Mrs Francesca Dorothy. b 52. Cam Univ MA73 Birm Univ DipTh83. Qu Coll Birm 81. **dss** 84 **d** 87 **p** 94. W Bromwich All SS *Lich* 84-94; Par Dn 87-94; C 94; Chapl Burrswood Chr Cen *Roch* 95; Perm to Offic *Chich* from 97. *46 Arun Vale, Coldwaltham, Pulborough RH20 1LP* Tel (01798) 872177

DIXON, John Kenneth (Ken). b 40. Linc Th Coll 79. **d** 81 **p** 82. C Goldington *St Alb* 81-85; V Cardington 85-94; RD Elstow 89-94; R Clifton 94-95; P-in-c Southill 94-95; R Clifton and Southill 95-05; RD Shefford 95-01; rtd 05. *7 Milton Fields, Brixham TQ5 0BH* Tel (01803) 854396 E-mail eidyn@cainnech.fsworld.co.uk

DIXON, John Martin. b 43. York Univ DMS96 ACMI96. Kelham Th Coll Lich Th Coll. **d** 72 **p** 73. C Ellesmere Port *Ches* 72-74; C Bredbury St Barn 74-75; P-in-c Greenlands *Blackb* 75-78; Chapl Victoria Hosp Blackpool 75-78; Chapl RAF 78-81; Asst Chapl HM Pris Featherstone 81-85; Dep Chapl HM Pris Wormwood Scrubs 85-87; Chapl HM Pris Rudgate and Thorp Arch 87-89; Chapl HM Pris Leeds 89-93; Chapl HM Pris Stafford from 93. *HM Prison, 54 Gaol Road, Stafford ST16 3AW* Tel (01785) 773033 *or* 773284 Fax 773001

DIXON, John Scarth. b 69. Aber Univ MA92. Westcott Ho Cam CTM98. **d** 98 **p** 99. C Walney Is *Carl* 98-01; R Harrington from 01. *The Rectory, Rectory Close, Harrington, Workington CA14 5PN* Tel (01946) 830215 E-mail jjcdixon@btinternet.com

DIXON, Kenneth. *See* DIXON, John Kenneth

DIXON, Lorraine. b 65. Leeds Univ BA96. CA Tr Coll Dip Evang 89 Qu Coll Birm BD98. **d** 98 **p** 99. C Potternewton *Ripon* 98-01; Chapl Ches Coll of HE *Ches* from 01; Min Can Ches Cathl from 04; Deanery Missr *Birm* from 05. *288A Ladypool Road, Birmingham B12 8JU* E-mail l.dixon65@btopenworld.com

DIXON, Michael. *See* DIXON, Edward Michael

DIXON, Nicholas Scarth. b 30. G&C Coll Cam BA54 MA63. Westcott Ho Cam 54. **d** 56 **p** 57. C Walney Is *Carl* 56-59; CF 59-62; V Whitehaven Ch Ch w H Trin *Carl* 62-70; R Blofield w Hemblington *Nor* 70-77; P-in-c Bowness *Carl* 77-79; R 79-81; V Frizington and Arlecdon 81-87; V Barton, Pooley Bridge and Martindale 87-95; rtd 95; Perm to Offic *Carl* from 95. *7 Mayburgh Avenue, Penrith CA11 8PA* Tel (01768) 892864

DIXON, Canon Peter. b 36. Qu Coll Ox BA58 MA62 Birm Univ BD65 PhD75. Qu Coll Birm DipTh60. **d** 60 **p** 61. C Mountain Ash *Llan* 60-63; C Penrhiwceiber w Matthewstown and Ynysboeth 63-68; P-in-c 68-70; V Bronllys w Llanfilo *S & B* 70-02; Bp's Chapl for Readers 80-02; Bp's Chapl for Th Educn 83-02; Warden of Readers 92-02; RD Hay 90-02; Can Res Brecon Cathl 98-02; rtd 02. *22 Caerpound, Hay-on-Wye, Hereford HR3 5DU*

DIXON, Peter David. b 48. Edin Univ BSc71 MIMechE. Edin Dioc NSM Course 75. **d** 79 **p** 80. NSM Prestonpans *Edin* 79-89; NSM Musselburgh 79-89; NSM Edin St Luke 90; P-in-c Edin St Barn from 91. *8 Oswald Terrace, Prestonpans EH32 9EG* Tel (01875) 812985

DIXON, Philip. b 48. Leeds Univ BSc69 Open Univ BA91. St Jo Coll Nottm 77. **d** 80 **p** 81. C Soundwell *Bris* 80-82; C Stoke Bishop 82-84; TV Hemel Hempstead *St Alb* 84-85; Chapl Westonbirt Sch from 85; Perm to Offic *Bris* from 86. *East Lodge, Westonbirt School, Tetbury GL8 8QG* Tel (01666) 880333

DIXON, Philip Roger. b 54. CCC Ox BA77 MA80. Oak Hill Th Coll BA80. **d** 80 **p** 81. C Droylsden St Mary *Man* 80-84; TV Rochdale 84-91; V Audenshaw St Steph from 91; AD Ashton-under-Lyne from 03. *St Stephen's Vicarage, 176 Stamford Road, Audenshaw, Manchester M34 5WW* Tel 0161-370 1863 E-mail ssaudenshaw@aol.com

DIXON, Robert. b 50. Univ of Wales (Lamp) BA80 Sussex Univ MA04. Chich Th Coll 80. **d** 81 **p** 82. C Maidstone St Martin *Cant* 81-84; Chapl HM Youth Cust Cen Dover 84-88; C All Hallows by the Tower etc *Lon* 88-90; P-in-c Southwick H Trin *Dur* 90-97; R 97; R Etchingham *Chich* from 97; V Hurst Green from 97. *9 McMichaels Way, Hurst Green, Etchingham TN19 7HJ* Tel (01580) 860105 Mobile 07779-121169 E-mail sussexrob@aol.com

DIXON, Roger John. b 33. Magd Coll Cam BA58 MA61. EAMTC 78. **d** 79 **p** 80. NSM Fakenham w Alethorpe *Nor* 79-82; C Brandeston w Kettleburgh *St E* 82-84; P-in-c 84-99; Asst Chapl Framlingham Coll 82-99; RD Loes *St E* 97-98; rtd 99; Perm to Offic *Nor* 99-05. *9 The Crescent, Fairwater, Cardiff CF5 3DF*

DIXON, Ms Sheila. b 46. Open Univ BA78 Trent Poly CertEd79. St Jo Coll Nottm 93. **d** 93 **p** 94. Par Dn Ordsall *S'well* 93-94; C 94-97; P-in-c Sutton w Carlton and Normanton upon Trent etc from 97; P-in-c Norwell w Ossington, Cromwell and Caunton from 05. *The Vicarage, Main Street, Norwell, Newark NG23 6JT* Tel (01636) 636329 E-mail sdixonrev@aol.com

DIXON, Stephen William. b 53. Nottm Univ BA75 Man Metrop Univ PGCE88 Liv Univ MTh00. N Ord Course 96. **d** 99 **p** 00. NSM Meltham *Wakef* from 99; Lic Preacher *Man* from 01. *83 Totties, Holmfirth HD9 1UJ* Tel (01484) 687376

DIXON, Mrs Teresa Mary. b 61. Southn Univ BSc82 Ball Coll Ox PGCE83. EAMTC 99. **d** 02 **p** 03. NSM Sutton and Witcham w Mepal *Ely* 02-04; C Littleport from 04. *Ash Tree Farm, A Furlong Drove, Little Downham, Ely CB6 2EW* Tel (01353) 699552 E-mail teresa.dixon@ely.anglican.org

DIZERENS, Charles Robert (Frère François). b 18. Lausanne Univ. **d** 97. Asst Chapl Montreux w Gstaad *Eur* from 97. *Avenue de Valmont 16, Lausanne 1010, Switzerland* Tel (0041) (21) 653 1090 *or* 963 43654 Fax 963 4391

DNISTRIANSKYJ, Stefan Mykola. b 61. Leic Univ BSc82 Chester Coll of HE BTh02. N Ord Course 99. **d** 02 **p** 03. C Halliwell St Luke *Man* from 02. *Karis, Stowell Street, Bolton BL1 3RQ* Tel (01204) 522810 Mobile 07931-785598 E-mail dnist@hotmail.com

DOBB, Canon Arthur Joseph. b 31. ARIBA54 ACertCM80 Hon FGCM93. Oak Hill Th Coll 56. **d** 58 **p** 59. C Bolton St Paul *Man* 58-60; C Rawtenstall St Mary 60-62; V Bircle 62-72; V Harwood 72-84; Hon Can Man Cathl 81-96; V Wingates 84-96; rtd 96; Perm to Offic *Man* from 96. *97 Turton Heights, Bromley Cross, Bolton BL2 3DU* Tel (01204) 308419

DOBB, Christopher. b 46. Dur Univ BA68. Cuddesdon Coll 68. **d** 70 **p** 71. C Portsea St Mary *Portsm* 70-73; Lic to Offic *S'wark* 73-77; Perm to Offic *Bris* 77-79; Lic to Offic 79-81; V Swindon St Aug 81-98; rtd 98. *Kingsbury Hall, The Green, Calne SN11 8DG* Tel (01249) 821521 Fax 817246 E-mail kingsburyhallcd@aol.com

DOBBIE, Charles William Granville. b 49. OBE92. Wycliffe Hall Ox 94. **d** 96 **p** 97. C Morriston *S & B* 96-00; Asst Chapl Morriston Hosp/Ysbyty Treforys NHS Trust 97-00; V Lyonsdown H Trin *St Alb* from 00. *Holy Trinity Vicarage, 18 Lyonsdown Road, Barnet EN5 1JE* Tel (020) 8216 3786 E-mail charles@holytrinitylyonsdown.org.uk

DOBBIE, Gary William. b 51. St Andr Univ MA75 BD77 Magd Coll Cam CertEd80 FRSA98 FSAScot. Coll of Resurr Mirfield 83. **d** 83 **p** 83. Kimbolton Sch Cambs 83-84; Hon C Kimbolton *Ely* 83-84; Sen Chapl Ch Hosp Horsham 86-96; Asst Chapl 96-03; Housemaster 93-03; Chapl Shrewsbury Sch from 03. *Shrewsbury School, Kingsland, Shrewsbury SY3 7BA* Tel (01743) 280550 Mobile 07879-426056 E-mail chaplain@shrewsbury.org.uk

DOBBIN, Canon Charles Philip. b 51. Jes Coll Cam BA73 MA77 Oriel Coll Ox BA75 MA88. St Steph Ho Ox 74. **d** 76 **p** 77. C New Addington *Cant* 76-79; C Melton Mowbray w Thorpe Arnold *Leic* 79-83; V Loughb Gd Shep 83-89; V Ashby-de-la-Zouch St Helen w Coleorton 89-00; RD Akeley W 93-00; Hon Can Leic Cathl 94-00; TR Moor Allerton *Ripon* from 00. *St John's Rectory, 1 Fir Tree Lane, Leeds LS17 7BZ* Tel 0113-268 4598 E-mail cdobbin@aol.com

DOBBIN, Harold John. b 47. Liv Univ BSc69. St Steph Ho Ox 70. **d** 73 **p** 74. C Newbold w Dunston *Derby* 73-77; C Leckhampton SS Phil and Jas w Cheltenham St Jas *Glouc* 77-80; V Hebburn St Cuth *Dur* 80-86; R Barlborough *Derby* 86-95; P-in-c Alfreton 95-00; V 00-04; RD Alfreton 02-04; P-in-c Clifton from 04; P-in-c Norbury w Snelston from 04. *Heron House, Chapel Lane, Clifton, Ashbourne DE6 2GL*

DOBBIN, Miss Penelope Jane. b 59. Slough Coll GRSC88. St Alb and Ox Min Course 96. **d** 99 **p** 00. C Bideford, Northam, Westward Ho, Appledore etc *Ex* 99-05; TV from 05. *The Rectory, Weare Gifford, Bideford EX39 4QP* Tel (01237) 429468 E-mail penny@entropytoo.freeserve.co.uk

DOBBINS, Lorraine Sharon. b 72. Ripon Coll Cuddesdon BTh01. **d** 01 **p** 02. C Talbot Village *Sarum* 01-05; TV Preston w Sutton Poyntz and Osmington w Poxwell from 05. *The Vicarage, 58 Littlemoor Road, Weymouth DT3 6AA* Tel (01305) 835921 *or* 815366 E-mail lorrainedobbins@hotmail.com

DOBBS, George Christopher. b 43. Linc Th Coll 66. **d** 68 **p** 69. C Hykeham *Linc* 68-71; Asst Master Heneage Sch Grimsby 71-78; Perm to Offic *S'well* 78-80; TV Chelmsley Wood *Birm* 80-84; TV Rochdale *Man* 84-99; V Sudden St Aidan from 00; C Castleton Moor from 00. *St Aidan's Vicarage, 498 Manchester Road, Rochdale OL11 3HE* Tel (01706) 631812 E-mail g3rjv@gqpr.demon.co.uk

DOBBS, Matthew Joseph. b 62. St Mich Coll Llan BTh04. **d** 04 **p** 05. C Llantwit Major *Llan* from 04. *Minas Tirith, 42 Llanmead Gardens, Rhoose, Barry CF62 3HX* Tel (01446) 719508 E-mail matthew@mdobbs.freeserve.co.uk

DOBBS, Michael John. b 48. Linc Th Coll 74. **d** 77 **p** 78. C Warsop *S'well* 77-82; V Worksop St Paul 82-89; P-in-c Mansfield St Mark 89-03; V Kirk Hallam *Derby* from 03. *The Vicarage, 71 Ladywood Road, Ilkeston DE7 4NF* Tel 0115-932 2402

DOBELL, Richard Frank. b 53. Ex Univ BA83 PGCE84 ARCO83. WMMTC 96. **d** 99 **p** 00. Asst Master Alcester Gr Sch 85-02; Bursar from 02; NSM Alveston *Cov* 99-03; NSM Alcester and Arrow w Oversley and Weethley from 03. *40 Fairwater Crescent, Alcester B49 6RB* Tel (01789) 762584 *or* 762494

DOBLE, Mrs Maureen Mary Thompson. b 44. RGN65. S Dios Minl Tr Scheme CECM93. **d** 93 **p** 94. NSM Kingston St Mary w Broomfield etc *B & W* from 93. *Rosebank, Lyngford Lane, Taunton TA2 7LL* Tel (01823) 286772

DOBLE, Peter. b 29. Univ of Wales (Cardiff) BA51 Fitzw Coll Cam BA54 MA58 St Edm Hall Ox MA68 Leeds Univ PhD92. Wesley Ho Cam 52. **d** 55 **p** 58. In Ch of S India 55-60; In Meth Ch 60-64; Hd of RE Qu Mary Sch Lytham St Annes *Blackb* 64-67; Lect RS Culham Coll Abingdon *Ox* 67-69; Sen Lect 69-74; Prin Lect and Hd Relig Studies 74-80; Perm to Offic *York* from 80; Dir York RE Cen 80-94; Sen Fell Th and RS Leeds Univ *Ripon* 95-98; Hon Lect from 98. *6 Witham Drive, Huntington, York YO32 3YD* Tel (01904) 761288 E-mail peter.doble@btinternet.com

DOBSON, Christopher John. b 62. Univ of Wales (Abth) BA83. Wycliffe Hall Ox BA88. **d** 89 **p** 90. C Biggin Hill *Roch* 89-92; C Tunbridge Wells St Jas w St Phil 92-95; USPG Zimbabwe 95-99; V Paddock Wood *Roch* from 00. *The Vicarage, 169 Maidstone Road, Paddock Wood, Tonbridge TN12 6DZ* Tel and fax (01892) 833917 *or* tel 837617 E-mail cdobson@supanet.com

DOBSON, Geoffrey Norman. b 46. ACP70. Leeds Univ CertEd68 BA77 Open Univ BA73. Wells Th Coll 71. **d** 74 **p** 75. C S Woodford H Trin CD *Chelmsf* 74-76; Colchester Adnry Youth Chapl 76-78; C Halstead St Andr w H Trin and Greenstead Green 76-78; Asst Dir Educn (Youth) *Carl* 78-82; P-in-c Kirkandrews-on-Eden w Beaumont and Grinsdale 78-82; V Illingworth *Wakef* 82-86; V Roxton w Gt Barford *St Alb* 86-93; Chapl N Man Health Care NHS Trust 93-98; P-in-c Newton Heath St Wilfrid and St Anne *Man* 93-97; C Newton Heath 97-98; P-in-c Alconbury w Alconbury Weston *Ely* 98-00; P-in-c Buckworth 98-00; P-in-c Gt w Lt Stukeley 98-00; Perm to Offic from 02. *30 Lees Lane, Southoe, Huntingdon PE19 5YG* Tel (01480) 475474

DOBSON, John Richard. b 64. Van Mildert Coll Dur BA87. Ripon Coll Cuddesdon 87. **d** 89 **p** 90. C Benfieldside *Dur* 89-92; C Darlington St Cuth 92-96; C-in-c Blackwell All SS and Salutation CD 96-98; V Blackwell All SS and Salutation from 98; P-in-c Coniscliffe from 04; AD Darlington from 01. *104 Blackwell Lane, Darlington DL3 8QQ* Tel (01325) 354503 E-mail john.dobson@durham.anglican.org

DOBSON, Kenneth Shuard. b 26. Oak Hill Th Coll 53. **d** 56 **p** 57. C Hatcham St Jas *S'wark* 56-59; C Wimbledon 59-62; R W Lynn *Nor* 62-66; Lic to Offic 66-68; P-in-c Deopham w Hackford 68-74; Chapl Eccles Hall Sch Quidenham 74-78; R Elvedon *St E* 78-84; R Eriswell 78-84; R Icklingham 78-84; RD Mildenhall 80-81; RD Newmarket 80-81; rtd 84; Chapl Wayland Hosp Norfolk 84-87; Lic to Offic *Nor* 84-97. *St Joseph's, 14 Salthouse Close, Crofty, Swansea SA4 3SN* Tel (01792) 851652

DOBSON, Philip Albert. b 52. Lanc Univ BA73 CertEd74. Trin Coll Bris 89. **d** 89 **p** 90. C Grenoside *Sheff* 89-92; C Cove St Jo *Guildf* 92-93; TV 93-96; V Camberley St Martin Old Dean from 96. *St Martin's Vicarage, Hampshire Road, Camberley GU15 4DW* Tel (01276) 23958 E-mail philip.dobson@ntlworld.com

DOBSON, Stuart Joseph. b 51. Westmr Coll Ox BA85. Chich Th Coll 86. **d** 88 **p** 89. C Costessey *Nor* 88-90; C Chaddesden St Phil *Derby* 90-92; C Friern Barnet St Jas *Lon* 92-93; TV Plymouth Em, Efford and Laira *Ex* 93-96; P-in-c Laira 96; R Withington St Crispin *Man* 96-98; P-in-c Beguildy and Heyope *S & B* 98-00; P-in-c Llangynllo and Bleddfa 99-00; TV Bruton and Distr *B & W* 00-01. *Whitecroft, Ulsta, Yell, Shetland ZE2 9BG* Tel (01957) 722391 E-mail stuart.dobson@btinternet.com

DOCHERTY, William Sales Hill. b 54. Callendar Park Coll of Educn Falkirk DipEd75 Open Univ BA96. TISEC 98. **d** 05. C Broughty Ferry *Bre* from 05. *27 Seafield Road, Broughty Ferry, Dundee DD5 3AH* Tel (01382) 731914 E-mail therevdoc@btinternet.com

✠**DOCKER, The Rt Revd Ivor Colin.** b 25. Birm Univ BA46 St Cath Soc Ox BA49 MA52. Wycliffe Hall Ox 46. **d** 49 **p** 50 **c** 75. C Normanton *Wakef* 49-52; C Halifax St Jo Bapt 52-54; Area Sec (Dios Derby Linc and S'well) CMS 54-58; Metrop Sec (S) 58-59; V Midhurst *Chich* 59-64; RD Midhurst 61-64; R Woolbeding 61-64; V Seaford w Sutton 64-71; RD Seaford 64-71; Can and Preb Chich Cathl 66-91; V Eastbourne St Mary 71-75; RD Eastbourne 71-75; Suff Bp Horsham 75-84; Area Bp Horsham 84-91; rtd 91; Asst Bp Ex from 91. *Braemar, Bradley Road, Bovey Tracey, Newton Abbot TQ13 9EU* Tel (01626) 832468

DODD, Alan Henry. b 42. Man Univ BA70 MA79. Chich Th Coll 82. **d** 82 **p** 83. C Fareham H Trin *Portsm* 82-84; TV 84-89; V Osmotherley w Harlsey and Ingleby Arncliffe *York* from 89; RD Mowbray 02-04; Chapl Northallerton Health Services NHS Trust from 92. *Orchard House, Ingleby Arncliffe, Northallerton DL6 3LN* Tel (01609) 882189

DODD, Andrew Patrick. b 68. Hatf Poly BEng91 Selw Coll Cam BTh00. Westcott Ho Cam 97. **d** 00 **p** 01. C New Addington *S'wark* 00-04; R Newington St Mary from 04. *The Rectory, 57 Kennington Park Road, London SE11 4JQ* Tel (020) 7735 1894 E-mail apdodd@fish.co.uk

DODD, Charles Nathanael. b 30. Westcott Ho Cam. **d** 57 **p** 58. C Milton *Portsm* 57-62; Australia 62-91; P-in-c Bretby w Newton Solney *Derby* 91-96; Bp's Ind Adv 91-00; rtd 00; Perm to Offic *Lon* from 02. *6 Sylvia Avenue, Hatch End, Pinner HA5 4QE* Tel (020) 8428 3275 E-mail chrl@popanva.freeserve.co.uk

DODD, James Henry Birchenough. b 25. CPsychol AFBPsS Ox Univ MA. Westcott Ho Cam 85. **d** 85 **p** 86. NSM Epping Upland *Chelmsf* 85-95; NSM Epping Distr 95-96; Perm to Offic from 96. *The Chequers, Epping Upland, Epping CM16 6PH* Tel (01992) 572561

DODD, Jane. b 33. Loughb Univ ALA51 FLA51. LNSM course 97. **d** 98 **p** 99. OLM Wroxham w Hoveton and Belaugh *Nor* from 98. *Locheil, Tunstead Road, Hoveton, Norwich NR12 8QN* Tel (01603) 782509

DODD, Mrs Jean. b 47. LNSM course 95. **d** 98 **p** 99. OLM Irlam *Man* from 98. *75 Harewood Road, Manchester M44 6DL* Tel 0161-775 9125

DODD, John Dudley. b 15. Liv Univ BA36 Lon Univ BD51 DipEd54. Westcott Ho Cam 54. **d** 54 **p** 55. C Jersey St Helier *Win* 54-78; rtd 78; P-in-c Jersey Gouray St Martin *Win* 78-93; NSM Jersey St Luke 94-96; Perm to Offic from 96. *10 Clos de Gouray, Gorey Village, Jersey JE3 9EN* Tel (01534) 854713

DODD, John Stanley. b 24. Huron Coll Ontario 46. **d** 50 **p** 51. C Kitchener Canada 50-52; Leeds St Jo Ev *Ripon* 52-54; C High

Harrogate Ch Ch 54-58; V Stainburn 58-65; V Weeton 58-64; V Meanwood 65-89; rtd 89; Perm to Offic *Ripon* from 89. *3 Shawdene, Burton Crescent, Leeds LS6 4DN* Tel 0113-278 9069

DODD, Malcolm Ogilvie. b 46. Dur Univ BSc67 Loughb Univ MSc90. Edin Th Coll 67. **d** 70 **p** 71. C Hove All SS *Chich* 70-73; C Crawley 73-78; P-in-c Rusper 79-83; Chapl Brighton Coll Jun Sch 83; Chapl Stancliffe Hall Sch 84-97; rtd 01. *Résidence Dodd, 210 Chemin des Villecrozes, Buis les Baronnies, 26170 Drome, France* Tel (0033) (4) 7528 0599 E-mail m.et.j.dodd@wanadoo.fr

DODD, Michael Christopher. b 33. Ch Coll Cam BA55 MA59. Ridley Hall Cam 57. **d** 59 **p** 60. C Stechford *Birm* 59-62; V Quinton Road W St Boniface 62-72; TV Paston *Pet* 72-77; TR Hodge Hill *Birm* 77-89; rtd 90; Perm to Offic *Birm* from 90. *39 Regency Gardens, Birmingham B14 4JS* Tel 0121-474 6945

DODD, Canon Peter Curwen. b 33. St Jo Coll Cam BA57 FRSA93. Linc Th Coll 58 Wm Temple Coll Rugby 59. **d** 60 **p** 61. C Eastwood *Sheff* 60-63; Ind Chapl 63-67; Ind Chapl *Newc* 67-98; RD Newc E 78-83 and 92-95; Hon Can Newc Cathl 82-98; rtd 98; Perm to Offic *Newc* from 98. *Glenesk, 26 The Oval, Benton, Newcastle upon Tyne NE12 9PP* Tel 0191-266 1293

DODDS, Alan Richard. b 46. Greenwich Univ BA92 K Coll Lon MA94. **d** 95 **p** 96. C Deal St Geo *Cant* 95-99; C-in-c Deal, The Carpenter's Arms 98-99; Prin OLM Course 99-01; TV Cullompton, Willand, Uffculme, Kentisbeare etc *Ex* from 02. *The Vicarage, Bridge Street, Uffculme, Cullompton EX15 3AX* Tel (01884) 841001 E-mail alan.and.chris@tesco.net

DODDS, Brian Martin. b 37. AKC62. **d** 63 **p** 64. C Morpeth *Newc* 63-67; Guyana 67-71; V Willington *Newc* 71-74; TV Brayton *York* 75-79; V Gravelly Hill *Birm* 79-83; V Winterton *Linc* 83-85; V Winterton Gp 85-90; V Gainsborough St Jo 90-96; V Morton 95-96; R Walesby 96-00; rtd 00; Perm to Offic *Linc* from 01. *69 Pennell Street, Lincoln LN5 7TD* Tel (01522) 512593 E-mail bmdodds@talk21.com

DODDS, Preb Graham Michael. b 58. York Univ PGCE81 Liv Univ MA01 LTCL80 GTCL80. Trin Coll Bris 84. **d** 84 **p** 85. C Reigate St Mary *S'wark* 84-91; P-in-c Bath Walcot *B & W* 91-93; R 93-96; Lay Tr Adv from 96; Dir Reader Studies from 96; Asst Dir Min Development from 01; Preb Wells Cathl from 03. *25 Wood Close, Wells BA5 2GA* Tel (01749) 677531 *or* 670777 Fax 674240 E-mail general@bathwells.anglican.org

DODDS, Canon Neil Sutherland. b 35. ARCO59 Keble Coll Ox BA59 DipTh61 MA63. Linc Th Coll 60. **d** 62 **p** 63. C Handsworth St Jas *Birm* 62-65; V Highters Heath 65-75; V Olton 75-00; RD Solihull 79-89; Hon Can Birm Cathl 82-00; rtd 00; Perm to Offic *Birm* and *Cov* from 00. *29 Stuart Close, Warwick CV34 6AQ* Tel (01926) 402909 E-mail neil.jean.dodds@talk21.com

DODDS, Canon Norman Barry. b 43. Open Univ BA. CITC 73. **d** 76 **p** 77. C Ballynafeigh St Jude *D & D* 76-80; I Belfast St Mich *Conn* from 80; Chapl HM Pris Belf from 84; Can Belf Cathl from 98. *5 Sunningdale Park, Belfast BT14 6RU* Tel and fax (028) 9071 5463 E-mail doddscavehill@yahoo.com

DODDS, Peter. b 35. WMMTC 88 Qu Coll Birm 88. **d** 91 **p** 92. NSM Hartshill *Cov* 91-93; NSM Nuneaton St Mary 94-95; Hon Chapl Geo Eliot Hosp NHS Trust Nuneaton from 95; Hon Chapl Mary Ann Evans Hospice from 95; NSM Camp Hill w Galley Common *Cov* 99-01; Perm to Offic from 02. *Wem House, 51 Magyar Crescent, Nuneaton CV11 4SQ* Tel (024) 7638 4061

DODGE, Robin Dennis. b 58. Cornell Univ NY BA80 Boston Univ JD83. Virginia Th Sem MDiv99. **d** 98 **p** 99. C Arlington St Mary USA 98-02; C Bris St Mary Redcliffe w Temple etc *Bris* 02-05; R Washington St Dav USA from 05. *St David's Episcopal Church, 5150 Macomb Street NW, Washington, DC 20016, USA* Tel (001) (202) 966 2093 Fax 966 3437

DODGSON, Ronald. b 27. Sarum & Wells Th Coll 72. **d** 74 **p** 75. Sub Warden Barn Fellowship Blandford Forum 74-85; Hon C Canford Magna *Sarum* 78-85; C Hartley Wintney, Elvetham, Winchfield etc *Win* 85-92; rtd 92. *84 Tavistock Road, Fleet, Aldershot GU51 4EZ* Tel (01252) 624991

DODHIA, Hitesh Kishorilal. b 57. Cranmer Hall Dur 85. **d** 88 **p** 89. C Leamington Priors All SS *Cov* 88-91; Chapl HM YOI Glen Parva 91-92; Asst Chapl 94-98; Chapl HM Pris Roch 92-94; Chapl HM Pris The Mount 98-01; Chapl HM Pris Wormwood Scrubs from 01; Perm to Offic *St Alb* from 02. *HM Prison Wormwood Scrubs, Du Cane Road, London W12 0TU* Tel (020) 8588 3331 E-mail dodhias@hotmail.com

DODSON, Canon Gordon. b 31. Em Coll Cam BA54 MA58 LLB55 LLM01 Barrister 56. Ridley Hall Cam 57. **d** 59 **p** 60. C Belhus Park *Chelmsf* 59-60; C Barking St Marg 60-63; CMS 63-67; C New Malden and Coombe *S'wark* 67-69; V Snettisham *Nor* 69-81; RD Heacham and Rising 76-81; P-in-c Reepham and Hackford w Whitwell and Kerdiston 81-83; P-in-c Salle 81-83; P-in-c Thurning w Wood Dalling 81-83; R Reepham, Hackford w Whitwell, Kerdiston etc 83-94; Hon Can Nor Cathl 85-94; rtd 94; Perm to Offic *Nor* from 94. *Poppygate, 2 The Loke, Cromer NR27 9DH* Tel (01263) 511811

DODSON, James Peter. b 32. Lich Th Coll 58. **d** 61 **p** 62. C Chasetown *Lich* 61-63; C Hednesford 63-68; V Halifax St Hilda *Wakef* 68-76; V Upperthong 76-85; TV York All SS Pavement w St Crux and St Martin etc *York* 85-90; rtd 92; Perm to Offic *Ripon* from 92. *Roseville, Studley Road, Ripon HG4 2QH* Tel (01765) 602053

DODSWORTH, George Brian Knowles. b 34. Univ of Wales DipTh62 Birm Univ DPS66 Open Univ AdDipCrim92 BSc94. St Mich Coll Llan 59. **d** 62 **p** 63. C Kidderminster St Mary *Worc* 62-67; Asst Chapl HM Pris Man 67-68; Chapl HM Pris Eastchurch 68-70; Chapl HM Pris Wakef 70-74; Chapl HM Pris Wormwood Scrubs 74-83; Asst Chapl Gen of Pris (SE) 83-90; Asst Chapl Gen of Pris (HQ) 90-94; Chapl HM Pris Brixton 94-95; Lic to Offic *Lon* 83-94 and *S'wark* from 94; rtd 99. *19 Farnsworth Court, West Parkside, London SE10 0QF* Tel and fax (020) 8305 0283 E-mail brian.gbkd@lineone.net

DOE, Martin Charles. b 54. Lon Univ BSc(Econ)75 PGCE87 MA95. St Steph Ho Ox 89. **d** 91 **p** 92. C Portsea St Mary *Portsm* 91-94; Chapl Abbey Grange High Sch Leeds 94-00; Sen Angl Chapl Scarborough and NE Yorks Healthcare NHS Trust from 00. *Scarborough Hospital, Woodlands Drive, Scarborough YO12 6QL* Tel (01723) 342500 E-mail martin.doe@acute.sney.nhs.uk

✠**DOE, The Rt Revd Michael David.** b 47. St Jo Coll Dur BA69 Bath Univ Hon LLD02. Ripon Hall Ox 69. **d** 72 **p** 73 **c** 94. C St Helier *S'wark* 72-76; Youth Sec BCC 76-81; C-in-c Blackbird Leys CD *Ox* 81-88; V Blackbird Leys 88-89; RD Cowley 86-89; Soc Resp Adv *Portsm* 89-94; Can Res Portsm Cathl 89-94; Suff Bp Swindon *Bris* 94-04; Gen Sec USPG from 04; Hon Asst Bp S'wark from 04. *USPG, Partnership House, 157 Waterloo Road, London SE1 8XA* Tel (020) 7928 8681 Fax 7928 3713 E-mail michaeld@uspg.org.uk

DOE, Mrs Priscilla Sophia. b 41. LRAM61. SEITE 97. **d** 00 **p** 01. NSM Maidstone All SS and St Phil w Tovil *Cant* from 00. *Mount St Laurence, High Street, Cranbrook TN17 3EW* Tel (01580) 712330

DOEL, Patrick Stephen. b 71. Wycliffe Hall Ox BA03. **d** 03 **p** 04. C Blackheath St Jo *S'wark* from 03. *Flat A, 15 St John's Park, London SE3 7TD* Tel (020) 8305 0520 E-mail steve.doel@ntlworld.com

DOGGETT, Margaret Ann. b 36. Open Univ BA78 Homerton Coll Cam PGCE79. LNSM course 94. **d** 96 **p** 97. OLM Pulham Market, Pulham St Mary and Starston *Nor* 96-99; OLM Dickleburgh and The Pulhams 99-01; rtd 02; Perm to Offic *Nor* from 02. *Antares, Station Road, Pulham St Mary, Diss IP21 4QT* Tel and fax (01379) 676662 Mobile 07710-621547 E-mail john.doggett@btinternet.com

DOHERTY, Mrs Christine. b 46. SEN72. STETS 97. **d** 00 **p** 01. NSM Framfield *Chich* 00-03; C Seaford w Sutton from 03. *St Luke's House, 16 Saltwood Road, Seaford BN25 3SP* Tel (01323) 892969 E-mail christinedoherty@chyngton.fsnet.co.uk

DOHERTY, Deana Rosina Mercy. b 21. St Aid Coll Dur BA55. **dss** 82 **d** 87 **p** 94. Sutton St Jas and Wawne *York* 82-95; Par Dn 87-94; C 94-95; Perm to Offic 95-99; rtd 98. *18 Gerard Road, Weston-super-Mare BS23 2RF* Tel (01934) 429149

DOHERTY, Terence William. b 30. Shoreditch Coll Lon TCert St Jo Coll Dur BA56. Ripon Hall Ox 56. **d** 58 **p** 59. C Church Stretton *Heref* 58-60; C Halesowen *Worc* 60-62; Lic to Offic 62-64 and 69-78; R Hagley 64-69; Warden Dioc Conf Cen *Ches* 69-78; Lic to Offic *B & W* 70-78; TR Sutton St Jas and Wawne *York* 78-99; rtd 99. *18 Gerard Road, Weston-super-Mare BS23 2RF* Tel (01934) 429149

DOHERTY, Thomas Alexander. b 48. Chich Th Coll 73. **d** 76 **p** 77. V Choral Derry Cathl *D & R* 76-79; C Llandaff w Capel Llanilltern *Llan* 79-80; PV Llan Cathl 80-84; V Penmark w Porthkerry 84-90; R Merthyr Dyfan 90-02; V Margam from 02. *Margam Vicarage, 59A Bertha Road, Margam, Port Talbot SA13 2AP* Tel (01639) 891067

DOICK, Paul Stephen James. b 70. Ripon Coll Cuddesdon 03. **d** 05. C Hove *Chich* from 05. *30 Bigwood Avenue, Hove BN3 6FQ* Tel (01273) 725811 Mobile 07742-868602 E-mail p.doick@btinternet.com

DOIDGE, Charles William. b 44. Univ Coll Lon BSc65 MSc67 PhD72. EMMTC 93. **d** 93 **p** 94. NSM Blaby *Leic* 93-96; P-in-c Willoughby Waterleys, Peatling Magna etc 96-04; rtd 04. *21 Brunel Mews, Solsbro Road, Torquay TQ2 6QA* Tel (01803) 690548 E-mail doidge@dmu.ac.uk

DOIDGE, Valerie Gladys. b 49. STETS 98. **d** 01 **p** 02. NSM St Leonards St Ethelburga *Chich* 01-04; C from 04. *6 Collinswood Drive, St Leonards-on-Sea TN38 0NU* Tel (01424) 425651 E-mail valrod@rdoidge.freeserve.co.uk

DOIG, Allan George. b 51. Univ of BC BA69 K Coll Cam BA73 MA80 PhD82 FSA98. Ripon Coll Cuddesdon 86. **d** 88 **p** 89. C Abingdon *Ox* 88-91; Chapl LMH Ox from 91; Fell from 96; Select Preacher *Ox* 95-96. *Lady Margaret Hall, Oxford OX2 6QA* Tel (01865) 274300 Fax 511069 E-mail allan.doig@lmh.ox.ac.uk

DOLAN, Miss Louise. b 68. St Paul's Cheltenham BA89 Reading Univ PGCE90. Aston Tr Scheme 92 Linc Th Coll 94 Westcott Ho Cam MA95. **d** 96 **p** 97. C N Stoneham *Win* 96-99. *19 Ipswich Grove, Norwich NR2 2LU* Tel (01603) 469865

DOLBY, Mrs Christine Teresa. b 54. Nottm Univ MA01 SRN80. EMMTC 98. **d** 01 **p** 02. C Cropwell Bishop w Colston Bassett, Granby etc *S'well* from 01. *The Curate's House, 4 Granby Hill, Granby, Nottingham NG13 9PQ* Tel (01949) 850127 Mobile 07818-123136 E-mail chri270@aol.com

DOLL, Peter Michael. b 62. Yale Univ BA84 Ch Ch Ox DPhil89. Cuddesdon Coll BA94 DipMin95. **d** 95 **p** 96. C Cowley St Jo *Ox* 95-99; Chapl Worc Coll Ox 98-02; TV Abingdon *Ox* from 02. *39 The Motte, Abingdon OX14 3NZ* Tel (01235) 520297

DOLLERY, Anne Mary Elizabeth. b 55. Hull Univ BA78. Ridley Hall Cam 02. **d** 04. C Thundersley *Chelmsf* from 04. *14 Grangeway, Benfleet SS7 3RP* Tel (01268) 771047 E-mail annedollery@yahoo.co.uk

DOLMAN, Derek Alfred George Gerrit. b 40. ALCD64. **d** 64 **p** 65. C St Alb St Paul *St Alb* 65-68; C Bishopwearmouth St Gabr *Dur* 68-72; R Jarrow Grange 72-80; V New Catton St Luke *Nor* 80-98; V New Catton St Luke w St Aug 98-00; R S Croxton Gp *Leic* from 00. *The Rectory, 19 Main Street, South Croxton, Leicester LE7 3RJ* Tel (01664) 840245

DOMINIC MARK, Brother. *See* IND, Dominic Mark

DOMINY, Canon Peter John. b 36. Qu Coll Ox BA60 MA64 Aber Univ MLitt83. Oak Hill Th Coll 60. **d** 62 **p** 63. C Bedworth *Cov* 62-66; Nigeria 67-84; Sudan United Miss 67-72; V Jos St Piran 72-84; R Broadwater St Mary *Chich* 84-92; TR 92-98; P-in-c Danehill 98-99; V 99-03; Can and Preb Chich Cathl 93-03; RD Uckfield 00-03; rtd 03; Perm to Offic *Sarum* from 03. *5 St Nicholas Gardens, Durweston, Blandford Forum DT11 0QH* Tel (01258) 450975

DOMMETT, Canon Richard Radmore. b 19. St Jo Coll Ox BA41 MA45. Wells Th Coll 41. **d** 43 **p** 44. C E Dulwich St Jo *S'wark* 43-48; C Peckham St Jo 48-52; V Clapham St Pet 52-60; R Caister *Nor* 60-81; P-in-c Saxthorpe and Corpusty 81-85; P-in-c Oulton SS Pet and Paul 81-85; P-in-c Blickling w Ingworth 81-85; P-in-c Heydon w Irmingland 82-85; Hon Can Nor Cathl 77-85; rtd 85; Perm to Offic *Nor* and *St E* from 85. *14 Norwich Road, Halesworth IP19 8HN* Tel (01986) 873778

DOMMETT, Simon Paul. b 58. Warwick Univ BSc79. St Jo Coll Nottm MA99. **d** 99 **p** 00. C Weston Favell *Pet* 99-02; P-in-c Gt w Lt Harrowden and Orlingbury from 02; P-in-c Isham w Pytchley from 05. *The Vicarage, 18 Kings Lane, Little Harrowden, Wellingborough NN9 5BL* Tel (01933) 678225 E-mail thedommetts@fish.co.uk

DONAGHY, Paul Robert Blount. b 56. Guildf Dioc Min Course 97. **d** 00 **p** 01. OLM Goldsworth Park *Guildf* from 00. *5 Knightswood, Woking GU21 3PU* Tel (01483) 835503 E-mail p.donaghy1@ntlworld.com

DONALD, Andrew William. b 19. St Jo Coll Morpeth 47 ACT ThL50. **d** 49 **p** 50. C Claremont Australia 49-50; C Perth Cathl 50-52; R Wyalkatchem 52-56; Perm to Offic *Lon* 57-58; Chapl Gothenburg *Eur* 58-65; Chapl Lausanne 65-68; Asst P Mt Lawley Australia 68-70; R Bellevue and Darlington 70-79; R Toodyay and Goomalling 79-84; rtd 84. *Eriswell, 18A Cobham Way, Westfield Park, W Australia 6111* Tel (0061) (8) 9390 8425

DONALD, Brother. *See* GREEN, Donald Pentney

DONALD, Dennis Curzon. b 38. Oak Hill Th Coll 68. **d** 70 **p** 71. C Carl St Jo *Carl* 70-73; Lic to Offic 73-77; Warden Blaithwaite Ho Chr Conf Cen Wigton 73-90; Chapl Cumberland Infirmary 85-92; Chapl Eden Valley Hospice Carl 92-98; Perm to Offic *Carl* from 77; rtd 03. *Windyfell, Raughton Head, Carlisle CA5 7DG* Tel (01697) 476246

DONALD, Robert Francis. b 49. St Jo Coll Nottm BTh75 LTh. **d** 75 **p** 76. C New Barnet St Jas *St Alb* 75-79; C St Alb St Paul 79-86; C St Alb St Mary Marshalswick 86-87; Lic to Offic from 87; Dir Chr Alliance Housing Assn Ltd 87-98. *24 Meadowcroft, St Albans AL1 1UD* Tel (01727) 841647 Mobile 07973-208289

DONALD, Rosemary Anne. b 52. STETS 99. **d** 02 **p** 03. NSM Blendworth w Chalton w Idsworth *Portsm* from 02. *3 Havant Road, Horndean, Waterlooville PO8 0DB* Tel (023) 9259 1719 E-mail rdonald@fish.co.uk

DONALD, Steven. b 55. CertEd76 Hull Univ MA99. Oak Hill Th Coll BA88. **d** 88 **p** 89. C Cheadle All Hallows *Ches* 88-91; C Ardsley *Sheff* 91; V Kendray 92-99; P-in-c Chadderton Ch Ch *Man* 99-03; V 03-05; V Carl St Jo *Carl* from 05. *St John's Vicarage, London Road, Carlisle CA1 2QQ* Tel (01228) 521601 E-mail stevedon1@aol.com

DONALD, William. b 30. Lon Univ DipTh61. Tyndale Hall Bris 58. **d** 61 **p** 62. C Stapenhill w Cauldwell *Derby* 61-63; Perm to Offic *Ox* 63-66; Lic to Offic *Bris* 66-70; C Cheltenham St Mark *Glouc* 70-77; C Glouc St Jas 77-82; Lic to Offic 82-95; rtd 95; Perm to Offic *Glouc* from 95. *82 Forest View Road, Gloucester GL4 0BY* Tel (01452) 506993

DONALDSON, Miss Elizabeth Anne. b 55. Univ of Wales (Ban) BSc76 Surrey Univ MSc80 Nottm Univ BA82. St Jo Coll Nottm 80. **dss** 83 **d** 87 **p** 94. Guildf Ch Ch *Guildf* 83-86; Cuddington 86-90; C 87-90; C Keresley and Coundon *Cov* 90-99; V Gt Amwell w St Margaret's and Stanstead Abbots *St Alb* from 00. *The Vicarage, 25 Hoddesdon Road, Stanstead Abbotts, Ware SG12 8EG* Tel (01920) 870115 Pager 07666-545248 E-mail vicar@3churches.net *or* anne.donaldson@ntlworld.com

DONALDSON, Mrs Janet Elizabeth. b 53. GTCL74 Whitelands Coll Lon CertEd75. EAMTC 95. **d** 98 **p** 99. NSM Tolleshunt Knights w Tiptree and Gt Braxted *Chelmsf* 98-02; V Knights and Hospitallers Par from 02. *The Rectory, Church Street, Great Maplestead, Halstead CO9 2RG* Tel (01787) 463106 E-mail janet@amdonaldson.freeserve.co.uk

DONALDSON, Malcolm Alexander. b 48. Cranmer Hall Dur 84. **d** 86 **p** 87. C Heworth H Trin *York* 86-89; Chapl York Distr Hosp 86-89; C Marfleet *York* 89-90; TV 90-96; R Collyhurst *Man* 96-05; rtd 05. *12 Clove Court, Tweedmouth, Berwick-upon-Tweed TD15 2FJ*

DONALDSON, Maurice Coburne. b 19. Univ of Wales BA40 Lon Univ BD47. St Mich Coll Llan 41. **d** 42 **p** 43. C Blaenau Ffestiniog *Ban* 42-44; C Conwy w Gyffin 44-47; C Llandysilio 47-49; P-in-c Llanfachraeth 49-53; V Ynyscynhaearn w Penmorfa 53-57; V Ysbyty Ystwyth w Ystradmeurig *St D* 57-70; V Ruabon *St As* 70-77; V Abergele 77-84; rtd 84; Perm to Offic *St As* from 84; Perm to Offic *Ban* from 84. *7 Llys Mair, Bryn Eithinog, Bangor LL57 2LA* Tel (01248) 354589

DONALDSON, Canon Roger Francis. b 50. Jes Coll Ox BA71 MA75. Westcott Ho Cam 72. **d** 74 **p** 75. C Mold *St As* 74-78; V Denio w Abererch *Ban* 78-95; R Llanbeblig w Caernarfon and Betws Garmon etc from 95; AD Arfon from 04; Hon Can Ban Cathl from 04. *The Rectory, 4 Ffordd Menai, Caernarfon LL55 1LF* Tel (01286) 673750

DONALDSON, William Richard. b 56. St Cath Coll Cam BA78 MA81. Ridley Hall Cam 79. **d** 82 **p** 83. C Everton St Sav w St Cuth *Liv* 82-85; C Reigate St Mary *S'wark* 85-89; V Easton H Trin w St Gabr and St Lawr and St Jude *Bris* 89-99; V W Ealing St Jo w St Jas *Lon* from 99. *23 Culmington Road, London W13 9NJ* Tel (020) 8566 3462 *or* 8566 3507 E-mail will.donaldson@stjohnsealing.org.uk

DONCASTER, Archdeacon of. *See* FITZHARRIS, The Ven Robert Aidan

DONCASTER, Suffragan Bishop of. *See* ASHTON, The Rt Revd Cyril Guy

DONE, Mrs Margaret. b 43. LNSM course 84 Linc Th Coll 91. **d** 92 **p** 94. OLM Coningsby w Tattershall *Linc* from 92. *43 Park Lane, Coningsby, Lincoln LN4 4SW* Tel (01526) 343013

DONE, Nigel Anthony. b 68. Wye Coll Lon BSc89. St Jo Coll Dur BA98. **d** 98 **p** 99. C Pilton w Croscombe, N Wootton and Dinder *B & W* 98-02; R Hardington Vale from 02. *The Rectory, Vicarage Lane, Norton St Philip, Bath BA2 7LY* Tel (01373) 834447 E-mail nigel.done@btinternet.com

DONEGAN-CROSS, Guy William. b 68. St Aid Coll Dur BA90. Trin Coll Bris BA98. **d** 99 **p** 00. C Swindon Ch Ch *Bris* 99-03; V Saltburn-by-the-Sea *York* from 03. *The Vicarage, Greta Street, Saltburn-by-the-Sea TS12 1LS* Tel (01287) 622007 E-mail guy@donegan-cross.freeserve.co.uk

DONELLA, Sister. *See* MATHIE, Patricia Jean

DONEY, Malcolm Charles. b 50. Lon Univ BA71 Middx Univ BA05. NTMTC 02. **d** 05. NSM Tufnell Park St Geo and All SS *Lon* from 05. *26 Womersley Road, London N8 9AN* Tel (020) 8340 2060 Mobile 07812-566520 E-mail malcolmdoney@blueyonder.co.uk

DONKERSLEY, Mrs Christine Mary. b 44. STETS 98. **d** 01 **p** 02. NSM Baltonsborough w Butleigh, W Bradley etc *B & W* from 01. *Pinewood, Church Street, Barton St David, Somerton TA11 6BX* Tel (01458) 850695 Fax as telephone E-mail cm.donkersley@route56.co.uk

DONKIN, Robert. b 50. St Mich Coll Llan 71. **d** 74 **p** 75. C Mountain Ash *Llan* 74-77; C Coity w Nolton 77-79; V Oakwood 79-84; V Aberaman and Abercwmboi 84-91; V Aberaman and Abercwmboi w Cwmaman 91-99; R Penarth w Lavernock 99-04; R Penarth and Llandough from 04. *The Rectory, 13 Hickman Road, Penarth CF64 2AJ* Tel (029) 2070 9463 E-mail robert.donkin@ntlworld.com *or* robert@rectory.fsworld.co.uk

DONNE, Miranda. **d** 04 **p** 05. NSM Whitchurch *Ex* from 04. *Whitchurch House, Whitchurch, Tavistock PL19 9EL* Tel (01822) 614552

DONNELLY, Ms Juliet Ann. b 70. K Coll Lon BD92 AKC92 PGCE93. Ripon Coll Cuddesdon 01. **d** 05. C Bexley St Jo *Roch* from 05. *13 The South Glade, Bexley DA5 3NY* Tel 07910-166491 (mobile) E-mail juliet.blessed@virgin.net

DONNELLY, Trevor Alfred. b 71. K Coll Lon BA93 AKC93. Cuddesdon Coll 94. **d** 97 **p** 98. C Southgate Ch Ch *Lon* 97-01; V Hinchley Wood *Guildf* from 01. *The Vicarage, 98 Manor Road North, Esher KT10 0AE* Tel (020) 8786 6391 E-mail revtrev.blessed@virgin.net

DONOHOE, Olive Mary Rose. b 58. TCD BA79 BTh94 MA95 CPA83. CITC 91. **d** 95 **p** 96. C Bandon Union *C, C & R* 95-98; I Mountmellick w Coolbanagher, Rosenallis etc *M & K* from 98. *The Rectory, Mountmellick, Portlaoise, Co Laois, Irish Republic* Tel (00353) (502) 24143 E-mail revol@elive.ie

DONOVAN, Mrs Rosalind Margaret. b 48. Birm Univ LLB69 Bedf Coll Lon DASS73. St Alb and Ox Min Course 95. **d** 98 **p** 99. NSM Seer Green and Jordans *Ox* 98-03; P-in-c Wexham from 03. *The Rectory, 7 Grangewood, Wexham, Slough SL3 6LP* Tel (01753) 523852 E-mail rosdonovan@tiscali.co.uk

DONOVAN, Mrs Rosemary Ann. b 71. La Sainte Union Coll BTh92 Birm Univ PGCE93. Qu Coll Birm MA01. **d** 01. C Kings Heath *Birm* 01-04; C Moseley St Mary from 04; C Moseley St Anne from 04. *The Vicarage, 15 Park Hill, Birmingham B13 8DU* Tel 0121-449 1071 E-mail rosemary@donovan123.freeserve.co.uk

DONSON, Miss Helen Cripps. b 32. Somerville Coll Ox DipEd55 MA58. Dalton Ho Bris 58 Gilmore Ho 69. **dss** 79 **d** 87. Staines St Pet *Lon* 80-83; Staines St Mary and St Pet 83-90; Par Dn 87-90; Par Dn Herne Bay Ch Ch *Cant* 90-92; rtd 93; Hon Par Dn Bexhill St Aug *Chich* 93-97; Perm to Offic from 97. *2 St Augustine's Close, Cooden Drive, Bexhill-on-Sea TN39 3AZ* Tel (01424) 734640

DOODES, Peter John. b 45. STETS 98. **d** 01. NSM Ninfield and Hooe *Chich* 01-02; NSM Hastings H Trin from 02. *Catslide, The Common, Hooe, Battle TN33 9ET* Tel (01424) 892329 Mobile 07718-302115 E-mail pjdoodes@hotmail.com

DOOGAN, Simon Edward. b 70. Univ of Wales (Abth) LLB92 Univ of Wales (Cardiff) LLM01 TCD BTh97. CITC 94. **d** 97 **p** 98. C Cregagh *D & D* 97-01; Dom Chapl to Bp Horsham *Chich* 01-04; I Aghalee *D & D* from 04. *The Rectory, 39 Soldierstown Road, Aghalee, Craigavon BT67 0ES* Tel (028) 9265 1233 E-mail simon_doogan@hotmail.com

DOOLAN, Leonard Wallace. b 57. St Andr Univ MA79 Ox Univ BA82 MA88. Ripon Coll Cuddesdon 80. **d** 83 **p** 84. C High Wycombe *Ox* 83-85; C Bladon w Woodstock 85-88; C Wootton by Woodstock 85-88; P-in-c 88-90; C Kiddington w Asterleigh 85-88; P-in-c 88-90; P-in-c Glympton 88-90; R Wootton w Glympton and Kiddington 90-91; TR Halesworth w Linstead, Chediston, Holton etc *St E* 91-98; RD Halesworth 95-98; TR Ifield *Chich* from 98. *The Vicarage, Ifield Street, Ifield, Crawley RH11 0NN* Tel (01293) 520187 *or* 520843 Fax 537578 E-mail ifield_parish@lineone.net

DOOR, Hazel Lesley. b 48. Open Univ BSc99. EAMTC 01. **d** 05. C Poitou-Charentes *Eur* from 05. *Fortran, 86400 Linazay, France* Tel (0033) (5) 49 87 71 45 E-mail rev.hazel@wanadoo.fr

DOORES, Miss Jennifer Mary. b 78. Hull Univ BA99 St Jo Coll Dur BA03. Cranmer Hall Dur 01. **d** 04 **p** 05. C Old Swinford Stourbridge *Worc* from 04. *58 Arlington Court, Stourbridge DY8 1NN* Tel (01384) 373286

DOORES, Peter George Herbert. b 46. DipYESTB71 Hull Univ BSc67 Birm Univ PGCE68. Linc Th Coll 92. **d** 92 **p** 93. C N Stoneham *Win* 92-96; V St Leonards and St Ives 96-03; P-in-c Alton St Lawr from 03. *St Lawrence's Vicarage, Church Street, Alton GU34 2BW* Tel (01420) 83234

DORAN, Clive. b 58. St Jo Coll Nottm 99. **d** 01 **p** 02. C Maghull *Liv* from 01. *6 Deyes End, Maghull, Liverpool L31 6DP* Tel 0151-286 3063 E-mail revclive@yahoo.com

DORAN, Edward Roy. b 47. St Jo Coll Nottm. **d** 85 **p** 86. C Roby *Liv* 85-88; V Ravenhead from 88. *St John's Vicarage, Crossley Road, Ravenhead, St Helens WA10 3ND* Tel (01744) 23601 E-mail revroydoran@ravenhead.fsnet.co.uk

DORANS, Robert Marshall. b 47. Open Univ BA82 Ex Univ MEd85 Dur Univ MA96. **d** 01 **p** 02. OLM Longhorsley and Hebron *Newc* from 01. *14 The Grange, Nedderton Village, Bedlington NE22 6BQ* Tel (01670) 832022 *or* 534300 E-mail bdorans@tiscali.co.uk

DORBER, The Very Revd Adrian John. b 52. St Jo Coll Dur BA74 K Coll Lon MTh91. Westcott Ho Cam 76. **d** 79 **p** 80. C Easthampstead *Ox* 79-85; P-in-c Emmer Green 85-88; Chapl Portsm Poly *Portsm* 88-92; Chapl Portsm Univ 92-97; Lect 91-97; Public Orator 92-97; Hon Chapl Portsm Cathl 92-97; P-in-c Brancepeth *Dur* 97-01; Dir Min and Tr from 97; Hon Can Dur Cathl 97-05; Dean Lich from 05. *The Deanery, 16 The Close, Lichfield WS13 7LD* Tel (01543) 306250 Fax 306251 E-mail adrian.dorber@lichfieldcathedral.org

DORCHESTER, Area Bishop of. *See* FLETCHER, The Rt Revd Colin William

DORÉ, Eric George. b 47. S Dios Minl Tr Scheme 87. **d** 90 **p** 91. NSM Hove Bp Hannington Memorial Ch *Chich* 90-92; C Burgess Hill St Andr 92-95; R Frant w Eridge 95-00; V Framfield from 00. *The Vicarage, Framfield, Uckfield TN22 5NH* Tel (01825) 890365 Fax 891064 E-mail ericdore@onetel.com

DOREY, Trevor Eric. b 30. ACIS53. S Dios Minl Tr Scheme 87. **d** 90 **p** 91. NSM E Woodhay and Woolton Hill *Win* 90-96; P-in-c Manaccan w St Anthony-in-Meneage and St Martin *Truro* 96-99; rtd 99; Perm to Offic *Sarum* from 01. *Pear Tree House, 40 Saint Martin's, Marlborough SN8 1AS* Tel (01672) 511958

DORGU, Woyin Karowei. b 58. MB, BS85. Lon Bible Coll BA93 Oak Hill Th Coll DipHE95. **d** 95 **p** 96. C Tollington *Lon* 95-98; C Upper Holloway 98-00; TV from 00. *St John's Vicarage, 51 Tytherton Road, London N19 4PZ* Tel and fax (020) 7272 5309 E-mail karmos.timsim@virgin.net

DORKING, Archdeacon of. *Vacant*

DORKING, Suffragan Bishop of. *See* BRACKLEY, The Rt Revd Ian James

DORLING, Philip Julian. b 69. Edin Univ BSc90. Ripon Coll Cuddesdon 03. **d** 05. C Ulverston St Mary w H Trin *Carl* from 05. *18 Church Walk, Ulverston LA12 7EN* Tel (01229) 586133

DORMANDY, Richard Paul. b 59. Univ Coll Lon BA81 St Edm Ho Cam BA88. Ridley Hall Cam 86. **d** 89 **p** 90. C Sydenham H Trin *S'wark* 89-93; V 93-01; V Westminster St Jas the Less *Lon* from 01. *56 Tachbrook Street, London SW1V 2NA* Tel (020) 7828 9242 *or* 7630 6282 E-mail richard@dormandy.co.uk *or* richard.dormandy@stjtl.org

DORMER, Christopher Robert. b 39. Bris Univ BA61. Lich Th Coll 61. **d** 63 **p** 64. C Sheff St Cecilia Parson Cross *Sheff* 63-67; C Greenford H Cross *Lon* 67-69; Brotherhood of St Barn Australia 69-74; Area Sec (Ireland) USPG 74-75; R Catton *York* 75-78; R Stamford Bridge Gp 78-81; RD Pocklington 80-81; Itinerant Priest *Mor* 81-98; P-in-c Lochalsh 81-98; P-in-c Poolewe 81-98; P-in-c Ullapool 81-98; P-in-c Kishorn 81-98; Miss to Seamen 81-98; Can St Andr Cathl Inverness *Mor* 94-98; R Kelso *Edin* 98-04; Lic to Offic *Mor* from 04. *1 Fraser Place, Ullapool IV26 2UX* Tel (01854) 613373

DORMOR, Duncan James. b 67. Magd Coll Ox BA88 Lon Univ MSc89. Ripon Coll Cuddesdon BA94 DipMin95. **d** 95 **p** 96. C Wolverhampton *Lich* 95-98; Chapl St Jo Coll Cam 98-02; Fell and Dean from 02. *St John's College, Cambridge CB2 1TP* Tel (01223) 338633 E-mail djd28@cam.ac.uk

DORMOR, Preb Duncan Stephen. b 36. St Edm Hall Ox BA60. Cuddesdon Coll 60. **d** 62 **p** 63. C Headington *Ox* 62-66; USA 66-72; R Hertford St Andr *St Alb* 72-88; RD Hertford 77-83; TR Tenbury *Heref* 88-01; R Burford I 88-01; R Burford II w Greete and Hope Bagot 88-01; R Burford III w Lt Heref 88-01; V Tenbury St Mich 94-01; RD Ludlow 96-01; Preb Heref Cathl 99-02; C Tenbury 01-02; C Burford I 01-02; C Burford II w Greete and Hope Bagot 01-02; C Burford III w Lt Heref 01-02; C Tenbury St Mich 01-02; rtd 02; Perm to Offic *Heref* from 02. *Brantwood, Hereford Road, Leominster HR6 8JU* Tel (01568) 610897

DORRINGTON, Brian Goodwin. b 32. Leeds Univ CertEd55. St Deiniol's Hawarden 65. **d** 66 **p** 67. C Poynton *Ches* 66-71; Perm to Offic *Truro* 71-78; Hd Master Veryan Sch Truro 71-84; Hon C Veryan *Truro* 78-84; C N Petherwin 84-87; C Boyton w N Tamerton 84-87; TV Bolventor 87-90; R Kilkhampton w Morwenstow 90-97; RD Stratton 92-97; rtd 97; Perm to Offic *Truro* from 00. *Southcroft, 18 Elm Drive, Bude EX23 8EZ* Tel (01288) 352467

DORRINGTON, Richard Bryan. b 48. Linc Th Coll 79. **d** 81 **p** 82. C Streetly *Lich* 81-84; C Badger 84-85; R 85-88; C Ryton 84-85; R 85-88; C Beckbury 84-85; R 85-88; V Geddington w Weekley *Pet* 88-98; P-in-c Bradworthy *Ex* 98-00; P-in-c Abbots Bickington and Bulkworthy 98-00; R Bradworthy, Sutcombe, Putford etc from 00; RD Holsworthy from 99. *The Rectory, St Peterswell Lane, Bradworthy EX22 7TQ* Tel (01409) 241411 E-mail therector@bradworthy.co.uk

DORSET, Archdeacon of. *See* MAGOWAN, The Ven Alistair James

DORSETT, Mark Richard. b 63. Univ of Wales (Lamp) BA84 MTh86 Birm Univ PhD90. Ripon Coll Cuddesdon 91. **d** 93 **p** 94. C Yardley St Edburgha *Birm* 93-96; Chapl K Sch Worc from 96; Min Can Worc Cathl *Worc* from 96. *12A College Green, Worcester WR1 2LH* Tel (01905) 25837

DOSSOR, John Haley. b 41. Leeds Univ BA62. EAMTC 87. **d** 90 **p** 91. NSM Hadleigh *St E* 90-01; P-in-c Ipswich St Mary at the Elms from 01. *The Vicarage, 68 Black Horse Lane, Ipswich IP1 2EF* Tel (01473) 216484 Mobile 07876-126676 E-mail haley@dossor.org

DOSSOR, Timothy Charles. b 70. Birm Univ BEng94. Ridley Hall Cam BTh99. **d** 99 **p** 00. C Ipswich St Jo *St E* 99-03; Asst Ldr Iwerne Holidays Titus Trust from 03. *31 Southdale Road, Oxford OX2 7SE* Tel (01865) 553226 *or* 310513 Mobile 07748-184503 E-mail tim@dossor.org

DOTCHIN, Andrew Steward. b 56. Federal Th Coll S Africa. **d** 84 **p** 85. S Africa 84-01; C Standerton w Evender 84-87; Asst P St Martin's-in-the-Veld 87-89; R Belgravia St Jo the Divine 89-94; Chapl St Martin's Sch Rosettenville 94-01; TV Blyth Valley *St E* 01-04; P-in-c Whitton and Thurleston w Akenham from 04. *The Rectory, 176 Fircroft Road, Ipswich IP1 6PS* Tel (01473) 741389 Mobile 07814-949828 E-mail andrew.dotchin@stedmundsbury.anglican.org

DOTCHIN, Canon Joan Marie. b 47. NEOC 84. **d** 87 **p** 94. C Newc St Gabr *Newc* 87-92; TD Willington 92-94; TV 94-95; TR 95-03; V Fenham St Jas and St Basil from 03; Hon Can Newc Cathl from 01. *St James and St Basil Vicarage, Wingrove Road North, Newcastle upon Tyne NE4 9EJ* Tel 0191-274 5078 Fax 287 3178 E-mail revj.dotchin@goldserve.net

DOUBLE, Richard Sydney (Brother Samuel). b 47. K Coll Lon BD69 AKC69. St Aug Coll Cant 69. **d** 70 **p** 71. C Walton St Mary *Liv* 70-74; SSF from 75; Guardian Hilfield Friary Dorchester 92-01; Can and Preb Sarum Cathl *Sarum* 95-01; V Cambridge St Benedict *Ely* from 01. *St Francis House, 14 Botolph Lane, Cambridge CB2 3RD* Tel (01223) 353903 E-mail samuelssf@franciscans.org.uk

DOUBTFIRE, Canon Barbara. b 39. LMH Ox BA61 MA65. **d** 91 **p** 94. Par Development Adv *Ox* 88-04; NSM Kidlington w Hampton Poyle 91-04; Hon Can Ch Ch 98-04; rtd 04. *6 Meadow Walk, Woodstock OX20 1NR* Tel (01993) 812095 E-mail spidir@oxford.anglican.org

DOUBTFIRE, Samuel. b 33. Edin Th Coll 63. **d** 66 **p** 66. C Knottingley *Wakef* 66-68; V Ripponden 68-76; V Crosthwaite Keswick *Carl* 76-81; V Barrow St Matt 81-87; R N Reddish *Man* 87-92; rtd 92; Perm to Offic *Bradf* from 92. *Greenacre, Station Road, Threshfield, Skipton BD23 5EP* Tel (01756) 752260

DOUGALL, David Brian. b 23. CBE. Oak Hill Th Coll. **d** 81 **p** 82. C Sandringham w W Newton *Nor* 81-83; P-in-c Fritton St Edm 83-84; R Somerleyton w Ashby 83-84; R Somerleyton w Ashby, Fritton and Herringfleet 84-92; rtd 92; Perm to Offic *Bris* from 92. *Somerley, The Green, Dauntsey, Chippenham SN15 4HY* Tel (01666) 510759

DOUGHTY, The Ven Andrew William. b 56. K Coll Lon BD AKC. Westcott Ho Cam 80. **d** 82 **p** 83. C Alton St Lawr *Win* 82-85; TV Basingstoke 85-91; V Chilworth w N Baddesley 91-95; R Warwick St Mary V Bermuda from 95; Adn Bermuda from 04. *PO Box WK 530, Warwick WK BX, Bermuda* Tel (001) (441) 236 5744 Fax 236 3667 E-mail adoughty@ibl.bm

DOUGLAS, Canon Alexander Joseph. b 18. TCD BA45 MA61. CITC 45. **d** 45 **p** 46. C Belfast St Mary *Conn* 45-49; I Connor St Sav 49-51; I Magheralin *D & D* 51-63; I Orangefield w Moneyreagh 63-86; rtd 86. *6 Rannoch Road, Holywood BT18 0NA* Tel (028) 9042 3661

DOUGLAS, Ann Patricia. b 49. Lon Univ CertEd71. Oak Hill NSM Course 85. **d** 88 **p** 94. Par Dn Chorleywood Ch Ch *St Alb* 88-94; V Oxhey All SS 94-02; TR Woodley *Ox* from 02. *The Rectory, 36 Church Road, Woodley, Reading RG5 4QJ* Tel 0118-969 2316 *or* 969 7956 Mobile 07885-022155 E-mail annidouglas@btopenworld.com

DOUGLAS, Anthony Victor. b 51. St Jo Coll Nottm 74. **d** 76 **p** 77. C Gt Crosby St Luke *Liv* 76-79; TV Fazakerley Em 79-84; TR Speke St Aid 84-90; TR Gt and Lt Coates w Bradley *Linc* 90-97; TR E Ham w Upton Park St Alb *Chelmsf* 97-02; R Holkham w Egmere w Warham, Wells and Wighton *Nor* from 02. *The Rectory, Church Street, Wells-next-the-Sea NR23 1JB* Tel (01328) 710107

DOUGLAS, Charles David. b 29. Leeds Univ BSc50. Linc Th Coll 68. **d** 70 **p** 71. C Royton St Anne *Man* 70-73; V Edenfield 73-83; V Spotland 83-88; P-in-c Calderbrook 88-95; P-in-c Shore 92-95; rtd 95; Perm to Offic *Man* from 95 and *Liv* from 00. *11 Harrison Crescent, Blackrod, Bolton BL6 5EX* Tel (01204) 667595

DOUGLAS, Gavin Allan. b 52. OBE00. St Mich Coll Llan 03. **d** 05. C Week St Mary w Poundstock and Whitstone *Truro* from 05. *4 Market Place, Week St Mary, Holsworthy EX22 6XT* Tel (01288) 341089 E-mail gavinadouglas@yahoo.co.uk

DOUGLAS, Ian Alexander. b 11. St Aug Coll Cant 71. **d** 71 **p** 72. C Palmers Green St Jo *Lon* 71-81; rtd 81; Perm to Offic *Lon* from 82. *105 The Chine, London N21 2EG* Tel (020) 8360 3472

DOUGLAS, Miss Janet Elizabeth. b 60. SS Paul & Mary Coll Cheltenham BEd83. Cranmer Hall Dur 88. **d** 90 **p** 94. Par Dn Yardley St Edburgha *Birm* 90-93; Par Dn Hamstead St Paul 93-94; C 94-00; Perm to Offic 00-04; C Birm St Martin w Bordesley St Andr from 04. *6 Baxter Court, 96 School Road, Moseley, Birmingham B13 9TP* Tel 0121-449 3763

DOUGLAS, John Howard Barclay. b 23. St Jo Coll Dur BA48. Bps' Coll Cheshunt 48. **d** 50 **p** 51. C Hartlepool St Hilda *Dur* 50-53; C Woodhouse *Wakef* 53-55; PC Gateshead St Edm *Dur* 55-60; V Thirkleby w Kilburn and Bagby *York* 60-88; rtd 88; Perm to Offic *York* from 88. *6 St Giles Close, York Road, Thirsk YO7 3BU* Tel (01845) 524573

DOUGLAS, Michael Williamson. b 51. Birm Univ BSc72 Liv Univ PGCE74. Trin Coll Bris 00. **d** 02 **p** 03. C Macclesfield Team Par *Ches* from 02. *7 Brocklehurst Way, Macclesfield SK10 2HY* Tel (01625) 617680 Mobile 07801-817061 E-mail mikedougie@yahoo.co.uk

DOUGLAS, Pamela Jean. *See* WELCH, Mrs Pamela Jean

DOUGLAS, Peter Melvyn. b 47. **d** 96 **p** 97. NSM Prestwick *Glas* 96-01; Chapl HM Pris Dovegate 01-03. *Whinnyknowe, Newmilns KA16 9LR* Tel (01560) 320007

DOUGLAS, Richard Norman Henry. b 37. St Alb and Ox Min Course 94. **d** 97 **p** 98. NSM Watercombe *Sarum* 97-02; rtd 02; Perm to Offic *Sarum* 02-04 and *Ox* from 04. *6 Vale Avenue, Grove, Wantage OX12 7LU* Tel (01235) 767753 E-mail dickandnan@onetel.com

DOUGLAS LANE, Charles Simon Pellew. b 47. BNC Ox MA71 MCIPD79. Oak Hill Th Coll 91. **d** 94 **p** 95. C Whitton St Aug *Lon* 94-97; P-in-c Hounslow W Gd Shep 97-02; V 02-05; TV Riverside *Ox* from 05. *The Vicarage, 55 Welley Road, Wraysbury, Staines TW19 5ER* Tel (01784) 481258 E-mail simondouglaslane@tiscali.co.uk

DOUGLASS, Michael Crone. b 49. Open Univ BA96. NEOC 02. **d** 05. NSM Gosforth St Nic *Newc* from 05. *44 Regent Road, Newcastle upon Tyne NE3 1ED* Tel and fax 0191-285 0977 E-mail m.douglass@blueyonder.co.uk

DOUGLASS, Preb Philip. b 48. Open Univ BA88. St Steph Ho Ox 87. **d** 89 **p** 90. C Peterlee *Dur* 89-92; V Crowan w Godolphin *Truro* 92-97; V Crowan and Treslothan from 98; P-in-c Penponds from 01; Preb St Endellion from 02. *Crowan Vicarage, 37 Trethannas Gardens, Praze, Camborne TR14 0LL* Tel and fax (01209) 831009 E-mail philip@thedouglasses.freeserve.co.uk

DOULIN, Patrick Brian Harry. b 36. Linc Th Coll 67. **d** 70 **p** 71. C Hurstpierpoint *Chich* 70-73; C Albourne 71-73; Australia 73-00; Papua New Guinea from 00. *PO Box 5845, Boroka, Papua New Guinea*

DOULL, Iain Sinclair. b 43. Univ of Wales (Cardiff) DPS88. St Mich Coll Llan 86. **d** 88 **p** 89. C Malpas *Mon* 88-91; P-in-c Newport All SS 91-98; V 98-02; V Newport Ch Ch from 02. *The Vicarage, Christchurch, Newport NP18 1JJ* Tel (01633) 420701

DOULTON, Dick. b 32. St Cath Coll Cam BA60 MA64. Ridley Hall Cam 61. **d** 63 **p** 64. C Gedling *S'well* 63-65; C Danbury *Chelmsf* 65; Lic to Offic *Ox* 88-90; Lic to Offic *L & K* from 90. *Ballygriffin, Kenmare, Killarney, Co Kerry, Irish Republic* Tel (00353) (64) 41743

DOULTON, Roderick John. b 55. Oak Hill Th Coll DipHE93. **d** 93 **p** 94. C Hoddesdon *St Alb* 93-96; P-in-c Caldecote All SS 96-98; P-in-c Old Warden 97-98; V Caldecote, Northill and Old Warden 98-99; TV Macclesfield Team Par *Ches* from 99; Chapl W Park Hosp Macclesfield from 99. *261 Oxford Road, Macclesfield SK11 8JY* Tel (01625) 423851 E-mail roddoulton@aol.com

DOVE, Canon Reginald George James Thomas. b 16. Leeds Univ BA38. Coll of Resurr Mirfield 38. **d** 40 **p** 41. C Blyth St Mary *Newc* 40-43; S Africa 43-52 and from 72; C Orlando and Pimville 43-47; P-in-c Pimville Miss Distr 47-52; Basutoland 52-66; Lesotho 66-72; R Leribe and Dir Hlotse Miss 52-72; Can Maseru 59-72; Asst P Kimberley Cathl 72-74; R Edenvale St Chad 74-88; rtd 88. *PO Box 2263, Edenvale, 1610 South Africa* Tel (0027) (11) 609 4257

DOVE, Richard. b 54. EMMTC DipTh99. **d** 99 **p** 00. NSM Dronfield w Holmesfield *Derby* from 99. *29 Hollins Spring Avenue, Dronfield S18 1RN* Tel (01246) 412502 E-mail rdove1553@aol.com *or* dick.dove@dwhparish.org.uk

DOVER, Suffragan Bishop of. *See* VENNER, The Rt Revd Stephen Squires

DOW, Andrew John Morrison. b 46. Univ Coll Ox BA67 MA71. Oak Hill Th Coll 69. **d** 71 **p** 72. C Watford St Luke *St Alb* 71-74; C Chadderton Ch Ch *Man* 75-78; V Leamington Priors St Paul *Cov* 78-88; V Knowle *Birm* 88-97; RD Solihull 95-97; V Clifton Ch Ch w Em *Bris* 97-04; P-in-c Cheltenham St Mary, St Matt, St Paul and H Trin *Glouc* from 04. *The Rectory, Windrush Cottage, Thorncliffe Drive, Cheltenham GL51 6PY* Tel (01242) 701580 E-mail andrewdow@blueyonder.co.uk

✠DOW, The Rt Revd Geoffrey Graham. b 42. Qu Coll Ox BA63 BSc65 MA68 MSc81 Birm Univ DPS74 Nottm Univ MPhil82. Clifton Th Coll 66. **d** 67 **p** 68 **c** 92. C Tonbridge SS Pet and Paul *Roch* 67-72; Chapl St Jo Coll Ox 72-75; Lect St Jo Coll Nottm 75-81; V Cov H Trin *Cov* 81-92; Can Th Cov Cathl 88-92; Area Bp Willesden *Lon* 92-00; Bp Carl from 00. *Rose Castle, Dalston, Carlisle CA5 7BZ* Tel (01697) 476274 Fax 476550 E-mail bishop.carlisle@carlislediocese.org.uk

DOWD, Garfield George. b 60. QUB BSc. **d** 86 **p** 87. C Monkstown *D & G* 86-90; I Carlow w Urglin and Staplestown *C & O* 90-05; Can Ossory Cathl 96-05; I Glenageary *D & G* from 05. *St Paul's Vicarage, Silchester Road, Glenageary, Co Dublin, Irish Republic* Tel (00353) (1) 280 1616 Fax 280 9459 Mobile 87-926 6558 E-mail glenageary@dublin.anglican.org

DOWDEN, Gordon Frederick. b 25. Selw Coll Cam BA51 MA55. Chich Th Coll 51. **d** 53 **p** 54. C Salisbury St Mich *Sarum* 53-56; C St Neots and Gt w Lt Paxton and Toseland *Ely* 56-58; R Hulme St Phil *Man* 58-70; R Hulme Ascension 70-78; RD Hulme 73-78; P-in-c Holybourne cum Neatham *Win* 78-82; RD Alton 79-82; C Man Gd Shep *Man* 82-91; AD Ardwick 82-90; Chapl Ancoats Hosp Man 85-90; rtd 91; Perm to Offic *Man* from 91. *41 Rozel Square, Manchester M3 4FQ* Tel 0161-832 5592

DOWDING, Ms Clare Alice Elizabeth. b 74. Ch Ch Coll Cant BA98 Greenwich Univ PGCE99. Westcott Ho Cam BA02. **d** 03 **p** 05. USA 03-04; C Longsight St Luke *Man* from 04. *61 Armitage Court, Kniveton Close, Manchester M12 5JH* Tel 0161-231 5072 Mobile 07903-553113 E-mail caedowding@hotmail.com

DOWDING, Edward Brinley. b 47. St Mich Coll Llan 70 St D Coll Lamp BA71. **d** 72 **p** 73. C Canton St Cath *Llan* 72-75; C Aberdare 75-78; V Aberavon H Trin 78-85; R Sully from 85; RD Penarth and Barry 98-04. *The Rectory, 26 South Road, Sully, Penarth CF64 5TG* Tel (029) 2053 0221

DOWDING, Mrs Elizabeth Jean. b 43. Bath Coll of HE TCert67. St Alb and Ox Min Course 00. **d** 04 **p** 05. NSM Goring w S Stoke *Ox* from 04. *30 Milldown Avenue, Goring, Reading RG8 0AS* Tel (01491) 873140 E-mail elizdowding@aol.com

DOWDING, Jeremy Charles. b 51. RMN72. St Steph Ho Ox 89. **d** 91 **p** 92. C Newport St Steph and H Trin *Mon* 91-94; C Risca 94-96; P-in-c Whitleigh *Ex* 96-05; P-in-c Thorpe-le-Soken *Chelmsf* from 05. *The Vicarage, Mill Lane, Thorpe-le-Soken, Clacton-on-Sea CO16 0ED* Tel (01255) 861234

DOWDING, Stanley Frederick. b 10. ALCD32 St Jo Coll Dur BA33 LTh33. **d** 34 **p** 35. C Bris St Silas *Bris* 34-37; C Downend 37-39; C Portland All SS w St Pet *Sarum* 39-42; OCF 39-42; P-in-c Weston Mill *Ex* 42-46; V Preston St Luke *Blackb* 46-55; Chapl HM Pris Preston 51-52; V Nelson in Lt Marsden *Blackb* 55-75; Chapl Reedyford Hosp 64; RD Burnley 68-70; RD Pendle 70-75; rtd 75; Lic to Offic *Blackb* 76-93; Perm to Offic from 93. *4 Hillside Avenue, Reedley, Burnley BB10 2NF* Tel (01282) 693030

DOWDLE, Canon Cynthia. b 48. Cranmer Hall Dur 88. **d** 90 **p** 94. C Allerton *Liv* 90-94; TR Halewood 94-00; V Knowsley from 00; Dean of Women's Min from 01; Hon Can Liv Cathl from 01. *The Vicarage, Tithebarn Road, Prescot L34 0JA* Tel 0151-546 4266 Fax 546 3897
E-mail cynthiadowdle@hotmail.com

DOWDY, Simon Mark Christopher. b 67. Trin Hall Cam BA89 MA93. Wycliffe Hall Ox 93. **d** 96 **p** 97. C Beckenham Ch Ch *Roch* 96-00; C St Helen Bishopsgate w St Andr Undershaft etc *Lon* from 00; P-in-c St Botolph without Aldersgate from 02. *110 Woodwarde Road, London SE22 8UT* Tel (020) 8299 3009 *or* 7283 2231 E-mail s.dowdy@st-helens.org.uk

DOWIE, Canon Winifred Brenda McIntosh. b 57. Callendar Park Coll of Educn Falkirk DipEd78 Trin Coll Bris ADPS96. BA91. **d** 92 **p** 94. Par Dn Downend *Bris* 92-94; C 94-95; Chapl Asst Southmead Health Services NHS Trust 95-98; Chapl St Pet Hospice Bris from 98; Hon Can Bris Cathl *Bris* from 02. *St Peter's Hospice, St Agnes Avenue, Knowle, Bristol BS4 2DU* Tel 0117-977 4605 *or* 915 9462 Fax 915 9473

DOWLAND, Martin John. b 48. Lon Univ BD70 Southn Univ PGCE71. Wycliffe Hall Ox 75. **d** 77 **p** 78. C Jesmond Clayton Memorial *Newc* 77-80; C Chadderton Ch Ch *Man* 80-85; R Haughton St Mary from 85. *Haughton Green Rectory, Meadow Lane, Denton, Manchester M34 7GD* Tel 0161-336 4529 Fax as telephone E-mail mdowland@aol.com

DOWLAND-OWEN, Edward Farrington. b 73. St D Coll Lamp BA95 Trin Coll Carmarthen PGCE96 FVCM99. S Wales Ord Course 00 St Mich Coll Llan 03. **d** 04 **p** 05. C Llandaff *Llan* from 04. *2 The White House, The Cathedral Green, Llandaff, Cardiff CF5 2EB* Tel (029) 2055 2313
E-mail fredowlandowen@aol.com

DOWLEN, Edward Mark. b 25. DLC47 Cranfield Inst of Tech MSc49. St Jo Coll Dur 79. **d** 79 **p** 80. C Rhyl w St Ann *St As* 79-82; C Warton St Paul *Blackb* 83-90; rtd 90; Lic to Offic *Sarum* from 90; Lic to Offic *Mor* from 93. *33 Hythe Road, Poole BH15 3NN* Tel (01202) 737699 *or* 770636

DOWLEN, Isabella McBeath. b 45. Man Univ CertEd86 Bournemouth Univ DMS91. STETS DipTh99. **d** 99 **p** 01. NSM Branksome St Aldhelm *Sarum* from 99. *33 Hythe Road, Poole BH15 3NN* Tel (01202) 737699

DOWLER, Robert Edward Mackenzie. b 67. Ch Ch Ox BA89 Selw Coll Cam BA93. Westcott Ho Cam 91. **d** 94 **p** 95. C Southgate Ch Ch *Lon* 94-97; C Somers Town 97-01; Tutor and Dir Past Th St Steph Ho Ox from 01; Vice Prin from 03. *St Stephen's House, 16 Marston Street, Oxford OX4 1JX* Tel (01865) 247874 Fax 794338

DOWLING, Donald Edward. b 43. St Andr Univ MA66. Cranmer Hall Dur. **d** 74 **p** 75. C Thame w Towersey *Ox* 74-77; C Norton *St Alb* 77-80; V Wilbury 81-99; V Stevenage St Nic and Graveley from 99. *St Nicholas House, 2A North Road, Stevenage SG1 4AT* Tel (01438) 354355
E-mail don.dowling@ntlworld.com

DOWLING, Kingsley Avery Paul. b 60. Open Univ BA Leeds Univ DipM91. Aston Tr Scheme 93 Ripon Coll Cuddesdon DipMin97. **d** 97 **p** 98. C Headingley *Ripon* 97-99; C Far Headingley St Chad 99-01; V Wortley de Leeds from 01. *Wortley Vicarage, Dixon Lane Road, Leeds LS12 4RU* Tel 0113-263 8867
E-mail kd@homeuser1.freeserve.co.uk

DOWLING, Paul Martin. b 55. ACA G&C Coll Cam MA79. Cranmer Hall Dur 88. **d** 90 **p** 91. C Redhill St Jo *S'wark* 90-94; V Wakef St Jo *Wakef* from 94. *St John's Vicarage, 65 Bradford Road, Wakefield WF1 2AA* Tel and fax (01924) 371029
E-mail dowling@fish.co.uk

DOWMAN, Peter Robert. b 52. City Univ BSc76. Wycliffe Hall Ox 82. **d** 84 **p** 85. C Cheltenham Ch Ch *Glouc* 84-87; C Danbury *Chelmsf* 87-90; R Woodham Ferrers and Bicknacre 90-95; Consultant E England CPAS 95-03; R Warboys w Broughton and Bury w Wistow *Ely* from 03. *The Rectory, 15 Church Road, Warboys, Huntingdon PE28 2RJ* Tel (01487) 824612
E-mail pdowman@bigfoot.com

DOWN, Martin John. b 40. Jes Coll Cam BA62 MA68. Westcott Ho Cam 63. **d** 65 **p** 66. C Bury St Mary *Man* 65-68; C Leigh St Mary 68-70; R Fiskerton *Linc* 70-75; V Irnham w Corby 75-79; RD Beltisloe 76-84; P-in-c Swayfield and Creeton w Swinstead 78-79; V Corby Glen 79-84; Good News Trust 84-88; Perm to Offic *Linc* 84-88 and *Pet* 86-88; P-in-c Ashill w Saham Toney *Nor* 88-94; R 94-00; C Watton w Carbrooke and Ovington 00-05; rtd 05; Perm to Offic *Nor* from 05. *22 Lee Warner Road, Swaffham PE37 7GD* Tel and fax (01760) 336492

DOWN, Peter Michael. b 54. K Coll Lon BD78 AKC. Coll of Resurr Mirfield 78. **d** 79 **p** 80. C Swindon Ch Ch *Bris* 79-82; C Southmead 82-84; TV Cannock *Lich* 84-92; V Coleford w Holcombe *B & W* 92-01; Hon C Westfield 01-02. *Address temp unknown*

DOWN, The Ven Philip Roy. b 53. R Melbourne Inst of Tech Dip Applied Science 76 Hull Univ MA93. Melbourne Coll of Div BTh82 MTh88. **d** 89 **p** 89. C Gt Grimsby St Mary and St Jas *Linc* 89-91; TV 91-95; R Hackington *Cant* 95-02; AD Cant 99-02; Adn Maidstone from 02. *The Old Rectory, The Street, Pluckley, Ashford TN27 0QT* Tel (01233) 840291 Fax 840759
E-mail pdown@archdeacmaid.org

✠**DOWN, The Rt Revd William John Denbigh.** b 34. St Jo Coll Cam BA57 MA61 FNI91. Ridley Hall Cam 57. **d** 59 **p** 60 **c** 90. C Fisherton Anger *Sarum* 59-63; Miss to Seamen 63-90; Australia 71-74; Dep Gen Sec Miss to Seamen 75; Gen Sec 76-90; Hon C Gt Stanmore *Lon* 75-90; Chapl St Mich Paternoster Royal 76-90; Perm to Offic *St Alb* 78-90; Hon Can Gib Cathl *Eur* 85-90; Hon Can Kobe Japan from 87; Bp Bermuda 90-95; Asst Bp Leic 95-01; P-in-c Humberstone 95-01; P-in-c Thurnby Lodge 01; rtd 01; Hon Asst Bp Ox from 01. *54 Dark Lane, Witney OX28 6LX* Tel (01993) 706615

DOWN AND DROMORE, Bishop of. *See* MILLER, The Rt Revd Harold Creeth

DOWN, Archdeacon of. *See* McCAMLEY, The Ven Gregor Alexander

DOWN, Dean of. *See* DINNEN, The Very Revd John Frederick

DOWNER, Barry Michael. b 58. STETS 99. **d** 02. NSM Shanklin St Sav *Portsm* from 02; NSM Lake from 02. *1 Rocklands Cottages, Woolverton Road, Ventnor PO38 1XW* Tel and fax (01983) 855970

DOWNER, Cuthbert John. b 18. S'wark Ord Course 60. **d** 74 **p** 75. Hon C Kirdford *Chich* 74-76; C Halesworth w Linstead and Chediston *St E* 76-79; P-in-c Knodishall w Buxlow 79-80; P-in-c Friston 79-80; R Bacton w Wyverstone 80-83; P-in-c Cotton and Wickham Skeith 80-83; R Bacton w Wyverstone and Cotton 83-84; rtd 84; Perm to Offic *St Alb* 84-87; *B & W* 88-95 and 97-98. *6 The Maples, Princes Road, Shepton Mallet BA4 5HL* Tel (01749) 344102

DOWNES, Gregory Charles. b 69. Roehampton Inst BSc91 Hughes Hall Cam PGCE92. Wycliffe Hall Ox BA95. **d** 96 **p** 97. C Hazlemere *Ox* 96-99; Chapl HM Pris Ashfield 99-01; Lect Lon Bible Coll 01-04; Chapl Pemb Coll Ox 04-05. *Address temp unknown* E-mail gregdownes@email.com

DOWNES, Richard John. b 63. Cranmer Hall Dur CTM94. **d** 94 **p** 95. C Bishopwearmouth St Gabr *Dur* 94-97; CF from 97. *c/o MOD Chaplains (Army)* Tel (01980) 615804 Fax 615800

DOWNEY, Canon John Stewart. b 38. QUB CertEd60 Open Univ BA76. Oak Hill Th Coll 63. **d** 66 **p** 67. C Londonderry St Aug *D & R* 66-71; I Dungiven w Bovevagh 71-82; Bp's Dom Chapl 75-82; V Bishopwearmouth St Gabr *Dur* 82-91; V New Malden and Coombe *S'wark* from 91; Hon Can S'wark Cathl from 97. *The Vicarage, 93 Coombe Road, New Malden KT3 4RE* Tel (020) 8942 0915

DOWNHAM, Canon Peter Norwell. b 31. Man Univ BA52. Ridley Hall Cam 54. **d** 56 **p** 57. C Cheadle *Ches* 56-62; V Rawtenstall St Mary *Man* 62-68; Chapl Rossendale Gen Hosp 62-68; V Denton Holme *Carl* 68-79; V Reading Greyfriars *Ox* 79-95; Hon Can Ch Ch 90-95; rtd 95; Hon C Cotehill and Cumwhinton *Carl* 95-00; Perm to Offic from 98. *19 The Green, Dalston, Carlisle CA5 7QB* Tel (01228) 711850

DOWNHAM, Simon Garrod. b 61. Solicitor 87 K Coll Lon LLB84. Wycliffe Hall Ox BA93 DipMin94. **d** 94 **p** 95. C Brompton H Trin w Onslow Square St Paul *Lon* 94-99; P-in-c Hammersmith St Paul from 00. *14 Lena Gardens, London W6 7PZ* Tel (020) 7603 9662 *or* 8748 3855
E-mail simon.downham@stph.org.uk

DOWNING, Francis Gerald. b 35. Qu Coll Ox BA56 MA60. Linc Th Coll. **d** 58 **p** 59. C Filwood Park CD *Bris* 58-60; Tutor Linc Th Coll 60-64; V Unsworth *Man* 64-80; Tutor N Ord Course 80-82; Vice-Prin 82-90; V Bolton SS Simon and Jude *Man* 90-97; rtd 97; Perm to Offic *Blackb* from 97. *33 Westhoughton Road, Chorley PR7 4EU* Tel (01257) 474240

DOWNS, Caroline Rebecca. b 58. UWIST BA80 Univ of Wales (Cardiff) PGCE81. St Mich Coll Llan 98. **d** 02 **p** 03. C Roath *Llan* from 02. *6 Newminster Road, Roath, Cardiff CF23 5AP* Tel (029) 2049 5699 E-mail carolinerebecca.downs@btinternet.com

DOWNS, Miss Geinor. b 47. UEA BA72 Southn Univ BTh89. Chich Th Coll 85. **d** 87 **p** 94. Par Dn Wellingborough All SS *Pet* 87-89; Development Officer Chich Th Coll 89-92; C Durrington *Chich* 92-95; Chapl City Hosp NHS Trust Birm from 95. *Chaplaincy Department, City Hospital NHS Trust, Dudley Road, Birmingham B18 7QH* Tel 0121-554 3801 ext 4055 *or* 567 5628 Fax 523 0951

DOWNS, John Alfred. b 58. MIBiol80 CBiol80 Leic Univ BSc79 PGCE80. EMMTC 90. **d** 93 **p** 94. NSM Barlestone *Leic* 93-96; NSM Markfield 96-99; NSM Thornton, Bagworth and Stanton 96-99; NSM Markfield, Thornton, Bagworth and Stanton etc from 99. *29 Meadow Road, Barlestone, Nuneaton CV13 0JG* Tel (01455) 290195

DOWNS, Mrs Lynsay Marie. b 75. Hull Univ BA98. Ripon Coll Cuddesdon BTh05. **d** 05. C Tettenhall Wood and Perton *Lich* from 05. *12 Windmill Lane, Wolverhampton WV3 8HJ* Tel (01902) 763160

DOWSE, Edgar. b 10. Dur Univ LTh35 Lon Univ BD37 Fitzw Coll Cam BA72 MA74 Lon Univ MPhil90. Clifton Th Coll 32 Cen Sch of Religion MA ThD. **d** 35 **p** 36. Asst Chapl and Tutor Clifton Th Coll 35-36; C Chippenham St Andr w Tytherton Lucas *Bris* 36-40; Tutor St Andr Th Coll Whittlesford 40-41; C Bournemouth St Mich *Win* 41-45; P-in-c Bournemouth H Epiphany 45-51; R Freemantle 51-57; V Bethnal Green St Bart *Lon* 57-71; Lect Lon Bible Coll 60-61; Lect St Mich Cornhill 60-63; St Steph Walbrook 65-68; P-in-c Acton Green St Alb *Lon* 71-72; V 72-75; rtd 75; Perm to Offic *Lon* 75-96 and from 00. *87 College Road, Isleworth TW7 5DP* Tel (020) 8568 2548

DOWSE, Ivor Roy. b 35. ARHistS MRSL. St Deiniol's Hawarden 66. **d** 68 **p** 70. C Harrow St Pet *Lon* 68-69; C Sudbury St Andr 69-71; C Weeke *Win* 71-73; Min Can Ban Cathl *Ban* 73-78; V Hollym w Welwick and Holmpton *York* 78-81; R Bearwood *Ox* 81-82; P-in-c Rothesay *Arg* 83-86; C Boxmoor St Jo *St Alb* 86-92; Hon C Cowes H Trin and St Mary *Portsm* 92-94; Perm to Offic 94-98; P-in-c St Hilary w Perranuthnoe *Truro* 98-00; rtd 01; Perm to Offic *S & M* and *Truro* from 05. *14 Close Famman, Port Erin, Isle of Man IM9 6BJ* Tel (01624) 837392

DOWSETT, Alan Charles. b 27. Selw Coll Cam BA51 MA55 Bris Poly CQSW76. Cuddesdon Coll 51. **d** 53 **p** 54. C Portsea St Mary *Portsm* 53-57; C Wokingham All SS *Ox* 57-60; V Water Orton *Birm* 60-64; Chapl Colston's Sch Bris 64-65; C Stoke Bishop *Bris* 65-68; Lic to Offic 69-89; rtd 89. *23 Upper Cranbrook Road, Bristol BS6 7UW* Tel 0117-924 3227

DOWSETT, Ian Peter. b 71. Liv Univ BA95 Lon Inst of Educn PGCE96. Wycliffe Hall Ox BA01. **d** 02. C Kensington St Helen w H Trin *Lon* from 02. *St Francis House, Dalgarno Way, London W10 5EL* Tel (020) 8968 4733 Mobile 07985-726465 E-mail irdowsett@talk21.com

DOWSETT, Marian Ivy Rose. b 40. **d** 88 **p** 97. NSM Rumney *Mon* 88-94; C St Mellons and Michaelston-y-Fedw 94-96; C St Mellons 96-03; V Llanrumney from 03. *114 Ridgeway Road, Rumney, Cardiff CF3 4AB* Tel (029) 2079 2635

DOWSON, Roger Christopher. b 32. Clifton Th Coll 60. **d** 63 **p** 64. C Virginia Water *Guildf* 63-66; C Darfield *Sheff* 66-68; V Thorpe Edge *Bradf* 68-80; V Wyke 80-91; rtd 91; Hon C Coley *Wakef* from 91; Perm to Offic *Bradf* 93-99 and from 03. *1 Windsor Villas, Norwood Green, Halifax HX3 8QS* Tel (01274) 674557

DOWSON, Simon Paul. b 63. Bris Univ BSc85 Cam Univ PGCE89. Cranmer Hall Dur 95. **d** 97 **p** 98. C Bradf St Aug Undercliffe *Bradf* 97-99; C Werrington *Pet* 99-04; V Skirbeck H Trin *Linc* from 04. *Holy Trinity Vicarage, 64 Spilsby Road, Boston PE21 9NS* Tel (01205) 363657 E-mail sifi@dowzim.fsnet.co.uk

DOXSEY, Roy Desmond. b 41. St D Coll Lamp 64. **d** 67 **p** 68. C Pembroke St Mary w St Mich *St D* 67-70; C Milford Haven 70-73; C Loughton *Ox* 73-75; Chapl Llandovery Coll 75-81 and 92-96; Zambia 81-86; Chapl Epsom Coll 86-92; V Roath St German *Llan* from 96. *St Germans Vicarage, Metal Street, Roath, Cardiff CF24 0LA* Tel (029) 2049 4488

DOYE, Andrew Peter Charles. b 64. BNC Ox BA85. Trin Coll Bris BA93. **d** 93 **p** 94. C Surbiton St Matt *S'wark* 93-96; C Bourne *Guildf* 96-99; C The Bourne and Tilford 99-00; R Wheathampstead *St Alb* from 00. *The Rectory, Old Rectory Gardens, Wheathampstead, St Albans AL4 8AD* Tel (01582) 833144 E-mail andrewdoye@hotmail.com

DOYLE, Canon Alan Holland. b 22. JP72. Lon Univ BD55 Birm Univ MA86 Buckingham Univ DPhil93. Wycliffe Hall Ox 52. **d** 52 **p** 53. C Braddan *S & M* 52-54; C Douglas St Geo 54-55; R Oldham St Andr *Man* 55-59; Chapl Ruzawi Prep Sch S Rhodesia 59-62; V Chaddesley Corbett *Worc* 62-66; CF (TA) 63-67; V Kidderminster St Jo *Worc* 66-67; R Salwarpe 67-74; RD Droitwich 69-78; P-in-c Himbleton w Huddington 74-78; Hon Can Worc Cathl 74-87; P-in-c Ombersley w Doverdale 78-83; R 83-87; rtd 87; Perm to Offic *Worc* from 87. *3 Graham Court, Graham Road, Malvern WR14 2HX* Tel (01684) 891816

DOYLE, Andrew Michael. b 63. K Coll Lon BD85 AKC85. Ripon Coll Cuddesdon 86. **d** 88 **p** 89. C Lytchett Minster *Sarum* 88-92; TV Kirkby *Liv* 92-97; V Rotherhithe H Trin *S'wark* from 97; RD Bermondsey from 00. *Holy Trinity Vicarage, Bryan Road, London SE16 5HF* Tel (020) 7237 4098

DOYLE, Brian William. b 31. FRSH. Sarum Th Coll 87. **d** 87 **p** 88. NSM Heene *Chich* 87-91; Chapl Qu Alexandra's Hosp Worthing 89-91; C W Tarring *Chich* 91-93; C Hangleton 93-95; rtd 95; Perm to Offic *Chich* from 96. *56A Langdale Gardens, Hove BN3 4HH* Tel (01273) 727910

DOYLE, Edward Michael. b 70. Univ of Wales (Cardiff) DipTh91. St Mich Coll Llan BTh93. **d** 94 **p** 95. C Sketty *S & B* 94-96; C Llwynderw 96-00; R Rogate w Terwick and Trotton w Chithurst *Chich* from 00. *The Vicarage, Fyning Lane, Rogate, Petersfield GU31 5EE* Tel (01730) 821576

DOYLE, Graham Thomas. b 48. St Barn Coll Adelaide ThL73 ThSchol77 Worc Coll Ox BA85 MA90. **d** 73 **p** 74. Australia 73-83; Perm to Offic *Ox* 83-85; C Cobbold Road St Sav w St Mary *Lon* 86; P-in-c Bradf St Oswald Chapel Green *Bradf* 86-91; Chapl Belgrade w Zagreb *Eur* 91-93; Chapl Belgrade 93-97; Taiwan 97-00; I Killeshandra w Killegar and Derrylane *K, E & A* 00-03; I Athlone w Benown, Kiltoom and Forgney *M & K* from 03. *St Mary's C of I Rectory, Bonavalley, Athlone, Co Westmeath, Irish Republic* Tel (00353) (90) 647 8350 Fax 647 6720 E-mail gtdoyleathlone@eircom.net

DOYLE, Nigel Paul. b 55. MHort(RHS)82. St Mich Coll Llan 00. **d** 03 **p** 04. NSM Treboeth *S & B* from 03; NSM Landore from 03. *3 Ael-y-Bryn, Penclawdd, Swansea SA4 3LF* Tel (01792) 850659 E-mail tadnigel@yahoo.co.uk

DOYLE, Robin Alfred. b 43. Dur Univ BA65. Westcott Ho Cam 66. **d** 68 **p** 69. C Edgbaston St Geo *Birm* 68-70; C Erdington St Barn 70-73; P-in-c Oldbury 73-81; R Maker w Rame *Truro* from 81. *The Vicarage, Fore Street, Kingsand, Torpoint PL10 1NB* Tel (01752) 822302

DOYLE, Mrs Tracey Elizabeth. b 58. Open Univ BA00. St Alb and Ox Min Course 94. **d** 97 **p** 98. OLM Winslow w Gt Horwood and Addington *Ox* 97-99; C 00-04; P-in-c Ivinghoe w Pitstone and Slapton from 04. *The Vicarage, Station Road, Ivinghoe, Leighton Buzzard LU7 9EB* Tel (01296) 668260 Mobile 07814-538208 E-mail mick.doyle@virgin.net

DOYLE, William. *See* DOYLE, Brian William

DRACKLEY, John Oldham. b 36. Em Coll Cam BA57 MA61. Wells Th Coll 57. **d** 59 **p** 60. C Eckington *Derby* 59-62; C Lee Gd Shep w St Pet *S'wark* 62-63; C Derby St Thos *Derby* 63-67; C Matlock and Tansley 67-77; P-in-c Radbourne 77-82; P-in-c Dalbury, Long Lane and Trusley 77-82; P-in-c Longford 77-82; Sec Dioc Cttee for Care of Chs 82-98; rtd 95; Perm to Offic *Derby* from 98. *26 Highfield Drive, Matlock DE4 3FZ* Tel (01629) 55902

DRAFFAN, Canon Ian William. b 42. Aston Univ BSc65 MSc66 FBCS77 CEng88. N Ord Course 83. **d** 86 **p** 87. NSM Millhouses H Trin *Sheff* 86-04; NSM Endcliffe from 04; Hon Can Sheff Cathl from 05. *8 Silverdale Crescent, Sheffield S11 9JH* Tel 0114-236 4523

DRAIN, Walter. b 39. JP75. Open Univ BA76 ACP66. NW Ord Course 76. **d** 79 **p** 80. NSM Cheadle *Ches* 79-81; C 81-84; V Chatburn *Blackb* 84-02; Sub Chapl HM Pris Preston 94-02; rtd 02; Perm to Offic *Blackb* from 02. *Angels, 28 The Croft, Euxton, Chorley PR7 6LH* Tel (01257) 249646

DRAKE, Frances Maud. b 43. Brentwood Coll of Educn TCert67 Sussex Univ BEd74 Birkbeck Coll Lon DipRS93. S'wark Ord Course 90. **d** 93 **p** 94. NSM Fryerning w Margaretting *Chelmsf* 93-01; P-in-c Margaretting w Mountnessing and Buttsbury from 01. *Little Pump House, Ongar Road, Kelvedon Hatch, Brentwood CM15 0LA* Tel and fax (01277) 364383 E-mail revfrances.drake@tiscali.co.uk

DRAKE, Graham. b 46. Linc Th Coll 81. **d** 83 **p** 85. C Alford w Rigsby *Linc* 83-84; Perm to Offic *Wakef* 84-85; Hon C Purston cum S Featherstone 85-89; NSM Castleford All SS 89-92; C Cudworth 92-95. *Flat 3, Woodland House, 5 Mill Hill, Pontefract WF8 4HR* Tel (01977) 708713 *or* 683324

DRAKE, Canon Graham Rae. b 45. Fitzw Coll Cam BA68 MA72. Qu Coll Birm 70. **d** 73 **p** 74. C New Windsor *Ox* 73-77; TV 77-78; P-in-c Bath Ascension *B & W* 78-81; TV Bath Twerton-on-Avon 81-86; P-in-c Buxton w Oxnead *Nor* 86-90; P-in-c Lammas w Lt Hautbois 86-90; RD Ingworth 88-94; R Buxton w Oxnead, Lammas and Brampton 90-95; P-in-c Cockley Cley w Gooderstone 95-01; P-in-c Gt and Lt Cressingham w Threxton 95-01; P-in-c Didlington 95-01; P-in-c Hilborough w Bodney 95-01; P-in-c Oxborough w Foulden and Caldecote 95-01; P-in-c Mundford w Lynford 99-01; P-in-c Ickburgh w Langford 99-01; P-in-c Cranwich 99-01; Hon Can Nor Cathl from 99; V Thorpe St Matt from 01. *St Matthew's Vicarage, Albert Place, Norwich NR1 4JL* Tel (01603) 620820 E-mail gdrake@freeuk.com

DRAKE, John Paul. b 19. Qu Coll Ox BA41 MA44. Cuddesdon Coll 46. **d** 47 **p** 48. C Stepney St Dunstan and All SS *Lon* 47-54; V Brighton All So *Chich* 54-59; Chapl St Edw Sch Ox 59-69; V Stewkley *Ox* 69-75; V Stewkley w Soulbury and Drayton Parslow 75-85; RD Mursley 77-83; rtd 85; Perm to Offic *St Alb* from 85. *3 The Cloisters, Welwyn Garden City AL8 6DU* Tel (01707) 325379

DRAKE, Leslie Sargent. b 47. Boston Univ BA69 MTh72 Hull Univ BPhil74 Anglia Poly Univ MSc93. Coll of Resurr Mirfield 78. **d** 78 **p** 79. C Oldham *Man* 78-81; TV Rochdale 81-83; V Palmers Green St Jo *Lon* 83-89; St Mary's Sch Cheshunt 89-91; Hd RE St Mary's Sch Hendon 91-99; TV Wimbledon *S'wark* 99-03; V Clay Hill St Jo and St Luke *Lon* from 03. *St Luke's Vicarage, 92 Browning Road, Enfield EN2 0HG* Tel (020) 8363 6055 E-mail isdrake@aol.com

DRAKELEY, Stephen Richard Francis. b 51. Aston Univ BSc73. Chich Th Coll 76. **d** 76 **p** 77. C Yardley Wood *Birm* 76-79; V Rednal 79-89; TV Bodmin w Lanhydrock and Lanivet *Truro* 89-99; P-in-c Falmouth All SS from 99. *All Saints' Vicarage,*

72 Dracaena Avenue, Falmouth TR11 2EN Tel and fax (01326) 317474 E-mail srfd@compuserve.com

DRAPER, The Ven Alfred James. b 23. Natal Univ BA50. St Aug Coll Cant DipTh59 St Paul's Coll Grahamstown LTh54. **d** 54 **p** 54. S Africa 54-63 and 75-87; V Tile Cross *Birm* 63-72; V Olton 72-75; Adn Durban 79-87; R S Ferriby *Linc* 87-93; V Horkstow 87-93; R Saxby All Saints 87-93; rtd 93; Perm to Offic *Ches* from 93. *4 Rugby Close, Macclesfield SK10 2HW* Tel (01625) 619033

DRAPER, Charles James. b 59. Dur Univ BSc80 Cam Univ BA86. Ridley Hall Cam 84. **d** 87 **p** 88. C Wareham *Sarum* 87-90; C Maltby *Sheff* 90-93; R The Claydons *Ox* 93-99; R Chinnor w Emmington and Sydenham etc 99-02; P-in-c Gt Faringdon w Lt Coxwell from 02. *The Vicarage, Coach Lane, Faringdon SN7 8AB* Tel (01367) 240106 E-mail 6drapers@cdraper.fslife.co.uk

DRAPER, Derek Vincent. b 38. Linc Th Coll 65. **d** 68 **p** 69. C Orpington All SS *Roch* 68-72; C Bramley *Guildf* 72-74; P-in-c Kempston All SS *St Alb* 74-76; Min Kempston Transfiguration CD 77-79; V Kempston Transfiguration 79-84; RD Bedford 79-84; V Bromham w Oakley 84-88; P-in-c Stagsden 84-88; V Bromham w Oakley and Stagsden 88-03; RD Elstow 00-02; Chapl Bromham Hosp 84-03; rtd 03; Perm to Offic *Ely* and *St Alb* from 03. *24 Wilkinson Close, Eaton Socon, St Neots PE19 8HJ* Tel (01480) 384031

DRAPER, Elizabeth Ann. *See* BRADLEY, Mrs Elizabeth Ann

DRAPER, Ivan Thomas. b 32. Aber Univ MB, ChB56 FRCP FRCPGlas. St Jo Coll Nottm 87. **d** 90 **p** 91. NSM Glas St Bride *Glas* from 90; P-in-c 96-97. *13/1 Whistlefield Court, 2 Canniesburn Road, Bearsden, Glasgow G61 1PX* Tel 0141-943 0954 E-mail murieldra@clara.net

DRAPER, James. *See* DRAPER, The Ven Alfred James

DRAPER, Jean Margaret. b 31. **d** 80 **p** 97. NSM Pontnewydd *Mon* 80-83; BRF 82-83; NSM Llantilio Pertholey w Bettws Chpl etc *Mon* 83-94; NSM Newport St Andr 94-03. *Govilon House, Merthyr Road, Govilon, Abergavenny NP7 9PT* Tel (01873) 830380

DRAPER, John William. b 54. Aston Tr Scheme 86 Qu Coll Birm 88. **d** 90 **p** 91. C Stepney St Dunstan and All SS *Lon* 90-94; C Leigh Park and Warren Park *Portsm* 94-96; R Rowner from 96; V Bridgemary from 04. *The Rectory, 174 Rowner Lane, Gosport PO13 9SU* Tel and fax (023) 9258 1834 *or* 9258 7934 Mobile 07802-730742 E-mail smrowner@netscapeonline.co.uk

DRAPER, Canon Jonathan Lee. b 52. Gordon Coll Mass BA76 St Jo Coll Dur BA78 PhD84. Ripon Coll Cuddesdon 83. **d** 83 **p** 84. C Baguley *Man* 83-85; Dir Academic Studies Ripon Coll Cuddesdon 85-92; V Putney St Mary *S'wark* 92-00; Can Res York Minster *York* from 00. *3 Minster Court, York YO1 7JJ* Tel (01904) 625599 E-mail jonathan.draper3@btinternet.com

DRAPER, Canon Martin Paul. b 50. OBE98. Birm Univ BA72 Southn Univ BTh79. Chich Th Coll 72. **d** 75 **p** 76. C Primrose Hill St Mary w Avenue Road St Paul *Lon* 75-78; C Westmr St Matt 79-84; Chapl Paris St Geo *Eur* 84-02; Adn France 94-02; Can Gib Cathl 94-02. *25 rue Vicq D'azir, 75010 Paris, France*

DRAPER, Patrick Hugh. b 43. S Dios Minl Tr Scheme 91. **d** 94 **p** 95. NSM Boscombe St Jo *Win* 94-99; P-in-c Southbourne St Chris 99-02; rtd 02; Perm to Offic *Win* from 02. *82 Tuckton Road, Bournemouth BH6 3HT* Tel (01202) 420190

DRAPER, Canon Paul Richard. b 64. Glas Univ MA87 TCD BTh90. **d** 90 **p** 91. C Drumragh w Mountfield *D & R* 90-94; I Ballydehob w Aghadown *C, C & R* from 94; Can Cork and Ross Cathls from 98; Bp's Dom Chapl from 99. *The Rectory, Ballydehob, Co Cork, Irish Republic* Tel (00353) (28) 37117

DRAPER, Peter Raymond. b 57. Leeds Poly BSc86 Leeds Univ CertEd88 Hull Univ PhD94 SRN80. NEOC 01. **d** 04 **p** 05. NSM S Cave and Ellerker w Broomfleet *York* from 04. *49 The Stray, South Cave, Brough HU15 2AN* Tel (01430) 422144 Mobile 07956-531002 E-mail p.r.draper@hull.ac.uk

DRAPER, Raymond James. b 48. Ex Coll Ox BA70 MA75 Em Coll Cam BA73 MA78. Ridley Hall Cam 71. **d** 74 **p** 75. C Sheff Manor *Sheff* 74-78; Ind Chapl 78-82; R Wickersley 82-00; V Leytonstone St Jo *Chelmsf* from 00. *St John's Vicarage, 44 Hartley Road, London E11 3BL* Tel (020) 8257 2792

DRAPER, Mrs Sylvia Edith. b 39. ARCM60. N Ord Course 86. **d** 89 **p** 94. C Aughton St Mich *Liv* 89-92; Par Dn Wigan St Jas w St Thos 92-94; Asst Chapl Wigan and Leigh Health Services NHS Trust 92-97; C Wigan St Jas w St Thos *Liv* 94-97; TV Walton-on-the-Hill 97-02; rtd 02; Perm to Offic *Liv* from 03. *6 Brookfield Lane, Aughton, Ormskirk L39 6SP* Tel (01695) 422138

DRAX, Elizabeth Margaret. *See* ANSON, Mrs Elizabeth Margaret

DRAY, John. b 66. St Chad's Coll Dur BSc87. St Steph Ho Ox BTh95. **d** 95 **p** 96. C Byker St Ant *Newc* 95-98; C Cullercoats St Geo 98-01; P-in-c Platt *Roch* 01-05; Chapl to the Deaf 01-05. *51 Widmore Lodge Road, Bromley BR1 2QE* E-mail john.dray@bigfoot.com

DRAYCOTT, John. b 53. Sheff Univ BA84 Dip Community Educn 82. Br Isles Nazarene Coll DipTh77 Linc Th Coll 85. **d** 85 **p** 86. In Wesleyan Reform Union 77-82; C Wombwell *Sheff* 85-87; V W Bessacarr 87-92; V Erith Ch Ch *Roch* from 92; P-in-c Erith St Jo 92-95. *Christ Church Vicarage, Victoria Road, Erith DA8 3AN* Tel (01322) 334729 Fax as telephone

DRAYCOTT, John Edward. b 54. EMMTC 99. **d** 01 **p** 02. C Calverton *S'well* from 01; C Epperstone from 01; C Gonalston from 01; C Oxton from 01. *21 Dunhelm Avenue, Calverton, Nottingham NG14 6NN* Tel 0115-910 3675

DRAYCOTT, Philip John. b 27. Sarum & Wells Th Coll. **d** 83 **p** 84. C Bishop's Cleeve *Glouc* 83-86; V Chedworth, Yanworth and Stowell, Coln Rogers etc 86-93; rtd 94; Perm to Offic *B & W* from 94. *April Cottage, Newton Road, North Petherton, Bridgwater TA6 6NA* Tel (01278) 662487

DRAYSON, Nicholas James Quested. b 53. Keble Coll Ox BA75 MA83. Wycliffe Hall Ox DipTh83. **d** 79 **p** 79. SAMS Argentina 79-82 and 92-00; Pastor Tartacal and Chapl to Chorote Indians 79-82; P-in-c Seville Ascension Spain 83-91; Adn Andalucia 89-91; Translations Co-ord 92-98; Pastor Salta St Andr 92-98; C Beverley Minster *York* from 00. *34 Carter Drive, Beverley HU17 9GL* E-mail nickd@fish.co.uk

DRAYTON, James Edward. b 30. St Deiniol's Hawarden 81. **d** 84 **p** 86. Hon C Heald Green St Cath *Ches* 84-88; C Bollington St Jo 88-92; P-in-c Lt Leigh and Lower Whitley 92-96; P-in-c Aston by Sutton 92-96; P-in-c Antrobus 92-96; rtd 96; Perm to Offic *York* from 96. *87 Wharfedale, Filey YO14 0DP*

DREDGE, David John. b 32. Cranmer Hall Dur 69. **d** 71 **p** 72. C Goole *Sheff* 71-74; P-in-c Eastoft 74-77; V Whitgift w Adlingfleet 74-77; V Whitgift w Adlingfleet and Eastoft 77-78; V Walkley 78-81; TV Bicester w Bucknell, Caversfield and Launton *Ox* 81-86; V N Brickhill and Putnoe *St Alb* 86-90; P-in-c Sarratt 90-95; rtd 95; Perm to Offic *Lich* from 95. *19 Waterdale, Wombourne, Wolverhampton WV5 0DH* Tel (01902) 897467

DREDGE, David Julian. b 36. ALA74 Sheff Univ BA59. Cranmer Hall Dur 61 Ban Ord Course 85. **d** 87 **p** 88. NSM Dwygyfylchi *Ban* 87-92; R Llanllechid 92-97; rtd 97; Perm to Offic *Ban* from 97. *Westfield, Treforris Road, Penmaenmawr LL34 6RH* Tel (01492) 623439 Mobile 07721-941861 Fax 0870-056 7258 E-mail david@djd-emd-chrstn.demon.co.uk

DREW, Gerald Arthur. b 36. Bps' Coll Cheshunt 59. **d** 61 **p** 62. C Lyonsdown H Trin *St Alb* 61-67; C Tring 67-71; R Bramfield w Stapleford and Waterford 71-78; V Langleybury St Paul 78-90; P-in-c Hormead, Wyddial, Anstey, Brent Pelham etc 90-95; V 95-01; rtd 01; Perm to Offic *St Alb* and *St E* from 01. *33 The Glebe, Lavenham, Sudbury CO10 9SN* Tel (01787) 248133

DREW (née ROY), Mrs Jennifer Pearl. b 53. SRN75 CSS91. Cranmer Hall Dur. **d** 01 **p** 02. C Hebburn St Jo and Jarrow Grange *Dur* 01-05; NSM Broom Leys *Leic* from 05. *84 Blackwood, Coalville LE67 4RF* Tel (01530) 831439 E-mail jennieroy@bigfoot.com

DREW, Joseph Harold. b 09. St D Coll Lamp BA30. St Mich Coll Llan 30. **d** 32 **p** 33. C Blaenavon w Capel Newydd *Mon* 32-35; C Roath St Sav *Llan* 35-38; C Newport St Jo Bapt *Mon* 38-39; V 39-50; Chapl HM Borstal Feltham 50-55; Chapl HM Pris Man 55-58; Chapl HM Pris Pentonville 58-64; Chapl and Sec Pris Chapl Coun 64-74; Asst Chapl Gen of Pris 64-74; rtd 74; Perm to Offic *S'wark* 82-02. *50 Kingsley Court, Pincott Road, Bexleyheath DA6 7LA* Tel (020) 8298 1216

DREW, Michael Edgar Cecil. b 31. Oriel Coll Ox BA55 MA59. St Steph Ho Ox 55. **d** 57 **p** 58. C Plymouth St Pet *Ex* 57-63; Missr Pemb Coll Cam Miss Walworth 63-67; Asst Chapl All Hallows Sch Rousdon 67-75; Chapl 80-81; Chapl Ex Sch 81-83; V Scraptoft *Leic* 83-97; V Hungarton 83-87; P-in-c Leic St Eliz Nether Hall 87-97; rtd 97. *28 St Mary's Paddock, Wellingborough NN8 1HJ* Tel (01933) 277407

DREW, Canon Rosemary. b 43. SRN64. EAMTC 90. **d** 93 **p** 94. NSM Gt Dunmow *Chelmsf* 93-96; NSM Gt Dunmow and Barnston from 96; Hon Can Chelmsf Cathl from 01; Area Adv for Healing and Deliverance Min from 04. *The Bowling Green, 8 The Downs, Dunmow CM6 1DT* Tel and fax (01371) 872662 E-mail bruce.drew@btinternet.com

DREW, Simon Mark. b 68. Liv Univ BEng89 CEng94 MICE94. St Jo Coll Nottm MA98 DipMM99. **d** 99 **p** 00. C Torquay St Matthias, St Mark and H Trin *Ex* 99-03; V Marshfield w Cold Ashton and Tormarton etc *Bris* from 03. *The Vicarage, Church Lane, Marshfield, Chippenham SN14 8NT* Tel (01225) 891850 E-mail simon@smdrew.freeserve.co.uk

DREWERY, Graeme Robert. b 66. St Jo Coll Cam BA88 MA92 PhD94 FRCO89. Linc Th Coll MDiv94. **d** 94 **p** 95. C Paston *Pet* 94-97; C Cottingham *York* 97-00; V Middlesbrough St Jo the Ev 00-05; R Brotton Parva from 05. *St Margaret's Rectory, 9 Crispin Court, Brotton, Saltburn-by-the-Sea TS12 2XL* Tel (01287) 676275

DREWETT, Canon Mervyn Henry. b 27. Wadh Coll Ox BA50 MA53. Linc Th Coll 52. **d** 54 **p** 55. C Filwood Park CD *Bris* 54-58; C Bishopston 58-61; V Brislington St Chris 61-67; V Henbury 67-80; RD Westbury and Severnside 79-80; TR Gtr Corsham 80-94; Hon Can Bris Cathl 80-94; RD Chippenham 82-88; rtd 94; Perm to Offic *Bris* and *Sarum* from 94. *14 The Beeches, Shaw, Melksham SN12 8EP* Tel (01225) 702726

DREYER, Rodney Granville. b 55. Lon Univ MPhil91 AKC91. St Paul's Coll Grahamstown DipTh81. **d** 81 **p** 82. S Africa 81-84 and 94-98; NSM Headstone St Geo *Lon* 84-86; NSM Northolt St Mary 86-87; C Portsea St Mary *Portsm* 87-90; V Sudbury St Andr *Lon* 90-94; Adn W and S Free State 94-95; V Hawkhurst *Cant* from 98. *The Vicarage, Moor Hill Road, Hawkhurst, Cranbrook TN18 4QB* Tel (01580) 753397 E-mail rodneydreyer@onetel.com

DRISCOLL, Canon David. b 42. Lon Univ BSc64 Nottm Univ DipTh69. Linc Th Coll 68. **d** 71 **p** 72. C Walthamstow St Jo *Chelmsf* 71-76; Chapl NE Lon Poly 71-79; C-in-c Plaistow St Mary 76-79; P-in-c Stratford St Jo and Ch Ch w Forest Gate St Jas 79-89; V Theydon Bois 89-01; RD Epping Forest 92-01; Hon Can Chelmsf Cathl 01; C All Hallows by the Tower etc *Lon* from 01. *159 Wapping High Street, London E1W 3NQ* Tel (020) 7481 0901

DRIVER, Arthur John Roberts. b 44. SS Coll Cam MA70 FCIPA73. Linc Th Coll 73. **d** 76 **p** 77. C S'wark H Trin w St Matt *S'wark* 76-80; TV N Lambeth 80-85; CMS Sri Lanka 86-92; V Putney St Marg *S'wark* 92-97; V Streatham St Paul from 97. *St Paul's Vicarage, 63 Chillerton Road, London SW17 9BE* Tel (020) 8672 5536 E-mail ajrdriver@btinternet.com

DRIVER, Bruce Leslie. b 42. Lon Univ LLB73 Nottm Univ DipTh77. Linc Th Coll 76. **d** 78 **p** 79. C Dunstable *St Alb* 78-81; TV 81-86; V Rickmansworth 86-98; RD Rickmansworth 91-98; V Northwood Hills St Edm *Lon* from 98. *St Edmund's Vicarage, 2 Pinner Road, Northwood HA6 1QS* Tel (020) 8866 9230 E-mail bldriver@tiscali.co.uk

DRIVER, Geoffrey. b 41. Chich Th Coll 86. **d** 88 **p** 89. C Pontefract St Giles *Wakef* 88-91; V Glass Houghton 91-97; Chapl Pontefract Hosps NHS Trust 97-99; R Southwick H Trin *Dur* 99-03; TR N Wearside from 03. *The Team Rectory, Rotherham Road, Sunderland SR5 5QS* Tel 0191-549 1261 E-mail fathergeoff@lineone.net

DRIVER, Geoffrey Lester. b 59. Liv Poly BA83. Chich Th Coll 86. **d** 89 **p** 90. C Walton St Mary *Liv* 89-92; C Walton-on-the-Hill 92; C Selsey *Chich* 92-95; V Cowfold from 95. *The Vicarage, Cowfold, Horsham RH13 8AH* Tel (01403) 864296

DRIVER, Gordon Geoffrey. b 32. Garnett Coll Lon Dip Teaching59. Trin Coll Bris. **d** 95 **p** 96. NSM Radipole and Melcombe Regis *Sarum* 95-03; rtd 03; Perm to Offic *Sarum* from 03. *11 Greenway Close, Weymouth DT3 5BQ* Tel (01305) 812784

DRIVER (née FRENCH), Janet Mary. b 43. Leeds Univ BA65 PGCE66 Surrey Univ BA98. Linc Th Coll 74. **dss** 80 **d** 92 **p** 94. St Paul's Cathl *Lon* 80-82; N Lambeth *S'wark* 80-85; CMS Sri Lanka 86-92; NSM Putney St Marg *S'wark* 92-97; Hon C Streatham St Paul from 97. *St Paul's Vicarage, 63 Chillerton Road, London SW17 9BE* Tel (020) 8672 5536

DRIVER, John. *See* DRIVER, Arthur John Roberts

DRIVER, Canon Penelope May. b 52. N Ord Course. **d** 87 **p** 94. Dioc Youth Adv *Newc* 86-88; C Cullercoats St Geo 87-88; Youth Chapl *Ripon* 88-96; Dioc Adv Women's Min from 91; Asst Dir of Ords 96-98; Dioc Dir of Ords from 98; Min Can Ripon Cathl from 96; Hon Can from 98. *The Parish House, 16 Orchard Close, Sharow, Ripon HG4 5BE* Tel and fax (01765) 607017 E-mail pdrvr@globalnet.co.uk

DRIVER, Roger John. b 64. Trin Coll Bris BA88. **d** 90 **p** 91. C Much Woolton *Liv* 90-93; C Fazakerley Em 93-94; TV 94-00; P-in-c Bootle St Matt 00-03; P-in-c Bootle St Leon 00-03; P-in-c Litherland St Andr 00-03; TR Bootle from 04. *The Vicarage, 70 Merton Road, Bootle L20 7AT* Tel 0151-922 3316 E-mail rogerdriver@btinternet.com

DROMORE, Archdeacon of. *See* SCOTT, The Ven William John

DROMORE, Dean of. *See* LOWRY, The Very Revd Stephen Harold

DROWLEY, Arthur. b 28. Oak Hill Th Coll 54. **d** 56 **p** 57. C Longfleet *Sarum* 56-59; C Wallington H Trin *S'wark* 59-62; V Taunton St Jas *B & W* 62-73; RD Taunton N 72-73; V Rodbourne Cheney *Bris* 73-87; R Bigbury, Ringmore and Kingston *Ex* 87-94; rtd 94; Perm to Offic *Ex* 94-02 and *Man* from 03. *4 Inglis Road, Park Hall, Oswestry SY11 4AN* Tel (01691) 671994

DROWN, Richard. b 19. BNC Ox BA41 MA43. Wycliffe Hall Ox 41. **d** 42 **p** 43. C St Helens St Helen *Liv* 42-45; Chapl K Coll Budo Uganda 46-65; Hd Master St Andr Sch Turi Kenya 65-73; Hd Master Edin Ho Sch New Milton 73-84; rtd 84; Hon C Brockenhurst *Win* from 85. *3 Waters Green Court, Brockenhurst SO42 7QR* Tel (01590) 624038

DRUCE, Brian Lemuel. b 31. MRICS55. Bps' Coll Cheshunt 58. **d** 60 **p** 61. C Whitton St Aug *Lon* 60-63; C Minehead *B & W* 63-66; R Birch St Agnes *Man* 66-70; V Overbury w Alstone, Teddington and Lt Washbourne *Worc* 70-81; Ind Chapl 81-91; rtd 91; Perm to Offic *Worc* from 91. *Park Cottage, Elmley Castle, Pershore WR10 3HU* Tel (01386) 710577 E-mail brian.druce@talk21.com

DRUCE, John Perry. b 34. Em Coll Cam BA57 MA61 Lambeth STh97 ALCM86. Wycliffe Hall Ox 57. **d** 59 **p** 60. C Wednesbury St Bart *Lich* 59-62; C Bushbury 62-64; V Walsall Wood 64-74; R Farnborough *Roch* 74-87; R E Bergholt *St E* 87-99; P-in-c Bentley w Tattingstone 95-99; rtd 99. *9 Fullers Close, Hadleigh, Ipswich IP7 5AS* Tel (01473) 827242 E-mail jgdruce@realemail.co.uk

DRUMMOND, Canon Christopher John Vaughan. b 26. Magd Coll Ox MA51 Magd Coll Cam MA56. Ridley Hall Cam 51. **d** 53 **p** 54. C Barking St Marg *Chelmsf* 53-56; Tutor Ridley Hall Cam 56-59; Lic to Offic *Ely* 57-62; Chapl Clare Coll Cam 59-62; Nigeria 63-69; V Walthamstow St Jo *Chelmsf* 69-74; P-in-c Stantonbury *Ox* 74-75; R 75-84; P-in-c Ducklington 84-88; Dioc Ecum Officer 84-88; Can Ibadan from 87; Home Sec Gen Syn Bd for Miss and Unity 88-91; rtd 91; P-in-c Colton *Lich* 91-94; Perm to Offic *Lich* 94-99 and *Guildf* from 97. *77 Markham Road, Capel, Dorking RH5 5JT* Tel (01306) 712637 Mobile 07966-518681

DRUMMOND, John Malcolm. b 44. Nottm Univ CertEd65. Edin Th Coll 68. **d** 71 **p** 72. C Kirkholt *Man* 71-74; C Westleigh St Pet 74-76; Hd of RE Leigh High Sch from 76; Lic Preacher from 76; Hon C Leigh St Jo 84-90; Hon C Tonge Moor from 90. *14 Bull's Head Cottages, Turton, Bolton BL7 0HS* Tel (01204) 852232 E-mail sdrummond@deanery.wigan.sch.uk

DRUMMOND, Josceline Maurice Vaughan. b 29. Lon Univ BD70. Wycliffe Hall Ox 55. **d** 58 **p** 59. C Tunbridge Wells St Jo *Roch* 58-60; C Walthamstow St Mary *Chelmsf* 60-62; V Oulton *Lich* 62-68; V Leyton St Cath *Chelmsf* 71-85; Gen Dir CMJ 85-94; Public Preacher *St Alb* 88-94; rtd 94; Perm to Offic *St Alb* from 94. *3 Fryth Mead, St Albans AL3 4TN* Tel (01727) 857620

DRURY, Anthony Desmond. b 42. Liv Poly FTC63. N Ord Course. **d** 99 **p** 00. NSM New Ferry *Ches* from 99. *61 Church Road, Bebington, Wirral CH63 3DZ* Tel 0151-334 4797

DRURY, Mrs Carol. b 61. SRN83. Trin Coll Bris 00. **d** 01 **p** 02. NSM Soundwell *Bris* 01-03; Miss Partner CMS from 04. *Address temp unknown* E-mail its-mrs-d@drury28@freeserve.co.uk

DRURY, Mrs Caroline Nora. b 60. St Alb and Ox Min Course 00. **d** 03 **p** 04. C Leavesden All SS *St Alb* from 03. *44 Haydon Road, Watford WD19 4DD* Tel (01923) 236894 E-mail caroline.drury@btinternet.com

DRURY, Desmond. *See* DRURY, Anthony Desmond

DRURY, The Very Revd John Henry. b 36. Trin Hall Cam MA66. Westcott Ho Cam 61. **d** 63 **p** 64. C St John's Wood *Lon* 63-66; Chapl Down Coll Cam 66-69; Chapl Ex Coll Ox 69-73; Can Res Nor Cathl *Nor* 73-79; Vice-Dean 78-79; Lect Sussex Univ 79-81; Dean K Coll Cam 81-91; Dean Ch Ch *Ox* 91-03; rtd 03; Chapl and Fell All So Coll Ox from 03. *All Souls College, Oxford OX1 4AL* Tel (01865) 279379 Fax 279299

DRURY, Michael Dru. b 31. Trin Coll Ox BA55 MA59. Wycliffe Hall Ox DipTh57. **d** 58 **p** 59. C Fulham St Mary N End *Lon* 58-62; C Blackheath St Jo *S'wark* 62-64; Chapl and Asst Master Canford Sch Wimborne 64-80; Chapl and Teacher Fernhill Manor Sch New Milton 80-81; P-in-c Stowe *Ox* 82-92; Asst Master Stowe Sch Bucks 82-92; R Rampton w Laneham, Treswell, Cottam and Stokeham *S'well* 92-96; rtd 96; Perm to Offic *Sarum* from 96. *Tanfield, Giddylake, Wimborne BH21 2QT* Tel (01202) 881246

DRURY, Richard Alexander. b 63. Lon Univ BD85 Avery Hill Coll PGCE86 ACII91. Trin Coll Bris MA00. **d** 00 **p** 01. C Kingswood *Bris* 00-03; Miss Partner CMS from 04. *Address temp unknown* E-mail richard@drury86.freeserve.co.uk

DRURY, Valerie Doreen. b 40. MBATOD80 Univ of Wales (Cardiff) BA62 K Coll Lon PGCE63 Lon Inst of Educn ADEDC80. Oak Hill Th Coll 85. **d** 87 **p** 94. NSM Becontree St Alb *Chelmsf* 87-89; NSM Becontree S 89-02; rtd 02; Perm to Offic *Chelmsf* from 02. *63 Tilney Road, Dagenham RM9 6HL* Tel (020) 8592 7285 E-mail valerie@lockyer40.freeserve.co.uk

DRYDEN, Barry Frederick. b 44. Chester Coll of HE BTh00. N Ord Course 97. **d** 00 **p** 01. C Formby St Pet *Liv* 00-03; V Woolston from 03. *The Vicarage, 20 Warren Lane, Woolston, Warrington WA1 4ES* Tel (01925) 813083 E-mail barjan@fish.co.uk

DRYDEN, Canon Leonard. b 29. MIEE59 MIMechE59 Lon Univ BD64 Bath Univ MSc73. Ridley Hall Cam. **d** 61 **p** 62. C Luton w E Hyde *St Alb* 61-65; C-in-c Bedminster *Bris* 65-74; Bp's Soc and Ind Adv 65-74; Chapl Bris Cathl 66-70; Hon Can Bris Cathl 70-74; Dir CORAT 74-76; Sec from 76; Team Ldr and Convener Lon Ind Chapl *Lon* 77-85; V Frindsbury w Upnor *Roch* 85-91; rtd 91; P-in-c Sevenoaks Weald *Roch* 91-95; Perm to Offic *Win* from 95. *1 King Alfred Terrace, Winchester SO23 7DE* Tel (01962) 852170

DRYE, Douglas John. b 37. Man Univ BSc61. Clifton Th Coll. **d** 63 **p** 64. C Whalley Range St Edm *Man* 63-66; C Drypool St Columba w St Andr and St Pet *York* 66-68; V Worsbrough Common *Sheff* 68-86; R Armthorpe 86-92; rtd 92; Perm to Offic *Pet* from 92. *25 Willow Crescent, Oakham LE15 6EQ* Tel (01572) 770429

DUBLIN (Christ Church), Dean of. *See* HARMAN, The Very Revd Robert Desmond

DUBLIN (St Patrick's), Dean of. *See* MacCARTHY, The Very Revd Robert Brian

DUBLIN, Archbishop of, and Bishop of Glendalough. *See* NEILL, The Most Revd John Robert Winder

DUBLIN, Archdeacon of. *See* PIERPOINT, The Ven David Alfred

DUCE, Canon Alan Richard. b 41. St Pet Coll Ox BA65 MA68 Enfield Poly CQSW75. Cuddesdon Coll 65. **d** 67 **p** 68. C Boston *Linc* 67-71; Chapl St Geo Hosp Lon 71-73; Hon C Harringay St Paul *Lon* 73-75; Chapl HM Pris Pentonville 75-76; Chapl HM Pris The Verne 76-81; Chapl HM Pris Linc 81-03; Gen Preacher *Linc* 81-03; rtd 03; Can and Preb Linc Cathl *Linc* from 02; Ed *Justice Reflections* from 02; Perm to Offic from 03. *2 Temple Gardens, Lincoln LN2 1NP* Tel (01522) 529468 Fax 514831 E-mail alanduce@hotmail.com

DUCK, Mrs Jacqueline. b 44. Ches Coll of HE BTh00 ACMA70. N Ord Course 97. **d** 00 **p** 01. NSM Ormskirk *Liv* 00-04; C Sutton from 04. *Sutton Vicarage, 40 Eaves Lane, St Helens WA9 3UB* Tel and fax (01744) 812347 E-mail jduck@surefish.co.uk

DUCKETT, Canon Brian John. b 45. ALCD70. **d** 70 **p** 71. C S Lambeth St Steph *S'wark* 70-73; C Norwood St Luke 73-75; C Bushbury *Lich* 75-77; TV 77-79; V Dover St Martin *Cant* 79-92; TR Swindon Dorcan *Bris* 92-00; RD Highworth 95-99; Hon Can Bris Cathl from 98; V Clifton H Trin, St Andr and St Pet from 00. *Holy Trinity Vicarage, 6 Goldney Avenue, Bristol BS8 4RA* Tel 0117-973 4751 E-mail office@hthotwells.fsnet.co.uk

DUCKETT, Ms Helen Lorraine. b 71. Keble Coll Ox BA92 Sheff Univ MA94 Birm Univ MPhil98. Qu Coll Birm 95. **d** 98 **p** 99. C Cannock *Lich* 98-01; TV Wednesfield from 01. *167 Colman Avenue, Wolverhampton WV11 3RU* Tel (01902) 630094 E-mail duckett.h@tinyworld.co.uk

DUCKETT, John Dollings. b 41. Nottm Univ BA62 BTh81. Linc Th Coll 79. **d** 81 **p** 82. C Boston *Linc* 81-84; V Baston 84-86; V Langtoft Gp 86-88; V Sutterton and Wigtoft 88-89; R Sutterton w Fosdyke and Algarkirk 89-92; P-in-c Chapel St Leonards w Hogsthorpe 92-97; V 97-00; V Bracebridge from 00. *The Vicarage, 60 Chiltern Road, Lincoln LN5 8SE* Tel (01522) 532636

DUCKETT, Keith Alexander. b 69. Worc Coll of Educn BA93 Birm Univ BD97 MA98. Qu Coll Birm 95. **d** 98 **p** 99. C Willenhall H Trin *Lich* 98-01; TV Blakenall Heath 01-03; Asst Chapl Sandwell Health Care NHS Trust from 03. *Sandwell General Hospital, Lyndon, West Bromwich B71 4HJ* Tel 0121-553 1831 *or* (01902) 732763 E-mail keith.duckett@swbh.nhs.uk *or* duckettk@fish.co.uk

DUCKETT, Lee Christopher James. b 67. Wycliffe Hall Ox BTh04. **d** 04 **p** 05. C Cranham Park *Chelmsf* from 04. *72 Marlborough Gardens, Upminster RM14 1SG* Tel (01708) 225604 Fax 223253 Mobile 07782-171320 E-mail rev.leeduckett@ntlworld.com

DUCKETT, Raphael Thomas Marie James. b 65. N Staffs Poly BA87. Cranmer Hall Dur 01. **d** 03 **p** 04. C Madeley *Heref* from 03. *7 Mellor Close, Madeley, Telford TF7 5SS* Tel (01952) 413674 E-mail raphael@fish.co.uk

DUCKWORTH, Mrs Annette Jacqueline. b 54. **d** 00 **p** 01. OLM Moxley *Lich* from 00. *1 Sutton Road, Wednesbury WS10 8SG* Tel (01902) 650656

DUCKWORTH, Brian George. b 47. Edin Th Coll 85. **d** 87 **p** 88. C Sutton in Ashfield St Mary *S'well* 87-95; C Sutton in Ashfield St Mich 89-95; P-in-c 95-98; TV Hucknall Torkard 98-03; R S Ockendon and Belhus Park *Chelmsf* from 03. *The Vicarage, 121 Foyle Drive, South Ockendon RM15 5HF* Tel and fax (01708) 853246 E-mail bduck@fish.co.uk

DUCKWORTH, Derek. b 29. Fitzw Ho Cam BA52 MA58 Lon Univ PGCE66 Lanc Univ PhD72. Oak Hill Th Coll 52. **d** 54 **p** 55. C Preston All SS *Blackb* 54-57; C Sutton *Liv* 57-58; Hon C Wakef St Jo *Wakef* 58-60; Public Preacher *Blackb* 60-64; C Whalley 64-73; Hon C Newbury *Ox* 73-80; Perm to Office *Ox* 80-81; *Cant* 81-84 and 85-86; P-in-c Dymchurch w Burmarsh and Newchurch *Cant* 84-85; Chapl Leybourne Grange Hosp W Malling 85-86; P-in-c Rampton w Laneham, Treswell, Cottam and Stokeham *S'well* 86-89; R 89-91; rtd 91; Perm to Offic *Cant* from 91. *10 Sharps Field, Headcorn, Ashford TN27 9UF* Tel (01622) 890143

DUDDING, Edward Leslie (Father Gregory). b 30. Auckland Univ MSc52 St Jo Coll Auckland LTh56. **d** 57 **p** 57. New Zealand 57-60; Lic to Offic *Chich* from 62; CSWG from 62; Father Superior from 73. *Monastery of The Holy Trinity, Crawley Down, Crawley RH10 4LH* Tel (01342) 712074

DUDLEY, Harold George. b 14. St Mich Coll Llan 68. **d** 70 **p** 70. C Fleur-de-Lis *Mon* 70-73; V Goldcliffe and Whitson and Nash 73-83; rtd 83; Lic to Offic *Mon* from 83. *Mayfield, Llanthewy Road, Newport NP20 4JZ*

DUDLEY, Mrs Janet Carr. b 36. EMMTC 86. **d** 89 **p** 94. NSM Countesthorpe w Foston *Leic* 89-94; NSM Arnesby w Shearsby and Bruntingthorpe 94-01; rtd 01; Perm to Offic *Leic* 01-02; NSM Market Harborough and The Transfiguration etc from 02. *13 The Broadway, Market Harborough LE16 7LZ* Tel (01858) 467619

DUDLEY, John Donald Swanborough. b 34. Edin Univ DipAgr53 Ox Univ BTh95. St Alb and Ox Min Course 96. **d** 97 **p** 98. NSM Emmer Green *Ox* 97-02; Perm to Offic from 02. *26 Russet Glade, Caversham, Reading RG4 8UJ* Tel 0118-954 6664 Fax as telephone

DUDLEY, Martin Raymond. b 53. K Coll Lon BD77 AKC77 MTh78 PhD94 FRHistS95 FSA97. St Mich Coll Llan 78. **d** 79 **p** 80. C Whitchurch *Llan* 79-83; V Weston *St Alb* 83-88; P-in-c Ardeley 87-88; V Owlsmoor *Ox* 88-95; Lect Simon of Cyrene Th Inst 92-95; R Smithfield St Bart Gt *Lon* from 95. *Church House, Cloth Fair, London EC1A 7JQ* Tel (020) 7606 5171 *or* 7628 3644 Fax 7600 6909 E-mail st.bartholomew@btinternet.com

DUDLEY, Miss Wendy Elizabeth. b 46. City of Sheff Coll CertEd68. Cranmer Hall Dur 79. **dss** 81 **d** 87 **p** 94. Cumnor *Ox* 81-87; Par Dn 87-89; Par Dn Hodge Hill *Birm* 89-94; C 94-95; TV 95-98; TV Bucknall *Lich* from 98. *The Vicarage, Dawlish Drive, Stoke-on-Trent ST2 0ET* Tel (01782) 260876 *or* 279300 E-mail wed.btm@tinyworld.co.uk

DUDLEY-SMITH, James. b 66. Fitzw Coll Cam BA89 MA92. Wycliffe Hall Ox BTh94. **d** 97 **p** 98. C New Borough and Leigh *Sarum* 97-01; C Hove Bp Hannington Memorial Ch *Chich* from 01. *43 Hogarth Road, Hove BN3 5RH* Tel (01273) 725642

✠**DUDLEY-SMITH, The Rt Revd Timothy.** b 26. OBE03. Pemb Coll Cam BA47 MA51 Lambeth MLitt91. Ridley Hall Cam 48. **d** 50 **p** 51 **c** 81. C Erith St Paul *Roch* 50-53; Lic to Offic *S'wark* 53-62; Hd of Cam Univ Miss Bermondsey 53-55; Chapl 55-60; Ed Sec Evang Alliance and Ed *Crusade* 55-59; Asst Sec CPAS 59-65; Gen Sec 65-73; Adn Nor 73-81; Suff Bp Thetford 81-91; rtd 92. *9 Ashlands, Ford, Salisbury SP4 6DY* Tel (01722) 326417

DUDLEY, Archdeacon of. *See* TRETHEWEY, The Ven Frederick Martyn

DUDLEY, Suffragan Bishop of. *See* WALKER, The Rt Revd David Stuart

DUERDEN, Martin James. b 55. Liv Poly BA77. Oak Hill Th Coll 86. **d** 88 **p** 89. C Tunbridge Wells St Jas *Roch* 88-92; V Southport SS Simon and Jude *Liv* 92-98; P-in-c Maghull 98-02; TR from 02. *The Rectory, 20 Damfield Lane, Liverpool L31 6DD* Tel 0151-526 5017 E-mail martin-duerden@bigfoot.com

DUERR, Robert Kenneth. b 54. Univ of S California BMus77 MMus80. Ridley Hall Cam 99. **d** 04. NSM Cambridge Gt St Mary w St Mich *Ely* from 04. *Great St Mary's Church, St Mary's Passage, Cambridge CB2 3PQ* Tel (01233) 741721 E-mail rd299@cam.ac.uk

DUFF, Alison. *See* FINCH, Mrs Alison

DUFF, Andrew John. b 57. MIOT. Sarum & Wells Th Coll 92. **d** 92 **p** 93. C Banbury *Ox* 92-95; C Bracknell 95-96; TV 96-98; CF 98-04; Chapl RN from 04. *Royal Naval Chaplaincy Service, Room 203, Victory Building, HM Naval Base, Porstmouth PO1 3LS* Tel (01705) 727903 Fax 727112

DUFF, Garden Ian. b 34. ACGI56 Imp Coll Lon BScEng56. Sarum & Wells Th Coll 92. **d** 93 **p** 94. NSM Ashton Gifford *Sarum* 93-97; TV Upper Wylye Valley 97-03; rtd 03. *Trinity Trees Cottage, 58 Upton Lovell, Warminster BA12 0JP* Tel (01985) 850291 Fax as telephone

DUFF, Jillian Louise Calland. b 72. Ch Coll Cam BA93 MA97 Worc Coll Ox DPhil96. Wycliffe Hall Ox BA02. **d** 03. C Litherland St Phil *Liv* from 03. *3 Harrington Road, Litherland, Liverpool L21 7NA* Tel 0151-222 5819 E-mail jillduff@fish.co.uk

DUFF, John Alexander. b 57. York Univ BA78. EMMTC DTPS94. **d** 94 **p** 95. NSM Linc St Geo Swallowbeck *Linc* 94-00; Perm to Offic *Ripon* from 02. *37 Mornington Crescent, Harrogate HG1 5DL* Tel (01423) 549987

DUFF, Michael Ian. b 63. Ox Univ BA85. Trin Coll Bris BA98 MA99. **d** 99 **p** 00. C Southsea St Jude *Portsm* 99-03; CMS Bandung Indonesia from 03. *Jalan Gunung Batu 10, Bandung, 40142, West Java, Indonesia* Tel (0062) (22) 203 3713 E-mail all@theduffs.me.uk

DUFF, Timothy Cameron. b 40. G&C Coll Cam BA62 LLM63 MA66 Solicitor 65. NEOC 90. **d** 93 **p** 94. NSM Tynemouth Priory *Newc* 93-96; NSM N Shields 96-00; Hon TV 00-05; rtd 05. *26 The Drive, North Shields NE30 4JW* Tel 0191-257 1463 Fax 296 1904 E-mail timothy@dufftyne.freeserve.co.uk

DUFFETT, Canon Paul Stanton. b 33. Keble Coll Ox BA55 MA59. Ripon Hall Ox DipTh58. **d** 59 **p** 60. C Portsea St Cuth *Portsm* 59-63; S Africa 63-80; Hon Can Zululand from 87; Accredited Rep Zululand and Swaziland Assn from 89; P-in-c Greatham w Empshott *Portsm* 80-85; R 85-88; R Papworth Everard *Ely* 88-98; Chapl Papworth Hosps 88-98; rtd 98; Hon Chapl Mothers' Union from 97; Perm to Offic *Ely* from 99. *11 Roman Hill, Barton, Cambridge CB3 7AX* Tel (01223) 262831

DUFFETT-SMITH (née RUSHTON), Ms Patricia Mary. b 54. Lon Univ BPharm76 Anglia Poly Univ MA99 MRPharmS77. EAMTC 94. **d** 97 **p** 98. NSM Haddenham and Wilburton *Ely* 97-00; Asst Chapl Hinchingbrooke Health Care NHS Trust from 99. *41 Denmark Road, Cottenham, Cambridge CB4 8QS* Tel 07788-668900 (mobile) E-mail trishads@hotmail.com

DUFFIELD, Ian Keith. b 47. K Coll Lon BD71 AKC71 MTh73. NY Th Sem DMin84. **d** 73 **p** 74. C Broxbourne *St Alb* 73-77; C Harpenden St Nic 77-81; TV Sheff Manor *Sheff* 81-87; V

Walkley 87-02; V Sheff St Leon Norwood from 02. *St Leonard's Vicarage, Everingham Road, Sheffield S5 7LE* Tel 0114-243 6689

DUFFIELD, John Ernest. b 55. BA86. Oak Hill Th Coll 83. **d** 86 **p** 87. C Walton Breck Ch Ch *Liv* 86-89; TV Fazakerley Em 89-00; Chapl N Cheshire Hosps NHS Trust from 00. *Warrington Hospital, Lovely Lane, Warrington WA5 1QG* Tel (01925) 662146 Fax 662048 E-mail john.duffield@nch.nhs.uk

DUFFIELD, Ronald Bertram Charles. b 26. Hull Univ Coll BA49 TCert50. Sarum & Wells Th Coll 91. **d** 92 **p** 93. NSM E Knoyle, Semley and Sedgehill *Sarum* 92-94; P-in-c 94-95; rtd 95; Perm to Offic *York* 95-99 and from 01; P-in-c Isfield *Chich* 99-01. *16 Wylies Road, Beverley HU17 7AP* Tel (01482) 880983

DUFFUS, Barbara Rose. *See* HOBBS, Mrs Barbara Rose

DUGDALE, Angela Marion. b 33. DL92. ARCM52 GRSM54 UEA Hon MA89. LNSM course 96. **d** 97 **p** 98. OLM Weybourne Gp *Nor* 97-03; rtd 03; Perm to Offic *Nor* from 03. *Beck House, Kelling, Holt NR25 7EL* Tel (01263) 588389 Fax 588594

DUGMORE, Barry John. b 61. STETS. **d** 01 **p** 02. C Cowplain *Portsm* 01-04; C-in-c Whiteley CD from 04; Dioc Ecum Officer from 04. *20 Sheridan Gardens, Whiteley, Fareham PO15 7DY* E-mail b.dugmore@ukgateway.net

DUGUID, Alison Audrey. b 52. STETS 99. **d** 02 **p** 03. C Appledore w Brookland, Fairfield, Brenzett etc *Cant* from 02. *Puddleglum, Appledore Road, Brenzett, Romney Marsh TN29 9UG* Tel (01797) 344125 Mobile 07880-711202 E-mail ali@dogooders.co.uk

DUGUID, Reginald Erskine. b 29. S'wark Ord Course. **d** 88 **p** 89. NSM Notting Hill All SS w St Columb *Lon* from 88. *53 Sandbourne, Dartmouth Close, London W11 1DS* Tel (020) 7221 4436

DUKE, Canon Alan Arthur. b 38. Tyndale Hall Bris 59. **d** 64 **p** 65. C Whalley Range St Marg *Man* 64-67; C Folkestone H Trin w Ch Ch *Cant* 67-71; V Queenborough 71-76; V Bearsted w Thurnham 76-86; P-in-c Torquay St Luke *Ex* 86-91; R Barham w Bishopsbourne and Kingston *Cant* 91-00; Dioc Communications Officer 91-95; Hon Can Cant Cathl 99-03; Chapl to Bp Dover 00-03; Bp's Media Link Officer 00-03; rtd 03; Perm to Offic *Cant* from 03. *Roundways, Derringstone Hill, Barham, Canterbury CT4 6QD* Tel (01227) 831817 E-mail aduke@fish.co.uk

DUKE, David Malcolm. b 40. Ch Ch Ox BA61 DipTh64 MA65 Newc Poly MPhil80 CQSW81. Cuddesdon Coll 63. **d** 65 **p** 66. C Sunderland Pennywell St Thos *Dur* 65-68; C Dur St Oswald 68-70; C Harton 70-74; Perm to Offic 85-96; Hon C Hedworth from 96. *43 Coquet Street, Jarrow NE32 5SW* Tel 0191-430 1200 Mobile 07979-036977 Fax 0191-537 4409

DUKE, Miss Judith Mary. b 47. Leeds Univ LLB68. Cranmer Hall Dur 03. **d** 04 **p** 05. NSM Buckrose Carrs *York* from 04. *13 Sledgate Garth, Rillington, Malton YO17 8JS* Tel (01944) 758305 Mobile 07929-825891 E-mail judy@buckrose.org.uk

DULFER, John Guidi. b 37. Lich Th Coll 62. **d** 64 **p** 65. C Fenny Stratford and Water Eaton *Ox* 64-67; C Cheshunt *St Alb* 67-68; C Kennington Cross St Anselm *S'wark* 68-74; C N Lambeth 74-76; P-in-c Kensington St Phil Earl's Court *Lon* 76-79; V 79-84; Chapl Odstock Hosp Salisbury 84; USA from 84; rtd 02. *135 West 22 Street #2, New York, NY 10011, USA* Tel (001) (212) 604 9040 E-mail johndulfer@hotmail.com

DULLEY, Arthur John Franklyn. b 32. Mert Coll Ox BA54 MA57. St Jo Coll Nottm 69. **d** 71 **p** 72. Lect St Jo Coll Nottm 71-96; Hon C Attenborough w Chilwell *S'well* 71-73; C Penn Fields *Lich* 73-74; Chapl Aldenham Sch Herts 74-79; Chapl HM Pris Ashwell 79-87; V Langham *Pet* 79-96; rtd 96; Perm to Offic *Ely* 96-98. *8 Prickwillow Road, Ely CB7 4QP* Tel (01353) 664381

DUMAT, Mrs Jennifer. b 42. ARCM62. Qu Coll Birm 80 EMMTC 82. **dss** 83 **d** 87 **p** 94. Chapl Asst Pilgrim Hosp Boston 83-94; P-in-c Friskney *Linc* 94-04; rtd 04. *11 Sea Lane, Butterwick, Boston PE22 0EY* Tel (01205) 760883

✠**DUMPER, The Rt Revd Anthony Charles.** b 23. Ch Coll Cam BA45 MA48. Westcott Ho Cam. **d** 47 **p** 48 **c** 77. C E Greenwich Ch Ch w St Andr and St Mich *S'wark* 47-49; Malaya 49-63; Malaysia 63-64; Dean Singapore 64-70; V Stockton St Pet *Dur* 70-77; P-in-c Stockton H Trin 76-77; RD Stockton 70-77; Suff Bp Dudley *Worc* 77-93; rtd 93; Hon Asst Bp Birm from 93. *117 Burberry Close, Birmingham B30 1TB* Tel 0121-458 3011

DUNBAR, Peter Lamb. b 46. Bede Coll Dur DipEd68. Lambeth STh77 N Ord Course 78. **d** 81 **p** 82. NSM Knaresborough *Ripon* 81-82; C Knaresborough 82-84; R Farnham w Scotton, Staveley, Copgrove etc 84-92; V Upper Nidderdale from 92; Chapl St Aid Sch Harrogate 86-94. *The Vicarage, Church Street, Pateley Bridge, Harrogate HG3 5LQ* Tel (01423) 711414 E-mail lionlamb@dircon.co.uk

DUNCAN, Canon Bruce. b 38. MBE93. Leeds Univ BA60 FRSA. Cuddesdon Coll 65. **d** 67 **p** 68. C Armley St Bart *Ripon* 67-69; Dir Children's Relief Internat 69-71; Chapl Vienna w Budapest and Prague *Eur* 71-75; V Crediton *Ex* 75-82; R Crediton and Shobrooke 82-86; RD Cadbury 76-81 and 84-86; Can Res Man Cathl *Man* 86-95; Prin Sarum Coll 95-02; Can and Preb Sarum Cathl *Sarum* 95-02; rtd 02; Perm to Offic *Sarum* from 02. *Church Path Cottage, St David's Hill, Exeter EX4 4DU* Tel and fax (01392) 420988 Mobile 07949-268541 E-mail churchpath@fsmail.net

DUNCAN, Christopher Robin. b 41. AKC71. **d** 72 **p** 73. C Allington *Cant* 72-77; P-in-c Wittersham 77-82; R Wittersham w Stone-in-Oxney and Ebony 82-85; V Chilham 85-92; P-in-c Challock w Molash 87-92; RD W Bridge 92-95 and 02-03; V Chilham w Challock and Molash from 92. *The Vicarage, 3 Hambrook Close, Chilham, Canterbury CT4 8EJ* Tel (01227) 730235 E-mail chris.duncan@chil-vic.co.uk

DUNCAN, Colin Richard. b 34. SS Coll Cam BA58 MA60. Ripon Coll Cuddesdon 83. **d** 85 **p** 86. C Stafford *Lich* 85-89; C Wednesfield 89-90; TV 90-99; rtd 99; Perm to Offic *Glouc* from 99. *Fir Tree Cottage, Union Road, Bakers Hill, Coleford GL16 7QB*

DUNCAN, Graham Charles Dewar. b 65. Sheff Univ BSc87. NTMTC 95. **d** 98 **p** 99. NSM Dawley St Jerome *Lon* 98-00; NSM Sheff St Mary Bramall Lane *Sheff* from 00; Manager St Mary's Ch Community Cen from 00. *11 Coverdale Road, Sheffield S7 2DD* Tel 0114-258 7275 *or* 272 5596 Fax 275 3892

DUNCAN, The Very Revd Gregor Duthie. b 50. Glas Univ MA72 Clare Coll Cam PhD77 Oriel Coll Ox BA83. Ripon Coll Cuddesdon 81. **d** 83 **p** 84. C Oakham, Hambleton, Egleton, Braunston and Brooke *Pet* 83-86; Edin Th Coll 87-89; R Largs *Glas* 89-99; Dean Glas from 96; R Glas St Ninian from 99. *St Ninian's Rectory, 32 Glencairn Drive, Glasgow G41 4PW* Tel 0141-423 1247 Fax 424 3332 E-mail dean@glasgow.anglican.org

DUNCAN, James Montgomerie. b 29. Edin Th Coll 53. **d** 56 **p** 57. C Edin St Pet *Edin* 56-59; C Edin Old St Paul 59-60; S Africa 60-65; Prov Youth Org Scotland 65-69; R Edin St Salvador *Edin* 69-86; Chapl HM Pris Saughton 69-86; R Aberlour *Mor* 86-98; R Fochabers 86-98; rtd 98. *East Scores House, 24 East Scores, St Andrews KY16 9BE* Tel (01334) 472295 E-mail heduncan@onetel.net.uk

DUNCAN, John. b 22. Open Univ BA. Roch Th Coll 64. **d** 66 **p** 67. C Gainsborough All SS *Linc* 66-68; C Boultham 68-71; V W Pinchbeck 72-76; Canada 76-81; R Ridgewell w Ashen, Birdbrook and Sturmer *Chelmsf* 81-88; rtd 88; Perm to Offic *Pet* from 91. *20 Westcott Way, Northampton NN3 3BE* Tel (01604) 30797

DUNCAN, The Ven John Finch. b 33. Univ Coll Ox BA57 MA63. Cuddesdon Coll 57. **d** 59 **p** 60. C S Bank *York* 59-61; SSF 61-62; C Birm St Pet *Birm* 62-65; Chapl Birm Univ 65-76; V Kings Heath 76-85; Hon Can Birm Cathl 83-85; Adn Birm 85-01; rtd 01; Perm to Offic *Birm* from 01. *66 Glebe Rise, King's Sutton, Banbury OX17 3PH* Tel (01295) 812641

DUNCAN, Peter Harold Furlong. b 25. AKC52 Lon Univ BA68 Goldsmiths' Coll Lon BA71 MPhil79. **d** 53 **p** 54. C Sheff St Geo and St Steph *Sheff* 53-56; C Wealdstone H Trin *Lon* 56-57; V Battersea St Pet *S'wark* 57-64; Nigeria 64-66; Hon C All Hallows by the Tower etc *Lon* 67-73; Ind Chapl Lon Docks 67-73; Sen Lect in Sociology City of Lon Poly 73-87; Hon C Gt Ilford St Andr *Chelmsf* 73-80; P-in-c Gt Canfield 80-87; P-in-c N Woolwich w Silvertown 87-93; rtd 93; Perm to Offic *York* from 93. *179 Windsor Drive, Haxby, York YO32 2YD* Tel and fax (01904) 769888 E-mail duncanpeteing@aol.com

DUNCAN, Thomas James. b 37. **d** 97 **p** 98. NSM Poplar *Lon* from 97. *1 Chardwell Close, London E6 5RR* Tel (020) 7474 9965 *or* 7538 9198 Mobile 07732-066434

DUNCAN, The Ven William Albert. b 30. TCD BA53 MA61 BD66. CITC 54. **d** 54 **p** 55. C Bangor Abbey *D & D* 54-57; C Larne and Inver *Conn* 57-61; Hd of Trin Coll Miss Belf 61-66; I Rasharkin w Finvoy 66-78; I Ramoan w Ballycastle and Culfeightrin 78-96; Adn Dalriada 93-96; rtd 96. *8 Beech Hill, Ballymoney BT53 6DB* Tel (028) 7066 4285

DUNCANSON, Derek James. b 47. TD93. AKC69 Open Univ BA80 Lon Univ MA(Ed)93 FCollP94. St Aug Coll Cant 69. **d** 70 **p** 71. C Norbury St Oswald *Cant* 70-72; CF (TAVR) 71-76 and 79-95; C Woodham *Guildf* 72-76; CF 76-79; V Burneside *Carl* 79-84; R Coppull St Jo *Blackb* 84-86; Chapl Bloxham Sch 86-99; V Pet St Mary Boongate *Pet* 99-04; RD Pet 01-04; Chapl Pet Regional Coll 00-04; Chapl Heathfield Sch Ascot from 04. *25 Ormathwaites Corner, Warfield, Bracknell RG42 3XX* Tel and fax (01344) 486603 E-mail duncansonderek@hotmail.com

DUNCOMBE, Maureen Barbara. *See* WHITE, Mrs Maureen Barbara

DUNDAS, Edward Paul. b 67. NUU BSc88. TCD Div Sch BTh91. **d** 91 **p** 92. C Portadown St Mark *Arm* 91-95; I Ardtrea w Desertcreat 95-00; Dioc Youth Adv to Abp Armagh 99-00; I Belfast St Aid *Conn* 00-05; I Lisburn Ch Ch from 05. *Christ Church Rectory, 27 Hillsborough Road, Lisburn BT28 1JL* Tel (028) 9266 2163 *or* 9267 3271 Mobile 07740-589465 E-mail paul_dundas@yahoo.com

DUNDAS, Edward Thompson. b 36. TCD BA63. **d** 64 **p** 65. C Conwall *D & R* 64-67; I Kilbarron 67-78; I Donagheady 78-84; I Kilmore St Aid w St Sav *Arm* 84-04; rtd 04. *114 Brownstown Road, Portadown, Craigavon BT62 3PZ* Tel (028) 3833 4474 Mobile 07989-842709

DUNDEE, Provost of. *See* BYRNE, The Very Revd Miriam Alexandra Frances

DUNFORD, Malcolm. b 34. FCA74. EMMTC 73. **d** 76 **p** 77. NSM Frodingham *Linc* from 76. *57 Rowland Road, Scunthorpe DN16 1SP* Tel (01724) 840879

DUNGAN, Hilary Anne. b 46. TCD BA98 ARCM68. CITC 98. **d** 00 **p** 01. C Arm St Mark *Arm* 00-03; I Maryborough w Dysart Enos and Ballyfin *C & O* from 03; Chapl Midlands Portlaoise Pris from 03. *The Rectory, Coote Street, Porlaoise, Co Laois, Irish Republic* Tel (00353) (502) 21154 E-mail portlaoise@leighlin.anglican.org

DUNK, Michael Robin. b 43. Oak Hill Th Coll BA82. **d** 82 **p** 83. C Northampton All SS w St Kath *Pet* 82-86; Ind Chapl *Birm* 86-96; P-in-c Warley Woods 96; V from 96; AD Warley from 01. *St Hilda's Vicarage, Abbey Road, Smethwick, Warley B67 5NQ* Tel 0121-429 1384 Fax 420 2386 E-mail michael.dunk@talk21.com

DUNK, Peter Norman. b 43. Sarum Th Coll 67. **d** 69 **p** 70. C Sheff St Mary w St Simon w St Matthias *Sheff* 69-71; C Margate St Jo *Cant* 71-74; Dioc Youth Officer *Birm* 74-78; R Hulme Ascension *Man* 78-83; V E Farleigh and Coxheath *Roch* 83; P-in-c Linton w Hunton 83; R Coxheath w E Farleigh, Hunton and Linton 83-88; Australia from 88; R Swanbourne 88-99; rtd 00. *7 Raffan View, Gwelup, W Australia 6018* Tel (0061) (8) 9447 8877 Fax as telephone

DUNKERLEY, James Hobson. b 39. Seabury-Western Th Sem BD69 STh70. **d** 64 **p** 65. C Stirchley *Birm* 64-66; C Perry Barr 66-70; R Chicago St Pet USA from 70. *6033 N Sheridan Road, Unit 44B, Chicago, IL 60660, USA* Tel (001) (772) 275 2773

DUNKLEY, Christopher. b 52. Edin Univ MA74 Ox Univ BA77 MA81. St Steph Ho Ox 75. **d** 78 **p** 79. C Newbold w Dunston *Derby* 78-82; C Chesterfield St Mary and All SS 82; Chapl Leic Univ *Leic* 82-85; TV Leic Ascension 85-92; Chapl Leics Hospice 85-87; V Leic St Aid 92-97; V Holbrooks *Cov* from 97. *St Luke's Vicarage, Rotherham Road, Coventry CV6 4FE* Tel (024) 7668 8604 E-mail kitdunkley@tiscali.co.uk

DUNKLEY, Reginald Alfred Lorenz. b 13. Clifton Th Coll 56. **d** 58 **p** 59. C Meopham *Roch* 59-60; C Belvedere All SS 60-64; R Longfield 64-78; rtd 78. *33 Sheriff Drive, Chatham ME5 9PU* Tel (01634) 862143

DUNKLING, Miss Judith Mary. b 77. Westcott Ho Cam 01. **d** 04 **p** 05. C Holbeach *Linc* from 04. *33 Spalding Road, Holbeach, Spalding PE12 7HG* Tel (01406) 490310 E-mail judith.dunkling@virgin.net

DUNLOP, Canon Arthur John. b 27. AKC52. **d** 53 **p** 54. C Loughton St Jo *Chelmsf* 53-57; C-in-c Chelmsf All SS CD 57-65; R Laindon w Basildon 65-72; RD Basildon 65-72; V Maldon All SS w St Pet 72-92; RD Maldon 73-82; Hon Can Chelmsf Cathl 80-92; RD Maldon and Dengie 89-92; rtd 92; Perm to Offic *Chelmsf* and *St E* from 92. *Maeldune, 64 Highfield Road, Sudbury CO10 2QJ* Tel (01787) 881699

DUNLOP, Canon Ian Geoffrey David. b 25. FSA New Coll Ox BA48 MA56. Linc Th Coll 54. **d** 56 **p** 57. C Bp's Hatfield *St Alb* 56-60; Chapl Westmr Sch 60-62; C Bures *St E* 62-72; Can Res and Chan Sarum Cathl *Sarum* 72-92; Dir Post-Ord Tr 72-92; Dir of Ords 73-92; Lect Sarum & Wells Th Coll 76-92; rtd 92; Hon C Selkirk *Edin* from 99. *Gowanbrae, The Glebe, Selkirk TD7 5AB* Tel (01750) 20706

DUNLOP, Peter John. b 44. TCD BA68 MA72 Dur Univ DipTh70 CertEd71. Cranmer Hall Dur. **d** 71 **p** 72. C Barking St Marg w St Patr *Chelmsf* 71-75; C Gt Malvern Ch Ch *Worc* 75-78; Chapl K Sch Tynemouth 78-89; V Monkseaton St Pet *Newc* 90-96; rtd 96; Perm to Offic *Newc* from 96. *19 Cliftonville Gardens, Whitley Bay NE26 1QJ* Tel 0191-251 0983

DUNN, Canon Alastair Matthew Crusoe. b 40. Lon Univ LLB64 AKC64. Wycliffe Hall Ox 78. **d** 80 **p** 81. C Yardley St Edburgha *Birm* 80-83; R Bishop's Sutton and Ropley and W Tisted *Win* 83-90; V Milford 90-04; Hon Can Win Cathl 03-04; C Harrogate St Mark *Ripon* 04-05; Hon C from 05; rtd 05. *58 Almsford Drive, Harrogate HG2 8EE* Tel (01423) 810357 E-mail asdunn@talk21.com

DUNN, Mrs Anne. b 36. **d** 03 **p** 04. OLM Weymouth H Trin *Sarum* from 03. *6 Ilchester Road, Weymouth DT4 0AW* Tel (01305) 770066 E-mail annedunn@uk2.net

DUNN, Mrs Barbara Anne. b 42. Man Univ BA72 Sheff Univ CQSW76. N Ord Course 92. **d** 95 **p** 96. NSM Stretford St Matt *Man* 95-02; Perm to Offic from 02. *71 Manley Road, Whalley Range, Manchester M16 8WF* Tel 0161-881 6929 E-mail bnsdunn@btinternet.com

DUNN, Brian. b 40. St Aid Birkenhead 66. **d** 69 **p** 70. C Over Darwen H Trin *Blackb* 69-71; C Burnley St Pet 71-74; V Darwen St Barn 74-84; V S Shore H Trin 84-02; Chapl Arnold Sch Blackpool 84-02; rtd 02; Perm to Offic *Blackb* from 02. *11 Kingsway, Blackpool FY4 2DF*

DUNN, Christopher George Hunter. b 28. Pemb Coll Cam BA49 MA53. Oak Hill Th Coll 51. **d** 53 **p** 54. C Tunbridge Wells H Trin *Roch* 53-54; C Broadwater St Mary *Chich* 54-58; R Garsdon w Lea and Cleverton *Bris* 59-74; Chapl Marie Curie Foundn (Tidcombe Hall) 74-95; V Tiverton St Geo *Ex* 74-01; RD Tiverton 84-91; rtd 01; Perm to Offic *Sarum* from 02. *8 Counter Close, Blandford Forum DT11 7XJ* Tel (01258) 456843

DUNN, David James. b 47. Leeds Univ CertEd79 BA82 Bris Univ DipHE90. Trin Coll Bris 88. **d** 90 **p** 91. C Magor w Redwick and Undy *Mon* 90-92; Chapl Toc H from 90; C St Mellons and Michaelston-y-Fedw *Mon* 92-93; V Pontnewydd from 93. *The Vicarage, 44 Church Road, Pontnewydd, Cwmbran NP44 1AT* Tel (01633) 482300

DUNN, David Michael. b 47. AKC70. St Aug Coll Cant 70. **d** 71 **p** 72. C Padgate *Liv* 71-74; C Halliwell St Marg *Man* 74-76; V Lever Bridge 76-84; V Bradshaw 84-01; TR Turton Moorland Min from 01. *St Maxentius Rectory, Bolton Road, Bolton BL2 3EU* Tel and fax (01204) 304240

DUNN, David Whitelaw Thomas. b 34. Trin Coll Carmarthen CertEd54. St Mich Coll Llan 87 St Deiniol's Hawarden 83. **d** 83 **p** 85. NSM Brecon St Mary and Battle w Llanddew *S & B* 83-87; Min Can Brecon Cathl 87-88; V Llanfihangel Crucorney w Oldcastle etc *Mon* 88-98; rtd 98. *The Craig, Cwmyoy, Abergavenny NP7 7NF* Tel (01873) 890092

DUNN, Derek William Robert. b 48. Open Univ BA81 MA01 Stranmillis Coll CertEd70 AMusTCL74 LTCL75. **d** 85 **p** 87. Aux Min Carnalea *D & D* 85-97; Aux Min Bangor Abbey 97-05; C Ballymena w Ballyclug *Conn* from 05. *13 Wandsworth Park, Carnalea, Bangor BT19 1BD* Tel (028) 9145 6898 E-mail derek@mambolo.freeserve.co.uk

DUNN, Florence Patricia (Pat). b 37. Chester Coll of HE BTh02. N Ord Course 99. **d** 02 **p** 03. NSM Basford *Lich* from 02. *213 Newcastle Road, Trent Vale, Stoke-on-Trent ST4 6PU* Tel (01782) 846417

DUNN, John Frederick. b 44. Trin Coll Bris 71. **d** 74 **p** 75. C Carl St Jo *Carl* 74-77; C Tooting Graveney St Nic *S'wark* 77-82; V Attleborough *Cov* 85; Perm to Offic *Cant* 86-02; V Tipton St Martin and St Paul *Lich* from 02. *St Martin's Vicarage, 1 Dudley Port, Tipton DY4 7PR* Tel 0121-557 1902

DUNN, Julian. b 46. Open Univ BA84. K Coll Lon 67 St Aug Coll Cant 70. **d** 71 **p** 72. C Hanworth All SS *Lon* 71-74; C Kidlington *Ox* 74-76; C-in-c Cleethorpes St Fran CD *Linc* 76-77; TV Cleethorpes 77-85; Chapl Friarage and Distr Hosp Northallerton 85-88; Chapl Broadmoor Hosp Crowthorne 88; Ind Chapl *York* 88-89; P-in-c Micklefield 88-89; Perm to Offic *Ox* from 91. *timbles brewery (*sic*), 1 Lewington Close, Great Haseley, Oxford OX44 7LS* Tel (01844) 279687 E-mail eisendora@aol.com

DUNN, Kevin Lancelot. b 62. Newc Univ BSc83. St Steph Ho Ox 89. **d** 92 **p** 93. C Tynemouth Cullercoats St Paul *Newc* 92-95; C Newc St Matt w St Mary 95-97; P-in-c Kirkholt *Man* 97-00; Chapl Rochdale Healthcare NHS Trust 00-02; Chapl Pennine Acute Hosps NHS Trust from 02. *17 Rochester Avenue, Prestwich, Manchester M25 0LF* Tel 0161-772 0717

DUNN, Kevin Samuel. b 31. Toronto Univ MDiv74. **d** 73 **p** 74. USA 73-90 and from 92; I Rathkeale w Askeaton and Kilcornan *L & K* 90-92. *20683 Waalew Road #118, Apple Valley, CA 92307, USA*

DUNN, Michael Henry James. b 34. Em Coll Cam BA56 MA62. Cuddesdon Coll 57 and 62. **d** 62 **p** 63. C Chatham St Steph *Roch* 62-66; C Bromley SS Pet and Paul 66-70; V Roch St Justus 70-83; P-in-c Malvern Wells and Wyche *Worc* 83-85; P-in-c Lt Malvern, Malvern Wells and Wyche 85-97; rtd 97; Perm to Offic *Worc* from 97. *253 Oldbury Road, Worcester WR2 6JT* Tel (01905) 429938

DUNN, Pat. *See* DUNN, Florence Patricia

DUNN, Paul James Hugh. b 55. Dur Univ PhD93. Ripon Coll Cuddesdon. **d** 83 **p** 84. C Wandsworth St Paul *S'wark* 83-87; C Richmond St Mary w St Matthias and St Jo 88-92; TV Wimbledon 92-98; V Ham St Rich from 98. *The Vicarage, Ashburnham Road, Ham, Richmond TW10 7NL* Tel (020) 8948 3758 E-mail revpdunn@aol.com

DUNN, Reginald Hallan. b 31. Oak Hill NSM Course 79. **d** 82 **p** 83. NSM Enfield St Andr *Lon* 82-88; NSM Forty Hill Jes Ch 88-92; NSM Enfield Chase St Mary 92-97; rtd 97; Perm to Offic *Lon* from 97. *3 Conway Gardens, Enfield EN2 9AD* Tel (020) 8366 3982

DUNN, Sharon Louise. *See* GOBLE, Mrs Sharon Louise

DUNN, Canon Struan Huthwaite. b 43. Ch Coll Hobart 66 Moore Th Coll Sydney ThL68 Clifton Th Coll 68. **d** 70 **p** 71. C Orpington Ch Ch *Roch* 70-74; C Cheltenham St Mary *Glouc* 74-76; C Cheltenham St Mary, St Matt, St Paul and H Trin 76; C Welling *Roch* 76-79; Chapl Barcelona w Casteldefels *Eur* 79-83; R Addington w Trottiscliffe *Roch* 83-89; P-in-c Ryarsh w Birling 83-89; P-in-c S Gillingham 89-90; TR 90-96; RD Gillingham 91-96; R Meopham w Nurstead from 96; Hon Can Roch Cathl from 97. *The Rectory, Shipley Hills Road, Meopham, Gravesend DA13 0AD* Tel (01474) 815259

DUNN, Thomas. *See* DUNN, David Whitelaw Thomas

DUNNAN, Donald Stuart. b 59. Harvard Univ AB80 AM81 Ch Ch Ox BA85 MA90 DPhil91. Gen Th Sem (NY) 86. **d** 86 **p** 87. USA 86-87 and from 92; Lib Pusey Ho 87-89; Lic to Offic

Ox 87-92; Perm to Offic *Cant* 87-92; Chapl Linc Coll Ox 90-92. *St James School, St James, MD 21781, USA* E-mail dsdunnan@stjames.edu

DUNNE, Canon Dermot Patrick Martin. b 59. Cert Psychotherapy 95. St Patr Coll Maynooth 78 CITC 98. **d** 83 **p** 84. In RC Ch 83-95; Dean's V Ch Ch Cathl Dublin *D & G* 99-01; I Crosspatrick Gp *C & O* from 01; Prec Ferns Cathl from 04. *The Rectory, Tinahely, Arklow, Co Wicklow, Irish Republic* Tel (00353) (402) 28922 Mobile 87-137 1955 E-mail crosspatrick@ferns.anglican.org

DUNNE, Kevin Headley. b 43. Cranmer Hall Dur 85. **d** 87 **p** 88. C Chester le Street *Dur* 87-90; V S Hetton w Haswell 90-94; P-in-c Oxclose 94-02; AD Chester-le-Street 97-02; R Chester le Street from 02. *The Rectory, Lindisfarne Avenue, Chester le Street DH3 3PT* Tel 0191-388 4027 Fax 388 9770 E-mail revdunne@aol.com

DUNNE, Nigel Kenneth. b 66. TCD BA88 BTh90 MA00 MPhil00. **d** 90 **p** 91. C Dublin St Bart w Leeson Park *D & G* 90-93; C Taney 93-95; I Blessington w Kilbride, Ballymore Eustace etc 95-03; Can Ch Ch Cathl Dublin 01-03; I Bandon Union *C, C & R* from 03. *The Rectory, Castle Road, Bandon, Co Cork, Irish Republic* Tel and fax (00353) (23) 41259 E-mail nidunne@oceanfree.net

DUNNETT, John Frederick. b 58. CQSW82 SS Coll Cam MA84 Worc Coll Ox MSc83. Trin Coll Bris BA87. **d** 88 **p** 89. C Kirkheaton *Wakef* 88-93; V Cranham Park *Chelmsf* from 93. *St Luke's Vicarage, 201 Front Lane, Upminster RM14 1LD* Tel (01708) 222122 E-mail jd@johndunnett.co.uk

DUNNETT, Keith Owen. b 66. Cranfield Inst of Tech BSc87. Trin Coll Bris BA00. **d** 00 **p** 01. C Walton and Trimley *St E* 00-03; V Clayton *Bradf* from 03. *The Vicarage, Clayton Lane, Clayton, Bradford BD14 6AX* Tel (01274) 880373 Mobile 07779-832286 E-mail keith.dunnett@virgin.net

DUNNETT, Robert Curtis. b 31. SS Coll Cam BA54 MA58. Oak Hill Th Coll 56. **d** 58 **p** 59. C Markfield *Leic* 58-60; C Bucknall and Bagnall *Lich* 60-73; Perm to Offic *Birm* from 72; Chapl and Tutor Birm Bible Inst 72-79; Vice-Prin 84-92; Hon Vice-Prin from 92; rtd 96. *30 Station Road, Harborne, Birmingham B17 9LY* Tel 0121-428 3945 Fax 428 3370

DUNNILL, Canon John David Stewart. b 50. UEA BA72 Ox Univ CertEd76 Birm Univ DipTh82 PhD88. Ripon Coll Cuddesdon 86. **d** 88 **p** 89. C Tupsley *Heref* 88-92; Lect Glouc Sch for Min 89-91; Sen Lect Murdoch Univ Australia from 92; Dir Bibl and Th Studies Angl Inst of Th from 92; Can Perth from 99. *School of Social Inquiry, Murdoch University, Murdoch, W Australia 6150* Tel (0061) (8) 9360 6369 *or* 9383 4403 Fax 9360 6480 E-mail dunnill@socs.murdoch.edu.au

DUNNING, Adam Jonathan. b 73. Regent's Park Coll Ox BA95 MA99 Birm Univ PhD00. Westcott Ho Cam 97. **d** 99 **p** 00. C Evesham w Norton and Lenchwick *Worc* 99-02; C Hamstead St Paul *Birm* 02-03; Hon C Moseley St Mary from 03. *97 Institute Road, Birmingham B14 7EU* Tel 0121-444 5551 E-mail a.dunning@ukonline.co.uk

DUNNING, John Stanley. b 19. Lon Univ BSc41. EMMTC 78. **d** 81 **p** 82. NSM Nottingham St Pet and St Jas *S'well* 81-85; rtd 85; Perm to Offic *S'well* from 85. *Broadgate Nursing Home, Broadgate, Beeston, Nottingham NG9 2GG* Tel 0115-922 4627

DUNNING, Martyn Philip. b 51. Reading Univ MSc79 Dur Univ MA95 MRTPI77. St Jo Coll Dur 89. **d** 92 **p** 93. C Beverley Minster *York* 92-96; P-in-c Brandesburton 96-97; P-in-c Leven w Catwick 96-97; R Brandesburton and Leven w Catwick 97-02; RD N Holderness 97-02; P-in-c Scarborough St Mary w Ch Ch and H Apostles 02-04; V from 04; RD Scarborough from 04. *St Mary's Vicarage, 1 North Cliff Gardens, Scarborough YO12 6PR* Tel (01723) 371354

DUNNINGS, Reuben Edward. b 36. Clifton Th Coll 62. **d** 66 **p** 67. C Longfleet *Sarum* 66-70; C Melksham 70-73; TV 73-78; R Broughton Gifford w Gt Chalfield 78-84; V Holt St Kath 78-84; R Broughton Gifford, Gt Chalfield and Holt 85-86; V Salisbury St Fran 86-99; P-in-c Stratford sub Castle 98-99; V Salisbury St Fran and Stratford sub Castle 99-01; rtd 01; Perm to Offic *Sarum* from 01. *11 Cornbrash Rise, Hilperton, Trowbridge BA14 7TS* Tel (01225) 768834

DUNSETH, George William. b 52. Multnomah Sch of the Bible Oregon BRE79. Oak Hill Th Coll BA85. **d** 85 **p** 86. C Cheadle All Hallows *Ches* 85-88; C New Borough and Leigh *Sarum* 88-91; V Thurnby w Stoughton *Leic* from 91. *The Vicarage, Thurnby, Leicester LE7 9PN* Tel 0116-241 2263 E-mail george.dunseth@btinternet.com

DUNSTAN, Gregory John Orchard. b 50. Cam Univ MA75 TCD BTh90. CITC 87. **d** 90 **p** 91. C Ballymena w Ballyclug *Conn* 90-93; I Belfast St Matt from 93. *Shankill Rectory, 51 Ballygomartin Road, Belfast BT13 3LA* Tel and fax (028) 9071 4325

DUNSTAN, Kenneth Ian. b 40. ACP Goldsmiths' Coll Lon BEd71. Oak Hill NSM Course 86. **d** 88 **p** 89. NSM Creeksea w Althorne, Latchingdon and N Fambridge *Chelmsf* 88-94; P-in-c Woodham Mortimer w Hazeleigh 94-98; P-in-c Woodham Walter 94-98; NSM Bradwell on Sea 99-05; rtd 05. *35 Ely Close, Southminster CM0 7AQ* Tel (01621) 772199 E-mail ken@kdunstan.go-plus.net

DUNSTAN, Mark Philip. b 70. Middx Univ BSc93. Oak Hill Th Coll BA03. **d** 03 **p** 04. C Stranton *Dur* from 03. *41 Arncliffe Gardens, Hartlepool TS26 9JG* Tel (01429) 277591 E-mail dunstan_mark@hotmail.com

DUNSTAN-MEADOWS, Victor Richard. b 63. Chich Th Coll BTh90. **d** 90 **p** 91. C Clacton St Jas *Chelmsf* 90-93; C Stansted Mountfitchet 93-95; CF 95-00; Chapl RAF from 00. *Chaplaincy Services (RAF), HQ, Personnel and Training Command, RAF Innsworth, Gloucester GL3 1EZ* Tel (01452) 712612 ext 5164 Fax 510828

DUNTHORNE, Paul. b 63. K Coll Lon LLB85 Paris Sorbonne 85 St Jo Coll Dur BA90 Dur Univ MA98. Cranmer Hall Dur 88. **d** 91 **p** 92. C Heacham and Sedgeford *Nor* 91-95; C Eastbourne H Trin *Chich* 95-98; P-in-c Preston and Ridlington w Wing and Pilton *Pet* 98-00; Local Min Officer 98-00; CME Officer *Heref* from 00. *7 Devereux Close, Hereford HR1 1QR* Tel (01432) 267918 E-mail paul@dunthorne55.freeserve.co.uk

DUNWICH, Suffragan Bishop of. *See* YOUNG, The Rt Revd Clive

DUNWOODY, Stephen John Herbert. b 71. Glam Univ BA92. St Steph Ho Ox BTh96. **d** 96 **p** 97. C Skewen *Llan* 96-98; C Roath 98-99; C Stanley *Liv* 99-02; TV Colyton, Southleigh, Offwell, Widworthy etc *Ex* 02-03; V Offwell, Northleigh, Farway, Cotleigh etc 03-05; CF from 05. *c/o MOD Chaplains (Army)* Tel (01980) 615804 Fax 615800 E-mail stephendunwoody@hotmail.com

DUNWOODY, Thomas Herbert Williamson. b 35. TCD BA58 MA64. TCD Div Sch Div Test59. **d** 59 **p** 60. C Newcastle *D & D* 59-61; Asst Missr Ballymacarrett St Martin 61-63; C Lurgan Ch the Redeemer 63-66; I Ardglass w Dunsford 66-74; Offg Chapl RAF 66-74; V Urmston *Man* 74-85; I Wexford w Ardcolm and Killurin *C & O* 85-93; Can Ferns Cathl 88-93; I Newry *D & D* 93-02; rtd 02. *3 Eden Court, Markethill, Co Armagh BT60 1LH* Tel (028) 3755 2893 E-mail thw_dunwoody@tiscali.co.uk

DUPLOCK, Canon Peter Montgomery. b 16. OBE76. Qu Coll Cam BA38 MA42. Ridley Hall Cam 38. **d** 40 **p** 41. C Morden *S'wark* 40-43; CF (EC) 43-47; R Nottingham St Nic *S'well* 47-52; R Loddington w Harrington *Pet* 52-55; V Kettering St Andr 55-64; Chapl Geneva *Eur* 64-71; Chapl Brussels w Charleroi, Liege and Waterloo 71-81; Chan Brussels Cathl 81; Adn NW Eur 81; rtd 81; Hon Can Brussels Cathl *Eur* from 81; R Breamore *Win* 81-86; Perm to Offic 86-95; Perm to Offic *Sarum* 86-98. *9 Capel Court, The Burgage, Prestbury, Cheltenham GL52 3EL* Tel (01242) 580518

DUPREE, Hugh Douglas. b 50. Univ of the South (USA) BA72 Virginia Th Sem MDiv75 Ch Ch Ox MA86 Ball Coll Ox DPhil88. **d** 75 **p** 76. USA 75-80; Hon C Ox St Mich w St Martin and All SS *Ox* 80-87; Asst Chapl Ball Coll Ox 84-87; Chapl from 87; Chapl HM Pris Ox 88-97. *Balliol College, Oxford OX1 3BJ* Tel (01865) 277777 *or* 721261

DUPUY, Alan Douglas William. b 48. Kent Univ Dip Chr Th 00. SEITE 98. **d** 00 **p** 01. NSM Forest Hill St Aug *S'wark* 00-01; NSM S Dulwich St Steph 01-04; NSM Perry Hill St Geo w Ch Ch and St Paul from 04. *16 Dominic Court, 43 The Gardens, London SE22 9QR* Tel (020) 8695 5769 Mobile 07960-226518 Fax 8693 4175 E-mail alandupuy@compuserve.com

DURAND, Noel Douglas. b 33. Jes Coll Cam BA57 MA61 BD76. Westcott Ho Cam 72. **d** 74 **p** 75. C Eaton *Nor* 74-78; V Cumnor *Ox* 78-01; rtd 01; Perm to Offic *Nor* from 01. *21 Nelson Road, Sheringham NR26 8BU* Tel (01263) 822388

DURAND, Stella Evelyn Brigid, Lady. b 42. TCD BA64 Sorbonne Univ Paris DèS65 St Jo Coll Dur DipTh70. CITC BTh99. **d** 00. C Kiltegan w Hacketstown, Clonmore and Moyne *C & O* 00-03; I from 03. *The Rectory, Kiltegan, Co Wicklow, Irish Republic* Tel and fax (00353) (59) 647 3368 E-mail stelladurand@eircom.net

DURANT, Miss Helen Mary. b 53. Saffron Walden Coll TCert74. Trin Coll Bris BA04. **d** 04 **p** 05. C S Croydon Em *S'wark* from 04. *35 Whitemead Close, South Croydon CR2 7AZ* Tel (020) 8680 1135 E-mail helen@emmanuelcroydon.org

DURANT, Robert-Ashton. b 23. OSB St D Coll Lamp BA47. Bp Burgess Hall Lamp. **d** 48 **p** 49. C Brynmawr *S & B* 48-49; C Fleur-de-Lis *Mon* 49-51; C Bassaleg 51-56; CF (TA) 53-55; V Trellech and Cwmcarvan *Mon* 56-69; Priest Tymawr Convent 56-69; V Slapton *Ex* 69-81; V Strete 69-81; R E Allington, Slapton and Strete 81-92; rtd 92; Perm to Offic *Ex* from 92. *18 Grosvenor Avenue, Torquay TQ2 7LA* Tel (01803) 613710

DURANT, William John Nicholls. b 55. K Coll Lon BA76 DipTh DPS. St Jo Coll Nottm 77. **d** 80 **p** 81. C Norwood St Luke *S'wark* 80-83; C Morden 83-88; TV 88-92; V Frindsbury w Upnor *Roch* 92-00; CF from 00. *c/o MOD Chaplains (Army)* Tel (01980) 615804 Fax 615800

DURBIN, Roger. b 41. Bris Sch of Min 83. **d** 85 **p** 86. NSM Bedminster *Bris* 85-91; NSM Henbury 91-94; NSM Clifton All SS w St Jo from 94. *13 Charbury Walk, Bristol BS11 9UU* Tel 0117-985 8404

DURELL, Miss Jane Vavasor. b 32. Bedf Coll Lon BSc55 Lambeth STh64. Gilmore Ho 61. **dss** 86 **d** 87 **p** 94. Banbury *Ox* 86-92; Par Dn 87-92; rtd 92; Perm to Offic *Nor* 92-94 and from 02; NSM Norwich St Mary Magd w St Jas 94-02. *25 Brakendon Close, Norwich NR1 3BX* Tel (01603) 627949

DURHAM, Mrs Eleanore Jane. b 62. St Andr Univ MTheol84. Trin Coll Bris MA01. **d** 01 **p** 02. C Childwall All SS *Liv* from 01. *80 Green Lane North, Childwall, Liverpool L16 8NL* Tel 0151-737 2214 E-mail janedurham@onetel.com

DURHAM, Archdeacon of. *See* CONWAY, The Ven Stephen David

DURHAM, Bishop of. *See* WRIGHT, The Rt Revd Nicholas Thomas

DURHAM, Dean of. *See* SADGROVE, The Very Revd Michael

DURIE, David James. b 63. Cen Lancs Univ BA93 St Martin's Coll Lanc MA99. Carl and Blackb Dioc Tr Inst 97. **d** 99 **p** 00. C Briercliffe *Blackb* 99-01; P-in-c Edin St Dav *Edin* from 02. *38 Silverknowes Drive, Edinburgh EH4 5HH* Tel 0131-538 6262 E-mail david.durie@btopenworld.com

DURING, Arthur Christopher. b 59. Sierra Leone Th Hall 80. **d** 83 **p** 85. Sierra Leone 83-86; Perm to Offic *S'wark* from 00. *22 Challice Way, London SW2 3RD* Tel (020) 8671 7678

DURKAN, Miss Barbara Isobel Mary. b 43. Kent Univ BSc71 MPhil00 Ch Ch Coll Cant MA95 Sarum Dioc Tr Coll CertEd65. SEITE 99. **d** 01 **p** 02. Aux Chapl HM Pris Standford Hill from 01. *HM Prison Standford Hill, Church Road, Eastchurch, Sheerness ME12 4AA* Tel (01795) 884559 Fax 880267

DURKIN, Anthony Michael. b 45. Sarum & Wells Th Coll 87. **d** 89 **p** 90. C Faversham *Cant* 89-92; V St Margarets-at-Cliffe w Westcliffe etc from 92. *The Vicarage, Sea Street, St Margarets-at-Cliffe, Dover CT15 6AR* Tel (01304) 852179 Fax 853898 E-mail anthony-durkin@care4free.net

DURLEY, Jonathan. St Mich Coll Llan. **d** 05. C Canton Cardiff *Llan* from 05. *60 Plasturton Gardens, Cardiff CF11 9HJ* Tel (029) 2031 0043

DURNDELL, Miss Irene Frances. b 43. Nottm Univ DipRE78. Trin Coll Bris DipHE86. **dss** 86 **d** 87 **p** 94. Erith Ch Ch *Roch* 86-93; Par Dn 87-93; Par Dn Erith St Paul 93-94; C 94-98; Asst Dir of Tr 93-98; V Falconwood from 98. *The Vicarage, The Green, Welling DA16 2PD* Tel (020) 8298 0065 Fax as telephone

DURNELL, John. b 32. St Aid Birkenhead 64. **d** 66 **p** 67. C Newport w Longford *Lich* 66-69; P-in-c Church Aston 69-72; R 72-77; V Weston Rhyn 77-82; P-in-c Petton w Cockshutt and Weston Lullingfield etc 82-83; R Petton w Cockshutt, Welshampton and Lyneal etc 83-97; rtd 97; Perm to Offic *Lich* from 97. *Fronlwyd, Hirnant, Penybontfawr, Oswestry SY10 0HP* Tel (01691) 870686

DURNFORD, Canon Catherine Margaret. b 36. St Mary's Coll Dur BA57. Gilmore Course 78 NW Ord Course 77. **d** 87 **p** 94. Area Sec USPG *York* and *Ripon* 82-89; Par Dn Whitby *York* 89-92; Par Dn Redcar 92-94; C Selby Abbey 94-97; V New Marske and Wilton 97-03; Can and Preb York Minster 01-03; rtd 03; Perm to Offic *York* from 03. *18 Canongate, Cottingham HU16 4DG* Tel (01482) 844868

DURNFORD, John Edward. b 30. CCC Cam BA53 MA61. Linc Th Coll 53. **d** 55 **p** 56. C Selby Abbey *York* 55-58; C Newland St Jo 58-62; S Rhodesia 62-65; Rhodesia 65-76; V Hebden Bridge *Wakef* 76-84; RD Calder Valley 82-84; P-in-c Blanchland w Hunstanworth *Newc* 84-90; P-in-c Edmundbyers w Muggleswick *Dur* 84-90; RD Corbridge *Newc* 88-93; R Blanchland w Hunstanworth and Edmundbyers etc 90-94; rtd 94; Perm to Offic *Newc* from 94. *7 Islestone Drive, Seahouses NE68 7XB* Tel (01665) 721032

DURNFORD, Comdr Peter Jeffrey. b 20. Bps' Coll Cheshunt 63. **d** 65 **p** 66. C Edmonton St Alphege *Lon* 65-67; Chapl Bonn w Cologne *Eur* 67-69; R St Just in Roseland *Truro* 70-82; P-in-c Ruan Lanihorne w Philleigh 70-82; P-in-c St Mewan 82-85; Chapl Mount Edgcumbe Hospice 82-88; rtd 85; Perm to Offic *Truro* from 85. *8 Tredenham Road, St Mawes, Truro TR2 5AN* Tel (01326) 270793

DURRAN, Ms Margaret. b 47. Surrey Univ MSc96 Lady Spencer Chu Coll of Educn CertEd70. S'wark Ord Course 88. **d** 91 **p** 94. Par Dn Brixton St Matt *S'wark* 91-94; C Streatham St Leon 94-95; V Walworth St Chris 95-99; Hon C S'wark St Geo w St Alphege and St Jude from 99; Hist Churches Project Officer *Lon* from 99. *2 St Alphege House, Pocock Street, London SE1 0BJ* Tel and fax (020) 7401 8808 Mobile 07739-988742 E-mail maggie.durran@virgin.net

DURRANT, Melvyn Richard Bloomfield. b 59. Leeds Univ BA82 St Luke's Coll Ex PGCE86. Trin Coll Bris 01. **d** 03 **p** 04. C Watercombe *Sarum* from 03; C Moreton and Woodsford w Tincleton from 03. *51 Binghams Road, Crossways, Dorchester DT2 8BW* Tel (01305) 853338 E-mail mel@durranthome.freeserve.co.uk

DURSTON, Canon David Michael Karl. b 36. Em Coll Cam BA60 MA64. Clifton Th Coll 61. **d** 63 **p** 64. C Wednesfield Heath *Lich* 63-66; Project Officer Grubb Inst 67-78; Ind Chapl *Lich* 78-84; P-in-c W Bromwich St Paul 78-82; V 82-84; Adult Educn Officer 84-92; Preb Lich Cathl 89-92; Can Res and Chan Sarum Cathl *Sarum* 92-03; Can and Preb from 03; TR Wylye and Till Valley from 03. *The Rectory, Duck Street, Steeple Langford, Salisbury SP3 4NH* Tel (01722) 790198 E-mail david.durston@btinternet.com

DUSSEK, Jeremy Neil James Christopher. b 70. St Jo Coll Dur BA92 DipTh. Westcott Ho Cam 96. **d** 97 **p** 98. C Whickham *Dur* 97-00; C Fareham H Trin *Portsm* 00-01; TV from 01. *The Vicarage, Hillson Drive, Fareham PO15 6PF* Tel (01329) 843705 *or* 232688 E-mail jeremy@dussek.fsnet.co.uk

DUST, Simon Philip. b 63. Oak Hill Th Coll BA95. **d** 95 **p** 96. C Chesham Bois *Ox* 95-00; C-in-c Bushmead CD *St Alb* 00-04; V Bushmead from 04. *Church House, 73 Hawkfields, Luton LU2 7NW* Tel and fax (01582) 487327 E-mail simondust@ntlworld.com

DUTFIELD, Canon Alan. b 20. Linc Th Coll 54. **d** 55 **p** 56. C Kimberworth *Sheff* 55-60; V New Rossington 60-71; R Old Brumby *Linc* 71-77; TR 77-86; Can and Preb Linc Cathl 81-86; RD Manlake 82-86; rtd 86; Perm to Offic *Linc* 89-94 and from 01; Perm to Offic *S'well* from 03. *30 Barnes Green, Scotter, Gainsborough DN21 3RW* Tel (01724) 764220

DUTHIE, Elliot Malcolm. b 31. Clifton Th Coll 63. **d** 66 **p** 67. C Eccleston St Luke *Liv* 66-69; Malaysia 70-75; P-in-c Bootle St Leon *Liv* 76-78; V 78-81; V Charlton Kings H Apostles *Glouc* 81-94; rtd 94; Perm to Offic *Glouc* 94-00 and *Ex* 02-05. *11 Fairisle Close, Oakwood, Derby DE21 2SJ* Tel (01332) 668238 E-mail m.duthie@tesco.net

DUTHIE, John. **d** 04. NSM Aberdeen St Pet *Ab* from 04. *Moraine, Inchmarlo, Banchory AB31 4BR* Tel (01330) 824108

DUTTON, Andrew Rivers George. b 49. Bris Univ BSc71 PGCE72 Reading Univ MSc79 Open Univ DMEd92. EAMTC 98. **d** 98 **p** 99. NSM Kettering SS Pet and Paul *Pet* 98-03; NSM Broughton w Loddington and Cransley etc from 04; Chapl Bp Stopford Sch from 99. *10 Beardsley Gardens, Kettering NN15 5UB* Tel (01536) 392401

DUTTON, Leonard Arthur. b 35. Bps' Coll Cheshunt 63. **d** 66 **p** 67. C Knighton St Jo *Leic* 66-70; C Chilvers Coton w Astley *Cov* 70-73; R Hathern *Leic* 73-79; V Ashby-de-la-Zouch H Trin 79-04; rtd 04. *8 Merganser Way, Coalville LE67 4QA* Tel (01530) 815420

DUTTON, Sandra Rosemary. b 50. Ripon Coll Cuddesdon 03. **d** 04 **p** 05. NSM Chatham St Steph *Roch* from 04. *130 City Way, Rochester ME1 2AF* Tel (01634) 404175 E-mail sandydutton@hotmail.com

DUVAL, Canon Philip Ernest. b 18. MBE45. Mert Coll Ox BA45 MA45. Westcott Ho Cam 47. **d** 47 **p** 48. C Tooting All SS *S'wark* 47-51; C Raynes Park St Sav 51-55; V Balham St Mary 55-66; R Merstham and Gatton 66-86; Hon Can S'wark Cathl 78-86; rtd 86; Perm to Offic *Cant* from 88. *2 The Holt, Frogs Hill, Newenden, Hawkhurst TN18 5PX* Tel (01797) 252578

DUVALL, Michael James. b 31. **d** 79 **p** 80. Hon C Kings Langley *St Alb* 79-89; Hon C Selworthy and Timberscombe and Wootton Courtenay *B & W* 89-95; Hon C Luccombe 89-95; Hon C Selworthy, Timberscombe, Wootton Courtenay etc 95-97; rtd 97; Perm to Offic *B & W* from 97. *Dovery Edge, 19 Hawkcombe View, Porlock, Minehead TA24 8NB* Tel (01634) 862834

DUXBURY, Clive Robert. b 49. St Jo Coll Nottm 90. **d** 92 **p** 93. C Horwich and Rivington *Man* 92-96; P-in-c Bury St Paul and Bury Ch King 98-00; P-in-c Freethorpe, Wickhampton, Halvergate w Tunstall *Nor* 00-02; P-in-c Reedham w Cantley w Limpenhoe and Southwood 00-02; R Freethorpe, Wickhampton, Halvergate etc from 02; RD Blofield 04-05; R High Ongar w Norton Mandeville *Chelmsf* from 05. *The Rectory, The Street, High Ongar, Ongar CM5 9NQ* Tel (01277) 362593 E-mail clive@cduxbury.freeserve.co.uk

DUXBURY, Canon James Campbell. b 33. Tyndale Hall Bris 58. **d** 61 **p** 62. C Southport SS Simon and Jude *Liv* 61-65; V Tittensor *Lich* 65-70; V W Bromwich Gd Shep w St Jo 70-75; P-in-c Wellington w Eyton 75-80; V 80-85; V Padiham *Blackb* 85-01; Hon Can Blackb Cathl 97-01; rtd 01; Can Emer Blackb Cathl *Blackb* from 01; Perm to Offic from 01. *1 Gills Croft, Clitheroe BB7 1LJ* Tel (01200) 429261 E-mail duxbury@ribble-valley.co.uk

DUXBURY, Miss Margaret Joan. b 30. JP81. DipEd52. St Jo Coll Nottm 83. **dss** 84 **d** 87 **p** 94. Thornthwaite w Thruscross and Darley *Ripon* 84-86; Middleton St Cross 86-90; C 87-90; Par Dn Dacre w Hartwith and Darley w Thornthwaite 90-94; C 94-96; rtd 97; NSM Bishop Monkton and Burton Leonard *Ripon* 97-02; Perm to Offic from 01. *Scot Beck House, Low Lane, Darley, Harrogate HG3 2QN* Tel (01423) 780451

DYALL, Henry. b 19. MRICS51 Lon Univ BSc51 LLB58. S'wark Ord Course 81. **d** 82 **p** 83. Hon C St Mary Cray and St Paul's Cray *Roch* 82-84; Perm to Offic 84-86; Hon C Sidcup Ch Ch 86-02; rtd 02; Perm to Offic *Roch* from 02. *2 Hillsley Court, 8 Elm Road, Sidcup DA14 6AB* Tel (020) 8308 0769

DYAS, Stuart Edwin. b 46. Lon Univ BSc67. Ridley Hall Cam 78. **d** 80 **p** 81. C Bath Weston St Jo w Kelston *B & W* 80-83; C

Tunbridge Wells St Jas *Roch* 83-90; V Nottingham St Jude *S'well* 90-99; AD Nottingham Cen 93-98; V Long Eaton St Jo *Derby* 99-05; rtd 05. *179 Bye Pass Road, Beeston, Nottingham NG9 5HR* Tel 0115-922 5844

DYAS, Sylvia Denise (Dee). b 51. Bedf Coll Lon BA72 Nottm Univ PhD99. St Jo Coll Nottm 98. **d** 00 **p** 01. Tutor St Jo Coll Nottm from 00; Perm to Offic *Derby* from 00. *179 Bye Pass Road, Beeston, Nottingham NG9 5HR* Tel 0115-922 5844 E-mail d.dyas@stjohns-nottm.ac.uk

DYE, Mrs Margaret Mary. b 48. N Ord Course 95. **d** 98 **p** 99. C Morley St Pet w Churwell *Wakef* 98-02; TV Morley from 02. *The Vicarage, 4 Lewisham Street, Morley, Leeds LS27 0LA* Tel 0113-252 3783 E-mail s.m.dye@btinternet.com

DYE, Stephen. b 49. N Ord Course 01. **d** 04 **p** 05. C Gildersome *Wakef* from 04. *St Andrew's Vicarage, 4 Lewisham Street, Morley, Leeds LS27 0LA* Tel 0113-252 3783 E-mail s.m.dye@btinternet.com

DYER, Canon Anne Catherine. b 57. St Anne's Coll Ox MA80 Lon Univ MTh89. Wycliffe Hall Ox 84. **d** 87 **p** 94. NSM Beckenham St Jo *Roch* 87-88; NSM Beckenham St Geo 88-89; Hon Par Dn Luton Ch Ch 89-94; Chapl for Evang 93-98; NSM Istead Rise 94-98; Min Development Officer 98-04; Hon Can Roch Cathl 00-04; Warden Cranmer Hall Dur from 05. *16 Briardene, Durham DH1 4QU* Tel 0191-384 0048 E-mail adyer82120@aol.com

DYER, Ms Catherine Jane. b 46. Westf Coll Lon BA68. Ox NSM Course 85. **d** 88 **p** 94. NSM Wokingham All SS *Ox* 88-90; C 90-95; TV W Slough 95-01; P-in-c Linslade from 01; AD Mursley from 03. *Linslade Vicarage, Vicarage Road, Leighton Buzzard LU7 2LP* Tel (01525) 372149 E-mail cdyer@fish.co.uk

DYER, Canon Christine Anne. b 53. Nottm Univ BEd75. EMMTC 81. **dss** 84 **d** 87 **p** 94. Mickleover St Jo *Derby* 85-87; Par Dn 87-90; Dioc Voc Adv 86-90; Par Educn Adv 90-98; Dioc Youth Officer from 91; P-in-c Morton and Stonebroom 98-99; P-in-c Shirland 98-99; R Morton and Stonebroom w Shirland from 99; Hon Can Derby Cathl from 02. *The Rectory, Main Road, Shirland, Alfreton DE55 6BB* Tel (01773) 836003 E-mail c.a.dyer@talk21.com

DYER, Mrs Gillian Marie. b 50. Sheff Univ BA71 Leic Univ PGCE72 Dip Counselling 99. S Dios Minl Tr Scheme 81. **dss** 84 **d** 87 **p** 94. Witney *Ox* 84-85; Carl St Cuth w St Mary *Carl* 86-89; Par Dn 87-89; Dioc Communications Officer 86-89; Par Dn Kirkbride w Newton Arlosh 89-91; Par Dn Carl H Trin and St Barn 91-94; TV 94-97; P-in-c Arbroath *Bre* 01-03; P-in-c Lower Darwen St Jas *Blackb* from 03. *The Vicarage, Stopes Brow, Lower Darwen, Darwen BB3 0QP* Tel (01254) 677903 E-mail tergill@aol.com

DYER, Canon James Henry. b 14. ALCD39. **d** 39 **p** 40. C S Hackney St Jo w Ch Ch *Lon* 39-43; C New Malden and Coombe *S'wark* 43-50; New Zealand from 50; V Murchison 50-56; V Collingwood 56-59; V Spring Creek 59-67; V Amuri 67-70; V Motupiko 70-77; Hon Can Nelson Cathl 85. *7 Talbot Street, Richmond, Nelson, New Zealand* Tel (0064) (3) 554 8638 E-mail james.dyer@xtra.co.nz

DYER, Janet. b 35. LNSM course 77. **dss** 85 **d** 86 **p** 94. Balerno *Edin* 85-86; NSM 86-93; Chapl Edin R Infirmary 88-93; Dn-in-c Roslin (Rosslyn Chpl) *Edin* 93-94; P-in-c 94-97; NSM Livingston LEP 97-00; Angl Chapl Livingstone St Jo Hosp 97-00; NSM Dalmahoy from 02. *499 Lanark Road West, Balerno EH14 7AL* Tel 0131-449 3767 E-mail adrian@dyer499.freeserve.co.uk

DYER, John Alan. b 31. Linc Coll Ox BA53 MA57 Lon Univ BD58. Tyndale Hall Bris 53. **d** 56 **p** 57. C Weston-super-Mare Ch Ch *B & W* 56-60; V Battersea St Geo w St Andr *S'wark* 60-69; Australia from 69; C-in-c Narraweena 69-74; R 74-96; AD Warringah 85-92; rtd 96. *5 Crisallen Street, Port Macquarie, NSW, Australia 2444* Tel (0061) (2) 6584 2868 E-mail johndy@ozemail.com.au

DYER, Ronald Whitfield. b 29. Solicitor 51. Guildf Dioc Min Course 91. **d** 95 **p** 96. NSM Fleet *Guildf* 95-99; rtd 99; Perm to Offic *Guildf* from 99. *7 Dukes Mead, Fleet GU51 4HA* Tel (01252) 621457

DYER, Stephen Roger. b 57. Brunel Univ BSc. Wycliffe Hall Ox 83. **d** 86 **p** 87. C Beckenham St Jo *Roch* 86-89; C Luton Ch Ch 89-94; V Istead Rise 94-01; V Frindsbury w Upnor 01-04. *16 Briardene, Durham DH1 4QU* Tel 0191-384 0048

DYER, Miss Sylvia Mary. b 30. Westf Coll Lon BA66. Ab Dioc Tr Course 90. **d** 95 **p** 98. NSM Turriff *Ab* from 95. *The Sheiling, Westfield Road, Turriff AB53 4AF* Tel (01888) 562530

DYER, Terence Neville. b 50. Sheff Univ BEng71 Leic Univ PGCE72. Carl Dioc Tr Course 86. **d** 89 **p** 90. NSM Kirkbride w Newton Arlosh *Carl* 89-91; NSM Carl H Trin and St Barn 91-97; NSM Arbroath *Bre* 01; P-in-c Monifieth 01-03; P-in-c Over Darwen St Jas *Blackb* from 03. *The Vicarage, Stopes Brow, Lower Darwen, Darwen BB3 0QP* Tel (01254) 677903 E-mail tergill@aol.com

DYKE, Mrs Elizabeth Muriel. b 55. St Mary's Coll Dur BSc77 St Martin's Coll Lanc PGCE78. Oak Hill Th Coll 92. **d** 94 **p** 95. C High Wycombe *Ox* 94-95; C W Wycombe w Bledlow Ridge, Bradenham and Radnage 95-97; TV Bedworth *Cov* 97-02; V Dunchurch from 02. *The Vicarage, 11 Critchley Drive, Dunchurch, Rugby CV22 6PJ* Tel (01788) 810274

DYKE, George Edward. b 22. TCD BA65 BCom65 MA80. CITC. **d** 79 **p** 80. NSM Dublin St Geo *D & G* 79-82; NSM Tallaght 83-89; NSM Killiney Ballybrack 89-90; Bp's C Dublin St Geo and St Thos and Finglas 90-95; Bp's C Dublin St Geo and St Thos 95-96; Chapl Mountjoy Pris 90-96; Chapl Arbour Hill Pris 90-96; rtd 96. *45 Thornhill Road, Mount Merrion, Co Dublin, Irish Republic* Tel (00353) (1) 288 9376

DYKES, John Edward. b 33. Trin Coll Bris 82. **d** 84 **p** 85. C Rushden w Newton Bromswold *Pet* 84-87; R Heanton Punchardon w Marwood *Ex* 87-97; rtd 97; Perm to Offic *Guildf* 98-01 and *B & W* from 02. *42 Ashley Road, Taunton TA1 5BP* Tel (01823) 282507 E-mail johnandvickyd@tiscali.co.uk

DYKES, Mrs Katrina Mary. b 66. Trin Coll Bris BA90. Guildf Dioc Min Course 03. **d** 04 **p** 05. NSM Windlesham *Guildf* from 04. *61 Goldney Road, Camberley GU15 1DW* Tel (01276) 514451 Fax 678015 E-mail katrinadykes@tiscali.co.uk

DYKES, Michael David Allan. b 42. Chich Th Coll 68. **d** 71 **p** 72. C Pocklington w Yapham-cum-Meltonby, Owsthorpe etc *York* 72-75; C Howden 75-77; V Eskdaleside w Ugglebarnby and Sneaton 77-85; R Stokesley 85-04; P-in-c Seamer in Cleveland 85-04; P-in-c Hilton in Cleveland 85-95; R Stokesley w Seamer from 05. *The Rectory, Leven Close, Stokesley, Middlesbrough TS9 5AP* Tel (01642) 710405 E-mail mdykes@fish.co.uk

DYKES, Philip John. b 61. Loughb Univ BSc83 DIS83. Trin Coll Bris Dip Th Studies 90 ADPS91. **d** 91 **p** 92. C Morden *S'wark* 91-95; C St Helier 95-98; TV Camberley St Paul *Guildf* 98-99; V Camberley Heatherside from 99. *61 Goldney Road, Camberley GU15 1DW* Tel (01276) 514451 Fax 678015 E-mail phil.dykes@ntlworld.com

DYMOND, Rosemary Carmen. b 70. Ox Univ MEng94 Aber Univ MSc95 Bremen Univ Dr rer nat 99. Wycliffe Hall Ox BA02. **d** 03 **p** 04. C The Hague *Eur* from 03. *Burgermeester Patijnlaan 680, 2585 CC The Hague, The Netherlands* Tel (00331) (70) 338 8617 E-mail rosiedymond@yahoo.com

DYSON, Mrs Clare Louise. b 63. WMMTC 02. **d** 05. C Tupsley w Hampton Bishop *Heref* from 05. *57 Quarry Road, Hereford HR1 1SL* Tel (01432) 352996

DYSON, Frank. b 28. Oak Hill Th Coll 60. **d** 62 **p** 63. C Parr *Liv* 62-65; V Newchapel *Lich* 65-77; R Bunwell w Carleton Rode *Nor* 77-79; P-in-c Tibenham 78-80; R Bunwell w Carleton Rode and Tibenham 80-81; R Pakefield 81-93; rtd 93; Perm to Offic *Nor* from 93. *12 Viburnum Green, Lowestoft NR32 2SN* Tel (01502) 574898

DYSON, Peter Whiteley. b 51. Man Univ BA73 LLB75. Qu Coll Birm 77. **d** 81 **p** 82. C Swindon Ch Ch *Bris* 81-84; P-in-c Brislington St Luke 84-91; V Bourne *Guildf* 91-92; Perm to Offic 02-04; P-in-c Herriard w Winslade and Long Sutton etc *Win* from 04; P-in-c Newnham w Nately Scures w Mapledurwell etc from 04. *The Vicarage, Church Street, Upton Grey, Basingstoke RG25 2RB* Tel (01256) 861750 E-mail pwdyson@onetel.com

DYTHAM, Linda Alison. b 52. STETS 02. **d** 05. NSM Savernake *Sarum* from 05. *55 Ailesbury Way, Burbage, Marlborough SN8 3TD* Tel (01672) 810972 Mobile 07921-123422 E-mail ladytham@btinternet.com

E

EADE, John Christopher. b 45. Ch Coll Cam BA68 MA72. Linc Th Coll 68. **d** 70 **p** 71. C Portsea N End St Mark *Portsm* 70-73; C Henleaze *Bris* 73-77; V Slad *Glouc* 77-82; V N Bradley, Southwick and Heywood *Sarum* 82-91; R Fovant, Sutton Mandeville and Teffont Evias etc from 91. *The Rectory, Brookwood House, Fovant, Salisbury SP3 5JA* Tel (01722) 714826 E-mail john@eade47.freeserve.co.uk

EADES, David Julian John. b 74. Univ of Wales BA95 Birm Univ DipTh97. St Jo Coll Dur BA99 Cranmer Hall Dur. **d** 00 **p** 01. C Walbrook Epiphany *Derby* 00-04; Chapl Essex Univ *Chelmsf* from 04. *Mariners, Rectory Hill, Wivenhoe, Colchester CO7 9LB* Tel (01206) 820806 E-mail rightrev@btopenworld.com

EADES, Jonathan Peter. b 51. Dundee Univ MA74 Edin Univ BD77. Coates Hall Edin 74. **d** 77 **p** 78. Chapl St Paul's Cathl Dundee *Bre* 77-88; Chapl Dundee Univ 79-88; TV Leek and Meerbrook *Lich* 88-96; RD Leek 93-96; TR Wolstanton from 96. *Wolstanton Rectory, Knutton Road, Newcastle ST5 0HU* Tel (01782) 717561

EADY, David Robert. b 43. Salford Univ BSc Birm Univ DSS. Glouc Th Course 82. **d** 85 **p** 86. NSM Highnam, Lassington, Rudford, Tibberton etc *Glouc* 85-95; NSM Stratton, N Cerney, Baunton and Bagendon 95-99; P-in-c Swindon w Uckington and Elmstone Hardwicke from 99. *The Rectory, Rectory Lane, Swindon, Cheltenham GL51 9RD* Tel (01242) 239069 E-mail davideady@hotmail.com

EADY, Timothy William. b 57. Open Univ BA. Cranmer Hall Dur 82. **d** 85 **p** 86. C Boulton *Derby* 85-88; C Portchester *Portsm* 88-92; Relig Progr Adv Ocean Sound Radio from 88; R Brighstone and Brooke w Mottistone *Portsm* from 92. *The Rectory, Rectory Lane, Brighstone, Newport PO30 4QH* Tel (01983) 740267 E-mail timothy_eady@yahoo.co.uk

EAGER, Ms Rosemary Anne McDowall. b 65. St Andr Univ MA87 Strathclyde Univ 88. Ridley Hall Cam 92. **d** 95 **p** 96. C Walthamstow St Mary w St Steph *Chelmsf* 95-98; C Walthamstow 98-01; TV Bushbury *Lich* 01-05; Perm to Offic from 05. *The Management Centre, 14 Kempthorne Avenue, Wolverhampton WV10 9JG* Tel (01902) 556348 Fax 552993

EAGGER, Mrs Christine Mary. b 32. **d** 94 **p** 95. NSM Upper w Lower Gravenhurst *St Alb* 94-03; Perm to Offic from 03. *43 Cainhoe Road, Clophill, Bedford MK43 4AQ* Tel (01525) 860973 E-mail eagger@fish.co.uk

EAGLE, Canon Julian Charles. b 32. Qu Coll Cam BA56 MA60. Westcott Ho Cam. **d** 58 **p** 59. C Billingham St Aid *Dur* 58-61; C Eastleigh *Win* 61-65; Ind Chapl 65-97; Hon Can Win Cathl 83-97; rtd 97; Perm to Offic *Win* from 97. *123 Cranleigh Road, Bournemouth BH6 5JY* Tel (01202) 429639

EAGLES, Peter Andrew. b 59. K Coll Lon BA82 AKC82 Ox Univ BA88. St Steph Ho Ox 86. **d** 89 **p** 90. C Ruislip St Martin *Lon* 89-92; CF from 92; Perm to Offic *Ripon* from 92. *c/o MOD Chaplains (Army)* Tel (01980) 615804 Fax 615800

EALES, Geoffrey Pellew. b 50. Trin Coll Bris 95. **d** 97 **p** 98. C Uphill *B & W* 97-00; C Weston super Mare Em 00-05; Chapl Weston Area Health Trust 00-05; V Milton *B & W* from 05. *St Peter's Vicarage, Baytree Road, Weston-super-Mare BS22 8HG* Tel (01934) 624247 E-mail geoffeales@aol.com

EALES, Howard Bernard. b 46. Sarum & Wells Th Coll 73. **d** 76 **p** 77. C Timperley *Ches* 76-78; C Stockport St Thos 78-82; V Wythenshawe Wm Temple Ch *Man* 82-95; V Cheadle Hulme All SS *Ches* from 95; RD Cheadle from 02. *All Saints' Vicarage, 27 Church Road, Cheadle Hulme, Cheadle SK8 7JL* Tel 0161-485 3455

EAMAN, Michael Leslie. b 47. Ridley Hall Cam 87. **d** 89 **p** 90. C Wharton *Ches* 89-93; V Buglawton 93-98; TV Congleton from 98. *St John's Vicarage, Buxton Road, Congleton CW12 2DT* Tel (01260) 273294 E-mail revmike@btopenworld.com

✠**EAMES, The Most Revd and Rt Hon Lord (Robert Henry Alexander).** b 37. QUB LLB60 PhD63 Hon LLD89 TCD Hon LLD92 Cam Univ Hon DD94 Lanc Univ Hon LLD94 Aber Univ Hon DD97 Ex Univ Hon DD99 Hon FGCM88. TCD Div Sch Div Test 60. **d** 63 **p** 64 **c** 75. C Bangor St Comgall *D & D* 63-66; I Gilnahirk 66-74; Bp's Dom Chapl 70-72; I Dundela St Mark 74-75; Bp D & R 75-80; Bp D & D 80-86; Abp Arm from 86. *The See House, Cathedral Close, Armagh BT61 7EE* Tel (028) 3752 7144 Fax 3752 7823 E-mail archbishop@armagh.anglican.org

EARDLEY, John. b 38. Ch Coll Cam BA61. Ridley Hall Cam 60. **d** 62 **p** 63. C Barnston *Ches* 62-65; C Wilmslow 65-67; V Hollingworth 67-75; V Leasowe 75-91; Chapl Leasowe Hosp 75-82; RD Wallasey 86-91; V Church Hulme and Chapl Cranage Hall Hosp 91-03; rtd 03; Perm to Offic *Ches* from 03. *7 Banks Road, Heswall, Wirral CH60 9JS* Tel 0151-342 9537

EARDLEY, Canon John Barry. b 35. MBE97. MEd87. AKC62. **d** 63 **p** 64. C Merton St Jas *S'wark* 63-66; C St Helier 66-69; C Bilton *Cov* 69-70; C Canley CD 70-74; P-in-c Church Lawford w Newnham Regis 74-80; P-in-c Leamington Hastings and Birdingbury 82-88; Dioc Educn Officer 82-00; Hon Can Cov Cathl 87-00; rtd 01; Perm to Offic *Cov* from 01. *8 Margaret's Close, Kenilworth CV8 1EN* Tel 024-7630 2345 *or* 7667 3467 E-mail johnbarry.eardley@ntlworld.com

EARDLEY, Robert Bradford. b 44. St Alb Minl Tr Scheme 90. **d** 93 **p** 94. NSM Digswell and Panshanger *St Alb* 93-96; NSM Wheathampstead 97-98; NSM Tewin 98-05; P-in-c 98-04; rtd 05; Perm to Offic *St Alb* from 05. *39 Lode Hill, Downton, Salisbury SP5 3PW* Tel (01725) 510622 E-mail rob.eardley@virgin.net

EARDLEY, William Robert. b 56. Oak Hill Th Coll DipHE96. **d** 96 **p** 97. C Whitfield *Derby* 96-99; TV Dronfield w Holmesfield from 99. *The Vicarage, Vicarage Close, Holmesfield, Dronfield S18 7WZ* Tel 0114-289 1425 E-mail william.eardley@dwhparish.org.uk

EAREY, Mark Robert. b 65. Loughb Univ BSc87 St Jo Coll Dur BA91. Cranmer Hall Dur 88. **d** 91 **p** 92. C Glen Parva and S Wigston *Leic* 91-94; C Luton Ch Ch *Roch* 94-97; Praxis Nat Educn Officer Sarum Coll 97-02; TR Morley *Wakef* from 02. *St Peter's Vicarage, Rooms Lane, Morley, Leeds LS27 9PA* Tel 0113-253 2052 E-mail morley.rector@fish.co.uk

EARIS, Stanley Derek. b 50. Univ Coll Dur BA71 BCL80. Ripon Hall Ox BA73 MA80. **d** 74 **p** 75. C Sutton St Jas and Wawne *York* 74-77; C Acomb St Steph 77-81; V Skelmanthorpe *Wakef* 81-87; R Market Deeping *Linc* 87-02; V N Walsham w Antingham *Nor* from 02; C Bacton w Edingthorpe w Witton and Ridlington from 04. *The Vicarage, 28A Yarmouth Road, North Walsham NR28 9AT* Tel (01692) 406380 E-mail derek.earis@ntlworld.com

EARL, Andrew John. b 61. Huddersfield Univ CertEd01 Ches Coll of HE BTh04. N Ord Course. **d** 04 **p** 05. NSM S Elmsall *Wakef* from 04. *The Chines, 22 Faith Street, South Kirkby, Pontefract WF9 3AL* Tel (01977) 658925 Mobile 07919-048689 E-mail aj-sc-earl@hotmail.com

EARL, David Arthur. b 34. Hartley Victoria Coll 63 Coll of Resurr Mirfield. **d** 83 **p** 83. In Meth Ch 67-83; P-in-c Paddock *Wakef* 83-84; C Huddersfield St Pet and All SS 84-99; rtd 99. *2 Clifton Court, Cleveland Road, Huddersfield HD1 4PU* Tel (01484) 535608

EARL, The Very Revd David Kaye Lee. b 28. TCD BA54. **d** 55 **p** 56. C Chapelizod *D & G* 55-58; I Rathkeale *L & K* 58-65; I Killarney 65-79; Prec Limerick Cathl 77-79; Dean Ferns *C & O* 79-94; I Ferns w Kilbride, Toombe, Kilcormack etc 79-94; rtd 94. *Random, Seafield, Tramore, Co Waterford, Irish Republic* Tel (00353) (51) 390503

EARL, Simon Robert. b 50. Culham Coll of Educn CertEd71 Open Univ BA82. Linc Th Coll 94. **d** 96 **p** 97. C Bexhill St Aug *Chich* 96-99; R Ninfield from 99; V Hooe from 99. *The Rectory, Church Lane, Ninfield, Battle TN33 9JW* Tel and fax (01424) 892308 E-mail srearl@btopenworld.com

EARL, Stephen Geoffrey Franklyn. b 53. Lon Univ BA76 Goldsmiths' Coll Lon PGCE77. Ridley Hall Cam 91. **d** 93 **p** 94. C Sawston *Ely* 93-96; V Burwell w Reach from 96; RD Fordham and Quy from 02. *The Vicarage, High Street, Burwell, Cambridge CB5 0HB* Tel and fax (01638) 741262 E-mail earls@fish.co.uk

EARLEY, Stephen John. b 48. Trin Coll Bris 91. **d** 93 **p** 94. C Stroud H Trin *Glouc* 93-98; C Leckhampton SS Phil and Jas w Cheltenham St Jas 98-02; V Nailsworth w Shortwood, Horsley etc from 02. *The Vicarage, Avening Road, Nailsworth, Stroud GL6 0BS* Tel (01453) 832181 E-mail stevearl@earleys.f9.co.uk

EARNEY, Preb Graham Howard. b 45. AKC67. **d** 68 **p** 69. C Auckland St Helen *Dur* 68-72; C Corsenside *Newc* 72-76; P-in-c 76-79; TV Willington 79-83; TR 83-87; Dioc Soc Resp Officer *B & W* 87-95; Dir Bp Mascall Cen *Heref* 95-02; Hon TV Ludlow, Ludford, Ashford Carbonell etc 95-02; Dioc Development Rep 96-02; Local Min Officer from 02; Preb Heref Cathl from 02; RD Condover from 03. *The Rectory, Wistanstow, Craven Arms SY7 8DG* Tel (01588) 672067

EARNSHAW, Alan Mark. b 36. CQSW81. Lon Coll of Div LTh60. **d** 60 **p** 61. C Fazakerley Em *Liv* 60-65; V Ovenden *Wakef* 65-79; NSM Halifax St Jude 79-90; V Coley 90-99; rtd 99; Perm to Offic *Wakef* from 00. *67 Smithy Clough Lane, Ripponden, Sowerby Bridge HX6 4LG* Tel (01422) 822833

EARNSHAW, Robert Richard. b 42. N Ord Course 78. **d** 81 **p** 82. NW Area Sec Bible Soc 78-85; NSM Liv All So Springwood *Liv* 81-85; R Hinton Ampner w Bramdean and Kilmeston *Win* 85-87; Chapl HM YOI Huntercombe and Finnamore 87-92; Chapl HM YOI Finnamore Wood Camp 87-92; R Spaxton w Charlynch, Goathurst, Enmore etc *B & W* 92-98; R Old Cleeve, Leighland and Treborough 98-03; rtd 03; Perm to Offic *Cov* from 03. *33 Westhill Road, Coventry CV6 2AD* Tel (024) 7659 1256 E-mail bobjen@sagainternet.co.uk

EARP, John William. b 19. Jes Coll Cam BA42 MA45. Ridley Hall Cam 42. **d** 43 **p** 44. C Portman Square St Paul *Lon* 43-46; Tutor Ridley Hall Cam 46-48; Chapl 48-51; Vice-Prin 51-56; Chapl Eton Coll 56-62; V Hartley Wintney and Elvetham *Win* 62-77; RD Odiham 76-83; V Hartley Wintney, Elvetham, Winchfield etc 77-88; rtd 88; Perm to Offic *Nor* from 89. *3 The Driftway, Sheringham NR26 8LD* Tel (01263) 825487

EARWAKER, John Clifford. b 36. Keble Coll Ox BA59 MA63 Man Univ MEd71. Linc Th Coll 59. **d** 61 **p** 62. C Ecclesall *Sheff* 61-64; Succ St Mary's Cathl *Edin* 64-65; Lic to Offic *Man* 65-69 and *Sheff* 69-93; Chapl and Lect Sheff Poly 81-92; Chapl and Lect Sheff Hallam Univ 92-93; rtd 93; Perm to Offic *Sheff* from 93. *89 Dransfield Road, Crosspool, Sheffield S10 5RP* Tel 0114-230 3487

EASEMAN, Robert Leslie. **d** 00 **p** 01. NSM Hunstanton St Mary w Ringstead Parva etc *Nor* from 00. *5 Lighthouse Close, Hunstanton PE36 6EL* Tel and fax (01485) 535258 Mobile 07941-323218 E-mail robert.easeman@virgin.net

EASON, Canon Cyril Edward. b 21. Leeds Univ BA43 MA67. Coll of Resurr Mirfield 43. **d** 45 **p** 46. C Tonge Moor *Man* 45-51; C Blackpool H Cross *Blackb* 51-53; V Lever Bridge *Man* 53-65; Area Sec USPG *B & W* 65-86; Area Sec USPG *Ex* and *Truro* 75-86; Perm to Offic *Truro* 75-86; Hon Can Mufulira from 85; rtd 86; P-in-c Tilshead, Orcheston and Chitterne *Sarum* 86-92; Perm to Offic *Truro* from 92 and *Ripon* from 95. *11 Bishop's Court, Williamson Drive, Ripon HG4 1AY* Tel (01765) 608300 E-mail edward.eason1@virgin.net

EAST, Bryan Victor. b 46. Oak Hill Th Coll DipHE93. **d** 93 **p** 94. C Waltham Cross *St Alb* 93-96; C Wotton St Mary *Glouc* 96-99;

V Humberston *Linc* from 99. *The Vicarage, 34 Tetney Road, Humberston, Grimsby DN36 4JF* Tel (01472) 813158 E-mail bryan.east@ntlworld.com

EAST, Mark Richard. b 57. Trin Coll Bris BA89. **d** 89 **p** 90. C Dalton-in-Furness *Carl* 89-93; TV Bucknall and Bagnall *Lich* 93-00; P-in-c Church Coniston *Carl* from 00; P-in-c Torver from 00. *St Andrew's Vicarage, Yewdale Road, Coniston LA21 8DX* Tel (01539) 441262 E-mail mark.east@lineone.net

EAST, Peter Alan. b 61. ACIB89 Southn Univ LLB82. Cranmer Hall Dur 90. **d** 93 **p** 94. C Combe Down w Monkton Combe and S Stoke *B & W* 93-97. *Address withheld by request*

EAST, Richard Kenneth. b 47. Oak Hill Th Coll 86. **d** 88 **p** 89. C Necton w Holme Hale *Nor* 88-92; R Garsdon, Lea and Cleverton and Charlton *Bris* from 92; RD Malmesbury 93-99. *The Rectory, The Street, Lea, Malmesbury SN16 9PG* Tel (01666) 823861 E-mail lea.rectory@btinternet.com

EAST, Stuart Michael. b 50. Chich Th Coll 86. **d** 88 **p** 89. C Middlesbrough St Martin *York* 88-92; R Upper Ryedale 92-97; V Macclesfield St Paul *Ches* 97-01; C Maidstone St Luke *Cant* 01-03; R Peopleton and White Ladies Aston w Churchill etc *Worc* from 03. *The Rectory, Peopleton, Pershore WR10 2EE* Tel (01905) 840243 Mobile 07754-244929 E-mail stuart@the-rectory.fsnet.co.uk

EAST KERALA, Bishop of. *See* SAMUEL, The Most Revd Kunnumpurathu Joseph

EAST RIDING, Archdeacon of. *See* HARRISON, The Ven Peter Reginald Wallace

EASTELL, Jane Rosamund. b 47. Sheff Univ BA68 DipArch71 RIBA73 Bris Univ BA99. Trin Coll Bris 97. **d** 99 **p** 00. C Backwell w Chelvey and Brockley *B & W* 99-03; NSM 99-00; C Chew Stoke w Nempnett Thrubwell from 03; C Chew Magna w Dundry and Norton Malreward from 03; Dioc Adv in Prayer and Spirituality from 04. *The Rectory, Pilgrims Way, Chew Stoke, Bristol BS40 8TX* Tel (01275) 332554 E-mail jane.eastell@btclick.com

EASTER, Canon Ann Rosemarie. SRN68 Cam Univ DipRS80 Univ of E Lon MBA94. Gilmore Ho 78. **dss** 80 **d** 87 **p** 94. Chapl Asst Newham Gen Hosp 80-89; Stratford St Jo and Ch Ch w Forest Gate St Jas *Chelmsf* 80-89; Par Dn 87-89; Perm to Offic from 89; Chief Exec The Renewal Programme from 95; AD Newham from 97; Hon Can Chelmsf Cathl from 99. *The Vicarage, Larkswood Road, London E4 9DS* Tel (020) 8524 1201 Mobile 07889-799290 Fax (020) 8529 5226 E-mail ann@renewalprogramme.freeserve.co.uk

EASTER, Brian James Bert. b 33. Lon Univ DipTh55 Birm Univ DPS75 PhD83. Tyndale Hall Bris 53 St Aug Coll Cant 56. **d** 57 **p** 58. C Tipton St Martin *Lich* 57-59; Midl Area Sec BCMS 59-64; V Barston *Birm* 64-72; Chapl Mentally Handicapped S Birm HA 72-94; Chapl Monyhull Hosp Birm 72-94; Lect Birm Univ 86-98; Chapl S Birm Mental Health NHS Trust 94-98; rtd 98; Perm to Offic *Birm* from 98. *24 Dingle Lane, Solihull B91 3NG* Tel 0121-705 8342 *or* 627 1627

EASTER, Stephen Talbot. b 22. St Cath Coll Cam BA47 MA53. Ely Th Coll. **d** 50 **p** 51. C Whitstable All SS *Cant* 50-53; S Rhodesia 53-56; V Womenswold *Cant* 56-61; C-in-c Aylesham CD 56-61; V St Margarets-at-Cliffe w Westcliffe etc 61-85; rtd 85; Perm to Offic *Cant* 85-02. *9-11 Blenheim Road, Deal CT14 7AJ* Tel (01304) 368021

EASTERN ARCHDEACONRY, Archdeacon of the. *See* CURRAN, The Ven Patrick Martin Stanley

EASTGATE, Canon John. b 30. Kelham Th Coll 47. **d** 54 **p** 55. C Ealing St Pet Mt Park *Lon* 54-58; C-in-c Leic St Gabr CD *Leic* 58-64; V Leic St Gabr 64-69; V Glen Parva and S Wigston 69-74; V Woodley St Jo the Ev *Ox* 74-83; V Hughenden 83-94; RD Wycombe 87-90; Hon Can Ch Ch 90-94; rtd 94. *12A Mowlem Court, Rempstone Road, Swanage BH19 1DR* Tel (01929) 421558 E-mail john@eastgate1702.fsnet.co.uk

EASTOE, Robin Howard Spenser. b 53. Lon Univ BD75 AKC75. Coll of Resurr Mirfield 77. **d** 78 **p** 79. C Gt Ilford St Mary *Chelmsf* 78-81; C Walthamstow St Sav 81-84; V Barkingside St Fran 84-92; V Leigh-on-Sea St Marg from 92; Chapl Southend Health Care NHS Trust from 96; RD Hadleigh *Chelmsf* from 00. *St Margaret's Vicarage, 1465 London Road, Leigh-on-Sea SS9 2SB* Tel (01702) 471773 E-mail eastoe@dialstart.net

EASTON, Christopher Richard Alexander. b 60. TCD BA81 DipTh84. **d** 84 **p** 85. C Belfast St Donard *D & D* 84-89; I Inishmacsaint *Clogh* 89-95; I Magheralin w Dollingstown *D & D* 95-01; I Coleraine *Conn* from 01. *St Patrick's Rectory, 28 Mountsandel Road, Coleraine BT52 1JE* Tel (028) 7034 3429 *or* tel and fax 7034 4213 E-mail ce.stpat@btopenworld.com

EASTON, Donald Fyfe. b 48. St Edm Hall Ox BA69 MA85 Nottm Univ CertEd70 Univ Coll Lon MA76 PhD90 Clare Hall Cam MA85. Westcott Ho Cam 89. **d** 90 **p** 91. NSM Fulham St Andr Fulham Fields *Lon* 90-97; Lic Preacher from 97. *12 Weltje Road, London W6 9TG* Tel (020) 8741 0233

EASTON, John. b 34. St Cath Soc Ox BA59 MA63. Chich Th Coll 59. **d** 61 **p** 62. C Rugeley *Lich* 61-64; TR 72-87; C Shrewsbury All SS 64-66; Ind Chapl *Sheff* 66-72; V Bolsover *Derby* 87-99; RD Bolsover and Staveley 93-98; rtd 99; Perm to Offic *Derby* from 99. *71 Wythburn Road, Chesterfield S41 8DP* Tel (01246) 555610

EASTON, John. b 41. Nor City Coll 71. LNSM course 95. **d** 97. OLM New Catton Ch Ch *Nor* from 97. *14 Carteford Drive, Norwich NR3 4DW* Tel (01603) 412589

EASTON, Richard Huntingford. b 26. Oriel Coll Ox BA51 MA51. Westcott Ho Cam 53. **d** 54 **p** 55. C Bris St Ambrose Whitehall *Bris* 54-57; New Zealand from 57. *271 Muriwai Road, RD1, Waimauku, Auckland 1250, New Zealand* Tel (0064) (9) 411 8320

EASTON, Robert Paul Stephen. b 62. Bris Univ BA84 Univ of Wales (Cardiff) Dip Journalism 85. St Steph Ho Ox BTh00. **d** 00 **p** 01. C Stoke Newington St Mary *Lon* 00-03; Chapl Brighton Coll from 03. *The Chaplaincy, Brighton College, Eastern Road, Brighton BN2 2AL* Tel (01273) 606524 E-mail roberteaston1@onetel.com

EASTON-CROUCH, Jonathan Brian. b 65. Univ Coll Lon DipHE96. SEITE 96. **d** 99 **p** 00. C Mitcham SS Pet and Paul *S'wark* 99-02; Hon C S Wimbledon H Trin and St Pet from 03. *19 Charminster Avenue, London SW19 3EL* Tel (020) 8544 0205

EASTWOOD, Colin Foster. b 34. Leeds Univ BA56 MA66. Linc Th Coll 65. **d** 67 **p** 68. C Cottingham *York* 67-70; C Darlington St Cuth *Dur* 70-75; V Eighton Banks 75-81; V Sutton St Jas *Ches* 81-99; rtd 99; Perm to Offic *Glouc* from 00. *14 Ross Close, Chipping Sodbury, Bristol BS37 6RS* Tel (01454) 317594

EASTWOOD, Harry. b 26. Man Univ BSc48. Ridley Hall Cam 81. **d** 82 **p** 83. NSM Barton Seagrave w Warkton *Pet* 82-00; Perm to Offic from 00. *22 Poplars Farm Road, Kettering NN15 5AF* Tel (01536) 513271

EASTWOOD, Miss Janet. b 54. Wycliffe Hall Ox 83. **dss** 86 **d** 87 **p** 94. Ainsdale *Liv* 86-90; Par Dn 87-90; TD Kirkby Lonsdale *Carl* 90-94; TV 94-95; Dioc Youth Officer 90-94; R Wavertree H Trin *Liv* from 95; P-in-c Wavertree St Thos 95-97; Chapl Blue Coat Sch Liv from 96. *Wavertree Rectory, Hunters Lane, Liverpool L15 8HL* Tel 0151-733 2172 E-mail janet@holytrinitywavertree.co.uk

EASTWOOD, Martin Russell. b 66. Edin Univ BMus88 LRSM02. Ripon Coll Cuddesdon BTh05. **d** 03 **p** 04. C Wymondham *Nor* from 03. *118 Tuttles Lane West, Wymondham NR18 0JJ* Tel (01953) 606775 E-mail wymondhamcurate@hotmail.com

EATOCK, John. b 45. Lanc Univ MA82. Lich Th Coll 67. **d** 70 **p** 71. C Crumpsall St Mary *Man* 70-73; C Atherton 73-74; C Ribbleton *Blackb* 74-77; V Ingol 77-83; V Laneside 83-92; RD Accrington 90-92; Perm to Offic from 92. *57 Heys Avenue, Haslingden, Rossendale BB4 5EE* Tel (01706) 222531 E-mail john@jeatock.freeserve.co.uk

EATON, Barry Anthony. b 50. St Martin's Coll Lanc MA98. Wilson Carlile Coll Dip Evang79 Carl and Blackb Dioc Tr Inst 94. **d** 97 **p** 98. C W Burnley All SS *Blackb* 97-99; Dep Chapl HM Pris Leeds 99-00; Chapl HM Pris Buckley Hall from 00. *HM Prison, Buckley Hall, Buckley Road, Rochdale OL12 9DP* Tel (01706) 8861610

EATON, Benjamin. *See* EATON, Canon Oscar Benjamin

EATON, David Andrew. b 58. Man Univ BSc79 ACA83. Trin Coll Bris BA89. **d** 89 **p** 90. C Barking St Marg w St Patr *Chelmsf* 89-92; C Billericay and Lt Burstead 92-95; P-in-c Vange 95-05; TV Sole Bay *St E* from 05. *The Vicarage, Parkgate, High Street, Wangford, Beccles NR34 8RL* Tel and fax (01502) 578827 E-mail davidaeaton@lineone.net

EATON, Canon David John. b 45. Nottm Univ LTh BTh74. St Jo Coll Nottm 70. **d** 74 **p** 75. C Headley All SS *Guildf* 74-77; Ind Chapl *Worc* 77-82; TV Halesowen 80-82; V Rowledge *Guildf* 82-89; V Leatherhead 89-01; R Leatherhead and Mickleham from 01; RD Leatherhead 93-98; Hon Can Guildf Cathl from 02. *The Vicarage, 3 St Mary's Road, Leatherhead KT22 8EZ* Tel (01372) 372313 E-mail parishoffice@tecres.net

✠**EATON, The Rt Revd Derek Lionel.** b 41. QSM85. Cert Français 69 Internat Inst Chr Communication Nairobi 74 Univ of Tunis CertFAI70 MA78. Trin Coll Bris DipTh66 WEC Miss Tr Coll DipTh66. **d** 71 **p** 71 **c** 90. C Barton Hill St Luke w Ch Ch *Bris* 71-72; Chapl Br Emb Tunisia 72-78; Provost All SS Cathl Cairo and Chapl Br Emb 78-83; Hon Can 85; New Zealand from 84; Assoc P Papanui St Paul 84; V Sumner-Redcliffs 85-90; Bp Nelson from 90. *PO Box 100, Nelson, New Zealand* Tel and fax (0064) (3) 548 8991 *or* tel 548 3124 Fax 548 2125 E-mail +derek@nn.ang.org.nz

EATON (née CRAIG), Mrs Julie Elizabeth. b 57. SEN81. Trin Coll Bris 87. **d** 89 **p** 94. Par Dn Gt Ilford St Andr *Chelmsf* 89-92; NSM Billericay and Lt Burstead 92-95; C 95-96; TV 96-01; Chapl Thameside Community Healthcare NHS Trust 92-95; Perm to Offic *Chelmsf* 01-05; TV Sole Bay *St E* from 05. *The Vicarage, Parkgate, High Street, Wangford, Beccles NR34 8RL* Tel (01502) 578827 E-mail juliecraigeaton@tiscali.co.uk

EATON, Mrs Margaret Anne. b 44. Ab Dioc Tr Course 82. **dss** 84 **d** 86 **p** 94. NSM Ellon *Ab* 84-95; NSM Cruden Bay 84-95; C Bridge of Don 95-00; Co-ord Scottish Episc Renewal Fellowship

(SERF) from 00; C Ellon 01-03; NSM Elgin w Lossiemouth *Mor* from 03. *8 Roseisle Place, Elgin IV30 4NX* Tel (01343) 541142 E-mail revmaggie12@aol.com

EATON, Canon Oscar Benjamin (Ben). b 37. Puerto Rico Th Coll STB66. **d** 66 **p** 67. Ecuador 66-69; C Wandsworth St Anne *S'wark* 69-71; C Aldrington *Chich* 71-73; TV Littleham w Exmouth *Ex* 74-79; R Alphington 79-84; Chapl Barcelona w Casteldefels *Eur* 84-88; Chapl Maisons-Laffitte 88-02; Can Malta Cathl from 96; rtd 02; P-in-c St Raphaël *Eur* from 02. *62 Hameau de Valescure, 83600 Fréjus, France* Tel (0033) (4) 94 40 48 61 E-mail htcml@aol.com

EATON, The Very Revd Peter David. b 58. K Coll Lon BA82 AKC82 Qu Coll Cam BA85 MA89 Magd Coll Ox MA90. Westcott Ho Cam 83. **d** 86 **p** 87. C Maidstone All SS and St Phil w Tovil *Cant* 86-89; Fells' Chapl Magd Coll Ox 89-91; Lic to Offic *Ox* from 89; USA from 91; Assoc R Salt Lake City St Paul 91-95; Hon Can Th Utah 91-01; R Lancaster St Jas Penn 95-01; Dean St Jo Cathl Denver from 02. *St John's Cathedral, 1350 Washington Street, Denver, CO 80203-2008, USA* Tel (001) (303) 831 7115 *or* 295 0956 Fax 831 7119
E-mail deansadmin@sjc-den.org

EATON, Miss Phyllis Mary. b 42. SRD Qu Eliz Coll Lon BSc63 Univ of S Africa BA79. WMMTC 87. **d** 90 **p** 94. NSM Washwood Heath *Birm* 90-91; NSM Edgbaston SS Mary and Ambrose 91-95; Perm to Offic from 95. *26 Blackthorne Road, Smethwick, Warley B67 6PZ* Tel 0121-552 4904 *or* 507 4085

EAVES, Alan Charles. b 37. Lon Univ DipTh64. Tyndale Hall Bris 62. **d** 65 **p** 66. C Southport SS Simon and Jude *Liv* 65-66; C Eccleston Ch Ch 66-70; V Earlestown 70-79; V Orpington Ch Ch *Roch* 79-02; rtd 02; Perm to Offic *Ely* from 03. *4 Chervil Close, Folksworth, Peterborough PE7 3SZ* Tel (01733) 241644 Mobile 07904-357476

EAVES, Brian Maxwell. b 40. Tyndale Hall Bris 66. **d** 69 **p** 70. C Wolverhampton St Jude *Lich* 69-72; C Fazeley 72-75; TV Ipsley *Worc* 75-79; Chapl Amsterdam *Eur* 79-86; Chapl Bordeaux w Riberac, Cahors, Duras etc 86-91; Monaco 91-93; TV Buckhurst Hill *Chelmsf* 93-96; R Culworth w Sulgrave and Thorpe Mandeville etc *Pet* 96-03; rtd 03. *17 Browning Road, Ledbury HR8 2GA* Tel (01531) 631582

EBBSFLEET, Suffragan Bishop of (Provincial Episcopal Visitor). *See* BURNHAM, The Rt Revd Andrew

EBELING, Mrs Barbara. b 44. Hull Univ BA67. St Alb Minl Tr Scheme 87. **d** 94 **p** 95. C Stevenage St Hugh and St Jo *St Alb* 94-99; R Blunham, Gt Barford, Roxton and Tempsford etc from 99. *The Vicrage, High Street, Great Barford, Bedford MK44 3JJ* Tel (01234) 870363
E-mail benefice@barfordmk44.freeserve.co.uk

ECCLES, James Henry. b 30. DLC64 Lon Univ Cert Psychology 70 DipEd. Wycliffe Hall Ox 86. **d** 87 **p** 88. NSM Llandudno *Ban* 87-91; rtd 91; NSM Llanrhos *St As* 94-00; Perm to Offic *Ban* from 97. *Lowlands, 7 St Seiriol's Road, Llandudno LL30 2YY* Tel (01492) 878524

ECCLES, Mrs Vivien Madeline. LNSM course. **d** 92 **p** 94. OLM Old Trafford St Bride *Man* from 92. *479 Barton Road, Stretford, Manchester M32 9TA* Tel 0161-748 9795

ECCLESTON, Mrs Frances Mary. b 61. Jes Coll Cam BA83 Sheff Univ CQSW88. N Ord Course 00. **d** 03 **p** 04. C Ranmoor *Sheff* from 03. *Flat 1, 5 Ranmoor Park Road, Sheffield S10 3GX* Tel 0114-230 5204 E-mail eccleston@clara.co.uk

ECCLESTONE, Gary Edward. b 73. Ex Univ BA95 PGCE96. Cuddesdon Coll BTh99. **d** 99 **p** 00. C Salisbury St Martin and Laverstock *Sarum* 99-03; P-in-c Hanslope w Castlethorpe *Ox* from 03. *The Vicarage, Park Road, Hanslope, Milton Keynes MK19 7LT* Tel (01908) 337936

ECHOLS, Mrs Janet Lyn Roberts. b 58. Coll of Charleston (USA) BA. Trin Episc Sch for Min Penn MDiv. **d** 95 **p** 96. Asst R Mt Pleasant Ch Ch USA 95-02; P-in-c Stapleford *Ely* from 02. *The Vicarage, Mingle Lane, Stapleford, Cambridge CB2 5SY* Tel (01223) 842150 Fax 841170 E-mail janetechols@yahoo.com

ECKERSLEY, Mrs Nancy Elizabeth. b 50. York Univ BA72 Leeds Univ CertEd73. NEOC 86. **d** 89 **p** 94. C Clifton *York* 89-00; Chapl York Distr Hosp 90-93; Lay Tr Officer *York* 93-00; V Heslington from 00. *The Vicarage, School Lane, Heslington, York YO10 5EE* Tel (01904) 410389

ECKERSLEY, Canon Richard Hugh. b 25. Trin Coll Cam BA48 MA50. Chich Th Coll 49. **d** 51 **p** 52. C Portsea St Jo Rudmore *Portsm* 51-57; C Portsea N End St Mark 57-62; V Paulsgrove 62-73; V Brighton St Nic *Chich* 73-84; Can Res Portsm Cathl *Portsm* 84-92; rtd 92; Perm to Offic *Portsm* from 92. *136 Kensington Road, Portsmouth PO2 0QY* Tel (023) 9265 3512

ECKHARD, Robert Leo Michael. b 60. Middx Poly BA87 La Sainte Union Coll PGCE88 Open Univ MA96. NTMTC 02. **d** 05. NSM Ealing St Paul *Lon* from 05. *4 Grosvenor Road, London W7 1HJ* Tel (020) 8840 4409 Mobile 07985-003057
E-mail bob.eckhard@stpauls-ealing.org

EDDISON, Frederick Donald Buchanan. b 19. Trin Coll Cam BA41 MA46. Ridley Hall Cam 47. **d** 48 **p** 49. C Fulham St Matt *Lon* 48-51; C St Marylebone All So w SS Pet and Jo 51-53; Asst Chapl and Asst Master Forres Sch Swanage 53-56; Chapl CSSM 56-65; V Tunbridge Wells St Jo *Roch* 65-80; rtd 80; Perm to Offic *Chich* 81-99. *c/o J M B Eddison Esq, 31 Hillside Road, Harpenden AL5 4BS* Tel (01582) 621180

EDDISON, Robert John Buchanan. b 16. Trin Coll Cam BA38 MA42. Ridley Hall Cam 38. **d** 39 **p** 40. C Tunbridge Wells St Jo *Roch* 39-43; Travelling Sec Scripture Union 42-80; rtd 81; Perm to Offic *Chich* from 81. *Durham Lodge, Gordon Road, Crowborough TN6 1EW* Tel (01892) 652606

EDE, The Ven Dennis. b 31. Nottm Univ BA55 Birm Univ MSocSc73. Ripon Hall Ox 55. **d** 57 **p** 58. C Sheldon *Birm* 57-60; C Castle Bromwich SS Mary and Marg 60-64; Chapl E Birm Hosp 60-76; C-in-c Hodge Hill CD *Birm* 64-70; V Hodge Hill 70-72; TR 72-76; Chapl Sandwell Distr Gen Hosp 76-90; V W Bromwich All SS *Lich* 76-90; P-in-c W Bromwich Ch Ch 76-79; RD W Bromwich 76-90; Preb Lich Cathl 83-90; Adn Stoke 90-97; rtd 97; Hon C Tilford *Guildf* 97-99; Hon C The Bourne and Tilford 99-02; Perm to Offic *Guildf* and *S'wark* from 03. *Tilford, 13 Park Close, Carshalton SM5 3EU* Tel (020) 8647 5891
E-mail dennisangelaede@aol.co.uk

EDEN, Grenville Mervyn. b 37. Bris Univ BA58 Lon Univ MPhil78. Ox Min Course 88. **d** 95 **p** 96. NSM Burnham w Dropmore, Hitcham and Taplow *Ox* from 95. *Langdale, Grays Park Road, Stoke Poges, Slough SL2 4JG* Tel (01753) 525962

EDEN, Henry. b 36. G&C Coll Cam BA59 MA64. Ox NSM Course. **d** 87 **p** 88. NSM Abingdon w Shippon *Ox* 87-88; Chapl Brentwood Sch Essex 88-95; TV Beaconsfield *Ox* 95-00; Perm to Offic *St E* from 01 and *Ely* from 03. *Ely Cottage, Denham, Bury St Edmunds IP29 5EQ* Tel (01284) 811884
E-mail heden@btinternet.com

EDEN, Mrs Lesley Patricia. b 54. Liv Univ MTh99. N Ord Course 93. **d** 96 **p** 97. C Wallasey St Hilary *Ches* 96-98; C Oxton 98-01; V Whitegate w Lt Budworth from 01; Min Review Officer from 01. *The Vicarage, Cinder Hill, Whitegate, Northwich CW8 2BH* Tel (01606) 882151 Fax as telephone
E-mail lesley_eden88@hotmail.com

EDEN, Leslie Thomas Ernest. b 19. ACII55. S'wark Ord Course. **d** 69 **p** 70. NSM Kidbrooke St Jas *S'wark* 69-94; rtd 94; Perm to Offic *S'wark* from 94. *47 Begbie Road, London SE3 8DA* Tel (020) 8856 3088

EDEN, Mervyn. *See* EDEN, Grenville Mervyn

EDEN, Michael William. b 57. Nottm Univ BTh86. Linc Th Coll 83. **d** 86 **p** 87. C Daventry *Pet* 86-89; TV Northampton Em 89-92; V Corby St Columba 92-03; P-in-c Stowmarket *St E* from 03. *The Vicarage, 7 Lockington Road, Stowmarket IP14 1BQ* Tel (01449) 678623 *or* 774652 Fax 774652
E-mail theedens@talk21.com

EDGAR, David. b 59. Newc Univ BA81. Linc Th Coll BTh86. **d** 86 **p** 87. C Wednesbury St Paul Wood Green *Lich* 86-91; V Winterton Gp *Linc* 91-00; C Linc St Swithin 00-01; P-in-c from 01; Chapl N Lincs Coll from 00. *1 St Giles Avenue, Lincoln LN2 4PE* Tel (01522) 528199 E-mail david.edgar1@tesco.net

EDGCUMBE, Irena Christine. *See* CZERNIAWSKA EDGCUMBE, Mrs Irena Christine

EDGE, Canon John Francis. b 32. Ex Coll Ox BA54 MA56. St Steph Ho Ox 54. **d** 58 **p** 59. C Oswestry H Trin *Lich* 58-62; V 64-79; Tutor Lich Th Coll 62-64; Malaysia 79-87; Hon Can Kuching from 88; TV Wolverhampton *Lich* 88-91; Chapl R Hosp Wolv 88-91; Subwarden St Deiniol's Lib Hawarden 91-93; C Briercliffe *Blackb* 93-96; C W Felton *Lich* 96-97; Res Min 97-01; rtd 97; Perm to Offic *Blackb* from 01. *24 Talbot Street, Briercliffe, Burnley BB10 2HW* Tel (01282) 429287

EDGE, John Nicholson. b 53. ONC73 HNC75. OLM course 96. **d** 99 **p** 00. OLM Flixton St Jo *Man* from 99. *5 Devon Road, Flixton, Manchester M41 6PN* Tel 0161-748 4736

EDGE, Michael MacLeod. b 45. St Andr Univ BSc68 Qu Coll Cam BA70 MA74. Westcott Ho Cam 68. **d** 72 **p** 73. C Allerton *Liv* 72-76; R Bretherton *Blackb* 76-82; P-in-c Kilpeck *Heref* 82-84; P-in-c St Devereux w Wormbridge 82-84; TR Ewyas Harold w Dulas, Kenderchurch etc 82-93; RD Abbeydore 84-90; V Enfield St Andr *Lon* from 93. *Enfield Vicarage, Silver Street, Enfield EN1 3EG* Tel (020) 8363 8676
E-mail michaeledge@freeuk.com
or enfieldparishchurch@zoom.co.uk

EDGE, Philip John. b 54. Ripon Coll Cuddesdon 77. **d** 80 **p** 81. C N Harrow St Alb *Lon* 80-83; C St Giles Cripplegate w St Bart Moor Lane etc 83-86; P-in-c Belmont 86-88; V 88-92; V Ellesmere and Welsh Frankton *Lich* 92-97; V Ellesmere from 97. *The Vicarage, Church Hill, Ellesmere SY12 0HB* Tel (01691) 622571

EDGE, Ms Renate Erika. b 50. Bonn Chamber of Commerce Translator's Dip 75 DIL77. Cranmer Hall Dur 86. **d** 88. Par Dn Leic H Spirit *Leic* 88-89; Asst Chapl Leic and Co Miss for the Deaf 88-89; Par Dn Leic H Apostles *Leic* 89-94. *6 Tideswell Bank, Glossop SK13 6HQ* Tel (01457) 855928

EDGE, Timothy Peter. b 55. Brighton Poly BSc80 CEng85 MIEE85 FRAS80. Westcott Ho Cam 85. **d** 88 **p** 89. C Norton *Ches* 88-91; C Bedworth *Cov* 91-96; TV Witney *Ox* 96-02; Asst

Chapl HM Pris Bullingdon from 02; NSM Cogges and S Leigh *Ox* from 03. *HM Prison Bullingdon, Patrick Haugh Road, Arncott, Bicester OX25 1PZ* Tel (01869) 353100 E-mail tim.edge@talk21.com

EDGELL, Hugh Anthony Richard. b 31. ARHistS84. AKC57. **d** 58 **p** 59. C N Lynn w St Marg and St Nic *Nor* 58-64; R S Walsham 64-74; V Upton w Fishley 64-74; R Hingham 74-81; R Hingham w Woodrising w Scoulton 81-85; V Horning 85-89; P-in-c Beeston St Laurence w Ashmanhaugh 85-89; R Horning w Beeston St Laurence and Ashmanhaugh 89-95; Prior St Benet's Abbey Horning 87-95; rtd 95; Perm to Offic *Nor* from 95. *Brambles, Brimbelow Road, Hoveton, Norwich NR12 8UJ* Tel (01604) 782206

EDGERTON, Ms Hilary Ann. b 66. R Holloway & Bedf New Coll Lon BSc88. Wycliffe Hall Ox BTh93. **d** 93 **p** 94. Par Dn S Cave and Ellerker w Broomfleet *York* 93-94; C 94-97; TV Howden 97-00; V Hayfield and Chinley w Buxworth *Derby* from 00. *8 Bluebell Close, Hayfield, High Peak SK22 2PG* Tel (01663) 743350 E-mail hilary@philippians3.totalserve.co.uk

EDIE, Jennifer Mary. b 40. Edin Univ MA62 Hong Kong Univ PGCE77. **d** 03 **p** 04. NSM Eyemouth *Edin* from 03. *Burnbank House, Foulden, Berwick-upon-Tweed TD15 1UH* Tel (01289) 386338 E-mail jennifermedie@hotmail.com

EDINBOROUGH, David. b 36. Nottm Univ BA58 MEd74. EMMTC 79. **d** 82 **p** 83. NSM Bramcote *S'well* 82-01; P-in-c 94-01; Dioc Officer for NSMs 89-94; rtd 01; Perm to Offic *S'well* 01-02; P-in-c Radford St Pet from 02. *105A Derby Road, Beeston, Nottingham NG9 3GZ* Tel 0115-925 1066 E-mail david.edinborough@btopenworld.com

EDINBURGH, Bishop of. *See* SMITH, The Rt Revd Brian Arthur

EDINBURGH, Dean of. *See* PEARSON, The Very Revd Kevin

EDINBURGH, Provost of. *See* FORBES, The Very Revd Graham John Thompson

EDIS, John Oram. b 26. ACIS50 ACP52 CDipAF78 FCollP89 Open Univ BA81. Ox NSM Course 85. **d** 88 **p** 89. Hon Warden and Chapl E Ivor Hughes Educn Foundn from 88; NSM Gt Chesham *Ox* 88-96; Perm to Offic *Lon* 96-03 and *Ox* from 96. *21 Greenway, Chesham HP5 2BW* Tel (01494) 785815

EDMEADS, Andrew. b 53. Linc Th Coll 84. **d** 86 **p** 87. C Sholing *Win* 86-89; R Knights Enham 89-97; rtd 97; Perm to Offic *Win* 97-99; Chapl St Mich Hospice Basingstoke from 00. *10 Altona Gardens, Andover SP10 4LG* Tel (01264) 391464

EDMONDS (née HARRIS), Mrs Catherine Elizabeth. b 52. Leic Coll of Educn CertEd73 ACP79 K Alfred's Coll Win 86 Basingstoke Coll of Tech 87. S Dios Minl Tr Scheme 91. **d** 95 **p** 96. NSM Basing *Win* 95-99; C Yeovil H Trin w Barwick *B & W* 99-01; Chapl Coll of SS Mark and Jo Plymouth *Ex* from 01. *Chaplain's House, College of St Mark and St John, Derriford Road, Plymouth PL6 8BH* Tel (01752) 789910 *or* 777188 ext 2047 E-mail pauledmonds@lineone.net

EDMONDS, Clive Alway. b 42. ACII. S'wark Ord Course 78. **d** 81 **p** 82. C Horsell *Guildf* 81-85; R Bisley and W End 85-92; RD Surrey Heath 90-92; R Haslemere 92-00; Chapl Wispers Sch Haslemere 92-00; P-in-c Westbury-on-Severn w Flaxley and Blaisdon *Glouc* 00-02; V Westbury-on-Severn w Flaxley, Blaisdon etc from 03. *The Vicarage, Westbury-on-Severn GL14 1LW* Tel (01452) 760592

EDMONDS (née MAGUIRE), Mrs Sarah Alison. b 65. Univ Coll Lon BSc87 Southn Univ MSc93. STETS 95. **d** 98 **p** 99. C Warwick St Paul *Cov* 98-02; P-in-c Hampton Lucy w Charlecote and Loxley from 02. *The Vicarage, Charlecote, Warwick CV35 9EW* Tel (01789) 840244 E-mail sedmonds@informs.co.uk

EDMONDS, Sidney. b 20. Oak Hill Th Coll. **d** 58 **p** 59. C Holborn St Geo w H Trin and St Bart *Lon* 58-61; Chapl HM Pris Liv 61-63; Dur 63-69; Parkhurst 69-74; Reading 74-85; V Aldworth and Ashampstead *Ox* 74-85; rtd 85. *22 Sandlea Park, Wirral CH48 0QF* Tel 0151-625 6147

EDMONDS, Tony Ernest. b 50. MSc PhD. EMMTC. **d** 05. NSM Barrow upon Soar w Walton le Wolds *Leic* from 05. *Mulberry Lodge, 8 Melton Road, Burton-on-the-Wolds, Loughborough LE12 5AG* Tel (01509) 881369 E-mail t.e.edmonds@btconnect.com

EDMONDS-SEAL, John. b 34. FFARCS63 Lon Univ MB, BS58. Ox NSM Course DipTh90. **d** 90 **p** 91. NSM Ox St Aldate w St Matt *Ox* 90-94; NSM Wheatley from 95. *Otway, Woodperry Road, Oxford OX3 9UY* Tel (01865) 351582 E-mail edmondsseal@doctors.org.uk

EDMONDSON, Christopher Paul. b 50. Dur Univ BA71 MA81. Cranmer Hall Dur. **d** 73 **p** 74. C Kirkheaton *Wakef* 73-79; V Ovenden 79-86; Bp's Adv on Evang 81-86; P-in-c Bampton w Mardale *Carl* 86-92; Dioc Officer for Evang 86-92; V Shipley St Pet *Bradf* 92-02; Warden Lee Abbey from 02. *Garden Lodge, Lee Abbey, Lynton EX35 6JJ* Tel (01598) 752621 *or* 754204 Fax 752619 E-mail warden@leeabbey.org.uk

EDMONDSON, The Very Revd John James William. b 55. St Jo Coll Dur BA83 MA91 PhD04. Cranmer Hall Dur 80. **d** 83 **p** 84. C Gee Cross *Ches* 83-86; C Camberley St Paul *Guildf* 86-88; TV 88-90; Chapl Elmhurst Ballet Sch 86-90; V Foxton w Gumley and Laughton and Lubenham *Leic* 90-94; R Bexhill St Mark *Chich* 94-05; Dioc Voc Adv 98-02; Asst Dir of Ords from 02; V Battle from 05; Dean Battle from 05; P-in-c Sedlescombe w Whatlington from 05. *The Deanery, Caldbec Hill, Battle TN33 0JY* Tel and fax (01424) 772693

EDMONTON, Area Bishop of. *See* WHEATLEY, The Rt Revd Peter William

EDMUND, Brother. *See* BLACKIE, Richard Footner

EDMUNDS, Andrew Charles. b 57. Whitelands Coll Lon BEd80 Croydon Coll DASS83 CQSW83. Oak Hill NSM Course 87. **d** 89 **p** 90. NSM Hawkwell *Chelmsf* 89-95; C Torquay St Matthias, St Mark and H Trin *Ex* 95-97; V Ripley *Derby* from 97. *The Vicarage, 26 Mount Pleasant, Ripley DE5 3DX* Tel (01773) 749641 E-mail acedmunds@allsaintsripley.freeserve.co.uk

EDMUNDS, Eric John. b 39. Univ of Wales TCert60. WMMTC 87. **d** 90 **p** 91. NSM Brewood *Lich* 90-93; Chapl St Pet Colleg Sch Wolv 91-93; R Llanerch Aeron w Ciliau Aeron and Dihewyd etc *St D* 93-97; R Aberporth w Tremain w Blaenporth and Betws Ifan 97-02; Bp's Adv on Tourism 95-02; Asst Dioc Dir of Educn 95-97 and 97-02; rtd 02. *15 Cwrt y Gloch, Peniel, Carmarthen SA32 7HW* Tel (01267) 221426

EDSON, The Ven Michael. b 42. Birm Univ BSc64 Leeds Univ BA71. Coll of Resurr Mirfield 69. **d** 72 **p** 73. C Barnstaple St Pet w H Trin *Ex* 72-77; TV Barnstaple and Goodleigh 77-79; TV Barnstaple, Goodleigh and Landkey 79-82; V Roxbourne St Andr *Lon* 82-89; AD Harrow 85-89; P-in-c S Harrow St Paul 86-89; Warden Lee Abbey 89-94; Lic to Offic *Ex* 89-94; Adn Leic 94-02; Bp's Insp of Par Registers and Records 94-02; TR Bideford, Northam, Westward Ho, Appledore etc *Ex* from 02. *The Rectory, Abbotsham Road, Bideford EX39 3AB* Tel (01237) 470228 *or* 474078 E-mail st.marys@easynet.co.uk

EDWARD, Brother. *See* LEES-SMITH, Christopher John

EDWARDS, Preb Albert. b 20. Univ of Wales (Lamp) BA48. St Mich Coll Llan 48. **d** 50 **p** 51. C Welshpool *St As* 50-54; V Stanton on Hine Heath *Lich* 54-58; R Hanley w Hope 58-64; RD Stoke N 63-64; V Tamworth 65-86; RD Tamworth 69-81; Preb Lich Cathl 73-86; rtd 86; Perm to Offic *Lich* 86-03; Perm to Offic *Heref* from 89. *Broom Cottage, Mount Street, Welshpool SY21 7LW* Tel (01938) 554008

EDWARDS, Aled. b 55. Univ of Wales (Lamp) BA77. Trin Coll Bris 77. **d** 79 **p** 80. C Glanogwen *Ban* 79-82; V Llandinorwig w Penisa'r-waen 82-85; R Botwnnog 85-93; V Cardiff Dewi Sant *Llan* 93-99; Nat Assembly Liaison Officer from 99; Hon Chapl Llan Cathl from 99. *20 Hilltop Avenue, Cilfynydd, Pontypridd CF37 4HZ* Tel (01443) 407310 E-mail aled@globalnet.co.uk

EDWARDS, Allen John. b 50. Univ of Wales (Cardiff) BSc72 Imp Coll Lon DIC81 PhD81 CEng81 EurIng88 FIMechE93 FINucE95 MIMgt95. St Alb and Ox Min Course 00. **d** 02 **p** 03. NSM Didcot All SS *Ox* from 02. *23 North Bush Furlong, Didcot OX11 9DY* Tel (01235) 519090

EDWARDS, Andrew Colin. b 55. ACA81 Pemb Coll Cam BA77 MA80. St Mich Coll Llan BD89. **d** 89 **p** 90. C Newport St Paul *Mon* 89-91; C Newport St Woolos 91-93; Min Can St Woolos Cathl 91-93; P-in-c Ynysddu 93-95; TV Mynyddislwyn 95-97; rtd 97. *197 Heritage Park, St Mellons, Cardiff CF3 0DU* Tel (029) 2079 2715

EDWARDS, Canon Andrew David. b 42. Tyndale Hall Bris 67. **d** 70 **p** 71. C Blackpool Ch Ch *Blackb* 70-73; C W Teignmouth *Ex* 73-76; P-in-c Ilfracombe SS Phil and Jas 76-85; C-in-c Lundy Is 79-89; V Ilfracombe SS Phil and Jas w W Down 85-89; TV Canford Magna *Sarum* 89-98; R Moresby *Carl* from 98; RD Calder from 02; Hon Can Carl Cathl from 05. *The Rectory, Low Moresby, Whitehaven CA28 6RR* Tel (01946) 693970 Fax 599501

EDWARDS, Andrew James. b 54. York Univ BA76. Wycliffe Hall Ox 77. **d** 80 **p** 81. C Beckenham St Jo *Roch* 80-83; C Luton Ch Ch 83-87; V Skelmersdale Ch at Cen *Liv* 87-95; V Netherton 95-02; V Southport St Phil and St Paul from 02; C Southport All SS and All So from 03. *37 Lethbridge Road, Southport PR8 6JA* Tel (01704) 531615 E-mail andrew@ajedwards.freeserve.co.uk

EDWARDS, Andrew Jonathan Hugo. b 56. Ex Univ BA78. Sarum & Wells Th Coll BTh93. **d** 93 **p** 94. C Honiton, Gittisham, Combe Raleigh, Monkton etc *Ex* 93-97; P-in-c Queen Thorne *Sarum* 97-01; Chapl Clayesmore Sch Blandford from 01. *Hambledon, Clayesmore School, Iwerne Minster, Blandford Forum DT11 8LJ* Tel (01747) 813064 E-mail joe.edwards@btinternet.com

EDWARDS, Anita Carolyn. *See* COLPUS, Mrs Anita Carolyn

EDWARDS, Mrs Anne Joan. b 67. Lanc Univ BA89. N Ord Course 97. **d** 00 **p** 01. C Elton All SS *Man* 00-04; Chapl Bolton Hosps NHS Trust 02-04; Chapl Team Ldr Wrightington Wigan and Leigh NHS Trust from 04. *St Paul's Vicarage, 10 Old Vicarage Gardens, Worsley, Manchester M28 3JR* Tel 0161-790 2483 E-mail anna.edwards@dsl.pipex.com

EDWARDS, Canon Arthur John. b 42. Qu Mary Coll Lon BA64 MPhil66. St Mich Coll Llan 66. **d** 68 **p** 69. C Newport St Woolos

Mon 68-71; V Llantarnam 71-74; Chapl Bp of Llan High Sch 74-78; V Griffithstown *Mon* 78-86; Dioc Dir RE 86-91; TR Cwmbran 86-95; Hon Can St Woolos Cathl 88-91; Can from 91; V Caerleon 95-02; V Caerleon w Llanhennock from 02; RD Newport from 98. *The Vicarage, Caerleon, Newport NP18 1AZ* Tel (01633) 420248

EDWARDS, Carl Flynn. b 63. Cranmer Hall Dur 03. **d** 05. C Scartho *Linc* from 05. *25 Waltham Road, Grimsby DN33 2LY* Tel (01472) 870373 E-mail carledwards@hotmail.co.uk

EDWARDS, Miss Carol Rosemary. b 46. Lon Univ DipTh76. Trin Coll Bris 74. **dss** 81 **d** 87 **p** 94. Hengrove *Bris* 81-82; Filton 82-85; Brislington St Chris 85-99; Dn-in-c 87-94; P-in-c 94-99; P-in-c Brislington St Chris and St Cuth 99-00; Hon Can Bris Cathl 93-00; P-in-c California *Ox* from 00. *California Vicarage, Vicarage Close, Finchampstead, Wokingham RG11 4JW* Tel 0118-973 0030

EDWARDS, Charles Grayson. b 37. Macalester Coll (USA) BSc59. Ripon Hall Ox 64. **d** 66 **p** 67. C Bletchley *Ox* 66-68; C Ware St Mary *St Alb* 68-73; TV Basingstoke *Win* 73-80; P-in-c Sandford w Upton Hellions *Ex* 80-82; R 82-94; Perm to Offic from 95; rtd 97. *The Peak, Higher Road, Crediton EX17 2EU* Tel (01363) 772530

EDWARDS, Christopher Alban. b 27. Hertf Coll Ox. Th Ext Educn Coll. **d** 89 **p** 92. S Africa 89-96; Pietersburg Ch Ch 89; Montagu 90-96; Harare Cathl Zimbabwe 96-01; Perm to Offic *Ripon* 01; *York* from 01. *1 Hastings House, Holyrood Lane, Ledsham, South Milford, Leeds LS25 5LL* Tel (01977) 682117 Mobile 07780-543114 E-mail chrisalban@btopenworld.com

EDWARDS, David Arthur. b 26. Wadh Coll Ox BA50 MA51. Wycliffe Hall Ox 50. **d** 52 **p** 53. C Didsbury St Jas and Em *Man* 52-55; Liv Sec SCM 55-58; Chapl Liv Univ *Liv* 55-58; R Burnage St Nic *Man* 58-65; V Yardley St Edburgha *Birm* 65-73; Org Sec CECS *Blackb, Carl* and *Man* 73-78; R Man Resurr *Man* 78-81; V Lorton and Loweswater w Buttermere *Carl* 81-87; USPG 87-92; Malaysia 87-92; rtd 92; Perm to Offic *Carl* from 00. *Wood Close, 11 Springs Road, Keswick CA12 4AQ* Tel (01768) 780274

EDWARDS, David John. b 60. Loughb Univ BA81 Homerton Coll Cam PGCE82 Kent Univ MA95. CA Tr Coll 86 EAMTC 94. **d** 95 **p** 96. C High Ongar w Norton Mandeville *Chelmsf* 95-98; Prin Taylor Coll Saint John Canada from 98; P-in-c Saint John St Jas 98-00; R Saint John St Jo from 00. *130 French Village Road, Saint John NB, Canada, E2N 1T1* E-mail edwa@nbnet.nb.ca

EDWARDS, The Very Revd David Lawrence. b 29. OBE95. Magd Coll Ox BA52 MA56 Lambeth DD90. Westcott Ho Cam 53. **d** 54 **p** 55. Fell All So Coll Ox 52-59; Tutor Westcott Ho Cam 54-55; SCM Sec 55-58; C Hampstead St Jo *Lon* 55-58; C St Martin-in-the-Fields 58-66; Ed SCM Press 59-66; Gen Sec SCM 65-66; Dean K Coll Cam 66-70; Six Preacher Cant Cathl *Cant* 69-76; Can Westmr Abbey 70-78; R Westmr St Marg 70-78; Chapl to Speaker of Ho of Commons 72-78; Sub Dean Westmr 74-78; Chmn Chr Aid 71-78; Dean Nor 78-83; Provost S'wark 83-94; rtd 94; Perm to Offic *Win* from 95; Hon Chapl Win Cathl from 95. *19 Crispstead Lane, Winchester SO23 9SF* Tel (01962) 862597

EDWARDS, Canon Diana Clare. b 56. SRN77 RSCN81 Nottm Univ BTh86. Linc Th Coll 83. **dss** 86 **d** 87 **p** 94. S Wimbledon H Trin and St Pet *S'wark* 86-87; Par Dn 87-90; Par Dn Lingfield and Crowhurst 90-94; C 94-95; Chapl St Piers Hosp Sch Lingfield 90-95; R Bletchingley *S'wark* 95-04; RD Godstone 98-04; Hon Can S'wark Cathl 01-04; Dean of Women's Min 03-04; Can Res Cant Cathl *Cant* from 04. *19 The Precincts, Canterbury CT1 2EP* Tel (01227) 865227 E-mail canonclare@canterbury-cathedral.org

EDWARDS, Erwyd. *See* EDWARDS, The Very Revd Thomas Erwyd Pryse

EDWARDS (née DALLISON), Canon Frances Mary. b 39. RSCN61 SRN64. St Mich Ho Ox CertRK68 Cranmer Hall Dur IDC71. **d** 92 **p** 94. NSM Skerton St Chad *Blackb* 92-97; Asst Chapl R Albert Hosp Lanc 92-94; Chapl 94-96; Regional Co-ord (NW) Ch Action on Disability 96-04; Hon Can Blackb Cathl *Blackb* 00-04; Perm to Offic from 04. *9 Rochester Avenue, Morecambe LA4 4RH* Tel (01524) 421224 Fax 413661 E-mail frances@floray.fsnet.co.uk

EDWARDS, Canon Geoffrey Lewis. b 14. Lon Univ BD39 AKC39. **d** 39 **p** 40. C Twickenham All Hallows *Lon* 39-44; C Bushey *St Alb* 44-47; V Mill End 47-72; V W Hyde St Thos 47-72; RD Watford 68-70; RD Rickmansworth 70-72; V Hockerill 72-84; RD Bishop's Stortford 74-84; Hon Can St Alb 76-84; rtd 84; Perm to Offic *Heref* 84-97 and *Ox* from 89. *91 Early Road, Witney OX28 1ET* Tel (01993) 704342

EDWARDS, Geraint. *See* EDWARDS, William Geraint

EDWARDS, Canon Geraint Wyn. b 47. Univ of Wales (Ban) BTh93. St D Coll Lamp DipTh70. **d** 71 **p** 72. C Llandudno *Ban* 71-73; C Ban St Mary 73-74; V Penisarwaen and Llanddeiniolen 74-77; V Llandinorwig w Penisarwaen and Llanddeiniolen 77-78; R Llanfechell w Bodewryd w Rhosbeirio etc from 78; RD Twrcelyn 94-01; AD from 01; Hon Can Ban Cathl 97-99; Prec from 99. *The Rectory, Penbodeistedd Estate, Llanfechell, Amlwch LL68 0RE* Tel (01407) 710356 E-mail geraint@rheithordy.fsnet.co.uk

EDWARDS, Canon Gerald Lalande. b 30. Bris Univ MEd72. Glouc Th Course 75. **d** 76 **p** 76. NSM Pittville All SS *Glouc* 76-79; NSM Cheltenham St Mich 79-96; Hon Can Glouc Cathl 91-96; rtd 96; Perm to Offic *Glouc* 96-97. *26 Monica Drive, Cheltenham GL50 4NQ* Tel (01242) 516863

EDWARDS, Gordon Henry. b 33. FRICS60 FCILA67 FCIArb72 Reading Univ PhD87. Ripon Coll Cuddesdon 89. **d** 90 **p** 91. NSM Sherston Magna, Easton Grey, Luckington etc *Bris* 90-92; NSM Yatton Keynell 92-96; NSM Chippenham St Paul w Hardenhuish etc 96-00; NSM Kington St Michael 96-00; Perm to Offic *Glouc* 00-01 and *Bris* from 00; NSM Badminton w Lt Badminton, Acton Turville etc *Glouc* 01-03; NSM Boxwell, Leighterton, Didmarton, Oldbury etc from 03; NSM Horton and Lt Sodbury from 03. *The Old Vicarage, Sherston, Malmesbury SN16 0LR* Tel (01666) 840405 Mobile 07889-132046 Fax (01666) 840683 E-mail gordonh.edwards@virgin.net

EDWARDS, Canon Graham Arthur. b 32. HNC53. St D Coll Lamp 56. **d** 61 **p** 62. C Betws w Ammanford *St D* 61-65; V Castlemartin and Warren 65-69; R Castlemartin w Warren and Angle etc 69-77; V St Clears w Llangynin and Llanddowror 77-83; CF (TAVR) 78-96; V St Clears w Llangynin and Llanddowror etc *St D* 83-94; Can St D Cathl 90-94; rtd 94. *Caswell, Station Road, St Clears, Carmarthen SA33 4BX* Tel (01994) 230342

EDWARDS, Graham Charles. b 40. Qu Coll Birm 80. **d** 82 **p** 83. C Baswich *Lich* 82-86; C Tamworth 86-88; R Hertford St Andr *St Alb* 88-05; RD Hertford and Ware 96-99; rtd 05. *2 The Old Forge, Main Road, Great Haywood, Stafford ST18 0RZ* Tel (01889) 882868

EDWARDS, Guy. *See* EDWARDS, Jonathan Guy

EDWARDS, Harold James. b 50. Lon Univ CertEd72. Ridley Hall Cam 84 Qu Coll Birm 78. **d** 81 **p** 82. NSM The Quinton *Birm* 81-84; C Highters Heath 84-85; V Llanwddyn and Llanfihangel-yng-Nghwynfa etc *St As* 85-88; V Ford *Heref* 88-97; V Alberbury w Cardeston 88-97; Chapl Shropshire and Mid-Wales Hospice from 96. *Shropshire and Mid-Wales Hospice, Bicton Heath, Shrewsbury SY3 8HS* Tel (01743) 236565 Mobile 07074-236236

EDWARDS, Harry Steadman. b 37. St Aid Birkenhead 64. **d** 66 **p** 67. Hon C Handsworth St Jas *Birm* 66-83; Hon C Curdworth w Castle Vale 83-85; P-in-c Small Heath St Greg 85-88; V High Crompton *Man* 88-98; rtd 98; Perm to Offic *Man* from 99. *42 Manor Road, Shaw, Oldham OL2 7JJ* Tel (01706) 672820

EDWARDS, Helen. *See* HINGLEY, Mrs Helen

EDWARDS, Helen Glynne. *See* WEBB, Mrs Helen Glynne

EDWARDS, The Ven Henry St John. b 30. Southn Univ DipEd. Ripon Hall Ox. **d** 59 **p** 60. C Wickford *Chelmsf* 59-62; Australia from 62; R Woodburn 62-65; Educn Officer Dio Grafton 65-69; Dean Grafton 69-78; V Mt Waverley St Steph 78-83; R Chelmer 83-89; Adn Moreton 85-89; Abp's Chapl 89-90; R Tamborine Mountain 90-95; Adn W Moreton 91-93; Adn Gold Coast 93-95; rtd 95. *PO Box 26, Wooli, NSW, Australia 2462* Tel (0061) (2) 6649 7626 E-mail stjohn@midcoast.com.au

EDWARDS, Canon Henry Victor. b 48. AKC71 Open Univ BA85 Middx Univ MSc00. St Aug Coll Cant 72. **d** 73 **p** 74. C W Leigh CD *Portsm* 73-77; V Cosham 77-84; V Reydon *St E* 84-86; V Blythburgh w Reydon 86-96; Chapl St Felix Sch Southwold 86-96; Chapl Blythburgh Hosp 86-96; Dioc Adv for Counselling and Past Care *St E* from 96; P-in-c Campsea Ashe w Marlesford, Parham and Hacheston 96-00; R from 00; Hon Can St E Cathl from 00. *The Rectory, Marlesford, Woodbridge IP13 0AT* Tel (01728) 746747 Fax 748175 Mobile 07710-417071 E-mail harry@psalm23.demon.co.uk

EDWARDS, Herbert Joseph. b 29. Nottm Univ BA51. Wells Th Coll 54. **d** 56 **p** 57. C Leic St Pet *Leic* 56-61; C-in-c Broom Leys CD 61-65; V Broom Leys 65-68; Lect Lich Th Coll 68-71; Rhodesia 71-79; Botswana 74-75; V Bloxwich *Lich* 80-84; R Asfordby *Leic* 84-92; R N w S Kilworth and Misterton 92-96; rtd 96; Perm to Offic *Leic* from 97 and *Lich* from 00. *St John's Hospital, St John Street, Lichfield WS13 6PB* Tel (01543) 416620

EDWARDS, Canon James Frederick. b 36. ALCD62. **d** 62 **p** 63. C Kenwyn *Truro* 62-68; V Tuckingmill 68-76; V St Columb Minor and St Colan 76-01; RD Pydar 84-93; Hon Can Truro Cathl 92-01; rtd 01; Perm to Offic *Truro* from 01. *45 Tretherras Road, Newquay TR7 2TF* Tel (01637) 870967

EDWARDS, Janet Margaret. b 41. TCert62 Lon Bible Coll BD73. WEMTC 98. **d** 01 **p** 02. NSM Coalbrookdale, Iron-Bridge and Lt Wenlock *Heref* from 01. *2 Madeley Wood View, Madeley, Telford TF7 5TF* Tel (01952) 583254

EDWARDS, Mrs Jill Kathleen. b 48. Man Univ BA69 Goldsmiths' Coll Lon CQSW72 Lon Univ DipRS85. S'wark Ord Course 90. **d** 93 **p** 95. NSM Grays Thurrock *Chelmsf* from

93; Ind Chapl from 93. *The Old Tennis Court, Allenby Crescent, Grays RM17 6DH* Tel (01375) 372887 E-mail jill@jilledwards.com

EDWARDS, John Ralph. b 50. Bris Univ BSc71 FCA74. St Alb and Ox Min Course 98. **d** 01 **p** 02. NSM California *Ox* from 01. *Green Hedges, 25 St John's Street, Crowthorne RG45 7NJ* Tel (01344) 774586 Mobile 07850-602488 Fax (01344) 774056 E-mail john.edwards@fish.co.uk

EDWARDS, Jonathan. *See* EDWARDS, Andrew Jonathan Hugo

EDWARDS, Jonathan Guy. b 63. Bris Univ BA85. Ridley Hall Cam BA93 MA96. **d** 94 **p** 95. C Preston Plucknett *B & W* 94-98; C Clevedon St Andr and Ch Ch 98-02; V Farrington Gurney from 02; V Paulton from 02. *The Vicarage, Church Street, Paulton, Bristol BS39 7LG* Tel (01761) 416581 E-mail guy.edwards1@tesco.net

EDWARDS, Joseph. *See* EDWARDS, Herbert Joseph

EDWARDS, Judith Sarah. *See* McARTHUR-EDWARDS, Mrs Judith Sarah

EDWARDS (née EVANS), Mrs Linda Mary. b 49. Univ of Wales (Cardiff) BA71 K Coll Lon BD74 AKC74. Yale Div Sch STM76. **dss** 76 **d** 80 **p** 99. Llanishen and Lisvane *Llan* 76-78; Wrexham *St As* 78-80; C 80-82; Chapl Maudsley Hosp Lon 82-84; Chapl Bethlem R Hosp Beckenham 82-84; Chapl Lon Univ *Lon* 84-87; NSM Llanfair-pwll and Llanddaniel-fab etc *Ban* 99-03; P-in-c Llangynog *St As* from 03. *Maes-y-Llan, Llangynog, Oswestry SY10 0HQ* Tel (01691) 860455 *or* tel and fax 860408 E-mail lme1@fish.co.uk

EDWARDS, Malcolm Ralph. b 27. Man Univ 49. Cranmer Hall Dur 57. **d** 59 **p** 60. C Withington St Paul *Man* 59-62; C Chadderton Em 62-64; R Longsight St Jo 64-70; V Halliwell St Thos 70-81; V Milnrow 81-92; rtd 92; Perm to Offic *Man* from 92. *20 Upper Lees Drive, Westhoughton, Bolton BL5 3UE* Tel (01942) 813279

EDWARDS, Mark Anthony. b 61. Moorlands Bible Coll Dip Th & Min 86 St Jo Coll Dur Cert Th & Min 95. **d** 95 **p** 97. C Ulverston St Mary w H Trin *Carl* 95-97; C Barrow St Jo 97-00; TV Barrow St Matt from 00. *St Francis House, 158 Schneider Road, Barrow-in-Furness LA14 5ER* Tel (01229) 839686 E-mail hayden@fox9411.freeserve.co.uk

EDWARDS, Mrs Mary. b 47. St Jo Coll York CertEd69 Birkbeck Coll Lon BSc74 New Coll Edin BD93. S Dios Minl Tr Scheme 96. **d** 96 **p** 97. NSM Avon Valley *Sarum* 96-00; TV Wexcombe 00-02; TV Savernake from 02. *The Vicarage, Church Street, Collingbourne Ducis, Marlborough SN8 3EL* Tel (01264) 852692 E-mail mary_avonvalley@hotmail.com

EDWARDS, Michael Norman William. b 34. Bp Gray Coll Cape Town 61 St Paul's Coll Grahamstown 62. **d** 63 **p** 65. S Africa 63-81; C Woodstock 63-66; C Plumstead 66-69; P-in-c Lansdowne All SS 69-72; R Hoetjes Bay 73-78; R Parow St Marg 78-80; Chaplain Tristan da Cunha 81-83; R Aston-on-Trent and Weston-on-Trent *Derby* 84-87; V Derby St Thos 87-95; P-in-c Blackwell 95-01; rtd 01; Perm to Offic *Win* from 02. *16 Ridley Close, Holbury, Southampton SO45 2NR* Tel (023) 8089 2924 E-mail mnwedwards.novaforest@btinternet.com

EDWARDS, Nicholas John. b 53. UEA BA75 Fitzw Coll Cam BA77 MA80. Westcott Ho Cam 75. **d** 78 **p** 79. C Kirkby *Liv* 78-81; V Cantril Farm 81-87; V Hale 87-94; R Chingford SS Pet and Paul *Chelmsf* 94-04; R Colyton, Musbury, Southleigh and Branscombe *Ex* from 04. *The Vicarage, Vicarage Street, Colyton EX24 6LJ* Tel (01297) 552307 E-mail nicholas_edwards@ntlworld.com

EDWARDS, Mrs Nita Mary. b 50. Univ of Wales (Ban) BD72 Nottm Univ PGCE73. Cranmer Hall Dur 93. **d** 93 **p** 94. C Ormesby *York* 93-95; C Billingham St Aid *Dur* 95-97; V 97-02; V Clayton *Lich* from 02. *The Vicarage, Clayton Lane, Newcastle ST5 3DW* Tel (01782) 614500 Fax as telephone E-mail nita.edwards@ntlworld.com

EDWARDS, Mrs Patricia Anne. b 52. EMMTC 76. **dss** 79 **d** 87 **p** 94. Hon Par Dn Clifton *S'well* 87-91; NSM Edwalton from 91. *Le Petit Champ, Widmerpool Road, Wysall, Nottingham NE12 6QW* Tel (01509) 880385

EDWARDS, Peter Clive. b 50. Lon Univ BA72. St Steph Ho Ox 83. **d** 85 **p** 86. C Lee St Aug *S'wark* 85-90; V Salfords 90-97; R Newington St Mary 97-03; Asst Chapl Costa Blanca *Eur* from 04. *Apdo Correos 158, 03420 Castalla, Alicante, Spain* Tel (0034) (96) 656 0716 E-mail pce11@yahoo.com

EDWARDS, Peter Richard Henderson. b 65. Nottm Univ BA86. St Steph Ho Ox 03. **d** 05. C Uppingham w Ayston and Wardley w Belton *Pet* from 05. *18 Siskin Road, Uppingham, Oakham LE15 9UL* Tel (01572) 820049 E-mail edwards.peter@tesco.net

EDWARDS, Canon Philip John. b 28. Lon Univ MRCS51 LRCP51. Chich Th Coll 58. **d** 60 **p** 61. C Orpington St Andr *Roch* 60-67; C Mayfield *Chich* 67-71; V Haywards Heath St Rich 71-91; Can and Preb Chich Cathl 84-91; rtd 91; Perm to Offic *Chich* from 91. *22 Hamsey Road, Sharpthorne, East Grinstead RH19 4PA* Tel (01342) 810210

EDWARDS, Philip Osbert Clifford. b 11. St Jo Coll Ox BA33 MA47. Wycliffe Hall Ox 35. **d** 35 **p** 36. C Bayswater *Lon* 35-38; C Chelsea St Luke 38-39; C Woburn Square Ch Ch 39-41; Chapl RAFVR 41-47; New Zealand 47-54; Chapl Oundle Sch 54-69; P-in-c Stoke Doyle *Pet* 60-63; Chapl St Chris Hospice Sydenham 69-74; Chapl Algarve *Eur* 74-77; rtd 77; Perm to Offic *Heref* 86-92. *8 The Old Orchard, Nash Meadows, South Warnborough, Hook RG29 1TR* Tel (01256) 862960

EDWARDS, Phillip Gregory. b 52. Lon Univ BSc73 Imp Coll Lon ARCS73 MSOSc90. Qu Coll Birm 78. **d** 81 **p** 82. C Lillington *Cov* 81-85; P-in-c Cov St Alb 85-86; TV Cov E 86-01; C Bury St Paul and Bury Ch King *Man* 01-03; Chapl Bolton Univ from 03; C Westhoughton and Wingates 04-05. *St James's Vicarage, 280 Walshaw Road, Bury BL8 1PY* Tel 0161-764 6217 Fax 762 5219 E-mail phil@edwards.clara.co.uk

EDWARDS, Raymond Lewis. Keble Coll Ox BA46 MA47 TCert48. St Deiniol's Hawarden 69. **d** 70 **p** 71. Prin Educn Cen Penmaenmawr 56-81; Hon C Dwygyfylchi *Ban* 70-81; P-in-c Llandwrog 81-82; R 82-90; Dioc Dir of Educn 84-92; rtd 90; Perm to Offic *Ban* from 90. *Bryn Llwyd, St Davids Road, Caernarfon LL55 1EL* Tel 07789-566370 (mobile)

EDWARDS, Richard John. b 47. Univ of Qld BA85. St Fran Coll Brisbane 83 McAuley Coll Brisbane DipRE85. **d** 85 **p** 85. Australia 85-87 and 88-96; C Olveston *Bris* 87-88; R Kingston St Mary w Broomfield etc *B & W* from 96. *The Rectory, Kingston St Mary, Taunton TA2 8HW* Tel (01823) 451257 Fax 451933 E-mail redwards@ukonline.co.uk

EDWARDS, Robert James. b 52. Cranmer Hall Dur 01. **d** 03 **p** 04. C Broadwater St Mary *Chich* from 03. *115 Shandon Road, Worthing BN14 9EA*

EDWARDS, Roger Brian. b 41. Sarum & Wells Th Coll 87. **d** 89 **p** 90. C Wellington and Distr *B & W* 89-92; V Hursley and Ampfield *Win* from 92. *The Vicarage, Knapp Lane, Ampfield, Romsey SO5 9BT* Tel (01794) 368291 E-mail ampfield-hursley.parish@virgin.net

EDWARDS, Rowland Thomas. b 62. Univ of Wales DipTh88 BTh91. St Mich Coll Llan 85. **d** 88 **p** 89. C Llangiwg *S & B* 88-90; C Morriston 90-91; V Llangorse, Cathedine, Llanfihangel Talyllyn etc 91-01; V Llyn Safaddan from 01; RD Hay from 02. *The Vicarage, Llangorse, Brecon LD3 7UG* Tel (01874) 658298

EDWARDS, Rupert Quintin. b 67. Bris Univ LLB89. Wycliffe Hall Ox BTh94. **d** 97 **p** 98. C Bromley Ch Ch *Roch* 97-00; C Hammersmith St Paul *Lon* 00-02. *342 Bluewater House, Smugglers Way, London SW18 1ED*

EDWARDS, Canon Ruth Blanche. b 39. Girton Coll Cam BA61 MA65 PhD68 Aber Coll of Educn PGCE75. Ab Dioc Tr Course 77. **d** 87 **p** 94. Lect Aber Univ *Ab* 77-90; Sen Lect 90-96; NSM Aberdeen St Jas 87-88; NSM Aberdeen St Jo 88-96; Lect Ripon Coll Cuddesdon 96-99; Hon Can St Andr Cathl *Ab* from 97; rtd 00; NSM Aberdeen St Jas *Ab* from 00. *99 Queen's Den, Aberdeen AB15 8BN* Tel (01224) 312688

EDWARDS, Mrs Sandra May. b 48. STETS 96. **d** 99 **p** 01. NSM Denmead *Portsm* from 99. *82 Drift Road, Clanfield, Waterlooville PO8 0NX* Tel (023) 9236 7228 *or* 9259 4968 E-mail sandra@pinoy.fsnet.co.uk

EDWARDS, Scott. b 71. Wolv Univ LLB93 St Jo Coll Dur BA00. Cranmer Hall Dur 97. **d** 00 **p** 01. C Halas *Worc* 00-03; V Frimley Green and Mytchett *Guildf* from 03. *The Vicarage, 37 Sturt Road, Frimley Green, Camberley GU16 6HY* Tel (01252) 835179

EDWARDS, Stephen. b 44. S'wark Ord Course. **d** 82 **p** 83. C Benhilton *S'wark* 82-86; P-in-c Clapham Ch Ch and St Jo 86-87; TV Clapham Team 87-94; Chapl HM Pris Wormwood Scrubs 94-96; Chapl HM Pris Maidstone 96-01; Chapl HM Pris Wandsworth 01-04; rtd 04; Perm to Offic *S'wark* from 04. *12 Bucharest Road, London SW18 3AR* Tel (020) 8870 1991

EDWARDS, Stephen Michael. b 72. Lanc Univ BSc93 Anglia Poly Univ MA99. Westcott Ho Cam 93. **d** 96 **p** 97. C Colwyn Bay *St As* 96-99; C Colwyn Bay w Brynymaen 99-02; P-in-c Birch-in-Rusholme St Agnes w Longsight St Jo etc *Man* from 02. *St Agnes's Rectory, Slade Lane, Manchester M13 0GN* Tel 0161-224 2596 E-mail frsme@btinternet.com

EDWARDS, Steven Charles. b 58. Lanc Univ BSc82 PhD86. Linc Th Coll 94. **d** 94 **p** 95. C Bradshaw *Man* 94-98; P-in-c Bolton Breightmet St Jas 98-04; TR Walkden and Lt Hulton from 04. *St Paul's Vicarage, 10 Old Vicarage Gardens, Worsley, Manchester M28 3JR* Tel 0161-790 2483 E-mail steve.edwards@dsl.pipex.com

EDWARDS, Stuart. b 46. Lanc Univ BA73. Kelham Th Coll 66. **d** 71 **p** 72. C Skerton St Luke *Blackb* 71-76; C Ribbleton 76-80; TV 80-82; V Blackb St Mich w St Jo and H Trin 82-91; V Blackpool H Cross from 91; RD Blackpool 93-94; P-in-c S Shore St Pet from 00. *Holy Cross Vicarage, Central Drive, Blackpool FY1 6LA* Tel (01253) 341263

EDWARDS, Mrs Susan. b 54. R Holloway Coll Lon BSc75 SS Hild & Bede Coll Dur PGCE76. Qu Coll Birm 78. **dss** 81 **d** 87 **p** 94. Lillington *Cov* 81-85; Cov E 85-01; Par Dn 87-94; C 94-01; P-in-c Woolfold *Man* from 01. *St James's Vicarage, 280 Walshaw Road, Bury BL8 1PY* Tel 0161-764 6217 Fax 762 5219 E-mail sue@edwards.clara.co.uk

EDWARDS, Mrs Susan Diane. b 48. St Alb Minl Tr Scheme 86 Cranmer Hall Dur 91. **d** 92 **p** 94. Par Dn Borehamwood *St Alb*

92-94; C 94-96; V Arlesey w Astwick from 96. *The Vicarage, 77 Church Lane, Arlesey SG15 6UX* Tel (01462) 731227 E-mail susan.d.edwards@ntlworld.com

EDWARDS, The Very Revd Thomas Erwyd Pryse. b 33. Univ of Wales (Lamp) BA56. St Mich Coll Llan 56. **d** 58 **p** 59. C Llanbeblig w Caernarfon *Ban* 58-63; Chapl Asst St Geo Hosp Lon 63-66; Lic to Offic *S'wark* 63-72; Chapl K Coll Hosp Lon 66-72; R Penmon and Llangoed w Llanfihangel Dinsylwy *Ban* 72-75; V Llandysilio 75-81; V Glanadda 81-85; Chapl St D Hosp Ban 81-84; Chapl Gwynedd Hosp Ban 84-86; V Ban St D and St Jas 86-88; Dean Ban 88-98; Hon Can Ban Cathl from 88; R Bangor 88-93; rtd 98; Perm to Offic *Ban* from 98. *61 Ffriddoedd Road, Bangor LL57 2TT* Tel (01248) 362108

EDWARDS, William Geraint. b 31. Liv Univ LLB53. Univ Sch Th Abth & Lamp BD56. **d** 03 **p** 03. NSM Chase *Sarum* from 03. *55 Runnymede Avenue, Bournemouth BH11 9SQ* Tel (01202) 579989 E-mail wgedwards1@hotmail.com

EDWARDSON, David Roger Hately. b 54. Stirling Univ BSc79 DipEd79 Edin Univ BD91. Edin Th Coll 88. **d** 91 **p** 92. C Edin St Jo *Edin* 91-93; R Kelso 93-98; Asst Chapl Oundle Sch from 98. *46A West Street, Oundle, Peterborough PE8 4EF* Tel (01832) 274405 Fax as telephone E-mail david.edwardson@lineone.net

EDWARDSON, Joseph Philip. b 28. Dur Univ BA52 Leeds Univ PGCE53. Wells Th Coll 61. **d** 63 **p** 64. C Macclesfield St Mich *Ches* 63-66; V Egremont St Jo 66-72; V Eastham 72-81; V Poulton 81-94; rtd 94; Perm to Offic *Ches* from 94. *Keppler, 38 Hazel Grove, Irby, Wirral CH61 4UZ* Tel 0151-648 2661

EDY, Robert James. b 48. Southn Univ BA70 CertEd71. Ox Min Course CBTS93. **d** 93 **p** 94. Dep Hd Master Henry Box Sch Witney from 90; NSM Ducklington *Ox* 93-99; P-in-c from 99. *The Rectory, 6 Standlake Road, Ducklington, Witney OX29 7XG* Tel (01993) 776625 E-mail bobedy21@hotmail.com

EDYE, Ian Murray. b 21. K Coll Lon BD AKC. S'wark Ord Course 66. **d** 69 **p** 70. NSM E Grinstead St Swithun *Chich* 69-00; Perm to Offic 00-02. *12 The Chancery, Bramcote, Nottingham NG9 3AJ* Tel 0115-943 6343

EFEMEY, Raymond Frederick. b 28. Ball Coll Ox BA51 MA64. Cuddesdon Coll 51. **d** 53 **p** 54. C Croydon St Mich *Cant* 53-57; C Hendford *B & W* 57-60; V Upper Arley *Worc* 60-66; Ind Chapl 60-66; P-in-c Dudley St Jas 66-69; V Dudley St Thos 66-69; V Dudley St Thos and St Luke 69-75; Hon C Stretford All SS *Man* 76-82; SSF from 81; P-in-c Weaste *Man* 82-87; V 87-93; rtd 93. *20 Groby Road, Chorlton-cum-Hardy, Manchester M21 1DD* Tel 0161-860 5416

EGAR, Miss Judith Anne. b 57. Somerville Coll Ox BA79 MA84 Solicitor 83. STETS 01. **d** 04 **p** 05. NSM Brighton St Nic *Chich* from 04. *15 St Peter's Place, Lewes BN7 1YP* Tel (020) 7898 1722 E-mail judith.egar@c-of-e.org.uk

EGERTON, George. b 28. S'wark Ord Course 70. **d** 73 **p** 74. NSM Shere *Guildf* 73-94; Perm to Offic from 94. *Weyside, Lower Street, Shere, Guildford GU5 9HX* Tel (01483) 202549

EGGERT, Max Alexander. b 43. AKC67 Birkbeck Coll Lon BSc74 Poly Cen Lon MA87 CPsychol90. **d** 67 **p** 68. C Whitton St Aug *Lon* 67-69; Hon C Hackney 72-74; Hon C Llantwit Major *Llan* 74-76; NSM Haywards Heath St Rich *Chich* 78-93; Lic to Offic from 93. *94 High Street, Lindfield, Haywards Heath RH16 2HP* Tel (01444) 483057

EGLIN, Ian Charles. b 55. St Jo Coll Dur BA76. Coll of Resurr Mirfield 77. **d** 79 **p** 80. C Cov St Mary *Cov* 79-83; TV Kingsthorpe w Northampton St Dav *Pet* 83-87; P-in-c Pitsford w Boughton 85-87; Chapl RN 87-03; V Ipplepen, Torbryan and Denbury *Ex* from 03. *The Rectory, Paternoster Lane, Ipplepen, Newton Abbot TQ12 5RY* Tel and fax (01803) 812215 E-mail ianeglin@btopenworld.com

EJIAKU, Sebastian Chidozie. b 58. Herts Univ MSc95. NTMTC 02. **d** 05. NSM Hoxton St Jo w Ch Ch *Lon* from 05. *116 Cann Hall Road, London E11 3NH* Tel (020) 8519 2555 Mobile 07952-950681 E-mail ejiakuo@aol.com

EKIN, Tom Croker. b 29. Linc Th Coll 59. **d** 60 **p** 61. C Leamington Priors All SS *Cov* 60-63; R Ilmington w Stretton-on-Fosse 63-72; S Africa 72-77; R Moreton-in-Marsh w Batsford *Glouc* 77-83; R Moreton-in-Marsh w Batsford, Todenham etc 83-94; rtd 95; Hon C Theale and Englefield *Ox* 96-04. *The Parsonage, Redcroft, Redhill, Bristol BS40 5SL* Tel and fax (01934) 862398

ELBOURNE, Keith Marshall. b 46. Nottm Univ BTh74 Lon Univ BD76. Westmr Past Foundn DAPC89 St Jo Coll Nottm 70. **d** 74 **p** 75. C Romford Gd Shep Collier Row *Chelmsf* 74-78; C Victoria Docks St Luke 78-81; P-in-c 81-92; V Walthamstow St Pet 92-02; TR Tettenhall Wood and Perton *Lich* from 02. *Christ Church Rectory, 7 Broxwood Park, Tettenhall Wood, Wolverhampton WV6 8LZ* Tel (01902) 751116 E-mail petros2@surfaid.org

ELBOURNE, Canon Raymond Nigel Wilson. b 43. Dur Univ BA66. Linc Th Coll 67. **d** 69 **p** 70. C Liscard St Mary *Ches* 69-72; V Hattersley 72-77; R Odd Rode 77-02; P-in-c Congleton St Jas 02-03; V from 03; RD Congleton 97-04; Hon Can Ches Cathl from 99. *St James's Vicarage, 116 Holmes Chapel Road, Congleton CW12 4NX* Tel (01260) 273722 E-mail elbourne@europe.com

ELBOURNE, Canon Timothy. b 60. Selw Coll Cam BA81 MA85 PGCE82. Westcott Ho Cam 84. **d** 86 **p** 87. C Tottenham H Trin *Lon* 86-88; Chapl York Univ *York* 88-94; P-in-c Thorp Arch w Walton 94-98; Dir of Educn *Ely* from 98; Hon Can Ely Cathl from 99. *19 The Oaks, Soham, Ely CB7 5FF* Tel and fax (01353) 723867 *or* tel 652711 Pager (04325) 320796 Fax (01353) 652700 E-mail tim.elbourne@ely.anglican.org

ELDER, Andrew John. b 49. Sunderland Poly BSc72 MSc76. NEOC 91. **d** 94 **p** 95. NSM Wallsend St Luke *Newc* 94-02; NSM Wallsend St Pet and St Luke 02-03; C Monkseaton St Pet from 03. *51 Rowantree Road, Newcastle upon Tyne NE6 4TE* Tel 0191-262 8795 E-mail andy.elder@btinternet.com

ELDER, David. b 28. Brechin NSM Ord Course 75. **d** 79 **p** 80. NSM Dundee St Salvador *Bre* 79-93; rtd 93; P-in-c Dundee St Martin *Bre* from 93. *Thistlemount, 21 Law Road, Dundee DD3 6PZ* Tel (01382) 827844

ELDER, Nicholas John. b 51. Hatf Poly BA73. Cuddesdon Coll 73. **d** 76 **p** 77. C Mill End and Heronsgate w W Hyde *St Alb* 76-79; TV Borehamwood 79-85; V Bedford St Mich 85-90; V Bedford All SS 90-00; V Camberwell St Geo *S'wark* from 00; Warden Trin Coll Cen Camberwell from 00. *St George's Vicarage, 115 Wells Way, London SE5 7SZ* Tel (020) 7703 2895 *or* 7703 9855 E-mail n.elder@virgin.net

ELDRID, John Gisborne Charteris. b 25. OBE97. AKC52. **d** 53 **p** 54. C St Geo-in-the-East w Ch Ch w St Jo *Lon* 53-56; C E Grinstead St Mary *Chich* 56-58; C St Steph Walbrook and St Swithun etc *Lon* 58-64 and 72-81; V Portsea All SS *Portsm* 64-71; P-in-c Portsea St Jo Rudmore 69-71; V Portsea All SS w St Jo Rudmore 71-72; Gen Consultant Cen Lon Samaritans 72-74; Dir The Samaritans 74-87; Gen Consultant-Dir 87-99; Consultant from 99; Lic to Offic *Lon* from 82; rtd 90; Perm to Offic *Portsm* from 90. *46 Marshall Street, London W1V 1LR* Tel (020) 7439 1406 Fax 7439 1233

ELDRIDGE, John Frederick. b 48. Loughb Univ BSc70 Golden Gate Sem (USA) MDiv83 Fuller Th Sem California DMin96. Oak Hill Th Coll 90. **d** 92 **p** 93. C Maidstone St Luke *Cant* 92-97; Min Prince's Park CD *Roch* 97-02; P-in-c Wickham Market w Pettistree *St E* from 02. *The Vicarage, Crown Lane, Wickham Market, Woodbridge IP13 0SA* Tel (01728) 746026 E-mail jeldridge@supanet.com

ELDRIDGE, John Kenneth Tristan. b 59. St Steph Ho Ox 90. **d** 92 **p** 93. C Brighton Resurr *Chich* 92-96; C Hangleton 96-98; TR Moulsecoomb 98-05; V W Worthing St Jo from 05; Chapl Sussex Beacon Hospice 00-05. *St John's Vicarage, 15 Reigate Road, Worthing BN11 5NF* Tel (01903) 247340

ELDRIDGE, Stephen William. b 50. Open Univ DipEurHum97 BA98. Chich Th Coll 87. **d** 89 **p** 90. C Stroud and Uplands w Slad *Glouc* 89-92; C Glouc St Mary de Crypt w St Jo and Ch Ch 92-95; C Glouc St Mary de Lode and St Nic 92-95; Bp's Chapl 92-93; P-in-c Kingswood w Alderley and Hillesley 95-00; P-in-c Cheltenham St Pet from 00. *St Peter's Vicarage, 375 Swindon Road, Cheltenham GL51 9LB* Tel (01242) 524369 Fax as telephone

ELEY, John Edward. b 49. Sarum & Wells Th Coll 74. **d** 77 **p** 78. C Sherborne w Castleton and Lillington *Sarum* 77-80; Min Can Carl Cathl *Carl* 80-84; V Bromsgrove All SS *Worc* 84-88; Perm to Offic *St E* 90-98; V Stourhead from 98. *The Rectory, Mill Road, Kedington, Haverhill CB9 7NN* Tel and fax (01440) 710216 Mobile 07785-575230 E-mail john.eley5@btopenworld.com

ELFORD, Keith Anthony. b 59. Em Coll Cam BA80 MA84. Wycliffe Hall Ox 87. **d** 90 **p** 91. C Chertsey *Guildf* 90-94; P-in-c Ockham w Hatchford 94-98; Bp's Chapl 94-98; Perm to Offic 98-00; Lic to Offic from 01. *15 Canford Drive, Addlestone KT15 2HH* Tel (01932) 885137 E-mail keith.elford@lineone.net

ELFORD, Canon Robert John. b 39. Man Univ MA71 Ex Univ PhD74. Brasted Th Coll 64 Ridley Hall Cam 66. **d** 68 **p** 69. C Denton St Lawr *Man* 68-71; P-in-c Gwinear *Truro* 71-74; R Phillack w Gwithian and Gwinear 74-78; Lect Man Univ 78-87; Hon C Withington St Paul *Man* 79-83; Warden St Anselm Hall 82-87; Lic to Offic 84-87; Pro-R Liv Inst of HE 88-99; Can Th Liv Cathl *Liv* 92-04; rtd 04. *1 North Quay, Wapping Quay, Liverpool L3 4BU* Tel 0151-709 0461

ELFRED, Michael William. b 48. BA76 MPhil. Linc Th Coll 77. **d** 79 **p** 80. C Boultham *Linc* 79-82; C Croydon H Sav *Cant* 82-84; C Upper Norwood All SS *S'wark* 84-88; V Sanderstead St Mary 88-01; P-in-c Tadworth from 01. *The Vicarage, 1 The Avenue, Tadworth KT20 5AS* Tel (01737) 813152 Mobile 07931-463661 E-mail michael.elfred@talk21.com

ELGAR, Richard John. b 50. Charing Cross Hosp Medical Sch MB, BS73 LRCP73 MRCS73 MRCGP80. St Jo Coll Nottm 92. **d** 92 **p** 93. NSM Derby St Alkmund and St Werburgh *Derby* 92-96; P-in-c Derby St Barn 96-01; V from 01; RD Derby N from 05. *St Barnabas' Vicarage, 122 Radbourne Street, Derby DE22 3BU* Tel (01332) 342553 E-mail relgar1015@aol.com

ELIZABETH CSF, Sister. *See* WEBB, Marjorie Valentine

ELIZABETH MARY CSD, Sister. *See* NOLLER, Hilda Elizabeth Mary

ELKINGTON, Mrs Audrey Anne. b 57. St Cath Coll Ox BA80 UEA PhD83 Nottm Univ DipTh86. St Jo Coll Nottm 85 EAMTC 86. **dss** 88 **d** 92 **p** 94. Monkseaton St Mary *Newc* 88-91; Ponteland 91-93; Par Dn 92-93; C Prudhoe 93-02; RD Corbridge 99-02; Bp's Adv for Women in Min from 01; Bp's Chapl from 02; Dir of Ords from 02. *16 Towers Avenue, Jesmond, Newcastle upon Tyne NE2 3QE* Tel 0191-281 0714 *or* 285 2220 Fax 284 6933 E-mail rev-elk@lineone.net *or* b.chap@tiscali.co.uk

ELKINGTON, Canon David John. b 51. Nottm Univ BTh76 Leic Univ MEd81. St Jo Coll Nottm 73. **d** 76 **p** 77. C Leic Martyrs *Leic* 76-78; C Kirby Muxloe 78-80; Asst Chapl Leic Univ 80-82; Hon C Leic H Spirit 82; Chapl UEA *Nor* 82-88; TV Newc Epiphany *Newc* 88-91; TR 91-93; P-in-c Prudhoe 93-98; V 98-02; Can Res Newc Cathl from 02. *16 Towers Avenue, Jesmond, Newcastle upon Tyne NE2 3QE* Tel 0191-281 0714 E-mail rev-elk@lineone.net

ELKINS, Alan Bernard. b 47. Sarum & Wells Th Coll 70. **d** 73 **p** 74. C Wareham *Sarum* 73-77; P-in-c Codford, Upton Lovell and Stockton 77-79; P-in-c Boyton w Sherrington 77-79; C Ashton Gifford 79; R Bishopstrow and Boreham 79-92; R Corfe Mullen 92-03; V W Byfleet *Guildf* from 03. *The Vicarage, 5 Dartnell Avenue, West Byfleet KT14 6PJ* Tel (01932) 345270 E-mail alanelkins@lineone.net

ELKINS, Mrs Joy Kathleen. b 45. Sarum Th Coll 93. **d** 96 **p** 97. NSM Corfe Mullen *Sarum* 96-03; NSM W Byfleet *Guildf* from 03. *The Vicarage, 5 Dartnell Avenue, West Byfleet KT14 6PJ* Tel (01932) 345270 E-mail joy-elkins@lineone.net

ELKINS, Canon Patrick Charles. b 34. St Chad's Coll Dur BA57 DipEd58 DipTh60. **d** 60 **p** 61. C Moordown *Win* 60-63; C Basingstoke 64-67; V Bransgore 67-04; Hon Can Win Cathl 89-04; rtd 04; Perm to Offic *Win* from 04. *1 Tyrrells Court, Bransgore, Christchurch BH23 8BU* Tel (01425) 673103

ELKS, Roger Mark. b 60. ACGI83 Imp Coll Lon BSc83. Wycliffe Hall Ox 89. **d** 92 **p** 93. C St Austell *Truro* 92-95; V Carbis Bay w Lelant 95-01; I Holywood *D & D* from 01. *The Vicarage, 156 High Street, Holywood BT18 9HT* Tel (028) 9042 2069 *or* 9042 3622 E-mail vicarroger@ntlworld.com

ELLACOTT, Alan Gren. b 58. Ripon Coll Cuddesdon 02. **d** 04 **p** 05. C Crewkerne w Wayford *B & W* from 04. *148 Park View, Crewkerne TA18 8JJ* Tel (01460) 73957 Mobile 07989-299063

ELLACOTT, David Alfred. b 35. SW Minl Tr Course 95. **d** 97 **p** 98. NSM Fremington *Ex* 97-02; Perm to Offic from 02. *2 Coppice Close, Fremington, Barnstaple EX31 2QE* Tel (01271) 373270

ELLAM, Stuart William. b 53. Westcott Ho Cam. **d** 85 **p** 86. C Ditton St Mich *Liv* 85-88; C Greenford H Cross *Lon* 88-91; Perm to Offic 91-94. *26 Church Road, Cowley, Uxbridge UB8 3NA* Tel (01895) 238815

ELLEANOR, David John. b 48. Leic Univ LLB70 St Jo Coll Dur BA88. Cranmer Hall Dur 85. **d** 88 **p** 89. C Consett *Dur* 88-90; P-in-c Ingleton 96-04; NSM from 04. *The Old Vicarage, Front Street, Ingleton, Darlington DL2 3JG* Tel (01325) 730928

ELLEM, Peter Keith. b 58. Nottm Univ BTh90 Leeds Univ MA99 CQSW. St Jo Coll Nottm 87. **d** 90 **p** 91. C Islington St Mary *Lon* 90-94; C Leeds St Geo *Ripon* 94-99; Australia from 99; R Yagoona from 00. *211 Auburn Road, Yagoona, NSW, Australia 2199* Tel (0061) (2) 9790 6281 Fax 9796 6201 E-mail prellen@smartchat.net.au

ELLENS, Gordon Frederick Stewart. b 26. FRAS Columbia Univ (NY) MPhil62 PhD68. K Coll Lon BD52 AKC52 St Boniface Warminster 52. **d** 53 **p** 54. C Old Street St Luke w St Mary Charterhouse etc *Lon* 53-55; C Chiswick St Mich 55-57; Canada 57-60; USA 62-66 and from 88; Japan 70-88; Asst Prof Relig St Sophia Univ Tokyo 70-75; Rikkyo Women's Univ 75-84; Prof Humanities Ueno Gakueu 84-88; rtd 92. *PO Box 1578, Santa Monica, CA 90406, USA* Tel (001) (310) 396 2062 Fax 396 5543

ELLERTON, Mrs Mary Diane. b 45. RGN67 Southn Univ RHV68 Huddersfield Poly Cert Health Educn 89. N Ord Course 90. **d** 93 **p** 94. NSM Upper Holme Valley *Wakef* from 93; Chapl Calderdale and Huddersfield NHS Trust from 01. *13 Liphill Bank Road, Holmfirth, Huddersfield HD9 2LQ* Tel (01484) 684207, 482266 *or* 343437 E-mail diane.ellerton@cht.nhs.uk

ELLERY, Arthur James Gabriel. b 28. St Jo Coll Dur BSc49. Linc Th Coll 51. **d** 53 **p** 54. C Milton next Sittingbourne *Cant* 53-56; C St Laur in Thanet 56-58; C Darlington St Cuth *Dur* 58-62; V Tanfield 62-70; Chapl St Olave's Sch York 70-78; V Gt Ayton w Easby and Newton in Cleveland *York* 78-81; Chapl Bancroft's Sch Woodford Green 81-86; V Chipperfield St Paul *St Alb* 86-93; rtd 93; Perm to Offic *Ely* 93-00; Perm to Offic *Pet* from 93. *7 Church Drive, Orton Waterville, Peterborough PE2 5EX* Tel (01733) 231800

ELLERY, Ian Martyn William. b 56. K Coll Lon BD AKC. Chich Th Coll. **d** 82 **p** 83. C Hornsey St Mary w St Geo *Lon* 82-85; V Choral York Minster *York* 85-89; Subchanter 86-89; R Patrington w Hollym, Welwick and Winestead 89-97; TR Howden 97-05; RD Howden 97-02; P-in-c Cawood w Ryther and Wistow from 05. *Cawood Vicarage, Rythergate, Cawood, Selby YO8 3TP* Tel (01757) 268273 E-mail jeimwe@aol.com

ELLIN, Lindsey Jane. *See* GOODHEW, Mrs Lindsey Jane Ellin

ELLINGTON, David John. b 39. Oriel Coll Ox BA63 MA. Cuddesdon Coll 63. **d** 65 **p** 66. C Sheff St Mark Broomhall *Sheff* 65-68; C Timperley *Ches* 68-72; P-in-c Altrincham St Jo 72-74; V 74-80; P-in-c Ashley 82-86; rtd 86; Perm to Offic *Ches* 87-00. *34 Cockpit Close, Woodstock OX20 1UH* Tel (01993) 815808

ELLIOT, Hugh Riversdale. b 25. Bps' Coll Cheshunt. **d** 62 **p** 65. C Swaffham *Nor* 62-64; C Kessingland 64-67; C Mutford w Rushmere 65-67; P-in-c 67-68; P-in-c Gisleham 67-68; P-in-c Welborne 68-72; P-in-c Yaxham 68-80; P-in-c N Tuddenham 72-80; R E w W Harling 80-90; R Bridgham and Roudham 81-90; R E w W Harling and Bridgham w Roudham 90-92; rtd 92; Perm to Offic *Nor* from 93. *Berryfields, 27 The Street, Alburgh, Harleston IP20 0DJ* Tel (01986) 86498

ELLIOT, Neil Robert Minto. b 63. Hatfield Poly BEng87 Herts Univ CertEd93. St Jo Coll Nottm 94. **d** 96 **p** 97. C Walbrook Epiphany *Derby* 96-00; Chapl Univ of Cen England in Birm 00-05; V Trail SS Andr and Geo Canada from 05. *St Andrew's Church, 1347 Pine Avenue, Trail BC, Canada, V1R 4E7* Tel (001) (250) 368 5581 E-mail rev.nelli@virgin.net

ELLIOT, William. b 33. Glouc Sch of Min 84. **d** 87 **p** 88. C Kington w Huntington, Old Radnor, Kinnerton etc *Heref* 87-90; C Heref H Trin 90-92; Chapl Corfu *Eur* 92-98; rtd 98; P-in-c Barlavington, Burton w Coates, Sutton and Bignor *Chich* from 98. *The Rectory, The Street, Sutton, Pulborough RH20 1PS* Tel (01798) 869220

ELLIOT, William Brunton. b 41. Edin Th Coll 90 Edin Dioc NSM Course 81. **d** 84 **p** 85. NSM Lasswade *Edin* 84-92; NSM Dalkeith 84-92; Assoc P Edin St Pet 92-94; R Selkirk from 94. *St John's Rectory, 23 Viewfield Park, Selkirk TD7 4LH* Tel (01750) 21364 E-mail sjselkirk@aol.com

ELLIOT-NEWMAN, Christopher Guy. b 43. Bede Coll Dur TCert67 Hull Univ BTh83 MEd87. Westcott Ho Cam 67. **d** 70 **p** 71. C Ditton St Mich *Liv* 70-73; C Hazlemere *Ox* 73-77; R Stockton-on-the-Forest w Holtby and Warthill *York* 77-87; Dir of Educn *Cant* 87-94; Perm to Offic *Newc* 95-99; P-in-c Warden w Newbrough 99-01. *15 Hextol Terrace, Hexham NE46 2DF* Tel (01434) 609612

ELLIOTT, Ben. *See* ELLIOTT, William Henry Venn

ELLIOTT, Brian. b 49. Dur Univ BA73. Coll of Resurr Mirfield 73. **d** 75 **p** 76. C Nunthorpe *York* 75-77; CF from 77. *c/o MOD Chaplains (Army)* Tel (01980) 615804 Fax 615800 E-mail brian@newpost.org

ELLIOTT, Charles Middleton. b 39. Linc Coll Ox BA60 Nuff Coll Ox DPhil62. Linc Th Coll 62. **d** 64 **p** 65. Lect Nottm Univ 63-65; C Wilford *S'well* 64-65; Zambia 65-69; Chapl Lusaka Cath 65-69; Asst Gen Sec Jt Cttee WCC 69-72; Asst Gen Sec Pontifical Commn Justice and Peace 69-72; Sen Lect UEA 72-77; Hon Min Can Nor Cathl *Nor* 73-77; Prof Development Studies Univ of Wales (Swansea) 77-82; Dir Chr Aid 82-84; Asst Gen Sec BCC 82-84; Prof Bris Univ 85-87; Australia 87-88; Visiting Prof K Coll Lon 88-89; Preb Lich Cathl *Lich* 88-97; Dean and Chapl Trin Hall Cam 90-01. *Address temp unknown* E-mail cme13@hermes.cam.ac.uk

ELLIOTT, Christopher John. b 44. Sarum Th Coll 66. **d** 69 **p** 70. C Walthamstow St Pet *Chelmsf* 69-71; C Witham 71-74; P-in-c Gt and Lt Bentley 74-80; R Colchester Ch Ch w St Mary V 80-85; R Sible Hedingham 85-93; V Leigh-on-Sea St Aid 93-98; P-in-c Thornton Gp *Linc* 98-01; RD Horncastle 98-01; P-in-c Gt Leighs *Chelmsf* 01-05; P-in-c Lt Leighs 01-05; P-in-c Lt Waltham 01-05; R Gt and Lt Leighs and Lt Waltham from 05; RD Chelmsf N from 04. *The Rectory, Brook Hill, Little Waltham, Chelmsford CM3 3LJ* Tel (01245) 360241 E-mail christopher.elliott@care4free.net

ELLIOTT, Christopher John. b 67. Southn Univ 93. Chich Th Coll 94. **d** 94 **p** 95. C Alton St Lawr *Win* 94-97; Perm to Offic *Guildf* 99-02. *77 Wickham Place, Church Crookham, Fleet GU52 6NQ* Tel 07788-195548 (mobile)

ELLIOTT, Colin David. b 32. AKC55. **d** 56 **p** 57. C W Wickham St Jo *Cant* 56-59; C Dover St Mary 59-64; V Linton 64-66; V Gillingham H Trin *Roch* 66-81; V Belvedere All SS 81-88; V Bromley St Jo 88-97; rtd 97; Perm to Offic *Roch* from 99. *Flat 3, 160 George Lane, London SE13 6JF* Tel (020) 8698 4901

ELLIOTT, David Reed. b 62. Lon Bible Coll BA91. Oak Hill Th Coll 91. **d** 93 **p** 94. C Luton Lewsey St Hugh *St Alb* 93-98; Dioc Communications Dept 98-00. *Address temp unknown*

ELLIOTT, Derek John. b 26. Pemb Coll Cam BA50 MA55. Oak Hill Th Coll 48. **d** 51 **p** 53. C Ealing Dean St Jo *Lon* 51-53; C New Milverton *Cov* 53-55; C Boscombe St Jo *Win* 55-57; V Biddulph *Lich* 57-63; R Rushden w Newton Bromswold *Pet* 63-68; RD Higham 66-68; Chapl Bedford Modern Sch 68-83; V Potten End w Nettleden *St Alb* 83-91; rtd 91; Hon C Twickenham St Mary *Lon* from 91; Perm to Offic *Guildf* from 99. *Westwinds, Ridgeway Road, Dorking RH4 3AT* Tel (01306) 876655

ELLIOTT, Miss Eveline Mary. b 39. Bedf Coll Lon BA60 Cam Univ 92 ALA63. EAMTC 92. **d** 95 **p** 96. NSM Bury St Edmunds St Mary *St E* 95-97; NSM Lark Valley from 97. *4 St Michael's Close, Northgate Street, Bury St Edmunds IP33 1HT* Tel (01284) 753592 E-mail me@larkvalley57.fsnet.co.uk

ELLIOTT, George Evan. b 17. Sarum Th Coll. **d** 58 **p** 59. C Padiham *Blackb* 58-61; C Cleveleys 61-63; V Kimblesworth *Dur* 63-71; V Sutton St James *Linc* 71-77; V Sutton St Edmund 71-77; R Wadingham w Snitterby 77-80; P-in-c Bishop Norton 77-80; R Bishop Norton, Wadingham and Snitterby 80-82; rtd 82; Perm to Offic *Nor* 82-98. *10 Ramsay Hall, 11-13 Byron Road, Worthing BN11 3HN* Tel (01903) 215480

ELLIOTT, Gordon. b 25. St Aid Birkenhead 63. **d** 65 **p** 66. C Latchford St Jas *Ches* 65-68; C Bollington St Jo 68-70; V Dukingfield St Mark 70-73; TV Tenbury *Heref* 74-78; V Bromfield 78-82; R Culmington w Onibury 78-82; V Stanton Lacy 78-82; P-in-c Withybrook w Copston Magna *Cov* 82-83; P-in-c Wolvey, Burton Hastings and Stretton Baskerville 82-83; V Wolvey w Burton Hastings, Copston Magna etc 83-90; rtd 90; Perm to Offic *Worc* from 90 and *Heref* 90-95. *12 Handbury Road, Malvern WR14 1NN* Tel (01684) 569388

ELLIOTT, Ian David. b 40. Qu Coll Cam BA61 MA65. Tyndale Hall Bris 64. **d** 66 **p** 67. C Halewood *Liv* 66-71; C Gt Crosby St Luke 71-74; C-in-c Dallam CD 74-80; V Dallam 80-83; TV Fazakerley Em 83-92; V Warrington H Trin 92-05; rtd 05. *Address temp unknown* E-mail rev-elliott@hotmail.com

ELLIOTT, John Andrew. b 44. ACIB68. St Alb and Ox Min Course 95. **d** 98 **p** 99. NSM Bedgrove *Ox* 98-01; C Modbury, Bigbury, Ringmore w Kingston etc *Ex* from 01. *The Church House, Ringmore, Kingsbridge TQ7 4HR* Tel (01548) 810565 E-mail johnaelliott@compuserve.com

ELLIOTT, John Philip. b 37. MIChemE61 MBIM Salford Univ CEng. Glouc Th Course 79. **d** 80 **p** 80. NSM Brimscombe *Glouc* 80-86; C Caverswall *Lich* 86-91; R Tredington and Darlingscott w Newbold on Stour *Cov* 91-97; rtd 97; Perm to Offic *Glouc* from 97. *Pipers Barn, 69 Bownham Park, Stroud GL5 5BZ*

ELLIOTT, Joseph William. b 37. Chich Th Coll. **d** 66 **p** 67. C Whickham *Dur* 66-72; V Lamesley 72-78; TR Usworth 78-93; P-in-c Belmont 93-95; V 95-98; rtd 98; Perm to Offic *Newc* from 01. *12 Harriot Drive, West Moor, Newcastle upon Tyne NE12 7EU* Tel 0191-256 6471

ELLIOTT, Capt Keith Alcock. b 51. St Jo Coll Dur 95 CA Tr Coll 83. **d** 95 **p** 96. C Chulmleigh, Chawleigh w Cheldon, Wembworthy etc *Ex* 95-99; TV Barnstaple from 99; C-in-c Roundswell CD from 99. *16 Mulberry Way, Roundswell, Barnstaple EX31 3QZ* Tel (01271) 375877 E-mail elliottkeith@btinternet.com

ELLIOTT (née JUTSUM), Mrs Linda Mary. b 56. St Pet Coll Birm CertEd77. WMMTC 92. **d** 95 **p** 96. NSM Longthorpe *Pet* 95-99; P-in-c Etton w Helpston and Maxey 99-04; Chapl Thorpe Hall Hospice from 04. *68 Bradwell Road, Peterborough PE3 9PZ* Tel (01733) 261793 E-mail rev_linda@lycos.co.uk

ELLIOTT, Mary. *See* ELLIOTT, Miss Eveline Mary

ELLIOTT, Maurice John. b 65. St Andr Univ MA87 TCD BTh92 MPhil93. CITC 89. **d** 93 **p** 94. C Coleraine *Conn* 93-98; I Greenisland 98-02; I Lurgan Ch the Redeemer *D & D* from 02. *Shankill Rectory, 62 Banbridge Road, Lurgan, Craigavon BT66 7HG* Tel (028) 3832 3341 *or* tel/fax 3832 5673 Mobile 07850-526505 E-mail maurice.elliott@lineone.net

ELLIOTT, Canon Michael Cowan. b 38. Auckland Univ BA63 Episc Th Sch Mass MDiv66 Massey Univ (NZ) MPhil82. St Jo Coll Auckland LTh61. **d** 61 **p** 62. New Zealand 61-65; C New Lynn 61-64; C Thames 65; USA 65-66; Warden Pemb Coll Miss Walworth *S'wark* 66-70; Dir St Luke's Cen Haifa Jerusalem 70-74; BCC 74-75; C Amersham *Ox* 74-75; Ecum Secretariat on Development NZ 76-84; Dir Chr Action NZ 84-87; Chapl City of Lon Poly *Lon* 87-89; Dir Inner City Aid 89-91; Tutor Westmr Coll Ox 91-98; Dir Ox Educn Trust 99-02; Dir Taught Progr Ox Cen for Miss Studies 00-02; Dir Min and Can Res Brecon Cathl *S & B* 02-03; rtd 03; Lect Univ of Wales (Lamp) *St D* from 03. *Orchard House, Chapel Road, Llanfihangel Talyllyn, Brecon LD3 7TH* Tel (01874) 658194 E-mail canonmcelliott@aol.com

ELLIOTT, Michael James. b 58. LTh. St Jo Coll Nottm 80. **d** 83 **p** 84. C Pontypridd St Cath *Llan* 83-86; C Leamington Priors St Paul *Cov* 86-89; Chapl RAF from 89; Perm to Offic *Ely* from 01. *Chaplaincy Services (RAF), HQ, Personnel and Training Command, RAF Innsworth, Gloucester GL3 1EZ* Tel (01452) 712612 ext 5164 Fax 510828

ELLIOTT, Nigel Harvey. b 55. St Jo Coll Nottm DCM92. **d** 92 **p** 93. C Radcliffe *Man* 92-95; V Kilnhurst *Sheff* from 95. *The Vicarage, Highthorne Road, Kilnhurst, Rotherham S64 5UU* Tel (01709) 589674 E-mail neil199076@aol.com

ELLIOTT, Norman. *See* ELLIOTT, William Norman

ELLIOTT, The Ven Peter. b 41. Hertf Coll Ox BA63 MA68. Linc Th Coll 63. **d** 65 **p** 66. C Gosforth All SS *Newc* 65-68; C Balkwell 68-72; V High Elswick St Phil 72-80; V N Gosforth 80-87; V Embleton w Rennington and Rock 87-93; RD Alnwick 89-93; Hon Can Newc Cathl 90-93; Adn Northd and Can Res Newc Cathl 93-05; rtd 05. *56 King Street, Seahouses NE68 7XS* Tel (01665) 721133

ELLIOTT, Peter Wolstenholme. b 31. CChem MRSC. NEOC 78. **d** 81 **p** 82. NSM Yarm *York* 81-02; Perm to Offic from 02. *48 Butterfield Drive, Eaglescliffe, Stockton-on-Tees TS16 0EZ* Tel (01642) 652698 E-mail revdpeter@hotmail.com

ELLIOTT, Philip. *See* ELLIOTT, John Philip

ELLIOTT, Mrs Rosemary Miriam. b 37. Toronto Univ BPaed62 Birm Univ BPhil86. **d** 04 **p** 05. Asst Chapl Birm Specialist Community Health NHS Trust from 04. *328 Highters Heath Lane, Birmingham B14 4TB* Tel 0121-430 6099 Mobile 07721-855007 E-mail rosemary.elliott@btinternet.com

ELLIOTT, Simon Richard James. b 66. Lon Univ BSc88. Cranmer Hall Dur BA95. **d** 95 **p** 96. C Hendon St Paul Mill Hill *Lon* 95-99; V Hull St Martin w Transfiguration *York* from 99. *St Martin's Vicarage, 942 Anlaby Road, Hull HU4 6AH* Tel (01482) 352995

ELLIOTT, Stanley Griffin. b 19. Lon Univ BA50. Ridley Hall Cam 50. **d** 52 **p** 53. C Astley Bridge *Man* 52-54; C Bedford Leigh 54-56; R Ordsall in Salford St Cypr 56-59; R Ashton-upon-Mersey St Martin *Ches* 59-80; V Tile Hill *Cov* 80-85; rtd 85; Perm to Offic *Win* 85-97; Perm to Offic *Sarum* from 85. *38 Melton Court, 37 Lindsay Road, Poole BH13 6BH* Tel (01202) 766080

ELLIOTT, William. *See* ELLIOTT, Joseph William

ELLIOTT, William. b 20. Lon Univ BA56. Ripon Hall Ox 60. **d** 61 **p** 62. C Kidderminster St Mary *Worc* 61-70; V Bewdley Far Forest 70-78; V Rock w Heightington w Far Forest 78-82; V Mamble w Bayton, Rock w Heightington etc 82-85; rtd 85; Perm to Offic *Heref* from 85; Perm to Offic *Worc* from 85. *8 Lea View, Cleobury Mortimer, Kidderminster DY14 8EE* Tel (01299) 270993 E-mail welliott@fish.co.uk

ELLIOTT, William Henry Venn (Ben). b 34. K Coll Cam BA55 MA59. Wells Th Coll 59. **d** 61 **p** 62. C Almondbury *Wakef* 61-66; V Bramshaw *Sarum* 66-81; P-in-c Landford w Plaitford 77-81; V Mere w W Knoyle and Maiden Bradley 81-99; rtd 99. *3 St George's Close, Salisbury SP2 8HA* Tel (01722) 338409

ELLIOTT, William James. b 38. Jes Coll Cam BA62 MA66 Birm Univ MA69 PhD74. Qu Coll Birm 62. **d** 64 **p** 65. C Hendon St Paul Mill Hill *Lon* 64-67; C St Pancras w St Jas and Ch Ch 67-69; P-in-c Preston St Paul *Blackb* 69-74; Chapl Preston R Infirmary 69-74; R Elstree *St Alb* 74-00; Research Fell Birm Univ *Birm* 00-03; rtd 03; Perm to Offic *Nor* from 00. *23 Neil Avenue, Holt NR25 6TG* Tel and fax (01263) 713853 E-mail bbillholt@aol.com

ELLIOTT, William Norman. b 20. Kelham Th Coll 37. **d** 43 **p** 44. C Tividale *Lich* 43-50; C Barnsley St Mary *Wakef* 50-55; V Smawthorpe St Mich 55-63; V S Crosland 64-85; rtd 85; Chapl Community of St Pet Horbury from 85; Perm to Offic *Wakef* from 85. *18 Woodlands, Horbury, Wakefield WF4 5HH* Tel (01924) 265547

ELLIOTT SMITH, Mark Charles. b 59. LRAM85 GRSM86 DipRAM87 ARCO88 Lon Univ MA96. St Steph Ho Ox 92. **d** 94 **p** 97. C W Hampstead St Jas *Lon* 94-95; In RC Ch 95-96; C Tottenham St Paul 96-01; P-in-c New Southgate St Paul 01-03; V from 03. *St Paul's Vicarage, 11 Woodland Road, London N11 1PN* Tel (020) 8361 1946 *or* (07815) 320761 E-mail frmarkelliottsmith@blueyonder.co.uk

ELLIS, Anthony. *See* ELLIS, John Anthony

ELLIS, Anthony Colin. b 56. Keble Coll Ox BA77 Man Univ PhD80. Linc Th Coll 80. **d** 81 **p** 82. C Mill Hill Jo Keble Ch *Lon* 81-83; Staff Tutor in RS Man Univ from 83; Dir of Centre for Continuing Educn from 99; C Stretford St Pet *Man* 83-87; NSM Shore 87-89; Lic Preacher from 89. *2 Crowther Terrace, Blackshaw, Hebden Bridge HX7 6DE* Tel (01422) 844242 *or* 0161-275 3302

ELLIS, Canon Bryan Stuart. b 31. Qu Coll Cam BA54 MA58. Ridley Hall Cam 55. **d** 57 **p** 58. C Ramsgate St Luke *Cant* 57-59; C Herne Bay Ch Ch 59-62; V Burmantofts St Steph and St Agnes *Ripon* 62-81; RD Wakef 81-96; V Wakef St Andr and St Mary 81-00; Hon Can Wakef Cathl 89-00; rtd 00; Perm to Offic *Ripon* from 01. *302 Oakwood Lane, Leeds LS8 3LE*

ELLIS, Charles Harold. b 50. N Ord Course 78. **d** 81 **p** 82. C Davyhulme St Mary *Man* 81-85; V Tonge w Alkrington 85-91; P-in-c Radcliffe St Thos and St Jo 91; P-in-c Radcliffe St Mary 91; TR Radcliffe 91-99; AD Radcliffe and Prestwich 96-99; P-in-c Newchurch 99-00; TR Rossendale Middle Valley 00-04; AD Rossendale 00-04; V Ingleton w Chapel le Dale *Bradf* from 04. *St Mary's Vicarage, Main Street, Ingleton, Carnforth LA6 3HF* Tel (01524) 241440 E-mail charlesandsue@compuserve.com

ELLIS, Christopher Charles. b 55. Edin Univ BD78 Hull Univ MA80 Societas Oecumenica 90. Edin Th Coll 76 Irish Sch of Ecum 78. **d** 79 **p** 80. C Selby Abbey *York* 79-82; C Fulford 82-85; Dioc Ecum Officer 81-98; Dioc Ecum Adv 90-98; Lect Ecum Th Hull Univ from 84; P-in-c Kexby w Wilberfoss *York* 85-90; Ecum Officer S Cleveland and N Yorks Ecum Coun 88-98; P-in-c Bulmer w Dalby, Terrington and Welburn 98-01; R Howardian Gp 01-05; P-in-c Sheriff Hutton, Farlington, Stillington etc from

05. *The Vicarage, Main Street, Sutton-on-the-Forest, York YO61 1DW* Tel (01347) 870336

ELLIS, Canon David Craven. b 34. Man Univ BA56 MA57. St Aid Birkenhead 59. **d** 61 **p** 62. C Gt Crosby St Luke *Liv* 61-65; Hong Kong 65-69; P-in-c Sawrey *Carl* 69-74; Dioc Youth Officer 69-74; V Halifax St Aug *Wakef* 74-84; R Greystoke, Matterdale and Mungrisdale *Carl* 84-87; R Watermillock 84-87; TR Greystoke, Matterdale, Mungrisdale etc 88-91; RD Penrith 87-91; TR Carl H Trin and St Barn 91-96; Hon Can Carl Cathl 91-96; rtd 96; Perm to Offic *Carl* 97-02 and from 04; NSM Cartmel Peninsula 02-04. *Calderstones, 5 Fellside, Allithwaite, Grange-over-Sands LA11 7RN* Tel (01539) 533974

ELLIS, Gay Winifred. b 48. Oak Hill Th Coll 94. **d** 96 **p** 97. NSM Nazeing *Chelmsf* 96-99; C 99-00; P-in-c Chingford St Anne 00-02; V 02-04; P-in-c Lambourne w Abridge and Stapleford Abbotts from 04. *The Rectory, 39 Hoe Lane, Abridge, Romford RM4 1AU* Tel (01992) 814390 E-mail gayellis@aol.com

ELLIS, Gillian Patricia. **d** 99 **p** 00. OLM Blymhill w Weston-under-Lizard *Lich* 99-00; OLM Lapley w Wheaton Aston from 00. *18 Ashleigh Crescent, Wheaton, Aston ST19 9PN* Tel (01785) 840925

ELLIS, Hugh William. b 54. Sussex Univ BSc76. Ridley Hall Cam 88. **d** 90 **p** 91. C Reading St Jo *Ox* 90-93; P-in-c Bradfield and Stanford Dingley 93-97; R 97-03; TR Langport Area Chs *B & W* from 03. *The Rectory, Huish Episcopi, Langport TA10 9QR* Tel (01458) 250480 E-mail hughelli@aol.com

ELLIS, Canon Ian Morton. b 52. QUB BD75 MTh82 TCD PhD89. CITC. **d** 77 **p** 78. C Portadown St Columba *Arm* 77-79; C Arm St Mark 79-85; Chapl Arm R Sch 79-85; Hon V Choral Arm Cathl 82-93; I Mullavilly 85-93; Dom Chapl to Abp Arm 86-93; Tutor for Aux Min (Arm) 90-93; Dioc Adv on Ecum 92-93; I Newcastle *D & D* from 93; Can Belf Cathl from 00; Ed *The Church of Ireland Gazette* from 01; Preb Newcastle St Patr Cathl Dublin from 01. *The Rectory, 1 King Street, Newcastle BT33 0HD* Tel (028) 4372 2439 E-mail ian.m.ellis@btinternet.com

ELLIS, Ian William. b 57. QUB BSc78 CertEd79 TCD BTh89. CITC 86. **d** 89 **p** 90. C Arm St Mark w Aghavilly *Arm* 89-91; I Loughgall w Grange 91-02; Sec Gen Syn Bd of Educn from 02. *Church of Ireland House, 61-67 Donegall Street, Belfast BT1 2QH* Tel (028) 9023 1202 Fax 9023 7802 E-mail edunorth@ireland.anglican.org

ELLIS, Jean Miriam. b 35. St Mich Coll Llan 92. **d** 95 **p** 97. NSM Llanelli *S & B* 95-98; NSM Rockfield and St Maughen's w Llangattock etc *Mon* 99-04; NSM Rockfield and Dingestow Gp from 05. *3 Plas Newydd, Llanarth, Raglan, Usk NP15 2AW* Tel (01873) 840023

ELLIS, John Anthony (Tony). b 47. Univ of Wales (Lamp) DipTh70 Open Univ BA80. Coll of Resurr Mirfield 70. **d** 72 **p** 73. C Sketty *S & B* 72-75; C Duston *Pet* 75-80; R Lichborough w Maidford and Farthingstone 80-85; V Stratfield Mortimer *Ox* 85-98; P-in-c Mortimer W End w Padworth 85-98; TR Kidlington w Hampton Poyle from 98; AD Ox from 04. *St Mary's Rectory, 19 Mill Street, Kidlington OX5 2EE* Tel and fax (01865) 372230 E-mail churchkid@tesco.net

ELLIS, John Beaumont. b 45. Univ of Wales (Lamp) BA67 LTh69. Bp Burgess Hall Lamp. **d** 69 **p** 70. C Abergavenny St Mary w Llanwenarth Citra *Mon* 69-72; C Swansea St Gabr *S & B* 72-75; V Llanbister and Llanbadarn Fynydd w Llananno 75-77; V Newport St Andr *Mon* 77-80; V Risca 80-84; V Cheadle Heath *Ches* 84-94. *12 Upper Hibbert Lane, Marple, Stockport SK6 7HX* Tel 0161-427 1963

ELLIS, John Franklyn. b 34. Leeds Univ BA58. Linc Th Coll 58. **d** 60 **p** 61. C Ladybarn *Man* 60-63; C Stockport St Geo *Ches* 63-66; V High Lane 66-81; V Chelford w Lower Withington 81-99; rtd 99; Perm to Offic *Ches* from 00. *3 Millers Croft, Adlington Street, Macclesfield SK10 1BD*

ELLIS, John Raymond. b 63. St Steph Ho Ox 95. **d** 97 **p** 98. C Clare w Poslingford, Cavendish etc *St E* 97-00; P-in-c Bury St Edmunds St Jo 00-02; P-in-c Bury St Edmunds St Geo 00-02; TV Bury St Edmunds All SS w St Jo and St Geo 02-04; Chapl RAF from 04. *HQ, Personnel and Training Command, RAF Innsworth, Gloucester GL3 1EZ* Tel (01452) 712612 ext 5164 Fax 510828

ELLIS, John Roland. b 32. Wells Th Coll 67. **d** 69 **p** 70. C Kettering SS Pet and Paul *Pet* 69-71; C Kingsthorpe 71-73; TV 73-74; TV Ebbw Vale *Mon* 74-76; V Llanddewi Rhydderch w Llanvapley etc 76-83; Miss to Seamen 79-86; V New Tredegar *Mon* 83-86; V Llanelli *S & B* 86-98; RD Crickhowell 91-98; rtd 99; P-in-c Rockfield and St Maughen's w Llangattock etc *Mon* 99-05; Hon C Rockfield and Dingestow Gp from 05. *3 Plas Newydd, Llanarth, Raglan, Usk NP15 2AW* Tel (01873) 840023

ELLIS, Canon John Wadsworth. b 42. MBE98. TCD BA64. **d** 66 **p** 67. C Lisburn Ch Ch Cathl *Conn* 66-69; C Norbiton *S'wark* 69-72; C New Clee *Linc* 72-85; V from 85; RD Grimsby and Cleethorpes 94-99; Can and Preb Linc Cathl from 98. *120 Queen Mary Avenue, Cleethorpes DN35 7SZ* Tel and fax (01472) 696521 *or* 329922 E-mail jwellis@ntlworld.com

ELLIS, Keith. b 39. Univ of Wales (Swansea) BSc60 Birm Poly BSc(Econ)74 Liv Univ CertEd61. St Jo Coll Nottm 95. **d** 96 **p** 97. NSM Marple All SS *Ches* 96-99; NSM Camelot Par *B & W* 99-03. *5 Lavender Close, Melksham SN12 6FW*

ELLIS, Kevin Stuart. b 67. Newc Univ BA91 Lon Bible Coll PhD97. Qu Coll Birm 99. **d** 01 **p** 02. C Matson *Glouc* 01-04; TV Maryport, Netherton and Flimby *Carl* from 04. *The Vicarage, Church Terrace, Maryport CA15 7PS* Tel (01900) 819886 E-mail kevinellis@fish.co.uk

ELLIS, Sister Lilian. b 44. Keswick Hall Coll TCert66. Wilson Carlile Coll Dip Evang90 Oak Hill Th Coll 95. **d** 96 **p** 97. C Vange *Chelmsf* 96-00; C Pitsea w Nevendon 00-02; rtd 02; Perm to Offic *Chelmsf* from 02. *9 The Poplars, Pitsea SS13 2ER* Tel (01268) 551018 E-mail lilian.ellis@tesco.net

ELLIS, Malcolm Railton. b 35. LTCL71 Univ of Wales (Lamp) BA56. Sarum Th Coll 56. **d** 58 **p** 59. C Llangynwyd w Maesteg *Llan* 58-61; C Llantrisant 61-67; V Troedrhiwgarth 67-70; PV Truro Cathl *Truro* 70-73; V Egloshayle 73-81; V Margam *Llan* 81-87; V Cardiff St Jo 87-00; TR Cen Cardiff 00-02; Prec and Can Llan Cathl 96-02; rtd 02. *41 Wendron Street, Helston TR13 8PT* Tel (01326) 574000

ELLIS, Preb Mark Durant. b 39. Ex Univ BA62. Cuddesdon Coll 62. **d** 64 **p** 65. C Lyngford *B & W* 64-67; V Weston-super-Mare St Andr Bournville 67-76; TV Yeovil 76-88; V Yeovil St Mich from 88; Preb Wells Cathl from 90; RD Yeovil 94-04. *St Michael's Vicarage, St Michael's Avenue, Yeovil BA21 4LH* Tel (01935) 475752 Fax as telephone

ELLIS, Paul. b 56. Man Poly HNC79. Aston Tr Scheme 88 Trin Coll Bris DipHE92. **d** 92 **p** 93. C Pennington *Man* 92-96; TV Deane from 96. *St Andrew's Vicarage, Over Hulton, Bolton BL5 1EN* Tel (01204) 651851 E-mail paul.ellis@stabolton.freeserve.co.uk

ELLIS, Peter Andrew. b 46. St D Coll Lamp 65. **d** 69 **p** 70. C Milford Haven *St D* 69-71; R Walwyn's Castle w Robeston W 71-74; Miss to Seafarers from 74; Hong Kong 74-75 and from 92; Singapore 75-82; The Tees and Hartlepool 82-92. *The Mariner's Club, 11 Middle Road, Kowloon, Hong Kong* Tel (00852) 2368 8261 Fax 2366 0928

ELLIS, Randolph John Keith. b 44. Univ of Wales MEd Man Univ CertEd. Westcott Ho Cam 98. **d** 01 **p** 02. C Glanogwen w St Ann's w Llanllechid *Ban* 01-04; Min Can Ban Cathl from 04. *Glan Arthur, Penisarwaun, Caernarfon LL55 3PW* Tel (01286) 873623 E-mail randolph@afoncegin.freeserve.co.uk

ELLIS, Richard. b 47. **d** 02 **p** 03. OLM Leiston *St E* from 02. *9 Kings Road, Leiston IP16 4DA* Tel (01728) 832168 Mobile 07759-349057 E-mail us@rellis41.freeserve.co.uk

ELLIS, Robert Albert. b 48. K Coll Lon BD70 AKC70. St Aug Coll Cant 70. **d** 72 **p** 73. C Liv Our Lady and St Nic w St Anne *Liv* 72-76; P-in-c Meerbrook *Lich* 76-80; Producer Relig Progr BBC Radio Stoke 76-80; V Highgate All SS *Lon* 80-81; P-in-c Longdon *Lich* 81-87; Dioc Communications Officer 81-01; Chapl Palma de Mallorca *Eur* from 01. *Nunez de Balboa 6, Son Armadans, 07014 Palma de Mallorca, Spain* Tel (0034) (971) 737279 Fax 454492 E-mail anglicanpalma@terra.es

ELLIS, The Ven Robin Gareth. b 35. Pemb Coll Ox BA57 BCL58 MA62. Chich Th Coll 58. **d** 60 **p** 61. C Swinton St Pet *Man* 60-63; Asst Chapl Worksop Coll Notts 63-66; V Swaffham Prior *Ely* 66-74; Asst Dir Educn 66-74; V Wisbech St Aug 74-82; V Yelverton *Ex* 82-86; Adn Plymouth 82-00; rtd 00; Perm to Offic *Ex* from 00. *24 Lyndhurst Road, Exmouth EX8 3DT* Tel (01395) 272891

ELLIS, Simon David. b 68. Univ of Wales (Cardiff) BSc89 Bris Univ PGCE90 MA00. St Steph Ho Ox BTh94. **d** 97 **p** 98. C Knowle H Nativity *Bris* 97-01; V Long Eaton St Laur *Derby* from 01. *The Vicarage, Regent Street, Long Eaton, Nottingham NG10 1JX* Tel 0115-973 3154 E-mail ellis.family@ukgateway.net

ELLIS, Susannah Margaret. b 44. Open Univ BA82 New Coll Dur CertEd88. EAMTC 93. **d** 96 **p** 97. NSM S Elmham and Ilketshall *St E* 96-98; Warden Quiet Waters Chr Retreat Ho 96-98; C Worlingham w Barnby and N Cove *St E* 98-01; C Beccles St Mich 98-01; P-in-c Worlingham w Barnby and N Cove 01-03; R from 03. *27 Lowestoft Road, Worlingham, Beccles NR34 7DZ* Tel (01502) 715403

ELLIS, The Ven Timothy William. b 53. AKC75. St Aug Coll Cant 75. **d** 76 **p** 77. C Old Trafford St Jo *Man* 76-80; V Pendleton St Thos 80-87; Chapl Salford Coll of Tech 80-87; V Sheff St Leon Norwood *Sheff* 87-01; P-in-c Shiregreen St Hilda 94-01; RD Ecclesfield 94-99; Hon Can Sheff Cathl 00-01; Adn Stow *Linc* from 01; Can and Preb Linc Cathl from 01. *The Archdeacon's House, Main Street, Hackthorn, Lincoln LN2 3PF* Tel (01673) 860382 Fax 860015 E-mail arch.stowlind@virgin.net

ELLISDON, Patrick Leon Shane. b 61. St Jo Coll Nottm 99. **d** 01 **p** 02. C Margate St Phil *Cant* 01-04; P-in-c Cliftonville from 04. *18 Devonshire Gardens, Margate CT9 3AF* Tel (01843) 226832 Mobile 07932-734932 E-mail panddellisdon@aol.com

✠**ELLISON, The Rt Revd John Alexander.** b 40. ALCD67. **d** 67 **p** 68 **c** 88. C Woking St Paul *Guildf* 67-70; SAMS from 71;

Argentina 80-83; R Aldridge *Lich* 83-88; Bp Paraguay from 88. *Iglesia Anglicana Paraguaya, Casilla 1124, Asuncin, Paraguay* Tel (00595) (21) 224028

ELLISON, Ms Sandra Anne. b 53. Anglia Poly Univ BA96 RMN74. EAMTC 99. **d** 02 **p** 03. C Hunstanton St Mary w Ringstead Parva etc *Nor* 02-05; R Ashmanhaugh, Barton Turf etc from 05. *11 Pinewood Drive, Horning, Norwich NR12 8LZ* Tel (01692) 630216

ELLISON, Simon John. b 51. SEITE 99. **d** 02 **p** 03. NSM Caterham *S'wark* from 02. *24 Bunce Drive, Caterham CR3 5FF* Tel (01883) 370751 E-mail father.simon@tiscali.co.uk

ELLISTON, John Ernest Nicholas. b 37. ALCD61. **d** 61 **p** 62. C Gipsy Hill Ch Ch *S'wark* 61-64; C Whitton and Thurleston w Akenham *St E* 64-68; P-in-c New Clee *Linc* 68-71; V 75-76; V Grimsby St Steph 71-75; P-in-c Mildenhall *St E* 77-79; RD Mildenhall 81-84; R Barton Mills, Beck Row w Kenny Hill etc 80-84; V Ipswich St Aug 84-96; R Guernsey St Peter Port *Win* 96-02; Chapl Princess Eliz Hosp Guernsey 96-02; rtd 02; Perm to Offic *St E* from 03. *27 Wyvern Road, Ipswich IP3 9TJ* Tel (01473) 726617 *or* 720036

ELLMORE, Peter Robert. b 44. Portsm Univ MA. Sarum & Wells Th Coll 84. **d** 86 **p** 87. C Bridgemary *Portsm* 86-89; C Portsea N End St Mark 89-91; Asst Chapl St Mary's Hosp Portsm 91-92; Chapl Qu Alexandra Hosp Portsm 91-93; Chapl Team Ldr Portsm Hosps NHS Trust 93-97; P-in-c Cosham *Portsm* 97-99; Angl Chapl Univ Coll Lon Hosps NHS Trust 99-01; Chapl Team Ldr United Bris Healthcare NHS Trust 01-04; Lead Chapl (S) *Caring for the Spirit* NHS Project from 04. *Jenner House, Unit E3 Avon Way, Langley Park, Chippenham SN15 1GG* E-mail peter.ellmore@lineone.net *or* peter.ellmore@ubht.swest.nhs.uk

ELLOR, Michael Keith. b 52. St Jo Coll Nottm 92. **d** 94 **p** 95. C Stafford St Jo and Tixall w Ingestre *Lich* 94-97; TV Bucknall and Bagnall 97-03; TR Bucknall from 03; RD Stoke from 02. *The Rectory, 151 Werrington Road, Bucknall, Stoke-on-Trent ST2 9AQ* Tel (01782) 280667 *or* 279300 E-mail ellors@bucknall12.fsnet.co.uk

ELLSLEY, Howard. b 23. Roch Th Coll 65. **d** 67 **p** 68. C Glas St Marg *Glas* 67-71; R Dalbeattie 71-77; TV Melton Mowbray w Thorpe Arnold *Leic* 77-78; R Balcombe *Chich* 78-83; R Airdrie *Glas* 83-88; R Gartcosh 83-88; rtd 88. *Auchencraig, Lower Barcaple, Ringford, Castle Douglas DG7 2AP* Tel (01557) 820228

ELLSON, Miss Deborah Louise. b 61. Brentwood Coll of Educn BEd84 Loughb Univ MA01. EAMTC 98. **d** 00 **p** 01. NSM Lowestoft St Marg *Nor* 00-04; P-in-c Langleybury St Paul *St Alb* from 04. *The Vicarage, 1 Langleybury Lane, Kings Langley WD4 8QQ* Tel (01923) 270634 E-mail revlou@fish.co.uk

ELLSON, Montague Edward. b 33. Birm Univ BA56 Cam Univ AdCertEd67. EAMTC 84. **d** 87 **p** 88. Hon C Freethorpe w Wickhampton, Halvergate etc *Nor* 87-90; C Gaywood, Bawsey and Mintlyn 90-92; Miss to Seafarers from 90; R Pulham *Nor* 92-94; P-in-c Starston 93-94; Dioc NSM Officer 94-97; R Pulham Market, Pulham St Mary and Starston 94-97; RD Redenhall 95-97; rtd 97; Perm to Offic *Nor* from 97. *Barn Cottage, Neatishead Road, Horning, Norwich NR12 8LB*

ELLSWORTH, Lida Elizabeth. b 48. Columbia Univ (NY) BA70 Girton Coll Cam PhD76. EMMTC 85. **d** 88 **p** 94. NSM Bakewell *Derby* from 88. *Apple Croft, Granby Gardens, Bakewell DE45 1ET* Tel (01629) 814255 Fax as telephone

ELLWOOD, Keith Brian. b 36. AIGCM58 FRSA65 DipRIPH&H65 ACP66 FCollP83 Curwen Coll Lon BA58 MMus65 Bede Coll Dur CertEd59 Hon DD99. Bps' Coll Cheshunt 64. **d** 64 **p** 65. Asst Master R Wanstead Sch 60-66; Chapl 64-66; C Wanstead St Mary *Chelmsf* 64-66; CF 66-70; OCF 70-71 and 76-79; Hong Kong 70-71; P-in-c Bicknoller *B & W* 71-73; Chapl Roedean Sch Brighton 73-76; Perm to Offic *B & W* 74-79; W Germany 76-79; Chapl Trin Coll Glenalmond 79-81; Hd Master St Chris Sch Burnham-on-Sea 82-86; Hon C Burnham *B & W* 82-86; R Staple Fitzpaine, Orchard Portman, Thurlbear etc 86-89; P-in-c Hugill *Carl* 89-93; Educn Adv 89-93; P-in-c Coldwaltham and Hardham *Chich* 93-95; rtd 96; Perm to Offic *Chich* 96-04 and *Sheff* from 04. *21 Fiddlers Drive, Armthorpe, Doncaster DN3 3TS* Tel (01302) 834031 E-mail k.b.e@btinternet.com

ELMAN, Simon Laurie. b 57. NTMTC. **d** 99 **p** 00. C Loughton St Jo *Chelmsf* 99-01; C Tye Green w Netteswell from 01. *86 Theydon Grove, Epping CM16 4QA* Tel (01992) 579532 E-mail simon@elman42.freeserve.co.uk

ELMES, Sister Evelyn Sandra. b 61. **d** 97 **p** 98. CA from 89; C Southchurch H Trin *Chelmsf* 97-00; Perm to Offic *Win* from 01. *18 Chawton Close, Winchester SO22 6HY* Tel (01926) 880928 E-mail eveelmes@tesco.net

ELMORE, Graeme Martin. b 47. Sarum & Wells Th Coll 71. **d** 74 **p** 75. C Norbury St Oswald *Cant* 74-77; P-in-c St Allen *Truro* 77-79; P-in-c St Erme 77-79; V Newlyn St Pet 79-85; CF (TA) 80-86; R Redruth w Lanner *Truro* 85-86; Chapl RN from 86. *Royal Naval Chaplaincy Service, Room 203, Victory Building, HM Naval Base, Portsmouth PO1 3LS* Tel (023) 9272 7903 Fax 9272 7111

ELPHICK, Robin Howard. b 37. ALCD63. **d** 64 **p** 65. C Clapham Common St Barn *S'wark* 64-67; C Woking St Pet *Guildf* 67-71; R Rollesby w Burgh w Billockby *Nor* 71-80; P-in-c Ashby w Oby, Thurne and Clippesby 79-80; R Rollesby w Burgh w Billockby w Ashby w Oby etc 80-84; R Frinton *Chelmsf* 84-94; P-in-c W w E Mersea and Peldon w Gt and Lt Wigborough 94-02; rtd 02; Perm to Offic *Nor* from 02. *1 Barn Cottages, Dodma Road, Weasenham, King's Lynn PE32 2TJ* Tel (01328) 838340 E-mail robin@relphick.fsnet.co.uk

ELPHICK, Canon Vivien Margaret. b 53. Solicitor 77 Kent Univ BA74. Trin Coll Bris BA90. **d** 90 **p** 94. C Oulton Broad *Nor* 90-94; P-in-c Burlingham St Edmund w Lingwood, Strumpshaw etc from 94; RD Blofield 98-04; Hon Can Nor Cathl from 03. *The Rectory, Barn Close, Lingwood, Norwich NR13 4TS* Tel (01603) 713880

ELPHIN AND ARDAGH, Archdeacon of. *See* FORSTER, The Ven Andrew James

ELPHIN AND ARDAGH, Dean of. *See* WILLIAMS, The Very Revd Arfon

ELSDON, Bernard Robert. b 29. Roch Th Coll 65. **d** 67 **p** 68. C Wallasey St Hilary *Ches* 67-71; C Liv Our Lady and St Nic w St Anne *Liv* 71-72; V Anfield St Marg 73-89; Dioc Exec Dir for Chr Resp 80-83; rtd 89; Perm to Offic *Man* and *Ches* from 89. *31 Douglas Road, Hazel Grove, Stockport SK7 4JE* Tel 0161-292 1858 E-mail bernard.hillcrest@ntlworld.com

ELSDON, Mrs Janice Margaret. b 49. CITC 92. **d** 95 **p** 96. NSM Cloughfern *Conn* 95-99; NSM Ahoghill w Portglenone 99-02; NSM Belfast St Thos from 02. *St Bartholomew's Rectory, 16 Mount Pleasant, Belfast BT9 5DS* Tel (028) 9066 9995 E-mail jelsdon@madasafish.com

ELSDON, Ronald. b 44. St Jo Coll Cam BA66 Trin Hall Cam PhD69 K Coll Lon BD86 Milltown Inst Dub PhD. CITC 97. **d** 99 **p** 00. C Ballymena w Ballyclug *Conn* 99-02; I Belfast St Bart from 02. *St Bartholomew's Rectory, 16 Mount Pleasant, Belfast BT9 5DS* Tel (028) 9066 9995 E-mail elsdon.rj@nireland.com *or* stbartholomew@connor.anglican.org

ELSMORE, Canon Guy Charles. b 66. Edin Univ BSc88. Ridley Hall Cam 93. **d** 93 **p** 94. C Huyton St Mich *Liv* 93-98; V Hough Green St Basil and All SS from 98; AD Widnes from 03; Hon Can Liv Cathl from 03. *All Saints' Vicarage, Hough Green Road, Widnes WA8 9SZ* Tel 0151-420 4963 E-mail allst_hg@hotmail.com

ELSON, Christopher John. b 52. K Coll Lon BD75 AKC75. St Aug Coll Cant. **d** 76 **p** 77. C New Haw *Guildf* 76-79; C Guildf H Trin w St Mary 79-82; C Hale 85-87; V Ripley from 87; Sub Chapl HM Pris Send 88-92. *The Vicarage, High Street, Ripley, Woking GU23 6AE* Tel (01483) 211460 Mobile 07956-103289 E-mail christopher.elson@tesco.net

ELSON, John Frederick. Roch Th Coll 62. **d** 64 **p** 65. C Tenterden St Mildred w Smallhythe *Cant* 64-68; P-in-c Chart next Sutton Valence 68-71; V Fletching *Chich* 71-93; Chapl Wivelsfield Green Hospice 91-93; rtd 93; Perm to Offic *Chich* from 93. *Fernbank, 36 Olive Meadow, Uckfield TN22 1QY* Tel (01825) 760663

ELSON, Sharon Anne. b 50. WEMTC 99. **d** 00 **p** 01. OLM Heref St Pet w St Owen and St Jas *Heref* from 00. *26 Craig House, Sudbury Avenue, Hereford HR1 1XU* Tel (01432) 370417 Mobile 07718-481318

ELSTOB, Stephen William. b 57. Sarum & Wells Th Coll. **d** 86 **p** 87. C Sunderland Springwell w Thorney Close *Dur* 86-88; C Upholland *Liv* 88-89; TV 89-96; V Cinnamon Brow from 96. *The Vicarage, 1 Briers Close, Fearnhead, Warrington WA2 0DN* Tel (01925) 823108

ELSTON, James Ian. b 70. City Univ BSc95. SEITE 01. **d** 04 **p** 05. NSM Old St Pancras *Lon* from 04. *8 Mansfield Road, London NW3 2HN* Tel (020) 7482 4056 E-mail jamesielston@aol.com

ELSTON, Philip Herbert. b 35. RD80 and Bar 90. Leeds Univ MA76 K Coll Lon AKC63 Leic Coll of Educn CertEd67. St Boniface Warminster 63. **d** 64 **p** 65. C Thurnby Lodge *Leic* 64-66; Hon C 66-67; Chapl RNR 67-90; Chapl Malosa Sch Malawi 68-75; Hon C Far Headingley St Chad *Ripon* 75-79; V Knowl Hill w Littlewick *Ox* 79-84; Chapl RN Sch Haslemere 85-89; C Felpham w Middleton *Chich* 89-90; Asst S Regional Dir Miss to Seamen 91-93; Dep S Regional Dir 93-97; S Regional Dir 97-00; Perm to Offic *Win* from 93; *Cant* 94-00; *Chich* from 97; Corps Chapl Sea Cadet Corps 83-95; rtd 00; Hon C Witchampton, Stanbridge and Long Crichel etc *Sarum* 00-04; Hon Chapl Miss to Seafarers from 00. *East Farm Cottage, Dinton Road, Wylye, Warminster BA12 0RE*

ELTON, Canon Derek Hurley. b 31. Lon Univ BSc52. Wycliffe Hall Ox 53. **d** 55 **p** 56. C Ashton-on-Ribble St Andr *Blackb* 55-57; India 58-70; R Wickmere w Lt Barningham and Itteringham *Nor* 71-79; R Lt w Gt Ellingham 79-83; P-in-c Rockland All SS and St Andr w St Pet 81-83; R Lt w Gt Ellingham w Rockland 83-88; Chapl Wayland Hosp Norfolk 84-88; Miss to Seamen 89-98; Algeria 89-94; Eritrea 94-98; rtd 96; Perm to Offic *Nor* from 00. *22 Alfred Road, Cromer NR27 9AN* Tel (01263) 511730 E-mail jedclef@paston.co.uk

ELTRINGHAM, Mrs Fiona Ann. b 48. CertEd69. NEOC 86. **d** 89 **p** 94. Par Dn Willington *Newc* 89-92; Chapl HM YOI

Castington 92-97; Chapl HM Pris Dur from 97. *HM Prison Durham, Old Elvet, Durham DH1 3HU* Tel 0191-386 2621 Fax 386 2524

ELVERSON, Ronald Peter Charles. b 50. St Edm Hall Ox BA73 MA86. St Jo Coll Nottm 84. **d** 86 **p** 87. C Whitnash *Cov* 86-90; V Dunchurch 90-01; R Dersingham w Anmer and Shernborne *Nor* 01-05; P-in-c Ore Ch Ch *Chich* from 05. *5 Cookson Gardens, Hastings TN35 5QH* Tel (01424) 715193
E-mail ronelverson@theelversons.fsnet.co.uk

ELVEY, Ms Charlotte Evanthia. b 44. St Anne's Coll Ox BA66 Bris Univ CertEd67. S'wark Ord Course 91. **d** 94 **p** 95. C Sydenham St Bart *S'wark* 94-98; P-in-c Worcester Park Ch Ch w St Phil 98-03; V from 03. *The Vicarage, 1E Lindsay Road, Worcester Park KT4 8LF* Tel (020) 8337 1327
E-mail c.elvey@btinternet.com

ELVIN, Jonathan Paul Alistair. b 65. Bris Univ BSc90 Fitzw Coll Cam BA94. Ridley Hall Cam CTM95. **d** 95 **p** 96. C Gravesend St Geo *Roch* 95-98; C Ex St Leon w H Trin *Ex* from 98. *63 Cedars Road, Exeter EX2 4NB* Tel and fax (01392) 432607
E-mail jonnyelvin@aol.com

ELVY, Canon Peter David. b 38. Lon Univ BA62 Fitzw Ho Cam BA64 MA68 Edin Univ PhD95. Ridley Hall Cam. **d** 65 **p** 66. C Herne *Cant* 65-66; C New Addington 66-68; C Addiscombe St Mildred 69-71; Youth Chapl *Chelmsf* 71-80; V Gt Burstead 75-92; Can Chelmsf Cathl 80-92; V Chelsea All SS *Lon* 92-05; Can Ughelli from 98; Preb St Paul's Cathl *Lon* from 05; rtd 05; Perm to Offic *Lon* from 05. *2 Honiton Mansions, 145 Kings Road, London SW3 5TU* Tel 07941-318889 (mobile)
E-mail peterelvy@compuserve.com

ELWIN, Ernest John. b 31. Selw Coll Cam BA54 MA58. Ridley Hall Cam 54. **d** 56 **p** 57. C Wandsworth All SS *S'wark* 56-59; C Harlow New Town w Lt Parndon *Chelmsf* 59-61; Asst Teacher Tidworth Down Sch Dorset 61-63; V Soundwell *Bris* 63-66; Asst Teacher Seldown Sch Dorset 66-68; Wareham Modern Sch 68-69; Perm to Offic *Sarum* from 67; Lect S Dorset Tech Coll Weymouth 70-85; Weymouth Coll 85-88; Sub Chapl HM Youth Cust Cen Portland from 93. *4 Portesham Hill, Portesham, Weymouth DT3 4EU* Tel (01305) 871358

ELWIS, Malcolm John. b 42. Melbourne Univ DipEd74. St Jo Coll Morpeth 69 ACT LTh73. **d** 70 **p** 72. Australia 70-80; Perm to Offic *Chich* from 80; Chapl Hellingly and Amberstone Hosps 88-93; Chapl Eastbourne and Co Healthcare NHS Trust from 93; Sub Chapl HM Pris Lewes 92-04; Chapl from 04. *Puddledock, Boreham Lane, Wartling, Hailsham BN27 1RS* Tel (01323) 833233

ELWOOD, Alan Roy. b 54. Sarum & Wells Th Coll 90. **d** 92 **p** 93. C Street w Walton *B & W* 92-96; V Kingsbury Episcopi w E Lambrook, Hambridge etc from 96. *The Vicarage, Folly Road, Kingsbury Episcopi, Martock TA12 6BH* Tel (01935) 824605

ELY, Nigel Patrick. b 62. Thames Poly BA83 Southn Univ BTh92. Chich Th Coll 89. **d** 92 **p** 93. C Rustington *Chich* 92-93; C Bexhill St Pet 93-96; Chapl St Geo Post 16 Cen *Birm* 96-99; Perm to Offic from 02. *57 Cherry Orchard Road, Birmingham B20 2LD* Tel 0121-554 6340

ELY, Archdeacon of. *See* BEER, The Ven John Stuart

ELY, Bishop of. *See* RUSSELL, The Rt Revd Anthony John

ELY, Dean of. *See* CHANDLER, The Very Revd Michael John

EMBERTON, John Nicholas. b 45. FCA69. Oak Hill NSM Course 85. **d** 88 **p** 89. NSM Purley Ch Ch *S'wark* 88-94; Vineyard Min Internat (UK) from 96. *49 Oakwood Avenue, Purley CR8 1AR* Tel (020) 8668 2684

EMBLETON, Harold. b 21. Ch Coll Cam BA47 MA52. Qu Coll Birm 47. **d** 49 **p** 50. C Kidderminster St Mary *Worc* 49-52; CF (TA) 50-52; C Wimbledon *S'wark* 52-53; Chapl RN 53-76; QHC 74-76; V Bognor *Chich* 76-84; RD Arundel and Bognor 77-82; V Skirwith, Ousby and Melmerby w Kirkland *Carl* 84-87; rtd 87; Perm to Offic *Carl* 87-93; Perm to Offic *Chich* from 93. *Flat 3, 7 Chatsworth Gardens, Eastbourne BN20 7JP* Tel (01323) 411426

EMBLIN, Richard John. b 48. BEd71 MA81. S Dios Minl Tr Scheme 83. **d** 86 **p** 87. C S w N Hayling *Portsm* 86-89; P-in-c Wootton 89-95; V Cowes H Trin and St Mary from 95; RD W Wight from 01. *The Vicarage, Church Road, Cowes PO31 8HA* Tel (01983) 292509 E-mail cowesvic@yahoo.com

EMBRY, Miss Eileen Margaret. b 38. Westf Coll Lon BA60 Bris Univ DipSS62 Lon Univ BD71. Lon Bible Coll DipTh67. **dss** 81 **d** 87 **p** 94. Lect Trin Coll Bris 71-83; Bishopsworth *Bris* 83-89; Par Dn 87-89; Tutor Trin Coll Bris 91-95; rtd 95; Perm to Offic *Bris* 91-98 and *B & W* from 98. *14 Saxby Close, Clevedon BS21 7YF* Tel (01275) 343533

EMERSON, Arthur Edward Richard. b 24. Lich Th Coll 69. **d** 72 **p** 73. C Barton upon Humber *Linc* 72-74; V Chapel St Leonards 75-88; P-in-c Hogsthorpe 77-88; V Chapel St Leonards w Hogsthorpe 88-91; rtd 91; Perm to Offic *Linc* from 91. *47 Highfields, Nettleham, Lincoln LN2 2SZ* Tel (01522) 754175

EMERSON, Mrs Jan Vivien. b 44. S Dios Minl Tr Scheme 89. **d** 92 **p** 95. NSM Chich St Paul and St Pet *Chich* 92-94; NSM Bosham from 94. *Lea-Rig, Crede Lane, Bosham, Chichester PO18 8PD* Tel (01243) 574948

EMERTON, Andrew Neil. b 72. York Univ BSc93 Qu Coll Ox DPhil96 Anglia Poly Univ BTh05. Ridley Hall Cam 02. **d** 05. C Brompton H Trin w Onslow Square St Paul *Lon* from 05. *St Paul's Church Flat, Onslow Square, London SW7 3NX* Tel 07956-500787 (mobile)

EMERTON, Prof John Adney. b 28. CCC Ox BA50 MA54 CCC Cam MA55 BD60 St Jo Coll Cam DD73 Edin Univ Hon DD77 FBA79. Wycliffe Hall Ox 50. **d** 52 **p** 53. C Birm Cathl *Birm* 52-53; Asst Lect Th Birm Univ 52-53; Lect Hebrew and Aramaic Dur Univ 53-55; Lect Div Cam Univ 55-62; Fell St Pet Coll Ox 62-68; Reader in Semitic Philology Ox Univ 62-68; Regius Prof Hebrew Cam Univ 68-95; Fell St Jo Coll Cam from 70; Hon Can Jerusalem from 84; Perm to Offic *Ely* from 98. *34 Gough Way, Cambridge CB3 9LN* Tel (01223) 363219

EMERY, Ms Karen Maureen. b 53. R Holloway Coll Lon BA74. St Alb Minl Tr Scheme 88. **d** 92 **p** 94. Par Dn Royston *St Alb* 92-94; C 94-96; TV Chipping Barnet w Arkley 96-02; P-in-c Heddon-on-the-Wall *Newc* from 02; Chapl Northumbria Police from 02. *St Andrew's Vicarage, The Towne Gate, Heddon-on-the-Wall, Newcastle upon Tyne NE15 0DT* Tel (01661) 853142

EMM, Robert Kenneth. b 46. K Coll Lon BD68 AKC68. **d** 69 **p** 70. C Hammersmith SS Mich and Geo White City Estate CD *Lon* 69-72; C Keynsham *B & W* 72-75; C Yeovil 75-80; TV Gt Grimsby St Mary and St Jas *Linc* 80-85; R N Thoresby 85-94; R Grainsby 85-94; V Waithe 85-94; R The North-Chapel Parishes from 94. *The Rectory, Church Lane, North Thoresby, Grimsby DN36 5QG* Tel and fax (01472) 840029
E-mail bob@bobemm.demon.co.uk

EMMEL, Canon Malcolm David. b 32. Qu Coll Birm DipTh58. **d** 58 **p** 59. C Hessle *York* 58-62; Canada 62-66; V Catterick *Ripon* 66-73; V Pateley Bridge and Greenhow Hill 73-77; P-in-c Middlesmoor w Ramsgill 76-77; V Upper Nidderdale 77-88; RD Ripon 79-86; Hon Can Ripon Cathl 84-97; R Bedale 88-97; P-in-c Leeming 88-97; rtd 97; Perm to Offic *Bradf* from 98. *29 Greystone Close, Burley in Wharfedale, Ilkley LS29 7RS* Tel (01943) 865047

EMMERSON, Peter Barrett. b 29. Fitzw Ho Cam BA54 MA58. Tyndale Hall Bris 50. **d** 54 **p** 57. Canada 54-58; V Fazakerley St Nath *Liv* 59-64; Distr Sec BFBS (Northd and Dur) 64-70; Distr Sec BFBS (Warks, Staffs and Birm) 70-74; W Midl Regional Sec BFBS 72-74; Hon C Boldmere *Birm* 71-74; C-in-c Crown E CD *Worc* 74-77; P-in-c Crown E and Rushwick 77-81; R Stoke Prior, Wychbold and Upton Warren 81-93; rtd 93; Perm to Offic *Worc* from 93. *Fir Tree Cottage, Ivy Lane, Fernhill Heath, Worcester WR3 8RW* Tel (01905) 456416
E-mail emmersonpb@beeb.net

✠**EMMERSON, The Rt Revd Ralph.** b 13. AKC38 Lon Univ BD38. Westcott Ho Cam 38. **d** 38 **p** 39 **c** 72. C Leeds St Geo *Ripon* 38-41; C-in-c Seacroft CD 41-48; C Methley 48-49; P-in-c 49-52; R 52-56; P-in-c Mickletown 49-52; R 52-56; V Headingley 56-66; Hon Can Ripon Cathl 64-66; Can Res Ripon Cathl 66-72; Suff Bp Knaresborough 72-79; rtd 79; Asst Bp Ripon and Leeds *Ripon* from 86. *Flat 1, 15 High St Agnes Gate, Ripon HG4 1QR* Tel (01765) 701626

EMMETT, Kerry Charles. b 46. St Jo Coll Dur BA68. St Jo Coll Nottm 71. **d** 73 **p** 74. C Attenborough w Chilwell *S'well* 73-75; C Chilwell 75-76; C Wembley St Jo *Lon* 76-79; V Hanworth St Rich 79-89; R Ravenstone and Swannington *Leic* 89-04; RD Akeley S 97-03; P-in-c Mountsorrel Ch Ch and St Pet from 04. *Christ Church Vicarage, 4 Rothley Road, Mountsorrel, Loughborough LE12 7JU* Tel 0116-230 2235

EMMETT, Thomas. b 40. Chich Th Coll 67. **d** 70 **p** 71. C Shiremoor *Newc* 70-73; C Haltwhistle 73-75; V Newc Ch Ch 75-80; P-in-c Newc St Anne 77-80; V Newc Ch Ch w St Ann 81-87; V Bywell from 87; P-in-c Mickley from 97. *Bywell Vicarage, Meadowfield Road, Stocksfield NE43 7PY* Tel (01661) 842272 Fax as telephone
E-mail tomemmett@toon99.fsnet.co.uk

EMMOTT, David Eugene. b 41. St Chad's Coll Dur BA63. **d** 66 **p** 67. C Bingley H Trin *Bradf* 66-69; C Anfield St Marg *Liv* 69-70; C Kirkby 70-75; Chapl Newc Poly *Newc* 75-78; Hon C Toxteth Park St Marg *Liv* 78-80; TV Upholland 80-88; V Southfields St Barn *S'wark* 88-99; TV Liv Our Lady and St Nic w St Anne *Liv* from 99. *6A Eastern Drive, Liverpool L19 0NB* Tel 0151-281 5493 *or* 236 5287 Fax 236 4118
E-mail davidemmott@livpc.co.uk *or* davidemmott@mac.com

EMMOTT, Douglas Brenton. b 45. K Coll Lon BD78 AKC78 York Univ MA97. Linc Th Coll 79. **d** 80 **p** 81. C Kingston upon Hull St Alb *York* 80-83; V Scarborough St Sav w All SS 83-91; V York St Chad 91-99; V Leeds All So *Ripon* from 99. *All Souls' Vicarage, Blackman Lane, Leeds LS2 9EY* Tel 0113-245 3078 Mobile 07812-852667 E-mail allsouls.leeds@virgin.net

EMMOTT, John Charles Lionel. b 32. SEITE 96. **d** 96 **p** 97. NSM Tenterden St Mich *Cant* 96-02; rtd 02; Perm to Offic *Cant* from 02. *58 Grange Crescent, St Michaels, Tenterden TN30 6DZ* Tel (01580) 762092 E-mail emmott@connectfree.co.uk

EMPEY, Canon Clement Adrian. b 42. TCD BA64 MA68 PhD71. CITC. **d** 74 **p** 75. C Dublin St Ann *D & G* 75-76; I Kells-Inistioge Gp *C & O* 76-84; Preb Tassagard St Patr Cathl Dublin from 82; I Clane w Donadea and Coolcarrigan *M & K* 84-88; Hon Chapl Miss to Seafarers from 88; Sen Chapl Miss to Seamen (Irish Republic) from 97; I Dublin St Ann and St Steph *D & G* 88-01; Treas St Patr Cathl Dublin 89-91; Chan 91-96; Prec 96-01; Chapl Rotunda Hosp from 98; Prin CITC from 01; Prec Ch Ch Cathl Dublin *D & G* from 01. *CITC, Braemor Park, Rathgar, Dublin 14, Irish Republic* Tel (00353) (1) 492 3506 *or* 405 5056 Fax 492 3082 *or* 405 5025 E-mail adrian.emp@eircom.net *or* principal@ireland.edu.anglican.org

✠**EMPEY, The Rt Revd Walton Newcome Francis.** b 34. TCD BA57 Hon FGCM02. K Coll (NS) BD68. **d** 58 **p** 59 **c** 81. C Glenageary *D & G* 58-60; Canada 60-66; Bp's C Grand Falls New Brunswick 60-63; I Madawaska 63-66; I Stradbally *C & O* 66-71; Dean Limerick *L & K* 71-81; I Limerick St Mich 71-81; Preb Taney St Patr Cathl Dublin 73-81; Bp L & K 81-85; Bp M & K 85-96; Abp Dublin *D & G* 96-02; Preb Cualaun St Patr Cathl Dublin 96-02; rtd 02. *Rathmore Lodge, Rathmore, Tullow, Co Carlow, Irish Republic* Tel (00353) (59) 916 1891 E-mail lempey@iol.ie

EMSLEY, John Stobart. b 13. Qu Coll Birm 39. **d** 41 **p** 41. C Norwood St Luke *S'wark* 41-44; C Charlton St Luke w St Paul 44-46; C Ilkley St Marg *Bradf* 46-51; V Bradf St Oswald Chapel Green 51-71; V Yeadon St Andr 71-79; rtd 79. *11 Bishop Garth, Pateley Bridge, Harrogate HG3 5LL* Tel (01423) 711835

EMSON, Stanley George. b 26. Glouc Sch of Min. **d** 89 **p** 90. NSM Cirencester *Glouc* 89-92; NSM Coates, Rodmarton and Sapperton etc 92-96; Perm to Offic 96-04; C-in-c Rodmarton CD from 04. *The School House, 31 Rodmarton, Cirencester GL7 6PE* Tel (01285) 841348

EMTAGE, Miss Susan Raymond. b 34. St Mich Ho Ox 63. **dss** 79 **d** 87 **p** 94. SW Area Sec CPAS Women's Action 75-82; Leic St Chris *Leic* 82-86; Bramerton w Surlingham *Nor* 86-88; C 87-88; C Rockland St Mary w Hellington, Bramerton etc 88-89; Par Dn W Bromwich St Jas and St Paul 89-94; C 94; rtd 94; Hon C Stapleton *Bris* 96-04. *23 Capel Court, The Burgage, Prestbury, Cheltenham GL52 3EL* Tel (01242) 577535 E-mail sue.emtage@ukonline.co.uk

ENDALL, Peter John. b 38. Linc Th Coll 83. **d** 85 **p** 86. C Burley in Wharfedale *Bradf* 85-88; V Thwaites Brow 88-03; RD S Craven 96-02; rtd 03; Hon C Tamworth *Lich* from 04. *The Parsonage, Church Drive, Hopwas, Tamworth B78 3AL* Tel (01827) 54599

ENDEAN, Michael George Devereux. b 33. Ox NSM Course. **d** 84 **p** 85. NSM Wantage Downs *Ox* 84-93. *87 Brookmead Drive, Wallingford OX10 9BH* Tel (01491) 824231

ENDICOTT, Michael John. b 45. **d** 97. NSM Pontnewydd *Mon* 97; NSM The Well Cen from 97. *The Well Centre, Station Road, Pontnewydd, Cwmbran NP44 1NZ* Tel (01633) 483660

ENEVER, John William. b 44. MBE92. Open Univ BA80. NTMTC AdDipPTS97. **d** 97 **p** 98. NSM Waltham H Cross *Chelmsf* 97-02; NSM Gt Ilford St Andr from 02. *St Andrew's Vicarage, St Andrew's Road, Ilford IG1 3PE* Tel (020) 8554 3858 E-mail rosemaryenever@onetel.com

ENEVER, Mrs Rosemary Alice Delande. b 45. Oak Hill Th Coll 86. **d** 88 **p** 94. NSM Gt Ilford St Jo *Chelmsf* 88-94; TV Waltham H Cross 94-02; Asst Area Dean Epping Forest 00-01; V Gt Ilford St Andr from 02. *St Andrew's Vicarage, St Andrew's Road, Ilford IG1 3PE* Tel (020) 8554 3858 E-mail rosemaryenever@onetel.com

ENEVER, Mrs Susan Elizabeth. b 33. WMMTC 87. **d** 92 **p** 94. NSM Rugby St Andr *Cov* 92-97; Perm to Offic *Cov* from 97; *Pet* from 98; and *Worc* from 00. *7 Rocheberie Way, Rugby CV22 6EG* Tel (01788) 813135

ENEVER, Vivian John. b 61. Collingwood Coll Dur BA82 Cam Univ PGCE85 Man Univ BPhil97. Westcott Ho Cam 88. **d** 91 **p** 92. C Gt Crosby St Faith *Liv* 91-95; C Cantril Farm 95-97; TV Halas *Worc* 97-03; TR Newark *S'well* from 03. *The Rectory, 6 Bede House Lane, Newark NG24 1PY* Tel (01636) 704513

ENGEL, Jeffrey Davis. b 38. Man Univ BA59 Liv Univ PGCE60 Keele Univ ADC69 Aston Univ MSc82 FCP83. St Deiniol's Hawarden 86. **d** 89 **p** 90. NSM Formby St Pet *Liv* 89-92; C Prescot 92-94; P-in-c Hale 94-03; Dioc Adv for Past Care and Counselling 94-03; rtd 04. *58 Viceroy Court, Lord Street, Southport PR8 1PW* Tel (01704) 535546 *or* 0151-430 6535

ENGELSEN, Christopher James. b 57. Nottm Univ BTh86. Linc Th Coll 83. **d** 86 **p** 87. C Sprowston *Nor* 86-89; C High Harrogate Ch Ch *Ripon* 89-92; TV Seacroft 92-95; P-in-c Foulsham w Hindolveston and Guestwick *Nor* 95-01; P-in-c Hevingham w Hainford and Stratton Strawless from 01. *The Rectory, Westgate Green, Hevingham, Norwich NR10 5RF* Tel (01603) 754240 E-mail christopher.engelsen@btopenworld.com

ENGLAND (formerly LEFROY), Mrs Kathleen Christine. b 33. Newton Park Coll Bris TCert53. St Mich Ho Ox 56 Trin Coll Bris 90. **d** 90 **p** 02. Personnel Sec SAMS 83-91; Asst Gen Sec 87-92; rtd 92; NSM Eastbourne H Trin *Chich* 90-02; NSM Eastbourne St Jo from 02; Chmn SEAN (Internat) and SOMA (UK) from 91; Dioc Voc Adv from 92. *11 Holywell Close, Eastbourne BN20 7RX* Tel (01323) 640294 E-mail katieengland@macunlimited.net

ENGLAND, Tarie. *See* CARLYON, Mrs Jessie Marguerite Tarie

ENGLAND-SIMON, Haydn Henry. b 57. Llan Dioc Tr Scheme 92. **d** 96 **p** 97. NSM Penydarren *Llan* 96-97; C Caerphilly 97-01; V Pentre from 01. *The Vicarage, 7 Llewellyn Street, Pentre CF41 7BY* Tel (01443) 433651

ENGLER, Mrs Margaret Dorothy. b 44. Lon Univ TCert77. S'wark Ord Course 90. **d** 93 **p** 94. NSM Harlesden All So *Lon* 93-97; Dep Chapl HM Pris Wandsworth 97; Acting Chapl HM Pris Wormwood Scrubs 97-98; Chapl HM Pris High Down 98-04; rtd 04. *Address temp unknown*

ENGLISH, Peter Gordon. b 31. Edin Univ MA55. Ripon Hall Ox 59. **d** 61 **p** 62. C Bingley All SS *Bradf* 61-64; V Cottingley 64-66; Uganda 66-72; rtd 86; Perm to Offic *Sarum* from 96. *9 Carlton Row, Trowbridge BA14 0RJ* Tel (01225) 752243

ENGLISH, Peter Redford. b 26. Ridley Hall Cam 70. **d** 72 **p** 73. C Tyldesley w Shakerley *Man* 72-74; C Worsley 74-76; R Levenshulme St Mark 76-81; R Heytesbury and Sutton Veny *Sarum* 81-91; rtd 91; NSM Redmarley D'Abitot, Bromesberrow w Pauntley etc *Glouc* 91-97; Perm to Offic *Sarum* from 95 and *Ex* from 01. *69 Tyrrell Mead, Sidmouth EX10 9TR* Tel (01395) 513578

ENGLISH, Philip Trevor. b 37. Dur Univ BSc60 FLIA81 MITPA84. Cranmer Hall Dur 60. **d** 62 **p** 63. C Hall Green Ascension *Birm* 62-66; Chapl St Jo Cathl Hong Kong 66-67; V Dorridge *Birm* 67-72; Perm to Offic *Ox* from 04. *Churchlands, Appletree Road, Chipping Warden, Banbury OX17 1LN* Tel (01295) 660222 Mobile 07831-446421 Fax (01295) 660725 E-mail pteifs@aol.com

ENNION, Peter. b 56. Aston Tr Scheme 85 Coll of Resurr Mirfield 87. **d** 89 **p** 90. C Middlewich w Byley *Ches* 89-91; C Aylestone St Andr w St Jas *Leic* 91-92; C Coppenhall *Ches* 92-94; P-in-c Newton in Mottram 94-99; P-in-c Tranmere St Paul w St Luke 99-04; V Torrisholme *Blackb* from 04. *The Ascension Vicarage, 63 Michaelson Avenue, Morecambe LA4 6SF* Tel (01524) 413144

ENNIS, Mrs Lesley. b 47. Bp Lonsdale Coll CertEd68 Open Univ BA84. OLM course 97. **d** 99 **p** 00. NSM Sowerby Bridge w Norland *Wakef* from 99. *26 Springfield, Sowerby Bridge HX6 1AD* Tel (01422) 832747 Mobile 07703-628897 Fax 842747 E-mail lesleyennis@care4free.net

ENNIS, Martin Michael. b 58. Man Univ BSc80 MCollP84. Sarum & Wells Th Coll 87. **d** 89 **p** 90. C Newquay *Truro* 89-92; C Tewkesbury w Walton Cardiff *Glouc* 92-95; P-in-c Brockworth 95-96; V 96-03. *44 Green Acre, Brockworth, Gloucester GL3 4NQ*

ENOCH, William Frederick Palmer. b 30. EMMTC 76. **d** 79 **p** 80. NSM Ilkeston St Mary *Derby* 79-85; P-in-c Ilkeston H Trin 85-95; rtd 95; Perm to Offic *Derby* from 95. *82 Derby Road, Ilkeston DE7 5EZ* Tel 0115-944 3003

ENSOR, Paul George. b 56. Ripon Coll Cuddesdon. **d** 82 **p** 83. C Newington St Mary *S'wark* 82-87; TV Croydon St Jo 87-91; P-in-c Brandon and Santon Downham *St E* 91-92; R Brandon and Santon Downham w Elveden 92-95; V Mitcham St Olave *S'wark* from 95. *St Olave's Vicarage, 22 Church Walk, London SW16 5JH* Tel (020) 8764 2048 E-mail pedrazzini@ukgateway.net

ENSOR, Canon Terence Bryan. b 45. K Coll Lon BD78 AKC78. Westcott Ho Cam 78. **d** 79 **p** 80. C Bermondsey St Hugh CD *S'wark* 79-82; Seychelles 82-85; V Northampton St Benedict *Pet* 85-90; Uruguay 90-93; Fieldworker USPG *Blackb, Bradf, Carl* and *Wakef* 93-96; V Blackb St Jas *Blackb* 96-02; Assoc P Caracas Venezuela 02-03; Hon Can Venezuela and Curazao from 02; TV Ribbleton *Blackb* from 03. *Ascension Vicarage, 450 Watling Street Road, Ribbleton, Preston PR2 6UA* Tel (01772) 700568

ENTICOTT, Ian Peter. b 59. Sheff Univ BA82 St Jo Coll Dur MA00. All Nations Chr Coll DipM87 Cranmer Hall Dur DMS99. **d** 99 **p** 00. C Higher Bebington *Ches* 99-02; P-in-c Kelsall from 02. *St Philip's Vicarage, Chester Road, Kelsall, Tarporley CW6 0SA* Tel (01829) 751472 E-mail ian_enticott@clergy.net

ENTWISTLE, Christopher John. b 47. N Ord Course 79. **d** 82 **p** 83. NSM Colne H Trin *Blackb* 82-84; C Poulton-le-Fylde 84-87; V Blackpool St Paul 87-96; RD Blackpool 94-96; P-in-c Overton 96-01; V Ashton-on-Ribble St Andr from 01; AD Preston from 04. *The Vicarage, 240 Tulketh Road, Ashton-on-Ribble, Preston PR2 1ES* Tel (01772) 726848

ENTWISTLE, Frank Roland. b 37. Dur Univ BA59 DipTh60. Cranmer Hall Dur 59. **d** 61 **p** 62. C Harborne Heath *Birm* 61-65; S Area Sec BCMS 65-66; Educn Sec 66-73; Hon C Wallington H Trin *S'wark* 68-73; UCCF 73-02; Hon C Ware Ch Ch *St Alb* 73-76; Hon C Leic H Trin w St Jo *Leic* 76-02; rtd 02. *Three Gables, Tews Lane, Bickington, Barnstaple EX31 2JU* Tel (01271) 321861 E-mail entwistles@cwcom.net

ENTWISTLE, Howard Rodney. b 36. Ball Coll Ox BA61. Linc Th Coll 61. **d** 63 **p** 64. C Langley St Aid CD *Man* 63-64; C Langley All SS and Martyrs 64-66; V Wythenshawe St Martin 66-73; R Stretford St Matt 73-99; rtd 99. *3 Coombes Avenue, Marple, Stockport SK6 7BW* Tel 0161-427-6294

ENWUCHOLA, Benjamin Ameh. b 56. Lon Bible Coll BA94. **d** 95 **p** 98. NSM S Tottenham St Ann *Lon* 96-99; NSM W

Kilburn St Luke w St Simon and St Jude from 99; Chapl Nigerian Congregation from 99. *82 Keslake Road, London NW6 6DG* Tel and fax (020) 8969 2379 E-mail benwuchola@yahoo.co.uk *or* nigerianchaplaincy@yahoo.co.uk

EPPS, Christopher Derek. b 54. ACII79. Linc Th Coll 95. **d** 95 **p** 96. C Clevedon St Jo *B & W* 95-98; R St John w Millbrook *Truro* 98-03; P-in-c Truro St Geo and St Jo from 03; P-in-c Truro St Paul and St Clem from 03. *St George's Vicarage, St George's Road, Truro TR1 3NR* Tel (01872) 272630 Fax 823559 E-mail frcdepps@btinternet.com

EPPS, Gerald Ralph. b 31. Open Univ BA79. Oak Hill Th Coll 52 K Coll Lon 54. **d** 57 **p** 58. C Slade Green *Roch* 57-60; V Freethorpe w Wickhampton *Nor* 60-70; P-in-c Halvergate w Tunstall 62-67; V 67-70; R Pulham St Mary Magd 70-80; P-in-c Alburgh 76-77; P-in-c Denton 76-77; P-in-c Pulham St Mary V 76-80; R Pulham 80-91; rtd 91; Perm to Offic *Nor* from 91. *10 Lime Close, Harleston IP20 9DG* Tel (01379) 854532

EQUEALL, Canon David Edward Royston. b 41. Open Univ BA. St Mich Coll Llan 68. **d** 71 **p** 72. C Mountain Ash *Llan* 71-74; C Gabalfa 74-77; Chapl Asst Univ Hosp of Wales Cardiff 74-77; Chapl 77-79; Chapl N Gen Hosp Sheff 79-94; Chapl N Gen Hosp NHS Trust Sheff 94-02; Chapl Manager Sheff Teaching Hosps NHS Trust from 02; Hon Can Sheff Cathl *Sheff* from 98. *Northern General Hospital, Herries Road, Sheffield S5 7AU* Tel 0114-271 5056 *or* 243 4343 E-mail david.equeall@sth.nhs.uk

ERIKSSON, Olaf Lennart. b 62. Ridley Hall Cam 03. **d** 05. C Cockerton *Dur* from 05. *213 Brinkburn Road, Darlington DL3 9LE* Tel (01325) 358389

ERLEBACH, Jonathan Bartholomew (Bart). b 77. York Univ BSc99. Oak Hill Th Coll BA05. **d** 05. C Hove Bp Hannington Memorial Ch *Chich* from 05. *47 Nevill Avenue, Hove BN3 7NB* Tel (01273) 739144 Mobile 07714-379836 E-mail bartbev@erlebach.org.uk

ERRIDGE, David John. b 45. Lon Univ DipTh68. Tyndale Hall Bris 66. **d** 69 **p** 70. C Bootle St Matt *Liv* 69-72; C Horwich H Trin *Man* 72-77; R Blackley St Andr 77-00; AD N Man 85-94; V Acomb St Steph *York* from 00. *The Vicarage, 32 Carr Lane, York YO26 5HX* Tel (01904) 798106

ERRINGTON, Mrs Sarah. b 67. UEA BA90. Wycliffe Hall Ox BTh94. **d** 97 **p** 98. C Gateacre *Liv* 97-02; TV Halewood from 02. *22 Kenton Road, Liverpool L26 9TS* Tel 0151-486 1159 E-mail revsarah@fish.co.uk

ESAU, John Owen. b 39. St Mich Coll Llan 93. **d** 95 **p** 96. Min Can St D Cathl *St D* 95-97; V Llanpumsaint w Llanllawddog 97-01; V Cydweli and Llandyfaelog 01-03; R Aberporth w Tremain w Blaenporth and Betws Ifan 03-04; rtd 04. *28 Cwrt y Gloch, Peniel, Carmarthen SA32 7HW* Tel (01267) 220549

ESCOLME, Miss Doreen. b 29. St Jo Coll Nottm 82. **dss** 83 **d** 87 **p** 94. Hunslet Moor St Pet and St Cuth *Ripon* 83-87; C 87-88; Par Dn Wyther Ven Bede 88-94; C 94; rtd 94; Perm to Offic *Ripon* from 94. *6 Heather Gardens, Leeds LS13 4LF* Tel 0113-257 9055

ESCRITT, Canon Margaret Ruth. b 37. Selly Oak Coll IDC62. **d** 87 **p** 94. Dioc Adv for Diaconal Mins *York* 85-91; Hon C Selby Abbey 87-90; C Kexby w Wilberfoss 93-94; Asst Chapl HM Pris Full Sutton 92-94; Chapl HM Pris Everthorpe 95-98; Can and Preb York Minster *York* 95-01; rtd 97; Perm to Offic *York* from 01. *73 Heslington Lane, York YO10 4HN* Tel (01904) 639444

ESCRITT, Michael William. b 35. Qu Coll Birm 64. **d** 67 **p** 68. C Huntington *York* 67-69; Abp's Dom Chapl 69-72; V Bishopthorpe 72-83; V Acaster Malbis 73-83; V Selby Abbey 83-90; TR Haxby w Wigginton 90-98; rtd 98; Perm to Offic *York* from 98. *73 Heslington Lane, York YO10 4HN* Tel (01904) 639444

ESDAILE, Canon Adrian George Kennedy. b 35. Mert Coll Ox BA57 MA61. Wells Th Coll 59. **d** 61 **p** 62. C St Helier *S'wark* 61-64; C Wimbledon 64-68; V Hackbridge and N Beddington 68-80; RD Sutton 76-80; TR Chipping Barnet w Arkley *St Alb* 80-01; RD Barnet 89-94; Hon Can St Alb 94-01; rtd 01; Perm to Offic *S'wark* from 01 and *Guildf* from 02. *29 Hereford Close, Epsom KT18 5DZ* Tel (01372) 723770 E-mail esdaile@fish.co.uk

ESHUN, Daniel Justice. b 69. Cape Coast Univ Ghana BA93 K Coll Lon MA97 PhD00 St Jo Coll Dur MA03. Cranmer Hall Dur 00. **d** 03 **p** 04. C Staines Ch Ch *Lon* from 03. *Peterhouse, 14 Thames Side, Staines TW18 2HA* Tel (01784) 450861 *or* 469155 Mobile 07743-923846 E-mail daniel.j.eshun@talk21.com *or* daniel@stainesparish.com

ESPIN-BRADLEY, Richard John. b 61. Lanc Univ BSc84. Oak Hill Th Coll 93. **d** 95 **p** 96. C Brundall w Braydeston and Postwick *Nor* 95-98; C St Helier *S'wark* 98-02; V Wolverhampton St Luke *Lich* from 02. *St Luke's Vicarage, 122 Goldthorn Hill, Wolverhampton WV2 3HU* Tel (01902) 340261 E-mail richardeb@blueyonder.co.uk

ESSER, Lindsay Percy David. b 53. BA. Oak Hill Th Coll. **d** 84 **p** 85. C Barnsbury St Andr and H Trin w All SS *Lon* 84-87; Chapl Paris St Mich *Eur* 87-90; C Spring Grove St Mary *Lon* 90-95; Mauritius from 95. *The Rectory, St Barnabas Church, Royal Road, Pamplemousses, Mauritius* Tel (00230) 243 3549 E-mail st.barnabas@intnet.mu

ESSEX, Mary Rose. b 50. **d** 02 **p** 03. NSM E and W Leake, Stanford-on-Soar, Rempstone etc *S'well* from 02. *The Rectory, Main Street, Stanford on Soar, Loughborough LE12 5PY* Tel (01509) 215191 E-mail rev.maryessex@btopenworld.com

ETCHELLS, Peter. b 26. Kelham Th Coll 48. **d** 52 **p** 53. C Chesterton St Geo *Ely* 52-55; C Leic St Marg *Leic* 55-58; R Willoughby Waterleys, Peatling Magna etc 58-96; rtd 96. *29 Upperfield Drive, Felixstowe IP11 9LS*

ETCHES, Haigh David. b 45. St Jo Coll Dur BA71 DipTh72. **d** 73 **p** 74. C Whitnash *Cov* 73-77; C Wallingford *Ox* 77-79; C Wallingford w Crowmarsh Gifford etc 79-83; P-in-c Bearwood 83-86; R from 86. *The Rectory, 6 St Catherine's Close, Sindlesham, Wokingham RG41 5BZ* Tel 0118-979 4364

ETHERIDGE, Canon Richard Thomas. b 32. Lon Univ BD62. ALCD61. **d** 62 **p** 63. C Wilmington *Roch* 62-65; C Rainham 65-69; V Langley St Jo *Birm* 69-01; P-in-c Oldbury 83-01; P-in-c Langley St Mich 95-01; Hon Can Birm Cathl 97-01; rtd 01; Perm to Offic *Birm* from 01 and *Worc* from 02. *23 Scobell Close, Pershore, Worcester WR10 1QJ* Tel (01386) 554745

ETHERIDGE, Terry. b 44. Wells Th Coll 68. **d** 70 **p** 71. C Barrow St Jo *Carl* 70-73; C Wilmslow *Ches* 73-76; V Knutsford St Cross 76-85; R Malpas and Threapwood from 85. *The Rectory, Church Street, Malpas SY14 8PP* Tel (01948) 860209

ETHERINGTON, Mrs Ferial Mary Gould. b 44. FILEx83. St Alb Minl Tr Scheme 86. **d** 93 **p** 94. NSM Luton St Chris Round Green *St Alb* 93-04; Selection Sec and Co-ord for OLM Min Division 97-04; rtd 04; Perm to Offic *Carl* from 04. *Northview, Durdar, Carlisle CA2 4TX* Tel (01228) 537676 E-mail ferial.etherington@virgin.net

ETHERINGTON, Robert Barry. b 37. Man Univ BA62. Linc Th Coll 62. **d** 64 **p** 65. C Linc St Jo *Linc* 64-67; C Frodingham 67-69; V Reepham 69-78; Ind Chapl 70-78; Ind Chapl *St Alb* 78-88; V Luton St Chris Round Green 88-04; RD Luton 98-02; rtd 04. *Northview, Durdar, Carlisle CA2 4TX* Tel (01228) 537676

ETHERTON, Geoffrey Robert. b 74. Univ of Cen England in Birm BMus96. Trin Coll Bris BA01. **d** 02 **p** 03. C Trentham and Hanford *Lich* 02-03; C Hanley H Ev from 03. *45 The Parkway, Hanley, Stoke-on-Trent ST1 3BB* Tel (01782) 874194 E-mail geoffetherton@theparkway.org.uk

ETTERLEY, Peter Anthony Gordon. b 39. Kelham Th Coll 63 Wells Th Coll 66. **d** 68 **p** 69. C Gillingham St Aug *Roch* 68-71; Papua New Guinea 71-80; V Cleeve w Chelvey and Brockley *B & W* 80-84; V Seaton Hirst *Newc* 84-86; TR 86-96; P-in-c Longframlington w Brinkburn 96-00; V 00-04; P-in-c Felton 96-00; V 00-04; rtd 04. *4 Clive Terrace, Alnwick NE66 1LQ* Tel (01665) 606252 E-mail peter.etterley@boltblue.com

ETTRICK, Peter Alured. b 14. OBE67 TD56 and Bars. Ch Coll Cam BA36 MA41. Qu Coll Birm 36. **d** 37 **p** 38. C Werneth *Man* 37-39; P-in-c Blackley St Pet 39-40; P-in-c Ashton Ch Ch 40-42; CF (EC) 42-47; R Heaton Norris Ch w All SS *Man* 47-52; Sen CF (TA) 48-62; Dep Asst Chapl Gen 62-66; R Flixton St Mich *Man* 52-61; V Gaydon w Chadshunt *Cov* 61-65; Asst Dir RE 61-65; V Radford 65-70; V Bisley *Glouc* 70-79; rtd 79; Perm to Offic *Glouc* from 80. *Meiktila, The Ridge, Bussage, Stroud GL6 8BB* Tel (01453) 883272

EUROPE, Bishop of Gibraltar in. *See* ROWELL, The Rt Revd Douglas Geoffrey

EUROPE, Suffragan Bishop in. *See* HAMID, The Rt Revd David

EUSTICE, Peter Lafevre. b 32. AKC56. **d** 57 **p** 58. C Finsbury Park St Thos *Lon* 57-60; C Redruth *Truro* 60-63; V Treslothan 63-71; V Falmouth All SS 71-76; R St Stephen in Brannel 76-97; rtd 97; Perm to Offic *Truro* from 97. *21 Gloucester Avenue, Carlyon Bay, St Austell PL25 3PT* Tel (01726) 817343

EVA, Canon Owen Vyvyan. b 17. MBE83. Selw Coll Cam BA39 MA43. Ridley Hall Cam 46. **d** 47 **p** 48. C Garston *Liv* 47-51; V Edge Hill St Cath 51-57; Hong Kong 57-61; P-in-c Warrington H Trin *Liv* 61-62; R Halewood 62-83; TR 83-86; RD Farnworth 71-81; Hon Can Liv Cathl 74-86; rtd 86; Perm to Offic *Ches* and *Liv* from 87. *10 Saddler's Rise, Norton, Runcorn WA7 6PG* Tel (01928) 717119

EVANS, Miss Alison Jane. b 66. Sheff Univ BSc87 Bris Univ PGCE93. Trin Coll Bris BA04. **d** 04 **p** 05. C Finham *Cov* from 04. *65 Cotswold Drive, Coventry CV3 6EZ* Tel (024) 7641 0327 E-mail aevans@talktalk.net

EVANS, The Ven Alun Wyn. b 47. Down Coll Cam BA70 MA73. Cuddesdon Coll 70. **d** 72 **p** 73. C Bargoed w Brithdir *Llan* 72-74; C Bargoed and Deri w Brithdir 74-75; C Coity w Nolton 75-77; V Cwmavon 77-81; Warden of Ords 80-81; V Llangynwyd w Maesteg 81-86; Prov Officer for Soc Resp 86-93; V Cardiff Ch Ch 93-99; V Swansea St Mary w H Trin *S & B* 99-00; TR Cen Swansea 00-04; Can Res Brecon Cathl 00-04; V Cynwil Elfed and Newchurch *St D* from 04; Adn Carmarthen from 04. *The Vicarage, Cynwyl Elfed, Carmarthen SA33 6TU* Tel (01267) 281605

EVANS, Mrs Amanda Jane. b 49. Lon Univ CertEd70 W Sussex Inst of HE DAES86. STETS Dip Chr Th and Min 97. **d** 97 **p** 98. C Faversham *Cant* 97-01; TV Whitstable from 01. *The Rectory,*

69 Swalecliffe Court Drive, Whitstable CT5 2NF Tel (01227) 792826 E-mail amanda@a-j-evans.fsnet.co.uk

EVANS, Andrew. *See* EVANS, John Andrew

EVANS, Andrew. b 57. Southn Univ BEd80. S Dios Minl Tr Scheme 88. **d** 91 **p** 92. NSM Cricklade w Latton *Bris* 91-97; C Yatton Keynell 97-99; TV By Brook 99-00; R Hullavington, Norton and Stanton St Quintin from 00; Bp's Adv for Rural Min from 00; OCF from 00. *The Rectory, 1 Rectory Close, Stanton St Quintin, Chippenham SN14 6DT* Tel and fax (01666) 837187 Mobile 07931-616329 E-mail andrew@evansa63.fsnet.co.uk

EVANS, Andrew Eric. b 58. Sheff Univ LLB80 Solicitor 83. Trin Coll Bris 01. **d** 03 **p** 04. C Gt Bookham *Guildf* from 03. *19 The Lorne, Great Bookham, Leatherhead KT23 4JY* Tel (01372) 453729 E-mail andrew@evansabove.supanet.com

EVANS, Mrs Anne. b 47. **d** 05. OLM Loppington w Newtown *Lich* from 05. *The Fields Farm, Welshampton, Ellesmere SY12 0NP* Tel (01948) 710206 E-mail aldersal@chesternet.co.uk

EVANS, Canon Anthony Nigel. b 53. Nottm Univ BA74 Fitzw Coll Cam BA76. Westcott Ho Cam 74. **d** 77 **p** 78. C Sneinton St Cypr *S'well* 77-80; C Worksop Priory 80-83; V Nottingham St Geo w St Jo 83-88; R Ordsall 88-95; P-in-c Sutton in Ashfield St Mary from 95; AD Newstead from 01; Hon Can S'well Minster from 04. *St Mary's Vicarage, Church Avenue, Sutton-in-Ashfield NG17 2EB* Tel (01623) 554509 E-mail frtony@care4free.net

EVANS, Ashley Francis. b 58. Birm Univ BA79. WEMTC 00. **d** 03 **p** 04. C Kington w Huntington, Old Radnor, Kinnerton etc *Heref* from 03. *5 Gravel Hill Drive, Kington HR5 3AE* Tel (01544) 231821 Mobile 07763-070177 E-mail ashley@castlefrome.freeserve.co.uk

EVANS, Aylmer. *See* EVANS, David Aylmer

EVANS, Barrie. *See* EVANS, The Ven John Barrie

EVANS, Brian. b 34. Univ of Wales (Cardiff) DipTh58 Open Univ BA86. St Deiniol's Hawarden 70. **d** 71 **p** 72. C Porthkerry *Llan* 71-72; C Barry All SS 72-75; V Abercynon 75-82; V Pendoylan w Welsh St Donats 82-87; R Maentwrog w Trawsfynydd *Ban* 87-99; rtd 99; Perm to Offic *Ban* from 99. *Madryn, 46 Glan Ysgethin, Talybont LL43 2BB* Tel (01341) 247965

EVANS, Caroline Mary. b 46. Ban Coll CertEd69 Liv Univ Dip Counselling 96. St Jo Coll Nottm DipTh86 Selly Oak Coll 72. **d** 86 **p** 97. C Llanbeblig w Caernarfon and Betws Garmon etc *Ban* 86-88; Dn-in-c Bodedern w Llechgynfarwy and Llechylched etc 88-97; V 97; RD Llifon and Talybolion 96-97; R Llanfairfechan w Aber from 97. *The Rectory, Aber Road, Llanfairfechan LL33 0HN* Tel (01248) 680591

EVANS, Charles Wyndham. b 28. Univ of Wales (Ban) BA49 St Cath Soc Ox BA51 MA55. St Steph Ho Ox 49. **d** 52 **p** 53. C Denbigh *St As* 52-56; Lic to Offic *St D* 56-79; Chapl Llandovery Coll 56-67; Chapl and Sen Lect Trin Coll Carmarthen 67-79; V Llanrhaeadr-yng-Nghinmeirch and Prion *St As* 79-98; Chapl Ruthin Sch 79-86; Dioc RE Adv *St As* 82-98; Tutor St Deiniol's Lib Hawarden 84-86; RD Denbigh *St As* 84-98; rtd 98. *Parciau, 12 The Close, Llanfairfechan, Conwy LL33 0AG* Tel (01248) 681766

EVANS, Prof Christopher Francis. b 09. CCC Cam BA32 MA38 Ox Univ MA48 Southn Univ Hon DLitt77 Glas Univ Hon DD85 FBA91 FKC70. Linc Th Coll 33. **d** 34 **p** 35. C Southampton St Barn *Win* 34-38; Tutor Linc Th Coll 38-44; Chapl and Lect Linc Dioc Tr Coll 44-48; Chapl and Fell CCC Ox 48-58; Select Preacher Ox Univ 55-57; Select Preacher Cam Univ 59-60; Lightfoot Prof Div Dur Univ 58-62; Can Res Dur Cathl *Dur* 58-62; Prof NT Studies K Coll Lon 62-77; rtd 77. *4 Church Close, Cuddesdon, Oxford OX44 9EX* Tel (01865) 874406

EVANS, Christopher Idris. b 51. Chich Th Coll 74. **d** 77 **p** 78. C Gelligaer *Llan* 77-80; C St Andrews Major w Michaelston-le-Pit 80-81; V Llangeinor 81-87; V Watlington w Pyrton and Shirburn *Ox* 87-97; R Icknield from 97. *The Vicarage, Hill Road, Watlington OX49 5AD* Tel (01491) 612494 E-mail icknield@aol.com

EVANS, Christopher Jonathan. b 43. AKC67 AKC88. **d** 68 **p** 69. C Wednesfield St Thos *Lich* 68-71; C Dorridge *Birm* 71-74; V Marston Green 74-81; V Acocks Green 81-86; RD Yardley 84-86; V Hill 86-88; Area Officer COPEC Housing Trust 88-91; V Harborne St Pet from 91. *St Peter's Vicarage, Old Church Road, Birmingham B17 0BB* Tel 0121-681 5446 *or* 681 1940 Fax 681 9186 E-mail jo@evansj84.fsnet.co.uk

EVANS, Claire Elizabeth Phoebe. b 78. St Steph Ho Ox BTh02. **d** 02 **p** 03. C Whitchurch *Llan* 02-04; Lic to Offic from 04. *Address temp unknown* Tel 07813-767956 (mobile) E-mail claireevans2k@hotmail.com

EVANS, Clive Richard. b 49. WEMTC 99. **d** 00 **p** 01. OLM Heref S Wye *Heref* from 00. *14 St Vincents Cross, Lower Bullingham, Hereford HR2 6EL* Tel (01432) 270838 *or* 353717 E-mail s.wye.team.ministry@talk21.com

EVANS, Clive Roger. b 59. Worc Coll Ox BA80 MA84. St Jo Coll Nottm 94. **d** 94 **p** 95. C Barton Seagrave w Warkton *Pet* 94-97; V Long Buckby w Watford from 97; P-in-c W Haddon w Winwick and Ravensthorpe from 03; RD Brixworth from 01. *The Vicarage, 10 Hall Drive, Long Buckby, Northampton NN6 7QU* Tel (01327) 842909 Fax as telephone E-mail clive@evans1359.freeserve.co.uk

EVANS, Canon Colin Rex. b 24. Reading Univ BA49. Linc Th Coll. **d** 57 **p** 58. C Boultham *Linc* 57-59; C Linc St Nic w St Jo Newport 59-62; V Linc St Mary-le-Wigford w St Martin 62-66; P-in-c Linc St Faith 63-66; R Bassingham 66-74; V Aubourn w Haddington 66-74; V Carlton-le-Moorland w Stapleford 66-74; R Skinnand 66-74; R Thurlby w Norton Disney 66-74; RD Graffoe 69-74; RD Elloe E 74-89; Can and Preb Linc Cathl 74-89; V Holbeach 74-89; rtd 90; Hon C Dawlish *Ex* 90-97; RD Kenn 95-97; Perm to Offic from 97. *87 West Cliff Park Drive, Dawlish EX7 9EL* Tel (01626) 865191

EVANS, Daniel Barri. b 70. St Steph Ho Ox 01. **d** 03 **p** 04. C Weymouth H Trin *Sarum* from 03. *Weldon Lodge, 65 Rodwell Road, Weymouth DT4 8QX* Tel (01305) 779088 Mobile 07952-679760 E-mail mary-dan.evans@virgin.net

EVANS, Miss Daphne Gillian. b 41. Bible Tr Inst Glas 67 Trin Coll Bris IDC75. **dss** 83 **d** 87. Wenlock *Heref* 83-88; TD 87-88; rtd 88. *Address temp unknown*

EVANS, Canon David. b 37. Keble Coll Ox BA60 MA65 Lon Univ BD64. Wells Th Coll 62. **d** 64 **p** 65. Min Can Brecon Cathl *S & B* 64-68; C Brecon w Battle 64-68; C Swansea St Mary and H Trin 68-71; Chapl Univ of Wales (Swansea) 68-71; Bp's Chapl for Samaritan and Soc Work *Birm* 71-75; Jt Gen Sec Samaritans 75-84; Gen Sec 84-89; R Heyford w Stowe Nine Churches *Pet* 89-96; R Heyford w Stowe Nine Churches and Flore etc 96-01; Chapl Northants Police 89-01; RD Daventry 96-00; Can Pet Cathl 97-01; rtd 01; Perm to Offic *Ex* from 01. *Curlew River, The Strand, Starcross, Exeter EX6 8PA* Tel (01626) 891712

EVANS, David. b 37. Open Univ BA73 FRSA95. St Mich Coll Llan 65. **d** 67 **p** 68. C Swansea St Pet *S & B* 67-70; C St Austell *Truro* 70-75; R Purley *Ox* 75-90; RD Bradfield 85-90; R Bryanston Square St Mary w St Marylebone St Mark *Lon* 90-99; P-in-c St Marylebone Ch Ch 90-91; R Nuthurst and Mannings Heath *Chich* from 99. *The Rectory, Nuthurst Street, Nuthurst, Horsham RH13 6LH* Tel (01403) 891449

EVANS, David Aylmer. b 28. Lon Univ CertEd62. St D Coll Lamp BA49 LTh51. **d** 51 **p** 52. C Brecon St David w Llanspyddid and Llanilltyd *S & B* 51-53; C Colwyn Bay *St As* 53-54; C Macclesfield St Mich *Ches* 54-56; V Lostock Gralam 56-59; Chapl Endsleigh Sch 59-65; Wokingham Gr Sch 65-72; Cllr S Molton Sch and Community Coll 73-87; V Middlezoy and Othery and Moorlinch *B & W* 87-93; rtd 93; Perm to Offic *Ex* and *B & W* from 94. *2 Higher Mead, Hemyock, Cullompton EX15 3QH* Tel (01823) 680974

EVANS (or BURTON EVANS), David Burton. b 35. Open Univ BA87 Goldsmiths' Coll Lon BMus93. K Coll Lon 58 Edin Th Coll 60. **d** 62 **p** 63. C Leeds St Hilda *Ripon* 62-63; C Cross Green St Sav and St Hilda 63-67; Min Can Dur Cathl *Dur* 67-71; Prebendal Sch Chich and PV Chich Cathl 71-74; R Lynch w Iping Marsh *Chich* 74-79; V Easebourne 79-86; Chapl K Edw VII Hosp Midhurst 77-86; R St Mich Cornhill w St Pet le Poer etc *Lon* 86-96; rtd 96; Pau *Eur* 96-01. *7 Forbes Place, King George Gardens, Chichester PO19 6LF* Tel (01243) 773266

EVANS, David Elwyn. b 43. St Mich Coll Llan 71. **d** 73 **p** 74. C Llandybie *St D* 73-75; C Llanelli 75-78; V Tre-lech a'r Betws w Abernant and Llanwinio 78-02; rtd 02. *8 Ger y Llan, The Parade, Carmarthen SA31 1LY*

EVANS, David Frederick Francis. b 35. Univ of Wales BSc59. Wells Th Coll 59. **d** 61 **p** 62. C Eltham St Jo *S'wark* 61-64; C Banbury *Ox* 64-69; V Brize Norton and Carterton 69-73; V Tilehurst St Geo 73-84; V Lydney w Aylburton *Glouc* 84-95; V Lydney 95-02; RD Forest S 90-95; Chapl Severn NHS Trust 94-02; rtd 02. *2 Bodforis, Bethesda, Bangor LL57 3PU* Tel (01248) 601994

EVANS, David John. b 49. Univ of Wales (Ban) BSc72 Bath Univ CertEd73 Leeds Univ DipTh77. Coll of Resurr Mirfield 75. **d** 78 **p** 79. C Wandsworth St Anne *S'wark* 78-81; C Angell Town St Jo 81-82; TV Catford (Southend) and Downham 82-90; P-in-c Broughton *Ely* 90-91; P-in-c Somersham w Pidley and Oldhurst 90-91; R 91-98; R Hilgay from 98; R Southery from 98. *The Rectory, Church Road, Hilgay, Downham Market PE38 0JL* Tel (01366) 384418 E-mail g4ynd@aol.com *or* david.evans@ely.anglican.org

EVANS, David Leslie Bowen. b 28. Univ of Wales (Lamp) BA52 LTh54. **d** 54 **p** 55. C Cardigan *St D* 54-57; C Llangathen w Llanfihangel Cilfargen 57-58; C Betws w Ammanford 58-60; V Betws Ifan 60-64; V Burry Port and Pwll 64-76; V Cardiff Dewi Sant *Llan* 76-86; Asst Chapl HM Pris Cardiff 76-86; V Llan-llwch w Llangain and Llangynog *St D* 86-95; Can St D Cathl 89-90; rtd 95. *35 Ger y Capel, Llangain, Carmarthen SA33 5AQ* Tel (01267) 241916

EVANS, David Richard. b 47. St Steph Ho Ox 68. **d** 72 **p** 73. C Cardiff St Jo *Llan* 72-76; PV Llan Cathl 76-80; V Cleeve Prior and The Littletons *Worc* from 80. *The Vicarage, South Littleton, Evesham WR11 8TJ* Tel and fax (01386) 830397 E-mail father.richard@tesco.net

✠**EVANS, The Rt Revd David Richard John.** b 38. G&C Coll Cam BA63 MA66. Clifton Th Coll 63. **d** 65 **p** 66 **c** 78. C Enfield Ch Ch Trent Park *Lon* 65-68; SAMS Argentina 69-77; Peru 77-88; Bp Peru 78-88; Bp Bolivia 82-88; Asst Bp Bradf 88-93; Gen Sec SAMS 93-03; Hon Asst Bp Chich 94-97; Hon Asst Bp Roch 95-97; Hon Asst Bp Birm 97-03; rtd 03; Hon Asst Bp Cov from 03; Hon C Alderminster and Halford from 03; Hon C Butlers Marston and the Pillertons w Ettington from 03. *The Vicarage, Alderminster, Stratford-upon-Avon CV37 8PE* Tel (01789) 450198 E-mail bishop.drjevans@virgin.net

EVANS, David Russell. b 36. Liv Univ BA57. Ripon Hall Ox 59. **d** 61 **p** 62. C Netherton CD *Liv* 61-65; Chapl Canon Slade Sch Bolton 65-93; Lic Preacher *Man* from 65; Perm to Offic *Liv* 76-03; rtd 00. *2 Rushford Grove, Bolton BL1 8TD* Tel (01204) 592981

EVANS, David Victor (formerly David John Parker Smith). b 47. Bris Univ Dip Counselling 97. S'wark Ord Course 83. **d** 86 **p** 95. SSF 71-94; Hon C Stepney St Dunstan and All SS *Lon* 86-89; Adult Educn Development Officer 86-89; Guardian Hilfield Friary Dorchester 89-91; Novice Guardian Liv 91-93; Birm 93-94; NSM Southmead *Bris* 94-98; TR Uttoxeter Area *Lich* from 98; RD Uttoxeter 02-04. *The Vicarage, 12 Orchard Close, Uttoxeter ST14 7DZ* Tel (01889) 563651 *or* 562915 E-mail dvictorevans@aol.com

EVANS, Derek. b 38. St As Minl Tr Course 93. **d** 97 **p** 98. NSM Llangollen w Trevor and Llantysilio *St As* 97-00; NSM Corwen and Llangar w Gwyddelwern and Llawrybetws 00-02; NSM Betws Gwerful Goch w Llangwm, Gwyddelwern etc from 02. *Fern Mount, 68 Berwyn Street, Llangollen LL20 8NA* Tel (01978) 861893

EVANS, Canon Derek. b 45. St D Coll Lamp. **d** 68 **p** 69. C Pembroke Dock *St D* 68-74; V Ambleston, St Dogwells, Walton E and Llysyfran 74-78; V Wiston w Ambleston, St Dogwells and Walton E 78-81; V Wiston w Ambleston, St Dogwells, Walton E etc 81-85; R Haverfordwest St Mary and St Thos w Haroldston from 85; Dep Dioc Dir of Educn 92-97; Dir from 97; Can St D Cathl from 99; RD Roose 00-04. *The Rectory, Scarrowscant Lane, Haverfordwest SA61 1EP* Tel and fax (01437) 763170 E-mail derek.evans0@talk21.com

EVANS, Preb Derek Courtenay. b 29. Down Coll Cam BA52 MA56. St Aid Birkenhead 55. **d** 57 **p** 58. C Taunton St Mary *B & W* 57-61; V Trull 61-77; RD Taunton S 72-77; P-in-c Walton 77; R Street 77; Preb Wells Cathl 77-94; R Street w Walton 78-94; RD Glastonbury 79-82; R Greinton 81-93; rtd 94; Perm to Offic *B & W* from 94. *41 Moorham Road, Winscombe BS25 1HS* Tel (01934) 843150

EVANS, Desmond. b 26. Univ of Wales (Lamp) BA48 St Cath Soc Ox BA50 MA54. St Steph Ho Ox 48. **d** 51 **p** 52. C Clydach *S & B* 51-54; V 82-87; Chapl Cranleigh Sch Surrey 54-59; Lic to Offic *Ban* 59-78; St Mary's Coll Ban 59-78; V Llanwrtyd w Llanddulas in Tir Abad etc *S & B* 78-82; RD Builth 79-82; V Abercraf and Callwen 87-95; rtd 95. *26 Palleg Road, Lower Cwmtwrch, Swansea SA9 2QE* Tel (01639) 845389

EVANS, Edward John. b 47. Univ of Wales (Cardiff) DipTh71. St Mich Coll Llan 67. **d** 71 **p** 72. C Llantwit Fardre *Llan* 71-77; R Eglwysilan 77-88; V Laleston w Tythegston and Merthyr Mawr from 88; RD Bridgend 94-04. *The Vicarage, Rogers Lane, Laleston, Bridgend CF32 0LB* Tel and fax (01656) 654254 Mobile 07968-044583 E-mail edward@lal-vicarage.freeserve.co.uk

EVANS, Elaine. *See* EVANS, Jennifer Elaine

EVANS, Ms Elaine. b 63. St Mich Coll Llan BTh02. **d** 02 **p** 03. C Llantwit Major *Llan* 02-05; C Penarth All SS from 05. *84 Coleridge Avenue, Penarth CF64 2SR* Tel (029) 2070 8044

EVANS, Elwyn David. b 36. Keble Coll Ox BA58 MA62. St Steph Ho Ox 58 St Mich Coll Llan 60. **d** 61 **p** 62. C Aberystwyth H Trin *St D* 61-63; C Llanelli St Paul 63-66; C Roath St German *Llan* 66-69; V Crynant 69-78; R Llanilid w Pencoed 79-95; rtd 95; Perm to Offic *Llan* and *S & B* from 95. *23 Christopher Rise, Pontlliw, Swansea SA4 9EN* Tel (01792) 891961

EVANS, Ernest Maurice. b 28. JP70. MIMechE66. St As Minl Tr Course 84. **d** 86 **p** 87. NSM Hope *St As* 86-89; P-in-c Corwen and Llangar w Gwyddelwern and Llawrybetws 89-90; R 90-95; rtd 95; Perm to Offic *Ban* from 97. *43 Cil-y-Graig, Llanfairpwllgwyngyll LL61 5NZ* Tel (01248) 712169 E-mail e.mauriceevans@btinternet.com

EVANS, Evan Walter. b 16. MBE66. St D Coll Lamp BA36. **d** 39 **p** 40. C Narberth *St D* 39-40; C Cardigan 40-42; CF (EC) 42-47; R Didmarton w Oldbury-on-the-Hill and Sopworth *Glouc* 47-52; CF 52-72; Chapl R Hosp Chelsea 72-81; Perm to Offic *St D* from 85. *3 Cilgwyn Row, Llandysul SA44 4BD* Tel (01559) 362275

EVANS, Frank Owen. b 23. Univ of Wales BA44. St D Coll Lamp 44. **d** 46 **p** 63. C Hubberston *St D* 46; C Llanelli 63-81; Hd Master Coleshill Secondary Sch Dyfed 74-82; Hon C Cydweli and Llandyfaelog *St D* 81-82; V Martletwy w Lawrenny and Minwear and Yerbeston 82-87; rtd 87. *35 Stradey Park Avenue, Llanelli SA15 3EG* Tel (01554) 777149

EVANS, Ms Freda Christine. b 48. MBE89. NTMTC 96. **d** 99 **p** 00. C Hampton Hill *Lon* 99-02; V Kingshurst *Birm* from 02. *St Barnabas' Vicarage, 51 Overgreen Drive, Birmingham B37 6EY* Tel 0121-770 3972 Fax as telephone E-mail freda@fish.co.uk

EVANS, Mrs Freda Mary Ann (Frieda). b 54. St D Coll Lamp DipTh96. **d** 00. OLM Malpas *Mon* from 00. *3 The Firs, Malpas, Newport NP20 6YD* Tel (01633) 850600 Mobile 0411-650088 E-mail frieda@evafirs.freeserve.co.uk

EVANS, Frederick James Stephens. b 21. Qu Coll Cam BA42 MA46. St D Coll Lamp LTh44. **d** 44 **p** 45. C Shirley *Birm* 44-47; R Scotter w E Ferry *Linc* 47-65; CF (TA) 48-51; R Chalfont St Peter *Ox* 65-78; V Rustington *Chich* 78-86; rtd 86; Perm to Offic *Chich* from 86. *45 Falmer Avenue, Goring-by-Sea, Worthing BN12 4SY* Tel (01903) 503905

EVANS, Canon Frederick John Margam. b 31. Magd Coll Ox BA53 MA57. St Mich Coll Llan 53. **d** 54 **p** 55. C New Tredegar *Mon* 54-58; C Chepstow 58-60; Asst Chapl United Sheff Hosps 60-62; Chapl Brookwood Hosp Woking 62-70; V Crookham *Guildf* 70-98; RD Aldershot 78-83; Hon Can Guildf Cathl 89-98; rtd 98; Perm to Offic *Guildf* from 98. *4 Radford Close, Farnham GU9 9AB* Tel (01252) 710594 Fax as telephone E-mail johnjunee@aol.com

EVANS, Gareth Clive. b 68. Univ of Wales (Cardiff) DipTh91. Ripon Coll Cuddesdon BTh96. **d** 96 **p** 97. C Gosforth All SS *Newc* 96-00; USA from 00. *HDS Student, Harvard Divinity School, 45 Francis Avenue, Cambridge, MA 02138, USA* Tel (001) (617) 495 4518

EVANS, Gareth Milton. b 39. Bris Univ LLB60 St Cath Coll Ox BA62 MA66. Ripon Hall Ox 60. **d** 63 **p** 64. C Hengrove *Bris* 63-65; Min Can Bris Cathl 65-68; C Bishopston 68-71; C Notting Hill *Lon* 71-83; V Bayswater from 83. *St Matthew's Vicarage, 27 St Petersburgh Place, London W2 4LA* Tel (020) 7229 2192

EVANS, Gareth Rae. b 48. MIPD. Ripon Coll Cuddesdon DipMin98. **d** 98 **p** 99. C Chepstow *Mon* 98-00; TV Cwmbran from 00. *The Vicarage, 292 Llantarnam Road, Llantarnam, Cwmbran NP44 3BW* Tel (01633) 489280

EVANS, Genevieve Sarah. b 62. Univ of Wales (Cardiff) BA04. St Mich Coll Llan 02. **d** 04 **p** 05. C Whalley Range St Edm and Moss Side etc *Man* from 04. *68 Dudley Road, Manchester M16 8DS* Tel 0161-226 8502 E-mail gennievans@tiscali.co.uk

EVANS, Canon Geoffrey Bainbridge. b 34. St Mich Coll Llan 56 Lambeth MA94. **d** 58 **p** 59. C Llan All SS CD *Llan* 58-60; C Llandaff N 60-67; Guyana 67-73; Chapl Izmir (Smyrna) w Bornova *Eur* 73-94; Adn Aegean 78-94; Can Malta Cathl 78-00; Chapl Ankara 85-91; Chapl Istanbul 87-89; Chapl Rome 94-99; Chapl Moscow 99; P-in-c Ankara from 00. *Sehit Ersan Caddesi 32/12, Cankaya, Ankara 06680, Turkey* Tel (0090) (312) 467 8276 E-mail gb_evans@hotmail.com

EVANS, Geoffrey David. b 44. Ex Univ PGCE74. K Coll Lon BD69 AKC69 St Aug Coll Cant 69. **d** 70 **p** 71. C Lawrence Weston *Bris* 70-73; Chapl Grenville Coll Bideford 74-79; Chapl Eastbourne Coll 79-82; Chapl Taunton and Somerset Hosp 83-91; Chapl Musgrove Park Hosp 83-91; Chapl Taunton Sch 92-04. *Address temp unknown*

EVANS, Gerald Arthur. b 35. Univ of Wales (Swansea) BA57. S'wark Ord Course 74. **d** 77 **p** 78. NSM Balcombe *Chich* 77-81; NSM Cuckfield 81-87; R Tillington 87-93; R Duncton 87-93; R Up Waltham 87-93; R W Chiltington 93-98; Dioc Ecum Officer 93-98; RD Storrington 93-98; rtd 98; Perm to Offic *Chich* 98-00. *49 Regent's Riverside, Brigham Road, Reading RG1 8QS* Tel 0118-956 1889

EVANS, Mrs Gillian. b 39. Imp Coll Lon BSc61. Mon Dioc Tr Scheme 84. **d** 88 **p** 94. NSM Penallt and Trellech *Mon* 88-89; NSM Overmonnow w Wonastow and Michel Troy 89-92; C Ludlow *Heref* 92-93; C Ludlow, Ludford, Ashford Carbonell etc 93-95; Dioc Ecum Officer 92-95; Pakistan 95-96; Perm to Offic *Heref* from 96; Hon C Dawlish *Ex* 97-98; TV Golden Cap Team *Sarum* 98-01; rtd 01. *Great Hillshone Barn, Ganarew, Monmouth NP25 3SS* Tel (01600) 891351

EVANS, Canon Glyn. b 10. Univ of Wales BA33. St Steph Ho Ox 33. **d** 34 **p** 35. C Dolgellau *Ban* 34-39; C Llanfairfechan 39-43; R Llanallgo w Llaneugrad 43-55; V St Issells *St D* 55-80; RD Narberth 65-80; Can St D Cathl 69-80; Treas 77-80; rtd 80. *3 Flemish Close, St Florence, Tenby SA70 8LT* Tel (01834) 871434

EVANS, Glyn. b 59. Nene Coll Northampton BA80 Leic Univ BA80 Ch Ch Coll Cant CertEd82 Kent Univ PGCE82 Birm Univ DipTh87. Qu Coll Birm 85. **d** 88 **p** 89. C Denton *Newc* 88-92; V Choppington 92-97; P-in-c Longhorsley and Hebron 97-01; Chapl HM Pris Acklington 97-01; P-in-c Newc St Andr and St Luke *Newc* from 01; City Cen Chapl from 01. *12 The Glebe, Stannington, Morpeth NE61 6HW* Tel 0191-232 7935 *or* 222 0259 E-mail citychap@fish.co.uk

EVANS, Canon Glyn Peter. b 54. Leeds Univ BA75. Ripon Coll Cuddesdon 76. **d** 77 **p** 78. C Binley *Cov* 77-80; C Clifton upon Dunsmore w Brownsover 80-84; P-in-c Lacock w Bowden Hill *Bris* 84-89; P-in-c Lt Compton w Chastleton, Cornwell etc *Ox* 89-00; Agric Chapl 89-00; Dioc Rural Officer from 00; Hon Can

Ch Ch from 05. *Stonewalls, Sibford Gower, Banbury OX15 5RT* Tel (01295) 280664 Mobile 07870-405241 E-mail glynevansrro@tiscali.co.uk *or* glynevans@goldserve.net

EVANS, Godfrey. *See* EVANS, Joseph Henry Godfrey

EVANS, Canon Gwyneth Mary. b 43. Gilmore Ho 69 Linc Th Coll 70. **dss** 74 **d** 87 **p** 94. Stamford Hill St Thos *Lon* 74-79; Chapl Asst R Free Hosp Lon 79-89; Chapl Salisbury Health Care NHS Trust 89-01; Can and Preb Sarum Cathl *Sarum* 96-01; rtd 01; Perm to Offic *Sarum* from 01. *39 The Close, Salisbury SP1 2EL* Tel (01722) 412546

EVANS, Canon Henry Thomas Platt. b 28. Selw Coll Cam BA51 MA55. Linc Th Coll 51. **d** 53 **p** 54. C Lt Ilford St Barn *Chelmsf* 53-56; C-in-c Stocking Farm CD *Leic* 56-58; V Stocking Farm 58-67; R Stretford St Matt *Man* 67-73; V Knighton St Mary Magd *Leic* 73-83; Hon Can Leic Cathl 76-93; RD Christianity S 81-83; Warden Launde Abbey 83-93; P-in-c Loddington 83-92; rtd 93; Perm to Offic *Leic* from 93. *16 Central Avenue, Leicester LE2 1TB* Tel 0116-270 2169

EVANS (née TAYLOR), Mrs Hilary Elizabeth. b 57. **d** 03 **p** 04. OLM Reddish *Man* from 03. *13 Lindfield Road, Stockport SK5 6SD* Tel 0161-442 3023 E-mail hilary@mojomusica.freeserve.co.uk

EVANS, Hilary Margaret. b 49. Redland Coll of Educn TDip71 Ches Coll of HE BTh97. N Ord Course 94. **d** 97 **p** 98. NSM Heald Green St Cath *Ches* 97-98; C 98-00; P-in-c Davyhulme Ch Ch *Man* 00-03; P-in-c Blackley St Pet from 03. *St Peter's Vicarage, 14 Hill Lane, Manchester M9 6PE* Tel 0161-740 2124 E-mail hmevans@boltblue.com

EVANS, Huw David. b 68. Sheff Univ BEng90 PGCE91. Trin Coll Bris BA98. **d** 98 **p** 02. C Sherborne w Castleton and Lillington *Sarum* 98-99; NSM Martock w Ash *B & W* 01-04; CF from 04. *c/o MOD Chaplains (Army)* Tel (01980) 615804 Fax 615800

EVANS, Mrs Jane. b 59. W Midl Coll of Educn BEd81. **d** 03 **p** 04. OLM Lilleshall, Muxton and Sheriffhales *Lich* from 03. *5 Collett Way, Priorslee, Telford TF2 9SL* Tel (01952) 291340 E-mail eeyore@rmplc.co.uk

EVANS, Mrs Jennifer. b 41. Ilkley Coll DipEd62. Sarum Th Coll 88. **d** 88. Par Dn Bramshott *Portsm* 88-91; C Bramshott and Liphook 91-92; Par Dn Whippingham w E Cowes 92-95; Par Dn Sarisbury from 95; rtd 01. *Honeycombs, 1A Addison Road, Sarisbury Green, Southampton SO31 7ER* Tel (01489) 572129 E-mail jennie.honeycombs@virgin.net

EVANS, Mrs Jennifer. b 43. **d** 01. NSM New Tredegar *Mon* from 01. *26 Glynsifi, Elliots Town, New Tredegar NP24 6DE* Tel (01443) 836798

EVANS, Jennifer Elaine. b 59. Wolv Univ BA92. Qu Coll Birm 00. **d** 02 **p** 03. C Stafford St Jo and Tixall w Ingestre *Lich* from 02. *42 Longhurst Drive, Stafford ST16 3RG* Tel (01785) 213196

EVANS, Jill. *See* EVANS, Mrs Gillian

EVANS, Mrs Joan. b 36. Nor Tr Coll TCert57 UEA BEd94. **d** 02 **p** 03. OLM Loddon, Sisland, Chedgrave, Hardley and Langley *Nor* from 02. *20 Norton Road, Loddon, Norwich NR14 6JN* Tel (01508) 528656 E-mail jevansolm@tiscali.co.uk

EVANS, John. *See* EVANS, Canon Frederick John Margam

EVANS, John Andrew. b 53. Hull Univ BSc74 Univ of Wales MSc75 Bris Univ BA96. Trin Coll Bris 94. **d** 96 **p** 97. C Walton H Trin *Ox* 96-98; C Caversham St Pet and Mapledurham etc 98-01; R Bradford Abbas and Thornford w Beer Hackett *Sarum* from 01. *The Rectory, Church Road, Thornford, Sherborne DT9 6QE* Tel (01935) 872382 E-mail rectorbradfordabbas@supaworld.com

EVANS, The Ven John Barrie. b 23. Univ of Wales (Lamp) BA47 St Edm Hall Ox BA49 MA54. St Mich Coll Llan 50. **d** 51 **p** 52. C Trevethin *Mon* 51-57; V Caerwent w Dinham and Llanfair Discoed 57-64; V Chepstow 64-79; Can St Woolos Cathl 71-77; Adn Mon 77-86; R Llanmartin w Wilcrick and Langstone 79-83; R Llanmartin 83-86; Adn Newport 86-93; rtd 93; Lic to Offic *Mon* from 93; Perm to Offic *Glouc* from 93. *Rockfield, Coleford Road, Tutshill, Chepstow NP16 7BU* Tel (01291) 626147

EVANS, John David Vincent. b 41. CQSW78. Lich Th Coll 66. **d** 68 **p** 70. C Kingsthorpe *Pet* 68-69; C Corby Epiphany w St Jo 69-72; Bp's Adv in Children's Work 72-74; Perm to Offic 88-90; R Green's Norton w Bradden 90-91; R Greens Norton w Bradden and Lichborough 91-96; V Northampton Ch Ch from 96. *Christ Church Vicarage, 3 Christ Church Road, Northampton NN1 5LL* Tel (01604) 633254 E-mail revjohnevans@mgownersclub.net

EVANS, Canon John Griffiths. b 37. Glouc Th Course 76. **d** 77 **p** 77. Hd Master Corse Sch Glos from 70; C Hartpury w Corse and Staunton *Glouc* 77-79; P-in-c from 79; Hon Can Glouc Cathl from 96; P-in-c Maisemore from 01. *Elm House, Gadfield Elms, Staunton, Gloucester GL19 3PA* Tel (01452) 840302

EVANS, John Laurie. b 34. Pretoria Univ BSc54 Imp Coll Lon BSc55 Rhodes Univ BA59. Ripon Coll Cuddesdon 84. **d** 86 **p** 87. C Bruton and Distr *B & W* 86-89; P-in-c Ambrosden w Merton and Piddington *Ox* 89-91; C Pet St Mary Boongate *Pet* 91-93; V Michael *S & M* 93-96; R Ballaugh 93-96; rtd 96; Chapl Allnutt's Hosp Goring Heath 96-99; P-in-c Fochabers *Mor* 99-00; P-in-c Strathnairn St Paul 00-03; TV Langtree *Ox* from 03. *The Vicarage, Crabtree Corner, Ipsden, Wallingford OX10 6BN* Tel and fax (01491) 682832 Mobile 07909-986369 E-mail jonevans@fish.co.uk

EVANS, John Miles. b 39. Yale Univ BA61 JD67 St Cath Coll Cam BA64 MA68. NY Th Sem MDiv93. **d** 95 **p** 95. Chapl St Jo Cathl Oban *Arg* 95-97; USA from 97; Interim R Lynbrook Ch Ch 98-99; R Davidsonville All Hallows from 99. *809 West Central Avenue, PO Box 103, Davidsonville, MD 21035, USA* Tel (001) (410) 798 1900 Fax as telephone E-mail 76765.633@compuserve.com

EVANS, John Rhys. b 45. Hull Univ BSc66. Sarum & Wells Th Coll 77. **d** 79 **p** 80. C Alton St Lawr *Win* 79-82; C Tadley St Pet 82-85; V Colden 85-91; V Bitterne Park 91-01; C Ringwood from 01; Chapl R Bournemouth and Christchurch Hosps NHS Trust from 01. *3 Waterside Close, Poulner, Ringwood BH24 1SB* Tel (01425) 483370

EVANS, John Ronald. b 16. Univ of Wales BA40. St Mich Coll Llan 41. **d** 42 **p** 44. C Rhosllannerchrugog *St As* 42-45; C Holywell 45-54; V Glyndyfrdwy 54-81; RD Edeyrnion 64-81; Dioc Sec SPCK 66-81; rtd 81. *21 Bryn Hyfryd, Johnstown, Wrexham LL14 1PR* Tel (01978) 842300

EVANS, John Stuart. b 57. Univ of Wales (Abth) BA78 Bretton Hall Coll PGCE81. Trin Coll Bris BA98. **d** 98 **p** 99. C Connah's Quay *St As* 98-02; V Rhosllannerchrugog from 02; AD Llangollen from 05. *16 Delyn, Johnstown, Wrexham LL14 1UY* Tel (01978) 840809 E-mail jsevans@surfaid.org

EVANS, Canon John Thomas. b 43. Univ of Wales DipTh66 DPS67. St Mich Coll Llan 66. **d** 67 **p** 68. C Connah's Quay *St As* 67-71; C Llanrhos 71-74; Chapl Rainhill Hosp Liv 74-78; TV Wrexham *St As* 78-83; V Holywell 83-96; RD Holywell 95-96; V Colwyn Bay 96-99; V Colwyn Bay w Brynymaen 99-02; RD Rhos 00-02; R Caerwys and Bodfari from 02; Can Cursal St As Cathl from 96. *The Rectory, Pen-y-Cefn Road, Caerwys, Mold CH7 5AQ* Tel (01352) 720223 E-mail johnevans@jtevans.freeserve.co.uk

EVANS, The Very Revd John Wyn. b 46. FSA88 FRHistS94 Univ of Wales (Cardiff) BA68 BD71. St Mich Coll Llan 68. **d** 71 **p** 72. C St D Cathl *St D* 71-72; Min Can St D Cathl 72-75; Perm to Offic *Ox* 75-77; Dioc Archivist *St D* 76-82; R Llanfallteg w Clunderwen and Castell Dwyran etc 77-82; Warden of Ords 78-83; Dioc Dir of Educn 82-92; Chapl Trin Coll Carmarthen 82-90; Dean of Chpl 90-94; Hd Th and RS 91-94; Hon Can St D Cathl *St D* 88-90; Can St D Cathl 90-94; Dean St D from 94; V St D Cathl 94-01; TR Dewisland from 01. *The Deanery, St Davids, Haverfordwest SA62 6RH* Tel (01437) 720202 Fax 721885

EVANS, Jonathan Alan. b 53. Fitzw Coll Cam BA75 PGCE77 MA79. St Jo Coll Nottm MA95. **d** 95 **p** 96. C Drypool *York* 95-98; V Beverley St Nic from 98. *St Nicholas' Vicarage, 72 Grovehill Road, Beverley HU17 0ER* Tel (01482) 881458 E-mail evansfamily@macunlimited.net

EVANS, Joseph Henry Godfrey. b 31. Univ of Wales (Lamp) BA50 St Mary's Coll Chelt CertEd75 Kingston Poly 89. Qu Coll Birm 53. **d** 55 **p** 56. C Hackney St Jo *Lon* 55-58; C Stonehouse *Glouc* 58-60; V Selsley 60-65; V Cheltenham St Pet 65-74; R Willersey w Saintbury 74-77; Chapl Tiffin Sch Kingston 77-94; rtd 95; Perm to Offic *S'wark* from 01. *300 Raeburn Avenue, Surbiton KT5 9EF* Tel (020) 8390 0936

EVANS, Mrs Judith Ann. b 55. DipN79. SEITE 99. **d** 02 **p** 03. C Crayford *Roch* from 02. *1A Iron Mill Place, Dartford DA1 4RT* Tel (01322) 552884 Mobile 07929-978523

EVANS, Canon Keith. b 57. Trin Coll Carmarthen CertEd81 BEd82. St D Coll Lamp BA84 Sarum & Wells Th Coll 84. **d** 85 **p** 86. C Swansea St Thos and Kilvey *S & B* 85-87; C Gorseinon 87-89; V Oxwich w Penmaen and Nicholaston 89-94; Dir Post-Ord Tr from 93; R Ystradgynlais 94-98; V Oystermouth from 98; Hon Can Brecon Cathl from 04. *The Vicarage, 9 Western Close, Mumbles, Swansea SA3 4HF* Tel (01792) 369971

EVANS, Kenneth. b 50. Bp Burgess Hall Lamp. **d** 74 **p** 75. C Llanaber w Caerdeon *Ban* 74-79; C Upper Clapton St Matt *Lon* 79-82; P-in-c Tottenham St Phil 82-95; V from 95. *St Philip's Vicarage, 226 Philip Lane, London N15 4HH* Tel and fax (020) 8808 4235 E-mail fr_kenmjd@tiscali.co.uk

✠**EVANS, The Rt Revd Kenneth Dawson.** b 15. Clare Coll Cam BA37 MA41. Ripon Hall Ox 37. **d** 38 **p** 39 **c** 68. C Northampton St Mary *Pet* 38-41; C Northampton All SS w St Kath 41-45; R Ockley *Guildf* 45-49; V Ranmore 49-57; V Dorking 49-57; V Dorking w Ranmore 57-63; RD Dorking 57-63; Hon Can Guildf Cathl 55-63 and 79-85; Can Res Guildf Cathl 63-68; Adn Dorking 63-68; Suff Bp Dorking 68-85; rtd 85. *3 New Inn Lane, Guildford GU4 7HN* Tel (01483) 567978

EVANS, Kenneth Roy. b 47. Lon Univ BSc FRSA96. Ridley Hall Cam 79. **d** 81 **p** 81. C Stratford-on-Avon w Bishopton *Cov* 81-82; C Trunch *Nor* 82-85; Chapl Mapperley Hosp Nottm 85-89; Chapl Nottm Mental Illness and Psychiatric Unit 85-94; Chapl Notts Healthcare NHS Trust from 94; Lic to Offic *S'well* from 85; Dir Scarborough Psychotherapy Tr Inst from 03. *117 Columbus Ravine, Scarborough YO12 7QU* Tel (01723) 376246 E-mail ken@kenevans.fsnet.co.uk

EVANS, Kevin Stuart. b 56. Bris Poly CQSW80. Qu Coll Birm DipTh95. **d** 95 **p** 96. C Madeley *Heref* 95-98; P-in-c Wombridge *Lich* from 98. *Wombridge Vicarage, Wombridge Road, Telford TF2 6HT* Tel (01952) 613334

EVANS, Linda Mary. *See* EDWARDS, Mrs Linda Mary

EVANS, Miss Madeleine Thelma Bodenham. b 30. K Coll Lon BD76 AKC76. Gilmore Course 80. **dss** 85 **d** 87 **p** 94. Chapl Pipers Corner Sch 85-91; Par Dn Calne and Blackland *Sarum* 91-94; C 94-00; Chapl St Mary's Sch Calne 91-99; rtd 00; Perm to Offic *Sarum* from 00. *11 Fairway, Rookery Park, Calne SN11 0LB* Tel and fax (01249) 814755

EVANS, Ms Margaret Elizabeth. b 48. Leeds Univ BA69 Lon Inst of Educn CertEd70. Oak Hill Th Coll 91. **d** 94 **p** 95. NSM Canonbury St Steph *Lon* from 94. *St Stephen's Canonbury, 17 Canonbury Road, London N1 2DF* Tel (020) 7226 7526 *or* 7359 4343 E-mail margareteevans@hotmail.com

EVANS, Mark Roland John. b 55. St Cath Coll Cam MA81 Bris Univ PGCE78. WEMTC 01. **d** 04 **p** 05. NSM Frenchay and Winterbourne Down *Bris* from 04. *60 High Street, Thornbury, Bristol BS35 2AN* Tel (01454) 414101 Mobile 07702-289385 E-mail mark.evans@bathwells.anglican.org

EVANS, Martin Lonsdale. b 69. Man Univ BA91. Ripon Coll Cuddesdon DipMin95. **d** 95 **p** 96. C Morpeth *Newc* 95-98; Chapl RN from 98. *Royal Naval Chaplaincy Service, Room 203, Victory Building, HM Naval Base, Portsmouth PO1 3LS* Tel (023) 9272 7903 Fax 9272 7111 E-mail ml.evans@virgin.com

EVANS, Matthew Scott. b 72. Grey Coll Dur BA93. Cranmer Hall Dur DMS98. **d** 98 **p** 99. C Fountains Gp *Ripon* 98-03; P-in-c Dacre w Hartwith and Darley w Thornthwaite from 03. *The Vicarage, Dacre Banks, Harrogate HG3 4ED* Tel (01423) 780262

EVANS, Michael. b 49. St Jo Coll Nottm 88. **d** 90 **p** 91. C Beeston *S'well* 90-93; P-in-c Kirkby in Ashfield St Thos 93-97; V from 97; Chapl Notts Healthcare NHS Trust from 93. *The Vicarage, 109 Diamond Avenue, Kirkby-in-Ashfield, Nottingham NG17 7LX* Tel (01623) 755131 E-mail mummamonk@aol.com

EVANS, Michael John. b 53. **d** 00 **p** 01. OLM Longnor, Quarnford and Sheen *Lich* 00-04; OLM Ipstones w Berkhamsytch and Onecote w Bradnop from 04. *Lower Marnshaw Head, Barrowmoor, Longnor, Buxton SK17 0QR* Tel (01298) 83293

EVANS, Neil Robert. b 54. Lon Univ MA93. Coll of Resurr Mirfield. **d** 84 **p** 85. C Bethnal Green St Jo w St Bart *Lon* 84-86; C St Jo on Bethnal Green 87-88; P-in-c Stoke Newington Common St Mich 88-95; V 95-98; V Twickenham All Hallows 98-05; Kensington Area CME Officer 98-05; Par Min Development Adv (Willesden Area) from 05. *St Anselm's Vicarage, 101 Nield Road, Hayes UB3 1SQ* Tel (020) 8573 0958 E-mail neil.evans@london.anglican.org

EVANS, Nicholas Anthony Paul. b 60. Sheff Univ BA81 Liv Univ PGCE86. Qu Coll Birm 81. **d** 84 **p** 87. C Ludlow *Heref* 84-85; C Sunbury *Lon* 86-92; Hd RE Guildf Co Sch 93-99; NSM Crookham *Guildf* 94-99; CF 99-02; V Shenley Green *Birm* from 02. *St David's Vicarage, 49 Shenley Green, Birmingham B29 4HH* Tel 0121-475 4874 Mobile 07769-550204 E-mail evnsnick@aol.com

EVANS, Nigel William Reid. b 70. Sheff Hallam Univ BEd96. Ridley Hall Cam BTh01. **d** 01 **p** 02. C Ossett and Gawthorpe *Wakef* 01-05; V Loddon, Sisland, Chedgrave, Hardley and Langley *Nor* from 05. *The Vicarage, 4 Market Place, Loddon, Norwich NR14 6EY* Tel (01508) 520251

EVANS, Norman Cassienet. b 30. Keble Coll Ox MA54. Guildf Dioc Min Course 91. **d** 95 **p** 96. OLM Seale, Puttenham and Wanborough *Guildf* 95-00; Perm to Offic from 00. *Tree Tops, Seale Lane, Puttenham, Guildford GU3 1AX* Tel (01483) 810677 E-mail norman@thereverend.fsnet.co.uk

EVANS, Mrs Patricia Rosemary. b 47. **d** 01. Par Dn Panteg *Mon* 01-03; Par Dn Panteg w Llanfihangel Pontymoile from 03. *Pentwyn Farm, Glascoed, Pontypool NP4 0TX* Tel and fax (01495) 785285 Mobile 07814-783714

EVANS, The Ven Patrick Alexander Sidney. b 43. Linc Th Coll 70. **d** 73 **p** 74. C Lyonsdown H Trin *St Alb* 73-76; C Royston 76-78; V Gt Gaddesden 78-82; V Tenterden St Mildred w Smallhythe *Cant* 82-89; Adn Maidstone 89-02; Hon Can Cant Cathl 89-02; Dir of Ords 89-93; Adn Cant and Can Res Cant Cathl from 02. *Chillenden Chambers, 29 The Precincts, Canterbury CT1 2EP* Tel (01227) 865238 Fax 785209 E-mail patricke@canterbury-cathedral.org

EVANS, Peter. b 35. St Aid Birkenhead 57. **d** 60 **p** 61. C Higher Bebington *Ches* 60-63; C W Kirby St Bridget 63-66; P-in-c Lower Tranmere 66-68; V Flimby *Carl* 68-74; V Kirkby Ireleth 74-79; P-in-c Kirkbride w Newton Arlosh 79-80; R 80-85; V Beckermet St Jo and St Bridget w Ponsonby 85-97; rtd 97; Perm to Offic *Carl* from 98. *26 Gelt Close, Carlisle CA3 0HJ*

EVANS, Peter. b 40. S'wark Ord Course 75. **d** 75 **p** 76. C Welling *S'wark* 75-78; C Sutton New Town St Barn 78-81; C Kingston All SS w St Jo 81-87; V Croydon Woodside 87-99; TV Sanderstead All SS 99-03; rtd 03. *174 Main Street, Stanton-under-Bardon, Markfield LE67 9TP* Tel (01530) 245470

EVANS, Peter Anthony. b 36. Imp Coll Lon BScEng57 St Cath Coll Ox DipTh59. St Steph Ho Ox 58. **d** 60 **p** 61. C Surbiton St Mark *S'wark* 60-63; Asst Chapl Lon Univ *Lon* 63-64; C S Kensington St Luke 64-68; C Surbiton St Andr and St Mark *S'wark* 68-69; C Loughton St Jo *Chelmsf* 69-74; P-in-c Becontree St Geo 74-82; Perm to Offic 82-89; NSM Romford St Alb 89-93; NSM Coopersale 93-95; NSM Epping Distr 95-96; rtd 97; Perm to Offic *Chelmsf* from 97. *6 Woodhall Crescent, Hornchurch RM11 3NN* Tel (01708) 509399

EVANS, Peter Gerald. b 41. Man Univ BA71. AKC65. **d** 65 **p** 66. C Kidbrooke St Jas *S'wark* 65-68; C Fallowfield *Man* 68-71; C Brockley Hill St Sav *S'wark* 71-73; P-in-c Colchester St Botolph w H Trin and St Giles *Chelmsf* 74-79; V 79-92; Perm to Offic from 93. *97 Northgate Street, Colchester CO1 1EY* Tel (01206) 543297

EVANS, Peter Kenneth Dunlop. b 38. Ch Coll Cam BA60. St D Coll Lamp 72. **d** 74 **p** 75. C Roath *Llan* 74-77; V Buttington and Pool Quay *St As* 77-87; V Llanfair Caereinion w Llanllugan 87-03; rtd 03. *Stepaside, Llanfair Caereinion, Welshpool SY21 0HU* Tel (01686) 627076

EVANS, Richard. *See* EVANS, David Richard

EVANS, Richard Edward Hughes. b 14. Univ of Wales BA44. St Mich Coll Llan. **d** 45 **p** 46. C Nantymoel *Llan* 45-48; C Pontyberem *St D* 48-50; C Llandeilo Fawr 50-53; V Ysbyty Cynfyn 53-64; V Llanybydder and Llanwenog w Llanwnnen 64-72; V Llanychaiarn 72-79; rtd 79. *23 Gwarfelin, Llanilar, Aberystwyth SY23 4PE* Tel (01974) 241357

EVANS, Richard Edward Victor. b 21. Linc Th Coll 66. **d** 68 **p** 69. C Aston cum Aughton *Sheff* 68-71; C Prestwich St Mary *Man* 71-74; R Moston St Jo 74-83; R Failsworth H Family 83-91; rtd 91; Perm to Offic *Man* from 91. *508 Edge Lane, Droylesden, Manchester M43 6JW* Tel 0161-370 1947

EVANS, Richard Gregory. b 50. Univ of Wales (Cardiff) DipTh72. St Mich Coll Llan 69. **d** 73 **p** 74. C Oystermouth *S & B* 73-76; C Clydach 76-79; CF 78-81; V Llanddew and Talachddu *S & B* 79-83; Youth Chapl 79-83; Hon Min Can Brecon Cathl 79-83; New Zealand from 83. *Wanganui Collegiate School, Wanganui, New Zealand* Tel (0064) (6) 349 0281 ext 8750 Fax 348 8302 E-mail rgevans@collegiate.school.nz

EVANS, Richard Neville. b 15. Qu Coll Cam BA36 MA44. Ripon Hall Ox 36. **d** 38 **p** 39. C E Wickham *S'wark* 38-43; Chapl RNVR 43-46; C Surbiton St Andr *S'wark* 46-47; R Southacre *Nor* 47-55; V Westacre 47-55; V Castle Acre w Newton 49-55; Chapl R Free Hosp Lon 55-60; V Cambridge St Andr Gt *Ely* 60-72; V Waterbeach 72-74; Perm to Offic 75-86; rtd 84; Perm to Offic *Truro* 86-95. *2 Hounster Drive, Millbrook, Torpoint PL10 1BZ* Tel (01752) 822811

EVANS, Richard Trevor. b 33. Jes Coll Ox MA58 DipEd58. St And Dioc Tr Course 73. **d** 76 **p** 76. NSM Leven *St And* 76-95; NSM St Andrews St Andr from 95. *33 Huntingtower Park, Whinnyknowe, Glenrothes KY6 3QF* Tel and fax (01592) 741670 E-mail revans9973@aol.com

EVANS, Robert. *See* EVANS, Simon Robert

EVANS, Canon Robert Arthur. b 24. Univ of Wales (Cardiff) BA48. St Mich Coll Llan 48. **d** 50 **p** 51. C Aberdare St Fagan *Llan* 50-52; C Roath 52-57; C Llandaff w Capel Llanilltern 57-61; Asst Chapl Mersey Miss to Seamen 61-62; Chapl Supt Mersey Miss to Seamen 62-74 and 79-89; Chapl RNR 67-89; V Rainhill *Liv* 74-79; Perm to Offic *Ches* 79-91; Hon Can Liv Cathl *Liv* 88-89; rtd 89; Perm to Offic *Liv* from 89. *1 Floral Wood, Riverside Gardens, Liverpool L17 7HR* Tel 0151-727 3608

EVANS, Robert Charles. b 55. K Coll Lon BA77 AKC77 MA78 MTh89 Qu Coll Cam BA80 MA83 CertEd85. Westcott Ho Cam 79. **d** 81 **p** 87. C St Breoke *Truro* 81-83; C St Columb Minor and St Colan 83-84; Chapl Rob Coll Cam 87-92; Lect Ches Coll of HE *Ches* from 92. *Chester College, Parkgate Road, Chester CH1 4BJ* Tel (01244) 375444

EVANS, Robert George Roger. b 49. Cam Univ MA. Trin Coll Bris 74 St Jo Coll Nottm 94. **d** 77 **p** 78. C Bispham *Blackb* 77-80; C Chadwell *Chelmsf* 80-84; V Ardsley *Sheff* from 84; P-in-c Kendray from 04; Chapl Barnsley Community & Priority Services NHS Trust 98-00. *The Vicarage, Doncaster Road, Barnsley S71 5EF* Tel (01226) 203784 E-mail rgrevans@compuserve.com

EVANS, Robert Stanley. b 51. Univ of Wales (Lamp) BA72 Univ of Wales (Cardiff) PGCE73. St Mich Coll Llan DPS92. **d** 92 **p** 93. C Penarth All SS *Llan* 92-95; R Gelligaer 95-99; V Roath 99-04; R Coychurch, Llangan and St Mary Hill from 04. *The Rectory, 9 Heol-Cae-Tyla, Coychurch, Bridgend CF35 5HR* Tel (01656) 656313

EVANS, Ronald. b 47. St Mich Coll Llan 85. **d** 87 **p** 88. C Flint *St As* 87-91; TV Wrexham 91-97; V Rhosymedre 97-99; V Rhosymedre w Penycae 99-05; PV Connah's Quay from 05. *8 Eurgain Avenue, Connah's Quay, Deeside CH5 4PW* Tel (01244) 812101 E-mail ronatrhosymedre@compuserve.com

EVANS, Ronald Wilson. b 47. Windsor Univ Ontario BA69 Dalhousie Univ MA83. Trin Coll Toronto MDiv73. **d** 72 **p** 73. Canada 72-98; R Springhill 73-76; Chapl Univ of Prince Edw Is 76-79; Lect 82-85; Chapl King's-Edgehill Sch 85-87; R Clements

87-98; Lect Bilgi Univ Istanbul 98-00; Asst Chapl Izmir (Smyrna) w Bornova *Eur* 00-03; P-in-c 03-04; Chapl from 04. *PK 1005, Pasaport, Izmir 35120, Turkey* Tel and fax (0090) (232) 464 5753 Mobile 535-734 1051 E-mail seljuk85@hotmail.com

EVANS, Roy Clifford. b 39. Qu Coll Birm 04. **d** 05. SSF from 91; Chapl Univ Hosp Birm NHS Foundn Trust from 05; NSM Billesley Common *Birm* from 05. *92 Creynolds Lane, Shirley, Solihull B90 4ER* Tel 0121-744 7547 Mobile 07791-398923 Pager 07623-614575 E-mail brother.evans@tesco.co.uk

EVANS, Mrs Sheila Jean. b 40. **d** 99 **p** 01. OLM Tollard Royal w Farnham, Gussage St Michael etc *Sarum* 99-01; OLM Chase from 01. *Church Mead, Harley Lane, Gussage All Saints, Wimborne BH21 5HD* Tel (01258) 840182

EVANS, Simon. b 55. Newc Univ BA77. St Steph Ho Ox 78. **d** 80 **p** 81. C Pet St Jude *Pet* 80-84; C Wantage *Ox* 84-87; V W Leigh *Portsm* 87-96; V Ruislip St Martin *Lon* from 96. *The Vicarage, 13 Eastcote Road, Ruislip HA4 8BE* Tel (01895) 633040 *or* 625456 E-mail frsimon@waitrose.com

EVANS, Simon Andrew. b 59. Sarum & Wells Th Coll 81. **d** 84 **p** 85. C Norbury St Steph and Thornton Heath *S'wark* 84-88; C Putney St Mary 88-92; P-in-c Telford Park St Thos 92-94; V 94-04; V Ensbury Park *Sarum* from 04. *St Thomas's Vicarage, 42 Coombe Avenue, Bournemouth BH10 5AE* Tel (01202) 519735 E-mail simon@evansonline.info

EVANS, Simon Robert (Bob). b 58. Reading Univ BSc79. N Ord Course 99. **d** 02 **p** 03. C Pudsey St Lawr and St Paul *Bradf* 02-04; P-in-c Low Moor from 04. *The Vicarage, 6 Vicarage Close, Wyke, Bradford BD12 8QW* Tel (01274) 678216 E-mail bob@becs2000.freeserve.co.uk

EVANS, Stanley George. b 43. CITC 00. **d** 03 **p** 04. Aux Min Killaloe w Stradbally *L & K* 03-04; Aux Min Killarney w Aghadoe and Muckross from 04. *St Mary's Rectory, Rookery Close, Killarney, Co Kerry, Irish Republic* Tel and fax (00353) (64) 31832 Mobile 87-636 9473 E-mail stanevans@eircom.net

EVANS, Stanley Munro. b 30. AKC53. **d** 54 **p** 55. C Norbury St Oswald *Cant* 54-57; C St Laur in Thanet 57-63; V Bredgar 63-71; V Bredgar w Bicknor and Huckinge 71-72; V Westgate St Sav 72-01; rtd 01; Perm to Offic *Cant* from 01. *40 Queen Bertha Road, Ramsgate CT11 0ED* Tel (01843) 594459

EVANS, Canon Stephen John. b 60. Dartmouth RN Coll 81 St Steph Ho Ox BA85 MA89 Aber Univ MPhil94. **d** 86 **p** 87. Prec St Andr Cathl Inverness *Mor* 86-89; R Montrose *Bre* 89-91; P-in-c Inverbervie 89-91; Miss to Seamen 89-91; V Northampton St Paul *Pet* 91-98; Continuing Minl Educn Officer 94-00; Liturg Officer 96-03; P-in-c Ecton 98-00; Warden Ecton Ho 98-00; R Uppingham w Ayston and Wardley w Belton *Pet* from 00; Can Pet Cathl from 03; RD Rutland from 03. *The Rectory, London Road, Uppingham, Oakham LE15 9TJ* Tel (01572) 823381 Fax as telephone E-mail evanssj@globalnet.co.uk *or* stephen.evans@rutnet.co.uk

EVANS, Steven Edward. b 52. Carl and Blackb Dioc Tr Inst 97. **d** 00 **p** 01. NSM Caton w Littledale *Blackb* 00-05; NSM Hornby w Claughton and Whittington etc from 05. *Swallows Nest, Melling, Carnforth LA6 2RA* Tel (01524) 222124

EVANS, Stuart. *See* EVANS, John Stuart

EVANS, Ms Susan Mary. b 55. St Jo Coll Dur BA76 CertEd77 Nottm Univ BCombStuds84. Linc Th Coll 81. **dss** 84 **d** 87 **p** 94. Weaste *Man* 84-88; Par Dn 87-88; Par Dn Longsight St Luke 88-92; Par Dn Claydon and Barham *St E* 92-94; C 94-99; P-in-c Henley 98-99; Chapl HM YOI Hollesley Bay Colony 99-02; NSM Henley, Claydon and Barham *St E* from 02. *The Rectory, 7 Back Lane, Claydon, Ipswich IP6 0EB* Tel (01473) 830362

EVANS, Tenniel. *See* EVANS, Walter Tenniel

EVANS, Terence. b 35. St Mich Coll Llan 67. **d** 69 **p** 70. C Loughor *S & B* 69-73; C Gowerton w Waunarlwydd 73-77; V Llanbister and Llanbadarn Fynydd w Llananno 77-82; V Llanyrnewydd 82-01; rtd 01. *28 Orchard Court, New Orchard Street, Swansea SA1 5EN*

EVANS, Terence Robert. b 45. N Ord Course 82. **d** 85 **p** 86. C Warrington St Elphin *Liv* 85-88; V Cantril Farm 88-94; V Rainhill 94-03; R Odd Rode *Ches* from 03. *Odd Rode Rectory, Church Lane, Scholar Green, Stoke-on-Trent ST7 3QN* Tel (01270) 882195 Fax as telephone E-mail terencerevans@aol.com

EVANS, Thomas Norman. b 30. K Coll Lon BA51 BD53 AKC56. **d** 56 **p** 57. C Handsworth *Sheff* 56-59; C Mexborough 59-61; V Denaby Main 61-65; V Wythenshawe Wm Temple Ch *Man* 65-78; RD Withington 72-78; R Prestwich St Mary 78-85; AD Radcliffe and Prestwich 78-85; Hon Can Man Cathl 79-85; R Skelton w Upleatham *York* 87-99; RD Guisborough 91-99; rtd 99; Perm to Offic *York* from 00. *4 Castelo Grove, Pickering YO18 7JV* Tel (01751) 476628

EVANS, Canon Timothy Simon. b 57. York Univ BA79 Sussex Univ MA81 Fitzw Coll Cam BA85 MA88. Ridley Hall Cam 83. **d** 87 **p** 88. C Whitton St Aug *Lon* 87-90; C Ealing St Steph Castle Hill 90-93; P-in-c Shireshead *Blackb* 93-97; Asst Chapl Lanc Univ 93-97; Dep Prin Carl and Blackb Dioc Tr Inst from 97; P-in-c Natland *Carl* from 97; RD Kendal 00-03; Hon Can Carl Cathl from 00. *The Vicarage, Natland, Kendal LA9 7QQ* Tel (01539) 560355 E-mail evansosmaston@clara.co.uk

EVANS, Trevor Owen. b 37. Univ of Wales BSc59. Coll of Resurr Mirfield 59. **d** 61 **p** 62. C Llanaber w Caerdeon *Ban* 61-64; C Llandudno 64-70; TV 70-75; V Llanidloes w Llangurig 75-89; RD Arwystli 75-89; Can and Preb Ban Cathl 82-98; Dioc Adv on Spirituality 84-03; R Trefdraeth 89-90; Dir of Min 89-98; R Llanfairpwll w Penmynydd 90-98; Dean Ban 98-03; RD Ogwen 99-00; rtd 03. *Hafan, 3 Coed y Castell, Bangor LL57 1PH* Tel (01248) 352855 E-mail revtrev@fish.co.uk

EVANS, Walter James. b 29. Huron Coll Ontario LTh58. **d** 58 **p** 59. Canada 58-63; C Toronto Redeemer 58-60; I Manvers 60-61; C Cobourg 61-63; C Wolborough w Newton Abbot *Ex* 63-65; R Chilthorne Domer, Yeovil Marsh and Thorne Coffin *B & W* 65-70; V Chalford *Glouc* 70-91; rtd 91; Perm to Offic *Glouc* 91-97. *67 Mandara Grove, Gloucester GL4 9XT* Tel (01452) 385157

EVANS, Walter Tenniel. b 26. Ox NSM Course. **d** 84 **p** 85. NSM Beaconsfield *Ox* 84-95; Perm to Offic from 95. *Candlemas, Seer Green Lane, Jordans, Beaconsfield HP9 2ST* Tel (01494) 873165

EVANS, William James Lynn. b 30. St D Coll Lamp 73. **d** 75 **p** 76. P-in-c Penbryn and Blaenporth *St D* 75-77; V Penbryn and Betws Ifan w Bryngwyn 77-79; V Penrhyncoch and Elerch 79-83; V Cynwil Elfed and Newchurch 83-87; V Llandybie 87-95; rtd 95. *5 Dolau Tywi, Manordeilo, Llandeilo SA19 7BL* Tel (01550) 777944

EVANS, Wyn. *See* EVANS, The Very Revd John Wyn

EVANS-PUGHE, Thomas Goronwy. b 29. TCD. Wycliffe Hall Ox 59. **d** 61 **p** 62. C Grassendale *Liv* 61-63; P-in-c Mossley Hill St Matt and St Jas 63-64; C 64-65; Prec Chelmsf Cathl *Chelmsf* 65-69; R Birchanger 69-94; rtd 94; Perm to Offic *Glouc* from 94. *Bath Orchard, Blockley, Moreton-in-Marsh GL56 9HU* Tel (01386) 701223

EVANS-SMITH, Brian. **d** 02 **p** 03. OLM S Ramsey St Paul *S & M* from 02. *707 King's Court, Ramsey, Isle of Man IM8 1LW* Tel (01624) 817322

EVASON, Stuart Anthony. b 44. Salford Univ BSc. Chich Th Coll 79. **d** 81 **p** 82. C Heref St Martin *Heref* 81-85; TV Cleethorpes *Linc* 85-87; TV Howden *York* 87-92; V Heywood St Jas *Man* 92-03; P-in-c Barrow St Jas *Carl* from 03. *St James's Vicarage, 36 Thorncliffe Road, Barrow-in-Furness LA14 5PZ* Tel (01229) 821475 E-mail stuart_evason@bigfoot.com

EVE, Cedric Robert Sutcliff. b 18. Lon Coll of Div 63. **d** 65 **p** 66. C Plumstead St Jas w St Jo *S'wark* 65-68; C Plumstead St Jo w St Jas and St Paul 68-69; C Ipsley *Worc* 69-73; TV 73-78; P-in-c Harvington and Norton and Lenchwick 78-84; rtd 84; Perm to Offic *Chich* from 85; *Guildf* 93-99. *Manormead Residential Home, Tilford Road, Hindhead GU26 6RA* Tel (01428) 604107

EVE, David Charles Leonard. b 45. AKC74 St Aug Coll Cant 74. **d** 75 **p** 76. C Hall Green Ascension *Birm* 75-79; TV Kings Norton 79-84; V Rowley Regis 84-93; Perm to Offic *Heref* 94-98 and from 01; NSM Hallow and Grimley w Holt *Worc* from 98. *Cleanlyseat Farm, Neen Savage, Cleobury Mortimer, Kidderminster DY14 8EN* Tel (01299) 270510 E-mail d.eve@virgin.net

EVE, Hilary Anne. *See* FIFE, Hilary Anne

EVE, Canon Ian Halliday. b 33. St Paul's Coll Grahamstown LTh59. **d** 59 **p** 60. S Africa 59-80 and from 81; P-in-c Salcombe *Ex* 80-81; Can Cape Town from 86. *Christ Church Rectory, Main Road, Constantia, 7800 South Africa* Tel (0027) (21) 794 6352 *or* 794 5051 Fax 794 1065

EVELEIGH, Raymond. b 36. Univ of Wales (Cardiff) BSc58. NW Ord Course 73. **d** 76 **p** 77. NSM S Cave and Ellerker w Broomfleet *York* 76-79; P-in-c Kingston upon Hull St Mary 79-82; Chapl Hull Coll of FE 79-01; V Anlaby Common St Mark *York* 82-94; V Langtoft w Foxholes, Butterwick, Cottam etc 94-01; rtd 01; Perm to Offic *York* from 04. *Pasture Lodge, West End, Kilham, Driffield YO25 4RR* Tel (01262) 420060 E-mail rev@revray.co.uk

EVENS, Jonathan Adrian Harvey. b 63. Middx Poly BA84 Middx Univ BA03 ACIPD90. NTMTC 00. **d** 03 **p** 04. C Barking St Marg w St Patr *Chelmsf* from 03. *48 Sunningdale Avenue, Barking IG11 7QF* Tel (020) 8227 1131 E-mail jon.evens@ntlworld.com

EVENS, Philip Alistair. b 36. Leic Univ BA61 Birm Univ MPhil02. Trin Coll Bris 84. **d** 86 **p** 87. C Aston SS Pet and Paul *Birm* 86-89; V Tyseley 89-99; rtd 99; Perm to Offic *Birm* from 99. *39 Douglas Road, Acocks Green, Birmingham B27 6HH* Tel 0121-708 1686

EVENS, Robert Alan. b 51. **d** 00 **p** 01. NSM Sharnbrook and Knotting w Souldrop *St Alb* 00-03; P-in-c from 05; P-in-c Wymington w Podington 03-05; P-in-c Felmersham from 05. *The Rectory, 81 High Street, Sharnbrook, Bedford MK44 1PE* Tel (01234) 782000 E-mail robert.evens@lineone.net

✠**EVENS, The Rt Revd Robert John Scott.** b 47. ACIB74. Trin Coll Bris 74. **d** 77 **p** 78 **c** 04. C Southsea St Simon *Portsm* 77-79; C Portchester 79-83; V Locks Heath 83-96; RD Fareham 93-96; Adn Bath and Preb Wells Cathl *B & W* 96-04; Suff Bp Crediton

Ex from 04. *32 The Avenue, Tiverton EX16 4HW* Tel (01884) 250002 Fax 258454
E-mail bishop.of.crediton@exeter.anglican.org

EVENSON, Bruce John. b 46. Wittenberg Univ Ohio BA68. Lutheran Sch of Th Chicago MDiv72. **d** 98 **p** 98. C Charleston Grace Ch USA 98-02; Chapl Porter-Gaud Sch Charleston 01-02; Chapl Stockholm w Gävle and Västerås *Eur* 02-05. *Address temp unknown*

EVEREST, Prof Graham Robert. b 57. Bedf Coll Lon BSc80 K Coll Lon PhD83. EAMTC 02. **d** 05. NSM Cringleford and Colney *Nor* from 05. *1 Thistle Close, Norwich NR5 9HR* Tel (01603) 744475 E-mail graham@geverest.freeserve.co.uk

EVEREST, Harold William. b 26. Lon Univ BD54. Tyndale Hall Bris 51. **d** 54 **p** 55. C Crookes St Thos *Sheff* 54-57; C Leyland St Andr *Blackb* 57-59; V Darwen St Barn 59-67; V Sheff St Jo *Sheff* 67-78; V Tinsley 78-91; Ind Chapl 78-91; rtd 91; Perm to Offic *S'well* from 03. *19 Carlton Fold, Nottingham NG2 4ER* Tel 0115-924 1837

EVEREST, Canon John Cleland. b 45. Sarum Th Coll 66. **d** 68 **p** 69. C Moulsecoomb *Chich* 68-71; C Easthampstead *Ox* 71-74; C Southwick St Mich *Chich* 74-77; Dioc Soc Services Adv *Worc* 77-84; Ind Chapl 84-93; R Worc City St Paul and Old St Martin etc 84-93; RD Worc E 89-93; Hon Can Worc Cathl from 90; TR Halas from 93; RD Dudley 95-98. *The Rectory, Bundle Hill, Halesowen B63 4AR* Tel and fax 0121-550 1158
E-mail halasoffice@ic24.net

EVERETT, Alan Neil. b 57. St Cath Coll Ox BA79 DPhil96 SS Coll Cam BA84. Westcott Ho Cam 82. **d** 85 **p** 86. C Hindley All SS *Liv* 85-88; Chapl Qu Mary Coll *Lon* 88-91; V S Hackney St Mich w Haggerston St Paul from 94. *97 Lavender Grove, London E8 3LR* Tel (020) 7249 4440 *or* tel and fax 7249 2627
E-mail alan@n16.org.uk

EVERETT, Anthony William. b 60. S Bank Poly BA82. Oak Hill Th Coll BA89. **d** 89 **p** 90. C Hailsham *Chich* 89-92; C New Malden and Coombe *S'wark* 92-97; V Streatham Park St Alb 97-02; V Herne Bay Ch Ch *Cant* from 02. *Christ Church Vicarage, 38 Beltinge Road, Herne Bay CT6 6BU* Tel (01227) 374906 *or* 366640 E-mail anthony@fayland.freeserve.co.uk

EVERETT, Mrs Christine Mary. b 46. St Osyth Coll of Educn CertEd67. Westcott Ho Cam 90. **d** 92 **p** 94. Par Dn Ipswich St Fran *St E* 92-94; C 94-95; C Gt and Lt Bealings w Playford and Culpho 96; P-in-c 96-02; P-in-c Creeting St Mary, Creeting St Peter etc from 02. *190 Hawthorne Drive, Ipswich IP2 0QQ* Tel (01473) 688339 Mobile 07980-023236
E-mail chrstevr@aol.com

EVERETT, Colin Gerald Grant. b 44. Open Univ BA77 Keswick Hall Coll CertEd. Ripon Coll Cuddesdon 79. **d** 81 **p** 82. C Aston cum Aughton *Sheff* 81-84; R Fornham All SS and Fornham St Martin w Timworth *St E* 84-92; P-in-c Old Newton w Stowupland 92-94; C Ipswich All Hallows 94-95; TV Ipswich St Fran 95-97; TV Ipswich St Mary at Stoke w St Pet and St Fran from 97. *190 Hawthorne Drive, Ipswich IP2 0QQ* Tel (01473) 688339

EVERETT, David Gordon. b 45. Pemb Coll Ox BA67 MA. Lon Coll of Div LTh68. **d** 70 **p** 71. C Hatcham St Jas *S'wark* 70-73; C Reading St Jo *Ox* 73-77; TV Fenny Stratford and Water Eaton 77-82; Hon C Bletchley 82-87; C Loughton 84-85; NSM Stantonbury and Willen 87-92; Chapl Ox Brookes Univ 92-96; NSM Iffley 93-96; C Treslothan *Truro* 96-97; C Crowan and Treslothan 98-02; Chapl Camborne Pool Redruth Coll 98-02; P-in-c Ketton w Tinwell *Pet* 02; P-in-c Easton on the Hill, Collyweston w Duddington etc 02; R Ketton, Collyweston, Easton-on-the-Hill etc from 03. *The Vicarage, 4 Edmonds Drive, Ketton, Stamford PE9 3TH* Tel (01780) 720228

EVERETT, Canon John Wilfred. b 37. Qu Coll Cam BA61 MA65. Cuddesdon Coll 64. **d** 66 **p** 67. C St Helier *S'wark* 66-69; C Yeovil St Jo w Preston Plucknett *B & W* 69-73; R Wincanton 73-82; R Pen Selwood 80-82; V Ashford *Cant* 82-02; Hon Can Cant Cathl 90-02; rtd 02; Perm to Offic *Cant* from 02. *Stream Cottage, 17 Gladstone Road, Willesborough, Ashford TN24 0BY* Tel (01233) 640736

EVERETT, Robert Henry. b 60. Em Coll Cam BA82 MA86 Ox Univ BA85 MA90 Ex Univ MPhil95. St Steph Ho Ox 83. **d** 86 **p** 87. C Ex St Thos and Em *Ex* 86-88; C Plymstock 88-91; R St Dominic, Landulph and St Mellion w Pillaton *Truro* 91-96; P-in-c Reading All SS *Ox* 96-98; V from 98. *All Saints' Vicarage, 14 Downshire Square, Reading RG1 6NH* Tel 0118-957 2000
E-mail frhenry@allsaints.fsnet.co.uk

EVERETT, Robin Nigel. b 34. Dur Univ BA55 DipTh59. Cranmer Hall Dur 57. **d** 59 **p** 60. C New Humberstone *Leic* 59-62; C Humberstone 62-66; V Quorndon 66-74; V Castle Donington 74-82; P-in-c Lockington w Hemington 81-82; V Castle Donington and Lockington cum Hemington 82-86; Antigua 86-87; R Ibstock w Heather *Leic* 87-98; rtd 98; Perm to Offic *Derby* 98-01 and *Leic* 99-01. *90 Sevenlands Drive, Boulton Moor, Derby DE24 5AQ* Tel (01332) 751879

EVERETT, Simon Francis. b 58. Oak Hill Th Coll BA89. **d** 89 **p** 90. C Wroughton *Bris* 89-93; TV Wexcombe *Sarum* 93-98; P-in-c The Iwernes, Sutton Waldron and Fontmell Magna 98-01; V Iwerne Valley from 01; RD Milton and Blandford from 01. *The Vicarage, Iwerne Minster, Blandford Forum DT11 8NF* Tel and fax (01747) 811291 E-mail everett@classicfm.net

EVERETT-ALLEN, Canon Clive. b 47. AKC70. St Aug Coll Cant 69. **d** 70 **p** 71. C Minera *St As* 70-72; C Hatcham St Cath *S'wark* 72-75; C Beaconsfield *Ox* 75; TV 75-83; R Southwick St Mich *Chich* 83-98; V E Grinstead St Swithun from 98; Can and Preb Chich Cathl from 98; RD E Grinstead from 05; Chapl Qu Victoria Hosp NHS Trust East Grinstead from 98. *St Swithun's Vicarage, Church Lane, East Grinstead RH19 3AZ* Tel (01342) 323307 E-mail revclive@aol.com

EVERINGHAM, Georgina Wendy (formerly WALLACE, Godfrey Everingham). b 32. Tyndale Hall Bris BA57. **d** 58 **p** 59. C Broadwater St Mary *Chich* 58-61; V Shipton Bellinger w S Tidworth *Win* 61-70; V Bournemouth St Paul 70-84; V Throop 84-95; rtd 95; Perm to Offic *Worc* from 96. *3 Harlech Close, Berkeley Alford, Worcester WR4 0JU* Tel (01905) 754394
E-mail gina@wordoflife.uk.com

EVERITT, Mark. b 34. Linc Coll Ox BA58 MA62. Wells Th Coll. **d** 60 **p** 61. C Hangleton *Chich* 60-63; Chapl Mert Coll Ox 63-02; rtd 02. *48 Annandale Avenue, Bognor Regis PO21 2EX* Tel (01243) 823852

EVERITT, Michael John. b 68. K Coll Lon BD90 AKC90. Qu Coll Birm 90 English Coll Rome 91. **d** 92 **p** 93. C Cleveleys *Blackb* 92-95; S Africa 95-98; Succ Bloemfontein Cathl 95-98; Prec 96-98; Chapl and Asst Lect Univ of Orange Free State 96-98; Sen Chapl St Martin's Coll *Blackb* 98-02; Asst Dir of Ords 00-02; R Standish from 02; AD Chorley from 04. *The Rectory, 13 Rectory Lane, Standish, Wigan WN6 0XA* Tel (01257) 421396 E-mail rector@standish.org.uk

EVERITT, William Frank James. b 38. FCA63 Dur Univ BA68 DipTh69. Cranmer Hall Dur 65. **d** 69 **p** 70. C Leic St Phil *Leic* 69-73; P-in-c Prestwold w Hoton 73-77; R Settrington w N Grimston and Wharram *York* 77-84; RD Buckrose 80-84; V Cheltenham St Pet *Glouc* 84-99; rtd 99; Perm to Offic *Ripon* from 03. *27 Lark Hill Crescent, Ripon HG4 2HN* Tel (01765) 603683
E-mail reveritt@yahoo.com

EVERY, Canon Edward. b 09. Mert Coll Ox BA30 MA46. Linc Th Coll 36. **d** 36 **p** 37. C Caistor w Holton le Moor and Clixby *Linc* 36-38; C Burnley St Pet *Blackb* 38-40; C Glouc St Paul *Glouc* 40-41; Chapl RAFVR 41-46; Field Officer Chr Reconstruction in Eur Greece 46-47; C St Helier *S'wark* 48-49; Jerusalem 50-79; Can Res 52-79; Acting Dean 78-79; rtd 79; Perm to Offic *Lon* 82-86; *S'wark* 86-91. *College of St Barnabas, Blackberry Lane, Lingfield RH7 6NJ* Tel (01342) 870806

EVES, Barry. b 51. Sunderland Poly DipHum86. Cranmer Hall Dur 86. **d** 88 **p** 89. C Tadcaster w Newton Kyme *York* 88-91; C York St Paul 91-93; V Bubwith w Skipwith 93-04. *Address temp unknown*

EWART, John. b 66. QUB BA89. CITC BTh02. **d** 02 **p** 03. C Derryloran *Arm* from 02. *51 Oldtown Street, Cookstown BT80 8EE* Tel (028) 8676 6046 E-mail ewartj@btinternet.com

EWBANK, Mark Robert. b 59. Qu Coll Ox MA86. Westcott Ho Cam 84. **d** 86 **p** 87. Zimbabwe 86-00; Asst P N End St Marg Bulawayo 87-88; P-in-c Pumula St Luke 88-96; R Famona St Mary 96-00; C Chalfont St Peter *Ox* from 00. *All Saints' Parsonage, Oval Way, Chalfont St Peter SL9 8PZ* Tel (01753) 883839 E-mail mre.vre@virginnet.co.uk

EWBANK, The Very Revd Robert Arthur Benson. b 22. Qu Coll Ox BA45 MA48. Cuddesdon Coll 46. **d** 48 **p** 49. C Boston *Linc* 48-52; Chapl Uppingham Sch 52-56; Zimbabwe 57-00; Prin Cyrene Secondary Sch Bulawayo 57-82; P-in-c Figtree CD 60-82; Can Bulawayo 64-80; Can Th 80-82; Dean Bulawayo 82-90; rtd 97; Perm to Offic *Ely* from 01. *15 Egremont Street, Ely CB6 1AE* Tel (01353) 654981

EWBANK, Canon Robin Alan. b 42. Ex Coll Ox BA64 MA88 Lon Univ BD68. Clifton Th Coll 66. **d** 69 **p** 70. C Woodford Wells *Chelmsf* 69-72; Warden Cam Univ Miss Bermondsey 72-76; TV Sutton St Jas and Wawne *York* 76-82; R Bramshott *Portsm* 82-91; R Bramshott and Liphook 91-99; Chmn IDWAL *Chich, Guildf* and *Portsm* 90-99; Hon Can Koforidua from 96; P-in-c Hartley Wintney, Elvetham, Winchfield etc *Win* 99-02; V from 02; RD Odiham from 04. *The Vicarage, Church Lane, Hartley Wintney, Basingstoke RG27 8DZ* Tel (01252) 842670 Fax 845583 E-mail robin_ewbank@lineone.net *or* stjohns_hw@talk21.com

EWBANK, The Ven Walter Frederick. b 18. Ball Coll Ox BA45 MA45 BD52. Bps' Coll Cheshunt. **d** 46 **p** 47. C Windermere St Martin *Carl* 46-49; V Hugill 49-52; V Casterton H Trin 52-62; V Raughton Head w Gatesgill 62-66; Hon Can Carl Cathl 66-78 and 83-84; V Carl St Cuth 66-71; Adn Westmorland and Furness 71-77; V Winster 71-78; Adn Carl 78-84; Can Res Carl Cathl 78-82; rtd 84; Perm to Offic *Carl* 84-94. *7 Castle Court, Castle Street, Carlisle CA3 8TP* Tel (01228) 810293

EWEN, Keith John McGregor. b 43. Sarum & Wells Th Coll 77. **d** 79 **p** 80. C Kington w Huntington *Heref* 79-82; C Kington w Huntington, Old Radnor, Kinnerton etc 82-83; P-in-c Culmington w Onibury 83-89; P-in-c Bromfield 83-89; P-in-c

Stanton Lacy 83-89; R Culmington w Onibury, Bromfield etc 90-01; R Llangenni and Llanbedr Ystrad Yw w Patricio *S & B* from 01. *The Rectory, Llangenny, Crickhowell NP8 1HD* Tel (01873) 812557

EWER, Edward Sydney John (Jonathan). b 36. Univ of New England BA69 Lanc Univ MPhil91. St Mich Th Coll Crafers ThL63. **d** 62 **p** 63. Australia 62-83; SSM from 68; Perm to Offic *Blackb* 83-84; Lic to Offic *Dur* 84-98; Prior SSM Priory Dur 85-98; Dioc Dir of Ords 94-98; Perm to Offic *S'wark* from 00; Hon C Pimlico St Mary Bourne Street *Lon* from 05; Hon C Pimlico St Barn from 05. *SSM Priory, 30 Bourne Street, London SW1W 8JJ* Tel (020) 7259 0499 E-mail j_ewer@yahoo.com

EWINGTON, John. b 43. MRICS65. Chich Th Coll 74. **d** 78 **p** 79. C Walthamstow St Jo *Chelmsf* 78-81; Papua New Guinea 81-87; V Southend St Sav Westcliff *Chelmsf* 87-96; TV Bideford, Northam, Westward Ho, Appledore etc *Ex* from 96. *The Vicarage, Meeting Street, Appledore, Bideford EX39 1RJ* Tel (01237) 470469 E-mail john@vicars.co.uk

EXCELL, Robin Stanley. b 41. AKC64. St Boniface Warminster 64. **d** 65 **p** 66. C Ipswich St Mary Stoke *St E* 65-68; C Melton Mowbray w Thorpe Arnold *Leic* 68-70; TV 70-71; R Gt and Lt Blakenham w Baylham *St E* 71-76; R Gt and Lt Blakenham w Baylham and Nettlestead 76-86; RD Bosmere 84-86; NSM Sproughton w Burstall 91-94; R Rattlesden w Thorpe Morieux, Brettenham etc 94-05; rtd 05; Perm to Offic *St E* from 05. *Hollywater, Upper Street, Baylham, Ipswich IP6 8JR* Tel (01473) 830228 E-mail robin.excell@tesco.net

EXELL, Ernest William Carter. b 28. Qu Coll Cam BA52 MA53. Tyndale Hall Bris 49. **d** 52 **p** 53. C Sydenham H Trin *S'wark* 52-54; C E Ham St Paul *Chelmsf* 54-57; Uganda 57-65; Tanzania 66-70; R Abbess and Beauchamp Roding *Chelmsf* 70-71; P-in-c White Roding w Morrell Roding 70-71; R Abbess Roding, Beauchamp Roding and White Roding 71-94; RD Roding 75-79; rtd 94; Perm to Offic *St E* from 94. *8 Ickworth Drive, Bury St Edmunds IP33 3PX* Tel (01284) 724726

EXELL, Michael Andrew John. b 45. FHCIMA MRIPHH67 MICA70. Sarum & Wells Th Coll 87. **d** 89 **p** 90. C Ryde H Trin *Portsm* 89-93; C Swanmore St Mich w Havenstreet 89-92; C Swanmore St Mich 92-93; P-in-c Carisbrooke St Mary 93-99; V from 99; P-in-c Carisbrooke St Nic 93-99; V from 99. *The Vicarage, 56 Castle Road, Carisbrooke, Newport PO30 1DT* Tel (01983) 522095

EXETER, Archdeacon of. *See* GARDNER, The Ven Paul Douglas

EXETER, Bishop of. *See* LANGRISH, The Rt Revd Michael Laurence

EXETER, Dean of. *See* MEYRICK, The Very Revd Cyril Jonathan

EXLEY, Malcolm. b 33. Cranmer Hall Dur. **d** 67 **p** 68. C Sutton St Jas *York* 67-73; V Mappleton w Goxhill 73-77; V Market Weighton 77-90; P-in-c Goodmanham 77-78; R 78-90; V Bridlington Em 90-98; rtd 98; Perm to Offic *York* from 00. *11 The Chase, Driffield YO25 7FJ* Tel (01377) 272312

EXLEY-STIEGLER, Canon George Ebdon. b 16. Syracuse Univ BS51. Berkeley Div Sch STM53. **d** 53 **p** 54. USA 53-79 and from 89; R Camden Trin NY 53-57; R Brockport St Luke NY 57-64; R Rochester Calvary-St Andr NY 64-79; rtd 79; Hon C Knowsley *Liv* 80-81; Hon C Upholland 81-89; Lect Upholland N Inst 80-84. *168 Dalaker Drive, Rochester, NY 14624, USA* E-mail geoes@frontiernet.net

EXON, Helier John Philip. b 44. MBE87. BSc70 CEng87 MIEE87. STETS 96. **d** 99 **p** 00. NSM Milton Abbas, Hilton w Cheselbourne etc *Sarum* 99-05; NSM Piddletrenthide w Plush, Alton Pancras etc 02-05; NSM Piddle Valley, Hilton, Cheselbourne etc from 05. *The Monk's House, Hilton, Blandford Forum DT11 0DG* Tel (01258) 880396 E-mail helier@exon.demon.co.uk

EYDEN, Christopher David. b 59. St Steph Ho Ox 88. **d** 91 **p** 92. C Tottenham St Paul *Lon* 91-93; C Ealing St Pet Mt Park 93-96; TV Wimbledon *S'wark* 96-04; Perm to Offic from 04. *All Saints' Vicarage, 70 Fulham High Street, London SW6 3LG* Tel (020) 7384 0115 Mobile 07951-600923 E-mail chriseyden@talk21.com

EYEONS, Keith James. b 70. Clare Coll Cam BA92 MA96 Lon Inst of Educn PGCE95. St Jo Coll Nottm MA(MM)03. **d** 01 **p** 02. C Iffley *Ox* 01-03; Chapl Down Coll Cam from 03. *Downing College, Cambridge CB2 1DQ* Tel (01223) 334800 E-mail eyeons@hotmail.com

EYERS, Frederick Thomas Laurence. b 12. Ridley Coll Melbourne LTh39. **d** 39 **p** 40. Australia 39-46, 50-73 and from 82; Perm to Offic *York* 46-50; SSM from 50. *Seniors House, 18 Victoria Street, Camberwell, Vic, Australia 3124* Tel (0061) (3) 9882 9597

EYLES, Anthony John. b 34. Bris Univ BSc57. Sarum Th Coll 61. **d** 63 **p** 64. C Wellington w W Buckland *B & W* 63-67; C Wilton 67-74; Ind Chapl *Dur* 74-85; Ind Chapl *Worc* 85-90; P-in-c Bickenhill w Elmdon *Birm* 90; P-in-c Bickenhill 90-00; Chapl Birm Airport 90-00; rtd 00; Perm to Offic *Ex* from 00. *5 Kersbrook Lane, Kersbrook, Budleigh Salterton EX9 7AD* Tel (01395) 446084

EYLES, David William. b 45. Sarum & Wells Th Coll 75. **d** 77 **p** 78. C Knaresborough *Ripon* 77-80; C Chapel Allerton 80-82; P-in-c W Tanfield and Well w Snape and N Stainley 82-83; R 83-91; P-in-c Middleham w Coverdale and E Witton 93-94; R 94-01; P-in-c Thornton Watlass w Thornton Steward 94-01; P-in-c Markington w S Stainley and Bishop Thornton 01-05; rtd 05. *The Vicarage, Westerns Lane, Markington, Harrogate HG3 3PB* Tel (01765) 677123

EYNON, John Kenneth. b 56. Nottm Univ BA77 BArch80. LNSM course 93. **d** 96 **p** 97. OLM Croydon Ch Ch *S'wark* from 96. *33 Fairlands Avenue, Thornton Heath CR7 6HD* Tel (020) 8684 9866 Mobile 0956-640328 Fax 8665 9871 E-mail johneynon@btinternet.com

EYNSTONE, Ms Sarah Francesca Louise. b 75. Univ Coll Lon BA96 Fitzw Coll Cam BA04. Westcott Ho Cam 02. **d** 05. C Hampstead St Jo *Lon* from 05. *1 Holly Bush Vale, London NW3 6TX* Tel (020) 7794 6838 Mobile 07906-406160 E-mail sarah.eynstone@cantab.net

EYRE, The Very Revd Richard Montague Stephens. b 29. Oriel Coll Ox BA53 MA56. St Steph Ho Ox 53. **d** 56 **p** 57. C Portsea N End St Mark *Portsm* 56-59; Tutor Chich Th Coll 59-61; Chapl 61-62; Chapl Eastbourne Coll 62-65; V Arundel w Tortington and S Stoke *Chich* 65-73; V Brighton Gd Shep Preston 73-75; Dir of Ords 75-79; Adn Chich 75-81; Can Res and Treas Chich Cathl 78-81; Dean Ex 81-95; rtd 95; Perm to Offic *B & W* 95-00; P-in-c Pau *Eur* 01-03. *Hathersage, Enmore, Bridgwater TA5 2DP* Tel (01278) 671790

EYRE, Canon Richard Stuart. b 48. Bris Univ BEd81 Nottm Univ MTh86. Linc Th Coll 74. **d** 77 **p** 78. C Henbury *Bris* 77-81; C Bedminster 81-82; TV 82-84; Chapl Bp Grosseteste Coll Linc 84-95; Sen Tutor 89-95; P-in-c Long Bennington w Foston *Linc* 95; P-in-c Saxonwell 95-97; R 97-01; RD Grantham 96-01; TR Hykeham from 01; RD Graffoe from 02; Can and Preb Linc Cathl from 03. *The Rectory, Mill Lane, North Hykeham, Lincoln LN6 9PA* Tel (01522) 882880 Fax 883100 E-mail richard.eyre3@ntlworld.com

F

FACCINI (née LEGG), Sandra Christine. b 55. Surrey Univ BSc78 PhD82. **d** 04 **p** 05. OLM Howell Hill w Burgh Heath *Guildf* from 04. *21 Wellesford Close, Banstead SM7 2HL* Tel (020) 8224 7361 Mobile 07743-675633 E-mail sandra@faccinis.freeserve.co.uk

FACER, Miss Rosemary Jane. b 44. Hull Univ BA65 Reading Univ CertEd66 LTCL72. Trin Coll Bris DipHE80. **dss** 80 **d** 87 **p** 98. St Paul's Cray St Barn *Roch* 80-88; Par Dn 87-88; C Cheltenham St Mark *Glouc* 88-01; C Clifton *York* from 01. *2 Doe Park, Clifton Moor, York YO30 4UQ* Tel (01904) 691474 E-mail r.rj.facer@talk21.com

FACEY, Andrew John. b 57. Trin Coll Cam BA79 MA83 Barrister-at-Law 80. Trin Coll Bris BA92. **d** 92 **p** 93. C Egham *Guildf* 92-96; P-in-c E Molesey St Paul 96-01; P-in-c Epsom Common Ch Ch 01-02; V from 02; Dioc Inter Faith Adv from 96. *Christ Church Vicarage, 20 Christ Church Road, Epsom KT19 8NE* Tel and fax (01372) 720302 E-mail andrew.facey@virgin.net

FAGAN, Jeremy David. b 75. Qu Coll Ox BA98 Wycliffe Hall Ox 99. **d** 01 **p** 02. C Chell *Lich* 01-04; TV Kirkby *Liv* from 04. *St Martin's Vicarage, Peatwood Avenue, Liverpool L32 7PR* Tel 0151-546 2387 E-mail faganj@yahoo.com

FAGAN, John Raymond. b 32. Lon Univ BD69. Ripon Hall Ox 71. **d** 72 **p** 73. C Stalybridge *Man* 72-74; C Madeley *Heref* 74-79; V Amington *Birm* 79-91; P-in-c Stonnall *Lich* 91-97; Chapl HM YOI Swinfen Hall 91-97; rtd 97; C Stonnall *Lich* 97; Res Min Elford from 98. *The Rectory, Church Road, Elford, Tamworth B79 9DA* Tel (01827) 383212

FAGAN, Thomas. b 27. MCIOB67 Man Univ CertEd70. NW Ord Course 78. **d** 81 **p** 82. NSM Rainhill *Liv* 81-90; NSM Prescot 90-97; rtd 97; Perm to Offic *Liv* 97-03. *4 Wensleydale Avenue, Prescot L35 4NR* Tel 0151-426 4788

FAGBEMI, Olubunmi Ayobami (Bunmi). b 57. Lagos Univ LLB78 LSE LLM81 Qu Mary Coll Lon PhD91 Solicitor 79. Ripon Coll Cuddesdon 95. **d** 97 **p** 98. C Enfield St Andr *Lon* 97-01; V Tottenham H Trin from 01. *Holy Trinity Vicarage, Philip Lane, London N15 4GZ* Tel (020) 8801 3021 E-mail bunmif@aol.com

FAGBEMI, Canon Stephen Ayodeji Akinwale. b 67. St Jo Coll Nottm BTh96 Kent Univ PhD04. Immanuel Coll Ibadan 87. **d** 90 **p** 91. C Iyere St Jo Nigeria 90-91; C Owo St Patr 91-92; P-in-c Wakajaye-Etile Ch Ch 92-93; V Emure-Ile St Sav 96-00; Can Owo from 99; Perm to Offic *Cant* 00-03; Hon C Murston w Bapchild and Tonge 03-05; Chapl Sunderland Univ *Dur* from 05; C Sunderland from 05. *Univeristy of Sunderland, Johnson Building, Chester Road, Sunderland SR1 3SD* Tel 0191-515 2933 Mobile 07796-643468 E-mail saaf95@hotmail.com *or* saaf90@yahoo.co.uk

FAGERSON, Joseph Leonard Ladd. b 35. Harvard Univ BA57 Lon Univ DipTh62. Ridley Hall Cam 61. **d** 63 **p** 64. C Tonbridge SS Pet and Paul *Roch* 63-67; Afghanistan 67-74; P-in-c Marbury *Ches* 74-75; P-in-c Kinloch Rannoch *St And* 75-00; Chapl Rannoch Sch Perthshire 75-00; rtd 00. *Westgarth, Tomnacroich, Fortingall, Aberfeldy PH15 2LJ* Tel (01887) 830569

FAHIE, Mrs Stephanie Bridget. b 48. St Jo Coll Nottm 85. **d** 87 **p** 94. Par Dn Leic St Chris *Leic* 87-90; Chapl Scargill Ho 90-95; P-in-c Hickling w Kinoulton and Broughton Sulney *S'well* 95-00; R from 00. *The Rectory, 41 Main Street, Kinoulton, Nottingham NG12 3EA* Tel (01949) 81657 E-mail kinoulton.rectory@virgin.net

FAINT, Paul Edward. b 38. Qu Coll Birm 85. **d** 87 **p** 88. C Cradley *Worc* 87-90; V Hanley Castle, Hanley Swan and Welland 90-94; V Northwood H Trin *Lon* 94-97; Miss to Seafarers from 97; Chapl Larnaca Cyprus 97-01; rtd 01; Perm to Offic *Ox* from 01; Hon Chapl Miss to Seafarers from 02. *17 Priory Orchard, Wantage OX12 9EL* Tel (01235) 772297 E-mail thefaints@lineone.net

FAIRALL, Michael John. b 45. SW Minl Tr Course 88. **d** 90 **p** 91. NSM Southway *Ex* from 90. *132 Lakeview Close, Tamerton Foliot, Plymouth PL5 4LX* Tel (01752) 707694 E-mail m.j.fairall@talk21.com

FAIRBAIRN, Francis Stephen. b 41. LNSM course 94. **d** 98 **p** 99. Hon C Orrell *Liv* from 98. *27 Greenslate Road, Billinge, Wigan WN5 7BQ* Tel (01695) 623127 *or* (01722) 812176 Fax (01722) 815398

FAIRBAIRN, John Alan. b 46. Trin Coll Cam BA67 MA72. Wycliffe Hall Ox 84. **d** 86 **p** 87. C Boscombe St Jo *Win* 86-89; C Edgware *Lon* 89-95; R Gunton St Pet *Nor* from 95; Chapl Jas Paget Healthcare NHS Trust from 96. *The Rectory, 36 Gunton Church Lane, Lowestoft NR32 4LF* Tel (01502) 580707

FAIRBAIRN, Stella Rosamund. **d** 87 **p** 94. NSM Banbury *Ox* 87-99; Perm to Offic *Pet* 88-94. *Hillside, Overthorpe, Banbury OX17 2AF* Tel (01295) 710648

FAIRBAIRN, Stephen. *See* FAIRBAIRN, Francis Stephen

FAIRBANK, Brian Douglas Seeley. b 53. AKC75. St Steph Ho Ox 77. **d** 78 **p** 79. C Newton Aycliffe *Dur* 78-81; C Stocking Farm *Leic* 81-84; TV Ratby cum Groby 84-91; Chapl RN 91-04; R Bramfield, Stapleford, Waterford etc *St Alb* from 04. *The Rectory, Church Lane, Watton-at-Stone, Hertford SG14 3RD* Tel (01920) 830575

FAIRBROTHER, Robin Harry. b 44. Univ of Wales DipTh68. Ho of Resurr Mirfield 64 Wells Th Coll 68. **d** 69 **p** 70. C Wrexham *St As* 69-74; C Welshpool w Castle Caereinion 74-77; V Bettws Cedewain and Tregynon 77-80; V Betws Cedewain and Tregynon and Llanwyddelan 80-92; TR Marshwood Vale *Sarum* 92-98; TR Golden Cap Team from 98. *The Rectory, Whitchurch Canonicorum, Bridport DT6 6RQ* Tel (01297) 489223 E-mail robin.fairbrother@talk21.com

FAIRCLOUGH, Clive Anthony. b 54. TISEC 01. **d** 04 **p** 05. C Nadder Valley *Sarum* from 04. *7 Church Street Close, Tisbury, Salisbury SP3 6QY* Tel (01747) 870790 Mobile 07962-023882 E-mail cfairclough@tisbury.entpdsl.com

FAIRCLOUGH, John Frederick. b 40. St Jo Coll Dur BA63 MA68 MBIM DMS78. Coll of Resurr Mirfield 81. **d** 83 **p** 84. C Horninglow *Lich* 83-87; V Skerton St Luke *Blackb* 87-94; V Thornton-le-Fylde 94-00; rtd 00; Perm to Offic *Blackb* from 01. *18 Crossfield Avenue, Bury BL9 5NX* Tel (01706) 825664

FAIRHURST, Canon Alan Marshall. b 30. Clare Coll Cam BA52 MA56 Lon Univ BD56. Tyndale Hall Bris 53 Hask's Th Academy Istanbul 54 Wycliffe Hall Ox 55. **d** 56 **p** 57. Tutor St Jo Coll Dur 56-60; C Stockport St Geo *Ches* 60-62; Ceylon 62-66; R Ashley w Silverley *Ely* 67-71; R Stockport St Mary *Ches* 71-95; Chapl Stockport Acute Services NHS Trust 76-95; Hon Can Ches Cathl *Ches* 81-95; RD Stockport 86-95; rtd 95; Perm to Offic *Ches* from 95. *50 Ridge Park, Bramhall, Stockport SK7 2BL* Tel 0161-439 3126

FAIRHURST, John Graham. b 39. Linc Th Coll 86. **d** 88 **p** 89. C Whiston *Sheff* 88-91; V Elsecar 91-04; AD Tankersley 01-04; Chapl Barnsley Community & Priority Services NHS Trust 98-04; rtd 04; Perm to Offic *Sheff* from 04. *30 Barberry Way, Ravenfield, Rotherham S65 4RE* Tel (01709) 548206

FAIRHURST, Ms Rosemary Anne. b 63. Newnham Coll Cam BA85 MA85 Lon Inst of Educn PGCE86. Wycliffe Hall Ox BA92. **d** 93 **p** 94. C Hackney Marsh *Lon* 93-97; C Islington St Mary 97-02; Dir Miss and Min Ripon Coll Cuddesdon from 02. *Ripon College, Cuddesdon, Oxford OX44 9EX* Tel (01865) 874404 Fax 875431 E-mail rosyfairhurst@ripon-cuddesdon.ac.uk

FAIRLAMB, Neil. b 49. Univ of Wales (Ban) BA71 Jes Coll Ox BPhil73 Pemb Coll Cam CertEd74. S'wark Ord Course 90. **d** 93 **p** 94. Hon C Dulwich St Barn *S'wark* 93-95; P-in-c Elerch w Penrhyncoch w Capel Bangor and Goginan *St D* 95-96; V 96-98; R Arthog w Fairbourne w Llangelynnin w Rhoslefain *Ban* 98-03; R Beaumaris from 03. *The Rectory, 5 Tros yr Afon, Beaumaris LL58 8BN* Tel (01248) 811402 Fax as telephone E-mail rheithor@aol.com

FAIRLESS (née CARTER), Mrs Elizabeth Jane. b 57. Derby Univ BSc00. St Jo Coll Nottm MTh02. **d** 02 **p** 03. C Leek and Meerbrook *Lich* from 02. *Old Timbers, 5 Stockwell Street, Leek ST13 6DH* Tel (01538) 383590 Mobile 07968-033489 E-mail lizfairless@hotmail.com

FAIRWEATHER, David James. b 35. Keele Univ BEd79. Wycliffe Hall Ox 70. **d** 72 **p** 73. C Trentham *Lich* 72-76; C Cheddleton 76; C Hanley H Ev 77-79; C Rugeley 79-86; V Brown Edge 86-03; rtd 03. *19 Brindley Bank Road, Rugeley WS15 2EY* Tel (01889) 586486

FAIRWEATHER, John. b 39. K Coll Lon AKC66 BD72. **d** 67 **p** 68. C Plymouth St Jas Ham *Ex* 67-69; C Townstal w St Sav and St Petrox w St Barn 69-73; R Corringham w Springthorpe *Linc* 73-78; P-in-c Blyborough 76-78; P-in-c Heapham 76-78; P-in-c Willoughton 76-78; V Pinchbeck 78-82; V Exwick *Ex* 82-04; rtd 04. *52 Woodman's Crescent, Honiton EX14 2DY* Tel (01404) 549711

FAIRWEATHER, Miss Sally Helen. b 69. St Hilda's Coll Ox BA91. Cranmer Hall Dur 94. **d** 97 **p** 98. C Illingworth *Wakef* 97-01; Warden H Rood Ho and C Thirsk *York* 01-02; Chapl Northallerton Health Services NHS Trust 01-02; C Sheff St Mark Broomhill *Sheff* 02-04; Mental Health Chapl Sheff Care Trust from 04. *4 Riverdale, Main Road, Grindleford, Hope Valley S32 2JN* Tel (01433) 639401

FALASCHI-RAY, Sonia Ofelia. Surrey Univ BSc79 Wolfs Coll Cam BA02 CEng86. Ridley Hall Cam 03. **d** 05. NSM Fowlmere, Foxton, Shepreth and Thriplow *Ely* from 05. *27 Church Lane, Barkway, Royston SG8 8EJ* Tel (01763) 849057 Mobile 07747-844265 E-mail sonia.falaschi'ray@virgin.net

FALCONER, Ian Geoffrey. b 40. BNC Ox BA62 Newc Univ MA93. Cuddesdon Coll 62. **d** 64 **p** 65. C Chiswick St Nic w St Mary *Lon* 64-68; C-in-c Hounslow Gd Shep Beavers Lane CD 68-76; P-in-c Hammersmith St Matt 76-84; P-in-c Byker St Silas *Newc* 84-93; V 93-95; P-in-c Newc St Phil and St Aug 95-98; P-in-c Newc St Matt w St Mary 95-98; P-in-c Newc St Phil and St Aug and St Matt w St Mary 98-00; V Seghill from 00. *Seghill Vicarage, Mares Close, Seghill, Cramlington NE23 7EA* Tel 0191-237 1228 E-mail fr-ian@excite.com

FALKNER, Jonathan Michael Shepherd. b 47. Open Univ BA74. Cranmer Hall Dur. **d** 79 **p** 80. C Penrith w Newton Reigny *Carl* 79-81; C Penrith w Newton Reigny and Plumpton Wall 81-82; C Dalton-in-Furness 82-84; V Clifton 84-90; P-in-c Dean 85-89; R 89-90; P-in-c Rumburgh w S Elmham w the Ilketshalls *St E* 90-92; R S Elmham and Ilketshall 92-99; RD Beccles and S Elmham 94-99; Hon Can St E Cathl 98-99; P-in-c W Newton and Bromfield w Waverton *Carl* 99-02; P-in-c Holme Cultram St Mary and St Cuth 00-02; TR Solway Plain from 02. *The Vicarage, Langrigg, Wigton CA7 3NA* Tel (01697) 320261 E-mail jonathan.falkner@talk21.com

FALL, Harry. b 17. Leeds Univ BA40 BD51 Dur Univ BA42 MA48. **d** 42 **p** 43. C Eccles St Mary *Man* 42-44; C Heaton Norris Ch Ch 44-45; C Linthorpe *York* 45-49; V Danby 49-54; V Harden *Bradf* 54-57; R Scrayingham *York* 57-71; R York H Trin w St Jo Micklegate and St Martin 71-84; rtd 84; Perm to Offic *York* from 84. *20 Weaponness Valley Road, Scarborough YO11 2JF* Tel (01723) 361822

FALLA, Miles. b 43. MCIM. EAMTC 93. **d** 96 **p** 97. NSM Buckden *Ely* 96-98; P-in-c Gretton w Rockingham *Pet* 98-99; V Gretton w Rockingham and Cottingham w E Carlton 99-04; RD Corby 01-02; rtd 04. *Bowlings, Silver Street, Buckden, St Neots PE19 5TS* Tel (01480) 811335 E-mail gretton@mfalla.fsnet.co.uk

FALLONE, Christopher. b 55. Aston Tr Scheme 85 Oak Hill Th Coll 87. **d** 90 **p** 91. C Rochdale *Man* 90-93; P-in-c Thornham w Gravel Hole 93-94; TV Middleton w Thornham from 94. *St John's Vicarage, 1177 Manchester Road, Rochdale OL11 2XZ* Tel (01706) 631825 Mobile 07976-624124 Fax 631645 E-mail chrisfallone@bigfoot.com

FALLOWS, Stuart Adrian. b 50. Moray Ho Edin 75. **d** 78 **p** 79. Hon C Forres w Nairn *Mor* 78-81; Hon C Elgin w Lossiemouth 81-86; Hon Dioc Chapl 86; C Brighton St Geo w St Anne and St Mark *Chich* 86-89; V Wivelsfield 89-98; P-in-c Kieth, Huntly and Aberchirder *Mor* 98-02; P-in-c Ringwould w Kingsdown *Cant* 02-04; R Ringwould w Kingsdown and Ripple etc from 05. *The Rectory, Upper Street, Kingsdown, Deal CT14 8BJ* Tel (01304) 373951 E-mail afallows@beeb.net

FALSHAW, Simon Meriadoc. b 60. Leeds Univ BSc82. Oak Hill Th Coll BA93. **d** 93 **p** 94. C Stapleford *S'well* 93-99; Miss Partner

Crosslinks 99-00; P-in-c The Lye and Stambermill *Worc* from 01; RD Stourbridge from 04. *Christ Church Vicarage, High Street, Lye, Stourbridge DY9 8LF* Tel (01384) 423142 *or* 894948 E-mail christchurchlye@classicfm.net

FANE, Clifford Charles. b 39. Kelham Th Coll 62. **d** 67 **p** 68. C Heston *Lon* 67-73; C Bedminster St Mich *Bris* 73-76; P-in-c 76-77; C Gaywood, Bawsey and Mintlyn *Nor* 77-81; V Bolton St Jo *Man* 81-90; rtd 90. *10 Booth Road, Little Lever, Bolton BL3 1JY* Tel (01204) 709420

FANTHORPE, Robert Lionel. b 35. Open Univ BA80 CertEd63 FCMI81 FCP90. Llan Dioc Tr Scheme. **d** 87 **p** 88. NSM Roath St German *Llan* 87-00; Lic to Offic from 00. *Rivendell, 48 Claude Road, Roath, Cardiff CF24 3QA* Tel (029) 2049 8368 Mobile 07767-207289 Fax (029) 2049 6832 E-mail fanthorpe@aol.com

FARADAY, John. b 49. Leeds Univ BSc71 MICE78. Oak Hill Th Coll 81. **d** 83 **p** 84. C Sutton *Liv* 83-86; C Rainhill 86-89; Chapl Whiston Hosp 86-89; V Over Darwen St Jas *Blackb* 89-02; TR S Rochdale *Man* from 02. *St Mary's Vicarage, The Sett, Badger Lane, Rochdale OL16 4RQ* Tel (01706) 649886 E-mail vicarj@btinternet.com

FARAH, Mones Anton. b 64. Trin Coll Bris BA88. **d** 88 **p** 89. C Aberystwyth *St D* 88-91; Chapl St D Coll Lamp 91-98; TV Gt Baddow *Chelmsf* from 98. *The Vicarage, 42 Riffhams Drive, Great Baddow, Chelmsford CM2 7DD* Tel (01245) 471516 E-mail monesf@yahoo.com

FARBRIDGE, Nicholas Brisco. b 33. FCA. Sarum & Wells Th Coll 75. **d** 77 **p** 78. C Gt Bookham *Guildf* 77-80; C Ewell 80-83; V Addlestone 83-89; R Shere 89-95; rtd 96; Perm to Offic *Guildf* from 96. *55 Curling Vale, Guildford GU2 7PH* Tel (01483) 531140 E-mail nickfarbridge@beeb.net

FARDON, Jean Audrey May. b 24. Westf Coll Lon BA45 Lon Inst of Educn DipEd46. Gilmore Ho DipTh69. **dss** 79 **d** 87 **p** 94. St Alb St Pet *St Alb* 79-92; Hon Par Dn 87-92; NSM Powick *Worc* 92-94; Perm to Offic from 94. *17 The Greenway, Powick, Worcester WR2 4RZ* Tel (01905) 830472

FARDON, Raymond George Warren. b 30. St Pet Hall Ox BA52 MA56. Ridley Hall Cam 54. **d** 59 **p** 60. C High Wycombe All SS *Ox* 59-63; Chapl Bedford Secondary Modern Sch 63-68; Hd Master K Sch Grantham 72-82; Travelling Ev 82-95; Hon C Longfleet *Sarum* 82-83; Perm to Offic 83-03; rtd 95. *9 Somerby Court, Bramcote, Nottingham NG9 3NB* Tel 0115-928 0810

FAREY, David Mark. b 56. St Jo Coll Dur BA85. Cranmer Hall Dur 82. **d** 86 **p** 87. C Brackley St Pet w St Jas *Pet* 86-89; TV Kingsthorpe w Northampton St Dav 89-96; R Laughton w Ripe and Chalvington *Chich* from 96; Chapl to Bp Lewes from 96. *The Rectory, Church Lane, Laughton, Lewes BN8 6AH* Tel (01323) 811642 Fax as telephone

FARGUS, Gavin James Frederick. b 30. AKC54. K Coll Lon. **d** 55 **p** 57. C Salisbury St Mark *Sarum* 55-57; C Wareham w Arne 57-60; C Marlborough 60-63; P-in-c Davidstow w Otterham *Truro* 63-65; R Nether Lochaber *Arg* 65-81; R Kinlochleven 65-81; rtd 81; Lic to Offic *Arg* 82-94. *61 Loan Fearn, Ballachulish, Argyll PH49 4JB* Tel (01855) 811851

FARGUS, Maxwell Stuart. b 34. Linc Coll Ox BA57 MA61 Leeds Univ DipAdEd79. Cuddesdon Coll 57. **d** 59 **p** 60. C Newc St Fran *Newc* 59-62; C Rothbury 62-64; Dioc Youth Officer *Ripon* 64-76; R Kirkby Wiske 64-76; Community Educn Officer Barnsley MBC 76-88; Perm to Offic *Sheff*; *Wakef* and *York* 77-88; V Rudston w Boynton and Kilham *York* 88-93; rtd 93; Perm to Offic *York* from 93. *56 Fir Tree Drive, Filey YO14 9NR* Tel and fax (01723) 513511

FARISH, Alan John. b 58. Lanc Univ BA. St Jo Coll Nottm LTh86 DPS86. **d** 86 **p** 87. C Bishopwearmouth St Gabr *Dur* 86-89; C Fatfield 89-98; P-in-c Preston on Tees 98-03; V Preston-on-Tees and Longnewton from 03. *The Vicarage, Quarry Road, Eaglescliffe, Stockton-on-Tees TS16 9BD* Tel (01642) 789814

FARLEY, Claire Louise. *See* MADDOCK, Ms Claire Louise

FARLEY, David Stuart. b 53. Univ Coll Dur BA75 Westmr Coll Ox MTh00 Nottm Univ DipTh82 Dip Counselling 99. St Jo Coll Nottm. **d** 84 **p** 85. C Bath Weston All SS w N Stoke *B & W* 84-87; Chapl Scargill Ho 87-90; Min Hedge End N CD *Win* 90-94; V Hedge End St Luke 94-00; Dep Chapl HM Pris Belmarsh 00-01; Chapl HM Pris Shrewsbury from 01. *HM Prison, The Dana, Shrewsbury SY1 2HR* Tel (01743) 352511 ext 325

FARLEY, Ian David. b 56. Linc Coll Ox BA78 MA87 Dur Univ PhD88. Cranmer Hall Dur 84. **d** 87 **p** 88. C Thorpe Acre w Dishley *Leic* 87-92; V S Lambeth St Steph *S'wark* 92-99; V Bacton w Edingthorpe w Witton and Ridlington *Nor* 99-03; Ind Chapl 99-03; TR Buckhurst Hill *Chelmsf* from 03. *St John's Rectory, High Road, Buckhurst Hill IG9 5RX* Tel (020) 8504 1931 E-mail mags@brewup.freeserve.co.uk

FARLEY, James Trevor. b 37. IEng MIEE FRSA. EMMTC 80. **d** 82 **p** 83. NSM Grantham *Linc* from 82. *Highfield Cottage, Station Road, Bottesford, Nottingham NG13 0EN* Tel (01949) 843646 Fax 843860 E-mail jimandroma@highfield40.fsnet.co.uk

FARLEY, Ronald Alexander. b 30. Oak Hill NSM Course. **d** 79 **p** 80. NSM Stoke Newington St Faith, St Matthias and All SS *Lon* 79-97; NSM Upper Clapton St Matt 99-04; rtd 04. *2 St James Close, Bishop Street, London N1 8PH* Tel (020) 7354 2231

FARLEY-MOORE, Peter James. b 72. Sheff Univ BA94. Ridley Hall Cam MA00. **d** 00 **p** 01. C Chapeltown *Sheff* 00-03; CMS from 03. *Church Mission Society, Partnership House, 157 Waterloo Road, London SE1 8UU* Tel (020) 7928 8681 E-mail farley-moore@tinyworld.co.uk

FARMAN, Joanne Margaret. b 46. Birkbeck Coll Lon BA81 Southlands Coll Lon PGCE82. SEITE 97. **d** 00 **p** 01. NSM Limpsfield and Titsey *S'wark* 00-04; Chapl St Geo Healthcare NHS Trust Lon from 00; Lead Chapl R Hosp for Neuro-Disability from 04. *10 Detillens Lane, Limpsfield, Oxted RH8 0DJ* Tel (01883) 713086 *or* (020) 8725 3070

FARMAN, Robert Joseph. b 54. Ridley Hall Cam 86. **d** 88 **p** 89. C Sutton St Nic *S'wark* 88-90; C Cheam Common St Phil 90-92; R Wootton w Glympton and Kiddington *Ox* 92-00; TV Kings Norton *Birm* 00-04; Chapl St Mary's Hospice 04-05; Chapl R Orthopaedic Hosp NHS Trust from 05. *58 Station Road, Kings Norton, Birmingham B30 1DA* Tel 0121-451 1234 *or* 685 4000 Mobile 07766-054137 E-mail robfarman@evemail.net

FARMAN, Mrs Roberta. b 48. Aber Univ MA70 Cam Univ CertEd72. Qu Coll Birm 78. **dss** 82 **d** 87 **p** 01. Ovenden *Wakef* 80-82; Scargill Ho 83-84; Coulsdon St Jo *S'wark* 85-86; Hon Par Dn Cambridge St Mark *Ely* 86-88; Hon Par Dn Sutton St Nic *S'wark* 88-92; Hon Par Dn Wootton w Glympton and Kiddington *Ox* 92-00; NSM Kings Norton *Birm* 01-04; Chapl Univ Hosp Birm NHS Foundn Trust from 01. *58 Station Road, Kings Norton, Birmingham B30 1DA* Tel 0121-451 1234 *or* 627 1627 E-mail bj@robfarman.evesham.net

FARMBOROUGH, James Laird McLelland (Mac). b 22. MBE90. Magd Coll Cam BA49 MA54. Tyndale Hall Bris. **d** 52 **p** 53. C Wolverhampton St Luke *Lich* 52-55; C Holloway St Mary w St Jas *Lon* 55-56; C Broadwater St Mary *Chich* 56-58; Chapl All SS Niteroi Brazil 58-64; Org Sec SAMS 65-70; V Marple All SS *Ches* 70-80; Chapl Vina del Mar St Pet Chile 80-92; Miss to Seamen 80-92; rtd 92. *5 Gracey Court, Woodland Road, Broadclyst EX5 3LP* Tel (01392) 462574

✠**FARMBROUGH, The Rt Revd David John.** b 29. Linc Coll Ox BA51 MA53. Westcott Ho Cam 51. **d** 53 **p** 54 **c** 81. C Bp's Hatfield *St Alb* 53-57; P-in-c 57-63; V Bishop's Stortford St Mich 63-74; RD Bishop's Stortford 73-74; Adn St Alb 74-81; Suff Bp Bedford 81-93; rtd 94; Hon Asst Bp St Alb from 94. *St Michael Mead, 110 Village Road, Bromham, Bedford MK43 8HU* Tel (01234) 825042

FARMER, Diane Marcia (Diana). b 61. Warwick Univ BSc82 PGCE83. WMMTC 97 Cranmer Hall Dur 00. **d** 01 **p** 02. C Allesley Park and Whoberley *Cov* from 01. *14 Harewood Road, Coventry CV5 8BQ* Tel (024) 7667 6839 E-mail diana@whoberley.org.uk

FARMER, George Wilson. b 37. Lich Th Coll 61. **d** 65 **p** 66. C Kingston All SS *S'wark* 65-69; C Heston *Lon* 69-74; C Southmead *Bris* 74-75; C Bedminster 75-80; TV Langley Marish *Ox* 80-86; R Wexham 86-03; rtd 03. *Chalfont Lodge, Denham Lane, Chalfont St Peter, Gerrards Cross SL9 0QQ* Tel (01753) 888002

FARMER, Lorelie Joy. Southn Univ BA65 MA68 Mass Univ EdD88. Cranmer Hall Dur. **d** 99 **p** 00. C Newbury *Ox* 99-03; C Stratford-upon-Avon, Luddington etc *Cov* from 03. *Holy Trinity Church, Maidenhead Road, Stratford-upon-Avon CV37 6XX* Tel (01789) 266316 E-mail loreliefarmer@dunelm.org.uk

FARMER, Robert John Thayer. b 62. Kent Univ BA84 SSC. St Steph Ho Ox 91. **d** 93 **p** 94. C Leigh St Clem *Chelmsf* 93-96; P-in-c Wellingborough St Mary *Pet* 96-00; V from 00; Chapl Northants Healthcare NHS Trust from 99. *St Mary's Vicarage, 193 Midland Road, Wellingborough NN8 1NG* Tel (01933) 225626 E-mail vicar@stmarywellingborough.org.uk

FARMER, Simon John. b 60. Birm Univ BSc82. St Jo Coll Nottm 86. **d** 89 **p** 90. C Ulverston St Mary w H Trin *Carl* 89-92; CF 92-97; Chapl HM Pris Lowdham Grange 97-00; CF (TA) from 99; Perm to Offic *S'well* from 00; Operations Dir (Africa) ACCTS Mil Min Internat from 00. *26 Halloughton Road, Southwell NG25 0LR* Tel (01636) 813599 E-mail sjfarmer@ntlworld.com

FARMER, Canon William John Cotton. b 19. St Jo Coll Dur LTh42 BA43. St Aid Birkenhead. **d** 43 **p** 44. C Ipswich St Aug *St E* 43-45; C Warwick St Mary *Cov* 45-49; C Solihull *Birm* 49-54; V Blackheath 54-64; V Packwood w Hockley Heath 64-81; Hon Can Birm Cathl 80-81; rtd 84. *12 Bowling Green Court, Hospital Road, Moreton-in-Marsh GL56 0BX* Tel (01608) 651082

FARMILOE, Preb Trevor James. b 42. Sarum & Wells Th Coll. **d** 82 **p** 82. C S Petherton w the Seavingtons *B & W* 82-85; R Norton St Philip w Hemington, Hardington etc 85-93; Chapl Rural Affairs Wells Adnry 87-92; RD Frome 89-93; V Martock w Ash from 93; RD Ivelchester 95-01 and from 04; Preb Wells Cathl from 96. *The Vicarage, 10 Water Street, Martock TA12 6JN* Tel and fax (01935) 826113 E-mail revtrev.martock@virgin.net

FARNHAM, Douglas John. b 30. SS Mark & Jo Coll Plymouth TCert52 Ex Univ AdDipEd66 MEd75. S Dios Minl Tr Scheme 80. **d** 83 **p** 84. Lect Bp Otter Coll Chich 70-78; Sen Lect W Sussex Inst of HE 78-92; NSM Barnham and Eastergate *Chich* 83-85; NSM Aldingbourne, Barnham and Eastergate 85-92; R 92-96; rtd 96; Perm to Offic *Chich* from 96. *16 Henty Close, Walberton, Arundel BN18 0PW* Tel (01243) 555992

FARNWORTH, Ms Joanna Helen. b 66. Jes Coll Cam BA88 MA92. St Jo Coll Nottm BTh98 MA99. **d** 99 **p** 00. C Middleton w Thornham *Man* 99-03; C Ashton 03-05; TV from 05. *St James's Vicarage, Union Street, Ashton-under-Lyne OL6 9NQ* Tel 0161-330 4925 E-mail joannafarnworth@aol.com

FARNWORTH, Roger. b 60. Man Univ BSc81. St Jo Coll Nottm MA99. **d** 99 **p** 00. C Tonge w Alkrington *Man* 99-03; TV Ashton 03-05; TR from 05. *St James's Vicarage, Union Street, Ashton-under-Lyne OL6 9NQ* Tel 0161-330 2771 E-mail rogerfarnworth@aol.com

FARQUHAR, Preb Patricia Ann. b 42. **dss** 78 **d** 87 **p** 94. S Hackney St Jo w Ch Ch *Lon* 80-01; Par Dn 87-94; C 94-01; Preb St Paul's Cathl 97-01; rtd 01. *5A Coronation Close, Norwich NR6 5HF* Tel (01603) 417554

FARQUHARSON, The Very Revd Hunter Buchanan. b 58. ALAM LLAM. Edin Th Coll 85. **d** 88 **p** 89. C Dunfermline *St And* 88-91; R Glenrothes 91-97; R Leven 95-97; R Dunfermline 97-99; Provost St Ninian's Cathl Perth from 99. *St Ninian's Cathedral, North Methven Street, Perth PH1 5PP* Tel and fax (01738) 850987 *or* tel 632053 Fax 639811 E-mail hbf1@compuserve.com *or* stninians.cathedral@btinernet.com

FARR, Arthur Ronald. b 24. JP77. Llan Dioc Tr Scheme 77. **d** 80 **p** 81. NSM Penarth All SS *Llan* 80-90; rtd 90; Perm to Offic *Llan* from 90. *3 Cymric Close, Ely, Cardiff CF5 4GR* Tel (029) 2056 1765

FARR (née ROSE), Margaret. b 37. Man Univ BDS, LDS60 Birm Univ MB, ChB69 MD85. WMMTC 99. **d** 02 **p** 03. NSM Handsworth St Jas *Birm* from 02. *35 West Drive, Handsworth, Birmingham B20 3ST* Tel 0121-554 0909

FARR, Mark Julian Richard. b 60. **d** 87 **p** 88. C Clapham Team *S'wark* 87-91; TV Wimbledon 91-95; USA from 96. *Sojourners, 2401 15th Street NW, Washington, DC 20009, USA*

FARR, Richard William. b 55. Ridley Hall Cam. **d** 83 **p** 84. C Enfield Ch Ch Trent Park *Lon* 83-87; C Eastbourne H Trin *Chich* 87-90; P-in-c Henham and Elsenham w Ugley *Chelmsf* from 90. *The Vicarage, Carters Lane, Henham, Bishop's Stortford CM22 6AQ* Tel (01279) 850281 E-mail dickthevic@netscapeonline.co.uk

FARRAN, Canon George Orman. b 35. Worc Coll Ox BA58 MA62. Wycliffe Hall Ox 58. **d** 60 **p** 61. C Tyldesley w Shakerley *Man* 60-62; Tutor Wycliffe Hall Ox 62-64; V Netherton *Liv* 64-73; R Sefton 69-73; R Credenhill w Brinsop, Mansel Lacey, Yazor etc *Heref* 73-83; RD Heref Rural 81-83; R Ditcheat w E Pennard and Pylle *B & W* 83-94; Dir of Ords 86-89; Can and Chan Wells Cathl 85-97; rtd 97; Perm to Offic *B & W* 97-00 and from 01. *Bethany, Ashton Hill, Corston, Bath BA2 9EY* Tel (01225) 872348

FARRANCE, William Kenneth. b 22. Univ of Wales (Ban) 46. Bps' Coll Cheshunt 49. **d** 52 **p** 53. C Newc St Gabr *Newc* 52-58; V Newsham 58-63; V Heddon-on-the-Wall 63-78; Chapl Tynemouth Hosps 79-82; AP Tynemouth Ch Ch 79-82; rtd 82; Perm to Offic *Newc* from 82. *32 Garden Terrace, Earsdon, Whitley Bay NE25 9LQ* Tel 0191-251 1599

FARRANT, David Stuart. b 38. Ripon Coll Cuddesdon 82. **d** 84 **p** 85. C Woodford St Mary w St Phil and St Jas *Chelmsf* 84-87; R Clymping and Yapton w Ford *Chich* 87-92; Dioc Schs Admin Officer 92-95; Chapl Qu Alexandra Hosp Home Worthing 95-04; P-in-c Amberley w N Stoke and Parham, Wiggonholt etc *Chich* from 04. *The New Vicarage, School Road, Amberley, Arundel BN18 9NA* Tel (01798) 831500

FARRANT, Canon John Frederick Ames. b 30. Aber Univ MA51 BD58 MTh80. Edin Th Coll 51. **d** 53 **p** 54. C Dundee St Mary Magd *Bre* 53-58; R Clydebank *Glas* 58-65; R Motherwell 65-70; Papua New Guinea 70-73 and 81-84; R Glas St Bride *Glas* 73-81; Can St Mary's Cathl 77-81; Provost Rabaul 81-84; R Penicuik *Edin* 85-96; R W Linton 85-96; Can St Mary's Cathl 92-96; Chapl Madeira *Eur* 96-98; rtd 98; Hon Asst P St Mary le Strand w St Clem Danes *Lon* from 98; Perm to Offic from 01. *20 Defoe House, London EC2Y 8DN* Tel (020) 7638 3963

FARRANT, Canon Martyn John. b 38. AKC61. **d** 62 **p** 63. C Hampton St Mary *Lon* 62-65; C Shere *Guildf* 65-67; V Stoneleigh 67-75; V Addlestone 75-83; V Dorking w Ranmore 83-98; RD Dorking 89-94; Hon Can Guildf Cathl 96-98; rtd 98; Perm to Offic *Guildf* from 98; Chapl Phyllis Tuckwell Hospice Farnham 98-01. *42 Hampstead Road, Dorking RH4 3AE* Tel (01306) 740916

FARRAR, Canon James Albert. b 27. TCD BA55 MA57. CITC 56. **d** 56 **p** 57. C Dublin Drumcondra w N Strand *D & G* 56-59; C Dublin Rathmines 59-61; I Ballinaclash 61-72; I Dunganstown w Redcross 72-79; Warden Ch Min of Healing 79-95; Hon Clerical V Ch Ch Cathl Dublin 79-92; Can Ch Ch Cathl Dublin from 92; rtd 95. *15 Hillside, Greystones, Co Wicklow, Irish Republic* Tel (00353) (1) 287 2706

FARRAR, Prof Roy Alfred. b 39. Imp Coll Lon BSc60 PhD67 DIC60 FWeldI85. Wycliffe Hall Ox 99. **d** 00 **p** 01. NSM Portswood St Denys *Win* 00-04; P-in-c Lille *Eur* from 04. *9 rue Léonard de Vinci, 59700 Marcq en Baroeul, France*

FARRAR, Ruth. b 43. Matlock Coll of Educn CertEd64. **d** 04 **p** 05. OLM Leesfield *Man* from 04. *Belvoir, 43 Coverhill Road, Grotton, Oldham OL4 5RE* Tel 0161-633 0374

FARRELL, Miss Katherine Lucy Anne. b 61. Westcott Ho Cam 00. **d** 02 **p** 03. C Forest Gate Em w Upton Cross *Chelmsf* 02-03; C Lt Ilford St Mich from 03. *52 Bolton Road, London E15 4JY*

FARRELL, Ms Margaret Ruth. b 57. Linc Inst Melbourne BAppSc(OT)78. **d** 02 **p** 03. C Bury St Edmunds All SS w St Jo and St Geo *St E* from 02. *140 Abbot Road, Bury St Edmunds IP33 3UW* Tel (01284) 768317 Mobile 07855-996831 E-mail farrell@fish.co.uk

FARRELL, Peter Godfrey Paul. b 39. Sarum & Wells Th Coll 72. **d** 74 **p** 75. C St Just in Roseland *Truro* 74-77; C Kenwyn 77-80; V Knighton St Jo *Leic* 80-86; TR Clarendon Park St Jo w Knighton St Mich 86-89; V Woodham *Guildf* 89-99; V Wells St Cuth w Wookey Hole *B & W* from 99. *The Vicarage, 1 St Cuthbert Street, Wells BA5 2AW* Tel (01749) 673136 Fax as telephone E-mail peter.farrell2@ukonline.co.uk

FARRELL, Robert Edward. b 54. Univ of Wales (Abth) BA74 Jes Coll Ox BA77 MA81. Qu Coll Birm 85. **d** 86 **p** 87. C Llanrhos *St As* 86-88; C Prestwich St Marg *Man* 89-91; V Moulsham St Luke *Chelmsf* 91-98; V Thorpe Bay from 98. *The Vicarage, 86 Tyrone Road, Southend-on-Sea SS1 3HB* Tel (01702) 587597 E-mail robert_farrell21@hotmail.com

FARRELL, Ronald Anthony. b 57. Edin Univ BD84 Birm Univ MA86. Qu Coll Birm 84. **d** 86 **p** 87. C Shard End *Birm* 86-87; C Shirley 87-89; Bp's Officer for Schs and Young People 89-93; V Kingstanding St Mark 93-01; TR Swinton and Pendlebury *Man* 01-05; P-in-c Lower Broughton Ascension 02-05; V W Bromwich St Fran *Lich* from 05. *Friar Park Vicarage, Freeman Road, Wednesbury WS10 0HJ* Tel 0121-556 5823

FARRELL, Thomas Stanley. b 32. Lon Univ BD71. Ridley Hall Cam 69. **d** 71 **p** 72. C Much Woolton *Liv* 71-73; C Gt Sankey 73-74; Asst Chapl Dulwich Coll 74-76; Chapl 76-81; P-in-c Wonersh *Guildf* 81-86; V 86-90; RD Cranleigh 87-90; R St Marg Lothbury and St Steph Coleman Street etc *Lon* 90-00; P-in-c St Botolph without Aldersgate 90-97; rtd 00; Hon C Burford w Fulbrook, Taynton, Asthall etc *Ox* 00-04; Perm to Offic from 04. *Westfarthing Cottage, 1 Lawrence Lane, Burford OX18 4RP* Tel (01993) 823951

FARRER, Canon Carol Elizabeth. b 47. Open Univ BA88. Cranmer Hall Dur 81. **dss** 83 **d** 87 **p** 94. Newbarns w Hawcoat *Carl* 83-86; Egremont and Haile 86-91; Par Dn 87-91; TD Penrith w Newton Reigny and Plumpton Wall 91-94; TV 94-01; Dioc Lay Min Adv 87-88; Assoc Dir of Ords 88-97; Dir of Ords 97-00; Dioc OLM Officer from 00; Hon Can Carl Cathl from 01; TV S Barrow from 01. *The Vicarage, 98A Roose Road, Barrow-in-Furness LA13 9RL* Tel (01229) 826489 Fax as telephone E-mail revcarol@fish.co.uk

FARRER, Canon Michael Robert Wedlake. b 22. St Pet Hall Ox BA52 MA57. Tyndale Hall Bris 47. **d** 52 **p** 53. C Ox St Ebbe *Ox* 52-56; Tutor Clifton Th Coll 56-65; R Barton Seagrave *Pet* 65-73; R Barton Seagrave w Warkton 73-78; V Cambridge St Paul *Ely* 78-92; RD Cambridge 84-89; Hon Can Ely Cathl 88-92; rtd 92; Bp's Sen Chapl *Ely* 92-95; Perm to Offic from 92. *2 Houghton Gardens, Ely CB7 4JN* Tel (01353) 665654

FARRER, Simon James Anthony. b 52. St Cath Coll Cam MA77 K Coll Lon BD78 MTh92. AKC78 Coll of Resurr Mirfield 78. **d** 79 **p** 80. C St John's Wood *Lon* 79-84; C N Harrow St Alb 84-87; P-in-c Hammersmith St Luke 87-93; USPG 93-99; Zambia 94-99; P-in-c Stoke Newington Common St Mich *Lon* 99-02; V from 02. *St Michael's Vicarage, 55 Fountayne Road, London N16 7ED* Tel (020) 8806 4225

FARRINGTON, Canon Christine Marion. b 42. Birkbeck Coll Lon BA65 Nottm Univ DASS66 Middx Poly MA75. St Alb Minl Tr Scheme 79. **dss** 82 **d** 87 **p** 94. Redbourn *St Alb* 82-87; Dir Past Studies Linc Th Coll 86-87; HM Pris Linc 86-87; Dir Sarum Chr Cen 87-93; Dn Sarum Cathl *Sarum* 87-93; Co-Dir of Ords and Dir of Women's Min *Ely* 93-02; Hon Can Ely Cathl 93-02; C Cambridge Gt St Mary w St Mich 93-96; V Cambridge St Mark 96-02; Chapl Wolfs Coll Cam 97-02; Perm to Offic *St Alb* 97-04; Chapl to The Queen from 98; rtd 02; RD Wheathampstead *St Alb* from 04. *30 Lybury Lane, Redbourn, St Albans AL3 7HY* Tel (01582) 793409

FARRINGTON, Lynda. WMMTC. **d** 01 **p** 02. NSM Cannock *Lich* from 01. *Blithford Farm, Blithbury, Rugeley WS15 3JB* Tel (01283) 840253 *or* 502131 E-mail farringtontowers@compuserve.com

FARROW, Edward. b 38. Sarum Th Coll 69. **d** 71 **p** 72. C Parkstone St Pet w Branksea *Sarum* 71-74; R Tidworth 74-79; P-in-c W and E Lulworth 79-80; P-in-c Winfrith Newburgh w Chaldon Herring 79-80; R The Lulworths, Winfrith Newburgh and Chaldon 80-83; V Ensbury Park 83-03; Chapl Talbot Heath

Sch Bournemouth 83-97; rtd 03. *21 avenue de Bourgogne, 13006 La Ciotat, France* Tel (0033) (4) 42 83 03 20

FARROW, Elizabeth Maura. b 43. Edin Th Coll. **d** 91 **p** 96. NSM Glas H Cross *Glas* 91-96; TV Bearsden 96-00 and from 03; TP Milngavie from 03. *5 Campsie Road, Strathblane G63 9AB* Tel (01360) 770936

FARROW, Ian Edmund Dennett. b 38. S'wark Ord Course 70. **d** 72 **p** 73. C Tunbridge Wells St Jo *Roch* 72-78; Chapl N Cambs Gen Hosp Gp 78-92; P-in-c Walsoken *Ely* 78-80; R 80-92; V Bisley, Oakridge, Miserden and Edgeworth *Glouc* 92-04; rtd 04. *Wellspring, Brook Lane, Stonesfield, Witney OX29 8PR* Tel (01993) 891293

FARROW, Keith. b 59. N Ord Course 02. **d** 05. C Sprotbrough *Sheff* from 05. *31 Ambleside Crescent, Sprotbrough, Doncaster DN5 7PR* Tel (01302) 561978 E-mail keithfarrow@blueyonder.co.uk

FARROW, Peter Maurice. b 44. St Chad's Coll Dur BSc65. **d** 68 **p** 69. C Gt Yarmouth *Nor* 68-71; C N Lynn w St Marg and St Nic 71-75; P-in-c Sculthorpe w Dunton and Doughton 75-77; Perm to Offic 78-89; TV Lowestoft and Kirkley 89-94; Ind Miss 89-94; Sen Ind Chapl 94-99; TV Gaywood 95-02; P-in-c Mundford w Lynford from 02; P-in-c Ickburgh w Langford from 02; P-in-c Cranwich from 02. *The Rectory, St Leonard's Street, Mundford, Thetford IP26 5HG* Tel (01842) 878220 E-mail farrpm@dialstart.net

FARROW, Robin Thomas Adrian. b 72. K Coll Lon BA93 AKC93. St Steph Ho Ox 94. **d** 96 **p** 97. C Lancing w Coombes *Chich* 96-00; R W Blatchington from 00. *St Peter's Rectory, 23 Windmill Close, Hove BN3 7LJ* Tel (01273) 732459

FARTHING, Michael Thomas. b 28. St Cuth Soc Dur 48. Lambeth STh81 St Steph Ho Ox. **d** 58 **p** 59. C St Marylebone St Mark w St Luke *Lon* 58-63; C Newport Pagnell *Ox* 63-69; R Standlake 69-76; R Yelford 69-76; R Lower Windrush 76-82; V Wheatley w Forest Hill and Stanton St John 82-95; rtd 95; Perm to Offic *Ox* from 95. *32 Falstaff Close, Eynsham, Oxford OX29 4QA* Tel (01865) 883805

FARTHING, Paul Andrew. b 58. McGill Univ Montreal BA80 STM82. Montreal Dioc Th Coll DipMin83. **d** 83 **p** 84. Canada 83-99; C Montreal W St Phil 83-85; R Montreal St Jo Divine 85-96; R Montreal St Jo Ev 96-99; P-in-c Burton *Lich* from 99. *The Vicarage, Rangemore Street, Burton-on-Trent DE14 2ED* Tel (01283) 544054 E-mail paul@pafarthing.clara.co.uk

FARTHING, Ronald Edward. b 27. Oak Hill Th Coll. **d** 58 **p** 59. C Tollington Park St Anne *Lon* 58-61; C Tollington Park St Mark 58-61; V Clodock and Longtown w Craswell and Llanveyno *Heref* 61-67; R Langley *Cant* 67-72; V Bapchild w Tonge and Rodmersham 72-80; TV Widecombe, Leusden and Princetown etc *Ex* 80-84; P-in-c Riddlesworth w Gasthorpe and Knettishall *Nor* 84-87; P-in-c Garboldisham w Blo' Norton 84-87; P-in-c Brettenham w Rushford 84-87; R Garboldisham w Blo' Norton, Riddlesworth etc 88-92; rtd 92; Perm to Offic *Nor* and *St E* from 92. *23 Home Close, Great Ellingham, Attleborough NR17 1HW* Tel (01953) 456750

FASS, Michael John. b 44. Trin Coll Cam MA75. Edin Dioc NSM Course 89. **d** 95 **p** 95. NSM Penicuik *Edin* 95-97; NSM W Linton 95-97; NSM Roslin (Rosslyn Chpl) from 97. *60 Braid Road, Edinburgh EH10 6AL* Tel 0131-447 8106 Fax 447 7367 E-mail mjfass@blueyonder.co.uk

FATHERS, Canon Derek Esmond. b 27. Magd Coll Ox MA50 DipEd52. St Aid Birkenhead DipTh56. **d** 56 **p** 57. Tutor St Aid Birkenhead 56-59; C W Kirby St Bridget *Ches* 59-63; V Thornton Hough 63-86; RD Wirral S 78-86; Hon Can Ches Cathl 82-92; C Woodchurch 86-89; Chapl Arrowe Park Hosp Wirral 86-92; rtd 92; Perm to Offic *Ches* from 92. *6 Ashton Drive, West Kirby, Wirral CH48 0RQ* Tel 0151-625 1181

FATHERS, Jeremy Mark. b 54. Crewe & Alsager Coll BEd78. WMMTC 93. **d** 96 **p** 97. NSM Baxterley w Hurley and Wood End and Merevale etc *Birm* 96-00; C Sheldon 00-03; Chapl N Warks NHS Trust 00-02; R Chelmsley Wood *Birm* from 03. *The Vicarage, Pike Drive, Birmingham B37 7US* Tel 0121-770 5155 *or* 770 1511 Mobile 07769-780306 E-mail j.fathers@virgin.net

FAULDS, Ian Craig. **d** 03 **p** 04. NSM Maughold *S & M* from 03. *The Lynague, Ramsey Road, Lynague, Peel, Isle of Man IM5 2AQ* Tel (01624) 842045

FAULDS, John Parker. b 33. Edin Th Coll 55. **d** 57 **p** 58. C Edin St Dav *Edin* 57-58; C Edin St Jo 58-60; Chapl Dundee Hosps 60-63; Chapl Qu Coll Dundee 60-63; Dioc Supernumerary *Bre* 60-63; Lic to Offic *Birm* 65-66; P-in-c Aston Brook 66-69; V Handsworth St Pet 69-87; Perm to Offic 87-98; rtd 99. *Address withheld by request*

FAULKES, Edmund Marquis. *See* MARQUIS-FAULKES, Edmund

FAULKNER, Mrs Anne Elizabeth. b 38. **d** 00 **p** 01. NSM Aylesbury w Bierton and Hulcott *Ox* 00-04; Chapl to Bp Buckingham 02-04; rtd 04; Hon C Wroxall *Portsm* from 04. *13 Western Road, Shanklin PO37 7NF* Tel (01983) 862291 E-mail aefpcf@aol.com

FAULKNER, Brian Thomas. b 48. S Dios Minl Tr Scheme. **d** 84 **p** 85. C W Leigh *Portsm* 84-88; R Foulsham w Hindolveston and Guestwick *Nor* 88-93; P-in-c Erpingham w Calthorpe, Ingworth, Aldborough etc 93-94; R from 94. *The Rectory, School Road, Erpingham, Norwich NR11 7QX* Tel (01263) 768073 E-mail brian-faulkner@lineone.net

FAULKNER, Mrs Catherine Evelyn. b 43. Man Poly RHV82. Dioc OLM tr scheme 98. **d** 01 **p** 02. OLM Urmston *Man* from 01. *5 Barnfield, Urmston, Manchester M41 9EW* Tel 0161-748 3226 E-mail cath@northwood1.freeserve.co.uk

FAULKNER, David Ernest. b 43. Univ of Wales (Lamp) DipTh65. St Mich Coll Llan 65. **d** 66 **p** 67. C Aberystwyth St Mich *St D* 66-68; C Tenby and Gumfreston 68-69; C Burry Port and Pwll 69-73; R Jeffreyston w Reynalton and E Williamston 73-79; R Jeffreyston w Reynoldston and E Williamston etc 79-89; V Whitland w Cyffig and Henllan Amgoed etc 89-96; V Llawhaden w Bletherston and Llanycefn from 96. *The Vicarage, Rock Road, Llawhaden, Narberth SA67 8HL* Tel (01437) 541225

FAULKNER, Henry Odin. b 35. G&C Coll Cam BA56 MA59. St Jo Coll Nottm 70. **d** 74 **p** 75. C Heigham H Trin *Nor* 74-76; C Heeley *Sheff* 76-80; TV Netherthorpe 80-84; Perm to Offic *St Alb* from 84; rtd 00. *69 Holywell Hill, St Albans AL1 1HF* Tel (01727) 854177 Mobile 07719-642479

FAULKNER, Margaret Evelyn. *See* WHITFORD, Mrs Margaret Evelyn

FAULKNER, Peter Graham. b 47. Lon Univ CertEd69. Oak Hill Th Coll BA87. **d** 82 **p** 83. C Crofton *Portsm* 87-89; R Mid Marsh Gp *Linc* 89-98; V S Cave and Ellerker w Broomfleet *York* from 98; RD Howden from 05. *The Vicarage, 10 Station Road, South Cave, Brough HU15 2AA* Tel (01430) 423693 E-mail peter@faulknerzp.karoo.co.uk

FAULKNER, Canon Roger Kearton. b 36. AKC62. **d** 63 **p** 64. C Oxton *Ches* 63-67; C Ellesmere Port 67-69; V Runcorn H Trin 69-73; TV E Runcorn w Halton 73-76; V Altrincham St Geo 76-90; Chapl Altrincham Gen Hosp 80-96; Hon Can Ches Cathl *Ches* 88-96; V Higher Bebington 90-96; rtd 96; Perm to Offic *Ches* 96-98. *58 Albermarle Road, Wallasey, Wirral CH44 6LX*

FAULKNER, Ms Susan Ann. b 70. Lanc Univ BA96. Ripon Coll Cuddesdon 97. **d** 99 **p** 00. C Scotswood *Newc* 99-03; P-in-c Byker St Silas from 03. *St Wilfrid's House, Trevelyan Drive, Newcastle upon Tyne NE5 4DA* Tel 0191-271 1866 Mobile 07786-265422 E-mail revsuefaulkner@aol.com

FAULKS, David William. b 45. EMMTC 82. **d** 86 **p** 87. C Market Harborough *Leic* 86-88; C Wootton Bassett *Sarum* 88-90; R Clipston w Naseby and Haselbech w Kelmarsh *Pet* from 90. *The Rectory, 18 Church Lane, Clipston, Market Harborough LE16 9RW* Tel (01858) 525342 Fax as telephone E-mail david.faulks@btinternet.com

FAULL, The Very Revd Cecil Albert. b 30. TCD BA52 MA87. **d** 54 **p** 55. C Dublin Zion Ch *D & G* 54-57; C Dublin St Geo 57-59; Hon Clerical V Ch Ch Cathl Dublin 58-63; C Dun Laoghaire 59-63; I Portarlington w Cloneyhurke and Lea *M & K* 63-71; I Dublin St Geo and St Thos *D & G* 71-80; I Clondalkin w Rathcoole 81-91; Can Ch Ch Cathl Dublin 90-91; I Dunleckney w Nurney, Lorum and Kiltennel *C & O* 91-96; Dean Leighlin 91-96; P-in-c Leighlin w Grange Sylvae, Shankill etc 91-96; rtd 96. *136 Beech Park, Lucan, Co Dublin, Irish Republic* Tel (00353) (1) 628 0593

FAULL, The Very Revd Vivienne Frances. b 55. St Hilda's Coll Ox BA77 MA82 Clare Coll Cam MA90. St Jo Coll Nottm BA81 DPS82. **dss** 82 **d** 87 **p** 94. Mossley Hill St Matt and St Jas *Liv* 82-85; Chapl Clare Coll Cam 85-90; Chapl Glouc Cathl *Glouc* 90-94; Can Res Cov Cathl *Cov* 94-00; Vice-Provost 95-00; Provost Leic 00-02; Dean Leic from 02. *The Cathedral Centre, 21 St Martin's, Leicester LE1 5DE* Tel 0116-262 5294 Fax 262 5295 E-mail viv.faull@leccofe.org

FAULL, William Baines. b 29. FRCVS70 Lon Univ BSc51. NW Ord Course 77. **d** 79 **p** 80. NSM Willaston *Ches* 79-80; NSM Neston 80-82; P-in-c Harthill and Burwardsley 82-86; Perm to Offic 87-91; from 96; Sen Fell Liv Univ from 89; V Ashton Hayes *Ches* 91-96; Chapl Hospice of the Good Shepherd Backford from 99. *Tioman, Briardale Road, Willaston, Neston CH64 1TD* Tel 0151-327 4424

FAULTLESS, Mrs Patricia Doreen. b 53. **d** 05. OLM Glascote and Stonydelph *Lich* from 05. *40 Stephenson Close, Glascote, Tamworth B77 2DQ* Tel (01827) 287171 Mobile 07980-434897 E-mail patfaultless@hotmail.com

FAURE WALKER, Edward William. b 46. RMA. St Alb and Ox Min Course 01. **d** 04. NSM Stevenage All SS Pin Green *St Alb* from 04. *Sandon Bury, Sandon, Buntingford SG9 0QY* Tel and fax (01763) 287753 Mobile 07801-175009 E-mail e.faure.walker@farming.me.uk

FAVELL, Brian Jeffrey. b 23. Cuddesdon Coll 64. **d** 66 **p** 67. C Rubery *Birm* 66-69; Lic to Offic 70-76; V Cwmtillery *Mon* 76-86; P-in-c Six Bells 77-86; RD Blaenau Gwent 83-86; V Cwmcarn 86-88; rtd 88; Perm to Offic *Worc* from 88. *3 Church Street, Fladbury, Pershore WR10 2QB* Tel (01386) 860585

FAWCETT, Mrs Diane Elizabeth. b 49. Cant Univ (NZ) BA72 Kent Univ MA03. Westcott Ho Cam 03. **d** 04. C Egerton w

Pluckley *Cant* from 04. *St James's Vicarage, Glebeland, Egerton, Ashford TN27 9DH* Tel (01233) 756224 E-mail fawcett38@hotmail.com

FAWCETT, Canon Frederick William. TCD BA49 MA52. CITC 50. **d** 50 **p** 51. C Belfast St Aid *Conn* 50-52; C-in-c Draperstown *D & R* 52-59; I 59-60; I Cumber Upper w Learmount 60-87; Can Derry Cathl 86-99; I Camus-juxta-Mourne 87-99; rtd 99. *Springbank, 73 Moneysallin Road, Kilrea, Coleraine BT51 5SR* Tel (028) 2954 1744

FAWCETT, Mrs Joanna Mary. b 45. SRN67 SCM69. EAMTC 01. **d** 04 **p** 05. NSM Blakeney w Cley, Wiveton, Glandford etc *Nor* from 04. *14 The Cornfields, Langham, Holt NR25 7DQ* Tel (01328) 830415 Mobile 07979-070562 E-mail jmfawcett@btinternet.com

FAWCETT, Canon Pamela Margaret. b 29. Univ Coll Lon BA51 DipEd75. EAMTC 83. **dss** 86 **d** 87 **p** 94. Stiffkey and Cockthorpe w Morston, Langham etc *Nor* 86-90; Hon C 87-90; Hon Asst Min Repps Deanery 91-92; Hon C Trunch 92-01; Asst Dir of Ords 93-99; Bp's Consultant for Women's Min 93-01; Hon Can Nor Cathl 94-01; Perm to Offic from 01. *Seekings, 47A High Street, Mundesley, Norwich NR11 8JL* Tel (01263) 721752

FAWCETT, Timothy John. b 44. K Coll Lon BD66 AKC67 PhD71. **d** 67 **p** 68. C Blackpool St Steph *Blackb* 67-70; Hon C St Marylebone All SS *Lon* 68-70; C Southgate St Mich 70-72; Sacr Dur Cathl *Dur* 72-75; V Wheatley Hill 75-79; V Torrisholme *Blackb* 79-84; V Thaxted *Chelmsf* 84-89; Perm to Offic *Nor* 89-94; NSM Holt Deanery from 94. *Dowitchers, 14 The Cornfield, Langham, Holt NR25 7DQ* Tel (01328) 830415

FAWNS, Lynne. b 56. Thames Valley Univ BA95. NTMTC 97. **d** 00 **p** 01. C Hillingdon All SS *Lon* 00-03; V London Colney St Pet *St Alb* from 03. *The Vicarage, Riverside, London Colney, St Albans AL2 1QT* Tel (01727) 769797 E-mail lynne@ffamily.freeserve.co.uk

FAYERS, Robert Stanley. b 48. DipFD SSC. St Steph Ho Ox 82. **d** 84 **p** 85. C Deptford St Paul *S'wark* 84-88; V Beckenham St Mich w St Aug *Roch* 88-00; V Brighton St Mich *Chich* from 00. *St Michael's Vicarage, 6 Montpelier Villas, Brighton BN1 3DH* Tel (01273) 727362 E-mail smb@supanet.com

FAYLE, David Charles Wilfred. b 51. Sarum & Wells Th Coll. **d** 83 **p** 84. C Parkstone St Pet w Branksea and St Osmund *Sarum* 83-87; TV Dorchester 87-96; P-in-c Taunton All SS *B & W* 96-97; V from 97. *All Saints' Vicarage, Roman Road, Taunton TA1 2DE* Tel (01823) 324730 E-mail dfayle@freeserve.co.uk

FAZZANI, Keith. b 47. Portsm Poly BSc70. Cant Sch of Min 93. **d** 96 **p** 97. NSM Appledore w Brookland, Fairfield, Brenzett etc *Cant* 96-01 and from 05; Asst Chapl E Kent Hosps NHS Trust from 01. *Oakhouse Farm, Appledore, Ashford TN26 2BB* Tel (01233) 758322 *or* (01227) 864095 E-mail kfazzani@btinternet.com

FEAK, Christopher Martin. b 52. Keele Univ BA75 Trent Poly DCG76. Trin Coll Bris DipHE94. **d** 94 **p** 95. C Handsworth St Mary *Birm* 94-97; P-in-c Perry Common 97-00; V from 00; AD Aston from 01. *St Martin's Vicarage, 148 Witton Lodge Road, Birmingham B23 5AP* Tel 0121-382 7666 E-mail chris.feak@ukonline.co.uk

FEARN, Anthony John. b 34. Lich Th Coll 58. **d** 61 **p** 62. C Redditch St Steph *Worc* 61-64; C Bladon w Woodstock *Ox* 64-66; V Ruscombe and Twyford 67-85; P-in-c Westmill w Gt Munden *St Alb* 85-87; Asst Dioc Stewardship Adv 85-87; Chr Giving Adv *Heref* 87-99; rtd 99; Perm to Offic *Heref* from 99. *49 Centurion Way, Credenhill, Hereford HR4 7FF* Tel (01432) 760060 E-mail john_fearn@bigfoot.com

FEARN, Michael Wilfrid. b 47. MBIM MIHT. Sarum & Wells Th Coll. **d** 94 **p** 95. C Blandford Forum and Langton Long *Sarum* 94-98; TV Wylye and Till Valley 98-04; R Flint *St As* from 04. *The New Rectory, Allt Goch, Flint CH6 5NF* Tel and fax (01352) 733274 E-mail mikebeverley.fearn@btinternet.com

FEARNLEY, Jeffrey Malcolm. b 46. Newc Univ BSc69. St Jo Coll Nottm DCM92. **d** 92 **p** 93. C Bispham *Blackb* 92-95; C Bolton w Ireby and Uldale *Carl* 95-00; TV Binsey 00-02; C from 02. *The Vicarage, Ireby, Wigton CA7 1EX* Tel (01697) 371307

FEARNSIDE, Mary Ingrid. b 44. OLM course 98. **d** 98 **p** 99. OLM Shelton and Oxon *Lich* from 98; Chapl R Shrewsbury Hosps NHS Trust 98-04; Chapl Shrewsbury and Telford NHS Trust from 04. *23 Eastwood Road, Shrewsbury SY3 8YJ* Tel (01743) 353290 Pager 01743-261000 E-mail mary.fearnside@fsmail.net

FEARON, Mrs Doris Ethel Elizabeth. b 26. Gilmore Ho 66. **dss** 72 **d** 87. Lingfield *S'wark* 68-75; Farnborough *Roch* 75-77; Bitterne *Win* 78-86; rtd 86; Bexhill St Pet *Chich* 86-87; Hon Par Dn 87-89; Perm to Offic 89-95; New Zealand from 96; Hon Asst Dn One Tree Hill St Oswald from 99. *The Haven, 2/66 Moana Avenue, One Tree Hill, Auckland 6, New Zealand* Tel (0064) (9) 636 6147

FEARON, Mrs Irene. b 51. Carl and Blackb Dioc Tr Inst 00. **d** 03 **p** 04. NSM Maryport, Netherton and Flimby *Carl* from 03. *Kirkborough Lodge, Ellenborough, Maryport CA15 7RD* Tel (01900) 813108 E-mail kirklodge@tiscali.co.uk

FEATHERSTON, Margery. *See* GRANGE, Mrs Alice Margery

FEATHERSTONE, Andrew. b 53. St Chad's Coll Dur BA74 MA93. Sarum & Wells Th Coll 78. **d** 80 **p** 81. C Newc H Cross *Newc* 80-83; C Seaton Hirst 83-86; TV 86-87; R Crook *Dur* 87-99; V Stanley 87-99; AD Stanhope 94-99; V Stockton from 99. *61 Bishopton Road, Stockton-on-Tees TS18 4PD* Tel (01642) 617420 *or* tel and fax 611734 E-mail andrew.featherstone@durham.anglican.org

FEATHERSTONE, Gray. b 42. Stellenbosch Univ BA62 LLB64. Cuddesdon Coll 65. **d** 67 **p** 68. C Woodstock S Africa 67-70; Asst Master Waterford Sch Swaziland 70-72; P-in-c Maputo St Steph and St Lawr Mozambique 73-76; Miss to Seamen 73-80; V Upper Clapton St Matt *Lon* 80-83; V Stamford Hill St Thos 80-89; Chr Aid Area Sec (N & W Lon) from 89; Perm to Offic *Lon* from 97. *137 Leslie Road, London N2 8BH* Tel (020) 8444 1975 *or* 7496 1690 E-mail gfeatherstone@christian-aid.org

FEATHERSTONE, John. b 32. Man Univ BA53 St Cath Soc Ox MTh59 Dur Univ DipEd66. Wycliffe Hall Ox 57. **d** 60 **p** 61. C Newland St Aug *York* 60-62; C Kidderminster St Jo and H Innocents *Worc* 62-65; Hd RE Co Gr Sch Pet 66-70; Hd RE Qu Anne Gr Sch York 70-85; Chapl Tangier *Eur* 86-87 and 90-93; Chapl Pau w Biarritz 87-88; C Mexborough *Sheff* 88-90; rtd 93; Perm to Offic *York* from 93. *39 Cambridge Avenue, Marton-in-Cleveland, Middlesbrough TS7 8EH* Tel (01642) 318181

FEATHERSTONE, Robert Leslie. b 54. Leeds Univ MA04 LLCM74 Lon Univ CertEd75. Chich Th Coll 84. **d** 86 **p** 87. C Crayford *Roch* 86-89; V Belvedere St Aug 89-94; V Crowborough St Jo *Chich* 94-01; P-in-c New Brompton St Luke *Roch* from 01. *St Luke's Vicarage, Sidney Road, Gillingham ME7 1PA* Tel (01634) 853060 Mobile 07702-062296 E-mail frrobertf@hotmail.com

FEAVER, Nigel Conway McDonald. b 51. Leeds Univ BA73 Brunel Univ MA76 CQSW76. Ripon Coll Cuddesdon 03. **d** 05. C Oxton *Ches* from 05. *36 Noctorum Dell, Prenton CH43 9UL* Tel 0151-513 5837 E-mail revnigelfeaver@surefish.co.uk

FEENEY, Damian Prescott Anthony. b 62. Grey Coll Dur BA83 PGCE84 ALCM81. Chich Th Coll BTh94. **d** 94 **p** 95. C Harrogate St Wilfrid *Ripon* 94-96; C Preston St Jo and St Geo *Blackb* 96-99; Bp's Miss P to Longsands 99-01; TR Ribbleton 01-04; V Woodplumpton from 04. *Woodplumpton Vicarage, Sandy Lane, Lower Bartle, Preston PR4 0RX* Tel (01772) 690355 E-mail frdfeeney@aol.com

FEHRENBACH, Donald Joseph. b 17. Selw Coll Cam BA49 MA53. Qu Coll Birm 49. **d** 51 **p** 52. C Beverley Minster *York* 51-54; Min Can Sarum Cathl *Sarum* 54-59; Min Can Windsor 59-65; V Sandford-on-Thames *Ox* 65-84; rtd 84; Perm to Offic *Ox* from 84. *2 Walbury, Bracknell RG12 9JB* Tel (01344) 640062

FEIST, Canon Nicholas James. b 45. Solicitor 70. St Jo Coll Nottm LTh76. **d** 76 **p** 77. C Didsbury St Jas *Man* 76-80; TV Didsbury St Jas and Em 80; V Friarmere 80-88; R Middleton 88-94; TR Middleton w Thornham from 94; Hon Can Man Cathl from 98; AD Heywood and Middleton from 99. *St Leonard's Rectory, Mellalieu Street, Middleton, Manchester M24 3DN* Tel 0161-643 2693

FEIT, Michael John. b 24. FICE68 FIStructE68. S'wark Ord Course. **d** 69 **p** 71. C Feltham *Lon* 69-76; C Ashford St Matt 76-78; C Hykeham *Linc* 78-81; V Cranwell 81-85; R Leasingham 81-85; R Bishop Norton, Wadingham and Snitterby 85-90; rtd 90; Hon C Surrey Epiphany Canada from 91. *14717-109A Avenue, Surrey BC, Canada, V3R 1Y7* Tel (001) (604) 582 5889

FELCE, Brian George. b 30. Jes Coll Ox BA54 MA57. Oak Hill Th Coll. **d** 58 **p** 59. C E Twickenham St Steph *Lon* 58-60; C Ramsgate St Luke *Cant* 60-64; R Bedingfield w Southolt *St E* 64-73; V Preston All SS *Blackb* 73-86; rtd 86. *11 St Barnabas Road, Sutton SM1 4NL* Tel (020) 8642 7885

FELIX, David Rhys. b 55. Univ of Wales (Cardiff) LLB76 Solicitor 81. Ripon Coll Cuddesdon 83. **d** 86 **p** 87. C Bromborough *Ches* 86-89; V Grange St Andr 89-99; Chapl Halton Gen Hosp NHS Trust 95-99; P-in-c Runcorn H Trin *Ches* 96-99; RD Frodsham 98-99; V Daresbury from 99; Sen Ind Chapl from 00. *All Saints' Vicarage, Daresbury Lane, Daresbury, Warrington WA4 4AE* Tel (01925) 740348 Fax 740799 E-mail david.felix@btinternet.com

FELL, Canon Alan William. b 46. Ball Coll Ox BA69 Leeds Univ DipTh70. Coll of Resurr Mirfield 68. **d** 71 **p** 72. C Woodchurch *Ches* 71-74; C Man Clayton St Cross w St Paul *Man* 74-75; C Prestwich St Marg 75-77; V Hyde St Thos *Ches* 77-80; R Tattenhall and Handley 80-86; V Sedbergh, Cautley and Garsdale *Bradf* from 86; Hon C Firbank, Howgill and Killington from 86; Hon Can Bradf Cathl from 96; RD Ewecross from 00. *The Vicarage, Loftus Hill, Sedbergh LA10 5SQ* Tel (01539) 620283

FELL, Stephen. b 18. St Jo Coll Dur LTh41 BA42. Oak Hill Th Coll 38. **d** 42 **p** 43. C Preston Em *Blackb* 42-45; C Tottenham All Hallows *Lon* 45-49; C Luton St Mary *St Alb* 49-52; R Toddington 52-58; R Castleford All SS *Wakef* 58-83; rtd 83; Perm to Offic *Ripon* from 83. *255 Lower Mickletown, Methley, Leeds LS26 9AN* Tel (01977) 515530

FELLOWS, Grant. b 56. K Coll Lon BD77 AKC77. Coll of Resurr Mirfield 79. **d** 80 **p** 81. C Addington *Cant* 80-84; C S

Gillingham *Roch* 84-86; V Heath and Reach *St Alb* 86-94; V Radlett 94-03; RD Aldenham 98-03; V Leighton Buzzard w Eggington, Hockliffe etc from 03. *The Vicarage, Pulford Road, Leighton Buzzard LU7 1AB* Tel (01525) 373217 E-mail grant@gfellows.f9.co.uk

FELLOWS, Ian Christopher. b 73. Univ Coll Ox BA94 MA98 St Jo Coll Dur BA99. Cranmer Hall Dur 96. **d** 99 **p** 00. C Bucknall and Bagnall *Lich* 99-03; TV Broughton *Man* from 03. *St John's Vicarage, 237 Great Clowes Street, Salford M7 2DZ* Tel 0161-792 9161 E-mail ianfellows@yahoo.co.uk

FELLOWS, John Lambert. b 35. LTCL67 SS Mark & Jo Coll Chelsea CertEd58. Portsm Dioc Tr Course 86. **d** 88. NSM Portsea St Cuth *Portsm* 88-94; NSM Farlington 94-05; Perm to Offic from 05. *7 Court Lane, Portsmouth PO6 2LG* Tel (023) 9237 7270

FELLOWS, John Michael. b 46. Oriel Coll Ox MA77. Coll of Resurr Mirfield 74. **d** 77 **p** 78. C Kings Heath *Birm* 77-80; TV E Ham w Upton Park St Alb *Chelmsf* 80-85; P-in-c Wormingford 85-90; P-in-c Mt Bures 85-90; P-in-c Lt Horkesley 85-90; V Wormingford, Mt Bures and Lt Horkesley 90; R Compton w Shackleford and Peper Harow *Guildf* from 90; Chapl Prior's Field Sch from 90. *The Rectory, The Street, Compton, Guildford GU3 1ED* Tel (01483) 810328 E-mail johnfellows@comptonrec.fslife.co.uk

FELLOWS, Peter William. b 48. CertEd70 DipEd79. Chich Th Coll 86. **d** 88 **p** 89. C Westmr St Steph w St Jo *Lon* 88-93; R Deptford St Paul *S'wark* from 93. *The Rectory, Mary Anne Gardens, London SE8 3DP* Tel (020) 8692 0989

FELLOWS, Mrs Susan Elizabeth. b 46. ATCL65 LTCL66 GTCL67. St Alb and Ox Min Course 99. **d** 02 **p** 03. NSM Weston Turville *Ox* from 02. *65 Craigwell Avenue, Aylesbury HP21 7AG* Tel (01296) 424982 Mobile 07712-226999 E-mail susan@sefellows.freeserve.co.uk

FELTHAM, Keith. b 40. Lon Univ DipTh66. **d** 75 **p** 76. In Bapt Ch 66-75; C Plympton St Mary *Ex* 75-79; TV Northam w Westward Ho! and Appledore 79-82; TR Lynton, Brendon, Countisbury, Lynmouth etc 82-85; P-in-c Bickleigh (Plymouth) 85-86; TR 86-91; Chapl R Bournemouth Gen Hosp 91-95; P-in-c Whimple, Talaton and Clyst St Lawr *Ex* 95-00; rtd 00; Perm to Offic *Ex* from 00. *6 The Heathers, Woolwell, Plymouth PL6 7QT* Tel (01792) 774447

FELTHAM-WHITE, Antony James. b 67. Ox Brookes Univ BSc92 Reading Univ MA94. Wycliffe Hall Ox 99. **d** 01 **p** 02. C Bernwode *Ox* 01-05; CF from 05. *c/o MOD Chaplains (Army)* Tel (01980) 615804 Fax 615800 E-mail antony@revelation-racing.org.uk

FENBY, Andrew Robert. b 66. Loughb Univ BSc88. St Steph Ho Ox 03. **d** 05. C Leigh-on-Sea St Marg *Chelmsf* from 05. *45 Eaton Road, Leigh-on-Sea SS9 3PF* E-mail afenby@mac.com

FENBY, Mrs Sarah Louise. b 66. Kent Univ BA88 Lon Bible Coll BA96. Trin Coll Bris MA00. **d** 00 **p** 01. C Stoke Gifford *Bris* 00-04; C S Croydon Em *S'wark* from 04. *St Francis House, 146 Tedder Road, South Croydon CR2 8AH* Tel (020) 8657 7864 E-mail sarahfenby@fsmail.net

FENN, Norman Alexander. b 20. Kelham Th Coll 37. **d** 43 **p** 44. C Tunstall Ch Ch *Lich* 43-47; C Leek St Edw 47-51; V Tilstock 51-55; V Milton 55-61; V Ellesmere 61-85; V Welsh Frankton 62-85; RD Ellesmere 70-85; rtd 85; Perm to Offic *Lich* from 85. *1 Larkhill Road, Oswestry SY11 4AW* Tel (01691) 659411

FENN, Roy William Dearnley. b 33. FRHistS70 FCP86 FSA88 Jes Coll Ox BA54 MA59 BD68. St Mich Coll Llan 54. **d** 56 **p** 57. C Swansea St Mary and H Trin *S & B* 57-59; C Cardiff St Jo *Llan* 59-60; C Coity w Nolton 60-63; V Glascombe w Rhulen and Gregrina *S & B* 63-68; V Glascwm and Rhulen 68-74; P-in-c Letton w Staunton, Byford, Mansel Gamage etc *Heref* 75-79; Perm to Offic *S & B* 80-85; Perm to Offic *Heref* 85-95; rtd 98. *9 Victoria Road, Kington HR5 3BX* Tel (01544) 230018

FENNELL, Canon Alfred Charles Dennis. b 15. Bp's Coll Calcutta 35. **d** 38 **p** 39. India 38-48; C Kensington St Helen w H Trin *Lon* 48-50; Min Queensbury All SS 50-54; V 54-62; Prec Birm Cathl *Birm* 62-65; V Yardley St Cypr Hay Mill 65-80; Hon Can Birm Cathl 78-80; rtd 80; Perm to Offic *Birm* and *Worc* from 80. *6 Merrievale Court, Barnards Green Road, Malvern WR14 3NE* Tel (01684) 560613

FENNELL, Anthony Frederick Rivers. b 26. Pemb Coll Cam BA50 MA55 York Univ BPhil76 Leic Univ PGCE51. Ab Dioc Tr Course 90. **d** 90 **p** 91. NSM Braemar *Ab* 90-96; NSM Ballater 90-96; NSM Aboyne 90-96; rtd 96. *19 Craigendarroch Circle, Ballater AB35 5ZA* Tel (01339) 755048

FENNEMORE, Canon Nicholas Paul. b 53. Wycliffe Hall Ox 76. **d** 79 **p** 80. C N Mymms *St Alb* 79-82; C Chipping Barnet w Arkley 82-83; TV 83-84; TV Preston w Sutton Poyntz and Osmington w Poxwell *Sarum* 84-86; Chapl St Helier Hosp Carshalton 86-90; Chapl Jo Radcliffe Hosp Ox 90-94; Chapl Ox Radcliffe Hosp NHS Trust 94-96; Sen Chapl Ox Radcliffe Hosps NHS Trust from 96; Hon Can Ch Ch *Ox* from 03. *John Radcliffe Hospital, Headington, Oxford OX3 9DU* Tel (01865) 741166 *or* 221732

FENNING, John Edward. b 32. CITC 86. **d** 88 **p** 89. NSM Douglas Union w Frankfield *C, C & R* 88-89; Chapl Ashton Sch Cork 88-96; NSM Moviddy Union *C, C & R* 89-99; rtd 99. *1 Kingston College, Mitchelstown, Co Cork, Irish Republic* Tel (00353) (25) 85587 E-mail revdjohne@eircom.net

FENSOME, Canon Anthony David. b 49. DipYL74 Open Univ BA89. Sarum & Wells Th Coll 82. **d** 84 **p** 85. C Gtr Corsham *Bris* 84-88; P-in-c Lyddington w Wanborough 88-91; P-in-c Bishopstone w Hinton Parva 88-91; V Lyddington and Wanborough and Bishopstone etc 91-93; V Chippenham St Pet from 93; RD Chippenham 94-99; Hon Can Bris Cathl from 98. *St Peter's Vicarage, Lords Mead, Chippenham SN14 0LL* Tel (01249) 654835 Fax as telephone E-mail tonyfens@aol.com

FENTIMAN, David Frank. b 43. RIBA74 Poly Cen Lon DipArch72 Roehampton Inst PGCE94. S Dios Minl Tr Scheme 90. **d** 93 **p** 94. NSM Hastings St Clem and All SS *Chich* 93-98; P-in-c Blacklands Hastings Ch Ch and St Andr 98-01; V from 01. *4 Barnfield Close, Hastings TN34 1TS* Tel (01424) 421821

FENTON, Barry Dominic. b 59. Leeds Univ BA85. Coll of Resurr Mirfield 85. **d** 87 **p** 88. C Leigh Park *Portsm* 87-90; Chapl and Prec Portsm Cathl 90-95; Min Can and Prec Westmr Abbey 95-02; Chapl N Middx Hosp NHS Trust from 02; PV Westmr Abbey from 04. *North Middlesex Hospital, Sterling Way, London N18 1QX* Tel (020) 8887 2000 *or* 8887 2724 E-mail dominic.fenton@nmh.nhs.uk

FENTON, Christopher Miles Tempest. b 28. Qu Coll Cam BA50 LLB51 MA55 LLM. Ridley Hall Cam 52. **d** 54 **p** 55. C Welling *Roch* 54-57; Chapl Malsis Prep Sch Keighley 57-63; C Hove Bp Hannington Memorial Ch *Chich* 63-65; V Ramsgate Ch Ch *Cant* 65-71; Hd Dept of Gp Studies Westmr Past Foundn 71-83; P-in-c Mottingham St Andr *S'wark* 71-73; Sen Tutor Cambs Consultancy in Counselling 73-85; Co-ord of Tr St Alb Past Foundn 80-88; Dir St Anne's Trust for Psychotherapy Ledbury from 85; Perm to Offic *Heref* from 85; rtd 93. *The Leys, Aston, Kingsland, Leominster HR6 9PU* Tel (01568) 708632

FENTON, Geoffrey Eric Crosland. b 54. St Jo Coll Ox BA75 MSc76. WEMTC 98. **d** 01 **p** 02. NSM Wedmore w Theale and Blackford *B & W* from 01. *Grove Cottage, Redmans Hill, Blackford, Wedmore BS28 4NG* Tel (01934) 713083 E-mail geoffrey.fenton@ukonline.co.uk

FENTON, Heather. b 48. Trin Coll Bris. **d** 87 **p** 97. C Corwen and Llangar *St As* 87-89; C Corwen and Llangar w Gwyddelwern and Llawrybetws 89-98; Dioc Rural Min Co-ord 87-98; Lic to Offic from 98; Asst P Penllyn Deanery 01-03; P-in-c Bryneglwys from 03. *Coleg y Groes, The College, Corwen LL21 0AU* Tel (01490) 412169

FENTON, Ian Christopher Stuart. b 40. AKC62. **d** 63 **p** 64. C Banstead *Guildf* 63-67; V N Holmwood 67-84; RD Dorking 80-84; V Witley 84-00; Perm to Offic *Ex* from 00; rtd 05. *Sweet Coppin Cottage, Bickington, Newton Abbot TQ12 6JR* Tel (01626) 821880

FENTON, Canon John Charles. b 21. Qu Coll Ox BA43 MA47 BD53 Lambeth DD01. Linc Th Coll 43. **d** 44 **p** 45. C Hindley All SS *Liv* 44-47; Chapl Linc Th Coll 47-51; Sub-Warden 51-54; Prin Lich Th Coll 58-65; V Wentworth *Sheff* 54-58; Prin St Chad's Coll Dur 65-78; Can Res Ch Ch *Ox* 78-91; Hon Can 91-92; rtd 91. *8 Rowland Close, Oxford OX2 8PW* Tel (01865) 554099

FENTON, Keith John. b 54. Coll of Resurr Mirfield 01. **d** 03 **p** 04. C St Annes St Anne *Blackb* from 03. *2 Vicarage Close, Lytham St Annes FY8 3BQ* Tel (01254) 54421 Mobile 07773-630784

FENTON, Michael John. b 42. Linc Th Coll 67. **d** 69 **p** 70. C Guiseley *Bradf* 69-72; C Heswall *Ches* 72-75; TV Birkenhead Priory 75-81; V Alvanley 81-91; Chapl Crossley Hosp Cheshire 82-91; V Holbrook and Lt Eaton *Derby* 91-03; V Allenton and Shelton Lock from 03. *St Edmund's Vicarage, Sinfin Avenue, Allenton, Derby DE24 9JA* Tel (01332) 701194

FENTON, Miss Penelope Ann. b 41. Leic Univ BSc64. Cant Sch of Min 92. **d** 95 **p** 96. NSM Eastling w Ospringe and Stalisfield w Otterden *Cant* 95-00; P-in-c from 00; Asst to Bp's Officer for NSM from 99. *9 Brogdale Road, Faversham ME13 8SX* Tel (01795) 536366 E-mail penny.fenton@lineone.net

FENTON, Vincent Thompson. b 52. 94. **d** 96 **p** 97. C Heworth St Mary *Dur* 96-99; C-in-c Bishop Auckland Woodhouse Close CD from 99; Chapl S Durham Healthcare NHS Trust from 01. *18 Watling Road, Bishop Auckland DL14 6RP* Tel (01388) 604086 E-mail vincent.fenton@durham.anglican.org

FENTON, Canon Wallace. b 32. TCD. **d** 64 **p** 65. C Glenavy *Conn* 64-67; I Tullaniskin w Clonoe *Arm* 67-87; Bp's C Sallaghy *Clogh* 87-96; Warden of Readers 91-96; Preb Clogh Cathl 95-96; I Kilwarlin Upper w Kilwarlin Lower *D & D* 96-99; rtd 99. *2 Beech Green, Doagh, Ballyclare BT39 0QB* Tel (028) 9334 0576

FENWICK, Canon Jeffrey Robert. b 30. Pemb Coll Cam BA53 MA57. Linc Th Coll 53. **d** 55 **p** 56. C Upholland *Liv* 55-58; S Rhodesia 58-64; Area Sec USPG *Ox* 64-65; Rhodesia 65-78; Adn Charter 73-75; Dean and Adn Bulawayo 75-78; Can Res Worc Cathl *Worc* 78-89; R Guernsey St Peter Port *Win* 89-95; Dean Guernsey 89-95; Hon Can Win Cathl 89-95; Pres Guernsey Miss to Seamen 89-95; rtd 95; Zimbabwe 95-04; S Africa from 04. *3 Suid Street, Alexandria, 6185 South Africa*

FENWICK, John Robert Kipling. b 51. Van Mildert Coll Dur BSc72 Nottm Univ BA74 MTh78 K Coll Lon PhD85 Lambeth STh84. St Jo Coll Nottm 72. **d** 77 **p** 78. C Dalton-in-Furness *Carl* 77-80; Lect Trin Coll Bris 80-88; Chapl 80-87; Abp Cant's Asst Sec for Ecum Affairs 88-92; NSM Purley Ch Ch *S'wark* 88-92; R Chorley St Laur *Blackb* 92-01; Perm to Offic *Carl* from 02. *16 Windsor Crescent, Ulverston LA12 9NP* Tel (01229) 584997 E-mail phoenix51@tiscali.co.uk

FENWICK, Canon Malcolm Frank. b 38. Cranmer Hall Dur 62. **d** 65 **p** 66. C Tynemouth Cullercoats St Paul *Newc* 65-68; C Bywell 68-73; V Alnmouth 73-75; CF (TAVR) 75-83; V Lesbury w Alnmouth *Newc* 75-80; V Delaval 80-91; RD Bedlington 83-88; V Riding Mill 91-01; P-in-c Whittonstall 91-01; Chapl Shepherd's Dene Retreat Ho from 91; RD Corbridge 93-99; P-in-c Slaley 97-99; P-in-c Healey 99-01; Hon Can Newc Cathl 97-01; rtd 01; Perm to Offic *Newc* from 01. *21 Welburn Close, Ovingham, Prudhoe NE42 6BD* Tel (01661) 835565

FENWICK, The Very Revd Richard David. b 43. Univ of Wales (Lamp) BA66 MA86 TCD MusB79 MA92 Univ of Wales (Lamp) PhD95 FLCM68 FTCL76 Hon FGCM04. Ridley Hall Cam 66. **d** 68 **p** 69. C Skewen *Llan* 68-72; C Penarth w Lavernock 72-74; PV, Succ and Sacr Roch Cathl *Roch* 74-78; Min Can St Paul's Cathl *Lon* 78-79; Min Can and Succ 79-83; Warden Coll Min Cans 81-83; PV Westmr Abbey 83-90; V Ruislip St Martin *Lon* 83-90; Can Res and Prec Guildf Cathl *Guildf* 90-97; Sub-Dean 96-97; Dean Mon from 97; V Newport St Woolos from 97; Warden Guild of Ch Musicians from 98. *The Deanery, Stow Hill, Newport NP20 4ED* Tel and fax (01633) 263338

FEREDAY, Adrian Paul. b 57. Huddersfield Poly CQSW88 DipSW88 Open Univ BSc96. Coll of Resurr Mirfield 92. **d** 94 **p** 95. C Gleadless *Sheff* 94-96; TV Aston cum Aughton w Swallownest, Todwick etc 96-01; R Firbeck w Letwell from 01; V Woodsetts from 01. *The Rectory, 4A Barker Hades Road, Letwell, Worksop S81 8DF* Tel (01909) 730346 E-mail fereday@apfereday.demon.co.uk

FEREDAY, Harold James Rodney. b 46. Sheff Univ CEIR76. St Jo Coll Nottm 87. **d** 89 **p** 90. C Rastrick St Matt *Wakef* 89-92; V Siddal 92-99; Dir Chr Care from 99; rtd 01; Perm to Offic *Wakef* and *York* from 01. *311 Filey Road, Scarborough YO11 3AF*

FERGUS, David. b 52. Imp Coll Lon BSc74. St Jo Coll Nottm 00. **d** 02 **p** 03. C Ilkeston St Mary *Derby* from 02. *1 Sparrow Close, Ilkeston DE7 4PW* Tel 0115-930 1978 E-mail fergii95@aol.com

FERGUSON, Canon Aean Michael O'Shaun. b 39. CITC 87. **d** 90 **p** 91. NSM Kilmallock w Kilflynn, Kilfinane, Knockaney etc *L & K* 90; NSM Killaloe w Stradbally 90-94; NSM Adare and Kilmallock w Kilpeacon, Croom etc 94-97; C Killala w Dunfeeny, Crossmolina, Kilmoremoy etc *T, K & A* 97-00; I 00; I Skreen w Kilmacshalgan and Dromard from 00; Dioc Information Officer from 04; Can Killala Cathl from 05. *The Rectory, Skreen, Co Sligo, Irish Republic* Tel (00353) (71) 916 6941 Fax 916 6989 Mobile 87-812 1020 E-mail skreen@killala.anglican.org

FERGUSON, Alastair Stuart. b 45. Lon Univ MB, BS69 Ball Coll Ox BA78 MA82 LRCP69 MRCS69. St Steph Ho Ox 80. **d** 82 **p** 83. NSM Dengie w Asheldham *Chelmsf* 82-86; NSM Mayland 86-89; NSM Steeple 86-89; Perm to Offic 89-91; R Mvurwi St Andr Zimbabwe 91-00; V Lastingham w Appleton-le-Moors, Rosedale etc *York* from 00. *The Vicarage, Lastingham, York YO62 6TN* Tel (01751) 417344 Mobile 07967-588776 E-mail vicarage@lastinghamchurch.org.uk

FERGUSON, Anthony David Norman. b 51. Wycliffe Hall Ox 75. **d** 78 **p** 79. C Tipton St Matt *Lich* 78-79; USA from 79; Chapl SAMS 79-80; R Marion St Jo 80-84; P-in-c Charlotte St Marg 84-89; R 89-93; R Jacksonville St Pet from 93. *5042 Timuquana Road, Jacksonville, FL 32210, USA* Tel (001) (904) 778 1434 Fax 778 1437 E-mail adnfs51@hotmail.com

FERGUSON, David Edward. d 04 p 05. Aux Min Antrim All SS *Conn* from 04. *7 Three Trees Manor, Broughshane, Ballymena BT43 7GY* Tel (028) 2586 2994

FERGUSON, Edith Constance May (Joy). b 37. Ch of Ireland Tr Coll DipEd60. CITC 99. **d** 02 **p** 03. NSM Bandon Union *C, C & R* from 02. *Telkador, Kinure, Oysterhaven, Co Cork, Irish Republic* Tel (00353) (21) 477 0663 Mobile 86-350 3138

FERGUSON, Canon Ian John. b 51. Aber Univ BD77. Trin Coll Bris 77. **d** 78 **p** 79. C Foord St Jo *Cant* 78-82; C Bieldside *Ab* 82-86; Dioc Youth Chapl 82-86; P-in-c Westhill 86-96; R from 96; Can St Andr Cathl from 01. *1 Westwood Drive, Westhill, Skeene AB32 6WW* Tel (01224) 740007 E-mail ianferguson@freenet.co.uk

FERGUSON, John Aitken. b 40. Glas Univ BSc64 Strathclyde Univ PhD74 CEng MICE ARCST64. Linc Th Coll 79. **d** 81 **p** 82. C Morpeth *Newc* 81-85; V Whittingham and Edlingham w Bolton Chapel 85-96; rtd 00. *Cold Harbour Cottage, Cold Harbour, Berwick-upon-Tweed TD15 2TQ*

FERGUSON, Joy. *See* FERGUSON, Edith Constance May

FERGUSON, Mrs Kathleen. b 46. LMH Ox BA68 MA72 ALA76. St As Minl Tr Course 86. **d** 88 **p** 97. NSM Llanidloes w Llangurig *Ban* 88-01; P-in-c Llandinam w Trefeglwys w Penstrowed 01-02; V 02-04; RD Arwystli 02-04; NSM Shelswell *Ox* from 04. *10C St Michaels Close, Fringford, Bicester OX27 8DW* Tel (01869) 278972 E-mail kathy.ferguson@dsl.pipex.com

FERGUSON, Michelle Dorothy Marie. b 58. Ottawa Univ BA78. Cranmer Hall Dur 93. **d** 95 **p** 96. NSM Gt Aycliffe *Dur* 95-97; Chapl Asst HM Pris Holme Ho 97-98; NSM Heighington *Dur* 99-04; R Hurworth from 04; R Dinsdale w Sockburn from 04. *The Rectory, 3 Croft Road, Hurworth, Darlington DL2 2HD* Tel (01325) 720362

FERGUSON, The Ven Paul John. b 55. New Coll Ox BA76 MA80 K Coll Cam BA84 MA88 FRCO75. Westcott Ho Cam 82. **d** 85 **p** 86. C Ches St Mary *Ches* 85-88; Sacr and Chapl Westmr Abbey 88-92; Prec 92-95; Can Res and Prec York Minster *York* 95-01; Adn Cleveland from 01; Can and Preb York Minster from 01; Warden of Readers from 04. *2 Langbaurgh Road, Hutton Rudby, Yarm TS15 0HL* Tel (01642) 706095 Fax 706097 E-mail ppmja@btinternet.com

FERGUSON, Richard Archie. b 39. Dur Univ BA62. Linc Th Coll 62. **d** 64 **p** 65. C Stretford St Matt *Man* 64-68; Bp's Dom Chapl *Dur* 68-69; C Newc St Geo *Newc* 69-71; V Glodwick *Man* 71-77; V Tynemouth Ch Ch *Newc* 77-82; V Tynemouth Ch Ch w H Trin 82-87; P-in-c Tynemouth St Aug 82-87; TR N Shields 87-90; TR Upton cum Chalvey *Ox* 90-95; V Kirkwhelpington, Kirkharle, Kirkheaton and Cambo *Newc* 95-04; AD Morpeth 95-04; rtd 04. *6 Green Close, Stannington, Morpeth NE61 6PE* Tel (01670) 789795 E-mail frgsno@aol.com

FERGUSON, Robert Garnett Allen. b 48. Leeds Univ LLB70 Clare Coll Cam. Cuddesdon Coll 71. **d** 73 **p** 74. C Wakef Cathl *Wakef* 73-76; V Lupset 76-83; Chapl Cheltenham Coll 83-87; Sen Chapl Win Coll from 87. *Winchester College, Winchester SO23 9NA* Tel (01962) 884056 *or* 840592

FERGUSON, Robin Sinclair. b 31. Worc Coll Ox BA53 MA57 Lon Univ CertEd63. ALCD55 Wycliffe Coll Toronto 55. **d** 57 **p** 58. C Brompton H Trin *Lon* 57-60; C Brixton St Matt *S'wark* 60-63; Hon C Framlingham w Saxtead *St E* 63-65; Hon C Haverhill 65-67; Chapl St Mary's Sch Richmond 67-75; C Richmond St Mary *S'wark* 68-76; P-in-c Shilling Okeford *Sarum* 76-87; Chapl Croft Ho Sch Shillingstone 76-87; R Milton Abbas, Hilton w Cheselbourne etc *Sarum* 87-96; rtd 96; Perm to Offic *Sarum* from 98. *11 Stowell Crescent, Wareham BH20 4PT* Tel (01929) 551340

FERGUSON, Ronald Leslie. b 36. Open Univ BA86 BA89 Newc Poly CertFT90. Chich Th Coll 65. **d** 68 **p** 69. C Toxteth Park St Marg *Liv* 68-72; C Oakham w Hambleton and Egleton *Pet* 72-74; Asst Chapl The Dorothy Kerin Trust Burrswood 74-76; V Castleside *Dur* 76-96; C Washington 96-99; Chapl Gateshead Healthcare NHS Trust 96-98; Chapl Gateshead Health NHS Trust from 98; P-in-c Eighton Banks *Dur* from 99. *St Thomas's Vicarage, 8 Norwood Court, Gateshead NE9 7XF* Tel 0191-487 6927 *or* 416 2895

FERGUSON, Wallace Raymond. b 47. Qu Coll Birm BTheol CITC 76. **d** 78 **p** 79. C Lurgan Ch the Redeemer *D & D* 78-80; I Newtownards w Movilla Abbey 80-84; I Mullabrack w Markethill and Kilcluney *Arm* 84-00; Hon V Choral Arm Cathl from 86; Dioc Chapl to Rtd Clergy from 92; I Carnteel and Crilly from 00. *St James's Rectory, 22 Carnteel Road, Aughnacloy BT69 6DU* Tel (028) 8555 7682

FERGUSON FLATT, Roy Francis. *See* FLATT, The Very Revd Roy Francis Ferguson

FERGUSON-STUART, Hamish. b 51. Open Univ BA92 RGN. OLM course 97. **d** 99 **p** 00. OLM Burton St Chad *Lich* from 99. *210 Derby Road, Burton-on-Trent DE14 1RN* Tel (01283) 510447

FERMER, Michael Thorpe. b 30. Lon Univ BSc52 ARCS52 St Cath Soc Ox BA54. Wycliffe Hall Ox 52. **d** 54 **p** 55. C Upper Holloway All SS *Lon* 54-57; C Plymouth St Andr *Ex* 57-59; V Tamerton Foliot 59-63; Asst Chapl United Sheff Hosps 63-64; Chapl 64-66; Lic to Offic *Sheff* 66-73; V Holmesfield *Derby* 73-79; TR Old Brampton and Loundsley Green 79-83; V Brightside St Thos and St Marg *Sheff* 83; V Brightside w Wincobank 83-89; V Loscoe *Derby* 89-94; rtd 94; Perm to Offic *Derby* from 94. *123 Bacons Lane, Chesterfield S40 2TN* Tel (01246) 555793

FERMER, Richard Malcolm. b 71. St Pet Coll Ox BA94 K Coll Lon MA95 PhD02 Surrey Univ PGCE96. Coll of Resurr Mirfield 00. **d** 02 **p** 03. C Palmers Green St Jo *Lon* 02-05; USPG Brazil from 05. *USPG, Partnership House, 157 Waterloo Road, London SE1 8XA* Tel (020) 7928 8681 Fax 7928 3713 E-mail richard.fermer@tiscali.co.uk

FERN, John. b 36. Nottm Univ BA57 DipRE64 MA88. Coll of Resurr Mirfield 57. **d** 59 **p** 60. C Carlton *S'well* 59-61; C Hucknall Torkard 61-68; V Rainworth 68-97; rtd 97; Perm to Offic *S'well* from 03. *17 Wharfedale Gardens, Mansfield NG18 3GZ* Tel (01623) 420165

FERNANDEZ, Mrs Valerie Anne. b 48. WMMTC 03. **d** 05. C Mile Cross *Nor* from 05. *Glebe House, 140 Mile Cross Road, Norwich NR3 2LD* Tel (01603) 417352

FERNANDEZ-VICENTE, Lorenzo Michel Manuel. b 68. Louvain Univ BA92 MA97 STL97. **d** 97 **p** 97. C Battersea St Mary *S'wark* from 04. *35 Kerrison Road, London SW11 2QG* Tel 07780-914434 (mobile) E-mail lfv@btopenworld.com

FERNANDO, Percy Sriyananda. b 49. Dundee Coll Dip Community Educn 81. St And Dioc Tr Course 85. **d** 88 **p** 89. NSM Blairgowrie *St And* from 88; NSM Coupar Angus from 89; NSM Alyth from 89. *Gowrie Cottage, Perth Road, Blairgowrie PH10 6QB*

FERNELEY, Alastair John. b 69. Roehampton Inst BA93 K Coll Lon MA94 Birm Univ MPhil98 St Jo Coll Dur MA02. Cranmer Hall Dur 00. **d** 02 **p** 03. C Skipton Ch Ch *Bradf* from 02. *61 Roughaw Road, Skipton BD23 2QA* Tel (01756) 798927

FERNS, Stephen Antony Dunbar. b 61. St Chad's Coll Dur BA84 MA94. Ripon Coll Cuddesdon BA87 MA91. **d** 88 **p** 89. C Billingham St Cuth *Dur* 88-90; Chapl Dur Univ 91; Chapl Van Mildert and Trevelyan Colls Dur 91-95; V Norton St Mary 95-97; Bp's Dom Chapl *Blackb* 97-01; Voc Officer and Selection Sec Min Division from 01. *Ministry Division, Church House, Great Smith Street, London SW1P 3NZ* Tel (020) 7898 1399 Fax 7898 1421 E-mail stephen.ferns@c-of-e.org.uk

FERNS, Archdeacon of. *See* MOONEY, The Ven Paul Gerard

FERNS, Dean of. *See* FORREST, The Very Revd Leslie David Arthur

FERNYHOUGH, Timothy John Edward. b 60. Leeds Univ BA81. Linc Th Coll 81. **d** 83 **p** 84. C Daventry *Pet* 83-86; Chapl Tonbridge Sch 86-92; Chapl Dur Sch 92-02; Hd RS and Asst Chapl Radley Coll from 02. *Radley College, Radley, Abingdon OX14 2HR* Tel (01235) 543000 Fax 543106

FERRIDAY, Donald Martin. b 30. Univ of Wales (Lamp) BA55. Qu Coll Birm 55. **d** 57 **p** 58. C Stockport St Sav *Ches* 57-59; C Heswall 59-64; V Cheadle Hulme All SS 64-72; V Ches 72-76; TR Ches Team 76-77; R W Kirby St Bridget 77-98; rtd 98; Perm to Offic *Ches* from 98. *142A Banks Road, West Kirby, Wirral CH48 0RB* Tel 0151-625 3910

FERRIS, Amanda Jane. b 61. RGN83. St Alb and Ox Min Course 00. **d** 03 **p** 04. NSM Letchworth St Paul w Willian *St Alb* from 03. *Rivendell, 33B Stotfold Road, Arlesey SG15 6XL* Tel (01462) 834627 Mobile 07780-670651 E-mail amanda.ferris@btinternet.com

FERRIS, Samuel Albert. b 41. Open Univ BA80. S & M Dioc Tr Inst 98. **d** 99 **p** 00. OLM Douglas All SS and St Thos *S & M* from 99. *27 Hillberry Meadows, Governors Hill, Douglas, Isle of Man IM2 7BJ* Tel (01624) 619631 Fax as telephone

FERRIS, Samuel Christopher. b 77. Univ of Wales (Lamp) BA98. Trin Coll Bris 02. **d** 04 **p** 05. C Tunbridge Wells St Mark *Roch* from 04. *11 Ramslye Road, Tunbridge Wells TN4 8LT* Tel (01892) 534061 E-mail chrisandhee@ferris4000.fsnet.co.uk

FERRITER, Felicity Eunicé Myfanwy. b 54. Sheff Univ BA76 Nottm Univ MA98. EMMTC 95. **d** 98 **p** 99. NSM Retford *S'well* 98-03; Asst Chapl Rampton Hosp Retford 99-01; Asst Chapl Notts Healthcare NHS Trust 01-02; Chapl 02-03; Asst to AD Retford 03-04; NSM Rampton w Laneham, Treswell, Cottam and Stokeham *S'well* from 04; NSM N and S Leverton from 04. *The Gables, Treswell Road, Rampton, Retford DN22 0HU* Tel (01777) 248580 E-mail felicityferriter@yahoo.com

FERRY, Canon David Henry John. b 53. TCD BTh88. **d** 88 **p** 89. C Enniskillen *Clogh* 88-90; I Leckpatrick w Dunnalong *D & R* 90-01; Bp's Dom Chapl from 96; I Donagheady from 01; Can Derry Cathl from 05. *Earlsgift Rectory, 33 Longland Road, Dunamanagh, Strabane BT82 0PH* Tel (028) 7139 8017

FERRY, Malcolm Ronald Keith. b 66. QUB BEd88. CITC BTh96. **d** 96 **p** 97. C Agherton *Conn* 96-99; I Kilwaughter w Cairncastle and Craigy Hill 99-03; I Castlerock w Dunboe and Fermoyle *D & R* from 03. *The Rectory, 52 Main Street, Castlerock, Coleraine BT51 4RA* Tel (028) 7084 8242 E-mail castlerock@derry.anglican.org

FESSEY, Mrs Annis Irene. b 40. St Mary's Coll Chelt CertEd60. Ripon Coll Cuddesdon 88. **d** 90 **p** 94. Par Dn Bris St Andr Hartcliffe *Bris* 90-94; C The Lydiards 94-95; C Penhill 95-00; rtd 00; Perm to Offic *Bris* 00-03 and *Portsm* from 03. *Tintern, 17 Mayfield Road, Ryde PO33 3PR* Tel (01983) 616466

FESSEY, Canon Brian Alan. b 39. Bris Univ CertEd61 Leeds Univ DipEd71. Ripon Coll Cuddesdon 88. **d** 90 **p** 91. Hon C Bishopsworth *Bris* 90; C Withywood CD 91-94; V Purton 94-03; Hon Can Bris Cathl 01-03; rtd 03; Perm to Offic *Portsm* from 03. *Tintern, 17 Mayfield Road, Ryde PO33 3PR* Tel (01983) 616466

FEWKES, Jeffrey Preston. b 47. Derby Univ MA99 DMin04. Wycliffe Hall Ox 72. **d** 75 **p** 76. C Chester le Street *Dur* 75-78; C Kennington St Mark *S'wark* 78-81; V Bulwell St Jo *S'well* 81-98; V Stapleford 98-02; Dep Co-ord Victim Support Nottm City N from 02. *3 Monks Close, Ilkeston DE7 5EY* Tel 0115-844 5093 E-mail j.fewkes@btopenworld.com

FFRENCH (née WILLIAMS), Mrs Janet Patricia (Trish). b 59. Bradf Univ BTech81. Trin Coll Bris BA02. **d** 02 **p** 03. C Quinton Road W St Boniface *Birm* from 02. *1 Four Acres, Quinton, Birmingham B32 1RY* Tel 0121-421 3530 Mobile 07801-257959 E-mail jtrishw@blueyonder.co.uk

FFRENCH, Timothy Edward. b 58. Ball Coll Ox MA86. Trin Coll Bris BA01 MA03. **d** 03 **p** 04. C Pedmore *Worc* from 03. *1 Four Acres, Birmingham B32 1RY* Tel 0121-421 3530 Mobile 07801-492126 E-mail timffrench@yahoo.co.uk

FICKE, Michael John. b 46. LNSM course 96. **d** 97 **p** 98. OLM Marnhull *Sarum* from 97. *13 Plowman Close, Marnhull, Sturminster Newton DT10 1LB* Tel (01258) 820509

FIDDYMENT, Alan John. b 40. Cant Sch of Min 91. **d** 94 **p** 95. NSM Chatham St Wm *Roch* 94-96; NSM Spalding *Linc* 96-99; R Barkston and Hough Gp from 99. *The Rectory, Barkston Road, Marston, Grantham NG32 2HN* Tel and fax (01400) 250875 Mobile 07930-434126 E-mail alanfid@hotmail.com

✠**FIDÈLE, The Most Revd Dirokpa Balufuga.** Bp Bukavu; Abp Congo from 02. *BP 134, Cyangugu, Rwanda* Tel (00250) 841 7697 E-mail anglicandiobkv@yahoo.com *or* dirokpa1@hotmail.com

FIDLER, John Harvey. b 49. Hatf Poly BSc72. St Alb Minl Tr Scheme 84. **d** 87 **p** 88. NSM Royston *St Alb* from 87; Perm to Offic *Ely* from 00. *8 Stamford Avenue, Royston SG8 7DD* Tel (01763) 241886

FIELD, Brian Hedley. b 31. St Jo Coll York CertEd53 DipPE54 ACP66 FCP84. **d** 99 **p** 00. NSM Maidstone St Luke *Cant* 99-04; Perm to Offic from 04. *Shebri, 21 Fauchons Close, Bearsted, Maidstone ME14 4BB* Tel (01622) 730117 Mobile 07785-156606

FIELD, David Hibberd. b 36. K Coll Cam BA58. Oak Hill Th Coll 58. **d** 60 **p** 61. C Aldershot H Trin *Guildf* 60-63; C Margate H Trin *Cant* 63-66; Sec Th Students Fellowship 66-68; Tutor Oak Hill Th Coll 68-93; Vice Prin 79-93; Dean Minl Tr Course 88-93; Dir Professional Min Div CPAS 94-00; Patr Sec CPAS 94-00; Perm to Offic *Cov* from 94; rtd 00. *25 Field Barn Road, Hampton Magna, Warwick CV35 8RX* Tel (01926) 410291

FIELD, Geoffrey Alder. b 13. Ely Th Coll. **d** 47 **p** 48. C King Cross *Wakef* 47-50; C Ely 50-54; V Whittlesey St Andr 54-75; V Foxton 75-80; rtd 81; Perm to Offic *Ely* 81-02. *14 Poplar Close, Great Shelford, Cambridge CB2 5LX* Tel (01223) 842099

FIELD, Gerald Gordon. b 54. K Coll Lon BD75 AKC75. Coll of Resurr Mirfield 76. **d** 77 **p** 78. C Broughton *Blackb* 77-79; C Blackpool St Steph 79-82; V Skerton St Luke 82-86; NSM Westleigh St Pet *Man* 92-93; V Shap w Swindale and Bampton w Mardale *Carl* 93-97; P-in-c Netherton 97; V 98-01; I Tullamore w Durrow, Newtownfertullagh, Rahan etc *M & K* from 01. *St Catherine's Rectory, Church Avenue, Tullamore, Co Offaly, Irish Republic* Tel and fax (00353) (506) 21731 Mobile 87-956 9188 E-mail tullamore@meath.anglican.org

FIELD, James Lewis. b 46. Open Univ BSc96. SEITE 94. **d** 97 **p** 98. NSM Chatham St Mary w St Jo *Roch* 97-00; R Gravesend H Family w Ifield from 00. *Burr Lea, Church Hill, Dartford DA2 7EH* Tel 07840-087056 (mobile)

FIELD, Martin Richard. b 55. Keswick Hall Coll CertEd76 Leic Univ MA87. St Jo Coll Nottm BTh82 LTh. **d** 82 **p** 83. C Gaywood, Bawsey and Mintlyn *Nor* 82-85; Perm to Offic *Leic* 85-87; Hon C S'well Minster *S'well* 87-88; Hon C Stand *Man* 88-89; Dioc Press and Communications Officer 88-91; CUF 91-95; Perm to Offic *Cant* 96-99. *7 Fosbrook House, Davidson Gardens, London SW8 2XH* Tel (020) 7627 1640

FIELD, Miss Olwen Joyce. b 53. St Jo Coll Nottm 86. **d** 88 **p** 94. Par Dn Kensal Rise St Mark and St Martin *Lon* 88-91; Par Dn Northwood H Trin 91-94; C 94-95; Chapl Mt Vernon Hosp 91-99; P-in-c W Drayton 99-03; V from 03; Dean of Women's Min Willesden Area from 01; AD Hillingdon from 03. *The Vicarage, 4 Beaudesert Mews, West Drayton UB7 7PE* Tel (01895) 442194 E-mail olwen@swanroad.go-plus.net

FIELD, Richard Colin. b 33. St Cath Soc Ox BA54 MA63. Clifton Th Coll 63. **d** 65 **p** 66. C Highbury Ch Ch *Lon* 65-70; V Hanger Lane St Ann 70-85; V Leytonstone St Jo *Chelmsf* 85-98; rtd 98; Perm to Offic *Chich* from 99. *21 Rufus Close, Lewes BN7 1BG* Tel (01273) 472884

FIELD, Canon Susan Elizabeth. b 59. York Univ BA80 Birm Univ CertEd81 Ox Univ MTh98. Qu Coll Birm 84. **d** 87 **p** 94. C Coleshill *Birm* 87-90; Chapl Loughb Univ *Leic* 91-98; TV Loughborough Em and St Mary in Charnwood from 98; Dir Post-Ord Tr 95-04; Bp's Adv for Women's Min 97-04; Dir of Ords from 04; Hon Can Leic Cathl from 04. *134 Valley Road, Loughborough LE11 3QA* Tel (01509) 234472 E-mail sue.field1@tesco.net

FIELD, William Jenkin. b 25. St Deiniol's Hawarden. **d** 66 **p** 67. C Cardiff St Jo *Llan* 66-72; V Llancarfan w Llantrithyd 72-94; rtd 94; Perm to Offic *Llan* from 94. *20 Whitmore Park Drive, Barry CF62 8JL* Tel (01446) 701027

FIELDEN, Elizabeth Ann. b 42. TCert63. LNSM course 98. **d** 99 **p** 00. OLM Broughton Gifford, Gt Chalfield and Holt *Sarum* from 99. *393 Ham Green, Holt, Trowbridge BA14 6PX* Tel (01255) 782509 Fax 783152 E-mail winesource@saqnet.co.uk

FIELDEN, Hugh. b 66. BNC Ox BA88 Birm Univ PGCE90. Qu Coll Birm 91. **d** 93 **p** 94. C Sholing *Win* 93-97; TV Bramley *Ripon* 97-02; TV Bingley All SS *Bradf* from 02. *Winston Grange, Otley Road, Bingley BD16 3EQ* Tel (01274) 568266

FIELDEN, Mrs Janice. b 46. Warwick Univ BEd82 MEd89. St Alb and Ox Min Course 99. **d** 02 **p** 03. NSM Chipping Norton *Ox* from 02. *The Vicarage, Church Lane, Charlbury OX7 3PX* Tel and fax (01608) 810286 E-mail parishoff@aol.com

FIELDEN, Robert. b 32. Linc Th Coll 65. **d** 67 **p** 68. C Bassingham *Linc* 67-72; R Anderby w Cumberworth 72-88; P-in-c Huttoft 72-88; P-in-c Mumby 77-88; R Fiskerton 88-90; rtd 90; Perm to Offic *Carl* 91-99 and *Linc* from 91. *Woodlands, 8 Fiskerton Road, Reepham, Lincoln LN3 4EB* Tel (01522) 750480 E-mail robert@rfielden.freeserve.co.uk

FIELDER, Joseph Neil. b 67. Univ of Wales BSc89. Wycliffe Hall Ox 93. **d** 96 **p** 97. C Cheadle All Hallows *Ches* 96-00; V Preston St Steph *Blackb* from 00. *St Stephen's Vicarage, 60 Broadgate, Preston PR1 8DU* Tel (01772) 555762 E-mail the.fielders@blueyonder.co.uk

FIELDGATE, John William Sheridan. b 44. St Jo Coll Dur BA68. Ox NSM Course 75. **d** 79 **p** 80. NSM Haddenham w Cuddington, Kingsey etc *Ox* 79-90; C Northleach w Hampnett and Farmington *Glouc* 90-92; C Cold Aston w Notgrove and Turkdean 90-92; P-in-c Upper and Lower Slaughter w Eyford and Naunton 92-01; P-in-c The Guitings, Cutsdean and Farmcote 92-01; V Acton w Gt Waldingfield *St E* from 01. *The Vicarage, Melford Road, Acton, Sudbury CO10 0BA* Tel and fax (01787) 377287 E-mail jandjfieldgate@ukonline.co.uk

FIELDING, John Joseph. b 29. TCD BA53 MA65 QUB DipEd57. TCD Div Sch Div Test 54. **d** 54 **p** 55. C Belfast St Luke *Conn* 54-57; C Belfast St Mary Magd 57-60; Chapl Windsor Boys' Sch Hamm 61-69; Chapl St Edw Sch Ox 69-73; V Highgate St Mich *Lon* 73-95; rtd 95; Perm to Offic *Guildf* from 95 and *S'wark* 99-04. *30 Sackville Mews, Sackville Road, Sutton SM2 6HS* E-mail j.j.fielding@btinternet.com

FIELDING, Stephen Aubrey. b 67. Ulster Univ BSc89 TCD BTh93. CITC 90. **d** 93 **p** 94. C Bangor Abbey *D & D* 93-97; I Templepatrick w Donegore *Conn* from 97. *926 Antrim Road, Templepatrick, Ballyclare BT39 0AT* Tel (028) 9443 2300 E-mail templepatrick@connor.anglican.org

FIELDSEND, John Henry. b 31. Nottm Univ BSc54 Lon Univ BD61. Lon Coll of Div ALCD59. **d** 61 **p** 62. C Pennington *Man* 61-64; C Didsbury Ch Ch 64-66; P-in-c Bayston Hill *Lich* 66-67; V 67-88; UK Dir CMJ 89-91; Dir and Min at Large CMJ 91-96; rtd 96; Perm to Offic *St Alb* 96-00; Hon C Thame *Ox* from 01. *58 Cedar Crescent, Thame OX9 2AU* Tel (01844) 212559 E-mail john@tehillah.freeserve.co.uk

FIELDSON, Robert Steven. b 56. Qu Coll Cam BA78 MA81 Wye Coll Lon MSc79 Nottm Univ BA86. St Jo Coll Nottm 84. **d** 87 **p** 88. C Walmley *Birm* 87-90; Chapl Protestant Ch in Oman 90-95; P-in-c Cofton Hackett w Barnt Green *Birm* 95-98; V from 98; AD Kings Norton from 00. *The Vicarage, 8 Cofton Church Lane, Barnt Green, Birmingham B45 8PT* Tel 0121-445 1269 E-mail rob@fieldson.co.uk

FIENNES, The Very Revd the Hon Oliver William. b 26. New Coll Ox BA54 MA55. Cuddesdon Coll 52. **d** 54 **p** 55. C Milton *Win* 54-58; Chapl Clifton Coll Bris 58-63; R St Mary-at-Lambeth *S'wark* 63-68; RD Lambeth 68; Can and Preb Linc Cathl *Linc* 69-97; Dean Linc 69-89; rtd 89; Perm to Offic *Pet* and *St E* from 89; *Linc* 99-02. *Home Farm House, Colsterworth, Grantham NG33 5HZ* Tel (01476) 860811

FIFE (née EVE), Hilary Anne. b 57. Lon Univ BEd80. Ripon Coll Cuddesdon 89. **d** 91 **p** 94. Par Dn Coulsdon St Andr *S'wark* 91-94; C 94-95; Chapl Croydon Coll 92-94; Asst Chapl Mayday Healthcare NHS Trust Thornton Heath 94-02; Sen Chapl from 02; Chapl Harestone Marie Curie Cen Caterham 94-98. *19 Greenview Avenue, Croydon CR0 7QW* Tel (020) 8654 8685 *or* 8401 3105

FIFE, Janet Heather. b 53. Sussex Univ BA77 Man Univ MPhil98. Wycliffe Hall Ox 84. **d** 87 **p** 94. Chapl Bradf Cathl *Bradf* 87-89; Par Dn York St Mich-le-Belfrey *York* 89-92; Chapl Salford Univ *Man* 92-00; Hon TV Pendleton St Thos w Charlestown 92-95; Hon TV Pendleton 95-96; V Upton Priory *Ches* from 00. *The Vicarage, Churchway, Macclesfield SK10 3HT* Tel (01625) 827761 E-mail j.fife@virgin.net

FIGG, Robin Arthur Rex. b 62. RN Eng Coll Plymouth BScEng84. Westcott Ho Cam CTM94. **d** 94 **p** 95. C Old Cleeve, Leighland and Treborough *B & W* 94-97; C Gt Berkhamsted *St Alb* 97-01; V Kildwick *Bradf* from 01. *The Vicarage, Kildwick, Keighley BD20 9BB* Tel (01535) 633307 E-mail vicar@kildwick.org.uk

FILBERT-ULLMANN, Mrs Clair. b 44. Leuven Univ Belgium BTh94 MA94. Virginia Th Sem 95. **d** 94 **p** 96. USA 94-95; Asst Chapl Charleroi *Eur* 95-00; P-in-c Leuven 99-02; Asst Chapl Tervuren w Liège 99-01; Perm to Offic from 02. *Muhlbach am Hochkonig 437, A-5505, Austria* Tel (0043) (6467) 20107 E-mail crullmann2001@yahoo.com

FILBY, The Ven William Charles Leonard. b 33. Lon Univ BA58. Oak Hill Th Coll 53. **d** 59 **p** 60. C Eastbourne All SS *Chich* 59-62; C Woking St Jo *Guildf* 62-65; V Richmond H Trin *S'wark* 65-71; V Hove Bp Hannington Memorial Ch *Chich* 71-79; R Broadwater St Mary 79-83; RD Worthing 80-83; Can and Preb Chich Cathl 81-83; Adn Horsham 83-02; rtd 02. *Kymber Cottage, Hale Hill, Westburton, Pulborough RH20 1HE* Tel (01798) 831269 E-mail williamfilby@btopenworld.com

FILER, Victor John. b 43. Sheff Univ MMin95. Sarum Th Coll 66. **d** 69 **p** 70. C Mortlake w E Sheen *S'wark* 69-74; SSF 75-82; P-in-c Plaistow SS Phil and Jas w St Andr *Chelmsf* 80-83; Chapl Plaistow Hosp 81-83; TV Beaconsfield *Ox* 84-90; TR Maltby *Sheff* 90-98; V Abbeydale St Jo from 98. *The Vicarage, 6 Kenwell Drive, Bradway, Sheffield S17 4PJ* Tel 0114-236 0786

FILLERY, William Robert. b 42. Univ of Wales (Swansea) BA65 Surrey Univ MA96. St D Coll Lamp CPS68 BD69 PGCE72. **d** 68 **p** 69. C Llangyfelach and Morriston *S & B* 68-71; C Morriston 71-72; Lic to Offic *Ox* 73-76; Chapl Windsor Girls' Sch Hamm W Germany 76-81; OCF 79-81; Chapl Reed's Sch Cobham 81-86; V Oxshott *Guildf* 86-89; P-in-c Seale 89-91; P-in-c Puttenham and Wanborough 89-91; Hd of RE Streatham Hill & Clapham Sch for Girls 91-03; V Llanybydder and Llanwenog w Llanllwni *St D* from 03. *The Vicarage, Llanllwni, Pencader SA39 9DR* Tel (01559) 395413

FILLINGHAM, Richard James. b 58. Man Univ BA80 Sheff Univ MA03 ACA83. All Nations Chr Coll Wycliffe Hall Ox. **d** 98 **p** 99. C Brinsworth w Catcliffe and Treeton *Sheff* 98-01; C Ecclesall 01-05. *92 Greystones Road, Sheffield S11 7BQ* Tel 0114-266 1804

FILMER, Paul James. b 58. Open Univ BA88. Aston Tr Scheme 95 Oak Hill Th Coll DipHE95. **d** 97 **p** 98. C Petham and Waltham w Lower Hardres etc *Cant* 97-00; P-in-c Patrixbourne w Bridge and Bekesbourne from 00. *The Vicarage, 23 High Street, Bridge, Canterbury CT4 5JZ* Tel (01227) 830250 E-mail revpfilmer@btinternet.com

FINCH, Mrs Alison. b 59. SEN79. Sarum & Wells Th Coll 90. **d** 92 **p** 94. Par Dn Banbury *Ox* 92-94; C 94-95; C Wokingham All SS 95-98; C Binfield 98-99; C St Peter-in-Thanet *Cant* 99-02; R Kirkwall and P-in-c Stromness *Ab* 02-05; Ind Chapl *Chelmsf* from 05; C Colchester St Pet and St Botolph from 05. *St Botolph's Vicarage, 50B Priory Street, Colchester CO1 2QB* Tel (01206) 868043 Mobile 07762-744977 E-mail alisonfinch@surefish.co.uk

FINCH, Barry Marshall. *See* PALMER-PALMER-FFYNCHE, Barry Marshall

FINCH, Christopher. b 41. Lon Univ BA63 AKC63 BD69. Sarum Th Coll 63. **d** 65 **p** 66. C High Wycombe *Ox* 65-69; Prec Leic Cathl *Leic* 69-73; R Lt Bowden St Nic 73-81; V Evington 81-99; P-in-c Leic St Phil 95-99; P-in-c Lower Dever Valley *Win* 99-00; R from 00. *The Rectory, 10 Pigeon House Field, Sutton Scotney, Winchester SO21 3NJ* Tel (01962) 760240

FINCH, David Walter. b 40. Cam Univ MA74 FIBMS69. Ridley Hall Cam. **d** 91 **p** 92. C Ixworth and Bardwell *St E* 91-92; C Blackbourne 92-94; P-in-c Stoke by Nayland w Leavenheath 94-00; P-in-c Polstead 95-00; P-in-c Fressingfield, Mendham etc from 00; RD Hoxne from 00. *The Vicarage, Christmas Lane, Metfield, Harleston IP20 0JY* Tel (01379) 586488

FINCH, Canon Edward Alfred. b 23. Lon Univ BSc50. Sarum Th Coll 50. **d** 52 **p** 53. C Wealdstone H Trin *Lon* 52-55; C E Grinstead St Swithun *Chich* 55-59; V Walthamstow St Pet *Chelmsf* 59-70; Can Res Chelmsf Cathl 70-85; Dir Interface Assn 85-90; rtd 90; Perm to Offic *Chelmsf* from 90 and *St E* from 91. *St Clare, The Street, Pakenham, Bury St Edmunds IP31 2JU* Tel and fax (01359) 230949 E-mail finch-travelfriends@talk21.com

FINCH, Frank. b 33. Qu Coll Birm 72. **d** 74 **p** 75. C Bilston St Leon *Lich* 74-78; R Sudbury and Somersal Herbert *Derby* 78-87; Chapl HM Pris Sudbury 78-87; HM Det Cen Foston Hall 80-87; V Lilleshall and Sheriffhales *Lich* 87-90; R The Ridwares and Kings Bromley 90-98; rtd 98; Perm to Offic *Lich* from 00. *11 Ferrers Road, Yoxall, Burton-on-Trent DE13 8PS* Tel (01543) 472065

FINCH, Jeffrey Walter. b 45. Man Univ BA(Econ)66 Liv Univ DASE80. Linc Th Coll 82. **d** 84 **p** 85. C Briercliffe *Blackb* 84-87; P-in-c Brindle 87-93; Asst Dir of Educn 87-93; V Laneside 93-00; TV Fellside Team from 00. *The Vicarage, Church Lane, Bilsborrow, Preston PR3 0RL* Tel (01995) 640269

FINCH, John. b 20. Bps' Coll Cheshunt 59. **d** 61 **p** 62. C Middlesbrough St Paul *York* 61-64; V Easington w Skeffling and Kilnsea 64-68; V Habergham Eaves St Matt *Blackb* 68-75; V Garstang St Helen Churchtown 75-86; rtd 86; Perm to Offic *Blackb* from 86. *55 Worcester Avenue, Garstang, Preston PR3 1FJ* Tel (01995) 602386

FINCH, Morag Anne Hamilton. b 64. EAMTC 97. **d** 00 **p** 01. C Cranham *Chelmsf* 00-05; V Gidea Park from 05. *St Michael's Vicarage, Main Road, Romford RM2 5EL* Tel (01708) 741084 E-mail thefinches@ntlworld.com

FINCH, Paul William. b 50. Oak Hill Th Coll DipTh73 Lon Bible Coll. **d** 75 **p** 76. C Hoole *Ches* 75-78; C Charlesworth *Derby* 78-87; C Charlesworth and Dinting Vale 87-88; TV Radipole and Melcombe Regis *Sarum* 88-01; V Malvern St Andr and Malvern Wells and Wyche *Worc* from 01. *St Andrew's Vicarage, 48 Longridge Road, Malvern WR14 3JB* Tel (01684) 573912 E-mail paul@finchnest.freeserve.co.uk

FINCH, Richard William. b 62. Westcott Ho Cam 95. **d** 97 **p** 98. C Saffron Walden w Wendens Ambo and Littlebury *Chelmsf*

97-00; C Elm Park St Nic Hornchurch 00-01; V from 01. *St Michael's Vicarage, Main Road, Romford RM2 5EL* Tel (01708) 741084 E-mail finches@aic.co.uk

FINCH, Ronald. b 15. Qu Coll Birm 79. **d** 80 **p** 80. Hon C Welford w Weston and Clifford Chambers *Glouc* 80-85; Perm to Offic *Ches* 85-03 and *Sheff* from 03. *55 Folds Crescent, Sheffield S8 0EP* Tel 0114-249 9029

FINCH, Miss Rosemary Ann. b 39. Leeds Univ CertEd60. **d** 93 **p** 94. OLM S Elmham and Ilketshall *St E* 93-00; Asst Chapl Ipswich Hosp NHS Trust from 00. *Ipswich Hospital, Heath Road, Ipswich IP4 5PD* Tel (01473) 712233 E-mail rosiestmse@aol.com

FINCH, Canon Stanley James. b 31. Mert Coll Ox BA55 MA58. Wells Th Coll 55. **d** 57 **p** 58. C Lancaster St Mary *Blackb* 57-61; C Leeds St Pet *Ripon* 61-65; V Habergham All SS *Blackb* 65-73; V S Shore H Trin 73-84; V Broughton 84-98; RD Preston 86-92; Hon Can Blackb Cathl 91-98; rtd 98; P-in-c Alderton, Gt Washbourne, Dumbleton etc *Glouc* 98-02; Perm to Offic from 02. *14 Bellflower Road, Walton Cardiff, Tewkesbury GL20 7SB* Tel (01684) 850544

FINCH, Thomas. b 20. Lon Univ BD57. Edin Th Coll 48. **d** 51 **p** 51. Chapl St Andr Cathl *Ab* 51-55; C St Marylebone St Cypr *Lon* 55-58; V Warmington *Pet* 58-67; RD Oundle 62-67; V Wellingborough St Mary 67-88; rtd 88; Perm to Offic *Blackb* from 88. *18 Royal Avenue, Leyland, Preston PR25 1BQ* Tel (01772) 433780

FINCHAM, Nicholas Charles. b 56. St Jo Coll Dur BA78 MA80. Westcott Ho Cam 80 Bossey Ecum Inst Geneva 81. **d** 82 **p** 83. C Seaham w Seaham Harbour *Dur* 82-85; C Lydney w Aylburton *Glouc* 85-87; C Isleworth All SS *Lon* 87-95; P-in-c Chiswick St Mich from 95. *St Michael's Vicarage, 60 Elmwood Road, London W4 3DZ* Tel (020) 8994 3173 E-mail nicholas.fincham@talk21.com

FINDLAY, Brian James. b 42. Wellington Univ (NZ) BA62 MA63 BMus66 Magd Coll Ox MA75. Qu Coll Birm DipTh71. **d** 72 **p** 73. C Deptford St Paul *S'wark* 72-75; Chapl and Dean of Div Magd Coll Ox 75-84; V Tonge Moor *Man* 84-02; Hon Can Man Cathl 00-03; R Monks Eleigh w Chelsworth and Brent Eleigh etc *St E* from 03. *The Rectory, The Street, Monks Eleigh, Ipswich IP7 7AU* Tel (01449) 740244

FINDLAY, James. b 68. Bp Otter Coll BA90 Westmr Coll Ox PGCE92. Wycliffe Hall Ox 02. **d** 04 **p** 05. C Gillingham St Mark *Roch* from 04. *The Garden House, Vicarage Road, Gillingham ME7 5JA* Tel (01634) 575280 Mobile 07814-558687 E-mail jim@findlay3519.freeserve.co.uk

FINDLAYSON, Roy. b 44. Man Univ CQSW69 MA89. Sarum & Wells Th Coll 80. **d** 82 **p** 83. C Benwell St Jas *Newc* 82-83; Hon C 83-85; C Morpeth 85-88; C N Gosforth 88; TV Ch the King 88-94; V Newc St Fran 94-98; Asst Chapl Newcastle upon Tyne Hosps NHS Trust from 98; Chapl Marie Curie Cen Newc from 98. *Marie Curie Centre, Marie Curie Drive, Newcastle upon Tyne NE4 6SS* Tel 0191-219 5560 *or* 273 8811

FINDLEY, Peter. b 55. Trin Coll Ox BA77 MA80 Barrister-at-Law (Gray's Inn) 78. Trin Coll Bris DipHE92. **d** 92 **p** 93. C Yateley *Win* 92-97; V Westwood *Cov* from 97. *St John's Vicarage, Featherbed Lane, Coventry CV4 7DD* Tel (024) 7647 0515 *or* 7669 5026 E-mail peterfindley@stjohnswestwood.freeserve.co.uk

FINDON, John Charles. b 50. Keble Coll Ox BA71 MA75 DPhil79. Ripon Coll Cuddesdon. **d** 77 **p** 78. C Middleton *Man* 77-80; Lect Bolton St Pet 80-83; V Astley 83-91; V Baguley 91-98; P-in-c Bury St Mary 98-05; R from 05. *St Mary's Rectory, Tithebarn Street, Bury BL9 0JR* Tel 0161-764 2452

FINKENSTAEDT, Harry Seymour. b 23. Yale Univ BA49 Mass Univ MA68. Episc Th Sch Cam Mass BD50. **d** 53 **p** 54. USA 53-71; C Hazlemere *Ox* 71-73; C Huntingdon St Mary w St Benedict *Ely* 73-75; R Castle Camps 75-84; R Shudy Camps 75-84; P-in-c W Wickham 79-84; P-in-c Horseheath 79-81; P-in-c Gt w Lt Stukeley 84-88; rtd 88; Perm to Offic *Ely* 88-01. *13761 Charismatic Way, Gainesville, VA 20155, USA* Tel (001) (703) 743 5787

FINLAY, Alison Mary. *See* CAW, Alison Mary

FINLAY, Christopher John. b 46. FCII71. WMMTC 95. **d** 98 **p** 99. NSM Coln St Aldwyns, Hatherop, Quenington etc *Glouc* from 98. *Coombe House, Calcot, Cheltenham GL54 3JZ* Tel (01285) 720806

FINLAY, Canon Hueston Edward. b 64. TCD BA85 BAI85 BTh89 MA92 Cam Univ MA98 Lon Univ PhD98. CITC 86. **d** 89 **p** 90. C Kilkenny w Aghour and Kilmanagh *C & O* 89-92; Bp's Dom Chapl 89-92; Lib and Registrar Kilkenny Cathl 89-92; Bp's V Ossory Cathl 90-92; Chapl Girton Coll Cam 92-95; C Cambridge Gt St Mary w St Mich *Ely* 92-95; Chapl and Fell Magd Coll Cam 95-99; Dean of Chpl 99-04; Can Windsor from 04. *8 The Cloisters, Windsor Castle, Windsor SL4 1NJ* Fax (01753) 833806 E-mail h.finlay@stgeorges-windsor.org

FINLAY, Michael Stanley. b 45. N Ord Course 78. **d** 81 **p** 82. C Padgate *Liv* 81-85; V Newton-le-Willows 85-90; V Orford St Marg 90-98; P-in-c Warrington St Elphin 98-00; R from 00. *The Rectory, Church Street, Warrington WA1 2TL* Tel (01925) 635020

FINLAY, Nicholas. b 47. Regent Coll Vancouver MCS00. St Jo Coll Nottm 01. **d** 02 **p** 03. C Haydock St Mark *Liv* 02-03; C Bootle 03-04; Lic to Adn Warrington 04-05; V Sittingbourne St Mary and St Mich *Cant* from 05. *The Vicarage, 26 Valenciennes Road, Sittingbourne ME10 1EN* Tel (01795) 427874 E-mail nickfinlay@aol.com

FINLAYSON, Duncan. b 24. LNSM course 73. **d** 76 **p** 76. NSM Bridge of Allan *St And* 76-94; NSM Alloa 77-94; NSM Dollar 77-94; Hon AP Hillfoots Team 80-87; rtd 94. *29 Cawder Road, Bridge of Allan, Stirling FK9 4JJ* Tel (01786) 833074

FINLAYSON, Grantley Adrian. b 55. Wilson Carlile Coll 74 Chich Th Coll 87. **d** 89 **p** 90. C Watford St Mich *St Alb* 89-92; TV W Slough *Ox* 92-97; Dioc Officer for Race Relations *Glouc* 97-02; V Luton St Andr *St Alb* from 02. *St Andrew's Vicarage, 11 Blenheim Crescent, Luton LU3 1HA* Tel (01582) 732380 Fax 481711 E-mail grantley@gfinlayson.fsworld.co.uk

FINLINSON, Paul. b 58. St Chad's Coll Dur BA79 St Martin's Coll Lanc PGCE81. Carl Dioc Tr Course 86. **d** 89 **p** 90. NSM Kirkby Lonsdale *Carl* 89-99; Chapl Worksop Coll Notts from 99. *Worksop College, Sparken Hill, Worksop S80 3AP* Tel (01909) 537109 *or* (01524) 69652

FINN, Gordon Frederick. b 33. Dur Univ BA60. Ely Th Coll 60. **d** 62 **p** 63. C Kingswinford St Mary *Lich* 62-65; C Northampton St Mary *Pet* 65-67; Chapl Barnsley Hall Hosp Bromsgrove 67-71; Chapl Lea Hosp Bromsgrove 67-71; C Swanage *Sarum* 71-73; P-in-c Ford End *Chelmsf* 73-79; V S Shields St Oswin *Dur* 79-98; rtd 98. *58 Hutton Lane, Guisborough TS14 8AW*

FINN, Ian Michael. b 58. AKC. Chich Th Coll 81. **d** 82 **p** 83. C Habergham All SS *Blackb* 82-83; C W Burnley All SS 83-85; C Torrisholme 85-87; V Lancaster Ch Ch w St Jo and St Anne 87-91; P-in-c Tillingham and Dengie w Asheldham *Chelmsf* 91-97; Chapl R Gr Sch Worc 97-99; P-in-c Denston w Stradishall and Stansfield *St E* 99-01; P-in-c Wickhambrook w Lydgate, Ousden and Cowlinge 00-01; R Bansfield from 02. *The Vicarage, Church Road, Wickhambrook, Newmarket CB8 8XH* Tel (01440) 820288 E-mail ifinn@ifinn98.freeserve.co.uk

FINN, Miss Sheila. b 30. LMH Ox BA68 MA69. Gilmore Ho 68. **dss** 78 **d** 87 **p** 94. Tettenhall Wood *Lich* 78-86; Dioc Ecum Officer 86-95; The Ridwares and Kings Bromley 86-87; Par Dn 87-94; C 94-95; rtd 95; Perm to Offic *Lich* from 97. *15 Leacroft Road, Penkridge, Stafford ST19 5BU* Tel (01785) 716018

FINNEMORE, James Christopher. b 59. Pemb Coll Cam BA81 MA85. Coll of Resurr Mirfield. **d** 85 **p** 86. C Manston *Ripon* 85-88; C Hessle *York* 88-92; R Bishop Wilton w Full Sutton, Kirby Underdale etc 92-99; R Garrowby Hill from 99. *The Rectory, Bishop Wilton, York YO42 1SA* Tel (01759) 368230

FINNEY, Canon David. b 41. St Mich Coll Llan 68. **d** 70 **p** 71. C Wythenshawe Wm Temple Ch *Man* 70-73; C Bedford Leigh 73-75; V Royton St Anne 75-81; V Dearnley 81-94; TV Rochdale from 94; Hon Can Man Cathl from 04. *The Vicarage, 89 Clement Royds Street, Rochdale OL12 6PL* Tel and fax (01706) 646272 E-mail davidfinney@tinyworld.co.uk

FINNEY, Canon Fred. b 17. Bris Univ BA38 DipEd39. Wycliffe Hall Ox 61. **d** 62 **p** 63. C Gt Crosby St Luke *Liv* 62-66; V Ashton-in-Makerfield St Thos 66-86; Hon Can Liv Cathl 83-86; rtd 86; Perm to Offic *Blackb* and *Liv* from 86. *1 Howard Drive, Tarleton, Preston PR4 6DA* Tel (01772) 812598

FINNEY, Canon John Thomas. b 27. Sheff Univ BA51 DipEd52. Ripon Hall Ox 60. **d** 62 **p** 63. C Leigh St Mary *Man* 62-65; V 83-97; V Peel 65-69; Chapl Hockerill Coll Bishop's Stortford 69-74; V Astley *Man* 74-83; AD Leigh 85-93; Hon Can Man Cathl 87-97; rtd 97; Perm to Offic *Man* from 97. *36 Station Road, Blackrod, Bolton BL6 5BW* Tel (01204) 698010

✠**FINNEY, The Rt Revd John Thornley.** b 32. Hertf Coll Ox BA55. Wycliffe Hall Ox 56. **d** 58 **p** 59 **c** 93. C Highfield *Ox* 58-61; C Weston Turville 61-65; R Tollerton *S'well* 65-71; V Aspley 71-80; Bp's Adv on Evang 80-89; Bp's Research Officer 88-89; Hon Can S'well Minster 84-89; Officer for Decade of Evang in C of E 90-93; Suff Bp Pontefract *Wakef* 93-98; rtd 98; Hon Asst Bp S'well from 98. *Greenacre, Crow Lane, South Muskham, Newark NG23 6DZ* Tel and fax (01636) 679791 E-mail john.finney2@ntlworld.com

FINNEY, Ms Melva Kathleen. b 24. LTh76. St Jo Coll Auckland 47 Gilmore Ho 56. **dss** 57 **d** 78. E Dulwich St Jo *S'wark* 56-59; Community of Sisters of the Love of God Ox 59-61; New Zealand from 61; Asst Chapl Christchurch 61-62; Fendalton St Barn 62-63; Asst Chapl Womens and Templeton Hosp 63-72; Asst Chapl Princess Marg Hosp Christchurch 63-72; Chapl 72-86; rtd 86. *22 Gunns Crescent, Cashmere, Christchurch 8002, New Zealand* Tel (0064) (3) 332 7100

FINNIE, Canon Robert. b 20. **d** 84 **p** 84. NSM Aberdeen St Andr *Ab* from 84; NSM Aberdeen St Ninian 84-97; Hon Can St Andr Cathl from 97. *10 Cairngorm Crescent, Aberdeen AB12 5BL* Tel (01224) 874669

FINNIMORE, Keith Anthony. b 36. AKC59. **d** 60 **p** 61. C Wanstead H Trin Hermon Hill *Chelmsf* 60-63; C Kingswood *S'wark* 63-65; V Bolney *Chich* 65-67; V Elmstead *Chelmsf* 67-73;

R Pentlow, Foxearth, Liston and Borley 73-77; NSM Cockfield w Bradfield St Clare, Felsham etc *St E* 89-91; R Hawstead and Nowton w Stanningfield etc 91-96; P-in-c 96-01; rtd 96; Perm to Offic *St E* from 01. *Larkhill, Rede Road, Whepstead, Bury St Edmunds IP29 4SS* Tel (01284) 735291

FIRBANK, Michael John. b 73. R Holloway Coll Lon BA94 St Mary's Coll Twickenham PGCE94. St Jo Coll Nottm MTh05. **d** 05. C St Illogan *Truro* from 05. *Church House, 46 Bosmeor Park, Redruth TR15 3JN* Tel (01209) 218753 Mobile 07888-711645 E-mail mjfirbank@hotmail.com

FIRMIN, Canon Dorrie Eleanor Frances. b 19. LNSM course. **d** 88 **p** 94. NSM Ellon *Ab* 88-99; NSM Cruden Bay 88-99; Hon Can St Andr Cathl from 97; rtd 99. *Minas Tirith, 7 Slains Avenue, Ellon AB41 9ZA* Tel (01358) 721623

FIRMIN, Paul Gregory. b 57. ACIB80. Trin Coll Bris BA87. **d** 87 **p** 88. C Swindon Ch Ch *Bris* 87-91; V Shrewsbury H Trin w St Julian *Lich* 91-99; V Astley, Clive, Grinshill and Hadnall 99-01; V Southampton St Mary Extra *Win* from 01. *The Vicarage, 65 Peartree Avenue, Bitterne, Southampton SO19 7JN* Tel (023) 8043 7192 E-mail nimrifs@btinternet.com

FIRMSTONE, Ian Harry. b 44. Qu Coll Birm. **d** 82 **p** 83. C Warminster St Denys *Sarum* 82-84; C N Stoneham *Win* 84-88; R Freemantle 88-90; V Littleport *Ely* 90-91; TV Stanground and Farcet 91-97; P-in-c Holme w Conington 95-96; rtd 97. *Binibquer Vell 216, Carrer des Timo, Sant Lluis, 07711 Menorca, Spain* Tel (0034) 6062 83760

FIRTH, Mrs Ann Neswyn. b 40. St As Minl Tr Course 95. **d** 98 **p** 99. NSM Llanidloes w Llangurig *Ban* 98-05; Perm to Offic from 05. *Springfield, Westgate Street, Llanidloes SY18 6HJ* Tel (01686) 413098
E-mail davidandneswyn@firth19.freeserve.co.uk

FIRTH, Barry. b 37. ACA60 FCA71. NW Ord Course 74. **d** 77 **p** 78. NSM Brighouse *Wakef* 77-81; P-in-c Batley St Thos 81-85; V 85-88; V Rastrick St Matt 88-95; RD Brighouse and Elland 92-96; TV Brighouse and Clifton 95-97; rtd 97; Perm to Offic *Wakef* from 97. *51 Bolehill Park, Hove Edge, Brighouse HD6 2RS* Tel (01484) 710227

FIRTH, Christopher John Kingsley. b 37. St Mich Coll Llan DipTh66. **d** 66 **p** 67. C Sutton in Ashfield St Mary *S'well* 66-70; V Langold 70-74; C Falmouth K Chas *Truro* 74-77; P-in-c Mabe 77-81; V 81-95; RD Carnmarth S 90-94; rtd 99. *The Gables, Trewin Road, Budock Water, Falmouth TR11 5EA* Tel (01326) 377539

FIRTH, Graham Alfred. b 38. Man Univ BA60. Ripon Hall Ox. **d** 62 **p** 63. C Norton Woodseats St Paul *Sheff* 62-65; C-in-c Kimberworth Park CD 65-69; V Kimberworth Park 69-71; P-in-c Egmanton and Laxton *S'well* 71-77; V Sibthorpe 77-04; R Elston w Elston Chapelry 77-04; R E Stoke w Syerston 77-04; R Shelton 91-04; rtd 04; Perm to Offic *S'well* from 04. *Fairview House, Sutton-cum-Beckingham, Lincoln LN5 0RE*

FIRTH, Neswyn. *See* FIRTH, Mrs Ann Neswyn

✠**FIRTH, The Rt Revd Peter James.** b 29. Em Coll Cam BA52 MA63. St Steph Ho Ox 53. **d** 55 **p** 56 **c** 83. C Barbourne *Worc* 55-58; C Malvern Link St Matthias 58-62; R Abbey Hey *Man* 62-66; Asst Network Relig Broadcasting BBC Man 66-67; Sen Producer/Org Relig Progr TV & Radio BBC Bris 67-83; Hon Can Bris Cathl *Bris* 74-83; Suff Bp Malmesbury 83-94; Angl Adv HTV West 84-94; rtd 94; Hon Asst Bp Glouc from 03. *Mill House, Silk Mill Lane, Winchcombe, Cheltenham GL54 5HZ* Tel (01242) 603669 E-mail peter@firth7.fsbusiness.co.uk

FISH, Mrs Jacqueline Wendy. b 42. NTMTC 02. **d** 04 **p** 05. NSM Enfield Chase St Mary *Lon* from 04. *41 Churchbury Lane, Enfield EN1 3TX* Tel (020) 8366 2235
E-mail jacquiefishie@aol.com

FISH, Michael. b 61. Carl and Blackb Dioc Tr Inst 01. **d** 04 **p** 05. NSM Blackb St Thos w St Jude *Blackb* from 04; NSM Blackb St Mich w St Jo and H Trin from 04. *48 St Martin's Drive, Blackburn BB2 5HU* Tel (01254) 609532 Mobile 07867-760110
E-mail mikefish@ntlworld.com

FISH, Winthrop. b 40. Dalhousie Univ Canada BA63 BEd Birm Univ BPhil76 MEd78. K Coll (NS) 62. **d** 64 **p** 65. Canada 64-74; Perm to Offic *Birm* 74-77; Asst Chapl Solihull Sch 77-79; Chapl Wroxall Abbey Sch 79-82; C Newquay *Truro* 82-84; V Highertown and Baldhu 84-89; P-in-c Newlyn St Newlyn 89-97; Dioc Children's Adv 89-97; Dioc Adv in RE 95-97; rtd 98; Perm to Offic *Ex* from 98. *2 Vicarage Road, East Budleigh, Budleigh Salterton EX9 7EF* Tel (01395) 445371

FISHER, Adrian Charles Proctor. b 24. TCD BA48 MA62. TCD Div Sch Div Test47. **d** 49 **p** 50. C Carlow *C & O* 49-52; C Tintern 49-52; C Killesk 49-52; CF 52-57 and 62-69; I Fethard w Killesk, Tintern and Templetown *C & O* 57-62; P-in-c N Stoke w Mongewell and Ipsden *Ox* 70-83; V 83-92; Chapl Oratory Prep Sch 73-80; rtd 92; Perm to Offic *Ox* from 99. *Aldermaston Soke, Silchester, Reading RG7 2PB* Tel 0118-970 0246

FISHER, Mrs Alison. b 48. Cranmer Hall Dur 04. **d** 05. NSM The Thorntons and The Otteringtons *York* from 05. *The Vicarage, 4 Endican Lane, Thorton le Moor, Northallerton DL7 9FB* Tel (01609) 761806 E-mail ali@endican.gotadsl.co.uk

FISHER, Andrew John. b 72. St Jo Coll Nottm BA02. **d** 02 **p** 03. C Ilkeston St Jo *Derby* from 02. *51 Doris Road, Ilkeston DE7 5DP* Tel 0115-852 9138

FISHER, Brian Robert. b 36. **d** 02 **p** 03. OLM Sole Bay *St E* from 02. *Greengates, Main Street, Walberswick, Southwold IP18 6UH* Tel (01502) 723023 Mobile 07766-216111
E-mail emite99660@aol.com

FISHER, David Stephen. b 66. Cuddesdon Coll BTh98. **d** 98 **p** 99. C Stockport SW *Ches* 98-01; V Gatley from 01. *St James's Vicarage, 11 Northenden Road, Cheadle SK8 4EN* Tel 0161-428 4764 E-mail daifisher@aol.com

FISHER, Mrs Diana Margaret. b 44. EMMTC DipTh94. **d** 94 **p** 95. NSM E and W Leake, Stanford-on-Soar, Rempstone etc *S'well* 94-97; NSM W Bridgford 97-98; NSM Aberfoyle and Callander *St And* 99; C Spalding St Jo w Deeping St Nicholas *Linc* 99-01; R Hallaton w Horninghold and Allexton, Tugby etc *Leic* from 01. *The Rectory, Churchgate, Hallaton, Market Harborough LE16 8TY* Tel (01858) 555363

FISHER, Eric Henry George. b 48. NTMTC 94. **d** 97 **p** 98. NSM Heydon, Gt and Lt Chishill, Chrishall etc *Chelmsf* 97-03; P-in-c Gt Oakley w Wix and Wrabness from 03. *The Rectory, Wix Road, Great Oakley, Harwich CO12 5BJ* Tel (01255) 880230
E-mail eric.fisher@ukgateway.net

FISHER, Eric William. b 30. Birm Univ BA53. Coll of Resurr Mirfield 70. **d** 72 **p** 73. C Styvechale *Cov* 72-75; C Chesterfield St Mary and All SS *Derby* 75-78; Chapl Buxton Hosps 78-84; TV Buxton w Burbage and King Sterndale *Derby* 78-84; R Shirland 84-89; V Sheff St Matt *Sheff* 89-95; rtd 95; Perm to Offic *Lich* 95-02. *6 Wickstead Row, Main Road, Betley, Crewe CW3 9AB*

FISHER, Frank. *See* FISHER, Canon Kenneth Francis McConnell

FISHER, George Arnold. b 54. Lon Univ BD75. N Ord Course 81. **d** 84 **p** 85. C Conisbrough *Sheff* 84-92; V Blackpool St Thos *Blackb* from 92. *St Thomas's Vicarage, 80 Devonshire Road, Blackpool FY3 8AE* Tel and fax (01253) 392544 *or* 399276
E-mail george@stthomaschurch.co.uk

FISHER, Gordon. b 44. NW Ord Course 74. **d** 77 **p** 78. NSM Airedale w Fryston *Wakef* 77-81; C Barkisland w W Scammonden 81-84; C Ripponden 81-84; V Sutton St Mich *York* 84-87; V Marton-in-Cleveland 87-96; R Kettering SS Pet and Paul *Pet* 96-02; rtd 02. *8 Mount Pleasant Avenue, Marske-by-the-Sea, Redcar TS11 7BW* Tel (01642) 489489
E-mail rector@sspp.co.uk

FISHER, Henry John. b 25. Lich Th Coll 64. **d** 66 **p** 67. C Kings Norton *Birm* 66-70; C Weston-super-Mare St Jo *B & W* 70-75; C Weston-super-Mare H Trin 72-75; P-in-c Leigh upon Mendip 75-78; P-in-c Stoke St Michael 75-78; P-in-c Leigh upon Mendip w Stoke St Michael 78-80; C Wilton 80-88; C Street w Walton 88-90; rtd 90; Perm to Offic *B & W* from 90. *18 Hawkers Lane, Wells BA5 3JL* Tel (01749) 677092

FISHER, Humphrey John. b 33. Harvard Univ AB55 Ox Univ DPhil59. Heythrop Coll Lon MA. **d** 91 **p** 92. NSM Bryngwyn and Newchurch and Llanbedr etc *S & B* from 91. *Rose Cottage, Newchurch, Kington, Hereford HR5 3QF* Tel (01544) 370632

FISHER, Ian St John. b 59. Down Coll Cam BA80 MA84 Leic Univ PhD84. St Steph Ho Ox BA88. **d** 88 **p** 89. C Colwall w Upper Colwall and Coddington *Heref* 88-91; Chapl Surrey Univ *Guildf* 92-97; V Hurst *Man* 97-04; V N Shoebury *Chelmsf* from 04. *The Vicarage, 2 Weare Gifford, Shoeburyness, Southend-on-Sea SS3 8AB* Tel (01702) 584053
E-mail ian.fisher@btclick.com

FISHER, Mrs Joan. b 52. **d** 00 **p** 01. NSM Blackpool St Mark *Blackb* 00-04; NSM Blackpool St Thos from 04. *St Thomas's Vicarage, 80 Devonshire Road, Blackpool FY3 8AE* Tel and fax (01253) 392544 E-mail joan@stthomaschurch.co.uk

FISHER, John Andrew. b 63. Bath Univ BSc85 MA97. Wycliffe Hall Ox BA93. **d** 94 **p** 95. C Rayleigh *Chelmsf* 94-98; V Burton Joyce w Bulcote and Stoke Bardolph *S'well* from 98; AD Gedling 00-05. *The Vicarage, 9 Chestnut Grove, Burton Joyce, Nottingham NG14 5DP* Tel 0115-931 2109
E-mail john.a.fisher@btinternet.com

FISHER, Canon Kenneth Francis McConnell (Frank). b 36. K Coll Lon 57. **d** 61 **p** 62. C Sheff St Geo and St Steph *Sheff* 61-63; Chapl Sheff Univ 64-69; Chapl Lon Univ *Lon* 69-75; P-in-c Dean *Carl* 75-80; Soc Resp Officer 75-80; TR Melksham *Sarum* 80-90; P-in-c Stapleford *Ely* 90-01; Dioc Ecum Officer 90-01; RD Shelford 94-03; Hon Can Ely Cathl from 98; rtd 01; P-in-c Grantchester *Ely* from 01. *The Vicarage, 44 High Street, Grantchester, Cambridge CB3 9NF* Tel (01223) 840460
E-mail thelmafisher@waitrose.com

FISHER, Mark Simon. b 52. K Coll Lon BD76 AKC76 Trin Coll Ox MA82 DPhil83. Kelham Th Coll 70 Perkins Sch of Th (USA) 76. **d** 78 **p** 78. SSF 78-80; Hon C Victoria Docks Ascension *Chelmsf* 78-79; Lic to Offic *Eur* and *Lon* 78-80; *Ox* 78-87; Chapl LMH Ox 80-86; R Glas St Matt *Glas* 87-89; Hon Asst P W Derby St Jo *Liv* from 97. *29A Rodney Street, Liverpool L1 9EH* Tel 0151-707 9748

FISHER, Canon Michael Harry. b 39. Ex Univ BA61. St Steph Ho Ox 61. **d** 63 **p** 64. C Wolverhampton St Pet *Lich* 63-67; C Newquay *Truro* 67-70; V Newlyn St Pet 70-75; P-in-c Launceston St Steph w St Thos 75-82; V Carbis Bay w Lelant 82-95; V Newquay 95-99; Hon Can Truro Cathl 85-99; RD Penwith 88-93; Chapl Costa del Sol W *Eur* 99-00; rtd 00; Perm to Offic *Truro* from 00 and *Eur* from 04. *Chymedda, Southway, Windmill, Padstow PL28 8RN* Tel (01841) 521544 Mobile 07970-865049 E-mail mfisher39@aol.com

FISHER, Michael John. b 43. Leic Univ BA64 Keele Univ MA67. Qu Coll Birm 75. **d** 78 **p** 79. NSM Stafford St Mary and St Chad *Lich* 78-79; NSM Stafford from 79. *35 Newland Avenue, Stafford ST16 1NL* Tel (01785) 245069

FISHER, Paul Vincent. b 43. Worc Coll Ox BA66 MA70 ARCM73. Qu Coll Birm DipTh68. **d** 70 **p** 71. C Redditch St Steph *Worc* 70-73; C Chorlton upon Medlock *Man* 73-79; Chapl Man Univ 73-79; Exec Sec Community Affairs Division BCC 79-81; Asst Dir of Tr and Dir of Lay Tr *Carl* 81-86; P-in-c Raughton Head w Gatesgill 81-85; Lay Tr Team Ldr *S'wark* 86-90; Dir of Tr 90-94; V Kingswood 94-00; rtd 00; Perm to Offic *Bradf* from 01. *3 Buxton Park, Langcliffe, Settle BD24 9NQ* Tel (01729) 824058 E-mail paul.fisher@ukonline.co.uk

FISHER, Peter Francis Templar. b 36. CCC Cam BA60 MA. Wells Th Coll 62. **d** 63 **p** 64. C Gt Ilford St Mary *Chelmsf* 63-67; C Colchester St Mary V 67-70; C-in-c Basildon St Andr CD 70-72; P-in-c Edstaston *Lich* 83-87; P-in-c Whixall 83-87; P-in-c Tilstock 84-87; V Shelton and Oxon 87-97; rtd 97. *8 Cecil Road, Dronfield S18 2GU* Tel 0114-258 1455

FISHER, Canon Peter Timothy. b 44. Dur Univ BA68 MA75. Cuddesdon Coll 68. **d** 70 **p** 71. C Bedford St Andr *St Alb* 70-74; Chapl Surrey Univ *Guildf* 74-78; Sub-Warden Linc Th Coll 78-83; R Houghton le Spring *Dur* 83-94; RD Houghton 87-92; Prin Qu Coll Birm 94-02; V Maney *Birm* from 02; Hon Can Birm Cathl from 00. *The Vicarage, Maney Hill Road, Sutton Coldfield B72 1JJ* Tel 0121-354 2426 E-mail pfisher@fish.co.uk

FISHER, Richard John. b 60. K Coll Lon BA82 AKC82 Selw Coll Cam BA87 Cam Univ MA95. Ridley Hall Cam 85. **d** 88 **p** 89. C Woodley St Jo the Ev *Ox* 88-91; C Acomb St Steph *York* 91-95; Chapl Preston Acute Hosps NHS Trust 98-02; Chapl Lanc Teaching Hosps NHS Trust from 02. *Royal Preston Hospital, Sharoe Green Lane North, Fulwood, Preston PR2 4HT* Tel (01772) 523730 *or* 716565 Fax 522447 E-mail richard.fisher@lthtr.nhs.uk

FISHER, Roy Percy. b 22. SS Mark & Jo Coll Chelsea TCert50 Univ of Wales MTh00. Linc Th Coll 51. **d** 53 **p** 54. C Lewisham St Jo Southend *S'wark* 53-56; Clare Coll Miss Rotherhithe 56-59; V Boughton under Blean *Cant* 59-66; V Westgate St Sav 66-71; R Staplegrove *B & W* 71-79; TR Eckington w Handley and Ridgeway *Derby* 79-87; rtd 87; Perm to Offic *Llan* from 87. *258 New Road, Porthcawl CF36 5BA* Tel (01656) 788682

FISHER, Mrs Sheila Janet. b 50. WEMTC 01. **d** 04 **p** 05. NSM Cam w Stinchcombe *Glouc* from 04. *1 Ashmead Court, Ashmead, Cam, Dursley GL11 5EN* Tel (01453) 544656 E-mail ashmead.fishers@btinternet.com

FISHER, Simon John Plumley. b 80. St Jo Coll Dur BA01. Ripon Coll Cuddesdon BA04. **d** 05. C Bath Bathwick *B & W* from 05. *64 St John's Road, Bathwick, Bath BA2 6PT* Tel (01225) 318488 E-mail sjpf@hotmail.com

FISHER, Stephen Newson. b 46. Univ of Wales (Swansea) BSc67 CEng82 MIEE82. Linc Th Coll 84. **d** 86 **p** 87. C Nunthorpe *York* 86-89; P-in-c Middlesbrough St Oswald 89-90; V 90-94; V Redcar 94-02; P-in-c The Thorntons and The Otteringtons from 02. *The Vicarage, 4 Endican Lane, Thornton le Moor, Northallerton DL7 9FB* Tel (01609) 761806 Fax 08701-634640 E-mail stephen@endican.gotadsl.co.uk

FISHER, Thomas Andrew. b 35. Southn Univ HNC57. Sarum & Wells Th Coll 84. **d** 86 **p** 87. C Win Ch Ch *Win* 86-89; Chapl Salisbury Coll of Tech *Sarum* 89-94; Chapl Salisbury Coll of FE 89-94; Perm to Offic *Sarum* 94-99; rtd 00; NSM Salisbury St Mark *Sarum* from 99. *Mombasa, Manor Farm Road, Salisbury SP1 2RR* Tel (01722) 335155

FISHER, Thomas Ruggles. b 20. Cranmer Hall Dur 58. **d** 60 **p** 61. C Melton Mowbray w Thorpe Arnold *Leic* 60-63; R Husbands Bosworth 63-74; R Husbands Bosworth w Mowsley and Knaptoft 74-79; R Husbands Bosworth w Mowsley and Knaptoft etc 79-82; Perm to Offic 82-96; Perm to Offic *Pet* from 83; rtd 85. *12 The Dell, Oakham LE15 6JG* Tel (01572) 757630

FISHER-BAILEY, Mrs Carol. b 56. **d** 96 **p** 97. C Eccleshill *Bradf* 96-99; TV Sutton St Jas and Wawne *York* from 99. *Wawne Vicarage, 50 Main Street, Wawne, Hull HU7 5XH* Tel (01482) 370414 E-mail carol@fisherbailey.fsnet.co.uk

FISHLOCK, Mrs Margaret Winifred (Peggy). b 28. Cant Sch of Min 87. **d** 97 **p** 98. NSM Deal St Leon and St Rich and Sholden *Cant* 97-04; Perm to Offic from 04. *58 Gilford Road, Deal CT14 7DQ* Tel (01304) 365841

FISHWICK, Alan. b 48. Chich Th Coll 87. **d** 89 **p** 90. C Laneside *Blackb* 89-92; C Accrington 92-93; TV 93-96; V Blackb St Aid 96-02; V Scorton and Barnacre and Calder Vale 02-05; P-in-c Coppull St Jo from 05. *St John's Vicarage, Darlington Street, Coppull, Chorley PR7 5AB* Tel (01257) 791258

FISHWICK, Mrs Ann. b 40. St Barn Coll Adelaide 91 Trin Coll Melbourne 93. **d** 91 **p** 94. Australia 91-97 and from 02; Chapl Charters Towers Hosp and Home 91-94; Dn Charters Towers St Paul 91-94; Asst P 94-97; Perm to Offic *Heref* 98-99; NSM Worthen 99-02; NSM Hope w Shelve 99-02; NSM Middleton 99-02. *PO Box 544, Weipa, Qld, Australia 4874* Tel (0061) (7) 4069 7228 E-mail capeyorkp@bigpond.com.au

FISHWICK, Ian Norman. b 54. Lanc Univ BEd E Lon Univ MA99. **d** 82 **p** 83. C High Wycombe *Ox* 82-87; V Walshaw Ch Ch *Man* 87-93; Area Voc Adv 88-93; V W Ealing St Jo w St Jas *Lon* 93-98; Dir of Ords Willesden Area 94-98; E Region Area Co-ord for CA 98-99; Operations Dir 99-04; Par Development Adv *Ox* from 05. *89 Carver Hill Road, High Wycombe HP11 2UB* Tel (01494) 598775 E-mail ian.fishwick@oxford.anglican.org

FISHWICK, Raymond Allen. b 42. St Fran Coll Brisbane 93 N Queensland Coll of Min ACP96. **d** 91 **p** 92. Australia 91-97 and from 02; R Charters Towers St Paul 91-97; P-in-c Worthen *Heref* 98-02; P-in-c Hope w Shelve 98-02; P-in-c Middleton 98-02; P-in-c Weipa St Luke from 02; CF from 02. *PO Box 544, Weipa, Qld, Australia 4874* Tel (0061) (7) 4069 7228 E-mail capeyorkp@bigpond.com.au

FISKE, Paul Francis Brading. b 45. St Jo Coll Dur BA68 PhD72. Wycliffe Hall Ox DipTh72. **d** 73 **p** 74. C Sutton *Liv* 73-76; TV Cheltenham St Mary, St Matt, St Paul and H Trin *Glouc* 76-80; C-in-c Hartplain CD *Portsm* 80-84; Hd of Miss UK CMJ 84-86; Hon C Edgware *Lon* 84-86; R Broughton Gifford, Gt Chalfield and Holt *Sarum* 86-95; TV Bourne Valley 95-97; Adv Chr Action 95-97; P-in-c Princes Risborough w Ilmer *Ox* 97-98; TR Risborough from 98. *The Rectory, Church Lane, Princes Risborough HP27 9AW* Tel (01844) 344784 Fax as telephone E-mail fiske@tiscali.co.uk

FISON, Geoffrey Robert Martius. b 34. Dur Univ BA59. Ely Th Coll 59. **d** 61 **p** 62. C Heavitree *Ex* 61-64; Australia 64-69; BSB 64-69; C Southampton Maybush St Pet *Win* 70-73; TV Strood *Roch* 73-79; TV Swindon Dorcan *Bris* 79-83; P-in-c Brislington St Cuth 83-99; rtd 99; Perm to Offic *Glouc* and *Bris* from 99. *88 Oakleaze Road, Thornbury, Bristol BS35 2LP* Tel (01454) 850678

FITCH, Capt Alan John. b 45. Open Univ BA82 Warwick Univ MA84. Wilson Carlile Coll 64 Qu Coll Birm 92. **d** 92 **p** 93. CA from 66; C Glouc St Jas and All SS *Glouc* 92-97; NSM Wotton St Mary 93-97; V Douglas All SS and St Thos *S & M* 97-02; Chapl HM Pris Is of Man 97-02; TR Walbrook Epiphany *Derby* from 02; Dioc Adv on Racial Justice from 02. *St Augustine's Rectory, 155 Almond Street, Derby DE23 6LY* Tel (01332) 766603 E-mail a.fitch@virgin.net

FITCH, Canon John Ambrose. b 22. CCC Cam BA44 MA48. Wells Th Coll 45. **d** 47 **p** 48. C Newmarket All SS *St E* 47-50; Chapl St Felix Sch Southwold 51-69; V Reydon *St E* 51-70; R Brandon and Santon Downham 70-80; Hon Can St E Cathl 75-87; RD Mildenhall 78-80; R Monks Eleigh w Chelsworth and Brent Eleigh etc 80-87; rtd 87; Perm to Offic *St E* and *Chelmsf* from 87. *The Oak House, High Street, Great Yeldham, Halstead CO9 4EX* Tel (01787) 237058

FITTER, Matthew Douglas. b 59. City of Lon Poly BSc81. Trin Coll Bris MA03. **d** 03 **p** 04. C Purley Ch Ch *S'wark* from 03. *132 Whytecliffe Road North, Purley CR8 2AS* Tel (020) 8763 8505 E-mail matthewfitter@hotmail.com

FITZ, Lionel Alfred. b 24. **d** 87 **p** 88. NSM Cheltenham St Mary, St Matt, St Paul and H Trin *Glouc* 87-94; Perm to Offic from 94. *9 Foxgrove Drive, Cheltenham GL52 6TQ* Tel (01242) 243405

FITZGERALD, Gerald. b 26. **d** 54 **p** 55. C Salford St Phil *Man* 54-57; New Zealand from 57. *8 Searidge Lane, Scarborough, Christchurch, New Zealand* Tel (0064) (3) 326 6112 Fax 326 6186

FITZGERALD, John Edward. b 44. Leic Univ MSc98 Dip Counselling. Oak Hill Th Coll DPS74. **d** 76 **p** 77. C Rainham *Chelmsf* 76-79; C Cambridge St Andr Less *Ely* 79-86; V Holmesfield *Derby* 86-88; Chapl HM Pris Wakef 88-90; Chapl HM Pris Whatton 90-93; Chapl HM Pris Nottm 90-98; Chapl HM YOI Glen Parva from 98. *HM Young Offender Institution, Glen Parva, Tiger's Road, Wigston LE18 4TN* Tel 0116-264 3100 ext 3339

FITZGERALD, Miss Melanie Anne. b 52. Sheff Univ BMus75. Westcott Ho Cam 96. **d** 98 **p** 99. C Rotherham *Sheff* 98-01; C Stannington 01-02; P-in-c Walkley from 02. *St Mary's Vicarage, 150 Walkley Road, Sheffield S6 2XQ* Tel 0114-234 5029 E-mail mfitzg@tesco.net

FITZGERALD CLARK, Mrs Diane Catherine. b 54. Rhode Is Univ BA76. Gen Th Sem NY MDiv86. **d** 86 **p** 87. USA 86-95; NSM Hampstead Em W End *Lon* 96-99; Chapl St Alb High Sch for Girls from 98; Assoc Min St Alb Abbey *St Alb* from 98; Perm to Offic *Lon* from 00. *13 Eleanor Avenue, St Albans AL3 5TA* Tel (01727) 860099

FITZGIBBON, Kevin Peter. b 49. St Jo Coll Nottm BTh81. **d** 81 **p** 82. C Corby St Columba *Pet* 81-85; V Newborough 85-99; V Eaton Socon *St Alb* from 99. *St Mary's Vicarage, 34 Drake Road, Eaton Socon, St Neots PE19 8HS* Tel (01480) 212219 E-mail k.fitzgibbon@care4free.net

FITZHARRIS, Barry. b 47. Lon Univ BA69 W Ontario Univ MA70 K Coll Lon BD72 AKC72. St Aug Coll Cant 72. **d** 73 **p** 74. C Whitstable All SS *Cant* 73-75; C Whitstable All SS w St Pet 75-76; Hon C Clapham Old Town *S'wark* 77-79; Asst Chapl Abp Tenison's Sch Kennington 78-84; Chapl and Hd RS 87-89; Hon C Streatham Ch Ch *S'wark* 80-84; R Radwinter w Hempstead *Chelmsf* 84-87; Hon C Streatham St Pet *S'wark* 87-89 and 97-98. *196 Davidson Road, Croydon CR0 6DP*

FITZHARRIS, The Ven Robert Aidan. b 46. Sheff Univ BDS71. Linc Th Coll 87. **d** 89 **p** 90. C Dinnington *Sheff* 89-92; V Bentley 92-01; RD Adwick 95-01; Hon Can Sheff Cathl 98-01; Adn Doncaster from 01. *Fairview House, 14 Armthorpe Lane, Doncaster DN2 5LZ* Tel (01302) 325787 *or* (01709) 309110 Mobile 07767-355357 Fax (01709) 309107 E-mail archdeacons.office@sheffield.anglican.org

FITZMAURICE, Arthur William John. b 65. AGSM89 Lon Inst of Educn PGCE92 Leeds Univ BA. Coll of Resurr Mirfield 97. **d** 99 **p** 00. C Spondon *Derby* 99-02; P-in-c Emscote *Cov* 02-03; TV Warwick from 03. *All Saints' Vicarage, Vicarage Fields, Warwick CV34 5NJ* Tel (01926) 492073 E-mail john@fmaurice.freeserve.co.uk

FITZPATRICK, Paul Kevin. b 60. Open Univ BA99 Univ of Wales (Lamp) MTh05. Cuddesdon Coll 96. **d** 98 **p** 99. C Okehampton w Inwardleigh, Bratton Clovelly etc *Ex* 98-02; P-in-c Whipton 02-04; V from 04. *The Vicarage, 9 Summer Lane, Exeter EX4 8BY* Tel (01392) 462206

FITZSIMONS, Canon Kathryn Anne. b 57. Bedf Coll of Educn CertEd78. NEOC 87. **d** 90. NSM Bilton *Ripon* 90-01; Soc Resp Development Officer Richmond Adnry 92-99; Urban Min Officer from 99; Hon Can Ripon Cathl from 04. *52 Newton Court, Leeds LS8 2PM* Tel 0113-248 5011 E-mail kathrynfitzsimons@hotmail.com

FLACH (née ROLLINS), Mrs Deborah Mary Rollins. b 54. Trin Coll Bris DipHE81 Sarum & Wells Th Coll 88. **d** 94 **p** 97. C Chantilly *Eur* 94-96; C Maisons-Laffitte 96-04; Asst Chapl from 04. *63 rue de Boissy, 60340 St Leu d'Esserent, France* Tel (0033) (3) 44 56 76 08 Fax 44 56 64 24 E-mail debjerflach@wanadoo.fr

FLACK, Miss Heather Margaret. b 47. **d** 95 **p** 96. C Shenley Green *Birm* 95-00; TV Kings Norton from 00. *195 Monyhull Hall Road, Birmingham B30 3QN* Tel 0121-458 3483

✠FLACK, The Rt Revd John Robert. b 42. Leeds Univ BA64. Coll of Resurr Mirfield 64. **d** 66 **p** 67 **c** 97. C Armley St Bart *Ripon* 66-69; C Northampton St Mary *Pet* 69-72; V Chapelthorpe *Wakef* 72-81; V Ripponden 81-85; V Barkisland w W Scammonden 81-85; V Brighouse 85-88; TR Brighouse St Martin 88-92; RD Brighouse and Elland 86-92; Hon Can Wakef Cathl 89-92; Adn Pontefract 92-97; Suff Bp Huntingdon *Ely* 97-03; Hon Can Ely Cathl 97-03; Abp's Rep H See and Dir Angl Cen Rome from 03; Hon Asst Bp Pet from 03; Perm to Offic *Ely* from 03; Hon Asst Bp Eur from 04. *Anglican Centre, Palazzo Doria Pamphilj, Piazza del Collegio Romano 2, 00186 Rome, Italy* Tel (0039) (06) 678 0302 Fax 678 0674 E-mail acr@anglicancentreinrome.org

FLAGG, David Michael. b 50. CCC Cam BA71 MA75. St Jo Coll Nottm BA76 Dip Past Counselling 94. **d** 77 **p** 78. C Hollington St Leon *Chich* 77-80; C Woodley St Jo the Ev *Ox* 80-86; Chapl The Dorothy Kerin Trust Burrswood 86-94; R Knockholt w Halstead *Roch* 94-99; Dir Chapl Services Mildmay UK 99-02; Hd Chapl Services Qu Eliz Hosp NHS Trust from 02. *Queen Elizabeth Hospital, Stadium Road, London SE18 4QH* Tel (020) 8836 6831 *or* 8836 6000 bleep 370 E-mail david.flagg@nhs.net

✠FLAGG, The Rt Revd John William Hawkins (Bill). b 29. **d** 59 **p** 61 **c** 69. Paraguay 59-63; Argentina 64-73; Adn N Argentina 65-69; Bp Paraguay and N Argentina 69-73; Asst Bp Chile 73-77; Bp Peru 73-77; Asst Bp Liv 78-86; V Toxteth St Cypr w Ch Ch 78-85; P-in-c Litherland Ch Ch 85-86; Gen Sec SAMS 86-93; Asst Bp Roch 87-92; Asst Bp S'well 92-96; Dioc Stewardship Adv 93-96; Dioc Adv in Rural Affairs 93-96; Dioc Adv for Overseas Affairs 94-96; rtd 97; Hon Asst Bp S'well from 97. *c/o A J Flagg Esq, 1 Denshaw, Up Holland, Wigan WN8 0AY* E-mail bill@southwell.anglican.org

FLAHERTY, Jane Venitia. *See* ANDERSON, Mrs Jane Venitia

FLAHERTY, Ms Mandy Carol. b 63. Ches Coll of HE BA86 Leic Univ PGCE87. St Jo Coll Nottm MTh04. **d** 04 **p** 05. C Oadby *Leic* from 04. *62 Fairstone Hill, Oadby, Leicester LE2 5RJ* Tel 0116-271 5265 E-mail mandycf@btopenworld.com

FLANAGAN, Miss Vivienne Lesley. b 66. Liv Poly BA89 Nottm Univ PGCE90. St Jo Coll Nottm MA98. **d** 98 **p** 99. C Huthwaite *S'well* 98-02; P-in-c Lenton Abbey from 02. *St Barnabas' Vicarage, Derby Road, Beeston, Nottingham NG9 2SN* Tel 0115-925 5488 E-mail vivienne@flanagan7719.freeserve.co.uk

FLATHER, Peter George. b 29. Sarum Th Coll. **d** 59 **p** 60. C Fordingbridge w Ibsley *Win* 59-63; C Lyndhurst 63-65; R E w W Bradenham *Nor* 65-72; P-in-c Speke All SS *Liv* 72-73; R Gunthorpe w Bale *Nor* 73-87; P-in-c Sharrington 73-87; P-in-c Gt w Lt Snoring 77-83; R Gunthorpe w Bale w Field Dalling, Saxlingham etc 87-89; rtd 89; Perm to Offic *Nor* 89-99. *29 Jannys Close, Aylsham, Norwich NR11 6DL* Tel (01263) 733548

FLATT, Donald Clifford. b 15. Worc Ord Coll 63. **d** 65 **p** 66. C Tring *St Alb* 65-67; V Wigginton 67-75; Chapl HM Pris Bedf 75-80; V Biddenham *St Alb* 75-82; rtd 83; P-in-c Oare w Culbone *B & W* 83-86; Perm to Offic from 86. *The Stables Cottage, Lamb Court, Dulverton TA22 9HB* Tel (01398) 323088

FLATT, The Very Revd Roy Francis Ferguson. b 47. Edin Th Coll 78. **d** 80 **p** 81. C St Andrews St Andr *St And* 80-82; C Elie and Earlsferry 80-82; C Pittenweem 80-82; Dioc Supernumerary 82-83; Dioc Sec *Arg* 83-87; Dioc Youth Chapl 83-94; R Lochgilphead from 83; R Kilmartin from 83; P-in-c Inveraray from 83; Dean Arg from 99. *Bishopton House, Bishopton Road, Lochgilpead PA31 8PY* Tel (01546) 602315 Fax 602519 Mobile 07775-852115 E-mail lochgilphead@argyll.anglican.org *or* dean.sedati@virgin.net

FLATT, Stephen Joseph. b 57. SRN79 RSCN81 NDN83. Sarum & Wells Th Coll 92. **d** 92 **p** 93. C Limpsfield and Titsey *S'wark* 92-96; TV Pewsey *Sarum* 96-97; Staff Nurse R Free Hampstead NHS Trust 97-99; Charge Nurse from 99; Perm to Offic *S'wark* 98-99; Lic to Offic from 99; Asst Chapl Univ Coll Lon Hosps NHS Trust 00-01; Chapl 01-03; Lead Chapl St Mary's NHS Trust Paddington from 03. *Chaplain's Office, St Mary's Hospital, Praed Street, London W2 1NY* Tel (020) 7886 1508 E-mail stephen.flatt@st-marys.nhs.uk

FLATTERS, Clive Andrew. b 56. Sarum & Wells Th Coll 83. **d** 86 **p** 88. C Weston Favell *Pet* 86-87; C Old Brumby *Linc* 88-91; C Syston *Leic* 91-93; TV 93-99; V Knottingley *Wakef* 99-02; TR Knottingley and Kellington w Whitley from 02. *The Vicarage, Chapel Street, Knottingley WF11 9AN* Tel (01977) 672267

FLAVELL, Paul William Deran. b 44. Univ of Wales (Ban) DipTh66. St Mich Coll Llan DPS68. **d** 68 **p** 69. Australia 68-71; C Blaenavon w Capel Newydd *Mon* 71-74; V Ynysddu 74-84; R Llanaber w Caerdeon *Ban* 84-00; V Llanstadwel *St D* from 00. *The Vicarage, 68 Church Road, Llanstadwel, Milford Haven SA73 1EB* Tel (01646) 600227

FLEET, Daniel James Russell. b 60. Wye Coll Lon BSc84 Keele Univ PGCE02. St Jo Coll Nottm LTh88 DPS89. **d** 89 **p** 90. C Boldmere *Birm* 89-92; C Caverswall and Weston Coyney w Dilhorne *Lich* 92-95; V Alton w Bradley-le-Moors and Oakamoor w Cotton 95-01; rtd 01; Perm to Offic *Lich* from 01. *124 Byrds Lane, Uttoxeter ST14 7RD* Tel (01889) 560214 E-mail dan.fleet@lineone.net

FLEMING, The Ven David. b 37. Kelham Th Coll 58. **d** 63 **p** 64. C Walton St Marg Belmont Road *Liv* 63-67; Chapl HM Borstal Gaynes Hall 68-76; V Gt Staughton *Ely* 68-76; RD St Neots 72-76; V Whittlesey 76-85; RD March 77-82; Hon Can Ely Cathl 82-01; P-in-c Ponds Bridge 83-85; Adn Wisbech 84-93; V Wisbech St Mary 85-89; Chapl Gen of Pris 93-01; Chapl to The Queen from 95; Perm to Offic *Ely* from 01. *Fair Haven, 123 Wisbech Road, Littleport, Ely CB6 1JJ* Tel (01353) 862498

FLEMING, Elizabeth Julie. b 57. Westhill Coll Birm CertEd79 Chester Coll of HE BTh00. N Ord Course 97. **d** 00 **p** 01. C Widnes St Jo *Liv* 00-03; P-in-c Walton Breck Ch Ch 03-04; V Walton Breck from 04. *Christ Church Vicarage, 157 Hartnup Street, Liverpool L5 1UW* Tel 0151-263 2518 E-mail joolz@merseymail.com

FLEMING, George. b 39. CITC. **d** 78 **p** 79. C Donaghcloney w Waringstown *D & D* 78-80; C Newtownards 80; I Movilla 80; C Heref St Pet w St Owen and St Jas *Heref* 80-85; V Holmer w Huntington 85-96; P-in-c Worfield 96-98; V 98-04; rtd 04. *The Chanters, St Breock, Wadebridge PL27 7JS* Tel (01208) 814811

FLEMING, Mrs Kathryn Claire. b 60. Trin Coll Cam BA82 MA91 Montessori TDip92. WEMTC 01. **d** 04 **p** 05. C Charlton Kings St Mary *Glouc* from 04. *20 Glynrosa Road, Charlton Kings, Cheltenham GL53 8QS* Tel (01242) 248858 Mobile 07775-630922 E-mail kathrynfleming@tiscali.co.uk

FLEMING, Mrs Penelope Rawling. b 43. Glas Univ MA63. Westcott Ho Cam 87. **d** 89 **p** 94. C Bourne *Guildf* 89-94; R Wotton and Holmbury St Mary 94-01; Dioc Voc Adv from 94; RD Dorking 99-01; R Gt Bookham from 01. *The Rectory, 2A Fife Way, Bookham, Leatherhead KT23 3PH* Tel (01372) 452405 E-mail pennyflem@aol.com

FLEMING, Ronald Thorpe. b 29. Codrington Coll Barbados 52. **d** 56 **p** 57. Barbados 56-61; C Delaval *Newc* 61-64; V Cambois 64-69; V Ancroft w Scremerston 69-81; V Longhirst 81-84; Chapl Preston Hosp N Shields 84-94; Chapl N Tyneside Hosps 84-94; rtd 94; Perm to Offic *Newc* 94-04. *49 Woodside Drive, Forres IV36 2UF* Tel (01309) 671101

FLEMING, Mrs Victoria Rosalie. b 58. WEMTC 01. **d** 04 **p** 05. NSM St Breoke and Egloshayle *Truro* from 04. *The Chanters, St Breock, Wadebridge PL27 7JS* Tel (01208) 814811

FLEMING, William Edward Charlton. b 29. TCD BA51 MA65. CITC 52. **d** 52 **p** 53. C Dublin Santry *D & G* 52-56; C Arm St Mark *Arm* 56-61; I Tartaraghan 61-80; Prov Registrar 79-96; I Tartaraghan w Diamond 80-96; Can Arm Cathl 86-96; Treas Arm Cathl 88-92; Chan Arm Cathl 92-96; rtd 96. *65 Annareagh Road, Drumorgan, Richhill, Armagh BT61 9JT* Tel (028) 3887 9612

FLENLEY, Benjamin Robert Glanville. b 50. Sarum & Wells Th Coll 86. **d** 88 **p** 89. C Eastleigh *Win* 88-92; V Micheldever and E

Stratton, Woodmancote etc 92-03; R Bentworth, Lasham, Medstead and Shalden from 03. *The Rectory, Bentworth, Alton GU34 5RB* Tel and fax (01420) 563218 E-mail flenbenley@aol.com

FLETCHER, Anthony. *See* FLETCHER, James Anthony

FLETCHER, Anthony Peter Reeves. b 46. Bede Coll Dur CertEd Nottm Univ BTh78. Kelham Th Coll 63 Ridley Hall Cam. **d** 74 **p** 75. C Luton St Mary *St Alb* 74-78; Chapl RAF 78-00; P-in-c Lyneham w Bradenstoke *Sarum* 98-99; P-in-c Kyrenia St Andr and Chapl N Cyprus 00-04; P-in-c Lyneham w Bradenstoke *Sarum* from 04. *17 Webbs Court, Lyneham, Chippenham SN15 4TR* Tel (01249) 892250

FLETCHER, Arthur William George. b 24. Leeds Univ BA50. Coll of Resurr Mirfield 50. **d** 52 **p** 53. C Bush Hill Park St Mark *Lon* 52-55; Chapl RAF 55-58 and 61-72; V Topcliffe *York* 58-61; R Challoch w Newton Stewart *Glas* 73-75; R Kilmacolm 75-82; R Bridge of Weir 75-82; R Largs 82-89; rtd 89; Perm to Offic *Glas* from 89. *c/o The Revd P G M Fletcher, 8 Golf Road, Glasgow G76 7LZ* Tel 0141-577 0196

FLETCHER, Miss Barbara. b 41. ALAM79. WMMTC 93. **d** 96 **p** 97. NSM Smethwick *Birm* 96-97; C 97-02; Perm to Offic from 02. *231 Abbey Road, Smethwick, Warley B67 5NN* Tel 0121-429 9354 Mobile 07711-972075 E-mail bfletcher@warleywoods.fsnet.co.uk

FLETCHER, Christopher Ian. b 43. BSc PhD. Glouc Sch of Min. **d** 89 **p** 90. C Tenbury *Heref* 89-93; R Bredenbury w Grendon Bishop and Wacton etc from 93; RD Bromyard from 99. *The Rectory, Bredenbury, Bromyard HR7 4TF* Tel (01885) 482236 E-mail fletcherc.m@talk21.com

FLETCHER, Colin John. b 46. Chich Th Coll. **d** 83 **p** 84. C Lt Ilford St Mich *Chelmsf* 83-86; C Hockerill *St Alb* 86-89; V New Cantley *Sheff* 89-95; C Kenton *Lon* 95-01; C Heavitree w Ex St Paul *Ex* 01-02; C Heavitree and St Mary Steps from 02. *10 Sherwood Close, Heavitree, Exeter EX2 5DX* Tel (01392) 677153 E-mail abcon@kenton62.freeserve.co.uk

✠**FLETCHER, The Rt Revd Colin William.** b 50. OBE00. Trin Coll Ox BA72 MA76. Wycliffe Hall Ox 72. **d** 75 **p** 76 **c** 00. C Shipley St Pet *Bradf* 75-79; Tutor Wycliffe Hall Ox 79-84; Hon C Ox St Andr *Ox* 79-84; V Margate H Trin *Cant* 84-93; RD Thanet 88-93; Abp's Chapl 93-00; Hon Can Dallas from 93; Area Bp Dorchester *Ox* from 00. *Arran House, Sandy Lane, Yarnton, Kidlington OX5 1PB* Tel (01865) 375541 Fax 379890 E-mail bishopdorchester@oxford.anglican.org

FLETCHER, David Clare Molyneux. b 32. Worc Coll Ox BA55 MA59 DipTh56. Wycliffe Hall Ox 56. **d** 58 **p** 59. C Islington St Mary *Lon* 58-62; Hon C 62-83; Field Worker Scripture Union 62-86; R Ox St Ebbe w H Trin and St Pet *Ox* 86-98; rtd 98. *51 Charlbury Road, Oxford OX2 6UX* Tel (01865) 552420

FLETCHER, David Ernest. b 53. Worc Coll of Educn BEd76 Open Univ MTh01. St Jo Coll Nottm 99. **d** 01 **p** 02. C Mixenden *Wakef* 01-04; P-in-c from 04. *The Old Sweet Factory, 1 Wheatley City, Halifax HX3 5LG* Tel (01422) 367713 Mobile 07702-385885 E-mail de.fletcher@btopenworld.com

FLETCHER, David Mark. b 56. Chich Th Coll 84. **d** 87 **p** 88. C Taunton St Andr *B & W* 87-91; P-in-c Chard, Furnham w Chaffcombe, Knowle St Giles etc 91-95; P-in-c Tiverton St Andr *Ex* from 95; RD Tiverton from 02; Chapl Mid Devon Primary Care Trust from 95. *St Andrew's Vicarage, Blackmore Road, Tiverton EX16 4AR* Tel (01884) 257865 E-mail dmfletcher@standrewstiv.fsnet.co.uk

FLETCHER, Douglas. b 40. Coll of Resurr Mirfield 67. **d** 68 **p** 69. C Notting Hill St Jo *Lon* 68-73; C Cambridge St Mary Less *Ely* 73-74; C Fulham St Jo Walham Green *Lon* 74-76; C Walham Green St Jo w St Jas 76-84; P-in-c Kensal Town St Thos w St Andr and St Phil 84-92; V from 92. *St Thomas's Vicarage, 231 Kensal Road, London W10 5DB* Tel (020) 8960 3703 *or* 8969 2810 E-mail admin@st-thomas.kensington-chelsea.sch.uk

FLETCHER, Capt Frank. b 40. Wilson Carlile Coll 71 EAMTC 94. **d** 96 **p** 96. Asst Chapl HM Pris Highpoint 90-97; Chapl HM Pris Wealstun 97-05; rtd 05. *52 South Parade, Northallerton DL7 8SL* Tel (01609) 778818

FLETCHER, George Henry Yorke. b 11. Wycliffe Hall Ox 58. **d** 59 **p** 60. C Yardley Wood *Birm* 59-62; V Hursley *Win* 62-67; V Hall Green St Pet *Birm* 67-75; V Clive w Grinshill *Lich* 75-80; rtd 80; Perm to Offic *Lich* from 80. *4 Croft Close, Bomere Heath, Shrewsbury SY4 3PZ* Tel (01939) 290337

FLETCHER, Gordon Wolfe (Robin). b 31. Edin Th Coll. **d** 62 **p** 63. C Eston *York* 62-65; C Harton Colliery *Dur* 65-68; V Pelton 68-81; V Ryhope 81-96; rtd 96. *23 Swinburne Road, Darlington DL3 7TD* Tel (01325) 265994 E-mail gordon.fletcher@btinternet.com

FLETCHER, James Anthony. b 36. St Edm Hall Ox BA60 DipTh61 MA66. St Steph Ho Ox 60. **d** 62 **p** 63. C Streatham St Pet *S'wark* 62-65; C Hobs Moat CD *Birm* 65-68; C Cowley St Jo *Ox* 68-77; V Hanworth All SS *Lon* 77-02; P-in-c Hanworth St Geo 89-91; rtd 02; Perm to Offic *Cant* from 02. *19 Strand Street, Sandwich, Kent CT13 9OX* Tel (01304) 620506

FLETCHER, James Arthur. b 71. Reading Univ BA99. Trin Coll Bris 03. **d** 05. C Bexleyheath Ch Ch *Roch* from 05. *50 Martin Dene, Bexleyheath DA6 8NA* Tel (020) 8298 1682

FLETCHER, Miss Janet. b 59. Cranmer Hall Dur. **d** 00 **p** 01. C Ainsdale *Liv* 00-04; TV Walton-on-the-Hill from 04; Hon Chapl Liv Cathl from 04. *St Nathaniel's Vicarage, 65 Fazakerley Road, Liverpool L9 2AJ* Tel 0151-525 7720 E-mail j.fletcher@xalt.co.uk

FLETCHER, Canon Jeremy James. b 60. Dur Univ BA81. St Jo Coll Nottm DipTh86. **d** 88 **p** 89. C Stranton *Dur* 88-91; C Nottingham St Nic *S'well* 91-94; P-in-c Skegby 94-00; P-in-c Teversal 96-00; Bp's Dom Chapl 00-02; Can Res and Prec York Minster *York* from 02. *2 Minster Court, York YO1 7JJ* Tel (01904) 624965 *or* 557205 E-mail jeremyf@tiscali.co.uk *or* precentor@yorkminster.org

FLETCHER, Canon John Alan Alfred. b 33. Oak Hill Th Coll 58. **d** 61 **p** 62. C Erith St Paul *Roch* 61-64; C Rushden *Pet* 64-67; R Hollington St Leon *Chich* 67-86; V Chadwell Heath *Chelmsf* 86-00; RD Barking and Dagenham 91-00; Chapl Chadwell Heath Hosp Romford 86-93; Chapl Redbridge Health Care NHS Trust 93-00; Hon Can Chelmsf Cathl *Chelmsf* 99-00; rtd 00; Perm to Offic *Chich* from 01. *87 Hoads Wood Road, Hastings TN34 2BB* Tel (01424) 712345 Mobile 07860-128912 E-mail john/pam@fletchers17.freeserve.co.uk

FLETCHER, Jonathan James Molyneux. b 42. Hertf Coll Ox BA66 MA68. Wycliffe Hall Ox 66. **d** 68 **p** 69. C Enfield Ch Ch Trent Park *Lon* 68-72; C Cambridge St Sepulchre *Ely* 72-76; C St Helen Bishopsgate w St Martin Outwich *Lon* 76-81; Min Wimbledon Em Ridgway Prop Chpl *S'wark* from 82. *Emmanuel Parsonage, 8 Sheep Walk Mews, London SW19 4QL* Tel (020) 8946 4728

FLETCHER, Keith. b 47. Man Univ DipTh72. Chich Th Coll 79. **d** 80 **p** 81. C Hartlepool St Paul *Dur* 80-82; V Eighton Banks 82-85; V Haydon Bridge *Newc* 85-96; RD Hexham 93-96; P-in-c Beltingham w Henshaw 93-96; R Ashmanhaugh, Barton Turf etc *Nor* 96-99; rtd 99. *2 Churchill Terrace, Sherburn Hill, Durham DH6 1PF* Tel 0191-372 0362

FLETCHER, Linden Elisabeth. b 50. Lon Univ BEd73 MA80. St Jo Coll Nottm 87. **d** 89 **p** 94. C Fakenham w Alethorpe *Nor* 89-93; C Cumnor *Ox* 93-02; P-in-c Ringshall w Battisford, Barking w Darmsden etc *St E* from 02; P-in-c Somersham w Flowton and Offton w Willisham from 02. *The Rectory, Main Road, Willisham, Ipswich IP8 4SP* Tel and fax (01473) 657768

FLETCHER, Mrs Margaret. b 44. **d** 04 **p** 05. NSM Thurstaston *Ches* from 04. *1 Coombe Road, Wirral CH61 4UN* Tel 0151-648 1025

FLETCHER, Mark. b 72. Staffs Poly BSc93. Oak Hill Th Coll BA00. **d** 00 **p** 01. C Paddington Em Harrow Road *Lon* 00-03; C W Kilburn St Luke w St Simon and St Jude 00-03; C Barnsbury from 04. *43 Matilda Street, London N1 0LA* Tel (020) 7278 5208 E-mail mark@midwinter.org.uk

FLETCHER, Martin. b 60. Bradf Univ BEng83. Ripon Coll Cuddesdon. **d** 00 **p** 01. C Oatlands *Guildf* 00-04; R Tolleshunt Knights w Tiptree and Gt Braxted *Chelmsf* from 04. *The Rectory, Rectory Road, Tiptree, Colchester CO5 0SX* Tel (01621) 815260 E-mail fletcher_martin@yahoo.co.uk

FLETCHER, Maurice. *See* FLETCHER, Ralph Henry Maurice

FLETCHER, Mrs Patricia. b 34. K Alfred's Coll Win CertEd74. Chich Th Coll 94. **d** 94. NSM Droxford *Portsm* 94-97; NSM Meonstoke w Corhampton cum Exton 94-97; Perm to Offic 97-00; NSM Blendworth w Chalton w Idsworth 00-04; rtd 04; Perm to Offic *Portsm* from 04. *17 Maylings Farm Road, Fareham PO16 7QU* Tel (01329) 311489

FLETCHER, Paul Gordon MacGregor. b 61. St Andr Univ MTh84. Edin Th Coll 84. **d** 86 **p** 87. C Cumbernauld *Glas* 86-89; C-in-c Glas H Cross 89-93; P-in-c Milngavie 93-99; R Clarkston from 99. *8 Golf Road, Clarkston, Glasgow G76 7LZ* Tel 0141-577 0196 E-mail paulmcgregorfletcher@hotmail.com

FLETCHER, Ralph Henry Maurice. b 43. St Steph Ho Ox 71. **d** 74 **p** 75. C Chislehurst Annunciation *Roch* 74-77; Chapl Quainton Hall Sch Harrow 77-87 and 94-00; Hon C Hillingdon All SS *Lon* 87-94; Perm to Offic *Lon* 94-00 and *Roch* 00-02. *7 Park View, Kingstone, Barnsley S70 6NB* Tel (01226) 779928

FLETCHER, Robert Alexander. b 52. Ridley Hall Cam. **d** 84 **p** 85. C Chalfont St Peter *Ox* 84-88; C Bushey *St Alb* 88-93; TV Digswell and Panshanger 93-00; P-in-c Aldenham 00-05; TV Aldenham, Radlett and Shenley from 05. *The Vicarage, Church Lane, Aldenham, Watford WD25 8BE* Tel (01923) 855905 *or* tel and fax 854209 E-mail r.a.fletcher@talk21.com

FLETCHER, Robin. *See* FLETCHER, Gordon Wolfe

FLETCHER, Canon Robin Geoffrey. b 32. Nottm Univ BA57. Ridley Hall Cam 57. **d** 59 **p** 60. C S Mimms Ch Ch *Lon* 59-64; V Wollaton Park *S'well* 64-71; V Clifton *York* 71-97; Chapl Clifton Hosp York 71-88; RD City of York 86-97; Can and Preb York Minster 89-00; rtd 98; Perm to Offic *York* from 00. *14 South Avenue, Fartown, Huddersfield HD2 1BY* Tel (01484) 510266 E-mail rgfletcher@tiscali.co.uk

FLETCHER, Mrs Sheila Elizabeth. b 35. Nottm Univ BA57 CertEd58. NEOC 84. **d** 87 **p** 94. NSM Dringhouses *York* 87-90;

Par Dn 90-94; C 94-97; P-in-c Sutton on the Forest 97-02; rtd 02; Perm to Offic *York* from 02. *68 Huntsman's Walk, York YO24 3LA* Tel (01904) 796876 E-mail rgeoff@soo.co.uk

FLETCHER, Stephen. b 57. Man Univ BA79 MA84. St Jo Coll Nottm 82. **d** 84 **p** 85. C Didsbury St Jas and Em *Man* 84-88; R Kersal Moor 88-01; TR Horwich and Rivington from 01. *The Rectory, Chorley Old Road, Horwich, Bolton BL6 6AX* Tel and fax (01204) 468263 E-mail stephen@fletchers.freeserve.co.uk

FLETCHER, Stephen William. b 62. Wolv Poly BA84 Birm Univ DipTh87. Qu Coll Birm 85. **d** 88 **p** 89. C Rainham *Roch* 88-91; C Shottery St Andr *Cov* 91-97; Min Bishopton St Pet 91-97; V Llanrumney *Mon* 97-02; V Adderbury w Milton *Ox* from 02. *The Vicarage, Dog Close, Adderbury, Banbury OX17 3EF* Tel (01295) 810309

FLETCHER, Steven John Carylon. b 60. NCTJ83. Aston Tr Scheme 89 Ripon Coll Cuddesdon 89. **d** 92. C Newquay *Truro* 92-93. *Address temp unknown*

FLETCHER, Timothy John. b 63. Sheff Univ BA88 St Jo Coll Dur MA04. Cranmer Hall Dur 01. **d** 03 **p** 04. C Four Marks *Win* from 03. *25 Badger Close, Four Marks, Alton GU34 5HB* Tel (01420) 568277 E-mail tim@fletcherchester.fsnet.co.uk

FLETCHER-CAMPBELL, Walter John Fletcher. b 12. Magd Coll Ox BA33 BSc38 MA44. Wells Th Coll 37. **d** 38 **p** 39. C Portsea St Mary *Portsm* 38-45; V Sarisbury 45-47; V Milton 47-60; RD Portsm 55-60; Metrop Sec USPG *Lon* and *Chelmsf* 60-66; Promotion and Tr Sec 66-68; Dep Home Sec 68-70; V Stanton Harcourt w Northmoor *Ox* 70-75; RD Witney 71-76; P-in-c Bampton Aston w Shifford 75-76; P-in-c Bampton Proper w Bampton Lew 75-76; rtd 77; RD Abingdon *Ox* 80-87; C Radley and Sunningwell 89-93. *153 Upper Road, Kennington, Oxford OX1 5LR* Tel (01865) 730467

FLEWKER, David William. b 53. Birm Univ BA75. Wycliffe Hall Ox 76. **d** 78 **p** 79. C Netherton *Liv* 78-82; C Prescot 82-84; V Seaforth 84-88; TV Whitstable *Cant* 88-96; Miss to Seamen 88-96; V Bethersden w High Halden *Cant* from 96; Asst Dir of Ords from 02. *The Vicarage, Bull Lane, Bethersden, Ashford TN26 3HA* Tel (01233) 820266 E-mail dawsle@yahoo.com

FLEWKER-BARKER, Miss Linda. b 68. Redcliffe Coll BA02 St Jo Coll Dur MA04. Cranmer Hall Dur 02. **d** 04 **p** 05. C Cheltenham Ch Ch *Glouc* from 04. *Hazelhurst, 26 Eldorado Road, Cheltenham GL50 2PT* Tel (01242) 522091 E-mail lindafbarker@yahoo.com

FLIGHT, Michael John. b 41. Sarum Th Coll 68. **d** 71 **p** 72. C Wimborne Minster *Sarum* 71-75; R Tarrant Gunville, Tarrant Hinton etc 75-78; P-in-c Tarrant Rushton, Tarrant Rawston etc 77-78; R Tarrant Valley 78-80; V Westbury 80-00; RD Heytesbury 83-87 and 96-00; R Broad Town, Clyffe Pypard, Hilmarton etc from 00; RD Calne from 03. *The Rectory, Wood Lane, Clyffe Pypard, Swindon SN4 7PY* Tel (01793) 739044 E-mail flightvic@aol.com

FLINDALL, Roy Philip. b 39. K Coll Lon AKC61 BD64 MPhil71 Keswick Hall Coll PGCE71. St Boniface Warminster 62. **d** 63 **p** 64. C Gt Yarmouth *Nor* 63-68; V Nor St Sav w St Paul 68-70; C-in-c Nor St Clem and St Geo 68-70; Lic to Offic *Ely* 90-92; *S'wark* 92-95; Chapl Pet High Sch 95-03; P-in-c Thorney Abbey *Ely* from 03. *The Vicarage, The Green, Thorney, Peterborough PE6 0QD* Tel (01733) 270388

FLINN, Canon John Robert Patrick. b 30. CITC. **d** 65 **p** 66. C Dublin Rathfarnham *D & G* 65-67; I Baltinglass w Ballynure etc *C & O* 67-76; I Castlepollard and Oldcastle w Loughcrew etc *M & K* 76-84; rtd 84; Treas Ossory and Leighlin Cathls *C & O* 90-92; Chan Ossory and Leighlin Cathls 96-01. *The Old School House, Kells, Co Kilkenny, Irish Republic* Tel (00353) (56) 772 8297

FLINT, Howard Michael. b 59. Edge Hill Coll of HE BEd81. Cranmer Hall Dur 95. **d** 97 **p** 98. C Chipping Campden w Ebrington *Glouc* 97-00; V Upper Wreake *Leic* from 00; RD Framland from 02. *The Vicarage, 2 Carrfields Lane, Frisby on the Wreake, Melton Mowbray LE14 2NT* Tel (01664) 434878 E-mail howard.flint@btopenworld.com

FLINT, Nicholas Angus. b 60. Chich Th Coll 84. **d** 87 **p** 88. C Aldwick *Chich* 87-91; Bp's Asst Chapl for the Homeless *Lon* 91-92; TV Ifield *Chich* 92-96; R Rusper w Colgate from 96. *The Rectory, High Street, Rusper, Horsham RH12 4PX* Tel (01293) 871251

FLINTHAM, Alan Jenkinson. b 45. Leeds Univ BSc66 PGCE67 MEd74. EMMTC 98. **d** 00 **p** 01. NSM Melbourne *Derby* from 00. *50 Burlington Way, Mickleover, Derby DE3 9BD* Tel (01332) 512293 E-mail flintham@flinthams.org.uk

FLINTOFT, Ian Hugh. b 74. Pemb Coll Cam BA97 MA99 MPhil98. Westcott Ho Cam 01. **d** 04 **p** 05. C Newc St Geo *Newc* from 04. *Tower House, St George's Close, Newcastle upon Tyne NE2 2TF* Tel 0191-281 3871 E-mail ianflintoft@hotmail.com

FLINTOFT-CHAPMAN, Margaret. *See* CHAPMAN, Mrs Margaret

FLINTOFT-CHAPMAN, Mrs Margaret. b 47. Leeds Univ BA68. NTMTC 03. **d** 05. NSM Barkingside St Cedd *Chelmsf* from 05. *84 Roding Lane North, Woodford Green IG8 8NG* Tel (020) 8504 6750

FLIPPANCE, Miss Kim Sheelagh May. b 64. RGN85 RM88. Trin Coll Bris 97. **d** 99 **p** 00. C Alderbury Team *Sarum* 99-01; C Clarendon 01-02; Asst Chapl Salisbury Health Care NHS Trust from 02. *The Chaplain's Office, Salisbury District Hospital, Salisbury SP2 8BJ* Tel (01722) 336262 E-mail chaplains.department@shc-tr.swest.nhs.uk

FLOATE, Herbert Frederick Giraud. b 25. Keble Coll Ox BA50 MA54. Qu Coll Birm 50. **d** 61 **p** 62. Seychelles 61; Hon C Quarrington w Old Sleaford *Linc* 63-65; P-in-c Mareham le Fen 65-66; Australia 66-72; R Stroxton *Linc* 72-74; R Harlaxton w Wyville and Hungerton 72-74; Lect Shenston New Coll Worcs 74-78; P-in-c Redditch St Geo *Worc* 78-79; Lic to Offic 80-84; R Upton Snodsbury and Broughton Hackett etc 84-89; Chapl Mojacar *Eur* 89-91; rtd 91; Perm to Offic *Heref* from 97. *15 Progress Close, Ledbury HR8 2QZ* Tel (01531) 635509

FLOATE, Miss Rhona Cameron. b 59. Univ of Wales (Cardiff) BA80. Trin Coll Bris 01. **d** 03 **p** 04. C Lighthorne *Cov* from 03; C Chesterton from 03; C Newbold Pacey w Moreton Morrell from 03. *5 Chestnut Grove, Moreton Morrell, Warwick CV35 9DG* Tel (01926) 650093 E-mail rhonafloate@hotmail.com

FLOCKHART, Mrs Ruth. b 56. TISEC 96. **d** 99 **p** 00. NSM Strathpeffer *Mor* from 99; NSM Dingwall from 99. *Kilmuir Farm Cottage, North Kessock, Inverness IV1 3ZG* Tel (01463) 731580 E-mail ruth@ancarraig.clara.co.uk

FLOOD, Kenneth. b 75. St Chad's Coll Dur BSc96 St Steph Ho Ox BTh01. **d** 01 **p** 02. C Hulme Ascension *Man* from 01. *35 Millington Walk, Hulme, Manchester M15 4DF* Tel 0161-226 4199 E-mail kenneth.flood@usa.net

FLOOD, Nicholas Roger. b 42. FCA. Ripon Hall Ox 71. **d** 92 **p** 93. NSM Romsey *Win* 92-94; Chapl Win and Eastleigh Healthcare NHS Trust from 94. *Royal Hampshire County Hospital, Romsey Road, Winchester SO22 5DG* Tel (01962) 824906 *or* 863535

FLORANCE, James Andrew Vernon. b 44. MCIOB. Linc Th Coll 84. **d** 86 **p** 87. C Lt Ilford St Mich *Chelmsf* 86-90; TV Becontree S 90-93; R Orsett and Bulphan and Horndon on the Hill 93-97; P-in-c Liscard St Mary w St Columba *Ches* 97-02; RD Wallasey 99-02; Chapl St D Foundn Hospice Care Newport 02-03; P-in-c Abersychan and Garndiffaith *Mon* from 03. *The Vicarage, Abersychan, Pontypool NP4 8PX* Tel (01495) 772213

FLORANCE (née WAINWRIGHT), Mrs Pauline Barbara. b 40. St Deiniol's Hawarden 83. **dss** 84 **d** 87 **p** 94. New Ferry *Ches* 84-90; Par Dn 87-90; Par Dn Hallwood 90-94; C 94-00; rtd 00; Perm to Offic *Ches* 00-03 and *Mon* from 04. *The Vicarage, Vicarage Lane, Abersychan, Pontypool NP4 8PX* Tel (01495) 772213 E-mail jim.florance@tiscali.co.uk

FLORY, John Richard. b 35. Clare Coll Cam BA59 MA63. Westcott Ho Cam 69. **d** 71 **p** 72. C Shirehampton *Bris* 71-74; V Patchway 74-82; R Lydiard Millicent w Lydiard Tregoz 82-86; TR The Lydiards 86-93; R Box w Hazlebury and Ditteridge 93-01; rtd 01; Perm to Offic *Derby* from 02. *Beechbank, 3 Ivonbrook Close, Darley Bridge, Matlock DE4 2JX* Tel (01629) 734707

FLOWER, David. b 48. IPFA75. EMMTC DTPS95. **d** 95 **p** 99. NSM Ashby-de-la-Zouch H Trin *Leic* 95-05; NSM Ashby-de-la-Zouch and Breedon on the Hill from 05. *29 Money Hill, Ashby-de-la-Zouch LE65 1JA* Tel (01530) 414939 E-mail david.flower@tesco.net

FLOWERDAY, Andrew Leslie. b 53. Imp Coll Lon BSc75. St Jo Coll Nottm DipTh. **d** 90 **p** 91. C Farnborough *Guildf* 90-95; TV Morden *S'wark* from 95. *140 Stonecot Hill, Sutton SM3 9HQ* Tel (020) 8330 6566 *or* 8337 6421

FLOWERDEW, Martin James. b 56. Herts Coll CertEd78 Pemb Coll Cam BEd79 UEA CertCS82. Sarum & Wells Th Coll 89. **d** 91 **p** 92. C Leagrave *St Alb* 91-95; C Radlett 95-99; TV Wilford Peninsula *St E* 99-01; V St Osyth *Chelmsf* from 01. *The Vicarage, The Bury, St Osyth, Clacton-on-Sea CO16 8NX* Tel (01255) 820348 E-mail theblacksheep@tinyworld.co.uk

FLOWERS, John Henry. b 33. Qu Coll Birm 63. **d** 65 **p** 66. C Aberdare St Fagan *Llan* 65-68; C Llantrisant 68-72; V Nantymoel w Wyndham 72-76; Asst Chapl HM Pris Wormwood Scrubs 76-78; Chapl HM Pris Birm 78-80; Chapl HM Pris Albany 80-93; rtd 93; Perm to Offic *Portsm* from 93. *1 Ulster Crescent, Newport PO30 5RU* Tel (01983) 525493

FLUX, Brian George. b 39. Oak Hill Th Coll 68. **d** 71 **p** 72. C Chadderton Ch Ch *Man* 71-74; C Preston All SS *Blackb* 74-76; Min Preston St Luke 76-81; CF (TA) from 78; R Higher Openshaw *Man* 81-88; Chapl HM Pris Haverigg 88-92; rtd 92. *65 Crosby Street, Maryport CA15 6DR* Tel (01900) 810635

FLYNN, Alexander Victor George. b 45. DTh. **d** 90 **p** 91. C Kilsaran w Drumcar, Dunleer and Dunany *Arm* 90-91; P-in-c 91-94; I 94-98; I Clonenagh w Offerlane, Borris-in-Ossory etc *C & O* 98-00. *Shalom, Ridge Road, Portlaoise, Co Laois, Irish Republic*

FLYNN, Peter Murray. b 35. Oak Hill Th Coll 76. **d** 79 **p** 80. Hon C Finchley St Mary *Lon* 79-83; Hon C Mill Hill Jo Keble Ch 84-86; C Mill End and Heronsgate w W Hyde *St Alb* 86-92; V Chessington *Guildf* from 92; rtd 05; Perm to Offic *Roch* from 05. *16 The Street, Plaxtol, Sevenoaks TN15 0QQ* Tel (01732) 811304 E-mail revpeterflynn@btopenworld.com

FOALE, Rosemary. *See* MASON, Sheila Rosemary

FODEN, Eric. Local Minl Tr Course. **d** 93 **p** 94. OLM New Bury *Man* 93-96. *45 Stetchworth Drive, Worsley, Manchester M28 1FU* Tel 0161-790 4627

FODEN, Mrs Janice Margaret. b 54. Sheff Univ BA76 Sheff City Poly PGCE77. N Ord Course 98. **d** 01 **p** 02. NSM Kimberworth *Sheff* 01-05; P-in-c Barnby Dun from 05. *The Vicarage, Stainforth Road, Barnby Dun, Doncaster DN3 1AA* Tel (01302) 882835 E-mail kf@kfoden.free-online.co.uk

FODEN-CURRIE, Mary Agnes. b 43. Bp Grosseteste Coll BEd64. St Jo Coll Nottm MA97. **d** 98 **p** 99. NSM Skegby *S'well* 98-02; NSM Skegby w Teversal 02-03; rtd 03; Perm to Offic *S'well* from 03. *40 Harvey Road, Mansfield NG18 4ES* Tel (01623) 479838

FOGDEN, Canon Elizabeth Sally. b 40. MBE04. MCSP61. Qu Coll Birm 76. **dss** 78 **d** 87 **p** 94. Chevington w Hargrave and Whepstead w Brockley *St E* 78-84; Honington w Sapiston and Troston 84-92; Par Dn 87-92; Par Dn Euston w Barnham, Elvedon and Fakenham Magna 90-92; TD Blackbourne 92-94; TV from 94; Chapl Center Parc Elvedon from 90; Dioc Adv Women's Min from 90; Hon Can St E Cathl from 92. *The Rectory, Church Road, Honington, Bury St Edmunds IP31 1RG* Tel and fax (01359) 269265 Mobile 07860-101980 E-mail honingtonrectory@freeserve.co.uk

FOGDEN, Mrs Patricia Lily Margaret. b 51. SRN73. **d** 03 **p** 04. OLM Orlestone w Snave and Ruckinge w Warehorne etc *Cant* from 03. *Harewood, Wey Street, Snave, Ashford TN26 2QH* Tel (01233) 733388 Mobile 07885-285636 E-mail patricia.fogden@zoom.co.uk

FOGG, Cynthia Mary (Sister Mary Clare). b 34. Bp Grosseteste Coll TCert54 CertRK54. LNSM course 94. **d** 95 **p** 96. NSM Westgate Common *Wakef* from 95. *St Peter's Convent, Dovecote Lane, Horbury, Wakefield WF4 6BD* Tel (01924) 272181 Fax 261225

FOGG, Mrs Margaret. b 37. Carl and Blackb Dioc Tr Inst 04. **d** 05. NSM Allonby, Cross Canonby and Dearham *Carl* from 05. *Green Pastures, 59 Sycamore Road, Maryport CA15 7AE* Tel (01900) 816203 E-mail margaret.fogg@btinternet.com

FOIZEY, Michael John. b 24. Trin Coll Cam BA45 MA65. Westcott Ho Cam 45. **d** 47 **p** 48. C Munster Square St Mary Magd *Lon* 47-53; V Willesden St Matt 53-60; R Lon Docks St Pet w Wapping St Jo 60-82; V Ealing Ch the Sav 82-89; Preb St Paul's Cathl 83-89; rtd 89; Perm to Offic *Worc* from 89. *157 Birmingham Road, Kidderminster DY10 2SL* Tel (01562) 823277

FOLEY, Geoffrey Evan. b 30. Univ of New England BA71 DipEd73 MEd79. St Jo Coll Morpeth 51. **d** 53 **p** 54. Australia 53-90 and from 91; Perm to Offic *S'wark* 90-91; Chapl Hamburg w Kiel *Eur* 91; C Stoke-upon-Trent *Lich* 91; rtd 93; Dioc Archivist *Grafton* from 97. *198 Dawson Street, Lismore, NSW, Australia 2480* Tel (0061) (2) 6621 4684 E-mail gefoley@bigpond.net.au

FOLEY, James Frank. b 50. MBE91. Reading Univ BSc72 Edin Univ DMS83. STETS DTM98. **d** 99 **p** 00. C St Illogan *Truro* 99-03; P-in-c Droxford *Portsm* from 03; P-in-c Meonstoke w Corhampton cum Exton from 03. *The Rectory, Rectory Lane, Meonstoke, Southampton SO32 3NF*

✠**FOLEY, The Rt Revd Ronald Graham Gregory.** b 23. St Jo Coll Dur BA49 DipTh50. **d** 50 **p** 51 **c** 82. C S Shore H Trin *Blackb* 50-54; V Blackb St Luke 54-60; Dir RE *Dur* 60-71; R Brancepeth 60-71; Hon Can Dur Cathl 65-71; Hon Can Ripon Cathl *Ripon* 71-82; V Leeds St Pet 71-82; Chapl to The Queen 77-82; Suff Bp Reading *Ox* 82-87; Area Bp Reading 87-89; rtd 89; Hon Asst Bp York from 95. *3 Poplar Avenue, Kirkbymoorside, York YO62 6ES* Tel (01751) 432439

FOLKARD, Oliver Goring. b 41. Nottm Univ BA63. Lich Th Coll 64. **d** 66 **p** 67. C Carlton *S'well* 66-67; C Worksop Priory 67-68; C Brewood *Lich* 68-71; C Folkingham w Laughton *Linc* 72-75; P-in-c Gedney Hill 76-77; V 77-84; V Whaplode Drove 76-84; V Sutton St Mary 84-94; RD Elloe E 89-94; P-in-c Scotter w E Ferry 94-99; R from 99; R Scotton w Northorpe from 99. *The Rectory, Church Lane, Scotter, Gainsborough DN21 3RZ* Tel (01724) 762951

FOLKS, Andrew John. b 42. St Jo Coll Dur BA65 DipTh69. **d** 69 **p** 70. C Stranton *Dur* 69-72; Chapl Sandbach Sch 73-80; Lic to Offic *Carl* 80-85; Chapl Casterton Sch Lancs 80-85; Hd Master Fernhill Manor Sch New Milton 85-97; Perm to Offic *Win* 85-97; NSM Langdale *Carl* from 97. *Langdale Vicarage, Chapel Stile, Ambleside LA22 9JG* Tel (01539) 437267

FOLKS, Peter William John. b 30. FRCO56 ARCM. Launde Abbey 72. **d** 72 **p** 73. C Leic St Aid *Leic* 72-76; V Newfoundpool 76-84; V Whetstone 84-94; rtd 94; Perm to Offic *Leic* from 94. *34 Triumph Road, Glenfield, Leicester LE3 8FR* Tel 0116-287 3177

FOLLAND, Mark Wilkins. b 59. Southn Univ BTh88. Sarum & Wells Th Coll 86. **d** 88 **p** 00. C Kirkby *Liv* 88-91; Chapl Asst Man R Infirmary 91-93; Chapl Cen Man Healthcare NHS Trust 93-00; Trust Chapl Team Ldr Cen Man/Man Children's Univ Hosp NHS Trust 00-04; Lead Chapl (NW) *Caring for the Spirit* NHS Project from 04. *Mellor House, Corporation Street, Stafford ST16 3SR* E-mail mfolland@central.cmht.nwest.nhs.uk

FOLLETT, Jeremy Mark. b 60. Jes Coll Cam BA82. St Jo Coll Nottm 90. **d** 91 **p** 92. C Newark *S'well* 91-95; C Hellesdon *Nor* 95-01; V St Alb Ch Ch *St Alb* from 01. *Christ Church Vicarage, 5 High Oaks, St Albans AL3 6DJ* Tel (01727) 857592

FOLLETT, Neil Robert Thomas. b 50. RMCS BSc75 Open Univ BA85. EAMTC 86. **d** 89 **p** 90. C Godmanchester *Ely* 89-92; V 92-00; V Wilton Place St Paul *Lon* 00; rtd 00. *Address withheld by request*

FOLLIN, Michael Stuart. b 62. UMIST BSc84. St Jo Coll Nottm MTh02. **d** 02 **p** 03. C Aughton Ch Ch *Liv* from 02. *25 Peet Avenue, Ormskirk L39 4SH* Tel (01695) 577958 Mobile 07813-794252 E-mail michael.follin@tiscali.co.uk

FOLLIS, Bryan Andrew. b 61. Ulster Poly BA83 QUB PhD90 TCD BA98. CITC 95. **d** 98 **p** 99. C Portadown St Mark *Arm* 98-01; I Belfast All SS *Conn* from 01. *All Saints Rectory, 25 Rugby Road, Belfast BT7 1PT* Tel (028) 9032 3327 E-mail bryan.follis@tiscali.co.uk

FOLLIS, Raymond George Carlile. b 23. DFC45. Lich Th Coll 63. **d** 65 **p** 66. C Walsall Wood *Lich* 65-69; R New Fishbourne *Chich* 69-88; P-in-c Appledram 84-88; rtd 88; Perm to Offic *Chich* from 88. *8 Old Rectory Gardens, Felpham, Bognor Regis PO22 7EP* Tel (01243) 825388

FONTAINE, Mrs Marion Elizabeth. b 39. RN61 RM62. St Alb and Ox Min Course 96. **d** 99 **p** 00. OLM Thatcham *Ox* from 99. *33 Druce Way, Thatcham RG19 3PF* Tel (01635) 827746

FOOKES, Roger Mortimer. b 24. VRD63 and Bar 73. Ch Ch Ox BA49 MA53. Wells Th Coll 48. **d** 50 **p** 51. C Westbury-on-Trym H Trin *Bris* 50-53; Chapl RNVR 51-58; Chapl RNR 58-74; C Frome St Jo *B & W* 53-55; R Barwick 55-62; R Closworth 55-62; V Midsomer Norton 62-78; RD Midsomer Norton 72-78; P-in-c Stratton on the Fosse 74-78; P-in-c Clandown 75-78; V Wotton-under-Edge w Ozleworth and N Nibley *Glouc* 78-89; RD Dursley 85-89; rtd 89; Perm to Offic *B & W* 90-99 and *Ex* 90-05. *Lyme Wood Nursing Home, Woodhouse Lane, Uplyme, Lyme Regis DT7 3SQ* Tel (01297) 445444

FOOKS, George Edwin. b 25. Trin Hall Cam BA49 MA52 Reading Univ AdDipEd70. Linc Th Coll 49. **d** 51 **p** 52. C Portsea St Cuth *Portsm* 51-53; C Fareham SS Pet and Paul 53-55; Chapl Earnseat Sch Carl 55-59; V Sheff St Cuth *Sheff* 59-64; Hd Careers Fairfax Gr Sch Bradf 64-66; Hd RE/Careers Buttershaw Comp Sch Bradf 66-70; Counsellor Ifield Sch Crawley 70-73; Hd Guidance Hengrove Sch Bris 73-78; Counsellor w Hearing Impaired Children (Avon) 78-89; Perm to Offic *Bris* from 83; Chapl Southmead Hosp Bris 89-90; Chapl Qu Eliz Hosp Bris 90-96; Chapl Thornbury Hosp from 90; rtd 90; Perm to Offic *Glouc* 90-97. *26 Rudgeway Park, Rudgeway, Bristol BS35 3RU* Tel (01454) 614072

FOOT, Adam Julian David. b 58. Thames Poly BSc80 Garnett Coll Lon CertEd87. Trin Coll Bris DipHE95. **d** 97 **p** 98. C Luton Ch Ch *Roch* 97-00; V Welling from 00. *St John's Vicarage, Danson Lane, Welling DA16 2BQ* Tel (020) 8303 1107 E-mail adam_foot@lineone.net

FOOT, Daniel Henry Paris. b 46. Peterho Cam BA67 MA74. Ridley Hall Cam 77. **d** 79 **p** 80. C Werrington *Pet* 79-82; P-in-c Cranford w Grafton Underwood 82; R Cranford w Grafton Underwood and Twywell from 83; P-in-c Slipton from 94. *The Rectory, Rectory Hill, Cranford, Kettering NN14 4AH* Tel (01536) 330231

FOOT, Elizabeth Victoria Anne. b 55. St Mich Coll Sarum BEd77. Trin Coll Bris BA04. **d** 04 **p** 05. C Linkinhorne *Truro* from 04; C Stoke Climsland from 04. *The Vicarage, Linkinhorne, Callington PL17 7LY* Tel (01579) 363009 E-mail linkvic@hotmail.com

FOOT, Keith George. b 45. Surrey Univ BSc70 Lon Univ PhD73 MRSC CChem. NTMTC 96. **d** 99 **p** 00. C New Thundersley *Chelmsf* 99-03; Min Prince's Park CD *Roch* from 03. *6 Thrush Close, Chatham ME5 7TG* Tel (01634) 685828 E-mail keith.foot@ukgateway.net

FOOT, Leslie Robert James. b 33. Bris Univ BSc54. Wells Th Coll 67. **d** 69 **p** 70. Hon C Yeovil *B & W* 69-76; Lic to Offic from 76. *45 The Roman Way, Glastonbury BA6 8AB* Tel (01458) 832247

FOOT, Lynda. b 43. Reading Univ BEd75 Loughb Univ MSc82 Nottm Univ MA00. EMMTC 97. **d** 00 **p** 01. NSM Coalville and Bardon Hill *Leic* 00-03; NSM Hickling w Kinoulton and Broughton Sulney *S'well* 04-05; NSM Bingham from 05. *34 White Furrows, Cotgrave, Nottingham NG12 3LD* Tel 0115-989 9724 Mobile 07799-662852 E-mail lyndachurch@aol.com

FOOT, Paul. b 41. Lon Univ BA64. Chich Th Coll 65. **d** 67 **p** 68. C Portsea N End St Mark *Portsm* 67-72; C Grimsbury *Ox* 72-74; V Cury w Gunwalloe *Truro* 74-80; P-in-c Port Isaac 80-83; P-in-c St Kew 80-83; V St Day 83-91; rtd 95. *Aeaea, 39 New Road, Llandovery SA20 0EA* Tel (01550) 720140

FOOTE, Desmond. b 46. S Dios Minl Tr Scheme. **d** 82 **p** 83. NSM Furze Platt *Ox* 82-88; NSM Ruscombe and Twyford 88-05;

NSM Woolhampton w Midgham and Beenham Valance from 05; NSM Aldermaston w Wasing and Brimpton from 05. *The Rectory, Birds Lane, Midgham, Reading RG7 5UL* Tel 0118-971 2186

FOOTE, John Bruce. b 18. G&C Coll Cam BA39 MA43 MD51 FRCPath. St Jo Coll Nottm 78. **d** 79 **p** 80. NSM Crookes St Thos *Sheff* 79-88; rtd 88; Perm to Offic *Sheff* from 88 and *Derby* from 79. *67 St Thomas Road, Sheffield S10 1UW* Tel 0114-266 5021

✠**FOOTTIT, The Rt Revd Anthony Charles.** b 35. K Coll Cam BA57 MA70. Cuddesdon Coll 59. **d** 61 **p** 62 **c** 99. C Wymondham *Nor* 61-64; C Blakeney w Lt Langham 64-67; P-in-c Hindringham w Binham and Cockthorpe 67-71; P-in-c Yarlington *B & W* 71-76; R N Cadbury 71-75; P-in-c S Cadbury w Sutton Montis 75-76; TR Camelot Par 76-81; RD Cary 79-81; Dioc Missr *Linc* 81-87; Can and Preb Linc Cathl 86-87; Dioc Rural Officer *Nor* 87; Adn Lynn 87-99; Suff Bp Lynn 99-03; rtd 03; Perm to Offic *Nor* from 04; Hon Asst Bp Nor from 04. *Ivy House, Whitwell Street, Reepham, Norwich NR10 4RA* Tel (01603) 870340

FORAN, Andrew John. b 55. Aston Tr Scheme 84 Linc Th Coll 86. **d** 88 **p** 89. C Epping St Jo *Chelmsf* 88-92; TV Canvey Is 92-97; C Dorking w Ranmore *Guildf* 97-99; Chapl HM Pris Send from 97. *HM Prison, Ripley Road, Send, Woking GU23 7LJ* Tel (01483) 223048 ext 325 Fax 223173

FORBES, Mrs Angela Laura. b 47. Ox Min Course 91. **d** 94 **p** 96. NSM Cowley St Jo *Ox* 94-04; Perm to Offic from 04. *6 Elm Crescent, Charlbury, Chipping Norton OX7 3PZ* Tel (01608) 819121

FORBES, The Very Revd Graham John Thompson. b 51. CBE04. Aber Univ MA73 Edin Univ BD76. Edin Th Coll 73. **d** 76 **p** 77. C Edin Old St Paul *Edin* 76-82; Can St Ninian's Cathl Perth *St And* 82-90; R Stanley 82-88; Provost St Ninian's Cathl Perth 82-90; R Perth St Ninian 82-90; Provost St Mary's Cathl *Edin* from 90; R Edin St Mary from 90. *8 Lansdowne Crescent, Edinburgh EH12 5EQ* Tel 0131-225 2978 *or* 225 6293 Mobile 07711-199297 Fax 0131-226 1482 *or* 225 3181 E-mail provost@cathedral.net

FORBES, Iain William. b 56. Ex Univ BA81. Chich Th Coll 83. **d** 85 **p** 86. C Upper Norwood St Jo *S'wark* 85-88; C Lewisham St Mary 88-90; Chapl St Martin's Coll of Educn *Blackb* 90-94; P-in-c Woodplumpton 94-99; Dioc Voc Adv 94-99; V Woodham *Guildf* from 99. *The Vicarage, 25 Woodham Waye, Woking GU21 5SW* Tel (01483) 762857

FORBES, Canon John Francis. b 29. CITC Dip Ecum 85. **d** 88 **p** 90. C Ferns w Kilbride, Toombe, Kilcormack etc *C & O* 88-90; NSM Gorey w Kilnahue, Leskinfere and Ballycanew from 90; Treas Ferns Cathl 98-03; Chan Ferns Cathl from 03. *Ballinabarna House, Enniscorthy, Co Wexford, Irish Republic* Tel (00353) (54) 33353 Mobile 87-237 9319

FORBES, The Very Revd John Franey. b 33. AKC57. **d** 58 **p** 59. C Darlington H Trin *Dur* 58-62; S Africa from 62; Dean Pietermaritzburg from 76. *The Deanery, PO Box 1639, Pietermaritzburg, 3200 South Africa* Tel (0027) (331) 425848 *or* 941567 Fax 948785

FORBES, Joyce Brinella. b 52. **d** 03 **p** 04. OLM Norbury St Steph and Thornton Heath *S'wark* from 03. *36 Dalmeny Avenue, London SW16 4RT* Tel (020) 8240 0283 E-mail petnard36@aol.com

FORBES, Patrick. b 38. Lon Univ Dip Sociology 74 Open Univ BA82. Linc Th Coll 64. **d** 66 **p** 67. C Yeovil *B & W* 66-69; C Plumstead Wm Temple Ch Abbey Wood CD *S'wark* 69-70; Thamesmead Ecum Gp 70-73; TV Thamesmead 73-78; Dioc Communications Officer *St Alb* 78-90; P-in-c Offley w Lilley 78-82; Info Officer Communications Dept Ch Ho Lon 91-95; Press Officer Miss to Seamen 95-99; rtd 99; Perm to Offic *St Alb* from 04. *18 Francis Road, Hinxworth, Baldock SG7 5HL* Tel and fax (01462) 742015 E-mail patrickforbes@waitrose.com

FORBES, Raymond John. b 34. ALCD58. **d** 58 **p** 59. C Wandsworth St Steph *S'wark* 58-61; C Kewstoke *B & W* 61-63; V Fordcombe *Roch* 63-73; R Ashurst 64-73; P-in-c Morden w Almer and Charborough *Sarum* 73-76; P-in-c Bloxworth 73-76; V Red Post 76-84; P-in-c Hamworthy 84-92; P-in-c Symondsbury and Chideock 92-96; rtd 96; Perm to Offic *Sarum* from 96. *65A Millhams Road, Bournemouth BH10 7LJ* Tel (01202) 582966

FORBES, Stuart. b 33. Lon Univ BD59. Oak Hill Th Coll 56. **d** 61 **p** 62. C Halliwell St Pet *Man* 61-64; P-in-c Wicker w Neepsend *Sheff* 64-69; V Stainforth 69-77; V Salterhebble All SS *Wakef* 77-89; V Toxteth Park St Mich w St Andr *Liv* 89-98; rtd 98; Perm to Offic *Lich* from 00. *29 Firbeck Gardens, Wildwood, Stafford ST17 4QR* Tel (01785) 663658

FORBES ADAM, Stephen Timothy Beilby. b 23. Ball Coll Ox. Chich Th Coll 59. **d** 61 **p** 62. C Guisborough *York* 61-64; R Barton in Fabis *S'well* 64-70; V Thrumpton 65-70; P-in-c S Stoke *B & W* 74-81; C Combe Down w Monkton Combe and S Stoke 81-83; Perm to Offic *B & W* 83-86; *Ox* 86-87; *York* from 88; NSM Epwell w Sibford, Swalcliffe and Tadmarton *Ox* 87-92; rtd 88. *Woodhouse Farm, Escrick, York YO19 6HT* Tel (01904) 878827

FORBES STONE, Elizabeth Karen. b 61. Birm Univ MB, BCh85 MRCGP89. Ridley Hall Cam BA99. **d** 00 **p** 01. C Brentford *Lon* 00-02; C Shaw cum Donnington *Ox* from 02. *The Rectory, 64 Northcroft Lane, Newbury RG14 1BN* Tel (01635) 35320 Mobile 07980-431710 E-mail buff@dandb.org.uk

FORCE-JONES, Graham Roland John. b 41. Sarum Th Coll 65. **d** 68 **p** 69. C Calne and Blackland *Sarum* 68-73; TV Oldbury 73-78; R 78-80; TR Upper Kennet 80-94; RD Marlborough 90-94; P-in-c Atworth w Shaw and Whitley from 94; Chapl Stonar Sch Melksham from 01. *The Vicarage, Corsham Road, Shaw, Melksham SN12 8EH* Tel (01706) 703335 E-mail g.force@shaw-vic.fsnet.co.uk

FORD, Adam. b 40. Lanc Univ MA72 K Coll Lon BD63 AKC63. **d** 65 **p** 65. C Cirencester *Glouc* 65-70; V Hebden Bridge *Wakef* 70-76; Chapl St Paul's Girls' Sch Hammersmith 77-01; Lic to Offic *Lon* 77-98; P in O 84-91. *55 Bolingbroke Road, London W14 0AH* Tel (020) 7602 5902

FORD, Ms Amanda Kirstine. b 61. Middx Univ BA83 Open Univ MA97. St Steph Ho Ox 98. **d** 00 **p** 01. C Leic Resurr *Leic* 00-05; Dioc CUF Officer 04-05; P-in-c Beaumont Leys from 05. *The Vicarage, 10 Parkside Close, Leicester LE4 1EP* Tel 0116-235 2667 E-mail aford@leicester.anglican.org

FORD, Mrs Avril Celia. b 43. St Mary's Coll Dur BSc64 Chelsea Coll Lon PGCE65. LNSM course 85. **d** 92 **p** 94. OLM Horncastle w Low Toynton *Linc* 92-98; NSM from 98; OLM High Toynton 92-98; NSM from 98; OLM Greetham w Ashby Puerorum 92-98; NSM from 98. *Frolic, Reindeer Close, Horncastle LN9 5AA* Tel (01507) 526234 *or* 525600

FORD, Benjamin Pierson. b 22. Princeton Univ AB48. Gen Th Sem (NY) MDiv51. **d** 51 **p** 52. USA 51-85 and from 87; C Gt Grimsby St Mary and St Jas *Linc* 85-87. *8897 Aztec Road, Albuquerque, NM 87111, USA*

FORD, Brian. b 40. OBE89. Imp Coll Lon BSc62 Nottm Univ MSc66 PhD74 Ox Univ MA74 CMathFIMA ARCS. St Alb and Ox Min Course 96. **d** 99 **p** 00. NSM Witney *Ox* 99-02; NSM Ramsden, Finstock and Fawler, Leafield etc from 02. *Ramsden Farmhouse, Ramsden, Oxford OX7 3AU* Tel (01993) 868343 Fax 868322 E-mail brian@nag.co.uk

FORD (née HARRISON-WATSON), Mrs Carole. b 44. Reading Univ BSc66 St Martin's Coll Lanc PGCE79 Cam Univ DipRS91. Carl Dioc Tr Inst 92. **d** 95 **p** 96. NSM Windermere *Carl* 95-98; NSM Borrowdale 98-01; NSM Thornthwaite cum Braithwaite, Newlands etc from 01. *The Vicarage, Borrowdale, Keswick CA12 5XQ* Tel (01768) 777238

FORD, Canon Christopher Simon. b 51. Leeds Univ MPhil86 PhD91. AKC74. **d** 75 **p** 76. C Wythenshawe Wm Temple Ch *Man* 75-77; C New Bury 77-80; R Old Trafford St Jo 80-94; R Moston St Jo 94-05; P-in-c Davyhulme St Mary from 05; Bp's Adv on Archives from 93; AD N Man 94-00; Hon Can Man Cathl from 04. *St Mary's Vicarage, 13 Vicarage Road, Urmston, Manchester M41 5TP* Tel 0161-748 2210 E-mail christopher.ford5@btinternet.com

FORD, David John. b 38. Lon Coll of Div BD68. **d** 69 **p** 70. C Blackheath St Jo *S'wark* 69-71; C Westlands St Andr *Lich* 71-75; V Sheff St Steph w St Phil and St Ann *Sheff* 75-77; R Netherthorpe 77-80; TR 80-84; R Thrybergh 82-84; R Thrybergh w Hooton Roberts 84-94; Ind Chapl 86-87; TV Parkham, Alwington, Buckland Brewer etc *Ex* 94-01; rtd 03; Hon C Knaresborough *Ripon* 01-05. *10 Grove Hill Road, Filey YO14 9NL* Tel (01723) 518292 E-mail revdford@fish.co.uk

FORD, Mrs Deborah Perrin. b 59. Leeds Univ BA81 Birm Univ MSocSc85 Univ of Wales (Ban) BTh CQSW85. EAMTC 00. **d** 03 **p** 04. NSM Cambridge St Benedict *Ely* from 03. *102 Millington Lane, Cambridge CB3 9HA* Tel (01223) 329321 E-mail deborahford@myrealbox.com

FORD, Derek Ernest. b 32. St Mich Coll Llan 56. **d** 58 **p** 59. C Roath St Martin *Llan* 58-61; C Newton Nottage 61-67; V Abercanaid 67-70; Perm to Offic *Win* 70-80; SSF from 72; Lic to Offic *Sarum* 73-80; Lic to Offic *Newc* 75-80; USA from 80; Min Prov American Province SSF 02-05. *St Elizabeth's Friary, 1474 Bushwick Avenue, Brooklyn, NY 11207, USA* Tel (001) (718) 455 5963 Fax 443 3437 E-mail broderekssf@aol.com

FORD, Eric Charles. b 31. Ely Th Coll 56. **d** 59 **p** 60. C Kettering St Mary *Pet* 59-65; R Bowers Gifford *Chelmsf* 65-69; V Walthamstow St Barn and St Jas Gt 69-76; V Chingford St Edm 76-97; rtd 97; Perm to Offic *Chelmsf* from 02. *c/o The Manager, Forest Place Home, Forest Place, Roebuck Lane, Buckhurst Hill IG9 5QL* Tel (020) 8505 2063

FORD, Eric Copeland. b 20. Linc Th Coll 68. **d** 70 **p** 71. C Lupset *Wakef* 70-73; V Cornholme 73-78; V Wragby w Sharlston 78-85; P-in-c Hightown 85-87; V 87-88; V Hartshead and Hightown 88-90; rtd 90; P-in-c Halifax St Jo *Wakef* 90-91; Chapl Las Palmas *Eur* 91-97; Perm to Offic *Blackb* 98-03. *Flat 11, Fosbrooke House, Clifton Drive, Lytham St Annes FY8 5QY*

FORD, Canon Henry Malcolm. b 33. Em Coll Cam BA54 MA58. Ely Th Coll 58. **d** 59 **p** 69. C Ipswich St Matt *St E* 59-61; Hon C

Bury St Edmunds St Jo 66-76; Hon C Hawstead and Nowton w Stanningfield etc 76-89; Hon Can St E Cathl 86-97; NSM Cockfield w Bradfield St Clare, Felsham etc 89-98. *Thatch on the Green, Cross Green, Cockfield, Bury St Edmunds IP30 0LG* Tel (01284) 828479

FORD, John. *See* FORD, William John

FORD, Canon John Albert. b 13. TCD BA35 MA38. CITC 36. **d** 36 **p** 37. C Derryloran *Arm* 36-39; C Arm St Mark 39-44; I Portadown St Sav 44-61; I Drumcree 61-83; Can Arm Cathl 75-83; rtd 83. *84 Bleary Road, Portadown BT63 5NF* Tel (028) 3834 5484

FORD, Canon John Frank. b 52. Chich Th Coll 76. **d** 79 **p** 80. C Forest Hill Ch Ch *S'wark* 79-82; V Lee St Aug 82-91; V Lower Beeding *Chich* 91-94; Dom Chapl to Bp Horsham 91-94; Dioc Missr 94-00; Can and Preb Chich Cathl 97-00; Prec and Can Res Chich Cathl from 00. *4 Vicars' Close, Canon Lane, Chichester PO19 1PT* Tel and fax (01444) 414658

FORD, Jonathan Laurence. *See* ALDERTON-FORD, Jonathan Laurence

FORD, Joyce. b 42. Qu Coll Birm 97. **d** 00 **p** 01. NSM Bentley *Lich* 00-04; NSM Wednesfield from 04. *33 Bowness Grove, Willenhall WV12 5DB* Tel (01922) 408420
E-mail joyce.ford@bigfoot.com

FORD, Mrs Nancy Celia. b 48. FCIPD00 Open Univ BA02. STETS 98. **d** 01 **p** 02. NSM Crookham *Guildf* 01-04; NSM Aldershot St Mich from 04; Asst Dioc Dir of Ords from 04. *34 Rowhill Avenue, Aldershot GU11 3LS* Tel (01252) 677995
E-mail sidnancy.ford@ntlworld.com

FORD, Peter. b 46. Bede Coll Dur TCert72 ACP75 York Univ MA96. Linc Th Coll 76. **d** 78 **p** 79. OGS from 72; C Hartlepool H Trin *Dur* 78-81; Dioc Youth Officer *Wakef* 81-84; C Mirfield Eastthorpe St Paul 82-84; C Upper Hopton 82-84; V Dodworth 84-88; Chapl and Hd RS Rishworth Sch W Yorks 88-97; Ho Master 94-97; P-in-c Accrington St Mary *Blackb* 97-99; C Torrisholme 99-01; V Warton St Paul from 01; Dioc Ecum Officer from 01. *The Vicarage, Church Road, Warton, Preston PR4 1BD* Tel (01772) 632227 Fax 632351
E-mail pford@ogs.net

FORD, Canon Peter Hugh. b 43. St Cath Coll Cam BA65 MA69. Cuddesdon Coll 65. **d** 67 **p** 68. C Is of Dogs Ch Ch and St Jo w St Luke *Lon* 67-70; Canada 70-91; C Tillsonburg St Jo 70-71; St Catharine's St Thos 71-73; P-in-c Thorold 71-73; R Port Colborne St Brendan 73-78; R Milton 78-80; Can Pastor Ch Ch Cathl Hamilton 80-86; Adn Lincoln 86-91; R Niagara-on-the-Lake St Mark 86-91; Montserrat 91; Saba 92-98; Perm to Offic *Chich* 98-99 and from 01; V Newchurch *Portsm* from 99; V Arreton from 99. *The Vicarage, Newchurch, Sandown PO36 0NN* Tel (01983) 865504 E-mail ph.ford@virgin.net

FORD, Richard Graham. b 39. AKC65 Open Univ BA96. **d** 66 **p** 67. C Morpeth *Newc* 66-71; C Fordingbridge w Ibsley *Win* 71-73; TV Whorlton *Newc* 73-80; Chapl RNR 75-92; V Choppington *Newc* 80-92; V Tynemouth Priory 92-04; rtd 04. *43 Farriers Rise, Shilbottle, Alnwick NE66 2EN* Tel (01665) 581115

FORD, Roger James. b 33. Sarum & Wells Th Coll 81. **d** 83 **p** 84. C Sidcup St Jo *Roch* 83-86; V Darenth 86-98; rtd 98; Perm to Offic *Cov* 02-04. *21 Hawthorn Way, Shipston-on-Stour CV36 4FD* Tel (01608) 664875 E-mail margaretandroger@hotmail.com

FORD, Roger Lindsay. b 47. Ex Univ LLB68. Llan Dioc Tr Scheme 87. **d** 91 **p** 92. NSM Fairwater *Llan* 91-96; NSM Llandaff 96-01. *93 Cardiff Road, Caerphilly CF83 1WS* Tel (029) 2088 2441

FORD, Mrs Shirley Elsworth. b 40. Open Univ BA88. Sarum & Wells Th Coll 89. **d** 91 **p** 94. C Farnham *Guildf* 91-96; V Wrecclesham 96-04; rtd 04. *North House, Queen's Park Mews, Queen's Park Rise, Brighton BN2 9YY*

FORD, Simone Louise. *See* BENNETT, Ms Simone Louise

FORD, William John. b 50. Linc Th Coll 89. **d** 91 **p** 92. C Marton-in-Cleveland *York* 91-94; V Whorlton w Carlton and Faceby 94-02; P-in-c Stainton w Hilton from 02; RD Stokesley from 03. *The Vicarage, 21 Thornton Road, Stainton, Middlesbrough TS8 9DS* Tel (01642) 288131
E-mail revjohn.ford@ntlworld.com

FORD-WHITCOMBE, William. *See* WHITCOMBE, William Ashley

FORDE, Stephen Bernard. b 61. Edin Univ BSc TCD DipTh. **d** 86 **p** 87. C Belfast St Mary *Conn* 86-89; Chapl QUB 89-95; Min Can Belf Cathl 89-91; Bp's Dom Chapl *Conn* 90-95; I Dublin Booterstown *D & G* 95-99; Dean of Res UCD 95-99; I Larne and Inver *Conn* from 99; I Glynn w Raloo from 99. *The Rectory, 8 Lower Cairncastle Road, Larne BT40 1PQ* Tel (028) 2827 2788 *or* 2827 4633 E-mail sbforde@cofiatlarne.fsnet.co.uk

FORDER, The Ven Charles Robert. b 07. Ch Coll Cam BA28 MA32. Ridley Hall Cam 28. **d** 30 **p** 31. C Hunslet Moor St Pet *Ripon* 30-33; C Burley 33-34; V Wibsey *Bradf* 34-40; V Bradf St Clem 40-47; V Drypool St Andr and St Pet *York* 47-55; Chapl HM Pris Hull 49-51; Chapl HM Borstal Hull 51-52; R Routh *York* 55-57; V Wawne 55-57; Adn York 57-72; Can and Preb York Minster 57-76; R Sutton upon Derwent 57-63; R York H Trin w St Jo Micklegate and St Martin 63-66; rtd 72; Perm to Offic *York* from 76. *Dulverton Hall, Esplanade, Scarborough YO11 2AR* Tel (01723) 340112

FORDHAM, Mrs June Erica. b 28. DCR52. Oak Hill Th Coll 83. **dss** 86 **d** 87 **p** 94. Digswell and Panshanger *St Alb* 86-87; Par Dn 87-90; TD 91-93; rtd 93; NSM Lemsford *St Alb* 93-01; Perm to Offic from 01. *22 Crossway, Welwyn Garden City AL8 7EE* Tel (01707) 326997

FORDHAM, Richard George. b 34. AIMarE60 TEng(CEI)71 FBIM74. **d** 91 **p** 92. NSM Cookham *Ox* 91-94; NSM Hedsor and Bourne End 94-01; Perm to Offic 01-04. *Address temp unknown*

FORDYCE, Andrew Ian. b 70. K Alfred's Coll Win BA94 Southn Univ PGCE96. Trin Coll Bris BA03. **d** 03 **p** 04. C Bramshott and Liphook *Portsm* from 03. *2 Meadow End, Liphook GU30 7UA* Tel (01428) 722142 Mobile 07884-010376
E-mail fordyce@fsmail.net

FOREMAN, Joseph Arthur. b 26. ACIB. S Dios Minl Tr Scheme 83. **d** 86 **p** 87. NSM Win St Bart *Win* 86-96; Perm to Offic from 96. *4 Denham Close, Winchester SO23 7BL* Tel (01962) 852138

FOREMAN, Canon Patrick Brian. b 41. CertEd. St Jo Coll Nottm 77. **d** 79 **p** 80. C Gainsborough All SS *Linc* 79-83; V Thornton St Jas *Bradf* 83-91; R Hevingham w Hainford and Stratton Strawless *Nor* 91-99; RD Ingworth 94-99; V Heacham from 99; Hon Can Nor Cathl from 03. *The Vicarage, Church Lane, Heacham, King's Lynn PE31 7HJ* Tel (01485) 570268

FOREMAN, Roy Geoffrey Victor. b 31. Oak Hill Th Coll 62. **d** 64 **p** 65. C Chitts Hill St Cuth *Lon* 64-67; C Rodbourne Cheney *Bris* 67-70; C Walthamstow St Mary w St Steph *Chelmsf* 71-92; TV 92-96; rtd 96; Perm to Offic *S'wark* from 97. *1 Vicarage Road, Croydon CR0 4JS* Tel (020) 8681 6200

FOREMAN, Timothy. b 56. K Coll Lon BD77. SEITE 97. **d** 99 **p** 00. C Camberwell St Giles w St Matt *S'wark* 99-02; R Buckland in Dover w Buckland Valley *Cant* from 02; Hon Min Can Cant Cathl from 04. *St Andrew's Rectory, London Road, Dover CT17 0TF* Tel (01304) 201324
E-mail fr.tim@ntlworld.com

FOREMAN, Vanessa Jane. *See* LAWRENCE, Mrs Vanessa Jane

FORGAN, Eleanor. b 44. St Andr Univ MA66 Aber Univ DipEd67. St And Dioc Tr Course. **d** 89 **p** 95. NSM Alloa *St And* from 89. *18 Alexandra Drive, Alloa FK10 2DQ* Tel (01259) 212836 *or* 724550 E-mail eforgan@fish.co.uk

FORMAN, Alastair Gordon. b 48. St Jo Coll Nottm 78. **d** 80 **p** 81. C Pennycross *Ex* 80-83; C Woking St Jo *Guildf* 83-88; V Luton Lewsey St Hugh *St Alb* 88-95; P-in-c Jersey Millbrook St Matt *Win* 95-01; P-in-c Jersey St Lawr 95-01. *Farnham Vineyard, 1 The Borough, Farnham GU9 7NA* Tel (01252) 737586
E-mail onformok@super.net.uk

FORMAN, Miss Diana Blanche Grant. b 19. Edin Dioc NSM Course 79. **dss** 83 **d** 86 **p** 94. Edin St Jo *Edin* 83-91; NSM 86-91; rtd 91. *Strathmore House, 4/3 Church Hill, Edinburgh EH10 4BQ* Tel 0131-447 4463

FORRER, Michael Dennett Cuthbert. b 34. St Pet Hall Ox BA59 MA63. Wycliffe Hall Ox 59. **d** 60 **p** 61. C Westwood *Cov* 60-63; C Cov Cathl 63-71; Ind Chapl 63-69; Sen Ind Chapl 69-71; Hon C All Hallows by the Tower etc *Lon* 76-99; Perm to Offic *Sarum* from 99 and *Ox* 01-02; Hon C Sonning *Ox* from 02; rtd 04. *6 Park View Drive South, Charvil, Reading RG10 9QX* Tel 0118-934 1989

FORREST, Canon Kenneth Malcolm. b 38. Linc Coll Ox BA61 MA65. Wells Th Coll 60. **d** 62 **p** 63. C Walton St Mary *Liv* 62-65; Asst Chapl Liv Univ 65-67; Chapl Blue Coat Sch Liv 67-75; R Wavertree H Trin *Liv* 67-75; R Wigan All SS 75-03; Hon Can Liv Cathl 87-03; AD Wigan E 89-02; rtd 03. *135 Chorley Road, Standish, Wigan WN1 2TE* Tel (01257) 425860

FORREST, The Very Revd Leslie David Arthur. b 46. TCD BA68 MA86. CITC 70. **d** 70 **p** 71. C Conwall *D & R* 70-73; I Tullyaughnish 73-80; I Galway w Kilcummin *T, K & A* 80-95; Dir of Ords 84-95; Can Tuam Cathl 86-95; Provost Tuam 91-95; Preb Tassagard St Patr Cathl Dublin from 91; Dean Ferns *C & O* from 95; I Ferns w Kilbride, Toombe, Kilcormack etc from 95. *The Deanery, Ferns, Enniscorthy, Co Wexford, Irish Republic* Tel (00353) (54) 66124 Fax 66985
E-mail ldaforrest@eircom.net

FORREST, Michael Barry Eric. b 38. Lon Univ BA87 MA89. NZ Bd of Th Studies LTh62 Chich Th Coll 64. **d** 66 **p** 67. C Beckenham St Jas *Roch* 66-70; Papua New Guinea 70-76; C Altarnon and Bolventor *Truro* 76-78; TV N Hill w Altarnon, Bolventor and Lewannick 78-79; R St Martin w E and W Looe 79-84; V Kensington St Phil Earl's Court *Lon* 84-04; rtd 04. *12 Riley Road, Brighton BN2 4AH* Tel (01273) 690231

FORREST, Canon Robin Whyte. b 33. Edin Th Coll 58. **d** 61 **p** 62. C Glas St Mary *Glas* 61-66; R Renfrew 66-70; R Motherwell 70-79; R Wishaw 75-79; R Forres *Mor* 79-98; R Nairn 79-92; Can St Andr Cathl Inverness 88-98; Hon Can from 98; Syn Clerk 91-92; Dean Mor 92-98; rtd 98. *Landeck, Cummingston, Elgin IV30 5XY* Tel and fax (01343) 835539

FORREST-REDFERN, Mrs Susan Michéle. b 57. S Bank Poly BEd86. St Jo Coll Nottm 01. **d** 03 **p** 04. C Lostock St Thos and St Jo *Man* from 03. *12 Salterton Drive, Bolton BL3 3RG* Tel (01204) 652977 E-mail revsuefr@tiscali.co.uk

FORRESTER, Herbert Howarth. b 19. Liv Univ LLB46. Wycliffe Hall Ox 65. **d** 67 **p** 68. C Blundellsands St Nic *Liv* 67-70; V Liv St Phil 70-76; V Liv St Phil w St Dav 76-85; rtd 85; Perm to Offic *Liv* 85-03. *5 Kenilworth Road, Liverpool L16 7PS* Tel 0151-722 1365

FORRESTER, Ian Michael. b 56. Chich Th Coll. **d** 82 **p** 83. C Leigh-on-Sea St Marg *Chelmsf* 82-84; Min Can, Succ and Dean's V Windsor 84-86; Perm to Offic *Ox* 84-86; Chapl Distinguished Conduct Medal League 86-95; Chapl Gallantry Medallists' League from 95; Prec and Chapl Chelmsf Cathl *Chelmsf* 86-91; Perm to Offic 91-99; Chapl Lancing Coll 91-99; P-in-c Boxgrove *Chich* from 99. *The Vicarage, Boxgrove, Chichester PO18 0ED* Tel (01243) 774045 E-mail iforrester@hotmail.com

FORRESTER, James Oliphant. b 50. SS Coll Cam BA72 MA76. Wycliffe Hall Ox 73. **d** 76 **p** 77. C Hull St Jo Newland *York* 76-80; C Fulwood *Sheff* 80-87; V Lodge Moor St Luke 87-90; V Ecclesfield 90-01; AD Ecclesfield 99-01; P-in-c Kingston upon Hull H Trin *York* 01-02; V and Lect from 02. *Holy Trinity Vicarage, 66 Pearson Park, Hull HU5 2TQ* Tel (01482) 342292

FORRESTER, Mrs Joyce. b 33. Thornbridge Hall Coll of Educn TCert53 ACP84 DACE85 Crewe & Alsager Coll MSc88. St Jo Coll Nottm 94. **d** 94 **p** 95. NSM Endon w Stanley *Lich* 94-00; Assoc Min Stonnall from 00. *The Vicarage, 3 St Peter's Close, Stonall, Walsall WS9 9EN* Tel (01543) 360395

FORRESTER, Matthew Agnew. b 31. Univ of Wales (Cardiff) BA64 Lon Univ DipTh72. Trin Coll Bris 70. **d** 72 **p** 73. C Tonbridge SS Pet and Paul *Roch* 72-77; Chapl Elstree Sch Woolhampton 77-78; Chapl Duke of York's R Mil Sch Dover 78-96; rtd 96; Perm to Offic *Cant* from 96. *4 Abbots Place, Canterbury CT1 2AH* Tel (01304) 823758

FORRESTER, Robin William. b 43. Kent Univ MA84 Aston Univ MSc90. All Nations Chr Coll 64. **d** 04 **p** 05. NSM Wharton *Ches* from 04. *27 Leven Avenue, Winsford CW7 3TA* Tel (01606) 862470 E-mail robin@wmforrester.fsnet.co.uk

FORRYAN, Canon John Edward. b 31. Wells Th Coll 58. **d** 60 **p** 61. C Leckhampton SS Phil and Jas *Glouc* 60-63; C Cirencester 63-68; V Glouc St Paul 68-78; R Rodborough 78-91; P-in-c Deerhurst, Apperley w Forthampton and Chaceley 91-95; V 95-97; Hon Can Glouc Cathl 94-97; rtd 97; Perm to Offic *Glouc* from 97. *26 Wye Road, Brockworth, Gloucester GL5 4PP* Tel (01452) 863578

FORRYAN, Thomas Quested. b 64. Pemb Coll Cam BA85 DipTh86. Wycliffe Hall Ox 87. **d** 90 **p** 91. C Cheadle Hulme St Andr *Ches* 90-93; C Aberavon *Llan* 93-94; UCCF 94-98. *1 Grosvenor Road, Watford WD1 2QS*

FORSE, Reginald Austin. b 43. Oak Hill Th Coll 77. **d** 79 **p** 80. C Crofton *Portsm* 79-84; NSM Gosport Ch Ch 91-96; NSM Alverstoke from 96. *40 Osprey Gardens, Lee-on-the-Solent PO13 8LJ* Tel (023) 9255 3395 E-mail regforse@yahoo.co.uk

FORSHAW, David Oliver. b 27. Trin Coll Cam BA50 MA52. Qu Coll Birm. **d** 53 **p** 54. C Glen Parva and S Wigston *Leic* 53-55; Singapore 55-59; V Heptonstall *Wakef* 59-66; V Whitehaven St Nic *Carl* 66-76; P-in-c Whitehaven Ch Ch w H Trin 73-76; V Benchill *Man* 76-89; C Elton All SS 89-92; rtd 92; Perm to Offic *Carl* from 92. *Tynashee, Church Street, Broughton-in-Furness LA20 6HJ* Tel (01229) 716068

FORSHAW, Canon Eric Paul. b 42. Lon Univ BSc63 Birm Univ MA78 Zürich Univ ThD90. Ridley Hall Cam 67 Gossner Inst Mainz 73. **d** 70 **p** 71. C Yardley St Edburgha *Birm* 70-72; Ind Chapl 72-78; Hon C Edgbaston St Geo 72-78; Bp's Adv on Ind Soc *S'well* 78-90; Perm to Offic 78-82; Assoc Min Nottm St Pet and St Jas 82-94; Hon Can S'well Minster 86-04; Bp's Research Officer 90-92; Progr Dir Nottm Common Purpose 92-94; TR Clifton 94-04. *33 Upton Close, Castle Donington, Derby DE74 2GN* Tel (01332) 858267 E-mail eric@forshaw.surfaid.org

FORSHAW, Mrs Frances Ann. b 52. Edin Univ BSc74 Glas Univ MN91 RGN76 SCM78. Moray Ord Course 91. **d** 98 **p** 02. NSM Elgin w Lossiemouth *Mor* 98-01; NSM Perth St Jo *St And* from 01. *1 Cairnies House, Glenalmond College, Glenalmond, Perth PH1 3RY* Tel (01738) 880777

FORSTER, The Ven Andrew James. QUB BA89. CITC BTh92. **d** 92 **p** 93. C Willowfield *D & D* 92-95; Dean of Res QUB 95-02; C of I Adv Downtown Radio Newtownards 96-02; I Drumcliffe w Lissadell and Munninane *K, E & A* from 02; Adn Elphin and Ardagh from 02. *The Rectory, Drumcliffe, Co Sligo, Irish Republic* Tel (00353) (71) 916 3125 E-mail andrew@theforsters.org

FORSTER, Bennet Fermor. b 21. BNC Ox BA48 MA53. Cuddesdon Coll. **d** 51 **p** 52. C Stepney St Dunstan and All SS *Lon* 51-53; C Petersfield w Sheet *Portsm* 53-57; V Portsea St Cuth 57-65; Chapl Bedford Sch 65-72; C Bedford St Pet *St Alb* 72-73; Lic to Offic 73-78; P-in-c Froxfield w Privett *Portsm* 78-81; V 81-88; P-in-c Hawkley w Prior's Dean 78-81; V 81-88; rtd 88; Perm to Offic *Worc* from 88. *39 Parkview, Abbey Road, Malvern WR14 3HG* Tel (01684) 567915

FORSTER, Gregory Stuart. b 47. Worc Coll Ox BA69 MA73 Dip Soc Anthropology 70. Wycliffe Hall Ox 69. **d** 72 **p** 73. C Bath Walcot *B & W* 72-74; C Bolton Em *Man* 74-76; C Bolton St Paul w Em 77-79; R Northenden from 79. *The Rectory, Ford Lane, Northenden, Manchester M22 4NQ* Tel 0161-998 2615

FORSTER, Ian Duncan. b 51. St Mich Coll Llan 95. **d** 97 **p** 98. C Lampeter Pont Steffan w Silian *St D* 97-00; C Llandysul w Bangor Teifi w Henllan etc 00-03; V Llangrannog w Llandysiliogogo w Penbryn from 03. *The Vicarage, Pontgarreg, Llandysul SA44 6AJ* Tel (01239) 654943

FORSTER, Kenneth. b 27. St Jo Coll Cam BA50 MA52 Salford Univ MSc77 PhD80. NEOC 83. **d** 86 **p** 87. NSM Hessle *York* 86-92; Chapl Humberside Poly 87-91; Chapl Humberside Univ 92; rtd 92; NSM Hull St Mary Sculcoates *York* 92-95; Perm to Offic from 95. *1 Peel Court, Longwick Road, Princes Risborough HP27 9EZ* Tel (01844) 343050

✠**FORSTER, The Rt Revd Peter Robert.** b 50. Mert Coll Ox MA73 Edin Univ BD77 PhD85. Edin Th Coll 78. **d** 80 **p** 81 **c** 96. C Mossley Hill St Matt and St Jas *Liv* 80-82; Sen Tutor St Jo Coll Dur 83-91; V Beverley Minster *York* 91-96; C Routh 91-96; Bp Ches from 96. *Bishop's House, 1 Abbey Street, Chester CH1 2JD* Tel (01244) 350864 Fax 314187 E-mail bpchester@chester.anglican.org

FORSTER, Thomas Shane. b 72. QUB BA93. CITC BTh93. **d** 96 **p** 97. C Drumglass w Moygashel *Arm* 96-99; Hon V Choral Arm Cathl 97-99; I Donaghmore w Upper Donaghmore from 99; Dioc Communications Officer from 02. *St Michael's Rectory, 66 Main Street, Castlecaulfield, Dungannon BT70 3NP* Tel (028) 8776 1214 E-mail donaghmore@armagh.anglican.org *or* dco@armagh.anglican.org

FORSTER, The Ven Victor Henry. b 17. TCD BA45 MA49. **d** 45 **p** 46. C Magheralin *D & D* 45-47; C-in-c Garrison w Slavin *Clogh* 47-51; Bp's C Ballybay 51-52; I Killeevan 52-59; I Rathgraffe *M & K* 59-67; I Aghalurcher w Tattykeeran, Cooneen etc *Clogh* 67-89; Preb Clogh Cathl 80-83; Adn Clogh 83-89; rtd 89; Lic to Offic *D & D* from 90. *4 Ard-Na-Ree, Groomsport, Bangor BT19 2JL* Tel (028) 9146 4548

FORSTER, William. b 50. Liv Poly HNC71. N Ord Course 92. **d** 95 **p** 96. C Ashton-in-Makerfield St Thos *Liv* 95-00; TR Fazakerley Em from 00. *Emmanuel Rectory, Higher Lane, Liverpool L9 9DJ* Tel 0151-525 2689 E-mail william.forster1@btopenworld.com

FORSYTH, Jeanette Mary Shaw. b 48. Aber Coll of Educn ACE78. Moray Ho Edin Dip Primary Educn 67 Ab Dioc Tr Course 83 St Jo Coll Nottm CertCS89. **d** 89. NSM Old Deer *Ab* 89-92; NSM Longside 89-92; NSM Strichen 89-92; NSM Fraserburgh 92-94; Tanzania 95-96, 97-98 and 99-00. *Moss-side of Strichen, Bogensourie, Strichen AB43 7TU* Tel (01771) 637230 E-mail jeanetteforsyth@hotmail.com

FORSYTH, John Warren. b 38. Edin Univ DPS76 Univ of W Aus BA62. Princeton Th Sem DMin98. **d** 65 **p** 66. Australia 65-74 and from 76; C Edin St Pet *Edin* 74-76; C Busselton 65-68; R Kondinin 68-72; C Warw 72-74; R E Fremantle and Palmyra 76-79; R Midland 82-89. *40B Cookham Road, Lathlain, W Australia 6100* Tel (0061) (8) 9472 1893 *or* 9224 2482 Fax 9472 1893 *or* 9224 3511 E-mail john.forsyth@rph.health.wa.gov.aau

FORSYTHE, John Leslie. b 27. CITC. **d** 65 **p** 66. C Cloughfern *Conn* 65-67; C Carnmoney 67-71; I Mossley 71-80; I Antrim All SS 80-95; Preb Conn Cathl 94-95; rtd 95. *96 Hopefield Road, Portrush BT56 8HF* Tel (028) 7082 2623

FORTNUM, Brian Charles Henry. b 48. Hertf Coll Ox MA Imp Coll Lon MSc. Wycliffe Hall Ox 82. **d** 84 **p** 85. C Tonbridge St Steph *Roch* 84-87; V Shorne 87-94; P-in-c Speldhurst w Groombridge and Ashurst 94-98; R 98-01; V Tunbridge Wells St Mark from 01. *The Vicarage, 1 St Mark's Road, Tunbridge Wells TN2 5LT* Tel (01892) 526069 Fax as telephone E-mail brian.fortnum@btinternet.com

FORWARD, Canon Eric Toby. b 50. Nottm Univ BEd72 Hull Univ MA93. Cuddesdon Coll 74. **d** 77 **p** 78. C Forest Hill Ch Ch *S'wark* 77-80; Chapl Goldsmiths' Coll Lon 80-84; Chapl Westwood Ho Sch Pet 84-86; V Brighton St Aug and St Sav *Chich* 86-90; Perm to Offic *York* 90-95; V Kingston upon Hull St Alb 95-05; Can Res and Prec Liv Cathl *Liv* from 05. *3 Cathedral Close, Liverpool L1 7BR* Tel 0151-708 0934

FORWARD, Miss Frances Mary. b 43. Bp Otter Coll Chich TCert64. SEITE DipTM99. **d** 99 **p** 00. NSM Ham St Andr *S'wark* from 99. *66 Tudor Drive, Kingston on Thames KT2 5QF* Tel (020) 8546 1833

FORWARD, Canon Ronald George. b 25. Selw Coll Cam BA50 MA54. Ridley Hall Cam 50. **d** 52 **p** 53. C Denton Holme *Carl* 52-55; C-in-c Mirehouse St Andr CD 55-61; V Mirehouse 61-66; V Kendal St Thos 66-90; V Crook 78-90; Hon Can Carl Cathl 79-90; rtd 90; Perm to Offic *Carl* from 90. *51 Mayo Park, Cockermouth CA13 0BJ* Tel (01900) 824359

FORWARD, Toby. *See* FORWARD, Canon Eric Toby
FOSBUARY, David Frank. b 32. Leeds Univ BA63. Coll of Resurr Mirfield 63. **d** 65 **p** 66. C Fleetwood St Pet *Blackb* 65-68; Lesotho 69-76; C Dovercourt *Chelmsf* 76-78; TV 78-79; TV Basildon St Martin w H Cross and Laindon etc 79-82; R Colsterworth *Linc* 82-84; R Colsterworth Gp 84-90; RD Beltisloe 89-90; R Lawshall w Shimplingthorne and Alpheton *St E* 90-96; rtd 96; Perm to Offic *St E* from 96. *56 Lindisfarne Road, Bury St Edmunds IP33 2EH* Tel (01284) 767687
FOSDIKE, Lewis Bertram. b 23. Keble Coll Ox BA52 MA56. Wells Th Coll 52. **d** 54 **p** 55. C Westbury-on-Trym H Trin *Bris* 54-58; V Bedminster St Fran 58-64; V Summertown *Ox* 64-76; TR Wolvercote w Summertown 76-89; rtd 89; Chapl St Hugh's Coll Ox 89-97. *18 Osberton Road, Oxford OX2 7NU* Tel (01865) 515817
FOSKETT, Eric William. b 29. Qu Coll Birm 75. **d** 78 **p** 79. NSM Billesley Common *Birm* 78-82; V Allens Cross 82-95; Chapl Hollymoor Hosp Birm 90-95; rtd 95; Perm to Offic *Birm* from 95. *1 Warmington Road, Hollywood, Birmingham B47 5PE* Tel (01564) 526181
FOSKETT, Canon John Herbert. b 39. St Cath Coll Cam BA62. Chich Th Coll 62. **d** 64 **p** 65. C Malden St Jo *S'wark* 64-70; P-in-c Kingston St Jo 70-76; Chapl Maudsley Hosp Lon 76-94; Chapl Bethlem R Hosp Beckenham 76-94; Hon Can S'wark Cathl *S'wark* 88-94; rtd 94; Perm to Offic *B & W* 95-01. *Victoria Cottage, 8 Cornwall Road, Dorchester DT1 1RT* Tel (01305) 751572
FOSS, David Blair. b 44. Bris Univ BA65 Dur Univ MA66 Fitzw Coll Cam BA68 MA72 K Coll Lon PhD86. St Chad's Coll Dur 68. **d** 69 **p** 70. C Barnard Castle *Dur* 69-72; Sierra Leone 72-74; Chapl St Jo Coll York 74-75; Chapl Ch Ch Coll of HE Cant 75-80; Chapl Elmslie Girls' Sch Blackpool 80-83; Tutor Coll of Resurr Mirfield 83-88; V Battyeford *Wakef* 88-99; V Ryde All SS *Portsm* 99-01; TR Rochdale *Man* from 01. *The Vicarage, Sparrow Hill, Rochdale OL16 1QT* Tel (01706) 645014
FOSSETT, Michael Charles Sinclair. b 30. Dur Univ BSc54 CEng59 MIMechE59. NEOC 82. **d** 90 **p** 91. NSM Nether w Upper Poppleton *York* from 90. *20 Fairway Drive, Upper Poppleton, York YO26 6HE* Tel (01904) 794712
FOSTEKEW, Dean James Benedict. b 63. Bulmershe Coll of HE BEd86. Chich Th Coll 89. **d** 92 **p** 93. C Boyne Hill *Ox* 92-95; P-in-c Lockerbie *Glas* 95-97; P-in-c Annan 95-97; P-in-c Dalmahoy *Edin* 97-02; Miss Co-ord from 97; Jt Prov Miss 21 Co-ord from 98; TV Edin St Mary from 02. *33 Manor Place, Edinburgh EH3 7EB* Tel 0131-226 3389 Mobile 07968-099470 E-mail mission21@edinburgh.anglican.org
FOSTER, Anthony Stuart. b 47. K Coll Cam BD69 Peterho Cam BA72 MA74 Lon Inst of Educn PGCE70. Pontifical Beda Coll Rome 82. **d** 85 **p** 86. In RC Ch 85-98; NSM Leighton-cum-Minshull Vernon *Ches* from 05. *2 Foxes Hollow, Crewe CW1 4NX* Tel (01270) 250480 E-mail revtonyfoster@btinternet.com
FOSTER, Antony John. b 39. Down Coll Cam BA61 MA65. Ridley Hall Cam 65. **d** 66 **p** 67. C Sandal St Helen *Wakef* 66-69; Uganda 69-74; V Mount Pellon *Wakef* 74-92; rtd 92; Perm to Offic *Wakef* from 92. *32 Savile Drive, Halifax HX1 2EU* Tel (01422) 344152
FOSTER, Basil. *See* FOSTER, William Basil
✠**FOSTER, The Rt Revd Christopher Richard James.** b 53. Univ Coll Dur BA75 Man Univ MA77 Trin Hall Cam BA79 MA83 Wadh Coll Ox MA83. Westcott Ho Cam 78. **d** 80 **p** 81 **c** 01. C Tettenhall Regis *Lich* 80-82; Chapl Wadh Coll Ox 82-86; C Ox St Mary V w St Cross and St Pet *Ox* 82-86; V Southgate Ch Ch *Lon* 86-94; CME Officer 88-94; Can Res and Sub-Dean St Alb 94-01; Suff Bp Hertford from 01. *Hertford House, Abbey Mill Lane, St Albans AL3 4HE* Tel (01727) 866420 Fax 811426 E-mail bishophertford@stalbans.anglican.org
FOSTER, David Brereton. b 55. Selw Coll Cam BA77 MA81 Ox Univ BA80. Wycliffe Hall Ox 78. **d** 81 **p** 82. C Luton St Mary *St Alb* 81-84; C Douglas St Geo and St Barn *S & M* 84-87; V S Ramsey St Paul 87-91; Dir Dioc Tr Inst 88-91; Asst Dir Buckingham Adnry Chr Tr Scheme *Ox* 91-95; Dir Buckingham Adnry Chr Tr Sch 95-97; C W Wycombe w Bledlow Ridge, Bradenham and Radnage 91-97; TV High Wycombe from 97. *15 The Brackens, High Wycombe HP11 1EB* Tel (01494) 451762 *or* 529668 E-mail david.foster@st-andrews.wycombechurches.org.uk
FOSTER, Donald Wolfe. b 24. St Cath Coll Cam BA48 MA50 TCD BD56. **d** 50 **p** 51. C Dunleckney *C & O* 50-52; C Coseley Ch Ch *Lich* 52-54; C Newland St Aug *York* 54-58; Chapl HM Borstal Hull 58-62; V Kingston upon Hull St Mary *York* 58-62; V Osbaldwick w Murton 62-67; Asst Chapl Loughborough Gr Sch 67-80; Chapl 80-87; Perm to Offic *Leic* from 81; rtd 87. *73 Park Road, Loughborough LE11 2HD* Tel (01509) 212782
FOSTER, Edward James Graham. b 12. St Jo Coll Cam BA34 MusBac35 MA38. Wells Th Coll 35. **d** 37 **p** 38. C Kidderminster St Mary *Worc* 37-43; C Feckenham w Astwood Bank 43-45; Chapl and Lect Dioc Tr Coll Chester 45-51; V Balby w Hexthorpe *Sheff* 51-67; V Ashford w Sheldon *Derby* 67-78; rtd 78; Perm to Offic *Derby* from 78. *Beckside, Baslow Road, Ashford-in-the-Water, Bakewell DE45 1QA* Tel (01629) 812868
FOSTER, Edward Philip John. b 49. Trin Hall Cam BA70 MA74. Ridley Hall Cam 76. **d** 79 **p** 80. C Finchley Ch Ch *Lon* 79-82; C Marple All SS *Ches* 82-86; P-in-c Cambridge St Matt *Ely* 86-90; V from 90. *St Matthew's Vicarage, 24 Geldart Street, Cambridge CB1 2LX* Tel (01223) 363545 Fax 512304 E-mail pf.smp@dial.pipex.com
FOSTER, Frances Elizabeth. *See* TYLER, Mrs Frances Elizabeth
FOSTER, Francis Desmond. b 11. ALCD33. **d** 34 **p** 35. C Norbury St Phil *S'wark* 34-39; C Faversham *Cant* 39-48; V Throwley 48-75; P-in-c Stalisfield w Otterden 73-75; V Throwley w Stalisfield and Otterden 75-77; rtd 77; Perm to Offic *Chich* from 78. *43 Milton Road, Eastbourne BN21 1SH* Tel (01323) 639430
FOSTER, Canon Gareth Glynne. b 44. Open Univ BA. Chich Th Coll 66. **d** 69 **p** 70. C Fairwater *Llan* 69-71; C Merthyr Tydfil 71-72; C Merthyr Tydfil and Cyfarthfa 72-76; TV 76-87; Dioc Soc Resp Officer from 87; P-in-c Abercanaid from 87; Exec Officer Dioc Bd Soc Resp from 95; Can Llan Cathl from 00. *19 The Walk, Merthyr Tydfil CF47 8RU,* or *Diocesan Office, Heol Fair, Llandaff, Cardiff CF5 2EE* Tel (029) 2057 8899 Mobile 07850-823038 E-mail garethfoster.dbf.llandaff@churchinwales.org.uk
FOSTER, Mrs Geraldine. b 55. RGN77. St Alb and Ox Min Course 00. **d** 03 **p** 04. C Flackwell Heath *Ox* from 03. *15 The Brackens, High Wycombe HP11 1EB* Tel (01494) 444995 *or* (01628) 53304 Fax (01494) 451762 E-mail gerryrgn@aol.com
FOSTER, Graham Paul. b 66. Univ of W Aus BSc86 DipEd87 BEd88 Murdoch Univ Aus BD99 Qu Coll Ox MSt00 DPhil02. **d** 04. Lect NT Edin Univ from 03; NSM Edin St Mary *Edin* from 04. *27/1 Hopetoun Street, Edinburgh EH7 4NF*
FOSTER, James. b 29. Man Univ BA52 MA55 Lon Univ CertEd53 Leeds Univ MEd74. NEOC 82. **d** 85 **p** 86. NSM Aldborough w Boroughbridge and Roecliffe *Ripon* 85-91; P-in-c Kirby-on-the-Moor, Cundall w Norton-le-Clay etc 91-97; rtd 97; Perm to Offic *Ripon* from 97. *Lylands Farm, Ouseburn, York YO26 9TU* Tel (01423) 330276
FOSTER, Mrs Joan Alison. b 46. ARMCM67. N Ord Course 95. **d** 98 **p** 99. NSM Blundellsands St Nic *Liv* 98-02; Asst Chapl Southport and Ormskirk NHS Trust 98-02; V N Harrow St Alb *Lon* from 02. *St Alban's Vicarage, Church Drive, Harrow HA2 7NS* Tel (020) 8868 6567 Mobile 07713-819012 E-mail revjoan@fish.co.uk *or* revjoanstalbans@fish.co.uk
FOSTER, Jonathan Guy Vere. b 56. Goldsmiths' Coll Lon BA78. Wycliffe Hall Ox 83. **d** 86 **p** 87. C Hampreston *Sarum* 86-90; Chapl Chantilly *Eur* 90-97; V Branksome St Clem *Sarum* from 97. *The Vicarage, 7 Parkstone Heights, Branksome, Poole BH14 0QE* Tel (01202) 748058 E-mail jonjane@fish.co.uk
FOSTER, Joseph James Frederick. b 22. SS Paul & Mary Coll Cheltenham CertEd42 Birm Univ DipEd59. **d** 88 **p** 88. NSM Elstead *Guildf* 88-94; Perm to Offic 94-03. *2 The Oakhurst, 21 The Knoll, Beckenham BR3 5UD* Tel (020) 8658 4559
FOSTER, Leslie. b 49. Linc Th Coll 89. **d** 91 **p** 92. C Coseley Ch Ch *Lich* 91-93; C Coseley Ch Ch *Worc* 93-95; V Firbank, Howgill and Killington *Bradf* 95-00; Hon C Sedbergh, Cautley and Garsdale 95-00; Dioc Rural Adv 96-00; P-in-c Ruyton XI Towns w Gt and Lt Ness *Lich* from 00. *The Vicarage, The Village, Ruyton Eleven Towns, Shrewsbury SY4 1LQ* Tel (01939) 261234 E-mail lesfoster@lunevic.freeserve.co.uk
FOSTER, Michael John. b 52. St Steph Ho Ox 76. **d** 79 **p** 80. C Wood Green St Mich *Lon* 79-82; TV Clifton *S'well* 82-85; P-in-c Aylesbury *Ox* 85-87; Dep Warden Durning Hall Chr Community Cen 87-89; V Lydbrook *Glouc* 89-97; R Hemsby, Winterton, E and W Somerton and Horsey *Nor* 97-99; P-in-c Tarrant Valley *Sarum* 99-01; P-in-c Tollard Royal w Farnham, Gussage St Michael etc 99-01; R Chase from 01. *The Rectory, Church Hill, Tarrant Hinton, Blandford Forum DT11 8JB* Tel (01258) 830764 E-mail drmike@church.prestel.co.uk
FOSTER, Paul. *See* FOSTER, Graham Paul
FOSTER, Paul. b 60. MAAT80. Oak Hill Th Coll DipHE93. **d** 93 **p** 94. C New Clee *Linc* 93-96; P-in-c Aldington w Bonnington and Bilsington *Cant* 96-02; P-in-c Lympne w W Hythe 00-02; Chapl HM Pris Aldington 96-02; Chapl HM YOI Feltham from 02. *HM Young Offender Institution, Bedfont Road, Feltham TW13 4ND* Tel (020) 8890 0061 *or* 8844 5325 E-mail pfozzy@hotmail.com *or* paul.foster01@hmps.gsi.gov.uk
FOSTER, Ronald George. b 25. Bris Univ BSc51 AKC51. **d** 52 **p** 53. C Lydney w Aylburton *Glouc* 52-54; C Leighton Buzzard *St Alb* 54-60; Chapl Bearwood Coll Wokingham 60-83; R Wantage Downs *Ox* 83-91; rtd 91; RD Wantage *Ox* 92-95; Perm to Offic from 92. *Ascension Cottage, Horn Lane, East Hendred, Wantage OX12 8LD* Tel (01235) 820790
FOSTER, Miss Samantha. b 80. Sunderland Univ BA01 St Jo Coll Dur BA04. Cranmer Hall Dur 01. **d** 04 **p** 05. C Fulford *York* from 04. *3 Maida Grove, York YO10 4EU* Tel (01904) 641924
FOSTER, Simon John Darby. b 57. Qu Mary Coll Lon BSc78. Wycliffe Hall Ox 85. **d** 88 **p** 89. C Bedgrove *Ox* 88-92; C Glyncorrwg w Afan Vale and Cymmer Afan *Llan* 92-94; R

Breedon cum Isley Walton and Worthington *Leic* 94-98; R Anstey from 98. *The Rectory, 1 Hurd's Close, Anstey, Leicester LE7 7GH* Tel 0116-236 2176 E-mail sfoster@leicester.anglican.org

FOSTER, Stephen. b 47. Leeds Univ CertEd69. NEOC 83. **d** 86 **p** 87. NSM Kingston upon Hull St Nic *York* 86-87; NSM Aldbrough, Mappleton w Goxhill and Withernwick 87-98; TV Howden 98-05; RD Howden 02-05; Chapl HM Pris Wolds 03-05; rtd 05; Perm to Offic *York* from 05. *Wycliffe, 6 Victoria Terrace, Robin Hoods Bay, Whitby YO22 4RJ* Tel (01947) 880055

FOSTER, Canon Stephen Arthur. b 54. Lon Univ BMus75 BA78 Potchefstroom Univ PhD98. Coll of Resurr Mirfield 75. **d** 78 **p** 79. C Ches H Trin *Ches* 78-82; C Tranmere St Paul w St Luke 82-83; V Grange St Andr 83-88; V Cheadle Hulme All SS 88-94; P-in-c Stockport St Matt 94-00; Asst Dir of Ords 96-04; V Sale St Anne 00-04; Can Res Leic Cathl *Leic* from 04; Prec Leic Cathl from 04. *15 Rockery Close, Leicester LE5 4DQ* Tel 0116-246 1230 Mobile 07715-560669 E-mail stephen.foster@leccofe.org

FOSTER, Steven. b 52. Wadh Coll Ox BA75 MA80. Ridley Hall Cam 76. **d** 79 **p** 80. C Ipsley *Worc* 79-83; TV Woughton *Ox* 83-94; V Walshaw Ch Ch *Man* from 94. *Christ Church Vicarage, 37 Gisburn Drive, Walshaw, Bury BL8 3DH* Tel 0161-763 1193 Fax 08707-052490 E-mail mail@alimus.plus.com

FOSTER, Steven Francis. b 55. Lon Univ BD76 AKC76 Open Univ BA91 FRSA90. Coll of Resurr Mirfield 77. **d** 78 **p** 79. C Romford St Edw *Chelmsf* 78-80; C Leigh St Clem 80-83; Ed Mayhew McCrimmon Publishers 84-86; Hon C Southend 85-86; P-in-c Sandon 86-90; R 90-91; R Wanstead St Mary 91-93; R Wanstead St Mary w Ch Ch 93-00; Perm to Offic 00-05; Asst to Master R Foundn of St Kath in Ratcliffe 00-04; P-in-c Brighton Annunciation *Chich* from 05. *Annunciation Vicarage, 89 Washington Street, Brighton BN2 9SR* Tel (01273) 681341 E-mail stevenffoster@aol.com

FOSTER, Stuart Jack. b 47. Oak Hill Th Coll BA80 Lambeth STh86. **d** 80 **p** 81. C Worting *Win* 80-84; C-in-c Kempshott CD 84-88; R Hook 88-95; Chapl and Warden Bp Grosseteste Coll Linc 95-99; R Kirton in Lindsey w Manton *Linc* from 99; R Grayingham from 99; OCF 99-04; Chapl ATC from 04. *The Vicarage, 28 South Cliff Road, Kirton Lindsey, Gainsborough DN21 4NR* Tel and fax (01652) 648009 Mobile 07885-701876 E-mail sjfoster.standrew@virgin.net

FOSTER, Susan. b 58. Nottm Univ BMedSci80 BM, BS82. WEMTC 00. **d** 03 **p** 05. NSM Tenbury *Heref* from 03. *Little Oaks Cottage, Hope Bagot, Ludlow SY8 3AE* Tel (01584) 891092 E-mail thefosters@littleoakshb.fsnet.uk

FOSTER, Susan Anne. b 53. Trin Coll Bris BA97. **d** 98 **p** 99. C Watton w Carbrooke and Ovington *Nor* 98-02; Min S Wonston CD *Win* from 02; P-in-c Micheldever and E Stratton, Woodmancote etc from 05. *6 Green Close, South Wonston, Winchester SO21 3EE* Tel (01962) 880650

FOSTER, Thomas Andrew Hayden. b 43. CITC 70. **d** 73 **p** 74. C Dublin Clontarf *D & G* 73-78; I Drumcliffe w Clare Abbey and Kildysart *L & K* 78-80; P-in-c Polstead *St E* 78; I Kilscoran w Killinick and Mulrankin *C & O* 80-85; I Fanlobbus Union *C, C & R* 85-86; R Lasswade and Dalkeith *Edin* 86-87; C Woodford St Mary w St Phil and St Jas *Chelmsf* 87-88; I New w Old Ross, Whitechurch, Fethard etc *C & O* 89-91; Dioc Info Officer (Ferns) 90-91; I Whitehouse *Conn* from 03. *The Rectory, 283 Shore Road, Newtownabbey BT37 9SR* Tel (028) 9085 1622 E-mail hfoster@ireland.com

FOSTER, Thomas Arthur. b 23. St D Coll Lamp BA47. Cuddesdon Coll 47. **d** 49 **p** 50. C Risca *Mon* 49-52; C Win H Trin *Win* 52-55; C Rumney *Mon* 55-56; V Cwmtillery 56-59; R Llanfoist and Llanellen 59-92; rtd 92; Perm to Offic *Mon* from 98. *The Bungalow, 5 The Bryn, Llangattock-juxta-Usk, Abergavenny NP7 9AG* Tel (01873) 840516

FOSTER, William Basil. b 23. Worc Ord Coll 65. **d** 67 **p** 68. C Folkingham w Laughton *Linc* 67-71; P-in-c Gedney Hill 71-75; V Whaplode Drove 71-75; R Heydour w Culverthorpe, Welby and Londonthorpe 75-77; P-in-c Ropsley 75-79; R 79-93; R Sapperton w Braceby 79-93; R Old Somerby 82-93; rtd 93. *31 Hedgefield Road, Barrowby, Grantham NG32 1TA* Tel (01476) 575925

FOSTER-CLARK, Mrs Sarah Hazel. b 75. Man Univ BA97 Heythrop Coll Lon MA99. Wycliffe Hall Ox 98. **d** 00 **p** 01. C Walmsley *Man* 00-01; C Turton Moorland Min 01; C Horwich and Rivington 01-04; C Halliwell from 04. *101 Cloister Street, Bolton BL1 3HA* Tel (01204) 841731 Mobile 07909-916741 E-mail revdf-c@xalt.co.uk

FOTHERBY, Miss Doreen. **d** 05. OLM Shipdham w E and W Bradenham *Nor* from 05. *6 Pound Green Lane, Shipdham, Thetford IP25 7LF* Tel (01362) 821481

FOTHERGILL, Richard Patrick. b 61. Newc Univ BA83. Trin Coll Bris 91. **d** 95 **p** 96. C E Twickenham St Steph *Lon* 95-97; Assoc R Kirstenhof S Africa 97-04; Network Miss P *Bris* from 04. *Flossie Cottage, South Stoke, Bath BA2 7ED* Tel (01225) 834579

FOUGNER, Tor Even. b 65. Lutheran Sch of Th Oslo 84. **p** 92. Norway 92-01; NSM Walkley *Sheff* 02-03; C Sheff St Leon Norwood from 03. *73 Providence Road, Sheffield S6 5BG* Tel 0114-233 3828 Mobile 07966-670207 E-mail fougner@online.no

FOULDS, John Stuart. b 64. Lanc Univ BA87 Southn Univ BTh91. Chich Th Coll 88. **d** 91 **p** 92. C Eastcote St Lawr *Lon* 91-95; C Wembley Park 95-99; P-in-c Meir *Lich* from 99. *The Vicarage, 715 Uttoxeter Road, Stoke-on-Trent ST3 5PY* Tel (01782) 313347

FOULGER, Bernard Darwin. b 28. Cant Sch of Min 86. **d** 89 **p** 90. OLM Sittingbourne H Trin w Bobbing *Cant* 89-97; rtd 97; Perm to Offic *Cant* from 97. *30 Frederick Street, Sittingbourne ME10 1AU* Tel (01795) 422724

FOULIS BROWN, Graham Douglas. b 50. JP87. St Steph Ho Ox 80. **d** 82 **p** 83. C Hungerford and Denford *Ox* 82-84; Chapl Hungerford Hosp 83-84; C Bicester w Bucknell, Caversfield and Launton *Ox* 84-85; TV 85-90; V Kidmore End and Sonning Common 90-03; P-in-c Rotherfield Peppard 02-03; R Rotherfield Peppard and Kidmore End etc from 03. *The Rectory, Kidmore End, Reading RG4 9AY* Tel 0118-972 3987 Fax 972 4202 E-mail gdfb.vicarage@lineone.net

FOULKES, Chan Meurig. b 21. St D Coll Lamp BA46. St Mich Coll Llan 46. **d** 47 **p** 48. C Llanbeblig w Caernarfon *Ban* 47-55; Bp's Private Chapl 55-58; V Harlech and Llanfair juxta Harlech 58-66; RD Ardudwy 64-76; R Llanaber w Caerdeon 66-76; Can Ban Cathl 71-89; Treas 74-83; Chan 83-89; R Llandegfan and Beaumaris w Llanfaes w Penmon etc 76-89; rtd 90; Perm to Offic *Ban* from 90. *Llanaber, 11 Gogarth Avenue, Penmaenmawr LL34 6PY* Tel (01492) 623011

FOULKES, Simon. b 58. Ox Poly BA81. Oak Hill Th Coll BA89. **d** 89 **p** 90. C St Austell *Truro* 89-92; C Boscombe St Jo *Win* 92-94; P-in-c Portswood St Denys 94-99; Par Evang Adv *Wakef* 99-04; TR Almondbury w Farnley Tyas 02-05. *53 Littlestone Road, Littlestone, New Romney TN28 8LN* Tel (01797) 364517 Mobile 07870-190620

FOUNTAIN, David Roy (Brother Malcolm). b 48. Qu Coll Birm 85. **d** 87 **p** 88. SSF from 72; NSM Handsworth St Mich *Birm* 87-92; Lic to Offic *Sarum* 92-95; Perm to Offic *Worc* 95-00, *Newc* 00-02, *Lon* 02-03; V Bentley *Sheff* from 03. *The Vicarage, 3A High Street, Bentley, Doncaster DN5 0AA* Tel (01302) 876272

FOUNTAIN, John Stephen. b 43. RAF Coll Cranwell 65 Solicitor 80. LNSM course 91. **d** 93 **p** 94. NSM Nacton and Levington w Bucklesham and Foxhall *St E* 93-03; NSM Taddington, Chelmorton and Flagg, and Monyash *Derby* from 03. *The Old School, Chelmorton, Buxton SK17 9SG* Tel (01298) 85009

FOUNTAIN, Miss Stephanie Ann Cecilia. b 58. Lon Univ BMus81 Roehampton Inst PGCE88. Westcott Ho Cam 00. **d** 02 **p** 03. C Tadworth *S'wark* from 02. *22 Station Approach Road, Tadworth KT20 5AD* Tel (01737) 817872 E-mail stephaniefountain@yahoo.co.uk

FOUTS, Arthur Guy. b 44. Washington Univ BA72 Seabury-Western Th Sem DMin98. Ridley Hall Cam 78. **d** 81 **p** 82. C Alperton *Lon* 81-84; R Pinxton *Derby* 84-87; USA from 88; R Dublin St Patr 88-89; Pastor Warren St Mark 90-91; R Silver Spring St Mary Magd 91-99; Chapl St Andr Sch 99-00; P-in-c Point of Rocks St Paul from 01. *15809 Quince Orchard Road, Gaithersburg, MD 20878, USA* E-mail rubberduck301@yahoo.com

FOWELL, Graham Charles. b 48. Southn Univ BTh85. Chich Th Coll. **d** 82 **p** 83. C Clayton *Lich* 82-86; C Uttoxeter w Bramshall 86-90; V Oxley 90-95; P-in-c Shifnal from 95. *St Andrew's Vicarage, Manor Close, Shifnal TF11 9AJ* Tel (01952) 463694 E-mail graham@shifvic.fsnet.co.uk

FOWLER, Anthony Lewis. b 57. Oak Hill Th Coll BA93. **d** 93 **p** 94. C Walton *St E* 93-96; P-in-c Combs 96-00; P-in-c Hitcham w Lt Finborough 98-00; R Combs and Lt Finborough 00-04; Chapl Suffolk Coll 00-04; Chapl HM Pris Coldingley from 04. *HM Prison Coldingley, Shaftesbury Road, Bisley, Woking GU24 9EX* Tel (01483) 804370 E-mail tony.fowler@hmps.gsi.gov.uk *or* alfowler@supanet.com

FOWLER, Canon Colin. b 40. Linc Th Coll 80. **d** 82 **p** 83. C Barbourne *Worc* 82-85; TV Worc St Martin w St Pet, St Mark etc 85-86; TV Worc SE 86-92; P-in-c Moulton *Linc* 92-95; Chapl Puerto de la Cruz Tenerife *Eur* 95-01; Hon Can Madrid Cathl from 99; R Tangmere and Oving *Chich* 01-05. *St Andrew's Vicarage, 21 Gibson Road, Tangmere, Chichester PO20 2JA* Tel (01243) 785089

FOWLER, Canon David Mallory. b 51. Lancs Coll of Agric OND72. Brasted Th Coll 74 Trin Coll Bris 75. **d** 78 **p** 79. C Rainhill *Liv* 78-81; C Houghton *Carl* 81-84; P-in-c Grayrigg 84-89; P-in-c Old Hutton w New Hutton 84-89; V Kirkoswald, Renwick and Ainstable 89-99; P-in-c Gt Salkeld w Lazonby 98-99; R Kirkoswald, Renwick, Gt Salkeld and Lazonby from 00; RD Penrith from 99; Hon Can Carl Cathl from 99. *The Vicarage, Kirkoswald, Penrith CA10 1DQ* Tel (01768) 898176 E-mail revdmf@aol.com

FOWLER, Mrs Janice Karen Brenda. b 56. Middx Univ BA97. Oak Hill Th Coll 91. **d** 93 **p** 94. NSM Walton *St E* 93-96; Chapl

Ipswich Hosp NHS Trust 94-00; NSM Combs *St E* 96-00; NSM Hitcham w Lt Finborough 98-00; C Combs and Lt Finborough 00-04; P-in-c 04; C S Hartismere from 04. *10A Red House Yards, Thornham Magna, Eye IP23 8HH* Tel 07720-262201 (mobile)

FOWLER, John Ronald. b 30. Ely Th Coll 55. **d** 58 **p** 59. C Surbiton St Andr *S'wark* 58-61; Guyana 61-70 and 83-89; V Sydenham All SS *S'wark* 70-81; V Wood End *Cov* 81-83; Can St Geo Cathl 86-89; Adn Demerara 86-89; V Bedford St Mich *St Alb* 90-95; rtd 95. *21 Painters Lane, Sutton, Ely CB6 2NS* Tel (01353) 776268

FOWLER, John Thomas. b 42. EAMTC. **d** 01 **p** 02. NSM Stoke by Nayland w Leavenheath and Polstead *St E* from 01. *Warners, Thorington Street, Stoke by Nayland, Colchester CO6 4SP* Tel and fax (01206) 337229 E-mail jm@albys2.freeserve.co.uk

FOWLES, Canon Christopher John. b 31. Lich Th Coll 54. **d** 58 **p** 59. C Englefield Green *Guildf* 58-63; C Worplesdon 63-69; V Chessington 69-77; V Horsell 77-95; RD Woking 92-94; Hon Can Guildf Cathl 94-95; rtd 95; Perm to Offic *Guildf* from 95. *78 St Jude's Road, Egham TW20 0DF* Tel (01784) 439457

FOX, Albert. b 06. MBE. **d** 73 **p** 74. C Bris St Ambrose Whitehall *Bris* 73-75; Hon C E Bris 75-79; rtd 79. *20 New Brunswick Avenue, Bristol BS5 8PW* Tel 0117-967 2632

FOX, Mrs Carole Ann. b 36. TISEC 98. **d** 99 **p** 00. NSM Ellon *Ab* from 99. *4 Mavis Bank, Newburgh, Ellon AB41 6FB* Tel (01358) 789693 E-mail charles.fox@tiscali.co.uk

FOX, Charles Edward. b 36. Lich Th Coll 62. **d** 66 **p** 67. C S Bank *York* 66-69; C Stokesley 69-72; P-in-c Ugthorpe 72-82; V Egton w Grosmont 72-82; P-in-c Newbold Verdon *Leic* 82-83; R Newbold de Verdun and Kirkby Mallory 84-04; rtd 04. *White Rose Cottage, 6 Brascote Lane, Newbold Verdon, Leicester LE9 9LF* Tel (01455) 822103

FOX, Colin George. b 46. TD. Southn Univ DipTh75. Sarum & Wells Th Coll 73. **d** 75 **p** 76. C N Hammersmith St Kath *Lon* 75-79; CF (TA) 76-90; C Heston *Lon* 79-81; TV Marlborough *Sarum* 81-90; P-in-c Pewsey 90-91; TR 91-98; TR Pewsey and Swanborough 98-03; Chapl Pewsey Hosp 90-95; P-in-c Avon Valley *Sarum* from 03. *The Vicarage, High Street, Netheravon, Salisbury SP4 9QP* Tel (01980) 670326 E-mail foxy.col@talk21.com

FOX, Cynthia. b 39. Ripon Coll of Educn CertEd59 Man Univ MEd72 Sheff Univ PhD81 Bradf Univ MSc83 Leeds Univ MA87 Westmr Coll Ox BTh98. N Ord Course 03. **d** 04 **p** 05. NSM Battyeford *Wakef* 04-05; NSM Brighouse and Clifton from 05. *Foxdene, 134 Nab Lane, Mirfield WF14 9QJ* Tel (01924) 499112 E-mail cynthia@nablane.fsnet.co.uk

FOX, Harvey Harold. b 27. Lich Th Coll 58. **d** 60 **p** 61. C Birchfield *Birm* 60-62; C Boldmere 62-65; V Sparkbrook Em 65-71; V Dordon 71-77; V Four Oaks 77-82; V Packwood w Hockley Heath 82-90; rtd 90; Perm to Offic *Cov* from 90. *37 Meadow Road, Henley-in-Arden B95 5LB* Tel (01564) 795302

FOX, Canon Herbert Frederick. b 26. Leeds Univ BA50. Coll of Resurr Mirfield 50. **d** 52 **p** 53. C Bury St Thos *Man* 52-55; V Unsworth 55-61; V Turton 61-72; V Farnworth and Kearsley 72-78; RD Farnworth 77-84; TR E Farnworth and Kearsley 78-84; Hon Can Man Cathl 81-84; V Ashford Hill w Headley *Win* 84-91; rtd 91; Perm to Offic *Man* from 91. *9 Highfield Road, Blackrod, Bolton BL6 5BP* Tel (01204) 698368

FOX, Canon Ian James. b 44. Selw Coll Cam BA66 MA70. Linc Th Coll 66. **d** 68 **p** 69. C Salford St Phil w St Steph *Man* 68-71; C Kirkleatham *York* 71-73; TV Redcar w Kirkleatham 73-77; V Bury St Pet *Man* 77-85; V Northallerton w Kirby Sigston *York* 85-03; RD Northallerton 85-91; Chapl Friarage and Distr Hosp Northallerton 88-92; Chapl Northallerton Health Services NHS Trust 92-03; V Barlby w Riccall *York* from 03; Can and Preb York Minster from 95. *The Vicarage, York Road, Barlby, Selby YO8 5JP* Tel (01757) 702384

FOX, Preb Jacqueline Frederica. b 43. Ripon Coll of Educn CertEd66 Leeds Univ MEd84 HonRCM85. S Dios Minl Tr Scheme 83. **dss** 85 **d** 87 **p** 94. RCM *Lon* 85-86; Dioc FE Officer 87-96; Hon C Acton St Mary 87-96; R from 96; Dean of Women's Min from 96; Dir of Ords Willesden Area from 01; Preb St Paul's Cathl from 01. *The Rectory, 14 Cumberland Park, London W3 6SX* Tel (020) 8992 8876 *or* 8993 0422 Fax 8896 3754 E-mail jackie.fox@london.anglican.org *or* stmary.acton@virgin.net

FOX, Mrs Jane. b 47. Open Univ BA91 Bp Otter Coll Chich CertEd75 ALA70. S Dios Minl Tr Scheme 92. **d** 95 **p** 96. NSM W Blatchington *Chich* 95-98; C Peacehaven and Telscombe Cliffs 98-01; C Telscombe w Piddinghoe and Southease 98-01; TV Hitchin *St Alb* from 01. *Holy Saviour Vicarage, St Anne's Road, Hitchin SG5 1QB* Tel (01462) 456140

FOX (née COULDRIDGE), Mrs Janice Evelyn. b 49. Bognor Regis Coll of Educn CertEd71. Glouc Sch of Min 89. **d** 92 **p** 94. C Tupsley w Hampton Bishop *Heref* 92-96; P-in-c Orleton w Brimfield 96-01; Dioc Ecum Officer 96-01; TV Worc SE *Worc* from 01; rtd 05. *4 Mcintyre Road, Worcester WR2 5LG* E-mail janfox7@netscape.net

FOX, Jeremy Robin. b 68. St Chad's Coll Dur BA89 MA92 Leeds Univ BA94. Coll of Resurr Mirfield 92. **d** 95 **p** 96. C S Shields All SS *Dur* 95-99; C Tottenham St Paul *Lon* 99-04; C Edmonton St Mary w St Jo 99-04; Chapl Belgrade *Eur* from 04. *c/o FCO (Belgrade), King Charles Street, London SW1A 2AH* Tel (00381) (11) 402315

FOX, John Brian. b 38. **d** 94 **p** 95. NSM Phillack w Gwithian and Gwinear *Truro* 94-96; NSM Godrevy 96-03; Chapl St Mich Mt from 04. *Abbeydale, 26 Tresdale Parc, Connor Downs, Hayle TR27 5DX* Tel (01736) 753935

FOX, Jonathan Alexander. b 56. St Jo Coll Nottm LTh77 BTh78. **d** 81 **p** 82. C Chasetown *Lich* 81-85; TV Fazakerley Em *Liv* 85-89; TV Madeley *Heref* 97-02. *Address temp unknown* E-mail jonathan@foxjaf.freeserve.co.uk

FOX, Leonard. b 41. AKC66. **d** 67 **p** 68. C Salford Stowell Memorial *Man* 67-68; C Hulme St Phil 68-72; C Portsea All SS w St Jo Rudmore *Portsm* 72-75; V Oakfield St Jo 75-92; P-in-c Portsea All SS from 92; Dir All SS Urban Miss Cen from 92. *All Saints' Vicarage, 51 Staunton Street, Portsmouth PO1 4EJ* Tel (023) 9287 2815 *or* 9282 9119 Fax 9283 8116 E-mail lf.rjf@virgin.net

FOX, Mrs Lynn. b 51. EMMTC 92. **d** 92 **p** 94. Assoc P Clifton *S'well* 92-96; TV 96-98. *Address temp unknown*

FOX, Maurice Henry George. b 24. Lon Univ BD58. St Aid Birkenhead 47. **d** 49 **p** 50. C Eccleshill *Bradf* 49-52; C Bingley All SS 52-56; V Cross Roads cum Lees 56-62; V Sutton 62-79; V Grange-over-Sands *Carl* 79-88; rtd 89. *7 Manor Close, Topcliffe, Thirsk YO7 3RH* Tel (01845) 578322

FOX, Michael Adrian Orme. b 47. Bris Univ BSc68 PhD72. WMMTC 01. **d** 04 **p** 05. NSM Codsall *Lich* from 04. *30 Bromley Gardens, Codsall, Wolverhampton WV8 1BE* Tel (01902) 843442 E-mail mike@maofox.me.uk

FOX, The Ven Michael John. b 42. Hull Univ BSc63. Coll of Resurr Mirfield 64. **d** 66 **p** 67. C Becontree St Elisabeth *Chelmsf* 66-70; C Wanstead H Trin Hermon Hill 70-72; V Victoria Docks Ascension 72-76; V Chelmsf All SS 76-88; P-in-c Chelmsf Ascension 85-88; RD Chelmsf 86-88; R Colchester St Jas, All SS, St Nic and St Runwald 88-93; Hon Can Chelmsf Cathl 91-93; Adn Harlow 93-95; Adn W Ham from 95. *86 Aldersbrook Road, London E12 5DH* Tel (020) 8989 8557 Fax 8530 1311 E-mail a.westham@chelmsford.anglican.org

FOX, Michael John Holland. b 41. Lon Univ BD68. Oak Hill Th Coll 64. **d** 69 **p** 70. C Reigate St Mary *S'wark* 69-73; NSM 76-01; C Guildf St Sav *Guildf* 73-76; Asst Chapl Reigate Gr Sch 76-81; Chapl from 81; NSM Reigate St Pet CD *S'wark* 96-01; P-in-c Reigate St Luke w Doversgreen from 01. *St Luke's Vicarage, Church Road, Reigate RH2 8HY* Tel (01737) 246302 E-mail mikejh.fox@virgin.net

FOX, Nigel Stephen. b 35. Sarum Th Coll 59. **d** 62 **p** 63. C Rainbow Hill St Barn *Worc* 62-65; C Kidderminster St Geo 65-67; C-in-c Warndon CD 67-69; V Warndon 69-74; R S Hill w Callington *Truro* 74-85; RD E Wivelshire 78-81; R St Martin w E and W Looe 85-95; rtd 95; Perm to Offic *Truro* from 95. *Newlair, 4 Bindown Court, Nomansland, Widegates, Looe PL13 1PX* Tel (01503) 240584

FOX, Norman Stanley. b 39. Wolv Univ LLB97. St Mich Coll Llan 61. **d** 64 **p** 65. C Brierley Hill *Lich* 64-67; C Tettenhall Regis 67-70; V Cradley *Worc* 70-73; Asst Chapl HM Pris Wakef 73-74; Chapl HM Pris The Verne 74-76; R Clayton W w High Hoyland *Wakef* 76-81; R Cumberworth 81-84; C Tettenhall Wood *Lich* 85-89; TV 89-91; V Pensnett 91-93; rtd 99. *54 Lyndon Road, Solihull B92 7RQ* Tel 0121-707 8216 E-mail nsfox@evemail.net

✠**FOX, The Rt Revd Peter John.** b 52. AKC74. St Aug Coll Cant 74. **d** 75 **p** 76 **c** 02. C Wymondham *Nor* 75-79; Papua New Guinea 79-85 and from 02; P-in-c Tattersett *Nor* 85-88; P-in-c Houghton 85-88; P-in-c Syderstone w Barmer and Bagthorpe 85-88; P-in-c Tatterford 85-88; P-in-c E w W Rudham 85-88; R Coxford Gp 88-89; TR Lynton, Brendon, Countisbury, Lynmouth etc *Ex* 89-95; RD Shirwell 93-95; P-in-c Harpsden *Ox* 95-02; Gen Sec Melanesian Miss 95-02; Bp Port Moresby from 02. *PO Box 6491, Boroko, NCD, Port Moresby, Papua New Guinea* Tel (00675) 323 2489 Fax 326 2493 E-mail acpngpom@global.net.pg *or* foxfamily@daltron.com.pg

FOX, Canon Raymond. b 46. QUB BSc69. CITC 71. **d** 71 **p** 72. C Holywood *D & D* 71-75; C Min Can Down Cathl 75-78; I Killinchy w Kilmood and Tullynakill 78-81; I Belfast St Mary *Conn* 81-88; I Killaney w Carryduff *D & D* 88-02; Can Down Cathl 98-02; Chapter Clerk and V Choral Belf Cathl 00-02; I Donegal w Killymard, Lough Eske and Laghey *D & R* from 02. *The Rectory, Ballyshannon Road, Donegal, Irish Republic* Tel (00353) (73) 972 1075 E-mail donegal@raphoe.anglican.org

FOX, Robert. b 54. Man Univ BEd76. N Ord Course 89. **d** 91 **p** 92. NSM Stalybridge *Man* 91; NSM Ashton St Mich 91-96; NSM Stalybridge from 96. *36 Norman Road, Stalybridge SK15 1LY* Tel 0161-338 8481 E-mail rob@foxesbrige.freeserve.com.uk

FOX, Robin. *See* FOX, Jeremy Robin

FOX, Sidney. b 47. Nottm Univ BTh79 PhD93. Linc Th Coll 75. **d** 79 **p** 80. C Middlesbrough St Oswald *York* 79-81; P-in-c 81-86; V 86-87; V Newby 87-92; R Brechin and Tarfside *Bre* 92-05; P-in-c Auchmithie 92-00; Can St Paul's Cathl Dundee 98-05; V

Broughton *Blackb* from 05. *The Vicarage, 410 Garstang Road, Broughton, Preston PR3 5JB* Tel (01772) 862330 E-mail revsfox@tiscali.co.uk

FOX, Timothy William Bertram. b 37. CCC Cam BA61. Qu Coll Birm 66. **d** 68 **p** 69. C Cannock *Lich* 68-72; C Bilston St Leon 72-75; V Essington 75-81; R Buildwas and Leighton w Eaton Constantine etc 81-92; RD Wrockwardine 88-92; R Bradeley, Church Eaton and Moreton 92-04; rtd 04. *The Vicarage, Church Lane, Hanbury, Burton-on-Trent DE13 8TF* Tel (01283) 813357

FOX-WILSON, Francis James. b 46. Nottm Univ BTh73. Linc Th Coll 69. **d** 73 **p** 74. C Eastbourne St Eliz *Chich* 73-76; C Seaford w Sutton 76-78; P-in-c Hellingly 78-79; P-in-c Upper Dicker 78-79; V Hellingly and Upper Dicker 79-85; V Goring-by-Sea 85-93; R Alfriston w Lullington, Litlington and W Dean from 93. *The Rectory, Sloe Lane, Alfriston, Polegate BN26 5UY* Tel (01323) 870376

FOXWELL, Rupert Edward Theodore. b 54. Magd Coll Cam BA76 MA80 Solicitor 79. Wycliffe Hall Ox 91. **d** 93 **p** 94. C Tonbridge SS Pet and Paul *Roch* 93-98. *24 Cheviot Close, Tonbridge TN9 1NH* Tel (01732) 358535 Fax as telephone E-mail foxwell@harvester.org.uk

FOY, Malcolm Stuart. b 48. ACP80 FCollP FRSA Univ of Wales (Lamp) BA71 Magd Coll Cam CertEd72 K Coll Lon MA89. Ox NSM Course 84. **d** 87 **p** 88. NSM Tilehurst St Mich *Ox* 87-90; C Ireland Wood *Ripon* 90-96; Adv RE Leeds Adnry 90-96; Dir Educn *Bradf* 96-99; C Otley 99; Perm to Offic from 00. *45 The Chase, Keighley BD20 6HU* Tel (01535) 665112

FRAIS, Jonathan Jeremy. b 65. Kingston Poly LLB87. Oak Hill Th Coll BA92. **d** 92 **p** 93. C Orpington Ch Ch *Roch* 92-96; Asst Chapl Moscow *Eur* 96-99; Chapl Kiev 99-05; R Bexhill St Mark *Chich* from 05. *The Rectory, 11 Coverdale Avenue, Bexhill-on-Sea TN39 4TY* Tel (01424) 843733

FRAMPTON, Miss Marcia Ellen. b 36. SRN65 SCM66. Ripon Coll Cuddesdon 86. **d** 88 **p** 95. Par Dn Paston *Pet* 88-89; Par Dn Burford w Fulbrook and Taynton *Ox* 90-92; Par Dn Witney 92-93; NSM Heref S Wye *Heref* 94-01; rtd 01; Perm to Offic *Heref* from 02. *15 Waterfield Road, Hereford HR2 7DD* Tel (01432) 278955 E-mail ellenkate@beeb.net

FRAMPTON-MORGAN, Anthony Paul George. *See* MORGAN, Anthony Paul George

FRANCE, Alistair. *See* FRANCE, Robert Alistair

FRANCE, Andrew. *See* FRANCE, John Andrew

FRANCE, Charles Malcolm. b 48. ACA71 FCA76. EAMTC 94. **d** 97 **p** 98. C Gt Grimsby St Mary and St Jas *Linc* 97-02; P-in-c Skegness and Winthorpe 02-04; P-in-c Ingoldmells w Addlethorpe 02-04; R Skegness Gp from 04. *20 Drake Road, Skegness PE25 3BH* Tel (01754) 612079 E-mail malcolmfrance@aol.com

FRANCE (née PIERCY), Mrs Elizabeth Claire. b 66. Qu Mary Coll Lon BSc87. Wycliffe Hall Ox 97. **d** 99 **p** 00. C Dronfield w Holmesfield *Derby* 99-03; V Allestree 03-05. *The Rectory, Rectory Close, Etchingham Road, Burwash, Etchingham TN19 7BH* Tel (01435) 882301 E-mail lizcfrance@tiscali.co.uk

FRANCE, Evan Norman Lougher. b 52. Jes Coll Cam BA74 MA78. Wycliffe Hall Ox 76. **d** 79 **p** 80. C Hall Green Ascension *Birm* 79-82; CMS 82-84; C Bexhill St Pet *Chich* 84-87; V Westfield from 87. *The Vicarage, Vicarage Lane, Westfield, Hastings TN35 4SD* Tel (01424) 751029

FRANCE, Geoffrey. b 37. S Dios Minl Tr Scheme 87. **d** 90 **p** 91. NSM Uckfield *Chich* 90-92; C 92-94; R Warbleton and Bodle Street Green 94-02; rtd 02. *Little Croft, 19 James Avenue, Herstmonceux, Hailsham BN27 4PB* Tel (01323) 831840

FRANCE, John Andrew. b 68. Edin Univ MA90 Leeds Univ BA00. Coll of Resurr Mirfield 98. **d** 00 **p** 01. C Hartlepool H Trin *Dur* 00-04; Co-ord Chapl HM Pris Low Newton 04-05; V Earsdon and Backworth *Newc* from 05. *The Vicarage, 5 Front Street, Earsdon, Whitley Bay NE25 9JU* Tel 0191-252 9393 E-mail andrewfrance1968@hotmail.com

FRANCE, Malcolm. *See* FRANCE, Charles Malcolm

FRANCE, Malcolm Norris. b 28. Ch Ch Ox BA53 MA57 Essex Univ PhD75. Westcott Ho Cam 53. **d** 55 **p** 56. C Ipswich St Mary le Tower *St E* 55-58; V Esholt *Bradf* 58-64; Chapl Essex Univ *Chelmsf* 64-73; Perm to Offic *Chich* 77-87; P-in-c Starston *Nor* 87-93; rtd 93; Perm to Offic *Nor* from 93. *The Old Swan, Townsend, Wylye, Warminster BA12 0RZ* Tel (01985) 248189

FRANCE, Canon Richard Thomas. b 38. Ball Coll Ox BA60 MA63 Lon Univ BD62 Bris Univ PhD67. Tyndale Hall Bris 60. **d** 66 **p** 67. C Cambridge St Matt *Ely* 66-69; Nigeria 69-73 and 76-77; Hon Can Ibadan from 94; Lib Tyndale Ho Cam 73-76; Warden 78-81; Vice-Prin Lon Bible Coll 81-88; Prin Wycliffe Hall Ox 89-95; R Wentnor w Ratlinghope, Myndtown, Norbury etc *Heref* 95-99; rtd 99; Perm to Offic *Ban* from 00. *Tyn-y-twll, Llangelynnin, Llwyngwril LL37 2QL* Tel (01341) 250596 E-mail rtfrance@lineone.net

FRANCE, Robert Alistair. b 71. Ox Poly BA92. Oak Hill Th Coll BA94. **d** 97 **p** 98. C Hartford *Ches* 97-02; P-in-c Stokenchurch and Ibstone *Ox* from 02. *The Vicarage, Wycombe Road, Stokenchurch, High Wycombe HP14 3RG* Tel (01494) 483384 Mobile 07929-147552 E-mail revalistair@aol.com

FRANCE, Robert Lyle. b 47. Univ of Mississippi BS69 Univ of Cincinnati MD73. Trin Coll Bris BA03. **d** 03 **p** 04. C Mangotsfield *Bris* 03-04; USA from 04. *PO Box 21, Duncan, MS 38740, USA* Tel (001) (662) 395 2579

FRANCE, Stephen Mark. b 66. Wycliffe Hall Ox BTh00. **d** 00 **p** 01. C Newbold w Dunston *Derby* 00-03; P-in-c Darley Abbey 03-05; Dioc Duty Press Officer 03-04; P-in-c Burwash *Chich* from 05. *The Rectory, Rectory Close, Etchingham Road, Burwash, Etchingham TN19 7BH* Tel (01435) 882301 E-mail revfrance@tiscali.co.uk

FRANCE, William Michael. b 43. Sydney Univ BA68 Lon Univ BD72 Chas Sturt Univ NSW MEd96. Moore Th Coll Sydney LTh70. **d** 73 **p** 73. Australia 73-76 and from 78; C Barton Seagrave w Warkton *Pet* 76-78. *6 Wesson Road, West Pennant Hills, NSW, Australia 2125* Tel (0061) (2) 9875 2987 *or* 9286 9605 Mobile 411-276050 Fax 9286 9632 E-mail b.j.b@optusnet.com.au *or* wfrance@sacs.nsw.edu.au

FRANCE, Archdeacon of. *See* WELLS, The Ven Anthony Martin Giffard

FRANCES, Nicolas Francis. b 61. MBE98. Portsm Poly HND82. N Ord Course 92. **d** 95 **p** 96. NSM Anfield St Columba *Liv* 95-98; Australia from 98; Acting Dir Health and Welfare Chapls Melbourne 98-99; Exec Dir Brotherhood of St Laur from 99. *15 Traill Street, Northcote, Vic, Australia 3070* Tel (0061) (3) 9481 7373 *or* 9483 1347 Fax 9486 9724 E-mail nic@bsl.org.au

FRANCES ANNE, Mother. *See* COCKER, Mrs Frances Rymer

FRANCIS, Miss Annette. b 44. DCR66. Trin Coll Bris DipHE93. **d** 93 **p** 94. NSM Belmont *Lon* 93; C 94-97; C Swansea St Pet *S & B* 97-99; V Llanelli from 99. *Llanelly Rectory, Abergavenny Road, Gilwern, Abergavenny NP7 0AD* Tel (01873) 830280

FRANCIS, Claude Vernon Eastwood. b 15. Univ of Wales BA38. Ripon Hall Ox 38. **d** 40 **p** 41. C Cilybebyll *Llan* 40-44; C Treorchy 44-46; C Whitchurch 46-49; C Winscombe *B & W* 49-55; R E Pennard w Pylle 55-75; R Ditcheat w E Pennard and Pylle 75-81; rtd 81; Perm to Offic *B & W* from 81. *The Garden Flat, Sexey's Hospital, Bruton BA10 0AS* Tel (01749) 812147

FRANCIS, David Carpenter. b 45. Southn Univ BSc66 Loughb Univ MSc71 Sussex Univ MA83. Westcott Ho Cam 85. **d** 87 **p** 88. C Ealing St Mary *Lon* 87-90; Chapl Ealing Coll of HE 87-90; Chapl Clayponds Hosp Ealing 88-90; P-in-c Wembley St Jo *Lon* 90-93; Chapl Wembley Hosp 90-93; V Platt *Roch* 93-01; Post Ord Tr Officer 93-98; RD Shoreham 99-01; R Stow on the Wold, Condicote and The Swells *Glouc* from 01. *The Rectory, Sheep Street, Stow on the Wold, Cheltenham GL54 1AA* Tel (01451) 830607 Mobile 07799-410370 Fax (01451) 830903 E-mail david@francisatthevicarage.freeserve.co.uk

FRANCIS, David Everton Baxter. b 45. St Deiniol's Hawarden 76. **d** 77 **p** 78. C Llangyfelach *S & B* 77-78; C Llansamlet 78-80; V Llanrhaeadr-ym-Mochnant, Llanarmon, Pennant etc *St As* 80-85; V Penrhyncoch and Elerch *St D* 85-93; V Borth and Eglwys-fach w Llangynfelyn 93-02; V Garthbeibio w Llanerfyl w Llangadfan *St As* from 02; AD Caereinion from 02. *Ty'r Eglwys, Pont Robert, Meifod SY22 6HY* Tel (01938) 500454

FRANCIS, Miss Gillian Cartwright. b 40. CertEd61. Dalton Ho Bris Trin Coll Bris DipTh71. **dss** 85 **d** 87 **p** 94. Blackheath *Birm* 86-94; Par Dn 87-94; P-in-c Stechford 94-03; rtd 03; Perm to Offic *Glouc* from 03. *22 Ince Castle Way, Gloucester GL1 4DT* Tel (01452) 503059

FRANCIS, Canon Graham John. b 45. St Mich Coll Llan 66. **d** 70 **p** 71. C Llanblethian w Cowbridge and Llandough etc *Llan* 70-76; V Penrhiwceiber w Matthewstown and Ynysboeth 76-02; V Cardiff St Mary and St Steph w St Dyfrig etc from 02; V Grangetown from 05; Can Llan Cathl from 02. *St Mary's Vicarage, 2 North Church Street, Cardiff CF10 5HB* Tel and fax (029) 2048 7777 E-mail fathergraham@aol.com

FRANCIS, Canon James More MacLeod. b 44. Edin Univ MA65 BD68 PhD74 Yale Univ STM69. New Coll Edin 65. **d** 87 **p** 87. Sen Lect RS Sunderland Univ *Dur* from 82; NSM Sunderland St Chad 87-98; TV Sunderland from 98; Tutor NEOC 89-98; Bp's Adv for NSM *Dur* from 99; Prin Dioc OLM Course from 02; Hon Can Dur Cathl from 00. *8 Cooke's Wood, Broompark, Durham DH7 7RL* Tel 0191-384 9638 E-mail jamesfrancis@mac.com

FRANCIS, James Stephen. b 66. Univ of Wales (Ban) DipTh85 FInstD97. SEITE DipTM99. **d** 99. NSM St Botolph Aldgate w H Trin Minories *Lon* 99-02; NSM Brixton Road Ch Ch *S'wark* 99-01; Perm to Offic *Derby* and *S'wark* from 01; Hon Par Dn Soho St Anne w St Thos and St Pet *Lon* from 02. *26 Rosewood House, Vauxhall Grove, London SW8 1TB* Tel (020) 7587 0562 *or* 7702 5629 E-mail jamesfrancis@trb.info

FRANCIS, Canon James Woodcock. b 28. OBE97. Wilberforce Univ Ohio AB57 Payne Th Sem Ohio BD58. Bexley Hall Div Sch Ohio 59. **d** 59 **p** 60. USA 59-84; Bermuda from 85; Can Res Bermuda 85-99; R Devonshire Ch Ch from 99. *PO Box HM 627, Hamilton HM CX, Bermuda* Tel (001809) 295 1125 Fax 292 5421

FRANCIS, Jeffrey Merrick. b 46. Bris Univ BSc69. Qu Coll Birm 72. **d** 76 **p** 77. C Bris Ch the Servant Stockwood *Bris* 76-79; C

Bishopston 79-82; V Bris St Andr Hartcliffe 82-93; TV Bris St Paul's 93-00; P-in-c Barton Hill St Luke w Ch Ch and Moorfields 00-02; Perm to Offic from 02. *32 Burfoot Gardens, Stockwood, Bristol BS14 8TE* Tel (01275) 831020

FRANCIS, Jeremy Montgomery. b 31. BNC Ox BA53 MA56. Glouc Sch of Min 84. **d** 87 **p** 88. NSM Chedworth, Yanworth and Stowell, Coln Rogers etc *Glouc* 87-90; NSM Coates, Rodmarton and Sapperton etc 90-01; NSM Daglingworth w the Duntisbournes and Winstone 95-97; NSM Brimpsfield w Birdlip, Syde, Daglingworth etc 97-00; Perm to Offic from 01. *Old Barnfield, Duntisbourne Leer, Cirencester GL7 7AS* Tel (01285) 821370

FRANCIS, John. b 56. Bris Poly BA78 MCIH81. LNSM course 95. **d** 98 **p** 99. OLM Hatcham Park All SS *S'wark* from 98. *Flat 2, 133 Deptford High Street, London SE8 4NS* Tel (020) 8691 3145 *or* 8875 5942 E-mail franci@threshold.org.uk

FRANCIS, John Sims. b 25. Fitzw Ho Cam BA54 MA58. St D Coll Lamp BA47 LTh49. **d** 49 **p** 50. C Swansea St Barn *S & B* 49-52; C Chesterton St Andr *Ely* 52-54; C Swansea St Mary and H Trin *S & B* 54-58; V Newbridge-on-Wye and Llanfihangel Brynpabuan 58-65; R Willingham *Ely* 65-82; RD N Stowe 78-82; R Rampton 82; P-in-c Buckden 82-85; V 85-91; rtd 91; Perm to Offic *Linc* 92-01. *3 The Brambles, Bourne PE10 9TF* Tel (01778) 426396

FRANCIS, Julian Montgomery. b 60. Selw Coll Cam BA83 MA83. S'wark Ord Course 88. **d** 91 **p** 92. C S Wimbledon H Trin and St Pet *S'wark* 91-95; V Cottingley *Bradf* 95-99; Minority Ethnic Angl Concerns Officer *Lich* 99-02; Assoc Min W Bromwich St Andr w Ch Ch 99-02; TR Coventry Caludon *Cov* from 02. *Stoke Rectory, 365A Walsgrave Road, Coventry CV2 4BG* Tel (024) 7663 5731 *or* 7644 3691 E-mail stoke.st.michael@fish.co.uk

FRANCIS, Kenneth. b 30. Em Coll Cam BA56 MA60. Coll of Resurr Mirfield. **d** 58 **p** 59. C De Beauvoir Town St Pet *Lon* 58-61; Zambia 62-70; V Harlow St Mary Magd *Chelmsf* 70-76; V Felixstowe St Jo *St E* 76-97; rtd 98. *33 Cordy's Lane, Trimley, Felixstowe IP10 0UD*

FRANCIS, Kenneth Charles. b 22. Oak Hill Th Coll 46. **d** 50 **p** 51. C Wandsworth All SS *S'wark* 50-53; V Deptford St Nic w Ch Ch 53-61; V Summerstown 61-77; R Cratfield w Heveningham and Ubbeston etc *St E* 77-87; rtd 87; Perm to Offic *Truro* from 87. *Wheal Alfred, Chapel Hill, Bolingey, Perranporth TR6 0DQ* Tel (01872) 571317

FRANCIS, Canon Leslie John. b 47. Pemb Coll Ox BA70 MA74 BD90 Nottm Univ MTh76 Qu Coll Cam PhD76 ScD97 Lon Univ MSc77 FBPsS88 FCP94. Westcott Ho Cam 70. **d** 73 **p** 74. C Haverhill *St E* 73-77; P-in-c Gt Bradley 78-82; P-in-c Lt Wratting 79-82; Research Officer Culham Coll Inst 82-88; P-in-c N Cerney w Bagendon *Glouc* 82-85; Perm to Offic 85-95; Fell Trin Coll Carmarthen 89-99; Dean of Chpl 95-99; Prof Th Univ of Wales (Lamp) 92-99; Prof Th Univ of Wales (Ban) from 99; Perm to Offic *Ox* 95-01; Hon Can St D Cathl *St D* from 98. *University of Wales, Neuadd Ardudwy, Holyhead Road, Bangor LL57 2PX* Tel (01248) 382566 Fax 383954 E-mail l.j.francis@bangor.ac.uk

FRANCIS, Martin Rufus. b 37. Pemb Coll Ox BA60 MA64. Linc Th Coll 60. **d** 63 **p** 64. C W Hartlepool St Paul *Dur* 63-67; C Yeovil St Jo w Preston Plucknett *B & W* 67-69; Chapl Tonbridge Sch 69-83; Chapl and Dep Hd St Jo Sch Leatherhead 83-94; R Herstmonceux and Wartling *Chich* 94-01; rtd 01; Perm to Offic *Sarum* from 02. *50 Lower Bryanston, Blandford Forum DT11 0DR* Tel (01258) 488619

FRANCIS, Paul Edward. b 52. Southn Univ BTh84. Sarum & Wells Th Coll 78. **d** 81 **p** 82. C Biggin Hill *Roch* 81-85; R Fawkham and Hartley 85-90; V Aylesford 90-99; V Riverhead w Dunton Green from 99; Chapl Dioc Assn of Readers from 01; RD Sevenoaks from 05. *The Vicarage, Riverhead, Sevenoaks TN13 3BS* Tel (01732) 455736

FRANCIS, Peter Brereton. b 53. St Andr Univ MTh77. Qu Coll Birm 77. **d** 78 **p** 79. C Hagley *Worc* 78-81; Chapl Qu Mary Coll *Lon* 81-87; R Ayr *Glas* 87-92; Miss to Seamen 87-92; Provost St Mary's Cathl *Glas* 92-96; R Glas St Mary 92-96; Warden and Lib St Deiniol's Lib Hawarden from 97. *St Deiniol's Library, Church Lane, Hawarden, Deeside CH5 3LT* Tel (01244) 532350 E-mail deiniol.visitors@btinternet.com

FRANCIS, Peter Philip. b 48. St Jo Coll Dur BA73. Wycliffe Hall Ox 73. **d** 75 **p** 76. C Foord St Jo *Cant* 75-78; C Morden *S'wark* 78-83; P-in-c Barford St Martin, Dinton, Baverstock etc *Sarum* 83-88; P-in-c Fovant, Sutton Mandeville and Teffont Evias etc 83-86; R Newick *Chich* from 88. *The Rectory, Church Road, Newick, Lewes BN8 4JX* Tel (01825) 722692

FRANCIS, Philip Thomas. b 58. TD03. St D Coll Lamp BA81 Regent's Park Coll Ox MTh99. Chich Th Coll 81. **d** 82 **p** 83. C Llanelli St Paul *St D* 82-84; C Barnsley St Mary *Wakef* 84-87; V Burton Dassett *Cov* from 87; V Gaydon w Chadshunt from 87; CF (TA) from 88. *Burton Dassett Vicarage, Northend, Southam CV47 2TH* Tel (01295) 770400 E-mail philip.francis@regents.ox.ac.uk

FRANCIS, Younis. b 66. **d** 95 **p** 95. C Addington *S'wark* from 05. *56 Viney Bank, Courtwood Lane, Croydon CR0 9JT* Tel (020) 8688 2663 E-mail younis_francis@hotmail.com

FRANCIS-DEHQANI, Gulnar Eleanor (Guli). b 66. Nottm Univ BA89 Bris Univ MA94 PhD99. SEITE 95. **d** 98 **p** 99. C Mortlake w E Sheen *S'wark* 98-02; Chapl R Academy of Music *Lon* 02-04; Chapl St Marylebone C of E Sch 02-04; Perm to Offic *Pet* from 04. *The Vicarage, Vicarage Road, Oakham LE15 6EG* Tel and fax (01572) 722108 Mobile 07771-948190 E-mail guli@uwclub.net

FRANCIS-DEHQANI, Lee Thomas. b 67. Nottm Univ BA89. Sarum & Wells Th Coll 92 Trin Coll Bris BA95. **d** 95 **p** 96. C Putney St Mary *S'wark* 95-98; TV Richmond St Mary w St Matthias and St Jo 98-04; P-in-c Oakham, Hambleton, Egleton, Braunston and Brooke *Pet* from 04; P-in-c Langham from 04; C Teigh w Whissendine and Market Overton from 04; C Cottesmore and Barrow w Ashwell and Burley from 04. *The Vicarage, Vicarage Road, Oakham LE15 6EG* Tel and fax (01572) 722108 Mobile 07867-503059 E-mail oakhamvicarage@uwclub.net

FRANÇOIS, Frère. *See* DIZERENS, Charles Robert

FRANK, Derek John. b 49. ACGI70 Imp Coll Lon BScEng70 Warwick Univ MSc71. Cranmer Hall Dur 83. **d** 85 **p** 86. C Clay Cross *Derby* 85-87; C Crookes St Thos *Sheff* 87-90; TV 90-93; Chapl Vevey w Château d'Oex and Villars *Eur* 93-02. *Address temp unknown*

FRANK, Penelope Edith. b 45. WMMTC 96. **d** 99 **p** 00. NSM Edgbaston St Geo *Birm* 99-02; Perm to Offic *Cov* 03-04; NSM Deanery of Kenilworth from 04; CPAS from 87. *CPAS, Athena Drive, Tachbrook Park, Warwick CV3 6NG* Tel (01926) 458446 E-mail pfrank@cpas.org.uk

FRANK, Canon Richard Patrick Harry. b 40. St Chad's Coll Dur BA66 DipTh68. **d** 68 **p** 69. C Darlington H Trin *Dur* 68-72; C Monkwearmouth St Andr 72-74; C-in-c Harlow Green CD 74-79; R Skelton and Hutton-in-the-Forest w Ivegill *Carl* 79-86; V Carl St Luke Morton 86-92; RD Carl 88-89; P-in-c Thursby 89-90; P-in-c Kirkbride w Newton Arlosh 89-92; TR Greystoke, Matterdale, Mungrisdale etc 92-98; P-in-c Patterdale 95-98; TR Gd Shep TM 98-99; RD Penrith 96-99; Hon Can Carl Cathl 97-99; rtd 99; Perm to Offic *Carl* 00-02; *York* from 02. *11 Risby Place, Beverley HU17 8NT* Tel (01482) 679540 E-mail richardandann.frank@virgin.net

FRANK, Richard Stephen. b 70. Keble Coll Ox MEng93 Fitzw Coll Cam MA98. Ridley Hall Cam 96. **d** 99 **p** 00. C Cranham Park *Chelmsf* 99-04; P-in-c St Margaret's-on-Thames *Lon* from 05. *295 St Margarets Road, Twickenham TW1 1PN* Tel (020) 8891 3504 Mobile 07973-719730 E-mail richardfrank@allsoulschurch.org.uk

FRANKLAND, Angela Tara. b 69. Lon Bible Coll BA96 MA98. EAMTC 97. **d** 99 **p** 00. C Hornchurch St Andr *Chelmsf* 99-03; TV Wickford and Runwell from 03. *8 Friern Walk, Wickford SS12 0HZ* Tel (01268) 734077 E-mail tfrankland@btinternet.com

FRANKLIN, Hector Aloysius. b 32. N Ord Course 94. **d** 97 **p** 98. NSM Chapeltown *Sheff* 97-99; P-in-c Sheff St Paul 99-02; rtd 02; Perm to Offic *Sheff* from 04. *108 Mackenzie Crescent, Burncross, Sheffield S35 1US* Tel 0114-245 7160

FRANKLIN, Joan Mary. b 20. St Andr Ho Portsm 47. **dss** 61 **d** 87. Scunthorpe St Jo *Linc* 66-70; Gt Grimsby St Mary and St Jas 70-86; rtd 86. *41 Ferry Road, Scunthorpe DN15 8QF* Tel (01724) 846685

FRANKLIN, Canon Lewis Owen. b 46. Natal Univ BSc67. S'wark Ord Course 68. **d** 73 **p** 74. S Africa 73-99; C Durban St Paul 74-75; R Newcastle H Trin 76-79; Dir St Geo Cathl Cen Cape Town 80-83; Chapl St Geo Gr Sch 84-86; R Sea Pt H Redeemer 87-89; R Cape Town St Paul 89-90; Subdean and Prec Kimberley Cathl 91-94 and 96-99; Hon Can from 93; Dioc Sec Kimberley and Kuruman 94-96; C Altrincham St Geo *Ches* 99-00; P-in-c Newcastle St Paul *Lich* from 00. *St Paul's Vicarage, Hawkstone Close, Newcastle ST5 1HT* Tel (01782) 617913 E-mail owenf@4u2give.com

FRANKLIN, Richard Charles Henry. b 48. Ch Ch Coll Cant CertEd70. Sarum & Wells Th Coll 75. **d** 78 **p** 79. C Pershore w Pinvin, Wick and Birlingham *Worc* 78-80; Educn Chapl 80-85; V Wollescote 85-92; V Fareham SS Pet and Paul *Portsm* 92-98; V Luton All SS w St Pet *St Alb* from 98; RD Luton from 02. *All Saints' Vicarage, Shaftesbury Road, Luton LU4 8AH* Tel (01582) 720129 E-mail richardfranklin@mail2world.com

FRANKLIN, Canon Richard Heighway. b 54. Southn Univ BA75 MPhil83. Sarum & Wells Th Coll 75. **d** 78 **p** 79. C Thame w Towersey *Ox* 78-81; Asst Chapl Southn Univ *Win* 81-83; Dir of Studies Chich Th Coll 83-89; P-in-c Stalbridge *Sarum* 89-94; V Weymouth H Trin from 94; Can and Preb Sarum Cathl from 02; RD Weymouth from 04. *Holy Trinity Vicarage, 7 Glebe Close, Weymouth DT4 9RL* Tel (01305) 760354 *or* 774597 E-mail richardfranklin@iname.com

FRANKLIN (née WESTMACOTT), Mrs Rosemary Margaret. b 41. WEMTC 03. **d** 05. NSM Cirencester *Glouc* from 05.

Waterton Farm House, Ampney Crucis, Cirencester GL7 5RR Tel (01285) 654282 E-mail rosemary@franklin509.freeserve.co.uk

FRANKLIN, Simon George. b 54. Bris Univ BA75. Ridley Hall Cam 77. **d** 79 **p** 80. C Woodmansterne *S'wark* 79-83; C St Peter-in-Thanet *Cant* 83-86; R Woodchurch 86-96; P-in-c Ottery St Mary, Alfington, W Hill, Tipton etc *Ex* 96-99; TR from 99. *The Vicar's House, 7 College Road, Ottery St Mary EX11 1DQ* Tel (01404) 812062 E-mail stpaul_church@lineone.net *or* safranklin@btopenworld.com

FRANKLIN, Stephen Alaric. b 58. Lon Univ BD87. Sarum & Wells Th Coll 87. **d** 89 **p** 90. C Chenies and Lt Chalfont, Latimer and Flaunden *Ox* 89-93; CF from 93. *c/o MOD Chaplains (Army)* Tel (01980) 615804 Fax 615800

FRANKLIN, William Henry. b 50. Macquarie Univ (NSW) BA78 Birkbeck Coll Lon MA82. Moore Th Coll Sydney 76 Melbourne Coll of Div 83 Chich Th Coll 85. **d** 86 **p** 87. C S Leamington St Jo *Cov* 86-89; Chapl RN from 89. *Royal Naval Chaplaincy Service, Room 203, Victory Building, HM Naval Base, Portsmouth PO1 3LS* Tel (023) 9272 7903 Fax 9272 7111

FRANKS, John Edward. b 29. **d** 61 **p** 62. C Plymouth St Matthias *Ex* 61-66; V Upton Grey w Weston Patrick and Tunworth *Win* 66-77; V Upton Grey, Weston Patrick, Tunworth etc 77-79; P-in-c Wolverton cum Ewhurst and Hannington 79-80; R Baughurst, Ramsdell, Wolverton w Ewhurst etc 81-94; rtd 94. *57 Victoria, Santa Lucija, Naxxar, NXR 02, Malta* Tel (00356) 2143 7006

FRANKS, John William. b 45. K Alfred's Coll Win BEd87 DAES94 MISM89. STETS 97. **d** 00 **p** 01. NSM Fareham H Trin *Portsm* 00-03; Hon Chapl Pitmore Sch Chandler's Ford 00-01; Hon Chapl Fareham Coll of F&HE 01-03; C Rowner *Portsm* from 03; C Bridgemary from 05. *St Matthew's Vicarage, 7 Duncton Way, Gosport PO13 0FD* Tel (01329) 828858

FRANKUM, Matthew David Hyatt. b 65. Leic Poly BSc87. Trin Coll Bris DipHE99. **d** 99 **p** 00. C Bath St Luke *B & W* 99-03; TV Worle from 03. *The Vicarage, 21 Westmarch Way, Weston-super-Mare BS22 7JY* Tel (01934) 513294 E-mail m.frankum@fish.co.uk

FRANSELLA, Cortland Lucas. b 48. Trin Hall Cam BA70 MA74 Heythrop Coll Lon MA00. NTMTC AdDipTh98 ADPS98. **d** 98 **p** 99. NSM Palmers Green St Jo *Lon* 98-03; NSM Hornsey St Mary w St Geo from 03. *17 Warner Road, London N8 7HB* Tel and fax (020) 8340 7706 E-mail fransella@btinternet.com

FRANZ, Canon Kevin Gerhard. b 53. Edin Univ MA74 BD79 PhD92. Edin Th Coll 76. **d** 79 **p** 80. C Edin St Martin *Edin* 79-83; R Selkirk 83-90; Provost St Ninian's Cathl Perth *St And* 90-99; R Perth St Ninian 90-99; Gen Sec Action of Churches Together in Scotland from 99; Hon Can St Ninian's Cathl Perth from 00. *Scottish Churches House, Kirk Street, Dunblane FK15 0AJ* Tel (01786) 823588 Fax 825844 E-mail kevinfranz@acts-scotland.org

FRASER, Alister Douglas. b 26. Qu Coll Cam BA49 MA55. Tyndale Hall Bris 50. **d** 68 **p** 69. C Weymouth St Jo *Sarum* 68-72; R Kingswood *Glouc* 72-80; V Woodside St Steph 80-84; RD Forest S 84-88; V Cinderford St Steph w Littledean 84-90; rtd 90; Perm to Offic *Ex* from 91. *4 Stevens Cross Close, Sidmouth EX10 9QJ* Tel (01395) 579568

FRASER, Andrew Thomas. b 52. Newc Univ Aus BA81. St Jo Coll (NSW) ThL79. **d** 81 **p** 82. Australia 81-87; C Prestbury *Glouc* 87-91; C Wotton St Mary 91-92. *79 Victoria Street, Gloucester GL1 4EP* Tel (01452) 381082

FRASER, Christine Nancy. b 61. TISEC 98. **d** 02 **p** 03. NSM St Ninian's Cathl Perth *St And* from 02. *9 Balvaird Place, Perth PH1 5EA* Tel (01738) 623827 E-mail cnfraser@btinternet.com

FRASER, David Ian. b 32. Em Coll Cam BA54 MA58. Oak Hill Th Coll 56. **d** 58 **p** 59. C Bedford St Jo *St Alb* 58-61; C Cheadle Hulme St Andr *Ches* 61-64; R Fringford w Hethe and Newton Purcell *Ox* 64-67; V Preston St Luke *Blackb* 67-71; V Surbiton Hill Ch Ch *S'wark* 71-91; rtd 91; Perm to Offic *Ox* from 97. *7 Godwyn Close, Abingdon OX14 1BU* Tel (01235) 532049

FRASER, Geoffrey Michael. b 29. Sarum Th Coll. **d** 59 **p** 60. C Thames Ditton *Guildf* 59-63; C Shere 63-65; C Dunsford and Doddiscombsleigh *Ex* 65-70; V Uffculme 70-92; rtd 92; Perm to Offic *Worc* from 92. *46 Priory Road, Malvern WR14 3DB* Tel (01684) 576302

FRASER, Giles Anthony. b 64. Newc Univ BA84 Ox Univ BA92 MA97 Lanc Univ PhD99. Ripon Coll Cuddesdon. **d** 93 **p** 94. C Streetly *Lich* 93-97; C Ox St Mary V w St Cross and St Pet *Ox* 97-00; Chapl Wadh Coll Ox 97-00; V Putney St Mary *S'wark* 00-04; TR from 04. *The Vicarage, 45 St John's Avenue, London SW15 6AL* Tel (020) 8788 4575

FRASER, Canon Jane Alicia. b 44. Man Univ BA. Glouc Sch of Min 86. **d** 89 **p** 94. NSM Upton on Severn *Worc* 89-00; NSM Ripple, Earls Croome w Hill Croome and Strensham 97-00; Faith Adv Dept of Health's Adv Gp on Teenage Pregnancy from 00; NSM Upton-on-Severn, Ripple, Earls Croome etc *Worc* from 00; Hon Can Worc Cathl from 05. *Sunnybank House, Holly Green, Upton-upon-Severn, Worcester WR8 0PG* Tel (01684) 594715 E-mail ministry@revjane.demon.co.uk

FRASER, Leslie. b 34. ALCD62. **d** 62 **p** 63. C St Helens St Matt Thatto Heath *Liv* 62-64; C Fazakerley Em 64-67; R Collyhurst St Oswald and St Cath *Man* 67-72; P-in-c Collyhurst St Jas 67-72; R Collyhurst 72-74; RNLI 75-92; rtd 95; Hon C Bispham *Blackb* 95-98; Perm to Offic 98-00; P-in-c Bridekirk *Carl* 99-04. *Bridesbeck Cottage, Dovenby, Cockermouth CA13 0PG* Tel (01900) 821282

FRASER, Leslie John. b 60. OLM course 96. **d** 99 **p** 00. NSM Thamesmead *S'wark* 99-04; Perm to Offic from 05. *4 Goldcrest Close, London SE28 8JA* Tel (020) 8473 4736 E-mail les.fraser@lineone.net

FRASER, Mark Adrian. b 69. Warwick Univ BSc90 Birm Univ MSc91. St Jo Coll Nottm MTh04. **d** 05. C Astley Bridge *Man* from 05. *St Paul's Vicarage, Halliwell Road, Bolton BL1 8BP* Tel (01204) 497260 Mobile 07963-397688 E-mail markandcatherine@care4free.net

FRASER-SMITH, Keith Montague. b 48. St Jo Coll Dur BA70. Trin Coll Bris. **d** 73 **p** 74. C Bishopsworth *Bris* 73-75; CMS 76-84; Egypt 76-80; Jerusalem 80-84; Asst Chapl Marseille w St Raphaël, Aix-en-Provence etc *Eur* 84-90; Media Dir Arab World Min 84-92; E Area Dir 92-97; Dep Internat Dir 97-98; NSM Worthing Ch the King *Chich* 90-93; Cyprus 93-97; NSM Tranmere St Cath *Ches* 97-98; P-in-c Barnton 98-03; Dir Global Mobilisation Arab World Min from 03; Perm to Offic *Ches* from 03. *33 Lord Street, Crewe CW2 7DH* Tel (01270) 214212 E-mail keithfs@domini.org

FRAY, Bernard Herbert. b 44. Worc Coll of Educn CertEd65 Open Univ BA73 LTCL67. Cranmer Hall Dur 02. **d** 03 **p** 04. NSM Long Marston *York* from 03; NSM Rufforth w Moor Monkton and Hessay from 03; NSM Healaugh w Wighill, Bilbrough and Askham Richard from 03; NSM Tockwith and Bilton w Bickerton from 03. *The Vicarage, 32 Westfield Road, Tockwith, York YO26 7PY* Tel (01423) 358998 E-mail bernardfray@hotmail.com

FRAY, Roger William. b 43. Philippa Fawcett Coll TCert69 Reading Univ BEd76. St Jo Coll Nottm MA95. **d** 95 **p** 96. C Grove *Ox* 95-99; P-in-c Brittany *Eur* from 99. *14A Le Lesnot, 56460 La Chapelle-Caro, France* Tel (0033) (2) 97 74 97 93 E-mail fraylesnot@aol.com

FRAY, Vernon Francis. b 41. Southn Coll of Tech HNC62 FCIOB79. S'wark Ord Course 91. **d** 94 **p** 95. NSM Heston *Lon* 94-96; NSM Twickenham All Hallows 96-02; NSM Teddington St Mark and Hampton Wick St Jo from 02. *198 Broom Road, Teddington TW11 9PQ* Tel (020) 8977 2068 E-mail vfray@btinternet.com

FRAY, Vivienne Jane. *See* KERNER, Vivienne Jane

FRAYLING, The Very Revd Nicholas Arthur. b 44. Ex Univ BA69 Liv Univ Hon LLD01. Cuddesdon Coll 69. **d** 71 **p** 72. C Peckham St Jo *S'wark* 71-74; V Tooting All SS 74-83; Can Res and Prec Liv Cathl *Liv* 83-87; R Liv Our Lady and St Nic w St Anne 87-90; TR 90-02; Hon Can Liv Cathl 89-02; Dean Chich from 02. *The Deanery, Canon Lane, Chichester PO19 1PX* Tel (01243) 812485 *or* 812494 E-mail dean@chichestercathedral.org.uk

FRAYNE, The Very Revd David. b 34. St Edm Hall Ox BA58 MA62 Birm Univ DipTh60. Qu Coll Birm 58. **d** 60 **p** 61. C E Wickham *S'wark* 60-63; C Lewisham St Jo Southend 63-67; V N Sheen St Phil and All SS 67-73; R Caterham 73-83; RD Caterham 80-83; Hon Can S'wark Cathl 82-83; V Bris St Mary Redcliffe w Temple etc *Bris* 83-92; RD Bedminster 86-92; Hon Can Bris Cathl 91-92; Provost Blackb 92-00; Dean Blackb 00-01; rtd 01; Perm to Offic *Sarum* from 02. *Newlands Cottage, Peacemarsh, Gillingham SP8 4HD* Tel (01747) 824065

FRAZER, David. b 60. QUB BSSc. TCD Div Sch. **d** 84 **p** 85. C Taney *D & G* 84-87; C Dublin Ch Ch Cathl Gp 87-88; I Clane w Donadea and Coolcarrigan *M & K* from 88. *Meath and Kildare Diocesan Centre, Moyglare, Maynooth, Co Kildare, Irish Republic* Tel (00353) 87-266 1587 (mobile) E-mail dfrazer@eircom.net

FRAZER, Ian Martin. b 44. QUB BTh. **d** 91 **p** 93. Lic to Offic *D & D* 91-98; NSM Orangefield w Moneyreagh from 98. *The Stacks, Deramore Park South, Belfast BT9 5JY* Tel (028) 9066 7100

FRAZER, Canon James Stewart. b 27. TCD Dip Bibl Studies. TCD Div Sch. **d** 57 **p** 58. C Belfast Whiterock *Conn* 57-59; C Belfast St Matt 59-61; I Lack *Clogh* 61-64; I Mullaglass *Arm* 64-65; I Milltown 65-70; Australia 70-74; I Heathcote w Axedale 70-72; I Kangaroo Par w Marong, Lockwood and Ravenswood 72-74; I Dromore *Clogh* 74-82; Bp Dom Chapl 82; I Derryvullen S w Garvary 82-90; Can Clogh Cathl 83-85; Preb 85-94; I Clogh w Errigal Portclare 90-94; Glebes Sec 91-94; Chan Clogh Cathl 93-94; rtd 94. *8 Carsons Avenue, Ballygowan, Newtownards BT23 5GD* Tel (028) 9752 1562

FREAR, Canon Philip Scott. b 45. Univ of Wales (Lamp) BA66. Bris & Glouc Tr Course 77. **d** 80 **p** 81. Hon C Purton *Bris* 80-81; C Rodbourne Cheney 81-85; V Hengrove 85-95; V Braddan *S & M* from 95; Perm to Offic *B & W* from 95; Chapl Isle of Man Dept of Health and Social Security from 98; Can St German's Cathl *S & M* from 04. *The Vicarage, Saddle Road, Braddan, Isle of Man IM4 4LB* Tel (01624) 675523

FREARSON, Andrew Richard. b 57. BA. Wycliffe Hall Ox. **d** 83 **p** 84. C Acocks Green *Birm* 83-86; C Moseley St Mary 86-89; P-in-c Holme *Blackb* 89-96; USA from 96. *3136 Lynnray Drive, Doraville, GA 30340, USA*

FREATHY, Nigel Howard. b 46. Lon Univ BA68 CertEd. Sarum & Wells Th Coll 79. **d** 81 **p** 82. C Crediton *Ex* 81-82; C Crediton and Shobrooke 82-84; TV Ex St Thos and Em 84-86; V Beer and Branscombe 86-01; P-in-c Stockland, Dalwood, Kilmington and Shute 01-03; V Kilmington, Stockland, Dalwood, Yarcombe etc from 03; RD Honiton 96-99. *The Vicarage, Kilmington, Axminster EX13 7RF* Tel (01297) 33156 E-mail nigel@freathy9813.freeserve.co.uk

FREDERICK, John Bassett Moore. b 30. Princeton Univ BA51 Birm Univ PhD73. Gen Th Sem (NY) MDiv54. **d** 54 **p** 55. USA 54-56 and 61-71; C All Hallows Barking *Lon* 56-58; C Ox SS Phil and Jas *Ox* 58-60; R Bletchingley *S'wark* 74-95; Reigate Adnry Ecum Officer 90-95; RD Godstone 92-95; rtd 95. *32 Chestnut Street, Princeton, NJ 08542, USA* Tel (001) (609) 924 7590 Fax 924 1694 E-mail jf9642@netscape.net

FREDERICK, Warren Charles. b 47. Illinois Univ BSc. Qu Coll Birm 86. **d** 88 **p** 89. C W Leigh *Portsm* 88-91; V N Holmwood *Guildf* 91-00; R Cumberland H Cross USA from 00. *612 Brookfield Avenue, Cumberland, MD 21502, USA* Tel (001) (301) 759 2688

FREDRIKSEN, Martin. b 47. St Chad's Coll Dur BA69 DipTh70 Univ of Wales (Lamp) MA03. **d** 70 **p** 71. C Bideford *Ex* 70-73; C Guildf St Nic *Guildf* 73-76; R Cossington *B & W* 76-82; V Woolavington 76-82; Asst Chapl K Coll Taunton 82-84; C Bp's Hatfield *St Alb* 84-94; P-in-c Broadstone *Sarum* 94; V from 94. *St John's Vicarage, Macaulay Road, Broadstone BH18 8AR* Tel (01202) 694109 E-mail fr.martin1@eggconnect.net

FREE, Canon James Michael. b 25. K Coll Lon BD50 AKC50. **d** 51 **p** 52. C Corsham *Bris* 51-54; Trinidad and Tobago 54-62; PC Knowle St Barn *Bris* 62-67; V Pilning 67-75; P-in-c Lydiard Millicent w Lydiard Tregoz 75-82; Hon Can Bris Cathl 76-82; Can Res, Prec and Sacr Bris Cathl 82-83; Can Treas 83-90; Bp's Adv for Miss 82-87; Bp's Officer for Miss and Evang 87-89; rtd 90; Perm to Offic *B & W* 90-03 and *Bris* from 90; P-in-c Haselbury Plucknett, Misterton and N Perrott *B & W* from 03. *The Rectory, New Street, North Perrott, Crewkerne TA18 7ST* Tel (01460) 271489

FREEBAIRN-SMITH, Canon Jane. b 36. K Coll Lon DipTh59. St Chris Coll Blackheath IDC60. **d** 88 **p** 94. NSM Uddingston *Glas* 88-91; NSM Cambuslang 88-91; Dioc Missr 88-92; Dioc Past Cllr 92-95; NSM Baillieston 91-92; C St Mary's Cathl 92-95; TV Hykeham *Linc* 95-03; Can and Preb Linc Cathl 02-03; rtd 04. *12 Bell Grove, Lincoln LN6 7PL* Tel (01522) 705421

FREEBORN, John Charles Kingon. b 30. G&C Coll Cam BA52 MA56. Ridley Hall Cam 53. **d** 55 **p** 56. C Doncaster St Geo *Sheff* 55-57; Tutor Wycliffe Hall Ox 57-61; R Flixton St Mich *Man* 61-72; C Leic H Apostles *Leic* 72-73; Teacher Greenacres Sch Oldham 73-75; C E Crompton *Man* 73-74; Hon C Ashton St Mich 74-76; Teacher St Jo Sch Ellesmere 75-79; Perm to Offic 77-80; Hd Master H Trin Sch Halifax 80-88; Teacher St Chad's Sch Hove Edge Wakef 88-91; Lic to Offic *Wakef* 80-83; Hon C Sowerby 83-94; NSM Halifax All SS from 94; rtd 95; Perm to Offic *Bradf* from 01. *27 Crossley Hill, Halifax HX3 0PL* Tel (01422) 342489

FREEMAN, Canon Alan John Samuel. b 27. SS Coll Cam BA48 MA52. Sarum Th Coll 50. **d** 52 **p** 53. C Tottenham Ch Ch W Green *Lon* 52-55; C Harpenden St Nic *St Alb* 55-60; R Aspley Guise 60-75; RD Fleete 67-70; RD Ampthill 70-75; Hon Can St Alb 74-92; V Boxmoor St Jo 75-92; Chapl Hemel Hempstead Gen Hosp (W Herts Wing) 75-92; RD Berkhamsted *St Alb* 85-92; rtd 92; Perm to Offic *St Alb* from 00. *3A Queen Street, Leighton Buzzard LU7 1BZ* Tel (01525) 384799

FREEMAN, Anthony John Curtis. b 46. Ex Coll Ox BA68 MA72. Cuddesdon Coll 70. **d** 72 **p** 73. C Worc St Martin *Worc* 72-74; C Worc St Martin w St Pet 74-75; Bp's Dom Chapl *Chich* 75-78; C-in-c Parklands St Wilfrid CD 78-82; V Durrington 82-89; P-in-c Staplefield Common 89-94; Bp's Adv on CME 89-93; Asst Dir of Ords 89-93. *4 Godolphin Close, Newton St Cyres, Exeter EX5 5BZ* Tel (01392) 851453 Fax as telephone E-mail anthony@imprint.co.uk

FREEMAN, Douglas James. b 20. Ox NSM Course 80. **d** 83 **p** 84. NSM Ellesborough *Ox* 83-91; NSM Ellesborough, The Kimbles and Stoke Mandeville 91-00 and from 04. *29 Chadley, Chalkshire Road, Butlers Cross, Aylesbury HP17 0TS* Tel (01296) 623240

FREEMAN, Gordon Bertie. b 37. CITC BTh95. **d** 95 **p** 96. C Lecale Gp *D & D* 95-98; I Ardara w Glencolumbkille, Inniskeel etc *D & R* from 98. *The Rectory, Ardara, Lifford, Co Donegal, Irish Republic* Tel (00353) (73) 954 1124 E-mail ardara@raphoe.anglican.org

FREEMAN, James Henry. b 14. **d** 79 **p** 80. Hon C Wandsworth St Steph *S'wark* 79-97. *53 Coombe Gardens, New Malden KT3 4AB*

FREEMAN, Jane. b 54. Dur Univ BA75 PhD80. Qu Coll Birm BD00. **d** 00 **p** 01. C Waterloo St Jo w St Andr *S'wark* 00-03; TV E Ham w Upton Park St Alb *Chelmsf* from 03. *The Rectory, Navarre Road, London E6 3AQ* Tel (020) 8470 8703 Mobile 07702-922818 E-mail email@janefreeman.org.uk

FREEMAN, Karl Fredrick. b 57. St Luke's Coll Ex BEd80. **d** 90 **p** 91. C Plymouth St Andr w St Paul and St Geo *Ex* 90-95; TV Plymouth St Andr and St Paul Stonehouse 95-96; Chapl Coll of SS Mark and Jo Plymouth 96-01; TR Plymouth Em, St Paul Efford and St Aug from 01. *The Rectory, 9 Seymour Drive, Plymouth PL3 5BG* Tel (01752) 248601 *or* 260317 E-mail revkarl@aol.com

FREEMAN, Malcolm Robin. b 48. Master Mariner 78. St And NSM Tr Scheme 85. **d** 88 **p** 89. NSM Kirkcaldy *St And* 88-94; NSM Westbury *Sarum* 99-02; R Tidworth, Ludgershall and Faberstown from 02. *The Rectory, 10 St James's Street, Ludgershall, Andover SP11 9QF* Tel (01264) 791202 Mobile 07810-862740 E-mail fgmastermariner@aol.com

FREEMAN (née ADAMS), Mrs Margaret Anne. b 27. AKC48. Gilmore Ho. **dss** 82 **d** 87 **p** 94. Gt Yarmouth *Nor* 80-87; rtd 87; Hon Par Dn Malborough w S Huish, W Alvington and Churchstow *Ex* 87-94; Hon C 94-96; Perm to Offic *Nor* 97-04. *9 Barton Way, Ormesby, Great Yarmouth NR29 5SD* Tel (01493) 730101

FREEMAN, Michael. *See* FREEMAN, Philip Michael

FREEMAN, Michael Charles. b 36. Magd Coll Cam BA61 MA68 Lon Univ BD69 PhD93. Clifton Th Coll 67. **d** 69 **p** 70. C Bedworth *Cov* 69-72; C Morden *S'wark* 72-77; P-in-c Westcombe Park St Geo 77-85; V Kingston Vale St Jo 85-94; rtd 99. *6 Wristland Road, Watchet TA23 0DH* Tel (01984) 634378 E-mail FreemMic@aol.com

FREEMAN, Michael Curtis. b 51. Lanc Univ BA72. Cuddesdon Coll 72. **d** 75 **p** 76. C Walton St Mary *Liv* 75-78; C Hednesford *Lich* 78-81; TV Solihull *Birm* 81-86; V Yardley Wood 86-90; V Farnworth *Liv* 90-03; AD Widnes 01-03; P-in-c Blundellsands St Mich from 03; P-in-c Gt Crosby All SS from 05. *St Michael's Vicarage, 41 Dowhills Road, Liverpool L23 8SJ* Tel 0151-924 9905 E-mail mcfreeman@freeuk.com

FREEMAN, Michael Raymond. b 58. Chu Coll Cam BA80 MA84 Ox Univ BA87. St Steph Ho Ox 85. **d** 88 **p** 89. C Clifton All SS w St Jo *Bris* 88-92; TV Elland *Wakef* 92-01; V Horninglow *Lich* from 01. *Horninglow Vicarage, 14 Rolleston Road, Burton-on-Trent DE13 0JZ* Tel (01283) 568613 E-mail cft-rfreeman@supanet.com

FREEMAN, Mrs Pamela Mary. b 45. WMMTC 83. **dss** 86 **d** 87 **p** 94. Cannock *Lich* 86-88; Par Dn 87-88; Min for Deaf (Salop Adnry) 88-95; Par Dn Shelton and Oxon 88-94; C 94-95; TV Stafford 95-00; P-in-c High Offley and Norbury 00-02; R Adbaston, High Offley, Knightley, Norbury etc from 02. *The Rectory, Newport Road, Woodseaves, Stafford ST20 0NP* Tel (01785) 284747 E-mail pmfreeman@bigfoot.com

FREEMAN, Peter Cameron Jessett. b 41. **d** 05. OLM Sturry w Fordwich and Westbere w Hersden *Cant* from 05. *29 Cedar Road, Sturry, Canterbury CT2 0HZ* E-mail fpeter@fish.co.uk

FREEMAN, Philip Martin (Brother Martin Philip). b 54. Westcott Ho Cam 76. **d** 79 **p** 80. C Stanley *Liv* 79-82; C Bromborough *Ches* 82-84; Chapl Halton Gen Hosp 84-91; V Runcorn H Trin *Ches* 84-91; R Ashton-upon-Mersey St Martin 91-96; SSF from 96; Perm to Offic *Sarum* 96-99 and *Birm* from 98. *Address temp unknown*

FREEMAN, Philip Michael. b 25. Jes Coll Cam BA50 MA54. Qu Coll Birm 50. **d** 52 **p** 53. C Gainsborough All SS *Linc* 52-58; V Messingham 58-65; V Goxhill 65-66; P-in-c Bottesford w Ashby 66-73; TR 73-75; P-in-c Warwick St Nic *Cov* 75-76; TV Warwick 77-87; P-in-c Claverdon w Preston Bagot 87-90; rtd 90; Perm to Offic *Cov* from 90. *38 Cocksparrow Street, Warwick CV34 4ED* Tel (01926) 411431

FREEMAN, Richard Alan. b 52. Ripon Coll Cuddesdon. **d** 83 **p** 84. C Crayford *Roch* 83-86; V Slade Green 86-94; R Eynsford w Farningham and Lullingstone 94-01; P-in-c Shoreham from 01; Chapl St Mich Sch Otford from 01. *The Vicarage, Station Road, Shoreham, Sevenoaks TN14 7SA* Tel (01959) 522363 E-mail ricktherec@aol.com

FREEMAN, The Ven Robert John. b 52. St Jo Coll Dur BSc74 Fitzw Coll Cam BA76 MA. Ridley Hall Cam 74. **d** 77 **p** 78. C Blackpool St Jo *Blackb* 77-81; TV Chigwell *Chelmsf* 81-85; V Leic Martyrs *Leic* 85-99; Hon Can Leic Cathl 94-03; RD Christianity S 95-98; Nat Adv in Evang 99-03; Lic to Offic *Leic* 99-03; Adn Halifax *Wakef* from 03. *2 Vicarage Gardens, Brighouse HD6 3HD* Tel (01484) 714553 Fax 711897 E-mail robert@frmn.com *or* archdeacon.halifax@wakefield.anglican.org

FREEMAN, Rodney. *See* FREEMAN, William Rodney

FREEMAN, Rosemary. b 47. **d** 03 **p** 04. NSM Madeley *Heref* from 03. *5 Rowley Close, Madeley, Telford TF7 5RR* Tel (01952) 583460

FREEMAN, Terence. b 40. Wells Th Coll 67. **d** 70 **p** 71. C Hanham *Bris* 70-75; C Cockington *Ex* 75-77; R Sampford Spiney w Horrabridge 77-89; V Wembury from 89; Hon Chapl

RN from 89. *The Vicarage, 63 Church Road, Wembury, Plymouth PL9 0JJ* Tel (01752) 862319
E-mail revkarl.freeman@lineone.net

FREEMAN, William Rodney. b 35. Ch Coll Cam MA63 FCA73. **d** 95 **p** 96. OLM Chelmondiston and Erwarton w Harkstead *St E* 95-05; rtd 05; Perm to Offic *St E* from 05. *Lavender Cottage, Harkstead, Ipswich IP9 1BN* Tel (01473) 328381
E-mail revrod@lavcot.freeserve.co.uk

FREER, Andrew Selwyn Bruce. b 26. Wells Th Coll 55. **d** 57 **p** 58. C Yardley St Edburgha *Birm* 57-62; R Byfield *Pet* 62-71; V Brackley St Pet w St Jas 71-81; R Bincombe w Broadwey, Upwey and Buckland Ripers *Sarum* 81-91; rtd 91; Perm to Offic *Sarum* 91-02 and *St E* from 04. *Appletree Cottage, High Street, Walsham-le-Willows, Bury St Edmunds IP31 3AA* Tel (01359) 259819

FREETH, Barry James. b 35. Birm Univ BA60. Tyndale Hall Bris 60. **d** 62 **p** 64. C Selly Hill St Steph *Birm* 62-63; C Birm St Jo Ladywood 63-71; Chapl RAF 71-75; P-in-c Crudwell w Ashley *Bris* 75-81; P-in-c Lanreath *Truro* 81-84; R 84-87; P-in-c Pelynt 81-84; V 84-87; R Harvington and Norton and Lenchwick *Worc* 87-93; V Ramsden, Finstock and Fawler, Leafield etc *Ox* 93-99; rtd 99; Perm to Offic *Derby* from 99. *The Vicarage, High Street, Cropredy, Banbury OX17 1NG* Tel (01295) 750799

FREETH, John Stanton. b 40. Selw Coll Cam BA62 MA66. Ridley Hall Cam 64. **d** 66 **p** 67. C Gillingham St Mark *Roch* 66-72; TV Heslington *York* 72-80; Chapl York Univ 72-80; TR Wynberg St Jo S Africa from 80; Adn Athlone 88-93. *15 Wellington Road, Wynberg, 7800 South Africa* Tel (0027) (21) 761 0908

FREETH, Patricia. b 48. Wycliffe Hall Ox BTh95. **d** 95 **p** 96. NSM Ramsden, Finstock and Fawler, Leafield etc *Ox* 95-99; TV Buxton w Burbage and King Sterndale *Derby* 99-03; V Shires' Edge *Ox* from 03. *The Vicarage, High Street, Cropredy, Banbury OX17 1NG* Tel (01295) 750799 Mobile 07947-436751
E-mail patfreeth@objn.freeserve.co.uk

FREMMER, Ludger. b 56. Ridley Hall Cam 02. **d** 04 **p** 05. C Mattishall w Mattishall Burgh, Welborne etc *Nor* from 04. *The New Rectory, Rectory Road, Hockering, Dereham NR20 3HP* Tel (01603) 880199 Mobile 07753-213145
E-mail ludger.fremmer@tesco.net

FRENCH, Basil Charles Elwell. b 19. Edin Th Coll LTh44. **d** 45 **p** 46. C Falkirk *Edin* 45-46; C Bris St Aid *Bris* 46-49; C Hendford *B & W* 49-51; V Ash 51-58; P-in-c Long Load 57-58; S Rhodesia 59-65; Rhodesia 65-80; Zimbabwe 80-85; rtd 85; Hon C Wrington w Butcombe *B & W* 85-88; Perm to Offic *B & W* 88-92 and *Ex* from 92. *9 Elmbridge Gardens, Exeter EX4 4AE* Tel (01392) 215933

FRENCH, Clive Anthony. b 43. AKC70. St Aug Coll Cant 70. **d** 71 **p** 72. C Monkseaton St Mary *Newc* 71-73; Dioc Youth Adv 73-76; Chapl RN 76-97; Chapl RN Coll Greenwich 75-97; Dir of Ords RN 85-90; R Cheam *S'wark* from 97. *The Rectory, 33 Mickleham Gardens, Cheam, Sutton SM3 8QJ* Tel (020) 8641 4664

FRENCH, Daniel Alain. b 68. Kent Univ BSc91. St Jo Sem Wonersh BTh97. **d** 97 **p** 98. In RC Ch 97-01; P-in-c Aberdeen St Clem *Ab* from 03. *St Clement's Church House, Mastrick Drive, Aberdeen AB16 6UF* Tel (01224) 662247
E-mail stclements@tiscali.co.uk

FRENCH, Canon Dendle Charles. b 29. Lon Univ BD56. ALCD55. **d** 56 **p** 57. C Gt Yarmouth *Nor* 56-63; Jamaica 63-66; V Sedgeford w Southmere *Nor* 66-71; P-in-c Gt Ringstead 66-67; R 67-71; TV Thetford 71-74; Chapl Hockerill Coll Bishop's Stortford 74-78; P-in-c St Paul's Walden *St Alb* 78-85; V 85-94; RD Hitchin 84-89; Hon Can St Alb 91-94; rtd 94; Chapl Glamis Castle from 94. *Woodfaulds, 7 Braehead Road, Glamis, Angus DD8 1RW* Tel and fax (01307) 840485
E-mail dendle.french@talk21.com

FRENCH, Derek John. b 47. Man Univ BA03. Ripon Coll Cuddesdon DipMin95. **d** 95 **p** 96. C Stand *Man* 95-98; TV E Farnworth and Kearsley 98-00; P-in-c Halliwell St Marg from 00. *St Margaret's Vicarage, 1 Somerset Road, Bolton BL1 4NE* Tel (01204) 840850 E-mail rev.djf@btinternet.com

FRENCH, George Leslie. b 47. AIFST NE Lon Poly BSc70. S'wark Ord Course 86. **d** 89 **p** 90. NSM Reading St Barn *Ox* 89-99. *Hawthorne House, 2 Cutbush Close, Lower Earley, Reading RG6 4XA* Tel 0118-986 1886

FRENCH, Janet. b 54. EAMTC 99. **d** 02 **p** 03. C Thetford *Nor* from 02. *44 Monksgate, Thetford IP24 1BY* Tel and fax (01842) 753818 Mobile 07762-708818 E-mail frenchrevj@hotmail.com

FRENCH, Janet Mary. *See* DRIVER, Janet Mary

FRENCH, Jonathan David Seabrook. b 60. Westcott Ho Cam 84. **d** 87 **p** 88. C Loughton St Jo *Chelmsf* 87-90; Chapl St Bede's Ch for the Deaf Clapham 90-92; C Richmond St Mary w St Matthias and St Jo *S'wark* 92-95; TV 96-03; V Downham St Barn from 03; Chapl RAD 92-03; Dioc Adv for Min of Deaf and Disabled People *S'wark* from 03. *St Barnabas' Vicarage, 1 Churchdown, Bromley BR1 5PS* Tel (020) 8698 4851
E-mail seabrook.french@virgin.net

FRENCH, Ms Judith Karen. b 60. St D Coll Lamp BA89. St Steph Ho Ox 89. **d** 91 **p** 94. Par Dn Botley *Portsm* 91-94; C Bilton *Cov* 94-97; V Charlbury w Shorthampton *Ox* from 97. *The Vicarage, Church Lane, Charlbury, Chipping Norton OX7 3PX* Tel and fax (01608) 810286
E-mail vicar@stmaryscharlbury.co.uk

FRENCH, Michael Anders. b 61. Ch Coll Cam BA83 MA87 Ridley Hall Cam BA91 Man Univ MA(Econ)96. **d** 92 **p** 93. C Norbury *Ches* 92-96; Chapl Ches Coll of HE 96-01; Chapl Geneva *Eur* from 01. *105 route du Bois des Iles, La Bâtie, 1290 Versoix, Switzerland* Tel (0041) (22) 779 0465
E-mail frenchgeneva@hotmail.com *or* m.french@anglican.ch

FRENCH, Michael John. b 37. WEMTC 92. **d** 95 **p** 96. OLM Cheltenham St Pet *Glouc* 95-01; NSM from 01. *8 Alexandria Walk, Cheltenham GL52 5LG* Tel (01242) 236661

FRENCH, Peter Robert. b 65. Man Univ BTh87. Qu Coll Birm 88. **d** 90 **p** 91. C Unsworth *Man* 90-93; C Bury Ch King w H Trin 93-95; V Bury Ch King 95-98; V Handsworth St Andr *Birm* from 98. *St Andrew's Vicarage, 55 Laurel Road, Birmingham B21 9PB* Tel 0121-551 2097 Fax 554 1084 E-mail peterfrench55@aol.com

FRENCH, Philip Colin. b 50. Sarum & Wells Th Coll 81. **d** 83 **p** 84. C Llansamlet *S & B* 83-86; P-in-c Waunarllwydd 86-87; V 87-97; P-in-c Swansea St Barn 97-98; V from 98. *St Barnabas' Vicarage, 57 Sketty Road, Swansea SA2 0EN* Tel (01792) 298601

FRENCH, Richard John. b 34. Open Univ BA82. Tyndale Hall Bris 62. **d** 64 **p** 65. C Rustington *Chich* 64-68; C Walton H Trin *Ox* 68-72; V Grove 72-99; rtd 99; Perm to Offic *Chich* from 01. *5 Green Meadows, The Welkin, Haywards Heath RH16 2PE* Tel (01444) 487842

FRENCH, Stephen Robert James. b 52. St Jo Coll Nottm. **d** 87 **p** 88. C Chell *Lich* 87-91; TV 91-94; V Wednesfield Heath 94-01; TV Hemel Hempstead *St Alb* from 01. *The Vicarage, 436 Warners End Road, Hemel Hempstead HP1 3QF* Tel (01442) 251897 E-mail frenchys@fish.co.uk

FRERE, Christopher Michael Hanbury. b 21. Roch Th Coll 65. **d** 67 **p** 68. C Spilsby w Hundleby *Linc* 67-71; V N Kelsey 71-76; V Cadney 71-76; P-in-c Aisthorpe w W Thorpe and Scampton 75-79; P-in-c Brattleby 75-79; R Fillingham 76-78; V Ingham w Cammeringham 76-78; RD Lawres 78-84; V Ingham w Cammeringham w Fillingham 79-86; R Aisthorpe w Scampton w Thorpe le Fallows etc 79-86; rtd 86; Perm to Offic *Linc* from 86. *164 Newark Road, North Hykeham, Lincoln LN6 8LZ* Tel (01522) 806326 E-mail cmh.frere@ntlworld.com

FRESHNEY, June. b 46. EMMTC 95. **d** 98 **p** 99. NSM Washingborough w Heighington and Canwick *Linc* 98-05; Asst Chapl St Barn Hospice Linc 03-05; P-in-c Caythorpe *Linc* from 05. *The Rectory, 45B Old Lincoln Road, Caythorpe, Grantham NG32 3EJ* Tel (01400) 272728 Mobile 07798-840015
E-mail revjune@supanet.com

FRESTON, John Samuel Kern. b 28. Lich Th Coll 70. **d** 72 **p** 73. C Walsall *Lich* 72-75; TV Trunch w Swafield *Nor* 75-77; TV Trunch 77-82; R W Winch 82-91; Chapl St Jas Hosp King's Lynn 82-85; Chapl Qu Eliz Hosp King's Lynn 85-90; rtd 91; Perm to Offic *Ely* and *Nor* from 91. *71 Howdale Road, Downham Market PE38 9AH* Tel (01366) 385936

FRETT, Daniel Calvin. b 60. Univ of S Carolina 85. NTMTC 95 Oak Hill Th Coll BA99. **d** 98 **p** 99. NSM Clerkenwell St Jas and St Jo w St Pet *Lon* 98-00; NSM Chelsea St Jo w St Andr 00-05; NSM Tulse Hill H Trin and St Matthias *S'wark* from 05. *3 Patience Road, London SW11 2PY* Tel (020) 7652 2243
E-mail frettd@netscape.net

FRETWELL, Brian George. b 34. TD. CEng MIMechE. Chich Th Coll 79. **d** 81 **p** 82. C Bude Haven *Truro* 81-82; C Saltash 82-85; C Walthamstow St Sav *Chelmsf* 85-87; V Doncaster Intake *Sheff* 87-97; rtd 99. *65 Little Breach, Chichester PO19 5TY* Tel (01243) 775980

FRETWELL, Cynthia Mary. b 37. EMMTC 90. **d** 91 **p** 94. Chapl Asst Doncaster R Infirmary 91-92; Chapl Asst Tickhill Road and St Cath Hosps 91-92; Chapl Asst Doncaster R Infirmary and Montagu Hosp NHS Trust 92-95; Chapl 95-96; rtd 96. *65 Little Breach, Chichester PO19 5TY* Tel (01243) 775980

FREWIN, William Charles. b 46. Trin Coll Bris 84. **d** 86 **p** 87. C Southchurch H Trin *Chelmsf* 86-89; C Shrub End 89-91; R W Bergholt 91-00; P-in-c Gt Wakering w Foulness from 00. *The Vicarage, 2 New Road, Great Wakering, Southend-on-Sea SS3 0AH* Tel (01702) 217493 E-mail billfrewin@beeb.net

FREY, Christopher Ronald. b 44. AKC69 Uppsala Univ BD73 MTh77. St Aug Coll Cant 69. **d** 70 **p** 71. C Addington *Ox* 70-72; Lic to Offic *Eur* 73-78; Chapl Stockholm w Uppsala 78-85; Can Brussels Cathl 81-85; Chapl Casterton Sch Lancs 85-89; Chapl Epsom Coll 89-91; Chapl Worksop Coll Notts 91-94; rtd 96. *Koriandergaten 42, 261 61 Landskrona, Sweden* Tel (0046) (418) 20953

FRIARS, Ian Malcolm George. b 50. Sarum & Wells Th Coll 83. **d** 85 **p** 86. C Norton *St Alb* 85-88; C Ramsey *Ely* 88-90; TV The Ramseys and Upwood 90-93; P-in-c Cottenham 93-94; R 94-01; P-in-c Long Melford *St E* 01-02; R Chadbrook from 02. *The Rectory, The Green, Long Melford, Sudbury CO10 9DT* Tel (01787) 310845 Fax 313767
E-mail ian.friars@stedmundsbury.anglican.org

FRICKER, Canon David Duncan. b 27. Lon Univ BA53. Ridley Hall Cam 53. **d** 55 **p** 56. C Ecclesfield *Sheff* 55-58; C Luton St Mary *St Alb* 58-61; V Luton St Paul 61-64; R Bedford St Pet 64-75; RD Bedford 69-79; Hon Can St Alb 74-88; P-in-c Bedford St Paul 75-79; R Bedford St Pet w St Cuth 75-88; R Brightling, Dallington, Mountfield etc *Chich* 88-97; RD Dallington 88-95; rtd 97; Perm to Offic *Chich* from 97. *Merton, Langham Road, Robertsbridge TN32 5EP* Tel (01580) 880064

FRIEND, Adam Lyndon David. b 76. St Martin's Coll Lanc BA98. Cranmer Hall Dur 99. **d** 02 **p** 03. C Witton *Ches* 02-05; V Over St Chad from 05. *The Vicarage, 1 Over Hall Drive, Winsford CW7 1EY* Tel (01606) 593222
E-mail fr.friend@btopenworld.co.uk

FRIEND, Frederick James. b 41. BA. Oak Hill NSM Course. **d** 82 **p** 83. NSM Hughenden *Ox* from 82. *The Chimes, Cryers Hill Road, High Wycombe HP15 6JS* Tel (01494) 563168

FRIENDSHIP, Roger Geoffrey (John-Francis). b 46. ACII72. WMMTC 90. **d** 93 **p** 94. SSF 76-02; NSM Harborne St Faith and St Laur *Birm* 93-94; Asst Novice Guardian Hilfield Friary 94-97; Novice Guardian 97-99; Gen Sec SSF 99-01; C Clerkenwell H Redeemer and St Mark *Lon* 00-01; R Romford St Andr *Chelmsf* from 01. *The Rectory, 119 London Road, Romford RM7 9QD* Tel and fax (01708) 741256 Mobile 07808-500717 E-mail francis.jon@btinternet.com

FRIGGENS, Canon Maurice Anthony. b 40. Sheff Univ BA65. Westcott Ho Cam 65. **d** 67 **p** 68. C Stocksbridge *Sheff* 67-70; C St Buryan, St Levan and Sennen *Truro* 70-72; R 72-84; RD Penwith 82-84; R St Columb Major w St Wenn 84-91; Dioc Dir of Ords 87-93; Hon Can Truro Cathl 87-00; V St Cleer 91-00; rtd 00; Perm to Offic *Ban* from 00; *Eur* from 01. *Tŷ Cernyw, Rhiw, Pwllheli LL53 8AF* Tel (01758) 780365

FRITH, Canon Christopher John Cokayne. b 44. Ex Coll Ox BA65 MA69. Ridley Hall Cam 66. **d** 68 **p** 69. C Crookes St Thos *Sheff* 68-71; C Rusholme H Trin *Man* 71-74; R Haughton St Mary 74-85; R Brampton St Thos *Derby* 85-02; V Alvaston from 02; Hon Can Derby Cathl from 99. *The Vicarage, 8 Church Street, Alvaston, Derby DE24 0PR* Tel (01332) 571143
E-mail cjc@friths.freeserve.co.uk

FRITH, David William. b 65. K Coll Lon BD87 PGCE88 MA96 Lambeth STh90. Westcott Ho Cam 88. **d** 90 **p** 91. C St John's Wood *Lon* 90-93; C Maidstone All SS and St Phil w Tovil *Cant* 93-95; V E Wickham *S'wark* 96-03; Local Min Adv 98-00; RD Plumstead 01-03; TR Cen Wolverhampton *Lich* from 03. *St Peter's House, 4 Exchange Street, Wolverhampton WV1 1TS* Tel (01902) 428491 Fax 420014
E-mail centralparish@wolves94.fsnet.co.uk

FRITH, Mrs Gillian. b 43. EAMTC 99. **d** 02 **p** 03. NSM Chipping Ongar w Shelley *Chelmsf* from 02. *82 Upper Park, Harlow CM20 1TW* Tel (01279) 301400 Mobile 07890-376779
E-mail g.frith@ntlworld.com

FRITH, Canon Ivy Florence. b 24. CertEd56. Lambeth DipTh93 St Chris Coll Blackheath 48. **dss** 79 **d** 87 **p** 94. St Alb Abbey *St Alb* 79-82; Truro St Paul and St Clem *Truro* 82-84; Truro St Mary 84-94; Hon Par Dn 87-94; Dioc Lay Min Adv 85-95; Asst Dioc Dir of Ords 87-95; MU Chapl 91-94; Hon Can Truro Cathl 93-94; Hon C Feock 94-96; Perm to Offic *S'wark* 96-04 and *Lich* from 04. *St Peter's Rectory, 42 Park Road East, Wolverhampton WV1 4QA* Tel (01902) 423140

FRITH, Jonathan Paul (Jonty). b 72. Jes Coll Cam BA94 MA97. Wycliffe Hall Ox 95. **d** 97 **p** 98. C Houghton *Carl* 97-00; Chapl Cranleigh Sch Surrey 00-04; C Crowborough *Chich* from 04. *1 Croft Cottages, Church Road, Crowborough TN6 1ED* Tel (01892) 662909 E-mail jp@jpfrith.freeserve.co.uk

✠**FRITH, The Rt Revd Richard Michael Cokayne.** b 49. Fitzw Coll Cam BA72 MA76. St Jo Coll Nottm 72. **d** 74 **p** 75 **c** 98. C Mortlake w E Sheen *S'wark* 74-78; TV Thamesmead 78-83; TR Keynsham *B & W* 83-92; Preb Wells Cathl 91-98; Adn Taunton 92-98; Suff Bp Hull *York* from 98. *Hullen House, Woodfield Lane, Hessle HU13 0ES* Tel (01482) 649019 Fax 647449
E-mail richard@bishop.karoo.co.uk

FRITZE-SHANKS, Miss Annette. Sydney Univ BA86 DipEd87 LLB89 Solicitor. SEITE 01. **d** 04 **p** 05. NSM Kilburn St Mary w All So and W Hampstead St Jas *Lon* from 04. *21A Kylemore Road, London NW6 2PS* Tel 07771-544201 (mobile)
E-mail annettefritze-shanks@campbellhooper.com

FROGGATT, Mrs Alison. b 35. Dur Univ BA56 Bradf Univ MA79. N Ord Course 96. **d** 98 **p** 98. NSM Bingley H Trin *Bradf* 98-02; rtd 02; Perm to Offic *Bradf* from 02. *2 Gilstead Hall, Bingley BD16 3NP* Tel (01274) 565716
E-mail alison.froggatt@lineone.net

FROGGATT, Mrs Elaine Muriel. b 43. Dioc OLM tr scheme 97. **d** 00 **p** 01. OLM Skirwith, Ousby and Melmerby w Kirkland *Carl* 00-04; OLM Cross Fell Gp from 04. *The Old Corn Mill, Blencarn, Penrith CA10 1TX* Tel (01768) 88757

FROGGATT, Jeffrey. b 27. Ch Coll Cam BA48 MA52. Ridley Hall Cam 49. **d** 51 **p** 52. C Scunthorpe St Jo *Linc* 51-53; C Doncaster St Jas *Sheff* 53-56; V New Edlington 56-62; V Malin Bridge 62-73; Ind Chapl and V Wortley 73-79; R Todwick 79-85; V Dore 85-92; rtd 92; Perm to Offic *Sheff* from 92 and *Derby* 92-00. *20 Bocking Lane, Sheffield S8 7BH* Tel 0114-262 0914

FROGGATT, Peter Michael. b 65. St Hild Coll Dur BA86 PGCE88. Wycliffe Hall Ox BTh95. **d** 95 **p** 96. C Bebington *Ches* 95-00; V Rock Ferry from 00. *The Vicarage, St Peter's Road, Birkenhead CH42 1PY* Tel 0151-645 1622 *or* 643 1042
E-mail prfroggatt@talk21.com

FROOM, Ian Leonard John. b 42. Sarum Th Coll 69. **d** 71 **p** 72. C Gillingham and Fifehead Magdalen *Sarum* 71-75; C Parkstone St Pet w Branksea and St Osmund 75-78; V Sedgley St Mary *Lich* 78-85; TV Weston-super-Mare Cen Par *B & W* 85-94; Perm to Offic 94-97; V Truro St Geo and St Jo *Truro* 97-03; rtd 03; Perm to Offic *Truro* from 03. *11 Marlborough Crescent, Falmouth TR11 2RJ* Tel (01326) 311760

FROST, Alan Sydney. b 26. K Coll Lon BD50 AKC50. **d** 51 **p** 52. C Folkestone St Sav *Cant* 51-56; C Sneinton St Steph *S'well* 56-59; C Croydon Woodside *Cant* 60-63; Asst Chapl Mersey Miss to Seamen 63-66; rtd 91. *Address excluded by request*

FROST, David J. b 48. **d** 86 **p** 87. Hon C Upper Norwood All SS *S'wark* 86-89; C Battersea St Luke 90-94; V Shirley St Geo from 94. *St George's Vicarage, The Glade, Croydon CR0 7QJ* Tel (020) 8654 8747 Fax 8654 1102
E-mail revdavid@stgeorgeschurch.co.uk

FROST, David Richard. b 54. Ridley Hall Cam 84. **d** 86 **p** 87. C Burgess Hill St Andr *Chich* 86-90; TV Rye 90-94; V Bexhill St Steph from 94. *The Vicarage, 67 Woodsgate Park, Bexhill-on-Sea TN39 4DL* Tel and fax (01424) 211186
E-mail david@drfrost.worldonline.co.uk

FROST, Derek Charles. b 47. Lich Th Coll 69. **d** 71 **p** 72. C Woodley St Jo the Ev *Ox* 71-76; V Bampton w Clanfield 76-81; V Minster Lovell and Brize Norton 81-88; TV Upper Kennet *Sarum* 88-92; P-in-c Seend and Bulkington 92-97; P-in-c Poulshot 95-97; V Seend, Bulkington and Poulshot 97-01; V Derry Hill w Bremhill and Foxham from 01. *The New Vicarage, Church Road, Derry Hill, Calne SN11 9NN* Tel (01249) 812172

FROST, The Ven George. b 35. Dur Univ BA56 MA61. Linc Th Coll 57. **d** 60 **p** 61. C Barking St Marg *Chelmsf* 60-64; C-in-c Marks Gate CD 64-70; V Tipton St Matt *Lich* 70-77; V Penn 77-87; RD Trysull 84-87; Preb Lich Cathl 85-87; Adn Salop 87-98; V Tong 87-98; P-in-c Donington 97-98; Adn Lich and Can Res and Treas Lich Cathl 98-00; rtd 00; Perm to Offic *Lich* from 00. *23 Darnford Lane, Lichfield WS14 9RW* Tel (01543) 415109 E-mail gfrost@fish.co.uk

FROST, Jeremy James. b 74. New Coll Ox BA96 MA99. Wycliffe Hall Ox BA99. **d** 00 **p** 01. C Wellington, All SS w Eyton *Lich* 00-04; Min Can and Prec Cant Cathl *Cant* from 04. *5 The Precincts, Canterbury CT1 2EE* Tel (01227) 765843
E-mail jeremy@jamesfrost.fsnet.co.uk

FROST, Canon Jonathan Hugh. b 64. Aber Univ BD88 Nottm Univ MTh99 MSSTh91. Ridley Hall Cam 91. **d** 93 **p** 94. C W Bridgford *S'well* 93-97; Police Chapl Trent Division 94-97; R Ash *Guildf* 97-02; Tutor Dioc Min Course from 99; Chapl Surrey Univ from 02; Can Res Guildf Cathl from 02. *6 Cathedral Close, Guildford GU2 7TL* Tel (01483) 576380 Mobile 07870-277709
E-mail j.frost@surrey.ac.uk

FROST, Canon Julian. b 36. Bris Univ BA61 MA65 Lon Univ CertEd70 Solicitor 57. Clifton Th Coll 64. **d** 65 **p** 66. C Welling *Roch* 65-69; Hon C 70-73; Dep Dir Schs Coun RE Project Lanc Univ 73-78; V New Beckenham St Paul 78-01; Hon Can Roch Cathl 00-01; rtd 01; Perm to Offic *Blackb* from 01. *93 Scotforth Road, Lancaster LA1 4JN* Tel (01524) 841967

FROST, Michael John. b 42. Westmr Coll Ox TCert64. LNSM course 92. **d** 95 **p** 96. OLM Harwood *Man* from 95. *86 Harden Drive, Harwood, Bolton BL2 5BX* Tel (01204) 418596

FROST, Richard John. b 49. Ch Ch Coll Cant CertEd71 BA00. SW Minl Tr Course 95. **d** 97 **p** 98. NSM Bideford, Northam, Westward Ho, Appledore etc *Ex* 97-00; C 00-03; TV from 03. *The Rectory, Fore Street, Northam, Bideford EX39 1AW* Tel (01237) 476749

FROST, Ronald Andrew. b 48. Cam Univ DipRS77 Univ of S Carolina BTh81. Ridley Hall Cam 86. **d** 87 **p** 88. C Gt Wilbraham *Ely* 87-89; P-in-c Stow Longa 89-91; V from 91; P-in-c Kimbolton 89-91; V from 91. *The Vicarage, Kimbolton, Huntingdon PE28 0HB* Tel (01480) 860279 Mobile 07866-648493

FROST, Stanley. b 37. Univ of Wales BSc61 Liv Univ MSc65 PhD68 MIBiol66 CBiol66 FAEB82. N Ord Course 79. **d** 82 **p** 83. NSM Lower Kersal *Man* 82-87; NSM Patricroft 87-89; NSM Convenor *Man* 87-95; Lic Preacher 89-03; P-in-c Pittenweem and Elie and Earlsferry *St And* 03-04; rtd 04. *15 Ruston Close, Chesterfield S40 4RY* Tel (01246) 201908
E-mail s.frost@cussac.freeserve.co.uk

FROST, Preb William Selwyn. b 29. Wells Th Coll 61. **d** 62 **p** 63. C Cheddleton *Lich* 62-67; V Longdon-upon-Tern 67-81; R Rodington 67-81; RD Wrockwardine 77-84; Preb Lich Cathl 81-96; R Longdon-upon-Tern, Rodington, Uppington etc 81-84; R Whittington St Jo 84-86; C Trysull 86-89; TV Wombourne w Trysull and Bobbington 89-96; rtd 96; Perm to Offic *Heref* from 96. *Ty Ffos, Dilwyn, Hereford HR4 8HZ* Tel (01544) 318703

FROSTICK, Canon John George. b 23. Wells Th Coll 52. **d** 54 **p** 55. C Loughborough St Pet *Leic* 54-57; C Knighton St Mary Magd 57-58; V Frisby-on-the-Wreake w Kirby Bellars 58-71; V Shepshed 71-83; Hon Can Leic Cathl 80-83; R Kirton w Falkenham *St E* 83-90; rtd 90; Perm to Offic *Leic* from 91. *68 Melton Road, Barrow-upon-Soar, Loughborough LE12 8NX* Tel (01509) 620110

FROSTICK, Paul Andrew. b 52. Stockwell Coll of Educn CertEd73. Ripon Hall Ox 74. **d** 77 **p** 78. C Shepton Mallet *B & W* 77-80; TV Barton Mills, Beck Row w Kenny Hill etc *St E* 80-85; TV Mildenhall 85-86; TV Raveningham *Nor* 86-89; V Bottisham and P-in-c Lode and Longmeadow *Ely* 89-90; V Bottisham and Lode w Long Meadow 90-94; Hd RE Brittons Sch Romford 94-97; Hd RE The Grove Sch St Leonards 97-00; rtd 00; Assoc P Bexhill St Aug *Chich* from 99. *18 The Ridings, Bexhill-on-Sea TN39 5HU* Tel (01424) 218126 E-mail paul@frostickrev.freeserve.co.uk

FROUD, Andrew William. b 65. Mansf Coll Ox BA87 St Cath Coll Cam MPhil92. Westcott Ho Cam 90. **d** 93 **p** 94. C Almondbury w Farnley Tyas *Wakef* 93-96; P-in-c Wootton *Portsm* 96-00; R 00-01; V Thornton-le-Fylde *Blackb* from 01. *The Vicarage, Meadows Avenue, Thornton-Cleveleys FY5 2TW* Tel (01253) 855099 E-mail froud.family@virgin.net

FROUDE (née WOOLCOCK), Canon Christine Ann. b 47. ACIB73. S Dios Minl Tr Scheme 92. **d** 95 **p** 96. NSM Stoke Bishop *Bris* 95-99; Chapl United Bris Healthcare NHS Trust 99-01; P-in-c Shirehampton *Bris* from 01; Dean Women's Min from 00; Hon Can Bris Cathl from 01. *St Mary's Vicarage, 8 Priory Gardens, Bristol BS11 0BZ* Tel and fax 0117-985 5450 E-mail christinefroude@lineone.net

FROWLEY, Peter Austin. b 32. CEng61 MIMechE61. WMMTC 82. **d** 84 **p** 85. NSM Tardebigge *Worc* 84-87; P-in-c 87-88; NSM Redditch St Steph 84-87; Hong Kong 88-92; V St Minver *Truro* 92-96; rtd 96; Perm to Offic *Ex* from 96. *Bramblecrest, Fortescue Road, Salcombe TQ8 8AP* Tel (01548) 842515

FRY, Alison Jacquelyn. b 65. Newnham Coll Cam BA86 MA90 Hertf Coll Ox DPhil90. Cranmer Hall Dur BA95 Dip Minl Studies 96. **d** 96 **p** 97. C Milton *B & W* 96-00; V Batheaston w St Cath from 00. *Batheaston Vicarage, Bannerdown Road, Batheaston, Bath BA1 7ND* Tel (01225) 858192 E-mail ajfry@fish.co.uk

FRY, Canon Barry James. b 49. K Alfred's Coll Win MA03 ACIB. Ripon Coll Cuddesdon 81. **d** 83 **p** 84. C Highcliffe w Hinton Admiral *Win* 83-87; V Southampton St Barn from 87; Hon Can Ruvuma Cathl Tanzania from 02. *St Barnabas' Vicarage, 12 Rose Road, Southampton SO14 6TE* Tel (023) 8022 3107

FRY, Mrs Florence Marion. b 24. WMMTC 87. **d** 88 **p** 94. Chapl and Welfare Officer to the Deaf 70-94; Chapl Cov Cathl *Cov* 88-94; Chmn Cov Coun of Chs 88-91; rtd 94; Perm to Offic *St Alb* from 96. *37 Grace Gardens, Bishop's Stortford CM23 3EU* Tel (01279) 652315

FRY, Canon James Reinhold. b 30. St Cuth Soc Dur BSc53 MA70 Kent Univ MA04 Lambeth STh90. Oak Hill Th Coll 55. **d** 57 **p** 58. C Bromley St Jo *Roch* 57-60; V Deptford St Luke *S'wark* 60-66; V Chalk *Roch* 66-97; RD Gravesend 81-91; Hon Can Roch Cathl 87-97; rtd 97; Perm to Offic *Roch* from 99 and *Cant* from 00. *67 Park Lane, Birchington CT7 0AU* Tel and fax (01843) 843423 E-mail j.fry3@btinternet.com

FRY, Miss Joan Aileen. b 29. Bedf Coll Lon BA50. Qu Coll Birm 79. **dss** 82 **d** 87 **p** 94. Colindale St Matthias *Lon* 82-87; Hendon St Mary 84-87; Hon Par Dn Swanage and Studland *Sarum* 87-95; Hon C Bridport 95-99; rtd 99; Perm to Offic *Sarum* from 00. *21 St James's Park, Bridport DT6 3UR* Tel (01308) 458614

FRY, Lynn Jane. b 60. **d** 03 **p** 04. OLM E w W Harling, Bridgham w Roudham, Larling etc *Nor* from 03. *40 White Hart Street, East Harling, Norwich NR16 2NE* Tel (01953) 717423 E-mail fryfam@fish.co.uk

FRY, Marion. *See* FRY, Mrs Florence Marion

FRY, Michael John. b 59. Nottm Univ BA80 Sheff Univ CQSW83 Cam Univ BA85. Westcott Ho Cam 83. **d** 86 **p** 87. C Upholland *Liv* 86-89; C Dovecot 89-91; TV St Luke in the City from 91. *2 Minster Court, Liverpool L7 3QB* Tel 0151-709 9665

FRY, Nigel. b 49. Kent Univ BA95. SEITE 97. **d** 00 **p** 01. NSM Len Valley *Cant* 00-03; C Hollingbourne and Hucking w Leeds and Broomfield from 03; Chapl HM Pris E Sutton Park from 02. *The Vicarage, Upper Street, Hollingbourne, Maidstone ME17 1UJ* Tel (01622) 880243 E-mail nigel.fry1@btinternet.com

FRY, Nigel Edward. b 57. St Jo Coll Nottm 91. **d** 93 **p** 94. C Wellingborough All Hallows *Pet* 93-96; R Peakirk w Glinton and Northborough 96-05; V Pet Ch Carpenter from 05. *The Vicarage, Chestnut Avenue, Peterborough PE1 4PE* Tel (01733) 567140 E-mail enfry@romans5.fsnet.co.uk

FRY, Roger Joseph Hamilton. b 29. Em Coll Cam BA52 MA56. Clifton Th Coll 52. **d** 54 **p** 55. C Walcot *B & W* 54-57; C Gresley *Derby* 57-61; P-in-c Bowling St Bart and St Luke *Bradf* 61-65; V Bowling St Jo 61-87; V Ingleton w Chapel le Dale 87-95; rtd 95; Perm to Offic *Bradf* from 95. *5 Margerison Crescent, Ilkley LS29 8QZ* Tel (01943) 608738

FRY, Roger Owen. b 30. Sarum Th Coll 58. **d** 60 **p** 61. C Yeovil St Mich *B & W* 60-63; P-in-c Weston-in-Gordano 64-70; R Clapton-in-Gordano 64-70; R Portishead 64-80; V Weston Zoyland w Chedzoy 80-94; rtd 94; Perm to Offic *B & W* from 95. *14 Lewmond Avenue, Wells BA5 2TS*

FRYDAY, Canon Barbara Yvonne. b 47. Ch of Ireland Tr Coll TCert67. CITC 90. **d** 92 **p** 93. NSM Cashel w Magorban, Tipperary, Clonbeg etc *C & O* 93-96; C Kilcooley w Littleon, Crohane and Fertagh 96-99; I from 99; Can Ossory Cathl from 03. *The Rectory, Grange Barna, Thurles, Co Tipperary, Irish Republic* Tel and fax (00353) (56) 883 4147 Mobile 86-275 0735 E-mail frydayb@eircom.net *or* kilcooley@cashel.anglican.org

FRYER, Charles Eric John. b 14. Lon Univ BA54 PhD84. Linc Th Coll 62. **d** 63 **p** 64. C Finham *Cov* 63-66; Perm to Offic *S'well* 66-75; Lic to Offic 75-79; R Killin *St And* 79-94; R Lochearnhead 79-89; Min Can Cork Cathl *C, C & R* from 97. *25 Vicar Street, Cork, Irish Republic* Tel (00353) (21) 316397

FRYER, Mrs Ida Doris. b 31. Lon Univ BA53. **d** 95 **p** 96. OLM Brantham w Stutton *St E* 95-00; OLM Holbrook, Stutton, Freston, Woolverstone etc 00-01; rtd 01; Perm to Offic *St E* from 01. *The Grove, Stutton, Ipswich IP9 2SE* Tel (01473) 328230

FRYER, Mrs Jenifer Anne. b 43. N Ord Course 89. **d** 92 **p** 94. Par Dn Ecclesfield *Sheff* 92-94; C 94-95; Chapl R Hallamshire Hosp Sheff 92-96; Chapl Weston Park Hosp Sheff 94-96; Chapl Asst N Gen Hosp NHS Trust Sheff from 96. *Northern General Hospital, Herries Road, Sheffield S5 7AU* Tel 0114-243 4343 ext 5056 *or* 246 1027

FRYER, Michael Andrew. b 56. St Jo Coll Nottm 88. **d** 90 **p** 91. C Hull St Martin w Transfiguration *York* 90-95; V Kingston upon Hull St Aid Southcoates from 95. *St Aidan's Vicarage, 139 Southcoates Avenue, Hull HU9 3HF* Tel (01482) 374403 E-mail mick@fryerm.fsnet.co.uk

FUDGE, Prof Erik Charles. b 33. Ch Coll Cam BA55 MA59 Southn Univ CertEd58 Cam Univ PhD68. Ox Min Course 91. **d** 93 **p** 94. NSM Wokingham St Sebastian *Ox* from 93. *4 South Close, Wokingham RG40 2DJ* Tel 0118-978 6081

FUDGER, David John. b 53. Sheff Univ MMin96. K Coll Lon 73 Coll of Resurr Mirfield 76. **d** 77 **p** 78. C Sutton in Ashfield St Mary *S'well* 77-80; P-in-c Duston *Pet* 80-82; V Radford All So w Ch Ch and St Mich *S'well* 82-91; Min Bermondsey St Hugh CD *S'wark* 91-97; P-in-c Blackheath Ascension 97-04; Hon PV S'wark Cathl 91-01; P-in-c Mansfield SS Pet and Paul *S'well* from 04. *The Vicarage, Lindhurst Lane, Mansfield NG18 4JE* Tel (01623) 642546 *or* tel and fax 640250 E-mail revfudger@mistral.co.uk

FUDGER, Canon Michael Lloyd. b 55. K Coll Lon BD77 AKC77. Coll of Resurr Mirfield 77. **d** 78 **p** 79. C Weston Favell *Pet* 78-82; C Pet H Spirit Bretton 82-84; V Irchester 84-90; TV Darnall-cum-Attercliffe *Sheff* 90-96; TV Attercliffe, Darnall and Tinsley 96-97; TR 97-03; TR Attercliffe and Darnall 03-05; V from 05; Chapl Nine o'Clock Community from 04; RD Attercliffe 91-96; Hon Can Sheff Cathl from 00. *34 Mather Court, Sheffield S9 4HQ* Tel 0114-244 0167 E-mail fudgerml@yahoo.co.uk

FUGGLE, Francis Alfred. b 13. Selw Coll Cam BA34 MA38. Wells Th Coll 35. **d** 36 **p** 37. C Kingsbury St Andr *Lon* 36-38; S Africa from 38. *360A Florida Road, Durban, 4001 South Africa* Tel (0027) (31) 238923

FULFORD, Alison Jane. b 79. CCC Cam BA00 MA04. Ridley Hall Cam 01. **d** 04 **p** 05. C Old Catton *Nor* from 04. *45 Garrick Green, Norwich NR6 7AN* Tel (01603) 424684 E-mail alisonfulford_1@hotmail.com

FULFORD, Susan Yvonne. b 61. **d** 03. OLM Pemberton St Mark Newtown *Liv* from 03. *13 Mitchell Street, Wigan WN5 9BY* Tel (01942) 242369 E-mail sueandmike2003@yahoo.co.uk

FULHAM, Suffragan Bishop of. *See* BROADHURST, The Rt Revd John Charles

FULKER, Lois Valerie. b 42. Keele Univ BA64. Cranmer Hall Dur 03. **d** 04 **p** 05. NSM Egremont and Haile *Carl* from 04. *3 Mill Farm, Calderbridge, Seascale CA20 1DN* Tel (01946) 841475 E-mail fulker@onetel.com

FULLAGAR, Michael Nelson. b 35. SS Coll Cam BA57 MA61. Chich Th Coll 57. **d** 59 **p** 60. C Camberwell St Giles *S'wark* 59-61; C Northolt Park St Barn *Lon* 61-64; C Hythe *Cant* 64-66; R Chipata Zambia 66-70; P-in-c Livingstone 70-75; P-in-c Chingola 75-78; R Freemantle *Win* 78-87; P-in-c Westbury w Turweston, Shalstone and Biddlesden *Ox* 87-94; Chapl S Bucks NHS Trust 94-96; rtd 96; P-in-c Burwash Weald *Chich* 97-04. *1 Roffrey Avenue, Eastbourne BN22 0AE* Tel (01323) 503212

FULLALOVE, Brenda Hurst. *See* CRASTON, Mrs Brenda Hurst

FULLARD, Craig William. b 73. BA97. Westcott Ho Cam 97. **d** 99 **p** 00. C Tipton St Jo *Lich* 99-01; C Tividale 01-03; Asst Chapl R Wolv Hosps NHS Trust from 03. *The Chaplain's Office, New Cross Hospital, Wolverhampton WV10 0QP* Tel (01902) 307999 ext 3482 E-mail fullard@ukonline.co.uk

FULLARTON, Mrs Heather Mary. b 42. Whitelands Coll Lon TCert63. Qu Coll Birm 90. **d** 92 **p** 94. Par Dn Colwich w Gt Haywood *Lich* 92-94; C 94-97; P-in-c Swindon and Himley 97-01; V Prees and Fauls 01-02; rtd 02; Perm to Offic *Sarum* from 03. *3 Rivers Arms Close, Sturminster Newton DT10 1DL* Tel (01258) 471895 Mobile 07703-379684
E-mail hfullarton@aol.com

FULLER, Alison Jane. b 61. St Andr Univ MTheol84. Edin Th Coll 85. **d** 87 **p** 94. C Selkirk *Edin* 87-89; C Melrose 87-89; C Galashiels 87-89; C Edin H Cross 89-92; Dn-in-c Edin St Columba 92-94; R from 94; Chapl Edin Univ 96-00. *28 Castle Terrace, Edinburgh EH1 2EL* Tel and fax 0131-228 6470
E-mail rectory.stcolumbasbythecastle@btinternet.com

FULLER, Alistair James. b 66. Univ of Wales (Lamp) BA87. Ripon Coll Cuddesdon 88. **d** 90 **p** 91. C Thornton-le-Fylde *Blackb* 90-95; V Skerton St Luke 95-01; R Bowbrook N *Worc* from 01; RD Droitwich from 04. *The Rectory, Droitwich Road, Hanbury, Bromsgrove B60 4DB* Tel (01527) 821826
E-mail alistair@alistairfuller.fsnet.co.uk

FULLER, Christopher John. b 53. Chich Th Coll 85. **d** 87 **p** 88. C Swinton and Pendlebury *Man* 87-90; C Chiswick St Nic w St Mary *Lon* 90-92; V Hounslow W Gd Shep 92-96; V Stoke Newington St Faith, St Matthias and All SS 96-05; V Enfield St Geo from 05. *St George's Vicarage, 706 Hertford Road, Enfield EN3 6NR* Tel (01992) 762581

FULLER, Frederick Walter Tom. b 17. St Cath Coll Cam BA48 MA53 Bris Univ MLitt72 Ex Univ PhD74. Union Th Sem (NY) STM54 Cuddesdon Coll 49. **d** 51 **p** 52. C Helmsley *York* 51-53; Lect and Chapl St Luke's Coll Ex 59-78; Dep PV Ex Cathl *Ex* from 62; Hon C Swindon New Town *Bris* 79-82; rtd 82; Perm to Offic *Bris* from 89. *29 Oxford Road, Swindon SN3 4HP* Tel (01793) 824980

FULLER, Canon Graham Drowley. b 33. AKC58. **d** 59 **p** 60. C E Grinstead St Swithun *Chich* 59-62; C Coulsdon St Andr *S'wark* 62-64; Chapl RN 64-68; V Battersea St Luke *S'wark* 68-75; V S Stoneham *Win* 75-90; Bp's Ecum Officer 84-90; R Eversley 90-96; Hon Can Win Cathl 93-96; rtd 96; Perm to Offic *Portsm* from 03. *Brookside Dairy, Nunnery Lane, Newport PO30 1YR* Tel (01983) 525976

FULLER, Canon John James. b 38. SS Coll Cam BA63 SS Coll Cam MA66. Chich Th Coll 63 Union Th Sem (NY) STM64. **d** 65 **p** 66. C Westmr St Steph w St Jo *Lon* 65-71; Tutor Cuddesdon Coll 71-75; Tutor Ripon Coll Cuddesdon 75-77; Prin S Dios Minl Tr Scheme 77-96; Can and Preb Sarum Cathl *Sarum* 83-96; V Wheatley w Forest Hill and Stanton St John *Ox* 96-97; TR Wheatley 97-03; rtd 03. *11 Ratcliffs Garden, Shaftesbury SP7 8HJ* Tel (01747) 850079

FULLER, Matthew John. b 74. Birm Univ BA95 PGCE96. Oak Hill Th Coll BA05. **d** 05. C St Helen Bishopsgate w St Andr Undershaft etc *Lon* from 05. *49A Chester Way, London SE11 4UR* Tel (020) 7735 2494 Mobile 07903-045667
E-mail matt@thebibletalks.org

FULLER, Michael George. b 46. Chich Th Coll 90. **d** 92 **p** 93. C Fulham All SS *Lon* 92-94; C Kensington St Mary Abbots w St Geo from 94; Dir Post-Ord Tr Kensington Area 94-99; Bp Kensington's Liaison Officer to Metrop Police from 99. *32A Campden Hill Gardens, London W8 7AZ* Tel (020) 7727 9486 Fax 7460 8566 Mobile 07733-010935
E-mail frmichael@stgeorgescampdenhill.co.uk

FULLER, Canon Michael Jeremy. b 63. Worc Coll Ox BA85 MA89 DPhil89 Qu Coll Cam BA91. Westcott Ho Cam CTM92. **d** 92 **p** 93. C High Wycombe *Ox* 92-95; C Edin St Jo *Edin* 95-00; Prin TISEC from 00; Can St Mary's Cathl *Edin* from 00. *28 Blackford Avenue, Edinburgh EH9 2PH* Tel 0131-667 7273 *or* 220 2272 Fax 220 2294
E-mail michaelf@tisec.scotland.anglican.org

FULLER, Canon Reginald Horace. b 15. Cam Univ BA37 MA41 Seabury-Western Th Sem DD83. Qu Coll Birm 39. **d** 40 **p** 41. C Bakewell *Derby* 40-43; C Ashbourne w Mapleton 43-46; C Edgbaston St Bart *Birm* 46-50; Prof Th St D Coll Lamp 50-55; USA from 55; Lic to Offic *Derby* from 64; rtd 80; Hon Can St Paul's Cathl Burlington from 88. *Westminster-Canterbury House, Apt 320, 1600 Westbrook Avenue, Richmond, VA 23227, USA*

FULLER, Robert James. b 10. Lon Univ BD53. **d** 55 **p** 56. C Nottingham St Andr *S'well* 55; R Exford w Exmoor *B & W* 61-75; rtd 75. *c/o Messrs Longueville Gittens, DX 26603, Oswestry* Tel (01691) 652241 Fax 670074

FULLER, Robert Peter. b 49. Bernard Gilpin Soc Dur 71 Trin Coll Bris 72. **d** 75 **p** 76. C Tonbridge SS Pet and Paul *Roch* 75-79; C Welling 79-83; V Nottingham St Sav *S'well* 83-89; V Ripley *Derby* 89-97; Chapl Ripley Hosp 89-93; Chapl S Derbyshire Community Health Services NHS Trust 93-97; V Colchester St Jo *Chelmsf* from 97. *St John's Vicarage, Evergreen Drive, Colchester CO4 4HU* Tel (01206) 843232
E-mail stjohnschurch.col@talk21.com

FULLER, Canon Terence James. b 30. Bris Univ BA55. Clifton Th Coll 55. **d** 56 **p** 57. C Uphill *B & W* 56-60; V Islington St Jude Mildmay Park *Lon* 60-67; V Southgate *Chich* 67-80; R Stoke Climsland *Truro* 80-95; RD Trigg Major 85-91; P-in-c Lezant w Lawhitton and S Petherwin w Trewen 93-95; Hon Can Truro Cathl 94-96; rtd 96; Perm to Offic *Truro* from 96. *9 Westover Road, Callington PL17 7EW* Tel (01579) 384958

FULLERTON, Hamish John Neville. b 45. Ball Coll Ox BA68 MA73. S'wark Ord Course 76. **d** 79 **p** 80. NSM Clapham Old Town *S'wark* 79-82; Abp Tenison's Sch Kennington 79-88; Hon C Brixton Road Ch Ch *S'wark* 89-91; C Streatham Ch Ch 91-96; C Purley St Mark 96-98; Asst P Tooting St Aug 98-01; Perm to Offic from 01. *Flat 4, 21 Offerton Road, London SW4 0DJ* Tel (020) 7622 7890

FULLJAMES, Mrs Janet Kathleen Doris. b 43. Open Univ BA79 Birm Univ MA93. Qu Coll Birm 85. **d** 87 **p** 94. Par Dn Harborne St Pet *Birm* 87-93; Par Dn Smethwick SS Steph and Mich 93-94; C 94-95; C Smethwick Resurr 95-98; P-in-c Dudley St Thos and St Luke *Worc* 98-04; P-in-c Dudley St Jo 98-04; rtd 04; Perm to Offic *B & W* from 04. *12 Obridge Road, Taunton TA2 7PX* Tel (01823) 333585

FULLJAMES, Michael William. b 36. OBE94. K Coll Lon AKC60. St Boniface Warminster 60. **d** 61 **p** 62. C Armley St Bart *Ripon* 61-64; C E Wells *B & W* 64-67; Chapl Mendip Hosp Wells 64-67; R Stanningley St Thos *Ripon* 67-73; Chapl St Aug Hosp Cant 73-88; St Martin's Hosp 82-88; RD W Bridge *Cant* 87-88; Chapl Rotterdam *Eur* 88-94; Sen Chapl Rotterdam Miss to Seamen 88-94; Sen Chapl Burrswood Chr Cen *Roch* 94-01; rtd 01; Perm to Office *Cant* and *Roch* from 01. *40 Somner Close, Canterbury CT2 8LJ* Tel (01227) 766950
E-mail michaelfulljames@onetel.com

FULLJAMES, Peter Godfrey. b 38. BNC Ox BA60 MA64 Birm Univ PhD91. Qu Coll Birm DipTh62. **d** 62 **p** 63. C Mexborough *Sheff* 62-65; Chapl Union Chr Coll India 65-69; Asst Master Wednesfield High Sch Wolverhampton 69-71; Asst Master Moorside High Sch Werrington 71-79; NSM Nairobi St Mark Kenya 80-85; Asst Master Nairobi High Sch 80-85; Research Fell Qu Coll Birm 85-87; Tutor WMMTC 87-90; Vice-Prin 90-93; Tutor Qu Coll Birm 93-94; Tutor Crowther Hall CMS Tr Coll Selly Oak 94-00; Hon Lect Th Birm Univ 97-03; rtd 00; Perm to Offic *B & W* from 04. *12 Obridge Road, Taunton TA2 7PX* Tel (01823) 333585

FULTON, Miss Ann Elizabeth. b 47. SW Minl Tr Course 01. **d** 04 **p** 05. NSM Kingston St Mary w Broomfield etc *B & W* from 04. *105 Stoke Road, Taunton TA1 3EL* Tel (01823) 282544
E-mail ann@fulton105.freeserve.co.uk

FULTON, John William. b 49. Ex Coll Ox BA71 BPhil72 MA75 MPhil79. Wycliffe Hall Ox 72. **d** 76 **p** 77. C Bexleyheath Ch Ch *Roch* 76-79; C Ealing Dean St Jo *Lon* 79-83; V Aldborough Hatch *Chelmsf* 83-87; Chapl Chantilly *Eur* 87-90; R Hepworth, Hinderclay, Wattisfield and Thelnetham *St E* from 90. *The Rectory, Church Lane, Hepworth, Diss IP22 2PU* Tel (01359) 250285 Fax as telephone

FUNNELL, Preb Norman Richard James. b 40. Univ of Wales (Lamp) BA64. Ripon Hall Ox 64. **d** 66 **p** 67. C Hackney *Lon* 66-70; Hon C 71-85; TV 85-93; R S Hackney St Jo w Ch Ch from 93; Preb St Paul's Cathl from 05. *The Rectory, 9 Church Crescent, London E9 7DH* Tel (020) 8985 5145 *or* 7254 5063
E-mail nrjf@tesco.net

FURBER, Mrs Jennifer Margaret. b 50. WEMTC 98. **d** 01 **p** 02. NSM Malvern Link w Cowleigh *Worc* from 01. *The Vicarage, 8 Christchurch Road, Malvern WR14 3BE* Tel (01684) 574106
E-mail jfurber@parousia.fslife.co.uk

FURBER, Peter. b 43. Ex Univ BA. Sarum & Wells Th Coll 83. **d** 85 **p** 86. C Stanmore *Win* 85-88; TV Basingstoke 88-95; C Ringwood 95-98; P-in-c Gt Malvern Ch Ch *Worc* 98-99; V from 99. *The Vicarage, 8 Christchurch Road, Malvern WR14 3BE* Tel (01684) 574106 E-mail pfurber@parousia.fslife.co.uk

FURBEY, Mrs Linda Alice. b 49. Hockerill Coll of Educn CertEd70 Wolfs Coll Cam BEd71 Coll of Ripon & York St Jo MA03. N Ord Course 00. **d** 03 **p** 04. NSM Crosspool *Sheff* from 03. *20 Crimicar Avenue, Sheffield S10 4EQ* Tel 0114-230 6356

FURLONG, Andrew William Ussher. b 47. TCD BA69 Jes Coll Cam BA71. Westcott Ho Cam 70 CITC 72. **d** 72 **p** 73. C Dundela St Mark *D & D* 72-76; C Dublin St Ann w St Mark and St Steph *D & G* 76-83; Zimbabwe 83-94; Adn W Harare 88-89; Can Harare 89-94; Asst Chapl Leeds Teaching Hosps NHS Trust 94-97; Dean Clonmacnoise *M & K* 97-02; I Trim and Athboy Gp 97-02; Prec Kildare Cathl 98-02. *12 Tubbermore Road, Dalkey, Co Dublin, Irish Republic* Tel (00353) (1) 285 9817
E-mail tiripo@gofree.indigo.ie

FURLONG (née DAVIES), Mrs Catharine Mary. b 48. Philippa Fawcett Coll CertEd73. EMMTC 85. **d** 88 **p** 95. C Spalding *Linc* 88-92; Zimbabwe 92-94; C Gt w Lt Gidding and Steeple Gidding *Ely* 94-96; P-in-c from 96; P-in-c Brington w Molesworth and Old Weston from 96; P-in-c Leighton Bromswold from 96; P-in-c Winwick from 96. *Brington Rectory, Church Lane, Brington, Huntingdon PE28 5AE* Tel (01832) 710207

FURNELL, The Very Revd Raymond. b 35. Linc Th Coll 63. **d** 65 **p** 66. C Cannock *Lich* 65-69; V Clayton 69-75; RD Stoke N

75-81; R Shelton 75-77; TR Hanley H Ev 77-81; Provost St E 81-94; V St E Cathl Distr 81-94; Dean York 94-03; rtd 03; Perm to Offic *St E* from 03. *9 Well Street, Bury St Edmunds IP33 1EQ* Tel (01284) 706335 E-mail r.furnell@btinternet.com

FURNESS, Barry Keith. b 47. Open Univ BSc93. **d** 04 **p** 05. OLM High Oak, Hingham and Scoulton w Wood Rising *Nor* from 04. *Waveney House, 11 Low Street, Wicklewood, Wymondham NR18 9QG* Tel and fax (01953) 606437 Mobile 07836-669335 E-mail barryfurness@norwich.anglican.com

FURNESS, Colin. b 43. Lich Th Coll 65. **d** 68 **p** 69. C New Bentley *Sheff* 68; C Sheff St Cecilia Parson Cross 68-74; V Edlington 74-78; C Heavitree w Ex St Paul *Ex* 78-81; TV 81-89; R Sampford Spiney w Horrabridge 89-03; TV Chard and Distr *B & W* from 03. *The Rectory, Furnham Road, Chard TA20 1AE* Tel (01460) 61012 E-mail furness@fish.co.uk

FURNESS, Dominic John. b 53. Bris Univ BA76. Ridley Hall Cam 82. **d** 84 **p** 85. C Downend *Bris* 84-88; V Stoke Hill *Guildf* 88-05; V Milford *Win* from 05. *The Vicarage, Lymington Road, Milford on Sea, Lymington SO41 0QN* Tel (01590) 643289 E-mail dominic.furness@tiscali.co.uk

FURNESS, Edward Joseph. b 41. S'wark Ord Course 74. **d** 77 **p** 78. NSM S Lambeth St Steph *S'wark* 77-81; Warden Mayflower Family Cen Canning Town *Chelmsf* 82-96; P-in-c Aston St Jas *Birm* 96-00; V 00-05; rtd 05; Perm to Offic *Birm* from 05. *83 Pype Hayes Road, Birmingham B24 0LU* Tel 0121-382 1218

FURNESS, Edward Peter Alexander. b 29. St Edm Hall Ox BA52 MA56. St Aid Birkenhead 52. **d** 54 **p** 55. C Ashton-on-Ribble St Andr *Blackb* 54-57; C Storrington *Chich* 57-59; C Sullington 57-59; V Worsthorne *Blackb* 59-64 and 88-94; V Longridge 64-88; rtd 94; Perm to Offic *Blackb* from 94. *26 Severn Street, Longridge, Preston PR3 3ND* Tel (01772) 784092

FURNESS, John Alfred. b 31. Chich Th Coll 60. **d** 62 **p** 63. C Leeds St Aid *Ripon* 62-66; C Rickmansworth *St Alb* 66-73; R Wymington 73-75; P-in-c Podington w Farndish 74-75; R Wymington w Podington 75-79; V Waltham Cross 79-89; RD Cheshunt 84-89; R Swyncombe w Britwell Salome *Ox* 89-97; rtd 97; Perm to Offic *St Alb* from 97; Perm to Offic *S'wark* from 00. *9 The Quadrangle, Morden College, 19 St German's Place, London SE3 0PW* Tel (020) 8858 2838

FURST, John William. b 41. Bris Sch of Min Ripon Coll Cuddesdon. **d** 84 **p** 85. C Bris Ch the Servant Stockwood *Bris* 84-88; V Hanham 88-94; Perm to Offic *Llan* from 98; V Gosberton, Gosberton Clough and Quadring *Linc* from 99. *The Vicarage, 6 Wargate Way, Gosberton, Spalding PE11 4NH* Tel (01775) 840694

✠**FURUMOTO, The Rt Revd John Junichiro.** b 33. Tokushima Univ BEd56 Wycliffe Coll Toronto LTh BTh Hon DD97. Cen Th Coll Tokyo 62. **d** 63 **p** 64 **c** 92. R Kobe Ascension 63-91; Bp Kobe from 92; Primate of Nippon Seikokai 00-02. *65-3 Yaraicho, Shinjuku-ku, Tokyo, 162-0805, Japan* Tel (0081) (3) 5228 3171 Fax 5228 3175

FUTCHER, Christopher David. b 58. Edin Univ BD80 Lon Univ MTh04. Westcott Ho Cam 80. **d** 82 **p** 83. C Borehamwood *St Alb* 82-85; C Stevenage All SS Pin Green 85-88; V 88-96; V St Alb St Steph 96-00; R Harpenden St Nic from 00. *The Rectory, 9 Rothamsted Avenue, Harpenden AL5 2DD* Tel (01582) 712202 *or* 765524 Fax 713646 E-mail cdfutcher@surefish.co.uk

FUTERS, Michael Roger. b 58. Trin & All SS Coll Leeds BEd80. St Jo Coll Nottm 82. **d** 85 **p** 86. C Narborough and Huncote *Leic* 85-87; C Spondon *Derby* 87-90; P-in-c Derby St Jas 90-95; TV Walbrook Epiphany 95-99; Community Development Officer Home Housing from 99; Hon C Derby St Mark from 99. *3 St Pancras Way, Derby DE1 3TH* Tel (01332) 203075

FYFE, Gordon Boyd. b 63. Aber Univ BD93 Edin Univ MTh95. TISEC 94. **d** 96 **p** 97. C Ayr *Glas* 96-99; C Maybole 96-99; C Girvan 96-99; R Airdrie from 99; R Coatbridge from 99. *The Rectory, 24 Etive Drive, Airdrie ML6 9QQ* Tel and fax (01236) 756550 E-mail gordonfyfe@blueyonder.co.uk

FYFE, Stewart John. b 69. City Univ BSc91. Ridley Hall Cam 03. **d** 05. C Barony of Burgh *Carl* from 05. *7 Cross House Gardens, Great Orton, Carlisle CA5 6NA* Tel 07985-900477 (mobile) E-mail stewart_fyfe@hotmail.com

FYFFE, Canon Robert Clark. b 56. Edin Univ BD78 Napier Univ Edin MBA98. Edin Th Coll 74. **d** 79 **p** 80. C Edin St Jo *Edin* 79-83; Youth Chapl *B & W* 83-87; Prov Youth Officer Scottish Episc Ch 87-92; Co-ord Internat Angl Youth Network from 88; R Perth St Jo *St And* from 93; Can St Ninian's Cathl Perth from 96. *23 Comely Bank, Perth PH2 7HU* Tel (01738) 625394 Fax 443053 E-mail bobfyffe@btopenworld.com

FYFFE, Timothy Bruce. b 25. New Coll Ox MA54. Westcott Ho Cam 54. **d** 56 **p** 57. C Lewisham St Mary *S'wark* 56-60; Nigeria 60-68; TV Lowestoft St Marg *Nor* 69-80; Chapl HM Pris Blundeston 70-78; TV Tettenhall Regis *Lich* 80-85; Chapl Compton Hall Hospice Wolv 85-87; NSM Wolverhampton St Andr *Lich* from 88; rtd 90. *40 Glentworth Gardens, Wolverhampton WV6 0SG* Tel (01902) 716510

FYLES, Gordon. b 39. Trin Coll Bris 76. **d** 77 **p** 78. C Islington St Mary *Lon* 77-81; Ext Sec BCMS 81-88; C Wimbledon Em Ridgway Prop Chpl *S'wark* 88-97; I Crinken *D & G* 97-04; rtd 04. *7 Shore Street, Hilton, Tain IV20 1XD* Tel (01862) 832131 E-mail gordonandyvonne@yahoo.co.uk

FYSH, Leslie David. b 35. Glouc Sch of Min 88. **d** 91 **p** 92. NSM Stonehouse *Glouc* 91-95; Asst Chapl Wycliffe Coll Glos 91-95; NSM W Walton *Ely* 95-00; Perm to Offic from 00. *16 Tower Court, Tower Road, Ely CB7 4XS* Tel (01353) 659776

G

GABB-JONES, Adrian William Douglas. b 43. MRICS. Ripon Coll Cuddesdon 79. **d** 81 **p** 82. C Northolt Park St Barn *Lon* 81-84; C Ruislip St Martin 84-89; V Minster Lovell and Brize Norton *Ox* 89-03; V Minster Lovell from 03. *The Vicarage, Burford Road, Minster Lovell, Oxford OX29 0RA* Tel (01993) 776492

GABBADON, Kenneth Fitz Arthur. b 53. N Man Coll Cert Counselling 89. N Ord Course 97. **d** 99 **p** 00. C Burnage St Marg *Man* 99-01; C Bury St Jo w St Mark 01-03; P-in-c Newton Heath from 03. *All Saints' Rectory, 2 Culcheth Lane, Manchester M40 1LR* Tel 0161-681 3102 E-mail kgabba7036@aol.com

GABE, Eric Sigurd. b 15. Lon Univ BA52 PhD94. St Aid Birkenhead 54. **d** 55 **p** 55. C W Kirby St Andr *Ches* 55-57; C Hoylake 57-60; V Cricklewood St Mich *Lon* 60-72; V Brondesbury St Anne w Kilburn H Trin 72-80; rtd 80; Perm to Offic *St Alb* from 80 and *Lon* from 81. *21 Cromer Road, Barnet EN5 5HT* Tel (020) 8449 6779

GABLE, Michael David. b 70. Poly of Wales BEng92. St Mich Coll Llan BTh95. **d** 95 **p** 96. C Newton Nottage *Llan* 95-99; V Aberavon H Trin 99-01; TV Aberavon 01-05; P-in-c Rhydyfelin w Graig from 05. *St John's Vicarage, 28 Llantrisant Road, Graig, Pontypridd CF37 1LW* Tel (01443) 651810 E-mail michaelgable@hotmail.com

GABRIEL, Michael Hunt. b 29. BA. **d** 57 **p** 58. C Waterford Ch Ch *C & O* 57-60; C New Windsor H Trin *Ox* 60-62; C Albany Street Ch Ch *Lon* 62-63; R W and E Shefford *Ox* 63-67; C Hillingdon St Jo *Lon* 67-86; C Kingston Buci *Chich* 86-94; rtd 94. *Flat 1, 6 Dittons Road, Eastbourne BN21 1DN*

GADD, Alan John. b 44. Imp Coll Lon BSc65 PhD69 FRMetS67. S'wark Ord Course 68. **d** 71 **p** 72. Asst Chapl Lon Univ *Lon* 71-72; Perm to Offic *S'wark* 73-91; C Battersea Park All SS 91-95; P-in-c 95-96; C Battersea Fields 96-05; rtd 05. *24 Holmewood Gardens, London SW2 3RS* Tel (020) 8678 8977 E-mail holmewood24@surefish.co.uk

GADD, Brian Hayward. b 33. Hatf Coll Dur BA54 DipEd55. Glouc Sch of Min 82. **d** 85 **p** 87. NSM Cleobury Mortimer w Hopton Wafers etc *Heref* 85-98; rtd 98; Perm to Offic *Heref* from 99. *34 Lower Street, Cleobury Mortimer, Kidderminster DY14 8AB* Tel (01299) 270758

GADD, Bryan Stephen Andrew. b 56. Dur Univ BA Ox Univ CertEd. Chich Th Coll. **d** 81 **p** 82. C Newlyn St Pet *Truro* 81-86; R St Mawgan w St Ervan and St Eval 86-90; Chapl Summer Fields Sch Ox 90-02; Perm to Offic *Truro* 90-00. *Address temp unknown* E-mail bryan.gadd@lineone.net

GADEN, Timothy John. b 64. Melbourne Univ BA86 Monash Univ Aus PhD96. Melbourne Coll of Div BD90. **d** 91 **p** 91. Australia 91-96 and from 01; C Battersea St Mary *S'wark* 97; V 97-01; Dir Post-Ord Tr Kingston Area 99-01; R Camberwell St Jo from 01. *15 The Grove, Camberwell, Vic, Australia 3124* Tel (0061) (3) 9889 6456 *or* 9882 4851 Mobile 419-114697 Fax (3) 9882 0086 E-mail gaden@stjohnscamberwell.org.au

GAGE, Alan William. b 52. Univ of Wales (Cardiff) BMus72 PGCE73 Bris Univ MEd90. WEMTC 98. **d** 00 **p** 01. NSM Tuffley *Glouc* from 00. *Chadburn, 83 Dinglewell, Hucclecote, Gloucester GL3 3HT* Tel (01452) 614892 E-mail alan@leapyear.demon.co.uk

GAGE, Aëlla Rupert Fitzehardinge Berkeley. b 66. Reading Univ BEd92. Oak Hill Th Coll 98. **d** 00. C Muswell Hill St Jas w St Matt *Lon* from 00. *67 St James Lane, London N10 3QY* Tel (020) 8365 3194 *or* 8883 6277 E-mail aella.gage@st-james.org.uk

GAGE, Canon Robert Edward. b 47. Whitman Coll Washington BA69. Cuddesdon Coll BA75 MA81. **d** 76 **p** 77. C Cheshunt *St Alb* 76-79; C Harpenden St Nic 79-81; V S Mymms 81-82; P-in-c Ridge 81-82; V S Mymms and Ridge 82-97; Prec and Can Res Wakef Cathl *Wakef* from 96. *4 Cathedral Close, Wakefield WF1 2DP* Tel (01924) 210008 E-mail gage@tromba.freeserve.co.uk

GAINER, Jeffrey. b 51. Jes Coll Ox BA73 MA77 Univ of Wales LLM94. Wycliffe Hall Ox 74. **d** 77 **p** 78. C Baglan *Llan* 77-81; V Cwmbach 81-85; V Tonyrefail w Gilfach Goch and Llandyfodwg 85-87; Dir NT Studies and Dir Past Studies St Mich Coll Llan 87-92; V Meidrim and Llanboidy and Merthyr *St D* from 92; AD St Clears from 03. *The Vicarage, Meidrim, Carmarthen SA33 5QF* Tel (01994) 231378

GAIR, Andrew Kennon. b 62. Westcott Ho Cam 88. **d** 91 **p** 92. C Clare w Poslingford, Cavendish etc *St E* 91-95; R Debden and Wimbish w Thunderley *Chelmsf* from 95. *The Rectory, Mill Road, Debden, Saffron Walden CB11 3LB* Tel (01799) 540285 E-mail andrew.gair@btinternet.com

✠**GAISFORD, The Rt Revd John Scott.** b 34. St Chad's Coll Dur BA59 MA76 DipTh60. **d** 60 **p** 61 **c** 94. C Audenshaw St Hilda *Man* 60-62; C Bramhall *Ches* 62-65; V Crewe St Andr 65-86; RD Nantwich 74-85; Hon Can Ches Cathl 80-86; Adn Macclesfield 86-94; Suff Bp Beverley (PEV) *York* 94-00; Asst Bp Ripon and Leeds *Ripon* 96-00; rtd 00; Perm to Offic *Ches* from 00. *5 Trevone Close, Knutsford WA16 9EJ* Tel (01565) 633531 Mobile 07855-615469 E-mail jandg.gaisford@tiscali.co.uk

GAIT, David James. b 48. BNC Ox BA71 BSc72 MA77 MSc83. Ridley Hall Cam 71. **d** 74 **p** 75. C Litherland St Paul Hatton Hill *Liv* 74-77; C Farnworth 77-80; V Widnes St Jo from 80; Chapl Widnes Maternity Hosp 86-90. *St John's House, Greenway Road, Widnes WA8 6HA* Tel 0151-424 3134 E-mail dave.gait@btinternet.com

GAKURU, Griphus Stephen. Makerere Univ Kampala BSc81 PGDE83 Selw Coll Cam MPhil92 PhD. Bp Tucker Coll Mukono BD88. **d** 88 **p** 91. Uganda 89-91; Hon C Cambridge H Trin w St Andr Gt *Ely* 91-92; Hon C Cambridge H Trin 92-95; Chapl Selw Coll Cam 91-95; C Small Heath *Birm* 95-98; C Huyton St Mich *Liv* 98-01; P-in-c Brownswood Park *Lon* 01-03; Perm to Offic *St Alb* from 03. *51 Tollgate Road, Colney Heath, St Albans AL4 0PX* Tel (01727) 826973 E-mail ggakuru@aol.com

GALBRAITH, Alexander Peter James. b 65. Qu Coll Ox BA86 MA90. Wycliffe Hall Ox 87. **d** 90 **p** 91. C Southport Em *Liv* 90-94; C Mossley Hill St Matt and St Jas 94-97; V Kew from 97; Chapl Southport and Ormskirk NHS Trust from 97. *20 Markham Drive, Kew, Southport PR8 6XR* Tel (01704) 547758

GALBRAITH, Jane Alexandra. **d** 95 **p** 96. NSM Kildare w Kilmeague and Curragh *M & K* 95-97; NSM Newbridge w Carnalway and Kilcullen 97-99; C Limerick *L & K* from 03. *50 Ballinvoher, Father Russell Road, Dooradoyle, Limerick, Irish Republic* Tel and fax (00353) (61) 302038

GALBRAITH, John Angus Frame. b 44. Sarum Th Coll 68. **d** 71 **p** 72. C Richmond St Mary *S'wark* 71-74; Chapl W Lon Colls 74-79; R S'wark H Trin w St Matt 79-95; V New Addington 95-02; Asst Chapl HM Pris Wandsworth 02-04; Chapl from 04. *HM Prison Wandsworth, PO Box 757, Heathfield Road, London SW18 3HS* Tel (020) 8874 7292 ext 327 E-mail angusg@madasafish.com

GALBRAITH, Peter John. b 59. QUB BA MTh TCD DipTh. **d** 85 **p** 86. C Knockbreda *D & D* 85-88; C Ballynafeigh St Jude 88-91; I Broomhedge *Conn* from 91. *Broomhedge Rectory, 30 Lurganure Road, Broughmore, Lisburn BT28 2TR* Tel (028) 9262 1229

GALE, Ms Charlotte. b 70. Leeds Univ BEng92 Nottm Univ MA00. St Jo Coll Nottm 98. **d** 01 **p** 02. C Whitnash *Cov* 01-05; P-in-c Potters Green from 05. *St Philip's Vicarage, Ringwood Highway, Coventry CV2 2GF* Tel (024) 7661 7706 E-mail cgale@fish.co.uk

GALE, Canon Christopher. b 44. ALCD67. **d** 68 **p** 69. C Balderton *S'well* 68-72; C Bilborough St Jo 72-75; P-in-c Colwick 75-78; V Radford St Pet 78-84; V Sherwood 84-98; AD Nottingham N 90-98; P-in-c Bulwell St Mary 98-02; R from 02; Hon Can S'well Minster from 03. *Bulwell Rectory, Station Road, Nottingham NG6 9AA* Tel 0115-927 8468 E-mail rev.chris@bulwell75.fsnet.co.uk

GALE, Colin Edward. b 49. Lon Univ PGCE74. St Jo Coll Nottm BTh73. **d** 79 **p** 80. C Hoole *Ches* 79-82; C Woodley St Jo the Ev *Ox* 82-87; V Clapham St Jas *S'wark* 87-96; V Sutton Ch Ch from 96; R Burstow w Horne from 05. *The Rectory, 5 The Acorns, Smallfield, Horley RH6 9QJ* Tel (01342) 842224 E-mail revceg@aol.com

GALE, The Ven John. b 34. Univ of Wales (Lamp) 67. **d** 69 **p** 70. C Aberdare *Llan* 69-71; C Merthyr Dyfan 71-74; S Africa 74-00; R Walmer St Sav 74-82; R Knysna St Geo 82-00; Adn Knysna 93-00; Lic to Offic *St D* from 00. *3 Connacht Way, Pembroke Dock SA72 6FB* Tel and fax (01946) 622219

GALE, Keith George. b 44. St Jo Coll Lusaka 68 Sarum Th Coll 69. **d** 70 **p** 71. C Sheff St Cuth *Sheff* 70-77; P-in-c Brightside All SS 72-77; C Birm St Martin *Birm* 77-81; USPG 81-94; Malawi 81-94; Adn Lilongwe 89-92; TV Sampford Peverell, Uplowman, Holcombe Rogus etc *Ex* from 94. *The Rectory, Blackdown View, Sampford Peverell, Tiverton EX16 7BE* Tel (01884) 821879 E-mail keithggale@aol.com

GALE, Ms Lucille Catherine. b 67. Sarum & Wells Th Coll 92. **d** 94 **p** 95. C Welling *S'wark* 94-97; Chapl Univ of Greenwich 97-00; V Welling from 00. *St Mary's Vicarage, Sandringham Drive, Welling DA16 3QU* Tel (020) 8856 0684

GALE, Peter Simon. b 56. Welsh Coll of Music & Drama 73 K Alfred's Coll Win PGCE78. St Mich Coll Llan BD83. **d** 83 **p** 84. C Caerphilly *Llan* 83-89; Chapl RN 89-93; V Ystrad Rhondda w Ynyscynon *Llan* from 93. *St Stephen's Vicarage, Ystrad, Pentre CF41 7RR* Tel (01443) 434426

GALES, Alan. b 29. Sarum Th Coll 56. **d** 59 **p** 60. C Greenside *Dur* 59-60; C Peterlee 60-63; Ind Chapl 60-70; V Marley Hill 63-94; Asst Chapl HM Pris Dur 74-81; rtd 94. *46 Corsair, Whickham, Newcastle upon Tyne NE16 5YA* Tel 0191-488 7352

GALES, Bernard Henry. b 27. Lon Univ BSc(Econ)51 Open Univ BA02. Wells Th Coll 62. **d** 64 **p** 65. C Sholing *Win* 64-67; C Fordingbridge w Ibsley 67-71; C S Molton w Nymet St George *Ex* 71-73; C Thelbridge 73-77; P-in-c 77-78; P-in-c Creacombe 77-78; P-in-c W w E Worlington 77-78; P-in-c Meshaw 77-78; P-in-c Witheridge 77-78; C Witheridge, Thelbridge, Creacombe, Meshaw etc 79-80; R Bow w Broad Nymet 80-93; V Colebrooke 80-93; R Zeal Monachorum 80-93; RD Cadbury 90-93; rtd 93; Perm to Offic *Ex* from 93. *8 Old Rectory Gardens, Morchard Bishop, Crediton EX17 6PF* Tel (01363) 877601

GALES, Simon Richard. b 59. CEng87 MICE87 Jes Coll Cam BA81 MA84. Wycliffe Hall Ox 91. **d** 93 **p** 94. C Houghton *Carl* 93-97; V Lindow *Ches* from 97. *St John's Vicarage, 137 Knutsford Road, Wilmslow SK9 6EL* Tel (01625) 583251 *or* 586329 E-mail simon@srgales.freeserve.co.uk

GALILEE, Canon George David Surtees. b 37. Oriel Coll Ox BA60 MA64. Westcott Ho Cam 61. **d** 62 **p** 63. C Knighton St Mary Magd *Leic* 62-67; V Stocking Farm 67-69; Tutor Westcott Ho Cam and Homerton Coll 69-71; V Sutton *Ely* 71-80; P-in-c Addiscombe St Mildred *Cant* 80-81; V 81-84; V Addiscombe St Mildred *S'wark* 85-95; Can Res and Chan Blackb Cathl *Blackb* 95-04; rtd 04; Perm to Offic *Blackb* from 04. *Ivy Hatch, 25 Ryburn Avenue, Blackburn BB2 7AU* Tel (01254) 671540 Fax 689666

GALLAGHER, Adrian Ian. b 43. CITC 89. **d** 92 **p** 93. C Drumachose *D & R* 92-96; I Camus-juxta-Bann 96-00; TV Langley and Parkfield *Man* from 00. *The Vicarage, 5 Wentworth Close, Middleton, Manchester M24 4BD* Tel 0161-643 8701 Mobile 07796-022473

GALLAGHER, Canon Ian. BTh. **d** 90 **p** 91. C Annagh w Drumgoon, Ashfield etc *K, E & A* 90-93; I Drumcliffe w Lissadell and Munninane 93-01; Can Elphin Cathl 97-01; Dioc Sec (Elphin and Ardagh) 97-01; Preb Mulhuddart St Patr Cathl Dublin 98-01; I Stillorgan w Blackrock *D & G* from 01. *The Rectory, St Brigid's Church Road, Stillorgan, Blackrock, Co Dublin, Irish Republic* Tel (00353) (1) 288 1091 Fax 278 1833 Mobile 86-811 9544 E-mail stillorgan@dublin.anglican.org

GALLAGHER, Matthew Edward. b 51. Glas Univ BSc75. EAMTC. **d** 00 **p** 01. NSM Northampton St Jas *Pet* 00-02. *11 Penfold Gardens, Great Billing, Northampton NN3 9PG* Tel (01604) 416972 E-mail me.gallagher@virgin.net

GALLAGHER, Michael Collins. b 48. Dur Univ BA. Sarum Th Coll. **d** 82 **p** 83. C Bridport *Sarum* 82-86; V Downton 86-01; RD Alderbury 93-99; R Crewkerne w Wayford *B & W* from 01. *The Rectory, Gouldsbrook Terrace, Crewkerne TA18 7JA* Tel (01460) 271188 Fax 271194 E-mail m.gallagher@mail.com

GALLAGHER, Neville Roy. b 45. Birm Univ CertEd66 K Coll Lon AKC70 BD76 Open Univ BA97. **d** 71 **p** 72. C Folkestone St Mary and St Eanswythe *Cant* 71-74; Hon C Sutton Valence w E Sutton and Chart Sutton 74-76; TV Cen Telford *Lich* 76-78; P-in-c Gt Mongeham *Cant* 78-80; P-in-c Ripple 78-80; R Gt Mongeham w Ripple and Sutton by Dover 80-83; V Kennington 83-88; Chapl and Dep Hd Bedgebury Sch Kent 88-05; P-in-c Appledore w Brookland, Fairfield, Brenzett etc *Cant* from 05. *The Vicarage, Old Way, Appledore, Ashford TN26 2DB* Tel (01233) 758250 E-mail nrwg45@aol.com

GALLAGHER, Robert. b 43. St Chad's Coll Dur BSc65 DipTh67. **d** 67 **p** 68. C Crosland Moor *Wakef* 67-69; C Huddersfield SS Pet and Paul 69-71; Chapl Huddersfield Poly 72-79; Min Coulby Newham LEP *York* 79-90; V Toxteth St Marg *Liv* from 90. *St Margaret's Vicarage, 3 Princes Road, Liverpool L8 1TG* Tel 0151-709 1526

GALLAGHER, Stephen. b 58. Southn Univ BTh89. Chich Th Coll 86. **d** 89 **p** 90. C S Shields All SS *Dur* 89-92; C Hartlepool St Paul 92-94; Chapl Hartlepool Gen Hosp 92-94; R Loftus and Carlin How w Skinningrove *York* 94-97; P-in-c Lower Beeding *Chich* from 97; Dioc Youth Officer from 97. *The Vicarage, Plummers Plain, Lower Beeding, Horsham RH13 6NU* Tel (01403) 891367 E-mail fatherstephen@plummersplain.freeserve.co.uk

GALLANT, Mrs Joanna-Sue Sheena. b 62. St Alb and Ox Min Course 99. **d** 02 **p** 03. C Amersham on the Hill *Ox* from 02. *50 Frances Street, Chesham HP5 3ER* Tel (01494) 580077 Mobile 07813-886805 E-mail gallant.family@zoom.co.uk

GALLETLY, Thomas. b 23. St Chad's Coll Dur BA50 DipTh52. **d** 52 **p** 53. C Woodhorn w Newbiggin *Newc* 52-55; Chapl Aycliffe

Approved Sch Co Dur 56-57; Chapl Chailey Heritage Hosp and Sch Lewes 57-88; Lic to Offic *Chich* 59-88; rtd 88; Perm to Offic *Chich* from 88. *The Glen, Lewes Road, Scaynes Hill, Haywards Heath RH17 7PG* Tel (01444) 831510

GALLEY, Giles Christopher. b 32. Qu Coll Cam BA56 MA60. Linc Th Coll 56. **d** 58 **p** 59. C Gt Yarmouth *Nor* 58-62; C N Lynn w St Marg and St Nic 62-66; C Leeds St Pet *Ripon* 66-69; V N Hull St Mich *York* 70-79; V Strensall 79-00; RD Easingwold 82-97; rtd 00; Perm to Offic *York* from 00. *19 St John's Road, Stamford Bridge, York YO41 1PH* Tel (01759) 371592

GALLICHAN, Henry Ernest. b 45. Sarum Th Coll 70. **d** 72 **p** 73. C Kenton Ascension *Newc* 72-76; Tanzania 76-80; Lic to Offic *Truro* 80-83; Public Preacher from 83. *Karibu, Trevelmond, Liskeard PL14 4LZ* Tel (01579) 320530
E-mail karibu@iname.com

✠**GALLIFORD, The Rt Revd David George.** b 25. Clare Coll Cam BA49 MA51. Westcott Ho Cam. **d** 51 **p** 52 **c** 75. C Newland St Jo *York* 51-54; C Eton w Boveney *Ox* 54-56; Min Can Windsor 54-56; V Middlesbrough St Oswald *York* 56-61; R Bolton Percy 61-71; Dioc Adult Tr Officer 61-71; Can and Preb York Minster 69-70; Can Res and Treas 70-75; Suff Bp Hulme *Man* 75-84; Suff Bp Bolton 84-91; rtd 91; Hon Asst Bp York from 95. *Bishopgarth, Maltongate, Thornton Dale, Pickering YO18 7SA* Tel (01751) 474605

GALLIGAN, Ms Adrienne. TCD BA81 HDipEd82. CITC BTh03. **d** 03 **p** 04. C Seapatrick *D & D* from 03. *26 Larchwood Avenue, Banbridge BT32 3XH* Tel (028) 4066 9086

GALLON, Mrs Audrey Kay. b 41. SEITE 94. **d** 97 **p** 98. NSM Gt Mongeham w Ripple and Sutton by Dover *Cant* 97-98; NSM Eastry and Northbourne w Tilmanstone etc 97-98; NSM Walmer 98-04; Perm to Offic 04-05. *Address temp unknown*

GALLOWAY, Canon Charles Bertram. b 41. Lon Univ BA62. Qu Coll Birm 64. **d** 64 **p** 65. C Darlington H Trin *Dur* 64-68; Ind Chapl Teesside 68-77; Sen Ind Chapl *Liv* 77-87; Team Ldr and Convener Lon Ind Chapl *Lon* 87-93; P-in-c Gosforth w Nether Wasdale and Wasdale Head *Carl* 93-98; R 98-04; Chapl Sellafield 94-04; Hon Can Carl Cathl from 03; rtd 04. *27 Oakfield Close, Sunderland SR3 3RT* Tel 0191-528 8459
E-mail bert.galloway@btinternet.com

GALLOWAY, Michael Edward. b 41. Chich Th Coll 72. **d** 74 **p** 75. C Aldwick *Chich* 74-77; C Bournemouth St Clem w St Mary *Win* 78-82; V S Benfleet *Chelmsf* from 83. *St Mary's Vicarage, 105 Vicarage Hill, Benfleet SS7 1PD* Tel (01268) 792294
E-mail ceag@dialstart.net

GALLOWAY, Peter John. b 54. OBE96 JP89. Goldsmiths' Coll Lon BA76 K Coll Lon PhD87 FRSA88 FSA00. St Steph Ho Ox 80. **d** 83 **p** 84. C St John's Wood *Lon* 83-86; C St Giles-in-the-Fields 86-90; Warden of Readers (Lon Episc Area) 87-92; P-in-c Hampstead Em W End 90-95; V from 95; Hon Fell Goldsmiths' Coll Lon from 99; AD N Camden *Lon* from 02. *Emmanuel Vicarage, Lyncroft Gardens, London NW6 1JU* Tel (020) 7435 1911 Fax 7431 5521 E-mail peter.galloway@sja.org.uk

GALSWORTHY, Colin. b 44. St Mich Coll Llan 95. **d** 00 **p** 01. NSM Skewen *Llan* 00-01; NSM Resolven w Tonna 01-04; NSM Tonna from 04; NSM Cadoxton-juxta-Neath from 04. *29 Woodlands Park Drive, Cadoxton, Neath SA10 8DE* Tel (01639) 636128

GALT, Ian Ross. b 34. Leeds Univ BSc56. **d** 76 **p** 77. NSM Newport St Julian *Mon* 76-87; NSM Newport St Teilo 87-98. *47 BryngIas Avenue, Newport NP20 5LR* Tel (01633) 821499

GAMBLE, Bronwen. *See* GAMBLE, Mrs Edana Bronwen

GAMBLE, David Lawrence. b 34. AKC61. **d** 62 **p** 63. C-in-c Shrub End All SS CD *Chelmsf* 62-65; C Colchester St Jas, All SS, St Nic and St Runwald 65-69; V Chelmsf St Andr 69-73; P-in-c Hatfield Heath 69-73; C 74-77; TV Hemel Hempstead *St Alb* 77-82; P-in-c Renhold 82-90; Chapl HM Pris Bedf 82-90; P-in-c Petersham *S'wark* 90-96; Chapl HM Pris Latchmere Ho 90-96; P-in-c Portsea St Geo *Portsm* 96-99; rtd 99; Hon C Yarmouth and Freshwater *Portsm* 99-04. *Easterholme, Tennyson Road, Yarmouth PO41 0PR* Tel (01983) 761360

GAMBLE, Diane Mary. BSc. **d** 00 **p** 01. NSM Sanderstead All SS *S'wark* from 00. *14 Barnfield Road, Sanderstead CR2 0EY*

GAMBLE, Donald William. b 67. NUU BSc88. TCD Div Sch BTh91. **d** 91 **p** 92. C Belfast St Mich *Conn* 91-95; I Dromore *Clogh* 95-00; P-in-c Renewal and Outreach in the City *Conn* from 00. *5 Fernridge Road, Newtownabbey BT36 5SP* Tel (028) 9084 2171 E-mail don.gamble@rocbelfast.com

GAMBLE, Mrs Edana Bronwen. b 56. Hull Univ BSc(Econ)78 FCA82 Nottm Univ MA02. EMMTC 99. **d** 02 **p** 03. NSM Nuthall *S'well* from 02. *8 Turner Close, Stapleford, Nottingham NG9 7HQ* Tel 0115-939 3062
E-mail brongamble@hotmail.com

GAMBLE, Ian Robert. b 66. Ulster Univ BA90 MA98 TCD BTh93. CITC 90. **d** 93 **p** 94. C Bangor St Comgall *D & D* 93-96; C Bangor Primacy 93-96; Bp's C Belfast Whiterock *Conn* 96-99; R Donaghadee *D & D* from 99. *The Rectory, 3 The Trees, New Road, Donaghadee BT21 0EJ* Tel (028) 9188 2594

GAMBLE, Norman Edward Charles. b 50. TCD BA72 HDipEd73 PhD78. CITC 76. **d** 79 **p** 80. C Bangor St Comgall *D & D* 79-83; I Dunleckney w Nurney, Lorum and Kiltennel *C & O* 83-90; Warden of Readers 84-90; P-in-c Leighlin w Grange Sylvae, Shankill etc 89-90; Can Leighlin Cathl 89-90; Preb Ossory Cathl 89-90; I Malahide w Balgriffin *D & G* from 90; Abp's Dom Chapl 95-03. *The Rectory, Church Road, Malahide, Co Dublin, Irish Republic* Tel and fax (00353) (1) 845 4770 Mobile 86-815 3277
E-mail norman_gamble@hotmail.com

GAMBLE, Canon Robin Philip. b 53. Oak Hill Th Coll 74. **d** 77 **p** 78. C Kildwick *Bradf* 77-78; C Laisterdyke 78-80; C York St Paul *York* 80-82; V Bradf St Aug Undercliffe *Bradf* 82-95; Dioc Adv in Evang 93-01; Can Ev Man Cathl *Man* from 01. *30 Rathen Road, Manchester M20 4GH* Tel 0161-446 1099 *or* 438 2834 E-mail robin.gamble1@virgin.net

GAMBLE, Ronald George. b 41. Cant Sch of Min 92. **d** 95 **p** 96. NSM Loose *Cant* 95-00; P-in-c Boxley w Detling from 00; Chapl NHS Ambulance Trust from 99. *The Vicarage, The Street, Boxley, Maidstone ME14 3DX* Tel (01622) 758606 Mobile 07712-562491 E-mail ron.gamble@talk21.com

GAMBLES, Una Beryl. b 33. Man Univ BEd78. St Chris Coll Blackheath 59. **d** 87 **p** 94. NSM Upton Priory *Ches* 87-01; Chapl Parkside Hosp Ches 87-93; Chapl E Cheshire NHS Trust 93-01; Chapl HM Pris Styal 94-98; Perm to Offic *Ches* from 01. *23 Grangelands, Upton, Macclesfield SK10 4AB* Tel (01625) 421691

GAMESTER, Sidney Peter. b 27. SS Coll Cam BA51 MA55. Oak Hill Th Coll 56. **d** 58 **p** 59. C Surbiton Hill Ch Ch *S'wark* 58-61; C Worthing H Trin *Chich* 61-69; R Silverhill St Matt 69-86; R Bexhill St Mark 86-93; rtd 93; Perm to Offic *Chich* from 93. *18 Crofton Park Avenue, Bexhill-on-Sea TN39 3SE* Tel (01424) 842276

GAMMON, William Paul Lachlan. b 60. SS Hild & Bede Coll Dur BA82. St Steph Ho Ox 89. **d** 91 **p** 92. C Chalfont St Peter *Ox* 91-94; Lect Bolton St Pet *Man* 94-98; R Woodston *Ely* from 98; P-in-c Fletton from 98. *The Rectory, 2 Rectory Gardens, Peterborough PE2 8HN* Tel (01733) 562786

GANDIYA, Chad Nicholas. b 53. Nottm Univ BTh80 Univ of Zimbabwe MA84 Michigan State Univ MA95. St Jo Coll Nottm 77. **d** 80 **p** 81. C Avondale Zimbabwe 80-83; R Mabelreigh St Pet 83-85; Chapl Michigan Univ USA 86-87; Asst P Harare Cathl 88; Warden Bp Gaul Coll 88-91; USA 92-95; R Marlborough St Paul 95-96; Prin Bp Gaul Coll 96-01; Tutor United Coll of Ascension Selly Oak from 01. *1 Huddleston Way, Selly Oak, Birmingham B29 5AJ* Tel 0121-415 6829
E-mail c.gandiya@bham.ac.uk

GANDIYA, Leonard Farirayi (Lee). b 64. Colorado Coll 87 Boston Univ 90 MA92. Ridley Hall Cam 92. **d** 94 **p** 95. NSM Camberwell St Luke *S'wark* 94-95; C Lowestoft St Marg *Nor* 95-98; Dioc Rep for Black Anglican Concerns 96-98; CF from 98. *c/o MOD Chaplains (Army)* Tel (01980) 615804 Fax 615800

GANDON, Andrew James Robson. b 54. St Jo Coll Dur BA76. Ridley Hall Cam 76. **d** 78 **p** 79. C Aston SS Pet and Paul *Birm* 78-82; CMS 82-95; Zaïre 82-88; Kenya 89-94; V Harefield *Lon* from 95; Chapl R Brompton and Harefield NHS Trust from 95. *The Vicarage, 28 Countess Close, Harefield, Uxbridge UB9 6DL* Tel (01895) 825960 Fax 820705
E-mail andrew.gandon@london.anglican.org

GANDON, James Philip. b 31. ALCD56. **d** 56 **p** 57. C Westcliff St Mich *Chelmsf* 56-58; Canada from 58; rtd 92. *62 Cambria Road North, Goderich ON, Canada, N7A 2P3*
E-mail phil.gandon@odyssey.on.ca

GANDON, Percy James. b 22. ALCD53. **d** 53 **p** 54. C New Humberstone *Leic* 53-56; C Leic H Trin 56-57; Chapl Tororo Uganda 57-63; V 60-63; V Hoddesdon *St Alb* 63-83; RD Cheshunt 81-83; Perm to Offic *Nor* 83-85 and from 86; P-in-c Lyng w Sparham 85-86; rtd 87. *The Old Bakery, 34 The Street, Hindolveston, Dereham NR20 5DF* Tel (01263) 861325

GANDY, Nicholas John. b 53. Westf Coll Lon BSc75 Reading Univ MSc76 Ex Coll Ox CertEd78 CBiol79 MIBiol. St Steph Ho Ox 86. **d** 88 **p** 89. C Crowthorne *Ox* 88-89; C Tilehurst St Mary 89-93; P-in-c Didcot St Pet 93-97; V 97-03; V Brackley St Pet w St Jas *Pet* from 03; OGS from 96. *The Vicarage, Old Town, Brackley NN13 7BZ* Tel (01280) 702767
E-mail nicholas@ngandy.fsnet.co.uk

GANE, Canon Christopher Paul. b 33. Qu Coll Cam BA57 MA61. Ridley Hall Cam 57. **d** 59 **p** 60. C Rainham *Chelmsf* 59-62; C Farnborough *Guildf* 62-64; V Erith St Paul *Roch* 64-71; V Ipswich St Marg *St E* 71-88; Hon Can St E Cathl 82-98; R Hopton, Market Weston, Barningham etc 88-98; rtd 98; Perm to Offic *St E* from 98. *25 The Croft, Bardwell, Bury St Edmunds IP31 1AN* Tel (01359) 251868

GANE, Nicholas. b 57. St Jo Coll Nottm 93. **d** 95 **p** 96. C Keynsham *B & W* 95-99; TV 99-02. *10 Ludlow Court, Willsbridge, Bristol BS30 6HB* E-mail nick.gane@virgin.net

GANGA, Jeremy Franklin. b 62. Cape Town Univ BSocSc86 Lon Bible Coll BA92 St Jo Coll Nottm MA93. Ridley Hall Cam 93. **d** 95 **p** 96. C St Peter-in-Thanet *Cant* 95-98; Chapl Felsted Sch 98-00; Past Chapl St Paul's Sch Barnes 00-02; NSM Fulham

St Pet *Lon* 00-02; P-in-c from 02. *St Peter's Vicarage, St Peter's Terrace, London SW6 7JS* Tel (020) 7385 2045
E-mail jeremy.ganga@btinternet.com

GANJAVI, John Farhad. b 57. Imp Coll Lon BSc79 ACGI79. Ridley Hall Cam 79. **d** 82 **p** 83. C Yardley St Edburgha *Birm* 82-85; C Knowle 85-89; P-in-c Beaudesert and Henley-in-Arden w Ullenhall *Cov* 89-92; R from 92; RD Alcester 92-99. *The Rectory, Beaudesert Lane, Henley-in-Arden B95 5JY* Tel (01564) 792570 E-mail bdesert@btinternet.com

GANN, Canon Anthony Michael. b 37. TCD BA60 MA64 BD64. **d** 62 **p** 63. V Choral Derry Cathl *D & R* 62-66; Lesotho 66-74; Dioc Officer for Miss and Unity *Carl* 75-80; P-in-c Bampton and Mardale 75-80; TV Cen Telford *Lich* 80-89; TR Wolvercote w Summertown *Ox* 89-02; RD Ox 95-99; rtd 02; Perm to Offic *Worc* from 02. *Avalon, 84 Pickersleigh Road, Malvern WR14 2RS* Tel (01684) 568114

GANN, John West. b 29. Ex Coll Ox BA55 MA59. Wells Th Coll 55. **d** 57 **p** 58. C Wendover *Ox* 57-59; C Walton St Mary *Liv* 59-62; R Didcot *Ox* 62-70; R Newbury St Nic 70-78; TR Newbury 73-78; V Twickenham St Mary *Lon* 78-87; Dir of Ords 81-87; TR Bridport *Sarum* 87-94; RD Lyme Bay 89-92; rtd 94; Perm to Offic *Glouc* from 94; *Bris* from 96. *Three Gables, Charlton Road, Tetbury GL8 8DX* Tel (01666) 503965
E-mail gann.jh@btopenworld.com

GANNEY (née CHAMBERS), Mrs Rachel Jill. b 73. Hull Univ BSc94 MSc96 Selw Coll Cam BTh04. Ridley Hall Cam 01. **d** 04 **p** 05. C Sutton St Jas and Wawne *York* from 04. *7 Corinthian Way, Hull HU9 1UF* Tel (01482) 212216
E-mail rachel@ganney.net

GANT, Canon Brian Leonard. b 45. Ox Univ MTh01. K Coll Lon 72. **d** 73 **p** 74. C Hillmorton *Cov* 73-75; C Cov St Geo 76; P-in-c Maldon St Mary *Chelmsf* 76-79; R Muthill, Crieff and Comrie *St And* 79-81; V Walsall St Paul *Lich* 81-84; Chapl K Sch Worc and Min Can Worc Cathl *Worc* 84-89; V Tunbridge Wells K Chas *Roch* 89-95; Hon Can Kumasi from 94; V Wymondham *Nor* 95-01; P-in-c York All SS N Street *York* 01-03; TV Haxby w Wigginton from 03; CME Officer York Adnry from 01. *The Vicarage, 5 Back Lane, Wigginton, York YO32 2ZH* Tel (01904) 768178 E-mail brianlgant@aol.com

GANT, Peter Robert. b 38. BNC Ox BA60 MA64 G&C Coll Cam BA62 MA67. Ridley Hall Cam 61. **d** 63 **p** 64. C Portsea St Mary *Portsm* 63-67; V Blackheath *Birm* 67-73; Asst Master Harold Malley Gr Sch Solihull 73-75; Perm to Offic *Birm* 73-75 and *Guildf* from 75; rtd 93. *8 Sandon Close, Esher KT10 8JE* Tel (020) 8398 5107

GANZ, Timothy Jon. b 36. Univ Coll Ox BA58 MA62 ARCM63. St Steph Ho Ox 58. **d** 61 **p** 62. C Shrewsbury H Cross *Lich* 61-65; Asst Chapl Hurstpierpoint Coll 65-69; Chapl 69-73; Chapl Univ of Wales (Swansea) *S & B* 74-75; P-in-c Hanley All SS *Lich* 75-80; TV Stoke-upon-Trent 80-81; V Tutbury 81-04; rtd 04. *3 Warren Close, Stretton, Burton-on-Trent DE13 0DD* Tel (01283) 749171

GARBETT, Capt Phillip Ronald. b 52. EAMTC 95. **d** 97 **p** 98. CA from 80; C Ipswich St Mary at Stoke w St Pet and St Fran *St E* 97-00; TV Walton and Trimley from 00. *2 Blyford Way, Felixstowe IP11 2FW* Tel (01394) 213992 Mobile 07884-212218
E-mail philip.garbett@ntlworld.com

GARBUTT, Gerald. b 41. St Aid Birkenhead 65. **d** 67 **p** 68. C Stretford All SS *Man* 67-70; Lic to Offic 70-72; R Salford St Bart 72-74; V Lower Kersal 74-79; TR Bethnal Green St Jo w St Bart *Lon* 79-90; P-in-c Stepney St Pet w St Benet 85-87; Chapl Furness Gen Hosp 90-94; Chapl S Cumbria HA 90-94; Hosp Services Chapl Furness Hosps NHS Trust 94-98; Chapl Westmorland Hosps NHS Trust 94-98; Chapl Morecambe Bay Hosps NHS Trust from 98; rtd 03. *6 Dale Garth, Leece, Ulverston LA12 0QU* Tel (01229) 823852

GARBUTT, Mrs Mary Yvonne. b 45. Ripon Coll Cuddesdon 00. **d** 02 **p** 03. C Desborough, Brampton Ash, Dingley and Braybrooke *Pet* from 02. *134 Pioneer Avenue, Desborough, Kettering NN14 2PB* Tel (01536) 760651
E-mail revmgarbutt@aol.com

✠**GARCIA-MONTIEL, The Rt Revd Martiniano.** Bp Cuernavaca; Acting Primate of Mexico from 03. *Apartado Postal 538, Admon 4, CP 62431 Cuernavaca, Morelos, Mexico* Tel (0052) (73) 152870 Fax as telephone
E-mail diovca@giga.com.mx

GARDEN, Robert Andrew (Robin). b 26. Edin Univ BSc49 Kent Univ MA95 MInstP58 FIMA72. Cant Sch of Min 87. **d** 90 **p** 91. NSM Sandwich *Cant* 90-97; Chapl St Bart Hosp Sandwich 91-00; Perm to Offic *Cant* from 97. *Naini, 164 St George's Road, Sandwich CT13 9LD* Tel (01304) 612116

GARDHAM, Mrs Linda Elizabeth. b 49. Leeds Univ BA70 Warwick Univ PGCE71. Cranmer Hall Dur 04. **d** 05. NSM Monkseaton St Pet *Newc* from 05. *17 Dipton Road, Whitley Bay NE25 9UH* E-mail leg@lgardham.freeserve.co.uk

GARDINER, Anthony Reade. b 35. Univ of NZ BA59. Cuddesdon Coll 60. **d** 62 **p** 63. C Gosforth All SS *Newc* 62-65; New Zealand 65-93 and from 00; V Waikohu 65-69; V Edgecumbe 69-74; V Eltham 74-78; V Trentham 78-81; V Waipukurau 81-88; Chapl Nelson Cathl 88-92; C Highcliffe w Hinton Admiral *Win* 93-94; TV N Creedy *Ex* 94-00; rtd 00. *1 Puriri Street, Eastbourne, Wellington 6008, New Zealand*
E-mail nantony2@paradise.net.nz

GARDINER, Charles Graham. b 18. AKC49. St Boniface Warminster. **d** 50 **p** 51. C Clapham H Trin *S'wark* 50-54; S Africa from 54. *55 Weltevreden Avenue, Rondebosch, 7700 South Africa* Tel (0027) (21) 689 1111

GARDINER, James Carlisle. b 18. St Jo Coll Dur LTh48. Tyndale Hall Bris. **d** 49 **p** 50. C Blackpool Ch Ch *Blackb* 49-52; C Rushen *S & M* 52-56; R Ditton *Roch* 56-83; rtd 83; Perm to Offic *Roch* from 83. *8 Church Street, Tonbridge TN19 1HD* Tel (01732) 362323

GARDINER, Canon Kenneth Ashton. b 27. S'wark Ord Course 60. **d** 63 **p** 64. C Sydenham H Trin *S'wark* 63-67; C Macclesfield St Mich *Ches* 67-70; V Chatham St Phil and St Jas *Roch* 70-93; RD Roch 88-93; Hon Can Roch Cathl 88-93; rtd 93; Perm to Offic *Roch* from 93. *44 Trevale Road, Rochester ME1 3PA* Tel (01634) 844524 E-mail ken.gardiner@blueyonder.co.uk

GARDINER, Thomas Alfred. b 29. St Cuth Soc Dur BA52 MA56. Ridley Hall Cam 54. **d** 56 **p** 57. C Stockport St Geo *Ches* 56-60; Asst Chapl Brentwood Sch Essex 60-62; Chapl 62-88; R Greensted-juxta-Ongar w Stanford Rivers *Chelmsf* 88-00; rtd 00; Perm to Offic *St E* from 00. *Oakwood Cottage, The Street, Wenhaston, Halesworth IP19 9DP* Tel (01502) 478367

GARDINER, William Gerald Henry. b 46. Lon Univ BD72. Oak Hill Th Coll 68. **d** 72 **p** 73. C Beckenham St Jo *Roch* 72-75; C Cheadle *Ches* 75-81; P-in-c Swynnerton *Lich* 81-83; P-in-c Swynnerton and Tittensor 81-83; R Swynnerton and Tittensor 83-86; V Westlands St Andr from 86; RD Newcastle from 97. *St Andrew's Vicarage, 50 Kingsway West, Westlands, Newcastle ST5 3PU* Tel (01782) 619594

GARDNER, Canon Anthony Brian. b 32. Lon Coll of Div 62. **d** 64 **p** 65. C Stoke *Cov* 64-68; R Whitnash 68-98; RD Leamington 78-79; RD Warwick and Leamington 79-87; Hon Can Cov Cathl 83-98; rtd 98; Perm to Offic *Cov* from 99. *4 Mark Antony Drive, Heathcote, Warwick CV34 6XA* Tel (01926) 832690

GARDNER, Brian. **d** 04 **p** 05. OLM Bodicote *Ox* from 04. *11 Farm Way, Banbury OX16 9TB* Tel (01295) 253309

GARDNER, Christine. *See* GARDNER, Mary Christine

GARDNER, The Ven Clifton Gordon. b 15. Toronto Univ BA36 Lon Univ BD39 AKC39. **d** 39 **p** 40. C Maidenhead St Luke *Ox* 39-41 and 46-47; Chapl RNVR 41-46; V Furze Platt *Ox* 47-52; Canada 52-76; Can St Paul's Cathl Lon Ontario 64-74; Adn Middx Ontario 74-76; Perm to Offic *Chelmsf* from 77. *1 Shepherd's Way, Saffron Walden CB10 2AH* Tel (01799) 527890

GARDNER, Clive Bruce. b 67. Selw Coll Cam BA89 MA92 Wycliffe Hall Ox BA93. **d** 96 **p** 97. C Beverley Minster *York* 96-98; Bp's Dom Chapl *Liv* 98-01; V Cumnor *Ox* from 01. *The Vicarage, 1 Abingdon Road, Cumnor, Oxford OX2 9QN* Tel (01865) 865402 Fax as telephone
E-mail vicarofcumnor@tesco.net

GARDNER, David. b 57. Oak Hill Th Coll BA87. **d** 87 **p** 88. C Ogley Hay *Lich* 87-91; TV Mildenhall *St E* 91-98; P-in-c Woodbridge St Jo 98-00; V 00-03; P-in-c Bredfield 01-03; V Woodbridge St Jo and Bredfield from 03. *St John's Vicarage, St John's Hill, Woodbridge IP12 1HS* Tel (01394) 382083 *or* tel and fax 383162 E-mail stjohns.woodbridge@btinternet.com

GARDNER, Elizabeth Mary. b 47. Nottm Univ BA01. Trin Coll Bris 72 St Jo Coll Nottm 00. **d** 01 **p** 02. C Swindon Dorcan *Bris* 01-04; P-in-c Runcorn St Jo Weston *Ches* from 04. *The Vicarage, 225 Heath Road South, Weston, Runcorn WA7 4LY* Tel (01928) 573798 E-mail beth.gardner@bigfoot.com

GARDNER, Geoffrey Maurice. b 28. K Coll Lon BA51 Lon Inst of Educn PGCE52 Bris Univ DipEd74. Cranmer Hall Dur DipTh59. **d** 59 **p** 60. C Bowling St Jo *Bradf* 59-62; Nigeria 62-72; Hon C Bath St Luke *B & W* 72-73; Perm to Offic 73-90; and 94-99; NSM Bath Widcombe 90-94; rtd 94; Perm to Offic *Ex* from 99. *15 Bramley Gardens, Whimple, Exeter EX5 2SJ* Tel (01404) 823235

GARDNER, Helen Jane. b 39. Man Univ BSc61 PGCE62. WMMTC 93. **d** 96 **p** 97. NSM Stow on the Wold *Glouc* 96-00; NSM Stow on the Wold, Condicote and The Swells 00-03; NSM Upper and Lower Slaughter w Eyford and Naunton from 03; NSM The Guitings, Cutsdean, Farmcote etc from 03. *6 St Mary's Close, Lower Swell, Cheltenham GL54 1LJ* Tel (01451) 832553 E-mail jane@jgardner99.fsnet.co.uk

GARDNER, Ian Douglas. b 34. St Pet Hall Ox BA58 MA62. Oak Hill Th Coll 58. **d** 60 **p** 61. C Biddulph *Lich* 60-63; C Weston St Jo *B & W* 64; Nigeria 65-76; P-in-c Hurstbourne Tarrant and Faccombe *Win* 77-79; V Hurstbourne Tarrant, Faccombe, Vernham Dean etc 79-85; R Nursling and Rownhams 85-99; rtd 99. *Wilderness Cottage, Haroldston Hill, Broad Haven, Haverfordwest SA62 3JP* Tel (01437) 781592

GARDNER, Ian Norman. b 52. Open Univ BSc96. WEMTC 03. **d** 05. NSM Dursley *Glouc* from 05. *9 Chestal Lodge, Chestal, Dursley GL11 5AA* Tel (01453) 546895 Mobile 07960-287403
E-mail ian@chestal.freeserve.co.uk

GARDNER, Mrs Jacqueline Anne. b 49. Cheltenham & Glouc Coll of HE DipApTh98. WEMTC 95. **d** 98 **p** 99. NSM Fairford and Kempsford w Whelford *Glouc* 98-02; NSM Cirencester from 02. *10 Park Street, Cirencester GL7 2BN* Tel (01285) 655505

GARDNER, Jane. *See* GARDNER, Helen Jane

GARDNER, Canon John Phillip Backhouse. b 21. St Aid Birkenhead 49. **d** 52 **p** 53. C Ashtead *Guildf* 52-55; C Bromley SS Pet and Paul *Roch* 55-57; V New Hythe 57-63; V Roch St Justus 63-69; R Wisley w Pyrford *Guildf* 70-87; RD Woking 82-87; Hon Can Guildf Cathl 86-87; rtd 87; Perm to Offic *Pet* from 87 and *Guildf* from 98. *42 Godley Road, Byfleet, West Byfleet KT14 7ER* Tel (01932) 347431

GARDNER, Mrs Marian Elizabeth. b 50. Ripon Coll of Educn DipEd71. WMMTC 00. **d** 03 **p** 04. NSM Kirkleatham *York* from 03. *The Willows, 29 Newcomen Terrace, Redcar TS10 1DD* Tel (01642) 756933 Mobile 07736-350643 E-mail marian@thegardners.org.uk

GARDNER, Mark Douglas. b 58. TCD BA80 MA83 DipTh83. **d** 83 **p** 84. C Ballymacarrett St Patr *D & D* 83-87; C Belfast St Steph w St Luke *Conn* 87-89; C Hendon and Sunderland *Dur* 89-90; TV Sunderland 90-95; I Dublin Santry w Glasnevin and Finglas *D & G* 95-01; PV and Chapter Clerk Ch Ch Cathl Dublin from 96; Min Can St Patr Cathl Dublin 96; Treas V 96-01. *24 Wainsfort Manor Crescent, Terenure, Dublin 6W, Irish Republic* Tel (00353) (1) 499 1571 *or* 677 8099 Mobile 87-266 0228 E-mail markgardner@eircom.net

GARDNER, Mary Christine. b 42. SRN64 SCM66 Liv Univ HVCert71. St Jo Coll Nottm 80. **dss** 82 **d** 85 **p** 94. Ches St Paul *Ches* 82-87; Macclesfield St Mich 84-85; Macclesfield Team Par 85-87; Par Dn 87; Chapl Asst Nottm City Hosp 87-93; Chapl St Chris Hospice Lon 93-01; V Over St Jo *Ches* 01-03; rtd 03. *5 East Pallant, Chichester PO19 1TS*

GARDNER, Michael Ronald. b 53. Wilson Carlile Coll Dip Evang86 Trin Coll Bris 95. **d** 97 **p** 98. CA 86-00; C Stanmore *Win* 97-01; V from 01. *St Luke's Vicarage, Mildmay Street, Winchester SO22 4BX* Tel (01962) 865240 E-mail mike-vic@fish.co.uk

GARDNER, Neil Kenneth. Univ of Wales (Swansea) BA92 Peterho Cam BA00 Univ of Wales (Cardiff) PhD01. Westcott Ho Cam 98. **d** 01 **p** 02. C Wisbech SS Pet and Paul *Ely* from 01; C Wisbech St Aug 03-04; P-in-c from 04. *The Rectory, 35 Gorefield Road, Leverington, Wisbech PE13 5AS* Tel and fax (01945) 581486 Mobile 07855-111794 E-mail neil@hmpleasure.freeserve.co.uk

GARDNER, The Ven Paul Douglas. b 50. K Coll Lon BA72 AKC72 Reformed Th Sem Mississippi MDiv79 SS Coll Cam PhD89. Ridley Hall Cam 79. **d** 80 **p** 81. C Cambridge St Martin *Ely* 80-83; Lect Oak Hill Th Coll 83-90; V Hartford *Ches* 90-03; RD Middlewich 94-99; Adn Ex from 03. *St Matthew's House, 45 Spicer Road, Exeter EX1 1TA* Tel (01392) 425432 Fax 425783 E-mail archdeacon.of.exeter@exeter.anglican.org

GARDNER, Richard Beverley Twynam. b 11. Chich Th Coll 33. **d** 36 **p** 37. C Gainsborough St Jo *Linc* 36-38; C Linc St Giles 38-39; C Horsell *Guildf* 39-42; Chapl RNVR 42-47; C York Town St Mich *Guildf* 47-48; V E Molesey St Paul 48-54; V Botleys and Lyne 54-71; V Long Cross 56-71; V Ewshott 71-76; rtd 76; Perm to Offic *Guildf* 81-93. *16 Palace Gate, Odiham, Hook, Basingstoke RG29 1JZ* Tel (01256) 704563

GARDNER (née JAMES), Mrs Sandra Kay. b 66. Aston Tr Scheme 97 Westcott Ho Cam CTM99. **d** 99 **p** 00. C Whittlesey, Pondersbridge and Coates *Ely* 99-02; R Leverington 02-04; V Southea w Murrow and Parson Drove 02-04; R Leverington, Newton and Tydd St Giles from 05. *The Rectory, 35 Gorefield Road, Leverington, Wisbech PE13 5AS* Tel and fax (01945) 581486 E-mail sandra.gardner@ely.anglican.org

GARDNER, Stephen John. b 70. Southn Univ MEng92. St Jo Coll Nottm 00. **d** 02 **p** 03. C Brinsworth w Catcliffe and Treeton *Sheff* 02-03; C Rivers Team from 03; V Woodlands from 05. *All Saints' Vicarage, 9 Great North Road, Woodlands, Doncaster DN6 7RB* Tel (01302) 723268 Mobile 07740-200942 E-mail stephen@gardnerfamily.co.uk

GARDNER, Mrs Susan Carol. b 54. SRN75. St Jo Coll Nottm 02. **d** 04 **p** 05. C Abington *Pet* from 04. *15 Honeysuckle Way, Northampton NN3 3QE* Tel (01604) 637880 Mobile 07723-189485

GARDNER, Vincent Lyndon. b 62. K Coll Lon MA98 Robert Gordon Univ Aber BFA90. St Steph Ho Ox 02. **d** 04 **p** 05. C Carew *St D* from 04. *22 Glenview Avenue, Pembroke Dock SA72 6EJ* Tel (01646) 686158 E-mail vincent_gardner@hotmail.com

GARDOM, Francis Douglas. b 34. Trin Coll Ox BA55 MA59. Wells Th Coll 58. **d** 60 **p** 61. C Greenwich St Alfege w St Pet *S'wark* 60-68; C Lewisham St Steph and St Mark 68-76; Hon C from 76. *79 Maze Hill, London SE10 8XQ* Tel (020) 8858 7052 *or* 8852 1474 E-mail francisgardom@aol.com

GARDOM, James Theodore Douglas. b 61. St Anne's Coll Ox BA83 K Coll Lon PhD92. Ripon Coll Cuddesdon 88. **d** 90 **p** 91. C Witney *Ox* 90-92; Zimbabwe 92-97; Dean of Studies Bp Gaul Coll Harare 93-97; V Chesterton St Andr *Ely* from 97. *10 Lynfield Lane, Chesterton, Cambridge CB4 1DR* Tel and fax (01223) 303469 E-mail james.gardom@ely.anglican.org

GARLAND, Christopher John. b 47. Ex Univ BA69 PhD72. Qu Coll Birm 78. **d** 80 **p** 81. C Beckenham St Jas *Roch* 80-82; C Roch 82-84; Papua New Guinea 85-93; Australia 94-95; R Copford w Easthorpe and Messing w Inworth *Chelmsf* from 95. *The Vicarage, Kelvedon Road, Messing, Colchester CO5 9TN* Tel (01621) 815434 E-mail cngarland@fish.co.uk

GARLAND, Michael. b 50. St D Coll Lamp DipTh72 Sarum & Wells Th Coll 72. **d** 73 **p** 74. C Swansea St Thos and Kilvey *S & B* 73-76; C Boldmere *Birm* 76-79; V Kingshurst 79-88; P-in-c Curdworth w Castle Vale 88-90; R Curdworth 90-03; P-in-c Wishaw 99-00; V Charlton Kings St Mary *Glouc* from 03. *The Vicarage, 63 Church Street, Charlton Kings, Cheltenham GL53 8AT* Tel (01242) 253402 Mobile 07974-066929 E-mail michaelgarland@compuserve.com

GARLAND, Peter Stephen John. b 52. N Lon Poly Dip Librarianship 77 ALA79 Univ Coll Lon BA73 Univ of W Ontario MA74 Dur Univ PGCE75. Ripon Coll Cuddesdon 88. **d** 90 **p** 91. C Crookham *Guildf* 90-94; V Tongham 94-99; Chapl Farnborough Coll of Tech 94-99; V Spalding St Jo w Deeping St Nicholas *Linc* from 99. *St John's Vicarage, 66A Hawthorn Bank, Spalding PE11 1JQ* Tel and fax (01775) 722816 E-mail peter_garland@hotmail.com

GARLICK, Canon David. b 37. Nottm Univ BA62 Ox Univ DipPSA63. St Steph Ho Ox 62. **d** 64 **p** 65. C Kennington St Jo *S'wark* 64-66; Hon C Newington St Paul 66-68; P-in-c Vauxhall St Pet 68-79; V Lewisham St Mary from 79; RD E Lewisham 92-99; Hon Can S'wark Cathl from 93. *Lewisham Vicarage, 48 Lewisham Park, London SE13 6QZ* Tel and fax (020) 8690 2682 *or* 8690 1585 E-mail davidgarlick@smarysl.fsnet.co.uk

GARLICK, Dennis. b 26. ACIS. Qu Coll Birm. **d** 84 **p** 85. NSM Dronfield *Derby* 84-88; C 88-89; C-in-c Holmesfield 89-90; TV Dronfield w Holmesfield 90-93; rtd 93; Perm to Offic *Derby* from 93. *51 Holmesdale Road, Dronfield S18 2FA* Tel (01246) 418792

GARLICK, Preb Kathleen Beatrice. b 49. Leeds Univ BA71 Birm Univ PGCE72. Glouc Sch of Min 87. **d** 90 **p** 94. NSM Much Birch w Lt Birch, Much Dewchurch etc *Heref* 90-03; P-in-c from 03; Chapl Heref Sixth Form Coll 96-03; Preb Heref Cathl *Heref* from 99. *The Rectory, Birch Lodge, Much Birch, Hereford HR2 8HT* Tel (01981) 540666 Mobile 07812-995442 E-mail kaygarlick@hotmail.com

GARLICK, Canon Peter. b 34. AKC57. **d** 58 **p** 59. C Swindon New Town *Bris* 58-63; St Kitts-Nevis 63-66; V Heyside *Man* 66-73; R Stretford All SS 73-79; RD Wootton *Pet* 79-88; V Duston 79-91; TR Duston Team 91-94; Can Pet Cathl 85-94; rtd 94; Perm to Offic *Pet* from 94. *120 Worcester Close, Northampton NN3 9GD* Tel (01604) 416511 E-mail petergarlick@tinyworld.co.uk

GARLICK, William Frederick. b 51. LNSM course 95. **d** 98 **p** 99. OLM Bermondsey St Jas w Ch Ch and St Crispin *S'wark* from 98. *6 Hannah Mary Way, London SE1 5QG* Tel (020) 7237 8326

GARNER, Alistair Ross. b 58. Pemb Coll Ox BA81 MA86. St Jo Coll Nottm Dip Th Studies 92. **d** 92 **p** 93. C Ashton-upon-Mersey St Mary *Ches* 92-96; P-in-c Bredbury St Mark 96-01; V from 01. *St Mark's Vicarage, 61 George Lane, Bredbury, Stockport SK6 1AT* Tel 0161-406 6552 E-mail revrossgarner@hotmail.com

GARNER, Canon Carl. b 42. Rhodes Univ BA62 Keble Coll Ox BA65 MA70. St Paul's Coll Grahamstown 66. **d** 67 **p** 68. S Africa 67-84; Dioc Missr *St Alb* 84-98; Can Res St Alb 84-98; P-in-c Digswell and Panshanger from 98; Hon Can St Alb from 99; Jt RD Welwyn Hatfield 01-03. *354 Knightsfield, Welwyn Garden City AL8 7NG* Tel (01707) 326677 E-mail carl@stjohnsdigswell.freeserve.co.uk

GARNER, David Henry. b 40. Trin Coll Bris 70. **d** 73 **p** 74. C Tunstead *Man* 73-75; C Fazeley *Lich* 76-78; V Sparkhill St Jo *Birm* 78-85; V Blackheath 85-01; Deanery P Warley Deanery from 01. *94 Honeybourne Road, Halesowen B63 3HD* Tel 0121-550 2498 Mobile 07779-948333 E-mail david.h.garner@btinternet.com

GARNER, Geoffrey Walter. b 40. Ripon Hall Ox 69. **d** 71 **p** 72. C Stoke *Cov* 71-76; V Tile Hill 76-80; TV Hackney *Lon* 80-89; R Bow w Bromley St Leon from 89. *16 Tomlins Grove, London E3 4NX* Tel (020) 8981 6710

GARNER, John David. b 47. **d** 03. OLM Kirkdale St Lawr *Liv* from 03. *10 Doon Close, Liverpool L4 1XW* Tel 0151-284 0388

GARNER, John Howard. b 45. Univ of Wales (Swansea) BSc67 Univ of Wales (Ban) PhD75. Moorlands Bible Coll SW Minl Tr Course 95. **d** 98 **p** 99. NSM Upton *Ex* from 98. *Highgrove Lodge, Sunbury Hill, Upton, Torquay TQ1 3ED* Tel (01803) 293640 E-mail johngarner@onetel.com

GARNER, Martin Wyatt. b 39. Lon Coll of Div 60 Tyndale Hall Bris 63 Sarum Th Coll 66. **d** 66 **p** 67. C Coleraine *Conn* 66-70; C Cambridge St Martin *Ely* 70-72; V Edge Hill St Nath *Liv* 72-80; P-in-c Burton in Kendal *Carl* 80-87; R Burghclere w Newtown and Ecchinswell w Sydmonton *Win* 87-93; R Ewelme, Brightwell Baldwin, Cuxham w Easington *Ox* from 93. *The Rectory, Ewelme, Wallingford OX10 6HP* Tel (01491) 837823

GARNER, Canon Peter. b 35. Lon Univ BSc56 Leeds Univ MEd91. Wycliffe Hall Ox 56. **d** 58 **p** 59. C Walthamstow St Jo *Chelmsf* 58-61; V Hainault 61-70; R Theydon Garnon 70-73; P-in-c Kirby-le-Soken 73-74; V 74-82; P-in-c Fountains *Ripon* 82-88; P-in-c Kirkby Malzeard w Grewelthorpe and Mickley etc 82-88; Par Development Adv 88-93; P-in-c Birstwith 91-93; R Walkingham Hill 93-01; Hon Can Ripon Cathl 99-01; rtd 01; Perm to Offic *Ripon* from 02. *Laver House, 29 Hell Wath Grove, Ripon HG4 2JT* Tel (01765) 601543 Mobile 07734-088521 E-mail peter@hellwath29.fsnet.co.uk

GARNER, Rodney George. b 48. Lon Univ BA87 Hull Univ MPhil96 Man Univ PhD01 MCIPD75. Qu Coll Birm 75. **d** 78 **p** 79. C Tranmere St Paul w St Luke *Ches* 78-81; V Eccleston St Thos *Liv* 81-90; P-in-c Sculcoates St Paul w Ch Ch and St Silas *York* 90-95; Lay Tr Officer (E Riding Adnry) 90-95; P-in-c Southport H Trin *Liv* 95-96; V from 96; Dioc Th Consultant from 95. *24 Roe Lane, Southport PR9 9DX* Tel and fax (01704) 538560 E-mail anglican@garnerr.freeserve.co.uk

GARNER, Ross. *See* GARNER, Alistair Ross

GARNER, Thomas Richard. b 43. K Coll Lon. **d** 69 **p** 70. C Tynemouth Ch Ch *Newc* 69-73; C Fenham St Jas and St Basil 73-76; V Hamstead St Bernard *Birm* 76-80; V Greytown New Zealand 80-87; V Levin 87-96; Can Wellington 96-99; V Upper Riccarton w Yaldhurst 99-05; rtd 05. *91 Chester Road, Carterton, New Zealand*

GARNETT, The Ven David Christopher. b 45. Nottm Univ BA67 Fitzw Coll Cam BA69 MA73. Westcott Ho Cam 67. **d** 69 **p** 70. C Cottingham *York* 69-72; Chapl Selw Coll Cam 72-77; P-in-c Patterdale *Carl* 77-80; Dir of Ords 78-80; V Heald Green St Cath *Ches* 80-87; R Christleton 87-92; TR Ellesmere Port 92-96; Adn Chesterfield *Derby* from 96; Hon Can Derby Cathl from 96. *The Old Vicarage, Church Street, Baslow, Bakewell DE45 1RY* Tel (01246) 583928 Fax 583949 E-mail davidcgarnett@yahoo.co.uk

GARNETT, James Arthur. b 42. N Ord Course 77. **d** 80 **p** 81. C Kirkby *Liv* 80-91; P-in-c Liv St Phil w St Dav from 91. *The Vicarage, 55 Sheil Road, Liverpool L6 3AD* Tel 0151-263 6202

GARNETT, Preb Ralph Henry. b 28. Cuddesdon Coll 58. **d** 60 **p** 61. C Broseley w Benthall *Heref* 60-64; V Leintwardine 64-69; P-in-c Downton w Burrington and Aston and Elton 66-69; RD Ludlow 72-75; R Burford II w Greete and Hope Bagot 69-87; R Burford III w Lt Heref 69-87; P-in-c Burford I 72-74; R 74-87; V Tenbury 69-74; TR 74-87; Preb Heref Cathl 82-93; P-in-c Fownhope 87-93; P-in-c Brockhampton w Fawley 87-93; RD Heref Rural 92-93; rtd 93; Perm to Offic *Heref* from 93. *5 Hampton Manor Close, Hereford HR1 1TG* Tel (01432) 274985

GARNETT, Roger James. b 58. Dur Univ BA79. Wycliffe Hall Ox 89. **d** 91 **p** 92. C Forest Gate St Sav w W Ham St Matt *Chelmsf* 91-94; C Collier Row St Jas and Havering-atte-Bower 94-02; V from 02. *St James Vicarage, 24 Lower Bedfords Road, Romford RM1 4DG* Tel (01708) 749891 E-mail rogergarnett@hotmail.com

GARNSEY, George Christopher. b 36. Qu Coll Ox BA63. **d** 60 **p** 60. Lic to Offic *Wakef* 78-79; C Lupset 80; Australia from 80; Prin St Jo Coll Morpeth 80-91; R Gresford w Paterson 93-01; rtd 01; Lect St Jo Coll Morpeth from 01. *17 James Street, Morpeth, NSW, Australia 2321* Tel (0061) (2) 4934 2658 Fax 4921 6898 E-mail jan@maths.newcastle.edu.au

GARRARD, Mrs Christine Ann. b 51. Open Univ BA86 LCST75. EAMTC 87. **d** 90 **p** 94. Par Dn Kesgrave *St E* 90-94; C 94-96; V Ipswich All Hallows 96-02; R Higham, Holton St Mary, Raydon and Stratford from 02; Asst Dioc Dir of Ords from 03. *The Rectory, School Hill, Raydon, Ipswich IP7 5LH* Tel (01473) 311706 E-mail revdchris@aol.com

GARRARD, James Richard. b 65. Dur Univ BA88 Keble Coll Ox DPhil92 Leeds Univ MA01. Westcott Ho Cam. **d** 94 **p** 95. C Elland *Wakef* 94-97; TV Brighouse and Clifton 98-01; P-in-c Balderstone *Blackb* from 01; Warden of Readers from 01. *The Vicarage, Commons Lane, Balderstone, Blackburn BB2 7LL* Tel (01254) 812232 E-mail jamesgarrard@4-mat.net

GARRARD, Nicholas James Havelock. b 62. Leeds Univ BA83. Westcott Ho Cam 86. **d** 88 **p** 89. C Scotforth *Blackb* 88-91; C Eaton *Nor* 91-95; V Heigham St Thos from 95; RD Nor S from 03. *St Thomas's Vicarage, 77 Edinburgh Road, Norwich NR2 3RL* Tel (01603) 624390 E-mail nickgarr39@aol.com

✠**GARRARD, The Rt Revd Richard.** b 37. K Coll Lon BD60 AKC60. **d** 61 **p** 62 **c** 94. C Woolwich St Mary w H Trin *S'wark* 61-66; C Cambridge Gt St Mary w St Mich *Ely* 66-68; Chapl Keswick Hall Coll of Educn 68-74; Prin Wilson Carlile Coll of Evang 74-79; Can Res and Chan S'wark Cathl *S'wark* 79-87; Dir of Tr 79-87; Can Res St E Cathl *St E* 87-94; Dioc Adv for CME 87-91; Adn Sudbury 91-94; Suff Bp Penrith *Carl* 94-01; Hon Can Carl Cathl 94-01; Abp's Rep H See and Dir Angl Cen Rome 01-03; Hon Asst Bp Eur from 01; rtd 03; Perm to Offic *Nor* from 03; Hon Asst Bp Nor from 03. *26 Carol Close, Stoke Holy Cross, Norwich NR14 8NN* Tel (01508) 494165 E-mail garrard.r-a@tiscali.co.uk

GARRARD, Miss Valerie Mary. b 48. K Alfred's Coll Win TCert69 St Paul's Cheltenham BEd84. **d** 03 **p** 04. OLM Wylye and Till Valley *Sarum* from 03. *Cowslip Cottage, Wylye Road, Hanging Langford, Salisbury SP3 4NW* Tel (01722) 790739 E-mail cft-vgarrard@supanet.com

GARRATT, Alan. **d** 04 **p** 05. NSM Hazlemere *Ox* from 04. *127 Marys Mead, Hazlemere, High Wycombe HP15 7DY* Tel (01494) 711577

GARRATT, Bernard John. b 43. Lon Univ BA65 Linacre Coll Ox BA67 MA71. St Steph Ho Ox 65. **d** 68 **p** 69. C Notting Hill St Jo *Lon* 68-71; C Fareham SS Pet and Paul *Portsm* 71-73; Chapl City of Lon Poly *Lon* 73-79; R Trowbridge H Trin *Sarum* 79-81; TR 81-87; V Wootton Bassett 87-05; RD Calne 88-90; rtd 05. *66 Rowell Way, Chipping Norton OX7 5BD* Tel (01608) 644560

GARRATT, David. b 44. AKC68. **d** 69 **p** 70. C Nottingham St Andr *S'well* 69-71; C Ollerton and Boughton 71-75; V Esh and Hamsteels *Dur* 75-79; V Woodborough *S'well* 79-90; C Daybrook 90-91; Perm to Offic *Dur* 92-04; C Ferryhill from 04; C Cornforth from 04. *7 Thomas Street, Sacriston, Durham DH7 6NG* Tel 0191-371 1695

GARRATT, Malcolm John. b 52. Nottm Univ BSc73. Trin Coll Bris DipHE99. **d** 99 **p** 00. C Bawtry w Austerfield and Misson *S'well* 99-00; C Hucknall Torkard 00-03; P-in-c Clipstone from 03; Chapl Welbeck Coll from 04. *The Vicarage, Church Road, Clipstone, Mansfield NG21 9DG* Tel and fax (01623) 623916 E-mail malcolm@2garratts.freeserve.co.uk

GARRATT, Peter James. b 37. ALCD64. **d** 64 **p** 65. C Bingham *S'well* 64-67; C Mansfield SS Pet and Paul 67-69; V Purlwell *Wakef* 69-73; R Kirk Sandall and Edenthorpe *Sheff* 73-82; R Whippingham w E Cowes *Portsm* 82-87; V Soberton w Newtown 87-01; rtd 02; Perm to Offic *Portsm* from 02. *35 Fair Isle Close, Fareham PO14 3RT* Tel (01329) 661162

GARRATT, Roger Charles. b 50. St Jo Coll Dur BA72. Cranmer Hall Dur 72. **d** 74 **p** 75. C Leamington Priors St Paul *Cov* 74-77; Chapl Emscote Lawn Sch Warw 77-00; Chapl and Dep Hd Arden Lawn Sch 77-00; TV Warwick *Cov* 02-03; TV Warwick from 03. *St Nicholas' Vicarage, 184 Myton Road, Warwick CV34 6PS* Tel (01926) 492997 *or* 403940 E-mail roger.garratt@btopenworld.com

GARRETT, Ms Celia Joy. b 60. RGN81 RM85. Cant Sch of Min 92. **d** 95. C S Ashford St Fran *Cant* 95-98; NSM from 98. *Address withheld by request*

GARRETT, Christopher Hugh Ahlan. b 35. Sarum & Wells Th Coll 72. **d** 75 **p** 76. C Addiscombe St Mildred *Cant* 75-81; V Thornton Heath St Jude w St Aid *S'wark* 81-00; rtd 00; Perm to Offic *Glouc* from 01. *Edge View, 18 Gloucester Road, Painswick GL6 6RA* Tel (01452) 813688

GARRETT, Clive Robert. b 54. Sheff Univ BA75 PhD80 Ex Univ PGCE88. St Jo Coll Nottm MA98. **d** 98 **p** 99. C Bath Weston St Jo w Kelston *B & W* 98-02; R from 02. *The Rectory, 8 Ashley Avenue, Bath BA1 3DR* Tel (01225) 427206 E-mail crg@cix.co.uk

GARRETT, Miss Elizabeth Clare. b 46. Trin Coll Bris. **d** 94 **p** 95. C Ewyas Harold w Dulas, Kenderchurch etc *Heref* 94-96; C Tupsley w Hampton Bishop 96-00; TV Uttoxeter Area *Lich* from 00. *The New Vicarage, Uttoxeter Road, Checkley, Stoke-on-Trent ST10 4NB* Tel (01538) 722732 E-mail claregarrett@aol.com

GARRETT, Geoffrey David. b 57. Oak Hill Th Coll 83. **d** 86 **p** 87. C Trentham *Lich* 86-90; V Rhodes *Man* 90-00; P-in-c Bardsley 00-05; V from 05. *The Vicarage, Byrth Road, Oldham OL8 2TJ* Tel 0161-624 9004 E-mail garretts@tinyworld.co.uk

GARRETT, Ian Lee. b 60. MCSP Dip Physiotherapy 81. Sarum & Wells Th Coll 86. **d** 89 **p** 90. C Maidstone St Martin *Cant* 89-95; P-in-c S Ashford St Fran from 95. *St Francis House, Cryol Road, Ashford TN23 5AS* Tel (01233) 625555

GARRETT, John Watkins. b 09. St Chad's Coll Dur BA35 LTh36. **d** 36 **p** 37. C Leic St Mary *Leic* 36-38; C Win H Trin *Win* 38-42; C Staveley *Derby* 42-44; C Derby St Barn 44-48; R Aylestone Park *Leic* 48-59; Chapl Carlton Hayes Psychiatric Hosp Narborough 54-90; R Narborough 59-75; rtd 75; Lic to Offic *Leic* 75-81; Perm to Offic 81-95. *4 Walcot Lane, Folkingham, Sleaford NG34 0TP* Tel (01529) 497385

GARRETT, Kevin George. b 48. Oak Hill Th Coll BA86. **d** 86 **p** 87. C Hoddesdon *St Alb* 86-89; C Loughton St Mary and St Mich *Chelmsf* 89-90; TV 90-95; P-in-c Loughton St Mich 95-96; Public Preacher 97; V Dover St Martin *Cant* from 97. *St Martin's Vicarage, 339 Folkestone Road, Dover CT17 9JG* Tel (01304) 205391 E-mail kevingarrett48@hotmail.com

GARRETT, Timothy Michael. b 70. Univ of Wales (Abth) BA91. Wycliffe Hall Ox BA01. **d** 02 **p** 03. C Ox St Andr *Ox* from 02. *5 Squitchey Lane, Oxford OX2 7LD* Tel (01865) 553944 E-mail tim.garrett@standrewsoxford.org.uk

GARROD, Mrs Christine Anne. b 49. EAMTC. **d** 00 **p** 01. C N w S Wootton *Nor* 00-04; P-in-c Brinklow *Cov* from 04; P-in-c Harborough Magna from 04; P-in-c Monks Kirby w Pailton and Stretton-under-Fosse from 04; P-in-c Churchover w Willey from 04. *Kirby Moynes House, 1 Gate Farm Drive, Monks Kirby, Rugby CV23 0RY* Tel (01788) 832811

GARROW, Alan John Philip. b 67. Lon Bible Coll BA90 Wycliffe Hall Ox MPhil94 Jes Coll Ox DPhil00. **d** 93 **p** 94. C Waltham H Cross *Chelmsf* 93-97; C Akeman *Ox* 00-04; Tutor St Alb and Ox

Min Course 00-04; Dir Studies from 00. *13 The Runcie Buildings, Ripon College, Cuddesdon, Oxford OX44 9EY* Tel (01865) 873764 E-mail alan_garrow@lineone.net

GARRUD, Christopher Charles. b 54. Cranmer Hall Dur DipTh84. **d** 85 **p** 86. C Watford *St Alb* 85-89; C Ireland Wood *Ripon* 89-95; Chapl Cookridge Hosp Leeds 93-95; R Farnley 95-02. *Address temp unknown*

GARSIDE, Canon Howard. b 24. Leeds Univ BA49. Coll of Resurr Mirfield 49. **d** 51 **p** 52. C Barnsley St Pet *Wakef* 51-53; C Linthorpe *York* 53-56; V Middlesbrough St Aid 56-64; V Manston *Ripon* 64-78; RD Whitkirk 70-78; Hon Can Ripon Cathl 78-89; V Harrogate St Wilfrid 78-80; P-in-c Harrogate St Luke 78-80; V Harrogate St Wilfrid and St Luke 80-89; RD Harrogate 83-88; rtd 89; Perm to Offic *Ripon* from 89. *73 Kirkby Road, Ripon HG4 2HH* Tel (01765) 690625 Mobile 07714-454829 E-mail hjgarside@aol.com

GARSIDE, Melvin. b 42. N Ord Course 85. **d** 88 **p** 89. C Lindley *Wakef* 88-91; C Shelf *Bradf* 91-93; V Lundwood *Wakef* 93-97; V Hanging Heaton 97-01; V Woodhouse and Bp's Adv in Racial Justice 01-05; rtd 05. *45 Osgodby Hall Road, Scarborough YO11 3PX* Tel (01723) 583523 Mobile 07803-250258 E-mail melgarside@melgarside.demon.co.uk

GARTLAND, Christopher Michael. b 49. Man Univ BA78 Sheff Univ Dip Psychotherapy 92 Leeds Univ MEd99. Coll of Resurr Mirfield 82. **d** 84 **p** 85. C Almondbury w Farnley Tyas *Wakef* 84-87; P-in-c Upperthong 87-89; TV Upper Holme Valley 89-91; Chapl Stanley Royd Hosp Wakef 91-94; Chapl Wakef HA (Mental Health Services) 91-95; Chapl Wakef and Pontefract Community NHS Trust from 95. *Fieldhead Hospital, Ouchthorpe Lane, Wakefield WF1 3SP* Tel (01924) 327498

GARTON, Mrs Anne-Marie. b 48. BA MSW CQSW. **d** 02 **p** 03. NSM Caterham *S'wark* from 02. *51 Crescent Road, Caterham CR3 6LH* Tel (01883) 343188 E-mail anne-marie.garton@southwark.anglican.org

GARTON, Capt Jeremy. b 56. Wilson Carlile Coll 78 SEITE 94. **d** 96 **p** 97. C Clapham Team *S'wark* 96-00; P-in-c Caterham Valley 00-03; TV Caterham from 03. *St John's Vicarage, 51 Crescent Road, Caterham CR3 6LH* Tel (01883) 343188 Fax (020) 7863 4120 E-mail jerry@garton.com

✠**GARTON, The Rt Revd John Henry.** b 41. Worc Coll Ox BA67 MA. Cuddesdon Coll 67. **d** 69 **p** 70 **c** 96. CF 69-73; Lect Linc Th Coll 73-78; TR Cov E *Cov* 78-86; V Cuddesdon and Prin Ripon Coll Cuddesdon 86-96; Hon Can Worc Cathl *Worc* 87-96; Suff Bp Plymouth *Ex* 96-05; rtd 05. *52 Clive Road, Oxford OX4 3EL* Tel (01865) 771093

GARTSIDE, Philip Oswin. b 60. Pemb Coll Ox BA82 MA86 Leeds Univ BA92. Coll of Resurr Mirfield 93. **d** 93 **p** 94. C Walton-on-the-Hill *Liv* 93-97; CR from 97. *House of the Resurrection, Stocks Bank Road, Mirfield WF14 0BN* Tel (01924) 483327

GARVIE, Mrs Anna-Lisa Karen. b 48. Luton Univ BA99. St Alb Minl Tr Scheme 89. **d** 96 **p** 97. NSM Caddington *St Alb* 96-99; NSM St Paul's Walden 99-01; Chapl Chelsea and Westmr Healthcare NHS Trust 98-01; Co-ord Chapl Hinchingbrooke Health Care NHS Trust from 01. *Hinchingbrooke Hospital, Hinchingbrooke Park, Huntingdon PE29 6NT* Tel (01480) 416125 Fax 416416 E-mail anna.garvie@hinchingbrooke.nhs.uk

GARWOOD, Simon Frederick. b 62. Reading Univ BA85 Lon Univ PGCE93 Birm Univ BD99. Qu Coll Birm MA00. **d** 00 **p** 01. C Chelmsf All SS *Chelmsf* 00-03; TV Witham from 03. *57 Powers Hall End, Witham CM8 2HF* Tel (01376) 502772 E-mail sgarwood@surefish.co.uk

GASCOIGNE, Philip. b 27. Oak Hill Th Coll. **d** 62 **p** 63. C Blackpool Ch Ch *Blackb* 62-65; V Bootle St Leon *Liv* 65-71; Staff Evang CPAS 71-74; V St Helens St Mark *Liv* 74-77; V Blackpool Ch Ch *Blackb* 77-81; V Blackpool Ch Ch w All SS 81-97; rtd 98; Perm to Offic *Blackb* from 98. *6 King's Close, Staining, Blackpool FY3 0EJ* Tel (01253) 890045

GASH, Christopher Alan Ronald. b 39. St Andr Univ 57. EMMTC 83. **d** 86 **p** 87. C Thurmaston *Leic* 86-89; P-in-c Stoke Golding w Dadlington 89-01; rtd 01; Perm to Offic *Cov* 01-03 and *Sarum* from 03. *38 Cooks Lane, Mursley, Milton Keynes MK17 0RU* Tel (01296) 720350

GASH, Canon Wilfred John. b 31. St Aid Birkenhead 60. **d** 62 **p** 63. C St Mary Cray and St Paul's Cray *Roch* 62-65; C Bexley St Jo 65-67; R Levenshulme St Pet *Man* 67-72; V Clifton 72-94; AD Eccles 81-87; Hon Can Man Cathl 86-97; P-in-c Pendlebury Ch Ch and St Aug 86-87; TR Bolton St Paul w Em 94-96; C Urmston 96-97; Dioc Adv on Evang 89-97; rtd 98; Perm to Offic *Ches* from 98. *22 Appleby Drive, Barrowford, Nelson BB9 6EX* Tel (01282) 690789

GASKELL, David. b 48. Lon Univ BD76. Trin Coll Bris 72. **d** 76 **p** 77. C Eccleston Ch Ch *Liv* 76-80; C Rainhill 80-83; V Over Darwen St Jas *Blackb* 83-88; V Livesey 88-95; V Preston St Cuth 95-01; V Copp w Inskip from 01. *St Peter's Vicarage, Preston Road, Inskip, Preston PR4 0TT* Tel (01772) 690316

GASKELL, Canon Ian Michael. b 51. Nottm Univ BTh81. Linc Th Coll 77. **d** 81 **p** 82. C Wakef St Jo *Wakef* 81-83; Ind Chapl *Sheff* 83-86; V Cleckheaton St Luke and Whitechapel *Wakef* 86-93; V Birkenshaw w Hunsworth 93-98; RD Birstall 96-98; Can Res Wakef Cathl from 98; Dioc Soc Resp Adv from 98. *2 Elm Grove, Horbury, Wakefield WF4 5EP* Tel (01924) 315110 *or* 371802 Fax 315114 *or* 364834 E-mail bpsadvisersr@wakefield.anglican.org

GASKELL, Preb John Bernard. b 28. Jes Coll Ox BA52 MA58. Chich Th Coll 59. **d** 60 **p** 61. C Beckenham St Jas *Roch* 60-64; C St Marylebone All SS *Lon* 64-68; C-in-c Grosvenor Chpl 68-79; Warden Liddon Ho Lon 68-79; V Holborn St Alb w Saffron Hill St Pet *Lon* 79-93; AD S Camden 81-86; Preb St Paul's Cathl 85-93; rtd 93; Perm to Offic *Lon* 93-96; Hon C St Marylebone All SS from 02. *8 Margaret Street, London W1W 8RA* Tel (020) 7436 3287

GASKELL, Marion Ingrid. b 52. Wilson Carlile Coll 74 N Ord Course 96. **d** 99 **p** 00. C Thorpe Edge *Bradf* 99-02; TV Shelf w Buttershaw St Aid 02-04; TR from 04. *8 Redwing Drive, Bradford BD6 3YD* Tel (01274) 817978 E-mail marion.gaskell@tesco.net

GASKELL, Mary. b 50. Nottm Univ BTh81 Bradf and Ilkley Coll CertEd89. Linc Th Coll 77. **dss** 81 **d** 89 **p** 94. Wakef St Jo *Wakef* 81-83; NSM Cleckheaton St Luke and Whitechapel 89-93; NSM Birkenshaw w Hunsworth 93-95; Asst Chapl St Jas Univ Hosp NHS Trust Leeds 95-97; Chapl Rishworth Sch Ripponden 97-99; P-in-c Purlwell *Wakef* 00-01; Chapl Dewsbury Health Care NHS Trust 01-02; Chapl Mid Yorks Hosps NHS Trust from 02. *2 Elm Grove, Horbury, Wakefield WF4 5EP* Tel (01924) 315110 Fax 315114

GASKELL, Peter John. b 70. Bris Univ MS93 ChB93. Oak Hill Th Coll BA03. **d** 03. NSM Poulton Lancelyn H Trin *Ches* from 03. *28 Latham Way, Wirral CH63 9NX* Tel 0151-334 6618 Mobile 07769-682142 E-mail petegaskell@glod.co.uk

GASPER (née COHEN), Mrs Janet Elizabeth. b 47. Birm Univ CertEd70. WMMTC 93. **d** 96 **p** 97. NSM Leominster *Heref* 96-99; C Letton w Staunton, Byford, Mansel Gamage etc 99-01; Hon Chapl RAF 97-01; R Baxterley w Hurley and Wood End and Merevale etc *Birm* from 01; P-in-c Kingsbury from 04. *The Vicarage, Church Lane, Kingsbury, Tamworth B78 2LR* Tel (01827) 874252 E-mail mgasper1@hotmail.com

GASTON, Raymond Gordon. b 62. Leeds Univ BA94. Linc Th Coll MTh94. **d** 96 **p** 97. C Leeds Gipton Epiphany *Ripon* 96-99; V Leeds St Marg and All Hallows from 99. *All Hallows Vicarage, 24 Regent Terrace, Leeds LS6 1NP* Tel 0113-242 2205 Mobile 07751-155124 E-mail raymoira@gn.apc.org

GATENBY, Canon Denis William. b 31. Ex Coll Ox BA54 DipTh55 MA58 Man Univ DSPT82. Wycliffe Hall Ox 54. **d** 56 **p** 57. C Deane *Man* 56-60; C Bradf Cathl *Bradf* 60-63; V Bootle St Matt *Liv* 63-72; V Horwich H Trin *Man* 72-84; TR Horwich 84-93; TR Horwich and Rivington 93-99; Hon Can Man Cathl 91-99; AD Deane 87-98; rtd 99; Perm to Offic *Man* from 00. *10 Parkgate Drive, Bolton BL1 8SD* Tel (01204) 592290

GATENBY, Paul Richard. b 32. Dur Univ BA55. Qu Coll Birm DipTh64. **d** 64 **p** 65. C Wellingborough St Barn *Pet* 64-68; V Braunston w Brooke 68-71; C Langley Marish *Ox* 71-72; TV Basildon St Martin w H Cross and Laindon *Chelmsf* 73-76; R Isham w Pytchley *Pet* 77-97; rtd 97; Perm to Offic *Pet* from 98. *8 Ivy Lane, Finedon, Wellingborough NN9 5NE* Tel (01933) 398819 E-mail paul.gatenby@ntlworld.com

GATENBY, Simon John Taylor. b 62. Nottm Univ BA83. St Jo Coll Nottm 84. **d** 87 **p** 88. C Haughton St Mary *Man* 87-90; C Newburn *Newc* 90-93; P-in-c Brunswick *Man* 93-96; R from 96; AD Hulme 99-05. *The Rectory, Hartfield Close, Brunswick, Manchester M13 9YX* Tel 0161-273 2470 E-mail simon@brunswickchurch.freeserve.co.uk

GATES, Alan Raymond. b 46. EAMTC 98. **d** 01 **p** 02. C W w E Mersea and Peldon w Gt and Lt Wigborough *Chelmsf* 01-05; P-in-c Gt Barton *St E* from 05. *The Vicarage, Church Road, Great Barton, Bury St Edmunds IP31 2QR* Tel and fax (01284) 787274 Mobile 07974-020379 E-mail agates@fish.co.uk

GATES, Mrs Frances Margaret. b 44. STETS 01. **d** 04 **p** 05. NSM Portsea St Mary *Portsm* from 04; NSM Portsea St Geo from 04; NSM Portsea All SS from 04. *114 Kings Road, Southsea PO5 4DW* Tel (023) 9282 0326 Mobile 07951-062226

GATES, John Michael. b 35. Dur Univ BA56 DipTh60. Cranmer Hall Dur 58. **d** 60 **p** 61. C Felixstowe St Jo *St E* 60-67; R Boyton w Capel St Andrew and Hollesley 67-98; P-in-c Shottisham w Sutton 87-92; rtd 98. *9 Foxgrove Lane, Felixstowe IP11 7JS* Tel (01394) 276886

GATES, Richard James. b 46. BA85. Oak Hill Th Coll 82. **d** 85 **p** 86. C Heald Green St Cath *Ches* 85-89; V Norton 89-98; V Bunbury and Tilstone Fearnall from 98. *The Vicarage, Vicarage Lane, Bunbury, Tarporley CW6 9PE* Tel (01829) 260991 Mobile 07715-178750 E-mail rick@prayer.fsnet.co.uk

GATES, Simon Philip. b 60. St Andr Univ MA82 St Jo Coll Dur BA86. Cranmer Hall Dur 84. **d** 87 **p** 88. C Southall Green St Jo *Lon* 87-91; Assoc Min St Andr Ch Hong Kong 91-95; V Clapham Park St Steph *S'wark* from 96; P-in-c Telford Park St Thos from 05. *The Vicarage, 2 Thornton Road, London SW12 0JU* Tel (020) 8671 8276 E-mail sgates2207@aol.com

GATFORD, The Ven Ian. b 40. AKC65. **d** 67 **p** 68. C Clifton w Glapton *S'well* 67-71; R 71-75; V Sherwood 75-84; Can Res Derby Cathl *Derby* 84-99; Adn Derby from 93; Hon Can Derby Cathl from 93. *1 Thatch Close, Derby DE22 1EA* Tel (01332) 553455 *or* 382233 Fax 552322 *or* 292969
E-mail archderby@talk21.com

GATHERCOLE, The Ven John Robert. b 37. Fitzw Ho Cam BA59 MA63. Ridley Hall Cam 59. **d** 62 **p** 63. C Dur St Nic *Dur* 62-66; C Croxdale 66-69; Bp's Soc and Ind Adv 66-69; Ind Chapl *Worc* 69-87; RD Bromsgrove 77-85; Sen Chapl Worcs Ind Miss 85-01; Hon Can Worc Cathl 80-01; Adn Dudley 87-01; rtd 01; Perm to Offic *Worc* from 01. *Wisteria Cottage, Main Road, Ombersley, Droitwich WR9 0EL* Tel (01905) 620263

GATISS, Lee. b 72. New Coll Ox BA96. Oak Hill Th Coll BA00. **d** 01 **p** 02. C Barton Seagrave w Warkton *Pet* 01-04; C St Helen Bishopsgate w St Andr Undershaft etc *Lon* from 04. *15 Morgan Street, London E3 5AA* Tel (020) 7283 2231
E-mail lee@gatiss.net

GATLIFFE, David Spenser. b 45. Keble Coll Ox BA67 Fitzw Coll Cam BA69. Westcott Ho Cam 67. **d** 69 **p** 70. C Oxted *S'wark* 69-72; C Roehampton H Trin 72-75; C S Beddington St Mich 76-77; TV Clapham Old Town 78-87; P-in-c Clapham Ch Ch and St Jo 81-87; TV Clapham Team 87-89; V S Wimbledon H Trin and St Pet 89-01; R Lee St Marg from 01; Ldr Post Ord Tr Woolwich Area from 04. *The Rectory, Brandram Road, London SE13 5EA* Tel (020) 8297 1181 *or* 8318 9643
E-mail stmargarets-lee@fish.co.uk

GATRILL, Adrian Colin. b 60. Southn Univ BTh82. Linc Th Coll 83. **d** 85 **p** 86. C W Bromwich St Andr *Lich* 85-88; C W Bromwich St Andr w Ch Ch 88-89; Chapl RAF from 89; Perm to Offic *St D* 90-95 and *Ripon* from 00. *Chaplaincy Services (RAF), HQ, Personnel and Training Command, RAF Innsworth, Gloucester GL3 1EZ* Tel (01452) 712612 ext 5164 Fax 510828
E-mail thegatrills@yahoo.com

GAUGE, Canon Barrie Victor. b 41. St D Coll Lamp BA62 Selw Coll Cam BA64 MA74 Liv Univ CQSW81 DipSocSc81. Bp Burgess Hall Lamp DPS65. **d** 65 **p** 66. C Newtown w Llanllwchaiarn w Aberhafesp *St As* 65-68; C Prestatyn 68-73; R Bodfari 73-76; Dioc RE Adv 73-76; Perm to Offic *Ches* 76-84; V Birkenhead St Jas w St Bede 84-90; Dir of Resources 90-98; Hon Can Ches Cathl 94-98; C Lache cum Saltney 95-98; Par Development Adv *Derby* from 98; Can Res Derby Cathl from 99; Dioc Miss Adv 01-04. *The Vicarage, 2 Glebe Crescent, Stanley, Ilkeston DE7 6FL* Tel 0115-932 2267
E-mail barrie.gauge@talk21.com

GAUNT, Adam. b 79. St Jo Coll Dur BA00 MA02. St Steph Ho Ox 03. **d** 05. C Middlesbrough Ascension *York* from 05. *The Curate's House, Penrith Road, Middlesbrough TS3 7JR* Tel (01642) 217433 E-mail adamgauntma@hotmail.com

GAUNT (née COTTELL), Mrs Avril Jane. b 50. SRN72 SCM74 Lon Univ Dip Nursing 81 Southn Univ DipTh97. S Dios Minl Tr Scheme 92. **d** 95 **p** 97. NSM Yatton Moor *B & W* 95-96 and 97-02; NSM Bourne *Guildf* 96-97; Asst Chapl N Bris NHS Trust from 02. *Myrtle Cottage, Ham Lane, Kingston Seymour, Clevedon BS21 6XE* Tel (01934) 832995

GAUNT, Eric Emmerson. b 33. Sarum Th Coll 65. **d** 67 **p** 68. C Hatch End St Anselm *Lon* 67-74; V Neasden cum Kingsbury St Cath 74-80; V Neasden St Cath w St Paul from 80. *St Catherine's Vicarage, Tanfield Avenue, London NW2 7RX* Tel (020) 8452 7322 E-mail dianachapman@madasafish.com

GAUNTLETT, Gilbert Bernard. b 36. Oriel Coll Ox BA59 MA62. Wycliffe Hall Ox 59. **d** 61 **p** 62. C Maidenhead St Andr and St Mary *Ox* 61-64; C Ox St Ebbe w St Pet 64-68; R Nottingham St Nic *S'well* 68-72; Asst Master Leys High Sch Redditch 73-79; Asst Master Stourport High Sch 79-85; rtd 97. *The Tower, Brynygwin Isaf, Dolgellau LL40 1YA* Tel (01341) 423481

GAUSDEN, Canon Peter James. b 32. Qu Coll Birm 57. **d** 60 **p** 61. C Battersea St Pet *S'wark* 60-63; C St Peter-in-Thanet *Cant* 63-68; V Sturry 68-74; R Sturry w Fordwich and Westbere w Hersden 74-97; Dioc Ecum Officer 91-97; Hon Can Cant Cathl 96-97; rtd 97; Perm to Offic *Cant* 97-99; Hon C St Nicholas at Wade w Sarre and Chislet w Hoath 99-04. *2 The Paddocks, Collards Close, Monkton, Ramsgate CT12 4JZ* Tel (01843) 825374

GAVED, Kenneth John Drew. b 31. LNSM course 92. **d** 95 **p** 96. OLM W Wickham St Jo *S'wark* 95-04. *42 Queensway, West Wickham BR4 9ER* Tel (020) 8462 4326

GAVIGAN, Josephine Katherine. b 49. Univ Coll Chich BA00. Sarum Th Coll 93. **d** 96. NSM Boxgrove *Chich* 96-00; C 00-03; Dn-in-c Maybridge from 03; RD Worthing from 05. *56 The Boulevard, Worthing BN13 1LA* Tel (01903) 249463 Mobile 07760-277262 E-mail deaconjo@hotmail.com

GAVIN, David Guy. b 63. Birm Univ BA85 Dur Univ BA90. Cranmer Hall Dur 88. **d** 91 **p** 92. C Parr *Liv* 91-95; TV Toxteth St Philemon w St Gabr and St Cleopas 95-02; P-in-c from 02. *St Cleopas Vicarage, Beresford Road, Liverpool L8 4SG* Tel 0151-727 0633 E-mail d.gavin@3tc4u.net

GAVIN (née GREGORY), Mrs Judith Rosalind. b 61. Open Univ BA97. St Jo Coll Nottm 99. **d** 01 **p** 02. C Moss Side St Jas w St Clem *Man* 01-04; C Whalley Range St Edm 01-04; C Rhyl w St Ann *St As* from 04. *Glen Maye, 18B Dyserth Road, Rhyl LL18 4DP* Tel (01745) 332224
E-mail judithanddarrell.gavin@btinternet.com

GAWITH, Canon Alan Ruthven. b 24. Man Univ Soc Admin Cert 47. Lich Th Coll 54. **d** 56 **p** 57. C Appleby and Murton cum Hilton *Carl* 56-59; C Newton Aycliffe *Dur* 59-61; C-in-c Owton Manor CD 61-67; V Kendal St Geo *Carl* 67-74; Soc Resp Officer *Man* 74-89; Hon Can Man Cathl 82-89; Bp's Adv on AIDS 88-92; rtd 90; Perm to Offic *Man* from 90. *7 Redwaters, Leigh WN7 1JD* Tel (01942) 676641

GAWNE-CAIN, John. b 38. G&C Coll Cam BA61 MA66 CEng MICE. Cuddesdon Coll 74. **d** 76 **p** 77. C Cowley St Jas *Ox* 76-80; P-in-c Ox St Giles 80-85; V Ox St Giles and SS Phil and Jas w St Marg 85-92; P-in-c Uffington w Woolstone and Baulking 92-93; P-in-c Shellingford 92-93; R Uffington, Shellingford, Woolstone and Baulking 93-03; rtd 03. *5 Beauchamp Lane, Oxford OX4 3LF* Tel (01865) 718643
E-mail j.gawne-cain@ruralnet.org.uk

GAWTHROP-DORAN, Mrs Sheila Mary. b 37. Birm Univ CertEd. Dalton Ho Bris 68. **dss** 79 **d** 87. Halliwell St Paul *Man* 79-82; New Bury 82-89; Par Dn 87-89; Par Dn Tonge w Alkrington 89-94; rtd 94; Perm to Offic *York* from 95. *35 Swarthdale, Haxby, York YO32 3NZ* Tel (01904) 761247

GAY, Adam Garcia Hugh. b 57. STETS 02. **d** 05. C Bitterne *Win* from 05. *4 Aberdour Close, Southampton SO18 5PF* Tel (023) 8047 3436 E-mail adamgay@totalise.co.uk

GAY, Colin James. b 37. Univ of Wales (Lamp) BA63. Chich Th Coll 63. **d** 65 **p** 66. C W Hackney St Barn *Lon* 65-69; C Hitchin *St Alb* 69-74; P-in-c Apsley End 74-80; TV Chambersbury 80-85; V Barnet Vale St Mark 85-03; rtd 03; Perm to Offic *St Alb* from 03. *14 Barleyfield Way, Houghton Regis, Dunstable LU5 5ER* Tel (01582) 862309

GAY, John Dennis. b 43. St Pet Coll Ox BA64 MA68 DPhil69 MSc78. Ripon Hall Ox 64. **d** 67 **p** 68. C Paddington St Jas *Lon* 67-71; P-in-c 71-72; Lic to Offic *Ox* from 72; Chapl Culham Coll Abingdon 72-79; Lect Ox Univ 78-80; Dir Culham Coll Inst from 80; Perm to Offic *Chich* 87-89. *Culham College Institute, 15 Norham Gardens, Oxford OX2 6PY* Tel (01865) 284885 Fax 284886 E-mail john.gay@culham.ac.uk

GAY, Canon Perran Russell. b 59. St Cath Coll Cam BA81 MA85 Ex Univ PGCE82 FRGS97. Ripon Coll Cuddesdon BA86. **d** 87 **p** 88. C Bodmin w Lanhydrock and Lanivet *Truro* 87-90; Bp's Dom Chapl 90-94; Dioc Officer for Unity 90-94; Can Res and Chan Truro Cathl from 94; Prec from 01; Dir of Tr 94-99. *52 Daniell Road, Truro TR1 2DA* Tel (01872) 276782 *or* 276491 Fax 277788 E-mail perran@perrangay.com *or* perran@trurocathedral.org.uk

GAY, Stuart. b 66. Oak Hill Th Coll BA94. **d** 00 **p** 01. C Sunningdale *Ox* 00-04; V Margate St Phil *Cant* from 04. *St Philip's Vicarage, 82 Crundale Way, Margate CT9 3YH* Tel (01843) 221589 E-mail stuart.gay@virgin.net

GAYFORD, John. b 37. Lon Univ BDS61 MB, BS65 MD78 FDSRCS64 FRCPsych86. St Jo Sem Wonersh 02. **d** 03. NSM E Grinstead St Mary *Chich* from 03. *Third Acre, 217 Smallfield Road, Horley RH6 9LR* Tel (01342) 842752

GAYLER, Roger Kenneth. b 44. Lich Th Coll 68. **d** 70 **p** 71. C Chingford St Anne *Chelmsf* 70-75; P-in-c Marks Gate 75-81; V from 81; RD Barking and Dagenham from 04. *The Vicarage, 187 Rose Lane, Romford RM6 5NR* Tel (020) 8599 0415
E-mail rev@r-gayler.fsnet.co.uk

GAYNOR, Mrs Mieke Aaltjen Cornelia. b 43. UEA BA79. St Jo Coll Nottm 02. **d** 03 **p** 04. NSM Hambleden Valley *Ox* from 03. *5 Lodge Close, Marlow SL7 1RB* Tel (01628) 481704
E-mail mieke.gaynor@btopenworld.com

GAZE, Mrs Sally Ann. b 69. SS Coll Cam BA91 MA95 Birm Univ PGCE92 MPhil98. Qu Coll Birm 94. **d** 96 **p** 97. C Martley and Wichenford, Knightwick etc *Worc* 96-00; C Crickhowell w Cwmdu and Tretower *S & B* 00-02; TR Newton Flotman, Swainsthorpe, Tasburgh, etc *Nor* from 02. *The Rectory, Church Road, Newton Flotman, Norwich NR15 1QB* Tel (01508) 470762
E-mail sally@tasvalley.org

GBEBIKAN, Angela Maria Abîke. b 56. Westcott Ho Cam 02. **d** 04 **p** 05. C Norbury St Steph and Thornton Heath *S'wark* from 04. *23 Beechwood Avenue, Thornton Heath CR7 7DY* Tel 07801-065472 (mobile) E-mail gbebikan@hotmail.com

GEACH, Canon Michael Bernard. b 26. Qu Coll Cam BA51 MA56. Westcott Ho Cam 51. **d** 53 **p** 54. C Kenwyn *Truro* 53-56; C Bodmin 56-59; C Helland 56-59; R St Dominic 59-65; Chapl Cotehele Ho Chapl Cornwall 60-65; V Linkinhorne 65-84; R Veryan w Ruan Lanihorne 84-96; Hon Can Truro Cathl 92-96; rtd 96; Perm to Offic *Truro* from 96. *17 Paul's Row, Truro TR1 1HH* Tel (01872) 262927

GEACH, Mrs Sarah Jane. b 50. Trin Coll Carmarthen CertEd73 CertRS94. WEMTC DipHE99. **d** 99 **p** 00. C Pill w Easton in Gordano and Portbury *B & W* 99-02; TV Ross *Heref* from 02. *The Rectory, Brampton Abbotts, Ross-on-Wye HR9 7JD* Tel (01989) 562010 E-mail sarah.geach@rtm.org.uk

GEAKE, Peter Henry. b 17. Trin Hall Cam BA39 MA46. Cuddesdon Coll 45. **d** 47 **p** 48. C Portsea St Mary *Portsm* 47-50;

C Southbroom *Sarum* 50-52; R Clovelly *Ex* 52-55; Chapl Canford Sch Wimborne 55-62; V Tattenham Corner and Burgh Heath *Guildf* 62-72; R Fulbeck *Linc* 72-82; P-in-c Carlton Scroop w Normanton 72-82; rtd 82; Perm to Offic *Ox* 94-95 and *Sarum* from 98. *33 Abbey Mews, Amesbury, Salisbury SP4 7EX* Tel (01980) 624815

GEAR, John Arthur. b 37. St Aid Birkenhead 62. **d** 64 **p** 66. C Attleborough *Cov* 64-66; C Attercliffe *Sheff* 66-68; C Sheerness H Trin w St Paul *Cant* 68-73; Asst Youth Adv *S'wark* 73-78; Youth Chapl *Lich* 78-88; V Stafford St Jo and Tixall w Ingestre 88-92; Gen Sec NCEC 92-97; rtd 97; Perm to Offic *Lich* 01-02; P-in-c Shrewsbury H Cross 02-03. *Greenside, Lime Kiln Bank, Telford TF2 9NU* Tel (01952) 613487 *or* (01743) 232723

✠**GEAR, The Rt Revd Michael Frederick.** b 34. Dur Univ BA59 DipTh61. Cranmer Hall Dur 59. **d** 61 **p** 62 **c** 93. C Bexleyheath Ch Ch *Roch* 61-64; C Ox St Aldate w H Trin *Ox* 64-67; V Clubmoor *Liv* 67-71; Rhodesia 71-76; Tutor Wycliffe Hall Ox 76-80; V Macclesfield St Mich *Ches* 80-85; RD Macclesfield 84-88; TR Macclesfield Team Par 85-88; Hon Can Ches Cathl 86-88; Adn Ches 88-93; Suff Bp Doncaster *Sheff* 93-99; rtd 99; Hon Asst Bp Roch from 99; Hon Asst Bp Cant from 00. *10 Acott Fields, Yalding, Maidstone ME18 6DQ* Tel (01622) 817388 E-mail mike.gear@rochester.anglican.org

GEBAUER, George Gerhart. b 25. Sarum & Wells Th Coll 71. **d** 73 **p** 74. C Portsdown *Portsm* 73-78; V Purbrook 78-91; rtd 91; Perm to Offic *Portsm* from 91. *52 St John's Road, Locks Heath, Southampton SO31 6NF* Tel (01489) 575172

GEDDES, Canon Gordon David. b 38. St Chad's Coll Dur BA59. **d** 61 **p** 62. C Bishopwearmouth St Mary V w St Pet CD *Dur* 61-65; P-in-c Jarrow 65-68; Teacher Crewe Boys' Gr Sch 68-71; Hd of RS 71-78; Hd of RE Ruskin Sch Crewe 78-90; P-in-c Church Minshull w Leighton and Minshull Vernon *Ches* 90-91; V Leighton-cum-Minshull Vernon from 91; RD Nantwich from 01; Hon Can Ches Cathl from 04; Chapl Mid Cheshire Hosps Trust from 91. *The Vicarage, Middlewich Road, Minshull Vernon, Crewe CW1 4RD* Tel (01270) 522213 Fax 522694 E-mail revggeddes@aol.com

GEDDES, Peter Henry. b 51. Trin Coll Bris 84. **d** 86 **p** 87. C Blackpool St Mark *Blackb* 86-88; C Barnston *Ches* 88-92; V Haslington w Crewe Green 92-04; V Partington and Carrington from 04. *St Mary's Vicarage, Manchester Road, Partington, Manchester M31 4FB* Tel 0161-775 3542

GEDDES, Roderick Charles. b 47. Man Univ DipEd78 MPhil85. N Ord Course 88. **d** 91 **p** 93. C Alverthorpe *Wakef* 91-92; C S Ossett 92-94; R Andreas, V Jurby and V Andreas St Jude *S & M* 94-03; P-in-c Gargrave *Bradf* from 03. *The Vicarage, Mill Hill Lane, Gargrave, Skipton BD23 3NQ* Tel (01756) 748548 E-mail geddes@mcb.net

GEDGE, Lloyd Victor. b 23. Cuddesdon Coll 54. **d** 57 **p** 58. C Headington *Ox* 57-60; Canada 60-63, 66-82 and from 86; New Zealand 63-66; P-in-c N Creake *Nor* 82-83; P-in-c S Creake 82-83; R N and S Creake w Waterden 84-86; rtd 88. *PO Box 61, Bruce AB, Canada, T0B 0R0*

GEDGE, Simon John Francis. b 44. Keble Coll Ox BA67 MA73. Cuddesdon Coll 67. **d** 69 **p** 70. C Perry Barr *Birm* 69-73; C Handsworth St Andr 73-75; V Birm St Pet 75-81; Perm to Offic *Lon* 81-85; Hon C Croydon St Jo *S'wark* 85-87. *121 Albyn Road, London SE8 4EB* Tel (020) 8692 7328

GEE, Anne Alison. b 43. **d** 01 **p** 02. NSM Canford Magna *Sarum* from 01. *37 Floral Farm, Wimborne BH21 3AT* Tel (01202) 887078

GEE, Mrs Dorothy Mary. b 33. St Jo Coll Nottm 88. **d** 89 **p** 94. Chapl Asst Univ Hosp Nottm 89-95; NSM Plumtree *S'well* 95-97; P-in-c 97-01; rtd 01; Perm to Offic *S'well* from 01. *16 The Leys, Normanton-on-the-Wolds, Keyworth, Nottingham NG12 5NU* Tel 0115-937 4927 E-mail mary.gee@microhelpuk.net

GEE, Canon Edward. b 28. St Deiniol's Hawarden 59. **d** 61 **p** 62. C Hanging Heaton *Wakef* 61-65; V Brownhill 65-75; V Alverthorpe 75-84; R Castleford All SS 84-92; Hon Can Wakef Cathl 87-92; rtd 92; Perm to Offic *Bradf* and *Wakef* from 92. *1 Holme Ghyll, Colne Road, Glusburn, Keighley BD20 8RG* Tel (01535) 630060

GEE, Norman. b 11. Lon Univ BA33 St Cath Soc Ox BA35 MA42. Wycliffe Hall Ox 33. **d** 35 **p** 36. C Kilburn St Mary *Lon* 35-38; Youth Sec CMJ 38-41; P-in-c Woodside Park St Barn *Lon* 40-41; V 41-49; V Oakwood St Thos 49-58; V Bath St Bart *B & W* 58-73; V Curry Rivel 73-78; rtd 78; Perm to Offic *B & W* 79-97. *5 Barn Close, Nether Stowey, Bridgwater TA5 1PA* Tel (01278) 732317

GEEN, James William. b 50. Chich Th Coll 76. **d** 79 **p** 80. C Brandon *Dur* 79-84; C Sunderland Red Ho 84-86; P-in-c N Hylton St Marg Castletown 86-89; V 89-91; Dep Chapl HM Pris Dur 91-92; Chapl HM YOI Lanc Farms 92-95; Chapl HM Pris Long Lartin 95-01; Chapl HM Pris Blakenhurst from 01. *HM Prison Blakenhurst, Hewell Lane, Redditch B97 6QS* Tel (01527) 400612 E-mail jacobus@fsmail.net

GEERING, Preb Anthony Ernest. b 43. Lon Univ DipTh66 Columbia Pacific Univ BSc. Kelham Th Coll 62. **d** 68 **p** 69. C Cov St Mary *Cov* 68-71; New Zealand 71-75; P-in-c Brinklow *Cov* 75-77; R 77-81; V Monks Kirby w Pailton and Stretton-under-Fosse 77-81; R Harborough Magna 77-81; V Pilton w Ashford *Ex* 81-86; P-in-c Shirwell w Loxhore 83-86; R Crediton and Shobrooke 86-01; P-in-c Sandford w Upton Hellions 00-01; R Crediton, Shobrooke and Sandford etc 01; RD Cadbury 93-97; R Chagford, Drewsteignton, Hittisleigh etc from 01; RD Okehampton from 02; Preb Ex Cathl from 02. *The Rectory, Chagford, Newton Abbot TQ13 8BW* Tel (01647) 433014

GEESON, Brian Alfred. b 30. Qu Coll Ox BA51 Trin & All SS Coll Leeds PGCE76. Qu Coll Birm 54. **d** 55 **p** 56. C Newbold w Dunston *Derby* 55-59; PC Calow 59-64; R Broughton *Bradf* 64-71; TV Seacroft *Ripon* 71-77; Hon C Hanging Heaton *Wakef* 77-87; Hon C Purlwell 87-94; rtd 94; Perm to Offic *Wakef* from 94. *30 Ullswater Avenue, Dewsbury WF12 7PL* Tel (01924) 465621

GEILINGER, John Edward. b 27. Lon Univ BSc53 BD58 BA76 MPhil79. Tyndale Hall Bris. **d** 59 **p** 60. C Plymouth St Jude *Ex* 59-61; Lect Trin Th Coll Umuahia Nigeria 63-72; Lect Th Coll of N Nigeria 72-77; Perm to Offic *Portsm* from 79; rtd 92. *Emmaus House, Colwell Road, Freshwater PO40 9LY* Tel (01983) 753030

GEISOW, Hilary Patricia. b 46. Salford Univ BSc67 Warwick Univ PhD71 Nottm Univ PGCE94. St Jo Coll Nottm 01. **d** 03 **p** 04. C Linc St Faith and St Martin w St Pet *Linc* from 03. *74 Roman Wharf, Lincoln LN1 1SR* Tel (01522) 546022 E-mail hilary@geisow.freeserve.co.uk

GELDARD, Preb Mark Dundas. b 50. Liv Univ BA71 Bris Univ MA75. Trin Coll Bris 73. **d** 75 **p** 76. C Aughton Ch Ch *Liv* 75-78; Tutor Trin Coll Bris 78-84; V Fairfield *Liv* 84-88; Dir of Ords *Lich* from 88; C Lich St Mary w St Mich 95-96; C Lich St Mich w St Mary and Wall from 96; Preb Lich Cathl from 00. *10 The Brambles, Lichfield WS14 9SE* Tel (01543) 306192 *or* 306220 Fax 306229 E-mail sue.jackson@lichfield.anglican.org

GELL, Anne Elizabeth. b 63. St Hugh's Coll Ox BA85 MA01 R Free Hosp Sch of Medicine MB, BS90 Surrey Univ BA01. STETS 98. **d** 01 **p** 02. C Headley All SS *Guildf* 01-05; V Wrecclesham from 05. *The Vicarage, 2 King's Lane, Wrecclesham, Farnham GU10 4QB* Tel (01252) 716431 E-mail annegell@lineone.net

GELL, Miss Margaret Florence. b 30. **d** 00 **p** 01. NSM Madeley *Lich* 00-04; rtd 04; Perm to Offic *Lich* from 04. *19 Pear Tree Drive, Madeley, Crewe CW3 9EN* Tel (01782) 750669

GELLI, Frank Julian. b 43. Birkbeck Coll Lon BA78 K Coll Lon MTh82. Ripon Coll Cuddesdon 84. **d** 86 **p** 87. C Chiswick St Nic w St Mary *Lon* 86-89; Chapl Ankara *Eur* 89-91; C Kensington St Mary Abbots w St Geo *Lon* 91-99; rtd 03. *58 Boston Gardens, Brentford TW8 9LP* Tel (020) 8847 4533 E-mail numapomp@talk21.com

GELLING, Canon John Drury. b 22. Pemb Coll Ox BA44 MA48. Wycliffe Hall Ox 44. **d** 54 **p** 55. Hd Master Eccles High Sch 50-64; C Irlam *Man* 54-59; V Rushen *S & M* 64-77; RD Castletown 71-77; R Ballaugh 77-92; P-in-c Michael 77-78; V 78-92; Can St German's Cathl 80-92; rtd 92; Perm to Offic *S & M* from 93. *Uplands, Ballavitchell Road, Crosby, Isle of Man IM4 2DN* Tel (01624) 851223

GELSTON, Anthony. b 35. Keble Coll Ox BA57 MA60 DD85. Ridley Hall Cam 59. **d** 60 **p** 61. C Chipping Norton *Ox* 60-62; Lect Th Dur Univ *Dur* 62-76; Sen Lect 76-88; Dean Div Faculty 77-79; Reader 89-95; Lic to Offic 62-95; rtd 95. *Lesbury, Hetton Road, Houghton le Spring DH5 8JW* Tel 0191-584 2256 E-mail anthony.gelston@durham.ac.uk

GEMMELL, Canon Ian William Young. b 52. ALAM. St Jo Coll Nottm. **d** 77 **p** 78. C Old Hill H Trin *Worc* 77-81; C Selly Park St Steph and St Wulstan *Birm* 81-83; V Leic St Chris *Leic* 83-93; RD Christianity S 92-93; P-in-c Gt Bowden w Welham, Glooston and Cranoe 93-02; P-in-c Church Langton w Tur Langton, Thorpe Langton etc 93-99; P-in-c Church Langton cum Tur Langton etc 99-02; R Gt Bowden w Welham, Glooston and Cranoe etc from 02; RD Gartree I from 97; Hon Can Leic Cathl from 03. *The Rectory, Dingley Road, Great Bowdon, Market Harborough LE16 7ET* Tel (01858) 462032 E-mail bud.gemmell@btopenworld.com

GENDALL, Stephen Mark. b 63. Univ of Zimbabwe DipRS90. **d** 89 **p** 90. Lundi St Apollos Zimbabwe 89-01; Youth Chapl 93-01; Can Cen Zimbabwe 00-01; V Lingfield and Crowhurst *S'wark* from 02. *The Vicarage, Vicarage Road, Lingfield RH7 6HA* Tel (01342) 832021 Mobile 07752-063150 E-mail steve@thegendalls.freeserve.co.uk

GENDERS, Nigel Mark. b 65. Oak Hill Th Coll BA92. **d** 92 **p** 93. C New Malden and Coombe *S'wark* 92-96; C Enfield Ch Ch Trent Park *Lon* 96-98; P-in-c Eastry and Northbourne w Tilmanstone etc *Cant* 98-03; P-in-c Woodnesborough w Worth and Staple from 03. *The Vicarage, The Street, Woodnesborough, Sandwich CT13 0NQ* Tel (01304) 613056 E-mail therev@f2s.com

✠**GENDERS, The Rt Revd Roger Alban Marson (Anselm).** b 19. BNC Ox BA47 MA47. Coll of Resurr Mirfield 48. **d** 52 **p** 52 **c** 77. CR from 52; Lic to Offic *Wakef* 52-55; Barbados 55-65;

Rhodesia 66-75; Adn E Distr 70-75; Bp Bermuda 77-82; Asst Bp Wakef 83-93; rtd 84; Hon Asst Bp Wakef from 93. *House of the Resurrection, Stocks Bank Road, Mirfield WF14 0BN* Tel (01924) 483346

GENEREUX, Patrick Edward. b 47. William Carey Coll BSc73 Univ of the South (USA) MDiv78. **d** 78 **p** 79. USA 78-81 and from 82; C Spalding *Linc* 81-82. *621 North 5th Street, Burlington, IA 52601-0608, USA* Tel (001) (319) 754 6420 E-mail pgenereux@aol.com

GENT, David Robert. b 71. Surrey Univ BSc94. Qu Coll Birm BD97. **d** 98 **p** 99. C Wotton-under-Edge w Ozleworth and N Nibley *Glouc* 98-02; C Yeovil H Trin w Barwick *B & W* from 02; Chapl Yeovil Coll from 02. *The Vicarage, Church Lane, Barwick, Yeovil BA22 9TE* Tel (01935) 426866 E-mail rev_d_gent@hotmail.com

GENT, Mrs Miriam. b 29. Leeds Univ BA51. SW Minl Tr Course 84. **d** 87 **p** 94. NSM Pinhoe and Broadclyst *Ex* 87-02; Dioc Adv in Adult Tr 96-99; Perm to Offic from 02. *Moss Hayne Cottage, West Clyst, Exeter EX1 3TR* Tel (01392) 467288 Fax 462980

GENT, Miss Susan Elizabeth. SSC81 K Coll Lon LLB78 Brunel Univ BA95 Wycliffe Hall Ox MPhil96 DipMin97. **d** 97 **p** 98. C Notting Hill St Jo and St Pet *Lon* 97-00; Chapl to City law firms from 00; Hon Assoc P St Paul's Cathl from 00; Dioc Visitor from 01. *3B Amen Court, London EC4M 7BU* Tel (020) 7329 2702 Fax 7248 3104 E-mail susan.gent@ukgateway.net

GENTRY, Michael John. b 66. St Steph Ho Ox BTh95. **d** 98 **p** 99. C Bromley SS Pet and Paul *Roch* 98-02; V Langton Green from 02. *The Vicarage, The Green, Langton Green, Tunbridge Wells TN3 0JB* Tel (01892) 862072 E-mail frmichael@beeb.net

GEOFFREY, Brother. *See* PEARSON, Canon Harold

GEOGHEGAN, Prof Luke. b 62. SS Hild & Bede Coll Dur BA83 Bedf Coll Lon MSc87 CQSW87 FRSA93. St Alb and Ox Min Course 87. **d** 00 **p** 01. NSM Spitalfields Ch Ch w All SS *Lon* 00-03; NSM Gt Berkhamsted *St Alb* from 03; Warden Toynbee Hall from 98. *16 Gravel Path, Berkhamsted HP4 2EF*

GEORGE, Alexander Robert. b 46. K Coll Lon BD69 AKC69. St Aug Coll Cant. **d** 70 **p** 71. C Newmarket St Mary w Exning St Agnes *St E* 70-74; C Swindon Ch Ch *Bris* 74-76; C Henbury 76-79; Lic to Offic 79-80; TV Oldland 80-88; C Ipswich St Aug *St E* 89; C Hadleigh w Layham and Shelley 89-90; P-in-c Assington 90-91; R Assington w Newton Green and Lt Cornard 91-00; P-in-c Hundon 00-03; Hon C 03-04; Hon C Stour Valley from 04; Dioc Moderator for Reader Tr 95-03; Asst Liturg Officer (Formation and Educn) 00-03; rtd 03; Nat Moderator for Reader Tr from 04. *The Vicarage, 5 Armstrong Close, Hundon, Sudbury CO10 8HD* Tel (01440) 786617 E-mail alecrg@genie.co.uk

GEORGE, Charles Roy. b 32. St Edm Hall Ox BA55 MA59. Cuddesdon Coll 55. **d** 57 **p** 58. C Chorley St Laur *Blackb* 57-60; C Norton *Derby* 60-64; V Eltham St Barn *S'wark* 64-74; V Milton *Portsm* 74-90; R Rowner 90-96; rtd 96; Perm to Offic *Portsm* from 96. *46 The Thicket, Fareham PO16 8PZ* Tel (01329) 288185

GEORGE, David. b 64. Wycliffe Hall Ox 01. **d** 03 **p** 04. C Inkberrow w Cookhill and Kington w Dormston *Worc* from 03. *3 The Pleck, Inkberrow, Worcester WR7 4JB* Tel (01386) 791369 E-mail revdave.george@virgin.net

GEORGE, David Michael. b 45. Selw Coll Cam BA66 MA70. Chich Th Coll 70. **d** 73 **p** 74. C Chiswick St Nic w St Mary *Lon* 73-76; C Kensington St Mary Abbots w St Geo 76-78; C Northolt Park St Barn 78-81; Argentina from 81; Adn River Plate 84-02; R St Jo Cathl Buenos Aires from 00. *Avda Belgrano 568-7A, 1092 Buenos Aires, Argentina* Tel (0054) (1) 4331 9573 E-mail smtla@cvtci.com.ar

GEORGE, Mrs Elizabeth Ann. b 33. Westf Coll Lon BA56. S Dios Minl Tr Scheme 84. **d** 87 **p** 94. NSM Basingstoke *Win* from 87. *71 Camrose Way, Basingstoke RG21 3AW* Tel (01256) 464763 E-mail elizabethgeorge@compuserve.com

GEORGE, The Ven Frederick. b 39. St Luke's Coll Ex TCert61. Chich Th Coll 82. **d** 72 **p** 83. Australia 72-75; Brunei 75-80; The Gambia 80-82 and 83-88; Prin Angl Tr Cen Farafeni 85-88; P-in-c Ringsfield w Redisham, Barsham, Shipmeadow etc *St E* 89-92; R Wainford 92-97; V Jamestown St Helena 97-03; Adn St Helena 99-03; rtd 03; Perm to Offic *Chich* from 03. *Hut's Gate Vicarage, Box 80, St Helena, STHL 1ZZ, South Atlantic*

GEORGE, Preb John Thomas. b 17. St D Coll Lamp BA42 Selw Coll Cam BA44 MA47. Westcott Ho Cam 44. **d** 45 **p** 46. C Llanstadwel *St D* 45-48; C Eastville St Thos *Bris* 48-50; C Wells St Cuth *B & W* 50-52; PV Wells Cathl 50-52; Teacher Wells Cathl Sch 50-52; V Cheddar 52-57; P-in-c Priddy 55-57; CF 57-60; V Thornton w Allerthorpe *York* 60-62; R Backwell *B & W* 62-72; RD Portishead 68-72; V Wellington w W Buckland and Nynehead 72-76; TR Wellington and Distr 76-82; Preb Wells Cathl 78-86; rtd 82; Hon C Diptford, N Huish, Harberton and Harbertonford *Ex* 85-97; Perm to Offic from 97. *12 Woolcombe Lane, Ivybridge PL21 0UA* Tel (01752) 698284

GEORGE, Nicholas Paul. b 58. St Steph Ho Ox 86. **d** 89 **p** 90. C Leeds St Aid *Ripon* 89-92; C Leeds Richmond Hill 92-96; Chapl Agnes Stewart C of E High Sch Leeds 93-96; V Leeds Halton St Wilfrid *Ripon* 96-02; V Camberwell St Giles w St Matt *S'wark* from 02. *St Giles's Vicarage, 200 Benhill Road, London SE5 7LL* Tel and fax (020) 7703 4504 Mobile 07771-603217 E-mail nick.george@care4free.net

✠**GEORGE, The Rt Revd Randolph Oswald.** b 24. Codrington Coll Barbados 46. **d** 50 **p** 51 **c** 76. Barbados 50-53; C Leigh *Lich* 53-55; C Ardwick St Benedict *Man* 55-57; C Bedford Park *Lon* 57-58; C Lavender Hill Ascension *S'wark* 58-60; Trinidad and Tobago 60-71; Hon Can Trinidad 68-71; Guyana from 71; Dean Georgetown 71-76; Suff Bp Stabroek 76-80; Bp Guyana from 80. *Austin House, Kingston, Georgetown 1, Guyana* Tel (00592) (2) 63862 Fax 64183

GEORGE, Robert Henry. b 45. FCCA73. WEMTC 99. **d** 01 **p** 02. OLM S Cerney w Cerney Wick and Down Ampney *Glouc* from 01. *Jedems, Berkeley Close, South Cerney, Cirencester GL7 5UN* Tel (01285) 860973 E-mail jedems@fish.co.uk

GEORGE, Roy. *See* GEORGE, Charles Roy

GEORGE-JONES, Canon Gwilym Ifor. b 26. K Coll (NS) 56. **d** 57 **p** 57. R Seaforth St Jas Canada 57-61; V Kirton in Lindsey *Linc* 61-71; R Grayingham 61-71; R Manton 61-71; V Alford w Rigsby 71-92; R Maltby 71-92; R Well 71-92; V Bilsby w Farlesthorpe 71-92; R Hannah cum Hagnaby w Markby 71-92; R Saleby w Beesby 71-92; RD Calcewaithe and Candleshoe 77-85 and 87-89; Can and Preb Linc Cathl 81-01; rtd 92. *42 Kelstern Road, Lincoln LN6 3NJ* Tel (01522) 691896

GEORGE-ROGERS, Gillian Jean Richeldis. b 47. St Mich Coll Llan. **d** 99 **p** 02. C Llanishen *Llan* 99-05; P-in-c Rhondda Fach Uchaf from 05. *The Vicarage, Woodville Place, Ferndale CF43 4LS* Tel (01443) 732321 E-mail gillian@richeldis.fslife.co.uk

GERD, Sister. *See* SWENSSON, Sister Gerd Inger

GERRANS, Daniel. b 58. Em Coll Cam LLB80 MA83 Barrister-at-Law (Middle Temple) 81. SEITE 02. **d** 05. NSM De Beauvoir Town St Pet *Lon* from 05. *19 College Cross, London N1 1PT* E-mail daniel.gerrans@xxiv.co.uk

GERRARD, The Ven David Keith Robin. b 39. St Edm Hall Ox BA61. Linc Th Coll 61. **d** 63 **p** 64. C Stoke Newington St Olave *Lon* 63-66; C Primrose Hill St Mary w Avenue Road St Paul 66-69; V Newington St Paul *S'wark* 69-79; V Surbiton St Andr and St Mark 79-89; RD Kingston 84-88; Hon Can S'wark Cathl 85-89; Adn Wandsworth 89-04; rtd 05. *15 Woodbourne Drive, Claygate, Esher KT10 0DR* Tel (01372) 467295

GERRARD, George Ernest. b 16. FCIS60 DD94. Ridley Hall Cam 66. **d** 68 **p** 69. C Hilborough w Bodney *Nor* 68-70; C Ramsey *Ely* 70-75; rtd 81; Perm to Offic *Nor* 86-98. *46 Cornwallis Court, Hospital Road, Bury St Edmunds IP33 3NH* Tel (01284) 756900

GERRARD, Paul Christian Francis. b 58. St Steph Ho Ox 92. **d** 94 **p** 01. C Longton *Lich* 94-95; NSM New Radnor and Llanfihangel Nantmelan etc *S & B* 01-04; NSM Knighton, Norton, Whitton, Pilleth and Cascob from 04. *The Old Vicarage, Norton, Presteigne LD8 2EN* Tel (01544) 260038

GERRISH, David Victor. b 38. St Jo Coll Dur BSc61 MA65. Oak Hill Th Coll 61. **d** 64 **p** 65. C Fareham St Jo *Portsm* 64-66; Asst Chapl K Sch Roch 67-71; Asst Chapl Bryanston Sch 71-73; Chapl 73-77; Chapl Mon Sch 77-86; Chapl Warminster Sch 86-89; R Portland All SS w St Pet *Sarum* 89-96; Chapl Aquitaine *Eur* 96-00; rtd 00; Perm to Offic *Sarum* from 01. *Scribbage House, 1 Herbert Place, Weymouth DT4 8LR* Tel (01305) 789319

GERRY, Brian John Rowland. b 38. Oak Hill Th Coll 69. **d** 71 **p** 72. C Hawkwell *Chelmsf* 71-74; C Battersea Park St Sav *S'wark* 74-77; C Battersea St Geo w St Andr 74-77; V Axmouth w Musbury *Ex* 77-86; R Upton 86-04; rtd 04. *12 Fletcher Close, Torquay TQ2 6DD* Tel (01803) 614571

GERRY, Ulric James. b 67. Bris Univ BEng89. Wycliffe Hall Ox BA96. **d** 97 **p** 98. C Hemel Hempstead *St Alb* 97-00; Perm to Offic 01-02; Crosslinks Tanzania from 02. *Address temp unknown*

GHEST, Richard William Iliffe. b 31. Em Coll Cam BA53 MA57 Lon Univ BA66. Wells Th Coll 53. **d** 55 **p** 56. C Weston-super-Mare St Jo *B & W* 55-57; India 58-63; C Holborn St Geo w H Trin and St Bart *Lon* 63-67; Ceylon 67-68; C Combe Down *B & W* 68-73; C Combe Down w Monkton Combe 73-74; R Tickenham 74-96; rtd 96. *120 Cottrell Road, Roath, Cardiff CF24 3EX* Tel (029) 2048 1597

GHINN, Edward. b 45. Oak Hill Th Coll 71. **d** 74 **p** 75. C Purley Ch Ch *S'wark* 74-77; Chile 77-82; V Sevenoaks Weald *Roch* 82-86; Chapl HM Pris Hull 86-89; Chapl HM Pris Pentonville 89-91; Chapl HM Pris Maidstone 91-96; Brazil 96-98; Min Parkwood CD *Cant* 98-01; Chapl HM Pris Grendon and Spring Hill 01-03; Chapl HM Pris Stocken from 03. *HM Prison Stocken, Stocken Hall Road, Stretton, Oakham LE15 7RD* Tel (01780) 485281 Fax 410681 E-mail e.ghinn@virgin.net

GHOSH, Dipen. b 43. St Jo Coll Nottm 71. **d** 74 **p** 75. C Bushbury *Lich* 74-77; Hon C 86-89; C Wednesfield Heath 89-91; TV Wolverhampton 91-98; TV Bushbury 98-02; Chapl Compton Hall Hospice Wolv 98-02; V Wolverhampton St Matt *Lich* from 02. *St Matthew's Vicarage, 14 Sydenham Road, Wolverhampton WV1 2NY* Tel (01902) 453056

GIBB, David Richard Albert. b 68. Lon Bible Coll BA90 Cov Univ MPhil95. **d** 95 **p** 96. C Ox St Ebbe w H Trin and St Pet *Ox* 95-01; V Leyland St Andr *Blackb* from 01. *St Andrew's Vicarage, 1 Crocus Field, Leyland PR25 3DY* Tel (01772) 621645 E-mail david.gibb7@ntlworld.com

GIBBARD, Roger. b 48. Southn Univ BA73. Cuddesdon Coll 73. **d** 75 **p** 76. C Portsea St Mary *Portsm* 75-79; P-in-c New Addington *Cant* 79-81; C Ditton St Mich *Liv* 81-82; TV 82-88; Asst Chapl HM Pris Liv 88-89; Chapl HM YOI Hindley 89-92; Chapl HM Pris Risley 92-00; V Wigan St Mich *Liv* 01-04. *97 Barnsley Street, Wigan WN6 7HB* Tel (01942) 233465 E-mail thegibbards@lycos.co.uk

GIBBINS, John Grenville. b 53. Aston Tr Scheme 89 Linc Th Coll 89. **d** 91 **p** 92. C Market Harborough *Leic* 91-95; P-in-c Blaby from 95. *The Rectory, Wigston Road, Blaby, Leicester LE8 4FU* Tel 0116-277 2588 E-mail ggibbins@leicester.anglican.org

GIBBON, Matthew. b 79. Trin Coll Carmarthen BA00. St Steph Ho Ox BTh03. **d** 03 **p** 04. C Caerau w Ely *Llan* from 03. *79 Heol y Castell, Ely, Cardiff CF5 5LR* Tel (029) 2067 0096 E-mail gibbmatt23@hotmail.com

GIBBONS, David Austen. b 63. York Univ BSc84. Ch Div Sch of Pacific 93 Ripon Coll Cuddesdon BA94. **d** 94 **p** 95. C Ryde H Trin *Portsm* 94-97; C Swanmore St Mich 94-97; C Gosport Ch Ch 97-01; R Havant from 01. *St Faith's Rectory, 5 Meadowlands, Havant PO9 2RP* Tel (023) 9248 3485 E-mail d_gibbons@talk21.com

GIBBONS, David Robin Christian. b 36. Chich Th Coll 82. **d** 84 **p** 85. C Seaford w Sutton *Chich* 84-87; R Harting 87-93; R Harting w Elsted and Treyford cum Didling 93-04; rtd 04. *Richmond Villas, 102 East Street, Selsey, Chichester PO20 0BX* Tel (01243) 602978

GIBBONS, Eric. b 47. Sarum & Wells Th Coll 69. **d** 72 **p** 73. C New Haw *Guildf* 72-76; C Hawley H Trin 76-79; P-in-c Blackheath and Chilworth 79-90; V 90-98; C Shere, Albury and Chilworth 98-99; P-in-c Tongham 99-04; rtd 04. *38 Ambleside Close, Farnborough GU14 0LA*

GIBBONS, Harvey Lloyd. b 62. Harper Adams Agric Coll HND84. Ripon Coll Cuddesdon 97. **d** 99 **p** 00. C Verwood *Sarum* 99-00; C Gillingham 00-02; P-in-c Upavon w Rushall and Charlton from 02; Dioc Voc Adv from 02. *The Vicarage, 5A Vicarage Lane, Upavon, Pewsey SN9 6AA* Tel (01980) 630248 *or* (01722) 411944 E-mail vocations@salisbury.anglican.org *or* ghrv@fish.co.uk

GIBBONS, The Ven Kenneth Harry. b 31. Man Univ BSc52. Cuddesdon Coll 54. **d** 56 **p** 57. C Fleetwood St Pet *Blackb* 56-60; NE Sch Sec SCM 60-62; Hon C Leeds St Pet *Ripon* 60-62; C St Martin-in-the-Fields *Lon* 62-65; V New Addington *Cant* 65-70; V Portsea St Mary *Portsm* 70-81; RD Portsm 73-79; Hon Can Portsm Cathl 76-81; Dir Post-Ord Tr *Blackb* 81-83; Acting Chapl HM Forces Weeton 81-85; Dir of Ords 82-90; Adn Lancaster 81-97; P-in-c Weeton 81-85; V St Michaels-on-Wyre 85-97; rtd 97; P-in-c St Magnus the Martyr w St Marg New Fish Street *Lon* 97-03; P-in-c St Clem Eastcheap w St Martin Orgar from 99. *112 Valley Road, Kenley CR8 5BU* Tel (020) 8660 7502 E-mail margaret@gibbons440.fsnet.co.uk

GIBBONS (née TOZE), Ms Lissa Melanie. b 58. Birm Univ BA79. St Alb and Ox Min Course 98. **d** 01 **p** 02. C Risborough *Ox* from 01. *The Rectory, Thornborough Road, Padbury, Buckingham MK18 2AH* Tel (01280) 813162 E-mail lissa.toze@tesco.net

GIBBONS, Paul James. b 37. JP. Chich Th Coll 63. **d** 65 **p** 66. C Croydon St Mich *Cant* 65-72; V Maidstone St Mich from 72. *The Vicarage, 109 Tonbridge Road, Maidstone ME16 8JS* Tel (01622) 752710

GIBBONS, Mrs Susan Janet. b 51. St Mary's Coll Dur BA73 Birm Univ PGCE74. WMMTC 89. **d** 92 **p** 94. NSM Fladbury w Wyre Piddle and Moor etc *Worc* 92-00; Perm to Offic from 00. *The Old School, Bricklehampton, Pershore WR10 3HJ* Tel (01386) 710475

GIBBONS, Thomas Patrick. b 59. St Jo Coll Dur BA82. St Steph Ho Ox 88. **d** 90 **p** 91. C Whorlton *Newc* 90-94; C Gosforth St Nic 94-96; R Radley and Sunningwell *Ox* 96-04; P-in-c Lenborough from 04. *The Rectory, Thornborough Road, Padbury, Buckingham MK18 2AH* Tel (01280) 813162 E-mail tomandlissa@waitrose.com

GIBBONS, Mrs Valerie Mary Lydele. b 49. St Aid Coll Dur BA72 Solicitor 75. Wycliffe Hall Ox 98. **d** 03 **p** 04. OLM Cholsey and Moulsford *Ox* from 03. *Kilifi, Caps Lane, Cholsey, Wallingford OX10 9HF* Tel and fax (01491) 651377 E-mail val.gibbons@btinternet.com

GIBBONS, Canon William Simpson. b 32. TCD BA60 MA64. **d** 61 **p** 62. C Londonderry Ch Ch *D & R* 61-65; I Drumholm and Rossnowlagh 65-70; C Dublin St Ann w St Steph *D & G* 70-72; I Kill 72-95; Can Ch Ch Cathl Dublin 91-95; rtd 95. *Muthaiga, 8 Mount Bernard Drive, Castlederg BT81 7JA* Tel (028) 8167 0691 E-mail william@gibbons1666.freeserve.co.uk

GIBBS, Colin Hugh. b 35. St Mich Coll Llan 82. **d** 84 **p** 85. C Bistre *St As* 84-87; V Penycae 87-92; rtd 92. *Asaph, 26 Cil y Coed, Ruabon, Wrexham LL14 6TA* Tel (01978) 823550

GIBBS, Colin Wilfred. b 39. Man Univ BA62 Birm Univ CertEd63. St Jo Coll Nottm 71. **d** 73 **p** 74. C Crowborough *Chich* 73-76; C Rodbourne Cheney *Bris* 76-77; C Bickenhill w Elmdon *Birm* 77-80; CF 80-96; Dir Ichthus Ho Homestay from 96; Perm to Offic *Ex* from 96; Chapl Grenville Coll Bideford 99-02. *132 Bay View Road, Bideford EX39 1BJ* Tel (01237) 425348 Fax as telephone E-mail colin@thenet.co.uk

GIBBS, Darryl. b 73. Trin Coll Carmarthen BEd95. Cuddesdon Coll BTh98. **d** 98 **p** 99. C Llandysul w Bangor Teifi w Henllan etc *St D* 98-99; C Carmarthen St Pet 99-01; C Llanelli 01-03; V Llanwynno *Llan* 03-04. *Address temp unknown* Tel 07775-805919 (mobile) E-mail darrylgibbs@easynet.co.uk

GIBBS, David Norman. b 65. Cam Univ BA87 MA90. Oak Hill Th Coll BA98. **d** 99 **p** 00. C Virginia Water *Guildf* 99-02; C Leyton Ch Ch *Chelmsf* from 02. *37 Norlington Road, London E11 4BE* Tel (020) 8556 3295 E-mail davidgibbs@x5g.com

GIBBS, Edmund. b 38. Fuller Th Sem California DMin81. Oak Hill Th Coll BD62. **d** 63 **p** 64. C Wandsworth All SS *S'wark* 63-66; SAMS Chile 66-70; Educn Sec SAMS 70-77; Ch Progr Manager Bible Soc 77-84; USA from 84; Assoc Prof Evang and Ch Renewal Fuller Th Sem 84-93; Prof Ch Growth from 96; Assoc R Beverly Hills All SS 93-96. *1136 Crowne Drive, Pasadena, CA 91107, USA* Tel (001) (626) 794 6393 E-mail eddgibbs@fuller.edu

GIBBS (née DE ROBECK), Mrs Fiona Caroline. b 74. St Martin's Coll Lanc BA96. St Jo Coll Nottm MA(TS)99. **d** 00 **p** 01. C Bitterne *Win* 00-05; C Chandler's Ford from 05. *45 Pantheon Road, Chandler's Ford, Eastleigh SO53 2PD* Tel (023) 8026 8433

GIBBS, Mrs Fiorenza Silvia Elisabetta. b 49. SRN71 Surrey Univ DipHV72. St Alb Minl Tr Scheme 90. **d** 93 **p** 99. NSM Hitchin *St Alb* 93-96; NSM Pirton 97-99; Asst Chapl N Herts NHS Trust 99-00; Asst Chapl E and N Herts NHS Trust 00-02; Chapl from 02. *12 Bunyon Close, Pirton, Hitchin SG5 3RE* Tel (01462) 711846 *or* (01438) 781518

GIBBS, Ian Edmund. b 47. Lon Univ BEd69. St Steph Ho Ox 72. **d** 75 **p** 76. C Stony Stratford *Ox* 75-79; V Forest Town *S'well* 79-83; R Diddlebury w Munslow, Holdgate and Tugford *Heref* from 83; R Abdon from 83. *The Rectory, Munslow, Craven Arms SY7 9ET* Tel (01584) 841688

GIBBS, James Millard. b 28. Univ of Michigan BSE51 Nottm Univ PhD68. Seabury-Western Th Sem BD57. **d** 57 **p** 57. USA 57-60; Lic to Offic *S'well* 61-62 and 65-66; C Brandon *Dur* 62-64; Vice-Prin Lich Th Coll 66-71; Lic to Offic *Lich* 66-71; India 72-77; Tutor Qu Coll Birm 78-84; V Stechford *Birm* 84-93; rtd 93; Perm to Offic *Birm* from 93. *13 Lingfield Court, 60 High Street, Harbourne, Birmingham B17 9NE* Tel 0121-426 2108 E-mail jmanddagibbs@aol.com

✠**GIBBS, The Rt Revd John.** b 17. Bris Univ BA42 Lon Univ BD48. Linc Th Coll 55. **d** 55 **p** 56 **c** 73. C Brislington St Luke *Bris* 55-57; Chapl St Matthias's Coll Bris 57-64; Vice-Prin 61-64; Prin Keswick Hall Coll of Educn 64-73; Lic to Offic *Nor* 64-73; Hon Can Nor Cathl 68-73; Suff Bp Bradwell *Chelmsf* 73-76; Bp Cov 76-85; rtd 85; Hon Asst Bp Bris and Glouc from 85. *Farthingloe, Southfield, Minchinhampton, Stroud GL6 9DY* Tel (01453) 886211

GIBBS, Jonathan Robert. b 61. Jes Coll Ox MA89 Jes Coll Cam PhD90. Ridley Hall Cam 84. **d** 89 **p** 90. C Stalybridge H Trin and Ch Ch *Ches* 89-92; Chapl Basle w Freiburg-im-Breisgau *Eur* 92-98; R Heswall *Ches* from 98. *The Rectory, Village Road, Heswall, Wirral CH60 0DZ* Tel 0151-342 3471 Fax 342 2275 E-mail jgibbs@fish.co.uk

GIBBS, Mrs Patricia Louise. b 39. S'wark Ord Course 91. **d** 94 **p** 95. NSM Croydon H Sav *S'wark* from 94; Chapl Asst Mayday Healthcare NHS Trust Thornton Heath 94-05. *41 Sandringham Road, Thornton Heath CR7 7AX* Tel (020) 8684 9720

GIBBS, Peter Winston. b 50. Ex Univ BA72 CQSW75. St Jo Coll Nottm DipTh. **d** 90 **p** 91. C Hampreston *Sarum* 90-94; P-in-c Ipswich St Matt *St E* 94-99; Assoc P Attenborough *S'well* 99-01; V Toton from 01. *95 Stapleford Lane, Toton, Beeston, Nottingham NG9 6FZ* Tel 0115-877 4771 E-mail ladybird1@ntlworld.com

GIBBS, Canon Philip Roscoe. b 33. Codrington Coll Barbados 57. **d** 60 **p** 61. Br Honduras 60-73; Belize 73-74; Hon Can Br Honduras 71-73; Hon Can Belize from 73; V Stoke Newington Common St Mich *Lon* 74-87; New Zealand from 87; rtd 93. *10 Gardener Street, Levin 5500, New Zealand* Tel (0064) (6) 367 9884

GIBBS, Raymond George. b 55. NTMTC 94. **d** 97 **p** 98. NSM Becontree S *Chelmsf* 97-99; C Dedham 99-04; C Colchester St Mich Myland from 04; Area Youth Officer from 04. *352 Mill Road, Mile End, Colchester CO4 5JF* Tel (01206) 843926 E-mail raymond.gibbs@ntlworld.com

GIBBS, Richard James. b 68. St Paul's Cheltenham BSc90. St Jo Coll Nottm MTh01. **d** 01 **p** 02. C Southport Ch Ch *Liv* 01-05; Min Banks St Steph CD from 05. *33 Abington Drive, Banks, Southport PR9 8FL* Tel (01704) 546294

GIBBS, Stewart Henry. b 77. CCC Cam BA98 MA PGCE99 Anglia Poly Univ BTh05. Ridley Hall Cam 02. **d** 05. C Grays

Thurrock *Chelmsf* from 05. *11 Conrad Gardens, Grays RM16 2TN* Tel (01375) 390370 Mobile 07899-753559

GIBBS, Canon William Gilbert. b 31. Bps' Coll Cheshunt 55. **d** 58 **p** 59. C Wellington w W Buckland *B & W* 58-61; C Kensington St Mary Abbots w St Geo *Lon* 61-68; V Guilsborough *Pet* 68; V Guilsborough w Hollowell 68-74; V Guilsborough w Hollowell and Cold Ashby 74-98; Jt P-in-c Cottesbrooke w Gt Creaton and Thornby 83-98; Jt P-in-c Maidwell w Draughton, Lamport w Faxton 88-98; Can Pet Cathl 88-98; rtd 98; Perm to Offic *Pet* 98-01 and from 03; P-in-c W Haddon w Winwick and Ravensthorpe 01-03. *Paines Close, Maidwell, Northampton NN6 9JB* Tel (01604) 686424

GIBBS, William John Morris. b 71. Birm Univ BSc94. Ripon Coll Cuddesdon BTh00. **d** 00 **p** 01. C Staines St Mary and St Pet *Lon* 00-03; C Kensington St Mary Abbots w St Geo from 03. *Vicarage Cottage, Vicarage Gate, London W8 4HN* Tel and fax (020) 7937 2364 *or* tel 7937 2419
E-mail will.gibbs@stmaryabbotschurch.org

GIBBY, Thomas Rees. b 12. St D Coll Lamp BA33 BD42. St Mich Coll Llan 33. **d** 35 **p** 36. C Llangeinor *Llan* 35-39; C Llantrisant 39-44; C Bideford *Ex* 44-45; R Langtree 45-58; P-in-c Lt Torrington 49-55; R 55-58; V Bradworthy 58-62; P-in-c W w E Putford 59-62; V Ivybridge 62-75; R Harford 63-75; RD Plympton 66-71; rtd 75; Perm to Offic *St D* from 75. *Penlon, Cwmann, Lampeter SA48 8DU* Tel (01570) 422100

GIBLIN, Brendan Anthony. b 64. K Coll Lon BD86 AKC93 Leeds Univ MA95. Wycliffe Hall Ox 90. **d** 92 **p** 93. C Tadcaster w Newton Kyme *York* 92-96; R Stockton-on-the-Forest w Holtby and Warthill 96-02; P-in-c Middleham w Coverdale and E Witton etc *Ripon* 02-03; R from 03. *The Rectory, Wensley, Leyburn DL8 4HS* Tel (01969) 623736
E-mail rev.brendan@virgin.net

GIBLING, Derek Vivian. b 31. Wadh Coll Ox BA56 MA63. Wycliffe Hall Ox 70. **d** 72 **p** 73. C Fisherton Anger *Sarum* 72-74; C Yatton Keynell *Bris* 74-77; C Castle Combe 74-77; C Biddestone w Slaughterford 74-77; P-in-c Youlgreave *Derby* 77-82; P-in-c Stanton-in-Peak 77-82; V Youlgreave, Middleton, Stanton-in-Peak etc 82-88; P-in-c Hartington and Biggin 88-90; V Hartington, Biggin and Earl Sterndale 90-96; rtd 96; Perm to Offic *Linc* 96-02; RD Bolingbroke 00-02. *The Hawthorns, Church Lane, West Keal, Spilsby PE23 4BG* Tel (01790) 754762

GIBRALTAR IN EUROPE, Bishop of. *See* ROWELL, The Rt Revd Douglas Geoffrey

GIBRALTAR, Archdeacon of. *Vacant*

GIBRALTAR, Dean of. *See* WOODS, The Very Revd Alan Geoffrey

GIBSON, Alan. b 35. Birm Univ BSc56 Man Univ MSc72. NW Ord Course 71. **d** 74 **p** 75. C Sale St Anne *Ches* 74-77; V Runcorn St Mich 77-82; Educn Adv *Carl* 82-88; P-in-c Hugill 82-88; V Grange-over-Sands 88-97; rtd 97; Perm to Offic *Derby* from 01. *11 Ecclesbourne Drive, Buxton SK17 9BX* Tel (01298) 22621

GIBSON, Alexander Douglas. b 21. Wycliffe Hall Ox 60. **d** 62 **p** 63. C St Helens St Helen *Liv* 62-65; V Gresley *Derby* 65-77; V Hartington 77-78; V Biggin 77-78; V Hartington and Biggin 78-88; rtd 88; Perm to Offic *Derby* from 88. *Westmead, Aldern Way, Baslow Road, Bakewell DE45 1AJ* Tel (01629) 812723
E-mail doug.gibson2@virgin.net

GIBSON, Anthony Richard. b 43. Ridley Hall Cam 83. **d** 85 **p** 86. C Rushmere *St E* 85-88; R N Tawton, Bondleigh, Sampford Courtenay etc *Ex* 88-93; RD Okehampton 92-93; P-in-c Tiverton St Pet and Chevithorne w Cove 93-03; rtd 03. *Le Bourg, Fajolles 82210, France* Tel (0033) (5) 63 94 14 83

GIBSON, Brenda. b 55. St Mary's Coll Dur BSc77 PhD80 Hughes Hall Cam PGCE81 Surrey Univ BA04. STETS 01. **d** 04 **p** 05. NSM Wimborne Minster *Sarum* from 04. *12 Meadow Court, Leigh Road, Wimborne BH21 2BG* Tel (01202) 881472
E-mail brenda@p-b-gibson.demon.co.uk

GIBSON, Catherine Snyder. b 39. Parson's Sch of Design (NY) 57. Ab Dioc Tr Course 82 Edin Th Coll 92. **d** 86 **p** 94. Colombia 86-87; NSM Aberdeen St Marg *Ab* 87-88; Dioc Hosp Chapl 89-92; C Aberdeen St Mary 93-94; Bp's Chapl for Tr and Educn 93-94; P-in-c Ballater 95-96; R 96-98; P-in-c Aboyne 95-96; R 96-98; P-in-c Braemar 95-97; Assoc P Fort Lauderdale USA 98-04; I Fermoy Union *C, C & R* from 04. *The Rectory, Forglen Terrace, Fermoy, Co Cork, Irish Republic* Tel (00353) (25) 31016 Mobile 87-993 0023 E-mail kategib@iol.ie *or* fermoy@cloyne.anglican.org

GIBSON, Charles Daniel. b 48. **d** 03 **p** 04. OLM Wisley w Pyrford *Guildf* from 03. *The Corner Cottage, Send Marsh Road, Ripley, Woking GU23 6JN* Tel (01483) 225317 Fax 223681
E-mail charles@chasdi.freeserve.co.uk

GIBSON, Colin Taylor. b 54. Trin Coll Cam BA77. Oak Hill Th Coll 86. **d** 88 **p** 89. C Thrybergh w Hooton Roberts *Sheff* 88-91; P-in-c Tinsley 91-96; TV Attercliffe, Darnall and Tinsley 96-02; TR Walsall *Lich* from 02; Hon C Walsall St Paul from 05; Hon C Walsall Pleck and Bescot from 05. *St Matthew's Rectory, 48 Jesson Road, Walsall WS1 3AX* Tel (01922) 624012
E-mail c.t.gibson@btinternet.com

GIBSON, David Francis. b 36. Magd Coll Cam BA57 BChir60 MB61. SW Minl Tr Course 84. **d** 90 **p** 91. NSM Newport, Bishops Tawton and Tawstock *Ex* 90-95; Chapl N Devon Healthcare NHS Trust 95-96; Perm to Offic *Ex* from 96. *Little Beara, Marwood, Barnstaple EX31 4EH* Tel (01271) 814876

GIBSON, David Innes. b 31. NDD53. Oak Hill Th Coll 56. **d** 59 **p** 60. C S Croydon Em *Cant* 59-62; C Washfield *Ex* 62-63; Asst Master and Chapl Blundells Sch Tiverton 63-64; Chapl Sutton Valence Sch Maidstone 64-68; Chapl Dean Close Sch Cheltenham 68-75; Asst Chapl and Ho Master 75-85; Asst Master Brightlands Sch Newnham-on-Severn 85-90; C Cheltenham St Mary, St Matt, St Paul and H Trin *Glouc* 91-96; rtd 96; Perm to Offic *Glouc* 96-97; and from 01. *2 Withyholt Park, Charlton Kings, Cheltenham GL53 9BP* Tel (01242) 511612

GIBSON, Douglas. *See* GIBSON, Alexander Douglas

GIBSON, Douglas Harold. b 20. Portsm Dioc Tr Course. **d** 87. NSM Portsea St Luke *Portsm* 87-92; Perm to Offic from 92. *83 Middle Street, Southsea PO5 4BW* Tel (023) 9282 9769

GIBSON, Garry Stuart. b 36. Univ Coll Lon BA62 PhD75 Birkbeck Coll Lon BA79. Oak Hill Th Coll 62. **d** 64 **p** 65. C Watford St Mary *St Alb* 64-67; Lect Cambs Coll of Arts and Tech 67-69; Government of Israel Scholar Hebrew Univ 69-70; Asst Master Angl Sch Jerusalem 69-70; Sen Lect Middx Univ *Lon* 70-97; Hon C Sidmouth, Woolbrook, Salcombe Regis, Sidbury etc *Ex* 96-99; C Stockland, Dalwood, Kilmington and Shute 99-03; C Kilmington, Stockland, Dalwood, Yarcombe etc 03-04. *14 Argus Close, Honiton EX14 1UT* Tel (01404) 44083
E-mail garrygib@yahoo.co.uk

GIBSON, The Ven George Granville. b 36. Cuddesdon Coll 69. **d** 71 **p** 72. C Tynemouth Cullercoats St Paul *Newc* 71-73; TV Cramlington 73-77; V Newton Aycliffe *Dur* 77-85; R Bishopwearmouth St Mich w St Hilda 85-90; TR Sunderland 90-93; RD Wearmouth 85-93; Hon Can Dur Cathl 88-01; Adn Auckland 93-01; rtd 01. *12 West Crescent, Darlington DL3 7PR* Tel (01325) 462526
E-mail granville.gibson@durham.anglican.org

GIBSON, Henry Edward. b 15. Keble Coll Ox BA41 DipTh42 MA46. St Steph Ho Ox 41. **d** 43 **p** 44. C Summertown *Ox* 43-49; Warden Youth Ho and Youth Org Scottish Episc Ch 49-51; C Farlington *Portsm* 51-56; V Ryde H Trin 56-63; V Waterlooville 63-81; rtd 81; Perm to Offic *Portsm* 81-96 and *Chich* from 81. *8 Worcester Road, Chichester PO19 5DJ* Tel (01243) 779194

GIBSON, Ian. b 48. Open Univ BA85 MSc FCIPD MCMI. S Dios Minl Tr Scheme 82. **d** 85 **p** 86. NSM Uckfield *Chich* 85-88; NSM Lt Horsted 85-88; NSM Isfield 85-88; V Fairwarp 88-93; P-in-c 94-00; NSM 00-04; V High Hurstwood 88-93; P-in-c 94-00; RD Uckfield 03-04; Bp's Dom Chapl and Research Asst from 04. *Caigers Cottage, Westergate Street, Woodgate, Chichester PO20 3SQ* Tel (01243) 544534 Fax 531332
E-mail chaplainchichester@diochi.org.uk *or* tigtrain@aol.com

GIBSON, John Murray Hope. b 35. Dur Univ BA58 DipTh60. Cranmer Hall Dur 58. **d** 60 **p** 61. C Chester le Street *Dur* 60-63; C Stockton 63-68; V Denton and Ingleton 68-75; V Swalwell 75-00; Chapl Dunston Hill Hosp Gateshead 80-99; rtd 00; Perm to Offic *Dur* and *Newc* from 01. *50 Church Road, Gosforth, Newcastle upon Tyne NE3 1BJ* Tel 0191-285 2942

GIBSON, Canon John Noel Keith. b 22. MBE89. Ch Coll Cam MA48 Lon Univ BD59. Coll of Resurr Mirfield 45. **d** 47 **p** 48. C S Elmsall *Wakef* 47-51; Antigua 51-56; Virgin Is from 56; Can All SS Cathl 89-92; rtd 92. *PO Box 65, Valley, Virgin Gorda, British Virgin Islands* Tel (001284) 495 5587

GIBSON, Kenneth George Goudie. b 54. Glas Univ MA83 Edin Univ BD87 Strathclyde Univ PGCE95. Edin Th Coll 83. **d** 88 **p** 89. C Glas St Marg *Glas* 88-90; R E Kilbride 90-98; R Carnoustie *Bre* from 98. *Holy Rood Rectory, 58 Maule Street, Carnoustie DD7 6AB* Tel (01241) 852202
E-mail kenneth.gibson@ntlworld.com

GIBSON, Laura Mary. *See* WILFORD, Laura Mary

GIBSON, Mark. b 48. **d** 84. OSB from 67; Abbot of Alton 82-90; Perm to Offic *Win* 84-95; NSM Paddington St Sav *Lon* from 90; Acting Bp's Chapl 90-91; Perm to Offic 91-94; NSM Paddington St Mary from 95; NSM Paddington St Mary Magd from 98. *6 Park Place Villas, London W2 1SP* Tel (020) 7724 7444 *or* 7262 3787 E-mail abbotsfancy@aol.com

GIBSON, Nigel Stephen David. b 53. St Barn Coll Adelaide DipMin87. **d** 87 **p** 87. C N Adelaide Ch Ch Australia 87-89; Lect Boston *Linc* 90-91; P-in-c Stamford St Mary and St Mich 91-92; P-in-c Stamford Baron 91-92; R Stamford St Mary and St Martin 92-98; Perm to Offic 98-00; V Kempston Transfiguration *St Alb* 00-04; Chapl Milan w Genoa and Varese *Eur* from 04. *All Saints', via Solferino 17, 20121 Milan, Italy* Tel and fax (0039) (02) 655 2258
E-mail frnigel@boxingkangaroo.org.uk

GIBSON, Mrs Patricia Elizabeth. b 57. Nottm Univ MA02. EMMTC 99. **d** 02 **p** 03. C Wigston Magna *Leic* from 02. *163 Little Glen Road, Leicester LE2 9TX* Tel 0116-277 4275
E-mail tricia.gibson@talk21.com
or tgibson@leicester.anglican.org

GIBSON, Paul Saison. b 32. BA LTh Huron Coll Ontario Hon DD90. Coll of Em and St Chad Hon DD88 Vancouver Sch of Th Hon DD95 Montreal Dioc Th Coll Hon DD98 Trin Coll Toronto Hon DD99. **d** 56 **p** 57. C Bloomsbury St Geo w St Jo *Lon* 56-59; R Homer St Geo Canada 59-60; Chapl McGill Univ Montreal 60-66; Prin Hong Kong Union Th Coll 66-72; Consultant Angl Ch of Canada 72-82; Liturg Officer 82-98. *588 Millwood Road, Toronto ON, Canada, M4S 1K8* Tel (001) (416) 487 2008

GIBSON, Philip Nigel Scott. b 53. St Jo Coll Dur BA78. Cranmer Hall Dur 79. **d** 79 **p** 80. C Yardley St Edburgha *Birm* 79-82; C Stratford-on-Avon w Bishopton *Cov* 82-84; Chapl SW Hosp Lon 84-91; Chapl St Thos Hosp Lon 84-91; Assoc P Newington St Paul *S'wark* 91-92; Chapl Charing Cross Hosp Lon 92-93; Chapl R Lon Hosp (Whitechapel) 93-94; Chapl Bedford Hosp NHS Trust from 95. *Chaplain's Office, Bedford Hospital, South Wing, Kempston Road, Bedford MK42 9DJ* Tel (01234) 355122

GIBSON, Raymond. b 23. Ely Th Coll 60. **d** 62 **p** 63. C Leic St Jas *Leic* 62-67; Succ Leic Cathl 67-68; Chapl Leic R Infirmary 67-68; Chapl Nottm City Hosp 68-84; V Barlings *Linc* 84-88; rtd 88. *11 Cornell Drive, Nottingham NG5 8RF*

GIBSON, Raymond Frank. b 34. Toronto Bible Coll BTh61 Tyndale Hall Bris 62. **d** 64 **p** 65. C Gt Horton *Bradf* 64-67; C Otley 67-72; V Fairlight *Chich* 72-83; V Hallwood *Ches* 83-85; R Freethorpe, Wickhampton, Halvergate w Tunstall *Nor* 85-99; P-in-c Reedham w Cantley w Limpenhoe and Southwood 94-99; rtd 99; Perm to Offic *Nor* from 99. *8 Waters Avenue, Carlton Colville, Lowestoft NR33 8BJ* Tel (01502) 537522

GIBSON, Canon Robert Swinton. b 26. Wadh Coll Ox BA50 MA55. Wells Th Coll 50. **d** 53 **p** 54. C Greenwich St Alfege w St Pet *S'wark* 53-61; Ind Missr 55-62; Hon Chapl to Bp S'wark 56-67; Sen Chapl S Lon Ind Miss 62-67; Nigeria 67-69; R Guisborough *York* 69-83; RD Guisborough 73-83; TR Halifax *Wakef* 83-94; Hon Can Wakef Cathl 85-94; RD Halifax 86-92; rtd 94; Perm to Offic *Wakef* and *York* from 94. *The Cottage, Main Street, Hutton Buscel, Scarborough YO13 9LL* Tel (01723) 862133

GIBSON, The Ven Terence Allen. b 37. Jes Coll Cam BA61 MA65. Cuddesdon Coll 61. **d** 63 **p** 64. C Kirkby *Liv* 63-66; TV 72-75; TR 75-84; Warden Cen 63 66-75; Youth Chapl 66-72; RD Walton 79-84; Adn Suffolk *St E* 84-87; Adn Ipswich 87-05; rtd 05; Perm to Offic *St E* from 05. *5 Berry Close, Purdis Farm, Ipswich IP3 8SP* Tel (01473) 714756

GIBSON, Thomas Thomson. b 23. Sarum Th Coll 62. **d** 63 **p** 64. C E w W Harnham *Sarum* 63-66; V Rowde 66-74; R Poulshot 67-74; V Badminton w Acton Turville *Glouc* 74-84; P-in-c Hawkesbury 81-84; V Badminton w Lt Badminton, Acton Turville etc 84-93; rtd 93; Perm to Offic *Glouc* 93-96 and from 01; *B & W* and *Sarum* from 95; *Eur* from 99. *9 Lansdown Place West, Bath BA1 5EZ* Tel (01225) 337903 Fax 483676

GIDDENS, Leslie Vernon. b 29. Bps' Coll Cheshunt 54. **d** 56 **p** 57. C Harrow St Pet *Lon* 56-58; C Tottenham St Benet Fink 58-63; C-in-c Hayes St Nic CD 63-94; rtd 94; Perm to Offic *Lon* from 94. *6 Ashdown Road, Uxbridge UB10 0HY* Tel (01895) 232406

GIDDEY, Canon William Denys. b 17. Leeds Univ BA39. Coll of Resurr Mirfield 39. **d** 41 **p** 42. C Weymouth St Paul *Sarum* 41-43; C St Geo-in-the-East St Mary *Lon* 43-48; R Binbrook *Linc* 48-61; R Swinhope w Thorganby 48-61; Chapl Eastbourne Hosp Gp 61-83; Can and Preb Chich Cathl *Chich* 78-90; rtd 82; Perm to Offic *Chich* from 90. *c/o S C Giddey Esq, 21 Grange Road, Lewes BN7 1TS*

GIDDINGS, Mrs Jaqueline Mary. b 44. St Aid Coll Dur BA67. SW Minl Tr Course 91. **d** 94 **p** 95. C Plympton St Mary *Ex* 94-02; rtd 02. *Grange End, Harrowbeer Lane, Yelverton PL20 6EA* Tel (01822) 854825

GIFFORD, Ms Elizabeth Ann. b 47. St Kath Coll Liv CertEd72 Open Univ BSc96. STETS 99. **d** 02. NSM Trowbridge H Trin *Sarum* from 02. *14 Innox Mill Close, Trowbridge BA14 9BA* Tel (01225) 768536 Mobile 07903-269587 E-mail revgif@aol.com

GIFFORD-COLE, David Henry. b 30. San Francisco Th Sem DMin87 ALCD56. **d** 56 **p** 57. C Ashtead *Guildf* 56-59; C Farnham 59-60; Canada from 60. *225 Hoylake Road West, Qualicum Beach BC, Canada, V9K 1K5*

✠**GILBERD, The Rt Revd Bruce Carlyle.** b 38. Auckland Univ BSc59. St Jo Coll Auckland LTh64 STh74. **d** 62 **p** 64 **c** 85. New Zealand 62-71 and from 73; C Devonport 62-64; C Ponsonby and Grey Lynn 65; P Asst Panmure 66-68; V Avondale 68-71; Ind Chapl and C Eaglescliffe *Dur* 71-73; Dir Ind Miss Wellington 73-79; Dir Th Educn by Ext 80-85; Bp Auckland 85-94; P-in-c Albany Greenhithe 95-00; P-in-c Tamaki St Thos 96-00; Chapl K Sch 97-00; rtd 00. *81 Manaia Road, Tairua, via Thames, New Zealand* Tel (0064) (7) 864 8727

GILBERT, Anthony John David. b 54. LRSC83 Open Univ BA91. Ripon Coll Cuddesdon 83. **d** 86 **p** 87. C Exning St Martin w Landwade *St E* 86-89; Chapl RAF from 89. *Chaplaincy Services (RAF), HQ, Personnel and Training Command, RAF Innsworth, Gloucester GL3 1EZ* Tel (01452) 712612 ext 5164 Fax 510828

GILBERT, Arthur John. b 57. LTCL76 GBSM79 Reading Univ PGCE80. Coll of Resurr Mirfield 88. **d** 91 **p** 92. C Uppingham w Ayston and Wardley w Belton *Pet* 91-94; C Armley w New Wortley *Ripon* 94-96; V Doncaster St Jude *Sheff* from 96; AD W Doncaster from 00. *St Jude's Vicarage, 2 Riverside Close, Doncaster DN4 0HW* Tel (01302) 852057 Fax 310716 E-mail ajg@stjude.fsworld.co.uk

GILBERT, Barry. b 46. Leeds Univ BA67. Coll of Resurr Mirfield 67. **d** 69 **p** 70. C Malvern Link w Cowleigh *Worc* 69-73; P-in-c Bromsgrove All SS 73-81; V 81-83; P-in-c Lower Mitton 83-88; V 88-92; V Stourport and Wilden from 92; RD Stourport 93-00 and from 02. *The Vicarage, Church Avenue, Stourport-on-Severn DY13 9DD* Tel (01299) 822041 E-mail barry_gilbert@talk21.com

GILBERT, Caroline Margaret. b 62. Nottm Univ BTh90. St Jo Coll Nottm 87. **d** 90. Hon C Aston SS Pet and Paul *Birm* 90-93. *Address temp unknown*

GILBERT, Miss Christine Lesley. b 44. DipHE. Trin Coll Bris 79. **dss** 85 **d** 86 **p** 94. Par Dn Bilston *Lich* 87-94; TV Penkridge Team 94-98; Bp's Soc and Ind Adv *Bris* 98-03; Hon C Swindon All SS w St Barn 98-03; rtd 03; Perm to Offic *Sarum* from 03. *16 Ridgeway Court, East Street, Warminster BA12 9AT* Tel (01985) 216770 Mobile 07759-977794 E-mail chrisgilb@aol.com

GILBERT, Christopher Anthony. b 60. Aston Univ BSc82. St Jo Coll Nottm 86. **d** 89 **p** 90. C Aston SS Pet and Paul *Birm* 89-93; TV Parr *Liv* 93-97; TV Cannock *Lich* 97-01. *Address temp unknown*

GILBERT, Clive Franklyn. b 55. City of Liv Coll of HE CertEd76 BEd77. SEITE 01. **d** 02 **p** 03. C Paddock Wood *Roch* from 02. *3 Ashcroft Road, Paddock Wood, Tonbridge TN12 6LG* Tel (01892) 833194 Mobile 07752-676663 E-mail gilbert_clive@hotmail.com

GILBERT, Frederick Herbert. b 14. Worc Ord Coll 64. **d** 66 **p** 67. C Ex St Paul *Ex* 66-69; C Paignton Ch Ch 69-73; TV Offwell, Widworthy, Cotleigh, Farway etc 73-79; rtd 80; Lic to Offic *Ex* 80-95; Perm to Offic from 95. *17 Hoskings Court, Strode Road, Buckfastleigh TQ11 0PF* Tel (01364) 643321

GILBERT, Frederick Joseph. b 29. Lich Th Coll 58. **d** 59 **p** 60. C Westhoughton *Man* 59-62; V Goodshaw 62-68; R Crumpsall St Matt 68-75; RD Cheetham 70-74; RD N Man 74-75; V Rochdale St Aid 75-78; TV Rochdale 78-80; V Westhoughton 80-84; TR 84-87; AD Deane 85-87; R W Bowbrook *Worc* 87-89; R Bowbrook N 89-93; rtd 93; Perm to Offic *Worc* from 93. *Freshways, Main Road, Peopleton, Pershore WR10 2EG* Tel (01905) 841629

GILBERT, Howard Neil. b 73. Southn Univ BA96. Ripon Coll Cuddesdon BTh05. **d** 05. C Dulwich St Barn *S'wark* from 05. *70 Frankfurt Road, London SE24 9NY* Tel (020) 8693 1524 E-mail hgilbert@stbarnabasdulwich.com

GILBERT, John. *See* GILBERT, Arthur John

GILBERT, John Edwin. b 28. FCA62. Bps' Coll Cheshunt 54. **d** 57 **p** 58. C Luton Ch Ch *St Alb* 57-60; C Gt Berkhamsted 60-64; P-in-c Kemptee India 65-68; Hon Chapl Nagpur Cathl 68-70; Dioc Treas Nagpur 65-70; Perm to Offic *St Alb* 71-77; Lic to Offic 77-86; Hon C Sunnyside w Bourne End 86-89; TV Padgate *Liv* 89-94; rtd 94; Perm to Offic *Heref* from 94. *4 Westgate Drive, Bridgnorth WV16 4QF* Tel (01746) 762611

GILBERT, Joseph. b 12. Chich Th Coll 33. **d** 36 **p** 37. C Bolton St Mark *Man* 36-39; C Withington St Crispin 39-43; R Ardwick St Matt 43-49; V Heyside 49-65; V Lever Bridge 65-76; rtd 77; Perm to Offic *Man* from 77. *159 Bolton Road, Turton, Bolton BL7 0AF* Tel (01204) 852736

GILBERT, Mrs Margaret Ann. b 39. Dub Inst of Adult Educn Dip Past Min 89 TCD DipTh91. CITC 89. **d** 92 **p** 93. NSM Dublin Clontarf *D & G* 92-96; NSM Dublin Santry w Glasnevin and Finglas from 96. *67 Grange Park Road, Raheny, Dublin 5, Irish Republic* Tel (00353) (1) 848 1340

GILBERT, Mark. *See* GILBERT, Philip Mark

GILBERT, Ms Mary Rose. b 63. Ridley Hall Cam 94. **d** 97 **p** 97. C Walsall Wood *Lich* 97-00; TV Bilston from 00; AD Wolverhampton from 03. *St Chad's Vicarage, 8 Cumberland Road, Bilston WV14 6LT* Tel (01902) 497794 E-mail mgdartford@aol.com

GILBERT, Michael Victor. b 61. Dur Univ BA84. Trin Coll Bris 92. **d** 94 **p** 95. C Chapeltown *Sheff* 94-97; V Brightside w Wincobank from 97. *The Vicarage, 24 Beacon Road, Sheffield S9 1AD* Tel 0114-281 9360 E-mail mike@thegilberts.f9.co.uk

GILBERT, Philip Mark. b 62. Liv Univ BA84 SSC. Coll of Resurr Mirfield 84. **d** 87 **p** 88. C Frodsham *Ches* 87-89; C Stockton Heath 89-92; R Tangmere and Oving *Chich* 92-01; P-in-c Graffham w Woolavington from 01; Chapl Seaford Coll Petworth from 01. *The Rectory, Graffham, Petworth GU28 0NL* Tel (01798) 867247 *or* 867851 Mobile 07810-004062 E-mail frmark@mgilbert.clara.co.uk

GILBERT, Raymond. b 34. AKC61. **d** 62 **p** 63. C Newbold w Dunston *Derby* 62-66; PV and Succ S'wark Cathl *S'wark* 66-68; P-in-c Stuntney *Ely* 68-74; Prec and Sacr Ely Cathl 68-74; Min Can Cant Cathl *Cant* 74-79; Hon Min Can 79-00; P-in-c Patrixbourne w Bridge and Bekesbourne 79-81; V 81-00; RD E Bridge 92-98; rtd 00. *16 Green Acres, Eythorne, Dover CT15 4LX* Tel (01304) 831485

GILBERT, Raymond Frederick. b 44. LNSM course 91. **d** 93 **p** 94. OLM Stowmarket *St E* from 93. *3 Violet Hill Road, Stowmarket IP14 1NE* Tel (01449) 677700

GILBERT, Roger Charles. b 46. Ex Coll Ox BA69 MA74 Nottm Univ MEd81. St Steph Ho Ox 69. **d** 71 **p** 72. NSM Bridgwater St Mary w Chilton Trinity *B & W* 71-74; NSM Rugeley *Lich* 74-81; NSM Cannock 81-83; NSM Wednesbury St Jas and St Jo from 83. *41 Stafford Road, Cannock WS11 4AF* Tel (01543) 570531 *or* 0121-505 1188

GILBERT, Canon Roger Geoffrey. b 37. K Coll Lon BD69 AKC69. **d** 70 **p** 71. C Walton-on-Thames *Guildf* 70-74; R St Mabyn *Truro* 74-81; P-in-c Helland 74-81; P-in-c Madron 81-86; R Falmouth K Chas 86-02; Hon Can Truro Cathl 94-02; RD Carnmarth S 94-00; Chapl to The Queen from 95; rtd 02. *2 rue de Plouzon, 22690 Pleudihen-sur-Rance, France* Tel (0033) (2) 96 88 28 69

GILBERT, Roy Alan. b 48. Birm Univ BEd70 Lon Univ DipTh79. Ripon Coll Cuddesdon 74. **d** 76 **p** 77. C Moseley St Mary *Birm* 76-82; Australia from 82. *Guildford Grammar School, 11 Terrace Road, Guildford, W Australia 6055* Tel (0061) (8) 9377 9245, 9377 9222 *or* 9279 1135 Fax 9377 3140 E-mail rgilbert@ggs.wa.edu.au

GILBERT, Sidney Horace. b 34. Dur Univ BA58 MA69 Univ of Wales BD62 CertEd83. St Mich Coll Llan 58. **d** 61 **p** 62. C Colwyn Bay *St As* 61-63; C Llanrhos 63-69; R Penley and Bettisfield 69-78; V Brymbo and Bwlchgwyn 78-82; Univ of Wales (Swansea) *S & B* 82-83; R Beeston Regis *Nor* 84-97; Holiday Chapl 84-91; Sen Chapl 91-97; V Llanwddyn and Llanfihangel-yng-Nghwynfa etc *St As* 97-99; rtd 99; Perm to Offic *Ches* 01-04; Hon C Odd Rode from 04. *The Parsonage, 53 Heath Avenue, Rode Heath, Stoke-on-Trent ST7 3RY* Tel (01270) 872132

GILBERTSON, Michael Robert. b 61. New Coll Ox BA82 MA92 Dur Univ PhD97. St Jo Coll Dur BA91. **d** 97 **p** 98. C Surbiton St Matt *S'wark* 97-00; V Stranton *Dur* from 00; AD Hartlepool from 02. *The Vicarage, 34 Westbourne Road, Hartlepool TS25 5RE* Tel (01429) 263190 Fax 400118 E-mail mikegilbertson@supanet.com

GILCHRIST, Alison Roxanne. b 62. Cranmer Hall Dur 02. **d** 04 **p** 05. C Preston St Cuth *Blackb* from 04. *11 Royal Drive, Fulwood, Preston PR2 3AF* Tel (01772) 718163

GILCHRIST, David John. b 51. Mert Coll Ox BA75 MA79 Nottm Univ DipTh77. St Jo Coll Nottm DPS79. **d** 79 **p** 80. C Gt Ilford St Andr *Chelmsf* 79-81; C Buckhurst Hill 81-84; Chapl Dover Coll 84-95; Chapl Brentwood Sch Essex from 95; Perm to Offic *Chelmsf* from 96. *Brentwood School, Brentwood CM15 8AS* Tel (01277) 214580 E-mail djgilchrist@brentwood.essex.sch.uk

GILCHRIST, Gavin Frank. b 53. AKC74. Coll of Resurr Mirfield 76. **d** 77 **p** 78. C Newbold w Dunston *Derby* 77-80; C Addlestone *Guildf* 80-84; V Blackpool St Mary *Blackb* 84-92; P-in-c Carl St Herbert w St Steph *Carl* 92-97; V 97-01; V Tynemouth Cullercoats St Paul *Newc* from 01. *The Vicarage, 53 Grosvenor Drive, Whitley Bay NE26 2JR* Tel 0191-252 4916 Fax as telephone E-mail fr.gavin.gilchrist@virgin.net

GILCHRIST, Lawrence Edward. b 29. Liv Univ BSc52. NW Ord Course 74. **d** 76 **p** 77. NSM Buxton w Burbage and King Sterndale *Derby* 76-83; V Chinley w Buxworth 83-94; rtd 94; Perm to Offic *St E* 94-03. *9 Santingley Lane, New Crofton, Wakefield WF4 1LG* Tel (01924) 860262

GILCHRIST, Spencer. b 66. QUB BA88. BTh. **d** 91 **p** 92. C Ballynafeigh St Jude *D & D* 91-97; I Connor w Antrim St Patr *Conn* from 97. *Connor Rectory, Church Road, Kells, Ballymena BT42 3JU* Tel (028) 2589 1254

GILDING, James Peter. b 33. Leeds Univ BA64. Ely Th Coll 61. **d** 63 **p** 64. C Chorley St Pet *Blackb* 63-66; C Pemberton St Fran Kitt Green *Liv* 66-69; P-in-c Terrington St John *Ely* 69-74; P-in-c Walpole St Andrew 69-74; V Elm 74-81; TR Stanground and Farcet 81-89; V Haslingfield 89-95; R Harlton 89-95; R Haslingfield w Harlton and Gt and Lt Eversden 95-96; rtd 96; Perm to Offic *York* from 98. *14 Main Street, Bishop Wilton, York YO42 1RX* Tel (01759) 368510

GILES, Anthony John. b 50. Aston Univ BSc71 Surrey Univ MSc78 Homerton Coll Cam PGCE86 CEng80 MIEE80. St Alb and Ox Min Course 01. **d** 04. NSM Stevenage H Trin *St Alb* from 04. *8 Norton Road, Letchworth Garden City SG6 1AB* Tel (01462) 620142 E-mail agiles6203@aol.com

GILES, Anthony Richard. b 68. Nottm Univ MA00. St Jo Coll Nottm 98. **d** 01 **p** 02. C Chellaston *Derby* from 01. *30 Acrefield Way, Chellaston, Derby DE73 6PN* Tel (01332) 705946 E-mail ant.dianne@btopenworld.com

GILES, Canon Barry James. b 35. Kelham Th Coll 54. **d** 59 **p** 60. C Leytonstone St Marg w St Columba *Chelmsf* 59-62; Prec Gib Cathl *Eur* 62-66; V Darwen St Geo *Blackb* 66-69; V Forest Gate St Edm *Chelmsf* 69-73; R Jersey St Pet *Win* 73-00; Vice-Dean Jersey 84-00; Hon Can Win Cathl 93-00; rtd 00; Perm to Offic *Chich* from 00. *St Pierre, 5 Bracken Road, Eastbourne BN20 8SH* Tel (01323) 439240 E-mail beejaygee.giles@btopenworld.com

GILES, Brother. *See* SPRENT, Michael Francis

GILES, Edward Alban. b 34. Bps' Coll Cheshunt. **d** 58 **p** 59. C Colne St Bart *Blackb* 58-61; C Warrington St Paul *Liv* 61-63; C Knysna S Africa 63-66; R Eersterus w Silverton 66-70; Chapl HM Pris Camp Hill 70-75; Chapl HM Pris Stafford 75-83; Chapl HM YOI Hollesley Bay Colony 83-94; rtd 94; Sub-Chapl HM Pris Blundeston from 94; Perm to Offic *Nor* 94-00 and *St E* from 94. *The Hollies, Ferry Farm Drive, Sutton Hoo, Woodbridge IP12 3DR* Tel (01394) 387486 E-mail eagl@onetel.net.uk

GILES, Canon Eric Francis. b 34. Sarum Th Coll 61. **d** 63 **p** 64. C Plympton St Mary *Ex* 63-71; R Dumbleton w Wormington *Glouc* 71-77; P-in-c Toddington w Stanley Pontlarge 71-77; R Dumbleton w Wormington and Toddington 77-79; V Churchdown St Jo 79-99; Hon Can Glouc Cathl 95-99; rtd 99; Perm to Offic *Glouc* and *Worc* from 99. *25 Station Road, Pershore WR10 1PN* Tel (01386) 554246

GILES, Gordon John. b 66. Lanc Univ BA88 Magd Coll Cam MLitt95. Ridley Hall Cam BA95 CTM95. **d** 95 **p** 96. C Chesterton Gd Shep *Ely* 95-98; Min Can and Succ St Paul's Cathl *Lon* 98-03; V Enfield Chase St Mary from 03. *St Mary Magdalene Vicarage, 30 The Ridgeway, Enfield EN2 8QH* Tel (020) 8363 1875 E-mail vicar@saintmarymagdalene.org.uk *or* gjg@ggiles.net

GILES, Graeme John. b 56. Linc Th Coll 82. **d** 85 **p** 86. C Prestbury *Glouc* 85-88; C Paulsgrove *Portsm* 88-96; V Friern Barnet St Pet le Poer *Lon* 96-04. *Hillersden House, 22 Church Road, East Molesey KT8 9DS* Tel 07981-708606 (mobile) E-mail graeme@priest.com

GILES (née WILLIAMS), Mrs Gwenllian. b 34. RSCN55 SRN58 SCM60. WMMTC 88. **d** 92 **p** 94. NSM Bromsgrove St Jo *Worc* 92-00; Perm to Offic 00-03; P-in-c Clifton-on-Teme, Lower Sapey and the Shelsleys 03-04. *Highfield, Bakers Hill, Aveton Gifford, Kingsbridge TQ7 4LA* Tel (01548) 559164

GILES, Canon John Robert. b 36. Em Coll Cam BA60 MA65. Ripon Hall Ox 60. **d** 61 **p** 62. C Lowestoft St Marg *Nor* 61-65; Chapl UEA 65-72; R Kidbrooke St Jas *S'wark* 72-79; Sub-Dean Greenwich 74-79; V Sheff St Mark Broomhall *Sheff* 79-87; Ind Chapl 79-92; Can Res Sheff Cathl 87-92; V Lee Gd Shep w St Pet *S'wark* 92-98; rtd 98; Perm to Offic *St E* from 99. *25 The Terrace, Aldeburgh IP15 5HJ* Tel (01728) 452319

GILES, Kevin Norman. b 40. Lon Univ BD69 DipRE69 Dur Univ MA74 ACT ThD90. ThL67 MTh78. **d** 68 **p** 69. Australia 69-72 and from 75; TV Chester le Street *Dur* 73-74; Chapl Tubingen Univ W Germany 75; Chapl Armidale Univ 75-80; R Kensington 81-95; I N Carlton St Mich from 96. *44 Arnold Street, North Carlton, Vic, Australia 3054* Tel (0061) (3) 9387 7214 *or* 9380 6387 Fax 9388 9050 E-mail giles@melbpc.org.au

GILES, Peter Michael Osmaston. b 40. Solicitor 65. S Dios Minl Tr Scheme 85. **d** 88 **p** 89. Hon C Wootton Bassett *Sarum* 88-90; Lic to RD Calne from 91; RD Calne 98-03; Chapl St Mary's Sch Calne from 00. *The Old Vicarage, Honeyhill, Wootton Bassett, Swindon SN4 7DY* Tel (01793) 852643 Fax 853191 E-mail gilesoldvic@talk21.com

GILES, The Very Revd Richard Stephen. b 40. Newc Univ BA63 MLitt88 MRTPI71. Cuddesdon Coll 64. **d** 65 **p** 66. C Higham Ferrers w Chelveston *Pet* 65-68; Perm to Offic *Ox* 69; C Oakengates *Lich* 70; C Stevenage St Geo *St Alb* 71-75; P-in-c Howdon Panns *Newc* 75-76; TV Willington 76-79; Bp's Adv for Planning *Pet* 79-87; V Pet St Jude 79-87; Par Development Officer *Wakef* 87-99; P-in-c Huddersfield St Thos 87-93; V 93-99; Hon Can Wakef Cathl 94-99; Can Th Wakef Cathl 98-99; Dean Philadelphia USA from 99. *3723 Chestnut Street, Philadelphia, PA 19104-7701, USA* Tel (001) (215) 386 0234 Fax 386 5009 E-mail philadean@aol.com

GILES, Robert Medwin. b 37. Man Univ BA(Econ)58 PGCE59. Ripon Hall Ox 64. **d** 66 **p** 67. C Peel *Man* 66-69; C Alverstoke *Portsm* 69-71; P-in-c Edale *Derby* 71-79; Warden Champion Ho Youth Tr Cen 71-79; Sen Youth Officer *York* 79-86; P-in-c Shipley *Chich* 86-87; V 87-91; Area Sec USPG *Pet* and *St Alb* 91-92; R Broughton w Loddington and Cransley etc *Pet* 92-02; RD Kettering 99-02; rtd 02. *Stone Cottage, Croft Lane, Staverton, Daventry NN11 6JE* Tel (01327) 705193 E-mail bobgiles@bobgiles.demon.co.uk *or* bobandjoan@talk21.com

GILES, Susan Jane. b 58. BSc. **dss** 83 **d** 92 **p** 94. Balsall Heath St Paul *Birm* 83-85; Asst Chapl Southmead Hosp Bris 86-90; Asst Chapl HM Rem Cen Pucklechurch 90-96; Asst Chapl HM Pris Bris 92-98; Chapl HM Pris Shepton Mallet 98-01; P-in-c Stockton H Trin *Dur* from 01; Chapl Ian Ramsey Sch Stockton from 01. *4 Greymouth Close, Stockton-on-Tees TS18 5LF* Tel (01642) 585749

GILES, Timothy David. b 46. FCA69. Oak Hill Th Coll 88. **d** 90 **p** 91. C Ipswich St Marg *St E* 90-94; C Reigate St Mary *S'wark* 94-99; P-in-c W Wickham St Jo 99-03; V from 03. *The Rectory, 30 Coney Hill Road, West Wickham BR4 9BX* Tel and fax (020) 8462 4001 E-mail timgiles@fish.co.uk

GILFORD, George. b 49. St Kath Coll Liv CertEd72 LTCL86. N Ord Course 88. **d** 91 **p** 92. NSM Gt Crosby St Faith *Liv* 91-98; NSM Gt Crosby St Faith and Waterloo Park St Mary 98-01. *Flat 2, 17 Alexandra Road, Waterloo, Liverpool L22 1RJ* Tel 0151-920 5744

GILKES, Donald Martin. b 47. St Jo Coll Nottm 78. **d** 80 **p** 81. C Conisbrough *Sheff* 80-84; P-in-c Balne 84-86; P-in-c Hensall 84-86; TV Gt Snaith 86-88; V Whittle-le-Woods *Blackb* 88-02; V Normanton *Wakef* from 02. *The Vicarage, High Street, Normanton WF6 1NR* Tel and fax (01924) 893100 E-mail don.gilkes@allsaintsnormanton.org

GILKS, Peter Martin. b 51. SRN77 Nottm Univ BMus72. Ripon Coll Cuddesdon 82. **d** 84 **p** 85. C Bitterne Park *Win* 84-87; TV Basingstoke 87-93; R Abbotts Ann and Upper and Goodworth Clatford 93-98; V Boyatt Wood from 98. *St Peter's Church House, 53 Sovereign Way, Eastleigh SO50 4SA* Tel (023) 8064 2188 E-mail peter.gilks@ntlworld.com

GILL, Canon Alan Gordon. b 42. Sarum & Wells Th Coll 73. **d** 75 **p** 76. C Wimborne Minster *Sarum* 75-78; R Winterbourne Stickland and Turnworth etc 78-86; V Verwood 86-00; Can and Preb Sarum Cathl from 99; TR Gillingham 00-04; V Gillingham and Milton-on-Stour from 04. *The Rectory, High Street, Gillingham SP8 4AJ* Tel (01747) 822435 *or* 821598 E-mail erznmine@houseofgill.org

GILL, Miss Beatrice Clarabelle. b 57. Angl Th Inst Belize 96. **d** 02 **p** 03. C Belmopan St Ann Belize 02-03; Perm to Offic *Birm* from 04. *2 Vicarage Road, Kings Heath, Birmingham B14 7RA* E-mail beagill@hotmail.com

GILL, Mrs Carol Ann. b 42. Lady Mabel Coll TCert71. N Ord Course 96. **d** 99 **p** 00. NSM Hanging Heaton *Wakef* 99-02; P-in-c from 02. *The Vicarage, 150 High Street, Hanging Heaton, Batley WF17 6DW* Tel (01924) 461917 Mobile 07946-038562 E-mail rev@cgill2.fsnet.co.uk

GILL, Christopher John Sutherland. b 28. Selw Coll Cam BA52 MA70. Ely Th Coll 52. **d** 54 **p** 55. C Portslade St Nic *Chich* 54-58; C Goring-by-Sea 58-60; Chapl St Edm Sch Cant 60-76; Chapl Bennett Memorial Dioc Sch Tunbridge Wells 76-92; Hon C Tunbridge Wells K Chas *Roch* 77-93; rtd 93; Perm to Offic *Roch* from 93. *Flat 1, Hurstleigh, Hurstwood Lane, Tunbridge Wells TN4 8YA* Tel (01892) 528409

GILL, David Alan. b 64. Coll of Resurr Mirfield 98. **d** 00 **p** 01. C Devizes St Jo w St Mary *Sarum* 00-04; P-in-c Brockworth *Glouc* from 04. *The Vicarage, 42 Court Road, Brockworth, Gloucester GL3 4ET* Tel (01452) 862114 E-mail frdavid@houseofgill.org

GILL, David Brian Michael. b 55. Southn Univ BTh88. Sarum & Wells Th Coll 83. **d** 86 **p** 87. C Honiton, Gittisham, Combe Raleigh, Monkton etc *Ex* 86-89; C Teignmouth, Ideford w Luton, Ashcombe etc 89-91; TV Ex St Thos and Em from 91; P-in-c Tamerton Foliot from 05. *The Vicarage, Whitson Cross Lane, Tamerton Foliot, Plymouth PL5 4NT* Tel (01752) 771033 E-mail david@dbmg.freeserve.co.uk

GILL, Mrs Gabrielle Mary (Gay). **d** 90 **p** 94. NSM Timperley *Ches* 90-96; rtd 96; Perm to Offic *Ches* from 97. *The Croft, 3 Harrop Road, Hale, Altrincham WA15 9BU* Tel 0161-928 1800

GILL, Miss Helen Barbara. b 61. K Alfred's Coll Win BEd87. Cranmer Hall Dur. **d** 99 **p** 00. C Newc St Gabr *Newc* 99-04; P-in-c Tynemouth St Jo from 04. *St John's Vicarage, St John's Terrace, Percy Main, North Shields NE29 6HS* Tel 0191-257 1819 E-mail helen@gill1999.freeserve.co.uk

GILL, James Joseph. b 45. Pontifical Univ Maynooth BD78. **d** 77 **p** 78. In RC Ch 77-82; C Howden *York* 82-83; TV 83-86; P-in-c Wragby w Sharlston *Wakef* 86-88; V Sharlston 88-91; V Tilehurst St Geo *Ox* 91-98; P-in-c Eastney *Portsm* 98-05; rtd 05. *40 Henderson Road, Southsea PO4 9JG*

✠GILL, The Rt Revd Kenneth Edward. b 32. Hartley Victoria Coll. **d** 58 **p** 60 **c** 72. In Ch of S India 58-80; Bp Karnataka Cen 72-80; Asst Bp Newc 80-98; rtd 99; Hon Asst Bp Newc from 99. *Kingfisher Lodge, 41 Long Cram, Haddington EH41 4NS* Tel (01620) 822113 E-mail k.gill@newcastle.anglican.org

GILL, Mrs Mary. b 20. Nottm Univ BA42. St Jo Coll Nottm CertCS43. **d** 88 **p** 96. NSM Alston Team *Newc* 88-90; rtd 90; Perm to Offic *Newc* from 90. *Old School, Garrigill, Alston CA9 3DP* Tel (01434) 381594

GILL, Michael John. b 59. SSC K Coll Lon BA81 AKC81 Univ of Wales (Cardiff) BD85. St Mich Coll Llan 82. **d** 85 **p** 86. Min Can St Woolos Cathl *Mon* 85-90; Chapl St Woolos Hosp Newport 87-90; Succ Heref Cathl *Heref* 90-93; C Heref St Jo 90-93; TV Ebbw Vale *Mon* 93-96; V Tonypandy w Clydach Vale *Llan* from 96. *The Vicarage, Richards Terrace, Tonypandy CF40 2LD* Tel (01443) 437759

GILL, Paul Joseph. b 45. Ridley Coll Melbourne 73. Melbourne Coll of Div DipRE76. **d** 74 **p** 74. Australia 74-76 and from 89; C Perth St Dav 74-76; C Birm St Martin *Birm* 77-79; V Pype Hayes 79-89; Perm to Offic *Perth* 89-93; R Perth St Paul 93-00; Sen Chapl HM Min of Justice from 00. *118 Waddell Road, Bicton, W Australia 6157* Tel (0061) (8) 9317 3912 *or* 9411 5476 Mobile 416-021945 Fax 9411 5542 E-mail gill@global.com.au

GILL, Prof Robin Morton. b 44. K Coll Lon BD66 AKC66 Lon Univ PhD69 Birm Univ MSocSc72. **d** 68 **p** 69. C Rugby St Andr *Cov* 68-71; Papua New Guinea 71-72; Lect Th Edin Univ 72-86; Sen Lect 86-88; Assoc Dean Faculty of Div 85-88; P-in-c Edin SS Phil and Jas *Edin* 73-75; P-in-c Ford *Newc* 75-87; P-in-c Coldstream *Edin* 87-92; Perm to Offic *Newc* from 92; Wm Leech Prof Applied Th Newc Univ 88-92; Mich Ramsey Prof Modern Th Kent Univ from 92; Hon Prov Can Cant Cathl *Cant* from 92; AD N Downs from 02; P-in-c Hollingbourne and Hucking w Leeds and Broomfield from 03. *Hucking Court Barn, Church Road, Hucking, Maidstone ME17 1QT* Tel (01622) 884120 E-mail r.gill@ukc.ac.uk

GILL, Mrs Ruth Montcrieff. **d** 04. Aux Min Cloughjordan w Borrisokane etc *L & K* from 04. *Kilgolan House, Kilcormac, Birr, Co Offaly, Irish Republic* Tel (00353) (509) 35341

GILL, Simon David. b 66. Southn Univ BSc87 PhD91. St Jo Coll Nottm BTh00. **d** 01 **p** 02. C Frinton *Chelmsf* 01-05; P-in-c Sudbury w Ballingdon and Brundon *St E* from 05. *5 Clermont Avenue, Sudbury CO10 1ZJ* Tel (01787) 375334 E-mail sallie.simon@tinyworld.co.uk

GILL, Stanley. b 34. Sarum Th Coll 66. **d** 68 **p** 69. C Ipswich St Mary at Stoke w St Pet & St Mary Quay *St E* 68-73 and 78-80; TV Ipswich St Mary at Stoke w St Pet etc 80-82; V Bury St Edmunds St Geo 73-78; P-in-c Childe Okeford, Manston, Hammoon and Hanford *Sarum* 82-89; R The Lulworths, Winfrith Newburgh and Chaldon 89-94; R Hazelbury Bryan and the Hillside Par 94-99; rtd 99; Perm to Offic *Ex* 99-02 and *Sarum* 00-02. *Fosbrooke House, 8 Clifton Drive, Lytham St Annes FY8 5RQ*

GILL, Thomas. b 21. St Aid Birkenhead 62. **d** 63 **p** 64. C Newland St Aug *York* 63-67; V Burstwick w Thorngumbald 67-78; RD S Holderness 74-78; R Brandesburton 78-86; RD N Holderness 80-86; rtd 87; Perm to Offic *York* from 87. *Bellfield, Arnold Lane West, Arnold, Hull HU11 5HP* Tel (01964) 562282

GILL, Timothy Charles. b 66. Newc Univ BA88 Jes Coll Cam MPhil93. Westcott Ho Cam 89. **d** 92 **p** 93. C N Hull St Mich *York* 92-96; P-in-c Sculcoates St Paul w Ch Ch and St Silas 96-98; P-in-c Hull St Mary Sculcoates 96-98; V York St Luke 98-02; R Adel *Ripon* from 02. *The Rectory, 25 Church Lane, Adel, Leeds LS16 8DQ* Tel 0113-267 3676 E-mail ttimgill@aol.com

GILL, Wilson. St Alb and Ox Min Course. **d** 05. C Walton H Trin *Ox* from 05. *2 Rochford Gardens, Slough SL2 5XD* Tel (01753) 551697

GILLARD, David John. b 66. Ridley Hall Cam CTM98. **d** 98 **p** 99. C Seaford w Sutton *Chich* 98-02; P-in-c Eastbourne St Eliz from 02. *The Vicarage, 11 Baldwin Avenue, Eastbourne BN21 1UJ* Tel (01323) 694728

GILLESPIE, David Ivan. b 68. TCD BTh01. CITC 98. **d** 01 **p** 02. C Agherton *Conn* 01-04; I Moy w Charlemont *Arm* from 04. *St James's Rectory, 37 The Square, Moy, Dungannon BT71 7SG* Tel (028) 8778 4312 Mobile 07743-874727 E-mail digillespie15@aol.com *or* moy@armagh.anglican.org

GILLESPIE, George Henry. b 20. SS Coll Cam BA46 MA55. Cuddesdon Coll 46. **d** 48 **p** 49. C Wigan All SS *Liv* 48-53; C Ashbourne w Mapleton and Clifton *Derby* 53-55; V Allenton and Shelton Lock 56-71; Chapl Derby High Sch for Girls 58-71; V Bath Ascension *B & W* 71-78; P-in-c Norton St Philip w Hemington, Hardington etc 78-81; R 81-85; rtd 85; Perm to Offic *B & W* 86-02. *50 Wilton Way, Abbotskerswell, Newton Abbot TQ12 5PG* Tel (01626) 367386

GILLESPIE, Michael David. b 41. EMMTC 86. **d** 89 **p** 90. NSM Countesthorpe w Foston *Leic* from 89. *3 Penfold Drive, Countesthorpe, Leicester LE8 3TP* Tel 0116-278 1130 E-mail mick.gillespie@btinternet.com

GILLESPIE, Nancy Gillian. b 41. TCD MA68 NUI DipBS84. DipTh97. **d** 97 **p** 98. Lib Ossory Cathl *C & O* 97-00; C Kilkenny w Aghour and Kilmanagh 97-00; I Stradbally w Ballintubbert, Coraclone etc from 00; P-in-c Maryborough w Dysart Enos and Ballyfin from 02. *The Rectory, Stradbally, Co Laois, Irish Republic* Tel (00353) (502) 25173 Mobile 87-232 2574 E-mail ngilles@iol.ie

GILLETT, Brian Alan Michael. b 42. MRICS73. Chich Th Coll. **d** 82 **p** 83. C Tupsley *Heref* 82-86; R Kingstone w Clehonger, Eaton Bishop etc 86-97; V Baltonsborough w Butleigh, W Bradley etc *B & W* from 97; Sub-Warden of Readers Wells Adnry 00-02. *The Vicarage, Church Close, Butleigh, Glastonbury BA6 8SH* Tel (01458) 850409

✠GILLETT, The Rt Revd David Keith. b 45. Leeds Univ BA65 MPhil68. Oak Hill Th Coll 66. **d** 68 **p** 69 **c** 99. C Watford St Luke *St Alb* 68-71; Sec Pathfinders and CYFA N Area 71-74; Lect St Jo Coll Nottm 74-79; Ch of Ireland Renewal Cen 80-82; V Luton Lewsey St Hugh *St Alb* 82-88; Prin Trin Coll Bris 88-99; Hon Can Bris Cathl *Bris* 91-99; Suff Bp Bolton *Man* from 99. *Bishop's Lodge, Bolton Road, Hawkshaw, Bury BL8 4JN* Tel (01204) 882955 Fax 882988 E-mail david.gillett@ukgateway.net

GILLETT, Victor Henry John. b 31. Open Univ BA83 BTh87 MTh94. Clifton Th Coll 59. **d** 62 **p** 63. C Walton Breck *Liv* 62-65; C Wednesfield Heath *Lich* 65-68; V Tipton St Paul 68-76; V Moulton *Pet* 76-92; TV Worthing Ch the King *Chich* 92-98; Chapl Ramsay Hall 92-98; rtd 98; Perm to Offic *Leic* from 98. *Manoah, 50 Stoneygate Drive, Hinckley LE10 1TD* Tel (01455) 239082 E-mail vgillett@manoah.freeserve.co.uk

GILLETT, Vincent. b 30. Lon Univ BSc55 UEA MSc72 Open Univ BA01 FCollP81. Chich Th Coll 59. **d** 61 **p** 62. C Blackpool St Mich *Blackb* 61-63; Chapl Adisadel Coll Ghana 63-66; Chapl Kumasi Univ 66-72; Asst Master St Marg C of E High Sch

Aigburth Liv 72-75; Asst Master Halewood Comp Sch 75-79; Hd Master St Wilfrid's Sch Ex 79-84; R Atherington and High Bickington *Ex* 84-94; V Burrington 84-94; rtd 95. *Birchy Barton Lodge, 2 Honiton Road, Exeter EX1 3EA* Tel (01392) 436393 E-mail vincent@gillett4688.freeserve.co.uk

GILLEY, Margaret Mary. b 54. St Andr Univ MTheol76 Dur Univ PhD97. NEOC 97. **d** 00 **p** 01. C Birtley *Dur* 00-03; P-in-c Stockton St Mark 03; V from 03; V Elton from 03. *The Vicarage, 76 Fairfield Road, Stockton-on-Tees TS19 7BP* Tel (01642) 586179 E-mail meg.gilley@durham.anglican.org

GILLHAM, Martin John. b 45. Wilson Carlile Coll IDC66 Qu Coll Birm 72. **d** 75 **p** 76. C Whitley Ch Ch *Ox* 75-78; TV Crowmarsh Gifford w Newnham Murren 78-79; TV Wallingford w Crowmarsh Gifford etc 79-83; V Kintbury w Avington 83-94; Dioc Lay Min Adv and Warden of Readers 89-97; P-in-c W Wycombe w Bledlow Ridge, Bradenham and Radnage 94-00; R 00; Prov Chapl Third Order SSF 95-99; P-in-c Norham and Duddo *Newc* 00-04; V from 04; P-in-c Cornhill w Carham from 00; P-in-c Branxton from 00. *The Vicarage, Church Lane, Norham, Berwick-upon-Tweed TD15 2LF* Tel (01289) 382325

GILLHAM, Mrs Patricia Anne. b 40. Wilson Carlile Coll IDC66 Ox Min Course CBTS93. **d** 93 **p** 94. Par Dn Kintbury w Avington *Ox* 93-94; C 94-95; C W Wycombe w Bledlow Ridge, Bradenham and Radnage 95-00; rtd 00; Perm to Offic *Newc* from 00. *The Vicarage, Church Lane, Norham, Berwick-upon-Tweed TD15 2LF* Tel (01289) 382325

GILLHESPEY, Canon Clive. b 28. Lon Univ DipTh66 BD73. Cranmer Hall Dur 63. **d** 65 **p** 66. C Barrow St Geo w St Luke *Carl* 65-69; V Flookburgh 69-74; R Barrow St Geo w St Luke 74-81; TR 81-92; Hon Can Carl Cathl 84-92; rtd 92; Perm to Offic *Carl* from 92. *Canon's Court, 43 Holyoake Avenue, Barrow-in-Furness LA13 9LH* Tel (01229) 839041

GILLIAN, Ronald Trevor. b 57. Ulster Univ Dip Music77 MTD78 QUB BEd89 TCD BTh93. CITC 90. **d** 93 **p** 94. C Belfast St Donard *D & D* 93-96; I Aghalurcher w Tattykeeran, Cooneen etc *Clogh* from 96; Dir of Ords from 04. *St Ronan's Rectory, Owenskerry Lane, Killarbran, Fivemiletown BT75 0SR* Tel and fax (028) 8554 8547 Mobile 07866-681247 E-mail colebrooke_clogher@hotmail.com

GILLIBRAND, John Nigel. b 60. Ox Univ BA82 MA86 Lon Univ PGCE83. St Steph Ho Ox BTh97. **d** 88 **p** 89. C Dolgellau w Llanfachreth and Brithdir etc *Ban* 88-90; C Llanbeblig w Caernarfon and Betws Garmon etc 90-91; V Ffestiniog w Blaenau Ffestiniog 91-97; V Llandegfan w Llandysilio 97-02; Nat Co-ord (Wales) Nat Autistic Soc from 02; Lic to Offic *Llan* 02-04; P-in-c Llangeler w Pen-Boyr *St D* from 04. *The Vicarage, Llangeler, Llandysul SA44 5EX* Tel (01559) 371170

GILLIBRAND, Margaret Ann Jane. b 43. **d** 01 **p** 02. OLM Deal St Leon and St Rich and Sholden *Cant* 01-04; Perm to Offic *Eur* from 04. *La Maison de l'Évêque, Les Picardies, 16420 Lesterts, France* E-mail gillibrand@onetel.com.uk

GILLIES, Canon Robert Arthur. b 51. Edin Univ BD77 St Andr Univ PhD91. Edin Th Coll 73. **d** 77 **p** 78. C Falkirk *Edin* 77-80; C Edin Ch Ch 80-84; Chapl Napier Coll 80-84; Chapl Dundee Univ *Bre* 84-90; R St Andrews St Andr *St And* from 91; Dioc Dir of Ords from 96; Can St Ninian's Cathl Perth from 97. *St Andrew's Rectory, Queen's Terrace, St Andrews KY16 9QF* Tel and fax (01334) 473344 E-mail r.a.gillies@tesco.net

GILLING, John Reginald. b 25. Cam Univ BA49 MA51 MLitt55. Cuddesdon Coll 53. **d** 55 **p** 56. C Romford St Alb *Chelmsf* 55-58; C Cambridge St Mary Less *Ely* 58-62; Chapl Ch Ch Ox 62-71; V Pimlico St Mary Graham-street *Lon* 71-90; AD Westmr St Marg 79-85; rtd 90; Perm to Offic *Chich* from 90. *49 Westgate, Chichester PO19 3EZ* Tel (01243) 775169

GILLINGHAM, John Bruce. b 48. Ch Ch Ox BA69 MA74. St Jo Coll Nottm BA73. **d** 73 **p** 74. C Plymouth St Andr w St Paul and St Geo *Ex* 73-77; C Ox St Aldate w H Trin *Ox* 78; Chapl Jes Coll Ox 78-88; Chapl Ox Pastorate 79-88; Dioc Missr *Birm* 88-92; R Ox St Clem *Ox* from 92. *St Clement's Rectory, 58 Rectory Road, Oxford OX4 1BW* Tel (01865) 248735

GILLINGHAM, Michael John. b 46. Univ of Wales (Swansea) DipSoc&CtyEd80 Hull Univ MA90. Chich Th Coll 68. **d** 71 **p** 72. C Llanharan w Peterston-super-Montem *Llan* 71-73; C Skewen 73-76; Neath Deanery Youth Chapl 74-76; Perm to Offic 79-80; TV Kirkby *Liv* 76-77; Youth Chapl Woodchurch *Ches* 77-79; Sen Youth Worker (Bedfordshire) *St Alb* 80-83; TV Sheff Manor *Sheff* 83-88; R Frecheville from 88; Chapl Sheff Sea Cadets from 87; Chapl RNR 90-92; Chapl S Yorks Police *Sheff* from 93. *Frecheville Rectory, Brackenfield Grove, Sheffield S12 4XS* Tel 0114-239 9555 Mobile 07702-133809 E-mail mike@mgillingham.f9.co.uk

GILLINGS, The Ven Richard John. b 45. St Chad's Coll Dur BA67. Linc Th Coll 68. **d** 70 **p** 71. C Altrincham St Geo *Ches* 70-75; P-in-c Stockport St Thos 75-77; R 77-83; P-in-c Stockport St Pet 78-83; TR Birkenhead Priory 83-93; RD Birkenhead 85-93; V Bramhall from 93; Hon Can Ches Cathl 92-94; Adn Macclesfield from 94. *The Vicarage, Robin's Lane, Bramhall, Stockport SK7 2PE* Tel 0161-439 2254 Fax 439 0878 E-mail richard.gillings@chester.anglican.org

GILLION, Robert Alan. b 51. LRAM. Sarum & Wells Th Coll 81. **d** 83 **p** 84. C E Dereham *Nor* 83-86; C Richmond St Mary w St Matthias and St Jo *S'wark* 86-90; P-in-c Discovery Bay Ch Hong Kong 90-98; Chapl Shek Pik Pris 90-98; Bp Kensington's Adv for Evang *Lon* from 98; P-in-c Upper Chelsea 01-02; V from 02; AD Chelsea from 04. *St Simon Zelotes Vicarage, 34 Milner Street, London SW3 2QF* Tel (020) 7589 5747 Fax 7589 2247 E-mail rob.gillion@london.anglican.org

GILLIONS, Michael George. b 37. Ch Ch Ox MA65 Keele Univ PGCE74. WEMTC 93. **d** 96 **p** 97. NSM Dorrington w Leebotwood, Longnor, Stapleton etc *Heref* 96-00; NSM Condover w Frodesley, Acton Burnell etc from 00. *The Maltsters, Dorrington, Shrewsbury SY5 7JD* Tel (01743) 718550

GILLMAN, Noel Francis. b 26. St D Dioc Tr Course St D Coll Lamp St Mich Coll Llan. **d** 79 **p** 80. NSM Llanelli *St D* 79-83; C 83-85; TV Tenby 85-91; rtd 91. *4 Oaklands, Swiss Valley, Llanelli SA14 8DA* Tel (01554) 772663

GILLMOR, Canon Samuel Frederick. b 29. St Aid Birkenhead. **d** 62 **p** 63. C Carlow Union *C & O* 62-64; I Fenagh Union 64-68; I Maryborough w Dysart Enos 68-79; Can Ossory Cathl 78-79; Can Leighlin Cathl 78-79; I Clane w Donadea *M & K* 79-84; I Mullingar, Portnashangan, Moyliscar, Kilbixy etc 84-93; Can Meath 92-93; I Achonry w Tubbercurry and Killoran *T, K & A* 93-03; Can Achonry Cathl 93-03; rtd 04. *Back Acre, Carrowdubh, Strandhill, Co Sligo, Irish Republic* Tel (00353) (71) 916 8571

GILLUM, Thomas Alan. b 55. Ex Univ BSc76. Cranmer Hall Dur 87. **d** 89 **p** 90. C Brompton H Trin w Onslow Square St Paul *Lon* 89-94; P-in-c Paddington St Steph w St Luke 94-04; P-in-c S Kensington St Jude from 04. *St Jude's Vicarage, 18 Collingham Road, London SW5 0LX* Tel (020) 7370 1360 E-mail tom.gillum@stjudeschurch.com

GILMAN, Michael. b 35. Man Univ BA57 Sheff Univ PhD99. Ripon Hall Ox 59. **d** 61 **p** 62. C Old Trafford St Jo *Man* 61-64; C Englefield Green *Guildf* 64-69; Historic Buildings Division Gtr Lon Coun 66-86; English Heritage 86-89; rtd 00. *6 Osborne Road, Egham TW20 9RN* Tel (01784) 437106

GILMORE, David Samuel. b 70. Univ of Ulster BSc92 CQSW92 QUB MSSc95. EAMTC 01. **d** 03 **p** 04. C Basildon St Martin *Chelmsf* 03-04; C Danbury from 04. *40 Millfields, Danbury, Chelmsford CM3 4LE* Tel (01245) 227260 E-mail davidgilmore@btinternet.com

GILMORE, Canon Henry. b 51. Man Univ BA72 TCD BD82. CITC 75. **d** 75 **p** 76. C Arm St Mark w Aghavilly *Arm* 75-78; C Dublin St Patr Cathl Gp *D & G* 78-81; I Stranorlar w Meenglas and Kilteevogue *D & R* 81-84; I Achill w Dugort, Castlebar and Turlough *T, K & A* 84-91; I Moville w Greencastle, Donagh, Cloncha etc *D & R* from 91; Can Raphoe Cathl from 01. *The Rectory, Moville, Co Donegal, Irish Republic* Tel (00353) (74) 938 2572 E-mail hgilmore@eircom.net

GILMOUR, Ian Hedley. b 57. Ex Univ LLB Lon Univ BD. Wycliffe Hall Ox 80. **d** 83 **p** 84. C Harold Wood *Chelmsf* 83-86; C Thame w Towersey *Ox* 86-91; V Streatham Vale H Redeemer *S'wark* from 91. *The Vicarage, Churchmore Road, London SW16 5UZ* Tel (020) 8764 5808

GILMOUR, John Logan. b 14. Cuddesdon Coll 46. **d** 48 **p** 49. C Reading St Mary V *Ox* 48-51; Min St Barn CD Reading 51-55; Thailand 55-58; V Ellel *Blackb* 58-60; S Africa from 60. *2 Russell Lodge, Main Road, Constantia, 7800 South Africa* Tel (0027) (21) 794 1523

GILPIN, Jeremy David. b 59. Pemb Coll Ox BA80 CertEd82. Trin Coll Bris BA88. **d** 88 **p** 89. C Southsea St Jude *Portsm* 88-92; R Itchingfield w Slinfold *Chich* 92-96; Chapl St Hugh's Coll Ox from 97. *12 Bay Tree Close, Iffley, Oxford OX4 4DT* Tel (01865) 770471 Fax as telephone E-mail gilpins@compuserve.com

GILPIN, Canon Richard John. b 45. Lon Univ BSc66. Wells Th Coll 67. **d** 70 **p** 71. C Davyhulme Ch Ch *Man* 70-74; Pastor Gustav Adolf Berlin EKD 74-77; R Heaton Norris Ch w All SS 77-83; R Chorlton-cum-Hardy St Clem 83-99; AD Hulme 95-99; V Norley, Crowton and Kingsley *Ches* from 99; RD Frodsham from 03; Hon Can Ches Cathl from 04. *The Vicarage, Station Road, Crowton, Northwich CW8 2RQ* Tel (01928) 788310 *or* 788933 E-mail dick@crowton.f9.co.uk

GILPIN, The Ven Richard Thomas. b 39. Lich Th Coll 60. **d** 63 **p** 64. C Whipton *Ex* 63-66; C Tavistock and Gulworthy 66-69; V 73-91; V Swimbridge 69-73; Preb Ex Cathl from 82; RD Tavistock 87-90; Dioc Dir of Ords 90-91; Adv for Voc and Dioc Dir of Ords 91-96; Sub Dean Ex Cathl 92-96; Adn Totnes from 96; Can Res Ex Cathl from 01. *Blue Hills, Bradley Road, Bovey Tracey, Newton Abbot TQ13 9EU* Tel (01626) 832064 Fax 834947 E-mail archdeacon.of.totnes@exeter.anglican.org

GIMSON, Francis Herbert. b 54. Reading Univ BSc79 LTh. St Jo Coll Nottm 83. **d** 86 **p** 87. C Menston w Woodhead *Bradf* 86-89; C Barnoldswick w Bracewell 89-91; V Langleybury St Paul *St Alb* 91-02; P-in-c Downton *Sarum* from 02; P-in-c Redlynch and Morgan's Vale from 04. *The Vicarage, Barford Lane, Downton, Salisbury SP5 3QA* Tel (01725) 510326 E-mail fgimson@nildram.co.uk

GINEVER, Paul Michael John. b 49. AKC71. **d** 72 **p** 73. C Davyhulme Ch Ch *Man* 72-75; Australia 76-77; C Tettenhall

Wood *Lich* 77-80; C Halesowen *Worc* 80; TV 80-86; P-in-c Gt Malvern Ch Ch 86-98; V S Hayling *Portsm* from 98. *The Vicarage, 34 Church Road, Hayling Island PO11 0NT* Tel (023) 9246 2914 *or* 9263 7649
E-mail parishoffice@haylinganglicans.freeserve.co.uk

GINGELL, John Lawrence. b 27. Lon Univ BD55. ALCD55. **d** 55 **p** 56. C Normanton *Derby* 55-58; C Ilkeston St Bart CD 58-61; Toc H Staff Padre 61-70; Asst Chapl S Lon Ind Miss 61-64; Lic to Offic *S'wark* 61-66; Lic to Offic *Liv* 67-70; V Somercotes *Derby* 70-72; Bp's Ind Adv 72-80; rtd 92. *18 Bournville Road, London SE6 4RN* Tel (020) 8690 0148

GINGRICH, Dale Robert. b 64. Midland Lutheran Coll (USA) BSc86 Lutheran Th Sem Gettysburg MDiv93. EAMTC 03. **d** 04 **p** 05. NSM Shingay Gp *Ely* from 04. *7 Greenside Close, Swavesey, Cambridge CB4 5RF* Tel (01954) 231972 Mobile 07766-706773 E-mail drging@onetel.com

GINN, Daniel Vivian. b 33. Univ of Wales (Cardiff) BSc55 DipEd56. Llan Dioc Tr Scheme 79. **d** 82 **p** 83. NSM Llantwit Major and St Donat's *Llan* 82-83; NSM Llantwit Major 83-02; TV 88-02; RD Llantwit Major and Cowbridge 94-02; Perm to Offic from 02. *Chenet, 24 Voss Park Drive, Llantwit Major CF61 1YE* Tel (01446) 792774

GINN, Canon Richard John. b 51. Lon Univ BD77 Dur Univ MLitt05 ACIB73 Lambeth STh85. Oak Hill Th Coll 75 Cranmer Hall Dur 77. **d** 79 **p** 80. C Hornsey Ch Ch *Lon* 79-82; C Highgate St Mich 82-85; V Westleton w Dunwich *St E* from 85; V Darsham from 85; P-in-c Middleton cum Fordley and Theberton w Eastbridge from 01; P-in-c Yoxford, Peasenhall and Sibton from 01; Hon Can St E Cathl from 01. *The Vicarage, Darsham Road, Westleton, Saxmundham IP17 3AQ* Tel (01728) 648271 E-mail r.ginn@btinternet.com

GINNO, Albert Charles. b 31. CA Tr Coll 51 Lon Coll of Div 66. **d** 68 **p** 69. C Kemp Town St Mark and St Matt *Chich* 68-72; P-in-c E Hoathly 72-83; V Westham 83-96; rtd 96; Perm to Offic *Chich* from 96. *106 Sorrel Drive, Eastbourne BN23 8BJ* Tel (01323) 761479 Fax 768920

GIRARD, Canon William Nicholas Charles. b 35. Coll of Resurr Mirfield 65. **d** 67 **p** 68. C Yate *Glouc* 67-70; C Westbury-on-Trym St Alb *Bris* 70-73; Chapl K Sch Ely 73-76; V Fenstanton *Ely* 76-85; V Hilton 76-85; R Balsham 85-99; P-in-c W Wickham 85-99; P-in-c Horseheath 85-96; RD Linton 93-94 and 96-99; Hon Can Ely Cathl 97-03; C Alconbury w Alconbury Weston 99-00; Hon C 00-03; C Buckworth 99-00; Hon C 00-03; C Gt w Lt Stukeley 99-00; Hon C 00-03; rtd 00; P-in-c Hamerton *Ely* 00-04; RD Leightonstone 00-02. *Ferrar House, Little Gidding, Huntingdon PE28 5RJ* Tel (01832) 293383

GIRLING, Andrew Martin. b 40. Em Coll Cam BA63 MA67. Wycliffe Hall Ox 63. **d** 65 **p** 66. C Luton w E Hyde *St Alb* 65-69; Chapl Hull Univ *York* 69-75; V Dringhouses 75-00; Can and Preb York Minster 97-00; P-in-c Thurlestone w S Milton *Ex* 00-02; R Thurlestone, S Milton, W Alvington etc from 02. *The Rectory, Homefield, Thurlestone, Kingsbridge TQ7 3LF* Tel (01548) 562219

GIRLING, David Frederick Charles. b 33. Kelham Th Coll 49 Edin Th Coll 58. **d** 61 **p** 62. C Caister *Nor* 61-65; C Leigh St Clem *Chelmsf* 65-66; CF 66-83; V Prittlewell St Luke *Chelmsf* 83-98; rtd 98; Perm to Offic *Nor* from 98. *37 Dell Road East, Lowestoft NR33 9LA* Tel (01502) 567426

GIRLING, Francis Richard (Vincent). b 28. Worc Coll Ox BA52 MA56 Lon Univ BD65. Coll of Resurr Mirfield 55. **d** 57 **p** 59. CR from 57; rtd 98; Lic to Offic *Wakef* from 98. *House of the Resurrection, Stocks Bank Road, Mirfield WF14 0BN* Tel (01924) 494318

GIRLING, Ian John. b 53. Oak Hill Th Coll 03. **d** 05. C Hubberston *St D* from 05. *95 Waterloo Road, Hakin, Milford Haven SA73 3PE* Tel (01646) 697649
E-mail iangirling@yahoo.co.uk

GIRLING, Stephen Paul. b 61. Southn Univ BSc83. Trin Coll Bris BA91. **d** 91 **p** 92. C Ogley Hay *Lich* 91-95; TV S Molton w Nymet St George, High Bray etc *Ex* 95-01; RD S Molton 97-01; V Crofton *Portsm* from 01. *The Vicarage, 40 Vicarage Lane, Stubbington, Fareham PO14 2JX* Tel (01329) 662007 Fax as telephone E-mail girlingsp@aol.com

GIRLING, Timothy Havelock. b 43. St Aid Birkenhead 63. **d** 67 **p** 68. C Wickford *Chelmsf* 67-70; C Luton w E Hyde *St Alb* 70-74; Chapl Luton and Dunstable Hosp 74-80; C Luton All SS w St Pet *St Alb* 74-80; R Northill w Moggerhanger 80-89; Chapl Glenfield Hosp NHS Trust Leic 89-00; Chapl Glenfrith Hosp 89-93; Chapl Univ Hosps Leic NHS Trust 00-04; Hon Can Leic Cathl *Leic* 97-04; rtd 04; Chapl Leics Partnership NHS Trust from 04. *36 Winton Avenue, Leicester LE3 1DH* Tel 0116-291 3795 Mobile 07879-418721 E-mail tgirling@ntlworld.com

GIRLING, Vincent. *See* GIRLING, Francis Richard

GIRTCHEN, John Christopher. b 54. Linc Th Coll 94. **d** 96 **p** 97. C Bourne *Linc* 96-00; V Barrow and Goxhill from 00. *The Vicarage, Thornton Street, Barrow-upon-Humber DN19 7DG* Tel (01469) 530357 E-mail jcgirtchen@lineone.net

GISBOURNE, Michael Andrew. b 65. Leeds Univ BA87. St Jo Coll Nottm BTh91. **d** 92 **p** 93. C Gateacre *Liv* 92-95; C Marton *Blackb* 95-98; V Freckleton 98-03; V Garstang St Thos from 03. *St Thomas's Vicarage, Church Street, Garstang, Preston PR3 1PA* Tel and fax (01995) 602162 E-mail revgis@fish.co.uk

✠**GITARI, The Most Revd David Mukuba.** b 37. K Coll Lon BA64 BD71 Ashland Univ (USA) Hon DD83 Kent Univ Hon DD98. Tyndale Hall Bris 68. **d** 71 **p** 72 **c** 75. Gen Sec Bible Soc Kenya 71-75; Bp Mt Kenya E 75-90; Bp Kirinyaga 90-97; Dean of Angl Ch of Kenya 94-97; Abp Kenya 96-02. *PO Box 607, 60100 Embu, Kenya* Tel (00254) (0161) 30832 Fax (0161) 30824
E-mail davidgitari@insightkenya.com

GITTINGS, Graham. b 46. Qu Coll Birm 75. **d** 78 **p** 79. C Caverswall *Lich* 78-81; C Wolverhampton St Matt 81-82; C Walthamstow St Mary w St Steph *Chelmsf* 82-83; C Dagenham 83-89; V Earl Shilton w Elmesthorpe *Leic* from 89. *The Vicarage, Maughan Street, Earl Shilton, Leicester LE9 7BA* Tel (01455) 843961 E-mail ggvicar@aol.com

GITTOES, Julie Anne. b 76. Trevelyan Coll Dur BA98 Graduate Soc Dur MA99 Selw Coll Cam PhD04. Westcott Ho Cam 99. **d** 03 **p** 04. C Hampton Hill *Lon* from 03. *82 Pigeon Lane, Hampton TW12 1AF* Tel (020) 8941 4424 Mobile 07941-871570
E-mail jag46@fish.co.uk

GIVEN, Harold Richard. b 54. Oak Hill Th Coll 75. **d** 78 **p** 79. C Belfast St Clem *D & D* 78-80; C Belfast St Donard 80-83; I Tamlaght O'Crilly Upper w Lower *D & R* 83-92; I Tamlaghtfinlagan w Myroe from 92. *Finlagan Rectory, 77 Ballykelly Road, Limavady BT49 9DS* Tel (028) 7176 2743

GLADSTONE, Robert Michael. b 60. Ch Ch Ox BA82 MA86. Wycliffe Hall Ox DipMin94. **d** 94 **p** 95. C Trentham *Lich* 94-97; C Heigham H Trin *Nor* 97-01; V Rothley *Leic* from 01. *The Vicarage, 128 Hallfields Lane, Rothley, Leicester LE7 7NG* Tel 0116-230 2241 E-mail gladrob@clara.net

✠**GLADWIN, The Rt Revd John Warren.** b 42. Chu Coll Cam BA65 MA68. Cranmer Hall Dur DipTh66. **d** 67 **p** 68 **c** 94. C Kirkheaton *Wakef* 67-71; Tutor St Jo Coll Dur 71-77; Dir Shaftesbury Project 77-82; Sec Gen Syn Bd for Soc Resp 82-88; Preb St Paul's Cathl *Lon* 84-88; Provost Sheff 88-94; Angl Adv Yorkshire TV 88-94; Bp Guildf 94-03; Bp Chelmsf from 03. *Bishopscourt, Main Road, Margaretting, Ingatestone CM4 0HD* Tel (01277) 352001 Fax 355374

GLADWIN, Thomas William. b 35. St Alb Minl Tr Scheme 78. **d** 81 **p** 82. NSM Hertford St Andr *St Alb* 81-82; NSM Digswell and Panshanger 82-86; C 86-96; rtd 96; Perm to Offic *St Alb* from 96. *99 Warren Way, Welwyn AL6 0DL* Tel (01438) 714700

GLAISTER, James Richard. b 30. Oak Hill Th Coll 81. **d** 83 **p** 84. NSM Shrub End *Chelmsf* 83-85; NSM Lawshall w Shimplingthorne and Alpheton *St E* 85-87; NSM Lavenham 87-88; C Felixstowe St Jo 88-95; rtd 95; Perm to Offic *St E* 95-01; *Carl* 00-02; *Blackb* 02-05. *Les Planchettes, 61350 St Roche sur Egrenne, France*

GLAISYER, The Ven Hugh. b 30. Oriel Coll Ox BA51 MA55. St Steph Ho Ox 51. **d** 56 **p** 56. C Tonge Moor *Man* 56-62; C Sidcup St Jo *Roch* 62-64; V Milton next Gravesend Ch Ch 64-81; RD Gravesend 74-81; V Hove All SS *Chich* 81-91; Can and Preb Chich Cathl 82-91; RD Hove 82-91; P-in-c Hove St Jo 87-91; Adn Lewes and Hastings 91-97; rtd 97; Perm to Offic *Chich* from 97. *Florence Villa, Hangleton Lane, Ferring, Worthing BN12 6PP* Tel and fax (01903) 244688 Mobile 07712-317118
E-mail h.glaisyer@virgin.net

GLANVILLE-SMITH, Canon Michael Raymond. b 38. Leeds Univ MA95. AKC61. **d** 62 **p** 63. C St Marylebone St Mark w St Luke *Lon* 62-64; C Penzance St Mary *Truro* 64-68; R Worc St Andr and All SS w St Helen *Worc* 68-74; Dioc Youth Chapl 68-74; V Catshill 74-80; P-in-c Worc St Martin w St Pet 80-81; TR Worc St Martin w St Pet, St Mark etc 81-86; TR Worc SE 86-90; Hon Can Worc Cathl 83-90; Can Res Ripon Cathl *Ripon* from 90; RD Ripon 96-97. *St Wilfrid's House, Minster Close, Ripon HG4 1QP* Tel (01765) 600211

GLARE, Michael Francis. b 28. Southn Univ BA54. St Steph Ho Ox 56. **d** 57 **p** 58. C Withycombe Raleigh *Ex* 57-62; C-in-c Goodrington CD 62-65; C Tamerton Foliot 65-70; R Weare Giffard w Landcross 70-76; RD Hartland 74-76; P-in-c Babbacombe 76-80; V 80-87; V Ilsington 87-93; rtd 93; Perm to Offic *Ex* from 94. *Poplar Lodge, 23 Albion Street, Shaldon, Teignmouth TQ14 0DF* Tel (01626) 872679

GLASBY, Alan Langland. b 46. St Jo Coll Nottm 74. **d** 77 **p** 78. C Erith St Paul *Roch* 77-80; C Moor Allerton *Ripon* 80-81; TV 81-87; V Middleton St Mary 87-92; V Bilton 92-00; V Barton and Manfield and Cleasby w Stapleton 00-04; TR E Richmond from 04. *The Vicarage, Silver Garth, Barton, Richmond DL10 6NG* Tel (01325) 377274 Mobile 07970-712484
E-mail alanglasby@btinternet.com

GLASGOW AND GALLOWAY, Bishop of. *See* JONES, The Rt Revd Idris

GLASGOW AND GALLOWAY, Dean of. *See* DUNCAN, The Very Revd Gregor Duthie

GLASGOW, Provost of. *See* DINES, The Very Revd Philip Joseph

GLASS, Kenneth William. b 23. FRSA68. **d** 57 **p** 58. C Ipswich St Matt *St E* 57-59; R Glemsford 59-63; P-in-c Somerton 59-63; V Ipswich St Nic 63-73; P-in-c Ipswich St Helen 73; R

Sproughton w Burstall 74-76; rtd 83; Perm to Offic *St E* 01-04. *19 Chalkeith Road, Needham Market, Ipswich IP6 8HA* Tel (01449) 720393

GLASS, Mrs Yvonne Elizabeth. b 58. EMMTC 94. **d** 97 **p** 98. NSM Bingham *S'well* 97-00; Asst Chapl Nottm City Hosp NHS Trust from 00. *30 Willoughby Road, West Bridgford, Nottingham NG2 6EZ* Tel 0115-846 2125

GLASSPOOL, John Martin. b 59. RGN87 Kent Univ BA83 Heythrop Coll Lon MTh95. Westcott Ho Cam 88. **d** 90 **p** 91. C Forest Gate Em w Upton Cross *Chelmsf* 90-93; P-in-c Theydon Garnon 93-95; Chapl St Marg Hosp Epping 93-99; TV Epping Distr *Chelmsf* 95-99; Asst Chapl R Free Hampstead NHS Trust 99-02; Chapl Surrey and Sussex Healthcare NHS Trust from 02. *Chaplaincy Department, East Surrey Hospital, Canada Avenue, Redhill RH1 5RH* Tel (01737) 768511 ext 6120 E-mail john.glasspool@sash.nhs.uk

GLAZEBROOK, William Leng. b 29. Edin Th Coll 76. **d** 76 **p** 77. C Dollar *St And* 76-82; Dioc Supernumerary 83; Chapl Trin Coll Glenalmond 84; P-in-c Glencarse *Bre* 84-87; Dioc Sec 84-87; Chapl HM Pris Perth 85-87; V Broughton Poggs w Filkins, Broadwell etc *Ox* 87-94; rtd 94; Perm to Offic *Bre* from 94; Hon C Perth St Jo *St And* from 98. *10 Rose Terrace, Perth PH1 5HA* Tel (01738) 624913

GLEADALL, John Frederick. b 39. Ripon Hall Ox 66 Sarum Th Coll 69. **d** 70 **p** 71. C S Ashford Ch Ch *Cant* 70-76; P-in-c Hothfield 76-83; P-in-c Eastwell w Boughton Aluph 81-83; P-in-c Westwell 81-83; V Westwell, Hothfield, Eastwell and Boughton Aluph 84-03; rtd 03; Hon C Old Leake w Wrangle *Linc* from 03; Chapl HM Pris N Sea Camp from 03. *Field House, Walcot Road, Billinghay, Lincoln LN4 4EG*

GLEAVES, John. b 39. Alsager Coll of Educn CertEd60 Westmr Coll Ox BTh03. N Ord Course 99. **d** 00 **p** 01. NSM Alsager St Mary *Ches* 00-03; P-in-c Alvanley from 03. *The Vicarage, 47 Ardern Lea, Alvanley, Frodsham WA6 9EQ* Tel (01928) 722012

GLEDHILL, Alan. b 43. Lon Univ BSc(Econ). N Ord Course 81. **d** 84 **p** 85. C Knaresborough *Ripon* 84-87; P-in-c Easby 87-88; P-in-c Bolton on Swale 87-88; V Easby w Brompton on Swale and Bolton on Swale 88-96; Teacher St Fran Xavier Sch Richmond from 96; Perm to Offic *Ripon* from 96. *15 White Lands, Richmond DL10 7DR* Tel (01748) 826973 *or* 823414

GLEDHILL, Canon James William. b 27. Dur Univ BA52. Westcott Ho Cam 52. **d** 56 **p** 57. C Mexborough *Sheff* 56-59; CF 59-61; C Bywell *Newc* 61-65; V Warden w Newbrough 65-98; RD Hexham 78-88; Hon Can Newc Cathl 88-98; rtd 98; Perm to Offic *Newc* from 98. *Castleview, Castlegate, Jedburgh TD8 6BD* Tel (01835) 862834

✠**GLEDHILL, The Rt Revd Jonathan Michael.** b 49. Keele Univ BA72 Bris Univ MA75. Trin Coll Bris 72. **d** 75 **p** 76 **c** 96. C Marple All SS *Ches* 75-78; C Folkestone H Trin w Ch Ch *Cant* 78-83; V Cant St Mary Bredin 83-96; Tutor Cant Sch of Min 83-96; RD Cant 88-94; Hon Can Cant Cathl 92-96; Suff Bp Southampton *Win* 96-03; Bp Lich from 03. *22B The Close, Lichfield WS13 7LG* Tel (01543) 306000 Fax 306009 E-mail bishop.lichfield@lichfield.anglican.org

GLEDHILL, Peter. b 29. Ball Coll Ox BA53 MA54. Cuddesdon Coll 54. **d** 56 **p** 57. C Balham St Mary *S'wark* 56-58; C Loughton St Jo *Chelmsf* 58-63; Jamaica 63-66; Barbados 66-67; Asst Master Cheadle Gr Sch 68-70; Lic to Offic *Lich* 70-71; P-in-c Kingstone w Gratwich 71-83; P-in-c Llanyblodwel and Trefonen 83-84; R 84-89; C Menai and Malltraeth Deanery *Ban* 90-94; NSM 95-96; rtd 94; Perm to Offic *Ban* from 96. *Yr Hen Felin, Pwllfanogl, Llanfairpwllgwyngyll LL61 6PD* Tel (01248) 714434

GLEESON, Robert Godfrey. b 49. Man Univ CQSW74. Qu Coll Birm 83. **d** 85 **p** 86. C Hall Green St Pet *Birm* 85-88; Asst Chapl Mental Health & Elderly Care Services Birm HA 88-90; Chapl 90-94; Chapl Moseley Hall Hosp Birm 90-94; Chapl S Birm Mental Health NHS Trust 94-03; Perm to Offic *Birm* from 03. *180 Pineapple Road, Birmingham B30 2TY* Tel 0121-444 2793 Mobile 07966-188006

GLEN, Robert Sawers. b 25. Qu Coll Cam BA49 MA56. Sarum & Wells Th Coll 79. **d** 81 **p** 82. Chapl Sherborne Sch 81-86; C Yetminster w Ryme Intrinseca and High Stoy *Sarum* 86-95; RD Sherborne 92-95; rtd 95; Perm to Offic *Sarum* from 95. *Devan Haye, North Road, Sherborne DT9 3BJ* Tel (01935) 812018

GLENDALOUGH, Archdeacon of. *See* SWANN, The Ven Edgar John

GLENFIELD, Samuel Ferran. b 54. QUB BA76 TCD MLitt90 MA94 Ox Univ MTh99. Wycliffe Hall Ox 88. **d** 91 **p** 92. C Douglas Union w Frankfield *C, C & R* 91-94; I Rathcooney Union 94-96; I Kill *D & G* from 96. *The Rectory, Kill o' the Grange, Blackrock, Co Dublin, Irish Republic* Tel (00353) (1) 280 1721 *or* tel and fax 289 6442

GLENNON, James Joseph. b 37. St Mary's Coll Strawberry Hill TCert69 BA70. Franciscan Ho of Studies. **d** 62 **p** 63. C S Woodford *Chelmsf* 64-65; NSM Hadleigh w Layham and Shelley *St E* 88-95; C Hadleigh 95-02; rtd 02; Perm to Offic *St E* from 02. *21 Carlford Court, 112 Parliament Road, Ipswich IP4 5EL* Tel (01473) 721072

GLOUCESTER, Archdeacon of. *See* SIDAWAY, The Ven Geoffrey Harold

GLOUCESTER, Bishop of. *See* PERHAM, The Rt Revd Michael Francis

GLOUCESTER, Dean of. *See* BURY, The Very Revd Nicholas Ayles Stillingfleet

GLOVER, Alan. b 47. SW Minl Tr Course DTPS99. **d** 99 **p** 00. NSM Bideford, Northam, Westward Ho, Appledore etc *Ex* from 99. *West Fordlands, Heywood Road, Northam, Bideford EX39 3QA* Tel (01237) 479542

GLOVER, David Charles. b 66. St Jo Coll Dur BA87 St Jo Coll Cam MPhil91. Ridley Hall Cam 87. **d** 90 **p** 91. C Wath-upon-Dearne w Adwick-upon-Dearne *Sheff* 90-92; Chapl Hatf Coll Dur 92-00; P-in-c Dur St Marg *Dur* 95-00; R Dur St Marg and Neville's Cross St Jo from 00. *St Margaret's Rectory, South Street, Durham DH1 4QP* Tel 0191-384 3623 Mobile 07932-683745 E-mail david.glover17@btinternet.com

GLOVER, Mrs Diana Mary. b 50. Kent Univ BA73 MA75. St Alb and Ox Min Course. **d** 01 **p** 02. C Aylesbury w Bierton and Hulcott *Ox* 01-05; P-in-c Amersham on the Hill from 05. *The Vicarage, 70 Sycamore Road, Amersham HP6 5DR* Tel (01494) 727553 E-mail diana.glover@btinternet.com

GLOVER, Elisabeth Ann. b 53. Univ Coll Ches BTh99. **d** 98 **p** 99. NSM Thurstaston *Ches* 98-99; C Stockton Heath 00-04; V Eastham from 04. *The Vicarage, 29 Ferry Road, Eastham, Wirral CH62 0AJ* Tel 0151-327 2182 E-mail glover01@btinternet.com

GLOVER, Henry Arthur. b 32. Lon Univ BSc58. Wycliffe Hall Ox 59. **d** 61 **p** 62. C Fareham St Jo *Portsm* 61-63; C Liv Our Lady and St Nic *Liv* 63-64. *15 Thorncliffe Road, Wallasey CH44 3AA* Tel 0151-638 6018

GLOVER, Janet Mary. b 58. Natal Univ BSc79 UED80. EAMTC 98. **d** 01 **p** 02. NSM Cambridge St Phil *Ely* 01-04; NSM Histon from 04; NSM Impington from 04. *35 Garlic Row, Cambridge CB5 8HW* Tel (01223) 563585 E-mail janet.glover@ntlworld.com

GLOVER, John. b 48. Kelham Th Coll 67. **d** 71 **p** 72. C Foley Park *Worc* 71-75; TV Sutton *Liv* 75-79; P-in-c Churchill w Blakedown *Worc* 79-84; R 84-87; R Belbroughton w Fairfield and Clent 87-91; Chapl Children's Family Trust from 91; NSM Flint *St As* 92-93; R Halkyn w Caerfallwch w Rhesycae 93-97; V Rhyl w St Ann from 97. *The Vicarage, 31 Bath Street, Rhyl LL18 3LU* Tel (01745) 353732

GLOVER, Mrs Judith Rosalind. b 53. NEOC DipHE95. **d** 95 **p** 96. C Glendale Gp *Newc* 95-99; P-in-c Alwinton w Holystone and Alnham 99-04; R Upper Coquetdale from 04. *The Vicarage, Alwinton, Morpeth NE65 7BE* Tel (01669) 650203 E-mail judy@alwinton.net

GLOVER, Michael John Myers. b 28. CEng MICE MSAICE Bradf Tech Coll Dip Civil Engineering 48 Lon Univ BSc48. Cuddesdon Coll 54. **d** 56 **p** 57. C Leic St Pet *Leic* 56-60; S Africa 60-73 and from 86; TR Northampton Em *Pet* 74-86; Bp's Chapl E Area Northn 73-74; rtd 93. *PO Box 447, Nongoma, 3950 South Africa* Tel (0027) (358) 310044 Fax 310457

GLOVER, Richard John. b 47. Nottm Univ BTh77. Linc Th Coll 73. **d** 77 **p** 78. C Barrow St Geo w St Luke *Carl* 77-79; C Netherton 79-80; P-in-c Addingham 80-83; P-in-c Edenhall w Langwathby and Culgaith 80-83; V Addingham, Edenhall, Langwathby and Culgaith 83-84; V Bishops Hull *B & W* 84-89; V Shilbottle *Newc* 89-96; V Whittingham and Edlingham w Bolton Chapel 96-00; P-in-c Barton, Pooley Bridge and Martindale *Carl* 00-04; Dioc Adv for Spiritual Direction and Healing 00-04; R Lower Swale *Ripon* from 04. *The Rectory, Manor Lane, Ainderby Steeple, Northallerton DL7 9PY* Tel (01609) 773346 E-mail richard@glov.fsnet.co.uk

GLYN-JONES, Alun. b 38. JP. CCC Cam BA59 MA63. Bps' Coll Cheshunt 60. **d** 61 **p** 62. C Portsea St Mary *Portsm* 61-65; Chapl Hampton Sch Middx 65-76; Hd Master Abp Tenison Gr Sch Croydon 76-88; V Twickenham St Mary *Lon* 88-01; rtd 01; Perm to Offic *B & W*; *Bris*; *Sarum* and *Eur* from 01. *10 Fitzmaurice Close, Bradford-on-Avon BA15 1UE* Tel (01225) 866874

GLYNN, Simon Adrian. b 59. Van Mildert Coll Dur BSc80 Univ Coll Ches BTh99. N Ord Course 96. **d** 99 **p** 00. NSM Carr Mill *Liv* 99-04; C Burscough Bridge from 04. *3 Thistle Court, Burscough, Ormskirk L40 4AW* Tel (01704) 896040 E-mail simon@simonglynn.plus.com

GOALBY, George Christian. b 55. Leeds Univ BA77. St Jo Coll Nottm DPS81. **d** 81 **p** 82. C Wakef St Andr and St Mary *Wakef* 81-84; Asst Chapl HM Pris Wakef 84-85; Chapl HM Youth Cust Cen Deerbolt 85-87; Chapl HM Pris Frankland 87-89; V Swinderby *Linc* from 89. *All Saints' Vicarage, 27 Station Road, Swinderby, Lincoln LN6 9LY* Tel and fax (01522) 868430 E-mail family.goalby@virgin.net

GOATCHER, Mrs Sara Jacoba Helena. b 46. Oak Hill NSM Course 86. **d** 89 **p** 94. NSM S Croydon Em *S'wark* 89-95; C 95-96; R Sutton St Nic from 96. *The Rectory, 34 Robin Hood Lane, Sutton SM1 2RG* Tel (020) 8642 3499 E-mail sara@richardandsara.demon.co.uk

GOATER, Michael Robert. b 46. York Univ BA MA. N Ord Course 89. **d** 92 **p** 93. C Norton *Sheff* 92-94; V Endcliffe 94-99;

Chapl Sheff Ind Miss 94-95; Assoc Chapl Sheff Hallam Univ 95-99; Asst Post-Ord Tr Officer 95-99; Dioc Voc Officer 96-99; C Stratford-upon-Avon, Luddington etc *Cov* 99-02; P-in-c Gt Shelford *Ely* from 02; RD Shelford from 04. *The Vicarage, 12 Church Street, Great Shelford, Cambridge CB2 5EL* Tel (01223) 843654 *or* 843274
E-mail mickthevic@btopenworld.com

GOBBETT, Michael George Timothy. b 64. St Chad's Coll Dur BSc86. St Steph Ho Ox BA89 MA98. **d** 90 **p** 91. C Hartlepool St Aid *Dur* 90-94; P-in-c Norton St Mich 94-95; V from 95. *St Michael's Vicarage, 13 Imperial Avenue, Norton, Stockton-on-Tees TS20 2EW* Tel (01642) 553984
E-mail michael@mgobbett.freeserve.co.uk

GOBEY, Ian Clifford. b 48. WEMTC 94. **d** 96 **p** 97. NSM Whiteshill and Randwick *Glouc* 96-00; NSM The Edge, Pitchcombe, Harescombe and Brookthorpe 00-01; NSM Painswick, Sheepscombe, Cranham, The Edge etc from 01. *The Rectory, Edge, Stroud GL6 6PF* Tel (01452) 812319
E-mail ian.gobey@tesco.net

GOBLE, Christopher. b 75. Univ of Wales (Lamp) BA96. Trin Coll Bris 96. **d** 98 **p** 99. C St Jo in Bedwardine *Worc* 98-01; P-in-c Worc St Clem 01-02; R Brington w Whilton and Norton etc *Pet* from 02. *The Rectory, Main Street, Great Brington, Northampton NN7 4JB* Tel (01604) 770402
E-mail chris@spencerbenefice.freeserve.co.uk

GOBLE, Clifford David. b 41. Oak Hill Th Coll 69. **d** 72 **p** 73. C Erith St Paul *Roch* 72-76; C Tunbridge Wells St Jas 76-79; R Southfleet 79-05; RD Gravesend 94-05; Hon Can Roch Cathl 99-05; rtd 05. *57 Bishops Way, Canterbury CT2 8DS* Tel (01227) 784502

GOBLE (née DUNN), Mrs Sharon Louise. b 71. Univ of Wales (Swansea) BA93 Fitzw Coll Cam BA97. Ridley Hall Cam CTM98. **d** 98 **p** 99. C Malpas *Mon* 98-01; C Cyncoed 01-02; R Heyford w Stowe Nine Churches and Flore etc *Pet* 02-04; Perm to Offic from 04. *The Rectory, Main Street, Great Brington, Northampton NN7 4JB* Tel (01604) 770402
E-mail rev@dunnsl.freeserve.co.uk

GODBER, Canon Francis Giles. b 48. Open Univ BA88. Ridley Hall Cam 72. **d** 75 **p** 76. C Blackheath *Birm* 75-78; C Wolverhampton St Matt *Lich* 78-80; TV Washfield, Stoodleigh, Withleigh etc *Ex* 80-85; R Shenley and Loughton *Ox* 85-88; TR Watling Valley 88-96; Chapl Heatherwood and Wexham Park Hosp NHS Trust 96-00; P-in-c Geddington w Weekley *Pet* from 00; Dioc Ecum Officer from 00; Can Pet Cathl from 03. *The Vicarage, 25 West Street, Geddington, Kettering NN14 1BD* Tel (01536) 742200 E-mail gilbar@telco4u.net

GODDARD, Andrew John. b 67. St Jo Coll Ox BA88 MA93 DPhil96. Cranmer Hall Dur 94. **d** 96 **p** 97. C Cogges and S Leigh *Ox* 96-99; Tutor Wycliffe Hall Ox from 99. *Wycliffe Hall, 54 Banbury Road, Oxford OX2 6PW* Tel (01865) 274200
E-mail andrew.goddard@wycliffe.ox.ac.uk

GODDARD, Canon Charles Douglas James. b 47. CITC 67. **d** 70 **p** 71. C Orangefield *D & D* 70-73; C Stormont 73-75; Miss to Seafarers from 75; Sen Chapl and Sec N Ireland from 77; Can Belf Cathl from 05. *7 Abercorn Drive, Carnreagh Road, Hillsborough BT26 6LB* Tel (028) 9268 3592 *or* 9075 1131
E-mail flying@angel.dnet.co.uk

GODDARD, Christopher. b 45. Sarum & Wells Th Coll 79. **d** 81 **p** 82. C Whitehaven *Carl* 81-83; C Barrow St Geo w St Luke 83-85; P-in-c Hayton St Mary 85-90; V Brigham 90-98; V Mosser 90-98; Perm to Offic 00-03; Hon C Cockermouth w Embleton and Wythop 03-05; TV from 05. *The Vicarage, 14 Harrot Hill, Cockermouth CA13 0BL* Tel (01900) 824383
E-mail chris.goddard@parishofcockermouth.org.uk

GODDARD, Derek George. b 38. St Martin's Coll Lanc BA97 CEng FIMechE FIMarE FCMI. Cranmer Hall Dur 94 Carl and Blackb Dioc Tr Inst DipTh95. **d** 97 **p** 98. NSM Windermere St Mary and Troutbeck *Carl* 97-01; P-in-c Leven Valley from 01. *The Vicarage, Haverthwaite, Ulverston LA12 8AJ* Tel (01539) 531476 E-mail d.d.goddard@talk21.com

GODDARD, Mrs Doris. b 48. St Mary's Coll Twickenham CertEd70 Open Univ BA80. S'wark Ord Course 93. **d** 96 **p** 97. Chapl John Nightingale Sch W Molesley 96-00; NSM Addlestone *Guildf* 96-98; NSM Botleys and Lyne 98-04; NSM Long Cross 98-04; NSM Chertsey, Lyne and Longcross 04-05; NSM Blackdown *B & W* from 05. *Address temp unknown*
E-mail jimgd@strodes.edex.co.uk

GODDARD, Douglas. *See* GODDARD, Canon Charles Douglas James

GODDARD, Mrs Elaine Clare. b 53. K Alfred's Coll Win CertEd78. WEMTC 96. **d** 99 **p** 00. C Leominster *Heref* 99-04; P-in-c St Weonards w Orcop, Garway, Tretire etc from 04. *The Vicarage, Mount Way, St Weonards, Hereford HR2 8NN* Tel (01981) 580307

GODDARD, Elisabeth Ann. b 64. St Hugh's Coll Ox BA89 MA99. Cranmer Hall Dur 94. **d** 96 **p** 97. C Cogges and S Leigh *Ox* 96-99; Chapl Jes Coll Ox 99-04; Tutor Wycliffe Hall Ox from 04; Hon C Ox St Andr *Ox* from 04. *Wycliffe Hall, 54 Banbury Road, Oxford OX2 6PW* Tel (01865) 274200

GODDARD, Canon Frederick Paul Preston. b 24. Jes Coll Cam BA49 MA51. Westcott Ho Cam 49. **d** 51 **p** 52. C Bp's Hatfield *St Alb* 51-57; New Zealand 57-61; V Abbots Langley *St Alb* 61-68; Chapl Yeatman and Coldharbour Hosp Dorset 69-87; V Sherborne w Castleton and Lillington *Sarum* 69-87; RD Sherborne 73-77; Can and Preb Sarum Cathl 75-87; rtd 87; Perm to Offic *Truro* from 92. *56 West Street, Polruan, Fowey PL23 1PL* Tel (01726) 870339

GODDARD, Giles William. b 62. Clare Coll Cam MA84. S'wark Ord Course 92. **d** 95 **p** 96. C N Dulwich St Faith *S'wark* 95-98; TR Walworth St Pet from 98; RD S'wark and Newington from 02. *St Peter's Rectory, Liverpool Grove, London SE17 2HH* Tel (020) 7703 3139 E-mail giles.goddard@virgin.net

GODDARD, Canon Harold Frederick. b 42. Keble Coll Ox BA63 MA69 DipTh65. Cuddesdon Coll 64. **d** 66 **p** 67. C Birm St Pet *Birm* 66-70; Chapl Dudley Road Hosp Birm 66-70; C Alverstoke *Portsm* 70-72; Chapl Gosport Cottage Hosp Portsm 70-72; P-in-c Portsea St Geo CD 72-76; Chapl Portsm Cathl 73-76; P-in-c Stoke Prior *Worc* 76-78; P-in-c Wychbold and Upton Warren 77-78; R Stoke Prior, Wychbold and Upton Warren 78-80; Chapl Forelands Orthopaedic Hosp Worc 77-80; Chapl R Marsden Hosp Lon and Surrey 80-83; R Martley and Wichenford *Worc* 83-88; P-in-c Knightwick w Doddenham, Broadwas and Cotheridge 85-88; R Martley and Wichenford, Knightwick etc 89-90; Bp's Adv on Min of Healing 84-99; Chapl St Rich Hospice Worc 87-94; RD Martley and Worc W *Worc* 88-90; Chapl Kidderminster Gen Hosp 90-92; P-in-c Hallow *Worc* 91-92; P-in-c Sedgeberrow w Hinton-on-the-Green 92-00; Chapl Evesham Community Hosp Worc 93-00; Co-ord Chapl Worcs Community Healthcare NHS Trust 97-00; Co-ord W Midl Healing Advisers 94-99; RD Evesham *Worc* 97-00; TR Kidderminster St Jo and H Innocents from 00; Hon Can Worc Cathl from 03. *The Vicarage, 9 Sutton Park Road, Kidderminster DY11 6LE* Tel and fax (01562) 822186 *or* 751914 Mobile 07768-106287 E-mail h.goddard@easicom.com

GODDARD, John David. b 42. Guy's Hosp Medical Sch MB, BS64 MRCP73. **d** 03 **p** 04. OLM Morden *S'wark* from 03. *58 Queen Mary Avenue, Morden SM4 4JR* Tel (020) 8540 5082
E-mail jdg13@blueyonder.co.uk

✠**GODDARD, The Rt Revd John William.** b 47. St Chad's Coll Dur BA69. **d** 70 **p** 71 **c** 00. C S Bank *York* 70-74; C Cayton w Eastfield 74-75; V Middlesbrough Ascension 75-82; RD Middlesbrough 81-87; V Middlesbrough All SS 82-88; Can and Preb York Minster 87-88; Vice-Prin Edin Th Coll 88-92; TR Ribbleton *Blackb* 92-00; Suff Bp Burnley from 00; Bp's Adv on Hosp Chapls from 01. *Dean House, 449 Padiham Road, Burnley BB12 6TE* Tel (01282) 470360 Fax 470361
E-mail bishop.burnley@ntlworld.com

GODDARD, Mrs Margaret. **d** 01 **p** 02. NSM Cockermouth w Embleton and Wythop *Carl* from 01. *The Vicarage, 14 Harrot Hill, Cockermouth CA13 0BL* Tel (01900) 824383 *or* 826151

GODDARD, Ms Marion. b 54. Sarum & Wells Th Coll 87. **d** 89 **p** 94. Par Dn Lewisham St Swithun *S'wark* 89-94; C 94-95; Chapl Brook Gen Hosp Lon 95-96; TV Thamesmead *S'wark* 96-04; rtd 04. *1 Hollows Close, Salisbury SP2 8JU* Tel (01722) 338562

GODDARD, Matthew Francis. b 45. Kelham Th Coll 65. **d** 69 **p** 70. C Mansfield St Mark *S'well* 69-72; C Northolt Park St Barn *Lon* 72-78; P-in-c Acton Green St Pet 78-87; R Norwood St Mary 87-96. *27 Hounslow Avenue, Hounslow TW3 2DZ* Tel (020) 8230 6591

GODDARD, Mrs Pamela Gay. b 53. LSE BSc(Econ)74 CQSW77. St Alb and Ox Min Course 95 EAMTC 97. **d** 98 **p** 99. C New Catton St Luke w St Aug *Nor* 98-03; Perm to Offic 03-05. *The Rectory, 1 St Michael's Close, Poole BH15 4QT* Tel (01202) 674878 E-mail pamgoddard@ic24.net

GODDARD, Mrs Rosemary Joy. b 48. Philippa Fawcett Coll CertEd69. EAMTC 00. **d** 03 **p** 04. C Linc St Nic w St Jo Newport *Linc* from 03. *14 Nettleham Close, Lincoln LN2 1SJ* Tel (01522) 511335 Mobile 07740-203149
E-mail rosemaryjg@aol.com

GODDARD, Stuart David. b 53. Cen Sch of Art Lon BA76 Middx Poly PGCE82. Trin Coll Bris 91. **d** 93 **p** 94. C Watling Valley *Ox* 93-97; P-in-c Bowthorpe *Nor* 97-00; TV 00-05; P-in-c Hamworthy *Sarum* from 05. *The Rectory, 1 St Michael's Close, Poole BH15 4QT* Tel (01202) 674878
E-mail stuart@goddard7.fsbusiness.co.uk

GODDARD, Canon Sydney Thomas. b 16. St Aid Birkenhead 46. **d** 49 **p** 50. C Ravenhead *Liv* 49-52; C St Helens St Helen 52-55; V Widnes St Ambrose 55-59; Warden World Friendship Ho 59-83; Chapl Liv Maternity Hosp 59-81; V Liv St Sav *Liv* 59-71; Hon Can Liv Cathl 69-83; rtd 83; Perm to Offic *Ban* from 84. *Ynys Thomas, Bronaber, Trawsfynydd, Blaenau Ffestiniog LL41 4UR* Tel (01766) 540413

GODDEN, Peter David. b 47. Leeds Univ BA69 MA04 ARCO70. Linc Th Coll 85. **d** 87 **p** 88. C Bearsted w Thurnham *Cant* 87-90; C Hykeham *Linc* 90-91; Hon PV Linc Cathl 90-99; TV Hykeham 91-95; P-in-c Linc St Pet-at-Gowts and St Andr 95-99; R Armthorpe *Sheff* 99-00; R Owmby Gp *Linc* from 00. *The*

Rectory, Owmby Cliff Road, Owmby-by-Spital, Market Rasen LN8 2HL Tel and fax (01673) 878275 E-mail peter@owmbygroup.co.uk

GODDEN, Timothy Richard James. b 62. Univ Coll Lon BA84. St Jo Coll Nottm 89. **d** 89 **p** 90. C Tulse Hill H Trin and St Matthias *S'wark* 89-93; TV Horsham *Chich* 93-01; TR Bishopsworth and Bedminster Down *Bris* from 01. *St Peter's Vicarage, 61 Fernsteed Road, Bristol BS13 8HE* Tel and fax 0117-964 2734 E-mail tim@cgodden.fsnet.co.uk

GODECK, John William George. b 30. Chich Th Coll 57. **d** 60 **p** 61. C Wadhurst *Chich* 60-62; C Tidebrook 60-62; C Eastbourne 62-63; R Bondleigh *Ex* 63-78; R Zeal Monachorum 63-78; P-in-c Broadwoodkelly 65-67; R 68-78; R Dunchideock and Shillingford St George w Ide 78-96; RD Kenn 83-89; rtd 96; Perm to Offic *Ex* from 96. *Boxgrove, 6 Barley Lane, Exeter EX4 1TE* Tel (01392) 424224

GODFREY, Ann Veronica. *See* MacKEITH, Mrs Ann Veronica

GODFREY, Canon Brian Ernest Searles. b 37. Lon Univ BSc60 MSc63 PhD72. S'wark Ord Course 78. **d** 81 **p** 82. NSM Hayes *Roch* 81-86; C 86-88; R Kingsdown 88-93; R Sundridge w Ide Hill 93-02; RD Sevenoaks 95-00; Hon Can Roch Cathl from 99; rtd 02; Perm to Offic *Sarum* from 03. *Rowans, Kingcombe Road, Toller Porcorum, Dorchester DT2 0DG* Tel (01300) 320833 E-mail godfrey@centrenet.co.uk

GODFREY, David Samuel George. b 35. CITC 64. **d** 66 **p** 67. C Londonderry Ch Ch *D & R* 66-68; I Tomregan w Drumlane *K, E & A* 68-72; I Cloonclare 72-79; I Templebreedy *C, C & R* 79-85; I Bray *D & G* 85-97; Can Ch Ch Cathl Dublin 95-97; Dean Kilmore *K, E & A* 97-04; I Kilmore w Ballintemple 97-04; Preb Mulhuddart St Patr Cathl Dublin 01-04; rtd 04. *37 Earlsfort Meadows, Earlsfort, Lucan, Co Dublin, Irish Republic* Tel (00353) 86-238 9686 E-mail dgodfrey@iol.ie

GODFREY, Edward Colin. b 30. Wells Th Coll 63. **d** 65 **p** 66. C Lyndhurst and Emery Down *Win* 65-69; C Paignton Ch Ch *Ex* 69-73; V Stockland w Dalwood 73-77; Chapl HM Pris Man 77-78; Chapl HM Pris Cant 78-83; Chapl HM Pris Highpoint 83-85 and 90-95; Chapl HM YOI Glen Parva 85-90; rtd 95; Perm to Offic *St E* from 95. *11 De Burgh Place, Clare, Sudbury CO10 8QL* Tel (01787) 277690

✠**GODFREY, The Rt Revd Harold William.** b 48. AKC71. St Aug Coll Cant 71. **d** 72 **p** 73 **c** 87. C Warsop *S'well* 72-75; TV Hucknall Torkard 75-86; Dioc Ecum Officer 81-82; USPG from 86; R and Adn Montevideo and Can Buenos Aires 86-88; Asst Bp Argentina and Uruguay 87-88; Bp Uruguay 88-98; Bp Peru from 98. *Calle Alcal 336, Urb la Castellana, Santiago de Surco, Lima 33, Peru* Tel (0051) (1) 422 9160 *or* 448 4855 Fax as telephone E-mail wgodfrey@amauta.rcp.net.pe

GODFREY, Ian. b 56. **d** 01 **p** 02. NSM Mill Hill Jo Keble Ch *Lon* from 01. *Sirocco, 40 Hillside Grove, London NW7 2LR* Tel (020) 8959 5123 Fax 8959 1434 E-mail igodfrey@ukonline.co.uk

GODFREY, Jennifer Olwen. **d** 02 **p** 03. C Lasswade *Edin* 02-03; NSM from 03; C Dalkeith 02-03; NSM from 03. *131 Newbattle Abbey Crescent, Dalkeith EH22 3LP* Tel 0131-660 6145 Mobile 07720-959028 E-mail jennie@godfrey25.freeserve.co.uk

GODFREY, John Frederick. b 31. Lon Univ LLB53 AKC54 Solicitor 57. Cuddesdon Coll 59. **d** 61 **p** 62. C Battersea St Luke *S'wark* 61-65; Min Reigate St Phil CD 65-72; Public Preacher *St Alb* 73-03; Perm to Offic from 03. *3 Davidge Place, Knotty Green, Beaconsfield HP9 2SR* Tel (01494) 689925 Fax 672930

GODFREY, Matthew Fenton. b 69. Univ Coll Dur BA91 K Coll Lon MA94. Ripon Coll Cuddesdon MTh04. **d** 04 **p** 05. C Bodmin w Lanhydrock and Lanivet *Truro* from 04. *23 Tanwood View, Bodmin PL31 2PN* Tel (01208) 75847 E-mail nitrogen_narcosis@hotmail.com

GODFREY, Michael. b 49. K Coll Lon BD70 AKC72. **d** 72 **p** 73. C Birtley *Dur* 72-75; Ind Chapl 76-79; Ind Chapl *Lich* 79-93; TV Bilston St Mary 79; TV Bilston 80-86; TV Wolverhampton 86-93; Preb Lich Cathl 87-93; Perm to Offic *Worc* from 04. *2 Beechcombe Close, Pershore WR10 1PW* Tel (01386) 555612

GODFREY, Michael James. b 50. Sheff Univ BEd77. St Jo Coll Nottm 79. **d** 82 **p** 83. C Walton H Trin *Ox* 82-86; C Chadderton Ch Ch *Man* 86-91; V Woodlands *Sheff* 91-03; V Wythall *Birm* from 03. *15 Hawthorne Drive, Hollywood, Birmingham B47 5QT* Tel 0121-430 2775 E-mail mikegodfrey@btinternet.com

GODFREY, Myles. *See* GODFREY, Rumley Myles

GODFREY, Nigel Philip. b 51. Ripon Coll Cuddesdon BA78 MA84 Lon Guildhall Univ MBA00 Bris Poly Dip Town Planning73 S Bank Univ DMS98 MRTPI76. Ripon Coll Cuddesdon 77. **d** 79 **p** 80. C Kennington St Jo w St Jas *S'wark* 79-89; Community of Ch the Servant 84-93; V Brixton Road Ch Ch *S'wark* 89-01; Prin OLM Scheme from 01; Chapl S'wark Cathl from 02. *47 Curtis Way, London SE1 5XW* Tel (020) 7564 9252 *or* 7378 7506 Fax 7403 6497 E-mail nigel.godfrey@southwark.anglican.org

GODFREY, Mrs Patricia Ann. b 54. SEITE 01. **d** 04 **p** 05. NSM Dover St Mary *Cant* from 04. *8 Longfield Road, Dover CT17 9QU* Tel (01304) 206019 E-mail trish@godfrey88.screaming.net

GODFREY (née ROGERS), Mrs Pauline Ann. b 58. LMH Ox BA79 MA83 Ox Univ Inst of Educn PGCE80. S Dios Minl Tr Scheme 89. **d** 92 **p** 94. NSM Headley All SS *Guildf* 92-96; C 96-99; Past Tutor Dioc Min Course from 96; P-in-c Wyke 99-01; V from 01. *Wyke Vicarage, Guildford Road, Normandy, Guildford GU3 2DA* Tel (01483) 811332 E-mail pag@yerfdog1.screaming.net

GODFREY, Rumley Myles. b 48. S'wark Ord Course. **d** 83 **p** 84. NSM Dorchester *Ox* from 83. *The Old Malthouse, Warborough OX10 7DY* Tel (01865) 858627 E-mail myles@warborough.fsnet.co.uk

GODFREY, Mrs Sarah Joy. b 64. Southn Univ BSc85 Bath Univ PGCE86. STETS 02. **d** 05. NSM Puddletown, Tolpuddle and Milborne w Dewlish *Sarum* from 05. *Bankfield House, Pound Lane, Dewlish, Dorchester DT2 7LZ* Tel (01258) 839067 E-mail docandrew@tiscali.co.uk

GODFREY, Simon Henry Martin. b 55. TD00. K Coll Lon BD80 AKC80. St Steph Ho Ox 80. **d** 81 **p** 82. C Kettering SS Pet and Paul *Pet* 81-84; R Crick and Yelvertoft w Clay Coton and Lilbourne 84-89; V Northampton All SS w St Kath 89-98; R Northampton All SS w St Kath and St Pet from 98. *All Saints' Rectory, 6 Albion Place, Northampton NN1 1UD* Tel (01604) 621854 *or* tel and fax 632194 E-mail simongodfrey@breathemail.net

GODFREY, Stanley William. b 24. CEng MIEE67. Qu Coll Birm 71. **d** 74 **p** 74. C Sutton Coldfield St Chad *Birm* 74-78; Hon C Handsworth St Andr 78-86; Hon C Worc City St Paul and Old St Martin etc *Worc* 86-89; Hon C Droitwich Spa 89-96; Perm to Offic from 96. *2 The Pippins, Eckington, Pershore WR10 3PY* Tel (01386) 751184

GODIN, Mrs Mary Louise. b 42. SRN64 QN66. Oak Hill NSM Course 89. **d** 92 **p** 94. NSM Surbiton Hill Ch Ch *S'wark* 92-97; Chapl Kingston and Distr Community NHS Trust 97-01; Team Chapl SW Lon and St George's Mental Health NHS Trust 01-03; Chapl Taunton and Somerset NHS Trust from 03. *Taunton and Somerset NHS Trust, Musgrove Park Hospital, Taunton TA1 5DA* Tel (01823) 333444 ext 2515 E-mail mary.godin@fsmail.net

GODSALL, Andrew Paul. b 59. Birm Univ BA81. Ripon Coll Cuddesdon 86. **d** 88 **p** 89. C Gt Stanmore *Lon* 88-91; C Ealing All SS 91-94; V Hillingdon All SS 94-01; Dir of Ords Willesden Area 99-01; Bp's Dom Chapl *Ex* from 01; PV Ex Cathl from 04. *2 West Avenue, Pennsylvania, Exeter EX4 4SD* Tel (01392) 676714 *or* 272362 Fax 430923 E-mail andrew.godsall@exeter.anglican.org

GODSALL, Canon Ralph Charles. b 48. Qu Coll Cam BA71 MA75. Cuddesdon Coll 73. **d** 75 **p** 76. C Sprowston *Nor* 75-78; Chapl Trin Coll Cam 78-84; V Hebden Bridge *Wakef* 84-93; V Westmr St Steph w St Jo *Lon* 93-01; Can Res Roch Cathl *Roch* from 01. *Easter Garth, The Precinct, Rochester ME1 1SX* Tel (01634) 405265 *or* 843366 Mobile 07919-534601 Fax (01634) 401410 E-mail precentor@rochestercathedraluk.org

GODSELL, David Brian. b 40. Lon Univ BA62. Coll of Resurr Mirfield 65. **d** 67 **p** 68. C Middlesbrough All SS *York* 67-73; C Stainton-in-Cleveland 73-75; V Byker St Ant *Newc* 75-90; P-in-c Brandon *Dur* 90-94; V 94-04; V Brandon and Ushaw Moor from 04. *The Vicarage, Sawmill Lane, Brandon, Durham DH7 8NS* Tel 0191-378 0845

GODSELL, Kenneth James Rowland. b 22. Birm Univ DipTh50 Birm Coll of Educn Dip Teaching50. Qu Coll Birm 75. **d** 76 **p** 77. Sen Lect Westhill Coll of HE Birm 74-85; Hon C Selly Hill St Steph *Birm* 76-81; Hon C Selly Park St Steph and St Wulstan 81-90; rtd 90; Lic to Offic *Birm* 90-96; Perm to Offic *Worc* from 96. *The Quest, Dock Lane, Tewkesbury GL20 7LN* Tel (01684) 772469

GODSON, Alan. b 31. Ch Coll Cam BA61 MA65. Clifton Th Coll 61. **d** 63 **p** 64. C Preston All SS *Blackb* 63-66; Lic to Offic *Man* 66-69; Asst Chapl Emb Ch Paris 69; Dioc Ev *Liv* 69-01; P-in-c Edge Hill St Mary 72-78; V 78-01; rtd 01; Perm to Offic *Liv* from 01. *28 Handley Court, Aigburth, Liverpool L19 3QS* Tel 0151-427 0255

GODSON, Mark Rowland. b 61. K Coll Lon BD83 AKC83 CertEd84. Linc Th Coll 84. **d** 86 **p** 87. C Hurst Green *S'wark* 86-88; C Fawley *Win* 88-90; TV Wimborne Minster and Holt *Sarum* 90-95; P-in-c Horton and Chalbury 90-95; P-in-c Stalbridge 95-96; Chapl Forest Healthcare NHS Trust Lon 96-00; P-in-c Bicton, Montford w Shrawardine and Fitz *Lich* from 00; Chapl Shropshire Co Primary Care Trust from 01. *The Rectory, 15 Brookside, Bicton, Shrewsbury SY3 8EP* Tel (01743) 851306 *or* 261000 E-mail sparky15@ntlworld.com

GODWIN, Canon David Harold. b 45. Kelham Th Coll 67. **d** 71 **p** 72. C Camberwell St Phil and St Mark *S'wark* 71-75; Asst Chapl The Lon Hosp (Whitechapel) 75-79; Chapl R E Sussex Hosp Hastings 79-86; Chapl Over Hosp Glouc 86-92; Chapl Glos R Hosp 86-94; Chapl Glos R Hosp NHS Trust 94-02; Chapl Glos Hosps NHS Trust 02-05; Hon Can Glouc Cathl 03-05; rtd 05; Perm to Offic *Glouc* from 05. *Mews Two, Wallsworth Hall, Sandhurst Lane, Sandhurst, Gloucester GL2 9PA* Tel (01452) 730435 E-mail davidhgodwin@hotmail.co.uk

GODWIN, Canon Michael Francis Harold. b 35. Nottm Univ BSc57. Ely Th Coll 59. **d** 61 **p** 62. C Farnborough *Guildf* 61-65; V Epsom St Barn 66-85; V Bramley and Grafham 85-98; Hon Can Guildf Cathl 89-98; rtd 00. *14 Lemmington Way, Horsham RH12 5JG* Tel (01403) 273411

GOFF, Philip Francis Michael. b 52. K Coll Lon BD73 AKC73 FBS00. St Aug Coll Cant 74. **d** 75 **p** 76. C Ruislip St Martin *Lon* 75-79; Chapl Aldenham Sch Herts 79-82; V Tokyngton St Mich *Lon* 82-89; In RC Ch 89-91; Primary Care Cllr NHS 91-98; Perm to Offic *Lon* 99-00; Chapl to Bp Edmonton 00-04; P-in-c Highgate St Aug from 04. *24 Redhill Street, London NW1 4DQ* Tel (020) 7388 0580 Mobile 07768-920506 E-mail phildress@blueyonder.co.uk

GOFTON, Canon William Alder. b 31. Dur Univ BA54. Coll of Resurr Mirfield 59. **d** 61 **p** 62. C Benwell St Aid *Newc* 61-64; C N Gosforth 64-69; V Seaton Hirst 69-77; V Newc H Cross 77-89; RD Newc W 85-89; Hon Can Newc Cathl 88-96; R Bolam w Whalton and Hartburn w Meldon 89-96; P-in-c Nether Witton 89-95; V 95-96; Chapl Kirkley Hall Coll 90-96; rtd 96; Perm to Offic *Newc* from 96. *4 Crossfell, Ponteland, Newcastle upon Tyne NE20 9EA* Tel (01661) 820344 E-mail aggofton@yahoo.co.uk

GOGGIN, Philip Frederick de Jean. b 46. **d** 05. NSM Sandbach Heath w Wheelock *Ches* from 05. *Hillcrest House, 4 Valley Road, Crewe CW2 8JU* E-mail p.f.goggin@mmu.ac.uk

GOLBOURNE, Winston George. b 30. Univ of W Indies BA53. Virginia Th Sem STM69 Sarum & Wells Th Coll 71. **d** 73 **p** 74. C Bitterne Park *Win* 73-76; Jamaica 76-79; C Handsworth St Andr *Birm* 79-83; V Perry Hill St Geo *S'wark* 83-00; rtd 00; Perm to Offic *Roch* and *S'wark* from 00. *17 Bromley College, London Road, Bromley BR1 1PE*

GOLD, Guy Alastair Whitmore. b 16. TD50. Trin Coll Cam BA38 MA48. Qu Coll Birm 55. **d** 55 **p** 56. C Prittlewell St Pet *Chelmsf* 55-57; Bp's Dom Chapl 58-61; R Wickham Bishops 62-69; R Hasketon *St E* 69-76; rtd 76; Perm to Offic *St E* 76-89. *Grove Court, Beech Way, Woodbridge IP12 4BW* Tel (01394) 383277

GOLDENBERG, Ralph Maurice. b 45. City Univ FBCO67 FBOA67. Trin Coll Bris DipHE90. **d** 90 **p** 91. C Kinson *Sarum* 90-93; C Edgware *Lon* 93-97; TV Roxeth 97-01; V Bayston Hill *Lich* from 01. *The Vicarage, 42 Eric Lock Road West, Bayston Hill, Shrewsbury SY3 0QA* Tel (01743) 872164 E-mail rgoldenberg@btopenworld.com

GOLDER, Rebecca Marie. *See* ROGERS, Mrs Rebecca Marie

GOLDIE, James Stuart. b 46. Edin Univ BTh73 BEd73. ALCD69. **d** 69 **p** 70. C Blackpool St Paul *Blackb* 69-70; C Gt Sankey *Liv* 70-73; Asst Chapl Greystone Heath Sch 70-73; Chapl Kilmarnock Academy 73-75; V Flixton St Jo *Man* 75-78; Chapl Friars Sch Man 75-78; V Skelmersdale St Paul *Liv* 78-80; Chapl Trin Sch Liv 78-80; Lect Man Bible Coll and Dir Man City Miss 80-83; Chapl Westbrook Hay Sch Hemel Hempstead 83-89; V Pennington w Lindal and Marton *Carl* 89-90; Chapl Bp Wand Sch *Lon* 90-95; Chapl Queenswood Sch Herts 96-97; Hd Master Westcliff Prep Sch 97-03; V Red Sea Area Egypt from 04; Prin El Gouna Internat Sch from 04. *23 Ffordd Naddyn, Glan Conway, Colwyn Bay LL28 4NH* Tel (01924) 892254

GOLDIE, Katrina Ruth. *See* SCOTT, Katrina Ruth

GOLDING, Neil Christopher. b 47. Warwick Univ BA69. S'wark Ord Course 92. **d** 95 **p** 96. C Mitcham Ascension *S'wark* 95-00; P-in-c Croydon Woodside from 00. *St Luke's Vicarage, Portland Road, London SE25 4RB* Tel (020) 8654 9841 Fax as telephone E-mail rev_neil@btopenworld.com

GOLDING, Piers Edwin Hugh. b 26. RD76. St Aug Coll Cant 48 Edin Th Coll 50. **d** 53 **p** 54. C Guildf Ch Ch *Guildf* 53-55; C Enfield St Andr *Lon* 55-58; Chapl RN 58-62; Chapl RNR 62-93; V S Bermondsey St Aug *S'wark* 62-93; rtd 93; Perm to Offic *St E* and *S'wark* from 93. *6 White Lion House, Broad Street, Eye IP23 7AF* Tel (01379) 871253

GOLDING, The Ven Simon Jefferies. b 46. CBE02. Brasted Place Coll 70. Linc Th Coll 72. **d** 74 **p** 75. C Wilton *York* 74-77; Chapl RN 77-97; Chapl of the Fleet 97-98 and 00-02; Adn for the RN 97-02; Dir Gen Naval Chapl Service 00-02; QHC from 97; Hon Can Gib Cathl *Eur* 98-02; rtd 02; Perm to Offic *Ripon* from 02. *Arlanza, Hornby Road, Appleton Wiske, Northallerton DL6 2AF* Tel (01609) 881185

GOLDING, Stephen. b 57. Keele Univ BA79 CertEd79 Lon Bible Coll BA86. Cant Sch of Min 93. **d** 95 **p** 96. NSM Ramsgate St Luke *Cant* 95-98; Chapl St Lawr Coll Ramsgate 95-98; Chapl Berkhamsted Colleg Sch Herts from 98. *Adelbert House, Mill Street, Berkhamsted HP4 2BA* Tel (01442) 878190 *or* 358201

GOLDINGAY, Prof John Edgar. b 42. Keble Coll Ox BA64 Nottm Univ PhD83 Lambeth DD97. Clifton Th Coll 64. **d** 66 **p** 67. C Finchley Ch Ch *Lon* 66-69; Lect St Jo Coll Nottm 70-75; Dir Studies 76-79; Registrar 79-85; Vice-Prin 85-88; Prin 88-97; Prof OT Fuller Th Sem Pasadena from 97. *111 South Orange Grove, Apartment 108, Pasadena, CA 91105, USA* Tel (001) (626) 405 0626 E-mail johngold@fuller.edu

GOLDSMITH, Brian Derek. b 36. Leeds Univ BA64. Coll of Resurr Mirfield 64. **d** 66 **p** 67. C Littlehampton St Mary *Chich* 66-69; C Guildf St Nic *Guildf* 69-73; V Aldershot St Aug 73-81; C-in-c Leigh Park St Clare CD *Portsm* 82-85; C Rowner 85-96; rtd 97; C Catherington and Clanfield *Portsm* 97-01; Perm to Offic *Win* from 98. *27 White Dirt Lane, Catherington, Waterlooville PO8 0NB* Tel (023) 9259 9462

GOLDSMITH, Christopher David. b 54. York Univ BA76 DPhil79. NTMTC 97. **d** 00 **p** 01. NSM Pitsea w Nevendon *Chelmsf* 00-04; V Warley Ch Ch and Gt Warley St Mary from 04. *Christ Church Vicarage, 79 Mount Crescent, Warley, Brentwood CM14 5DD* Tel (01277) 220428 Mobile 07981-912576 E-mail c.goldsmith@btinternet.com

GOLDSMITH, John Oliver. b 46. K Coll Lon BD69 AKC69. St Aug Coll Cant 69. **d** 70 **p** 71. C Dronfield *Derby* 70-73; C Ellesmere Port *Ches* 73-74; TV Ellesmere Port 74-81; P-in-c Pleasley *Derby* 81-87; P-in-c Pleasley Hill *S'well* 83-87; V Matlock Bank *Derby* 87-97; RD Wirksworth 92-97; P-in-c Kirk Hallam 97-01; V 01-02; P-in-c Taddington, Chelmorton and Flagg, and Monyash from 02; P-in-c Hartington, Biggin and Earl Sterndale from 02; RD Buxton from 02. *The Vicarage, Church Street, Monyash, Bakewell DE45 1JH* Tel (01629) 812234

GOLDSMITH, Lesley Anne. NTMTC 02. **d** 05. C E Ham w Upton Park St Alb *Chelmsf* from 05. *2 Norman Road, London E6 6HN* Tel (020) 8503 4734 E-mail lesley.goldsmith@btinternet.com

GOLDSMITH, Malcolm Clive. b 39. Birm Univ BSocSc60 Aston Univ MSc01. Ripon Hall Ox 60. **d** 62 **p** 63. C Balsall Heath St Paul *Birm* 62-64; Chapl Aston Univ 64-72; Bp's Adv on Ind Soc *S'well* 72-79; R Nottingham St Pet and St Jas 79-85; Gen Sec IVS 85-88; Bp's Personal Exec Asst *Bradf* 88-91; Research Fell Stirling Univ *St And* 91-94; R Edin St Cuth *Edin* 94-02; Dioc Dir of Ords 95-01; rtd 02. *34 Cumberland Street, Edinburgh EH3 6SA* Tel 0131-558 9434 Mobile 07795-122622 E-mail malcolm.goldsmith123@btopenworld.com

GOLDSMITH, Mrs Mary Louie. b 48. K Coll Lon BA70 AKC70. Qu Coll Birm 91. **d** 93 **p** 94. NSM Matlock Bank *Derby* 93-97; NSM Kirk Hallam 97-02; NSM Taddington, Chelmorton and Flagg, and Monyash from 00. *The Vicarage, Church Street, Monyash, Bakewell DE45 1JH* Tel (01629) 812234

GOLDSMITH, Mrs Pauline Anne. b 40. Linc Th Coll 82. **dss** 84 **d** 87 **p** 94. Waddington *Linc* 86-88; Par Dn 87-88; Par Dn Gt and Lt Coates w Bradley 88-94; TV 94-96; TV Kidderminster St Mary and All SS w Trimpley etc *Worc* 96-01; rtd 01; Perm to Offic *Derby* and *Sheff* from 01. *143 Ravencar Road, Eckington, Sheffield S21 4JR* Tel (01246) 430083

GOLDSMITH, Stephen. b 32. Edin Th Coll. **d** 76 **p** 77. SPCK Staff 53-97; Bookshops Regional Manager SPCK 87-97; NSM Penicuik *Edin* 76-81; NSM Linc St Nic w St Jo Newport *Linc* 81-90; NSM Gt and Lt Coates w Bradley 90-96; NSM Kidderminster St Mary and All SS w Trimpley etc *Worc* 96-01; Perm to Offic *Derby* and *Sheff* from 01. *143 Ravencar Road, Eckington, Sheffield S21 4JR* Tel (01246) 430083

GOLDSPINK, David. b 35. Open Univ BA81. Lon Coll of Div 62. **d** 65 **p** 66. C Mile Cross *Nor* 65-68; C St Austell *Truro* 68-70; TV Bramerton w Surlingham *Nor* 70-73; Min Gunton St Pet 73-75; R Mutford w Rushmere w Gisleham w N Cove w Barnby 75-81; Asst Chapl HM Pris Man 81-82; Chapl HM Youth Cust Cen Hollesley Bay Colony 82-84; Chapl HM Pris Blundeston 84-88; Perm to Offic *St E* 87-01; rtd 88; Perm to Offic *Nor* from 88. *14 Deepdale, Carlton Colville, Lowestoft NR33 8TU* Tel (01502) 537769

GOLDSTONE-CREASEY, Graham. b 51. Trent Poly BA. Cranmer Hall Dur 80. **d** 83 **p** 84. C Birstall and Wanlip *Leic* 83-87; C-in-c Wheatley Park St Paul CD *Sheff* 87-92; V Wheatley Park 92-95; P-in-c Gleadless Valley 95-98. *Address temp unknown*

GOLDSTRAW, William Henry. b 15. Lich Th Coll 60. **d** 61 **p** 62. C Stone St Mich *Lich* 61-68; V Alton 68-82; V Bradley-in-the-Moors 68-82; V Alton w Bradley-le-Moors 82-84; rtd 84; Perm to Offic *Lich* from 84. *36 The Avenue, Cheddleton, Leek ST13 7JB* Tel (01538) 360204

GOLDTHORPE, Ms Shirley. b 42. Linc Th Coll 70. **dss** 76 **d** 87 **p** 94. Thornhill Lees *Wakef* 76-78; Birkenshaw w Hunsworth 78-80; Batley St Thos 80-85; Batley All SS 80-85; Purlwell 80-92; Par Dn 87-88; Dn-in-c 88-92; Dn-in-c Horbury Junction 92-94; P-in-c 94-01; rtd 02; Perm to Offic *Wakef* from 02. *10 Orchid View, Alverthorpe, Wakefield WF2 0FG* Tel (01924) 383181 Mobile 07885-462837

GOLLEDGE, Christopher John. b 66. St Mich Coll Llan DipTh92. **d** 92 **p** 93. C Newton Nottage *Llan* 92-95; Perm to Offic *Chich* from 95. *32 Bennett Road, Brighton BN3 5JL*

GOLLEDGE, Miss Patricia Anne. b 55. Trin Coll Bris BA00. **d** 00 **p** 01. C Pontypool *Mon* 00-03; TV from 03. *The Vicarage, Freeholdland Road, Pontnewynydd, Pontypool NP4 8LW* Tel (01495) 763159

GOLLOP, Michael John. b 58. Keble Coll Ox BA81 MA85. St Mich Coll Llan BD85. **d** 85 **p** 86. C Newport St Mark *Mon* 85-87; C Bassaleg 87-91; V St Hilary Greenway 91-93; V Itton and St Arvans w Penterry and Kilgwrrwg etc from 93. *The Vicarage, St Arvans, Chepstow NP16 6EU* Tel (01291) 622064

GOLTON, Alan Victor. b 29. St Jo Coll Ox BA51 MA54 DPhil54. LNSM course 84. **d** 85 **p** 86. P-in-c Barston *Birm* 87-95; Perm to Offic 95-96; Hon C Grenoble *Eur* 97-00. *Chant du Matin, Les Michallons, 38250 St Nizier du Moucherotte, France* Tel (0033) (4) 76 53 43 77 E-mail avgolton@hotmail.com

GOMERSALL, Ian Douglass. b 56. Birm Univ BSc77 Fitzw Coll Cam BA80 MA85 Dur Univ MA94. Westcott Ho Cam 78. **d** 81 **p** 82. C Darlington St Mark w St Paul *Dur* 81-84; C Barnard Castle w Whorlton 84-86; Chapl HM YOI Deerbolt 85-90; P-in-c Cockfield *Dur* 86-88; R 88-90; Dep Chapl HM Pris Wakef 90-91; Chapl HM Pris Full Sutton 91-97; P-in-c Kexby w Wilberfoss *York* 93-97; TV Man Whitworth *Man* 97-03; P-in-c Man Victoria Park from 98; Chapl Man Univ 97-03; Hon Chapl from 03; Chapl Man Metrop Univ 97-03; Hon Chapl from 03. *St Chrysostom's Rectory, 38 Park Range, Manchester M14 5HQ* Tel 0161-224 6971 Mobile 07711-670225 E-mail fatherian@priest.com

GOMERSALL, Richard. b 45. FCA68. N Ord Course 90. **d** 93 **p** 94. NSM Thurcroft *Sheff* 93-96; NSM Sheff St Matt 96-03; Ind Chapl 98-03; C-in-c Southey Green St Bernard CD from 03. *Dale View House, 14 Wignall Avenue, Wickersley, Rotherham S66 2AX* Tel (01709) 546441 Fax 701900 E-mail fr.gomersall@btinternet.com

GOMES, Jules Francis. b 66. Bombay Univ BA86 United Th Coll Serampore MTh97 Selw Coll Cam PhD04. Union Bibl Sem Serampore BD94. **d** 98 **p** 98. India 98-04; Co-ord Chapl Univ of Greenwich *S'wark* from 04. *35 Elmdene Road, London SE18 6TZ* Tel (020) 8316 0344 Mobile 07981-570384 E-mail j.gomes@gre.ac.uk

✠**GOMEZ, The Most Revd Drexel Wellington.** b 37. Dur Univ BA59. Codrington Coll Barbados 55. **d** 59 **c** 72. Tutor Codrington Coll Barbados 64-68; Bp Barbados 72-93; Bp Coadjutor Nassau and Bahamas 95-96; Dioc Bp 96-01; Bp Bahamas and Turks and Caicos Is from 01; Abp W Indies from 98. *PO Box N-7107, Nassau, Bahamas* Tel (001242) 322 3015 Fax 322 7943 E-mail primate@batelnet.bs

GOMM, Timothy Frank. b 64. St Jo Coll Nottm 00. **d** 02 **p** 03. C Kinson *Sarum* 02-04; C Heatherlands St Jo from 04; Community Chapl Rossmore Community Coll from 04. *63 Good Road, Poole BH12 3HP* Tel (01202) 246426 E-mail tim.gomm@ntlworld.com

GOMPERTZ, Canon Peter Alan Martin. b 40. ALCD63. **d** 64 **p** 65. C Eccleston St Luke *Liv* 64-69; Scripture Union 69-73; C Yeovil *B & W* 73-75; V Northampton St Giles *Pet* 75-96; Can Pet Cathl from 88; R Aynho and Croughton w Evenley etc from 96. *The Rectory, Croughton Road, Aynho, Banbury OX17 3BG* Tel (01869) 810903 Mobile 07771-615364 Fax (01869) 811240 E-mail canon.gompertz@virgin.net

GONIN, Christopher Willett. b 33. Man Univ DACE87 MBA92. AKC59. **d** 60 **p** 61. C Camberwell St Geo *S'wark* 60-64; C Stevenage H Trin *St Alb* 64-69; C Bletchley *Ox* 70-73; R Newington St Mary *S'wark* 73-76; Perm to Offic *Bris* 76-77; Hon C Horfield H Trin 77-89; Hon C City of Bris 89-91; V Milton Ernest *St Alb* 92-97; V Thurleigh 92-97; rtd 97; Perm to Offic *St E* from 97. *15 The Gables, Leiston IP16 4UZ* Tel (01728) 635549 E-mail christopher@gonin.wanadoo.co.uk

GOOCH, John Ellerton. b 46. Natal Univ BEcon70. Trin Coll Bris 73. **d** 75 **p** 76. Chapl S Africa 75-98; Perm to Offic *Chelmsf* 98-00; Casablanca *Eur* from 98. *Place Leclerc, Angle rue de Vanneaux 1, Oasis 20100, Casablanca, Morocco* Tel and fax (00212) (2) 257120 E-mail john.gooch@cwcom.net

GOOCH, Michael Anthony. b 44. Nottm Coll of Educn TCert66. Cant Sch of Min 90. **d** 93 **p** 94. NSM New Romney w Old Romney and Midley *Cant* 93-97; P-in-c Teynham w Lynsted and Kingsdown 97-98; P-in-c from 98; Bp's Officer for NSM 98-03. *The Vicarage, 76 Station Road, Teynham, Sittingbourne ME9 9SN* Tel (01795) 522510 E-mail mgooch@connectfree.co.uk

GOOD, Alan Raymond. b 39. Bris Sch of Min 83. **d** 85 **p** 86. NSM Horfield St Greg *Bris* 85-97; Chapl Asst Southmead Health Services NHS Trust 97-99; Chapl Asst N Bris NHS Trust from 99. *Southmead Hospital, Westbury-on-Trym, Bristol BS10 5NB* Tel 0117-959 5447, 950 5050 *or* (01454) 415778

GOOD, Andrew Ronald. b 60. Bris Univ BA82. Linc Th Coll 83. **d** 85 **p** 86. C Epping St Jo *Chelmsf* 85-88; C Cheshunt *St Alb* 88-91; R Spixworth w Crostwick *Nor* 91-92; R Frettenham w Stanninghall 91-92; R Spixworth w Crostwick and Frettenham 92-04; Perm to Offic from 04. *20 Ebbisham Drive, Norwich NR4 6HN*

GOOD, Anthony Ernest. b 28. ARIBA51 Heriot-Watt Univ MSc73. Wells Th Coll 54. **d** 56 **p** 57. C Maidstone All SS *Cant* 56-60; C Reading St Mary V *Ox* 60-62; R Sandhurst 62-70; Perm to Offic *Ex* 71-82; TR Wallingford w Crowmarsh Gifford etc *Ox* 82-92; RD Wallingford 85-91; rtd 92; Perm to Offic *Ex* from 92. *Cotts Weir Quay, Bere Alston, Yelverton PL20 7BX* Tel (01822) 840524

GOOD, David Howard. b 42. Glouc Sch of Min 84. **d** 87 **p** 88. NSM Bromyard *Heref* 87-92; C Pontesbury I and II 92-95; P-in-c Ditton Priors w Neenton, Burwarton etc 95-98; R Ditton Priors w Neenton, Burwarton etc 98-02; rtd 02; Perm to Offic *Heref* from 02. *26 Farjeon Close, Ledbury HR8 2FU* Tel (01531) 636474

GOOD, Geoffrey. b 27. St Aid Birkenhead. **d** 61 **p** 62. C Roby *Liv* 61-65; V Staincliffe *Wakef* 65-79; V Thornes St Jas w Ch Ch 79-93; rtd 93; Perm to Offic *Wakef* from 93. *147 Thornes Road, Wakefield WF2 8QN* Tel (01924) 378273

GOOD, George Fitzgerald. b 19. TCD BA41. CITC 42. **d** 42 **p** 43. C Drumglass *Arm* 42-45; Clerical V Ch Ch Cathl Dublin *D & G* 45-49; I Inniskeel w Lettermacaward *D & R* 49-60; I Raphoe w Raymochy 60-67; Can Raphoe Cathl 60-62; Dean Raphoe 62-67; Dean Derry 67-84; I Templemore 67-84; rtd 84. *Cliff Cottage, Portnoo, Co Donegal, Irish Republic*

GOOD, Preb John Hobart. b 43. Bps' Coll Cheshunt 66 Coll of Resurr Mirfield 68. **d** 69 **p** 70. C Ex St Jas *Ex* 69-73; C Cockington 73-75; C Wolborough w Newton Abbot 75-78; P-in-c Exminster 78-80; P-in-c Kenn 78-80; R Exminster and Kenn 80-95; RD Kenn 89-95; TR Axminster, Chardstock, All Saints etc from 95; Preb Ex Cathl from 02; Chapl All Hallows Sch Rousdon from 98. *The Rectory, Church Street, Axminster EX13 5AQ* Tel (01297) 32264 E-mail jhgood_minster@hotmail.com

✠**GOOD, The Rt Revd Kenneth Raymond.** b 52. TCD BA74 Nottm Univ BA76 NUI HDipEd81 MEd84. St Jo Coll Nottm 75. **d** 77 **p** 78 **c** 02. C Willowfield *D & D* 77-79; Chapl Ashton Sch Cork 79-84; I Dunganstown w Redcross and Conary *D & G* 84-90; I Lurgan Ch the Redeemer *D & D* 90-02; Adn Dromore 97-02; Bp D & R from 02. *The See House, 112 Culmore Road, Londonderry BT48 8JF* Tel (028) 7135 1206 *or* 7126 2440 Fax 7135 2554 E-mail bishop@derry.anglican.org

GOOD, The Ven Kenneth Roy. b 41. K Coll Lon BD66 AKC66. **d** 67 **p** 68. C Stockton St Pet *Dur* 67-70; Chapl Antwerp Miss to Seamen *Eur* 70-74; Japan 74-79; Hon Can Kobe from 74; Asst Gen Sec Miss to Seamen 79-85; Asst Chapl St Mich Paternoster Royal *Lon* 79-85; V Nunthorpe *York* 85-93; RD Stokesley 90-93; Adn Richmond *Ripon* from 93. *Hoppus House, Smith Lane, Hutton Conyers, Ripon HG4 5DX* Tel (01765) 604342 Fax as telephone E-mail good.richmond@sagainternet.co.uk

GOOD, Robert Stanley. b 24. TCD BA45 BD47 Kent Univ MA82. TCD Div Sch Div Test 46. **d** 47 **p** 48. C Lurgan Ch the Redeemer *D & D* 47-49; CMS 50-60; Kenya 50-60; Perm to Offic *Cant* from 61; Sen Div Master Maidstone Gr Sch 62-64; Sen Lect Ch Ch Coll Cant 64-78; Fiji 83-87; Par Educn Officer Herne Bay Ch Ch *Cant* 88-94; rtd 94. *Njiani, 44 Ivanhoe Road, Herne Bay CT6 6EG* Tel (01227) 363561

GOOD, Stuart Eric Clifford. b 37. Wycliffe Hall Ox 63. **d** 64 **p** 65. C Walton H Trin *Ox* 64-67; Australia from 66; Dir Chapl Services Angl Homes Inc 85-05; rtd 05. *6 Enright Circuit, Stanford Gardens, Beeliar, W Australia 6164* Tel (0061) 418-943337 (mobile) E-mail sbargood@bigpond.net.au

GOOD, Canon William Thomas Raymond. b 13. TCD BA39 MA45. **d** 39 **p** 40. C Castlecomer *C & O* 39-43; Dioc C (Cork) *C, C & R* 43-45; I Kilnagross 45-52; I Castleventry w Kilmean 52-60; I Rathcooney 60-73; Can Cloyne Cathl 67-69; Prec 69-82; I Carrigrohane Union 73-82; Can Cork Cathl 79-82; rtd 82. *Woodley, Main Road, Shankill, Co Dublin, Irish Republic* Tel (00353) (1) 272 0921

GOODACRE, Canon David Leighton. b 36. Birm Univ DPS69. AKC59. **d** 60 **p** 61. C Stockton St Chad *Dur* 60-63; C Birtley 63-68; Chapl Sunderland Gen Hosp 69-74; P-in-c Ryhope *Dur* 75-81; V Ovingham *Newc* 81-01; Hon Can Newc Cathl 92-01; rtd 01; Perm to Offic *Newc* from 01. *9 Wilmington Close, Newcastle upon Tyne NE3 2SF* Tel 0191-271 4382

GOODAIR, Janet. *See* CHEESEMAN, Ms Janet

GOODALL, George. b 24. LCP. **d** 86 **p** 87. NSM Bretby w Newton Solney *Derby* 86-94; Perm to Offic from 94. *6 Brizlincote Lane, Burton-on-Trent DE15 0PR* Tel (01283) 562467

GOODALL, John William. b 45. Hull Univ BA69. Ripon Hall Ox 69. **d** 71 **p** 72. C Loughborough Em *Leic* 71-74; C Dorchester *Ox* 74-75; TV 75-80; Tutor Sarum & Wells Th Coll 80-88; Vice Prin S Dios Minl Tr Scheme 80-88; P-in-c Gt Wishford *Sarum* 80-83; P-in-c Colehill 88-96; V from 96; Dioc Dir of Readers 88-95. *The Vicarage, Smugglers Lane, Colehill, Wimborne BH21 2RY* Tel (01202) 883721

GOODALL, Jonathan Michael. b 61. R Holloway Coll Lon BMus83. Wycliffe Hall Ox 86. **d** 89 **p** 90. C Bicester w Bucknell, Caversfield and Launton *Ox* 89-92; Asst Chapl HM Pris Bullingdon 90-92; Min Can, Chapl, and Sacr Westmr Abbey 92-98; Bp's Chapl and Research Asst *Eur* from 98; Hon C Westmr St Matt *Lon* 99-03; PV Westmr Abbey from 04; Abp's Chapl and Ecum Officer *Cant* from 05. *Lambeth Palace, London SE1 7JU* Tel (020) 7898 1200 E-mail jonathan.goodall@c-of-e.org.uk

GOODALL, Malcolm. b 39. Newc Univ MA93. Carl Dioc Tr Inst 80. **d** 85 **p** 86. NSM Allonby and Cross Canonby *Carl* 85-88; C Auckland St Andr and St Anne *Dur* 88-90; V Grindon and Stillington 90-98; P-in-c Wolsingham and Thornley 98-03; R from 03. *The Rectory, 14 Rectory Lane, Wolsingham, Bishop Auckland DL13 3AJ* Tel (01388) 527340 E-mail malcolm.goodall@durham.anglican.org

GOODBODY, Ruth Vivien. b 68. Surrey Univ BA02. Wycliffe Hall Ox 96 STETS 00. **d** 02 **p** 03. C Bourne Valley *Sarum* from 02. *26 Winterslow Road, Porton, Salisbury SP4 0LR* Tel (01980) 610838 E-mail the.goodbodies@virgin.net

GOODBODY, Steven John. b 70. Univ of Wales (Cardiff) BD92. Wycliffe Hall Ox 00. **d** 02 **p** 03. C Tunbridge Wells St Jo *Roch* from 02. *112 Stephen's Road, Tunbridge Wells TN4 9QA* Tel (01892) 521767 Mobile 07768-645172 E-mail sjgoodbody@csi.com

GOODBODY, Timothy Edward. b 66. York Univ BA89 Surrey Univ DipTran90. Wycliffe Hall Ox BTh98. **d** 98 **p** 99. C Blandford Forum and Langton Long *Sarum* 98-02; NSM Bourne Valley from 02. *26 Winterslow Road, Porton, Salisbury SP4 0LR* Tel (01980) 610838 E-mail the.goodbodies@virgin.net

GOODBURN, David Henry. b 41. S'wark Ord Course 73. **d** 76 **p** 77. NSM Enfield SS Pet and Paul *Lon* 76-82; Perm to Offic 83-85; NSM Potters Bar *St Alb* 85-88; Chapl RN 88-96; V Luton St Sav *St Alb* from 96. *St Saviour's Vicarage, St Saviour's Crescent, Luton LU1 5HG* Tel (01582) 730445

GOODCHILD, Andrew Philip. b 55. CertEd80. Oak Hill Th Coll BA85. **d** 85 **p** 86. C Barnston *Ches* 85-88; C Hollington St Leon *Chich* 88-89; P-in-c Millbrook *Ches* 89-94; Chapl and Hd RE Kimbolton Sch Cambs from 94. *Kimbolton School, Kimbolton, Huntingdon PE28 0EA* Tel (01480) 862209 Fax 860386 E-mail melandi@talk21.com

GOODCHILD, Canon John McKillip. b 42. Clare Coll Cam BA64 MA68 Oriel Coll Ox CertEd69. Wycliffe Hall Ox 67. **d** 69 **p** 70. C Clubmoor *Liv* 69-72; Nigeria 72-83; Hon Can Aba from 74; V Ainsdale *Liv* 83-89; TR Maghull 89-98; Prin OLM Tr Scheme *Nor* from 98. *Emmaus House, 65 The Close, Norwich NR1 4DH* Tel (01603) 611196 *or* 632041 Fax 766476 E-mail johngoodchild@norwich.anglican.org

GOODCHILD, Roy John. b 30. Wycliffe Hall Ox 60. **d** 61 **p** 62. C Hayes *Roch* 61-64; C S w N Bersted *Chich* 64-68; R Birdham w W Itchenor 68-73; V Saltdean 74-83; V Hollington St Jo 83-90; V Ticehurst and Flimwell 90-97; RD Rotherfield 95-97; rtd 97; Perm to Offic *Chich* from 97. *8 Caburn Court, Station Street, Lewes BN7 2DA* Tel (01273) 478484

GOODDEN, John Maurice Phelips. b 34. Sarum & Wells Th Coll 70. **d** 72 **p** 75. C Weymouth H Trin *Sarum* 72-74; C Harlow New Town w Lt Parndon *Chelmsf* 74-78; Ind Chapl and Chapl Princess Alexandra Hosp Harlow 78-82; V Moulsham St Jo *Chelmsf* 86-90; R Chipstead and Adv Rural Min *S'wark* 90-04; rtd 04. *The Homestead, Sutton End, Crockerton, Warminster BA12 8BG* Tel (07984) 158093 E-mail jgoodden@madasafish.com

GOODE, Anthony Thomas Ryall (Tom). b 42. Ex Coll Ox BA64 MA71. Cuddesdon Coll 65. **d** 67 **p** 68. C Wolvercote *Ox* 67-71; P-in-c Edith Weston w Normanton *Pet* 72-74; Chapl RAF 71-91; Asst Chapl-in-Chief 91-97; Chapl to The Queen 95-97; Chapl Abu Dhabi St Andr UAE 97-00; V Hurstbourne Tarrant, Faccombe, Vernham Dean etc *Win* from 00. *The Vicarage, Hurstbourne Tarrant, Andover SP11 0AH* Tel (01264) 736222 Fax 736148 E-mail spetroshbt@aol.com

GOODE, John Laurence. b 48. W Cheshire Coll of Tech TEng70 Federal Univ Minas Gerais Brazil Dip Teaching78. Chich Th Coll 81. **d** 83 **p** 84. C Crewe St Andr *Ches* 83-86; USPG 87-94; Brazil 91-94; TV Ches Team *Ches* 94-00; V Latchford Ch Ch from 00. *Christ Church Vicarage, Wash Lane, Warrington WA4 1HT* Tel (01925) 630846

GOODE, Jonathan. b 67. St Martin's Coll Lanc BA89. Qu Coll Birm. **d** 00 **p** 01. C Middleton St Mary *Ripon* 00-04; P-in-c Hartlepool St Hilda *Dur* from 04; Chapl St Hilda's Sch from 04. *The Rectory, Church Close, Hartlepool TS24 0PW* E-mail revjgoode@yahoo.com

GOODE, Michael Arthur John. b 40. K Coll Lon BD AKC63. **d** 64 **p** 65. C Sunderland Springwell w Thorney Close *Dur* 64-68; C Solihull *Birm* 68-70; R Fladbury, Wyre Piddle and Moor *Worc* 70-75; P-in-c Foley Park 75-81; V 81-83; RD Kidderminster 81-83; TR Crawley *Chich* 83-93; TR Abingdon *Ox* from 93; V Shippon 93-05. *The Rectory, St Helen's Court, Abingdon OX14 5BS* Tel (01235) 520144 E-mail st.helens@tesco.net

GOODE, Canon Peter William Herbert. b 23. Oak Hill Th Coll 60. **d** 62 **p** 63. C Woodford Wells *Chelmsf* 62-65; V Harold Hill St Paul 65-76; V Gt Warley Ch Ch 76-93; RD Brentwood 89-93; Hon Can Chelmsf Cathl 90-93; rtd 93; Perm to Offic *St Alb* from 93. *52 Slimmons Drive, St Albans AL4 9AP* Tel (01727) 852166

GOODE, Thomas. *See* GOODE, Anthony Thomas Ryall

GOODER, Canon Martin Lee. b 37. Sheff Univ BSc58. Oak Hill Th Coll 58. **d** 60 **p** 61. C Barrow St Mark *Carl* 60-63; C Halliwell St Pet *Man* 63-66; R Chorlton on Medlock St Sav 66-71; R Brunswick 71-92; P-in-c Bacup Ch Ch 92-02; Hon Can Man Cathl 98-02; rtd 02; Perm to Offic *Man* from 02. *12 Walton Close, Bacup OL13 9RE* Tel (01706) 872418 E-mail gooder@btopenworld.com

GOODERHAM, Daniel Charles. b 24. St Fran Coll Brisbane 49. **d** 52 **p** 53. Australia 52-60; C Staveley *Derby* 60-61; C Ipswich St Thos *St E* 61-64; V Ipswich St Bart 64-71; R Drinkstone 71-78; R Rattlesden 71-78; RD Lavenham 75-78; V Beckenham St Mich w St Aug *Roch* 78-87; P-in-c Whiteparish *Sarum* 87-89; rtd 89; Perm to Offic *St E* from 89. *58 Millfield, Eye IP23 7DE* Tel (01379) 871589

GOODERICK, Peter Handley. b 26. Down Coll Cam BA50 MA52. Linc Th Coll 51. **d** 53 **p** 54. C Brighouse *Wakef* 53-56; Prec Gib Cathl *Eur* 56-58; Chapl Izmir 58-59; C Wimbledon *S'wark* 59-63; CF (TAVR) 59-74; V Streatham St Paul *S'wark* 63-68; V Merton St Jas 68-80; P-in-c Baginton *Cov* 80-81; P-in-c Stoneleigh w Ashow 80-81; R Stoneleigh w Ashow and Baginton 81-88; RD Kenilworth 83-90; R Berkswell 88-91; rtd 91; Chapl Malaga w Almunecar and Nerja *Eur* 91-92; Perm to Offic *Cov* from 93. *9 Margetts Close, Kenilworth CV8 1EN* Tel (01926) 859855

GOODEY, Philip Julian Frank. b 61. Glos Coll of Arts & Tech HND83. Aston Tr Scheme 87 Trin Coll Bris DipTh92. **d** 92 **p** 93. C Iver *Ox* 92-94; C Hornchurch St Andr *Chelmsf* 94-99; V Wickham Market w Pettistree *St E* 99-01; TR Parkham, Alwington, Buckland Brewer etc *Ex* from 01; P-in-c Lundy Is from 01. *The Rectory, Parkham, Bideford EX39 5PL* Tel (01237) 451204 Fax 452162 E-mail phil.goodey@zetnet.co.uk

GOODFELLOW, Ian. b 37. St Cath Coll Cam BA61 MA65 Lon Univ PGCE76 Dur Univ PhD83. Wells Th Coll 61. **d** 63 **p** 64. C Dunstable *St Alb* 63-67; Chapl Haileybury Coll 67-71; Asst Chapl St Bede Coll Dur 71-74; Lect and Tutor 71-75; Sen Lect and Tutor SS Hild and Bede Coll Dur 75-78; Sen Cllr Open Univ (SW Region) 78-97; Perm to Offic *Ex* from 89; rtd 02. *Crosslea, 206 Whitchurch Road, Tavistock PL19 9DQ* Tel (01822) 612069 E-mail goodfellow1@lineone.net

GOODFIELD, Dudley Francis. b 40. AKC65. **d** 66 **p** 67. C Bath Twerton-on-Avon *B & W* 66-69; C Lache cum Saltney *Ches* 69-71; C Portishead *B & W* 71-76; V Weston-super-Mare St Andr Bournville 76-82; V Ruishton w Thornfalcon 82-05; rtd 05. *4 Gillards Close, Rockwell Green, Wellington TA21 9DX* Tel (01823) 660533

GOODGER, Kenneth Andrew. b 67. Univ of Qld BA96. St Fran Coll Brisbane BTh97. **d** 93 **p** 96. Australia 93-99 and from 02; C Milton 93-96; C Caloundra 96-99; C Pimlico St Pet w Westmr Ch Ch *Lon* 99-02; R Moorooka and Salisbury from 02. *28 Piers Street, Moorooka, Qld, Australia 4105* Tel (0061) (7) 3892 2508 E-mail m.sanglican@uqconnect.net

GOODHAND, Richard. b 51. Sarum & Wells Th Coll 88. **d** 90 **p** 91. C Wollaton *S'well* 90-93; P-in-c Clarborough w Hayton 93-98; Sub-Chapl HM Pris Ranby 93-96; Asst Chapl 96-98; P-in-c Blidworth *S'well* 98-02; P-in-c Rainworth 98-02; V Blidworth w Rainworth from 02. *The Vicarage, 27 St Peter's Drive, Rainworth, Mansfield NG21 0BE* Tel (01623) 798980 E-mail richard.goodhand@ntlworld.com

GOODHEW, David John. b 65. Collingwood Coll Dur BA86 CCC Ox DPhil92 St Jo Coll Dur BA92. Cranmer Hall Dur 90. **d** 93 **p** 94. C Bedminster *Bris* 93-96; Chapl and Fell St Cath Coll Cam 96-01; V Fulford *York* from 01; P-in-c York St Denys 01-04. *The Vicarage, 1 Fulford Park, Fulford, York YO10 4QE* Tel (01904) 633261 E-mail dj.goodhew@ukonline.co.uk

GOODHEW, Mrs Lindsey Jane Ellin. b 66. UEA BA87 St Jo Coll Dur BA92 Dip Minl Studies 93. Cranmer Hall Dur 90. **d** 93 **p** 94. C Bishopsworth *Bris* 93-96; Perm to Offic *Ely* 96-97; NSM Cambridge St Mark 97-01; Perm to Offic *York* from 01. *The Vicarage, 1 Fulford Park, Fulford, York YO10 4QE* Tel (01904) 633261

GOODHEW, Roy William. b 41. Reading Univ BA. S Dios Minl Tr Scheme. **d** 89 **p** 90. C Southampton Maybush St Pet *Win* 89-94; V Hound from 94. *The Vicarage, Grange Road, Netley Abbey, Southampton SO31 5FF* Tel (023) 8045 2209

GOODING, Canon Ian Eric. b 42. Leeds Univ BSc63 BCom65 MIProdE68 CEng69. St Jo Coll Nottm 70 Lon Coll of Div LTh72 DPS73. **d** 73 **p** 74. C Wandsworth All SS *S'wark* 73-77; Bp's Ind Adv *Derby* from 77; P-in-c Stanton-by-Dale w Dale Abbey 77-87; R 87-00; P-in-c Risley 94-00; R Stanton-by-Dale w Dale Abbey and Risley from 00; RD Erewash from 98; Hon Can Derby Cathl from 02. *The Rectory, Stanhope Street, Stanton-by-Dale, Ilkeston DE7 4QA* Tel and fax 0115-932 4585 Mobile 07768-917385 E-mail iangooding@zoom.co.uk

GOODING, Ian Peter Slade. b 56. Imp Coll Lon BScEng77 MBCS88. Qu Coll Birm 90. **d** 92 **p** 93. C Swindon Dorcan *Bris* 92-96; TV Langley Marish *Ox* 96-02. *5 Pipston Green, Kents Hill, Milton Keynes MK7 6HT* Tel (01908) 673651 E-mail goodingip@clara.co.uk

GOODING, John Henry. b 47. St Jo Coll Nottm. **d** 84 **p** 85. C Charles w Plymouth St Matthias *Ex* 84-88; C Leeds St Geo *Ripon* 88-93; TV Liskeard, St Keyne, St Pinnock, Morval etc *Truro* 93-94; Lon and SE Consultant CPAS from 94; Perm to Offic *Guildf* 94-96; *S'wark* 94-00; *Cant, Chich, Lon,* and *Roch* from 94; Hon C Egham *Guildf* from 96; Dioc Par Resource Officer 00-03; Dioc Dir Miss, Evang and Par Development from 03. *Diocesan House, Quarry Street, Guildford GU1 3XG* Tel (01483) 571826 ext 206 *or* (01932) 560407 E-mail john.gooding@cofeguildford.org.uk

GOODLAD, Canon Martin Randall. b 39. Sheff City Coll of Educn TDip60. Linc Th Coll 63. **d** 66 **p** 67. C Bramley *Ripon* 66-69; TV Daventry *Pet* 69-71; Asst Dioc Youth Officer 69-71; Asst Dir of Educn *Wakef* 71-74; Youth Work Officer Gen Syn Bd of Educn 74-83; P-in-c Cheam Common St Phil *S'wark* 83-85; V 85-97; RD Sutton 90-97; Hon Chapl St Raphael's Hospice 87-97; V Coulsdon St Andr *S'wark* 97-05; Hon Can S'wark Cathl 96-05; rtd 05. *3 Cromer Mansions, Cheam Road, Sutton SM1 2SR* Tel (020) 8915 0555 E-mail hornes27@aol.com

GOODLAND, Michael Eric. b 53. WEMTC 97. **d** 97 **p** 98. NSM Ilminster and Distr *B & W* 97-02; NSM Crewkerne w Wayford from 02. *26 Bincombe Drive, Crewkerne TA18 7BE* Tel (01460) 72363 *or* 76151 E-mail mike07@themail.co.uk

GOODLEY, Christopher Ronald. b 47. K Coll Lon BD72 AKC72. **d** 73 **p** 74. C Shenfield *Chelmsf* 73-77; C Hanley H Ev *Lich* 77-78; TV 78-83; Chapl Whittington Hosp Lon 83-86; Chapl St Crispin's Hosp Northampton 88-94; Chapl Northampton Community Healthcare NHS Trust 94-01; Chapl Northants Healthcare NHS Trust from 01. *Princess Marina Hospital, Duston, Northampton NN5 6UH* Tel (01604) 595087 *or* 752323 Fax 583795 E-mail chris.goodley@nchc-tr.anglox.nhs.uk

GOODMAN, Ms Alice Abigail. b 58. Harvard Univ BA80 Girton Coll Cam BA82 MA86 Boston Univ MDiv97. Ripon Coll Cuddesdon 00. **d** 01 **p** 03. C Redditch, The Ridge *Worc* 01-02; C Kidderminster St Mary and All SS w Trimpley etc from 02. *10 James Road, Kidderminster DY10 2TR* Tel (01562) 748274 E-mail goodhill@macunlimited.net

GOODMAN, Andrew Francis Malby. b 56. Lon Univ BA79 Birm Univ MSocSc88 CQSW88. Qu Coll Birm 01. **d** 03 **p** 04. C Hamstead St Paul *Birm* from 03. *119 Lechlade Road, Birmingham B43 5NE* Tel 0121-357 1428 E-mail goodmanco@yahoo.co.uk

GOODMAN, Preb Denys Charles. b 24. Selw Coll Cam BA49 MA56. Linc Th Coll 49. **d** 51 **p** 52. C Leigh St Mary *Man* 51-54; C Pendlebury St Aug 54-57; V Hollinwood 57-70; R Bath Bathwick St Mary *B & W* 70-78; P-in-c Bath Bathwick St Jo 76-78; R Bath Bathwick 78-91; RD Bath 81-90; Preb Wells Cathl 82-96; Sub-Dean Wells 82-96; rtd 91; Perm to Offic *B & W* from 96. *Hollinwood, Johnson Close, Wells BA5 3NN* Tel (01749) 675011

GOODMAN, Canon Derek George. b 34. Keble Coll Ox BA57 MA60. Ridley Hall Cam 59. **d** 61 **p** 62. C Attenborough *S'well* 61-65; R Eastwood 65-84; Dioc Insp of Schs 65-89; V Woodthorpe 84-89; Dioc Dir of Educn *Leic* 89-96; Hon Can Leic Cathl 90-96; rtd 96; Perm to Offic *Leic* from 96. *1 Brown Avenue, Quorn, Loughborough LE12 8RH* Tel (01509) 415692

GOODMAN, John. b 20. Selw Coll Cam BA42 MA46. Linc Th Coll 47. **d** 49 **p** 50. C Kidderminster St Jo *Worc* 49-53; C Marlborough *Sarum* 53-56; V Wootton Bassett 56-65; C Broad Town 56-65; C Salisbury St Mark 65-68; V 68-83; R Wool and E Stoke 83-88; rtd 88; Perm to Offic *Sarum* from 88. *141 Avon Road, Devizes SN10 1PY* Tel (01380) 721267

GOODMAN, John Dennis Julian. b 35. Sarum & Wells Th Coll 74. **d** 76 **p** 77. C Cotmanhay *Derby* 76-79; TV Old Brampton and Loundsley Green 79-86; R Finningley w Auckley *S'well* 86-96; rtd 96; Perm to Offic *Pet* from 96. *6 Mason Close, Thrapston, Kettering NN14 4UQ* Tel (01832) 731194

GOODMAN, Mrs Mairion Kim (Mars). b 73. Leeds Univ BA95. Trin Coll Bris BA03. **d** 05. NSM Redland *Bris* from 05. *12 Downend Road, Horfield, Bristol BS7 9PF* Tel 0117-946 4693 E-mail mars@redland.org.uk

GOODMAN, Canon Mark Alexander Scott. b 61. Lanc Univ BA84 Nottm Univ BTh90 New Coll Edin MTh97. Linc Th Coll 87. **d** 90 **p** 91. C Denton St Lawr *Man* 90-93; R Dalkeith *Edin* from 93; R Lasswade from 93; Can St Mary's Cathl from 02; Syn Clerk from 02. *The Rectory, 7 Anrum Bank, Dalkeith EH22 3AY* Tel and fax 0131-663 7000 Mobile 07711-547927 E-mail markgoodman@beeb.net

GOODMAN, Peter William (Bill). b 60. St Cath Coll Cam BA82. St Jo Coll Nottm 85. **d** 89 **p** 90. C Stapenhill w Cauldwell *Derby* 89-92; C Ovenden *Wakef* 92-94; V Halifax St Aug 94-98; Crosslinks Ethiopia from 98. *c/o Crosslinks, 251 Lewisham Way, London SE4 1XF*

GOODMAN, Canon Sidney William. b 10. Kelham Th Coll 27. **d** 33 **p** 34. C Wigan St Mich *Liv* 33-36; C Gt Grimsby St Mary and St Jas *Linc* 36-39; V Fulstow 39-44; V Habrough 44-55; V Immingham 44-55; V Habrough Gp 55-71; RD Grimsby N 57-64; RD Haverstoe 64-76; Can and Preb Linc Cathl 69-79; P-in-c Wold Newton w Hawerby 71-78; rtd 78; Perm to Offic *Linc* from 78. *28 Grosvenor Road, Louth LN11 0BB* Tel (01507) 603798

GOODMAN, Victor Terence. b 46. Liv Univ BSc67 CEng92 MBCS74. EMMTC 82. **d** 85 **p** 86. NSM Barwell w Potters Marston and Stapleton *Leic* 85-89; NSM Croft and Stoney Stanton 89-94; P-in-c Whetstone 94-03; TV Hugglescote w Donington, Ellistown and Snibston from 03. *St James's Vicarage, Highfield Street, Coalville LE67 3BN* Tel (01530) 832679 E-mail vgoodman@leicester.anglican.org

GOODMAN, Mrs Victoria Elizabeth Stuart. b 51. RGN74. Trin Coll Bris DipTS98. **d** 98 **p** 99. C Ilminster and Distr *B & W* 98-02; R Blagdon w Compton Martin and Ubley from 02; Dioc Chapl Mothers' Union from 01. *The Rectory, High Street, Blagdon, Bristol BS40 7TA* Tel (01761) 462495

GOODMAN, William. *See* GOODMAN, Peter William

GOODRICH, Derek Hugh. b 27. Selw Coll Cam BA48 MA54. St Steph Ho Ox 50. **d** 52 **p** 53. C Willesden St Andr *Lon* 52-57; Guyana 57-00; Adn Berlice 81-84; V Gen Dio Guyana 82-94; Dean Georgetown 84-93; P-in-c St Aloysius 93-00; rtd 00. *The College of St Barnabas, Blackberry Lane, Lingfield RH7 6NJ* Tel (01342) 871630

GOODRICH, Canon Peter. b 36. Dur Univ BA58. Cuddesdon Coll 60. **d** 62 **p** 63. C Walton St Jo *Liv* 62-66; C Prescot 66-68; V Anfield St Marg 68-72; V Gt Crosby St Faith 72-83; P-in-c Seaforth 76-80; RD Bootle 78-83; TR Upholland 83-94; R Halsall 94-02; Dir Dioc OLM Scheme 94-02; Hon Can Liv Cathl 89-02; rtd 03; Perm to Offic *Liv* from 03. *Dunelm, 16 Hillside Avenue, Ormskirk L39 4TD* Tel (01695) 573285

GOODRIDGE, Paul Charles. b 54. Leic Univ MSc98 MCIPD88. **d** 04. OLM Cheam *S'wark* from 04. *47 Chatsworth Road, Sutton SM3 8PL* Tel (020) 8641 8011 Mobile 07793-048377 E-mail paul.goodridge1@btinternet.com

GOODRIDGE, Canon Peter David. b 32. Yale Univ STM84 FRSA92. AKC57. **d** 58 **p** 59. C Eastcote St Lawr *Lon* 58-64; V Tottenham St Phil 64-71; V W Drayton 71-85; P-in-c St Michael Penkevil *Truro* 85-88; P-in-c Lamorran and Merther 85-88; Dir of Educn 85-97; Hon Can Truro Cathl 87-96; Can Lib Truro Cathl 96-00; Perm to Offic from 01. *16 Crescent Rise, Truro TR1 3ER* Tel (01872) 270940 *or* 274352 Fax 222510 E-mail frpdg@btinternet.com

✠**GOODRIDGE, The Rt Revd Sehon Sylvester.** b 37. K Coll Lon BD66 AKC91 Gen Th Sem NY DD95. Huron Coll Ontario DD77 Codrington Coll Barbados 59. **d** 63 **p** 64 **c** 94. St Lucia 64-66; Chapl Univ of W Indies Jamaica 66-71; Warden and Dep Prin United Th Coll W Indies 69-71; Barbados 71-89; Prin Codrington Coll 71-82; Warden, Cllr and Sen Lect Univ of W Indies 83-89; Hon Can Barbados from 76; Prin Simon of Cyrene Th Inst 89-94; Chapl to The Queen 93-94; Bp Windward Is 94-02; rtd 02. *80 Prior Park Terrace, 6th Avenue, St James, Barbados, West Indies* Tel (001) (784) 457 1942 *or* 457 0775

GOODRUM, Mrs Alice. b 30. Lightfoot Ho Dur 58. **dss** 80 **d** 87 **p** 94. Fenham St Jas and St Basil *Newc* 80-91; C 87-91; rtd 91; Perm to Offic *Dur* and *Newc* from 91. *58 West Avenue, South Shields NE34 6BD* Tel 0191-425 3629

GOODSELL, Patrick. b 32. BA88. Linc Th Coll 62. **d** 64 **p** 65. C Thornton Heath St Jude *Cant* 64-65; C Croydon St Jo *S'wark* 65-70; V Tenterden St Mich *Cant* 70-78; P-in-c Sellindge w Monks Horton and Stowting 78-84; P-in-c Lympne w W Hythe 82-84; V Sellindge w Monks Horton and Stowting etc 84-92; V Nonington w Wymynswold and Goodnestone etc 92-98; rtd 98; Perm to Offic *Cant* from 98. *3 James Close, Lyminge, Folkestone CT18 8NL* Tel (01303) 863976 E-mail pat_goodsell@btinternet.com

GOODWIN, Barry Frederick John. b 48. Birm Univ BSc69 PhD77. St Jo Coll Nottm 86. **d** 88 **p** 89. C Ware Ch Ch *St Alb* 88-91; P-in-c Stanstead Abbots 91-96; P-in-c Gt Amwell w St Marg 95-96; V Gt Amwell w St Margaret's and Stanstead Abbots 96-99; RD Hertford and Ware 96-99; V Clapham Park All SS *S'wark* 99-05; RD Clapham 02-05; Soc Resp (Par Development) Adv Croydon Adnry from 05. *48 Northampton Road, Croydon CR0 7HT* Tel (020) 8681 5496 *or* 8681 5496 E-mail barry.goodwin@ukgateway.net

GOODWIN, Daphne Mary. b 35. Lon Univ MB, BS60. STETS 94. **d** 97 **p** 98. NSM Ifield *Chich* from 97. *150 Buckswood Drive, Gossops Green, Crawley RH11 8JF* Tel (01293) 612906 E-mail dapheter.goodwin@ukgateway.net

GOODWIN, David Wayne. b 71. Univ of Wales BD95. Cranmer Hall Dur 95. **d** 97 **p** 98. C Ches H Trin *Ches* 97-00; Dep Chapl HM Pris Dur 00-01; Chapl HM YOI Thorn Cross 01-04; Chapl HM Pris Liv from 04. *HM Prison Liverpool, 68 Hornby Road, Liverpool L9 3DF* Tel 0151-530 4127

GOODWIN, Mrs Gillian Sheila. b 54. N Ord Course MTh99. **d** 99 **p** 00. C Penkridge Team *Lich* 99-02; TV Wrockwardine Deanery from 02. *The Rectory, Wrockwardine, Telford TF6 5DD* Tel (01902) 240969

GOODWIN, Canon John Fletcher Beckles. b 20. Jes Coll Cam BA43 MA46. Ridley Hall Cam 42. **d** 45 **p** 46. C Southall H Trin *Lon* 45-48; C Drypool *York* 48-49; Niger 50-57; Vice-Prin Ripon Hall Ox 57-62; V Merton *Ox* 62-70; V Heanor *Derby* 70-74; V Hazlewood 74-85; V Turnditch 74-85; Adv for In-Service Tr and Chapl to Bp 74-88; Hon Can Derby Cathl 81-85; rtd 85; Perm to Offic *Derby* 85-99. *1 Kirby Place, Oxford OX4 2RX* Tel (01865) 712356

GOODWIN, Ronald Victor. b 33. S'wark Ord Course. **d** 86 **p** 87. NSM Wickford and Runwell *Chelmsf* 86-98; Perm to Offic

98-01; NSM W Hanningfield 01-03; P-in-c from 03. *164 Southend Road, Wickford SS11 8EH* Tel (01268) 734447

GOODWIN, Stephen. b 58. Sheff Univ BA80. Cranmer Hall Dur 82. **d** 85 **p** 86. C Lytham St Cuth *Blackb* 85-87; C W Burnley All SS 88-90; TV Headley All SS *Guildf* 90-98; NSM Leek and Meerbrook *Lich* 98-03; Chapl Univ Hosp of N Staffs NHS Trust from 03. *2 Lordshire Mews, Armshead Road, Werrington, Stoke-on-Trent ST9 0HJ* Tel (01782) 302418 E-mail goodwin@mcmail.com

GOODWIN, Mrs Susan Elizabeth. b 51. Leeds Poly BSc74 Leeds Univ MSc76. St Jo Coll Dur 82. **dss** 84 **d** 87 **p** 94. Norton Woodseats St Chad *Sheff* 84-87; Par Dn 87; Chapl Scargill Ho 87-89; NSM W Burnley All SS *Blackb* 89-90; NSM Headley All SS *Guildf* 90-98; Past Asst Acorn Chr Healing Trust 91-93; P-in-c Wetley Rocks *Lich* from 98. *2 Lordshire Mews, Armshead Road, Werrington, Stoke-on-Trent ST9 0HJ* Tel (01782) 302418

GOODWIN HUDSON, Brainerd Peter de Wirtz. b 34. K Coll Lon BD57 AKC57. Westcott Ho Cam 57. **d** 59 **p** 60. C Morden *S'wark* 59-60; Australia 61-65; Asst Sec CCCS 65-68; Chapl St Lawr Coll Ramsgate 68-74; Chapl Repton Sch Derby 74-94; Chapl Santiago Chile 94-01; rtd 99; Hon C Broadwell, Evenlode, Oddington, Adlestrop etc *Glouc* from 02. *The Vicarage, Bledington, Chipping Norton OX7 6UR* Tel (01608) 658102 E-mail brainerd@freeuk.com

GOODWINS, Christopher William Hedley. b 36. St Jo Coll Cam BA58 MA62. Linc Th Coll 62. **d** 64 **p** 65. C Lowestoft Ch Ch *Nor* 64-69; V Tamerton Foliot *Ex* 69-98; P-in-c Southway 78-82; rtd 98; P-in-c Isleham *Ely* 99-04. *102 The Causeway, Isleham, Ely CB7 5ST* Tel (01638) 780284 E-mail christopher@isleham.freeserve.co.uk

GOODYER, Canon Edward Arthur. b 42. Witwatersrand Univ BA63 SS Coll Cam BA67 MA70 Rhodes Univ MTh91. St Paul's Coll Grahamstown 68. **d** 68 **p** 69. S Africa 69-92; Can Cape Town 80-84; R Alverstoke *Portsm* from 92; P-in-c Gosport Ch Ch 97-01; Hon Can Wusasa Nigeria from 99. *The Rectory, Little Anglesey Road, Alverstoke, Gosport PO12 2JA* Tel and fax (023) 9258 1979 *or* 9258 0551 Mobile 07947-884714 E-mail ego.lizg@virgin.net

GOOLD, Peter John. b 44. Lon Univ BD74. St Steph Ho Ox 67. **d** 70 **p** 71. C Chiswick St Nic w St Mary *Lon* 70-73; Chapl Asst R Masonic Hosp Lon 73-74; Chapl Asst Basingstoke Distr Hosp 74-77; Chapl R Marsden Hosp Lon and Surrey 77-80; Chapl N Hants Hosp 80-94; Chapl N Hants Hosps NHS Trust from 94; Chapl N Hants Loddon Community NHS Trust from 94; Perm to Offic *Guildf* from 94. *The North Hampshire Hospital, Aldermaston Road, Basingstoke RG24 9NA* Tel (01256) 473202 *or* 314901

GORDON, Alan Williamson. b 53. Strathclyde Univ BA75 MCIBS79. Wycliffe Hall Ox 98. **d** 98 **p** 99. C Win Ch Ch *Win* 98-02; R King's Worthy from 02; R Headbourne Worthy from 02. *The Rectory, Campion Lane, King's Worthy, Winchester SO23 7QP* Tel (01962) 882166 E-mail alan.gordon98@ntlworld.com

GORDON, The Very Revd Alexander Ronald. b 49. Nottm Univ BPharm71. Coll of Resurr Mirfield 74. **d** 77 **p** 78. C Headingley *Ripon* 77-80; C Fareham SS Pet and Paul *Portsm* 80-83; V Cudworth *Wakef* 83-85; P-in-c Tain *Mor* 85-87; P-in-c Lairg Miss 87-01; P-in-c Brora and Dornoch 88-01; Dioc Dir of Ords 89-01; Can St Andr Cathl Inverness 95-01; Hon Can 02-05; Chapl Strasbourg *Eur* 02-05; Provost St Andr Cathl Inverness *Mor* from 05. *St Andrew's Lodge, 15 Ardross Street, Inverness IV3 5NS* Tel (01463) 233535 Mobile 07917-668918 E-mail canonalexgordon@btinternet.com

GORDON, Anne. *See* LE BAS, Ms Jennifer Anne

✠**GORDON, The Rt Revd Archibald Ronald McDonald.** b 27. Ball Coll Ox BA50 MA52. Cuddesdon Coll 50. **d** 52 **p** 53 **c** 75. C Stepney St Dunstan and All SS *Lon* 52-55; Chapl Cuddesdon Coll 55-59; Lic to Offic *Ox* 57-59; V Birm St Pet *Birm* 59-68; Lect Qu Coll Birm 60-62; Can Res Birm Cathl *Birm* 67-71; V Ox St Mary V w St Cross and St Pet *Ox* 71-75; Bp Portsm 75-84; Bp at Lambeth (Hd of Staff) *Cant* 84-91; Asst Bp S'wark 84-91; Bp HM Forces 85-90; Can Res and Sub-Dean Ch Ch *Ox* 91-96; Asst Bp Ox from 91; rtd 96. *16 East St Helen Street, Abingdon OX14 5EA* Tel (01235) 526956

GORDON, Bruce Harold Clark. b 40. Edin Univ MTh96. Cranmer Hall Dur 65. **d** 68 **p** 69. C Edin St Jas *Edin* 68-71; C Blackheath St Jo *S'wark* 71-74; R Duns *Edin* 74-90; R Lanark and Douglas *Glas* 90-05; rtd 05. *52 Foxknowe Place, Livingston EH54 6TX* E-mail sunnysock@ntlworld.com

GORDON, David John. b 65. Edin Th Coll CECM93. **d** 93 **p** 94. Chapl St Andr Cathl *Ab* 93-95; P-in-c Alexandria *Glas* 95-00; Chapl NE Lincs NHS Trust 00-01; Chapl Tayside Univ Hosps NHS Trust from 01. *Chaplain's Office, Ninewells Hospital, Dundee DD1 9SY* Tel (01382) 632755 *or* 660111 E-mail david.j.gordon@tuht.scot.nhs.uk

GORDON, Donald Ian. b 30. Nottm Univ BA52 PhD64. Westcott Ho Cam 71. **d** 71 **p** 72. NSM Newport *Chelmsf* 71-75; NSM Creeksea w Althorne, Latchingdon and N Fambridge 76-00; rtd 00; Perm to Offic *Chelmsf* from 01. *Holden House, Steeple Road, Latchingdon, Chelmsford CM3 6JX* Tel (01621) 740296

GORDON, Edward John. b 32. Univ of Wales BA52. St Mich Coll Llan 52. **d** 55 **p** 56. C Baglan *Llan* 55-61; C Newcastle w Laleston and Tythegston 61-65; V Ynyshir 65-69; C Bramhall *Ches* 69-72; V Cheadle Hulme All SS 72-79; V Tranmere St Paul w St Luke 79-88; V Sandbach Heath 88-97; Chapl Arclid Hosp 90-93; RD Congleton *Ches* 92-97; P-in-c Wheelock 95-97; rtd 97; Perm to Offic *B & W* from 97. *55 Greenslade Gardens, Nailsea, Bristol BS48 2BJ* Tel (01275) 853404

GORDON, John Michael. b 30. CITC. **d** 83 **p** 84. NSM Dublin St Geo *D & G* 83-85; NSM Dublin Irishtown w Donnybrook from 85. *Ferndale House, Rathmichael, Shankill, Co Dublin, Irish Republic* Tel (00353) (1) 282 2421 Fax 282 2954

GORDON, Jonathan Andrew. b 61. Keele Univ BA83 MPhil98 Southn Univ BTh88. Sarum & Wells Th Coll. **d** 87 **p** 88. C Wallingford w Crowmarsh Gifford etc *Ox* 87-91; C Tilehurst St Mich 91-93; TV Stoke-upon-Trent *Lich* 93-97; Chapl Southn Inst of HE *Win* 98-05; P-in-c Northchurch and Wigginton *St Alb* from 05. *St Mary's Rectory, 80 High Street, Northchurch, Berkhamsted HP4 3QW* Tel (01442) 865312

GORDON, Keith Adrian. b 49. Surrey Univ BSc71 Birm Univ MA02. Open Th Coll 95. **d** 98 **p** 99. Venezuela 98-03; C Caracas St Mary 98-99; Bp's Chapl Dioc Chpl 99-03; P-in-c Tenerife Sur *Eur* from 03. *Residencial Sonia #17, Calle El Mojon, Callao Salvaje, Adeje, 38678 Tenerife* Tel and fax (0034) (922) 742045 Mobile 679-660277 E-mail kagordon40@hotmail.com

GORDON, Canon Kenneth Davidson. b 35. Edin Univ MA57. Tyndale Hall Bris 58. **d** 60 **p** 61. C St Helens St Helen *Liv* 60-66; V Daubhill *Man* 66-71; R Bieldside *Ab* 71-01; Can St Andr Cathl 81-01; Syn Clerk 96-01; rtd 01; Hon Can St Andr Cathl *Ab* from 01; Perm to Offic *Blackb* and *Liv* from 01. *The Old Schoolhouse, Hurst Green, Mawdesley, Ormskirk L40 2QT* Tel and fax (01704) 823084 Mobile 07715-169548 E-mail canonken@btopenworld.com

GORDON, Kristy. *See* PATTIMORE, Mrs Kristy

GORDON, Mrs Pamela Anne. b 48. Brighton Coll of Educn CertEd69 BEd70. St Alb and Ox Min Course 99. **d** 02 **p** 03. NSM Wargrave w Knowl Hill *Ox* from 02. *Rebeny, 2A Hawthorn Road, Caversham, Reading RG4 6LY* Tel 0118-947 8676 Fax 954 3076 E-mail pam.gordon@ntlworld.com

GORDON, Sister Patricia Ann. b 44. St Alb and Ox Min Course. **d** 00 **p** 01. Professed CSMV from 80; NSM Didcot St Pet *Ox* from 00. *St Mary's Convent, Challow Road, Wantage OX12 9DJ* Tel and fax (01235) 767112 Mobile 07884-196004 E-mail smlcsmv@fish.co.uk

GORDON, Robert Andrew. b 42. Llan Dioc Tr Scheme 82. **d** 84 **p** 85. C Bargoed and Deri w Brithdir *Llan* 84-87; V Aberpergwm and Blaengwrach 87-94; R Johnston w Steynton *St D* 94-97; R Cosheston w Nash and Upton 97-04; TV Carew from 04. *The Rectory, St Michael's House, Cosheston, Pembroke Dock SA72 4UD* Tel (01646) 682477

GORDON, Robert John. b 56. Edin Univ MA81. Wycliffe Hall Ox 87. **d** 89 **p** 90. C Wilnecote *Lich* 89-91; C Bideford *Ex* 91-95; P-in-c Feniton, Buckerell and Escot 95-05; P-in-c Tiverton St Pet and Chevithorne w Cove from 05. *St Peter's Vicarage, 29 Moorlands, Tiverton EX16 6UF* Tel (01884) 254079 E-mail robert.j.gordon@btopenworld.com

GORDON, Ronald. *See* GORDON, The Rt Revd Archibald Ronald McDonald

GORDON, Thomas William. b 57. QUB BEd80 Univ of Ulster MA86 TCD BTh89 DPS89 Dip Counselling 96. CITC 85. **d** 89 **p** 90. C Ballymacash *Conn* 89-91; Min Can Belf Cathl 91-95; Chapl and Tutor CITC 91-96; Dir Extra-Mural Studies from 96; Lect Past Th and Liturgy from 01; PV Ch Ch Cathl Dublin *D & G* from 96; Co-ord Relig Progr RTE from 99. *CITC, Braemor Park, Dublin 14, Irish Republic* Tel (00353) (1) 492 3506 *or* 492 3695 Fax 492 3082 E-mail tommi@eircom.net *or* tgordon@tcd.ie

GORDON CLARK, John Vincent Michael. b 29. FCA DipRS. S'wark Ord Course 73. **d** 76 **p** 77. NSM Guildf H Trin w St Mary *Guildf* 76-81; NSM Albury w St Martha 81-91; Dioc Chapl to MU 92-95; Lic to Offic 95-99; Hon C Guildf Cathl 91-99; Perm to Offic from 99. *Hillfield, 8 Little Warren Close, Guildford GU4 8PW* Tel (01483) 569027

GORDON-CUMMING, Henry Ian. b 28. Barrister-at-Law (Gray's Inn) 56. Oak Hill Th Coll 54. **d** 57 **p** 58. C Southsea St Jude *Portsm* 57-60; Uganda 61-68; V Virginia Water *Guildf* 68-78; R Busbridge 78-87; R Lynch w Iping Marsh and Milland *Chich* 87-94; rtd 94; Perm to Offic *Chich* from 94. *Bay Cottage, Brookside, Runcton, Chichester PO20 1PX* Tel (01243) 783395

GORDON-KERR, Canon Francis Alexander. b 39. Dur Univ BA64 MA67 Hull Univ PhD81 DipEd. Wycliffe Hall Ox 65. **d** 67 **p** 68. C Heworth St Mary *Dur* 67-70; Chapl Newc Poly *Newc* 70-75; Chapl Hull Univ *York* 75-82; V Welton w Melton 82-92; Clergy Tr Officer E Riding 82-92; AD W Hull 87-96; RD Hull 89-96; Can and Preb York Minster 89-98; V Anlaby St Pet 92-98; R Crowland *Linc* 98-04; rtd 04. *Alberic Cottage, Low Road, Barrowby, Grantham NG32 1DD* Tel (01476) 574961

GORDON-TAYLOR, Benjamin Nicholas. b 69. St Jo Coll Dur BA90 MA92 Leeds Univ BA94 FRSA99. Coll of Resurr Mirfield 92. **d** 95 **p** 96. C Launceston *Truro* 95-97; C Northampton St Matt *Pet* 97-99; Fell and Chapl Univ Coll Dur 99-04; Lect and Tutor Coll of Resurr Mirfield from 05. *College of the Resurrection, Stocks Bank Road, Mirfield WF14 0BW* Tel (01924) 490441 E-mail bgordon-taylor@mirfield.org.uk

GORDON-WALKER, Caroline. b 37. LMH Ox BA59. Cranmer Hall Dur 01. **d** 02 **p** 03. NSM Poitou-Charentes *Eur* 02-05; C Aquitaine from 05. *18 Rue Pierre Pestereau, 86400 Civray, France* Tel (0033) (5) 49 87 97 36 E-mail carolinegw@wanadoo.fr

GORE, Canon John Charles. b 29. Leeds Univ BA52. Coll of Resurr Mirfield 52. **d** 54 **p** 55. C Middlesbrough St Jo the Ev *York* 54-59; N Rhodesia 59-64; Zambia 64-75; Can Lusaka 70-75; R Elland *Wakef* 75-84; TR 84-86; RD Brighouse and Elland 77-86; V Wembley Park St Aug *Lon* 86-95; P-in-c Tokyngton St Mich 89-90; AD Brent 90-95; rtd 95; P-in-c Heptonstall *Wakef* 95-99; Perm to Offic *Bradf* from 99. *3 Navigation Square, Skipton BD23 1XB* Tel (01756) 792297

GORE, Canon John Harrington. b 24. Em Coll Cam BA49 MA52. Westcott Ho Cam 49. **d** 51 **p** 52. C Deane *Man* 51-54; C Whitstable All SS w St Pet *Cant* 54-59; CF 59-62; V Womenswold *Cant* 62-67; C-in-c Aylesham CD 62-67; R Deal St Leon 67-75; RD Sandwich 70-78; P-in-c Sholden 74-75; R Deal St Leon w Sholden 75-80; R Southchurch H Trin *Chelmsf* 80-90; RD Southend-on-Sea 84-89; Hon Can Chelmsf Cathl 86-90; rtd 90; Perm to Offic *St E* and *Chelmsf* from 90. *8 De Burgh Place, Clare, Sudbury CO10 8QL* Tel (01787) 278558

GORHAM, Andrew Arthur. b 51. Bris Univ BA73 Birm Univ DipTh78 MA87. Qu Coll Birm 77. **d** 79 **p** 80. C Plaistow St Mary *Roch* 79-82; Chapl Lanchester Poly *Cov* 82-87; TV Warwick 87-95; Chapl Birm Univ *Birm* 95-00; Bp's Dom Chapl from 00. *Bishop's Croft, Old Church Road, Harborne, Birmingham B17 0BE* Tel 0121-427 2295 *or* 427 1163 Fax 426 1322 E-mail bishopschaplain@birmingham.anglican.org

GORHAM, Miss Karen Marisa. b 64. Trin Coll Bris BA95. **d** 95 **p** 96. C Northallerton w Kirby Sigston *York* 95-99; P-in-c Maidstone St Paul *Cant* from 99; Asst Dir of Ords from 02; AD Maidstone from 03. *St Paul's Vicarage, 130 Boxley Road, Maidstone ME14 2AH* Tel (01622) 691926 E-mail revdkaren@aol.com

GORICK, David Charles. b 32. Reading Univ BA55 Nottm Univ DipEd72. EMMTC 81. **d** 84 **p** 85. NSM W Bridgford *S'well* 84-89; C Gotham 89-97; C Kingston and Ratcliffe-on-Soar 89-97; C Barton in Fabis 89-97; C Thrumpton 89-97; P-in-c Gotham 97-99; rtd 99; Perm to Offic *S'well* from 03. *11 Brookfields Way, East Leake, Loughborough LE12 6HD* Tel (01509) 856960

GORICK, Janet Margaret. b 30. Reading Univ BA54. EMMTC 84. **dss** 86 **d** 87 **p** 94. Hon Par Dn W Bridgford *S'well* 87-95; NSM Gotham 95-99; NSM Barton in Fabis 95-99; NSM Kingston and Ratcliffe-on-Soar 95-99; NSM Thrumpton 95-99; rtd 99; Perm to Offic *S'well* from 03. *11 Brookfields Way, East Leake, Loughborough LE12 6HD* Tel (01509) 856960

GORICK, Martin Charles William. b 62. Selw Coll Cam BA84 MA88. Ripon Coll Cuddesdon 85. **d** 87 **p** 88. C Birtley *Dur* 87-91; Bp's Dom Chapl *Ox* 91-94; V Smethwick *Birm* 94-01; AD Warley 97-01; R Stratford-upon-Avon, Luddington etc *Cov* from 01. *The Vicarage, 7 Old Town, Stratford-upon-Avon CV37 6BG* Tel (01789) 266022 *or* 266316 E-mail office@stratford-upon-avon.org

GORING, Charles Robert. b 60. Nottm Univ BA91. Linc Th Coll Cert Min & Miss 93. **d** 93 **p** 94. C Thornbury *Glouc* 93-96; Perm to Offic *Chich* 97-98; Facilitator Demined Trust from 98; C Mayfield 98-00; V The Hydneye from 00; Chapl E Sussex Hosps NHS Trust from 01. *St Peter's House, The Hydneye, Eastbourne BN22 9BY* Tel and fax (01323) 504392 E-mail demined@onetel.com

GORRIE, Richard Bingham. b 27. Univ Coll Ox BA49 MA51. Ridley Hall Cam 49. **d** 51 **p** 52. C Ox St Clem *Ox* 51-54; C Morden *S'wark* 54-56; Scripture Union Rep (Scotland) 56-92; Chapl Fettes Coll Edin 60-74; Dir Inter-Sch Chr Fellowship (Scotland) 74-80; rtd 92; Perm to Offic *Glas* from 92. *17 Auchlochan Courtyard, New Trows Road, Lesmahagow, Lanark ML11 0JS* Tel (01555) 895076 E-mail gorries@silas57.freeserve.co.uk

GORRINGE, Prof Timothy Jervis. b 46. St Edm Hall Ox BA69 MPhil75. Sarum Th Coll 69. **d** 72 **p** 73. C Chapel Allerton *Ripon* 72-75; C Ox St Mary V w St Cross and St Pet *Ox* 76-78; India 79-86; Chapl St Jo Coll Ox 86-96; Reader St Andr Univ from 96; Prof Th Ex Univ from 99. *Department of Theology, Exeter University, Queen's Building, The Queen's Drive, Exeter EX4 4QH* Tel (01392) 264242 E-mail t.j.gorringe@exeter.ac.uk

GORTON, Anthony David Trevor. b 39. Lon Univ BSc65. Oak Hill Th Coll 78. **d** 81 **p** 82. NSM Colney Heath St Mark *St Alb* 81-00; NSM Watford St Pet from 00. *Waterdell, Lane End, Hatfield AL10 9AG* Tel (01707) 263605 E-mail tonygorton@hotmail.com

GORTON, Ian Charles Johnson. b 62. Bp Otter Coll BA84 Sarum & Wells Th Coll 86. **d** 89 **p** 90. C Wythenshawe Wm Temple Ch *Man* 89-92; C Man Apostles w Miles Platting 92-95; P-in-c Abbey Hey 95-03; P-in-c Moston St Chad from 03; P-in-c Blackley St Mark White Moss from 05. *St Chad's Rectory, 30 Hawthorn Road, Manchester M40 3RH* Tel 0161-681 3203

GORTON (née CARTER), Sarah Helen Buchanan. b 44. St Andr Univ BSc65 DipEd66. TISEC 93. **d** 96 **p** 98. NSM Lenzie *Glas* 96-01; P-in-c Alexandria from 01. *The Rectory, Queen Street, Alexandria G83 0AS* Tel (01389) 752633 E-mail sally@sgorton.freeserve.co.uk

GOSDEN, Timothy John. b 50. Open Univ BA86. Chich Th Coll 74. **d** 77 **p** 78. C Cant All SS *Cant* 77-81; Asst Chapl Loughb Univ *Leic* 81-85; Lic to Offic *Cant* 85-87; Chapl Ch Ch Coll of HE Cant 85-87; Sen Chapl Hull Univ 87-94; V Taunton Lyngford *B & W* 94-98; V Harrow St Mary *Lon* from 98. *St Mary's Vicarage, Church Hill, Harrow HA1 3HL* Tel (020) 8422 2652 E-mail timgosden@tiscali.co.uk *or* stmaryharrow@aol.com

GOSHAI, Miss Veja Helena. b 32. SRN57 SCM59 Midwife Teacher's Dip 66 City Univ BSc99. Trin Coll Bris 75. **d** 87 **p** 94. Asst Chapl St Bart Hosp Lon 87-97; rtd 92; Perm to Offic *S'wark* 99-03. *Grace, 26 Bilston Road, Crawford, Cape Town, 7780 South Africa*

GOSLING, David. b 27. St Alb and Ox Min Course 95. **d** 98 **p** 99. OLM High Wycombe *Ox* 98-03; Perm to Offic from 02. *72 Hatters Lane, High Wycombe HP13 7NJ* Tel (01494) 443947 E-mail dgosling027@btopenworld.com

GOSLING, David Lagourie. b 39. Man Univ MSc63 Fitzw Coll Cam MA69 Lanc Univ PhD74 MInstP69 CPhys84. Ridley Hall Cam 63. **d** 73 **p** 74. Hon C Lancaster St Mary *Blackb* 73-74; Hon C Kingston upon Hull St Matt w St Barn *York* 74-77; Hon C Cottingham 78-83; Asst Chapl Geneva *Eur* 84-89; C Cambridge Gt St Mary w St Mich *Ely* 89-90; C Dry Drayton 90-94; USPG India 95-99; Perm to Offic *York* from 95 and *Ely* from 01; Fell Clare Hall Cam from 01. *Clare Hall, Herschel Road, Cambridge CB3 9AL* Tel (01223) 352450 Fax 332333

GOSLING, James Albert. b 41. Oak Hill Th Coll 81. **d** 84 **p** 85. NSM Victoria Docks St Luke *Chelmsf* 84-96; Hon C Gt Mongeham w Ripple and Sutton by Dover *Cant* 96-01; Hon C Eastry and Northbourne w Tilmanstone etc 96-01; C Kenton, Mamhead, Powderham, Cofton and Starcross *Ex* 01-02. *2 Wordsworth Close, Exmouth EX8 5SQ* Tel (01395) 225278 E-mail jimandjan@jimandjan.fsnet.co.uk

GOSLING, John William Fraser. b 34. St Jo Coll Dur BA58 DipTh60 MA71 Ex Univ PhD78. Cranmer Hall Dur 58. **d** 60 **p** 61. C Plympton St Mary *Ex* 60-68; V Newport 68-78; Org Sec CECS *St Alb* and *Ox* 78-82; C Stratford sub Castle *Sarum* 83-86; Adv on CME 83-86; Perm to Offic 86-91 and from 95; C Swindon Ch Ch *Bris* 91-95; rtd 95. *1 Wiley Terrace, Wilton, Salisbury SP2 0HN* Tel (01722) 742788 E-mail jgosling@fish.co.uk

GOSNEY, Jeanette Margaret. b 58. Bath Univ BA81 Nottm Univ PGCE82. St Jo Coll Nottm BTh93 MPhil95. **d** 95 **p** 96. C Ipswich St Marg *St E* 95-98; Asst Chapl Loughb Univ *Leic* 98; Sen Chapl 98-01; Tutor Trin Coll Bris 01-04; Chapl Repton Sch Derby 04-05; P-in-c Braughing w Furneux Pelham and Stocking Pelham *St Alb* from 05. *St Mary's Rectory, 7A Green End, Braughing, Ware SG11 2PG* Tel (01920) 822619 E-mail vicar@braughing.org.uk

GOSS, David James. b 52. Nottm Univ BCombStuds. Linc Th Coll. **d** 83 **p** 84. C Wood Green St Mich w Bounds Green St Gabr etc *Lon* 83-86; TV Gleadless Valley *Sheff* 86-89; TR 89-95; V Wheatley Hills from 95. *The Vicarage, 18 Central Boulevard, Doncaster DN2 5PE* Tel (01302) 342047 E-mail geese@talk21.com

GOSS, Kevin Ian. b 56. LRAM75 LTCL76 GRSM77 LGSM80 Hughes Hall Cam PGCE78. S Dios Minl Tr Scheme 89. **d** 92 **p** 93. NSM Ardingly *Chich* 92-98; Asst Chapl Ardingly Coll 92-98; Min Can, Prec and Sacr Cant Cathl *Cant* 98-03; P-in-c Hockerill *St Alb* from 04. *Hockerill Vicarage, 4A All Saints Close, Bishop's Stortford CM23 2EA* Tel (01279) 834407

GOSS, Michael John. b 37. Chich Th Coll 62. **d** 65 **p** 66. C Angell Town St Jo *S'wark* 65-68; C Catford St Laur 68-71; P-in-c Lewisham St Swithun 71-81; V Redhill St Jo 81-88; V Dudley St Thos and St Luke *Worc* 88-98; C Small Heath *Birm* 98-02; rtd 02; Perm to Offic *Birm* from 02. *8 Mayland Road, Birmingham B16 0NG* Tel 0121-429 6022

GOSSWINN, Nicholas Simon. b 50. Birm Poly FGA80. St D Coll Lamp DipTh73. **d** 73 **p** 77. C Abergavenny St Mary *Mon* 73-74; C-in-c Bassaleg 74-80; TV Barrow St Geo w St Luke *Carl* 81-87; C Usworth *Dur* 89-90; TV 90-96; P-in-c Sunderland Red Ho 96-02; P-in-c Stockport St Matt *Ches* 02-03. *Alnwick, Queens Park, Millom LA18 5DY*

GOSTELOW (née THOMPSON), Mrs Ruth Jean. b 47. St Alb Minl Tr Scheme 85. **d** 90 **p** 94. Par Dn Stonebridge St Mich *Lon* 90-94; C Ealing St Paul 94-96; TV W Slough *Ox* 96-03; V New Haw *Guildf* from 03. *The Vicarage, 149 Woodham Lane, New*

Haw, Addlestone KT15 3NJ Tel and fax (01932) 343187 E-mail reverendruth@aol.com

GOSWELL, Geoffrey. b 34. SS Paul & Mary Coll Cheltenham CertEd68. Glouc Th Course 70. **d** 71 **p** 72. C Cheltenham Em *Glouc* 71-73; C Lydney w Aylburton 73-76; P-in-c Falfield w Rockhampton 76-79; Chapl HM Det Cen Eastwood Park 76-79; Area Sec CMS *Ely* 79-81; *Linc* and *Pet* 79-86; Dep Regional Sec (UK) CMS 86-97; P-in-c Orton Waterville *Ely* 90-96; TV The Ortons, Alwalton and Chesterton 96-97; rtd 97; Perm to Offic *Pet* from 01. *9 Kimble Close, Northampton NN4 0RF* Tel (01604) 709512

GOTELEE, Peter Douglas. b 28. K Coll Lon 50. **d** 54 **p** 55. C Croydon St Pet S End *Cant* 54-57; C Camberley St Paul *Guildf* 57-65; P-in-c Badshot Lea CD 65-75; P-in-c Bisley 75-76; V W End 75-76; R Bisley and W End 76-85; V Yarcombe w Membury and Upottery *Ex* 85-93; P-in-c Cotleigh 85-93; rtd 93; Perm to Offic *Ex* from 93. *3 Sharpitor Close, Paignton TQ3 1AR* Tel (01803) 559150

GOTHARD, Mrs Anne Marie. b 51. STETS. **d** 00. NSM E Meon and Langrish *Portsm* 00-04; NSM Catherington and Clanfield from 04. *27 Green Lane, Clanfield, Waterlooville PO8 0JU* Tel (023) 9259 6315 Mobile 07939-472796 E-mail anne@gothard.freeserve.co.uk

GOTT, Stephen. b 61. St Jo Coll Nottm Dip Th & Min 94. **d** 94 **p** 95. C Mount Pellon *Wakef* 94-97; V Greetland and W Vale from 97. *The Vicarage, 2 Goldfields Way, Greetland, Halifax HX4 8LA* Tel (01422) 372802 E-mail stephen.gott@btinternet.com

GOUGH, Andrew Stephen. b 60. Sarum & Wells Th Coll 83. **d** 86 **p** 87. C St Leonards Ch Ch and St Mary *Chich* 86-88; C Broseley w Benthall *Heref* 88-90; V Ketley and Oakengates *Lich* 90-93; TV Bickleigh (Plymouth) *Ex* 93; TV Bickleigh and Shaugh Prior 94; P-in-c St Day *Truro* 94-96; V Chacewater w St Day and Carharrack from 96. *The Vicarage, Pink Moors, St Day, Redruth TR16 5NN* Tel (01209) 820275 E-mail stpaulchacewater@churchserve.net

GOUGH, Andrew Walter. b 55. Bris Univ BA78. Trin Coll Bris 90. **d** 92 **p** 93. C Mossley Hill St Matt and St Jas *Liv* 92-94; C Wavertree H Trin 94-96; Chapl Warw Sch from 96. *9 Griffin Road, Warwick CV34 6QX* Tel (01926) 400533 *or* 776416 E-mail awg@warwickschool.org

GOUGH, Anthony Walter. b 31. Lon Univ DipTh68 Leic Univ MA76. Chicago Th Sem DMin81 Oak Hill Th Coll 57. **d** 60 **p** 61. C Southsea St Simon *Portsm* 60-64; R Peldon *Chelmsf* 64-71; V Rothley *Leic* 71-80; USA 80-81; Chapl St Jo Hosp Aylesbury 81-82; Perm to Offic *Leic* 82-96; rtd 96. *410 Hinckley Road, Leicester LE3 0WA* Tel and fax 0116-285 4284 E-mail tg1@ntlworld.com

GOUGH, Colin Richard. b 47. St Chad's Coll Dur BA69. Cuddesdon Coll 73. **d** 75 **p** 76. C Lich St Chad *Lich* 75-78; C Codsall 78-84; V Wednesbury St Paul Wood Green 84-92; TR Tettenhall Wood 92-99; TR Tettenhall Wood and Perton 99-01; P-in-c Stannington *Newc* from 01; Dioc Adv for CME from 01. *The Vicarage, Beechlea, Stannington, Morpeth NE61 6HL* Tel (01670) 789122 *or* 0191-270 4153 Fax 0191-270 4101 E-mail colingough@onetel.com *or* c.gough@newcastle.anglican.org

GOUGH, David Norman. b 42. Oak Hill Th Coll 70. **d** 70 **p** 71. C Penn Fields *Lich* 70-73; C Stapenhill w Cauldwell *Derby* 73-77; V Heath 77-86; P-in-c Derby St Chad 86-95; TV Walbrook Epiphany 95-03; P-in-c Codnor from 03; P-in-c Loscoe from 03. *The Vicarage, 20 Denby Lane, Codnor, Ripley DE5 9SN* Tel (01773) 742516 E-mail gough@heyho.fsnet.co.uk

GOUGH, Derek William. b 31. Pemb Coll Cam BA55 MA59. St Steph Ho Ox 55. **d** 57 **p** 58. C E Finchley All SS *Lon* 57-60; C Roxbourne St Andr 60-66; V Edmonton St Mary w St Jo 66-98; rtd 98; Perm to Offic *Chelmsf* from 98 and *St Alb* from 00. *11 Church Lane, Letchworth Garden City SG6 1AJ* Tel (01462) 680683

GOUGH, Mrs Elizabeth. b 54. Carl and Blackb Dioc Tr Inst. **d** 00 **p** 01. OLM Brampton and Farlam and Castle Carrock w Cumrew *Carl* 00-02; OLM Hayton w Cumwhitton 00-02; OLM Irthington, Crosby-on-Eden and Scaleby 00-02; OLM Eden, Gelt and Irthing from 02. *Brackenside Barn, Brampton CA8 2QX* Tel (01697) 746252

GOUGH, Canon Ernest Hubert. b 31. TCD BA53 MA57. TCD Div Sch Div Test 54. **d** 54 **p** 55. C Glenavy *Conn* 54-57; C Lisburn Ch Ch 57-61; P-in-c Belfast St Ninian 61-62; I 62-71; I Belfast St Bart 71-85; I Templepatrick w Donegore 85-97; Can Conn Cathl from 91; rtd 97. *The Cairn, 15 Swilly Road, Portstewart BT55 7DJ* Tel (028) 7083 3253 E-mail ehg@thecairn.fsnet.co.uk

GOUGH, Frank Peter. b 32. Lon Coll of Div 66. **d** 68 **p** 69. C Weymouth St Mary *Sarum* 68-70; C Attenborough w Chilwell *S'well* 70-73; R Barrow *Ches* 73-77; P-in-c Summerstown *S'wark* 77-88; RD Tooting 80-88; Dioc Past Sec 88-93; Tutor and Chapl Whittington Coll Felbridge 93-98; rtd 98. *18 Bromley College, London Road, Bromley BR1 1PE* Tel (020) 8290 1090 Mobile 07970-199135

GOUGH, Jonathan Robin Blanning. b 62. Univ of Wales (Lamp) BA83 Westmr Coll Ox MTh96 FRSA03. St Steph Ho Ox 83. **d** 85 **p** 86. C Braunton *Ex* 85-86; C Matson *Glouc* 86-89; CF 89-01 and from 05; Abp's Officer for Ecum *Cant* 01-05; Can Gib Cathl *Eur* 02-05; Public Preacher *Win* 02-05. *c/o MOD Chaplains (Army)* Tel (01980) 615804 Fax 615800

GOUGH, Miss Lynda Elizabeth. b 54. RGN83 SS Hild & Bede Coll Dur BA94. Wycliffe Hall Ox 97. **d** 99 **p** 00. C Stranton *Dur* 99-03; V Spennymoor, Whitworth and Merrington from 03. *10 Merrington Close, Kirk Merrington, Spennymoor DL16 7HU* Tel (01388) 815471

GOUGH, Martyn John. b 66. Univ of Wales (Cardiff) BTh87 Univ of Wales (Lamp) MA05 FRSA04. St Steph Ho Ox 88. **d** 90 **p** 91. C Port Talbot St Theodore *Llan* 90-92; C Roath 92-94; Asst Chapl Milan w Genoa and Varese *Eur* 95-98; Chapl RN from 98. *Royal Navy Chaplaincy Service, Room 203, Victory Building, HM Naval Base, Portsmouth PO1 3LS* Tel (023) 9272 7903 Fax 9272 7111

GOUGH, Robert. b 50. S'wark Ord Course 79. **d** 82 **p** 83. C Heston *Lon* 82-83; C Feltham 83-86; TV Hemel Hempstead *St Alb* 86-90; NSM Kingston All SS w St Jo *S'wark* 90-91; Perm to Offic *S'wark* 91-94; *St As* 95-00; P-in-c Corwen and Llangar w Gwyddelwern and Llawrybetws *St As* 00-02; P-in-c Betws Gwerful Goch w Llangwm, Gwyddelwern etc 02-03. *Pen y Gaer Uchaf, Llanfihangel Glyn Myfyr, Corwen LL21 9UH* Tel (01490) 420791

GOUGH, Stephen William Cyprian. b 50. Alberta Univ BSc71. Cuddesdon Coll BA80. **d** 79 **p** 80. C Walton St Mary *Liv* 79-83; V New Springs 83-87; V Childwall St Dav from 87; V Stoneycroft All SS from 04. *St David's Vicarage, Rocky Lane, Liverpool L16 1JA* Tel 0151-722 4549

GOULD, Alan Charles. b 26. Lon Univ DipTh53. **d** 62 **p** 63. C Bromborough *Ches* 62-67; V Audlem and Burleydam 67-80; V Knowbury and P-in-c Coreley and Doddington *Heref* 80-83; P-in-c Cound and Berrington w Betton Strange 83-91; rtd 91; Perm to Offic *Heref* and *Lich* from 91. *32 Mytton Oak Road, Shrewsbury SY3 8UD* Tel (01743) 244820

GOULD, David Robert. b 59. Cov Poly BA81. Cranmer Hall Dur 87. **d** 90 **p** 91. C Rugby St Andr *Cov* 90-93; CF 93-94; Perm to Offic *Cov* 01-05; TV Kings Norton *Birm* from 05. *53 Wychall Park Grove, Birmingham B38 8AG* Tel 0121-459 5144 Mobile 07913-546870 E-mail gould2@freewire.co.uk

GOULD, Preb Douglas Walter. b 35. St Jo Coll Cam BA59 MA63. Ridley Hall Cam 59. **d** 61 **p** 62. C Clifton *York* 61-64; C Bridgnorth w Tasley *Heref* 64-67; C Astley Abbotts w Linley 64-67; R Acton Burnell w Pitchford 67-73; P-in-c Cound 68-73; Asst Dioc Youth Officer 68-73; P-in-c Frodesley 69-73; V Bromyard 73-00; P-in-c Stanford Bishop 73-00; RD Bromyard 73-99; Chapl Bromyard Community Hosp 73-92; Chapl Herefordshire Community Health NHS Trust 92-00; P-in-c Ocle Pychard *Heref* 76-88; P-in-c Ullingswick 76-88; P-in-c Stoke Lacy, Moreton Jeffries w Much Cowarne etc 76-83; Preb Heref Cathl 83-00; rtd 00; Perm to Offic *Heref* from 00. *Highwood Croft, Marden, Hereford HR1 3EW* Tel and fax (01432) 880084 E-mail waltergould@waitrose.com

GOULD, Ms Janet. b 63. LTCL85. Westcott Ho Cam 92. **d** 95 **p** 96. C Pet St Mary Boongate *Pet* 95-98; C Fleet *Guildf* 98-04; C St Mellons *Mon* from 04. *Ty'r Capel, 54A Cardiff Road, Llandaff, Cardiff CF5 2DT* Tel (029) 2056 3116 E-mail jan.gould2@btinternet.com

GOULD, John Barry. b 38. MICE68. S'wark Ord Course 77. **d** 77 **p** 78. C Streatham St Leon *S'wark* 77-80; V Upper Tooting H Trin 80-87; P-in-c Brockham Green 87-90; P-in-c Betchworth and Buckland 87-95; C-in-c Roundshaw St Paul CD 95-03; RD Sutton 00-03; rtd 03. *16 Highlands, Potterne, Devizes SN10 5NS* Tel (01380) 730292

GOULD, Jonathan George Lillico. b 58. Bris Univ LLB79. Wycliffe Hall Ox 86. **d** 89 **p** 91. Australia 89-93; Schs Worker Scripture Union Independent Schs 93-95; Perm to Offic *S'wark* 93-95; Min Hampstead St Jo Downshire Hill Prop Chpl *Lon* from 95. *The Parsonage, 64 Pilgrim's Lane, London NW3 1SN* Tel (020) 7794 8946 *or* tel and fax 7435 8404 E-mail jonathan@sjdh.org

GOULD, Mrs Pamela Rosemarie. **d** 01 **p** 02. NSM New Bilton *Cov* 01-03; Asst Chapl HM YOI Onley 01-03; NSM Clifton upon Dunsmore and Newton *Cov* 03-05; P-in-c from 05. *19 Church Road, Church Lawford, Rugby CV23 9EG* Tel (024) 7654 5745 E-mail revpamgould@aol.com

GOULD, Peter Richard. b 34. Univ of Wales BA57. Qu Coll Birm DipTh62. **d** 62 **p** 63. C Rothwell *Ripon* 62-68; V Allerton Bywater 68-73; Lic to Offic *S'well* 73-76; Chapl Lic Victuallers' Sch Ascot 76-93; V Aberavon H Trin *Llan* 93-99; rtd 99. *Amber Cottage, 1 Load Lane, Weston Zoyland, Bridgwater TA7 0EQ* Tel (01278) 691029

GOULD, Robert Ozburn. b 38. Williams Coll Mass BA59 St Andr Univ PhD63. **d** 78 **p** 83. NSM Edin St Columba *Edin* 78-80; TV from 83; Hon Dioc Supernumerary 80-83; Hon Chapl Edin Univ from 00. *33 Charterhall Road, Edinburgh EH9 3HS* Tel 0131-667 7230 *or* 650 9502 E-mail gould@ed.ac.uk

GOULD, Susan Judith. *See* MURRAY, Mrs Susan Judith
GOULD, Walter. *See* GOULD, Preb Douglas Walter
GOULDER, Canon Catherine Helen. b 44. Hull Univ BA65 MA67 Ox Univ DipEd68. NEOC 96. **d** 98 **p** 99. NSM Sutton St Mich *York* 98-02; P-in-c N Cave w Cliffe from 02; P-in-c Hotham from 02; Can and Preb York Minster from 05. *The Vicarage, Church Lane, North Cave, Brough HU15 2GJ* Tel (01430) 470716 E-mail kgoulder@fish.co.uk
GOULDING, John Gilbert. b 29. Univ Coll Dur BA54 MA59. **d** 88 **p** 89. NSM Kemsing w Woodlands *Roch* 88-91; Hon Nat Moderator for Reader Tr ACCM 90-91; ABM 91-94; NSM Sevenoaks St Luke CD 91-96; Perm to Offic from 97. *Springwood, 50 Copperfields, Kemsing, Sevenoaks TN15 6QG* Tel (01732) 762558
GOULDING, Nicolas John. b 56. Southn Univ BSc78 PhD82. NTMTC 94. **d** 97 **p** 98. NSM St Bart Less *Lon* from 97; Chapl St Bart's and RLSMD Qu Mary and Westf Coll from 97; Perm to Offic *St Alb* from 99. *5 Greatfield Close, Harpenden AL5 3HP* Tel (01582) 461293 *or* (020) 7882 6128 Fax (020) 7982 6076 E-mail n.j.goulding@qmul.ac.uk
GOULDSTONE, Canon Timothy Maxwell. b 46. Ex Univ BSc68 MSc76 PhD02 Lon Univ BD94 MSOSc87. Trin Coll Bris 76. **d** 78 **p** 79. C Ware Ch Ch *St Alb* 78-81; P-in-c Ansley *Cov* 81-82; V 82-85; V St Keverne *Truro* 85-95; Preb St Endellion 90-99; P-in-c St Michael Penkevil 95-02; P-in-c Lamorran and Merther 95-02; Dir Lay Tr 95-02; RD Powder 96-01; Hon Can Truro Cathl 99-02; Chapl UEA *Nor* 02-05; Dir Nor Cathl Inst 02-05; P-in-c Beckington w Standerwick, Berkley, Rodden etc *B & W* from 05. *8 Church Street, Beckington, Frome BA11 6TG* Tel (01373) 830314 E-mail t.gouldstone@btopenworld.com
GOULDTHORPE, Rachel Carolyn. b 72. Bp Otter Coll 00. **d** 03. NSM Hove *Chich* 03-05; C Moulsecoomb from 05. *The Vicarage, Selham Drive, Brighton BN1 9EL* Tel (01273) 601854
GOULSTON, Jeremy Hugh. b 68. St Aid Coll Dur BA90. Ripon Coll Cuddesdon 01. **d** 03 **p** 04. C Henfield w Shermanbury and Woodmancote *Chich* from 03. *Glebe House, 41 Furners Mead, Henfield BN5 9JA* Tel (01273) 492690
GOULSTONE, Thomas Richard Kerry. b 36. Univ of Wales (Lamp) BA57. St Mich Coll Llan 57. **d** 59 **p** 60. C Llanbadarn Fawr *St D* 59-61; C Carmarthen St Pet 61-64; V 84-93; V Whitchurch w Solva and St Elvis 64-67; V Gors-las 67-76; V Burry Port and Pwll 76-84; Chapl W Wales Gen Hosp Carmarthen 84-93; Can St D Cathl *St D* 86-93; Hon Can St D Cathl from 93; RD Carmarthen 88-92; Adn Carmarthen 91-93; Dean and Lib St As Cathl *St As* 93-01; rtd 01. *80 Sandpiper Road, Llanelli SA15 4SH* Tel (01554) 746117
GOUNDREY-SMITH, Stephen John. b 67. Brighton Poly BSc88 MRPharmS89 City Univ MSc94. Aston Tr Scheme 96 Wycliffe Hall Ox BTh01. **d** 99 **p** 00. C Happisburgh, Walcott, Hempstead w Eccles etc *Nor* 99-01; Perm to Offic *Pet* 02-03; NSM Middleton Cheney w Chacombe 03-04; NSM Chenderit from 04. *1 The Walnuts, Main Street, Charlton, Banbury OX17 3DR* Tel (01295) 816887 Mobile 07771-741009 E-mail stephen@goundrey-smith.freeserve.co.uk
GOUNDRY, Canon Ralph Walter. b 31. St Chad's Coll Dur BA56 DipTh58. **d** 58 **p** 59. C Harton Colliery *Dur* 58-62; Prec Newc Cathl *Newc* 62-65; V Sighill 65-72; V Long Benton 72-96; Hon Can Newc Cathl 94-96; rtd 96; Perm to Offic *York* 96-98. *16 Old Manor Way, Chislehurst BR7 5XS* Tel (020) 8249 9992
GOUPILLON, Mrs Jane Elizabeth. b 50. Univ of Wales (Lamp) BA92 Trin Coll Carmarthen PGCE94. St Mich Coll Llan. **d** 03 **p** 04. C Carmarthen St Dav *St D* from 03. *The Parsonage, 26 Knoll Gardens, Carmarthen SA31 3EJ* Tel (01267) 222865
GOURDIE, Mrs Janice Elizabeth. b 65. Univ of Wales (Ban) BTh04. **d** 04 **p** 05. C Botwnnog w Bryncroes *Ban* from 04. *Maelor, 6 Nant y Felin, Nefyn, Pwllheli LL53 6LH* Tel (01758) 721047 Mobile 07969-655497 E-mail janicegourdie@hotmail.com
GOURLEY, Malcolm Samuel. b 37. MRPharmS58. NEOC 94. **d** 98 **p** 98. NSM Gt Smeaton w Appleton Wiske and Birkby etc *Ripon* 98-00; NSM Ainderby Steeple w Yafforth and Kirby Wiske etc 00-02; NSM Herrington, Penshaw and Shiney Row *Dur* from 02. *10 Weymouth Drive, Houghton le Spring DH4 7TQ* Tel 0191-385 4076
GOURLEY, William Robert Joseph. b 48. K Coll Lon BD74. CITC 68. **d** 75 **p** 76. C Newtownards *D & D* 75-78; I Currin w Drum and Newbliss *Clogh* 78-81; I Dublin St Geo and St Thos, Finglas and Free Ch *D & G* 81-88; I Dublin Zion Ch from 88. *The Rectory, 18 Bushy Park Road, Rathgar, Dublin 6, Irish Republic* Tel (00353) (1) 492 2365 *or* 406 4730 E-mail wilbertgourley@ireland.com
GOVAN, Kesh Rico. b 66. St Jo Coll Dur BA96. Cranmer Hall Dur 93. **d** 96 **p** 97. C Astley Bridge *Man* 96-00; TV Walkden and Lt Hulton 00-04; I Blessington w Kilbride, Ballymore Eustace etc *D & G* from 04. *The Rectory, Blessington, Co Wicklow, Irish Republic* Tel (00353) (45) 865178
GOVENDER, Rogers Morgan. b 60. Natal Univ BTh97. St Paul's Coll Grahamstown DipTh85. **d** 85 **p** 86. S Africa 85-00; C Overport Ch Ch 85-87; R Greyville St Mary 88-92; R Hayfields St Matt 93-98; Adn Pietermaritzburg 97-98; R Berea St Thos 99-00; P-in-c Didsbury Ch Ch *Man* from 01; P-in-c Withington St Chris from 03; AD Withington from 04. *Christ Church Rectory, 35 Darley Avenue, Manchester M20 2ZD* Tel 0161-445 4152 E-mail rogersg@darleyave.fsnet.co.uk
GOW, Iain Douglas. b 60. Denver Univ USA BA83 MIM85. Trin Coll Bris DipHE92 MA94. **d** 94 **p** 95. C Kenilworth St Jo *Cov* 94-97; C Birm St Martin w Bordesley St Andr *Birm* from 97; AD Birm City Cen 02-04. *59 Featherstone Road, Kings Heath, Birmingham B14 6BD* Tel 0121-443 1400 *or* 443 4822 E-mail iain@bullring.org
GOW, Peter Draffin. b 52. Bede Coll Dur BEd76. St Jo Coll Nottm 83. **d** 85. C Kingston Hill St Paul *S'wark* 85-86; rtd 86. *Chatsworth Wing, Royal Hospital for Neuro-disability, London SW15 3SW* Tel (020) 8788 5158 E-mail petergow@waacis.edex.co.uk
GOWDEY, Michael Cragg. b 32. Oriel Coll Ox BA56 MA58 Keele Univ CertEd73. Qu Coll Birm DipTh57. **d** 58 **p** 59. C Ashbourne w Mapleton and Clifton *Derby* 58-63; V Chellaston 63-69; Asst Chapl Ellesmere Coll 69-74; Chapl Trent Coll Nottm 74-81; Educn Chapl *Worc* 81-97; Chapl K Edw Sixth Form Coll Worc 81-97; rtd 97; P-in-c Beeley and Edensor *Derby* 97-02; Perm to Offic from 02. *18 Moorhall Estate, Bakewell DE45 1FP* Tel (01629) 814121
GOWEN, John Frank. b 30. **d** 87 **p** 89. NSM Lecale Gp *D & D* 87-91; NSM Cregagh 87-91; Lic to Offic 89-99; NSM Stormont 99-01; NSM Knock from 01. *36 Downshire Road, Belfast BT6 9JL* Tel (028) 9070 1640
GOWER, Canon Christopher Raymond. b 45. Nottm Univ BA73 Heythrop Coll Lon MA96 Univ of Wales MTh02 FRSA84. St Jo Coll Nottm 70. **d** 73 **p** 74. C Hounslow H Trin *Lon* 73-76; Hon C N Greenford All Hallows 76-77; P-in-c Willesden Green St Gabr 77-83; P-in-c Brondesbury St Anne w Kilburn H Trin 81-82; Perm to Offic 82-84; P-in-c Yiewsley 84-96; R St Marylebone w H Trin from 97; P-in-c St Marylebone St Cypr from 99; Hon Can Ilesa from 04. *21 Beaumont Street, London W1G 6DQ* Tel (020) 7935 8965 *or* 7935 7315 Fax 7486 5493 E-mail office@stmarylebone.org
GOWER, Denys Victor. b 33. Cant Sch of Min 85. **d** 87 **p** 88. NSM Gillingham H Trin *Roch* 87-91; NSM Gillingham St Aug 89-91; C Perry Street 91-93; P-in-c Wateringbury w Teston and W Farleigh 93-96; R 96-00; rtd 00; Perm to Offic *Roch* 00-02; Ind Chapl from 02; Perm to Offic *Cant* from 03. *4 Locarno Avenue, Gillingham ME8 6ET* Tel (01634) 375765 Mobile 07930-820441
GOWER, Nigel Plested. b 37. SS Coll Cam BA62 MA65 Lon Univ PGCE68. Ridley Hall Cam 61. **d** 63 **p** 64. C Walthamstow St Jo *Chelmsf* 63-66; CMS Nigeria 67-78; P-in-c Loscoe *Derby* 78-79; V 79-88; RD Heanor 84-88; R Bamford 88-98; Dioc World Development Officer 90-96; P-in-c Bradwell 96-98; Assoc P Alfreton Deanery 98-02; rtd 02; Perm to Offic *Heref* from 02. *New Cottage, Llanbister Road, Llandrindod Wells LD1 5UW* Tel (01547) 550318
GOWER, Miss Patricia Ann. b 44. Wilson Carlile Coll IDC79 Sarum & Wells Th Coll 88. **d** 88 **p** 94. Chapl Bris Univ *Bris* 88-91; Hon Par Dn Clifton St Paul 88-91; Par Dn Spondon *Derby* 91-94; C 94-95; P-in-c Hatton 95-98; Asst Chapl HM Pris Sudbury 95-98; Chapl 98-04; rtd 04; Perm to Offic *Derby* from 04. *19 Heronswood Drive, Spondon, Derby DE21 7AX* Tel (01332) 671031
GOWER, Miss Paulette Rose-Mary de Garis. b 70. Plymouth Univ BEd93. Cranmer Hall Dur 01. **d** 03 **p** 04. C Shrewsbury St Geo w Greenfields *Lich* from 03. *5 Bayford Drive, Shrewsbury SY1 3XQ* Tel (01743) 289122
GOWER, Archdeacon of. *See* WILLIAMS, The Ven Robert John
GOWING-CUMBER, Alexander John. b 72. Fitzw Coll Cam MA00 Moorlands Th Coll BA94. Ridley Hall Cam 98. **d** 00 **p** 03. C Vange *Chelmsf* 00-02; C Rayleigh 02-05; TV Grays Thurrock from 05. *The Vicarage, Clockhouse Lane, Grays RM16 6YW* Tel (01375) 482252 E-mail countdarcy@hotmail.com
GOYMOUR, Mrs Joanna Leigh. b 58. Reading Univ BA79. Dioc OLM tr scheme 99. **d** 02 **p** 03. OLM Bures w Assington and Lt Cornard *St E* from 02. *Dorking Tye House, Dorking Tye, Bures CO8 5JY* Tel (01787) 227494 E-mail jo@acgoymour.freeserve.co.uk
GOYMOUR, Michael Edwyn. b 29. Selw Coll Cam BA51 McGill Univ Montreal BD53. Montreal Dioc Th Coll 51 Wells Th Coll 53. **d** 53 **p** 54. C Bury St Edmunds St Jo *St E* 53-56; C Ipswich St Bart 56-60; R Gamlingay *Ely* 60-68; rtd 92; Perm to Offic *Ely* and *Pet* from 92. *56 Church Drive, Orton Waterville, Peterborough PE2 5HE* Tel (01733) 231535
GRACE, Capt David Leonard. b 55. Wilson Carlile Coll Dip Evang 92 Ripon Coll Cuddesdon DipMin99. **d** 99 **p** 00. CA from 92; C St Leonards and St Ives *Win* 99-04; V from 04. *The Vicarage, 30 Pine Drive, St Ives, Ringwood BH24 2LN* Tel (01425) 476198
GRACE, Mrs Irene. b 36. Nottm Univ BSc58. Guildf Dioc Min Course 96. **d** 98 **p** 99. OLM Stoneleigh *Guildf* from 98.

33 Woodstone Avenue, Stoneleigh, Epsom KT17 2JS Tel (020) 8393 7280

GRACE, Kenneth. b 24. Leeds Univ BA49. Wycliffe Hall Ox 62. **d** 63 **p** 64. C Tonge w Alkrington *Man* 63-66; R Thwing *York* 66-70; V Wold Newton 66-70; Chapl St Andr Sch Worthing 70-76; R Berwick w Selmeston and Alciston *Chich* 76-81; P-in-c Kingston Buci 81-85; R Westbourne 85-90; rtd 90; Perm to Offic *Chich* from 90. *17 Ramsay Hall, 11-13 Byron Road, Worthing BN11 3HN* Tel (01903) 230611

GRACE, Ms Louise Sarah. b 68. Girton Coll Cam BA89. Ripon Coll Cuddesdon BA97 Ch Div Sch of Pacific 97. **d** 98 **p** 99. C Wordsley *Worc* 98-02; R Teme Valley N from 03. *The Rectory, Lindridge, Tenbury Wells WR15 8JQ* Tel (01584) 881331 E-mail louisegrace@fsmail.net

GRACE, Richard Maurice. b 29. St Chad's Coll Dur BA53. Chich Th Coll 53. **d** 55 **p** 56. C Toxteth Park St Agnes *Liv* 55-58; C Wolverhampton St Pet *Lich* 58-62; V W Bromwich St Fran 62-78; P-in-c Salt 78-84; P-in-c Sandon w Burston 82-84; V Salt and Sandon w Burston 84-93; rtd 94; Perm to Offic *Ches* from 94. *Little Owls, 1 Trinity Close, Crewe CW2 8FD* Tel (01270) 662221

GRACE, Wilfrid Windsor. b 15. ACA39 FCA60. Westcott Ho Cam 52. **d** 53 **p** 54. C Chippenham St Andr w Tytherton Lucas *Bris* 53-57; V Minety w Oaksey 57-71; V Oldland 71-76; V Abbots Leigh w Leigh Woods 76-80; Chapl Ham Green Hosp 79-87; rtd 80; Perm to Offic *B & W* from 81; Hon Chapl Cheshire Home Axbridge from 81. *Hurn Mead, 71 Woodborough Road, Winscombe BS25 1BA* Tel (01934) 843362

GRACIE, Anthony Johnstone. b 25. Ch Coll Cam BA48 MA51. Linc Th Coll 57. **d** 59 **p** 60. C Edgbaston St Geo *Birm* 59-62; R Lyndon w Manton and Martinsthorpe *Pet* 62-76; R N Luffenham 66-76; V Odiham w S Warnborough and Long Sutton *Win* 76-85; Perm to Offic *Bris* 85-88; rtd 88. *Colt Corner, Horn Lane, East Hendred, Wantage OX12 8LD* Tel (01235) 821509 E-mail a.gracie@btconnect.com

GRACIE, Canon Bryan John. b 45. Open Univ BA81. AKC67. **d** 68 **p** 69. C Whipton *Ex* 68-72; Chapl St Jo Sch Tiffield 72-73; Chapl HM Borstal Stoke Heath 74-78; Asst Chapl HM Pris Liv 74; Chapl HM Youth Cust Cen Feltham 78-85; Chapl HM Pris Birm from 85; Hon Can Birm Cathl *Birm* from 05. *Chaplain's Office, HM Prison, Winson Green Road, Birmingham B18 4AS* Tel 0121-554 3838 ext 325 Fax 554 7990

GRAEBE, Canon Denys Redford. b 26. Qu Coll Cam BA48 MA51. Westcott Ho Cam 50. **d** 51 **p** 52. C Hitchin St Mary *St Alb* 51-57; R Gt Parndon *Chelmsf* 57-72; V Norton *St Alb* 72-83; R Kimpton w Ayot St Lawrence 83-92; RD Wheathampstead 87-92; Hon Can St Alb Abbey 90-92; rtd 92; Perm to Offic *St E* from 92. *5 Sancroft Way, Fressingfield, Eye IP21 5QN* Tel (01379) 588178 E-mail dgraebe@fish.co.uk

GRAESSER, Adrian Stewart. b 42. Tyndale Hall Bris 63. **d** 67 **p** 68. C Nottingham St Jude *S'well* 67-69; C Slaithwaite w E Scammonden *Wakef* 69-72; CF 72-75; V Earl's Heaton *Wakef* 75-81; R Norton Fitzwarren *B & W* 81-86; R Bickenhill w Elmdon *Birm* 86-90; R Elmdon St Nic 90-00; P-in-c Dolton *Ex* from 00; P-in-c Iddesleigh w Dowland from 00; P-in-c Monkokehampton from 00; RD Torrington 02-05. *The Rectory, Rectory Road, Dolton, Winkleigh EX19 8QT* Tel (01805) 804264 E-mail graesser.dolton@tinyworld.co.uk

GRAHAM, Alan Robert. b 44. St Edm Hall Ox BA67 MA71. St Steph Ho Ox 67. **d** 70 **p** 71. C Clifton All SS *Bris* 70-74; C Tadley St Pet *Win* 74-77; P-in-c Upper Clatford w Goodworth Clatford 77-79; R Abbotts Ann and Upper and Goodworth Clatford 79-84; V Lyndhurst and Emery Down 84-92; P-in-c Over Wallop w Nether Wallop 92-02; rtd 02; Perm to Offic *Win* from 02. *4 Sutton Place, Brockenhurst SO42 7TX* Tel (01590) 622324

GRAHAM, Alexander. *See* GRAHAM, The Rt Revd Andrew Alexander Kenny

GRAHAM, Alfred. b 34. Bris Univ BA57. Tyndale Hall Bris. **d** 58 **p** 59. C Chaddesden St Mary *Derby* 58-61; C Bickenhill w Elmdon *Birm* 61-64; V Kirkdale St Lawr *Liv* 64-70; V Stapleford *S'well* 70-83; V Burton Joyce w Bulcote 83-95; V Burton Joyce w Bulcote and Stoke Bardolph 95-97; rtd 97; Perm to Offic *S'well* from 03. *2 Hobsons Acre, Gunthorpe, Nottingham NG14 7FF* Tel 0115-966 3912

GRAHAM, Alistair. *See* GRAHAM, Michael Alistair

✠**GRAHAM, The Rt Revd Andrew Alexander Kenny (Alec).** b 29. St Jo Coll Ox BA52 DipTh53 MA57 Lambeth DD95. Ely Th Coll 53. **d** 55 **p** 56 **c** 77. C Hove All SS *Chich* 55-58; Chapl, Lect Th, and Tutor Worc Coll Ox 58-70; Warden Linc Th Coll 70-77; Can and Preb Linc Cathl *Linc* 70-77; Suff Bp Bedford *St Alb* 77-81; Bp Newc 81-97; Chmn ACCM 84-87; Chmn Doctrine Commn 87-95; rtd 97; Hon Asst Bp Carl from 97. *Fell End, Butterwick, Penrith CA10 2QQ* Tel (01931) 713147

GRAHAM, Canon Anthony Nigel. b 40. Univ of Wales (Abth) BA62 CertEd70. Ripon Hall Ox 62. **d** 64 **p** 65. C Heref H Trin *Heref* 64-67; C Birm St Martin *Birm* 67-69; C Selly Oak St Mary 71-75; V Edgbaston SS Mary and Ambrose 75-83; CMS Miss Partner Nigeria 84-88; Hon Can Jos from 88; V Highworth w Sevenhampton and Inglesham etc *Bris* 88-95; RD Highworth 93-95; P-in-c Coalpit Heath 95-99; V 99-00; rtd 00. *19 Dormer Road, Cheltenham GL51 0AX*

GRAHAM, Anthony Stanley David. b 34. SS Coll Cam BA56 MA60. Cuddesdon Coll 58. **d** 60 **p** 61. C Welwyn Garden City *St Alb* 60-64; Asst Chapl Ipswich Sch 64-65; C Margate St Jo *Cant* 65-68; Chr Aid Area Sec *Chich* 68-99; Perm to Offic *Cant* from 68; rtd 99. *48 Springfield Road, Crawley RH11 8AH* Tel (01293) 526279 E-mail tonygraham@satyagraha.fsnet.co.uk

GRAHAM, Bruce. *See* GRAHAM, William Bruce

GRAHAM, Christopher John. EMMTC. **d** 03 **p** 04. NSM Ripley *Derby* from 03. *41 Lathkill Drive, Ripley DE5 8HW* Tel (01773) 747223

GRAHAM, Clifton Gordon. b 53. ARCM72 GRSM74 FRCO75 Coll of Ripon & York St Jo PGCE76. St Steph Ho Ox 90. **d** 92 **p** 93. C Northfield *Birm* 92-93; C Perry Beeches 93-97; P-in-c S Yardley St Mich 97-00; V from 00. *St Michael's Vicarage, 60 Yew Tree Lane, Birmingham B26 1AP* Tel 0121-706 2563 E-mail frclifton@st-michaels.co.uk

GRAHAM, David. *See* GRAHAM, George David

GRAHAM, Canon Frederick Lawrence. b 35. TCD BA65 DCCD88. CITC 66. **d** 66 **p** 67. C Belfast St Matt *Conn* 66-69; TV Chelmsley Wood *Birm* 69-73; Ch of Ireland Youth Officer 73-78; Bp's C Stoneyford *Conn* 78-88; Bp's C Fahan Lower and Upper *D & R* 88-91; Can Raphoe Cathl 90-01; I Donagheady 91-01; Can Derry Cathl 95-01; rtd 01. *Thuma Mina, 80 Altnahinch Road, Loughguile, Ballymena BT44 9JS* Tel (028) 2764 1016 E-mail freka@thuma.fsnet.co.uk

GRAHAM, Frederick Louis Roth. b 20. Selw Coll Cam BA47 MA49. Ridley Hall Cam 48. **d** 50 **p** 51. C Shirley *Win* 50-53; R Old Trafford St Jo *Man* 53-61; R Wombwell *Sheff* 61-71; V Thorne 71-77; P-in-c Chilton-super-Polden w Edington *B & W* 77-82; P-in-c Catcott 77-82; V W Poldens 82-86; RD Glastonbury 82-86; rtd 86; Perm to Offic *Win* from 86. *73 Newlands Avenue, Southampton SO15 5EQ* Tel (023) 8078 9353

GRAHAM, George David. b 42. Jes Coll Cam BA64 MA68. St Jo Coll Nottm LTh Lon Coll of Div 66. **d** 71 **p** 72. C Corby St Columba *Pet* 71-74; C Deptford St Jo *S'wark* 74-77; P-in-c Deptford St Pet 77-82; C-in-c Wheatley Park St Paul CD *Sheff* 82-87; TV Dunstable *St Alb* 87-92; V Bromley Common St Luke *Roch* 92-02; R Hayes from 02. *The Rectory, Hayes Street, Bromley BR2 7LH* Tel (020) 8462 1373

GRAHAM, Canon George Edgar. b 55. QUB BA91. Sarum & Wells Th Coll 74 CITC 77. **d** 78 **p** 79. C Lisburn Ch Ch *Conn* 78-81; C Mossley 81-83; I Broomhedge 83-91; I Derriaghy w Colin 91-96; I Ballywillan 96-05; I Dunluce from 05; Can Conn Cathl from 05. *Dunluce Rectory, 17 Priestland Road, Bushmills BT57 8QP* E-mail g.k.graham@btinternet.com

GRAHAM, George Gordon. b 17. OBE96. St Chad's Coll Dur BA48 DipTh50 MSc71. **d** 50 **p** 51. C Luton Ch Ch *St Alb* 50-53; C Bakewell *Derby* 53-56; P-in-c Wheatley Hill *Dur* 56-69; V Hunwick 69-88; Chapl Homelands Hosp Dur 80-94; Chapl Bishop Auckland Hospitals NHS Trust 94-98; Chapl S Durham Healthcare NHS Trust from 98; rtd 88. *3 The Willows, Bishop Auckland DL14 7HH* Tel (01388) 602758

GRAHAM, George Gordon. b 34. Harvard Univ BA55 MDiv JD71. **d** 96 **p** 97. Aux Min Seapatrick *D & D* 97-99; Aux Min Lecale Gp 99-03; P-in-c Castlewellan w Kilcoo from 03. *10 Castlebridge Court, Newcastle BT33 0RF* Tel (028) 4062 2612 *or* 4372 6175 E-mail gorbargrah@aol.com

GRAHAM, Gordon Cecil. b 31. JP. Ch Coll Cam BA53 MA57. Ripon Hall Ox 53. **d** 55 **p** 56. C Didsbury St Jas and Em *Man* 55-58; C Rochdale 58-60; R Heaton Mersey 60-67; Chapl Hulme Gr Sch Oldham 67-74; Lic to Offic *Ches* 72-92; rtd 92. *21 The Crescent, Davenport, Stockport SK3 8SL* Tel 0161-483 6011

GRAHAM, Harry John. b 52. Magd Coll Cam BA75 MA86. Trin Coll Bris BA94. **d** 96 **p** 97. C Walkden and Lt Hulton *Man* 96-99; Chapl Salford Coll of Tech 96-99; P-in-c Edgeside *Man* 99-00; TV Rossendale Middle Valley 00-02; Gen Sec Miss without Borders (UK) Ltd from 02. *69 Eyre Court, Finchley Road, London NW8 9TX* Tel (020) 7586 8336

GRAHAM, Ian Maxwell. b 50. CertEd76. Chich Th Coll 86. **d** 88 **p** 89. C Middlesbrough St Thos *York* 88-90; C Stainton-in-Cleveland 90-93; V Hemlington 93-00; V Grangetown from 00. *The Vicarage, Clynes Road, Grangetown, Middlesbrough TS6 7LY* Tel (01642) 453704 E-mail casahild@lineone.net

GRAHAM, James Hamilton. b 54. Trin Hall Cam BA76 MA80 Solicitor 78. Ripon Coll Cuddesdon BA83 MA87. **d** 84 **p** 85. C Harlescott *Lich* 84-88; C Adderley 88-93; C Drayton in Hales 88-93; C Moreton Say 88-93; R Hodnet w Weston under Redcastle 93-00; RD Hodnet 97-00; V Eccleshall from 00. *The Vicarage, Church Street, Eccleshall, Stafford ST21 6BY* Tel (01785) 850351

GRAHAM, John Galbraith. b 21. MBE05. K Coll Cam BA43 MA46. Ely Th Coll 46. **d** 48 **p** 49. C E Dulwich St Jo *S'wark* 48-49; Chapl St Chad's Coll *Dur* 49-52; C Aldershot St Mich

Guildf 52-55; C-in-c Beaconsfield St Mich CD *Ox* 55-62; Chapl Reading Univ 62-72; C Pimlico St Pet w Westmr Ch Ch *Lon* 72-74; R Houghton w Wyton *Ely* 74-78; rtd 86; Lic to Offic *St E* from 86; Perm to Offic *Ely* from 93. *31 Rectory Lane, Somersham, Huntingdon PE28 3EL* Tel (01487) 842737

GRAHAM, Kevin. *See* GRAHAM, Terence Kevin Declan

GRAHAM, Mrs Marion McKenzie. b 39. St As Minl Tr Course. **d** 89 **p** 97. NSM Bagillt *St As* 89-93; NSM Flint 93-99 and from 00; C 99-00. *Sharondale, Bryntirion Road, Bagillt CH6 6BZ* Tel (01352) 734139

GRAHAM, Canon Matthew. b 30. Univ Coll Dur BSc54. K Coll (NS) BD71 Ridley Hall Cam 54. **d** 56 **p** 57. C Littleover *Derby* 56-59; C Fazakerley Em *Liv* 59-61; V Huyton St Geo 61-65; Canada 65-71; V Sutton Coldfield St Columba *Birm* 71-85; V Warley Woods 85-95; RD Warley 87-93; Hon Can Birm Cathl 90-95; rtd 95; Perm to Offic *Worc* from 95. *18 The Drive, Checketts Lane, Worcester WR3 7JS* Tel (01905) 458151

GRAHAM, Michael. b 30. Westcott Ho Cam 61. **d** 61 **p** 62. C Withington St Paul *Man* 61-64; V Lawton Moor 64-87; R Mobberley *Ches* 87-99; rtd 99; Perm to Offic *Ches* from 00. *16 Wood Lane, Timperley, Altrincham WA15 7QB* Tel 0161-904 8335

GRAHAM, Michael. b 51. CITC BTh95. **d** 95 **p** 96. C Cork St Fin Barre's Union *C, C & R* 95-98; Min Can Cork Cathl 97-98; I Drogheda w Ardee, Collon and Termonfeckin *Arm* from 98; Ch of Ireland Internet Co-ord 99-05. *St Peter's Rectory, Drogheda, Co Louth, Irish Republic* Tel (00353) (41) 987 0073
E-mail drogheda@armagh.anglican.org

GRAHAM, Michael Alistair. b 47. CITC 67. **d** 70 **p** 71. C Dublin Clontarf *D & G* 71-75; C Ox St Mich w St Martin and All SS *Ox* 76-78; P-in-c Dublin Sandymount *D & G* 80-86; I Stillorgan w Blackrock 86-00; Soc Worker E Health Bd Dub from 00. *15 Rock Lodge, Killiney, Co Dublin, Irish Republic* Tel (00353) (1) 285 6635

GRAHAM, Nigel. *See* GRAHAM, Canon Anthony Nigel

GRAHAM, Ms Olivia Josephine. b 56. UEA BA84. St Alb and Ox Min Course 94. **d** 97 **p** 98. NSM Wheatley *Ox* 97-98; C Risborough 98-01; TV Burnham w Dropmore, Hitcham and Taplow from 01. *Burnham Rectory, The Precincts, Burnham, Slough SL1 7HU* Tel (01628) 604173
E-mail graham.glenny@virgin.net

GRAHAM, Peter. b 32. CEng MIMechE. **d** 86 **p** 87. NSM Minchinhampton *Glouc* 86-96; Perm to Offic 96-97; NSM Alderminster and Halford *Cov* 98-02; NSM Butlers Marston and the Pillertons w Ettington 98-02; rtd 02; Perm to Offic *Cov* from 02. *10 Banbury Road, Ettington, Stratford-upon-avon CV37 7TB* Tel (01789) 740335

GRAHAM, Peter Bartlemy. b 23. K Coll Cam BA47 MA52. Ely Th Coll 50. **d** 52 **p** 53. C St Alb Abbey *St Alb* 52-55; V Eaton Bray 55-64; R Harpenden St Nic 64-73; V Aylesbury *Ox* 73-82; Hon Can Ch Ch 79-82; R Elford *Lich* 82-88; Dioc Adv Past Care and Counselling 82-88; rtd 88; Perm to Offic *Sarum* from 88. *Carriers Cottage, Buckland Newton, Dorchester DT2 7DW* Tel (01300) 345287

GRAHAM, Richard William. b 63. Poly of Wales BA86 ACA91. Trin Coll Bris 03. **d** 05. C Savernake *Sarum* from 05. *6 Henrys Garth, Burbage, Marlborough SN8 3TE*
E-mail randmgraham@hotmail.com

GRAHAM, Robert John. b 70. Wycliffe Hall Ox BTh99. **d** 99 **p** 00. C Nailsea H Trin *B & W* 99-04. *60 Stocken Close, Hucclecote, Gloucester GL3 3UL* E-mail revrgraham@btinternet.com

GRAHAM, Ronald Fleming. b 33. Edin Th Coll 67. **d** 69 **p** 69. Chapl St Andr Cathl *Ab* 69-73; R Glas Gd Shep *Glas* 73-75; R Glas Gd Shep and Ascension 75-76; CF (TA) 74-76; R Peterhead *Ab* 76-80; Chapl RAF 76-80; Bp's Dom Chapl *Arg* 80-84; Itinerant Priest 80-84; R Lanark *Glas* 84-89; R Douglas 84-89; rtd 89; Hon C Glas St Ninian *Glas* 90-98. *77 Merryvale Avenue, Giffnock, Glasgow G46 6DE* Tel 0141-569 5090

GRAHAM, Ronald Gaven. b 27. **d** 90 **p** 91. NSM Adare w Kilpeacon and Croom *L & K* 90-92; Dioc Info Officer (Limerick) 91-95; NSM Rathkeale w Askeaton and Kilcornan 92-96; NSM Wexford w Ardcolm and Killurin *C & O* from 97. *8 Chestnut Grove, Fernyhill, Killinick, Co Wexford, Irish Republic* Tel (00353) (53) 43013 *or* 58369

GRAHAM, Roy Richard Arthur. b 39. Lon Univ BD63 Open Univ BA78. ALCD62. **d** 63 **p** 64. C Southsea St Jude *Portsm* 63-66; C Morden *S'wark* 66-70; V Tittensor *Lich* 70-79; R Hurworth and Dinsdale w Sockburn *Dur* 79-02; rtd 02. *The School House, Eaglesfield, Lockerbie DG11 3PA* Tel (01461) 500499 E-mail rragraham@onenet.co.uk

GRAHAM, Stig. *See* GRAHAM, William Stig

GRAHAM, Mrs Susan Lochrie. b 46. Sheff Univ PhD01. Yale Div Sch MDiv90. **d** 90 **p** 91. Canada 90-96; Cow Head Par 90-92; P-in-c Kingsway All SS, St Hilary, Bolton etc 92-96; NSM Ilminster and Distr *B & W* 96-97; Perm to Offic 97-03; NSM Glastonbury w Meare from 03. *The Vicarage, Holy Well Road, Edington, Bridgwater TA7 9LE* Tel (01278) 723055
E-mail s.l.graham@exeter.ac.uk

GRAHAM, Terence Kevin Declan. b 67. NUI BSc89 TCD BTh02. CITC 99. **d** 02 **p** 03. C Knock *D & D* 02-05; I Carrowdore w Millisle from 05. *Carrowdore Rectory, 40 Woburn Road, Millisle, Newtownards BT22 2HY* Tel (028) 9186 2219 Mobile 07973-257193 E-mail carrowdore@down.anglican.org

GRAHAM, Mrs Wendy. **d** 01 **p** 02. OLM Chalfont St Peter *Ox* from 01. *The Box, Hillfield Road, Chalfont St Peter, Gerrards Cross SL9 0DU* Tel (01753) 885066

GRAHAM, William Bruce. b 37. Univ of New Mexico BA60 Yale Univ MDiv90. **d** 90 **p** 91. Canada 90-97; P-in-c W Poldens *B & W* from 97; P-in-c Greinton from 05; RD Glastonbury from 03. *The Vicarage, Holy Well Road, Edington, Bridgwater TA7 9LE* Tel (01278) 722055 Fax 722962
E-mail rural.dean@btinternet.com

GRAHAM, William Stig. b 53. Newc Univ BSc75. NEOC. **d** 99 **p** 00. C W Acklam *York* 99-02; Chapl Myton Hamlet Hospice from 02. *2 Winyates Road, Lighthorne Heath, Leamington Spa CV33 9TU* Tel (01926) 640811 *or* 492518
E-mail stiggraham@netscape.net
or stig.graham@mytonhospice.org

GRAHAM-BROWN, John George Francis. b 34. CA60. Wycliffe Hall Ox 60. **d** 63 **p** 64. C Darlington St Cuth *Dur* 63-67; C Rufforth w Moor Monkton and Hessay *York* 67-73; Sec York Dioc Redundant Chs Uses Cttee 69-89; Asst Sec DBF 73-84; Dioc Past Cttee 73-89; Hon C York St Barn 73-85; P-in-c 85-92; TV Marfleet 92-99; rtd 99; Perm to Offic *St Alb* from 00. *40 Hunters Oak, Hemel Hempstead HP2 7SW* Tel (01482) 402226 E-mail f.graham-brown@tinyonline.co.uk

GRAHAM-ORLEBAR, Ian Henry Gaunt. b 26. New Coll Ox BA49 MA56. Cuddesdon Coll 60. **d** 62 **p** 63. C Hemel Hempstead *St Alb* 62-70; R Barton-le-Cley w Higham Gobion 70-80; R Barton-le-Cley w Higham Gobion and Hexton 80-92; rtd 92; Perm to Offic *Ex* from 94. *Hole Farm, Bickington, Newton Abbot TQ12 6PE* Tel (01626) 821298

GRAINGER, Canon Bruce. b 37. Nottm Univ BA62 Hull Univ MA83. Cuddesdon Coll 62. **d** 64 **p** 65. C Bingley All SS *Bradf* 64-67; Chapl K Sch Cant 67-72; Hon Min Can Cant Cathl *Cant* 69-72; V Baildon *Bradf* 72-88; V Oxenhope 88-04; Hon Can Bradf Cathl 84-04; Dir of Ords 88-96; Dioc Ecum Officer 96-04; Lect Bradf Univ from 99; RD S Craven 02-03; rtd 04. *Aspen Lodge, Low Shann Farm, High Spring Gardens Lane, Keighley BD20 6LN* Tel (01535) 611989 E-mail grainger@nildram.co.uk

GRAINGER, Horace. b 34. Carl Dioc Tr Course 82. **d** 85 **p** 86. NSM Barrow St Matt *Carl* 85-89; C Carl St Herbert w St Steph 89-91; TV Penrith w Newton Reigny and Plumpton Wall 91-96; P-in-c Holme Cultram St Mary 96-00; P-in-c Holme Cultram St Cuth 96-00; rtd 00; NSM Barrow St Aid *Carl* 01-03; NSM S Barrow from 03. *15 Maylands Avenue, Barrow-in-Furness LA13 0AL* Tel (01229) 828603

GRAINGER, Ian. b 66. Barrow-in-Furness Coll of FE BTEC NC86. Cranmer Hall Dur 89. **d** 92 **p** 93. C Whitehaven *Carl* 92-94; C Walney Is 94-97; P-in-c Barrow St Aid 97-02; V Camerton, Seaton and W Seaton from 02. *The Vicarage, Ling Beck Park, Seaton, Workington CA14 1JQ* Tel (01900) 602162
E-mail revd.ian@grainger89.fsnet.co.uk

GRAINGER, Michael Noel Howard. b 40. Trin Coll Carmarthen. **d** 91 **p** 92. NSM Haverfordwest St Martin w Lambston *St D* 91-95; V Maenclochog and New Moat etc 95-05; rtd 05. *1 Empasse Edith Piaf, Kerbregent, Plumeliau 56930, France*

GRAINGER, Prof Roger Beckett. b 34. Birm Univ MA70 Leeds Univ PhD79 Lon Univ BA80 DD90 Huddersfield Poly MPhil88 Bris Univ PhD92 Leeds Metrop Univ BSc98 PhD(Educ)01 Lambeth STh83 FRSA85 FRAI85 British Psychological Soc Statement of Equivalence 96 CPsychol96 AFBPsS99. Lich Th Coll 64. **d** 66 **p** 69. C W Bromwich All SS *Lich* 66-68; C Walsall 69-73; Chapl Stanley Royd Hosp Wakef 73-90; rtd 91; Hon C Wakef St Jo *Wakef* from 93; Dioc Drama Adv from 98; Prof Extraordinary Potchefstroom Univ S Africa from 01; Hon Chapl Wakef Cathl from 02. *7 Park Grove, Horbury, Wakefield WF4 6EE* Tel (01924) 272742

GRAINGER-SMITH, James Edward. b 71. Nottm Univ BA92. St Jo Coll Nottm MA02. **d** 02 **p** 03. C Hordle *Win* from 02. *Church Cottage, Sway Road, Tiptoe, Lymington SO41 6FR* Tel (01425) 616670 E-mail j.j.grainger-smith@lineone.net

GRANDELL, Canon Peter Frank. b 59. Wagner Coll NY BS81 Gen Th Sem NY MDiv95. **d** 95 **p** 95. USA 95-96 and from 98; Asst to Dean St Paul's Cathl Burlington VT 95-96; C St John's Wood *Lon* 96-98; Can Prec SS Pet and Paul Cathl Washington DC from 99. *4000 Massachusetts Avenue NW, Washington, DC 20016, USA*

GRANGE (née FEATHERSTON), Mrs Alice Margery. b 55. Teesside Univ BA97. N Ord Course. **d** 99 **p** 00. C Pickering w Lockton and Levisham *York* 99-02; TV Crosslacon *Carl* from 02. *The Vicarage, Arlecdon, Frizington CA26 3UB* Tel and fax (01946) 861353 E-mail alicegrange@tiscali.co.uk

GRANNER, Mrs Linda. b 52. Westmr Coll Ox BTh00. WMMTC 01. **d** 03 **p** 04. NSM Bearwood *Birm* from 03. *36 Roman Way, Birmingham B15 2SJ* Tel 0121-472 4330 Mobile 07745-396412
E-mail linda@theoattitude.freeserve.co.uk

GRANT, Alistair Sims. b 25. SS Coll Cam BA49 MA53. Sarum Th Coll 49. **d** 51 **p** 52. C Northampton St Jas *Pet* 51-54; C Conisbrough *Sheff* 54-57; Org Sec (E Anglia) CECS 57-58; V Haddenham *Ely* 58-65; rtd 90; Perm to Offic *Ely* 90-00. *56 The Causeway, Burwell, Cambridge CB5 0DU* Tel (01638) 741670

GRANT, Canon Andrew Richard. b 40. Univ of Wales BA62. Chich Th Coll 63. **d** 65 **p** 66. C Kennington St Jo *S'wark* 65-68; Hon C 70-72; Hon C Stockwell Green St Andr 68-70; V Nunhead St Antony 72-79; TR N Lambeth 79-92; USPG Ghana 92-99; Hon Can Kumasi from 02; C Paddington St Jo w St Mich *Lon* 99-01; P-in-c Stockwell St Mich *S'wark* 01-03; P-in-c Stockwell St Andr and St Mich 03-04; V from 04. *St Michael's Vicarage, 78 Stockwell Park Road, London SW9 0DA* Tel (020) 7274 6357

GRANT, Anthony David. b 54. **d** 05. NSM Bardsley *Man* from 05. *33 Wakeling Road, Denton, Manchester M34 6FR* Tel 0161-320 8874 E-mail tony.grant@quista.net

GRANT, Antony Richard Charles. b 34. Ch Ch Ox BA59 MA64. Coll of Resurr Mirfield 72. **d** 74 **p** 75. C St John's Wood *Lon* 74-77; Novice CR 77-79; CR from 79; Lic to Offic *Wakef* from 80; Perm to Offic *Lon* from 98; rtd 99. *House of the Resurrection, Stocks Bank Road, Mirfield WF14 0BN* Tel (01924) 483332 Fax 490489 E-mail agrant@mirfield.org.uk

GRANT, Arthur Glyndŵr Webber (Glyn). b 28. K Coll Lon RTC47 St Luke's Coll Ex CertEd49. Wells Th Coll 52. **d** 54 **p** 55. C Cannock *Lich* 54-57; S Rhodesia 57-63; C Paignton St Jo *Ex* 63-68; C Brighton Gd Shep Preston *Chich* 68-76; C Moulsecoomb 76-80; Chapl HM Pris Northeye 80-83; P-in-c Wartling *Chich* 80-83; C Seaford w Sutton 83-87; Sub-Chapl HM Pris Lewes 86-92; rtd 92; Perm to Offic *Ex* 93-95 and from 98. *33 Occombe Valley Road, Paignton TQ3 1QX* Tel (01803) 522722

GRANT, Eric. *See* GRANT, William Frederick

GRANT, Canon Geoffrey. b 27. Lich Th Coll 55. **d** 58 **p** 59. C Swindon New Town *Bris* 58-62; V Eastville St Thos 62-67; V Sherston Magna w Easton Grey 67-75; P-in-c Luckington w Alderton 71-75; P-in-c Woolcott Park 75-78; V Cotham St Mary 76-78; V Cotham St Sav w St Mary 78-81; TR Yate New Town 81-88; Hon Can Bris Cathl 82-92; Dir St Jo Home Bris 89-92; rtd 92; Perm to Offic *Bris* 92-97; Chapl Beaulieu-sur-Mer *Eur* 97-00. *1266 Chemin des Espinets, 06570 St Paul de Vence, France* Tel (00334) (9) 358 7849

GRANT, Canon Geoffrey Leslie. b 33. Trin Coll Cam BA57 MA61. Ridley Hall Cam 57. **d** 59 **p** 60. C Chelsea St Luke *Lon* 59-64; Chapl Orwell Park Sch Nacton from 64; R Nacton w Levington *St E* 64-78; P-in-c Bucklesham w Brightwell and Foxhall 75-76; R Nacton and Levington w Bucklesham and Foxhall from 78; P-in-c Kirton w Falkenham from 96; RD Colneys from 86; Hon Can St E Cathl from 94. *The Rectory, Nacton, Ipswich IP10 0HY* Tel (01473) 659232 E-mail canon@nildram.co.uk

GRANT, Glyn. *See* GRANT, Arthur Glyndwr Webber

GRANT, James Neil. b 57. Toorak Coll of Educn BEd80. Trin Coll Melbourne BTh84. **d** 85 **p** 86. C E Frankston Australia 85-87; C Feltham *Lon* 87-89; Chapl Peninsula Sch Mt Eliza Melbourne 89-03; Assoc P Mt Eliza 99-03; Assoc P Richmond St Steph from 04. *21 Bent Street, East Malvern, Vic, Australia 3145* Tel (0061) (3) 5976 1773 Mobile 425-721962 E-mail frjames.ststephens@keypoint.com.au

GRANT, John Brian Frederick. b 47. Bris Univ BSc68 MB, ChB71 MD76 FRCS76. Coll of Resurr Mirfield 91. **d** 93 **p** 94. C Doncaster Ch Ch *Sheff* 93-95; C Doncaster H Trin 95-96; Asst Chapl Salford R Hosps NHS Trust from 96. *Chaplains' Office, Hope Hospital, Stott Lane, Salford M6 8HD* Tel 0161-787 5167 *or* 789 7373

GRANT, Ms Kerry Jean. b 65. SEITE 00. **d** 03 **p** 04. NSM Eltham St Sav *S'wark* from 03; Chapl Lewisham Hosp NHS Trust from 05. *76 Kinveachy Gardens, London SE7 8EJ* Tel (020) 8473 7676 Mobile 07866-690527 E-mail kes@waitrose.com

GRANT, Canon Malcolm Etheridge. b 44. Edin Univ BSc66 BD69. Edin Th Coll 66. **d** 69 **p** 70. C St Mary's Cathl *Glas* 69-72; C Grantham w Manthorpe *Linc* 72; TV Grantham 72-78; P-in-c Invergordon St Ninian *Mor* 78-81; Provost St Mary's Cathl *Glas* 81-91; R Glas St Mary 81-91; Provost St Andr Cathl Inverness *Mor* 91-02; R Inverness St Andr 91-02; P-in-c Culloden St Mary-in-the-Fields 91-97; R Strathnairn St Paul 91-97; Hon Can St Andr Cathl Inverness from 02; V Eaton Bray w Edlesborough *St Alb* from 02; RD Dunstable from 04. *The Vicarage, 11 High Street, Eaton Bray, Dunstable LU6 2DN* Tel (01525) 220261

GRANT, Murray William. b 36. Chich Th Coll 64. **d** 66 **p** 67. C Stanley *Liv* 66-70; C Munster Square St Mary Magd *Lon* 70-74; C Westmr St Sav and St Jas Less 74-82; P-in-c Albany Street Ch Ch 82; P-in-c Hammersmith H Innocents 83-94; V 94-99; Chapl Naples w Sorrento, Capri and Bari *Eur* 99-03; rtd 04. *5 rue des Agrumes, La Corniche, Bizerte, 7000, Tunisia*

GRANT, Patrick Iain Douglas. b 67. K Alfred's Coll Win BA88. Cuddesdon Coll BTh93. **d** 96 **p** 97. C Croydon Woodside *S'wark* 96-99; V S Beddington St Mich from 99. *St Michael's Vicarage, Milton Road, Wallington SM6 9RP* Tel (020) 8647 1201 E-mail grant.saintmichael@tesco.net

GRANT, Canon Rodney Arthur. b 26. AKC52. K Coll Lon St Boniface Warminster. **d** 53 **p** 54. C Edin St Jas *Edin* 53-56; C Musselburgh 56-59; P-in-c Prestonpans 59-60; P-in-c Edin St Aid Miss Niddrie Mains 60-72; R Edin St Jas 72-80; R Edin Ch Ch 72-80; R Edin Ch Ch-St Jas 80-86; R Edin SS Phil and Jas 86-92; Chapl St Columba's Hospice Edin 86-92; Hon Can St Mary's Cathl from 91; rtd 92; P-in-c Edin St Vin *Edin* from 98. *1F1, 29 Bruntsfield Gardens, Edinburgh EH10 4DY* Tel 0131-229 1857

GRANT, Stephen David. b 77. Univ of Wales (Lamp) BA99. Ripon Coll Cuddesdon BTh04. **d** 04. C Colwyn Bay w Brynymaen *St As* from 04. *11 Rhiw Road, Colwyn Bay LL29 7TE* Tel 07870-680535 (mobile) E-mail sgrant77@hotmail.com

GRANT, William Frederick (Eric). b 23. Fitzw Ho Cam BA48 MA50 Cam Univ CertEd50. Wycliffe Hall Ox 51. **d** 53 **p** 54. C Islington St Paul Ball's Pond *Lon* 53-57; V Islington All SS 57-60; Head RE Therfield Sch Leatherhead 60-84; Perm to Offic *Guildf* from 66 and *S'wark* from 89; rtd 88. *Kingfishers, 24 The Avenue, Brockham, Betchworth RH3 7EN* Tel (01737) 842551

GRANT, The Very Revd William James. b 29. **d** 58 **p** 59. Asst Missr S Ch Miss Ballymacarrett *D & D* 58-60; C Belfast St Geo *Conn* 60-63; Canada 63-66; Miss to Seamen 66-70; I Fethard w Tintern and Killesk *C & O* 70-77; I Cong, Ballinrobe and Aasleagh *T, K & A* 77-81; Adn Tuam 80-93; I Tuam w Cong and Aasleagh 81-93; Dean Tuam 81-93; rtd 93. *48 Brazabon House, Sandymount, Dublin 4, Irish Republic* Tel (00353) (1) 269 5071

GRANTHAM, Michael Paul. b 47. Linc Th Coll. **d** 84 **p** 85. C Gainsborough All SS *Linc* 84-87; R S Kelsey Gp 87-94; R Dunster, Carhampton and Withycombe w Rodhuish *B & W* from 94; RD Exmoor 03-05. *The Rectory, St George's Street, Dunster, Minehead TA24 6RS* Tel (01643) 821812 E-mail michael@rectoryrecordings.fsnet.co.uk

GRANTHAM, Suffragan Bishop of. *Vacant*

GRASBY, Derek. b 56. Bris Univ BA80 MA82. Wesley Coll Bris 77 EAMTC 95. **d** 95 **p** 96. C Harlescott *Lich* 95-96; C W Bromwich St Andr w Ch Ch 96-98; R Newton Heath *Man* 98-02; Chapl UWE *Bris* 02-03; R Farnley *Ripon* from 03. *The Rectory, 16 Cross Lane, Leeds LS12 5AA* Tel 0113-263 8064 Mobile 07958-089156 Fax 08701-339312 E-mail graz@clara.co.uk

GRATTON, Patricia Margaret. *See* MAGUIRE, Mrs Patricia Margaret

GRATY, Canon John Thomas. b 33. Univ Coll Ox BA58 MA60. Coll of Resurr Mirfield 58. **d** 60 **p** 61. C Cov St Mark *Cov* 60-63; C Hitchin St Mary *St Alb* 63-67; R Cov St Alb *Cov* 67-75; P-in-c Radway w Ratley 75-77; P-in-c Warmington w Shotteswell 75-77; RD Dassett Magna 76-79; R Warmington w Shotteswell and Radway w Ratley 77-84; Hon Can Cov Cathl 80-96; P-in-c Nuneaton St Mary 84-89; V 89-96; rtd 96; Perm to Offic *Cov* from 96. *48 Shakespeare Street, Stratford-upon-Avon CV37 6RN* Tel (01789) 298856

GRAVELL, Canon John Hilary. b 45. Univ of Wales (Abth) BA65 DipEd66. Burgess Hall Lamp 66. **d** 68 **p** 69. C Aberystwyth *St D* 68-72; R Llangeitho w Blaenpennal 72-81; V Betws Leuci 73-81; V Llan-non 81-95; Can St D Cathl from 92; V Llandybie from 95; RD Dyffryn Aman from 01. *The Vicarage, 77 Kings Road, Llandybie, Ammanford SA18 2TL* Tel (01269) 850337

GRAVES, Jonathan Mark. b 57. BEd. St Steph Ho Ox. **d** 84 **p** 85. C St Leonards Ch Ch and St Mary *Chich* 84-88; C-in-c N Langley CD 88-95; V Stone Cross St Luke w N Langney 95-02; Chapl St Wilfrid's Hospice Eastbourne 94-02; Chapl Grenville Coll Bideford 02-04. *6 Jervis Avenue, Eastbourne BN23 6DU* Tel (01323) 728601 E-mail fr.jonathan@jgraves.fslife.co.uk

GRAVES, Peter. b 33. RMN STD FInstSMM. EMMTC 78. **d** 81 **p** 82. NSM Roughey *Chich* 81-89; NSM Itchingfield w Slinfold 89-98; Perm to Offic *S'well* from 98. *5 Fletcher Court, The Woodlands, Farnsfield, Newark NG22 8LY* Tel (01623) 882987 E-mail gravespeter@bluecarrots.com

GRAY, Alan. b 25. LRAM52 Dip Community Educn 75. Qu Coll Birm 51. **d** 54 **p** 55. C Monkseaton St Pet *Newc* 54-56; C Sighill 56-61; C-in-c Balkwell CD 61-66; R Callander *St And* 66-74; R Killin 66-74; R Lochearnhead 66-74; R Alloa 74-77; Community Educn Officer 76-85; Lic to Offic 77-85; R Alyth 85-90; R Blairgowrie 85-90; R Coupar Angus 85-90; rtd 90. *12B Park Terrace, Stirling FK8 2JT* Tel (01786) 479616

GRAY, Alan Eric. b 18. Lich Th Coll 38. **d** 41 **p** 42. C Sampford Peverell *Ex* 41-44; CR 44-52; Miss P Penhalonga S Rhodesia 47-51; R St Mark's S Africa 52-56; R Shabani S Rhodesia 56-61; V Lower Beeding *Chich* 61-70; rtd 83. *14 Frederick Road, Malvern WR14 1RS* Tel (01684) 572453 E-mail rjgray@waitrose.com

GRAY, Canon Angela Margery. b 46. St D Coll Lamp DipTh73. **dss** 73 **d** 80 **p** 97. Aberystwyth *St D* 73-80; C Dafen and Llwynhendy 80-90; C-in-c 90-97; V Llwynhendy from 97; Hon

Can St D Cathl from 01. *Clergy House, 10 Bryn Isaf, Llwynhendy, Llanelli SA14 9EX* Tel (01554) 774213

GRAY, Brett Christopher. b 71. Lon Bible Coll BA95. Ridley Hall Cam 02. **d** 04 **p** 05. C Sunnyside w Bourne End *St Alb* from 04. *2 Lombardy Drive, Berkhamsted HP4 2LG* Tel (01442) 876394 E-mail brett_gray@yahoo.co.uk

GRAY, Charles Malcolm. b 38. SSC. Lich Th Coll 67. **d** 69 **p** 70. C St Geo-in-the-East St Mary *Lon* 69-72; C Bush Hill Park St Mark 72-75; V Winchmore Hill H Trin from 75. *Holy Trinity Vicarage, King's Avenue, London N21 3NA* Tel and fax (020) 8360 2947 *or* 8364 2724 Mobile 07721-664178 E-mail frcmg.wh@btopenworld.com

GRAY, Ms Christine Angela (Kit). b 46. Nottm Univ BA67 CertEd68 Dur Univ DipTh73. Cranmer Hall Dur 71. **dss** 80 **d** 87 **p** 94. Rawthorpe *Wakef* 74-81; Chapl Nottm Univ *S'well* 81-88; C Rushmere *St E* 88-94; P-in-c Ringshall w Battisford, Barking w Darmsden etc 94-00; P-in-c Nayland w Wiston from 00. *The Vicarage, Bear Street, Nayland, Colchester CO6 4LA* Tel (01206) 262316

GRAY, Dale Armitage. b 42. Edin Th Coll 62. **d** 92 **p** 93. Dioc Missr *Arg* 92-98; Chapl St Jo Cathl Oban 92-95; P-in-c Cumbrae (or Millport) 95-98; rtd 98. *Address temp unknown*

GRAY, David. b 55. Oak Hill Th Coll. **d** 00 **p** 01. C Bestwood Em w St Mark *S'well* 00-04; P-in-c Bulwell St Jo from 04. *St John's Vicarage, Snape Wood Road, Bulwell, Nottingham NG6 7GH* Tel 0115-927 8025 E-mail davidgray72@hotmail.com

GRAY, David Bryan. b 28. RD77. Roch Th Coll 59. **d** 61 **p** 62. C Linc St Giles *Linc* 61-65; V Thurlby 65-67; P-in-c Ropsley 67-75; P-in-c Sapperton w Braceby 67-75; P-in-c Somerby w Humby 67-75; R Trimley *St E* 75-82; R Orford w Sudbourne, Chillesford, Butley and Iken 82-94; rtd 94; Perm to Offic *St E* from 94. *25 Southgate House, Rougham Road, Bury St Edmunds IP33 2RN*

GRAY, David Cedric. b 53. RMN77 Hollings Coll Man 79. LNSM course 94. **d** 97 **p** 98. OLM Gorton Em w St Jas *Man* from 97. *39 Jessop Street, Gorton, Manchester M18 8TZ* Tel 0161-355 6605 Pager 017623-725682

GRAY, David Michael. b 57. ACIBS80 St Jo Coll Dur BA99. CA Tr Coll 90 Cranmer Hall Dur 97. **d** 99 **p** 00. C Newc H Cross *Newc* 99-02; V Long Benton St Mary from 02. *St Mary's Vicarage, Blackfriars Way, Newcastle-upon-Tyne NE12 8ST* Tel 0191-266 2326 E-mail revdavegray@aol.com

GRAY, Canon Donald Cecil. b 24. K Coll Lon 46. Linc Th Coll 49. **d** 50 **p** 51. C Abington *Pet* 50-53; C Bedford St Paul *St Alb* 53-56; Chapl Bedf Gen Hosp 53-56; C Wilton Place St Paul *Lon* 56-59; V N Holmwood *Guildf* 59-67; RD Dorking 63-67; Chapl Cobgates Hosp and Farnham Hosp Guildf 67-89; R Farnham 67-89; RD Farnham 69-74; Hon Can Guildf Cathl 71-89; rtd 89; Perm to Offic *Win* from 89. *13 Benenden Green, Alresford SO24 9PE* Tel (01962) 734234

GRAY, Canon Donald Clifford. b 30. CBE98 TD70. Liv Univ MPhil81 Man Univ PhD85 FRHistS88. AKC55. **d** 56 **p** 57. C Leigh St Mary *Man* 56-60; CF (TA) 58-67; V Westleigh St Pet *Man* 60-67; V Elton All SS 67-74; CF (TAVR) 67-77; QHC 74-77; R Liv Our Lady and St Nic w St Anne *Liv* 74-87; RD Liv 75-81; Hon Can Liv Cathl 82-87; Chapl to The Queen 82-00; Can Westmr Abbey 87-98; R Westmr St Marg 87-98; Chapl to Speaker of Ho of Commons 87-98; rtd 98; Perm to Offic *Linc* from 98. *3 Barn Hill Mews, Stamford PE9 2GN* Tel (01780) 765024 Fax 756183

GRAY, Evan William. b 43. Oak Hill Th Coll 86. **d** 88 **p** 89. C Street w Walton *B & W* 88-92; V Blackpool St Mark *Blackb* 92-03; V Ellel w Shireshead from 03. *The Vicarage, Chapel Lane, Ellel, Lancaster LA2 0PW* Tel (01524) 752017 E-mail sianevan@evan20.freeserve.co.uk

GRAY, Frank Harold Castell. b 14. ALCD41. **d** 41 **p** 42. C Northwood Em *Lon* 41-45; P-in-c Nottingham St Ann *S'well* 45-47; V Gatten St Paul *Portsm* 47-53; V Prestonville St Luke *Chich* 53-66; V Watford St Luke *St Alb* 66-79; rtd 79; Perm to Offic *B & W* 80-98 and from 00. *9 Southwell Close, Trull, Taunton TA3 7EU* Tel (01823) 282567

GRAY, Canon Geoffrey Thomas. b 23. Oak Hill Th Coll 40 and 46. **d** 46 **p** 47. C Havering-atte-Bower *Chelmsf* 46-48; C Dovercourt 48-49; C Ches Square St Mich w St Phil *Lon* 49-51; V Lee Gd Shep *S'wark* 51-56; P-in-c Eltham St Pet 52-56; R Bermondsey St Mary w St Olave and St Jo 56-59; P-in-c Bermondsey St Luke 57-59; V Yalding *Roch* 59-66; RD Malling 64-66; V Gillingham St Mary 66-75; RD Gillingham 66-75; Perm to Offic 75-80; V Strood St Nic w St Mary 80-87; Hon Can Roch Cathl 82-87; Chapl Huggens Coll Northfleet 87-91; rtd 88; Hon Bp's Chapl *Roch* from 90; Hon PV Roch Cathl from 91; Perm to Offic from 00. *Deanery Lodge, The Precinct, Rochester ME1 1TG* Tel (01634) 844165

GRAY, James William. St Alb and Ox Min Course. **d** 05. NSM Crich and S Wingfield *Derby* from 05. *Holmleigh, Market Place, Crich, Matlock DE4 5DD* Tel (01773) 857921

GRAY (née ROBERTS), Mrs Jennifer. b 55. R Holloway Coll Lon BA76 Somerville Coll Ox PGCE77. St Alb and Ox Min Course 00. **d** 03 **p** 04. C Welwyn Garden City *St Alb* from 03. *62 Attimore Road, Welwyn Garden City AL8 6LP* Tel (01707) 321177 E-mail jennygraywgc@aol.com

GRAY, Joan. *See* BURKITT-GRAY, Mrs Joan Katherine

GRAY, John David Norman. b 38. Oak Hill Th Coll DipHE86. **d** 86 **p** 87. C Portsdown *Portsm* 86-88; C Worthing St Geo *Chich* 88-91; TV Swanborough *Sarum* 91-98; rtd 98; Perm to Offic *Ex* 00-03 and *Portsm* from 03. *15 Charminster Court, 46 Craneswater Park, Southsea PO4 0NU* Tel (023) 9285 1299

GRAY, John Howard. b 39. St Aid Birkenhead 61. **d** 65 **p** 66. C Old Trafford St Cuth *Man* 65-68; C Urmston 68-74; V Oldham Moorside from 74. *The Vicarage, 1 Glebe Lane, Oldham OL1 4SJ* Tel 0161-652 6452

GRAY, Mrs Joy Dora. b 24. SRN46 SCM48 HVCert. Gilmore Ho 79. **dss** 81 **d** 87 **p** 95. Newick *Chich* 81-87; Hon Par Dn 87-94; NSM Fletching 94-98; Perm to Offic from 98. *10 High Hurst Close, Newick, Lewes BN8 4NJ* Tel (01825) 722965

GRAY, Julian Francis. b 64. Univ of Wales (Lamp) BA86. Coll of Resurr Mirfield 86. **d** 88 **p** 89. Min Can and C St Woolos Cathl *Mon* 88-91; C Bassaleg 91-93; V Overmonnow w Wonastow and Michel Troy 93-98; V King's Sutton and Newbottle and Charlton *Pet* 98-00; V Usk and Monkswood w Glascoed Chpl and Gwehelog *Mon* 00-03; V Usk and Gwehelog w Llantrisant w Llanllowell from 03. *The Vicarage, Castle Parade, Usk NP15 1AA* Tel (01291) 671441 E-mail usk.vicarage@btinternet.com

GRAY, Malcolm. *See* GRAY, Charles Malcolm

GRAY, The Ven Martin Clifford. b 44. Westcott Ho Cam 78. **d** 80 **p** 81. C Gaywood, Bawsey and Mintlyn *Nor* 80-84; V Sheringham 84-94; P-in-c Lowestoft and Kirkley 94; TR Lowestoft St Marg 94-99; Chapl Lothingland Hosp 95-99; RD Lothingland *Nor* 97-99; Adn Lynn from 99. *Holly Tree House, Whitwell Road, Sparham, Norwich NR9 5PN* Tel and fax (01362) 688032 E-mail archdeacon.lynn@4frontmedia.co.uk

GRAY, Maurice William Halcro. b 27. Hertf Coll Ox BA48 MA60. Coll of Resurr Mirfield. **d** 60 **p** 61. C Cricklade w Latton *Bris* 60-63; Chapl Ellesmere Coll 63-92; Lic to Offic *Lich* 63-93; rtd 92; Hon C Ellesmere *Lich* from 93; RD Ellesmere 95-98. *Finstown, 6 Teal Drive, Ellesmere SY12 9PX* Tel (01691) 623353

GRAY, Melvyn Dixon. b 38. Lon Univ BD86 Dur Univ MA89. NEOC 84. **d** 87 **p** 88. C Richmond w Hudswell *Ripon* 87-90; P-in-c Downholme and Marske 88-90; P-in-c Forcett and Aldbrough and Melsonby 90-91; R 91-00; R Mobberley *Ches* 00-04; rtd 04. *19 Windgroves, Chilton, Ferryhill DL17 0RS* Tel (01388) 721870 E-mail windgroves2004@yahoo.co.uk

GRAY, Neil Kenneth. b 48. Kelham Th Coll 67. **d** 71 **p** 72. C Chorley St Laur *Blackb* 71-74; C S Shore H Trin 74-78; P-in-c Preston St Oswald 78-83; C Blackpool St Steph 83-87; Chapl Bolton HA from 87; Chapl Bolton Hosps NHS Trust from 90; Co-ord Spiritual and Cultural Care 90-03; Hd of Chapl from 04. *The Chaplains' Office, Royal Bolton Hospital, Minerva Road, Farnworth, Bolton BL4 0JR* Tel (01204) 390770 *or* 390390 E-mail neil.gray@boltonh-tr.nwest.nhs.uk

GRAY, Neil Ralph. b 53. MA. St Steph Ho Ox. **d** 82 **p** 83. C Kennington St Jo w St Jas *S'wark* 82-85; C Somers Town *Lon* 85-88. *3 Parsonage Close, High Wycombe HP13 6DT* Tel (01494) 531875

GRAY, Mrs Patricia Linda. b 51. Univ of Wales (Swansea) BA73 Chester Coll of HE BTh02. N Ord Course 99. **d** 02 **p** 03. NSM Glazebury w Hollinfare *Liv* 02-04; C from 04. *10 Hesnall Close, Glazebury, Warrington WA3 5PB* Tel (01942) 603161 Mobile 07747-772345 E-mail pat.gray@virgin.net

GRAY, Patrick. *See* GRAY, Sidney Patrick

GRAY, Penelope Jane. *See* GRAYSMITH, Mrs Penelope Jane

GRAY, Percy. b 28. OBE94 TD71. Lon Univ BA53 St Cath Soc Ox BA55 MA59. Oak Hill Th Coll 50. **d** 55 **p** 56. C Sutton *Liv* 55-58; C Chelsea Ch Ch *Lon* 58-59; V Bermondsey St Crispin w Ch Ch *S'wark* 59-99; CF (TA) 59-67; CF (TAVR) from 67; CF (ACF) from 76; rtd 99; Perm to Offic *S'wark* from 04; OCF from 04. *12 King Edward III Mews, Paradise Street, London SE16 4QH* Tel (020) 7394 7127 E-mail percyvic@aol.com

GRAY, Canon Philip Charles. b 67. Nottm Univ BA91. St Steph Ho Ox 91. **d** 93 **p** 94. C Scarborough St Martin *York* 93-97; TV Leek and Meerbrook *Lich* 97-01; Bp's Dom Chapl *Blackb* from 02; Hon Can Ho Ghana from 04. *79 Ribchester Road, Blackburn BB1 9HT* Tel (01254) 248234 E-mail chaplain@bishopofblackburn.org.uk

GRAY, Philip Thomas. b 41. Lon Univ BA65. Chich Th Coll 66. **d** 68 **p** 69. C Leigh St Clem *Chelmsf* 68-74; P-in-c Wickham Skeith *St E* 86-97; V Mendlesham from 74. *The Vicarage, Old Station Road, Mendlesham, Stowmarket IP14 5RS* Tel (01449) 766359

GRAY, Canon Robert James. b 70. TCD BA92 HDipEd93 MA95 Irish Sch of Ecum MPhil97. CITC 94. **d** 96 **p** 97. C Clooney w Strathfoyle *D & R* 96-99; Hon Sec Gen Synod Cttee for Chr Unity from 98; I Ardamine w Kiltennel, Glascarrig etc *C & O* from 99; Treas Ferns Cathl from 04. *Ardamine Rectory, Courtown Harbour, Gorey, Co Wexford, Irish Republic* Tel and fax (00353) (55) 25423 Mobile 86-684 7621 E-mail rjgray@esatclear.ie

GRAY, Sidney Patrick. b 19. Worc Ord Coll. **d** 63 **p** 63. C Skegness *Linc* 63-65; V Dunholme 65-71; R Cliffe at Hoo w Cooling *Roch* 72-78; V Gillingham St Aug 78-84; rtd 84; Perm to Offic *Cant* and *Roch* from 84. *September Cottage, 168 Loose Road, Maidstone ME15 7UD*

GRAY, Stephen James Norman. b 66. Lon Univ BA89 Hughes Hall Cam PGCE91. Ridley Hall Cam MA00. **d** 00 **p** 01. C Cheltenham Ch Ch *Glouc* 00-03; Chapl RN 03-04; Chapl Sherborne Sch from 04. *Rosslyn House, Acreman Street, Sherborne DT9 3NU* Tel (01935) 813846

GRAY, Mrs Ursula Mary. b 33. K Coll Lon BD56 AKC91 Univ of Wales (Lamp) MA02. **d** 04. NSM Shaston *Sarum* from 04. *Southdowns, 33 Layton Lane, Shaftesbury SP7 8EY* Tel (01747) 850955 E-mail jmg@argonet.co.uk

GRAY-STACK, Martha Mary Stewart. b 35. QUB BA57. **d** 90 **p** 91. NSM Limerick City *L & K* 90-93; Warden of Readers 90-93; NSM Clara w Liss, Moate and Clonmacnoise *M & K* 93-00; Chapl Kingston Coll Co Cork from 00. *16 Kingston College, Mitchelstown, Co Cork, Irish Republic* Tel and fax (00353) (25) 258 5975

GRAYSHON, Matthew Richard. b 47. St Jo Coll Nottm BTh81. **d** 81 **p** 82. C Beverley Minster *York* 81-85; V Hallwood *Ches* 85-93; R Hanwell St Mary w St Chris *Lon* from 93. *The Rectory, 91 Church Road, London W7 3BJ* Tel (020) 8567 6185 Fax 8579 8755 E-mail matthewgrayshon@tesco.net

GRAYSHON, Paul Nicholas Walton (Nick). b 50. St Jo Coll Dur 81. **d** 83 **p** 84. C Walkden Moor *Man* 83-87; V Radcliffe St Andr from 87. *St Andrew's Vicarage, St Andrew's View, Radcliffe, Manchester M26 4HE* Tel 0161-723 2427 Fax as telephone E-mail nickgrayshon@btopenworld.com

GRAYSMITH (née GRAY), Mrs Penelope Jane. b 63. SS Hild & Bede Coll Dur BA85 Em Coll Cam MPhil88. Westcott Ho Cam 86. **d** 89 **p** 94. Par Dn Evington *Leic* 89-92; Par Dn Cannock *Lich* 92-94; C 94-96; Chapl Asst Mid Staffs Gen Hosps NHS Trust from 96; Chapl Kath Ho Hospice Stafford from 96. *The Vicarage, 97 Baswich Lane, Stafford ST17 0BN* Tel (01785) 251057 *or* 230930 E-mail graysmit@fish.co.uk

GRAYSMITH, Peter Alexander. b 62. UEA BSc83. Westcott Ho Cam 85. **d** 88 **p** 89. C Tettenhall Regis *Lich* 88-89; C Cannock 89-92; TV 92-99; V Rocester and Croxden w Hollington 99-01; V Baswich from 01. *The Vicarage, 97 Baswich Lane, Stafford ST17 0BN* Tel (01785) 251057 E-mail graysmit@fish.co.uk

GRAYSON, Canon Robert William. b 24. Worc Coll Ox BA48 MA49 DipTh50. Wycliffe Hall Ox 49. **d** 50 **p** 51. C N Meols *Liv* 50-53; India 53-57; P-in-c Litherland St Paul Hatton Hill *Liv* 57-61; V Knowsley 61-66; V Stanwix *Carl* 66-79; RD Carl 71-79; Hon Can Carl Cathl 76-89; V Appleby 79-89; R Ormside 81-89; rtd 89; Perm to Offic *Carl* 89-99 and from 01. *Panorama, North End, Burgh-by-Sands, Carlisle CA5 6BD* Tel (01228) 576863

GRAYSON, Robin John. b 53. Mert Coll Ox BA74 DPhil78. Wycliffe Hall Ox 00. **d** 02 **p** 03. C Beaconsfield *Ox* from 02. *26 Candlemas Mead, Beaconsfield HP9 1AP* Tel (01494) 675083 Mobile 07801-280475 E-mail r.j.grayson@btinternet.com

GREADY, Andrew John. b 63. Univ Coll Lon BSc84 Newc Univ MA93 Surrey Univ BSc05. Cranmer Hall Dur 86. **d** 89 **p** 90. C Monkwearmouth St Andr *Dur* 89-92; S Africa 92-99; C Bramley St Cath 92-96; R Sunninghill St Steph 96-99; Chapl St Pet Prep Sch 99; V Shottermill *Guildf* from 00; Chapl Amesbury Sch from 01. *The Vicarage, Vicarage Lane, Shottermill, Haslemere GU27 1LQ* Tel (01428) 645878 Fax 645880 E-mail andrew@greadyfamily.fsnet.co.uk

GREANY, Canon Richard Andrew Hugh. b 44. Qu Coll Ox BA67 MA83. Coll of Resurr Mirfield 67. **d** 69 **p** 70. C Hartlepool St Oswald *Dur* 69-72; C Clifton All SS *Bris* 72-75; Tutor Coll of Resurr Mirfield 75-78; V Whitworth w Spennymoor *Dur* 78-83; P-in-c Byers Green 78-79; Asst Prin St Alb Minl Tr Scheme 83-88; V Flamstead *St Alb* 83-88; V Hessle *York* 88-94; V Cambridge St Mary Less *Ely* from 94; Dioc Spirituality Officer from 99; Hon Can Ely Cathl from 05. *St Mary the Less Vicarage, 4 Newnham Terrace, Cambridge CB3 9EX* Tel (01223) 350733 *or* 366202 E-mail andrew.greany@ely.anglican.org

GREANY, Mrs Virginia Clare. b 52. Bris Univ BA74 PGCE75 Hull Univ Dip Counselling 93 MSc94. Westcott Ho Cam 96 EAMTC 97. **d** 98. Bp's Dn to Local Government *Ely* 98-99; Asst to Dean Trin Hall Cam 98-00. *Trinity Hall, Cambridge CB2 1TJ* Tel (01223) 332500

GREAR, Hugh Massey. b 60. Bris Univ LLB82. SEITE. **d** 00 **p** 01. C Warlingham w Chelsham and Farleigh *S'wark* 00-04; V Upper Tooting H Trin w St Aug from 04. *Holy Trinity Vicarage, 14 Upper Tooting Park, London SW17 7SW* Tel (020) 8672 4790 E-mail hughgrear@x-stream.co.uk

GREASLEY, James Kenneth. b 39. K Coll Lon BD66 AKC66. **d** 67 **p** 68. C Stoke upon Trent *Lich* 67-70; P-in-c Lusaka St Pet Zambia 70-76; V Gt Staughton *Ely* 76-81; Chapl HM Borstal Gaynes Hall 76-81; V Melbourn and Meldreth *Ely* 81-96; RD Shingay 82-96; R Chalfont St Peter *Ox* 96-04; rtd 04. *Bank Cottage, Norton, Presteigne LD8 2EN* Tel (01544) 267567 E-mail jk.greasley@btinternet.com

GREATBATCH, John Charles. b 56. N Staffs Poly BA80. Coll of Resurr Mirfield 80. **d** 83 **p** 84. C Wednesbury St Paul Wood Green *Lich* 83-88; C Codsall 88-94; V Tipton St Jo 94-97; V Charlestown *Truro* from 97; Chapl Cornwall Healthcare NHS Trust 98-02; Chapl Cen Cornwall Primary Care Trust from 02. *The Vicarage, Church Road, Charlestown, St Austell PL25 3NS* Tel (01726) 75688 Mobile 07799-078164 E-mail john@obadiah19.fsnet.co.uk

GREATOREX, Mrs Susan Kathleen. b 58. St Hilda's Coll Ox BA79 MA04 Univ of Wales (Cardiff) PGCE80. WEMTC 01. **d** 04 **p** 05. C Keynsham *B & W* from 04. *88 Chandag Road, Keynsham, Bristol BS31 1QE* E-mail susangreatorex@hotmail.com

GREATREX, Richard Quintin. b 65. K Coll Lon BD86 Surrey Univ BA02. STETS 99. **d** 02 **p** 03. NSM Westbury-on-Trym St Alb *Bris* from 02. *The Garden Flat, 97B Pembroke Road, Clifton, Bristol BS8 3EE* Tel 0117-974 3607

GREATREX, Warren Robert. b 21. Qu Univ Kingston Ontario BCom41. Trin Coll Toronto LTh50 BD51. **d** 50 **p** 51. Canada 50-78; Perm to Offic *Heref* 78-98; *Ely* from 99. *16 Westberry Court, Cambridge CB3 9BG* Tel (01223) 369335

GREAVES, Canon John Neville. b 29. Newc Univ MA96 Dur Univ MLitt03 AAAI56. St Aid Birkenhead 58. **d** 61 **p** 62. C Pendleton St Ambrose *Man* 61-62; P-in-c 62-63; C Benchill 63-65; C-in-c Wythenshawe St Rich CD 65-71; V Wythenshawe St Rich 71-73; R Sadberge *Dur* 73-78; V Dur St Cuth 78-94; Chapl New Coll Dur 78-92; Lect NEOC 79-84; Chapl Dur Co Fire Brigade 85-94; RD Dur 80-93; Hon Can Dur Cathl 91-94; rtd 94; Perm to Offic *Ches* 94-97; P-in-c Salt and Sandon w Burston *Lich* 97-00; Past Aux Eccleshall Deanery 00-01; Perm to Offic *Lich* 01-02 and *Heref* from 03. *3 Sitwell Close, Bucknell SY7 0DD* Tel (01547) 530152

GREED, Frederick John. b 44. Trin Coll Bris 79. **d** 81 **p** 82. C Yateley *Win* 81-85; R Ore *Chich* 85-95; R Street w Walton *B & W* from 95. *The Rectory, Vestry Close, Street BA16 0HZ* Tel (01458) 442671 E-mail john.greed@tesco.net

GREEDY, Tegryd Joseph. b 31. St D Coll Lamp 59. **d** 61 **p** 62. C Newbridge *Mon* 61-64; C Bassaleg 64-66; V Newport St Teilo 66-74; Hon C Newport St Mark 80-83; V Goldcliffe and Whitson and Nash 83-90; Ind Chapl 83-90; V Marshfield and Peterstone Wentloog etc 90-96; rtd 96. *42 Churchward Drive, Newport NP19 4SB* Tel (01633) 282159

GREEN, Alan John Enrique. b 56. Worc Coll Ox BA78 MA83. Linc Th Coll 83. **d** 85 **p** 86. C Kirkby *Liv* 85-88; TV 88-94; Chapl Knowsley Community Coll 87-90; Chapl Worc Coll Ox 94-98; C Ox St Giles and SS Phil and Jas w St Marg *Ox* 94-98; TR St Jo on Bethnal Green *Lon* from 98. *St John's Rectory, 30 Victoria Park Square, London E2 9PB* Tel and fax (020) 8980 1742 E-mail alan.green@virgin.net

GREEN, Alison Mary. b 51. Boro Road Teacher Tr Coll BEd74 Wesley Coll Bris MA03. STETS 02. **d** 04 **p** 05. NSM Bath St Barn w Englishcombe *B & W* from 04. *Tower House, 297 Bloomfield Road, Bath BA2 2NU* Tel (01225) 830514 Fax 833001 Mobile 07884-260127 E-mail alig9@btinternet.com

GREEN, Anthony Brian. b 39. Sussex Univ MA88 Birm Univ CertEd60 ACP66. Bps' Coll Cheshunt 62. **d** 64 **p** 65. C Batheaston w St Cath *B & W* 64-67; Chapl Aiglon Coll and Villars *Eur* 67-71; Hd Master Battisborough Sch Holbeton 71-81; Chapl R Gr Sch Worc 81-83; Hd Master Frewen Coll Rye 83-96; P-in-c New Groombridge *Chich* from 97. *The Vicarage, Corsley Road, Groombridge, Tunbridge Wells TN3 9SE* Tel and fax (01892) 864265 E-mail fidgreen@aol.com

GREEN, Arthur Edward. b 27. Chich Th Coll 58. **d** 59 **p** 60. C Malden St Jas *S'wark* 59-62; C Caterham 62-67; R Burgh Parva w Briston *Nor* 67-75; V Middleton 75-76; V Middleton w E Winch 76-84; R Neatishead w Irstead 84-90; V Barton Turf 84-90; R Neatishead, Barton Turf and Irstead 90-92; rtd 92; Perm to Offic *Portsm* from 92. *10 James Butcher Court, 16 Eastern Villas Road, Southsea PO4 0TD* Tel (023) 9275 0701

GREEN, Barrie. b 51. SS Coll Cam BA72 MA76. Wycliffe Hall Ox 75. **d** 78 **p** 79. C Castle Vale *Birm* 78-81; V W Heath 81-96; RD Kings Norton 87-95; TR Dronfield w Holmesfield *Derby* from 96. *The Rectory, Church Street, Dronfield S18 1QB* Tel (01246) 411531 *or* 412328 Fax 08707-065540 E-mail barrie.green@dwhparish.org.uk

GREEN, Benedict. *See* GREEN, Humphrey Christian

GREEN, Brian Robert. b 31. Bris Univ BA55. Tyndale Hall Bris 52. **d** 56 **p** 57. C Toxteth Park St Philemon *Liv* 56-58; V Toxteth Park St Philemon w St Silas 58-69; P-in-c Toxteth Park St Gabr 64-69; P-in-c Toxteth Park St Jo and St Thos 64-69; P-in-c Toxteth Park St Jas and St Matt 68-69; V Elsenham *Chelmsf* 69-85; V Henham 69-85; P-in-c Ugley 84-85; V Henham and Elsenham w Ugley 85-89; RD Newport and Stansted 87-89; Perm to Offic *Ex* 90-91; V Tidenham w Beachley and Lancaut *Glouc* 91-97; RD Forest S 95-97; rtd 97; Perm to Offic *Ex* from 97. *1 The Square, Offwell, Honiton EX14 9SA* Tel (01404) 831795

GREEN, Catherine Isabel. *See* HITCHENS, Mrs Catherine Isabel

GREEN, Christopher Frederick. b 46. Nottm Univ BTh75 Birm Univ DipEd85 Univ of Wales (Abth) MEd94. Bp Otter Coll

CertEd69 Linc Th Coll 71. **d** 75 **p** 76. C Hodge Hill *Birm* 75-77; C S Lafford *Linc* 77-79; P-in-c Worc St Mich *Worc* 79-82; Hd RS and Lib RNIB New Coll Worc 82-96; V Clipstone *S'well* 96-02; rtd 02; Perm to Offic *Linc* from 03. *Cobwebs, Middlefield Lane, Glentham, Market Rasen LN8 2ET* Tel (01673) 878633

GREEN, Christopher Martyn. b 58. New Coll Edin BD80. Cranmer Hall Dur 82. **d** 83 **p** 84. C Virginia Water *Guildf* 83-87; C Bromley Ch Ch *Roch* 87-91; Study Asst the Proclamation Trust 91-92; C Surbiton Hill Ch Ch *S'wark* 92-00; Vice Prin Oak Hill Th Coll from 00; Perm to Offic *Lon* from 02. *Oak Hill Theological College, Chase Side, London N14 4PS* Tel (020) 8449 0467 *or* 8441 0315

GREEN, Mrs Clare Noreen. b 30. SW Minl Tr Course 84. **d** 88. NSM Bideford *Ex* 88-90; Perm to Offic from 90. *6 Balmoral Gardens, Topsham, Exeter EX3 0DJ* Tel (01392) 875118

GREEN, Daphne Mary. b 55. K Coll Cam BA77 Bradf Univ MBA91 Leeds Univ PhD01 Lon Inst of Educn PGCE79. N Ord Course 95. **d** 98 **p** 99. C Headingley *Ripon* 98-02; Chapl Leeds Metrop Univ 00-02; R Stanningley St Thos from 02. *50 Lane End, Pudsey LS28 9AD* Tel 0113-255 0909 *or* 256 6535 Mobile 07796-084264 Fax 0113-255 0910
E-mail daphne@stanningleyparish.org.uk

GREEN, David Allen. b 61. Sheff City Poly BA90. Cranmer Hall Dur 00. **d** 02 **p** 03. C Huyton St Geo *Liv* from 02. *31 Endmoor Road, Huyton, Liverpool L36 3UH* Tel 0151-489 4086
E-mail david.green@huytondeanery.org

GREEN, Canon David John. b 54. DCR, MU. SW Minl Tr Course 82. **d** 85 **p** 86. C St Marychurch *Ex* 85-89; C Laira 89-90; V Maughold *S & M* from 90; RD Ramsey from 98; Dioc Dir of Ords from 05; Can St German's Cathl from 05. *The Vicarage, Maughold, Isle of Man IM7 1AS* Tel (01624) 812070
E-mail dgreen@mcb.net

GREEN, David Norman. b 37. Magd Coll Cam BA60. Clifton Th Coll 60. **d** 62 **p** 63. C Islington St Mary *Lon* 62-65; C Burley *Ripon* 65-68; Kenya 69-80; P-in-c Brimscombe *Glouc* 81-90; R Woodchester and Brimscombe 90-96; P-in-c Coberley w Cowley 96-97; P-in-c Colesborne 96-97; P-in-c Coberley, Cowley, Colesbourne and Elkstone 97-04; Dioc Rural Adv 96-04; rtd 04; Tanzania from 04. *c/o Dr A D Green, 23 Burton Street, Loughborough LE11 2DT* Tel (01509) 231209

GREEN, David William. b 53. CertEd75 Nottm Univ BCombStuds84. Linc Th Coll 81. **d** 84 **p** 85. C S Merstham *S'wark* 84-88; C Walton-on-Thames *Guildf* 88-91; V Gillingham H Trin *Roch* 91-99; Chapl Lennox Wood Elderly People's Home 91-99; V Strood St Nic w St Mary from 99. *The Vicarage, 3 Central Road, Strood, Rochester ME2 3HF* Tel (01634) 719052
E-mail revdavidgreen@lineone.net

GREEN, Canon Derek George Wilson. b 27. Bris Univ BA53 MA58. Tyndale Hall Bris 48. **d** 53 **p** 54. C Weymouth St Mary *Sarum* 53-55; Chapl RAF 55-58; R N Pickenham w Houghton on the Hill *Nor* 58-89; R S Pickenham 58-89; R N Pickenham w S Pickenham etc 89-93; Hon Can Nor Cathl 78-93; E Region Co-ord Scripture Union 80-92; rtd 93; Perm to Offic *Sarum* from 93. *5 Hawkins Meadow, College Fields, Marlborough SN8 1UA* Tel (01672) 511713

GREEN, Donald Henry. b 31. Selw Coll Cam BA54 Lon Inst of Educn PGCE55. Qu Coll Birm 81. **d** 83 **p** 84. C Dudley St Aug Holly Hall *Worc* 83-85; V Dudley St Barn 85-90; rtd 96. *The Cuckoo's Nest, 12 Mill Green, Knighton LD7 1EE* Tel (01547) 528289

GREEN, Donald Pentney (Brother Donald). b 25. Leeds Univ BA50. Coll of Resurr Mirfield 50. **d** 52 **p** 53. C Ardwick St Benedict *Man* 52-55; SSF from 55; Sec for Miss SSF 78-96; Lic to Offic *Chelmsf* 58-60 and 69-72; Papua New Guinea 60-63; Chapl HM Pris Kingston (Portsm) 72-76; Lic to Offic *Edin* 76-77; Org Sec Catholic Renewal 77; Lic to Offic *Lich* from 78; rtd 95. *85 Crofton Road, London E13 8QT* Tel (020) 7474 5863
E-mail donaldssf@aol.com

GREEN, Mrs Dorothy Mary. b 36. Westf Coll Lon BA58. Selly Oak Coll 60. **dss** 83 **d** 87 **p** 94. Ryde All SS *Portsm* 83-87; C 87-91; Hon C Hempnall *Nor* 91-96; rtd 96; Perm to Offic *B & W* from 97. *Oneida, Charnwood Drive, Cheddar BS27 3HD* Tel (01934) 742167

GREEN, Douglas Edward. b 17. Sarum Th Coll 47. **d** 50 **p** 51. C Glouc St Paul *Glouc* 50-53; C Malvern Link St Matthias *Worc* 53-56; R Tolladine 56-58; V Bosbury *Heref* 58-78; R Coddington 59-79; V Wellington Heath 59-79; Hon C Minsterley 78-80; rtd 82; Perm to Offic *Worc* from 83. *21 The Quadrangle, Newland, Malvern WR13 5AX* Tel (01684) 568335

GREEN, Canon Duncan Jamie. b 52. Sarum & Wells Th Coll 82. **d** 84 **p** 85. C Uckfield *Chich* 84-87; Dioc Youth Officer *Chelmsf* 87-96; Warden and Chapl St Mark's Coll Res Cen 93-96; TR Saffron Walden w Wendens Ambo, Littlebury etc from 96; Hon Can Chelmsf Cathl from 03; RD Saffron Walden from 05. *The Rectory, 17 Borough Lane, Saffron Walden CB11 4AG* Tel (01799) 500947 E-mail rector.saffronwalden@ntlworld.com

GREEN, Edward John. b 35. Lich Th Coll. **d** 59 **p** 60. C Longford *Cov* 59-61; C Wigston Magna *Leic* 61-65; V 73-00; V Ellistown 65-73; rtd 00; Perm to Offic *Leic* 00-03. *Holly Mount, 27 Greendale Road, Glen Parva, Leicester LE2 9HD* Tel 0116-277 2479

GREEN, Edward Marcus. b 66. Mert Coll Ox BA88 MA92. Wycliffe Hall Ox 90. **d** 94 **p** 95. C Glyncorrwg w Afan Vale and Cymmer Afan *Llan* 94-96; C Aberystwyth *St D* 96-99; P-in-c Pontypridd St Cath w St Matt *Llan* 00-01; V Pontypridd St Cath from 01. *St Catherine's Vicarage, Gelliwastad Grove, Pontypridd CF37 2BS* Tel (01443) 402021
E-mail marcusgreen@manutd.com

GREEN, Canon Edward Michael Bankes. b 30. Ex Coll Ox BA53 MA56 Qu Coll Cam BA57 MA61 BD66 Toronto Univ DD92 Lambeth DD96. Ridley Hall Cam 55. **d** 57 **p** 58. C Eastbourne H Trin *Chich* 57-60; Tutor Lon Coll of Div 60-69; Prin St Jo Coll Nottm 69-75; Hon Can Cov Cathl *Cov* 70-78; R Ox St Aldate w H Trin *Ox* 75-82; R Ox St Aldate w St Matt 82-86; Canada 87-92; Prof Evang Regent Coll Vancouver 87-92; Abps' Adv Springboard for Decade of Evang 92-96; Six Preacher Cant Cathl *Cant* 93-99; rtd 96; Sen Research Fell Wycliffe Hall Ox from 97; Perm to Offic *Ox* from 99. *7 Little Acreage, Marston, Oxford OX3 0PS* Tel (01865) 248387

GREEN, Mrs Elizabeth Pauline Anne. b 29. Lon Coll of Div DipRK70. **dss** 76 **d** 87 **p** 94. Chorleywood Ch Ch *St Alb* 76-87; Par Dn 87-90; C Chipping Sodbury and Old Sodbury *Glouc* 90-95; Asst Dioc Missr 90-95; rtd 95; NSM Chipping Sodbury and Old Sodbury *Glouc* 95-99; Perm to Offic *Glouc*; *Bris* from 99. *The Old House, The Common, Chipping Sodbury, Bristol BS37 6PX* Tel (01454) 311936 E-mail p.green@care4free.net

GREEN, Eric Kenneth. b 18. Tyndale Hall Bris 40. **d** 45 **p** 47. C Heatherlands St Jo *Sarum* 45-48; C Radipole 48-49; C Bucknall and Bagnall *Lich* 49-50; V Halwell w Moreleigh *Ex* 50-53; V Wakef St Mary *Wakef* 53-55; R Peldon *Chelmsf* 55-57; P-in-c Leaden Roding 57-58; R 58-63; V Aythorpe Roding and High Roding 60-63; R All Cannings w Etchilhampton *Sarum* 63-75; V Over Kellet *Blackb* 75-83; rtd 83; Perm to Offic *Bradf* 91-98. *1 Capel Court, The Burgage, Prestbury, Cheltenham GL52 3EL*

GREEN, Ernest James. b 31. Pemb Coll Cam BA55 MA62. Linc Th Coll 55. **d** 57 **p** 58. C Rawmarsh *Sheff* 57-60; Sec Th Colls Dept SCM 60-62; Prec and Sacr Bris Cathl *Bris* 62-65; Min Can 62-65; V Churchill *B & W* 65-78; RD Locking 72-78; V Burrington and Churchill 78-82; Preb Wells Cathl 81-82; V Ryde All SS *Portsm* 82-91; P-in-c Ryde H Trin 82-86; RD E Wight 83-88; TR Hempnall *Nor* 91-96; rtd 96; Perm to Offic *B & W* from 97. *Oneida, Charnwood Drive, Cheddar BS27 3HD* Tel (01934) 742167 E-mail egreen@fish.co.uk

GREEN, Ms Fiona Jenifer. b 67. Rob Coll Cam BA89 MA93. Ridley Hall Cam 02. **d** 05. C Highbury Ch Ch w St Jo and St Sav *Lon* from 05. *7 Lyndon Court, 67A Kelvin Road, London N5 2PP* Tel 07786-541559 (mobile) E-mail fionajgreen@yahoo.co.uk

GREEN, Fleur Estelle. b 72. Univ of Wales (Ban) BD94. Ripon Coll Cuddesdon DipMin95. **d** 97 **p** 98. C Blackpool St Jo *Blackb* 97-00; C Lancaster St Mary w St John and St Anne 00-03; P-in-c Blackb St Luke w St Phil 03-04; P-in-c Witton 03-04; V Blackb Christ the King from 04. *St Mark's Vicarage, Buncer Lane, Blackburn BB2 6SY* Tel (01254) 676615

GREEN, Frank Gilbert. b 23. Kelham Th Coll 46. **d** 50 **p** 51. C Sheff St Cecilia Parson Cross *Sheff* 50-56; SSM from 52; C Nottingham St Geo w St Jo *S'well* 56-58; Basutoland 59-62; S Africa 62-69 and 84-88; Lesotho 69-84; Lic to Offic *Ox* from 88; rtd 93. *Society of the Sacred Mission, 1 Linford Lane, Willen, Milton Keynes MK15 9DL* Tel (01908) 234546

GREEN, Gareth David. b 60. Worc Coll Ox BA82 MA86 FRCO79 FLCM87 ARCM75 Leeds Univ MA98. N Ord Course 94. **d** 97 **p** 98. NSM Lupset *Wakef* 97-00; V W Ardsley 00-03. *Address temp unknown* E-mail gareth@gareth73.freeserve.co.uk

GREEN, Gary Henry. b 64. Univ of Wales (Cardiff) BD87. St Mich Coll Llan 93. **d** 95 **p** 96. C Baglan *Llan* 95-97; C Neath w Llantwit 97-01; TV Neath 01-02; V Llangiwg *S & B* from 02. *The Vicarage, 10 Uplands Road, Pontardawe, Swansea SA8 4AH* Tel (01792) 862003

GREEN, George James. b 26. Cuddesdon Coll 69. **d** 69 **p** 70. C Handsworth St Mary *Birm* 69-76; R Croughton w Evenley *Pet* 76-88; R Aynho and Croughton w Evenley 88-95; rtd 95; Perm to Offic *Cov* from 95. *Dibbinsdale, Langley Road, Claverdon, Warwick CV35 8PU*

GREEN, Gillian. b 41. Balls Park Coll Hertford TCert61 Open Univ BA83. EAMTC 03. **d** 05. NSM Stour Valley *St E* from 05. *Lady's Green Cottage, Lady's Green, Ousden, Newmarket CB8 8TU* Tel (01284) 850605 E-mail gill@g-green.fsnet.co.uk

GREEN, Mrs Gloria. b 49. STETS 00. **d** 03 **p** 04. NSM Jersey St Brelade *Win* from 03; Asst Chapl Jersey Gen Hosp 03-04. *29 La Verte Rue, Mont ès Croix, St Brelade, Jersey JE3 8EL* Tel (01534) 744804 Fax 08700-941104 E-mail glo@glogreen.com

GREEN, Gordon Sydney. b 33. Ridley Hall Cam 77. **d** 79 **p** 80. C Ipswich St Marg *St E* 79-83; TV Barton Mills, Beck Row w Kenny Hill etc 83-85; TV Mildenhall 85-86; rtd 86; Perm to Offic *Pet* from 87 and *St E* from 97. *28 Upton Close, Ipswich IP4 2QQ* Tel (01473) 252188

GREEN, Graham Herbert. b 53. City Univ BSc74. Westcott Ho Cam 75. **d** 78 **p** 79. C Hatcham St Cath *S'wark* 78-82; C S

Ashford Ch Ch *Cant* 82-88; V Cheriton All So w Newington 88-97; P-in-c Milton next Sittingbourne 97-02; V from 02. *The Vicarage, Vicarage Road, Milton Regis, Sittingbourne ME10 2BL* Tel (01795) 472016 E-mail graham@green90.fsnet.co.uk

GREEN, Graham Reginald. b 48. Sarum & Wells Th Coll 71. **d** 74 **p** 75. C Chorley St Laur *Blackb* 74-76; C Padiham 76-79; V Osmondthorpe St Phil *Ripon* 79-94. *3 Northwood Gardens, Colton, Leeds LS15 9HH* Tel 0113-264 3558

GREEN, Humphrey Christian (Benedict). b 24. Mert Coll Ox BA49 MA52. Cuddesdon Coll 50. **d** 51 **p** 52. C Northolt St Mary *Lon* 51-56; Lect Th K Coll Lon 56-60; Lic to Offic *Wakef* from 61; CR from 62; Vice-Prin Coll of Resurr Mirfield 65-75; Prin 75-84; rtd 94. *House of the Resurrection, Stocks Bank Road, Mirfield WF14 0BN* Tel (01924) 494318 *or* 483328

GREEN, Imogen Elizabeth. *See* VIBERT, Imogen Elizabeth

GREEN, Jeffrey. b 43. Chich Th Coll 76. **d** 78 **p** 79. C Crewkerne w Wayford *B & W* 78-81; C Cockington *Ex* 81-83; P-in-c Ripple *Worc* 83; P-in-c Ripple, Earls Croome w Hill Croome and Strensham 83; R 83-87; Perm to Offic *Glouc* 02-03; Hon C Boxwell, Leighterton, Didmarton, Oldbury etc from 03; Hon C Nailsworth w Shortwood, Horsley etc from 03. *The Vicarage, Horsley Hill, Horsley, Stroud GL6 0PW* Tel (01453) 833310

GREEN, Miss Jennifer Mary. b 55. SEN78 SRN81 RM84. Trin Coll Bris DipHE88 ADPS89. **d** 90 **p** 95. C Tong *Bradf* 90-93; Chapl Bradf Cathl 93; CMS from 94; Uganda from 94. *Muhabura Diocese, PO Box 22, Kisoro, Uganda*

GREEN, Jeremy Nigel. b 52. St Andr Univ MA Nottm Univ DipTh. St Jo Coll Nottm 80. **d** 83 **p** 84. C Dorridge *Birm* 83-86; V Scrooby *S'well* 86-94; V Bawtry w Austerfield and Misson from 94; AD Bawtry from 01. *The Vicarage, Martin Lane, Bawtry, Doncaster DN10 6NJ* Tel (01302) 710298 E-mail jngreen@lineone.net

GREEN, John. *See* GREEN, Edward John

GREEN, John. b 28. AKC54. **d** 55 **p** 56. C Poulton-le-Fylde *Blackb* 55-57; C St Annes St Thos 57-63; V Inskip 63-75; V Fairhaven 75-87; rtd 87; Perm to Offic *Blackb* from 87. *42 Westwood Road, Lytham, Lytham St Annes FY8 5NX* Tel (01253) 739288

GREEN, John. b 53. Nottm Univ BCombStuds83. Linc Th Coll 80. **d** 83 **p** 84. C Watford St Mich *St Alb* 83-86; C St Alb St Steph 86-91; Chapl RN from 91. *Royal Naval Chaplaincy Service, Room 203, Victory Building, HM Naval Base, Portsmouth PO1 3LS* Tel (023) 9272 7903 Fax 9272 7111

GREEN, John David. b 29. Lon Univ BD66. Roch Th Coll 63. **d** 66 **p** 66. C Roch St Pet w St Marg *Roch* 66-72; V Oxshott *Guildf* 72-85; R Weybridge 85-94; rtd 94; Perm to Offic *Guildf* from 94. *103 Bitterne Drive, Woking GU21 3JX* Tel (01483) 727936

GREEN, John Francis Humphrey. b 44. Ex Univ BA65 Heythrop Coll Lon MA96. Westcott Ho Cam 91. **d** 93 **p** 94. C Tadworth *S'wark* 93-96; Chapl St Geo Sch Harpenden 96-01; P-in-c Flamstead *St Alb* from 01; P-in-c Markyate Street from 01. *The Vicarage, 50 Trowley Hill Road, Flamstead, St Albans AL3 8EE* Tel (01582) 842040 E-mail johnhumphreygreen@hotmail.com

GREEN, Canon John Henry. b 44. K Coll Lon BD72 AKC. **d** 73 **p** 74. C Tupsley *Heref* 73-77; Asst Chapl Newc Univ *Newc* 77-79; V Stevenage St Hugh Chells *St Alb* 79-85; V St Jo in Bedwardine *Worc* 85-92; P-in-c Guarlford and Madresfield w Newland 92-99; Dir of Ords from 92; Hon Can Worc Cathl from 94; C Fladbury w Wyre Piddle and Moor etc from 99. *The Vicarage, Main Street, Cropthorne, Pershore WR10 3NB* Tel (01386) 861304 E-mail jgreen@cofe-worcester.org.uk *or* ddomalvern@aol.com

GREEN, John Herbert Gardner-Waterman. b 21. Trin Hall Cam BA48 MA58. Wells Th Coll 58. **d** 59 **p** 60. C New Romney w Hope *Cant* 59-63; V Hartlip 63-68; R Sandhurst w Newenden 68-90; RD W Charing 74-81; rtd 90; Perm to Offic *Cant* from 90 and *Chich* from 98. *Littlefield House, Maytham Road, Rolvenden Layne, Cranbrook TN17 4NS* Tel (01580) 241579

GREEN, Preb John Stanley. b 12. Keble Coll Ox BA33 MA37. Wells Th Coll 33. **d** 35 **p** 36. C Stockport St Matt *Ches* 35-39; C Bournemouth St Mary *Win* 39-46; PV Ex Cathl *Ex* 46-49; Dep PV 49-77; R Ex St Jas 49-77; Preb Ex Cathl 69-84; rtd 77; Perm to Offic *Ex* 84-04. *265 Hinton Way, Great Shelford, Cambridge CB2 5AN* Tel (01223) 844170

GREEN, Joseph Hudson. b 28. TD76. Dur Univ TCert73. Kelham Th Coll 48. **d** 53 **p** 54. C Norton St Mich *Dur* 53-56; C Heworth St Mary 56-62; V Harton Colliery 62-69; Chapl S Shields Gen Hosp 62-69; CF (TA) 63-67; CF (TAVR) 67-77; V Leadgate *Dur* 69-78; V Dudleston *Lich* 78-85; V Criftins 78-85; R Hodnet w Weston under Redcastle 85-93; RD Hodnet 86-93; rtd 93; Perm to Offic *Lich* from 93. *3 The Paddocks, Market Drayton TF9 3UE* Tel (01630) 658887

GREEN, Julia Ann. *See* CARTWRIGHT, Julia Ann

GREEN, Miss Karina Beverley. b 61. Ripon Coll Cuddesdon 87. **d** 90 **p** 94. C Lee-on-the-Solent *Portsm* 90-93; Dioc Youth Officer *Guildf* 94-99; Youth and Children's Work Adv *Portsm* 99-03; P-in-c Portsea St Geo from 03; CME Officer from 03. *The Vicarage, 8 Queen Street, Portsmouth PO1 3HL* Tel (023) 9283 8713 E-mail youth@portsmouth.anglican.org

✠**GREEN, The Rt Revd Laurence Alexander.** b 45. K Coll Lon BD68 AKC68. DMin82 NY Th Sem STM69 St Aug Coll Cant 70. **d** 70 **p** 71 **c** 93. C Kingstanding St Mark *Birm* 70-73; V Erdington St Chad 73-83; Prin Aston Tr Scheme 83-89; Hon C Birchfield *Birm* 84-89; TR Poplar *Lon* 89-93; Area Bp Bradwell *Chelmsf* from 93. *The Bishop's House, Orsett Road, Horndon-on-the-Hill, Stanford-le-Hope SS17 8NS* Tel (01375) 673806 Fax 674222 E-mail lauriegreen@globalnet.co.uk

GREEN, Mrs Linda Anne. b 60. Avery Hill Coll DipHE84. Westcott Ho Cam 84. **dss** 86 **d** 87 **p** 94. Borehamwood *St Alb* 86-89; Par Dn 87-89; Par Dn Sheff St Cuth *Sheff* 89-90; Chapl Asst N Gen Hosp Sheff 89-90; Chapl 90-96; Chapl Qu Mary's Sidcup NHS Trust from 96. *Queen Mary's Hospital, Frognal Avenue, Sidcup DA14 6LT* Tel (020) 8302 2678

GREEN, Mrs Linda Jeanne. b 50. R Holloway Coll Lon BSc72 RGN74 RCNT79. St Alb and Ox Min Course 01. **d** 04 **p** 05. C Headington Quarry *Ox* from 04. *20 Binswood Avenue, Headington, Oxford OX3 8NZ* Tel (01865) 741768 Mobile 07973-802863 E-mail linda@green121.fsnet.co.uk

GREEN, Marcus. *See* GREEN, Edward Marcus

GREEN, Mrs Margaret Elizabeth. b 34. DipYL65. St Mich Ho Ox 60. **dss** 84 **d** 87 **p** 94. Ecclesall *Sheff* 84-87; Par Dn 87-90; C Doncaster St Jas 90-94; rtd 95; Perm to Offic *Sheff* from 95. *91 Littemoor Lane, Doncaster DN4 0LQ* Tel (01302) 365884

✠**GREEN, The Rt Revd Mark.** b 17. MC45. Linc Coll Ox BA40 MA44 Aston Univ Hon DSc80. Cuddesdon Coll 40. **d** 40 **p** 41 **c** 72. C Glouc St Cath *Glouc* 40-42; CF (EC) 43-46; V Newland St Jo *York* 48-53; CF 53-56; V S Bank *York* 56-58; R Cottingham 58-64; Can and Preb York Minster 63-72; Hon Chapl to Abp York 64-72; V Bishopthorpe 64-72; V Acaster Malbis 64-72; RD Ainsty 64-68; Suff Bp Aston *Birm* 72-82; Dioc Dir of Ords 80-82; rtd 82; Asst Bp Chich from 82. *27 Selwyn House, Selwyn Road, Eastbourne BN21 2LF* Tel (01323) 642707

GREEN, Martin Charles. b 59. Bris Univ BA81 MPhil86. Wycliffe Hall Ox 82. **d** 84 **p** 85. C Margate H Trin *Cant* 84-88; V Kingston upon Hull St Aid Southcoates *York* 88-94; P-in-c Bishop's Itchington *Cov* from 94; Dioc Children's Officer 94-05; P-in-c Radford Semele from 05. *The Vicarage, Bishop's Itchington, Leamington Spa CV47 2QJ* Tel (01926) 613466 E-mail revmcg@aol.com

GREEN, Martyn. b 41. FCA. Ridley Hall Cam 78. **d** 80 **p** 81. C Wetherby *Ripon* 80-83; V Leeds St Cypr Harehills 83-90; V Ossett cum Gawthorpe *Wakef* 90-99; TR Haxby w Wigginton *York* from 99. *The Rectory, 3 Westfield Close, Wigginton, York YO32 2JG* Tel (01904) 760455 Fax as telephone

GREEN, Mrs Maureen. b 49. Avery Hill Coll CertEd70 Lon Univ BEd71. EAMTC 95. **d** 98 **p** 02. NSM Ipswich St Jo *St E* from 98; Asst Chapl Ipswich Hosp NHS Trust 98-05; Asst Chapl Local Health Partnerships NHS Trust 98-02; Asst Chapl Cen Suffolk Primary Care Trust 02-05. *Rose Cottage, 41 Cowper Street, Ipswich IP4 5JB* Tel (01473) 434330 E-mail maureengreen@talk21.com

GREEN, Canon Maurice Paul. b 34. MCIMA60. Wells Th Coll 68. **d** 70 **p** 71. C Eaton *Nor* 70-74; R N w S Wootton 74-90; RD Lynn 83-89; Hon Can Nor Cathl 88-96; V Swaffham 90-96; rtd 96; Perm to Offic *St E* from 96. *6 Wimborne Avenue, Ipswich IP3 8QW* Tel (01473) 711061 E-mail m.green25@ntl.com

GREEN, Michael. *See* GREEN, Canon Edward Michael Bankes

GREEN, Muriel Hilda. b 38. SEITE 94. **d** 96 **p** 97. NSM Ealing St Barn *Lon* 96-98; C 98-00; Hon C Elmstead *Chelmsf* 00-04; P-in-c from 04. *3 Laurence Close, Elmstead Market, Colchester CO7 7EJ* Tel (01206) 825401 E-mail murielgreen@onetel.com

GREEN, Neil Howard. b 57. New Coll Ox BA80 PGCE81. Wycliffe Hall Ox 87. **d** 90 **p** 91. C Finchley St Paul and St Luke *Lon* 90-94; C Muswell Hill St Jas w St Matt 94-98; V Eastbourne All So *Chich* from 98. *The Vicarage, 53 Susan's Road, Eastbourne BN21 3TH* Tel (01323) 731366

GREEN, Norman. b 20. St Pet Hall Ox BA48 BCL50 MA53. Wycliffe Hall Ox 51. **d** 52 **p** 53. C Mossley Hill St Matt and St Jas *Liv* 52-55; Chapl Liv Coll 55-64; Prin Cathl Sch Lahore Pakistan 64-70; Chapl R Masonic Sch for Girls Rickmansworth 70-80; Prin Edwardes Coll Pakistan 80-82; rtd 82; Perm to Offic *B & W* from 82. *Badgers' Way, Holton, Wincanton BA9 8AL* Tel (01963) 33363

GREEN, Paul. b 25. RD. Sarum & Wells Th Coll 72. **d** 74 **p** 75. C Pinhoe *Ex* 74-77; P-in-c 77-79; V 79-85; P-in-c Bishopsteignton 85-88; P-in-c Ideford, Luton and Ashcombe 85-88; rtd 88; Perm to Offic *Ex* from 88. *58 Maudlin Drive, Teignmouth TQ14 8SB* Tel (01626) 777312

GREEN, Paul John. b 48. Sarum & Wells Th Coll 72. **d** 73 **p** 74. C Tuffley *Glouc* 73-76; C Prestbury 76-82; P-in-c Highnam w Lassington and Rudford 82-83; P-in-c Tibberton w Taynton 82-83; R Highnam, Lassington, Rudford, Tibberton etc 84-92; Hon Min Can Glouc Cathl 85-96; V Fairford 92-96; RD Fairford 93-96; rtd 96; Perm to Offic *Glouc* from 98. *19 Prices Road, Abbeymead, Gloucester GL4 4PD* Tel (01452) 614259

GREEN, Pauline. *See* GREEN, Mrs Elizabeth Pauline Anne

GREEN, Peter. b 38. Ex Univ BSc59. Sarum Th Coll 59. **d** 61 **p** 62. C Romford St Edw *Chelmsf* 61-66; Chapl Trin Coll Kandy

Ceylon 66-70; V Darnall *Sheff* 71-80; TV Stantonbury *Ox* 80-87; TV Stantonbury and Willen 87-91; Dep Chapl HM Pris Belmarsh 91-92; Chapl HM Pris Woodhill 92-03; rtd 03; Perm to Offic *Ox* from 04. *34 North Twelfth Street, Milton Keynes MK9 3BT* Tel (01908) 240634 Mobile 07808-556213 Fax (01908) 240635 E-mail petergspp@aol.com

GREEN, Canon Peter Edwin. b 33. Lich Th Coll. **d** 62 **p** 63. C Sprowston *Nor* 62-65; C-in-c Heartsease St Fran CD 65-73; V Loddon w Sisland 73-91; Hon Can Nor Cathl 86-92; rtd 92; Perm to Offic *Nor* 92-96 and *St E* from 96. *Ambleside, Lowestoft Road, Beccles NR34 7DG* Tel (01502) 717740

GREEN, Peter Geoffrey. b 59. St Andr Univ MA83 Open Univ MA01. Coll of Resurr Mirfield 85. **d** 88 **p** 89. C Pershore w Pinvin, Wick and Birlingham *Worc* 88-91; V Dudley St Barn 91-99; V W Bromwich St Fran *Lich* 99-04; RD W Bromwich 02-04; Chapl Abbots Bromley Sch from 04. *Duttons House, High Street, Abbots Bromley, Rugeley WS15 3BN* Tel (01283) 840528 E-mail chaplain@abbotsbromley.staffs.sch.uk

GREEN, Peter Jamie. b 63. Aston Tr Scheme 87 Oak Hill Th Coll BA93. **d** 93 **p** 94. C Brigg *Linc* 93-97; C Brigg, Wrawby and Cadney cum Howsham 97; P-in-c Billinghay 97-01; V Carr Dyke Gp 01-02; R Kelsey Gp from 02. *The Rectory, Grange Lane, North Kelsey, Market Rasen LN7 6EZ* Tel and fax (01652) 678924

GREEN, Philip Charles. b 53. N Ord Course 91. **d** 94 **p** 95. C Southport Em *Liv* 94-98; P-in-c Crossens 98-03; TV N Meols 03-05; TR from 05. *St John's Vicarage, Rufford Road, Southport PR9 8JH* Tel (01704) 227662 E-mail revphilgreen@crossens1.freeserve.co.uk

GREEN, Canon Philip Harry. b 19. ALCD50. **d** 50 **p** 51. C Keighley *Bradf* 50-53; V Everton St Sav *Liv* 53-57; V Barnoldswick w Bracewell *Bradf* 57-64; V Shipley St Paul 64-77; Hon Can Bradf Cathl 77-82; V Gargrave 77-82; rtd 82; Perm to Offic *Bradf* 82-94 and *Carl* from 82. *102 Kentsford Road, Grange-over-Sands LA11 7BB* Tel (01539) 532950

GREEN, Richard Alistair. b 76. Ex Univ BA97. St Steph Ho Ox BA01. **d** 01 **p** 02. C Cockerton *Dur* 01-05; TV Ludlow, Ludford, Ashford Carbonell etc *Heref* from 05; Chapl Shropshire Co Primary Care Trust from 05. *St Mary's Vicarage, Donkey Lane, Ashford Carbonel, Ludlow SY8 4DA* Tel (01584) 831113 E-mail richardgreen@ashfordcarbonell.co.uk

GREEN, Richard Charles. b 49. K Coll Lon 68 St Aug Coll Cant 73. **d** 74 **p** 75. C Broseley w Benthall *Heref* 74-79; TV Heref St Martin w St Fran 80-95; C Heref S Wye 95-99; rtd 99; Hon Chapl Heref S Wye *Heref* 99-02; Chapl from 02. *5 Bardolph Close, Hereford HR2 7QA* Tel (01432) 354588 *or* 353717 Mobile 07976-910881 E-mail rghswtm@aol.com

GREEN, Robert Henry. b 57. K Coll Lon BD79. Wycliffe Hall Ox 81. **d** 83 **p** 84. C Norbury *Ches* 83-86 and from 91; C Knutsford St Jo and Toft 86-88; rtd 88. *122 Cavendish Road, Hazel Grove, Stockport SK7 6JH* Tel (01625) 858680 E-mail rob.green122@ntlworld.com

GREEN, Robert Leonard. b 44. Sarum & Wells Th Coll. **d** 84 **p** 85. C Battersea St Luke *S'wark* 84-89; CF 89-04; P-in-c Southwick w Boarhunt *Portsm* from 05. *The White House, High Street, Southwick, Fareham PO17 6EB* Tel (023) 9237 7568

GREEN, Robert Stanley. b 42. Dur Univ BA65. Wells Th Coll 65. **d** 67 **p** 68. C Ashford *Cant* 67-73; R Otham 73-80; V Bethersden w High Halden 80-87; R Winterbourne Stickland and Turnworth etc *Sarum* 87-99; R Monkton Farleigh, S Wraxall and Winsley 99-05; rtd 05. *The Bungalow, Wootton Grove, Sherborne DT9 4DL* Tel (01935) 817066 E-mail albertgoat@aol.com

GREEN, Robin Christopher William. b 43. Leeds Univ BA64 Fitzw Ho Cam BA67. Ridley Hall Cam 65. **d** 68 **p** 69. C S'wark H Trin *S'wark* 68-71; C Englefield Green *Guildf* 71-73; Chapl Whitelands Coll of HE *S'wark* 73-78; Team Ldr Dioc Lay Tr Team 78-84; V W Brompton St Mary w St Pet *Lon* 84-87; USPG 87-90; Perm to Offic *S'wark* 88-90; rtd 03. *The Catch, 53 Sandown Road, Deal CT14 6PE* Tel (01304) 389050

GREEN, Rodney William. b 52. LNSM course 90. **d** 93 **p** 94. OLM Flixton St Jo *Man* from 93. *85 Arundel Avenue, Flixton, Manchester M41 6MG* Tel 0161-748 7238

GREEN, Roger Thomas. b 43. Oak Hill Th Coll. **d** 79 **p** 80. C Paddock Wood *Roch* 79-83; R High Halstow w All Hallows and Hoo St Mary 83-89; Chapl HM Pris Brixton 89-90; Chapl HM Pris Standford Hill 90-94; Chapl HM Pris Swaleside 94-00; Chapl HM Pris Roch 99-03; Chapl HM Pris Blantyre Ho 03; Chapl HM Pris Brixton from 03. *HM Prison Brixton, PO Box 369, Jebb Avenue, London SW2 5XF* Tel (020) 8674 9811

GREEN, Preb Ronald Henry. b 27. Lambeth MA86 Bps' Coll Cheshunt 53. **d** 55 **p** 56. C St Marylebone Ch Ch w St Barn *Lon* 55-58; R 58-62; Dioc Youth Tr Officer 62-64; C St Andr Holborn 62-64; RE Adv 63-73; V Hampstead St Steph 64-73; RD N Camden 67-73; V Heston 73-80; Preb St Paul's Cathl 75-83; Jt Dir Lon and S'wark Bd of Educn 79-83; Dir of Educn *Sarum* 83-86; R Chiddingfold *Guildf* 86-91; rtd 91; Perm to Offic *Nor* 91-92; Master St Nic Hosp Salisbury 92-97; Perm to Offic *Sarum* from 98. *20 Ayleswade Road, Salisbury SP2 8DR* Tel (01722) 327660

GREEN (née JARMAN), Mrs Rosemary Susan. b 44. St Alb and Ox Min Course 99. **d** 01 **p** 02. OLM Bradfield and Stanford Dingley *Ox* from 01. *1 Buscot Copse, Bradfield, Reading RG7 6JB* Tel 0118-974 4640 Fax 974 4910 E-mail rosemary.s.green@talk21.com

GREEN, Ruth Valerie. *See* JAGGER, Mrs Ruth Valerie

GREEN, Ryan. b 77. Nottm Univ BA99. St Steph Ho Ox MTh05. **d** 05. C The Cookhams *Ox* from 05. *53 Broomhill, Cookham, Maidenhead SL6 9LH* Tel (01628) 520184 E-mail rybob3000@hotmail.com

GREEN, Sidney Leonard. b 44. K Coll Lon MTh86 Montessori DipEd84. Oak Hill Th Coll BD72. **d** 72 **p** 73. C Skelmersdale St Paul *Liv* 72-74; C Denton Holme *Carl* 74-76; In Bapt Min 76-85; Chapl Qu Eliz Gr Sch Blackb 85-91; Chapl Epsom Coll 91-01; P-in-c Sway *Win* 01-03; V 03-04; rtd 04. *Bethany, 31 Maesbury Circuit, Sturt, Adelaide, S Australia 5047* E-mail sidneygreen@onetel.com

GREEN, Ms Stella Louise. b 61. Kent Univ BA84. St Mich Coll Llan 01. **d** 03 **p** 04. C Stamford Hill St Thos *Lon* from 03. *20 Moresby Road, London E5 9LF* Tel (020) 8806 2430 Mobile 07815-089704 E-mail stellalgreen@hotmail.com

GREEN, Stephen Keith. b 48. Ex Coll Ox BA69 Mass Inst of Tech MSc75. N Ord Course 84. **d** 87 **p** 88. Hong Kong 87-93; Perm to Offic *Lon* 93-00; NSM Kensington St Barn from 01. *8 Canada Square, London E14 5HQ* Tel (020) 7992 3600 Fax 7991 4344

GREEN, Steven Douglas. b 57. Univ of Wales (Ban) DipTh81 Dip Counselling 99 Univ of Wales BA97. Sarum & Wells Th Coll 81. **d** 82 **p** 83. C Hawarden *St As* 82-86; V Mostyn 86-93; V Ffynnongroew 86-93; V Mostyn w Ffynnongroyw 93-99; R Trefnant w Tremeirchion 99-01; R Cefn w Trefnant w Tremeirchion from 01. *The Rectory, Trefnant, Denbigh LL16 5UG* Tel (01745) 730584 E-mail s.d.green@talk21.com

GREEN, Ms Susan Denise. b 66. TCD BA89 HDipEd90. **d** 92 **p** 93. C Antrim All SS *Conn* 92-95; Dioc Youth Officer (Cashel) *C & O* 95-00; Chapl Adelaide and Meath Hosp Dublin from 00. *Castleknock Rectory, 12 Hawthorn Lawn, Castleknock, Dublin 15, Irish Republic* Tel (00353) (1) 821 3083 Fax 820 4505 E-mail greenorr@esatclear.ie

GREEN, Mrs Susan Margaret. b 54. Univ of Wales (Abth) BSc75. SW Minl Tr Course 92. **d** 95 **p** 96. NSM Wiveliscombe w Chipstable, Huish Champflower etc *B & W* from 95; Sub-Warden of Readers Taunton Adnry from 00. *North Rodden Cottage, Maundown, Wiveliscombe, Taunton TA4 2BU* Tel (01984) 623809 E-mail suegreen@mountain.freeserve.co.uk

GREEN, Miss Sylvia. b 45. Bris Univ LLB66. WEMTC 97. **d** 00 **p** 01. NSM W Heref from 00. *23 Tower Road, Hereford HR4 0LF* Tel (01432) 264599 *or* 373300 Mobile 07970-287394 Fax (01432) 352952 E-mail diooffice@hereford.anglican.org

GREEN, Trevor Geoffrey Nash. b 45. BA. Oak Hill Th Coll 81. **d** 84 **p** 85. C Stalybridge H Trin and Ch Ch *Ches* 84-89; V 89-96; V Lache cum Saltney from 96. *St Mark's Vicarage, 5 Cliveden Road, Chester CH4 8DR* Tel (01244) 671702 *or* 675372 Fax 677818 E-mail trevoratmarks@aol.com

GREEN, Trevor Howard. b 37. Sarum & Wells Th Coll 72. **d** 74 **p** 75. C Bloxwich *Lich* 74-77; C Willenhall St Steph 77-79; P-in-c 79-80; V 80-82; V Essington 82-90; V Bishopswood and Brewood 90-02; P-in-c Coven 00-02; RD Penkridge 94-01; rtd 02. *113 Stafford Street, Cannock WS12 2EN* Tel (01543) 271159

GREEN, William. b 44. Newc Univ BA66 DipEd67 MA77. N Ord Course 87. **d** 90 **p** 91. NSM Utley *Bradf* 90-97; P-in-c Scarborough St Jas w H Trin *York* 97-00; V Thornton St Jas *Bradf* from 00. *The Vicarage, 300 Thornton Road, Thornton, Bradford BD13 3AB* Tel (01274) 833200 E-mail billgreen@vicarage24.freeserve.co.uk

GREENACRE, Canon Roger Tagent. b 30. Ordre national du Merite 98. Clare Coll Cam BA52 MA56 Lambeth DD01. Coll of Resurr Mirfield 52. **d** 54 **p** 55. C Hanworth All SS *Lon* 54-59; Chapl Ely Th Coll 59-60; Chapl Summer Fields Sch Ox 60-61; C N Audley Street St Mark *Lon* 62-63; Chapl Liddon Ho Lon 63-65; Chapl Paris St Geo *Eur* 65-75; RD France 70-75; Dioc Ecum Officer *Chich* 75-88; Lect Chich Th Coll 75-89; Can Res Chich Cathl *Chich* 75-00; Chan 75-97; Prec 97-00; Select Preacher Ox Univ 95; Chmn Chich Dioc Eur Ecum Cttee 89-99; rtd 00; P-in-c Beaulieu-sur-Mer *Eur* from 00. *Le Saint Michel, 9 rue Paul-Doumer, 06310 Beaulieu-sur-Mer, France* Tel and fax (0033) (4) 93 01 45 61 E-mail vanessagarnham@base.mc

GREENALL, Canon Ronald Gilbert. b 41. St Aid Birkenhead 61. **d** 64 **p** 65. C Adlington *Blackb* 64-67; C Ribbleton 67-69; R Coppull St Jo 69-84; V Garstang St Thos 84-99; RD Garstang 89-96; Hon Can Blackb Cathl 95-99; rtd 99; Perm to Offic *Blackb* from 99. *40 Duckworth Drive, Catterall, Preston PR3 1YS* Tel (01995) 606135

GREENAWAY-ROBBINS, Mark. b 72. Ox Univ BA95. Qu Coll Birm 96. **d** 99 **p** 00. C Redruth w Lanner and Treleigh *Truro* 99-01; Consultant on Other Faiths 00-01; TV Whitchurch *Llan* from 02. *3 Lon Ganol, Cardiff CF14 6EB*

GREENE, Prof Colin John David. b 50. QUB BA73 Fitzw Coll Cam MA75 Nottm Univ PhD. St Jo Coll Nottm 78. **d** 80 **p** 81. NSM Sandiacre *Derby* 80-81; C Loughborough Em *Leic* 81-84; V Thorpe Acre w Dishley 84-89; Evang Tr Consultant Bible Soc 89-91; Tutor Trin Coll Bris 91-95; Th Consultant Bible Soc and Springdale Coll 95-96; Hd Th and Public Policy Bible Soc 96-03; Dean Th and Prof Seattle Pacific Univ USA from 03. *Seattle Pacific University, 3307 Third Avenue W, Seattle, WA 98119, USA* Tel (001) (206) 281 2000

GREENE, David Arthur Kirsopp. b 36. St Pet Coll Ox BA60 MA64 FE TCert81. Tyndale Hall Bris 61. **d** 63 **p** 64. C Southgate *Chich* 63-66; C Kirby Grindalythe *York* 66-69; C N Grimston w Wharram Percy and Wharram-le-Street 66-69; R Folke, N Wootton and Haydon w Long Burton *Sarum* 69-75; R Long Burton, Folke, N Wootton, Haydon etc 75-80; P-in-c Thornford w Beer Hackett 80-84; P-in-c High Stoy 81-84; R Bradford Abbas and Thornford w Beer Hackett 84-00; rtd 00; Perm to Offic *Sarum* from 01 and *B & W* from 03. *Little Orchards, Priestlands, Sherborne DT9 4HW* Tel (01935) 813467

GREENE, John Howe. b 22. K Coll Lon AKC48 BD49. **d** 49 **p** 50. C Drayton in Hales *Lich* 49-52; C Stoke upon Trent 52-56; V Wilnecote 56-62; V Lodsworth *Chich* 62-69; R Selham 62-69; R Burwash 69-75; R Petworth 75-88; RD Petworth 76-88; P-in-c Egdean 76-80; R 80-88; rtd 88; Perm to Offic *Chich* from 88. *37 Wilderness Road, Hurstpierpoint, Hassocks BN6 9XD* Tel (01273) 833651

GREENE, Paul David O'Dwyer. b 53. Brunel Univ BSc78 Southn Univ DASS81 CQSW81. Oak Hill NSM Course 90. **d** 93 **p** 94. NSM Northwood Em *Lon* from 93. *50 The Drive, Northwood HA6 1HP* Tel (01923) 829605 Mobile 07870-237104 Fax (01923) 828867 E-mail paul@pgreene.demon.co.uk

GREENER, The Ven Jonathan Desmond Francis. b 61. Trin Coll Cam BA83 MA87. Coll of Resurr Mirfield 89. **d** 91 **p** 92. C S'wark H Trin w St Matt *S'wark* 91-94; Bp's Dom Chapl *Truro* 94-96; V Brighton Gd Shep Preston *Chich* 96-03; Adn Pontefract *Wakef* from 03. *24 Pledwick Lane, Sandal, Wakefield WF2 6DN* Tel (01924) 240547 Fax 251921
E-mail archdeacon.pontefract@wakefield.anglican.org

GREENFIELD, Canon Martin Richard. b 54. Em Coll Cam MA75. Wycliffe Hall Ox MA78. **d** 79 **p** 80. C Enfield Ch Ch Trent Park *Lon* 79-83; CMS from 84; Nigeria 85-94; Hon Can Aba from 89; C Langdon Hills *Chelmsf* 94-95; R Brampton *Ely* from 95; RD Huntingdon 99-04. *The Rectory, 15 Church Road, Brampton, Huntingdon PE28 4PF* Tel (01480) 453341
E-mail m.greenfield@ntlworld.com

GREENFIELD, Norman John Charles. b 27. Leeds Univ BA51. Chich Th Coll 51. **d** 53 **p** 54. C Portsea St Cuth *Portsm* 53-56; C Whitley Ch Ch *Ox* 56-60; V Moorends *Sheff* 60-65; V Littleworth *Ox* 65-71; Asst Stewardship Adv 65-70; V New Marston 71-79; Dioc Stewardship Adv *Chich* 79-88; P-in-c Amberley w N Stoke 79-83; R Guestling and Pett 88-94; rtd 94; Perm to Offic *Chich* from 94. *5 Marlborough Close, Eastbourne BN23 8AN* Tel (01323) 769494

GREENHALGH, David Murray. b 13. Jes Coll Cam BA34 MA38 Lon Univ BD47. Ridley Hall Cam 34. **d** 36 **p** 37. C Worsley *Man* 36-38; C Pennington 38-43; R Newton Heath St Anne 43-49; V Guilden Morden *Ely* 49-55; V Terrington St Clement 55-59; V Shirley *Win* 59-78; rtd 78. *12 St Christopher's Home, Abington Park Crescent, Northampton NN3 3AD* Tel (01604) 232087

GREENHALGH, Eric. b 20. Tyndale Hall Bris. **d** 63 **p** 64. C Preston St Mary *Blackb* 63-66; P-in-c 66-68; V 68-72; V Partington and Carrington *Ches* 72-81; V Inskip *Blackb* 81-85; rtd 85; Perm to Offic *Blackb* and *Carl* from 85. *Maranatha, 4 Rydal Close, Millom LA18 4QR* Tel (01229) 770995

GREENHALGH, Ian Frank. b 49. Wycliffe Hall Ox 74. **d** 77 **p** 78. C Parr *Liv* 77-80; V Wigan St Barn Marsh Green 80-84; Chapl RAF 84-04; V Clapham-with-Keasden and Austwick *Bradf* from 04. *The Vicarage, Clapham Road, Austwick, Lancaster LA2 8BE* Tel (01524) 251313

GREENHALGH, Philip Adrian. b 52. Dur Univ MA05. Ian Ramsey Coll 75 Wycliffe Hall Ox 76. **d** 79 **p** 80. C Gt Clacton *Chelmsf* 79-82; P-in-c Stalmine *Blackb* 82-86; Rep Leprosy Miss E Anglia 86-87; Area Org CECS 88-90; NSM Alston Team *Newc* 90-92; NSM Chulmleigh *Ex* 92-93; NSM Chawleigh w Cheldon 92-93; NSM Wembworthy w Eggesford 92-93; P-in-c Gilsland w Nether Denton *Carl* 93-95; V Millom 95-00; P-in-c Heatherycleugh *Dur* 00-04; P-in-c Westgate 00-04; P-in-c St John in Weardale 00-04; P-in-c Stanhope w Frosterley 02-04; P-in-c Eastgate w Rookhope 02-04; R Upper Weardale from 04; AD Stanhope from 00. *The Rectory, 48 Front Street, Stanhope, Bishop Auckland DL13 2UE* Tel (01388) 528449

GREENHALGH, Stephen. b 53. Dip Counselling 97 Man Univ MA99. Trin Coll Bris 77 Lon Bible Coll BA81. **d** 81 **p** 82. C Horwich H Trin *Man* 81-84; C Horwich 84-85; Chapl RAF 85-89; Perm to Offic *Blackb* 96-01 and *Carl* from 01. *2 Old Chapel Lane, Levens, Kendal LA8 8PX* Tel (01539) 737856

GREENHILL, Anthony David. b 39. Bris Univ BSc59. Tyndale Hall Bris 61. **d** 63 **p** 64. C Southsea St Jude *Portsm* 63-65; India 65-78; C Kinson *Sarum* 78-81; V Girlington *Bradf* 81-97; C Platt Bridge *Liv* 97-00; rtd 00; Perm to Offic *Bradf* from 01. *65 Lymbridge Drive, Blackrod, Bolton BL6 5TH* Tel (01204) 696509 E-mail admp@greenhill.me.uk

GREENHOUGH, Alan Kenneth. b 40. St D Coll Lamp. **d** 66 **p** 67. C Allestree *Derby* 66-70; C Ilkeston St Mary 70-73; V Bradwell 73-85; R Twyford w Guist w Bintry w Themelthorpe etc *Nor* 85-95; P-in-c Stibbard 94-95; R Twyford, Guist, Bintree, Themelthorpe etc from 95. *The Rectory, Norwich Road, Guist, Dereham NR20 5LU* Tel (01362) 683255

GREENHOUGH, Andrew Quentin. b 68. E Lon Poly BSc89. Wycliffe Hall Ox BTh94. **d** 94 **p** 95. C Partington and Carrington *Ches* 94-98; C Davenham from 98; P-in-c Moulton from 01. *The Vicarage, 66 Jack Lane, Moulton, Northwich CW9 8NR* Tel (01606) 593355 E-mail andy@macvicar.org.uk

GREENHOUGH, Arthur George. b 30. Fitzw Ho Cam BA52 MA56. Tyndale Hall Bris 55. **d** 57 **p** 58. C Wakef St Andr *Wakef* 57-63; R Birkin w Haddlesey *York* 63-85; RD Selby 77-84; P-in-c Hambleton 84-85; R Haddlesey w Hambleton and Birkin 85-00; rtd 01; Perm to Offic *York* from 01. *16 Grange Road, Camblesforth, Selby YO8 8HF* Tel (01757) 617347

GREENHOUGH, Geoffrey Herman. b 36. Sheff Univ BA57 Lon Univ BD71. St Jo Coll Nottm 74. **d** 75 **p** 76. C Cheadle Hulme St Andr *Ches* 75-78; R Tilston and Shocklach 78-82; V Hyde St Geo 82-87; V Pott Shrigley 87-00; rtd 00; Perm to Offic *Ches* from 01. *9 Spey Close, Winsford CW7 3BP* Tel (01606) 556275
E-mail geoffrey@ggreenhough.freeserve.co.uk

GREENISH, Brian Vivian Isitt. b 20. LRCP MRCS Lon Univ MB BS. **d** 89 **p** 89. NSM Bedford St Pet w St Cuth *St Alb* 89-91; Perm to Offic from 91. *69 Chaucer Road, Bedford MK40 2AL* Tel (01234) 352498

GREENLAND, Martin. b 65. Warwick Univ BSc87. Westcott Ho Cam 94. **d** 97 **p** 98. C Scarborough St Martin *York* 97-00; TV Bramley and Ravenfield w Hooton Roberts etc *Sheff* 00-04; V Ravenfield, Hooton Roberts and Braithwell from 04. *The Rectory, Micklebring Lane, Braithwell, Rotherham S66 7AS* Tel (01709) 812665

GREENLAND, Paul Howard. b 59. Bath Univ BA80 ACA85. Trin Coll Bris. **d** 00 **p** 01. C Caverswall and Weston Coyney w Dilhorne *Lich* 00-03; P-in-c Chelmsf St Andr *Chelmsf* from 03. *The Vicarage, 88 Chignal Road, Chelmsford CM1 2JB* Tel and fax (01245) 496722 Pager 07669-017638
E-mail paulhgreenland@care4free.net

GREENLAND, Roy Wilfrid. b 37. St Steph Ho Ox 71. **d** 73 **p** 74. C Wanstead St Mary *Chelmsf* 73-76; V Harlow St Mary Magd 76-83; P-in-c Huntingdon All SS w St Jo *Ely* 83-84; P-in-c Huntingdon St Barn 83-84; P-in-c Huntingdon St Mary w St Benedict 83-84; Bermuda 84-89; V Northampton St Alb *Pet* 89-92; R Waldron *Chich* 92-02; rtd 02. *2 The Glebe, Flore, Northampton NN7 4LX* Tel (01327) 349877

GREENMAN, David John. b 35. Lon Univ BA59. Oak Hill Th Coll 57. **d** 61 **p** 62. C Wandsworth St Steph *S'wark* 61-63; C Bishopwearmouth St Gabr *Dur* 63-66; C-in-c Bedgrove CD *Ox* 66-74; P-in-c Macclesfield Ch Ch *Ches* 74-77; V 77-81; P-in-c Glouc All SS *Glouc* 81-85; V Glouc St Jas 81-85; V Bare *Blackb* 85-91; V Market Lavington and Easterton *Sarum* 91-99; rtd 99; Perm to Offic *Sarum* and *Win* from 00. *3 Bure Lane, Christchurch BH23 4DJ* Tel (01425) 241034

GREENMAN (née CHESTER), Mrs Irene Mary. b 51. Dioc OLM tr scheme 97. **d** 99 **p** 00. OLM Cornholme *Wakef* 99-00; OLM Cornholme and Walsden from 00. *8 Glenview Street, Cornholme, Todmorden OL14 8LT* Tel and fax (01706) 817296
E-mail irene@stmicks99.freeserve.co.uk

GREENSLADE, Gillian Carol. b 43. Leic Univ BA64 Nottm Univ PGCE65 Essex Univ MA78. EAMTC 93. **d** 96 **p** 97. NSM Dovercourt and Parkeston w Harwich *Chelmsf* 96-00; NSM Colchester, New Town and The Hythe 00-02; R Broxted w Chickney and Tilty etc from 02; Adv for Women's Min (Colchester Area) from 05. *The Rectory, Park Road, Little Easton, Dunmow CM6 2JJ* Tel (01371) 872509

GREENSLADE, Keith James Inglis. b 27. St Mich Coll Llan 60. **d** 62 **p** 63. C Bishopsworth *Bris* 62-65; C Chippenham St Paul w Langley Burrell 65-68; V Upper Stratton 68-95; rtd 95; Perm to Offic *Bris* and *Sarum* from 95. *65 Shakespeare Road, Wootton Bassett, Swindon SN4 8HF* Tel (01793) 853253

GREENSLADE, Peter Michael. b 37. Bp Burgess Hall Lamp 69. **d** 71 **p** 72. C Llanwnda w Goodwick and Manorowen *St D* 71-73; C Lydiate *Liv* 73-75; V Wigan St Cath 75-76; Chapl Newsham Gen Hosp Liv 76-78; C Knotty Ash St Jo *Liv* 76-78; C Lache cum Saltney *Ches* 78-80; V Barnton 80-84; C Warburton 85-86; Warden Petroc Chr Guest Ho 86-90; rtd 90. *8 Ash Grove Close, Bodenham, Hereford HR1 3LT* Tel (01658) 797210

GREENSLADE, Timothy Julian. b 63. St Jo Coll Ox BA86. Oak Hill Th Coll BA95. **d** 95 **p** 96. C Broadwater St Mary *Chich* 95-99; TV Radipole and Melcombe Regis *Sarum* from 99. *The Vicarage, 106 Spa Road, Weymouth DT3 5ER* Tel (01305) 771938

GREENSTREET, Mark George. b 68. St Jo Coll Dur BA97. Cranmer Hall Dur 94. **d** 97 **p** 98. C St Alb St Pet *St Alb* 97-99; C Stevenage St Hugh and St Jo 99-01; C Dorridge *Birm* 01-04; V

Halton *Ches* from 04. *The Vicarage, Castle Road, Halton, Runcorn WA7 2BE* Tel (01928) 563636
E-mail mark-greenstreet@lineone.net

GREENWAY, John. b 32. Bps' Coll Cheshunt 68 Qu Coll Birm 69. **d** 69 **p** 70. C Luton Ch Ch *St Alb* 69-74; C Pulloxhill w Flitton 75-76; P-in-c Marston Morteyne 76-79; P-in-c Lidlington 77-79; P-in-c Marston Morteyne w Lidlington 80-81; R 81-97; rtd 97; Perm to Offic *Portsm* from 98. *73 Northmore Road, Locks Heath, Southampton SO31 6ZW* Tel (01489) 886791

GREENWAY, John Michael. b 34. **d** 96 **p** 97. OLM Gt Yarmouth *Nor* 96-04; Perm to Offic from 04. *17 Hamilton Road, Great Yarmouth NR30 4ND* Tel (01493) 853558

GREENWAY, Margaret Hester. b 26. **d** 87. Downend *Bris* 75-79; Oldland 79-82; Stratton St Margaret w S Marston etc 82-86; rtd 86; Perm to Offic *B & W* 87-95. *5 Weston Lodge, Lower Bristol Road, Weston-super-Mare BS23 2PJ* Tel (01934) 623561

GREENWELL, Christopher. b 49. Linc Th Coll 79. **d** 81 **p** 82. C Scarborough St Martin *York* 81-84; V S Bank 84-89; R Bolton by Bowland w Grindleton *Bradf* 89-92; V Nether Hoyland St Andr *Sheff* 92-96; V Kirkleatham *York* from 96. *Kirkleatham Vicarage, 130 Mersey Road, Redcar TS10 4DF* Tel (01642) 482073 E-mail chris@greenwell49.freeserve.co.uk

GREENWELL, Paul. b 60. Magd Coll Ox BA81 MA85. St Steph Ho Ox 82. **d** 85 **p** 86. C Hendon and Sunderland *Dur* 85-88; Min Can and Prec Ripon Cathl *Ripon* 88-93; Chapl Univ Coll of Ripon and York St Jo 88-93; V Hunslet St Mary *Ripon* 93-02; Asst Chapl Harrogate Health Care NHS Trust from 02; Convenor Dioc Adv Gp for Chr Healing *Ripon* from 03. *Harrogate District Hospital, Lancaster Park Road, Harrogate HG2 7SX* Tel (01423) 553045
E-mail chaplaincy@hhc-tr.northy.nhs.uk

GREENWOOD, David. *See* GREENWOOD, Norman David

GREENWOOD, Elizabeth. *See* GREENWOOD, Mrs Margaret Elizabeth

GREENWOOD, Canon Gerald. b 33. Leeds Univ BA57 Sheff Poly MSc81 Surrey Univ Hon MA93. Linc Th Coll 57. **d** 59 **p** 60. C Rotherham *Sheff* 59-62; V Elsecar 62-70; V Wales 70-77; P-in-c Thorpe Salvin 74-77; Dioc Sch Officer 77-84; P-in-c Bramley and Ravenfield 77-78; P-in-c Hooton Roberts 77-78; R 78-84; Hon Can Sheff Cathl 80-84; Dioc Dir of Educn 81-84; Hon Can S'wark Cathl *S'wark* 84-97; Dir of Educn 84-97; rtd 97; Perm to Offic *Cant* from 97. *Home Farm Cottage, Westmarsh, Canterbury CT3 2LW* Tel (01304) 812160

GREENWOOD, Gordon Edwin. b 44. Trin Coll Bris 78. **d** 80 **p** 81. C Bootle St Matt *Liv* 80-83; V Hunts Cross 83-93; V Skelmersdale St Paul from 93; P-in-c Skelmersdale Ch at Cen from 02. *The Vicarage, Church Road, Skelmersdale WN8 8ND* Tel (01695) 722087
E-mail gordongreenwood@stpaulskem.freeserve.co.uk

GREENWOOD, James Peter. b 61. Univ Coll Lon BSc83 St Jo Coll Dur BA90 RIBA87. Cranmer Hall Dur 88. **d** 91 **p** 92. C Belper *Derby* 91-94; CMS Pakistan 95-01; V Islamabad St Thos 95-00; V Silsden *Bradf* from 01; Dioc Spirituality Adv from 05. *The Vicarage, Briggate, Silsden, Keighley BD20 9JS* Tel (01535) 652204 E-mail jpetergreenwood@hotmail.com

GREENWOOD, John Newton. b 44. St Chad's Coll Dur BA69 DipTh70. **d** 70 **p** 71. C Hartlepool H Trin *Dur* 70-72; Lic to Offic from 72; Hd Master Archibald Primary Sch Cleveland 84-97; Asst Chapl HM Pris Holme Ho from 99. *1 Brae Head, Eaglescliffe, Stockton-on-Tees TS16 9HP* Tel (01642) 783200

GREENWOOD, Leslie. b 37. Dur Univ BA59 DipTh61. St Jo Coll Dur. **d** 61 **p** 62. C Birstall *Wakef* 61-63; C Illingworth 64-70; Chapl H Trin Sch Halifax 64-89; V Charlestown 70-91; TV Upper Holme Valley 91-97; Perm to Offic from 97; rtd 00. *2 Trenance Gardens, Greetland, Halifax HX4 8NN* Tel (01422) 373926 E-mail kyandles@aol.com

GREENWOOD, Mrs Margaret Elizabeth. b 34. St Mary's Coll Chelt TCert65 Surrey Univ MA93. St Mich Ho Ox 60. **d** 00. NSM Shepperton *Lon* 00-01; NSM Whitton SS Phil and Jas from 01. *Bundoran Cottage, Vicarage Lane, Laleham, Staines TW18 1UE* Tel (01784) 458115
E-mail wedderburn.phoebe@talk21.com

GREENWOOD, Michael Eric. b 44. Oak Hill Th Coll 78. **d** 80 **p** 81. C Clubmoor *Liv* 80-83; V Pemberton St Mark Newtown 83-94; V Grassendale 94-00; V Ashton-in-Makerfield St Thos from 00. *The Vicarage, 18 Warrington Road, Ashton-in-Makerfield, Wigan WN4 9PL* Tel (01942) 727275
E-mail mikeg@tinyonline.co.uk

GREENWOOD, Norman David. b 52. Edin Univ BMus74 Lon Univ BD78 Nottm Univ MPhil90. Oak Hill Th Coll 76. **d** 78 **p** 79. C Gorleston St Andr *Nor* 78-81; SAMS 81-83; C Cromer *Nor* 83-84; R Appleby Magna and Swepstone w Snarestone *Leic* 84-94; P-in-c Chesterfield H Trin *Derby* 94-95; P-in-c Chesterfield Ch Ch 94-95; R Chesterfield H Trin and Ch Ch 95-99; V S Ramsey St Paul *S & M* from 99; Dir of Ords from 01; Chapl HM Pris Is of Man from 05. *St Paul's Vicarage, Walpole Drive, Ramsey, Isle of Man IM8 1NA* Tel (01624) 812275

GREENWOOD, Peter. *See* GREENWOOD, James Peter

GREENWOOD, Canon Robin Patrick. b 47. St Chad's Coll Dur BA68 MA71 DipTh69 Birm Univ PhD92. **d** 70 **p** 71. C Adel *Ripon* 70-73; Min Can and Succ Ripon Cathl 73-78; V Leeds Halton St Wilfrid 78-86; Dioc Can Res Glouc Cathl *Glouc* 86-95; Dioc Missr and Dir Lay and Post-Ord Tr 86-95; Dir of Min and Hon Can Chelmsf Cathl *Chelmsf* 95-00; Prov Officer for Min Ch in Wales 01-05; Hon C Canton St Jo *Llan* 02-05; V Monkseaton St Mary *Newc* from 05. *St Mary's Vicarage, 77 Holywell Avenue, Whitley Bay NE26 3AG* Tel 0191-252 2484

GREENWOOD, Roy Douglas. b 27. Tyndale Hall Bris 58. **d** 60 **p** 61. C Ox St Matt *Ox* 60-62; V Ulpha *Carl* 62-63; V Seathwaite w Ulpha 63-72; P-in-c Haverthwaite 72-74; C Ulverston St Mary w H Trin 74-78; V Egton w Newland 78-86; Assoc Chapl Palma de Mallorca and Balearic Is *Eur* 86-93; Assoc Chapl Palma de Mallorca 93-95; rtd 95. *La Finquita, Apartado 78, Pollensa, Palma de Mallorca 07460, Spain* Tel (0034) (71) 530966

GREER, Eric Gordon. b 52. Pepperdine Univ BA74. Princeton Th Sem MDiv80. **d** 93 **p** 94. C Southgate St Andr *Lon* 93-96; C Camden Square St Paul 96-00; V Grange Park St Pet from 00. *The Vicarage, Langham Gardens, London N21 1DN* Tel (020) 8360 2294 E-mail egreer@talk21.com

GREER, Robert Ferguson. b 34. TCD BA56 MA59. Div Test 60. **d** 60 **p** 61. C Dundela St Mark *D & D* 60-65; I Castlewellan 65-77; I Castlewellan w Kilcoo 77-02; Can Dromore Cathl 90-02; Prec 93-02; rtd 02. *Dromore, Townsend, Harwell, Didcot OX11 0DX* Tel (01235) 835639 Fax 820473
E-mail rfgreer@ukonline.co.uk

GREETHAM, Canon William Frederick. b 40. Bede Coll Dur CertEd. Cranmer Hall Dur 63. **d** 66 **p** 67. C St Annes St Thos *Blackb* 66-69; C Ashton-on-Ribble St Andr 69-71; Chapl Aysgarth Sch 71-82; C Bedale *Ripon* 72-75; V Crakehall, Hornby and Patrick Brompton and Hunton 75-82; V Kirkby Stephen *Carl* 82-90; R Kirkby Stephen w Mallerstang etc 90-96; RD Appleby 86-91; P-in-c Crosthwaite Kendal 96-05; P-in-c Cartmel Fell 96-05; P-in-c Winster 96-05; P-in-c Witherslack 96-05; Hon Can Carl Cathl 89-05; rtd 05; Perm to Offic *Blackb* and *Carl* from 05. *2 Crosslands, Whittington, Carnforth LA6 2NX* Tel (015242) 71521 E-mail canonbillg@hotmail.co.uk

GREEVES, Roger Derrick. b 43. TCD BA66 MA70 Fitzw Coll Cam BA68 MA73. Wesley Ho Cam 66 Westcott Ho Cam 98. **d** 98 **p** 99. In Methodist Ch 68-98; NSM Cam St Edw *Ely* 98-00; Chapl Oakington Immigration Reception Cen 00-01; Chapl Peterho Cam 00-01; Dean Clare Coll Cam from 01. *28 Bateman Street, Cambridge CB2 1NB* Tel (01223) 571699 *or* 333240 Mobile 07719-863772 Fax (01223) 571705
E-mail rdg20@cam.ac.uk

GREG, John Kennedy. b 24. Trin Coll Cam BA46 MA61. Chich Th Coll 46. **d** 49 **p** 50. C Walmsley *Man* 49-51; C Carl H Trin *Carl* 51-55; V Lanercost w Kirkcambeck 55-62; V Cumwhitton 62-75; C Carl St Barn 75; TV 75-80; Chapl Strathclyde Ho Hosp Carl 80-85; TV Carl H Trin and St Barn *Carl* 80-85; rtd 85; Perm to Offic *Carl* 86-93. *113 Wigton Road, Carlisle CA2 7EL* Tel (01228) 538837

GREGG, David William Austin. b 37. Lon Univ BD66 Bris Univ MA69. Tyndale Hall Bris 63. **d** 68 **p** 69. C Barrow St Mark *Carl* 68-71; P-in-c Lindal w Marton 71-75; Communications Sec Gen Syn Bd for Miss and Unity 76-81; Prin Romsey Ho Coll Cam 81-88; V Haddenham w Cuddington, Kingsey etc *Ox* 88-96; P-in-c Newton Longville w Stoke Hammond and Whaddon 96-02; rtd 03; Perm to Offic *Carl* from 03. *Lowick Farm House, Lowick Green, Ulverston LA12 8DX* Tel (01229) 885258

GREGORY, Alan Paul Roy. b 55. K Coll Lon BD77 MTh78 AKC. Ripon Coll Cuddesdon 78. **d** 79 **p** 80. C Walton-on-Thames *Guildf* 79-82; Tutor and Dir Studies Sarum & Wells Th Coll 82-88; USA from 88. *3817 Red River Street, Austin, TX 78751, USA*

GREGORY, Andrew Forsythe. b 71. St Jo Coll Dur BA92. Wycliffe Hall Ox BA96 MA00 DPhil01. **d** 97 **p** 98. C E Acton St Dunstan w St Thos *Lon* 97-99; Asst Chapl Keble Coll Ox 97-99; Chapl Linc Coll Ox 99-03; Research Fell Keble Coll Ox from 03. *Keble College, Oxford OX1 3PG* Tel (01865) 280723
E-mail andrew.gregory@theology.ox.ac.uk

GREGORY, Brian. b 43. Trin Coll Bris. **d** 82 **p** 83. C Burscough Bridge *Liv* 82-85; V Platt Bridge 85-92; V Ben Rhydding *Bradf* from 92. *The Vicarage, Ben Rhydding, Ilkley LS29 8PT* Tel (01943) 607363 *or* 601430
E-mail brian@bgregory.freeserve.co.uk

GREGORY, Clive Malcolm. b 61. Lanc Univ BA84 Qu Coll Cam BA87 MA89 Warwick Univ Hon MA99. Westcott Ho Cam 85. **d** 88 **p** 89. C Margate St Jo *Cant* 88-92; Chapl Warw Univ *Cov* 92-98; TR Cov E from 98. *St Peter's Rectory, Charles Street, Coventry CV1 5NP* Tel (024) 7622 5907
E-mail clive@coveastteam.clara.co.uk

GREGORY, Father. *See* DUDDING, Edward Leslie

GREGORY, Graham. b 36. Open Univ BA78. Tyndale Hall Bris 63. **d** 66 **p** 67. C Wandsworth St Mich *S'wark* 66-71; C Hastings Em and St Mary in the Castle *Chich* 71-75; V Douglas St Ninian *S & M* 75-91; Dioc Youth Officer 78-88; Chapl HM Pris Douglas 82-86; RD Douglas *S & M* 86-91; V Wollaton Park *S'well* 91-95; V Lenton Abbey 91-95; rtd 95; Perm to Offic *York* from 98. *15 Keble Drive, Bishopthorpe, York YO23 2TA* Tel (01904) 701679

GREGORY, Ian Peter. b 45. Open Univ BA82 Plymouth Univ PGCE92. Bernard Gilpin Soc Dur 66 Chich Th Coll 67. **d** 70 **p** 71. C Tettenhall Regis *Lich* 70-73; C Shrewsbury H Cross 73-76; P-in-c Walsall St Mary and All SS Palfrey 76-80; R Petrockstowe, Petersmarland, Merton, Meeth etc *Ex* 80-87; TV Ex St Thos and Em 87-91; Hon C S Wimbledon All SS *S'wark* 94-00. *142 Monkleigh Road, Morden SM4 4ER* Tel (020) 8401 6148

GREGORY, John Frederick. b 33. Glouc Sch of Min 75. **d** 78 **p** 78. NSM S Cerney w Cerney Wick *Glouc* 78-81; NSM Coates, Rodmarton and Sapperton etc 81-88; P-in-c Kempsford w Welford 88-98; rtd 98; Perm to Offic *B & W* from 99. *Mount Cottage, Skilgate, Taunton TA4 2DQ*

GREGORY, Judith Rosalind. *See* GAVIN, Mrs Judith Rosalind

GREGORY, Mary Emma. b 70. Birm Univ BA92 St Jo Coll Dur BA04. Cranmer Hall Dur 02. **d** 05. C Hatfield *Sheff* from 05. *10 Grange Close, Hatfield, Doncaster DN7 6QR* Tel (01302) 841617 Mobile 07734-052524 E-mail maryegregory@tiscali.co.uk

GREGORY, Peter. b 35. Cranmer Hall Dur 59. **d** 62 **p** 63. C Pennington *Man* 62-65; C N Ferriby *York* 65-68; V Tonge Fold *Man* 68-72; V Hollym w Welwick and Holmpton *York* 72-77; P-in-c Foston w Flaxton 77-80; P-in-c Crambe w Whitwell and Huttons Ambo 77-80; R Whitwell w Crambe, Flaxton, Foston etc 81-94; rtd 94. *6 High Terrace, Northallerton DL6 1BG* Tel (01609) 776956

GREGORY, Richard Branson. b 33. Fitzw Ho Cam BA58 MA62. Sarum Th Coll 58 Ridley Hall Cam 59. **d** 60 **p** 61. C Sheff St Cuth *Sheff* 60-62; Asst Chapl Leeds Univ *Ripon* 62-64; V Yeadon St Jo *Bradf* 64-71; R Keighley 71-74; TR Keighley St Andr 74-82; Hon Can Bradf Cathl 71-82; RD S Craven 71-73 and 78-82; P-in-c Broadmayne, W Knighton, Owermoigne etc *Sarum* 82-85; R 85-98; rtd 98; Perm to Offic *Sarum* from 98. *2 Huish Cottages, Sydling, Dorchester DT2 9NS* Tel (01300) 341835

GREGORY, Canon Stephen Simpson. b 40. Nottm Univ BA62 CertEd63. St Steph Ho Ox. **d** 68 **p** 69. C Aldershot St Mich *Guildf* 68-71; Chapl St Mary's Sch Wantage 71-74; R Edgefield *Nor* 74-88; R Holt 74-94; R Holt w High Kelling 94-95; RD Holt 79-84 and 93-95; Hon Can Nor Cathl 94-95; V Prestbury *Glouc* 95-03; TR Prestbury and All SS from 03; P-in-c Pittville All SS 99-03; RD Cheltenham from 00; Hon Can Glouc Cathl from 04. *The Vicarage, Tatchley Lane, Prestbury, Cheltenham GL52 3DQ* Tel (01242) 244373 E-mail prestbur@globalnet.co.uk

GREGORY, Timothy Stephen. b 48. Sheff City Coll of Educn CertEd70. N Ord Course 96. **d** 99 **p** 00. NSM Deepcar *Sheff* from 99. *33 St Margaret Avenue, Deepcar, Sheffield S36 2TE* Tel 0114-288 4198 E-mail tim.gregory@virgin.net

GREGORY-SMITH, Hew Quentin. b 69. Univ of Wales (Abth) BSc93. St Mich Coll Llan 98. **d** 01 **p** 02. C Pembroke Gp *St D* 01-04; C Henfynyw w Aberaeron and Llanddewi Aberarth etc from 04. *Dyffryn, Lampeter Road, Aberaeron SA46 0ED* Tel (01545) 571579

GREGSON, Gillian Amy. b 33. Westmr Coll Ox BTh02 CQSW78. **d** 98 **p** 99. OLM Coulsdon St Jo *S'wark* 98-05; Perm to Offic from 05. *3 Coulsdon Road, Coulsdon CR5 2LG* Tel (020) 8660 0304

GREGSON, Peter John. b 36. Univ Coll Dur BSc61. Ripon Hall Ox 61. **d** 63 **p** 64. C Radcliffe St Thos *Man* 63-65; C Baguley 65-67; Chapl RN 68-91; V Ashburton w Buckland in the Moor and Bickington *Ex* 91-01; RD Moreton 95-98; rtd 01; Perm to Offic *Sarum* from 01. *Beech Tree Cottage, 18 Rectory Road, Broadmayne, Dorchester DT2 8EG* Tel (01305) 852478

GREIFF, Andrew John. b 64. Huddersfield Univ BA98 Leeds Univ PGCE99 St Jo Coll Dur BA05. Cranmer Hall Dur 03. **d** 05. C Pudsey St Lawr and St Paul *Bradf* from 05. *18 West Park, Pudsey LS28 7SN* Tel 0113-257 4582 E-mail andrew@greiff.freeserve.co.uk

GREIG, George Malcolm. b 28. CA53 St Andr Univ BD95. LNSM course 75. **d** 81 **p** 82. NSM Dundee St Mary Magd *Bre* 81-84; NSM Dundee St Jo 82-84; P-in-c Dundee St Ninian 84-85; Chapl St Paul's Cathl Dundee 85-98; rtd 98; Hon C Dundee St Salvador *Bre* from 98. *61 Charleston Drive, Dundee DD2 2HE* Tel (01382) 566709 E-mail gmg28@btinternet.com

GREIG, John Kenneth. b 38. Natal Univ BA57. **d** 61 **p** 62. C Durban St Thos S Africa 61-65; C Sheldon 65-66; C Friern Barnet St Jas *Lon* 66-69; C Kenton 69-71; Asst Chapl Dioc Coll Rondebosch S Africa 71-76; Chapl 76-78; Chapl Whitelands Coll of HE *S'wark* 78-84; V Purley St Swithun 84-04; Area Ecum Officer (Croydon) 84-04; rtd 04; Perm to Offic *S'wark* from 05. *29 Clive Road, London SW19 2JA* Tel (020) 8715 2784 E-mail jkgreig@hotmail.com

GREIG, Martin David Sandford. b 45. Bris Univ BSc67. St Jo Coll Nottm 72. **d** 75 **p** 76. C Keresley and Coundon *Cov* 75-79; C Rugby St Andr 79-83; TV 83-86; V Cov St Geo 86-93; TV Southgate *Chich* 93-01; R Maresfield from 01; P-in-c Nutley from 01. *16 The Paddock, Maresfield, Uckfield TN22 2HQ* Tel (01825) 764536 E-mail martin.greig@ntlworld.com *or* martin.greig@dsl.pipex.com

GREIG, Michael Lawrie Dickson. b 48. Shuttleworth Agric Coll NDA70. All Nations Chr Coll 78 St Jo Coll Nottm 94. **d** 96 **p** 97. C Hunningham *Cov* 96-00; C Wappenbury w Weston under Wetherley 96-00; C Offchurch 96-00; C Long Itchington and Marton 96-00; P-in-c Napton-on-the-Hill, Lower Shuckburgh etc from 00. *The Vicarage, Butt Hill, Napton, Rugby CV47 8NE* Tel (01926) 812383 E-mail mg@biggles99.freeserve.co.uk

GRELLIER, Brian Rodolph. b 34. AKC61. **d** 62 **p** 63. C Wandsworth St Paul *S'wark* 62-66; Japan 66-72; Miss to Seamen 72-76; V Freiston w Butterwick *Linc* 76-97; Chapl HM Pris N Sea Camp 89-96; rtd 97; Perm to Offic *Chich* from 99. *4 Fairfield Crescent, Hurstpierpoint, Hassocks BN6 9SE* Tel (01273) 833437

GRENFELL, James Christopher. b 69. Qu Coll Ox BA93 MA96 MPhil95 Ox Univ DPhil00. Westcott Ho Cam 98. **d** 00 **p** 01. C Kirkby *Liv* 00-03; Jt P-in-c Sheff Manor *Sheff* from 03. *St Aidan's Vicarage, 2 Manor Lane, Sheffield S2 1UF* Tel 0114-272 4676 E-mail james.grenfell@btinternet.com

GRENFELL, Joanne Woolway. b 72. Oriel Coll Ox BA93 DPhil97 Univ of BC MA94. Westcott Ho Cam 98. **d** 00 **p** 01. C Kirkby *Liv* 00-03; Jt P-in-c Sheff Manor *Sheff* from 03. *St Aidan's Vicarage, 2 Manor Lane, Sheffield S2 1UF* Tel 0114-272 4676 E-mail joanne.grenfell@btinternet.com

GRENHAM-TOZE, Mrs Sharon Carmel. b 66. Reading Univ LLB87 Solicitor 92. Trin Coll Bris 94 St Alb and Ox Min Course 96. **d** 98 **p** 00. C Buckingham *Ox* 98-00; C Milton Keynes 00-02; Miss Adv USPG *Lon*, *Ox* and *St Alb* 02-03; NSM Wilshamstead and Houghton Conquest *St Alb* 03-04; Chapl Oakhill Secure Tr Cen from 04. *Oakhill Secure Training Centre, Chalgrove Field, Otterburn Crescent, Milton Keynes MK5 6AH* Tel (01908) 866067 E-mail sgtoze@btopenworld.com *or* grassrootsp@aol.com

GRESHAM, Karen Louise. *See* SMEETON, Mrs Karen Louise

GRETTON, Tony Butler. b 29. St Jo Coll Dur BA53. **d** 54 **p** 55. C W Teignmouth *Ex* 54-57; R Norton Fitzwarren *B & W* 57-68; rtd 68; Chapl Glouc Docks Mariners' Ch *Glouc* 73-92; P-in-c Brookthorpe w Whaddon 79-82; Hon C The Edge, Pitchcombe, Harescombe and Brookthorpe 82-89; Perm to Offic from 89. *18 Clover Drive, Hardwicke, Gloucester GL2 4TG* Tel (01452) 721505

GREW, Nicholas David. b 52. Surrey Univ BSc74 MSc75. Wycliffe Hall Ox 93. **d** 95 **p** 96. C Biddulph *Lich* 95-99; P-in-c Knaphill *Guildf* 99-00; V Knaphill w Brookwood from 00. *Trinity House, Trinity Road, Knaphill, Woking GU21 2SY* Tel (01483) 473489 E-mail nickthevic@onetel.com

GREW, Richard Lewis. b 32. Clare Coll Cam BA54 MA58. Wycliffe Hall Ox 67. **d** 68 **p** 70. C Repton *Derby* 68-73; Asst Chapl Repton Sch Derby 74-93; Lic to Offic *Derby* 73-93; rtd 93; Perm to Offic *Sarum* from 94. *5 Priory Gardens, Spetisbury, Blandford Forum DT11 9DS* Tel (01258) 857613

GREWCOCK, Peter Joseph. b 28. Sarum Th Coll. **d** 58 **p** 59. C Mitcham St Barn *S'wark* 58-60; C Kingswood 60-62; V Howe Bridge *Man* 62-72; P-in-c Werrington, St Giles in the Heath and Virginstow *Truro* 72-73; V Leic St Chad *Leic* 73-76; P-in-c Trotton w Chithurst *Chich* 76-80; C Broadstone *Sarum* 80-84; TV Gillingham 84-88; P-in-c Milborne St Andrew w Dewlish 88-92; rtd 92; Perm to Offic *Sarum* 92-98. *9 Hambledon Close, Blandford Forum DT11 7SA* Tel (01258) 450893

GREY, Canon Edward Alwyn. b 23. Univ of Wales (Swansea) BA48. St D Coll Lamp. **d** 50 **p** 51. C Wrexham *St As* 50-58; R Llanfynydd 58-69; R Flint 69-89; RD Holywell 73-89; Can St As Cathl 76-89; rtd 89. *60 Gronant Road, Prestatyn LL19 9NE* Tel (01745) 855302

GREY, Richard Thomas. b 50. TD94. St D Coll Lamp BA73 Ripon Hall Ox 73. **d** 75 **p** 76. C Blaenavon w Capel Newydd *Mon* 75-77; Ind Chapl 77-02; C Newport St Paul 77-80; CF (TA) from 78; Chapl Aberbargoed Hosp 80-88; V Bedwellty *Mon* 80-88; R Llanwenarth Ultra 88-92; R Govilon w Llanfoist w Llanelen 92-02; RD Abergavenny 98-02; V Brynmawr *S & B* from 02. *The Vicarage, Dumfries Place, Brynmawr, Ebbw Vale NP23 4RA* Tel (01495) 310405

GREY, Canon Roger Derrick Masson. b 38. AKC61. **d** 62 **p** 63. C Darlington H Trin *Dur* 62-63; C Bishopwearmouth St Mich 63-67; V Mabe *Truro* 67-70; Dioc Youth Chapl 67-70; Youth Chapl *Glouc* 70-77; V Stroud H Trin 77-82; Dioc Can Res Glouc Cathl 82-03; Dir of Educn 82-94; Bp's Chapl 94-03; rtd 03; Clergy Widows' Officer (Glouc Adnry) *Glouc* from 03; Perm to Offic from 04. *12 Buckingham Close, Walton Cardiff, Tewkesbury GL20 7QB* Tel (01684) 275742

GREY, Stephen Bernard. b 56. Linc Th Coll 86. **d** 88 **p** 89. C Worsley *Man* 88-93; V Bamford 93-04; P-in-c Rochdale St Geo w St Alb 99-04; P-in-c Preesall *Blackb* 04-05; P-in-c Hambleton w Out Rawcliffe 04-05; V Waterside Par from 05. *St Oswald's Vicarage, Lancaster Road, Knott End-on-Sea, Poulton-le-Fylde FY6 0DU* Tel (01253) 810297

GREY, Canon Thomas Hilton. b 18. St D Coll Lamp BA39 Keble Coll Ox BA41 MA46. St Mich Coll Llan 41. **d** 42 **p** 43. C

Aberystwyth H Trin *St D* 42-49; R Ludchurch and Templeton 49-64; R Haverfordwest St Thos and Haroldston E St Issell 64-77; Can St D Cathl 72-84; Treas St D Cathl 80-84; RD Roose 74-84; R Haverfordwest St Mary and St Thos w Haroldston 77-84; rtd 85. *3 Gwscwm Park, Burry Port SA16 0DX* Tel (01554) 833629

GREY-SMITH, Donald Edward. b 31. ACT ThL64. **d** 64 **p** 65. Australia 64-68 and from 71; W Germany 68-69; C Weeke *Win* 69-71; rtd 96. *6/317 Military Road, Semaphore Park, S Australia 5019* Tel (0061) (8) 8449 4420

GRIBBEN, John Gibson. b 44. K Coll Lon BD75 QUB MTh81. CITC 73. **d** 75 **p** 76. C Dunmurry *Conn* 75-78; CR from 79; Lic to Offic *Wakef* from 83. *House of the Resurrection, Stocks Bank Road, Mirfield WF14 0BN* Tel (01924) 490441

GRIBBIN, Canon Bernard Byron. b 35. Bradf Univ MPhil84. St Aid Birkenhead 58. **d** 60 **p** 61. C Maghull *Liv* 60-63; C Prescot 63-65; V Denholme Gate *Bradf* 65-71; V Bankfoot 71-79; Dioc Stewardship Adv 79-86; Prec and Chapl Choral Ches Cathl *Ches* 86-91; V Ringway 91-96; Dioc Tourism Officer 91-96; Hon Can Ches Cathl 91-96; rtd 96; Perm to Offic *Bradf* from 96. *5 Heather Court, Ilkley LS29 9TZ* Tel (01943) 816253

GRIBBLE, Howard Frank. b 27. Magd Coll Cam BA50 MA56. Ely Th Coll 50. **d** 52 **p** 53. C Leytonstone St Marg w St Columba *Chelmsf* 52-56; N Rhodesia 56-59; Metrop Area Sec UMCA 59-62; V Harlow St Mary Magd *Chelmsf* 62-70; R Lawhitton *Truro* 70-81; R Lezant 70-81; RD Trigg Major 75-79; P-in-c S Petherwin w Trewen 77-79; Chapl R Cornwall Hosps Trust 81-84; rtd 84; Perm to Offic *Truro* from 84. *Westerlies, Marine Drive, Widemouth Bay, Bude EX23 0AQ* Tel (01288) 361528

GRIBBLE, Malcolm George. b 44. Chu Coll Cam BA67 MA71. Linc Th Coll 79. **d** 81 **p** 82. C Farnborough *Roch* 81-84; V Bostall Heath 84-90; V Bexleyheath Ch Ch 90-02; P-in-c Hever, Four Elms and Mark Beech from 02. *The Rectory, Rectory Lane, Hever, Edenbridge TN8 7LH* Tel (01732) 862249 E-mail malcolm@gribule.net

GRICE, Charles. b 24. MBE83. **d** 58 **p** 59. C Stocksbridge *Sheff* 58-61; R Armthorpe 61-66; Ind Missr 66-69; Ind Chapl 69-76; V Tinsley 69-73; V Oughtibridge 73-76; Gen Sec Ch Lads' and Ch Girls' Brigade 77-91; R Braithwell w Bramley *Sheff* 88-91; rtd 89; Perm to Offic *Sheff* from 89. *57 Deepdale Road, Rotherham S61 2NR* Tel (01709) 557551

GRICE, Canon David Richard. b 32. Keble Coll Ox BA55 MA59. St Steph Ho Ox 55. **d** 57 **p** 58. C Leeds St Aid *Ripon* 57-61; C Middleton St Mary 61-62; V Woodlesford 62-69; V Leeds St Wilfrid 69-78; TR Seacroft 78-93; Hon Can Ripon Cathl 92-99; P-in-c Thorner 93-95; V 95-99; rtd 99; Perm to Offic *Ripon* from 00. *15 Mead Road, Leeds LS15 9JR* Tel 0113-260 4371 E-mail david@grice12.freeserve.co.uk

GRIER, James Emerson. b 74. St Pet Coll Ox BA95 MA01. Wycliffe Hall Ox 96. **d** 98 **p** 99. C Ox St Andr *Ox* 98-02; C Harborne Heath *Birm* from 02. *33 Margaret Road, Harborne, Birmingham B17 0EU* Tel 0121-241 5145 Mobile 07947-834365 E-mail jamesgrier@stjohns-church.co.uk

GRIERSON, Peter Stanley. b 42. Lon Univ BD68 Leeds Univ MPhil74. Linc Th Coll 68. **d** 69 **p** 70. C Clitheroe St Mary *Blackb* 69-71; C Aston cum Aughton *Sheff* 71-74; V Preston St Jude w St Paul *Blackb* 74-81; V Blackb St Luke w St Phil 89-97; RD Blackb 91-97; V Burnley St Matt w H Trin 97-02; Perm to Offic *Bradf* from 03. *2 Spindle Mill, Skipton BD23 1NY* Tel (01756) 797175

GRIEVE, David Campbell. b 51. St Jo Coll Dur BA74. Wycliffe Hall Ox 74. **d** 76 **p** 77. C Upton (Overchurch) *Ches* 76-80; C Selston *S'well* 80-82; V Pelton *Dur* 82-89; rtd 89. *The Rectory, 107 Front Street, Cockfield, Bishop Auckland DL13 5AA* Tel (01388) 718447 E-mail davidgrieve@cix.co.uk

GRIEVE (née PIERSSENÉ), Frances Jane. b 55. St Jo Coll Dur BA76. Cranmer Hall Dur 99. **d** 01 **p** 02. C Barnard Castle w Whorlton *Dur* 01-05; P-in-c Cockfield from 05; P-in-c Lynesack from 05. *The Rectory, 107 Front Street, Cockfield, Bishop Auckland DL13 5AA* Tel (01388) 718447 E-mail davidgrieve@cix.co.uk

GRIEVE, Mrs Judith Margaret. b 52. Goldsmiths' Coll Lon CertEd73. NEOC 91. **d** 94 **p** 96. NSM Choppington *Newc* 94-99; P-in-c Woodhorn w Newbiggin from 99. *The Vicarage, 34A Front Street, Newbiggin-by-the-Sea NE64 6PS* Tel (01670) 817220

GRIEVES, Anthony Michael. b 47. St Alb Minl Tr Scheme 81. **d** 84 **p** 85. NSM Stevenage St Mary Shephall *St Alb* 84-86; NSM Stevenage St Mary Shephall w Aston 86-95; Perm to Offic from 95. *27 Falcon Close, Stevenage SG2 9PG* Tel (01438) 727204

GRIEVES, Ian Leslie. b 56. Bede Coll Dur CertEd77 BEd78. Chich Th Coll 82. **d** 84 **p** 85. C Darlington St Mark w St Paul *Dur* 84-87; C Whickham 87-89; V Darlington St Jas from 89. *St James's Vicarage, Vicarage Road, Darlington DL1 1JW* Tel (01325) 465980 E-mail father_grieves@lineone.net

GRIFFIN, Alan Howard Foster. b 44. TCD BA66 MA69 Peterho Cam PhD71. Sarum & Wells Th Coll 75. **d** 78 **p** 79. Lect Ex Univ 78-01; Asst to Lazenby Chapl 78-92; Sub-Warden Duryard Halls 78-81; Warden 81-84; Sen Warden 84-98; Perm to Offic *Ex* 92-98; C Heavitree w Ex St Paul 98-01; Ex Campus Chapl Plymouth Univ 98-01; R St Andr-by-the-Wardrobe w St Ann, Blackfriars *Lon* from 01; R St Jas Garlickhythe w St Mich Queenhithe etc from 01; CME Officer (Two Cities Area) from 01. *St Andrew's House, 35 St Andrew's Hill, London EC4V 5DE* Tel (020) 7248 7546 Fax 7329 3632

GRIFFIN, Christopher Donald. b 59. Reading Univ BA80 CertEd81. Wycliffe Hall Ox DipTh85. **d** 85 **p** 86. C Gerrards Cross *Ox* 85-88; Chapl Felsted Sch 88-98; Perm to Offic *Chelmsf* 88-98; Chapl Sedbergh Sch from 98; Lic to Offic *Bradf* from 98. *Sedburgh School, Sedburgh LA10 5HG* Tel (01539) 620535

GRIFFIN, Dennis Gordon. b 24. Worc Ord Coll 66. **d** 68 **p** 69. C Cradley *Worc* 68-69; V Rainbow Hill St Barn 69-74; R Broughton St Jo *Man* 74-79; V Pendlebury Ch Ch 79-86; rtd 89. *20 The Quadrangle, The Beauchamp Community, Newland, Malvern WR13 5AX* Tel (01684) 563371

GRIFFIN, Gerald Albert Francis. b 31. Qu Coll Birm 74. **d** 77 **p** 78. NSM Bushbury *Lich* 77-83; Ind Chapl *Dur* 83-88; Chapl HM Pris Man 88-89; Chapl HM Pris Featherstone 89-93; C Toxteth St Philemon w St Gabr and St Cleopas *Liv* 93-96; rtd 96; NSM W Bromwich Deanery *Lich* from 00. *7 Chartwell Drive, Bushbury, Wolverhampton WV10 8JL* Tel (01902) 836414

GRIFFIN, Harold Rodan Bristow. b 12. Jes Coll Cam BA33 LLB34 MA43. Ridley Hall Cam 43. **d** 45 **p** 46. C Kirby Moorside w Gillamoor *York* 45-49; C Linthorpe 49-52; C Boylestone *Derby* 52; R Hulland, Atlow and Bradley 52-61; V Framsden *St E* 61-71; R Helmingham 61-71; rtd 77; Perm to Offic *Ely* 91-99. *Highlands, Fitzgerald Road, Woodbridge IP12 1EN* Tel (01394) 383090

GRIFFIN, Joan Angela. b 35. Qu Coll Birm 82. **dss** 85 **d** 92 **p** 94. Moseley St Mary *Birm* 85-92; NSM from 92. *389 Wake Green Road, Birmingham B13 0BH* Tel 0121-777 8772 *or* 449 2243 Fax 449 2243

GRIFFIN, Canon John Henry Hugh. b 13. St Cath Coll Cam BA35 MA39. Linc Th Coll 35. **d** 38 **p** 39. C Bramford w Burstall *St E* 38-42; P-in-c Halesworth 42-46; R Stratford St Mary 46-72; V Higham 46-72; C Hadleigh w Layham and Shelley 72-73; P-in-c Gt and Lt Glemham 73-79; P-in-c Blaxhall w Stratford St Andrew and Farnham 73-79; Hon Can St E Cathl 78-79; rtd 79; Perm to Offic *St E* 79-98. *3 Church Street, Hadleigh, Ipswich IP7 5DT* Tel (01473) 823100

GRIFFIN, Canon Joseph William. b 48. St Mich Coll Llan 70. **d** 74 **p** 75. C Killay *S & B* 74-78; C Swansea St Thos and Kilvey 78-81; V Troedrhiwgarth *Llan* 81-91; V Llanrhidian w Llanmadoc and Cheriton *S & B* 91-99; RD W Gower 94-99; V Swansea St Nic 99-04; RD Swansea 02-04; P-in-c SW Gower from 04; Hon Can Brecon Cathl from 98. *The Rectory, Port Eynon, Swansea SA3 1NL* Tel (01792) 390456

GRIFFIN, Keith. b 66. Nottm Trent Univ BA88. Cranmer Hall Dur BA94. **d** 95 **p** 96. C Gedling *S'well* 95-98; V Barkingside St Geo *Chelmsf* 99-02; TV Upper Holme Valley *Wakef* from 02. *The Vicarage, 3 Vicarage Meadows, Holmfirth HD9 1DZ* Tel (01484) 682644 E-mail revdkg@fish.co.uk

GRIFFIN, Kenneth Francis. b 21. Lon Univ BSc64. St Jo Coll Nottm 72. **d** 73 **p** 74. C Bexleyheath Ch Ch *Roch* 73-77; R Kingsdown 77-82; rtd 86. *Woodlands, Palmers Cross Hill, Rough Common, Canterbury CT2 9BL* Tel (01227) 457314

GRIFFIN, Malcolm Roger. b 46. Goldsmiths' Coll Lon TCert67 Open Univ BA73 DipMgt90 MCIPD91. S'wark Ord Course. **d** 83 **p** 84. NSM Romford St Andr *Chelmsf* 83-87; NSM Romford St Jo 87-91; P-in-c 98-00; NSM Gt Ilford St Alb 91-97; Perm to Offic 97-98; P-in-c Cratfield w Heveningham and Ubbeston etc *St E* 00-02; Perm to Offic *Nor* and *St E* from 02. *4 Old Forge Court, Brockdish, Diss IP21 4JE* Tel (01379) 669252

GRIFFIN, Mark Richard. b 68. Trin Coll Bris BA93. Westcott Ho Cam 94. **d** 96 **p** 97. C Walmer *Cant* 96-00; V Wingham w Elmstone and Preston w Stourmouth from 00. *St Mary's House, 5 St Mary's Meadow, Wingham, Canterbury CT3 1DF* Tel (01227) 721530 E-mail revd.mark.griffin@talk21.com

GRIFFIN, Michael. b 59. **d** 01 **p** 01. C Kirkdale St Lawr *Liv* 01-02; P-in-c 02-05; V from 05. *St Lawrence's Vicarage, 21 Westminster Close, Liverpool L4 1XB* Tel 0151-922 5794 Fax 944 2667 E-mail mike.j.griffin@amserve.net

GRIFFIN, Canon Michael Richard. b 19. CD78. Trin Coll Bris 43. **d** 44 **p** 44. C Tonbridge St Steph *Roch* 44-45; C Tunbridge Wells H Trin 45-47; V Hindley St Pet *Liv* 47-51; Canada from 51; Can Huron from 64. *68 Caledonia Street, Stratford ON, Canada, N5A 5W6*

GRIFFIN, Niall Paul. b 37. TCD BA61 Div Test61. **d** 61 **p** 62. C Newtownards *D & D* 61-63; C Arm St Mark *Arm* 63-64; Jamaica 64-66; C Lurgan Ch the Redeemer *D & D* 66-69; Chapl RAF 69-84; Missr Chr Renewal Cen *D & D* 84-89; Nat Dir (Ireland) SOMA UK from 89. *7 Cloughmore Park, Rostrevor, Newry BT34 3AX* Tel and fax (028) 4173 8959 E-mail n&g@griffin.go-plus.net

GRIFFIN, Nigel Robert. b 50. Univ of Wales (Lamp) BA71. Ripon Hall Ox 71. **d** 73 **p** 74. C Burry Port and Pwll *St D* 73-77; C Carmarthen St Pet 77-79; Youth Chapl 79-86; V Whitland and Kiffig 80-89; Warden of Ords 86-91; V Llangunnor w Cwmffrwd

89-92; RD Carmarthen 91-92; R Aberporth w Tremain and Blaenporth 92-95; R Aberporth w Tremain w Blaenporth and Betws Ifan 95-96; Chapl Morriston Hosp/Ysbyty Treforys NHS Trust 96-99; Chapl Swansea NHS Trust from 99. *Morriston Hospital, Heol Maes Eglwys, Cwmrhydyceirw, Swansea SA6 8EL* Tel (01792) 702222

GRIFFIN, Canon Rutland Basil. b 16. ALCD41. **d** 41 **p** 42. C Aylesbury *Ox* 41-45; C Bp's Hatfield *St Alb* 45-50; V Biggleswade 50-61; V Dartford H Trin *Roch* 61-84; RD Dartford 64-84; Hon Can Roch Cathl 70-84; rtd 84; Perm to Offic *Roch* and *Cant* 84-95; *Cov* from 97. *10 Upper Stables, Parkfield Way, Haywards Heath RH16 4TA* Tel (01444) 474440

GRIFFIN, The Very Revd Victor Gilbert Benjamin. b 24. MRIA TCD BA46 MA57 Hon DD92. CITC 47. **d** 47 **p** 48. C Londonderry St Aug *D & R* 47-51; C Londonderry Ch Ch 51-57; I 57-68; Preb Howth St Patr Cathl Dublin 62-68; Dean St Patr Cathl Dublin 68-91; rtd 91. *7 Tyler Road, Limavady BT49 0DW* Tel (028) 7176 2093

GRIFFISS, Helen Mary. b 48. Univ of Wales (Ban) CertEd69 K Alfred's Coll Win MA98. STETS 97. **d** 00 **p** 01. Miss Adv USPG *Bris, Sarum* and *Win* 00-03; NSM Bransgore *Win* 00-03; C Milton from 04. *St Peter's House, 25 Ashley Common Road, New Milton BH25 5AJ* Tel and fax (01425) 612644 E-mail helengriffiss@surefish.co.uk

GRIFFITH, Brian Vann. b 34. Univ Sch Th Abth & Lamp DipTh82 BTh91 MTh94 St D Dioc Tr Course 81. **d** 82 **p** 83. NSM C Aberystwyth *St D* 82-87; NSM Llanfihangel w Llanafan and Llanwnnws etc 87-88; NSM C Llanbadarn Fawr w Capel Bangor and Goginan 88-93; Public Preacher 93-96; NSM Machynlleth w Llanwrin and Penegoes *Ban* 97-99; rtd 99; Perm to Offic *St D* from 00. *14 Ystwyth Close, Penparcau, Aberystwyth SY23 3RU*

GRIFFITH, The Ven David Vaughan. b 36. St D Coll Lamp BA60. Lich Th Coll 60. **d** 62 **p** 63. C Llanfairfechan *Ban* 62-66; C Dolgellau 66-70; R Llanfair Talhaiarn *St As* 70-82; R Llanfairtalhaiarn and Llansannan 82-85; P-in-c Llangernyw, Gwytherin and Llanddewi 77-85; V Colwyn 85-98; Warden of Readers 91-99; Can Cursal St As Cathl 95-98; P-in-c Berriew and Manafon 98-99; V 99-02; Preb St As Cathl and Adn Montgomery 98-02; rtd 02. *1 Bishop's Walk, St Asaph LL17 0SU* Tel (01745) 582903

GRIFFITH, Donald Bennet. b 17. Dur Univ LTh40. St Aid Birkenhead 36. **d** 40 **p** 41. C Collyhurst St Oswald *Man* 40-43; C Pendlebury St Jo 43-45; P-in-c Pendleton 45-47; V Everton St Cuth *Liv* 47-52; V Lathom 52-58; R Frating w Thorrington *Chelmsf* 58-66; R Lawford 66-73; R Theydon Garnon 73-77; P-in-c Bradfield 77-82; rtd 82; Perm to Offic *Chelmsf* from 82. *Porto Cristo, Mill Lane, Thorpe-le-Soken, Clacton-on-Sea CO16 0ED* Tel (01255) 861766

GRIFFITH, Frank Michael. b 24. Bris Univ BSc50 Lon Univ DipTh60. St Aid Birkenhead 58. **d** 60 **p** 61. C Leamington Priors H Trin *Cov* 60-63; C Stratford-on-Avon w Bishopton 63-67; V Rounds Green *Birm* 67-70; R Barford *Cov* 70-78; V Wasperton 70-78; RD Stratford-on-Avon 77-79; R Barford w Wasperton and Sherbourne 78-89; RD Fosse 79-87; rtd 90; Perm to Offic *Cov* from 90. *Wusi, Armscote Road, Tredington, Shipston-on-Stour CV36 4NP* Tel (01608) 661621

GRIFFITH, Glyn Keble Gethin. b 37. St D Coll Lamp BA59. Ridley Hall Cam 67. **d** 69 **p** 70. C Derby St Aug *Derby* 69-72; C Coity w Nolton *Llan* 72-75; P-in-c Heage *Derby* 75-81; V Allestree St Nic 81-92; R Wilne and Draycott w Breaston 92-01; rtd 01; Perm to Offic *Mon* and *Heref* from 02; *Glouc* from 04. *3 Cornford Close, Osbaston, Monmouth NP25 3NT* Tel (01600) 719740

GRIFFITH, Canon Hugh Emrys. b 24. St D Coll Lamp BA53. **d** 54 **p** 55. C Welshpool *St As* 54-56; C Abergele 56-58; R Llanfair Talhaiarn 58-61; R Llangeinwen w Llangaffo and Llanfair-yn-y-Cwmwd *Ban* 61-75; R Llanllyfni 75-81; R Amlwch 81-94; RD Twrcelyn 82-94; Can Ban Cathl from 89; rtd 94; Perm to Offic *Ban* from 94. *Llys Caerwynt, Rhos-y-bol, Amlwch LL68 9PR* Tel (01407) 831917

GRIFFITH, Canon John Vaughan. b 33. LTh73. St D Coll Lamp 53. **d** 58 **p** 59. C Holyhead w Rhoscolyn *Ban* 58-63; R Maentwrog w Trawsfynydd 63-68; Chapl RAF 68-72; V Winnington *Ches* 72-76; V Northwich St Luke and H Trin 76-81; V Sandiway 81-98; Dioc Communications Officer 84-86; Ed Ches Dioc News 84-92; Hon Can Ches Cathl 89-98; rtd 98; Perm to Offic *Ches* from 99. *41 Moss Lane, Cuddington, Northwich CW8 2PT*

GRIFFITH, Michael. *See* GRIFFITH, Frank Michael

GRIFFITH, Peter Malcolm. b 43. FRICS71. EAMTC 94. **d** 97 **p** 98. NSM Stilton w Denton and Caldecote etc *Ely* 97-99; R Sawtry and Glatton from 00. *The Rectory, Church Causeway, Sawtry, Huntingdon PE28 5TD* Tel (01487) 830215 E-mail rev.griffith@tiscali.co.uk

GRIFFITH, Sandra. b 44. Open Univ BA94. EAMTC 01. **d** 04 **p** 05. NSM The Ortons, Alwalton and Chesterton *Ely* from 04. *The Rectory, Church Causeway, Sawtry, Huntingdon PE28 5TD* Tel (01487) 830215 E-mail sandra@griffith422.freeserve.co.uk

GRIFFITH, Stephen. *See* GRIFFITH, William Stephen

GRIFFITH, Steven Ellsworth. b 63. St Steph Ho Ox. **d** 87 **p** 88. C Holyhead w Rhoscolyn w Llanfair-yn-Neubwll *Ban* 87-90; CF from 90. *c/o MOD Chaplains (Army)* Tel (01980) 615804 Fax 615800

GRIFFITH, Mrs Wendy Margaret. b 41. **d** 01 **p** 02. NSM Sixpenny Handley w Gussage St Andrew etc *Sarum* from 01. *2 Corner Cottages, Pound Hill, Witchampton, Wimborne BH21 5AW* Tel (01258) 840557 Mobile 07720-942996 E-mail wendy@michaelblyth.uk

GRIFFITH, William Stephen. b 50. MBE02. Univ of Wales (Ban) BA71 FRAS92. Westcott Ho Cam 71. **d** 73 **p** 74. C Llandudno *Ban* 73-76; C Calne and Blackland *Sarum* 76-78; P-in-c Broadwindsor w Burstock and Seaborough 78-79; TV Beaminster Area 79-81; Perm to Offic 81-83; Chapl St Pet Sch York 83-87; C Leeds St Pet *Ripon* 87; Chapl Bearwood Coll Wokingham 87-92; CMS Jordan 92-95; Sen Chapl Univ of Wales (Cardiff) *Llan* 95-96; Chapl Damascus 96-02; P-in-c Yerevan, Baku and Tbilisi *Eur* 03; V Denton *Newc* from 04. *The Vicarage, Dunblane Crescent, Newcastle upon Tyne NE5 2BE* Tel 0191-267 2058 Mobile 07729-278294 E-mail denton.vicar@btinternet.com

GRIFFITH-JONES, Robin Guthrie. b 56. New Coll Ox BA78 Ch Coll Cam BA88. Westcott Ho Cam 86. **d** 89 **p** 90. C Cantril Farm *Liv* 89-92; Chapl Linc Coll Ox 92-99; Master of The Temple from 99. *The Master's House, Temple, London EC4Y 7BB* Tel (020) 7353 8559 E-mail master@templechurch.com

GRIFFITHS, Ainsley. *See* GRIFFITHS, John Mark Ainsley

GRIFFITHS, Alan Charles. b 46. Dur Univ BA67. Cranmer Hall Dur 66. **d** 69 **p** 70. C Leic H Apostles *Leic* 69-72; Lic to Offic *York* 73-77; V Lea Hall *Birm* 77-87; Asst Dir of Educn *Sheff* 87-92; V W Bessacarr 92-02; V Conisbrough from 02. *The Vicarage, 8 Castle Avenue, Conisbrough, Doncaster DN12 3BT* Tel (01709) 864695 E-mail alan.c.griffiths@virgin.net

GRIFFITHS, Alec. b 42. St Chad's Coll Dur BA63 DipTh65. **d** 65 **p** 66. C Glas St Ninian *Glas* 65-68; C Greenock 68-72; R Glas H Cross 72-79; V Birchencliffe *Wakef* 79-83; Chapl Kingston Hosp Surrey 83-99; rtd 99; Perm to Offic *S'wark* 99-00; Hon C W Acton St Martin *Lon* from 00; Hon C Ealing All SS from 00. *St Martin's Cottage, Hale Gardens, London W3 9SQ* Tel and fax (020) 8896 9009 E-mail alec.griffiths@btopenworld.com

GRIFFITHS, Andrew Taylor. b 68. Jes Coll Ox BA92 MA96. Cranmer Hall Dur 98. **d** 00 **p** 01. C Paris St Mich *Eur* 00-04; C Galleywood Common *Chelmsf* 04-05; V from 05. *Galleywood Vicarage, 450 Beehive Lane, Chelmsford CM2 8RN* Tel (01245) 353922 Mobile 07969-605059 E-mail andy@angelserve.net

GRIFFITHS, Arthur Evan. b 27. ACP66. St Deiniol's Hawarden. **d** 69 **p** 70. Hon C Cleobury Mortimer w Hopton Wafers *Heref* 69-83; C 84-86; P-in-c Coreley and Doddington 86-88; P-in-c Knowbury 86-88; rtd 89; Perm to Offic *Heref* from 93. *Maryn, Catherton Road, Cleobury Mortimer, Kidderminster DY14 8EB* Tel (01299) 270489

GRIFFITHS, Beatrice Mary. b 29. Chelsea Coll Lon CertEd60. Westcott Ho Cam 85. **dss** 86 **d** 87 **p** 94. W Bridgford *S'well* 86-87; NSM Wilford Hill 87-99; rtd 99; Perm to Offic *S'well* from 99. *7 Stella Avenue, Tollerton, Nottingham NG12 4EX* Tel 0115-937 4155

GRIFFITHS, Caroline. *See* PRINCE, Caroline Heidi Ann

GRIFFITHS (née MITCHELL), Mrs Clare. **d** 01 **p** 02. C Caerleon w Llanhennock *Mon* 01-03; Chapl Malvern Girls' Coll from 03. *Malvern Girls' College, Avenue Road, Malvern WR14 3BA* Tel (01684) 892288

GRIFFITHS, Canon David. b 38. St Mich Coll Llan DipTh67. **d** 67 **p** 68. C Llangollen *St As* 67-71; C Rhyl 71-74; V Kerry 74-77; V Kerry and Llanmerewig 77-82; R Caerwys and Bodfari 82-87; V Gresford 87-03; V Holt 97-03; RD Wrexham 97-01; RD Gresford 01-03; Can St As Cathl 98-03; rtd 03. *16 Heol-y-Wal, Bradley, Wrexham LL11 4BY*

GRIFFITHS, David Bruce. b 44. Sussex Univ BA69 Hull Univ MA83. Linc Th Coll. **d** 82 **p** 83. C Springfield All SS *Chelmsf* 82-84; TV Horwich *Man* 84-92; V Heaton Ch Ch 92-03; P-in-c Ainsworth from 03. *The Vicarage, Ainsworth Hall Road, Ainsworth, Bolton BL2 5RY* Tel (01204) 398567 E-mail dbgriff@fish.co.uk

GRIFFITHS, David John. b 53. Bromsgrove F E Coll HND76. St Jo Coll Nottm BTh93 DipMM94. **d** 94 **p** 95. C Retford St Sav *S'well* 94-96; NSM Thwaites Brow *Bradf* 96-98; P-in-c Oakenshaw cum Woodlands 98-03; Asst Chapl Airedale NHS Trust 96-03; V Buttershaw St Paul *Bradf* from 03. *St Paul's Vicarage, 42A Wibsey Park Avenue, Bradford BD6 3QA* Tel (01274) 676359

GRIFFITHS, David Mark. b 41. Univ of Wales (Cardiff) BA67 CertEd71. St Mich Coll Llan DMS92. **d** 94 **p** 95. C Llwynderw *S & B* 94-96; R Llanbadarn Fawr, Llandegley and Llanfihangel etc 96-02; V Slebech and Uzmaston w Boulston *St D* from 02. *The Vicarage, Uzmaston, Haverfordwest SA62 4AE* Tel (01437) 762325

GRIFFITHS, David Mark. b 59. Kent Univ BA80. Chich Th Coll 81. **d** 83 **p** 84. C Clydach *S & B* 83-84; C Llwynderw 84-88; V Swansea St Nic 88-98; Chapl Swansea Inst of HE 88-98; V Swansea St Gabr from 98; Chapl Swansea NHS Trust from 98. *St Gabriel's Vicarage, Bryn Road, Brynmill, Swansea SA2 0AP* Tel (01792) 464011

GRIFFITHS, The Ven David Nigel. b 27. RD77. Worc Coll Ox BA52 MA56 Reading Univ PhD91 FSA. Linc Th Coll 56. **d** 58 **p** 59. C Northampton St Matt *Pet* 58-61; SPCK HQ Staff 61-67; Chapl RNR 63-77; Hon C Bromley St Andr *Roch* 65-67; V Linc St Mich *Linc* 67-73; R Linc St Mary Magd w St Paul 67-73; Vice Chan and Lib Linc Cathl 67-73; TR New Windsor *Ox* 73-87; RD Maidenhead 77-82 and 84-87; Chapl to The Queen 77-97; Hon Can Ch Ch *Ox* 83-87; Adn Berks 87-92; rtd 92; Chapl St Anne's Bede Houses Linc 93-00; Perm to Offic *Linc* from 00. *2 Middleton's Field, Lincoln LN2 1QP* Tel (01522) 525753 E-mail bibliophile@britishlibrary.net

GRIFFITHS, David Percy Douglas. b 25. St Mich Coll Llan. **d** 78 **p** 79. C Betws w Ammanford *St D* 78-80; V Llanarth w Mydroilyn, Capel Cynon, Talgarreg etc 80-84; V Llanarth and Capel Cynon w Talgarreg etc 84-86; V Newcastle Emlyn w Llandyfriog and Troed-yr-aur 86-95; rtd 95. *The Poplars, Ebenezer Street, Newcastle Emlyn SA38 9BS* Tel (01239) 711448

GRIFFITHS, David Rowson Hopkin. b 38. Oak Hill Th Coll 59. **d** 62 **p** 63. C Barrow St Mark *Carl* 62-65; OMF Internat from 66; Japan 66-88; Philippines from 88; rtd 03. *c/o Mrs Bronwen Coe, 52 Shepherds Way, Cirencester GL7 2ET* Tel (01285) 885841

GRIFFITHS, David Wynne. b 47. Univ of Wales (Cardiff) BD73 PGCE77 MA85 MEd93 PhD97. St Mich Coll Llan 69. **d** 73 **p** 74. C Gabalfa *Llan* 73-76; Lic to Offic 77-79; Hon C Tonypandy w Clydach Vale 79-80; Hon C Pontypridd St Cath 80-87; Perm to Offic from 87. *5 Heol-y-Wern, Rhiwbina, Cardiff CF14 6NG*

GRIFFITHS, Ms Elizabeth Leigh. b 61. St Hugh's Coll Ox BA83 MA87 Warwick Univ PGCE84. Ripon Coll Cuddesdon 96. **d** 98 **p** 99. C Bettws *Mon* 98-99; C Maindee 99-01; TV Cen Swansea and Dioc Chapl Tertiary Educn *S & B* 01-03; C St Martin-in-the-Fields *Lon* from 03. *6 St Martin's Place, London WC2N 4JJ* Tel (020) 7766 1102 Fax 7839 5163 E-mail lizgriff@fish.co.uk *or* clergy@smitf.org

GRIFFITHS, Eric. b 33. **d** 02 **p** 04. NSM St Andr-by-the-Wardrobe w St Ann, Blackfriars *Lon* from 02; NSM St Jas Garlickhythe w St Mich Queenhithe etc from 02. *The Charterhouse, Charterhouse Square, London EC1M 6AN* Tel (020) 7490 1025 E-mail egcharterhouse@yahoo.co.uk

GRIFFITHS, Garrie Charles. b 53. St Jo Coll Nottm. **d** 77 **p** 78. Canada 77-78; C Stalybridge H Trin and Ch Ch *Ches* 78-81; C Moreton 81-84; V Godley cum Newton Green 84-89; V Bayston Hill *Lich* 89-01; TR Mildenhall *St E* 01-04; V Hadfield *Derby* from 04. *St Andrew's Vicarage, 122 Hadfield Road, Hadfield, Glossop SK13 2DR* Tel (01457) 852431 E-mail garriegriff@whsmithnet.co.uk

GRIFFITHS, Gerald Brian. b 41. Open Univ BA88. SEITE 97. **d** 00 **p** 01. NSM Cliftonville *Cant* 00-03; TV St Laur in Thanet from 04. *St Christopher's House, Kimberley Road, Ramsgate CT12 6HH* Tel (01843) 594160 E-mail geebeegee@tiscali.co.uk

GRIFFITHS, Gerald Lewis. b 38. Westmr Coll Ox MTh97. Qu Coll Birm. **d** 88 **p** 89. C Wrexham *St As* 88-91; TV 91-95; R Hope 95-00; rtd 00. *10 Ryder Close, Wrexham LL13 9GS* Tel (01978) 355244

GRIFFITHS, Gordon John. b 31. Univ of Wales (Cardiff) BA53. S'wark Ord Course 72. **d** 75 **p** 76. NSM Sutton St Nic *S'wark* 75-78; Asst Chapl Eastbourne Coll 78-81; Perm to Offic *Chich* from 81. *15 Buckhurst Close, Willingdon, Eastbourne BN20 9EF* Tel (01323) 505547

GRIFFITHS, Griff. *See* GRIFFITHS, Stephen David

GRIFFITHS, Harvey Stephen. b 35. Linc Coll Ox BA58 MA62. Linc Th Coll 62. **d** 62 **p** 63. C Frodingham *Linc* 62-65; C Darlington St Cuth *Dur* 65-70; Chapl RN 70-92; P-in-c Southwick w Boarhunt *Portsm* 92-05; rtd 05; Perm to Offic *Portsm* from 05. *27 Burnham Wood, Fareham PO16 7UD* Tel (01329) 232915 Mobile 07747-093365 E-mail harvey@hsgriffiths.fsnet.co.uk

GRIFFITHS, Mrs Jean Rose. b 36. Avery Hill Coll TCert56. S'wark Ord Course 93. **d** 95 **p** 96. NSM Charlton *S'wark* 95-03; Asst Chapl HM Pris Brixton 95-03; Chapl 03-04; rtd 04; Perm to Offic *S'wark* from 04. *32 Weyman Road, London SE3 8RY* Tel (020) 8319 8676 *or* 8588 6051 E-mail jpg@fish.co.uk

GRIFFITHS, John Alan. b 48. CPsychol AFBPsS Univ of Wales BSc72 Cape Town Univ MSc76. St Mich Coll Llan 87. **d** 89 **p** 90. C Neath w Llantwit *Llan* 89-93; V Roath St German 93-95. *All Pine Grange, Bath Road, Bournemouth BH1 2PF* Tel (01202) 314120

GRIFFITHS, John Gareth. b 44. Lich Th Coll 68. **d** 71 **p** 72. C Shotton *St As* 71-73; C Rhyl w St Ann 73-76; V Llanasa 76-95; RD Holywell 89-95; V Rhuddlan from 95. *The Vicarage, Vicarage Lane, Rhuddlan, Rhyl LL18 2UE* Tel (01745) 591568

GRIFFITHS, John Mark Ainsley. b 68. Man Univ BSc90 MSc91 PGCE92 Ox Univ BA97. Ripon Coll Cuddesdon 95. **d** 98 **p** 99. Min Can Bangor *Ban* 98-01; P-in-c Denio w Abererch 01-02; V from 02. *The Vicarage, Ala Road, Pwllheli LL53 5BL* Tel (01758) 612305 E-mail ainsley@fish.co.uk

GRIFFITHS, Malcolm. b 47. St Alb Minl Tr Scheme. **d** 82 **p** 83. NSM Hemel Hempstead *St Alb* 82-86; C 86-87; TV Liskeard, St Keyne, St Pinnock, Morval etc *Truro* 87-96; V Landrake w St Erney and Botus Fleming from 96. *The Vicarage, School Road, Landrake, Saltash PL12 5EA* Tel (01752) 851801

GRIFFITHS, Margaret. *See* MacLACHLAN, Mrs Margaret

GRIFFITHS, Mrs Margarett. b 29. ATCL47 LRAM48. CA Tr Coll 50. **dss** 81 **d** 87. Hackington *Cant* 81-83; Ashford 84-89; Par Dn 87-89; rtd 89. *39 Newington Way, Craven Arms SY7 9PS* Tel (01588) 673848

GRIFFITHS, Mark. *See* GRIFFITHS, David Mark

GRIFFITHS, Canon Martyn Robert. b 51. Nottm Univ BTh74 St Martin's Coll Lanc PGCE75. Kelham Th Coll 70. **d** 74 **p** 75. C Kings Heath *Birm* 74-77; C-in-c Elmdon Heath CD 77-79; TV Solihull 79-81; Asst Admin Shrine of Our Lady of Walsingham 81-85; V Oldham St Steph and All Martyrs *Man* 85-89; TR Swinton and Pendlebury 89-98; Hon Can Man Cathl 96-98; R Preston St Jo and St Geo *Blackb* 98-05; Hon Can Blackb Cathl 00-05; R Henley w Remenham *Ox* from 05. *St Mary's Rectory, Hart Street, Henley-on-Thames RG9 2AU* Tel and fax (01491) 577340 E-mail rector.hwr@lineone.net

GRIFFITHS, Meirion. b 38. Clifton Th Coll 63. **d** 66 **p** 67. C Upper Holloway St Pet *Lon* 66-68; C Taunton St Jas *B & W* 68-70; C Radipole *Sarum* 70-74; R Chich St Pancras and St Jo *Chich* 74-82; R Corwen and Llangar *St As* 82-88; RD Edeyrnion 82-88; Australia from 88; C Albany 88; R Collie 89-93; P-in-c Maddington 97-00; rtd 00. *27 Coachwood Way, Maddington, W Australia 6109* Tel (0061) (8) 9459 2920 Fax 9452 2720 E-mail meirion4@aol.com

GRIFFITHS, Mervyn Harrington. b 15. Ripon Hall Ox 53. **d** 54 **p** 55. C Aigburth *Liv* 54-56; C Grassendale 56-58; C Findon *Chich* 58-59; R Bighton *Win* 59-78; V Bishop's Sutton 59-78; rtd 80; Perm to Offic *Ex* from 80. *7 Barnards Farm, Beer, Seaton EX12 3NF* Tel (01297) 22382

GRIFFITHS, Morgan Emlyn. b 17. St D Coll Lamp BA38 St Mich Coll Llan 39. **d** 43 **p** 44. C Loughor *S & B* 43-45; C Defynnog w Rhydybriw and Llandeilo'r Fan 45-47; Barbados 47-59; R Cwmdu and Tretower *S & B* 60-78; V Crickhowell w Cwmdu and Tretower 78-83; rtd 83. *10 St John's, Pendre Close, Brecon LD3 9ED* Tel (01874) 611125

GRIFFITHS, Neville. b 39. Univ of Wales BA63. St D Coll Lamp LTh66. **d** 66 **p** 67. C Newport St Mark *Mon* 66-68; C Cardiff St Jo *Llan* 68-70; Chapl Greystoke Coll Carl 70-76; C Greystoke w Matterdale *Carl* 70-75; TV Greystoke, Matterdale and Mungrisdale 75-76; Chapl Grey Coll Dur 76-81; C Croxdale *Dur* 76-81; R Didsbury Ch Ch *Man* 81-83; P-in-c Lowther and Askham *Carl* 83-84; R 84-88; V Guernsey St Matt *Win* 88-93; R Guernsey St Pierre du Bois 93-02; R Guernsey St Philippe de Torteval 93-02; Vice-Dean Guernsey 99-02; rtd 03. *6 Howlcroft Villas, Neville's Cross, Durham DH1 4DU* Tel 0191-386 4778

GRIFFITHS, Paul Edward. b 48. St Jo Coll Nottm 86. **d** 88 **p** 89. C Ipswich St Andr *St E* 88-92; P-in-c Tollerton *S'well* 92-00; P-in-c Plumtree 95-97; Ind Chapl and Dioc Adv on Ind Soc 97-00; V Hellesdon *Nor* from 00. *The Vicarage, Broom Avenue, Hellesdon, Norwich NR6 6LG* Tel (01603) 426902

GRIFFITHS, Percy. *See* GRIFFITHS, David Percy Douglas

GRIFFITHS, Richard Barre Maw. b 43. CCC Ox BA65 MA69. Cranmer Hall Dur DipTh71 BA71. **d** 71 **p** 72. C Fulwood *Sheff* 71-74; Hon C Sheff St Jo 74-76; Fell Dept of Bibl Studies Sheff Univ 74-76; C Fulham St Matt *Lon* 76-78; P-in-c 78-83; R Chich St Pancras and St Jo *Chich* from 83. *St Pancras's Rectory, 9 St John Street, Chichester PO19 1UR* Tel (01243) 536390 *or* 536387 E-mail stpancraschichester@hotmail.com

GRIFFITHS, Prof Richard Mathias. b 35. K Coll Cam BA57 MA61 PhD62 BNC Ox MA66 FIL91 FKC95. Ox Min Course 89 St Alb and Ox Min Course 96. **d** 97 **p** 98. Prof French K Coll Lon 90-00; NSM W Woodhay w Enborne, Hampstead Marshall etc *Ox* 97-00; NSM Llantrisant *Llan* from 01. *Waltham House, Bradford Place, Penarth CF64 1AG* Tel (029) 2070 7828 Fax 2070 9699 E-mail richard.griffiths@newbury.net

GRIFFITHS, Canon Robert Herbert. b 53. Chich Th Coll 75. **d** 76 **p** 77. C Holywell *St As* 76-80; CF (TA) 79-87; P-in-c Gyffylliog *St As* 80-84; V Llanfair Dyffryn Clwyd 80-84; V Llanfair DC, Derwen, Llanelidan and Efenechtyd 84-88; Asst Dioc Youth Chapl 81-86; Dioc Youth Chapl 86-91; PV St As and Tremeirchion w Cefn 88-97; Chapl H M Stanley Hosp 88-97; Bp's Visitor and Dioc RE Adv *St As* 88-93; Chapl Glan Clwyd Distr Gen Hosp 93-97; V Llanrhos *St As* from 97; Can St As Cathl from 98; Chapl NW Wales NHS Trust from 97. *Llanrhos Vicarage, 2 Vicarage Road, Llandudno LL30 1PT* Tel (01492) 876152

GRIFFITHS, Robert James. b 52. Nottm Univ BTh82. St Jo Coll Nottm 79. **d** 82 **p** 83. C Kettering St Andr *Pet* 82-85; C Collier Row St Jas and Havering-atte-Bower *Chelmsf* 86-89; R High Ongar w Norton Mandeville 89-97; R Ilmington w Stretton-on-Fosse etc *Cov* 97-99; V Newport *Chelmsf* 99-03; V Newport and

Widdington from 03. *The Vicarage, 5 Meadowford, Newport, Saffron Walden CB11 3QL* Tel (01799) 540339 E-mail robert.griffiths@btinternet.com

GRIFFITHS, Roger. b 46. Trin Coll Bris 70. **d** 74 **p** 75. C Normanton *Derby* 74-77; C Bucknall and Bagnall *Lich* 77-80; TV 80-83; TV Aberystwyth *St D* 83-86; R Letterston w Llanfair Nant-y-Gof etc from 86; RD Dewisland and Fishguard from 01. *The Rectory, 122 St David's Road, Letterston, Haverfordwest SA62 5SE* Tel (01348) 840336

GRIFFITHS, Roger Michael. b 47. Wycliffe Hall Ox 83. **d** 86 **p** 87. Min Can St D Cathl *St D* 86-88; V Pen-boyr 88-94; V Fishguard w Llanychar and Pontfaen w Morfil etc 94-03. *Trebover Farmhouse, Llanychaer, Fishguard SA65 9SA* Tel (01348) 873963 E-mail roger@rogriff.freeserve.co.uk

GRIFFITHS, Russell Howard. b 22. Glouc Th Course 75. **d** 77 **p** 78. NSM Fownhope w Fawley *Heref* 77-80; NSM Brockhampton 77-80; P-in-c Bridstow w Peterstow 80-81; TV Ross w Brampton Abbotts, Bridstow and Peterstow 81-87; rtd 87; Perm to Offic *Heref* from 91. *Flat 1, Weirside House, 29 Bridge Avenue, Otley LS21 2AA*

GRIFFITHS, Shane Owen. b 63. Ripon Coll Cuddesdon 01. **d** 04 **p** 04. C Icknield *Ox* from 04. *Church Cottage, 30 Church Street, Watlington OX49 5QR* Tel (01491) 614003 E-mail shaneowengriffiths@hotmail.com

GRIFFITHS, Shirley Thelma. b 48. Univ of Wales (Ban) CertEd69 Open Univ BA83 Coll of Ripon & York St Jo MA01. St Deiniol's Hawarden 79. **d** 82 **p** 95. NSM Dyserth and Trelawnyd and Cwm *St As* 82-91; RE Officer 89-95; Min Can St As Cathl 91-95; P-in-c The Cowtons *Ripon* 95-02; RE Adv 95-02; V Abergele *St As* from 02. *The Vicarage, 28 Lon Dirion, Abergele LL22 8PX* Tel (01745) 833132 Fax as telephone E-mail stg@fish.co.uk

GRIFFITHS, Simon Mark. b 62. Ch Ch Coll Cant BA84 Kent Univ MA95. Chich Th Coll. **d** 87 **p** 88. C Cardiff St Jo *Llan* 87-91; Sub-Chapl HM Pris Cardiff 87-91; Chapl and Succ Roch Cath *Roch* 91-96; Chapl Univ Coll Chich 96-01; V Sheff St Matt *Sheff* from 01. *St Matthew's Vicarage, 29 Winchester Road, Sheffield S10 4EE* Tel 0114-230 5641

GRIFFITHS, Canon Stanley Arthur. b 17. Lon Univ BSc38. Cuddesdon Coll 46. **d** 47 **p** 48. C Southsea St Matt *Portsm* 47-48; C Southsea H Spirit 48-51; C Cowley St Jas *Ox* 51-55; V Northbourne 55-65; V St Neots *Ely* 65-77; RD St Neots 76-82; Hon Can Ely Cathl 76-82; V Buckden 77-82; rtd 82; Perm to Offic *Ely* 82-96 and *York* from 82. *17 York Road, Malton YO17 6AX* Tel (01653) 697324

GRIFFITHS, Stephen David (Griff). b 70. Oak Hill Th Coll BA96 Trin Coll Bris. **d** 00 **p** 01. C Cranleigh *Guildf* 00-04; TV Thetford *Nor* from 04. *24 Foxglove Road, Thetford IP24 2XF* Tel (01842) 764601 Mobile 07708-414952 E-mail revgriff@tesco.net

GRIFFITHS, Stephen Mark. b 67. Nottm Univ BTh93 PhD00. St Jo Coll Nottm 90. **d** 93 **p** 94. C Glascote and Stonydelph *Lich* 93-96; P-in-c Stratford New Town St Paul *Chelmsf* 96-02; P-in-c Steeple Bumpstead and Helions Bumpstead from 02; Tutor Ridley Hall Cam from 01. *The Vicarage, North Street, Steeple Bumpstead, Haverhill CB9 7DP* Tel (01440) 730128 Mobile 07905-861234 E-mail revsgriff@aol.com

GRIFFITHS, Stephen Robert. b 78. Oak Hill Th Coll BA00. Ridley Hall Cam 02. **d** 04 **p** 05. C Normanton *Derby* from 04. *18 Lawnlea Close, Sunnyhill, Derby DE23 1XQ* Tel (01332) 602724 E-mail steph78griff@hotmail.com

GRIFFITHS, Mrs Susan Angela. b 61. St Jo Coll Nottm BTh94. **d** 94 **p** 95. C Ingrow cum Hainworth *Bradf* 94-98; V Wyke 98-03; C Buttershaw St Paul from 03. *St Paul's Vicarage, 42A Wibsey Park Avenue, Bradford BD6 3QA* Tel (01274) 676359

GRIFFITHS, Canon Sylvia Joy. b 50. Gipsy Hill Coll of Educn CertEd71. St Jo Coll Nottm 85. **dss** 86 **d** 87 **p** 94. Woodthorpe *S'well* 86-90; Par Dn 87-90; Min Bestwood/Rise Park LEP 90-94; TD Bestwood 90-94; TR 94-99; P-in-c Sherwood 99-01; V from 01; Hon Can S'well Minster from 04. *St Martin's Vicarage, Trevose Gardens, Sherwood, Nottingham NG5 3FU* Tel 0115-960 7547 E-mail sylvia.griffiths1@btopenworld.com

GRIFFITHS, Thomas. b 31. AKC57. **d** 58 **p** 59. C Cheadle Hulme All SS *Ches* 58-61; C Oxton 61-63; V Micklehurst 63-72; V Ringway 73-91; V Liscard St Mary w St Columba 91-96; rtd 96; Perm to Offic *Ches* from 96 and *Lich* from 01. *14A High Street, Ellesmere SY12 0EP* Tel (01691) 623589

GRIFFITHS, Tudor Francis Lloyd. b 54. Jes Coll Ox BA76 MA81 Leeds Univ PhD99. Wycliffe Hall Ox 76. **d** 79 **p** 80. C Brecon w Battle *S & B* 79-81; Min Can Brecon Cathl 79-81; C Swansea St Mary w H Trin 81-83; R Llangattock and Llangyndir 83-88; CMS Uganda 89-95; C Newton St Pet *S & B* 96; Dioc Missr *Mon* from 96; V Goldcliffe and Whitson and Nash 96-98; TV Magor 98-03; TR Hawarden *St As* from 03. *The Rectory, 2 Birch Rise, Hawarden CH5 3DD* Tel (01244) 520091

GRIFFITHS, Vyrnach Morgan. b 24. Univ of Wales (Lamp) BA50. St Mich Coll Llan 52. **d** 54 **p** 55. C Llantrisant *Llan* 54-56; C Ystradyfodwg 56-60; C Cwmavon 60-61; V Clydach Vale 61-63; R Llanfair Talhaiarn *St As* 63-70; V Dinas w Penygraig *Llan* 70-74; R Llanddulas *St As* 74-80; R Llanddulas and Llysfaen 80-89; rtd 89. *10 Cilfan, Pensarn, Abergele LL22 7RD*

GRIFFITHS, William Bevan. b 13. AKC37. **d** 37 **p** 38. C Llangyfelach and Morriston *S & B* 37-50; R Llanbadarn Fawr and Llandegley 50-59; R Braunston *Pet* 59-79; rtd 79; Perm to Offic *Llan* from 79. *73 Glannant Way, Cimla, Neath SA11 3YP* Tel (01639) 770527

GRIFFITHS, Canon William David Aled. b 52. Univ of Wales (Abth) BA74 Man Univ AHA77. St Mich Coll Llan DipTh83. **d** 83 **p** 84. C Carmarthen St Pet *St D* 83-87; Asst Warden of Ords 84-91; Warden of Ords from 91; V Llansadwrn w Llanwrda and Manordeilo 87-92; V Llangunnor w Cwmffrwd from 92; Can St D Cathl from 01. *The Vicarage, Llangunnor Road, Carmarthen SA31 2HY* Tel (01267) 236435

GRIFFITHS, William David Maldwyn. b 23. St D Coll Lamp BA47. **d** 50 **p** 51. C Cardigan *St D* 50-54; C Henfynyw w Aberaeron 54-57; P-in-c Llechryd 57-59; V Mathri, St Edrens and Llanrheithan 59-67; V Llanfihangel Genau'r Glyn 67-89; RD Llanbadarn Fawr 87-89; rtd 89. *Bro Enlli, Lower Regent Street, Aberaeron SA46 0HZ* Tel (01545) 570176

GRIFFITHS, William Thomas Gordon. b 48. York Univ BA70 Fitzw Coll Cam BA79. Ridley Hall Cam 78. **d** 80 **p** 81. C Dulwich St Barn *S'wark* 80-83; C Egglescliffe *Dur* 83-85; Ind Chapl 85-90; V Stockton St Jas 90-98; NSM Leamington Hastings and Birdingbury *Cov* 98-03; NSM Grandborough w Willoughby and Flecknoe 98-03; NSM Leam Valley from 03. *The Vicarage, Lower Street, Willoughby, Rugby CV23 8BX* Tel (01788) 890309

GRIGG, Simon James. b 61. Warwick Univ BA82 MA83 Southn Univ BTh90. Chich Th Coll 87. **d** 90 **p** 91. C Cowley St Jas *Ox* 90-94; C W Hampstead St Jas *Lon* 94-95; V Munster Square Ch Ch and St Mary Magd from 95. *8 Laxton Place, London NW1 3PT* Tel (020) 7388 3095 Mobile 07958-472568 E-mail simon.grigg@btopenworld.com

GRIGG, Canon Terence George. b 34. Kelham Th Coll 54. **d** 59 **p** 60. C Brookfield St Anne, Highgate Rise *Lon* 59-62; Chapl Lee Abbey 63-66; Chapl and Lect St Luke's Coll Ex 66-70; V Stainton-in-Cleveland *York* 70-83; R Cottingham 83-04; Hon Can Koforidua from 84; Can and Preb York Minster *York* 90-04; rtd 04. *Sachristan Cottage, Zeal Monachorum, Crediton EX17 6DF* Tel (01363) 82719

GRIGG, William John Frank. b 27. SSC. Ripon Hall Ox. **d** 66 **p** 67. C Wigan All SS *Liv* 66-67; C Leek St Luke *Lich* 67-69; C Fenton 69-74; C St Stephen by Saltash *Truro* 74-76; TV Redruth 76-79; TV Laneast w St Clether and Tresmere 79-81; P-in-c Wendron 81-85; TV Helston and Wendron 85-91; rtd 91. *St Germoe, 23 Dunheved Fields, Launceston PL15 7HS* Tel (01566) 772878

GRIGGS, Canon Alan Sheward. b 33. Trin Hall Cam BA56 MA60. Westcott Ho Cam 58. **d** 60 **p** 61. C Arnold *S'well* 60-63; Succ S'wark Cathl *S'wark* 63-66; Ind Chapl 66-71; C Leeds H Trin *Ripon* 71-81; V 81-91; Soc and Ind Adv 71-81; Hon Can Ripon Cathl 84-98; Soc Resp Officer 91-98; rtd 98; Perm to Offic *Ripon* from 98. *32 St Chad's Avenue, Leeds LS6 3QF* Tel 0113-275 8100 E-mail alan@griggs32.freeserve.co.uk

GRIGGS, Mrs Anthea Mary. b 37. Homerton Coll Cam TCert57 New Coll Edin BA86. St Alb and Ox Min Course. **d** 00 **p** 01. NSM Sunningdale *Ox* from 00. *Shrub House, 1 Coworth Road, Sunningdale SL5 0NX* Tel (01344) 623450 E-mail a.m.griggs@talk21.com

GRIGGS, Frederick John. b 20. Peterho Cam BA48 MA53. Linc Th Coll. **d** 50 **p** 51. C Stand *Man* 50-53; C Writtle *Chelmsf* 53-55; P-in-c The Chignals w Mashbury 55-58; V Chelmsf St Andr 58-62; R Colne Engaine 62-80; P-in-c Frating w Thorrington 80-83; rtd 85. *6 Church View, Holton, Halesworth IP19 8PB* Tel (01986) 875298

✠**GRIGGS, The Rt Revd Ian Macdonald.** b 28. Trin Hall Cam BA52 MA56. Westcott Ho Cam. **d** 54 **p** 55 **c** 87. C Portsea St Cuth *Portsm* 54-59; Dioc Youth Chapl *Sheff* 59-64; Bp's Dom Chapl 59-64; V Sheff St Cuth 64-71; V Kidderminster St Mary *Worc* 71-82; Hon Can Worc Cathl 77-84; TR Kidderminster St Mary and All SS, Trimpley etc 82-84; Preb Heref Cathl *Heref* 84-94; Adn Ludlow 84-87; P-in-c Tenbury St Mich 84-87; Suff Bp Ludlow 87-94; rtd 94; Hon Asst Bp Carl from 94. *Rookings, Patterdale, Penrith CA11 0NP* Tel (01768) 482064 E-mail ian.griggs@virgin.net

GRIGOR, Miss Alice Moira (Tirsh). b 49. Ripon Coll Cuddesdon 94. **d** 96 **p** 97. C Curry Rivel w Fivehead and Swell *B & W* 96-98; C Nailsea Ch Ch w Tickenham 98-00; TV Ross *Heref* from 00. *The Rectory, Weston under Penyard, Ross-on-Wye HR9 7QA* Tel (01989) 562926

GRIGOR, David Alexander. b 29. Lon Univ DipTh54. St Aid Birkenhead 51. **d** 54 **p** 55. C Hengrove *Bris* 54-57; C Marshfield w Cold Ashton 57-60; V Newport *Ex* 60-67; V Paignton St Paul Preston 67-73; Brazil 73-74; Hon C Heavitree *Ex* 74-77; Chapl Ex Sch 74-77; Chapl Brighton Coll 77-89; Chapl Warminster Sch 89-93; rtd 93; Perm to Offic *Win* from 02 and *Portsm* from 03. *13 College Close, Hamble, Southampton SO41 4QU* Tel (023) 8045 3946

GRIGSBY, Peter Edward. b 31. Magd Coll Cam MA56 CertEd56. NEOC 85. **d** 88 **p** 89. NSM Haxby w Wigginton *York* 88-90; C Brayton 90-92; TV 92-97; rtd 97; Perm to Offic *Chich* 98-01. *4 The Hop Garden, South Harting, Petersfield GU31 5QL* Tel (01730) 825295

GRIGSON, Richard John Stephen. b 60. Man Univ BA83. Qu Coll Birm 86. **d** 88 **p** 89. C W Bromwich St Fran *Lich* 88-92; V Smallthorne from 92; P-in-c Brown Edge from 05. *St Saviour's Vicarage, Ford Green Road, Stoke-on-Trent ST6 1NX* Tel (01782) 835941 Fax (07092) 214726 E-mail richard.grigson@lichfield.anglican.org

GRIMASON, The Very Revd Alistair John. b 57. CITC 76. **d** 79 **p** 80. C Belfast H Trin *Conn* 79-82; C Dublin Drumcondra w N Strand *D & G* 82-84; I Navan w Kentstown, Tara, Slane, Painestown etc *M & K* 84-91; Dioc Youth Officer (Meath) 90-94; Dioc Info Officer (Meath) 90-96; I Tullamore w Durrow, Newtownfertullagh, Rahan etc 91-00; Preb Tipper St Patr Cathl Dublin 92-00; Can Meath *M & K* 92-00; Chan Kildare Cathl 98-00; Dean Tuam *T, K & A* from 00; I Tuam w Cong and Aasleagh from 00. *Deanery Place, Cong, Claremorris, Co Mayo, Irish Republic* Tel and fax (00353) (94) 954 6017

GRIME, Arthur Michael. b 28. Kelham Th Coll 48. **d** 52 **p** 53. Basutoland 52-55; C Ealing St Barn *Lon* 55-57; C Pimlico St Gabr 57-59; C Greenford H Cross 59-62; V Fulham St Pet 62-66; V Chiswick St Paul Grove Park 66-88; rtd 89; Perm to Offic *Chich* from 89. *29 Eton Close, Datchet, Slough SL3 9BE* Tel (01753) 545802

GRIME, William John Peter. b 38. St Jo Coll Ox BA60 MA66. Cuddesdon Coll 69. **d** 70 **p** 71. C Blackb St Jas *Blackb* 70-74; Chapl St Martin's Coll of Educn 74-77; V Seascale *Carl* 77-78; P-in-c Irton w Drigg 77-78; V Seascale and Drigg 78-05; rtd 05. *c/o The Vicarage, Belbrough Lane, Hutton Rudby, Yarm TS15 0HY* E-mail wjpg@ontel.com

GRIMLEY, The Very Revd Robert William. b 43. Ch Coll Cam BA66 MA70 Wadh Coll Ox BA68 MA76. Ripon Hall Ox 66. **d** 68 **p** 69. C Radlett *St Alb* 68-72; Chapl K Edw Sch Birm 72-84; Hon C Moseley St Mary *Birm* 72-84; V Edgbaston St Geo 84-97; Dean Bris from 97. *The Deanery, 20 Charlotte Street, Bristol BS1 5PZ* Tel 0117-926 2443 *or* 926 4879 Fax 925 3678 E-mail dean@bristol.anglican.org

GRIMSBY, Suffragan Bishop of. *See* ROSSDALE, The Rt Revd David Douglas James

GRIMSDALE, Mrs Margaret. b 24. Sister-Tutor's Dip 48 Lon Univ STD55. Gilmore Course 80. **dss** 82 **d** 87. Stoke Poges *Ox* 82-88; Hon Par Dn 87-88; Hon Par Dn Burrington and Churchill *B & W* 88-90; rtd 90; Perm to Offic *B & W* 90-94. *Address temp unknown*

GRIMSHAW, Eric Fenton Hall. b 34. Bris Univ BA57. Tyndale Hall Bris 54. **d** 58 **p** 59. C Moss Side St Jas *Man* 58-61; C Leyland St Andr *Blackb* 61-64; V Preston St Mark 64-72; V Mirehouse *Carl* 72-91; Hon Can Carl Cathl 86-91; V Knowsley *Liv* 91-99; rtd 99; Perm to Offic *Liv* from 99. *22 Lynwood Avenue, Aughton, Ormskirk L39 5BB* Tel (01695) 424864

GRIMSTER, Barry John. b 49. Ex Univ BA70. Trin Coll Bris 72. **d** 74 **p** 75. C S Lambeth St Steph *S'wark* 74-77; C New Malden and Coombe 77-82; P-in-c Deptford St Jo 82-84; V Deptford St Jo w H Trin 84-89; V Woking St Pet *Guildf* 89-01; TR from 02. *The Rectory, 28 High Street, Old Woking, Woking GU22 9ER* Tel (01483) 762707

GRIMWADE, Canon John Girling. b 20. Keble Coll Ox BA48 MA52. Cuddesdon Coll 48. **d** 50 **p** 51. C Kingston All SS *S'wark* 50-53; C Ox St Mary V *Ox* 53-56; PC Londonderry *Birm* 56-62; R Caversham *Ox* 62-81; Hon Can Ch Ch 73-90; Chapl to The Queen 80-90; R Caversham St Pet and Mapledurham etc *Ox* 81-83; P-in-c Stonesfield 83-89; rtd 89; Perm to Offic *Glouc* and *Ox* from 89. *88 Alexander Drive, Cirencester GL7 1UJ* Tel (01285) 885767

GRIMWADE, Leslie Frank. b 24. FBIM60. Trin Coll Bris 74. **d** 77 **p** 78. C Taunton St Jas *B & W* 77-80; C Polegate *Chich* 80-83; R Swainsthorpe w Newton Flotman *Nor* 83-90; rtd 90; Hon Min Malmesbury Abbey *Bris* 90-97; Chapl Malmesbury Hosp 90-97; Perm to Offic *Sarum* and *Ex* from 97; *B & W* from 01. *4 St George's Mews, The Mount, Taunton TA1 3TA* Tel (01823) 254887

GRIMWOOD, Andrew Stuart. b 68. Ex Univ BA89. St Mich Coll Llan BD97. **d** 98 **p** 99. C Llangynwyd w Maesteg *Llan* 98-01; P-in-c Rhyl w St Ann *St As* 01-04; R Newtown w Llanllwchaiarn w Aberhafesp from 04. *The Rectory, 3 Old Barn Lane, Newtown SY16 2PT* Tel (01686) 622260

GRIMWOOD, Canon David Walter. b 48. Lon Univ BA70 K Coll Lon BD73 AKC73. **d** 74 **p** 75. C Newc St Geo *Newc* 74-78; C Whorlton 78-80; TV Totton *Win* 80-93; Adv to Coun for Soc Resp *Roch* and *Cant* 93-02; Chief Exec Ch in Soc *Roch* and *Cant* from 02; Hon Can Roch Cathl *Roch* from 97. *56 Postley Road, Maidstone ME15 6TR* Tel (01622) 764625 *or* 755014 Fax 693531 E-mail david@csr.org.uk

GRINDELL, James Mark. b 43. Nottm Univ BA66 Bris Univ MA69. Wells Th Coll 66. **d** 68 **p** 69. C Bushey Heath *St Alb* 68-72; C Ex St Dav *Ex* 72-74; Chapl St Audries Sch W Quantoxhead 74-83; Chapl Berkhamsted Colleg Sch Herts 83-86; Chapl Denstone Coll Uttoxeter 86-91; Chapl Portsm Gr Sch 91-03; rtd 03; Hon Chapl Portsm Cathl *Portsm* from 91. *60 Cottage Grove, Southsea PO5 1EW* Tel (023) 9229 1318

✠**GRINDROD, The Most Revd John Basil Rowland.** b 19. KBE90. Qu Coll Ox BA49 MA54. Linc Th Coll 49 DTh51. **d** 51 **p** 52 **c** 66. C Hulme St Mich *Man* 51-54; R Ancoats All SS 56-60; Australia from 60; Adn Rockhampton 60-65; Bp Riverina 66-71; Bp Rockhampton 71-80; Abp Brisbane 80-90; rtd 90. *14B Thomas Street, Murwillumbah, NSW, Australia 2484* Tel (0061) (2) 6672 6640

GRINHAM, Garth Clews. b 36. Oak Hill Th Coll 61. **d** 64 **p** 65. C Beckenham Ch Ch *Roch* 64-68; C Wallington H Trin *S'wark* 68-71; V Erith St Paul *Roch* 71-76; Asst Sec CPAS 76-81; Hon C Knockholt *Roch* 76-81; V Southport Ch Ch *Liv* 81-94; V Douglas St Ninian *S & M* 94-01; rtd 01; Perm to Offic *Liv* from 01. *8 Ottery Close, Southport PR9 9GE* Tel (01704) 213468

GRINHAM, Julian Clive. b 39. Birkbeck Coll Lon BA65. Oak Hill Th Coll 79. **d** 81 **p** 82. C Blackb Ch Ch w St Matt *Blackb* 81-83; Nat Sec Pathfinders CPAS 83-89; Dir CYPECS 89-94; V Normanton *Derby* 94-00; rtd 00; Perm to Offic *Nor* from 01. *85 Gwyn Crescent, Fakenham NR21 8NE* Tel (01328) 853068

GRINSELL, Robert Paul. b 62. Ch Ch Coll Cant BA86 PGCE89. Trin Coll Bris MA03. **d** 03 **p** 04. C Foord St Jo *Cant* from 03. *2 Chalk Close, Folkestone CT19 5TD* Tel (01303) 245281 E-mail grinsell@btopenworld.com

GRINSTED, Richard Anthony. b 43. Leic Univ BSc65. Oak Hill Th Coll 67. **d** 70 **p** 71. C Egham *Guildf* 70-73; C Woodford Wells *Chelmsf* 73-76; P-in-c Havering-atte-Bower 76-84; R Ditton *Roch* 84-94; R Chulmleigh *Ex* 94-96; R Chawleigh w Cheldon 94-96; R Wembworthy w Eggesford 94-96; R Chulmleigh, Chawleigh w Cheldon, Wembworthy etc 96-00; rtd 00. *Stonehouse, Christow, Exeter EX6 7NE* Tel (01647) 252653

GRISCOME, David. b 47. Oak Hill Th Coll BA88 TCD Div Sch 89. **d** 89 **p** 90. C Glendermott *D & R* 89-91; I Clondehorkey w Cashel 91-95; I Mevagh w Glenalla 91-95; Bp's C Calry *K, E & A* 95-97; I 97-00; Dean Elphin and Ardagh 99-04; I Sligo w Knocknarea and Rosses Pt 99-04; Perm to Offic *Cant* from 04. *23 Elmleigh Road, Littlebourne, Canterbury CT3 1UE* Tel (01227) 721599

✠**GRISWOLD, The Most Revd Frank Tracy.** b 37. Harvard Univ AB59 Oriel Coll Ox BA62 MA66. Gen Th Sem NY 59 Hon DD85 Seabury-Western Th Sem Hon DD85. **d** 62 **p** 63 **c** 85. C Bryn Mawr Redeemer 63-67; R Yardley St Andr 67-74; R Philadelphia St Martin-in-the-Fields 74-85; Bp Coadjutor Chicago 85-87; Bp Chicago 87-97; Presiding Bp from 98. *Episcopal Church Center, 815 Second Avenue, New York, NY 10017, USA* Tel (001) (212) 716 6276 *or* 867 8400 Fax 490 3298 E-mail pboffice@episcopalchurch.org

GRITTEN, Desmond Digby. b 17. ALCD54. **d** 54 **p** 55. C Blackheath St Jo *S'wark* 54-58; V Kenilworth St Jo *Cov* 58-87; RD Kenilworth 63-73; rtd 87; Perm to Offic *Cant* from 87; *Ex* from 92 and *Chelmsf* and *Cant* from 97. *54 Claremont Road, London E7 0PZ* Tel (020) 8257 1301

GROARKE, Ms Nicola Jane. b 62. Lanc Univ BA84. Ridley Hall Cam. **d** 00 **p** 01. C Balham Hill Ascension *S'wark* from 00. *22 Rochelle Close, London SW11 2RX* Tel (020) 8871 1118 *or* 8675 8626 E-mail nikki@groarke.fsnet.co.uk

GROEPE, Canon Thomas Matthew Karl. b 51. St Pet Coll Natal 76. **d** 78 **p** 79. S Africa 78-83 and from 88; Hon C Waterloo St Jo w St Andr *S'wark* 83-88. *PO Box 1932, Cape Town, 8000 South Africa* Tel and fax (0027) (21) 465 4946 *or* tel 461 9566 E-mail karlgroepe@mweb.co.za

GROOCOCK, Christopher John. b 59. St Jo Coll Nottm 89. **d** 92 **p** 93. C Shawbury *Lich* 92-95; V Hengoed w Gobowen 95-00; CF from 00. *c/o MOD Chaplains (Army)* Tel (01980) 615804 Fax 615800

GROOCOCK, Craig Ronald. WMMTC 03. **d** 05. C Kenilworth St Nic *Cov* from 05. *145 Albion Street, Kenilworth CV8 2FY* Tel (01926) 858169 Mobile 07811-395169 E-mail craiggroocock@aol.com

GROOM, Mrs Susan Anne. b 63. Univ of Wales BA85 Hughes Hall Cam MPhil86 Lon Bible Coll MA94 Open Univ MPhil00. St Jo Coll Nottm 94. **d** 96 **p** 97. C Harefield *Lon* 96-99; C Eastcote St Lawr 99-01; P-in-c Yiewsley 01-03; V from 03. *The Vicarage, 93 High Street, Yiewsley, West Drayton UB7 7QH* Tel (01895) 442093 E-mail vicar@stmatthews-yiewsley.org.uk

GROSSCURTH, Stephen. b 55. Sarum & Wells Th Coll 81. **d** 84 **p** 85. C Southport H Trin *Liv* 84-87; C Amblecote *Worc* 87-89; V Walton St Jo *Liv* 89-95; Chapl S Man Univ Hosps NHS Trust from 95. *Wythenshawe Hospital, Southmoor Road, Manchester M23 9LT* Tel 0161-291 2298 *or* (01925) 821124 Fax 0161-946 2603

GROSSE, Anthony Charles Bain. b 30. Oak Hill Th Coll 58. **d** 61 **p** 62. C Chislehurst Ch Ch *Roch* 61-65; C Washfield *Ex* 65-71; TV Washfield, Stoodleigh, Withleigh etc 71-73; R Hemyock 73-86; P-in-c Clayhidon 76-86; R Hemyock w Culm Davy and Clayhidon 87-93; R Hemyock w Culm Davy, Clayhidon and

Culmstock 93-96; rtd 96; Perm to Offic *Ex* from 98. *17 Frog Street, Bampton, Tiverton EX16 9NT* Tel (01398) 331981 E-mail acgrosse@btinternet.com

GROSSE, Peter George. b 43. St Steph Ho Ox 02. **d** 03 **p** 04. NSM Reading St Matt *Ox* from 03. *18 Rangewood Avenue, Reading RG30 3NN* Tel 0118-959 4573 E-mail petergrosse@supanet.com

GROSSE, Richard William. b 52. Solicitor 77 Mid Essex Tech Coll LLB73. Ridley Hall Cam 86. **d** 88 **p** 89. C Soham *Ely* 88-91; C Bedale *Ripon* 91-93; C-in-c Thornton Watlass w Thornton Steward 91-93; V Barton and Manfield w Cleasby 93-95; V Barton and Manfield and Cleasby w Stapleton 95-99; R Keelby Gp *Linc* 99-04; R Callander *St And* from 04; R Aberfoyle from 04. *St Mary's Rectory, Main Street, Aberfoyle, Stirling FK8 3UJ* Tel and fax (01877) 382887 E-mail richard_grosse@hotmail.com

GROSU, Iosif. b 60. Iasi Univ BTh92. RC Inst Iasi DipTh89. **d** 89 **p** 89. In RC Ch 89-93; C Darlington St Cuth *Dur* 96-99; C Stockton St Jo and Stockton St Jas 99-02; TV Ch the K from 02. *6 Badgers Wood, Stanley DH9 0HR* Tel (01207) 237732 E-mail i.grosu@ntlworld.com

GROSVENOR, Royston Johannes Martin. b 47. K Coll Lon BD70 AKC. **d** 71 **p** 72. C Pontesbury I and II *Heref* 71-75; C Bishopston *Bris* 75-79; P-in-c Croydon St Pet S End *Cant* 79-81; V Croydon St Pet 81-84; V Croydon St Pet *S'wark* 85-87; R Merstham and Gatton 87-97; V Tidenham w Beachley and Lancaut *Glouc* from 97; P-in-c St Briavels w Hewelsfield from 05; RD Forest S from 04. *Tidenham Vicarage, Gloucester Road, Tutshill, Chepstow NP16 7DH* Tel (01291) 622442 E-mail roystongrosvenor@tidenham42.freeserve.co.uk

GROVE, Lynn. b 43. Lon Univ MB, BS67. Cranmer Hall Dur 03. **d** 04 **p** 05. NSM Pickering w Lockton and Levisham *York* from 04. *The Poplars, Scarborough Road, Rillington, Malton YO17 8LQ* Tel (01944) 758698 E-mail lynngrove43@hotmail.com

GROVE, Ronald Edward. b 32. Oak Hill Th Coll 60. **d** 63 **p** 64. C Bromley St Jo *Roch* 63-66; V Stratford New Town St Paul *Chelmsf* 66-94; rtd 97; Perm to Offic *Chich* from 97 and *Cant* from 00. *27 Bromley College, London Road, Bromley BR1 1PE* Tel (020) 8290 0381

GROVER, Wilfrid John. b 29. Lich Th Coll 55. **d** 58 **p** 59. C Northampton St Alb *Pet* 58-61; C Boyne Hill *Ox* 61-65; V Cookham 65-85; RD Maidenhead 82-85; Warden Christchurch Retreat Ho *Glouc* 85-93; rtd 89; Hon C Jedburgh *Edin* from 93. *Cairnbrook, Bemersyde, Melrose TD6 9DP* Tel (01835) 822054

GROVES, Elizabeth Ann. Bp Otter Coll 94. **d** 97. NSM Soberton w Newtown *Portsm* 97-01; NSM Botley from 01; NSM Curdridge from 01; NSM Durley from 01. *33 Vectis Road, Alverstoke, Gosport PO12 2QD* Tel (023) 9258 2841 *or* (01489) 782445 E-mail akeagroves@aol.com

GROVES, James Alan. b 32. CCC Cam BA58 MA62. Wells Th Coll 58. **d** 60 **p** 61. C Milton next Gravesend Ch Ch *Roch* 60-64; C Beckenham St Jas 64-66; V Orpington St Andr 66-98; rtd 98; Perm to Offic *Chich* from 98. *9 Wykeham Road, Hastings TN34 1UA* Tel (01424) 200839

GROVES, Mrs Jill. b 61. Univ Coll Lon BSc82. St Jo Coll Nottm Dip Th Studies 91 MA93. **d** 93 **p** 94. C Tenbury *Heref* 93-98; P-in-c Hope Bowdler w Eaton-under-Heywood from 98; P-in-c Cardington from 98; P-in-c Rushbury from 98. *The Rectory, Hope Bowdler, Church Stretton SY6 7DD* Tel (01694) 722918 E-mail jill@grovesfamily.org.uk

GROVES, Justin Simon John. b 69. Lon Bible Coll BA93. Ridley Hall Cam 00. **d** 02 **p** 03. C Glouc St Cath *Glouc* from 02. *35 St Mary Square, Gloucester GL1 2QT* Tel (01452) 310810

GROVES, Margaret Ann. b 49. Nottm Univ BEd71 BPhil88. EMMTC 95. **d** 98 **p** 99. NSM Farnsfield *S'well* from 98; NSM Bilsthorpe from 98. *Churchill House, Church Hill, Bilsthorpe, Newark NG22 8RU* Tel (01623) 870679

GROVES, Peter John. b 70. New Coll Ox BA92 MA96 DPhil96. Westcott Ho Cam 95. **d** 97 **p** 98. C Leigh-on-Sea St Marg *Chelmsf* 97-99; P Lib Pusey Ho Ox 99-01; Asst Chapl and Tutor Keble Coll Ox 01-02; Chapl and Fell BNC Ox from 02; Hon C Ox St Mary Magd *Ox* 01-04; P-in-c from 05. *15 Beaumont Street, Oxford OX1 2NA* Tel (01865) 247836 *or* tel and fax 277833 E-mail peter.groves@theology.ox.ac.uk

GROVES, Canon Philip Neil. b 62. Man Univ BA84. St Jo Coll Nottm 86. **d** 88 **p** 89. C Holbeck *Ripon* 88-91; CMS 91-99; Tanzania 93-98; Hon Can Mpwampwa from 98; TV Melton Mowbray *Leic* from 99. *1 Palmerston Road, Melton Mowbray LE13 0SS* Tel (01664) 564229 E-mail rev.phil@ntlworld.com

GROVES, Robert John. b 42. Trin Coll Bris 74. **d** 76 **p** 77. C Norwood St Luke *S'wark* 76-79; P-in-c Clapham Park All SS 79-86; V Anerley *Roch* 86-95; TV Canford Magna *Sarum* 95-98; TR Tollington *Lon* 98-02; rtd 02; Perm to Offic *Cant* and *Roch* from 02. *12 Oatfield Close, Cranbrook TN17 3NH* Tel (01580) 715756 E-mail bob_groves@lineone.net

GROWNS, John Huntley. b 28. Chich Th Coll 57. **d** 60 **p** 61. C Hayes St Mary *Lon* 60-64; C Addlestone *Guildf* 64-67; C-in-c Kempston Transfiguration CD *St Alb* 67-74; R Stevenage St Geo 74-82; R Felpham w Middleton *Chich* 82-88; P-in-c Westmill w Gt Munden *St Alb* 88-89; Dioc Stewardship Adv 88-93; P-in-c Westmill 89-93; rtd 93; Perm to Offic *Chich* 93-04 and *St Alb* 93-00. *147 Woodlands Lane, Chichester PO19 5PB* Tel (01243) 780206

GRUBB, Greville Alexander (Alex). b 36. Saltley Tr Coll Birm CertEd60 Leeds Univ DipPE61. St Jo Coll Nottm 72. **d** 74 **p** 75. C Rushden w Newton Bromswold *Pet* 74-77; Chapl St D Coll Llandudno 77-89; Chapl Casterton Sch Lancs 90-96; rtd 96; Perm to Offic *Blackb* from 96 and *Bradf* from 02. *Beckstones, 21 Littledale Road, Brookhouse, Lancaster LA2 9PH* Tel (01524) 770512

GRUNDY, Anthony Brian. b 36. Pemb Coll Cam BA62 MA87. Ridley Hall Cam 61. **d** 63 **p** 64. C Hatcham St Jas *S'wark* 63-66; C Margate H Trin *Cant* 66-68; C Brixton Hill St Sav *S'wark* 68-70; V Assington *St E* 70-76; TV Much Wenlock w Bourton *Heref* 76-81; TV Wenlock 81-82; TR 82-88; RD Condover 86-88; R Burghfield *Ox* 88-02; rtd 02. *29 Gerald Road, Worthing BN11 5QQ* Tel (01903) 507213

GRUNDY, Christopher John. b 49. ACA72. Trin Coll Bris 74. **d** 77 **p** 78. C Maidstone St Luke *Cant* 77-81; Argentina 81-82; Chile 82-84; Perm to Offic *Guildf* 84-96; NSM Guildf Ch Ch w St Martha-on-the-Hill 96-99; C Shere, Albury and Chilworth from 99. *The Vicarage, Brook Road, Chilworth, Guildford GU4 8ND* Tel (01483) 454070 E-mail chris@grundy.org.uk *or* chris@grundy49.fsnet.co.uk

GRUNDY, David. *See* GRUNDY, Julian David

GRUNDY, Jocelyn Pratchitt. b 22. Trin Coll Cam MA. Westcott Ho Cam 64. **d** 66 **p** 67. C Guildf H Trin w St Mary *Guildf* 66-68; R Shere 68-73; V Fleet 73-83; C Aldershot St Mich 83-87; rtd 87; Perm to Offic *Guildf* from 87. *Richmond Cottage, School Hill, Seale, Farnham GU10 1HY* Tel (01252) 782238

GRUNDY, Mrs Judith Michal Towers Mynors. b 54. Lady Spencer Chu Coll of Educn CertEd76 Ox Univ BEd77. Trin Coll Bris DipHE87. **d** 93 **p** 94. NSM Kensal Rise St Mark and St Martin *Lon* 93-95; NSM Snettisham w Ingoldisthorpe and Fring *Nor* 95-04; R Denver and Ryston w Roxham and W Dereham etc *Ely* from 04. *The Rectory, Ryston Road, Denver, Downham Market PE38 0DP* Tel (01366) 383226

GRUNDY, Julian David. b 60. St Andr Univ MA83. Trin Coll Bris BA88. **d** 89 **p** 90. C Lancaster St Thos *Blackb* 89-92; C Kensal Rise St Mark and St Martin *Lon* 92-95; R Snettisham w Ingoldisthorpe and Fring *Nor* 95-03. *The Rectory, Ryston Road, Denver, Downham Market PE38 0DP* Tel (01366) 387727 E-mail david@grundyd.fslife.co.uk

GRUNDY, Malcolm Leslie. b 44. AKC68 Open Univ BA76. **d** 69 **p** 70. C Doncaster St Geo *Sheff* 69-72; Ind Chapl 72-80; Dir of Educn *Lon* 80-86; TR Huntingdon *Ely* 86-91; Hon Can Ely Cathl 88-94; Dir Avec 91-94; Adn Craven *Bradf* 94-05; Dir Foundn for Ch Leadership from 05. *4 Portal Road, York YO26 6BQ* Tel (01904) 787387 E-mail director@churchleadershipfoundation.org

GRUNDY, Paul. b 55. BD77 AKC. Linc Th Coll 79. **d** 80 **p** 81. C Ryhope *Dur* 80-82; C Ferryhill 82-85; TV Cramlington *Newc* 85-87; TV Swinton and Pendlebury *Man* 87-90; V Wingate Grange *Dur* 90-95; R Willington and Sunnybrow from 95. *The Rectory, Willington, Crook DL15 0DE* Tel (01388) 746242

GRÜNEBERG, Keith Nigel. b 72. CCC Ox BA93 MA96 St Jo Coll Dur BA97. Cranmer Hall Dur 95. **d** 01 **p** 02. C Pangbourne w Tidmarsh and Sulham *Ox* 01-04; Dir Studies Dioc Bd Stewardship from 04. *47 Stockey End, Abingdon OX14 2NF* Tel (01235) 528661 E-mail keith.gruneberg@oxford.anglican.org

GRÜNEWALD, Gottfried Johannes. b 38. Loyola Univ Chicago MPS92. Th Faculty Frankfurt 66. **d** 69 **p** 69. Denmark 70-95; C Dunbar *Edin* 95-97; R Dollar *St And* 98-05; rtd 05. *Address temp unknown* E-mail gk.grunewald@virgin.net

GRYLLS, Ms Catherine Anne. b 70. **d** 00 **p** 01. C Hall Green St Pet *Birm* 00-04; P-in-c Balsall Heath St Paul from 04; P-in-c Edgbaston SS Mary and Ambrose from 04. *15 Raglan Road, Birmingham B5 7RA* Tel 0121-440 2196

GRYLLS, Canon Michael John. b 38. Qu Coll Cam BA62 MA66. Linc Th Coll 62. **d** 64 **p** 65. C Sheff Gillcar St Silas *Sheff* 64-67; C-in-c Dunscroft CD 67-70; V Herringthorpe 70-78; V Amport, Grateley, Monxton and Quarley *Win* 78-89; RD Andover 85-89; V Whitchurch w Tufton and Litchfield 89-03; Hon Can Win Cathl 01-03; rtd 03; Perm to Offic *Worc* from 04. *41 Church Street, Evesham WR11 1DY* Tel (01386) 442086

GUBBINS, Andrew Martin. b 65. York Univ BA86 Keele Univ 93. St Jo Coll Nottm LTh93. **d** 96 **p** 97. C Harrogate St Mark *Ripon* 96-00; P-in-c Osmondthorpe St Phil 00-03; V Leeds All SS w Osmondthorpe from 03. *St Philip's Vicarage, 68 Osmondthorpe Lane, Leeds LS9 9EF* Tel 0113-249 7371 E-mail gubbins@fish.co.uk

GUBBINS (née O'BRIEN), Mrs Mary. b 68. Leeds Univ BSc90. St Jo Coll Nottm BTh93. **d** 94 **p** 95. C Middleton St Mary *Ripon* 94-96; C Bilton 96-99; Perm to Offic from 99. *St Philip's Vicarage, 68 Osmondthorpe Lane, Leeds LS9 9EF* Tel 0113-249 7371

GUDGEON, Canon Michael John. b 40. Qu Coll Cam BA63 MA67. Chich Th Coll 65. **d** 66 **p** 67. C Kings Heath *Birm* 66-72; Asst Chapl K Edw Sch Birm 69-72; Chapl and Tutor Cuddesdon Coll 72-75; V Hawley H Trin *Guildf* 75-80; V Minley 75-80; Adult Educn Adv *Chich* 80-87; Can Res Portsm Cathl *Portsm* 87-90; Dioc Dir of Educn 87-90; V Hove St Thos *Chich* 90-93; TV Hove 93-94; Perm to Offic 94-98; Bp's Chapl *Eur* 94-98; Dir of Ords 94-97; Can Gib Cathl from 96; P-in-c Worthing St Andr *Chich* from 98. *St Andrew's Vicarage, 21 Victoria Road, Worthing BN11 1XB* Tel (01903) 233442 Fax as telephone E-mail michaelgudgeon@aol.com

GUERNSEY, Dean of. *See* MELLOR, The Very Revd Kenneth Paul

✠**GUERRERO, The Rt Revd Orlando.** b 45. Episc Sem of Ecuador. **p** 80 **c** 95. P Puerto la Cruz H Trin 80-93; Interim P Caracas St Mary 80-84; Bp Venezuela from 95. *Apartado 49-143, Avenida Caron 100, Colinas de Bello Monte, Caracas 1042-A, Venezuela* Tel (0058) (2) 753 0723 Fax 751 3180

GUEST, David. b 41. Dur Univ BA62. Coll of Resurr Mirfield 70. **d** 72 **p** 73. C Horsforth *Ripon* 72-75; C Richmond 75-76; C Richmond w Hudswell 76-78; R Middleham 78-81; R Middleham and Coverham w Horsehouse 81-86; V W Rainton and E Rainton *Dur* 86-03; RD Houghton 92-94 and 96-97; rtd 03. *Lindisfarne, 3 New Croft, Horsforth, Leeds LS18 4TD* Tel 0113-258 0521

GUEST, David Andrew. b 61. Portsm Coll of Tech NDTJ82. Chich Th Coll BTh92. **d** 92 **p** 93. C Prenton *Ches* 92-94; C Ches H Trin 94-97; Assoc P Douglas All SS and St Thos *S & M* 97-00; Dioc Communications Officer 97-00; Relig Adv Manx Radio 97-00; Bp's Dom Chapl 98-00; Dioc Communications Officer *Chich* from 00; C Hove 00-03; C Southwick St Mich 03-04; C Southwick from 04. *St Peter's House, 107A Gardner Road, Portslade, Brighton BN41 1PN* Tel (01273) 592125 *or* 421021 Fax 421041 E-mail david.guest@diochi.org.uk

GUEST, Derek William. b 55. N Ord Course 90. **d** 93 **p** 94. C Cheadle Hulme St Andr *Ches* 93-99; V from 99. *2 Orrishmere Road, Cheadle Hulme, Cheadle SK8 5HP* Tel 0161-486 9306 E-mail revdguest@yahoo.co.uk

GUEST, Ernest Anthony. b 64. NTMTC 99. **d** 02 **p** 03. C Gt Ilford St Jo *Chelmsf* from 02. *25 Valentines Road, Ilford IG1 4RZ* Tel (020) 8518 3982 Mobile 07810-516356 E-mail ernie@eguest.fsnet.co.uk

GUEST, Mrs Helen. b 54. Totley Thornbridge Coll CertEd75 Nottm Univ MA02. EMMTC 99. **d** 02 **p** 03. NSM Brimington *Derby* 02-05; C Hatton from 05. *2A Eaton Close, Hatton, Derby DE56 5ED* Tel (01283) 520424 E-mail revsguest@surefish.co.uk

GUEST, John. b 36. Trin Coll Bris 59. **d** 61 **p** 62. C Barton Hill St Luke w Ch Ch *Bris* 61-64; C Liv St Sav *Liv* 65-66; USA from 66; rtd 01. *30 Myrtle Hill Road, Sewickley, PA 15143, USA*

GUEST, John Andrew Kenneth. b 55. Univ of Wales (Lamp) BA78. Wycliffe Hall Ox 78. **d** 80 **p** 81. C Eastwood *S'well* 80-84; TV Toxteth St Philemon w St Gabr and St Cleopas *Liv* 84-89; C Cranham Park *Chelmsf* 89-93; P-in-c Stanford-le-Hope w Mucking 93-03; R from 03. *The Rectory, The Green, Stanford-le-Hope SS17 0EP* Tel (01375) 672271 E-mail gof4god@aol.com

GUEST, Michael. b 52. FTC73. EMMTC. **d** 99 **p** 00. NSM Heath *Derby* from 99. *33 Gloucester Road, Stonegravels, Chesterfield S41 7EF* Tel (01246) 230048

GUEST, Simon Llewelyn. b 56. Univ of Wales (Lamp) BA78 CertEd79. St Mich Coll Llan 83. **d** 85 **p** 86. C Bassaleg *Mon* 85-88; C Cwmbran 88-89; TV 89-91; V Raglan w Llandenny and Bryngwyn 91-05; V Rockfield and Dingestow Gp from 05; AD Raglan-Usk 01-05. *The Vicarage, Dingestow, Monmouth NP25 4DY* Tel (01600) 740206

GUEST-BLOFELD, Thomas. b 35. St D Coll Lamp BA59. Cranmer Hall Dur 59. **d** 62 **p** 63. C Maltby *Sheff* 62-63; C Goole 63-66; C Pocklington w Yapham-cum-Meltonby, Owsthorpe etc *York* 67-68; C Ely 68-70; C Pemberton St Jo *Liv* 70-72; V Walton St Jo 72-74; V Barkisland w W Scammonden *Wakef* 74-80; V Smallbridge *Man* 80-82; C Irlam 83-86; rtd 87. *Mooban Sahakorn, 102l5 Nong Han, S0170 M005, Amper San Sai, Chiang Mai 50290, Thailand*

GUILDFORD, Bishop of. *See* HILL, The Rt Revd Christopher John

GUILDFORD, Dean of. *See* STOCK, The Very Revd Victor Andrew

GUILFORD, John Edward. b 50. S & M Dioc Tr Inst 94. **d** 99 **p** 00. OLM Lonan *S & M* from 99; OLM Laxey from 99. *Tremissary House, Strathallan Road, Douglas, Isle of Man IM2 4PN* Tel and fax (01624) 672001 Mobile 07624-494274 E-mail revjohnnyg@manx.net

GUILLAN, Miss Barbara Doris. b 19. S'wark Ord Course 45. **d** 87. NSM St Stythians w Perranarworthal and Gwennap *Truro* 87-89; rtd 89; Perm to Offic *Truro* 89-94. *Address temp unknown*

GUILLE, The Ven John Arthur. b 49. Southn Univ BTh79. Sarum & Wells Th Coll 73. **d** 76 **p** 77. C Chandler's Ford *Win* 76-80; P-in-c Bournemouth St Jo 80-84; P-in-c Bournemouth St Mich 83-84; V Bournemouth St Jo w St Mich 84-89; R Guernsey St Andr 89-99; Adn Win from 99; Can Res Win Cathl from 99. *6 The Close, Winchester SO23 9LS* Tel (01962) 857263 *or* 857241 Fax 857242 E-mail john.guille@winchester-cathedral.org.uk

GUILLEBAUD, Mrs Jette Margaret. b 48. Ex Univ BA70 UWE Hon MA98 FRSA95. Ripon Coll Cuddesdon 03. **d** 05. NSM Sarum Cathl *Sarum* from 05. *The Dovecot, Mount Sorrel, Broad Chalke, Salisbury SP5 5HQ* Tel (01722) 781281 Mobile 07985-576739 E-mail maggieguillebaud@lycos.co.uk

GUILLEBAUD, Miss Margaret Jean. b 43. Edin Univ BSc66. All Nations Chr Coll DipRS79 Cranmer Hall Dur 79. **dss** 80 **d** 87 **p** 94. New Malden and Coombe *S'wark* 80-84; Carlton Colville w Mutford and Rushmere *Nor* 84-91; Par Dn 87-91; Par Dn Rodbourne Cheney *Bris* 91-94; C 94-95; Rwanda from 95. *BP 426, Kigali, Rwanda*

GUINNESS, Alexander. *See* GUINNESS, Graham Alexander

GUINNESS, Christopher Paul. b 43. Lon Coll of Div 64. **d** 67 **p** 68. C Farnborough *Guildf* 67-70; C Tulse Hill H Trin *S'wark* 70-74; C Worting *Win* 74-78; P-in-c S Lambeth St Steph *S'wark* 78-89; V 89-91; RD Lambeth 86-90; C Ches Square St Mich w St Phil *Lon* 91-97; Living Waters Trust 98-00; Chapl Ealing Hosp NHS Trust from 00. *Ealing Hospital, Uxbridge Road, Southall UB1 3HW* Tel (020) 8574 2444 *or* 8846 1041 Fax 8846 1056 E-mail chaplain@hhnt.org *or* lisa@goldsboro.fsnet.co.uk

GUINNESS, Canon Garry Grattan. b 40. Em Coll Cam BA64 MA68. Ridley Hall Cam 64. **d** 66 **p** 67. C Wallington H Trin *S'wark* 66-69; C St Marylebone All So w SS Pet and Jo *Lon* 69-72; P-in-c Clifton H Trin, St Andr and St Pet *Bris* 72-79; V Watford St Luke *St Alb* 79-90; TR Worthing Ch the King *Chich* 90-05; Hon Can Kigeme from 02; rtd 05. *37 Stowell Crescent, Wareham BH20 4PT* Tel (01929) 550215 E-mail gguinness@fish.co.uk

GUINNESS, Graham Alexander. b 60. Jordan Hill Coll Glas DCE82 Edin Univ LTh85. Edin Th Coll 82. **d** 85 **p** 86. Dioc Youth Chapl *Mor* 85-88; C Elgin w Lossiemouth 85-88; Asst P Glas St Ninian *Glas* 88-90; R Tighnabruaich *Arg* 90-91 and 94-99; R Dunoon 90-99; Miss to Seamen 90-99; R Fort William *Arg* from 99. *St Andrew's Rectory, Parade Road, Fort William PH33 6BA* Tel and fax (01397) 702979 E-mail ftwilliam@argyll.anglican.org

GUINNESS, Canon Peter Grattan. b 49. Man Univ BSc71 CertEd73. St Jo Coll Nottm 80. **d** 82 **p** 83. C Normanton *Wakef* 82-87; V Fletchamstead *Cov* 87-91; V Lancaster St Thos *Blackb* from 91; Hon Can Blackb Cathl from 04. *St Thomas's Vicarage, 33 Belle Vue Terrace, Lancaster LA1 4TY* Tel (01524) 590410 E-mail peter@st.tees.org.uk

GUINNESS, Canon Robin Gordon. b 38. St Jo Coll Cam MA61. Ridley Hall Cam 63. **d** 63 **p** 64. C Bedworth *Cov* 63-66; CMS 66-68; Canada from 68. *47 Prospect Street, Westmount PQ, Canada, H3Z 1W5* Tel (001) (514) 931 6796

GUISE, John Christopher. b 29. Cheltenham & Glouc Coll of HE MA94 MRPharmS51. WMMTC 80 Dip Miss87. **d** 83 **p** 84. NSM Alfrick, Lulsley, Suckley, Leigh and Bransford *Worc* 83-94; NSM Martley and Wichenford, Knightwick etc 94-00; Perm to Offic from 00. *Marsh Cottage, Leigh, Worcester WR6 5LE* Tel (01886) 832336

GUISE, Stephen. b 48. Win Sch of Art BA75. Chich Th Coll 85. **d** 87 **p** 88. C Bexhill St Pet *Chich* 87-90; TV Haywards Heath St Wilfrid 90-94; V Kirdford 94-97; Chapl Community of Servants of the Cross 97-01; P-in-c Amberley w N Stoke and Parham, Wiggonholt etc *Chich* 99-03; TV Bridport *Sarum* from 03. *Allington Vicarage, Parsonage Road, Bridport DT6 5ET* Tel (01308) 424698 E-mail s.guise@amserve.com

GUITE, Ayodeji Malcolm. b 57. Pemb Coll Cam BA80 MA84 Newc Poly PGCE82 Dur Univ PhD93. Ridley Hall Cam 88. **d** 90 **p** 91. C Ely 90-93; TV Huntingdon 93-98; Chapl Anglia Poly Univ 98-03; Chapl Girton Coll Cam from 03. *Girton College, Cambridge CB3 0JG* Tel (01223) 338999 E-mail mg320@cam.ac.uk

GUITE, Canon Margaret Ann. b 53. Girton Coll Cam BA74 MA78 St Jo Coll Dur PhD81. Cranmer Hall Dur 75. **dss** 79 **d** 87 **p** 94. Warlingham w Chelsham and Farleigh *S'wark* 79-82; Cherry Hinton St Jo *Ely* 82-86; Tutor Westcott Ho Cam 82-90; Tutor Wesley Ho Cam 87-90; NSM Ely 90-93; NSM Chettisham 90-93; NSM Prickwillow 90-93; NSM Huntingdon 93-99; V Fenstanton from 99; V Hilton from 99; Hon Can Ely Cathl from 04; RD Huntingdon from 05. *The Vicarage, 16 Church Street, Fenstanton, Huntingdon PE28 9JL* Tel (01480) 463334 E-mail mguite@bigfoot.com

GUIVER, Paul Alfred (George). b 45. St Chad's Coll Dur BA68. Cuddesdon Coll 71. **d** 73 **p** 74. C Mill End and Heronsgate w W Hyde *St Alb* 73-76; P-in-c Bishop's Frome *Heref* 76-82; P-in-c Castle Frome 76-82; P-in-c Acton Beauchamp and Evesbatch 76-82; CR from 85; Superior from 02; Lic to Offic *Wakef* from 85. *House of the Resurrection, Stocks Bank Road, Mirfield WF14 0BN* Tel (01924) 483301 E-mail gguiver@mirfield.org.uk

GUIVER, Roger William Antony. b 53. Edin Univ MA75 St Chad's Coll Dur BA78. Coll of Resurr Mirfield. **d** 82 **p** 83. C

Rekendyke *Dur* 82-85; Chapl Middlesbrough Gen Hosp 85-93; P-in-c Middlesbrough St Columba w St Paul *York* 85-94; V Acomb Moor 94-97; V Middlesbrough St Thos 97-00. *Swang Farm, Glaisdale, Whitby YO21 2QZ* Tel (01947) 897210

GULL, William John. b 42. Ripon Hall Ox 63. **d** 65 **p** 66. C Worksop Priory *S'well* 65-69; C Newark St Mary 69-71; P-in-c Mansfield St Lawr 71-77; V 77-78; Chapl HM YOI Lowdham Grange 78-90; R Lambley *S'well* 78-91; V Sneinton St Cypr 91-99; rtd 99; Perm to Offic *S'well* from 03. *37 Hazel Grove, Mapperley, Nottingham NG3 6DQ* Tel 0115-920 8071 E-mail wjgull@btopenworld.com

GULLAND, John Robertson. b 46. ACIB Avery Hill Coll CertEd70 Open Univ BA76 Chelsea Coll Lon MA82. Oak Hill Th Coll 88. **d** 90 **p** 91. NSM Woodside Park St Barn *Lon* 90-92; Lic to Offic *S & M* from 91; NSM Castletown from 92; Chapl K Wm Coll from 92. *Anchor House, Queens Road, Port St Mary, Isle of Man IM9 5ES* Tel (01624) 834548

GULLIDGE, Philip Michael Nowell. b 60. Univ of Wales (Swansea) BSc82 Univ of Wales (Cardiff) BD93. St Mich Coll Llan 90. **d** 93 **p** 94. C Neath w Llantwit *Llan* 93-97; V Treharris w Bedlinog 97-03; V Treharris, Trelewis and Bedlinog from 04. *The Vicarage, 13 The Oaks, Quakers Yard, Treharris CF46 5HQ* Tel (01443) 410280

GULLIFORD, Mrs Susan Diane. b 49. W Midl Coll of Educn BEd86. WMMTC 97. **d** 00 **p** 01. NSM Tettenhall Regis *Lich* 00-02; C Wednesfield 02-04; Perm to Offic from 04. *2 James Street, Willenhall WV13 1SS* E-mail sue.gulliford@btinternet.com

GULLIFORD, William Douglas FitzGerald. b 69. Selw Coll Cam BA91 MA95. Westcott Ho Cam. **d** 94 **p** 95. C Banstead *Guildf* 94-97; C Wilton Place St Paul *Lon* 97-00; Chapl Guildhall Sch of Music and Drama 97-01; P-in-c St Dunstan in the West from 00; Gen Sec Angl and E Churches Assn from 00; Bp's Chapl *Lon* 00-02; R St Mary le Strand w St Clem Danes from 02; Bp's Chapl for E Orthodox Affairs from 02; Dioc Dir of Ords *Eur* from 03. *184A Fleet Street, London EC4A 2HD* Tel and fax (020) 7405 1929 E-mail william.gulliford@london.anglican.org

GULLY, Mrs Carol Glenys. b 57. Coll of Ripon & York St Jo BEd79. N Ord Course 02. **d** 05. NSM Castleton Moor *Man* from 05. *The Vicarage, 389 Bury and Rochdale Old Road, Heywood OL10 4AT* Tel (01706) 369610 E-mail revdcggully@aol.com

GULLY, Paul David. b 59. Shoreditch Coll Lon BEd81. Trin Coll Bris BA95. **d** 95 **p** 96. C Radcliffe *Man* 95-99; TV New Bury from 99; P-in-c Rochdale St Geo w St Alb from 05; P-in-c Bamford from 05. *The Vicarage, 389 Bury and Rochdale Old Road, Heywood OL10 4AT* Tel (01706) 369610 E-mail revdpaulgully@aol.com

GULVIN, Philip Christopher. b 53. BSc76. St Jo Coll Nottm 82. **d** 85 **p** 86. C Northwood H Trin *Lon* 85-89; TV Sanderstead All SS *S'wark* 89-96; V Croydon St Matt 96-99; C W Wickham St Fran 99-02; C W Wickham St Fran and St Mary 02-04; rtd 04. *The Vicarage, 2 The Grove, West Wickham BR4 9JS* Tel (020) 8777 6010 E-mail gulvip@aol.com

GUMBEL, Nicholas Glyn Paul. b 55. Trin Coll Cam MA76 BA85. Wycliffe Hall Ox 83. **d** 86 **p** 87. C Brompton H Trin w Onslow Square St Paul *Lon* from 86. *13 Macaulay Road, London SW4 0QP* Tel (020) 7498 1472 *or* 7052 0263 E-mail juliet.sloggett@htb.org.uk

GUMMER, Dudley Harrison. b 28. Roch Th Coll 61. **d** 63 **p** 64. C Deptford St Paul *S'wark* 63-65; C Melton Mowbray w Thorpe Arnold *Leic* 65-68; C-in-c E Goscote CD 68-75; V E Goscote 75-78; V Luton St Anne *St Alb* 78-88; R Albury w St Martha *Guildf* 88-95; rtd 95; Perm to Offic *Chich* from 95; *Portms* from 03. *Wyndham House, The Gardens, West Ashling, Chichester PO18 8DX* Tel (01243) 573002

GUNN, Jeffrey Thomas. b 47. St Chad's Coll Dur BA77 Kent Univ MA95. Coll of Resurr Mirfield 77. **d** 79 **p** 80. C Prestbury *Glouc* 79-82; P-in-c Coldham, Elm and Friday Bridge *Ely* 82-87; V Larkfield *Roch* 87-94; P-in-c Leybourne 87-94; V Petts Wood 94-99; Dean Ballarat Australia 99-04; V Eastbourne St Sav and St Pet *Chich* from 05. *St Saviour's Vicarage, Spencer Road, Eastbourne BN21 4PA* Tel (01323) 722317

GUNN, Robert. b 35. Oak Hill Th Coll 59. **d** 62 **p** 63. C Upper Holloway St Jo *Lon* 62-66; C Woking St Jo *Guildf* 66-69; Scripture Union 69-71; R Necton w Holme Hale *Nor* 71-77; V Tottenham St Jo *Lon* 77-81; V Gt Cambridge Road St Jo and St Jas 82-85; V Luton St Fran *St Alb* 85-90; Chapl Luton Airport 90-95; rtd 95; Perm to Offic *St Alb* from 95. *95 Edgewood Drive, Luton LU2 8ER* Tel (01582) 416151

GUNN-JOHNSON, The Ven David Allan. b 49. Lambeth STh85 MA95. St Steph Ho Ox 79. **d** 81 **p** 82. C Oxhey St Matt *St Alb* 81-84; C Cheshunt 84-88; TR Colyton, Southleigh, Offwell, Widworthy etc *Ex* 88-03; RD Honiton 90-96; Preb Ex Cathl 99-03; Adn Barnstaple from 03; Dioc Warden of Readers from 04. *Stage Cross, Sanders Lane, Bishops Tawton, Barnstaple EX32 0BE* Tel (01271) 375475 Fax 377934 E-mail archdeacon.of.barnstaple@exeter.anglican.org

GUNNER, Canon Laurence François Pascal. b 36. Keble Coll Ox BA59 MA63. Wells Th Coll 59. **d** 61 **p** 62. C Charlton Kings St Mary *Glouc* 61-65; C Hemel Hempstead *St Alb* 65-69; Chapl Bloxham Sch 69-86; Sen Chapl Marlborough Coll 86-96; Can Windsor from 96; Steward from 97. *6 The Cloisters, Windsor Castle, Windsor SL4 1NJ* Tel (01753) 848767 E-mail laurence.gunner@stgeorges-windsor.org

GUNSTONE, Canon John Thomas Arthur. b 27. St Chad's Coll Dur BA48 MA55. Coll of Resurr Mirfield 50. **d** 52 **p** 53. C Walthamstow St Jas Gt *Chelmsf* 52-53; C Forest Gate St Edm 53-58; C-in-c Rush Green St Aug CD 58-71; Chapl Barn Fellowship Winterborne Whitechurch 71-75; Tutor Sarum & Wells Th Coll 71-75; Sec Gtr Man Co Ecum Coun 75-92; Lic to Offic *Man* 75-80; Hon Can Man Cathl 80-92; rtd 92; Perm to Offic *Man* 03. *12 Deneford Road, Didsbury, Manchester M20 2TD* Tel 0161-434 8351

GUNTER, Timothy Wilson. b 37. Leeds Univ BA59 St Jo Coll Cam BA62 MA66. Ridley Hall Cam 59. **d** 62 **p** 63. C Beverley Minster *York* 62-65; C Hornsea and Goxhill 65-70; V Silsden *Bradf* 70-80; V Sunninghill *Ox* 80-03; rtd 03; Perm to Offic *Worc* from 04. *2 Hillstone Court, Victoria Road, Malvern WR14 2TE* Tel (01684) 899377 E-mail gunters@gmail.com

GUNYON, Stephen Francis. b 14. Selw Coll Cam BA38 MA48. Linc Th Coll 38. **d** 40 **p** 41. C Greenhill St Jo *Lon* 40-43; SSF 43-44; CF 44-48; C Westmr St Steph w St Jo *Lon* 48-50; V Thornaby on Tees St Paul *York* 50-57; Res Chapl Middx Hosp Lon 57-66; Gen Sec Hosp Chapl Fellowship 57-66; V Hinchley Wood *Guildf* 66-71; V Hindhead 71-80; rtd 80; Perm to Offic *Pet* 80-94. *c/o Mrs M M Hayns, 4 The Gateway, Sicklesmere Road, Bury St Edmunds IP33 2BN*

GUPPY, Kenneth Henry Stanley. b 29. Univ of Wales (Lamp) BA54. St Mich Coll Llan 54. **d** 56 **p** 57. C Rumney *Mon* 56-61; Chapl Shirley Ho Sch Watford 61-63; V Llangwm Uchaf and Llangwm Isaf w Gwernesney etc *Mon* 63-85; rtd 85; Lic to Offic *Ox* 88-92; Perm to Offic *B & W* 94-00. *11 St Thomas's Court, Woodbury Avenue, Wells BA5 2XY*

GURD, Brian Charles (Simon). b 44. Sarum & Wells Th Coll 72. **d** 74 **p** 75. OSP from 67; Lic to Offic *Win* 74-82; Prior Alton Abbey 79-82; C Shepherd's Bush St Steph w St Thos *Lon* 82-84; NSM Willesborough *Cant* 85-87; V Bethersden w High Halden 87-95; R Etchingham *Chich* 95-97; V Hurst Green 95-97; V Langney 97-01; R Yarm *York* from 01. *The Rectory, 6 Westgate, Yarm TS15 9BU* Tel (01642) 781115

GURDON, Mrs June Mary. b 38. Sarum Th Coll 83. **dss** 86 **d** 87 **p** 94. Jersey St Sav *Win* 85-86; Jersey St Mary 86-88; Par Dn 87-88; Par Dn Jersey St Brelade 88-94 and from 94. *The Glade, La rue des Pres, Jersey JE3 3EH* Tel (01534) 864282

GURNEY, Miss Ann. b 27. Lon Univ DipTh48 STh92. Gilmore Ho 45. **dss** 54 **d** 87 **p** 94. Lewisham St Jo Southend *S'wark* 54-56; Warden Berridge Ho Coll of Educn 56-59; Prin Gilmore Ho 59-70; Bp's Adv for Lay Min *Lon* 70-87; rtd 87; Hon C Eltham H Trin *S'wark* 94-98; Perm to Offic from 98. *3 Brecon Court, Greenacres, London SE9 5BG* Tel (020) 8850 4083

GURNEY, Canon Dennis Albert John. b 31. OBE02. Lon Coll of Div. **d** 67 **p** 68. C Boscombe St Jo *Win* 67-69; V Hurstbourne Tarrant and Faccombe 70-77; R Jersey St Ouen w St Geo 77-84; Hon Chapl Miss to Seafarers from 84; Chapl ICS UAE 84-01; Can Bahrain from 98; rtd 01; Perm to Offic *Ex* and *B & W* from 02. *3 Stevens Cross Close, Sidford, Sidmouth EX10 9QJ* Tel (01395) 515362 Mobile 07789-111226

GURR, Mrs Mary Sandra. b 42. St Alb and Ox Min Course 95. **d** 98 **p** 99. C Easthampstead *Ox* 98-02; TV High Wycombe from 02. *The Vicarage, 245 Micklefield Road, High Wycombe HP13 7HU* Tel (01494) 520323 E-mail marygurr@stmichaelshouse.freeserve.co.uk

GURR, Ralph Sydney. b 27. AKC55. **d** 57 **p** 58. C Lewisham St Mary *S'wark* 57-63; Chapl Lewisham Hosp 61-63; C Cheam *S'wark* 63-69; V Wyke *Bradf* 69-72; V Edmonton St Mich *Lon* 72-79; R Fordingbridge w Ibsley *Win* 79-82; V Fordingbridge 82-84; C N Stoneham 84-94; P-in-c 89-90; rtd 94; Perm to Offic *Win* from 94. *1 Grosvenor Mansions, Grosvenor Square, Polygon, Southampton SO15 2GQ* Tel (023) 8033 9243

GURR, Stephen John. b 72. Kent Univ BA94. Trin Coll Bris MLitt94. **d** 97 **p** 98. C Ore *Chich* 97-00; C Goring-by-Sea 00-03; V Findon w Clapham and Patching from 03. *The Rectory, School Hill, Findon, Worthing BN14 0TR* Tel (01903) 873601

GUSH, Laurence Langley. b 23. Lon Univ BSc44. NW Ord Course 73. **d** 76 **p** 77. NSM Sheff St Matt *Sheff* 76-82; NSM Aston cum Aughton 82-84; NSM Aston cum Aughton and Ulley 84-89; rtd 89. *3 New Court, Eyam, Hope Valley S32 5RL* Tel (01433) 631818

GUSSMAN, Canon Robert William Spencer Lockhart. b 50. Ch Ch Ox BA72 MA76. Coll of Resurr Mirfield BA74. **d** 75 **p** 76. C Pinner *Lon* 75-79; C Northolt W End St Jos 79-81; P-in-c Sutton *Ely* 81-82; V 82-89; P-in-c Witcham w Mepal 81-82; R 82-89; RD Ely 86-89; V Alton St Lawr *Win* 89-02; Hon Can Win Cathl 99-02; rtd 02; Perm to Offic *Win* from 02. *6A Patrick's Close, Liss GU33 7ER* Tel (01730) 893545

GUTHRIE, Adrian Malcolm. b 57. Goldsmiths' Coll Lon BEd80. Wycliffe Hall Ox 01. **d** 03 **p** 04. C Ickenham *Lon* 03-05; R from 05. *St Giles's Rectory, 38 Swakeley's Road, Ickenham, Uxbridge UB10 8BE* Tel (01895) 622970 E-mail am.guthrie@virgin.net

GUTHRIE, Nigel. b 60. LRAM78 ARCO80 ARCM81 Bris Univ BA82 Ox Univ BA87 MA91. Ripon Coll Cuddesdon 85. **d** 88 **p** 89. C Cov St Jo *Cov* 88-91; Chapl Cov Cathl 91-94; V Chellaston *Derby* 94-02; RD Melbourne 99-02; R Crediton, Shobrooke and Sandford etc *Ex* from 02. *The Vicarage, Church Street, Crediton EX17 2AQ* Tel (01363) 772669 *or* 773226

GUTSELL, Canon David Leonard Nicholas. b 35. Sheff Univ BA59 LTh74. ALCD61. **d** 61 **p** 62. C Clapham Common St Barn *S'wark* 61-65; V Upper Tulse Hill St Matthias 65-76; RD Clapham and Brixton 74-75; V Patcham *Chich* 76-93; Can and Preb Chich Cathl 89-00; V Polegate 93-00; rtd 00; C Peacehaven and Telscombe Cliffs *Chich* 01-05; C Southease 01-05; C Piddinghoe 01-05; Perm to Offic from 05. *30 Balsdean Road, Brighton BN2 6PF* Tel (01273) 301085 E-mail gutselldln@davidln.fsnet.co.uk

GUTSELL, Eric Leslie. b 44. Goldsmiths' Coll Lon TCert65 Ox Univ Special Dip Educn Studies 87. Ox NSM Course 79. **d** 82 **p** 83. NSM Gt Faringdon w Lt Coxwell *Ox* 82-88; NSM Shrivenham w Watchfield and Bourton 82-99; Asst Chapl HM Pris Wormwood Scrubs 99-00; Chapl HM Pris Coldingley 00-03; Chapl HM Pris Erlestoke 03-04; rtd 04. *54 Folly View Road, Faringdon SN7 7DH* Tel (01367) 240886 E-mail ericgutsell@virgin.net

GUTTERIDGE, David Frank. b 39. Man Univ BSc61 Lon Inst of Educn PGCE62 DipEd67 Birkbeck Coll Lon MSc73. WMMTC 82. **d** 85 **p** 87. NSM Droitwich *Worc* 85-87; NSM Droitwich Spa 87-93; C Shrawley, Witley, Astley and Abberley 93-98; Chapl Abberley Hall Sch Worc 93-97; Dioc Tertiary Educn Officer *Worc* 97-99; NSM Ombersley w Doverdale 98-99; TV Malvern Link w Cowleigh 99-02; rtd 02. *79 Tan House Lane, Malvern WR14 1LQ* Tel (01886) 833578 E-mail dgutteridge@cofe-worcester.org.uk

GUTTERIDGE, John. b 34. Oak Hill Th Coll 60. **d** 63 **p** 64. C Deptford St Luke *S'wark* 63-66; C Southgate *Chich* 66-70; P-in-c Brixton Road Ch Ch *S'wark* 70-73; P-in-c Manuden w Berden *Chelmsf* 73-76; Distr Sec (N Lon, Herts and Essex) BFBS 76-82; Hon C Walthamstow St Gabr 79-82; V 82-95; Chapl Thorpe Coombe Psycho-Geriatric Hosp 83-95; rtd 95; Perm to Offic *Chelmsf* from 95. *52 Hatch Road, Pilgrims Hatch, Brentwood CM15 9PX* Tel (01277) 375401 E-mail john_gutteridge@hotmail.com

GUTTERIDGE, John Philip. b 52. QUB BA74. Chich Th Coll 75. **d** 78 **p** 79. C Leeds St Aid *Ripon* 78-82; C Manston 82-85; P-in-c Beeston Hill H Spirit 85-00; Perm to Offic from 03. *4 Amberton Garth, Leeds LS8 3JW*

GUTTRIDGE (née EVANS), Mrs Frances Margaret Bethan. b 54. Reading Univ BSc75 Univ of Wales (Cardiff) PGCE76. STETS. **d** 00 **p** 01. C Weston-super-Mare St Andr Bournville *B & W* 00-04; V from 04. *7 Boundary Close, Weston-super-Mare BS23 4LY* Tel (01934) 627818 Mobile 07778-137454 E-mail bethanguttridge@hotmail.com

GUTTRIDGE, John Arthur. b 26. Trin Hall Cam BA51 MA55. Westcott Ho Cam 51. **d** 53 **p** 54. C Rugby St Andr *Cov* 53-59; Lect Wells Th Coll 59-61; Chapl 61-63; Vice-Prin 63-66; Bp's Dom Chapl *Wakef* 66-68; Dir Post-Ord Tr 66-68; Dir of Further Tr *Dur* 68-74; Dir Studies Sarum & Wells Th Coll 74-78; C Bilston St Leon *Lich* 78-79; TV Bilston 80-84; V Wall 84-90; V Stonnall 84-90; rtd 91. *The Charterhouse, Charterhouse Square, London EC1M 6AN* Tel (020) 7251 6357

GUTWEIN, Martin. b 45. Hobart Coll (NY) BA67. Episc Th Sch Cam Mass MA69 MDiv72. **d** 72 **p** 72. USA 72-78 and from 80; C Toxteth St Marg *Liv* 78-80. *527 North 2nd Street, Camden, NJ 08102, USA* Tel (001) (856) 365 2664 *or* 365 5880

GUY, Mrs Alison. b 43. CQSW69. WMMTC 95. **d** 98 **p** 99. NSM Minchinhampton *Glouc* 98-04; P-in-c Bisley, Chalford, France Lynch, and Oakridge from 04. *7 Tooke Road, Minchinhampton, Stroud GL6 9DA* Tel (01453) 883906 E-mail alisonguy@metronet.co.uk

GUY, Ian Towers. b 47. Newc Univ MB, BS70 MSc89 MRCGP. NEOC. **d** 83 **p** 84. NSM Saltburn-by-the-Sea *York* 83-88; NSM Skelton w Upleatham 88-92; Perm to Offic from 92. *14 North Terrace, Skelton-in-Cleveland, Saltburn-by-the-Sea TS12 2ES* Tel (01287) 650309 Mobile 07092-298033 E-mail ian.guy@gp-a81630.nhs.uk

GUY, John Richard. *See* MORGAN-GUY, John Richard

GUY, Kate Anne. b 26. LNSM course 87. **d** 88 **p** 94. OLM Welton *Linc* 88-92; OLM Welton and Dunholme w Scothern 92-96; Perm to Offic 96-02. *2 Eastfield Close, Welton, Lincoln LN2 3NB* Tel (01673) 860285

GUY, Peter-John. b 71. Bournemouth Univ BA93. Oak Hill Th Coll BA03. **d** 03 **p** 04. C Eastbourne All So *Chich* from 03. *Wellesley House, Longstone Road, Eastbourne BN21 3SL* Tel (01323) 749915 E-mail pjgerdaguy@hotmail.com

GUY, Simon Edward Walrond. b 39. St Andr Univ MA61. St D Coll Lamp LTh67. **d** 67 **p** 68. C Bris St Mary Redcliffe w Temple etc *Bris* 67-68; C Knowle St Martin 68-71; C Bishopston 71-75; V Westwood *Sarum* 75-81; TV Melksham 81-82; TV Wednesfield *Lich* 82-90; R Heaton Moor *Man* 90-02; P-in-c Heaton Norris Ch w All SS 99-01; TV Heatons 02-04; rtd 04. *1 Holley Close, Exminster, Exeter EX6 8SS* Tel (01392) 823084 E-mail sewguy@supanet.com

GUYANA, Bishop of. *See* GEORGE, The Rt Revd Randolph Oswald

GUYMER, Canon Raymond John. b 41. AKC64. **d** 65 **p** 66. C W Bromwich All SS *Lich* 65-70; Chapl HM Pris Wormwood Scrubs 70-71; Chapl HM Borstal Portland 71-78; Chapl HM Youth Cust Cen Hollesley Bay Colony 78-84; Chapl HM Pris Wormwood Scrubs 84-93; Chapl HM Pris Win 93-01; Hon Can Win Cathl *Win* from 99; Hon C Upper Itchen from 02. *24 Arle Close, Alresford SO24 9BG* Tel (01962) 734022

GWILLIAM, Christopher. b 44. St Chad's Coll Dur BA65 DipTh67. **d** 67 **p** 68. C Chepstow *Mon* 67-70; C Risca 70-72; V Cwmtillery 72-75; V Hartlepool St Oswald *Dur* 75-82; Relig Progr Producer Radio Tees 82-87; C Stockton w St Jo 82-83; R Longnewton w Elton 83-87; Relig Progr Producer Radio Nottm *S'well* 87-93; Relig Progr Producer BBC Network Radio 93-95; rtd 04. *13 Kilburn Road, Stockton-on-Tees TS18 4HA* Tel (01642) 614205 E-mail gwilliam@nildram.co.uk

GWILLIAMS (formerly HARTLEY), Mrs Dianna Lynn. b 57. California Univ BA78 K Coll Lon MA01. S'wark Ord Course 89. **d** 92 **p** 94. NSM Peckham St Sav *S'wark* 92-97; C Dulwich St Barn 97-99; V from 99; AD Dulwich from 05; Chapl Alleyn's Foundn Dulwich from 99. *St Barnabas's Vicarage, 38 Calton Avenue, London SE21 7DG* Tel (020) 8693 1524 *or* 8693 2936 Fax 8693 0203 E-mail dgwilliams@stbarnabasdulwich.com

GWILLIM, Allan John. b 51. Coll of Resurr Mirfield 87. **d** 89 **p** 90. C Skerton St Luke *Blackb* 89-94; P-in-c Ellel 94-98; V Fleetwood St Pet from 98. *St Peter's Vicarage, 39 Mount Road, Fleetwood FY7 6EX* Tel (01253) 771642

GWILT, Stephen Gary. b 59. **d** 88 **p** 89. S Africa 88-94; Chapl Glouc Docks Mariners' Ch *Glouc* 95-00; C Moreton *Ches* 00-03; R High Halstow w All Hallows and Hoo St Mary *Roch* from 03. *The Rectory, 2 Cooling Road, High Halstow, Rochester ME3 8SA* Tel (01634) 250637

GWINN, Brian Harvey. b 35. MIQA75. St Alb Minl Tr Scheme 83. **d** 86 **p** 87. NSM Wheathampstead *St Alb* 86-88; Ind Chapl 88-95; RD Hatfield 93-95; P-in-c Watton at Stone 95-99; P-in-c Bramfield w Stapleford and Waterford 96-99; R Bramfield, Stapleford, Waterford etc 99-01; rtd 01; Perm to Offic *St Alb* from 01. *32 Wick Avenue, Wheathampstead, St Albans AL4 8QB* Tel (01582) 629903 Mobile 07966-469754 E-mail gwinns@ntlworld.com

GWYNN, Phillip John. b 57. Univ of Wales BA87 Univ of Wales (Cardiff) DPS89. St Mich Coll Llan 87. **d** 89 **p** 90. C Clydach *S & B* 89-93; V Swansea St Thos and Kilvey 93-00; V Tycoch from 00; Hon Chapl Miss to Seafarers from 93. *The Vicarage, 26 Hendrefoilan Road, Swansea SA2 9LS* Tel and fax (01792) 204476 Mobile 07803-059629 E-mail rev.gwynn@virgin.net

GWYNNE, Robert Durham. b 44. Birm Univ DipTh70. Qu Coll Birm 67. **d** 70 **p** 72. C N Hammersmith St Kath *Lon* 70-75; C Ramsey *Ely* 76-78; TV Old Brumby *Linc* 78-81; P-in-c Goxhill and Thornton Curtis 81-83; C Edmonton All SS w St Mich *Lon* 83-84; rtd 86. *127 Eastfield Road, Louth LN11 7AS* Tel (01507) 600966

GWYTHER, Canon Geoffrey David. b 51. St D Coll Lamp DipTh73. **d** 74 **p** 75. C Pembroke Dock *St D* 74-77; C Milford Haven 77-81; V Llawhaden w Bletherston and Llanycefn 81-88; R Prendergast w Rudbaxton from 88; RD Daugleddau from 01; Can St D Cathl from 01. *Prendergast Rectory, 5 Cherry Grove, Haverfordwest SA61 2NT* Tel (01437) 762625

GWYTHER, Ronald Lloyd. b 23. Lon Univ BA85 Southn Univ MA97. St Fran Coll Brisbane ThL47. **d** 47 **p** 48. Australia 48-50; Perm to Offic *Ox* 50-51; Australia 51-56; C Broadstairs *Cant* 56-60; R Pinxton *Derby* 60-73; CF (TA) 71-88; V Swanley St Mary *Roch* 73-89; rtd 89; Perm to Offic *Portsm* from 89. *St Helen's, 20 Maylings Farm Road, Fareham PO16 7QU* Tel (01329) 230990

GYLE, Alan Gordon. b 65. Aber Univ MA87 Ox Univ BA91 FRSA99. St Steph Ho Ox. **d** 92 **p** 93. C Acton Green *Lon* 92-94; Min Can, Succ and Dean's V Windsor 94-99; Chapl Imp Coll and R Coll of Art 99-04; P-in-c Wilton Place St Paul *Lon* 01-03; V from 03. *St Paul's Vicarage, 32 Wilton Place, London SW1X 8SH* Tel and fax (020) 7201 9990 *or* tel 7201 9999 E-mail alan@stpaulsknightsbridge.org

GYLES, Ms Sonia. b 76. TCD BTh01. CITC 98. **d** 01 **p** 02. C Taney *D & G* 01-04; I Dublin Sandford w Milltown from 04. *The Rectory, Sandford Close, Ranelagh, Dublin 6, Irish Republic* Tel (00353) (1) 497 2983 Fax 496 4789 E-mail sgyles@eircom.net

GYTON, Robert Wilfred. b 21. N Ord Course. **d** 78 **p** 79. NSM Repps *Nor* 78-79; C Trunch 79-83; TV 83-88; rtd 88; Perm to Offic *Nor* 88-94 and from 97; P-in-c Castleacre w Newton, Rougham and Southacre 94-97. *Yamato, 47 Fir Park, Ashill, Thetford IP25 7DE* Tel (01760) 440305

H

HAARHOFF, Robert Russell. b 46. St Paul's Coll Grahamstown 89 Th Ext Educn Coll 91. **d** 90 **p** 91. Zimbabwe 91-02; Harare Cathl 91-94; I Makonde 94-02; P-in-c Astley, Clive, Grinshill and Hadnall *Lich* from 02. *The Vicarage, Shrewsbury Road, Hadnall, Shrewsbury SY4 4AG* Tel (01939) 210241 E-mail robhaarhoff@tiscali.co.uk

HABERMEHL, Canon Kenneth Charles. b 22. Em Coll Cam BA46 MA48. Chich Th Coll 47. **d** 49 **p** 50. C Luton St Chris Round Green CD *St Alb* 49-53; C Luton Ch Ch 53-56; V Caddington 56-65; V Kempston All SS 65-87; Hon Can St Alb 81-87; rtd 87; Perm to Offic *St Alb* 87-93 and from 00. *34 Bedford Road, Aspley Guise, Milton Keynes MK17 8DH* Tel (01908) 584710

HABERSHON, Kenneth Willoughby. b 35. MBE01. New Coll Ox BA57 MA60 DipTh58. Wycliffe Hall Ox 57. **d** 59 **p** 60. C Finchley Ch Ch *Lon* 59-66; Sec CYFA 66-74; CPAS Staff 74-90; Hon C Slaugham *Chich* from 84; Ldr Mayfield CYFA 90-00; Sec Ch Patr Trust and Peache Trustees from 90; rtd 00. *Truckers Ghyll, Horsham Road, Handcross, Haywards Heath RH17 6DT* Tel (01444) 400274 Fax 401293

✠HABGOOD, The Rt Revd and Rt Hon Lord (John Stapylton). b 27. PC83. K Coll Cam BA48 MA51 PhD52 Dur Univ Hon DD75 Cam Univ Hon DD84 Aber Univ Hon DD88 Huron Coll Hon DD90. Cuddesdon Coll 53. **d** 54 **p** 55 **c** 73. C Kensington St Mary Abbots w St Geo *Lon* 54-56; Vice-Prin Westcott Ho Cam 56-62; R Jedburgh *Edin* 62-67; Prin Qu Coll Birm 67-73; Hon Can Birm Cathl *Birm* 71-73; Bp Dur 73-83; Abp York 83-95; rtd 95. *18 The Mount, Malton YO17 7ND*

HABGOOD, Simon. *See* LAWRENCE, Simon Peter

HABGOOD, Stephen Roy. b 52. Univ of Wales (Cardiff) DipTh77 Open Univ MBA95 Fitzw Coll Cam MSt01. St Mich Coll Llan 75. **d** 77 **p** 78. C Whitchurch *Llan* 77-80; Perm to Offic *Worc* 85-91. *Yew Tree Cottage, Wharf Road, Gnosall, Stafford ST20 0DA* Tel (01785) 824244

HABIBY, Canon Samir Jamil. b 33. Phillips Univ BA55 MA56. Ch Div Sch of Pacific MDiv58 Episc Th Sem Kentucky DD. **d** 58 **p** 59. R Hinesville St Phil USA 58-98 and from 04; P-in-c Lausanne *Eur* 98-04; rtd 04. *24 Sawyers Crossing Road, Swanzey, NH 03446, USA* Tel and fax (001) (603) 357 8778

HACK, Canon Rex Hereward. b 28. ACA56 FCA67 Pemb Coll Cam BA50 MA56. Ripon Hall Ox 58. **d** 59 **p** 60. C Ashton-upon-Mersey St Mary *Ches* 59-62; C Ellesmere Port 62-65; V Norton Cuckney *S'well* 65-69; V Bramhall *Ches* 69-93; RD Cheadle 87-92; Hon Can Ches Cathl 90-93; rtd 93; Perm to Offic *Ches* from 93. *Marshmead, 8A Pownall Avenue, Bramhall, Stockport SK7 2HE* Tel 0161-439 0300

✠HACKER, The Rt Revd George Lanyon. b 28. Ex Coll Ox BA52 MA56. Cuddesdon Coll 52. **d** 54 **p** 55 **c** 79. C Bris St Mary Redcliffe w Temple *Bris* 54-59; Chapl St Boniface Coll Warminster 59-64; V Bishopwearmouth Gd Shep *Dur* 64-71; R Tilehurst St Mich *Ox* 71-79; Suff Bp Penrith *Carl* 79-94; Hon Can Carl Cathl 79-94; Episc Adv for the Angl Young People's Assn 87-94; rtd 94; Hon Asst Bp Carl from 94. *Keld House, Milburn, Penrith CA10 1TW* Tel (01768) 361506 E-mail bishhack@btopenworld.com

HACKER HUGHES, Katherine Lucy. b 60. York Univ BA81. Westcott Ho Cam 90. **d** 92 **p** 94. Par Dn S Woodham Ferrers *Chelmsf* 92-94; C 94-95; NSM Maldon All SS w St Pet 95-98; Chapl Chelmsf Cathl 98-01; P-in-c Gt Waltham w Ford End 01-05; Adv relationship and family issues (Bradwell Area) 01-03; Perm to Offic from 05. *1 Swiss Avenue, Chelmsford CM1 2AD* Tel (01245) 600969 E-mail katyhh@lineone.net

HACKETT, Bryan Malcolm. b 66. Magd Coll Ox BA88 MA93 Cam Univ BA92 MA03. Westcott Ho Cam 90. **d** 93 **p** 94. C Willington *Newc* 93-97; TV Radcliffe *Man* 97-03; P-in-c Prestwich St Mary from 03. *The Rectory, Church Lane, Prestwich, Manchester M25 1AN* Tel 0161-773 2912 E-mail bryan.hackett@btinternet.com

HACKETT, Canon Frank James. b 33. AMIMechE68 MBIM72 MIIM79 HNC54 DMS72 Birm Univ MA77. Bps' Coll Cheshunt 62. **d** 64 **p** 65. C Feltham *Lon* 64-69; Ind Chapl *Lich* 69-73; Ind Chapl Port of Lon *Chelmsf* 73-98; P-in-c N Ockendon 79-93; Hon Can Chelmsf Cathl 93-98; Ind Chapl 93-98; rtd 98; Perm to Offic *Lon* 98-02 and *Chelmsf* from 99. *11 Fairfield Avenue, Upminster RM14 3AZ* Tel (01708) 221461

HACKETT, Glyndwr. *See* HACKETT, The Ven Ronald Glyndwr

HACKETT, John Nigel. b 32. Trin Hall Cam BA55 MA59. Ely Th Coll. **d** 59 **p** 60. C Handsworth St Mary *Birm* 59-66; V Handsworth St Jas 66-82; P-in-c Balsall Common 82-83; V 83-95; Perm to Offic *B & W* from 96; rtd 97. *Honeymead, Duck Lane, Kenn, Clevedon BS21 6TP* Tel (01275) 876591

HACKETT, Peter Edward. b 25. Magd Coll Ox BA48 MA51 ALCD60. **d** 60 **p** 61. C Lenton *S'well* 60-62; C Attenborough w Bramcote 62-63; V Lenton Abbey 63-67; R Acton Beauchamp and Evesbatch w Stanford Bishop *Heref* 67-71; V Choral Heref Cathl 72-76; P-in-c St Weonards w Orcop 76-79; P-in-c Tretire w Michaelchurch and Pencoyd 76-79; P-in-c Garway 76-79; P-in-c Welsh Newton w Llanrothal 77-79; V Rounds Green *Birm* 79-87; C Sutton Coldfield H Trin 87-90; rtd 90; NSM Shipton Moyne w Westonbirt and Lasborough *Glouc* 91-94; Perm to Offic *Birm* and *Worc* 94-99; *Heref* from 00. *96 The Pastures, Lower Bullingham, Hereford HR2 6EX* Tel (01432) 272462

HACKETT, The Ven Ronald Glyndwr. b 47. Hatf Coll Dur BA70. Cuddesdon Coll 70. **d** 72 **p** 73. C Pembroke St Mary w St Mich *St D* 72-75; C Bassaleg *Mon* 75-78; V Blaenavon w Capel Newydd 78-84; Chapl R Gwent Hosp 84-90; V Newport St Paul *Mon* 84-90; V Newport Ch Ch 90-01; Adn Mon from 01; R Mamhilad and Llanfihangel Pontymoile 01-03; R Mamhilad w Monkswood and Glascoed Chapel from 03. *The Rectory, 1 Millbrook Court, Little Mill, Pontypool NP4 0HT* Tel (01495) 785528

HACKETT, Victoria Anne. b 52. St Gabr Coll Lon CertEd73 Open Univ BA91 Surrey Univ DipTh00. SEITE 97. **d** 00 **p** 01. NSM Earlsfield St Andr *S'wark* from 00. *40 Freshford Street, London SW18 3TF* Tel (020) 8947 3755 E-mail v.ah@btopenworld.com

HACKING, Philip Henry. b 31. St Pet Hall Ox BA53 MA57. Oak Hill Th Coll 53. **d** 55 **p** 56. C St Helens St Helen *Liv* 55-58; C-in-c Edin St Thos *Edin* 59-68; V Fulwood *Sheff* 68-97; rtd 97; Perm to Offic *Sheff* from 98. *61 Sefton Court, Sefton Road, Sheffield S10 3TP* Tel 0114-230 4324

HACKING, Rodney Douglas. b 53. K Coll Lon BD74 AKC74 Man Univ MA83. St Aug Coll Cant 75. **d** 76 **p** 78. C Byker St Mich *Newc* 76-77; C Eltham St Jo *S'wark* 77-79; Ind Chapl *Ripon* 80-85; R Upwell St Pet and Outwell *Ely* 85-88; Vice Prin S Dios Minl Tr Scheme 89-93; V Bolton-le-Sands *Blackb* 93-97; R The Wainfleet Gp *Linc* from 03. *The Rectory, Vicarage Lane, Wainfleet St Mary, Skegness PE24 4JJ* Tel (01754) 880401 E-mail rdnyhacking@aol.com

HACKING, Stuart Peter. b 60. St Pet Coll Ox BA82 MA. Oak Hill Th Coll 83. **d** 85 **p** 86. C Shipley St Pet *Bradf* 85-88; C Darfield *Sheff* 88-91; V Thornton St Jas *Bradf* 91-00; P-in-c Frizinghall St Marg from 00. *7 Redbeck Vale, Shipley BD18 3BN* Tel (01274) 580166 Fax (07020) 972854 E-mail stuart.hacking@breathemail.net

HACKL, Aileen Patricia. b 41. Wycliffe Hall Ox 00. **d** 01 **p** 02. Hon Asst Chapl Vienna *Eur* from 01. *Hardtmuthgasse 28/3/20, A-1100 Vienna, Austria* Tel and fax (0043) (1) 600 3083 E-mail aileen_hackl@hotmail.com

HACKNEY, Archdeacon of. *See* DENNEN, The Ven Lyle

HACKSHALL, Brian Leonard. b 33. K Coll Lon BD53 AKC53. **d** 57 **p** 58. C Portsea St Mary *Portsm* 57-62; C Westbury-on-Trym St Alb *Bris* 62-64; V Avonmouth St Andr 64-71; Miss to Seamen 71-79; C Crawley *Chich* 79; TV 79-98; Ind Chapl 89-98; rtd 98. *5 St Michael Street, Brecon LD3 9AB* Tel (01874) 611319

HACKWOOD, The Ven Paul Colin. b 61. Huddersfield Poly BSc84. Qu Coll Birm 86. **d** 89 **p** 90. C Horton *Bradf* 89-93; Soc Resp Adv *St Alb* 93-97; V Thornbury *Bradf* from 97; Adn Loughborough *Leic* from 05. *The Archdeaconry, 21 Church Road, Glenfield, Leicester LE3 8DP* Tel 0116-231 1632 Fax 232 1593

HADDLETON, Peter Gordon. b 53. UEA BA74 Southn Univ BTh80. Sarum & Wells Th Coll 76. **d** 79 **p** 80. C Thamesmead *S'wark* 79-83; TV Bridgnorth, Tasley, Astley Abbotts, etc *Heref* 83-91; TV Heref S Wye 91-98; TR from 98. *The Rectory, 91 Ross Road, Hereford HR2 7RJ* Tel (01432) 277234 *or* 353717 Fax 352142 E-mail peter.haddleton@talk21.com or s.wye.team.ministry@talk21.com

HADDOCK, Malcolm George. b 27. Univ of Wales (Cardiff) DipTh53 BA56 CertEd73. St Deiniol's Hawarden 87. **d** 80 **p** 81. NSM Newport Ch Ch *Mon* 80-85; NSM Risca 85-87; C 87-89; C Caerleon 89-96; rtd 96; Lic to Offic *Mon* from 96. *48 Cambria Close, Caerleon, Newport NP18 1LF* Tel (01633) 422960

HADDON-REECE (née STREETER), Mrs Christine Mary. b 50. St Jo Coll Nottm BTh81 LTh81. **dss** 83 **d** 87 **p** 94. Monkwearmouth St Andr *Dur* 83-85; Stranton 85-87; Par Dn 87-90; Par Dn Lastingham w Appleton-le-Moors, Rosedale etc *York* 90-94; C 94-97; V Topcliffe, Baldersby w Dishforth, Dalton etc from 97. *St Columba's Vicarage, Front Street, Topcliffe, Thirsk YO7 3RU* Tel (01845) 577939

HADFIELD, Prof Brigid. b 50. Edin Univ LLB72 QUB LLM77 Essex Univ PhD03. EAMTC 02. **d** 03 **p** 04. NSM Wivenhoe *Chelmsf* from 03. *12 Thornton Drive, Colchester CO4 5WB* Tel (01206) 843426 E-mail bhadf@essex.ac.uk

HADFIELD, Christopher John Andrew Chad. b 39. Jes Coll Cam BA61. Wells Th Coll 63. **d** 65 **p** 66. C Wigton w Waverton *Carl* 65-68; Teacher Newlands Sch 70-99; Lic to Offic *Mor* from 92; Perm to Offic *Chich* from 96. *15 The Fridays, East Dean, Eastbourne BN20 0DH* Tel (01323) 422050

HADFIELD, Derek. b 34. **d** 01 **p** 02. OLM Folkestone H Trin w Ch Ch *Cant* 01-04; OLM Sandgate St Paul w Folkestone St Geo

01-04; rtd 04; Perm to Offic *Cant* from 04. *49 Collingwood Court, Collingwood Rise, Folkestone CT20 3PX* Tel (01303) 246808 E-mail derekandruth@dhadfield20.freeserve.co.uk

HADFIELD, Douglas. b 22. K Coll Cam BA44 MA49. St Jo Coll Nottm 84. **d** 88 **p** 89. Hon C Lenzie *Glas* 88-92; rtd 92; Perm to Offic *Glas* from 92; Perm to Offic *Pet* from 94. *8 Church Street, Helmdon, Brackley NN13 5QJ* Tel (01295) 760679

HADFIELD, Graham Francis. b 48. Bris Univ BSc69. Cranmer Hall Dur 69. **d** 73 **p** 74. C Blackpool St Thos *Blackb* 73-76; CF 76-99; Asst Chapl Gen 99-04; QHC 02-04; P-in-c Nottingham St Jude *S'well* from 04. *St Jude's Vicarage, Woodborough Road, Nottingham NG3 5HE* Tel 0115-960 4102 E-mail graham@hadf48.fsnet.co.uk

HADFIELD, Jonathan Benedict Philip John. b 43. Lon Univ BA64 Jes Coll Cam BA67 MA72. Edin Th Coll 66. **d** 68 **p** 69. C Fort William *Arg* 68-70; Chapl K Sch Glouc from 70; Hon Min Can Glouc Cathl *Glouc* from 70. *Dulverton House, King's School, Pitt Street, Gloucester GL1 2BG* Tel (01452) 521251

HADFIELD, Norman. b 39. Doncaster Coll of Educn TEng78. St Mich Coll Llan 89 Llan Dioc Tr Scheme 83. **d** 86 **p** 87. NSM Ferndale w Maerdy *Llan* 86-90; C Llanblethian w Cowbridge and Llandough etc 90-92; V Resolven w Tonna 92-04; RD Neath 01-03; rtd 04. *42 Lakeside, Cwmdare, Aberdare CF44 8AX* Tel (01685) 872764

HADJIOANNOU, John. b 56. Ch Coll Cam BA78 MA81. St Alb and Ox Min Course 95. **d** 97 **p** 98. C Linslade *Ox* 97-00; V Kinsley w Wragby *Wakef* from 00. *Kinsley Vicarage, Wakefield Road, Fitzwilliam, Pontefract WF9 5BX* Tel (01977) 610497 E-mail john@minster.co.uk

HADLEY, Ann. *See* HADLEY, Preb Elizabeth Ann

HADLEY, Charles Adrian. b 50. Trin Coll Cam BA71 MA75. Cuddesdon Coll 73. **d** 75 **p** 76. C Hadleigh w Layham and Shelley *St E* 75-78; C Bracknell *Ox* 78-82; R Blagdon w Compton Martin and Ubley *B & W* 82-92; RD Chew Magna 88-92; R Somerton w Compton Dundon, the Charltons etc 92-04; Chapl Ex Univ *Ex* from 04. *2 Velwell Road, Exeter EX4 4LE* Tel (01392) 435384

HADLEY, David Charles. b 42. **d** 02 **p** 03. NSM Kenley *S'wark* from 02. *21 Park Road, Kenley CR8 5AQ* Tel (020) 8763 6206

HADLEY, Donald Thomas. b 30. Lich Th Coll 55. **d** 58 **p** 59. C Saltley *Birm* 58-61; C-in-c S Yardley St Mich CD 61-66; V S Yardley St Mich 66-70; V Tonge Moor *Man* 70-84; C Selly Oak St Mary *Birm* 85-90; rtd 90; Perm to Offic *Birm* from 90 and *Worc* from 00. *175 Studley Road, Redditch B98 7HG* Tel (01527) 522658

HADLEY, Preb Elizabeth Ann. b 33. DipTh83. St Jo Coll Nottm 80. **dss** 81 **d** 87 **p** 94. Aspley *S'well* 81-85; Stone St Mich w Aston St Sav *Lich* 85-92; Par Dn 87-92; P-in-c Myddle 92-97; R 97-99; P-in-c Broughton 92-97; V 97-99; Dioc Voc Officer 92-99; Preb Lich Cathl 97-99; rtd 99; P-in-c Harvington *Worc* 99-00; Perm to Offic from 00. *6 Peninsular Road, Norton, Worcester WR5 2SE* Tel (01905) 353710

HADLEY, John Spencer Fairfax. b 47. Ch Ch Ox BA70 MA73. Coll of Resurr Mirfield BA72. **d** 73 **p** 74. C Stoke Newington St Mary *Lon* 73-77; C High Wycombe *Ox* 77-81; TV 82-87; P-in-c Clifton St Paul *Bris* 87-91; Sen Chapl Bris Univ 87-91; Chapl Hengrave Hall Ecum Cen 91-94; Ecum Assoc Min Chelsea Methodist Ch 94-97; Hon C Chelsea St Luke and Ch Ch *Lon* 94-97; Chapl Westcott Ho Cam 97-02; P-in-c Horfield H Trin *Bris* from 02. *Horfield Rectory, Wellington Hill, Bristol BS7 8ST* Tel 0117-924 6185 E-mail spencer@fairfax2.fsnet.co.uk

HADLEY, Stuart James. b 55. K Coll Lon BD76 AKC76. St Steph Ho Ox 77. **d** 78 **p** 79. C Mansfield St Mark *S'well* 78-82; V Cowbit *Linc* 82-86; Perm to Offic 86-88; NSM W w E Allington and Sedgebrook 88-95; NSM Saxonwell 95-96; NSM Woolsthorpe 88-95; NSM Harlaxton Gp 95-96; Perm to Offic 97-99; NSM Barkston and Hough Gp from 99. *35 Wensleydale Close, Grantham NG31 8FH* Tel (01476) 575854 E-mail hadleystuart@hotmail.com

HADLOW, Mrs Jennifer Lesley. b 48. **d** 01 **p** 02. OLM Herne *Cant* from 01. *2 Hicks Forstal Cottages, Hicks Forstal Road, Hoath, Canterbury CT3 4NA* Tel (01227) 711516 E-mail jennyhadlow@hotmail.com

HAGAN, Canon Kenneth Raymond. b 40. Fairfax Univ Australia BA97. St Jo Coll Morpeth 62. **d** 64 **p** 65. C Charlestown Australia 64-69; C Cessnock 69-70; R E Pilbara 70-75; C Portsea St Mary *Portsm* 75-78; P-in-c Wolvey, Burton Hastings and Stretton Baskerville *Cov* 78-81; P-in-c Withybrook w Copston Magna 78-81; P-in-c Shilton w Ansty 78-81; OCF 78-81; Dir St Mungo Community 82-88; R Hamilton Australia 89-98; R Portland 98-05; Can Ballarat from 99; rtd 05; P-in-c Heveningham *St E* from 04. *Willowbank, Walpole, Halesworth IP19 9AT* Tel (01986) 784603

HAGGAN, David Anthony. b 25. QUB LLB49 Barrister-at-Law 70. S'wark Ord Course 87. **d** 89 **p** 90. NSM Reigate St Mary *S'wark* 89-05; Perm to Offic from 05. *2 Fairford Close, Reigate RH2 0EY* Tel (01737) 246197

HAGGAR, Keith Ivan. b 38. MRPharmS61. Cant Sch of Min 87. **d** 90 **p** 91. NSM Woodnesborough w Worth and Staple *Cant* 90-98; Perm to Offic from 98; Chapl St Bart Hosp Sandwich 00-03. *Burtree Cottage, The Street, Worth, Deal CT14 0DE* Tel (01304) 613599

HAGGER, Jonathan Paul. b 59. St Jo Coll Nottm BTh95. **d** 95 **p** 96. C Newsham *Newc* 95-97; C Newc St Gabr 97-00; P-in-c Cresswell and Lynemouth 00-02; C Newc St Fran from 02. *18 Cotswold Gardens, Newcastle upon Tyne NE7 7AE* Tel 0191-281 2059

HAGGIE, Deborah. *See* HOLMYARD, Mrs Deborah

HAGGIS, Richard. b 66. Ch Ch Ox BA88 MA95 Nottm Univ MA95. Linc Th Coll. **d** 95 **p** 96. C Romford St Edw *Chelmsf* 95-98; Chapl Trin Coll Cam 98-00; C St Giles-in-the-Fields *Lon* 00-03. *45D Christchurch Street, London SW3 4AS* Tel (020) 7376 5911 E-mail rh.giles@btopenworld.com

HAGGIS, Timothy Robin. b 52. New Coll Ox BA75 MA79. St Jo Coll Nottm. **d** 82 **p** 83. C Chilwell *S'well* 82-86; TV Hucknall Torkard 86-94; Chapl Trent Coll Nottm from 94. *Trent College, Long Eaton, Nottingham NG10 4AD* Tel 0115-849 4980 E-mail tim.haggis@trentcollege.net

HAGON, Roger Charles. b 58. Nottm Univ BA80. St Steph Ho Ox 82. **d** 85 **p** 86. C Charlton St Luke w H Trin *S'wark* 85-88; C St Helier 88-95; V Kenley from 95; P-in-c Purley St Barn from 01. *The Vicarage, 3 Valley Road, Kenley CR8 5DJ* Tel (020) 8660 3263

HAGUE, David Hallett. b 59. Univ Coll Lon BScEng81 MSc82. Ridley Hall Cam CTM93. **d** 93 **p** 94. C Luton St Mary *St Alb* 93-96; V Stevenage St Pet Broadwater from 96. *St Peter's House, 1 The Willows, Stevenage SG2 8AN* Tel (01438) 238236 E-mail vicar@stpeter-stevenage.co.uk

HAHNEMAN, Geoffrey Mark. b 54. Baylor Univ (USA) BA77 Virginia Th Sem MDiv80 Ox Univ DPhil87. **d** 80 **p** 80. C Boston Advent USA 80-84; Hon C Ox St Mary Magd *Ox* 85-87; Asst Chapl Brussels *Eur* 87-90; Can Minneapolis Cathl USA 90-94; R Portsmouth Trin Ch 95-00. *St Columba's, 55 Vaucluse Avenue, Middletown, RI 02872, USA* Tel (001) (401) 847 5571 E-mail ghahneman@msn.com

HAIG, Alistair Matthew. b 39. K Coll Lon BD63 AKC63. **d** 64 **p** 65. C Forest Gate St Edm *Chelmsf* 64-67; C Laindon w Basildon 67-71; V S Woodham Ferrers 71-78; P-in-c Bath H Trin *B & W* 78-83; R 83-89; R Bocking St Mary *Chelmsf* 89-95; Dean Bocking 89-95; rtd 00. *17 Maidenburgh Street, Colchester CO1 1UB* Tel (01206) 795275

HAIG, Andrew Livingstone. b 45. Keble Coll Ox BA67. Coll of Resurr Mirfield 67. **d** 69 **p** 70. C Elton All SS *Man* 69-75; R Brantham *St E* 75-76; R Brantham w Stutton 76-82; RD Samford 81-82; P-in-c Haverhill 82; TR Haverhill w Withersfield, the Wrattings etc 82-90; RD Clare 84-87; Chapl Qu Eliz Hosp King's Lynn 90-94; Chapl King's Lynn and Wisbech Hosps NHS Trust from 94. *The Chaplain's Office, Queen Elizabeth Hospital, Gayton Road, King's Lynn PE30 4ET* Tel (01553) 613613 ext 2642

HAIG, Canon Murray Nigel Francis. b 39. Univ of Wales (Lamp) BA62. Kelham Th Coll 62. **d** 66 **p** 67. C Felixstowe St Jo *St E* 66-72; C Morpeth *Newc* 72-74; V Byker St Mich 74-79; V Byker St Mich w St Lawr 79-81; I Benwell St Jas 81-85; TR Benwell 85-91; TR Cramlington 91-97; Hon Can Newc Cathl 95-05; P-in-c Alnwick 97-98; V 98-05; rtd 05. *4 Farm Well Place, Prudhoe NE42 5FB* Tel (07801) 495616 E-mail d.haig@abbeyfield.com

HAIGH, Alan Bernard. b 42. NEOC 87. **d** 90 **p** 91. NSM Thorner *Ripon* from 90. *4 The Paddock, Thorner, Leeds LS14 3JB* Tel 0113-289 2870

HAIGH, Colin. b 15. St Chad's Coll Dur BA40 DipTh41 MA43. **d** 41 **p** 42. C Linthwaite *Wakef* 41-44; C Featherstone 44-45; C Streatham St Pet *S'wark* 45-48; C Benhilton 48-50; C Ipswich St Bart *St E* 50-52; C Leigh St Clem *Chelmsf* 52-56; R Fobbing 56-64; P-in-c Rawreth 64-68; V Romford St Alb 68-80; rtd 80; Perm to Offic *Chelmsf* from 80. *159 King's Road, Glemsford, Sudbury CO10 7QX* Tel (01787) 281715

HAIGH, John Gibson. b 47. Chich Th Coll 88. **d** 90 **p** 91. C Swinton and Pendlebury *Man* 90-93; C Richmond w Hudswell *Ripon* 93-96; C Downholme and Marske 93-96; R Nuthurst *Chich* 96-99; V Burnley St Mark *Blackb* from 99. *St Mark's Vicarage, 9 Rossendale Road, Burnley BB11 5DQ* Tel and fax (01282) 428178 E-mail revjhaigh@hotmail.com

HAIGH, Nicholas James. b 71. Sheff Univ BA00 St Jo Coll Dur MA04. Cranmer Hall Dur 02. **d** 04 **p** 05. C Bredbury St Mark *Ches* from 04. *12 St Mark's Street, Bredbury, Stockport SK6 1AR* Tel 0161-355 1147 Mobile 07876-782888 E-mail nickhaigh@breathemail.net

HAIGH, Richard Michael Fisher. b 30. Dur Univ BA57 Birm Univ DPS71. Cranmer Hall Dur DipTh59. **d** 59 **p** 60. C Stanwix *Carl* 59-62; CMS 62-70; India 63-67 and 68-70; R Salford St Clem w St Cypr Ordsall *Man* 71-75; R Holcombe 75-85; V Unsworth 85-93; R Brough w Stainmore, Musgrave and Warcop *Carl* 93-97; rtd 97; Perm to Offic *Carl* from 98. *21 Templand*

Park, Allithwaite, Grange-over-Sands LA11 7QS Tel (01539) 532312 E-mail richard@randshaigh.freeserve.co.uk

HAILES, Derek Arthur. b 38. Coll of Resurr Mirfield. **d** 82 **p** 83. C Sneinton St Cypr *S'well* 82-84; V Kneesall w Laxton 84-85; P-in-c Wellow 84-85; V Kneesall w Laxton and Wellow 85-88; V Sneinton St Steph w St Alb 88-95; P-in-c Bury H Trin *Man* 95-03; rtd 03. *14 Manor Road, Carlton, Nottingham NG4 3AY* Tel 0115-987 3314

HAILS, Canon Brian. b 33. JP71. ACMA62 FCMA76. NEOC 77. **d** 81 **p** 82. NSM Harton *Dur* 81-87; Ind Chapl 87-99; Hon Can Dur Cathl 93-99; TR Sunderland 96-99; rtd 99. *Inhurst, 5 Hepscott Terrace, South Shields NE33 4TH* Tel 0191-456 3490 E-mail canon-hails@ukonline.co.uk

HAINES, Andrew Philip. b 47. LSE BSc68. Oak Hill Th Coll 84. **d** 87 **p** 88. C Enfield Ch Ch Trent Park *Lon* 87-91; V Hillmorton *Cov* from 91. *The Vicarage, Hoskyn Close, Hillmorton, Rugby CV21 4LA* Tel (01788) 576279 E-mail andrew@cahaines.fsnet.co.uk

HAINES, Daniel Hugo. b 43. TD89. MRCS73 DRCOG78 Lon Univ BDS68 Witwatersrand Univ 78. **d** 79 **p** 84. Swaziland 79-80; Falkland Is 80-82; Hon C Hatcham St Cath *S'wark* 84-99; Perm to Offic from 99. *56 Vesta Road, London SE4 2NH* Tel (020) 7635 0305 E-mail 113270.506@compuserve.com

HAINES, Canon Robert Melvin. b 31. Coll of Resurr Mirfield 71. **d** 73 **p** 74. C Derringham Bank *York* 73-76; P-in-c Newport St Steph 76-79; TV Howden 80-82; R Turriff *Ab* 82-97; R Cuminestown 82-97; R Banff 82-97; P-in-c Portsoy 94-97; P-in-c Buckie 94-97; rtd 97; NSM Turriff *Ab* from 97; Hon Can St Andr Cathl from 01. *Ceol-na-Mara, 11 Scotstown, Banff AB45 1LA* Tel (01261) 818258

HAINES, Stephen Decatur. b 42. Freiburg Univ MA68 Fitzw Coll Cam BA70 MA74. **d** 71 **p** 72. C Fulham St Dionis Parson's Green *Lon* 71-76; C Finchley St Mary 76-78; Hon C Clapham Old Town *S'wark* 83-87; Hon C Clapham Team 87-88; Hon C Camberwell St Giles w St Matt 88-94; Hon Chapl S'wark Cathl from 92. *3 Lyndhurst Square, London SE15 5AR* Tel (020) 7703 4239

HAIR, James Eric. b 48. Lon Univ BA69 MPhil92. St Steph Ho Ox 69. **d** 72 **p** 73. C Fishponds St Jo *Bris* 72-75; C Bushey *St Alb* 75-79; P-in-c Lake *Portsm* 79-81; V 81-88; P-in-c Shanklin St Sav 79-81; V 81-88; TV Totton *Win* 88-95; C Portchester *Portsm* 96-97; Community Mental Health Chapl Portsm Health Care NHS Trust 97-02; Community Mental Health Chapl Hants Partnerships NHS Trust from 02; Chapl Team Ldr E Hants Primary Care Trust from 99; Asst to RD Fareham *Portsm* 97-98 and 99. *219 West Street, Fareham PO16 0ET* Tel (01329) 825231

HAITH, James Rodney. b 69. Ex Univ BA. Ridley Hall Cam 02. **d** 04 **p** 05. C Brompton H Trin w Onslow Square St Paul *Lon* from 04. *11 Onslow Gardens, London SW7 3AP* Tel 08456-447533 Mobile 07833-705271 E-mail jamie.haith@htb.org.uk

HALAHAN, Maxwell Crosby. b 30. Lon Univ BSc52 Southn Univ CertEd78 W Sussex Inst of HE AdCertEd83. Westcott Ho Cam 54. **d** 56 **p** 57. C Forton *Portsm* 56-60; C Liv Our Lady and St Nic *Liv* 60-62; Dom Chapl to Bp Nassau and the Bahamas 62-64; C Widley w Wymering *Portsm* 64-66; C-in-c Cowes St Faith CD 66-70; V Cowes St Faith 70-77; Hon C Portsea St Sav 77-84; rtd 84; Perm to Offic *Portsm* 84-94. *4 Coach House Mews, Old Canal, Southsea PO4 8HD*

HALE, Antony Jolyon (Jon). b 56. MRTPI89 Newc Univ BA79. Sarum & Wells Th Coll 86. **d** 88 **p** 89. C Monkseaton St Mary *Newc* 88-92; P-in-c Tandridge *S'wark* 92-97; C Oxted 92-97; C Oxted and Tandridge 97-98; V Crawley Down All SS *Chich* from 98. *The Vicarage, Vicarage Road, Crawley Down, Crawley RH10 4JJ* Tel (01342) 714922 E-mail aj@jkcahale.plus.com

HALE, David Nigel James. b 43. SEITE 00. **d** 03 **p** 04. NSM Aylesham w Adisham *Cant* from 03; NSM Nonington w Wymynswold and Goodnestone etc from 03. *Chilton House, 43 The Street, Ash, Canterbury CT3 2EN* Tel (01304) 813161 E-mail halenigelval@hotmail.com

HALE, Canon Dennis Ernest (Jim). b 26. MBE02. Southn Univ MA(Ed)66. Sarum & Wells Th Coll 74. **d** 77 **p** 78. NSM N Stoneham *Win* 77-86; Assoc Chapl Southn Univ 86-99; NSM Swaythling 90-99; rtd 99; Hon Can Win Cathl *Win* from 01; Perm to Offic from 02. *12 Field Close, Southampton SO16 3DY* Tel and fax (023) 8055 4538

HALE, John Frederick. b 29. Fitzw Ho Cam BA54 MA58. Tyndale Hall Bris. **d** 55 **p** 56. C Heigham H Trin *Nor* 55-58; C Paddington St Jas *Lon* 58-61; V St Leonards St Ethelburga *Chich* 61-79; C Prestonville St Luke 79-90; R Rotherfield w Mark Cross 90-92; rtd 92; Perm to Offic *Chich* from 92. *51 Brangwyn Drive, Brighton BN1 8XB* Tel (01273) 554944

HALE, Jon. *See* HALE, Antony Jolyon

HALE, Keith John Edward. b 53. Sheff Poly BSc75. St Jo Coll Nottm MA94. **d** 91 **p** 92. C Greasbrough *Sheff* 91-94; P-in-c Tankersley 94-95; R Tankersley, Thurgoland and Wortley from 95; Ind Chapl 96-01; Bp's Rural Adv from 01. *The Rectory, 9 Chapel Road, Tankersley, Barnsley S75 3AR* Tel (01226) 744140

HALE (née McKAY), Mrs Margaret McLeish (Greta). b 37. RN76. WEMTC 92. **d** 95 **p** 96. OLM Bream *Glouc* 95-01; NSM 01-04; NSM Newland and Redbrook w Clearwell from 04. *1 The Bungalow, High Street, Clearwell, Coleford GL16 8JS* Tel (01594) 832400

HALE, Nigel. *See* HALE, David Nigel James

HALE, Roger Anthony. b 41. MCIH85. Brasted Th Coll 68 Oak Hill Th Coll 70. **d** 72 **p** 73. C Blackb Sav *Blackb* 72-75; C Burnley St Pet 75-77; Chapl Burnley Gen Hosp 75-77; V Fence in Pendle *Blackb* 77-82; Chapl Lancs Ind Miss 77-82; NSM Tottenham St Mary *Lon* 88-91; R Cheddington w Mentmore and Marsworth *Ox* from 91. *The Rectory, 29 Mentmore Road, Cheddington, Leighton Buzzard LU7 0SD* Tel (01296) 661358

HALES, Jan. *See* STEVENSON, Ms Jan

HALES, Sandra Louise. Lon Univ BSc94 Univ Coll Lon MSc96 TCD BTh02 RGN. CITC. **d** 02 **p** 03. C Lucan w Leixlip *D & G* from 02. *280 River Forest, Leixlip, Co Kildare, Irish Republic* Tel (00353) (1) 601 4679 E-mail slhales@eircom.net

HALEY, Thomas Arthur. b 52. NTMTC 98. **d** 98 **p** 99. NSM Old Ford St Paul and St Mark *Lon* 98-02; NSM Hackney Marsh from 02. *4 Vivian Road, London E3 5RF* Tel (020) 8981 1656 E-mail tomarcie@aol.com

HALFORD, David John. b 47. JP84. Open Univ DipEd86 Didsbury Coll Man CertEd69 Open Univ BA75 Man Univ MEd79 ACP72. LNSM course 96. **d** 96 **p** 97. OLM Royton St Anne *Man* from 96. *33 Broadway, Royton, Oldham OL2 5DD* Tel 0161-633 4650 Fax as telephone

HALFPENNY, Brian Norman. b 36. CB90. St Jo Coll Ox BA60 MA64. Wells Th Coll 60. **d** 62 **p** 63. C Melksham *Sarum* 62-65; Chapl RAF 65-83; Sen Chapl RAF Coll Cranwell 82-83; Asst Chapl-in-Chief RAF 83-88; Chapl-in-Chief RAF 88-91; QHC 85-91; Offg Chapl RAF from 91; Can and Preb Linc Cathl *Linc* 89-91; TR Redditch, The Ridge *Worc* 91-01; rtd 01; Perm to Offic *Glouc* from 02. *80 Roman Way, Bourton-on-the-Water, Cheltenham GL54 2EW* Tel (01451) 821589

HALIFAX, Archdeacon of. *See* FREEMAN, The Ven Robert John

HALKES, Canon John Stanley. b 39. SW Minl Tr Course 87. **d** 90 **p** 91. NSM St Buryan, St Levan and Sennen *Truro* 90-92; P-in-c Lanteglos by Fowey 92-04; P-in-c Lansallos 03-04; Hon Can Truro Cathl from 03; rtd 04. *Reading Room Cottage, Mixton Farm, Lerryn, Lostwithiel PL22 0QE*

HALL, Alan Maurice Frank. b 28. FCCA. Sarum & Wells Th Coll 86. **d** 89 **p** 90. NSM Winterbourne Stickland and Turnworth etc *Sarum* 89-97; Perm to Offic *Sarum* 97-00 and *St Alb* from 00. *2 Barnes Road, Wooton, Bedford MK43 9FA* Tel (01234) 764676

✠**HALL, The Rt Revd Albert Peter.** b 30. St Jo Coll Cam BA53 MA56. Ridley Hall Cam 53. **d** 55 **p** 56 **c** 84. C Birm St Martin *Birm* 55-60; S Rhodesia 60-65; Rhodesia 65-70; R Birm St Martin *Birm* 70-84; Hon Can Birm Cathl 75-84; Suff Bp Woolwich *S'wark* 84-91; Area Bp Woolwich 91-96; Chmn ACUPA 90-96; rtd 96; Asst Bp Birm from 96. *27 Jacey Road, Birmingham B16 0LL* Tel 0121-455 9240

HALL, Canon Alfred Christopher. b 35. Trin Coll Ox BA58 MA61. Westcott Ho Cam 58. **d** 61 **p** 62. C Frecheville *Derby* 61-64; C Dronfield 64-67; V Smethwick St Matt *Birm* 67-70; V Smethwick St Matt w St Chad 70-75; Can Res Man Cathl *Man* 75-83; Hon Can 83-90; Dioc Adult Educn Officer 75-83; Dioc World Development Officer 76-88; V Bolton St Pet 83-90; Co-ord Chr Concern for One World 90-00; rtd 96; Hon Can Ch Ch *Ox* 00-01. *The Knowle, Philcote Street, Deddington, Banbury OX15 0TB* Tel (01869) 338225 Fax 337766 E-mail achall@globalnet.co.uk

HALL, Mrs Ann Addington. b 34. Ex Univ CertEd71. SW Minl Tr Course 82. **dss** 85 **d** 87 **p** 94. Ex St Mark *Ex* 85-90; Hon Par Dn 87-90; Perm to Offic 90-92; NSM Cen Ex from 92. *5 Harringcourt Road, Exeter EX4 8PQ* Tel (01392) 278717

HALL, Arthur John. b 23. Bris Univ BSc48. Sarum & Wells Th Coll 74. **d** 76 **p** 77. NSM Portishead *B & W* 76-88; Perm to Offic from 88; Chapl St Brandon's Sch Clevedon 86-91. *34 Beechwood Road, Portishead, Bristol BS20 8EP* Tel (01275) 842603

HALL, Barry George. b 38. Solicitor 62. Oak Hill Th Coll 78. **d** 81 **p** 82. NSM Stock Harvard *Chelmsf* 81-90; NSM W Hanningfield 90-02; P-in-c 93-02. *Harvard Cottage, Swan Lane, Stock, Ingatestone CM4 9BQ* Tel (01277) 840387

HALL, Brian. b 59. Aston Tr Scheme 90 Oak Hill Th Coll DipHE94. **d** 94 **p** 95. C Mansfield St Jo *S'well* 94-96; C Skegby 96-99; P-in-c Sutton in Ashfield St Mich 99-04; R Carlton-in-the-Willows from 04. *St Paul's Rectory, Church Street, Nottingham NG4 1BJ* Tel 0115-961 1644 E-mail brian.hall2@ntlworld.com

HALL, Canon Brian Arthur. b 48. Ex Univ BEd70. Cuddesdon Coll 73. **d** 75 **p** 76. C Hobs Moat *Birm* 75-79; V Smethwick 79-93; R Handsworth St Mary from 93; AD Handsworth 99-05; Hon Can Birm Cathl from 05. *Handsworth Rectory, 288 Hamstead Road, Birmingham B20 2RB* Tel 0121-554 3407 E-mail brian.a.hall@btinternet.com

HALL, Charles Bryan. b 37. Liv Univ BA59. St Mich Coll Llan 59. **d** 62 **p** 63. C Prestatyn *St As* 62-64; C Cardiff St Mary *Llan*

64-67; V 73-75; C Hawarden *St As* 67-72; TV 72-73 and 84-86; P-in-c Cardiff St Steph *Llan* 73-75; V Cardiff St Mary w St Steph 75-81; V Penycae *St As* 81-84; R Llandegla and Llanarmon yn Ial 86-02; rtd 02. *11 Maes Robert, Cefn, St Asaph LL17 0HR* Tel (01745) 582908

HALL, Charles John. b 40. JP. ALCD68. **d** 68 **p** 69. C Upton (Overchurch) *Ches* 68-72; C Morden *S'wark* 72-76; V Hyson Green *S'well* 76-84; V Stapleford 84-97; RD Beeston 90-97; TR Thetford *Nor* 97-05; RD Thetford and Rockland 99-03; rtd 05; Perm to Offic *Nor* from 05. *24 Mill Road, Reepham, Norwich NR10 4JU* Tel (01603) 879194 E-mail hallthetrec@tesco.net

HALL, Christine Mary. b 45. K Coll Lon BD67 MPhil86. **d** 87. NSM Bickley *Roch* 87-92; Vice-Prin Chich Th Coll 92-95; Lic to Offic *Chich* from 95. *The Old School, East Marden, Chichester PO18 9JE* Tel (01243) 535244

HALL, Christopher. *See* HALL, Canon Alfred Christopher

HALL, David Anthony. b 43. Reading Univ BA66. Qu Coll Birm 79. **d** 81 **p** 82. C Norton *St Alb* 81-85; TV Hitchin 85-93; P-in-c Bidford-on-Avon *Cov* 93; V from 93; RD Alcester from 05. *The Vicarage, 5 Howard Close, Bidford-on-Avon, Alcester B50 4EL* Tel (01789) 772217 E-mail davidahall@onetel.com

HALL, David Martin. b 66. Greenwich Univ BA89. Oak Hill Th Coll BA00. **d** 00 **p** 01. C Bebington *Ches* 00-03; P-in-c Danehill *Chich* from 03. *The Vicarage, Lewes Road, Danehill, Haywards Heath RH17 7ER* Tel (01825) 790269

HALL, Denis. b 43. Lon Coll of Div 65. **d** 69 **p** 70. C Netherton *Liv* 69-71; C Roby 72-75; V Wigan St Steph 75-90; V Newton-le-Willows from 90. *The Vicarage, 243 Crow Lane East, Newton-le-Willows WA12 9UB* Tel (01925) 290545 E-mail allsaints@3tc4u.net

HALL, Derek. *See* HALL, Canon John Derek

HALL, Derek Guy. b 26. Tyndale Hall Bris 50. **d** 51 **p** 52. C Preston All SS *Blackb* 51-54; C Halliwell St Pet *Man* 54-56; C-in-c Buxton Trin Prop Chpl *Derby* 56-58; V Blackb St Jude *Blackb* 58-67; R Fazakerley Em *Liv* 67-74; TR 74-81; V Langdale *Carl* 81-86; rtd 86; Perm to Offic *Carl* from 86. *14 Gale Park, Ambleside LA22 0BN* Tel (01539) 433144

HALL, Edwin George. b 40. Sarum & Wells Th Coll 88. **d** 91 **p** 92. NSM Purton *Bris* 91-97; rtd 97; Perm to Offic *Bris* 97-01. *Address temp unknown*

HALL, Elaine Chegwin. b 59. RGN82 Liv Univ MTh01. N Ord Course 94. **d** 97 **p** 98. C Frankby w Greasby *Ches* 97-01; V Stretton and Appleton Thorn from 01; RD Gt Budworth from 03. *The Vicarage, Stretton Road, Stretton, Warrington WA4 4NT* Tel (01925) 730276 E-mail petera.hall@care4free.net

HALL, Fiona Myfanwy Gordon. b 63. NNEB84 Regents Th Coll BA95 Roehampton Inst PGCE96. Ridley Hall Cam 02. **d** 04 **p** 05. C Southampton Maybush St Pet *Win* from 04. *All Saints' House, 60 Brookwood Road, Southampton SO16 9AJ* Tel (023) 8078 1228

HALL, Frances. *See* SHOESMITH, Mrs Judith Frances

HALL, Geoffrey Hedley. b 33. Bris Univ BA55. St Steph Ho Ox 63. **d** 65 **p** 66. C Taunton H Trin *B & W* 65-67; CF 67-80; Sen CF 80-86; P-in-c Ambrosden w Arncot and Blackthorn *Ox* 72-75; V Barnsley St Edw *Wakef* 86-98; rtd 98; Perm to Offic *St And* from 98 and *Bre* from 99. *Montana Villa, 39 Heston Crescent, Perth PH2 7XD* Tel (01738) 636802 Mobile 07803-578499 E-mail geoffrey.hall@icscotland.net

HALL, George. *See* HALL, Edwin George

HALL, George Richard Wyndham. b 49. Ex Univ LLB71. Wycliffe Hall Ox BA74 MA78. **d** 75 **p** 76. C Walton H Trin *Ox* 75-79; C Farnborough *Guildf* 79-84; Bp's Chapl *Nor* 84-87; R Saltford w Corston and Newton St Loe *B & W* from 87; Chapl Bath Coll of HE 88-90; RD Chew Magna *B & W* 97-03. *The Rectory, 12 Beech Road, Saltford, Bristol BS31 3BE* Tel (01225) 872275 Fax as telephone E-mail richardhall@blueyonder.co.uk

HALL, Canon George Rumney. b 37. LVO99 CVO03. Westcott Ho Cam 60. **d** 62 **p** 63. C Camberwell St Phil *S'wark* 62-65; C Waltham Cross *St Alb* 65-67; R Buckenham w Hassingham and Strumpshaw *Nor* 67-74; Chapl St Andr Hosp Thorpe 67-72; Chapl HM Pris Nor 72-74; V Wymondham *Nor* 74-87; RD Humbleyard 86-87; R Sandringham w W Newton 87-94; P-in-c Flitcham 87-94; P-in-c Wolferton w Babingley 87-94; R Sandringham w W Newton and Appleton etc 95-03; P-in-c Castle Rising 87-03; P-in-c Hillington 87-03; Hon Can Nor Cathl 87-03; RD Heacham and Rising 89-01; Dom Chapl to The Queen 87-03; Chapl to The Queen from 89; rtd 03; Perm to Offic *Nor* from 03. *Town Farm Cottage, Lynn Road, Bircham, King's Lynn PE31 6RJ* Tel (01485) 576134

HALL, Mrs Gillian Louise. b 45. N Ord Course 87. **d** 90 **p** 94. NSM Earby *Bradf* 90-96; NSM Gisburn 96-01; NSM Hellifield 96-01; Perm to Offic from 01; Chapl Airedale NHS Trust from 02. *244 Colne Road, Barnoldswick, Colne BB18 6TD* Tel (01282) 842593

HALL, Canon Godfrey Charles. b 43. Linc Coll Ox BA66 MA72. Cuddesdon Coll 66. **d** 68 **p** 69. C St Helier *S'wark* 68-72; Asst Chapl Ch Hosp Horsham 72-82; Hd Master Prebendal Sch Chich from 82; Can and Preb Chich Cathl *Chich* from 93. *53 West Street, Chichester PO19 1RT* Tel (01243) 782026

HALL, Harold Henry Stanley Lawson. b 23. Qu Coll Birm 56. **d** 58 **p** 59. C Bishopwearmouth Ch Ch *Dur* 58-61; C Winlaton 61-65; V Cockerton 65-69; V Newton Aycliffe 69-76; R Whitburn 76-89; rtd 89. *9 Balmoral Terrace, East Herrington, Sunderland SR3 3PR* Tel 0191-528 0108

HALL, Harry. b 41. Open Univ BA93. Chich Th Coll 91. **d** 91 **p** 92. C Boston *Linc* 91-92; C Bourne 92-94; P-in-c Sutterton w Fosdyke and Algarkirk 94-97; R Sutterton, Fosdyke, Algarkirk and Wigtoft 97-99; V Barnsley St Edw *Wakef* 99-05; Chapl ATC 99-05; I Ardstraw w Baronscourt, Badoney Lower etc *D & R* from 05. *Address temp unknown* E-mail slk248@hotmail.com

HALL, Henry. *See* DEANE-HALL, Henry Michael

HALL, Canon Hubert William Peter. b 35. Ely Th Coll 58. **d** 60 **p** 61. C Louth w Welton-le-Wold *Linc* 60-62; C Gt Grimsby St Jas 62-69; C Gt Grimsby St Mary and St Jas 69-71; Hon Chapl Miss to Seafarers 71-01; V Immingham *Linc* 71-01; RD Haverstoe 86-01; Can and Preb Linc Cathl 89-01; rtd 01; Perm to Offic *Linc* from 01. *6 Abbey Rise, Barrow-upon-Humber DN17 7IF* Tel (01469) 531504 E-mail peterhall@freeuk.com

HALL, Ian Alfred. b 60. Sheff Univ BA96. Ushaw Coll Dur 81 N Ord Course 98. **d** 85 **p** 86. In RC Ch 86-98; C Whitkirk *Ripon* 99-02; TV Swinton and Pendlebury *Man* from 02. *St Augustine's Vicarage, 23 Hospital Road, Pendlebury, Swinton, Manchester M27 4EY* Tel 0161-794 4298 E-mail carolian86@yahoo.co.uk

HALL, Ian Michael. b 48. Mansf Coll Ox MA70 Leeds Univ CertEd71. Carl Dioc Tr Course 85. **d** 88 **p** 89. NSM Eskdale, Irton, Muncaster and Waberthwaite *Carl* from 88. *Fisherground Farm, Boot, Holmrook CA19 1TF* Tel (01946) 723319

HALL, James. b 28. Wollongong Univ BA78. CITC 53. **d** 56 **p** 57. C Belfast St Mich *Conn* 56-59; I Cleenish *Clogh* 59-62; R Openshaw *Man* 63-68; Australia 68-89; R Morley w Deopham, Hackford, Wicklewood etc *Nor* 89-92; R High Oak 92-93; rtd 93. *54 Sunnybank Crescent, Horsley, NSW, Australia 2530* Tel (0061) (2) 4262 7881

HALL, Canon James Robert. b 24. TCD BA48 MA54. **d** 49 **p** 50. C Seagoe *D & D* 49-51; C Lisburn Ch Ch *Conn* 51-59; I Belfast St Mich 59-66; I Finaghy 66-89; Can Belf Cathl 82-89; rtd 89. *3 Coachman's Way, Hillsborough BT26 6HQ* Tel (028) 9268 9678

HALL, Mrs Jean Margaret. b 38. Bris Univ CertEd59 AdCertEd73. Bris Sch of Min 84. **d** 88 **p** 94. NSM Bris St Andr w St Bart *Bris* 88; NSM E Bris 88-91; Par Dn Plympton St Mary *Ex* 91-93; Asst Chapl E Kent Community NHS Trust 93-98; P-in-c Brompton Regis w Upton and Skilgate *B & W* 98-00; rtd 00; Hon C Bratton, Edington and Imber, Erlestoke etc *Sarum* 00-05. *26 Summer Shard, South Petherton TA13 5DP* Tel (01460) 240099 E-mail jean.hall@bigfoot.com

HALL, Jeffrey Ernest. b 42. Linc Th Coll 73. **d** 75 **p** 76. C Brampton St Thos *Derby* 75-78; C Whittington and New Whittington 78-81; TV Riverside *Ox* 81-90; R Anstey *Leic* 90-97; TR Hugglescote w Donington, Ellistown and Snibston from 97. *The Rectory, Grange Road, Hugglescote, Coalville LE67 2BQ* Tel (01530) 832557

HALL, The Ven John Barrie. b 41. Sarum & Wells Th Coll 82. **d** 84 **p** 85. Chapl St Edward's Hosp Cheddleton 84-88; C Cheddleton *Lich* 84-88; V Rocester 88-94; V Rocester and Croxden w Hollington 94-98; RD Uttoxeter 91-98; Adn Salop from 98; V Tong from 98; P-in-c Donington from 98. *Tong Vicarage, Shifnal TF11 8PW* Tel (01902) 372622 Fax 374021 E-mail archdeacon.salop@lichfield.anglican.org

HALL, John Bruce. b 33. St Louis Covenant Th Sem MTh80 DMin85 Lon Coll of Div ALCD60. **d** 60 **p** 61. C Kingston upon Hull H Trin *York* 60-67; C Beverley Minster 67-68; V Clapham Park St Steph *S'wark* 68-76; R Tooting Graveney St Nic 76-03; rtd 03; Perm to Offic *S'wark* from 03. *44 Mayford Road, London SW12 8SD* Tel (020) 8673 6839 E-mail jbewhall@macunlimited.net

HALL, John Charles. b 46. Hull Univ BA71 Spurgeon's Coll MTh05. Ridley Hall Cam 71. **d** 73 **p** 74. C Bromley Common St Aug *Roch* 73-77; C Westbury-on-Trym St Alb *Bris* 78-80; Oman 80-82; C-in-c Bishop Auckland Woodhouse Close CD *Dur* 82-90; P-in-c Gt and Lt Glemham, Blaxhall etc *St E* 90-91; P-in-c Rodney Stoke w Draycott *B & W* 91-01; Dioc Ecum Officer 91-01; V Southmead *Bris* from 01. *St Stephen's Vicarage, Wigton Crescent, Bristol BS10 6DR* Tel 0117-950 7164 Mobile 07811-316249 E-mail revjon@ukonline.co.uk

HALL, John Curtis. b 39. CEng73 MIMechE73. Coll of Resurr Mirfield 80. **d** 82 **p** 83. C Pet Ch Carpenter *Pet* 82-86; TV Heavitree w Ex St Paul *Ex* 86-93; R Bow w Broad Nymet 93-04; V Colebrooke 93-04; R Zeal Monachorum 93-04; RD Cadbury 97-02; rtd 04. *37 Lawn Drive, Chudleigh, Newton Abbot TQ13 0LS* Tel (01626) 853245

HALL, Canon John Derek. b 25. St Cuth Soc Dur BA50. Linc Th Coll 50. **d** 52 **p** 53. C Redcar *York* 52-54; C Newland St Jo 54-57; V Boosbeck w Moorsholm 57-61; V Middlesbrough St Oswald 61-68; Chapl St Luke's Hosp Middlesbrough 61-67; V York St Chad *York* 68-90; Chapl Bootham Park Hosp 68-85; Can and Preb York Minster *York* 85-90; rtd 90; Chapl Castle Howard

90-02; Perm to Offic *York* from 98. *25 Fairfields Drive, Skelton, York YO30 1YP* Tel (01904) 470978

HALL, John Edmund. b 49. Birm Poly CQSW76 Open Univ BA84. Trin Coll Bris BA89. **d** 89 **p** 90. C Winchmore Hill St Paul *Lon* 89-92; V Edmonton St Aldhelm 92-01; Dir Soc Resp *Cov* from 01. *The Rectory, Spring Hill, Bubbenhall, Coventry CV8 3BD* Tel (024) 7630 2345 *or* 7671 0500 Fax 7671 0550 E-mail john.hall@covcofe.org

HALL, Canon John Kenneth. b 32. Qu Coll Birm 61. **d** 63 **p** 64. C Ilminster w Whitelackington *B & W* 63-66; P-in-c Mackworth St Fran *Derby* 66-69; V Blackford *B & W* 69-76; R Chapel Allerton 69-76; New Zealand from 77; Can St Pet Cathl Waikato 85-91; rtd 93. *24 Pohutukawa Drive, Athenree, Katikati RD1, New Zealand* Tel (0064) (7) 863 4465 Fax as telephone

HALL, John MacNicol. b 44. Glas Univ BSc65 MB, ChB69 MRCGP75 St Jo Coll Cam BA73 MA76 Nottm Univ MTh88. Westcott Ho Cam 71. **d** 86 **p** 86. NSM Knighton St Jo *Leic* 86; NSM Clarendon Park St Jo w Knighton St Mich 86-89; Perm to Offic *Ely* 89-91; *St Alb* 90-92; *Birm* 91-00; Lic to Offic *Birm* from 00. *HM Prison, Winson Green Road, Birmingham B18 4AS* Tel 0121-554 3838 Fax 554 7990 E-mail rev.john.hall@tinyworld.co.uk

HALL, John Michael. b 47. BD. Oak Hill Th Coll 68. **d** 73 **p** 74. C Walthamstow St Mary w St Steph *Chelmsf* 73-76; C Rainham 76-79; P-in-c Woodham Mortimer w Hazeleigh 79-93; P-in-c Woodham Walter 79-93; Ind Chapl 79-93; R Fairstead w Terling and White Notley etc from 93; RD Witham from 01. *The Rectory, New Road, Terling, Chelmsford CM3 2PN* Tel (01245) 233256 E-mail revjohnhall@tinyworld.co.uk

HALL, Canon John Michael. b 62. Leeds Univ BA. Coll of Resurr Mirfield 83. **d** 86 **p** 87. C Ribbleton *Blackb* 86-89; C Carnforth 89-92; V Lt Marsden 92-98; V Lt Marsden w Nelson St Mary 98; V Warton St Oswald w Yealand Conyers from 98; Hon Can Bloemfontein Cathl from 01. *St Oswald's Vicarage, Warton, Carnforth LA5 9PG* Tel and fax (01524) 732946 E-mail johnbloem@aol.com

HALL, John Redvers. b 25. Dur Univ BA59 DipTh62 Man Univ CertEd74. **d** 61 **p** 62. C Lutterworth w Cotesbach *Leic* 61-63; C Loughborough Em 63-66; Lic to Offic 66-70; Lic to Offic *Blackb* 70-81; P-in-c Ingoldmells w Addlethorpe *Linc* 81-83; V Cholsey *Ox* 83-92; rtd 92; Perm to Offic *Chich* from 92. *3 Peak Coach House, Cotmaton Road, Sidmouth EX10 8SY*

HALL, Canon John Robert. b 49. St Chad's Coll Dur BA71. Cuddesdon Coll 73. **d** 75 **p** 76. C Kennington St Jo *S'wark* 75-78; P-in-c S Wimbledon All SS 78-84; V Streatham St Pet 84-92; Dioc Dir of Educn *Blackb* 92-98; Hon Can Blackb Cathl 92-94 and 98-00; Can Res 94-98; Gen Sec Nat Soc from 98; Chief Educn Officer and Gen Sec C of E Bd of Educn 98-02; Hd Educn Division Abps' Coun from 03; Hon C S Norwood St Alb *S'wark* from 03. *25 Goodenough Road, London SW19 3QW* Tel and fax (020) 8543 7428 E-mail jrh54@fsmail.net

HALL, John Terence Peter. b 67. St Jo Coll Dur BA98. Cranmer Hall Dur. **d** 98 **p** 99. C Towcester w Easton Neston *Pet* 98-01; P-in-c Blakesley w Adstone and Maidford etc from 01. *The Vicarage, Collswell Lane, Blakesley, Towcester NN12 8RB* Tel (01327) 860507 E-mail john@beneficeofbamf.f9.co.uk

HALL, Jonathan. b 62. Ch Ch Coll Cant BA83 MIPD94. STETS BTh99. **d** 99 **p** 00. C Weymouth H Trin *Sarum* 99-03; R Whippingham w E Cowes *Portsm* from 03. *The Rectory, 69 Victoria Grove, East Cowes PO32 6DL* Tel (01983) 200107

HALL, Kenneth Robert James. b 59. St Jo Coll Nottm 95. **d** 98 **p** 99. NSM Derryloran *Arm* 98-02; C Drumglass w Moygashel 02-03; I Brackaville w Donaghendry and Ballyclog from 03. *Holy Trinity Rectory, 82 Dungannon Road, Coalisland, Dungannon BT71 4HT* Tel (028) 8774 0243 E-mail krjhall@btinternet.com

HALL, Keven Neil. b 47. Auckland Univ BSc PhD74. K Coll Lon BD AKC79. **d** 79 **p** 80. New Zealand 79-87; NSM Shepherd's Bush St Steph w St Thos *Lon* 91-95 and 98-00; NSM W Acton St Martin 96-98; Chapl Nat Soc for Epilepsy 91-03; Chapl Cen Middx Hosp NHS Trust from 00. *3 Roman Close, London W3 8HE* Tel (020) 8752 0543 *or* 8965 5733 Fax 8453 2199 E-mail kevenhall@hotmail.com

HALL, Leslie. b 37. Man Univ BSc59. EMMTC 83. **d** 86 **p** 87. NSM Freiston w Butterwick and Benington *Linc* 86-02; Perm to Offic from 02; Dioc NSM Officer 94-97. *29 Brand End Road, Butterwick, Boston PE22 0ET* Tel (01205) 760375

HALL, Mrs Lilian Evelyn Mary. b 42. SW Minl Tr Course 02. **d** 05. NSM Ludgvan, Marazion, St Hilary and Perranuthnoe *Truro* from 05. *Pillar House, Ludgvan, Penzance TR20 8EY* Tel (01736) 740824 E-mail johnandlily.hall@btinternet.com

HALL, Mrs Linda Charlotte. b 50. Cam Inst of Educn CertEd72. St Alb Minl Tr Scheme 85 Oak Hill Th Coll 91. **d** 92 **p** 94. NSM St Alb St Steph *St Alb* 92-98; NSM Sandridge 98-99; C Ipswich All Hallows *St E* 99-00; Perm to Offic 01; TV Cwmbran *Mon* from 01. *St Mary's Vicarage, 87 Bryn Eglwys, Cwmbran NP44 2LF* Tel (01633) 483945

HALL, Mrs Margaret Mercia. b 39. Bedf Coll Lon BA61 Cam Univ DipRS78. Gilmore Ho 73. **dss** 80 **d** 87 **p** 94. Gt Chesham *Ox* 81-00; Par Dn 87-94; C 94-00; rtd 00; Perm to Offic *Ox* from 01. *The Elms, 94 Fullers Hill, Chesham HP5 1LR* Tel (01494) 784479

HALL, Mrs Marigold Josephine. b 29. Linc Th Coll 81. **dss** 83 **d** 87. Chapl Asst Hellesdon Hosp Nor 83-94; Nor St Pet Parmentergate w St Jo *Nor* 83-87; C 87-94; rtd 90; Perm to Offic *Nor* from 94. *36 Cavendish House, Recorder Road, Norwich NR1 1BW* Tel (01603) 625933

HALL, Ms Melanie Jane. b 55. Ex Univ BA78. Ripon Coll Cuddesdon 01. **d** 03 **p** 04. C Stepney St Dunstan and All SS *Lon* from 03. *6 Arbour Square, London E1 0SH* Tel and fax (020) 7790 9961 E-mail melanie.jh@btopenworld.com

HALL, Michael Alan. b 76. Univ of Wales (Lamp) BA98. Ripon Coll Cuddesdon 99. **d** 01 **p** 02. C Wellington Ch Ch *Lich* 01-05; V Chelmsf All SS *Chelmsf* from 05. *All Saints' Vicarage, 76A Kings Road, Chelmsford CM1 4HP* Tel (01245) 281706 E-mail revd.michael@btinternet.com

HALL, Canon Michael Anthony. b 41. St Paul's Coll Grahamstown LTh64. **d** 64 **p** 65. S Africa 64-01; C E London St Alb 65-67; C Queenstown St Mich 67-69; R Port Elizabeth All SS 70-78; R E London All SS 78-81; R Queenstown St Mich w Tarkastad St Mary 81-91; Adn Aliwal N 81-01; R Barkly E St Steph and P-in-c Dordrecht St Aug 91-01; Hon Can Grahamstown from 01; P-in-c Lapford, Nymet Rowland and Coldridge *Ex* 01-03; TV N Creedy from 03. *The Rectory, Lapford, Crediton EX17 6PX* Tel and fax (01363) 83321 Mobile 07751-798670 E-mail micksandhall@btopenworld.com

HALL, Michael Edward. b 32. Fitzw Ho Cam BA57 MA61. Ridley Hall Cam 68. **d** 69 **p** 70. C Aspley *S'well* 69-73; P-in-c Bulwell St Jo 73-75; V 75-81; P-in-c Tyler's Green *Ox* 81-90; V 90-00; rtd 00. *The Round House, 107 High Street, Brampton, Huntingdon PE28 4TQ*

HALL, Murray. b 34. K Coll Lon. **d** 61 **p** 62. C Eaton *Nor* 61-64; C Shalford *Guildf* 64-67; V Oxshott 67-72; P-in-c Runham *Nor* 72-80; R Filby w Thrigby w Mautby 72-80; P-in-c Stokesby w Herringby 72-80; R Filby w Thrigby, Mautby, Stokesby, Herringby etc 80-94; rtd 94; Perm to Offic *Nor* from 94. *64 Nursery Close, Acle, Norwich NR13 3EH* Tel (01493) 751287

HALL, Nicholas Charles. b 56. **d** 86 **p** 87. C Hyde St Geo *Ches* 86-89; C Cheadle 89-91; NSM from 91. *5 Brooklyn Crescent, Cheadle SK8 1DX* Tel 0161-491 6758 Fax 491 0285 E-mail nick@domini.org

HALL, Canon Nigel David. b 46. Univ of Wales (Cardiff) BA67 BD76 Lon Univ CertEd68. St Mich Coll Llan 73. **d** 76 **p** 77. C Cardiff St Jo *Llan* 76-81; R Llanbadarn Fawr, Llandegley and Llanfihangel etc *S & B* 81-95; RD Maelienydd 89-95; V Builth and Llanddewi'r Cwm w Llangynog etc from 95; Can Brecon Cathl from 94; Prec 99-00; Treas 00-04; Chan from 04; AD Builth from 04. *The Vicarage, 1 North Road, Builth Wells LD2 3BT* Tel (01982) 552355

HALL (née WANSTALL), Canon Noelle Margaret. b 53. Wolfs Coll Cam BEd76. Sarum & Wells Th Coll 84. **dss** 86 **d** 87 **p** 94. Hythe *Cant* 86-89; Par Dn 87-89; Par Dn Reculver and Herne Bay St Bart 89-94; C 94-95; Dioc Adv in Women's Min 92-99; Asst Dir Post-Ord Tr 94-97; P-in-c Sittingbourne St Mary 95-00; Hon Can Cant Cathl from 96; P-in-c Cant St Martin and St Paul 00-02; R from 02. *The Rectory, 13 Ersham Road, Canterbury CT1 3AR* Tel (01227) 462686 E-mail noelle@thinker117.freeserve.co.uk

HALL, Peter. *See* HALL, Canon Hubert William Peter

HALL, Peter. *See* HALL, The Rt Revd Albert Peter

HALL, Peter Douglas. b 60. Ox Poly HND81. Oak Hill Th Coll BA92. **d** 92 **p** 93. C Bromyard *Heref* 92-96; C Dorridge *Birm* 96-01; V Fareham St Jo *Portsm* from 01. *St John's Vicarage, 3A Upper St Michael's Grove, Fareham PO14 1DN* Tel (01329) 284203 *or* 280762 E-mail peter@revhall.freeserve.co.uk

HALL, Philip Edward Robin. b 36. Oak Hill Th Coll 64. **d** 67 **p** 68. C Ware Ch Ch *St Alb* 67-70; C Rayleigh *Chelmsf* 70-73; R Leven w Catwick *York* 73-85; P-in-c Mayfield *Lich* 85-95; P-in-c Ilam w Blore Ray and Okeover 89-95; Res Min Canwell, Hints and Drayton Bassett 95-01; rtd 01; Perm to Offic *Sheff* from 01 and *Derby* from 02. *45 St Alban's Road, Sheffield S10 4DN* Tel 0114-229 5032

HALL, Richard. *See* HALL, George Richard Wyndham

HALL, Richard Alexander Bullock. b 71. Ex Univ BA93 Edin Univ MTh95 BD98. Edin Th Coll 98. **d** 98 **p** 99. C Boxmoor St Jo *St Alb* 98-01; CF from 01. *c/o MOD Chaplains (Army)* Tel (01980) 615804 Fax 615800 E-mail rhall13572@aol.com

HALL, Robert Arthur. b 35. Lon Univ BSc66. NW Ord Course 74. **d** 77 **p** 78. C York St Paul *York* 77-79; R Elvington w Sutton on Derwent and E Cottingwith 79-82; Chapl Tiffield Sch Northants 82-84; V Bessingby and Carnaby *York* 84-88; V Fulford 88-00; P-in-c York St Denys 97-00; rtd 00; Perm to Offic *York* from 00. *11 Almond Grove, Filey YO14 9EH* Tel (01723) 518355 E-mail robertandjune@cwctv.net

HALL, Robert Stainburn. b 72. Qu Coll Cam BA93. St Steph Ho Ox 96. **d** 98 **p** 99. C Worc SE *Worc* 98-01; TV Halas from 01. *St Margaret's Vicarage, 55 Quarry Lane, Halesowen B63 4PD* Tel 0121-550 8744

HALL, Roger John. b 53. MBE97. Linc Th Coll. **d** 84 **p** 85. C Shrewsbury St Giles w Sutton and Atcham *Lich* 84-87; CF from 87; Warden Amport Ho 98-01; Chapl Guards Chpl Lon 01-03; Asst Chapl Gen from 03; Dir Ords 98-02 and Warden of Readers from 98. *c/o MOD Chaplains (Army)* Tel (01980) 615804 Fax 615800 E-mail revrjhall@aol.com

HALL, Ronald Cecil. b 20. St Aid Birkenhead 63. **d** 65 **p** 66. C Tamworth *Lich* 65-69; R Talke 69-74; V Birstwith *Ripon* 74-90; P-in-c Thornthwaite w Thruscross and Darley 76-77; rtd 90. *Wickham House, Kingsmead, Farm Road, Bracklesham Bay, Chichester PO20 8JU* Tel (01243) 671190

HALL, Mrs Sonia Winifred. b 44. Nottm Univ BSc66 Leeds Univ MSc68. Ox Min Course DipMin94. **d** 94 **p** 95. NSM Ox St Andr *Ox* 94-95; C Buckland 96-98; C Gainfield 98-99. *Alcudia, Bilbrook Lane, Minehead TA24 6HE* Tel 07930-558882 (mobile)

HALL, Stephen Clarence. b 23. Kelham Th Coll 46. **d** 51 **p** 52. C Killingworth *Newc* 51-53; C Newc H Cross 53-56; Rhodesia 56-77; S Africa from 77; R Makoni 56-69; P-in-c Bonda 59-62; R Mabelreign 62-68; Chapl Univ Coll of Rhodesia 68-77; Chapl Michaelhouse Sch 77-86; R Richard's Bay St Andr 86-97; rtd 97. *PO Box 102124, Meer-en-See, Zululand, 3901 South Africa* Tel (0027) (351) 32293

HALL, Stephen Philip. b 56. Ripon Coll Cuddesdon. **d** 84 **p** 85. C Camberwell St Giles *S'wark* 84-88; Chapl Brighton Poly *Chich* 88-92; TV Bicester w Bucknell, Caversfield and Launton *Ox* 92-02; Sub Chapl HM Pris Bullingdon 92-02; TV Southampton (City Cen) *Win* from 02. *The Deanery, 100 Chapel Road, Southampton SO14 5GL* Tel (023) 8063 3134

HALL, Prof Stuart George. b 28. New Coll Ox BA52 MA55 BD72. Ripon Hall Ox 53. **d** 54 **p** 55. C Newark w Coddington *S'well* 54-58; Tutor Qu Coll Birm 58-62; Lect Th Nottm Univ 62-73; Sen Lect 73-78; Prof Ecclesiastical Hist K Coll Lon 78-90; Perm to Offic *St Alb* 80-86 and *S'wark* 86-90; R Pittenweem *St And* 90-98; R Elie and Earlsferry 90-98; rtd 93. *Hopedene, 15 High Street, Elie, Leven KY9 1BY* Tel and fax (01333) 330145 E-mail sgh1@st-andrews.ac.uk

HALL, Thomas Bartholomew Berners. b 39. St Fran Coll Brisbane 63 ThL65. **d** 65 **p** 66. Australia 65-75 and from 82; C Townsville Cathl 65-66; C Rockhampton Cathl 66-69; P-in-c Emerald 69-70; R 70-75; P-in-c Whitehawk *Chich* 75-82; V Inglewood and Texas 82-89; V Pine Rivers S 85-89; R Strathpine from 89. *2 Lindale Court, Cashmere, Qld, Australia 4500* Tel (0061) (7) 3882 0880 *or* 3881 2090 Mobile 428-711719 E-mail tombbhall@ozemail.com.au

HALL, Timothy Patrick. b 65. Bucks Coll of Educn BSc87 Oak Hill Th Coll BA93. Trin Coll Bris 99. **d** 01 **p** 02. C Kingsnorth and Shadoxhurst *Cant* 01-04; P-in-c Crowfield w Stonham Aspal and Mickfield *St E* from 04; P-in-c Coddenham w Gosbeck and Hemingstone w Henley from 04. *The Rectory, The Street, Stonham Aspal, Stowmarket IP14 6AQ* Tel (01449) 711409 E-mail tph@tesco.net

HALL, Timothy Robert. b 52. Dur Univ BA74. St Jo Coll Nottm LTh87. **d** 87 **p** 88. C Hawarden *St As* 87-89; Chapl St D Coll Llandudno from 90. *Woodpecker Cottage, St David's College, Llandudno LL30 1RD* Tel (01492) 581224

HALL, William. b 34. Hull Univ BSc(Econ)56 St Jo Coll Dur CertRS88. NEOC 89. **d** 92 **p** 93. NSM Bishopwearmouth St Nic *Dur* 92-01; rtd 01. *31 Nursery Road, Silksworth Lane, Sunderland SR3 1NT* Tel 0191-528 4843

HALL, Canon William Cameron. b 40. K Coll Lon 60. **d** 65 **p** 66. C Thornaby on Tees St Paul *York* 65-68; Chapl to Arts and Recreation *Dur* from 68; V Grindon 71-80; Hon Can Dur Cathl from 84; Sen Chapl Actors' Ch Union 89-04; Perm to Offic *York* from 89; Hon Sen Research Fell Sunderland Univ *Dur* from 98. *1 Stafford Villas, Gateshead NE9 7SL* Tel and fax 0191-419 4883 E-mail billhalluk@yahoo.co.uk

HALL, William Nawton Sinclair. b 17. Kelham Th Coll 35. **d** 41 **p** 42. C Gateshead St Cuth *Dur* 41-43; C Notting Hill All SS w St Columb *Lon* 43-46; C Clewer St Andr *Ox* 46-50; PC Gateshead St Aid *Dur* 50-55; R Witton Gilbert 55-61; R Lowther w Askham *Carl* 61-84; rtd 83; Perm to Offic *Carl* 84-99. *1 Ambler Grove, Holmfield Park, Halifax HX2 9TR*

HALL-CARPENTER, Leslie Thomas Frank. b 19. Lich Th Coll 55. **d** 57 **p** 58. C Methley w Mickletown *Ripon* 57-59; V Kirkby Ravensworth w Dalton 59-61; India 61-63; V Ellingham w S Charlton *Newc* 63-67; V Horsford and Horsham St Faith w Newton St Faith *Nor* 67-69; R Lochgilphead *Arg* 69-70; Area Sec USPG *York* 70-73; P-in-c Well *Ripon* 73-74; V Kirk Hammerton 74-75; R Hunsingore w Cowthorpe 74-75; V Nun Monkton 74-75; R Kirk Hammerton w Nun Monkton and Hunsingore 75-77; P-in-c Hackness w Harwood Dale *York* 77-79; V Melbecks and Muker *Ripon* 79-82; R Twyford w Guist w Bintry w Themelthorpe etc *Nor* 82-84; rtd 84; Perm to Offic *Nor* 90-96. *c/o A Hall-Carpenter Esq, West End Cottage, High Street, Shipdham, Thetford IP25 7PA*

HALL-MATTHEWS, Preb John Cuthbert Berners. b 33. Univ of Qld BA55 K Coll Lon PGCE65. Coll of Resurr Mirfield 58. **d** 60 **p** 61. C Woodley St Jo the Ev *Ox* 60-63; C Is of Dogs Ch Ch and St Jo w St Luke *Lon* 63-65; Asst Chapl Ch Hosp Horsham 65-72; Chapl R Hosp Sch Holbrook 72-75; V Tupsley *Heref* 75-90; P-in-c Hampton Bishop and Mordiford w Dormington 77-90; RD Heref City 84-90; Preb Heref Cathl 85-90; TR Wolverhampton *Lich* 90-98; TR Cen Wolverhampton 98-02; Preb Lich Cathl from 01; rtd 02. *Hillcrest, Corvedale Road, Halford, Craven Arms SY7 9BT* Tel (01588) 672706 E-mail jotricia@hall-matthews.freeserve.co.uk

HALL-THOMPSON, Colin Lloyd. b 51. JP. TCD. **d** 84 **p** 85. C Dublin Rathfarnham *D & G* 84-86; Bp's C Clonmel Union *C, C & R* 86-91; Chapl Fort Mitchel Pris 86-91; Chapl Port of Cork 86-89; I Kilbride *Conn* 91-03; I Ballymacarrett *D & D* from 03; Hon Chapl Miss to Seafarers from 91. *The Vicarage, 155 Upper Newtownards Road, Belfast BT4 3HX* Tel (028) 9065 7180 E-mail colin.hall-thompson@ntlworld.com

HALLAM, Lawrence Gordon. b 31. Lich Th Coll 61. **d** 63 **p** 64. C Brighton St Martin *Chich* 63-68; R Cocking w Bepton 68-71; V Eastbourne Ch Ch 71-84; V Bexhill St Barn 84-87; rtd 87; Perm to Offic *Chich* 87-92. *18 Eaton Court, Eaton Gardens, Hove BN3 3PL* Tel (01273) 772328

HALLAM, Mrs Marilyn. **d** 03 **p** 04. NSM Hayes *Roch* from 03. *83 Pickhurst Rise, West Wickham, Bromley BR4 0AE* Tel (020) 8777 2246

HALLAM, Nicholas Francis. b 48. MRCPath91 Univ Coll Ox BA71 MA81 Glas Univ PhD76 MB, ChB81. Ox NSM Course 84. **d** 87 **p** 88. NSM Ox St Clem *Ox* 87-93; NSM Balerno *Edin* from 93. *11 Ravelrig Park, Edinburgh EH14 7DL* Tel 0131-449 5341 *or* 536 6329

HALLAM, Canon Peter Hubert. b 33. Trin Hall Cam BA56 MA60. Westcott Ho Cam 56. **d** 58 **p** 59. C St Annes St Thos *Blackb* 58-62; Asst Chapl and Tutor St Bede Coll Dur 62-67; V Briercliffe *Blackb* 67-98; Hon Can Blackb Cathl 92-98; rtd 98; Perm to Offic *Blackb* from 02. *57 Grassington Drive, Burnley BB10 2SP* Tel (01282) 441070

HALLAM, Stuart Peter. b 66. St Martin's Coll Lanc BA92 Wolfs Coll Cam BTh99. Westcott Ho Cam 96. **d** 99 **p** 00. C Battersea St Mary *S'wark* 99-02; Chapl RN from 02. *Royal Naval Chaplaincy Service, Room 203, Victory Building, HM Naval Base, Portsmouth PO1 3LS* Tel (01705) 727903 E-mail revhallam@aol.com

✠**HALLATT, The Rt Revd David Marrison.** b 37. Southn Univ BA59 St Cath Coll Ox BA62 MA66. Wycliffe Hall Ox 59. **d** 63 **p** 64 **c** 94. C Maghull *Liv* 63-67; PC Totley *Derby* 67-75; R Didsbury St Jas *Man* 75-80; R Barlow Moor 76-80; TR Didsbury St Jas and Em 80-89; Adn Halifax *Wakef* 89-94; Area Bp Shrewsbury *Lich* 94-01; Asst Bp Sheff from 01; rtd 02. *1 Merbeck Grove, High Green, Sheffield S35 4HE* Tel 0114-284 4440 E-mail david.hallatt@sheffield.anglican.org

HALLATT, John Leighton. b 34. St Pet Coll Ox BA58 MA62. Wycliffe Hall Ox 58. **d** 60 **p** 61. C Ipswich St Jo *St E* 60-63; C Warrington St Paul *Liv* 63-66; V Wadsley *Sheff* 66-72; V Hindley St Pet *Liv* 72-75; Area Sec (Scotland and Dios Newc and Dur) CMS 75-83; N Sec CMS 78-83; TR Cramlington *Newc* 83-90; V Monkseaton St Mary 90-99; rtd 99; Perm to Offic *Newc* from 99. *16 Eastfield Avenue, Whitley Bay NE25 8LT* Tel 0191-252 9518

HALLETT, Miss Caroline Morwenna. b 51. Nottm Univ BSc72 PGCE74 Univ of Wales (Ban) BTh05. EAMTC 03. **d** 05. C Sole Bay *St E* from 05. *31 The Firs, Reydon, Southwold IP18 6YS* E-mail challett@myself.com

HALLETT, Howard Adrian. b 43. Man Univ MPhil90. Oak Hill Th Coll BA81. **d** 81 **p** 82. C Walshaw Ch Ch *Man* 81-84; V Stoke sub Hamdon *B & W* 84-99; RD Ivelchester 91-95; V Kea *Truro* 99-05; rtd 05; Perm to Offic *Truro* from 05. *Tremanda, La Vague, Feock, Truro TR3 6RQ* Tel (01872) 862564

HALLETT, Miss Jacqueline Victoria (Lyn). b 54. Ex Univ BA75 PGCE76. Linc Th Coll 94. **d** 94 **p** 95. C Crook and Stanley *Dur* 94-99; P-in-c Crook 99-01; R 01-04; P-in-c Castleside from 04. *The Vicarage, 6 Hillcrest, Castleside, Consett DH8 9EB* Tel (01207) 590086

HALLETT, Keith Philip. b 37. Tyndale Hall Bris 61. **d** 64 **p** 65. C Higher Openshaw *Man* 64-68; C Bushbury *Lich* 68-71; P-in-c Drayton Bassett 71-72; R 72-90; V Fazeley 71-90; P-in-c Hints 78-83; V 83-90; C-in-c Canwell CD 78-83; V Canwell 83-90; RD Tamworth 81-90; P-in-c Buckhurst Hill *Chelmsf* 90-93; TR 93-02; rtd 02; Perm to Offic *B & W* from 03. *46 Balmoral Way, Worle, Weston-super-Mare BS22 9AL* Tel (01934) 413711 E-mail kph@webtribe.net

HALLETT, Peter. b 49. Bath Univ BSc72. Oak Hill Th Coll DPS. **d** 76 **p** 77. C Brinsworth w Catcliffe *Sheff* 76-79; P-in-c Doncaster St Jas 80-81; V 81-86; R Henstridge and Charlton Horethorne w Stowell *B & W* from 86. *The Vicarage, Henstridge, Templecombe BA8 0QE* Tel (01963) 362266 Fax as telephone E-mail halatvic@aol.com

HALLETT, Peter Duncan. b 43. CCC Cam BA66 MA68. Westcott Ho Cam 69. **d** 71 **p** 72. C Sawston *Ely* 71-73; C Lyndhurst and Emery Down *Win* 73-78; C Skegness and Winthorpe *Linc* 78-80; P-in-c Samlesbury *Blackb* 80-91; Asst Dir RE 80-00; C Leyland St Ambrose 91-94; V Lostock Hall from 00; P-in-c Farington Moss from 03. *St James's Vicarage, 76A Brownedge Road, Lostock Hall, Preston PR5 5AD* Tel (01772) 335366 E-mail peter.hallett@blackburn.anglican.org

HALLETT, Raymond. b 44. EMMTC 85. **d** 88 **p** 89. NSM Hucknall Torkard *S'well* 88-01; NSM Basford St Leodegarius 01-03. *26 Nursery Close, Hucknall, Nottingham NG15 6DQ* Tel 0115-953 7677

HALLIDAY, Christopher Norton Robert. b 48. Bradf Univ PhD99. N Ord Course 82. **d** 85 **p** 86. C Davyhulme St Mary *Man* 85-87; Lect Bolton St Pet 87-90; I Rathdrum w Glenealy, Derralossary and Laragh *D & G* 90-00; R Valley Lee St Geo USA 00-05. *21360 Little St Anne's Lane, Leonardtown, MD 20650, USA* Tel (001) (301) 862 2247 E-mail christopher@olg.com

HALLIDAY, Mrs Diana Patricia. b 40. ALA66. N Ord Course 89. **d** 92 **p** 94. NSM Burley in Wharfedale *Bradf* 92-95; NSM Harden and Wilsden 95-97; P-in-c Cullingworth from 97. *The Vicarage, Halifax Road, Cullingworth, Bradford BD13 5DE* Tel (01535) 272434 Mobile 07774-235844

HALLIDAY, Edwin James. b 35. NW Ord Course 70. **d** 73 **p** 74. C New Bury *Man* 73-76; V Bolton St Phil 76-82; Dioc Communications Officer 82-88; V Radcliffe St Thos and St Jo 82-90; R Gt Lever 90-02; rtd 02; Perm to Offic *Man* from 02. *8 Oxford Close, Farnworth, Bolton BL4 0NF* Tel (01204) 792347

HALLIDAY, Geoffrey Lewis. b 40. Lon Coll of Div LTh66. **d** 66 **p** 67. C W Bridgford *S'well* 66-72; V Woodborough 72-78; P-in-c St Dav Bermuda 78-80; V Rampton *S'well* 80-81; P-in-c Laneham 80-81; P-in-c Treswell and Cottam 80-81; V Rampton w Laneham, Treswell and Cottam 81-85; V Attenborough 85-88; Perm to Offic *Derby* 91-92; NSM Ilkeston St Mary from 92; rtd 03. *Frog Hollow, 323 Heanor Road, Ilkeston DE7 8TN* Tel 0115-930 8607 Mobile 07799-111093 E-mail fayandgeoff@froghollow.f9.co.uk

HALLIDAY, Jean Douglas. b 47. NTMTC 99. **d** 01 **p** 02. NSM Forest Gate Em w Upton Cross *Chelmsf* 01-02; NSM E Ham w Upton Park St Alb from 02. *St John's Flat, 522A Goresbrook Road, Dagenham RM9 4XB* Tel and fax (020) 8593 0616 E-mail jeandhalliday@aol.com

HALLIDAY, Louisa. b 42. Open Univ BA77 BA94. STETS. **d** 00 **p** 01. NSM Wylye and Till Valley *Sarum* from 00. *Station House, Great Wishford, Salisbury SP2 0PA* Tel (01722) 790618

HALLIDAY, Paula Patricia. b 50. Man Univ MEd83 TCD BTh94. **d** 94 **p** 95. C Killala w Dunfeeny, Crossmolina, Kilmoremoy etc *T, K & A* 94-97; I Crosspatrick Gp *C & O* 97-00; R Leonardtown St Andr USA from 00. *21360 Little St Anne's Lane, Leonardtown, MD 20650, USA* Tel (001) (301) 862 2247 E-mail revpaula@olg.com

✠HALLIDAY, The Rt Revd Robert Taylor. b 32. Glas Univ MA54 BD57. Edin Th Coll 55. **d** 57 **p** 58 **c** 90. C St Andrews St Andr *St And* 57-60; R 83-90; C Glas St Marg *Glas* 60-63; Lect NT Edin Th Coll 63-74; R Edin H Cross *Edin* 63-83; Tutor Edin Univ 69-71; Can St Mary's Cathl *Edin* 73-83; R St Andrews St Andr *St And* 83-90; Tutor St Andr Univ 84-90; Bp Bre 90-96; rtd 96. *28 Forbes Road, Edinburgh EH10 4ED* Tel 0131-221 1490

HALLIDIE SMITH, Andrew. b 31. Pemb Coll Cam BA54 MA58. Ely Th Coll 55. **d** 56 **p** 57. C Pype Hayes *Birm* 56-58; Sec Albany Trust Lon 58-60; Canada 60-63 and 67-70 and 79-81 and from 91; V Elmstead *Chelmsf* 63-67; R Alresford 70-79; V Elsecar *Sheff* 81-91; rtd 91. *PO Box 765, Big River SK, Canada, S0J 0E0* Tel (001) (306) 469 4417 Fax 469 5662

HALLING, William Laurence. b 43. Linc Coll Ox BA64 MA68 Lon Univ BD68. Tyndale Hall Bris 66. **d** 68 **p** 69. C Beckenham St Jo *Roch* 68-72; C Walton H Trin *Ox* 72-78; V Barrow St Mark *Carl* 78-86; R Kirkheaton *Wakef* 86-04; Chapl Mill Hill Hosp Huddersfield 86-04; rtd 04. *56 Westborough Drive, Halifax HX2 7QL* Tel (01422) 320829 E-mail halling@fish.co.uk

HALLIWELL, Christopher Eigil. b 57. Newc Univ BA78. Trin Coll Bris DipHE91. **d** 91 **p** 92. C Mildenhall *St E* 91-94; R Wrentham w Benacre, Covehithe, Frostenden etc 94-97; TV Sileby, Cossington and Seagrave *Leic* 97-01; V Preston St Cuth *Blackb* from 01. *St Cuthbert's Vicarage, 20 Black Bull Lane, Fulwood, Preston PR2 3PX* Tel (01772) 717346 E-mail challiwell@fish.co.uk *or* vicarstcuthberts@fish.co.uk

HALLIWELL, Ivor George. b 33. St Cath Coll Cam BA57 MA60. Wells Th Coll 58. **d** 60 **p** 60. C Hanworth St Geo *Lon* 60-62; C Willenhall *Cov* 62-65; C-in-c Whitley St Jas CD 65-68; V Whitley 68-72; V Corton *Nor* 72-77; P-in-c Hopton 72-74; V 74-77; Asst Chapl HM Pris Pentonville 77; Chapl HM Pris Ex 77-83; Chapl HM Pris Wakef 83-85; P-in-c Bickington *Ex* 85-87; P-in-c Ashburton w Buckland-in-the-Moor 85-87; V Ashburton w Buckland in the Moor and Bickington 87-90; Chapl HM Pris Channings Wood 90-97; Lic to Offic *Ex* 90-97; rtd 97; Perm to Offic *Ex* from 97. *Anastasis, Avenue Road, Bovey Tracey, Newton Abbot TQ13 9BQ* Tel (01626) 834899 E-mail ivor@ivorhalliwell.com

HALLIWELL, Canon Michael Arthur. b 28. St Edm Hall Ox BA50 MA53. Ely Th Coll 52. **d** 54 **p** 55. C Welling *S'wark* 54-57; C Bournemouth St Alb *Win* 57-59; Asst Gen Sec C of E Coun on Foreign Relns 59-62; C St Dunstan in the West *Lon* 60-62; Chapl Bonn w Cologne *Eur* 62-67; Chapl RAF 66-67; V Croydon St Andr *Cant* 67-71; R Jersey St Brelade *Win* 71-96; Chapl HM Pris Jersey 75-80; Vice-Dean Jersey *Win* 85-99; Tutor S Dios Minl Tr Scheme 92-96; rtd 96; Hon C Jersey Grouville *Win* 96-99; Hon Can Win Cathl 98-99; Perm to Offic from 99. *1 Alliance Cottages, Awbridge Hill, Romsey SO51 0HF* Tel (01794) 830395 E-mail halliwells@jerseymail.co.uk

HALLOWS, John Martin. b 50. Birm Univ BA78 Lon Univ PGCE82 E Lon Univ MSc93. Oak Hill Th Coll 92. **d** 94 **p** 95. C Boxmoor St Jo *St Alb* 94-98; TV Bracknell *Ox* 98-01; V Barrowford and Newchurch-in-Pendle *Blackb* from 01. *St Thomas's Vicarage, Wheatley Lane Road, Barrowford, Nelson BB9 6QS* Tel and fax (01282) 613206 E-mail jhallows@compuserve.com

HALLS, Canon Peter Ernest. b 38. Bris Univ BA62. Tyndale Hall Bris 59. **d** 64 **p** 65. C Blackb St Barn *Blackb* 64-67; C Bromley Ch Ch *Roch* 67-70; V Halvergate w Tunstall *Nor* 70-79; V Freethorpe w Wickhampton 71-79; P-in-c Beighton and Moulton 77-79; V Tuckswood 79-90; RD Nor S 86-90; R Brooke, Kirstead, Mundham w Seething and Thwaite 90-03; RD Depwade 91-97 and 01-03; Hon Can Nor Cathl 99-03; rtd 03; Perm to Offic *Nor* from 03. *1 Church Farm Close, Weston Longville, Norwich NR9 5JY* Tel (01603) 880835

HALLS, Susan Mary. *See* HEMSLEY HALLS, Susan Mary

HALMSHAW, Mrs Stella Mary. b 36. Brighton Coll of Educn TCert57. St Alb Minl Tr Scheme 81. **dss** 84 **d** 87 **p** 96. Radlett *St Alb* 84-01; Par Dn 87-93; Hon C 93-01; Chapl Herts Univ 93-96; rtd 96; P-in-c Wittersham w Stone-in-Oxney and Ebony *Cant* from 01. *The Rectory, The Street, Wittersham, Tenterden TN30 7EA* Tel (01797) 270142

HALSALL, Graham. b 61. Sheff Univ BA82 Westmr Coll Ox PGCE84. St Steph Ho Ox MTh00. **d** 00 **p** 01. C Preston St Jo and St Geo *Blackb* 00-02; C Torrisholme 02-04; P-in-c Bamber Bridge St Sav from 04. *St Saviour's Vicarage, Church Road, Bamber Bridge, Preston PR5 6AJ* Tel (01772) 335374 E-mail graham@halsall4461.reeserve.co.uk

HALSALL, Mrs Isobel Joan. b 47. Liv Univ CertEd71. Local Minl Tr Course 91. **d** 94 **p** 95. OLM Walshaw Ch Ch *Man* from 94. *42 Knowsley Road, Bolton BL2 5PU* Tel (01204) 394171

HALSALL, Michael John. b 61. Salford Univ BSc83. Wycliffe Hall Ox 88. **d** 91 **p** 92. C Cowley St Jo *Ox* 91-93; CF 93-99; P-in-c Prittlewell St Luke *Chelmsf* 99-00; V from 00. *The Vicarage, St Luke's Road, Southend-on-Sea SS2 4AB* Tel (01702) 467620 E-mail m.j.hallsall@talk21.com

HALSE, Raymond Stafford. b 19. Lon Univ BA49. Oak Hill Th Coll 46. **d** 50 **p** 51. C Rodbourne Cheney *Bris* 50-52; C Farnborough *Guildf* 52-54; V Islington St Jude Mildmay Park *Lon* 54-59; V Over Stowey w Aisholt *B & W* 59-68; V Ramsgate St Luke *Cant* 68-85; P-in-c Ramsgate Ch Ch 85; rtd 85; Hon C Hordle *Win* 85-89; Perm to Offic *Sarum* 90-01. *Berkeley Lodge Nursing Home, 42 Shelley Road, Worthing BN11 4DA* Tel (01903) 235111

HALSEY, Anthony Michael James. b 35. K Coll Cam BA56 MA62 Solicitor 64. St Jo Coll Nottm 73. **d** 75 **p** 76. C Derby St Werburgh *Derby* 75-77; Chapl Canford Sch Wimborne 78-87; TV Sanderstead All SS *S'wark* 87-89; Perm to Offic *Portsm* from 89; rtd 00. *Woodlands, South Road, Liphook GU30 7HS* Tel (01428) 724459 E-mail halseys@southroad.fsbusiness.co.uk

✠HALSEY, The Rt Revd Henry David. b 19. K Coll Lon BA38. Sarum Th Coll 40. **d** 42 **p** 43 **c** 68. C Petersfield w Sheet *Portsm* 42-45; Chapl RN 46-47; C Plymouth St Andr *Ex* 47-50; V Netheravon w Fittleton *Sarum* 50-53; C-in-c Chatham St Steph CD *Roch* 53-59; V Chatham St Steph 59-62; V Bromley SS Pet and Paul 62-68; Chapl Bromley Hosp 62-68; Hon Can Roch Cathl *Roch* 64-68; RD Bromley 65-66; Adn Bromley 66-68; Suff Bp Tonbridge 68-72; Bp Carl 72-89; rtd 89; Hon Asst Bp Portsm from 91. *Bramblecross, Gully Road, Seaview PO34 5BY* Tel (01983) 613583

HALSEY, Brother John Walter Brooke. b 33. Cam Univ BA57 Edin Univ Dip Past Th 67. Westcott Ho Cam 61. **d** 61 **p** 62. C Stocksbridge *Sheff* 61-65; Community of the Transfiguration Midlothian from 65; Ind Chapl Edin 65-69. *Hermitage of the Transfiguration, 23 Manse Road, Roslin EH25 9LF*

HALSON, Bryan Richard. b 32. Jes Coll Cam BA56 MA60 Liv Univ MA72 Geneva Univ 59. Ridley Hall Cam 57. **d** 59 **p** 60. C Coulsdon St Andr *S'wark* 59-62; Lic to Offic *Ches* 63-68; Tutor St Aid Birkenhead 63-65; Sen Tutor 65-68; Vice-Prin 68-69; Lect Alsager Coll of Educn 69-72; Prin Lect Crewe and Alsager Coll of HE 72-90; Perm to Offic *Ches* from 97. *1 Victoria Mill Drive, Willaston, Nantwich CW5 6RR*

HALSTEAD, Stuart. b 67. NTMTC 02. **d** 05. C Houghton Regis *St Alb* from 05. *The Clergy House, Lowry Drive, Houghton Regis, Dunstable LU5 5SJ* Tel (01582) 863292 E-mail stuart.halstead@btopenworld.com

✠HAMBIDGE, The Most Revd Douglas Walter. b 27. Lon Univ BD58. ALCD53 Angl Th Coll (BC) DD70. **d** 53 **p** 54 **c** 69. C Dalston St Mark w St Bart *Lon* 53-56; Canada 56-93 and from 95; R Cassiar 56-58; R Smithers 58-64; R Fort St John 64-69; Can Caledonia 65-69; Bp Caledonia 69-80; Bp New Westmr 80; Abp New Westmr and Metrop BC 81-93; Prin St Mark's Th Coll Dar es Salaam 93-95; Asst Bp Dar es Salaam 93-95; Chan

Vancouver Sch of Th from 95. *1621 Golf Club Drive, Delta BC, Canada, V4M 4E6* Tel (001) (604) 948 1931
E-mail hambidge@vst.edu

HAMBIDGE, John Robert. b 29. Birm Univ MA02. Sarum Th Coll. **d** 55 **p** 56. C Tynemouth H Trin W Town *Newc* 55-57; C Middlesbrough St Jo the Ev *York* 58-63; C Clerkenwell H Redeemer w St Phil *Lon* 63-64; C Richmond St Mary *S'wark* 64-66; V Richmond St Jo 66-76; R Swanscombe *Roch* 76-84; V Aberedw w Llandeilo Graban and Llanbadarn etc *S & B* 84-91; P-in-c Sibson w Sheepy and Ratcliffe Culey *Leic* 91-94; P-in-c Orton-on-the-Hill w Twycross etc 92-94; R The Sheepy Gp 95-97; rtd 97; Perm to Offic *Lich* from 99. *99 Elizabeth Drive, Tamworth B79 8DE* Tel (01827) 61526
E-mail john@hambidge.org.uk

HAMBLEN, John William Frederick. b 24. Sarum Th Coll 64. **d** 65 **p** 66. C Weymouth H Trin *Sarum* 66-68; C Marlborough 68-70; V Chardstock 70-77; P-in-c Lytchett Matravers 77-83; P-in-c Burpham *Chich* 83-89; Dioc Stewardship Adv 83-89; rtd 89; Perm to Offic *Ex* from 89. *73 West Cliff Road, Dawlish EX7 9QX*

HAMBLETON, Ronald Dalzell. b 27. Ripon Hall Ox 61. **d** 62 **p** 63. C Stokesay *Heref* 62-65; V Knowbury 65-75; P-in-c Weston under Penyard 75-79; P-in-c Hope Mansell 75-79; R Weston-under-Penyard w Hope Mansel and The Lea 79-92; rtd 92; NSM Portree *Arg* 92-95; Perm to Offic *Heref* from 96. *21 Pentaloe Close, Mordiford, Hereford HR1 4LS* Tel (01432) 870622

HAMBLIN, Derek Gordon Hawthorn. b 35. SW Minl Tr Course 94. **d** 96 **p** 97. Hon C S Brent and Rattery *Ex* from 96. *Little Sand Park, Chapel Fields, South Brent TQ10 9BS* Tel (01364) 72388

HAMBLIN, John Talbot. b 38. St Steph Ho Ox 64. **d** 66 **p** 67. C Newc St Jo *Newc* 66-70; C Covent Garden St Paul *Lon* 70-71; C St Marylebone Ch Ch w St Barn 71-72; C St Marylebone Ch Ch w St Paul 72-73; C Hendon St Mary 73-76; P-in-c Hornsey St Pet 76-77; V Tottenham Ch Ch W Green 76-77; V W Green Ch Ch w St Pet 77-96; rtd 98. *Terry's Cross House, Brighton Road, Woodmancote, Henfield BN5 9SX* Tel (01273) 491256

HAMBLIN, Canon Roger Noel. b 42. Ripon Hall Ox 67. **d** 70 **p** 71. C Scotforth *Blackb* 70-73; C Altham w Clayton le Moors 73-76; V Cockerham w Winmarleigh 76-87; V Cockerham w Winmarleigh and Glasson 87-00; P-in-c Wray w Tatham and Tatham Fells 00-03; V E Lonsdale from 03; Hon Can Blackb Cathl from 04. *The Vicarage, Main Street, Wray, Lancaster LA2 8QF* Tel (01524) 221030

HAMBORG, Graham Richard. b 52. Bris Univ BSc73 Nottm Univ BA76 MTh77. St Jo Coll Nottm 74. **d** 77 **p** 78. C Tile Cross *Birm* 77-80; C Upton cum Chalvey *Ox* 80-82; TV 82-86; V Ruscombe and Twyford 86-04; AD Sonning 03-04; CME Adv *Chelmsf* from 04; NSM Gt Baddow from 04. *The Rectory, Colam Lane, Little Baddow, Chelmsford CM3 4SY* Tel (01245) 222454
E-mail revghamborg@hotmail.com

HAMBREY, Canon Frank Bernard. b 14. Leeds Univ BA42. Coll of Resurr Mirfield 43. **d** 44 **p** 45. C W Bromwich St Andr *Lich* 44-46; C Edgmond 46-51; V Bury St Thos *Man* 51-57; Area Sec (Dios Man and Liv) SPG 57-64; USPG 65-68; V Colton *Carl* 68-70; Can Res Bermuda 70-75; Perm to Offic *Carl* 77-99; rtd 79. *Bully Cottage, Embleton, Cockermouth CA13 9YA* Tel (01768) 776379

HAMBREY, Frederick Charles. b 19. Leeds Univ BA41. Coll of Resurr Mirfield 41. **d** 43 **p** 45. C Bloxwich *Lich* 43-45; C Willenhall St Giles 45-49; C Hednesford 49-54; V W Bromwich Gd Shep 54-59; V Hanbury 59-70; V Colton *Carl* 70-71; V Satterthwaite and Rusland 70-71; V Colton w Satterthwaite and Rusland 71-84; rtd 84; Perm to Offic *Carl* from 85. *Underknott, Blease Road, Threlkeld, Keswick CA12 4RX* Tel (01768) 779604

HAMBROOK, Peter John. b 37. **d** 01 **p** 02. OLM Gt Mongeham w Ripple and Sutton by Dover *Cant* 01-04; OLM Deal St Leon w St Rich and Sholden etc from 04; OLM Ringwould w Kingsdown and Ripple etc from 05. *4 Brewery Cottages, Northbourne Road, Great Mongeham, Deal CT14 0HA* Tel (01304) 364457 E-mail peter@4brewerycotts.fsnet.co.uk

HAMEL COOKE, Ian Kirk. b 17. Birm Univ BA39. Chich Th Coll 39. **d** 41 **p** 42. C Bedminster St Fran *Bris* 41-43; C Alton All SS *Win* 43-48; V N Baddesley 48-55; R Hartest w Boxted *St E* 55-63; V Addlestone *Guildf* 63-75; R Tittleshall w Godwick and Wellingham *Nor* 75-76; R Tittleshall w Godwick, Wellingham and Weasenham 76-82; rtd 82; Perm to Offic *Nor* from 82. *Crugmeer, Croft Yard, Wells-next-the-Sea NR23 1JS* Tel (01328) 710358

HAMER, David Handel. b 41. Cape Town Univ BA61 Trin Coll Ox BA66. Coll of Resurr Mirfield 62. **d** 66 **p** 67. S Africa 66-73; C Claremont 66-70; Chapl St Paul's Coll Grahamstown 70-73; Chapl Blundell's Sch Tiverton 73-01; rtd 01. *Jaspers Green, Uplowman, Tiverton EX16 7DP* Tel (01884) 829130

HAMER, Irving David. b 59. **d** 84 **p** 85. C Newton Nottage *Llan* 84-88; C Roath 88-90; V Llansawel, Briton Ferry 90-00; V Roath St Martin from 00; Miss to Seafarers from 90. *St Martin's Vicarage, Strathnairn Street, Roath, Cardiff CF24 3JL* Tel (029) 2048 2295 E-mail irving.hamer@ic24.net

HAMER, Mrs Penelope Ann. MA FIBMS. **d** 00 **p** 01. NSM Hartpury w Corse and Staunton *Glouc* from 00. *Catsbury Cottage, Corsend Road, Hartpury GL19 3BP* Tel (01425) 700314

HAMER, Canon Val. b 52. Leeds Univ BA74. S'wark Ord Course 83. **dss** 86 **d** 87 **p** 94. Warlingham w Chelsham and Farleigh *S'wark* 86-88; Par Dn 87-88; Par Dn Caterham 88-94; C 94-96; RD Caterham 95-96; Sub Chapl HM Pris Wandsworth 88-95; V Addiscombe St Mildred *S'wark* 96-02; Ldr Post Ord Tr Croydon Area 94-99; Can Res and Chan Heref Cathl *Heref* from 02. *2 Cathedral Close, Hereford HR1 2NG* Tel and fax (01432) 278672 E-mail chancellor@herefordcathedral.co.uk *or* val_hamer@hotmail.com

HAMERTON, Thomas Patrick. b 13. St Edm Hall Ox BA35 DipTh36 MA50. Cuddesdon Coll 37. **d** 38 **p** 39. C Bury St Mary *Man* 38-40; C Southbourne St Kath *Win* 40-42; India 42-44; C Parkstone St Pet w Branksea *Sarum* 44-52; V Weedon Lois w Plumpton *Pet* 52-58; R Abthorpe 52-58; R Slapton 52-58; V Weedon Lois w Plumpton and Moreton Pinkney 58-63; R Abington 63-76; V Welton w Ashby St Ledgers 76-83; rtd 83; Perm to Offic *Glouc* 83-95. *c/o Mrs F Dale, 63 Clifton Road, Rugby CV21 3QG*

HAMEY, Geoffrey Allan. b 25. Lon Univ BSc47. S'wark Ord Course 75. **d** 78 **p** 79. NSM Pinner *Lon* 78-83; P-in-c Fincham *Ely* 83-84; P-in-c Marham 83-84; P-in-c Shouldham 83-84; P-in-c Shouldham Thorpe 83-84; V 84-88; rtd 88; Hon C Winkleigh *Ex* 88-96; Perm to Offic *Ex* 96-02; *Lich* from 02. *15 Victoria Gardens, Lichfield WS13 8BG* Tel (01543) 416079

✠**HAMID, The Rt Revd David.** b 55. McMaster Univ Ontario BSc78. Trin Coll Toronto MDiv81. **d** 81 **p** 82 **c** 02. Canada 81-96; C Burlington St Chris 81-83; R Burlington St Jo 83-87; Miss Co-ord Gen Syn of Angl Ch of Canada 87-96; Hon Can Santo Domingo 93-02; Dir Ecum Affairs ACC 96-02; Suff Bp Eur from 02. *14 Tufton Street, London SW1P 3QZ* Tel (020) 7898 1160 Fax 7898 1166
E-mail david.hamid@europe.c-of-e.org.uk

HAMIL, Sheila. b 49. TCert71. NEOC DipHE95. **d** 95 **p** 98. NSM Wallsend St Luke *Newc* 95-97; NSM Long Benton St Mary 97-02; NSM Willington from 02. *5 Kings Road, Wallsend NE28 7QT* Tel 0191-287 3449
E-mail sheila@sheilahamil.co.uk

HAMILL-STEWART, Simon Francis. b 32. Pemb Coll Cam BA56. N Ord Course 77. **d** 80 **p** 81. NSM Neston *Ches* 80-83; C 83-86; V Over St Jo 86-00; Dioc Ecum Officer 92-00; rtd 00; Perm to Offic *Ches* 00-01; C Middlewich w Byley 01-03. *87 Warmingham Lane, Middlewich CW10 0DJ* Tel (01606) 737329

HAMILTON, Canon Edgar Reid. b 27. TCD BA49 MA52. CITC 51. **d** 51 **p** 52. C Belfast St Donard *D & D* 51-55; Dean's V Belf Cathl 55-59; C-in-c Stormont *D & D* 60-64; I 64-93; Can Belf Cathl 85-91; Preb Wicklow St Patr Cathl Dublin 90-93; rtd 93. *13 Massey Park, Belfast BT4 2JX* Tel (028) 9076 3835

HAMILTON, Gerald Murray Percival. b 14. Ch Coll Cam BA37 MA41. Ridley Hall Cam 37. **d** 39 **p** 40. C Shirley *Win* 39-40; Bp's Dom Chapl 40-41; C Odiham w S Warnborough and Long Sutton 41-44; C Leeds St Pet *Ripon* 44-46; V Ashton-upon-Mersey St Mary *Ches* 46-51; Relig Broadcasting Org BBC N Region 52-65; Lic to Offic *Ches* 51-65; Can Res Newc Cathl *Newc* 65-67; Bp's Ind and Community Adv 65-67; Prin Lect Coll of Ripon & York St Jo 67-79; R Crayke w Brandsby and Yearsley *York* 78-82; rtd 82; Perm to Offic *York* from 82. *31 St Andrewgate, York YO1 7BR* Tel (01904) 632506 Fax 623288 E-mail peter@standrewgate.demon.co.uk

HAMILTON, Graham. *See* HAMILTON, William Graham

HAMILTON, James Davy. b 20. Hatf Coll Dur 38. Edin Th Coll 40. **d** 43 **p** 45. C Kirkcaldy *St And* 43-46; C Wokingham St Paul *Ox* 46-49; Chapl RAF 49-55; C St Athan *Llan* 49-50; C Boscombe Down 50-52; C Amersham *Ox* 55-62; R Sandford w Upton Hellions *Ex* 62-79; P-in-c Ashprington 79-81; P-in-c Cornworthy 79-81; R Ashprington, Cornworthy and Dittisham 81-83; C Weymouth St Paul *Sarum* 83-85; rtd 85; Perm to Offic *Ex* from 85. *21 Langaton Lane, Exeter EX1 3SP* Tel (01392) 466747

HAMILTON, John Frederick. b 57. Leeds Univ BA78. Edin Th Coll 78. **d** 80 **p** 81. C Whitkirk *Ripon* 80-83; C Leeds Belle Is St Jo and St Barn 83-86; V Oulton w Woodlesford 86-94; V Cookridge H Trin from 94. *Cookridge Vicarage, 53 Green Lane, Cookridge, Leeds LS16 7LW* Tel 0113-267 4921 Mobile 07780-677341 Fax 0113-261 2102
E-mail sulaco57@btopenworld.com

HAMILTON, John Hans Patrick. b 44. K Coll Lon BD66 AKC67 Lon Univ DipAdEd76 FCMI96. St Boniface Warminster 66. **d** 67 **p** 68. C Cleobury Mortimer w Hopton Wafers *Heref* 67-69; C Sanderstead All SS *S'wark* 69-73; V Battersea St Mary-le-Park 73-75; Perm to Offic *Ely* 75-90; Dir of Educn *Derby* 90-95; P-in-c Cliddesden and Ellisfield w Farleigh Wallop etc *Win* 95-00; Perm to Offic 00-03; P-in-c The Caundles w Folke and Holwell *Sarum* from 03; P-in-c Dungeon Hill from 03. *The Rectory, Holwell, Sherborne DT9 5LF* Tel (01963) 23035
E-mail john@montoid2.fsnet.co.uk

HAMILTON, John Nicholas. b 49. Trin Coll Cam BA71 MA75. Ridley Hall Cam 72. **d** 75 **p** 76. C Ealing Dean St Jo *Lon* 75-79; C Stoughton *Guildf* 79-83; R Denton St Lawr *Man* 83-88; R The Sherbornes w Pamber *Win* from 88. *The Rectory, Vyne Road, Sherborne St John, Basingstoke RG24 9HX* Tel (01256) 850434 E-mail jnh@btinternet.com

HAMILTON, Canon Noble Ridgeway. b 23. TD66. TCD BA45 MA49. **d** 47 **p** 48. C Dundela St Mark *D & D* 47-51; C Holywood 51-55; I Belfast St Clem 55-61; I Seapatrick 61-89; Can Dromore Cathl 66-89; Prec 75-84; Chan 84-89; rtd 89; Lic to Offic *D & D* from 90. *67 Meadowvale, Waringstown, Craigavon BT66 7RL* Tel (028) 3888 2064

HAMILTON, Paul Stuart. b 69. Univ of Wales (Ban) BTh02. EAMTC. **d** 02 **p** 03. C Hawkwell *Chelmsf* from 02. *44 Hawkwell Park Drive, Hockley SS5 4HB* Tel (01702) 204547 E-mail pshamilton@btinternet.com

HAMILTON, Richard Alexander. b 46. Pemb Coll Cam BA67 MA87 Brunel Univ PGCE97. S Dios Minl Tr Scheme 82. **d** 85 **p** 86. NSM Guernsey St Sampson *Win* 85-89; C Highgate St Mich *Lon* 89-91; P-in-c Tottenham H Trin 91-96; Master Denbigh High Sch Luton 96-98; TV The Ortons, Alwalton and Chesterton *Ely* from 98. *The Rectory, 67 Church Drive, Orton Waterville, Peterborough PE2 5HE* Tel (01733) 238877 Mobile 07958-317512 Fax (01733) 239885 E-mail hamvic@aol.com

HAMILTON, Robert Hair. b 26. Oak Hill Th Coll 75. **d** 76 **p** 77. C Bootle St Matt *Liv* 76-78; C Horwich H Trin *Man* 78-81; R Whalley Range St Marg 81-86; Lect Em Bible Coll Birkenhead 86-97; Perm to Offic *Ches* from 86; rtd 91. *Akolutos, 27 Wimbourne Avenue, Thingwall, Wirral CH61 7UL* Tel 0151-648 4014

HAMILTON, Samuel Derek. b 34. Bris Univ BA58. Tyndale Hall Bris 54. **d** 59 **p** 60. C Dublin St Cath *D & G* 59-61; C Dublin Booterstown 61-63; I Drumcliffe w Lissadell *K, E & A* 63-69; I Cahir *C & O* 69-78; Bp's C Sallaghy *Clogh* 79-83; rtd 83. *The Old Rectory, 6 Dupplin Terrace, Perth PH2 7DG* Tel (01738) 623948

HAMILTON, William Graham. b 63. New Coll Ox BA86. Wycliffe Hall Ox BA95. **d** 95 **p** 96. C Ivybridge w Harford *Ex* 95-99; V Bovey Tracey SS Pet, Paul and Thos w Hennock from 99. *The Vicarage, Coombe Cross, Bovey Tracey, Newton Abbot TQ13 9EP* Tel (01626) 833813 E-mail revgraham.hamilton@btopenworld.com

HAMILTON, William Joseph Taylor. b 40. DMA64 Univ Coll Ches MTh00. **d** 97 **p** 98. NSM Ches Team *Ches* 97-02; C Malborough w S Huish, W Alvington and Churchstow *Ex* 02; C Thurlestone, S Milton, W Alvington etc from 02. *The Vicarage, Townsend Road, West Alvington, Kingsbridge TQ7 3PZ* Tel (01548) 857658 E-mail bill@hamiltonb.freeserve.co.uk

HAMILTON-BROWN, James John. b 35. Lon Univ BSc59. Trin Coll Bris AdDipTh90 Ridley Hall Cam 59. **d** 61 **p** 62. C Attenborough w Bramcote *S'well* 61-67; V Bramcote 67-76; R and D Officer Abps' Coun on Evang 76-79; Lic to Offic *Sarum* 76-81 and 91-95; TR Dorchester 81-91; Sec Par and People 91-95; P-in-c Tarrant Valley 95-99; C Tollard Royal w Farnham, Gussage St Michael etc 99-00; rtd 00; Perm to Offic *Sarum* from 00. *The Old Mill, Spetisbury, Blandford Forum DT11 9DF* Tel (01258) 453939 E-mail jumperhb@aol.com

HAMILTON MANON, Phillip Robert Christian. b 49. BA88. St Steph Ho Ox 89. **d** 90 **p** 91. C Norton St Mary *Dur* 90-94; P-in-c Cleadon Park 94-95; V 95-97; TV Lewes All SS, St Anne, St Mich and St Thos *Chich* 97-00; R Lewes St Anne from 00. *St Anne's Rectory, 57 St Anne's Crescent, Lewes BN7 1SD* Tel (01273) 472545

HAMLET, Paul Manning. b 42. Open Univ BA81 Ex Univ MEd96 Univ of Wales (Lamp) MTh04 Lambeth STh84 FCollP96. Kelham Th Coll 61. **d** 66 **p** 67. C Rumboldswyke *Chich* 66-69; C Ely 69-73; Hon C Ipswich St Bart *St E* 73-84; Chapl Wellington Sch Somerset 84-94; Chapl Ipswich Sch 94-02; CF (TAVR) 88-99; CF (ACF) from 99; rtd 02; Perm to Offic *St E* from 02. *5 Wincanton Close, Ipswich IP4 3EE* Tel (01473) 724413 E-mail paul.hamlet@btopenworld.com

HAMMERSLEY, Peter. b 41. Lon Univ BD78 Birm Univ MEd87 PhD97. Kelham Th Coll 60. **d** 65 **p** 66. C Oadby *Leic* 65-69; R Linstead Jamaica 70-73; Chapl and Hd RE DeCarteret Coll Mandeville 73-77; Chapl K Sch and Min Can Worc Cathl *Worc* 77-84; V Foley Park 84-90; TV Kidderminster St Jo and H Innocents 90-91; Hon Lect Sch of Educn Dioc Warden of Readers 91; Vice-Prin Aston Tr Scheme 91-97; Birm Univ *Birm* from 98; Adult RE Researcher St Pet Saltley Trust 98-99; Chapl HM Pris Hewell Grange from 98. *52 Hanbury Road, Droitwich WR9 8PR* Tel (01905) 798590 *or* (01527) 552216 Fax (01527) 552001 E-mail peter.hammersley@tiscali.co.uk

HAMMERSLEY, Peter Angus Ragsdale. b 35. Linc Th Coll 74. **d** 76 **p** 77. C Stafford *Lich* 76-79; P-in-c W Bromwich St Andr 79-83; V 83-88; P-in-c W Bromwich Ch Ch 85-88; V Streetly 88-98; RD Walsall 90-98; C Ledbury *Heref* 98-00; Team Chapl W Heref 98-00; rtd 01; Assoc TV Ledbury *Heref* 01-04. *15 Pound Close, Tarrington, Hereford HR1 4AZ* Tel (01432) 890609

HAMMETT, The Ven Barry Keith. b 47. Magd Coll Ox BA71 MA74. St Steph Ho Ox 71. **d** 74 **p** 75. C Plymouth St Pet *Ex* 74-77; Chapl RN 77-02; Chapl of the Fleet and Adn for the RN from 02; Dir Gen Naval Chapl Service from 02; QHC from 99; Hon Can Portsm Cathl *Portsm* from 02; Can Gib Cathl *Eur* from 03. *Royal Naval Chaplaincy Service, Room 203, Victory Building, HM Naval Base, Portsmouth PO1 3LS* Tel (023) 9272 7900 Fax 9272 7111

HAMMON, David Edward. b 48. St Mich Coll Llan 99. **d** 01 **p** 02. C Pembroke Dock *St D* 01-04. *Address temp unknown* Tel 07779-711239 (mobile) E-mail davidhammon@lineone.net

HAMMOND, Mrs Barbara Watson. b 33. ACP70 Lanc Univ MA79. Bp Otter Coll TCert53 S'wark Ord Course DipRS92. **d** 92 **p** 94. NSM Upper Norwood St Jo *S'wark* 92-94; Hon C Spring Park All SS 94-97; Perm to Offic *S'wark* 97-02 and *Portsm* from 98. *27 Maisemore Gardens, Emsworth PO10 7JU* Tel (01243) 370531 E-mail barbara@br2811.demon.co.uk

HAMMOND, Canon Brian Leonard. b 31. Bris Univ BSc54. Wells Th Coll 56. **d** 58 **p** 59. C Clapham H Trin *S'wark* 58-62; V Walworth All SS and St Steph 62-72; V S Merstham 72-87; RD Reigate 80-86; Hon Can S'wark Cathl 83-97; V Spring Park All SS 87-97; rtd 97; Perm to Offic *S'wark* 97-02 and *Portsm* from 98. *27 Maisemore Gardens, Emsworth PO10 7JU* Tel (01243) 370531 Mobile 07802-482974 E-mail brian@br2811.demon.co.uk

HAMMOND, Carolyn John-Baptist. b 64. St Jo Coll Ox MA90 Univ Coll Ox DPhil93 CCC Ox BA97. Westcott Ho Cam CTM98. **d** 98 **p** 99. C Gamlingay w Hatley St Geo and E Hatley *Ely* 98-99; C Gamlingay and Everton 99-01; R from 01. *The Rectory, Stocks Lane, Gamlingay, Sandy SG19 3JP* Tel (01767) 652181 *or* 651204 E-mail revcally@ukonline.co.uk

HAMMOND, Charles Kemble. b 10. TCD BA33 MA37. TCD Div Sch Div Test33. **d** 34 **p** 35. C Willowfield *D & D* 35-37; C Belfast St Donard 37; Australia from 37; C Summer Hill 37-38; C-in-c Golden Grove 38-40; Dir Educn *Sydney* 40-49; R Carlingford 49-52; R Heyfield 52-58; Chapl St Vin and Prince Henry Hosps 58-59; Chapl Alfred Hosp 59-64; Chapl Parramatta Psychiatric Hosp 64-66; Dir of Chapl Dio Melbourne 66-78; rtd 78. *69 Courtlands, 15 Gloucester Avenue, North Parramatta, NSW, Australia 2151* Tel (0061) (2) 9360 1064

HAMMOND, David Geoffrey. b 80. **d** 04 **p** 05. NSM Preston-on-Tees and Longnewton *Dur* from 04. *5 The Close, Long Newton, Stockton-on-Tees TS21 1DW* Tel (01642) 570878

HAMMOND, Diana Mary. b 46. **d** 99 **p** 00. OLM Bishopstrow and Boreham *Sarum* 99-04; OLM Upper Wylye Valley from 04. *41 Bishopstrow, Warminster BA12 9HN* Tel (01985) 214495

HAMMOND, Frank. b 49. Linc Th Coll 75. **d** 77 **p** 78. C Sutton *Liv* 77-79; C Blundellsands St Nic 80-83. *Address temp unknown*

HAMMOND, Canon Jacob Aryee. b 47. St Nic Th Coll Ghana LTh85. **d** 84 **p** 85. Ghana 84-97; Hon Can Koforidua from 95; C Merthyr Tydfil St Dav *Llan* 97-04. *Address temp unknown*

HAMMOND, Lindsay John. b 57. Southn Univ BA83. Sarum & Wells Th Coll 84. **d** 86 **p** 87. C Ashford *Cant* 86-90; V Appledore w Brookland, Fairfield, Brenzett etc 90-03; P-in-c Stone-in-Oxney 95-03; RD S Lympne 95-01; P-in-c Westwell, Hothfield, Eastwell and Boughton Aluph from 03; Hon Min Can Cant Cathl from 93. *The Vicarage, Eastwell Lane, Westwell, Ashford TN25 4LQ* Tel (01233) 712576 E-mail applevic@clara.co.uk

HAMMOND, Martin James. b 62. St Jo Coll Nottm. **d** 05. C Walmley *Birm* from 05. *90 Walmley Ash Road, Sutton Coldfield B76 1JB* Tel 0121-681 4742 E-mail curate@stjohnswalmley.co.uk

HAMMOND, Peter Clark. b 27. Linc Coll Ox BA49 MA53. Wells Th Coll 51. **d** 52 **p** 53. C Willesborough *Cant* 52-55; C Croydon St Jo 55-59; R Barham 60-66; V Walmer 66-85; V Rolvenden 85-89; rtd 89; Perm to Offic *Ely* from 89. *19 Hardwick Street, Cambridge CB3 9JA* Tel (01223) 467425

HAMNETT, Herbert Arnold. b 22. K Coll Lon BSc49. Qu Coll Birm 49. **d** 51 **p** 52. C Greenhill St Jo *Lon* 51-54; C Horsham *Chich* 55-60; R Yapton w Ford 60-87; rtd 87; Perm to Offic *St E* 87-97. *Clarence House, Stradbrooke Road, Fressingfield, Eye IP21 5PP* Tel (01379) 588082

HAMPEL, Canon Michael Hans Joachim. b 67. Univ Coll Dur BA89 St Chad's Coll Dur MA02 FRSA02. Westcott Ho Cam 90. **d** 93 **p** 94. C Whitworth w Spennymoor *Dur* 93-97; Min Can, Prec and Sacr Dur Cathl 97-02; Sen Tutor St Chad's Coll Dur 02-04; Can Res St E Cathl *St E* from 04. *1 Abbey Precincts, Bury St Edmunds IP33 1RS* Tel (01284) 761982 Fax 768655 Mobile 07947-070210 E-mail michael.hampel@dunelm.org.uk

HAMPSON, Claude Eric. b 25. Rhodes Univ BA49. St Paul's Coll Grahamstown LTh50. **d** 50 **p** 51. C Pietermaritzburg Cathl S Africa 50-54; C Greenford H Cross *Lon* 54-58; Sec Fellowship of SS Alb and Sergius 58-60; Australia 60-74 and 77-04; R Mt Isa and Adn of the W 67-74; P-in-c Mekong Vietnam 74-75; V Kilburn St Aug w St Jo *Lon* 75-77; R Branxton 77-82; rtd 85. *PO Box 107, Edgecliffe, NSW, Australia 2027*

HAMPSON, David. b 46. Chich Th Coll 69. **d** 72 **p** 73. C Penrith *Carl* 72-78; V Crosscrake 78-95; V Crosscrake and Preston Patrick 95; P-in-c Arnside 95-97; rtd 97. *81 Rectory Road, North Ashton, Wigan WN4 0QD* Tel (01942) 728760

HAMPSON, Miss Judith Elizabeth. b 50. I M Marsh Coll of Physical Educn Liv BEd72 Open Univ BA89. Ripon Coll Cuddesdon 90. **d** 92 **p** 94. C Alnwick *Newc* 92-96; R Allendale w Whitfield 96-05; V Haydon Bridge and Beltingham w Henshaw from 05. *The Vicarage, Haydon Bridge, Hexham NE47 6LL* Tel (01434) 684152 E-mail rev.jude@dsl.pipex.com

HAMPSON, Michael John. b 67. Jes Coll Ox BA88. Ripon Coll Cuddesdon 88. **d** 91 **p** 92. C W Burnley All SS *Blackb* 91-93; C Harlow St Mary Magd *Chelmsf* 93-00; V Church Langley 00-04. *Station House, Arkholme, Carnforth LA6 1AZ* Tel 07712-477003 (mobile) E-mail michael@michaelhampson.freeserve.co.uk

HAMPSON, Robert Edward. b 58. LSE BSc80 Heythrop Coll Lon BA91 MTh93. Ridley Hall Cam. **d** 97 **p** 98. C Chingford SS Pet and Paul *Chelmsf* 97-01; V Wanstead H Trin Hermon Hill from 01. *Holy Trinity Vicarage, 185 Hermon Hill, London E18 1QQ* Tel (020) 8530 3029 E-mail roberthampson@btopenworld.com

HAMPSTEAD, Archdeacon of. *See* LAWSON, The Ven Michael Charles

HAMPTON, Alison Jean. b 61. St Mary's Coll Twickenham BA98. SEITE. **d** 01 **p** 02. C Notting Dale St Clem w St Mark and St Jas *Lon* 01-04; P-in-c Burrough Hill Pars *Leic* from 04; Chapl Brooksby Melton Coll from 04. *The Rectory, 1 High Street, Somerby, Melton Mowbray LE14 2PZ* Tel (01664) 454318 E-mail alison@clementjames.co.uk

HAMPTON, Carla Irene. b 47. ARCM67 GRSM68. NTMTC 96. **d** 99 **p** 00. Asst Chapl Mid-Essex Hosp Services NHS Trust 98-02; Chapl 02-04; NSM Chelmsf St Andr *Chelmsf* 99-04; NSM Gt and Lt Leighs and Lt Waltham from 04. *280 Broomfield Road, Chelmsford CM1 4DY* Tel (01245) 356287 *or* 514069 E-mail revcarla@fish.co.uk

HAMPTON, Canon John Waller. b 28. Linc Coll Ox BA51 MA58. Westcott Ho Cam 51. **d** 53 **p** 54. C Rugby St Andr *Cov* 53-56; Chapl St Paul's Sch Hammersmith 56-65; Chapl St Paul's Girls' Sch Hammersmith 60-65; V Gaydon w Chadshunt *Cov* 65-69; Asst Dir RE 65-70; C-in-c Warwick St Nic 69-75; Fell Qu Coll Birm 75-76; P-in-c Wetton *Lich* 76-82; P-in-c Alstonfield 76-82; P-in-c Sheen 76-80; RD Alstonfield 80-82; P-in-c Butterton 80-82; P-in-c Warslow and Elkstones 80-82; P-in-c Broadway *Worc* 82-91; V 91-93; RD Evesham 87-93; Hon Can Worc Cathl 88-93; rtd 93; Perm to Offic *Ab* from 93. *41 Craigton Terrace, Aberdeen AB15 7RN* Tel (01224) 310074

HAMPTON, Stephen William Peter. b 72. Magd Coll Cam BA93 MA97 Ex Coll Ox MSt99 DPhil02. Wycliffe Hall Ox BA95 MA98. **d** 96 **p** 97. C St Neots *Ely* 96-98; Chapl and Fell Ex Coll Ox 98-03; Sen Tutor St Jo Coll Dur from 04; Hon Min Can Dur Cathl *Dur* from 05. *St John's College, 3 South Bailey, Durham DH1 3RJ* Tel 0191-334 3881 E-mail s.p.hampton@durham.ac.uk

HAMPTON, Terence Alastair Godfrey Macpherson. b 38. Bris Univ PGCE73. Lon Coll of Div ALCD63 BD68. **d** 64 **p** 65. C Clifton Ch Ch w Em *Bris* 64-66; C Ickenham *Lon* 66-67; C Patchway *Bris* 67-73; TV Jersey St Brelade *Win* 73-83; R Jersey Grouville 83-94; rtd 00. *Jersey Cheshire Home, Rope Walk, St Helier, Jersey JE2 4UU* Tel (01534) 285858

HAMPTON DAVIES, David Arthur Guy. *See* DAVIES, David Arthur Guy Hampton

HAMPTON-SMITH, David Charles. b 22. Ch Ch Ox BA48 MA48. Cuddesdon Coll 48. **d** 50 **p** 51. C Shrewsbury St Chad *Lich* 50-53; C Kingswood *S'wark* 53-56; V Howe Bridge *Man* 56-62; Chapl Woodbridge Sch 62-65; Australia from 65; rtd 87. *139 Esplanade, Port Noarlunga South, S Australia 5167* Tel (0061) (8) 8386 1284

HANAWAY, Peter Louis. b 47. Open Univ BA85 Middx Univ BA02. NTMTC 99. **d** 02 **p** 03. NSM Westmr St Matt *Lon* from 02. *711 Duncan House, Dolphin Square, London SW1V 3PP* Tel (020) 7798 8478 Mobile 07947-722219 E-mail peter.hanaway@cwctv.com

HANCE, Mrs Joy. b 47. Cam Inst of Educn. St Alb and Ox Min Course 99. **d** 02 **p** 03. NSM Cherbury w Gainfield *Ox* from 02. *The Vicarage, Buckland, Faringdon SN7 8QN* Tel (01367) 870618 Mobile 07752-187014 E-mail joysmail@talk21.com

HANCE, Mrs Marion. **d** 01 **p** 02. OLM Cheddington w Mentmore and Marsworth *Ox* from 01. *20 New Street, Cheddington, Leighton Buzzard LU7 0RL* Tel (01296) 661761

HANCE, Stephen John. b 66. Portsm Poly BSc89 Nottm Univ BTh92 MA93. St Jo Coll Nottm 90. **d** 93 **p** 94. C Southsea St Jude *Portsm* 93-96; TV Tollington *Lon* 96-99; V Balham Hill Ascension *S'wark* from 99. *Ascension Vicarage, 22 Malwood Road, London SW12 8EN* Tel (020) 8673 7666 *or* 8675 8626 Fax 8516 9429 *or* 8673 3796 E-mail stephen.hance@virgin.net

HANCOCK, Mrs Barbara. b 40. TCert60. EMMTC 93. **d** 96 **p** 04. NSM Caythorpe *Linc* from 96. *Fulbeck Cottage, Sudthorpe Hill, Fulbeck, Grantham NG32 3LE* Tel (01400) 272644 E-mail bchancock@lineone.net

HANCOCK, Christopher David. b 54. Qu Coll Ox BA75 MA80 St Jo Coll Dur BA78 PhD84. Cranmer Hall Dur. **d** 82 **p** 83. C Leic H Trin w St Jo *Leic* 82-85; Chapl Magd Coll Cam 85-88; USA 88-94; V Cambridge H Trin *Ely* 94-02; Dean Bradf 02-04. *3 College Farm Cottages, Garford, Abingdon OX13 5PF* Tel (01865) 392804 E-mail chancock@btinternet.com

HANCOCK, David Richard. b 48. Chich Th Coll. **d** 89 **p** 90. C Maidstone All SS and St Phil w Tovil *Cant* 89-93; CF 90-93; P-in-c Sellindge w Monks Horton and Stowting etc *Cant* 93-99; Perm to Offic from 99; Thailand from 99. *73/5 Moo 2 Patak Road, Karon Subdistrict, Muang District, Phuket 83100, Thailand* Tel (0066) (76) 284163 Fax 284193 E-mail yohan@phuket.ksc.co.th

HANCOCK, Mrs Eleanor Mary Catherine. b 55. Huddersfield Univ CertEd91. Carl and Blackb Dioc Tr Inst. **d** 05. C Carl H Trin and St Barn *Carl* from 05. *14 Hartington Place, Carlisle CA1 1HL* Tel and fax (01228) 527106 Mobile 07763-482542 E-mail emhancock@hartington.fsworld.co.uk

HANCOCK, Ivor Michael. b 31. Lon Univ BD60. Linc Th Coll 65. **d** 66 **p** 67. C Havant *Portsm* 66-69; V Gosport Ch Ch 69-76; P-in-c Southend St Alb *Chelmsf* 76-80; V Hawley H Trin *Guildf* 80-96; V Minley 80-96; RD Aldershot 83-88; rtd 96; Perm to Offic *Ox* from 98. *Assisi, 15 Whaley Road, Wokingham RG40 1QA* Tel 0118-962 9976

HANCOCK, Canon John Clayton. b 36. Dur Univ BA58. Cranmer Hall Dur DipTh60. **d** 60 **p** 61. C Newbarns w Hawcoat *Carl* 60-65; V Church Coniston 65-76; R Torver 66-76; P-in-c Heversham 76-77; V 77-93; V Heversham and Milnthorpe from 93; Hon Can Carl Cathl from 98. *The Vicarage, Woodhouse Lane, Heversham, Milnthorpe LA7 7EW* Tel (01539) 563125

HANCOCK, John Martin. b 55. Ealing Coll of Educn BA78. Wycliffe Hall Ox 97. **d** 99 **p** 00. C Bedford St Jo and St Leon *St Alb* 99-04; V Old Hill H Trin *Worc* from 04. *The Vicarage, 58 Wrights Lane, Cradley Heath B64 6RD* Tel (01384) 412987

HANCOCK, Canon John Mervyn. b 38. St Jo Coll Dur BA61 DipTh64 MA70 Hertf Coll Ox BA63 MA66. Cranmer Hall Dur 63. **d** 64 **p** 65. C Bishopwearmouth St Gabr *Dur* 64-67; V Hebburn St Jo 67-87; RD Jarrow 83-92; V S Westoe 87-03; C-in-c S Shields St Aid w St Steph 92-95; Hon Can Dur Cathl 88-03; rtd 03. *9 Railway Cottages, Dubmire, Houghton le Spring DH4 6LE* Tel 0191-385 7491 E-mail kda77@dial.pipex.com

HANCOCK, Leonard George Edward. b 28. Open Univ BA81 Leic Univ MEd84. ALCD52. **d** 52 **p** 56. C Bilston St Leon *Lich* 52-53; C Sheff St Swithun *Sheff* 56-58; C Ecclesfield 58; C-in-c Ecclesfield St Paul CD 58-63; V Sheff St Mary w St Simon w St Matthias 63-72; V Michael *S & M* 72-76; R Loughborough All SS *Leic* 76-83; R Loughborough All SS and H Trin 83-93; rtd 93; Perm to Offic *Leic* from 93. *5 Rumsey Close, Quorn, Loughborough LE12 8EZ* Tel (01509) 827258

HANCOCK, Malcolm James. b 50. Leeds Univ MA02 AGSM73. Sarum & Wells Th Coll 85. **d** 87 **p** 88. C Sandhurst *Ox* 87-90; P-in-c Bradbourne and Brassington *Derby* 90-92; TV Wirksworth 92-95; V Tunbridge Wells K Chas *Roch* 95-02; R Beckenham St Geo from 02. *The Rectory, 14 The Knoll, Beckenham BR3 5JW* Tel (020) 8650 0983 *or* 8663 6996 Fax 8658 4914 E-mail malcolm.j.hancock@btinternet.com

HANCOCK, Martin. *See* HANCOCK, John Martin

HANCOCK, Ms Mary Joy. b 40. Auckland Univ BA61 Auckland Teachers' Coll PGCE62 Man Univ CQSW69. S'wark Ord Course 91. **d** 94 **p** 95. NSM Merton St Mary *S'wark* 94-01; NSM Colliers Wood Ch Ch from 01. *55 Huntspill Street, London SW17 0AA* Tel (020) 8946 8984

HANCOCK, Nigel John. b 35. K Coll Cam BA63 MA67. EAMTC 86. **d** 89 **p** 91. NSM Cambridge St Mary Less *Ely* 89-00; PV St Jo Coll Cam 95-99; Perm to Offic *Ely* from 00. *5 Atherton Close, Cambridge CB4 2BE* Tel (01223) 355828

HANCOCK, Preb Paul. b 43. AKC66. **d** 67 **p** 68. C Wednesbury St Paul Wood Green *Lich* 67-70; C Rugeley 70-73; V Rickerscote 73-75; R Blisland w St Breward *Truro* 75-78; V Mansfield St Lawr *S'well* 78-82; P-in-c Charleton *Ex* 82-83; P-in-c E Portlemouth, S Pool and Chivelstone 82-83; R Charleton w Buckland Tout Saints etc 83-95; RD Woodleigh 88-95; P-in-c Plymouth Crownhill Ascension 95-99; V from 99; Preb Ex Cathl from 03. *The Vicarage, 33 Tavistock Road, Plymouth PL5 3AF* Tel (01752) 783617 E-mail hazelnut33@aol.com

HANCOCK, Paul Byron. b 51. Bris Univ BA71 MA73. Ripon Hall Ox 72. **d** 75 **p** 76. C Croydon St Jo *Cant* 75-78; USA from 78. *3200 Woodland Ridge Boulevard, Baton Rouge, LA 70816, USA* E-mail hancockp@ehsbr.org

HANCOCK, The Ven Peter. b 55. Selw Coll Cam BA76 MA79. Oak Hill Th Coll BA80. **d** 80 **p** 81. C Portsdown *Portsm* 80-83; C Radipole and Melcombe Regis *Sarum* 83-87; V Cowplain *Portsm* 87-99; RD Havant 93-98; Hon Can Portsm Cathl from 97; Adn The Meon from 99; Dioc Dir Miss from 03. *Victoria Lodge, 36 Osborn Road, Fareham PO16 7DS* Tel (01329) 828100 *or* 280101 Mobile 07974-008134 Fax (01329) 281603 E-mail phancock@fish.co.uk

HANCOCK, Peter Ernest. b 33. Man Univ BA54. Qu Coll Birm 54. **d** 56 **p** 57. C Wigston Magna *Leic* 56-59; C Hucknall Torkard *S'well* 59-61; V Sutton in Ashfield St Mich 61-65; Dioc Youth Officer *Portsm* 65-73; R Broughton Astley *Leic* 73-86; Dioc Adv for Min of Health and Healing *B & W* 86-93; rtd 94; Perm to

Offic *B & W* from 98. *24 Mulberry Road, Congresbury, Bristol BS49 5HD* Tel (01934) 838920

HANCOCK, Peter Thompson. b 31. G&C Coll Cam BA54 MA58. Ridley Hall Cam 54. **d** 56 **p** 57. C Beckenham Ch Ch *Roch* 56-59; Chapl St Lawr Coll Ramsgate 59-62; Chapl Stowe Sch 62-67; Asst Chapl and Lect Br Embassy Ch Paris *Eur* 67-70; V Walton H Trin *Ox* 70-80; Canada 80-84; V Northwood H Trin *Lon* 84-94; rtd 94; Perm to Offic *Ox* from 99. *Roughwood Oak, Deadhearn Lane, Chalfont St Giles HP8 4HG* Tel (01494) 872324

HANCOCK, Reginald Legassicke (Rex). b 28. Trin Coll Cam BA51 MA57. Clifton Th Coll 60. **d** 61 **p** 62. C Finchley Ch Ch *Lon* 61-63; CF 63-82; R Quantoxhead *B & W* 82-93; rtd 93; Perm to Offic *B & W* from 94. *Stowleys, Bossinton Lane, Porlock, Minehead TA24 8HD* Tel (01643) 862327

HANCOCK, Richard Manuel Ashley. b 69. LRPS02. Linc Th Coll 94 Westcott Ho Cam 95. **d** 97 **p** 98. C Didcot St Pet *Ox* 97-00; P-in-c Shrivenham w Watchfield and Bourton 00-03; V Shrivenham and Ashbury from 03. *St Andrew's Vicarage, Shrivenham, Swindon SN6 8AN* Tel (01793) 780183 E-mail vicar@standrews-shrivenham.fsnet.co.uk

HANCOCK, Ronald Edward. b 24. MRCS49 LRCP49. **d** 78 **p** 79. Hon C Highbury Ch Ch w St Jo *Lon* 78-82; R Puddletown and Tolpuddle *Sarum* 82-90; rtd 90; Perm to Offic *Sarum* from 90. *27 Clarendon Avenue, Weymouth DT3 5BG* Tel (01305) 812436

HANCOCK, Mrs Vittoria Ruth. b 74. Univ of Wales (Ban) BSc95 BD99. Cranmer Hall Dur 91. **d** 01 **p** 02. C Llanberis w Llanrug *Ban* 01-04; C Dolgellau w Llanfachreth and Brithdir etc from 04. *Ty'r Ficer, Pencefn Road, Dolgellau LL40 2ER* Tel (01341) 423538 E-mail revvit@fish.co.uk

HANCOCKS, Graeme. b 58. Univ of Wales (Ban) BD79 Oslo Univ 87. Linc Th Coll 79. **d** 81 **p** 82. C Denbigh and Nantglyn *St As* 81-84; Asst Chapl Oslo St Edm *Eur* 84-88; Chapl Stockholm 88-89; Chapl Marseille w St Raphaël, Aix-en-Provence etc 89; Chapl Gothenburg w Halmstad, Jönköping etc 90-93; Chapl Southn Univ Hosps NHS Trust 93-98; Chapl Trafford Healthcare NHS Trust 98-02; Chapl Leeds Teaching Hosps NHS Trust from 02. *St James University Hospital, Beckett Street, Leeds LS9 7TF* Tel 0113-243 3144

HANCOX, Granville Leonard. b 32. Lich Th Coll 67. **d** 70 **p** 71. C Caverswall *Lich* 70-73; C Norton in the Moors 73-76; P-in-c Leek St Luke 76-79; TV Leek 79-83; V Priors Lee and St Georges 83-97; rtd 97; Perm to Offic *Lich* from 00. *4 Cedarwood Drive, Muxton, Telford TF2 8SH* Tel (01952) 604018

✠**HAND, The Rt Revd Geoffrey David.** b 18. CBE75 KBE84. Oriel Coll Ox BA41 MA46. Cuddesdon Coll 40. **d** 42 **p** 43 **c** 50. C Heckmondwike *Wakef* 42-46; Papua New Guinea 46-83; Bp Coadjutor New Guinea 50-63; Adn N New Guinea 50-63; Bp Papua New Guinea 63-77; Abp Papua New Guinea 77-83; Bp Port Moresby 77-83; rtd 83; P-in-c E w W Rudham *Nor* 83-85; P-in-c Houghton 83-85. *121 Brackenbury Road, London W6 0BQ*

HAND, Michael. *See* HAND, Peter Michael

HAND, Michael Anthony (Tony). b 63. SROT York Univ BA84 DipCOT88. St Jo Coll Nottm MA95. **d** 95 **p** 96. C Lutterworth w Cotesbach *Leic* 95-98; C Lutterworth w Cotesbach and Bitteswell 99-01; V Acomb H Redeemer *York* from 01; Chapl Manor Sch from 01. *The Vicarage, 108 Boroughbridge Road, York YO26 6AB* Tel (01904) 798593 E-mail holyredeemer01@hotmail.com

HAND, Nigel Arthur. b 54. St Jo Coll Nottm. **d** 84 **p** 85. C Birm St Luke *Birm* 84-88; C Walton H Trin *Ox* 88-89; TV 89-97; C Selly Park St Steph and St Wulstan *Birm* 97-04; P-in-c Selly Park Ch Ch from 04; AD Moseley from 04. *927 Pershore Road, Selly Oak, Birmingham B29 7PS* Tel 0121-472 2514 E-mail nigejudy@hansbham.freeserve.co.uk

HAND, Peter Michael. b 42. Univ Coll Ox BA63 Lon Univ BSc75. Sarum & Wells Th Coll 77. **d** 80 **p** 81. NSM Shaston *Sarum* 80-81; C Tisbury 81-83; C Glastonbury St Jo w Godney *B & W* 83-84; C Glastonbury w Meare, W Pennard and Godney 84-87; V High Littleton 87-99; RD Midsomer Norton 92-98; R Winford w Felton Common Hill from 99; Warden of Readers Wells Adnry from 98. *The Rectory, 4 Parsonage Lane, Winford, Bristol BS40 8DG* Tel (01275) 474636

HAND, Philip Ronald. b 53. Spurgeon's Coll BA78. **d** 03 **p** 04. NSM Southampton (City Cen) *Win* from 03. *52 Cranbury Avenue, Southampton SO14 0LT* Tel (023) 8049 4490 E-mail hand1@fish.co.uk

✠**HANDFORD, The Most Revd George Clive.** b 37. Hatf Coll Dur BA61. Qu Coll Birm DipTh63. **d** 63 **p** 64 **c** 90. C Mansfield SS Pet and Paul *S'well* 63-67; Lebanon 67-74; Dean Jerusalem 74-78; UAE 78-83; Adn Gulf 78-83; V Kneesall w Laxton *S'well* 83-84; P-in-c Wellow 83-84; RD Tuxford and Norwell 83-84; Adn Nottingham 84-90; Suff Bp Warw *Cov* 90-96; Bp Cyprus and the Gulf from 96; Pres Bp Episc Ch Jerusalem and Middle E from 02. *PO Box 22075, 1517 Nicosia, Cyprus* Tel (00357) (22) 671220 Fax 674553 E-mail bishop@spidernet.com.cy *or* cygulf@spidernet.com.cy

HANDFORD, John Richard. b 32. Sydney Univ BSc52 Univ Coll Lon MSc58 Surrey Univ MA84 Heythrop Coll Lon MTh96 Lon Univ PhD04. Lon Coll of Div 68. **d** 69 **p** 70. Asst Chapl Wellington Coll Berks 69-80; Hon C Windlesham *Guildf* 87-92; Perm to Offic from 92. *Desiderata, 33 Chertsey Road, Windlesham GU20 6EW* Tel (01276) 472397

HANDFORD, Maurice. b 25. Oak Hill Th Coll 48. **d** 52 **p** 53. C Dublin Miss Ch *D & G* 52-55; Org & Deputation Sec ICM (N & Midl) 55-58; C-in-c Buxton Trin Prop Chpl *Derby* 58-87; I Clondevaddock w Portsalon and Leatbeg *D & R* 87-90; Bp's Dom Chapl 88-90; rtd 90; Perm to Offic *Ches* from 90 and *Derby* from 92. *9 Birtlespool Road, Cheadle Hulme, Cheadle SK8 5JZ* Tel 0161-485 3134

HANDFORTH, Canon Richard Brereton. b 31. St Pet Coll Ox BA55 MA60. Westcott Ho Cam 63. **d** 64 **p** 65. C Hornchurch St Andr *Chelmsf* 64-65; Hong Kong 65-73; Chapl CMS Fellowship Ho Chislehurst 73-75; Hon C Chislehurst St Nic *Roch* 73-75; Home Educn Sec CMS 75-83; V Biggin Hill *Roch* 83-88; Inter-change Adv CMS 88-96; Hon C Plaistow St Mary *Roch* from 95; Hon Can Lagos from 95; rtd 96. *67 Murray Avenue, Bromley BR1 3DJ* Tel (020) 8460 0238

HANDLEY, The Ven Anthony Michael. b 36. Selw Coll Cam BA60 MA64. Chich Th Coll 60. **d** 62 **p** 63. C Thorpe *Nor* 62-66; C Gaywood, Bawsey and Mintlyn 66-72; V Hellesdon 72-81; RD Nor N 80-81; Adn Nor 81-93; Adn Norfolk 93-02; rtd 02; Perm to Offic *Nor* from 02. *25 New Street, Sheringham NR26 8EE* Tel (01263) 820928

HANDLEY, Dennis Francis. b 57. MIE79 TEng(CEI)80. Coll of Resurr Mirfield 82. **d** 85 **p** 86. C Headingley *Ripon* 85-88; C Rothwell 88-92; V Liversedge *Wakef* 92-97; V Ripponden from 97; V Barkisland w W Scammonden from 97; Dioc Rural Officer from 04. *St Bartholomew's Vicarage, Ripponden, Sowerby Bridge HX6 4DF* Tel (01422) 822239 E-mail dennisandcatherine@ripponden.fslife.co.uk

HANDLEY, John. b 38. Oak Hill Th Coll. **d** 83 **p** 84. C Witton w Brundall and Braydeston *Nor* 83-86; R Reedham w Cantley w Limpenhoe and Southwood 86-93; P-in-c E w W Harling and Bridgham w Roudham 93-95; R E w W Harling, Bridgham w Roudham, Larling etc 95-05; P-in-c Garboldisham w Blo' Norton, Riddlesworth etc 94-96; RD Thetford and Rockland 95-98; rtd 05; Perm to Offic *Nor* from 05. *6 Barton Close, Swaffham PE37 7SB* Tel (01760) 336328

HANDLEY, Michael. *See* HANDLEY, The Ven Anthony Michael

HANDLEY, Neil. b 40. St Aid Birkenhead 64. **d** 67 **p** 68. C Ashton Ch Ch *Man* 67-70; C Stretford All SS 70-73; C Tonge 73; C-in-c Bolton St Jo Breightmet CD 74-79; V Bolton St Jo 79-80; R Broughton St Jo 80-87; Perm to Offic *Eur* from 90. *La Taire du Grel, 24250 Domme, France* Tel (0033) 53 28 23 42

HANDLEY, Terence Anthony. b 55. Open Univ BA89. Trin Coll Bris 85. **d** 87 **p** 88. C Meole Brace *Lich* 87-91; V Stafford St Paul Forebridge 91-94. *Address temp unknown*

HANDLEY MACMATH, Terence. b 59. Goldsmiths' Coll Lon BA80 K Coll Cam MA98. Westcott Ho Cam 91. **d** 94 **p** 95. NSM Southwold *St E* 94-95; Perm to Offic *St Alb* 96-99; C St Alb St Pet 99-05; V Harrow Weald All SS *Lon* from 05. *All Saints' Vicarage, 175 Uxbridge Road, Harrow HA3 6TP* Tel (020) 8954 0247 E-mail terence@harrowweald.org

HANDS, Graeme. b 35. Cranmer Hall Dur. **d** 61 **p** 62. C Atherstone *Cov* 61-63; Chapl Aldwickbury Sch Harpenden 63-66; C Cov St Alb *Cov* 66-68; P-in-c Warwick St Paul 68-80; V Radford 80-98; RD Cov N 87-93; rtd 98; Perm to Offic *Nor* and *Cov* from 99. *Rose Cottage, The Hill, Walsingham NR22 6DP* Tel (01328) 820288

HANDSCOMBE, Canon Richard John. b 23. Cuddesdon Coll 58. **d** 60 **p** 61. C Shrub End *Chelmsf* 60-63; V Fingringhoe 63-86; P-in-c E Donyland 75-77; R Fingringhoe w E Donyland 86-90; R Fingringhoe w E Donyland and Abberton etc 90-02; Hon Can Chelmsf Cathl 89-02; rtd 02; Perm to Offic *Chelmsf* from 03. *The Rectory, Church Road, Fingringhoe, Colchester CO5 7BN* Tel (01206) 729383

HANFORD, Canon William Richard. b 38. Keble Coll Ox BA60 MA64 Lon Univ BD66 Univ of Wales LLM95. St Steph Ho Ox 60. **d** 63 **p** 64. C Roath St Martin *Llan* 63-66; C Llantwit Major 67-68; PV Llan Cathl 68-72; Chapl RN 72-76; Hon Chapl Gibraltar Cathl *Eur* 74-76; Hon C Eastbourne St Sav and St Pet *Chich* 76-77; C Brighton St Pet 77-78; Can Res and Prec Guildf Cathl *Guildf* 78-83; Hon Can from 03; V Ewell from 83; Tutor and Lect Chich Th Coll 79-86. *St Mary's Vicarage, 14 Church Street, Ewell, Epsom KT17 2AQ* Tel (020) 8393 2643 E-mail wrhanford@btopenworld.com *or* stmarysewell@btopenworld.com

HANKE, Canon Hilary Claire. b 53. Qu Coll Birm BTheol93. **d** 93 **p** 94. C Kempsey and Severn Stoke w Croome d'Abitot *Worc* 93-97; TV Wordsley 97-99; Convenor for Women's Min from 98; Hon Can Worc Cathl from 98; P-in-c Reddal Hill St Luke from 01; RD Dudley from 04. *St Luke's Vicarage, Upper High Street, Cradley Heath, Warley B64 5HX* Tel and fax (01384) 569940 E-mail hchanke@btinternet.com

HANKEY, Miss Dorothy Mary. b 38. CertEd65. Trin Coll Bris 75. **dss** 78 **d** 87 **p** 94. Wigan St Jas w St Thos *Liv* 78-84; Middleton *Man* 84-85; Litherland Ch Ch *Liv* 85-89; Par Dn 87-89; Par Dn Blackpool St Mark *Blackb* 89-94; C 94-95; C Blackpool St Paul 95-98; rtd 98; Perm to Offic *Blackb* from 98. *89 Rutland Avenue, Poulton-le-Flyde FY6 7RX* Tel (01253) 890635

HANKINS, Clifford James. b 24. Chich Th Coll 70 SSC87. **d** 72 **p** 73. C Henfield *Chich* 72-76; V Fernhurst 76-84; V Mithian w Mount Hawke *Truro* 84-89; rtd 89; Hon C W Wittering and Birdham w Itchenor *Chich* from 90. *2 Kestrel Close, East Wittering, Chichester PO20 8PQ* Tel (01243) 672164

HANLEY, Mirt Joseph. b 74. Univ Coll Ches BA95. CITC BTh03. **d** 03 **p** 04. Aux Min Tralee w Kilmoyley, Ballymacelligott etc *L & K* from 03. *20 Cloghar L, Tralee, Co Kerry, Irish Republic* Tel (00353) (66) 718 1861 Mobile 87-619 4733 E-mail mairtjhanley@hotmail.com

HANLON, Michael James. b 50. St Jo Coll Nottm 96. **d** 98 **p** 99. C Tamworth *Lich* 98-00; C Melbourne St Jo Australia from 00. *25 The Eyrie, Lilydale, Vic, Australia 3140* Tel (0061) (3) 9739 5235 *or* 9739 3541 E-mail mikeruth@alphalink.com.au

HANLON, Thomas Kyle. b 72. QUB BA94 TCD BTh97. **d** 97 **p** 98. C Bangor St Comgall *D & D* 97-00; I Dromore *Clogh* from 00; Chapl to Bp Clogh from 03. *The Rectory, 19 Galbally Road, Dromore, Omagh BT78 3EE* Tel (028) 8289 8300 E-mail k.hanlon@tiscali.co.uk

HANMER, Sister Phoebe Margaret. b 31. Edin Univ MA54. **d** 96 **p** 97. S Africa 96-97; Perm to Offic *Ox* 99-00 and *Birm* from 04. *366 High Street, Smethwick B66 3PD* Tel and fax 0121-558 0094

HANMER, Canon Richard John. b 38. Peterho Cam BA61 MA65. Linc Th Coll 62. **d** 64 **p** 65. C Sheff St Swithun *Sheff* 64-69; Bp's Chapl *Nor* 69-73; V Cinderhill *S'well* 73-81; V Eaton *Nor* 81-94; Dioc Chapl MU 91-04; Hon Can Nor Cathl 93-94; Can Res Nor Cathl 94-04; P-in-c Nor St Mary in the Marsh 94-04; rtd 04; Perm to Offic *Nor* from 04. *The Cottage, 15 The Green, Felbrigg, Norwich NR11 8PW*

HANNA, Miss Elizabeth. b 50. QUB BA73 Lon Bible Coll BA79 Milltown Inst Dub MA01. CITC 99. **d** 01 **p** 02. C Bangor Abbey *D & D* 01-04; I Magherally w Annaclone from 04. *Magherally Rectory, 46 Kilmacrew Road, Banbridge BT32 4EP* Tel (028) 4062 9944 Mobile 07801-946909 E-mail magherally@dromore.anglican.org

HANNA, John. b 44. Lon Bible Coll BA83. Westcott Ho Cam 86. **d** 87 **p** 88. C Denton Ch Ch *Man* 87-91; V Higher Walton *Blackb* 91-98; C Marple All SS *Ches* 98-02; TV Burrington, Chawleigh, Cheldon, Chulmleigh etc *Ex* from 02; RD S Molton from 03. *The Vicarage, The Square, Witheridge, Tiverton EX16 8AE* Tel (01884) 860768

HANNA, Patricia Elizabeth. TCD BA HDipEd QUB BD NUU MA. **d** 99 **p** 00. Aux Min Nenagh *L & K* from 99; Aux Min Drumcliffe w Kilnasoolagh from 00. *St Columba's Rectory, Bindon Street, Ennis, Co Clare, Irish Republic* Tel and fax (00353) (65) 682 0109 E-mail patriciahanna.ennis@eircom.net

HANNA, Peter Thomas. b 45. ACII66 GIFireE75. CITC 85. **d** 88 **p** 89. NSM Cork St Fin Barre's Union *C, C & R* 88-95; Min Can Cork Cathl from 92; Dioc Info Officer 94-95; Aux Min Cork St Luke Union 95-00; Aux Min Kinsale Union 00-04; Aux Min Douglas Union w Frankfield from 04. *Mount Windsor, Farnahoe, Inishannon, Co Cork, Irish Republic* Tel and fax (00353) (21) 477 5470 E-mail hanna7@gofree.indigo.ie

HANNA, Canon Robert Charles. b 49. Oak Hill Th Coll 75. **d** 77 **p** 78. C Coleraine *Conn* 77-82; I Convoy w Monellan and Donaghmore *D & R* 82-94; Can Raphoe Cathl 88-94; I Drumcliffe w Kilnasoolagh *L & K* from 94; Can Limerick, Killaloe and Clonfert Cathls from 00; Chan from 04. *St Columba's Rectory, Bindon Street, Ennis, Co Clare, Irish Republic* Tel and fax (00353) (65) 682 0109 E-mail bobhanna@eircom.net

HANNA, Steven John. b 70. Oak Hill Th Coll BA02. **d** 02 **p** 03. C Dagenham *Chelmsf* from 02. *8 Church Lane, Dagenham RM10 9UL* Tel (020) 8517 2664 E-mail stevenhanna@yahoo.com

HANNAFORD, Prof Robert. b 53. Ex Univ BEd76 MA78 PhD87. St Steph Ho Ox 78. **d** 80 **p** 81. C Ex St Jas *Ex* 80-83; Chapl Ex Univ 83-88; Tutor St Steph Ho Ox 89-92; Sen Lect Ch Ch Coll Cant 92-99; Prof Chr Th Univ Coll Chich 99-01; Hon C Bury w Houghton and Coldwaltham and Hardham *Chich* 99-01; Th Consultant Bp Horsham 99-01; Can and Preb Chich Cathl 00-01; Prof Th St Martin's Coll Lanc from 02; Hon C Tunstall w Melling and Leck *Blackb* 02-03; Hon C E Lonsdale from 03. *The Vicarage, Church Lane, Tunstall, Carnforth LA6 2RQ* Tel (01524) 274376 E-mail robert@hannafor.freeserve.co.uk

HANNAH, Darrell Dale. b 62. Grand Canyon Univ BA85 S Bapt Th Sem MDiv89 Regent Coll Vancouver ThM92 Magd Coll Cam PhD96. WMMTC 00. **d** 03 **p** 03. NSM Edgbaston St Geo *Birm* 03-04; NSM Iffley *Ox* from 04. *Church House, The Oval, Oxford OX4 4SE* Tel (01865) 747857 E-mail darrell.hannah@theology.ox.ac.uk

HANNAH, Kimberley Victoria. *See* WILLIAMS, Mrs Kimberley Victoria

HANNEN, Robert John. *See* DAVIES-HANNEN, Robert John

✠**HANNON, The Rt Revd Brian Desmond Anthony.** b 36. TCD BA59 MA62. TCD Div Sch Div Test61. **d** 61 **p** 62 **c** 86. C Clooney *D & R* 61-64; I Desertmartin 64-69; I Londonderry Ch Ch 69-82; I Enniskillen *Clogh* 82-86; Preb Clogh Cathl 82-84; Dean Clogh 85-86; Bp Clogh 86-01; rtd 01. *Drumconnis Top, 202 Mullaghmeen Road, Ballinamallard, Enniskillen BT94 2DZ* Tel (028) 6638 8557 Fax 6638 8086 E-mail bdah@btinternet.com

HANNY, Mrs Annette Elizabeth. b 49. Keele Univ MA95. WMMTC 02. **d** 05. NSM Langley St Mich *Birm* from 05; NSM Langley St Jo from 05; NSM Oldbury from 05; NSM Londonderry from 05. *93 St Mary's Road, Smethwick B67 5DG* Tel 0121-420 2858 Mobile 07970-841662 E-mail annette.hanny@hobtpct.nhs.uk

HANOVA, Ms Petra. b 70. Chas Univ Prague BA97. Ridley Hall Cam 00. **d** 03. C Toxteth St Philemon w St Gabr and St Cleopas *Liv* from 03. *40 Madryn Street, Liverpool L8 3TT* Tel 0151-726 0581

HANSELL, Peter Michael. b 76. Qu Coll Birm. **d** 05. C Moseley St Mary *Birm* from 05. *4 Woodrough Drive, Birmingham B13 9EP* Tel 0121-449 5950

HANSEN, Mrs Moira Jacqueline. b 55. K Coll Lon BSc76. Oak Hill Th Coll BA88. **d** 88 **p** 96. Par Dn Finchley Ch Ch *Lon* 88-91; Par Dn Broadwater St Mary *Chich* 91-94; Chapl Oak Hill Th Coll 94-00; P-in-c Stanton *St E* 00-04; P-in-c Hopton, Market Weston, Barningham etc 00-04; R Stanton, Hopton, Market Weston, Barningham etc from 04. *The Rectory, The Street, Stanton, Bury St Edmunds IP31 2DQ* Tel (01359) 250239 E-mail moira@hansenj.fsnet.co.uk

HANSEN, Neil Bertram. b 29. **d** 53 **p** 54. C Plymouth St Pet *Ex* 53-55; New Zealand from 55. *3 Mascot Street, Tawa, Wellington, New Zealand* Tel (0064) (4) 232 9983

HANSFORD, Gordon John. b 40. Southn Univ BSc61. Trin Coll Bris 77. **d** 79 **p** 80. C Ex St Leon w H Trin *Ex* 79-82; C Shirley *Win* 82-87; R Landcross, Littleham, Monkleigh etc *Ex* 87-96; TV Bideford, Northam, Westward Ho!, Appledore etc 96-99; P-in-c Monkleigh 96-99; RD Hartland 96-99; V Paul *Truro* from 99. *The Vicarage, 1 St Pol-de-Leon View, Paul, Penzance TR19 6US* Tel (01736) 731261

HANSFORD, Ruth Patricia. b 68. K Coll Lon BSc90 Surrey Univ MSc96 Sch of Pharmacy Lon PhD00. Trin Coll Bris BA02. **d** 03 **p** 04. C Parkham, Alwington, Buckland Brewer etc *Ex* from 03. *Lupins, 5 Manor Court, Parkham, Bideford EX39 5PG* Tel and fax (01237) 451779 *or* tel 452120 Mobile 07718-765936 E-mail maggiethecat@waitrose.com

HANSON, Christopher. b 48. Ox Univ BA(Theol)02. Birm Bible Inst DipMin75 Wycliffe Hall Ox 87. **d** 89 **p** 90. C Heref St Pet w St Owen and St Jas *Heref* 89-91; C Plymouth St Andr w St Paul and St Geo *Ex* 91-93; C Devonport St Mich 93-94; TV Shebbear, Buckland Filleigh, Sheepwash etc 94-97; TV Langley Marish *Ox* from 97. *The Vicarage, Parlaunt Road, Langley, Slough SL3 8BB* Tel (01753) 545167

HANSON, Dale Robert. b 57. Fitzw Coll Cam BA78 MA81 Univ of BC MA80. Ridley Hall Cam 81. **d** 84 **p** 85. C Much Woolton *Liv* 84-87; Hong Kong 87-91; TV Billingham St Aid *Dur* 91-95; C Dur St Nic 95-98; V from 98. *St Nicholas' Vicarage, Kepier Villas, Durham DH1 1JP* Tel 0191-384 6066 E-mail dale.hanson@virgin.net

HANSON, Edward William. b 51. Salem State Coll (USA) BA73 Tufts Univ (USA) MA78 Boston Coll (USA) PhD92. Episc Div Sch (USA) MDiv00 Ripon Coll Cuddesdon 00. **d** 01 **p** 02. C Linc St Botolph and Linc St Pet-at-Gowts and St Andr *Linc* 01-04; P-in-c Orsett and Bulphan and Horndon on the Hill *Chelmsf* from 04. *1 Southview Cottages, Rectory Road, Orsett, Grays RM16 3JX* Tel (01375) 891254 E-mail rector@hobnob.org.uk

HANSON, Canon John Westland. b 19. OBE74. St Jo Coll Dur BA41 DipTh43 MA44. **d** 43 **p** 44. C Louth w Welton-le-Wold *Linc* 43-50; Chapl and Lect RAF Flying Coll Manby 50-76; R Grimoldby w Manby 50-76; RD E Louthesk 60-68; Chief Examiner Relig Studies Cam Univ 66-82; Can and Preb Linc Cathl 67-02; RD Louthesk 68-77; V Woodhall Spa and Kirkstead 76-88; P-in-c Langton w Woodhall 76-88; rtd 88. *Brookfield, 28 Tor-o-Moor Road, Woodhall Spa LN10 6TD* Tel (01526) 352554

HANSON, Keith. b 59. Cranmer Hall Dur 99. **d** 01 **p** 02. C Armley w New Wortley *Ripon* 01-04; C Whitkirk from 04. *26 Hollyshaw Lane, Whitkirk, Leeds LS15 7BD* Tel 0113-226 0396 E-mail revkeef@hotmail.com

HANSON, Mrs Margaret Patricia. b 45. Ripon Coll Cuddesdon 04. **d** 05. NSM Ifield *Chich* from 05. *Birch Cottage, 7 Barnwood, Crawley RH10 7TH* Tel (01293) 535569 E-mail margaret.hanson1@tesco.net

HANSON, Michael Beaumont. b 49. Ox Univ MA. N Ord Course 81. **d** 84 **p** 85. NSM Leeds St Geo *Ripon* 84-98; Chapl

Leeds Gr Sch 84-99; rtd 99; Perm to Offic *Carl* from 00. *5 The Crofts, Crosby, Maryport CA15 6SP* Tel (01900) 816630 E-mail mc@hansons.plus.com

HANSON, Peter Richard. b 45. ARCM. Chich Th Coll 72. **d** 75 **p** 76. C Forest Gate St Edm *Chelmsf* 75-79; C Chingford SS Pet and Paul 79-81; V Leytonstone H Trin Harrow Green 81-86; Dep Chapl HM Pris Wandsworth 86-88; Chapl HM Pris Lewes 88-91; rtd 91; Perm to Offic *Chich* from 91. *Flat 2, 39 St Anne's Crescent, Lewes BN7 1SB* Tel (01273) 471714

HANSON, Robert Arthur. b 35. Keele Univ BA57. St Steph Ho Ox 57 St Mich Coll Llan 59. **d** 60 **p** 61. C Longton St Mary and St Chad *Lich* 60-65; Chapl St Mary's Cathl *Edin* 65-69; R Glas St Matt *Glas* 69-79; R Paisley H Trin 79-87; V Walsall St Andr *Lich* 87-93; Perm to Offic *Worc* 94-97; C Kentish Town *Lon* 97-01; rtd 02. *St Benet's Church House, Ospringe Road, London NW5 2JB* Tel (020) 7267 4720 Mobile 07951-154384 E-mail bob.hanson@tiscali.co.uk

HANSON, Timothy David. b 68. Oak Hill Th Coll BA95. **d** 95 **p** 96. C Boscombe St Jo *Win* 95-00; V Wharton *Ches* from 00. *The Vicarage, 165 Crook Lane, Winsford CW7 3DR* Tel (01606) 593215 *or* 861860 E-mail tiohanson@aol.com

HANWELL, David John. b 46. Leic Univ CertEd74 UEA BEd94. **d** 98 **p** 99. OLM Mundford w Lynford *Nor* 98-04; OLM Cranwich 98-04; OLM Ickburgh w Langford 98-04; OLM Cockley Cley w Gooderstone 99-04; P-in-c from 04; OLM Gt and Lt Cressingham w Threxton 99-04; C from 04; OLM Hilborough w Bodney 99-04; C from 04; OLM Oxborough w Foulden and Caldecote 99-04; C from 04. *The Rectory, Elm Place, Gooderstone, King's Lynn PE33 9BX* Tel (01366) 328856 E-mail david.hanwell@btopenworld.com

HAOKIP (formerly YAM), David Tongkhoyam. b 60. Serampore Univ BTh89 Madras Univ MDiv92. H Cross Coll Rangoon. **d** 84 **p** 85. Burma 83-93; India 93-95; Korea 96-97; Perm to Offic *S'wark* 99; TV Southampton (City Cen) *Win* 00-05; V E Ham St Geo *Chelmsf* from 05. *The Vicarage, Buxton Road, London E6 3NB* Tel (020) 8472 2111 E-mail haokip@fish.co.uk

HAPGOOD-STRICKLAND, Canon Peter Russell. b 57. St Steph Ho Ox BA83. **d** 83 **p** 84. C Ashford *Cant* 83-86; C Sheerness H Trin w St Paul 86-90; V Blackb St Thos w St Jude *Blackb* 90-97; P-in-c Burnley St Andr w St Marg 97; V Burnley St Andr w St Marg and St Jas from 98; Hon Can Blackb Cathl from 05. *St Andrew's Vicarage, 230 Barden Lane, Burnley BB10 1JD* Tel (01282) 423185 E-mail standrews@marsdens.net

HARBIDGE, The Ven Adrian Guy. b 48. St Jo Coll Dur BA70. Cuddesdon Coll 73. **d** 75 **p** 76. C Romsey *Win* 75-80; V Bournemouth St Andr 80-86; V Chandler's Ford 86-99; RD Eastleigh 93-99; Adn Bournemouth from 99. *Glebe House, 22 Bellflower Way, Chandler's Ford, Eastleigh SO53 4HN* Tel and fax (023) 8026 0955 E-mail adrian.harbidge@dial.pipex.com

HARBORD, Paul Geoffrey. b 56. JP99. Keble Coll Ox BA78 MA86. Chich Th Coll 81. **d** 83 **p** 84. C Rawmarsh w Parkgate *Sheff* 83-86; C Doncaster St Geo 86-90; C-in-c St Edm Anchorage Lane CD 90-95; V Masbrough 95-03; Bp's Chapl from 03. *4 Clarke Drive, Sheffield S10 2NS* Tel 0114-266 1932 Mobile 07898-485428 E-mail pgh56@beeb.net

HARBORD, Philip James. b 56. St Cath Coll Ox BA77. Cranmer Hall Dur 78. **d** 80 **p** 81. C Enfield St Andr *Lon* 80-83; CMS 84-88; Pakistan 84-88; C Clay Hill St Jo and St Luke *Lon* 88-91; Chapl Wexham Park Hosp Slough 91-92; Chapl Upton Hosp Slough 91-92; Chapl Heatherwood and Wexham Park Hosp NHS Trust 92-95; Chapl Leic Gen Hosp NHS Trust 95-98; Chapl Fosse Health NHS Trust 98-99; Chapl Leics and Rutland Healthcare NHS Trust 99-01; P-in-c Cosby *Leic* from 01; P-in-c Whetstone from 03. *The Vicarage, Church Lane, Whetstone, Leicester LE8 6BA* Tel 0116-284 8713 E-mail philipharbord@btinternet.com

HARBOTTLE, Anthony Hall Harrison. b 25. LVO79. Ch Coll Cam BA50 MA53. Wycliffe Hall Ox 50. **d** 52 **p** 53. C Boxley *Cant* 52-54; C St Peter-in-Thanet 54-60; R Sandhurst w Newenden 60-68; Chapl in Windsor Gt Park 68-81; Chapl to The Queen 68-95; R E Dean w Friston and Jevington *Chich* 81-95; rtd 95; P-in-c E Dean w Friston and Jevington *Chich* 95-96. *44 Summerdown Road, Eastbourne BN20 8DQ* Tel (01323) 730881

HARBRIDGE, Philip Charles Anthony. b 65. K Coll Lon LLB88 AKC88 Ch Coll Cam BA98 MA02. Westcott Ho Cam. **d** 99 **p** 00. C Hampton All SS *Lon* 99-02; Chapl Ch Coll Cam from 02. *Christ's College, Cambridge CB2 3BU* Tel (01223) 334922 E-mail pcah2@cam.ac.uk

HARCOURT, Canon Giles. b 36. Westcott Ho Cam 68. **d** 71 **p** 72. C Bishopwearmouth St Mich w St Hilda *Dur* 71-73; C Fishponds St Mary *Bris* 73-75; Bp's Dom Chapl *S'wark* 75-78; Lic to Offic 78-79; V S Wimbledon H Trin and St Pet 79-88; V Greenwich St Alfege 88-04; Hon Chapl RN Coll Greenwich 89-99; RD Greenwich Thameside *S'wark* 94-98; Boro Dean Greenwich 94-98; Hon Can S'wark Cathl 96-04; rtd 05; Perm to Offic *Chich* from 05. *1A Trinity Trees, Eastbourne BN21 3LA* Tel (01323) 638790

HARCOURT, Paul George. b 67. Em Coll Cam BA88 MA92. Wycliffe Hall Ox BA91. **d** 92 **p** 93. C Moreton *Ches* 92-95; C Woodford Wells *Chelmsf* 95-00; V from 00. *All Saints' Vicarage, 4 Inmans Row, Woodford Green IG8 0NH* Tel (020) 8504 0266 Fax 8504 9640 E-mail pharcourt@btconnect.com

HARCOURT-NORTON, Michael Clive. *See* NORTON, Michael Clive Harcourt

HARCUS, Canon Arthur Reginald (Reg). b 38. Lon Univ BD71 MPhil78. Kelham Th Coll 58. **d** 63 **p** 64. C Charlton St Luke w St Paul *S'wark* 63-69; C Felpham w Middleton *Chich* 78-80; P-in-c Donnington 80-85; V Fernhurst 85-91; V Bolney and Tutor Lay Educn and Tr 91-02; TV Crawley 02-05; Hon Can Koforidua from 91; rtd 05. *Peterhouse, 128 Ifield Road, Crawley RH11 7BW* Tel (01293) 520921

HARDACRE (née BROOKFIELD), Patricia Anne. b 50. St Mary's Coll Dur BA72 St Jo Coll Dur MA74. Cranmer Hall Dur. **dss** 84 **d** 87 **p** 94. Kingston upon Hull St Nic *York* 84-86; Acomb St Steph 86-96; Par Dn 87-94; C 94-96; TV Preston Risen Lord *Blackb* from 96. *St Mary's Vicarage, St Mary's Close, Preston PR1 4XN* Tel (01772) 794222 E-mail anne@hipporage.fsnet.co.uk

HARDAKER, Canon Ian Alexander. b 32. K Coll Lon BD59 AKC59. **d** 60 **p** 61. C Beckenham St Geo *Roch* 60-65; R Eynsford w Lullingstone 65-70; V Chatham St Steph 70-85; RD Roch 78-85; Hon Can Roch Cathl 83-98; Clergy Appts Adv 86-98; Chapl to The Queen 94-02; rtd 99; Perm to Offic *B & W* from 00. *The Old Post Office, Huish Champflower, Taunton TA4 2EY* Tel (01984) 623409

HARDCASTLE, Ian Kenneth Dalton. b 56. Auckland Univ BE78 ME80. St Jo Coll Nottm MTh04. **d** 04 **p** 05. C Denton Holme *Carl* from 04. *118 Dalston Road, Carlisle CA2 5PJ* Tel (01228) 522938 E-mail ian@castlewd.co.uk

HARDCASTLE, Nigel John. b 47. Reading Univ BSc68. Qu Coll Birm. **d** 72 **p** 73. C Weoley Castle *Birm* 72-75; C Handsworth St Andr 75-78; V Garretts Green 78-86; Exec Sec Ch Computer Project BCC 86-89; R Emmer Green *Ox* 89-99; V Reading St Luke w St Bart from 99. *St Luke's Vicarage, 14 Erleigh Road, Reading RG1 5LH* Tel 0118-926 2372 Fax as telephone E-mail nigel@hardcastle33.fsnet.co.uk

HARDCASTLE, Roger Clive. b 52. Southn Univ BSc73. Qu Coll Birm. **d** 78 **p** 79. C Walton St Mary *Liv* 78-82; V Pemberton St Fran Kitt Green 82-94; TV Padgate 94-96; V Birchwood from 96. *The Vicarage, Admiral's Road, Birchwood, Warrington WA3 6QG* Tel (01925) 811906 E-mail rhardcastle@btopenworld.com

HARDIE, John Blair. b 16. MBE46. LDS FDS MRCS38 MRCSE66. Edin Th Coll 73. **d** 76 **p** 76. Chapl St Paul's Cathl Dundee *Bre* 76-86; rtd 86; Hon C Carnoustie *Bre* from 86. *4 Lammerton Terrace, Dundee DD4 7BW* Tel (01382) 860836

HARDIE, Canon Stephen. b 41. AKC67. **d** 68 **p** 69. C Roxbourne St Andr *Lon* 68-73; C Colchester St Mary V *Chelmsf* 73-76; R Wivenhoe 76-92; TR Dovercourt and Parkeston 92-96; P-in-c Harwich 92-96; R Dovercourt and Parkeston w Harwich 96-04; TR Harwich Peninsula from 04; P-in-c Ramsden Crays w Ramsden Bellhouse from 02; RD Harwich 97-04; Hon Can Chelmsf Cathl from 02. *The Rectory, 51 Highfield Avenue, Harwich CO12 4DR* Tel (01255) 502033

HARDING, Alan. b 45. St Jo Coll Ox BA67 MA73 Pemb Coll Ox DPhil92. Oak Hill NSM Course 89. **d** 93 **p** 94. NSM Lt Heath *St Alb* 93-99; P-in-c S Mymms and Ridge 99-05; rtd 05. *The Old Guildhall, Mill Street, Gislingham, Eye IP23 8JT* Tel (01379) 783361

HARDING, Alec James. b 61. St Andr Univ MA83 DTh. Cranmer Hall Dur 86. **d** 89 **p** 90. C Thirsk *York* 89-93; TV Heref St Martin w St Fran *Heref* 93-95; TV Heref S Wye 95-00; V Barnard Castle w Whorlton *Dur* from 00; AD Barnard Castle from 03. *The Vicarage, Parson's Lonnen, Barnard Castle DL12 8ST* Tel (01833) 637018 E-mail aleckim@barney16.fsnet.co.uk

HARDING, Andrew Barry. b 66. Trent Poly HND88 Birm Univ DipHE97. Westcott Ho Cam CTM99. **d** 99 **p** 00. C Rainham *Roch* 99-03; V Hoo St Werburgh from 03. *The Vicarage, Vicarage Lane, Hoo, Rochester ME3 9BB* Tel (01634) 250291 E-mail ardy@abh123.freeserve.co.uk

HARDING, Canon Brenda Kathleen. b 39. Bedf Coll Lon BA60 K Coll Lon BD62 Lon Inst of Educn PGCE65. St Deiniol's Hawarden 91. **d** 92 **p** 94. NSM Lancaster Ch Ch *Blackb* from 92; Acting Vice-Prin Carl and Blackb Dioc Tr Inst 04-05; Hon Can Blackb Cathl *Blackb* from 05. *14 Ascot Close, Lancaster LA1 4LT* Tel (01524) 66071

HARDING, Canon Brian Edward. b 38. ALCD65. **d** 65 **p** 66. C Chislehurst Ch Ch *Roch* 65-68; P-in-c Baxenden *Blackb* 68-70; V 70-88; V Douglas from 88; Hon Can Blackb Cathl from 96. *The Vicarage, 5 Tan House Lane, Parbold, Wigan WN8 7HG* Tel (01257) 462350 Fax 464827 E-mail brian.hardfam@virgin.net

HARDING, Clifford Maurice. b 22. Leeds Univ BA47. Coll of Resurr Mirfield 46. **d** 48 **p** 49. C Tonge Moor *Man* 48-54; Nyasaland 54-56; CF 56-59; V Oldham St Jo *Man* 59-65; Lic to Offic *Blackb* 65-87; rtd 87; Perm to Offic *Blackb* from 87. *31 Riley Avenue, Lytham St Annes FY8 1HZ* Tel (01253) 725138

HARDING, Colin Ronald Stansby. b 32. RGN71 FVCM92 Dip Th & Min. Bp Otter Coll 94. **d** 97. NSM Aldingbourne, Barnham and Eastergate *Chich* from 97. *Spindle Trees, 67 Elm Grove, Barnham, Bognor Regis PO22 0HJ* Tel (01243) 552579

HARDING, Derek Gordon Edward. b 50. Open Univ BA89 MIAP95. **d** 01 **p** 02. OLM Godstone and Blindley Heath *S'wark* from 01. *68 Lagham Road, Godstone RH9 8HB* Tel (01342) 893892

HARDING, Frederick Arthur. b 16. S'wark Ord Course 75. **d** 77 **p** 78. NSM Oxted *S'wark* 77-97; NSM Oxted and Tandridge 97-03. *Orchard Court, East Grinstead Road, Lingfield RH7 6ET* Tel (01342) 834444

HARDING, John Stuart Michael. b 45. St Jo Coll Nottm 79. **d** 81 **p** 82. C Clifton *S'well* 81-87; V Broxtowe 87-98; Consultant to Churches 98-00; Perm to Offic *Chelmsf* 98-01 and *M & K* from 01. *Address temp unknown* E-mail rflexnserv@aol.com

HARDING, John William Christopher. b 31. St Jo Coll Dur BA55. **d** 58 **p** 59. C Wigan St Cath *Liv* 58-60; C Much Woolton 60-63; V Whiston 63-73; V Birkdale St Jo 73-97; rtd 97; Perm to Offic *Liv* from 98. *17 Baytree Close, Southport PR9 8RE* Tel (01704) 507654

HARDING, Ms Lesley Anne. b 58. Westcott Ho Cam 98 SEITE 99. **d** 01 **p** 02. C Walmer *Cant* 01-03; C Broadstairs 03-04; Perm to Offic from 05. *9 Bakers Court, Church Road, Ramsgate CT11 8RG* Tel (01843) 585902
E-mail lesley.harding@ukgateway.net

HARDING, Lyndon Albert. b 60. Trin Coll Bris 00. **d** 02 **p** 03. C Hollington St Leon *Chich* from 02. *158 Old Church Road, St Leonards-on-Sea TN38 9HD* Tel (01424) 852496

HARDING, Mrs Marion. b 33. Gilmore Course 75. **dss** 85 **d** 87 **p** 94. Hertford St Andr *St Alb* 85-87; Par Dn 87-93; rtd 93; NSM Lt Amwell *St Alb* 93-97; Perm to Offic from 97. *41 Calton Avenue, Hertford SG14 2ER*

HARDING, Mrs Mary Elizabeth. b 46. SRN67. STETS 97. **d** 00 **p** 01. NSM Shaston *Sarum* from 00; Chapl Westmr Memorial Hosp Shaftesbury from 02. *The Old Mill, Manor Farm, Fontmell Magna, Shaftesbury SP7 0NW* Tel (01747) 811731
E-mail mary@harding6.freeserve.co.uk

HARDING, Michael Anthony John. b 37. Brasted Th Coll 67 Sarum Th Coll 68. **d** 71 **p** 72. C Forest Hill Ch Ch *S'wark* 71-72; C Catford St Laur 72-74; C Leominster *Heref* 74-77; R Neenton and V Ditton Priors 77-86; P-in-c Aston Botterell w Wheathill and Loughton 77-86; P-in-c Burwarton w N Cleobury 77-86; R Ditton Priors w Neenton, Burwarton etc 86-94; V E Budleigh w Bicton and Otterton *Ex* 94-03; rtd 03; Perm to Offic *Sarum* from 03. *The Beaches, 22 Middlehill Road, Colehill, Wimborne BH21 2SD* Tel (01202) 884775
E-mail michaelharding@onetel.com

HARDING, Preb Michael David. b 38. Man Univ BA61. Lich Th Coll 61. **d** 63 **p** 64. C Hednesford *Lich* 63-67; C Blurton 67-70; V Newcastle St Paul 70-99; RD Newcastle 87-97; Preb Lich Cathl 89-99; rtd 99; Perm to Offic *Lich* from 00. *7 Staines Court, Stone ST15 8XF* Tel (01785) 811737
E-mail mdharding@argonet.co.uk

HARDING, Peter Gordon. b 45. Lon Univ BA70 Open Univ BA88 MA90. Cranmer Hall Dur DipTh79. **d** 79 **p** 80. C Kirkheaton *Wakef* 79-82; NSM New Sleaford *Linc* 90-00. *67 The Drove, Sleaford NG34 7AS* Tel (01529) 307231
E-mail pgharding@lineone.net

HARDING, Peter Richard. b 46. AKC69. St Aug Coll Cant 69. **d** 70 **p** 71. C Chorley St Pet *Blackb* 70-73; C Ribbleton 73-74; C St Marylebone w H Trin *Lon* 74-80; P-in-c St Marylebone St Cypr 80-82; V 82-98; AD Westmr St Marylebone 83-92; Sub-Warden Guild of St Raphael 88-98; rtd 98; Perm to Offic *Chich* 98-99; Asst to RD Brighton from 00. *27A Chichester Place, Brighton BN2 1FF* Tel (01273) 685323

HARDING, Richard Michael. b 42. St Alb Minl Tr Scheme 80. **d** 83 **p** 84. C Pershore w Pinvin, Wick and Birlingham *Worc* 83-86; V Longdon, Castlemorton, Bushley, Queenhill etc 86-95; P-in-c Catshill and Dodford 95-97; V 97-02; P-in-c Stokenham w Sherford and Beesands, and Slapton *Ex* 02-05; R from 05. *The Vicarage, Stokenham, Kingsbridge TQ7 2ST* Tel (01548) 580385

HARDING, Rolf John. b 22. Oak Hill Th Coll 41 Lon Coll of Div 46. **d** 49 **p** 50. C Sydenham H Trin *S'wark* 49-52; C Harold Wood *Chelmsf* 52-53; Min Harold Hill St Paul CD 53-61; V Coopersale 61-91; Chapl St Marg Hosp Epping 73-91; Chapl W Essex HA 86-91; rtd 91; Perm to Offic *B & W* from 91; Asst Chapl R United Hosp Bath NHS Trust 92-94. *11 Westbrook Park, Weston, Bath BA1 4DP* Tel (01225) 484968

HARDING, Miss Sylvia. b 23. St Mich Ho Ox 55. **dss** 64 **d** 87. Rodbourne Cheney *Bris* 57-66; Midl Area Sec CPAS 66-71; Patchway 71-78; Sec Coun of Women's Min Bris 77-84; rtd 84; Westbury-on-Trym St Alb *Bris* 86-92; Hon Par Dn 87-92; Perm to Offic *Bris* and *B & W* from 92. *53 Brampton Way, Portishead, Bristol BS20 6YW* Tel (01275) 847046 *or* 848638

HARDINGHAM, Paul David. b 52. Lon Univ BSc74 Fitzw Coll Cam BA77. Ridley Hall Cam 75. **d** 78 **p** 79. C Cambridge St Martin *Ely* 78-81; C Jesmond Clayton Memorial *Newc* 81-88; C Harborne Heath *Birm* 88-91; R Ipswich St Matt *St E* 91-04; V Halliwell St Pet *Man* from 04. *St Peter's Vicarage, 1 Sefton Road, Bolton BL1 6HT* Tel (01204) 848567
E-mail paul@hardingham60.freeserve.co.uk

HARDMAN, Bryan Edwin. b 29. Lon Univ BD60 Selw Coll Cam PhD64 K Coll Lon MTh75. Moore Th Coll Sydney. **d** 55 **p** 55. C Hurstville Australia 55-60; Perm to Offic *Ely* 60-65; V Cambridge St Andr Less 65-68; Prin Bible Coll of S Australia 68-83; Prin Karachi Dioc Sem Pakistan 83-86; Prin Discipleship Tr Cen Singapore 87-94; Nat Dir Interserve Korea 94-97; Visiting Prof Tyndale Univ Canada 99-00; rtd 01. *U197/1215 Grand Junction Road, Hope Valley, S Australia 5090*
E-mail bryanhardman@hotmail.com

HARDMAN, The Ven Christine Elizabeth. b 51. Lon Univ BSc(Econ)73. St Alb Minl Tr Scheme 81. **dss** 84 **d** 87 **p** 94. Markyate Street *St Alb* 84-87; Par Dn 87-88; Tutor St Alb Minl Tr Scheme 88-91; Course Dir 91-96; C Markyate Street 94-96; V Stevenage H Trin 96-01; RD Stevenage 99-01; Adn Lewisham *S'wark* from 01. *129A Honor Oak Park, London SE23 3LD* Tel (020) 7939 9408
E-mail christine.hardman@southwark.anglican.org

HARDMAN, Geoffrey James. b 41. Birm Univ BA63. N Ord Course 77. **d** 80 **p** 81. NSM Latchford St Jas *Ches* 80-93; NSM Haydock St Jas *Liv* from 94. *48 Denbury Avenue, Stockton Heath, Warrington WA4 2BW* Tel (01925) 264064
E-mail geoff@ghardman.freeserve.co.uk

HARDMAN, Mrs Pamela. b 39. **d** 01 **p** 02. NSM Bramhall *Ches* from 01. *38 Deva Close, Poynton, Stockport SK12 1HH* Tel (01625) 877936 E-mail revpamela@tiscali.co.uk

HARDMAN, Canon Peter George. b 35. Man Univ BSc56. Ridley Hall Cam 58. **d** 60 **p** 61. C Oldham St Paul *Man* 60-63; NW England Area Sec SCM 63-64; NW England Area Sec CEM 64-67; Asst Chapl Marlborough Coll 67-72; Chapl 72-79; P-in-c Wareham *Sarum* 79-80; TR 80-00; Chapl Wareham Hosp 80-92; Chapl Dorset Health Care NHS Trust 92-00; Can and Preb Sarum Cathl *Sarum* 87-00; RD Purbeck 89-99; rtd 00; Perm to Offic *Sarum* from 00 and *B & W* from 02. *55 Palairet Close, Bradford-on-Avon BA15 1US* Tel (01225) 867198
E-mail peterhardman@onetel.com

HARDWICK, Canon Christopher George. b 57. Open Univ BA94 Birm Univ MA96 PhD00 ACIB79 DASSc94. Ripon Coll Cuddesdon 90. **d** 92 **p** 93. C Worc SE *Worc* 92-95; R Ripple, Earls Croome w Hill Croome and Strensham 95-00; R Upton-on-Severn, Ripple, Earls Croome etc from 00; RD Upton 97-05; Hon Can Worc Cathl from 03. *The Rectory, Old Street, Upton-upon-Severn, Worcester WR8 0JQ* Tel and fax (01684) 591241
E-mail chrishardwick@uptonparishoffice.org.uk

HARDWICK, Dennis Egerton. b 27. St Deiniol's Hawarden. **d** 82 **p** 83. NSM Lache cum Saltney *Ches* 82-85; P-in-c Backford 85-88; P-in-c Capenhurst 87-88; R Backford and Capenhurst 88-93; rtd 93; Perm to Offic *Chich* from 93. *11 Prime Close, Walberton, Arundel BN18 0PL*

HARDWICK, Canon Graham John. b 42. Qu Coll Birm 68. **d** 70 **p** 71. C Watford St Mich *St Alb* 70-73; C N Mymms 73-75; Youth Officer Cov Cathl *Cov* 75-81; Chapl Lanchester Poly 76-81; V Nuneaton St Nic 81-95; P-in-c New Bilton from 95; Ind Chapl from 95; Hon Can Cov Cathl from 04. *St Oswald's Vicarage, New Street, Rugby CV22 7BE* Tel (01788) 544011 Fax 333256 E-mail revgjh@talk21.com

HARDWICK, John Audley. b 28. Em Coll Cam BA51 MA55. Westcott Ho Cam 51. **d** 53 **p** 54. C Selby Abbey *York* 53-56; Chapl St Edm Sch Hindhead 56-60; Chapl Aysgarth Sch 60-62; Chapl St Edm Sch Hindhead 62-86; Asst Hd Master 73-90; Lic to Offic *Guildf* 63-90; rtd 93; Perm to Offic *Ches* 95-05. *4 Stratford Court, Avon Road, Farnham GU9 8PG*

HARDWICK, Robert. b 56. St Jo Coll Nottm DCM93. **d** 93 **p** 94. C Beeston *S'well* 93-97; V Scawby, Redbourne and Hibaldstow *Linc* 97-01; RD Yarborough 00-01; R Swift Current St Steph Canada from 01. *108 Second Avenue NE, Swift Current SK, Canada, S9H 2C7* Tel (001) (306) 773 4007 Fax 773 3641
E-mail rob.hardwick@sasktel.net

HARDWICK, Canon Susan Frances. b 44. Warwick Univ BA81. Qu Coll Birm 82. **dss** 85 **d** 87 **p** 94. Chilvers Coton w Astley *Cov* 85-91; C 87-91; Dioc Disabilities Officer 91-96; Chapl Hereward Coll 91-96; Chapl FE Colls from 94; Hon C New Bilton 96-98; FE Field Officer Team Co-ord (W Midl) from 97; Chapl Rainsbrook Secure Tr Cen from 99; Hon Can Cov Cathl *Cov* from 04. *St Oswald's Vicarage, New Street, Rugby CV22 7BE* Tel (01788) 544011 *or* 528800 Fax 333256 *or* 815056
E-mail susan.hardwick@gslglobal.com

HARDWICKE, Stephen Michael. b 57. Herts Coll BA85 Lon Bible Coll MA87 K Coll Lon MTh92. Westcott Ho Cam 93. **d** 95 **p** 96. C Leagrave *St Alb* 95-01; P-in-c Cowley *Lon* 01-03; R from 03. *St Laurence Rectory, Church Road, Cowley, Uxbridge UB8 3NB* Tel and fax (01895) 232728
E-mail stevehardwicke660@hotmail.com

HARDY, Ms Alison Jane. b 61. St Anne's Coll Ox BA82 MA96. N Ord Course 92. **d** 95 **p** 96. C Flixton St Mich *Man* 95-98; Lect Bolton St Pet 98-00; P-in-c Irlam 00-05; R Stand from 05.

38 Dovehouse Close, Whitefield, Manchester M45 7PE Tel 0161-766 2619 E-mail alisonhardy@fsmail.net

HARDY, Anthony. b 36. **d** 86 **p** 87. NSM Malden St Jas *S'wark* from 86. *48 Blake's Lane, New Malden KT3 6NR* Tel (020) 8949 0703

HARDY, Anthony William. b 56. Man Univ BEd79 MEd86 Open Univ BSc00. St Jo Coll Nottm 86. **d** 88 **p** 89. C Pennington *Man* 88-91; V Eccleston St Luke *Liv* 91-00; NW Regional Consultant CPAS from 00; Dioc Evang *Liv* from 00. *33 Church Street, Marple, Stockport SK6 6BW* E-mail tonyh@cpas.org.uk

HARDY, Canon Brian Albert. b 31. St Jo Coll Ox BA54 DipTh55 MA58. Westcott Ho Cam 55. **d** 57 **p** 58. C Rugeley *Lich* 57-62; Chapl Down Coll Cam 62-66; C-in-c Livingston Miss *Edin* 66-74; Preb Heref Cathl *Heref* 74-78; Ch Planning Officer Telford 74-78; RD Telford Severn Gorge 75-78; Chapl Edin Th Coll 78-82; Chapl Edin R Infirmary 82-86; R Edin St Columba *Edin* 82-91; Dean Edin 86-91; Hon Can St Mary's Cathl from 91; R St Andrews All SS *St And* 91-96; rtd 96. *3/3 Starbank Road, Edinburgh EH5 3BN* Tel 0131-551 6783 E-mail bhardy@fish.co.uk

HARDY, Christopher Richard. b 52. R Holloway Coll Lon BMus77 Southn Univ BTh90. Chich Th Coll 87. **d** 90 **p** 91. C Kenton *Lon* 90-95; V E Finchley All SS from 95. *All Saints' Vicarage, Twyford Avenue, London N2 9NH* Tel and fax (020) 8883 9315 Mobile 07785-728272 E-mail christopherhardy@btinternet.com

HARDY, Prof Daniel Wayne. b 30. Haverford Coll (USA) BA52. Gen Th Sem (NY) STB55 STM63. **d** 55 **p** 56. USA 55-61 and 90-95; Fell and Tutor Gen Th Sem 59-61; Lic to Offic *Ox* 61-65; Lect Modern Th Thought Birm Univ 65-75; Sen Lect 75-86; Hon C Londonderry *Birm* 67-86; Van Mildert Prof Div Dur Univ 86-90; Can Res Dur Cathl *Dur* 86-90; Dir Cen Th Inquiry 90-95; rtd 96; Perm to Offic *Ely* from 96. *101 Millington Lane, Cambridge CB3 9HA* Tel (01223) 312302 Fax 303609 E-mail dwhardy@compuserve.com

HARDY, Miss Janet Frances. b 59. Newc Univ BA81 CertEd82. Trin Coll Bris 87. **d** 89 **p** 94. Par Dn Sheff St Paul *Sheff* 89-92; TD Gt Snaith 92-94; TV 94-96; V Pitsmoor Ch Ch 96-01; V Thorpe Hesley from 01. *The Vicarage, 30 Barnsley Road, Thorpe Hesley, Rotherham S61 2RR* Tel 0114-246 3487

HARDY, John Charles. b 22. Sheff Univ BA48 DipEd49 Lon Univ DipTh53. St Deiniol's Hawarden 66. **d** 67 **p** 68. Hon C Chorley St Laur *Blackb* 67-87; rtd 87; Perm to Offic *Blackb* from 87. *4 Glamis Drive, Chorley PR7 1LX* Tel (01257) 265743

HARDY, John Christopher. b 61. St Jo Coll Dur BA83 Dur Univ MA95 New Coll Edin BD92 Ox Univ MLitt00. Coates Hall Edin 89 Aston Tr Scheme 87. **d** 92 **p** 93. C Walker *Newc* 92-95; Fell Chapl Magd Coll Ox 95-98; TV Benwell *Newc* 98-03; R Alston Moor from 03. *The Parsonage House, Brampton Road, Alston CA9 3AA* Tel (01434) 382558

HARDY, Canon John Lewis Daniel. b 26. St Chad's Coll Dur BA51 DipTh52. **d** 52 **p** 53. C Hucknall Torkard *S'well* 52-58; V Harworth 58-65; V Sutton in Ashfield St Mary 65-85; R Keyworth 85-93; P-in-c Stanton-on-the-Wolds 85-93; RD S Bingham 91-93; Hon Can S'well Minster 92-93; rtd 93; Perm to Offic *S'well* from 93. *10 Redhill Lodge Drive, Nottingham NG5 8JH* Tel 0115-926 7370

HARDY, Mrs Lesley Anne. b 53. Nottm Univ BA75 St Luke's Coll Ex PGCE76. **d** 05. OLM Lydd *Cant* from 05. *All Saints' Rectory, Park Street, Lydd, Romney Marsh TN29 9AY* Tel (01797) 320345

HARDY, Michael Frederick Bryan. b 36. Selw Coll Cam BA60 MA64. Linc Th Coll 60. **d** 62 **p** 63. C Pontefract St Giles *Wakef* 62-66; C Lightcliffe 66-69; V Hightown 69-78; V Birkby 78-85; C Boultham *Linc* 88-89; V Misterton and W Stockwith *S'well* 89-01; rtd 01; Perm to Offic *S'well* from 01. *23 Anderson Way, Lea, Gainsborough DN21 5EF* Tel (01427) 614468

HARDY, Michael Henry. b 33. Qu Coll Birm 85. **d** 86 **p** 87. C Leic St Jas *Leic* 86-88; R Arnesby w Shearsby and Bruntingthorpe 88-94; RD Guthlaxton I 91-94; TV Bradgate Team 94-99; rtd 99; Perm to Offic *Leic* and *Pet* from 99. *14 Dean's Street, Oakham LE15 6AF* Tel (01572) 722591

HARDY, Michael John. b 35. Keble Coll Ox BA58 MA66. Cuddesdon Coll 59. **d** 61 **p** 62. C Dalton-in-Furness *Carl* 61-64; C Harborne St Pet *Birm* 64-68; Min Can Ripon Cathl *Ripon* 68-73; Appt and Tr Sec USPG 73-80; R Stretford St Pet *Man* 80-91; P-in-c Newton Hall *Dur* 91-96; TR Keighley St Andr *Bradf* 96-00; rtd 00; Perm to Offic *Wakef* from 01. *5 Outlane, Netherthong, Huddersfield HD9 3EQ* Tel (01484) 683655

HARDY, Canon Paul Richard. b 30. K Coll Cam BA52 MA56. St Steph Ho Ox 57. **d** 59 **p** 60. C Corringham *Chelmsf* 59-61; C Prittlewell All SS 61-64; USPG 64-95; Tanzania 64-95; Can Dar-es-Salaam 74-88; Can Zanzibar and Tanga 88-95; Hon Can from 95; rtd 95; Perm to Offic *Roch* from 95. *22 Bromley College, London Road, Bromley BR1 1PE* Tel (020) 8290 1289 E-mail paul@hardy84.fsnet.co.uk

HARDY, Miss Pauline. b 41. CertEd. Linc Th Coll 85. **d** 87 **p** 94. Par Dn Walsall Wood *Lich* 87-89; Par Dn Buckingham *Ox* 89-93; C Buckingham w Radclive cum Chackmore 93-97; C Nash w Thornton, Beachampton and Thornborough 96-97; C Buckingham 97-03; C Watling Valley from 03. *The Rectory, Pitcher Lane, Loughton, Milton Keynes MK5 8AU* Tel (01908) 691288 E-mail pannahardy@waitrose.com

✠**HARDY, The Rt Revd Robert Maynard.** b 36. CBE01. Clare Coll Cam BA60 MA64 Hull Univ Hon DD92. Cuddesdon Coll 60. **d** 62 **p** 63 **c** 80. C Langley St Aid CD *Man* 62-64; C Langley All SS and Martyrs 64-65; Chapl and Lect Th Selw Coll Cam 65-72; V Boreham Wood All SS *St Alb* 72-75; Dir St Alb Minl Tr Scheme 75-80; P-in-c Aspley Guise *St Alb* 75-79; P-in-c Husborne Crawley w Ridgmont 76-79; R Aspley Guise w Husborne Crawley and Ridgmont 80; Suff Bp Maidstone *Cant* 80-87; Bp Linc 87-01; Bp HM Pris 85-01; rtd 01; Hon Asst Bp Carl from 01. *Carleton House, Back Lane, Langwathby, Penrith CA10 1NB* Tel (01768) 881210

HARDY, Sam Richard Ian. b 71. Wall Hall Coll Aldenham BEd95 Open Univ MA00. Wycliffe Hall Ox BTh04. **d** 04. C Parr *Liv* from 04. *St Peter's Vicarage, Delta Road, St Helens WA9 2DZ* Tel (01744) 735925 E-mail sam.hardy@tiscali.co.uk

HARDY, Stephen John Arundell. b 49. Spurgeon's Coll DipTh74. SEITE 95. **d** 97 **p** 98. NSM Marden *Cant* 97-00; P-in-c Lydd from 00; AD Romney from 03. *All Saints' Rectory, Park Street, Lydd, Romney Marsh TN29 9AY* Tel (01797) 320345 E-mail stephenhardy@macmail.com

HARE, Christopher Sumner. b 49. Solicitor 73. WEMTC 92. **d** 95 **p** 96. NSM Saltford w Corston and Newton St Loe *B & W* 95-01; P-in-c Timsbury and Priston from 01. *The Rectory, South Road, Timsbury, Bath BA2 0EJ* Tel (01761) 479660

HARE, David. b 46. Qu Coll Birm. **d** 83 **p** 83. SSF 67-94; Bp's Dom Chapl *Birm* 83-87; V Handsworth St Mich 87-97; R Newton Regis w Seckington and Shuttington 97-03; rtd 03; Perm to Offic *Birm* from 03. *118 Southam Road, Birmingham B28 0AD* Tel 0121-777 3493 E-mail dandjhare@hallgreen118.fsnet.co.uk

HARE, Douglas Stewart. b 27. Bris Univ BA51 Lon Inst of Educn PGCE52. Wycliffe Hall Ox 82. **d** 96 **p** 97. NSM Margate H Trin *Cant* 96-99; rtd 99; Perm to Offic *Sarum* from 00. *8 Lady Down View, Tisbury, Salisbury SP3 6LL* Tel (01747) 871544

HARE, Frank Richard Knight. b 22. Trin Hall Cam BA46 MA48. Cuddesdon Coll 46. **d** 48 **p** 49. C Dennington *St E* 48-51; C Eastbourne St Mary *Chich* 51-54; R Rotherfield 54-62; V Steyning 62-70; R Ashurst 62-70; TV Raveningham *Nor* 70-71; TR Barnham Broom 71-79; V Buxton w Oxnead 79-86; R Lammas w Lt Hautbois 79-86; rtd 86; Perm to Offic *St E* from 86. *14 Lee Road, Aldeburgh IP15 5HG* Tel (01728) 453372

HARE, Michael John. b 41. Lon Univ MD71 Cam Univ MA77. EAMTC 00. **d** 02 **p** 03. NSM E Leightonstone *Ely* from 02; NSM Alconbury w Alconbury Weston from 04; NSM Buckworth from 04. *Manor House, 66 Main Street, Hartford, Huntingdon PE29 1YA* Tel (01480) 453172 Mobile 07850-845004 Fax (01480) 451731 E-mail john@hare.waitrose.com

HARE, Richard William. b 66. Bris Univ BSc88 PhD94. Cranmer Hall Dur BA95. **d** 95 **p** 96. C Coulsdon St Jo *S'wark* 95-98; C Coventry Caludon *Cov* 98-99; TV from 99; AD Cov E from 01. *The Vicarage, Wyken Croft, Coventry CV2 3AD* Tel (024) 7660 2332 E-mail thehares@ic24.net

✠**HARE, The Rt Revd Thomas Richard.** b 22. Trin Coll Ox BA48 MA53. Westcott Ho Cam 48. **d** 50 **p** 51 **c** 71. C Haltwhistle *Newc* 50-52; Bp's Dom Chapl *Man* 52-59; Can Res Carl Cathl *Carl* 59-65; R Barrow St Geo w St Luke 65-69; Adn Westmorland and Furness 65-71; Hon Can Carl Cathl 65-71; V Winster 69-71; Suff Bp Pontefract *Wakef* 71-92; rtd 92. *Wood Cottage, Mirehouse, Underskiddaw, Keswick CA12 4QE* Tel (01768) 772996

✠**HARE DUKE, The Rt Revd Michael Geoffrey.** b 25. Trin Coll Ox BA49 MA51 St Andr Univ Hon DD94. Westcott Ho Cam 50. **d** 52 **p** 53 **c** 69. C St John's Wood *Lon* 52-56; V Bury St Mark *Man* 56-62; Past Dir Clinical Th Assn Nottm 62-64; Past Consultant 64-69; V Daybrook *S'well* 64-69; Bp St And 69-94; rtd 94. *2 Balhousie Avenue, Perth PH1 5HN* Tel (01738) 622642 E-mail bishmick@aol.com

HARES, David Ronald Walter. b 40. Qu Coll Cam BA63 MA67 CertEd. Westcott Ho Cam 64. **d** 66 **p** 67. C Cannock *Lich* 66-69; Chapl Peterho Cam 69-72; Asst Master Chesterton Sch Cam 72-74; V Kesgrave *St E* 74-98; R Lt Barningham, Blickling, Edgefield etc *Nor* 98-05; rtd 05; Perm to Offic *Nor* from 05. *17 Trory Street, Norwich NR2 2RH* Tel (01603) 626392 E-mail dh@davidhares.freeserve.co.uk

HAREWOOD, John Rupert. b 24. Man Univ BA48. Sarum & Wells Th Coll 76. **d** 79 **p** 80. NSM Taunton St Jas *B & W* 79-82; TV Camelot Par 82-89; rtd 89; Perm to Offic *Ex* from 92. *19 Swains Road, Budleigh Salterton EX9 6HU* Tel (01395) 445802

HARFORD, Julian Gray. b 29. Univ Coll Ox BA52 MA59 Lon Univ PGCE58. Qu Coll Birm DipTh64. **d** 64 **p** 65. C W End *Win* 64-67; C Chearsley w Nether Winchendon *Ox* 67-77; C Chilton All SS 72-77; R Westbury w Turweston, Shalstone and Biddlesden 77-86; C Chenies and Lt Chalfont 86-87; C Chenies and Lt Chalfont, Latimer and Flaunden 87-95; rtd 95; Perm to Offic *Sarum* from 95. *14 Dial Close, Seend, Melksham SN12 6NP* Tel (01380) 828306

HARFORD, The Ven Michael Rivers Dundas. b 26. Trin Coll Cam BA49 MA51. Westcott Ho Cam 50. **d** 52 **p** 53. C Ashton-on-Ribble St Andr *Blackb* 52-55; Perm to Offic *Edin* 55-56; Malaya 56-63; Malaysia 63-66; V Childwall St Dav *Liv* 66-71; Australia from 71; Adn Albany 76-79; Adn Swan 86-89; Adn Mitchell 90-91; rtd 91. *Unit 12, 18 Bridges Road, Melville, W Australia 6156* Tel (0061) (8) 9319 1538 Mobile 410-566896 E-mail michael.harford@perth.anglican.org

HARFORD, Timothy William. b 58. Nottm Univ BTh89. Linc Th Coll 86. **d** 89 **p** 90. C Minehead *B & W* 89-93; R Knebworth *St Alb* 93-03; Children's Soc from 03. *The Children's Society, Edward Rudolf House, Margery Street, London WC1X 0JL* Tel (020) 7841 4400 E-mail tim@harford1.freeserve.co.uk

HARGER, Robin Charles Nicholas. b 49. BTh. Sarum & Wells Th Coll 78. **d** 81 **p** 82. C Charlton Kings St Mary *Glouc* 81-85; C Folkestone St Mary and St Eanswythe *Cant* 85-89; TV Langley and Parkfield *Man* 89-95; TV Bournemouth St Pet w St Swithun, H Trin etc *Win* from 95. *The Vicarage, 2A St Anthony's Road, Bournemouth BH2 6PD* Tel (01202) 554355 E-mail robin.harger2@btopenworld.com

HARGRAVE, Canon Alan Lewis. b 50. Birm Univ BSc73 PhD77. Ridley Hall Cam 87. **d** 89 **p** 90. C Cambridge H Trin w St Andr Gt *Ely* 89-92; C Cambridge H Trin 92-93; C-in-c Fen Ditton 93-94; V Cambridge H Cross 94-04; Can Res Ely Cathl from 04. *Powchers Hall, The College, Ely CB7 4DL* Tel (01353) 660304 E-mail alan.hargrave@cathedral.ely.anglican.org

HARGREAVE, James David. b 44. ALCM89 LTCL90 Lon Univ BA66. **d** 73 **p** 74. C Houghton le Spring *Dur* 73-77; C Gateshead St Cuth w St Paul 77-79; V Trimdon 79-87; C-in-c Stockton Green Vale H Trin CD 87-94; V Hedon w Paull *York* 94-02; rtd 02; Perm to Offic *York* from 03. *1 The Avenue, Crescent Street, Cottingham HU16 5QT* Tel (01482) 844297

HARGREAVES, Arthur Cecil Monsarrat. b 19. Trin Hall Cam BA42 MA46. Westcott Ho Cam 47. **d** 49 **p** 50. C Wembley St Jo *Lon* 49-52; India 52-61 and 70-76; Asia Sec CMS 61-69; Gen Sec Conf of Br Miss Socs 76-79; Hon C Croydon St Aug *Cant* 79-81; V Marden 81-86; rtd 86; Perm to Offic *S'wark* from 86. *Windrush Cottage, 87 Downscourt Road, Purley CR8 1BJ* Tel (020) 8668 8871

HARGREAVES, Arthur Walsh. b 34. FRCSE FRCS Man Univ MB, ChB FRCSGlas. St Deiniol's Hawarden 89. **d** 90 **p** 91. NSM Baguley *Man* 90-00; Perm to Offic from 00. *Greenaways, Woodbourne Road, Sale M33 3SX* Tel 0161-973 7674

HARGREAVES, John. b 43. St Jo Coll Nottm 86. **d** 88 **p** 89. C Werneth *Man* 88-91; TV Rochdale 91-96; C Man Gd Shep 96-97; Perm to Offic *Liv* 96-97; C Manchester Gd Shep and St Barn *Man* 97-98; rtd 98. *15 Ambleside Avenue, Rawtenstall, Rossendale BB4 6RY*

HARGREAVES, Canon John Henry Monsarrat. b 11. Trin Coll Cam BA33 MA37. Westcott Ho Cam 35. **d** 37 **p** 38. C Bishopwearmouth Ch Ch *Dur* 37-39; C Hunslet St Mary *Ripon* 39-43; Nigeria 43-57; CMS Miss 43-49; Tutor Union Th Coll 49-51; Tutor Melville Hall Ibadan 51-54; Sec CMS 54-57; C Brompton H Trin *Lon* 57-58; C St Alb St Mich *St Alb* 58-60; Warden Buwalasi Th Coll Uganda 61-63; CMS 63-65; Min Sevenoaks St Luke CD *Roch* 65-83; RD Sevenoaks 74-79; Hon Can Roch Cathl 81-83; rtd 83; Perm to Offic *Guildf* from 91. *c/o Miss C F Hargreaves, 36 Royal Albert Road, Bristol BS6 7NY*

HARGREAVES, John Rodney. b 36. Open Univ BA74. Didsbury Methodist Coll 59 St Deiniol's Hawarden 74. **d** 75 **p** 75. In Methodist Ch 63-74; C Pontypool *Mon* 75-77; C Llanedeyrn 77-79; Chapl HM Pris Aylesbury 79-83; Sen Chapl HM Pris Stafford 83-88; Asst Chapl Gen of Pris (N) 88-90; Asst Chapl Gen of Pris 90-96; R Stone St Mich and St Wulfad w Aston St Sav *Lich* 96-01; rtd 01; Master St Jo Hosp Lich 01-04; Perm to Offic from 04. *217 Newcastle Road, Stone ST15 8LF* Tel (01785) 814765 E-mail jrhargreaves@easynet.co.uk

HARGREAVES, John Wilson. b 46. Aber Univ BScFor67 Birm Poly DipVG73. Westcott Ho Cam 84. **d** 86 **p** 87. C Rugby St Andr *Cov* 86-90; TV Daventry, Ashby St Ledgers, Braunston etc *Pet* 90-97; Chapl Daventry Tertiary Coll 94-97; P-in-c Pinxton *Derby* 97-01; R 01-02; TR E Scarsdale from 02. *The Rectory, Rectory Road, Upper Langwith, Mansfield NG20 9RE* Tel (01623) 748505

HARGREAVES, Ms Marise. b 60. Leeds Univ BA81. Cranmer Hall Dur 82. **dss** 85 **d** 94 **p** 95. Yeadon St Jo *Bradf* 85-87; NSM Bradf St Clem 94-96; NSM Buttershaw St Paul 96-00; C Eccleshill 00-03; Perm to Offic from 03. *45 Lodore Road, Bradford BD2 4JH* Tel (01274) 641420

HARGREAVES, Mark Kingston. b 63. Oriel Coll Ox BA85 MA89 Rob Coll Cam PhD91 W Lon Inst of HE PGCE86. Ridley Hall Cam 87. **d** 91 **p** 92. C Highbury Ch Ch w St Jo and St Sav *Lon* 91-94; C Ealing St Steph Castle Hill 94-97; C Notting Hill St Jo and St Pet 97-02; V Notting Hill St Pet from 03. *48 Ladbroke Road, London W11 3NW* Tel (020) 7221 9841 E-mail mark@nottinghillchurch.org.uk

HARGREAVES-STEAD, Terence Desmond. b 32. Edin Th Coll 60. **d** 63 **p** 64. C Walney Is *Carl* 63-66; Chapl Withington Hosp Man 66-72; V Westleigh St Paul *Man* from 72; Chapl Wigan and Leigh Health Services NHS Trust 96-01; Chapl Wrightington Wigan and Leigh NHS Trust from 01. *St Paul's Vicarage, Westleigh Lane, Leigh WN7 5NW* Tel (01942) 882883 *or* 672333

HARINGTON, Roger John Urquhart. b 48. Trin Hall Cam BA70 MA71. Coll of Resurr Mirfield 72. **d** 75 **p** 76. C Liv Our Lady and St Nic w St Anne *Liv* 75-78; Asst Chapl Leeds Univ and Poly *Ripon* 78-81; TV Moor Allerton 81-86; Dioc Drama Adv (Jabbok Theatre Co) 86-95; V Leeds Gipton Epiphany 95-02. *21 Spencer Place, Leeds LS7 4DQ* Tel 0113-240 0769 E-mail jabbok@gn.apc.org

HARKER, Harold Aidan. b 35. **d** 82 **p** 83. OSB from 53; C Reading St Giles *Ox* 82-83; Lic to Offic 83-87; C Halstead St Andr w H Trin and Greenstead Green *Chelmsf* 87-89; P-in-c Belchamp St Paul 89-97; R Belchamp Otten w Belchamp Walter and Bulmer etc 97-00; rtd 00; Lic to Offic *Chelmsf* from 00. *38 Sheppard's College, London Road, Bromley BR1 1PE* Tel (020) 8464 1206

HARKER, Ian. b 39. Dur Univ BA61. Lich Th Coll Moray Ho Edin 66. **d** 63 **p** 64. C Knottingley *Wakef* 63-66; Perm to Offic 66-70; C Notting Hill *Lon* 70-75; Chapl Newc Univ *Newc* 75-83; Master Newc St Thos Prop Chpl 75-83; Perm to Offic *Chelmsf* 99-01; C Plaistow and N Canning Town 01; C Loughton St Jo 01-02; V Leytonstone H Trin Harrow Green from 02. *The Vicarage, 4 Holloway Road, London E11 4LD* Tel and fax (020) 8539 7760 E-mail harkatvic@aol.com

HARKER, John Hadlett. b 37. Dur Univ BSc59 Newc Univ PhD67 CEng MIChemE64 MInstE64 CChem MRSC65 FIChemE80. NEOC 81. **d** 84 **p** 85. C Earsdon *Newc* 84-87; P-in-c Long Horsley 87-91; V Bassenthwaite, Isel and Setmurthy *Carl* 91-94; TR Howden *York* 94-96; P-in-c Willerby w Ganton and Folkton 96-98; rtd 98; Perm to Offic *Newc* 98-01 and from 04; Hon C Newc St Andr and St Luke 01-04. *13 The Oval, Woolsington, Newcastle upon Tyne NE13 8AS* Tel 0191-286 6441 E-mail harker@thestell.freeserve.co.uk

HARKER, Stephan John. b 47. Em Coll Cam BA68 MA72. Westcott Ho Cam 70. **d** 72 **p** 73. C Marton *Blackb* 72-76; C Preston St Matt 76-79; C Fleetwood St Pet 79-80; Chapl Charterhouse Sch Godalming from 81. *Lower Oakhurst, Frith Hill Road, Godalming GU7 2ED* Tel (01483) 422155

HARKIN, John Patrick. b 53. Open Univ BA92. Oak Hill Th Coll DipHE89. **d** 89 **p** 90. C Wisley w Pyrford *Guildf* 89-93; P-in-c Mickleham 93-98; Chapl Box Hill Sch Surrey 93-98; R Jersey St Ouen w St Geo *Win* from 98; Vice-Dean Jersey from 01; Hon Chapl ATC from 02. *The Rectory, La Route du Marais, St Ouen, Jersey JE3 2GG* Tel (01534) 481800 Fax 484202 E-mail harkin@jerseymail.co.uk

HARKIN, Terence James. b 46. Lon Bible Coll BA82 New Coll Edin MTh94. **d** 95 **p** 96. In Bapt Min 86-95; C Edin H Cross *Edin* 95-96; C S Queensferry 95-96; P-in-c from 96. *6 Wellhead Close, South Queensferry EH30 9WA* Tel 0131-319 1099 *or* 331 1958 E-mail tjharkin@nildram.co.uk

HARKINS, James Robert. b 27. Minnesota Univ BA49. Seabury-Western Th Sem MTh53. **d** 52 **p** 52. USA 52-60, 72-79 and 91-93; Colombia 60-72; Dominica 79-85; Venezuela 85-91; Chapl Venice w Trieste *Eur* 94-99; P-in-c Menton 99-01; rtd 01. *Soleil du Menton, 2 Sent Pigautier, 06500 Menton, France* Tel (0033) (4) 9357 2025

HARKNETT, David Philip. b 74. St Pet Coll Ox BA97. Oak Hill Th Coll BA03. **d** 03 **p** 04. C Radipole and Melcombe Regis *Sarum* from 03. *1 Campion Close, Weymouth DT4 7UE* Tel (01305) 788202 E-mail davidharknett@hotmail.com *or* davix@mygfa.org

HARKNETT, Linda. b 48. Open Univ BA81 Croydon Coll CertEd92. SEITE 97. **d** 00 **p** 01. NSM Sutton St Nic *S'wark* 00-03; Chapl Epsom and St Helier NHS Trust 00-03; Chapl Whitelands Coll Surrey Univ Roehampton *S'wark* from 03. *Chaplain's Office, Whitelands College, West Hill, London SW15 3SN* Tel (020) 8392 3516 E-mail l.harknett@roehampton.ac.uk

HARLAND, Canon Harold William James. b 35. Hertf Coll Ox BA59 MA63. Clifton Th Coll 59. **d** 61 **p** 62. C Reigate St Mary *S'wark* 61-64; C Farnborough *Guildf* 64-68; V Walmley *Birm* 68-74; V Bromley Ch Ch *Roch* 74-86; V Foord St Jo *Cant* 86-00; Dir Post-Ord Tr 93-97; Hon Can Cant Cathl 94-00; rtd 00; Perm to Offic *Cant* from 00. *121 Station Road West, Canterbury CT2 8DE* Tel (01227) 764699 E-mail harlandh992@aol.com

✠**HARLAND, The Rt Revd Ian.** b 32. Peterho Cam BA56 MA60. Wycliffe Hall Ox 58. **d** 60 **p** 61 **c** 85. C Melton Mowbray w Thorpe Arnold *Leic* 60-63; V Oughtibridge *Sheff* 63-72; V Sheff St Cuth 72-75; P-in-c Brightside All SS 72-75; RD Ecclesfield 73-75; V Rotherham 75-79; RD Rotherham 76-79; Adn Doncaster 79-85; P-in-c Dunscroft Ch Ch 81-83; Hon Can Blackb Cathl *Blackb* 85-89; Suff Bp Lancaster 85-89; Bp Carl 89-00; rtd 00; Hon Asst Bp Eur from 00. *White House, 11 South Street, Gargrave, Skipton BD23 3RT* Tel (01756) 748623 E-mail isharland.gargrave@amserve.net

HARLEY, Brother Brian Mortimer. b 25. K Coll Lon 48. **d** 53 **p** 54. C Bris St Agnes w St Simon *Bris* 53-56; Lic to Offic *Sarum* 56-62; SSF from 56; Chapl St Fran Sch Hooke 58-61; Papua New Guinea 61-79; Australia from 87; Min Gen SSF from 91; rtd 95. *The Hermitage of St Bernadine, PO Box 46, Stroud, NSW, Australia 2425* Tel (0061) (2) 4994 5372 Fax 4994 5527

HARLEY, Canon Brian Nigel. b 30. Clare Coll Cam BA53 MA57. Cuddesdon Coll 53. **d** 55 **p** 56. C Basingstoke *Win* 55-60; TV 71-73; TR 73-80; C W End 60-61; C-in-c Southn St Chris Thornhill CD 61-71; V Eastleigh 80-93; RD Eastleigh 85-93; rtd 93; Perm to Offic *Win* from 93; Bp's Dom Chapl 94-96. *18 Phillimore Road, Southampton SO16 2NR* Tel (023) 8055 1049

HARLEY, Mrs Carol Anne. b 46. **d** 00 **p** 01. OLM Tettenhall Wood and Perton *Lich* from 00. *27 Tyrley Close, Compton, Wolverhampton WV6 8AP* Tel (01902) 755316
E-mail allynharley@lineone.net

HARLEY, Christopher David. b 41. Selw Coll Cam BA63 MA69 Bris Univ PGCE64 Columbia Bible Sem DMin92 Utrecht Univ PhD02. Clifton Th Coll 64. **d** 66 **p** 67. C Finchley Ch Ch *Lon* 66-69; Hon C 75-78; Ethiopia 70-75; Hd of UK Miss CMJ 75-78; Lect All Nations Chr Coll Ware 78-85; Prin 85-93; Chmn Lon Inst of Contemporary Christianity 88-89; Chmn CMJ 89-90; Crosslinks from 93; Gen Dir OMF Internat from 93; NSM Bromley Ch Ch *Roch* 93-96; NSM Singapore from 96. *2 Cluny Road, Singapore 259570* Tel (0065) 473 6180 *or* 473 5755
E-mail harleydavid@omf.net

HARLEY, David Bertram. b 22. Down Coll Cam BA50 MA55. Westcott Ho Cam 55. **d** 56 **p** 58. Asst Master Bedford Sch 50-58; C Biddenham *St Alb* 56-58; Chapl Stamford Sch 58-87; rtd 87; Confrater Browne's Hosp Stamford from 87; Lic to Offic *Linc* 59-94; Perm to Offic from 94. *Beggars' Roost, Priory Road, Stamford PE9 2ES* Tel (01780) 763403

HARLEY, Michael. b 50. AKC73 Ch Ch Coll Cant CertEd74 Lambeth STh92 Kent Univ MPhil95. St Aug Coll Cant 74. **d** 75 **p** 76. C Chatham St Wm *Roch* 75-78; C-in-c Weeke *Win* 78-81; V Southampton St Mary Extra 81-86; V Hurstbourne Tarrant, Faccombe, Vernham Dean etc 86-99; ACORA Link Officer 91-94; Dioc Rural Officer 95-97; RD Andover 95-99; V Chandler's Ford from 99. *The Vicarage, 30 Hursley Road, Chandler's Ford, Eastleigh SO53 2FT* Tel (023) 8025 2597
E-mail vicar@parishofchandlersford.fsnet.co.uk

HARLEY, Nigel. *See* HARLEY, Canon Brian Nigel

HARLEY, Robert Patterson. b 53. St Andr Univ MA75 Cam Univ CertEd76 Glas Univ PhD89 Edin Univ BD97. **d** 97 **p** 98. C Edin St Thos *Edin* 97-00; Chapl Lothian Univ Hosps NHS Trust 98-00; P-in-c Kirriemuir *St And* from 00. *128 Glengate, Kirriemuir DD8 4JG* Tel (01575) 575515
E-mail robertharley@tiscali.co.uk

HARLEY, Roger Newcomb. b 38. Ely Th Coll 61. **d** 64 **p** 65. C Plymouth St Pet *Ex* 64-66; C Heston *Lon* 66-69; C Maidstone All SS w St Phil and H Trin *Cant* 69-73; R Temple Ewell w Lydden 73-79; P-in-c Shirley St Geo 79-81; V 81-85; V Croydon H Sav *S'wark* 85-95; V Forest Row *Chich* 95-03; rtd 03; Perm to Offic *Cant* from 03. *7 Roman Way, St Margarets-at-Cliffe, Dover CT15 6AH* Tel (01304) 851720
E-mail roger.harley@btinternet.com

HARLING, Timothy Charles. b 80. Fitzw Coll Cam BA04. Westcott Ho Cam 02. **d** 05. C Romsey *Win* from 05. *15 Mount Temple, Romsey SO51 5UW*

HARLOW, Antony Francis. b 24. Pemb Coll Cam BA50 MA55 DipTh55. Oak Hill Th Coll 84. **d** 85 **p** 86. NSM Watford St Luke *St Alb* 85-86; CMS 86-91; Uganda 86-91; Perm to Offic *St Alb* 90-98; NSM Watford St Pet 92-96; Perm to Offic *B & W* from 98. *1 Jubilee Homes, Langford Road, Langford, Bristol BS40 5HU* Tel (01934) 862605

HARLOW, Canon Derrick Peter. b 30. St Jo Coll Cam BA53 MA57. Ridley Hall Cam 53. **d** 55 **p** 56. C Barking St Marg *Chelmsf* 55-58; V Leyton Em 58-63; V Goodmayes All SS 63-75; R Thundersley 76-83; TR Saffron Walden w Wendens Ambo and Littlebury 83-95; Hon Can Chelmsf Cathl 84-95; rtd 95; Perm to Offic *Ely* from 95 and *Chelmsf* from 98. *26 Kintbury, Duxford, Cambridge CB2 4RR* Tel (01223) 721405

HARLOW, Mrs Elizabeth Gilchrist. b 27. MSc50 DipTh60. Oak Hill Th Coll 85. **d** 91 **p** 94. NSM St Alb St Luke *St Alb* 91-94; NSM Watford St Luke 94-96; Perm to Offic *St Alb* 96-98 and *B & W* from 98. *1 Jubilee Homes, Langford Road, Langford Road, Bristol BS40 5HU* Tel (01934) 862605

HARLOW-TRIGG, Richard John St Clair. b 63. Cam Univ BA85 MA88. Cranmer Hall Dur 87. **d** 89 **p** 90. C Hyson Green *S'well* 89-91; C Basford w Hyson Green 91-94; C Mansfield SS Pet and Paul 94-97; TV Newark 97-01; Chapl Mid Sussex NHS Trust 01-02; St Pet and St Jas Hospice N Chailey from 02; Chapl Brighton and Sussex Univ Hosps NHS Trust from 02. *The Princess Royal Hospital, Lewes Road, Haywards Heath RH16 4EX* Tel (01444) 441881 ext 4232
E-mail richard.harlow-trigg@bsuh.nhs.uk

HARLOW, Archdeacon of. *See* TAYLOR, The Ven Peter Flint

HARMAN, Kathleen Joyce. b 49. **d** 03 **p** 04. C Llangynwyd w Maesteg *Llan* from 03. *21 Cwm Farteg, Bryn, Port Talbot SA13 2SS* Tel (01639) 899522

HARMAN, Leslie Davies. b 46. Nottm Univ BTh76. St Jo Coll Nottm LTh75. **d** 76 **p** 77. C Wandsworth All SS *S'wark* 76-78; C Godstone 78-82; V Thorncombe w Winsham and Cricket St Thomas *B & W* 82-87; TV Hitchin *St Alb* 87-95; V Royston from 95; RD Buntingford 96-01. *The Vicarage, 31 Baldock Road, Royston SG8 5BJ* Tel (01763) 243145 *or* 246371
E-mail lesharman@beeb.net

HARMAN, Michael John. b 48. Chich Th Coll 71. **d** 74 **p** 75. C Blackpool St Steph *Blackb* 74-79; Chapl RN from 79. *Royal Naval Chaplaincy Service, Room 203, Victory Building, HM Naval Base, Portsmouth PO1 3LS* Tel (023) 9272 7903 Fax 9272 7111

HARMAN, The Very Revd Robert Desmond. b 41. TCD BA65 MA71. TCD Div Sch 67. **d** 67 **p** 68. C Taney Ch Ch *D & G* 67-73; I Dublin Santry w Glasnevin 73-86; I Dublin Sandford w Milltown 86-04; Can Ch Ch Cathl Dublin 91-04; Treas 02-04; Hon Sec Gen Syn from 99; Dean Ch Ch Cathl Dublin from 04; I Dublin Ch Ch Cathl Gp from 04. *The Deanery, St Werburgh Street, Dublin 8, Irish Republic* Tel (00353) (1) 478 1797 *or* 677 8099 Mobile 87-297 1077 Fax (1) 475 3442 *or* 679 8991
E-mail dean@dublin.anglican.org

HARMAN, Theodore Allan. b 27. Linc Coll Ox BA52 MA56 Hatf Coll Dur MA90. Wells Th Coll 52. **d** 54 **p** 55. C Hawkshead and Low Wray *Carl* 54-55; C Kirkby Stephen w Mallerstang 55-57; Asst Chapl Sedbergh Sch 57-84; Sen Chapl 84-87; Tutor Hatf Coll Dur from 88; Admissions Tutor 89-90; Lib and Coll Officer 91-02; Acting Chapl 99-00; Fell from 00; Perm to Offic *Dur* from 88. *Flat D1, Hatfield College, North Bailey, Durham DH1 3RQ* Tel 0191-334 2626 Fax 334 3101
E-mail t.a.harman@durham.ac.uk

HARMER, Timothy James. b 47. Birm Univ CertEd68. St Jo Coll Nottm BA95. **d** 95 **p** 96. C Studley *Cov* 95-98; V Tanworth *Birm* from 98. *The Vicarage, Vicarage Hill, Tanworth-in-Arden, Solihull B94 5EB* Tel (01564) 742565 Fax 741817
E-mail revtim.harmer@virgin.net

HARMSWORTH, Canon Roger James. b 46. Univ of W Ontario BA87. Huron Coll Ontario MDiv90. **d** 90 **p** 90. Canada 90-96; I Maryborough w Dysart Enos and Ballyfin *C & O* 96-01; I Killanne w Killegney, Rossdroit and Templeshanbo from 01; Treas Ferns Cathl 03-04; Chan from 04. *The Rectory, Clonroche, Enniscorthy, Co Wexford, Irish Republic* Tel and fax (00353) (54) 44180 E-mail therev@iol.ie

HARNDEN, Peter John. b 63. Coll of Resurr Mirfield 96. **d** 98 **p** 99. C Staplehurst *Cant* 98-02; V Tokyngton St Mich *Lon* from 02. *The Vicarage, St Michael's Avenue, Wembley HA9 6SL* Tel (020) 8902 3290 E-mail harny@cwcom.net *or* harny@boltblue.net

HARNEY, Janice. b 56. Man OLM Scheme 99. **d** 02 **p** 03. OLM Pennington *Man* from 02. *29 Green Lane, Leigh WN7 2TL* Tel and fax (01942) 671481 Mobile 07811-764355
E-mail jan.harney@btinternet.com

HARNISH, Robert George. b 64. Univ of Ottawa BSc87 Worc Coll Ox DPhil90 MA92. Wycliffe Hall Ox 90. **d** 93 **p** 94. C Chinnor w Emmington and Sydenham etc *Ox* 93-95; Chapl and Dean of Div New Coll Ox 96-01; Chapl Eliz Coll Guernsey from 01. *11 Saumarez Street, St Peter Port, Guernsey GY1 2PT* Tel (01481) 713298 *or* 726544

HARONSKI, Boleslaw. b 46. Pemb Coll Ox BA68 MA72 DPhil73. St Mich Coll Llan 80 Westcott Ho Cam 82. **d** 82 **p** 83. C Maindee *Mon* 82-85; V Llanishen w Trellech Grange and Llanfihangel etc 85-89; V Blackwood 89-92. *45 St Julian's Road, Newport NP9 7GN*

✠**HARPER, The Rt Revd Alan Edwin Thomas.** b 44. OBE96. Leeds Univ BA65. CITC 75. **d** 78 **p** 79 **c** 02. C Ballywillan *Conn* 78-80; I Moville w Greencastle, Upper Moville etc *D & R* 80-82; I Londonderry Ch Ch 82-86; I Belfast Malone St Jo *Conn* 86-02; Preb St Audoen St Patr Cathl Dublin 90-01; Adn Conn 96-02; Prec Belf Cathl 96-02; Bp Conn from 02. *Bishop's House, 113 Upper Road, Greenisland, Carrickfergus BT38 8RR* Tel (028) 9086 3165, 9032 3188 *or* 9032 2268 Fax 9036 4266
E-mail aharper@fish.co.uk

HARPER, Preb Alan Peter. b 50. Man Univ BA73 FCA83. Ripon Coll Cuddesdon 86. **d** 88 **p** 89. C Newport w Longford and Chetwynd *Lich* 88-91; P-in-c Wilnecote 91-94; V 94-98; V Codsall from 98; Preb Lich Cathl from 02. *The Vicarage, 52 Church Road, Codsall, Wolverhampton WV8 1EH* Tel (01902) 842168 E-mail rev.alan.harper@lineone.net

HARPER, Barry. *See* HARPER, Canon Malcolm Barry

HARPER, Brian John. b 61. Liv Univ BA82 TCD DipTh85. **d** 85 **p** 86. C Portadown St Columba *Arm* 85-88; C Drumglass 88-89; I Errigle Keerogue w Ballygawley and Killeshil 89-93; I Mullavilly from 93. *89 Mullavilly Road, Tandragee, Craigavon BT62 2LX* Tel (028) 3884 0221 *or* 3884 1918
E-mail mullavilly@btinternet.com

HARPER, Clive Stewart. b 35. FCIS71. Ridley Hall Cam 80. **d** 82 **p** 83. C Bromyard *Heref* 82-85; P-in-c Bredenbury and Wacton w

Grendon Bishop 85-89; P-in-c Edwyn Ralph and Collington w Thornbury 85-89; P-in-c Pencombe w Marston Stannett and Lt Cowarne 85-89; R Bredenbury w Grendon Bishop and Wacton etc 89-92; R Bilton *Cov* 92-02; rtd 02; Hon C Churchover w Willey *Cov* from 02. *Kairos, 18 Whimbrel Close, Rugby CV23 0WG* Tel (01788) 541041

HARPER, David Laurence. b 51. Qu Coll Cam BA73 MA77 PhD78. Wycliffe Hall Ox BA80. **d** 80 **p** 81. C Mansfield SS Pet and Paul *S'well* 80-84; C Wollaton 84-87; V Brinsley w Underwood 87-94; R Bingham from 94; AD Bingham 00-03; AD E Bingham from 03. *The Rectory, Bingham, Nottingham NG13 8DR* Tel (01949) 837335 E-mail dl.harper@btopenworld.com

HARPER, Geoffrey. b 32. Hertf Coll Ox BA55 MA59. Coll of Resurr Mirfield. **d** 57 **p** 58. C Cov St Pet *Cov* 57-60; C Handsworth St Mich *Birm* 60-62; C-in-c Kingstanding St Mark CD 62-71; V Kingstanding St Mark 71-73; R Sheviock *Truro* 73-80; R Antony w Sheviock 80-82; V Paul 82-98; Dioc Development Rep 86-98; rtd 98; Perm to Offic *Truro* 99-04. *24 Mill Road, Basingstoke RG24 9SL*

HARPER, Geoffrey Roger. b 57. Jes Coll Cam BA MA. St Jo Coll Nottm 81. **d** 84 **p** 85. C Belper *Derby* 84-87; C Birstall and Wanlip *Leic* 87-90; TV Tettenhall Regis *Lich* 90-97; C Aldridge 97-02; Perm to Offic from 02; Chapl Douglas MacMillan Hospice Stoke-on-Trent from 04. *50 Lichfield Road, Walsall WS4 2DJ* Tel (01922) 611484 E-mail roger.harper@virgin.net

HARPER, Gordon. b 32. Oak Hill Th Coll 64. **d** 66 **p** 67. C Halliwell St Pet *Man* 66-71 and 84-99; P-in-c Brinsworth *Sheff* 71-75; V Brinsworth w Catcliffe 76-84; rtd 99. *15 New Church Road, Bolton BL1 5QP* Tel (01204) 849413

HARPER, Gordon William Robert. b 48. Wellington Univ (NZ) BA70 St Chad's Coll Dur BA74 Nottm Univ PhD89. Coll of Resurr Mirfield 74. **d** 75 **p** 76. C Battyeford *Wakef* 75-76; New Zealand 76-80; P-in-c Byers Green *Dur* 80-83; V Evenwood 83-89; R Wolviston 89-00; V Billingham St Mary 97-01; P-in-c Winlaton from 01. *The Rectory, Winlaton, Blaydon-on-Tyne NE21 6PL* Tel 0191-414 3165 Fax as telephone E-mail drgwr&jharper@westbill.freeserve.co.uk

HARPER, Ian. b 54. AKC78. Oak Hill Th Coll 79. **d** 80 **p** 81. C Sidcup St Jo *Roch* 80-83; C Bushey *St Alb* 83-87; TV Thamesmead *S'wark* 87-92; TR N Lambeth 92-00; V Homerton St Luke *Lon* from 00; AD Hackney from 04. *St Luke's Vicarage, 23 Cassland Road, London E9 7AL* Tel (020) 8525 0950 *or* 8985 2263 E-mail sluke.hackney@london.anglican.org

HARPER, James. b 35. St Luke's Coll Ex TDip57. SW Minl Tr Course DipTh89. **d** 90 **p** 91. NSM Pendeen w Morvah *Truro* 90-97; Perm to Offic *Win* from 01. *1 Millstream Mews, 50 Beaconsfield Road, Christchurch BH23 1QT* Tel (01202) 477138

HARPER, John Anthony. b 46. AKC69. **d** 70 **p** 71. C Pet St Mary Boongate *Pet* 70-73; C Abington 73-75; V Grendon w Castle Ashby 75-82; Asst Dioc Youth Chapl 75-82; R Castor w Sutton and Upton 82-94; TV Riverside *Ox* 94-04; V Meppershall and Shefford *St Alb* from 04. *The Rectory, Church Road, Meppershall, Shefford SG17 5NA* Tel (01462) 813334 E-mail j.harper@ukgateway.net

HARPER, John Hugh. b 34. ALAM62 Hertf Coll Ox BA57 MA61. Wells Th Coll 57. **d** 59 **p** 60. C Twerton *B & W* 59-62; R Chapel Allerton 62-69; V Blackford 62-69; V Halsetown *Truro* 69-91; RD Penwith 84-88; P-in-c S Brent *Ex* 91; V S Brent and Rattery 91-99; rtd 99; Perm to Offic *Chelmsf* 00-04. *19 Winston Rise, Four Marks, Alton GU34 5HP* Tel (01420) 563227

HARPER, Joseph Frank. b 38. Hull Univ BA60 MA86 MPhil98. Linc Th Coll 80. **d** 81 **p** 82. C Preston St Cuth *Blackb* 81-83; C Lancaster St Mary 83-87; V Bamber Bridge St Aid 87-92; V Kinsley w Wragby *Wakef* 92-99; R Newhaven *Chich* 99-04; rtd 04. *30 Greenways, Consett DH8 7DE* Tel (01207) 590962

HARPER, Canon Malcolm Barry. b 37. Dur Univ BSc59. Wycliffe Hall Ox 59. **d** 61 **p** 62. C Harold Wood *Chelmsf* 61-65; C Madeley *Heref* 65-68; V Slaithwaite w E Scammonden *Wakef* 68-75; V Walmley *Birm* 75-03; Hon Can Birm Cathl 96-03; rtd 03; Perm to Offic *Birm* from 03. *1 Welcombe Drive, Sutton Coldfield B76 1ND* Tel 0121-351 3990 E-mail canonbarryharper@tiscali.co.uk

HARPER, Mrs Margaret. b 51. Nottm Coll of Educn TCert73 Nottm Univ BEd74. St Alb and Ox Min Course 98. **d** 01 **p** 02. C Slough *Ox* 01-05; P-in-c Leeds St Cypr Harehills *Ripon* from 05; P-in-c Burmantofts St Steph and St Agnes from 05. *St Agnes Vicarage, 21 Shakespeare Close, Leeds LS9 7UQ* Tel 0113-248 2648

HARPER, Martin Nigel. b 48. FRICS88 PGCE95. S Dios Minl Tr Scheme. **d** 85 **p** 86. NSM St Leonards Ch Ch and St Mary *Chich* 85-93; NSM Rye 94-95. *Bexhill High School, Down Road, Bexhill-on-Sea TN39 4HT*

HARPER, Canon Maurice. b 20. St Steph Ho Ox 60. **d** 62 **p** 63. C Upminster *Chelmsf* 62-67; V Gt Ilford St Mary 67-71; R Upminster 71-85; RD Havering 80-85; Hon Can Chelmsf Cathl 84-85; rtd 85; Perm to Offic *Chelmsf* and *Nor* from 85; *St E* from 87. *30 Cookham Dene, Buckhurst Road, Bexhill-on-Sea TN40 1RU* Tel (01424) 222189 E-mail mauriceh@fish.co.uk

HARPER, Michael Sydney. b 36. Portsm Dioc Tr Course 86. **d** 87. NSM Leigh Park St Clare CD *Portsm* 87-88; NSM Warren Park from 88; NSM Leigh Park from 96. *17 Hampage Green, Warren Park, Havant PO9 4HJ* Tel (023) 9245 4275

HARPER, Richard Michael. b 53. Lon Univ BSc75 Univ of Wales PhD78. St Steph Ho Ox BA80 MA87. **d** 81 **p** 82. C Holt *Nor* 81-84; C-in-c Grahame Park St Aug CD *Lon* 84-88; Sub-Warden and Dir Studies St Mich Coll Llan 88-93; Lect Ch Hist Univ of Wales (Cardiff) 88-93; R St Leonards Ch Ch and St Mary *Chich* 94-03; RD Hastings 02-03; V Weymouth St Paul *Sarum* from 03. *St Paul's Vicarage, 58 Abbotsbury Road, Weymouth DT4 0BJ* Tel (01305) 778821 E-mail frrweymouthstp@beeb.net

HARPER, Roger. *See* HARPER, Geoffrey Roger

HARPER, Roger. b 43. Man Univ BSc FCA. **d** 87 **p** 88. NSM Onchan *S & M* 87-97; NSM Douglas St Geo from 97. *Lhergydhoo Farm, Lhergydhoo, Peel, Isle of Man IM5 2AE* Tel (01624) 842466

HARPER, Rosemary Elizabeth. b 55. Birm Univ BA76 ARCM75 DipRAM78. NTMTC 96. **d** 99 **p** 00. C Amersham *Ox* 99-03; P-in-c Gt Missenden w Ballinger and Lt Hampden from 03. *The Rectory, Church Street, Amersham HP7 0BD* Tel (01494) 728988 E-mail rosie51619@aol.com

HARPER, Thomas Reginald. b 31. Dur Univ BA57 MA67. **d** 58 **p** 59. C Corbridge w Halton *Newc* 58-60; C Byker St Mich 60-62; V Ushaw Moor *Dur* 62-67; Asst Chapl HM Pris Dur 62-67; N Sec CMS 67-74; V Thornthwaite *Carl* 74-75; V Thornthwaite cum Braithwaite and Newlands 76-90; TV Bellingham/Otterburn Gp *Newc* 90-91; TV N Tyne and Redesdale 91-92; TR 92-98; RD Bellingham 93-98; rtd 98; Perm to Offic *Carl* from 98. *Dunelm, Old Lake Road, Ambleside LA22 0DH* Tel (01539) 433556

HARPER, Timothy James Lincoln. b 54. LRAM Lon Univ BMus76 CertEd DipP&C MA96. Wycliffe Hall Ox 84. **d** 86 **p** 87. C Morden *S'wark* 86-90; V Deptford St Pet 90-97; R Amersham *Ox* from 97. *The Rectory, Church Street, Amersham HP7 0DB* Tel (01494) 724426 *or* 729380 Fax 08701-639596 E-mail tjlharper@aol.com

HARPHAM, Mrs Diana Joan. b 44. MCSP66. St Alb Minl Tr Scheme 94. **d** 98 **p** 99. NSM Harrold and Carlton w Chellington *St Alb* 98-01; NSM Bromham w Oakley and Stagsden from 01. *The Old Police House, 40 Stagsden Road, Bromham, Bedford MK43 8PT* Tel (01234) 823222 Fax 825577 E-mail di@harpham.com

HARRATT, Preb Philip David. b 56. Magd Coll Ox BA79 MA83. Ripon Coll Cuddesdon 82. **d** 85 **p** 86. C Ewyas Harold w Dulas, Kenderchurch etc *Heref* 85-88; V Chirbury from 88; V Marton from 88; V Trelystan from 88; RD Pontesbury from 01; P-in-c Middleton from 02; Preb Heref Cathl from 03. *The Vicarage, Chirbury, Montgomery SY15 6BN* Tel (01938) 561218 Fax as telephone E-mail philip@chirvic.freeserve.co.uk

HARREX, David Brian. b 54. DipHE89. Trin Coll Bris 87. **d** 89 **p** 90. C Bedminster St Mich *Bris* 89-93; V Pilning w Compton Greenfield 93-00; RD Westbury and Severnside 97-99; AD Bris W 99-00; TR Yate New Town from 00. *The Rectory, 97 Canterbury Close, Yate, Bristol BS37 5TU* Tel (01454) 311483 E-mail davidharrex@hotmail.com

HARRIES, Canon Gwilym David. b 41. Univ of Wales (Lamp) BA63. St Mich Coll Llan 63. **d** 65 **p** 66. C Llangiwg *S & B* 65-68; C Llangyfelach and Morriston 68-71; TV Aberystwyth *St D* 71-76; R Hubberston 76-82; R Hubberston w Herbrandston and Hasguard etc 82-84; V Burry Port and Pwll from 84; Hon Can St D Cathl from 00. *The Vicarage, 134 Pencoed Road, Burry Port SA16 0PS* Tel (01554) 832936

HARRIES, Henry Rayner Mackintosh. b 30. MBE67. Chich Th Coll 53. **d** 55 **p** 56. C Hastings H Trin *Chich* 55-58; Chapl RAF 58-79; Asst Chapl-in-Chief RAF 79-84; QHC 83-84; P-in-c Gt Brickhill w Bow Brickhill and Lt Brickhill *Ox* 84-86; R 86-94; RD Mursley 91-94; rtd 95; Perm to Offic *Chelmsf* from 94. *2 Fyfield Road, Ongar CM5 0AH* Tel (01277) 363741

HARRIES, John Edward. b 60. Bris Univ BSc81 PhD84. Wycliffe Hall Ox 94. **d** 96 **p** 97. C Hyde St Geo *Ches* 96-00; P-in-c Walton from 00; C Latchford St Jas from 00; Chapl Sir Thos Boteler High Sch from 03. *St John's Vicarage, Chester Road, Higher Walton, Warrington WA4 6TJ* Tel (01925) 662939

HARRIES, Mrs Judith Janice. b 43. SRN67 Trin Coll Bris BA93 Bris Univ PGCE94. WEMTC 99. **d** 01 **p** 02. NSM Bath St Sav w Swainswick and Woolley *B & W* 01-03; Hon C Farmborough, Marksbury and Stanton Prior from 03. *19 Victoria Buildings, Bath BA2 3EH* Tel (01225) 332418 E-mail judithharries@hotmail.com

HARRIES, Malcolm David. b 44. BA99. Oak Hill Th Coll 94. **d** 96 **p** 97. C Rock Ferry *Ches* 96-00; P-in-c Godley cum Newton Green 00-04. *Address temp unknown*

HARRIES, Rayner. *See* HARRIES, Henry Rayner Mackintosh

✠**HARRIES, The Rt Revd Richard Douglas.** b 36. Selw Coll Cam BA61 MA65 Lon Univ Hon DD94 FKC83 FRSL96. Cuddesdon Coll 61. **d** 63 **p** 64 **c** 87. C Hampstead St Jo *Lon* 63-69; Chapl Westf Coll Lon 67-69; Tutor Wells Th Coll 69-71; Warden Sarum & Wells Th Coll 71-72; V Fulham All SS *Lon*

72-81; Dean K Coll Lon 81-87; Consultant to Abps Cant and York on Inter-Faith Relns from 86; Bp Ox from 87. *Bishop's House, 27 Linton Road, Oxford OX2 6UL* Tel (01865) 208222 Fax 790470 E-mail bishopoxon@oxford.anglican.org

HARRINGTON, John Christopher Thomas. b 43. Qu Coll Birm 71. **d** 74 **p** 75. C Northampton St Mich *Pet* 74-76; C Paston 76-79; R Doddington *Ely* 79-82; R Benwick St Mary 79-82; R Doddington w Benwick 82-83; CF (TA) 75-85; Chapl Doddington Co Hosp 79-83; V Eastbourne St Mich *Chich* 83-02; R Selsey from 02; Chapl RNLI from 03. *The Rectory, 75 St Peter's Crescent, Selsey, Chichester PO20 0NA* Tel (01243) 601984 E-mail jcharrington@tiscali.co.uk

HARRINGTON, William Harry. b 33. AKC57. **d** 58 **p** 59. C Childwall All SS *Liv* 58-60; C Sutton 60-64; V Ditton St Mich 64-76; V Mossley Hill St Barn 76-83; V Highfield 83-01; rtd 01; Perm to Offic *Liv* from 03. *4 Crowther Drive, Winstanley, Wigan WN3 6LY* Tel (01942) 225021

HARRIS, Arthur Emlyn Dawson. b 27. Ex Univ BSc47 Lon Univ DipRS86. S'wark Ord Course 83. **d** 86 **p** 87. NSM Frant w Eridge *Chich* 86-87; P-in-c Withyham St Mich 87-95; rtd 95; Perm to Offic *Sarum* from 96. *53A The Close, Salisbury SP1 2EL* Tel (01722) 339886 E-mail closecelts@aol.com

HARRIS, Bernard Malcolm. b 29. Leeds Univ BA54. Coll of Resurr Mirfield 54. **d** 56 **p** 57. C Shrewsbury St Chad *Lich* 56-60; C Porthill 60-61; V Birches Head 61-66; V W Bromwich St Jas 66-78; V Sedgley All SS 78-93; rtd 93; Perm to Offic *Worc* from 93. *6 Beacon Lane, Sedgley, Dudley DY3 1NB* Tel (01902) 663134 E-mail bernard.harris@care4free.co.uk

HARRIS, Brian. *See* HARRIS, The Ven Reginald Brian

HARRIS, Brian. b 33. Man Univ BSc. Qu Coll Birm 79. **d** 80 **p** 81. C Lich St Chad *Lich* 80-81; Perm to Offic *Ches* 82-87; NSM Warburton 87-88; P-in-c 88-92; R Gt and Lt Casterton w Pickworth and Tickencote *Pet* 92-98; RD Barnack 94-98; rtd 98; Perm to Offic *Pet* from 99. *Meadowbrook, Carlby Road, Greatford, Stamford PE9 4PR* Tel (01778) 560978

HARRIS, Brian William. b 38. K Coll Lon BD61 AKC61. St Boniface Warminster 61. **d** 62 **p** 63. C Liversedge *Wakef* 62-65; C Kirkby *Liv* 65-70; V Dalton 70-79; V Aberford w Saxton *York* 79-91; V Hemingbrough 91-95; rtd 95; Perm to Offic *York* from 95; Dom Chapl to Bp Selby 95-03; Rtd Clergy and Widows Officer (York Adnry) from 99. *2 Furness Drive, Rawcliffe, York YO30 5TD* Tel (01904) 638214 E-mail harrischap@tiscali.co.uk

HARRIS, Catherine Elizabeth. *See* EDMONDS, Mrs Catherine Elizabeth

HARRIS, Charles Edward. b 20. Roch Th Coll 63. **d** 65 **p** 66. C Hertford St Andr *St Alb* 65-71; R Sywell w Overstone *Pet* 71-90; rtd 90; Perm to Offic *Chich* from 92 and *St Alb* from 00. *College of St Barnabas, Blackberry Lane, Lingfield RH7 6NJ* Tel (01342) 870607

HARRIS, Cyril Evans. b 30. Linc Th Coll 61. **d** 63 **p** 64. C Beaconsfield *Ox* 63-68; V Stoke Poges 68-98; rtd 98; Perm to Offic *Ox* from 99. *The Gables, 8 De Parys Avenue, Bedford MK40 2TW* Tel (01234) 344927

HARRIS, David. b 52. AKC76. St Steph Ho Ox 76. **d** 77 **p** 79. C Wimbledon *S'wark* 77-80; C Coalbrookdale, Iron-Bridge and Lt Wenlock *Heref* 80-82; V Highters Heath *Birm* 82-84; Perm to Offic *Lon* 85-88. *Address temp unknown*

HARRIS, David Rowland. b 46. Ch Ch Ox BA69 DipTh71 MA72. Wycliffe Hall Ox 70. **d** 73 **p** 74. C Virginia Water *Guildf* 73-76; C Clifton Ch Ch w Em *Bris* 76-79; Scripture Union 79-85; V Bedford Ch Ch *St Alb* 85-99; R Ex St Leon w H Trin *Ex* from 99. *St Leonard's Rectory, 27 St Leonard's Road, Exeter EX2 4LA* Tel (01392) 255681 *or* 255449 E-mail dandsharris@hotmail.com

HARRIS, Derrick William. b 21. **d** 63 **p** 64. C Birkdale St Jo *Liv* 63-67; V Billinge 67-81; V Walton *Ches* 81-87; rtd 88; Perm to Offic *Ches* and *Liv* from 88. *3 Melrose Avenue, Southport PR9 9UY* Tel (01704) 213828

HARRIS, Duncan Roy. b 46. **d** 89 **p** 90. Chapl Miss to Seamen 89-98; UAE 89-92; Cyprus 92-97; P-in-c Patrington w Hollym, Welwick and Winestead *York* from 98. *The Rectory, Northside, Patrington, Hull HU12 0PA* Tel (01964) 630327 Fax 630366 E-mail fr.duncan@tiscali.co.uk

HARRIS, Mrs Elaine Sarah. b 43. SW Minl Tr Course 02. **d** 03 **p** 04. NSM Dyffryn *Llan* from 03. *15 Fforest Goch, Rhos, Pontardawe SA8 3JB* Tel (01792) 862299 E-mail fforestgoch@hotmail.com

HARRIS, Ernest John. b 46. Lon Univ DipTh74 QUB BD75. **d** 75 **p** 76. C Lisburn Ch Ch *Conn* 75-78; C Coleraine 78-83; I Belfast St Kath 83-90; I Ballinderry from 90. *The Rectory, 124 Ballinderry Road, Ballinderry Upper, Lisburn BT28 2NL* Tel (028) 9265 1310

HARRIS, Frank Edward. b 33. ACT ThL69 St Fran Coll Brisbane 65. **d** 68 **p** 69. Australia 68-71 and 73-76; C Plymstock *Ex* 71-72; C E Acton St Dunstan w St Thos *Lon* 72-73; C Bodmin *Truro* 76-77; P-in-c Menheniot 77-79; V Winton *Man* 79-87; Guinea 87-89; R Blisland w St Breward *Truro* 90-96; rtd 98. *4 Gwel Marten, Headland Road, Carbis Bay, St Ives TR26 2PB* Tel (01736) 793280

HARRIS, Geoffrey Daryl. b 39. Open Univ BA83. St Aid Birkenhead 63. **d** 66 **p** 67. C Eston *York* 66-70; C Iffley *Ox* 70-75; V Bubwith *York* 75-78; V Bubwith w Ellerton and Aughton 78-79; P-in-c Stillingfleet w Naburn 79-80; R Escrick and Stillingfleet w Naburn 80-95; Chapl Qu Marg Sch York 83-94; Hon C Okehampton w Inwardleigh, Bratton Clovelly etc *Ex* 96-99; P-in-c Ashwater, Halwill, Beaworthy, Clawton etc 99-01; R 01-03; rtd 03. *5 Strawberry Fields, North Tawton EX20 2GX* Tel (01837) 880292 E-mail the.harrisclan1@tinyonline.co.uk

HARRIS, George. b 36. Sarum Th Coll 66. **d** 68 **p** 69. C Shildon *Dur* 68-70; CF 70-74; P-in-c Doddington *Ely* 74-75; R 75-78; R Benwick St Mary 74-78; V Shotton *Dur* 78-86; V Stockton St Mark 86-87; V Chilton Moor 87-94; P-in-c Lyons 96; R 96-99; rtd 99. *49 Dunelm Drive, Houghton le Spring DH4 5QQ* Tel 0191-584 8608

HARRIS, Harriet Anne. b 68. Oriel Coll Ox BA90 New Coll Ox DPhil94. St Steph Ho Ox. **d** 00 **p** 01. C Ox St Mary V w St Cross and St Pet *Ox* from 00; Chapl Wadh Coll Ox from 00. *33 Minster Road, Oxford OX4 1LY* Tel (01865) 202835 *or* 277905 E-mail harriet.harris@wadh.ox.ac.uk

HARRIS, James. b 54. CITC 99. **d** 02 **p** 03. Aux Min Ballybeen *D & D* 02-05; C Belfast St Brendan from 05. *8 Grangewood Avenue, Dundonald, Belfast BT16 1GA* Tel (028) 9050 6074 Mobile 07761-066421 E-mail harrisj639@aol.com

HARRIS, Canon James Nigel Kingsley. b 37. St D Coll Lamp BA60. Sarum Th Coll. **d** 62 **p** 63. C Painswick *Glouc* 62-65; C Glouc St Paul 65-67; V Slad 67-77; V Cam 77-78; P-in-c Stinchcombe 77-78; V Cam w Stinchcombe 78-82; V Stonehouse 82-02; Chapl Glos R Hosp NHS Trust 92-02; rtd 02; Hon Can Antsiranana Madagascar from 00; Perm to Offic *Glouc* from 03. *14 Shalford Close, Cirencester GL7 1WG* Tel (01285) 885641

HARRIS, James Philip. b 59. Westf Coll Lon BA82 Univ of Wales PGCE97. St Mich Coll Llan BD86. **d** 86 **p** 87. C Newport St Paul *Mon* 86-89; C Bedwellty 89-91; V Newport St Matt 91-96; Chapl Univ of Wales Inst Cardiff *Llan* 97-99; Chapl Glam Univ 99-03; V Gwernaffield and Llanferres *St As* from 03. *The Vicarage, Cilcain Road, Gwernaffield, Mold CH7 5DQ* Tel (01352) 740205 E-mail jharris3@glam.ac.uk

HARRIS, Jeremy Michael. b 64. Gwent Coll of HE HNC86. St Steph Ho Ox BTh93. **d** 93 **p** 94. C Newport St Julian *Mon* 93-95; C Ebbw Vale 95-97; Dioc Youth Chapl 96-98; TV Ebbw Vale 97-98; TV Bracknell *Ox* from 98. *St Andrew's Vicarage, 25 Stoney Road, Bracknell RG42 1XY* Tel (01344) 425229 E-mail jeremy_m_harris@compuserve.com

HARRIS, The Very Revd John. b 32. Univ of Wales (Lamp) BA55. Sarum Th Coll 55. **d** 57 **p** 58. V Pontnewynydd *Mon* 57-60; C Bassaleg 60-63; V Penmaen 63-69; V Newport St Paul 69-84; RD Newport 77-93; V Maindee 84-93; Can St Woolos Cathl 84-93; Dean Brecon *S & B* 93-98; V Brecon St Mary and Battle w Llanddew 93-98; rtd 98; Lic to Offic *Mon* from 98. *40 Mounton Drive, Chepstow NP16 5EH* Tel (01291) 621233

HARRIS, Canon John. b 45. St Steph Ho Ox 72. **d** 75 **p** 76. C Wanstead St Mary *Chelmsf* 75-84; V Penponds *Truro* 84-91; V St Gluvias from 91; RD Carnmarth S from 00; Hon Can Truro Cathl from 01. *The Vicarage, St Gluvias, Penryn TR10 9LQ* Tel (01326) 373356

HARRIS, John. b 54. Leeds Univ BSc75. St Jo Coll Nottm LTh86. **d** 86 **p** 87. C S Ossett *Wakef* 86-90; V Moldgreen 90-97; P-in-c S Ossett from 97. *36 Manor Road, Ossett, Wakefield WF5 0AU* Tel (01924) 263311 *or* 281732 E-mail johnharris@ccso.fsnet.co.uk

HARRIS, John Brian. b 53. Hertf Coll Ox BA76. Ripon Coll Cuddesdon 87. **d** 89 **p** 90. C Witton *Ches* 89-93; R Thurstaston 93-99; V Stockton Heath 99-04; P-in-c Gt Saughall from 04. *The Vicarage, Church Road, Saughall, Chester CH1 6EN* Tel (01244) 880213 E-mail brian@jbharris.fsnet.co.uk

HARRIS, Canon John Peter. b 33. St D Coll Lamp BA57. **d** 58 **p** 59. Chapl St Woolos Hosp Newport 58-63; C Newport St Woolos *Mon* 58-60; Chapl St Woolos Cathl 60-63; CF (TA) 59-63; CF 63-82; V Chepstow *Mon* 82-98; RD Chepstow 85-97; Can St Woolos Cathl 93-98; rtd 98; Lic to Offic *Mon* from 98. *7 Victoria Way, Undy, Magor, Newport NP26 3NW* Tel (01633) 882423

HARRIS, John Stuart. b 29. Hertf Coll Ox BA52 MA56. Wells Th Coll 52. **d** 54 **p** 55. C Epsom St Martin *Guildf* 54-58; C Guildf H Trin w St Mary 58-63; R Bentley 63-72; V Milford 72-87; R Walton-on-the-Hill 87-98; Dioc Ecum Officer 87-92; rtd 98; Perm to Offic *Roch* from 00. *6 Pearse Place, Lamberhurst, Tunbridge Wells TN3 8EJ* Tel (01892) 890582

HARRIS, Mrs Judith Helen. b 42. Chelsea Coll Lon TCert64 Westmr Coll Ox MTh03. St Alb Minl Tr Scheme 83. **dss** 86 **d** 87 **p** 94. Leagrave *St Alb* 86-87; Hon Par Dn 87-91; TD Dunstable 91-94; TV 94-03; rtd 03; Perm to Offic *Truro* from 03. *Belmont, Fore Street, Porthleven, Helston TR13 9HN* Tel (01326) 563090 E-mail revdjhharris@ntlworld.com

HARRIS, Canon Kenneth. b 28. NW Ord Course 70. **d** 72 **p** 73. NSM Upton Ascension *Ches* 72-77; NSM Eccleston and

Pulford 77-80; P-in-c Hargrave 80-81; V 81-94; Exec Officer Dioc Bd for Soc Resp 84-94; Hon Can Ches Cathl 91-94; rtd 94; Perm to Offic *Ches* from 94; P-in-c Ashton Hayes 96-98; P-in-c Alvanley 98-99. *Delsa, Willington Road, Willington, Tarporley CW6 0ND* Tel (01829) 751880

HARRIS, Lawrence Rex Rowland. b 35. St Cath Coll Cam BA59 MA63. Ely Th Coll. **d** 61 **p** 62. C Carrington *S'well* 61-63; Chapl Rampton Hosp Retford 63-66; V Sturton w Littleborough *S'well* 66-71; V Bole w Saundby 66-71; R Clowne *Derby* 71-04; RD Bolsover and Staveley 81-86; rtd 04. *131 North Road, Clowne, Chesterfield S43 4PQ*

HARRIS, Leslie Gerald Conley Eyre. b 44. Culham Coll of Educn CertEd66 St Jo Coll Nottm LTh00 FRGS83. Wycliffe Hall Ox 71. **d** 75 **p** 76. Kenya 75-99; Chapl Banda Sch Nairobi 75-99; NSM Karen St Fran 75-99; NSM Kiambu St Paul 84-99; NSM Limuru All SS 90-99; C Sawley *Derby* 00-03; R Pinxton from 03. *The Rectory, 49 Town Street, Pinxton, Nottingham NG16 6HH* Tel (01773) 580024

HARRIS, Linda Margaret. b 55. Man Univ BSc76 UMIST MSc78 Birkbeck Coll Lon MSc98. Wycliffe Hall Ox 03. **d** 05. C Cannock *Lich* from 05. *23 Gloucester Way, Cannock WS11 7YN* Tel (01543) 277548 E-mail lmh3lindaharris@netscape.net

HARRIS, Margaret Claire (Sister Margaret Joy). b 53. RGN85 Homerton Coll Cam BEd78. Ridley Hall Cam CTM92. **d** 92. Par Dn Stevenage All SS Pin Green *St Alb* 92-93; C 93-95; CSMV 95-99; OSB from 99. *St Mary's Abbey, 52 Swan Street, West Malling ME19 6JX* Tel (01732) 843309

HARRIS, Mark Jonathan. b 66. St Cath Coll Cam BA88 MA92 PhD92. Ripon Coll Cuddesdon BA01. **d** 02 **p** 03. C Cowley St Jas *Ox* 02-04; Chapl Oriel Coll Ox from 04. *Oriel College, Oxford OX1 4EW* Tel (01865) 276580 E-mail chaplain@oriel.ox.ac.uk

HARRIS, Martin John. b 54. Trin Coll Cam BA76 MA. Wycliffe Hall Ox 82. **d** 85 **p** 86. C Lindfield *Chich* 85-88; C Galleywood Common *Chelmsf* 88-91; V Southchurch Ch Ch from 91; RD Southend-on-Sea from 00. *Christ Church Vicarage, 58 Colbert Road, Southend-on-Sea SS1 3BP* Tel (01702) 582585 E-mail martin.harris@messages.co.uk

HARRIS, Michael. b 34. ACP65 MIL76 St Mark & St Jo Coll Lon CertEd56. Qu Coll Birm. **d** 83 **p** 84. NSM Bournville *Birm* 83-90; NSM Stirchley 90-96; Chapl Univ of Cen England in Birm 92-99; Dean NSMs 96-99; rtd 00; Perm to Offic *Birm* and *Cov* from 00. *33 Bosley Close, Shipston-on-Stour CV36 4QA* Tel and fax (01608) 661672 Mobile 07811-489713 E-mail revmichael@harrisann.fsnet.co.uk

HARRIS, Michael Andrew. b 53. Ian Ramsey Coll 74 Trin Coll Bris 75. **d** 78 **p** 79. C St Paul's Cray St Barn *Roch* 78-82; C Church Stretton *Heref* 82-87; Res Min Penkridge w Stretton *Lich* 87-90; Res Min Penkridge Team 90-92; V Amington *Birm* from 92. *The Vicarage, 224 Tamworth Road, Amington, Tamworth B77 3DE* Tel (01827) 62573 E-mail mike.harris26@ntlworld.com

HARRIS, Nicholas Bryan. b 60. Down Coll Cam BA81 MA85. Ridley Hall Cam 82. **d** 85 **p** 86. C Walney Is *Carl* 85-88; C S'wark Ch Ch *S'wark* 88-92; Perm to Offic *Chich* from 92. *82 Hurst Road, Eastbourne BN21 2PW* Tel (01323) 731922

HARRIS, Owen. b 50. Univ of Wales (Swansea) BSc(Econ)71 PGCE72. St Mich Coll Llan DipTh94. **d** 94 **p** 95. C Bassaleg *Mon* 94-98; TV Cwmbran 98-01; V Maindee 01-02; rtd 02. *2 Marine Cottages, Ferryside SA17 5SB* Tel (01267) 267095

✠**HARRIS, The Rt Revd Patrick Burnet.** b 34. Keble Coll Ox BA58 MA63. Clifton Th Coll 58. **d** 60 **p** 61 **c** 73. C Ox St Ebbe w St Pet *Ox* 60-63; SAMS 63-81; Adn N Argentina 70-73; Bp 73-80; R Kirkheaton *Wakef* 81-85; Asst Bp Wakef 81-85; Sec C of E Partnership for World Miss 86-88; Asst Bp Ox 86-88; Bp S'well 88-99; rtd 99; Hon Asst Bp Eur from 99; Asst Bp Linc from 99. *Apartment B, Ireton House, Pavilion Gardens, Cheltenham GL50 2SR* E-mail patrickharris@owet.freeserve.co.uk

HARRIS, Paul. b 55. St Paul's Cheltenham BEd79. Oak Hill Th Coll 82. **d** 84 **p** 85. C Billericay and Lt Burstead *Chelmsf* 84-87; TV Cheltenham St Mary, St Matt, St Paul and H Trin *Glouc* 87-93; V Bitterne *Win* 93-97; UK Evang Co-ord Evang Alliance 97-02; C Portswood Ch Ch *Win* 02-04; TR Cheltenham St Mark *Glouc* from 04. *St Mark's Rectory, Fairmount Road, Cheltenham GL51 7AQ* Tel (01242) 255110 E-mail harrisrevpaul@aol.com

HARRIS, Paul Ian. b 45. MSc. Qu Coll Birm. **d** 82 **p** 83. C The Quinton *Birm* 82-86; V Atherstone *Cov* from 86. *40 Holte Road, Atherstone CV9 1HN* Tel (01827) 713200 E-mail paulih@ntlworld.com

HARRIS, Paul Michael. b 58. Chelsea Coll Lon BSc79 Oak Hill Th Coll BA89 Bath Coll of HE CertEd82. **d** 89. C Finchley Ch Ch *Lon* 89-90; Asst Master St Luke's Sch W Norwood 90-91; Master and Asst Chapl Brent Internat Sch Manila 91-92; Volunteer Miss Movement Sunningdale 93-94; Past Asst St Joseph's RC Ch Dorking 94-95; Form Master Merton Court Prep Sch Sidcup 95-97; Asst Master Clewborough Ho Prep Sch Camberley 98-01; Asst Master St Nic Sch for Girls Church Crookham from 01. *66 Horsham Road, Owlsmoor, Sandhurst GU47 0YZ* Tel (01344) 771376

HARRIS, Peter Frank. b 43. WMMTC 89. **d** 92 **p** 93. NSM Lich Ch Ch *Lich* 92-96; NSM Ogley Hay 96-00; NSM Rushall 00-03; Perm to Offic from 03. *94 Ogley Hay Road, Burntwood WS7 2HU* Tel (01543) 319163

HARRIS, Peter Malcolm. b 52. Em Coll Cam BA74 MA79. Trin Coll Bris. **d** 80 **p** 81. C Upton (Overchurch) *Ches* 80-83; BCMS 83-93; Crosslinks Portugal from 83. *c/o A Rocha Trust, Connansknowe, Kirkton, Dumfries DG1 1SX* Tel (01387) 710286 E-mail peterharris@compuserve.com

HARRIS, Peter Samuel. b 68. Dundee Univ BA98 St Jo Coll Dur BA04. Cranmer Hall Dur 02. **d** 04 **p** 05. C Walton and Trimley *St E* from 04. *27 Treetops, Felixstowe IP11 9ER* Tel (01394) 282654 E-mail psh@fish.co.uk

HARRIS, Raymond. b 36. Nottm Univ BA58. Lich Th Coll 58. **d** 60 **p** 61. C Clifton St Fran *S'well* 60-63; C Davyhulme St Mary *Man* 63-66; V Bacup Ch Ch 66-82; R Dunsby w Dowsby *Linc* 82-87; R Rippingale 82-87; R Rippingale Gp 87-94; rtd 94. *2 The Bungalow, High Street, Swaton, Sleaford NG34 0JU* Tel (01529) 421343

HARRIS, Canon Raymond John. b 29. Leeds Univ BA51. Coll of Resurr Mirfield 51. **d** 53 **p** 54. C Workington St Mich *Carl* 53-59; V New Swindon St Barn Gorse Hill *Bris* 59-94; Hon Can Bris Cathl 80-94; RD Cricklade 82-88; rtd 94; Perm to Offic *Glouc* from 94. *46 Courtbrook, Fairford GL7 4BE* Tel (01285) 713965

HARRIS, Rebecca Jane. *See* SWYER, Mrs Rebecca Jane

HARRIS (née LEE), Mrs Rebecca Susan. b 62. Man Univ BA85 S Glam Inst HE 86. Trin Coll Bris DipHE95. **d** 95 **p** 96. C Cirencester *Glouc* 95-99; TV Gt Chesham *Ox* from 99. *Christ Church Vicarage, 95 Latimer Road, Chesham HP5 1QQ* Tel (01494) 773318 Fax as telephone

HARRIS, The Ven Reginald Brian. b 34. Ch Coll Cam BA58 MA61. Ridley Hall Cam. **d** 59 **p** 60. C Wednesbury St Bart *Lich* 59-61; C Uttoxeter w Bramshall 61-64; V Bury St Pet *Man* 64-70; V Walmsley 70-80; RD Walmsley 70-80; Adn Man 80-98; Can Res Man Cathl 80-98; rtd 98; Perm to Offic *Derby* from 98. *9 Cote Lane, Hayfield, Stockport SK22 2HL* Tel (01663) 746321

HARRIS, Robert Douglas. b 57. BEd. Chich Th Coll 80. **d** 82 **p** 83. C Portsea St Mary *Portsm* 82-87; V Clevedon St Jo *B & W* 87-92; R Felpham w Middleton *Chich* 92-99; R Felpham 99-04; RD Arundel and Bognor 98-04; P-in-c Southwick from 04. *The Rectory, 22 Church Lane, Southwick, Brighton BN42 4GB* Tel (01273) 592389

HARRIS, Robert James. b 45. Nottm Univ MA02 ALCD73. St Jo Coll Nottm 69. **d** 72 **p** 73. C Sheff St Jo *Sheff* 72-76; C Goole 76-78; V Bramley and Ravenfield 78-91; P-in-c Boulton *Derby* 91-99; RD Melbourne 96-99; P-in-c Hazlewood 99-02; P-in-c Hazlewood and Milford 02-05; V Hazelwood, Holbrook and Milford from 05. *The Vicarage, Hob Hill, Hazelwood, Belper DE56 4AL* Tel (01332) 840161 E-mail robert@kneetinnit.fsnet.co.uk

HARRIS, Robin. **d** 05. Aux Min Carnalea *D & D* from 05. *109 Cairnburn Road, Belfast BT4 2PF* Tel (028) 9076 8085

HARRIS, Mrs Ruth. b 60. Hull Univ BA82 Liv Univ MArAd84. N Ord Course 01. **d** 04 **p** 05. C Kinsley w Wragby *Wakef* from 04; C Felkirk from 05. *13 Little Hemsworth, Hemsworth, Ponterfract WF9 4BH* Tel (01977) 625596 E-mail ruth.harris11@btinternet.com

HARRIS, Thomas William. b 54. Univ of Wales (Lamp) MA04 AKC76. Linc Th Coll 77. **d** 78 **p** 79. C Norton Woodseats St Chad *Sheff* 78-81; V Barnby Dun 81-91; P-in-c Kirk Bramwith and Fenwick 81-85; Chapl RN 91-94; R Draycot *Bris* 94-02; P-in-c Cawston w Booton and Brandiston etc *Nor* from 02; Chapl Norfolk and Nor Univ Hosp NHS Trust from 02. *The Rectory, Ames Court, Cawston, Norwich NR10 4AN* Tel (01603) 871282 E-mail tomwharris@tiscali.co.uk

HARRIS, William Edric Mackenzie. b 46. Sarum & Wells Th Coll 72. **d** 75 **p** 76. C Langney *Chich* 75-79; C Moulsecoomb 80-81; TV 81-85; R W Grinstead from 85. *The Rectory, Steyning Road, West Grinstead, Horsham RH13 8LR* Tel (01403) 710339 E-mail williamem.harris@virgin.net

HARRIS, William Fergus. b 36. CCC Cam BA59 MA63 Edin Univ DipEd70. Yale Div Sch 59 Westcott Ho Cam 60. **d** 62 **p** 63. C St Andrews St Andr *St And* 62-64; Chapl Edin Univ *Edin* 64-71; R Edin St Pet 71-83; R Perth St Jo *St And* 83-90; Hon C from 90; rtd 90; Prov Archivist from 91. *35 St Mary's Drive, Perth PH2 7BY* Tel (01738) 621379

HARRIS-DOUGLAS, John Douglas. b 34. Ripon Hall Ox 65. **d** 66 **p** 67. C Ringwood *Win* 66-67; C Baswich *Lich* 67-71; R St Tudy *Truro* 71-74; R St Tudy w Michaelstow 74-76; Adv in Children's Work and Asst Dir Educn 71-76; R Fiskerton *Linc* 76-79; Dir of Educn and Adv RE 76-79; P-in-c Thormanby *York* 79-84; V Brafferton w Pilmoor and Myton-on-Swale 79-84; V Brafferton w Pilmoor, Myton-on-Swale etc 84-97; rtd 97; Perm to Offic *York* from 97. *Tanglewood Cottage, Newton-upon-Ouse, York YO30 2BN* Tel (01347) 848219

HARRIS-EVANS, William Giles. b 46. AKC68. Bangalore Th Coll DipTh70. **d** 70 **p** 71. C Clapham H Trin *S'wark* 70-74; Sri

Lanka 75-78; V Benhilton *S'wark* 78-86; TR Cov E *Cov* 86-93; TR Brighouse and Clifton *Wakef* 93-99; V Petersfield *Portsm* from 99; R Buriton from 99. *The Vicarage, Shackleford House, 12 Dragon Street, Petersfield GU31 4AB* Tel and fax (01730) 264138 *or* 260213 E-mail petersfield@stpeters.fsbusiness.co.uk

HARRIS-WHITE, John Emlyn. b 34. St Aid Birkenhead 59. **d** 62 **p** 63. C Cricklade w Latton *Bris* 62-63; C Kingswood 63-66; C Ashton-on-Ribble St Andr *Blackb* 66-69; V Heyhouses 69-71; Chapl Roundway Hosp Devizes 71-77; Chapl R Variety Children's Hosp 77-89; Chapl K Coll and Belgrave Hosps Lon 77-89; Regional Community Relns Co-ord 89-93; rtd 94; Hon C Folkestone St Pet *Cant* 97-01. *40 Tippet Knowes Road, Winchburgh, Broxburn EH52 6UL*

HARRISON, Alan George. b 20. Leeds Univ BA49. Coll of Resurr Mirfield 49. **d** 51 **p** 52. C Wellingborough St Mary *Pet* 51-55; R Corozal Br Honduras 55-61; V Bournemouth St Fran *Win* 61-68; V Eastleigh 68-72; Chapl Guild of Health Lon 72-76; Chapl St Mich Convent Ham 73-86; Sec Coun for Relig Communities 76-86; rtd 86; Perm to Offic *S'wark* from 86. *10 The Quadrangle, Morden College, London SE3 0PW* Tel (020) 8858 5134

HARRISON, Alastair Lee. b 22. ALCD51. **d** 51 **p** 52. C Stoke Damerel *Ex* 51-54; Chapl RAF 54-67; Chapl Miss to Seamen 67-77; Lic to Offic *D & G* 77-83; Lic to Offic *M & K* 77-83; C Dublin St Ann w St Mark and St Steph *D & G* 83-92; rtd 92. *8 Grosvenor Place, Rathgar, Dublin 6, Irish Republic* Tel (00353) (1) 497 6053

HARRISON, Mrs Alison Edwina. b 53. Newc Univ BEd75. Linc Th Coll 84. **dss** 86 **d** 87 **p** 94. Loughborough Em *Leic* 86-87; Par Dn 87-89; C Stockton *Dur* 89-92; P-in-c Lynesack 92-95; P-in-c Cockfield 92-95; P-in-c Ebchester 95-96; R 96-97; V Medomsley 96-97; V Newc H Cross *Newc* 97-01; P-in-c Ulgham from 01; P-in-c Widdrington from 01. *The Vicarage, Grangemoor Road, Widdrington, Morpeth NE61 5PU* Tel (01670) 790389 E-mail alison.harrison3@btopenworld.com

HARRISON, Mrs Barbara Ann. b 41. Man Univ BA63 Leic Univ CertEd64. EMMTC 85. **d** 88 **p** 94. C Immingham *Linc* 88-94; P-in-c Habrough Gp 94-99; V 99-01; rtd 02; Perm to Offic *Linc* from 02. *3 Windsor Mews, Louth LN11 9AY* Tel (01507) 610015

HARRISON, Canon Barbara Anne. b 34. Westf Coll Lon BA56 CertEd57 Hull Univ MA85. Linc Th Coll 76. **dss** 79 **d** 87 **p** 94. Lakenham St Jo *Nor* 79-80; Chapl York Univ *York* 80-88; TD Sheff Manor *Sheff* 88-93; Par Dn Holts CD *Man* 93-94; C-in-c 94-98; Dioc UPA Officer 93-98; Chapl Rochdale Healthcare NHS Trust 98-04; NSM Bury Ch King *Man* 98-99; C 00-01; NSM Bury St Paul 98-99; C 00-04; P-in-c Kirkholt 01-04; Hon Can Man Cathl 02-04; rtd 04. *66 Gainsborough Avenue, Rochdale OL11 2QT* Tel (01706) 639872

HARRISON, Bernard Charles. b 37. St Mich Coll Llan 61. **d** 64 **p** 65. C Toxteth Park St Marg *Liv* 64-69; C Hindley All SS 69-71; V Wigan St Geo 71-02; rtd 02. *66 Brookhouse Street, Wigan WN1 3EY* Tel (01942) 244500

HARRISON, Brian John. b 35. FCP. Glouc Sch of Min 83. **d** 86 **p** 89. NSM Broseley w Benthall *Heref* 86-93; Perm to Offic 94-97. *17 Hafren Road, Little Dawley, Telford TF4 3HJ* Tel (01952) 591891

HARRISON, Bruce. b 49. Linc Th Coll 86. **d** 88 **p** 89. C Syston *Leic* 88-90; C Whitby *York* 90-93; V Glaisdale 93-99; R Brotton Parva 99-04; V Coatham and Dormanstown from 04; Chapl Tees and NE Yorks NHS Trust from 04. *Coatham Vicarage, 9 Blenheim Terrace, Redcar TS10 1QP* Tel (01642) 482870 E-mail br218@hotmail.com

HARRISON, Bruce Mountford. b 49. AKC71. **d** 72 **p** 73. C Hebburn St Cuth *Dur* 72-75; C Bethnal Green St Jo w St Simon *Lon* 75-77; P-in-c Bethnal Green St Bart 77-78; TV Bethnal Green St Jo w St Bart 78-80; C-in-c Pennywell St Thos and Grindon St Oswald CD *Dur* 80-85; V Sunderland Pennywell St Thos 85-90; V Gateshead St Helen from 90. *The Vicarage, 7 Carlton Terrace, Gateshead NE9 6DE* Tel 0191-487 6510

HARRISON, Christine Amelia. b 47. Southn Univ DipTh97. STETS 94. **d** 98 **p** 99. NSM Goldsworth Park *Guildf* from 98. *Ravenscroft, Fernhill Lane, St John's, Woking GU22 0DR* Tel (01483) 750645 E-mail christine@revharrison.freeserve.co.uk

HARRISON, Christopher Dennis. b 57. Clare Coll Cam BA79 BA86. Westcott Ho Cam 84. **d** 87 **p** 88. C Camberwell St Geo *S'wark* 87-92; V Forest Hill 92-96; P-in-c Fenny Bentley, Kniveton, Thorpe and Tissington *Derby* 96-98; P-in-c Parwich w Alsop-en-le-Dale 96-98; R Fenny Bentley, Thorpe, Tissington, Parwich etc from 98; RD Ashbourne from 98. *The Vicarage, Parwich, Ashbourne DE6 1QD* Tel (01335) 390226 E-mail christopherharrison@ntlworld.com

HARRISON, Christopher Joseph. b 38. AKC61 Hull Univ CertEd68 Bris Univ BEd75. **d** 62 **p** 63. C Bottesford *Linc* 62-67; C Elloughton *York* 67-68; Asst Master Bishop's Cleeve Primary Sch 68-74; Sen Master 74-78; Dep Hd 78-96; P-in-c Farmington *Glouc* 69-73; C Tredington w Stoke Orchard and Hardwicke 74-86; rtd 96; Perm to Offic *Glouc* from 87. *Appledore, 93 Stoke Road, Bishops Cleeve, Cheltenham GL52 8RP* Tel (01242) 673452

HARRISON, Crispin. *See* HARRISON, Michael Burt

HARRISON, Sister Cécile. b 29. Bp Lonsdale Coll TCert51 Lon Univ DBRS73. St Steph Ho Ox 97. **d** 97 **p** 97. CGA from 66; Lic to Offic *Eur* from 97. *Prasada, Quartier Subrane, Montauroux, 83440 Fayence, France* Tel and fax (0033) (4) 94 47 74 26 E-mail cga.prasada@wanadoo.fr

HARRISON, David Daniel. b 62. St Paul's Cheltenham BA84 Leeds Univ MA85 Westmr Coll Ox PGCE88. Westcott Ho Cam 03. **d** 05. C Beckenham St Geo *Roch* from 05. *37 Rectory Road, Beckenham BR3 1HL* Tel (020) 8658 3195

HARRISON, David Henry. b 40. Tyndale Hall Bris 65. **d** 68 **p** 69. C Bolton St Paul *Man* 68-72; V Bircle 72-83; V Southport SS Simon and Jude *Liv* 83-91; TR Fazakerley Em 91-99; V Toxteth Park Ch Ch and St Mich w St Andr 99-05; rtd 05. *55 The Oval, Shevington, Wigan WN6 8EN* E-mail getrevdake@hotmail.com

HARRISON, David Samuel. b 44. Univ of Wales (Ban) BSc67. St Mich Coll Llan 67. **d** 70 **p** 71. C Canton St Jo *Llan* 70-74; C Witton *Ches* 74-78; V Sutton St Geo 78-96; P-in-c Henbury 96-01; V from 01. *St Thomas's Vicarage, Church Lane, Henbury, Macclesfield SK11 9NN* Tel (01625) 424113

HARRISON, Miss Doreen. b 32. Leeds Univ BA53 PGCE54 DipRE57 Lanc Univ MLitt78 MA(Ed)79. **d** 92 **p** 94. C Ambleside w Brathay *Carl* 92-96; Asst P Colton 96-01; P-in-c 01-02; Asst P Rusland 96-01; P-in-c 01-02; Asst P Satterthwaite 96-01; P-in-c 01-02; rtd 02; Perm to Offic *Carl* from 02. *Fox How, Ambleside LA22 9LL* Tel (01539) 433021

HARRISON, Francis Russell. b 20. EAMTC. **d** 82 **p** 83. NSM Felixstowe St Jo *St E* 82-85; Asst Chapl Ipswich Hosp 85-87; rtd 87; Perm to Offic *St E* 87-03. *The Strands, London Road, Copdock, Ipswich IP8 3JF* Tel (01473) 730292

HARRISON, Fred Graham. b 41. Lon Univ BSc62. Ridley Hall Cam 80. **d** 82 **p** 83. C Lenton *S'well* 82-85; V Ruddington 85-04; rtd 04. *18 Holly Bank, Hollingworth, Hyde SK14 8QL* Tel (01457) 765955 E-mail fgharrison@virgin.net

HARRISON, Guy Patrick. b 58. Dip Counselling 91 Ox Univ MTh99. Sarum & Wells Th Coll 92. **d** 94 **p** 95. C Wimborne Minster and Holt *Sarum* 94-96; C Wimborne Minster 96-97; Chapl Dorothy House Hospice Winsley 97-01; Chapl Stoke Mandeville Hosp NHS Trust from 01. *Stoke Mandeville Hospital NHS Trust, Mandeville Road, Aylesbury HP21 8AL* Tel (01296) 316677 Fax 316604 E-mail guy.harrison@smh.nhs.uk

HARRISON, Herbert Gerald. b 29. Oak Hill Th Coll 53. **d** 56 **p** 57. C Chesterfield H Trin *Derby* 56-59; C Cambridge St Andr Less *Ely* 59-64; Miss to Seamen 64-74; Kenya 64-68; Port Chapl Ipswich 68-74; V Ipswich All SS *St E* 74-81; P-in-c Elmsett w Aldham 81-88; P-in-c Kersey w Lindsey 81-88; R Horringer cum Ickworth 88-94; rtd 94; Perm to Offic *St E* from 94. *15 Lynwood Avenue, Felixstowe IP11 9HS* Tel (01394) 283764

HARRISON, Ian David. b 45. Imp Coll Lon BSc66. Oak Hill Th Coll 93. **d** 96 **p** 97. NSM Tunbridge Wells St Jo *Roch* 96-99; P-in-c Chiddingstone w Chiddingstone Causeway from 99. *The Rectory, Chiddingstone, Edenbridge TN8 7AH* Tel and fax (01892) 870478 E-mail ian@therectory.fsbusines.co.uk

HARRISON, Ian Wetherby. b 39. Kelham Th Coll 59. **d** 64 **p** 65. C Kennington Park St Agnes *S'wark* 64-67; C E Ham w Upton Park *Chelmsf* 67-71; V Walthamstow St Mich 71-78; Dioc Ecum Officer *Wakef* 78-87; P-in-c Upper Hopton 78-87; P-in-c Mirfield Eastthorpe St Paul 82-87; Succ St D Cathl *St D* 87-90; P-in-c Leic Ascension *Leic* 90-92; V Leic St Anne 92-04; rtd 04. *28 Oakfield Avenue, Birstall, Leicester LE4 3DQ* E-mail iwharri@aol.com

HARRISON (née HOLLINRAKE), Mrs Jean Margaret. b 28. Leeds Univ DSS51 Bolton Teacher Tr Coll TCert64. Wakef Dioc Reader Tr 82. **d** 93 **p** 96. NSM Perth St Ninian *St And* 93-96; NSM Stanley 96-98; Bp's Chapl 95-99. *14 Valley View, Heptonstall, Hebden Bridge HX7 7LP* Tel (01442) 845822

HARRISON, John. b 49. Fitzw Coll Cam BA71 MA74. Westcott Ho Cam 74. **d** 77 **p** 78. C Nunthorpe *York* 77-81; C Acomb St Steph 81-83; C-in-c St Aid 81-83; V Heptonstall *Wakef* 83-91; R Stamford Bridge Gp *York* 91-02; V Easingwold w Raskelf from 02; RD Easingwold from 05. *The Vicarage, Church Hill, Easingwold, York YO61 3JT* Tel (01347) 821394

HARRISON, John Northcott. b 31. St Jo Coll Cam BA54. Westcott Ho Cam 54. **d** 56 **p** 57. C Moor Allerton *Ripon* 56-59; C Bedale 59-61; V Hudswell w Downholme 61-64; Youth Chapl *Dur* 64-68; V Auckland St Andr and St Anne 68-76; Community Chapl Stockton-on-Tees 76-83; TR Southampton (City Cen) *Win* 83-88; V Bris Ch the Servant Stockwood *Bris* 88-96; RD Brislington 89-95; Chapl St Brendan's Sixth Form Coll 90-96; rtd 96; Perm to Offic *B & W* and *Bris* from 96. *8 Moorham Road, Winscombe BS25 1HS* Tel (01934) 844403

HARRISON, Josephine Mary. b 42. Southn Univ DTM97. **d** 97 **p** 98. NSM Yatton Keynell *Bris* 97-99; NSM By Brook 99-01; Perm to Offic *B & W* 01-02; NSM Wellington and Distr from 02. *Pippins, 18 Cox Road, Wellington TA21 9RD* Tel (01823) 669525 Fax as telephone

HARRISON, Keith. *See* HARRISON, Peter Keith

HARRISON, Lyndon. b 47. St Mich Coll Llan 91. **d** 93 **p** 94. C Ebbw Vale *Mon* 93-96; TV 96-01; TV Caldicot 01-05; TR from

05. *The Vicarage, 19 Main Road, Portskewett, Caldicot NP26 5SG* Tel (01291) 420313

HARRISON, Martin. b 58. Bris Univ BA89. Trin Coll Bris 86. **d** 89 **p** 90. C Heworth H Trin *York* 89-94; Chapl York Distr Hosp 89-94; P-in-c Skelton w Shipton and Newton on Ouse *York* 94-95; R 95-01; V Strensall from 01; RD Easingwold 00-05. *The Vicarage, 10 York Road, Strensall, York YO32 5UN* Tel (01904) 490683 E-mail martin.harrison1@tesco.net

HARRISON, Mary Furley. b 21. MBE63. Westf Coll Lon BA42. Moray Ho Edin CertEd43 Edin Dioc NSM Course 79. **dss** 83 **d** 86. Edin H Cross *Edin* 83-86; NSM from 86; rtd 89. *Barnhill, 33 Barnton Avenue, Edinburgh EH4 6JJ* Tel 0131-336 2226

HARRISON, Matthew Henry. b 64. Univ Coll Dur BA85 Union Th Sem (NY) STM93. St Steph Ho Ox BA88 MA92. **d** 89 **p** 90. C Whickham *Dur* 89-92; C Owton Manor 93-95; USA 92-93; Asst Chapl Paris St Geo *Eur* 95-02; Perm to Offic 02-04; C Paddington St Jas *Lon* from 04. *61 Pembroke House, Hallfield Estate, London W2 6HQ* Tel (020) 7706 1248

HARRISON, Michael Anthony. b 48. Westhill Coll Birm CertCYW72 Huddersfield Poly CertEd88 Leeds Poly BA91 Leeds Univ MA98. N Ord Course 94. **d** 97 **p** 98. NSM Thornhill and Whitley Lower *Wakef* 97-99; TV Wrexham *St As* 99-03; V Ruabon from 03. *The Vicarage, Park Street, Ruabon, Wrexham LL14 6LF* Tel (01978) 810176 E-mail whernside@aol.com

HARRISON, Michael Burt (Crispin). b 36. Leeds Univ BA59 Trin Coll Ox BA62 MA66. Coll of Resurr Mirfield 59. **d** 63 **p** 64. C W Hartlepool St Aid *Dur* 63-64; C Middlesbrough All SS *York* 64-66; Lic to Offic *Wakef* 67-69 and 78-87; CR from 68; S Africa 69-77 and 87-97; Registrar Coll of the Resurr Mirfield 78-84; Vice-Prin 84-87; Superior CR 97-02. *St Peter's Priory, PO Box 991, Southdale, 2135 South Africa* Tel (0027) (11) 434 2504 Fax 434 4556 E-mail crpriory@acenet.co.za

HARRISON, Michael Robert. b 63. Selw Coll Cam BA84 K Coll Lon PhD97 Bradf Univ MA99. Ripon Coll Cuddesdon BA89 Union Th Sem (NY) STM90. **d** 90 **p** 91. C S Lambeth St Anne and All SS *S'wark* 90-94; Chapl Bp's Chapl to Students *Bradf* 94-98; Chapl Bradf Univ 94-98; Chapl Bradf and Ilkley Community Coll 94-98; P-in-c Eltham H Trin *S'wark* 98; V from 98; RD Eltham and Mottingham from 05. *Holy Trinity Vicarage, 59 Southend Crescent, London SE9 2SD* Tel (020) 8850 1246 E-mail mikeharrison7@hotmail.com

HARRISON, Canon Noel Milburn. b 27. Leeds Univ MPhil75 PhD80. St Aid Birkenhead 54. **d** 57 **p** 58. C Doncaster St Jas *Sheff* 57-60; Chapl Yorkshire Res Sch for Deaf Doncaster 60-68; C Woodlands *Sheff* 60-62; Chapl to the Deaf 60-68; Hd Master Elmete Hall Sch Leeds 68-84; Hon C Whitgift w Adlingfleet and Eastoft 83-84; Hon C Abbeydale St Jo 84-86; Dioc Dir of Educn 84-94; R Tankersley 86-94; Hon Can Sheff Cathl 88-94; rtd 94; Perm to Offic *Sheff* from 94 and *Linc* 95-99. *Aidan House, 118 High Street, Crowle, Scunthorpe DN17 4DR*

HARRISON, Mrs Nona Margaret. b 50. Open Univ BA80. S Dios Minl Tr Scheme 92. **d** 95 **p** 96. NSM E w W Wellow and Sherfield English *Win* 95-99; NSM Barton Stacey and Bullington etc 99; NSM Hurstbourne Priors, Longparish etc from 00. *The Rectory, Longparish, Andover SP11 6PG* Tel (01264) 720215

HARRISON, Oliver. b 71. SS Paul & Mary Coll Cheltenham BA93. St Jo Coll Nottm MA95. **d** 97 **p** 98. Asst Chapl The Hague *Eur* 97-00; C Walmley *Birm* 00-04; C-in-c Grove Green LEP *Cant* from 04. *7 Samphire Close, Weavering, Maidstone ME14 5UD* Tel (01622) 739294 E-mail oliver.harrison@tiscali.co.uk

HARRISON, Miss Patricia Mary. b 35. St Kath Coll Lon CertEd65 Dip Primary Educn 70 Open Univ BA74. St Mich Ho Ox IDC59. **dss** 85 **d** 87 **p** 94. Nunthorpe *York* 85-87; NSM 87-98; rtd 95; Perm to Offic *York* from 98. *22 Lamonby Close, Nunthorpe, Middlesbrough TS7 0QG* Tel (01642) 313524

HARRISON, Paul Graham. b 53. Sarum & Wells Th Coll 76. **d** 79 **p** 80. C Brixham w Churston Ferrers *Ex* 79-82; C Portsea N End St Mark *Portsm* 82-87; V Tiverton St Andr *Ex* 87-94; Chapl Tiverton and Distr Hosp 90-94; P-in-c Astwood Bank *Worc* 94-05; TV Redditch Ch the K from 05; Chapl to the Deaf from 94; Perm to Offic *Cov* from 94. *The Vicarage, 16 Church Road, Astwood Bank, Redditch B96 6EH* Tel (01527) 892489 *or* 894257 Fax 894795 E-mail p.g.harrison@btinternet.com *or* dda@cofe-worcester.org.uk

HARRISON, Paul Thomas. b 57. Nor Sch of Art BA80 Leic Poly PGCE88 Coll of Ripon & York St Jo MA99. Qu Coll Birm 95. **d** 97 **p** 98. C Northallerton w Kirby Sigston *York* 97-01; TV Usworth *Dur* from 01. *14 Prestwick Close, Washington NE37 2LP* Tel 0191-416 7604

HARRISON, Peter. *See* HARRISON, Robert Peter

HARRISON, Peter Keith. b 44. Open Univ BA85. St Aid Birkenhead. **d** 68 **p** 69. C Higher Bebington *Ches* 68-71; C Walmsley *Man* 71-74; V Lumb in Rossendale 74-79; V Heywood St Marg 79-87; V Hey 87-95; AD Saddleworth 93-95; Chapl Athens w Kifissia *Eur* 95-98; V Aston Cantlow and Wilmcote w Billesley *Cov* 98-02; V W Burnley All SS *Blackb* from 02. *All Saints' Vicarage, Padiham Road, Burnley BB12 6PA* Tel (01282) 775629 Fax as telephone E-mail harrison.ssc@virgin.net

HARRISON, The Ven Peter Reginald Wallace. b 39. Selw Coll Cam BA62. Ridley Hall Cam 62. **d** 64 **p** 65. C Barton Hill St Luke w Ch Ch *Bris* 64-69; Chapl Greenhouse Trust 69-77; Dir Northorpe Hall Trust 77-84; Lic to Offic *Wakef* 77-84; TR Drypool *York* 84-98; AD E Hull 88-98; Can and Preb York Minster from 94; Adn E Riding from 98. *Brimley Lodge, 27 Molescroft Road, Beverley HU17 7DX* Tel (01482) 881659 Fax as telephone E-mail peterrwharrison@breathemail.net

HARRISON, Canon Philip Hubert. b 37. Sarum & Wells Th Coll 77. **d** 79 **p** 80. C Wymondham *Nor* 79-83; V Watton w Carbrooke and Ovington 83-92; R Drayton w Felthorpe 92-02; Hon Can Nor Cathl 99-02; rtd 02; Perm to Offic *Nor* from 02. *The Fairstead, 1 Back Street, Horsham St Faith, Norwich NR10 3JP* Tel (01603) 893087

HARRISON, Mrs Rachel Elizabeth. b 53. NEOC 98. **d** 01 **p** 02. C Skelton w Upleatham *York* 01-04; P-in-c New Marske from 04; P-in-c Wilton from 04; Ind Chapl from 04. *9 Blenheim Terrace, Redcar TS10 1QP* Tel (01642) 482870 E-mail rachelhere@hotmail.com

HARRISON, Richard Kingswood. b 61. Linc Coll Ox BA83 MA88 Leeds Univ BA90. Coll of Resurr Mirfield 88. **d** 91 **p** 92. C Reading St Giles *Ox* 91-93; Asst Chapl Merchant Taylors' Sch Northwood 93-96; Chapl Ardingly Coll 96-02; R Shill Valley and Broadshire *Ox* 02-04; Chapl Uppingham Sch from 04. *48 High Street West, Uppingham, Oakham LE15 9QD* Tel (01572) 822144 E-mail rkh@uppingham.co.uk

HARRISON, Robert Peter. b 28. Chich Th Coll. **d** 60 **p** 61. C Ealing Ch the Sav *Lon* 60-64; C Hammersmith SS Mich and Geo White City Estate CD 64-66; P-in-c Fulham St Pet 66-73; V 73-94; rtd 94; Perm to Offic *Chich* from 94. *8 Broadwater Way, Worthing BN14 9LP* Tel (01903) 217073

HARRISON, Robert William. b 62. Mansf Coll Ox BA84. Qu Coll Birm 87. **d** 89 **p** 90. C Sholing *Win* 89-93; Communications Adv to Bp Willesden *Lon* 93-97; C Cricklewood St Gabr and St Mich 93-97; V Hillingdon St Jo from 97. *St John's Vicarage, Royal Lane, Uxbridge UB8 3QR* Tel (01895) 461945 E-mail rob.harrison@london.anglican.org

HARRISON, Rodney Lovel Neal. b 46. MBE87. Dur Univ BA67. Ripon Coll Cuddesdon DipMin95. **d** 95 **p** 96. C N w S Wootton *Nor* 95-98; P-in-c Gt and Lt Bedwyn and Savernake Forest *Sarum* 98-02; TV Savernake from 02. *The Vicarage, Church Street, Great Bedwyn, Marlborough SN8 3PF* Tel (01672) 870779 E-mail rodney@rlnh-ejhh.demon.co.uk

HARRISON, Rosemary Jane. b 53. Bradf Coll of Educn CertEd76. Trin Coll Bris DipHE85. **d** 87 **p** 94. NSM Southway *Ex* 87-89; NSM Kinson *Sarum* 89-96. *41 North Lane, Buriton, Petersfield GU31 5RS* Tel (01730) 269390

HARRISON, Roy. *See* HARRISON, Canon William Roy

HARRISON, Russell. *See* HARRISON, Francis Russell

HARRISON, Miss Ruth Margaret. b 33. BEM85. FRSA94. Ripon Coll Cuddesdon 02. **d** 02 **p** 03. NSM Baddiley and Wrenbury w Burleydam *Ches* from 02. *2 Heywood Cottages, Heywood Lane, Audlem, Crewe CW3 0EX* Tel (01270) 812010

HARRISON, Mrs Shirley Ann. b 56. Leic Univ BA76. N Ord Course 02. **d** 05. NSM Saddleworth *Man* from 05. *86 Beaufort Road, Ashton-under-Lyne OL6 6NU* Tel 0161-308 2045 Mobile 07748-637217 E-mail shirleya.harrison@btopenworld.com

HARRISON, Steven John. b 47. Univ of Wales (Abth) BSc68 PhD74 FRMetS74. St And Dioc Tr Course 87. **d** 90 **p** 91. NSM Alloa *St And* 90-94; NSM Bridge of Allan 94-02; NSM Spittal *Newc* from 02; NSM Scremerston from 02. *St John's Vicarage, 129 Main Street, Spittal, Berwick-upon-Tweed TD15 1RP* Tel (01289) 307342 E-mail sjhl@stir.ac.uk *or* johnandaveril@aol.com

HARRISON, Walter William. b 28. St Jo Coll Nottm. **d** 71 **p** 72. C Lenton *S'well* 71-74; R Carlton-in-the-Willows 74-93; rtd 93; Perm to Offic *S'well* from 00. *20 Conway Gardens, Nottingham NG5 6LR* Tel 0115-920 0766

HARRISON, Canon William Roy. b 34. Dur Univ BA58 DipTh59. Cranmer Hall Dur 57. **d** 59 **p** 60. C Kingswood *Bris* 59-62; Kenya 62-65; P-in-c Gt Somerford *Bris* 66; V Soundwell 66-99; Hon Can Bris Cathl 92-99; rtd 99; Perm to Offic *Bris* from 99. *20 Pool Road, Bristol BS15 1XL* Tel 0117-967 9802

HARRISON-WATSON, Carole. *See* FORD, Mrs Carole

HARRISSON, John Anthony Lomax. b 47. Ex Univ BA72. Qu Coll Birm 72. **d** 74 **p** 75. C Loughton St Jo *Chelmsf* 74-81; V Chingford St Anne 81-98; TV Aldrington *Chich* 98-04; TV Golden Cap Team *Sarum* from 04. *The Vicarage, West Hill Road, Lyme Regis DT7 3LW* Tel (01297) 443134

HARROLD, Canon Jeremy Robin. b 31. Hertf Coll Ox BA54 BSc56 MA58. Wycliffe Hall Ox. **d** 59 **p** 60. C Rushden *Pet* 59-61; Bp's Chapl *Lon* 61-64; Australia 64-67; V Harlesden St Mark *Lon* 67-72; V Hendon St Paul Mill Hill 72-84; V Stowmarket *St E* 84-96; RD Stowmarket 90-96; Hon Can St E Cathl 94-96; rtd 96; Perm to Offic *St E* from 96. *18 Wilkinson Way, Woodbridge IP12 1SS* Tel (01394) 380127

HARRON, Gareth Andrew. b 71. QUB BA92. CITC BTh95. **d** 95 **p** 96. C Willowfield *D & D* 95-98; C Dromore Cathl 98-02; I Magheralin w Dollingstown from 02. *The Rectory, 12 New Forge Road, Magheralin, Craigavon BT67 0QJ* Tel (028) 9261 1273 E-mail gareth@gharron.freeserve.co.uk

HARRON, James Alexander. b 37. GIMechE61 HNC59. St Aid Birkenhead 63. **d** 65 **p** 66. C Willowfield *D & D* 65-69; I Desertmartin *D & R* 69-80; Dep Sec BCMS (Ireland) 80-84; I Aghalee *D & D* 84-03; Preb Dromore Cathl 02-03; Chapl HM Pris Maghaberry 86-03; rtd 03. *8 Churchill Avenue, Lurgan, Craigavon BT66 7BW* Tel and fax (028) 3834 6543

HARROP, Stephen Douglas. b 48. St Jo Coll York CertEd74 Man Univ DipAdEd90. Edin Th Coll 77. **d** 79 **p** 82. C Middlesbrough St Martin *York* 79-80; C Cayton w Eastfield 80-81; C Oldham *Man* 82-84; V Oldham St Barn 84-89; P-in-c Em Ch Hong Kong 89-93; Ind Chapl and TV Kidderminster St Mary and All SS w Trimpley etc *Worc* 93-95; Chapl Kidderminster Coll 93-95; Sandwell Chs Link Officer *Birm* 95-96; Dep Chapl HM Pris Brixton 96-97; Chapl Taichung St Jas Taiwan 97-98; R Lower Merion St Jo USA 98-99; R Essington St Jo 99-03; Perm to Offic *Man* 03-04; C Elton St Steph 04-05; P-in-c from 05. *The Vicarage, 14 Springside Road, Bury BL9 5JE* Tel 0161-797 9273 E-mail sharropsd@aol.com

HARRY, Bruce David. b 40. JP77. Culham Coll Ox CertEd60. N Ord Course 83. **d** 86 **p** 87. NSM Liscard St Thos *Ches* 86-91; NSM Eastham 91-94; C New Brighton St Jas 94-96; C New Brighton Em 94-96; C New Brighton St Jas w Em 96-98; NSM 98-02; NSM New Brighton All SS 98-02; P-in-c 02-03; Perm to Offic from 03. *21 Sandymount Drive, Wallasey CH45 0LJ* Tel 0151-639 7232

HART, Allen Sydney George. b 38. Chich Th Coll 64. **d** 67 **p** 68. C N Wembley St Cuth *Lon* 67-71; C W Bromwich All SS *Lich* 71-74; TV Hucknall Torkard *S'well* 74-80; V Annesley Our Lady and All SS 80-86; V Bilborough St Jo 86-99; RD Nottingham W 94-99; P-in-c Clarborough w Hayton 99-03; Asst Chapl HM Pris Ranby 99-03; rtd 03; Perm to Offic *S'well* from 03. *3 Castleton Close, Hucknall, Nottingham NG15 6TD* Tel 0115-955 2067 E-mail margartal@care4free.net

HART, André Hendrik. b 62. Cape Town Univ BA86. St Steph Ho Ox 89. **d** 91 **p** 92. C Newbold w Dunston *Derby* 91-95; P-in-c Clifton and Norbury w Snelston 95-02; Chapl S Derbyshire Community Health Services NHS Trust 95-02; V Westbury-on-Trym H Trin *Bris* from 02. *Holy Trinity Vicarage, 44 Eastfield Road, Westbury-on-Trym, Bristol BS9 4AG* Tel 0117-962 1536 *or* 950 8644 E-mail ahart001@fish.co.uk

HART, Anthony. b 35. St Mich Coll Llan 77. **d** 79 **p** 80. NSM Jersey St Helier *Win* 79-81; C Heref All SS *Heref* 81-82; C Kingstone 82-84; C Eaton Bishop 82-84; C Clehonger 82-84; R Sutton St Nicholas w Sutton St Michael 84-88; R Withington w Westhide 84-88; R Jersey St Mary *Win* 88-01; rtd 01; Perm to Offic *Win* from 02. *Villa Rapallo, Mont de la Trinite, St Helier, Jersey JE2 4NJ* Tel (01534) 739146 Mobile 07797-750435 E-mail hart@localdial.com

HART, Colin Edwin. b 45. Leeds Univ BA66 PGCE67 MPhil89 Fitzw Coll Cam BA73 MA77 K Coll Lon MTh76 Man Univ PhD98. Trin Coll Bris 74. **d** 74 **p** 75. C Ware Ch Ch *St Alb* 74-78; TV Sheff Manor *Sheff* 78-80; V Wombridge *Lich* 80-87; Lect St Jo Coll Nottm 87-01; Public Preacher *S'well* 87-01; Hon C Chilwell 87-91; Hon C Trowell 91-01. *Address temp unknown*

HART, Dagogo. b 50. Birm Bible Inst Dip Systematic Th 79 LicTh81. **d** 82 **p** 83. Nigeria 82-01; C Niger Delta St Cypr 82-88; V 93-96; Bp's Chapl *Niger Delta* 83-88; Res Min Niger Delta Ch Ch 89-92; Can Res St Steph Cathl 97-00; C W Bromwich St Jas w St Paul *Lich* from 01. *3 Tiverton Drive, West Bromwich B71 1DA* Tel 0121-553 0601

HART, David. b 48. Edge Hill Coll of HE BEd80 Liv Inst of Educn AdDipEd84 Liv Univ MEd87 Chester Coll of HE BPhil94. N Ord Course 91. **d** 94 **p** 95. NSM Ashton-in-Makerfield St Thos *Liv* 94-02; NSM Wigan W Deanery from 02. *12 Ratcliffe Road, Aspull, Wigan WN2 1YE* Tel (01942) 832918

HART, David Alan. b 54. Keble Coll Ox BA75 MPhil78 Union Th Sem (NY) STM79. Westcott Ho Cam 83. **d** 83 **p** 84. Asst Chapl Gresham's Sch Holt 83-84; Chapl Nor Sch 84-85; Chapl Shrewsbury Sch 85-87; Chapl St Jo Coll Sch Cam 87-88; C Camberwell St Giles w St Matt *S'wark* 88-90; Chapl Loughb Univ *Leic* 90-97; Relig and Roehampton Inst *S'wark* 97-98; Past Services Development Co-ord Derby Univ *Derby* 98-02; Sen Lect K Alfred Coll *Win* from 03. *King Alfred's College, Winchester SO22 4NR* Tel (01962) 841515 Mobile 07876-620514 Fax (01962) 842280 E-mail davidhart@wkac.ac.uk

HART, David Alan. b 54. Rhodes Univ BTh86 MTh89 PhD92. **d** 81 **p** 82. S Africa 81-99; R Auckland Park St Pet 82-86; Sub Dean Kimberley Cathl 86-90; Chapl Cape Town Univ 90-94; NSM Cape Town Cathl 94-98; Chapl Bournemouth and Poole Coll of FE *Sarum* from 99. *21B Laidlaw Close, Poole BH12 5EW* Tel (01202) 595383 E-mail dhart@bournemouth.ac.uk

HART, David Leonard. b 42. Ripon Hall Ox 68. **d** 71 **p** 72. C Castle Vale *Birm* 71-73; Chapl All SS Hosp Birm 73-94; Chapl Services Manager N Birm Mental Health Trust 94-03; Manager Past Care Birm and Solihull Mental Health Trust from 03. *12 Dorchester Drive, Birmingham, B17 0SW,* or *Highcroft Hospital, 71 Fentham Road, Birmingham B23 6AL* Tel 0121-427 7828 *or* 623 5500

HART, David Maurice. b 35. Univ Coll Dur BSc57. Clifton Th Coll 59. **d** 61 **p** 62. C Bolton St Paul *Man* 61-64; C Hamworthy *Sarum* 64-70; R W Dean w E Grimstead 70-81; R Farley w Pitton and W Dean w E Grimstead 81-90; V Steeple Ashton w Semington and Keevil 90-03; rtd 03. *9 Field Close, Westbury BA13 3AG* Tel (01373) 827912

HART, Canon Dennis Daniel. b 22. Linc Th Coll 45. **d** 48 **p** 49. C Abbots Langley *St Alb* 48-49; C Bedford St Paul 49-53; CF 53-55; V St Alb St Sav *St Alb* 55-92; Hon Can St Alb 74-92; RD St Alb 84-90; rtd 92. *7 Bassett Close, Redbourn AL3 7JY* Tel (01582) 794464

HART, Dennis William. b 30. JP. Open Univ BA. Oak Hill Th Coll 75. **d** 78 **p** 79. NSM Clacton St Paul *Chelmsf* from 78. *15 Albert Gardens, Clacton-on-Sea CO15 6QN* Tel (01255) 431794

HART, Edwin Joseph. b 21. Oak Hill Th Coll 56. **d** 58 **p** 59. C Harlow New Town w Lt Parndon *Chelmsf* 58-60; C Leyton 60-61; C-in-c Cranham Park St Luke CD 61-69; V Cranham Park 69-71; R Markfield *Leic* 71-89; rtd 89; Perm to Offic *Leic* from 89. *135 Grace Dieu Road, Thringstone, Coalville LE67 5AP* Tel (01530) 222767

HART, Geoffrey Robert. b 49. TISEC 93. **d** 95 **p** 96. P-in-c Edin St Salvador *Edin* 96-98; C Edin St Cuth 96-98; Lic to Offic 98-00; TV Edin St Marg from 00. *27 Links View, Port Seton, Prestonpans EH32 0EZ* Tel (01875) 811147 Mobile 07963-463551 E-mail geoff@lovehart.demon.co.uk

HART, Canon Geoffrey William. b 27. Ex Coll Ox BA51 MA55. Ridley Hall Cam 51. **d** 54 **p** 55. C Islington St Mary *Lon* 54-58; C Leeds St Geo *Ripon* 58-59; V Harold Wood *Chelmsf* 59-65; V Southport Ch Ch *Liv* 65-73; R Cheltenham St Mary *Glouc* 73-76; TR Cheltenham St Mary, St Matt, St Paul and H Trin 76-93; Hon Can Glouc Cathl 78-93; rtd 93; Chapl All Hallows Sch Rousdon 94-96; Perm to Offic *Ex* 94-02 and *Ox* from 02. *2 Little Lane, Eynsham, Witney OX29 4LG* Tel (01865) 884055

HART, Mrs Gillian Mary. b 57. Sheff City Poly BA79. Carl Dioc Tr Inst 92. **d** 95 **p** 96. C Burgh-by-Sands and Kirkbampton w Kirkandrews etc *Carl* 95-99; C Aikton 95-99; C Orton St Giles 95-99; Dioc Youth Officer 99-03; Chapl St Martin's Coll Carl 99-03; R Barony of Burgh *Carl* from 03. *The Rectory, Burgh-by-Sands, Carlisle CA5 6AW* Tel (01228) 576324 E-mail hart.gill@btopenworld.com

HART, Graham Cooper. b 36. S Dios Minl Tr Scheme 88. **d** 91 **p** 92. NSM Filton *Bris* 91-93; NSM Downend 93-01. *11 West Hill, Portishead, Bristol BS20 6LQ* Tel (01275) 840363

HART, Canon Graham Merril (Merry). b 23. Ridley Coll Melbourne 65. **d** 77 **p** 77. Tanzania 69-84; CMS 72-83; Can Musoma from 85; Chapl Ostend w Knokke and Bruges *Eur* 84-93; Miss to Seamen 84-93; rtd 93; Perm to Offic *S'wark* from 93. *Morden College, 7 Alexander Court, Kidbrook Grove, London SE3 0LH* Tel (020) 8858 3731

HART, James. b 53. MIL84 Dur Univ BA75 DipEd76 DipHE88 Lon Univ BD98. Oak Hill Th Coll 86. **d** 88 **p** 89. C Starbeck *Ripon* 88-90; SAMS Argentina 90-96; Chapl Bishop's Stortford Coll 96-00; Chapl Felsted Sch from 00; Dioc FE Officer *Chelmsf* from 00. *Austens, Bury Chase, Felsted, Great Dunmow CM6 3DQ* Tel (01371) 820414 E-mail jh@felsted.org

HART, John Peter. b 39. Bris Sch of Min 80. **d** 84 **p** 85. NSM Malmesbury w Westport and Brokenborough *Bris* 84-88; C Yatton Moor *B & W* 89-90; V Bridgwater H Trin 90-96; Chapl HM Pris The Mount 96-01; P-in-c Sarratt *St Alb* 96-04; P-in-c Chipperfield St Paul 01-04; rtd 04. *4 Waverley Gardens, Stamford PE9 1BH*

HART, Mark. b 61. Chu Coll Cam BA82 Cam Univ MA86 PhD86. Trin Coll Bris BA98. **d** 98 **p** 99. C Bromborough *Ches* 98-02; V Plemstall w Guilden Sutton from 02. *The Vicarage, Wicker Lane, Guilden Sutton, Chester CH3 7EL* Tel (01244) 300306 E-mail hart@mkgfr.freeserve.co.uk

HART, Merril. *See* HART, Canon Graham Merril

HART, Canon Michael Anthony. b 50. AKC71. St Aug Coll Cant 72. **d** 73 **p** 74. C Southwick St Columba *Dur* 73-76; C Hendon St Alphage *Lon* 76-78; P-in-c Eltham Park St Luke *S'wark* 78-83; V 83-85; R Newington St Mary 85-96; P-in-c Camberwell St Mich w All So w Em 85-96; RD S'wark and Newington 93-96; P-in-c Chaldon 96-97; P-in-c Caterham 96-97; TR 98-05; RD Caterham 98-05; Hon Can S'wark Cathl 01-05; Can Missr for Ch in Soc from 05. *507 Butlers Wharf, 36 Shad Thames, London SE1 2YE* Tel (020) 7403 6607 E-mail michael.hart@southwark.anglican.org

HART, Preb Michael Stuart. b 39. Univ of Wales (Lamp) BA61 Lanc Univ MA72. Wycliffe Hall Ox 61. **d** 63 **p** 64. C W Bromwich St Jas *Lich* 63-66; C Tarrington w Stoke Edith *Heref* 66-67; C Putney St Mary *S'wark* 67-70; V Accrington St Mary *Blackb* 70-82; RD Accrington 76-82; Hon Can Blackb Cathl

81-91; V Walton-le-Dale 82-91; TR Heavitree w Ex St Paul *Ex* 91-02; P-in-c Ex St Mary Steps 01-02; TR Heavitree and St Mary Steps from 02; P-in-c Exwick *Ex* from 05; Preb Ex Cathl from 02. *St Mary Steps Rectory, 10 Victoria Park Road, Exeter EX2 4NT* Tel (01392) 677150
E-mail sacerdotal@eurobell.co.uk

HART, Peter. *See* HART, John Peter

HART, Peter Osborne. b 57. St Jo Coll Nottm. **d** 92 **p** 93. C Shipley St Pet *Bradf* 92-97; TV Walsall *Lich* 97-03; TV Cannock from 03. *St Luke's Vicarage, 18 Queen Street, Cannock WS11 1AE* Tel (01543) 579660

HART, Peter William. b 60. Liv Univ BA82 Université de Haute Normandie MèsL84 Univ of Wales (Swansea) MPhil92. Sarum & Wells Th Coll 86. **d** 88 **p** 89. C Llansamlet *S & B* 88-89; C Sketty 89-92; P-in-c Warndon St Nic *Worc* 92-97; R Berkhamsted St Mary *St Alb* 97-04; V Kew St Phil and All SS w St Luke *S'wark* from 04. *St Philip's Vicarage, 70 Marksbury Avenue, Richmond TW9 4JF* Tel (020) 8392 1425 *or* 8332 1324
E-mail pwhart1@aol.com

HART, Richard. b 49. St D Coll Lamp BA82 Oriel Coll Ox MPhil84. Qu Coll Birm 84. **d** 85 **p** 86. C Sketty *S & B* 85-87; P-in-c Llanbister w Llanbadarn Fynydd w Llananno 87-88; V 88-92; P-in-c Preston and Dymock w Donnington and Kempley *Glouc* 92-00; P-in-c Beguildy and Heyope and Llangynllo and Bleddfa *S & B* from 01. *The Vicarage, Beguildy, Knighton LD7 1YE* Tel (01547) 510252

HART, Robert William. b 76. R Holloway & Bedf New Coll Lon BSc97 Leeds Univ BA01 MA04. Coll of Resurr Mirfield 99. **d** 02 **p** 03. C Haydock St Jas *Liv* from 02. *27 Homestead Avenue, Haydock, St Helens WA11 0ND* Tel (01744) 633312 Mobile 07970-229469 E-mail rwhart@orange.net

HART, Ronald George. b 46. BSc Lon Univ DASS77 CQSW77. Sarum & Wells Th Coll. **d** 85 **p** 86. C Sittingbourne St Mich *Cant* 85-88; C Walton H Trin *Ox* 88-89; TV 89-96; R Broughton Gifford, Gt Chalfield and Holt *Sarum* from 96; Chapl UWE *Bris* from 05. *The Octagon, Frenchay Campus, Coldharbour Lane, Bristol BS16 1QY* Tel 0117-328 2334
E-mail ronhart1@compuserve.com

HART, Tony. b 36. CCC Cam BA59 MA63. Cuddesdon Coll 59. **d** 61 **p** 62. C Middlesbrough All SS *York* 61-64; Bp's Dom Chapl *Dur* 64-67; Hon Chapl 67-72; C Owton Manor CD 67-70; V Harton Colliery 70-71; TR S Shields All SS 71-83; RD Jarrow 77-83; Can Res Dur Cathl 83-92; V Easingwold w Raskelf *York* 92-97; V 97-01; RD Easingwold 97-00; rtd 01; Perm to Offic *Newc* from 02. *13 Stobhill Villas, Morpeth NE61 2SH* Tel (01670) 519017

HART, Prof Trevor Andrew. b 61. St Jo Coll Dur BA82 Aber Univ PhD89. **d** 88 **p** 88. NSM Bieldside *Ab* 88-95; NSM St Andrews St Andr *St And* from 95; Prof Div St Mary's Coll St Andr Univ from 95; Prin St Mary's Coll from 01. *St Mary's College, South Street, St Andrews KY16 9JU* Tel (01334) 462864
E-mail tah@st-andrews.ac.uk

HARTE, Frederick George. b 25. AKC53. **d** 54 **p** 55. C Lewisham St Jo Southend *S'wark* 54-57; C Eltham H Trin 57-60; V Bellingham St Dunstan 60-73; V Plumstead St Nic 73-84; V Sutton Bridge *Linc* 84-90; rtd 90; Master St Jo Hosp Bath and P-in-c of Chpl 90-00; Perm to Offic *Guildf* from 00. *Heartsease, 5 Vale Road, Claygate, Esher KT10 0NJ* Tel and fax (01372) 802548 E-mail hartefamily1@cwctv.net

HARTE, The Ven Matthew Scott. b 46. TCD BA70 MA74. CITC 71. **d** 71 **p** 72. C Bangor Abbey *D & D* 71-74; C Ballynafeigh St Jude 74-76; I Ardara w Glencolumbkille, Inniskeel etc *D & R* 76-98; I Dunfanaghy, Raymunterdoney and Tullaghbegley from 98; Adn Raphoe from 83. *The Rectory, Horn Head Road, Dunfanaghy, Letterkenny, Co Donegal, Irish Republic* Tel (00353) (74) 913 6187 Fax 913 6051
E-mail archdeacon@raphoe.anglican.org

HARTERINK, Mrs Joy Frances. b 49. DCEG82 Essex Univ BA71 Hughes Hall Cam CertEd72 Lon Univ MSc87. Oak Hill NSM Course 89. **d** 92 **p** 94. NSM Richmond H Trin and Ch Ch *S'wark* from 92; Chapl Richmond Coll 97-01. *9 Sandringham House, Courtlands, Sheen Road, Richmond TW10 5BG* Tel (020) 8948 7579

HARTLAND, David Robson. b 33. Qu Coll Birm 64. **d** 66 **p** 67. C Brierley Hill *Lich* 66-71; V Hartshill 71-76; V Moxley 76-85; V Willenhall St Steph 85-99; rtd 99; Perm to Offic *Lich* and *Worc* from 00. *80 Clifton Street, Bilston WV14 9HB* Tel (01902) 563262

HARTLAND, Ian Charles. b 49. K Coll Lon BD72 AKC72 PGCE73 MTh76. Sarum & Wells Th Coll 83. **d** 84 **p** 85. C Orpington All SS *Roch* 84-87; Sen Lect Ch Ch Coll Cant 87-95; Adv for RE Kent Co Coun from 96. *Ivy Lodge, 4 The Terrace, Canterbury CT2 7AJ* Tel (01227) 760789 Fax 768978
E-mail ian.hartland@kent.gov.uk

HARTLESS, Mrs Berengaria Isabella de la Tour. b 52. Univ of Wales (Cardiff) BSc74 Goldsmiths' Coll Lon PGCE76 Liv Univ MA03. Ox Min Course CBTS93. **d** 93 **p** 94. Par Dn High Wycombe *Ox* 93-94; C 94-97; P-in-c Seer Green and Jordans 97-00; OLM Tr Officer (Bucks) 97-00; Dioc Prin of OLM from 00. *27 Don Bosco Close, Oxford OX4 2LD* Tel (01865) 717986
E-mail beren.hartless@oxford.anglican.org

HARTLEY, Mrs Anne Theresa. b 52. St Cuth Soc Dur BSc74 Worc Coll of Educn PGCE75. **d** 03 **p** 04. OLM Shipton-under-Wychwood w Milton, Fifield etc *Ox* from 03. *The Old House, Upper Milton, Milton-under-Wychwood, Chipping Norton OX7 6EX* Tel (01993) 830160 Mobile 07976-025101
E-mail annethartley@hotmail.com

HARTLEY, Brian. b 41. N Ord Course 82. **d** 85 **p** 86. NSM Royton St Paul *Man* 85-91; NSM Oldham St Steph and All Martyrs 91-94; TV E Farnworth and Kearsley 94-97; TR New Bury from 97; P-in-c Gt Lever from 03; AD Farnworth from 98. *New Bury Rectory, 130A Highfield Road, Farnworth, Bolton BL4 0AJ* Tel (01204) 572334
E-mail brian_hartley@tiscali.co.uk

HARTLEY, Colin Redfearn. b 60. Cant Ch Ch Univ Coll BA98. Ridley Hall Cam 02. **d** 04 **p** 05. C Herne Bay Ch Ch *Cant* from 04. *66 Linden Avenue, Herne Bay CT6 8TZ* Tel (01227) 371457
E-mail rev.hartley@btinternet.com

HARTLEY, Daniel George. b 73. Leeds Univ BA95. Coll of Resurr Mirfield 96. **d** 99 **p** 00. C Richmond w Hudswell *Ripon* 99-03; Chapl HM YOI Deerbolt from 03. *HM YOI Deerbolt, Bowes Road, Barnard Castle DL12 9BG* Tel (01833) 633325
E-mail daniel.hartley@hmps.gsi.gov.uk

HARTLEY, Diann Lynn. *See* GWILLIAMS, Mrs Dianna Lynn

HARTLEY, Graham William Harrington. b 21. Ripon Hall Ox 61. **d** 62 **p** 63. C N Meols *Liv* 62-65; Nigeria 65-66; V Knowsley *Liv* 66-72; V Langdale *Carl* 72-81; TV Egremont and Haile 81-85; TV Whitehaven 85-88; rtd 88; Perm to Offic *Carl* from 88. *6 Meadowside, Chapel Stile, Ambleside LA22 9JE* Tel (01539) 437322

HARTLEY, Helenann Macleod. b 73. St Andr Univ MTheol95 Princeton Th Sem ThM96 Worc Coll Ox MPhil00 DPhil05. St Alb and Ox Min Course 03. **d** 05. C Wheatley *Ox* from 05. *43 Fairfax Gate, Holton, Oxford OX33 1QE* Tel 07981-914832 (mobile) E-mail helemann.hartley@hmc.ox.ac.uk

HARTLEY, Herbert. b 28. AKC52. **d** 53 **p** 54. C Blackpool H Cross *Blackb* 53-55; C Reading St Giles *Ox* 55-58; V Ruscombe and Twyford 58-66; Chapl RN 66-73; C Langley Marish *Ox* 73-77; R Hedsor and Bourne End 77-93; rtd 93. *The College of St Barnabas, Blackberry Lane, Lingfield RH7 6NJ* Tel (01342) 870260

HARTLEY, John Peter. b 56. Cam Univ BA78 Leeds Univ PhD82 Dur Univ BA84. Cranmer Hall Dur 82. **d** 85 **p** 86. C Spring Grove St Mary *Lon* 85-88; C Bexleyheath St Pet *Roch* 88-91; P-in-c Hanford *Lich* 91-00; Faith in the City Officer (Potteries) 91-00; V Eccleshill *Bradf* from 00. *The Vicarage, 2 Fagley Lane, Bradford BD2 3NS* Tel (01274) 636403 Mobile 07811-915320 E-mail vicar@stluke-eccleshill.org.uk

HARTLEY, John William. b 47. St Jo Coll Dur BA69. Linc Th Coll 70. **d** 72 **p** 73. C Poulton-le-Fylde *Blackb* 72-76; C Lancaster St Mary 76-79; V Barrowford 79-87; V Salesbury from 87; AD Whalley from 01. *St Peter's Vicarage, 49A Ribchester Road, Blackburn BB1 9HU* Tel (01254) 248072
E-mail john@salesbury49a.freeserve.co.uk

HARTLEY, Julian John. b 57. Oak Hill Th Coll BA85. **d** 85 **p** 86. C Eccleston Ch Ch *Liv* 85-89; V Goose Green 89-00; P-in-c Mosley Common *Man* from 00. *St John's Vicarage, Mosley Common Road, Worsley, Manchester M28 4AN* Tel 0161-790 2957 Fax 799 0314 E-mail rev.hartley@hartley.me.uk

HARTLEY, Michael Leslie. b 56. Leeds Univ BSc77. Ripon Coll Cuddesdon 87. **d** 89 **p** 90. C Standish *Blackb* 89-93; V Bamber Bridge St Aid 93-98; TR Colne and Villages from 98. *The Vicarage, Keighley Road, Colne BB8 7HF* Tel (01282) 83511
E-mail mike@hartley00.freeserve.co.uk

HARTLEY, Nigel John. b 48. Portsm Poly BA. St Jo Coll Nottm. **d** 83 **p** 84. C Ipswich St Marg *St E* 83-86; P-in-c Hintlesham w Chattisham 86-95; Dioc Radio Officer 86-95; P-in-c Gt Finborough w Onehouse, Harleston, Buxhall etc 95-04; RD Stowmarket 96-99; V Aldeburgh w Hazlewood from 04. *The Vicarage, Church Walk, Aldeburgh IP15 5DU* Tel (01728) 452223 E-mail nigel.hartley@stedmundsbury.anglican.org

HARTLEY, Paul. b 51. Nottm Univ BTh88. Linc Th Coll 85. **d** 88 **p** 89. C Clitheroe St Mary *Blackb* 88-91; TV Guiseley w Esholt *Bradf* 91-97; R Ackworth *Wakef* from 97. *The Rectory, Cross Hill, Ackworth, Pontefract WF7 7EJ* Tel (01977) 602751

HARTLEY, Canon Peter. b 44. Avery Hill Coll PGCE67 Ox Univ DipRE74 St Cath Coll Cam BA66 MA69. Sarum & Wells Th Coll 77. **d** 78 **p** 79. Hon C Freemantle *Win* 78-79; Chr Educn Officer *Pet* 79-81; Dir of Educn 81-90; Dir Coun of Educn and Tr *Chelmsf* from 90; Hon Can Chelmsf Cathl from 92; Perm to Offic *Nor* from 04. *St Clare, Links Drive, Chelmsford CM2 9AW* Tel (01245) 251461 E-mail hartleyp@chelmsford.anglican.org

HARTLEY, Peter Mellodew. b 41. Qu Coll Cam BA63 MA66 Lon Univ MSc71 DipTh83 FICE. S'wark Ord Course 80. **d** 83 **p** 84. NSM Salfords *S'wark* 83-97; Chapl Surrey and Sussex Healthcare NHS Trust 97-02; rtd 02; Perm to Offic *Chich* from 00 and *S'wark* from 02. *Old Timbers, North Lane, West Hoathly RH19 4QF* Tel (01342) 811238

HARTLEY, Stephen William Mark. b 50. St Chad's Coll Dur BA71. Westcott Ho Cam 72. **d** 74 **p** 75. C Holbrooks *Cov* 74-76; C Styvechale 76-79; P-in-c Snitterfield w Bearley 79-81; V 81-83; V Exhall 83-88; V Tilehurst St Cath *Ox* 88-95; TR Cowley St Jas from 95. *Cowley Rectory, 11 Beauchamp Lane, Oxford OX4 3LF* Tel (01865) 747680 Fax 395896
E-mail stephen.hartley@btinternet.com

HARTLEY, Stewart John Ridley. b 47. St Jo Coll Nottm 78. **d** 80 **p** 81. C Altham w Clayton le Moors *Blackb* 80-84; P-in-c Nelson St Phil 84-91; V 91-98; V Gt Marsden w Nelson St Phil 99-03; Hon Can Blackb Cathl 99-03; V Bermondsey St Anne and St Aug *S'wark* from 03; V Bermondsey St Jas w Ch Ch and St Crispin from 03. *St Anne's Vicarage, 10 Thorburn Square, London SE1 5QH* Tel (020) 7237 3950
E-mail stewarthartley@btinternet.com

HARTLEY, Susan Mary. b 49. Newc Univ MB, BS73 MRCGP77. SEITE 99. **d** 02 **p** 03. NSM Spitalfields Ch Ch w All SS *Lon* from 02. *35 Buxton Street, London E1 5EH* Tel (020) 7247 1344 Mobile 07890-901249
E-mail sue@hartley1662.fsnet.co.uk

HARTNELL, Canon Bruce John. b 42. Ex Univ BA64 Linacre Coll Ox BA66 MA. Ripon Hall Ox 64. **d** 66 **p** 67. C S Stoneham *Win* 66-69; Chapl and Tutor Ripon Hall Ox 69-74; V Knowl Hill w Littlewick *Ox* 74-78; Chapl Southn Univ *Win* 78-83; V Sholing from 83; AD Southampton 93-01; Hon Can Win Cathl from 93. *The Vicarage, 41 Station Road, Southampton SO19 8FN* Tel (023) 8044 8337 E-mail bruce.hartnell@ukgateway.net

HARTOPP, Mrs Penelope Faye. b 55. Ripon Coll Cuddesdon. **d** 03 **p** 04. C Studley *Cov* 03-04; C Cov E from 04. *70 Leicester Road, Bedworth CV12 8AG* Tel (024) 7645 2493

HARTREE, Steven John. b 45. FFA78. WMMTC 96. **d** 99 **p** 00. NSM Highbridge *B & W* 99-03; P-in-c Tintinhull w Chilthorne Domer, Yeovil Marsh etc from 03. *The Rectory, Vicarage Street, Tintinhull, Yeovil BA22 8PY* Tel (01935) 822655

HARTROPP, Andrew James. b 59. Southn Univ BSc80 PhD85. Oak Hill Th Coll BA95. **d** 98 **p** 99. C Watford *St Alb* 98-01; C Watford Ch Ch from 01; Teacher Henrietta Barnett Sch from 01. *77 Northfield Gardens, Watford WD24 7RF* Tel (01923) 225411
E-mail a.hartropp@clara.net

HARVEY, Alan Douglas. b 25. FRSH82. Melbourne Coll of Div 78. **d** 79 **p** 81. Australia 79-86; Perm to Offic *Ely* 86-87; V Wiggenhall St Germans and Islington 88-95; V Wiggenhall St Mary Magd 88-95; rtd 95; Perm to Offic *Cant* from 95. *17 Day View Road, Broadstairs CT10 2EA* Tel (01843) 862794

HARVEY, Alison Christine Vera. b 57. Open Univ BA97 Nottm Univ MA03. EMMTC 01. **d** 03 **p** 04. C Horncastle w Low Toynton *Linc* from 03; C High Toynton from 03; C Greetham w Ashby Puerorum from 03. *St Mary's House, 6 Park Road, Horncastle LN9 5EF* Tel (01507) 527312 Mobile 07789-835039
E-mail alison@harvey8086.freeserve.co.uk

HARVEY, Canon Anthony Ernest. b 30. Worc Coll Ox BA53 MA56 DD83. Westcott Ho Cam 56. **d** 58 **p** 59. C Chelsea Ch Ch *Lon* 58-62; Ch Ch Ox 62-69; Warden St Aug Coll Cant 69-75; Lect Th Ox Univ 76-82; Chapl Qu Coll Ox 77-82; Can and Lib Westmr Abbey 82-99; Sub-Dean and Adn Westmr 87-99; rtd 99; Perm to Offic *Glouc* from 00. *Mendelssohn Cottage, Broadway Road, Willersey, Broadway WR12 7BH* Tel (01386) 859260

HARVEY, Arthur Ernest. b 30. Lon Univ DipTh58 MSc80. Oak Hill Th Coll 54. **d** 57 **p** 58. C Rayleigh *Chelmsf* 57-60; C Morpeth *Newc* 60-63; R Pitsea *Chelmsf* 63-74; Bp's Ind Officer 73-80; R Bobbingworth 74-81; Chapl Bordeaux w Riberac, Cahors, Duras etc *Eur* 82-86; V Barnsbury St Andr and H Trin w All SS *Lon* 86-90; TR Barnsbury 90-97; rtd 97; Perm to Offic *Chich* from 01. *Prompt Corner, 4A Arundel Road, Eastbourne BN21 2EL* Tel (01323) 642982

HARVEY, Brian. b 51. Hatf Poly BA74. St As Minl Tr Course 02. **d** 05. NSM Cilcain and Nannerch and Rhydymwyn *St As* from 05. *The Rectory, 9 Pen y Coed, Nannerch, Mold CH7 5RS* Tel (01352) 741376 Fax 07831-623289
E-mail brianharvey@mac.com

HARVEY, Christopher John Alfred. b 41. S'wark Ord Course 66. **d** 69 **p** 70. C Grays Thurrock *Chelmsf* 69-73; C Gt Baddow 73-75; V Berechurch St Marg w St Mich 75-94; R Tendring and Lt Bentley w Beaumont cum Moze 94-00; P-in-c Alresford from 00. *The Rectory, St Andrew's Close, Alresford, Colchester CO7 8BL* Tel (01206) 823163 E-mail cjharvey@ukonline.co.uk

HARVEY, The Ven Cyril John. b 30. Univ of Wales (Lamp) BA51. Coll of Resurr Mirfield 51. **d** 53 **p** 54. C Caerau w Ely *Llan* 53-57; C Milford Haven *St D* 57-61; V Castlemartin and Warren 61-65; R Begelly w Kilgetty 65-73; V Haverfordwest St Martin w Lambston 73-88; Can St D Cathl from 85; R Tenby 88-96; Adn St D 91-96; rtd 96. *10 Oakwood Grove, Slade Lane, Haverfordwest SA61 2HF* Tel (01437) 768036

HARVEY, Canon Debra Eileen. b 54. SW Minl Tr Course. **d** 94 **p** 95. NSM Camborne *Truro* from 94; Chapl w Deaf People from 94; Hon Can Truro Cathl from 03. *Ankorva Salow, Tehidy Road, Camborne TR14 0NA* Tel (01209) 716282 Mobile 07774-975268 Fax and minicom as telephone
E-mail hippo@ankorva.freeserve.co.uk

HARVEY, Desmond Victor Ross. b 37. QUB BA59. Princeton Th Sem ThM63 Fuller Th Sem California DMin93 St Mich Coll Llan 95. **d** 95 **p** 96. Presbyterian Min 65-95; C Cwmbran *Mon* 95-97; TV 97; Perm to Offic from 97; Offg Chapl RAF from 98. *Mallory, Llanmaes, Llantwit Major CF61 2XR* Tel and fax (01446) 792753

HARVEY, John. b 30. S'wark Ord Course. **d** 65 **p** 66. C Lewisham St Jo Southend *S'wark* 65-73; V Bellingham St Dunstan 73-78; TV Bourne Valley *Sarum* 78-81; TR 81-87; R Kilkhampton w Morwenstow *Truro* 87-90; rtd 90; Perm to Offic *Roch* 90-99. *18 Ramsay Hall, 11-13 Byron Road, Worthing BN11 3HN*

HARVEY, John Christopher. b 65. Univ of Wales (Lamp) BA86 Nottm Univ BTh89. Linc Th Coll 86. **d** 89 **p** 90. C Dwygyfylchi *Ban* 89-93; V Llangrannog w Llandysiliogogo w Penbryn *St D* 93-02; RD Glyn Aeron 99-02; P-in-c Llangystennin *St As* 02-04; R from 04. *The Rectory, Glyn y Marl Road, Llandudno Junction LL31 9NS* Tel (01492) 583579

HARVEY, John Mark. b 64. QUB BEd87 TCD BTh93. CITC 90. **d** 93 **p** 94. C Portadown St Columba *Arm* 93-96; I Monaghan w Tydavnet and Kilmore *Clogh* 96-01; Dioc Communications Officer 97-00; Miss Officer (Ireland) CMS 01-05; I Ballybeen *D & D* from 05. *1 Grahamsbridge Road, Dundonald, Belfast BT16 0DB* Tel (028) 9048 9297
E-mail dco@clogher.anglican.org

HARVEY, Lt Col John William Arthur. b 43. Guildf Dioc Min Course 98. **d** 01 **p** 02. OLM Aldershot St Aug *Guildf* from 01. *59 Knoll Road, Fleet GU51 4PT* Tel (01252) 622793
E-mail john@harvey59.freeserve.co.uk

HARVEY, Lance Sydney Crockford. b 25. Ridley Hall Cam 67. **d** 69 **p** 70. C Mortlake w E Sheen *S'wark* 69-74; P-in-c Woolwich St Thos 75-86; V Lee Gd Shep w St Pet 86-92; RD E Lewisham 87-91; rtd 92; Perm to Offic *Truro* from 92. *17 Lariggan Road, Penzance TR18 4NJ*

HARVEY, Margaret Claire. b 41. Univ of Wales (Abth) BA62 DipEd63 Lon Univ BD68. Dalton Ho Bris 66. **dss** 68 **d** 80 **p** 97. Flint *St As* 68-74; Lect Trin Coll Bris 74-80; Connah's Quay *St As* 79-80; C 80-86; Bp's Adv for Continuing Clerical Educn 86-98; Hon C Corwen and Llangar 86-87; Dn-in-c Bryneglwys 87-97; P-in-c 97-02; rtd 02. *Coleg y Groes, The College, Corwen LL21 0AU* Tel (01490) 412169 E-mail colegygroes@talk21.com

HARVEY, Mark. *See* HARVEY, John Mark

HARVEY, Maurice. b 31. CITC 70. **d** 70 **p** 71. C Lisburn St Paul *Conn* 70-72; C Ballymacarrett St Patr *D & D* 72-77; I Ballyphilip w Ardquin 77-79; I Ardmore w Craigavon 79-87; I Killyman *Arm* 87-94; Bp's C Acton and Drumbanagher 94-97; rtd 97. *Flat 1, 16 Cathedral Close, Armagh BT61 7EE* Tel (028) 3752 3971

HARVEY, Murray Alexander. b 63. Univ of Qld BA85 Deakin Univ Australia DHSc03 MAPsS87. St Fran Coll Brisbane BTh91. **d** 91 **p** 92. Australia 91-02; C Milton 92-93; C Stafford 94-95; P-in-c Tamborine Mt St Geo 95-02; V Glen Gp *Linc* from 02. *The Vicarage, 19 Spalding Road, Pinchbeck, Spalding PE11 3UD* Tel and fax (01775) 725698
E-mail murray.harvey@spaldingchurches.org

HARVEY, Canon Norman Roy. b 43. Nottm Univ DipAE86. Wycliffe Hall Ox 66. **d** 69 **p** 70. C Clay Cross *Derby* 69-72; C Dronfield 72-76; TV 76-79; P-in-c Rowsley 79-89; Dioc Youth Officer 79-83; Dioc Adv in Adult and Youth Educn 83-89; TR Eckington w Handley and Ridgeway 89-01; R Eckington and Ridgeway from 01; RD Bolsover and Staveley 00-05; Hon Can Derby Cathl from 00. *The Rectory, 17 Church Street, Eckington, Sheffield S21 4BG* Tel and fax (01246) 432196
E-mail norman.harvey2@btopenworld.com

HARVEY, Oliver Paul. b 33. Magd Coll Ox BA55 MA59. Cuddesdon Coll 57. **d** 59 **p** 60. C S Norwood St Mark *Cant* 59-61; C Hythe 61-64; Zambia 64-71; Chapl Cant Coll of Tech 71-77; Hon C Cant St Martin and St Paul *Cant* 73-77; Chapl K Sch Roch 77-88; C Roch 88-90; V Gillingham St Mary 90-00; RD Gillingham 98-00; rtd 00; Perm to Offic *Roch* 00-03. *11 Henley Road, Taunton TA1 5BN* Tel (01823) 272825

HARVEY, Miss Pamela Betty. b 33. Dalton Ho Bris IDC59 CertRK59. **dss** 68 **d** 87 **p** 95. Nottingham St Ann *S'well* 68-72; Bestwood St Matt 72-76; CPAS Staff 76-93; Dir Consultants Division CPAS 93-99; rtd 99; Hon C Glenfield *Leic* 95-04; Perm to Offic from 04. *72 Chestnut Road, Glenfield, Leicester LE3 8DB* Tel 0116-232 2959
E-mail pam.harvey@ukgateway.net

HARVEY, Mrs Patricia Ann. b 45. Qu Coll Birm. **dss** 82 **d** 87 **p** 94. Gospel Lane St Mich *Birm* 82-85; Exhall *Cov* 85-89; C 87-89; TD Droitwich Spa *Worc* 89-94; TV 94-97; P-in-c Finstall 97-00; V 00-02; rtd 02; Perm to Offic *Heref* from 02 and *Worc* from 04. *15 Mount Orchard, Tenbury Wells WR15 8DW* Tel (01584) 819444 E-mail patricia.harvey3@virgin.net

HARVEY, Canon Patrick Arnold. b 58. TCD BA MA. CITC 82. **d** 85 **p** 86. C Bandon Union *C, C & R* 85-88; Dean's V Limerick St Mich *L & K* 88-91; Dioc Info Officer 88-91; I Abbeyleix w Ballyroan etc *C & O* from 91; Can Ossory Cathl from 97. *The Rectory, Abbeyleix, Portlaoise, Co Laois, Irish Republic* Tel and fax (00353) (502) 31243 E-mail abbeyleix@leighlin.anglican.org

HARVEY, Paul. *See* HARVEY, Oliver Paul

HARVEY, Robert Martin. b 30. S'wark Ord Course 69. **d** 70 **p** 71. C Sutton New Town St Barn *S'wark* 70-75; C Leatherhead *Guildf* 76-78; V Wadworth w Loversall *Sheff* 78-96; RD W Doncaster 94-97; rtd 96; Perm to Offic *Sheff* from 96. *44 Castlegate, Tickhill, Doncaster DN11 9QU* Tel (01302) 746532

HARVEY, Robin Grant. b 43. Clare Coll Cam BA64 MA68 Univ of NSW PhD74. Linc Th Coll 85. **d** 87 **p** 88. C Keynsham *B & W* 87-91; R E w W Harptree and Hinton Blewett 91-97; Chapl Surrey Univ *Guildf* 98-02; P-in-c Cuddington from 02. *St Mary's Vicarage, St Mary's Road, Worcester Park KT4 7JL* Tel (020) 8337 5025 *or* 8337 4026 Fax 8337 6680 E-mail rgharvey@fish.co.uk

HARVEY, Roland. b 68. St Jo Coll Nottm 99. **d** 01 **p** 02. C Skelmersdale St Paul *Liv* 01-05; P-in-c Pemberton St Fran Kitt Green from 05. *The Vicarage, 42 Sherborne Road, Orrell, Wigan WN5 0JA* Tel (01942) 213227 Mobile 07817-901455 E-mail revdrol@fish.co.uk

HARVEY, Simon John. b 63. Trin Coll Bris BA00. **d** 00 **p** 01. C Walsall St Paul *Lich* 00-03; TV Oadby *Leic* from 03. *St Paul's House, Hamble Road, Oadby, Leicester LE2 4NX* Tel 0116-271 0519 E-mail simon@sjharvey.org.uk

HARVEY, Steven Charles. b 58. Reading Univ BA79 Ox Univ BA83 MA88 FRSA03. Ripon Coll Cuddesdon 81. **d** 84 **p** 85. C Oldham *Man* 84-87; Chapl and Hd RS St Pet Sch York 87-96; Sen Dep Hd Kingswood Sch Bath 96-03; Sen Provost Woodard Corp from 03; Perm to Offic *Lich* from 03. *The Provost's Lodging, High Street, Abbots Bromley, Rugeley WS15 3BW* Tel (01283) 840670 *or* 840120 E-mail scharvey@surfaid.org

HARVEY, Trevor John. b 43. Sheff Univ BA64 K Coll Lon MA94. Coll of Resurr Mirfield 64. **d** 66 **p** 67. C Kingswinford St Mary *Lich* 66-72; V Upper Gornal 72-77; V Meir 77-86; Chapl St Geo Sch Windsor 86-99; Min Can Windsor 86-99; Chapl Ellesmere Coll 99-03; rtd 03; C Meir Heath *Lich* 03-04; C Meir Heath and Normacot from 04. *1 Rolt Close, Stone ST15 8YX* Tel (01785) 813266 E-mail revdtjharvey@yahoo.co.uk

HARVEY, Mrs Verity Margaret. b 48. Bris Univ BA69 Saltley Tr Coll Birm DipEd70. St Alb and Ox Min Course 99. **d** 02 **p** 03. NSM Radlett *St Alb* 02-05; NSM Aldenham, Radlett and Shenley from 05. *28 Field Road, Watford WD19 4DR* Tel (01923) 492863

HARVEY-NEILL, Nicola Lisa Jane. b 69. QUB BD91 TCD MPhil95. CITC BTh94. **d** 95 **p** 96. Dioc C *T, K & A* 95-96; C Galway w Kilcummin 96-97; Dioc Youth Adv (Limerick) *L & K* 97-01; Chapl Villier's Sch Limerick 98-01; Chapl Limerick Univ 98-01; Perm to Offic from 01. *Modreeny Rectory, Cloughjordan, Co Tipperary, Irish Republic* Tel and fax (00353) (505) 42183 Mobile 87-250 0570 E-mail nickihn@eircom.net *or* smneill@iol.ie

HARVIE, Robert. b 53. **d** 04 **p** 05. OLM Godalming *Guildf* from 04. *7 Ockford Ridge, Godalming GU7 2NP* Tel (01483) 415931 E-mail robert.harvie@btinternet.com

HARWOOD, Frederick Ronald. b 21. Wells Th Coll 61. **d** 63 **p** 64. C Devonport St Mark Ford *Ex* 63-66; V Hessenford *Truro* 66-71; V Hayle 71-87; rtd 87; Hon C Madron *Truro* 88-92; Prec Gib Cathl and Port Chapl *Eur* 92-95; Perm to Offic *Truro* from 95. *Ferncliffe, 5 Harbour View, Hayle TR27 4LB* Tel (01736) 753690

HARWOOD (formerly SOUTH), Mrs Gillian. b 51. NEOC 87. **d** 90 **p** 94. C Rothbury *Newc* 90-93; C Morpeth 93-97; V Amble from 97. *The Vicarage, Straffen Court, Amble, Morpeth NE65 0HA* Tel (01665) 710273 E-mail gillysouth@btopenworld.com

HARWOOD, Canon John Rossiter. b 26. Selw Coll Cam BA51 MA55. Wycliffe Hall Ox 51. **d** 53 **p** 54. C Handsworth St Mary *Birm* 53-55; Tutor Trin Coll Umuahia Nigeria 57-64; Warden Minl Tr Cen Freetown Sierra Leone and Bp's Dom Chapl 64-67; Home Educn Sec CMS 67-75; V Cheltenham Ch Ch *Glouc* 75-91; RD Cheltenham 84-89; Hon Can Glouc Cathl 85-91; rtd 91; Perm to Offic *Ex* 91-99; *Chich* and *Portsm from 00. 8 Kingsey Avenue, Emsworth PO10 7HP* Tel (01243) 372215

HARWOOD, Peter James. b 64. Birm Univ MB88 ChB88. Wycliffe Hall Ox BA93. **d** 94 **p** 95. C Cov H Trin *Cov* 94-97; C Kensington St Barn *Lon* 97-02; V Woking Ch Ch *Guildf* from 02. *Christ Church Vicarage, 10 Russetts Close, Woking GU21 4BH* Tel (01483) 762100 E-mail peter@christchurchwoking.org

HASELHURST (née STERLING), Mrs Anne. b 51. Macalester Coll (USA) BA73. EAMTC 89. **d** 92 **p** 94. Par Dn Bury St Edmunds St Jo *St E* 92-94; C 94-95; V Fordham St Pet *Ely* from 95; P-in-c Kennett from 95. *The Vicarage, 24 Mildenhall Road, Fordham, Ely CB7 5NR* Tel (01638) 720266 E-mail annehaselhurst@compuserve.com

HASELOCK, Canon Jeremy Matthew. b 51. York Univ BA73 BPhil74. St Steph Ho Ox BA82 MA86. **d** 83 **p** 84. C Pimlico St Gabr *Lon* 83-86; C Paddington St Jas 86-88; Bp's Dom Chapl *Chich* 88-91; P-in-c Boxgrove 91-94; V 94-98; Dioc Adv on Liturgy 91-98; Can and Preb Chich Cathl 94-98; Can Res and Prec Nor Cathl *Nor* from 98. *34 The Close, Norwich NR1 4DZ* Tel (01603) 619169 Fax 766032

HASKETT, Mrs Fiona Ann. b 55. SEITE 01. **d** 04 **p** 05. NSM Leigh *Roch* from 04. *11 Oaklands Way, Hildenborough, Tonbridge TN11 9DA* Tel (01732) 832467 E-mail fiona.haskett@btopenworld.com

HASKEY, Alyn Rex. b 51. EMMTC 02. **d** 04 **p** 05. NSM Sneinton St Chris w St Phil *S'well* from 04; NSM Nottingham St Sav from 04; NSM Nottingham St Nic from 04. *Flat 1, 6 Vickers Street, Nottingham NG3 4LD* Tel 0115-960 5489 E-mail alynhaskey@freedomministries.freeserve.co.uk

HASKINS, Canon Thomas. b 41. TCD BA72. CITC 71. **d** 73 **p** 74. C Larne and Inver *Conn* 73-78; C Antrim All SS 78-83; I Belfast St Mark 83-90; I Dublin Clontarf *D & G* 90-02; I Dublin St Ann and St Steph from 02; Can Ch Ch Cathl Dublin from 99. *St Ann's Vicarage, 88 Mount Anville Wood, Dublin 14, Irish Republic* Tel (00353) (1) 288 0663

HASLAM, Andrew James. b 57. Univ Coll Dur BSc78 Coll of Ripon & York St Jo PGCE79. Lambeth STh84 Trin Coll Bris 80. **d** 83 **p** 84. C Leyland St Andr *Blackb* 83-86; C Hartford *Ches* 86-88; V Grimsargh *Blackb* 88-98; V St Helens St Mark *Liv* from 98. *St Mark's Vicarage, 160 North Road, St Helens WA10 2TZ* Tel (01744) 23806 E-mail andrewhaslam@st-h.freeserve.co.uk

HASLAM, Canon Frank. b 26. Bris Univ BA50. Tyndale Hall Bris 49. **d** 51 **p** 52. C Halliwell St Paul *Man* 51-55; Uganda 56-60; C Wednesfield Heath *Lich* 60-61; V Wolverhampton St Matt 61-65; V Blackpool Ch Ch *Blackb* 65-70; V Macclesfield St Mich *Ches* 71-80; Dir of Resources 80-91; Hon Can Ches Cathl 81-91; rtd 91; Perm to Offic *Ches* from 91; P-in-c Bistre *St As* 99-00. *Brackendale, Chester Road, Buckley CH7 3AH* Tel (01244) 549291

HASLAM, James Robert. b 31. Open Univ BA74. Bps' Coll Cheshunt 55. **d** 57 **p** 58. C Penwortham St Mary *Blackb* 57-63; V Cockerham 63-74; V Cockerham w Winmarleigh 74-76; V Gt Harwood St Bart 76-88; V Fairhaven 88-95; rtd 95; Perm to Offic *Blackb* from 95. *5 Willow Trees Drive, Blackburn BB1 8LB* Tel (01254) 697092

HASLAM, Mrs Jane. b 70. Leeds Poly BA92. Trin Coll Bris BA97. **d** 97 **p** 98. C Minehead *B & W* 97-00; Perm to Offic *Newc* 00-03; C Balkwell 03-04; P-in-c Purton *Bris* from 04. *The Vicarage, 2 Kingsacre, Hyde Lane, Purton, Swindon SN5 4DU* Tel (01793) 770210 E-mail jane.haslam@virgin.net

HASLAM, John Gordon. b 32. Birm Univ LLB53. Qu Coll Birm 75. **d** 77 **p** 77. Hon C Bartley Green *Birm* 77-79; Hon C Moseley St Mary 79-96; Chapl to The Queen 89-02; Perm to Offic *Heref* from 97. *16 Mill Street, Ludlow SY8 1BE* Tel (01584) 876663 Fax as telephone

HASLAM, Michael Henry. b 72. Buckingham Univ BA93. Trin Coll Bris BA94 MA94. **d** 97 **p** 98. C Minehead *B & W* 97-00; Chapl Newc Univ *Newc* 00-04; Dioc Ecum Officer *Bris* from 04; C Purton from 04. *The Vicarage, 2 Kingsacre, Hyde Lane, Purton, Swindon SN5 4DU* Tel (01793) 770210 Mobile 07817-703929 E-mail mike.haslam@bristoldiocese.org

HASLAM, Robert John Alexander. b 34. CCC Cam BA58. Coll of Resurr Mirfield 58. **d** 60 **p** 61. C Rawmarsh w Parkgate *Sheff* 60-66; Perm to Offic *Edin* 66-73; Perm to Offic *Carl* 73-77; P-in-c Peebles *Edin* 77-81; V Darnall *Sheff* 81-85; Hon C Bermondsey St Hugh CD *S'wark* 86-88; R Clydebank *Glas* 88-98; Chapl Mlaga *Eur* 98-03. *Plaza de las Descalzas 2l3C, 29200 Mlaga, Spain* Tel and fax (0034) (95) 221 9396

HASLAM-JONES, Christopher John. b 28. ALCD53. **d** 53 **p** 54. C Walthamstow St Jo *Chelmsf* 53-57; C High Wycombe All SS *Ox* 57-62; V Parkfield in Middleton *Man* 62-68; V Radcliffe St Andr 68-86; R Colchester Ch Ch w St Mary V *Chelmsf* 86-93; rtd 93; Perm to Offic *Sarum* from 93. *Ramla, 4A Belle Vue Road, Poole BH14 8TW* Tel and fax (01202) 717674 E-mail c.jhaslamjones@tiscali.co.uk

HASLER, John Joseph (Joe). b 45. Univ of Wales (Cardiff) MPhil99. Qu Coll Birm 89. **d** 90 **p** 91. C Horfield H Trin *Bris* 90-93; V Bris St Andr Hartcliffe 93-01; V Bris Lockleaze St Mary Magd w St Fran from 01; AD City from 03. *The Vicarage, Copley Gardens, Bristol BS7 9YE* Tel 0117-951 2516

HASSALL, William Edwin. b 41. St Jo Coll Nottm 75. **d** 77 **p** 78. C Wellington w Eyton *Lich* 77-80; C Farewell 80-82; V 82-93; C Gentleshaw 80-82; V 82-93; P-in-c Cheddleton 93-94; Perm to Offic *Lich* from 97; Chapl Asst Birm Heartlands and Solihull NHS Trust 98-01; Chapl Team Ldr from 01. *Birmingham Heartlands Hospital, Bordesley Green East, Birmingham B9 5SS* Tel 0121-424 1369 *or* (01543) 275087

HASSELL, David Edwin. b 38. WMMTC 87. **d** 90 **p** 91. NSM Worc SE *Worc* 90-93; C Abberton, Naunton Beauchamp and Bishampton etc 93-94; P-in-c 94; R Abberton, The Flyfords, Naunton Beauchamp etc 94-04; rtd 04; Perm to Offic *Worc* from 04. *14 Napleton Lane, Kempsey, Worcester. WR5 3PT* Tel (01905) 828096

HASSELL, John Charles. b 44. FCA. Sarum & Wells Th Coll 81. **d** 83 **p** 84. C Tottenham St Paul *Lon* 83-86; C Fingringhoe w E Donyland *Chelmsf* 86-90; V Moulsham St Jo 90-00; TR Grays

Thurrock from 00; RD Thurrock 01-03. *The Rectory, 10 High View Avenue, Grays RM17 6RU* Tel (01375) 377379 E-mail john@hassell2000.fsnet.co.uk

HASTE, James Victor William. b 36. St Mich Th Coll Crafers 64. **d** 68 **p** 70. C Ormond Australia 68-69; C Roehampton H Trin *S'wark* 70-72; P-in-c Boroko Papua New Guinea 72-76; Sec ABM Vic Australia 76-81; I Armadale w Hawksburn 81-86; I Vermont S 86-89; Inter-Ch Trade and Ind Chapl 89-99; rtd 01; Lic to Offic The Murray 99-05; Perm to Offic Melbourne from 05. *17 Park View Drive, Aspendale, Vic, Australia 3195* Tel (0061) (3) 9588 2805 Mobile 407-044086 E-mail baha@picknowl.com.au

HASTED, Marcus Arthur David. b 35. Qu Coll Birm 63. **d** 66 **p** 67. C Woodchurch *Ches* 66-69; C W Kirby St Bridget 69-72; V Farndon 72-76; V Farndon and Coddington 76-79; Perm to Offic 98-00 and from 02; NSM Liscard St Mary w St Columba 00-02. *62 South Road, West Kirby, Wirral CH48 3HQ* Tel 0151-625 0428

HASTEY, Erle. b 44. St Mich Coll Llan 66. **d** 68 **p** 69. C Pontefract St Giles *Wakef* 68-71; C Almondbury 71-74; V Purlwell 74-79; P-in-c Batley Carr 76-79; V Ynyshir *Llan* 79-86; V Tylorstown w Ynyshir 86-87; V Tonyrefail w Gilfach Goch 87-97; P-in-c Llandyfodwg 87-97; V Tonyrefail w Gilfach Goch and Llandyfodwg 97-99; V Pyle w Kenfig 99-04; rtd 04. *2 Cambray Close, Porthcawl CF36 3PY* Tel (01656) 783935

HASTIE-SMITH, Timothy Maybury. b 62. Magd Coll Cam MA84. Wycliffe Hall Ox 85. **d** 88 **p** 89. C Ox St Ebbe w H Trin and St Pet *Ox* 88-91; Chapl Stowe Sch 91-98; Hd Master Dean Close Sch Cheltenham from 98; Perm to Offic *Glouc* from 99. *Dean Close House, Landsdown Road, Cheltenham GL51 6QD* Tel (01242) 512537 *or* 522640 Fax 258003

HASTINGS, David Kerr. b 40. St Luke's Coll Ex CertEd63. Ox NSM Course 84. **d** 87 **p** 88. Hd Master St Edburg's Sch Bicester 82-89; Asst Chapl HM Pris Grendon and Spring Hill 87-89; NSM Bicester w Bucknell, Caversfield and Launton *Ox* 87-89; Chapl HM Pris Reading 90-92; P-in-c Gt Wishford *Sarum* 92; P-in-c S Newton 92; P-in-c Stapleford w Berwick St James 92; P-in-c Winterbourne Stoke 92; R Lower Wylye and Till Valley 92-95; Chapl HM Pris Ex 96-01; Perm to Offic *Ex* from 01; rtd 01. *26 Hoopern Street, Exeter EX4 4LY* Tel (01392) 498233

HASTINGS, Canon Gary Lea. b 56. New Univ of Ulster BA82 MA87 TCD BTh93. CITC 90. **d** 93 **p** 94. C Galway w Kilcummin *T, K & A* 93-95; Dom Chapl to Bp Tuam from 94; I Aughaval w Achill, Knappagh, Dugort etc from 95; Can Tuam Cathl from 00. *The Rectory, Newport Road, Westport, Co Mayo, Irish Republic* Tel (00353) (98) 25127 E-mail gary@anu.ie

HASTROP, Paul. b 39. Wells Th Coll 70. **d** 72 **p** 73. C Parkstone St Osmund *Sarum* 72-76; C Penzance St Mary w St Paul *Truro* 76-79; V St Blazey 79-87; TV Bournemouth St Pet w St Swithun, H Trin etc *Win* 87-94; TV Thornaby on Tees *York* 94-96; P-in-c Portsea St Sav *Portsm* 96-03; rtd 03; Hon C Paignton St Jo *Ex* from 05. *St Andrew's House, 73 Dartmouth Road, Paignton TQ4 5AF*

HASTWELL, James Sydney. b 37. Roch Th Coll 67. **d** 69 **p** 70. C Croydon St Aug *Cant* 69-73; C Hurstpierpoint *Chich* 73-75; P-in-c Twineham 76; P-in-c Sayers Common 76; P-in-c Albourne 76; R Albourne w Sayers Common and Twineham 76-88; V Forest Row 88-94; rtd 97; Perm to Offic *Chich* from 97. *54 Ridgewood Gardens, Bexhill-on-Sea TN40 1TS*

HATCH, Canon George Andrew. b 29. Leeds Univ BA. Coll of Resurr Mirfield 51. **d** 53 **p** 54. C S Farnborough *Guildf* 53-55; Windward Is 55-63; Barbados from 63; R St Mary Barbados 63-73; Assoc Dir Chr Action Development in Caribbean 73-83; R St Jas Barbados 83-94; rtd 94. *St James, Barbados* Tel (001809) 432 0700

HATCH, Richard Francis. b 36. Qu Coll Cam BA60 MA64. Cuddesdon Coll 60. **d** 62 **p** 63. C Leigh St Mary *Man* 62-66; PC Peel Green 66-71; V Barton w Peel Green 71-75; Dioc Broadcasting Officer 73-85; R Birch St Jas and Fallowfield 75-78; Lic Preacher from 78; rtd 01. *24 Denison Road, Manchester M14 5SQ* Tel 0161-225 0799

HATCHETT, Michael John. b 49. Enfield Coll BSc72 K Coll Lon BD77 AKC77. Linc Th Coll 77. **d** 78 **p** 79. C Halstead St Andr *Chelmsf* 78-79; C Halstead St Andr w H Trin and Greenstead Green 79-81; C Greenstead 81-85; V Gt Totham 85-01; R Gt Totham and Lt Totham w Goldhanger from 01; RD Witham 96-01. *The Vicarage, 1 Hall Road, Great Totham, Maldon CM9 8NN* Tel and fax (01621) 893150 E-mail mikehatchett2004@yahoo.co.uk

HATCHETT, Mrs Ruth Merrick. b 54. K Coll Lon BD77 AKC77 Open Univ BA92. EAMTC 03. **d** 05. NSM Tolleshunt Knights w Tiptree and Gt Braxted *Chelmsf* from 05. *The Vicarage, 1 Hall Road, Great Totham, Maldon CM9 8NN* Tel and fax (01621) 893150 E-mail rmhatchett@yahoo.com

HATCHLEY, Canon Walter John. b 24. Lon Univ BA65. Coll of Resurr Mirfield 64. **d** 66 **p** 67. C Monkseaton St Pet *Newc* 66-69; C Gosforth All SS 69-72; C Cullercoats St Geo 72; TV 72-78; V Newc St Fran 78-93; RD Newc E 83-92; Hon Can Newc Cathl 90-93; rtd 93; Perm to Offic *Newc* from 93. *4 Woodthorne Road, Jesmond, Newcastle upon Tyne NE2 3PB*

HATCHMAN, Ms Elizabeth Mary. b 63. St Andr Univ MA85. Selly Oak Coll Qu Coll Birm BD92. **d** 93 **p** 94. C Aston SS Pet and Paul *Birm* 93-96; C Rowley Regis 96-00; Chapl St Geo Post 16 Cen 00-04; Perm to Offic from 05. *21 Westfield Road, Birmingham B14 7SX* Tel 0121-236 9177 Fax 236 7021

HATCHMAN, Hugh Alleyne. b 28. Qu Coll Cam BA52 MA56. Ridley Hall Cam 52. **d** 54 **p** 55. C E Twickenham St Steph *Lon* 54-56; C Morden *S'wark* 56-59; E Midl Area Sec CPAS 59-63; V New Catton St Luke *Nor* 63-79; Chapl Bexley Hosp Kent 79-93; rtd 93. *Braemar, North Lyminge, Lyminge, Folkestone CT18 8EF* Tel (01303) 862369

HATFIELD, Rebecca Alison. b 76. St Andr Univ MTheol99. Cranmer Hall Dur 02. **d** 04 **p** 05. C Haughton le Skerne *Dur* from 04. *18 Corbridge Crescent, Darlington DL1 2QH* Tel (01325) 366697 Mobile 07930-631936

HATHAWAY, Canon David Alfred Gerald. b 48. St Mich Coll Llan. **d** 72 **p** 73. C Newport St Julian *Mon* 72-74; P-in-c Oakham w Hambleton and Egleton *Pet* 74-77; V Newport St Matt *Mon* 77-83; CF (TA) from 78; V Abertillery *Mon* 83-88; V Rumney from 88; Hon Can St Woolos Cathl 91-05; Can from 05. *The Vicarage, 702 Newport Road, Rumney, Cardiff CF3 4DF* Tel (029) 2079 7882

HATHAWAY, John Albert. b 24. Sarum Th Coll 59. **d** 60 **p** 61. C Fleet *Guildf* 60-64; C Cowley St Jas *Ox* 64-66; V Holmwood *Guildf* 66-71; V Westborough 71-74; V Newmarket All SS *St E* 74-82; V Acton w Gt Waldingfield 82-85; R W Downland *Sarum* 85-90; rtd 90; Perm to Offic *Sarum* from 94. *12 St Edwards Court, Shaftesbury SP7 8LZ* Tel (01747) 851950

HATHAWAY, Martin Charles. b 48. St Jo Coll Nottm 93. **d** 95 **p** 96. C Weddington and Caldecote *Cov* 95-99; V Potters Green 99-04; C The Heyfords w Rousham and Somerton *Ox* 04-05; C Fritwell w Souldern and Ardley w Fewcott 04-05; Lic to Offic Bicester and Islip Deanery from 05. *8 Soden Road, Upper Heyford, Bicester OX25 5LR* Tel (01869) 233083 E-mail martin_hathaway@lineone.net

HATHAWAY, Vivienne Ann. b 57. Bucks Chilterns Univ Coll BSc96. Westcott Ho Cam 00. **d** 02 **p** 03. C Bp's Hatfield *St Alb* from 02. *Church Cottage, 2 Church Street, Hatfield AL9 5AP* Tel (01707) 261949 E-mail vivienne@vhathaway.freeserve.co.uk

HATHERLEY, Peter Graham. b 46. Univ of Wales (Cardiff) BSc67 PhD70. St Mich Coll Llan 70. **d** 72 **p** 73. C Ystrad Mynach *Llan* 72-75; Hon C Tonyrefail 75-88; Perm to Offic from 88. *Treetops, The Derwen, Bridgend CF35 6HD* Tel (01656) 662196

HATHERLEY, Victor Charles. b 17. St Aug Coll Cant 63. **d** 64 **p** 64. C Crewkerne *B & W* 64-68; R E Harptree 68-73; R E w W Harptree 73-76; R E w W Harptree and Hinton Blewett 76-82; rtd 82; Perm to Offic *B & W* 83-91 and *Sarum* from 91. *10 Fairview Road, Broadstone BH18 9AX* Tel (01202) 692855

HATHORNE (née MARSH), Mrs Carol Ann. b 44. W Midl Coll of Educn BA83. WMMTC 88. **d** 91 **p** 94. Par Dn Wednesbury St Paul Wood Green *Lich* 91-93; NSM Pensnett *Worc* 93-97; TV Cannock *Lich* 97-01; NSM Willenhall H Trin from 05. *The Vicarage, 129 Essington Road, Willenhall WV12 5DT* Tel (01922) 409460

HATHORNE, Mark Stephen. b 51. Boston Univ MDiv76. **d** 00 **p** 00. C Willenhall H Trin *Lich* 00-01; TV from 01. *The Vicarage, 129 Essington Road, Willenhall WV12 5DT* Tel (01922) 409460 E-mail m.s.hathorne@virgin.net

HATHWAY, Ross Arthur. b 56. DATh87. Moore Th Coll Sydney BTh86. **d** 86 **p** 87. C Tamworth St Pet Australia 87-88; C Corby St Columba *Pet* 89-92; R Trull w Angersleigh *B & W* 92-02; R Kellyville St Steph Australia from 03. *12 Falkirk Court, Kellyville, NSW, Australia 2155*

HATREY, David Nigel. b 57. SS Mark & Jo Coll Plymouth CertEd79 Cert Science 87 BEd90 Ex Univ MA01. SW Minl Tr Course 90. **d** 93 **p** 94. NSM S Hill w Callington *Truro* 93-01; Hon C Street w Walton *B & W* from 01. *Pilgrims Way, Chilton Polden Hill, Edington, Bridgwater TA7 9AL* Tel (01278) 723616 E-mail hatreys@micehouse.fsnet.co.uk

HATTAN, Jeffrey William Rowland. b 49. Cranmer Hall Dur 83. **d** 85 **p** 86. C Eston w Normanby *York* 85-89; TV 89-95; V Hunmanby w Muston from 95. *The Vicarage, 6 Northgate, Hunmanby, Filey YO14 0NT* Tel (01723) 890294 E-mail jeff@all-saints.freeserve.co.uk

HATTER, Canon David George. b 21. Lich Th Coll. **d** 57 **p** 58. C Carrington *S'well* 57-61; V Clipstone 61-67; V Mansfield St Mark 67-81; V Sutton w Carlton and Normanton upon Trent etc 81-86; P-in-c Caunton 84-86; Hon Can S'well Minster 84-86; RD Tuxford and Norwell 84-86; rtd 86; Perm to Offic *S'well* 86-00 and from 03. *1 North End, Farndon, Newark NG24 3SX* Tel (01636) 76960

HATTON, Jane Elizabeth. b 53. St Alb and Ox Min Course CBTS98. **d** 98 **p** 99. NSM Stevenage St Pet Broadwater *St Alb* 98-04; Asst Chapl E and N Herts NHS Trust from 04. *2 Dancote, Park Lane, Knebworth SG3 6PB* Tel (01438) 811039 E-mail janehatton@dial.pipex.com

HATTON, Jeffrey Charles. b 49. K Coll Lon BD70 Bris Univ MA72. Westcott Ho Cam 73 Episc Th Sch Cam Mass 74. **d** 74 **p** 75. C Nor St Pet Mancroft *Nor* 74-78; C Earlham St Anne 78-79; Relig Broadcasting Asst IBA 79-82; Hon C Kensington St Barn *Lon* 79-84; Hon C Fulham All SS 85-89; R Win All SS w Chilcomb and Chesil *Win* 89-94; Dioc Communications Officer 89-94; P-in-c Salisbury St Thos and St Edm *Sarum* 94-99; R 99-05; rtd 05. *4 Longhill Drive, Salisbury SP2 8TD* E-mail charlesh@cix.co.uk

HATTON, Michael Samuel. b 44. St Jo Coll Dur BA72 DipTh74. **d** 74 **p** 75. C Dudley St Jas *Worc* 74-75; C N Lynn w St Marg and St Nic *Nor* 75-77; C Walsall Wood *Lich* 78-79; Min Shelfield St Mark CD 79-89; V Middleton St Cross *Ripon* 89-97; V Ingol *Blackb* from 97. *St Margaret's Vicarage, 1A St Margaret's Close, Ingol, Preston PR2 3ZU* Tel (01772) 727208 E-mail spike.ingol@virgin.net

HATTON, Trevor. b 55. Oak Hill Th Coll BA86. **d** 86 **p** 87. C Chilwell *S'well* 86-90; R Trowell 90-95; Chapl Nottm Trent Univ 95-99; P-in-c Nottingham St Nic 99-02; R from 02. *37 Lyme Park, West Bridgford, Nottingham NG2 7TR* Tel 0115-982 0407 E-mail trevor@stnics.org

HATWELL, Timothy Rex. b 53. Oak Hill Th Coll BA85. **d** 85 **p** 86. C Tonbridge St Steph *Roch* 85-90; V Cudham and Downe from 90. *The Vicarage, Cudham Lane South, Cudham, Sevenoaks TN14 7QA* Tel (01959) 572445 Mobile 07799-601546 Fax 08701-256898 E-mail tim.hatwell@pcd.org.uk

HAUGHAN, John Francis (Frank). b 28. Tyndale Hall Bris 56. **d** 60 **p** 61. C Tonbridge St Steph *Roch* 60-63; C Cheltenham St Mark *Glouc* 63-67; V Tewkesbury H Trin 67-92; rtd 92; Perm to Offic *Glouc* from 92 and *Worc* from 04. *1 Farmers Lane, Childswickham, Broadway WR12 7HN* Tel (01386) 852268

HAUGHTON, Peter Steele. b 57. K Coll Lon BD84 MA90 Fitzw Coll Cam DipTh85. Westcott Ho Cam 84. **d** 86 **p** 87. C Cheam Common St Phil *S'wark* 86-90; Chapl Lon Univ Medical Schs 90-94; Educn Adv Lon Univ Medical Schs 94-95; P-in-c Kingston Vale St Jo 95-03; Adv in Ethics and Law K Coll Lon from 03. *95 Bullar Road, Southampton SO18 1GT* Tel 07815-803920 (mobile) E-mail peter.haughton@btinternet.com

HAVARD, Alan Ernest. b 27. Qu Coll Birm 79. **d** 81 **p** 82. NSM Rugby St Matt *Cov* 81-84; C Portishead *B & W* 84-86; V Mickleover All SS *Derby* 86-96; rtd 96; Perm to Offic *Derby* from 96. *7 Headingley Court, Littleover, Derby DE3 6XS*

HAVARD, David William. b 56. Man Univ BA84. Qu Coll Birm 84. **d** 85. C Man Clayton St Cross w St Paul *Man* 85-88; Canada 88-02; Perm to Offic *Sheff* from 03. *33 Hallcar Street, Sheffield S4 7JY* Tel 0114-272 9695 E-mail deacondave@onetel.com

HAVELL, Edward Michael. b 38. Dur Univ BA65. Ridley Hall Cam 66. **d** 68 **p** 69. C Ecclesall *Sheff* 68-71; C Roch St Justus *Roch* 71-74; P-in-c Holbeach Hurn *Linc* 74-75; C Hollington St Jo *Chich* 75-85; TV Rye 85-92; C E Dereham and Scarning *Nor* 92; rtd 93; Perm to Offic *Chich* from 99. *4 Gammons Way, Sedlescombe, Battle TN33 0RQ* Tel (01424) 870864

HAVENS, Mrs Anita Sue. b 44. Mass Univ BSEd67 Clark Univ (USA) MA72 Hughes Hall Cam BA79. Cranmer Hall Dur MA83. **dss** 84 **d** 87 **p** 94. Gateshead Hosps 84-87; Par Dn Cen Telford *Lich* 87-90; Ind Chapl 87-90; Ind Chapl *Liv* 90-96; TV Man Whitworth *Man* 96-99; Chapl Man Univ 96-99; R Birch St Agnes w Longsight St Jo w St Cypr 99-01; rtd 01; Perm to Offic *Carl* from 03. *Stone Cottage, Kirkby Thore, Penrith CA10 1UE* Tel (01768) 362682 E-mail sue.havens@lineone.net

HAVEY, Kenneth Richard. b 61. St Steph Ho Ox 95. **d** 97 **p** 98. C Corringham *Chelmsf* 97-98; C Leigh St Clem 98-02; R from 02. *St Clement's Rectory, 80 Leigh Hill, Leigh-on-Sea SS9 1AR* Tel (01702) 475967 E-mail frkenneth@stclement.plus.com

HAVILAND, Andrew Mark James. b 65. Leeds Univ BEd87. STETS 02. **d** 05. NSM N Holmwood *Guildf* from 05. *28 Bentsbrook Park, North Holmwood, Dorking RH5 4JN* Tel and fax (01306) 740861 Mobile 07855-823255 E-mail andrew@haviland.fslife.co.uk

HAVILAND, Edmund Selwyn. b 24. K Coll Cam BA49 MA51. Wells Th Coll 49. **d** 51 **p** 52. C St Helier *S'wark* 51-55; C-in-c Bermondsey St Hugh CD 55-58; V Ockbrook *Derby* 58-68; V E Peckham *Roch* 68-78; R E Peckham and Nettlestead 78-84; S Africa 84-85; Dep Chapl HM Pris Brixton 85-89; rtd 89; Perm to Offic *Guildf* from 89. *Hill Farm, Thursley, Godalming GU8 6QQ* Tel (01252) 702115

HAWES, Andrew Thomas. b 54. Sheff Univ BA77 Em Coll Cam MA79. Westcott Ho Cam 77. **d** 80 **p** 81. C Gt Grimsby St Mary and St Jas *Linc* 80-84; P-in-c Gedney Drove End 84-86; P-in-c Sutton St Nicholas 84-86; V Lutton w Gedney Drove End, Dawsmere 86-89; V Edenham w Witham on the Hill 89-00; V Edenham w Witham on the Hill and Swinstead from 00; RD Beltisloe from 97. *The Vicarage, Church Lane, Edenham, Bourne PE10 0LS* Tel and fax (01778) 591358

HAWES, The Ven Arthur John. b 43. UEA BA86 Birm Univ DPS72 DLA75. Chich Th Coll 65. **d** 68 **p** 69. C Kidderminster St Jo *Worc* 68-72; P-in-c Droitwich 72-76; R Alderford w Attlebridge and Swannington *Nor* 76-92; Chapl Hellesdon and David Rice Hosps and Yare Clinic 76-92; RD Sparham *Nor* 81-91; Mental Health Act Commr 86-94; Hon Can Nor Cathl *Nor* 88-95; TR Gaywood 92-95; Adn Linc from 95; Can and Preb Linc Cathl from 95. *Archdeacon's House, Northfield Road, Quarrington, Sleaford NG34 8RT* Tel (01529) 304348 *or* (07803) 249834 Fax (01529) 304354 E-mail ad.oflincoln@virgin.net

HAWES, Joseph Patricius. b 65. St Chad's Coll Dur BA87. St Steph Ho Ox 88. **d** 91 **p** 92. C Clapham Team *S'wark* 91-96; P-in-c Barnes St Mich 96-97; TV Barnes 97-03; V Fulham All SS *Lon* from 03. *All Saints' Vicarage, 70 Fulham High Street, London SW6 3LG* Tel (020) 7736 6301 E-mail angelos@surfaid.org *or* vicarasfulham@aol.com

HAWES, Mary Elizabeth. b 56. SEITE 94. **d** 00 **p** 01. Dioc Children's Adv *Lon* from 98; NSM Streatham St Leon *S'wark* from 00. *9 Roman Rise, London SE19 1JG* Tel (020) 8761 0231 E-mail therevs@fish.co.uk *or* mary.hawes@london.anglican.org

HAWES, Michael Rowell. b 31. AKC61. **d** 62 **p** 63. C Epsom St Martin *Guildf* 62-65; Chapl RAF 65-86; R Newnham w Nately Scures w Mapledurwell etc *Win* 86-97; rtd 97; Perm to Offic *Win* from 97. *7 Holly Lane, Ashley, New Milton BH25 5RF* Tel (01425) 620698

HAWKEN, Andrew Robert. b 58. K Coll Lon BD81 AKC81. St Steph Ho Ox 83. **d** 85 **p** 86. C Ex St Dav *Ex* 85-88; TV Witney *Ox* 88-93; V Benson from 93; AD Aston and Cuddesdon from 02. *The Vicarage, Church Road, Benson, Wallingford OX10 6SF* Tel and fax (01491) 201668 Mobile 07711-664877 E-mail andrew.hawken@ntlworld.com

HAWKEN, Rosalind Mary. b 56. York Univ BA77 Univ of Wales (Cardiff) BTh02. St Mich Coll Llan 99. **d** 02 **p** 03. C Swansea St Thos and Kilvey *S & B* 02-03; C Gorseinon from 03. *28 Bryneithin Road, Gorseinon, Swansea SA4 4XA* Tel (01792) 897062

HAWKER, The Ven Alan Fort. b 44. Hull Univ BA65 Lon Univ DipTh68. Clifton Th Coll 65. **d** 68 **p** 69. C Bootle St Leon *Liv* 68-71; C Fazakerley Em 71-73; V Goose Green 73-81; TR Southgate *Chich* 81-98; Can and Preb Chich Cathl 91-98; RD E Grinstead 94-98; Hon Can Bris Cathl *Bris* from 98; Adn Swindon 98-99; Adn Malmesbury from 99. *Church Paddock, Church Lane, Kington Langley, Chippenham SN15 5NR* Tel (01249) 750085 Fax 750086 E-mail alan@venjen.fsnet.co.uk

HAWKER, Brian Henry. b 34. AKC61 St Boniface Warminster 61. **d** 62 **p** 63. C Hemel Hempstead *St Alb* 62-66; R Stone w Hartwell w Bishopstone *Ox* 66-69; Chapl St Jo Hosp Stone 66-69; V W Wycombe 69-72; Past Consultant Clinical Th Assn 72-83; Past Consultant 83-94; Public Preacher *S'well* 72-76; rtd 94; Perm to Offic *B & W* 76-83; *Truro* 83-90; and *Leic* from 99. *12 Burfield Avenue, Loughborough LE11 3AZ* Tel (01509) 261439

HAWKER, Canon Peter John. b 37. OBE96. Ex Univ BA59. Wycliffe Hall Ox 69. **d** 70 **p** 71. Asst Chapl Berne *Eur* 70-76; Chapl Berne w Neuchâtel 76-89; Adn Switzerland 86-04; Chapl Zürich w St Gallen, Baden and Zug 90-00; Can Brussels Cathl 86-04. *Schulgasse 10, 3280 Murten, Switzerland* Tel (0041) (26) 670 6221 Fax 670 6219 E-mail phawker@anglican.ch

HAWKES, Mrs Cecilia Mary (Cilla). b 48. Reading Univ BSc69 Canley Coll of Educn DipEd71. EAMTC 99. **d** 02 **p** 03. NSM Takeley w Lt Canfield *Chelmsf* from 02. *Greenfields, Felsted, Dunmow CM6 3LF* Tel and fax (01371) 856480 E-mail pandchawkes@aol.com

HAWKES, Mrs Elisabeth Anne. b 56. GRNCM78 PGCE80 Kent Univ MA97. Linc Th Coll 86. **d** 88 **p** 97. Hon Par Dn Finham *Cov* 88-90; Hon Par Dn Bexhill St Pet *Chich* 90-97; Asst to RD Oundle *Pet* 97-98; NSM Oundle 98-00; NSM Benefield and Southwick w Glapthorn 99-00; Perm to Offic *Cant* 00-04; NSM Reculver and Herne Bay St Bart from 04; Hon Min Can Cant Cathl from 03. *The Vicarage, 25 Dence Park, Herne Bay CT6 6BQ* Tel and fax (01227) 360948 E-mail liz@hawkes48.freeserve.co.uk

HAWKES, Mrs Helen Vanda. b 50. Surrey Univ BA01. STETS 98. **d** 01 **p** 02. NSM N Hayling St Pet *Portsm* from 01; NSM Hayling Is St Andr from 01. *67 East Lodge Park, Farlington, Portsmouth PO16 1BZ* Tel (023) 9221 9005 Mobile 07719-828113 E-mail vanda.hawkes@btinternet.com

HAWKES, Keith Andrew. b 28. Oak Hill Th Coll 72. **d** 74 **p** 75. C Gt Yarmouth *Nor* 74-77; C-in-c Bowthorpe CD 77; Chapl Düsseldorf *Eur* 77-83; TV Quidenham *Nor* 83-88; TR 88-90; RD Thetford and Rockland 86-90; R Wickmere w Lt Barningham, Itteringham etc 90-96; Dioc Rural Officer 90-94; P-in-c Saxthorpe w Corpusty, Blickling, Oulton etc 94-96; R Lt Barningham, Blickling, Edgefield etc 96-98; Bp's Chapl 98; rtd 98; Perm to Offic *Nor* 98-00 and from 04; P-in-c Guiltcross 00-03; Chapl Norwich Primary Care Trust 00-02; Chapl Riddlesworth Hall Sch Nor from 04. *Peel Cottage, West Church Street, Kenninghall, Norwich NR16 2EN* Tel and fax (01953) 888533 E-mail revkahawkes@aol.com

HAWKES, Martyn John. b 71. Nottm Univ BA94 St Jo Coll Dur BA01. Cranmer Hall Dur 99. **d** 02 **p** 03. C Is of Dogs Ch Ch and St Jo w St Luke *Lon* 02-05; C Brownswood Park from 05; C

Stoke Newington St Mary from 05. *St John's Vicarage, 2A Gloucester Drive, London N4 2LW* Tel (020) 8211 0729 E-mail mj_hawkes@yahoo.co.uk

HAWKES, Nigel Anthony Robert. b 59. UEA BSc80 Edin Univ MSc82. Ripon Coll Cuddesdon 00. **d** 02 **p** 03. C Chase *Ox* 02-04; C Chipping Norton 04-05; TV Dorchester from 05. *The Vicarage, 49 The Green North, Warborough, Wallingford OX10 7DW* Tel (01865) 858381 E-mail revnige@fish.co.uk

HAWKES, Ronald Linton. b 54. St Jo Coll York CertEd75 Leeds Univ BEd76 Kent Univ MA96. Linc Th Coll 85. **d** 87 **p** 88. C Finham *Cov* 87-90; TV Bexhill St Pet *Chich* 90-97; V Oundle *Pet* 97-00; P-in-c Benefield and Southwick w Glapthorn 99-00; Dir Post-Ord Tr 98-00; Chapl St Edm Sch Cant 00-03; V Reculver and Herne Bay St Bart *Cant* from 03; Hon Min Can Cant Cathl from 01. *The Vicarage, 25 Dence Park, Herne Bay CT6 6BQ* Tel and fax (01227) 360948 E-mail revronald@hotmail.com

HAWKES, Vanda. *See* HAWKES, Mrs Helen Vanda

HAWKETT, Graham Kenneth. b 20. Bps' Coll Cheshunt 61. **d** 63 **p** 64. C Farncombe *Guildf* 63-67; V Wyke 67-85; rtd 85; Perm to Offic *Guildf* from 85. *Bede House, Beech Road, Haslemere GU27 2BX* Tel (01428) 656430

HAWKINGS, Timothy Denison. b 55. Ex Univ BA78 Nottm Univ BA80. St Jo Coll Nottm 78. **d** 81 **p** 82. C Penn *Lich* 81-85; TV Stafford 85-94; TR Stratton St Margaret w S Marston etc *Bris* from 94. *The Rectory, Kenwin Close, Swindon SN3 4NY* Tel (01793) 822793 E-mail thawkings@strattonsm.fsnet.co.uk

HAWKINS, The Very Revd Alun John. b 44. K Coll Lon BA66 AKC66 Univ of Wales (Ban) BD81. St Deiniol's Hawarden 78. **d** 81 **p** 82. C Dwygyfylchi *Ban* 81-84; R Llanberis 84-89; Tutor Ban Dioc NSM Course 85-90; Dir of Ords *Ban* 86-90; V Knighton and Norton *S & B* 89-93; Chapl Knighton Hosp 89-93; R Bangor *Ban* from 93; Adult Educn Officer from 93; Sec Dioc Bd of Miss from 93; Can Res and Can Missr Ban Cathl 93-00; Adn Ban 00-04; Dean Ban from 04. *The Deanery, Cathedral Close, Glanrafon, Bangor LL57 1LH* Tel (01248) 362840 Fax 353882

HAWKINS, Andrew Robert. b 40. St Andr Univ BSc64. St Chad's Coll Dur BA68 DipTh69. **d** 69 **p** 70. C Sutton St Nic *S'wark* 69-73; C Wimbledon 73-77; TV Cramlington *Newc* 77-81; R Clutton w Cameley *B & W* 81-89; Chapl City of Bath Coll of FE from 89; Perm to Offic *B & W* from 90. *18 Wally Court Road, Chew Stoke, Bristol BS40 8XN* Tel (01275) 332422 E-mail andrewr.hawkins@virgin.net

HAWKINS, Canon Bruce Alexander. b 44. Qu Coll Ox BA66 MA71. Sarum Th Coll 66. **d** 68 **p** 69. C Epsom St Martin *Guildf* 68-71; Dioc Youth Chapl *Cant* 72-81; Hon Min Can Cant Cathl 75-99; Dep Dir of Educn 81-86; V Walmer 86-05; RD Sandwich 94-00; Hon Can Cant Cathl 99-05; rtd 05; Perm to Offic *Cant* from 05. *88 The Gateway, Dover CT16 1LQ* Tel (01304) 240820

HAWKINS, Mrs Christine Ann. b 56. SEITE. **d** 01 **p** 02. NSM Epping Distr *Chelmsf* 01-02; C Woodford St Mary w St Phil and St Jas from 02; P-in-c Hatfield Broad Oak and Bush End from 05; Ind Chapl to Harlow from 05. *The Vicarage, Feathers Hill, Hatfield Broad Oak, Bishop's Stortford CM22 7HD* Tel (01279) 718274 Mobile 07944-431794 E-mail revchris.hawkins@btopenworld.com

HAWKINS, Canon Clive Ladbrook. b 53. DHSA79 St Pet Coll Ox BA76 MA79 DipTh82. Trin Coll Bris 80. **d** 82 **p** 83. C Win Ch Ch *Win* 82-86; R Eastrop from 86; AD Basingstoke from 00; Hon Can Win Cathl from 05. *Eastrop Rectory, 2A Wallis Road, Basingstoke RG21 3DW* Tel (01256) 355507 *or* 464249 E-mail clive.hawkins@stmarys-basingstoke.org.uk

✠**HAWKINS, The Rt Revd David John Leader.** b 49. Nottm Univ BTh73 LTh. St Jo Coll Nottm 69 ALCD73. **d** 73 **p** 74 **c** 02. C Bebington *Ches* 73-76; Nigeria 76-82; C Ox St Aldate w St Matt *Ox* 83-86; V Leeds St Geo *Ripon* 86-99; TR 99-02; Area Bp Barking *Chelmsf* from 02. *Barking Lodge, 35A Verulam Avenue, London E17 8ES* Tel (020) 8509 7377 Fax 8521 4097 E-mail bishopdavid@chelmsford.anglican.org

HAWKINS, David Kenneth Beaumont. b 36. Em Coll Saskatoon LTh63. **d** 63 **p** 64. Canada 63-85; C St Alb St Paul *St Alb* 85-87; C Hednesford *Lich* 87-92; R Buildwas and Leighton w Eaton Constantine etc 92-95; TV Wrockwardine Deanery 95-01; rtd 01. *PO Box 454, 131 Westward Crescent, Wellington ON, Canada, K0K 3L0*

HAWKINS, Donald John. b 39. K Coll Lon BD62 AKC62. St Boniface Warminster 62. **d** 63 **p** 64. C Winlaton *Dur* 63-66; C Gateshead St Mary 66-69; C Ryhope 69-71; R Cockfield 71-79; Chapl N Staffs R Infirmary Stoke-on-Trent 79-89; Chapl Stoke-on-Trent City Gen Hosp 89-93; Chapl N Staffs Hosp NHS Trust 93-99; Chapl Co-ord 94-99; rtd 99; Perm to Offic *Lich* from 99. *12 The Avenue, Hartshill, Stoke-on-Trent ST4 6BJ* Tel and fax (01782) 620691 E-mail hawkins@12ave.freeserve.co.uk

HAWKINS, Canon Francis John. b 36. Ex Coll Ox BA61 MA63. Chich Th Coll 59. **d** 61 **p** 62. C Tavistock and Gulworthy *Ex* 61-64; Lect Chich Th Coll 64-73; Vice-Prin 73-75; V E Grinstead St Mary *Chich* 75-81; Can Res and Treas Chich Cathl 81-01; V Sidlesham 81-89; Dir of Ords 89-01; rtd 01. *6 Priory Road, Chichester PO19 1NS* Tel (01243) 771921

HAWKINS, Ian Clinton. b 27. Roch Th Coll 63. **d** 65 **p** 66. C Boulton *Derby* 65-68; V Cotmanhay 68-77; V Ospringe *Cant* 77-85; P-in-c Eastling 77-85; P-in-c Goodnestone H Cross w Chillenden and Knowlton 85; P-in-c Womenswold 85; V Nonington w Wymynswold and Goodnestone etc 85-92; rtd 92; Perm to Offic *Derby* from 92. *7 Main Road, Bradwell, Hope Valley S33 9JG* Tel (01433) 621360 E-mail ian.hawkins4@virgin.net

HAWKINS, James Reginald. b 39. Ex Univ BA61 Hull Univ MA00. Westcott Ho Cam 61. **d** 63 **p** 64. C Cannock *Lich* 63-66; C Wem 66-67; C Cheddleton 67-69; R Yoxall 69-77; R The Quinton *Birm* 77-84; V Bosbury w Wellington Heath etc *Heref* 84-96; P-in-c Ancaster Wilsford Gp *Linc* 96-99; R 99-04; RD Loveden 97-03; rtd 04. *14 Pound Pill, Corsham SN13 9JA* Tel (01249) 715353 E-mail james.hawkins39@btopenworld.com

HAWKINS, John. b 27. Ox Poly DipArch52. S'wark Ord Course 84. **d** 87 **p** 88. NSM Carshalton Beeches *S'wark* 87-89; Perm to Offic 89-04. *44 Castlemaine Avenue, South Croydon CR2 7HR* Tel (020) 8688 9685

HAWKINS, John Arthur. b 45. Kelham Th Coll 64. **d** 69 **p** 70. C Cov St Alb *Cov* 70-73; C Fletchamstead 73-77; V Whitley 77-81; TV Northampton Em *Pet* 81-90; TV Gt Chesham *Ox* 90-98; C Thorpe *Nor* from 98. *8 Hampton Drive, Thorpe St Andrew, Norwich NR7 0UT* Tel (01603) 431868

HAWKINS, John Charles Lacey. b 18. Linc Th Coll 40. **d** 42 **p** 43. C Dalton-in-Furness *Carl* 42-44; C Workington St Mich 44-48; V Allonby w W Newton 48-53; V Thornton w Allerthorpe *York* 53-60; R Stockton-on-the-Forest w Holtby and Warthill 60-77; R Sigglesthorne and Rise w Nunkeeling and Bewholme 77-83; rtd 83; Perm to Offic *York* 83-96. *4 Bromley College, London Road, Bromley BR1 1PE* Tel (020) 8460 1469

HAWKINS, John Colin. b 50. SEITE 97. **d** 00 **p** 01. NSM W Wickham St Jo *S'wark* 00-04; P-in-c Burwash Weald *Chich* from 04. *The Vicarage, Burwash Common, Etchingham TN19 7NA* Tel (01435) 883287 E-mail john.c.hawkins@btinternet.com

HAWKINS, John Edward Inskipp. b 63. K Coll Lon BD85. Qu Coll Birm 86. **d** 88 **p** 89. C Birchfield *Birm* 88-92; C Poplar *Lon* 92-93; TV 93-99; V W Hendon St Jo from 99; AD W Barnet from 04. *St John's Vicarage, Vicarage Road, London NW4 3PX* Tel and fax (020) 8202 8606 E-mail jeih.stj@aladdinscave.net

HAWKINS, Nicholas Milner. b 45. Univ of Wales (Swansea) BA MSc. **d** 01. Par Dn Dingestow and Llangovan w Penyclawdd etc *Mon* 01-02; Perm to Offic *Ban* 02-03; NSM Nefyn w Tudweiliog w Llandudwen w Edern from 03. *Bryn Mor, Llangwnadl, Pwllheli LL53 8NS* Tel (01758) 770582 Mobile 07870-264385 Fax (01758) 770228 E-mail nick.hawkins@btinternet.com

HAWKINS, Noel. b 46. St Jo Coll Nottm 82. **d** 84 **p** 85. C Worksop St Jo *S'well* 84-86; C Wollaton Park 86-89; TV Billericay and Lt Burstead *Chelmsf* 89-95; TV Keynsham *B & W* 95-00; V Brislington St Chris and St Cuth *Bris* from 00. *The Vicarage, 35 Wick Crescent, Bristol BS4 4HG* Tel 0117-977 6351

HAWKINS, Miss Patricia Sally. b 59. LMH Ox BA80 MA84 Ex Univ BPhil85 CQSW85. St Steph Ho Ox 99. **d** 01 **p** 02. C Stafford *Lich* 01-04; V Oxley from 04. *The Vicarage, Lymer Road, Oxley, Wolverhampton WV10 6AA* Tel (01902) 783342 Mobile 07929-975651

HAWKINS, Paul Henry Whishaw. b 46. Ex Coll Ox BA68 MA74 SS Coll Cam MA84. St Steph Ho Ox 70. **d** 72 **p** 73. C Fawley *Win* 72-75; C Ealing St Steph Castle Hill *Lon* 75-77; P-in-c Dorney *Ox* 77-78; TV Riverside 78-81; Chapl SS Coll Cam 82-87; V Plymstock *Ex* 87-97; RD Plymouth Sutton 91-96; TR Plymstock and Hooe 97-00; Preb Ex Cathl 98-00; P-in-c St Pancras w St Jas and Ch Ch *Lon* 00-02; V from 02. *St Pancras Vicarage, 6 Sandwich Street, London WC1H 9PL* Tel (020) 7388 1630 *or* tel and fax 7388 1461 E-mail st.pancras@lineone.net

HAWKINS, Peter Edward. b 35. Leeds Univ BA60. Coll of Resurr Mirfield 60. **d** 62 **p** 63. C Forest Gate St Edm *Chelmsf* 62-65; C Sevenoaks St Jo *Roch* 65-68; Chapl Metrop Police Cadet Corps Tr Sch 68-73; P-in-c Knowle H Nativity *Bris* 73; TV Knowle 73-79; V Westbury-on-Trym H Trin 79-87; TR Solihull *Birm* 87-96; Hon Can Birm Cathl 92-96; rtd 00. *Back Street Cottage, 15 St Andrew's Road, Stogursey, Bridgwater TA5 1TE* Tel (01278) 733635 Fax as telephone E-mail peh.stogursey@tiscali.uk

HAWKINS, Peter Michael. b 38. Kelham Th Coll 58. **d** 63 **p** 64. India 63-69; C Manningham St Paul and St Jude *Bradf* 70-72; C Bradf Cathl 72-75; V Allerton 75-90; V Pet H Spirit Bretton *Pet* from 90; P-in-c Marholm 90-95. *23 Westhawe, Bretton, Peterborough PE3 8BE* Tel (01733) 264418 *or* 842508 Mobile 07952-805657 Fax (01733) 332544 E-mail holyspiritchurch@fish.co.uk *or* hawkinspp@aol.com

HAWKINS, Richard Randal. b 39. **d** 65 **p** 66. C Bushbury *Lich* 65-68; C Woodford St Mary *Chelmsf* 68-71; S Africa from 71; rtd 04. *PO Box 1433, Wandsbeck, 3631 South Africa*

✠**HAWKINS, The Rt Revd Richard Stephen.** b 39. Ex Coll Ox BA61 MA65 Ex Univ BPhil76. St Steph Ho Ox 61. **d** 63 **p** 64

c 88. C Ex St Thos *Ex* 63-66; C Clyst St Mary 66-75; TV Clyst St George, Aylesbeare, Clyst Honiton etc 75-78; TV Cen Ex 78-81; Bp's Officer for Min and Jt Dir Ex and Truro NSM Scheme 78-81; Dioc Dir of Ords 79-81; Adn Totnes 81-88; P-in-c Oldridge and Whitestone 81-87; Suff Bp Plymouth 88-96; Suff Bp Crediton 96-04; rtd 04; Hon Asst Bp Ex from 05. *Applegarth, Longmeadow Road, Lympstone, Exmouth EX8 5LF* Tel (01395) 265434

HAWKINS, Richard Whishaw. b 51. Coll of Resurr Mirfield 93. **d** 95 **p** 96. C Weymouth H Trin *Sarum* 95-99; P-in-c Hey *Man* from 99; AD Saddleworth from 03. *St John's Vicarage, 1 Owen Fold, Oldham OL4 3DT* Tel 0161-626 3630 E-mail richard.hawkins107@ntlworld.com

HAWKINS, Roger David William. b 33. K Coll Lon BD58 AKC58. **d** 59 **p** 60. C Twickenham St Mary *Lon* 59-61; C Heston 61-64; C Dorking w Ranmore *Guildf* 64-65; V Mitcham St Mark *S'wark* 65-74; V Redhill St Matt 74-91; P-in-c Warlingham w Chelsham and Farleigh 91-97; TR 97-98; rtd 98. *2 Grove Court, Falkland Grove, Dorking RH4 3DL* Tel (01306) 885817

HAWKINS, Roger Julian. b 32. Ripon Hall Ox 59. **d** 61 **p** 62. C-in-c Newall Green CD *Man* 61-63; Chapl RAF 63-67; R Mawgan in Pyder *Truro* 67-75; R Lanteglos by Camelford w Advent 75-78; R Newmarket St Mary w Exning St Agnes *St E* 78-85; P-in-c Coltishall w Gt Hautbois *Nor* 85-87; R Coltishall w Gt Hautbois and Horstead 87-90; Chapl Whiteley Village *Guildf* 90-94; rtd 97; Perm to Offic *Win* 01-02 and *Sarum* from 02. *42 St Ann Place, Salisbury SP1 2SU* Tel (01722) 415979

HAWKINS, Steven Andrew. b 51. Nottm Univ BEd75 Open Univ BSc91 Bris Poly ADEd90. STETS 95. **d** 98 **p** 99. C Horfield H Trin *Bris* 98-02; V Brislington St Anne from 02. *The Vicarage, 23 First Avenue, Bristol BS4 4DU* Tel 0117-983 0283 Mobile 07900-242443 E-mail steven@hawkins96.freeserve.co.uk

HAWKINS, Susan. b 47. Doncaster Coll of Educn CertEd69 Chester Coll of HE BTh99. N Ord Course 95. **d** 99 **p** 00. NSM Prestbury *Ches* 99-02; P-in-c Marthall from 02; Chapl David Lewis Cen for Epilepsy from 02. *The Vicarage, Sandlebridge Lane, Marthall, Knutsford WA16 7SB* Tel (01625) 860981 E-mail dvs.hawkins@btinternet.com

HAWKINS, Timothy St John. b 59. CCC Ox BA82. Trin Coll Bris BA87. **d** 87 **p** 88. C Cheltenham St Mary, St Matt, St Paul and H Trin *Glouc* 87-90; C Cowplain *Portsm* 90-94; V Pennycross *Ex* 94-96; P-in-c St Keverne *Truro* from 96. *The Vicarage, St Keverne, Helston TR12 6NG* Tel (01326) 280227 E-mail helen.hawkins@tesco.net

HAWKINS, William Arthur. b 18. Clifton Th Coll 50. **d** 53 **p** 54. C Ellacombe *Ex* 53-54; C Totnes 54-58; R Ashill w Broadway *B & W* 58-74; R Herstmonceux *Chich* 74-83; rtd 83; Perm to Offic *Chich* from 84. *Three Gables, 17 Heighton Road, Newhaven BN9 0RB* Tel (01273) 513694

HAWKSBEE, Canon Derek John. b 28. Lon Univ BSc49. S'wark Ord Course 70. **d** 71 **p** 72. C Norbiton *S'wark* 71-75; Cand and S Area Sec SAMS 71-79; Overseas Sec 73-79; Hon Can Paraguay from 73; Hon C Tunbridge Wells St Jo *Roch* 75-79; USA 79-87; R Ravendale Gp *Linc* 88-96; rtd 96; Perm to Offic *Roch* from 99. *205 Upper Grosvenor Road, Tunbridge Wells TN1 2EG* Tel (01892) 533485

HAWKSWORTH, Maldwyn Harry. b 45. Aston Univ CertEd74. St Jo Coll Nottm 87. **d** 89 **p** 90. C Penn *Lich* 89-94; TV Bloxwich from 94. *6 Cresswell Crescent, Bloxwich, Walsall WS3 2UW* Tel (01922) 476647

HAWKSWORTH, Peter John Dallas. b 54. Solicitor 79 St Jo Coll Ox BA75 MA79. Sarum & Wells Th Coll 89. **d** 91 **p** 92. C Warminster St Denys, Upton Scudamore etc *Sarum* 91-95; P-in-c Salisbury St Mark 95-99; V from 99; RD Salisbury from 03. *St Mark's Vicarage, 62 Barrington Road, Salisbury SP1 3JD* Tel (01722) 323767 E-mail confluence@btinternet.com

HAWLEY, Canon Anthony Broughton. b 41. St Pet Coll Ox BA67 MA71. Westcott Ho Cam 67. **d** 69 **p** 70. C Wolverhampton St Pet *Lich* 69-72; C-in-c Bermondsey St Hugh CD *S'wark* 73-84; Hon PV S'wark Cathl 83-84; TR Kirkby *Liv* 84-02; AD Walton 93-02; Hon Can Liv Cathl 96-02; Can Res Liv Cathl from 02. *2 Cathedral Close, Liverpool L1 7BR* Tel 0151-708 0932 *or* 709 6271 E-mail canon.hawley@liverpoolcathedral.org.uk

HAWLEY, Georgina. b 45. **d** 01 **p** 02. Australia 01-02; NSM Chippenham St Pet *Bris* 02-03; Perm to Offic from 03. *2 Coopers Meadow, Yatton Keynell, Chippenham SN14 7PZ* Tel (01249) 782858 Fax as telephone E-mail ghawley@brookes.ac.uk

HAWLEY, The Ven John Andrew. b 50. K Coll Lon BD71 AKC71. Wycliffe Hall Ox 72. **d** 74 **p** 75. C Kingston upon Hull H Trin *York* 74-77; C Bradf Cathl Par *Bradf* 77-80; V Woodlands *Sheff* 80-91; TR Dewsbury *Wakef* 91-02; Hon Can Wakef Cathl 98-02; Adn Blackb from 02. *19 Clarence Park, Blackburn BB2 7FA* Tel (01254) 262571 Pager 07623-110608 Fax (01254) 263394 E-mail archdeacon.blackburn@milestonenet.co.uk

HAWLEY, Nigel David. b 51. Coll of Resurr Mirfield 77. **d** 80 **p** 81. C Birch w Fallowfield *Man* 80-84; P-in-c Moston St Jo 84-85; R 85-93; R Reddish from 93. *St Elisabeth's Rectory, 28 Bedford Street, Stockport SK5 6DJ* Tel 0161-432 3033 E-mail frnigel@stelisabeths.fsnet.co.uk

HAWLEY, William David Llewellyn. b 41. Univ of W Aus BCom77 Curtin Univ Aus DPA88 Murdoch Univ Aus BD94. **d** 92 **p** 95. Australia 92-00; Hon C Bullcreek w Bateman 92-94; Hon C Kwinana 94-95; Dioc Registrar 95-98; Assoc P Spearwood w Hilton 95-98; R Hilton 98-00; TV By Brook *Bris* from 01. *2 Coopers Meadow, Yatton Keynell, Chippenham SN14 7PZ* Tel (01249) 782858 Fax as telephone

HAWNT, John Charles Frederick. b 30. St Paul's Cheltenham. Selly Oak Coll 52 Westwood Cen Zimbabwe 72. **d** 75 **p** 76. Rhodesia 75-80; Zimbabwe 80-81; C Rugby St Andr *Cov* 81-85; R Lydeard St Lawrence w Brompton Ralph etc *B & W* 85-00; rtd 00; S Africa from 00. *39 St Andrew Road, Houghton, Johannesburg, 2198 South Africa*

HAWORTH, Mrs Betsy Ellen. b 24. Wm Temple Coll Hawarden 50. **dss** 80 **d** 89. Walkden Moor *Man* 80-81; Third Ch Estates Commr 81-88; Lic to Offic 88-89; NSM Astley Bridge 89-99. *14 Sharples Hall Fold, Bolton BL1 7EH* Tel (01204) 591588

HAWORTH (née ARMSTRONG), Fiona Heather. b 65. Reading Univ BSc86 Nottm Univ PhD90. St Jo Coll Nottm BTh94. **d** 97 **p** 98. C Sutton in Ashfield St Mary *S'well* 97-02; TV Kidderminster St Mary and All SS w Trimpley etc *Worc* from 02. *The Vicarage, 50 Nursery Grove, Kidderminster DY11 5BG* Tel (01562) 748016 E-mail haworth@fish.co.uk

HAWORTH, Mark Newby. b 50. Aber Univ BSc73 MICFor81. Westcott Ho Cam 88. **d** 90 **p** 91. C Cherry Hinton St Andr *Ely* 90-93; C Teversham 90-93; P-in-c Swaffham Bulbeck and Swaffham Prior w Reach 93-94; V 94-02; Sub Warden of Readers 95-02; RD Fordham 96-02; Chapl Framlingham Coll 03; Chapl to Bp Pet 03-05; TR Pendleton *Man* from 05. *The Rectory, 92 Fitzwarren Street, Salford M6 5RS* Tel 0161-745 7608 Mobile 07932-160009 E-mail father.mark@virgin.net

HAWORTH, Paul. b 47. G&C Coll Cam BA68 MA72. Westcott Ho Cam 75. **d** 78 **p** 79. C Hornchurch St Andr *Chelmsf* 78-81; C Loughton St Mary and St Mich 81-88; TV Waltham H Cross 88-92; TR Becontree S 92-00; P-in-c S Woodham Ferrers from 00. *The Vicarage, 18 Victoria Road, South Woodham Ferrers, Chelmsford CM3 5LR* Tel (01245) 322134 E-mail preacherman@pewend.org

HAWORTH, Stanley Robert. b 48. St Jo Coll Dur BA69. Sarum & Wells Th Coll 71. **d** 73 **p** 74. C Skipton H Trin *Bradf* 73-76; C Bradf Cathl 76-78; C Grantham *Linc* 78; TV 78-82; V Deeping St James 82-96; V Middlewich w Byley *Ches* 96-01; P-in-c Forcett and Aldbrough and Melsonby *Ripon* from 01. *The Vicarage, 1 Appleby Close, Aldbrough St John, Richmond DL11 7TT* Tel (01325) 374634 E-mail stantherevman@hotmail.com

HAWORTH, Stuart. b 43. Local Minl Tr Course 91. **d** 94 **p** 95. OLM Bradshaw *Man* 94-01; OLM Turton Moorland Min from 01. *178 Turton Road, Bolton BL2 3EE* Tel (01204) 594506

HAWTHORN, The Ven Christopher John. b 36. Qu Coll Cam BA60 MA64. Ripon Hall Ox 60. **d** 62 **p** 63. C Sutton St Jas *York* 62-66; V Kingston upon Hull St Nic 66-72; V E Coatham 72-79; V Scarborough St Martin 79-91; RD Scarborough 82-91; Can and Preb York Minster 87-01; Adn Cleveland 91-01; rtd 01; Perm to Offic *York* from 01. *43 Barley Rise, Strensall, York YO32 5AB* Tel (01904) 492060

HAWTHORN, David. b 63. Chich Th Coll 87. **d** 90 **p** 91. C Hartlepool H Trin *Dur* 90-94; C Middlesbrough All SS *York* 94-95; P-in-c Thornaby on Tees 95-96; V S Thornaby 96-02; P-in-c Brighton Annunciation *Chich* 02-04; V Hollinwood and Limeside *Man* from 04. *St Margaret's Vicarage, 61 Chapel Road, Oldham OL8 4QQ* Tel and fax 0161-681 4541 E-mail hawthorn@supanet.com

HAWTHORN, Thomas Russell. b 18. MBE90. Imp Coll Lon BSc48 Lon Univ ACGI48. **d** 82 **p** 82. Mexico 82-84; Perm to Offic *Nor* from 84; Sub Chapl HM Pris Blundeston 86-94. *82 Wollaston Road, Lowestoft NR32 2PF* Tel (01502) 518741

HAWTHORNE, Canon Andrew. b 68. Jes Coll Ox BA89 MA93 K Coll Lon PhD04. Chich Th Coll BTh93. **d** 93 **p** 94. C Christchurch *Win* 93-97; TV Dorchester *Sarum* 97-00; rtd 00; Hon Can Kinkizi from 04; C Christchurch *Win* from 05. *68 Arnewood Road, Southbourne, Bournemouth BH6 5DN* Tel (01202) 569163 E-mail andrewahawthorne@aol.com

HAWTHORNE, John William. b 32. St Aug Coll Cant 74. **d** 77 **p** 78. C Boxley *Cant* 77-80; P-in-c Otham 80-82; P-in-c Langley 80-82; R Otham w Langley 82-83; TR Preston w Sutton Poyntz and Osmington w Poxwell *Sarum* 83-87; R Tetbury w Beverston *Glouc* 87-01; rtd 01; Perm to Offic *Ex* from 02. *19 Long Street, Devizes SN10 1NN* Tel (01380) 728056 E-mail honitonhawthorne@aol.com

HAWTHORNE, Canon William James (Jim). b 46. MBE01. TCD 66 Ch of Ireland Tr Coll 66. **d** 69 **p** 70. C Gilnahirk *D & D* 69-72; Asst Chapl Miss to Seamen 72-76; C Boultham *Linc* 76-78; C Bracebridge Heath 78-90; Dioc Adv for Relig Broadcasting 80-90; Chapl Palma de Mallorca and Balearic Is *Eur* 90-93; Chapl Palma de Mallorca 93-01; P-in-c Menorca 97-98; Can Gib Cathl 97-01; rtd 01. *16-08 Victoria Centre, Milton Street, Nottingham NG1 3PL* Tel 0115-840 7913 E-mail williamjameshawthorne@hotmail.com

✠**HAWTIN, The Rt Revd David Christopher.** b 43. Keble Coll Ox BA65 MA70. Wm Temple Coll Rugby 65 Cuddesdon Coll 66. **d** 67 **p** 68 **c** 99. C Pennywell St Thos and Grindon St Oswald CD *Dur* 67-71; C Stockton St Pet 71-74; C-in-c Leam Lane CD 74-79; R Washington 79-88; Dioc Ecum Officer 88-91; Adn Newark *S'well* 92-99; Suff Bp Repton *Derby* from 99. *Repton House, Lea, Matlock DE4 5JP* Tel (01629) 534644 Fax 534003 E-mail bishop.repton@btinternet.com

HAY, David Frederick. b 38. MA67. Qu Coll Birm 82. **d** 84 **p** 85. C Prenton *Ches* 84-88; V Stockport St Sav 88-96; P-in-c Gt Saughall 96-03; rtd 03; Hon Min Can Ches Cathl *Ches* from 04. *2 Moel View Road, Buckley CH7 2BT* Tel (01244) 541342

HAY, Ian Gordon. b 52. Dundee Univ MA73 Edin Univ BD76 CertEd84. Edin Th Coll 73. **d** 76 **p** 77. C Dumfries *Glas* 76-79; Dioc Chapl *Bre* 79-81; R Brechin 81-85; Asst Chapl H Trin Sch Halifax 85-88; Dioc Youth Officer *Carl* 89-98; Sen Development Worker Youth Link Scotland from 98. *The Ross House, Pittendreich, Kinross KY13 9HD* Tel (01592) 840820 E-mail youthlink-scot@sol.co.uk

HAY, Jack Barr. b 31. Bps' Coll Cheshunt 57. **d** 60 **p** 61. C Byker St Ant *Newc* 60-63; C Killingworth 63-68; V Cowgate 68-77; V Woodhorn w Newbiggin 77-96; rtd 96; Perm to Offic *Newc* from 96. *7 Glebelands, Corbridge NE45 5DS* Tel (01434) 632979

HAY, Joanna Jane Louise. b 61. Coll of Ripon & York St Jo BEd83. NEOC 98. **d** 01 **p** 02. NSM Scalby *York* 01-04; V Bridlington Em from 04; P-in-c Skipsea w Ulrome and Barmston w Fraisthorpe from 04. *Emmanuel Vicarage, 72 Cardigan Road, Bridlington YO15 3JT* Tel (01262) 604948 E-mail jjlhay@yahoo.co.uk

HAY, John. b 43. St D Coll Lamp 63. **d** 67 **p** 68. C Ynyshir *Llan* 67-70; C Cardiff St Mary and St Steph w St Dyfrig etc 70-74; V Llanwynno 74-78; P-in-c Weston-super-Mare All SS *B & W* 78-80; TV Weston-super-Mare Cen Par 80-85; P-in-c Handsworth St Mich *Birm* 85-86; NSM Eastbourne St Sav and St Pet *Chich* 88-91; V Buckley *St As* 91-96; P-in-c Ardwick St Benedict *Man* 96-99; C Hollinwood and Oldham St Chad Limeside 99-01; rtd 01. *11 Mayfair Court, 357 Park Road, Blackpool FY1 6QR*

HAY, The Very Revd John. b 45. CITC 77. **d** 79 **p** 80. C Newtownards *D & D* 79-81; I Galloon w Drummully *Clogh* 81-89; I Donacavey w Barr 89-03; Can Clogh Cathl 91-03; Dean Raphoe *D & R* from 03; I Raphoe w Raymochy and Clonleigh from 03. *Maranatha, The Deanery, Raphoe, Lifford, Co Donegal, Irish Republic* Tel (00353) (74) 914 5226 *or* (028) 8284 0377 E-mail dean@raphoe.anglican.org *or* johnhayraphoe@eircom.net

HAY, Margaret Ann. b 47. STETS. **d** 05. NSM Elson *Portsm* from 05. *Bodinnick, 12 Longwater Drive, Gosport PO12 2UP*

HAY, Nicholas John. b 56. Sheff Poly BSc85 DPS88. St Jo Coll Nottm 85. **d** 88 **p** 89. C Blackb Redeemer *Blackb* 88-91; C Hellesdon *Nor* 91-95; R Widford *Chelmsf* 95-01; Sen Chapl HM Pris Ashfield from 01. *HM Prison and YOI Ashfield, Shortwood Road, Pucklechurch, Bristol BS16 9QJ* Tel 0117-303 8128 *or* 303 8000 E-mail chaplaincy@premiercustodial.com

HAY, Richard. b 42. CMG92. Ball Coll Ox BA63. Cranmer Hall Dur 94. **d** 96 **p** 97. C Hastings St Clem and All SS *Chich* 96-99; V Addlestone *Guildf* from 99; RD Runnymede from 02. *The Vicarage, 140 Church Road, Addlestone KT15 1SJ* Tel (01932) 842879 E-mail randmhay@compuserve.com

HAYBALL, Douglas Reginald. b 18. Oak Hill Th Coll 66. **d** 68 **p** 69. C Ilkley All SS *Bradf* 68-72; V Parr Mt *Liv* 72-75; P-in-c Sheepey w Ratcliffe Culey *Leic* 75-76; R Sibson w Sheepy and Ratcliffe Culey 76-86; rtd 86; Perm to Offic *B & W* from 86. *57 Parklands Way, Somerton TA11 6JG* Tel (01458) 273312

HAYCRAFT, Roger Brian Norman. b 43. Oak Hill Th Coll 69. **d** 73 **p** 74. C Belsize Park *Lon* 73-76; C Yardley St Edburgha *Birm* 76-79; V Hornchurch H Cross *Chelmsf* 79-03; rtd 03. *12 Hannards Way, Hainault IG6 3TB* Tel (020) 8501 1718

HAYDAY, The Very Revd Alan Geoffrey David. b 46. Kelham Th Coll 65. **d** 69 **p** 70. C Evington *Leic* 69-72; C Spalding *Linc* 72-78; V Cherry Willingham w Greetwell 78-86; RD Lawres 84-86; TR Brumby 86-02; RD Manlake 93-99; Can and Preb Linc Cathl 00-02; Dean St Chris Cathl Bahrain from 02. *St Christopher's Cathedral, PO Box 36, Manama, Bahrain* Tel (00973) 253 3866 E-mail decani@batelco.com.bh

HAYDEN, Carol Toni. b 64. N Ord Course. **d** 05. NSM Ainsworth *Man* from 05. *38 Launceston Road, Radcliffe, Manchester M26 3UN* Tel 0161-724 0514 E-mail revchayden@aol.com

HAYDEN, The Ven David Frank. b 47. Lon Univ BD71. Tyndale Hall Bris 67. **d** 71 **p** 72. C Silverhill St Matt *Chich* 71-75; C Galleywood Common *Chelmsf* 75-79; R Redgrave cum Botesdale w Rickinghall *St E* 79-84; RD Hartismere 81-84; V Cromer *Nor* 84-02; P-in-c Gresham 84-98; Chapl Cromer and Distr Hosp Norfolk 84-94; Chapl Norfolk and Nor Health Care NHS Trust 94-00; Chapl Fletcher Hosp Norfolk 85-00; RD Repps *Nor* 95-02; Hon Can Nor Cathl from 96; Adn Norfolk from 02. *8 Boulton Road, Thorpe St Andrew, Norwich NR17 0DF* Tel and fax (01603) 702477 E-mail archdeacon.norfolk@4frontmedia.co.uk

HAYDEN, Eric Henry Ashmore. b 26. ACII65. Sarum & Wells Th Coll 71. **d** 73 **p** 74. C Horsham *Chich* 73-78; V Cuckfield 78-92; rtd 92; P-in-c Tilshead, Orcheston and Chitterne *Sarum* 92-97; Perm to Offic *Ox* from 98; *Sarum* from 98. *2 Parsonage Lane, Hungerford RG17 0JB* Tel (01488) 686584

✠**HAYDEN, The Rt Revd John Donald.** b 40. Lon Univ BD62. Tyndale Hall Bris 63. **d** 65 **p** 66 **c** 04. C Macclesfield Ch Ch *Ches* 65-68; C H Spirit Cathl Dodoma Tanzania 68-69; V Moshi 70-77; Home Sec USCL 77-83; TV Ipswich St Mary at Stoke w St Pet *St E* 83-94; P-in-c Bury St Edmunds St Mary 94-99; V 99-04; Asst Bp Mt Kilimanjaro from 04. *45 Birkenhead Road, Meols, Wirral CH47 5AF* Tel 07973-737682 (mobile) E-mail johnhayden@dsl.pipex.com

HAYDEN, Mark Joseph James. b 68. St Thos Aquinas Pontifical Univ Rome BD93 Clonliffe Coll DipHum89. H Cross Coll Clonliffe 86. **d** 92 **p** 93. In RC Ch 92-99; C Monkstown *D & G* 99-01; I Gorey w Kilnahue, Leskinfere and Ballycanew *C & O* from 01. *The Rectory, The Avenue, Gorey, Co Wexford, Irish Republic* Tel and fax (00353) (55) 21383 E-mail gorey@ferns.anglican.org

HAYDOCK, Canon Alan. b 41. Kelham Th Coll 60. **d** 65 **p** 66. C Rainworth *S'well* 65-68; C Hucknall Torkard 68-71; TV 71-74; V Bilborough St Jo 74-80; R E Bridgford 80-82; R E Bridgford and Kneeton from 82; RD Bingham 84-94; Hon Can S'well Minster from 86. *The Rectory, Kirk Hill, East Bridgford, Nottingham NG13 8PE* Tel (01949) 20218

HAYDON, Mrs Christine Mary. b 45. K Alfred's Coll Win CertEd66. NTMTC 93. **d** 96 **p** 97. NSM Aylesford *Roch* from 96. *44 Bramley Road, Snodland ME6 5DY* Tel (01634) 241821

HAYDON, Keith Frank. b 46. Cuddesdon Coll 73. **d** 75 **p** 76. C De Beauvoir Town St Pet *Lon* 75-77; C Wells St Thos w Horrington *B & W* 77-80; TV Weston-super-Mare Cen Par 80-84; TV Cowley St Jas *Ox* 84-87; TR 87-95; V Walsingham, Houghton and Barsham *Nor* 95-96; P-in-c 96-99; rtd 01. *Address withheld by request*

HAYE, Alfred Kirby. **d** 05. OLM Delaval *Newc* from 05. *1 Muirfield, Whitley Bay NE25 9HY* Tel 0191-291 3480

HAYES, Brian Richard Walker. b 33. Qu Coll Birm 81. **d** 83 **p** 84. C Cheadle Hulme All SS *Ches* 83-87; C Sheff St Cecilia Parson Cross *Sheff* 87-88; C Sheff St Leon Norwood 88-91; V Gazeley w Dalham, Moulton and Kentford *St E* 91-02; P-in-c Higham Green 98-02; rtd 02; Hon C W Felton *Lich* from 02. *The Rectory, Fox Lane, West Felton, Oswestry SY11 4EN* Tel (01691) 610228 E-mail brianhayes@cwcom.net

HAYES, Bruce John. b 75. UCD BA97 TCD BTh01. CITC 98. **d** 01 **p** 02. C Cregagh *D & D* 01-04; I Abbeystrewry Union *C, C & R* from 04. *The Rectory, Coronea Drive, Skibbereen, Co Cork, Irish Republic* Tel (00353) (28) 21234 E-mail abbeystrewry@eircom.net

HAYES, Christopher John. b 64. Univ of Wales BN RGN Leeds Univ MA. Cranmer Hall Dur. **d** 96 **p** 97. C Burton Fleming w Fordon, Grindale etc *York* 96-99; R Buckrose Carrs from 99; P-in-c Weaverthorpe w Helperthorpe, Luttons Ambo etc from 03. *The Vicarage, Low Moorgate, Rillington, Malton YO17 8JW* Tel (01944) 758891 E-mail chris@buckrose.org.uk

HAYES, David Malcolm Hollingworth. b 42. K Coll Lon BD68 AKC68 MPhil97. **d** 69 **p** 70. C Upper Teddington SS Pet and Paul *Lon* 69-70; C Ruislip St Martin 70-75; P-in-c Ludford *Heref* 75-80; P-in-c Ashford Carbonell w Ashford Bowdler 75-80; V Eastcote St Lawr *Lon* 80-90; R Cant St Pet w St Alphege and St Marg etc *Cant* from 90; P-in-c Blean from 03; Master Eastbridge Hosp from 90; Guardian of the Greyfriars from 97. *The Master's Lodge, 58 St Peter's Street, Canterbury CT1 2BE* Tel (01227) 462395 E-mail davmon@eastbridge.fsnet.co.uk

HAYES, David Roland Payton. b 37. Hertf Coll Ox BA62 MA66. Coll of Resurr Mirfield 62. **d** 64 **p** 65. C Woodley St Jo the Ev *Ox* 64-67; C Emscote *Cov* 67-69; C Farnham Royal *Ox* 69-75; P-in-c 75-78; P-in-c Lathbury 78-79; P-in-c Newport Pagnell 78-79; R Newport Pagnell w Lathbury 79-85; RD Newport 80-85; Chapl Renny Lodge Hosp 85-87; R Newport Pagnell w Lathbury and Moulsoe *Ox* 85-86; P-in-c 86-87; P-in-c Bucknell w Buckton, Llanfair Waterdine and Stowe *Heref* 87-91; V Bucknell w Chapel Lawn, Llanfair Waterdine etc 91-94; RD Clun Forest 91-94; P-in-c Presteigne w Discoed, Kinsham and Lingen 94-00; P-in-c Knill 97-00; R Presteigne w Discoed, Kinsham, Lingen and Knill 00-01; rtd 01; Perm to Offic *Heref* from 01. *3 Redcar Avenue, Hereford HR4 9TJ* Tel (01432) 261466

HAYES, Denise Angela. b 62. N Ord Course 02. **d** 05. C Ashton-in-Makerfield St Thos *Liv* from 05. *79 Greenfields Crescent, Ashton-in-Makerfield, Wigan WN4 8QY* Tel (01942) 272681 Mobile 07736-523168 E-mail denisehayes4@aol.com

HAYES, John Henry Andrew. b 52. BSc. Wycliffe Hall Ox 82. **d** 84 **p** 85. C Moreton *Ches* 84-87; R Barrow 87-94; Bp's Chapl 87-94; P-in-c Runcorn St Mich 94-04; P-in-c Runcorn All SS from 94; P-in-c Runcorn H Trin from 04. *The Vicarage, 1 Highlands Road, Runcorn WA7 4PS* Tel (01928) 572417 E-mail revjohnhayes@ntlworld.com

HAYES, Kenneth Richard. b 50. Cen Sch of Art Lon DipAD72 RCA(Lon). Qu Coll Birm 95. **d** 97 **p** 98. C Gravesend H Family w Ifield *Roch* 97-01; V Gillingham St Mary from 01. *The Vicarage, 27 Gillingham Green, Gillingham ME7 1SS* Tel (01634) 850529

HAYES, Mrs Marion Anne. b 51. Liv Inst of Educn CertEd72 Leeds Univ BA05. N Ord Course 02. **d** 05. NSM Runcorn All SS *Ches* from 05; NSM Runcorn H Trin from 05. *The Vicarage, 1 Highlands Road, Runcorn WA7 4PS* Tel (01928) 572417

HAYES, Michael Gordon William. b 48. St Cath Coll Cam BA69 MA73 PhD73. Ridley Hall Cam 73. **d** 75 **p** 76. C Combe Down w Monkton Combe *B & W* 75-78; C Cambridge H Trin *Ely* 78-81; V Bathampton *B & W* 81-88; V Clevedon St Andr and Ch Ch 88-95; C Belper *Derby* 95-00; P-in-c Drayton in Hales *Lich* from 00; RD Hodnet from 01. *The Vicarage, Mount Lane, Market Drayton TF9 1AQ* Tel (01630) 652527 E-mail mhhayes@freeuk.com

HAYES, Michael John. b 52. Lanc Univ BA73. Coll of Resurr Mirfield 75. **d** 78 **p** 79. C Notting Hill *Lon* 78-81; C-in-c Hammersmith SS Mich and Geo White City Estate CD 81-88; Perm to Offic 98-00; NSM Norwood St Mary 00-03. *Address temp unknown*

HAYES, Richard. b 39. K Coll Lon BD68 AKC68. **d** 69 **p** 70. C Dartford H Trin *Roch* 69-72; C S Kensington St Steph *Lon* 72-76; V Ruislip Manor St Paul 76-82; V Ealing St Pet Mt Park 82-91; R St Edm the King and St Mary Woolnoth etc 91-99; rtd 99; Perm to Offic *Lich* 99-04 and *Heref* from 00; Hon C Shrewsbury St Alkmund *Lich* from 04. *26 St John's Hill, Shrewsbury SY1 1JJ* Tel (01743) 244668 E-mail rhayes@beeb.net

HAYES, Richard Henry. b 65. Bp Otter Coll St Jo Coll Nottm 89. **d** 92 **p** 93. C Southborough St Pet w Ch Ch and St Matt *Roch* 92-95; C Downend *Bris* 95-97; V Gravesend St Mary *Roch* 97-02; R Clymping and Yapton w Ford *Chich* from 02. *The Rectory, St Mary's Meadow, Yapton, Arundel BN18 0EE* Tel (01243) 552962 Mobile 07944-804933 E-mail hayesrev@supanet.com

HAYES, Mrs Rosemarie Eveline. b 51. Brighton Coll of Educn CertEd72. N Ord Course 88. **d** 91 **p** 94. Par Dn Manston *Ripon* 91-94; C 94-95; C Beeston 95-00; V Horsforth from 00. *St Margaret's Vicarage, Church Lane, Horsforth, Leeds LS18 5LA* Tel 0113-258 2481 E-mail rosemarie@hayes2482.fsnet.co.uk

HAYES, Stephen Anthony. b 57. St Jo Coll Dur BA80 S Bank Univ PGCE96. St Alb and Ox Min Course 97. **d** 99 **p** 00. NSM Kingham w Churchill, Daylesford and Sarsden *Ox* 99-01; Chapl Kingham Hill Sch Oxon from 99; NSM Chipping Norton *Ox* from 01. *Severn House, Kingham Hill School, Kingham, Chipping Norton OX7 6TW* Tel and fax (01608) 658341 E-mail steve@hayesfamily.freeuk.com

HAYES, Timothy James. b 62. **d** 89 **p** 90. C Lache cum Saltney *Ches* 89-94; P-in-c Dukinfield St Jo 94-99; V from 99. *37 Harald Avenue, Dukinfield SK16 5NH* Tel 0161-308 4708

HAYHOE, Geoffrey John Stephen. b 57. Portsm Univ BSc00. Qu Coll Birm 01. **d** 03 **p** 04. C Felixstowe St Jo *St E* from 03. *20 Russell Road, Felixstowe IP11 2BD* Tel (01394) 278592 Mobile 07946-379678 E-mail john@hayhoe.net

HAYLER, Peter John. b 65. R Holloway Coll Lon BSc87 Univ of Wales MPhil02. Wilson Carlile Coll 89 St Mich Coll Llan 99. **d** 00 **p** 04. Ind Chapl *Mon* 95-03; C Pontnewydd 00-03; C Magor from 03. *6 Old Barn Court, Undy, Caldicot NP26 3TE* Tel (01633) 882551 E-mail haylers@dialstart.net

HAYLES, Graham David. b 39. Clifton Th Coll 64. **d** 67 **p** 68. C Gipsy Hill Ch Ch *S'wark* 67-70; C Heatherlands St Jo *Sarum* 70-74; V W Streatham St Jas *S'wark* 74-90; TR Hinckley H Trin *Leic* 90-03; rtd 03; Perm to Offic *S'wark* from 04. *19 Park Road, Redhill RH1 1BT* Tel (01737) 761732

HAYLLAR, Bruce Sherwill. b 23. Trin Hall Cam BA47 MA53. Cuddesdon Coll 48. **d** 50 **p** 51. C Almondbury *Wakef* 50-53; India 53-63; V Peacehaven *Chich* 63-72; Zambia 72-75; V Moulsecoomb *Chich* 76-81; TR 81-83; R Rotherfield w Mark Cross 83-90; RD Rotherfield 87-90; rtd 90; Perm to Offic *Chich* from 90. *Moses Farm Cottage, Piltdown, Uckfield TN22 3XN* Tel (01825) 722006

HAYMAN, Mrs Audrey Doris. b 41. St Mary's Coll Chelt 61 Bris Univ CertEd61 Cov Coll of Educn 65. Glouc Sch of Min 88. **d** 91 **p** 94. NSM Matson *Glouc* 91-98; P-in-c Falfield w Rockhampton 98-02; P-in-c Oldbury-on-Severn 98-02; Perm to Offic 02-04; NSM Barnwood from 04. *32 Corncroft Lane, Matson, Gloucester GL7 2BN* Tel (01452) 411786 E-mail audrey.hayman@hotmail.com

HAYMAN, Canon Robert Fleming. b 31. Princeton Univ BA53. Gen Th Sem (NY) MDiv56. **d** 56 **p** 56. USA 56-88; I Drumcliffe w Lissadell and Munninane *K, E & A* 88-92; Preb Elphin Cathl 88-92; rtd 92. *1102 East Boston Street, Seattle, WA 98102, USA* Tel (001) (206) 860 7565

HAYNES, Anthony. *See* HAYNES, Michael Anthony

HAYNES, Miss Catherine Mary. b 68. Man Univ BA90. St Mich Coll Llan BD95 Dip Past Th 96. **d** 96 **p** 97. C Llantwit Major *Llan* 96-99; C Coity w Nolton 99-01; P-in-c Llangammarch w Llanganten and Llanlleonfel etc *S & B* 01-03; P-in-c Irfon Valley from 03. *The Rectory, Maesglas, Llangammarch Wells LD4 4EE* Tel (01591) 620482 E-mail cmhaynes@compuserve.com

HAYNES, Clifford. b 33. Cam Univ MA60. Linc Th Coll 80. **d** 82 **p** 83. C Lightcliffe *Wakef* 82-85; V Bradshaw 85-98; rtd 98; Perm to Offic *Carl* from 98. *East Lyn, Lazonby, Penrith CA10 1BX* Tel (01768) 897018

HAYNES, Cyril Michael. b 26. Univ of Wales BEd64. **d** 84 **p** 85. NSM Wenlock *Heref* 84-96; Perm to Offic 96-99. *Address temp unknown*

HAYNES (née RYDER), Mrs Jennifer Ann. b 40. Bath Spa Univ Coll BSc99. **d** 04. OLM Potterne w Worton and Marston *Sarum* from 04. *15 Mill Road, Worton, Devizes SN10 5SF* Tel (01380) 723911 E-mail jhaynes1@fish.co.uk

HAYNES, Canon John Richard. b 35. Ely Th Coll 60. **d** 63 **p** 64. C Bollington St Jo *Ches* 63-67; C Ches St Jo 67-68; C Davenham 68-70; Rhodesia 70-80; Zimbabwe 80-90; Sub-Dean Bulawayo Cathl 78-83; Hon Can Matabeleland from 90; V Bishop's Stortford *St Alb* 90-00; rtd 00; Perm to Offic *B & W* from 01. *53 Stag Way, Glastonbury BA6 9PR* Tel (01458) 830686

HAYNES, John Stanley. b 30. WMMTC. **d** 82 **p** 83. NSM Westwood *Cov* 82-84; C Radford Semele and Ufton 84-85; V 85-95; rtd 95; Perm to Offic *Cov* from 95. *64 Rugby Road, Cubbington, Leamington Spa CV32 7JF* Tel (01926) 330016

HAYNES, Leonard Thomas. b 17. **d** 69 **p** 70. C Lutterworth w Cotesbach *Leic* 69-73; C-in-c Swinford w Catthorpe, Shawell and Stanford 73-74; V 74-83; rtd 83; Perm to Offic *Leic* 83-02; *Birm* 95-97. *Seale Pastures House, Burton Road, Acresford, Swadlincote DE12 8AP* Tel (01283) 761024

HAYNES, Michael Anthony (Tony). b 47. Heythrop Coll Lon MA95 Univ of Wales LLM03. NTMTC 98. **d** 00 **p** 01. NSM Tottenham St Paul *Lon* from 00. *51 Lorraine Court, Clarence Way, London NW1 8SG* Tel (020) 7916 0370

HAYNES, Canon Michael Thomas Avery. b 32. AKC61. St Boniface Warminster 61. **d** 62 **p** 63. C Hebden Bridge *Wakef* 62-64; C Elland 64-68; V Thornhill Lees 68-82; V Lindley 82-97; Hon Can Wakef Cathl 82-97; rtd 97. *Longwood Edge Cottage, 86 Lamb Hall Road, Huddersfield HD3 3TJ*

HAYNES, The Very Revd Peter. b 25. Selw Coll Cam BA49 MA54. Cuddesdon Coll 50. **d** 52 **p** 53. C Stokesley *York* 52-54; C Hessle 54-58; V Drypool St Jo 58-63; Asst Dir RE *B & W* 63-70; Youth Chapl 63-70; V Glastonbury St Jo 70-72; V Glastonbury St Jo w Godney 72-74; Adn Wells, Can Res and Preb Wells Cathl 74-82; Dean Heref and V Heref St Jo *Heref* 82-92; rtd 92; Perm to Offic *B & W* 92-04. *5 St John Street, Hereford HR1 2NB* Tel (01432) 342271

HAYNES, Peter Nigel Stafford. b 39. Hertf Coll Ox BA62 MA66. Cuddesdon Coll 62. **d** 64 **p** 65. C Norwood All SS *Cant* 64-68; C Portsea N End St Mark *Portsm* 68-72; Asst Chapl Brussels *Eur* 72-76; TV Banbury *Ox* 76-80; Asst Sec (Internat Affairs) Gen Syn Bd Soc Resp 80-85; P-in-c E Peckham and Nettlestead *Roch* 85-92; R Bredgar w Bicknor and Frinsted w Wormshill etc *Cant* 92-99; rtd 99. *1 Vesper Cottage, Cage Lane, Smarden, Ashford TN27 8QD* Tel (01233) 770367

HAYNES, Valerie Elizabeth. b 53. St Steph Ho Ox 03. **d** 05. C Sheerness H Trin w St Paul *Cant* from 05. *The Vicarage, North Road, Queenborough ME11 5HA* Tel (01795) 662648 Mobile 07803-798475

HAYSMORE, Geoffrey Frederick. b 39. Bps' Coll Cheshunt 63. **d** 66 **p** 67. C St Marylebone St Mark w St Luke *Lon* 66-69; C Stockton St Chad *Dur* 69-72; C-in-c Town End Farm CD 72-77; Perm to Offic *York* from 95; rtd 01. *139 Lambton Road, Middlesbrough TS4 2ST* Tel (01642) 275259

HAYTER, Mary Elizabeth. *See* BARR, Mary Elizabeth

HAYTER, Raymond William. b 48. Oak Hill Th Coll 74. **d** 77 **p** 78. C Bermondsey St Jas w Ch Ch *S'wark* 77-80; C Sydenham H Trin 81-83; Asst Chapl HM Pris Brixton 83-84; Chapl HM Youth Cust Cen Stoke Heath 84-88; Chapl HM Pris Maidstone 88-91; CF from 91. *c/o MOD Chaplains (Army)* Tel (01980) 615804 Fax 615800

HAYTER, Ronald William Joseph. b 19. Keble Coll Ox BA40 MA44. Wells Th Coll 40. **d** 42 **p** 43. C Honiton *Ex* 42-45; C Ex St Mark 45-47; C Ex St Thos 47-51; C Paignton St Jo 51-55; V Countess Wear 55-87; rtd 87; Perm to Offic *Ex* 92-98. *2D Imperial Court, Parkhill Road, Torquay TQ1 2EP*

HAYTER, Sandra. *See* RAILTON, Sandra

HAYTHORNTHWAITE, Robert Brendan. b 31. Solicitor 59 TCD BA53 LLB56 MA64 QUB DipEd71. Edin Th Coll 63. **d** 64 **p** 65. C Belfast St Jo Laganbank w Orangefield *D & D* 64-66; C Belfast St Thos *Conn* 66-68; Lic to Offic 68-75; C Belfast Malone St Jo 75-89; I Shinrone w Aghancon etc *L & K* 89-98; Dom Chapl to Bp of Killaloe and Clonfert 89-98; rtd 98. *La Nauvrasse, 17270 St Pierre du Palais, Montguyon, Charente-Maritime, France* Tel (0033) (5) 46 04 56 58

HAYTON, John Anthony. b 45. TD81. Heythrop Coll Lon MA00 ACII70. Oak Hill Th Coll 93. **d** 96 **p** 97. NSM St Alb St Mich *St Alb* from 96; OCF from 02. *89 Harpenden Road, St Albans AL3 6BY* Tel (01727) 761719 *or* 835037 Fax 765832 *or* 811744 E-mail johntish.hayton@lineone.net

HAYTON, Mark William. b 59. St Steph Ho Ox 85. **d** 88 **p** 89. C Sittingbourne St Mich *Cant* 88-91; C Kennington 91-94; R Broadstairs from 94; RD Thanet 96-01. *The Rectory, Nelson Place, Broadstairs CT10 1HQ* Tel (01843) 862921 E-mail markhayton@supanet.com

HAYTON, Norman Joseph Patrick. b 32. MRICS57. Sarum Th Coll 69. **d** 71 **p** 72. C Lytham St Cuth *Blackb* 71-74; V Wesham 74-79; V Chorley St Geo 79-80; NSM Kells *Carl* 84-85; P-in-c Flimby 85-90; V Barrow St Jas 90-94; TV Egremont and Haile 94-97; P-in-c Distington 97-00; rtd 00; P-in-c Charnock Richard *Blackb* from 01. *The Vicarage, 132 Church Lane, Charnock Richard, Chorley PR7 5NA* Tel (01257 791385 E-mail normanhayton@hotmail.com

HAYWARD, Canon Alan Richard. b 25. Open Univ BA72. Wycliffe Hall Ox 54. **d** 56 **p** 57. C Dudley St Fran *Worc* 56-59; C-in-c Wollescote CD 59-65; V Wollescote 65-85; Hon Can Worc Cathl 85-91; R Alvechurch 85-91; rtd 91; Perm to Offic *Worc* 91-01. *2 St Kenelm's Court, St Kenelm's Road, Romsley, Halesowen B62 0NF* Tel (01562) 710749

HAYWARD, Canon Christopher Joseph. b 38. TCD BA63 MA67. Ridley Hall Cam 63. **d** 65 **p** 66. C Hatcham St Jas *S'wark* 65-69; Warden Lee Abbey Internat Students' Club Kensington 69-74; Chapl Chelmsf Cathl *Chelmsf* 74-77; P-in-c Darlaston All SS *Lich* 77-83; Ind Chapl 77-83; Can Res Bradf Cathl *Bradf* 83-92; Sec Bd Miss 83-92; R Linton in Craven 92-03; P-in-c Burnsall w Rylstone 97-03; RD Skipton 93-98; Hon Can Bradf Cathl 92-03; rtd 03. *28A North Parade, Burley in Wharfedale, Ilkley LS29 7JR* Tel (01943) 865850

HAYWARD, Derek. *See* HAYWARD, The Ven John Derek Risdon

HAYWARD, Jane. *See* HAYWARD, Ms Pamela Jane

HAYWARD, Canon Jeffrey Kenneth. b 47. Nottm Univ BTh74. St Jo Coll Nottm LTh73. **d** 74 **p** 75. C Stambermill *Worc* 74-77; C Woking St Jo *Guildf* 77-83; V Springfield H Trin *Chelmsf* 83-98; Chapl HM Pris Chelmsf 86-00; Area RD Chelmsf 86-88; RD Chelmsf 88-93; RD Chelmsf N 93-95; Hon Can Chelmsf Cathl 93-98; Chapl HM Pris Wakef from 00. *HM Prison, Love Lane, Wakefield WF2 9AG* Tel (01924) 378282 ext 463 Fax 384391

HAYWARD, Mrs Jennifer Dawn. b 38. WMMTC 85. **d** 88 **p** 94. NSM Gt Malvern St Mary *Worc* 88-90; NSM Gt Malvern Ch Ch 88-90; Par Dn 90-94; C 94-96; TV Wirksworth *Derby* 96-04; rtd 04; Perm to Offic *Worc* from 04. *26 Barley Crescent, Long Meadow, Worcester WR4 0HW* Tel (01905) 29545 E-mail revd.j.d.hayward@fish.co.uk

HAYWARD, John Andrew. b 63. MHCIMA83 Nottm Univ BTh89. Linc Th Coll 86. **d** 89 **p** 90. C Seaford w Sutton *Chich* 89-92; C St Pancras H Cross w St Jude and St Pet *Lon* 92-95; V Kentish Town St Martin w St Andr from 95. *St Martin's Vicarage, 26 Vicar's Road, London NW5 4NL* Tel and fax (020) 7485 3807 E-mail smartingospeloak@aol.com

HAYWARD, The Ven John Derek Risdon. b 23. OBE00. Trin Coll Cam BA56 MA64. Westcott Ho Cam 56. **d** 57 **p** 58. C Sheff St Mary w St Simon w St Matthias *Sheff* 57-59; V Sheff Gillcar St Silas 59-63; V Isleworth All SS *Lon* 64-94; Adn Middx 74-75; Gen Sec Lon Dio 75-93; rtd 94; Perm to Offic *B & W* from 94. *29A Great Pulteney Street, Bath BA2 4BU* Tel (01225) 336305 Fax 421862

HAYWARD, Preb John Talbot. b 28. Selw Coll Cam BA52 MA56. Wells Th Coll 52. **d** 54 **p** 55. C S Lyncombe *B & W* 54-58; R Lamyatt 58-71; V Bruton w Wyke Champflower and Redlynch 58-71; RD Bruton 62-71; R Weston-super-Mare St Jo 71-75; Preb Wells Cathl from 73; TR Weston-super-Mare Cen Par 75-92; rtd 92; Perm to Offic *B & W* from 92. *5 Chelswood Avenue, Weston-super-Mare BS22 8QP* Tel (01934) 628431

HAYWARD, Ms Pamela Jane. b 52. RGN82. Westcott Ho Cam 84. **d** 87 **p** 94. Par Dn Northampton St Mary *Pet* 87-90; Par Dn Bris St Mary Redcliffe w Temple etc *Bris* 90-94; C 94-96; V Eastville St Anne w St Mark and St Thos from 96. *St Anne's Vicarage, 75 Greenbank Road, Bristol BS5 6HD* Tel and fax 0117-952 0202

HAYWARD, Peter Noel. b 26. Leeds Univ BA48 BD78. Coll of Resurr Mirfield 48. **d** 50 **p** 51. C S Elmsall *Wakef* 50-56; C Sheldon *Birm* 56-60; C-in-c Garretts Green CD 60-69; V Garretts Green 69-70; V N Cave w Cliffe *York* 70-00; R Hotham 70-00; RD Howden 78-86; P-in-c Newbald 97-00; rtd 00; Perm to Offic *Carl* from 00; Hon C Solway Plain from 02. *The Old Chapel, Allonby, Maryport CA15 6QH* Tel (01900) 881466

HAYWARD, William Richmond. b 42. JP98. NY Th Sem BA90 NY Th Sem MPS91. Chich Th Coll 88. **d** 88 **p** 90. Bermuda from 88; Miss to Seafarers from 91. *8 Seabright Avenue, Paget DV 04, Bermuda* Tel (001441) 236 3221 Fax as telephone

HAYWOOD, James William. b 36. Chich Th Coll 69. **d** 73 **p** 74. C Leeds Halton St Wilfrid *Ripon* 73-76; C Workington St Jo *Carl* 76-78; V Clifton 78-84; P-in-c Barrow St Jas 84-85; V 85-89; V Crosby Ravensworth 89-94; R Asby 89-94; V Bolton 89-94; rtd 98. *19 Bramham Road, Whitwood, Castleford WF10 5PA*

HAYWOOD, Keith Roderick. b 48. Oak Hill Th Coll 84. **d** 86 **p** 87. C Fazeley *Lich* 86-90; TV Leek and Meerbrook 90-01; Acting TR Hanley H Ev 01-03; TR from 03. *Hanley Rectory, 35 Harding Road, Hanley, Stoke-on-Trent ST1 3BQ* Tel (01782) 266066 E-mail krhaywood@xalt.co.uk

HAZEL, Sister. *See* SMITH, Sister Hazel Ferguson Waide

HAZELL, The Ven Frederick Roy. b 30. Fitzw Ho Cam BA53 MA59. Cuddesdon Coll 54. **d** 56 **p** 57. C Ilkeston St Mary *Derby* 56-59; C Heanor 59-62; V Marlpool 62-63; Chapl Univ of W Indies 63-66; C St Martin-in-the-Fields *Lon* 66-68; V Croydon H Sav *Cant* 68-84; RD Croydon 72-78; Hon Can Cant Cathl 73-84; P-in-c Croydon H Trin 77-80; Adn Croydon *S'wark* 84-93; rtd 93; P-in-c Chard, Furnham w Chaffcombe, Knowle St Giles etc *B & W* 95-99; P-in-c Tardebigge *Worc* 00-03; Perm to Offic *Birm* from 00 and *Worc* from 04. *Cotswold Cottage, School Lane, Alvechurch, Birmingham B48 7SA* Tel 0121-445 1318

HAZELL, Thomas Jeremy. b 35. Bris Univ LLB56 PhD01. St D Coll Lamp 56. **d** 58 **p** 59. C Newport St Paul *Mon* 58-61; C Derby St Jo *Derby* 61-64; V Arksey *Sheff* 64-69; Sen Student Cllr Univ of Wales (Cardiff) *Llan* 69-89; rtd 95. *Castlewood Barn, Ponde, Llandefalle, Brecon LD3 0NR* Tel (01874) 754030

HAZELTON, John. b 35. St Cath Coll Cam BA56 MA60 Bris Univ MLitt74 Newc Univ BPhil80. Wells Th Coll 59. **d** 61 **p** 62. C Twerton *B & W* 61-65; V Pitcombe w Shepton Montague 65-72; Lect SS Hild and Bede Dur 72-79; Asst Master Dame Allan's Schs Newc 79-88; Chapl 88-95; rtd 95; Perm to Offic *Dur* from 97. *36 Orchard Drive, Durham DH1 1LA* Tel 0191-384 6606

HAZELTON, Michael John. b 53. UEA BA76 Bedf Coll Lon PhD81 Heythrop Coll Lon BD89. **d** 90 **p** 91. Asst Chapl Helsinki *Eur* 94-95; Asst Chapl Zürich w Winterthur 95-98; R Mablethorpe w Trusthorpe *Linc* 98-02; R Saxonwell 02-05; V Danby *York* from 05; P-in-c Westerdale from 05. *The Vicarage, Yall Flats Lane, Danby, Whitby YO21 2NQ* Tel (01287) 660388 E-mail mjh_uk@hotmail.com

HAZELTON, Robert Henry Peter. b 22. Wells Th Coll 65. **d** 67 **p** 68. C Eastover *B & W* 67-69; C Milton 69-76; V Peasedown St John 76-80; V Peasedown St John w Wellow 80-89; rtd 90; Perm to Offic *B & W* from 90. *37 High Meadows, Midsomer Norton, Bath BA3 2RY* Tel (01761) 419675

HAZELWOOD, Ms Jillian. b 32. Bp Otter Coll CertEd52 St Alb Minl Tr Scheme 82. **d** 87 **p** 94. NSM Wheathampstead *St Alb* 87-02; Perm to Offic from 02. *14 Butterfield Road, Wheathampstead, St Albans AL4 8PU* Tel and fax (01582) 833146

HAZLEDINE, Basil William. b 18. St Pet Hall Ox BA42 MA45. Wycliffe Hall Ox 42. **d** 43 **p** 44. C Highfield *Ox* 43-46; C Gerrards Cross 46-51; V Barking St Patr *Chelmsf* 51-55; R Twineham and V Sayers Common *Chich* 55-60; V Stoughton *Guildf* 60-70; V Westlands St Andr *Lich* 70-77; P-in-c Whatfield w Semer *St E* 77-78; R 78-81; P-in-c Nedging w Naughton 77-81; R Whatfield w Semer, Nedging and Naughton 81-84; rtd 84. *1 David Gresham House, 226 Pollards Oak Road, Oxted RH8 0JP* Tel (01883) 717763

HAZLEHURST, Anthony Robin. b 43. Man Univ BSc64. Tyndale Hall Bris 65. **d** 68 **p** 69. C Macclesfield Ch Ch *Ches* 68-71; C Bushbury *Lich* 71-75; P-in-c New Clee *Linc* 75-85; TV Deane *Man* 85-96; V Harwood from 96. *The Vicarage, Stitch mi Lane, Bolton BL2 4HU* Tel (01204) 525196 E-mail robinhaz@fish.co.uk

HAZLEHURST, David. b 32. Liv Univ BSc54. St Steph Ho Ox 55. **d** 57 **p** 58. C Sheff Arbourthorne *Sheff* 57-59; C Doncaster Ch Ch 59-61; C W Wycombe *Ox* 61-63; P-in-c Collyhurst St Jas *Man* 66-67; V Blackrod 67-79; V Halliwell St Marg 79-84; R Sutton St Nic *S'wark* 84-94; rtd 94; Perm to Offic *S'wark* from 95; Perm to Offic *Guildf* 95-99. *3 Up The Quadrangle, Morden College, 19 St Germans Place, London SE3 0PW* Tel (020) 8853 1180

HAZLEHURST, David John Benedict (Benny). b 63. Trin Coll Bris 88. **d** 91 **p** 92. C Plumstead St Jo w St Jas and St Paul *S'wark* 91-98; Estates Outreach Worker (S'wark Adnry) 98-02; V Brixton Road Ch Ch from 02. *The Vicarage, 96 Brixton Road, London SW9 6BE* Tel (020) 7793 0621 Mobile 07973-498590 E-mail christchurchnb@tiscali.co.uk

HAZLEHURST, Robin. *See* HAZLEHURST, Anthony Robin

HAZLETT, Stephen David. b 56. TCD BTh88. CITC. **d** 88 **p** 89. C Ballywillan *Conn* 88-90; I Rathcoole 90-95; I Dunluce 95-00; TV Sunderland *Dur* from 00; Ind Chapl from 00. *14 The Oaks West, Sunderland SR2 8HZ* Tel 0191-565 4121 E-mail stephen.hazlett@lineone.net

HAZLEWOOD, Andrew Lord. b 54. BSc. Wycliffe Hall Ox. **d** 82 **p** 83. C Leckhampton SS Phil and Jas w Cheltenham St Jas *Glouc* 82-85; C Waltham H Cross *Chelmsf* 85-89; R Pedmore *Worc* from 89. *The Rectory, Pedmore Lane, Stourbridge DY9 0SW* Tel (01562) 884856 *or* 887287 E-mail andrewhazlewood@hotmail.com *or* stpeterspedmore@hotmail.com

HAZLEWOOD, David Paul. b 47. Sheff Univ MB, ChB70 Campion Hall Ox BA72 MA77. Wycliffe Hall Ox 70. **d** 73 **p** 74. C Chapeltown *Sheff* 73-75; Singapore 76; Indonesia 76-88; R Ipswich St Helen *St E* 88-97; V Shirley *Win* from 97. *The*

Vicarage, 2B Wordsworth Road, Southampton SO15 5LX Tel (023) 8077 4329 E-mail david.hazlewood@ukgateway.net

HAZLEWOOD, William Peter Guy. b 71. De Montfort Univ BA97. St Steph Ho Ox BTh01. **d** 01 **p** 02. C Knowle H Nativity and Easton All Hallows *Bris* 01-04; P-in-c Iver Heath *Ox* from 04. *The Rectory, 2 Pinewood Close, Iver SL0 0QS* Tel (01753) 654470 E-mail frwill@onetel.com

HEAD, David Nicholas. b 55. Pemb Coll Cam BA77 MA81 Westmr Coll of Educn MTh01. Westcott Ho Cam 78. **d** 81 **p** 82. C Surbiton St Andr and St Mark *S'wark* 81-84; C St Marylebone w H Trin *Lon* 84-89; TV Clapham Team *S'wark* 89-96; Chapl Trin Hospice Lon 89-96; Chapl Princess Alice Hospice Esher 96-03; R Lyng, Sparham, Elsing, Bylaugh, Bawdeswell etc *Nor* from 03. *The Rectory, Rectory Road, Lyng, Norwich NR9 5RA* Tel and fax (01603) 872381 E-mail davidhead@tiscali.co.uk

HEAD, Canon Derek Leonard Hamilton. b 34. ALCD58. **d** 58 **p** 59. C Bexleyheath Ch Ch *Roch* 58-61; C Wisley w Pyrford *Guildf* 61-66; C-in-c Ewell St Paul Howell Hill CD 66-73; R Headley All SS 73-81; TR 81-82; RD Farnham 80-82; V Chertsey 82-99; Hon Can Guildf Cathl 83-99; RD Runnymede 88-93; Dir Post-Ord Tr 90-94; rtd 99; Perm to Offic *Win* from 00. *9 Tangmere Close, Mudeford, Christchurch BH23 4LZ* Tel (01425) 276545 E-mail headd@onetel.com

HEAD, Canon Ivan Francis. b 53. Univ of W Aus BA75 Glas Univ PhD85. Melbourne Coll of Div BD78. **d** 79 **p** 79. Australia 79-81 and from 85; C Uddingston *Glas* 81-85; C Cambuslang 81-85; Dir Angl Inst Theol Perth 85-91; Warden Ch Coll Tasmania Univ 91-94; Warden St Paul's Coll Sydney Univ from 95. *St Paul's College, University of Sydney, NSW, Australia 2006* Tel (0061) (2) 9550 7444 *or* 9557 1447 Fax 9519 7246 E-mail ihead@mail.usyd.edu.au

HEAD, Peter Ernest. b 38. Lon Univ BSc59. Ridley Hall Cam 61. **d** 63 **p** 64. C Fulwood *Sheff* 63-66; C Belper *Derby* 66-68; Hd RE Shoeburyness Sch Southend-on-Sea 69-74; Hd RE Bilborough Coll 74-79; Public Preacher *S'well* 74-79; NSM Bramcote 74-79; Vice-Prin Totton Coll Southn 79-93; Hon C Hordle *Win* 94-02; rtd 03; Perm to Offic *Win* from 02. *44 Lentune Way, Lymington SO41 3PF* Tel and fax (01590) 678097 E-mail peter_head@bigfoot.com

HEAD, William Peter. b 18. St Edm Hall Ox BA46 MA51. Cuddesdon Coll 46. **d** 48 **p** 49. C Beeston *S'well* 48-52; CF 52-56; V Wellingborough St Barn *Pet* 56-61; Chapl Highfield Sch Liphook 61-74; rtd 83; Perm to Offic *Chich* from 83. *3 Ferndale Road, Chichester PO19 6QJ* Tel (01243) 527075

HEADING, Margaret Anne. b 66. Leeds Univ BSc88 Man Univ PhD91 Aston Univ PGCE99. Wycliffe Hall Ox BA01. **d** 02 **p** 03. C Fletchamstead *Cov* from 02. *466 Tile Hill Lane, Coventry CV4 9DY* Tel (024) 7647 3281 E-mail heading@fish.co.uk

HEADING, Canon Richard Vaughan. b 43. ARCS65 Lon Univ BSc65. Coll of Resurr Mirfield 66. **d** 68 **p** 69. C Heref St Martin *Heref* 68-75; P-in-c Birches Head *Lich* 75-77; P-in-c Northwood 75-77; TV Hanley H Ev 77-82; V Heref H Trin *Heref* 82-92; TR Bedminster *Bris* from 92; Hon Can Bris Cathl from 01; AD Bris S from 01. *Bedminster Rectory, 287 North Street, Bristol BS3 1JP* Tel 0117-966 4025 Fax 963 1209 E-mail heading@surfaid.org

HEADLAND, James Frederick. b 20. Clifton Th Coll 51. **d** 53 **p** 54. C Barnsbury St Andr *Lon* 53-55; C Spitalfields Ch Ch w All SS 55-57; V Upper Tulse Hill St Matthias *S'wark* 57-65; R Church Pulverbatch *Heref* 65-81; P-in-c Smethcott w Woolstaston 65-81; R Reedham w Cantley w Limpenhoe and Southwood *Nor* 81-86; rtd 86; Perm to Offic *Heref* from 86 and *Lich* 88-00. *3 Ashford Avenue, Pontesbury, Shrewsbury SY5 0QN* Tel (01743) 790565

HEADLEY, Miss Carolyn Jane. b 50. K Coll Lon MA94 MCSP71. Oak Hill Th Coll BA83. **dss** 83 **d** 87 **p** 94. Kensal Rise St Mark and St Martin *Lon* 83-87; Par Dn Uxbridge 87-90; TD 90-92; Warden of Readers (Willesden Area) 88-92; Tutor Wycliffe Hall Ox 94-05; P-in-c W Meon and Warnford *Portsm* from 05. *The Rectory, Doctors Lane, West Meon, Petersfield GU32 1LR* Tel (01730) 829226 E-mail carolyn@headley1.plus.com

HEADS, John. b 27. Bps' Coll Cheshunt 60. **d** 62 **p** 63. C Beamish *Dur* 61-64; C Monkwearmouth St Andr 64-65; C Stockton St Chad 65-70; rtd 94. *18 Green Crescent, Golcar, Huddersfield HD7 4RF* Tel (01484) 651232

HEAGERTY, Alistair John. b 42. MBE86. Oriel Coll Ox BA63 MA67. Lon Coll of Div BD68. **d** 68 **p** 69. C Margate H Trin *Cant* 68-72; CF 72-97; Chapl R Memorial Chpl Sandhurst 92-97; TV Kingswood *Bris* from 97. *60 Lavers Close, Kingswood, Bristol BS15 9ZG* Tel 0117-935 2658 E-mail alistair@heagerty.freeserve.co.uk

HEAK, Philip George. b 70. QUB BA92. CITC BTh95. **d** 95 **p** 96. C Ballymacash *Conn* 95-98; C Galway w Kilcummin *T, K & A* 98-00; Dioc Youth Officer (Cashel) *C & O* from 00. *2 Colonnade Cottages, St Canice's Cathedral, Co Kilkenny, Irish Republic* Tel (00353) 86-817 2356 (mobile) E-mail pheak@eircom.net

HEAL, David Walter. b 37. Ox Univ MA63. Trin Coll Carmarthen 87. **d** 90 **p** 91. NSM Henfynyw w Aberaeron and Llanddewi Aberarth *St D* 90-96; Hon Asst Chapl Algarve *Eur* 96-98; Chapl Madeira 98-03; rtd 03; Perm to Offic *St D* from 04. *Cae Gwair Bach, Llanon SY23 5LZ* Tel (01974) 202596

HEAL, Miss Felicity Joan. b 42. Brighton Poly Dip Counselling 88. Portsm Dioc Tr Course 89. **d** 92. NSM Bramshott and Liphook *Portsm* 92-95; NSM Blendworth w Chalton w Idsworth 95-97; Perm to Offic from 97. *40 Rushes Road, Petersfield GU32 3BW* Tel (01730) 260410 Mobile 07712-249608 E-mail felicity@felicityheal.fsnet.co.uk

HEAL, Geoffrey. b 28. Linc Th Coll 54. **d** 56 **p** 57. C Camberwell St Giles *S'wark* 56-59; C Rotherhithe St Mary w All SS 59-62; V Peckham St Jo 62-75; V Southfields St Barn 75-88; rtd 88; Perm to Offic *Ex* 89-98. *Digby Cottage, 5 Hind Street, Ottery St Mary EX11 1BW* Tel (01404) 814729

HEALD, William Roland. b 40. St Jo Coll Auckland 72. **d** 74 **p** 75. C Howick New Zealand 74; C Kaitaia 75; C Auckland St Paul Symonds Street 76-78; V 84-93; C Bournville *Birm* 78-79; V Henderson New Zealand 79-82; V S Kensington St Luke *Lon* from 93. *12 Wharfedale Street, London SW10 9AL* Tel (020) 7244 0425 *or* 7370 0338 E-mail bill.heald@virgin.net

HEALE, Nicholas James. b 67. St Cath Coll Ox BA89 DPhil95 Leeds Univ BA94. Coll of Resurr Mirfield 95. **d** 95 **p** 96. C Syston *Leic* 95-99; V Blackpool St Mich *Blackb* from 99. *St Michael's Vicarage, Calvert Place, Blackpool FY3 7RU* Tel (01253) 397755

HEALE, Walter James Grenville. b 40. Wycliffe Hall Ox 77. **d** 79 **p** 80. C Walsall *Lich* 79-82; TV Marfleet *York* 82-89; TR 89-94; R Easington w Skeffling, Kilnsea and Holmpton from 94; P-in-c Owthorne and Rimswell w Withernsea from 00. *The Rectory, Hull Road, Easington, Hull HU12 0TE* Tel (01964) 650203

HEALES, John. b 48. K Coll Lon BD71 AKC71 PGCE72 DPS76. St Mich Coll Llan 75. **d** 76 **p** 77. C Cwmbran *Mon* 76-78; Chapl Rendcomb Coll Cirencester 78-82; Chapl Mon Sch 84-88; V Penhow, St Brides Netherwent w Llandavenny etc *Mon* from 88. *Flat 1, The Rectory, Llanfaches, Newport NP26 3AY* Tel (01633) 400901

HEALEY, James Christopher. b 44. Linc Th Coll 84. **d** 86 **p** 87. C Boultham *Linc* 86-90; TV Gt Grimsby St Mary and St Jas 90-91; I Narraghmore and Timolin w Castledermot etc *D & G* 91-93; I New Ross *C & O* 93-97; Dean Lismore 97-99; I Lismore w Cappoquin, Kilwatermoy, Dungarvan etc 97-99; Chan Cashel Cathl 97-99; Prec Waterford Cathl 97-99; Can Ossory Cathl 97-99; I Arvagh w Carrigallen, Gowna and Columbkille *K, E & A* 99-02; P-in-c Winthorpe and Langford w Holme *S'well* 02-03; R Coddington and Winthorpe and Langford w Holme 03-05; rtd 05. *12 Ridgeway, Nettleham, Lincoln LN2 2TL* Tel (01522) 753622

HEALEY, Michael Harry Edmund. b 74. Mansf Coll Ox MA01 Leeds Univ BA03. Coll of Resurr Mirfield 01. **d** 04 **p** 05. C Norton *Sheff* from 04. *6 Hazlebarrow Close, Sheffield S8 8AL* Tel 0114-237 5355 E-mail mhehealey@hotmail.com

HEANEY, Canon James Roland. b 59. **d** 85 **p** 86. C Ballynafeigh St Jude *D & D* 85-88; C Lisburn Ch Ch Cathl *Conn* 88-90; I Dunganstown w Redcross and Conary *D & G* from 90; Can Ch Ch Cathl Dublin from 05. *The Rectory, Redcross, Co Wicklow, Irish Republic* Tel and fax (00353) (404) 41637 E-mail heaneyr@indigo.ie

HEANEY, Michael Roger. b 43. TCD BA66 HDipEd67 MA69 DCG83. CITC 74. **d** 76 **p** 77. Chapl St Columba's Coll Dub from 76. *Montana, Scholarstown Road, Dublin 16, Irish Republic* Tel (00353) (1) 493 1167 *or* 493 2219 E-mail mheaney@iol.ie

HEANEY, Robert Stewart. **d** 01 **p** 02. C Dunboyne Union *M & K* 01-04. *46 Court Place Gardens, Iffley, Oxford OX4 4EW* Tel (01865) 715996 E-mail heaney2000@eircom.net *or* robert.heaney@theology.ox.ac.uk

HEANEY, Samuel Stewart. b 44. Open Univ BA79 Ulster Univ BEd83 Lon Univ BD93 QUB MPhil99. St Deiniol's Hawarden 92. **d** 92 **p** 93. In Presbyterian Ch 85-92; C Knockbreda *D & D* 92-96; I Belfast H Trin and St Silas *Conn* 96-02; I Ballyrashane w Kildollagh from 02. *9 Sandelwood Avenue, Coleraine BT52 1JW* Tel (028) 7034 3061

HEANEY, Timothy Daniel. b 59. Trin Coll Bris BA04. **d** 04 **p** 05. C Dursley *Glouc* from 04. *1 Riversmill Walk, Dursley GL11 5GL* Tel (01453) 546697 E-mail tim@heaney.org.uk

HEANEY, Wendy Anne. b 42. St Alb Minl Tr Scheme 90. **d** 95 **p** 96. NSM Clifton and Southill *St Alb* 95-99; Asst Chapl HM Pris Bedf 95-99; Chapl 99-02; Lic to Offic *St Alb* 99-02; rtd 02; Perm to Offic *St Alb* from 03. *34 Meadow Way, Letchworth Garden City SG6 3JB* Tel (01462) 641303

HEANS, Simon John. b 56. Peterho Cam BA77 MA81. St Steph Ho Ox 92. **d** 94 **p** 95. Asst Chapl Lancing Coll 94-99; NSM Lancing St Mich *Chich* 94-99; Chapl R Gr Sch Worc 99-00; C Brighton Resurr *Chich* 00-04; V Beckenham St Barn *Roch* from 04. *St Barnabas' Vicarage, Oakhill Road, Beckenham BR3 6NG* Tel (020) 8650 3332 Fax 8658 2429 E-mail simon@heans.fsnet.co.uk

HEAP, David Leonard. b 58. Man Univ BA79. Cranmer Hall Dur 82. **d** 85 **p** 86. C Clitheroe St Jas *Blackb* 85-88; C Blackb St Gabr 88-92; V Bare from 92. *St Christopher's Vicarage, 12 Elm Grove, Morecambe LA4 6AT* Tel (01524) 411363 E-mail davidheap@readingroom.freeserve.co.uk

HEAPS, Richard Peter. b 35. Bernard Gilpin Soc Dur 58 Qu Coll Birm 58. **d** 61 **p** 62. C Castle Bromwich SS Mary and Marg *Birm* 61-65; C-in-c Erdington St Chad CD 65-70; V Nechells 70-81; RD Aston 75-81; V Marston Green 81-86; P-in-c Shrawley and Witley w Astley *Worc* 86-92; R Shrawley, Witley, Astley and Abberley 92-01; rtd 01; Perm to Offic *Worc* from 01. *9 Timberdyne Close, Rock, Kidderminster DY14 9RT* Tel (01299) 832376

HEARD, Charles. b 19. S'wark Ord Course 62. **d** 65 **p** 66. C Plumstead St Nic *S'wark* 65-71; C Blackheath All SS 71-72; V Barnes H Trin 72-84; rtd 84; Hon C E Wickham *S'wark* from 84. *Flat 5, Elmfield Court, Wickham Street, Welling DA16 3DF* Tel (020) 8855 9809

HEARD, Stephen Edward. b 53. NTMTC 02. **d** 04. NSM Bush Hill Park St Mark *Lon* from 04. *43 Speed House, Barbican, London EC2Y 8AT* Tel (020) 7638 9501 Mobile 07939-263657 E-mail stephen.heard3@btinternet.com

HEARN, John Henry. b 49. Trin Coll Bris. **d** 82 **p** 83. C Epsom Common Ch Ch *Guildf* 82-85; C Ringwood *Win* 85-88; Chapl Basingstoke Distr Hosp 88-91; Chapl Luton and Dunstable Hosp 91-96; C Ampthill w Millbrook and Steppingley *St Alb* 96-99; P-in-c Wymington w Podington 99-03; V W Acklam *York* from 03. *St Mary's Vicarage, 50 Church Lane, Middlesbrough TS5 7EB* Tel (01642) 817150 E-mail john.hearn@tesco.net

HEARN, Jonathan. b 58. Leeds Univ BA81 GradIPM85. Westcott Ho Cam 89. **d** 91 **p** 92. C Tuffley *Glouc* 91-94; C Milton *Win* 94-02; P-in-c Warwick St Paul *Cov* 02-03; TV Warwick from 03. *St Paul's Vicarage, 33 Stratford Road, Warwick CV34 6AS* Tel (01926) 419814

HEARN, Canon Peter Brian. b 31. St Jo Coll Dur 52. **d** 55 **p** 56. C Frodingham *Linc* 55-59; R Belton SS Pet and Paul 59-64; PC Manthorpe w Londonthorpe 59-64; V Billingborough 64-73; V Sempringham w Pointon and Birthorpe 64-73; V Flixborough w Burton upon Stather 73-96; RD Manlake 87-93; Can and Preb Linc Cathl 92-01; rtd 96; Perm to Offic *Linc* from 01. *7 St Andrews Drive, Burton-upon-Stather, Scunthorpe DN15 9BY* Tel (01724) 720510

HEARN, Thomas Peter. b 18. Selw Coll Cam BA40 MA45. Linc Th Coll 40. **d** 42 **p** 43. C Oxhey St Matt *St Alb* 42-45; C Cirencester *Glouc* 45-52; V Childswyckham 52-62; R Aston Somerville 52-62; RD Winchcombe 60-62; R Stratton w Baunton 62-75; V France Lynch 75-83; rtd 84; Perm to Offic *Glouc* from 84. *9 Cotswold Close, Cirencester GL7 1XP* Tel (01285) 655627 E-mail hearn.petvon@amserve.net

HEARN, Trevor. b 36. Sarum Th Coll 61. **d** 64 **p** 65. C Hounslow St Steph *Lon* 64-67; Miss to Seafarers 67-01; UAE 92-01; rtd 01; Perm to Offic *Bris* from 01. *37 Elberton Road, Bristol BS9 2PZ* Tel 0117-983 6526 E-mail tandv@hearn3136.fsnet.co.uk

HEARTFIELD, Canon Peter Reginald. b 27. Chich Th Coll 61. **d** 63 **p** 64. C Hurstpierpoint *Chich* 63-67; V Brighton St Alb Preston 67-73; Chapl Kent and Cant Hosp 73-92; Chapl Nunnery Fields Hosp Cant 73-92; Six Preacher Cant Cathl *Cant* 79-84; Hon Can Cant Cathl 84-92; rtd 92; Perm to Offic *Cant* from 00. *13 Lanfranc Gardens, Harbledown, Canterbury CT2 8NJ* Tel (01227) 451621

HEASLIP, William John (Jack). b 44. TCD BA66. CITC 79. **d** 80 **p** 81. Chapl Mt Temple Sch Dub 80-86; Bp's C Aughaval w Burrishoole, Knappagh and Louisburgh *T, K & A* 86-88; I Aughaval w Achill, Knappagh, Dugort etc 88-95; Radio Officer (Tuam) 90-95; I Cork St Luke Union *C, C & R* 95-98; Colann Renewal Min *T, K & A* from 98. *Cloghadockan, Turlough, Castlebar, Co Mayo, Irish Republic* Tel (00353) (94) 902 5282 E-mail jackheaslip@eircom.net

HEATH, Mrs Cynthia Grace. b 46. ARCM66 GRSM68 St Mark & St Jo Coll Lon TCert68 Open Univ BA85. WMMTC 94. **d** 97 **p** 98. NSM Penkridge Team *Lich* 97-00; TV from 00. *The Vicarage, Top Road, Acton Trussell, Stafford ST17 0RQ* Tel (01785) 711154 Fax as telephone E-mail cheath@fish.co.uk

HEATH, Henry. b 40. FCII77. Oak Hill Th Coll 77. **d** 80 **p** 81. NSM Lexden *Chelmsf* 80-86; C Colne Engaine 86; NSM Halstead St Andr w H Trin and Greenstead Green 86-90; NSM W w E Mersea 90-95; R Stanway 95-02; rtd 02; Perm to Offic *Chelmsf* 02-05; P-in-c Wormingford, Mt Bures and Lt Horkesley from 05. *The Vicarage, Church Road, Wormingford, Colchester CO6 3AZ* Tel and fax (01787) 227398 E-mail heathatquayside@aol.com

HEATH, Mrs Janet. b 45. EMMTC 89. **d** 91 **p** 94. Par Dn Rainworth *S'well* 91-94; C 94-96; C Mansfield Woodhouse 96-99; rtd 00; Perm to Offic *S'well* from 00. *17 The Hollies, Sherwood Park, Rainworth, Mansfield NG21 0FZ* Tel (01623) 490422 E-mail janheath@supanet.com

HEATH, John Henry. b 41. Chich Th Coll 69. **d** 71 **p** 72. C Crediton *Ex* 71-74; C Tavistock and Gulworthy 74-76; C Brixham 76-77; C Brixham w Churston Ferrers 77-79; R Bere Ferrers 79-85; P-in-c Moretonhampstead, N Bovey and Manaton 85-88; R 88-93; P-in-c Lifton 93-99; P-in-c Kelly w Bradstone 93-99; P-in-c Broadwoodwidger 93-99; R Lifton, Broadwoodwidger, Coryton, Stowford etc 99-01; V Lifton, Broadwoodwidger, Stowford etc 01-03; rtd 03. *19 Closure Place, Peterchurch, Hereford HR2 0RS* Tel (01981) 550242

HEATH, Canon Peter Henry. b 24. Kelham Th Coll 40. **d** 47 **p** 48. C Derby St Anne *Derby* 47-49; C Staveley 49-52; C Brampton St Thos 52-54; C-in-c Brampton St Mark CD 54-59; V New Whittington 59-66; V Glossop 66-92; RD Glossop 83-89; Hon Can Derby Cathl 84-92; rtd 92; Perm to Offic *Derby* from 92. *Birchinlea, 15 Park Crescent, Glossop SK13 7BQ* Tel (01457) 862047

HEATH, Mrs Wendy Hillary. b 47. WMMTC 95. **d** 98 **p** 99. NSM Rugeley *Lich* 98-99; C 00-01; P-in-c Brereton from 01. *The Vicarage, 72 Main Road, Brereton, Rugeley WS15 1DU* Tel (01889) 582466 E-mail wen_heath@hotmail.com

HEATH, William Walter. b 11. St Jo Coll Ox BA32. **d** 72 **p** 73. Hon C Petworth *Chich* 72-90; Perm to Offic from 90. *Malthouse, Lurgashall, Petworth GU28 9ET* Tel (01428) 707212

HEATH-WHYTE, David Robert. b 68. Fitzw Coll Cam BA89. Wycliffe Hall Ox BTh98. **d** 98 **p** 99. C Gt Chesham *Ox* 98-02; V Frogmore *St Alb* from 02. *Holy Trinity Vicarage, 39 Frogmore, St Albans AL2 2JU* Tel (01727) 872172 E-mail david@hotfrog.info

HEATHCOTE, Warwick Geoffrey. b 46. St Paul's Coll Grahamstown 97. **d** 00 **p** 01. C Grahamstown Cathl S Africa 00-03; C Cirencester *Glouc* from 03. *The Parsonage, 32 Watermoor Road, Cirencester GL7 1JR* Tel (01285) 652299 E-mail warwick@htcw.fsnet.co.uk

HEATHER, Dennis Eric. b 34. LNSM course 95. **d** 98 **p** 99. OLM Hook *S'wark* from 98. *276 Hook Road, Chessington KT9 1PF* Tel (020) 8397 0063

HEATHER, Mark Duncan Grainger. b 62. Leic Poly LLB83 Leeds Univ BA99. Coll of Resurr Mirfield 97. **d** 99 **p** 00. C Leeds St Aid *Ripon* 99-03; V Leeds Halton St Wilfrid from 03. *St Wilfrid's Vicarage, Selby Road, Leeds LS15 7NP* Tel 0113-264 7000 E-mail mark.heather@bigfoot.com

HEATHER, Sally Patricia. b 51. Avery Hill Coll BEd73. STETS 99. **d** 02 **p** 03. NSM Michelmersh and Awbridge and Braishfield etc *Win* from 02. *Narnia, 2 Airlie Road, Winchester SO22 4NQ* Tel (01962) 622305 E-mail spheather@narnians.freeserve.co.uk

HEATHFIELD, Simon David. b 67. Birm Univ BMus88. Ridley Hall Cam BTh99. **d** 99 **p** 00. C Heswall *Ches* 99-02; Voc and Min Adv CPAS from 02. *27 Chestnut Tree Avenue, Coventry CV4 9FZ* Tel and fax (024) 7646 7410 E-mail srheath@fish.co.uk

HEATLEY, Cecil. *See* HEATLEY, Canon William Cecil

HEATLEY, David Henry. b 50. Kent Univ BA72. Qu Coll Birm 86. **d** 88 **p** 89. C Liss *Portsm* 88-91; V Newchurch and Arreton 91-99; R Greatham w Empshott and Hawkley w Prior's Dean from 99; Dioc Rural Officer from 98. *The Vicarage, Hawkley, Liss GU33 6NF* Tel (01730) 827459 E-mail dhheatley@aol.com

HEATLEY, Henry Daniel. b 24. CITC DipTh68. **d** 68 **p** 69. C Belfast St Matt *Conn* 68-72; C-in-c Layde 72-78; C Belfast St Mary 78-80; I Belfast St Barn 80-92; rtd 92. *Ebenezer, 91 Larne Road, Carrickfergus BT38 7NH* Tel (028) 9336 5382

HEATLEY, Canon William Cecil. b 39. QUB BA61. Ridley Hall Cam 62. **d** 64 **p** 65. C Ballymacarrett St Patr *D & D* 64-69; C Herne Hill St Paul *S'wark* 69-74; TV Sanderstead All SS 75-82; P-in-c Peckham St Sav 82-87; V from 87; RD Dulwich 97-02; Hon Can S'wark Cathl from 01. *173 Choumert Road, London SE15 4AW* Tel (020) 7639 5072 *or* 7732 3435

HEATON, Alan. b 36. K Coll Lon BD64 AKC64 Nottm Univ MTh76. **d** 65 **p** 66. C Stockton St Chad *Dur* 65-68; C Englefield Green *Guildf* 68-70; C Winlaton *Dur* 70-74; Chapl Derby Lonsdale Coll *Derby* 74-79; V Alfreton 79-87; RD Alfreton 81-86; TR Clifton *S'well* 87-93; P-in-c Rolleston w Fiskerton, Morton and Upton 93-96; rtd 97; Perm to Offic *Liv* from 97. *29 The Parchments, Newton-le-Willows WA12 0DX* Tel (01925) 292209

HEATON, Sister Elizabeth Ann. b 65. Bath Coll of HE BSc87. Ripon Coll Cuddesdon. **d** 00 **p** 01. C Lostwithiel, St Winnow w St Nectan's Chpl etc *Truro* 00-03; CSF from 03. *The Community of St Francis, Compton Durville, South Petherton TA13 5ES* Tel (01460) 240473 E-mail liz.hn@btopenworld.com

HEATON, Julian Roger. b 62. LSE BSc(Econ)83. St Steph Ho Ox BA86 MA92. **d** 87 **p** 88. C Stockport St Thos w St Pet *Ches* 87-90; Chapl Asst Qu Medical Cen and Univ Hosp Nottm 90-92; V Knutsford St Cross 92-01; P-in-c Altrincham St Jo 01-05; Voc Officer (Macclesfield Adnry) 01-05; V Sale St Anne from 05. *St Anne's Vicarage, Church Road West, Sale M33 3GD* Tel 0161-973 4145 E-mail julian@heatonfamily.freeserve.co.uk

HEATON, Nicholas Mark. b 70. Leeds Metrop Univ BEd92 Ches Coll of HE BTh04. N Ord Course 01. **d** 04 **p** 05. C Linthorpe *York* from 04. *23 Linden Grove, Middlesbrough TS5 5NF* Tel (01642) 723046 E-mail nickheaton@wwjcd.fsnet.co.uk

HEAVER, Derek Cyril. b 47. St Jo Coll Nottm BTh69. **d** 73 **p** 74. C Win Ch Ch *Win* 73-77; CF 77-02; rtd 02. *Orchard Cottage, 2 Myrtle Close, Puncknowle, Dorchester DT2 9EH* Tel and fax (01308) 898466 E-mail delsaun@eurobell.co.uk

HEAVISIDES, Canon Neil Cameron. b 50. Selw Coll Cam BA72 MA76 Ox Univ BA74 MA85. Ripon Hall Ox 72. **d** 75 **p** 76. C Stockton St Pet *Dur* 75-78; Succ S'wark Cathl *S'wark* 78-81; V Seaham w Seaham Harbour *Dur* 81-88; P-in-c Edington and Imber, Erlestoke and E Coulston *Sarum* 88-89; R 89-93; Can Res Glouc Cathl *Glouc* from 93. *7 College Green, Gloucester GL1 2LX* Tel (01452) 523987

HEAWOOD, Canon Alan Richard. b 32. G&C Coll Cam BA54 MA58. Union Th Sem (NY) BD56 Ripon Hall Ox 56. **d** 57 **p** 58. C Horwich H Trin *Man* 57-59; C Weaste 59-60; C Beverley Minster *York* 60-62; Chapl and Lect St Pet Coll Saltley 62-65; R Hockwold w Wilton *Ely* 65-72; R Weeting 65-72; V Melbourn 72-80; V Meldreth 72-80; P-in-c Teversham 80-90; Adult Educn Sec 80-89; Dir of Educn 80-98; Hon Can Ely Cathl 80-98; rtd 98; Perm to Offic *Ely* from 98. *10 Westberry Court, Grange Road, Cambridge CB3 9BG* Tel (01223) 460088

HEAZELL, Pamela Fletcher. b 50. NTMTC 96. **d** 99 **p** 00. NSM Hayes St Nic CD *Lon* 99-01; NSM N Greenford All Hallows 01-04; P-in-c from 04. *72 Horsenden Lane North, Greenford UB6 0PD* Tel (020) 8933 7700 E-mail pfheazell@aol.com

HEBBLETHWAITE, Canon Brian Leslie. b 39. Magd Coll Ox BA61 MA67 Magd Coll Cam BA63 MA68 BD84. Westcott Ho Cam 62. **d** 65 **p** 66. C Elton All SS *Man* 65-68; Chapl Qu Coll Cam 68; Dean of Chpl and Fell 69-94; Asst Lect Div Cam Univ 73-77; Lect 77-99; Can Th Leic Cathl *Leic* 82-00; rtd 99; Perm to Offic *Ely* from 02. *The Old Barn, 32 High Street, Stretham, Ely CB6 3JQ* Tel (01353) 648279 Mobile 07740-307568 E-mail blh1000@cam.ac.uk

HEBBLETHWAITE, Emma Sian. b 65. CCC Cam BA88 MA91 PhD92. Westcott Ho Cam. **d** 94 **p** 95. C Framlingham w Saxtead *St E* 94-96; Chapl K Coll Cam 96-01. *The Old Barn, 32 High Street, Stetham, Ely CB6 3JQ* Tel (0353) 648279 E-mail esh12@cam.ac.uk

HEBBLEWHITE, David Ernest. b 52. Hull Univ BA81 Nottm Univ MA82 CQSW82. St Jo Coll Nottm MA95. **d** 97 **p** 98. C Melton Mowbray *Leic* 97-00; TV Cannock *Lich* from 00. *226 Hednesford Road, Heath Hayes, Cannock WS12 3DZ* Tel (01543) 450481

HEBBORN, Roy Valentine Charles. S Dios Minl Tr Scheme 83. **d** 86 **p** 87. NSM Lewes All SS, St Anne, St Mich and St Thos *Chich* 86-00; NSM Lewes St Anne 00-01; rtd 01. *3 St Anne's Terrace, Western Road, Lewes BN7 1RH* Tel (01273) 474063

HEBDEN, Mrs Cynthia Margaret. b 47. Univ of Wales (Ban) BTh94. **d** 94 **p** 97. NSM Llanfairpwll w Penmynydd *Ban* 94-95; C Twrcelyn Deanery 95-96; C Knighton St Mary Magd *Leic* 96-99; P-in-c Higham-on-the-Hill w Fenny Drayton and Witherley 99-02; P-in-c Stoke Golding w Dadlington 01-02; R Fenn Lanes Gp 02-03; V Shepshed and Oaks in Charnwood from 03. *The Vicarage, 30A Brick Kiln Lane, Shepshed, Loughborough LE12 9EL* Tel (01509) 508550 E-mail hebdens@lineone.net

HEBDEN, John Percy. b 18. Sheff Univ 46 Lon Univ 67. St Aid Birkenhead 58. **d** 60 **p** 60. C Skipton H Trin *Bradf* 60-62; R Kirby Misperton *York* 63-67; V Laxey *S & M* 70-83; V Lonan 80-83; rtd 84; Hon C Douglas St Geo and St Barn *S & M* 84-95. *Begra, Clayhead Road, Baldrine, Isle of Man IM4 6DN* Tel (01624) 861296

HEBDEN, Peter. b 43. Wigan Coll of Tech MICE67. St As Minl Tr Course 92. **d** 95 **p** 96. NSM Twrcelyn Deanery *Ban* 95-96; NSM Glen Magna cum Stretton Magna etc *Leic* 96-98; Chapl to Asst Bp Leic 98-99; NSM Barwell w Potters Marston and Stapleton 00-02; Perm to Offic from 02. *The Vicarage, 30A Brick Kiln Lane, Shepshed, Loughborough LE12 9EL* Tel (01509) 508550 E-mail hebdens@leicester.anglican.org

HEBER, Andrew John. b 63. Nottm Univ BA86 MA89 CQSW89 Dip Counselling 97. Trin Coll Bris BA99. **d** 99 **p** 00. C Parr *Liv* 99-03; TV Kirkby from 03. *St Andrew's Vicarage, 9 Redwood Way, Liverpool LL33 4DU* Tel 0151-548 7969 E-mail gill.heber@bigfoot.com

HEBER PERCY, Canon Christopher John. b 41. St Jo Coll Cam BA64 MA68. Wells Th Coll 66. **d** 68 **p** 69. C Leigh St Mary *Man* 68-71; Asst Ind Chapl 71-80; P-in-c Oldham St Andr 75-78; TV Oldham 78-80; Ind Chapl *Win* 80-90; N Humberside Ind Chapl *York* from 90; AD E Hull from 98; Can and Preb York Minster from 05. *19 Bellfield Avenue, Hull HU8 9DS* Tel (01482) 702033

HECTOR, Noel Antony. b 61. Sheff Univ LLB83 Barrister-at-Law 84. Oak Hill Th Coll BA91. **d** 91 **p** 92. C Rodbourne Cheney *Bris* 91-92; C Bris St Mary Redcliffe w Temple etc 92-95; R Wrington w Butcombe *B & W* 95-03; R E Clevedon w Clapton in Gordano etc from 03; Chapl N Bris NHS Trust from 03. *The Rectory, All Saints' Lane, Clevedon BS21 6AU* Tel and fax (01275) 873257 E-mail eastcleveub@blueyonder.co.uk

HEDDLE, Duncan. b 34. Wadh Coll Ox BA57 MA61 DPhil64. **d** 86 **p** 86. Chapl Aber Univ *Ab* from 86; P-in-c Bucksburn from 90. *2 Douglas Place, High Street, Aberdeen AB24 3EA* Tel (01224) 485975 *or* 272888

HEDGE, Peter Andrew. b 62. New Coll Ox MA90. Coll of Resurr Mirfield 90. **d** 93 **p** 94. C Thornbury *Bradf* 93-97; V Queensbury from 97. *7 Russell Hall Lane, Queensbury, Bradford BD13 2AJ* Tel (01274) 815516

HEDGER, Canon Graham. b 57. Lon Bible Coll BA79. Ridley Hall Cam 81. **d** 83 **p** 84. C Walton *St E* 83-86; TV Mildenhall 86-91; R Swainsthorpe w Newton Flotman *Nor* 91-94; Dioc Evang Officer 91-94; Perm to Offic *St E* 95-99; Bp's Chapl and Liaison Officer from 99; Hon Can St E Cathl from 04. *14 St Peter's Close, Charsfield, Woodbridge IP13 7RG* Tel (01473) 277042 *or* 252829 Fax 737820 *or* 232552 E-mail graham@stedmundsbury.anglican.org

HEDGES, Mrs Anne Violet. b 53. Ripon Coll Cuddesdon 87. **d** 89 **p** 94. C Thetford *Nor* 89-94; Chapl Riddlesworth Hall Sch Nor 93-00; P-in-c Garboldisham w Blo' Norton, Riddlesworth etc *Nor* 94-97; R Guiltcross 97-00; Dep Chapl HM Pris Leeds 00-01; Chapl HM Pris Leic from 01. *HM Prison, Welford Road, Leicester LE2 7AJ* Tel 0116-228 3000 Fax 228 3001 E-mail anne.hedges@hmps.gsi.gov.uk

HEDGES, Canon Dennis Walter. b 29. Sarum Th Coll. **d** 62 **p** 63. C Walton-on-Thames *Guildf* 62-66; C Westborough 66-69; V Blackheath and Chilworth 69-79; R Farncombe 79-94; RD Godalming 84-89; Hon Can Guildf Cathl 92-94; rtd 94; Perm to Offic *Guildf* and *Win* from 94; *Portsm* from 99. *21 Lincoln Green, Alton GU34 1SX* Tel and fax (01420) 542624 Mobile 07989-110454 E-mail dennisw.hedges@lineone.net

HEDGES, Ian Charles. b 55. Sarum & Wells Th Coll 79. **d** 82 **p** 83. C Chessington *Guildf* 82-85; C Fleet 85-90; Dioc Adv on Homelessness from 87; V S Farnborough from 90; Tr Officer for Past Assts 91-00. *The Vicarage, 1 St Mark's Close, Farnborough GU14 6PP* Tel (01252) 544711

HEDGES, Canon Jane Barbara. b 55. St Jo Coll Dur BA78. Cranmer Hall Dur 78. **dss** 80 **d** 87 **p** 94. Fareham H Trin *Portsm* 80-83; Southampton (City Cen) *Win* 83-87; Par Dn 87-88; Dioc Stewardship Adv *Portsm* 88-93; Can Res Portsm Cathl 93-01; P-in-c Honiton, Gittisham, Combe Raleigh, Monkton etc *Ex* 01-03; TR from 03; RD Honiton from 03. *The Rectory, Rookwood Close, Honiton EX14 1BH* Tel (01404) 42925 *or* 44035 Fax 47841 E-mail hedges@eclipse.co.uk

HEDGES, Mrs Jane Rosemary. b 44. RGN65. S Dios Minl Tr Scheme 86. **d** 89 **p** 94. NSM Gillingham *Sarum* 89-04; NSM Gillingham and Milton-on-Stour from 04. *Dene Hollow, Wyke, Gillingham SP8 4NG* Tel (01747) 822812

HEDGES, John Michael Peter. b 34. Leeds Univ BA60. Ripon Hall Ox 60. **d** 61 **p** 62. C Weaste *Man* 61-65; V Ashton St Pet 65-74; C Easthampstead *Ox* 74-85; V Tilehurst St Geo 85-91; C Thatcham 91-94; TV 94-99; rtd 99; Perm to Offic *Ox* from 99. *39 Mallard Way, Grove, Wantage OX12 0QG* Tel (01235) 766834

HEDGES, Leslie Norman. b 26. Bris Univ BA51 Lon Univ BD56. Clifton Th Coll 48. **d** 53 **p** 54. C Summerstown *S'wark* 53-55; C Wolverhampton St Luke *Lich* 55-56; C Reigate St Mary *S'wark* 56-59; V Clapham Park All SS 59-70; V Findern *Derby* 70-82; V Willington 70-82; V Trowbridge St Thos and W Ashton *Sarum* 82-91; rtd 91; Perm to Offic *Truro* from 91. *16 Penwerris Road, Truro TR1 3QS* Tel (01872) 279858

HEDLEY, Charles John Wykeham. b 47. R Holloway Coll Lon BSc69 PhD73 Fitzw Coll Cam BA75 MA79. Westcott Ho Cam 73. **d** 76 **p** 77. C Chingford St Anne *Chelmsf* 76-79; C St Martin-in-the-Fields *Lon* 79-84 and 85-86; P-in-c 84-85; Chapl Ch Coll Cam 86-90; TR Gleadless *Sheff* 90-99; R Westmr St Jas *Lon* from 99. *St James's Rectory, 197 Piccadilly, London W1J 9LL* Tel (020) 7734 4511 Fax 7734 7449 E-mail ch@chsplace.freeserve.co.uk

HEDLEY, Mrs Julia Margaret. b 56. Goldsmiths' Coll Lon BA78 Bedf Coll Lon MSc85 Liv Univ MTh03 SRN80 Lon Univ DipN82. N Ord Course 97. **d** 00 **p** 01. C Altrincham St Geo *Ches* 00-04; PV Ches Cathl from 04. *Cromwell Lodge, 156 Foregate Street, Chester CH1 1HJ* Tel (01244) 345543 E-mail julia.hedley1@btinternet.com

HEDLEY, William Clifford. b 35. Tyndale Hall Bris 65. **d** 67 **p** 68. C Hensingham *Carl* 67-69; C Rainhill *Liv* 69-71; C St Helens St Helen 71-73; V Low Elswick *Newc* 73-81; V Kingston upon Hull St Aid Southcoates *York* 81-87; TV Heworth H Trin 87-94; V Norton juxta Malton 94-97; C Newburn *Newc* 97-01; rtd 01. *21 Laburnum Grove, Sunniside, Newcastle upon Tyne NE16 5LY* Tel 0191-488 2908

HEDWORTH, Paul Simon James. b 56. Worc Coll of Educn BEd78. Qu Coll Birm BA(Theol)84. **d** 04 **p** 05. NSM Bacup and Stacksteads *Man* from 04; Chapl Qu Eliz Gr Sch Blackb from 04. *49 Rockcliffe Road, Bacup OL13 9QG* Tel (01706) 870165 Mobile 07966-503194 E-mail hedworth@ntlworld.com

HEELEY, Mrs Janet. b 45. **d** 00 **p** 01. OLM Lich St Chad *Lich* from 00. *43 High Grange, Lichfield WS13 7DU* Tel (01543) 251600 *or* 416595

HEFFER, Thomas Patrick Peter. b 69. K Coll Lon BD90 AKC90 Univ of Wales (Cardiff) LLM03. Ripon Coll Cuddesdon 94.

d 96 p 97. C Sprowston w Beeston *Nor* 96-98; Bp's Chapl and Press Officer 98-01; Min Sec Miss to Seafarers from 01; Lic to Offic *Lon* from 01; Perm to Offic *Ox* and *St Alb* from 01. *The Mission to Seafarers, St Michael Paternoster Royal, College Hill, London EC4R 2RL* Tel (020) 7248 5202 Fax 7248 4761 E-mail ministry@missiontoseafarers.org

HEFFER, William John Gambrell. b 30. AKC55. **d** 56 **p** 57. C Biggleswade *St Alb* 56-59; C Clacton St Jas *Chelmsf* 59-61; V Langford *St Alb* 61-67; V Luton All SS 67-73; P-in-c Eaton Socon 73-75; V 75-77; Lic to Offic 78-81; R Wingrave w Rowsham, Aston Abbotts and Cublington *Ox* 81-88; R Wilden w Colmworth and Ravensden *St Alb* 88-91; C Leighton Buzzard w Eggington, Hockliffe etc 91-94; rtd 94; Perm to Offic *St Alb* 94-00 and from 01; *Ox* 97-01; P-in-c Empingham and Exton w Horn w Whitwell *Pet* 00-01. *Domus, 35 Pebblemoor, Edlesborough, Dunstable LU6 2HZ* Tel (01525) 220618

HEFFERNAN, Anna Elizabeth. b 65. Cuddesdon Coll DipMin95. **d** 97 **p** 98. C Limpsfield and Titsey *S'wark* 97-00; C Warlingham w Chelsham and Farleigh 00-03; TV from 03. *St Christopher's Vicarage, Chelsham Road, Warlingham CR6 9EQ* Tel (01883) 624494

HEFFERNAN, Ms May Olive. b 52. Maria Grey Coll Lon CertEd74 Lon Univ BD93. Aston Tr Scheme 88 Westcott Ho Cam 93. **d** 93 **p** 94. C Duddeston w Nechells *Birm* 93-97; P-in-c Ward End 97-03; rtd 03. *71 Sonning Gardens, Hampton TW12 3PN*

HEGARTY, Gerald. b 52. QUB BA74 BD81. Union Th Coll Belf 78. **d** 86 **p** 87. NSM Leic H Trin w St Jo *Leic* 86-87; P-in-c Sibson w Sheepy and Ratcliffe Culey 87-90; Tutor Wycliffe Hall Ox 90-95; Chapl St Edm Hall Ox 90-96 and from 04; Tutor St Alb and Ox Min Course *Ox* 96-99; Vice Prin from 00. *39 Lakeside, Oxford OX2 8JF* Tel (01865) 557847

HEIDT, John Harrison. b 32. Yale Univ BA54 Ox Univ BLitt67 DPhil75. Nashotah Ho BD57 MDiv69. **d** 56 **p** 57. USA 57-75 and from 96; C Ox St Mary Magd *Ox* 75-80; V Up Hatherley *Glouc* 80-96; P-in-c Cheltenham St Steph 89-95; rtd 97. *204 North Rosemont Avenue, Dallas, TX 75208, USA* Tel (001) (214) 948 3442 Fax 941 0339

HEIDT, Michael Lewis. b 65. K Coll Lon BD86. St Steph Ho Ox 88. **d** 90 **p** 91. C Reading St Luke w St Bart *Ox* 90-94; R Bladensburg St Luke USA from 00. *4002 53rd Street, Bladensburg, MD 20710, USA* Tel (001) (301) 927 6466

HEIGHTON, Miss Janet Elizabeth. b 67. Leeds Poly BSc92. Ripon Coll Cuddesdon. **d** 00 **p** 01. C Leeds Gipton Epiphany *Ripon* 00-04; P-in-c from 04. *154 Amberton Road, Leeds LS9 6SP* Tel 0113-249 4356 Mobile 07970-036524 E-mail heighton@fish.co.uk

HEIL, Canon Janet. b 53. Liv Univ BEd75 St Jo Coll Dur BA84. Cranmer Hall Dur. **dss** 85 **d** 87 **p** 94. Ashton Ch Ch *Man* 85-91; Par Dn 87-91; Par Dn Scotforth *Blackb* 91-94; C 94-95; V Gt Harwood St Bart from 95; P-in-c Gt Harwood St Jo from 02; Hon Can Blackb Cathl from 04. *St Bartholomew's Vicarage, 1 Church Lane, Great Harwood, Blackburn BB6 7PU* Tel (01254) 884039

HEINZE, Canon Rudolph William. b 31. Concordia Coll (USA) BSc56 CertEd56 De Paul Univ (USA) MA59 Univ of Iowa PhD65. **d** 86 **p** 87. NSM London Colney St Pet *St Alb* 86-98; Lect Oak Hill Th Coll 86-98; Sen Tutor 88-94; Vice-Prin 94-97; Visiting Scholar from 99; Hon Can Port Sudan from 94; Hon Prof Middx Univ *Lon* from 98; Perm to Offic *St Alb* from 98. *1714D Lakecliffe Drive, Briarcliffe Lakes, Wheaton, IL 60187, USA* Tel (001) (630) 588 8954 E-mail revrudi@aol.com

HELEN, Sister. *See* LODER, Sister Helen

HELEY, John. b 28. Lon Univ BA72. Bps' Coll Cheshunt 54. **d** 56 **p** 57. S Africa 57-61; C Wimborne Minster *Sarum* 61-62; V Narborough w Narford *Nor* 62-67; R Pentney St Mary Magd w W Bilney 62-67; V Catton 67-69; Lic to Offic *Ox* 69-72; R E w W Rudham *Nor* 72-75; P-in-c Houghton 72-74; V 74-75; V Hunstanton St Edm 75-82; V Hunstanton St Edm w Ringstead 82-83; rtd 88. *Meadow Cottage, Cradle Hall Farm, Burnham Market, Kings Lynn PE31 8JX* Tel (01485) 518686

HELFT, Gunter. b 23. Lon Univ BA48. Ely Th Coll 46. **d** 48 **p** 49. Chapl Essex Home Sch Chelmsf 48-52; C Chelmsf Ascension *Chelmsf* 48-49; C Billesley Common *Birm* 52-53; Miss to Seamen 53-62; Japan 53-57; Sec HQ 57-62; Sudan 57; Bp's Youth Officer *Ox* 62-65; Tr Officer C of E Youth Coun 65-67; Hd Master Abp Temple's Sch Lambeth 67-71; Hd Master Don Valley High Sch S Yorkshire 71-80; rtd 80; Perm to Offic *Worc* from 87. *19 Kenwood Avenue, Worcester WR4 9BD* Tel (01905) 29797 E-mail ghelft@tiscali.co.uk

HELLARD, Dawn Yvonne Lorraine. b 47. St Mich Coll Llan 89. **d** 91 **p** 97. C Llantwit Major *Llan* 91-95; TV Cowbridge from 95. *The Vicarage, St Hilary, Cowbridge CF71 7DP* Tel (01446) 772460

HELLEWELL, John. b 63. Bris Univ BSc86 BTh93 Nottm Univ MA94. St Jo Coll Nottm 93. **d** 94 **p** 95. C Greasbrough *Sheff* 94-98; P-in-c High Hoyland, Scissett and Clayton W *Wakef* 98-04; V Mount Pellon from 04. *The Vicarage, Church Lane, Halifax HX2 0EF* Tel (01422) 365027 E-mail john@revjhell.freeserve.co.uk

HELLICAR, Hugh Christopher. b 37. Birm Univ DPS70. Qu Coll Birm 69. **d** 70 **p** 71. C Bromyard *Heref* 70-73; C Bishop's Castle w Mainstone 73-75; Perm to Offic *S'wark* 77-85 and *Chich* 83-93; NSM Hove *Chich* 93-98; rtd 02. *74 Marina, St Leonards-on-Sea TN38 0BJ* Tel (01424) 444072

HELLIER, Jeremy Peter. b 53. K Coll Lon BD75 AKC75 Westmr Coll Ox DipRE98. St Aug Coll Cant 75. **d** 76 **p** 77. C Walton *St E* 76-79; C Ipswich St Fran 79-80; C Wolborough w Newton Abbot *Ex* 80-82; CF 82-84; R Pendine w Llanmiloe and Eglwys Gymyn w Marros *St D* 84-89; TR Widecombe-in-the-Moor, Leusdon, Princetown etc *Ex* 89-94; CF (TAVR) from 90; RD Moreton *Ex* 91-94; Chapl and Hd RE Wellington Sch Somerset from 94. *Wellington School, Wellington TA21 8NT* Tel (01823) 668827 *or* 668837 Fax 668844 E-mail jph@wellington-school.org.uk

HELLIWELL (née SWALLOW), Mrs Judith Hazel. b 46. Dioc OLM tr scheme 99. **d** 01 **p** 02. OLM Meltham *Wakef* from 01. *3 Upper Wilshaw, Meltham, Holmfirth HD9 4EA* Tel (01484) 851158

HELLMUTH, Miss Lynn. b 61. Lon Bible Coll BA82 Birm Univ PGCE83. Wycliffe Hall Ox 00. **d** 02 **p** 03. C Twickenham Common H Trin *Lon* 02-05; TV Crawley *Chich* from 05. *St Richard's Vicarage, 1 Crossways, Crawley RH10 1QF* Tel (01293) 533727 E-mail lynnhellmuth@yahoo.co.uk

HELLYER, Ian Anthony. b 66. Lanc Univ BSc91 Nottm Univ BTh95. Linc Th Coll 92. **d** 95 **p** 96. C Poulton-le-Fylde *Blackb* 95-01; R Moretonhampstead, Manaton, N Bovey and Lustleigh *Ex* from 01. *The Rectory, 3 Grays Meadow, Moretonhampstead, Newton Abbot TQ13 8NB* Tel (01647) 441098 E-mail hellyer@surfaid.org

HELLYER, Stephen John. b 56. St Cath Coll Cam BA77 MA81. Wycliffe Hall Ox 82. **d** 84 **p** 85. C Plymouth St Andr w St Paul and St Geo *Ex* 84-88; Chapl Lee Abbey 88-89; Lon and SE Consultant CPAS 90-94; C Nottingham St Nic *S'well* 94-98; P-in-c Ox St Matt *Ox* from 98. *St Matthew's Vicarage, Marlborough Road, Oxford OX1 4LW* Tel (01865) 243434 E-mail steve@hellyers.fsworld.co.uk

HELM, Alistair Thomas. b 53. Aston Univ BSc75. EAMTC 88. **d** 91 **p** 92. NSM Leic St Jas *Leic* 91-95; NSM Humberstone 95-03; NSM Ascension TM 03-04; NSM Aylestone Park CD from 04. *20 Stoughton Drive North, Leicester LE5 5UB* Tel 0116-273 0613 E-mail ahelm@leicester.anglican.org

HELM, Catherine Mary. b 64. St Martin's Coll Lanc BEd86. St Jo Coll Nottm 03. **d** 05. C Heswall *Ches* from 05. *The Croft, Croftsway, Wirral CH60 9JP* Tel 0151-342 3224 E-mail helmcatherine@yahoo.co.uk

HELM, Nicholas. b 57. Surrey Univ BSc81. St Jo Coll Nottm 85. **d** 88 **p** 89. C Old Ford St Paul w St Steph and St Mark *Lon* 88-92; TV Netherthorpe *Sheff* 92-93; V Sheff St Bart 93-98; Bp's Chapl 99-03; Bp's Adv in Spirituality from 99; Chapl Whirlow Grange Conf Cen Sheff from 99. *23 Hill Turrets Close, Sheffield S11 9RE* Tel 0114-235 0191 Fax 235 2275 E-mail nick@bishopscroft.idps.co.uk

HELMS, David Clarke. b 50. Boston Univ AB72. Yale Div Sch MDiv77. **d** 77 **p** 77. USA 77-88; Ind Chapl *Worc* 88-97; Ind Chapl Teesside *York* 97-02. *17 Gilesgate, Durham DH1 1QW*

HELYER, Patrick Joseph Peter. b 15. FRGS83. ALCD39 Wycliffe Hall Ox 38. **d** 38 **p** 39. C Maidstone St Paul *Cant* 38-41; Asst Chapl Miss to Seamen 41-42; Chapl RNVR 42-46; V St Nicholas at Wade w Sarre *Cant* 46-50; Australia 51-61; V Rolvenden *Cant* 62-66; R Frome St Quintin w Evershot and Melbury Bubb *Sarum* 66-71; Falkland Is 71-75; Hon Can Port Stanley 72-75; R Streat w Westmeston *Chich* 75-78; Tristan da Cunha 78-81; rtd 81; Perm to Offic *Heref* 84-00; *Glouc* from 84. *Tristan, 4 Gorse Lane, Sling, Coleford GL16 8JH* Tel (01594) 834990

HEMINGWAY, Peter. b 32. S'wark Ord Course 72. **d** 75 **p** 76. NSM Belmont *S'wark* 75-79; C Herne Hill St Paul 79-81; V Headstone St Geo *Lon* 81-92; V N Harrow St Alb 87-02; rtd 02. *Chelmerton, 138 Winthrope Road, Bury St Edmunds IP33 3XW* Tel (01284) 705070

HEMMING, Terry Edward. b 47. Calvin Coll Michigan MA84 S Dios Minl Tr Scheme 88. **d** 90 **p** 91. NSM Win All SS w Chilcomb and Chesil *Win* from 90; Chapl St Swithun's Sch Win from 95. *15 Gordon Avenue, Winchester SO23 0QE* Tel (01962) 855701 *or* 835717 E-mail revhemm@yahoo.co.uk *or* hemmingt@stswithuns.com

HEMMING-CLARK, Stanley Charles. b 29. Peterho Cam BA52 MA56. Ridley Hall Cam 52. **d** 54 **p** 55. C Redhill H Trin *S'wark* 54-56; C Woking St Jo *Guildf* 56-59; V Crockenhill All So *Roch* 59-97; rtd 97; Perm to Offic *Guildf* from 97. *St Anthony's, 22 Ashcroft, Shalford, Guildford GU4 8JT* Tel (01483) 568197

HEMMINGS, Ms Jane Marie. b 68. Lon Univ BD91 AKC91 Heythrop Coll Lon MTh95. NTMTC 01. **d** 03 **p** 04. C Bishop's Waltham *Portsm* from 03; C Upham from 03. *15 Denewulf*

Close, Bishops Waltham, Southampton SO32 1GZ Tel (01489) 896976 E-mail dauphin.jg@tiscali.co.uk

HEMMINGS, Keith. b 43. **d** 97. Par Dn Bedwellty *Mon* from 97. *Penydarren, Park Drive, Bargoed CF81 8PJ* Tel (01443) 830662

HEMMINGS, Roy Anthony. b 48. Univ of Wales (Cardiff) BD85 MTh00. St Mich Coll Llan 82. **d** 86 **p** 87. C Rhyl w St Ann *St As* 86-90; CF from 90. *c/o MOD Chaplains (Army)* Tel (01980) 615804 Mobile 07710-774431 Fax (01980) 615800 E-mail ryghemm@aol.com

HEMPHILL, John James. b 44. TCD BA68 MA72. Oak Hill Th Coll 71. **d** 73 **p** 74. C Dundonald *D & D* 73-78; I Balteagh w Carrick *D & R* 78-02; I Ballyhalbert w Ardkeen *D & D* from 02. *Ballyeasboro Rectory, 187 Main Road, Portavogie, Newtownards BT22 1DA* Tel (028) 4277 1234 Mobile 07779-928666

HEMSLEY, David Ridgway. b 36. AKC61. **d** 61 **p** 62. C Penhill *Bris* 61-64; C Highworth w Sevenhampton and Inglesham etc 64-66; C Surbiton St Andr *S'wark* 67-70; P-in-c Tingewick w Water Stratford *Ox* 70-75; P-in-c Radclive 72-75; PM N Marston w Granborough etc 75-81; P-in-c Quainton 75-81; TV Schorne 81-90; P-in-c Lt Missenden 90-93; V 93-01; rtd 01. *27 Overn Avenue, Buckingham MK18 1LG* Tel (01280) 814636

HEMSLEY HALLS, Susan Mary. b 59. Cranmer Hall Dur 93. **d** 95 **p** 96. C Wilnecote *Lich* 95-00; P-in-c Attenborough *S'well* from 00; Dioc Chapl amongst Deaf People from 00. *Vale Cottage, 19 Church Lane, Attenborough, Beeston NG9 6AS* Tel 0115-925 9602 E-mail office@stmarysattenboro.f9.co.uk

HEMSTOCK, Julian. b 51. Trent Poly BSc74 CEng MIProdE. Sarum & Wells Th Coll 89. **d** 91 **p** 92. C Carrington *S'well* 91-94; C Basford St Aid 94-97; Asst Chapl Qu Medical Cen Nottm Univ Hosp NHS Trust 97-03; Chapl from 03. *Queen's Medical Centre Univ Hospital, Derby Road, Nottingham NG7 2UH* Tel 0115-924 9924 ext 43799 E-mail julian.hemstock@qmc.nhs.uk

HEMSTOCK, Mrs Pat. b 51. Sarum & Wells Th Coll 89. **d** 91 **p** 95. Par Dn Carrington *S'well* 91-94; Par Dn Basford St Aid 94-95; C 95-97; P-in-c 97-05; V Calverton from 05. *The Vicarage, Crookdole Lane, Calverton, Nottingham NG14 6GF* Tel 0115-965 2552 E-mail pat.hemstock@btinternet.com

HEMSWORTH, John Alan. b 45. FGA67. Man OLM Scheme 99. **d** 02 **p** 03. OLM Droylsden St Andr *Man* from 02. *13 Keston Avenue, Droylsden, Manchester M43 6BL* Tel 0161-292 7356

HENCHER, John Bredon. b 31. Lich Th Coll 58. **d** 60 **p** 61. C Pershore w Wick *Worc* 60-62; Bp's Dom Chapl 63-64; V Amblecote 64-70; Perm to Offic *Glouc* 72-74; Dioc RE Adv *Heref* 74-80; Lic to Offic 80-87; Perm to Offic *Mon* 87-00; Asst Chapl Mon Sch 87-00; Chapl from 00. *The Tank House, Weston, Pembridge, Leominster HR6 9JE* Tel (01544) 388540

HENDERSON, Canon Alastair Roy. b 27. BNC Ox BA51 MA54. Ridley Hall Cam 52. **d** 54 **p** 55. C Ex St Leon w H Trin *Ex* 54-57; Travelling Sec IVF 57-60; C St Mary le Bow w St Pancras Soper Lane etc *Lon* 58-60; V Barton Hill St Luke w Ch Ch *Bris* 60-68; P-in-c Bris St Phil and St Jacob w Em 67-68; V Stoke Bishop 68-92; Lect Clifton Th Coll 69-71; Lect Trin Coll Bris 71-73; RD Westbury and Severnside *Bris* 73-79; Hon Can Bris Cathl 80-92; rtd 92; Perm to Offic *Ex* from 92. *3 Garden Court, Cricketfield Lane, Budleigh Salterton EX9 6PN* Tel (01395) 446147

HENDERSON, Andrew Douglas. b 36. Trin Coll Cam BA60 MA64 Ox Univ DipPSA63 Liv Univ DASS65 MBASW. Cuddesdon Coll 60. **d** 62 **p** 63. C Newington St Paul *S'wark* 62-64; Hon C Camberwell St Luke 65-80; Perm to Offic *Lon* from 85. *178 Lancaster Road, London W11 1QU* Tel (020) 7229 6790

HENDERSON, Ashley. *See* HENDERSON, Peter Ashley

HENDERSON, Colin. *See* HENDERSON, Francis Colin

HENDERSON, David. *See* HENDERSON, Robert David Druitt

HENDERSON, David. b 35. Oak Hill NSM Course. **d** 83 **p** 84. NSM Rush Green *Chelmsf* 83-00; Perm to Offic from 00. *Le Strange Cottages, 2-8 Hunstanton Road, Heacham, King's Lynn PE31 7HH* Tel (01485) 572150

HENDERSON, Elizabeth. b 42. Cert Counselling & Learning Support Cert Ecum. **d** 99 **p** 00. C Ballymacash *Conn* from 99; Asst Chapl R Group of Hosps Health and Soc Services Trust from 99; C Finaghy *Conn* from 00. *39 Garvey Court, Lisburn BT27 4DG* Tel (028) 9260 7146

HENDERSON, Francis Colin. b 35. St Cath Coll Cam BA59 MA63. Cuddesdon Coll 60. **d** 62 **p** 63. C Croydon St Jo *Cant* 62-67; V Westwood *Cov* 67-75; V Chilvers Coton w Astley 75-80; P-in-c Wolston 80; P-in-c Church Lawford w Newnham Regis 80; V Wolston and Church Lawford 80-85; USA from 85; rtd 00. *1364 Katella Street, Laguna Beach, CA 92651, USA* Tel (001) (949) 497 2239 E-mail echenderson@earthlink.net

HENDERSON, James. b 22. Chich Th Coll 51. **d** 54 **p** 55. C Burnage St Nic *Man* 54-56; C Prestwich St Mary 56-59; V Waterfoot 59-64; P-in-c Rawtenstall St Jo 61-64; V Bolton St Geo 64-70; V Newhey 70-87; rtd 87; Perm to Offic *Man* from 87. *17 Swift Road, Rochdale OL11 5RF* Tel (01706) 522228

HENDERSON, Canon Janet. b 57. St Jo Coll Dur BA88 RGN82. Cranmer Hall Dur 85. **d** 88 **p** 94. Par Dn Wisbech SS Pet and Paul *Ely* 88-90; Par Dn Bestwood *S'well* 90-93; Tutor St Jo Coll Nottm 92-97; Lect Worship 93-97; NSM Bramcote *S'well* 94-97; Lect Worship and Tutor Ridley Hall Cam 97-01; Dir Studies 00-01; P-in-c Nuthall *S'well* from 01; Dean of Women's Min from 01; Hon Can S'well Minster from 03. *24 Watnall Road, Nuthall, Nottingham NG16 1DU* Tel 0115-938 9923 E-mail j.henderson2@btinternet.com

HENDERSON, Judith Ann. b 37. **d** 89 **p** 94. NSM Sheringham *Nor* 89-92; NSM Brampton St Thos *Derby* 92-00; Perm to Offic *Sarum* from 00. *Blackmore House, Stone Lane, Wimborne BH21 1HD* Tel (01202) 881422

HENDERSON, Canon Julian Tudor. b 54. Keble Coll Ox BA76 MA81. Ridley Hall Cam 77. **d** 79 **p** 80. C Islington St Mary *Lon* 79-83; V Hastings Em and St Mary in the Castle *Chich* 83-92; V Claygate *Guildf* from 92; RD Emly 96-01; Hon Can Guildf Cathl from 02. *The Vicarage, Church Road, Claygate, Esher KT10 0JP* Tel (01372) 463603 Fax 464894 E-mail julianhenderson@aol.com

HENDERSON, Nicholas Paul. b 48. Selw Coll Cam BA73 MA77. Ripon Hall Ox 73. **d** 75 **p** 76. C St Alb St Steph *St Alb* 75-78; Warden J F Kennedy Ho Cov Cathl 78-79; C Bow w Bromley St Leon *Lon* 79-85; P-in-c W Acton St Martin 85-96; V from 96; P-in-c Ealing All SS 89-95; V from 96. *The Parishes Office, 25 Birch Grove, London W3 9SP* Tel (020) 8992 2333 *or* 8248 0608 Fax 8993 5812 E-mail nicholashenderson@btinternet.com

HENDERSON, Noel. *See* HENDERSON, Samuel James Noel

HENDERSON, Olive Elizabeth. b 48. St Jo Coll Nottm CertCS. **d** 97 **p** 98. Aux Min Tallaght *D & G* 97-99; P-in-c Moviddy Union *C, C & R* 99-01; P-in-c Rathdrum w Glenealy, Derralossary and Laragh *D & G* 01-04; C from 04. *The Rectory, Rathdrum, Co Wicklow, Irish Republic* Tel (00353) (404) 43814 Mobile 87-218 1891 E-mail rathdrum@glendalough.anglican.org

HENDERSON, Patrick James. b 57. R Holloway Coll Lon BA78 Surrey Univ PGCE01. St Steph Ho Ox 83. **d** 86 **p** 87. C Hornsey St Mary w St Geo *Lon* 86-90; V Whetstone St Jo 90-95; In RC Ch 95-01; Perm to Offic 01-02; C Hornsey H Innocents from 02; C Stroud Green H Trin 02-04; P-in-c from 04; Chapl Greig City Academy from 02. *Holy Trinity Vicarage, Granville Road, London N4 4EL* Tel (020) 8340 2051 Mobile 07947-714893 E-mail pjhenderson2001@yahoo.co.uk

HENDERSON, Peter Ashley. b 59. St Martin's Coll Lanc PGCE00. Carl and Blackb Dioc Tr Inst 02. **d** 05. NSM Arnside *Carl* from 05. *2 Lowther Park, Kendal LA9 6RS* Tel (01539) 736079 E-mail janash@btinternet.com

✠**HENDERSON, The Rt Revd Richard Crosbie Aitken.** b 57. Magd Coll Ox MA84 DPhil84. St Jo Coll Nottm 83. **d** 86 **p** 87 **c** 98. C Chinnor w Emmington and Sydenham etc *Ox* 86-89; I Abbeystrewry Union *C, C & R* 89-95; I Ross Union 95-98; Dean Ross 95-98; Chan Cork Cathl 95-98; Bp T, K & A from 98. *Bishop's House, Knockglass, Crossmolina, Ballina, Co Mayo, Irish Republic* Tel (00353) (96) 31317 Fax 31775 E-mail bishop@tuam.anglican.org

HENDERSON, Robert. b 43. TCD 66 Ulster Univ DipG&C87 Lambeth STh94. **d** 69 **p** 70. C Drumglass *Arm* 69-72; Chapl Miss to Seamen 72-78; Kenya 77-78; I Mostrim w Granard, Clonbroney, Killoe etc *K, E & A* 78-82; I Belfast St Matt *Conn* 82-92; I Kilroot and Templecorran 92-98; rtd 98. *39 Garvey Court, Lisburn BT27 4DG* Tel (028) 9260 7146

HENDERSON, Robert David Druitt. b 41. St Edm Hall Ox MA64 Brunel Univ MA77 K Alfred's Coll Win PGCE88. **d** 03 **p** 04. OLM Wylye and Till Valley *Sarum* from 03. *Orchard House, Salisbury Road, Steeple Langford, Salisbury SP3 4NQ* Tel (01722) 790388 E-mail henderson.family@virgin.net

HENDERSON, Samuel James Noel. b 16. Hertf Coll Ox BA39 MA42. **d** 42 **p** 43. C Seagoe *D & D* 42-45; C Donaghadee 45-46; P-in-c Clabby *Clogh* 46-47; C Ipswich All SS *St E* 47-48; C Heacham *Nor* 48-49; C Ingoldisthorpe 48-49; R E w W Lexham 49-53; R Gt Dunham 49-53; R Nor St Aug w St Mary 53-56; V Eastbourne Ch Ch *Chich* 56-65; V Hickling *Nor* 65-82; rtd 82; Perm to Offic *Nor* from 82. *96 Church Lane, Beeston Regis, Sheringham NR26 8EY* Tel (01263) 825686

HENDERSON, Mrs Shirley Claire. b 49. Surrey Univ BA02. Bp Otter Coll 94. **d** 96 **p** 02. NSM Gatcombe, Chale and Shorwell w Kingston *Portsm* 96-00; NSM Whitwell, Niton and St Lawrence 00-03; P-in-c Shedfield from 03. *The Vicarage, 52 Brooklynn Close, Waltham Chase, Southampton SO32 2RZ* Tel (01489) 896637 Fax as telephone E-mail rev_shirley@hotmail.com

HENDERSON, Terry James. b 45. Warwick Univ Dip Counselling 97. St Deiniol's Hawarden 76. **d** 77 **p** 77. C Wrexham *St As* 77-79; Wilson Carlile Coll of Evang 79-81; TV Langtree *Ox* 81-87; P-in-c Aston Cantlow and Wilmcote w Billesley *Cov* 87-90; V 90-97; V St Peter-in-Thanet *Cant* 97-02; R Elmley Castle w Bricklehampton and Combertons *Worc* from 02. *The Rectory, 22 Parkwood, Elmley Castle, Pershore WR10 3HT* Tel (01386) 710394 E-mail terryhenderson@onetel.com

HENDERSON, William Desmond. b 27. TCD BA56 Div Test 56 MA64. **d** 56 **p** 57. C Derryloran *Arm* 56-59; C Conwall *D & R* 59-62; I Killoughter *K, E & A* 62-64; I Kilrush *C & O* 64-66; I Tubbercurry w Kilmactigue *T, K & A* 66-75; rtd 75. *8 Kingston College, Mitchelstown, Co Cork, Irish Republic*

HENDERSON, William Ernest. b 53. CEng81 MICE81 Southn Univ BSc75. St Jo Coll Nottm 87. **d** 89 **p** 90. C Win Ch Ch *Win* 89-93; V Stanley *Wakef* from 93. *The Vicarage, 379 Aberford Road, Stanley, Wakefield WF3 4HE* Tel (01924) 822143 *or* 835746 E-mail bill@stpeters-stanley.org.uk

HENDERSON, William Ralph. b 32. Oak Hill Th Coll 65. **d** 67 **p** 68. C Littleover *Derby* 67-68; C Nottingham St Sav *S'well* 68-74; V Alne *York* 75-92; Chapl York Distr Hosp 86-92; rtd 92; Perm to Offic *York* from 92. *15 Drakes Close, Huntington, York YO32 9GN* Tel (01904) 761741

HENDEY, Clifford. b 30. K Coll Lon BD53 AKC53. **d** 54 **p** 55. C S Wimbledon All SS *S'wark* 54-58; Trinidad and Tobago 58-71 and 81-82; V Spratton *Pet* 72-77; V Leeds All So *Ripon* 77-80; R Corringham *Linc* 80-81; V Alkham w Capel le Ferne and Hougham *Cant* 82-95; rtd 95; Perm to Offic *Cant* from 95. *308 Dover Road, Folkestone CT19 6NZ*

HENDRICKSE, Canon Clarence David. b 41. CEng MIMechE71 Nottm Univ PGCE73. St Jo Coll Nottm 71. **d** 74 **p** 75. C St Helens St Helen *Liv* 74-76; C Netherley Ch Ch CD 76-77; TV 78-87; V Liv Ch Ch Norris Green 87-93; V Eccleston Ch Ch from 93; Hon Can Liv Cathl from 96. *The Vicarage, Chapel Lane, Eccleston, St Helens WA10 5DA* Tel (01744) 22698 Fax as telephone

HENDRY, Mrs Helen Clare. b 58. Lanc Univ BA79 Cam Univ PGCE80. Reformed Th Sem Mississippi MA85 Oak Hill Th Coll 94. **d** 95. Lect Oak Hill Th Coll from 86; NSM Muswell Hill St Jas w St Matt *Lon* from 95. *44 The Grove, London N13 5JR* Tel (020) 8882 2186 *or* 8883 6277 E-mail clareh@oakhill.ac.uk

HENDRY, Leonard John. b 34. Univ of Wales Cert Past Th68. St D Coll Lamp DipTh68. **d** 68 **p** 69. C Minchinhampton *Glouc* 68-71; C Bishop's Cleeve 71-74; V Cheltenham St Mich 74-78; V Horsley and Newington Bagpath w Kingscote 78-82; Chapl Salonika *Eur* 82-91; rtd 94. *Stratigi 34, Pilea, Salonika 543 52, Greece* Tel (0030) (31) 281193

HENDY, Canon Graham Alfred. b 45. St Jo Coll Dur BA67 MA75 Fitzw Coll Cam CertEd. Sarum Th Coll 67. **d** 70 **p** 71. C High Wycombe *Ox* 70-75; TV 75-78; R Upton cum Chalvey 78-83; TR 83-90; R S Walsham and Upton *Nor* 90-97; Dioc Lay Tr Officer 90-97; Can Res S'well Minster *S'well* 97-02; R Upper Itchen *Win* from 02. *The Rectory, Cheriton, Alresford SO24 0QH* Tel (01962) 771226 E-mail graham@grahamhendy.fsnet.co.uk

HENEY, William Butler. b 22. Potchefstroom Univ BA99. CITC. **d** 60 **p** 61. C Seagoe *D & D* 60-63; I Carrickmacross *Clogh* 64-73; I Newbridge w Carnalway and Kilcullen *M & K* 73-95; Treas Kildare Cathl 81-86; Can Kildare Cathl 81-95; Adn Kildare 86-94; rtd 95; Chapl Mageough Home *D & G* from 96. *14 Trees Road, Mount Merrion, Blackrock, Co Dublin, Irish Republic* Tel (00353) (1) 288 9773

HENLEY, Claud Michael. b 31. Keble Coll Ox BA55 MA59. Chich Th Coll 55. **d** 57 **p** 58. C Cowley St Jas *Ox* 57-60; C Wetherby *Ripon* 60-63; C Brighton St Pet *Chich* 63-69; V Brighton St Jo 69-75; V New Groombridge 75-96; rtd 96; Perm to Offic *Chich* from 97. *12 Barn Stables, De Montfort Road, Lewes BN7 1ST* Tel (01273) 472467

HENLEY, David Edward. b 44. Sarum & Wells Th Coll 69. **d** 72 **p** 73. C Fareham H Trin *Portsm* 72-76; C-in-c Leigh Park St Clare CD 76-78; R Freshwater 78-87; RD W Wight 83-87; R Meonstoke w Corhampton cum Exton 87-02; R Droxford 87-02; RD Bishop's Waltham 93-98; Hon Can Portsm Cathl 96-02; TR Chalke Valley *Sarum* from 02. *The Vicarage, Newtown, Broad Chalke, Salisbury SP5 5DS* Tel (01722) 780262

HENLEY, Dean. b 64. St Chad's Coll Dur BA93. Westcott Ho Cam 95. **d** 95 **p** 96. C Farncombe *Guildf* 95-99; TV Hale w Badshot Lea from 99. *The Vicarage, 12 Badshot Lea Road, Badshot Lea, Farnham GU9 9LD* Tel (01252) 327044 E-mail deanhenley@waitrose.com

HENLEY, John Francis Hugh. b 48. SS Mark & Jo Coll Chelsea CertEd69. St Mich Coll Llan DipTh82. **d** 82 **p** 83. C Griffithstown *Mon* 82-85; V St Hilary Greenway 85-90; P-in-c Fulham St Etheldreda w St Clem *Lon* from 90. *St Etheldreda's Vicarage, Doneraile Street, London SW6 6EL* Tel (020) 7736 3809

HENLEY, Michael. *See* HENLEY, Claud Michael

✠**HENLEY, The Rt Revd Michael Harry George.** b 38. CB91. Lon Coll of Div. **d** 61 **p** 62 **c** 95. C St Marylebone w H Trin *Lon* 61-64; Chapl RN 64-68 and 74-89; Chapl of the Fleet and Adn for the RN 89-93; Dir Gen Naval Chapl Services 92-93; Chapl St Andr Univ *St And* 68-72; Chapl R Hosp Sch Holbrook 72-74; QHC 89-93; Hon Can Gib Cathl *Eur* 89-93; P-in-c Pitlochry *St And* 94-95; Bp St And 95-04; rtd 04. *Afton House, Kennedy Gardens, St Andrews KY16 9DJ* Tel (01334) 473167

HENLY, Francis Michael. b 25. Sarum Th Coll. **d** 67 **p** 68. C E w W Harnham *Sarum* 67-70; P-in-c Stour Provost w Todbere 70-75; P-in-c Rowde 75-79; V 79-83; R Poulshot 79-83; V Bishop's Cannings, All Cannings etc 83-92; rtd 92; Perm to Offic *Sarum* from 92. *Oldbury View, Middle Lane, Cherhill, Calne SN11 8XX* Tel (01249) 815191

HENNING, Mrs Judy. b 49. Portsm Univ MSc99. S Dios Minl Tr Scheme 85. **d** 88 **p** 97. C Catherington and Clanfield *Portsm* 88-91; C Leigh Park 91-92; Perm to Offic 94-96; Min in Whiteley and Asst to RD Fareham 96-99; C-in-c Whiteley CD 99-04; P-in-c Old Cleeve, Leighland and Treborough *B & W* from 04. *The Rectory, Old Cleeve, Minehead TA24 6HN* Tel (01984) 640576 E-mail judy.henning@btinternet.com

HENRY, Miss Jacqueline Margaret. b 40. Open Univ BA82. Trin Coll Bris DipHE79. **dss** 83 **d** 87 **p** 94. Deptford St Jo *S'wark* 79-82; Catshill and Dodford *Worc* 83-86; The Lye and Stambermill 86-87; Par Dn 87-89; Educn Chapl 89-93; C Tolleshunt Knights w Tiptree and Gt Braxted *Chelmsf* 94-97; Chapl amongst Deaf People 94-97; TV Stantonbury and Willen *Ox* 97-02; rtd 02; Perm to Offic *Cant* from 02. *72 St Nicholas Road, Faversham ME13 7PB* Tel (01795) 538785

HENRY, Peter. b 49. BTh. St Jo Coll Nottm. **d** 84 **p** 85. C Sinfin Moor *Derby* 84-89; C Blagreaves St Andr CD 84-89; V Guernsey St Jo *Win* 89-97; P-in-c Sawley *Derby* 97-01; R from 01. *The Rectory, 561 Tamworth Road, Long Eaton, Nottingham NG10 3FB* Tel 0115-973 4900

HENRY, Canon Stephen Kenelm Malim. b 37. Brasted Th Coll 58 Bps' Coll Cheshunt 60. **d** 62 **p** 63. C Leic St Phil *Leic* 62-67; CF 67-70; V Woodhouse *Wakef* 70-01; Hon Can Wakef Cathl 00-01; rtd 01; Perm to Offic *Wakef* from 01. *1 Yorkstone, Crosland Moor, Huddersfield HD4 5NQ* Tel (01484) 644807 Fax as telephone

HENSHALL, Keith. *See* HENSHALL, Ronald Keith

✠**HENSHALL, The Rt Revd Michael.** b 28. St Chad's Coll Dur BA54. **d** 56 **p** 57 **c** 76. C Sewerby w Marton *York* 56-59; C Bridlington Quay H Trin 56-59; C-in-c Micklehurst CD *Ches* 59-62; V Micklehurst 62-63; V Altrincham St Geo 63-76; Hon Can Ches Cathl 72-76; Suff Bp Warrington *Liv* 76-96; rtd 96; Perm to Offic *Liv* 96-03 and *York* 96-99; Hon Asst Bp York from 99. *28 Hermitage Way, Sleights, Whitby YO22 5HG* Tel (01947) 811233

HENSHALL, Canon Nicholas James. b 62. Wadh Coll Ox BA84 MA88. Ripon Coll Cuddesdon 85. **d** 88 **p** 89. C Blyth St Mary *Newc* 88-92; V Scotswood 92-02; Can Res Derby Cathl *Derby* from 02. *24 Kedleston Road, Derby DE22 1GU* Tel (01332) 343523 E-mail precentor@btopenworld.com

HENSHALL, Ronald Keith. b 54. Loughb Coll of Educn CertEd76. Chich Th Coll 87. **d** 89 **p** 90. C Ribbleton *Blackb* 89-92; TV 95-98; USPG St Kitts-Nevis 92-95; V Ellel w Shireshead *Blackb* 98-02; Cyprus 02-05; Chapl R Alexandra and Albert Sch Reigate from 05. *Royal Alexandra and Albert School, Gatton Park, Reigate RH2 0TD* Tel (01737) 649000 E-mail keithofpaphos@msn.com

HENSHAW, Nicholas Newell. b 49. Rhodes Univ BA72. Cuddesdon Coll 73. **d** 75 **p** 76. C Beaconsfield *Ox* 75-78; Chapl Wellington Coll Berks 78-80; C Pimlico St Pet w Westmr Ch Ch *Lon* 80-82; Chapl Sevenoaks Sch from 82; Hon C Sevenoaks St Nic *Roch* from 82. *Sevenoaks School, High Street, Sevenoaks TN13 1HU* Tel (01732) 456710

HENSON, Carolyn. b 44. Bedf Coll Lon BA65 Nottm Univ MTh88 PhD97 Solicitor 75. EMMTC 82. **dss** 85 **d** 87 **p** 94. Braunstone *Leic* 85-89; Par Dn 87-89; Adult Educn and Tr Officer *Ely* 89-91; NSM Sutton and Witcham w Mepal 89-95; Chapl Gt Ormond Street Hosp for Children NHS Trust 95-96; NSM Cainscross w Selsley *Glouc* 96-97; Vice Prin EMMTC *S'well* 97-01; R Morley w Smalley and Horsley Woodhouse *Derby* from 02. *The Vicarage, 80 Main Road, Smalley, Ilkeston DE7 6EF* Tel (01332) 880380 E-mail carolyn.henson@virgin.net

HENSON, John David. b 49. EMMTC. **d** 00 **p** 01. NSM Beckingham w Walkeringham *S'well* 00-02; NSM Gringley-on-the-Hill 00-02; NSM Misterton and W Stockwith from 02; Asst Chapl HM Pris Whatton from 00; Sen Police Chapl *S'well* from 03. *The Vicarage, Church Lane, Misterton, Doncaster DN10 4AL* Tel (01427) 890270 E-mail jd.henson@btinternet.com

HENSON, Canon John Richard. b 40. Selw Coll Cam BA62 MA66. Ridley Hall Cam 62. **d** 65 **p** 66. C Ollerton *S'well* 65-68; Univs Sec CMS 68-73; Chapl Scargill Ho 73-78; V Shipley St Paul *Bradf* 78-83; TR Shipley St Paul and Frizinghall 83-91; V Ilkeston St Mary *Derby* 91-99; V Mickleover St Jo from 99; Dioc Ecum Officer from 96; Hon Can Derby Cathl from 00. *St John's Vicarage, 7 Onslow Road, Mickleover, Derby DE3 9JJ* Tel and fax (01332) 516545 E-mail john.henson3@ntlworld.com

HENSON, Richard Clive. b 41. Univ of Wales (Cardiff) BSc63 PhD66. S'wark Ord Course 77. **d** 88 **p** 89. NSM Lee St Mildred *S'wark* 88-97; NSM Donington *Lich* 97-99; rtd 99. *Address temp unknown*

HENSON, Shaun Christopher. b 64. E Nazarene Coll (USA) BA94 Duke Univ (USA) MDiv98. Wycliffe Hall Ox 03. **d** 04 **p** 05. C Bladon w Woodstock *Ox* 04-05; C Blenheim from 05.

19 Park Close, Bladon, Woodstock OX20 1RN Tel (01993) 813603 Mobile 07795-547555 E-mail hensonshaunc@aol.com

HENSTRIDGE, Edward John. b 31. Ex Coll Ox BA55 MA59 FCIPD77. Wells Th Coll 55. **d** 57 **p** 58. C Milton *Portsm* 57-62; V Soberton w Newtown 62-69; Lic to Offic *Derby* 69-71; Perm to Offic *Guildf* 72-84 and from 02; Lic to Offic 84-02; Bp's Officer for NSMs 97-01. *The White House, Thursley Road, Elstead, Godalming GU8 6LW* Tel (01252) 702272 Fax 702747 E-mail johnhn@globalnet.co.uk

HENTHORNE, Thomas Roger. b 30. EAMTC. **d** 79 **p** 80. Hd Master St Mary's Sch St Neots 67-93; Hon C St Neots *Ely* from 79. *Stapeley, 45 Berkley Street, Eynesbury, St Neots PE19 2NE* Tel (01480) 472548 E-mail roger.henthorne@tesco.net

HENTON, John Martin. b 48. AKC71 St Luke's Coll Ex DipEd72. St Aug Coll Cant 74. **d** 74 **p** 75. C Woolwich St Mary w H Trin *S'wark* 74-77; C Cotham St Mary *Bris* 77-78; C Cotham St Sav w St Mary 78-80; R Filton 80-87; Chapl Ex Sch 87-91; Chapl St Marg Sch Ex 87-91; V Ex St Dav *Ex* from 91. *St David's Vicarage, 95 Howell Road, Exeter EX4 4LH* Tel (01392) 254396 E-mail j.henton@tesco.net

HENWOOD, Mrs Gillian Kathleen. b 56. ABIPP81 Lanc Univ MA97. Carl and Blackb Dioc Tr Inst 94. **d** 97 **p** 98. NSM Whitechapel w Admarsh-in-Bleasdale *Blackb* 97-01; Rural Chapl 00-03; Bp's Adv for Leisure and Tourism 01-03; C Westmr St Jas *Lon* 03-04; V Nunthorpe *York* from 04. *St Mary's Vicarage, Church Lane, Nunthorpe, Middlesbrough TS7 0PD* Tel (01642) 316570 E-mail gillhenwood@hotmail.com

HENWOOD, Martin John. b 58. DL05. Glas Univ BD81. Ripon Coll Cuddesdon. **d** 85 **p** 86. C Dartford H Trin *Roch* 85-88; C St Martin-in-the-Fields *Lon* 88-93; V Dartford H Trin *Roch* from 93. *The Vicarage, High Street, Dartford DA1 1RX* Tel (01322) 222782

HENWOOD, Canon Peter Richard. b 32. St Edm Hall Ox BA55 MA69. Cuddesdon Coll 56. **d** 57 **p** 58. C Rugby St Andr *Cov* 57-62; C-in-c Gleadless Valley CD *Sheff* 62-71; V Plaistow St Mary *Roch* 71-97; RD Bromley 79-96; Hon Can Roch Cathl 88-97; rtd 97. *Wayside, 1 Highfield Close, Sandling Road, Saltwood, Hythe CT21 4QP* Tel (01303) 230039

HENWOOD (née OAKLEY), Mrs Susan Mary. b 55. Salford Univ BSc76. St Jo Coll Nottm LTh86 DPS87. **d** 87 **p** 94. Par Dn Armthorpe *Sheff* 87-91; C Howell Hill *Guildf* 91-96; Perm to Offic *Cov* 02-04; NSM Bidford-on-Avon from 04. *5 Blenheim Close, Bidford-on-Avon, Alcester B50 4HW* Tel (01789) 490630

HEPPER, Christopher Michael Alan. b 55. St Jo Coll Nottm 90. **d** 92 **p** 93. C High Harrogate Ch Ch *Ripon* 92-95; Bp's Dom Chapl 95-99; Chapl Poitou-Charentes *Eur* from 99. *29 rue Pierre Pestureau, 86400 Civray, France* Tel (0033) (5) 49 97 04 22 Mobile (6) 85 05 34 62 Fax 49 97 04 37 E-mail michael.hepper@wanadoo.fr

HEPPER, William Raymond. b 62. Kingston Poly BA83. Trin Coll Bris BA98. **d** 98 **p** 99. C Spring Grove St Mary *Lon* 98-01; CMS Egypt 01-04; NSM Greenford H Cross *Lon* from 05. *St Edward's House, 12A Medway Drive, Greenford UB6 8LN* Tel (020) 8997 4953 E-mail heppers@dataxprs.com.eg

HEPPLE, Gordon. b 32. Edin Th Coll. **d** 63 **p** 68. C Billingham St Cuth *Dur* 63-64; C Ryhope 64; Perm to Offic 66-68; C Wingate Grange 68-69; C Heworth St Mary 69; C Gateshead St Mary 69-71; P-in-c Low Team 71-72; R Lyons 72-79; V Basford St Aid *S'well* 79-84; V Blackhill *Dur* 84-95; rtd 97; Perm to Offic *Win* from 97. *66B Ringwood Road, Christchurch BH23 5RE* Tel (01425) 279068

HEPTINSTALL, Mrs Lillian. b 49. EMMTC 99. **d** 02 **p** 03. NSM Chilwell *S'well* from 02. *8 Cranston Road, Bramcote, Nottingham NG9 3GU* Tel 0115-916 4588 E-mail heptinstall@ntlworld.com

HEPWORTH, Canon Ernest John Peter. b 42. K Coll Lon BD65 AKC65 Hull Univ MA87. **d** 66 **p** 67. C Headingley *Ripon* 66-69; Asst Chapl St Geo Hosp Lon 69-71; C Gt Grimsby St Mary and St Jas *Linc* 71-72; TV 72-74; V Crosby 74-80; V Barton upon Humber 80-04; RD Yarborough 86-92; Can and Preb Linc Cathl 94-04; rtd 04. *63 Ferriby Road, Barton-upon-Humber DN18 5LQ* Tel (01652) 661363 E-mail ernest@hepworth2000.fsnet.co.uk

HEPWORTH, Michael David Albert. b 37. Em Coll Cam BA59 MA63 Lon Inst of Educn PGCE60. Ridley Hall Cam 65. **d** 67 **p** 68. C Eastbourne All SS *Chich* 67-69; Teacher Eastbourne Coll 67-69; Asst Chapl Bedford Sch 69-72; Chapl 72-83; Hd Master Birkdale Sch 83-98; Perm to Offic *Derby* and *Sheff* from 83. *29 Stumperlowe Park Road, Sheffield S10 3QP* Tel 0114-230 6016 Fax 263 0714 E-mail hepworth@onet.co.uk

HEPWORTH, Michael Edward. b 29. Leeds Univ BA51. NW Ord Course 74. **d** 77 **p** 78. Hon C Timperley *Ches* 77-98; Hon Chapl RAF from 77; Perm to Offic *Ches* from 00. *56 Ridgeway Road, Timperley, Altrincham WA15 7HD* Tel 0161-980 5104

HERAPATH, Jonathan James. b 67. Westmr Coll Ox BTh96 Ox Brookes Univ PGCE02. St Steph Ho Ox 03. **d** 05. C Cowley St Jo *Ox* from 05. *58 Magdalen Road, Oxford OX4 1RB* Tel 07745-405150 (mobile) E-mail jonathanherapath@02.co.uk

HERBERT, Anthony. b 19. Bris Univ. Qu Coll Birm 46. **d** 48 **p** 49. C Frodingham *Linc* 48-51; C Liv St Bride *Liv* 51-54; Chapl Liv Univ 51-54; C Liv St Sav 54-55; C Stapleton *Bris* 55-58; V Hamer *Man* 58-64; Chapl HM YOI Buckley Hall 58-64; V Dur St Cuth *Dur* 64-78; Chapl Low Newton Rem Cen 68-77; V Barrow upon Soar *Leic* 78-83; R Barrow upon Soar w Walton le Wolds 83-84; rtd 84; Perm to Offic *B & W* from 85. *12 Valley View, Clutton, Bristol BS39 5SN* Tel (01761) 452494

HERBERT, Christopher John. b 37. Dur Univ BA60 DipTh62. Cranmer Hall Dur 60. **d** 62 **p** 63. C Huyton Quarry *Liv* 62-65; C Rainford 65-68; V Impington *Ely* 68-78; RD N Stowe 76-78; V Gt Shelford 78-97; RD Shelford 80-85; rtd 97. *North Place, Crown Street, Great Bardfield, Braintree CM7 4ST* Tel (01371) 810516

✠**HERBERT, The Rt Revd Christopher William.** b 44. Univ of Wales (Lamp) BA65. Wells Th Coll 65. **d** 67 **p** 68 **c** 95. C Tupsley *Heref* 67-71; Dioc RE Adv 71-76; Dioc Dir RE 76-81; Preb Heref Cathl 76-81; V Bourne *Guildf* 81-90; Hon Can Guildf Cathl 85-95; Adn Dorking 90-95; Bp St Alb from 95. *Abbey Gate House, 4 Abbey Mill Lane, St Albans AL3 4HD* Tel (01727) 853305 Fax 846715 E-mail bishop@stalbans.anglican.org

HERBERT, Clair Geoffrey Thomas. b 36. Tyndale Hall Bris 61. **d** 64 **p** 65. C Nottingham St Sav *S'well* 64-67; C Harwell *Ox* 67-70; C Chilton All SS 67-70; V Bucklebury w Marlston 70-80; Chapl Brighton Coll Jun Sch 80-83; Hon C Upton (Overchurch) *Ches* 85-86; C 86-88; V Collier Row St Jas and Havering-atte-Bower *Chelmsf* 88-01; rtd 01; Perm to Offic *Ripon* from 01. *24 Birstwith Grange, Birstwith, Harrogate HG3 3AH* Tel (01423) 771315

HERBERT, Clare Marguerite. b 54. Bris Univ CASS85 St Hild Coll Dur BA76 New Coll Edin MTh78. Linc Th Coll 79. **dss** 81 **d** 87 **p** 94. Clifton St Paul *Bris* and Asst Chapl Bris Univ 81-84; Hon Par Dn Bris St Mary Redcliffe w Temple etc *Bris* 87-90; Dioc Past Care Adv *Lon* 92-95; Hon C Clapham Team *S'wark* 94-96; C St Martin-in-the-Fields *Lon* 96-98; R Soho St Anne w St Thos and St Pet from 98; Dean of Women's Min Two Cities Area from 01. *St Anne's Rectory, 55 Dean Street, London W1D 6AF* Tel (020) 7437 5006 *or* tel and fax 7437 8039 E-mail stannes.soho@virgin.net

HERBERT, Canon David Alexander Sellars. b 39. Bris Univ BA60. St Steph Ho Ox 65. **d** 67 **p** 68. C St Leonards Ch Ch *Chich* 67-80; C St Leonards Ch Ch and St Mary 81; V Bickley *Roch* from 81; Hon Can Roch Cathl from 92. *The Vicarage, Bickley Park Road, Bromley BR1 2BE* Tel (020) 8467 3809 Fax as telephone E-mail david.herbert@lineone.net

HERBERT, David Roy. b 51. K Coll Lon BD73 AKC73. **d** 74 **p** 75. C Sheff St Aid w St Luke *Sheff* 74-76; C Sheff Manor 76-78; TV Gleadless Valley 78-83; TV Ellesmere Port *Ches* 83-93; V Tarvin from 93; Continuing Minl Tr Officer from 03. *St Andrew's Vicarage, Tarvin, Chester CH3 8EB* Tel (01829) 740354 E-mail davidrherbert@tiscali.co.uk

HERBERT, Mrs Denise Bridget Helen. b 42. SRN72 SCM74. Ripon Coll Cuddesdon DipMin95. **d** 95 **p** 96. S Africa 95-00; NSM Ocean View 95-97; NSM Grahamstown Cathl 97-99; Sub-Dean 99-00; R Jedburgh *Edin* from 00. *The Rectory, 46 Castlegate, Jedburgh TD8 6BB* Tel and fax (01835) 863892 E-mail denise-herbert@beeb.net

HERBERT, Geoffrey. *See* HERBERT, Clair Geoffrey Thomas

HERBERT, Geoffrey William. b 38. Ox Univ MA62 Birm Univ PhD72. Qu Coll Birm 80. **d** 82 **p** 83. C Hall Green Ascension *Birm* 82-85; R Sheldon 85-95; rtd 95; Perm to Offic *Birm* from 95; Co-ord for Spiritual Direction 00-05. *28 Lulworth Road, Birmingham B28 8NS* Tel 0121-777 2684 E-mail gandjherbert@tesco.net

HERBERT, Graham Paul. b 54. Birm Univ BA75 CertEd76 Ox Univ BA80 MA. Wycliffe Hall Ox 78. **d** 81 **p** 82. C Crowborough *Chich* 81-85; Chapl Monkton Combe Sch Bath 85-98; C Claygate *Guildf* 99-01. *Address temp unknown*

HERBERT, Graham Victor. b 61. Nottm Univ BA02. St Jo Coll Nottm 00. **d** 02 **p** 03. C Strood St Nic w St Mary *Roch* from 02. *12 Cadnam Close, Rochester ME2 3TS* Tel (01634) 321592

HERBERT, Jonathan Patrick. b 62. Bris Univ BA86. Linc Th Coll 86. **d** 88 **p** 89. C Kirkby *Liv* 88-91; TV Blakenall Heath *Lich* 91-96; Pilsdon Community from 96. *Pilsdon Manor, Pilsdon, Bridport DT6 5NZ* Tel (01308) 868308 Fax 868161

HERBERT, Kenneth Cyril. b 20. Univ of Wales (Abth) BA41. St D Coll Lamp LTh43. **d** 43 **p** 44. C Carmarthen St Pet *St D* 43-56; V Llangorwen 56-89; RD Llanbadarn Fawr 80-86; rtd 89. *68 Ger-y-llan, Penrhyncoch, Aberystwyth SY23 3HQ* Tel (01970) 828207

HERBERT, Malcolm Francis. b 53. K Coll Lon BD74 AKC74 St Mary's Coll Chelt CertEd75. Trin Coll Bris 76. **d** 77 **p** 78. C Wotton-under-Edge w Ozleworth and N Nibley *Glouc* 77-79; C Milton *B & W* 79-80; C Worle 80-85; V Woking Ch Ch *Guildf* 86-02; RD Woking 94-99; Dioc Dir of Ords *Bris* from 02; C Kington St Michael and Chippenham St Paul w Hardenhuish etc 02-05; C Chippenham St Pet from 05. *3 Stapleford Close, Chippenham SN15 3FZ* Tel (01249) 765827 E-mail ddo.bristol@btopenworld.com

HERBERT, Michael. b 35. Nottm Univ BA57. St D Coll Lamp 59. **d** 61 **p** 62. C Paston *Pet* 61-65; C Northampton All SS w

St Kath 65-67; R Sutton w Upton 67-72; Asst Youth Chapl 67-72; Ind Chapl 72-84; P-in-c Pitsford 79-84; Ind Chapl *Worc* 84-01; TV Redditch, The Ridge 84-01; Chapl NE Worcs Coll 86-01; rtd 01; Perm to Offic *Worc* from 01. *33 Abbey Road, Redditch B97 4BL* Tel and fax (01527) 69975

HERBERT, Canon Ronald. b 53. Worc Coll Ox BA75 MA80 Lon Univ BD78 W Kentucky Univ MA79. Oak Hill Th Coll 75. **d** 79 **p** 80. C Welling *Roch* 79-89; V Falconwood 89-90; V Becontree St Mary *Chelmsf* from 90; Hon Can Chelmsf Cathl from 02. *The Vicarage, 191 Valence Wood Road, Dagenham RM8 3AH* Tel (020) 8592 2822 E-mail ronald.herbert@virgin.net

HERBERT, Mrs Rosemary. b 44. Westf Coll Lon BSc65. Qu Coll Birm 81. **dss** 85 **d** 87. Malvern Link w Cowleigh *Worc* 85-91; Hon Par Dn 87-91; NSM Malvern H Trin and St Jas from 91. *4 Cedar Avenue, Malvern WR14 2SG* Tel (01684) 572497

HERBERT, Stephen Edward. b 54. Hastings Coll Nebraska BA76 Bemidji State Univ MA81. Seabury-Western Th Sem MDiv87. **d** 87 **p** 87. V Lake City Grace Ch USA 87-90; Asst P Vancouver St Jas Canada 90-00; TV Wythenshawe *Man* from 00. *St Richard's Vicarage, 42 Lomond Road, Manchester M22 5JD* Tel 0161-499 2022 E-mail stephenherbert@supanet.com

HERBERT, Canon Timothy David. b 57. Man Univ BA78 MPhil88 PhD04. Ridley Hall Cam 79. **d** 81 **p** 82. C Macclesfield St Mich *Ches* 81-85; V Wharton 85-93; Asst CME Officer 90-93; P-in-c Thanington *Cant* 93-98; Dir of Ords 93-98; Dir Dioc Tr Inst *Carl* from 99; C Cotehill and Cumwhinton 99-00; Hon Can Carl Cathl from 99; C Scotby and Cotehill w Cumwhinton from 00. *The Vicarage, Cotehill, Carlisle CA4 0DY* Tel (01228) 561745 Fax 562366 E-mail therbert@globalnet.co.uk

✠**HERD, The Rt Revd William Brian.** b 31. Clifton Th Coll 55. **d** 58 **p** 59 **c** 76. C Wolverhampton St Luke *Lich* 58-61; Uganda 61-77; Adn Karamoja 70-75; Bp Karamoja 76-77; Deputation Sec (Ireland) BCMS 77-89; C Harrow Trin St Mich *Lon* 89-93; V Gresley *Derby* 93-98; rtd 98; Perm to Offic *Sarum* from 98. *Karibu, 13 Ambleside, Weymouth DT3 5HH* Tel (01305) 770257

HEREFORD, Archdeacon of. *See* COLMER, The Ven Malcolm John

HEREFORD, Bishop of. *See* PRIDDIS, The Rt Revd Anthony Martin

HEREFORD, Dean of. *See* TAVINOR, The Very Revd Michael Edward

HEREWARD, John Owen. b 53. FRCSE82 Lon Univ MB, BS77. Ridley Hall Cam 89. **d** 91 **p** 92. C W Ealing St Jo w St Jas *Lon* 91-95; P-in-c Hanwell St Mellitus w St Mark from 95; Dir Post-Ord Tr from 97; AD Ealing 98-03. *St Mellitus Vicarage, 1 Church Road, London W7 3BA* Tel (020) 8567 6535 E-mail john@jhereward.fsnet.co.uk

HEREWARD-ROTHWELL, Canon Michael John. b 46. MA Tulane Univ (USA) DPhil03. Chich Th Coll 74. **d** 78 **p** 79. C Chelmsf All SS *Chelmsf* 78-82; C Clacton St Jas 82-85; V Thorpe *Guildf* from 85; Hon Can Guildf Cathl from 99. *The Vicarage, Church Approach, Egham TW20 8TQ* Tel and fax (01932) 565986 E-mail mjh.r@fish.co.uk

HERITAGE, Barry. b 35. Clifton Th Coll 59. **d** 61 **p** 62. C Wolverhampton St Jude *Lich* 61-65; C Chaddesden St Mary *Derby* 65-67; V Kidsgrove *Lich* 67-76; NE Area Sec CPAS 76-89; V Elloughton and Brough w Brantingham *York* 89-93; C York St Paul 93-00; rtd 00; Perm to Offic *York* from 00. *32 St Swithins Walk, York YO26 4UF* Tel (01904) 786077

HERKES, Richard Andrew. b 54. Kent Univ BA75. STETS 99. **d** 02 **p** 03. NSM Polegate *Chich* from 02. *31 Wannock Lane, Eastbourne BN20 9SB* Tel (01323) 488328 E-mail rherkes@hotmail.com

HERKLOTS, Canon John Radu. b 31. Trin Hall Cam BA53 MA61. Westcott Ho Cam 54. **d** 55 **p** 56. C Attercliffe w Carbrook *Sheff* 55-60; C Stoke Damerel *Ex* 60-65; V Devonport St Bart 65-72; V Denmead *Portsm* 72-97; RD Havant 82-87; Hon Can Portsm Cathl 86-97; rtd 97; Perm to Offic *Heref* 97-02 and *Portms* from 03. *14 Derwent Road, Lee-on-the-Solent PO13 8JG* Tel (023) 9255 2652

HERMAN, Jean-Pierre. b 59. Louvain Univ MA83 BPh83. Namur Dioc Sem BTh87. **d** 86 **p** 87. In RC Ch (Belgium) 86-00; Perm to Offic *Eur* 01-02; C Brussels 02-04; P-in-c Leuven from 04; P-in-c Charleroi from 04. *10 rue d'Harscamp, B-5380 Novilles-les-Bois, Belgium* Tel and fax (0032) (81) 657576 Mobile 475-684665 E-mail jean.pierre.herman@skynet.be

HERON, David George. b 49. AKC72. **d** 73 **p** 74. C Stockton St Chad *Dur* 73-77; C Beamish 77-81; R Willington and Sunnybrow 81-95; V Dipton and Leadgate from 95. *The Vicarage, St Ives Road, Leadgate, Consett DH8 7SN* Tel (01207) 503918

HERON, George Dobson. b 34. TD. Cranmer Hall Dur 58. **d** 61 **p** 62. C Benfieldside *Dur* 61-65; C Winlaton 65-68; V Dunston St Nic 68-77; P-in-c Dunston Ch Ch 74-77; V Dunston 77-82; V Gateshead St Helen 82-89; rtd 94; Perm to Offic *Dur* 94-96 and *Newc* from 94. *36 Woodlands Road, Shotley Bridge, Consett DH8 0DE* Tel (01207) 507733

HERON, Nicholas Peter. b 60. Man Univ BA81 Southn Univ BTh86. Sarum & Wells Th Coll. **d** 84 **p** 85. C Brinnington w Portwood *Ches* 84-87; Chapl RAF from 87. *Chaplaincy Services (RAF), HQ, Personnel and Training Command, RAF Innsworth, Gloucester GL3 1EZ* Tel (01452) 712612 ext 5164 Fax 510828

HERRICK, Andrew Frederick. b 58. Univ of Wales (Lamp) BA80. Wycliffe Hall Ox 80. **d** 82 **p** 83. C Aberystwyth *St D* 82-85; P-in-c Llangeitho and Blaenpennal w Betws Leucu etc 85-86; R 86-88; Youth Chapl 86-88; R Aberporth w Tremain and Blaenporth 88-91; Succ St D Cathl 91-94; V Betws w Ammanford 94-00; TV Aberystwyth from 00. *Fenton, Queens Square, Aberystwyth SY23 2HL* Tel (01970) 624537

HERRICK, David William. b 52. Middx Poly BSc73. St Jo Coll Nottm 79. **d** 82 **p** 83. C Ipswich St Matt *St E* 82-85; C Nor St Pet Mancroft w St Jo Maddermarket *Nor* 85-88; V Bury St Edmunds St Geo *St E* 88-96; P-in-c Gt Barton 96-99; Dir Studies Dioc Min Course from 99; Vice Prin from 04. *24 Cromwell Road, Ely CB6 1AS* Tel (01353) 662909 Fax 662056

HERRICK (formerly COWLEY), Mrs Jean Louie Cameron. b 39. Sarum Dioc Tr Coll CertEd59. St Alb and Ox Min Course 94. **d** 96 **p** 97. NSM Chorleywood Ch Ch *St Alb* 96-02; NSM Hermitage *Ox* 02-05; Perm to Offic *Glouc* from 05. *52 Cambrian Road, Walton Cardiff, Tewkesbury GL20 7RP* E-mail jean.herrick@tesco.net

HERRICK (née RENAUT), Canon Vanessa Anne. b 58. York Univ BA80 Fitzw Coll Cam MA96 LTCL75. St Jo Coll Nottm 80 Ridley Hall Cam 94. **d** 96 **p** 97. C St E Cathl Distr *St E* 96-99; Chapl Fitzw Coll Cam 99-02; Fell 01-02; Tutor Ridley Hall Cam 99-02; Dir Min and Vocation *Ely* from 03; Hon Can Ely Cathl from 03. *24 Cromwell Road, Ely CB6 1AS* Tel (01353) 662909 Fax 662056 Mobile 07778-496340 E-mail vanessa.herrick@ely.anglican.org

HERROD, Mrs Kathryn. b 59. Warwick Univ BSc80 Matlock Coll of Educn PGCE81. St Jo Coll Nottm MA97. **d** 97 **p** 98. C Wollaton *S'well* 97-01; R Warsop from 01. *The Rectory, Church Road, Warsop, Mansfield NG20 0SL* Tel (01623) 843290

HERRON, Robert Gordon John. b 36. MCIPD75 Dip Counselling CPC. Wycliffe Hall Ox 65. **d** 77 **p** 78. C Ditton St Mich *Liv* 77-80; C W Kirby St Bridget *Ches* 80-82; R Gorton St Mary and St Thos *Man* 82-00; rtd 00. *The Gables, 13 West Road, Bowden, Altrincham WA14 2LD*

HERSCHEL, Richard James. b 27. Villanova Univ USA MA72. **d** 57 **p** 57. USA 57-81 and 84-97; TV Cannock *Lich* 82-84; rtd 92. *80B King Street, Norwich NR1 1PG* Tel (01603) 614873

HERTFORD, Archdeacon of. *See* JONES, The Ven Trevor Pryce

HERTFORD, Suffragan Bishop of. *See* FOSTER, The Rt Revd Christopher Richard James

HERVÉ, Canon John Anthony. b 49. TD94. Open Univ BA81 Wolv Univ PGCE95. Lich Th Coll 70. **d** 73 **p** 74. C Middlesbrough All SS *York* 73-76; CF 76-81; P-in-c Handsworth St Andr *Birm* 81-86; Hon C Cowley St Jo *Ox* 86-90; Tutor St Steph Ho Ox 86-90; V Sparkbrook St Agatha w Balsall Heath St Barn *Birm* from 90; P-in-c Highgate from 05; Hon Can Birm Cathl from 05. *The Vicarage, 120 Stanhope Street, Birmingham B12 0XB* Tel 0121-440 4605 E-mail fr.john@saintagathas.org.uk

HERVEY, Mrs Mary Diana (Di). b 41. St Hugh's Coll Ox BA63. St And Dioc Tr Course 83 TISEC 96. **d** 92 **p** 94. Par Dn Cupar *St And* 92-94; Asst Chapl St Andr Univ 94-97; Asst P Cen Fife Team 94-97; C Ulverston St Mary w H Trin *Carl* 97-00; P-in-c Barrow St Jo from 00. *St John's Vicarage, James Watt Terrace, Barrow-in-Furness LA14 2TS* Tel (01229) 821101 E-mail revdih@aol.com

HERYET, Dudley. b 18. AKC42. **d** 42 **p** 43. C Southampton St Alb *Win* 42-45; C Finsbury Park St Thos *Lon* 45-48; C Hackney Wick St Mary of Eton w St Aug 48-50; C St Geo-in-the-East St Mary 50-53; V 53-58; V Edmonton St Mich 58-62; V Blean *Cant* 62-73; V Kennington 73-83; rtd 83; Perm to Offic *Cant* 83-96 and from 05. *27 Homespire House, Knotts Lane, Canterbury CT1 2AB* Tel (01227) 451511

HESELTINE, Mrs Barbara Joan. b 42. Keele Univ BA65. S'wark Ord Course 85. **d** 88 **p** 94. NSM Addington *S'wark* 88-98; Perm to Offic *Truro* from 98; NSM Feock from 02. *The Lodge, Penpol, Devoran, Truro TR3 6NA* Tel and fax (01872) 870039 Mobile 07767-264060 E-mail barbara.hesletine@tesco.net

HESELWOOD, Eric Harold. b 43. Oak Hill Th Coll 84. **d** 86 **p** 87. C Farnborough *Roch* 86-88; V Biggin Hill 88-96; V Orpington All SS 96-98; V Bromley Common St Aug from 98. *St Augustine's Vicarage, Southborough Lane, Bromley BR2 8AT* Tel (020) 8467 1351 Fax as telephone E-mail eric.heselwood@talk21.com

HESELWOOD, Mrs Hilda. b 39. CA Tr Coll 61. **dss** 85 **d** 87 **p** 94. CA from 63; Bromley Common St Luke *Roch* 85-00; Par Dn 87-94; C 94-00; rtd 00; Perm to Offic *Roch* from 00. *St Augustine's Vicarage, Southborough Lane, Bromley BR2 8AT* Tel (020) 8467 1351 Fax as telephone

HESFORD-LOCKE, Richard Nigel. b 61. Coll of Resurr Mirfield 92. **d** 94 **p** 95. C Middlesbrough Ascension *York* 94-97; C Paignton St Jo *Ex* 97-98; rtd 98. *2 Windyhill Drive, Bolton BL3 4TH*

HESKETH, Canon Philip John. b 64. K Coll Lon BD86 AKC86 PhD94 Richmond Fellowship Coll Dip Human Relns 90. Ripon Coll Cuddesdon 92. **d** 94 **p** 95. C Bearsted w Thurnham *Cant* 94-98; V Chatham St Steph *Roch* from 98; Can Res Roch Cathl from 05. *St Stephen's Vicarage, 55 Pattens Lane, Chatham ME4 6JR* Tel (01634) 849791

HESKETH, Robin Adams Lempriere. b 18. St Cath Soc Ox BA43 MA47. St Steph Ho Ox 43. **d** 45 **p** 46. C Babbacombe *Ex* 45-48; Perm to Offic 48-51; C Dawlish 51-55; C Brixham 55-61; V S Petherwin w Trewen *Truro* 61-72; V Lewannick 62-71; P-in-c Penponds 72-73; V 73-83; rtd 84; Perm to Offic *Truro* from 84. *Camelview, Marshall Road, Nanstallon, Bodmin PL30 5LD* Tel (01208) 831892

HESKETH, The Ven Ronald David. b 47. Bede Coll Dur BA68 Univ of Wales (Cardiff) DPS71. Ridley Hall Cam 69 St Mich Coll Llan 71. **d** 71 **p** 72. C Southport H Trin *Liv* 71-74; Asst Chapl Miss to Seamen 74-75; Chapl RAF 75-98; Command Chapl RAF 98-01; Chapl-in-Chief RAF from 01; QHC from 01; Can and Preb Linc Cathl *Linc* from 01. *Chaplaincy Services (RAF), HQ, Personnel and Training Command, RAF Innsworth, Gloucester GL3 1EZ* Tel (01452) 712612 ext 5164 Fax 510828 E-mail vera&ron.hesketh@dunelm.org.uk

HESKINS, Georgiana Mary. b 48. K Coll Lon BD81 AKC81 MTh93. Westcott Ho Cam 81. **dss** 83 **d** 87 **p** 94. Cobbold Road St Sav w St Mary *Lon* 83-85; St Botolph Aldgate w H Trin Minories 85-87; Par Dn 87; Perm to Offic *S'wark* 88-93; Par Dn Kidbrooke St Jas 93-95; Tutor S'wark Ord Course 93-94; Tutor SEITE 94-98; Hon Chapl S'wark Cathl *S'wark* from 95; Teacher Eltham Coll 98-02; Asst Chapl Qu Eliz Hosp NHS Trust from 03. *Queen Elizabeth Hospital NHS Trust, Stadium Road, London SE18 4QH* Tel (020) 8836 6831 Mobile 07776-122350 E-mail georgiana@lineone.net

HESKINS, Jeffrey George. b 55. AKC78 Heythrop Coll Lon MA94 Princeton Th Sem DMin00. Chich Th Coll 80. **d** 81 **p** 82. C Primrose Hill St Mary w Avenue Road St Paul *Lon* 81-85; Enfield Deanery Youth Officer 85-88; C Enfield Chase St Mary 85-88; TV Kidbrooke St Jas *S'wark* 88-95; R Charlton St Luke w H Trin 95-02; P-in-c Old Charlton St Thos 02; R Charlton from 02. *The Rectory, 185 Charlton Church Lane, London SE7 7AA* Tel (020) 8858 0791 Fax 8305 1297 E-mail heskins@lineone.net

HESLAM, Peter Somers. b 63. Hull Univ BA89 Keble Coll Ox DPhil94 Trin Coll Cam BA96 MA01. Ridley Hall Cam 93. **d** 96 **p** 97. C Huntingdon *Ely* 96-99; Min Stukeley Meadows LEP 99; Dir Studies EAMTC 99-00; Tutor Ridley Hall Cam from 99; Dir Capitalism Project Lon Inst of Contemporary Chr 00-04; Hon C Cherry Hinton St Jo *Ely* from 00; Fell Faculty of Div Cam Univ from 05. *Glebe House, 64A Glebe Road, Cambridge CB1 7SZ* Tel (01223) 722822 E-mail psh20@cam.ac.uk

HESLOP, Alan. *See* HESLOP, James Alan

HESLOP, Andrew James. b 66. Man Univ BA87 PGCE88. **d** 03 **p** 04. OLM Turton Moorland Min *Man* from 03. *677 Tonge Moor Road, Bolton BL2 3BW*

HESLOP, David Anthony. b 45. BSc DipEd DipTh MTh Birm Univ MLitt97. St Jo Coll Nottm 81. **d** 83 **p** 84. C Willenhall H Trin *Lich* 83-86; V Gresley *Derby* 86-92; V Marston on Dove w Scropton 92-95; Chapl Derby Univ 95-99; V Castle Donington and Lockington cum Hemington *Leic* 99-03; Chapl E Midl Airport 99-03; Prin OLM and Integrated Tr *Sarum* from 03. *25 Lime Kiln Way, Salisbury SP2 8RN* Tel (01722) 417616 *or* 411944 Fax 08701-301824 E-mail david.heslop@salisbury.anglican.org *or* revdave@heslops.co.uk

HESLOP, Harold William. b 40. Leeds Univ BA62 Open Univ BA72. Ox NSM Course 75. **d** 78 **p** 79. NSM Stoke Mandeville *Ox* 78-91; NSM Wendover 82-00; NSM Ellesborough, The Kimbles and Stoke Mandeville 91-94. *7 Chiltern Road, Wendover, Aylesbury HP22 6DB* Tel (01296) 624812

HESLOP, James Alan. b 37. Codrington Coll Barbados 61. **d** 64 **p** 65. C Bartica Guyana 64-68; P-in-c Long Is Nassau 68-71; C Ch Ch Cathl 71-72; C Haxby w Wigginton *York* 72-74; TV 74-76; V York St Olave w St Giles 76-87; V Northampton All SS w St Kath *Pet* 87-88; R Felpham w Middleton *Chich* 88-92; TR Howden *York* 92-94; Warden Coll of St Barn Lingfield 94-95; Warden Morley Retreat and Conf Ho Derby 95-98; R Kirkbride and V Lezayre St Olave Ramsey *S & M* 98-99; P-in-c Woburn w Eversholt, Milton Bryan, Battlesden etc *St Alb* 99-03; rtd 03; Chapl Soc of St Marg 04-05; P-in-c Pau *Eur* from 05. *Anglican Chaplaincy, 3 bis rue Pasteur, 64000 Pau, France* Tel (0033) (5) 59 02 82 55

HESLOP, Michael Andrew. b 47. Trin Coll Bris 73. **d** 76 **p** 77. C Burmantofts St Steph and St Agnes *Ripon* 76-80; V Thorpe Edge *Bradf* 80-87; TV Penrith w Newton Reigny and Plumpton Wall *Carl* 87-91; V Silloth 91-01; V Kettlewell w Conistone, Hubberholme etc *Bradf* from 01. *The Vicarage, Westgate, Kettlewell, Skipton BD23 5QU* Tel (01756) 760237

HESS, John. b 44. Liv Poly BSc70. SEITE 95. **d** 98 **p** 99. C Margate All SS *Cant* 98-03; C The Brents and Davington w Oare and Luddenham 03-05; rtd 05; Perm to Offic *Cant* from 05. *46 Stonebridge Way, Faversham ME13 7SB* Tel (01795) 535970 E-mail john.hess@connectfree.co.uk

HESS, Paul Austin. b 67. Cape Town Univ BA89. St Bede's Coll Umtata. **d** 93 **p** 93. C Matroosfontein S Africa 92-94; NSM Eythorne and Elvington w Waldershare etc *Cant* 95-96; C Storrington *Chich* 96-99; Chapl Hurstpierpoint Coll 99-05; Chapl Eton Coll from 05. *Eton College, Windsor SL4 6DW* Tel (01753) 671161 E-mail pahess@tiscali.co.uk

HESTER, Canon John Frear. b 27. St Edm Hall Ox BA48 MA52. Cuddesdon Coll 51. **d** 52 **p** 53. C Southall St Geo *Lon* 52-55; C Clerkenwell H Redeemer w St Phil 55-58; Sec Actors' Ch Union 58-63; Sen Chapl 70-75; Chapl Soc of Sisters of Bethany Lloyd Square 59-62; Dep Min Can St Paul's Cathl 62-75; R Soho St Anne w St Thos and St Pet 63-75; P-in-c Covent Garden St Paul 69-75; P-in-c Brighton St Jo *Chich* 75-80; V Brighton St Pet 75-78; Can and Preb Chich Cathl 76-85; Can Res and Prec Chich Cathl 85-97; RD Brighton 76-85; RD Kemp Town 76-83; RD Preston 76-83; P-in-c Brighton Chpl Royal 77-78; V Brighton St Pet w Chpl Royal 78-80; V Brighton St Pet w Chpl Royal and St Jo 80-85; P-in-c Brighton St Nic 84-85; Chapl to The Queen 84-97; rtd 97; Perm to Offic *Chich* from 97. *The Hovel, Church Lane, Oving, Chichester PO20 2DE* Tel (01243) 782071 E-mail thehovel@bigfoot.com

HETHERINGTON, Andrew. b 50. Sheff Univ BSc71. Wycliffe Hall Ox 71. **d** 74 **p** 75. C Leic H Trin w St Jo *Leic* 74-78; C Leic H Apostles 78-82; V Bootle St Mary w St Paul *Liv* 82-93; TR W Swindon and the Lydiards *Bris* 93-01; P-in-c Chebsey, Ellenhall and Seighford-with-Creswell *Lich* from 01. *The Vicarage, Seighford, Stafford ST18 9PQ* Tel (01785) 282829

HETHERINGTON, Mrs Charlotte Elizabeth. b 52. Girton Coll Cam BA74 Maria Grey Coll Lon PGCE75 Heythrop Coll Lon MA02. St Alb and Ox Min Course 95. **d** 98 **p** 99. NSM Stratfield Mortimer and Mortimer W End etc *Ox* 98-04; C Portsea St Mary *Portsm* from 04. *2 Glebe Flats, Nutfield Place, Portsmouth PO1 4JF* Tel (023) 9282 6892 E-mail charlottehetherington@hotmail.com

HETHERINGTON, Dermot Hugh. b 42. SRN63 RMN65 Worc Coll of Educn BSc. **d** 78 **p** 79. NSM Raveningham *Nor* 78-90; Perm to Offic from 90. *1 Whiteways, Wheatacre, Beccles NR34 0AU* Tel (01502) 677467

HETHERINGTON, Mrs Glynis Catherine. b 48. EMMTC 93. **d** 93 **p** 94. NSM E and W Leake, Stanford-on-Soar, Rempstone etc *S'well* 93-99; R from 99. *The Rectory, 3 Bateman Road, East Leake, Loughborough LE12 6LN* Tel (01509) 852228

HETHERINGTON, John Carl. b 52. Linc Th Coll. **d** 84 **p** 85. C Crosby *Linc* 84-88; TV Cleethorpes 88-93; Chapl RAF from 93. *Chaplaincy Services (RAF), HQ, Personnel and Training Command, RAF Innsworth, Gloucester GL3 1EZ* Tel (01452) 712612 ext 5164 Fax 510828

HETLING, William Maurice. b 37. AKC61. **d** 62 **p** 63. C Eltham St Barn *S'wark* 62-66; C Horley 66-71; Jamaica 71-75; C-in-c Farnham Royal S CD *Ox* 75-78; TV W Slough 78-80 and 88-91; TR 80-88; TV Parkstone St Pet w Branksea and St Osmund *Sarum* 91-96; P-in-c Reading St Barn *Ox* 96-99; rtd 99; Perm to Offic *Chich* from 99. *12 Manor Close, Storrington, Pulborough RH20 4LF*

HEWES, John. b 29. Nottm Univ BA50. Chich Th Coll 79. **d** 81 **p** 82. C Buckland in Dover w Buckland Valley *Cant* 81-84; P-in-c Elmsted w Hastingleigh 84-89; P-in-c Crundale w Godmersham 84-89; RD W Bridge 88-89; R Lydd 89-95; RD S Lympne 89-95; rtd 95; Perm to Offic *Cant* from 95. *Brambledown, Tamley Lane, Hastingleigh, Ashford TN25 5HW* Tel (01233) 750214

HEWES, Timothy William. b 50. Sheff Univ BDS74. St Alb and Ox Min Course 98. **d** 01. NSM Abingdon *Ox* from 01. *55 Lower Radley, Abingdon OX14 3AY* Tel (01235) 523963 Mobile 07771-880117 E-mail tim@rdlf.uninet.co.uk

HEWETSON, The Ven Christopher. b 37. Trin Coll Ox BA60 MA64. Chich Th Coll 67. **d** 69 **p** 70. C Leckhampton St Pet *Glouc* 69-71; C Wokingham All SS *Ox* 71-73; V Didcot St Pet 73-82; R Ascot Heath 82-90; RD Bracknell 86-90; P-in-c Headington Quarry 90-94; Hon Can Ch Ch 92-94; RD Cowley 94; Adn Ches 94-02; rtd 02; Bp's Adv for Spirituality *Ex* from 03. *The Old Estate House, The Square, North Molton, South Molton EX36 3HP* Tel (01598) 740573

HEWETSON, David Geoffrey. b 31. S'wark Ord Course 71. **d** 74 **p** 75. NSM Brighton St Mich *Chich* from 74. *Flat 1, 166 Dyke Road, Brighton BN1 5PU* Tel (01273) 275776

HEWETSON, Canon Robin Jervis. b 39. AKC63 K Coll Lon MA93. **d** 64 **p** 65. C Thorpe *Nor* 64-67; C E Dereham w Hoe 67-69; TV Mattishall w Mattishall Burgh 69-72; R Ingham w Sutton 72-78; R Catfield 75-78; R Taverham w Ringland 78-89; P-in-c Marsham 89-92; P-in-c Burgh 89-92; Dioc Ecum Officer 89-04; Exec Officer Norfolk Ecum Coun 89-04; R Marsham w Burgh-next-Aylsham 92-04; Hon Can Nor Cathl 01-04; rtd 04; Perm to Offic *Nor* from 04. *83 Soame Close, Aylsham, Norwich NR11 6JF* Tel (01263) 734325

HEWETSON, Canon Valerie Patricia. b 44. St Mary's Coll Dur BSc66 MSc70 Leeds Univ MA75. Linc Th Coll 89. **d** 91 **p** 94. C Kingston upon Hull St Nic *York* 91-94; V Barmby Moor w

Allerthorpe, Fangfoss and Yapham 94-98; V Barmby Moor Gp from 98; Can and Preb York Minster from 01; RD S Wold from 01. *The Vicarage, St Helen's Square, Barmby Moor, York YO42 4HF* Tel (01759) 305971 E-mail hewetson@fish.co.uk

HEWETT, Andrew David. b 63. Univ of Wales (Lamp) BA. Chich Th Coll 84. **d** 86 **p** 87. C Caldicot *Mon* 86-90; Chapl RAF from 90. *Chaplaincy Services (RAF), HQ, Personnel and Training Command, RAF Innsworth, Gloucester GL3 1EZ* Tel (01452) 712612 ext 5164 Fax 510828

HEWETT, Maurice Gordon. b 28. Lon Univ BA53. Oak Hill Th Coll 49. **d** 54 **p** 55. C Gipsy Hill Ch Ch *S'wark* 54-57; C Maidstone St Faith *Cant* 57-60; R Chevening *Roch* 60-95; rtd 95; Perm to Offic *Roch* from 95; Hon Wing Chapl ATC 96-04. *Rosings, 12 The Thicketts, Sevenoaks TN13 3SZ* Tel and fax (01732) 464734

HEWETT, Roger Leroy. b 45. St Mich Coll Llan DipTh95. **d** 95 **p** 96. C Whitchurch *Llan* 95-98; R Blaina and Nantyglo *Mon* from 98. *The Rectory, Station Road, Blaina NP13 3BW* Tel (01495) 290130

HEWISON, Alan Stuart. b 30. SS Mark & Jo Coll Plymouth BEd82. K Coll Lon. **d** 57 **p** 58. C S Mymms K Chas *Lon* 57-60; C Bourne *Guildf* 60-63; Chapl RN 63-79; Perm to Offic *Ex* from 79; rtd 95. *8 Hazelwood Crescent, Plymouth PL9 8BL*

HEWITSON, John Kenneth. b 48. Curtin Univ Aus BA Flinders Univ Aus MA96 DSS84. Adelaide Coll of Div ThL70 ACT ThSchol83. **d** 71 **p** 72. C Swindon Ch Ch *Bris* 71-74; Australia from 74; C Spearwood 74-76; R Balga 76-77; Chapl Royal Perth Hosp 79-83; R Lockridge 83-86; R Eliz 92-97; Chapl Trin Coll 93-98; Chapl Kormilda Coll Darwin from 99; R Freds Pass from 00. *PO Box 346, Humpty Doo, NT, Australia 0836* Tel (0061) (8) 8983 3947 Fax 8983 3951 E-mail jah@octa4.net.au

HEWITT, Christopher James Chichele (Chich). b 45. Witwatersrand Univ BSc68 UNISA BA78 MTh92 LTCL69. St Paul's Coll Grahamstown DipTh79. **d** 78 **p** 79. S Africa 78-99; Chapl St Paul's Coll Grahamstown 84-86; Warden 86-92; Can Grahamstown Cathl 88-93; Chan 92; Sub-Dean 93; Dean and Adn Grahamstown 93-98; USA 99; TR Radcliffe *Man* from 00; AD Radcliffe and Prestwich from 02. *St Thomas's Vicarage, Heber Street, Radcliffe, Manchester M26 2TG* Tel 0161-723 2123 E-mail gill-chich@heberstreet.freeserve.co.uk

HEWITT, Colin Edward. b 52. Man Poly BA80 Em Coll Cam BA82 MA86. Westcott Ho Cam 80. **d** 83 **p** 84. C Radcliffe St Thos and St Jo *Man* 83-84; C Langley and Parkfield 84-86; R Byfield w Boddington *Pet* 86-89; R Byfield w Boddington and Aston le Walls 89-91; Chapl RAF from 91. *Chaplaincy Services (RAF), HQ, Personnel and Training Command, RAF Innsworth, Gloucester GL3 1EZ* Tel (01452) 712612 ext 5164 *or* (01845) 815387 Fax 510828

HEWITT, David Warner. b 33. Selw Coll Cam BA56 MA60. Wells Th Coll 57. **d** 59 **p** 60. C Longbridge *Birm* 59-61; C Sheldon 61-64; V Smethwick Old Ch 64-70; V Smethwick 70-78; P-in-c Littlehampton St Jas *Chich* 78-85; P-in-c Wick 78-85; V Littlehampton St Mary 78-85; TR Littlehampton and Wick 86-89; Perm to Offic *Eur* from 95; rtd 98; Hon Asst Chapl Gtr Athens *Eur* 00-03. *PO Box 7822, Limenas, 640 04 Thassos, Greece* E-mail tangulls@the.forthnet.gr

HEWITT, Canon Francis John Adam. b 42. St Chad's Coll Dur BA64. **d** 66 **p** 67. C Dewsbury Moor *Wakef* 66-69; C Huddersfield St Jo 69-73; V King Cross 73-81; V Lastingham w Appleton-le-Moors, Rosedale etc *York* 81-94; RD Helmsley 85-94; V Pickering 94-95; V Pickering w Lockton and Levisham from 95; RD Pickering from 94; Can and Preb York Minster from 97. *The Vicarage, Hatcase Lane, Whitby Road, Pickering YO18 7HD* Tel and fax (01751) 472983
E-mail francis.hewitt@btopenworld.com

HEWITT, Garth Bruce. b 46. St Jo Coll Dur BA68. Lon Coll of Div LTh70. **d** 70 **p** 71. C Maidstone St Luke *Cant* 70-73; Staff Evang CPAS 73-79; Hon C W Ealing St Jo w St Jas *Lon* 73-81; Dir Amos Trust 88-96; World Affairs Adv *Guildf* 94-96; Regional Co-ord (Lon and SE) Chr Aid from 96; Perm to Offic *S'wark* 96-04; P-in-c All Hallows Lon Wall *Lon* 97-99; V from 99. *Christian Aid, All Hallows on the Wall, 83 London Wall, London EC2M 5ND* Tel (020) 7496 1680 *or* 7588 2638 Fax 7496 1684
E-mail ghewitt@christian-aid.org

HEWITT, Geoffrey Williams. b 48. Leeds Univ BA69. Wells Th Coll 70. **d** 72 **p** 73. C Heywood St Luke *Man* 72-74; Ind Chapl 74-77; P-in-c Hulme St Geo 74-77; R Mamhilad and Llanfihangel Pontymoile *Mon* 77-80; Ind Chapl 77-80; V Arthog w Fairbourne *Ban* 80-89; R Llangelynnin w Rhoslefain 87-89; TV Bangor 89-94; Dioc Soc Resp Officer 89-02; P-in-c Pentir 94-02; Hon Can Ban Cathl 99-02; RD Ogwen 00-02; P-in-c Draycot *Bris* from 02. *The Rectory, Church Road, Christian Malford, Chippenham SN15 4BW* Tel and fax (01249) 720070 Mobile 07950-497580
E-mail geoffrey@revhewitt.freeserve.co.uk

HEWITT, Guy Arlington Kenneth. b 67. Univ of W Indies BSc91 MSc93. SEITE 00. **d** 03. *11 Cupar Road, London SW11 4JW* Tel (020) 7622 4925 E-mail gakhewitt@hotmail.com

HEWITT, Harold William. b 12. Fitzw Ho Cam BA35 MA39. Wycliffe Hall Ox 36. **d** 38 **p** 39. C Westhoughton *Man* 38-40; C Kersal Moor 40-43; V Oldham St Paul 43-52; R Droylsden St Mary 52-66; V Gt Bowden w Welham *Leic* 66-77; rtd 77; Perm to Offic *Ches* from 77. *20 Rectory Close, Bowling Green Court, Nantwich CW5 5SW* Tel (01270) 626660

HEWITT, James Herbert. b 17. Ch Coll Cam BA39 MA42. Ridley Hall Cam 40. **d** 41 **p** 42. C Heworth H Trin *York* 41-43; C York St Mary Castlegate w St Mich Spurriergate 41-43; C Tulse Hill H Trin *S'wark* 43-45; CMS India 45-47; Pakistan 47-60; Vice-Prin CMS Tr Coll Chislehurst 61-65; C Spitalfields Ch Ch w All SS *Lon* 64-65; V New Beckenham St Paul *Roch* 65-71; R Mereworth w W Peckham 71-75; V Bradf St Aug Undercliffe *Bradf* 75-82; rtd 82; Perm to Offic *Glas* from 82. *73 Georgetown Road, Dumfries DG1 4DG* Tel (01387) 263973

HEWITT, John Kaffrell. b 34. St Aid Birkenhead 60. **d** 63 **p** 64. C Woking Ch Ch *Guildf* 63-66; P-in-c Sudbury w Ballingdon and Brundon *St E* 66-70; V 70-80; V Portsdown *Portsm* 80-96; rtd 96; Perm to Offic *Win* from 97. *45 Knowland Drive, Milford-on-Sea, Lymington SO41 0RH* Tel (01590) 644473

HEWITT, Kenneth Victor. b 30. Lon Univ BSc49 CertEd51 MSc53. Cuddesdon Coll 60. **d** 62 **p** 63. C Maidstone St Martin *Cant* 62-64; C Croydon St Mich 64-67; P-in-c S Kensington St Aug *Lon* 67-73; V 73-95; Asst Chapl Lon Univ 67-73; rtd 95; Perm to Offic *Roch* from 95. *Lower Treasurer's House, 41 Bromley College, London Road, Bromley BR1 1PE* Tel (020) 8464 0014

HEWITT, Michael David. b 49. K Coll Lon BD79 AKC79 CertEd. Qu Coll Birm 79. **d** 80 **p** 81. C Bexleyheath Ch Ch *Roch* 80-84; C Buckland in Dover w Buckland Valley *Cant* 84-89; R Ridgewell w Ashen, Birdbrook and Sturmer *Chelmsf* from 89. *The Rectory, Church Lane, Ridgewell, Halstead CO9 4SA* Tel (01440) 785355

HEWITT, Patrick. *See* HEWITT, Canon William Patrick

HEWITT, Paul Stephen Patrick. b 59. BA DipTh. **d** 86 **p** 87. C Ballymacash *Conn* 86-89; Sen C Ballymena w Ballyclug 89-91; I Glencraig *D & D* from 91; Dir of Ords 98-04. *Glencraig Vicarage, 3 Seahill Road, Craigavad, Holywood BT18 0DA* Tel (028) 9042 2225 E-mail paul-hewitt@beeb.net

HEWITT, Peter. *See* HEWITT, Thomas Peter James

HEWITT, Robert Samuel. b 51. QUB BSc73. CITC 77. **d** 80 **p** 81. C Dundela St Mark *D & D* 80-84; R Donaghadee 84-92. *3 The Trees, New Road, Donaghadee BT21 0EJ* Tel (028) 9188 2594

HEWITT, Stephen Wilkes. b 49. Fitzw Coll Cam MA71. St Jo Coll Nottm 88. **d** 90 **p** 91. C Eaton *Nor* 90-93; V Warwick St Paul *Cov* 93-01; Perm to Offic *Newc* 01-02; P-in-c High Spen and Rowlands Gill *Dur* from 02. *2 Beechwood, High Spen, Rowlands Gill NE39 2BL* Tel (01207) 542815
E-mail sandshewitt@hotmail.com

HEWITT, Thomas Peter James. b 24. St Andr Univ MA50. St Steph Ho Ox 50. **d** 52 **p** 53. C Ellesmere Port *Ches* 52-56; C Leytonstone St Marg w St Columba *Chelmsf* 56-60; V Barlby *York* 60-65; V Godshill *Portsm* 65-93; rtd 93. *c/o C L Wiggins Esq, Jerome and Co Solicitors, 98 High Street, Newport PO30 1BD*

HEWITT, Timothy James. b 67. St D Coll Lamp BD. Ripon Coll Cuddesdon. **d** 91 **p** 92. C Milford Haven *St D* 91-94; C Llanelli 94-96; P-in-c Llan-non 96-97; V Clydach *S & B* from 98. *The Vicarage, 53 Bryntawe Road, Ynystawe, Swansea SA6 5AD* Tel (01792) 843203

HEWITT, Canon William Patrick. b 48. Nottm Univ BTh79. Linc Th Coll 75. **d** 79 **p** 80. C Workington St Jo *Carl* 79-83; V Flookburgh 83-87; V Barrow St Matt 87-90; V Lowick and Kyloe w Ancroft *Newc* 90-96; R Ford and Etal 90-96; RD Norham 91-96; I Fanlobbus Union *C, C & R* from 96; Can Cork Cathl from 00; Can Cloyne Cathl from 00. *The Rectory, Sackville Street, Dunmanway, Co Cork, Irish Republic* Tel and fax (00353) (23) 45151 E-mail fanlobbus@cork.anglican.org *or* fanlobbus@eircom.net

HEWITT-HORSMAN, Simon. b 76. Brunel Univ BSc99. St Steph Ho Ox BA01. **d** 02 **p** 05. C Warren Park and Leigh Park *Portsm* 02-04; C Walthamstow St Sav *Chelmsf* from 04. *212 Markhouse Road, London E17 8EP* Tel (020) 8988 6323
E-mail frsimonhewitt@hotmail.com
or simonhewitthorsman@fsmail.net

HEWLETT, Mrs Caroline Joan. b 68. Coll of Ripon & York St Jo BEd92 St Jo Coll Dur BA01. Cranmer Hall Dur 99. **d** 01 **p** 02. C Leeds St Geo *Ripon* 01-04; Chapl Leeds Combined Court Cen 03-04; C Aldborough w Boroughbridge and Roecliffe from 04. *Rollinson House, Ladywell Road, Boroughbridge, York YO51 9HL* Tel 07866-750211 (mobile)
E-mail carolinehewlett@hotmail.com

HEWLETT, David Bryan. b 49. Bris Univ BEd72. Qu Coll Birm 77. **d** 79 **p** 80. C Ludlow *Heref* 79-81; TV 81-84; V Marden w Amberley and Wisteston 84-92; Lect Glouc Sch for Min 84-92; Field Officer for Lay Min *Heref* 84-91; CME Officer 86-92; Dir Post-Ord Tr 91-92; Hd Master St Fran Sch Pewsey 92-94; Co-ord Chapl Frenchay Healthcare NHS Trust Bris 94-00; Dir Past Studies OLM Scheme and CME Adv *Linc* 00-04; Par

Development Adv (South) 00-04; R Pontesbury I and II *Heref* from 04. *The Deanery, Main Road, Pontesbury, Shrewsbury SY5 0PS* Tel (01743) 792221 E-mail david.hewlett3@btopenworld.com

HEWLETT, David Jonathon Peter. b 57. Dur Univ BA79 PhD83. Ridley Hall Cam 82. **d** 83 **p** 84. C New Barnet St Jas *St Alb* 83-86; Lect CITC 86-90; P-in-c Feock *Truro* 91-95; Jt Dir SW Minl Tr Course 91-95; Prin SWMTC 95-03; Adv Local Ord Min 91-95; Hon Can Truro Cathl *Truro* 01-03; Prin Qu Coll Birm from 03. *71 Farquhar Road, Edgbaston, Birmingham B15 2QP* Tel 0121-452 2612 *or* 454 8171 E-mail dhewlett@queens.ac.uk

HEWLETT, Guy Edward. b 59. Thames Poly CertEd89 Open Univ BA90. Oak Hill Th Coll 96. **d** 96 **p** 97. NSM Sudbury St Andr *Lon* 96-99; C Harrow Trin St Mich 99-05; V Harrow Weald St Mich from 05. *74 Bishop Ken Road, Harrow HA3 7HR* Tel (020) 8861 1710 E-mail guyhewlett@lineone.net

HEWLINS, Pauline Elizabeth. *See* SEAMAN, Mrs Pauline Elizabeth

HEWSON, Mrs Rose Raylene. b 47. St Alb and Ox Min Course 96. **d** 99 **p** 00. NSM High Wycombe *Ox* 99-02; NSM Burnham w Dropmore, Hitcham and Taplow from 02. *Hitcham Vicarage, 1 The Precincts, Burnham, Slough SL1 7HU* Tel (01628) 602881 E-mail rosie@hewsons.net

HEWSON, Thomas Robert. b 45. Man Univ BA66. S'wark Ord Course 85. **d** 89 **p** 90. C Chinnor w Emmington and Sydenham etc *Ox* 89-92; TV Burnham w Dropmore, Hitcham and Taplow from 92. *Hitcham Vicarage, 1 The Precincts, Burnham, Slough SL1 7HU* Tel and fax (01628) 602881 E-mail trh@hewsons.net

HEYCOCKS, Christian John. b 71. Univ of Wales (Ban) BA93 MA96 Cam Univ CTM97. Westcott Ho Cam 94 CITC 97. **d** 97 **p** 98. C Rhyl w St Ann *St As* 97-00; Chapl RN 00-04; Chapl HMS Drake from 04. *Royal Naval Chaplaincy Service, Room 203, Victory Building, HM Naval Base, Portsmouth PO1 3LS* Tel (023) 9272 7903 Fax 9272 7111

HEYES, Andrew Robin. b 61. Man Univ BA93. St Steph Ho Ox 93. **d** 95 **p** 96. C Tonge Moor *Man* 95-00; V Glodwick from 00. *St Mark's Vicarage, 1 Skipton Street, Oldham OL8 2JF* Tel 0161-624 4964

HEYES, Robert John. b 46. STETS 00. **d** 03 **p** 04. NSM Bramley and Grafham *Guildf* from 03. *Juniper Cottage, 22 Eastwood Road, Bramley, Guildford GU5 0DS* Tel (01483) 893706 Fax 894001 E-mail heyes@tiscali.co.uk

HEYGATE, Stephen Beaumont. b 48. Loughb Univ BSc71 CQSW73 PhD89. St Jo Coll Nottm LTh88. **d** 88 **p** 89. C Aylestone St Andr w St Jas *Leic* 88-90; V Cosby 90-00; V Evington from 00; P-in-c Leic St Phil 00-04; Bp's Adv for Healing and Deliverance from 04. *Evington Vicarage, Stoughton Lane, Stoughton, Leicester LE2 2FH* Tel 0116-271 2032 E-mail sheygate@leicester.anglican.org

HEYHOE, Jonathan Peter. b 53. Man Univ BA75. Trin Coll Bris 77. **d** 80 **p** 81. C Woking St Pet *Guildf* 80-83; C Heatherlands St Jo *Sarum* 83-91; Chr Renewal Cen Rostrevor 91-95; Perm to Offic *D & D* 91-97; I Ballybay w Mucknoe and Clontibret *Clogh* from 98. *The Rectory, Knocknamaddy, Ballybay, Co Monaghan, Irish Republic* Tel (00353) (42) 974 1102 Mobile 87-418 1427 E-mail ballybay@clogher.anglican.org *or* jheyhoe@esatclear.ie

HEYWOOD, Mrs Anne Christine. b 44. Sarum Th Coll. **d** 97 **p** 98. C Talbot Village *Sarum* 97-01; TV Shaston from 01. *St James's Vicarage, 34 Tanyard Lane, Shaftesbury SP7 8HW* Tel (01747) 852193

HEYWOOD, David Stephen. b 55. Selw Coll Cam BA76 MA80 SS Hild & Bede Coll Dur PhD89. St Jo Coll Dur 80. **d** 86 **p** 87. C Cheltenham St Luke and St Jo *Glouc* 86-90; TV Sanderstead All SS *S'wark* 90-98; V Edensor *Lich* 98-03; Deanery and Min Development Officer from 03. *22 Red Bank, Stoke-on-Trent ST3 4EY* Tel (01782) 321257

HEYWOOD, Deiniol John Owen. *See* KEARLEY-HEYWOOD, Deiniol John Owen

HEYWOOD, Geoffrey Thomas. b 26. St Mich Coll Llan 60. **d** 62 **p** 63. C Porthmadog *Ban* 62-64; C Llandudno 64-67; V Caerhun w Llangelynin 67-74; Asst Chapl HM Pris Liv 74-75; Chapl HM Pris Ex 75-77; Chapl HM Pris Wakef 77-79; Chapl HM YOI Eastwood Park 79-90; Chapl HM Pris Leyhill 79-90; rtd 90; Perm to Offic *Glouc* from 94. *5 Meadow Road, Leyhill, Wotton-under-Edge GL12 8HW*

HEYWOOD, Michael Herbert. b 41. Liv Univ BSc63. Clifton Th Coll 63. **d** 65 **p** 66. C Low Elswick *Newc* 65-68; C St Helens St Mark *Liv* 68-75; Leprosy Miss Area Org NE & Cumbria 75-85; S Lon, Surrey and Berks 85-91; Internat Publicity and Promotional Co-ord from 91. *390 Kingston Road, New Malden KT3 3RX* Tel (020) 8287 9192 Fax 8569 7292 E-mail mikeh@temint.org

HEYWOOD, Peter. b 46. Cranmer Hall Dur 72. **d** 75 **p** 76. C Blackley St Andr *Man* 75-78; C Denton Ch Ch 78-80; V Constable Lee 80-01; rtd 01; Perm to Offic *Man* from 01. *12 Heys Close, Cloughfold, Rossendale BB4 7LW* Tel (01706) 222069

HEZEL, Adrian. b 43. Chelsea Coll Lon BSc64 PhD67. N Ord Course 78. **d** 81 **p** 82. NSM Mirfield *Wakef* 81-89; C 89-90; V Shelley and Shepley 90-99; V Hoylake *Ches* from 99. *The Vicarage, 1 Stanley Road, Hoylake, Wirral CH47 1HL* Tel 0151-632 3897

HIBBARD, John. **d** 03 **p** 04. NSM Stewkley w Soulbury and Drayton Parslow *Ox* from 03. *Chapel Side, 6 Nearton End, Swanbourne, Milton Keynes MK17 0SL*

HIBBERD, Brian Jeffery. b 35. Fitzw Coll Cam MA62 Southn Univ MA84. Ridley Hall Cam 58. **d** 60 **p** 61. C Cambridge H Trin *Ely* 60-63; C Doncaster St Mary *Sheff* 63-66; Asst Master Price's Sch Fareham 66-69; Warblington Sch Havant 69-71; Hd Soc and RS Carisbrooke High Sch 71-84; Distr Health Promotion Officer Is of Wight 84-88; SW Herts 88-90; Hd RS Goffs Sch Cheshunt 90-95; rtd 95; Teacher Qu Sch Bushey 95-97; Teacher R Masonic Sch for Girls Rickmansworth 97-00; Hon C Abbots Langley *St Alb* 00-01; Perm to Offic from 01. *50 Rosehill Gardens, Abbots Langley WD5 0HF* Tel (01923) 267391

HIBBERD, Carol Anne. b 59. Kent Univ BA80. S'wark Ord Course 89. **d** 92 **p** 94. NSM Gospel Lane St Mich *Birm* 92-94; C 94-98; C Coleshill 98-02; Chapl Marie Curie Cen Warren Pearl from 02. *Marie Curie Centre Warren Pearl, 911-913 Warwick Road, Solihull B91 3ER* Tel 0121-254 7800 *or* 770 5844 E-mail carol.hibberd@mariecurie.org.uk

HIBBERD, John. b 60. Wadh Coll Ox MA82. Trin Coll Bris BA89. **d** 89 **p** 90. C Northolt St Mary *Lon* 89-92; C-in-c Southall Em CD 92-94; Min of Miss Through Faith Miss *Ely* from 95. *Celandine, 1 School Lane, Swavesey, Cambridge CB4 5RL* Tel (01954) 200285 Fax as telephone E-mail john.hibberd@ntlworld.com

HIBBERD, John Charles. b 38. Bernard Gilpin Soc Dur 62 Chich Th Coll 63. **d** 66 **p** 67. C W Drayton *Lon* 66-70; C Noel Park St Mark 70-72; C Ealing St Steph Castle Hill 72-75; V Gunnersbury St Jas 75-84; V Whitton SS Phil and Jas 84-86; Finance and Trust Sec Lon Dioc Fund 87-98; Perm to Offic 87-98; rtd 98. *18 Pursley Close, Sandown PO36 9QP* Tel (01983) 401036

HIBBERT, Miss Anne Mary Elizabeth. Southn Univ BA81. Trin Coll Bris 81. **dss** 83 **d** 87 **p** 94. Muswell Hill St Jas w St Matt *Lon* 83-86; Leic H Trin w St Jo *Leic* 86-87; Par Dn 87-90; Perm to Offic *Cov* from 90; Evang Co-ord and Adv CPAS 90-98; Churches Millennium Exec 98-99; Miss & Spirituality Adv BRF 99-03; Dir Well Chr Healing Cen from 03. *The Well Christian Healing Centre, PO Box 3407, Leamington Spa CV32 6ZH* Tel 07973-563667 (mobile) E-mail anne@thewellhealingcentre.org.uk

HIBBERT, Charles Dennis. b 24. Linc Th Coll 69. **d** 70 **p** 71. C Radcliffe-on-Trent *S'well* 70-73; P-in-c Ladybrook 73-77; V 77-79; V Boughton 79-85; V Ollerton 79-85; R Nuthall 85-89; rtd 89; Perm to Offic *S'well* from 89. *27 Nottingham Road, Kimberley, Nottingham NG16 2NB* Tel 0115-938 6302

HIBBERT, Peter John. b 43. Hull Univ BA71 Lon Univ CertEd72 MA79. Sarum & Wells Th Coll 85. **d** 88 **p** 89. C Newsome and Armitage Bridge *Wakef* 88-92; P-in-c Newton Flowery Field *Ches* 92-00; P-in-c Hyde St Thos 97-00; V Handsworth St Jas *Birm* from 00. *St James's Vicarage, 21 Austin Road, Birmingham B21 8NU* Tel 0121-554 4151

HIBBERT, Prof Peter Rodney. b 53. Man Univ LLB74 Liv Univ DipArch83 Nottm Univ MA99 Solicitor 77. EMMTC 96. **d** 99 **p** 00. C Knighton St Mary Magd *Leic* 99-01; Perm to Offic *Leic* from 01 and *Birm* from 03. *Grange Cottage, 37 Rushes Lane, Lubenham, Market Harborough LE16 9TN* Tel (01858) 433174

HIBBERT, Richard Charles. b 62. Trin Coll Bris BA93. **d** 96 **p** 97. C Luton St Mary *St Alb* 96-00; V Bedford Ch Ch from 00. *Christ Church Vicarage, 115 Denmark Street, Bedford MK40 3TJ* Tel (01234) 359342 Fax as telephone E-mail vicar@christchurchbedford.org.uk

HIBBINS, Neil Lance. b 60. St Anne's Coll Ox BA82 MA87. St Mich Coll Llan DPS83. **d** 85 **p** 86. C Griffithstown *Mon* 85-87; C Pontypool 87-88; TV Pontypool 88-92; Walsall Hosps NHS Trust 92-96; Asst Chapl Manor Hosp Walsall 92-96; R Norton Canes *Lich* from 96. *The Rectory, 81 Church Road, Norton Canes, Cannock WS11 9PQ* Tel (01543) 278969 E-mail neil_hibbins@lycos.com

HICHENS, Anthony. b 29. AKC59. **d** 60 **p** 61. C Ashford St Hilda *Lon* 60-64; C Leeds St Wilfrid *Ripon* 64-66; Guyana 67-75; P-in-c Stratton Audley w Godington *Ox* 76-83; P-in-c Finmere w Mixbury 76-78; P-in-c Fringford w Hethe and Newton Purcell 78-83; R Stratton Audley and Godington, Fringford etc 83-95; rtd 95; Perm to Offic *Pet* from 95. *86 Horton Drive, Middleton Cheney, Banbury OX17 2LL* Tel (01295) 712826

HICKES, Roy Edward. b 31. Lon Univ DipTh60. St Aid Birkenhead 56. **d** 59 **p** 60. C New Bury *Man* 59-63; C Wyther Ven Bede *Ripon* 63-65; R Oldham St Andr *Man* 65-69; V Smallbridge 69-79; R Winford *B & W* 79-81; R Winford w Felton Common Hill 81-88; RD Chew Magna 85-88; Chapl Costa Blanca *Eur* 88-92; rtd 92; Perm to Offic *B & W* and *Bris* from 92; Hon C Wrington w Butcombe *B & W* 97-98. *17 Haycombe, Bristol BS14 0AJ* E-mail royhickes@blueyonder.co.uk *or* randwhickes@blueyonder.co.uk

HICKEY, Canon Francis Joseph (Tony). b 20. AKC49. **d** 50 **p** 51. C Portsea St Mary *Portsm* 50-58; V Tilbury Docks *Chelmsf* 58-87; RD Orsett and Grays 70-83; Hon Can Chelmsf Cathl 79-87; rtd 87; Perm to Offic *Portsm* from 90; *Guildf* 95-00; *Chelmsf* from 03. *202 Parkside House, Malvern Road, Southsea PO5 2LD* Tel (023) 9275 0301

HICKFORD, Michael Francis. b 53. Edin Th Coll 84. **d** 86 **p** 87. Chapl St Jo Cathl Oban *Arg* 86-89; R Alexandria *Glas* 89-95; P-in-c Dingwall and Strathpeffer *Mor* 95-03; Dean Mor 98-03; R Inverness St Andr and Provost St Andr Cathl Inverness 03-04; Chapl NHS Highland from 04. *New Craigs Hospital, 8 Leachkin Road, Inverness IV3 8NP* Tel (01463) 704000 ext 2426 Mobile 07795-238928

HICKLING, Canon Colin John Anderson. b 31. K Coll Cam BA53 MA57. Chich Th Coll 56. **d** 57 **p** 58. C Pallion *Dur* 57-61; Asst Tutor Chich Th Coll 61-65; Asst Lect K Coll Lon 65-68; Lect 68-84; Hon C Munster Square St Mary Magd *Lon* 68-69; Dep Min Can St Paul's Cathl 69-78; Hon C E Dulwich St Jo *S'wark* 70-84; Dep P in O 71-74; P in O 74-84; Can Th Leic Cathl *Leic* 81-96; Tutor Qu Coll Birm 84-85; Lect Linc Th Coll 85-86; V Arksey *Sheff* 86-98; Hon Lect Bibl Studies Sheff Univ from 86; rtd 98; Hon C Sprotbrough *Sheff* 98-04. *College of St Barnabas, Blackberry Lane, Lingfield RH7 6NJ* Tel (01342) 871649

HICKLING, John. b 34. Handsworth Coll Birm 56. Launde Abbey 69. **d** 69 **p** 70. In Methodist Ch 59-69; C Melton Mowbray w Thorpe Arnold *Leic* 69-71; TV 71-75; R Waltham on the Wolds w Stonesby and Saltby 75-84; R Aylestone St Andr w St Jas 84-93; R Husbands Bosworth w Mowsley and Knaptoft etc 93-96; rtd 96; Perm to Offic *Leic* from 99. *28 Oxford Drive, Melton Mowbray LE13 0AL* Tel (01664) 560770

HICKMAN, George May. b 11. AKC33. **d** 35 **p** 36. C Hayes St Mary *Lon* 35-36; C Stepney St Aug w St Phil 36-39; C Bray *Ox* 40-41; V Beedon 41-45; V Rotherhithe H Trin *S'wark* 45-50; R Nettlecombe *B & W* 50-68; R Withycombe 68-84; rtd 84; Perm to Offic *B & W* 85-91. *1 The Causeway, Withycombe, Minehead TA24 6PZ* Tel (01984) 640227

HICKMAN, John William. b 38. Barrister-at-Law (Middle Temple) 69 Qu Coll Cam LLM81. Oak Hill Th Coll 92. **d** 95 **p** 96. NSM Sevenoaks St Nic *Roch* 95-98; P-in-c Stedham w Iping *Chich* 98-04; rtd 04. *Bywood, Selham Road, West Lavington, Midhurst GU29 0EG* Tel (01730) 810821

HICKS, Miss Barbara. b 42. Cranmer Hall Dur BA71. **dss** 85 **d** 87 **p** 94. Norton Woodseats St Paul *Sheff* 85-87; Par Dn Sheff St Jo 87-94; C 94-02; Chapl Shrewsbury Hosp 96-02; rtd 02. *87 Underwood Road, Sheffield S8 8TG* Tel 0114-255 8087

HICKS, Ms Eunice. b 41. Trin Coll Bris BA00. WEMTC 01. **d** 01 **p** 02. NSM Chew Magna w Dundry and Norton Malreward *B & W* from 01. *4 The Crescent, Chew Magna, Bristol BS40 8RH* Tel (01275) 331536 E-mail heunice@fish.co.uk

HICKS, Francis Fuller. b 28. Sarum & Wells Th Coll 71. **d** 74 **p** 75. C Broadstone *Sarum* 74-78; P-in-c Kington Magna and Buckhorn Weston 78-79; TV Gillingham 79-86; P-in-c Portland St Jo 86-89; V 89-93; rtd 93; Perm to Offic *B & W* and *Sarum* from 93. *Windyridge, 21 Castle Road, Sherborne DT9 3RW* Tel (01935) 814837

HICKS, Miss Joan Rosemary. b 60. Homerton Coll Cam BEd83. Westcott Ho Cam 87. **d** 90 **p** 94. C Wendover *Ox* 90-95; C Earley St Pet 95-98; P-in-c Beech Hill, Grazeley and Spencers Wood 98-05; P-in-c Cox Green from 05. *The Vicarage, 9 Warwick Close, Maidenhead SL6 3AL* Tel (01628) 622139
E-mail joanhicks@compuserve.com

HICKS, John Michael. b 67. Crewe & Alsager Coll BA89 K Coll Lon MA01 K Alfred's Coll Win PGCE90. NTMTC 02. **d** 05. NSM Grosvenor Chpl *Lon* from 05. *167 John Ruskin Street, London SE5 0PQ* Tel 07971-670092 (mobile)
E-mail jnhx@hotmail.com

HICKS, Richard Barry. b 32. Dur Univ BA55. Sarum Th Coll 59. **d** 61 **p** 62. C Wallsend St Luke *Newc* 61-64; C Tynemouth Ch Ch 64-69; V Tynemouth St Jo 69-75; V Prudhoe 75-82; TV Swanborough *Sarum* 82-86; R Hilperton w Whaddon and Staverton etc 86-97; rtd 97; Perm to Offic *Newc* from 97 and *Carl* from 98. *Lane House, Sawmill Lane, Brampton CA8 1DA* Tel (01697) 72156

HICKS, Stuart Knox. b 34. Univ of W Ontario BA56 Huron Coll LTh59 Ox Univ DipEd67. **d** 58 **p** 60. Canada 58-65; C Allerton *Liv* 65-66; Hon C Rye Park St Cuth *St Alb* 68-72; Lic to Offic *B & W* 72-87 and 88-95; Chapl Magdalen Chpl Bath 80-86; Chapl Partis Coll Bath 88-90; rtd 99. *Folly Orchard, The Folly, Saltford, Bristol BS31 3JW* Tel (01225) 873391

HICKS, Mrs Valerie Joy. b 47. SRN69 HVCert70. Cant Sch of Min 82. **dss** 85 **d** 87 **p** 94. Roch 85-89; Hon Par Dn 87-89; Par Dn Thatcham *Ox* 89-93; TD Aylesbury w Bierton and Hulcott 93-94; TV 94-00; P-in-c Dordon *Birm* from 00; Dioc Chapl Mothers' Union from 01. *St Leonard's Vicarage, Watling Street, Dordon, Tamworth B78 1TE* Tel (01827) 892294
E-mail val.hicks@tesco.net

HICKS, William Trevor. b 47. Hull Univ BA68 Fitzw Coll Cam BA70 MA74. Westcott Ho Cam 68. **d** 70 **p** 71. C Cottingham *York* 70-73; C Elland *Wakef* 73-76; V Walsden 76-81; V Knottingley 81-92; R Castleford All SS 92-96; P-in-c Womersley and Kirk Smeaton 96-00; RD Pontefract 94-99; V Bolsover *Derby* from 00; RD Bolsover and Staveley from 05. *The Vicarage, Church Street, Bolsover, Chesterfield S44 6HB* Tel (01246) 824888

HIDE, Timothy John. b 71. Roehampton Inst BA95. St Steph Ho Ox 97. **d** 99 **p** 00. C Woodford St Mary w St Phil and St Jas *Chelmsf* 99-01; C Upminster 01-05; C Chingford SS Pet and Paul from 05. *The Vicarage, 220A Larkshall Road, London E4 6NP* Tel (020) 8529 4740 Fax 08707-622402
E-mail frtimhide@200a.co.uk

HIDER, David Arthur. b 46. Lon Univ BSc67. Sarum & Wells Th Coll 86. **d** 89 **p** 90. NSM Southbourne w W Thorney *Chich* 89-91; C Goring-by-Sea 91-94; P-in-c Peacehaven and Telscombe Cliffs 94-99; V from 99; P-in-c Telscombe w Piddinghoe and Southease 94-99; V Telscombe Village from 99; V Piddinghoe from 99; V Southease from 99. *The Vicarage, 41 Bramber Avenue, Peacehaven BN10 8HR* Tel and fax (01273) 583149 E-mail revd_d_hider@msn.com

HIGDON, Lewis George. b 36. Dur Univ BA58. Cranmer Hall Dur DipTh60. **d** 60 **p** 61. C Leeds St Pet *Ripon* 60-65; C Shipley St Paul *Bradf* 65-66; V Esholt 67-75; V Kirkstall *Ripon* 75-79; V Stanwix *Carl* 79-87; V Ambleside w Brathay 87-95; rtd 95. *Springtime, 17 Priory Crescent, Grange-over-Sands LA11 7BL* Tel (01539) 532864

HIGGINBOTTOM, Richard. b 48. Lon Univ BD74. Oak Hill Th Coll. **d** 74 **p** 75. C Kenilworth St Jo *Cov* 74-77; C Finham 77-79; P-in-c Attleborough 79-81; V 81-84; Asst Chapl HM Pris Brixton 84-85; Chapl HM Pris Roch 85-92; Chapl HM Pris Camp Hill 92-00; Chapl HM YOI Dover 00-03; rtd 03; Perm to Offic *Cant* from 03. *c/o Crockford, Church House, Great Smith Street, London SW1P 3NZ* Tel 07779-775081 (mobile)

HIGGINBOTTOM, Richard William. b 51. Man Univ BA73 MA75. Edin Th Coll 83. **d** 85 **p** 86. C Knighton St Mary Magd *Leic* 85-87; C Northleach w Hampnett and Farmington *Glouc* 87-89; V Hayfield *Derby* 89-93; Consultant NW England and Scotland CPAS from 93; Perm to Offic *Blackb* from 93; *St A* from 98; *Edin* from 01. *2 Highfield Place, Bankfoot, Perth PH1 4AX* Tel (01738) 787429
E-mail rhigginbottom@cpas.org.uk

HIGGINS, Anthony Charles. b 46. LNSM course 96. **d** 97 **p** 98. OLM Swanage and Studland *Sarum* from 97. *The Old School House, School Lane, Studland, Swanage BH19 3AJ* Tel (01929) 450691

HIGGINS, Bernard. b 42. Leic Poly BPharm63 PhD66 MRPharmS68. St Jo Coll Nottm 89. **d** 91 **p** 92. C Stockport St Geo *Ches* 91-94; C Stockport SW 94-95; P-in-c Dunham Massey St Marg and St Mark 95-98; V 98-00; rtd 00; Perm to Offic *Blackb* and *Carl* from 01. *Woodbine Cottage, Promenade, Arnside, Carnforth LA5 0HD* Tel (01524) 761000

HIGGINS, Frank Roylance. b 34. Open Univ BA74 MEd83. Bps' Coll Cheshunt 59. **d** 62 **p** 63. C Sunderland *Dur* 62-64; C S Westoe 64-66; P-in-c Smethwick St Mich *Birm* 66-67; V 67-70; V Garretts Green 70-75; Lic to Offic *Worc* 76-84; Perm to Offic *Birm* 81-87; Hon C Feckenham w Bradley *Worc* 84-87; R Ripple, Earls Croome w Hill Croome and Strensham 87-95; RD Upton 92-95; rtd 95; P-in-c Church Lench w Rous Lench and Abbots Morton *Worc* 95-00; Perm to Offic from 00. *Verona, Abberton Road, Bishampton, Pershore WR10 2LU* Tel and fax (01386) 462694

HIGGINS, Geoffrey Minta. b 27. New Coll Ox BA52 MA56. Cuddesdon Coll 52. **d** 54 **p** 55. C Pet St Mary Boongate *Pet* 54-56; CF 56-77; Hong Kong from 77. *12-C Far East Consortium Building, 29 On Lok Road, Yuen Long, New Territories, Hong Kong* Tel (00852) 479 9374

HIGGINS, Canon Godfrey. b 39. St Chad's Coll Dur BA61 DipEd63. **d** 63 **p** 64. C Brighouse *Wakef* 63-66; C Huddersfield St Jo 66-68; R High Hoyland w Clayton W 68-75; V Marsden 75-83; V Pontefract St Giles 83-04; Hon Can Wakef Cathl 93-04; rtd 04. *2 Holme View, Ilkley LS29 9EL* Tel (01943) 603861

HIGGINS, John. b 44. Lon Bible Coll MTh98. Trin Coll Bris 71. **d** 73 **p** 74. C Clapham St Jas *S'wark* 73-74; C Ruskin Park St Sav and St Matt 74-77; C Hamworthy *Sarum* 77-80; V Bordesley St Andr *Birm* 80-83; V Bishop Sutton and Stanton Drew and Stowey *B & W* from 83. *The Vicarage, Sutton Hill Road, Bishop Sutton, Bristol BS39 5UR* Tel (01275) 333385

HIGGINS, John Leslie. b 43. Open Univ BA79 Birm Univ MEd89 Univ of Cen England in Birm CQSW75. Lich Th Coll 64. **d** 66 **p** 67. C Sale St Anne *Ches* 66-69; C Bredbury St Mark 69-72; V Wharton 72-74; Hon C Annan and Lockerbie *Glas* 75-79; V Coseley Ch Ch *Lich* 79-89; R Arthuret *Carl* 89-96; Soc Resp Officer and Child Protection Co-ord 96-00; C Brampton and Farlam and Castle Carrock w Cumrew 96-00; Hon Can Carl Cathl 96-00; rtd 00; Hon C Annan *Glas* from 00; Perm to Offic *Carl* from 01. *Green Croft Cottage, The Haggs, Ecclefechan, Lockerbie DG11 3ED* Tel (01576) 300796 Fax 300790 Mobile 07867-505644 E-mail john_l_higgins@lineone.net

HIGGINS, Kenneth. b 56. TCD BTh93. CA Tr Coll Dip Evang83 CITC 90. **d** 93 **p** 94. C Cregagh *D & D* 93-96; Bp's C Movilla 96-00; I from 01. *34 Hollymount Road, Newtownards B23 7DL* Tel (028) 9181 0787

HIGGINS, The Very Revd Michael John. b 35. Birm Univ LLB57 G&C Coll Cam LLB59 PhD62. Ridley Hall Cam 63. **d** 65 **p** 65. C Ormskirk *Liv* 65-67; Selection Sec ACCM 67-74; Hon C St Marylebone St Mark w St Luke *Lon* 69-74; P-in-c Woodlands *B & W* 74-80; V Frome St Jo 74-80; TR Preston St Jo *Blackb* 80-91; Dean Ely 91-03; rtd 03. *Twin Cottage, North Street, Great Dunham, King's Lynn PE32 2LR* Tel (01328) 701058

HIGGINS, Richard Ellis. b 63. Univ of Wales BA84. St Mich Coll Llan DipTh88 DPS89. **d** 89 **p** 90. C Bargoed and Deri w Brithdir *Llan* 89-92; Zimbabwe 92-94; V Penmaen and Crumlin *Mon* 94-99; Chapl Glan Hafren NHS Trust 94-99; V Rhymney *Mon* 99-02; Angl Chapl Pet Hosps NHS Trust from 03. *11 Bryniau Cottages, Pant, Merthyr Tydfil CF48 2DW*

HIGGINS, Rupert Anthony. b 59. Man Univ BA80. Wycliffe Hall Ox 82. **d** 85 **p** 86. C Plymouth St Andr w St Paul and St Geo *Ex* 85-90; C-in-c St Paul 88-90; Assoc V Clifton Ch Ch w Em *Bris* 90-95; V S Croydon Em *S'wark* 95-02; C Langham Place All So *Lon* from 02. *2 St Paul's Court, 56 Manchester Street, London W1U 3AF* Tel (020) 7486 0006 E-mail rupert.higgins@allsouls.org

HIGGINS, Canon Timothy John. b 45. Bris Univ BEd70 Lanc Univ MA74 St Jo Coll Dur DipTh79. **d** 79 **p** 80. C Northampton All SS w St Kath *Pet* 79-82; V Whitton St Aug *Lon* 82-90; AD Hampton 86-90; TR Aylesbury w Bierton and Hulcott *Ox* from 90; RD Aylesbury 94-04; Hon Can Ch Ch from 00. *The Rectory, Parson's Fee, Aylesbury HP20 2QZ* Tel (01296) 424276

HIGGINSON, Andrew John. b 62. Bradf Univ BTech85. Trin Coll Bris 02. **d** 04 **p** 05. C Quarrington w Old Sleaford *Linc* from 04; C Silk Willoughby from 04. *56 Clay Hill Road, Sleaford NG34 7TF* Tel (01529) 415154 E-mail andrewj.higginson@btopenworld.com

HIGGINSON, Gerald Scott. b 29. Keele Univ BA54 Birm Univ PhD57. NW Ord Course 73. **d** 76 **p** 77. NSM York St Mary Bishophill Junior w All SS *York* 76-84; P-in-c 84-86; P-in-c York H Trin w St Jo Micklegate and St Martin 84-86; R Micklegate H Trin and Bishophill Junior St Mary 86-99; rtd 00; Perm to Offic *York* from 00. *35 Aldwark, York YO1 7BX* Tel (01904) 635707

HIGGINSON, Richard Andrew. b 53. St Jo Coll Cam BA74 Man Univ PhD82. EAMTC 02. **d** 04 **p** 05. NSM Cambridge St Phil *Ely* from 04. *15 Guest Road, Cambridge CB1 2AL* Tel (01223) 315667 E-mail rah41@cam.ac.uk

HIGGON, David. Univ of Wales (Swansea) BA75 Birm Univ MBA96 Nottm Univ MA99. EMMTC 96. **d** 00 **p** 01. NSM Crich and S Wingfield *Derby* 00-04; Chapl HM Pris Dovegate from 04. *HM Prison Dovegate, Uttoxeter ST14 8XR* Tel (01283) 820000 E-mail dhiggon@btopenworld.com

HIGGS, Andrew Richard Bowen. b 53. Man Univ BSc75. St Jo Coll Nottm 81. **d** 85 **p** 86. C Droylsden St Mary *Man* 85-88; C Harlow Town Cen w Lt Parndon *Chelmsf* 88-95; TV 95-02; Chapl Princess Alexandra Hosp NHS Trust 96-02; R Stifford *Chelmsf* from 02. *The Rectory, High Road, North Stifford, Grays RM16 5UE* Tel (01375) 372733 E-mail andy@higgs4a.fsnet.co.uk

HIGGS, Michael John. b 53. Sarum & Wells Th Coll 76. **d** 80 **p** 81. C Cant St Martin and St Paul *Cant* 80-84; C Maidstone St Martin 84-88; R Egerton w Pluckley 88-03; rtd 03. *8 Robinsons Mill, Mellis, Eye IP23 8DW* Tel (01379) 783926

HIGGS, Owen Christopher Goodwin. b 63. St Anne's Coll Ox BA84 MA88. St Steph Ho Ox 90. **d** 93 **p** 94. C Teddington St Mark and Hampton Wick St Jo *Lon* 93-96; C Lon Docks St Pet w Wapping St Jo 96-00; V Petts Wood *Roch* from 00. *The Vicarage, Willett Way, Orpington BR5 1QE* Tel (01689) 829971

HIGHAM, Gerald Norman. b 40. St Aid Birkenhead 64. **d** 68 **p** 69. C Garston *Liv* 68-71; C Blundellsands St Nic 71-73; V Bolton All So w St Jas *Man* 73-78; V Tonge w Alkrington 78-84; P-in-c Edenfield 84-86; P-in-c Stubbins 84-86; V Edenfield and Stubbins 86-03; rtd 03. *71 Cherry Tree Way, Rossendale BB4 4JZ* Tel (01706) 210143 E-mail revg.higham@rotary1280.org

HIGHAM, Canon Jack. b 33. Linc Coll Ox BA56 MA60 Union Th Sem (NY) STM61 Birm Univ DipTh59. Qu Coll Birm 58. **d** 60 **p** 61. C Handsworth *Sheff* 60-64; V Handsworth Woodhouse 64-70; USA 70-78; R Stoke Bruerne w Grafton Regis and Alderton *Pet* 78-83; RD Towcester 82-83; Can Res, Chan and Lib Pet Cathl 83-03; rtd 03; Perm to Offic *S'well* from 04. *44 Alma Hill, Kimberley, Nottingham NG16 2JF* Tel 0115-938 6063

HIGHAM, John Leonard. b 39. Wycliffe Hall Ox 62. **d** 65 **p** 66. C Prescot *Liv* 65-71; V Hollinfare 71-74; Adult and Youth Service Adv Knowsley 74-76; TV Padgate 76-84; V Farnworth 84-89; TR Sutton 89-02; rtd 02; Perm to Offic *Liv* from 03. *86 Ormskirk Road, Rainford, St Helens WA11 8DB*

HIGHAM (née ANNS), Mrs Pauline Mary. b 49. Bris Univ BEd71. EMMTC 87. **d** 90 **p** 94. Par Dn Wirksworth w Alderwasley, Carsington etc *Derby* 90-92; Par Dn Lt Berkhamsted and Bayford, Essendon etc *St Alb* 92-94; C 94-96; P-in-c from 96; RD Hertford and Ware from 05. *1 Little Berkhamsted Lane, Little Berkhamsted, Hertford SG13 8LU* Tel (01707) 875940 Fax 875289

HIGHTON, Philip William. b 70. Liv Univ BSc91 Nottm Univ MSc92. Oak Hill Th Coll BA05. **d** 05. C Knutsford St Jo and Toft *Ches* from 05. *92 Grove Park, Knutsford WA16 8QB*

HIGHTON, William James. b 31. St Deiniol's Hawarden. **d** 82 **p** 83. NSM Thornton Hough *Ches* 82-84; C Cheadle 84-88; V Walton 88-99; rtd 99; Perm to Offic *Carl* from 01. *15 Mowbray Drive, Burton-in-Kendal, Carnforth LA6 1NF* Tel (01524) 782073

HIGTON, Anthony Raymond. b 42. Lon Univ BD65. Oak Hill Th Coll 65. **d** 67 **p** 68. C Newark Ch Ch *S'well* 67-69; C Cheltenham St Mark *Glouc* 70-75; R Hawkwell *Chelmsf* 75-99; Gen Dir CMJ from 99; Public Preacher *St Alb* from 99. *CMJ, 30C Clarence Road, St Albans AL1 4JJ* Tel (01727) 833114 Fax 848312 E-mail tonyh@cmj.org.uk

HILARY, Sister. *See* JORDINSON, Vera

HILBORN, David Henry Kyte. b 64. Nottm Univ BA85 PhD94 Mansf Coll Ox MA88. **d** 02 **p** 02. C Acton St Mary *Lon* from 02. *39 Derwentwater Road, London W3 6DF* Tel (020) 8896 1306 *or* 8993 0422 Fax 8896 2944 E-mail dhilborn@btconnect.com

HILBORN, Mrs Mia Alison Kyte. b 63. City Univ BSc84 Mansf Coll Ox MA87. **d** 02 **p** 02. Chapl Team Ldr Guy's and St Thos' Hosps NHS Trust Lon from 01; NSM N Lambeth *S'wark* from 02; Perm to Offic *Lon* from 02. *39 Derwentwater Road, London W3 6DF* Tel (020) 8896 1306 *or* 7188 5588 Mobile 07740-779585 E-mail mia.hilborn@gstt.sthames.nhs.uk

HILDITCH, Canon Janet. b 59. St Andr Univ MTh81 PhD87. N Ord Course 92. **d** 94 **p** 95. C Kirkholt *Man* 94-98; Chapl Rochdale Healthcare NHS Trust 97-98; Chapl N Man Health Care NHS Trust 98-00; Chapl Tameside and Glossop Acute Services NHS Trust from 00; Hon Can Man Cathl *Man* from 04. *Tameside General Hospital, Fountain Street, Ashton-under-Lyne OL6 9EW* Tel 0161-331 6000

HILDRED, David. b 61. Bath Univ BSc83 CertEd83. Wycliffe Hall Ox 86. **d** 89 **p** 90. C Westcliff St Mich *Chelmsf* 89-92; C Rayleigh 92-96; V Sidcup St Andr *Roch* from 96; AD Sidcup from 03. *The Vicarage, St Andrew's Road, Sidcup DA14 4SA* Tel (020) 8300 4712 E-mail david@hildred.freeserve.co.uk

HILDRETH, Sarah Frances. b 72. St Mich Coll Llan BTh05. **d** 05. C Hawarden *St As* from 05. *3 Ffordd Tegid, St David's Park, Ewloe, Deeside CH5 3UD* Tel (01244) 530788 Mobile 07752-261931

HILES, Janet Rita. b 39. St Alb and Ox Min Course 96. **d** 98 **p** 99. OLM Dorchester *Ox* 98-03; rtd 03; Perm to Offic *Portsm* from 04. *Malabar, The Broadway, Totland Bay PO39 0AN* Tel (01983) 752765 E-mail chrishiles@4thenet.co.uk

HILES, John Michael. b 32. Qu Coll Cam BA57 MA61. Sarum Th Coll 57. **d** 59 **p** 60. C Clifton St Jas *Sheff* 59-62; V Bramley St Fran 62-69; Hon C Holmfirth *Wakef* 69-89; Hon C Upper Holme Valley 89-91; Lic to Offic 91-97; Perm to Offic *Wakef* 97-03 and *Sarum* from 03. *22 Oldfield Road, Bishopdown, Salisbury SP1 3GQ* Tel (01722) 349951

HILL, Alexander Francis. b 71. St Mary's Coll Twickenham BA(QTS)94 Leeds Univ MA97. Coll of Resurr Mirfield 95. **d** 97 **p** 98. C Notting Hill All SS w St Columb *Lon* 97-02; V Willesden St Matt from 02. *St Matthew's Vicarage, St Mary's Road, London NW10 4AU* Tel (020) 8965 3748 E-mail fralex@thehills.demon.co.uk

HILL, Mrs Anne Doreen. b 40. **d** 88 **p** 94. Par Dn Bexleyheath St Pet *Roch* 88-90; Sub-Chapl HM Pris Belmarsh 91-96; Dep Chapl 96-99; Hon C Lee St Mildred *S'wark* 93-04; rtd 04. *Address temp unknown*

HILL, Barry Leon. b 79. Wycliffe Hall Ox BTh05. **d** 05. C Loughborough Em and St Mary in Charnwood *Leic* from 05. *47 Brookfield Avenue, Loughborough LE11 3LN* Tel (01509) 237246 E-mail barry@hill-home.co.uk

HILL, Mrs Bridget Ann. b 54. Open Univ BA82 CertEd75. EMMTC 83. **dss** 86 **d** 87 **p** 94. Gt and Lt Coates w Bradley *Linc* 86-88; Hon Par Dn 87-88; Par Dn Louth 88-91; TD 91-94; TV 94-98; Chapl Louth Co Hosp 89-98; P-in-c Saltfleetby and Theddlethorpe *Linc* 98-99; R 99-03; TV E Dereham and Scarning *Nor* from 03; Chapl Mothers' Union from 05. *1 De Narde Road, Dereham NR19 1HQ* Tel (01362) 692982 E-mail bridget.hill@ntlworld.com

HILL, Carol Ann. b 48. St Paul's Univ Ottawa BTh94. **d** 95 **p** 95. Canada 95-98; C Westboro Ottawa All SS 95-98; C Altham w Clayton le Moors *Blackb* 98-01; TV Hawarden *St As* from 01. *St Mary's Vicarage, Church Road, Broughton CH4 0QB* Tel (01244) 520148

HILL, Canon Charles Bernard. b 50. Sheff Univ BA71 Qu Coll Ox DPhil76. Cant Sch of Min 91. **d** 94 **p** 95. NSM Sandgate St Paul w Folkestone St Geo *Cant* 94-98; NSM Folkestone H Trin w Ch Ch 98-04; Perm to Offic from 04; Eur Sec Coun for Chr Unity from 99; Can Gib Cathl *Eur* from 03. *18 Audley Road, Folkestone CT20 3QA,* or *Church House, Great Smith Street, London SW1P 3NZ* Tel (01303) 253270 *or* (020) 7898 1474 Fax (020) 7898 1483 E-mail cbh@cbhill.demon.co.uk

HILL, Charles Merrick. b 52. Strathclyde Univ BA74. Qu Coll Birm. **d** 80 **p** 81. C Silksworth *Dur* 80-83; C Stockton St Pet 83-85; TV Southampton (City Cen) *Win* 85-87; V Portsea St Geo *Portsm* 87-94; P-in-c Bodenham w Hope-under-Dinmore, Felton etc *Heref* 94-04; P-in-c Hellingly and Upper Dicker *Chich* 04-05; V from 05. *The Vicarage, 14 Orchard Grange, Lower Dicker, Hailsham BN27 3PA* Tel (01323) 440246

HILL, Charles Winston. b 78. Lanc Univ BA99. St Steph Ho Ox 00. **d** 03 **p** 04. C Lt Marsden w Nelson St Mary *Blackb* 03-04; C Blackb St Thos w St Jude from 04; C Blackb St Mich w St Jo and H Trin from 04. *Bank Cottage, Eanam Wharf, Blackburn BB1 5BL*

✠**HILL, The Rt Revd Christopher John.** b 45. K Coll Lon BD67 AKC67 MTh68. **d** 69 **p** 70 **c** 96. C Tividale *Lich* 69-73; C Codsall 73-74; Abp's Asst Chapl on Foreign Relns *Cant* 74-81; ARCIC from 74; Sec 74-90; Abp's Sec for Ecum Affairs *Cant* 82-89; Hon Can Cant Cathl 82-89; Chapl to The Queen 87-96; Can Res and Prec St Paul's Cathl *Lon* 89-96; Select Preacher Ox Univ 90; Area Bp Stafford *Lich* 96-04; Bp Guildf from 04; Clerk of the Closet from 05. *Willow Grange, Woking Road, Guildford GU4 7QS* Tel (01483) 590500 Fax 590501
E-mail bishop.christopher@cofeguildford.org.uk

HILL, The Ven Colin. b 42. Leic Univ BSc64 Open Univ PhD88. Ripon Hall Ox 64. **d** 66 **p** 67. C Leic Martyrs *Leic* 66-69; C Braunstone 69-71; Lect Ecum Inst Thornaby Teesside 71-72; V Worsbrough St Thos and St Jas *Sheff* 72-78; Telford Planning Officer *Lich* 78-96; RD Telford and Telford Severn Gorge *Heref* 80-96; Preb Heref Cathl 83-96; Can Res Carl Cathl *Carl* 96-04; Dioc Sec 96-04; Adn W Cumberland from 04. *50 Stainburn Road, Stainburn, Workington CA14 1SN* Tel (01900) 66190
E-mail archdeacon.west@carlislediocese.org.uk

HILL, Canon Colin Arnold Clifford. b 29. OBE96. Bris Univ 52 Univ of Wales (Ban) MPhil03. Ripon Hall Ox 55. **d** 57 **p** 58. C Rotherham *Sheff* 57-61; V Brightside St Thos 61-64; R Easthampstead *Ox* 64-73; Chapl RAF Coll Bracknell 68-73; V Croydon St Jo *Cant* 73-84; V Croydon St Jo *S'wark* 85-94; Chapl Abp Whitgift Foundn 73-94; Hon Can Cant Cathl *Cant* 75-84; Hon Can S'wark Cathl *S'wark* 85-94; Chapl to The Queen 90-99; rtd 94. *Silver Birches, 70 Preston Crowmarsh, Wallingford OX10 6SL* Tel and fax (01491) 836102
E-mail colin.sb@btopenworld.com

HILL, Canon David. b 25. AKC54. **d** 55 **p** 56. C Kingsbury H Innocents *Lon* 55-58; C Putney St Mary *S'wark* 58-62; V Battersea St Mich 62-89; RD Battersea 69-76; Hon Can S'wark Cathl 74-89; rtd 89; Perm to Offic *Chelmsf* 89-98. *70 Gloucester Avenue, Maldon CM9 6LA* Tel (01621) 855384

HILL, David Rowland. b 34. Lon Univ BSc55. Qu Coll Birm. **d** 59 **p** 60. C Upper Tooting H Trin *S'wark* 59-61; C Cheam 61-63; C Richmond St Mary 63-68; V Sutton St Nicholas *Linc* 68-82; V Pinchbeck 82-99; rtd 99; Perm to Offic *Linc* 99-02. *24 London Road, Spalding PE11 2TA* Tel (01775) 768912

HILL, Derek Stanley. b 28. AKC53. **d** 53 **p** 54. C Rushmere *St E* 53-55; S Africa 55-57; C Boreham Wood All SS *St Alb* 57-59; V Crowfield *St E* 59-67; P-in-c Stonham Aspal 59-61; R 61-67; V Bury St Edmunds St Geo 67-73; P-in-c Ampton w Lt Livermere and Ingham 68-73; V Gazeley w Dalham 73-75; P-in-c Lidgate w Ousden 73-74; P-in-c Gt Bradley 74-78; V Gazeley w Dalham and Moulton 75-78; V Gt Barton 78-86; V Bury St Edmunds All SS 86-93; rtd 93; Perm to Offic *St E* from 93. *Whinwillow, 38 Maltings Garth, Thurston, Bury St Edmunds IP31 3PP* Tel (01359) 230770

HILL, Elizabeth Jayne Louise. *See* DAVENPORT, Elizabeth Jayne Louise

HILL, Ernest. *See* HILL, George Ernest

HILL, Eugene Mark. b 48. Univ of Wales (Lamp) BA71. Sarum Th Coll 71. **d** 73 **p** 74. C Sutton St Nic *S'wark* 73-77; Hon C 77-80; Asst Chapl Em Sch Wandsworth 77-87; Chapl 87-04; Hon C St Helier *S'wark* 83-84; Hon C Caterham 84-98; Dir Chr Studies Course 85-04; Perm to Offic from 98. *22 Bramley Hill, South Croydon CR2 6LT* Tel (020) 8688 1387

HILL, Geoffrey Dennison. b 31. Tyndale Hall Bris DipTh55. **d** 56 **p** 57. C Denton Holme *Carl* 56-59; R Asby w Ormside 59-63; R Arthuret 63-71; V Arnside 71-76; P-in-c Torver 76-79; rtd 91. *Holywath, Coniston LA21 8HN*

HILL, Geoffrey Lionel. b 45. WEMTC 96. **d** 03 **p** 04. OLM Thornbury and Oldbury-on-Severn w Shepperdine *Glouc* from 03. *2 Solent Way, Thornbury, Bristol BS35 2XD* Tel (01454) 416851 Mobile 07968-229912 E-mail gl.hill@bigfoot.com

HILL, George Ernest. b 25. St Jo Coll Nottm. **d** 85 **p** 87. OLM Selston *S'well* 85-95; Perm to Offic from 95. *105 Main Road, Jacksdale, Nottingham NG16 5HR* Tel (01773) 603446

HILL, Giles. *See* HILL, The Rt Revd Michael John Giles

HILL, Canon Gillian Beryl. b 53. Open Univ BA86. S Dios Minl Tr Scheme 87. **d** 90 **p** 94. NSM Southsea St Jude *Portsm* 90-95; C Southsea St Pet 95-01; V Catherington and Clanfield from 01; Hon Can Portsm Cathl from 03. *The Vicarage, 330 Catherington Lane, Catherington, Waterlooville PO8 0TD* Tel (023) 9259 3228 *or* 3139 E-mail gillhill@inglisrd.freeserve.co.uk

HILL, Harold Gordon Haynes. b 15. Tyndale Hall Bris 36. **d** 39 **p** 40. C Aldridge *Lich* 39-42; Org Sec (N and Midl) ICM 42-46; Cen Sec S 46-48; R Whinburgh w Westfield *Nor* 48-81; R Reymerston 48-81; P-in-c Cranworth w Letton and Southbergh 78-79; rtd 81. *11 Pilgrims Way, Great Finborough, Stowmarket IP14 3AY* Tel (01449) 614335

HILL, Ian Maxwell. b 60. Loughb Univ BSc81 MCIT85. EMMTC DipTh95. **d** 95 **p** 96. NSM Thurnby Lodge *Leic* 95-00; NSM Thurmaston from 00. *Shady Ash, 4 Sturrock Close, Thurnby, Leicester LE7 9QP* Tel 0116-243 1609

HILL, James. *See* HILL, Kenneth James

HILL, James Arthur. b 47. Ulster Univ BEd85. CITC 69. **d** 72 **p** 73. C Ballymena w Ballyclug *Conn* 72-74; C Arm St Mark w Aghavilly *Arm* 74-78; C Derg w Termonamongan *D & R* 78-79; I Inver w Mountcharles, Killaghtee and Killybegs 79-87. *53 Dufferin Avenue, Bangor BT20 3AB* Tel (028) 9146 9090

HILL, Mrs Jennifer Clare. b 50. City Univ BSc71 FBCO72. EAMTC 94. **d** 97 **p** 98. NSM Bottesford and Muston *Leic* 97-98; C Glen Parva and S Wigston 98-01; C Walsall Wood *Lich* from 01; AD Walsall from 05. *Church House, 25 Green Lane, Shelfield, Walsall WS4 1RN* Tel (01922) 692550

HILL, John. b 56. S'wark Ord Course. **d** 89 **p** 90. NSM Upper Norwood St Jo *S'wark* 89-94; Chapl RN from 94. *Royal Naval Chaplaincy Service, Room 203, Victory Building, HM Naval Base, Portsmouth PO1 3LS* Tel (023) 9272 7903 Fax 9272 7111

HILL, John Michael. b 34. FCA. Oak Hill NSM Course 81. **d** 85 **p** 86. NSM Rayleigh *Chelmsf* 85-96; Perm to Offic *Lon* 85-92; Chapl Rochford Gen Hosp 93-95; Chapl Southend Health Care NHS Trust 95-99; NSM Rochford *Chelmsf* from 96. *25D Belchamps Way, Hockley SS5 4NT* Tel (01702) 203287

HILL, Mrs Judith Anne. b 47. RGN68. STETS 99. **d** 02 **p** 03. OLM Wool and E Stoke *Sarum* from 02. *9 High Street Close, Wool, Wareham BH20 6BW* Tel (01929) 462888
E-mail reverendjudy@tiscali.co.uk

HILL, Kenneth. b 27. Wycliffe Coll Toronto LTh. **d** 58 **p** 59. Canada 58-61; C Newc St Matt w St Mary *Newc* 61-62; SSF 62-64; C Burslem St Werburgh *Lich* 64-67; C Walsall St Gabr Fulbrook 67-70; P-in-c Hanley St Jude 70-79; P-in-c Chacewater *Truro* 79-92; rtd 92; Perm to Offic *Truro* from 92. *Carbis Barn, Church Road, Stithians, Truro TR3 7DH* Tel (01209) 861070

HILL, Kenneth James (Jim). b 43. Leic Univ BA64 Lon Univ BD68. Oak Hill Th Coll 65. **d** 69 **p** 70. C Southall Green St Jo *Lon* 69-72; C Blackheath Park St Mich *S'wark* 72-75; C Bath Abbey w St Jas *B & W* 75-83; P-in-c Bath St Mich w St Paul 75-82; R 82-83; R Huntspill 83-91; Omega Order 91-98; Perm to Offic *B & W* and *Bris* 91-98; C Somerton w Compton Dundon, the Charltons etc *B & W* from 98. *The Parsonage, Charlton Adam, Somerton TA11 7AS* Tel (01458) 223061
E-mail kjhill@tiscali.co.uk

HILL, Laurence Bruce. b 43. AKC67. **d** 69 **p** 70. C Feltham *Lon* 69-72; C-in-c Hampstead St Steph 72-77; V Finchley H Trin from 77. *Holy Trinity Vicarage, 91 Church Lane, London N2 0TH* Tel and fax (020) 8883 8720 E-mail frlaurencehill@yahoo.co.uk

HILL, Leslie Hugh. b 23. Westcott Ho Cam 73. **d** 73 **p** 74. NSM Holbrook and Lt Eaton *Derby* 73-79; NSM Loscoe 79-85; P-in-c Denby 85-88; P-in-c Horsley Woodhouse 87-88; rtd 88; Perm to Offic *Derby* from 88. *1 Hunter Drive, Kilburn, Derby DE56 0ND* Tel (01332) 881081

HILL, Malcolm Crawford. b 43. Lon Univ DipTh70. Oak Hill Th Coll 68. **d** 71 **p** 72. C Maidstone St Luke *Cant* 71-74; C Longfleet *Sarum* 74-79; V Bexleyheath St Pet *Roch* 79-90; V Lee St Mildred *S'wark* 90-04; rtd 04. *64 St Mary's Road, Poole BH15 2LL* Tel (01202) 666076

HILL, Mrs Marjorie Ann. b 38. MCSP60. St Jo Coll Nottm 92. **d** 94 **p** 95. C Hull St Martin w Transfiguration *York* 94-99; P-in-c Willerby w Ganton and Folkton 99-03; rtd 03; Perm to Offic *York* from 03. *16 Autherd Garth, Walkington, Beverley HU17 8RZ* Tel (01482) 865188 E-mail marjhill@fish.co.uk

HILL, Mark. *See* HILL, Eugene Mark

HILL, Martyn William. b 43. Man Univ BSc64 Univ of Wales (Ban) PhD70 CPhys85 MInstP68. Westcott Ho Cam CTM92. **d** 92 **p** 93. C Horninglow *Lich* 92-95; TV Hawarden *St As* 95-00; V Bistre from 00. *Bistre Vicarage, Mold Road, Buckley CH7 2NH* Tel (01244) 550947

HILL, Matthew Anthony Robert. b 71. Leeds Univ BA93 Univ of Wales (Cardiff) BD96. St Mich Coll Llan 94. **d** 97 **p** 98. C Cardiff St Jo *Llan* 97-00; Min Can Llan Cathl 00-04; P-in-c Dowlais and Penydarren 04-05; R from 05. *The Rectory, Gwernllwyn Road, Dowlais, Merthyr Tydfil CF48 3NA* Tel (01685) 722118

HILL, Michael. *See* HILL, John Michael

HILL, Michael. b 32. TD77. AKC55. **d** 56 **p** 57. C Tynemouth Cullercoats St Paul *Newc* 56-59; C Drayton in Hales *Lich* 59-61; V Milton 61-64; V Preston Gubbals 64-73; V Leaton 64-76; CF (TA) 65-67; CF (TAVR) 67-87; V Oswestry St Oswald *Lich* 76-87; P-in-c Trefonen 80-83; V Sunningdale *Ox* 87-97; rtd 97; Perm to Offic *Lich* from 97. *20 Winterton Way, Montford Grange, Bicton Heath, Shrewsbury SY3 5PA* Tel (01743) 341076

✠**HILL, The Rt Revd Michael Arthur.** b 49. Ridley Hall Cam 74. **d** 77 **p** 78 **c** 98. C Addiscombe St Mary *Cant* 77-81; C Slough *Ox*

81-83; P-in-c Chesham Bois 83-90; R 90-92; RD Amersham 89-92; Adn Berks 92-98; Area Bp Buckm 98-03; Bp Bris from 03. *Wethered House, 11 The Avenue, Clifton, Bristol BS8 3HG* Tel 0117-973 0222 Fax 923 9670 E-mail bishop@bristoldiocese.org

HILL, The Rt Revd Michael John Giles. b 43. S Dios Minl Tr Scheme 82. **d** 84 **p** 86. Community of Our Lady and St John from 67; Abbot from 90; Perm to Offic *Win* 84-92; Lic to Offic from 92; Perm to Offic *Portsm* from 04. *Alton Abbey, Abbey Road, Beech, Alton GU34 4AP* Tel (01420) 562145 *or* 563575 Fax 561691

HILL, Nora. b 47. Univ of Wales BA95 PGCE97. St Mich Coll Llan 00. **d** 03 **p** 04. NSM Llandogo w Whitebrook Chpl and Tintern Parva *Mon* from 03. *3 Warwick Close, Chepstow NP16 5BU* Tel (01291) 626784

HILL, Norman William. b 14. Ch Coll Cam BA36 MA40. Linc Th Coll 43. **d** 45 **p** 46. C Hitchin St Mary *St Alb* 45-49; C St Alb Abbey 49-60; V Rickmansworth 60-74; P-in-c Northill 74-78; P-in-c Moggerhanger 74-78; P-in-c Northill w Moggerhanger 78-79; RD Biggleswade 75-79; rtd 80; Perm to Offic *Newc* from 80. *4 Overstone Gardens, Elvaston Road, Hexham NE46 2HH* Tel (01434) 609715

HILL, Patricia Frances. b 49. RGN90. SEITE DipTM99. **d** 99 **p** 00. NSM Hythe *Cant* 99-01; Asst Chapl E Kent Hosps NHS Trust 99-00; Team Ldr Chapl from 01. *Springville, Sandling Road, Saltwood, Hythe CT21 4QJ* Tel (01303) 266649 E-mail patricia.hill@ekht.nhs.uk

HILL, Peppie. *See* HILL, Stephanie Jane

HILL, Canon Peter. b 36. AKC60. St Boniface Warminster 60. **d** 61 **p** 62. C Gt Berkhamsted *St Alb* 61-67; R Bedford St Mary 67-69; P-in-c 69-70; V Goldington 69-79; V Biggleswade 79-90; RD Biggleswade 80-85; Hon Can St Alb 85-90; V Holbeach *Linc* 90-01; RD Elloe E 94-99; P-in-c The Suttons w Tydd 99-01; rtd 01; Perm to Offic *Nor* from 01. *Rayner Cottage, Low Street, Sloley, Norwich NR12 8HD* Tel (01692) 538744

HILL, Canon Peter. b 50. Man Univ BSc71 Nottm Univ MTh90. Wycliffe Hall Ox 81. **d** 83 **p** 84. C Porchester *S'well* 83-86; V Huthwaite 86-95; P-in-c Calverton 95-04; RD S'well 97-01; Dioc Chief Exec from 04; Hon Can S'well Minster from 01. *15 Adams Row, Southwell NG25 0FF* Tel (01636) 816445 E-mail ce@southwell.anglican.org

HILL, Ralph Jasper. b 15. Tyndale Hall Bris 38. **d** 41 **p** 42. C Stambermill *Worc* 41-44; C Harmondsworth *Lon* 44-45; C Wandsworth St Steph *S'wark* 45-48; Org Sec SAMS 49-59; Asst Master Hove Gr Sch 65-78; rtd 80; Perm to Offic *Chich* from 82. *29 Gorham Way, Telscombe Cliffs, Newhaven BN10 7BA* Tel (01273) 583729

HILL, Richard Brian. b 47. Dur Univ BA68 DipTh70. Cranmer Hall Dur 68 Westcott Ho Cam 70. **d** 71 **p** 72. C Cockermouth All SS w Ch Ch *Carl* 71-74; C Barrow St Geo w St Luke 74-76; V Walney Is 76-83; Dir of Clergy Tr 83-90; P-in-c Westward, Rosley-w-Woodside and Welton 83-90; V Gosforth All SS *Newc* from 90. *All Saints' Vicarage, 33 Brackenfield Road, Newcastle upon Tyne NE3 4DX* Tel 0191-285 6345 *or* 213 0450 Fax 246 2548 E-mail r.b.hill@lineone.net

HILL, Richard Hugh Oldham. b 52. CCC Ox BA74 BA77 MA78. Wycliffe Hall Ox 75. **d** 78 **p** 79. C Harold Wood *Chelmsf* 78-81; C Hampreston *Sarum* 81-86; TV N Ferriby *York* 86-97; V Swanland from 97. *The Vicarage, St Barnabas Drive, Swanland, North Ferriby HU14 3RL* Tel (01482) 631271 E-mail stbrhoh@aol.com

HILL, Robert Arthur. b 59. Trent Poly BSc83 Open Univ BA93. ACT 96. **d** 01 **p** 02. Sen Chapl Miss to Seafarers Australia 95-03; C Kettering SS Pet and Paul *Pet* from 03. *19 Greenhill Road, Kettering NN15 7LW* Tel and fax (01536) 523603 E-mail robert@peterandpaul.org.uk

HILL, Robert Joseph. b 45. Oak Hill Th Coll BA81. **d** 81 **p** 82. C W Derby St Luke *Liv* 81-84; P-in-c Devonport St Mich *Ex* 84-97; Chapl Morden Coll Blackheath 97-99; TV Manningham *Bradf* 99-04; P-in-c Davyhulme Ch Ch *Man* from 04. *Christ Church Vicarage, 14 Welbeck Avenue, Urmston, Manchester M41 0GJ* Tel 0161-748 2018 E-mail rjh@credo-ergo-sum.fsnet.co.uk

HILL, Robin. b 35. Cranmer Hall Dur 59. **d** 62 **p** 63. C Aspley *S'well* 62-65; V Mansfield St Aug 65-71; R Hulland, Atlow and Bradley *Derby* 71-76; Australia 76-86; P-in-c Alkmonton, Cubley, Marston, Montgomery etc *Derby* 86-93; P-in-c Ticknall, Smisby and Stanton-by-Bridge 93-99; P-in-c Barrow-on-Trent w Twyford and Swarkestone 94-99; rtd 99. *34 Samson Street, White Gum Valley, W Australia 6162* Tel (0061) (8) 9335 9652

HILL, Rodney Maurice. b 44. Leeds Univ BA67 FCIPD. Ripon Coll Cuddesdon 04. **d** 05. NSM N Hinksey and Wytham *Ox* from 05. *13 Hobson Road, Oxford OX2 7JX* Tel (01865) 426804 E-mail rodneymauricehill@hotmail.com

HILL, Canon Roger Anthony John. b 45. Liv Univ BA67 Linacre Coll Ox BA69 MA. Ripon Hall Ox 67. **d** 70 **p** 71. C St Helier *S'wark* 70-74; C Dawley Parva *Lich* 74-75; C Cen Telford 76-77; TV 77-81; TR 81-88; TR Newark w Hawton, Cotham and Shelton *S'well* 88-89; TR Newark 89-02; RD Newark 90-95; Hon Can S'well Minster 98-02; R Man St Ann *Man* from 02; Hon Can Man Cathl from 02; AD Hulme from 05; Chapl to The Queen from 01. *The Rectory, 296 Wilbraham Road, Chorlton-cum-Hardy, Manchester M21 0UU* Tel 0161-881 1229

HILL, Simon George. b 53. Reading Univ BSc75 MSc78. S'wark Ord Course 80. **d** 83 **p** 84. NSM Croydon St Aug *Cant* 83-84; Swaziland 84-86; Fiji 86-88; NSM Croydon St Aug *S'wark* 88-90; Tanzania 90-94; Uganda 94-96; Swaziland 96-98; Perm to Offic *Chich* and *S'wark* 99-02; P-in-c Cockfield w Bradfield St Clare, Felsham etc *St E* 02-04; R Bradfield St Clare, Bradfield St George etc from 04. *The Rectory, Howe Lane, Cockfield, Bury St Edmunds IP30 0HA* Tel (01284) 828385 Mobile 07747-022903 E-mail revsimon@dial.pipex.com

HILL, Simon James. b 64. Sheff Univ BA85 Ex Univ PGCE88. Ripon Coll Cuddesdon BA84 DipMin95. **d** 95 **p** 96. C Manston *Ripon* 95-98; TV Dorchester *Ox* 98-03; Dir Berinsfield Progr Ripon Coll Cuddesdon 98-03; R Backwell w Chelvey and Brockley *B & W* from 03. *The Rectory, 72 Church Lane, Backwell, Bristol BS48 3JJ* Tel (01275) 462391

HILL, Stephanie Jane (Peppie). b 67. K Coll Lon LLB88. Wycliffe Hall Ox BTh05. **d** 05. C Loughborough Em and St Mary in Charnwood *Leic* from 05. *47 Brookfield Avenue, Loughborough LE11 3LN* Tel (01509) 237246 E-mail pep@hill-home.co.uk

HILL, Stuart Graeme. b 64. Ripon Coll Cuddesdon BTh97. **d** 97 **p** 98. C Usworth *Dur* 97-99; C Monkwearmouth 99-01; TV from 01. *St Peter's Vicarage, St Peter's Way, Sunderland SR6 0DY* Tel 0191-567 3726 E-mail stuart.hill@durham.anglican.org

HILL, Trevor Walton. b 30. Leeds Univ BA57. Coll of Resurr Mirfield. **d** 59 **p** 60. C Bollington St Jo *Ches* 59-62; C Woodchurch 62-64; V Addingham *Carl* 64-67; V Carl H Trin 67-71; R Wetheral w Warwick 71-80; P-in-c Doddington w Wychling *Cant* 80-82; P-in-c Newnham 80-82; rtd 95. *59 Medina Avenue, Newport PO30 1HG*

HILL, William. b 44. Man Univ BSc66 CEng73 MICE73. SEITE 95. **d** 98 **p** 99. NSM Farnham *Guildf* 98-01; P-in-c Smallburgh w Dilham w Honing and Crostwight *Nor* 01-05; rtd 05; Perm to Offic *Nor* from 05. *Grange Farm House, Yarmouth Road, Worstead, North Walsham NR28 9LX* Tel and fax (01692) 403402 E-mail w_hill_ss@hotmail.com

HILL, William Henry George. b 21. S'wark Ord Course 66. **d** 69 **p** 70. C Welling *S'wark* 69-73; C Reigate St Luke S Park 73-76; R Norton and V Lynsted w Kingsdown *Cant* 76-87; rtd 87; Perm to Offic *Sarum* 87-05. *Diana House, Manor Road, Brackley NN13 6AJ* Tel (01280) 840244 Mobile 07817-821709

HILL-BROWN, Timothy Duncan. b 65. Westmr Coll Ox BA87. Wycliffe Hall Ox DPS92. **d** 93 **p** 94. C Sparkhill w Greet and Sparkbrook *Birm* 93-97; C Sutton Coldfield H Trin 97-99; P-in-c Short Heath 99-00; V from 00. *St Margaret's Vicarage, Somerset Road, Birmingham B23 6NQ* Tel 0121-373 9209 E-mail duncan@ukonline.co.uk

HILL-TOUT, Mark Laurence. b 50. AKC73. **d** 74 **p** 75. C Brighton Resurr *Chich* 74-77; C New Shoreham 77-79; C Old Shoreham 77-79; Dioc Stewardship Adv Lewes and Hastings 79-84; P-in-c Stonegate 79-83; R Horsted Keynes 84-89; V St Helens *Portsm* 89-95; V Sea View 89-95; P-in-c Widley w Wymering 95-99; V from 99. *The Vicarage, Medina Road, Portsmouth PO6 3NH* Tel (023) 9237 6307 E-mail mark.hilltout@tesco.net

HILLARY, Leslie Tyrone James. b 59. Cranmer Hall Dur 84. **d** 87 **p** 88. C Middlesbrough All SS *York* 87-89; C Stainton-in-Cleveland 89-91; CF from 91. *c/o MOD Chaplains (Army)* Tel (01980) 615804 Fax 615800

HILLAS, Ms Patricia Dorothy. b 66. E Lon Univ BA91 Middx Univ BA02. NTMTC 98. **d** 02 **p** 03. C Kensal Rise St Mark and St Martin *Lon* from 02; V Northolt Park St Barn from 05. *The Vicarage, Raglan Way, Northolt UB5 4SX* Tel and fax (020) 8422 3775 E-mail tricia@thillas.freeserve.co.uk

HILLEBRAND, Frank David. b 46. AKC68. St Boniface Warminster 68. **d** 69 **p** 70. C Wood Green St Mich *Lon* 69-72; C Evesham *Worc* 72-75; V Worc H Trin 75-80; V Kidderminster St Jo 80-90; TR Kidderminster St Jo and H Innocents 90-91; TV High Wycombe *Ox* 91-95; TR 95-00; Team Chapl Portsm Hosps NHS Trust from 00. *Chaplaincy Office, Queen Alexandra Hospital, Portsmouth PO6 3LY* Tel (023) 9228 6408 E-mail fhillebrand@sovereign32.freeserve.co.uk

HILLEL, Laurence Christopher Francis. b 54. Bris Univ BA76 Sheff Univ PGCE78 SOAS Lon MA84. Cuddesdon Coll 98. **d** 98 **p** 99. C Pinner *Lon* 98-00; NSM Eastcote St Lawr 01-04; Chapl Bp Ramsey Sch 01-04; NSM Brondesbury St Anne w Kilburn H Trin *Lon* from 04. *49 Keslake Road, London NW6 6DH* Tel (020) 8968 3898 E-mail revhillel@aol.com

HILLIAM, Mrs Cheryl. b 49. EMMTC DipTh94. **d** 94 **p** 95. C Linc St Faith and St Martin w St Pet *Linc* 94-98; P-in-c S Ormsby Gp from 98. *The Rectory, South Ormsby, Louth LN11 8QT* Tel (01507) 480236

HILLIARD, David. b 57. TCD BTh91. CITC 88. **d** 91 **p** 92. C Holywood *D & D* 91-94; C Seagoe 94-96; I Tartaraghan w

Diamond *Arm* from 96. *The Rectory, 5 Tarthlogue Road, Portadown BT62 1RB* Tel and fax (028) 3885 1289 E-mail tartaraghan@armagh.anglican.org

HILLIARD, Canon George Percival St John. b 45. TCD BA67. **d** 69 **p** 70. C Seapatrick *D & D* 69-73; C Carrickfergus *Conn* 73-76; I Fanlobbus Union *C, C & R* 76-85; Dean Cloyne 85-02; Prec Cork Cathl 85-02; I Cloyne Union 85-02; Chapl Univ Coll Cork from 02; Can Cork and Cloyne Cathls from 02. *The Chaplaincy, Iona, College Road, Cork, Irish Republic* Tel (00353) (21) 490 2444 E-mail gchilliard@hotmail.com *or* gphilliard@ucc.ie

HILLIARD, Robert Godfrey. b 52. Univ of Wales DipTh75 Portsm Univ BA(Ed)97 MA02. St Mich Coll Llan 72. **d** 75 **p** 76. C Whitchurch *Llan* 75-80; Chapl RNR 77-80; Chapl RN from 80; Hon Chapl Portsm Cathl *Portsm* from 03. *Royal Naval Chaplaincy Service, Room 203, Victory Building, HM Naval Base, Portsmouth PO1 3LS* Tel (023) 9272 7903 Fax 9272 7111

HILLIARD, Russell Boston. b 57. N Carolina Univ BA82 Vanderbilt Univ (USA) PhD95. St Jo Coll Nottm 01. **d** 03 **p** 04. C Zürich *Eur* from 03. *Rebweg 12, 8309 Nuerensdorf, Switzerland* Tel and fax (0041) (1) 836 9245 Mobile 79-501 4904 E-mail rhilliard@anglican.ch

HILLIER, Andrew. b 68. RGN92. SW Minl Tr Course 99. **d** 02 **p** 03. C Castle Cary w Ansford *B & W* from 02. *The Church House, Ansford Road, Castle Cary BA7 7HG* Tel (01963) 350245 Mobile 07980-743799 E-mail andrewhillier@bigfoot.com.

HILLIER, Derek John. b 30. Sarum Th Coll 61. **d** 63 **p** 64. C Salisbury St Mark *Sarum* 63-65; C Weymouth H Trin 65-66; R Caundle Bishop w Caundle Marsh and Holwell 66-75; P-in-c Pulham 70-78; R The Caundles and Holwell 75-81; R The Caundles w Folke and Holwell 81-02; rtd 02; Perm to Offic *Sarum* and *B & W* from 02. *Sarum House, Bishop's Caundle, Sherborne DT9 5ND* Tel and fax (01963) 23243

HILLIER, John Frederick. b 43. ARIBA67. **d** 01 **p** 02. OLM Merton St Mary *S'wark* from 01. *36 Watery Lane, London SW20 9AD* Tel (020) 8540 4160 Mobile 07802-646374 Fax (020) 8715 8123 E-mail jfhillier@fish.co.uk

HILLIER (née CHAPMAN), Mrs Linda Rosa. b 54. Middx Univ BA04. NTMTC 01. **d** 04 **p** 05. C W Drayton *Lon* from 04. *79 Torbay Road, Harrow HA2 9QG* Tel (020) 8864 5728 E-mail lindarosahillier@msn.com

HILLIER, The Ven Michael Bruce. b 49. St Barn Coll Adelaide ThD73. **d** 74 **p** 75. Australia 74-80; C Tewkesbury w Walton Cardiff *Glouc* 81-86; Australia from 86; P-in-c Whyalla from 94; Adn Eyre Peninsula from 01. *37 Wood Terrace, PO Box 244, Whyalla, S Australia 5600* Tel (0061) (8) 8644 0391 Fax 8644 0657 E-mail mjhillier@dove.net.au

HILLIER, Timothy John. b 55. Westmr Coll Ox CertEd77. Oak Hill Th Coll DipHE96. **d** 96 **p** 97. C Chertsey *Guildf* 96-00; V 00-04; V Chertsey, Lyne and Longcross from 04. *The Vicarage, London Street, Chertsey KT16 8AA* Tel and fax (01932) 563141 E-mail hillier@timp33.freeserve.co.uk

HILLMAN, Clive Ralph. b 71. York Univ BSc92. St Steph Ho Ox BA93. **d** 96 **p** 97. C Kingston upon Hull St Alb *York* 96-00; TV Ifield *Chich* 00-02; Chapl St Jo Coll Cam from 02. *St John's College, Cambridge CB2 1TP* Tel (01223) 338617 E-mail crh41@cam.ac.uk

HILLMAN, John Anthony. b 32. St Chad's Coll Dur BA53. St Mich Coll Llan 54. **d** 55 **p** 56. C Llangollen *St As* 56-60; C Silvertown S Africa 60-64; P-in-c Matroosfontein 64-72; R Noorder Paarl 72-75; R Durbanville 75-80; R Somerset W 80-86; TV Wolstanton *Lich* 86-91; P-in-c E Goscote w Ratcliffe and Rearsby *Leic* 91-93; TV Syston 93-98; rtd 98. *7 Hafod Road West, Penrhyn Bay, Llandudno LL30 3PN* Tel (01492) 541374

HILLMAN, Jonathan. b 68. Man Univ BEng90. Ridley Hall Cam. **d** 00 **p** 01. C N Wingfield, Clay Cross and Pilsley *Derby* 00-03; TV Cove St Jo *Guildf* from 03. *Fircroft, 21 St John's Road, Farnborough GU14 9RL* Tel (01252) 543502 E-mail stjohns@parishofcove.org.uk

HILLMAN, Miss Sarah Catherine. b 68. Selw Coll Cam BA90 MA94. St Jo Coll Nottm 01. **d** 03 **p** 04. C Sandy *St Alb* from 03. *14 Pyms Way, Sandy SG19 1BZ* Tel (01767) 683201 E-mail sarah_hillman@ntlworld.com

HILLS, Mrs Christine Ann. NTMTC. **d** 05. NSM Romford Gd Shep Collier Row *Chelmsf* from 05. *323 Pettits Lane North, Romford RM1 4PH*

HILLS, Elaine. b 45. RN67. Mon Dioc Tr Scheme 02. **d** 04. NSM Caerleon w Llanhennock *Mon* from 04. *6 Anthony Drive, Caerleon, Newport NP18 3DS* Tel (01633) 421248 Mobile 07967-349096 E-mail elainehills@tiscali.co.uk

HILLS, Kenneth Hugh. b 30. Univ of NZ BCom54. Ripon Hall Ox 55. **d** 57 **p** 58. C Handsworth St Mary *Birm* 57-59; V Wanganui Paroch Distr New Zealand 59-61; V Porirua 61-67; Ind Chapl *Birm* 67-74; Chapl Aston Univ 74-82; rtd 91; Community Member Cluny Hill Coll 93-00. *Flat 5, 5 Ardmore Terrace, Holywood BT18 9BH* Tel (028) 9042 1545 E-mail ken.hills@findhorn.org *or* k_h@onetel.com

HILLS, Michael John. b 58. BA82. Westcott Ho Cam 87. **d** 88 **p** 89. C Workington St Jo *Carl* 88-91; C Gosforth All SS *Newc* 91-93; TV Seaton Hirst 93-98; Chapl RN from 98. *Royal Navy Chaplaincy Service, Room 203, Victory Building, HM Naval Base, Portsmouth PO1 3LS* Tel (023) 9272 7903 Fax 9272 7111

HILLS, Michael Rae Buchanan. b 52. Univ of Wales (Lamp) BA81 Ex Univ BPhil83 CQSW83. St Steph Ho Ox. **d** 94 **p** 95. C Kingston upon Hull St Nic *York* 94-97; V Newington w Dairycoates 97-03; P-in-c from 03; N Humberside Ind Chapl from 03; P-in-c Kingston upon Hull St Nic from 05. *St John's Vicarage, 203 St George's Road, Hull HU3 3SP* Tel (01482) 214551 E-mail vicar@kanga.karoo.co.uk

HILLS, Michael William John. b 54. Univ of Wales (Lamp) BA84. Westcott Ho Cam 85. **d** 87 **p** 88. C Reddish *Man* 87-91; V Bolton St Phil 91-00; V Northampton St Mich w St Edm *Pet* from 00; P-in-c Northampton H Sepulchre w St Andr and St Lawr from 04. *St Michael's House, 631 Wellingborough Road, Northampton NN3 3HR* Tel (01604) 406197 *or* tel and fax 230316 Mobile 07932-141428 E-mail mickkhills@btconnect.com

HILLS, Richard Leslie. b 36. Qu Coll Cam BA60 MA63 DIC64 UMIST PhD68 FMA83. St Deiniol's Hawarden 85. **d** 87 **p** 88. C Urmston *Man* 87-89; C Gt Yarmouth *Nor* 89-90; NSM Mottram in Longdendale *Ches* 90-01; Perm to Offic from 01. *Stamford Cottage, 47 Old Road, Mottram, Hyde SK14 6LW* Tel (01457) 763104

HILLS, Roger Malcolm. b 42. Oak Hill Th Coll 83. **d** 86 **p** 87. Hon C Mill Hill Jo Keble Ch *Lon* 86-98; NSM Mill Hill St Mich 86-98; Perm to Offic 98-00; V Queensbury All SS from 00. *The Vicarage, 24 Waltham Drive, Edgware HA8 5PQ* Tel (020) 8952 4536 *or* 8952 0744 E-mail allsaints.queensbury@btinternet.com

HILLS, Stephen Alan. b 59. Sheff Univ BA81. Ridley Hall Cam 97. **d** 99 **p** 00. C Southborough St Pet w Ch Ch and St Matt etc *Roch* 99-02; TV from 02. *The Rectory, Rectory Drive, Bidborough, Tunbridge Wells TN3 0UL* Tel (01892) 528081 E-mail stephen.hills5@virgin.net

HILLYER, Charles Norman. b 21. Lon Univ BD48. Lambeth STh67 ALCD48. **d** 48 **p** 49. C Finchley Ch Ch *Lon* 48-51; C New Malden and Coombe *S'wark* 51-54; V Hanley Road St Sav w St Paul *Lon* 54-59; Chapl City of Lon Maternity Hosp 54-59; V Ponsbourne *St Alb* 59-70; Chapl Tolmers Park Hosp 59-70; Lib Tyndale Ho Cam 70-73; Org Ed UCCF 73-79; Sec Tyndale Fellowship Bibl Research Cam 73-75; P-in-c Hatherleigh *Ex* 79-81; V 81-86; rtd 86; Perm to Offic *Sarum* 89-03 and *Leic* from 03. *10 Smyth Close, Market Harborough LE16 7NS* Tel (01858) 432179 E-mail norman.hillyer@btinternet.com

HILTON, Clive. b 30. K Coll Lon 54. **d** 58 **p** 59. C Wythenshawe Wm Temple Ch CD *Man* 58-61; C Newton Heath All SS 61-62; C-in-c Oldham St Chad Limeside CD 62-65; V Oldham St Chad Limeside 65-70; P-in-c Gravesend H Family *Roch* 70-71; R Killamarsh *Derby* 71-88; R Broughton w Loddington and Cransley etc *Pet* 88-91; rtd 92; Perm to Offic *Man* 92-95; *Ches* 95-99; *Linc* 89-01; *Ely* from 05. *73A Tattershall Drive, Market Deeping, Peterborough PE6 8BZ* Tel (01778) 346217

HILTON, Ian Anthony. b 57. St Jo Coll Nottm 83. **d** 86 **p** 87. C Nottingham St Sav *S'well* 86-90; C Aspley 90-97; P-in-c Colchester, New Town and The Hythe *Chelmsf* 97-02; R from 02. *The Rectory, 24 New Town Road, Colchester CO1 2EF* Tel (01206) 530320 E-mail ian.hilton@ntlworld.com

HILTON, John. b 49. Ex Univ BA70. Cuddesdon Coll 71. **d** 73 **p** 74. C W Derby St Jo *Liv* 73-79; V Orford St Andr 79-96; V Leeds St Wilfrid *Ripon* from 96. *St Wilfrid's Vicarage, Chatsworth Road, Leeds LS8 3RS* Tel 0113-249 7724 E-mail john@the-oak-403.demon.co.uk

HILTON, John Read. b 41. Lon Univ BD63 AKC65 LSE BSc73. **d** 65 **p** 66. C Cov H Trin *Cov* 65-69; C Hemel Hempstead *St Alb* 69-70; Hon C Catford St Andr *S'wark* 70-81. *275 Folkestone Road, Dover CT17 9LL* Tel (01304) 206794

HILTON-TURVEY, Geoffrey Michael. b 34. Oak Hill Th Coll 80. **d** 81 **p** 82. C Bispham *Blackb* 81-85; V Inskip 85-99; rtd 99; Perm to Offic *Heref* from 00. *20 Cralves Mead, Tenbury Wells WR15 8EX* Tel (01584) 811153 E-mail gmh-t@gmh-t.freeserve.co.uk

HILTON-TURVEY, Keith Geoffrey Michael. b 59. Oak Hill Th Coll BA03. **d** 03 **p** 04. C S Mimms Ch Ch *Lon* from 03. *8 Wentworth Road, Barnet EN5 4NT* Tel (020) 8441 0645 E-mail kht@fideste.freeserve.co.uk

HINA, Christine Magdeleine. b 66. St Alb and Ox Min Course. **d** 01 **p** 02. C Stevenage St Hugh and St Jo *St Alb* from 01. *1 Vallansgate, Stevenage SG2 8PY* Tel (01438) 236536 E-mail christine@anih.freeserve.co.uk

HINCHCLIFFE, Garry Anthony Frank. b 68. New Coll Edin BD94. Edin Th Coll 90. **d** 94 **p** 95. C Dumfries *Glas* 94-97; P-in-c Motherwell and Wishaw 97-00; V Hampsthwaite and Killinghall *Ripon* 00-04; V Hampsthwaite and Killinghall and Birstwith from 04. *The Vicarage, Church Lane, Hampsthwaite, Harrogate HG3 2HB* Tel (01423) 770337 E-mail gsahinch@compuserve.com

HINCHEY, Peter John. b 30. LTCL53. Chich Th Coll 55. **d** 58 **p** 59. C Malden St Jo *S'wark* 58-61; V Rosherville *Roch* 61-67; V Gillingham St Aug 67-72; V Bromley St Andr 72-74; Hon Chapl to Bp 74-78; Hon C Lamorbey H Redeemer 76-78; R Foots Cray 78-81; Perm to Offic *Chich* 92-94; rtd 94; Hon C Rotherhithe St Mary w All SS *S'wark* 94-98; Perm to Offic *Chelmsf* from 95; *St E* from 97; *Chich* from 03. *16 Collington Grove, Bexhill-on-Sea TN39 3UB* Tel (01424) 846238 E-mail hincheypj@hotmail.com

HINCKLEY, Paul Frederick. b 61. Cranfield Inst of Tech MSc85 Farnborough Tech Coll HND83. Ridley Hall Cam CTM94. **d** 94 **p** 95. C Ovenden *Wakef* 94-99; TV Billericay and Lt Burstead *Chelmsf* from 99. *Christ Church Vicarage, 10 Chestwood Close, Billericay CM12 0PB* Tel (01277) 652659 E-mail paul@billericaychurches.org

✠**HIND, The Rt Revd John William.** b 45. Leeds Univ BA66. Cuddesdon Coll 70. **d** 72 **p** 73 **c** 91. C Catford (Southend) and Downham *S'wark* 72-76; V Forest Hill Ch Ch 76-82; P-in-c Forest Hill St Paul 81-82; Prin Chich Th Coll 82-91; Wiccamical Preb Chich Cathl *Chich* 82-91; Area Bp Horsham 91-93; Bp Eur 93-01; Asst Bp Chich 93-01; Bp Chich from 01. *The Palace, Chichester PO19 1PY* Tel (01243) 782161 Fax 531332 E-mail bishchichester@diochi.org.uk

HIND, Mrs Ruth Elizabeth. b 71. Cen Lancs Univ BA93. St Jo Coll Nottm MTh01. **d** 02 **p** 03. C Caldbeck, Castle Sowerby and Sebergham *Carl* from 02. *The Vicarage, Church Lane, Thursby, Carlisle CA5 6PF* Tel (01228) 712949 E-mail ruthehind@supanet.com

HIND, Canon Stanley Maurice. b 29. AKC53. **d** 54 **p** 55. C Haydock St Jas *Liv* 54-57; C Elland *Wakef* 57-60; V Mirfield Eastthorpe St Paul 60-67; V Carleton 67-78; V E Hardwick 72-78; V Morley St Pet w Churwell 78-86; V Womersley 86-87; P-in-c Kirk Smeaton 86-87; V Womersley and Kirk Smeaton 87-94; Hon Can Wakef Cathl 89-94; rtd 94; Perm to Offic *Wakef* from 94. *1 The Lilacs, Carleton Road, Pontefract WF8 3RW* Tel (01977) 700386

HINDER, Doreen Patterson. b 38. Open Univ BA95. Selly Oak Coll 60 Bris Bapt Coll 68. **d** 97 **p** 98. NSM Stanwix *Carl* 97-99; P-in-c Glenurquhart *Mor* 99-03; rtd 03. *Hardies Byre, Kirkhill, Inverness IV5 7PP* Tel (01463) 831729 E-mail dghinder@madasafish.com

HINDLE, Miss Penelope Jane Bowyn. b 45. Trin Coll Bris 76. **dss** 84 **d** 87 **p** 94. Stoneycroft All SS *Liv* 84-89; Par Dn 87-89; Asst Chapl Broadgreen Hosp Liv 87-89; Asst Chapl R Free Hosp Lon 89-93; Chapl N Herts NHS Trust 93-02; rtd 02. *19 Park Lane, Knebworth SG3 6PD* Tel (01438) 811584

HINDLEY, Canon Andrew David. b 59. Univ of Wales (Lamp) BA. Sarum & Wells Th Coll. **d** 82 **p** 83. C Huddersfield St Pet *Wakef* 82-84; C Huddersfield St Pet and All SS 84-86; P-in-c Holmfield 86-91; R Ribchester w Stidd *Blackb* 91-96; Bp's Adv for Leisure and Tourism 91-96; Chapl Ribchester Hosp from 91; Can Res Blackb Cathl from 96. *22 Billinge Avenue, Blackburn BB2 6SD* Tel (01254) 261152 *or* 51491 Fax 689666 E-mail andrew.hindley@blackburn.anglican.org

HINDLEY, Canon Anthony Talbot. b 41. Bernard Gilpin Soc Dur 61 Oak Hill Th Coll 62. **d** 66 **p** 67. C Stoke next Guildf St Jo *Guildf* 66-69; C Eldoret Kenya 70-72; V Menengai 72-78; C Redhill H Trin *S'wark* 78-79; P-in-c Eastbourne All So *Chich* 79-83; V 83-86; V S Malling 86-98; R Wainford *St E* from 98; RD Beccles and S Elmham 00-03; Hon Can St E Cathl from 05. *The Rectory, 27 School Road, Ringsfield, Beccles NR34 8NZ* Tel (01502) 717862 Mobile 07766-546601 E-mail anthony.hindley@stedmundsbury.anglican.org

HINDLEY, John Philip Talbot. b 76. Ex Univ BA96 Oak Hill Th Coll BA01. **d** 01 **p** 02. C Astley Bridge *Man* 01-04; Assoc Miss Partner Crosslinks from 04. *5 Haydn Avenue, Manchester M14 4DJ* Tel 0161-226 6860 Mobile 07790-007390 E-mail john@theplant.net

HINDLEY, Michael Alexander. b 72. Man Metrop Univ BA94. Wycliffe Hall Ox BTh05. **d** 05. C Clubmoor *Liv* from 05. *38 Paget Road, Oxford OX4 2TD* Tel (01865) 711080 Mobile 07980-912768 E-mail mike_kate@tesco.net

HINDLEY, Roger Dennis. b 48. Birm Univ BA70 Ox Univ BA77 MA83. Ripon Coll Cuddesdon 75 Qu Coll Birm 77. **d** 78 **p** 79. C Rubery *Birm* 78-81; C Henbury *Bris* 81-83; V Erdington St Chad *Birm* 83-89; V Hill 89-05; AD Sutton Coldfield 96-02; Hon Can Birm Cathl 00-05; TR Willington *Newc* from 05. *St Mary's Vicarage, 67 Churchill Street, Wallsend NE28 7TE* Tel 0191-262 8208 E-mail rdhindley@yahoo.co.uk

HINDLEY, Thomas Richard. b 31. ARIBA54 Sheff Univ BA53 Lon Univ BD66. Clifton Th Coll 61. **d** 63 **p** 64. C Kenilworth St Jo *Cov* 63-67; C Cheadle *Ches* 67-70; R Harpurhey Ch Ch *Man* 70-95; R Harpurhey St Steph 72-95; rtd 96; Perm to Offic *Man* from 96. *15 Twyford Close, Didsbury, Manchester M20 2YR* Tel 0161-438 0387

HINDS, Kenneth Arthur Lancelot. b 30. K Coll Lon BA00 Birkbeck Coll Lon MA04. Bps' Coll Cheshunt. **d** 64 **p** 65. C Sawbridgeworth *St Alb* 64-67; C Gt Berkhamsted 67-71; V Boreham Wood St Mich 71-75; Trinidad and Tobago 75-79; P-in-c Gt Ilford St Luke *Chelmsf* 79-81; V 81-95; rtd 95; Perm to Offic *Chelmsf* from 95. *214 Aldborough Road South, Ilford IG3 8HF* Tel (020) 8598 2963 E-mail frkalhinds@ntlworld.com

HINE, John Victor. b 36. Open Univ BA82. Carl Dioc Tr Course 85. **d** 88 **p** 89. NSM Dean *Carl* 88-92; NSM Clifton 88-92; C Millom 92-94; P-in-c Gt Broughton and Broughton Moor 94-02; P-in-c Brigham 99-02; rtd 02; Perm to Offic *Carl* from 02. *4 The Paddocks, Thursby, Carlisle CA5 6PB* Tel (01228) 712704 E-mail hine.hine@virgin.net

HINE, Keith Ernest. b 50. Bradf Univ BA Leeds Univ CertEd. N Ord Course 89. **d** 89 **p** 90. C Wilmslow *Ches* 89-94; V Bowdon from 94. *The Vicarage, Church Brow, Bowdon, Altrincham WA14 2SG* Tel 0161-928 2468 Fax 929 5956 E-mail keith@hine24.freeserve.co.uk

HINES, Richard Arthur. b 49. Imp Coll Lon MSc73 PhD76 K Coll Lon MTh89. Oak Hill Th Coll 82. **d** 84 **p** 85. C Mile Cross *Nor* 84-87; Lect Oak Hill Th Coll 87-97; Vice-Prin NTMTC 94-97; R Happisburgh, Walcott, Hempstead w Eccles etc *Nor* from 97; C Bacton w Edingthorpe w Witton and Ridlington from 04. *The Rectory, Happisburgh, Norwich NR12 0PW* Tel (01692) 650313 E-mail hines@norfolkcoast.fsnet.co.uk

HINEY, Thomas Bernard Felix. b 35. MC61. RMA 56. Ridley Hall Cam 67. **d** 69 **p** 70. C Edgbaston St Aug *Birm* 69-71; CF 71-91; Chapl R Hosp Chelsea from 91; Chapl Mercers' Coll Holborn from 99. *The Royal Hospital Chelsea, Royal Hospital Road, London SW3 4SL* Tel (020) 7881 5234 Fax 7823 6871 E-mail thiney2199@aol.com

HINGE, Canon David Gerald Francis. b 30. FRSA57. Wells Th Coll 64. **d** 66 **p** 67. C Brookfield St Anne, Highgate Rise *Lon* 66-69; C N Greenford All Hallows 69-71; V Winton *Man* 71-78; R Etherley *Dur* 78-96; Hon Can Dur Cathl 90-00; rtd 96. *9 Hillside, Ingleton, Darlington DL2 3JH* Tel (01325) 732002

HINGE, Derek Colin. b 36. Imp Coll Lon BSc58 CChem60 MRSC60. St Alb Minl Tr Scheme 84. **d** 88 **p** 89. NSM Bishop's Stortford St Mich *St Alb* from 88. *12 Avenue Road, Bishop's Stortford CM23 5NU* Tel (01279) 652173 E-mail derek.hinge@ntlworld.com

HINGLEY, Christopher James Howard. b 48. Trin Coll Ox BA69 MA71. Wycliffe Hall Ox 81. **d** 80 **p** 81. Zimbabwe 80-81 and from 87; Lic to Offic *Ox* 85-87. *Whitestone School, Postbag 4, Hillside, Bulawayo, Zimbabwe*

HINGLEY (née EDWARDS), Mrs Helen. b 55. Natal Univ BSW75. St Steph Ho Ox 94. **d** 96 **p** 97. C Gravelly Hill *Birm* 96-01; TV Cen Wolverhampton *Lich* 01-05; P-in-c Hamstead St Bernard *Birm* from 05. *The Vicarage, 147 Hamstead Road, Great Barr, Birmingham B43 5BB* Tel 0121-358 1286 E-mail hhingley@fish.co.uk

HINGLEY, Robert Charles. b 46. Ball Coll Ox BA69 MA74 Birm Univ CertEd73. Qu Coll Birm DipTh72. **d** 73 **p** 74. C Charlton St Luke w H Trin *S'wark* 73-76; Asst Warden Iona Abbey 76-77; TV Langley Marish *Ox* 77-83; V Balsall Heath St Paul *Birm* 83-90; Perm to Offic 90-91; V Birm St Luke 91-96; Lic to Offic from 96; Perm to Offic *Lich* from 01. *The Vicarage, 147 Hamstead Road, Great Barr, Birmingham B43 5BB* Tel 0121-357 4534

HINGLEY, Roderick Stanley Plant. b 51. St Chad's Coll Dur BA72. St Steph Ho Ox 74. **d** 75 **p** 76. C Lower Gornal *Lich* 75-79; C Tividale 79-82; C Broseley w Benthall *Heref* 82-84; C Wanstead St Mary *Chelmsf* 84-92; V Romford St Alb from 92. *St Alban's Vicarage, 3 Francombe Gardens, Romford RM1 2TH* Tel (01708) 473580

HINKES, Sidney George Stuart. b 25. Lon Univ BA50 BD70. St Steph Ho Ox 50. **d** 52 **p** 53. C Burton St Paul *Lich* 52-54; C Leigh St Clem *Chelmsf* 54-58; C Upton cum Chalvey *Ox* 58-66; C-in-c Bayswater St Mary CD 66-82; V Headington St Mary 83-90; rtd 90; Perm to Offic *B & W* from 90-91; *Bris* from 92; *Glouc* 03-05; Rtd Clergy Officer Malmesbury Adnry *Bris* 93-04. *1 The Bungalow, Bremilham Road, Malmesbury SN16 0DQ* Tel (01666) 825249 E-mail sidney@fish.co.uk

HINKLEY, Maureen. b 41. **d** 04. NSM Hollington St Jo *Chich* from 04. *8 Wadhurst Close, St Leonards-on-Sea TN37 7AZ* Tel (01424) 754872

HINKS (née CHAMBERS), Mrs Marion Patricia. b 48. Univ of Wales BDS72. SW Minl Tr Course 97. **d** 97 **p** 98. NSM Plymstock and Hooe *Ex* from 97. *52 Southland Park Road, Wembury, Plymouth PL9 0HQ* Tel (01752) 862439 Mobile 07889-291228 E-mail marion@southlandpark.freeserve.co.uk

HINKSMAN, Adrian James Terence. b 43. Open Univ BA76 Lon Inst of Educn DipEd82. St Alb and Ox Min Course 96. **d** 99 **p** 00. NSM Hemel Hempstead *St Alb* 99-02; NSM St Alb St Mary Marshalswick from 02; Dioc CME Officer from 02. *83 The Ridgeway, St Albans AL4 9NU* Tel (01727) 751230 E-mail adrian_hinksman@hotmail.com

HINKSMAN, Barrie Lawrence James. b 41. K Coll Lon BD64 AKC64 Birm Univ PhD02. St Boniface Warminster 61. **d** 65 **p** 66. C Crosby *Linc* 65-67; Ecum Development Officer Scunthorpe Coun of Chs 67-69; C Chelmsley Wood *Birm* 69-72; TV 72-75; P-in-c Offchurch *Cov* 75-79; Bp's Adv for Lay Tr 75-79; Perm to Offic 89-90; Hon Chapl Cov Cathl from 90; Perm to Offic *Birm* from 01; Hon Sen Fell Warw Univ *Cov* from 02.

Needlers End Cottage, 32 Stoneton Crescent, Balsall Common, Coventry CV7 7QG Tel (01676) 530085 Fax as telephone E-mail b.hinksman@btopenworld.com

HINSLEY, Robert Charles. b 77. Univ of Wales (Abth) BTh98. Cranmer Hall Dur 03. **d** 05. C Carlton-in-Lindrick and Langold w Oldcotes *S'well* from 05. *St Luke's Vicarage, Church Street, Langold, Worksop S81 9NW* Tel (01909) 730796 E-mail roberthinsley@yahoo.co.uk

HINTON, Mrs Frances Mary. b 43. EN(G)85. EMMTC 89. **d** 92 **p** 94. Par Dn Hornsey Rise Whitehall Park Team *Lon* 92-94; C 94-97; C Upper Holloway 97; TV Barking St Marg w St Patr *Chelmsf* 97-04; rtd 04. *7 Austen Walk, Lincoln LN2 4LP* Tel (01522) 533151 E-mail revfran@fish.co.uk

HINTON, Geoffrey. b 34. Bede Coll Dur BA56 Em Coll Cam MA67 Sussex Univ PGCE72. Ridley Hall Cam 58. **d** 60 **p** 61. C Cheltenham St Mary *Glouc* 60-61; C Beverley Minster *York* 61-65; C Newark St Mary *S'well* 70-71; rtd 99. *1 Northmoor Place, Oxford OX2 6XB* Tel (01865) 510267

HINTON, James William. b 63. Cov Poly BSc84 Leeds Univ PGCE86. St Jo Coll Nottm 00. **d** 02 **p** 03. C Thornbury *Bradf* 02-05; P-in-c Bowling St Steph from 05; C Lt Horton from 05. *St Stephen's Vicarage, 48 Newton Street, Bradford BD5 7BH* Tel (01274) 720784 *or* 391537

HINTON, Michael Ernest. b 33. K Coll Lon 53 St Boniface Warminster 56. **d** 57 **p** 58. C Babbacombe *Ex* 57-60; S Africa 60-66; P-in-c Limehouse St Pet *Lon* 66-68; R Felmingham *Nor* 68-72; R Suffield 68-72; P-in-c Colby w Banningham and Tuttington 68-72; Bahamas 72-76; P-in-c Mylor w Flushing *Truro* 76-77; V 77-80; R The Deverills *Sarum* 82-87; Bermuda 87-89; Virgin Is 89-91; Chapl Sequoian Retreat and Conf Progr from 91; rtd 98; Perm to Offic *St E* 00-01; *Ex* from 02. *Le Petit Pain, St Ann's Chapel, Kingsbridge TQ7 4HQ* Tel (01548) 810124 E-mail lacton.int@virgin.net

HINTON, Michael George. b 27. Mert Coll Ox BA48 MA51 Reading Univ PhD59. S Dios Minl Tr Scheme 81. **d** 83 **p** 84. NSM Weston-super-Mare St Paul *B & W* 83-85; NSM Sibertswold w Coldred *Cant* 85-87; NSM Eythorne and Elvington w Waldershare etc 87-95; Perm to Offic from 95. *212 The Gateway, Dover CT16 1LL* Tel (01304) 204198 Fax as telephone E-mail michael@hintonm.demon.co.uk

HINTON, Nigel Keith. b 49. Univ Coll Lon BSc70 Worc Coll of Educn PGCE73 Lon Univ MA87. Oak Hill NSM Course 89. **d** 92 **p** 93. NSM Cudham and Downe *Roch* from 92; Perm to Offic *Lon* from 03. *2 Runciman Close, Pratts Bottom, Orpington BR6 7SZ* Tel (01689) 855348

HINTON, Paul Robin George. b 64. St Jo Coll Dur BA86. Qu Coll Birm BA05. **d** 05. C Rowley Regis *Birm* from 05. *194 Hanover Road, Rowley Regis B65 9EQ* Tel 0121-559 3830 Mobile 07854-039251 E-mail hintons@bearwood64.fsnet.co.uk

HINTON, Robert Matthew. b 69. Lanc Univ BA91. Cranmer Hall Dur BA97. **d** 97 **p** 98. C Lache cum Saltney *Ches* 97-99; C Cheadle Hulme St Andr 99-02; V Hale Barns w Ringway from 02. *Ringway Vicarage, Wicker Lane, Hale Barns, Altrincham WA15 0HQ* Tel 0161-980 3955 *or* 980 3234 E-mail revrobhinton@hotmail.com

HIPKINS, Leslie Michael. b 35. Univ Coll Dur BA57 ACIS60. Oak Hill Th Coll 78 Westcott Ho Cam 89. **d** 81 **p** 82. NSM Halstead St Andr w H Trin and Greenstead Green *Chelmsf* 81-87; C Tolleshunt Knights w Tiptree and Gt Braxted 87-89; P-in-c Cratfield w Heveningham and Ubbeston etc *St E* 89-00; rtd 00; Perm to Offic *St E* from 01. *Laundry Farm, Thorington, Halesworth IP19 9JF* Tel (01502) 478675

HIPPISLEY-COX, Stephen David. b 63. Sheff Univ BSc85 PhD92 Peterho Cam BA98. Westcott Ho Cam 96. **d** 99 **p** 00. C Ollerton w Boughton *S'well* 99-02; NSM Wilford Hill from 02. *43 Willow Road, West Bridgford, Nottingham NG2 7AY* Tel 0115-945 2714 E-mail s.d.hippisley-cox@bigfoot.com

HIPPLE, Mrs Maureen AtLee. b 53. Miami-Dade Community Coll. **d** 94 **p** 94. USA 94-96 and from 97; Asst Min Tunkhannock St Patr 94-95; Asst Min Towanda Ch Ch 95-97 and 97-98; R from 98; NSM Portarlington w Cloneyhurke and Lea *M & K* 96-97. *RR 5, Box 5069-A, Towanda, PA 18848, USA* E-mail christchurch@sosbbs.com

HIRONS, Malcolm Percy. b 36. Oriel Coll Ox BA59 MA62. Wycliffe Hall Ox 59. **d** 61 **p** 62. C Edgbaston St Aug *Birm* 61-64; Chapl Warw Sch 64-65; C Beverley Minster *York* 65-69; V Barnby upon Don *Sheff* 69-80; P-in-c Kirk Bramwith 75-80; P-in-c Fenwick 75-80; V Norton Woodseats St Paul 80-98; rtd 98; Perm to Offic *Nor* from 98. *Broome Lodge, 8 Lincoln Square, Hunstanton PE36 6DL* Tel (01485) 532385

HIRST, Alan. b 44. Leeds Univ CQSW74. Linc Th Coll 79. **d** 81 **p** 82. C Newton Heath All SS *Man* 81-84; Chapl to the Deaf 84-88; V Oldham St Chad Limeside 88-91; Dep Chapl HM Pris Liv 91-92; Chapl HM Pris Ranby 92-96 and from 00; Chapl HM Pris Wakef 96-99. *HM Prison, Ranby, Retford DN22 8EU* Tel (01777) 862000

HIRST, Anthony Melville (Anthony Mary). b 50. Cuddesdon Coll 74. **d** 77 **p** 78. C S Gillingham *Roch* 77-80; C Coity w Nolton *Llan* 80-83; OSB from 81; R Hallaton w Horninghold, Allexton, Tugby etc *Leic* 83-90; R Arthog w Fairbourne w Llangelynnin w Rhoslefain *Ban* 90-97; R Montgomery and Forden and Llandyssil *St As* 97-04; V Bedford Leigh *Man* from 04. *The Parish House, 121 Green Lane, Leigh WN7 2TW* Tel (01942) 673519 E-mail ahirst@avnet.co.uk

HIRST, Arnold. *See* HIRST, Reginald Arnold Archer

HIRST, David William. b 37. Man Univ BA78. Brasted Th Coll 59 St Aid Birkenhead 61. **d** 63 **p** 64. C Clayton *Man* 63-64; C Bury St Jo 64-66; C Wythenshawe Wm Temple Ch 67-70; V Oldham St Chad Limeside 70-79; V Friezland 79-91; R Ashton St Mich 91-95; Chapl HM Pris Buckley Hall 95-00; Chapl HM Pris Wolds 00-02; rtd 02. *8 Priory Mews, Lytham St Annes FY8 4FT* Tel 07833-353837 (mobile)

HIRST, Canon Godfrey Ian. b 41. MBIM Univ of Wales (Lamp) BA63. Chich Th Coll 63. **d** 65 **p** 66. C Brierfield *Blackb* 65-68; Ind Chapl *Liv* 68-71; TV Kirkby 71-75; Ind Chapl *Blackb* 75-94; P-in-c Treales 75-87; Hon Can Blackb Cathl from 83; Can Res Blackb Cathl 87-94; V Lytham St Cuth from 94; AD Kirkham from 98. *The Vicarage, Church Road, Lytham St Annes FY8 5PX* Tel and fax (01253) 736168 Mobile 07885-118331 E-mail ghirst1@compuserve.com *or* ghirst@stcuthbertslytham.co.uk

HIRST, John Adrian. b 49. St Jo Coll Nottm BTh78. **d** 78 **p** 79. C Cheltenham St Mark *Glouc* 78-84; TV 84-85; TV Swan *Ox* 85-89; R Denham from 89. *The Rectory, Ashmead Lane, Denham, Uxbridge UB9 5BB* Tel (01895) 832771

HIRST, Mrs Judith. b 54. St Mary's Coll Dur BA76 LMH Ox PGCE77 Hull Univ MA86. Cranmer Hall Dur BA94. **d** 94 **p** 95. Bp's Adv in Past Care and Counselling *Dur* 94-00; C Dur St Oswald 94-00; Dir Min Formation Cranmer Hall Dur from 00. *St John's College, 3 South Bailey, Durham DH1 3RJ* Tel 0191-374 3500 Fax 374 3573

HIRST, Malcolm. b 62. Ilkley Coll BA84. Moorlands Bible Coll 86 Trin Coll Bris BA00. **d** 00 **p** 01. C Bromley Common St Aug *Roch* 00-03; C Farnborough from 03. *Church House, Leamington Avenue, Orpington BR6 9QB* Tel (01689) 856931 E-mail malcolm@port-vale.freeserve.co.uk

HIRST, Mrs Rachel Ann. b 58. Portsm Poly BA79 Hull Univ PGCE81 ACII85. NEOC 99. **d** 02 **p** 03. NSM Clifton *York* 02-04; C from 04. *13 Florence Grove, Rawcliffe, York YO30 5UR* Tel (01904) 340856 E-mail rhirst@fish.co.uk

HIRST, Reginald Arnold Archer. b 36. St Paul's Coll Grahamstown. **d** 60 **p** 61. S Africa 60-88; R Wickham *Portsm* from 88. *The Rectory, Southwick Road, Wickham, Fareham PO17 6HR* Tel (01329) 832134 Fax 835434 E-mail arnold@wykhirst.demon.co.uk

HISCOCK, Donald Henry. b 26. St Mich Th Coll Crafers 50 ACT ThL56. **d** 53 **p** 54. Australia 53 and from 65; SSM 54-82; C Averham w Kelham *S'well* 56-58; Lic to Offic 58-59; S Africa 59-60; Basutoland 60-61; rtd 92. *12 Charsley Street, Willagee, W Australia 6156* Tel (0061) (8) 9314 5192 *or* 9364 8472

HISCOCK, Gary Edward. b 43. Dip Drama68 Lon Univ DipRS88. Oak Hill Th Coll BA90. **d** 90 **p** 91. C Cheltenham St Luke and St Jo *Glouc* 90-94; C Hardwicke, Quedgeley and Elmore w Longney 95-96; rtd 96. *25 Bournside Road, Cheltenham GL51 3AL* Tel (01242) 513002

HISCOCK, Peter George Harold. b 31. Wadh Coll Ox BA54 MA66. Ely Th Coll 54. **d** 58 **p** 59. C Edgehill St Dunstan *Liv* 58-61; C Kirkby 61-64; C Southport St Luke 64-66; Asst Dean of Residence TCD 66-68; Dean of Res TCD 68-73; India 73-76; TV Jarrow *Dur* 77-82; Chapl Univ Coll Dur 82-87; RD Newc Cen *Newc* 87-94; P-in-c Dinnington 87-88; TV Ch the King 88-94; rtd 94; Perm to Offic *Lon* from 95. *8 Banbury Road, London E9 7DU* Tel (020) 8986 2252

HISCOCK, Phillip George. b 47. Southn Univ MPhil90 CertEd68 DipAdEd84 MIPD83. STETS 95. **d** 98 **p** 99. NSM Portchester and Chapl Portsm Docks *Portsm* 98-02; Chapl Dunkirk Miss to Seafarers *Eur* from 02. *Princess Alice House, 130 rue de l'Ecole Maternelle, 59140 Dunkerque, France* Tel (0033) (3) 28 59 04 36 Fax 28 66 09 05 E-mail phil.hiscock@mtsmail.org *or* flyingangelmtdk@netinfo.fr

HISCOCKS, Nicholas Robin Thomas. b 75. Keble Coll Ox BA96 MA01 Anglia Poly Univ MA01. Ridley Hall Cam 99. **d** 01 **p** 02. C Bromley Ch Ch *Roch* from 01. *56 Heathfield Road, Bromley BR1 3RW* Tel (020) 8466 9452 E-mail nrth@tinyworld.co.uk

HISCOX, Miss Denise. b 47. Lon Univ TCert68 Lanchester Poly BSc78. WMMTC 98. **d** 01 **p** 02. NSM Cov St Mary *Cov* 01-05; NSM Leamington Priors All SS from 05; NSM Leamington Spa H Trin and Old Milverton from 05. *48 Wainbody Avenue North, Coventry CV3 6DB* Tel (024) 7641 1034 E-mail denisehiscox@lineone.net

HISCOX, Jonathan Ronald James. b 64. Univ of Wales (Cardiff) DipTh85. Qu Coll Birm 87. **d** 89 **p** 90. C Wiveliscombe *B & W* 89-93; P-in-c Donyatt w Horton, Broadway and Ashill 93-94; TV Ilminster and Distr 94-02; R Rowde and Bromham *Sarum* from 02. *The Rectory, High Street, Bromham, Chippenham SN15 2HA* Tel (01380) 859750 E-mail hj56095@fish.co.uk

HISLOP, Martin Gregory. b 55. Jas Cook Univ Townsville BA78 Univ of S Aus MEd88. **d** 92 **p** 93. C N Mackay St Ambrose Australia 92-93; Dir Studies St Barn Coll of Min 93-94; Chapl Ballarat Univ 95-98; Asst Chapl St Mich Gr Sch and Assoc P E St Kilda 98; C Kingston St Luke *S'wark* 00-01; P-in-c 01-05; V from 05. *St Luke's Vicarage, 4 Burton Road, Kingston upon Thames KT2 5TE* Tel (020) 8546 4064 E-mail mhislop@btinternet.com

HITCH, Kim William. b 54. Leic Univ BSc75 K Coll Lon MA94. Trin Coll Bris 76. **d** 78 **p** 79. C Becontree St Mary *Chelmsf* 78-80; C Huyton Quarry *Liv* 80-83; V Hatcham St Jas *S'wark* 83-91; TR Kidbrooke 91-02; R Kidbrooke St Jas from 02; Dir Ords (Woolwich Area) from 05. *St James's Rectory, 62 Kidbrooke Park Road, London SE3 0DU* Tel (020) 8856 3438 Fax 08701-364983 E-mail hitchoffice@worldonline.co.uk

HITCHCOCK, David. b 37. MCIEH. S'wark Ord Course 70. **d** 73 **p** 74. NSM Milton next Gravesend Ch Ch *Roch* 73-94; NSM Chalk 96-98; CF (ACF) from 79; Perm to Offic *Lon* 93-02; NSM St Andr-by-the-Wardrobe w St Ann, Blackfriars from 02; NSM St Jas Garlickhythe w St Mich Queenhithe etc from 02. *148 Old Road East, Gravesend DA12 1PF* Tel (01474) 361091 E-mail hitch5@btinternet.com

HITCHENS (née GREEN), Mrs Catherine Isabel. b 48. Cant Sch of Min 89. **d** 92 **p** 94. C Willesborough *Cant* 92-96; Sen Asst P E Dereham and Scarning *Nor* 96-97; Asst Chapl HM Pris Wayland 96-97; Chapl HM Pris Leic 97-00; Chapl HM YOI Castington 00-02; Chapl HM Pris Cant from 02. *The Chaplain's Office, HM Prison, 46 Longport, Canterbury CT1 1PJ* Tel (01227) 862863

HITCHING, His Honour Judge Alan Norman. b 41. Ch Ch Ox BA62 MA66 BCL63 Barrister-at-Law (Middle Temple) 64. **d** 01 **p** 02. NSM High Ongar w Norton Mandeville *Chelmsf* from 01. *9 Monkhams Drive, Woodford Green IG8 0LG* Tel (020) 8504 4260 E-mail ahitching@lix.compulink.co.uk

HITCHINS, Graham Edward David. b 54. S Dios Minl Tr Scheme 91. **d** 94 **p** 95. C Bishop's Waltham *Portsm* 94-97; C Upham 94-97; C Honiton, Gittisham, Combe Raleigh, Monkton etc *Ex* 97-98; TV 98-03; Chapl RN from 03. *Royal Navy Chaplaincy Service, Room 203, Victory Building, HM Naval Base, Portsmouth PO1 3LS* Tel (023) 9272 7903 Fax 9272 7111

HITCHMAN, Keith John. b 62. Middx Univ BSc90. Trin Coll Bris BA95. **d** 95 **p** 96. C Bestwood *S'well* 95-99; Chapl Glos Univ 99-04; C Cheltenham St Mary, St Matt, St Paul and H Trin *Glouc* from 04. *27 Cleeve View Road, Cheltenham GL52 5NJ* Tel (01242) 575246 E-mail family.hitchman@virgin.net

HITCHMOUGH, William. b 30. N Ord Course. **d** 81 **p** 82. NSM Penketh *Liv* 81-83; Chapl Warrington Distr Gen Hosp 83-99; Perm to Offic *Liv* from 83 and *Guildf* from 00. *4 Rex Court, Haslemere GU27 1LJ* Tel (01428) 661504

HIZA, Douglas William. b 38. Richmond Univ Virginia BA60 MDiv63 Mankato State Univ MS70. Virginia Th Sem 60. **d** 63 **p** 64. USA 63-79; Chapl Hackney Hosp Gp Lon 80-95; Chapl Homerton Hosp Lon 80-95; Perm to Offic *Lon* from 96. *10 Meynal Crescent, London E9 7AS* Tel (020) 8985 7832

HJORTH, Rolf Gunnar Leer. b 25. St Jo Coll Ox BA46 MA50 AMICE. Wycliffe Hall Ox 61. **d** 62 **p** 63. C Cumnor *Ox* 62-65; V Bramfield and Walpole *St E* 65-69; V Oulton *Lich* 69-78; Chapl Ostend w Knokke and Bruges *Eur* 78-84; Chapl Düsseldorf 85-90; rtd 90; Perm to Offic *Lich* 99-03. *Carrer Dalma i Bernat 105, Begur, 17255 Girona, Spain* E-mail rolf.hjorth@carefree.net

HOAD, Anne Elizabeth. b 42. Bris Univ BA63. **dss** 69 **d** 94 **p** 95. Asst Chapl Imp Coll *Lon* 69-74; S'wark Lay Tr Scheme 74-77; Brixton St Matt *S'wark* 77-80; Charlton St Luke w H Trin 80-94; Project Worker Community of Women and Men 88-91; Voc Adv Lewisham from 91; Asst Chapl Lewisham Hosp 92-03; Hon C Lee Gd Shep w St Pet 94-03; C from 03. *14 Silk Close, London SE12 8DL* Tel (020) 8297 8761

HOAD, Miss Rosemary Claire. b 60. Cranmer Hall Dur 92. **d** 94 **p** 95. C Epsom St Martin *Guildf* 94-97; TV Brentford *Lon* from 97. *St Faith's Vicarage, 122 Windmill Road, Brentford TW8 9NA* Tel (020) 8560 3782 E-mail rosemary.hoad@btinternet.com

HOAR, George Stanley. b 20. Chich Th Coll 47. **d** 50 **p** 53. C Cullercoats St Geo *Newc* 50-52; C Old Brumby *Linc* 53-56; V Alvingham w N and S Cockerington 56-60; V Leake 60-71; V Castle Bytham 71-91; R Careby w Holywell and Aunby 73-91; R Lt Bytham 73-91; rtd 91; Perm to Offic *Pet* from 91. *1 Sulthorpe Road, Ketton, Stamford PE9 3SN* Tel (01780) 720817

HOARE, Carol. b 46. Lon Univ BA68 Birm Univ CertEd69. Qu Coll Birm 86 WMMTC 86. **d** 91 **p** 94. NSM Curdworth *Birm* 91-00; Perm to Offic from 00. *14 Elms Road, Sutton Coldfield B72 1JF* Tel 0121-354 1117

HOARE, David Albert Sylvester. b 47. **d** 95. C Gibraltar Cathl *Eur* 95-00. *3 Governor's Lane, Gibraltar*

HOARE, Canon David Marlyn. b 33. Bps' Coll Cheshunt 60. **d** 63 **p** 64. C Ampthill w Millbrook and Steppingley *St Alb* 63-67; C Bushey 67-70; V Harlington 70-76; V Oxhey All SS 76-81; V Hellesdon *Nor* 81-98; Hon Can Nor Cathl 95-98; rtd 98; Perm to Offic *Nor* from 98. *42 Starling Close, Aylsham, Norwich NR11 6XG* Tel (01263) 734565

HOARE, Diana Charlotte. Kent Univ BA78. WEMTC 02. **d** 05. C Bishop's Castle w Mainstone, Lydbury N etc *Heref* from 05. *The Vicarage, Lydbury North SY7 8AU* Tel (01588) 680609 Mobile 07989-432280 E-mail diana@stonescribe.com

HOARE (née CULLING), Elizabeth Ann. b 58. St Mary's Coll Dur BA76 St Jo Coll Dur PhD87 Rob Coll Cam BA88 PGCE80. Ridley Hall Cam 86. **d** 89 **p** 94. Par Dn S Cave and Ellerker w Broomfleet *York* 89-92; Tutor Cranmer Hall Dur 93-95; P-in-c Cherry Burton *York* 95-00; Abp's Sen Adv on Rural Affairs 95-98; Abp's Adv for Spiritual Direction 98-00; Chapl Bp Burton Coll York 95-00; Perm to Offic *York* 01-02; NSM Cowesby from 02; NSM Felixkirk w Boltby from 02; NSM Kirby Knowle from 02; NSM Leake w Over and Nether Silton and Kepwick from 02; Tutor and Lect Cranmer Hall Dur from 02. *Leake Vicarage, Knayton, Thirsk YO7 4AZ* Tel (01845) 537277 E-mail liz.wildgoose@bigfoot.com

HOARE, Janet Francis Mary. *See* MILES, Ms Janet Francis Mary

HOARE, Patrick Reginald Andrew Reid (Toddy). b 47. TD80 and Bar 88. Hull Univ MA90. Wycliffe Hall Ox 77. **d** 80 **p** 81. C Guisborough *York* 80-83; P-in-c Felixkirk w Boltby from 83; P-in-c Kirby Knowle from 83; P-in-c Leake w Over and Nether Silton and Kepwick from 83; P-in-c Cowesby from 83; CF (TA) 82-99. *Leake Vicarage, Knayton, Thirsk YO7 4AZ* Tel (01845) 537277

HOARE, Patrick Vernon Keymer. b 35. Oak Hill NSM Course 90. **d** 93 **p** 94. NSM Staines St Mary and St Pet *Lon* 93-96; P-in-c Littleton 95-99; rtd 00; Perm to Offic *Lon* from 03. *2 Saxonby Avenue, Sunbury-on-Thames TW16 5HP* Tel (01932) 700379

HOARE, Roger John. b 38. Tyndale Hall Bris 63. **d** 66 **p** 67. C Stoughton *Guildf* 66-70; C Chesham St Mary *Ox* 70-73; V Bath St Bart *B & W* 73-83; V Gt Faringdon w Lt Coxwell *Ox* 83-89; Deputation Appeals Org (NE Lon) Children's Soc 89-93; P-in-c Lambourne w Abridge and Stapleford Abbotts *Chelmsf* 93-03; Ind Chapl 93-03; rtd 03. *44 Anchor Road, Tiptree, Colchester CO5 0AP* Tel (01621) 817236 E-mail rogerhoare@aol.com

✠**HOARE, The Rt Revd Rupert William Noel.** b 40. Trin Coll Ox BA61 MA66 Fitzw Ho Cam BA64 MA84 Birm Univ PhD73. Kirchliche Hochschule Berlin 61 Westcott Ho Cam 62. **d** 64 **p** 65 **c** 93. C Oldham St Mary w St Pet *Man* 64-67; Lect Qu Coll Birm 68-72; Can Th Cov Cathl *Cov* 70-76; R Man Resurr *Man* 72-78; Can Res Birm Cathl *Birm* 78-81; Prin Westcott Ho Cam 81-93; Area Bp Dudley *Worc* 93-00; Hon Can Worc Cathl 93-00; Dean Liv from 00. *1 Cathedral Close, Liverpool L1 7BR* Tel 0151-708 0924 *or* 709 6271 Fax 702 7292

HOARE, Canon Simon Gerard. b 37. AKC61. **d** 62 **p** 63. C Headingley *Ripon* 62-65; C Adel 65-68; R Spofforth 68-71; R Spofforth w Kirk Deighton 71-77; V Rawdon *Bradf* 77-85; Hon Can Bradf Cathl 85-02; R Carleton and Lothersdale 85-02; Dioc Ecum Officer 85-94; rtd 02; Perm to Offic *Ripon* from 02. *Skell Villa, 20 Wellington Street, Ripon HG4 1PH* Tel (01765) 692187 E-mail sghoare@freenetname.co.uk

HOARE, Toddy. *See* HOARE, Patrick Reginald Andrew Reid

HOARE, Vernon. *See* HOARE, Patrick Vernon Keymer

HOBBS, Antony Ewan Talbot. b 25. Ripon Hall Ox 58. **d** 60 **p** 61. C Cuckfield *Chich* 62-64; V Staplefield Common 64-89; rtd 89; Perm to Offic *Chich* from 89. *Chippers, Chalvington, Hailsham BN27 3TE* Tel (01321) 811243

HOBBS (formerly DUFFUS), Mrs Barbara Rose. b 51. EMMTC. **d** 98 **p** 99. C Linc St Faith and St Martin w St Pet *Linc* 98-00; C Grantham 00-02; P-in-c Brothertoft Gp 02-04; Mental Health Chapl SE Lincs 02-04; P-in-c Hastings St Clem and All SS *Chich* from 04. *The Rectory, 7 High Street, Hastings TN34 3EY* Tel (01424) 422023 E-mail bduffus@fish.co.uk

HOBBS, Basil Ernest William. b 22. St Chad's Coll Dur BA49 DipTh50. **d** 51 **p** 52. C Mitcham St Mark *S'wark* 51-54; CF 54-68; Hon C Paddington H Trin w St Paul *Lon* 70-72; Asst Chapl St Mary's Hosp Praed Street Lon 69-72; Novice CR 72-74; Past Consultant Clinical Th Assn 74-84; Lic to Offic *S'well* 74-83; Chapl HM Pris Nottm 81-84; Hon C Nottingham St Andr *S'well* 83-84; C 84-86; TV Clifton 86-87; rtd 87; Perm to Offic *S'well* 87-00 and *Leic* from 99. *17 Stuart Court, High Street, Kibworth, Leicester LE8 0LR* Tel 0116-279 6367 E-mail bew.hobbs@zoom.co.uk

HOBBS, Christopher Bedo. b 61. Jes Coll Cam BA83 BTh90. Ridley Hall Cam 88. **d** 91 **p** 92. C Langham Place All So *Lon* 91-95; C Hull St Jo Newland *York* 95-00; V Selly Park St Steph and St Wulstan *Birm* from 00. *18 Sellywick Road, Birmingham B29 7JA* Tel 0121-472 0050 *or* 472 8253 E-mail ststephens@talk21.com *or* hoblet@compuserve.com

HOBBS, Christopher John Pearson. b 60. Sydney Univ BA82 K Coll Lon BD89 AKC89. Wycliffe Hall Ox 89. **d** 91 **p** 92. C S Mimms Ch Ch *Lon* 91-94; C Jesmond Clayton Memorial *Newc* 94-97; V Oakwood St Thos *Lon* from 97. *St Thomas's Vicarage, 2 Sheringham Avenue, London N14 4UE* Tel (020) 8360 1749 *or* tel and fax 8245 9152 E-mail christopher.hobbs@blueyonder.co.uk

HOBBS, Edward Quincey. b 74. Bris Univ BSc95. Wycliffe Hall Ox BA99. **d** 00 **p** 01. C Stapenhill w Cauldwell *Derby* 00-03; C

Newbury *Ox* from 03. *14 Strawberry Hill, Newbury RG14 1XJ* Tel (01635) 41922 E-mail e.q.hobbs@talk21.com

HOBBS, Ian. *See* HOBBS, Kenneth Ian

HOBBS, James. b 42. K Alfred's Coll Win CertEd64 Open Univ BA89 Hull Univ MA94 Lincs & Humberside Univ Dip Counselling 97. Linc Th Coll 66. **d** 68 **p** 69. C Moseley St Mary *Birm* 68-73; V Kingstanding St Mark 73-77; R Rushbrooke *St E* 77-78; R Bradfield St Geo 77-80; P-in-c Bradfield St Clare 77-80; P-in-c Felsham w Gedding 77-80; R Bradfield St George w Bradfield St Clare etc 80-84; P-in-c Gt and Lt Whelnetham 84-85; R Gt and Lt Whelnetham w Bradfield St George 85-90; Ecum Chapl for F&HE Grimsby *Linc* 90-97; Chapl Humberside Univ (Grimsby Campus) 90-97; Gen Preacher 92-97; V Ingham w Cammeringham w Fillingham 97-01; R Aisthorpe w Scampton w Thorpe le Fallows etc 97-01; P-in-c Burton by Linc 97-01; rtd 01; Perm to Offic *Linc* 01-04. *The Rectory, 7 High Street, Hastings TN34 3EY* Tel (01424) 422023 Mobile 08707-875032 E-mail jimhobbs@tiscali.co.uk

HOBBS, Mrs Joan Rosemary. b 39. Chelsea Coll Lon TDip61. WEMTC 97. **d** 00 **p** 01. NSM Cheltenham St Mary, St Matt, St Paul and H Trin *Glouc* 00-02; Perm to Offic 02-04; NSM Brimpsfield w Birdlip, Syde, Daglingworth etc from 04. *Manor Farmhouse, Woodmancote, Cirencester GL7 7EF* Tel and fax (01285) 831244 E-mail joan@hobbsjr.fsnet.co.uk

HOBBS, John Antony. b 36. S Dios Minl Tr Scheme. **d** 87 **p** 88. NSM Crowborough *Chich* from 87. *May Cottage, Alice Bright Lane, Crowborough TN6 3SQ* Tel (01892) 653909

HOBBS, Jonathan Noel Alan. b 70. Oak Hill Th Coll BA03. **d** 03. C Lindfield *Chich* from 03. *32 Noah's Ark Lane, Haywards Heath RH16 2LT* Tel (01444) 482989 E-mail jon@hobbs99.freeserve.co.uk

HOBBS, Kenneth Brian. b 47. Sussex Univ BA68 Lon Inst of Educn PGCE70. NTMTC 98. **d** 98 **p** 99. NSM Howell Hill *Guildf* 98-01; NSM Shere, Albury and Chilworth from 01. *Yeoman's Acre, Farley Green, Albury, Guildford GU5 9DN* Tel (01483) 202165 E-mail hobbs@farleygreen.net

HOBBS, Kenneth Ian. b 50. Oak Hill Th Coll 74. **d** 77 **p** 78. C Southborough St Pet w Ch Ch and St Matt *Roch* 77-80; C Hoole *Ches* 80-84; V Barnston 84-95; P-in-c Bedworth *Cov* 95; TR 95-01; RD Nuneaton 00-01; TR Radipole and Melcombe Regis *Sarum* from 01. *39 Icen Road, Weymouth DT3 5JL* Tel (01305) 785553 E-mail kih@fish.co.uk

HOBBS, Leslie. b 42. Sussex Univ BA64 Lon Bible Coll BD67. EAMTC. **d** 02 **p** 03. NSM Somerleyton, Ashby, Fritton, Herringfleet etc *Nor* from 02. *Nether End Cottage, Blacksmiths Loke, Lound, Lowestoft NR32 5LS* Tel (01502) 732536 Mobile 07833-753704

HOBBS, Ms Maureen Patricia. b 54. Surrey Univ BSc76 Warwick Univ 92. Westcott Ho Cam 95. **d** 97 **p** 98. C Shrewsbury St Chad w St Mary *Lich* 97-01; R Baschurch and Weston Lullingfield w Hordley from 01; Dioc Adv for Women in Min from 04. *The Rectory, Baschurch, Shrewsbury SY4 2EB* Tel (01939) 260305 E-mail hobbsmaureen@yahoo.co.uk

HOBBS, Michael Bedo. b 30. Fitzw Ho Cam BA58 MA62. Clifton Th Coll 58. **d** 60 **p** 61. C Southsea St Jude *Portsm* 60-63; Paraguay 63-65; Argentina 65-67; V Potters Green *Cov* 68-75; Distr Sec BFBS 75-82; R Plaxtol *Roch* 82-96; Dioc Miss Audits Consultant 90-96; rtd 96; Perm to Offic *Sarum* from 96. *Falcons, Barkers Hill, Semley, Shaftesbury SP7 9BH* Tel (01747) 828920

HOBBS, Ms Sarah Kathleen. b 72. Liv Univ BA94 UMIST BSc98 PGCE95. Wycliffe Hall Ox BA05. **d** 05. C W Ealing St Jo w St Jas *Lon* from 05. *41 Leighton Road, London W13 9EL* Tel (020) 8567 0241 Mobile 07808-580894 E-mail sarahkhobbs@hotmail.com

HOBBS, Sarah Louise. b 47. WEMTC 01. **d** 04 **p** 05. NSM Westbury-on-Severn w Flaxley, Blaisdon etc *Glouc* from 05. *Folly Cottage, Adsett Lane, Adsett, Westbury-on-Severn GL14 1PQ* Tel (01452) 760337 E-mail sarah@qhobbs.wanadoo.co.uk

HOBBS, Simon John. b 59. St Steph Ho Ox BA82 MA. **d** 83 **p** 84. C Middlesbrough Ascension *York* 83-85; C Stainton-in-Cleveland 85-88; C St Marylebone All SS *Lon* 88-90; P-in-c Paddington St Pet 90-94; C-in-c Grosvenor Chpl from 94; C Hanover Square St Geo from 94. *24 South Audley Street, London W1K 2PA* Tel and fax (020) 7499 1684 E-mail info@grosvenorchapel.force9.co.uk

HOBDAY, Peter Hugh Francis. b 34. IEng90. Oak Hill NSM Course 99. **d** 00 **p** 01. NSM Perivale *Lon* 00-05; Perm to Offic from 05. *41 Bilton Road, Greenford UB6 7BA* Tel (020) 8997 1250 Mobile 07778-007370 E-mail petehobday@aol.com

HOBDEN, Brian Charles. b 38. Oak Hill Th Coll 63. **d** 66 **p** 67. C S Lambeth St Steph *S'wark* 66-70; C Cheadle *Ches* 70-76; USA from 76; R Brandon 76-87; R Portsm St Jo 87-98; R Mesilla Park St Jas from 98; rtd 03. *3160 Executive Hills Road, Las Cruces, NM 88011, USA* Tel (001) (505) 521 9435 Fax 526 4821 E-mail stjames@lascruces.com

HOBDEN, Christopher Martin. b 49. Lon Univ BSc71. Oak Hill Th Coll 80. **d** 87 **p** 88. NSM St Marylebone All So w SS Pet and Jo *Lon* 87-88; NSM Langham Place All So 88-95. *10 Kent Terrace, London NW1 4RP*

HOBDEN, David Nicholas. b 54. K Coll Lon BD76 AKC76 Cam Univ PGCE. Ripon Coll Cuddesdon 77. **d** 78 **p** 79. C Marlborough *Sarum* 78-80; C Salisbury St Thos and St Edm 81-85; V Shalford *Guildf* 85-99; Asst Chapl R Surrey Co Hosp NHS Trust 99-00; Sen Chapl from 00. *Department of Pastoral Care, Royal Surrey County Hospital, Egerton Road, Guildford GU2 5XX* Tel (01483) 406835 *or* 571122 E-mail cmhobden@aol.com *or* dhobden@royalsurrey.nhs.uk

HOBDEN, Geoffrey William. b 46. DipTh. Trin Coll Bris 80. **d** 82 **p** 83. C Ex St Leon w H Trin *Ex* 82-86; V Weston-super-Mare Ch Ch *B & W* from 86; RD Locking 93-99. *Christ Church Vicarage, 18 Montpelier, Weston-super-Mare BS23 2RH* Tel (01934) 624376 Fax 641016 E-mail geoff@ccwsm.org.uk

HOBLEY, Ms Susan Elizabeth. b 51. Newc Univ BA74 Dur Univ PGCE75. NEOC 98. **d** 01 **p** 02. NSM Millfield St Mark and Pallion St Luke *Dur* 01-05; C Sheff St Mark Broomhill *Sheff* from 05. *9 Betjeman Gardens, Sheffield S10 3FW* Tel 0114-266 4343 E-mail sue@stmarkssheffield.co.uk

HOBROUGH, Mrs Margaret Edith. b 40. OBE97. Man Univ BA63 Newc Univ MEd75 K Coll Lon MTh80 FRSA94. STETS 01. **d** 03 **p** 04. NSM Godalming *Guildf* from 03. *257 Stoughton Road, Guildford GU2 9PQ* Tel (01483) 538390 Fax 562478 E-mail margarethobrough@v21.me.uk

HOBSON, Alexander. *See* HOBSON, John Alexander

HOBSON, Anthony Peter. b 53. St Jo Coll Cam BA74. St Jo Coll Nottm 75. **d** 77 **p** 78. C Brunswick *Man* 77-82; R Stretford St Bride 82-92; TR Hackney Marsh *Lon* 92-00; V Leic Martyrs *Leic* from 00. *The Vicarage, 17 Westcotes Drive, Leicester LE3 0QT* Tel 0116-254 6162 Fax as telephone E-mail martyrs@btconnect.com

HOBSON, Capt Barry Rodney. b 57. Open Univ BA98. Wilson Carlile Coll 82 EAMTC 97. **d** 98 **p** 99. CA from 85; C Warboys w Broughton and Bury w Wistow *Ely* 98-01; P-in-c Roxwell *Chelmsf* from 01. *The Vicarage, Vicarage Road, Roxwell, Chelmsford CM1 4NB* Tel (01245) 248157 E-mail b.hobson@btinternet.com

HOBSON, Jeremy Graeme. b 71. Lon Univ BMedSci95 MB, BS96. Oak Hill Th Coll BA03. **d** 03 **p** 04. C Eastbourne H Trin *Chich* from 03. *20 Chamberlain Road, Eastbourne BN21 1RU* Tel (01323) 642406 E-mail thehobsons@onetel.com

HOBSON, John Alexander (Alex). b 70. LMH Ox BA91 MA02 York Univ MA94. Wycliffe Hall Ox BA01. **d** 02 **p** 03. C Aynho and Croughton w Evenley etc *Pet* 02-05; Chapl RAF from 05. *Chaplaincy Services (RAF), HQ, Personnel and Training Command, RAF Innsworth, Gloucester GL3 1EZ* Tel (01452) 712612 ext 5164 Fax 510828 E-mail hobson@oxfree.com

HOBSON, Canon Patrick John Bogan. b 33. MC53. Magd Coll Cam BA56 MA60. S'wark Ord Course 75 Qu Coll Birm 77. **d** 79 **p** 80. C St Jo in Bedwardine *Worc* 79-81; R Clifton-on-Teme, Lower Sapey and the Shelsleys 81-88; TR Waltham H Cross *Chelmsf* 88-98; Hon Can Chelmsf Cathl 95-98; rtd 98. *24 Cunliffe Close, Oxford OX2 7BL* Tel (01865) 556206 Fax as telephone E-mail patrick.hobson@talk21.com

HOBSON, Peter. *See* HOBSON, Anthony Peter

HOBSON, Mrs Yvonne Mary. b 45. Ex Univ BTh03. SW Minl Tr Course 00. **d** 03 **p** 04. C St Illogan *Truro* from 03. *Church House, 46 Bosmeor Park, Redruth TR15 3JN* Tel (01209) 218753 E-mail revmeup@bosmeor.plus.com

HOCKEN, Glen Rundle. b 59. ACA84 Kent Univ BA80 Southlands Coll Lon PGCE90. Wycliffe Hall Ox 90. **d** 92 **p** 93. C Cogges *Ox* 92-94; C Cogges and S Leigh 94-96; C Boldmere *Birm* 96-99; TV Southgate *Chich* from 99. *Holy Trinity House, Titmus Drive, Crawley RH10 5EU* Tel (01293) 525809

HOCKEY (née LOOMES), Gaenor Mary. b 65. Hull Univ BA92 RGN86. St Jo Coll Nottm MPhil93. **d** 96 **p** 97. C Charles w Plymouth St Matthias *Ex* 96-00; C Devonport St Aubyn 00-05; Perm to Offic from 05. *St Aubyn's Vicarage, Chapel Street, Devonport, Plymouth PL1 4DP* Tel (01752) 565203 E-mail gaenor@fish.co.uk *or* gaenorloomes@hotmail.com

HOCKEY, Paul Henry. b 49. Oak Hill Th Coll BA86. **d** 86 **p** 87. C Dalton-in-Furness *Carl* 86-89; R Clifton, Brougham and Cliburn 89-94; V Fremington *Ex* from 94; Chapl Children's Hospice SW from 97. *The Vicarage, Fremington, Barnstaple EX31 2NX* Tel (01271) 373879

HOCKING, Canon Hugh Michael Warwick. b 12. VRD54. Ch Coll Cam BA34 MA38. Westcott Ho Cam 34. **d** 36 **p** 37. C Hackney St Jo *Lon* 36-37; C Stoke Damerel *Ex* 37-39; Chapl RNVR 39-46; V Madron w Morvah *Truro* 46-54; Chapl Poltair Hosp 50-54; V Bris St Ambrose Whitehall *Bris* 54-62; R Guildf H Trin w St Mary *Guildf* 62-77; Chapl St Luke's Hosp Guildf 63-77; Hon Can Guildf Cathl *Guildf* 68-77; rtd 77; Chapl W Cornwall Hosp Penzance 78-97; Perm to Offic *Ex* from 97. *23 Gracey Court, Woodland Road, Broadclyst, Exeter EX5 3GA* Tel (01392) 465170

HOCKING, Paul Frederick. b 43. Chich Th Coll 84. **d** 86 **p** 87. C Whitton and Thurleston w Akenham *St E* 86-89; V Ipswich All Hallows 89-91; P-in-c Gt Cornard 91-98; V 98; P-in-c Woolpit w Drinkstone 98-03; R 03-05; rtd 05; Perm to Offic *St E* from 05.

32 Spriteshall Lane, Trimley St Mary, Felixstowe IP11 9QY Tel (01394) 277600 E-mail mhock33733@aol.com

HOCKLEY, Paul William. b 47. Chu Coll Cam BA68 MA72 Nottm Univ BA73. St Jo Coll Nottm 71. **d** 74 **p** 75. C Chatham St Phil and St Jas *Roch* 74-78; C Tunbridge Wells St Jo 78-81; V Penketh *Liv* from 81. *St Paul's Vicarage, 6 Poplar Avenue, Penketh, Warrington WA5 2EH* Tel (01925) 723492 Fax 486945 E-mail paul-hockley@lineone.net

HOCKLEY, Canon Raymond Alan. b 29. LRAM53 Em Coll Cam MA71. Westcott Ho Cam 56. **d** 58 **p** 59. C Endcliffe *Sheff* 58-61; P-in-c Wicker w Neepsend 61-63; Chapl Westcott Ho Cam 63-68; Chapl Em Coll Cam 68-76; Can Res and Prec York Minster *York* 76-95; rtd 95; Perm to Offic *York* from 95. *College of St Barnabas, Blackberry Lane, Lingfield RH7 6NJ*

HOCKNULL, Mark Dennis. b 63. Surrey Univ BSc85 Univ Coll Lon PhD89. Cranmer Hall Dur BA93. **d** 94 **p** 95. C Prenton *Ches* 94-96; C Runcorn All SS and Runcorn St Mich 96-99; V Gt Meols 99-05; CME Officer *Linc* from 05; Lic Preacher from 05. *105 Nettleham Road, Lincoln LN2 1RU* E-mail mark.hocknull@btinternet.com

HOCKRIDGE, Joan. b 25. Girton Coll Cam BA47 MA50. St Steph Ho Ox 82. **dss** 83 **d** 87 **p** 94. Ealing Ascension Hanger Hill *Lon* 83-88; Hon C 87-88; Hon C Hanger Hill Ascension and W Twyford St Mary 88-92; Hon C Hillingdon St Jo 92-95; Perm to Offic 95-00. *17 Mead Way, Ruislip HA4 7QW* Tel (01895) 622643

HODDER, Christopher John. b 75. Huddersfield Univ BA96. St Jo Coll Nottm BTh00. **d** 01 **p** 02. C Loughborough Em and St Mary in Charnwood *Leic* 01-05; Chapl Derby Univ *Derby* from 05; Chapl Derby Cathl from 05. *1 Peet Street, Derby DE22 3RF* Tel (01332) 594172 *or* 591878 E-mail chrisandlou@clhodder.freeserve.co.uk *or* c.hodder@derby.ac.uk

HODDER, John Kenneth. b 45. Edin Univ MA68. Cuddesdon Coll 71. **d** 73 **p** 74. C Kibworth Beauchamp *Leic* 73-76; C Whittlesey *Ely* 76-80; R Downham 80-87; P-in-c Coveney 80-81; R 81-87; R Nunney and Witham Friary, Marston Bigot etc *B & W* from 87. *The Rectory, High Street, Nunney, Frome BA11 4LZ* Tel (01373) 836732

HODDER, Trevor Valentine. b 31. Bps' Coll Cheshunt 65. **d** 67 **p** 68. C Oxhey All SS *St Alb* 67-70; C Digswell 70-73; V Colchester St Anne *Chelmsf* 74-96; rtd 96; Perm to Offic *Chelmsf* from 00. *30 Drury Road, Colchester CO2 7UX* Tel (01206) 766480

HODGE, Albert. b 40. N Ord Course 84. **d** 87 **p** 88. C Huyton St Geo *Liv* 87-89; P-in-c Widnes St Paul 89-97; Chapl Halton Coll of FE 89-97; C Linton in Craven *Bradf* from 97; C Burnsall w Rylstone from 97; rtd 05. *The Rectory, Burnsall, Skipton BD23 6BP* Tel (01756) 720331

HODGE, Anthony Charles. b 43. AKC66. **d** 67 **p** 68. C Carrington *S'well* 67-69; C Bawtry w Austerfield 69-72; C Misson 69-72; Grenada 72-74; Trinidad and Tobago 74-76; V Tuckingmill *Truro* 76-78; V Worksop St Paul *S'well* 78-81; P-in-c Patrington w Hollym, Welwick and Winestead *York* 81-86; R 86-88; V York St Olave w St Giles from 88; V York St Helen w St Martin from 97; Chapl York Coll for Girls 88-96. *St Olave's Vicarage, 52 Bootham, York YO30 7BZ* Tel (01904) 625186 Mobile 07803-042987 E-mail anthony.hodge@stolave.org.uk

HODGE, Colin. b 39. Sarum & Wells Th Coll. **d** 83 **p** 84. NSM Wareham *Sarum* 84-87; C Parkstone St Pet w Branksea and St Osmund 87-89; V Lilliput 89-00; rtd 00; Perm to Offic *Sarum* from 01. *35 Stowell Crescent, Wareham BH20 4PT* Tel (01929) 553222

HODGE, Graham Anthony. b 49. Linc Th Coll 79. **d** 80 **p** 81. C Hale *Guildf* 80-82; C Christchurch *Win* 82-86; R Chawton and Farringdon 86-96; rtd 96. *6 Reads Field, Four Marks, Alton GU34 5DS* Tel (01420) 561782

HODGE, Canon Michael Robert. b 34. Pemb Coll Cam BA57 MA61. Ridley Hall Cam 57. **d** 59 **p** 60. C Harpurhey Ch Ch *Man* 59; C Blackpool St Mark *Blackb* 59-62; V Stalybridge Old St Geo *Man* 62-67; R Cobham w Luddesdowne and Dode *Roch* 67-81; Hon Can Roch Cathl 81-99; R Bidborough 81-99; rtd 99; Hon C Chale *Portsm* from 99; Hon C Gatcombe from 99; Hon C Shorwell w Kingston from 99; Asst to RD W Wight from 99. *Braxton Cottage, Halletts Shute, Norton, Yarmouth PO41 0RH* Tel and fax (01983) 761121 Mobile 07941-232983 E-mail michael.hodge.1954@pem.cam.ac.uk

HODGE, Nigel John. b 61. BTh83 Open Univ BSc97 Univ of Wales DPS85 MIBiol98. St Mich Coll Llan 83. **d** 85 **p** 86. C Mynyddislwyn *Mon* 85-87; C Machen 87-89; TV Ebbw Vale 89-91; V Abercarn 91-98; Lic to Offic from 99. *6 Maple Terrace, Abercarn, Newport NP11 5JF* Tel (01495) 249014

HODGES, Francis Reginald. b 26. Selw Coll Cam BA48 MA61. Chich Th Coll 48. **d** 50 **p** 51. C Portsea St Alb *Portsm* 50-56; Prior Ho of the Resurr Mirfield 56-58; C Heref All SS *Heref* 58-61; R St Breoke *Truro* 61-76; rtd 76; C St Kew *Truro* 77-78; P-in-c 78-80. *The Fore Dore Home, Trebathic, Wadebridge PL27 6SB* Tel (01208) 863471

HODGES, Ian. Ridley Hall Cam. **d** 05. C Llantrisant *Llan* from 05. *36 Danygraig Heights, Talbot Green, Pontyclun CF72 8FD* Tel (01443) 226508

HODGES, Jasper Tor. b 62. Leeds Univ BSc84 Sheff Univ MEng85 Lon Univ PGCE87. Trin Coll Bris BA94. **d** 94 **p** 95. C Holbeck *Ripon* 94-97; C Ealing St Steph Castle Hill *Lon* 97-04; V Arbourthorne and Norfolk Park *Sheff* from 04. *St Paul's and St Leonard's Vicarage, 458B East Bank Road, Sheffield S2 2AD* Tel 0114-239 8533 Fax 08701-687299 E-mail jasper@live.freeserve.co.uk

HODGES, Keith Michael. b 53. Southn Univ BTh82 Heythrop Coll Lon MA04. Chich Th Coll 77. **d** 80 **p** 81. C Sydenham St Phil *S'wark* 80-84; Perm to Offic 85; C Leatherhead *Guildf* 86-89; V Aldershot St Aug from 89. *St Augustine's Vicarage, Holly Road, Aldershot GU12 4SE* Tel (01252) 320840 E-mail father.keith@ntlworld.com

HODGES, Mrs Laura. b 53. St Alb and Ox Min Course 01. **d** 04 **p** 05. NSM Abingdon *Ox* from 04. *38 Baker Road, Abingdon OX14 5LW* Tel (01235) 527654 E-mail laura.hodges@btinternet.com

HODGES, Miss Stefanie Margaret. b 54. Trin Coll Bris DipHE95. **d** 97. C Croydon Ch Ch *S'wark* 97-99; C Sutton St Nic 99-02; TV Mildenhall *St E* from 02. *The Vicarage, 2 Oak Drive, Beck Row, Bury St Edmunds IP28 8UA* Tel (01638) 717331

HODGETTS, Alan Paul. b 54. Birm Poly BSc78 Heythrop Coll Lon MA96. St Steph Ho Ox 79. **d** 82 **p** 83. C Perry Barr *Birm* 82-85; C Broseley w Benthall *Heref* 85-87; V Effingham w Lt Bookham *Guildf* 87-96; R Merrow from 96. *The Rectory, 232 Epsom Road, Guildford GU4 7AA* Tel (01483) 504311 E-mail alanphodgetts@netscape.net

HODGETTS, Colin William John. b 40. St D Coll Lamp BA61 Ripon Hall Ox 61. **d** 63 **p** 64. C Hackney St Jo *Lon* 63-68; Hon C St Martin-in-the-Fields 70-76; C Creeksea w Althorne *Chelmsf* 76-79; Perm to Offic *Ex* 84-03; C Parkham, Alwington, Buckland Brewer etc from 03. *Quincott, Cheristowe, Hartland, Bideford EX39 6DA* Tel (01237) 441426 E-mail colin-julia@hartland.swinternet.co.uk

HODGETTS, Harry Samuel. b 30. Chich Th Coll 63. **d** 65 **p** 66. C Harton Colliery *Dur* 65-68; C Penzance St Mary *Truro* 68-70; V Penwerris 70-79; V Kettering St Mary *Pet* 79-94; rtd 95; Perm to Offic *Win* from 03. *20 Crofton Close, Christchurch BH23 2JN* Tel (01202) 474456

HODGINS, Miss Kylie Anne. b 68. SEITE 98. **d** 02 **p** 03. C Histon *Ely* from 02; C Impington from 02. *60 Impington Lane, Impington, Cambridge CB4 9NJ* Tel (01223) 236887 E-mail kylie.hodgins@dial.pipex.com

HODGINS, Philip Arthur. b 57. Lanc Univ BA78 Bradf Univ MBA90 MCIPD94. Linc Th Coll 82. **d** 85 **p** 86. C Norton *Ches* 85-88; C Whitkirk *Ripon* 88-89; Perm to Offic *Bradf* 89-90 and *Chich* 91-02; Hon C Chiddingly w E Hoathly *Chich* 02-04; P-in-c from 04. *The Rectory, Rectory Close, East Hoathly, Lewes BN8 6EG* Tel (01825) 840270 E-mail philhodgins@btinternet.com

HODGKINSON, Canon John. b 27. Trin Hall Cam BA51 MA55. Linc Th Coll 51. **d** 53 **p** 54. C Penrith St Andr *Carl* 53-56; C Linc St Nic w St Jo Newport *Linc* 56-58; C-in-c Lin St Jo Bapt CD 58-63; V Linc St Jo 63-66; R Old Brumby 66-71; V Kendal H Trin *Carl* 71-90; Hon Can Carl Cathl 84-90; rtd 90; Perm to Offic *Carl* from 90. *Boxtree Barn, Levens, Kendal LA8 8NZ* Tel (01539) 560806 E-mail boxtreebarn@hotmail.com

HODGKINSON, John David. b 57. Birm Univ BA78 Edin Univ BD89. Edin Th Coll 86. **d** 89 **p** 90. C Briercliffe *Blackb* 89-92; C Darwen St Cuth w Tockholes St Steph 92-94; R Harrington *Carl* 94-00; V Walney Is from 00. *The Vicarage, Promenade, Walney, Barrow-in-Furness LA14 3QU* Tel (01229) 471268

HODGKINSON, Oswald Merchant. b 21. Qu Coll Birm 68. **d** 69 **p** 70. C Shard End *Birm* 69-74; V 74-80; TV Wrexham *St As* 80-86; rtd 86; Perm to Offic *St As* and *Ban* from 86. *Brackenrigg, Bryn Pydew Road, Bryn Pydew, Llandudno Junction LL31 9JH* Tel (01492) 540395

HODGSON, Ms Amanda Jane. b 66. Westmr Coll Ox BA88 St Andr Univ Dip Div 93 Heythrop Coll Lon MA99. Westcott Ho Cam CTM96. **d** 96 **p** 97. C Epping Distr *Chelmsf* 96-01; TV Wythenshawe *Man* from 01. *St Luke's Vicarage, Brownley Road, Wythenshawe, Manchester M22 4PT* Tel 0161-998 2071 E-mail revmand@aol.com

HODGSON, Anthony Owen Langlois. b 35. Ripon Hall Ox 60. **d** 62 **p** 63. C Stiffkey w Morston and Blakeney w Lt Langham *Nor* 62-65; C Paddington Ch Ch *Lon* 66-70; Area Sec (Beds & Cambs) Chr Aid 70-74; (Herts & Hunts) 70-73; (Rutland & Northants) 73-74; V Gt w Lt Gidding and Steeple Gidding *Ely* 77-81; Warden Dovedale Ho 81-89; P-in-c Ilam w Blore Ray and Okeover *Lich* 81-89; Dir Chr Rural Cen 89-91; C Checkley and Stramshall 91-97; TV Uttoxeter Area 97-00; rtd 00. *Ferrar House, Little Gidding, Huntingdon PE28 5RJ*

HODGSON, Antony Robert. b 66. Dundee Univ MA88 Jes Coll Cam BA92 MA96 Lanc Univ MA04. Westcott Ho Cam 90 Ven English Coll Rome 92. **d** 93 **p** 94. C Chorley St Geo *Blackb*

93-96; C Lytham St Cuth 96-99; V St Annes St Marg from 99. *St Margaret's Vicarage, 24 Chatsworth Road, Lytham St Annes FY8 2JN* Tel (01253) 722648

HODGSON, Christopher. b 24. Oriel Coll Ox BA49 MA54. Qu Coll Birm 50. **d** 52 **p** 53. C Cheltenham Ch Ch *Glouc* 52-55; C Liv Our Lady and St Nic *Liv* 55-57; V Anfield St Columba 57-64; V Pembury *Roch* 64-82; Chapl Pembury Hosp Tunbridge Wells 66-82; R Aynho w Newbottle and Charlton *Pet* 82-85; Chapl Burrswood Cen for Divine Healing 85-94; C Castle Bromwich St Clem *Birm* 86-94; rtd 94. *6 The Covers, Seaford BN25 1DF* Tel (01323) 896461

HODGSON, Canon David George. b 54. Coll of Resurr Mirfield. **d** 82 **p** 83. C Stainton-in-Cleveland *York* 82-87; R Loftus 87; P-in-c Carlin How w Skinningrove 87; R Loftus and Carlin How w Skinningrove 87-93; V Middlesbrough Ascension from 93; P-in-c S Bank from 03; RD Middlesbrough from 98; Can and Preb York Minster from 01. *The Ascension Vicarage, Penrith Road, Middlesbrough TS3 7JR* Tel (01642) 244857

HODGSON, David Peter. b 56. Fitzw Coll Cam BA77 MA81 Nottm Univ BA82 MTh85. St Jo Coll Nottm 80. **d** 83 **p** 84. C Guiseley w Esholt *Bradf* 83-86; Asst Chapl Loughb Univ *Leic* 86-89; P-in-c Hatfield Broad Oak *Chelmsf* 89-90; P-in-c Bush End 89-90; P-in-c Hatfield Broad Oak and Bush End 90-97; Ind Chapl to Harlow 89-97; R Wokingham All SS *Ox* from 97; AD Sonning from 04. *The Rectory, 2A Norreys Avenue, Wokingham RG40 1TU* Tel 0118-979 2999
E-mail david@allsaints.prestel.co.uk

HODGSON, Derek. *See* HODGSON, The Ven John Derek

HODGSON, Derek Cyril. b 29. Hatf Coll Dur BA50. **d** 54 **p** 55. C Lindley *Wakef* 54-58; C-in-c Mixenden CD 58-62; V Thurlstone 62-75; V Mytholm Royd 75-97; rtd 97; Perm to Offic *York* from 98. *The Autumn Barn, Bishop Wilton, York YO42 1TF* Tel (01759) 368741

HODGSON, Gary Stuart. b 65. Ridley Hall Cam CTM98. **d** 98 **p** 99. C S Ossett *Wakef* 98-01; V Kirkburton from 01. *The Vicarage, 3B Shelley Lane, Kirkburton, Huddersfield HD8 0SJ* Tel (01484) 602188 E-mail gary@garyhodgson.freeserve.co.uk

HODGSON, George. b 36. Qu Coll Birm 75. **d** 78 **p** 79. NSM Wordsley *Lich* 78-93; NSM Wordsley *Worc* from 93; Perm to Offic 84-93. *1 Newfield Drive, Kingswinford DY6 8HY* Tel (01384) 292543 Mobile 07811-753160
E-mail george@hodgson25.freeserve.co.uk

HODGSON, Mrs Helen Mary. b 66. N Ord Course 01. **d** 04 **p** 05. C Flockton cum Denby Grange *Wakef* from 04; C Emley from 04. *The Vicarage, 3B Shelley Lane, Kirkburton, Huddersfield HD8 0SJ* Tel (01484) 602188
E-mail helen@helenhodgson.freeserve.co.uk

HODGSON, John. b 35. St Jo Coll Cam MA62 Lon Univ BD61. St Deiniol's Hawarden 80. **d** 81 **p** 82. Hon C Padiham *Blackb* 81-84; C W Burnley All SS 85-87; V 87-95; rtd 95; Perm to Offic *Worc* 95-02 and *Glouc* 98-02. *15 Acton Crescent, Felton, Morpeth NE65 9NF* Tel (01670) 787665

HODGSON, The Ven John Derek. b 31. St Jo Coll Dur BA53. Cranmer Hall Dur DipTh59. **d** 59 **p** 60. C Stranton *Dur* 59-62; C Monkwearmouth St Andr 62-64; V Stillington 64-66; V Consett 66-75; TR Gateshead 75-83; RD Gateshead 76-83; Hon Can Dur Cathl 78-83; Can Res Dur Cathl 83-97; Adn Auckland 83-93; Adn Dur 93-97; rtd 97. *45 Woodside, Barnard Castle, Durham DL12 8DZ* Tel (01833) 690557

HODGSON, Kenneth Jonah. b 36. Open Univ BA79 CQSW89. Oak Hill Th Coll. **d** 69 **p** 70. C Rainford *Liv* 69-72; C Fazakerley Em 72-74; TV 74-78; Soc Worker 78-96; CF 79-82; rtd 00; C Wallasey St Hilary *Ches* from 01. *134 Rake Lane, Wallasey, Merseyside CH45 1JW* Tel 0151-639 2980 Fax as telephone

HODGSON, Roger Vaughan. b 27. Magd Coll Cam BA49 MA54. Cuddesdon Coll 55. **d** 56 **p** 57. C Westmr St Matt *Lon* 56-59; C Pimlico St Pet w Westmr Ch Ch 59-65; R Lt Hadham *St Alb* 65-78; Chapl Oporto *Eur* 78-80; Chapl and Lect St Deiniol's Lib Hawarden 81-82; V Coldwaltham *Chich* 82-92; rtd 92; Asst Chapl Costa Blanca *Eur* 92-94; Perm to Offic *Chich* from 94. *2 Bakers Arms Hill, Arundel BN18 9DA* Tel (01903) 884708

HODGSON, The Ven Thomas Richard Burnham. b 26. FRMetS88. Lon Coll of Div BD52 ALCD52. **d** 52 **p** 53. C Crosthwaite Kendal *Carl* 52-55; C Stanwix 55-59; V Whitehaven St Nic 59-65; R Aikton 65-67; Bp's Dom Chapl and V Raughton Head w Gatesgill 67-73; Dir of Ords 70-74; Hon Can Carl Cathl 72-91; V Grange-over-Sands 73-79; RD Windermere 76-79; Adn W Cumberland 79-91; V Mosser 79-83; rtd 91; Perm to Offic *Carl* from 91. *58 Greenacres, Wetheral, Carlisle CA4 8LD* Tel (01228) 561159

HODGSON, Vernon Charles. b 34. MRPharmS58 Lon Univ BPharm58 Univ of Wales (Cardiff) DPS91. St Mich Coll Llan 90 Llan Dioc Tr Scheme 83. **d** 86 **p** 87. NSM Roath *Llan* 86-91; C Caerphilly 91-93; V Llanbister w Llanbadarn Fynydd w Llananno *S & B* 93-97; V Llanddewi Ystradenni 94-97; V Llanbister w Llanbadarn Fynydd w Llananno etc 97-01; rtd 01. *114 Carisbrooke Way, Cyncoed, Cardiff CF23 9HX* Tel (029) 2045 3403

HODKINSON, George Leslie. b 48. Qu Coll Birm 86. **d** 88 **p** 89. C Hall Green St Pet *Birm* 88-91; TV Solihull 91-96; P-in-c Billesley Common 96-00; V from 00; AD Moseley 01-02. *Holy Cross Vicarage, 29 Beauchamp Road, Birmingham B13 0NS* Tel 0121-444 1737

HODSON, Gordon George. b 35. St Chad's Coll Dur BA59 DipTh60. **d** 60 **p** 61. C Tettenhall Regis *Lich* 60-64; C Rugeley 64-68; V Shrewsbury St Mich 68-74; V Kinnerley w Melverley 74-87; P-in-c Knockin w Maesbrook 75-87; P-in-c Chebsey 87-91; P-in-c Seighford, Derrington and Cresswell 87-91; V Chebsey, Ellenhall and Seighford-with-Creswell 91-00; rtd 00; Perm to Offic *Lich* from 01. *27 Oak Drive, Oswestry SY11 2RU* Tel (01691) 662849

HODSON, Keith. b 53. Hatf Coll Dur BA74. Wycliffe Hall Ox 77. **d** 80 **p** 81. C Ashton-upon-Mersey St Mary *Ches* 80-84; C Polegate *Chich* 84-92; V Baddesley Ensor w Grendon *Birm* from 92. *The Vicarage, 75 Newlands Road, Baddesley Ensor, Atherstone CV9 2BY* Tel (01827) 715327
E-mail keithhodson@talk21.com

HODSON, Miss Margaret Christina. b 39. Linc Th Coll 88. **d** 90 **p** 94. Par Dn Old Trafford St Jo *Man* 90-94; C 94-95; P-in-c Calderbrook and Shore 95-01; rtd 01. *53 Lon Thelwal, Benllech, Tyn-y-Gongl LL74 8QH* Tel (01248) 852990

HODSON, Mrs Margot Rosemary. b 60. Bris Univ BSc82 PGCE83. All Nations Chr Coll 87 St Alb and Ox Min Course 99. **d** 01 **p** 02. C Grove *Ox* 01-04; Chapl Jes Coll Ox from 04. *Jesus College, Oxford OX1 3DW* Tel (01865) 279757
E-mail margot.hodson@jesus.ox.ac.uk

HODSON, Canon Raymond Leslie. b 42. St Chad's Coll Dur BSc64 DipTh66. **d** 66 **p** 67. C Adlington *Blackb* 66-68; C Cleveleys 68-72; V Ewood 72-77; V Nazeing *Chelmsf* 77-84; R Ampthill w Millbrook and Steppingley *St Alb* 84-95; Chapl Madrid *Eur* 95-04; Can Gib Cathl 02-04; rtd 04. *Mataro 1, 1 dcha, 28034 Madrid, Spain*

HODSON, William. b 42. Man Univ BA. Cranmer Hall Dur 81. **d** 82 **p** 83. C Ashton St Mich *Man* 82-86; V Tintwistle *Ches* 86-93; P-in-c Weston 93-99; rtd 99. *10 St Anne's Road, Horwich, Bolton BL6 7EJ* Tel (01204) 696172
E-mail bill.hodson@btopenworld.com

HOEY, David Paul. b 57. QUB BD79. CITC 79. **d** 81 **p** 82. C Belfast Whiterock *Conn* 81-83; C Portadown St Mark *Arm* 83-84; I Cleenish w Mullaghdun *Clogh* 84-90; I Magheracross 90-03; Dir of Ords 91-03; Can Clogh Cathl 95-03; Min Consultant for Ireland CPAS from 03. *44 Laragh, Ballycassidy, Enniskillen BT4 2JT* Tel (028) 6632 9655 Mobile 07712-873322
E-mail dphoey@btinternet.com *or* phoey@cpas.org.uk

HOEY, The Ven Raymond George. b 46. TCD BA70 MA. **d** 72 **p** 73. C Portadown St Mark *Arm* 72-78; I Camlough w Mullaglass from 78; Dom Chapl to Abp Arm from 86; Adn Arm from 92. *2 Maytown Road, Bessbrook, Newry BT35 7LY* Tel and fax (028) 3083 0301 E-mail archdeacon@armagh.anglican.org *or* rghoey@btinternet.com

HOEY, William Thomas. b 32. CITC 64. **d** 66 **p** 67. C Belfast St Mary *Conn* 66-68; C Lisburn Ch Ch 69-72; I Ballinderry 72-78; I Belfast St Simon w St Phil 78-02; rtd 02. *11 Carnshill Court, Belfast BT8 6TX* Tel (028) 9079 0595

HOFBAUER, Miss Andrea Martina. b 71. Johannes Gutenberg Univ Mainz. St Steph Ho Ox 00. **d** 02 **p** 03. C Teignmouth, Ideford w Luton, Ashcombe etc *Ex* from 02. *51 Higher Coombe Drive, Teignmouth TQ14 9LR* Tel (01626) 772098
E-mail andihof@hotmail.com

HOFFMAN, Canon Stanley Harold. b 17. St Edm Hall Ox BA39 MA43 Kent Univ MA82. Linc Th Coll 40. **d** 41 **p** 42. C New Windsor *Ox* 41-44; C Weston All SS *B & W* 44-47; C Chertsey *Guildf* 47-51; V Shottermill 51-65; Dir of Educn *Roch* 65-80; Hon Can Roch Cathl 65-80; Warden of Readers 73-80; Chapl to The Queen 76-88; rtd 80. *3 Ramsay Hall, Byron Road, Worthing BN11 3HN* Tel (01903) 217332

HOFFMANN, Jonathan Mark. b 60. Cranmer Hall Dur 95. **d** 97 **p** 99. C Eaton *Nor* 97-98; C Horsell *Guildf* 98-02; TV Aston cum Aughton w Swallownest and Ulley *Sheff* from 02. *The Vicarage, 27 Skipton Road, Swallownest, Sheffield S26 4NQ* Tel 0114-287 9271 E-mail holyhoff@aol.com.

HOGAN, Edward James Martin. b 46. Trin Coll Bris. **d** 85 **p** 86. C St Austell *Truro* 85-88; V Gt Broughton and Broughton Moor *Carl* 88-94; V St Stythians w Perranarworthal and Gwennap *Truro* from 94; RD Carnmarth N from 03. *The Vicarage, Old Vicarage Close, Stithians, Truro TR3 7DZ* Tel (01209) 860123
E-mail vicar@stythian.org

HOGAN, Miss Jennie. b 75. Goldsmiths' Coll Lon BA99 Fitzw Coll Cam BA03. Westcott Ho Cam 01. **d** 04 **p** 05. C Westmr St Steph w St Jo *Lon* from 04. *Flat C, Clergy House, Hide Place, London SW1P 4NJ* Tel (020) 7821 9991
E-mail jenniehogan@mac.com

HOGAN, John James. b 24. St Edm Hall Ox BA51 MA56. Wells Th Coll 51. **d** 53 **p** 54. C Cannock *Lich* 53-55; C Drayton in Hales 55-58; V Woore 58-84; P-in-c Norton in Hales 82-84; V Woore and Norton in Hales 84-89; rtd 89; Perm to Offic *Lich* 89-00. *Wrekin Prospect, Audlem Road, Woore, Crewe CW3 9RJ* Tel (01630) 647677

HOGAN, William Riddell. b 22. Qu Coll Birm 48. **d** 51 **p** 52. C Brighouse *Wakef* 51-54; Singapore 55-58; V Greetland *Wakef* 59-73; V Greetland and W Vale 73-80; V Kellington w Whitley 80-87; rtd 87. *15 The Pastures, Carlton, Goole DN14 9QF* Tel (01405) 862233

HOGARTH, Alan Francis. b 58. Oak Hill Th Coll BA89. **d** 89 **p** 90. C Felixstowe SS Pet and Paul *St E* 89-93; R Beckington w Standerwick, Berkley, Rodden etc *B & W* 93-04; P-in-c Basildon w Aldworth and Ashampstead *Ox* from 04. *The Vicarage, Pangbourne Road, Upper Basildon, Reading RG8 8LS* Tel (01491) 671223

HOGARTH, Foley James Myddelton. b 16. Ch Ch Ox BA38 MA42. Wells Th Coll 38. **d** 39 **p** 40. C Rainbow Hill St Barn *Worc* 39-41; C Charlton Kings H Apostles *Glouc* 41-42; CF 42-46; V Fordcombe *Roch* 47-52; Asst Hd Master Holmewood Ho Sch Kent 52-53; Australia from 53; rtd 81. *3 Chilton Court, 28 Buxton Street, North Adelaide, S Australia 5006* Tel (0061) (8) 8267 1759

HOGARTH, Joseph. b 32. Edin Th Coll 65. **d** 67 **p** 67. C Walney Is *Carl* 67-71; V Whitehaven St Jas 71-76; V Millom H Trin w Thwaites 76-82; V Maryport 82-91; V Consett *Dur* 91-97; rtd 97; Perm to Offic *Roch* from 99. *81 High Street, Crayford, Dartford DA1 4EJ* Tel (01322) 526733

HOGARTH, Peter Robert. b 61. Bath Univ MSc97 Bris Univ BA01. Trin Coll Bris 99. **d** 01 **p** 02. C Martock w Ash *B & W* 01-04; Asst Chapl Oslo w Bergen, Trondheim, Stavanger etc *Eur* from 04. *3A Dragabergvelen, 4085 Hundvag, Stavanger, Norway* Tel (0047) 5155 5488 E-mail prhogarth2000@yahoo.co.uk

HOGBEN, The Ven Peter Graham. b 25. Bps' Coll Cheshunt 60. **d** 61 **p** 62. C Hale *Guildf* 61-64; V Westborough 64-71; V Ewell 71-82; Hon Can Guildf Cathl 79-90; RD Epsom 80-82; Adn Dorking 82-90; rtd 90; Perm to Offic *Guildf* from 90. *3 School Road, Rowledge, Farnham GU10 4EJ* Tel (01252) 793533

HOGG, Mrs Ann Grant. b 46. St Andr Univ MA68 Hughes Hall Cam PGCE70. N Ord Course 99. **d** 02 **p** 03. NSM Bromborough *Ches* 02-04; Perm to Offic *St Alb* 04-05; NSM Watford Ch Ch from 05. *The Vicarage, Church Fields, Christchurch Crescent, Radlett WD7 8EE* Tel (01923) 856606 E-mail wijoho@aol.com

HOGG, Anthony. b 42. Univ of Wales (Lamp) BA63. Linc Th Coll 64 Chich Th Coll 78. **d** 78 **p** 79. NSM Ridgeway *Ox* 78-86; C 90-91; NSM W w E Hanney 86-88; Hd Master New Coll Sch Ox 88-89; P-in-c Hanney, Denchworth and E Challow *Ox* 91-92; V from 92. *The Vicarage, Winter Lane, West Hanney, Wantage OX12 0LF* Tel (01235) 868863 E-mail victory@ukgateway.net

HOGG, Neil Richard. b 46. BSc69. Ridley Hall Cam 82. **d** 84 **p** 85. C Bingham *S'well* 84-87; TV Bushbury *Lich* 87-00; V Worksop St Jo *S'well* from 00. *St John's Vicarage, 1B Shepherds Avenue, Worksop S81 0JD* Tel (01909) 489868 Mobile 07585-816697 E-mail shepherd1b@njhogg.fsnet.co.uk

HOGG, William John. b 49. New Coll Ox MA71 Lon Univ CertEd72 Crewe & Alsager Coll MSc88. Edin Th Coll 86. **d** 88 **p** 89. C Oxton *Ches* 88-93; R Bromborough 93-04; P-in-c Radlett *St Alb* 04-05; TR Aldenham, Radlett and Shenley from 05. *The Vicarage, Church Fields, Christchurch Crescent, Radlett WD7 8EE* Tel (01923) 856606 E-mail wijoho@aol.lcom

HOGG, William Ritson. b 47. Leeds Univ BSc69. Qu Coll Birm DipTh71. **d** 72 **p** 73. C Bordesley St Oswald *Birm* 72-76; TV Seacroft *Ripon* 76-82; V Hunslet St Mary 82-88; V Catterick 88-97. *Address temp unknown*

HOGGARD, Mrs Jean Margaret. b 36. NW Ord Course 76. **dss** 79 **d** 87 **p** 94. Northowram *Wakef* 79-94; Par Dn 87-94; C Ovenden 94-00; rtd 00; Perm to Offic *Wakef* from 01. *13 Joseph Avenue, Northowram, Halifax HX3 7HJ* Tel (01422) 201475

HOGWOOD, Brian Roy. b 38. Bps' Coll Cheshunt. **d** 65 **p** 92. NSM Thetford *Nor* 91-93; Hon C from 93; Chapl Addenbrooke's NHS Trust 98-99; Perm to Offic *Ely* from 98. *31 Byron Walk, Thetford IP24 1JX* Tel (01842) 753915

HOLBEN, Bruce Frederick. b 45. STETS 99. **d** 02 **p** 03. NSM W Wittering and Birdham w Itchenor *Chich* from 02. *3 Elmstead Gardens, West Wittering, Chichester PO20 8NG* Tel (01243) 514129 Mobile 07940-759060

HOLBROOK, Ms Barbara Mary. b 58. Nottm Trent Univ BA94 Nottm Univ MA04. EMMTC 02. **d** 04 **p** 05. C Chesterfield H Trin and Ch Ch *Derby* from 04. *Christ Church Vicarage, 89 Sheffield Road, Chesterfield S41 7JH* Tel (01246) 237022 Mobile 07766-732514 E-mail barbara.holbrook@fish.co.uk

HOLBROOK, Colin Eric Basford. *See* BASFORD HOLBROOK, Colin Eric

HOLBROOK, John Edward. b 62. St Pet Coll Ox BA83 MA87. Ridley Hall Cam 82. **d** 86 **p** 87. C Barnes St Mary *S'wark* 86-89; C Bletchley *Ox* 89-93; C N Bletchley CD 89-93; V Adderbury w Milton 93-02; RD Deddington 00-02; R Wimborne Minster *Sarum* from 02; P-in-c Witchampton, Stanbridge and Long Crichel etc from 02; RD Wimborne from 04; Chapl S and E Dorset Primary Care Trust from 02. *The Rectory, 17 King Street, Wimborne BH21 1DZ* Tel (01202) 882340 E-mail john.holbrook@ukonline.co.uk

HOLBROOKE-JONES, Canon Stanley Charles. b 27. Dur Univ BA58 DipTh60 MA77. Cranmer Hall Dur 58. **d** 60 **p** 61. C Gravesend St Jas *Roch* 60-63; C Streatham Immanuel w St Anselm *S'wark* 63-66; V W Bromwich H Trin *Lich* 66-79; V W Exe *Ex* 79-88; R Poole *Sarum* 88-97; Miss to Seafarers from 88; Can and Preb Sarum Cathl *Sarum* 96-97; rtd 97; Perm to Offic *Sarum* from 97. *27 Clarendon Road, Broadstone BH18 9HT* Tel (01202) 460433

HOLCOMBE, Canon Graham William Arthur. b 50. Open Univ BA99. St Mich Coll Llan DipTh80. **d** 80 **p** 81. C Neath w Llantwit *Llan* 80-84; Asst Youth Chapl 81-84; PV Llan Cathl 84-86; V Pentyrch 86-00; V Pentyrch w Capel Llanillterne 00-02; Can Llan Cathl from 02. *1 White House, Cathedral Green, Llandaff, Cardiff CF5 2EB* Tel (029) 2056 9521

HOLDAWAY, Simon Douglas. b 47. Lanc Univ BA73 Sheff Univ PhD81. N Ord Course 78. **d** 81 **p** 82. NSM Gleadless *Sheff* from 81; Sen Lect Sheff Univ from 81. *136 Totley Brook Road, Sheffield S17 3QU* Tel 0114-236 3711

HOLDAWAY, Canon Stephen Douglas. b 45. Hull Univ BA67. Ridley Hall Cam 67. **d** 70 **p** 71. C Southampton Thornhill St Chris *Win* 70-73; C Tardebigge *Worc* 73-78; Ind Chapl 73-78; Ind Chapl *Linc* 78-93; Co-ord City Cen Group Min 81-93; TR Louth from 93; RD Louthesk from 95; Can and Preb Linc Cathl from 00. *The Rectory, 49 Westgate, Louth LN11 9YE* Tel (01507) 603213 *or* 610247 Fax 602991 E-mail stephen.holdaway@btinternet.com

HOLDEN, Canon Arthur Stuart James. b 23. ALCD51. **d** 51 **p** 52. C Barking St Marg *Chelmsf* 51-54; P-in-c Berechurch 54-55; V 55-61; V Earls Colne 61-82; P-in-c White Colne 66-67; V 68-82; V Earls Colne and White Colne 82-88; Hon Can Chelmsf Cathl 80-88; rtd 88; Perm to Offic *Chelmsf* from 88. *10 Wroxham Close, Colchester CO3 3RQ* Tel (01206) 560845

HOLDEN, Geoffrey. b 26. FCII54. Oak Hill Th Coll 57. **d** 59 **p** 60. C Crookes St Thos *Sheff* 59-61; C Belper *Derby* 61-63; C Woking St Jo *Guildf* 63-66; R Bath St Mich w St Paul *B & W* 66-73; Chapl Bath Gp Hosps 73-91; rtd 91; Perm to Offic *B & W* from 91. *32 Crescent Gardens, Bath BA1 2NB* Tel (01225) 427933

HOLDEN, Geoffrey Ralph. b 25. Ripon Hall Ox 64. **d** 65 **p** 66. C Sparkhill St Jo *Birm* 65-68; C Walsall *Lich* 68-71; R Longton St Jas 71-75; rtd 90. *Aberscethin, Talybont LL43 2AR* Tel (01341) 247538

HOLDEN, Jack Crawford (Simon). b 30. Leeds Univ BA59. Coll of Resurr Mirfield 59. **d** 61 **p** 61. C Middlesbrough All SS *York* 61-64; Lic to Offic *Wakef* 65-69 and from 98; CR from 67; Asst Chapl Univ Coll *Lon* 69-74; rtd 98. *House of the Resurrection, Stocks Bank Road, Mirfield WF14 0BN* Tel (01924) 494318

HOLDEN, Canon John. b 33. MBE76. Sheff Univ MA02 ACMA62. Ridley Hall Cam 65 Selly Oak Coll 71. **d** 67 **p** 68. C Flixton St Jo CD *Man* 67-71; Uganda 71-75; V Aston SS Pet and Paul *Birm* 75-87; RD Aston 86-87; Hon Can Birm Cathl 86-87; R Ulverston St Mary w H Trin *Carl* 87-98; RD Furness 90-94; Hon Can Carl Cathl 91-94; rtd 98; Perm to Offic *Carl* from 98 and *Heref* from 99. *3 Alison Road, Church Stretton SY6 7AT* Tel (01694) 724167

HOLDEN, John Norman. b 35. Heythrop Coll Lon MA97. Oak Hill Th Coll 91. **d** 95 **p** 96. NSM Codicote *St Alb* 95-96; Perm to Offic *St Alb* from 96 and *Ely* from 00. *4 Chapel Row, Shay Lane, Upper Dean, Huntingdon PE28 0LU* Tel (01234) 708928 E-mail jnholden@ndirect.co.uk

HOLDEN, John Worrall. b 44. K Coll Lon AKC67 DPS. **d** 70 **p** 71. C Derby St Bart *Derby* 70-72; Lic to Offic 72-74; Hon C St Helier *S'wark* 74-77; Hon C St Marylebone All SS *Lon* 80-83; Hon C St Botolph Aldgate w H Trin Minories 84-95. *4 Foster Lane, London EC2V 6HH*

HOLDEN, Mark Noel. b 61. Collingwood Coll Dur BA82 Edin Univ CQSW85 Warwick Univ TCert93 Birm Univ MA95. Qu Coll Birm 93. **d** 95 **p** 96. C Brumby *Linc* 95-99; P-in-c Wragby 99-00; R Wragby Gp from 00. *The Vicarage, Church Street, Wragby, Lincoln LN8 5RA* Tel (01673) 857825

HOLDEN, Norman. *See* HOLDEN, John Norman

HOLDEN, Paul Edward. b 53. CEng79 MIM MIBF BSc75 DipHE84. Trin Coll Bris 82. **d** 86 **p** 87. C Harpurhey Ch Ch *Man* 86-88; C Harpurhey St Steph 88-93; Sen Min Harpurhey LEP 88-93. *2 Baywood Street, Harpurhey, Manchester M9 5XJ* Tel 0161-205 2938

HOLDEN, Richard Gary. **d** 04 **p** 05. C Louth *Linc* from 04. *15 Grosvenor Crescent, Louth LN11 0BD* Tel (01507) 603635

HOLDEN, Mrs Rita. b 45. St Alb and Ox Min Course 98. **d** 01 **p** 03. OLM Burghfield *Ox* 01-02; NSM Droitwich Spa *Worc* from 02. *40 Nightingale Close, Droitwich WR9 7HB* Tel (01905) 772787 Mobile 07814-621389 E-mail rita@openv.clara.co.uk

HOLDEN, Simon. *See* HOLDEN, Jack Crawford

HOLDEN, Stuart. *See* HOLDEN, Canon Arthur Stuart James

HOLDER, Canon John William. b 41. Chester Coll CertEd61 Open Univ BA73 Bath Univ MEd85. Trin Coll Bris MA94. **d** 87 **p** 88. C Brockworth *Glouc* 87-91; P-in-c Avening w Cherington 91-95; V Cinderford St Jo from 95; P-in-c Lydbrook 99-03; Hon Can Glouc Cathl from 03. *St John's Vicarage, 1 Abbots View, Cinderford GL14 3EG* Tel (01594) 825446 E-mail vicar@churchstjohn.org

HOLDER, Kenneth William. b 29. Sarum Th Coll 60. **d** 61 **p** 62. C Crawley *Chich* 61-65; C-in-c Wick CD 65-73; V Hangleton 73-79; R Rotherfield 79-81; R Rotherfield w Mark Cross 81-83; Chapl Eastbourne Coll 83-84; C Farnborough *Roch* 85; TV Mildenhall *St E* 87-92; R Redgrave cum Botesdale w Rickinghall 92-99; rtd 99; Perm to Offic *Chich* from 01. *Flat 3, 13 Granville Road, Eastbourne BN20 7HE* Tel (01323) 410868

HOLDER, Rodney Dennis. b 50. Trin Coll Cam BA71 MA75 Ch Ch Ox MA75 DPhil78 FRAS75 CPhys91 MInstP91 CMath95 FIMA95. Wycliffe Hall Ox BA96. **d** 97 **p** 98. C Long Compton, Whichford and Barton-on-the-Heath *Cov* 97-01; C Wolford w Burmington 97-01; C Cherington w Stourton 97-01; C Barcheston 97-01; Perm to Offic 01-02; P-in-c The Claydons *Ox* from 02. *The Rectory, Queen Catherine Road, Steeple Claydon, Buckingham MK18 2PY* Tel (01296) 738055 Fax as telephone E-mail rodney.holder@virgin.net

HOLDING, Kenneth George Frank. b 27. Sarum & Wells Th Coll 75. **d** 77 **p** 78. C Bexley St Mary *Roch* 77-80; Min Joydens Wood St Barn CD 80-85; R Mereworth w W Peckham 85-92; rtd 92; Perm to Offic *York* 92-04; P-in-c Willerby w Ganton and Folkton from 04. *Willerby Vicarage, Wains Lane, Staxton, Scarborough YO12 4SF* Tel (01944) 710364

HOLDRIDGE, The Ven Bernard Lee. b 35. Lich Th Coll 64. **d** 67 **p** 68. C Swinton *Sheff* 67-71; V Doncaster St Jude 71-81; R Rawmarsh w Parkgate 81-88; RD Rotherham 86-88; V Worksop Priory *S'well* 88-94; Adn Doncaster *Sheff* 94-01; rtd 01; Perm to Offic *Sheff* from 01. *354 Thorne Road, Doncaster DN2 5AN* Tel (01302) 341331

HOLDSTOCK, Adrian Charles. b 51. Peterho Cam BA MA74 CEng MIMechE MCMI. EMMTC 00. **d** 03 **p** 04. NSM Bosworth and Sheepy Gp *Leic* from 03. *34 Herald Way, Burbage, Hinckley LE10 2NX* Tel 07771-844073 (mobile) E-mail adrianchóldstock@yahoo.co.uk

HOLDSWORTH, Ian Scott. b 52. Sheff Poly BA75. Oak Hill Th Coll BA81. **d** 81 **p** 82. C Denham *Ox* 81-84; P-in-c S Leigh 84-89; P-in-c Cogges 84-88; V 88-89; Perm to Offic *Pet* 95; NSM Brackley St Pet w St Jas 96-99; P-in-c Northampton St Mary 99-04; V from 04. *St Mary's Vicarage, Towcester Road, Northampton NN4 9EZ* Tel (01604) 761104

HOLDSWORTH, The Ven John Ivor. b 49. Univ of Wales (Abth) BA70 Univ of Wales (Cardiff) BD73 MTh75. St Mich Coll Llan 70. **d** 73 **p** 74. C Newport St Paul *Mon* 73-77; CF (TAVR) 75-90; V Abercraf and Callwen *S & B* 77-86; Bp's Chapl for Th Educn 80-97; V Gorseinon 86-97; Hon Lect Th Univ of Wales (Swansea) 88-96; Prin and Warden St Mich Coll Llan 97-03; Lect Th Univ of Wales (Cardiff) 97-03; Adn St D from 03; V Steynton from 03. *The New Vicarage, Steynton, Milford haven SA73 1AW* Tel (01646) 692867

HOLDSWORTH, Kelvin. b 66. Man Poly BSc89 St Andr Univ BD92 Edin Univ MTh96. TISEC 95. **d** 97 **p** 98. C Perth St Ninian *St And* from 97; Prec St Ninian's Cathl Perth 97-00; R Bridge of Allan from 00; Chapl Stirling Univ from 00. *21 Fountain Road, Bridge of Allan FK9 4AT* Tel (01786) 832368 Fax 831223 E-mail kelvin@thurible.net *or* rector@st-saviour.org

HOLDSWORTH, Michael Andrew. b 65. Univ Coll Dur BA88. Ripon Coll Cuddesdon BA92 MA96. **d** 93 **p** 94. C Cannock *Lich* 93-97; TV Sheff Manor *Sheff* 97-99; Tutor Ripon Coll Cuddesdon 97-99. *39 Calcott Road, Knowle, Bristol BS4 2HB* Tel 0117-977 5769

HOLE, The Very Revd Derek Norman. b 33. De Montfort Univ Hon DLitt99 Leic Univ Hon LLD05. Linc Th Coll 57. **d** 60 **p** 61. C Knighton St Mary Magd *Leic* 60-62; S Africa 62-64; C Kenilworth St Nic *Cov* 64-67; R Burton Latimer *Pet* 67-73; V Leic St Jas *Leic* 73-92; Hon Can Leic Cathl 83-92; RD Christianity S 83-92; Provost Leic 92-99; Chapl to The Queen 85-93; rtd 99; Perm to Offic *Leic* from 00. *25 Southernhay Close, Leicester LE2 3TW* Tel 0116-270 9988 E-mail dnhole@leicester.anglican.org

HOLFORD, Andrew Peter. b 62. Nottm Univ BSc84. Cranmer Hall Dur 87. **d** 90 **p** 91. C Waltham Cross *St Alb* 90-93; C Northampton St Benedict *Pet* 93-95; V Pet Ch Carpenter 95-04; TR Baldock w Bygrave and Weston *St Alb* from 04. *The Rectory, 9 Pond Lane, Baldock SG7 5AS* Tel (01462) 894398 E-mail andrewholford@ukonline.co.uk

HOLFORD, Canon John Alexander. b 40. Chich Th Coll 65. **d** 67 **p** 68. C Cottingley *Bradf* 67-71; C Baildon 71-73; P-in-c Bingley H Trin 73-74; V 74-86; V Woodhall 86-93; C Shelf 93-94; TV Shelf w Buttershaw St Aid 94-99; rtd 99; P-in-c Embsay w Eastby *Bradf* 99-04; Hon Can Bradf Cathl 03-04. *3 Wheelwrights Court, Hellifield, Skipton BD23 4LX* Tel (01729) 851740

HOLFORD, Margaret Sophia. b 39. St Alb and Ox Min Course 95. **d** 98 **p** 99. NSM Stevenage St Andr and St Geo *St Alb* 98-03; NSM Ickleford w Holwell 03-05; NSM Holwell, Ickleford and Pirton from 05. *Icknield House, Westmill Lane, Ickleford, Hitchin SG5 3RN* Tel (01462) 432794 Fax 436618

HOLGATE, David Andrew. b 54. Cape Town Univ BA77 Port Eliz Univ BA89 Rhodes Univ MTh90 PhD94. All Nations Chr Coll 80. **d** 82 **p** 84. S Africa 82-93; C Uitenhage St Kath 82-84; Asst P Port Elizabeth St Hugh 84-87; P-in-c Somerset E All SS 88-89; St Paul's Coll Grahamstown 90-93; CME Officer *Chelmsf* 93-96; P-in-c Felsted 93-96; V Felsted and Lt Dunmow 96-97; Dean of Studies STETS from 97; Vice-Prin from 01. *19 The Close, Salisbury SP1 2EE* Tel (01722) 424820 Fax 424811 E-mail daholgate@stets.ac.uk

✠**HOLLAND, The Rt Revd Alfred Charles.** b 27. St Chad's Coll Dur BA50 DipTh52. **d** 52 **p** 53 **c** 70. C W Hackney St Barn *Lon* 52-54; Australia 55-78 and from 94; R Scarborough 55-70; Asst Bp Perth 70-77; Bp Newcastle 78-92; rtd 92; Chapl St Geo Coll Jerusalem 93-94. *21 Sullivan Crescent, Wanniassa, ACT, Australia 2903* Tel (0061) (2) 6231 8368 E-mail acjmholland@bigpond.com

✠**HOLLAND, The Rt Revd Edward.** b 36. AKC64. **d** 65 **p** 66 **c** 86. C Dartford H Trin *Roch* 65-69; C Mill Hill Jo Keble Ch *Lon* 69-72; Prec Gib Cathl *Eur* 72-74; Chapl Naples Ch Ch 74-79; Chapl Bromley Hosp 79-86; V Bromley St Mark *Roch* 79-86; Suff Bp Eur 86-95; Dean Brussels 86-95; Area Bp Colchester *Chelmsf* 95-01; rtd 01; Hon Asst Bp Lon from 02; Hon Asst Bp Eur from 02. *37 Parfrey Street, London W6 9EW* Tel (020) 8746 3636 E-mail ed.holland@btopenworld.com

HOLLAND, Frederick. *See* HOLLAND, Laurence Frederick Alfred

HOLLAND, Geoffrey. *See* HOLLAND, William Geoffrey Bretton

HOLLAND, Glyn. b 59. Hull Univ BA Bris Univ CertEd. Coll of Resurr Mirfield 83. **d** 85 **p** 86. C Brighouse St Martin *Wakef* 85-89; V Ferrybridge 89-96; Chapl Pontefract Gen Infirmary 89-96; V Middlesbrough All SS *York* from 96. *All Saints' Vicarage, Grange Road, Middlesbrough TS1 2LR* Tel (01642) 245035

HOLLAND, Jesse Marvin Sean. b 66. Westmr Coll Ox MTh03. Oak Hill Th Coll BA97. **d** 98 **p** 99. C Thundersley *Chelmsf* 98-02; P-in-c Tedburn St Mary, Whitestone, Oldridge etc *Ex* from 02. *The Rectory, 12 Church Lane, Whitestone, Exeter EX4 2JT* Tel (01392) 811406 E-mail northkennteam@aol.com

HOLLAND, John Stuart. b 52. Sarum & Wells Th Coll 77. **d** 80 **p** 81. C Wylde Green *Birm* 80-83; C Swanage and Studland *Sarum* 83-85; P-in-c Handley w Pentridge 85-88; TV Preston w Sutton Poyntz and Osmington w Poxwell 88-95; P-in-c Failsworth St Jo *Man* 95-01; V Ashton Ch Ch from 01. *Christ Church Vicarage, Vicarage Road, Ashton-under-Lyne OL7 9QY* Tel and fax 0161-330 1601 Mobile 07718-483817 E-mail john@holland245.freeserve.co.uk

HOLLAND, Laurence Frederick Alfred (Fred). b 21. Sarum & Wells Th Coll. **d** 87 **p** 88. NSM Beaminster Area *Sarum* 87-92; Perm to Offic from 94. *18 St Mary Well Street, Beaminster DT8 3BB* Tel (01308) 862426

HOLLAND, Mrs Linda. b 48. Sarum & Wells Th Coll DCM93. **d** 93 **p** 94. Par Dn Queensbury All SS *Lon* 93-94; C 94-96; C Enfield St Jas 96-01; V Coney Hill *Glouc* from 01. *St Oswald's Vicarage, Coney Hill, Gloucester GL4 7LX* Tel (01452) 523618 E-mail revlynne@batzion.fsnet.co.uk

HOLLAND, Matthew Francis. b 52. Lon Univ BA73. Qu Coll Birm DipTh78. **d** 79 **p** 80. C Ecclesall *Sheff* 79-83; TV Gleadless Valley 83-86; TR 86-88; V Sheff Gillcar St Silas 88-92; V Sheff St Silas Broomhall 92-98; V Southsea St Simon *Portsm* from 98. *St Simon's Vicarage, 6 Festing Road, Southsea PO4 0NG* Tel (023) 9273 3068 E-mail matts@fish.co.uk

HOLLAND, Paul William. b 55. Coll of Resurr Mirfield 78. **d** 80 **p** 81. C Parkstone St Pet w Branksea and St Osmund *Sarum* 80-83; CR 85-93; Asst Chapl Musgrove Park Hosp 93; Asst Chapl St Helier Hosp Carshalton 93-96; C Croydon St Jo *S'wark* 96-04; TV Barnes from 04. *39 Elm Bank Gardens, London SW13 0NX* Tel (020) 8876 5230 E-mail pauhold@mac.com

HOLLAND, Peter Christie. b 36. St Andr Univ BSc60 Dur Univ DipTh62. Cranmer Hall Dur 60. **d** 62 **p** 63. C Darlington St Jo *Dur* 62-64; C Bishopwearmouth Ch Ch 64-69; V Tudhoe 69-77; V New Seaham 77-89; V Totternhoe, Stanbridge and Tilsworth *St Alb* 89-01; rtd 02; Perm to Offic *Dur* from 02. *Bracken Ridge, Woodland, Bishop Auckland DL13 5RH* Tel (01388) 718881 E-mail hollandpeter90@supanet.com

HOLLAND, Simon Geoffrey. b 63. MHCIMA83 Dorset Inst of HE OND81. Trin Coll Bris DipHE90 BA. **d** 91 **p** 92. C Reigate St Mary *S'wark* 91-95; Chapl Lee Abbey 95-99; Lic to Offic *Ex* 95-99; C Guildf St Sav *Guildf* from 99. *16 Cunningham Avenue, Guildford GU1 2PE* Tel (01483) 562332 E-mail simon.holland@st-saviours.org.uk

HOLLAND, Simon Paul. b 56. Univ Coll Lon LLB77 Qu Coll Cam BA80 MA84 Edin Univ MTh94. Westcott Ho Cam 79. **d** 81 **p** 82. C Uckfield *Chich* 81-84; TV Lewes All SS, St Anne, St Mich and St Thos 84-88; TR 88-91; R Glas St Matt *Glas* 91-95; P-in-c Glas St Kentigern 95-96; R Aldingbourne, Barnham and Eastergate *Chich* from 96. *The Rectory, 97 Barnham Road, Barnham, Bognor Regis PO22 0EQ* Tel (01243) 554077 *or* 553955 Fax 554677 E-mail parishofabe@pavilion.co.uk

HOLLAND, Mrs Tessa Christine. b 59. Hull Univ BA81. STETS 00. **d** 03 **p** 04. NSM Storrington *Chich* from 03. *Wild Fortune, Sandgate Lane, Storrington, Pulborough RH20 3HJ* Tel (01903) 740487

HOLLAND, William Geoffrey Bretton. b 36. Magd Coll Cam BA59 MA63. Westcott Ho Cam 61. **d** 63 **p** 64. C Cannock *Lich* 63-66; C Paddington Ch Ch *Lon* 66-69; Chapl Magd Coll Cam 69-73; V Twyford *Win* 74-78; V Twyford and Owslebury and Morestead 78-84; Chapl Twyford Sch Win 84-90; rtd 01. *68A Warwick Way, London SW1V 1RZ*

HOLLANDS, Albert William. b 17. Roch Th Coll 60. **d** 62 **p** 63. C Aylsham *Nor* 62-66; R Syderstone 66-77; R Tattersett 67-83; P-in-c Tatterford 76-83; R Syderstone w Barmer 77-79; R Syderstone w Barmer and Bagthorpe 79-83; rtd 83; Perm to Offic *Nor* from 84. *25 Renwick Park East, West Runton, Cromer NR27 9LY* Tel (01263) 837352

HOLLANDS, Derek Gordon. b 45. Southn Univ DipTh. Brasted Th Coll Chich Th Coll 72. **d** 74 **p** 75. C Banstead *Guildf* 74-77; C Cranleigh 77-79; C Haywards Heath St Wilfrid *Chich* 79-80; TV 80-82; Chapl Hillingdon Area HA 82-86; Chapl W Suffolk Hosp Bury St Edm 86-95; Pres Coll Health Care Chapls 92-94; Sen Chapl R Cornwall Hosps Trust 95-98; rtd 99. *Oaklands Lodge, Lawshall Road, Hawstead, Bury St Edmunds IP29 5NR* Tel (01284) 386196 E-mail derek.hollands@tesco.net

HOLLANDS, Percival Edwin Macaulay. b 36. Edin Th Coll 57. **d** 60 **p** 61. C Greenock *Glas* 60-64; C Aberdeen St Mary *Ab* 64-65; P-in-c Aberdeen St Clem 65-68; R Cruden Bay 68-70; CF 70-82; C Ribbleton *Blackb* 82-83; TV 83-88; C Penwortham St Mary 88-92; V Farington 92-98; rtd 98; Perm to Offic *Nor* from 00. *30 Teasel Road, Attleborough NR17 1XX* Tel (01953) 457372

HOLLANDS, Ray Leonard. b 42. MRICS02 MASI MRSH MCIOB. S'wark Ord Course 68. **d** 71 **p** 72. NSM Hanworth All SS *Lon* 71-77, 85-91, 95-98 and 02-03; NSM Hanworth St Geo 77-85; NSM Marshwood Vale *Sarum* 81-91; NSM Upper Sunbury St Sav *Lon* 98-01; rtd 03. *Yew Tree Cottage, Marshwood, Bridport DT6 5QF* Tel (01297) 678566 E-mail rlh.ltd@virgin.net

HOLLETT, Catherine Elaine. *See* DAKIN, Mrs Catherine Elaine

HOLLEY, Canon Geoffrey Raymond. b 28. AKC51. **d** 52 **p** 53. C Gt Ilford St Clem *Chelmsf* 52-53; C Gt Burstead 53-56; V 56-75; Bp's Ecum Officer 71-82; R Loughton St Jo 75-91; TR 91-92; Can Chelmsf Cathl 78-92; RD Epping Forest 82-92; rtd 92; Perm to Offic *Chelmsf* from 92. *5 The Maltings, Park Street, Thaxted, Dunmow CM6 2NB* Tel (01371) 830902

HOLLEY, Preb Graham Frank. b 29. Sarum Th Coll 60. **d** 61 **p** 62. C Heref All SS *Heref* 61-63; C W Wycombe *Ox* 63-67; V Much Marcle *Heref* 67-94; P-in-c Lt Marcle 84-86; RD Ledbury 87-90; Preb Heref Cathl 87-94; rtd 94; R Gourock *Glas* from 94. *40 Barrhill Road, Gourock PA19 1LB* Tel (01475) 632487

HOLLEY, Paul Robert. b 65. St Jo Coll Dur 91. **d** 94 **p** 95. C Tonge w Alkrington *Man* 94-98; P-in-c Salford St Phil w St Steph 98-00; P-in-c Salford Sacred Trin 99-00; R Salford Sacred Trin and St Phil 00-03; P-in-c La Côte *Eur* from 03. *7 Chemin du Couchant, 1260 Nyon, Switzerland* Tel (0041) (22) 364 0030 E-mail paul.holley@lineone.net

HOLLIDAY, Andrew. b 62. St Steph Ho Ox 89. **d** 92 **p** 93. C Marton *Blackb* 92-95; C Poulton-le-Fylde 95-97; V Leyland St Jas 97-04; AD Leyland 02-04; P-in-c Darwen St Pet w Hoddlesden from 04. *The Rectory, St Peter's Close, Darwen BB3 2EA* Tel (01254) 702411

HOLLIDAY, Arthur. b 22. St Jo Coll Dur 80. **d** 81 **p** 82. Hon C Allerton *Bradf* 81-84; Hon C Thornton St Jas 84-91; Perm to Offic from 91. *9 Alston Close, Bradford BD9 6AN* Tel (01274) 487331

HOLLIDAY, Peter Leslie. b 48. FCA79 Birm Univ BCom70 MA92. Qu Coll Birm 81. **d** 83 **p** 84. C Burton *Lich* 83-87; P-in-c Longdon 87-93; PV and Subchanter Lich Cath 87-93; R Stratford-on-Avon w Bishopton *Cov* 93-00; Dir St Giles Hospice Lich from 00; Chan's V Lich Cathl *Lich* from 02. *St Giles Hospice, Fisherwick Road, Lichfield WS14 9LH* Tel (01543) 432031 E-mail plh@clara.net

HOLLIDAY, William. b 33. Qu Coll Cam BA56 MA60 McGill Univ Montreal BD58 LTh58. Montreal Dioc Th Coll 56 Linc Th Coll 58. **d** 58 **p** 59. C Stanningley St Thos *Ripon* 58-63; C Romaldkirk 63-64; India 64-77; V Thwaites Brow *Bradf* 77-86; RD S Craven 82-86; P-in-c Horton 86-98; P-in-c Bradf St Oswald Chapel Green 91-98; RD Bowling and Horton 95-98; rtd 98; Perm to Offic *Bradf* from 99. *61 Woodside Crescent, Bingley BD16 1RE* Tel (01274) 568413

HOLLIMAN, The Ven John James. b 44. St D Coll Lamp BA66. **d** 67 **p** 68. C Tideswell *Derby* 67-71; CF 71-99; QHC 94-99; Dep Chapl Gen 96-99; Adn for the Army 96-99; V Funtington and Sennicotts *Chich* from 99; R W Stoke from 99; RD Westbourne from 04. *The Vicarage, Church Lane, Funtington, Chichester PO18 9LH* Tel (01243) 575257 Fax 572303 E-mail venjjh@aol.com

HOLLIN, Ian. b 40. Open Univ BA76 DCC91. Sarum Th Coll 67. **d** 70 **p** 71. C Lancaster Ch Ch *Blackb* 70-72; C S Shore H Trin 72-75; C Marton Moss 72-75; V Morecambe St Lawr 75-78; V Blackpool St Mary 78-83; PV and Succ Ex Cathl *Ex* 83-87; Counsellor Coun for Chr Care and Tr 87-91; Admin Boniface Cen Ex 91-93; TV Maltby *Sheff* 93-96; R Handsworth from 96. *The Rectory, Handsworth Road, Handsworth, Sheffield S13 9BZ* Tel 0114-269 2403 E-mail ian.hollin@handsworth.org.uk

HOLLINGHURST, Canon Anne Elizabeth. b 64. Trin Coll Bris BA96. **d** 96 **p** 97. C Nottingham St Sav *S'well* 96-99; Chapl Derby Univ and Derby Cathl 99-05; Bp's Dom Chapl *Man* from 05; Can Res Man Cathl from 05. *Bishopscourt, Bury New Road, Salford M7 4LE* Tel 0161-792 2096 *or* 788 8461 Fax 792 6826 E-mail chaplain@bishopscourt.manchester.anglican.org

HOLLINGHURST, Stephen. b 59. Univ of Wales DipTh. St Jo Coll Nottm 81. **d** 83 **p** 84. C Hyde St Geo *Ches* 83-86; C Cropwell Bishop w Colston Bassett, Granby etc *S'well* 86-90; R Pembridge w Moor Court, Shobdon, Staunton etc *Heref* 90-02; R Presteigne w Discoed, Kinsham, Lingen and Knill from 02; RD Kington and Weobley 95-02. *The Rectory, St David's Street, Presteigne LD8 2BP* Tel (01544) 267777 E-mail steve.hollinghurst@lineone.net

HOLLINGHURST, Stephen Patrick. b 63. Hull Univ BA84. Trin Coll Bris BA93 MA93. **d** 96 **p** 97. C Nottingham St Sav *S'well* 96-99; Chapl Nottm Trent Univ 99-03; Perm to Offic *Derby* 00-04; Chapl Derby Cathl 04-05. *197A Lancaster Road, Salford M6 8NB* Tel 0161-788 8461

HOLLINGS, Ms Daphne. b 46. WMMTC 02. **d** 05. NSM Adbaston, High Offley, Knightley, Norbury etc *Lich* from 05. *247 Stone Road, Stafford ST16 1LA* Tel (01785) 211329 E-mail daphne.hollings@tiscali.co.uk

HOLLINGS, Miss Patricia Mary. b 39. CertEd59. S'wark Ord Course 84. **d** 87. Par Dn Wyke *Bradf* 87-94; C 94-96; rtd 96; Perm to Offic *Bradf* from 96. *1 Greenacre Way, Wyke, Bradford BD12 9DJ* Tel (01274) 677439

HOLLINGS, Robert George. b 48. St Jo Coll Nottm. **d** 94 **p** 95. C Cotmanhay *Derby* 94-97; TV Godrevy *Truro* 97-02; V Newhall *Derby* from 02. *St John's Vicarage, Church Street, Newhall, Swadlincote DE11 0HY* Tel (01283) 214685

HOLLINGSHEAD, Miss Pauline Carol. b 49. Local Minl Tr Course. **d** 94 **p** 95. OLM Colsterworth Gp *Linc* from 94. *The Lodge, Little Ponton, Grantham NG33 5BS* Tel and fax (01476) 530382 E-mail thelodge@madasafish.com

HOLLINGSHURST, Christopher Paul. b 63. St Chad's Coll Dur BA85 Westmr Coll Ox PGCE86 Anglia Poly Univ MA04. Ridley Hall Cam 96. **d** 99 **p** 00. C Bourn and Kingston w Caxton and Longstowe *Ely* 99-00; C Papworth 00-03; V Hook *S'wark* from 03. *The Vicarage, 278 Hook Road, Chessington KT9 1PF* Tel (020) 8397 3521 E-mail chris.hollingshurst1@btopenworld.com

HOLLINGSHURST, Robert Peter. b 38. Ridley Hall Cam 64. **d** 67 **p** 68. C Roxeth Ch Ch *Lon* 67-70; C Attenborough w Chilwell *S'well* 70-73; C Ramsgate St Luke *Cant* 74-75; Chapl to the Deaf 78-80; TV Louth *Linc* 80-84; Chapl to the Deaf *Sarum* 84-87; P-in-c Odstock w Nunton and Bodenham 84-96; P-in-c Britford and Charlton All Saints 89-96; R Gt and Lt Gaddesden *St Alb* 96-04; rtd 04. *Tudor Croft, 3 Tudor Close, Seaford BN25 2LU* Tel (01323) 892186 E-mail rpholl38@aol.com

HOLLINGSWORTH, Geoffrey. b 53. MCIPD85 Leeds Poly 74. N Ord Course 86. **d** 86 **p** 87. C Thorne *Sheff* 86-89; V Rawcliffe 89-96; V Airmyn, Hook and Rawcliffe from 96. *The Vicarage, 12 Church Lane, Hook, Goole DN14 5PN* Tel (01405) 763654

HOLLINGSWORTH, James William. b 69. Southn Univ BA91 SS Coll Cam BA96. Aston Tr Scheme 92 Ridley Hall Cam 94. **d** 97 **p** 98. C Mildenhall *St E* 97-01; R Barcombe *Chich* from 01. *The Rectory, 1 The Grange, Barcombe, Lewes BN8 5AT* Tel (01273) 400260 E-mail james@barcombe.net

HOLLINGSWORTH, Miss Paula Marion. b 62. Van Mildert Coll Dur BSc83. Trin Coll Bris BA91. **d** 91 **p** 94. C Keynsham *B & W* 91-95; C Balsall Heath St Paul *Birm* 95-98; Tutor Crowther Hall CMS Tr Coll Selly Oak 95-01; P-in-c Houghton-on-the-Hill, Keyham and Hungarton *Leic* from 01; Bp's Adv for CME 01-04. *The Rectory, 16 Main Street, Houghton-on-the-Hill, Leicester LE7 9GD* Tel 0116-241 2226 E-mail phollingsworth@leicester.anglican.org

HOLLINGTON, David Mark. b 61. DipEH83 MIEH83. Trin Coll Bris BA94. **d** 94. C Wednesbury St Paul Wood Green *Lich* 94-95; C Cannock 95-96. *19 Rylands Drive, Wolverhampton WV4 5SQ*

HOLLINRAKE, Jean Margaret. *See* HARRISON, Mrs Jean Margaret

HOLLINS, Mrs Beverley Jayne. b 68. Univ of Wales (Abth) BLib90. St Alb and Ox Min Course 00. **d** 03 **p** 04. C Milton Keynes *Ox* from 03. *2 Symington Court, Shenley Lodge, Milton Keynes MK5 7AN* Tel (01908) 230746 Fax 200216 E-mail beverley.hollins@ukf.net

HOLLINS, John Edgar. b 35. St Jo Coll Cam BA58 MA62. Oak Hill Th Coll 58. **d** 60 **p** 61. C Whalley Range St Edm *Man* 60-63; C Highbury Ch Ch *Lon* 63-66; C St Alb St Paul *St Alb* 66-71; Hon C Halliwell St Paul *Man* 71-72; C Ravenhill St Jo 72-73; Perm to Offic *Birm* 79-81; V Millbrook *Ches* 81-89; rtd 89; Perm to Offic *Truro* from 89. *Tresuan, Meadway, Looe PL13 1JT* Tel (01503) 264062

HOLLINS (formerly SHIPP), Patricia Susan. b 54. Univ of Wales BA76. St Paul's Coll Grahamstown 77 Linc Th Coll 81. **d** 83 **p** 94. C Cyncoed *Mon* 83-87; Par Dn Lawrence Weston *Bris* 89-91; Par Dn Henbury 91-94; P-in-c Longwell Green 94; V 94-99; Hon Can Bris Cathl 97-99; Chapl Mt Vernon and Watford Hosps NHS Trust 99-00; Sen Co-ord Chapl W Herts Hosps NHS Trust 00-04; Lead Chapl (E) *Caring for the Spirit* NHS Project from 04. *Beds and Herts Workforce Development, Tonman House, 63-77 Victoria Street, St Albans AL1 3ER* E-mail susan.hollins@bhsha.nhs.uk

HOLLIS, Anthony Wolcott Linsley. b 40. McGill Univ Montreal BA61 Long Is Univ MA76. Gen Th Sem NY MDiv64. **d** 64 **p** 65. USA 64-92; Bermuda from 92. *Address temp unknown*

HOLLIS, The Ven Arnold Thaddeus. b 33. JP87. Stockton State Coll New Jersey BA74 NY Th Sem MDiv74 STM76 DMin78. Codrington Coll Barbados 56. **d** 59 **p** 60. C Wakef St Jo *Wakef* 60-62; Br Guiana 62-64; P-in-c Horbury Bridge *Wakef* 64-66; C Loughton St Jo *Chelmsf* 66-69; USA 69-77; Bermuda from 77; Hon Chapl RN from 77; Chapl HM Pris from 77; Chapl Miss to Seafarers from 90; Hon Can Bermuda Cathl from 87; Adn Bermuda 96-03; rtd 03. *3 Middle Road, Sandys, Bermuda 5B 0Z* Tel (001441) 234 0834 *or* 234 2025 Fax 234 2723 E-mail athol@ibl.bm

HOLLIS, Christopher Barnsley. b 28. Clare Coll Cam BA52 MA59. Wells Th Coll 60. **d** 62 **p** 63. C Baildon *Bradf* 62-64; V Esholt 64-66; V Heaton St Barn 66-85; RD Airedale 73-82; Hon Can Bradf Cathl 77-85; Chapl HM YOI Medomsley 85-90; V Medomsley *Dur* 85-90; P-in-c Denholme Gate *Bradf* 90-95; rtd 95; Perm to Offic *Bradf* from 95. *52 Wilmer Drive, Bradford BD9 4AS* Tel (01274) 546722

HOLLIS, Derek. b 60. Loughb Univ BA82. Cranmer Hall Dur 83. **d** 86 **p** 87. C Evington *Leic* 86-89; C Arnold *S'well* 89-93; V Beckingham w Walkeringham 93-03; P-in-c Gringley-on-the-Hill 95-03; V Beckingham w Walkeringham and Gringley 03-05; Hon Chapl Miss to Seafarers 03-04; Bp's Adv on Rural Affairs *S'well* from 04; P-in-c Elston w Elston Chapelry from 05; P-in-c E Stoke w Syerston from 05; P-in-c Shelton from 05; P-in-c Sibthorpe from 05; P-in-c Staunton w Flawborough from 05; P-in-c Kilvington from 05. *The Rectory, Top Street, Elston, Newark NG23 5NP* Tel (01636) 525383 E-mail rural.adviser@southwell.anglican.org

HOLLIS, Douglas John. b 32. S Dios Minl Tr Scheme. **d** 84 **p** 85. NSM Haywards Heath St Wilfrid *Chich* 84-98; Perm to Offic from 98. *2 Northlands Avenue, Haywards Heath RH16 3RT* Tel (01444) 453688

HOLLIS, Canon Gerald. b 19. Ch Ch Ox BA42 MA45. Wells Th Coll 45. **d** 47 **p** 48. C Stepney St Dunstan and All SS *Lon* 47-50; C Rossington *Sheff* 50-54; R Armthorpe 54-60; V Rotherham 60-74; Hon Can Sheff Cathl 70-74; Adn Birm 74-84; Hon Can Birm Cathl 74-84; rtd 84; Perm to Offic *Sarum* from 87. *68 Britford Lane, Salisbury SP2 8AH* Tel (01722) 338154

HOLLIS, Howard Charles. b 16. Melbourne Univ MusBac40. Trin Coll Melbourne ThL43. **d** 45 **p** 46. Australia 45-47; C Croydon Woodside *Cant* 47-49; C S Kensington St Steph *Lon* 49-51; Min Can Westmr Abbey 51-59; Dep P in O 54-59; Chapl Westmr Sch 57-59; Australia 59-65 and from 76; V Primrose Hill St Mary w Avenue Road St Paul *Lon* 65-76; rtd 83. *18 Maud Street, North Balwyn, Vic, Australia 3104* Tel (0061) (3) 9859 3213

HOLLIS, Miss Rebecca Catherine. b 78. St Martin's Coll Lanc BA99. Ripon Coll Cuddesdon BTh03. **d** 03 **p** 04. C Broughton *Blackb* from 03. *25 Northway, Fulwood, Preston PR2 9TP* Tel (01772) 717072

HOLLIS, Timothy Knowles. b 28. RN Coll Dartmouth 45. St Steph Ho Ox 54. **d** 58 **p** 59. C Oatlands *Guildf* 58-60; C Crawley *Chich* 60-63; C Sotterley w Willingham *St E* 63-69; R Sotterley, Willingham, Shadingfield, Ellough etc 69-76; Gen Sec L'Arche UK 77-93; rtd 93; Perm to Offic *Chich* 93-02 and *Glouc* from 03. *9 Abbots Court Drive, Twyning, Tewkesbury GL20 6JJ* Tel (01684) 274903

HOLLIS, Mrs Valerie Elizabeth. b 40. **d** 92 **p** 94. NSM Kempston Transfiguration *St Alb* from 92. *33 Silverdale Street, Kempston, Bedford MK42 8BE* Tel (01234) 853397

HOLLOWAY, Canon David Dennis. b 43. Lich Th Coll 65. **d** 68 **p** 69. C Cricklade w Latton *Bris* 68-71; C Bris St Agnes w St Simon 71-72; C Bris St Agnes and St Simon w St Werburgh 72-74; V Bitton 74-78; TV E Bris 78-80; P-in-c Tormarton w W Littleton 80-83; Sub Chapl HM Pris Bris 80-92; Dioc Ecum Officer *Bris* 83-93; Hon C Bris St Mich 89-93; Hon Can Bris Cathl from 92; V Horfield St Greg 93-00; RD Horfield 97-99; Chapl St Monica Home Westbury-on-Trym from 00. *Gate Lodge, St Monica Home, Cote Lane, Bristol BS9 3UN* Tel 0117-949 4000

HOLLOWAY, David Ronald James. b 39. Univ Coll Ox BA62 MA66. Ridley Hall Cam 65. **d** 67 **p** 68. C Leeds St Geo *Ripon* 67-71; Tutor Wycliffe Hall Ox 71-72; V Jesmond Clayton Memorial *Newc* from 73. *The Vicarage, 7 Otterburn Terrace, Jesmond, Newcastle upon Tyne NE2 3AP* Tel 0191-281 2001 *or* 281 2139

HOLLOWAY, Graham Edward. b 45. Chich Th Coll 69. **d** 72 **p** 73. C W Drayton *Lon* 72-75; P-in-c Hawton *S'well* 75-80; V Ladybrook 80-85; P-in-c Babworth 85-87; R Babworth w Sutton-cum-Lound 87-97; RD Retford 88-93; C Mansfield Woodhouse 97-04; P-in-c Mansfield St Aug from 04; P-in-c Pleasley Hill from 04. *St Augustine's Vicarage, 46 Abbott Road, Mansfield NG19 6DD* Tel (01623) 621247 E-mail graham@manwood.freeserve.co.uk

HOLLOWAY, Keith Graham. b 45. Linc Coll Ox BA67 St Jo Coll Dur DipTh72. **d** 73 **p** 74. C Gt Ilford St Andr *Chelmsf* 73-78; Hon C Squirrels Heath 78-80; Min Chelmer Village CD 80-87; V E Springfield 87-89; P-in-c Gt Dunmow 89-96; R Gt Dunmow and Barnston 96-02; R Upper Colne from 02. *The Rectory, Church Road, Great Yeldham, Halstead CO9 4PT* Tel and fax (01787) 236055 E-mail kanddway@aol.com

HOLLOWAY, Michael Sinclair. b 50. UEA BSc74 Southn Univ PGCE75. STETS 99. **d** 02 **p** 03. NSM Catherington and Clanfield *Portsm* from 02. *15 Rosewood Gardens, Clanfield, Waterlooville PO8 0LT* Tel (023) 9259 9848 E-mail mike@thewolery.freeserve.co.uk

✠**HOLLOWAY, The Rt Revd Prof Richard Frederick.** b 33. Lon Univ BD63 NY Th Sem STM68 Strathclyde Univ DUniv94 Aber Univ Hon DD95 Napier Univ Edin DLitt00 Glas Univ DD01 FRSE95. Edin Th Coll 58. **d** 59 **p** 60 **c** 86. C Glas St Ninian *Glas* 59-63; P-in-c Glas St Marg 63-68; R Edin Old St Paul *Edin* 68-80; R Boston The Advent MA USA 80-84; V Ox St Mary Magd *Ox* 84-86; Bp Edin 86-00; Primus 92-00; rtd 00; Gresham Prof of Div 97-01. *6 Blantyre Crescent, Edinburgh EH10 5AE* Tel 0131-446 0696 Mobile 07710-254500 E-mail doc.holloway@virgin.net

HOLLOWAY, Roger Graham. b 33. OBE97. Selw Coll Cam BA58 MA61. S'wark Ord Course 75. **d** 78 **p** 80. Hong Kong 78-80 and 85-88; Japan 80-84; PV Westmr Abbey from 88; Nat Dir ICF 91-96; Lic to Offic *Lon* from 94; Preacher Gray's Inn from 97; Lic Preacher *Lon* from 97. *Flat 6, 2 Porchester Gardens, London W2 6JL* Tel (020) 7402 4937 Fax 7402 4683

HOLLOWAY, Simon Anthony. b 50. Sussex Univ BSc72. Trin Coll Bris 76. **d** 79 **p** 81. C Bushbury *Lich* 79-81; C Castle Church 81-84; P-in-c Sparkbrook Ch Ch *Birm* 84-91; V 91-02; AD Bordesley 92-02; TV Horley *S'wark* from 02. *St Wilfrid's Vicarage, Horley Row, Horley RH6 8DF* Tel (01293) 771869 Mobile 07986-274393 E-mail holloway.sparkbrook@charis.co.uk

HOLLOWOOD, Christopher George. b 54. K Alfred's Coll Win BEd76 Open Univ MA97. Ripon Coll Cuddesdon 83. **d** 86 **p** 87. C Tupsley *Heref* 86-89; R Much Birch w Lt Birch, Much Dewchurch etc 89-92; Hd RS Haywood High Sch Heref 92-97; Sen Teacher St Aug Upper Sch Ox 97-00; Dep Hd N Bromsgrove High Sch 00-02; Headmaster Bp Llan Ch in Wales High Sch Cardiff from 02. *170 Kings Road, Cardiff CF11 9DG* Tel (029) 2056 2485 E-mail c.hollowood@ntlworld.com

HOLLOWOOD, Graham. b 56. St Steph Ho Ox DipMin99. **d** 99 **p** 00. C Newport St Julian *Mon* 99-02; V Newport All SS from 02. *The Vicarage, Brynglas Road, Newport NP20 5QY* Tel (01633) 854657

HOLLOWOOD, Lewis William Rye. b 17. Dur Univ 37. Edin Th Coll 37. **d** 40 **p** 41. C St Paul's Cathl Dundee *Bre* 40-41; Chapl 41-43; C Ches St Jo *Ches* 43-44; R Fortrose *Mor* 44-46; R Cromarty 44-46; R Paisley H Trin *Glas* 46-47; R Renfrew 46-47; R Carnoustie *Bre* 47-49; Chapl K Coll Hosp Lon 49-50; V Mark Beech *Roch* 50-59; V New Groombridge *Chich* 59-67; V Hadlow Down 67-74; R Buxted and Hadlow Down 72-74; V Bexhill St Barn 75-81; Chapl Community Servants of the Cross Lindfield 81-97; rtd 82. *Holy Rood Cottage, Park Lane, Lindfield, Haywards Heath RH16 2QY* Tel (01444) 482090

HOLLYWELL, Julian Francis. b 70. Liv Univ BSc91 Leeds Univ MA05. N Ord Course 03. **d** 05. C Didsbury Ch Ch *Man* from 05; C Withington St Chris from 05. *257 Kingsway, Cheadle SK8 1LA* Tel 07963-420564 (mobile)

HOLMAN, Francis Noel. b 37. DSPT90. Sarum Th Coll 62. **d** 65 **p** 66. C Weston Favell *Pet* 65-68; C Eckington *Derby* 68-71; Asst Chapl St Thos Hosp Lon 72-77; Chapl Hope Hosp Salford 77-02; Chapl Salford R Hosp 77-93; Chapl Ladywell Hosp 77-99; Chapl Man and Salford Skin Hosp 88-94; rtd 02; Perm to Offic *Man* from 03. *90 Rocky Lane, Eccles, Manchester M30 9LY* Tel 0161-707 1180

HOLMAN, Geoffrey Gladstone. b 32. AKC56. **d** 57 **p** 58. C Eltham St Barn *S'wark* 57-60; CF 60-73; Dep Asst Chapl Gen 73-80; Asst Chapl Gen 80-84; QHC 82-84; V Wetwang and Garton-on-the-Wolds w Kirkburn *York* 84-92; RD Harthill 87-92; rtd 92; P-in-c Askham Bryan *York* 93-01; Perm to Offic from 01. *20 North Parade, Bootham, York YO30 7AB* Tel (01904) 624419 E-mail samegus@samegus.plus.com

HOLMDEN, Miss Maria Irene. b 50. Trent Poly TCert72 BEd73 Goldsmiths' Coll Lon Dip Primary Educn 84. Oak Hill Th Coll DipHE92. **d** 92 **p** 94. Par Dn Stratford St Jo and Ch Ch w Forest Gate St Jas *Chelmsf* 92-94; C 94-96; P-in-c Leyton All SS 96-01;

V from 01. *All Saints' Vicarage, 47 Melbourne Road, London E10 7HF* Tel (020) 8558 8139 E-mail mholmden@fish.co.uk

HOLME, Thomas Edmund. b 49. Selw Coll Cam BA71 MA75. Coll of Resurr Mirfield 71. **d** 73 **p** 74. C Wyther Ven Bede *Ripon* 73-76; C Wimbledon *S'wark* 76-78; TV 78-79; V Bermondsey St Anne 79-81; V Stamford Baron *Pet* 83-89; P-in-c Tinwell 83-89; Hon Min Can Pet Cathl 84-89; Prec Worc Cathl *Worc* 89-95; P-in-c Penshurst and Fordcombe *Roch* from 95. *The Rectory, High Street, Penshurst, Tonbridge TN11 8BN* Tel (01892) 870316

HOLMES, Alan Stewart. b 57. MInstPkg88 St Andr Univ BSc80. Ox NSM Course 85. **d** 88 **p** 89. NSM Shinfield *Ox* 88-95; NSM Beech Hill, Grazeley and Spencers Wood 95-98. *The Cottage, Church Lane, Three Mile Cross, Reading RG7 1HB* Tel 0118-988 2436

HOLMES, Andrew Keith. b 69. Univ of Wales BEng93. St Mich Coll Llan BTh96. **d** 96 **p** 97. C Clydach *S & B* 96-98; C Swansea St Thos and Kilvey 98-00; P-in-c New Radnor and Llanfihangel Nantmelan etc 00-03; V Penrhiwceiber, Matthewstown and Ynysboeth *Llan* from 03. *The Vicarage, Penrhiwceiber, Mountain Ash CF45 3YF* Tel (01443) 473716 E-mail andrew@akholmes.freeserve.co.uk

HOLMES (née PLATT), Mrs Anne Cecilia. b 46. Birm Univ BA67 Ox Univ DipEd68 MInstGA96. St Alb and Ox Min Course 99. **d** 02 **p** 03. NSM Marston w Elsfield *Ox* from 02; Chapl Headington Sch 02-04; Asst Chapl Oxon Mental Healthcare NHS Trust from 04. *59 Oxford Road, Old Marston, Oxford OX3 0PH* Tel (01865) 794916 Mobile 07831-254727 E-mail anne@acholmes.demon.co.uk

HOLMES, Anthony David Robert. b 38. Oak Hill Th Coll 75. **d** 77 **p** 78. C Iver *Ox* 77-81 and from 00; V Bucklebury w Marlston 81-00. *St Peter's House, Delaford Close, Iver SL0 9JX* Tel and fax (01753) 632846 E-mail tonyholmes@iver.nildram.co.uk

HOLMES, Brian. b 41. Sunderland Univ DipHE95. NEOC 92. **d** 95 **p** 96. NSM Darlington St Matt and St Luke *Dur* 95-98; V from 98. *The Vicarage, 32 Skeldale Grove, Darlington DL3 0GW* Tel (01325) 354669 E-mail brian.holmes@durham.anglican.org

HOLMES (née KENYON), Caroline Elizabeth. b 40. SRN62. N Ord Course 04. **d** 05. NSM Hale and Ashley *Ches* from 05. *17 Kensington Gardens, Hale, Altrincham WA15 9DP* E-mail caroline.holmes@btinternet.com

HOLMES, Clive Horace. b 31. Ox NSM Course. **d** 83 **p** 84. NSM Cumnor *Ox* 83-98; Perm to Offic from 98. *62 Westminster Way, Oxford OX2 0LW* Tel (01865) 249640

HOLMES, David Roy. b 34. FCIPD75. Ox NSM Course 81. **d** 84 **p** 85. NSM Ox SS Phil and Jas w St Marg *Ox* 84-85; NSM Ox St Giles and SS Phil and Jas w St Marg 85-99; Lic to Offic 99-00; Perm to Offic *St Alb* from 00. *90 Westfields, St Albans AL3 4LZ* Tel (01727) 857442

HOLMES, Frank. b 22. NW Ord Course 75. **d** 78 **p** 79. NSM Hyde St Geo *Ches* 78-81; C Poynton 81-87; rtd 87; Perm to Offic *Ches* from 87. *277 Stockport Road, Marple, Stockport SK6 6ES* Tel 0161-449 9289

HOLMES, Geoffrey. *See* HOLMES, Robert John Geoffrey

HOLMES, Geoffrey Robert. b 67. Nottm Univ BSc89. Ridley Hall Cam BA92. **d** 93 **p** 94. C Clifton St Jas *Sheff* 93-98; V Worsbrough St Thos and St Jas 98-05. *17 Vernon Road, Worsbrough, Barnsley S70 5BD* E-mail geoffrey.r.holmes@tesco.net

HOLMES, Grant Wenlock. b 54. St Steph Ho Ox BA78 MA83. **d** 79 **p** 80. C Benhilton *S'wark* 79-82; C-in-c S Kenton Annunciation CD *Lon* 82-86; Tutor Chich Th Coll 86-87; Bp's Dom Chapl *Chich* 86-88; V Mayfield 88-99; P-in-c Mark Cross 97-99; Asst Chapl Lewisham Hosp NHS Trust 99-01; Lead Chapl Kingston Hosp NHS Trust Surrey from 01; Hon C Barnes *S'wark* from 01. *Kingston Hospitals NHS Trust, Galsworthy Road, Kingston upon Thames KT2 7QB* Tel (020) 8546 7711 ext 2292 E-mail grant.holmes@kingstonhospital.nhs.uk

HOLMES, Canon John Robin. b 42. Leeds Univ BA64. Linc Th Coll 64. **d** 66 **p** 67. C Wyther Ven Bede *Ripon* 66-69; C Adel 69-73; V Beeston Hill St Luke 73-76; V Holbeck 76-86; RD Armley 82-86; V Manston 86-93; Hon Can Ripon Cathl 89-98; Dioc Missr 93-98; Can Missr *Wakef* from 98. *5 Kingfisher Grove, Sandal, Wakefield WF2 6SD* Tel (01924) 255832 Mobile 07712-044364 Fax 258761 E-mail john.holmes@wakefield.anglican.org

HOLMES, Jonathan Michael. b 49. Qu Coll Cam BA70 MA74 VetMB73 PhD78 MRCVS73. Ridley Hall Cam 87. **d** 88 **p** 89. Chapl Qu Coll Cam from 88; Dean of Chpl from 94. *Queens' College, Cambridge CB3 9ET* Tel (01223) 335545 Fax 335522 E-mail jmh38@cam.ac.uk

HOLMES, Nigel Peter. b 48. Nottm Univ BTh72 Lanc Univ CertEd72 Lon Univ BD76 Sheff Univ MEd84. Kelham Th Coll. **d** 72 **p** 73. C Barrow St Matt *Carl* 72-75; C Derby St Bart *Derby* 75-78; P-in-c Gt Barlow 78-84; V Carl St Herbert w St Steph *Carl* 84-91; V Keswick St Jo 91-94; V Mexborough *Sheff* 94-97; P-in-c Nether Hoyland St Pet 97-98; P-in-c Nether Hoyland St Andr 97-98; V Hoyland from 98; AD Tankersley from 04. *The Vicarage, 104 Hawshaw Lane, Hoyland, Barnsley S74 0HH* Tel (01226) 749231

HOLMES, Noel Edwin. b 26. Massey Univ (NZ) BA72. St Jo Coll Auckland 48 NZ Bd of Th Studies LTh65. **d** 51 **p** 52. New Zealand 51-56, 58-89 and from 90; C Lewisham St Mary *S'wark* 56-57; C Pallion *Dur* 57; Lisbon *Eur* 89-90. *Unit 4, Bambury Close, Point Chevalier, Auckland 1002, New Zealand* Tel (0064) (9) 846 0574

HOLMES, Mrs Patricia Ann. b 52. Bris Univ BA89 MA90. N Ord Course 96. **d** 97 **p** 98. C Almondbury w Farnley Tyas *Wakef* 97-00; V Northowram from 00. *The Vicarage, Church Walk, Northowram, Halifax HX3 7HF* Tel (01422) 202551 E-mail standort@surfaid.org

HOLMES, Peter Anthony. b 55. Univ of Wales (Ban) BA77 Brighton Poly CertEd78. Trin Coll Bris. **d** 88 **p** 89. C Croydon Ch Ch *S'wark* 88-93; V Norbiton from 93; RD Kingston 97-00. *The Vicarage, 21 Wolsey Close, Kingston upon Thames KT2 7ER* Tel (020) 8942 8330

HOLMES, Prof Peter Geoffrey. b 32. Bris Univ BSc59 MSc69 Leic Univ PhD74 CEng FIEE. St Deiniol's Hawarden 74. **d** 76 **p** 77. NSM Glen Parva and S Wigston *Leic* 76-02; Prof Nottm Poly 85-92; Prof Nottm Trent Univ 92-96; rtd 02; Perm to Offic *Leic* from 02. *19 Windsor Avenue, Glen Parva, Leicester LE2 9TQ* Tel 0116-277 4534 E-mail peterholmes@iee.org

HOLMES, Peter John. b 41. Reading Univ TCert63 Open Univ BA76 K Coll Lon BA96 AKC96 MA97 Glas Univ PhD02. St Steph Ho Ox 03. **d** 04 **p** 05. NSM Beaconsfield *Ox* from 04. *10 Park Lawn, Farnham Royal, Slough SL2 3AP* Tel (01753) 646673 E-mail peter.holmes@dial.pipex.com

HOLMES, Robert John Geoffrey. b 28. TCD BA53 MA57. Ely Th Coll 56. **d** 57 **p** 58. C Whitton St Aug CD *Lon* 57-59; C St Pancras w St Jas and Ch Ch 59-63; C Stepney St Dunstan and All SS 63-66; Chapl The Lon Hosp (Whitechapel) 63-68; C Stepney St Aug w St Phil *Lon* 66-68; S Africa 68-74; Perm to Offic *Ely* 74 and *Chich* 74-76; R Telscombe w Piddinghoe and Southease 76-93; P-in-c Barlavington, Burton w Coates, Sutton and Bignor 93-96; rtd 95; Perm to Offic *Chich* 95-01. *7 Buckhurst Road, Telscombe Cliffs, Peacehaven BN10 7AH*

HOLMES, Roger Cockburn. b 46. Jes Coll Ox BA70 MA84 Edin Univ BD76. Edin Th Coll 73. **d** 84 **p** 85. Canada 84-88; R Ditchingham w Pirnough *Nor* 88-90; R Hedenham 88-90; R Broome 88-90; R Ditchingham, Hedenham and Broome 90-93; V Helmsley *York* 93-97. *16 Heslington Road, York YO10 5AT* Tel (01904) 629640 E-mail fatherholmes@hotmail.com

HOLMES, Roy Grant. b 37. Ox NSM Course 83. **d** 86 **p** 87. NSM Wokingham St Paul *Ox* from 86. *58 Copse Drive, Wokingham RG41 1LX* Tel 0118-978 4141

HOLMES, Stanley Thomas. b 11. Selw Coll Cam BA34 MA46. St Steph Ho Ox 34. **d** 36 **p** 37. C Headington *Ox* 36-48; V Goring 48-84; rtd 84; Perm to Offic *Ox* from 84. *c/o Mrs D W Holmes, Lady Lucy Cottage, Coln St Aldwyns, Cirencester GL7 5AG* Tel (01285) 750216

HOLMES, Stephen. b 54. St Andr Univ MTheol84. Chich Th Coll 84. **d** 86 **p** 87. C Croydon St Jo *S'wark* 86-89; C Tewkesbury w Walton Cardiff *Glouc* 89-92; P-in-c Bournemouth St Luke *Win* 92-94; V from 94. *St Luke's Vicarage, 31 Lonsdale Road, Bournemouth BH3 7LY* Tel (01202) 516653

HOLMES, Stephen John. b 50. CertEd72 DipHE83. Trin Coll Bris 81 Sarum & Wells Th Coll 88. **d** 89 **p** 90. C Skegness and Winthorpe *Linc* 89-93; P-in-c Mablethorpe w Trusthorpe 93-97; V Hadleigh St Barn *Chelmsf* from 97. *St Barnabas' Vicarage, 169 Church Road, Hadleigh, Benfleet SS7 2EJ* Tel (01702) 554658

HOLMES, William John. b 49. **d** 97 **p** 98. Aux Min Billy w Derrykeighan *Conn* 97-02; Aux Min Ballymoney w Finvoy and Rasharkin from 02. *14 Glenlough Park, Coleraine BT52 1TY* Tel (028) 7035 5993

HOLMYARD, Mrs Deborah. b 58. Open Univ BA90 PGCE96. Th Ext Educn Coll 89. **d** 92 **p** 95. C Pretoria St Fran S Africa 92-93; Perm to Offic *S'wark* 93-94; NSM Merton St Mary 94-96; Asst Chapl HM Pris Brixton 96-97; P-in-c Barton Hill St Luke w Ch Ch and Moorfields *Bris* from 02. *St Luke's Vicarage, 60 Barton Hill Road, Bristol BS5 0AW* Tel 0117-955 5947 Mobile 07766-035131 E-mail dholmyard@yahoo.co.uk

HOLNESS, Edwin Geoffrey Nicholas. b 39. RGN. Sarum Th Coll 68. **d** 71 **p** 72. C Upper Beeding and Bramber w Botolphs *Chich* 71-74; C Munster Square St Mary Magd *Lon* 74-75; Perm to Offic *Chich* 75-76 and 77-99; C Brighton Annunciation 76-77; Chapl Brighton Hosp Gp 77-94; Chapl R Sussex Co Hosp Brighton 77-94; P-in-c Southwick St Pet *Chich* 99-02; rtd 02. *41 Wivelsfield Road, Saltdean, Brighton BN2 8FP* Tel (01273) 307025

HOLROYD, John Richard. b 54. Liv Univ BA75 PGCE77. Wycliffe Hall Ox 78. **d** 81 **p** 82. C Gt Stanmore *Lon* 81-84; Min Can, V Choral and Prec St E Cathl *St E* 84-89; TV Wolverton *Ox* 89-96; P-in-c Maidenhead St Luke from 96. *St Luke's Vicarage, 26 Norfolk Road, Maidenhead SL6 7AX* Tel (01628) 783033 E-mail rholroyd@dircon.co.uk

HOLROYD, Stephen Charles. b 56. UEA BA79. St Jo Coll Nottm 84. **d** 87 **p** 88. C Barton Seagrave w Warkton *Pet* 87-91; V Eye 91-97; V Silsoe, Pulloxhill and Flitton *St Alb* from 97. *The Vicarage, Firtree Road, Silsoe, Bedford MK45 4DU* Tel (01525) 862380 E-mail silsoe.vicarage@tesco.net

HOLT, Mrs Claire Frances. b 66. Bris Univ BSc88 Kingston Poly PGCE89. STETS 02. **d** 05. NSM N Farnborough *Guildf* from 05; Chapl HM Pris Coldingley from 05. *27 Church Road East, Farnborough GU14 6QJ* Tel (01252) 655010 Mobile 07900-583403 E-mail clairefholt@hotmail.com

HOLT, Canon David. b 44. St Jo Coll Dur BSc67 DipTh69. **d** 70 **p** 71. C Blackley St Pet *Man* 70-73; C Radcliffe St Thos 73-74; C Radcliffe St Thos and St Jo 74-75; V Ashton St Pet 75-79; Dioc Youth Officer *Guildf* 80-85; V Bagshot 85-97; RD Surrey Heath 92-97; V Fleet 97-03; RD Aldershot 98-03; Hon Can Guildf Cathl 99-03; rtd 03; Perm to Offic *Guildf* from 03. *62 Lynwood Drive, Mytchett, Camberley GU16 6BY* Tel (01276) 507538 Mobile 07974-354411 E-mail david.holt@ntlworld.com

HOLT, Canon Douglas Robert. b 49. MA. Ridley Hall Cam. **d** 82 **p** 83. C Cambridge St Barn *Ely* 82-84; P-in-c 84-86; V 86-91; V Ealing St Mary *Lon* 91-98; Can Res Bris Cathl *Bris* from 98; Dir Par Development Team from 98. *9 Leigh Road, Clifton, Bristol BS8 2DA* Tel 0117-973 7427

HOLT, Francis Thomas. b 38. Edin Th Coll 79. **d** 81 **p** 82. C Cullercoats St Geo *Newc* 81-83; C Ponteland 83-86; Chapl Worc Coll of HE 86-89; R Worc St Clem *Worc* 86-93; V Finstall 93-96; Chapl Menorca *Eur* 96-97; Perm to Offic *Worc* from 97; rtd 98. *10 Ash Close, Malvern WR14 2WF* Tel (01684) 575507

HOLT, Harold. b 20. **d** 52 **p** 52. Dioc Supernumerary *Ab* 52; P-in-c Burravoe 52-56; R Strichen 56-60; V Haslingden St Jo Stonefold *Blackb* 60-72; V Blackb St Aid 72-85; rtd 85; Perm to Offic *Blackb* from 85. *Lindens Rest Home, Higher Deardengate, Haslingden, Rossendale BB4 5PU* Tel (01978) 358084

HOLT, Jack Derek. b 38. Trin Coll Bris 71. **d** 73 **p** 74. C Daubhill *Man* 73-76; P-in-c Thornham w Gravel Hole 76-79; V 79-83; R Talke *Lich* 83-93; V Cotmanhay *Derby* 93-03; Chapl S Derbyshire Community and Mental Health Trust 93-03; rtd 03. *31 Hatherton Close, Newcastle ST5 7SN* Tel (01782) 560845

HOLT, James Edward. b 49. St Martin's Coll Lanc BA94 PGCE95. N Ord Course 99. **d** 02 **p** 04. NSM Holme-in-Cliviger w Worsthorne *Blackb* 02-03; NSM Whalley from 03. *5 Graham Street, Padiham, Burnley BB12 8RW* Tel (01282) 778319

HOLT, Keith. b 37. CPFA62. S'wark Ord Course. **d** 82 **p** 83. NSM Selsdon St Jo w St Fran *Cant* 82-84; NSM Selsdon St Jo w St Fran *S'wark* from 85. *12 Ridge Langley, South Croydon CR2 0AR* Tel (020) 8651 1815

HOLT, Mrs Lucinda Jane. b 65. Open Univ BSc00. Wycliffe Hall Ox 01. **d** 03 **p** 04. C Newton Longville and Mursley w Swanbourne etc *Ox* from 03. *The Rectory, Drayton Road, Newton Longville, Milton Keynes MK17 0BH* Tel (01908) 377847 E-mail andrew-lucy@tinyworld.co.uk

HOLT, Michael. b 38. Univ of Wales (Lamp) BA61. St D Coll Lamp. **d** 63 **p** 64. C Stand *Man* 63-69; V Bacup St Jo 69-03; AD Rossendale 98-00; rtd 03. *22 Windermere Road, Bacup OL13 9DN* Tel (01706) 877976

HOLT, Shirley Ann. LNSM course 97. **d** 98 **p** 99. OLM High Oak, Hingham and Scoulton w Wood Rising *Nor* from 98. *Westfields, Church Lane, Wicklewood, Wymondham NR18 9QH* Tel (01953) 603668 E-mail saholt@talk21.com

HOLT, Stuart Henry. b 57. Bath Coll of HE BEd78. Ridley Hall Cam 84. **d** 87 **p** 88. C Locks Heath *Portsm* 87-90; Chapl RAF 90-91; C Worthing St Geo *Chich* 91-93; C Portchester *Portsm* 93-95; Perm to Offic 02-03; P-in-c Soberton w Newtown from 03. *The Vicarage, Webbs Green, Soberton, Southampton SO32 3PY* Tel (01489) 877400 E-mail stuart.holt2@btopenworld.com

HOLT, Susan Mary. b 45. Coll of Ripon & York St Jo MA98. N Ord Course 97. **d** 97 **p** 98. NSM Longwood *Wakef* 97-00; NSM Liversedge w Hightown from 00. *229/231 Stainland Road, Holywell Green, Halifax HX4 9AJ* Tel (01422) 376481 E-mail susan@micromundi.net

HOLTAM, Nicholas Roderick. b 54. Collingwood Coll Dur BA75 K Coll Lon BD78 AKC78 Dur Univ MA89. Westcott Ho Cam 78. **d** 79 **p** 80. C Stepney St Dunstan and All SS *Lon* 79-83; Tutor Linc Th Coll 83-88; V Is of Dogs Ch Ch and St Jo w St Luke *Lon* 88-95; V St Martin-in-the-Fields from 95. *6 St Martin's Place, London WC2N 4JH* Tel (020) 7766 1100 Fax 7839 5163 E-mail clergy@smitf.org

HOLTH, Oystein Johan. b 31. Open Univ BA75. AKC54. **d** 54 **p** 55. C Greenford H Cross *Lon* 54-56; Br N Borneo and Sarawak 56-63; E Malaysia 63-67; Chapl OHP 67-75; Chapl St Hilda's Sch Whitby 67-75; P-in-c Pimlico St Barn *Lon* 75-97; Ind Chapl 75-97; rtd 97; Perm to Offic *Lon* from 97. *13 Dollis Park, London N3 1HJ* Tel (020) 8346 8131

HOLY, Ravi. b 69. Trin Coll Bris BA05. **d** 05. C Battersea St Luke *S'wark* from 05. *30 Canford Road, London SW11 6NZ* Tel (020) 8772 0463 Mobile 07930-401963 E-mail raviholy@aol.com

HOLYER, Vincent Alfred Douglas. b 28. Ex Univ BA54. Oak Hill Th Coll 54. **d** 56 **p** 57. C Bethnal Green St Jas Less *Lon* 56-58; C Braintree *Chelmsf* 58-61; V Islington All SS *Lon* 61-65; R St Ruan w St Grade *Truro* 65-85; V Constantine 85-91; rtd 91; Perm to Offic *Truro* from 91. *22 Warwick Avenue, Illogan, Redruth TR16 4DZ* Tel (01209) 842982

HOLZAPFEL, Peter Rudolph. b 51. St Jo Coll Nottm 84. **d** 86 **p** 87. C St Jo in Bedwardine *Worc* 86-89; R Kempsey and Severn Stoke w Croome d'Abitot from 99. *The Rectory, 3 Oakfield Drive, Kempsey, Worcester WR5 3PP* Tel (01905) 820202

HOMER, Alan Fellows. b 30. Ridley Hall Cam 61. **d** 63 **p** 64. C Heref St Jas *Heref* 63-66; V Brixton Hill St Sav *S'wark* 66-73; Dep Chapl HM Pris Brixton 66-70; CF (TA) 70-73; CF 73-76; V Heeley *Sheff* 75-87; R Cheveley *Ely* 87-95; R Ashley w Silverley 87-95; V Wood Ditton w Saxon Street 87-95; V Kirtling 87-95; RD Linton 94-95; rtd 95; Perm to Offic *Bris* from 95 and *Ox* 95-01. *62 The Willows, Highworth, Swindon SN6 7PH* Tel and fax (01793) 764023

HOMER, Antony James. b 72. La Sainte Union Coll BTh95 Leeds Univ MA02 Southn Univ PGCE96. Coll of Resurr Mirfield 00. **d** 02 **p** 03. C St Leonards Ch Ch and St Mary *Chich* from 02. *17 Alfred Street, St Leonards-on-Sea TN38 0HD* Tel (01424) 433614 E-mail frantonyh@hotmail.com

HOMEWOOD, Michael John. b 33. Wells Th Coll 69. **d** 71 **p** 72. C Ilfracombe H Trin *Ex* 71-72; C Ilfracombe, Lee and W Down 72-75; P-in-c Woolacombe 76-78; TV Ilfracombe, Lee, W Down, Woolacombe and Bittadon 78-82; TR S Molton w Nymet St George, High Bray etc 82-97; RD S Molton 93-95; rtd 97; Perm to Offic *Sarum* from 97. *5 Avon Drive, Wareham BH20 4EL* Tel (01929) 556216

HOMEWOOD, Peter Laurence de Silvie. b 58. Oriel Coll Ox BA80 MA84. St Steph Ho Ox 90. **d** 92 **p** 93. C Ruislip St Martin *Lon* 92-96; R Hayes St Mary from 96; P-in-c Hayes St Anselm from 03. *The Rectory, 170 Church Road, Hayes UB3 2LR* Tel (020) 8573 2470 E-mail peter@hayes-rectory.demon.co.uk

HOMFRAY, John Bax Tayler. b 29. Keble Coll Ox BA52 MA. Ridley Hall Cam 52. **d** 54 **p** 55. C Kingswood *Bris* 54-57; C Leckhampton St Pet *Glouc* 57-64; V Staverton w Boddington 64-86; V Staverton w Boddington and Tredington etc 87-95; rtd 95; Perm to Offic *Glouc* from 95. *Nazareth House, London Road, Cheltenham GL52 6YJ* Tel (01242) 516361

HOMFRAY, Kenyon Lee James. b 55. TCD BTh99 MA03 Univ of Wales (Cardiff) LLM02. CITC 96. **d** 99 **p** 00. C Convoy w Monellan and Donaghmore *D & R* 99-02; I 02-05; I Bunclody w Kildavin, Clonegal and Kilrush *C & O* from 05. *The Rectory, Bunclody, Enniscorthy, Co Wexford, Irish Republic* Tel (00353) (54) 77652

HONE, Canon Frank Leslie. b 11. Kelham Th Coll 32. **d** 38 **p** 39. C Sheff Arbourthorne *Sheff* 38-40; CF (EC) 40-45; C Sheff St Anne and St Phil *Sheff* 45-46; C Rotherham 46-49; V Brightside St Thos 49-53; R Attercliffe w Carbrook 53-60; P-in-c Sheff St Swithun 60-66; V Frodingham *Linc* 66-78; RD Manlake 69-76; Can and Preb Linc Cathl 72-78; rtd 78; Perm to Offic *Linc* from 78. *Morcote, 13 Roselea Avenue, Welton, Lincoln LN2 3RT* Tel (01673) 861548

HONES, Simon Anthony. b 54. Sussex Univ BSc75. Qu Coll Birm DipTh78. **d** 79 **p** 80. C Win Ch Ch *Win* 79-82; C Basing 82-88; Min Chineham CD 88-90; V Surbiton St Matt *S'wark* from 90. *St Matthew's Vicarage, 20 Kingsdowne Road, Surbiton KT6 6JZ* Tel (020) 8399 4853 E-mail shones@netcomuk.co.uk

HONEY, Canon Frederick Bernard. b 22. Selw Coll Cam BA48 MA72. Wells Th Coll 48. **d** 50 **p** 51. C S'wark St Geo *S'wark* 50-52; C Claines St Jo *Worc* 52-55; V Wollaston 55-87; RD Stourbridge 72-83; Hon Can Worc Cathl 75-87; rtd 87. *38 Park Farm, Bourton-on-the-Water, Cheltenham GL54 2HF* Tel (01451) 822218

HONEY, Thomas David. b 56. Lon Univ BA78. Ripon Coll Cuddesdon 80. **d** 83 **p** 84. C Mill End and Heronsgate w W Hyde *St Alb* 83-86; C Stepney St Dunstan and All SS *Lon* 86-89; TV High Wycombe *Ox* 89-95; P-in-c Headington Quarry from 95. *The Vicarage, Quarry Road, Headington, Oxford OX3 8NU* Tel (01865) 762931 E-mail tom.honey@ukonline.co.uk

HONG KONG ISLAND, Bishop of. *See* KWONG KONG KIT, The Most Revd Peter

HONG KONG SHENG KUNG HUI, Archbishop of. *See* KWONG KONG KIT, The Most Revd Peter

HONNER, Canon Robert Ralph. b 15. St Chad's Coll Dur BA37 DipTh38 MA40. **d** 38 **p** 39. C Gt Crosby St Faith *Liv* 38-41; P-in-c Wigan St Andr 41-44; C Rugby St Andr *Cov* 44-49; V Derby St Barn *Derby* 49-53; V Melbourne 54-72; RD Melbourne 54-67; Hon Can Derby Cathl 58-80; V Beeley and Edensor 72-80; RD Bakewell and Eyam 73-78; rtd 80; Perm to Offic *Derby* from 80. *5 Castle Mews, Blackwell Lane, Melbourne, Derby DE73 8LW* Tel (01332) 864356

HONNOR, Jonathan Michael Bellamy. b 62. Leeds Univ BA84 Kent Univ PGCE89. Stavanger Sch of Miss and Th 98. **p** 00. Norway 00-03; C Warren Park *Portsm* from 03; C Leigh Park from 03. *St Clare's House, Strouden Court Precinct, Havant PO9 4JX* Tel (023) 9245 1762

HONNOR, Mrs Marjorie Rochefort. b 27. Birm Univ BA48. Cranmer Hall Dur 79. **dss** 81 **d** 87 **p** 94. Church Oakley and Wootton St Lawrence *Win* 81-87; Par Dn 87-89; rtd 89; Perm to

Offic *Win* from 98. *33C Surrey Road, Bournemouth BH4 9HR* Tel (01202) 761021

HONOR MARGARET, Sister. *See* McILROY, Sister Honor Margaret

HONOUR, Colin Reginald. b 44. Lanc Univ CertEd69 Man Univ AdDipEd75 Newc Univ MEd80. N Ord Course 88. **d** 91 **p** 92. NSM Walmsley *Man* 91; C Middleton 92-94; R Holcombe 94-01; P-in-c Hawkshaw Lane 99-01; P-in-c Aldingham, Dendron, Rampside and Urswick *Carl* 01-03; R from 03. *The Vicarage, Church Road, Great Urswick, Ulverston LA12 0TA* Tel (01229) 581383 E-mail cnchonour@btinternet.com

HONOUR, Derek Gordon. b 59. Bath Univ BSc84. St Jo Coll Nottm. **d** 89 **p** 90. C High Wycombe *Ox* 89-91; C Brightside w Wincobank *Sheff* 91-94; P-in-c Dawley St Jerome *Lon* 94-01; C Derby St Alkmund and St Werburgh *Derby* from 01. *54 Park Grove, Derby DE22 1HF* Tel (01332) 331927 E-mail derekhonour@compuserve.com

HONOUR, Mrs Joanna Clare. b 61. Westmr Coll Ox BEd83. St Jo Coll Nottm LTh88 DPS89. **d** 89 **p** 94. Par Dn High Wycombe *Ox* 89-91; Par Dn Brightside w Wincobank *Sheff* 91-94; C 94; Perm to Offic *Lon* 94-96; Dep Chapl HM Pris Wandsworth 95-97; NSM Dawley St Jerome *Lon* 96-01; Chapl HM Pris The Mount 97; Perm to Offic *Derby* from 01; Chapl HM Pris Foston Hall from 01. *HM Prison Foston Hall, Foston, Derby DE65 5DN* Tel (01283) 584300

HONOUR, Jonathan Paul. b 68. Ox Brookes Univ BSc90 Greenwich Univ PGCE91. St Jo Coll Nottm MA98 DipMM99. **d** 99 **p** 00. C Tonbridge St Steph *Roch* 99-03; TV Woodley *Ox* from 03. *171 Hurricane Way, Woodley, Reading RG5 4UH* Tel 0118-969 2981 Mobile 07752-241255 E-mail jon.honour@ntlworld.com

HOOD, Mrs Doreen. b 38. Open Univ BA90 SRN59 RFN61. NEOC 90. **d** 93 **p** 94. NSM Cullercoats St Geo *Newc* 93-99; NSM Monkseaton St Pet 99-00; P-in-c Newc St Hilda 00-03; rtd 03. *24 Keswick Drive, North Shields NE30 3EW* Tel 0191-253 1762

HOOD, Leslie. b 23. NEOC. **d** 85 **p** 85. NSM Seaham w Seaham Harbour *Dur* 85-90; NSM Dalton le Dale 90-93; NSM Hawthorn 90-93; rtd 93; Perm to Offic *Dur* from 93. *3 Queen Street, Seaham SR7 7SR* Tel 0191-581 2658 E-mail leslie@hood71.freeserve.co.uk

HOOD, Peter Michael. b 47. Sheff Univ BSc68. Wycliffe Hall Ox 70. **d** 73 **p** 74. C Soundwell *Bris* 73-76; P-in-c Walcot St Andr CD 76-77; TV Swindon St Jo and St Andr 77-80; V Esh and Hamsteels *Dur* 80-88; V Stockton St Paul 88-00; P-in-c Herrington 00-05; P-in-c Penshaw 00-05; P-in-c Shiney Row 00-05; R Herrington, Penshaw and Shiney Row from 05. *All Saints' Rectory, Old Penshaw, Houghton le Spring DH4 7ER* Tel 0191-584 2631 E-mail peter.hood@rohlfing-hood.freeserve.co.uk

HOOD, Canon Thomas Henry Havelock. b 24. Chich Th Coll 51. **d** 54 **p** 55. C Stella *Dur* 54-57; Australia from 57; Hon Can Brisbane from 88; rtd 93. *18 Moonyean Street, Bellbird Park, Qld, Australia 4300* Tel (0061) (7) 3288 5106 E-mail havelock@gil.com.au

HOOGERWERF, John Constant. b 50. Bris Poly BA85 MCIH86. Oscott Coll (RC) 68. **d** 73 **p** 74. In RC Ch 73-84; NSM Davyhulme Ch Ch *Man* 84-93; Perm to Offic *Heref* 93-04; NSM Mold *St As* 04; Lic to Offic from 04. *2 Llys y Foel, Mold CH7 1EX* Tel (01352) 750701

HOOK, Ian Kevin. b 57. Trin Coll Bris DipHE95. **d** 95 **p** 96. C Dalton-in-Furness *Carl* 95-98; C Newbarns w Hawcoat 98-01; V Barrow St Mark from 01. *St Mark's Vicarage, Rawlinson Street, Barrow-in-Furness LA14 1BX* Tel (01229) 820405 E-mail ian@hooki.freeserve.co.uk

HOOK, Neil. b 73. Univ of Wales (Swansea) BA94 Univ of Wales (Cardiff) BD96. St Mich Coll Llan 94. **d** 97 **p** 98. C Brecon St Mary and Battle w Llanddew *S & B* 97-99; Min Can Brecon Cathl 97-99; P-in-c Llanllyr-yn-Rhos w Llanfihangel Helygen 99-00; V Upper Wye 00-05; V Trallwng w Bettws Penpont w Aberyskir etc from 05. *The Vicarage, Trallong, Brecon LD3 8HP* Tel (01874) 636549

HOOKER, Richard Malcolm Neil. b 38. Lon Univ BDS63 LDS63. Guildf Dioc Min Course. **d** 98 **p** 99. OLM Ashtead *Guildf* from 98. *Lanacre Cottage, 4 Farm Close, Fetcham KT22 9BJ* Tel (01372) 372446 Mobile 07802-961686 E-mail rmn@hooker13.freeserve.co.uk

HOOKWAY, John Leonard Walter. b 73. St Jo Coll Dur BSc95. St Jo Coll Nottm MTh04. **d** 04 **p** 05. C St Alb St Paul *St Alb* from 04. *46 Brampton Road, St Albans AL1 4PT* Tel (01727) 842227 Mobile 07932-691576 E-mail john.hookway@virgin.net

HOOLE, Charles. b 33. St Aid Birkenhead 61. **d** 63 **p** 64. C Skerton St Luke *Blackb* 63-65; P-in-c Preston St Jas 65-69; V Lostock Hall 69-73; Chapl HM Pris Eastchurch 74-75; V St Annes St Marg *Blackb* 75-81; V S Shore St Pet 81-92; C Laneside 92-94; rtd 95; Perm to Offic *Blackb* from 95. *32 Hanover Crescent, Blackpool FY2 9DL* Tel (01253) 353564

HOOPER, Preb Derek Royston. b 33. St Edm Hall Ox BA57 MA65. Cuddesdon Coll 57. **d** 59 **p** 60. C Gt Walsingham *Nor* 59-62; C Townstall w Dartmouth *Ex* 62-65; V Lynton and Brendon 65-69; C Littleham w Exmouth 70-72; TV 72-79; R Wrington w Butcombe *B & W* 79-94; Preb Wells Cathl 93-94; rtd 94; Perm to Offic *Ex* 95; B & W 95-00. *23 Dagmar Road, Exmouth EX8 2AN* Tel (01395) 272831

HOOPER, Geoffrey Michael. b 39. MBE00. K Coll Lon 61. **d** 66 **p** 67. C Chesterfield St Mary and All SS *Derby* 66-69; Chapl RAF 69-74; P-in-c Hook Norton w Swerford and Wigginton *Ox* 74-80; P-in-c Gt Rollright 75-80; R Hook Norton w Gt Rollright, Swerford etc 80-82; Warden Mansf Ho Univ Settlement Plaistow 82-00; Dir 86-00; rtd 03. *Ty'n Twil, Penbodias, Llaniestyn, Pwllheli LL53 8SD* Tel (01758) 730526 E-mail geoffreyhooper@lineone.net

HOOPER, Ian. b 44. St Jo Coll York CertEd67. Trin Coll Bris. **d** 88 **p** 89. C Martlesham w Brightwell *St E* 88-92; R Pakenham w Norton and Tostock from 92; RD Ixworth from 03. *The Vicarage, Church Hill, Pakenham, Bury St Edmunds IP31 2LN* Tel (01359) 230287 E-mail hooper@pakvic.freeserve.co.uk

✠**HOOPER, The Rt Revd Michael Wrenford.** b 41. Univ of Wales (Lamp) BA63. St Steph Ho Ox 63. **d** 65 **p** 66 **c** 02. C Bridgnorth St Mary *Heref* 65-70; P-in-c Habberley 70-78; R 78-81; V Minsterley 70-81; RD Pontesbury 75-80; Preb Heref Cathl 81-02; V Leominster 81-85; TR Leominster 85-97; P-in-c Eyton 81-85; RD Leominster 81-97; P-in-c Eye, Croft w Yarpole and Lucton 91-97; Adn Heref 97-02; Suff Bp Ludlow from 02; Adn Ludlow from 02. *Bishop's House, Corvedale Road, Craven Arms SY7 9BT* Tel (01588) 673571 Fax 673585 E-mail bishopofludlow@ukf.net

HOOPER, Paul Denis Gregory. b 52. Man Univ BA75 Ox Univ BA80 MA87. Wycliffe Hall Ox 78. **d** 81 **p** 82. C Leeds St Geo *Ripon* 81-84; Dioc Youth Officer 84-87; Bp's Dom Chapl 87-95; Dioc Communications Officer 87-97; V Harrogate St Mark from 95; AD Harrogate from 05. *The Vicarage, 15 Wheatlands Road, Harrogate HG2 8BB* Tel (01423) 504959 E-mail stmarks@hgate.freeserve.co.uk

HOOPER, Peter Guy. b 30. K Coll Lon 51. **d** 55 **p** 56. C Huddersfield St Pet *Wakef* 55-60; C Brompton H Trin *Lon* 60-67; R Hazelbury Bryan w Stoke Wake etc *Sarum* 72-84; R Yetminster w Ryme Intrinseca and High Stoy 84-93; RD Sherborne 87-91; rtd 93; Perm to Offic *B & W* and *Sarum* from 93. *Rose Villa, Long Street, Sherborne DT9 3DD* Tel (01935) 816819

HOOPER, Sydney Paul. b 46. QUB BA68 Lanc Univ CertEd69. **d** 85 **p** 87. NSM Killaney w Carryduff *D & D* 85-91; Lic to Offic from 91; NSM Belfast St Chris 01-03; NSM Ballymacarrett from 03. *26 Manse Park, Carryduff, Belfast BT8 8RX* Tel (028) 9081 5607 *or* 9056 6289

HOOPER, William Gilbert. b 38. Ex Univ BA60. St Mich Coll Llan. **d** 82 **p** 83. C Hubberston w Herbrandston and Hasguard etc *St D* 82-85; R Llangwm and Freystrop 85-97; R Llangwm w Freystrop and Johnston 97-04; rtd 04. *5 Pen y Ffordd, St Clears, Carmarthen SA33 4DX*

HOOTON, David James. b 50. St Kath Coll Liv CertEd73 DipRE81. N Ord Course 83. **d** 86 **p** 87. NSM Pemberton St Mark Newtown *Liv* 86-89; C Ashton-in-Makerfield St Thos 89-92; V Bryn from 92. *The Vicarage, 12 Bryn Road, Ashton-in-Makerfield, Wigan WN4 0AA* Tel (01942) 727114

HOPCRAFT, Jonathan Richard. b 34. Oriel Coll Ox BA55 DipEd66 MA66. Westcott Ho Cam 57. **d** 59 **p** 60. C Cannock *Lich* 59-63; N Rhodesia 63-64; S Rhodesia 64-65; Hon C Olton *Birm* 66-68; Antigua 68-72; C Gt Grimsby St Mary and St Jas *Linc* 72; TV 72-76; P-in-c E Stockwith 76-84; V Blyton w Pilham 76-84; P-in-c Laughton w Wildsworth 76-84; TV Bilston *Lich* 84-90; P-in-c Wolverhampton St Jo 90-98; C Wolverhampton 97-98; TV Cen Wolverhampton 98-00; rtd 00; Perm to Offic *Chelmsf* from 01. *13 Nabbott Road, Chelmsford CM1 2SW* Tel (01245) 263983 E-mail jonhopcraft@supanet.com

HOPE, Charles Henry. b 64. Regent's Park Coll Ox BA87 MA90. St Jo Coll Dur BA90. **d** 90 **p** 91. C Tynemouth St Jo *Newc* 90-94; V 94-03; P-in-c Prudhoe from 03. *The Vicarage, 5 Kepwell Court, Prudhoe NE42 5PE* Tel (01661) 836059 Mobile 07884-070619 E-mail charleshope@btopenworld.com

HOPE, Colin Frederick. b 49. St Mich Coll Llan 73. **d** 76 **p** 77. C Warrington St Elphin *Liv* 76-80; V Newton-le-Willows 80-84; CSWG from 84; Lic to Offic *Chich* from 88. *The Monastery, Crawley Down, Crawley RH10 4LH* Tel (01342) 712074

HOPE, Miss Edith. b 43. SRN64 SCM66 HVCert72 Lanc Univ MA86. Wycliffe Hall Ox 89. **d** 91 **p** 94. Par Dn Droylsden St Mary *Man* 91-94; Par Dn Ecclesall *Sheff* 94; C 94-01; V Crosspool from 01. *The Vicarage, 1 Barnfield Road, Sheffield S10 5TD* Tel 0114-230 2531 E-mail edith.hope@btclick.com

HOPE, Robert. b 36. Dur Univ BSc61. Clifton Th Coll 61. **d** 63 **p** 64. C Woking St Mary *Guildf* 63-66; C Surbiton Hill Ch Ch *S'wark* 66-68; Th Students' Sec IVF 68-71; Hon C Wallington H Trin *S'wark* 69-71; C Ox St Ebbe w St Pet *Ox* 71-74; V Walshaw Ch Ch *Man* 74-87; TR Radipole and Melcombe Regis *Sarum*

87-93; rtd 93; Perm to Offic *St D* from 93. *1A Swiss Valley, Felinfael, Llanelli SA14 8BS* Tel (01554) 759199

HOPE, Canon Susan. b 49. St Jo Coll Dur BA83. Cranmer Hall Dur 80. **dss** 83 **d** 87 **p** 94. Boston Spa *York* 83-86; Brightside w Wincobank *Sheff* 86-97; Par Dn 87-89; Dn-in-c 89-94; V 94-97; V Chapeltown 97-02; Dioc Missr from 02; RD Tankersley 00-02; Hon Can Sheff Cathl from 00; Six Preacher Cant Cathl *Cant* from 99. *42 Oswin Avenue, Balby, Doncaster DN4 0PA* Tel (01302) 858225 E-mail shope12443@aol.com

✠**HOPE OF THORNES, The Rt Revd and Rt Hon Lord (David Michael).** b 40. KCVO95 PC91. Nottm Univ BA62 Linacre Ho Ox DPhil65 Hon FGCM94. St Steph Ho Ox 62. **d** 65 **p** 66 **c** 85. C W Derby St Jo *Liv* 65-67 and 68-70; Chapl Bucharest *Eur* 67-68; V Orford St Andr *Liv* 70-74; Prin St Steph Ho Ox 74-82; V St Marylebone All SS *Lon* 82-85; Master of Guardians Shrine of Our Lady of Walsingham 82-93; Bp Wakef 85-91; Bp Lon 91-95; Dean of HM Chpls Royal and Prelate of OBE 91-95; Abp York 95-05; rtd 05; P-in-c Ilkley St Marg *Bradf* from 05; Asst Bp Bradf from 05. *St Margaret's Vicarage, The Lodge, Wells Road, Ilkley LS29 9JH* Tel (01943) 607015

HOPEWELL, Jeffery Stewart. b 52. Leic Univ BA75 ACA79. EMMTC 82. **d** 85 **p** 86. NSM Houghton on the Hill w Keyham *Leic* 85-88; NSM Houghton-on-the-Hill, Keyham and Hungarton 88-91; C Syston 91-93; TV Syston 93-97; Bp's Ecum Adv 91-97; P-in-c Wymeswold and Prestwold w Hoton 97-04; V Old Dalby, Nether Broughton, Saxelbye etc from 04; Dioc Ecum Officer from 03. *The Vicarage, Church Lane, Old Dalby, Melton Mowbray LE14 3LB* Tel (01664) 820064 E-mail jhopewell@leicester.anglican.org

HOPKIN, David James. b 67. Qu Coll Birm BTh94 Ripon Coll Cuddesdon DipMin99. **d** 99 **p** 00. C Wickford and Runwell *Chelmsf* 99-02; TV Penistone and Thurlstone *Wakef* from 02. *The Vicarage, Manchester Road, Thurlstone, Sheffield S36 9QS* Tel (01226) 370954 E-mail hopkin@tesco.net

HOPKIN, Gerallt. b 12. Univ of Wales BA36. Sarum Th Coll 37. **d** 38 **p** 39. C Aberdare St Fagan *Llan* 38-40; C Caerau St Cynfelin 40-44; C Gelligaer 44-50; V Penrhiwceiber 50-55; V Penrhiwceiber and Tyntetown w Ynysboeth 55-68; R St Fagans w Michaelston-super-Ely 68-77; rtd 77; Perm to Offic *Llan* from 79. *c/o R L Macarthy Esq, 59 Hereford Road, Monmouth NP25 3HQ*

HOPKINS, Mrs Angela Joan. b 42. Bp Otter Coll Chich CertEd64. S Dios Minl Tr Scheme 92. **d** 95 **p** 96. NSM Kingsbury H Innocents *Lon* from 95. *3 Regal Way, Harrow HA3 0RZ* Tel (020) 8907 1045 E-mail hopkinsangl@aol.com

HOPKINS, Miss Barbara Agnes. b 28. Lon Univ BSc60 Imp Coll Lon DIC66 MPhil67 DipRS80. St Alb Minl Tr Scheme 82. **dss** 85 **d** 87. Bedford All SS *St Alb* 85-86; Chapl Asst Bedf Gen Hosp 86-88; Bedford St Mich *St Alb* 86-88; Hon Par Dn 87-88; Chapl Asst N Lincs Mental Health Unit 89-91; rtd 91; Perm to Offic *Linc* 93-95. *1 St Anne's Bedehouses, Sewell Road, Lincoln LN2 5QS* Tel (01522) 513359

HOPKINS, Brenda Alison. b 63. St Martin's Coll Lanc BA95 Anglia Poly Univ MA97. Westcott Ho Cam 95. **d** 97 **p** 98. C Camberwell St Geo *S'wark* 97-00; Chapl Nor City Coll of F&HE *Nor* 00-03. *Rose Tree Cottage, The Green, Stokesby, Great Yarmouth NR29 3EX* E-mail bhopkins@ccn.ac.uk

HOPKINS, Christopher Freeman. b 41. Dur Univ BA63. Wells Th Coll 63. **d** 65 **p** 66. C Spring Park *Cant* 65-69; S Africa 69-78; Botswana 78-81; R Beckley and Peasmarsh *Chich* from 81. *The Rectory, School Lane, Peasmarsh, Rye TN31 6UW* Tel and fax (01797) 230255

HOPKINS, Ernest. b 16. Tyndale Hall Bris 68. **d** 69 **p** 70. C Walton Breck *Liv* 69-70; P-in-c Everton St Chrys 70-74; P-in-c Everton St Jo 70-74; P-in-c Everton Em 70-74; V Everton St Chrys 74-79; RD Walton 76-79; V Eccleston St Luke 79-83; rtd 83; Perm to Offic *St A* from 84 and *Ches* from 88. *12 Shetland Drive, Bromborough, Wirral CH62 7JZ* Tel 0151-334 4044

HOPKINS, Henry Charles. b 46. RD87. Edin Th Coll 65. **d** 71 **p** 72. C Dundee St Salvador *Bre* 71-74; C Dundee St Martin 71-74; Chapl RNVR from 72; R Monifieth *Bre* 74-78; Chapl Miss to Seamen Kenya 78-85; Singapore 85-92; Offg Chapl NZ Defence Force 89-92; Chapl Miss to Seamen Teesside 92-94; V Middlesbrough St Thos *York* 94-97; V N Thornaby from 97. *St Paul's Vicarage, 60 Lanehouse Road, Thornaby, Stockton-on-Tees TS17 8EA* Tel and fax (01642) 868086 E-mail harry.hopkins@ntlworld.com

HOPKINS, Hugh. b 33. TCD BA. **d** 62 **p** 63. C Ballymena *Conn* 62-64; C Belfast Ch Ch 64-67; I Ballintoy 67-72; I Belfast St Ninian 72-81; I Mossley 81-86; I Ballywillan 86-96; Can Belf Cathl 94-96; rtd 96. *2 Bush Gardens, Ballyness, Bushmills BT57 8AE* Tel (028) 2073 2981

HOPKINS, Ian Richard. b 70. Dur Univ BA92 Ox Univ BTh00. **d** 00 **p** 01. C Edin St Thos *Edin* 00-04; R from 04. *16 Belgrave Road, Edinburgh EH12 6NF* Tel 0131-334 4434 *or* 316 4292 E-mail office@saintthomas.org.uk

HOPKINS, John Dawson. b 39. Chich Th Coll 85. **d** 87 **p** 88. C Walker *Newc* 87-89; C Newc St Fran 89-92; V Horton 92-00; rtd 00; Perm to Offic *Newc* from 01. *Amen Cottage, 31 High Fair, Wooler NE71 6PA* Tel (07790) 915763

HOPKINS, John Edgar Alexander. b 19. TD65. Jes Coll Cam BA46 MA48. Wells Th Coll 46. **d** 48 **p** 49. C Forest Gate Em *Chelmsf* 48-50; P-in-c Nursling and Rownhams *Win* 50-55; Min Maybush St Pet CD 50-59; V Southampton Maybush St Pet 59-65; V Holdenhurst 65-71; C-in-c Holdenhurst St Barn CD 65-71; Chapl Stonar Sch Melksham 71-80; P-in-c Broad Town *Sarum* 80-81; P-in-c Clyffe Pypard and Tockenham 80-81; R Broad Town, Clyffe Pypard and Tockenham 81-85; rtd 85; Perm to Offic *Sarum* from 98. *17 Curzon Close, Calne SN11 0EU* Tel (01249) 819563

HOPKINS, Kenneth Victor John. b 45. Univ Coll Lon BA66 Lon Univ BD69 Hull Univ PhD84. Tyndale Hall Bris 66. **d** 69 **p** 70. C S Mimms Ch Ch *Lon* 69-72; C Branksome St Clem *Sarum* 72-75; P-in-c Trowbridge St Thos 75-76; V 76-81; R Wingfield w Rowley 76-81; Chapl and Lect NE Surrey Coll of Tech 81-84; Hd Student Services Essex Inst of HE 84-88; Kingston Poly 88-92; Kingston Univ 92-98; Dean of Students from 98; Pro Vice-Chan from 04. *Kingston University, Penrhyn Road, Kingston-upon-Thames KT1 2EE* Tel (020) 8547 7401

HOPKINS, Lionel. b 48. Open Univ BA82. St D Coll Lamp DipTh70. **d** 71 **p** 72. C Llandeilo Tal-y-bont *S & B* 71-74; C Morriston 74-78; P-in-c Waunarllwydd 78-80; V 80-86; Youth Chapl 84-86; V Llangyfelach 86-96; P-in-c Swansea Ch Ch 96-00; Chapl HM Pris Swansea from 96. *HM Prison, 200 Oystermouth Road, Swansea SA1 3SR* Tel (01792) 464030

HOPKINS, Miss Patricia Mary. b 46. Kingston Poly BEd78. Trin Coll Bris 83. **dss** 85 **d** 87 **p** 94. Gorleston St Andr *Nor* 85-87; C 87-88; C Woking St Jo *Guildf* 88-90; TD Barnham Broom *Nor* 90-94; TV 94-97; V Otford *Roch* from 97. *The Vicarage, The Green, Otford, Sevenoaks TN14 5PD* Tel (01959) 523185 E-mail st.bartholomews@otford.net

HOPKINS, Peter. b 54. Nottm Univ BSc75 Imp Coll Lon MSc79. Oak Hill Th Coll BA86. **d** 86 **p** 87. C Gee Cross *Ches* 86-90; R Gt Gonerby *Linc* 90-95; R Barrowby and Gt Gonerby from 95; RD Grantham from 01. *The Rectory, 7 Long Street, Great Gonerby, Grantham NG31 8LN* Tel and fax (01476) 565737 E-mail peterhoppy@worldonline.co.uk

HOPKINS, Richard Clive John. b 74. Nottm Univ BA95 Ex Univ PGCE97. Wycliffe Hall Ox BTh02. **d** 02 **p** 03. C Duffield *Derby* 02-05; C Duffield and Lt Eaton from 05. *2 Mayfair Court, Milford Road, Duffield, Belper DE56 4EL* Tel (01332) 843169 E-mail hopkins@richardcj.fsnet.co.uk

HOPKINS, Robert James Gardner. b 42. Bris Univ BSc64 ACA76 FCA81. St Alb Minl Tr Scheme. **d** 79 **p** 80. NSM Chorleywood Ch Ch *St Alb* 79-83; NSM Parr Mt *Liv* 83-97; NSM Crookes St Thos *Sheff* from 97; Dir Angl Ch Planting Initiatives from 92. *70 St Thomas Road, Sheffield S10 1UX* Tel and fax 0114-267 8266 *or* 278 9378 E-mail admin@acpi.org.uk

HOPKINSON, The Ven Barnabas John. b 39. Trin Coll Cam BA63 MA67. Linc Th Coll 63. **d** 65 **p** 66. C Langley All SS and Martyrs *Man* 65-67; C Cambridge Gt St Mary w St Mich *Ely* 67-71; Asst Chapl Charterhouse Sch Godalming 71-75; P-in-c Preshute *Sarum* 75-76; TV Marlborough 76-81; RD Marlborough 77-81; TR Wimborne Minster and Holt 81-86; Can and Preb Sarum Cathl 83-04; RD Wimborne 85-86; Adn Sarum 86-98; P-in-c Stratford sub Castle 87-98; Adn Wilts 98-04; rtd 04. *Tanners Cottage, 22 Frog Strret, Bampton, Tiverton EX16 9NT* Tel (01398) 331611

HOPKINSON, Benjamin Alaric. b 36. Trin Coll Ox BA59. Chich Th Coll 59. **d** 61 **p** 62. C Pallion *Dur* 61-66; Rhodesia 66-67; Botswana 67-74; Hon C Sherwood *S'well* 74-77; Hon C Carrington 74-77; V Lowdham 77-85; R Whitby *York* 85-95; Miss to Seafarers from 85; V Stainton w Hilton *York* 95-01; Chapl Cleveland Constabulary 95-01; rtd 01; Perm to Offic *Newc* from 01. *11 Watershaugh Road, Warkworth, Morpeth NE65 0TT* Tel and fax (01665) 714213 E-mail dumela@dial.pipex.com

HOPKINSON, Colin Edward. b 57. BA LLB. Ridley Hall Cam. **d** 84 **p** 85. C Chadwell *Chelmsf* 84-87; C Canvey Is 87-90; P-in-c E Springfield 90-98; RD Chelmsf N 95-99; R Langdon Hills from 98. *The Rectory, 105A Berry Lane, Basildon SS16 6AP* Tel (01268) 542156 E-mail cchopkinson@aol.com

HOPKINSON, David John. b 47. Ox NSM Course. **d** 79 **p** 80. NSM Wardington *Ox* 79-80; Hon C Didcot St Pet 80-83; C Headingley *Ripon* 83-87; P-in-c Leeds All So 87-91; R Middleton Tyas w Croft and Eryholme 91-95; V Leeds Belle Is St Jo and St Barn 95-98; rtd 98; Perm to Offic *Ripon* from 98. *17 Sheldrake Drive, Leeds LS10 3NB* Tel 0113-276 2798

HOPKINSON, Canon William Humphrey. b 48. Lon Univ BSc69 Dur Univ MA78 Nottm Univ MPhil84 Man Poly MSc90 California State Univ MEd00 ARIC73. Cranmer Hall Dur. **d** 77 **p** 78. C Normanton *Derby* 77-80; C Sawley 80-82; V Birtles *Ches* 82-87; Dir Past Studies N Ord Course 82-94; Dir Course Development 90-94; CME Officer *Ches* 87-94; P-in-c Tenterden St Mich *Cant* 94-96; Dir Min and Tr 94-02; Hon Can Cant Cathl from 01; Perm to Offic from 03; World Faith Manager Immigration Removal Cen Harmondsworth from 04. *3 Goldings*

Court, Nineacres, Ashford TN24 9JR Tel 07734-202750 (mobile) *or* (020) 8283 3929 E-mail whhopkinson@f25.com

HOPLEY, David. b 37. Wells Th Coll 62. **d** 65 **p** 66. C Frome St Jo *B & W* 65-68; R Staunton-on-Arrow w Byton and Kinsham *Heref* 68-81; P-in-c Lingen 68-81; P-in-c Aymestrey and Leinthall Earles w Wigmore etc 72-81; R Dungeon Hill *Sarum* 81-02; rtd 02. *Sunnyside, Clatworthy, Taunton TA4 2EH* Tel (01984) 623842

HOPLEY, Gilbert. b 40. Univ of Wales (Ban) BA62. St D Coll Lamp LTh65. **d** 65 **p** 66. C St As and Tremeirchion *St As* 65-73; Warden Ch Hostel Ban 73-76; Chapl Univ of Wales (Ban) *Ban* 73-76; V Meifod and Llangynyw *St As* 76-79; Chapl St Marg Sch Bushey 79-87; Hd Master St Paul's Cathl Choir Sch 87-97. *Plas Afon, Pentrefelin, Criccieth LL52 0PT* Tel (01766) 523588

HOPLEY, William James Christopher. b 50. AKC74. St Aug Coll Cant 74. **d** 75 **p** 76. C Kidderminster St Jo *Worc* 75-78; Ind Chapl 78-85; Co-ord Ind Chapl 85-94; TV Worc St Martin w St Pet, St Mark etc 85-86; TV Worc SE 86-94; Sen Chapl W Midl Police *Birm* from 94; Perm to Offic *Worc* from 02. *PO Box 52, Lloyd House, Colmore Circus Queensway, Birmingham B4 6NQ* Tel 0121-626 5071 Fax 626 5064 E-mail b.hopley@west-midlands.police.uk

HOPPER, Peter Edward. b 60. OLM course 96. **d** 99 **p** 00. OLM Bermondsey St Mary w St Olave, St Jo etc *S'wark* from 99. *56 Reverdy Road, London SE1 5QD* Tel (020) 7237 1543 *or* 7525 1831 E-mail phopper@phopper.screaming.net

HOPPER, Peter John. b 37. Univ Coll Dur BSc59 Lon Univ PGCE60. N Ord Course 89. **d** 91 **p** 91. C Aston cum Aughton and Ulley *Sheff* 91-93; C Aston cum Aughton w Swallownest, Todwick etc 93-94; P-in-c Braithwell w Bramley 94-95; TV Bramley and Ravenfield w Hooton Roberts etc 95-00; rtd 00; Perm to Offic *Worc* from 00. *21 Hornsby Avenue, Worcester WR4 0PN* Tel (01905) 731618 E-mail peterjhopper@supanet.com

HOPPER, Robert Keith. b 45. St Jo Coll Dur 74. **d** 77 **p** 78. C Oxclose *Dur* 77-80; C Hebburn St Jo 80-82; V Lobley Hill 82-04; P-in-c Marley Hill 02-04; V Hillside from 04. *All Saints' Vicarage, Rowanwood Gardens, Gateshead NE11 0DP* Tel and fax 0191-460 4409 Mobile 07960-754744 E-mail bob.hopper@durham.anglican.org

HOPPERTON, Thomas. b 33. SSC. Chich Th Coll 71. **d** 73 **p** 74. C Cheam *S'wark* 73-89; P-in-c St Alb Ch 76-89; P-in-c Rotherhithe St Kath w St Barn 89-92; P-in-c S Bermondsey St Bart 91-92; V Bermondsey St Kath w St Bart 92-01; rtd 01; Perm to Offic *York* from 03. *8 Croft Heads, Sowerby, Thirsk YO7 1ND* Tel (01845) 524210 E-mail fathert@nildram.co.uk

HOPTHROW, Mrs Elizabeth Rosemary Gladys. b 45. **d** 01 **p** 02. NSM Aylesham w Adisham *Cant* 01-04; NSM Nonington w Wymynswold and Goodnestone etc 01-04; NSM Barham w Bishopsbourne and Kingston from 04; Chapl Pilgrim's Hospice Cant from 01. *146 The Street, Kingston, Canterbury CT4 6JQ* Tel (01227) 830070 *or* 812610 E-mail lizziehopthrow@quista.net

HOPWOOD, Adrian Patrick. b 37. N Lon Poly BSc61 CBiol MIBiol MCIWEM. Ox Min Course 87. **d** 90 **p** 91. NSM Chesham Bois *Ox* 90-93; NSM Amersham 93-95; NSM Ridgeway 95-05; rtd 05. *The Glebe House, Childrey, Wantage OX12 9UP* Tel (01235) 751518

HOPWOOD OWEN, Mrs Karen. b 58. Padgate Coll of Educn CertEd79 St Martin's Coll Lanc DASE90. LNSM course 92. **d** 95 **p** 96. OLM Peel *Man* 95-99; OLM Walkden and Lt Hulton from 99. *168 Manchester Road, Tyldesley, Manchester M29 8WY* Tel (01942) 894850

HORAN, John Champain. b 52. WMMTC 95. **d** 98 **p** 99. NSM Leckhampton SS Phil and Jas w Cheltenham St Jas *Glouc* from 98; Dioc Communications Officer 01-02. *38 Leckhampton Road, Cheltenham GL53 0BB* Tel (01242) 235370 E-mail horan.jc@btinternet.com

HORBURY, Prof William. b 42. Oriel Coll Ox BA64 MA67 Clare Coll Cam BA66 PhD71 DD00 FBA97. Westcott Ho Cam 64. **d** 69 **p** 70. Fell Clare Coll Cam 68-72; CCC Cam from 78; R Gt w Lt Gransden *Ely* 72-78; Lect Div Cam Univ 84-98; Prof Jewish and Early Chr Studies from 98; P-in-c Cambridge St Botolph *Ely* from 90. *5 Grange Road, Cambridge CB3 9AS* Tel (01223) 363529 Fax 462751

HORDER, Mrs Catharine Joy. b 51. Battersea Coll of Educn CertEd72 UWE BA98. S Dios Minl Tr Scheme 92. **d** 95 **p** 96. C Burrington and Churchill *B & W* 95-00; TV Yatton Moor from 00. *1 Miller Road, Cleeve, Bristol BS49 4NL* Tel (01934) 833152 E-mail jfm2@fish.co.uk

HORDER, Peter Alan Trahair. b 43. LNSM course 95. **d** 97 **p** 98. OLM Madron *Truro* 97-01; OLM Gulval 99-01; OLM Gulval and Madron from 01. *Kourion, 38 Boscathnoe Way, Heamoor, Penzance TR18 3JS* Tel (01736) 360813

HORDERN, Peter John Calveley. b 35. Jes Coll Cam BA59 MA64 McMaster Univ Ontario PhD72. Linc Th Coll 59. **d** 61 **p** 62. C Billingham St Aid *Dur* 61-65; Canada from 65; rtd 00. *346 Aberdeen Avenue, Brandon MB, Canada, R7A 1N4* Tel (001) (204) 727 3324

HORE, Leslie Nicholas Peter. b 40. SW Minl Tr Course 99. **d** 02 **p** 03. OLM Treverbyn *Truro* from 02. *Tremore, Hallaze Road, Penwithick, St Austell PL26 8YW* Tel (01726) 851750 E-mail hore1@freeuk.com

HORE, Michael John. b 50. Man Univ BSc71. Linc Th Coll 75. **d** 78 **p** 79. C Maidstone St Martin *Cant* 78-81; C St Peter-in-Thanet 81-83; R Storrington *Chich* 83-93; RD Storrington 90-93; V Goring-by-Sea 93-02; R Cottenham *Ely* from 02. *The Rectory, 6 High Street, Cottenham, Cambridge CB4 8SA* Tel (01954) 250454 E-mail mrthore@yahoo.co.uk

HORLESTON, Kenneth William. b 50. BA86. Oak Hill Th Coll 84. **d** 86 **p** 87. C Wednesfield Heath *Lich* 86-89; V Blagreaves *Derby* 89-00; P-in-c Horsley 00-02; P-in-c Denby 00-02; V Horsley and Denby from 02. *The Vicarage, Church Street, Horsley, Derby DE21 5BR* Tel (01332) 880284 E-mail ken@horleston.freesrve.co.uk

HORLOCK, Andrew John. b 51. Bath Univ BSc74 Open Univ MPhil89 Nottm Univ PhD99. Ridley Hall Cam 03. **d** 05. C Crich and S Wingfield *Derby* from 05. *6 Dowie Way, Crich, Matlock DE4 5NJ* Tel (01773) 853923 Mobile 07952-180370 E-mail andrewhorlock@hotmail.com

HORLOCK, The Very Revd Brian William. b 31. OBE78. Univ of Wales (Lamp) BA55. Chich Th Coll 55. **d** 57 **p** 58. C Chiswick St Nic w St Mary *Lon* 57-61; C Witney *Ox* 61-62; V N Acton St Gabr *Lon* 62-68; Chapl Oslo w Bergen, Trondheim and Stavanger *Eur* 68-89; RD Scandinavia 75-79; Adn 80-89; Hon Can Brussels Cathl 80-89; Dean Gib 89-98; Chapl Gib 89-98; rtd 98; Perm to Offic *Eur* from 98; Hon C Wootton Bassett *Sarum* from 98. *1 Richard's Close, Wootton Bassett, Swindon SN4 7LE* Tel (01793) 848344 Fax 848378

HORLOCK, Peter Richard. b 76. UWE BA97. Oak Hill Th Coll BA04. **d** 04 **p** 05. C Rusholme H Trin *Man* from 04. *2 The Grange, Rusholme, Manchester M14 5NY* Tel 0161-224 1123 Mobile 07890-860022 E-mail peterhorlock@hotmail.com

HORN, Colin Clive. b 39. CEng MIMechE. Cant Sch of Min. **d** 83 **p** 84. NSM Yalding w Collier Street *Roch* 83-91; V Kemsing w Woodlands 91-98; RD Shoreham 94-98; rtd 99; Perm to Offic *B & W* from 00. *Roundhill Cottage, Tadhill, Leigh upon Mendip, Bath BA3 5QT* Tel and fax (01373) 812736 Mobile 07885-523190

HORNBY (née CHRISTIAN), Mrs Helen. b 47. K Coll Lon BA68 AKC68 Lon Inst of Educn PGCE69. Cranmer Hall Dur 00. **d** 02 **p** 03. C Briercliffe *Blackb* from 02. *16 Oakwood Close, Burnley BB10 2DY* Tel (01282) 452376

HORNE, Brian Edward. b 37. CEng68 MRAeS68 MIEE68 EurIng92 Lon Univ BSc62 PhD78. WEMTC 92. **d** 95 **p** 96. OLM Cheltenham St Mark *Glouc* from 95. *87A Rowanfield Road, Cheltenham GL51 8AF* Tel (01242) 236786

HORNE, Jack Kenneth. b 20. Linc Th Coll 68. **d** 70 **p** 71. C Danbury *Chelmsf* 70-75; V Frampton *Linc* 75-85; rtd 85; Perm to Offic *Linc* from 01. *154 Kenilworth Road, Grantham NG31 9UH* Tel (01476) 578867

HORNE, Mona Lyn Denison. b 38. Gipsy Hill Coll of Educn TCert58. WEMTC 98. **d** 99 **p** 00. OLM Cheltenham St Mark *Glouc* from 99. *87A Rowanfield Road, Cheltenham GL51 8AF* Tel (01242) 236786 Fax 691869

HORNE, Simon Timothy. b 62. Ball Coll Ox BA86 MA90 Southn Univ RN(MH)89 Birm Univ PhD99. Qu Coll Birm BD94. **d** 95 **p** 96. C Basingstoke *Win* 95-99; C Fordingbridge 99-01; TV Fordingbridge and Breamore and Hale etc from 01. *19 Falconwood Close, Fordingbridge SP6 1TB* Tel (01425) 650563 Fax as telephone E-mail simon.horne@fordingbridge.com

HORNER, Eric. b 43. EMMTC 87. **d** 90 **p** 91. C Boultham *Linc* 90-93; P-in-c Frampton w Kirton in Holland 93-97; V Kirton in Holland 97-04; rtd 05. *24 Hurn Close, Ruskington, Sleaford NG34 9FE* Tel (01526) 834043 E-mail erichorner04@aol.com

HORNER, John Henry. b 40. Leeds Univ BA62 Lon Univ DipRS74 Middx Poly MA87. Oak Hill Th Coll 76. **d** 79 **p** 80. Hon C Datchworth w Tewin *St Alb* 79-85; Hon C Ware St Mary 85-91; C S Ashford Ch Ch *Cant* 91-94; C Bp's Hatfield *St Alb* 94-99; V Sandridge 99-02; rtd 02; P-in-c Broxbourne w Wormley *St Alb* 03-04. *41 St Leonard's Road, Hertford SG14 3JW* Tel (01992) 423725 E-mail john.horner1@ntlworld.com

HORNER, Peter Francis. b 27. Jes Coll Ox BA51 MA55. Kelham Th Coll 52. **d** 54 **p** 55. Tutor Kelham Th Coll 54-73; Chapl 58-73; C Averham w Kelham *S'well* 54-56; Lic to Offic *S'well* 56-73 and *Ox* 74-87; SSM from 58; Australia 87-97; rtd 97. *St Antony's Priory, 77 Claypath, Durham DH1 1QT* Tel 0191-384 3747

HORNER, Richard Murray. b 61. Dur Univ BSc83. NTMTC 93. **d** 96 **p** 97. C Sherborne w Castleton and Lillington *Sarum* 96-99; Chapl Rugby Sch from 99. *11 Horton Crescent, Rugby CV22 5DJ* Tel (01788) 544939

HORNSBY, Edgar. b 23. AKC50. **d** 51 **p** 52. C Portsea St Mary *Portsm* 51-55; Chapl RAF 55-69; St Mary's Hall and Brighton Coll 69-74; Chapl St Swithun's Sch Win 74-88; rtd 88; Perm to Offic *B & W* from 88 and *Sarum* from 01. *The Manor Farmhouse, Littlewindsor, Beaminster DT8 3QU* Tel (01308) 868491

HORNSBY, William John. b 49. RIBA79. SEITE 98. **d** 01 **p** 02. C Faversham *Cant* 01-04; C Preston next Faversham, Goodnestone and Graveney 02-04; P-in-c Newington w Hartlip and Stockbury from 04. *The Vicarage, Church Lane, Newington, Sittingbourne ME9 7JU* Tel (01795) 844345
E-mail billhornsby@smoc.freeserve.co.uk

HOROBIN, Timothy John. b 60. St Jo Coll Nottm 92. **d** 94 **p** 95. C Nelson St Phil *Blackb* 94-98; P-in-c Blackpool St Paul 98-00; Perm to Offic from 05. *75 Main Street, Warton, Carnforth LA5 9PJ* Tel (01524) 733037 Mobile 07811-074063

HORREX, Mrs Gay Lesley. b 42. Guildf Dioc Min Course 90. **d** 96 **p** 97. OLM Walton-on-Thames *Guildf* from 96. *173 Sidney Road, Walton-on-Thames KT12 3SB* Tel (01932) 225742
E-mail jandghorrex@btinternet.com

HORROCKS, Judith Anne. b 53. Univ of Calgary BSc76 Keele Univ MA99. St Jo Coll Nottm. **dss** 82 **d** 87 **p** 94. Denton Ch Ch *Man* 82-85; Whalley Range St Edm 85-97; Par Dn 87-94; C 94-97; Chapl Man R Infirmary 88-90; Chapl Christie Hosp NHS Trust Man 95-03; Chapl S Man Univ Hosps NHS Trust 98-03; Lic Preacher *Man* 97-03; Hon Can Man Cathl 02-03; Multifaith Chapl Co-ord Sheff Hallam Univ *Sheff* from 03. *Emmanuel Vicarage, Edward Street, Bolton BL3 5LQ* Tel (01204) 393282
E-mail judie.horrocks@christie-tr.nwest.nhs.uk

HORROCKS, Oliver John. b 30. Clare Coll Cam BA53 MA57. Westcott Ho Cam 53. **d** 55 **p** 56. C Moss Side Ch Ch *Man* 55-58; C Arnold *S'well* 58-60; R Ancoats *Man* 60-67; R Barthomley *Ches* 67-96; rtd 96; Perm to Offic *Ches* from 98. *36 Station Road, Alsager, Stoke-on-Trent ST7 2PD* Tel (01270) 877284

HORROCKS, Robert James. b 56. Grey Coll Dur BSc78. St Jo Coll Nottm DipTh80 DPS82. **d** 82 **p** 83. C Denton Ch Ch *Man* 82-85; R Whalley Range St Edm 85-97; P-in-c Bolton St Paul w Em from 97. *Emmanuel Vicarage, Edward Street, Bolton BL3 5LQ* Tel (01204) 393282 Fax 0870-1247270
E-mail bob@horrocks.org.uk

HORROCKS, Stanley. b 22. Man Univ BA76. Coll of Resurr Mirfield 77. **d** 78 **p** 79. Hon C Man Miles Platting *Man* 78-81; Hon C Lower Broughton St Clem w St Matthias 81-87; rtd 87; NSM Higher Broughton *Man* 87-92; NSM Broughton St Jas w St Clem and St Matthias 92-93; Perm to Offic from 93. *80 Northumberland Street, Salford M7 4DG* Tel 0161-792 1037

HORSEMAN, Christopher Michael. b 54. Bris Sch of Min 84 Trin Coll Bris 87. **d** 88 **p** 89. C Weston-super-Mare Cen Par *B & W* 88-92; TV Yatton Moor 92-02; NSM from 02. *6 Westaway Park, Yatton, Bristol BS49 4JU* Tel (01934) 834537
E-mail cfhors@globalnet.co.uk

HORSEMAN, Colin. b 46. Lon Coll of Div ALCD69 BD70 STh75. **d** 70 **p** 71. C Higher Openshaw *Man* 70-74; C Darfield *Sheff* 75-78; V Stainforth 78-88; V Heeley 88-95; P-in-c Ducklington *Ox* 95-99; P-in-c Gt Horkesley *Chelmsf* 99-02; P-in-c W Bergholt 00-02; R W Bergholt and Gt Horkesley from 02; RD Dedham and Tey from 03. *The Rectory, Ivy Lodge Road, Great Horkesley, Colchester CO6 4EN* Tel (01206) 271242
E-mail revcolin@tiscali.co.uk

HORSEY, Maurice Alfred. b 30. ACIB. S'wark Ord Course 61. **d** 64 **p** 65. C Oxhey All SS *St Alb* 64-67; C Coulsdon St Jo *S'wark* 67-71; P-in-c Champion Hill St Sav 71-76; Hon C Lewisham St Swithun 84-86; P-in-c Woolwich St Thos 86-90; R 90-94; rtd 94; Chapl Costa del Sol W *Eur* 94-98; Perm to Offic from 99. *6/47 Marina de Casares, 29690 Casares, Malaga, Spain* Tel (0034) (95) 289 2166 E-mail dorothy@tiscali.es

HORSEY, Stanley Desmond. b 20. Ely Th Coll 46. **d** 49 **p** 50. C S Clevedon *B & W* 49-51; C Leigh-on-Sea St Marg *Chelmsf* 51-53; C Barbourne *Worc* 53-55; V Edgbaston St Jas *Birm* 55-60; V Brighton St Martin *Chich* 60-67; V Hove St Barn 67-77; V Hove St Barn and St Agnes 77-85; rtd 85; Perm to Offic *Chich* from 85. *27A Amesbury Crescent, Hove BN3 5RD* Tel (01273) 732081

HORSFALL, David John. b 55. Bris Poly BA77. Trin Coll Bris DipHE82 St Jo Coll Nottm DPS89. **d** 89 **p** 90. C Chaddesden St Mary *Derby* 89-92; V Swadlincote from 92; RD Repton from 99. *The Vicarage, Church Street, Swadlincote DE11 8LF* Tel (01283) 217756

HORSFALL, Keith. b 39. Tyndale Hall Bris 62. **d** 65 **p** 66. C Walton Breck *Liv* 65-68; C Fazakerley Em 68-70; C Mile Cross *Nor* 70-73; V Gayton 73-80; TR Parr *Liv* 80-90; V Leyland St Andr *Blackb* 90-00; P-in-c Willand *Ex* 00-01; TV Cullompton, Willand, Uffculme, Kentisbeare etc from 01. *The Rectory, Old Village, Willand, Cullompton EX15 2RH* Tel (01884) 32247 E-mail horsfall@xalt.co.uk

HORSHAM, Archdeacon of. *See* COMBES, The Ven Roger Matthew

HORSHAM, Area Bishop of. *See* URWIN, The Rt Revd Lindsay Goodall

HORSINGTON, Timothy Frederick. b 44. Dur Univ BA66. Wycliffe Hall Ox 67. **d** 69 **p** 70. C Halewood *Liv* 69-72; C Farnworth 72-75; C-in-c Widnes St Jo 72-75; P-in-c Llangarron w Llangrove *Heref* 75-82; P-in-c Whitchurch w Ganarew 77-82; R Llangarron w Llangrove, Whitchurch and Ganarew 83-84; R Highclere and Ashmansworth w Crux Easton *Win* from 84. *The Rectory, 2 Flexford Close, Highclere, Newbury RG20 9PE* Tel (01635) 253991

HORSLEY, Canon Alan Avery. b 36. St Chad's Coll Dur BA58 Pacific States Univ MA84 PhD85. Qu Coll Birm 58. **d** 60 **p** 61. C Daventry *Pet* 60-63; C Reading St Giles *Ox* 63-64; C Wokingham St Paul 64-66; V Yeadon St Andr *Bradf* 66-71; R Heyford w Stowe Nine Churches *Pet* 71-78; RD Daventry 76-78; V Oakham w Hambleton and Egleton 78-81; V Oakham, Hambleton, Egleton, Braunston and Brooke 81-86; Can Pet Cathl 79-86; V Lanteglos by Fowey *Truro* 86-88; Provost St Andr Cathl Inverness *Mor* 88-91; R Inverness St Andr 88-91; P-in-c Culloden St Mary-in-the-Fields 88-91; P-in-c Strathnairn St Paul 88-91; V Mill End and Heronsgate w W Hyde *St Alb* 91-01; RD Rickmansworth 00-01; Perm to Offic *Truro* from 98; rtd 01; Perm to Offic *Pet* from 03. *44 Furnace Drive, Daventry NN11 9FU* Tel (01327) 312550
E-mail alanahorsley@hotmail.co.uk

HORSLEY, Amelia Mary Elizabeth. b 69. K Alfred's Coll Win BEd91. St Jo Coll Nottm MA97. **d** 98 **p** 99. C Southampton Maybush St Pet *Win* 98-01; Teacher Mansel Infant Sch Southampton 01; Teacher Highfields Primary Sch Leic from 01; Dep Hd from 05. *95 Aylestone Drive, Leicester LE2 8SB* Tel 0116-283 7710 E-mail amehorsley@aol.com

HORSLEY, Peter Alec. b 56. Leeds Metrop Univ CertEd98. Cranmer Hall Dur 99. **d** 01 **p** 02. C Acomb St Steph *York* from 01. *36 Fellbrook Avenue, Acomb, York YO26 5PS* Tel (01904) 793240

HORSMAN, Andrew Alan. b 49. Otago Univ BA70 Man Univ MA72 PhD75. St Steph Ho Ox BA80 MA87. **d** 81 **p** 82. C Hillingdon All SS *Lon* 81-84; C Lt Stanmore St Lawr 84-87; TV Haxby w Wigginton *York* 87-98; V Acomb Moor from 98; P-in-c York All SS N Street from 03. *2 Sherringham Drive, York YO24 2SE* Tel (01904) 706047
E-mail andrew@jasdn.freeserve.co.uk

HORSWELL, Kevin George. b 55. Jes Coll Cam BA77 MA81 Nottm Univ BA81. St Jo Coll Nottm 79. **d** 82 **p** 83. C Bootle Ch Ch *Liv* 82-86; Chapl LMH Ox 86-91; C Ox St Giles and SS Phil and Jas w St Marg *Ox* 86-91; R Dodleston *Ches* 91-00; R Llanaber w Caerdeon *Ban* from 00. *The Rectory, Mynach Road, Barmouth LL42 1RL* Tel (01341) 280516

HORTA, Nelson Pinto. b 40. Lisbon Univ Lic80 Catholic Univ of Portugal LicTh92. **d** 65 **p** 69. Portugal from 65; V Setbal H Spirit 69-71; V Lisbon St Paul 71-96; Asst Chapl Gtr Lisbon *Eur* 97-00. *Quinta da Cerieira, rua C, Lote 261, Vale de Figueira-Sobreda, 2800 Almada, Portugal* Tel (00351) (1) 295 7943

HORTON, Alan Michael. b 47. Univ of Wales BScTech71. Linc Th Coll 92. **d** 92 **p** 93. C Bexleyheath Ch Ch *Roch* 92-95; P-in-c Slade Green 95-99; V 99-03; P-in-c Southborough St Thos from 03. *The Vicarage, 28 Pennington Road, Southborough, Tunbridge Wells TN4 0SL* Tel (01892) 529624 *or* 617398
E-mail alanhorton@easynet.co.uk

HORTON, Andrew Charles. b 50. Ex Univ BA71. Sarum Th Coll 71. **d** 73 **p** 74. C Westbury-on-Trym St Alb *Bris* 73-76; USA 76-90; P-in-c Battersea St Mich *S'wark* 90-92; V 92-98; Local Min Officer Kingston Episc Area 94-98; TR Selsdon St Jo w St Fran 98-03. *Address temp unknown*

HORTON, Anne. *See* HORTON, Canon Roberta Anne

HORTON, Cathy Lynne Bosworth. b 62. BA JD. SEITE. **d** 99 **p** 00. NSM Warlingham w Chelsham and Farleigh *S'wark* 99-03; Assoc P Shaker Heights USA from 03. *411 Chagrin Boulevard, Moreland Hills, OH 44022, USA*

HORTON, Canon Christopher Peter. b 26. Leeds Univ BA49. Coll of Resurr Mirfield 49. **d** 51 **p** 52. C Blyth St Mary *Newc* 51-55; C Delaval 55-59; V Grangetown *York* 59-91; Can and Preb York Minster 85-91; rtd 91; Perm to Offic *Newc* from 91. *51 Well Ridge Close, Seaton Grange, Whitley Bay NE25 9PN* Tel 0191-251 0742

HORTON, David Harold. b 49. St Jo Coll Dur BA72. NEOC 82. **d** 86 **p** 87. C Enfield St Jas *Lon* 86-90; Min Joydens Wood St Barn CD *Roch* 90-93; V Joydens Wood St Barn 93-99; P-in-c Rosherville 99-04; rtd 04. *20 Serviden Drive, Bromley BR1 2UB* Tel (020) 8695 7551 E-mail davidhhorton@yahoo.com

HORTON, Canon Jeremy Nicholas Orkney. b 44. Cranmer Hall Dur 64. **d** 68 **p** 69. C Dalton-in-Furness *Carl* 68-70; C Penrith 70-73; V Hudswell w Downholme and Marske *Ripon* 73-75; R Middleton Tyas and Melsonby 75-81; P-in-c Croft 78-81; P-in-c Eryholme 78-81; V Wortley de Leeds 81-93; V Middleton St Mary 93-98; RD Armley 96-98; V Kirby-on-the-Moor, Cundall w Norton-le-Clay etc from 98; Jt AD Ripon 01-04; Hon Can Ripon Cathl from 01. *The Vicarage, 13 The Croft, Kirby Hill, Boroughbridge, York YO51 9YA* Tel (01423) 326284
E-mail nick.horton@fish.co.uk

HORTON, John Ward. b 27. Leeds Univ BA50. Coll of Resurr Mirfield 50. **d** 52 **p** 53. C Balkwell CD *Newc* 52-55; C E Coatham *York* 55-58; C-in-c Acomb Moor CD 58-71; V Acomb Moor 71-93; rtd 93; Perm to Offic *Newc* from 93. *39 Billy Mill Lane, North Shields NE26 8BZ* Tel 0191-296 4082

HORTON, Mrs Joy. b 52. CertEd73 Kent Univ MA98. SEITE 94. **d** 97 **p** 98. C Dartford St Edm *Roch* 97-01; Chapl Bromley

Hosps NHS Trust 01-02; C Erith St Jo *Roch* 02-03; Perm to Offic from 03. *The Vicarage, 28 Pennington Road, Southborough, Tunbridge Wells TN4 0SL* Tel (01892) 529624 E-mail hjoy@fish.co.uk

HORTON, Melanie Jane. b 64. Univ of Cen England in Birm LLB85 Solicitor 88. Ripon Coll Cuddesdon BA96. **d** 96 **p** 97. C Lich St Chad *Lich* 96-00; Chapl R Masonic Sch for Girls Rickmansworth 00-03; Chapl St Edm Sch Cant from 03. *St Edmund's School, Canterbury CT2 8HU* Tel (01227) 454575

HORTON, Michael John. b 56. St Jo Coll Cam BA80 MA83 Univ of Wales (Swansea) PGCE83. Wycliffe Hall Ox BA88 MA92. **d** 89 **p** 90. C Northallerton w Kirby Sigston *York* 89-92; C Ulverston St Mary w H Trin *Carl* 92-94; V Lightwater *Guildf* 94-04; Chapl Wrekin Coll Telford from 04. *Five Gables, Prospect Road, Wellington, Telford TF1 3BE* Tel (01952) 415059 E-mail michael@hortonfamily.co.uk *or* mjhorton@wrekincollege.ac.uk

HORTON, Nicholas. *See* HORTON, Canon Jeremy Nicholas Orkney

HORTON, Ralph Edward. b 41. S'wark Ord Course 75. **d** 78 **p** 79. C Streatham St Leon *S'wark* 78-81; TV Catford (Southend) and Downham 81-88; V Ashford St Matt *Lon* from 88. *The Vicarage, 99 Church Road, Ashford TW15 2NY* Tel (01784) 252459

HORTON, Canon Roberta Anne. b 44. Leic Univ BSc66 CertEd67 Nottm Univ BCombStuds82. Linc Th Coll 79. **dss** 82 **d** 87 **p** 94. Cambridge St Jas *Ely* 82-86; Beaumont Leys *Leic* 86-87; Par Dn 87-91; Dioc Dir of Tr 91-00; P-in-c Swithland 94-99; R Woodhouse, Woodhouse Eaves and Swithland from 00; Hon Can Leic Cathl from 94. *The Rectory, 157 Main Street, Swithland, Loughborough LE12 8TQ* Tel and fax (01509) 891163 E-mail rahorton@leicester.anglican.org

HORWOOD, Graham Frederick. b 34. Univ of Wales (Cardiff) BA55. Coll of Resurr Mirfield 55. **d** 57 **p** 58. C Llantrisant *Llan* 57-61; C Roath St Sav 61-62; C Roath 62-66; V Clydach *S & B* 66-77; V Canton St Luke *Llan* 77-99; rtd 99. *26 Heol-yr-Onnen, Llanharry, Pontyclun CF72 9NJ* Tel (01443) 225777 E-mail ghorwood@freeuk.com

HOSKIN, Brian. *See* HOSKIN, Henry Brian

HOSKIN, Canon David William. b 49. Hatf Coll Dur BSc71. Wycliffe Hall Ox 72. **d** 75 **p** 76. C Bridlington Priory *York* 75-78; C Rodbourne Cheney *Bris* 78-79; C Bebington *Ches* 79-82; R Lockington and Lund and Scorborough w Leconfield *York* 82-88; V Beverley St Mary from 88; RD Beverley from 97; Can and Preb York Minster from 05. *St Mary's Vicarage, 15 Molescroft Road, Beverley HU17 7DX* Tel and fax (01482) 881437 E-mail office@stmarysbeverley.org.uk

HOSKIN, Canon Eric James. b 28. St Chad's Coll Dur BA50 DipTh52. **d** 52 **p** 53. C Coney Hill *Glouc* 52-54; C Stroud 54-57; R Ruardean 57-63; P-in-c Lydbrook 61-63; V Cheltenham Em 63-70; R Dursley 70-86; RD Dursley 77-85; Hon Can Glouc Cathl 81-86; R Easington w Liverton *York* 86-96; rtd 96; Perm to Offic *York* from 96. *37A Algarth Rise, Pocklington, York YO42 2HX* Tel (01759) 305798

HOSKIN, Henry Brian. b 32. NW Ord Course 72. **d** 75 **p** 76. NSM Chesterfield St Aug *Derby* 75-79; NSM Bolsover 79-83; NSM Old Brampton and Loundsley Green 83-88; P-in-c Gt Barlow 88-94; rtd 97; Perm to Offic *Derby* from 97. *25 Barn Close, Chesterfield S41 8BD* Tel (01246) 201550

HOSKING, Canon Harold Ernest. b 19. Lich Th Coll 51. **d** 53 **p** 54. C Penwerris *Truro* 53-56; R Mawgan in Pyder 56-61; V Newlyn St Pet 61-69; V Newquay 69-74; TR Redruth 74-80; R Redruth w Lanner 80-84; Hon Can Truro Cathl 78-84; rtd 84; Perm to Offic *Ex* and *Truro* 84-03; *Ely* from 03. *11 Greenfield Close, Stapleford, Cambridge CB2 5BT* Tel (01223) 840468

HOSKINS, Hugh George. b 46. S Dios Minl Tr Scheme. **d** 84 **p** 85. NSM Hilperton w Whaddon and Staverton etc *Sarum* 84-87; C Calne and Blackland 87-90; R W Lavington and the Cheverells 90-97; TR Upper Wylye Valley 97-04; RD Heytesbury 00-03; TR Pewsey and Swanborough from 04. *The Rectory, Church Street, Pewsey SN9 5DL* Tel (01672) 564357 Fax 563203 E-mail hahoskins@aol.com

HOSKINS, Mrs Rosemary Anne. b 56. Surrey Univ BA03. Wesley Coll Bris 99 STETS 01. **d** 02 **p** 03. NSM Camelot Par *B & W* from 02. *Springfields, Weston Bampfylde, Yeovil BA22 7HZ* Tel (01963) 440026 E-mail revrose@weston-bampfylde.freeserve.co.uk

HOSKYNS, John Algernon Peyton. b 20. Pemb Coll Cam BA41 MA45. Westcott Ho Cam 47. **d** 49 **p** 50. C Eastleigh *Win* 49-52; C Brompton H Trin *Lon* 52-54; V Hartley Wintney and Elvetham *Win* 54-62; R Worplesdon *Guildf* 62-72; V St Weonards w Orcop *Heref* 73-76; P-in-c Linton w Upton Bishop 76-78; P-in-c How Caple w Sollers Hope 76-85; P-in-c Sellack and King's Caple w Foy 81-85; rtd 85; Perm to Offic *Heref* 85-99. *The Coach House, Dinham House, St Minver, Wadebridge PL27 6RH* Tel (01208) 812516

HOST, Mrs Charmaine Anne. b 54. WMMTC 87. **d** 90 **p** 94. C Westwood *Cov* 90-94; C Whitnash 94-96; V Kineton from 96; V Combroke w Compton Verney from 96. *2 Little Pittern, Kineton, Warwick CV35 0LU* Tel (01926) 640248

HOTCHEN, Stephen Jeffrie. b 50. Bradf Coll of Educn. Linc Th Coll 85. **d** 87 **p** 88. C Morpeth *Newc* 87-90; TV High Wycombe *Ox* 90-91; R Dingwall and Strathpeffer *Mor* 91-94; V Rickerscote *Lich* 94-04; R Aylmerton, Runton, Beeston Regis and Gresham *Nor* from 04. *The Rectory, Cromer Road, West Runton, Cromer NR27 9QT* Tel (01263) 837279 Mobile 07976-387199 E-mail sjhotchen@aol.com

HOTCHIN, Mrs Hilary Moya. b 52. Birm Univ CertEd73. WMMTC 85. **d** 88 **p** 94. NSM Redditch St Steph *Worc* 88-91; Par Dn Handsworth *Sheff* 91-94; C 94-96; TV Maltby 96-98. *St George's Rectory, 33 Carden Avenue, Hull HU9 4RT* Tel (01482) 791291

HOUGH, Adrian Michael. b 59. Hertf Coll Ox BA80 MA84 DPhil84 MRSC CChem ACIPD. Ripon Coll Cuddesdon BA91. **d** 92 **p** 93. C Martley and Wichenford, Knightwick etc *Worc* 92-96; Asst P Evesham Deanery 96-97; V Badsey w Aldington and Offenham and Bretforton 97-04; C Lerwick and Burravoe *Ab* 04-05; Perm to Offic *Worc* from 05. *6 Burma Close, Evesham WR11 1GZ* Tel (01386) 48786 E-mail badseyvc@surfaid.org

HOUGH, Miss Carole Elizabeth. b 59. Lon Hosp SRN81. St Jo Coll Nottm DipMin91. **d** 91 **p** 94. C Beoley *Worc* 91-95; Asst Chapl Addenbrooke's NHS Trust 95-98; Chapl Milton Keynes Gen NHS Trust from 98; Chapl Milton Keynes Primary Care Trust from 98. *Milton Keynes General Hospital, Standing Way, Milton Keynes MK6 5LD* Tel (01908) 660033 ext 2215

HOUGH, Michael Jeremy. b 61. Wilson Carlile Coll Oak Hill Th Coll. **d** 02 **p** 03. C Redhill H Trin *S'wark* from 02. *3 Ringwood Avenue, Redhill RH1 2DY* Tel (01737) 762593 Mobile 07939-088867 E-mail mickhough@hotmail.com

HOUGH, Peter George. b 40. Dur Univ BA62. Wells Th Coll 62. **d** 64 **p** 65. C Stocking Farm CD *Leic* 64-68; V Leic St Aid 68-76; V Knutton *Lich* from 76; P-in-c Silverdale and Alsagers Bank 93-94; V Alsagers Bank from 01. *The Vicarage, Church Lane, Newcastle ST5 6DU* Tel (01782) 624282

HOUGH, Sharron Lesley. b 54. **d** 01 **p** 02. OLM Willenhall H Trin *Lich* 01-05; C Bentley from 05. *10 Pineneedle Croft, Willenhall WV12 4BY* Tel (01902) 410458

HOUGH, Sidney Stephen Valentine. b 27. G&C Coll Cam BA50 MA54. Ripon Hall Ox 55. **d** 57 **p** 58. C Goodmayes All SS *Chelmsf* 57-60; C Warwick St Mary *Cov* 60-62; V Messing *Chelmsf* 62-72; R Inworth 62-72; V Messing w Inworth 72-77; Chapl Warley Hosp Brentwood 78-79; R Alphamstone w Lamarsh and Pebmarsh *Chelmsf* 79-88; rtd 88. *27 Weavers Court, Weavers Lane, Sudbury CO10 1HY* Tel (01787) 374812

HOUGH, Wendy Lorraine. **d** 00 **p** 01. C The Hague *Eur* 00-03. *Keizersgracht 481, 1017DL Amsterdam, The Netherlands* Tel (0031) (20) 420 2007

HOUGHTON, Christopher Guy. b 64. W Surrey Coll of Art & Design BA86. Oak Hill Th Coll BA89. **d** 89 **p** 90. C Mossley Hill St Matt and St Jas *Liv* 89-92; C Ashton-in-Makerfield St Thos 92-95; C Southport St Phil and St Paul 95-96; Chapl Chorley and S Ribble NHS Trust 96-01; rtd 01; Perm to Offic *Blackb* from 03. *35 Deerfold, Chorley PR7 1UD*

HOUGHTON, David John. b 47. Edin Univ BSc(Econ)68. Cuddesdon Coll 69. **d** 71 **p** 72. C Prestbury *Glouc* 71-74; Prec Gib Cathl *Eur* 74-76; Chapl Madrid 76-78; C Croydon St Jo *Cant* 78-80; Chapl Warw Sch 80-85; P-in-c Isleworth St Fran *Lon* 85-90; USA 90-91; TV Clapham Team *S'wark* 91-01; RD Clapham 93-01; V Clapham H Spirit 02; Chapl Paris St Geo *Eur* from 02. *7 rue Auguste Vacquerie, 75116 Paris, France* Tel (0033) (1) 47 23 37 27 *or* 47 20 22 51 E-mail davidhoughton@wanadoo.fr *or* chaplain@stgeorgesparis.com

HOUGHTON, Mrs Evelyn Mabel. b 44. Stockwell Coll of Educn TCert65. Oak Hill NSM Course 92. **d** 94 **p** 95. NSM Bedford St Jo and St Leon *St Alb* 94-98; C Reading St Agnes w St Paul *Ox* from 98. *St Paul's House, 3 Whitley Wood Lane, Reading RG2 8PN* Tel 0118-987 4448

HOUGHTON, Geoffrey John. b 59. Ridley Hall Cam 87. **d** 90 **p** 91. C Sholing *Win* 90-94; P-in-c Jersey All SS 94-99; V from 99; P-in-c Jersey St Simon 94-99; V from 99; Vice-Dean Jersey from 99; Hon Chapl Jersey Hospice from 96. *All Saints' Vicarage, Savile Street, St Helier, Jersey JE2 3XF* Tel (01534) 768538 E-mail geoffhoughton@jerseymail.co.uk *or* gjh@super.net.uk

HOUGHTON, Graham. *See* HOUGHTON, Peter Graham

HOUGHTON, Hugh Alexander Gervase. b 76. St Jo Coll Cam MPhil98 MA01 Leeds Univ BA02. Coll of Resurr Mirfield 00. **d** 03 **p** 04. NSM Weoley Castle *Birm* from 03. *St Gabriels' Church, 34 Shenley Lane, Birmingham B29 5PL* Tel 0121-475 4283 *or* 414 5771 E-mail ssm@hagh.co.uk

HOUGHTON, Ian David. b 50. Lanc Univ BA71 Newc Univ CertEd74 Man Univ CertRS90. Sarum & Wells Th Coll 80. **d** 82 **p** 83. C Newc St Geo *Newc* 82-85; Chapl Newc Poly 85-92; Chapl Univ of Northumbria at Newc 92-95; Master Newc St Thos Prop Chpl 90-95; Black Country Urban Ind Miss *Lich* 95-04; Res Min Bilston 95-04; Chapl Pet City Cen *Pet* from 04; C Pet St Jo from 04. *19 Danes Close, Peterborough PE1 5LJ* Tel (01733) 763729 E-mail idh_bcuim@hotmail.com

HOUGHTON, James Robert. b 44. AKC67 St Luke's Coll Ex 73. St Boniface Warminster 67. **d** 68 **p** 69. C Herrington *Dur* 68-70; Asst Dioc Youth Chapl *Bris* 70-72; Perm to Offic *Ex* 73-74; C Heavitree 74-77; C Heavitree w Ex St Paul 78; Perm to Offic *Lon* 78-80 and 83-88; Hon C W Drayton 80-83; Chapl Greycoat Hosp Sch 83-88; Chapl Stonar Sch Melksham 88-95; Chapl St Mary and St Anne's Sch Abbots Bromley 95-99; R Buxted and Hadlow Down *Chich* 99-02; V Eastbourne St Mich from 02. *The Vicarage, 15 Long Acre Close, Eastbourne BN21 1UF* Tel (01323) 645740

HOUGHTON, Canon John Caswell. b 16. Dur Univ BA38 LTh38. St Boniface Warminster 34. **d** 39 **p** 40. C Wolverton St Geo *Ox* 39-42; Zambia 42-74; Warden Dioc Th Sem N Rhodesia 47-52; Can N Rhodesia 60-62; Adn N Rhodesia 62-64; Adn S Zambia 64-70; Can Lusaka 71-74; Promotions Sec Feed the Minds 74-81; rtd 81; Perm to Offic *Ox* from 82. *18 Cornelia Close, Bletchley, Milton Keynes MK2 3LX* Tel (01908) 370526

HOUGHTON, Michael Richard. b 29. CCC Cam BA52 MA56. Cuddesdon Coll 52. **d** 54 **p** 55. C Portsea N End St Mark *Portsm* 54-57; New Zealand from 57; Adn Tamaki 77-81. *Private Bag 12, Papakura, New Zealand* Tel (0064) (9) 292 2432

HOUGHTON, Peter Graham. b 51. St Jo Coll Nottm 85. **d** 87 **p** 88. C Toxteth Park St Clem *Liv* 87-91; Chapl Winwick Hosp Warrington 91-94; Chapl Warrington Community Health Care NHS Trust 94-98; Chapl HM Pris Styal 98-01; Chapl St Helens and Knowsley Hosps NHS Trust 04-05. *40 Grange Drive, Penketh, Warrington WA5 2JN*

HOUGHTON, Robert Sherwood. b 26. Trin Coll Melbourne BA48 Clare Coll Cam BA51 MA56 LLB59 Mercer Ho Melbourne DipEd62. Wells Th Coll 52. **d** 52 **p** 53. C Howe Bridge *Man* 52-54; Australia from 54; rtd 95. *Homestead Hostel, 11 Homestead Avenue, Wallington, Vic, Australia 3221* Tel (0061) (3) 9328 4221

HOUGHTON, Mrs Rosemary Margaret Anne. b 46. Dioc OLM tr scheme 98. **d** 00 **p** 01. OLM Earlham St Eliz *Nor* from 00. *74 St Mildred's Road, West Earlham, Norwich NR5 8RS* Tel (01603) 502752 Mobile 07808-774811 E-mail user@houghtonfamily.in2home.co.uk

HOUGHTON, Mrs Susan Jeanette. b 39. Qu Mary Coll Lon BSc61 Nottm Univ PGCE62. WMMTC 98. **d** 99 **p** 00. OLM Dursley *Glouc* 99-02; rtd 02; NSM Offwell, Northleigh, Farway, Cotleigh etc *Ex* from 02. *2 Combewater Cottages, Wilmington, Honiton EX14 9SQ* Tel (01404) 831887 E-mail susanhoughton@lineone.net *or* davidjohnhoughton@lineone.net

HOUGHTON, Thomas. b 17. NW Ord Course 71. **d** 74 **p** 75. NSM Newcastle w Butterton *Lich* 74-82; Perm to Offic from 82. *Fernyhough, Little Madeley, Crewe CW3 9JT* Tel (01782) 750275

HOUGHTON, Timothy John. b 56. Kingston Poly BSc88. Oak Hill Th Coll BA93. **d** 97 **p** 98. C Normanton *Derby* 97-03. *Picardy, Harsfold Road, Rustington, Littlehampton BN16 2QH* Tel (01903) 775064 E-mail timhough@ntlworld.com

HOULDEN, Prof James Leslie. b 29. Qu Coll Ox BA52 MA56. Cuddesdon Coll 53. **d** 55 **p** 56. C Hunslet St Mary and Stourton *Ripon* 55-58; Tutor Chich Th Coll 58-59; Chapl 59-60; Chapl Trin Coll Ox 60-70; Prin Cuddesdon Coll 70-75; Prin Ripon Coll Cuddesdon 75-77; V Cuddesdon *Ox* 70-77; Hon Can Ch Ch 76-77; Sen Lect NT Studies K Coll Lon 77-87; Prof Th 87-94; rtd 94; Perm to Offic *S'wark* 94-99. *5 The Court, Fen End Road West, Knowle, Solihull B93 0AN* Tel (01564) 777138 E-mail leslie.houlden@btopenworld.com

HOULDING, Preb David Nigel Christopher. b 53. AKC76 SSC. **d** 77 **p** 78. C Hillingdon All SS *Lon* 77-81; C Holborn St Alb w Saffron Hill St Pet 81-85; V Hampstead St Steph w All Hallows from 85; AD N Camden 01-02; Preb St Paul's Cathl from 04. *All Hallows' House, 52 Courthope Road, London NW3 2LD* Tel (020) 7267 7833 *or* 7267 6317 Mobile 07710-403294 Fax (020) 7267 6317 E-mail fr.houlding@lineone.net

HOULDSWORTH, Raymond Clifford. b 30. Bps' Coll Cheshunt 64. **d** 66 **p** 67. C Egham Hythe *Guildf* 66-70; C Cranbrook *Cant* 70-76; V Hernhill 76-82; V Minster w Monkton 82-95; rtd 95; Perm to Offic *Mon* from 95. *St Illtyd's, 11 Craig Road, Six Bells, Abertillery NP13 2LR* Tel (01495) 321934

HOULT, Roy Anthony. b 35. AKC58. **d** 59 **p** 60. C Walton St Mary *Liv* 59-63; Canada from 63; Hon Can Koot 75-79. *381 Huron Street, Toronto ON, Canada, M5S 2G5*

HOUNSFIELD, Thomas Paul. b 15. Lon Coll of Div 46. **d** 47 **p** 48. C Penn Fields *Lich* 47-50; R Treeton *Sheff* 50-61; V Donington *Lich* 61-80; rtd 80; Perm to Offic *Win* from 81. *10 Widden Close, Sway, Lymington SO41 6AX* Tel (01590) 682399

HOUSE, Graham Ivor. b 44. BA80. Oak Hill Th Coll 77. **d** 80 **p** 81. C Ipswich St Jo *St E* 80-84; V Ipswich St Andr 84-00; R Monks Eleigh w Chelsworth and Brent Eleigh etc 00-03; rtd 03; Perm to Offic *St E* from 03. *1 Scott Lane, Melton, Woodbridge IP12 1TJ* Tel (01394) 615710 Mobile 07966-169372

HOUSE, Jack Francis. b 35. Bris Univ BEd70 Lon Univ MA80 Univ of Wales MTh94. Bris & Glouc Tr Course 79. **d** 80 **p** 81. NSM Bedminster *Bris* 80-92; Perm to Offic 92-94; NSM Knowle H Nativity 94-03; NSM Easton All Hallows 98-03; NSM Brislington St Anne from 03. *48 Hendre Road, Bristol BS3 2LR* Tel 0117-966 1144 E-mail rhouse3766@aol.com

HOUSE, Mrs Janet. b 45. UEA BA67 Keswick Hall Coll PGCE68 Sussex Univ MA80. Ripon Coll Cuddesdon 93. **d** 95 **p** 96. C Swindon Ch Ch *Bris* 95-99; TV Worc SE *Worc* from 99. *The Vicarage, 4 Silverdale Avenue, Worcester WR5 1PY* Tel (01905) 353432 E-mail jhouse@waitrose.com

HOUSE, Miss Maureen Ruth (Mo). b 33. St Mich Ho Ox 56 LNSM course 95. **d** 98 **p** 99. NSM Charlton *S'wark* from 98. *88 Speedwell Street, London SE8 4AT* Tel (020) 8691 1637

HOUSE, Simon Hutchinson. b 30. Peterho Cam BA65 MA67. Cuddesdon Coll 61. **d** 64 **p** 65. C Sutton St Jas *York* 64-67; C Acomb St Steph 67-69; V Allestree St Nic *Derby* 69-81; RD Duffield 74-81; V Bitterne Park *Win* 81-91; rtd 91; Perm to Offic *Win* from 91. *22 Stanley Street, Southsea PO5 2DS* Tel (023) 9283 8592

HOUSE, Vickery Willis. b 45. MA. Kelham Th Coll. **d** 69 **p** 70. C Crediton *Ex* 69-76; TV Sampford Peverell, Uplowman, Holcombe Rogus etc 76-81; R Berwick w Selmeston and Alciston *Chich* 81-90; Chapl Ardingly Coll 90-94; V Brighton St Bart *Chich* from 94. *16 Richmond Terrace, Brighton BN2 9SA* Tel (01273) 685142 *or* 620491 Fax 572215 E-mail stbarts@fastnet.co.uk

HOUSEMAN, Patricia Adele. *See* CAMPION, Mrs Patricia Adele

HOUSLEY, Andrew Arthur. b 67. Wilson Carlile Coll 91 Ridley Hall Cam 00. **d** 02 **p** 03. C Ormskirk *Liv* from 02. *18 Lea Crescent, Ormskirk L39 1PQ* Tel (01695) 570876 E-mail andrewjohousley@ukonline.co.uk

HOUSMAN, Arthur Martin Rowand. b 53. MA CertEd. Trin Coll Bris 81. **d** 83 **p** 84. C Croydon Ch Ch Broad Green *Cant* 83-84; C Croydon Ch Ch *S'wark* 85-87; TV Stratton St Margaret w S Marston etc *Bris* 87-93; Chapl Peterhouse Sch Zimbabwe 93-98; Chapl Nor Sch from 98; Hon PV Nor Cathl *Nor* from 98. *Cottage Farm Cottage, Beccles Road, Raveningham, Norwich NR14 6NW* Tel (01508) 548991

HOUSTON, Canon Arthur James. b 54. Trin Coll Bris BA87. **d** 87 **p** 88. C Chatham St Phil and St Jas *Roch* 87-91; I Carrigaline Union *C, C & R* 91-99; Can Cork Cathl 95-99; Can Ross Cathl 95-99; Dir of Ords 96-99; V Margate H Trin *Cant* from 99; AD Thanet from 02; Hon Can Cant Cathl from 03. *The Vicarage, 5 Devonshire Gardens, Cliftonville, Margate CT9 3AF* Tel (01843) 294129 E-mail arthurhouston@btinternet.com

HOUSTON, David Wiliam James. b 52. DipTh98. **d** 93 **p** 95. S Africa 93-00; Lyttelton St Steph 93-96; R Sabie w Lydenburg 96-00; P-in-c Elmsted w Hastingleigh *Cant* from 00; P-in-c Petham and Waltham w Lower Hardres etc from 00. *The Rectory, Curtis Lane, Stelling Minnis, Canterbury CT4 6BT* Tel (01227) 709318 Fax as telephone E-mail davidwjhouston@ssgchurches.fsnet.co.uk

HOUSTON, Edward Davison. b 31. TCD BA56. **d** 57 **p** 58. C Conwall Union *D & R* 57-59; India 59-88; V Whittlebury w Paulerspury *Pet* 89-01; P-in-c Wicken 89-01; Perm to Offic from 01; rtd 01. *38 Meadow Street, Market Harborough LE16 7JZ*

HOUSTON, Helen Sarah. b 70. Bris Univ BA91. St Jo Coll Nottm MA95. **d** 95 **p** 96. C Bourne *Guildf* 95-98; Perm to Offic *Bris* 98-99; Hon C Chippenham St Pet 99-00; C Ballyholme *D & D* 02-04; C Stretton and Appleton Thorn *Ches* from 04. *48 Stansfield Drive, Grappenhall, Warrington WA4 3EA* Tel (01925) 211466 E-mail helen@davehouston.fsnet.co.uk

HOUSTON, Kenneth. *See* HOUSTON, Prof Samuel Kenneth

HOUSTON, Maurice Iain. b 48. TISEC 99. **d** 02 **p** 03. C Edin Old St Paul *Edin* 02-05; R Melrose from 05. *The Rectory, 20 High Cross Avenue, Melrose TD6 9SU* Tel (01896) 822626 Mobile 07866-074568 E-mail mors@fish.co.uk

HOUSTON, Michael Alexander. b 46. Lanc Univ MA92. Linc Th Coll 86. **d** 88 **p** 89. C Longton *Blackb* 88-91; C Woughton *Ox* 91-92; TV 92-98; TR 98-99; TR Gd Shep TM *Carl* from 99. *The Rectory, Greystoke, Penrith CA11 0TJ* Tel (01768) 483293 E-mail mike.greystoke@tiscali.co.uk

HOUSTON, Michael James. b 41. Dub Bible Coll St Jo Coll Nottm. **d** 95 **p** 97. Aux Min *D & D* 95-99; P-in-c Ballyphilip w Ardquin from 99. *Milltown House, 12 Kearney Road, Portaferry, Newtownards BT22 1QF* Tel (028) 4272 9997 Fax 9042 8199

HOUSTON, Prof Samuel Kenneth (Ken). b 43. FIMA73 QUB BSc64 PhD67 MILT. CITC 81. **d** 85 **p** 86. NSM Belfast St Jas w St Silas *Conn* 85-91; NSM Belfast St Andr from 91; Prof Mathematical Studies Ulster Univ from 96. *29 North Circular Road, Belfast BT15 5HB* Tel (028) 9077 1830 *or* 9036 6953 Fax 9036 6859 E-mail sk.houston@north-circular.demon.co.uk

HOUSTON, William Paul. b 54. QUB BSSc76 TCD BTh78. CITC 78. **d** 81 **p** 82. C Carrickfergus *Conn* 81-83; C Bangor St Comgall *D & D* 83-86; I Gilford 86-90; I Carnalea 90-99; I Clondalkin w Rathcoole *D & G* from 99; Min Can St Patr Cathl Dublin from 00. *The Rectory, 5 Monastery Road, Clondalkin, Dublin 22, Irish Republic* Tel (00353) (1) 459 2160

HOVENDEN, Gerald Eric. b 53. York Univ BA75 Ox Univ MA85. Wycliffe Hall Ox 78. **d** 81 **p** 82. C Pitsmoor w Ellesmere *Sheff* 81-85; Chapl Lyon w Grenoble and St Etienne *Eur* 85-90; TV S Gillingham *Roch* 90-98; TR Southborough St Pet w Ch Ch and St Matt 98-02; TR Southborough St Pet w Ch Ch and St Matt etc from 02. *The Vicarage, 86 Prospect Road, Southborough, Tunbridge Wells TN4 0EG* Tel (01892) 528534 E-mail geh@hovendens.freeserve.co.uk

HOVEY, Richard Michael. b 58. Imp Coll Lon BScEng79 ACGI79 Cranfield Inst of Tech MBA84 CEng83 MIEE83. Cranmer Hall Dur 93. **d** 95 **p** 96. C Cheddar *B & W* 95-99; TV Gtr Corsham *Bris* 99-01; TV Gtr Corsham and Lacock 01-05; CMS from 05. *CMS, Partnership House, 157 Waterloo Road, London SE1 8UU* Tel (020) 7928 8681 E-mail rmh@dawntreader.freeserve.co.uk

HOVIL, Jeremy Richard Guy. b 65. K Coll Lon BSc86 Spurgeon's Coll Lon MTh99. Wycliffe Hall Ox BTh95. **d** 95 **p** 96. C Kensington St Barn *Lon* 95-99; Crosslinks Uganda from 00. *PO Box 6016, Kampala, Uganda* Tel (00256) (41) 501972 *or* (77) 612230 E-mail hovils@spacenetuganda.com

HOVIL, Richard Guy. b 29. Ex Coll Ox BA51 MA57. Ridley Hall Cam. **d** 55 **p** 56. C Finchley Ch Ch *Lon* 55-58; Staff Worker Scripture Union 58-71; Chapl Monkton Combe Sch Bath 71-83; V Fremington *Ex* 83-94; rtd 94; Perm to Offic *Sarum* from 94. *37 Upper Marsh Road, Warminster BA12 9PN* Tel (01985) 214337 E-mail richard@hovil.fsnet.co.uk

HOW, Canon John Maxloe. b 15. Magd Coll Cam BA37 MA49. Westcott Ho Cam 39. **d** 39 **p** 40. C Norton St Mary *Dur* 39-44; P-in-c W Pelton 44-45; P-in-c Stella 46-47; V Thornley 47-51; V Monkwearmouth St Andr 51-59; V Barton w Pooley Bridge *Carl* 59-73; RD Penrith 61-73; Hon Can Carl Cathl 72-81; V Kirkby Lonsdale w Mansergh 73-76; TR Kirkby Lonsdale 76-81; rtd 81; Perm to Offic *Carl* from 81. *The Laurels, 3 Belle Isle Terrace, Grange-over-Sands LA11 6EA* Tel (01539) 534117

HOWARD, Alan James. b 45. Bris Univ BA69. Clifton Th Coll. **d** 71 **p** 72. C Welling *Roch* 71-74; C Cromer *Nor* 74-78; V Sidcup St Andr *Roch* 78-86; V Leyton St Cath *Chelmsf* 86-93; V Leyton St Cath and St Paul 93-00; rtd 05. *4 Bower Close, Romford RM5 3SR* Tel (01708) 760905

HOWARD, Andrew. b 63. Man Univ BA95 Leeds Univ MA97. Coll of Resurr Mirfield 95. **d** 97 **p** 98. C Worksop Priory *S'well* 97-01; V Hemlington *York* from 01. *St Timothy's House, 31 Coatham Close, Hemlington, Middlesbrough TS8 9JW* Tel (01642) 590496

HOWARD, Arthur Calvin. b 60. Leeds Univ LLB82 Barrister 83. Wycliffe Hall Ox 00. **d** 03. C Heswall *Ches* 03-04; C Weston from 04. *3 Knights Way, Shavington, Crewe CW2 5HU* Tel (01270) 664072

HOWARD, Charles William Wykeham. b 52. Southn Univ BTh81. Sarum & Wells Th Coll 76. **d** 79 **p** 80. C St Mary-at-Latton *Chelmsf* 79-82; Chapl RN from 82. *Royal Naval Chaplaincy Service, Room 203, Victory Building, HM Naval Base, Portsmouth PO1 3LS* Tel (023) 9272 7903 Fax 9272 7111

HOWARD, Clive Eric. b 65. Oak Hill Th Coll BA99. **d** 99 **p** 00. C Chipping Sodbury and Old Sodbury *Glouc* 99-03; V Tipton St Matt *Lich* from 03. *St Matthew's Vicarage, Dudley Road, Tipton DY4 8DJ* Tel 0121-557 1929 E-mail clive-howard@rev65.fsnet.co.uk

HOWARD, David John. b 47. Brasted Th Coll 68 Ripon Hall Ox 70. **d** 72 **p** 73. C Benchill *Man* 72-75; C Sedgley All SS *Lich* 75-77; C-in-c Lostock CD *Man* 77-85; V Lt Hulton 85-88; Perm to Offic 90-91; C E Leake *S'well* 91-92; C Costock 91-92; C Rempstone 91-92; C Stanford on Soar 91-92; C W Leake w Kingston-on-Soar and Ratcliffe-on-Soar 91-92; C E and W Leake, Stanford-on-Soar, Rempstone etc 92-94; P-in-c Bilborough w Strelley 94-98; Chapl HM YOI Werrington Ho 98-03; Chapl HM Pris Drake Hall from 03. *HM Prison and YOI Drake Hall, Eccleshall, Stafford ST21 6LQ* Tel (01785) 774144 E-mail david.howard3@hmps.gsi.gov.uk

HOWARD, David John. b 51. Lon Univ BSc73. Oak Hill Th Coll 74. **d** 77 **p** 78. C Radipole and Melcombe Regis *Sarum* 77-83; R Tredington and Darlingscott w Newbold on Stour *Cov* 83-90; P-in-c Binley 90-94; V 94-04; RD Cov E 95-99; V Potterne w Worton and Marston *Sarum* from 04. *The Vicarage, 4 Rookes Lane, Potterne, Devizes SN10 5NF* Tel (01380) 723189 E-mail howard@binleyvicarage.fsnet.co.uk

HOWARD, Canon Donald. b 27. K Coll Lon BD58 AKC58. **d** 59 **p** 60. C Saltburn-by-the-Sea *York* 59-62; S Africa 62-72; R Haddington *Edin* 72-78; Can St Andr Cathl *Ab* 78-91; Provost St Andr Cathl 78-91; R Aberdeen St Andr 78-91; Chapl Aber Univ 78-82; P-in-c Aberdeen St Ninian 80-91; Angl Adv Grampian TV 84-88; rtd 91; Hon Can St Andr Cathl *Ab* from 91; Perm to Offic *Ripon* from 91. *42 Waterside, Ripon HG4 1RA* Tel (01765) 692144 E-mail donaldripon@aol.com

HOWARD, Mrs Erika Kathryn. b 49. SRN70 SCM72. S Dios Minl Tr Scheme 88. **d** 91 **p** 94. NSM New Shoreham and Old Shoreham *Chich* 91-94; C Kingston Buci 94-03; V Sompting from 03. *The Vicarage, West Street, Sompting, Lancing BN15 0AP* Tel (01903) 234511 E-mail erikahoward@supanet.com

HOWARD, Canon Francis Curzon. b 27. Lon Univ DipTh57. St Aid Birkenhead 54. **d** 57 **p** 58. C Claughton cum Grange *Ches* 57-60; C Cheltenham St Paul *Glouc* 60-62; V Sheff St Barn *Sheff* 62-65; Bermuda 65-71; USA from 71; Asst Atone Westfield Massachusetts 71-76; R Tariffville Trin Connecticut 76-98; rtd 98; Can Kaduna from 95. *PO Box 423, 116 Terry's Plain Road, Simsbury, CT 06070, USA* Tel (001) (860) 658 1897

HOWARD, Frank Thomas. b 36. Lon Univ BSc57. Bps' Coll Cheshunt 59. **d** 61 **p** 62. C Macclesfield St Mich *Ches* 61-64; C Claughton cum Grange 64-66; V Lache cum Saltney 66-76; R Stanton *St E* 76-97; RD Ixworth 79-85; P-in-c Hempnall *Nor* 97-01; rtd 01; Perm to Offic *Nor* from 01. *55 Heywood Avenue, Diss IP22 4DN* Tel (01379) 640819

HOWARD, Geoffrey. b 30. Barrister-at-Law 83 Lon Univ LLB77. EMMTC. **d** 85 **p** 86. NSM Barton *Ely* 85-87; NSM Coton 85-87; C W Walton 87-92; TV Daventry, Ashby St Ledgers, Braunston etc *Pet* 92-97; rtd 97; Perm to Offic *Ely* 97-00. *11 Porson Court, Porson Road, Cambridge CB2 2ER* Tel (01223) 300738

HOWARD, George Granville. b 47. Trin Coll Bris. **d** 88 **p** 89. C Downend *Bris* 88-92; V Clifton H Trin, St Andr and St Pet 92-99; Bp's Officer for Miss and Evang 92-99; V W Streatham St Jas *S'wark* from 99; RD Tooting from 02. *St James's Vicarage, 236 Mitcham Lane, London SW16 6NT* Tel (020) 8664 6059 *or* 8677 3947

HOWARD, John. *See* HOWARD, Nicolas John

HOWARD, John Alexander. b 27. Wesley Coll Leeds 48 Coll of Resurr Mirfield 66. **d** 67 **p** 68. C Almondbury *Wakef* 67-71; V Skelmanthorpe 71-81; R Fortrose *Mor* 81-94; R Cromarty 81-94; R Arpafeelie 81-94; rtd 94; Perm to Offic *Glouc* from 94. *2 Webbs Cottages, Stratford Road, Mickleton, Chipping Campden GL55 6SW* Tel (01386) 438787

HOWARD, John Robert. b 60. NUI BA HDipEd TCD DipTh. **d** 84 **p** 85. C Donaghcloney w Waringstown *D & D* 84-88; I Belfast St Ninian *Conn* 88-94; Bp's Dom Chapl 88-94; Chapl Ulster Univ 88-94; I Annahilt w Magherahamlet *D & D* from 94; Chapl HM Pris Maghaberry from 96. *Annahilt Rectory, 15 Ballykeel Road, Hillsborough BT26 6NW* Tel (028) 9263 8218

HOWARD, Mrs Judith Marion. WEMTC 98. **d** 01 **p** 02. NSM Glouc St Jas and All SS *Glouc* from 01. *Paulmead, Wells Road, Bisley, Stroud GL6 7AG* Tel (01452) 770776

HOWARD, Keith. b 55. St Jo Coll Nottm 81. **d** 84 **p** 85. C Llanidloes w Llangurig *Ban* 84-87; R Llansantffraid Glan Conwy and Eglwysbach *St As* 87-00; V Heapey St Barnabas and Withnell St Paul *Blackb* from 00. *1 Balmoral Drive, Brinscall, Chorley PR6 8ST* Tel (01254) 832017

HOWARD, Martin John Aidan. b 68. Lon Univ BA90 Open Univ MA96. St Jo Coll Nottm MA97. **d** 97 **p** 98. C Billericay and Lt Burstead *Chelmsf* 97-01; TV Kinson *Sarum* from 01. *The Rectory, 51 Millhams Road, Bournemouth BH10 7LJ* Tel (01202) 571996 E-mail rev@howardhome.org.uk

HOWARD, Canon Michael Charles. b 35. Selw Coll Cam BA58 MA63 CQSW72. Wycliffe Hall Ox 58. **d** 60 **p** 61. C Stowmarket *St E* 60-64; CMS Nigeria 64-71; Hon Can Ondo 70-71; Hon C Southborough St Pet w Ch Ch and St Matt *Roch* 72-73; Perm to Offic *Ox* from 73; rtd 00. *17 Milton Road, Bloxham, Banbury OX15 4HD* Tel (01295) 720470

HOWARD, Natalie Delia. b 51. St Mich Coll Llan 99. **d** 02 **p** 03. NSM Magor *Mon* from 02. *8 The Meadows, Magor, Caldicot NP26 3LA* Tel (01633) 881714

HOWARD, Nicolas John. b 61. Nottm Univ BTh90. Aston Tr Scheme 85 Linc Th Coll 87. **d** 90 **p** 91. C Bracknell *Ox* 90-94; P-in-c Oldham St Chad Limeside *Man* 94-96; Perm to Offic *Birm* 96-99. *11 Chesterfield Court, Middleton Hall Road, Birmingham B30 1AF* Tel 0121-459 4975

HOWARD, Norman. b 26. AKC57. St Boniface Warminster 57. **d** 58 **p** 59. C Friern Barnet St Jas *Lon* 58-62; Jamaica 62-69; USA from 69; rtd 91. *766 Lake Forest Road, Clearwater, FL 33765, USA* Tel (001) (813) 799 3929

HOWARD, Paul David. b 47. Lanchester Poly BA69. St Jo Coll Nottm 74. **d** 77 **p** 78. C Bedworth *Cov* 77-83; V Newchapel *Lich* 83-93; V Stretton w Claymills 93-04; P-in-c Talke from 04. *The Rectory, 26 Crown Bank, Talke, Stoke-on-Trent ST7 1PU* Tel (01782) 782348 E-mail paul@howard510.freeserve.co.uk

HOWARD, Peter Leslie. b 48. Nottm Univ BTh77 Birm Univ MA80 Leeds Univ MEd91. St Jo Coll Nottm LTh77. **d** 77 **p** 78. C Gospel Lane St Mich *Birm* 77-81; P-in-c Nechells 81-85; V Stanley *Wakef* 85-92; P-in-c Nor Heartsease St Fran *Nor* from 92; Dioc UPA/CUF Link Officer from 02. *St Francis's Vicarage, 100 Rider Haggard Road, Norwich NR7 9UQ* Tel (01603) 702799 E-mail plhoward.stfrancis@tinyworld.co.uk

HOWARD, Reginald James. b 33. AKC60. **d** 61 **p** 62. C Shildon *Dur* 61-64; C Hurworth 64-66; V Morley St Paul *Wakef* 66-75; V Westgate Common 75-93; rtd 93; Perm to Offic *Wakef* from 98. *41 Oakleigh Avenue, Wakefield WF2 9DF* Tel (01924) 373020

HOWARD, Canon Robert Weston. b 28. Pemb Coll Cam BA49 MA53. Westcott Ho Cam 51. **d** 53 **p** 54. C Bishopwearmouth St Mich *Dur* 53-56; C Cambridge Gt St Mary w St Mich *Ely* 56-60; Hong Kong 60-66; V Prenton *Ches* 66-75; RD Frodsham 74-82; P-in-c Dunham-on-the-Hill 75-77; V Helsby and Ince

75-77; V Helsby and Dunham-on-the-Hill 77-82; Hon Can Ches Cathl 78-82; V Moseley St Mary *Birm* 82-88; V Chalke Valley W *Sarum* 88-93; rtd 93; Perm to Offic *St D* and *Heref* from 93. *The Coach House, 13 Clun Road, Aston-on-Clun, Craven Arms SY7 8EW* Tel (01588) 660630

HOWARD, Ronald. b 40. AMIBF65 AMICME01 EngTech91. Cranmer Hall Dur 86. **d** 88 **p** 89. C Baildon *Bradf* 88-92; P-in-c Sutton 92-96; P-in-c St Tudy w St Mabyn and Michaelstow *Truro* 96-00; P-in-c Keyingham w Ottringham, Halsham and Sunk Is *York* 00-03; R from 03; RD S Holderness from 04. *The Rectory, Ottringham Road, Keyingham, Hull HU12 9RX* Tel (01964) 622171 Fax 622907
E-mail fatherronald@btinternet.com

HOWARD, Simon Charles. b 60. Birm Univ BA81 Westhill Coll Birm CYCW86. Ridley Hall Cam 90. **d** 92 **p** 93. C Cambridge St Martin *Ely* 92-96; Chapl St Bede's Sch Cam 92-96; P-in-c Earley Trinity *Ox* 96-05; P-in-c Ruscombe and Twyford from 05. *The Vicarage, Ruscombe, Reading RG10 9UD* Tel 0118-934 1092 *or* 934 1685 E-mail revsimon@lineone.net

HOWARD, Stanley Reginald Kekewich. b 10. St Pet Hall Ox BA31 MA35. Ridley Hall Cam 31. **d** 33 **p** 34. C Battersea St Mich *S'wark* 33-36; C Watford St Andr *St Alb* 36-39; C Margate H Trin *Cant* 39-40; R Cuxton *Roch* 40-51; V Cheltenham St Paul *Glouc* 51-76; Chapl St Cath Ho 51-68; Chapl Cheltenham Boys' Home 51-56; Chapl Cheltenham Maternity and St Paul's Hosps 61-76; rtd 76; Perm to Offic *Win* from 81. *Grimston Rectory, Watery Lane, Grimston, King's Lynn PE32 1BQ* Tel (01485) 600353
E-mail srkh@grimston-rectory.freeserve.co.uk

HOWARD, Ms Susan. b 65. Lanc Univ BA86. Ripon Coll Cuddesdon 88. **d** 91 **p** 94. C Ditton St Mich *Liv* 91-94; C Kirkby 94-97; Adv for Youth and Young Adults *Man* 97-00; Governor HM Pris Styal from 01. *HM Prison, Styal, Wilmslow SK9 4HR* Tel (01625) 532141

HOWARD, Thomas Norman. b 40. St Aid Birkenhead 64. **d** 67 **p** 68. C Farnworth and Kearsley *Man* 67-70; C Prestwich St Marg 70-73; V Heyside 73-85; Warden Lamplugh Ho Angl Conf Cen 85-90; Hon C Langtoft w Foxholes, Butterwick, Cottam etc *York* 85-87; C 87-90; V Fence and Newchurch-in-Pendle *Blackb* 90-00; Dioc Ecum Officer 90-95; rtd 00; Hon C Stalybridge H Trin and Ch Ch *Ches* 01-03; Perm to Offic from 03. *Bethel Barn, Main Road, Nether Kellet, Carnforth LA6 1EF* Tel (01524) 736552

HOWARD, William Alfred. b 47. St Jo Coll Dur BA69. Wycliffe Hall Ox 74. **d** 77 **p** 79. C Norbiton *S'wark* 77-80; C Mile Cross *Nor* 80-84; R Grimston, Congham and Roydon from 84; Chapl Norfolk Constabulary from 00. *The Rectory, Watery Lane, Grimston, King's Lynn PE32 1BQ* Tel (01485) 600335
E-mail william.howard@dunelm.org.uk

HOWARD-COWLEY, Joseph Charles. b 27. Trin Coll Cam BA53 MA56. Wells Th Coll 53. **d** 55 **p** 56. C Newmarket All SS *St E* 55-58; Chapl Aycliffe Approved Sch Co Dur 58-61; V Aldringham *St E* 61-86; rtd 86; Perm to Offic *St E* 86-93 and *Truro* from 93. *36 Bath Road, Wootton Bassett, Swindon SN4 7DF*

HOWARD JONES, Preb Raymond Vernon. b 31. AKC54. **d** 55 **p** 56. C Hutton *Chelmsf* 55-58; CF 58-62; V Walpole St Andrew *Ely* 62-64; Chapl St Crispin's Hosp Northampton 64-70; V Brockhampton w Fawley *Heref* 70-86; V Fownhope 70-86; RD Heref Rural 77-81; Preb Heref Cathl 81-97; Communications Adv and Bp's Staff Officer 86-97; rtd 97; Perm to Offic *Heref* from 97. *Kingfishers, Breinton, Hereford HR4 7PP* Tel (01432) 279371

HOWARTH, Christopher. b 47. Ch Ch Coll Cant CertEd69 Open Univ BA76. S Dios Minl Tr Scheme. **d** 83 **p** 84. NSM Uckfield *Chich* from 83; NSM Lt Horsted from 83; NSM Isfield from 83. *137 Rocks Park Road, Uckfield TN22 2BD* Tel (01825) 765352

HOWARTH, Mrs Henriette. b 66. Utrecht Univ MTh94. Wycliffe Hall Ox 91. **d** 04 **p** 05. C Sparkbrook Ch Ch *Birm* from 04. *172 Woodlands Road, Sparkhill, Birmingham B11 4ET* Tel 0121-777 1989 E-mail hentob@aya.yale.edu

HOWARTH, Robert Francis Harvey. b 31. S'wark Ord Course 71. **d** 72 **p** 73. C St Marylebone All So w SS Pet and Jo *Lon* 72-73; C St Helen Bishopsgate w St Martin Outwich 73-78; V Harlow St Mary and St Hugh w St Jo the Bapt *Chelmsf* 78-88; P-in-c Victoria Docks Ascension 88-96; rtd 96. *Lochhill, Palnackie, Castle Douglas DG7 1PW* Tel (01556) 600363

HOWARTH, Canon Ronald. b 26. TCD BA51 MA54. Linc Th Coll 50. **d** 52 **p** 53. C Gannow *Blackb* 52-55; Nigeria 55-89; rtd 91. *4 Kingston Court, Walton Street, Oxford OX2 6ES* Tel (01865) 553046

HOWARTH, Toby Matthew. b 62. Yale Univ BA86 Birm Univ MA91 Free Univ of Amsterdam PhD01. Wycliffe Hall Ox 89. **d** 92 **p** 93. C Derby St Aug *Derby* 92-95; Crosslinks India 95-00; The Netherlands 00-02; Vice Prin and Tutor Crowther Hall CMS Tr Coll Selly Oak 02-04; P-in-c Springfield *Birm* from 04. *172 Woodlands Road, Sparkhill, Birmingham B11 4ET* Tel 0121-777 1989 E-mail hentob@aya.yale.edu

HOWAT, Jeremy Noel Thomas. b 35. Em Coll Cam BA59 MA62. Ridley Hall Cam 59. **d** 63 **p** 64. C Sutton *Liv* 63-65; C Kirk Ella *York* 65-66; C Bridlington Quay Ch Ch 66-69; R Wheldrake 69-78; Dioc Youth Officer 69-74; SAMS Argentina 78-81 and 90-97; P-in-c Newton upon Ouse *York* 81-82; V Shipton w Overton 81-82; P-in-c Skelton by York 81-82; R Skelton w Shipton and Newton on Ouse 82-89; C Elloughton and Brough w Brantingham 97-99; rtd 99; Perm to Offic *York* from 00. *18 Petersway, York YO30 6AR* Tel (01904) 628946
E-mail jnth@ntlworld.com

HOWDEN, Frank Newton. b 16. Connecticut Univ MS68 Univ of the South (USA) AB40. Gen Th Sem NY MDiv43. **d** 43 **p** 43. USA 43-85; Adn New Haven Co Connecticut 65-69; rtd 85; Lic to Offic *Roch* 85-99; Perm to Offic from 99. *9 Argyle Road, Southborough, Tunbridge Wells TN4 0SU* Tel (01892) 528838
E-mail fnhowden@aol.com

HOWDEN, Canon John Travis. b 40. RIBA62. Sarum Th Coll 66. **d** 69 **p** 70. C S Gillingham *Roch* 69-72; C Banbury *Ox* 72-73; Lic to Offic *York* 73-74; Hon C Hull St Jo Newland 74-81; Hon C Stock Harvard *Chelmsf* 82-86; R Doddinghurst and Mountnessing 86-91; P-in-c Pleshey and Warden Pleshey Retreat Ho 91-00; R Wickham Bishops w Lt Braxted 00-05; Hon Can Chelmsf Cathl 97-05; rtd 05; Perm to Offic *Chelmsf* from 05. *12A Back Road, Writtle, Chelmsford CM1 3PD* Tel (01245) 422023 E-mail johnhowden@realemail.co.uk

HOWDLE, Glyn. b 50. Bp Lonsdale Coll BEd72 Birm Univ DPSE84. St Alb Minl Tr Scheme 90. **d** 01 **p** 02. NSM Aspenden, Buntingford and Westmill *St Alb* from 01. *58 Ermine Street, Thundridge, Ware SG12 0SY* Tel and fax (01920) 469632 Mobile 07909-920437
E-mail glynjosealicia@howdle.fslife.co.uk

HOWE, Alan Raymond. b 52. Nottm Univ BTh79. St Jo Coll Nottm 76. **d** 80 **p** 81. C Southsea St Simon *Portsm* 80-83; C Bexleyheath St Pet *Roch* 83-86; TV Camberley St Paul *Guildf* 86-93; P-in-c Mansfield St Jo *S'well* 93-96; P-in-c Wollaton Park 96-02; V from 02; AD Nottingham W from 99. *St Mary's Vicarage, Wollaton Hall Drive, Nottingham NG8 1AF* Tel 0115-978 6988 E-mail alan@stmaryswp.fsnet.co.uk

HOWE, Anthony Graham. b 72. Qu Coll Ox BA93 MA99. St Steph Ho Ox BA00. **d** 01 **p** 02. C Newbury *Ox* 01-04; Bp's Chapl *Wakef* 04; Dioc Communications Officer from 04. *Craven House, 166 Horbury Road, Wakefield WF2 8BQ* Tel (01924) 384264 Mobile 07795-095157 E-mail fatherhowe@aol.com

HOWE, Charles. b 30. Lon Univ BD65 Open Univ BA79. Tyndale Hall Bris 55. **d** 58 **p** 59. C Willowfield *D & D* 58-60; C Derryloran *Arm* 60-64; C Belfast St Bart *Conn* 64-65; I Tullyaughnish w Kilmacrennan and Killygarvan *D & R* 65-72; I Londonderry St Aug 73-95; Can Derry Cathl 85-95; Dioc Org and Tutor for Aux Min 93-95; rtd 95. *2 Dunnwood Park, Londonderry BT47 2NN* Tel (028) 7131 2305
E-mail charleshowe1@hotmail.com

HOWE, Canon David Randall. b 24. St Jo Coll Cam BA51 MA55. Wells Th Coll 51. **d** 53 **p** 54. C Basingstoke *Win* 53-59; V Rotherwick, Hook and Greywell 59-70; R Bossington w Broughton 70-81; R Broughton w Bossington and Mottisfont 81-86; R Broughton, Bossington, Houghton and Mottisfont 86-89; Hon Can Win Cathl 87-89; rtd 89; Perm to Offic *Sarum* and *Win* 89-05. *Easter Cottage, 36 Britwell Road, Burnham, Slough SL1 8AG* Tel (01628) 603046

HOWE, Miss Frances Ruth. b 28. ACIB67. Cranmer Hall Dur IDC80. **dss** 80 **d** 87 **p** 94. Newc St Andr *Newc* 80-82; Chapl Asst R Victoria Infirmary Newc 80-87; Chapl Wylam and Fleming Ch Hosp 82-87; Chapl St Oswald's Hospice Newc 86-92; C Newc Epiphany *Newc* 87-90; rtd 92; Hon C Delaval *Newc* 92-98; Perm to Offic from 98. *18 Mason Avenue, Whitley Bay NE26 1AQ* Tel 0191-252 5163

HOWE, The Ven George Alexander. b 52. St Jo Coll Dur BA73. Westcott Ho Cam 73. **d** 75 **p** 76. C Peterlee *Dur* 75-79; C Norton St Mary 79-81; V Hart w Elwick Hall 81-85; R Sedgefield 85-91; RD Sedgefield 89-91; V Kendal H Trin *Carl* 91-00; RD Kendal 94-00; Hon Can Carl Cathl from 94; Adn Westmorland and Furness from 00; Bp's Adv for Ecum Affairs from 01. *The Vicarage, Windermere Road, Lindale, Grange-over-Sands LA11 6LB* Tel (01539) 534717 Fax 535090
E-mail archdeacon.south@carlislediocese.org.uk

HOWE, Canon John. b 36. Ex Coll Ox BA58 MA63. St Steph Ho Ox 58. **d** 61 **p** 62. C Horninglow *Lich* 61-64; C Sedgley All SS 64-66; V Ocker Hill 66-73; V Gnosall 73-79; P-in-c Hoar Cross 79-82; Preb Lich Cathl 83-88; V Hoar Cross w Newchurch 83-88; Can Res Lich Cathl 88-96; Master St Jo Hosp Lich 96-00; rtd 00; Perm to Offic *Lich* from 01. *9 Cherry Street, The Leys, Tamworth B79 7ED* Tel (01827) 57817

HOWE, Canon Nicholas Simon. b 60. Man Univ BA81 K Coll Lon MTh85. Ridley Hall Cam 86. **d** 88 **p** 89. C Lich St Chad *Lich* 88-92; TV Leeds City *Ripon* 92-01; Dioc Dir of Ords and Post-Ord Tr *Sheff* from 01; Chapl Sheff Cathl from 01; Can Res Sheff Cathl from 03. *47 Firth Park Avenue, Sheffield S5 6HF* Tel 0114-243 6013 *or* 263 6064
E-mail nick.howe@sheffield-cathedral.org.uk

HOWE, Canon Rex Alan. b 29. Ch Coll Cam BA53 MA57. Coll of Resurr Mirfield 53. **d** 55 **p** 56. C Barnsley St Pet *Wakef* 55-57; C Helmsley *York* 57-60; V Middlesbrough St Martin 60-67; V Redcar 67-73; V Kirkleatham 67-73; RD Guisborough 67-73; Dean Hong Kong 73-76; Adn 75-76; TR Grantham *Linc* 77-85; RD Grantham 78-85; Can and Preb Linc Cathl 81-85; V Canford Cliffs and Sandbanks *Sarum* 85-94; RD Poole 92-94; rtd 94; Perm to Offic *Sarum* from 94. *18 St Nicholas Hospital, 5 St Nicholas Road, Salisbury SP1 2SW* Tel (01722) 326677

HOWE, Roy William. b 38. ALCD67. **d** 66 **p** 67. C Bradf Cathl *Bradf* 66-70; C Barnoldswick w Bracewell 70-72; V Yeadon St Jo 72-79; P-in-c Bainton *York* 79-86; P-in-c Middleton-on-the-Wolds 79-86; P-in-c N Dalton 79-86; RD Harthill 81-87; C Watton w Beswick and Kilnwick 82-86; R Bainton w N Dalton, Middleton-on-the-Wolds etc 86-87; TV Penrith w Newton Reigny and Plumpton Wall *Carl* 87-92; Dioc Chapl to Agric and Rural Life 87-92; V Cornhill w Carham *Newc* 92-98; V Branxton 92-98; P-in-c Coddenham w Gosbeck and Hemingstone w Henley *St E* 98-03; rtd 03; Perm to Offic *St E* from 04. *Ballaclague, 2 Halvasso Vean, Longdowns, Penryn TR10 9DN* Tel (01209) 860552

HOWE, Ruth. *See* HOWE, Miss Frances Ruth

HOWE, William Ernest. b 25. MRICS51. Westcott Ho Cam 68. **d** 70 **p** 71. C Anston *Sheff* 70-73; V 84-92; C Woodsetts 70-73; V Greasbrough 73-84; rtd 92; Perm to Offic *Sheff* from 92 and *S'well* from 97. *21 Broad Bridge Close, Kiveton Park, Sheffield S26 6SL* Tel (01909) 773948

HOWELL, Alfred. b 32. Wells Th Coll 57. **d** 59 **p** 60. C Ferryhill *Dur* 59-61; C Tankersley *Sheff* 61-63; V New Edlington 63-66; V Sparkbrook Ch Ch *Birm* 66-73; Lic to Offic *Chelmsf* 73-83; P-in-c Brentwood St Geo 83-88; rtd 88; Perm to Offic *Chich* from 88. *Windy Corner, Grove Lane, Iden, Rye TN31 7QA* Tel (01797) 280564

HOWELL, Andrew John. b 44. Clifton Th Coll 68. **d** 71 **p** 72. C Halliwell St Pet *Man* 71-77; V Facit 77-95; P-in-c Smallbridge and Wardle from 95. *The Vicarage, 151 Wardle Road, Rochdale OL12 9JA* Tel (01706) 713529

HOWELL, Canon Basil Rayson. b 20. St Pet Hall Ox BA49 MA53. Wycliffe Hall Ox 49. **d** 51 **p** 52. C Worksop St Jo *S'well* 51-54; C-in-c Worksop St Paul CD 54-61; V Blundellsands St Nic *Liv* 61-81; RD Bootle 69-78; Hon Can Liv Cathl 78-81; rtd 81; Perm to Offic *Cov* from 81. *9 Arlington Court, Arlington Avenue, Leamington Spa CV32 5HR* Tel (01926) 314746

HOWELL, David. b 29. Clifton Th Coll 56. **d** 59 **p** 60. C Tipton St Martin *Lich* 59-62; V W Bromwich St Paul 62-71; V Deptford St Jo *S'wark* 71-81; Dir and Chapl Home of Divine Healing Crowhurst 81-89; rtd 90; Dir Ch Coun for Health and Healing 91-93; Hon Dioc Adv on Health and Healing *B & W* 93-00; Perm to Offic from 01. *60 Andrew Allan Road, Rockwell Green, Wellington TA21 9DY* Tel (01823) 664529

HOWELL (formerly WILLIAMS), David Paul. b 61. Coll of Resurr Mirfield 91. **d** 93 **p** 94. G Leic St Aid *Leic* 93-97; P-in-c Edvin Loach w Tedstone Delamere etc *Heref* from 97. *The Rectory, Whitbourne, Worcester WR6 5RP* Tel (01886) 821285

HOWELL, Donald Martin. b 32. Lon Univ BD56. **d** 95 **p** 96. NSM Aylmerton w Runton *Nor* 95-96; NSM Holt w High Kelling 96-99; rtd 00; Perm to Offic *Nor* from 00. *8 The Beeches, Station Road, Holt NR25 6AU* Tel (01263) 713397

HOWELL, Geoffrey Peter. b 52. Selw Coll Cam BA75 MA78 Leeds Univ MA01 K Alfred's Coll Win PGCE77 LTCL82. Cranmer Hall Dur 85. **d** 87 **p** 88. C Hartlepool St Luke *Dur* 87-90; TV Burford I *Heref* 90-94; TV Burford II w Greete and Hope Bagot 90-94; TV Burford III w Lt Heref 90-94; TV Tenbury 90-94; P-in-c Cradley w Mathon and Storridge 94-97; Succ Heref Cathl 97-99; Chapl Heref Cathl Jun Sch 97-99; Perm to Offic *Heref* from 99; Min Can St Woolos Cathl *Mon* from 02. *10 Clifton Road, Newport NP20 4EW* Tel (01633) 264805 E-mail geoffrey.howell@tesco.net

HOWELL, Mrs Heather Ellen. b 40. Bp Otter Coll Chich TCert60 Sussex Univ BA83. Ripon Coll Cuddesdon 00. **d** 01. NSM Newhaven *Chich* from 01. *1 Rookery Way, Bishopstone, Seaford BN25 2SA* Tel (01323) 898167

HOWELL, Martin John Hope. b 38. Bris Univ BA62. Tyndale Hall Bris 59. **d** 64 **p** 65. C Bolton St Paul *Man* 64-67; C Bishopsworth *Bris* 67-70; V Swindon St Aug 70-81; TR Stratton St Margaret w S Marston etc 81-93; RD Cricklade 88; RD Highworth 88-93; Chapl Lee Abbey 93-98; Chapl St Pet Via del Mar Chile 99-03; rtd 03; Hon C Salcombe and Malborough w S Huish *Ex* from 03. *26 Weymouth Park, Hope Cove, Kingsbridge TQ7 3HD* Tel (01548) 562402

HOWELL, Roger Brian. b 43. ALCD67. **d** 67 **p** 68. C Battersea Park St Sav *S'wark* 67-71; C Southgate *Chich* 71-76; V Pendeen and P-in-c Sancreed *Truro* 76-81; V Bedgrove *Ox* 81-91; R Purley from 91; RD Bradfield 94-04. *The Rectory, 1 Westridge Avenue, Purley, Reading RG8 8DE* Tel 0118-941 7727 E-mail rbh@bradean.fsnet.co.uk

HOWELL, Ronald William Fullerton. b 51. Man Univ BA72 CertEd Ox Univ BA78 MA. Ripon Coll Cuddesdon 76. **d** 79 **p** 80. C Newc St Fran *Newc* 79-81; C Warmsworth *Sheff* 81-82; Dioc Educn Officer 82-85; V Millhouses H Trin 85-93; R Thornhill and Whitley Lower *Wakef* 93-96. *East House, 10 Woodbridge Road East, Ipswich IP4 5PA* Tel (01473) 727309

HOWELL, Simon Gordon. b 63. Sheff Univ BMus84 Bath Coll of HE PGCE85 ACII90. Ridley Hall Cam 00. **d** 03 **p** 04. C Northwood Em *Lon* from 03. *10 Northwood Way, Northwood HA6 1AT* Tel (01923) 823718 *or* 845204 Fax 845209 E-mail simon.howell@ecn.org.uk

HOWELL, Preb Walter Ernest. b 17. St D Coll Lamp BA49. **d** 50 **p** 51. C Bromley St Mich *Lon* 50-56; V Somers Town 56-68; V Kentish Town St Benet and All SS 68-79; Preb St Paul's Cathl 78-84; V Alexandra Park St Sav 79-84; rtd 84; Perm to Offic *York* from 90. *6 Wattlers Close, Copmanthorpe, York YO23 3XR* Tel (01904) 702615

HOWELL-JONES, Canon Peter. b 62. Huddersfield Poly BMus84 Bretton Hall Coll PGCE85. St Jo Coll Nottm 90 MA96. **d** 93 **p** 94. C Walsall *Lich* 93-98; V Boldmere *Birm* 98-05; Can Res Birm Cathl from 05; Bp's Adv for Miss from 05. *Birmingham Cathedral, Colmore Row, Birmingham B3 2QB* Tel 0121-262 1840 Fax 262 1860

HOWELLS, Chan Arthur Glyn. b 32. Univ of Wales (Lamp) BA54. St Mich Coll Llan 54. **d** 56 **p** 57. C Oystermouth *S & B* 56-58; C Llangyfelach and Morriston 58-64; R Llandefalle and Llyswen w Boughrood etc 64-69; Youth Chapl 67-71; V Landore 70-80; Dioc Missr 80-89; Can Brecon Cathl 80-89; Can Treas 89-94; Dir St Mary's Coll Swansea 82-89; V Swansea St Jas *S & B* 89-98; Chan Brecon Cathl from 94; RD Swansea 96-98; rtd 98. *2 Lilliput Lane, West Cross, Swansea SA3 5AQ* Tel (01792) 402123

HOWELLS, David. b 55. Grey Coll Dur BA78. Ripon Coll Cuddesdon 79. **d** 81 **p** 82. C Birtley *Dur* 81-84; Canada from 84. *127 Glasgow Street North, Guelph ON, Canada, N1H 4W5* Tel (001) (519) 821 7419

HOWELLS, David Morgan. b 24. Qu Coll Birm 72. **d** 75 **p** 76. NSM Radford *Cov* 75-87; rtd 87; Perm to Offic *Cov* from 87; *Roch* from 98. *14 St Werburgh's Court, Pottery Road, Rochester ME3 9AP* Tel (01634) 251544

HOWELLS (formerly SMITHAM), Mrs Elizabeth Ann. b 62. St D Coll Lamp BA90 St Mich Coll Llan DPS91. **d** 92 **p** 97. C Llangiwg *S & B* 92-94; C Morriston 94-98; P-in-c Llanfair-is-gaer and Llanddeiniolen *Ban* 98-00; V 00-03; V Llanddeiniolen w Llanfair-is-gaer etc 03-04; V Clydau w Egremont and Llanglydwen etc *St D* from 04. *Trelech Vicarage, Penybont, Carmarthen SA33 6PJ* Tel (01994) 484335

HOWELLS, Euryl. b 60. Univ of Wales (Cardiff) BD93. St Mich Coll Llan 90. **d** 93 **p** 94. C Deanery of Emlyn *St D* 93-97; V Llangeler w Pen-Boyr 97-03; P-in-c Tre-lech a'r Betws w Abernant and Llanwinio from 03. *Trelech Vicarage, Penybont, Carmarthen SA33 6PJ* Tel (01994) 484335

HOWELLS, Garfield Edwin. b 18. K Coll Lon 53 St Boniface Warminster 53. **d** 54 **p** 55. C Sanderstead All SS *S'wark* 54-57; CF 57-60; R Kingsdown *Roch* 60-64; Australia from 64; rtd 83. *301/17 Hefron Street, Rockingham, W Australia 6168* Tel (0061) (8) 9592 8337

HOWELLS, Gordon. b 39. Univ of Wales (Cardiff) BSc61 DipEd62. Ripon Coll Cuddesdon 86. **d** 88 **p** 89. C Atherstone *Cov* 88-89; C Lillington 89-92; R Clymping and Yapton w Ford *Chich* 92-97; P-in-c Rackheath and Salhouse *Nor* 97-04; Chapl among Deaf People 97-04; rtd 04. *53 Abbey Road, Rhos on Sea, Colwyn Bay LL28 4NR* Tel (01492) 525899 E-mail g.howells.norwich@virgin.net

HOWELLS, Neil. b 23. Qu Mary Coll Lon BSc48. Bps' Coll Cheshunt 48. **d** 50 **p** 51. C Cowley St Jas *Ox* 50-54; C Forest Hill 54-56; Min Headington St Mary 56-60; V Maidenhead St Luke 60-68; Chapl Maidenhead Gen Hosp 60-68; R Welford w Wickham 68-73; R Welford w Wickham and Gt Shefford 73-77; RD Newbury 73-77; V Bray and Braywood 77-84; rtd 84; Perm to Offic *Sarum* from 85. *19 Loders, Bridport DT6 3SA* Tel (01308) 456490

HOWELLS, Richard Grant. b 62. Univ of Wales (Lamp) BA83. Westcott Ho Cam 83 and 92. **d** 93 **p** 94. NSM Harston w Hauxton and Newton *Ely* from 93. *The Old School House, 8 High Street, Harston, Cambridge CB2 5PX* Tel (01223) 871902 E-mail richard@oldschoolhouse.demon.co.uk

HOWELLS, Mrs Sandra Jane. b 52. FBDO77 Univ of Wales (Cardiff) DipRS97. LNSM course 90. **d** 93 **p** 97. NSM Caerwent w Dinham and Llanfair Discoed etc *Mon* 93-97; C Griffithstown 97-00; V Penallt and Trellech from 00. *The Vicarage, Penallt, Monmouth NP25 4SE* Tel (01600) 716622

HOWELLS, William Gordon. b 26. **d** 61 **p** 62. C Aberdare *Llan* 61-64; C Coity w Nolton 64-67; C Northam *Ex* 67-71; V Bishops Tawton 71-76; V Cofton w Starcross 76-80; R Aveton Gifford 80-86; V Modbury 80-86; TV Lynton, Brendon, Countisbury, Lynmouth etc 86-91; rtd 91; Perm to Offic *Ex* from 91 and *Linc* from 01. *3 St Nicholas Way, Lutton, Spalding PE12 9HR* Tel (01406) 363466

HOWES, Alan. b 49. Chich Th Coll 76. **d** 79 **p** 80. C Bilborough St Jo *S'well* 79-82; TV Newark w Hawton, Cotham and Shelton 82-89; TV Newark 89-94; P-in-c Coseley St Chad *Worc* 94-96; V from 96. *St Chad's Vicarage, 3 Oak Street, Coseley, Bilston WV14 9TA* Tel (01902) 882285 Mobile 07941-284048 E-mail alan@heavensdoor.co.uk

HOWES, David. b 30. Open Univ BA75. Roch Th Coll 62. **d** 64 **p** 65. C Highweek *Ex* 64-67; C Clyst St George 67-71; P-in-c Woolfardisworthy w Kennerleigh 71-72; P-in-c Washford Pyne w Puddington 71-72; TR N Creedy 72-73; Perm to Offic 74-77; C Walworth *S'wark* 77-78; C-in-c Roundshaw St Paul CD 78-83; R S'wark St Geo 83-90; P-in-c S'wark St Jude 84-90; P-in-c Risley *Derby* 90-93; Bp's Ind Adv 90-93; rtd 93; Perm to Offic *Derby* 93-00; *S'well* 95-00; *Win* from 01. *Drokensford, Chapel Road, Meonstoke, Southampton SO32 3NJ* Tel (01489) 878174

HOWES, Miss Judith Elizabeth. b 44. SRN RSCN. Ripon Coll Cuddesdon 83. **d** 89 **p** 94. Par Dn Ex St Sidwell and St Matt *Ex* 89-92; Par Dn Brixham w Churston Ferrers and Kingswear 92-94; C 94-95; TV E Darlington *Dur* 95-97; TR 97-02; P-in-c Washington 02-04; P-in-c S Shields St Simon from 04; C Hedworth from 04. *Boldon Rectory, Rectory Green, West Boldon, East Boldon NE36 0QD* Tel 0191-536 7370 E-mail judith.howes@durham.anglican.org

HOWES, Mrs Kathleen Valerie. b 44. Surrey Univ BA05. STETS 03. **d** 05. NSM Droxford *Portsm* from 05; NSM Meonstoke w Corhampton cum Exton from 05. *Drokensford, Chapel Road, Meonstoke, Southampton SO32 3NJ* Tel (01489) 878174 Mobile 07940-115927 E-mail valerie.howes@ukonline.co.uk

HOWES, Michael John Norton. b 43. Hull Univ BA66. Linc Th Coll 66. **d** 68 **p** 69. C Gt Berkhamsted *St Alb* 68-71; C Ampthill w Millbrook and Steppingley 71-72; Chapl RAF 72-88; V Thurlby w Carlby *Linc* 88-95; V Ness Gp 95-97; R Bassingham 97-00; V Aubourn w Haddington 97-00; V Carlton-le-Moorland w Stapleford 97-00; R Thurlby w Norton Disney 97-00; P-in-c Ashill w Saham Toney *Nor* 01-03; rtd 03. *182 Rookery Lane, Lincoln LN6 7PH* Tel (01522) 801514 E-mail mike.howes5@ntlworld.com

HOWES, Canon Norman Vincent. b 36. AKC61. **d** 62 **p** 63. C Radford *Cov* 62-66; V Napton on the Hill 66-72; V Exhall 72-83; R Walton d'Eiville and V Wellesbourne 83-03; RD Fosse 87-93; Hon Can Cov Cathl 89-03; rtd 03; Perm to Offic *Cov* from 03. *Harwood Cottage, Bottom Street, North End, Southam CV47 2TH* Tel (01295) 770303 E-mail norman@nhowes.freeserve.co.uk

HOWES, Valerie. *See* HOWES, Mrs Kathleen Valerie

HOWES, William John Lawrence. b 46. EAMTC. **d** 00 **p** 01. NSM Lexden *Chelmsf* 00-04; NSM Coggeshall w Markshall from 04. *26 Westfield Drive, Coggeshall, Colchester CO6 1PU* Tel and fax (01376) 561826 Mobile 07718-048574 E-mail frbill@tiscali.co.uk

HOWITT, Barbara Gillian. b 39. K Coll Lon BD60 PGCE61 MA95. EAMTC 99. **d** 00 **p** 01. NSM Longthorpe *Pet* from 00. *8 Wakerley Drive, Orton Longueville, Peterborough PE2 7WF* Tel (01733) 391092

HOWITT, Ivan Richard. b 56. Kent Univ BA81. Sarum & Wells Th Coll 83. **d** 85 **p** 86. C Herne Bay Ch Ch *Cant* 85-87; C St Laur in Thanet 87-90; R Owmby and Normanby w Glentham *Linc* 90-91; P-in-c Spridlington w Saxby and Firsby 90-91; R Owmby Gp 91-99; RD Lawres 96-99; Chapl Hull Miss to Seafarers 99-03; V Hedon w Paull *York* from 03. *The Vicarage, 44 New Road, Hedon, Hull HU12 8BS* Tel (01482) 897693 Mobile 07739-316019 E-mail ivanhowitt@ivanhowitt.karoo.co.uk

HOWITT, John Leslie. b 28. Lon Coll of Div 60. **d** 62 **p** 63. C Attenborough w Bramcote *S'well* 62-66; Chapl Rampton Hosp Retford 66-71; P-in-c Treswell and Cottam *S'well* 68-71; Chapl HM Pris Cardiff 71-75; Chapl HM Youth Cust Cen Dover 75-79; Chapl HM Pris Dartmoor 79-83; Chapl HM Pris Cant 83-87; Chapl HM Det Cen Aldington 83-87; Perm to Offic *Cant* 87-88; V Shobnall *Lich* 88-94; rtd 94; Perm to Offic *Chich* from 94. *6 Park View Road, Hove BN3 7BF*

HOWITZ (formerly TEDD), Christopher Jonathan Richard. b 74. Ch Ch Ox MEng96. Oak Hill Th Coll BA00. **d** 00 **p** 01. C Harpurhey Ch Ch *Man* 00-04; P-in-c Higher Openshaw from 05. *St Clement's Rectory, Ashton Old Road, Manchester M11 1HF* Tel 0161-370 1538

HOWLES, Kenneth. b 56. Oak Hill Th Coll 91. **d** 93 **p** 94. C Leyland St Andr *Blackb* 93-96; C Livesey 96-97; C Ewood 96-97; P-in-c 97-99; V 99-03; P-in-c Blackb Sav 01-03; V Chorley St Jas from 03. *St James's Vicarage, St James's Place, Chorley PR6 0NA* Tel (01257) 263153 E-mail kenhowles@btinternet.com

HOWLETT, Mrs Elizabeth Mary. b 58. Southn Univ BA80. WMMTC 99. **d** 01 **p** 02. C Salter Street and Shirley *Birm* 01-04; Bp's Adv for Lay Adult Educn and Tr from 04. *6 Greenside, Shirley, Solihull B90 4HH* Tel (01564) 702233

HOWLETT, Richard Laurence. b 56. Kent Univ BA79. Trin Coll Bris. **d** 94 **p** 95. C Louth *Linc* 94-98; R Marston Morteyne w Lidlington *St Alb* from 98; V Goldington from 05. *The Vicarage, Church Lane, Goldington, Bedford MK41 0AP* Tel (01234) 355024 E-mail richard@revhowlett.fslife.co.uk

HOWLETT, Victor John. b 43. S Dios Minl Tr Scheme 90. **d** 93 **p** 94. NSM Bris St Andr w St Bart *Bris* 93-95; Hon C Bris St Matt and St Nath 95-96; Hon C Bishopston 95-96; C Gtr Corsham 96-99; V Wick w Doynton and Dyrham from 99; AD Kingswood and S Glos from 02. *The Vicarage, 57 High Street, Wick, Bristol BS30 5QQ* Tel 0117-937 3581 E-mail victorhowlett@charis.co.uk

HOWMAN, Anne Louise. b 43. Lon Univ Dip Sociology 81 Ex Univ BA97. SW Minl Tr Course 97. **d** 99 **p** 00. NSM Ex St Dav *Ex* 99-02; C Salcombe and Malborough w S Huish from 02. *The Vicarage, Malborough, Kingsbridge TQ7 3RR* Tel (01548) 561234 E-mail alhow@btinternet.com

HOWORTH, Sister Rosemary. Newnham Coll Cam MA. Westcott Ho Cam. **d** 98 **p** 99. NSM Derby St Andr w St Osmund *Derby* from 98. *The Convent of the Holy Name, Morley Road, Oakwood, Derby DE21 6HP* Tel (01332) 671716

HOWSE, Elizabeth Ann. *See* SMITH, Mrs Elizabeth Ann

HOWSE, Martin David. b 58. St Steph Ho Ox 97. **d** 99 **p** 00. C Colchester St Jas and St Paul w All SS etc *Chelmsf* 99-03; V Rush Green from 03. *St Augustine's Vicarage, 78 Birkbeck Road, Romford RM7 0QP* Tel (01708) 741460 Mobile 07770-928167 Fax (01708) 732093 E-mail martin.howse@virgin.net

HOWSON, Christopher Stewart. b 69. Bradf Univ BA94 CQSW94 St Jo Coll Dur BA02. Cranmer Hall Dur 99. **d** 02 **p** 03. C Tong *Bradf* from 02. *St Christopher's Vicarage, 207 Broadstone Way, Bradford BD4 9BT* Tel (01274) 605256 E-mail chrishowson@yahoo.com

HOWSON, James Edward. b 62. Ridley Hall Cam 97 EAMTC 98. **d** 00 **p** 01. C Cogges and S Leigh *Ox* from 00. *44 Shakespeare Road, Eynsham, Witney OX29 4PY* Tel (01993) 703665

HOY, Michael John. b 30. Reading Univ BSc52. Oak Hill Th Coll 57. **d** 59 **p** 60. C Worthing St Geo *Chich* 59-62; C Tulse Hill H Trin *S'wark* 62-66; R Danby Wiske w Yafforth and Hutton Bonville *Ripon* 66-76; V Camelsdale *Chich* 76-87; V Gt Marsden *Blackb* 87-96; rtd 96. *35 Hardwick Park, Banbury OX16 1YF* Tel (01295) 268744

HOY, Stephen Anthony. b 55. Leeds Poly BA76. Linc Th Coll 92. **d** 94 **p** 95. C Glen Parva and S Wigston *Leic* 94-98; V Linc St Jo *Linc* from 98. *St John's Vicarage, 102 Sudbrooke Drive, Lincoln LN2 2EF* Tel (01522) 525621 E-mail stephen@hoy997.freeserve.co.uk

HOYAL, Richard Dunstan. b 47. Ch Ch Ox BA67 MA71 BA78. Ripon Coll Cuddesdon 76. **d** 79 **p** 80. C Stevenage St Geo *St Alb* 79-83; V Monk Bretton *Wakef* 83-89; V Ilkley St Marg *Bradf* 89-04; Dir of Ords 96-04; Hon Can Bradf Cathl 03-04; P-in-c Clifton All SS w St Jo *Bris* from 04; P-in-c Easton All Hallows from 04. *All Saints' Vicarage, 68 Pembroke Road, Bristol BS8 3ED* Tel 0117-974 1355 E-mail richard@rdhoyal.fsnet.co.uk

HOYE, Reginald George. b 16. Tyndale Hall Bris 58. **d** 60 **p** 61. C Penn Fields *Lich* 60-62; V Nottingham St Sav *S'well* 62-82; rtd 82; Perm to Offic *S'well* from 82. *1 White Acre, Burton Joyce, Nottingham NG14 5BU* Tel 0115-931 2485

HOYLAND, John Gregory. b 50. Sussex Univ BEd73. Wycliffe Hall Ox 75. **d** 78 **p** 79. C Pudsey St Lawr *Bradf* 78-81; P-in-c Long Preston 81-84; V Long Preston w Tosside 84; CPAS Staff 85-87; Chapl York St Jo Coll 87-01; Lect from 01; Perm to Offic *York* from 01. *5 White Cross Road, York YO31 8JR* Tel (01904) 632368 *or* 656771

HOYLE, David Fredric. b 46. Lon Bible Coll. **d** 02 **p** 03. NSM Northwood Em *Lon* from 02. *154 Hilliard Road, Northwood HA6 1SP* Tel (01923) 840678 *or* 845200 E-mail david.f.hoyle@lineone.net

HOYLE, Canon David Michael. b 57. CCC Cam BA80 MA83 PhD91. Ripon Coll Cuddesdon 84. **d** 86 **p** 87. C Chesterton Gd Shep *Ely* 86-88; Chapl and Fell Magd Coll Cam 88-91; Dean and Fell 91-95; V Southgate Ch Ch *Lon* 95-02; Dir Post-Ord Tr (Edmonton) 00-02; Dioc Officer for Min *Glouc* from 02; Dioc Can Res Glouc Cathl from 02. *4 College Green, Gloucester GL1 2LR* Tel (01452) 410022 ext 231 E-mail dhoyle@glosdioc.org.uk

HOYLE, Lawrence. b 27. St Aid Birkenhead 52. **d** 55 **p** 56. C Haley Hill *Wakef* 55-57; C Bromley SS Pet and Paul *Roch* 57-59; V Widnes St Ambrose *Liv* 59-61; R Lanteglos by Camelford w Advent *Truro* 61-66; V Wrose *Bradf* 66-70; R Thwing *York* 70-81; V Wold Newton 71-81; Warden Lamplugh Ho Angl Conf Cen 72-85; Dir Angl Renewal Min 81-89; Hon C Starbeck *Ripon* 87-89; rtd 89; Perm to Offic *Ex* 92-02 and *York* from 02. *2 Wheatcroft Court, Sea Cliff Road, Scarborough YO11 2XT* Tel (01723) 353919 Mobile 07817-256529 E-mail lawrencehoyle@onetel.com

HOYLE, Pamela Margaret. *See* CLOCKSIN, Mrs Pamela Margaret

HOYLE, Stephen Jonathan. b 64. Leeds Univ BA87. Ripon Coll Cuddesdon 88. **d** 90 **p** 91. C Lt Stanmore St Lawr *Lon* 90-93; C Lon Docks St Pet w Wapping St Jo 93-96; Perm to Offic 01-02; TV Withycombe Raleigh *Ex* from 02. *St John's Vicarage, 3 Diane Close, Exmouth EX8 5QG* Tel (01395) 270094

HRYZIUK, Petro. b 57. Lanc Univ BEd80 Open Univ MA95. St Jo Coll Nottm 89. **d** 90 **p** 91. C Huyton St Geo *Liv* 90-93; C Goose Green 93-96; C Wavertree H Trin 96-98; TV Maghull

98-05; Chapl Shrewsbury and Telford NHS Trust from 05. *Chaplaincy Department, Royal Shrewsbury Hospital, Mytton Oak Road, Shrewsbury SY3 8XQ* Tel (01743) 261000 E-mail petroh@hotmail.com

HUARD, The Ven Geoffrey Robert. b 43. Lon Univ DipTh71 DMin95. Clifton Th Coll 64 69. **d** 70 **p** 71. C Barking St Marg *Chelmsf* 70-73; C Everton St Ambrose w St Tim *Liv* 73-74; C Everton St Pet 74-76; Australia from 76; Adn Sydney and Cumberland 89-93; Adn Liverpool from 93. *PO Box Q190, QVB, Sydney, NSW, Australia 1230* Tel (0061) (2) 9558 5986 *or* 9265 1571 Fax 9265 1543 E-mail gchuard@dingoblue.net.au

HUBAND, Eric Bob. b 27. Bris Univ BSc50. Sarum Th Coll 50. **d** 52 **p** 53. C Lockleaze St Fran CD *Bris* 52-56; C Bishopsworth 56-60; V Greenbank 60-67; V Hengrove 67-77; R E Horsley *Guildf* 77-92; rtd 92; Perm to Offic *Bris* from 92; and *Sarum* from 98. *23 Hardens Mead, Chippenham SN15 3AE* Tel (01249) 661219

HUBAND, Richard William. b 39. Trin Coll Cam BA62 MA66. Qu Coll Birm 76. **d** 78 **p** 79. C Norton *St Alb* 78-81; R Aspley Guise w Husborne Crawley and Ridgmont 81-91; V Elstow 91-03; rtd 03. *5 Shooters Paddock, Layton Lane, Shaftesbury SP7 8AB* Tel (01747) 854741

HUBBARD, David Harris. b 33. St Pet Hall Ox BA57 MA61 K Coll Lon MTh88. Ridley Hall Cam 59. **d** 60 **p** 61. C Dalston St Mark w St Bart *Lon* 60-63; C Stoke Newington St Olave 63-67; Hon C 67-68; Asst Master Dalston Sch 67-75; Hon C Hornsey Ch Ch 69-70; V 70-82; AD W Haringey 78-85; V Highgate All SS 82-02; rtd 02; Hon C W Hampstead St Cuth *Lon* 02-04; Perm to Offic from 04. *35 Sheppards College, London Road, Bromley BR1 1PF* Tel (020) 8695 7477

HUBBARD, Mrs Elisabeth Ann. b 41. EAMTC 82. **dss** 85 **d** 87 **p** 94. Cambridge H Trin w St Andr Gt *Ely* 85-86; Cherry Hinton St Jo 86-92; Par Dn 87-92; Par Dn Milton 92-94; C 94-95; R Willingham and Rampton 95-00; rtd 00; NSM Ely from 01. *3 Lodge Gardens, Haddenham, Ely CB6 3TR* Tel (01353) 741472 E-mail geolis@fish.co.uk

HUBBARD, Ian Maxwell. b 43. FCollP83 ACP83 Surrey Univ BEd84 Goldsmiths' Coll Lon MA86. Sarum & Wells Th Coll 69. **d** 73 **p** 74. Hon C S'wark H Trin w St Matt *S'wark* 73-78; Hon C Camberwell St Mich w All So w Em 78-87; Hon C Dulwich St Barn 87-90; C Battersea St Mary 90-92; V Winscombe *B & W* 92-98; TR Yatton Moor from 98; RD Portishead from 02. *The Rectory, 1 Well Lane, Yatton, Bristol BS49 4HT* Tel (01934) 832184 E-mail ian@hubbardi.freeserve.co.uk

HUBBARD, The Ven Julian Richard Hawes. b 55. Em Coll Cam BA76 MA81. Wycliffe Hall Ox BA80 MA85. **d** 81 **p** 82. C Fulham St Dionis Parson's Green *Lon* 81-84; Chapl Jes Coll and Tutor Wycliffe Hall Ox 84-89; Selection Sec ACCM 89-91; Sen Selection Sec ABM 91-93; V Bourne *Guildf* 93-99; P-in-c Tilford 97-99; RD Farnham 96-99; Can Res Guildf Cathl and Dir Minl Tr 99-05; Adn Ox and Can Res Ch Ch *Ox* from 05. *Archdeacon's Lodging, Christ Church, Oxford OX1 1DP* Tel and fax (01865) 276185 E-mail archdoxf@oxford.anglican.org

HUBBARD, Laurence Arthur. b 36. Qu Coll Cam BA60 MA64. Wycliffe Hall Ox 60 CMS Tr Coll Chislehurst 65 CMS Tr Coll Selly Oak 93. **d** 62 **p** 63. C Widcombe *B & W* 62-65; CMS Kenya 66-73; V Pype Hayes *Birm* 73-79; P-in-c Norwich-over-the-Water Colegate St Geo *Nor* 79-85; P-in-c Nor St Aug w St Mary 79-85; CMS 85-97; Area Sec *Cant* and *Roch* 85-93; Chapl Damascus, Syria 93-97; Miss to Seamen Aqaba, Jordan 97-00; rtd 00; Perm to Offic *Glouc* from 01. *31 Saddlers Road, Quedgeley, Gloucester GL2 4SY* Tel (01452) 728061

HUBBARD, Peter James. b 72. York Univ BA93 Nottm Univ PGCE97. Trin Coll Bris BA03. **d** 04 **p** 05. C Hinckley H Trin *Leic* from 04. *2 Brascote Road, Hinckley LE10 0HE* Tel (01455) 610474 Mobile 07751-453845 E-mail peterdebbieuk@tiscali.co.uk

HUBBARD, Roy Oswald. b 32. Lich Th Coll 62. **d** 64 **p** 65. C Baswich *Lich* 64-68; P-in-c Ash 68-70; V Stevenage St Pet Broadwater *St Alb* 71-78; V Flitwick 78-90; RD Ampthill 87-90; R Sharnbrook and Knotting w Souldrop 90-96; rtd 96; Perm to Offic *St Alb* and *Pet* from 96. *11 Cowslip Close, Rushden NN10 0UD* Tel (01933) 419210

HUBBARD-JONES, Ms Judith Frances. b 49. St Alb Minl Tr Scheme 79. **dss** 82 **d** 87 **p** 94. Hemel Hempstead *St Alb* 82-86; Longden and Annscroft w Pulverbatch *Heref* 86-87; Hon C 87-91; Vice Prin WEMTC 91-97; Acting Prin 94-95; Hon C Leominster *Heref* 94-97; Cathl Chapl and Visitors' Officer *Glouc* 97-02; I Kinneigh Union *C, C & R* from 02. *The Rectory, Ballineen, Co Cork, Irish Republic* Tel (00353) (23) 47047 E-mail kinneigh@cork.anglican.org

HUBBLE, Canon Raymond Carr. b 30. Wm Temple Coll Rugby 60. **d** 61 **p** 62. C Newbold w Dunston *Derby* 61-64; Chapl RAF 64-80; Asst Chapl-in-Chief RAF 80-85; QHC 84-85; P-in-c Odiham w S Warnborough and Long Sutton *Win* 85; P-in-c Odiham 85-86; V 86-95; RD Odiham 88-95; Hon Can Win Cathl 94-95; rtd 95; Perm to Offic *Win* from 95. *Dormers, Centre Lane, Everton, Lymington SO41 0JP*

HUBBLE, Canon Trevor Ernest. b 46. Bernard Gilpin Soc Dur 69 Chich Th Coll 70. **d** 76 **p** 77. C Eltham St Barn *S'wark* 76-79; Lesotho 80-87; C St Agnes Mission Teyateyameng 80-81; R Quthing H Trin 81-85; Adn S Lesotho 84-87; Warden Ang Tr Cen and Dir Chr Educ 85-87; S Africa 87-00; Co-ord of Tr for Lay Min 87-89; R Matatiele St Steph 89-00; Adn Matatiele 91-00; V Gen Umzimvubu 95-00; Shared Min Tr Officer *Dur* from 00; C Esh from 00; C Hamsteels from 00; C Langley Park from 00; C Waterhouses from 00. *St Paul's Vicarage, 21 The Wynds, Esh Winning, Durham DH7 9DT* Tel 0191-373 4273 Mobile 07759-310524 E-mail tshubble@freenetname.co.uk

HUCKETT, Andrew William. b 50. AKC72. St Aug Coll Cant 72. **d** 73 **p** 74. C Chipping Sodbury and Old Sodbury *Glouc* 73-76; Miss to Seafarers from 76; Chapl Flushing 76-79; Chapl Teesside 79-82; Chapl Lagos Nigeria 82-85; Chapl Mombasa Kenya 85-86; Chapl Milford Haven 86-92; Chapl Medway Ports 92-03; Staff Chapl and Chapl Thames/Medway 03-05; Chapl Southampton from 05. *Southampton Seafarers' Centre, 12/14 Queens Terrace, Southampton SO14 3BP* Tel (023) 8033 3106 *or* 8071 4083 Mobile 07836-261324 E-mail southampton@mtsmail.org

HUCKLE, John Walford (Wally). b 39. EMMTC. **d** 89 **p** 90. C Nottingham St Pet and St Jas *S'well* 89-00; Commercial Chapl Nottingham City Cen 89-00; Dioc Adv on Ind Soc 96-97; rtd 00; Perm to Offic *S'well* from 00. *43 Bingham Road, Radcliffe-on-Trent, Nottingham NG12 2FY* Tel 0115-933 2278 E-mail wally.huckle@ntlworld.com

HUCKLE, Peter. b 46. Ox Univ Inst of Educn CertEd69 Auckland Univ DipPE71 DipEd71. Educn for Min (NZ). **d** 90 **p** 91. New Zealand 90-91; Hon C N Walsham w Antingham *Nor* 91-92; C Gt Yarmouth 92-94; TV 94-96; Min Can and Chapl St Paul's Cathl *Lon* 96-97; Asst Chapl Athens and Perm to Offic *Eur* 97; SSJE from 97; Superior from 02. *St Edward's House, 22 Great College Street, London SW1P 3QA* Tel (020) 7222 9234 Fax 7799 2641 E-mail superior@ssje.org.uk

HUCKLE, Stephen Leslie. b 48. Ch Ch Ox BA70 BA72 MA74. Coll of Resurr Mirfield 73. **d** 75 **p** 76. C Wednesbury St Paul Wood Green *Lich* 75-78; C Aylesbury *Ox* 78-85; C Farnham Royal w Hedgerley 85-88; V Fenny Stratford 88-98; V Stirchley *Birm* from 98. *The Vicarage, 18 Pineapple Grove, Birmingham B30 2TJ* Tel 0121-443 1371 E-mail stephen@ascension.fsbusiness.co.uk

HUCKLE, Walford. *See* HUCKLE, John Walford

HUDD, Philip Simon Gorman. b 68. Westmr Coll Ox BA90. Westcott Ho Cam 91. **d** 93 **p** 94. C Kirkby *Liv* 93-97; TV 97-99; V Lancaster Ch Ch *Blackb* from 99; AD Lancaster from 04. *Christ Church Vicarage, 1 East Road, Lancaster LA1 3EE* Tel (01524) 34430 E-mail phil@gorhudd.freeserve.co.uk

HUDDLESON, Robert Roulston. b 32. QUB BA55 TCD Div Test57. **d** 57 **p** 58. C Ballymena *Conn* 57-59; C Belfast St Jas 59-63; Ethiopia 65-69; Exec Asst WCC Geneva 69-75; Dep Sec Gen Syn Bd for Miss and Unity 75-81; Admin Sec *Dur* 81-86; Dioc Sec *Ex* 86-97; rtd 97; Perm to Offic *Ex* from 97. *Mount Pleasant, Tiverton Road, Bampton, Tiverton EX16 9DX* Tel (01398) 331412

HUDDLESTON, Geoffrey Roger. b 36. TCD BA63 MA67. Ridley Hall Cam 63. **d** 65 **p** 66. C Tonbridge SS Pet and Paul *Roch* 65-69; Chapl RAF 69-85; V Lyonsdown H Trin *St Alb* 85-00; RD Barnet 94-99; rtd 00; Perm to Offic *Lich* from 01. *The Granary, Bellamour Lodge Farm, Colton Road, Colton, Rugeley WS15 3NZ* Tel (01889) 574052

HUDGHTON, John Francis. b 56. BA. Cranmer Hall Dur 81. **d** 83 **p** 84. C Stockport St Geo *Ches* 83-85; C Witton 85-87; C Stockport St Alb Hall Street 87-90; V Thornton-le-Moors w Ince and Elton 90-95; Chapl RAF 95-01; P-in-c Burnby *York* 01-03; P-in-c Londesborough 01-03; P-in-c Nunburnholme and Warter and Huggate 01-03; P-in-c Shiptonthorpe and Hayton 01-03; TR Buxton w Burbage and King Sterndale *Derby* from 03. *The Rectory, 7 Lismore Park, Buxton SK17 9AU* Tel (01298) 22151

HUDSON, Andrew Julian. b 57. Cranmer Hall Dur 93. **d** 93 **p** 94. C Moldgreen *Wakef* 93-97; P-in-c Lundwood 97-01; V Dodworth 01-04; Ind Chapl *Chelmsf* from 04; C Aveley and Purfleet from 04. *St Stephen's Vicarage, London Road, Purfleet RM19 1QD* Tel (01708) 891242 Mobile 07989-988496 E-mail hudsonab@aol.com

HUDSON, Anthony George. b 39. N Ord Course. **d** 84 **p** 85. C Harrogate St Mark *Ripon* 84-87; P-in-c Hampsthwaite 87-96; P-in-c Killinghall 87-94; V Hampsthwaite and Killinghall 96-99; rtd 99; Perm to Offic *Ripon* from 00. *26 Beckwith Crescent, Harrogate HG2 0BQ* Tel (01423) 858740

HUDSON, Brainerd Peter de Wirtz Goodwin. *See* GOODWIN HUDSON, Brainerd Peter de Wirtz

HUDSON, Christopher John. b 45. Bedf Coll Lon BSc68 MCIH73. Cranmer Hall Dur. **d** 77 **p** 78. C Bath Weston St Jo *B & W* 77-80; Youth Chapl 77-80; P-in-c Baltonsborough w Butleigh and W Bradley 80-84; V 84-87; P-in-c Shirwell w Loxhore *Ex* 87-89; P-in-c Kentisbury, Trentishoe, E Down and Arlington 88-89; RD Shirwell 88-91; TR Shirwell, Loxhore,

Kentisbury, Arlington, etc 90-91; P-in-c Trentishoe 90-91; R Huntspill *B & W* 91-94; rtd 01; Perm to Offic *B & W* from 98. *62B Deane Drive, Taunton TA1 5PQ* Tel (01823) 324615 E-mail revchris320@aol.com

HUDSON, Clive. b 42. Nor City Coll CertEd66. Dioc OLM tr scheme 01. **d** 03 **p** 04. OLM Redenhall, Harleston, Wortwell and Needham *Nor* from 03. *9 Shotford Road, Harleston IP20 9JH* Tel (01379) 853284 E-mail hudson.harleston@virgin.net

HUDSON, Canon Gerald Ernest. b 20. Ex Coll Ox BA42 MA46. Westcott Ho Cam 42. **d** 43 **p** 44. C Deptford St Paul *S'wark* 43-47; C Raynes Park St Sav 47-51; V Catford St Laur 51-60; V Roehampton H Trin 60-71; Hon Can S'wark Cathl 68-80; Prin S'wark Ord Course 71-80; R St Mary le Bow w St Pancras Soper Lane etc *Lon* 80-85; rtd 85; Perm to Offic *Cant* 85-99; Dir Post-Ord Tr 86-88. *10 Medina Avenue, Whitstable CT5 4EN* Tel (01227) 276548

HUDSON, John. b 47. FRSA CertSS. Linc Th Coll. **d** 83 **p** 84. C Merton St Mary *S'wark* 83-86; C Kirk Ella *York* 86-88; P-in-c Lenborough *Ox* 88-93; V Lenborough 93-03; P-in-c Tingewick w Water Stratford, Radclive etc 89-93; P-in-c Water Stratford 93-00; P-in-c Reading St Matt from 03. *St Matthew's Vicarage, 205 Southcote Lane, Reading RG30 3AX* Tel 0118-957 3755

HUDSON, John. b 51. Oak Hill Th Coll 84. **d** 86 **p** 87. C Leyland St Andr *Blackb* 86-89; V Coppull from 89. *The Vicarage, Chapel Lane, Coppull, Chorley PR7 4NA* Tel (01257) 791218

HUDSON, Canon John Cecil. b 22. Selw Coll Cam BA46 MA48. Qu Coll Birm BD51. **d** 48 **p** 49. C Darlington St Cuth *Dur* 48-53; CF (TA) 50-57; TR Usworth *Dur* 53-57; V Padiham *Blackb* 57-68; RD Burnley 65-68; RD Whalley 68-83; V Clitheroe St Mary 68-85; Hon Can Blackb Cathl 79-85; rtd 85; Perm to Offic *Blackb* and *Bradf* from 85. *29 Eastfield Drive, West Bradford, Clitheroe BB7 4TQ* Tel (01200) 423531

HUDSON, Canon John Leonard. b 44. AKC66. **d** 67 **p** 68. C Dodworth *Wakef* 67-70; Prec Wakef Cathl 70-73; V Ravensthorpe 73-80; V Royston from 80; P-in-c Carlton from 90; RD Barnsley 93-04; Hon Can Wakef Cathl from 98. *The Clergy House, Church Street, Royston, Barnsley S71 4QZ* Tel (01226) 722410 E-mail john.hudson@uku.co.uk

HUDSON, John Peter. b 42. AKC64. St Boniface Warminster 64. **d** 65 **p** 66. C S Shields St Hilda w St Thos *Dur* 65-68; Chapl RN 68-84; V Mellor *Blackb* from 84. *The Vicarage, Church Lane, Mellor, Blackburn BB2 7JL* Tel (01254) 812324 Fax 814567 E-mail jpeterhudson@aol.com

HUDSON, Prof John Richard Keith. b 35. St Pet Coll Ox BA60 MA64 State Univ NY PhD83. Linc Th Coll 60. **d** 62 **p** 63. C Tettenhall Wood *Lich* 62-65; Chapl and Lect Bp Grosseteste Coll Linc 65-71; Staff Officer Gen Syn Bd of Educn 72-73; Australia 73-79; Lect Riverina Coll of Advanced Educn Wagga 73-74; Lect Mt Gravatt Coll of Advanced Educn Brisbane 74-79; Master and Chapl Yardley Court Sch Tonbridge 79-82; USA from 82; Teaching Asst State Univ NY 82-83; Asst Prof Louisiana State Univ Alexandria 83-85; Asst R Alexandria St Jas 84-85; R Camden St Paul Delaware from 85; Prof Wesley Coll Dover 85-92; Chapl Delaware Hospice 92-96; rtd 01. *1300 Morris Avenue, Villanova, PA 19085, USA* Tel (001) (610) 525 3131 E-mail jrkh65@msn.com

HUDSON, John Stephen Anthony. b 49. S Dios Minl Tr Scheme 85 Chich Th Coll 86. **d** 88 **p** 89. C Horsham *Chich* 88-91; TV Littlehampton and Wick from 91. *The Vicarage, 40 Beaconsfield Road, Wick, Littlehampton BN17 6LN* Tel (01903) 724990

HUDSON, Mrs Mary Gertrude. b 29. Univ Coll Lon BA51 CertEd52. Qu Coll Birm 82. **dss** 85 **d** 87 **p** 94. Kings Norton *Birm* 85-87; NSM 87-97; rtd 97; Perm to Offic *S'well* from 04. *1 Wentworth Way, Edwalton, Nottingham NG12 4DJ* Tel 0115-914 4070

HUDSON, Peter John. b 66. **d** 03 **p** 04. OLM Deptford St Paul *S'wark* from 03. *The New Rectory, Mary Ann Gardens, London SE8 3DP* Tel (020) 8692 0989 E-mail curate@paulsdeptford.org.uk

HUDSON, Philip Howard. b 50. St Steph Ho Ox 89. **d** 91 **p** 92. C Poulton-le-Fylde *Blackb* 91-95; V Blackpool St Wilfrid from 95. *St Wilfrid's Vicarage, 8 Langdale Road, Blackpool FY4 4RT* Tel (01253) 761532

HUDSON, Stephen. *See* HUDSON, John Stephen Anthony

HUDSON, Thomas George. b 32. TCD BA54. CITC Div Test54. **d** 55 **p** 56. C Belfast St Matt *Conn* 55-58; C Belfast Ch Ch 58-60; C Carlow *C & O* 60-61; I Hacketstown 61-69; I Kinneigh Union *C, C & R* 69-72; I Monasterevan *M & K* 72-83; I Mostrim w Granard, Clonbroney, Killoe etc *K, E & A* 83-97; Can Elphin Cathl 86-97; rtd 97. *34 Oak Court Grove, Palmerstown, Dublin 20, Irish Republic* Tel (00353) (1) 626 9854

HUDSON, Trevor. b 32. Dur Univ BA56. Cranmer Hall Dur. **d** 58 **p** 59. C Doncaster St Mary *Sheff* 58-62; C Attercliffe 62-64; V Stannington 64-79; V Abbeydale St Jo 79-88; V Worsbrough 88-95; rtd 95; Perm to Offic *Sheff* from 95. *Spring Villa Garden, 136A Langsett Road South, Oughtibridge, Sheffield S35 0HA* Tel 0114-286 3559

HUDSON, Walter Gerald. b 29. **d** 95 **p** 96. Hon C Eccleston Park *Liv* 95-99; Perm to Offic from 99. *31 Springfield Lane, Eccleston, St Helens WA10 5EW* Tel (01744) 24919

HUDSON, Wilfred. b 23. St Jo Coll Dur BA49. **d** 51 **p** 52. C Doncaster St Mary *Sheff* 51-56; V Brampton Bierlow 56-64; V Anston 64-74; V Woodsetts 64-74; V Sharrow St Andr 74-88; rtd 88; Perm to Offic *Sheff* from 88. *128 Totley Brook Road, Sheffield S17 3QU* Tel 0114-236 5558

HUDSON-WILKIN, Mrs Rose Josephine. b 61. WMMTC 89. **d** 91 **p** 94. Par Dn Wolverhampton St Matt *Lich* 91-94; C 94-95; C W Bromwich Gd Shep w St Jo 95-98; Black Anglican Concern 95-98; V Dalston H Trin w St Phil and Haggerston All SS *Lon* from 98. *The Vicarage, Livermere Road, London E8 4EZ* Tel (020) 7254 5062 E-mail revdrose@aol.com

HUDSPITH, Colin John. b 46. Nottm Univ BA67. SW Minl Tr Course 93. **d** 96 **p** 97. C Pilton w Ashford *Ex* 96-97; C Barnstaple 97-99; C Shirwell, Loxhore, Kentisbury, Arlington, etc 99-00; TV from 00. *The Rectory, Shirwell, Barnstaple EX31 4JU* Tel (01271) 850436 E-mail chudsp@netcomuk.co.uk

HUDSPITH, Ernest. b 26. Open Univ BA73 Birm Univ DipTh64. Qu Coll Birm 61. **d** 64 **p** 65. PV S'well Minster *S'well* 64-67; Prec Gib Cathl *Eur* 67-68; NSM Twickenham St Mary *Lon* 69-74; rtd 94; Perm to Offic *Chich* from 01. *Flat 3, 68 Warrior Square, St Leonards-on-Sea TN37 6BP* Tel (01424) 441760

HUDSPITH, Mrs Susan Mary. b 49. St Alb Minl Tr Scheme 79. **dss** 82 **d** 87 **p** 94. Luton St Chris Round Green *St Alb* 82-92; Par Dn 87-88; NSM 88-92; Perm to Offic 92-94 and 00-05; NSM Luton St Mary 94-00; NSM Stevenage St Pet Broadwater from 05. *15 Waverley Close, Stevenage SG2 8RU* Tel (01438) 725030 E-mail geoff-sue.hudspith@virgin.net

HUGGETT, Christopher Roy. b 49. Hull Univ BA72 CertEd73. Linc Th Coll 79. **d** 93 **p** 94. C Accrington St Jo w Huncoat *Blackb* 93-95; C Cleveleys 95-97; P-in-c Scorton 97-99; V Scorton and Barnacre and Calder Vale 99-02; P-in-c Leyburn w Bellerby *Ripon* from 02. *The Vicarage, I'Anson Close, Leyburn DL8 5LF* Tel (01969) 622251 E-mail c.huggett@freenet.co.uk

HUGGETT, David John. b 34. Lon Univ BSc56 Southn Univ PhD59. Clifton Th Coll 64. **d** 67 **p** 68. C Heatherlands St Jo *Sarum* 67-70; C Cambridge St Sepulchre *Ely* 70-73; R Nottingham St Nic *S'well* 73-92; Cyprus 93-99; rtd 99. *101 Admirals Walk, West Cliff Road, Bournemouth BH2 5HF* Tel (01202) 558199

HUGGETT, John Victor James. b 39. Dur Univ BA64. Tyndale Hall Bris 64. **d** 66 **p** 67. C Hailsham *Chich* 66-69; C Worthing St Geo 69-71; C Woking St Pet *Guildf* 71-73; C Buckhurst Hill *Chelmsf* 73-76; V Meltham Mills *Wakef* 76-78; V Wilshaw 76-78; rtd 79; Jt Ldr Breath Fellowship from 79; Perm to Offic *Wakef* 79-84 and *Roch* from 84. *Breath Ministries Healing Centre, Weald House, 10A High Street, Tunbridge Wells TN1 1UX* Tel (01892) 512520 E-mail cjphuggett@btopenworld.com

HUGGETT, Kevin John. b 62. St Jo Coll Dur BA83. Trin Coll Bris 88. **d** 91 **p** 92. C Gt Ilford St Andr *Chelmsf* 91-94; Regional Manager for Uganda and Sudan CMS 94-01; Hon C Tonbridge SS Pet and Paul *Roch* 98-01; Chapl Lanc Univ *Blackb* from 01. *11 Alderman Road, Lancaster LA1 5FW* Tel (01524) 843091 *or* 594082/71 E-mail k.huggett@lancaster.ac.uk

HUGGETT, Michael George. b 38. Bris Univ BA60 Birm Univ CertEd61 Nottm Univ DCE83. EMMTC 85. **d** 88 **p** 89. C Sawley *Derby* 88-92; C Chaddesden St Phil 92-93; P-in-c Alkmonton, Cubley, Marston, Montgomery etc 93-99; R 99-04; rtd 04. *15 Welland Close, Mickleover, Derby DE3 0RZ* Tel (01332) 511259

HUGGINS, Stephen David. b 53. Sussex Univ BEd75 Leic Univ DipEd79 K Coll Lon MA80. STETS. **d** 01 **p** 02. NSM Bexhill St Aug *Chich* 01-02; NSM Sedlescombe w Whatlington from 02. *The Rectory, Church Hill, Sedlescombe, Battle TN33 0QP* Tel (01424) 870233

HUGHES, Adrian John. b 57. Newc Univ BA78 Dur Univ BA82. Cranmer Hall Dur 80. **d** 83 **p** 84. C Shard End *Birm* 83-86; TV Solihull 86-90; TV Glendale Gp *Newc* 90-94; P-in-c Belford 94-95; V Belford and Lucker from 95; V Ellingham 95-02; AD Bamburgh and Glendale from 97; Asst Dioc Dir of Ords from 98. *The Vicarage, North Bank, Belford NE70 7LY* Tel (01668) 213545 Fax as telephone E-mail revdajh@aol.com

HUGHES, Alan. b 34. St D Coll Lamp BA54 St Mich Coll Llan 58. **d** 60 **p** 61. C Aberavon *Llan* 60-62; Chapl RAF 62-66; CF 66-76; USA from 76. *1408 South West 20th Street, Gresham, OR 97030, USA*

HUGHES, Alan. b 46. TD. Edin Th Coll 71. **d** 74 **p** 75. C Edin St Cuth *Edin* 74-76; P-in-c Edin St Luke 76-78; C Marske in Cleveland *York* 78-81; V New Marske 81-84; V Kirkbymoorside w Gillamoor, Farndale etc 84-94; CF 84-94; V Berwick H Trin and St Mary *Newc* from 94. *The Vicarage, Parade, Berwick-upon-Tweed TD15 1DF* Tel and fax (01289) 306136 Mobile 07941-757412 E-mail berwick.church@bigwig.net *or* skypilot@bigwig.net

HUGHES, Albert Ashbden. b 10. Univ of Wales BA37. St Mich Coll Llan 38. **d** 39 **p** 40. C Llangeinwen *Ban* 39-42; CF 43-44; C Llanfachraeth *Ban* 42-45; C Llandegai 45-49; R Blaina *Mon* 49-55; V Harlech and Llanfair juxta Harlech *Ban* 55-58; V Coldhurst *Man* 58-64; Chapl Oldham and Distr Gen Hosp

57-64; V Goostrey *Ches* 64-76; rtd 76; Perm to Offic *Ches* from 76. *50 Preston Road, Lytham St Annes FY8 5AA* Tel (01253) 795108

HUGHES, Albert William. b 48. S Dios Minl Tr Scheme 90. **d** 92 **p** 93. Community of Our Lady and St John from 70; Prior from 90; Perm to Offic *Win* from 96. *Alton Abbey, Abbey Road, Beech, Alton GU34 4AP* Tel (01420) 562145 *or* 563575 Fax 561691

HUGHES, Alexander James. b 75. Greyfriars Ox BA97 St Edm Coll Cam MPhil99. Westcott Ho Cam 98. **d** 00 **p** 01. C Headington Quarry *Ox* 00-03; Bp's Dom Chapl *Portsm* from 03. *11 Burnham Wood, Fareham PO16 7UD* Tel (01329) 280247 Fax 231538 E-mail bouverie@lineone.net

HUGHES, Allan Paul. b 45. Glam Coll of Educn CertEd69 Open Univ BA91. Abp's Sch of Min 01. **d** 02 **p** 03. Chapl St Olave's Sch York 02-05; NSM Skelton w Shipton and Newton on Ouse *York* 02-03; Asst to RD Easingwold 03-04; NSM York All SS Pavement w St Crux and St Mich from 04; NSM York St Denys from 04. *All Saints' Rectory, 52 St Andrewgate, York YO1 7BZ* Tel (01904) 466041

HUGHES, Andrew Terrell. b 29. Bris Univ BA56 DipEd. Coll of Resurr Mirfield 64. **d** 66 **p** 67. C Weston-super-Mare St Sav *B & W* 66-70; C Yeovil St Jo w Preston Plucknett 70-73; TV Yeovil 73-83; R Wincanton 83-88; rtd 89; Perm to Offic *Sarum* from 89. *2 Cove Street, Weymouth DT4 8TS* Tel (01305) 778639

HUGHES, Miss Angela Mary. b 52. Avery Hill Coll CertEd75. St Steph Ho Ox 90. **d** 92 **p** 94. Par Dn Kidderminster St Mary and All SS w Trimpley etc *Worc* 92-94; C 94-96; P-in-c Gilmorton w Peatling Parva and Kimcote etc *Leic* 96-01; RD Guthlaxton II 99-01; R Wyberton *Linc* from 01; V Frampton from 01; RD Holland W from 04. *The Rectory, Church Lane, Wyberton, Boston PE21 7AF* Tel (01205) 353593 Fax 311765 E-mail ahughes@webleicester.co.uk

HUGHES, Arthur John. b 41. MCIOB71 MRICS78. WEMTC 03. **d** 05. NSM Church Stretton *Heref* from 05. *Jacey, 2 Lawley Close, Church Stretton SY6 6EP* Tel (01694) 722582 E-mail jhnhughes6@aol.com

HUGHES, Arthur Lewis. b 36. St Deiniol's Hawarden 65 CA Tr Coll 61. **d** 68 **p** 69. C Holywell *St As* 68-71; Lect Watford St Mary *St Alb* 71-75; V Thornton in Lonsdale w Burton in Lonsdale *Bradf* 75-84; V Daubhill *Man* 84-89; V Castle Town *Lich* 89-00; Chapl Staffs Univ 91-00; rtd 00; Perm to Offic *Ches* from 00. *31 Hunt Close, Towcester NN12 7AD* Tel (01327) 358257

HUGHES, Arthur William Ronald. b 14. Ch Coll Cam BA36 MA40. St Mich Coll Llan 37. **d** 39 **p** 41. C Rhosddu *St As* 39-40; C Minera 40-42; C Wrexham 42-49; R Llangynyw 49-53; R Moston St Jo *Man* 53-57; V Coalbrookdale *Heref* 57-67; V Arthog w Fairbourne *Ban* 67-74; R Machynlleth and Llanwrin 74-77; rtd 77; Perm to Offic *St D* 77-01. *4 Millgate Street, Methwold, Thetford IP26 4NY*

HUGHES, Benjamin John. b 65. Golds Coll Lon BEd91. Cranmer Hall Dur BTh97. **d** 99 **p** 00. NSM Fulham St Matt *Lon* 99-03; Chapl RN from 03. *Royal Naval Chaplaincy Service, Room 203, Victory Building, HM Naval Base, Portsmouth PO1 3LS* Tel (023) 9272 7903 Fax 9272 7111

HUGHES, Bernard Patrick. b 35. Oak Hill Th Coll DipTh64. **d** 65 **p** 66. C Fulham St Matt *Lon* 65-69; Chapl St Steph Hosp Lon 69-89; Chapl St Mary Abbots Hosp Lon 69-97; Chapl Westmr Hosp Lon 89-94; Chapl Westmr Children's Hosp Lon 89-94; Sen Chapl Chelsea and Westmr Healthcare NHS Trust 94-97; rtd 97; Perm to Offic *Bris* and *Sarum* from 97. *Charis, 6 Priory Park, Bradford-on-Avon BA15 1QU* Tel (01225) 868679

HUGHES, Bertram Arthur Edwin. b 23. Clifton Th Coll 64. **d** 66 **p** 67. C Taunton St Jas *B & W* 66-68; C Ramsgate St Luke *Cant* 68-70; Australia 70-76; P-in-c Swanton Abbott w Skeyton *Nor* 76-80; P-in-c Scottow 76-80; Australia 80-83; R Reymerston w Cranworth, Letton, Southburgh etc *Nor* 83-84; rtd 84; Perm to Offic *Ex* from 90. *88 Winslade Road, Sidmouth EX10 9EZ* Tel (01395) 512452

HUGHES, Miss Carol Lindsay. b 51. Cam Inst of Educn CertEd72 Nottm Univ BEd86. Trin Coll Bris DipHE93. **d** 93 **p** 94. C Ilkeston St Mary *Derby* 93-97; P-in-c Langley Mill from 97; RD Heanor from 99. *The Vicarage, 214 Cromford Road, Langley Mill, Nottingham NG16 4HB* Tel (01773) 712441 E-mail lindsay@hugheshouse.freeserve.co.uk

HUGHES, Christopher Clarke. b 40. MRAC61. ALCD65. **d** 65 **p** 66. C Broadclyst *Ex* 65-68; C Chenies and Lt Chalfont *Ox* 68-70; TV Lydford w Bridestowe and Sourton *Ex* 70-72; TV Lydford, Brent Tor, Bridestowe and Sourton 72-74; V Buckland Monachorum 74-83; R Ashtead *Guildf* 83-98; R Aboyne and Ballater *Ab* 98-03; rtd 03. *Stone Farmhouse, Thorveton, Exeter EX5 5LL* Tel (01884) 855250

HUGHES, Clive. b 54. Univ of Wales BA77 MA82. St Mich Coll Llan BD95. **d** 95 **p** 96. C Carmarthen St Dav *St D* 95-97; TV Aberystwyth 97-04; P-in-c Hanmer, Bronington, Bettisfield, Tallarn Green *St As* from 04. *The Vicarage, Hanmer, Whitchurch SY13 3DE* Tel (01948) 830468

HUGHES, David Anthony. b 25. Trin Coll Cam BA48 MA55. Linc Th Coll 74. **d** 76 **p** 77. C Boston *Linc* 76-78; V Graffoe 78-90; rtd 90; Perm to Offic *Linc* from 91. *27 St Clement's Road, Ruskington, Sleaford NG34 9AF* Tel (01526) 832618

HUGHES, David Howard. b 55. Univ of Wales (Ban). St Mich Coll Llan. **d** 79 **p** 80. C Llanrhos *St As* 79-82; C Eckington w Handley and Ridgeway *Derby* 82-83; C Staveley and Barrow Hill 83-85; TV 85-89; V Whitworth St Bart *Man* 89-00. *2 Cromwell Road, Chesterfield S40 4TH* Tel (01246) 277361

HUGHES, David Michael. b 41. Oak Hill Th Coll BD67. **d** 68 **p** 69. C Tunbridge Wells St Jo *Roch* 68-73; C Crookes St Thos *Sheff* 73-81; V Normanton *Wakef* 81-90; TR Didsbury St Jas and Em *Man* from 90; AD Withington 00-04. *St James's Rectory, 9 Didsbury Park, Manchester M20 5LH* Tel 0161-434 2178 Fax 445 1388 E-mail davidhughes@stj-emm.org

HUGHES, Debbie Ann. *See* PEATMAN, Mrs Debbie Ann

HUGHES, Denis Charles. b 27. LNSM course 92. **d** 95 **p** 96. OLM S Merstham *S'wark* 95-02; rtd 02; Perm to Offic *S'wark* from 02. *1 South Close Green, Merstham, Redhill RH1 3DU* Tel (01737) 642652 Mobile 07889-679224 E-mail ajdch@aol.com

HUGHES, Elfed. b 53. St Mich Coll Llan BD75 PhD03. **d** 77 **p** 78. C Skewen *Llan* 77-80; TV Ystradyfodwg w Gelli, Rhigos and Tonpentre 80-81; P-in-c Pentre CD 81-85; V Pentre 85-87; Chapl Wales Poly 87-91; V Llantrisant 91-97; rtd 97; Perm to Offic *Llan* from 99; *Ban, St D* and *Mon* from 02; *Glouc* from 04; USPG Miss Adv for Ch in Wales from 02 and Glouc from 04. *19 Heol Brynteg, Tonyrefail, Porth CF39 8DL*

HUGHES, Mrs Elizabeth Jane. b 58. K Coll Lon BD81 AKC81. Ripon Coll Cuddesdon 81. **dss** 83 **d** 87 **p** 94. Chipping Barnet w Arkley *St Alb* 83-86; Dunstable 86-87; Hon Par Dn 87-93; NSM Boxmoor St Jo 93-03; Chapl Hospice of St Fran Berkhamsted from 99. *17 Lansdowne Road, Luton LU3 1EE* Tel (01582) 730722 E-mail liz.hughes@stfrancis.org.uk

HUGHES, Ms Eunice Nesta. b 14. K Coll Lon 38 CertEd51. Lambeth DipTh40 St Chris Coll Blackheath 34. **dss** 61 **d** 87. RE Teacher Darley Gate 62-64; Cheltenham Ladies' Coll 65-74; Cant St Martin and St Paul *Cant* 76-80; Westgate St Sav 80-87; Hon Par Dn 87; Perm to Offic 87-97. *Flat 1, 4 Cedric Road, Westgate-on-Sea CT8 8NZ* Tel (01843) 831746

HUGHES, The Ven Evan Arthur Bertram. b 25. St D Coll Lamp BA48 LTh50. **d** 50 **p** 51. C Abergwili w Llanfihangel-uwch-Gwili *St D* 50-53; C Llanelli 53-58; India 59-69; Adn Bhagalpur 65-66; C Llanstadwel *St D* 70-73; Pakistan 73-74; R Johnston w Steynton *St D* 74-80; Can St D Cathl 80-85; V Newcastle Emlyn 80-81; V Newcastle Emlyn w Llandyfriog and Troed-yr-aur 81-86; Adn Carmarthen 85-91; V Llanegwad w Llanfynydd 86-88; V Cynwil Elfed and Newchurch 88-91; rtd 91. *104 Bronwydd Road, Carmarthen SA31 2AW* Tel (01267) 237155

HUGHES, Canon Evelyn. b 31. Gilmore Ho 73. **dss** 79 **d** 87 **p** 94. Fetcham *Guildf* 79-82; Dioc Adv Lay Min 82-86; Farnborough 83-87; C 87-92; Bp's Adv for Women's Min 87-94; Dn-in-c Badshot Lea CD 92-94; C-in-c 94-96; Hon Can Guildf Cathl 94-96; rtd 96; Perm to Offic *Guildf* from 96. *4 Oaklands, Haslemere GU27 3RD* Tel (01428) 651576

HUGHES, Gareth Francis. b 73. St Jo Coll Dur MSc94 GInstP94. St Mich Coll Llan BD98. **d** 98 **p** 99. C Haughton le Skerne *Dur* 98-02; TV White Horse *Sarum* from 02. *The Vicarage, The Hollow, Dilton Marsh, Westbury BA13 4BU* Tel (01373) 822560 E-mail gareth.hughes@whitehorseteam.org

HUGHES, The Very Revd Geraint Morgan Hugh. b 34. Keble Coll Ox BA58 MA63. St Mich Coll Llan 58. **d** 59 **p** 60. C Gorseinon *S & B* 59-63; C Oystermouth 63-68; R Llanbadarn Fawr, Llandegley and Llanfihangel etc 68-76; R Llandrindod w Cefnllys 76-87; R Llandrindod w Cefnllys and Disserth 87-98; Can Brecon Cathl 89-98; Prec Brecon Cathl 95-98; RD Maelienydd 95-98; Dean Brecon 98-00; V Brecon St Mary and Battle w Llanddew 98-00; rtd 00. *Hafod, Cefnllys Lane, Penybont, Llandrindod Wells LD1 5SW* Tel (01597) 851830

HUGHES, Canon Gerald Thomas. b 30. Lon Univ BD63 MTh. Qu Coll Birm 72. **d** 72 **p** 73. Lic to Offic *Cov* 72-80; P-in-c Birdingbury 80-81; P-in-c Leamington Hastings 80-81; V Leamington Hastings and Birdingbury 81-82; V Dunchurch 82-89; RD Rugby 85-89; Can Res Cov Cathl 89-94; rtd 94; Perm to Offic *Cov* and *Worc* from 94. *Loafers' Cottage, Lazy Lane, Fladbury, Pershore WR10 2QL* Tel (01386) 860650

HUGHES, Gwilym Berw. b 42. St Mich Coll Llan DipTh68. **d** 68 **p** 69. C Conwy w Gyffin *Ban* 68-71; V Llandinorwig 71-75; TV Llandudno 75-80; V Dwygyfylchi 80-96; RD Arllechwedd 88-96; V Bodelwyddan *St As* from 96. *The Vicarage, Bodelwyddan, Rhyl LL18 5UR* Tel (01745) 583034

HUGHES, Gwilym Lloyd. b 48. Univ of Wales (Cardiff) BD76 MA79 DipTh74 Univ of Wales (Ban) CertEd84. St Mich Coll Llan 71. **d** 99 **p** 00. NSM Caerwys and Bodfari *St As* from 99; Warden of Readers 99-02. *Adlonfa, Bodfari, Denbigh LL16 4DA* Tel (01745) 710385

HUGHES, Canon Gwyndaf Morris. b 36. Univ of Wales (Lamp) BA57 St Cath Soc Ox 57. St Steph Ho Ox 58 St Mich Coll Llan 59. **d** 59 **p** 60. C Glanogwen *Ban* 59-62; Chapl RN 62-78; R Llanfairpwll w Penmynydd *Ban* 78-90; R Beaumaris 90-03; RD Tindaethwy 88-01; AD 01-03; Can Ban Cathl 95-99; Prec 97-99;

Preb 99-03; rtd 03. *Cae Pysgodlyn, Waterloo Port, Caernarfon LL55 1LW* Tel (01286) 677461

HUGHES, Canon Hazel. b 45. St Jo Coll Dur 75. **dss** 78 **d** 87 **p** 94. Lower Mitton *Worc* 78-81; Worc St Martin w St Pet, St Mark etc 82-87; Par Dn Worc SE 87-88; Dn-in-c Wribbenhall 88-94; V 94; P-in-c from 94; Chapl to Mentally Handicapped from 94; Hon Can Worc Cathl from 95. *Wribbenhall Vicarage, Trimpley Lane, Bewdley DY12 1JJ* Tel (01299) 402196 Mobile 07986-251938 E-mail hazel.hughes1@btopenworld.com

HUGHES, Heather Alice. b 48. Open Univ BA91 Kent Univ 97. SEITE DipTM99. **d** 99 **p** 00. NSM Pembury *Roch* from 99. *7 Henwoods Crescent, Pembury TN2 4LJ* Tel (01892) 822764 E-mail hughes@heather39.freeserve.co.uk

HUGHES, Hugh. b 13. St D Coll Lamp BA35 St Mich Coll Llan 35. **d** 36 **p** 37. C Llanfaethlu w Llanfwrog *Ban* 36-41; C Holyhead 41-45; V Dolwyddelan 45-56; R Llanbeulan w Llanfaelog and Tal-y-Llyn 56-69; R Llaneugrad w Llanallgo and Penrhosllugwy etc 73-82; RD Twrcelyn 80-82; rtd 82; Perm to Offic *Ban* from 86. *50 Craig-y-Don, Benllech, Tyn-y-Gongl LL74 8TB* Tel (01248) 853500

HUGHES, Canon Hywel Maldwyn. b 20. Univ of Wales (Swansea) BA42. St Mich Coll Llan 42. **d** 44 **p** 45. C Llangyfelach and Morriston *S & B* 44-47; C Builth w Alltmawr and Llanynys 46-48; Min Can Brecon Cathl 48-53; R Llanfeugan w Llanddetty and Glyncollwg 53-59; R Ystradgynlais 59-68; V Killay 68-87; RD Clyne 79; Can Brecon Cathl from 81; Treas Brecon Cathl 81; Chan 83-87; rtd 88; Canada from 95; Perm to Offic Toronto from 95. *142 Three Valleys Drive, Don Mills ON, Canada, M3A 3B9* Tel (001) (416) 445 8571

HUGHES, Ian. b 67. Aston Tr Scheme Trin Coll Bris BA00. **d** 00 **p** 01. C Halton *Ches* 00-04; P-in-c Seacombe from 04. *Seacombe Vicarage, 5 Brougham Road, Wallasey CH44 6PN* Tel 0151-638 3677 E-mail ihughes@hotmail.com

HUGHES, Preb Ivor Gordon. b 45. Culham Coll of Educn CertEd68 Westmr Coll Ox MTh94. Ripon Coll Cuddesdon 75. **d** 77 **p** 78. C Newport w Longford *Lich* 77-79; Children's Work Officer CMS 79-82; V Gt and Lt Bedwyn and Savernake Forest *Sarum* 82-86; P-in-c Urchfont w Stert 86-90; TR Redhorn 90-92; Nat Children's Officer Gen Syn Bd of Educn 92-95; R Yeovil w Kingston Pitney *B & W* from 95; Preb Wells Cathl from 02; RD Yeovil from 04; Chapl St Marg Hospice from 04. *The Rectory, 5 West Park, Yeovil BA20 1DE* Tel and fax (01935) 475396 E-mail ivor.hughes1@virgin.net

HUGHES, Mrs Jackie Louise. b 50. ACP81 Birm Poly BEd86. WMMTC 89. **d** 92. NSM Edgbaston St Geo *Birm* 92-95; Tutor Qu Coll Birm from 96. *267 Stoney Lane, Yardley, Birmingham B25 8YG* Tel 0121-628 4184 *or* 454 8597

HUGHES, James Thomas. b 74. St Anne's Coll Ox BA95 Liv Hope PGCE97. Oak Hill Th Coll BA02. **d** 03 **p** 04. C Virginia Water *Guildf* from 03. *6 Beechmont Avenue, Virginia Water GU25 4EY* Tel (01344) 849172 E-mail happierlarry@yahoo.co.uk

HUGHES, John. *See* HUGHES, Arthur John

HUGHES, John Chester. b 24. St Jo Coll Dur BA48 DipTh50 MA51. **d** 50 **p** 51. C Southend St Sav Westcliff *Chelmsf* 50-53; Succ Chelmsf Cathl 53-55; V New Humberstone *Leic* 55-61; V Croxton Kerrial w Branston by Belvoir 61-63; Provost Leic 63-78; V Bringhurst w Gt Easton 78-87; rtd 87; Perm to Offic *Leic* 87-99. *29 High Street, Hallaton, Market Harborough LE16 8UD* Tel (01858) 89622

HUGHES, John David. b 58. Leeds Univ BA79 Man Univ PGCE82. Ripon Coll Cuddesdon 97. **d** 99 **p** 00. C Wythenshawe *Man* from 99. *St Francis's Vicarage, Chalford Road, Manchester M23 8RD* Tel 0161-437 4605

HUGHES, Canon John Herbert Vivian. b 28. St D Coll Lamp BA51 LTh53. **d** 53 **p** 54. C Abergwili w Llanfihangel-uwch-Gwili *St D* 53-58; C Llanelli 58-62; V Newchurch and Merthyr 62-71; V Abergwili w Llanfihangel-uwch-Gwili etc 71-89; RD Carmarthen 82-88; Can St D Cathl 87-89; rtd 89. *104 Bronwydd Road, Carmarthen SA31 2AR* Tel (01267) 237155

HUGHES, John Malcolm. b 47. Man Univ BSc68. Coll of Resurr Mirfield 68. **d** 71 **p** 72. C Newton Nottage *Llan* 71-78; V Llanwynno 78-92; R Cadoxton-juxta-Barry from 92. *The Rectory, 21 Rectory Road, Cadoxton, Barry CF63 3QB* Tel and fax (01446) 406690 E-mail cjb@johnmhughes.free-online.co.uk

HUGHES, John Mark David. b 78. Jes Coll Cam BA00 MA04 Mert Coll Ox MSt02 Em Coll Cam PhD05. Westcott Ho Cam 01. **d** 05. C Ex St Dav *Ex* from 05. *Ty Dewi Sant, 44 Wrefords Close, Exeter EX4 5AY* Tel (01392) 498352 Mobile 07967-744035 E-mail jmdh3@cantab.net

HUGHES, Canon John Patrick. b 41. Sheff Univ Dip Leadership Renewal & Miss 98. Oak Hill Th Coll DipTh66. **d** 67 **p** 68. C Chorleywood St Andr *St Alb* 67-71; C E Twickenham St Steph *Lon* 71-76; TV High Wycombe *Ox* 77-92; Chapl Wycombe Hosp 77-83; V Harborne Heath *Birm* from 92; Hon Can Birm Cathl from 99. *St John's Vicarage, 99 Wentworth Road, Birmingham B17 9ST* Tel 0121-428 2093 *or* 427 4601 Fax 428 1934 E-mail jphughes@stjohns-church.co.uk

HUGHES, John Tudor. b 59. Nottm Univ BSc81 Univ of Wales (Cardiff) BD84. St Mich Coll Llan 81. **d** 84 **p** 85. C Mold *St As* 84-88; Asst Dioc Youth Chapl 86-90; Dioc Youth Chapl 90-97; Min Can St As Cathl 88-90; Min St As and Tremeirchion 88-90; V Holt 90-96; V Buckley 96-04; RD Mold 00-03; V Gresford from 04. *The Vicarage, Church Green, Gresford, Wrexham LL12 8RG* Tel (01978) 852236

HUGHES, John William George. b 48. MBE93. St Mich Coll Llan DipTh72. **d** 72 **p** 73. C Swansea St Pet *S & B* 72-76; V Cwmddauddwr w St Harmon's and Llanwrthwl 76-79; P-in-c Caereithin 79; V 80-86; Chapl RAF 86-02. *Address temp unknown*

HUGHES, Leonard Mordecai. b 50. St Jo Coll Nottm 95. **d** 97 **p** 98. NSM N Evington *Leic* from 97. *68 Trevino Drive, Leicester LE4 7PH* Tel 0116-266 9979

HUGHES, Lindsay. *See* HUGHES, Miss Carol Lindsay

HUGHES, Martin Conway. b 40. Ex Coll Ox BA61 MA67. Chich Th Coll. **d** 63 **p** 64. C Roehampton H Trin *S'wark* 63-67; C Addlestone *Guildf* 67-71; V Burpham 71-88; V Shamley Green 88-05; RD Cranleigh 90-95; rtd 05. *22 Siskin Close, Bishops Waltham, Southampton SO32 1RQ* Tel (01489) 890365 E-mail martin@mchughes.org.uk

HUGHES, Matthew James. b 66. K Coll Lon BD88. Westcott Ho Cam 89. **d** 91 **p** 92. C Heston *Lon* 91-94; C Fulham All SS 94-96; TV St Laur in Thanet *Cant* 96-01; R Farnborough *Roch* from 01. *The Rectory, Farnborough Hill, Orpington BR6 7EQ* Tel (01689) 856931 E-mail jmath@btinternet.com

HUGHES, Michael John Minto. b 50. Liv Univ MB, ChB74 DRCOG87 DGM88 Westmr Coll Ox MTh94. Wycliffe Hall Ox 76. **d** 79 **p** 80. C Stranton *Dur* 79-82; Chapl Intercon Ch Soc Peru 82-86; Perm to Offic *Dur* 86-87 and *Carl* 87-89; TV Thetford *Nor* 89-97; P-in-c Downham *Ely* 97-05; Hon C Ely from 05. *Georgian House, 6A Station Road, Ely CB7 4BS*

HUGHES, Nesta. *See* HUGHES, Ms Eunice Nesta

HUGHES, Neville Joseph. b 52. NUU BA79 MBIM93. CITC 97. **d** 91 **p** 92. NSM Mullabrack w Markethill and Kilcluney *Arm* 91-98; I from 00; C Portadown St Mark 98-00. *The Rectory, 6 Mullurg Road, Markethill BT60 1QN* Tel (028) 3755 1092

HUGHES, The Ven Paul Vernon. b 53. Ripon Coll Cuddesdon 79. **d** 82 **p** 83. C Chipping Barnet w Arkley *St Alb* 82-86; TV Dunstable 86-93; P-in-c Boxmoor St Jo 93-98; V 98-03; RD Hemel Hempstead 96-03; Adn Bedford from 03. *17 Landsowne Road, Luton LU3 1EE* Tel (01582) 730722 Fax 877354 E-mail archdbedf@stalbans.anglican.org

HUGHES, Mrs Penelope Patricia. b 47. Sheff Univ LLB. WMMTC 95. **d** 98 **p** 99. NSM Whitley *Cov* 98-01; NSM Leamington Spa H Trin and Old Milverton 01-03; P-in-c Berkswell from 03. *The Rectory, Meriden Road, Berkswell, Coventry CV7 7BE* Tel (01676) 533605 E-mail penhughes@aol.com

HUGHES, Peter John. b 43. Melbourne Univ BA67 Ch Ch Ox BPhil77. Trin Coll Melbourne 64 ACT 69. **d** 70 **p** 70. Australia 70-74 and 84-97; Perm to Offic *Ox* 75-77; Lic to Offic 77-79; Chapl Lon Univ *Lon* 79-84. *PO Box 626, North Sydney, NSW, Australia 2059*

HUGHES, Peter John. b 59. Wolv Poly BA83 Lon Univ PGCE85. Wycliffe Hall Ox 90. **d** 92 **p** 93. C Ecclesall *Sheff* 92-96; V Kimberworth 96-05; R Wickersley from 05. *The Rectory, 5 Church Lane, Wickersley, Rotherham S66 1ES* Tel (01709) 543111

HUGHES, Peter Knowles. b 61. Sarum & Wells Th Coll 87. **d** 90 **p** 91. C Whitchurch *Bris* 90-93; Perm to Offic *Worc* 93-97 and from 02; Chapl Univ Coll Worc 97-02. *Woodside Farmhouse, Blakes Lane, Guarlford, Malvern WR13 6NZ* Tel (01684) 311308

HUGHES, Philip. b 47. St Jo Coll Nottm 79. **d** 81 **p** 82. C Dolgellau w Llanfachreth and Brithdir etc *Ban* 81-83; Asst Youth Chapl 82-83; R Llaneugrad w Llanallgo and Penrhosllugwy etc 83-95; R Llanberis w Llanrug 95-03; Dioc Youth Chapl 93-98; RD Arfon 00-02; R Llanfair-pwll and Llanddaniel-fab etc from 03. *The Rectory, Ffordd Caergybi, Llanfairpwllgwyngyll LL61 5SX* Tel and fax (01248) 713746 E-mail revphilip@aol.com

HUGHES, Philip Stephen. b 34. Dur Univ BA59. Coll of Resurr Mirfield 59. **d** 62 **p** 63. C Horfield St Greg *Bris* 62-66; C Bedminster St Mich 66-69; P-in-c Chippenham St Pet 69-71; V 71-83; TR Bedminster 83-91; V Ashton Keynes, Leigh and Minety 91-00; rtd 00; Perm to Offic *Worc* from 00. *19 Fairways, Pershore WR10 1HA* Tel (01386) 552375

HUGHES, Richard Clifford. b 24. Pemb Coll Cam BA57 MA59. Ely Th Coll 48. **d** 50 **p** 51. C Wandsworth St Anne *S'wark* 50-53; S Rhodesia 53-65; S Africa 65-86; Adn Pinetown 75-80; Australia from 86; rtd 89. *1/184 Springfield Road, Blackburn North, Vic, Australia 3130* Tel (0061) (3) 9894 4889 E-mail cherryh@smart.net.au

HUGHES, Richard Jeffrey. b 47. Trin Coll Carmarthen CertEd68. St Mich Coll Llan 74. **d** 76 **p** 77. C Llanbeblig w Caernarfon and Betws Garmon etc *Ban* 76-78; Dioc Youth Chapl 78-82; TV Holyhead w Rhoscolyn w Llanfair-yn-Neubwll 78-83; R Llanfachraeth 83-92; R Llangefni w Tregaean and

Llangristiolus etc 92-95; R Llanbeblig w Caernarfon and Betws Garmon etc from 95. *Hafoty, 30 Bryn Rhos, Rhosbodrual, Caernarfon LL55 2BT* Tel (01286) 674181

HUGHES, Richard Millree. b 33. Univ of Wales BA56 MA79. St Mich Coll Llan 56. **d** 58 **p** 59. C Mold *St As* 58-61; V Choral St As Cathl 61-64; V Towyn 64-67; Asst Master Marlborough Sch Woodstock 77-79; R Whitchurch St Mary *Ox* 79-00; rtd 00. *Cae Canol Mawr, Cwm Teigl, Blaenau Ffestiniog LL41 4RF,* or *Le Village, St Antoine, 32340 Miradoux, France* Tel 07798-790369 (mobile) E-mail rmillree@aol.com

HUGHES, Robert Elistan-Glodrydd. b 32. Trin Coll Ox BA54 MA58 Birm Univ MLitt85. Westcott Ho Cam 55. **d** 57 **p** 58. C Stoke *Cov* 57-61; Ind Chapl *S'wark* 61-64; Birm Univ *Birm* 64-87; Chapl 64-69; Lodgings Warden and Student Welfare Adv 69-87; Dir Housing Study Overseas Students Trust 88-91; Perm to Offic *Ban* 88-94; V Harlech and Llanfair-juxta-Harlech etc 94-99; rtd 97. *Clogwyn Melyn, Talsarnau LL47 6TP* Tel (01766) 780257 E-mail shebob.clog@virgin.net

HUGHES, Robert Guy. b 64. York Univ BSc86 Reading Univ PhD89 Ox Univ BA92 MA96. Ripon Coll Cuddesdon 90. **d** 93 **p** 94. C Sandhurst *Ox* 93-95; Asst Chapl K Sch Ely 95-96; Chapl 96-99; Min Can Ely Cathl *Ely* 96-99. *Address temp unknown*

HUGHES, Robert Leslie. b 52. Qu Coll Birm 98. **d** 00 **p** 01. C The Quinton *Birm* from 00. *111 Glyn Farm Road, Quinton, Birmingham B32 1NJ* Tel 0121-422 3596 E-mail roberthughes@fish.co.uk

HUGHES, Rodney Thomas. b 39. Dur Univ BA60 St Cath Coll Ox DipTh61. Wycliffe Hall Ox 60. **d** 62 **p** 63. C Edin St Thos *Edin* 62-65; C Harlow New Town w Lt Parndon *Chelmsf* 65-67; R Haworth *Bradf* 67-74; R W Knighton w Broadmayne *Sarum* 74-77; R Broadmayne, W Knighton, Owermoigne etc 77-82; V Crosthwaite Keswick *Carl* 82-02; rtd 02; Perm to Offic *Carl* from 02. *2 Bewcastle Close, Carlisle CA3 0PU* Tel (01228) 401680

HUGHES, Roger. *See* HUGHES, William Roger

HUGHES, Ronald. *See* HUGHES, Arthur William Ronald

HUGHES, Mrs Sally Lorraine. b 59. Open Univ BA98. EAMTC 99. **d** 02 **p** 03. NSM Gretton w Rockingham and Cottingham w E Carlton *Pet* 02-05; Asst Chapl Kettering Gen Hosp NHS Trust 02-04; P-in-c Stoke Albany w Wilbarston and Ashley etc *Pet* from 05. *28 Rushton Road, Wilbarston, Market Harborough LE16 8QL* Tel (01536) 770998 Mobile 07740-171139 E-mail sally@hughes.uk.com

HUGHES, Mrs Sheila. b 52. Chester Coll of HE DipApTh96. N Ord Course 92. **d** 95 **p** 96. NSM Birkenhead Priory *Ches* 95-97; C 97-99; P-in-c Northwich St Luke and H Trin 99-01; V from 01; Bp's Adv for Women in Min from 00; Chapl Mid Cheshire Hosps Trust from 99. *St Luke's Vicarage, Dyar Terrace, Northwich CW8 4DN* Tel (01606) 74632 E-mail sheila@hughes1051.freeserve.co.uk

HUGHES, Steven Philip. b 52. MBE01. St Jo Coll Dur BA80. Ridley Hall Cam 80. **d** 82 **p** 83. C Chilvers Coton w Astley *Cov* 82-86; TV Kings Norton *Birm* 86-91; Perm to Offic *Eur* 92-96; Asst Chapl Bucharest 96-98; P-in-c Bucharest w Sofia 98-01; P-in-c Belgrade 98-00; P-in-c Hoole *Blackb* from 02. *The Rectory, 69 Liverpool Old Road, Much Hoole, Preston PR4 4GA* Tel (01772) 612267 E-mail stevenhughes@tiscali.co.uk

HUGHES, Trystan Owain. b 72. Univ of Wales (Ban) BD94 PhD98. Wycliffe Hall Ox MTh. **d** 05. C Llantwit Major *Llan* from 05. *8 Illtyd Avenue, Llantwit Major CF61 1TG* Tel (01446) 792476 E-mail trystan_hughes@hotmail.com

HUGHES, Ms Valerie Elizabeth. b 53. Birm Univ BA75 CertEd76. Wycliffe Hall Ox DipTh86. **d** 87 **p** 94. C Hallwood *Ches* 87-90; Par Dn Garston *Liv* 90-93; Asst Chapl Liv Univ 93; TD Gateacre 93-94; TV 94-00; C St Helens St Helen from 00. *75 King Edward Road, St Helens WA10 6LE*

HUGHES, William. *See* HUGHES, Albert William

HUGHES, William Piers Maximillian. b 76. Ex Univ BA99. Ripon Coll Cuddesdon 99. **d** 01 **p** 02. C Cley Hill Warminster *Sarum* from 01. *39 Manor Gardens, Warminster BA12 8PN* Tel (01985) 214953 E-mail will-hattie@lineone.net

HUGHES, William Roger. b 47. ACCA MCIPD MBIM. Trin Coll Carmarthen. **d** 91 **p** 92. NSM Llan-non *St D* 91-93; Dio Officer for Soc Resp from 93; V Llangathen w Llanfihangel Cilfargen etc from 93. *The Vicarage, Llangathen, Carmarthen SA32 8QD* Tel (01558) 668455

HUGHMAN, June Alison. b 58. Kingston Poly BSc81 Southn Univ PhD84. Trin Coll Bris DipHE88. **d** 89 **p** 94. Par Dn Penge St Jo *Roch* 89-93; C Woking Ch Ch *Guildf* 93-98; V Croydon Ch Ch *S'wark* 98-00; C Uxbridge *Lon* from 00; Town Cen Min from 00. *84 Harefield Road, Uxbridge UB8 1PN* Tel and fax (01895) 254121 *or* tel 258766 E-mail junehughman@tiscali.co.uk

HUGO, Canon Keith Alan. b 41. Nottm Univ BA62. Chich Th Coll 62. **d** 64 **p** 65. C Pontefract St Giles *Wakef* 64-68; C Chesterfield St Mary and All SS *Derby* 68-71; V Allenton and Shelton Lock 71-77; Dioc Communications Officer *Sarum* 77-89; V Worton 77-84; V Potterne 77-84; Can and Preb Sarum Cathl from 84; V Potterne w Worton and Marston 84-89; R Wyke Regis from 89; RD Weymouth 94-04. *The Rectory, 1 Portland Road, Weymouth DT4 9ES* Tel and fax (01305) 784649 E-mail keith.hugo@talk21.com

HUISH, Barnaby Thomas. b 71. St Chad's Coll Dur BA94 MA95. Cuddesdon Coll BA98. **d** 99 **p** 00. C Darlington H Trin *Dur* 99-02; Prec and Min Can St Alb Abbey *St Alb* from 02. *Flat 1, The Deanery, Sumpter Yard, St Albans AL1 1BY* Tel (01727) 890207

HUITSON, Christopher Philip. b 45. Keble Coll Ox BA66 MA70. Cuddesdon Coll 67. **d** 69 **p** 70. C Croydon St Sav *Cant* 69-71; Soc Service Unit St Martin-in-the-Fields Lon 71-73; C St Alb St Pet *St Alb* 73-77; V Cople 77-78; P-in-c Willington 77-78; V Cople w Willington 78-89; V Leavesden All SS 89-96; V Totteridge from 96; RD Barnet 99-05. *The Vicarage, 44 Totteridge Village, London N20 8PR* Tel (020) 8445 6787 Fax 8445 8757 E-mail c.huitson@btinternet.com

HULBERT, Hugh Forfar. b 22. Bris Univ BA49. Bible Churchmen's Coll Bris 46. **d** 50 **p** 51. C Summerstown *S'wark* 50-53; C Felixstowe SS Pet and Paul *St E* 53-55; Min Collier Row St Jas CD *Chelmsf* 55-59; SW Area Sec CPAS 59-63; V Portsea St Luke *Portsm* 63-75; V Worthing H Trin *Chich* 75-81; C-in-c Hove H Trin CD 81-85; C Hailsham 86-87; rtd 87; Perm to Offic *Chich* from 87. *8 Ramsay Hall, 11-13 Byron Road, Worthing BN11 3HN* Tel (01903) 209594

HULBERT, John Anthony Lovett. b 40. Trin Coll Cam BA63 MA67. Wells Th Coll 64. **d** 66 **p** 67. C Fareham H Trin *Portsm* 66-70; R Wickham 70-79; RD Bishop's Waltham 74-79; V Bedford St Andr *St Alb* 79-92; RD Bedford 87-92; V Leighton Buzzard w Eggington, Hockliffe etc 92-03; Hon Can St Alb 91-03; C Stansted *Chich* 03-04; P-in-c Lynch w Iping Marsh and Milland from 04. *Lynch Rectory, Fernhurst Road, Milland, Liphook GU30 7LU* Tel (01428) 741285 E-mail anthony@nhulbert.freeserve.co.uk

HULBERT, Canon Martin Francis Harrington. b 37. Dur Univ BSc58 MA62. Ripon Hall Ox 58. **d** 60 **p** 61. C Buxton *Derby* 60-63; C Eglingham *Newc* 63-67; C-in-c Loundsley Green Ascension CD *Derby* 67-71; P-in-c Frecheville 71-73; R Frecheville and Hackenthorpe *Sheff* 73-77; P-in-c Hathersage *Derby* 77-83; V 83-90; RD Bakewell and Eyam 81-90; R Brailsford w Shirley and Osmaston w Edlaston 90-93; V Tideswell 93-02; RD Buxton 96-99; Hon Can Derby Cathl 89-02; rtd 02; Perm to Offic *Derby* from 02. *16 Lismore Road, Buxton SK17 9AZ* Tel (01298) 79566 E-mail martin.hulbert1@btinternet.com

HULETT, Mrs Janet Elizabeth Mary. b 48. **d** 91 **p** 96. NSM Broadwater St Mary *Chich* 91-95; NSM Thame *Ox* from 96. *24 Clarendon Drive, Thame OX9 3XP* Tel (01844) 216457 E-mail janethulett@onet.co.uk

HULETT, Peter. b 31. CEng MIMechE62 Leeds Univ CertEd74. Wycliffe Hall Ox 75. **d** 77 **p** 78. C Eastwood *S'well* 77-80; C Granby w Elton 80-83; V Gilling and Kirkby Ravensworth *Ripon* 83-90; P-in-c Bishop Monkton and Burton Leonard 90-96; rtd 96; Perm to Offic *Bradf* from 96. *2 Cardan Drive, Ilkley LS29 8PH* Tel (01943) 604202

HULL, Mrs Bernadette Mary. b 46. E Lon Univ BA92 PGCE93. NTMTC 99. **d** 02 **p** 03. NSM Becontree S *Chelmsf* from 02. *46 Hall Road, Chadwell Heath, Romford RM6 4LJ* Tel (020) 8252 3540 *or* 8491 8765 Mobile 07990-730293 E-mail bmhull@ntlworld.com

HULL, David John. b 44. Linc Th Coll 88. **d** 90 **p** 91. C Mansfield Woodhouse *S'well* 90-93; P-in-c Mansfield St Lawr 93-00; V Mosbrough *Sheff* 00-03; V Elmton *Derby* from 03. *The Vicarage, 1 Elmton Road, Creswell, Worksop S80 4HD* Tel (01909) 721264

HULL, John Hammond. b 36. Brasted Th Coll 58 Sarum Th Coll 60. **d** 61 **p** 62. C Gt Clacton *Chelmsf* 61-66; Area Chapl (E Anglia) Toc H 66-70; (Midl Region) 70-75; Lic to Offic *Chelmsf* 66-75; Chapl Toc H HQ 75-82; Lic to Offic *Ox* from 75. *66 Grenville Avenue, Wendover, Aylesbury HP22 6AL* Tel (01296) 624487

HULL, Thomas Henry. b 55. QUB BD79. NTMTC 94. **d** 97 **p** 98. C Kidbrooke *S'wark* 97-99; TV 99-01; I Lecale Gp *D & D* from 01; Min Can Down Cathl from 03. *Lecale Rectory, 9 Quoile Road, Downpatrick BT30 6SE* Tel (028) 4461 3101 *or* 4461 4922 Fax 4461 4456 E-mail henryhull@downcathedral.org

HULL, Timothy David. b 60. Lon Bible Coll 87 K Coll Lon PhD97. St Jo Coll Nottm BTh90. **d** 90 **p** 91. C Leyton St Mary w St Edw *Chelmsf* 90-95; Chapl Havering Coll of F&HE 94-98; C Harold Hill St Geo *Chelmsf* 95-98; TV Becontree W from 98; Co-ord NTMTC 98-01; Registrar from 01. *St Peter's Vicarage, 29 Warrington Road, Dagenham RM3 3JH* Tel (020) 8597 7779 E-mail timhull@tiscali.co.uk

HULL, Suffragan Bishop of. *See* FRITH, The Rt Revd Richard Michael Cokayne

✠**HULLAH, The Rt Revd Peter Fearnley.** b 49. K Coll Lon BD71 AKC71 FRSA93. Cuddesdon Coll 73. **d** 74 **p** 75 **c** 99. Asst Chapl St Edw Sch Ox 74-77; C Summertown *Ox* 74-76; C Wolvercote w Summertown 76-77; Chapl Sevenoaks Sch 77-82; Hon C Sevenoaks St Nic *Roch* 77-82; Ho Master Internat Cen Sevenoaks Sch 82-87; Hon C Kippington 82-87; Sen Chapl K Sch and Hon Min Can Cant Cathl *Cant* 87-92; Hd Master Chetham's Sch of Music 92-99; Hon Can Man Cathl *Man* 96-99; Area Bp Ramsbury *Sarum* 99-05; Prin Northn Academy from

05; Hon Asst Bp Pet from 05. *The Northampton Academy, Billing Brook Road, Northampton NN3 8NH* Tel (01604) 402811 Fax 414265 E-mail bishop.peter@northampton-academy.org

HULLETT, Frederick Graham. St Jo Coll York CertEd53 Leeds Univ BA58. Coll of Resurr Mirfield 58. **d** 60 **p** 61. C Acton Green St Pet *Lon* 60-61; C W Hackney St Barn 61-64; C Paddington St Mary 64-67; Hon C 67-69; P-in-c Haggerston St Aug w St Steph 69-73; Lic to Offic 73-84; Perm to Offic *Linc* from 84; rtd 91. *2 Ryland Road, Welton, Lincoln LN2 3LU* Tel (01673) 860839

HULLYER, Paul Charles. b 68. Anglia Poly Univ MA98 Lambeth MA04 FRSA04. Aston Tr Scheme 92 Westcott Ho Cam 94. **d** 97 **p** 98. C Stoke Newington St Mary *Lon* 97-00; C Addlestone *Guildf* 00-03; V Hillingdon All SS *Lon* from 03. *All Saints' Vicarage, Ryefield Avenue, Uxbridge UB10 9BT* Tel (01895) 234947 E-mail hullyer@fish.co.uk

HULME, Alan John. b 60. Birm Univ BSc81. Wycliffe Hall Ox BA90. **d** 91 **p** 92. C Chilwell *S'well* 91-96; TV Roxeth *Lon* 96-02; V S Harrow St Paul from 02. *St Paul's Vicarage, Findon Close, Corbins Lane, Harrow HA2 8NJ* Tel and fax (020) 8864 0362 *or* tel 8422 2991 E-mail alanjhulme@aol.com

HULME (née ASHLEY), Mrs Jane Isobel. b 59. Birm Univ BSc81. **d** 05. NSM S Harrow St Paul *Lon* from 05. *St Paul's Vicarage, Findon Close, Corbins Lane, Harrow HA2 8NJ* Tel and fax (020) 8864 0362 *or* tel 8422 2991 E-mail janehulme@aol.com

HULME, Ms Juliette Mary. b 57. Whitelands Coll Lon BEd81. Cranmer Hall Dur 94. **d** 94 **p** 95. C Crayford *Roch* 94-98; C Leatherhead *Guildf* 98-01; CF from 02. *c/o MOD Chaplains (Army)* Tel (01980) 615804 Fax 615800 E-mail juliette.hulme@hotmail.com

HULME, Norman. b 31. Kelham Th Coll 50. **d** 54 **p** 55. C Blackb St Pet *Blackb* 54-57; C Blakenall Heath *Lich* 57-59; V Gannow *Blackb* 59-64; V Anwick *Linc* 64-74; V S Kyme 64-74; V Moulton 74-83; V Earl Shilton w Elmesthorpe *Leic* 83-88; Chapl Harperbury Hosp Radlett 88-96; rtd 96. *Moorcroft, 9 Birch Grove, Spalding PE11 2HL* Tel (01775) 710127 E-mail norjoan@yahoo.co.uk

HULME, Suffragan Bishop of. *See* LOWE, The Rt Revd Stephen Richard

HULSE, William John. b 42. Dur Univ BA65. Linc Th Coll 65. **d** 67 **p** 68. C S Westoe *Dur* 67-70; Lic to Offic *Newc* 70-72; C Far Headingley St Chad *Ripon* 72-76; R Swillington 76-88; V Shadwell 88-95; V Oulton w Woodlesford 95-02; P-in-c Spennithorne w Finghall and Hauxwell from 02; Chapl Mothers' Union from 03. *The Rectory, Spennithorne, Leyburn DL8 5PR* Tel (01969) 623010

HULT, Mrs Anna Eva Hildegard. b 73. Lund Univ Sweden MTh. Lund Inst Past Th 97. **p** 98. C Norrahammar Sweden 98-99; Asst V Ignaberga 99-00; Asst V Genard 00-03; Perm to Offic *Ely* 02-03; P-in-c Witchford w Wentworth from 03. *The Vicarage, 75 Main Street, Witchford, Ely CB6 2HQ* Tel (01353) 669420 Mobile 07986-923646 E-mail annahult@onetel.com

HUME, Miss Clephane Arrol. b 46. Open Univ BA87 Edin Univ MTh98 DipOT68. Edin Dioc NSM Course 88. **d** 92 **p** 94. NSM Edin St Jo *Edin* from 92. *30 Findhorn Place, Edinburgh EH9 2JP* Tel 0131-667 2996 Fax 668 3568 E-mail clephaneh@aol.com

HUME, Ernest. b 45. Linc Th Coll 77. **d** 79 **p** 80. C Ilkeston St Mary *Derby* 79-81; C Sheff Manor *Sheff* 81-82; TV 82-88; V Norton Woodseats St Chad 88-99; V Woodhouse St Jas 99-02; rtd 02. *Shadwell, 6 Canal Bridge, Killamarsh, Sheffield S21 1DJ* Tel 0114-248 1769 E-mail ehume@vicarage51.freeserve.co.uk

HUME, Martin. b 54. Coll of Resurr Mirfield 89. **d** 91 **p** 92. C Brentwood St Thos *Chelmsf* 91-94; P-in-c Corringham 94-04; V E Wickham *S'wark* from 04. *St Michael's Vicarage, Upper Wickham Lane, Welling DA16 3AP* Tel (020) 8304 1214 E-mail martinhume@aol.com

HUMMERSTONE, Jeremy David. Mert Coll Ox BA65 MA70. Wells Th Coll 70. **d** 72 **p** 73. C Helmsley *York* 72-75; C Pockley cum E Moors 72-75; P-in-c Manningford Bruce w Manningford Abbots *Sarum* 75; TV Swanborough 75-80; P-in-c Frithelstock *Ex* 80-81; P-in-c Gt Torrington 80-81; P-in-c Lt Torrington 80-81; V Gt and Lt Torrington and Frithelstock from 81. *The Vicarage, Calf Street, Torrington EX38 8EA* Tel (01805) 622166 E-mail hummerstone@bigfoot.com

HUMPHREY, Mrs Betty. b 37. St Mich Ho Ox 59. **d** 90 **p** 94. C Hardwicke, Quedgeley and Elmore w Longney *Glouc* 90-93; Dn-in-c Swindon w Uckington and Elmstone Hardwicke 93-94; P-in-c 94-96; R 96-98; rtd 98; Perm to Offic *Glouc* from 00. *11 Lower Orchard, Tibberton, Gloucester GL19 3AX* Tel (01452) 790790

HUMPHREY, David Lane. b 57. Maine Univ BA79. St Jo Coll Nottm 84. **d** 88 **p** 89. C Springfield All SS *Chelmsf* 88-91; C Thundersley 91-96; V Standon *St Alb* 96-04; RD Bishop's Stortford 01-04; R Portland St Matt USA from 04. *11229 NE Prescott Street, Portland, OR 97220, USA* Tel (001) (503) 252 5720 E-mail humphrey@iinet.com

HUMPHREY, Derek Hollis. b 37. Chich Th Coll 69. **d** 72 **p** 73. C Havant *Portsm* 72-75; C Southsea H Spirit 75-78; V Finsbury Park St Thos *Lon* 78-88; V S Patcham *Chich* 88-03; rtd 03; C Clayton w Keymer *Chich* from 03. *The Rectory, 1 The Crescent, Hassocks BN6 8RB* Tel (01273) 843570

HUMPHREY, Canon George William. b 38. Lon Bible Coll BD61 Lon Univ CertEd74 Man Univ Dip Educn Guidance 75. Oak Hill Th Coll 61. **d** 62 **p** 63. C Heigham H Trin *Nor* 62-64; P-in-c Buckenham w Hassingham and Strumpshaw 64-67; Chapl St Andr Hosp Norwich 64-67; Asst Master Mexborough Gr Sch 67-69; Hd RE Cheadle Gr Sch 69-76; Hon C Cheadle Hulme St Andr *Ches* 70-76; P-in-c Kellington w Whitley *Wakef* 76-80; Teacher Thurnscoe Comp Sch 76-80; RE Insp Glos Co Coun and Dio *Glouc* 80-93; Dioc RE Adv 93-99; Hon Can Glouc Cathl 95-99; rtd 00; Perm to Offic *Glouc* from 00. *11 Lower Orchard, Tibberton, Gloucester GL19 3AX* Tel (01452) 790790

HUMPHREY, Heather Mary. b 46. CertEd68. WMMTC 87. **d** 90 **p** 94. NSM Overbury w Teddington, Alstone etc *Worc* 90-96; NSM Berrow w Pendock, Eldersfield, Hollybush etc 96-98; C Coseley Ch Ch 98-00; V from 00. *The Vicarage, Church Road, Coseley, Bilston WV14 8YB* Tel (01902) 353551

HUMPHREY, Timothy Martin. b 62. Ex Univ BA83. St Jo Coll Nottm DipTh87. **d** 89 **p** 90. C Wallington H Trin *S'wark* 89-92; P-in-c 92-97; C Oakley w Wootton St Lawrence *Win* 97-02; Faith Development Field Officer 97-02; V Kensington St Barn *Lon* from 02. *St Barnabas's Vicarage, 23 Addison Road, London W14 8LH* Tel (020) 7471 7019 *or* 7471 7000 Fax 7471 7001 E-mail tim@stbk.org.uk

HUMPHREYS, Mrs Anne-Marie (Anna). b 44. SRN67 K Coll Lon BD92 AKC92 Man Univ MA96 Cert Counselling 99. N Ord Course 92. **d** 95 **p** 96. NSM Manchester Gd Shep and St Barn *Man* 95-98; NSM Burnage St Nic 98-03; Chapl Cen Man Healthcare NHS Trust 96-01; Chapl Cen Man/Man Children's Univ Hosp NHS Trust from 01. *413 Asia House, 82 Princess Streeet, Manchester M1 6BE* Tel 0161-228 6165 *or* 276 1234

HUMPHREYS, Brian Leonard. b 29. MChS51 SRCh. Bp Attwell Tr Inst. **d** 87 **p** 88. NSM Maughold *S & M* 87-91; NSM S Ramsey St Paul 91-92; NSM Andreas 92-94; Perm to Offic from 94. *Thie Cassan Yack, Jack's Lane, Port E Vullen, Ramsey, Isle of Man IM7 1AW* Tel (01624) 813694

HUMPHREYS, Daniel Robert. b 74. K Coll Lon BA95 AKC95 Leeds Univ BA99. Coll of Resurr Mirfield 97. **d** 00 **p** 01. C Scarborough St Martin *York* 00-02; C Kilburn St Aug w St Jo *Lon* from 02. *122 Dibdin House, Maida Vale, London W9 1QG* Tel (020) 7328 9301 E-mail drhumphreys@lineone.net

HUMPHREYS, George Bernard. b 10. AKC36. **d** 36 **p** 37. C Leigh St Mary *Man* 36-38; C Streatham St Pet *S'wark* 38-41; C Tarporley *Ches* 42-48; R Moreton Corbet *Lich* 48-53; V Dawley Parva 53-65; R Fobbing *Chelmsf* 65-78; rtd 78; Perm to Offic *Ex* from 78. *Prestercot, Butts Lane, Christow, Exeter EX6 7NN* Tel (01647) 252595

HUMPHREYS, James Graham. b 36. Liv Univ BEng57 PhD60. Trin Coll Bris 61. **d** 63 **p** 64. C Denton Holme *Carl* 63-66; C St Helens St Mark *Liv* 66-68; V Houghton *Carl* 68-79; V Bramcote *S'well* 79-93; RD Beeston 85-90; rtd 93; Perm to Offic *S'well* 93-01; Perm to Offic *Carl* from 01. *383 London Road, Carlisle CA1 3HA* Tel (01228) 597108

HUMPHREYS, Canon John Elwyn Price. b 15. OBE77 Portuguese Order of Merit 94. Univ of Wales BA37. St Mich Coll Llan 38. **d** 39 **p** 41. C Newtown *St As* 39-42; C Rhosymedre 42-43; Chapl RNVR 43-46; Chapl RN 46-51; Chapl Santa Cruz *Eur* 51-52; Chapl and Asst Master Reed's Sch Cobham 53-57; Lic to Offic *Guildf* 53-57; Chapl Estoril *Eur* 57-80; Can Gib Cathl 67-80; rtd 80. *Casa Contente, Av Sra do Monte da Saúde 341, 2765-452 Estoril, Portugal* Tel (00351) (21) 468 3238

HUMPHREYS, John Louis. b 51. Jes Coll Cam BA72 MA76 Nottm Univ BA75. St Jo Coll Nottm 73. **d** 76 **p** 77. C W Bromwich Gd Shep w St Jo *Lich* 76-79; C Woodford Wells *Chelmsf* 79-83; V Werrington *Lich* from 83; Chapl HM YOI Werrington Ho 83-98. *The Vicarage, 360 Ash Bank Road, Werrington, Stoke-on-Trent ST9 0JS* Tel (01782) 302441 Fax as telephone E-mail jlhumphreys@lineone.net

HUMPHREYS, Canon Kenneth Glyn. b 28. Bps' Coll Cheshunt 64. **d** 66 **p** 67. C New Windsor St Jo *Ox* 66-67; C Whitley Ch Ch 67-70; V Compton 70-74; V Compton w E Ilsley 74-75; R E Ilsley 74; C Wokingham All SS 75-77; Chapl Lucas Hosp Wokingham (Almshouses) 77-81; V California *Ox* 81-94; RD Sonning 86-88; Hon Can Ch Ch 91-94; rtd 95; Perm to Offic *Ox* from 96. *17 Snowberry Close, Wokingham RG41 4AQ* Tel 0118-977 2096

HUMPHREYS, Mrs Lydia Ann. b 60. CCSk90. Sarum & Wells Th Coll DCM93. **d** 93 **p** 94. C Gaywood *Nor* 93-95 and 95-97; TV Cov E *Cov* from 97. *St Margaret's Vicarage, 18 South Avenue, Coventry CV2 4DR* Tel (024) 7645 7344 Fax as telephone E-mail lydia@humphreys.clara.co.uk

HUMPHREYS, Canon Philip Noel. b 34. Bps' Coll Cheshunt 62. **d** 64 **p** 65. C Plymouth St Andr *Ex* 64-68; Chapl Lee Abbey 68-73; V Porchester *S'well* 73-82; RD W Bingham 82-87; P-in-c W Leake w Kingston-on-Soar and Ratcliffe-on-Soar 82-87; R W

Bridgford 82-00; Hon Can S'well Minster 93-00; rtd 00; Perm to Offic *S'well* from 01. *48 Windsor Avenue, Newark, Nottingham NG24 4JA* Tel (01636) 705317

HUMPHREYS, Canon Roger John. b 45. CertEd66 Open Univ BA76. Wycliffe Hall Ox 81. **d** 83 **p** 84. Chapl Dragon Sch Ox 83-87; C Ox St Andr *Ox* 83-87; V Carterton 87-94; R Bladon w Woodstock 94-05; TR Blenheim from 05; AD Woodstock from 01; Hon Can Ch Ch from 05. *The Rectory, Rectory Lane, Woodstock OX20 1UQ* Tel and fax (01993) 811415 E-mail rectorrog@aol.com

HUMPHREYS, Stephen Robert Beresford. b 52. K Coll Lon BA98. K Coll Lon 74. **d** 76 **p** 77. C Northwood Hills St Edm *Lon* 76-79; C Manningham St Mary and Bradf St Mich *Bradf* 79-81; Chapl Bradf R Infirmary 82-86; C Leeds St Pet *Ripon* 87-90; Perm to Offic *B & W* 94-99; Hon C Selworthy, Timberscombe, Wootton Courtenay etc from 02. *Stowey Farm, Timberscombe, Minehead TA24 7BW* Tel 07973-409536 (mobile) Fax 07967-494334

HUMPHREYS, William Alfred. b 18. Lich Th Coll 54. **d** 56 **p** 57. C Stone St Mich *Lich* 56-60; V Fazeley 60-65; V Prees 65-83; P-in-c Fauls 66-70; V 70-83; RD Wem and Whitchurch 80-83; rtd 83; Perm to Offic *Heref* 83-97. *Bryncroft, 4 Seabridge Meadow, Bucknell SY7 0AP* Tel (01547) 530597

HUMPHRIES, Anthony Roy. b 49. Lon Univ BSc73. Wycliffe Hall Ox. **d** 94 **p** 95. C Worksop St Jo *S'well* 94-96; C Retford St Sav 96-98; TV Grantham *Linc* 98-00; TV Bestwood *S'well* 00-03; V Branston w Tatenhill *Lich* from 03. *The Vicarage, Church Road, Branston, Burton-on-Trent DE14 3ER* Tel (01283) 568926 E-mail revtonyhumphries@hotmail.com

HUMPHRIES, Benjamin Paul. b 56. Man Univ BA77 FRGS85. Qu Coll Birm 82. **d** 85 **p** 86. C Hall Green Ascension *Birm* 85-88; P-in-c Belmont *Man* 88-96; Fieldworker USPG *Blackb*, *Bradf*, *Carl* and *Wakef* 96-98; Perm to Offic *Carl* 96-99; Area Co-ord Lic to Offic *Blackb* from 97; Chr Aid (Cumbria, Lancs and Isle of Man) from 98; Perm to Offic *Carl* from 02. *4 Tinniswood, Ashton-on-Ribble, Preston PR2 1EL* Tel (01772) 768694 *or* tel and fax 726770 E-mail bhumphries@christian-aid.org

HUMPHRIES, Betty. *See* HUMPHRIES, Miss Marion Betty

HUMPHRIES, Catherine Elizabeth. *See* NICHOLLS, Mrs Catherine Elizabeth

HUMPHRIES, Canon Christopher William. b 52. St Jo Coll Cam BA73 MA77 Lon Inst of Educn CertEd74. St Jo Coll Nottm 77. **d** 79 **p** 80. C Eccleshill *Bradf* 79-82; Chapl Scargill Ho 82-86; TV Guiseley w Esholt *Bradf* 86-91; V Filey *York* 91-05; RD Scarborough 98-04; Can Res Ches Cathl *Ches* from 05. *9 Abbey Street, Chester CH1 2JF* E-mail canon.humphries@chestercathedral.com

HUMPHRIES, David. *See* HUMPHRIES, William David

HUMPHRIES, David Graham. b 48. Univ of Wales (Cardiff) DipTh70. St Mich Coll Llan 67. **d** 71 **p** 72. C Neath w Llantwit *Llan* 71-72; C Bishop's Cleeve *Glouc* 81-83; C Cirencester 83-87; V Glouc St Steph 87-96; P-in-c Mickleton 96-03; Assoc P Up Hatherley from 03. *28 Davallia Drive, Up Hatherley, Cheltenham GL51 5XG* Tel (01242) 861261

HUMPHRIES, David John. b 51. BSc CertEd BD. Edin Th Coll. **d** 84 **p** 85. C Styvechale *Cov* 84-88; V Greetland and W Vale *Wakef* 88-96; V Shawbury *Lich* from 96; V Stanton on Hine Heath from 96; R Moreton Corbet from 96. *The Vicarage, Church Road, Shawbury, Shrewsbury SY4 4NH* Tel (01939) 250419

HUMPHRIES, Donald. b 43. Bris Univ BA66. Clifton Th Coll 66. **d** 68 **p** 69. C Selly Hill St Steph *Birm* 68-74; Chapl Warw Univ *Cov* 74-79; V Bedford Ch Ch *St Alb* 79-85; V Cambridge H Trin w St Andr Gt *Ely* 85-92; V Cambridge H Trin 92-94; rtd 94; Perm to Offic *Ely* from 94. *56 The Rowans, Milton, Cambridge CB4 6YU* Tel (01223) 562100

HUMPHRIES, Miss Dorothy Maud. b 22. Bedf Coll Lon BA44 Lon Univ DipEd45 Cam Univ DipTh50. Gilmore Course 85. **dss** 79 **d** 87 **p** 94. Kidderminster Deanery *Worc* 79-97; NSM 87-97; Perm to Offic from 98. *16 George Law Court, Anchorfields, Kidderminster DY10 1PZ* Tel (01562) 824459

HUMPHRIES, Frank Charles. b 40. St Chad's Coll Dur BA61 DipTh63. **d** 63 **p** 64. C Tottenham All Hallows *Lon* 63-66; C S Harrow St Paul 66-71; V Hillingdon All SS 71-80; V Preston Ascension 80-97; Dir of Ords 86-97; rtd 97; Perm to Offic *Lon* from 97. *1 Chantry Place, Headstone Lane, Harrow HA3 6NY* Tel (020) 8428 9944

HUMPHRIES, Grahame Leslie. b 44. Lon Coll of Div ALCD70 LTh. **d** 71 **p** 72. C Wandsworth St Mich *S'wark* 71-74; C Slough *Ox* 74-77; P-in-c Arley *Cov* 77-82; R 82-84; Norfolk Churches' Radio Officer *Nor* 84-96; P-in-c Bawdeswell w Foxley 84-96; P-in-c Mayfield *Lich* 96-02; Local Min Adv (Stafford) 96-02; RD Uttoxeter 98-02; P-in-c Blockley w Aston Magna and Bourton on the Hill *Glouc* from 02; Local Min Officer from 02. *The Vicarage, The Square, Blockley, Moreton-in-Marsh GL56 9ES* Tel (01386) 700283

HUMPHRIES, Mrs Janet Susan. b 56. St Alb and Ox Min Course 02. **d** 04. NSM Potton w Sutton and Cockayne Hatley *St Alb* from 04. *7 Shakespeare Drive, Upper Caldecote, Biggleswade SG18 9DD* Tel (01767) 220365 E-mail janet.humphries1@ntlworld.com

HUMPHRIES, John. b 49. Univ of Wales (Cardiff) DipTh76. St Mich Coll Llan 73. **d** 76 **p** 77. C Pontnewynydd *Mon* 76-78; C Ebbw Vale 78-81; V Pet Ch Carpenter *Pet* 81-86; P-in-c King's Cliffe 86-87; R King's Cliffe w Apethorpe 87-93; R King's Cliffe 93-97; V Finedon from 97; Chapl Northants Fire and Rescue Service from 03. *The Vicarage, Finedon, Wellingborough NN9 5NR* Tel (01933) 680285 Mobile 07976-370434 E-mail frjohn13@aol.com

HUMPHRIES, Miss Marion Betty. b 29. Open Univ BA84. Selly Oak Coll 51. **dss** 80 **d** 87 **p** 94. Newmarket St Mary w Exning St Agnes *St E* 80-82; Acomb St Steph *York* 83-86; Scarborough St Martin 86-93; Par Dn 87-93; C Cayton w Eastfield 94; rtd 94; Perm to Offic *Nor* from 95. *27 Wells Road, Walsingham NR22 6DL* Tel (01328) 820489

HUMPHRIES, Richard James Robert. b 44. FRAM95. EAMTC 99. **d** 01 **p** 02. NSM Heybridge w Langford *Chelmsf* 01-02; NSM Maldon All SS w St Pet from 02; Asst Chapl Mid-Essex Hosp Services NHS Trust 01-04; Chapl Essex Rivers Healthcare NHS Trust from 04. *1 Prince of Wales Road, Great Totham, Maldon CM9 8PX* Tel (01621) 892922 Mobile 07803-281036 E-mail richard.humphries1@btopenworld.com

HUMPHRIES, Robert William. b 36. Open Univ BA87. SW Minl Tr Course 96. **d** 99 **p** 00. OLM Kenwyn w St Allen *Truro* from 99. *27 Penhalls Way, Truro TR3 6EX* Tel (01872) 862827

HUMPHRIES, William David. b 57. QUB BEd DipTh LTCL. CITC. **d** 86 **p** 87. C Ballyholme *D & D* 86-90; Min Can Belf Cathl from 89; V Choral 90-93; C Belfast St Anne *Conn* 90-93; I Stormont *D & D* from 93. *St Molua's Rectory, 3 Rosepark, Belfast BT5 7RG* Tel (028) 9048 2292 *or* 9041 9171 E-mail stormont@down.anglican.org

HUMPHRIS, Richard. b 44. N Glos Tech Coll OND69. Sarum & Wells Th Coll 69. **d** 72 **p** 73. C Cheltenham St Luke and St Jo *Glouc* 72-77; C Lydney w Aylburton 77-82; Chapl RAF 82-85; TV Kippax w Allerton Bywater *Ripon* 85-92; RSPCA 92-95; rtd 95; Perm to Offic *York* from 98. *33 Cliff Terrace, Micklefield, Leeds LS25 4DF* Tel 0113-287 4446

HUMPHRISS, Canon Reginald George. b 36. Kelham Th Coll 56. **d** 61 **p** 62. C Londonderry *Birm* 61-63; Asst Dir RE *Cant* 63-66; Dioc Youth Chapl 63-66; V Preston next Faversham 66-72; P-in-c Goodnestone St Bart and Graveney 71-72; V Spring Park 72-76; R Cant St Martin and St Paul 76-90; RD Cant 82-88; Hon Can Cant Cathl 85-01; R Saltwood 90-01; RD Elham 93-00; rtd 01; Perm to Offic *Cant* from 01. *Winsole, Faussett, Lower Hardres, Canterbury CT4 7AH* Tel (01227) 765264

HUMPHRY, Toby Peter. b 66. Man Univ BA88. Ripon Coll Cuddesdon BA90 MA96 Qu Coll Birm 92. **d** 93 **p** 94. C Westhoughton *Man* 93-96; C Westhoughton and Wingates 97; TV Atherton 97-99; TV Atherton and Hindsford 99-02; TV Atherton and Hindsford w Howe Bridge 02-03; Chapl K Sch Ely from 03. *The King's School, Barton Road, Ely CB7 4DB* Tel (01353) 653905 E-mail chaplain@kings-ely.cambs.sch.uk

HUMPHRYES, Garry James. b 62. Coll of Resurr Mirfield 92. **d** 95 **p** 96. C Lt Marsden *Blackb* 95-98; C Darwen St Cuth w Tockholes St Steph 98-00; V Nelson St Bede 00-03; V Morecambe St Barn from 03; Dioc Race and Community Relns Officer 98-03. *St Barnabas' Vicarage, 101 Regent Road, Morecambe LA3 1AG* Tel (01524) 411283 *or* 401464

HUMPHRYS, Kevin Luke. b 73. Surrey Univ BA97. St Steph Ho Ox. **d** 99 **p** 00. C Moulsecoomb *Chich* 99-03. *148 Lyndhurst Road, Worthing BN11 2DW* Tel (01903) 230336 E-mail kevin.humphrys@bigfoot.com

HUMPHRYS, Laura Frances. b 53. Goldsmiths' Coll Lon PGCE77. STETS 00. **d** 03 **p** 04. NSM Shorwell w Kingston *Portsm* from 03; NSM Gatcombe from 03; NSM Chale from 03. *Address withheld by request*

HUNDLEBY, Alan. b 41. LNSM course 86. **d** 86 **p** 87. OLM Fotherby *Linc* 86-02; NSM Barnoldby le Beck from 02. *35 Cheapside, Waltham, Grimsby DN37 0HE* Tel (01472) 827159

HUNG, Frank Yu-Chi. b 45. Birm Univ BSc68 BA75 Liv Univ MSc71 Ox Univ DipTh77. Wycliffe Hall Ox 76. **d** 78 **p** 79. C Walton H Trin *Ox* 78-82; C Spring Grove St Mary *Lon* 82-85; TV Wexcombe *Sarum* 85-92; V Hatcham St Jas *S'wark* 92-98; Chapl Goldsmiths' Coll Lon 95-98; Chapl S Bank Univ from 98. *1 St Alphege Clergy House, Pocock Street, London SE1 0BJ* Tel (020) 7928 8912

HUNGERFORD, Robin Nicholas. b 47. Redland Coll of Educn CertEd74. Trin Coll Bris 86. **d** 88 **p** 89. C Swindon Dorcan *Bris* 88-92; TV Melbury *Sarum* 92-01; P-in-c Winterbourne Stickland and Turnworth etc 01-05; V Winterborne Valley and Milton Abbas from 05. *The Rectory, North Street, Winterborne Stickland, Blandford Forum DT11 0NL* Tel and fax (01258) 880482 E-mail rjnk@rhungerford.freeserve.co.uk

HUNNISETT, John Bernard. b 47. AKC73. **d** 73 **p** 74. C Charlton Kings St Mary *Glouc* 73-77; C Portsea St Mary *Portsm* 77-80; V

Badgeworth w Shurdington *Glouc* 80-87; R Dursley 87-99; TR Ross *Heref* from 99; RD Ross and Archenfield from 02. *The Rectory, Church Street, Ross-on-Wye HR9 5HN* Tel (01989) 562175 Fax 564387 E-mail team.rector@rtm.org.uk

HUNNYBUN, Martin Wilfrid. b 44. Oak Hill Th Coll 67. **d** 70 **p** 71. C Ware Ch Ch *St Alb* 70-74; C Washfield, Stoodleigh, Withleigh etc *Ex* 74-75; TV 75-80; R Braunston *Pet* 80-85; Asst Chapl HM Pris Onley 80-85; Australia 83 and 85-98 and from 00; Min Flinders Melbourne 83; R Berry and Kangaroo Valley Sydney 85-94; Sen Chapl Ang Retirement Villages 94-98; TV Parkham, Alwington, Buckland Brewer etc *Ex* 98-00; Dioc Ecum Adv 98-00; R Glebe Sydney from 00. *138A Glebe Point Road, PO Box 353, Glebe, NSW, Australia 2037* Tel (0061) (2) 9518 4063 *or* 9660 1818 Fax 9660 5696 E-mail mhunnybun@ozemail.com.au

HUNT, Alan. b 31. GIMechE51 GIPE51. St Mich Coll Llan 65. **d** 67 **p** 68. C Standish *Blackb* 67-72; V Clitheroe St Paul Low Moor 72-76; Lic to Offic 76-85; rtd 85; Perm to Offic *Blackb* from 85. *68 Coniston Drive, Walton-le-Dale, Preston PR5 4RQ* Tel (01772) 339554

HUNT, Andrew Collins. b 54. Reading Univ BA77 Hull Univ PGCE79. St Alb Minl Tr Scheme 82 Sarum & Wells Th Coll 89 WEMTC 99. **d** 00 **p** 01. NSM Cainscross w Selsley *Glouc* 00-02. *Address temp unknown*

HUNT, Ashley Stephen. b 50. St Jo Coll Nottm 81. **d** 83 **p** 84. C Southchurch H Trin *Chelmsf* 83-86; TV Droitwich *Worc* 86-87; USA 88-91; TV Melton Gt Framland *Leic* 92-93; TV Melton Mowbray 93-98; TV Grantham *Linc* 98-00; Chapl Mental Health 98-01; C Stamford All SS w St Jo 00-01; TV Mynyddislwyn *Mon* from 02. *The Vicarage, Commercial Road, Cwmfelinfach, Ynysddu, Newport NP11 7HW* Tel (01495) 200257 E-mail louhunt3@aol.com

HUNT, Mrs Christina. b 24. Qu Mary Coll Lon BSc45. S Dios Minl Tr Scheme 78. **dss** 81 **d** 87 **p** 94. Alderbury and W Grimstead *Sarum* 81-87; Hon Par Dn 87-91; Hon Par Dn Alderbury Team 91-94; rtd 94; Perm to Offic *Sarum* from 94. *The Heather, Southampton Road, Alderbury, Salisbury SP5 3AF* Tel (01722) 710601

HUNT, Christopher Paul Colin. b 38. Ch Coll Cam BA62 MA62. Clifton Th Coll 63. **d** 65 **p** 66. C Widnes St Paul *Liv* 65-68; Singapore 68-70; Malaysia 70-71; Hon C Foord St Jo *Cant* 72-73; Iran 74-80; Overseas Service Adv CMS 81-91; P-in-c Claverdon w Preston Bagot *Cov* 91-02; rtd 02; Perm to Offic *Worc* from 04. *Birchfield House, 18 Oaklands, Malvern WR14 4JE* Tel (01684) 578803

HUNT, David John. b 35. Kelham Th Coll 60. **d** 65 **p** 66. C Bethnal Green St Jo w St Simon *Lon* 65-69; C Mill Hill St Mich 69-73; R Staple Fitzpaine, Orchard Portman, Thurlbear etc *B & W* 73-79; P-in-c E Coker w Sutton Bingham 79-88; V E Coker w Sutton Bingham and Closworth 88-00; RD Merston 85-94; rtd 00; Perm to Offic *B & W* from 01. *Meadowside, Head Street, Tintinhull, Yeovil BA22 8QH* Tel (01935) 824554

HUNT, Derek Henry. b 38. ALCD61. **d** 62 **p** 63. C Roxeth Ch Ch *Lon* 62-66; C Radipole *Sarum* 66-70; P-in-c Shalbourne w Ham 70-72; V Burbage 72-73; V Burbage and Savernake Ch Ch 73-78; P-in-c Hulcote w Salford *St Alb* 78-88; R Cranfield 78-88; R Cranfield and Hulcote w Salford 88-95; rtd 95; Perm to Offic *St Alb* 95-98. *26 Jowitt Avenue, Kempston, Bedford MK42 8NW*

HUNT, Ernest Gary. b 36. Univ Coll Dur BA57. Carl Dioc Tr Inst 90. **d** 93 **p** 94. NSM Salesbury *Blackb* 93-95; NSM Blackb St Mich w St Jo and H Trin 95-98; NSM Balderstone 98-01; rtd 01; Perm to Offic *Blackb* from 01. *Dunelm, 10 Pleckgate Road, Blackburn BB1 8NN* Tel (01254) 52531

HUNT, Ernest William. b 09. St Jo Coll Dur BA31 MA34 Birm Univ BD46 St Cath Soc Ox BLitt51 Ox Univ MLitt90. St Jo Coll Dur DipTh32. **d** 32 **p** 33. C Gateshead Fell *Dur* 32-37; V Dunston Ch Ch 37-43; Succ Birm Cathl *Birm* 43-51; Lect Qu Coll Birm 46-51; Vice-Prin Lich Th Coll 51-57; Prof St D Coll Lamp 57-69; rtd 75. *16 Peachcroft Road, Abingdon OX14 2NA* Tel (01235) 521549

HUNT, Giles Butler. b 28. Trin Hall Cam BA51 MA55. Cuddesdon Coll 51. **d** 53 **p** 54. C N Evington *Leic* 53-56; C Northolt St Mary *Lon* 56-58; Bp's Dom Chapl *Portsm* 58-59; Bp's Chapl *Nor* 59-62; R Holt 62-67; R Kelling w Salthouse 63-67; C Pimlico St Pet w Westmr Ch Ch *Lon* 67-72; V Barkway w Reed and Buckland *St Alb* 72-79; V Preston next Faversham, Goodnestone and Graveney *Cant* 79-92; rtd 92; Perm to Offic *Nor* from 92. *The Cottage, The Fairstead, Cley-next-the-Sea, Holt NR25 7RJ* Tel (01263) 740471

HUNT, Canon Ian Carter. b 34. Chich Th Coll 61. **d** 64 **p** 65. C Plymouth St Pet *Ex* 64-67; C Daventry *Pet* 67-70; V Northampton St Paul 70-91; Can Pet Cathl 81-99; V Wellingborough All Hallows 91-99; rtd 99; Chapl Allnutt's Hosp Goring Heath from 99. *The Chaplaincy, Almshouses, Goring Heath, Reading RG8 7RS* Tel (01491) 680261

HUNT, James Allen. b 49. Linc Th Coll 92. **d** 92 **p** 93. C Huddersfield St Pet and All SS *Wakef* 92-95; V Longwood from 95. *St Mark's Vicarage, 313 Vicarage Road, Huddersfield HD3 4HJ* Tel and fax (01484) 314163 E-mail jimandcarol2002@yahoo.co.uk

HUNT, James Castle. b 66. Univ of Ulster BSc90 MRICS92. Wycliffe Hall Ox 02. **d** 04 **p** 05. C N Farnborough *Guildf* from 04. *14 Wilton Court, Farnborough GU14 7AP* Tel (01252) 517339 *or* tel and fax 513111 E-mail james@stpetersfarnborough.org.uk

HUNT, Jeremy Mark Nicholas. b 46. Open Univ BA73 Bris Univ DipEd FRGS70. Ridley Hall Cam 83. **d** 85 **p** 86. C Leckhampton SS Phil and Jas w Cheltenham St Jas *Glouc* 85-87; Asst Chapl Vevey w Château d'Oex and Villars *Eur* 87-89; Chapl Berne w Neuchâtel 89-90; Dep Chapl HM Pris Pentonville 94-95; Chapl HM Pris Highpoint 95-05; TV Bury St Edmunds All SS w St Jo and St Geo *St E* from 05. *2 Fen Way, Bury St Edmunds IP33 3ZA* Tel (01284) 752906

HUNT, John Barry. b 46. Lich Th Coll 70 Qu Coll Birm 72. **d** 73 **p** 74. C Auckland St Andr and St Anne *Dur* 73-77; C Consett 77-79; R Lyons 79-89; P-in-c Hebburn St Cuth 89-05; P-in-c Hebburn St Oswald 01-05; V Hebburn St Cuth and St Oswald from 05. *St Cuthbert's Vicarage, Argyle Street, Hebburn NE31 1RD* Tel 0191-422 1145

HUNT, John Edwin. b 38. ARCO Dur Univ BA60 DipEd. EMMTC 78. **d** 81 **p** 82. NSM Newbold w Dunston *Derby* 81-92; NSM Chesterfield St Mary and All SS 92-02. *4 Ardsley Road, Ashgate, Chesterfield S40 4DG* Tel (01246) 275141 E-mail fredwin@cwcom.net

HUNT, John Stewart. b 37. Nor Ord Course 75. **d** 78 **p** 79. NSM Hunstanton St Edm *Nor* 78-81; NSM Hunstanton St Mary w Ringstead Parva, Holme etc 81-86; NSM Sedgeford w Southmere 84-86; C Lowestoft and Kirkley 86-89; R Blundeston w Flixton and Lound 89-93; P-in-c Kessingland w Gisleham 93-99; R Kessingland, Gisleham and Rushmere 99-00; rtd 00; Perm to Offic *Nor* from 00. *10 Peddars Drive, Hunstanton PE36 6HF* Tel (01485) 533424

HUNT, Canon Judith Mary. b 57. MRCVS80 Bris Univ BVSc80 Lon Univ PhD85 Fitzw Coll Cam BA90. Ridley Hall Cam 88. **d** 91 **p** 94. Par Dn Heswall *Ches* 91-94; C 94-95; P-in-c Tilston and Shocklach 95-03; Bp's Adv for Women in Min 95-00; Can Res Ches Cathl from 03; Dioc Dir of Min from 03. *5 Abbey Street, Chester CH1 2JF* Tel (01244) 346893 *or* 620444 E-mail judy.hunt@chester.anglican.org

HUNT, Kevin. b 59. St Jo Coll Dur BA80 Ox Univ BA84 MA88. St Steph Ho Ox 81. **d** 84 **p** 85. C Mansfield St Mark *S'well* 84-85; C Hendon and Sunderland *Dur* 85-88; V Sunderland St Mary and St Pet 88-95; TR Jarrow 95-02; V Walker *Newc* from 02; Asst Dioc Dir of Ords from 03. *Walker Vicarage, Middle Street, Newcastle upon Tyne NE6 4DB* Tel 0191-262 3666 E-mail kevinht10@hotmail.com

HUNT, Mark. *See* HUNT, Jeremy Mark Nicholas

HUNT, Miss Nicola Mary. b 54. SRN77 RSCN77 RHV87. Ripon Coll Cuddesdon DipMin95. **d** 95 **p** 96. C Broughton Astley and Croft w Stoney Stanton *Leic* 95-98; C Plymouth Em, St Paul Efford and St Aug *Ex* 98-01; V Ermington and Ugborough from 01. *The Vicarage, Lutterburn Street, Ugborough, Ivybridge PL21 0NG* Tel (01752) 897360

HUNT, Paul. *See* HUNT, Christopher Paul Colin

HUNT, Paul Edwin. b 47. Ripon Coll Cuddesdon 93. **d** 95 **p** 96. C Cleobury Mortimer w Hopton Wafers etc *Heref* 95-98; P-in-c Fritwell w Souldern and Ardley w Fewcott *Ox* 98-05; TR Cherwell Valley from 05. *The Vicarage, 44 Forge Place, Fritwell, Bicester OX27 7QQ* Tel (01869) 346739 E-mail paul.hunt@breathemail.net

HUNT, Paul Firth. b 62. Ox Univ MA89 Edin Univ BD89. Edin Th Coll 86. **d** 89 **p** 90. C Leeds Halton St Wilfrid *Ripon* 89-92; C Leeds City 92-95; V Leeds Richmond Hill 95-01. *Address temp unknown* E-mail paul@phunt.fsnet.co.uk

HUNT, Paul Michael. b 57. St Chad's Coll Dur BA79 K Coll Lon PGCE80 MA96 Univ of Wales (Lamp) MTh04. Chich Th Coll 91. **d** 92 **p** 93. Chapl Brighton Coll 92-93; NSM St Leonards SS Pet and Paul *Chich* 92-93; Chapl Mill Hill Sch Lon 93-98; Hon C Hendon St Paul Mill Hill *Lon* 95-98; P in O 96-98; V Southgate St Andr *Lon* 98-05; Warden of Readers (Edmonton Area) 01-05; Chapl Em Sch Wandsworth from 05. *Emanuel School, Battersea Rise, London SW11 1HS* Tel (020) 8870 4171 E-mail pmh@emanuel.org.uk

HUNT, Canon Peter John. b 35. AKC58. St Boniface Warminster. **d** 59 **p** 60. C Chesterfield St Mary and All SS *Derby* 59-61; C Matlock and Tansley 61-63; Chapl Matlock Hosp 61-63; Lect Matlock Teacher Tr Coll 61-63; V Tottington *Man* 63-69; CF (TA) 65-67 and from 75; V Bollington St Jo *Ches* 69-76; R Wilmslow 76-98; Hon Can Ches Cathl 94-02; P-in-c Brereton w Swettenham 98-02; rtd 02; Perm to Offic *Ches* from 02. *1 Varden Town Cottages, Birtles Lane, Over Alderley, Macclesfield SK10 4RZ* Tel (01265) 829593 E-mail canonhari@aol.com

HUNT, Richard William. b 46. G&C Coll Cam BA67 MA71. Westcott Ho Cam 68. **d** 72 **p** 73. C Bris St Agnes and St Simon w St Werburgh *Bris* 72-77; Chapl Selw Coll Cam 77-84; V Birchfield *Birm* 84-01; R Chich St Paul and Westhampnett *Chich*

from 01. *The Rectory, Tower Close, Chichester PO19 1QN* Tel (01243) 531624 E-mail richard@hunts.fsnet.co.uk

HUNT, Ms Rosalind Edna Mary. b 55. Man Univ BA76. St Steph Ho Ox 86. **d** 88 **p** 94. Chapl Jes Coll Cam 88-92; Hon Chapl to the Deaf *Ely* 92-04; C Cambridge St Jas 00. *Flat 1, Thorne House, Wilmslow Road, Manchester M14 6DW* Tel 0161-257 0238 E-mail ros.hunt@virgin.net

HUNT, Canon Russell Barrett. b 35. NY Univ Virginia Univ Fitzw Ho Cam. Westcott Ho Cam 73. **d** 75 **p** 76. C Leic St Mary *Leic* 75-78; V Leic St Gabr 78-82; Chapl Leic Gen Hosp 82-95; Hon Can Leic Cathl *Leic* 88-95; rtd 95. *33 Braunstone Avenue, Leicester LE3 0JH* Tel 0116-254 9101

HUNT, Simon John. b 60. Pemb Coll Ox BA81 MA85. St Jo Coll Nottm 87. **d** 90 **p** 91. C Stalybridge St Paul *Ches* 90-93; C Heysham *Blackb* 93-99; V Higher Walton from 99. *The Vicarage, Blackburn Road, Higher Walton, Preston PR5 4EA* Tel (01772) 335406 E-mail shunt@aschurchhw.co.uk

HUNT, Stephen. b 38. Man Univ BSc61 MSc62 PhD64 DSc80. Carl Dioc Tr Inst 88. **d** 91 **p** 92. C Broughton *Blackb* 91-95; Chapl Preston Acute Hosps NHS Trust 94-95; V Preston Em *Blackb* 95-03; rtd 03. *8 Wallace Lane, Forton, Preston PR3 0BA*

HUNT, Timothy Collinson. b 65. ASVA91 Univ of Wales (Cardiff) BD95 Ox Univ MTh98. Ripon Coll Cuddesdon 95. **d** 97 **p** 98. C Ex St Dav *Ex* 97-01; Chapl Blundell's Sch Tiverton from 01. *1B Hillands, 39 Tidcombe Lane, Tiverton EX16 4EA* Tel (01884) 242343 E-mail tc@collhunt.fsnet.co.uk

HUNT, Vera Susan Henrietta. b 33. S Dios Minl Tr Scheme 88. **d** 91 **p** 94. Hon Chapl RAD from 91; Perm to Offic *Lon* from 03. *27 Redriff Close, Maidenhead SL6 4DJ* Tel (01628) 23909 E-mail vera@sh-hunt.fsnet.co.uk

HUNTER, Allan Davies. b 36. Univ of Wales (Lamp) BA57. Coll of Resurr Mirfield 57. **d** 59 **p** 60. C Cardiff St Jo *Llan* 59-68; V Llansawel 68-76; Youth Chapl 71-77; V Llansawel w Briton Ferry 76-79; V Canton St Cath 79-01; rtd 01. *9 Avonridge, Thornhill, Cardiff CF14 9AU* Tel (029) 2069 3054 E-mail allanhunter@talk21.com

HUNTER, David Hilliard Cowan. b 48. Massey Univ (NZ) BA92. St Jo Coll Auckland LTh74. **d** 73 **p** 74. New Zealand 73-03; C Stoke 73-75; C Christ Church Cathl 75-78; V Waimea 78-79; Chapl Tongariro Pris Farm 79-85; Chapl Waikune Pris 81-85; Chapl Rangipo Pris 81-85; Chapl Rimutuka Pris and Pris Staff Coll 86-92; P Asst Silverstream 86-92; Chapl NZ Army 88-92; P Asst Marton 92-97; P Asst Cambridge 97-01; Chapl Bruton Sch for Girls 02; P-in-c Stevington *St Alb* from 03. *Wimborne Grange, 19 Linden Road, Bedford MK40 2DQ* Tel (01234) 357370 E-mail david@stmarythevirgin.fsworld.co.uk

HUNTER, Edwin Wallace. b 43. NUI BA83 FCIM. CITC 91. **d** 94 **p** 95. NSM Cork St Fin Barre's Union *C, C & R* from 94; Min Can Cork Cathl from 95; Bp's Dom Chapl from 03. *Cedar Lodge, Church Road, Carrigaline, Co Cork, Irish Republic* Tel (00353) (21) 437 2338 E-mail enjhunter@eircom.net

HUNTER, Canon Frank <u>Geoffrey</u>. b 34. Keble Coll Ox BA56 MA60 Fitzw Coll Cam BA58 MA62. Ridley Hall Cam 57. **d** 59 **p** 60. C Bircle *Man* 59-62; C Jarrow Grange *Dur* 62-65; V Kingston upon Hull St Martin *York* 65-72; V Linthorpe 72-76; V Heslington 76-99; RD Derwent 78-98; Can and Preb York Minster 85-99; rtd 99; Perm to Offic *Wakef* from 01. *2 Flexbury Avenue, Morley, Leeds LS27 0RG* Tel 0113-253 9213

HUNTER, Ian Paton. b 20. Em Coll Cam BA46 MA50. Tyndale Hall Bris 40. **d** 43 **p** 47. C Harrington *Pet* 43-47; C Portman Square St Paul *Lon* 47-50; V Furneux Pelham w Stocking Pelham *St Alb* 50-54; V Moulton *Pet* 54-60; V Danehill *Chich* 60-67; R Plumpton w E Chiltington 67-77; V Burwash Weald 77-83; P-in-c Stonegate 83-85; rtd 85; Perm to Offic *Chich* from 86. *Edzell, 15 Harrow Close, Seaford BN25 3PE* Tel (01323) 899871

HUNTER, James. b 38. Bible Tr Inst Glas DipTh65 Union Th Coll Belf BD90. **d** 92 **p** 92. In Pb Ch of Ireland 82-92; V Werneth *Man* 92-98; V Woking St Paul *Guildf* from 98; Asst Chapl HM Pris Coldingley from 01. *St Paul's Vicarage, Pembroke Road, Woking GU22 7ED* Tel (01483) 772081 *or* 888611

HUNTER, John Crichton. b 38. Univ of Wales (Cardiff) BA59 DipEd60 LTCL. St Steph Ho Ox 98. **d** 99 **p** 00. NSM Walham Green St Jo w St Jas *Lon* from 99. *The Vicarage Flat, 40 Racton Road, London SW6 1LP* Tel (020) 7381 3368 Fax 7386 5004

HUNTER, Canon John Gaunt. b 21. St Jo Coll Dur BA49 Leeds Univ MA94. Ridley Hall Cam 49. **d** 51 **p** 52. C Bradf Cathl *Bradf* 51-54; C Compton Gifford *Ex* 54-56; V Bootle St Matt *Liv* 56-62; Uganda 62-65; Prin Bp Tucker Coll 62-65; Dioc Missr *Liv* 65-71; V Altcar 65-78; Abp York's Adv in Miss 71-78; Hon Can Liv Cathl 71-78; R Buckhurst Hill *Chelmsf* 78-79; TR 79-89; Dioc Adv in Evang *Bradf* 89-92; rtd 92; Perm to Offic *Bradf* from 92. *Westhouse Lodge, Westhouse, Ingleton LA6 3NZ* Tel (01524) 241305

HUNTER, Mrs Linda Margaret. b 47. STETS 95. **d** 98. NSM Wootton *Portsm* 98-02; NSM Chale, Gatcombe and Shorwell w Kingston 02-05; rtd 05. *100 Caesars Road, Newport PO30 5EA* Tel (01983) 529529

HUNTER, Lionel Lawledge Gleave. b 24. Liv Coll of Art NDD50. ALCD53. **d** 53 **p** 54. C Leic H Trin *Leic* 53-56; C Northampton St Giles *Pet* 56-58; C Everton St Chrys *Liv* 58-59; P-in-c Liv St Mich 59-61; Chile 61-72; R Diddlebury w Bouldon and Munslow *Heref* 72-75; P-in-c Abdon w Clee St Margaret 73-75; P-in-c Holdgate w Tugford 73-75; Canada 75-85; V N Elmham w Billingford *Nor* 85-89; R N Elmham w Billingford and Worthing 89-90; rtd 90; Perm to Offic *Heref* from 93. *Araucana, Wyson Lane, Brimfield, Ludlow SY8 4AN* Tel (01584) 711463

HUNTER, Michael John. b 45. CCC Cam BA67 MA71 PhD71 Ox Univ BA75. Wycliffe Hall Ox 73. **d** 76 **p** 77. C Partington and Carrington *Ches* 76-79; CMS 80-90; Uganda 80-89; C Penn Fields *Lich* 90-02; RD Trysull 97-02; V Dore *Sheff* from 02. *The Vicarage, 51 Vicarage Lane, Dore, Sheffield S17 3GY* Tel 0114-236 3335 E-mail dorevicar@aol.com

HUNTER, Canon Michael Oram. b 40. K Coll Lon BD64 AKC64. **d** 65 **p** 66. C Tividale *Lich* 65-68; C Harrogate St Wilfrid *Ripon* 68-70; V Hawksworth Wood 70-78; V Whitkirk 78-86; TR Gt Grimsby St Mary and St Jas *Linc* from 86; Can and Preb Linc Cathl from 89. *49 Park Drive, Grimsby DN32 0EG* Tel (01472) 342933 *or* 358610 Fax 250751 E-mail mo.hunter@virgin.net

HUNTER, Paul. b 55. Huddersfield Poly BEd82 Cliff Coll MA05. Chich Th Coll 86. **d** 88 **p** 90. C Weymouth H Trin *Sarum* 88-92; P-in-c Hucknall Torkard *S'well* 92; TV 92-96; V Thurcroft *Sheff* from 96. *The Vicarage, 122 Green Arbour Road, Thurcroft, Rotherham S66 9ED* Tel (01709) 542261

HUNTER, Peter Wells. b 52. Bris Univ BSc73. Trin Coll Bris BA91. **d** 91 **p** 92. C New Borough and Leigh *Sarum* 91-97; P-in-c Warminster Ch Ch from 97. *The Vicarage, 13 Avon Road, Warminster BA12 9PR* Tel (01985) 212219 E-mail peter.wh@btopenworld.com

HUNTER, Robert. b 36. Man Univ BSc60. Clifton Th Coll. **d** 63 **p** 64. C Chadderton Ch Ch *Man* 63-65; C Balderstone 65-69; C Newburn *Newc* 69-73; TV Sutton St Jas and Wawne *York* 73-81; V Bilton St Pet 81-82; Hon C N Hull St Mich 82-91; TV Howden 91-97; P-in-c Ashton St Pet *Man* 97-99; TV Ashton 00-01; rtd 01; Perm to Offic *Bradf* from 02. *50 Kendall Avenue, Shipley BD18 4DY* Tel (01274) 584884

HUNTER, Canon Rodney Squire. b 33. Ex Coll Ox BA56 MA61. Coll of Resurr Mirfield 56. **d** 58 **p** 59. C Forest Gate St Edm *Chelmsf* 58-61; Lib Pusey Ho Ox 61-65; Zambia 65-74; Malawi from 74; rtd 01. *Matamangwe House, Private Bag 17, Nkhotakota, Malawi*

HUNTER, Stephen Albert Paul. b 52. JP96. N Ord Course 01. **d** 04 **p** 05. NSM Ecclesall *Sheff* from 04. *Overhill, Townhead Road, Dore, Sheffield S17 3GE* Tel 0114-236 9978 Fax 275 9769 Mobile 07739-949473 E-mail stephen_hunter@btconnect.com

HUNTER SMART, Ian Douglas. b 60. St Jo Coll Dur BA83 MA99. Edin Th Coll 83. **d** 85 **p** 86. C Cockerton *Dur* 85-89; TV Jarrow 89-92; TV Sunderland 92-98; Chapl Sunderland Univ 92-98; Ecum Chapl Newcastle Coll of H&FE 98-00; Perm to Offic *Dur* from 98. *33 Barbary Drive, Sunderland SR6 0RB* Tel 0191-567 1966 E-mail ihs@dunelm.org.uk

HUNTER SMART, William David. b 75. Bris Univ BSc97. Wycliffe Hall Ox BA01. **d** 02 **p** 03. C Watford *St Alb* from 02. *8A Lammas Road, Watford WD18 0BA* Tel (01923) 232979 E-mail williamhuntersmart@tiscali.co.uk

HUNTINGDON, Archdeacon of. *See* McCURDY, The Ven Hugh Kyle

HUNTINGDON, Suffragan Bishop of. *See* INGE, The Rt Revd John Geoffrey

HUNTLEY, David Anthony. b 32. AMInstT56 MRTvS78 MILT98. Lon Bible Coll BA60 Fuller Sch of World Miss MTh81 Trin Coll Singapore 65. **d** 64 **p** 65. OMF Internat from 61; Singapore 61-71; Indonesia 72-73; Philippines 74-75; Hong Kong 77-81; Seychelles 82-87; Thailand 88-97; NSM S Croydon Em 76-77, 81-82, 87-88, 91-92 and 98-04. *42 Farnborough Avenue, South Croydon CR2 8HD* Tel (020) 8657 5673

HUNTLEY, Denis Anthony. b 56. Saltley Tr Coll Birm CertEd77. Qu Coll Birm 77. **d** 80 **p** 81. C Llanblethian w Cowbridge and Llandough etc *Llan* 80-83; TV Glyncorrwg w Afan Vale and Cymmer Afan 83-86; R 86-89; Chapl Asst Walsgrave Hosp Cov 89-92; Chapl Halifax Gen Hosp 92-94; Chapl Calderdale Healthcare NHS Trust 94-97; C Leeds City *Ripon* 97-02; Chapl to the Deaf 97-02; Chapl amongst Deaf People and Adv for Deaf Min from 02. *11 Bedford View, Leeds LS16 6DL* Tel 0113-267 2599 E-mail dhuntley56@hotmail.com

HUNTRESS, Franklin Elias. b 33. Berkeley Div Sch STM62. **d** 62 **p** 63. USA 62-65, 73-77, 81-91 and from 98; C Ches St Mary *Ches* 65-68; C Waltham Abbey *Chelmsf* 68-73; V Leic St Gabr *Leic* 77-81; C Skegness and Winthorpe *Linc* 91-93; P-in-c Long Bennington w Foston 93-94; rtd 98. *5C Independence Way, Glover Landing, Marble Head, MA 01945, USA* Tel (001) (781) 631 4785

HUNWICKE, John William. b 41. Hertf Coll Ox BA64 MA67. St Steph Ho Ox. **d** 67 **p** 68. C Beaconsfield *Ox* 67-70; C Newington St Paul *S'wark* 70-73; Hd of Th Lancing Coll 73-01;

rtd 01; C Lifton, Broadwoodwidger, Stowford etc *Ex* from 01. *The Rectory, Lewdown, Okehampton EX20 4DN* Tel (01566) 783493

HURCOMBE, Thomas William. b 45. BD74 AKC76. **d** 76 **p** 77. C Hampstead All So *Lon* 76-79; C Is of Dogs Ch Ch and St Jo w St Luke 79-83; C Bromley All Hallows 83-89; C E Greenwich Ch Ch w St Andr and St Mich *S'wark* 89-96; Ind Chapl 89-97; Dioc Urban Missr 90-96; Greenwich Waterfront Chapl 96-98; C Charlton St Luke w H Trin 97-98; P-in-c S Norwood St Mark from 98. *St Mark's Vicarage, 101 Albert Road, London SE25 4JE* Tel (020) 8656 6329 E-mail hurcomt@aol.com

HURD, Alun John. b 52. Edin Univ MTh97. Trin Coll Bris BA86. **d** 86 **p** 87. C Chertsey *Guildf* 86-90; Chapl St Pet Hosp Chertsey 86-90; V W Ewell *Guildf* 90-04; Chapl NE Surrey Coll Ewell 01-04; Min Distr P Lower Yorke Peninsular Australia from 05. *Minlaton Rectory, 23 First Street, Minlaton, S Australia 5575* Tel (0061) (8) 8853 2093 E-mail alun@hurdbass.fsnet.co.uk

HURD, Mrs Brenda Edith. b 44. Sittingbourne Coll DipEd75. Cant Sch of Min 87. **d** 92 **p** 94. NSM Birling, Addington, Ryarsh and Trottiscliffe *Roch* 92-02; P-in-c Wrotham from 02. *The Rectory, Borough Green Road, Wrotham, Sevenoaks TN15 7RA* Tel (01732) 882211 E-mail b.hurd@virgin.net

HURD, John Patrick. b 37. CertEd65 Open Univ BA73 Kent Univ MA92. S Dios Minl Tr Scheme 77. **d** 80 **p** 81. NSM Billingshurst *Chich* 80-82 and 89-94; NSM Itchingfield w Slinfold 82-89. *Groomsland Cottage, Parbrook, Billingshurst RH14 9EU* Tel (01403) 782167

HURFORD, Colin Osborne. b 33. Qu Coll Ox BA55 MA59. Wells Th Coll 55. **d** 57 **p** 58. C Barnoldswick w Bracewell *Bradf* 57-61; C Warrington St Elphin *Liv* 61-63; Malaysia 63-70; P-in-c Annscroft *Heref* 71-79; P-in-c Longden 71-79; P-in-c Pontesbury III 71-79; R Longden and Annscroft 79-85; P-in-c Church Pulverbatch 81-85; R Longden and Annscroft w Pulverbatch 85-86; Tanzania 86-87; TR Billingham St Aid *Dur* 87-96; rtd 96; Perm to Offic *Heref* from 96; *Lich* from 01. *14 Station Road, Pontesbury, Shrewsbury SY5 0QY* Tel (01743) 792605

✠**HURFORD, The Rt Revd Richard Warwick.** b 44. OAM99. Trin Coll Bris BA96 ACertCM71 Hon FGCM96 MACE81 Univ of Wales MTh02. St Jo Coll Morpeth ACT DipTh69 Sarum Th Coll DipTh71 Melbourne Coll of Div DipRE74. **d** 69 **p** 70 **c** 01. Australia 69-71 and from 78; Prec Grafton Cathl 69-70; P-in-c Tisbury *Sarum* 71-73; R 73-75; R Tisbury and Swallowcliffe w Ansty 75-76; P-in-c Chilmark 76-78; TR Tisbury 76-78; TR Coffs Harbour 78-83; Dean Grafton 83-97; Adn The Clarence and Hastings 85-87; Adn Grafton 87-92; R Sydney St Jas 97-01; Bp Bathurst from 01. *Bishopscourt, 288 William Street, PO Box 23, Bathurst, NSW, Australia 2795* Tel (0061) (2) 6331 3550 *or* 6331 1722 Fax 6331 3660 *or* 6332 2772 E-mail bxbishop@ix.net.au

HURLE, Canon Anthony Rowland. b 54. Lon Univ BSc Em Coll Cam PGCE. Wycliffe Hall Ox 80. **d** 83 **p** 84. C Ipswich St Mary at Stoke w St Pet *St E* 83-87; TV Barking St Marg w St Patr *Chelmsf* 87-92; V St Alb St Paul *St Alb* from 92; RD St Alb 95-05; Hon Can St Alb from 05. *St Paul's Vicarage, 7 Brampton Road, St Albans AL1 4PN* Tel and fax (01727) 836810 *or* tel 846281 E-mail tony@stpauls-stalbans.org *or* vicar@stpauls-stalbans.org

HURLE (née POWNALL), Mrs Lydia Margaret. b 53. SRN SCM. Wycliffe Hall Ox 78. **dss** 81 **d** 94 **p** 95. Ipswich St Mary at Stoke w St Pet etc *St E* 81-83; NSM St Alb St Paul *St Alb* from 93. *St Paul's Vicarage, 7 Brampton Road, St Albans AL1 4PN* Tel and fax (01727) 836810 E-mail tony.hurle@ntlworld.com

HURLEY, Daniel Timothy. b 37. St Mich Coll Llan 68. **d** 70 **p** 71. C Llanfabon *Llan* 70-73; CF 73-79; R W Walton *Ely* 79-86; V Cwmddauddwr w St Harmon's and Llanwrthwl *S & B* 86-02; rtd 02. *39 Ellesmere Orchard, Emsworth PO10 8TP* Tel (01243) 376923

HURLEY, Mark Tristan. b 57. Trin Coll Bris BA89. Sarum & Wells Th Coll 89. **d** 91 **p** 92. C Gainsborough All SS *Linc* 91-94; TV Grantham 94-00; V Donington and Bicker 00-02. *Address temp unknown*

HURLEY, Robert. b 64. Univ of Wales (Cardiff) BD86. Ridley Hall Cam 88. **d** 90 **p** 91. C Dagenham *Chelmsf* 90-93; C Egg Buckland *Ex* 93-96; C Devonport St Budeaux 96; P-in-c Camberwell All SS *S'wark* 96-99; V 99-02; Camberwell Deanery Missr 96-02; R Oldbury *Sarum* 02-04. *c/o Crockford, Church House, Great Smith Street, London SW1P 3NZ* E-mail janeandbobhurley@aol.com

HURLOCK, Ronald James. b 31. BSc PhD. St Deiniol's Hawarden. **d** 83 **p** 84. C Oxton *Ches* 83-87; Chapl Asst Man R Infirmary 87-91; rtd 91. *78 Garwood Close, Westbrook, Warrington WA5 5TF* Tel (01925) 444583

HURLSTON, Ronald Wilcox. b 30. St Deiniol's Hawarden 84. **d** 86 **p** 87. NSM Timperley *Ches* 86-90; C 90-95; rtd 95; Perm to Offic *Ches* from 95. *1 Heath Road, Timperley, Altrincham WA15 6BH* Tel 0161-283 2898

HURN, Mrs June Barbara. b 32. Birm Univ CertEd53. Cant Sch of Min 87. **d** 90 **p** 94. NSM Chislehurst St Nic *Roch* from 90. *Hawkswing, Hawkwood Lane, Chislehurst BR7 5PW* Tel (020) 8467 2320

HURRELL, John William. b 25. Ripon Hall Ox 65. **d** 66 **p** 67. C Painswick *Glouc* 66-68; C Glouc St Geo 68-70; C Thornbury 70-73; V Glouc St Steph 73-86; V Deerhurst, Apperley w Forthampton and Chaceley 86-90; rtd 90; Perm to Offic *B & W* from 90. *1 Church View, Porlock, Minehead TA24 8NA* Tel (01643) 862488

HURRELL, Lionel Rex. b 41. Southn Univ BA64. Coll of Resurr Mirfield 64. **d** 66 **p** 67. C St Marychurch *Ex* 66-69; C Dawlish 69-71; Dioc Youth Officer *Cov* 71-75; V Porthleven *Truro* 75-80; RD Kerrier 78-80; P-in-c Sithney 78-80; V Swindon New Town *Bris* 80-88; TR 88-97; RD Wroughton 93-97; Hon Can Bris Cathl 94-97; rtd 97. *331 Seaside, Eastbourne BN22 7PA* Tel (01323) 649597

HURREN, Timothy John. b 46. York Univ BA74 ACIB69. NEOC 99. **d** 02 **p** 03. NSM High Harrogate St Pet *Ripon* from 02. *1 South Park Road, Harrogate HG1 5QU* Tel (01423) 541696 E-mail timhurren@fish.co.uk

HURRY, Lynn Susan. b 59. Middx Univ BA05. NTMTC 02. **d** 05. C Southchurch H Trin *Chelmsf* from 05. *20 Wansfell Gardens, Southend-on-Sea SS1 3SW* Tel (01702) 586511

HURST, Alaric Desmond St John. b 24. New Coll Ox BA50 MA70. Wells Th Coll 48. **d** 51 **p** 53. C Huddersfield H Trin *Wakef* 51-52; C Leeds St Geo *Ripon* 52-54; Bp's Chapl for Rehabilitation *Roch* 55-56; C St Steph Walbrook and St Swithun etc *Lon* 57-59; V Pudsey St Paul *Bradf* 59-63; V Writtle *Chelmsf* 63-69; rtd 89. *9 Ganderton Court, Pershore WR10 1AW* Tel (01905) 840939

HURST, Antony. b 38. MA MSc. S'wark Ord Course 79. **d** 83 **p** 84. NSM S'wark H Trin w St Matt *S'wark* 83-89; NSM S'wark Ch Ch 89-96; NSM St Martin-in-the-Fields *Lon* from 96; Perm to Offic *S'wark* from 96. *33 Hugh Street, London SW1V 1QJ* Tel (020) 7828 2844 E-mail clergy@smitf.org

HURST, Brian Charles. b 58. Nottm Univ BA. Ripon Coll Cuddesdon 82. **d** 84 **p** 85. C Cullercoats St Geo *Newc* 84-87; C Prudhoe 87-88; TV Willington 88-95; V Denton 95-03; RD Newc W 97-98; TV Glendale Gp from 03. *2 Queens Road, Wooler NE71 6DR* Tel (01668) 281468 E-mail brian.hurst1@btopenworld.com

HURST, Canon Colin. b 49. Linc Th Coll 88. **d** 90 **p** 91. C Wavertree H Trin *Liv* 90-93; C Croft and Stoney Stanton *Leic* 93-95; TV Broughton Astley and Croft w Stoney Stanton 95-97; V Wigan St Andr *Liv* from 97; AD Wigan W from 03; Hon Can Liv Cathl from 03. *St Andrew's Vicarage, 3A Mort Street, Wigan WN6 7AU* Tel (01942) 243514 E-mail churst6000@aol.com

HURST, Colin. b 58. Westmr Coll Ox BA90. St Jo Coll Nottm MA95. **d** 95 **p** 96. C Warboys w Broughton and Bury w Wistow *Ely* 95-98; P-in-c Wisbech St Mary 98-04; P-in-c Guyhirn w Ring's End 98-04; V Wisbech St Mary and Guyhirn w Ring's End etc from 05. *The Vicarage, Church Road, Wisbech St Mary, Wisbech PE13 4RN* Tel and fax (01945) 410814 E-mail cehurst@globalnet.co.uk

HURST, Canon Jeremy Richard. b 40. Trin Coll Cam BA61 MA MPhil FCP. Linc Th Coll 62. **d** 64 **p** 65. C Woolwich St Mary w H Trin *S'wark* 64-69; Perm to Offic *Ex* 69-76 and *Ox* 76-84; TV Langley Marish *Ox* 84-85; TR 85-05; Hon Can Ch Ch from 05; Chapl Thames Valley Univ *Lon* 92-98; rtd 05. *Hortus Lodge, 22A Bolton Avenue, Windsor SL4 3JF* Tel (01753) 861158 E-mail jeremyhurst@lineone.net

HURST, John. b 31. NW Ord Course 76. **d** 79 **p** 80. C Flixton St Jo *Man* 79-82; P-in-c Hindsford 82-86; V 86-88; V Halliwell St Paul 88-93; rtd 93; Perm to Offic *Man* from 99. *26 Cornwall Avenue, Bolton BL5 1DZ* Tel (01204) 659233

HURT, Mrs Grenda Mary. b 36. JP91. LSE BSc63. STETS 96. **d** 99 **p** 01. NSM Freshwater *Portsm* from 99; NSM Yarmouth from 99; Asst Chapl Isle of Wight Healthcare NHS Trust from 03; Chapl Earl Mountbatten Hospice from 03. *Easterholme, Tennyson Road, Yarmouth PO40 9SP* Tel (01983) 761360 Mobile 07979-803127 E-mail grenda@lineone.net

✠**HURTADO, The Rt Revd Jorge A Perera.** b 34. **d** 57 **p** 58 **c** 94. Bp Cuba from 94. *Calle 6 No 273, Vedado, Plaza de la Revolucin, Havana 4, 10400, Cuba* Tel (0053) (7) 35655, 38003, 321120 *or* 312436 Fax 333293 E-mail episcopal@ip.etecsa.cu

HUSSEY, Martin John. b 46. STETS 96. **d** 99 **p** 00. NSM Thames Ditton *Guildf* from 99. *94 Wellington Close, Walton-on-Thames KT12 1BE* Tel (01932) 221914 E-mail martinhussey_uk@yahoo.co.uk

HUSTON, Mary Brigid. b 59. Hull Univ BA80 K Coll Lon MA98 RGN84 RM86. SEITE 95. **d** 98 **p** 99. C S Dulwich St Steph *S'wark* 98-02; TV Catford (Southend) and Downham from 02. *233 Bellingham Road, London SE6 1EH* Tel (020) 8695 6376 E-mail mary.huston@ukgateway.net

HUTCHENS, Holly Blair. b 42. Univ of Michigan BA64 Univ of Chicago MA69. Seabury-Western Th Sem MDiv88. **d** 88 **p** 88. USA 88-05; P-in-c Glenurquhart *Mor* from 05. *St Ninian's House, Glenurquhart, Inverness IV3 6TN* Tel (01456) 476264 E-mail hbhutchens@aol.com

HUTCHEON, Mrs Elsie. b 39. RGN63 CertEd UEA MEd98. EAMTC 89. **d** 92 **p** 94. NSM Heigham St Thos *Nor* 92-02;

P-in-c Heigham St Barn w St Bart from 02. *1 St Barnabas's Vicarage, Russell Street, Norwich NR2 4QT* Tel (01603) 627859 E-mail elsie@rev.demon.co.uk

HUTCHIN, David William. b 37. Man Univ MusB58 CertEd59 DipEd59 LRAM ARCM LTCL. Glouc Sch of Min 85. **d** 88 **p** 89. NSM Northleach w Hampnett and Farmington *Glouc* 88-94; NSM Cold Aston w Notgrove and Turkdean 88-94; NSM Chedworth, Yanworth and Stowell, Coln Rogers etc 94-01; RD Northleach 96-99; Perm to Offic *Leic* from 01 and *Derby* from 02. *44 Spinney Hill, Melbourne DE73 8LX* Tel (01332) 865134

HUTCHINGS, Colin Michael. b 36. Clifton Th Coll 66. **d** 68 **p** 69. C Worksop St Jo *S'well* 68-71; C Hampreston *Sarum* 71-76; TV Tisbury 76-82; R Waddesdon w Over Winchendon and Fleet Marston *Ox* 82-00; rtd 00; Perm to Offic *Pet* from 01. *Nimrod, 4 The Beeches, Pattishall, Towcester NN12 8LT* Tel (01327) 830563

HUTCHINGS, Ian James. b 49. Lon Univ DipTh72 Chester Coll of HE MA03. Clifton Th Coll 69 Trin Coll Bris 72. **d** 73 **p** 74. C Parr *Liv* 73-77; C Timperley *Ches* 77-81; V Partington and Carrington 81-96; V Huntington from 96; Chapl Bp's Blue Coat C of E High Sch from 96. *St Luke's Vicarage, 14 Celandine Close, Huntington, Chester CH3 6DT* Tel and fax (01244) 347345 *or* tel 344705 E-mail ihutchings@aol.com

HUTCHINGS, John Denis Arthur. b 29. Keble Coll Ox BA53 MA59 MSc59. Chich Th Coll 58. **d** 60 **p** 61. C St Pancras w St Jas and Ch Ch *Lon* 60-63; Asst Chapl Denstone Coll Uttoxeter 63-67 and 79-83; C Stepney St Dunstan and All SS *Lon* 67-78; V Devonport St Boniface *Ex* 83-86; TR Devonport St Boniface and St Phil 86-93; P-in-c Lydford and Brent Tor 93-95; rtd 96; Perm to Offic *Ex* from 96. *Maisonette, 40 Brook Street, Tavistock PL19 0HE* Tel (01822) 616946

HUTCHINS, Paul. b 79. Coll of Resurr Mirfield 99 N Ord Course 04. **d** 05. C Royton St Paul *Man* from 05. *136 Denbydale Way, Royton, Oldham OL2 5TE* Tel 0161-628 0141 Mobile 07818-022678

HUTCHINSON, Alison Joyce. b 62. Leeds Univ BA84 RMN90. Aston Tr Scheme 92 Ripon Coll Cuddesdon 94. **d** 97 **p** 98. C Benfieldside *Dur* 97-00; C Bishopwearmouth St Nic 00-02; Perm to Offic *Carl* from 02. *7 Park Close, Penrith CA11 8ND* Tel (01768) 867053 E-mail alison.hutchinson@btopenworld.com

HUTCHINSON, Canon Andrew Charles. b 63. Univ of Wales (Ban) BA84 MEd96. Aston Tr Scheme 85 Chich Th Coll 87. **d** 89 **p** 90. C Burnley St Cath w St Alb and St Paul *Blackb* 89-92; C Shrewsbury St Chad w St Mary *Lich* 92-94; Chapl Heref Cathl Sch 94-97; Succ Heref Cathl *Heref* 94-97; Chapl Solihull Sch from 97; Can St Jo Pro-Cathl Katakwa from 00. *2 St Alphege Close, Church Hill Road, Solihull B91 3RQ* Tel 0121-704 3708

HUTCHINSON, Andrew Paul. b 65. Trin Hall Cam BA87 MA91 Solicitor 90. Aston Tr Scheme 92 Ripon Coll Cuddesdon BTh97. **d** 97 **p** 98. C Stanley *Dur* 97-99; C Sunderland 99-01; TV 01-02; Chapl Sunderland Univ 99-02; TV Penrith w Newton Reigny and Plumpton Wall *Carl* from 02; Chapl Cumbria Campus Cen Lancs Univ from 02. *7 Park Close, Penrith CA11 8ND* Tel (01768) 867053 E-mail paul.hutchinson5@btopenworld.com

HUTCHINSON, Canon Cyril Peter. b 37. Dur Univ BA61. Wm Temple Coll Rugby 61. **d** 63 **p** 64. C Birm St Paul *Birm* 63-67; Prin Community Relns Officer 66-69; Perm to Offic 67-69; Dir Bradf SHARE 69-76; Perm to Offic *Bradf* 69-75; Hon C Manningham 75-76; V Clayton 76-83; RD Bowling and Horton 80-83; TR Keighley St Andr 83-94; Hon Can Bradf Cathl 84-03; rtd 94; Hon C Keighley All SS *Bradf* 94-03. *Wellcroft, Laycock Lane, Laycock, Keighley BD22 0PN* Tel (01535) 606145

HUTCHINSON, David. *See* HUTCHINSON, Canon William David

HUTCHINSON, David Bamford. b 29. QUB BSc53 TCD Div Test55 QUB DipEd57. **d** 55 **p** 56. C Lisburn Ch Ch *Conn* 55-57; Uganda 57-65; I Kilkeel *D & D* 66-75; I Willowfield 75-82; V Longfleet *Sarum* 82-94; rtd 94; Perm to Offic *Sarum* 94-99. *Bethany, 3 Panorama Road, Poole BH13 7RA* Tel (01202) 664964

HUTCHINSON, Hugh Edward. b 27. FICE CEng. Bps' Coll Cheshunt. **d** 61 **p** 62. C Limehouse St Anne *Lon* 61-64; C Townstall w Dartmouth *Ex* 64-67; V Ex St Mark 67-75; P-in-c Foston on the Wolds *York* 75-77; P-in-c N Frodingham 75-77; R Beeford w Lissett 75-77; R Beeford w Frodingham and Foston 77-80; RD N Holderness 79-80; P-in-c Appleton Roebuck w Acaster Selby 80-84; P-in-c Etton w Dalton Holme 84-91; rtd 91; Perm to Offic *York* from 91. *33 Limestone Grove, Burniston, Scarborough YO13 0DH* Tel (01723) 871116

HUTCHINSON, Jeremy Olpherts. b 32. Oriel Coll Ox BA55 MA60 St Jo Coll Dur DipTh57. **d** 57 **p** 58. C Shoreditch St Leon *Lon* 57-60; V Hoxton St Jo w Ch Ch 60-78; Hon C Hackney 78-85; C Highbury Ch Ch w St Jo and St Sav 85-91; P-in-c Hanley Road St Sav w St Paul 91-92; TV Tollington 92-96; rtd 96; Perm to Offic *Lon* from 96. *8 Casimir Road, London E5 9NU* Tel (020) 8806 6492

HUTCHINSON, John Charles. b 44. K Coll Lon 64. **d** 69 **p** 70. C Portsea All SS *Portsm* 69-73; TV Fareham H Trin 73-78; P-in-c Pangbourne *Ox* 78-86; P-in-c Tidmarsh w Sulham 84-86; R Pangbourne w Tidmarsh and Sulham 86-96. *90 Fir Tree Avenue, Wallingford OX10 0PL* Tel (01491) 832445

HUTCHINSON, Jonathan Graham. b 62. Bris Univ BA01. Trin Coll Bris 98. **d** 01 **p** 02. C Church Stretton *Heref* 01-04; P-in-c Aspley *S'well* from 04. *St Margaret's Vicarage, 319 Aspley Lane, Nottingham NG8 5GA* Tel 0115-929 2920 *or* tel and fax 929 8899 E-mail jghutchinson@onetel.com

HUTCHINSON, Jonathan Mark. b 45. Cant Sch of Min 85. **d** 89 **p** 90. NSM Wickham Market w Pettistree and Easton *St E* 89-93; V Thorington w Wenhaston, Bramfield etc 94-97; TV Ipswich St Mary at Stoke w St Pet and St Fran 97-02. *27 Milton Lane, Wells BA5 2QS* Tel (01749) 676096

HUTCHINSON, Canon Julie Lorraine. b 55. WMMTC 90. **d** 93 **p** 94. C Northampton St Mary *Pet* 93-95; P-in-c Morcott w Glaston and Bisbrooke 95-97; P-in-c Lyddington w Stoke Dry and Seaton w Caldecott 97-03; Dir of Ords and Dioc Voc Adv from 03; Can Pet Cathl from 04. *The Rectory, Stanwick, Wellingborough NN9 6PP* Tel (01933) 626203 E-mail stanwick@fish.co.uk

HUTCHINSON, Mrs Karen Elizabeth. b 64. LMH Ox BA85 MA89 Solicitor 89. Wycliffe Hall Ox. **d** 01 **p** 02. C Alton St Lawr *Win* from 01. *13 Walnut Close, Alton GU34 2BA* Tel (01420) 542288

HUTCHINSON, Mark. *See* HUTCHINSON, Jonathan Mark

HUTCHINSON, Moreen Anne. b 46. Ulster Univ BA84. CITC 98. **d** 01 **p** 02. NSM Larne and Inver *Conn* 01-04; P-in-c Ardclinis and Tickmacrevan w Layde and Cushendun from 04. *St Mary's Rectory, 76 Largy Road, Carnlough, Ballymena BT44 0JJ* Tel and fax (028) 2888 5593 E-mail moreenhutchinson@talk21.com

HUTCHINSON, Paul. *See* HUTCHINSON, Andrew Paul

HUTCHINSON, Paul Edward. b 33. K Coll Lon. **d** 59 **p** 60. C Bromley St Mich *Lon* 59-63; C Mill Hill St Mich 63-66; C Sandridge *St Alb* 66-73; V St Alb St Mary Marshalswick 73-80; V Tunstall *Lich* 80-91; RD Stoke N 82-91; V Lower Gornal 91-93; V Lower Gornal *Worc* 93-98; rtd 98; Perm to Offic *Lich* from 99. *55 Mill Hayes Road, Burslem, Stoke-on-Trent ST6 4JB* Tel (01782) 813361

HUTCHINSON, Miss Pauline. b 49. St Jo Coll Nottm 88. **d** 90 **p** 94. Par Dn Sherwood *S'well* 90-94; C 94-95; TV Newark from 95; Chapl Newark Hosp NHS Trust 95-04. *St Leonard's Vicarage, Lincoln Road, Newark NG24 2DQ* Tel (01636) 703691

HUTCHINSON, Peter. *See* HUTCHINSON, Canon Cyril Peter

HUTCHINSON, Peter Francis. b 52. Portsm Poly HND74. Sarum & Wells Th Coll 87. **d** 89 **p** 90. C Honiton, Gittisham, Combe Raleigh, Monkton etc *Ex* 89-93; V Valley Park *Win* from 93. *35 Raglan Close, Eastleigh SO53 4NH* Tel (023) 8025 5749 E-mail st.francis@ukgateway.net

HUTCHINSON, Philip Sheldon. b 32. Pemb Coll Cam BA56 MA59. Chich Th Coll 56. **d** 58 **p** 59. C Plumstead St Nic *S'wark* 58-60; C Roehampton H Trin 60-64; R Washington DC St Tim USA 64-65; R Charlton St Luke w St Paul *S'wark* 65-69; Australia from 69; P-in-c Marysville 69-70; R Alexandra 70-73; I Leopold 73-77; I St Kilda Ch Ch 77-97; rtd 97. *c/o Mrs S D Cohen, 64 Gordon Street, Naracoorte, S Australia 5271* Tel (0061) (8) 8762 0029

HUTCHINSON, Raymond John. b 51. Liv Univ BSc73. Westcott Ho Cam 73. **d** 76 **p** 77. C Peckham St Jo *S'wark* 76-78; C Peckham St Jo w St Andr 78-79; C Prescot *Liv* 79-81; V Edgehill St Dunstan 81-87; P-in-c Litherland Ch Ch 87-89; P-in-c Waterloo Park 87-89; V Waterloo Ch Ch and St Mary 90-97; Chapl Wigan and Leigh Health Services NHS Trust 97-01; Chapl Wrightington Wigan and Leigh NHS Trust from 01; P-in-c Wigan All SS *Liv* from 04; P-in-c Wigan St Geo from 05. *The Rectory, 6 Wrightington Street, Wigan WN1 2BX* Tel (01942) 244459 E-mail hutchinsons@glebehouse.fslife.co.uk

HUTCHINSON, The Very Revd Roland Louis. b 29. TCD BA51 MA61. **d** 52 **p** 53. C Mullabrack w Kilcluney *Arm* 52-54; C Dromore Cathl *D & D* 54-62; C-in-c Rathmullan w Tyrella 62-65; I 65-74; I Magheralin w Dollingstown 74-95; Treas Dromore Cathl 86-90; Prec 90-93; Dean Dromore 93-95; rtd 95. *Summerhill Lodge, 22 Summerhill, Lurgan, Craigavon BT66 7AW* Tel (028) 3888 1789

HUTCHINSON, Canon Stephen. b 38. St Chad's Coll Dur BA60 DipTh62. **d** 62 **p** 63. C Tividale *Lich* 62-68; V Walsall St Andr 68-73; R Headless Cross *Worc* 73-81; TR Redditch, The Ridge 81-91; RD Bromsgrove 85-91; V Stourbridge St Thos 91-03; Hon Can Worc Cathl 88-03; rtd 03; Perm to Offic *Worc* from 03. *251 Stourbridge Road, Kidderminster DY10 2XJ* Tel (01562) 631658

HUTCHINSON, Canon William David. b 27. Wycliffe Hall Ox 55. **d** 57 **p** 58. C Ipswich St Jo *St E* 57-60; R Combs 60-65; V Ipswich St Aug 65-76; R Ewhurst *Guildf* 76-81; V Aldeburgh w Hazlewood *St E* 81-92; RD Saxmundham 83-88; Hon Can St E Cathl 87-92; rtd 92. *Hazelwood, 1 Birch Close, Woodbridge IP12 4UA* Tel (01394) 383760

HUTCHINSON CERVANTES, Canon Ian Charles. b 62. Cant Univ (NZ) BSc84 Reading Univ MSc86 Jes Coll Cam BA89 MA92. Westcott Ho Cam 86. **d** 89 **p** 90. C Iffley *Ox* 89-92; USPG 92-04; Locum P Caracas Cathl Venezuela 93; P-in-c El Cayo St Andr Belize 93-97; USPG Staff 97-04; Hon Can El Redentor Cathl Madrid from 01; Hon Can Buenos Aires from 02; Chapl Madrid *Eur* from 04. *St George's Anglican Church, Nez de Balboa 43, 28001 Madrid, Spain* Tel (0034) (91) 576 5109

✠**HUTCHISON, The Most Revd Andrew Sandford.** b 38. Montreal Dioc Th Coll Hon DD93. Trin Coll Toronto. **d** 69 **p** 70 **c** 70. Canada from 69; Dean Montreal 84-90; Bp Montreal 90-04; Primate of Angl Ch of Canada from 04. *600 Jarvis Street, Toronto ON, Canada, M4Y 2J6* Tel (001) (416) 924 9119 Fax 924 0211 E-mail primate@national.anglican.ca

HUTCHISON, Geoffrey John. b 52. Trin Hall Cam MA76 Lon Univ CertEd76. Ridley Hall Cam 77. **d** 79 **p** 80. C Harold Wood *Chelmsf* 79-83; CF 83-89; Warden Viney Hill Chr Adventure Cen 89-96; P-in-c Viney Hill *Glouc* 89-96; V Wadsley *Sheff* from 96. *The Vicarage, 91 Airedale Road, Sheffield S6 4AW* Tel 0114-234 8481 E-mail johnhutch@classicfm.net

HUTT, Colin Villette. b 32. FCA. Glouc Sch of Min 87. **d** 89 **p** 90. NSM Ludlow *Heref* 89-93; C Ludlow, Ludford, Ashford Carbonell etc 93-94; TV Tenbury 94-01; rtd 01; Perm to Offic *Heref* from 01. *Broxwell, Livesey Road, Ludlow SY8 1EX* Tel (01584) 877959 Fax 831659 E-mail broxwell@hotmail.com

HUTT, Canon David Handley. b 38. Lambeth MA05 AKC68. **d** 69 **p** 70. C Bedford Park *Lon* 69-70; C Westmr St Matt 70-73; PV and Succ S'wark Cathl *S'wark* 73-78; Chapl K Coll Taunton 78-82; V Bordesley SS Alb and Patr *Birm* 82-86; V St Marylebone All SS *Lon* 86-95; Can Steward Westmr Abbey 95-05; Sub-Dean and Adn Westmr 99-05; rtd 05. *3CC Morpeth Terrace, London SW1P 1EW*

HUTTON, Elizabeth. *See* HUTTON, Susan Elizabeth

HUTTON, Griffith Arthur Jeremy. b 31. Trin Hall Cam BA56 MA59. Linc Th Coll 56. **d** 58 **p** 59. C Hexham *Newc* 58-60; C Gosforth All SS 60-65; V Whitegate *Ches* 65-71; V Whitegate w Lt Budworth 71-78; R Dowdeswell and Andoversford w the Shiptons etc *Glouc* 78-91; V Newnham w Awre and Blakeney 91-96; rtd 96; Perm to Offic *Heref* from 99. *Hill House, Stoke Lacy, Bromyard HR7 4RE* Tel (01432) 820423

HUTTON, Joseph Charles. b 21. DFC41. Westcott Ho Cam 63. **d** 65 **p** 66. C St Marychurch *Ex* 65-67; V Warborough *Ox* 67-70; V Earley St Pet 70-75; R Ludgvan *Truro* 75-79; rtd 79. *2 Baines Close, Bourton-on-the-Water, Cheltenham GL54 2PU*

HUTTON, Mrs Serena Quartermaine. b 35. Nottm Univ BA57 Lon Univ BA73 Stranmillis Coll PGCE68 FRSA87. St Alb and Ox Min Course 95. **d** 98 **p** 99. OLM Chinnor, Sydenham, Aston Rowant and Crowell *Ox* from 98. *Elma Cottage, The Green, Kingston Blount, Chinnor OX9 4SE* Tel (01844) 354173

HUTTON, Susan Elizabeth. b 70. Univ of Wales (Cardiff) BD91. Ripon Coll Cuddesdon 93. **d** 95 **p** 96. C W Parley *Sarum* 95-99; C Trowbridge H Trin 99-05; P-in-c from 05. *The Vicarage, 67A Drynham Road, Trowbridge BA14 0PF* Tel (01225) 751275 E-mail rev.beth@virgin.net

HUTTON-BURY, David. b 44. BA. **d** 94 **p** 95. NSM Geashill w Killeigh and Ballycommon *M & K* 94-97; NSM Clane w Donadea and Coolcarrigan 97-00; NSM Mullingar, Portnashangan, Moyliscar, Kilbixy etc from 00. *Chorleyville Farm, Tullamore, Co Offaly, Irish Republic* Tel (00353) (506) 21813

HUXHAM, Hector Hubert. b 29. Bris Univ BA55. Tyndale Hall Bris 52. **d** 56 **p** 57. C Eccleston St Luke *Liv* 56-58; C Heworth H Trin *York* 59-60; V Burley *Ripon* 61-66; Chapl St Jas Univ Hosp Leeds 67-94; rtd 94; Perm to Offic *Bradf* 94-98 and *Ripon* from 94. *3 Oakwell Oval, Leeds LS8 4AL* Tel 0113-266 8851

HUXHAM, Canon Peter Richard. b 38. Worc Coll Ox BA61 MA74. St Steph Ho Ox 61. **d** 63 **p** 64. C Gillingham *Sarum* 63-67; C Osmondthorpe St Phil *Ripon* 67-70; V Parkstone St Osmund *Sarum* 70-75; TR Parkstone St Pet w Branksea and St Osmund 75-92; RD Poole 85-92; Can and Preb Sarum Cathl 85-92; Chapl Taunton and Somerset NHS Trust 92-03; rtd 03. *Salterns House, 34 Brownsea View Avenue, Poole BH14 8LQ* Tel (01202) 707431

HUXLEY, Edward Jonathan. b 74. Bris Univ BEng95. Trin Coll Bris BA04. **d** 05. C Sea Mills *Bris* from 05. *10 Albert Road, Staple Hill, Bristol BS16 5LA* Tel 0117-377 0058 E-mail edwardhuxley@fish.co.uk

HUXLEY, Canon Stephen Scott. b 30. Linc Th Coll 53. **d** 56 **p** 57. C Cullercoats St Geo *Newc* 56-59; C Eglingham 59-60; C N Gosforth 60-63; V Nether Witton and Hartburn and Meldon 63-65; V Tynemouth Priory 65-74; V Warkworth and Acklington 74-78; P-in-c Tynemouth St Jo 78-81; V 81-87; Hon Can Newc Cathl 82-92; V Wylam 87-92; rtd 92; Perm to Offic *Newc* from 92. *35 Castle Street, Norham, Berwick-upon-Tweed TD15 2LQ* Tel (01289) 382356

HUXTABLE, Christopher Michael Barclay. b 61. Ex Univ BA83 Qu Coll Cam PGCE84. St Steph Ho Ox 93. **d** 95 **p** 96. C Chich 95-98; C Haywards Heath St Wilfrid 98-99; TV 99-01; Chapl Geelong Gr Sch (Timbertop) Australia 01-04; Chapl St Mary's Sch Wantage 04-05. *Address temp unknown* E-mail christopher.huxtable@virgin.net

HUXTABLE, Michael George. b 29. St Jo Coll Cam BA50 MA54. S Dios Minl Tr Scheme 87. **d** 90 **p** 91. NSM Fisherton Anger *Sarum* 90-01; Perm to Offic *Ex* from 01. *10 Trews Weir Reach, Exeter EX2 4EG* Tel (01392) 277332

HUXTABLE, Peter Alexander. b 68. Southn Univ BEng90. St Jo Coll Nottm MTh01. **d** 01 **p** 02. C Kidderminster St Geo *Worc* 01-05; V Bestwood Em w St Mark *S'well* from 05. *Emmanuel Vicarage, 10 Church View Close, Arnold, Nottingham NG5 9QP* Tel 0115-920 8879 E-mail huxbox@freeuk.com

HUYTON, Stuart. b 37. St D Coll Lamp BA62. **d** 63 **p** 64. C Kingswinford H Trin *Lich* 63-66; C Leek St Edw 66-69; V Wigginton 69-76; V Wombourne 76-89; RD Trysull 79-84; P-in-c Bobbington 85-89; TR Wombourne w Trysull and Bobbington 89-95; V Lt Aston 95-04; rtd 04. *14 Crosbie Close, Chichester PO19 8RZ* Tel (01243) 790119

HUYTON, Susan Mary. b 57. Birm Univ BA79 DipTh86. Qu Coll Birm 83. **d** 86 **p** 97. C Connah's Quay *St As* 86-89; C Wrexham 89-90; Dn-in-c 90-91; TV 91-99; V Gwersyllt from 99. *The Vicarage, Old Mold Road, Gwersyllt, Wrexham LL11 4SB* Tel (01978) 756391 E-mail suehyton@aol.com

HUZZEY, Peter George. b 48. Trin Coll Bris 74. **d** 76 **p** 77. C Bishopsworth *Bris* 76-79; V 86-96; C Downend 79-80; TV Kings Norton *Birm* 80-86; TR Bishopsworth and Bedminster Down *Bris* 97-00; RD Bedminster 98-99; TR Kingswood from 00. *Holy Trinity Vicarage, High Street, Kingswood, Bristol BS15 4AD* Tel 0117-967 3627 Fax as telephone E-mail huzzeypeter@hotmail.com

HYATT, Robert Keith. b 34. Em Coll Cam BA59 MA63. Ridley Hall Cam 58. **d** 60 **p** 61. C Cheltenham St Mary *Glouc* 60-63; Asst Chapl K Edw Sch Witley 63-65; C Godalming *Guildf* 65-69; Hong Kong 69-78; V Claygate *Guildf* 78-91; TV Whitton *Sarum* 91-96 and 99-00; TR 96-99; rtd 00; Perm to Offic *B & W* from 00 and *Bris* from 02; May Moore Chapl Malmesbury *Bris* 02-05; Chapl Kennet and N Wilts Primary Care Trust 02-05. *19 Dark Lane, Malmesbury SN16 0BB* Tel (01666) 829026 *or* 826666 E-mail bobnhelen@onetel.com

HYDE, Dennis Hugh. b 23. Leeds Univ BA56. Sarum Th Coll 60. **d** 60 **p** 61. C Farncombe *Guildf* 60-62; C Burgh Heath 62-65; V Shottermill 65-74; Past Consultant Clinical Th Assn 74-80; rtd 88. *32 Amis Avenue, New Haw, Addlestone KT15 3ET* Tel (01932) 345526

HYDE, Edgar Bonsor. b 29. Clifton Th Coll 59. **d** 61 **p** 62. C Weston-super-Mare Ch Ch *B & W* 61-66; C Chipping Campden *Glouc* 66-70; R Longborough w Condicote and Sezincote 70-78; R Longborough, Sezincote, Condicote and the Swells 78-99; rtd 99; Perm to Offic *Glouc* from 99. *1 Turnpike Close, Primrose Court, Moreton-in-Marsh GL56 0JJ* Tel (01608) 652456

HYDE, Jeremy Richard Granville. b 52. Sch of Pharmacy Lon BPharm75 PhD80. St Alb and Ox Min Course 01. **d** 04 **p** 05. NSM Furze Platt *Ox* from 04. *South Riding, Shoppenhangers Road, Maidenhead SL6 2PZ* Tel (01628) 621651 E-mail jeremyrhyde@aol.com

HYDE-DUNN, Keith Frederick. b 43. Sarum Th Coll. **d** 69 **p** 70. Rhodesia 69-72; C Horsham *Chich* 73-77; P-in-c Fittleworth 77-86; P-in-c Graffham w Woolavington 86-00; Perm to Offic from 01; rtd 04. *The Hermitage, Church Place, Pulborough RH20 1AF* Tel (01798) 873892

HYDER, Geoffrey Frank. b 28. St Jo Coll Dur 49. **d** 53 **p** 54. C Kingston upon Hull H Trin *York* 53-56; C Southend St Sav Westcliff *Chelmsf* 56-59; V Haggerston All SS *Lon* 59-65; V Southwick St Pet *Chich* 65-68; Regional Org (Gtr Lon) Chr Aid 68-74; R Keston *Roch* 74-83; R Speldhurst w Groombridge and Ashurst 83-93; RD Tunbridge Wells 86-91; rtd 93; Perm to Offic *Chich* and *Roch* from 93. *60 The Bourne, Hastings TN34 3AY* Tel (01424) 715350

HYDER-SMITH, Brian John. b 45. FInstAM MCMI MBIM. EAMTC 84. **d** 87 **p** 88. NSM Huntingdon *Ely* 87-90; P-in-c Abbots Ripton w Wood Walton 90-98; P-in-c Kings Ripton 90-98; C Whittlesey, Pondersbridge and Coates 98-99; TV 99-04; rtd 04. *La Cachette, Le Val Pien, Le Bosc Renoult, 61470 Le Sap, France* Tel (0033) (2) 33 12 57 51 E-mail cachette2@wanadoo.fr

HYDON, Ms Veronica Weldon. b 52. N Lon Poly BA73 Maria Grey Coll Lon CertEd74. Aston Tr Scheme 87 Westcott Ho Cam 89. **d** 91 **p** 94. Par Dn Poplar *Lon* 91-94; C 94-95; P-in-c Roxwell *Chelmsf* 95-00; Lay Development Officer 95-00; V Forest Gate Em w Upton Cross 00-03; Assoc V Timperley *Ches* from 03. *The Vicarage, 97 Park Road, Timperley, Altrincham WA15 6QG* Tel 0161-962 3017 E-mail vhydon@hotmail.com

HYETT, Dawn Barbara. b 53. Cyncoed Coll CertEd74 Open Univ BA79. WEMTC 99. **d** 02 **p** 03. NSM Bromyard *Heref* from 02. *Roberts Hill, Norton, Bromyard HR7 4PB* Tel (01885) 483747

HYETT, Derek Walter. b 79. Coll of Resurr Mirfield. **d** 05. C Edmonton St Alphege *Lon* from 05; C Ponders End St Matt from 05. *Flat 3, 84 South Street, Enfield EN3 4BF* Tel (020) 8805 1674

HYLAND, Cecil George. b 38. TCD BA62 MA78. CITC Div Test. **d** 63 **p** 64. C Belfast St Nic *Conn* 63-66; C Monkstown *D & G* 66-68; Ch of Ireland Youth Officer 68-73; Chapl TCD 73-79; I Tullow *D & G* 79-90; I Howth 90-05; Dir of Ords (Dub) 91-98; Can Ch Ch Cathl Dublin 91-05; Cen Dir of Ords 98-05; rtd 05. *34 The Vale, Skerries Road, Skerries, Co Dublin, Irish Republic* Tel (00353) (1) 810 6884 Mobile 86-838 5317 E-mail cecilhyland@hotmail.com

HYNDMAN, David Jonathan. b 65. Man Univ BA95. Wycliffe Hall Ox MTh95. **d** 97 **p** 98. C Cockermouth w Embleton and Wythop *Carl* 97-00; TV Congleton *Ches* 00-05; C Hartford from 05. *52 Stones Manor Lane, Hartford, Northwich CW8 1NU* Tel (01606) 77740 E-mail dhyndman@bun.com

HYSLOP, Mrs Catherine Graham Young. b 53. St Andr Univ CPSS75. Carl Dioc Tr Inst 90. **d** 92 **p** 94. NSM St Bees *Carl* 92-95; NSM Upperby St Jo 95-98; C 98-03; C S Carl TM from 03. *St John's Vicarage, Manor Road, Upperby, Carlisle CA2 4LH* Tel (01228) 523380 E-mail jim.hyslop@talk21.com

HYSLOP, Thomas James (Jim). b 54. St Andr Univ BD76. Edin Th Coll 76. **d** 78 **p** 79. C Whitehaven *Carl* 78-81; C Walney Is 81-83; P-in-c Gt Broughton and Broughton Moor 83-85; V 85-88; V Kells 88-95; P-in-c Upperby St Jo 95-97; V 97-03; TR S Carl TM from 03. *St John's Vicarage, Manor Road, Upperby, Carlisle CA2 4LH* Tel (01228) 523380 E-mail jim.hyslop@talk21.com

HYSON, Peter Raymond. b 51. Open Univ BA80 BA87. Oak Hill Th Coll 85. **d** 87 **p** 88. C Billericay and Lt Burstead *Chelmsf* 87-92; TV Whitton *Sarum* 92-99. *Address temp unknown*

I

I'ANSON, Frederic Mark. b 43. R Agric Coll Cirencester MRAC68. Carl Dioc Tr Inst 89. **d** 92 **p** 93. NSM Sedbergh, Cautley and Garsdale *Bradf* 92-98; P-in-c Kirkby-in-Malhamdale w Coniston Cold from 98. *The Vicarage, Kirkby Malham, Skipton BD23 4BS* Tel (01729) 830215 E-mail mark@mmia.demon.co.uk

IBADAN SOUTH, Bishop of. *See* AJETUNMOBI, The Rt Revd Jacob Ademola

IBALL, Charles Martin John. b 40. Lich Th Coll 67. **d** 69 **p** 70. C Dudley St Edm *Worc* 69-73; C W Bromwich St Jas *Lich* 73-76; V Oxley 76-80; Hon C Whittington w Weeford from 86; Hon C Clifton Campville w Edingale and Harlaston from 96; rtd 04. *75 Carlcroft, Stoneydelph, Tamworth B77 4DW* Tel (01827) 896644

IBBOTSON, Miss Tracy Alexandra. b 63. Cranmer Hall Dur 01. **d** 03 **p** 04. C Todmorden *Wakef* from 03. *12 Phoenix Court, Todmorden OL14 5SJ* Tel (01706) 816716

IDDON, Roy Edward. b 40. TCert61 Lanc Univ MA88. N Ord Course 83. **d** 83 **p** 84. Hd Teacher St Andr Primary Sch Blackb from 83; NSM Bolton St Matt w St Barn *Man* 83-88; Lic to AD Walmsley 88-93; NSM Walmsley 93-01; NSM Turton Moorland Min 01-04; NSM Bolton St Phil from 04. *28 New Briggs Fold, Egerton, Bolton BL7 9UL* Tel (01204) 306589

IDLE, Christopher Martin. b 38. St Pet Coll Ox BA62. Clifton Th Coll 62. **d** 65 **p** 66. C Barrow St Mark *Carl* 65-68; C Camberwell Ch Ch *S'wark* 68-71; P-in-c Poplar St Matthias *Lon* 71-76; R Limehouse 76-89; R N Hartismere *St E* 89-95; Perm to Offic *S'wark* 95-03 and *St E* 01-03; rtd 03; Perm to Offic *Roch* from 04. *16 Cottage Avenue, Bromley BR2 8LQ* Tel and fax (020) 8462 1749

IEVINS, Mrs Catherine Ruth. b 54. LMH Ox BA77 MA80 Solicitor 81. EAMTC 98. **d** 01 **p** 02. C Pet Ch Carpenter *Pet* from 01. *32 Ledbury Road, Peterborough PE3 9RH* Tel (01733) 269029

IEVINS, Peter Valdis. b 54. St Jo Coll Ox BA75 MA81 Solicitor 79. Westcott Ho Cam 86. **d** 88 **p** 89. C Sawston *Ely* 88-91; C Babraham 88-91; NSM Pet Ch Carpenter *Pet* from 01. *32 Ledbury Road, Peterborough PE3 9RH* Tel (01733) 269029

IGENOZA, Andrew Olu. b 50. Ife Univ Nigeria BA75 Man Univ PhD82. Immanuel Coll Ibadan 87. **d** 88 **p** 89. Nigeria 88-99; C Gorton St Phil *Man* 00-01. *17 Northmoor Road, Longsight, Manchester M12 4NF* Tel 0161-248 8758

IGWE, Oliver Chimezie. b 72. St Paul's Univ Coll Awka Nigeria BA90 St Jo Coll Dur MA01. **d** 96 **p** 97. Nigeria 96-02; Perm to Offic *Birm* from 03. *194 Hanover Road, Rowley Regis, Warley B65 9EQ* Tel 0121-559 1251 E-mail ekele21@yahoo.co.uk

IKIN, Gordon Mitchell. b 30. AKC57. **d** 58 **p** 59. C Leigh St Mary *Man* 58-61; V Westleigh St Paul 61-72; V Thornham St Jas 72-95; rtd 95; Perm to Offic *Man* from 95. *5 The Quadrangle, Newland, Malvern WR13 5AX* Tel (01684) 564948

ILES, Canon Paul Robert. b 37. FRCO65 Fitzw Coll Cam BA59 MA64 St Edm Hall Ox MA80. Sarum Th Coll 59. **d** 61 **p** 62. Chapl Bp Wordsworth Sch Salisbury 61-67; C Salisbury St Mich *Sarum* 61-64; Min Can Sarum Cathl 64-67; C Bournemouth St Pet *Win* 67-72; R Filton *Bris* 72-79; V Ox SS Phil and Jas w St Marg *Ox* 79-83; Can Res and Prec Heref Cathl *Heref* 83-03; rtd 03; Hon C Prestbury and All SS *Glouc* from 03. *24 Willowherb Close, Prestbury, Cheltenham GL52 5LP* Tel (01242) 579456

ILLING, Eric James. b 33. Kelham Th Coll 54 Chich Th Coll 55. **d** 57 **p** 58. C Leeds St Aid *Ripon* 57-60; C Leeds All SS 60-62; C E Grinstead St Swithun *Chich* 62-65; V Middleton St Mary *Ripon* 65-74; R Felpham w Middleton *Chich* 74-81; Chapl R Devon and Ex Hosp (Wonford) 81-91; TR Heavitree w Ex St Paul *Ex* 81-91; R Bradninch and Clyst Hydon 91-94; rtd 94; Perm to Offic *B & W* from 94 and *Eur* from 98. *25 Pikes Crescent, Taunton TA1 4HS* Tel (01823) 289203

ILLINGWORTH, John Patrick Paul. b 34. New Coll Ox BA59 MA63. Chich Th Coll 61. **d** 63 **p** 64. C Brighouse *Wakef* 63-66; C Willesden St Andr *Lon* 66-70; Chapl Gothenburg w Halmstad and Jönköping *Eur* 70-74; Perm to Offic *Chich* 74; V Ryhill *Wakef* 74-82; R Weston Longville w Morton and the Witchinghams *Nor* 82-04; P-in-c Alderford w Attlebridge and Swannington 94-04; RD Sparham 95-00; rtd 04; Perm to Offic *Nor* from 04. *1 The Paddock, Top Common, East Runton, Cromer NR27 9PR* Tel (01263) 515710

ILORI, Emmanuel. b 57. **d** 04. NSM New Addington *S'wark* from 04. *58 Sundale Avenue, South Croydon CR2 8RP* Tel 07734-929501 (mobile)

ILOTT, Philip Edwin. b 36. Roch Th Coll 66. **d** 68 **p** 69. C Leavesden All SS *St Alb* 68-71; C-in-c Godshill CD *Portsm* 71-77; V Mayfield *Chich* 77-81; V Bexhill St Barn 81-84; rtd 84; Perm to Offic *Chich* 85-97. *Durlock, 15 Shining Cliff, Hastings TN34 2GT*

ILSLEY (née ROGERS), Mrs Anne Frances. b 50. Guy's Hosp Medical Sch RGN72 Poly Cen Lon HDipHV78 Heythrop Coll Lon BA00. Wycliffe Hall Ox 00. **d** 02 **p** 03. NSM Harefield *Lon* from 02. *36 Kewferry Road, Northwood HA6 2PB* Tel (01923) 840871 Mobile 07956-374624 E-mail annefi36@aol.com

ILSON, John Robert. b 37. Leeds Univ BSc59 Lon Univ BD64 CertEd65. ALCD63. **d** 64 **p** 65. C Kennington St Mark *S'wark* 64-67; C Sydenham H Trin 67-70; Asst Dir RE *Sheff* 70-77; R Hooton Roberts 70-75; R Hooton Roberts w Ravenfield 75-77; P-in-c Kidderminster St Geo *Worc* 77-81; TR 81-85; P-in-c Powick 85-96; Chapl N Devon Healthcare NHS Trust 97-04. *88 Chanters Hill, Barnstaple EX32 8DG* Tel (01271) 379163 *or* 322577

ILTON, Mrs Jennifer Jane. b 38. S Dios Minl Tr Scheme 92. **d** 95 **p** 96. NSM Jersey St Sav *Win* from 95. *38 Maison St Louis, St Saviour, Jersey JE2 7LX* Tel (01534) 722327

ILYAS, Marilyn. b 51. Oak Hill Th Coll 92. **d** 95 **p** 96. C Roch 95-98; TV S Chatham H Trin 98-01; TR from 01. *26 Mayford Road, Chatham ME5 8SZ* Tel (01634) 660922 E-mail milyas@btinternet.com

IMPEY, Miss Joan Mary. b 35. Lon Univ CertRK69. Dalton Ho Bris 65. **dss** 74 **d** 87 **p** 94. Kennington St Mark *S'wark* 67-75; Barking St Marg w St Patr *Chelmsf* 75-81; Harwell w Chilton *Ox* 81-87; Par Dn 87-92; Par Dn Didcot All SS 92-94; C 94-97; rtd 98; Perm to Offic *Ox* from 99. *15 Loder Road, Harwell, Didcot OX11 0HR* Tel (01235) 820346

IMPEY, Canon Patricia Irene. b 45. Birm Univ BA67 Lanc Univ MPhil01. Carl Dioc Tr Course 88. **d** 90 **p** 94. Par Dn Blackpool St Paul *Blackb* 90-94; C 94-95; Chapl Asst Victoria Hosp Blackpool 94-95; Asst Chapl Norfolk and Nor Hosp 95-96; Hon C Sprowston w Beeston *Nor* 96; R King's Beck 96-02; V Ecclesfield *Sheff* from 02; Hon Can Sheff Cathl from 04. *The Vicarage, 230 The Wheel, Ecclesfield, Sheffield S35 9ZB* Tel 0114-257 0002

IMPEY, Richard. b 41. Em Coll Cam BA63 MA67 Harvard Univ ThM67. Ridley Hall Cam 67. **d** 68 **p** 69. C Birm St Martin *Birm* 68-72; Dir of Tr *B & W* 72-79; Dir of Ords 76-79; V Blackpool St Jo *Blackb* 79-95; RD Blackpool 84-90; Hon Can Blackb Cathl 89-95; Dioc Dir of Tr *Nor* 95-00; P-in-c Heigham St Barn w St Bart 00-02; V Wentworth *Sheff* from 02; Bp's Adv in Par Development from 04. *The Vicarage, 230 The Wheel, Ecclesfield, Sheffield S35 9ZB* Tel 0114-257 0002

INALL, Mrs Elizabeth Freda. b 47. MCSP69. St Alb Minl Tr Scheme 88. **d** 92 **p** 94. NSM Tring *St Alb* 92-01; C Harpenden St Nic from 01. *10 Cross Way, Harpenden AL5 4RA* Tel (01582) 713007 E-mail elizabeth.inall@ukf.net

INCE, Peter Reginald. b 26. Bp's Coll Calcutta 48. **d** 51 **p** 52. India 51-55; C Leek St Luke *Lich* 55-57; C Milton 57-59; C Lewisham St Jo Southend *S'wark* 59-62; R Loddington w Cransley *Pet* 62-75; V Snibston *Leic* 75-79; R Mickleham *Guildf* 79-92; rtd 92;

Perm to Offic *Guildf* from 92. *Bickerton, 8 Rockdale, Headley Road, Grayshott, Hindhead GU26 6TU* Tel (01428) 604694

IND, Dominic Mark. b 63. Lanc Univ BA87. Ridley Hall Cam 87. **d** 90 **p** 91. C Birch w Fallowfield *Man* 90-93; SSF 93-95; Perm to Offic *Glas* 95-96; C Byker St Martin *Newc* 96-98; C Walker 96-98; P-in-c Cambuslang *Glas* from 98; P-in-c Uddingston from 98. *The Rectory, 5 Brownside Road, Cambuslang, Glasgow G72 8NL* Tel 0141-641 1173 E-mail dom@alba9.fsnet.co.uk

IND, Philip William David. b 35. K Coll Lon BD82. Wycliffe Hall Ox 74 Cranmer Hall Dur 59. **d** 65 **p** 66. C Ipswich St Jo *St E* 65-67; C Charlton Kings St Mary *Glouc* 67-71; R Woolstone w Gotherington and Oxenton 71-74; Chapl Alleyn's Sch Dulwich 76-81; C Beckenham St Geo *Roch* 83-85; V Bromley St Jo 85-87; Perm to Offic *Ox* 88-91 and from 95; P-in-c Hurley 91-92; P-in-c Stubbings 91-92; rtd 92. *Stilegate, Tugwood Common, Cookham, Maidenhead SL6 9TT* Tel (01628) 477425 E-mail mtpipind@aol.com

✠**IND, The Rt Revd William.** b 42. Leeds Univ BA64. Coll of Resurr Mirfield 64. **d** 66 **p** 67 **c** 87. C Feltham *Lon* 66-71; C Northolt St Mary 71-73; TV Basingstoke *Win* 73-87; Vice-Prin Aston Tr Scheme 79-82; Dioc Dir of Ords *Win* 82-87; Hon Can Win Cathl 84-87; Suff Bp Grantham *Linc* 87-97; Dean Stamford 87-97; Can and Preb Linc Cathl 87-97; Bp Truro from 97. *Lis Escop, Feock, Truro TR3 6QQ* Tel (01872) 862657 Fax 862037 E-mail bishop@truro.anglican.org

INDER, Patrick John. b 30. K Coll Lon BD54 AKC54 Huddersfield Univ MA98. St Boniface Warminster. **d** 55 **p** 56. C St Margaret's-on-Thames *Lon* 55-57; C Golders Green 57-61; V Hanwell St Mellitus 61-77; R Rawmarsh w Parkgate *Sheff* 77-80; rtd 80; Hon C Sheff St Matt *Sheff* 82-88; Perm to Offic *Wakef* from 98 and *Win* from 02. *Roucoulement, rue de la Brigade, St Andrews, Guernsey GY6 8RQ* Tel (01481) 234343 E-mail roucoulement@cwgsy.net

INDIAN OCEAN, Archbishop of the Province of the. *See* RABENIRINA, The Most Revd Remi Joseph

INESON, David Antony. b 36. DPS. ALCD62. **d** 62 **p** 63. C Sandal St Helen *Wakef* 62-65; C Birm St Geo *Birm* 66-71; V Horton *Bradf* 71-80; RD Bowling and Horton 78-80; V Sedbergh, Cautley and Garsdale 80-86; C Firbank, Howgill and Killington 81-86; TV Langley and Parkfield *Man* 86-88; TR Banbury *Ox* 92-98; R 98-01; rtd 01; Perm to Offic *Ripon* from 01. *11 Church Close, Redmire, Leyburn DL8 4HF* Tel (01969) 624631 E-mail hdi@redmire.fslife.co.uk

INESON, Emma Gwynneth. b 69. Birm Univ BA92 MPhil93 PhD98. Trin Coll Bris BA99. **d** 00 **p** 01. C Dore *Sheff* 00-03; Chapl Lee Abbey from 03. *Lee Abbey Fellowship, Lee Abbey, Lynton EX35 6JJ* Tel (01598) 752621 E-mail revsineson@aol.com

INESON, Mathew David. b 69. Birm Univ BEng91. Trin Coll Bris BA99 MA00. **d** 00 **p** 01. NSM Dore *Sheff* 00-03; Chapl Lee Abbey from 03. *Lee Abbey Fellowship, Lee Abbey, Lynton EX35 6JJ* Tel (01598) 752621 E-mail revsineson@aol.com

INESON, Matthew. b 68. Leeds Univ BA00. Coll of Resurr Mirfield 97. **d** 00 **p** 01. C Owton Manor *Dur* 00-03; V Dalton *Sheff* from 03. *The Vicarage, 2 Vicarage Close, Dalton, Rotherham S65 3QL* Tel (01709) 850377 Mobile 07780-686310 E-mail frmatt_@excite.com

INGAMELLS, Ronald Sidney. b 32. FCIPD92. AKC56. **d** 57 **p** 58. C Leeds Gipton Epiphany *Ripon* 57-59; C Gt Yarmouth *Nor* 59-64; Dioc Youth Officer 64-79; Hon C Nor St Pet Mancroft 64-79; P-in-c Lemsford *St Alb* 79-02; Sec Tr Development and Chr Educn Nat Coun YMCAs 79-92; Consultant to Romania Euro Alliance YMCAs 93-97; rtd 02; Perm to Offic *Ely* from 03. *2 Aragon Close, Buckden, St Neots PE19 5TY* Tel (01480) 811608 E-mail ingamells@fish.co.uk

✠**INGE, The Rt Revd John Geoffrey.** b 55. St Chad's Coll Dur BSc77 MA94 PhD02 Keble Coll Ox PGCE79. Coll of Resurr Mirfield. **d** 84 **p** 85 **c** 03. Asst Chapl Lancing Coll 84-86; Jun Chapl Harrow Sch 86-89; Sen Chapl 89-90; V Wallsend St Luke *Newc* 90-96; Can Res Ely Cathl *Ely* 96-03; Vice-Dean 99-03; Suff Bp Huntingdon from 03. *14 Lynn Road, Ely CB6 1DA* Tel (01353) 662137 Fax 669357 E-mail suffragan@ely.anglican.org

INGHAM, Anthony William. b 55. Ven English Coll Rome PhB75 STB78 N Ord Course 98. **d** 78 **p** 79. In RC Ch 78-98; NSM Tottington *Man* 99-01; CF from 01. *c/o MOD Chaplains (Army)* Tel (01980) 615804 Fax 615800

INGHAM, Miss Dawn. b 48. **d** 04 **p** 05. C Brownhill *Wakef* from 04. *8A Amber Street, Batley WF17 8HH* Tel (01924) 472576

INGHAM, John Edmund. b 34. Reading Univ BA56. Clifton Th Coll 58. **d** 60 **p** 61. C Rodbourne Cheney *Bris* 60-63; C Tunbridge Wells St Jo *Roch* 63-67; V Sevenoaks Weald 67-82; V Farrington Gurney *B & W* 82-92; V Paulton 82-92; RD Midsomer Norton 88-91; R Aspley Guise w Husborne Crawley and Ridgmont *St Alb* 92-99; rtd 99; Perm to Offic *B & W* from 00. *10 Milton Lane, Wookey Hole, Wells BA5 1DG* Tel (01749) 677529

INGHAM, Malcolm John. b 68. Wycliffe Hall Ox BTh99. **d** 99 **p** 00. C Moreton-in-Marsh w Batsford, Todenham etc *Glouc* 99-03; C Leckhampton SS Phil and Jas w Cheltenham St Jas 03-04; TV The Ortons, Alwalton and Chesterton *Ely* from 04. *St Andrew's Rectory, 4 Alwalton Hall, Alwalton, Peterborough PE7 3UN* Tel (01733) 239289 E-mail rev@malcolm-ingham.fsnet.co.uk

INGHAM, Mrs Carol Helen. *See* PHARAOH, Carol Helen

INGHAM, Mrs Pamela. b 47. MBE96. NEOC 93. **d** 96 **p** 97. C Newc Epiphany *Newc* 96-99; C Fawdon 99-00; P-in-c from 00. *St Mary's Vicarage, 7 Fawdon Lane, Newcastle upon Tyne NE3 2RR* Tel 0191-285 5403 E-mail pimbe@aol.com

INGLE-GILLIS, William Clarke. b 68. Baylor Univ (USA) BA90 MA95 K Coll Lon PhD04. Westcott Ho Cam 02. **d** 04 **p** 05. C Caldicot *Mon* from 04. *30 Westway, Rogiet, Caldicot NP26 3SP* Tel and fax (01291) 424362 E-mail fr.will@clara.co.uk

INGLEBY, Canon Anthony Richard. b 48. Keele Univ BA72. Trin Coll Bris. **d** 83 **p** 84. C Plymouth St Jude *Ex* 83-88; R Lanreath *Truro* 88-97; V Pelynt 88-97; RD W Wivelshire 96-97; P-in-c Stoke Climsland from 97; P-in-c Linkinhorne from 03; P-in-c Liskeard and St Keyne from 05; Hon Can Truro Cathl from 04. *The Rectory, Church Street, Liskeard PL14 3AQ* Tel (01579) 342178 E-mail tony@ingleby100.freeserve.co.uk

INGLEDEW, Peter David Gordon. b 48. AKC77 Jo Dalton Coll Man CertEd73 Croydon Coll DASS92 CQSW92 Univ Coll Chich BA03. St Steph Ho Ox 77. **d** 78 **p** 79. C Whorlton *Newc* 78-81; C Poplar *Lon* 81-83; TV 83-85; V Tottenham H Trin 85-90; Perm to Offic *Chich* from 90. *11 St Luke's Terrace, Brighton BN2 2ZE* Tel (01273) 689765 Fax 389115

INGLESBY, Eric Vredenburg (Paul). b 15. Qu Coll Ox BA46 MA63. Wycliffe Hall Ox 63. **d** 64 **p** 64. C Plymouth Crownhill Ascension *Ex* 64-66; R Caythorpe *Linc* 66-70; C Scilly Is *Truro* 70-73; C Plymouth St Andr w St Paul and St Geo *Ex* 73-76; rtd 76. *43 Palmers Road, Glastonbury BA6 9PB* Tel (01458) 833591

INGLESBY, Richard Eric. b 47. Birm Univ BSc69 Bris Univ CertEd74. Wycliffe Hall Ox 85. **d** 87 **p** 88. C Cheltenham Ch Ch *Glouc* 87-92; P-in-c Paulton *B & W* 92-94; V 94-01; P-in-c Farrington Gurney 92-94; V 94-01; P-in-c Moxley *Lich* from 01; C Darlaston All SS from 01; C Darlaston St Lawr from 01; Ecum Adv (Wolverhampton Area) from 04; RD Wednesbury from 05. *The Vicarage, 5 Sutton Road, Moxley, Wednesbury WS10 8SG* Tel and fax (01902) 653084

INGLIS, Kelvin John. b 62. Ripon Coll Cuddesdon MTh00. **d** 00 **p** 01. C Southampton Maybush St Pet *Win* 00-04; V Whitchurch w Tufton and Litchfield from 04. *The Vicarage, Church Street, Whitchurch RG28 7AS* Tel (01256) 892535

INGRAM, Canon Bernard Richard. b 40. Lon Coll of Div 66. **d** 66 **p** 67. C Bromley Common St Aug *Roch* 66-70; C Gravesend St Geo 70-74; Chapl Joyce Green Hosp Dartford 75-83; V Dartford St Edm *Roch* 75-83; V Strood St Fran 83-04; RD Strood 91-97; Hon Can Roch Cathl from 00; rtd 04. *1 Hillview Cottage, Upper Colwall, Malvern WR13 6DH* Tel and fax (01684) 540475 E-mail st.francisstrood@cableinet.co.uk

INGRAM, Miss Emmeline Jessica Anne. b 26. Gilmore Ho 53. **dss** 54 **d** 87. Ind Chapl *Chelmsf* 68-82; rtd 86; Leigh-on-Sea St Jas *Chelmsf* 86-87; Hon Par Dn from 87. *73 Bohemia Chase, Leigh-on-Sea SS9 4PW* Tel (01702) 520276

INGRAM, Gary Simon. b 58. K Coll Lon BD AKC. Ripon Coll Cuddesdon. **d** 83 **p** 84. Chapl Nelson and Colne Coll 92-98; C Spalding *Linc* 83-87; C Heaton Ch Ch *Man* 87-89; V Colne H Trin *Blackb* 89-98; RD Pendle 96-98; R Poulton-le-Sands w Morecambe St Laur from 98; AD Lancaster 98-04. *The Rectory, Church Walk, Morecambe LA4 5PR* Tel and fax (01524) 410941 E-mail garyingram@care4free.net

INGRAM, Michael. b 28. St Jo Coll Dur 49. **d** 53 **p** 54. C Southend St Sav Westcliff *Chelmsf* 53-56; C Stoke Damerel *Ex* 56-60; Chapl RAF 60-76; P-in-c St Enoder *Truro* 76-79; rtd 90. *2 Cedar Drive, Shanklin PO37 7ED* Tel (01983) 868925

INGRAM, Canon Peter Anthony. b 53. N Ord Course 83. **d** 86 **p** 87. C Maltby *Sheff* 86-89; TV Gt Snaith 89-92; R Adwick-le-Street w Skelbrooke from 92; AD Adwick 01-05; V Millhouses H Trin from 05; Hon Can Sheff Cathl from 05. *The Vicarage, Millhouses Lane, Sheffield S7 2HB* Tel 0114-236 2838 E-mail revingram@lineone.net

INGRAMS, Peter Douglas. b 56. Wheaton Coll Illinois BA77 Ox Univ BA80. Wycliffe Hall Ox 78. **d** 83 **p** 84. C Rowner *Portsm* 83-86; C Petersfield w Sheet 86-90; V Sheet 90-96; V Locks Heath from 96. *The Vicarage, 125 Locks Heath Park Road, Locks Heath SO31 6LY* Tel (01489) 572497

INKPEN, Richard John. b 28. AKC56. **d** 58 **p** 59. C Willesden St Mary *Lon* 58-61; C Hendon St Mary 61-66; C-in-c S Kenton Annunciation CD 66-69; Chapl Montreux w Gstaad *Eur* 69-70; V Blackmoor *Portsm* 70-93; RD Petersfield 80-85; rtd 94; Perm to Offic *Ex* from 94. *69 St Luke's Road, Newton Abbot TQ12 4ND* Tel (01626) 204231

INKPIN, David Leonard. b 32. Liv Univ BSc54 CChem MRSC55. EMMTC 83. **d** 86 **p** 87. NSM Legsby, Linwood and Market Rasen *Linc* 86-04; Perm to Offic from 04. *Weelsby House, Legsby Road, Market Rasen LN8 3DY* Tel (01673) 843360 E-mail inkypens@yahoo.co.uk

INKPIN, Jonathan David Francis. b 60. Mert Coll Ox MA81 Dur Univ PhD96. Ripon Coll Cuddesdon BA85. **d** 86 **p** 87. C Hackney *Lon* 86-88; Tutor Ripon Coll Cuddesdon 88-90; C Cuddesdon *Ox* 88-90; TV Gateshead *Dur* 90-95; C Stanhope w Frosterley 95-01; C Eastgate w Rookhope 95-01; Dioc Rural Development Officer 95-01; Australia from 01. *78 Henry Parry Drive, PO Box 4255, Gosford East, NSW, Australia 2250* Tel (0061) (2) 4324 2630

INMAN, Malcolm Gordon. b 33. Edin Th Coll 58. **d** 60 **p** 61. C Lundwood *Wakef* 60-63; C Heckmondwike 63-70; V Wrenthorpe 70-75; Chapl Cardigan Hosp 70-73; Asst Chapl Pinderfields Gen Hosp Wakef 72-73; V Cleckheaton St Jo *Wakef* 75-98; rtd 98; Perm to Offic *Wakef* from 98. *14 Briestfield Road, Thornhill Edge, Dewsbury WF12 0PW* Tel (01924) 437171

INMAN, Mark Henry. b 31. Lon Univ BSc53. EAMTC 80. **d** 83 **p** 84. Hon C Orford w Sudbourne, Chillesford, Butley and Iken *St E* 83-85; Chapl HM YOI Hollesley Bay Colony 85-91; Hon C Alderton w Ramsholt and Bawdsey *St E* 85-92; P-in-c 92-00; P-in-c Shottisham w Sutton 92-00; TV Wilford Peninsula 00-01; rtd 01; Perm to Offic *Nor* from 01. *Mill Farm House, Newton Road, Sporle, King's Lynn PE32 2DB* Tel (01760) 722544

INMAN, Martin. b 50. K Coll Lon BD72 AKC73. St Aug Coll Cant 72. **d** 73 **p** 74. C Bridgnorth St Mary *Heref* 73-77; C Parkstone St Pet w Branksea and St Osmund *Sarum* 77-79; V Willenhall St Anne *Lich* 79-85; Chapl Yeovil Distr Gen Hosp 85-91; TV Yeovil *B & W* 85-88; R Barwick 88-91; Chapl Jersey Gen Hosp 91-99; Chapl Whittington Hosp NHS Trust 99-03; TV Smestow Vale *Lich* from 03. *The Vicarage, School Road, Trysull, Wolverhampton WV5 7HR* Tel (01902) 324537

INMAN, Paul Stuart. b 60. Nottm Univ BTh90 Man Univ MA94. Linc Th Coll 87. **d** 90 **p** 91. C Hulme Ascension *Man* 90-94; CMS 94-98; Dioc Missr (Owerri) Nigeria 94-98; V in charge Cathl of Transfiguration 95-98; P-in-c Colkirk w Oxwick w Pattesley, Whissonsett etc *Nor* 98-05; R Upper Wensum Village Gp from 05. *The Rectory, Market Hill, Colkirk, Fakenham NR21 7NU* Tel (01328) 863890

INMAN, Canon Thomas Jeremy. b 45. Rhodes Univ BA67. St Steph Ho Ox 67. **d** 69 **p** 70. C Deptford St Paul *S'wark* 69-72; C Bellville S Africa 72-73; R Malmesbury 73-76; P-in-c Donnington *Chich* 76-80; V Hangleton 80-86; V Bosham from 86; RD Westbourne 91-99; Can and Preb Chich Cathl from 00. *The Vicarage, Bosham Lane, Bosham, Chichester PO18 8HX* Tel (01243) 573228 Mobile 07941-834914 E-mail tjinman45@aol.com

INNES, Donald John. b 32. St Jo Coll Ox BA54 MA. Westcott Ho Cam 56. **d** 56 **p** 57. C St Marylebone St Mark Hamilton Terrace *Lon* 56-58; C Walton-on-Thames *Guildf* 58-67; Chapl Moor Park Coll Farnham 67-76; P-in-c Tilford *Guildf* 76-97; rtd 97; Perm to Offic *Guildf* from 97. *Watchetts, 67A Upper Hale Road, Farnham GU9 0PA* Tel (01252) 734597

INNES, Donald Keith. b 33. St Jo Coll Ox BA56 MA60 Lon Univ BD58 Bris Univ MPhil01. Clifton Th Coll 56. **d** 58 **p** 59. C Harold Hill St Paul *Chelmsf* 58-61; C Ealing Dean St Jo *Lon* 61-65; V Westacre *Nor* 65-70; R Gayton Thorpe w E Walton 65-70; V Woking St Paul *Guildf* 70-78; R Alfold and Loxwood 78-88; V Doddington w Wychling *Cant* 88-90; V Newnham 88-90; V Doddington, Newnham and Wychling 90-97; rtd 97; Perm to Offic *Chich* from 98. *High Elms, Lewes Road, Ringmer, Lewes BN8 5NE* Tel (01273) 814995

INNES, James Michael. b 32. Lon Univ BA56 BD59. Clifton Th Coll 59. **d** 59 **p** 60. C Blackpool St Thos *Blackb* 59-62; Tutor Clifton Th Coll 62-65; V Burton All SS *Lich* 65-73; V Ashton-upon-Mersey St Mary *Ches* 73-90; P-in-c Brereton w Swettenham 90-91; R 91-97; Dioc Clergy Widows and Retirement Officer 93-97; rtd 97; Perm to Offic *Derby* from 97. *22 Sandown Avenue, Mickleover, Derby DE3 0QQ* Tel (01332) 516691 E-mail jminnes.9@tiscali.co.uk

INNES, Canon Robert Neil. b 59. K Coll Cam BA82 MA85 St Jo Coll Dur BA91 Dur Univ PhD95. Cranmer Hall Dur 89. **d** 95 **p** 96. C Dur St Cuth *Dur* 95-97; Lect St Jo Coll Dur 95-99; C Sherburn w Pittington *Dur* 97-99; C Shadforth 97-99; P-in-c Belmont 99-00; V 00-05; Sen Chapl and Chan Brussels Cathl *Eur* from 05. *Allée de l'Aqueduc 23, 1410 Waterloo, Belgium* Tel (0032) (2) 511 7183

INNES, Ms Ruth. b 56. New Coll Edin BD00. TISEC 97. **d** 00 **p** 01. Prec St Ninian's Cathl Perth *St And* 00-02; P-in-c Linlithgow *Edin* from 02; P-in-c Bathgate from 02. *The Rectory, 85 Acredales, Linlithgow EH49 6JA* Tel (01506) 842384 E-mail revruth.innes@virgin.net

INSLEY, Michael George Pitron. b 47. Trin Coll Ox BA69 MA70 Nottm Univ MPhil85. Wycliffe Hall Ox 69. **d** 72 **p** 73. C Beckenham Ch Ch *Roch* 72-76; P-in-c Cowden 76-79; Lect St Jo Coll Nottm 79-85; V Tidebrook and Wadhurst *Chich* 85-98; P-in-c Stonegate 95-98; Can and Preb Chich Cathl 94-98; P-in-c Horsmonden and Dioc Rural Officer *Roch* 98-03; V Bromley Common St Luke from 03. *St Luke's Vicarage, 20 Bromley Common, Bromley BR2 9PD* Tel (020) 8464 2076 E-mail michaelinsley@compuserve.com

INSTON, Brian John. b 47. St Alb and Ox Min Course 95. **d** 98 **p** 99. C Bentley *Sheff* 98-01; V Balby from 01. *St John's Vicarage, 6 Greenfield Lane, Doncaster DN4 0PT* Tel and fax (01302) 853278 Mobile 07990-513120

INVERNESS, Provost of. *See* GORDON, The Very Revd Alexander Ronald

✠**INWOOD, The Rt Revd Richard Neil.** b 46. Univ Coll Ox BSc70 MA73 Nottm Univ BA73. St Jo Coll Nottm 71. **d** 74 **p** 75 **c** 03. C Fulwood *Sheff* 74-78; C St Marylebone All So w SS Pet and Jo *Lon* 78-81; V Bath St Luke *B & W* 81-89; R Yeovil w Kingston Pitney 89-95; Preb Wells Cathl 90-95; Adn Halifax *Wakef* 95-03; Suff Bp Bedford *St Alb* from 03; Cen Chapl Mothers' Union from 05. *Bishop's Lodge, Bedford Road, Cardington, Bedford MK44 3SS* Tel (01234) 831432 Fax 831484 E-mail bishopbedford@stalbans.anglican.org

IPGRAVE, The Ven Michael Geoffrey. b 58. Oriel Coll Ox BA78 MA94 St Chad's Coll Dur PhD00 SOAS Lon MA04. Ripon Coll Cuddesdon BA81. **d** 82 **p** 83. C Oakham, Hambleton, Egleton, Braunston and Brooke *Pet* 82-85; Asst P Chiba Resurr Japan 85-87; TV Leic Ascension *Leic* 87-90; TV Leic H Spirit 91-95; TR 95-99; P-in-c Leic St Mary 93-94; Bp's Adv on Relns w People of Other Faiths 91-99; Bp's Dom Chapl 92-99; Hon Can Leic Cathl 94-04; Adv Inter-Faith Relns Abp's Coun 99-04; Sec Ch's Commission Inter-Faith Relns 99-04; Hon C Leic Presentation *Leic* 02-04; Adn S'wark from 04. *49 Colombo Street, London SE1 8DP* Tel (020) 7939 9409 *or* 7771 2858 E-mail michael.ipgrave@southwark.anglican.org

IPSWICH, Archdeacon of. *Vacant*

IQBAL, Javaid. b 71. St Jo Coll Nottm BA97. **d** 97 **p** 99. C Lahore St Thos Pakistan 97-99; P-in-c Lahore Ch Ch 99-00; Dir Miss and Evang Raiwind 98-99; Perm to Offic *Leic* 00-05; C Evington from 05. *14 Fallowfield Road, Leicester LE5 6LQ* Tel and fax 0116-241 2833 Mobile 07782-169987 E-mail javaidiqbal7@aol.com

IREDALE, Simon Peter. b 56. Cam Univ BA78 MPhil80. Wycliffe Hall Ox 83. **d** 86 **p** 87. C Thirsk *York* 86-89; Asst Chapl Norfolk and Nor Hosp 89-90; P-in-c Kexby w Wilberfoss *York* 90-93; Sub-Chapl HM Pris Full Sutton 90-93; Chapl RAF from 93. *Chaplaincy Services (RAF), HQ, Personnel and Training Command, RAF Innsworth, Gloucester GL3 1EZ* Tel (01452) 712612 ext 5164 Fax 510828

IRELAND, David Arthur. b 45. Mert Coll Ox BA67 MA71 MICFM87. Cuddesdon Coll 67. **d** 69 **p** 70. C Chapel Allerton *Ripon* 69-72; C Harpenden St Nic *St Alb* 72-76; R Clifton 76-84; Perm to Offic *Guildf* 91-00; NSM Leatherhead and Mickleham from 01. *The Rectory, Old London Road, Mickleham, Dorking RH5 6EB* Tel (01372) 378335 E-mail rev.ireland43@btinternet.com

IRELAND, Leslie Sydney. b 55. York Univ BA76. St Jo Coll Nottm 83. **d** 86 **p** 87. C Harwood *Man* 86-89; C Davyhulme St Mary 89-90; V Bardsley 90-99; R Levenshulme St Andr and St Pet from 99; P-in-c Levenshulme St Mark from 05; AD Heaton from 04. *The Rectory, 27 Errwood Road, Levenshulme, Manchester M19 2PN* Tel 0161-224 5877 E-mail lesireland@compuserve.com

IRELAND, Mrs Lucy Annabel. b 53. Univ of Zimbabwe BSc74. St Jo Coll Nottm DPS85. **dss** 85 **d** 87 **p** 95. Mansfield St Jo *S'well* 85-87; Hon Par Dn Harwood *Man* 87-89; NSM Bardsley 90-99; C Levenshulme St Andr and St Pet from 99. *The Rectory, 27 Errwood Road, Levenshulme, Manchester M19 2PN* Tel 0161-224 5877 E-mail lesireland@compuserve.com

IRELAND, Mark Campbell. b 60. St Andr Univ MTh81 Sheff Univ MA01. Wycliffe Hall Ox 82. **d** 84 **p** 85. C Blackb St Gabr *Blackb* 84-87; C Lancaster St Mary 87-89; Chapl HM Pris Lanc 87-89; V Baxenden *Blackb* 89-97; Team Ldr Miss Division *Lich* from 98; TV Walsall from 98. *14 Gorway Gardens, Walsall WS1 3BJ* Tel (01922) 626010 Fax 625924 E-mail mark.ireland@lichfield.anglican.org

IRELAND, Mrs Mary Janet. b 52. EMMTC 96. **d** 99 **p** 00. NSM Kibworth and Smeeton Westerby and Saddington *Leic* 99-02; C Lutterworth w Cotesbach and Bitteswell from 02. *The Vicarage, Lutterworth Road, Bitteswell, Lutterworth LE17 4RX* Tel (01455) 552443 E-mail mary_ireland@talk21.com

IRELAND, Mrs Sharran. b 49. SEITE 95. **d** 98 **p** 99. C Appledore w Brookland, Fairfield, Brenzett etc *Cant* 98-01; TV St Laur in Thanet 01-03; TR from 03. *The Rectory, 2 Newington Road, Ramsgate CT11 0QT* Tel (01843) 592478 E-mail sharran@fish.co.uk

IRESON, David Christopher. b 45. Man Univ TCert67 Birm Univ BEd80. St Steph Ho Ox DipTh93. **d** 93 **p** 94. C Minehead *B & W* 93-97; V St Decumans from 97. *St Decuman's Vicarage, 47A Brendon Road, Watchet TA23 0HU* Tel (01984) 631228 E-mail david.ireson@btinternet.com

IRESON, Ms Gillian Dorothy. b 39. Gilmore Ho 67. **dss** 72 **d** 87 **p** 94. Stepney St Dunstan and All SS *Lon* 72-99; Par Dn 87-94; C 94-99; rtd 99; Perm to Offic *Nor* from 00. *67 Glebe Road, Norwich NR2 3JH* Tel (01603) 451969

IRESON, Philip. b 52. Newc Univ BSc73. St Jo Coll Nottm. **d** 84 **p** 85. C Owlerton *Sheff* 84-87; V The Marshland 87-94; Perm to Offic *Linc* 90-93; Chapl HM YOI Hatfield 91-92; Bp's Rural Adv *Sheff* 91-00; R Firbeck w Letwell 94-01; V Woodsetts 94-01; Chapl HM Pris and YOI Doncaster from 01. *HM Prison Doncaster, Marshgate, Doncaster DN5 8UX* Tel (01302) 760870 Fax 760851 E-mail philip@iresonr.freeserve.co.uk

IRESON, Richard Henry. b 46. Linc Th Coll 69. **d** 71 **p** 72. C Spilsby w Hundleby *Linc* 71-74; TV Grantham w Manthorpe 74-76; R Claypole 76-79; P-in-c Westborough w Dry Doddington and Stubton 76-77; R 77-79; R Bratoft w Irby-in-the-Marsh 79-86; V Burgh le Marsh 79-86; V Orby 79-86; R Welton-le-Marsh w Gunby 79-86; R Wyberton 86-01; RD Holland W 95-97; V Frampton 97-01; V Alford w Rigsby from 01; R Well from 01; R Saleby w Beesby and Maltby from 01; V Bilsby w Farlesthorpe from 01; R Hannah cum Hagnaby w Markby from 01. *The Vicarage, 15 Bilsby Road, Alford LN13 9EW* Tel (01507) 462791

IRETON, Paul. b 65. Cranmer Hall Dur 99. **d** 01 **p** 02. C Southway *Ex* from 01. *5 Treago Gardens, Plymouth PL6 7EJ* Tel (01752) 511481 E-mail revpireton@eurobell.co.uk

IRETON, Robert John. b 56. Bris Univ BEd. Oak Hill Th Coll BA. **d** 84 **p** 85. C Bromley Ch Ch *Roch* 84-87; TV Greystoke, Matterdale, Mungrisdale etc *Carl* 87-90; V Falconwood *Roch* 90-97; V Stanwix *Carl* 97-04; P-in-c Erith St Jo *Roch* from 04; Chapl Trin Sch Belvedere from 04. *St John's Church House, 100 Park Crescent, Erith DA8 3DZ* Tel (01322) 332555

IRONS, Barry. b 39. Wilson Carlile Coll 57 Coll of Resurr Mirfield 82. **d** 83 **p** 84. CA from 57; C Willersey, Saintbury, Weston-sub-Edge etc *Glouc* 83-85; R Scalford w Goadby Marwood and Wycombe etc *Leic* 85-88; P-in-c Clun w Chapel Lawn, Bettws-y-Crwyn and Newcastle *Heref* 88-91; Bp's Officer for Evang 91-94; P-in-c Breinton 91-94; P-in-c Weston-super-Mare Cen Par *B & W* 94-95; R Weston super Mare St Jo 96-04; rtd 04. *18 Beach Court, Beach Road, Weston-super-Mare BS23 1BD* Tel (01934) 621958 Mobile 07785-270848

IRONS, Nigel Richard. b 55. Aston Univ BSc77. St Jo Coll Nottm MA95. **d** 97 **p** 98. C Newchapel *Lich* 97-00; V Burton All SS w Ch Ch from 00. *All Saints' Vicarage, 242 Blackpool Street, Burton-on-Trent DE14 3AU* Tel (01283) 565134 E-mail mail@nigelirons.co.uk

IRONSIDE, John Edmund. b 31. Peterho Cam BA55 MA59. Qu Coll Birm 55. **d** 57 **p** 58. C Spring Park *Cant* 57-60; C Guernsey St Sampson *Win* 60-63; Thailand 63-66; V Guernsey St Jo *Win* 66-72; V Sholing 72-82; R Guernsey St Sampson 82-98; Miss to Seamen 82-98; rtd 98; Perm to Offic *Win* from 98; Vice-Dean Guernsey 99. *Le Petit Creux, Les Landes, Vale, Guernsey GY3 5JQ* Tel (01481) 249209 Fax 242776

IRVINE, Mrs Andrea Mary. b 49. Sussex Univ BA70 Ox Univ PGCE71. NTMTC 99. **d** 02. NSM Cov H Trin *Cov* from 02. *The Deanery, 11 Priory Row, Coventry CV1 5EX* Tel (024) 7663 1448 *or* 7652 1200 E-mail amirvine@lineone.net

IRVINE, Barry. *See* IRVINE, William Barry

IRVINE, Mrs Catherine Frances. b 70. K Coll Lon BA97. Ripon Coll Cuddesdon 99. **d** 01 **p** 02. C Romsey *Win* 01-05; TV Richmond St Mary w St Matthias and St Jo *S'wark* from 05. *St Matthias's House, 22 Cambrian Road, Richmond TW10 6JQ* Tel and fax (020) 8948 7217 E-mail cateirvine@fish.co.uk

IRVINE, Christopher Paul. b 51. Nottm Univ BTh75 Lanc Univ MA76 St Martin's Coll Lanc PGCE77. Kelham Th Coll 73. **d** 76 **p** 76. Chapl Lanc Univ *Blackb* 76-77; C Stoke Newington St Mary *Lon* 77-80; Chapl Sheff Univ *Sheff* 80-85; Chapl St Edm Hall Ox 85-90; Tutor St Steph Ho Ox 85-90; Vice-Prin 91-94; V Cowley St Jo *Ox* 94-98; Prin Coll of Resurr Mirfield from 98. *College of the Resurrection, Stocks Bank Road, Mirfield WF14 0BW* Tel (01924) 481908 Fax 492738 E-mail cirvine@mirfield.org.uk

IRVINE, David John. b 50. Trin Coll Cam BA72 MA75. N Ord Course 91. **d** 94 **p** 95. C Hexham *Newc* 94-99; P-in-c Blanchland w Hunstanworth and Edmundbyers etc from 99; P-in-c Slaley from 99; P-in-c Healey from 03; P-in-c Whittonstall from 03. *The Vicarage, Slaley, Hexham NE47 0AA* Tel (01434) 673609

IRVINE, Donald Andrew. b 45. Trin Coll Bris DipHE94. **d** 96 **p** 97. C Allington and Maidstone St Pet *Cant* 96-99; P-in-c Harrietsham w Ulcombe 99-02; P-in-c Lenham w Boughton Malherbe 00-02; R Len Valley from 02. *The Rectory, Church Road, Harrietsham, Maidstone ME17 1AP* Tel and fax (01622) 859466 E-mail revirvine@aol.com

IRVINE, Gerard Philip. b 30. QUB BA52. Edin Th Coll 56. **d** 56 **p** 57. Chapl St Andr Cathl *Ab* 56-58; Prec St Andr Cathl 58-59; C Belfast Malone St Jo *Conn* 61-66; Chapl Community of St Jo Ev Dublin 67-77; C Dublin Sandymount *D & G* 77-97; rtd 97. *12A Carraig na Greine House, Coliemore Road, Dalkey, Co Dublin, Irish Republic* Tel (00353) (1) 230 1430

IRVINE, James Clyde. b 35. QUB BA57 NUU BPhil(Ed)83. CITC 59. **d** 59 **p** 60. C Belfast St Luke *Conn* 59-62; C Lisburn Ch Ch Cathl 62-65; R Duneane w Ballyscullion 65-69; I Kilbride 69-74; Hd of RE Ballyclare High Sch 73-98; Bp's C Killead w Gartree 98-05; rtd 05. *1A Rathmena Avenue, Ballyclare BT39 9HX* Tel (028) 9332 2933 E-mail irvine@killead61.fsnet.co.uk

IRVINE, The Very Revd John Dudley. b 49. Sussex Univ BA70. Wycliffe Hall Ox BA80. **d** 81 **p** 82. C Brompton H Trin w Onslow Square St Paul *Lon* 81-85; P-in-c Kensington St Barn 85-94; V 94-01; Dean Cov from 01. *The Deanery, 11 Priory Row, Coventry CV1 5EX* Tel and fax (024) 7663 1448 *or* tel 7652 1200 E-mail john.irvine@coventrycathedral.org.uk

IRVINE, Preb John Graham Gerard Charles. b 20. Mert Coll Ox BA42 MA46. St Steph Ho Ox 42. **d** 45 **p** 46. C Knowle H Nativity *Bris* 45-48; C Longton St Mary and St Chad *Lich* 48-51; C Soho St Anne w St Thos and St Pet *Lon* 51-53; Lon Dioc Home Missr Cranford 53-61; V Earl's Court St Cuth w St Matthias 61-69; V Westmr St Matt 69-86; Preb St Paul's Cathl 82-86; rtd 86; Perm to Offic *Chich* from 86. *42 Montpelier Road, Brighton BN1 3BA* Tel (01273) 730039

IRVINE, The Very Revd John Murray. b 24. Magd Coll Cam BA45 MA49. Ely Th Coll 46. **d** 48 **p** 49. C Poplar All SS w St Frideswide *Lon* 48-53; Chapl SS Coll Cam 53-60; Selection Sec CACTM 60-65; Can Res and Chan Heref Cathl *Heref* 65-78; Dir of Ords 65-78; Provost S'well 78-91; P-in-c Edingley w Halam 78-91; P-in-c Rolleston w Fiskerton, Morton and Upton 90-91; rtd 91; Perm to Offic *Ex* from 92. *9 Salston Barton, Strawberry Lane, Ottery St Mary EX11 1RG* Tel (01404) 815901

IRVINE, Simon Timothy. b 74. CITC 00. **d** 03 **p** 04. C Dublin Ch Ch Cathl Gp *D & G* from 03. *32 Shandon Drive, Phibsborough, Dublin 7, Irish Republic* Tel (00353) (1) 838 0469 *or* 872 4154 Mobile 87-944 4113 Fax (1) 878 2615

IRVINE, Stanley. b 35. TCD. **d** 83 **p** 84. C Arm St Mark w Aghavilly *Arm* 83-85; I Kilmoremoy w Castleconnor, Easkey, Kilglass etc *T, K & A* 85-94; Dom Chapl to Bp Tuam 88-94; I Stranorlar w Meenglas and Kilteevogue *D & R* 94-05; Bp's Dom Chapl 01-05; Can Raphoe Cathl 02-05; rtd 05. *3 Inisfayle Crescent, Bangor BT19 1DT* Tel (028) 9146 2012

IRVINE, Mrs Suzanne. b 74. Huddersfield Univ BA96. St Jo Coll Nottm 99. **d** 03 **p** 04. C Wrose *Bradf* from 03. *24 Wrose Avenue, Bradford BD2 1HP* Tel (01274) 642883 E-mail chocsxxx@hotmail.com

IRVINE, William Barry. b 48. QUB BD75 Cheltenham & Glouc Coll of HE Dip Palliative Care 99. St Jo Coll Nottm 75. **d** 76 **p** 77. C Belfast St Mich *Conn* 76-80; C Mansfield SS Pet and Paul *S'well* 80-84; V Chapel-en-le-Frith *Derby* 84-90; Chapl Cheltenham Gen and Delancey Hosps 90-94; Chapl E Glos NHS Trust 94-02; Chapl Glos Hosps NHS Trust from 02. *Cheltenham General Hospital, Sandford Road, Cheltenham GL53 7AN* Tel (01242) 222222 ext 4286 *or* 274286

IRVINE-CAPEL, Luke Thomas. b 75. Greyfriars Ox BA97 MA01 Leeds Univ MA99 SSC. Coll of Resurr Mirfield 97. **d** 99 **p** 00. C Abertillery w Cwmtillery w Six Bells *Mon* 99-01; Chapl Gwent Tertiary Coll 99-01; Min Can St Woolos Cathl 01-03; Sub-Chapl HM Pris Cardiff 02-03; R Cranford *Lon* from 03. *The Rectory, 34 High Street, Cranford, Hounslow TW5 9RG* Tel (020) 8897 8836 E-mail frluke.capel@ntlworld.com

IRVING, Canon Andrew. b 27. St Deiniol's Hawarden 62. **d** 65 **p** 66. C Benwell St Jas *Newc* 65-69; C Langley Marish *Ox* 69-73; V Moulsford 73-81; Canada from 81; rtd 92. *204-4630 Ponderosa Drive, Peachland BC, Canada, V0H 1X5* Tel (001) (604) 767 9582

IRVING, Canon Donald Richard. b 31. Lon Univ BSc56. Lon Coll of Div 66. **d** 68 **p** 69. C Leic H Trin *Leic* 68-71; Asst Chapl HM Pris Leic 70-71; Chapl to Leic Students 70-71; E Regional Co-ord CPAS 71-76; Dir Ch Soc 76-82; Gen Sec ICS 82-92; Hon Can Brussels Cathl *Eur* from 83; rtd 92. *The Old Orchard, Manor House Gardens, Edenbridge TN8 5EG*

IRVING, Canon Michael John Derek. b 43. BEd80. Qu Coll Birm 80. **d** 81 **p** 82. C Coleford w Staunton *Glouc* 81-84; V Dean Forest H Trin 84-91; RD Forest S 88-91; P-in-c Hempsted 91-96; Dir of Ords 91-96; Hon Can Glouc Cathl from 94; R Minchinhampton from 96. *The Rectory, Butt Street, Minchinhampton, Stroud GL6 9JP* Tel (01453) 882289 E-mail irvings@enterprise.net

IRWIN, Albert Samuel. b 14. TCD BA38 MA44. CITC 38. **d** 38 **p** 39. C Bury St Pet *Man* 38-42; C Bolton St Pet 42-45; Lect 45-47; Chapl RNVR 47-48; C Gillingham *Sarum* 48-49; Argentina 49-54; V Apethorpe w Woodnewton *Pet* 54-59; R Clyst St Mary *Ex* 59-61; R Clyst St George 59-61; V Stamford Baron *Pet* 61-81; P-in-c Tinwell 77-81; rtd 81; Lic to Offic *Pet* 81-85; Perm to Offic from 85; *Linc* 91-00. *19 Water Street, Stamford PE9 2NJ*

IRWIN, John Nesbitt Cottier. b 27. Mert Coll Ox BA50 MA53 SEN79. SW Minl Tr Course 86. **d** 87 **p** 88. NSM Buckfastleigh w Dean Prior *Ex* from 87. *56 Plymouth Road, Buckfastleigh TQ11 0DH* Tel (01364) 643044

IRWIN, Mrs Patricia Jane. b 49. Carl and Blackb Dioc Tr Inst 02. **d** 05. NSM S Carl TM *Carl* from 05. *31 Blackwell Road, Carlisle CA2 4AB* Tel (01228) 526885

IRWIN, Patrick Alexander. b 55. BNC Ox BA77 MA81 Edin Univ BD81. Edin Th Coll 77 Liturgisches Inst Trier 79. **d** 81

p 82. Hon C Cambridge St Botolph *Ely* 81-84; Chapl BNC Ox 84-92; Lect Th 86-92; CF 92-99; Sen CF from 99; Chapl Guards Chpl Lon from 05; Dir of Ords from 05; Chapl Udruga Hvrata Sv Dominik Gorazde 94-95; Perm to Offic *D & G* from 87 and *Arm* from 96; Hon V Choral Arm Cathl *Arm* from 02. *c/o MOD Chaplains (Army)* Tel (01980) 615804 Fax 615800 E-mail patalexirwin@yahoo.co.uk

IRWIN, Stewart. b 53. Sarum & Wells Th Coll 80. **d** 83 **p** 84. C Brighouse *Wakef* 83-87; V Stockton St Jo *Dur* 87-95; V Howden-le-Wear and Hunwick from 95. *The Vicarage, Hunwick, Crook DL15 0JU* Tel (01388) 604456

IRWIN, Miss Susan Elizabeth. b 47. Cam Univ DipRS79. St Jo Coll Dur 77. **dss** 79 **d** 87 **p** 94. Harborne St Faith and St Laur *Birm* 79-82; Caterham *S'wark* 82-88; Par Dn 87-88; Par Dn Kidlington w Hampton Poyle *Ox* 88-94; C 94-95; TV Gt Marlow w Marlow Bottom, Lt Marlow and Bisham from 95. *18 Oak Tree Road, Marlow SL7 3EE* Tel (01628) 481722 E-mail sue.irwin@btopenworld.com

IRWIN, Victor. b 32. Lon Coll of Div 64. **d** 66 **p** 67. C Leic H Trin *Leic* 66-68; CF 68-72; V Quarry Bank *Lich* 72-81; P-in-c Hopesay w Edgton *Heref* 81-85; V Lydbury N 81-85; R Wickenby Gp *Linc* 85-88; R Gartcosh *Glas* 88-91; R Airdrie 88-91; I Garrison w Slavin and Belleek *Clogh* 91-97; rtd 97. *7 Cowan Heron House, Dromara Road, Dromore BT25 1DW* Tel (028) 9269 8086

IRWIN, Canon William George. b 53. QUB BSc77. CITC 80. **d** 80 **p** 81. C Lisburn St Paul *Conn* 80-83; C Seagoe *D & D* 83-85; C Newtownards w Movilla Abbey 85-88; I Ballymacash *Conn* from 88; Preb Conn Cathl from 04. *St Mark's Rectory, 97 Antrim Road, Lisburn BT28 3EA* Tel (028) 9266 2393 E-mail wgirwin@btopenworld.com

IRWIN-CLARK, Peter Elliot. b 49. Univ Coll Lon LLB71 Barrister 72. Cranmer Hall Dur BA80. **d** 81 **p** 82. C Kirkheaton *Wakef* 81-86; V Shirley *Win* 86-96; Perm to Office *Chich* 96-97 and *S'wark* 97; V Prestonville St Luke *Chich* 97-03; Missr Warham Trust and Faith Development Officer (Basingstoke Adnry) *Win* from 03. *Home Farm House, Malshanger, Basingstoke RG23 7ET* Tel and fax (01256) 781860 E-mail panddic@surfaid.org

ISAAC, Canon David Thomas. b 43. Univ of Wales BA65. Cuddesdon Coll 65. **d** 67 **p** 68. C Llandaff w Capel Llanilltern *Llan* 67-71; P-in-c Swansea St Jas *S & B* 71-73; Chapl Ch in Wales Youth Coun 73-77; V Llangiwg *S & B* 77-79; Dioc Youth Officer *Ripon* 79-83; Nat Officer for Youth Work Gen Syn Bd of Educn 83-90; Dioc Dir of Educn *Portsm* from 90; Can Res Portsm Cathl from 90. *1 Pembroke Close, Portsmouth PO1 2NX* Tel (023) 9281 8107 *or* 9282 2053 Mobile 07768-997220 Fax 9229 5081 E-mail dde@portsmouth.anglican.org

ISAAC, Edward Henry. b 20. Qu Coll Cam BA42 MA46. Ridley Hall Cam 45. **d** 47 **p** 48. C Wednesbury St Bart *Lich* 47-51; V Liv St Phil *Liv* 51-56; V Knowsley 56-61; V Garston 61-66; V Millom St Geo *Carl* 66-85; rtd 85; Perm to Offic *Carl* from 86. *31 Lowther Road, Millom LA18 4PE* Tel (01229) 772332

ISAACS, John Kenneth. b 36. Cam Univ MA. EAMTC. **d** 82 **p** 83. NSM Ely 82-85; Chapl K Sch Ely 85-94; Lic to Offic *Ely* 85-94; P-in-c Denver 94-02; P-in-c Ryston w Roxham 94-02; P-in-c W Dereham 94-02; R Denver and Ryston w Roxham and W Dereham etc 02-03; rtd 03; Perm to Offic *Ely* from 03. *18 Barton Road, Ely CB7 4DE* Tel (01366) 387727

ISAACSON, Alan Timothy. b 55. York Univ BA77 Sheff Univ PGCE84 Leeds Univ MA97. N Ord Course 94. **d** 96 **p** 97. C Kimberworth *Sheff* 96-99; TV Brinsworth w Catcliffe and Treeton 99-03; TV Rivers Team from 03. *The Rectory, Church Lane, Treeton, Rotherham S60 5PZ* Tel 0114-269 6542

ISABEL, Sister. *See* KEEGAN, Frances Ann

ISAM, Miss Margaret Myra Elizabeth (Wendy). b 35. Nottm Univ BEd73. EMMTC 78. **dss** 81 **d** 87 **p** 94. Humberston *Linc* 81-84; Gt Grimsby St Andr and St Luke 85-93; Dn-in-c 87-93; P-in-c Gt Grimsby St Andr w St Luke and All SS 94-97; V 97-00; rtd 00; Perm to Offic *Linc* from 00. *18 Grainsby Avenue, Cleethorpes DN35 9PA* Tel (01472) 699821 Mobile 07950-464542

ISBISTER, Charles. b 27. Chich Th Coll 58. **d** 60 **p** 61. C Tynemouth Ch Ch *Newc* 60-64; C Boyne Hill *Ox* 64-67; V Cookridge H Trin *Ripon* 67-93; rtd 93; Perm to Offic *Ripon* from 01. *2 Church Mount, Horsforth, Leeds LS18 5LE* Tel 0113-239 0813 Mobile 07714-356059

ISHERWOOD, David Owen. b 46. BA68 Lon Univ MA95 MPhil87. Ridley Hall Cam 76. **d** 78 **p** 79. C Sanderstead All SS *S'wark* 78-82; C Horley 82-84; TV 84-88; P-in-c Streatham Immanuel and St Andr 88-89; V 89-95; TR Clapham Team 95-01; V Clapham H Trin and St Pet from 02. *25 The Chase, London SW4 0NP* Tel (020) 7498 6879 *or* 7627 0941 Fax 7627 5065 E-mail david.htc@lineone.net

ISHERWOOD, Robin James. b 56. Hull Univ BA78 Uppsala Univ MDiv92. Ripon Coll Cuddesdon DipMin94. **d** 94 **p** 95. C Bramhall *Ches* 94-98; V Alsager St Mary from 98; Hon Chapl ATC from 99. *St Mary's Vicarage, 37 Eaton Road, Alsager, Stoke-on-Trent ST7 2BQ* Tel (01270) 875748 E-mail vicar@pit6.fsnet.co.uk

ISHERWOOD, Samuel Peter. b 34. Lon Coll of Div ALCD62 LTh74. **d** 62 **p** 63. C Bacup St Sav *Man* 62-65; C Man Albert Memorial Ch 65-67; V Livesey *Blackb* 67-79; V Handforth *Ches* 79-99; RD Cheadle 92-99; rtd 99; Perm to Offic *York* from 00. *1 Andrew Drive, Huntington, York YO32 9YF* Tel (01904) 438116

ISIORHO, David John Phillip. b 58. Liv Poly BA80 Warwick Univ MA93 Bradf Univ PhD98 Wolv Poly Dip Psychology 89. Westcott Ho Cam 87. **d** 90 **p** 91. C Nuneaton St Mary *Cov* 90-93; P-in-c Bradf St Oswald Chapel Green *Bradf* 93-96; P-in-c Brereton *Lich* 96-00; P-in-c Arthingworth, Harrington w Oxendon and E Farndon *Pet* 00-05; P-in-c Maidwell w Draughton, Lamport w Faxton 01-05; V Kempston All SS *St Alb* from 05. *The Vicarage, Cleveland Street, Kempston, Bedford MK42 8DW* Tel (01234) 854788 E-mail davidisiorho@catholic.org

ISIORHO (née NORTHALL), Mrs Linda Barbara. b 50. Birm Univ BA72 Worc Coll of Educn PGCE75. Qu Coll Birm 88. **d** 90 **p** 94. C Wood End *Cov* 90-91; Perm to Offic *Cov* 91-93 and *Bradf* 93-94; NSM Low Moor St Mark *Bradf* 94-96; Perm to Offic *Lich* 96-97; NSM Alrewas 97-00; Perm to Offic *Pet* 01-05. *The Vicarage, Cleveland Street, Kempston, Bedford MK42 8DW* Tel (01234) 854788

ISITT, Canon David Edgar Reid. b 28. K Coll Cam BA49 MA53. Wells Th Coll 51. **d** 53 **p** 54. C Westbury-on-Trym H Trin *Bris* 53-56; Chapl K Coll Cam 56-60; V Haslingfield *Ely* 60-68; R Harlton 60-68; Chapl St Edw K and Martyr Cam 68-77; Asst Chapl Trin Hall Cam 68-77; Can Res Bris Cathl *Bris* 77-86; Dir Dioc Sch of Min 77-86; P-in-c Bris Ch Ch w St Ewen and All SS 80-82; Dioc Dir of Ords 81-86; Lic to Offic *Ely* 87-93; Acting Dean Trin Hall Cam 89; Tutor Westcott Ho 90; Chapl Fitzw Coll Cam 90-93; rtd 93; Perm to Offic *Ely* from 99. *41 Fulbrooke Road, Cambridge CB3 9EE* Tel (01223) 571763

ISITT, Norman. b 34. St Jo Coll Dur BA56. Cranmer Hall Dur DipTh59. **d** 59 **p** 60. C Loughton St Mary *Chelmsf* 59-62; C Moulsham St Jo 62-64; Billericay Co Sch 64-90; Squirrels Heath Sch Romford 64-90; Althorpe and Keadby Co Sch 66-95; rtd 95. *21 Cambridge Avenue, Bottesford, Scunthorpe DN16 3LT* Tel (01724) 851489

ISLE OF WIGHT, Archdeacon of. *See* READER, The Ven Trevor Alan John

ISON, Andrew Phillip. b 60. Imp Coll Lon BEng82 Penn Univ MSE83 Univ Coll Lon PhD87 Bris Univ BA01 CEng92 MIChemE92. Trin Coll Bris 99. **d** 01 **p** 02. C Cleethorpes *Linc* 01-05; V Bestwood Park w Rise Park *S'well* from 05. *81 Cherry Orchard Mount, Nottingham NG5 5TJ* Tel 0115-920 9398 E-mail isonandrew@aol.com

ISON, Canon David John. b 54. Leic Univ BA76 Nottm Univ BA78 K Coll Lon PhD85. St Jo Coll Nottm 76. **d** 79 **p** 80. C Deptford St Nic and St Luke *S'wark* 79-85; Lect CA Tr Coll Blackheath 85-88; V Potters Green *Cov* 88-93; Jt Dir SW Minl Tr Course *Ex* 93-95; Dioc Officer for CME from 93; Bp's Officer for NSMs from 97; Can Res Ex Cathl from 95; Chan from 97. *12 Cathedral Close, Exeter EX1 1EZ* Tel and fax (01392) 499710 *or* tel 275745 E-mail ison@exeter-cathedral.org.uk *or* david.ison@talk21.com

ISON, Mrs Hilary Margaret. b 55. Leic Univ BA76 Nottm Univ DipTh78 E Lon Univ MA02. Gilmore Course 77 St Jo Coll Nottm DPS79. **d** 87 **p** 94. NSM Deptford St Nic and St Luke *S'wark* 87-88; NSM Potters Green *Cov* 88-90; C Rugby St Andr 90-93; Chapl Ex Hospiscare 93-00; C Ex St Mark, St Sidwell and St Matt *Ex* 99-02; Bp's Adv for Women in Min from 02; Area Tutor SWMTC from 03; PV Ex Cathl *Ex* from 04. *12 Cathedral Close, Exeter EX1 1EZ* Tel (01392) 275745 E-mail hilary.ison@talk21.com

ISRAEL, Martin Spencer. b 27. Witwatersrand Univ MB49 MRCP52. **d** 74 **p** 75. Hon C St Mich Cornhill w St Pet le Poer etc *Lon* 74-77; Hon C S Kensington H Trin w All SS 77-82; P-in-c 83-96; rtd 96. *21 Soudan Road, London SW11 4HH* Tel (020) 7622 5756

ISSBERNER, Norman Gunther Erich. b 34. Fitzw Ho Cam BA58 MA61. Clifton Th Coll 57. **d** 59 **p** 60. C Croydon Ch Ch Broad Green *Cant* 59-61; C Surbiton Hill Ch Ch *S'wark* 61-66; V Egham *Guildf* 66-75; V Wallington H Trin *S'wark* 75-86; UK Chmn Africa Inland Miss from 77; Adv on Miss and Evang *Chelmsf* 86-91; P-in-c Castle Hedingham 91-93; V Clacton St Paul 93-99; RD St Osyth 94-99; rtd 99; Perm to Offic *Chelmsf* from 99. *14 Darcy Close, Frinton-on-Sea CO13 0RR* Tel (01255) 673548

ITALY AND MALTA, Archdeacon of. *See* SIDDALL, The Ven Arthur

ITUMU, John Murithi. b 65. Lon Bible Coll 01. **d** 02 **p** 03. C Cricklewood St Gabr and St Mich *Lon* from 02. *31 Olive Road, London NW2 6TY* Tel (020) 8450 8707 Mobile 07946-000364 E-mail john.itumu@lst.ac.uk *or* joitumu@hotmail.com

IVE, Jeremy George Augustus. b 57. Rhodes Univ BA81 Ch Coll Cam PhD86 K Coll Lon MPhil95. Wycliffe Hall Ox DipTh91. **d** 91 **p** 92. NSM Ivybridge w Harford *Ex* 91-95; P-in-c Abbotskerswell 95-99; P-in-c Tudeley cum Capel w Five Oak Green *Roch* from 99; Dioc Lay Min Adv 99-01. *The Vicarage, Sychem Lane, Five Oak Green, Tonbridge TN12 6TL* Tel and fax (01892) 836653 E-mail jeremy@tudeley.org

IVE (née KNOTT), Mrs Pamela Frances. b 58. Bedf Coll of Educn BEd79. Wycliffe Hall Ox 88. **d** 90. Par Dn Ivybridge w Harford *Ex* 90-95; Par Dn Abbotskerswell 95-99; Par Dn Tudeley cum Capel w Five Oak Green *Roch* from 99. *The Vicarage, Sychem Lane, Five Oak Green, Tonbridge TN12 6TL* Tel and fax (01892) 836653 *or* tel 835548 E-mail pamela@tudeley.org

IVELL, Robert William. b 45. Lon Univ BSc71 Liv Univ CertEd. Ridley Hall Cam 83. **d** 85 **p** 86. C Wadsley *Sheff* 85-88; V Laughton w Throapham 88-96; V Wadworth w Loversall from 96. *The Vicarage, Vicarage Drive, Wadworth, Doncaster DN11 9BW* Tel (01302) 851974

IVES, Raymond Charles. b 27. St Mark & St Jo Coll Lon CertEd50. LNSM course 92. **d** 95 **p** 96. OLM Croydon St Pet *S'wark* 95-04. *60 Windermere Road, West Wickham BR4 9AW* Tel (020) 8777 4956

IVES, Mrs Susan Ethel. b 48. EAMTC. **d** 01 **p** 02. NSM Moulsham St Luke *Chelmsf* from 01. *47 Long Brandocks, Writtle, Chelmsford CM1 3JL* Tel (01245) 420325 E-mail sives@fish.co.uk

IVESON, Mrs Patricia Jill. b 35. Cam Univ CertEd55 Lon Univ DipTh70 K Coll Lon BD76 AKC76. **dss** 81 **d** 87 **p** 94. Wilmington *Roch* 81-87; Hon Par Dn 87-94; Hon C from 94; Chapl Dartford and Gravesham NHS Trust from 87. *The Birches, 15 Wallis Close, Wilmington, Dartford DA2 7BE* Tel (01322) 279100

IVESON, Robert George. b 70. Oak Hill Th Coll BA01. **d** 01 **p** 02. C Cheadle All Hallows *Ches* 01-04; C-in-c Cheadle Hulme Em CD from 04. *198 Bruntwood Lane, Cheadle Hulme, Cheadle SK8 6BE* Tel 0161-485 1154 E-mail rob_iveson@yahoo.co.uk

IVESON, Ronald Edward. b 68. Chester Coll of HE RMN92. Aston Tr Scheme 95 Oak Hill Th Coll BA00. **d** 00 **p** 01. C Lache cum Saltney *Ches* 00-03; V Bidston from 03. *The Vicarage, 6 Statham Road, Prenton CH43 7XS* Tel 0151-652 4852 *or* 653 4584

IVIN, Miss Maureen. b 34. Gilmore Ho 60. **dss** 85 **d** 87 **p** 94. Grays Thurrock *Chelmsf* 85-99; Par Dn 87-94; TV 94-99; rtd 99; Perm to Offic *Chelmsf* from 00. *40 Cleveland Drive, Westcliff-on-Sea SS0 0SU* Tel (01702) 346664

IVISON, Norman William. b 54. Hull Univ BA75 DipEd76. Trin Coll Bris. **d** 82 **p** 83. Ecum Liaison Officer BBC Radio Furness 82-85; C Barrow St Mark *Carl* 82-85; Chapl Barrow Sixth Form Coll 83-85; Dioc Broadcasting Officer *Lich* 85-91; Relig Progr Producer BBC Radio Stoke 85-91; Hon C Bucknall and Bagnall *Lich* 85-91; Asst Producer Relig Progr BBC TV Man 91-93; Producer Relig Progr BBC TV Man from 93; Perm to Offic *Man* 92-95; Lic to Offic 95-98; Perm to Offic *Blackb* from 98. *44 Peel Park Avenue, Clitheroe BB7 1JR* Tel (01200) 429306 *or* 0161-244 3238 Fax 244 3232 Mobile 0585-866317 E-mail norman.ivison@bbc.co.uk

IVORY, Christopher James. b 54. Reading Univ BSc76. Qu Coll Birm. **d** 81 **p** 82. C Waltham Cross *St Alb* 81-84; C Is of Dogs Ch Ch and St Jo w St Luke *Lon* 84-88; V Streatham Ch Ch *S'wark* 88-03; Lambeth Adnry Ecum Officer 90-95; RD Streatham 00-03; R King's Lynn St Marg w St Nic *Nor* from 03. *St Margaret's Vicarage, St Margaret's Place, King's Lynn PE30 5DL* Tel (01553) 772858 E-mail vicar@stmargaretskingslynn.org.uk

IWANUSCHAK, Victor. b 51. Coll of Ripon & York St Jo MA00. N Ord Course 97. **d** 00 **p** 01. C Pontefract All SS *Wakef* 00-03; P-in-c from 03. *All Saints' Vicarage, Grenton, South Baileygate, Pontefract WF8 2JL* Tel (01977) 695590 Mobile 07734-710254 E-mail info@iwanuschak@triom.net

IZOD, Mrs Wendy Janet. b 47. Sheff Univ BSc(Econ)68. SEITE 98. **d** 01 **p** 02. NSM Hever, Four Elms and Mark Beech *Roch* from 01; Chapl ATC from 01. *West Lodge, Stick Hill, Edenbridge TN8 5NJ* Tel (01342) 850738 Mobile 07703-107496 Fax (01342) 850077 E-mail izod.calligraphy@btinternet.com

IZZARD, David Antony. b 55. Trin Coll Bris DipHE94. **d** 94 **p** 95. C E Bris 94-98; V Sea Mills from 98. *St Edyth's Vicarage, Avon Leaze, Bristol BS9 2HV* Tel 0117-968 1912 *or* 968 6965 E-mail clan.izzard@ukgateway.net

IZZARD, Ms Susannah Amanda. b 59. Hatf Poly BA82 Birm Univ MEd93 Wolv Univ PGCE92. Trin Coll Bris BA86. **dss** 86 **d** 87 **p** 01. Birm St Martin w Bordesley St Andr *Birm* 86-89; Par Dn 87-89; C Handsworth St Jas 89-91; Asst Chapl Qu Eliz Hosp Birm 90-91; Lect Birm Univ 93-02; NSM Selly Oak St Mary from 01. *2 Hemyock Road, Birmingham B29 4DG* Tel 0121-243 3745 Fax as telephone E-mail susannah.izzard@blueyonder.co.uk

J

JACK, Alexander Richard. b 30. Leeds Univ BSc55 MSc66. Oak Hill Th Coll 69. **d** 71 **p** 72. C Penn Fields *Lich* 71-78; P-in-c 78-83; R Barnston and Lt Dunmow *Chelmsf* 83-95; RD Dunmow 88-95; rtd 95; Perm to Offic *Lich* from 95. *30 Bellencroft Gardens, Wolverhampton WV3 8DT* Tel (01902) 763481

JACK, Canon Henry Graham. b 21. K Coll Lon AKC48 BD49. **d** 49 **p** 50. C Hornsey Ch Ch *Lon* 49-50; C Steyning *Chich* 52-56; R Warbleton 56-61; V Alfriston and Lullington 61-65; RD Seaford 64-65; Chile 65-74; Hon Can Chile 66-74; R Trowbridge St Jas *Sarum* 74-87; Can and Preb Sarum Cathl 83-87; rtd 87; Perm to Offic *Sarum* from 87. *285A The Common, Holt, Trowbridge BA14 6QJ* Tel (01225) 782776

JACK, Judith Ann. b 54. Wycliffe Hall Ox 03. **d** 05. C Tetbury w Beverston *Glouc* from 05. *The Rectory, Shipton Moyne, Tetbury GL8 8PW* Tel (01666) 880132 E-mail jackpot@waitrose.com

JACK, Paul. b 65. QUB BSc92 Univ Coll Galway MSc94 TCD BTh99. CITC 96. **d** 99 **p** 00. C Jordanstown *Conn* 99-01; C Seagoe *D & D* from 01. *39 Seagoe Road, Portadown, Craigavon BT63 5HW* Tel (028) 3839 4315 E-mail curate.seagoe@dromore.anglican.org

JACK, Robin Watson. b 43. Westcott Ho Cam. **d** 90 **p** 91. C Debenham w Aspall and Kenton *St E* 90-93; P-in-c Bacton w Wyverstone and Cotton 93-00; R Bacton w Wyverstone, Cotton and Old Newton etc from 00. *The Rectory, Church Road, Bacton, Stowmarket IP14 4LJ* Tel (01449) 781245

JACKLIN, John Frederick. b 30. Oak Hill Th Coll 72. **d** 72 **p** 72. Chile 72-75; C Roxeth Ch Ch *Lon* 75-78; V Selston *S'well* 78-95; rtd 95; Perm to Offic *Derby* from 97. *5 Rose Avenue, Borrowash, Derby DE7 3GA* Tel (01332) 669670

JACKS, David. b 59. Nottm Univ BTh87 Birm Univ MA95. Linc Th Coll 84. **d** 87 **p** 88. C Oakham, Hambleton, Egleton, Braunston and Brooke *Pet* 87-90; V Weedon Bec w Everdon 90-98; P-in-c Dodford 96-98; V Weedon Bec w Everdon and Dodford 98-01; V Llandrillo-yn-Rhos *St As* from 01. *Llandrillo Vicarage, 36 Llandudno Road, Colwyn Bay LL28 4UD* Tel (01492) 548878 Mobile 07850-597891 E-mail david@llandrillo.fsbusiness.co.uk

JACKSON, Alan. b 44. Newc Univ BA67 DipEd68 MEd79. NEOC 79. **d** 81 **p** 82. NSM Jesmond H Trin *Newc* 81-82; Chapl Bp Wand Sch Sunbury-on-Thames 82-89; V Hanworth St Rich *Lon* from 89. *St Richard's Vicarage, 35 Forge Lane, Hanworth TW13 6UN* Tel (020) 8898 0241 E-mail alan.jackson@london.anglican.org

JACKSON, Canon Arthur Malcolm. b 31. TCD BA54 MA60. TCD Div Sch Div Test 54. **d** 54 **p** 55. C Templecorran Union *Conn* 54-57; C Dublin Santry Union *D & G* 57-58; Bp's V and Registrar *C & O* 58-61; I Monasterevan *M & K* 61-68; I Narraghmore w Fontstown and Timolin *D & G* 68-88; I Narraghmore and Timolin w Castledermot etc 88-91; I Killanne w Killegney, Rossdroit and Templeshanbo *C & O* 91-00; Preb Ferns Cathl 93-96; Bp's Dom Chapl 93-97; Chan Ferns Cathl 96-98; Prec Ferns Cathl 98-00; rtd 00. *2 Church Road, Bunclody, Enniscorthy, Co Wexford, Irish Republic* Tel (00353) (54) 75066

JACKSON, Barry. b 30. St Jo Coll Cam BA53 DipEd54 MA57. Westcott Ho Cam 63. **d** 65 **p** 66. C Stockport St Geo *Ches* 65-68; C Bridgwater St Mary, Chilton Trinity and Durleigh *B & W* 68-70; P-in-c Thurloxton 70-75; Chapl Wycliffe Coll Glos 75-88; V Heathfield *Chich* 88-97; rtd 97; Perm to Offic *Chich* from 98. *11 Glenleigh Walk, Robertsbridge TN32 5DQ* Tel (01580) 880067

JACKSON, The Very Revd Brandon Donald. b 34. Liv Univ LLB56 Bradf Univ Hon DLitt90. Wycliffe Hall Ox DipTh59. **d** 58 **p** 59. C New Malden and Coombe *S'wark* 58-61; C Leeds St Geo *Ripon* 61-65; V Shipley St Pet *Bradf* 65-77; Relig Adv Yorkshire TV 69-79; Provost Bradf 77-89; Dean Linc 89-97; rtd 97; Perm to Offic *Ripon* from 98. *Little Spigot, West Witton, Leyburn DL8 4LP* Tel (01969) 624589 E-mail bdj1@mlj2.freeserve.co.uk

JACKSON, Christopher John Wilson. b 45. St Pet Coll Ox BA67 MA87. Ridley Hall Cam 69. **d** 72 **p** 73. C Putney St Marg *S'wark* 72-76; C Battersea St Pet and St Paul 76-79; TV Preston St Jo *Blackb* 79-87; P-in-c Sandal St Cath *Wakef* 87-90; V Shenley Green *Birm* 90-01; AD Kings Norton 95-99; P-in-c Chesterfield H Trin and Ch Ch *Derby* from 01. *31 Newbold Road, Chesterfield S41 7PG* Tel (01246) 273508 E-mail jacks49@tiscali.co.uk

JACKSON, Miss Cynthia. b 42. CertMS90. S'wark Ord Course 93. **d** 96 **p** 97. NSM Wimbledon *S'wark* from 96. *39 Panmuir Road, London SW20 0PZ* Tel (020) 8947 5940 *or* 7361 2396

JACKSON, Canon David. b 33. Leeds Univ BA60. Coll of Resurr Mirfield 60. **d** 62 **p** 63. C Lewisham St Steph *S'wark* 62-65; P-in-c New Charlton H Trin 65-69; C Charlton St Luke w St Paul 69-72; Sen Tutor Coll of the Resurr Mirfield 72-75; R Clapham

H Trin 75-78; P-in-c Clapham St Pet 76-78; TR Clapham Old Town 78-84; Hon Can S'wark Cathl 80-96; V Battersea St Mary-le-Park 84-89; V Surbiton St Andr and St Mark 89-96; rtd 96; Chapl St Mich Convent Ham 96-03. *18 Tower Lane, Bearsted, Maidstone ME14 4JJ* Tel (01622) 730041

JACKSON, David. b 48. Open Univ BA85. Nazarene Th Coll Man DipTh73 St Deiniol's Hawarden 91. **d** 91 **p** 92. C Scotforth *Blackb* 91-95; C Banbury *Ox* 95-98; Chapl Ox Radcliffe Hosps NHS Trust 95-00; V Banbury St Hugh *Ox* from 98. *St Hugh's Vicarage, 4 Longfellow Road, Banbury OX16 9LB* Tel (01295) 264961 E-mail sthughban@aol.com

JACKSON, David Hilton. b 62. Stanford Univ BA84 Princeton Th Sem MDiv90 Ox Univ MSt94 Wycliffe Hall Ox DipTh95. **d** 95 **p** 96. C Ox St Andr *Ox* 95-98; TV Thame 98-00; USA from 00; Assoc R and Chapl Upland St Mark 01-03; Sen Assoc for Par Life Pasadena All SS from 03. *614 Occidental Drive, Claremont, CA 91711, USA* E-mail david.jackson@cgu.edu

JACKSON, David Reginald Estcourt. b 25. OBE. Qu Coll Cam BA45 MA49. St Jo Coll Dur 80. **d** 81 **p** 82. Hon C Douglas *Blackb* 81-82; C 82-87; rtd 90. *64 The Common, Parbold, Wigan WN8 7EA* Tel (01257) 462671

JACKSON, David Robert. b 51. Lon Univ BDS. Linc Th Coll 81. **d** 83 **p** 84. C Hatcham St Cath *S'wark* 83-87; V Sydenham St Bart 87-93; Perm to Offic *Lon* from 03. *168 Manor Park, London SE13 5RH* Tel (020) 8297 9132 E-mail djsaab@aol.com

JACKSON, David William. b 53. Goldsmiths' Coll Lon BA75 PGCE76. Cranmer Hall Dur 90. **d** 92 **p** 93. C Desborough *Pet* 92-95; C Eastham *Ches* 95-98; P-in-c Taverham w Ringland *Nor* 98-05; V Taverham from 05. *The Rectory, 173 Taverham Road, Taverham, Norwich NR8 6SG* Tel (01603) 868217

JACKSON, Canon Derek. b 26. Ex Coll Ox BA51 MA55. Westcott Ho Cam 51. **d** 53 **p** 54. C Radcliffe-on-Trent *S'well* 53-56; C Frome St Jo *B & W* 56-57; V Eaton Socon *St Alb* 57-63; V Boxmoor St Jo 63-74; V Bishop's Stortford St Mich 74-85; Hon Can St Alb 82-85; Bermuda 85-89; P-in-c Cerne Abbas w Godmanstone and Minterne Magna *Sarum* 89-95; rtd 95; Chapl Menorca *Eur* 95-96; Perm to Offic *St Alb* from 96 and *Chelmsf* from 97. *88 Stansted Road, Bishop's Stortford CM23 2DZ* Tel (01279) 652664

JACKSON, Canon Derek Reginald. b 49. K Coll Lon BD72 AKC72. **d** 73 **p** 74. C Westhoughton *Man* 73-75; C Kendal H Trin *Carl* 75-78; V Pennington w Lindal and Marton 78-83; Warden of Readers 82-92; V Kendal St Geo 83-94; Hon Can Carl Cathl 89-00; V Applethwaite 94-96; P-in-c Troutbeck 94-96; V Windermere St Mary and Troutbeck 96-00; RD Windermere 98-00; Can Res Bradf Cathl *Bradf* 00-03; P-in-c Bingley All SS from 03; RD Airedale from 05. *The Rectory, Hallbank Drive, Bingley BD16 4BZ* Tel (01274) 563113

JACKSON, Doreen May. b 35. SRN. S Dios Minl Tr Scheme. **d** 88 **p** 94. NSM Fareham H Trin *Portsm* from 88. *134 Oak Road, Fareham PO15 5HR* Tel (01329) 841429

JACKSON, Mrs Elizabeth Mary. b 41. Man Univ BA67 Leeds Univ MA01. Ox Min Course 90. **d** 92 **p** 94. Chapl Asst Reading Hosps 86-95; NSM Reading St Mary w St Laur *Ox* 92-94; Chapl R Berks and Battle Hosps NHS Trust 95-02; NSM Reading Deanery *Ox* from 02. *157 Bath Road, Reading RG30 2BD* Tel 0118-956 8330 E-mail mjack2bl@aol.com

JACKSON, Canon Frances Anne (Peggy). b 51. Somerville Coll Ox BA72 MA76 ACA76 FCA81. Ripon Coll Cuddesdon 85. **d** 87 **p** 94. C Ilkeston St Mary *Derby* 87-90; TM Hemel Hempstead *St Alb* 90-94; TV 94-98; TR Mortlake w E Sheen *S'wark* from 98; RD Richmond and Barnes 00-05; Hon Can S'wark Cathl from 03; Dean of Women's Min from 04. *The Rectory, 170 Sheen Lane, London SW14 8LZ* Tel (020) 8876 4816 E-mail pjackson@fish.co.uk

JACKSON, Miss Freda. b 41. Bp Otter Coll TCert61 LNSM course 89. **d** 92 **p** 94. OLM Middleton *Man* 92-94; OLM Middleton w Thornham from 94. *783 Manchester Old Road, Middleton, Manchester M24 4RE* Tel 0161-653 5876

JACKSON, Ms Gillian Rosemary. b 52. Newc Univ BA75 PGCE76 Aber Univ MLitt80 Nottm Univ MA04 AFBPsS. EMMTC 01. **d** 04 **p** 05. NSM Bosworth and Sheepy Gp *Leic* from 04. *Keeper's Cottage, Help out Mill, Shackerstone, Nuneaton CV13 0BT* Tel (01530) 264122 E-mail gill.jackson@leccofe.org

JACKSON, Harry Francis. b 30. K Coll Lon BD61 AKC61 Ex Univ BTh05 FBCO80. Sarum Th Coll 61. **d** 62 **p** 62. Bermuda 62-65; C Cobham *Guildf* 65-69; R Ash 69-96; Chapl RAF Farnborough 80-96; rtd 96; P-in-c Mawnan *Truro* 96-01; Perm to Offic from 02. *Rosnython, Treliever Road, Mabe Burnthouse, Penryn TR10 9EX* Tel (01326) 372532 E-mail harry.jackson4@btinternet.com

JACKSON, Hilary Walton. b 17. St Chad's Coll Dur BA40 MA48. **d** 46 **p** 47. C Selby Abbey *York* 46-49; C Middlesbrough All SS 49-51; V Thornley *Dur* 51-56; V Beamish 56-66; V Heighington 66-82; rtd 82. *127 Bates Avenue, Darlington DL3 0UE* Tel (01325) 243794 E-mail hilary.jackson@durham.anglican.org

JACKSON, Ian. b 53. Jes Coll Ox BA75. Linc Th Coll 76. **d** 78 **p** 79. C Holbeach *Linc* 78-82; V Newsome *Wakef* 82-85; V Newsome and Armitage Bridge 85-03; TR Em TM 03-04; P-in-c Corfe Castle, Church Knowle, Kimmeridge etc *Sarum* from 04. *The Rectory, East Street, Corfe Castle, Wareham BH20 5EE* Tel (01929) 480257

JACKSON, Mrs Janet Lesley. b 45. Newc Poly CQSW78 ACertC93. NEOC 93. **d** 96 **p** 97. NSM Whorlton *Newc* 96-98; Chapl St Oswald's Hospice Newc from 98. *The Vicarage, Thornhill Road, Ponteland, Newcastle upon Tyne NE20 9PZ* Tel (01661) 822140

JACKSON, Mrs Joan. b 44. Bolton Coll of Educn CertEd71 Lanc Univ MA98. Carl and Blackb Dioc Tr Inst 95. **d** 98 **p** 99. NSM Staveley, Ings and Kentmere *Carl* 98-00; Chapl Furness Hosps NHS Trust 98-00; Asst Chapl Bradf Hosps NHS Trust from 00; NSM Bingley H Trin *Bradf* from 03. *The Rectory, Hallbank Drive, Bingley BD16 4BZ* Tel (01274) 563113

JACKSON, John Edward. b 29. K Coll Lon BD57 AKC57. St Boniface Warminster 57. **d** 58 **p** 59. C Crofton Park St Hilda w St Cypr *S'wark* 58-61; V Bremhill w Foxham *Sarum* 61-69; V Netheravon w Fittleton 69-73; V Netheravon w Fittleton and Enford 73-85; OCF 69-85; V Salisbury St Mark *Sarum* 85-92; P-in-c Bryngwyn and Newchurch and Llanbedr etc *S & B* 92-96; rtd 96. *The Cloister, 1 Hermon Villas, Rhosgoch, Builth Wells LD2 3JY* Tel (01497) 851660

JACKSON, John Frazier. b 52. Cedarville Coll Ohio BA79 Capital Univ Ohio JD83 Reformed Th Sem Mississippi MA96 Worc Coll Ox DPhil02. St Alb and Ox Min Course 99. **d** 00 **p** 01. C Kidlington w Hampton Poyle *Ox* 00-04; Chapl Tudor Hall Sch from 04. *33 Hampden Drive, Kidlington OX5 2LR* Tel (01865) 424619 E-mail jfj@jackson4.demon.co.uk

JACKSON, John Reginald. b 25. Selw Coll Cam BA45 MA49. Ridley Hall Cam 45. **d** 48 **p** 49. C Doncaster St Jas *Sheff* 48-50; C Walcot *B & W* 50-53; C Cheltenham St Mark *Glouc* 53-56; R Down *Ex* 56-67; R Georgeham 67-73; V Abbotsley *Ely* 73-79; V Everton w Tetworth 73-79; V Waresley 73-79; P-in-c Garway *Heref* 79-85; P-in-c St Weonards w Orcop 79-85; P-in-c Tretire w Michaelchurch and Pencoyd 79-85; P-in-c Welsh Newton w Llanrothal 79-85; rtd 85; Perm to Offic *Heref* 85-97. *4 Rosemary Gardens, Hereford HR1 1UP* Tel (01432) 270271

JACKSON, Preb John Wilson. b 14. St Jo Coll Dur BA38. Wycliffe Hall Ox 38. **d** 40 **p** 41. C Bordesley H Trin *Birm* 40-41; C Sparkhill St Jo 41-44; C Walsall St Matt *Lich* 44-46; R Birm All SS *Birm* 46-50; V Bromley Common St Aug *Roch* 50-52; V Sparkhill St Jo *Birm* 52-64; Chapl Birm Women's Hosp 52-64; Hon Can Birm Cathl *Birm* 61-64; V Swindon Ch Ch *Bris* 64-68; Chapl Swindon Hosps 64-68; V Walsall *Lich* 68-81; RD Walsall 68-81; Preb Lich Cathl 72-81; rtd 81; Perm to Offic *Birm* from 82. *37 The Court, Fen End Road West, Knowle, Solihull B93 0AN* Tel (01564) 776179 Mobile 07812-913328

JACKSON, Miss Kathryn Dianne. b 64. Leeds Univ BA87 MA01. St Steph Ho Ox 87. **d** 90 **p** 94. Par Dn Headingley *Ripon* 90-94; C Hawksworth Wood 94-00; P-in-c Scarborough St Columba *York* from 00; Chapl St Cath Hospice Scarborough from 00. *160 Dean Road, Scarborough YO12 7JH* Tel (01723) 375070 E-mail kathryn.jackson@st-catherineshospice.org.uk

JACKSON, Kenneth William. b 30. MCSP53. Chich Th Coll 70. **d** 72 **p** 73. C Eastney *Portsm* 72-74; C Portchester 75-79; V Elson 79-95; rtd 95. *13 Jellicoe Avenue, Gosport PO12 2PA* Tel (023) 9258 7089

JACKSON, Malcolm. b 58. NEOC 01. **d** 04 **p** 05. C Guisborough *York* from 04. *16 Lealholm Way, Guisborough TS14 8LN* E-mail mal_jacko@hotmail.com

JACKSON, Margaret Elizabeth. b 47. Lon Univ BSc68 MSc95 FCIPD91. S'wark Ord Course DipRS83. **dss** 83 **d** 92 **p** 94. Surbiton Hill Ch Ch *S'wark* 83-84; Saffron Walden w Wendens Ambo and Littlebury *Chelmsf* 84-85; Dulwich St Barn *S'wark* 86-97; Hon C 92-97; Personal Asst to Bp S'wark 92-94; Selection Sec Min Division 96-00; NSM Churt *Guildf* 98-01; NSM The Bourne and Tilford from 01. *Rise Cottage, Hale House Lane, Churt, Farnham GU10 2JG* Tel (01428) 714411 *or* (01722) 413386 Fax (01428) 714426 E-mail k.m.jackson@btinternet.com

JACKSON, Mrs Margaret Elizabeth. b 47. Mon Dioc Tr Scheme. **d** 87 **p** 94. C Chepstow *Mon* 87-90; C Exhall *Cov* 90-92; C Leamington Priors All SS 92-96; R Hulme Ascension *Man* 96-99; V Alstonfield, Butterton, Ilam etc *Lich* from 99; RD Alstonfield 00-03. *The Vicarage, Alstonefield, Ashbourne DE6 2FX* Tel (01335) 310216 E-mail maggie.jackson@virgin.net

JACKSON, Canon Margaret Jane. b 50. RGN72 S Bank Poly HDipHV75. S'wark Ord Course 89. **d** 92 **p** 94. Par Dn Hatcham St Cath *S'wark* 92-94; C 94-98; V Mottingham St Edw from 98; Hon Can S'wark Cathl from 03. *St Edward's Vicarage, St Keverne Road, London SE9 4AQ* Tel (020) 8857 6278 E-mail margaretjjackson@compuserve.com

JACKSON, Ms Marie Ann. b 45. Nottm Univ BSc66. St Alb and Ox Min Course 98. **d** 98 **p** 99. OLM High Wycombe *Ox* from 98.

19 New Road, Sands, High Wycombe HP12 4LH Tel (01494) 530728

JACKSON, Mark Harding. b 51. Open Univ BA87. Sarum & Wells Th Coll 76. **d** 79 **p** 80. C Hobs Moat *Birm* 79-83; Chapl RN 83-04; Chapl RAF from 04. *Chaplaincy Services (RAF), HQ, Personnel and Training Command, RAF Innsworth, Gloucester GL3 1EZ* Tel (01452) 712612 ext 5164 *or* (01845) 815387 Fax (01452) 510828

JACKSON, Martin. b 56. Clare Coll Cam BA77 MA81 Dur Univ MA97. Cranmer Hall Dur BA80. **d** 81 **p** 82. C Houghton le Spring *Dur* 81-84; C Bishopwearmouth St Mich w St Hilda 84-86; TV Winlaton 86; V High Spen and Rowlands Gill 86-94; P-in-c Benfieldside 94-97; V from 97; AD Lanchester from 00. *St Cuthbert's Vicarage, Church Bank, Consett DH8 0NW* Tel (01207) 503019 Fax 588399
E-mail martin.jackson@durham.anglican.org

JACKSON, Matthew Christopher. b 75. Univ of Wales (Abth) BD96 MTh98. Ripon Coll Cuddesdon. **d** 01 **p** 02. C King's Lynn St Marg w St Nic *Nor* from 01. *29 Goodwins Road, King's Lynn PE30 5QX* Tel (01553) 692904
E-mail matthew-jackson@talk21.com

JACKSON, Mrs Melanie Jane Susann. b 60. Univ of W of England BA83 Leic Univ MA94. SW Minl Tr Course 97. **d** 00 **p** 01. C Ottery St Mary, Alfington, W Hill, Tipton etc *Ex* 00-04; Perm to Offic from 04. *8 St Michaels Hill, Clyst Honiton, Exeter EX5 2NB* Tel (01392) 366783
E-mail melaniejackson@amiajackson.fsnet.co.uk

✠**JACKSON, The Rt Revd Michael Geoffrey St Aubyn.** b 56. TCD BA79 MA82 St Jo Coll Cam BA81 MA85 PhD86 Ch Ch Ox MA89 DPhil89. CITC 86. **d** 86 **p** 87 **c** 02. C Dublin Zion Ch *D & G* 86-89; Chapl Ch Ch Ox 89-97; Student 93-97; Dean Cork *C, C & R* 97-02; I Cork St Fin Barre's Union 97-02; Chapl and Asst Lect Univ Coll Cork 98-02; Chapl Cork Inst of Tech 98-02; Bp Clogh from 02. *The See House, Ballagh Road, Fivemiletown BT75 0QP* Tel and fax (028) 8952 2475
E-mail bishop@clogher.anglican.org

JACKSON, Michael Ian. b 51. Southn Univ BA73. STETS 00. **d** 03 **p** 04. Dir St Jo Win Charity from 87; NSM Twyford and Owslebury and Morestead *Win* from 03. *Hill Farm Lodge, Morestead, Winchester SO21 1LZ* Tel (01962) 777277
E-mail mijackson@ukgateway.net

JACKSON, Michael James. b 44. Liv Univ BEng65 Newc Univ PhD84 CEng69 MICE69. NEOC 82. **d** 84 **p** 85. C Houghton le Spring *Dur* 84-87; V Millfield St Mark 87-95; V Ponteland *Newc* from 95; AD Newc W from 03. *The Vicarage, Thornhill Road, Ponteland, Newcastle upon Tyne NE20 9PZ* Tel (01661) 822140

JACKSON, Michael Richard. b 31. Selw Coll Cam BA54 MA58. Westcott Ho Cam 54. **d** 56 **p** 57. C Gosforth All SS *Newc* 56-62; R Dinnington *Sheff* 62-76; V Swinton 76-97; rtd 97; Perm to Offic *Sheff* from 97. *10 Elmhirst Drive, Rotherham S65 3ED* Tel (01709) 531065

JACKSON, Norman. b 14. St Jo Coll Dur BA39 DipTh40 MA42. **d** 40 **p** 41. C Chorley St Geo *Blackb* 40-42; C Poulton-le-Fylde 42-45; Distr Sec (Man Area) BFBS 45-49; V Bolton H Trin *Man* 49-53; V Norden w Ashworth 53-69; R St Mewan *Truro* 69-79; rtd 80; Perm to Offic *Carl* 82-93. *23 Riverbank Road, Kendal LA9 5JS*

JACKSON, Norman. b 20. CEng MIMechE53. S'wark Ord Course 74. **d** 77 **p** 78. NSM Erith Ch Ch *Roch* 77-82; NSM Bishopstoke *Win* 82-95; rtd 95; Perm to Offic *Win* from 95. *7 Otter Close, Eastleigh SO50 8NF* Tel (023) 8069 5045

JACKSON, Peggy. *See* JACKSON, Canon Frances Anne

JACKSON, Peter. *See* JACKSON, Thomas Peter

JACKSON, Peter. b 39. Open Univ BA81. St Jo Coll Nottm LTh85. **d** 85 **p** 86. C Clifton *York* 85-88; Chapl Clifton Hosp York 85-88; TV Moor Allerton *Ripon* 88-98; V Holbeck 98-04; rtd 04. *131 Sandringham Drive, Leeds LS17 8DQ* Tel 0113-269 8989 E-mail pandarjackson@email.msn.com

JACKSON, Peter Charles. b 71. Univ of Northumbria at Newc BA95. Oak Hill Th Coll BA01. **d** 02 **p** 03. C Lowestoft Ch Ch *Nor* from 02. *10 Station Road, Lowestoft NR32 4QF* Tel (01502) 508695

JACKSON, Peter Jonathan Edward. b 53. St Pet Coll Ox BA74 MA78 PGCE78. St Steph Ho Ox 79. **d** 79 **p** 80. Lect Westmr Coll Ox 79-80; Hon C Ox St Mich w St Martin and All SS *Ox* 79-80; C Malvern Link w Cowleigh *Worc* 79-82; Chapl Aldenham Sch Herts 82-89; Chapl and Hd RE Harrow Sch 89-01; Lect K Coll Lon 92-99; Dir Chr Educn and Assoc R Washington St Patr USA 01-03; V Southgate Ch Ch *Lon* from 03. *The Vicarage, 1 The Green, London N14 7EG* Tel (020) 8882 0917 *or* 8886 0384
E-mail peter.jackson@london.anglican.org

JACKSON, Peter Lewis. b 34. Bps' Coll Cheshunt 63. **d** 66 **p** 67. C Stockingford *Cov* 66-67; C Kenilworth St Nic 67-72; P-in-c Napton on the Hill 72-75; V 75-89; V Lower Shuckburgh 75-89; R Napton-on-the-Hill, Lower Shuckburgh etc 89-99; rtd 99; Perm to Offic *Cov* from 99. *66 Arthur Street, Kenilworth CV8 2HE* Tel (01926) 864234

JACKSON (née PRICE), Mrs Rachel Anne. b 57. Dioc OLM tr scheme 00. **d** 03 **p** 04. OLM Barnham Broom and Upper Yare *Nor* from 03. *Red Hall, Red Hall Lane, Southburgh, Thetford IP25 7TG* Tel (01362) 821032 Fax 820145
E-mail rachel@edwardjacksonltd.com

JACKSON, Richard Charles. b 61. Ch Ch Ox BA83 Cranfield Inst of Tech MSc85. Trin Coll Bris DipHE94. **d** 94 **p** 95. C Lindfield *Chich* 94-98; V Rudgwick from 98; RD Horsham from 05. *The Vicarage, Cox Green Close, Rudgwick, Horsham RH12 3DD* Tel (01403) 822127 E-mail rjac187233@aol.com

JACKSON, Richard Hugh. b 44. St Jo Coll York CertEd66 UEA MA84. LNSM course 96. **d** 98 **p** 99. OLM Stalham and E Ruston w Brunstead *Nor* 98-00; OLM Stalham, E Ruston, Brunstead, Sutton and Ingham from 00. *5 Rivermead, Stalham, Norwich NR12 9PH* Tel (01692) 581389

JACKSON, Robert. b 69. Nottm Univ BA01. St Jo Coll Nottm 98. **d** 01 **p** 02. C Altham w Clayton le Moors *Blackb* 01-03; C Blackb St Gabr 03-05; TV Westhoughton and Wingates *Man* from 05. *The Vicarage, 91 Chorley Road, Westhoughton, Bolton BL5 3PG* Tel (01942) 812119 Mobile 07703-824849
E-mail jacksonsrt@aol.com

JACKSON, Robert Brandon. b 61. Lanchester Poly BA86 Ox Univ BA88 MA95. Wycliffe Hall Ox 86. **d** 89 **p** 90. C Bromley Common St Aug *Roch* 89-92; P-in-c Stowe *Ox* 92-97; Asst Chapl Stowe Sch 92-97; Chapl Ld Wandsworth Coll Basingstoke 97-02; Chapl Stowe Sch from 02. *Stowe School, Buckingham MK18 5EH* Tel (01280) 818000 *or* 818144
E-mail rjackson@stowe.co.uk

JACKSON, Robert Fielden. b 35. St D Coll Lamp BA57. Sarum Th Coll 57. **d** 59 **p** 60. C Altham w Clayton le Moors *Blackb* 59-62; C Lytham St Cuth 62-64; V Skerton St Chad 64-69; V Preesall 69-90; RD Garstang 85-89; V Wray w Tatham and Tatham Fells 90-00; rtd 00; Perm to Offic *Blackb* from 01. *8 Squirrel's Chase, Lostock Hall, Preston PR5 5NE* Tel (01772) 338756

JACKSON, The Ven Robert William. b 49. K Coll Cam MA73 Man Univ MA. St Jo Coll Nottm 78. **d** 81 **p** 82. C Fulwood *Sheff* 81-84; V Grenoside and Chapl Grenoside Hosp 84-92; V Scarborough St Mary w Ch Ch and H Apostles *York* 92-01; Springboard Missr 01-04; Adn Walsall *Lich* from 04. *55B Highgate Road, Walsall WS1 3JE* Tel (01922) 620153 Fax 4445354 E-mail archdeacon.walsall@lichfield.anglican.org

JACKSON, Roger. b 57. Chich Th Coll 85. **d** 88 **p** 89. C Hale *Guildf* 88-92; V Barton w Peel Green *Man* 92-95; P-in-c Long Crendon w Chearsley and Nether Winchendon *Ox* 95-00; V from 00. *The Vicarage, 84A High Street, Long Crendon, Aylesbury HP18 9AL* Tel (01844) 208363 Fax as telephone
E-mail vicarlc@supanet.com

JACKSON, Canon Roger Brumby. b 31. Dur Univ BSc53 DipEd54. Ridley Hall Cam 57. **d** 59 **p** 60. C Rowner *Portsm* 59-61; C Drypool St Columba w St Andr and St Pet *York* 61-64; Asst Chapl HM Pris Hull 61-64; V Plumstead St Jas w St Jo *S'wark* 65-68; P-in-c Plumstead St Paul 65-68; V Plumstead St Jo w St Jas and St Paul 68-74; Sub-Dean Woolwich 71-74; Chapl Hulton Hosp Bolton 74-94; Chapl Bolton Hosp NHS Trust 94-01; V Deane *Man* 74-80; TR 80-01; AD Deane 80-85; Hon Can Man Cathl 90-01; rtd 01; Perm to Offic *Man* from 01. *17 Bentworth Close, Westhoughton, Bolton BL5 2GN* Tel (01942) 813209

JACKSON, Preb Roland Francis. b 20. Univ of Wales (Lamp) BA42. St Mich Coll Llan 42. **d** 44 **p** 45. C Risca *Mon* 44-49; C Chepstow St Arvan's w Penterry 49-54; R Haughton *Lich* 54-61; V Stafford St Paul Forebridge 61-72; RD Eccleshall 72-82; Chapl HM Pris Drake Hall 75-85; V Eccleshall *Lich* 72-85; Preb Lich Cathl 82-85; rtd 85; Perm to Offic *Lich* from 85. *Treginnis, 29 Meadow Drive, Haughton, Stafford ST18 9HQ* Tel (01785) 780571

JACKSON, Canon Ronald William. b 37. Lon Univ MA71 ALCD. **d** 69 **p** 70. C Crofton *Portsm* 69-74; V Wolverhampton St Matt *Lich* 74-85; V Bloxwich 85-89; C Tamworth 89-92; Bp's Officer for Par Miss and Development *Bradf* 92-98; Hon Can Bradf Cathl 94-98; rtd 98; Perm to Offic *Bradf* from 98. *94 Primrose Lane, Bingley BD16 4QP* Tel and fax (01274) 510642 E-mail rjackson@mattprint.vianw.co.uk

JACKSON, Ruth Ellen. b 69. Dub City Univ BBS91. CITC BTh02. **d** 02 **p** 03. C Portadown St Mark *Arm* from 02. *115 Brownstown Road, Portadown BT62 3PZ* Tel (028) 3833 5562

JACKSON, Miss Ruth Victoria. b 78. Univ Coll Dur BA99 Fitzw Coll Cam BA01 MA05. Ridley Hall Cam 99. **d** 02 **p** 03. C York St Mich-le-Belfrey *York* from 02; CF(V) 04-05; Chapl RAF from 05. *Chaplaincy Services (RAF), HQ, Personnel and Training Command, RAF Innsworth, Gloucester GL3 1EZ* Tel (01452) 712612 ext 5164 Fax 510828

JACKSON (née STAFF), Mrs Susan. b 59. Leeds Univ BA82. Ridley Hall Cam 88. **d** 90 **p** 94. Par Dn Mickleover All SS *Derby* 90-93; Par Dn Chatham St Wm *Roch* 93-94; C 94-97; TV Walton Milton Keynes *Ox* from 97. *The Rectory, London Road, Broughton, Milton Keynes MK10 9AA* Tel (01908) 667846

JACKSON, Thomas Peter. b 27. Univ of Wales (Lamp) BA50. St Mich Coll Llan 50. **d** 52 **p** 53. C Swansea St Mary and H Trin *S & B* 52-58; Area Sec (S Midl and S Wales) UMCA 58-60; V Glouc St Steph *Glouc* 60-73; R Upton St Leonards 73-92; RD Glouc N 82-91; rtd 92; Perm to Offic *Glouc* from 92. *44 Grebe Close, Gloucester GL4 9XL* Tel (01452) 533769

JACKSON, Wendy Pamela. b 45. Th Ext Educn Coll 99. **d** 00 **p** 02. S Africa 00-03; Community P Woodlands 02-03; C Crediton, Shobrooke and Sandford etc *Ex* from 03. *14 Linhay Park, Sandford, Crediton EX17 4LL* Tel (01363) 776342 E-mail wendy@davwen.freeserve.co.uk

JACKSON, William Stafford. b 48. Sunderland Poly DCYW83 Sunderland Univ CertEd96. Linc Th Coll 86. **d** 89 **p** 90. C Heworth St Mary *Dur* 89-91; C Tudhoe Grange 91-92; Churches' Regional Commn in the NE 97-01; NSM Dipton and Leadgate from 03. *10 Woodland Terrace, Nettlesworth, Chester-le-Street DH2 3PW* Tel 0191-371 1048 *or* 373 5998 Mobile 07956-421263 E-mail billjackson@faithinaction.fsnet.co.uk

JACKSON, Canon William Stanley Peter. b 39. St Mich Coll Llan 63. **d** 66 **p** 67. C Llandrindod w Cefnllys *S & B* 66-69; C Gowerton w Waunarlwydd 69-73; V Crickadarn w Gwenddwr and Alltmawr 73-79; R Llanfeugan w Llanthetty etc 79-04; Dioc GFS Chapl 84-92; Can Res Brecon Cathl 90-04; Prec 98-99; Treas 99-00; Chan 00-04; Dioc Communications Officer 92-94; RD Crickhowell 98-02; rtd 04. *9 St Peter's Avenue, Fforestfach, Swansea SA5 5BX* E-mail canonjacko@aol.com

JACKSON-STEVENS, Preb Nigel. b 42. St Steph Ho Ox. **d** 68 **p** 69. C Babbacombe *Ex* 68-73; P-in-c W Buckland 73-75; V Swimbridge 73-75; V Swimbridge and W Buckland 75-84; P-in-c Mortehoe 84-85; P-in-c Ilfracombe, Lee, W Down, Woolacombe and Bittadon 84-85; TR Ilfracombe, Lee, Woolacombe, Bittadon etc from 85; RD Barnstaple 93-97; Preb Ex Cathl from 95. *The Vicarage, St Brannock's Road, Ilfracombe EX34 8EG* Tel and fax (01271) 863467

JACOB, Mrs Amelia Stanley. b 52. Punjab Univ BA73. Oak Hill Th Coll. **d** 90 **p** 94. NSM Asian Chr Congregation All SS Tufnell Park *Lon* 90-92; NSM Alperton from 92. *62 Clifford Road, Wembley HA0 1AE* Tel (020) 8429 8633 *or* 8902 4592 E-mail stjames2000@breathemail.net

JACOB, John Lionel Andrew. b 26. Selw Coll Cam BA50 MA54. Westcott Ho Cam 50. **d** 52 **p** 53. C Brightside St Thos *Sheff* 52-55; C Maltby 55-58; V Doncaster Intake 58-67; V Sheff St Aid w St Luke 67-75; TR Sheff Manor 75-82; R Waddington *Linc* 82-91; rtd 91; Perm to Offic *Linc* 91-00. *8 Manormead, Tilford Road, Hindhead GU26 6RA* Tel (01428) 602559

JACOB, Canon Joseph. b 38. CITC 65. **d** 68 **p** 69. C Belfast St Aid *Conn* 68-70; Bp's Dom Chapl 70-71; I Kilscoran *C & O* 71-80; I Geashill *M & K* 80-83; Asst Warden Ch's Min of Healing 83-86; Gen Sec (Ireland) CMJ 87-91; I Ardamine, Kilnamanagh w Monamolin *C & O* 91-98; Preb Ferns Cathl 96-98; rtd 98. *Crannaulin, Clonmullen, Bunclody, Co Wexford, Irish Republic* Tel (00353) (54) 77532

JACOB, Neville Peter. b 60. Kent Univ BA82 Leeds Metrop Univ PGCE86. Ripon Coll Cuddesdon 94. **d** 96 **p** 97. C Market Harborough *Leic* 96-97; C Market Harborough Transfiguration 96-97; C Market Harborough and The Transfiguration etc 97-99; Chapl Miss to Seafarers 99-03; P-in-c Copythorne *Win* from 03; Chapl Ibex from 03. *The Vicarage, Pine Ridge, Romsey Road, Cadnam, Southampton SO40 2NN* Tel and fax (023) 8081 4769 E-mail raveknave@tinyworld.co.uk

JACOB, The Ven William Mungo. b 44. Hull Univ LLB66 Linacre Coll Ox BA69 MA73 Ex Univ PhD. St Steph Ho Ox 70. **d** 70 **p** 71. C Wymondham *Nor* 70-73; Asst Chapl Ex Univ *Ex* 73-75; Dir Past Studies Sarum & Wells Th Coll 75-80; Vice-Prin 77-80; Selection Sec and Sec Cttee for Th Educn ACCM 80-86; Warden Linc Th Coll 85-96; Can and Preb Linc Cathl *Linc* 86-96; Hon C Linc Minster Gp 88-96; Adn Charing Cross *Lon* from 96; Bp's Sen Chapl 96-00; R St Giles-in-the-Fields from 00. *15A Gower Street, London WC1E 6HW* Tel (020) 7636 4646 *or* 7323 1992 Fax 7937 2560 *or* 7323 4102 E-mail archdeacon.charingcross@london.anglican.org

JACOBS, Michael David. b 41. Ex Coll Ox BA63 MA67. Chich Th Coll 63. **d** 65 **p** 66. C Walthamstow St Pet *Chelmsf* 65-68; Chapl Sussex Univ *Chich* 68-72; Student Cllr Leic Univ *Leic* 72-84; Sen Lect 84-02; Dir Cen for Past Care and Counselling 84-91. *Address temp unknown*

JACOBS, Neville Robertson Eynesford. b 32. Lon Coll of Div ALCD59. **d** 59 **p** 60. C Chesham St Mary *Ox* 59-62; CMS 62-67; C Keynsham *B & W* 67-71; R Croscombe and Dinder 72-80; R Pilton w Croscombe, N Wootton and Dinder 80-83; V Biddenham *St Alb* 83-89; V Chipping Sodbury and Old Sodbury *Glouc* 89-97; RD Hawkesbury 91-94; rtd 97; Perm to Offic *S'wark* from 98. *22 Comforts Farm Avenue, Hurst Green, Oxted RH8 9DH* Tel (01883) 714127

JACOBS, Peter John. b 33. JP. CMIWSc MICFM. SEITE 96. **d** 96 **p** 97. NSM Boughton under Blean w Dunkirk and Hernhill *Cant* 96-99; NSM Murston w Bapchild and Tonge 99-02; rtd 02; Perm to Offic *Cant* from 02. *13 Crown Gardens, Canterbury CT2 8LQ* Tel (01227) 455733 E-mail peter@pjacobs72.freeserve.co.uk

JACOBSON, Ian Andrew. b 61. FRGS94. STETS 02. **d** 05. NSM Ewell St Fran *Guildf* from 05. *34 Woodlands Road, Epsom KT18 7HW* Tel (01372) 742281 E-mail andrew.jacobson@waitrose.com

JACQUES, Barry John. b 52. Open Univ BSc95. Wycliffe Hall Ox 00. **d** 02 **p** 03. NSM Attleborough *Cov* 02-03; C Weddington and Caldecote from 03. *Weddington Rectory, 49B Church Lane, Nuneaton CV10 0EX* Tel (024) 7635 3400 E-mail bjjacques@screaming.net *or* barry@bjjacques.screaming.net

JACQUES, Mrs Margaret Irene. b 53. St Jo Coll Nottm BA03. **d** 03 **p** 04. C W Hallam and Mapperley w Stanley *Derby* from 03. *8 The Crescent, Stanley Common, Ilkeston DE7 6GH* Tel 0115-944 1811 Mobile 07866-415116 E-mail jacamk@ajacques.fsworld.co.uk

JACQUES, Martin. b 62. Coll of Resurr Mirfield 00. **d** 02 **p** 03. C Margate St Jo *Cant* from 02. *173 Ramsgate Road, Margate CT9 4EY* Tel (01843) 293209 E-mail martin@jacques1078.freeserve.co.uk

JACQUET, Trevor Graham. b 56. Man Univ BSc77. Oak Hill Th Coll BA88. **d** 88 **p** 89. C Deptford St Nic and St Luke *S'wark* 88-92; Chapl HM Pris Brixton 92-95; Chapl HM Pris Elmley from 95; Perm to Offic *S'wark* 96-02. *HM Prison Elmley, Eastchurch, Sheerness ME12 4DZ* Tel (01795) 882000 E-mail trevor@jacquet2.freeserve.co.uk

JACSON, Edward Shallcross Owen. b 38. St Steph Ho Ox 61. **d** 64 **p** 65. C Yate *Glouc* 64-67; C Churchdown 67-70; P-in-c Sandhurst 70-75; V Sherborne w Windrush and the Barringtons 75-76; V Sherborne, Windrush, the Barringtons etc 76-80; TV Shaston *Sarum* 80-87; Lic to Offic 87-03; Perm to Offic from 03. *Grove Farm House, Melbury Abbas, Shaftesbury SP7 0DE* Tel (01747) 853688

JAGE-BOWLER, Christopher William. b 61. Nottm Univ BA83 Ch Ch Ox PGCE84 Down Coll Cam BA89 MA95. Ridley Hall Cam 87. **d** 90 **p** 91. C Downend *Bris* 90-94; Chapl Bris Univ 94-96; C Bris St Mich and St Paul 94-96; Asst Chapl Berlin *Eur* 96-97; Chapl from 97. *Goethestrasse 31, 13158 Berlin, Germany* Tel (0049) (30) 917 2248 Fax as telephone E-mail office@stgeorges.de

JAGGER, The Ven Ian. b 55. K Coll Cam BA77 MA81 St Jo Coll Dur BA80 MA87. Cranmer Hall Dur 78. **d** 82 **p** 83. C Twickenham St Mary *Lon* 82-85; P-in-c Willen *Ox* 85-87; TV Stantonbury and Willen 87-94; TR Fareham H Trin *Portsm* 94-98; Dioc Ecum Officer 94-96; RD Fareham 96-98; Can Missr 98-01; Adn Auckland *Dur* from 01; Dioc Rural Development Officer from 01. *2 Etherley Lane, Bishop Auckland DL14 7QR* Tel (01388) 451635 Fax 607502 E-mail archdeacon.of.auckland@durham.anglican.org

JAGGER, Peter John. b 38. Lambeth MA71 Leeds Univ MPhil76 PhD87 FRHistS78. Wesley Coll Leeds 62 Coll of Resurr Mirfield 67. **d** 68 **p** 69. C Leeds All SS *Ripon* 68-71; V Bolton w Redmire 71-77; Warden and Chief Lib St Deiniol's Lib Hawarden 77-97; Dir of Self Supporting Min 77-97; Lic to Offic *St As* 77-02; rtd 97; Perm to Offic *St E* from 03. *Redmire, 12 Eastlands, Stradbroke, Eye IP21 5JA* Tel (01379) 384292

JAGGER (née GREEN), Mrs Ruth Valerie. b 56. Ex Univ CertEd77. Ox NSM Course 87. **d** 90 **p** 94. NSM Stantonbury and Willen *Ox* 90-94; NSM Fareham H Trin *Portsm* 94-98; NSM Portsm Deanery 98-01; Perm to Offic *Dur* from 02. *2 Etherly Lane, Bishop Auckland DL14 7QR* Tel (01388) 451635 Fax 607502

JAGO, Alfred Douglas James. b 08. Leeds Univ BA30. Coll of Resurr Mirfield 30. **d** 32 **p** 33. C Plymouth St Pet *Ex* 32-42; C-in-c Honicknowle CD 42-57; V Honicknowle 57; V Penwerris *Truro* 57-65; RD Carnmarth S 63-65; R St Stephen in Brannel 65-76; RD St Austell 71-76; rtd 76; Hon C Charlestown *Truro* from 77. *22 Fairbourne Road, St Austell PL25 4NR* Tel (01726) 75208

JAGO, Christine May. b 52. SRN73. OLM course 92. **d** 94 **p** 95. OLM St Buryan, St Levan and Sennen *Truro* from 94. *Boscarne House, St Buryan, Penzance TR19 6HR* Tel (01736) 810374 Fax 810070 E-mail w-cjago@supanet.com

JAGO, David. b 48. Shoreditch Coll Lon CertEd69 Birm Univ BPhil77 Hull Univ Dip Counselling 93. St Steph Ho Ox DipMin95. **d** 97 **p** 98. C S Bank *York* 97-00; V Middlesbrough St Martin w St Cuth from 00. *St Martin's Vicarage, Kirby Avenue, Middlesbrough TS5 4LA* Tel (01642) 819634

JAKEMAN, Francis David. b 47. Leeds Univ BSc69 Ealing Coll of Educn DMS81. Cuddesdon Coll 71. **d** 74 **p** 75. C Gt Grimsby St Mary and St Jas *Linc* 74-77; Ind Chapl *Lon* 77-88; V Harrow Weald All SS 88-03; V Bexleyheath Ch Ch *Roch* from 03; AD Erith from 04. *57 Townley Road, Bexleyheath DA6 7HY* Tel (020) 8301 5086 Mobile 07734-436879 E-mail fjakeman@btopenworld.com

JALLAND, Hilary Gervase Alexander. b 50. Ex Univ BA72. Coll of Resurr Mirfield 74. **d** 76 **p** 77. C Ex St Thos *Ex* 76-80; C Ex St Thos and Em 80; C Portsea St Mary *Portsm* 80-86; V Hempton and Pudding Norton *Nor* 86-90; TV Hawarden *St As* 90-93; R Llandysilio and Penrhos and Llandrinio etc 93-03; V

Towyn and St George from 03. *7 Parc Gwellyn, Kinmel Bay, Rhyl LL18 5HN* Tel (01745) 356362 E-mail hgajalland@talk21.com

JAMES, Andrew Nicholas. b 54. BSc76. Trin Coll Bris 77. **d** 80 **p** 81. C Prescot *Liv* 80-83; C Upholland 83-85; V Hindley Green 85-91; V Dean Forest H Trin *Glouc* from 91; RD Forest S 97-03. *Holy Trinity Vicarage, Oakland Road, Harrow Hill, Drybrook GL17 9JX* Tel (01594) 542232 Fax as telephone E-mail andrew@dean-net.co.uk

JAMES, Andrew Peter. b 69. Glam Univ BSc96 Univ of Wales (Cardiff) BTh99. St Mich Coll Llan 96. **d** 99 **p** 00. C Roath *Llan* 99-01; C Radyr from 01. *32 Glyn Simon Close, Cardiff CF5 2RZ* Tel (029) 2069 3054 E-mail jamesfra@hotmail.com

JAMES, Anne Loraine. b 45. St Jo Coll Nottm CertCS TISEC Cert Miss Studies97. **d** 90 **p** 94. NSM Ellon *Ab* 90-99; NSM Cruden Bay 90-99; NSM Alford 99-02; P-in-c from 02. *St Andrew's House, 53 Main Street, Alford AB33 8PX* Tel (01975) 564006 E-mail revanne.alford@virgin.net

JAMES, Barry Paul. b 49. BSc. Sarum & Wells Th Coll. **d** 82 **p** 83. C Bitterne Park *Win* 82-86; V Southampton St Mary Extra 86-00; R Fawley from 00. *The Rectory, 1 Sheringham Close, Southampton SO45 1SQ* Tel (023) 8089 3552 E-mail bpjames@email.com

JAMES, Brian. *See* JAMES, The Ven David Brian

JAMES, Brother. *See* PICKEN, James Hugh

JAMES, Brunel Hugh Grayburn. b 70. Selw Coll Cam BA93 MA93. Wycliffe Hall Ox BA97 DipMin98. **d** 98 **p** 99. C Thornbury *Bradf* 98-02; R Barwick in Elmet *Ripon* from 02. *The Rectory, Main Street, Barwick in Elmet, Leeds LS15 4JQ* Tel 0113-281 2218 Mobile 07790-880220 E-mail brunel@fish.co.uk

JAMES, Miss Carolyn Anne. b 65. Coll of Ripon & York St Jo BA87 Nottm Univ BTh91 Leeds Univ MA03. Linc Th Coll 88. **d** 91 **p** 94. Par Dn Middleton St Mary *Ripon* 91-94; C Wetherby 94-97; V Kirkstall from 97; Chapl and Sen Warden Bp Grosseteste Coll Linc from 05. *7 Riseholme Road, Lincoln LN1 3SN* Tel (01522) 527347 E-mail carolynajames@kss99.freeserve.co.uk

✠**JAMES, The Rt Revd Colin Clement Walter.** b 26. K Coll Cam BA49 MA51. Cuddesdon Coll 50. **d** 52 **p** 53 **c** 73. C Stepney St Dunstan and All SS *Lon* 52-55; Asst Chapl Stowe Sch 55-56; Chapl 56-59; Asst in Relig Broadcasting BBC 59-60; Relig Broadcasting Org W Region BBC 60-67; V Bournemouth St Pet *Win* 67-73; P-in-c Bournemouth St Steph 70-73; Dir of Tr 72-77; Can Res Win Cathl 73-77; Suff Bp Basingstoke 73-77; Bp Wakef 77-85; Bp Win 85-95; rtd 95; Hon Asst Bp B & W 95-01; Hon Asst Bp Win from 03. *35 Christchurch Road, Winchester SO23 9SY* Tel and fax (01962) 868874

JAMES, Colin Robert. b 39. Magd Coll Ox BA61 MA65 DipEd62. St Alb and Ox Min Course 93. **d** 96 **p** 97. NSM Wokingham All SS *Ox* from 96. *7 Sewell Avenue, Wokingham RG41 1NT* Tel 0118-978 1515

JAMES, David. *See* JAMES, Richard David

JAMES, The Ven David Brian. b 30. FCA52 Univ of Wales (Swansea) BA63. St Mich Coll Llan 55. **d** 57 **p** 58. C Llandeilo Tal-y-bont *S & B* 57-59; C Swansea Ch Ch 59-63; V Bryngwyn and Newchurch and Llanbedr etc 63-70; R Llanfeugan w Llanthetty and Glyncollwng etc 70-79; V Ilston w Pennard 79-94; Hon Can Brecon Cathl 87-89; RD Gower 89-94; Can Brecon Cathl 89-94; Chan Brecon Cathl 93-94; Adn Brecon 94-99; P-in-c Llanllyr-yn-Rhos w Llanfihangel Helygen 94-99; Adn Gower 99-00; rtd 00. *1 Llys Ger-y-Llan, Pontarddulais, Swansea SA4 8HJ* Tel and fax (01792) 881323

✠**JAMES, The Rt Revd David Charles.** b 45. Ex Univ BSc66 PhD71. St Jo Coll Nottm BA73. **d** 73 **p** 74 **c** 98. C Portswood Ch Ch *Win* 73-76; C Goring-by-Sea *Chich* 76-78; Chapl UEA *Nor* 78-82; V Ecclesfield *Sheff* 82-90; RD Ecclesfield 87-90; V Portswood Ch Ch *Win* 90-98; Hon Can Win Cathl 98; Suff Bp Pontefract *Wakef* 98-02; Bp Bradf from 02. *Bishopscroft, Ashwell Road, Heaton, Bradford BD9 4AU* Tel (01274) 545414 Fax 544831 E-mail bishop@bradford.anglican.org

JAMES, David Clive. b 40. Bris Univ BA61 K Coll Lon DipEd87. Lich Th Coll 62 St Steph Ho Ox 64. **d** 65 **p** 66. C Portslade St Nic *Chich* 65-68; C Haywards Heath St Wilfrid 68-71; Chapl Brighton Poly 71-76; Perm to Offic from 76; Lic to Offic from 76. *22 Bradford Road, Lewes BN7 1RB* Tel and fax (01273) 471851 E-mail djjames@waitrose.com

JAMES, David Henry. b 45. Univ of Wales MB, BCh68 Univ of Wales (Swansea) MA92 MRCPsych75 DPM74. SW Minl Tr Course 95. **d** 98. NSM Truro Cathl *Truro* 98-00; rtd 00; Perm to Offic *Truro* 00-04. *Address temp unknown*

JAMES, Preb David Howard. b 47. Ex Univ BA70 MA73 Pemb Coll Cam CertEd72. Linc Th Coll 81. **d** 83 **p** 84. C Tavistock and Gulworthy *Ex* 83-86; C E Teignmouth 86-88; C W Teignmouth 86-88; P-in-c Bishopsteignton 88-89; P-in-c Ideford, Luton and Ashcombe 88-89; TV Teignmouth, Ideford w Luton, Ashcombe etc 90-95; P-in-c Sidmouth, Woolbrook, Salcombe Regis, Sidbury etc 95-97; TR from 97; Preb Ex Cathl from 99; RD Ottery from 03. *The Rectory, Glen Road, Sidmouth EX10 8RW* Tel (01395) 514223 E-mail dhj@sidvt.freeserve.co.uk

JAMES, David William. b 55. Birm Univ BA99. CA Tr Coll CertRS77 Coll of Resurr Mirfield 86. **d** 88 **p** 88. C New Rossington *Sheff* 88-90; V Yardley Wood *Birm* 90-95; P-in-c Allens Cross 95-96; V from 96. *St Bartholomew's Vicarage, 148 Frankley Beeches Road, Birmingham B31 5LW* Tel and fax 0121-475 8329 Mobile 07970-941023

JAMES, Derek George. b 27. Sarum & Wells Th Coll 72. **d** 74 **p** 75. C Petersfield w Sheet *Portsm* 74-77; P-in-c Gosport Ch Ch 77-81; V 81-96; RD Gosport 90-96; rtd 96; Perm to Offic *Portsm* from 96. *2 Pyrford Close, Alverstoke, Gosport PO12 2RP* Tel (023) 9258 4753

JAMES, Dewi Hirwaun. b 41. St Mich Coll Llan 66 Lich Th Coll 67. **d** 70 **p** 72. C Porthmadog St Jo w Borth-y-Gest and Tremadog *Ban* 70-73; C Llanbeblig w Caernarfon and Betws Garmon etc 83-85; C Bangor 88-89 and 90-94; C Sheff St Cecilia Parson Cross *Sheff* 89-90; Min Can Ban Cathl *Ban* 90-94; C Holyhead w Rhoscolyn w Llanfair-yn-Neubwll 94-95; C Holyhead 95-96; rtd 02. *30 Ambrose Street, Bangor LL57 1BH* Tel (01248) 354910

JAMES, Canon Eric Arthur. b 25. K Coll Lon AKC50 BD51 FKC78 Trin Coll Cam MA55 Lambeth DD93 FRSA92. **d** 51 **p** 52. C Westmr St Steph w St Jo *Lon* 51-55; Chapl Trin Coll Cam 55-59; Warden Trin Coll Miss Camberwell 59-64; V Camberwell St Geo *S'wark* 59-64; Dir Par and People 64-69; Can Res and Prec S'wark Cathl 66-73; Dioc Missr *St Alb* 73-83; Can Res St Alb 73-83; Hon Can 83-90; Preacher Gray's Inn 78-97; Dir Chr Action 79-90; Hon Dir from 90; Chapl to The Queen 84-95; Extra Chapl to The Queen from 95; rtd 90; Perm to Offic *S'wark* 90-02. *11 Denny Crescent, London SE11 6SF* Tel (020) 7582 3068

JAMES, Frank. *See* JAMES, Idris Frank

JAMES, Gerwyn. *See* JAMES, Joshua John Gerwyn

JAMES, Gillian Mary. b 49. **d** 99. OLM Bassaleg *Mon* from 99. *69 Hollybush Road, Cyncoed, Cardiff CF2 4SZ* Tel (029) 2073 2673

JAMES, Glyn. *See* JAMES, Henry Glyn

JAMES, Canon Godfrey Walter. b 36. Univ of Wales (Lamp) BA58 Univ of Wales (Cardiff) MA60 St Pet Coll Ox DipEd61 BA63 MA67. St Mich Coll Llan 63. **d** 64 **p** 65. C Canton St Jo *Llan* 64-71; V Williamstown 71-85; V Kenfig Hill 85-01; Hon Can Llan Cathl 96-01; rtd 01. *23 Crossfield Avenue, Porthcawl CF36 3LA*

✠**JAMES, The Rt Revd Graham Richard.** b 51. Lanc Univ BA72 Hon FGCM92. Cuddesdon Coll 72. **d** 75 **p** 76 **c** 93. C Pet Ch Carpenter *Pet* 75-79; C Digswell *St Alb* 79-82; TV Digswell and Panshanger 82-83; Sen Selection Sec and Sec Cand Cttee ACCM 83-87; Abp's Chapl *Cant* 87-93; Hon Can Dallas from 89; Suff Bp St Germans *Truro* 93-99; Bp Nor from 99. *The Bishop's House, Norwich NR3 1SB* Tel (01603) 629001 Fax 761613 E-mail bishop@bishopofnorwich.org

JAMES, Henley George. b 31. Sarum & Wells Th Coll 79. **d** 81 **p** 82. C Tottenham H Trin *Lon* 81-85; C Cricklewood St Pet 85-88; P-in-c 88-89; V Bearwood *Birm* 89-97; rtd 97. *11 Brosil Avenue, Birmingham B20 1LB* Tel 0121-523 4243

JAMES, Henry Glyn. b 26. Keble Coll Ox BA50 DipTh51 MA58 Toronto Univ MEd74. Wycliffe Hall Ox 50. **d** 52 **p** 53. C Edgbaston St Aug *Birm* 52-54; C Surbiton St Matt *S'wark* 54-57; Housemaster Kingham Hill Sch Oxon 57-62; Chapl St Lawr Coll Ramsgate 62-68; Canada 68-73; Hon C Kidmore End *Ox* 74-77; K Jas Coll of Henley 74-87; Hon C Remenham *Ox* 77-88; Chapl The Henley Coll 87-88; Chapl Toulouse *Eur* 88-91; rtd 91; Perm to Offic *Win* from 93. *13 Harbour Road, Bournemouth BH6 4DD* Tel (01202) 427697 E-mail glyn.james1@ntlworld.com

JAMES, Herbert Royston Joseph. b 22. Sarum Th Coll 65. **d** 67 **p** 68. C Whipton *Ex* 67-75; V Shaugh Prior 75-83; V Ipplepen w Torbryan 83-87; rtd 87; Perm to Offic *Ex* from 90. *188 Hamlin Lane, Exeter EX1 2SH*

JAMES, Prof Ian Nigel. b 48. Leeds Univ BSc69 Man Univ PhD74. St Alb and Ox Min Course 99. **d** 02 **p** 03. NSM Bracknell *Ox* 02-04; NSM Winkfield and Cranbourne from 04. *2 Kyle Close, Bracknell RG12 7DF* Tel (01344) 451155 Mobile 07808-207422 E-mail dr.i.n.james@btinternet.com

JAMES, Idris Frank. b 20. MISM69 AMBIM70. St D Coll Lamp 52. **d** 55 **p** 59. C Llangynwyd w Maesteg *Llan* 55-59; C Plaistow St Andr *Chelmsf* 59-61; C Chadwell Heath 61-62; V Dunton 62-79; P-in-c Bulphan 62-64; R 64-77; rtd 85. *7 Allerdene Walk, Whickham, Newcastle upon Tyne NE16 4LL* E-mail rev.ifj@clara.co.uk

JAMES, Jeffrey Aneurin. b 53. Univ of Wales (Cardiff) BScEcon80 Bris Univ MSc85 MHSM83. WEMTC 98. **d** 01 **p** 02. NSM Minchinhampton *Glouc* from 01. *Jays Cottage, Keble Road, France Lynch, Stroud GL6 8LW* Tel (01453) 882481 E-mail jeff@jayscott.globalnet.co.uk

JAMES, Jeremy Richard. b 52. Jes Coll Cam BA73 MA77 York Univ CertEd77. Cranmer Hall Dur 86. **d** 88 **p** 89. C Broxbourne w Wormley *St Alb* 88-91; C Hailsham *Chich* 91-99; V Wadhurst from 99; V Tidebrook from 99; P-in-c Stonegate from 99; RD

Rotherfield from 03. *The Vicarage, High Street, Wadhurst TN5 6AA* Tel (01892) 782083
E-mail jeremy@jrjames.freeserve.co.uk

JAMES, John Charles. b 35. Keble Coll Ox BA59. Linc Th Coll 68. **d** 70 **p** 71. C S Shields St Hilda w St Thos *Dur* 70-77; P-in-c Jarrow Docks 77-78; Adn Seychelles 78-92; V Mylor w Flushing *Truro* from 92. *The Vicarage, Mylor, Falmouth TR11 5UD* Tel (01326) 374408

JAMES, John David. b 23. CCC Cam MA. Wells Th Coll. **d** 50 **p** 51. C Romford St Edw *Chelmsf* 50-54; C Cannock *Lich* 54-56; R Wickham Bishops *Chelmsf* 56-61; V Stansted Mountfitchet 61-71; V Clacton St Jas 71-84; R Poulshot *Sarum* 84; V Rowde 84; R Rowde and Poulshot 84-88; rtd 88; Perm to Offic *Heref* from 92. *15 Beaconsfield Park, Ludlow SY8 4LY* Tel (01584) 873754

JAMES, John Hugh Alexander. b 56. St Jo Coll Dur BA78. St Mich Coll Llan. **d** 81 **p** 82. C Newton Nottage *Llan* 81-84; Prov Youth and Children's Officer Ch in Wales 84-92; V Llanfihangel-ar-arth *St D* 92-97; V Llanfihangel-ar-arth w Capel Dewi 97-04; RD Emlyn 01-04; V Cydweli and Llandyfaelog from 04; AD Cydweli from 05. *The Vicarage, Vicarage Lane, Kidwelly SA17 4SY* Tel (01554) 890295
E-mail hugh@ficerdy.freeserve.co

JAMES, John Morgan. b 21. Lon Univ BD43 MTh45. ALCD43. **d** 44 **p** 45. C Leyton St Mary w St Edw *Chelmsf* 44-47; C Southend St Sav Westcliff 47-50; Prec Chelmsf Cathl 50-53; V Kemp Town St Mark *Chich* 53-65; R Balcombe 65-67; V Sunbury *Lon* 67-77; RD Kemp Town *Chich* 55-65; Dir Coll of Preachers 77-85; Lic to Offic *Guildf* 77-86; rtd 85. *Fair Winds, 126 Pagham Road, Pagham, Bognor Regis PO21 4NN* Tel (01243) 264250

JAMES, John Paul. b 30. Sarum Th Coll 58. **d** 60 **p** 61. C Milton *Portsm* 60-65; C Stanmer w Falmer and Moulsecoomb *Chich* 65-69; PC Brighton H Trin 69-71; Canada from 71; R Saguenay St Jean 71; Dean Quebec 77-87; R Westmount St Matthias 87-96; rtd 96. *97 Huron Street #301, Stratford ON, Canada, N5A 5S7* Fax (001) (519) 273 9226
E-mail helenandpaul@rogers.com

JAMES, Joshua John Gerwyn. b 31. St D Coll Lamp BA52. **d** 54 **p** 55. C Haverfordwest St Mary w St Thos *St D* 54-56; C Llanaber w Caerdeon *Ban* 56-57; CF 57-76; V Tidenham w Beachley and Lancaut *Glouc* 76-80; R Aberdovey *Ban* 80-82; V Quinton w Marston Sicca *Glouc* 82-90; RD Campden 88-90; P-in-c Upper Chelsea St Simon *Lon* 90-96; rtd 96; Perm to Offic *S'wark* from 97. *25 The Watergardens, Warren Road, Kingston upon Thames KT2 7LF* Tel (020) 8974 6889

JAMES, Mrs Julie Margaret. b 55. Shenstone Coll of Educn BEd77. Qu Coll Birm 01. **d** 04 **p** 05. NSM Salwarpe and Hindlip w Martin Hussingtree *Worc* from 04. *Wyche Cottage, Plough Road, Tibberton, Droitwich WR9 7NQ* Tel (01905) 345688 Mobile 07751-465241 E-mail julie.m.james@btinternet.com.uk

JAMES, Keith Edwin Arthur. b 38. Sarum & Wells Th Coll 85. **d** 87 **p** 88. C Hempnall *Nor* 87-91; R Roughton and Felbrigg, Metton, Sustead etc 91-98; V Ascension Is 98-01; rtd 02; Chapl Laslett's *Worc* 02-04; Perm to Offic *Nor* from 05. *30 Woodland Rise, Tasburgh, Norwich NR15 1NF* Tel (01508) 470032

JAMES, Keith Nicholas. b 69. Leeds Univ BA91 Nottm Univ MA93. St Jo Coll Nottm 91. **d** 93 **p** 94. C Crosby *Linc* 93-96; P-in-c Cherry Willingham w Greetwell 96-00; R S Lawres Gp 00-03; RD Lawres 01-03; R Ribbesford w Bewdley and Dowles *Worc* from 03. *The Rectory, 57 Park Lane, Bewdley DY12 2HA* Tel (01299) 402275 *or* 404773 E-mail kn.james@btinternet.com

JAMES, Malcolm. b 37. CEng MICE MIStructE. N Ord Course 80. **d** 83 **p** 84. NSM Ripponden *Wakef* from 83. *Lower Stones, Bar Lane, Rishworth, Sowerby Bridge HX6 4EY* Tel (01422) 822483 Fax 825992
E-mail malcolm@mjconsultancy.demon.co.uk

JAMES, Mark Nicholas. b 55. Jes Coll Ox BA77 MA80 PGCE79. Ridley Hall Cam 03. **d** 05. C Gt Dunmow and Barnston *Chelmsf* from 05. *31 Woodlands Park Drive, Dunmow CM6 1WH* Tel 07884-185835 (mobile)

JAMES, Martin. b 40. ACII. **d** 94 **p** 95. OLM N Farnborough *Guildf* from 94. *43 Ashley Road, Farnborough GU14 7HB* Tel (01252) 544698 E-mail martinjean.james@ntlworld.com

JAMES, Michael John. b 29. ALA53 Strathclyde Univ CYCW74 Heriot-Watt Univ CQSW81. Ho of Resurr Mirfield 57. **d** 59 **p** 60. C Applethwaite *Carl* 59-61; C Carl H Trin 61-63; C-in-c Carl St Luke Morton CD 63-67; R Lambley w Knaresdale *Newc* 67-72; Rossie Sch Montrose 75-83; Prin Redding Ho Falkirk 83-86; rtd 93. *28 Windsor Street, Edinburgh EH7 5JR* Tel 0131-556 4935

JAMES, Noel Beddoe Walters. b 39. St Mich Coll Llan DipTh68. **d** 68 **p** 69. C Swansea St Nic *S & B* 68-70; C Swansea St Pet 70-72; Chapl RAF 72-93; P-in-c The Heyfords w Rousham and Somerton *Ox* 93-00; R 00-02; rtd 02. *Ivy-Lee, Llanfihangel-ar-Arth, Pencader SA39 9HX* Tel (01559) 384176

JAMES, Paul Maynard. b 31. Univ of Wales (Ban) BA52 Fitzw Ho Cam BA54 MA58. Ridley Hall Cam 56. **d** 57 **p** 58. C Newhaven *Chich* 57-60; Kenya 60-65; SW Area Sec CCCS 65-68; V Shrewsbury St Julian *Lich* 68-76; V Shrewsbury H Trin w St Julian 76-90; P-in-c Woore and Norton in Hales 90-98; Adn Salop's Adv on Evang 90-98; RD Hodnet 93-97; rtd 98; Perm to Offic *Heref* and *Lich* from 00. *Nettledene, Elms Lane, Little Stretton, Church Stretton SY6 6RD* Tel (01694) 722559

JAMES, Canon Peter David. b 42. Keble Coll Ox BA63 Lon Univ BD67. Tyndale Hall Bris 64. **d** 67 **p** 68. C Haydock St Mark *Liv* 67-69; C Ashton-in-Makerfield St Thos 69-74; V Whiston 74-80; V Harlech and Llanfair-juxta-Harlech etc *Ban* 80-94; R Botwnnog w Bryncroes from 94; R Aberdaron w Rhiw and Llanfaelrhys etc from 00; Hon Can Ban Cathl from 02. *The Rectory, Botwnnog, Pwllheli LL53 8PY* Tel (01758) 730450
E-mail peterjames@botwnnog.fsnet.co.uk

JAMES, Raymond John. b 36. Linc Th Coll 85. **d** 87 **p** 88. C Cov E *Cov* 87-91; V Wolvey w Burton Hastings, Copston Magna etc 91-01; rtd 01. *46 Cornmore, Pershore WR10 1HX* Tel (01336) 556537

JAMES, Richard Andrew. b 44. Mert Coll Ox BA67 MA70. Tyndale Hall Bris DipTh69. **d** 70 **p** 71. C Bebington *Ches* 70-73; C Histon *Ely* 73-77; Chapl Guildf Coll of Tech 77-80; C Guildf St Sav w Stoke-next-Guildford *Guildf* 77-80; Ecum Chapl Bedf Coll of HE *St Alb* 81-83; TV Ipsley *Worc* 84-89; R Mulbarton w Kenningham *Nor* 89-92; rtd 93. *5 Kirkby Close, Ripon HG4 2DS* Tel (01765) 604511

JAMES, Richard David. b 45. Cheltenham & Glouc Coll of HE MA97. Lon Coll of Div 66. **d** 70 **p** 71. C Boultham *Linc* 70-74; C New Waltham 74-77; TV Cleethorpes 77-87; TR E Bris 87-99; V E Bris St Ambrose and St Leon from 99. *St Ambrose Vicarage, 487 Whitehall Road, Bristol BS5 7DA* Tel 0117-951 2270 Mobile 07749-243407

JAMES, Richard David. b 65. Clare Coll Cam MA88 Lon Hosp MB, BChir90. Ridley Hall Cam 92. **d** 95 **p** 96. C Clifton Ch Ch w Em *Bris* 95-98; C Enfield Ch Ch Trent Park *Lon* 98-00; V from 00. *The Vicarage, 2A Chalk Lane, Cockfosters, Barnet EN4 9JQ* Tel (020) 8441 1230 *or* tel and fax 8449 0556
E-mail richard@ccc1.fsnet.co.uk

JAMES, Richard Lindsay. b 39. Kelham Th Coll 61. **d** 66 **p** 67. C Seacroft *Ripon* 66-74; rtd 04. *3 Cavendish Mews, Hove BN3 1AZ* Tel (01273) 324672

JAMES, Richard William. b 47. St D Coll Lamp DipTh75. **d** 75 **p** 76. C Hubberston *St D* 75-78; R Pendine w Llanmiloe and Eglwys Gymyn w Marros 78-83; V Caerwent w Dinham and Llanfair Discoed etc *Mon* 83-84; Chapl Gothenburg w Halmstad, Jönköping etc *Eur* 84-89; P-in-c Shooters Hill Ch Ch *S'wark* 89-97; V Plumstead St Mark and St Marg from 97. *St Mark's Vicarage, 11 Old Mill Road, London SE18 1QE* Tel (020) 8854 2973

JAMES, Robert William. b 79. Kent Univ BA01 SOAS Lon MA02 CCC Cam MPhil03. Westcott Ho Cam 02. **d** 05. C Bradfield St Clare, Bradfield St George etc *St E* from 05; C St Edm Way from 05. *53 Raynsford Road, Great Whelnetham, Bury St Edumnds IP30 0TN* Tel (01284) 386696
E-mail robdogcollar@yahoo.co.uk

JAMES, Roger Michael. b 44. K Coll Lon BD66 AKC66. **d** 69 **p** 70. C Frindsbury w Upnor *Roch* 69-72; Lic to Offic *St Alb* 73-78; C Digswell 78-81; R Knebworth 81-92; P-in-c Upper Tean and Local Min Adv (Stafford) *Lich* 92-99; Dir Cottesloe Chr Tr Progr *Ox* 99-03; R Cusop w Blakemere, Bredwardine w Brobury etc *Heref* from 03. *The Vicarage, Cusop, Hay-on-Wye, Hereford HR3 5RF* Tel (01497) 820634

JAMES, Sandra Kay. *See* GARDNER, Mrs Sandra Kay

JAMES, Stephen Lynn. b 53. Middx Poly DipHCM74 Dip Personnel Mgt 75. Oak Hill Th Coll BA86. **d** 86 **p** 87. C Heigham H Trin *Nor* 86-89; Canada 89-93; R Bebington *Ches* from 93. *The Rectory, Church Road, Bebington, Wirral CH63 3EX* Tel 0151-645 6478 Fax 643 9664
E-mail standrews@bebingtonparishchurch.supanet.com

JAMES, Stephen Nicholas. b 51. Reading Univ MA87 Bris Univ EdD95 LTCL72 ARCM72 FTCL73 FRSA00. St Alb and Ox Min Course 01. **d** 04 **p** 05. NSM Hanney, Denchworth and E Challow *Ox* from 04. *Broadlea, 16 The Croft, West Hanney, Wantage OX12 0LD* Tel (01235) 868686 Fax 868993
E-mail drsnjames@aol.com

JAMES, Mrs Susan Margaret. b 58. SRN81 RSCN81 St Jo Coll Dur BA04. Cranmer Hall Dur 00. **d** 04 **p** 05. NSM Derby St Paul *Derby* from 04. *267 Victoria Avenue, Ockbrook, Derby DE72 3RL* Tel (01332) 673551
E-mail suzejames@hotmail.com

JAMES, Mrs Veronica Norma. b 59. STETS 99. **d** 02 **p** 03. NSM Ashton Keynes, Leigh and Minety *Bris* 02-05; R Merriott w Hinton, Dinnington and Lopen *B & W* from 05. *The Rectory, Church Street, Merriott TA16 5PS* Tel (01460) 73226
E-mail flojoefred@hotmail.com

JAMES, William Glynne George. b 39. Trin Coll Carmarthen 82. **d** 85 **p** 86. NSM Gorseinon *S & B* from 85. *23 Cecil Road, Gowerton, Swansea SA4 3DF* Tel (01792) 872363

JAMESON, David Kingsbury. b 28. Mert Coll Ox BA50 MA55. Qu Coll Birm 50. **d** 53 **p** 54. C Leominster *Heref* 53-56; C Portsm Cathl *Portsm* 56-60; Dioc Youth Officer 58-61; V Gosport Ch Ch

60-65; V Portsea St Cuth 65-70; V Enfield Jes Chpl *Lon* 70-74; RD Nuneaton *Cov* 74-79; V Nuneaton St Nic 74-80; Org Sec (Leics and Northants) CECS 80-82; P-in-c Forty Hill Jes Ch *Lon* 82-87; V 87-91; rtd 91; Hon C Okehampton w Inwardleigh, Bratton Clovelly etc *Ex* 94-96; Hon C St Giles-in-the-Fields *Lon* 96-99; Perm to Offic *Chelmsf* 99-00 and *Cov* from 01. *20 Grasmere Crescent, Nuneaton CV11 6ED* Tel (024) 7674 6957

JAMESON, Canon Dermot Christopher Ledgard. b 27. TCD BA49 MA54. CITC 49. **d** 50 **p** 51. C Seagoe *D & D* 50-53; C Holywood 53-57; I Kilkeel 57-62; I Donaghcloney w Waringstown 62-79; Can Dromore Cathl 77-93; I Kilbroney 79-93; Treas Dromore Cathl 81-83; Prec Dromore Cathl 83-90; Chan Dromore Cathl 90-93; rtd 93. *Concord, 10B Kilbroney Road, Rostrevor, Newry BT34 3BH* Tel (028) 4173 9728

JAMESON, Geoffrey Vaughan. b 27. Culham Coll Ox CertEd51 St Luke's Coll Ex AdCertEd52. Wycliffe Hall Ox 68. **d** 70 **p** 71. C Buckingham *Ox* 70-73; R Exton w Whitwell *Pet* 73-86; V Marystowe, Coryton, Stowford, Lewtrenchard etc *Ex* 86-90; rtd 90; Perm to Offic *Portsm* from 91 and *Win* from 03. *18 Eglantine Walk, Cowplain, Waterlooville PO8 9BG* Tel (023) 9257 1112

JAMESON, Howard Kingsley. b 63. Warwick Univ BSc84. Trin Coll Bris 99. **d** 02 **p** 03. C Wareham *Sarum* from 02. *8 Wellstead Road, Wareham BH20 4EY* Tel (01929) 551494 E-mail howard.jameson@virgin.net

JAMESON, Peter. b 31. Trin Coll Cam BA54 MA60. Linc Th Coll. **d** 62 **p** 63. C Earl's Court St Cuth w St Matthias *Lon* 62-68; C Notting Hill St Clem 68-72; C Notting Hill St Clem and St Mark 72-74; TV Notting Hill 74-77; V Stoke Newington St Olave 77-95; rtd 95; Perm to Offic *Chich* from 95. *Colemans, Warren Lane, Cross in Hand, Heathfield TN21 0TB* Tel (01435) 863414

JAMIESON, Douglas. *See* JAMIESON, William Douglas

JAMIESON, Guy Stuart. b 66. Leeds Univ BA98. Ripon Coll Cuddesdon. **d** 00 **p** 01. C Woodhall *Bradf* 00-03; V Southowram and Claremount *Wakef* from 03. *St Anne's Vicarage, Church Lane, Southowram, Halifax HX3 9TD* Tel (01422) 365229 E-mail ragu@fish.co.uk

JAMIESON, Hugh Gollan. b 20. TCD BA49. CITC 49. **d** 49 **p** 50. C Limerick St Lawr w H Trin and St Jo *L & K* 49-51; I Ballynaclough Union 51-53; Sec BCMS 53-56; I Murragh Union *C, C & R* 56-60; R Birkin w Haddlesey *York* 60-63; I Derralossary *D & G* 63-69; I Mothel *C & O* 69-76; I Badoney Lower *D & R* 76-78; I Donagh w Tyholland and Errigal Truagh *Clogh* 78-82; I Killeshandra w Killegar and Derrylane *K, E & A* 82-87; rtd 87. *Rose Cottage, Killyboley, Glaslough, Monaghan, Irish Republic* Tel (00353) (47) 88231

JAMIESON, Kenneth Euan Oram. b 24. Lon Univ DipTh68. Roch Th Coll 60. **d** 62 **p** 63. C Bromley SS Pet and Paul *Roch* 62-66; R Colchester St Mary Magd *Chelmsf* 66-71; V Bexleyheath St Pet *Roch* 71-78; P-in-c Maidstone St Faith *Cant* 78-83; P-in-c Maidstone St Paul 78-83; Ind Chapl *St Alb* 83-89; rtd 89; Perm to Offic *B & W* from 89. *4 Ashley Road, Taunton TA1 5BP* Tel (01823) 289367

JAMIESON, Canon Marilyn. b 52. Cranmer Hall Dur IDC80. **d** 91 **p** 94. Par Dn Bensham *Dur* 91-93; Par Dn Ryton w Hedgefield 93-94; Chapl Metro Cen Gateshead 94-02; Bp's Sen Chapl from 02; Hon Can Dur Cathl from 97. *Barmoor House, 64 Main Road, Ryton NE40 3AJ* Tel 0191-413 4592

JAMIESON, Peter Grant. b 64. Liv Univ BA87. Coll of Resurr Mirfield 93. **d** 93 **p** 94. C Charlton Kings St Mary *Glouc* 93-96. *3 Belmont Mews, Upper High Street, Thame OX9 3EJ* Tel (01844) 212895

JAMIESON, Miss Rosalind Heather. b 49. CertEd71. St Jo Coll Dur 79. **dss** 81 **d** 87 **p** 94. Queensbury All SS *Lon* 81-85; Richmond H Trin and Ch Ch *S'wark* 85-87; Par Dn 87-91; Par Dn Burmantofts St Steph and St Agnes *Ripon* 91-94; C 94-99; TV Seacroft from 99. *St Richard's Vicarage, Ramshead Hill, Leeds LS14 1BX* Tel 0113-273 2527 E-mail jamheat2002@tiscali.co.uk

JAMIESON, Mrs Susan Jennifer. b 49. Liv Univ SRN71. Dioc OLM tr scheme 97. **d** 00 **p** 01. OLM Clubmoor *Liv* from 00. *15 Winsford Road, Liverpool L13 0BJ* Tel 0151-475 7562 Mobile 07879-425277 E-mail sujamo@cableinet.co.uk

JAMIESON, Thomas Lindsay. b 53. N Lon Poly BSc74. Cranmer Hall Dur. **d** 77 **p** 78. C Gateshead Fell *Dur* 77-80; C Gateshead 80-84; TV 84-90; P-in-c Gateshead St Cuth w St Paul 90-91; TV Bensham 91-93; P-in-c Ryton w Hedgefield 93-95; R 95-05; R Ryton from 05; AD Gateshead W 94-98. *Barmoor House, 64 Main Road, Ryton NE40 3AJ* Tel 0191-413 4592 E-mail atl.jamieson@talk21.com

JAMIESON, William Douglas. b 38. Oak Hill Th Coll 63. **d** 66 **p** 67. C Shrewsbury St Julian *Lich* 66-68; C Bucknall and Bagnall 68-70; C Otley *Bradf* 70-74; TV Keighley 74-81; V Utley 81-00; rtd 00; Perm to Offic *Ches* from 00. *11 The Quay, Frodsham, Warrington WA6 7JG* Tel (01928) 731085 Mobile 07974-947838 E-mail douglasjamieson@lineone.net

JAMIESON-HARVEY, Neil Benedict. b 44. Chich Th Coll 89. **d** 91 **p** 92. Bahamas 91-95; C Meir Heath *Lich* 95-96; P-in-c Cross Heath from 96. *St Michael's Presbytery, Linden Grove, Newcastle ST5 9LJ* Tel (01782) 617241 E-mail frneil@crossheath.co.uk

JANES, David Edward. b 40. Lon Univ BSc67. Glouc Sch of Min 86. **d** 89 **p** 90. NSM Church Stretton *Heref* 89-00; rtd 00; Perm to Offic *Heref* from 00. *15 Watling Street South, Church Stretton SY6 7BG* Tel (01694) 722253

JANICKER, Laurence Norman. b 47. SS Mark & Jo Coll Chelsea DipEd69. Ridley Coll Melbourne 77 St Jo Coll Nottm 83. **d** 85 **p** 86. C Beverley Minster *York* 85-89; R Lockington and Lund and Scorborough w Leconfield 89-94; V Cov St Geo *Cov* from 94. *St George's Vicarage, 101 Moseley Avenue, Coventry CV6 1HR* Tel (024) 7659 1994

JANSMA, Henry Peter. b 57. NE Bible Coll (USA) BA79 Westmr Th Sem (USA) MA85 St Jo Coll Dur PhD91. Linc Th Coll 89. **d** 91 **p** 92. C Spalding *Linc* 91-96; P-in-c Cleethorpes St Aid 96-97; V 97-01; R Haddon Heights St Mary USA from 01. *501 Green Street, Haddon Heights, NJ 08035, USA* Tel (001) (856) 547 0565 *or* 547 3240 Fax 310 0565 E-mail stmaryshh@juno.com

JANSSON, Maria Patricia. b 55. Milltown Inst Dub DipRE75 MRelSc92. CITC 00. **d** 01 **p** 02. C Galway w Kilcummin *T, K & A* 01-02; C Kilscoran w Killinick and Mulrankin *C & O* 02-04; C Wexford w Ardcolm and Killurin 02-04; I from 04. *The Rectory, Park, Wexford, Irish Republic* Tel and fax (00353) (53) 43013 E-mail miajansson@eircom.net

JANVIER, Philip Harold. b 57. Trin Coll Bris BA87. **d** 87 **p** 88. C Much Woolton *Liv* 87-90; TV Toxteth St Philemon w St Gabr and St Cleopas 90-97; TR Gateacre from 97. *St Stephen's Rectory, Belle Vale Road, Liverpool L25 2PQ* Tel and fax 0151-487 9338

JAONA, Ramahalefitra Hyacinthe Arsène. b 70. St Paul's Th Coll Ambatoharanana Madagascar CAP94. **d** 94 **p** 96. Madagascar 94-97 and from 98; C Caldicot *Mon* 97-98. *Mission Angelican, BP 126, 206 Antalaha, Antsiranana, Madagascar*

JAPAN, Primate of. *See* UNO, The Most Revd James Toru

JAQUES, Geoffrey Sanderson. b 48. Man Univ BSc. NEOC 94. **d** 97 **p** 98. NSM Gt Ayton w Easby and Newton in Cleveland *York* from 97. *132 Roseberry Crescent, Great Ayton, Middlesbrough TS9 6EW* Tel (01642) 722979 E-mail jaques@fish.co.uk

JARAM, Peter Ellis. b 45. Lon Univ BSc70 CEng77 MIEE77 MBIM88. Linc Th Coll 94. **d** 94 **p** 95. C Bridlington Priory *York* 94-96; C Rufforth w Moor Monkton and Hessay 96-97; C Healaugh w Wighill, Bilbrough and Askham Richard 96-97; P-in-c 97-01; Chapl Askham Bryan Coll 97-01; V Brompton by Sawdon w Hutton Buscel, Snainton etc *York* from 01. *The Vicarage, 4 Cayley Lane, Brompton-by-Sawdon, Scarborough YO13 9DL* Tel (01723) 862061 E-mail pej.parish@virgin.net

JARDIN, Kenneth. b 35. TCD 67. **d** 69 **p** 70. Chapl R Sch Arm 69-72; C Arm St Mark *Arm* 69-72; Chapl RAF 72-78; V Barlings *Linc* 78-83; P-in-c Stainton-by-Langworth 78; P-in-c Scothern w Sudbrooke 78; Chapl Monte Carlo *Eur* 83-87; P-in-c Sudbury and Somersal Herbert *Derby* 87-92; Dep Chapl HM Open Pris Foston Hall and Sudbury 87-92; P-in-c Kirk Langley 92-03; P-in-c Mackworth All SS 92-03; P-in-c Mugginton and Kedleston 92-03; rtd 03. *25-05 Victoria Centre, Nottingham NG1 3PW* Tel 0115-959 8844

JARDINE, Canon Anthony. b 38. Qu Coll Birm 64. **d** 67 **p** 68. C Baldock w Bygrave and Clothall *St Alb* 67-71; C N Stoneham *Win* 71-73; P-in-c Ecchinswell cum Sydmonton 73-79; P-in-c Burghclere w Newtown 78-79; R Burghclere w Newtown and Ecchinswell w Sydmonton 79-87; R Wonston and Stoke Charity w Hunton 87-97; P-in-c Chawton and Farringdon 97-04; Dioc Rural Officer 97-04; Hon Can Win Cathl 99-04; rtd 04; Hon C Knight's Enham and Smannell w Enham Alamein *Win* from 04. *The Rectory, Dunhills Lane, Enham Alamein, Andover SP11 6HU* Tel (01264) 352827 E-mail rev_jardine@hotmail.com

JARDINE, David Eric Cranswick. b 30. CCC Ox BA53 MA57. Wycliffe Hall Ox 53. **d** 55 **p** 56. C Wavertree St Mary *Liv* 55-58; C Liv All So Springwood 58-62; C Horley *S'wark* 62-65; V Mitcham Ch Ch 65-72; V Iford *Win* 72-89; R Smannell w Enham Alamein 89-96; rtd 96; Perm to Offic *Sheff* from 96. *387 Redmires Road, Sheffield S10 4LE* Tel 0114-230 8721 E-mail ema98dej@sheffield.ac.uk

JARDINE, David John (Brother David). b 42. QUB BA65. CITC 67. **d** 67 **p** 68. C Ballymacarrett St Patr *D & D* 67-70; Asst Chapl QUB 70-73; SSF from 73; Asst Chapl HM Pris Belf 75-79; Chapl 79-85; USA 85-88; Sen Asst Warden Ch of Ireland Min of Healing 88-92; Dir Divine Healing Min 92-99. *3 Richmond Park, Stranmillis, Belfast BT9 5EF* Tel (028) 9068 7692 *or* 9031 1532

JARDINE, Canon Norman. b 47. QUB BSc72. Trin Coll Bris 74. **d** 76 **p** 77. C Magheralin *D & D* 76-78; C Dundonald 78-80; Bp's C Ballybeen 80-88; I Willowfield 88-00; Dir Think Again 00-04; I Ballynafeigh St Jude from 04; Can Belf Cathl from 03. *10 Mornington, Belfast BT7 3JS* Tel (028) 9050 4976 E-mail norman.jardine2@ntlworld.com

JARDINE, Thomas Parker. b 44. Oak Hill Th Coll BA87. **d** 87 **p** 88. C Crowborough *Chich* 87-91; R Dersingham w Anmer and

Shernborne *Nor* 91-00; P-in-c Southport SS Simon and Jude *Liv* 00-03; V from 03; C Southport All SS and All So from 03. *The Vicarage, 128 Roe Lane, Southport PR9 7PJ* Tel (01704) 227095

JARMAN, Christopher (Kit). b 38. QUB BA63. Wells Th Coll 69. **d** 71 **p** 72. C Leckhampton SS Phil and Jas *Glouc* 71-73; Chapl RN 73-93; Chapl Rossall Sch Fleetwood 94; R Stirling *St And* 94-03; Chapl ATC 97-03; rtd 03; Warrant from 04. *Ground Floor Flat 2, 4 Branksome Park, Longsdale Road, Oban PA34 5JZ* Tel and fax (01631) 563535

JARMAN, John Geoffrey. b 31. IEng. S'wark Ord Course 75. **d** 78 **p** 79. NSM Chigwell *Chelmsf* 78-81; NSM Leytonstone St Marg w St Columba 81-87; C Walthamstow St Sav 87-89; V Gt Bentley 89-92; P-in-c Frating w Thorrington 89-92; C Wanstead St Mary 92-93; C Wanstead St Mary w Ch Ch 93-95; rtd 95; Perm to Offic *Chelmsf* from 95. *20 Stevens Way, Chigwell IG7 6HR* Tel (020) 8500 2161

JARMAN, Robert Joseph. b 59. Van Mildert Coll Dur BA90 Univ of Wales (Cardiff) DPS91. **d** 92 **p** 93. C Llanishen and Lisvane *Llan* 92-93; C Whitchurch 93-94. *47 Penydre, Rhiwbina, Cardiff CF14 6EJ*

JARMY, David Michael. b 49. Hughes Hall Cam PGCE90. Chich Th Coll 76. **d** 79 **p** 80. C St Leonards Ch Ch *Chich* 79-80; C St Leonards Ch Ch and St Mary 81-82; C St Leonards SS Pet and Paul 82-85; V Sidley 85-89; Lt Gidding Community 89-90; NSM Oundle *Pet* 90-98; Chapl Bp Stopford Sch Kettering 90-98; P-in-c Turners Hill *Chich* from 98; Angl Chapl Worth Sch from 98. *The Vicarage, Church Road, Turners Hill, Crawley RH10 4PB* Tel (01342) 715278 E-mail jarmy@tesco.net

JARRATT, Canon Robert Michael. b 39. K Coll Lon BD62 AKC62. NY Th Sem. **d** 63 **p** 64. C Corby St Columba *Pet* 63-67; Lay Tr Officer *Sheff* 67-71; Ind Chapl *S'wark* 72-80; P-in-c Betchworth 76-80; V Ranmoor *Sheff* 80-01; P-in-c Worsbrough and Dir Post-Ord Tr 01-05; RD Hallam 87-94; Hon Can Sheff Cathl 95-05; rtd 05. *42 Storthwood Court, Storth Lane, Sheffield S10 3HP* Tel 0114-230 7036 E-mail michael@jarrattnet.co.uk

JARRATT, Stephen. b 51. Edin Univ BD76 St Kath Coll Liv CertEd77. **d** 78 **p** 79. C Horsforth *Ripon* 78-81; C Stanningley St Thos 81-84; P-in-c Fishponds St Jo *Bris* 84-85; V 85-92; V Chapel Allerton *Ripon* 92-04; AD Allerton 97-04; TR Clifton *S'well* from 04. *The Rectory, 569 Farnborough Road, Nottingham NG11 9DG* Tel 0115-974 9388 E-mail steveandnicky@thejarratts.freeserve.co.uk

✠**JARRETT, The Rt Revd Martyn William.** b 44. K Coll Lon BD67 AKC67 Hull Univ MPhil91. **d** 68 **p** 69 **c** 94. C Bris St Geo *Bris* 68-70; C Swindon New Town 70-74; C Northolt St Mary *Lon* 74-76; V Northolt W End St Jos 76-81; V Hillingdon St Andr 81-83; P-in-c Uxbridge Moor 82-83; V Uxbridge St Andr w St Jo 83-85; Selection Sec ACCM 85-88; Sen Selection Sec 89-91; V Chesterfield St Mary and All SS *Derby* 91-94; Suff Bp Burnley *Blackb* 94-00; Hon Can Blackb Cathl 94-00; Suff Bp Beverley (PEV) *York* from 00; Hon Asst Bp Dur, Ripon and Sheff from 00; Hon Asst Bp Man, S'well and Wakef from 01; Hon Asst Bp Bradf from 02; Hon Asst Bp Liv from 03; Hon Can Wakef Cathl *Wakef* from 01. *3 North Lane, Roundhay, Leeds LS8 2QJ* Tel 0113-265 4280 Fax 265 4281 E-mail bishop-of-beverley@3-north-lane.fsnet.co.uk

JARRETT, Rene Isaac Taiwo. b 49. TCert79 Lon Inst of Educn BEd94. Sierra Leone Th Hall CPS83. **d** 83 **p** 85. Sierra Leone 83-89; Hon C St Pancras w St Jas and Ch Ch *Lon* from 89; Hon C Bloomsbury St Geo w Woburn Square Ch Ch from 95. *2 Woburn Mansions, Torrington Place, London WC1E 7HL* Tel (020) 7580 5165 *or* 7405 3044 E-mail jarrorene@yahoo.co.uk

JARROW, Suffragan Bishop of. *See* PRITCHARD, The Rt Revd John Lawrence

JARVIS, Ian Frederick Rodger. b 38. Bris Univ BA60. Tyndale Hall Bris 61. **d** 63 **p** 64. C Penge Ch Ch w H Trin *Roch* 63-67; C Bilston St Leon *Lich* 67-71; V Lozells St Silas *Birm* 71-76; V Chaddesden St Mary *Derby* 76-95; V Newhall 95-02; rtd 02; Perm to Offic *Derby* from 02. *29 Springfield Road, Midway, Swadlincote DE11 0BZ* Tel (01283) 551589

JARVIS, Jeffrey Wallace. b 45. Univ of Qld BEd96. Sarum & Wells Th Coll ThL73. **d** 75 **p** 76. C Cherry Hinton St Andr *Ely* 75-77; C Nottingham St Mary *S'well* 77-78; Australia from 78; R Greenwood 78-80; Chapl Ch Gr Sch 80-84; R Edgehill Cairns Gd Shep 84-86; Chapl Brisbane Boys' Coll 86-91; Chapl St Marg Angl Girls' Sch 91-94; Chapl RAN 94-96; Chapl Fraser Coast Angl Coll from 96. *14 Spence Street, Point Vernon, Qld, Australia 4655* Tel (0061) (7) 4124 4506 *or* 4124 5411 Fax 4124 5833 E-mail jjarvis@fcac.qld.edu.au

JARVIS, Mrs Lynda Claire. b 46. Southn Univ CQSW87. STETS 95. **d** 98 **p** 99. C Chandler's Ford *Win* 98-01; rtd 01. *Largo Santana 3, Tavira, 8800-701 Algarve, Portugal* Tel (00351) (281) 323553 Mobile 961-166240

JARVIS, Miss Mary. b 35. Leeds Univ BA57 Lon Univ CertEd59. Cranmer Hall Dur 78. **dss** 80 **d** 87 **p** 94. Low Harrogate St Mary *Ripon* 80-84; Wortley de Leeds 84-87; C 87-88; C Upper Armley 88-94; C Holbeck 94-95; rtd 95; Perm to Offic *Ripon* from 01. *71 Burnsall Croft, Leeds LS12 3LH* Tel 0113-279 7832

JARVIS, Mrs Pamela Ann. b 51. Sussex Univ BEd74. SW Minl Tr Course 97. **d** 00 **p** 01. C Braunton *Ex* 00-03; C Combe Martin, Berrynarbor, Lynton, Brendon etc 03-04; TV from 04. *The Rectory, Lee Road, Lynton EX35 6BP* Tel (01598) 753251 Mobile 07773-900523 E-mail pajarvis@ntlworld.com

JARVIS, Peter Timothy. b 64. St Jo Coll Nottm 02. **d** 04 **p** 05. C Thatcham *Ox* from 04. *47A Station Road, Thatcham RG19 4PU* Tel (01635) 867336 Mobile 07834-076988 E-mail revdpj@tiscali.co.uk

JARVIS, Rupert Charles Melbourn. b 69. St Andr Univ MA92 Univ of Wales (Swansea) MPhil96. Cuddesdon Coll 96. **d** 98 **p** 99. C Swansea St Mary w H Trin *S & B* 98-99; Min Can Brecon Cathl 99-01; CF from 01. *c/o MOD Chaplains (Army)* Tel (01980) 615804 Fax 615800

JASON, Mark Andrew. b 73. Madras Univ BA94 S Asia Inst for Advanced Chr Studies MA96. Gurukul Lutheran Th Coll & Research Inst BD00. **p** 01. India 01-03; Perm to Offic *Ab* from 03. *31 Gladstone Place, Aberdeen AB10 6UX* Tel (01224) 321714 E-mail m.a.jason@abdn.ac.uk

JASPER, Prof David. b 51. Jes Coll Cam BA72 MA76 Keble Coll Ox BD80 Dur Univ PhD83 Ox Univ DD02. St Steph Ho Ox BA75 MA79. **d** 76 **p** 77. C Buckingham *Ox* 76-79; C Dur St Oswald *Dur* 80; Chapl Hatf Coll Dur 81-88; Dir Cen Study of Lit and Th Dur 88-91; Prin St Chad's Coll Dur 88-91; Reader and Dir Cen Study of Lit and Th Glas Univ from 91; Vice-Dean of Div 95-98; Dean of Div from 98; Lic to Offic *Glas* from 91. *Netherwood, 124 Old Manse Road, Wishaw ML2 0EP* Tel and fax (01698) 373286 E-mail d.jasper@arts.gla.ac.uk

JASPER, David Julian McLean. b 44. Dur Univ BA66 Nottm Univ DipTh67. Linc Th Coll 66. **d** 68 **p** 69. C Redruth *Truro* 68-72; TV 72-75; V St Just in Penwith 75-86; P-in-c Sancreed 82-86; C Reading St Matt *Ox* 96-00; P-in-c 00-02; R S Petherton w the Seavingtons *B & W* from 02. *The Rectory, Hele Lane, South Petherton TA13 5DY* Tel (01460) 240377 Mobile 07767-814533 E-mail david.jasper@virgin.net

JASPER, James Roland. b 32. CA Tr Coll 56 NEOC 82. **d** 84 **p** 84. C Newburn *Newc* 84-86; V Ansley *Cov* 86-97; rtd 97; Perm to Offic *Leic* from 97 and *Cov* from 03. *69 Desford Road, Newbold Verdon, Leicester LE9 9LG* Tel (01455) 822567

JASPER, Jonathan Ernest Farley. b 50. AKC72 DPMSA85. St Aug Coll Cant 73. **d** 73 **p** 74. C Cheshunt *St Alb* 73-75; C Bedford St Paul 75-77; C Bedford St Pet w St Cuth 75-77; Chapl Southn Univ *Win* 77-80; Chapl Lon Univ Medical Students *Lon* 80-86; PV Chich Cathl *Chich* 86-89; P-in-c Earls Colne and White Colne *Chelmsf* 89-94; P-in-c Colne Engaine 89-94; R Earls Colne w White Colne and Colne Engaine 95-02; C Christchurch *Win* from 02. *49 Brabazon Drive, Christchurch BH23 4TL* Tel (01425) 280831

JAUNDRILL, John Warwick. b 47. MInstM81. Qu Coll Birm 86. **d** 88 **p** 89. C Bistre *St As* 88-91; P-in-c Towyn and St George 91-92; V 92-02. *20 Avon Court, Mold CH7 1JP* Tel (01352) 751632

JAY, Colin. b 62. Keble Coll Ox BA85 St Jo Coll Dur BA89. Cranmer Hall Dur 87. **d** 90 **p** 91. C Bishopwearmouth St Gabr *Dur* 90-94; C Newton Aycliffe 94; TV 94-96; TV Gt Aycliffe 96-03; AD Sedgefield 99-03; Chapl Co Dur & Darlington Priority Services NHS Trust from 03. *Earls House Hospital, Lanchester Road, Durham DH1 5RD* Tel 0191-333 6262 E-mail colsar@netscapeonline.co.uk

JAY, Ms Nicola Mary. b 37. SRN58. NEOC 88. **d** 91 **p** 94. Par Dn Whitburn *Dur* 91-94; C 94-95; P-in-c Sacriston and Kimblesworth 95-00; rtd 00. *29 Church Street, Sacriston, Durham DH7 6JL* Tel 0191-371 0152

JAY, Richard Hylton Michael. b 31. Bris Univ BEd75. Sarum & Wells Th Coll 77. **d** 79 **p** 80. NSM Bath St Barn w Englishcombe *B & W* 79-81; NSM Saltford w Corston and Newton St Loe 81-88; R Hatch Beauchamp w Beercrocombe, Curry Mallet etc 89-97; rtd 97; Perm to Offic *B & W* from 97. *Stableside, 5 Princess Road, Taunton TA1 4SY* Tel (01823) 335531

JAYNE, Martin Philip. b 49. Man Univ BA71 MRTPI73. Carl Dioc Tr Course 87. **d** 90 **p** 91. NSM Natland *Carl* from 90; Dioc Officer for NSM from 04. *12 Longmeadow Lane, Natland, Kendal LA9 7QZ* Tel (01539) 560942 E-mail jayne@which.net

JEANES, Gordon Paul. b 55. Ox Univ BA79 MA82 BD90 Univ of Wales (Lamp) PhD99. St Steph Ho Ox 80. **d** 82 **p** 83. C S Wimbledon H Trin and St Pet *S'wark* 82-85; C Surbiton St Andr and St Mark 85-90; Chapl St Chad's Coll Dur 90-93; Sub-Warden St Mich Coll Llan 94-98; Lect Th Univ of Wales (Cardiff) 94-98; V Wandsworth St Anne *S'wark* from 98; P-in-c Wandsworth St Faith from 05; Dioc Voc Adv from 99. *St Anne's Vicarage, 182 St Ann's Hill, London SW18 2RS* Tel (020) 8874 2809 E-mail gordon.jeanes@virgin.net

JEANS, The Ven Alan Paul. b 58. MIAAS84 MIBCO84 Southn Univ BTh89 Univ of Wales (Lamp) MA03. Sarum & Wells Th Coll 86. **d** 89 **p** 90. C Parkstone St Pet w Branksea and St Osmund *Sarum* 89-93; P-in-c Bishop's Cannings, All Cannings etc 93-98; Par Development Adv from 98; Can and Preb Sarum Cathl from 02; Adn Sarum from 03; RD Alderbury from 05. *Herbert House, 118 Lower Road, Salisbury SP2 9NW* Tel (01722) 336290 *or* (01380) 840373 Fax (01722) 411990 *or* (01380) 848247 E-mail adsarum@salisbury.anglican.org

JEANS, David Bockley. b 48. Mert Coll Ox BA71 MA80 PGCE73 Man Univ MPhil98. Trin Coll Bris. **d** 85 **p** 86. C Clevedon St Andr and Ch Ch *B & W* 85-88; V Wadsley *Sheff* 88-96; Dir of Studies Wilson Carlile Coll of Evang 96; Prin from 97. *Wilson Carlile College of Evangelism, 50 Cavendish Street, Sheffield S3 7RZ* Tel 0114-278 7020 E-mail d.jeans@sheffieldcentre.org.uk

JEAPES (née PORTER), Mrs Barbara Judith. b 47. Cam Inst of Educn TCert68. Carl Dioc Tr Inst 91. **d** 94 **p** 95. NSM Egremont and Haile *Carl* from 94. *15 Millfields, Beckermet CA21 2YY* Tel (01946) 841489 E-mail barbara@jeapesb.fsnet.co.uk

JEAVONS, Mrs Margaret Anne. b 51. Liv Poly BA72 Bris Univ BA01 St Kath Coll Liv PGCE74. Trin Coll Bris 99. **d** 01 **p** 02. C Totnes w Bridgetown, Berry Pomeroy etc *Ex* 01-05; V Sutton St Mich *York* from 05. *St Michael's Vicarage, 751 Marfleet Lane, Hull HU9 4TJ* Tel (01482) 374509 E-mail mjeavons@btopenworld.com

JEAVONS, Maurice. b 32. Ely Th Coll 60. **d** 62 **p** 63. C Longton St Jo *Lich* 62-68; V Wednesfield St Greg 68-81; V Lower Gornal 81-90; NSM Willenhall St Anne 92-93; C Tunstall 93-99; rtd 99; Hon C Wolverhampton St Steph *Lich* from 99. *17 Colaton Close, Wolverhampton WV10 9BB* Tel (01902) 351118

JEE, Jonathan Noel. b 63. BNC Ox BA84 MA88. Wycliffe Hall Ox 85. **d** 88 **p** 89. C Brampton St Thos *Derby* 88-92; TV Hinckley H Trin *Leic* 92-00; V Leamington Priors St Paul *Cov* from 00. *The Vicarage, 15 Lillington Road, Leamington Spa CV32 5YS* Tel (01926) 772132 *or* 427149 E-mail jonathan.jee@ntlworld.com

JEFF, Canon Gordon Henry. b 32. St Edm Hall Ox BA56 MA60. Wells Th Coll 59. **d** 61 **p** 62. C Sydenham St Bart *S'wark* 61-64; C Kidbrooke St Jas 64-66; V Clapham St Paul 66-72; V Raynes Park St Sav 73-79; RD Merton 77-79; V Carshalton Beeches 79-86; P-in-c Petersham 86-90; Chapl St Mich Convent 90-96; Hon Can S'wark Cathl 93-96; rtd 96. *9 Barnetts Well, Draycott, Cheddar BS27 3TF* Tel (01934) 744943

JEFFCOAT, Rupert Edward Elessing. b 70. St Cath Coll Cam BA92 MA96 FRCO91. WMMTC 02. **d** 05. NSM Brisbane Cathl Australia from 05. *GPO Box 421, Brisbane, Qld, Australia 4001* Tel (0061) (7) 3835 2231 E-mail rjeffcoat@freenetname.co.uk

JEFFERIES, Michael Lewis. b 45. St Jo Coll Nottm. **d** 87 **p** 88. C Pudsey St Lawr and St Paul *Bradf* 87-93; V Beckenham St Jo *Roch* 93-00; TV Modbury, Bigbury, Ringmore w Kingston etc *Ex* from 00. *The Vicarage, 3 Little Gate, Loddiswell, Kingsbridge TQ7 4RB* Tel (01548) 550841

JEFFERIES, Preb Phillip John. b 42. St Chad's Coll Dur BA65 DipTh67 MA91. **d** 67 **p** 68. C Tunstall Ch Ch *Lich* 67-71; C Wolverhampton St Pet 71-74; P-in-c Oakengates 74-80; V 80-82; P-in-c Ketley 78-82; V Horninglow 82-00; Bp's Adv on Hosp Chapl from 82; RD Tutbury 97-00; Preb Lich Cathl from 99; TR Stafford from 00. *The Rectory, 32 Rowley Avenue, Stafford ST17 9AG* Tel (01785) 258511 E-mail phillipjefferies@stmarystafford.fsnet.co.uk

JEFFERS, Cliff Peter. b 69. CITC BTh98. **d** 98 **p** 99. C Limerick City *L & K* 98-01; I Clonenagh w Offerlane, Borris-in-Ossory etc *C & O* 01-04; I Athy w Kilberry, Fontstown and Kilkea *D & G* from 04. *The Rectory, Church Road, Athy, Co Kildare, Irish Republic* Tel (00353) (59) 863 1446 Fax 863 1490 E-mail athy@glendalough.anglican.org

JEFFERSON, Charles Dudley. b 55. St Pet Coll Ox BA78 MA81. Ridley Hall Cam 79. **d** 81 **p** 82. C Chadkirk *Ches* 81-84; C Macclesfield St Pet 84-85; C Macclesfield Team Par 85-89; R Elworth and Warmingham 89-99; Chapl Framlingham Coll 99-01; Chapl Rendcomb Coll Cirencester from 01; P-in-c Rendcomb *Glouc* from 01. *The Rectory, Rendcomb, Cirencester GL7 7EZ* Tel (01285) 831319

JEFFERSON, David Charles. b 33. Leeds Univ BA57. Coll of Resurr Mirfield 57. **d** 59 **p** 60. C Kennington Cross St Anselm *S'wark* 59-62; C Richmond St Mary 62-64; Chapl Wilson's Gr Sch Camberwell 64-93; Chapl Wilson's Sch Wallington 75-99; Public Preacher *S'wark* 64-74; Hon C Carshalton Beeches 74-04; rtd 93; Perm to Offic *S'wark* from 04. *15 Sandown Drive, Carshalton SM5 4LN* Tel (020) 8669 0640

JEFFERSON, Michael William. b 41. K Coll Lon AKC64. WMMTC 96. **d** 98 **p** 99. C Four Oaks *Birm* 98-02; P-in-c Longdon *Lich* from 02; Local Min Adv (Wolverhampton) from 02. *The Vicarage, Longdon, Rugeley WS15 4PS* Tel (01543) 492871

JEFFERY, Graham. b 35. Qu Coll Cam BA58. Wells Th Coll 58. **d** 60 **p** 61. C Southampton Maybush St Pet *Win* 60-63; Australia 63-66; C E Grinstead St Swithun *Chich* 66-68; C-in-c The Hydneye CD 68-74; V Wick 74-76; C Hove 76-78; P-in-c Newtimber w Pyecombe 78-82; R Poynings w Edburton, Newtimber and Pyecombe 82-92; P-in-c Sullington and Thakeham w Warminghurst 92-95; rtd 96; NSM Poynings w Edburton, Newtimber and Pyecombe *Chich* 97-99; Perm to Offic from 00. *St Andrews, Rock Road, Ashington, Pulborough RH20 3AG* Tel (01903) 741268

JEFFERY (née CAW), Mrs Hannah Mary. b 69. Birm Univ BMus91. St Jo Coll Nottm MA95. **d** 95 **p** 96. C Northampton St Giles *Pet* 95-99; Hon C Hanger Hill Ascension and W Twyford St Mary *Lon* 99-04; TV Northampton Em *Pet* from 04. *9 Botmead Road, Northampton NN3 5JF* Tel (01604) 787954 E-mail jeffery@xalt.co.uk

JEFFERY, Mrs Jennifer Ann. b 45. Philippa Fawcett Coll CertEd66. STETS. **d** 02 **p** 03. NSM Wilton *B & W* from 02. *4 Southwell, Trull, Taunton TA3 7HU* Tel (01823) 286589 E-mail jenny@jajeffery.freeserve.co.uk

JEFFERY, Jonathan George Piers. b 63. Man Univ LLB84. Ripon Coll Cuddesdon 95. **d** 97 **p** 98. C Lee-on-the-Solent *Portsm* 97-01; V Leigh Park from 01; V Warren Park from 01. *The Vicarage, Riders Lane, Havant PO9 4QT* Tel (023) 9247 5276

JEFFERY, Kenneth Charles. b 40. Univ of Wales BA64 Linacre Coll Ox BA67 MA70. St Steph Ho Ox 64. **d** 67 **p** 68. C Swindon New Town *Bris* 67-68; C Summertown *Ox* 68-71; C Brighton St Pet *Chich* 71-77; V Ditchling 77-00; rtd 05. *62 Fruitlands, Malvern WR14 4XA* Tel (01684) 567042 E-mail kenneth@jeffery333.fslife.co.uk

JEFFERY, Michael Frank. b 48. Linc Th Coll 74. **d** 76 **p** 77. C Caterham Valley *S'wark* 76-79; C Tupsley *Heref* 79-82; P-in-c Stretton Sugwas 82-84; P-in-c Bishopstone 83-84; P-in-c Kenchester and Bridge Sollers 83-84; V Whiteshill *Glouc* 84-92; P-in-c Randwick 92; V Whiteshill and Randwick 93-02; TV Bedminster *Bris* from 02. *St Paul's Vicarage, 2 Southville Road, Bristol BS3 1DG* Tel 0117-908 6996

JEFFERY, Norman. b 42. Bps' Coll Cheshunt. **d** 67 **p** 68. C Putney St Marg *S'wark* 67-71; C Hoddesdon *St Alb* 71-74; P-in-c Roxton w Gt Barford 74-79; V 79-86; V Woburn Sands from 86; RD Ampthill from 96. *The Vicarage, Church Road, Woburn Sands, Milton Keynes MK17 8TR* Tel (01908) 582581

JEFFERY, Peter James. b 41. Leeds Univ BSc63. Oak Hill Th Coll 64. **d** 66 **p** 67. C Streatham Park St Alb *S'wark* 66-70; C Northampton St Giles *Pet* 70-73; C Rushden St Pet 73-76; C Rushden w Newton Bromswold 77-78; V Siddal *Wakef* 78-85; V Sowerby Bridge w Norland 85-98; P-in-c Cornholme 98-00; P-in-c Walsden 98-00; V Cornholme and Walsden 00-05; rtd 05. *12 Highcroft Road, Todmorden OL14 5LZ* E-mail jeffrey@cornden.freeserve.co.uk

JEFFERY, Peter Noel. b 37. Pemb Coll Ox BA60 MA64. Linc Th Coll 60. **d** 62 **p** 63. C W Smethwick *Birm* 62-64; P-in-c Bordesley St Andr 64-69; R Turvey *St Alb* 69-98; P-in-c Stevington 79-98; rtd 98. *Franconia Cottage, The Gardens, Adstock, Buckingham MK18 2JF* Tel (01296) 715770

JEFFERY, Richard William Christopher. b 43. Ex Univ BA65. Coll of Resurr Mirfield 66. **d** 68 **p** 69. C Widley w Wymering *Portsm* 68-71; C Salisbury St Mich *Sarum* 71-74; TV Ridgeway 74-80; V Stanford in the Vale w Goosey and Hatford *Ox* 80-89; V Topsham *Ex* from 89; RD Aylesbeare from 01. *The Vicarage, Globefields, Topsham, Exeter EX3 0EZ* Tel (01392) 876120 E-mail knocksink@eurobell.co.uk

JEFFERY, The Very Revd Robert Martin Colquhoun. b 35. K Coll Lon BD58 AKC58 Birm Univ Hon DD99 FRSA91. **d** 59 **p** 60. C Grangetown *Dur* 59-61; C Barnes St Mary *S'wark* 61-63; Asst Sec Miss and Ecum Coun Ch Assembly 64-68; Sec Dept Miss and Unity BCC 68-71; V Headington *Ox* 71-78; RD Cowley 73-78; P-in-c Tong *Lich* 78-83; V 83-87; Dioc Missr 78-80; Adn Salop 80-87; Dean Worc 87-96; Can Res and Sub-Dean Ch Ch *Ox* 96-02; Select Preacher Ox Univ 91, 97, 98 and 02; rtd 02. *47 The Manor House, Bennett Crescent, Cowley, Oxford OX4 2UG* Tel (01865) 749706 E-mail rmcj@btopenworld.com

JEFFERYES, June Ann. b 37. Dur Univ BA58. WMMTC 87. **d** 90 **p** 94. NSM Caverswall *Lich* 90-92; NSM Caverswall and Weston Coyney w Dilhorne 92-02; rtd 02. *24 Glen Drive, Alton, Stoke-on-Trent ST10 4DJ* Tel (01538) 702150

JEFFERYES, Preb Neil. b 37. St Andr Univ BSc60 Lon Univ BD62. Tyndale Hall Bris 60. **d** 63 **p** 64. C St Helens St Helen *Liv* 63-68; V Barrow St Mark *Carl* 68-77; RD Furness 74-77; P-in-c Tetsworth *Ox* 77-81; P-in-c Adwell w S Weston 77-81; P-in-c Stoke Talmage w Wheatfield 77-81; RD Aston 81-85; R Tetsworth, Adwell w S Weston, Lewknor etc 81-86; V Caverswall *Lich* 86-92; P-in-c Dilhorne 86-92; RD Cheadle 91-98; V Caverswall and Weston Coyney w Dilhorne 92-02; Preb Lich Cathl 97-02; rtd 02. *24 Glen Drive, Alton, Stoke-on-Trent ST10 4DJ* Tel (01538) 702150 E-mail neil@jefferyes.freeserve.co.uk

JEFFORD, Mrs Margaret June. b 50. Univ of Wales RGN81. St Mich Coll Llan 94. **d** 96 **p** 97. C Risca *Mon* 96-98; C Pontypool 98-00; TV 00-02; V Newbridge w Crumlin 02-04; V Newbridge from 04. *St Paul's Vicarage, High Street, Newbridge, Newport NP11 4FW* Tel (01495) 243975

JEFFORD, Peter Ernest. b 29. AKC53. **d** 54 **p** 55. C Berkeley *Glouc* 54-57; C Petersfield w Sheet *Portsm* 57-61; Chapl Churcher's Coll 57-61; R Rollesby w Burgh w Billockby *Nor* 62-71; V Watton 71-81; V Watton w Carbrooke and Ovington 81-82; Offg Chapl RAF 71-82; P-in-c Brampford Speke *Ex*

82-83; P-in-c Cadbury 82-83; P-in-c Thorverton 82-83; P-in-c Upton Pyne 82-83; TR Thorverton, Cadbury, Upton Pyne etc 83-92; rtd 92; Perm to Offic *Ox* 92-96 and from 03; Hon C Ox St Mary V w St Cross and St Pet 96-99; P-in-c Whitchurch St Mary 00-03; Chapl Plater Coll 96-05. *27 Ashlong Road, Headington, Oxford OX3 0NH* Tel (01865) 760593

JEFFORD, Ronald. b 46. Univ of Wales (Lamp) Univ of Wales (Cardiff) DPS. St Mich Coll Llan Dip Minl Studies. **d** 91 **p** 92. C Ebbw Vale *Mon* 91-94; TV 94-95; R Bedwas and Rudry 95-98; V Abersychan and Garndiffaith 98-03; TV Mynyddislwyn from 03. *The Vicarage, Central Avenue, Oakdale, Blackwood NP2 0JS* Tel (01495) 223043

JEFFREE, Robin. b 29. AKC54. **d** 55 **p** 56. C N Harrow St Alb *Lon* 55-59; C Hendon St Mary 59-62; V Manea *Ely* 62-67; V Hartford 67-83; R Denver 83-94; V Ryston w Roxham 83-94; V W Dereham 83-94; rtd 94; Perm to Offic *Nor* from 94. *3 Church Lane, Hindolveston, Dereham NR20 5BT* Tel (01263) 861857

JEFFREY, Katrina. *See* METZNER, Mrs Katrina

JEFFREYS, David John. b 45. S Dios Minl Tr Scheme 89. **d** 92 **p** 93. NSM Bexhill St Barn *Chich* 92-95; Chapl Hastings and Rother NHS Trust from 95. *The Conquest Hospital, The Ridge, St Leonards-on-Sea TN37 7RD* Tel (01424) 757088 *or* 843672 E-mail chaplaincy@mail.har-tr.sthames.nhs.uk

JEFFREYS (née DESHPANDE), Mrs Lakshmi Anant. b 64. Liv Univ BSc86 Ex Univ PGCE87. Wycliffe Hall Ox BTh94. **d** 94 **p** 95. C Long Eaton St Jo *Derby* 94-97; Chapl Nottm Trent Univ *S'well* 98-03; Perm to Offic *Derby* 03-04; Dioc Miss Adv from 04. *43 White Street, Derby DE22 1HB* Tel (01332) 224432 E-mail lakshmi.jeffreys@derby.anglican.org

JEFFREYS, Timothy John. b 58. Man Univ BSc79. Cranmer Hall Dur 83. **d** 86 **p** 87. C Goodmayes All SS *Chelmsf* 86-88; Perm to Offic *S'wark* 92-93; Hon C S Lambeth St Anne and All SS 93-96; C Croydon St Jo from 96. *Church House, Barrow Road, Croydon CR0 4EZ* Tel (020) 8688 7006

JEFFRIES, Frances Alyx. b 59. Bris Poly BA82 Solicitor 83. **d** 04 **p** 05. OLM Gainsborough and Morton *Linc* from 04. *33 Balfour Street, Gainsborough DN21 2LF* Tel (01427) 678569 E-mail frances@33gains.fsnet.co.uk

JEFFRIES, Keith. b 48. St Steph Ho Ox DipMin93. **d** 93 **p** 94. C St Marychurch *Ex* 93-96; TV Wood Green St Mich w Bounds Green St Gabr etc *Lon* 96-98; V The Hydneye *Chich* 98-00; Chapl Univ of Greenwich *Roch* 00-02; Chapl Kent Inst of Art and Design 00-02; Chapl Tenerife Sur *Eur* 02-03; Perm to Offic *Roch* 03-04; Bp's Adv on Chr/Muslim Relns *Birm* from 04. *9 Isbourne Way, Birmingham B9 4PL* Tel 0121-771 4593 E-mail fatherkeithjeffries@hotmail.com

JELF, Miss Pauline Margaret. b 55. Chich Th Coll 88. **d** 90 **p** 94. Par Dn Clayton *Lich* 90-94; C Knutton 94-98; P-in-c Silverdale and Alsagers Bank 94-98; Perm to Offic 98-02; C Clayton 02; C Betley and Madeley 02-04; C Trent Vale from 03. *11 Stafford Avenue, Newcastle ST5 3BN* Tel (01785) 639545

JELLEY, David. b 25. St Deiniol's Hawarden 86. **d** 87 **p** 88. NSM Evington *Leic* 87-93; P-in-c New Galloway *Glas* 93-97; rtd 97; Perm to Offic *Leic* from 00. *Address temp unknown*

JELLEY, Ian. b 54. Newc Univ MA94 Cert Counselling 97. NEOC 89. **d** 91 **p** 92. C Jarrow *Dur* 91-95; P-in-c Leam Lane 95-96; Chapl HM Pris Holme Ho 96-01; R Grindon, Stillington and Wolviston *Dur* 01-03; rtd 03. *8 Beverley Road, Billingham TS23 3RE*

JELLEY, James Dudley. b 46. Linc Th Coll 78. **d** 80 **p** 81. C Stockwell Green St Andr *S'wark* 80-85; V Camberwell St Phil and St Mark 85-93; Perm to Offic 93-96; V Camberwell St Luke from 96; RD Camberwell from 00. *St Luke's Vicarage, 30 Commercial Way, London SE15 5JQ* Tel (020) 7703 5587 Fax as telephone

JELLEY (née CAPITANCHIK), Mrs Sophie Rebecca. b 72. Leeds Univ BA93. Wycliffe Hall Ox MPhil97. **d** 97 **p** 98. C Shipley St Pet *Bradf* 97-00; CMS Uganda 00-03; C Churt and Hindhead *Guildf* from 03. *St John's Vicarage, Old Kiln Lane, Churt, Farnham GU10 2HX* Tel (01428) 713368 E-mail sophie@jelley.f9.co.uk

JENKIN, The Hon Charles Alexander Graham. b 54. BScEng. Westcott Ho Cam 81. **d** 84 **p** 85. C Binley *Cov* 84-88; TV Canvey Is *Chelmsf* 88-94; TR Melton Mowbray *Leic* from 94; RD Framland 98-02. *The Rectory, 67 Dalby Road, Melton Mowbray LE13 0BQ* Tel (01664) 480923 E-mail cjenkin@leicester.anglican.org

JENKIN, Christopher Cameron. b 36. BNC Ox BA61 MA64. Clifton Th Coll 61. **d** 63 **p** 64. C Walthamstow St Mary *Chelmsf* 63-68; C Surbiton Hill Ch Ch *S'wark* 68-78; V Newport St Jo *Portsm* 78-88; TR Newbarns w Hawcoat *Carl* 88-01; rtd 01; Perm to Offic *Carl* from 01. *Beckside, Orton, Penrith CA10 3RX* Tel (01539) 624410

JENKINS, Alan David. b 60. Bris Poly BA83 Wolv Poly DipTM87 DipM90 Spurgeon's Coll MTh02. All So Coll of Applied Th DipApTh85 Wycliffe Hall Ox 93. **d** 95 **p** 96. C Tunbridge Wells St Jas w St Phil *Roch* 95-01; TV S Gillingham from 01. *58 Parkwood Green, Gillingham ME8 9PP* Tel (01634) 300883 E-mail suzieandalan.jenkins@virgin.net

JENKINS, Allan Kenneth. b 40. Lon Univ BD63 AKC63 MTh69 PhD85. St Mich Coll Llan 63. **d** 64 **p** 65. C Llanblethian w Cowbridge *Llan* 64-70; India 70-76; V Llanarth w Clytha, Llansantffraed and Bryngwyn *Mon* 76-78; Dir of Studies Chich Th Coll 78-83; P-in-c Fowlmere *Ely* 83-87; P-in-c Thriplow 83-87; Sen Tutor EAMTC 84-87; Sen Chapl Cardiff Colls 87-95; Dioc Dir Post-Ord Tr *Llan* 88-95; P-in-c Sidlesham *Chich* from 95; Tutor Univ Coll Chich from 95. *The Vicarage, Church Farm Lane, Sidlesham, Chichester PO20 7RE* Tel (01243) 641237 E-mail a.jenkins@ucc.ac.uk

JENKINS, Miss Anne Christina. b 47. Birm Univ BA70 Hull Univ CertEd71 St Jo Coll Dur BA77 DipTh78. Cranmer Hall Dur 75. **dss** 78 **d** 87 **p** 94. E Coatham *York* 78-81; OHP 81-87; Perm to Offic *York* 81-87; Ghana 87-88; Par Dn Beeston *Ripon* 88-93; Par Dn Leeds Gipton Epiphany 93-94; V Leeds St Marg and All Hallows 94-99; rtd 99; Perm to Offic *York* from 00. *28 Hill Cottages, Rosedale East, Pickering YO18 8RG* Tel (01751) 417130

JENKINS, Audrey Joan. b 36. TCert61. St D Coll Lamp. **d** 01. Par Dn Marshfield and Peterstone Wentloog etc *Mon* from 01. *10 Lytham Grove, St Mellons, Cardiff CF3 0LU* Tel (029) 2036 0574 E-mail audrey@stmellons.co.uk

JENKINS, Catherine. **d** 05. NSM Silverton, Butterleigh, Bickleigh and Cadeleigh *Ex* from 05. *Butterleigh House, Butterleigh, Cullompton EX15 1PH* Tel (01884) 855379

JENKINS, Clifford Thomas. b 38. Westmr Coll Ox MTh02 IEng MIElecIE. Sarum & Wells Th Coll 74. **d** 77 **p** 78. Chapl Yeovil Coll 77-86; Hon C Yeovil w Kingston Pitney *B & W* 77-80; P-in-c 80-86; Chs FE Liaison Officer *B & W, Bris* and *Glouc* 87-90; Perm to Offic *B & W* 87-92 and from 93; FE Adv Gen Syn Bd of Educn and Meth Ch 90-98; rtd 98. *Bethany, 10 Grove Avenue, Yeovil BA20 2BB* Tel (01935) 475043 E-mail clifford.jenkins@virgin.net

JENKINS, Clive Ronald. b 57. Ripon Coll Cuddesdon 81. **d** 84 **p** 85. C E Grinstead St Swithun *Chich* 84-87; C Horsham 87-88; TV 88-90; Dioc Youth Chapl 90-96; P-in-c Amberley w N Stoke and Parham, Wiggonholt etc 93-96; V Southbourne w W Thorney from 96. *The Vicarage, 271 Main Road, Southbourne, Emsworth PO10 8JE* Tel (01243) 372436

JENKINS, David. *See* JENKINS, Canon William David

JENKINS, David. *See* JENKINS, Preb Richard David

✠**JENKINS, The Rt Revd David Edward.** b 25. Qu Coll Ox BA51 MA54 Dur Univ DD87. Linc Th Coll 52. **d** 53 **p** 54 **c** 84. C Birm Cathl *Birm* 53-54; Lect Qu Coll Birm 53-54; Chapl Qu Coll Ox 54-69; Lect Th Ox Univ 55-69; Can Th Leic Cathl *Leic* 66-82; Dir WCC Humanum Studies 69-73; Dir Wm Temple Foundn Man 73-78; Jt Dir 79-94; Prof Th and RS Leeds Univ 79-84; Bp Dur 84-94; rtd 94; Hon Asst Bp Ripon and Leeds *Ripon* from 94. *Ashbourne, Cotherstone, Barnard Castle DL12 9PR* Tel (01833) 650804 Fax 650714

JENKINS, Canon David Harold. b 61. SS Coll Cam BA84 MA87 Ox Univ BA88 MA94 FSAScot01. Ripon Coll Cuddesdon 86. **d** 89 **p** 90. C Chesterton Gd Shep *Ely* 89-91; C Earley St Pet *Ox* 91-94; V Blackpool St Mich *Blackb* 94-99; V Broughton 99-04; AD Preston 04; Can Res Carl Cathl *Carl* from 04; Dir of Educn from 04. *1 The Abbey, Carlisle CA3 8TZ* Tel (01228) 597614 *or* 538086 Fax 815409 E-mail director.education@carlislediocese.org.uk

JENKINS, David Noble. b 25. CCC Cam BA47 MA50. Cuddesdon Coll 48. **d** 50 **p** 51. C Northampton St Matt *Pet* 50-54; Chapl Hurstpierpoint Coll 54-59; USPG 60-65; Chapl Eastbourne Coll 66-74; V Jarvis Brook *Chich* 75-90; rtd 90; USA 90-92; Perm to Offic *Chich* from 92. *2 Littlebourne Cottages, London Road, Crowborough TN6 1SR* Tel (01892) 661179

JENKINS, David Roland. b 32. Kelham Th Coll 55. **d** 59 **p** 60. C Middlesbrough St Jo the Ev *York* 59-60; C Kingston upon Hull St Alb 60-64; C Roehampton H Trin *S'wark* 64-68; V Dawley St Jerome *Lon* 68-73; R Harlington 73-98; rtd 98; Perm to Offic *Lon* from 99. *21F Cleveland Road, Cowley, Uxbridge UB8 2DR* Tel (01895) 253761

JENKINS, David Thomas. b 43. Ox Univ MA94 RIBA70 Lon Univ DipTh79. S'wark Ord Course 76 Ripon Coll Cuddesdon 86. **d** 79 **p** 80. NSM Merthyr Tydfil and Cyfarthfa *Llan* 79-86; NSM Brecon St David w Llanspyddid and Llanilltyd *S & B* 86-91; P-in-c Llangiwg 91-92; V 92-01; Chapl Puerto de la Cruz Tenerife *Eur* from 02. *Apartado 68, Parque Taoro, Puerto de la Cruz, 38400 Tenerife, Canary Islands* Tel (0034) (922) 384038 Fax 388285

JENKINS, The Ven David Thomas Ivor. b 29. K Coll Lon BD52 AKC52 Birm Univ MA63. **d** 53 **p** 54. C Bilton *Cov* 53-56; V Wolston 56-61; Asst Dir RE *Carl* 61-63; V Carl St Barn 63-72; V Carl St Cuth 72-76; P-in-c Carl St Mary w St Paul 72-76; V Carl St Cuth w St Mary 76-91; Dioc Sec 84-95; Hon Can Carl Cathl 76-91; Can Res 91-95; Adn Westmorland and Furness 95-99; rtd 99; Perm to Offic *Carl* from 00. *Irvings House, Sleagill, Penrith CA10 3HD* Tel (01931) 714400

JENKINS, Canon Eric Neil. b 23. Univ of Wales BSc43 MSc47. Wycliffe Hall Ox 60. **d** 62 **p** 63. C Allerton *Liv* 62-65; V Hale 65-73; Bp's Adv on Soc and Scientific Affairs 73-88; V Hightown

73-88; Hon Can Liv Cathl 83-89; rtd 89; Perm to Offic *Liv* 89-03. *c/o Mrs B Rundell, 11 John Taylor Way, Moreton Morrell, Warwick CV35 9DH* Tel (01926) 651541

JENKINS, Eric Robert. b 52. Poly Cen Lon BSc74. STETS 97. **d** 00 **p** 01. C Weybridge *Guildf* 00-04; R Cobham and Stoke D'Abernon from 04. *The Vicarage, St Andrew's Walk, Cobham KT11 3EQ* Tel (01932) 862109 Mobile 07747-844689 E-mail er.jenkins@btinternet.com

JENKINS, The Very Revd Frank Graham. b 23. St D Coll Lamp BA47 Jes Coll Ox BA49 MA53. St Mich Coll Llan 49. **d** 50 **p** 51. C Llangeinor *Llan* 50-53; Min Can Llan Cathl 53-60; CF (TA) 56-61; V Abertillery *Mon* 60-64; V Risca 64-75; Can St Woolos Cathl 67-76; V Caerleon 75-76; Dean Mon 76-90; rtd 90; Lic to Offic *Mon* from 90. *Rivendell, 209 Christchurch Road, Newport NP19 7QL* Tel (01633) 255278

JENKINS, Frederick Llewellyn. b 14. St D Coll Lamp BA35 St Mich Coll Llan 36. **d** 37 **p** 38. C Gilfach Goch w Llandyfodwg *Llan* 37-40; C Bishop's Castle w Mainstone *Heref* 40-45; CF 45-64; CF (R of O) 64-69; Chapl R Masonic Sch Bushey 64-77; rtd 77; Perm to Offic *Lich* 77-95. *Address temp unknown*

JENKINS, Garry Frederick. b 48. Southn Univ BTh79. Chich Th Coll 75. **d** 79 **p** 80. C Kingsbury St Andr *Lon* 79-84; C Leigh St Clem *Chelmsf* 84-88; P-in-c Brentwood St Geo 88-94; V from 94. *The Vicarage, 28 Robin Hood Road, Brentwood CM15 9EN* Tel (01277) 213618 E-mail g.f.jenkins@amserve.net

JENKINS, Gary John. b 59. York Univ BA80 CertEd81. Oak Hill Th Coll BA89. **d** 89 **p** 90. C Norwood St Luke *S'wark* 89-94; P-in-c St Helier 94-95; V 95-01; V Redhill H Trin from 01. *4 Carlton Road, Redhill RH1 2BX* Tel (01737) 779917 E-mail garyjjenkins@hotmail.com

JENKINS, Canon George Patrick. b 36. Univ of Wales (Lamp) BA61. Lich Th Coll 61. **d** 63 **p** 64. C Dursley *Glouc* 63-66; C Stroud H Trin 66-69; V Churcham w Bulley 69-81; V Churcham w Bulley and Minsterworth 81-02; RD Forest N 79-95; Hon Can Glouc Cathl 90-02; rtd 02. *Meadow Bank, Cefnllys Lane, Penybont, Llandrindod Wells LD1 5TY* Tel (01597) 850027

JENKINS, Canon Jeanette. b 42. St Jo Coll Nottm 83. **dss** 84 **d** 86 **p** 94. NSM Kilmarnock *Glas* 84-94; NSM Irvine St Andr LEP 84-94; NSM Ardrossan 84-94; Asst Chapl Crosshouse Hosp 86-94; Chapl Ayrshire Hospice 90-02; Can St Mary's Cathl *Glas* from 99. *4 Gleneagles Avenue, Kilwinning KA13 6RD* Tel (01294) 553383 Mobile 07775-595901 E-mail ivanjen@lineone.net

JENKINS, John Francis. b 46. Ripon Hall Ox 77 Ripon Coll Cuddesdon 75. **d** 77 **p** 78. C Filton *Bris* 77-79; C Bris St Andr Hartcliffe 79-84; P-in-c Bris H Cross Inns Court 84-85; V 85-95; R Odcombe, Brympton, Lufton and Montacute *B & W* from 95. *The Rectory, Street Lane, Higher Odcombe, Yeovil BA22 8UP* Tel (01935) 863034

JENKINS, John Howard David. b 51. Birm Univ BA72. St Steph Ho Ox 72. **d** 74 **p** 75. C Milford Haven *St D* 74-77; PV Llan Cathl *Llan* 77-81; Chapl Lowther Coll and V Choral St As Cathl *St As* 81-84; C Neath w Llantwit *Llan* 84-86; Chapl Colston's Sch Bris 86-91; Chapl Blue Coat Sch Birm 91-04; Chapl R Masonic Sch for Girls Rickmansworth from 04. *Royal Masonic School, Rickmansworth Park, Rickmansworth WD3 4HF* Tel (01923) 725338 *or* 773593

JENKINS, John Morgan. b 33. Open Univ BA96. Mon Dioc Tr Scheme 82. **d** 85 **p** 86. NSM Cwmbran *Mon* 85-02; rtd 02. *5 Ridgeway Avenue, Newport NP20 5AJ* Tel (01633) 662231

JENKINS, John Raymond. b 26. K Coll Lon 52. **d** 53 **p** 54. C Wrexham *St As* 53-56; Hon C 77-82; C Welshpool 56-57; V Mochdre 57-65; V Llandysul *St D* 65-67; V Llanfair Caereinion w Llanllugan *St As* 67-70; V Llanychaearn w Llanddeiniol *St D* 82-91; rtd 91; Chapl Lanzarote *Eur* 95-97. *Manoravon, Main Street, Llanon SY23 5HJ* Tel (01974) 202212

JENKINS, John Richard. b 68. Dundee Univ LLB90 Leeds Univ MA98. St Steph Ho Ox BA94. **d** 94 **p** 95. C Brighouse and Clifton *Wakef* 94-97; C Barnsley St Mary 97-99; Perm to Offic *Lon* from 03; Dir Affirming Catholicism from 05. *St Matthew's House, 20 Great Peter Street, London SW1P 2BU* Tel (020) 7233 0235 E-mail directoraffcath@btinternet.com

JENKINS, Julian James. b 56. Bris Poly HND76 Univ of Wales (Cardiff) DMS98. St Mich Coll Llan 97. **d** 99 **p** 00. C Whitchurch *Llan* 99-01; TV Aberavon from 01. *77 Victoria Road, Aberavon, Port Talbot SA12 6QQ* Tel (01639) 892306

JENKINS, Lawrence Clifford. b 45. AKC70 Open Univ BA77. St Aug Coll Cant. **d** 71 **p** 72. C Osmondthorpe St Phil *Ripon* 71-74; C Monkseaton St Mary *Newc* 75-78; V Shiremoor 78-84; V Wheatley Hills *Sheff* 84-95; RD Doncaster 92-95; V Greenhill from 95. *St Peter's Vicarage, Reney Avenue, Sheffield S8 7FN* Tel 0114-237 7422 E-mail lawrie.jenkins@ukgateway.net

JENKINS, Patrick. *See* JENKINS, Canon George Patrick

JENKINS, Paul Morgan. b 44. Sussex Univ BEd68 Fitzw Coll Cam BA73 MA76. Westcott Ho Cam 71. **d** 74 **p** 75. C Forest Gate St Edm *Chelmsf* 74-77; Chapl Bryanston Sch 77-85; P-in-c Stourpaine, Durweston and Bryanston *Sarum* 77-83; Asst Chapl and Housemaster Repton Sch Derby 84-89; Dean of Chpl 89-91; R Singleton *Chich* 91-97; V E Dean 91-97; V W Dean 91-97; Dir St Columba's Retreat and Conf Cen from 97; Chapl Community of St Pet Woking from 03. *St Columba's House, Maybury Hill, Woking GU22 8AB* Tel (01483) 766498 Mobile 07973-848941 Fax (01483) 740441 E-mail retreats@stcolumbashouse.org.uk

JENKINS (née RICHARDSON), Pauline Kate. b 41. RGN62 Nottm Univ CertEd80 RNT83. St Jo Coll Nottm 91. **d** 94 **p** 98. Uganda 94-96; Perm to Offic *S'well* 96-98; NSM Selston 98-01; NSM Annesley w Newstead 01-03; rtd 03; Perm to Offic *S'well* from 03. *The Rookery, 130 Church Street, Eastwood, Nottingham NG16 3HT* Tel (01773) 713636 Mobile 07976-716955

JENKINS, Richard. *See* JENKINS, John Richard

JENKINS, Preb Richard David. b 33. Magd Coll Cam BA58 MA. Westcott Ho Cam 59. **d** 61 **p** 62. C Staveley *Derby* 61-64; C Billingham St Aid *Dur* 64-68; V Walsall Pleck and Bescot *Lich* 68-73; R Whitchurch 73-97; RD Wem and Whitchurch 85-95; P-in-c Tilstock and Whixall 92-95; Preb Lich Cathl 93-97; rtd 97; Perm to Offic *Lich* from 99. *The Council House, Council House Court, Castle Street, Shrewsbury SY1 2AU* Tel (01743) 270051

JENKINS, Richard Morvan. b 44. St Mich Coll Llan DipTh68 DPS69. **d** 69 **p** 70. C Tenby *St D* 69-73; V Llanrhian w Llanhywel and Carnhedryn 73-77; V Llanrhian w Llanhywel and Carnhedryn etc 77-80; R Johnston w Steynton 80-93; V St Ishmael's w Llan-saint and Ferryside from 93. *The Vicarage, Water Street, Ferryside SA17 5RT* Tel (01267) 267288

JENKINS, Robert. *See* JENKINS, Eric Robert

JENKINS, Canon Robert Francis. b 33. BNC Ox BA57 MA59. Wycliffe Hall Ox 57. **d** 59 **p** 60. C Hall Green Ascension *Birm* 59-63; V Dosthill and Wood End 63-71; V Brandwood 71-85; V Sutton Coldfield St Columba 85-97; Hon Can S Malawi from 87; rtd 97; Perm to Offic *Birm* from 97 and *Lich* from 00. *4 The Pines, Lichfield WS14 9XA* Tel (01543) 252176

JENKINS, Tanya Louise. b 66. Univ of Wales BD87 MPhil89 PhD93 PGCE94. Westcott Ho Cam 95. **d** 98 **p** 99. C Malltraeth Deanery *Ban* 98-01; P-in-c Llangefni w Tregaean *Ban* 01-04. *Drws y Coed, Penmynydd Road, Llangefni LL77 7HR* E-mail tanyacwmtawe@cyngar.fsnet.co.uk

JENKINS, Thomas Glennard Owen. b 22. St Jo Coll Ox BA48 MA52. Wells Th Coll 49 Wycliffe Hall Ox 50. **d** 50 **p** 51. Min Can St D Cathl *St D* 50-54; Chapl RN 54-58; Prec and Sacr Worc Cathl *Worc* 58-60; V Hailey w Crawley *Ox* 60-79; V Penbryn and Betws Ifan w Bryngwyn *St D* 79-87; rtd 87. *c/o Mrs R Jenkins, Coed-y-Wern, Sarnau, Llandysul SA44 6PX*

JENKINS, Thomas William. b 14. Univ of Wales BA40. St Mich Coll Llan 40. **d** 42 **p** 43. C Newport St Mark *Mon* 42-46; C Kidderminster St Mary and All SS, Trimpley etc *Worc* 46-48; V Walsall Pleck and Bescot *Lich* 48-67; V Shrewsbury H Trin w St Julian 67-75; Chapl Manor Hosp and St Jo Hosp 48-67; V Ruyton 75-80; rtd 80; Perm to Offic *Lich* 80-00. *4 Larkhill Road, Park Hall, Oswestry SY11 4AW* Tel (01691) 659304

JENKINS, Timothy David. b 52. Pemb Coll Ox BA73 MLitt77 MA82 St Edm Ho Cam BA84. Ridley Hall Cam 82. **d** 85 **p** 86. C Kingswood *Bris* 85-87; Sen Chapl Nottm Univ *S'well* 88-92; Dean Jes Coll Cam from 92. *50 Stanley Road, Cambridge CB5 8BL* Tel (01223) 363185 *or* 339339 E-mail tdj22@jesus.cam.ac.uk

JENKINS, Canon William David. b 42. Birm Univ BA63. St D Coll Lamp LTh65. **d** 65 **p** 66. C Gorseinon *S & B* 65-67; C Llanelli *St D* 67-72; V Clydach *S & B* 72-82; Chapl Gwynedd Hosp NHS Trust 82-97; V Llanrhos *St As* 82-97; RD Llanrwst 84-96; Can Cursal St As Cathl from 93; TR Tenby *St D* from 97. *The Rectory, Church Park, Tenby SA70 7EE* Tel (01834) 842068

JENKINSON, Margaret. b 40. MCSP62. Carl Dioc Tr Inst 89. **d** 92 **p** 94. NSM Preesall *Blackb* 92-96; NSM Lanercost, Walton, Gilsland and Nether Denton *Carl* 96-04; P-in-c Lorton and Loweswater w Buttermere from 04. *The Vicarage, Loweswater, Cockermouth CA13 0RU* Tel (01900) 85237 E-mail mgtandhenry@aol.com

JENKYNS, Preb Henry Derrik George. b 30. Sarum Th Coll 57. **d** 60 **p** 61. C Kettering SS Pet and Paul *Pet* 60-64; V Shrewsbury St Geo *Lich* 64-71; V Wednesbury St Paul Wood Green 71-76; V Stokesay *Heref* 76-86; P-in-c Acton Scott 76-86; RD Condover 80-86; Preb Heref Cathl 83-96; R Kington w Huntington, Old Radnor, Kinnerton etc 86-96; rtd 96; Perm to Offic *Heref* from 96. *Llantroft, Newcastle, Craven Arms SY7 8PD* Tel (01588) 640314

JENKYNS, John. *See* JENKYNS, Thomas John Blackwell

JENKYNS, John Thomas William Basil. b 30. Univ of Wales (Lamp) BA54 St Cath Coll Ox BA57 MA62. Wycliffe Hall Ox 54. **d** 57 **p** 58. C Neasden cum Kingsbury St Cath *Lon* 57-60; C S Lyncombe *B & W* 60-64; V Gt Harwood St Bart *Blackb* 64-66; R Colne St Bart 66-69; V Chard St Mary *B & W* 69-87; Preb Wells Cathl 87; V Swaffham *Nor* 87-89; V Overbury w Teddington, Alstone etc *Worc* 89-95; rtd 95. *2 Clos y Fran, Glais, Swansea SA7 9TH* Tel (01792) 842765

JENKYNS, Stephen. b 60. Univ of Wales (Cardiff) BTh02. St Mich Coll Llan 99. **d** 02 **p** 03. C Penarth w Lavernock *Llan* 02-04; C Penarth and Llandough from 04. *Church House, 153 Windsor Road, Penarth CF64 1JF* Tel (029) 2070 5485

JENKYNS, Thomas John Blackwell. b 31. Univ of Wales (Lamp) BA52. **d** 54 **p** 55. C Llanelli St Paul *St D* 54-58; C New Windsor

St Jo *Ox* 58-64; Chapl RAF 64-85; P-in-c Herriard w Winslade and Long Sutton etc *Win* 85-86; V 86-98; rtd 98; Perm to Offic *Ex* 98-04. *Brackenfield, 14 Heather Close, Woodhall Spa LN10 6YD* Tel (01526) 351330

JENNER, Miss Brenda Ann. b 54. Culham Coll Ox BEd80. St Jo Coll Nottm DPS88. **d** 88. Par Dn Leigh St Mary *Man* 88-92; Par Dn Leic Ch Sav *Leic* 92-94. *18 Chatsworth Avenue, Wigston, Leicester LE18 4LF*

JENNER, Michael Albert. b 37. Oak Hill Th Coll 75. **d** 77 **p** 78. C Mile Cross *Nor* 77-80; P-in-c Easton *Ely* 80-86; P-in-c Ellington 80-86; P-in-c Grafham 80-86; P-in-c Spaldwick w Barham and Woolley 80-86; Perm to Offic *Roch* from 01; rtd 02. *Heathgate Cottage, Langton Road, Langton Green, Tunbridge Wells TN3 0BA* Tel and fax (01892) 535136 Mobile 07831-826954

JENNER, Peter John. b 56. Chu Coll Cam BA77 PhD80 MA81. St Jo Coll Nottm 82. **d** 85 **p** 86. C Upperby St Jo *Carl* 85-88; Chapl Reading Univ *Ox* 88-96; P-in-c Mellor *Derby* 96-99; V from 99. *The Vicarage, Church Road, Mellor, Stockport SK6 5LX* Tel 0161-427 1203

JENNER, William George. b 37. Nottm Univ BSc59 K Coll Lon PGCE60. **d** 97 **p** 98. OLM Gillingham w Geldeston, Stockton, Ellingham etc *Nor* 97-05; Perm to Offic from 05. *3 Woodland Drive, Kirby Cane, Bungay NR35 2PT* Tel (01508) 518229

JENNETT, The Ven Maurice Arthur. b 34. St Jo Coll Dur BA60. Cranmer Hall Dur 60. **d** 62 **p** 63. C Marple All SS *Ches* 62-67; V Withnell *Blackb* 67-75; V Stranton *Dur* 75-91; Crosslinks Zimbabwe 92-99; Asst P Nyanga St Mary Magd 92-93; R 93-99; Can and Adn Manicaland N 97; rtd 99; Perm to Offic *Ripon* from 01. *2 Southfield Avenue, Ripon HG4 2NR* Tel (01765) 607842

JENNINGS, Anne. *See* SMITH, Mrs Anne

JENNINGS, Prof Barry Randall. b 39. Southn Univ BSc61 PhD64 DSc76 DEng01 FInstP70 FRSC95. SW Minl Tr Course 96. **d** 98 **p** 99. Prof Physics Reading Univ from 84; NSM St Germans *Truro* 98-00; NSM S Hill w Callington from 00. *Pitt Meadow, St Dominic, Saltash PL12 6SX* Tel (01579) 350940 Fax as telephone

JENNINGS, Clive John. b 57. Trin Coll Bris. **d** 00 **p** 01. C Milton *B & W* 00-02; C Clevedon St Andr and Ch Ch from 02. *34 Rippleside, Clevedon BS21 7JX* Tel (01275) 872134 E-mail cmj11a@ntlworld.com

✠**JENNINGS, The Rt Revd David Willfred Michael.** b 44. AKC66. **d** 67 **p** 68 **c** 00. C Walton St Mary *Liv* 67-69; C Christchurch *Win* 69-73; V Hythe 73-80; V Romford St Edw *Chelmsf* 80-92; RD Havering 85-92; Hon Can Chelmsf Cathl 87-92; Adn Southend 92-00; Suff Bp Warrington *Liv* from 00. *34 Central Avenue, Eccleston Park, Prescot L34 2QP* Tel 0151-426 1897 Fax 493 2479 E-mail bw@warringon75.freeserve.co.uk

JENNINGS, Canon Frederick David. b 48. K Coll Lon BD73 AKC73 Loughb Univ MPhil98. St Aug Coll Cant 73. **d** 74 **p** 75. C Halesowen *Worc* 74-77; Perm to Offic *Birm* 78-80; Perm to Offic *Leic* 78-80 and 85-87; P-in-c Snibston 80-85; Community Relns Officer 81-84; P-in-c Burbage w Aston Flamville 87-91; R from 91; Hon Can Leic Cathl from 03. *The Rectory, New Road, Burbage, Hinckley LE10 2AW* Tel (01455) 230512 Fax 250833 E-mail revdavidjennings@btinternet.com

JENNINGS, George. b 20. Lon Univ BD64 Lambeth STh89. Oak Hill Th Coll 46. **d** 51 **p** 52. C Laisterdyke *Bradf* 51-53; C Morden *S'wark* 53-56; V Houghton *Carl* 56-66; V Haydock St Mark *Liv* 66-77; V Newburgh 77-89; rtd 89; Perm to Offic *Liv* from 89 and *Heref* from 90. *Shalom, 97 Watling Street South, Church Stretton SY6 7BH* Tel (01694) 722145

JENNINGS, Harold Andrew. b 15. ATCL35 LTCL36 FTCL37 MRST39 LRAM39. St Deiniol's Hawarden 63. **d** 63 **p** 64. C Swansea St Gabr *S & B* 63-67; R Aberedw w Llandeilo Graban etc 67-79; V Knighton and Norton 79-85; Hon C Llanbister and Llanbadarn Fynydd w Llananno 85-87; rtd 87. *Finsbury, Beaufort Road, Llandrindod Wells LD1 5EL* Tel (01597) 824892

JENNINGS, Ian. b 47. Leeds Univ MA98. N Ord Course 95. **d** 97 **p** 97. NSM Hackenthorpe *Sheff* 97-01; Asst Chapl HM Pris Doncaster 97-98; Chapl HM Pris and YOI Doncaster 98-01; V Sheff St Cuth *Sheff* from 01. *The Vicarage, 7 Horndean Road, Sheffield S5 6UJ* Tel 0114-243 6506 E-mail ian@stcuthberts.net

JENNINGS, Janet. b 38. SCM71 SRN74. Oak Hill Th Coll BA87. **d** 88 **p** 97. Par Dn Stevenage St Pet Broadwater *St Alb* 88-90; Perm to Offic *St As* from 92. *Pound House, Forden, Welshpool SY21 8NU* Tel (01938) 580400

JENNINGS, Jonathan Peter. b 61. K Coll Lon BD83. Westcott Ho Cam 84. **d** 86 **p** 87. C Peterlee *Dur* 86-89; C Darlington St Cuth 89-92; Dioc Communications Officer *Man* 92-95; Broadcasting Officer Gen Syn 95-01; Perm to Offic *S'wark* 95-98; Hon C Banstead *Guildf* 98-04; Abp Cant's Press Sec from 01. *Lambeth Palace, London SE1 7JU* Tel (020) 7898 1224 Fax (020) 7261 9836 *or* 7261 1765 E-mail jonathan.jennings@c-of-e.org.uk *or* revjpj@aol.com

JENNINGS, The Very Revd Kenneth Neal. b 30. CCC Cam BA54 MA58. Cuddesdon Coll 54. **d** 56 **p** 57. C Ramsgate H Trin *Cant* 56-59; India 59-66; Vice-Prin Cuddesdon Coll 67-73; V Hitchin St Mary *St Alb* 73-76; TR Hitchin 77-83; Dean Glouc 83-96; rtd 96; Perm to Offic *Bradf* from 96. *The School House, Keasden, Clapham, Lancaster LA2 8EY* Tel (01524) 251455

JENNINGS, Mervyn. b 39. Sarum & Wells Th Coll 83. **d** 85 **p** 86. C Knowle *Bris* 85-89; P-in-c Cressing and Rural Youth Development Officer *Chelmsf* 89-93; V Barkingside St Fran from 93. *St Francis's Vicarage, 144 Fencepiece Road, Ilford IG6 2LA* Tel (020) 8500 2970 Fax 8270 3205 E-mail father.mervyn.jennings@ntlworld.com

JENNINGS, Peter James. b 28. Univ of Wales (Lamp) BA56. St D Coll Lamp LTh57. **d** 57 **p** 58. C Dudley St Jo *Worc* 57-60; C Dudley St Thos 61-64; Chapl HM Borstal Portland 64-66; Chapl HM Pris Wakef 66-70; Chapl HM Pris Liv 70-76; RD Walton *Liv* 75-76; Chapl HM Pris Styal 76-77 and 88-92; N Regional Chapl 76-82; Asst Chapl Gen (N) 82-88; Perm to Offic *Man* 77-89 and from 00; *Ches* from 79; rtd 93. *6 St Ann's Road South, Cheadle SK8 3DZ* Tel 0161-437 8828

JENNINGS, Robert Henry. b 46. St Jo Coll Dur BA69 MA79. Qu Coll Birm DipTh71. **d** 72 **p** 73. C Dursley *Glouc* 72-74; C Coleford w Staunton 75-78; TV Bottesford w Ashby *Linc* 78-83; TV Witney *Ox* 83-89; V Lane End w Cadmore End from 89. *The Vicarage, 7 Lammas Way, Lane End, High Wycombe HP14 3EX* Tel (01494) 881913

JENNINGS, Canon Thomas Robert. b 24. TCD BA47 MA51. **d** 48 **p** 49. C Drumragh *D & R* 48-51; CF 51-67; I Killeshandra *K, E & A* 67-70; I Newcastle w Newtownmountkennedy and Calary *D & G* 70-92; Can Ch Ch Cathl Dublin from 88; rtd 92. *66 Seacourt, Newcastle, Greystones, Co Wicklow, Irish Republic* Tel (00353) (1) 281 0777

JENNINGS, Walter James. b 37. Birm Univ BMus60 MA90. Qu Coll Birm 77. **d** 80 **p** 81. Hon C Hampton in Arden *Birm* 80-84; Chapl St Alb Aided Sch Highgate Birm 84-86; C Wotton-under-Edge w Ozleworth and N Nibley *Glouc* 86-89; V Pittville All SS 89-98; rtd 98; Chapl Beauchamp Community 98-00; Perm to Offic *Worc* from 98. *Flat 7, Leamington Court, Wells Road, Malvern WR14 4HF* Tel (01684) 561513 E-mail walter.linda@virgin.net

JENNO, Charles Henry. b 25. Wells Th Coll 65. **d** 66 **p** 67. C Shirehampton *Bris* 66-69; C Fishponds St Mary 69-73; V Thornes St Jas w Ch Ch *Wakef* 73-78; V Carleton 78-82; V E Hardwick 78-82; rtd 82; Perm to Offic *Wakef* from 82. *32 Tower Avenue, Upton, Pontefract WF9 1EE* Tel (01977) 640925

JENSEN, Alexander Sönderup. b 68. Tübingen Univ 94 St Jo Coll Dur PhD97 Ox Univ MTh01. St Steph Ho Ox 97. **d** 99 **p** 00. C Norton St Mich *Dur* 99-02; Lect CITC 02-05; Lect Murdoch Univ Australia from 05. *School of Soc Sciences & Humanities, Murdoch University, South Street, Murdoch, W Australia 6150* Tel (0061) (8) 9360 6625 Fax 9360 6480 E-mail a.jensen@murdoch.edu.au

JENSEN, Erik Henning. b 33. Copenhagen Univ BPhil51 Harvard Univ STM54 Worc Coll Ox BLitt58 DPhil69. Ripon Hall Ox 56. **d** 58 **p** 59. C Highwood *Chelmsf* 58-59; C Simanggang Sarawak 59-61; Borneo 61-62; Malaysia 63-03; rtd 02. *The Rock House, Maugersbury, Stow-on-the-Wold GL54 1HP* Tel (01451) 830171

✠**JENSEN, The Most Revd Peter Frederick.** b 43. Lon Univ BD70 Sydney Univ MA76 Ox Univ DPhil80. Moore Th Coll Sydney. **d** 69 **p** 70 **c** 01. C Broadway Australia 69-76; Perm to Offic *Ox* 76-79; Lect Moore Th Coll 73-76 and 80-84; Prin 85-01; Can Sydney 89-01; Abp Sydney from 01. *PO Box Q190, QVB PO, NSW, Australia 1230* Tel (0061) (2) 9265 1521 Fax 9265 1504

JENSON, Philip Peter. b 56. Ex Coll Ox BA78 MA82 Down Coll Cam BA80 MA86 PhD88. Ridley Hall Cam 80. **d** 87 **p** 88. C Gt Warley Ch Ch *Chelmsf* 87-89; Lect Trin Coll Bris from 89. *15 Henleaze Road, Henleaze, Bristol BS9 4EX,* or *Trinity College, Stoke Hill, Bristol BS9 1JP* Tel 0117-962 1861 *or* 968 2803 E-mail philip.jenson@trinity-bris.ac.uk

JEPPS, Philip Anthony. b 34. BNC Ox BA58 MA68. Wycliffe Hall Ox 58. **d** 60 **p** 73. C Elton All SS *Man* 60; Perm to Offic *Pet* 70-73; R Church w Chapel Brampton 74-80; P-in-c Harlestone 79-80; V Kettering St Andr 80-94; V Conisbrough *Sheff* 94-01; rtd 01; Perm to Offic *Heref* from 01. *2 Eagle Cottages, Church Lane, Orleton, Ludlow SY8 4HT* Tel (01568) 780517

JEPSON, Joanna Elizabeth. b 76. Trin Coll Bris BA99 Cam Univ MA03. Ridley Hall Cam 01. **d** 03. C Plas Newton *Ches* from 03. *13 Mannings Lane South, Chester CH2 3RX* Tel (01244) 313746 E-mail joeyjep@yahoo.com

JERMAN, Edward David. b 40. Trin Coll Carmarthen CertEd61. **d** 87 **p** 88. NSM Llandrygarn w Bodwrog and Heneglwys etc *Ban* from 87. *Tryfan, Trefor, Holyhead LL65 3YT* Tel (01407) 720856

JERMY, Jack. b 22. ACP65. Ripon Hall Ox 64. **d** 65 **p** 66. Hd Master SS Simon and Jude Primary Sch Bolton 62-80; C Bolton SS Simon and Jude *Man* 65-74; P-in-c Rivington 74-93; NSM Horwich and Rivington 93-95; Perm to Offic from 95. *Bent House, Long Lane, Heath Charnock, Chorley PR6 9EW* Tel (01257) 480466

JERMY, Stuart John. b 66. Middx Univ BEd90. Wycliffe Hall Ox 01. **d** 03 **p** 04. C New Thundersley *Chelmsf* from 03. *42 Bartley*

Road, Benfleet SS7 4DB Tel (01268) 795664 Mobile 07801-071443 E-mail stu-liz@fish.co.uk

JERSEY, Dean of. *See* KEY, The Very Revd Robert Frederick

JERUSALEM AND THE MIDDLE EAST, President Bishop of the Episcopal Church in. *See* HANDFORD, The Most Revd George Clive

JERVIS, Christopher. b 53. BEd Cam Univ DipTh. Wycliffe Hall Ox. **d** 82 **p** 83. C Woodford Wells *Chelmsf* 82-85; Chapl Felsted Sch 85-87; Chapl Canford Sch Wimborne from 87. *Merryvale, Canford Magna, Wimborne BH21 3AF* Tel (01202) 887722 *or* 841254

JERVIS, William Edward. b 47. MRICS74. Linc Th Coll 74. **d** 77 **p** 78. C W Bromwich All SS *Lich* 77-80; C Horsham *Chich* 80-86; R W Tarring from 86. *West Tarring Rectory, Glebe Road, Worthing BN14 7PF* Tel (01903) 235043

JESSETT, David Charles. b 55. K Coll Lon BD77 AKC77 MTh. Westcott Ho Cam 78. **d** 79 **p** 80. C Aveley *Chelmsf* 79-82; C Walthamstow St Pet 82-85; P-in-c Hunningham *Cov* 85-91; P-in-c Wappenbury w Weston under Wetherley 85-91; Progr Dir Exploring Chr Min Scheme 85-91; Dir CME 87-90; Perm to Offic 90-97; P-in-c Barford w Wasperton and Sherbourne from 97. *The Rectory, Church Lane, Barford, Warwick CV35 8ES* Tel (01926) 624238 E-mail david@jessetts.freeserve.co.uk

JESSIMAN, Timothy Edward. b 58. Oak Hill Th Coll DipHE91. **d** 91 **p** 92. C Baldock w Bygrave *St Alb* 91-95; C Bideford *Ex* 95-96; TV Bideford, Northam, Westward Ho, Appledore etc 96-00; Chapl Grenville Coll Bideford 95-00; Chapl N Devon Healthcare NHS Trust 98-00; P-in-c Hartplain *Portsm* from 00. *The Vicarage, 61 Hart Plain Avenue, Waterlooville PO8 8RG* Tel (023) 9226 4551 E-mail tim.jessiman@ntlworld.com

JESSON, Alan Francis. b 47. TD89. Ealing Coll of Educn 70 Loughb Univ MLS77 Selw Coll Cam MA87 ALA70 FLA91 MBIM82. EAMTC 88. **d** 91 **p** 92. NSM Swavesey *Ely* 91-95; NSM Fen Drayton w Conington and Lolworth etc 95-00; CF (ACF) 92-96; Sen Chapl ACF from 96; R Outwell *Ely* from 00; R Upwell St Pet from 00; Perm to Offic *Nor* from 01. *The Rectory, 5 New Road, Upwell, Wisbech PE14 9AB* Tel (01945) 772213 E-mail alan.jesson@ely.anglican.org

JESSON, George Albert Oswald (Ossie). b 54. NCA73. Trin Coll Bris DipHE92. **d** 92 **p** 93. C Thorpe Acre w Dishley *Leic* 92-01; C Chilwell *S'well* from 01. *Church House, Barncroft, Beeston, Nottingham NG9 4HU* Tel 0115-922 1879 E-mail revo.jesson@ntlworld.com

JESSON, Mrs Julia Margaret. b 54. St Matthias Coll Bris CertEd75 Nottm Univ MA04. EMMTC 01. **d** 04 **p** 05. NSM Stapleford *S'well* from 04. *The Church House, Barncroft, Beeston, Nottingham NG9 4HU* Tel 0115-922 1879 E-mail julia.jesson@ntlworld.com

JESSOP, Mrs Gillian Mary. b 48. Hatf Poly BSc71 Nottm Univ MEd85 Homerton Coll Cam PGCE80. EAMTC 91. **d** 94 **p** 95. C Gt Yarmouth *Nor* 94-97; R Gt w Lt Addington and Woodford *Pet* 97-02; Asst Dir Tr for Readers 00-02; R Paston from 02; Dir Tr for Readers from 02. *The Rectory, 236 Fulbridge Road, Peterborough PE4 6SN* Tel (01733) 578228 E-mail rev.gill@tesco.net

JESSOP, John Edward. b 46. RMCS BSc71 CEng78 MIEE78. S Dios Minl Tr Scheme 87 Ridley Coll Melbourne 89. **d** 90 **p** 90. Australia 90-02; C Mooroolbark 90-91; P-in-c S Yarra 92-93; I Blackburn St Jo 93-98; I Kew H Trin 98-02; P-in-c Brimpsfield w Birdlip, Syde, Daglingworth etc *Glouc* 02-04; R from 04. *The Rectory, Church Road, Daglingworth, Cirencester GL7 7AG* Tel and fax (01285) 640782

JESSUP, William Roy. b 27. Lon Univ BSc48 CertEd. Ridley Hall Cam 59. **d** 61 **p** 62. C Walton *St E* 61-64; R Tuddenham St Mary w Cavenham 64-83; P-in-c Eriswell 75-78; Assoc Min Ipswich All SS 83-85; R Toppesfield and Stambourne *Chelmsf* 85-92; rtd 92; Perm to Offic *Chelmsf* and *St E* from 92. *71 Brain Valley Avenue, Black Notley, Braintree CM77 8LT* Tel (01376) 322554

JESTY, Mrs Helen Margaret. b 51. York Univ BA72. Cranmer Hall Dur BA81. **dss** 82 **d** 87. S Lambeth St Steph *S'wark* 82-86; Norbiton 86-93; Par Dn 87-90; Hon Par Dn 91-93. *Fairfield, 1 Downside Road, Winchester SO22 5LT* Tel (01962) 849190

JEVONS, Preb Alan Neil. b 56. Ex Univ BA77 Selw Coll Cam BA80 MA84. Ridley Hall Cam. **d** 81 **p** 82. C Halesowen *Worc* 81-84; C Heywood St Luke w All So *Man* 84-87; TV Heref St Martin w St Fran *Heref* 87-93; P-in-c Much Birch w Lt Birch, Much Dewchurch etc 93-02; RD Ross and Archenfield 98-02; TR Tenbury from 02; Preb Heref Cathl from 02. *The Rectory, Burford, Tenbury Wells WR15 8HG* Tel (01584) 819748

JEVONS, Harry Clifford. b 46. Bp Otter Coll 01. **d** 04 **p** 05. C Ifield *Chich* from 04. *2 Lychgate Cottage, Ifield, Crawley RH11 0NN* Tel (01293) 511836 Mobile 07881-527050 E-mail harryjevons@supanet.com

JEWELL, Alan David John. b 59. St Cath Coll Ox MA86. Wycliffe Hall Ox 83. **d** 86 **p** 87. C Walton H Trin *Ox* 86-91; TV Sutton *Liv* 91-97; TV Halewood 97-01; TR from 01. *The Rectory, 3 Rectory Drive, Halewood, Liverpool L26 6LJ* Tel 0151-487 5610 E-mail alandjjewell@btopenworld.com

JEWELL, Charles John. b 15. Bps' Coll Cheshunt 46. **d** 49 **p** 50. C Swindon St Aug *Bris* 49-52; CF 52-58; C-in-c Patchway CD *Bris* 58-61; Tristan da Cunha 61 and 71-74; Area Sec (Ireland) USPG 62-69; Area Sec USPG *Ex* and *Truro* 69-71; S Africa 74-87; rtd 87; Perm to Offic *Ex* from 87. *11 Arundel Close, Exeter EX2 8UG* Tel (01392) 426781

JEWELL, Mrs Maureen Ann. b 34. Reading Univ CertEd72. Chich Th Coll 90. **d** 91 **p** 95. NSM Parklands St Wilfrid CD *Chich* 91-94; NSM Storrington 94-97; Perm to Offic from 97. *3 Garden Close, Storrington, Pulborough RH20 4PL* Tel (01903) 742780

JEWELL, Raymond Frederick. b 27. CA Tr Coll 56. **d** 05 **p** 05. NSM Tuffley *Glouc* from 05. *1 Bybrook Gardens, Tuffley, Gloucester GL4 0HQ*

JEWITT, Martin Paul Noel. b 44. AKC69. St Aug Coll Cant. **d** 70 **p** 71. C Usworth *Dur* 70-74; TV 77-78; Papua New Guinea 74-77; V Balham Hill Ascension *S'wark* 78-93; R N Reddish *Man* 93-99; V Thornton Heath St Paul *S'wark* from 99. *The Vicarage, 1 Norbury Avenue, Thornton Heath CR7 8AH* Tel (020) 8653 2762

JEYNES, Anthony James. b 44. AKC68. **d** 69 **p** 70. C Ellesmere Port *Ches* 69-73; C Birkenhead St Pet w St Matt 73-75; R Oughtrington 75-80; C Timperley 80-85; C Eastham 85-89; V New Brighton St Jas 89-96; P-in-c New Brighton Em 94-96; R Tarleton *Blackb* 96-04; P-in-c Kyrenia St Andr and Chapl N Cyprus from 04. *PO Box 22075, 1517 Nicosia, Cyprus* Tel (0090) (392) 815 4329 Fax 815 4486 E-mail standrew@kktc.net

JIGNASU, Nallinkumar Hiralal. b 28. Bombay Univ BA48. Bp Tucker Coll Mukono 68. **d** 68 **p** 69. Uganda 68-73; C Leamington Priors St Mary *Cov* 73-75; Nigeria 75-79; P-in-c New Humberstone *Leic* 80-94; rtd 94; Perm to Offic *Leic* from 94. *8 Somerby Road, Thurnby, Leicester LE7 9PR* Tel 0116-241 8541

JOACHIM, Margaret Jane. b 49. FGS91 St Hugh's Coll Ox BA70 MA74 W Midl Coll of Educn PGCE71 Birm Univ PhD77. S Dios Minl Tr Scheme 91. **d** 94 **p** 95. NSM Ealing St Barn *Lon* 94-97; NSM Ealing St Pet Mt Park from 97. *8 Newburgh Road, London W3 6DQ* Tel (020) 8723 4514 *or* 8754 4547 E-mail margaret.joachim@london.anglican.org

JOAN, Sister. *See* DAVIES, Sister Joan Margaret

JOB, Canon Evan Roger Gould. b 36. Magd Coll Ox BA60 MA64 ARCM55. Cuddesdon Coll 60. **d** 62 **p** 63. C Liv Our Lady and St Nic *Liv* 62-65; V New Springs 65-70; Min Can and Prec Man Cathl *Man* 70-74; Prec and Sacr Westmr Abbey 74-79; Can Res, Prec and Sacr Win Cathl *Win* 79-94; Vice-Dean Win 91-94; Select Preacher Ox Univ 74 and 91; rtd 01; Perm to Offic *Win* from 94 and *Portsm* from 04. *Kitwood Farmhouse, Kitwood Lane, Ropley, Alresford SO24 0DB* Tel (01962) 772303

JOBBER, Barry William. b 38. N Staffs Poly BA84. Cuddesdon Coll 73. **d** 75 **p** 76. C Fenton *Lich* 76-79; V Goldenhill 79-80; Perm to Offic *Ches* 90-02; NSM Middlewich w Byley from 02; rtd 03. *16 Angus Grove, Middlewich CW10 9GR* Tel (01606) 737386 Mobile 07974-380234 E-mail barry-jobber@supanet.com

JOBLING, Jeremy Charles. b 72. Natal Univ BSc95. Wycliffe Hall Ox 03. **d** 05. C Watford *St Alb* from 05. *8A Lammas Road, Watford WD18 0BA* Tel (01923) 232979 E-mail charli3boy@yahoo.co.uk

JOBSON, Clifford Hedley. b 31. St Jo Coll Dur BA54 DipTh56 MA81. **d** 56 **p** 57. C Hall Green Ascension *Birm* 56-59; C Ambleside w Rydal *Carl* 59-60; R Arthuret 60-62; CF 62-73; Dep Asst Chapl Gen 73-78; Asst Chapl Gen 78-84; QHC from 80; V Fleet *Guildf* 84-96; rtd 96; Perm to Offic *B & W* from 96. *Vine Cottage, 25 Silver Street, South Petherton TA13 5AL* Tel (01460) 241783

JOEL, Mrs Mary Tertia. b 35. **d** 99 **p** 00. OLM Blyth Valley *St E* from 99. *38 Saxmundham Road, Aldeburgh IP15 5JE* Tel (01728) 454886 Mobile 07790-910554 E-mail maryt@joel12.freeserve.co.uk

JOHANSEN, Paul Charles. b 33. Miami Univ BEd61 Univ of California Berkeley STB64. Yale Div Sch 61. **d** 64 **p** 64. USA 64-96 and from 98; rtd 96; P-in-c Adare w Kilpeacon and Croom *L & K* 96-98; P-in-c New Philadelphia Trin Ch from 01. *504 Third Avenue NW, New Philadelphia, OH 44663, USA* E-mail trinity@tusco.net

JOHN, Alexander Dominic. b 26. Madras Univ BA47. Episc Sem Austin Texas MDiv63. **d** 63 **p** 64. C Millhouses H Trin *Sheff* 63-65; Switzerland 65-68; India 68-78; Australia from 78; rtd 85. *12 Bentwood Avenue, Woodlands, W Australia 6018* Tel (0061) (8) 9445 3530 E-mail remo@space.net.au

JOHN, Andrew Thomas Griffith. b 64. Univ of Wales LLB. St Jo Coll Nottm BA. **d** 89 **p** 90. C Cardigan w Mwnt and Y Ferwig *St D* 89-91; C Aberystwyth 91-92; TV 92-99; V Henfynyw w Aberaeron and Llanddewi Aberarth etc from 99. *The Vicarage, Panteg Road, Aberaeron SA4 0EP* Tel (01545) 570433 E-mail andyjohn@andyjohn.freeserve.co.uk

JOHN, Canon Arun Andrew. b 54. **d** 77 **p** 78. India 77-96; S Africa 97-04; TV Manningham *Bradf* from 04. *St Paul's Rectory,*

63 St Paul's Road, Manningham, Bradford BD8 7LS Tel (01274) 490550 E-mail stpauls@legend.co.uk

JOHN, Barbara. b 34. Cam Univ DipTh67. Gilmore Ho. **dss** 67 **d** 80 **p** 97. Merthyr Tydfil *Llan* 67-71; Loughton St Jo *Chelmsf* 71-73; Newport St Woolos *Mon* 73-78; Asst Chapl Univ Hosp of Wales Cardiff 78-85; C Radyr *Llan* 85-00; rtd 00. *14 Pace Close, Cardiff CF5 2QZ* Tel (029) 2055 2989

JOHN, Canon Beverley Hayes. b 49. Qu Coll Birm 83. **d** 85 **p** 86. C Oystermouth *S & B* 85-87; C Morriston 87-88; V Cefn Coed w Vaynor from 88; RD Brecon from 99; Can Res Brecon Cathl from 04. *The Vicarage, Somerset Lane, Cefn Coed, Merthyr Tydfil CF48 2PA* Tel (01685) 374253

JOHN, Caroline Victoria. b 64. Cam Univ BA86 MA90. St Jo Coll Nottm DPS90. **d** 90. NSM Cardigan w Mwnt and Y Ferwig *St D* 90-91; NSM Aberystwyth 91-96. *The Vicarage, Panteg Road, Aberaeron SA46 0EP* Tel (01545) 570433

JOHN, Canon David Michael. b 36. Univ of Wales (Lamp) BA57. St Mich Coll Llan 57. **d** 59 **p** 60. C Pontypool *Mon* 59-61; C Roath *Llan* 61-66; Asst Chapl HM Pris Liv 66-67; Chapl HM Pris Ex 67-68; V Ystrad Rhondda *Llan* 68-76; V Pontyclun w Talygarn 76-84; R Newton Nottage 84-91; Can Llan Cathl 85-91; rtd 91; Perm to Offic *Llan* and *Mon* from 91. *1 Hornbeam Close, St Mellons, Cardiff CF3 0JA* Tel (029) 2079 7496

JOHN, David Wyndham. b 61. Lon Bible Coll. NTMTC. **d** 01 **p** 02. NSM Hampstead Em W End *Lon* 01-04; NSM W Hampstead St Cuth from 04. *13 Kingscroft Road, London NW2 3QE* Tel (020) 8452 1913 Mobile 07719-333389

JOHN, The Ven Elwyn Crebey. b 36. Univ of Wales (Lamp) BA57. St Mich Coll Llan 57. **d** 59 **p** 60. C Llangiwg *S & B* 59-62; C Llandrindod w Cefnllys 62-66; V Beguildy and Heyope 66-79; Youth Chapl 72-79; Chapl Agric and Rural Soc 77-03; V Builth and Llanddewi'r Cwm w Llangynog etc 79-95; Can Brecon Cathl 88-95; Can Res Brecon Cathl 95-03; Prec 94-95; Treas 95-98; Chan 98-03; V Brecon St Mary w Llanddew 95-01; Adn Brecon 99-03; rtd 03. *17 Cae Castell, Builth Wells LD2 3BE* Tel (01982) 551553

JOHN, The Ven Islwyn David. b 33. St D Coll Lamp BA56. **d** 58 **p** 59. C Brynamman *St D* 58-61; C Carmarthen St Dav 61-64; V 83-93; V Penbryn and Blaenporth 64-68; V Llandysul 68-83; Can St D Cathl 88-93; RD Carmarthen 92-93; Adn Carmarthen 93-99; V Cynwil Elfed and Newchurch 93-99; rtd 99. *Brookfield, 106 Bronwydd Road, Carmarthen SA31 2AW* Tel (01267) 237868

JOHN, Canon James Richard. b 21. Ch Coll Cam BA47 MA49. Cuddesdon Coll 47. **d** 49 **p** 50. C Sidcup Ch Ch *Roch* 49-52; V Gillingham St Mary 52-66; RD Gillingham 60-66; V Bolton St Jas w St Chrys *Bradf* 66-78; R Guiseley 78-83; RD Otley 80-86; P-in-c Esholt 82-83; TR Guiseley w Esholt 83-87; Hon Can Bradf Cathl 83-87; rtd 87; Perm to Offic *Bradf* from 87. *37 Croft House Drive, Otley LS21 2ER* Tel (01943) 461998

JOHN, The Very Revd Jeffrey Philip Hywel. b 53. Hertf Coll Ox BA75 Magd Coll Ox DPhil84. St Steph Ho Ox BA77 MA78. **d** 78 **p** 79. C Penarth w Lavernock *Llan* 78-80; Asst Chapl Magd Coll Ox 80-82; Fell and Dean of Div 84-91; Chapl and Lect BNC Ox 82-84; V Eltham H Trin *S'wark* 91-97; Chan and Can Th S'wark Cathl 97-04; Bp's Adv for Min 97-04; Dean St Alb from 04. *The Deanery, Sumpter Yard, St Albans AL1 1BY* Tel (01727) 890203 Fax 890227 E-mail dean@stalbanscathedral.org.uk

JOHN, Mrs Marie. b 48. **d** 04. OLM Camberwell St Geo *S'wark* from 04. *8 Caroline Gardens, Asylum Road, London SE15 2SQ* Tel (020) 7635 5534

JOHN, Mark Christopher. b 61. SS Mark & Jo Coll Plymouth BA83. St Steph Ho Ox 84. **d** 87 **p** 88. C Treboeth *S & B* 87-90; V Swansea St Mark and St Jo 90-94; Chapl HM Pris Swansea 91-94; Chapl HM Pris Usk and Prescoed 94-97; Chapl HM Pris Cardiff from 97; Lic to Offic *Mon* from 99. *HM Prison Cardiff, Knox Road, Cardiff CF24 0UG* Tel (029) 2043 3100 ext 3233 Fax 2043 3318

JOHN, Meurig Hywel. b 46. St D Coll Lamp 67. **d** 71 **p** 72. C Llanelli Ch Ch *St D* 71-74; V Penrhyncoch and Elerch 74-79; V Llanfihangel Aberbythych 79-81; R Cilgerran w Bridell and Llantwyd 81-83; V Gwaun-cae-Gurwen 83-89; V Llanfihangel Genau'r-glyn and Llangorwen 89-95; V Newcastle Emlyn w Llandyfriog etc 95-01; Assoc V Lampeter and Llanddewibrefi Gp 01-03; rtd 03. *Arosfa, Llanybri, Carmarthen SA33 5HQ* Tel (01267) 241096

JOHN, Napoleon. b 55. Punjab Univ BA76. Lahetysteologisen Inst Ryttyla Finland DipHE85 Oak Hill Th Coll BA93. **d** 93 **p** 94. C Leyton St Mary w St Edw *Chelmsf* 93-96; C Leyton St Mary w St Edw and St Luke 96-97; P-in-c Becontree St Elisabeth 97-04; V from 04. *The Vicarage, Hewett Road, Dagenham RM8 2XT* Tel (020) 8517 0355 E-mail nj7@totalise.co.uk

JOHN, Nigel. b 59. Univ of Wales (Cardiff) BA87 Selw Coll Cam MPhil90. Westcott Ho Cam 88. **d** 91 **p** 92. C Carmarthen St Pet *St D* 91-94; Chapl Roehampton Inst *S'wark* 94-96; V Gors-las *St D* 96-98; V Llanelli Ch Ch 98-02; Chapl Univ of Wales (Swansea) *S & B* from 02. *23 Mayals Avenue, Blackpill, Swansea SA3 5DE* Tel (01792) 401703

JOHN, Richard. *See* JOHN, Canon James Richard

JOHN, Robert Michael. b 46. Edin Univ BSc67 Man Univ MSc68 PhD70 Otago Univ BD78. St Jo Coll Auckland 76. **d** 78 **p** 79. New Zealand 78-87 and from 88; C Swansea St Jas *S & B* 87-88. *1 Barrymore Road, Mount Albert, Auckland 1003, New Zealand* Tel (0064) (9) 846 4812 *or* 379 7440

JOHN, Stephen Michael. b 63. Univ of Wales (Lamp) BA85. Coll of Resurr Mirfield 87. **d** 89 **p** 90. C Coity w Nolton *Llan* 89-91; C Merthyr Dyfan 91-94; V Tredegar St Geo *Mon* 94-99; Chapl HM Pris Gartree 99-04; TV Tenby *St D* from 04. *9 Lamack Vale, Tenby SA70 8DN* Tel (01834) 844330

JOHN-FRANCIS, Brother. *See* FRIENDSHIP, Roger Geoffrey

JOHNES, Philip Sydney. b 45. St Mich Coll Llan Dip Minl Studies 92. **d** 92 **p** 93. C Cardigan w Mwnt and Y Ferwig *St D* 92-95; V Llanegwad w Llanfynydd from 95. *Llanegwad Vicarage, Heol Alltyferin, Nantgaredig, Carmarthen SA32 7NE* Tel (01267) 290142 Fax as telephone E-mail pjohnes@aol.com

JOHNS, Adam Aubrey. b 34. TCD BA57 MA76 NUU BA75. CITC Div Test 58. **d** 58 **p** 59. C Aghalee *D & D* 58-61; C Derriaghy *Conn* 61-63; I Billy 63-77; I Billy w Derrykeighan 77-03; Can Conn Cathl 98-03; rtd 03. *26 Chatham Road, Armoy, Ballymoney BT53 8TT* Tel (028) 2075 1978

JOHNS, Canon Bernard Thomas. b 36. Birm Univ BSc58. St Mich Coll Llan 61. **d** 63 **p** 64. C Aberavon *Llan* 63-65; C St Andrews Major w Michaelston-le-Pit 65-70; V Cardiff St Andr and St Teilo 70-76; Asst Dioc Dir of Educn 72-91; V Roath 76-88; R Wenvoe and St Lythans 88-02; Dioc Dir Community Educn 91-02; Can Llan Cathl 96-02; rtd 02. *Bay Tree Cottage, 13 Badgers Meadow, Pwllmeyric, Chepstow NP16 6UE* Tel (01291) 623254 E-mail johnsbtj@fish.co.uk

JOHNS, James Dudley. b 09. Selw Coll Cam BA34 MA38. Ridley Hall Cam 34. **d** 36 **p** 37. C Moulsham St Jo *Chelmsf* 36-39; C Grays Thurrock 39-41; V Forest Gate All SS 41-49; Dioc Insp of Schs 46-53; Res Chapl Butlin's Camp Clacton 47-48; Chapl and Dean Selw Coll Cam 49-53; Staff Sec SCM (Cam Univ) 49-51; Chapl Barnard Castle Sch 53-64; Chapl St Geo Sch Harpenden 64-69; Chapl Harpenden St Jo *St Alb* 64-69; R Gt w Lt Wymondley 70-80; R Gt and Lt Wymondley w Graveley and Chivesfield 80-81; rtd 81; Perm to Offic *Nor* 82-94 and *Chelmsf* from 95. *25A Beeches Close, Saffron Walden CB11 4BU* Tel (01799) 527119

JOHNS, Mrs Patricia Holly. b 33. Girton Coll Cam BA56 MA60 Hughes Hall Cam PGCE57. Ox NSM Course 87. **d** 90 **p** 94. NSM Wantage *Ox* 90-94; NSM Marlborough *Sarum* 94-95; rtd 95; Perm to Offic *Sarum* from 95. *Flat 1, Priory Lodge, 93 Brown Street, Salisbury SP1 2BX* Tel (01722) 328007

JOHNS, Canon Ronald Charles. b 37. TD. Dur Univ BA59. Wells Th Coll 59. **d** 61 **p** 62. C Wigan All SS *Liv* 61-66; TV Kirkby 66-75; Ho Master Ruffwood Sch Kirkby 70-75; TV Maghull 75-79; Dep Hd Master Maghull Old Hall High Sch 75-79; P-in-c Borrowdale *Carl* 79-84; V 84-89; RD Derwent 81-89; Hon Can Carl Cathl 87-89; Can Res 89-94; R Caldbeck, Castle Sowerby and Sebergham 94-00; rtd 01; Perm to Offic *Nor* from 01. *3 Kings Road, Coltishall, Norwich NR12 7DX*

JOHNS, Thomas Morton. b 43. Oak Hill Th Coll 67. **d** 70 **p** 71. C N Meols *Liv* 70-73; C Farnborough *Guildf* 73-76; P-in-c Badshot Lea CD 76-83; Dep Chapl HM Pris Man 83; Chapl HM Youth Cust Cen Wellingborough 83-88; Chapl HM YOI Swinfen Hall 88-90; Chapl Tr Officer 88-95; Chapl HM Pris Service Coll 90-95; Asst Chapl Gen of Pris (HQ) 95-01; Acting Chapl Gen 00-01; P-in-c Colbury *Win* from 02; Chapl Hants Constabulary from 02. *The Vicarage, Deerleap Lane, Totton, Southampton SO40 7EH* Tel (023) 8029 2132 Mobile 07974-025478 E-mail tom@johns.evesham.net

JOHNS, Trevor Charles. b 33. St D Coll Lamp BA58. **d** 58 **p** 59. C Pembroke St Mary w St Mich *St D* 58-61; R Walwyn's Castle w Robeston W 61-67; CF 67-75; V Spittal and Treffgarne *St D* 75-79; C Tring *St Alb* 79-80; TV Tring 80-85; V Knighton and Norton *S & B* 85-86; V Merthyr Cynog and Dyffryn Honddu etc 86-98; rtd 98. *109 Hoel-y-Banc, Bancffosfelen, Llanelli SA15 5DF*

JOHNS, William Price. b 28. Keble Coll Ox BA51 DipTh52 MA56. St Mich Coll Llan 52. **d** 53 **p** 54. C Whitchurch *Llan* 53-56; C Pontypridd St Cath 56-59; Min Can Brecon Cathl *S & B* 59-62; V Wellington *Heref* 62-78; R Wellington w Pipe-cum-Lyde and Moreton-on-Lugg 78-93; P-in-c Ford 63-69; rtd 93; Perm to Offic *Llan* from 93. *12 Deepdale Close, Cardiff CF23 5LR* Tel (029) 2048 3762

JOHNSEN, Edward Andrew. b 67. Birm Univ BTheol89. Qu Coll Birm 95. **d** 97 **p** 98. C Birm St Luke *Birm* 97-01; C Handsworth St Mary 01-04; Perm to Offic from 05. *43 St Christophers, Handsworth Wood, Birmingham B20 1BP* Tel 0121-554 2551 E-mail johnsen@fish.co.uk

JOHNSON, Amanda Saffery. b 58. K Alfred's Coll Win BEd83. Wycliffe Hall Ox. **d** 97 **p** 98. C Oxhey All SS *St Alb* 97-00; C Bricket Wood 00-02; Teacher Bp Wand Sch Sunbury-on-Thames 02-04; C Dorking St Paul *Guildf* from 05. *6 Falkland Road, Dorking RH4 3AB* Tel 07905-893394 (mobile) E-mail amandola@tesco.net

JOHNSON, Andrew Paul. b 56. W Surrey Coll of Art & Design BA79 Kent Coll for Careers CertEd82 TCD BTh96. CITC 93. **d** 96 **p** 97. C Penarth w Lavernock *Llan* 96-99; R Walton W w Talbenny and Haroldston W *St D* from 99. *The Rectory, Walton West, Little Haven, Haverfordwest SA62 3UB* Tel (01437) 781279

JOHNSON, Andrew Peter. b 67. Westf Coll Lon BA89 St Jo Coll Nottm MA98 LTh99. Aston Tr Scheme 94. **d** 99 **p** 00. C Hitchin *St Alb* 99-03; V Batley All SS and Purlwell *Wakef* from 03. *The Vicarage, Churchfield Street, Batley WF17 5DL* Tel and fax (01924) 473049 E-mail johnsons@care4free.net

JOHNSON, Andrew Robert. b 68. Jes Coll Ox MA96 Univ of Wales (Abth) MLib93 PhD96. Cranmer Hall Dur 03. **d** 05. C Carmarthen St Pet *St D* from 05. *St Peter's Clergy House, 10A The Parade, Carmarthen SA31 1LY* E-mail andrewj@evemail.net

JOHNSON, Mrs Angela Carolyn Louise. b 52. RGN76. STETS 00. **d** 03 **p** 04. NSM Catherington and Clanfield *Portsm* from 03. *90 Downhouse Road, Waterlooville PO8 0TY* Tel (023) 9264 4595

JOHNSON, Anthony. *See* JOHNSON, Edward Anthony

JOHNSON, Anthony Arthur Derry. b 15. Kelham Th Coll 31. **d** 39 **p** 40. C Pinner *Lon* 39-42; C Willesden St Andr 42-44; C Winchmore Hill H Trin 44-49; V Brookfield St Anne, Highgate Rise 49-60; V Mill Hill St Mich 60-73; R Chalfont St Giles *Ox* 73-80; rtd 80; Perm to Offic *Sarum* from 80. *Garden Close, Long Street, Sherborne DT9 3DD* Tel (01935) 813469

JOHNSON, Anthony Peter. b 45. K Coll Lon BD76 AKC76 MTh79. Wells Th Coll 67. **d** 70 **p** 71. C Goldington *St Alb* 70-73; C Hainault *Chelmsf* 73-76; TV Loughton St Mary 76-81; V Scunthorpe All SS *Linc* 81-85; V Alkborough 85-87; Chapl Man Univ and TV Man Whitworth *Man* 87-96; P-in-c Chorlton-cum-Hardy St Werburgh 96-00; R 00-05; P-in-c Yardley St Cypr Hay Mill *Birm* from 05. *The Vicarage, 7 Fordrough, Yardley, Birmingham B25 8DL* Tel 0121-773 1278

JOHNSON, Canon Anthony Trevor. b 27. CCC Ox BA51 MA55. Cuddesdon Coll 51. **d** 53 **p** 54. C Wareham w Arne *Sarum* 53-57; C Melksham 57-60; R Tarrant Gunville, Tarrant Hinton etc 60-67; R Upton Scudamore 67-85; V Warminster St Denys 67-85; RD Heytesbury 71-76; Can and Preb Sarum Cathl 75-92; P-in-c Horningsham 76-85; P-in-c Semley and Sedgehill 85-86; R E Knoyle, Semley and Sedgehill 86-92; rtd 92; Perm to Offic *Sarum* from 92. *Coombe Warren, Hindon Lane, Tisbury, Salisbury SP3 6QQ* Tel (01747) 870130

JOHNSON, Anthony Warrington. b 40. Goldsmiths' Coll Lon CertEd60. St Jo Coll Nottm 86. **d** 88 **p** 89. C Lutterworth w Cotesbach *Leic* 88-92; V Countesthorpe w Foston from 92; P-in-c Arnesby w Shearsby and Bruntingthorpe 94-01. *The Vicarage, 102 Station Road, Countesthorpe, Leicester LE8 5TB* Tel 0116-278 4442 *or* 277 8643 E-mail tony@fish.co.uk

JOHNSON, Barry Charles Richard. b 48. EAMTC 96. **d** 99 **p** 00. NSM Billericay and Lt Burstead *Chelmsf* 99-01; C Gt Burstead 01-02; C Bowers Gifford w N Benfleet 02-04; P-in-c Woodham Mortimer w Hazeleigh from 04. *The Rectory, Maldon Road, Woodham Mortimer, Maldon CM9 6SN* Tel and fax (01621) 843373 E-mail bjohnson@chelmsford.anglican.org

JOHNSON, Beverley Charles. b 35. Bp Gray Coll Cape Town 59. **d** 61 **p** 62. S Africa 61-67 and from 91; C Woodstock St Mary 61-64; C Clanwilliam St Jo 64-65; C Plumstead St Mark 65-67; C Southsea St Pet *Portsm* 68-69; C Southwick St Cuth CD *Dur* 70-71; P-in-c Waterhouses 71-80; R Burnmoor 80-85; V Brandon 85-89; Australia 89-91; Asst P Sea Point St Jas 91-01; rtd 01. *43 Oxford Street, Goodwood, 7460 South Africa* Tel and fax (0027) (21) 592 1180 Mobile 82-202 5260

JOHNSON, Mrs Brenda Margaret. b 47. TISEC 93. **d** 00. NSM Edin St Salvador *Edin* 00-02; NSM Wester Hailes St Luke 00-02; NSM Dalmahoy from 02. *58 Ratho Park Road, Ratho, Newbridge EH28 8PQ* Tel 0131-333 1742 Mobile 07713-154744 E-mail brenmj@freeuk.com

JOHNSON, Brian. b 42. S'wark Ord Course 84. **d** 87 **p** 88. NSM Dulwich St Barn *S'wark* 87-92; NSM Herne Hill 92-94; Perm to Offic 94-96; Chapl HM Pris Man 96-01; P-in-c Rotterdam *Eur* 01-02; Operations Manager ICS 03; Perm to Offic *Ches* from 04. *11A Lynton Park Road, Cheadle Hulme, Cheadle SK8 6JA* Tel 0161-485 3787 E-mail revbfg@ntlworld.com

JOHNSON, Christopher Dudley. b 26. Worc Coll Ox BA44 MA51. Cuddesdon Coll 53. **d** 56 **p** 57. C Basingstoke *Win* 56-61; V Bethnal Green St Barn *Lon* 61-67; V Eton w Eton Wick and Boveney *Ox* 67-88; rtd 91; Perm to Offic *Sarum* from 96. *Lavinces Cottage, Netherbury, Bridport DT6 5LL*

JOHNSON, Christopher Frederick. b 43. MRICS67. Ripon Hall Ox 71. **d** 74 **p** 75. C Chatham St Steph *Roch* 74-78; V Slade Green 78-85; V Wilmington 85-95; R Chevening from 95. *Chevening Rectory, Homedean Road, Chipstead, Sevenoaks TN13 2RU* Tel (01732) 453555

JOHNSON, Christopher Paul. b 47. St Jo Coll Nottm BTh74. **d** 74 **p** 75. C Normanton *Wakef* 74-78; P-in-c Dewsbury St Mark 78-82; V Harden and Wilsden *Bradf* 82-88; P-in-c Holbeck *Ripon* 88-94; V 94-97; Asst Chapl Leeds Teaching Hosps NHS Trust 97-01; Chapl Bradf Hosps NHS Trust from 01. *Bradford Royal Infirmary, Duckworth Lane, Bradford BD9 6RJ* Tel (01274) 542200 E-mail c-johnson@ic24.net

JOHNSON, Christopher Robert. b 43. Lon Coll of Div 66. **d** 70 **p** 71. C Everton St Geo *Liv* 70-71; C Childwall All SS 71-75; TV Gateacre 75-76; TV Bushbury *Lich* 76-87; R Burslem from 87. *The Rectory, 16 Heyburn Crescent, Burslem, Stoke-on-Trent ST6 4DL* Tel (01782) 838932

JOHNSON, Canon Colin Gawman. b 32. Leeds Univ BA59. Coll of Resurr Mirfield 59. **d** 61 **p** 62. C Barrow St Matt *Carl* 61-67; V 90-96; V Addingham 67-71; V Carl H Trin 71-80; V Wigton 80-90; Hon Can Carl Cathl 85-96; rtd 96; Perm to Offic *Carl* from 97. *Hemp Garth, Ireby, Wigton CA7 1EA* Tel (01697) 371578

JOHNSON, Colin Leslie. b 41. Trin Coll Cam MA65. Cheshunt Coll Cam 62. **d** 93 **p** 94. Publications Dir Chr Educn Movement from 89; NSM Brailsford w Shirley and Osmaston w Edlaston *Derby* from 93. *33 The Plain, Brailsford, Ashbourne DE6 3BZ* Tel (01335) 360591 E-mail colin@retoday.org.uk

JOHNSON, Colin Stewart. b 46. SEITE 99. **d** 02 **p** 03. NSM Borden *Cant* 02-05; C Charlton-in-Dover from 05. *3 Monastery Avenue, Dover CT16 1AB* Tel (01304) 201143 E-mail colinj@kent119.freeserve.co.uk

JOHNSON, Cyril Francis. b 22. St Cath Coll Cam BA49 MA54. Ely Th Coll 50. **d** 52 **p** 53. C Twickenham All Hallows *Lon* 52-56; C Kingsthorpe *Pet* 56-61; R Harpole 61-87; rtd 87; Perm to Offic *Chich* from 01. *16 Blake's Way, Eastbourne BN23 6EW* Tel (01323) 723491

JOHNSON, David. *See* JOHNSON, John David

JOHNSON, David Alan. b 43. Lon Univ BSc63 PhD67. Trin Coll Bris 78. **d** 80 **p** 81. C Watford *St Alb* 80-85; V Idle H Trin *Bradf* from 85. *The Vicarage, 470 Leeds Road, Thackley, Bradford BD10 9AA* Tel (01274) 613300 *or* 615411 E-mail vicar@htidle.org.uk

JOHNSON, David Bryan Alfred. b 36. Kelham Th Coll 56. **d** 61 **p** 62. C Streatham St Paul *S'wark* 61-63; Malaysia 63-71; V Worc St Mich *Worc* 71-74; Warden Lee Abbey Internat Students' Club Kensington 74-77; V Plumstead St Mark and St Marg *S'wark* 77-86; Chapl W Park Hosp Epsom 86-96; Chapl Laslett's *Worc* 96-01; rtd 96. *3 St Birinus Cottages, Wessex Way, Bicester OX26 6DX* Tel (01869) 320839

JOHNSON, David Clark. b 15. Tyndale Hall Bris 61. **d** 62 **p** 63. C Chippenham St Paul *Bris* 62-64; C Chippenham St Paul w Langley Burrell 64-65; V Bishopsworth 65-74; V Stratton St Margaret 75-78; TR Stratton St Margaret w S Marston etc 78-80; rtd 80; Perm to Offic *Bris* from 80. *13 High Kingsdown, Bristol BS2 8EN* Tel 0117-929 8894

JOHNSON, David Francis. b 32. Univ Coll Ox BA55 MA59. Westcott Ho Cam 55. **d** 57 **p** 58. C Earlsdon *Cov* 57-59; C Willenhall 59-61; C Attenborough w Bramcote *S'well* 61-62; V Ravenstone w Weston Underwood *Ox* 62-66; V Crewe Ch Ch *Ches* 66-70; P-in-c Crewe St Pet 67-70; V Thornton w Allerthorpe *York* 70-79; V N Hull St Mich 79-81; V Leyburn w Bellerby *Ripon* 81-88; V Coxwold and Husthwaite *York* 88-97; rtd 97; Perm to Offic *York* 98-03. *Nursery Cottage, The Park, Wormelow, Hereford HR2 8EQ* Tel (01981) 540967

JOHNSON, David John. b 49. Lanc Univ BA72. Linc Th Coll 78. **d** 81 **p** 82. C Stockport St Thos *Ches* 81-84; OGS from 83; C Stockton Heath *Ches* 84-88; V Tranmere St Paul w St Luke 88-99; P-in-c Antrobus 99-02; P-in-c Aston by Sutton 99-02; P-in-c Lt Leigh and Lower Whitley 99-02; V Antrobus, Aston by Sutton, Lt Leigh etc from 02. *The Vicarage, Street Lane, Lower Whitley, Warrington WA4 4EN* Tel (01925) 730158

JOHNSON, David Richard. b 67. Birm Univ BSc88. Ripon Coll Cuddesdon BA92 MA97. **d** 94 **p** 95. C Horfield H Trin *Bris* 94-97; V Two Mile Hill St Mich 97-01; Asst Chapl Haileybury Coll 01-02; Chapl Dauntsey's Sch Devizes from 02. *20 High Street, West Lavington, Devizes SN10 4HQ* Tel (01380) 814573 E-mail johnsoda@dauntseys.wilts.sch.uk

JOHNSON, David William. b 40. Oak Hill Th Coll BD64. **d** 65 **p** 66. C Tunbridge Wells St Jas *Roch* 65-68; C Kirby Muxloe *Leic* 68-72; V Burton Joyce w Bulcote *S'well* 72-83; V Mitford and Chapl Northgate Mental Handicap Unit Morpeth 83-87; Asst Chapl R Victoria Infirmary Newc 87-89; Chapl R Shrewsbury Hosps NHS Trust 89-04; rtd 04. *42 Hartlands, Bedlington NE22 6JG* Tel (01670) 828693

JOHNSON, David William. b 53. Selw Coll Cam BA76. Ripon Coll Cuddesdon 76. **d** 78 **p** 79. C Fulham St Etheldreda w St Clem *Lon* 78-82; Communications Sec Gen Syn Bd for Miss and Unity 82-87; PV Westmr Abbey 85-87; R Gilmorton w Peatling Parva and Kimcote etc *Leic* 87-91; R Cogenhoe *Pet* 91-95; R Whiston 93-95; rtd 95; Perm to Offic *Ox* from 00. *Seaview Cottage, 115 Hurst Street, Oxford OX4 1HE* Tel (01865) 793393

JOHNSON, Preb Derek John. b 36. St Aid Birkenhead 65. **d** 68 **p** 69. C Eccleshall *Lich* 68-73; C Stafford St Mary 73-75; Chapl New Cross Hosp Wolv 75-96; Preb Lich Cathl *Lich* 83-96; rtd 96; Perm to Offic *St E* from 96. *6 St Paul's Close, Aldeburgh IP15 5BQ* Tel (01728) 452474

JOHNSON, Miss Diana Margaret. b 46. MCSP68 SRP68 Grad Dip Physiotherapy 68. Cranmer Hall Dur CTM94. **d** 94 **p** 95. C Birtley *Dur* 94-99; TV Gateshead from 99; AD Gateshead from 03. *Venerable Bede House, 3 Wordsworth Street, Gateshead NE8 3HE* Tel 0191-478 2730

JOHNSON, Mrs Diane Pearl. b 47. Leeds Univ BA68 Cam Univ PGCE69. EAMTC 95. **d** 98 **p** 99. NSM Gt Bowden w Welham, Glooston and Cranoe *Leic* 98-01; C Evington and Leic St Phil 01-04; P-in-c Leic St Phil from 04. *St Mary's Vicarage, 56 Vicarage Lane, Humberstone, Leicester LE5 1EE* Tel 0116-276 7281 Fax 276 4504 E-mail grahamanddiane@ntlworld.com

JOHNSON, Canon Donald Arnold. b 28. Linc Coll Ox BA51 MA59. Cuddesdon Coll 51. **d** 53 **p** 54. C Henfield *Chich* 53-55; C Horsham 55-59; V Oving w Merston 59-68; Bp's Dom Chapl 59-68; V Hellingly 68-78; V Upper Dicker 68-78; R W Stoke 78-98; V Funtington and Sennicotts 78-98; Can and Preb Chich Cathl 96-98; rtd 98; Perm to Offic *Chich* from 99. *Vectis, Commonside, Westbourne, Emsworth PO10 8TA* Tel (01243) 371433

JOHNSON, Mrs Dorothy. Leic Univ BSc89 Ox Univ MTh95 RGN NDN80 FRSH91. Qu Coll Birm 77. **dss** 80 **d** 87 **p** 94. Coventry Caludon *Cov* 80-81; Wolston and Church Lawford 81-86; NSM Stoneleigh w Ashow from 87; Bp's Asst Officer for Soc Resp 87-96. *The Firs, Stoneleigh Road, Bubbenhall, Coventry CV8 3BS* Tel and fax (024) 7630 3712 E-mail firsjohn@supanet.com

JOHNSON, Douglas Leonard. b 45. Trin Coll Bris 70 Lon Bible Coll MA95. **d** 73 **p** 74. C New Malden and Coombe *S'wark* 73-76; P-in-c Upper Tulse Hill St Matthias 76-82; CPAS Staff 82-88; Lect and Tutor CA Coll 88-91; Hon C Wimbledon Em Ridgway Prop Chpl *S'wark* from 83; Dir Crossways Chr Educn Trust from 92; Lect Cornhill Tr Course from 95. *11 Preston Road, London SW20 0SS* Tel (020) 8946 2136 Fax 8947 4146

JOHNSON, Edward Anthony (Tony). b 32. Univ of Wales (Swansea) BSc54. St Steph Ho Ox 79. **d** 81 **p** 82. C Wolvercote w Summertown *Ox* 81-84; P-in-c Ramsden 84-87; P-in-c Finstock and Fawler 84-87; P-in-c Wilcote 84-87; V Ramsden, Finstock and Fawler, Leafield etc 87-92; rtd 92; Hon C Kennington *Ox* 92-98; Perm to Offic from 98. *15 Cranbrook Drive, Kennington, Oxford OX1 5RR* Tel (01865) 739751

JOHNSON, Mrs Elizabeth Jane. b 47. St Hilda's Coll Ox MA69. Wycliffe Hall Ox 84. **dss** 86 **d** 87 **p** 94. NSM Ox St Aldate w St Matt *Ox* 86-91; NSM Marston 91-94; NSM Ox St Clem 94-95; NSM Islip w Charlton on Otmoor, Oddington, Noke etc 95-99; OLM Officer (Dorchester) 99-00; Asst Chapl Oxon Mental Healthcare NHS Trust 00-04; NSM Bladon w Woodstock *Ox* 99-04; NSM Shill Valley and Broadshire from 04. *The Vicarage, Filkins, Lechlade GL7 3JQ* Tel (01367) 860846 E-mail lizjohn@crecy.fsnet.co.uk

JOHNSON, Eric. b 38. Nottm Univ BSc60 Open Univ BA92 SS Paul & Mary Coll Cheltenham MA94 Leeds Univ DipFE72. Qu Coll Birm 74. **d** 77 **p** 78. Sen Lect Cov Tech Coll 66-91; NSM Earlsdon *Cov* 77-81; NSM Wolston and Church Lawford 81-86; NSM Stoneleigh w Ashow and Baginton 90-98; FE Liaison Officer *B & W*, *Bris* and *Glouc* 91-93; Dioc Dir of Educn *Worc* 93-98; rtd 98; Assoc CME Adv *Cov* from 98. *The Firs, Stoneleigh Road, Bubbenhall, Coventry CV8 3BS* Tel and fax (024) 7630 3712 E-mail firsjohn@supanet.com

JOHNSON, Mrs Frances Josephine. b 53. N Ord Course. **d** 05. C Hall Green St Pet *Birm* from 05. *The Vicarage, 7 Fordrough, Yardley, Birmingham B25 8DL* Tel 0121-773 1278

JOHNSON, Geoffrey Kemble. b 22. RD71. Roch Th Coll 62. **d** 64 **p** 65. C Hayes *Roch* 64-68; R Worlingham *St E* 68-84; rtd 84; Perm to Offic *Nor* 84-00 and *St E* from 84. *53 St Walstans Road, Taverham, Norwich NR8 6NG* Tel (01603) 860626

JOHNSON, Geoffrey Stuart. b 39. ALCD65 Wolv Poly DipEd Sussex Univ DPhil01. **d** 65 **p** 66. C Worksop St Jo *S'well* 65-68; Taiwan 68-71; Singapore 71-76; Aber Univ *Ab* 76-78; Perm to Offic *Heref* 78-82; P-in-c Hoarwithy, Hentland and Sellack 82-84; Chapl Horton Hosp Epsom 84-90; Distr Chapl Brighton HA 90-94; Managing Chapl Brighton Healthcare NHS Trust 94-99; Managing Chapl S Downs Health NHS Trust 94-99; Chapl from 99; rtd 99; Perm to Offic *Chich* from 01. *5 Garden Mews, 15 Beachy Head Road, Eastbourne BN20 7QP* Tel (01323) 644083

JOHNSON, Gillian Margaret. b 55. Bretton Hall Coll CertEd76 Coll of Ripon & York St Jo MA03. N Ord Course 00. **d** 03 **p** 04. C Thornhill and Whitley Lower *Wakef* from 03. *5 Wood Mount, Overton, Wakefield WF4 4SB* Tel (01924) 262181 Mobile 07880-901201 E-mail gilljohnson99@hotmail.com

JOHNSON, Gordon Edward. b 27. Oak Hill Th Coll 76. **d** 77 **p** 78. C Scarborough St Mary w Ch Ch and H Apostles *York* 77-82; V Hutton Cranswick w Skerne 82-86; P-in-c Watton w Beswick and Kilnwick 82-86; V Hutton Cranswick w Skerne, Watton and Beswick 86-88; V Bubwith w Skipwith 88-93; rtd 93; Perm to Offic *York* and *Ripon* from 93. *Greenacres, Lovesome Hill, Northallerton DL6 2PB* Tel (01609) 881512

JOHNSON, Graham. b 37. Westcott Ho Cam 66. **d** 68 **p** 69. C Stafford St Mary *Lich* 68-71; C Wombourne 71-74; Youth Chapl 74-77; P-in-c Tong 76-77; Res Min Wednesfield St Thos 77-78; TV 79-82; P-in-c Milwich and Weston upon Trent 82-88; P-in-c Gayton w Fradswell 84-88; V Fradswell, Gayton, Milwich and Weston 88-90; TV Wolstanton 90-96; V Oxley 96-02; rtd 03. *Ty Pab, 4 Church Street, Tremadog, Porthmadog LL49 9RA* Tel (01766) 513744 E-mail graham@typab.freeserve.co.uk

JOHNSON, Graham James. b 43. Leeds Univ BA67. Coll of Resurr Mirfield DipTh69. **d** 70 **p** 71. C Heckmondwike *Wakef* 70-73; C Pet St Jude *Pet* 73-76; V Gt w Lt Harrowden and Orlingbury 76-83; R Daventry 83-92; TR Daventry, Ashby St Ledgers, Braunston etc 92; RD Daventry 88-92; Chapl Danetre Hosp 83-93; P-in-c Loddington *Leic* 93-99; Warden Launde Abbey 93-99; RD Framland 94-96; Bp's Chapl and Interfaith Adv 00-02; P-in-c Humberstone 02-03; P-in-c Thurnby Lodge 02-03; TR Ascension TM from 03. *St Mary's Vicarage, 56 Vicarage Lane, Humberstone, Leicester LE5 1EE* Tel 0116-276 7281 Fax 276 4504 E-mail grahamanddiane@ntlworld.com

JOHNSON, Harriet Etta. LRAM DipEd40. Trin Coll Bris. **dss** 76 **d** 87. Burundi 76-80; Ipplepen w Torbryan *Ex* 81-87; Hon Par Dn 87-90; Perm to Offic from 90. *10 Fairfield West, Huxtable Hill, Torquay TQ2 6RN* Tel (01803) 690115

JOHNSON, Mrs Hilary Ann. b 51. RGN72 RHV74 DipRS85. S'wark Ord Course 82. **dss** 85 **d** 87 **p** 94. Hon Par Dn Salfords *S'wark* 85-90; Chapl St Geo Hosp Lon 90-94; Chapl St Geo Healthcare NHS Trust Lon from 94; Assoc P Wimbledon *S'wark* from 95. *St George's Hospital, Blackshaw Road, London SW17 0QT* Tel (020) 8725 3070, 8725 3071 *or* 8397 0952 Fax 8725 1621 E-mail hilary.johnson@stgeorges.nhs.uk

JOHNSON, Ian Lawrence. b 44. Wells Th Coll 68. **d** 71 **p** 72. C Benhilton *S'wark* 71-73; C Weymouth H Trin *Sarum* 73-76; R Pewsey 76-81; R Maiden Newton and Valleys 81-83; Youth Officer (Sherborne Area) 81-83; Dioc Youth Officer 83-88; TR Langley and Parkfield *Man* 88-95; P-in-c Haughton St Anne 95-99; Dioc Adv on Evang 95-99; TR Southampton (City Cen) *Win* from 99. *The Rectory, 32B Morris Road, Southampton SO15 2BR* Tel (023) 8023 5716 Fax 8057 9765 E-mail ianljohnson@zoom.co.uk *or* rectory@ic24.net

JOHNSON, Ian Leslie. b 51. Bede Coll Dur TCert73. Wycliffe Hall Ox DipMin93. **d** 93 **p** 94. C Evington *Leic* 93-96; Sub Chapl HM Pris Gartree 96-97; C Foxton w Gumley and Laughton and Lubenham *Leic* 96-97; C Foxton w Gumley and Laughton 97-00; P-in-c from 00; Sub Chapl HM Pris Gartree from 97. *The Vicarage, Vicarage Drive, Foxton, Market Harborough LE16 7RJ* Tel (01858) 545245 E-mail ijoh270951@aol.com

JOHNSON (née SILINS), Ms Jacqueline. b 62. Coll of Ripon & York St Jo BA85. Ripon Coll Cuddesdon 01. **d** 03 **p** 04. C Torpoint *Truro* from 03. *3 Grove Park, Torpoint PL11 2PP* Tel (01752) 812418 Mobile 07905-354723 E-mail jackie@sinl.fsnet.co.uk

✠**JOHNSON, The Rt Revd James Nathaniel.** b 32. Wells Th Coll 63. **d** 64 **p** 65 **c** 85. C Lawrence Weston *Bris* 64-66; P-in-c St Paul's Cathl St Helena 66-69; V 69-71; Hon Can from 75; Area Sec USPG *Ex* and *Truro* 72-74; R Combe Martin *Ex* 74-80; V Thorpe Bay *Chelmsf* 80-85; Bp St Helena 85-91; R Byfield w Boddington and Aston le Walls *Pet* 91-92; Asst Bp Pet 91-92; V Hockley *Chelmsf* 92-97; Asst Bp Chelmsf 92-97; Can Chelmsf Cathl 94-97; rtd 97; Hon Asst Bp Chelmsf 97-04; Hon Asst Bp Ox from 04. *St Helena, 28 Molyneux Drive, Bodicote, Banbury OX15 4AP* Tel (01295) 255357 E-mail bpjnj@onetel.com

JOHNSON, Canon John Anthony. b 18. Selw Coll Cam BA48 MA53 St Jo Coll Dur DipTh51. **d** 51 **p** 52. C Battersea St Mary *S'wark* 51-54; C Merton St Mary 54-56; V Balderton *S'well* 56-60; V Mansfield Woodhouse 60-70; V Beeston 70-85; RD Beeston 81-85; Hon Can S'well Minster 82-85; rtd 86; Perm to Offic *Blackb* 90-02. *Driftwood, Ireleth Road, Askam-in-Furness LA16 7JD* Tel (01229) 462291

JOHNSON, John Cecil. b 23. Peterho Cam BA48. Ely Th Coll 57. **d** 59 **p** 60. C Whitton SS Phil and Jas *Lon* 59-70; P-in-c Fulham St Andr Fulham Fields 70-73; V 73-88; rtd 88; Perm to Offic *Lich* from 88; Perm to Offic *Heref* from 90. *13 Selkirk Drive, Sutton Hill, Telford TF7 4JE* Tel (01952) 588407

JOHNSON, John David. b 38. Handsworth Coll Birm 60 Claremont Sch of Th 65 St Deiniol's Hawarden 71. **d** 71 **p** 72. C Heref St Martin *Heref* 71-73; P-in-c Ewyas Harold w Dulas 73-79; P-in-c Kilpeck 73-79; P-in-c St Devereux w Wormbridge 73-79; P-in-c Kenderchurch 73-79; P-in-c Bacton 78-79; TR Ewyas Harold w Dulas, Kenderchurch etc 79-81; R Kentchurch w Llangua, Rowlestone, Llancillo etc 79-81; Chapl Napsbury Hosp St Alb 81-96; Chapl Horizon NHS Trust Herts 96-00; Chapl Barnet Healthcare NHS Trust 96-00; Chapl Barnet and Chase Farm Hosps NHS Trust 00-05; Chapl Herts Partnerships NHS Trust 02-03; rtd 03. *24 Rushendon Furlong, Pitstone, Leighton Buzzard LU7 9QX* Tel (020) 8952 2381

JOHNSON, Joseph Clarke. b 10. Bps' Coll Cheshunt 46. **d** 48 **p** 49. C Carl H Trin *Carl* 48-50; V St John's in the Vale w Wythburn 51-57; V Beckermet St Bridget w Ponsonby 57-78; rtd

78; Perm to Offic *Carl* from 78. *High Moss, Calderbridge, Seascale CA20 1DQ* Tel (01946) 841289

JOHNSON, Josephine. *See* JOHNSON, Mrs Frances Josephine

JOHNSON, Mrs Julie Margaret. b 47. LNSM course 94. **d** 98 **p** 99. OLM Welton and Dunholme w Scothern *Linc* from 98. *7 St Mary's Avenue, Welton, Lincoln LN2 3LN* Tel (01673) 860650

JOHNSON, Kathryn Ann. d 03 **p** 04. C Wrexham *St As* 03-04; C Prestatyn from 04. *The Vicarage, First Avenue, 109 High Street, Prestatyn LL19 9AR* Tel (01745) 853780

JOHNSON, Keith Henry. b 64. Keele Univ BA91 CQSW91. Coll of Resurr Mirfield BA97. **d** 97 **p** 98. C W Bromwich St Fran *Lich* 97-00; P-in-c Willenhall St Giles 00-05; V from 05. *St Giles's Vicarage, Walsall Street, Willenhall WV13 2ER* Tel (01902) 605722 E-mail keith.johnson14@btinternet.com

JOHNSON, Keith Winton Thomas William. b 37. K Coll Lon BD63 AKC63. **d** 64 **p** 65. C Dartford H Trin *Roch* 64-69; Chapl Kuwait 69-73; V Erith St Jo *Roch* 73-80; V Bexley St Jo 80-91; V Royston *St Alb* 91-94; R Sandon, Wallington and Rushden w Clothall 94-97; Dean St Chris Cathl Bahrain 97-02; rtd 02; Hon C Balsham, Weston Colville, W Wickham etc *Ely* from 04. *The Vicarage, The Causeway, West Wratting, Cambridge CB1 5NA* Tel (01223) 291265 E-mail keith1412@hotmail.com

JOHNSON, Kenneth William George. b 53. Hull Univ BA76 PGCE77. EMMTC 92. **d** 95 **p** 96. NSM Ilkeston H Trin *Derby* 95-99; NSM Sandiacre from 99; Chapl Bluecoat Sch Nottm from 02. *18 Park Avenue, Awsworth, Nottingham NG16 2RA* Tel 0115-930 7830 E-mail kwjohnson@lineone.net

JOHNSON, Miss Lesley Denise. b 47. WMMTC 95. **d** 98 **p** 99. NSM Stockingford *Cov* 98-01; TV Cov E from 01. *St Alban's Vicarage, Mercer Avenue, Coventry CV2 4PQ* Tel (024) 7645 2493 Fax as telephone

JOHNSON, Malcolm Arthur. b 36. Univ Coll Dur BA60 MA64 Lon Metrop Univ Hon MA02. Cuddesdon Coll 60. **d** 62 **p** 63. C Portsea N End St Mark *Portsm* 62-67; Chapl Qu Mary Coll *Lon* 67-74; V St Botolph Aldgate w H Trin Minories 74-92; P-in-c St Ethelburga Bishopgate 85-89; AD The City 85-90; Master R Foundn of St Kath in Ratcliffe 93-97; Bp's Adv for Past Care and Counselling *Lon* 97-01; rtd 02. *Mill Eyot, Chertsey Road, Shepperton TW17 9LA* Tel (01932) 224365 Fax 226428

JOHNSON, Canon Malcolm Stuart. b 35. AKC60. **d** 61 **p** 62. C Catford St Laur *S'wark* 61-64; Hon C Hatcham St Cath 66-76; P-in-c Kingstanding St Luke *Birm* 76-77; V 77-82; P-in-c Peckham St Jo w St Andr *S'wark* 82-92; V 92-03; Hon Can Sabongidda-Ora from 98; rtd 04. *34 Sheppard's College, London Road, Bromley BR1 1PF* Tel (020) 8466 5276

JOHNSON, Canon Margaret Anne Hope. b 52. Homerton Coll Cam Open Univ BA81 Fitzw Coll Cam BA95. Ridley Hall Cam 93. **d** 95 **p** 96. C Northampton Em *Pet* 95-97; P-in-c 97-98; TR from 98; Adv in Women's Min from 03; Can Pet Cathl from 04. *13 Booth Lane North, Northampton NN3 6JG* Tel (01604) 648974 E-mail revmahj@aol.com

JOHNSON, Margaret Joan (Meg). b 41. S'wark Ord Course 92. **d** 95 **p** 96. NSM Sanderstead St Mary *S'wark* 95-04. *73 St Peter's Street, South Croydon CR2 7DG* Tel (020) 8686 1711 E-mail meg.johnson@southwark.anglican.org

JOHNSON, Mark. b 62. Leic Poly BSc84 Loughb Univ PhD88. Ripon Coll Cuddesdon 88. **d** 94 **p** 95. C Bishop's Cleeve *Glouc* 94-98; TV Heref S Wye *Heref* from 98. *The Vicarage, 1 Holme Lacy Road, Hereford HR2 6DD* Tel (01432) 353275 *or* 353717 Fax 352412 E-mail s.wye.team.ministry@talk21.com

JOHNSON, Michael. b 42. Birm Univ BSc63. S'wark Ord Course 68. **d** 71 **p** 72. C Kidbrooke St Jas *S'wark* 71-74; NSM Eynsford w Farningham and Lullingstone *Roch* 74-89; NSM Selling w Throwley, Sheldwich w Badlesmere etc *Cant* from 89. *1 Halke Cottages, North Street, Sheldwich, Faversham ME13 0LR* Tel (01795) 536583 E-mail onehalke@aol.com

JOHNSON, Canon Michael Anthony. b 51. Ex Univ BA76. Ripon Coll Cuddesdon 76 Ch Div Sch of the Pacific (USA) 77. **d** 78 **p** 79. C Primrose Hill St Mary w Avenue Road St Paul *Lon* 78-81; C Hampstead St Jo 81-85; TV Mortlake w E Sheen *S'wark* 85-93; V Wroughton *Bris* from 93; RD Wroughton 97-99; AD Swindon from 99; Hon Can Bris Cathl from 99. *The Vicarage, Church Hill, Wroughton, Swindon SN4 9JS* Tel (01793) 812301 Fax 814582 E-mail canonmike@hotmail.com

JOHNSON, Michael Colin. b 37. Lon Univ DipRS80. S'wark Ord Course 77. **d** 80 **p** 81. NSM New Eltham All SS *S'wark* 80-84; NSM Woldingham 84-98; rtd 98; Perm to Offic *Chich* from 99. *5 The Mount, Meads Road, Eastbourne BN20 7PX* Tel (01323) 730501 E-mail tandem@mountmeads.fsnet.co.uk

JOHNSON, Michael Gordon. b 45. Kelham Th Coll 64. **d** 68 **p** 69. C Holbrooks *Cov* 68-72; C Cannock *Lich* 72-75; V Coseley Ch Ch 75-79; P-in-c Sneyd 79-82; R Longton 82-88; Chapl Pilgrim Hosp Boston 88-96; TV Jarrow *Dur* 96-98; Chapl Monkton and Primrose Hill Hosp 96-98; R Burghwallis and Campsall *Sheff* from 98. *The Vicarage, High Street, Campsall, Doncaster DN6 9AF* Tel (01302) 700286

JOHNSON, Michael Robert. b 68. Aston Business Sch BSc90. Ridley Hall Cam CTM97. **d** 97 **p** 98. C E Greenwich *S'wark* 97-00; C Perry Hill St Geo 00-03; Chapl W Lon YMCA from 03. *YMCA, 25 St Mary's Road, London W5 5RE* Tel (020) 8799 4800 E-mail thebluegnu@yahoo.co.uk

JOHNSON, Mrs Nancy May. b 46. TCert67 Sheff Poly MA86. N Ord Course 00. **d** 02 **p** 03. NSM Sheff Cathl *Sheff* 02-04; Asst Chapl Sheff Teaching Hosps NHS Trust from 04. *121 Rustlings Road, Sheffield S11 7AB* Tel 0114-266 6456 E-mail nancy@121rustlings.freeserve.co.uk

JOHNSON, Nigel Edwin. b 41. AKC64 St Boniface Warminster 64. **d** 65 **p** 66. C Poulton-le-Sands *Blackb* 65-68; Chapl RN 68-93; Perm to Offic *Cant* 93-00 and *Carl* from 00; rtd 99. *Mell View, 9 Thirlmere Park, Penrith CA11 8QS* Tel (01768) 899865

JOHNSON, Nigel Victor. b 48. ARCM68 LTCL75 Cam Univ DipEd69. Linc Th Coll 80. **d** 82 **p** 83. C Lindley *Wakef* 82-85; P-in-c Upperthong 85-87; Perm to Offic *Derby* 88-89; NSM Calow and Sutton cum Duckmanton 89-90; R 90-00; RD Bolsover and Staveley 98-00; V Newbold w Dunston from 00; RD Chesterfield from 02. *Newbold Rectory, St John's Road, Chesterfield S41 8QN* Tel (01246) 450374 E-mail anselard@aol.com

JOHNSON, Peter Colin. b 64. SS Mark & Jo Coll Plymouth BEd87 Univ of Wales (Lamp) PhD00. SW Minl Tr Course 97. **d** 00 **p** 01. NSM Godrevy *Truro* from 00. *Seascape, Trewelloe Road, Praa Sands, Penzance TR20 9SU* Tel (01736) 763407 E-mail revdocpj@btinternet.com

JOHNSON, Canon Peter Frederick. b 41. Melbourne Univ BA63 Ch Ch Ox BA68 MA72. St Steph Ho Ox 68. **d** 69 **p** 70. C Banbury *Ox* 69-71; Tutor St Steph Ho Ox 71-74; Chapl St Chad's Coll Dur 74-80; Vice-Prin 78-80; Chapl K Sch Cant 80-90; Perm to Offic *Cant* 80-81; Hon Min Can Cant Cathl 81-90; Can Res Bris Cathl *Bris* from 90. *41 Salisbury Road, Bristol BS6 7AR* Tel 0117-944 4464 E-mail pfjohnson@blueyonder.co.uk

JOHNSON, Prof Peter Stewart. b 44. Nottm Univ BA65 PhD70. Cranmer Hall Dur 01. **d** 03 **p** 04. NSM Dur St Nic *Dur* from 03. *126 Devonshire Road, Durham DH1 2BH* Tel 0191-386 6334 Mobile 07949-680467

JOHNSON, Philip Anthony. b 69. All Nations Chr Coll BA97 MA98 FIBMS94. Ridley Hall Cam 00. **d** 02 **p** 03. C Witham *Chelmsf* from 02. *23 Forest Road, Witham CM8 2PS* Tel (01376) 517170 E-mail revdphilip@aol.com

JOHNSON (née DAVIES), Rhiannon Mary Morgan. b 69. St Anne's Coll Ox BA90 MA96 Univ of Wales (Cardiff) PhD94 BD96 Dip Past Th 97. St Mich Coll Llan 94. **d** 97 **p** 98. C Whitchurch *Llan* 97-99; NSM Walton W w Talbenny and Haroldston W *St D* 99-00; Chapl Trin Coll Carmarthen 00; NSM Walton W w Talbenny and Haroldston W *St D* from 00. *The Rectory, Walton West, Little Haven, Haverfordwest SA62 3UB* Tel (01437) 781279 E-mail rhiannonmm@tesco.net

JOHNSON, Richard Miles. b 59. Bris Univ BSc82. St Jo Coll Nottm 87. **d** 90 **p** 91. C Bromley SS Pet and Paul *Roch* 90-94; USPG/CMS Philippines 94-97; C Bexleyheath Ch Ch *Roch* from 97; Ind Chapl from 97. *69 Garden Avenue, Bexleyheath DA7 4LE* Tel and fax (020) 8303 9509 *or* tel 8304 6887 E-mail dickim@globalnet.co.uk

JOHNSON, Robert Kenneth. b 48. N Ord Course 83. **d** 86 **p** 87. C Hattersley *Ches* 86-88; C Brinnington w Portwood 88-90; V Gospel Lane St Mich *Birm* 90-97; P-in-c Birm St Geo from 97. *St George's Rectory, 100 Bridge Street West, Birmingham B19 2YX* Tel 0121-359 2000 Fax 359 8163 E-mail robj@cofe-newtown.fsnet.co.uk

JOHNSON, Canon Robin Edward Hobbs. b 39. Fitzw Ho Cam BA61 MA65. Ripon Hall Ox 61. **d** 63 **p** 64. C Tyldesley w Shakerley *Man* 63-66; Lic to Offic *Leic* 66-71; V Castleton Moor *Man* 71-77; Dir of Ords 76-81; V Prestwich St Gabr 77-81; V Heaton Ch Ch 81-91; Hon Can Man Cathl 86-91; TR Dorchester *Sarum* 91-00; RD Dorchester 99-00; rtd 00; Chapl Torrevieja *Eur* 00-03. *The Chaplain's House, St Oswald's Close, The Tything, Worcester WR1 1HR* Tel (01905) 616619

JOHNSON, Ronald. b 40. Sunderland Poly NDD61 Liv Coll of Art ATD62. Wycliffe Hall Ox 69. **d** 72 **p** 73. C Deane *Man* 72-74; C N Meols *Liv* 74-75; Chapl St Jo Sch Tiffield 75-82; TV Riverside *Ox* 82-84; Asst Chapl Eton Coll 82-84; Warden Eton Coll Dorney Project 82-84; Chapl Eastbourne Coll 85-99; rtd 99; Perm to Offic *Dur* from 99. *55 Cutlers Hall Road, Consett DH8 8RE* Tel (01207) 582109

JOHNSON, Ronald George. b 33. Chich Th Coll 75. **d** 76 **p** 77. Hon C Shipley *Chich* 76-79; C Brighton St Matthias 79-82; P-in-c Barlavington 82; P-in-c Burton w Coates 82; P-in-c Sutton w Bignor 82; R Barlavington, Burton w Coates, Sutton and Bignor 82-93; rtd 93; Perm to Offic *Chich* from 93. *1 Highdown Drive, Littlehampton BN17 6HJ* Tel (01903) 732210

JOHNSON, The Very Revd Samuel Hugh Stowell Akinsope. b 30. K Coll Lon BD61. Lich Th Coll 52. **d** 55 **p** 56. C Whitechapel St Paul w St Mark *Lon* 55-58; C Sunbury 58-59; C Lisson Grove w St Marylebone St Matt w Em 59-60; C St Martin-in-the-Fields 60-62; Nigeria from 63; Provost Lagos Cathl 70-95; rtd 95. *1 Oba Nle Aro Crescent, Ilupeju, PO Box 10021, Marina, Lagos, Nigeria*

JOHNSON (née ROWE), Mrs Shiela. b 43. Cert Child Care 66. CITC 93. **d** 96 **p** 97. Aux Min Urney w Denn and Derryheen *K, E & A* 96-97; Aux Min Boyle and Elphin w Aghanagh, Kilbryan etc 97-01; Aux Min Roscommon w Donamon, Rathcline, Kilkeevin etc 97-01; Aux Min Clondevaddock w Portsalon and Leatbeg *D & R* from 02. *Ballymore Rectory, Port-na-Blagh, Letterkenny, Co Donegal, Irish Republic* Tel (00353) (74) 913 6185 E-mail clondehorkey@raphoe.anglican.org

JOHNSON, Stanley. b 42. QUB BSc63 TCD BTh89. CITC 86. **d** 89 **p** 90. C Kilmore w Ballintemple, Kildallan etc *K, E & A* 89-97; Adn Elphin and Ardagh 97-01; Can Elphin Cathl 97-01; I Templemichael w Clongish, Clooncumber etc 97-01; I Clondehorkey w Cashel *D & R* from 01. *Ballymore Rectory, Port-na-Blagh, Letterkenny, Co Donegal, Irish Republic* Tel (00353) (74) 913 6185
E-mail clondehorkey@raphoe.anglican.org
or johnsons@esatclear.ie

JOHNSON, Stephen. b 57. Cranmer Hall Dur. **d** 00 **p** 01. C Longton *Blackb* 00-02; C Longridge 03-04; V Preston Em from 04. *Emmanuel Vicarage, 2 Cornthwaite Road, Fulwood, Preston PR2 3DA* Tel (01772) 717136 Mobile 07790-917504

JOHNSON, Stephen William. b 63. Trent Poly BEd86 Keele Univ MA94 Univ Coll Ches BA05 ALCM85. N Ord Course 02. **d** 05. NSM Keele *Lich* from 05; NSM Silverdale from 05; NSM Madeley from 05; NSM Betley from 05. *86 Dunnocksfold Road, Alsager, Stoke-on-Trent ST7 2TW* Tel (01270) 874066 Mobile 07766-411090
E-mail stephenjohnson@cheddleton18.freeserve.co.uk

JOHNSON, Stuart. *See* JOHNSON, Geoffrey Stuart

JOHNSON, Mrs Susan Constance. b 46. EAMTC 01. **d** 03 **p** 04. NSM Heald Green St Cath *Ches* from 03. *11A Lynton Park Road, Cheadle Hulme, Cheadle SK8 6JA* Tel 0161-485 3787
E-mail bjohnson@ics-uk.org.

JOHNSON, Terence John. b 44. Cov Poly BA89. Lon Coll of Div ALCD70 LTh74. **d** 69 **p** 70. C Woodside *Ripon* 69-72; C Leeds St Geo 72-76; C Heworth H Trin *York* 76-81; V Budbrooke *Cov* 81-97; Chapl Wroxall Abbey Sch 83-93; V Stone Ch Ch and Oulton *Lich* 97-02; P-in-c Collingtree w Courteenhall and Milton Malsor *Pet* from 02. *The Rectory, Barn Corner, Collingtree, Northampton NN4 0NF* Tel (01604) 705620
E-mail terence@johnson7142.fsnet.co.uk

JOHNSON, Thomas Bernard. b 44. BA CertEd. Oak Hill Th Coll. **d** 84 **p** 85. C Birkenhead St Jas w St Bede *Ches* 84-88; R Ashover and Brackenfield *Derby* 88-01; P-in-c Wessington 99-01; R Ashover and Brackenfield w Wessington 01-03; Hon Chapl Derbyshire St Jo Ambulance from 91; RD Chesterfield 97-02; V Swanwick and Pentrich from 03. *The Vicarage, 4 Broom Avenue, Swanwick, Alfreton DE55 1DQ* Tel (01773) 602684
E-mail t.b.johnson@virgin.net

JOHNSON, Victor Edward. b 45. Linc Th Coll 83. **d** 85 **p** 86. C Garforth *Ripon* 85-90; Dioc Video Officer 90-92; V Wyther Ven Bede 92-00; V Shelley and Shepley *Wakef* 00-01; rtd 01; Perm to Offic *Bradf* from 02. *12 Rosie's Brae, Isle of Whithorn, Newton Stewart DG8 8LT* Tel (01988) 500511 E-mail vej@onetel.com

JOHNSTON, Alan Beere. b 14. Leeds Univ BA36. Coll of Resurr Mirfield 36. **d** 38 **p** 39. C Manningham St Chad *Bradf* 38-40; C Middlesbrough St Paul *York* 40-43; Perm to Offic 43-45; C Crawley *Chich* 45-47; C Portsea N End St Mark *Portsm* 47-48; C Marske in Cleveland *York* 48-50; P-in-c Carlin How w Skinningrove 50-52; V 52-57; V Clifton 57-62; V Kingston upon Hull St Mary 62-68; Asst Master Sir Henry Cooper High Sch Hull 68-70; Waltham Toll Bar Sch Waltham 70-71; Tutor Workers' Educn Assn 71-81; rtd 81; Perm to Offic *Eur* from 83; Asst Chapl Istanbul 89-90; Perm to Offic *Chich* from 93. *6 Arlington Close, Goring-by-Sea, Worthing BN12 4ST* Tel (01903) 426590

JOHNSTON, Alexander Irvine. b 47. Keele Univ BA70 LRAM. St Alb Minl Tr Scheme 77. **d** 80 **p** 81. NSM Hockerill *St Alb* 80-95; NSM High Wych and Gilston w Eastwick 95-96; TV Bottesford w Ashby *Linc* 96-01; P-in-c St Germans *Truro* from 01. *The Vicarage, Quay Road, St Germans, Saltash PL12 5LY* Tel and fax (01503) 230690
E-mail alec@johnston2000.fsnet.co.uk

JOHNSTON, Allen Niall. b 61. Southn Univ BTh92 Kent Univ MA97 AMBIM87 MISM87 MInstD00. Sarum & Wells Th Coll 89. **d** 92 **p** 93. C Roehampton H Trin *S'wark* 92-95; Dir Past Services Richmond, Twickenham and Roehampton NHS Trust 95-98; Tutor SEITE 95-97; Perm to Offic *Ely* from 03 and *D & R* from 04. *Suite 700, Westminster House, 7 Millbank, London SW1P 3JA* E-mail niall@nialljohnston.org

JOHNSTON, Austin. b 50. Huddersfield Poly CertEd76 BEd90. Chich Th Coll Dip Th & Min 94. **d** 94 **p** 95. C Peterlee *Dur* 94-97; C Stockton St Pet 97-00; TR Stanley and Tanfield 00-01; TR Ch the K from 01. *The Rectory, Church Bank, Stanley DH9 0DU* Tel (01207) 233936

JOHNSTON, Charles Walter Barr. b 38. Lon Univ BSc61. Oak Hill Th Coll 62. **d** 64 **p** 65. C Holloway St Mark w Em *Lon* 64-68; Argentina from 68; SAMS 70-03; rtd 03. *c/o A Johnston Esq, 27 Cloister Crofts, Leamington Spa CV32 6QG* Tel (01926) 336 136

JOHNSTON, David. *See* JOHNSTON, Thomas David

JOHNSTON, David George Scott. b 66. Avery Hill Coll BA88. SEITE 00. **d** 03 **p** 04. C Frindsbury w Upnor and Chattenden *Roch* from 03. *18 Honeypot Close, Rochester ME2 3DU* Tel (01634) 321239 E-mail cathryn.johnston@ntlworld.com

JOHNSTON, Canon Donald Walter. b 28. Trin Coll Melbourne BA51 Lon Univ PGCE52 Em Coll Cam BA63 MA67. Ridley Hall Cam 64. **d** 64 **p** 65. C Cottingham *York* 64-66; Australia from 66; Min Nunawading Melbourne 67-69; Chapl Brighton Gr Sch Melbourne 70-73; Chapl Melbourne C of E Gr Sch 74-84; Angl Bd of Miss 85-90; Chapl H Name Sch Dogura 85; Hd Martyrs' Memorial Sch Popondetta 86-89; Hon Commissary from 91; Can Papua New Guinea from 90; rtd 91. *22 Albert Street, PO Box 114, Point Lonsdale, Vic, Australia 3225* Tel (0061) (3) 5258 2139 *or* 9690 0549 Fax 5258 3994
E-mail dncjohnston@al.com.au

JOHNSTON, Duncan Howard. b 63. Hull Univ BA85 Nottm Univ MA93. St Jo Coll Nottm 91. **d** 93 **p** 94. C Werrington *Pet* 93-96; V Gt Doddington and Wilby 96-01; Dioc Adv in Local Miss *Dur* 02-03; R Fremont St Jo USA from 03. *346 East Main Street, Fremont, MI 49412, USA* Tel (001) (231) 924 7120
E-mail djepisc@joimal.com

JOHNSTON, Edith Violet Nicholl. b 28. **d** 87. Par Dn Bentley *Sheff* 87-88; rtd 88; Perm to Offic *Sheff* from 88. *32 Tennyson Avenue, Mexborough S64 0AX* Tel (01709) 570189

JOHNSTON, Elizabeth Margaret. b 37. QUB BA58 DipEd69 Serampore Univ BD87 Lon Univ DipTh62. Dalton Ho Bris. **d** 81 **p** 94. BCMS India 62-92; C Belfast St Chris *D & D* 93-94; Bp's C 94-03; Can Down Cathl 01-03; rtd 03. *103 Ballydorn Road, Killinchy, Newtownards BT23 6QB* Tel (028) 9754 2518 Mobile 07980-123181
E-mail elizabeth_johnston@amserve.com

JOHNSTON, Frank. *See* JOHNSTON, William Francis

JOHNSTON, The Very Revd Frederick Mervyn Kieran. b 11. TCD BA33 MA52. **d** 34 **p** 36. C Castlecomer *C & O* 34-36; C Cork St Luke *C, C & R* 36-38; I Kilmeen 38-40; I Drimoleague 40-45; I Cork St Mich 45-58; Can Cork and Cloyne Cathls 55-59; I Bandon 58-67; Treas Ross Cathl 59-60; Adn Cork 59-66; Dean Cork 66-71; rtd 71. *24 Lapps Court, Hartlands Avenue, Cork, Irish Republic* Tel (00353) (21) 313264

JOHNSTON, Geoffrey Stanley. b 44. Aston Univ MBA81 Birm Univ CertEd78. Kelham Th Coll 64. **d** 68 **p** 69. C Blakenall Heath *Lich* 68-72 and 73-75; C St Buryan, St Levan and Sennen *Truro* 72-73; P-in-c Willenhall St Steph *Lich* 75-76; C W Bromwich All SS 76-77; Lect W Bromwich Coll of Commerce and Tech 78-82; Ind Chapl *Worc* 82-94; TV Halesowen 82-94; NSM Dudley St Fran 94-99; P-in-c from 99; P-in-c Dudley St Edm from 04. *St Francis's Vicarage, 50 Laurel Road, Dudley DY1 3EZ* Tel and fax (01384) 350422
E-mail geoff.johnston@blueyonder.co.uk

JOHNSTON, Mrs Helen Kay. b 48. SRN70. St Alb and Ox Min Course 95. **d** 98 **p** 99. OLM Banbury St Paul *Ox* 98-01; P-in-c Flimby *Carl* 01-03; C Netherton 01-03. *2 Clough Mill, Slack Lane, Little Hayfield, High Peak SK22 2NJ* Tel (01663) 741900
E-mail kaybees@supanet.com

JOHNSTON, Miss Henrietta Elizabeth Ann. b 59. St Jo Coll Dur BA03. Cranmer Hall Dur 01. **d** 03. C Cov H Trin *Cov* from 03. *85 Stoney Road, Coventry CV3 6HH* Tel (024) 7650 4141 Mobile 07796-948904 E-mail hennie.johnston@tiscali.co.uk

JOHNSTON, Kay. *See* JOHNSTON, Mrs Helen Kay

JOHNSTON, Malcolm. *See* JOHNSTON, William Malcolm

JOHNSTON, Michael David Haigh. b 44. S Dios Minl Tr Scheme 88. **d** 91 **p** 92. NSM Wootton *Portsm* 91-95; NSM Ryde H Trin 95-99; NSM Swanmore St Mich 95-99; P-in-c Cowes St Faith 99-03; Asst Chapl Isle of Wight Healthcare NHS Trust from 03; Chapl HM Pris Kingston (Portsm) from 03. *HM Prison Kingston, 122 Milton Road, Portsmouth PO3 6AS* Tel (023) 9289 1100 E-mail rvdmikej@fastmail.fm

JOHNSTON, Michael Edward. b 68. TCD BA97. CITC BTh00. **d** 00 **p** 01. Bp's V Kilkenny Cathl *C & O* 00-03; C Kilkenny w Aghour and Kilmanagh 00-03; V Waterford w Killea, Drumcannon and Dunhill from 03. *Christ Church Rectory, Church Road, Tramore, Co Waterford, Irish Republic* Tel (00353) (51) 391263 E-mail vicar@waterford.anglican.org

JOHNSTON, Niall. *See* JOHNSTON, Allen Niall

JOHNSTON, Canon Robert John. b 31. Oak Hill Th Coll 64. **d** 64 **p** 65. C Bebington *Ches* 64-68; I Lack *Clogh* 68-99; Can Clogh Cathl 89-99; rtd 99. *2 Beechcroft, Semicock Road, Ballymoney BT53 6NF* Tel (028) 2766 9317

JOHNSTON, Thomas Cosbey. b 15. Em Coll Cam BA40 MA44. Ridley Hall Cam 40. **d** 42 **p** 43. C Handsworth St Mary *Birm* 42-48; New Zealand from 48. *254 Main Road, Moncks Bay, Christchurch, New Zealand 8008* Tel (0064) (3) 384 1224

JOHNSTON, Thomas David. b 52. Salford Univ BSc78 TCD MPhil03. N Ord Course 98. **d** 98 **p** 99. Dioc Communications Officer *Man* 96-00; NSM Bolton St Paul w Em 98-00; I Sixmilecross w Termonmaguirke *Arm* 00-03; Dir Communications *Liv* from 03. *671 Chorley New Road, Horwich,*

Bolton BL6 6HR Tel (01204) 698748 *or* 0151-705 2150 Mobile 07967-105999 E-mail david.johnston@liverpool.anglican.org

JOHNSTON, Trevor Samuel. b 72. Ulster Univ BMus96 TCD BTh01. CITC 98. **d** 01 **p** 02. C Carrickfergus *Conn* 01-04; C Jordanstown from 04; Chapl Jordanstown and Belf Campuses Ulster Univ from 04. *7 Macroom Gardens, Carrickfergus BT38 8NB* Tel (028) 9336 2552 E-mail trevor.j@excite.com *or* t.johnston@ulst.ac.uk

JOHNSTON, Canon Wilfred Brian. b 44. TCD BA67 MA70. Div Test 68. **d** 68 **p** 70. C Seagoe *D & D* 68-73; I Inniskeel *D & R* 73-82; I Castlerock w Dunboe and Fermoyle 82-02; Dioc Registrar from 89; Can Derry Cathl from 92; Preb from 99; Bp's C Gweedore, Carrickfin and Templecrone from 02. *2 The Apple Yard, Coleraine BT51 3PP,* or *The Rectory, Bunbeg, Co Donegal, Irish Republic* Tel (028) 7032 6406 *or* (00353) (74) 953 1043 E-mail b.johnston@talk21.com

JOHNSTON, William Derek. b 40. CITC 68. **d** 68 **p** 69. V Choral Derry Cathl *D & R* 68-70; I Swanlinbar w Templeport *K, E & A* 70-73; I Billis Union 73-84; Glebes Sec (Kilmore) 77-03; I Annagh w Drumaloor and Cloverhill 84-87; Preb Kilmore Cathl 85-89; I Annagh w Drumgoon, Ashfield etc 87-99; Adn Kilmore 89-03; I Lurgan w Billis, Killinkere and Munterconnaught 99-03; rtd 03. *Ballaghanea, Mullagh Road, Virginia, Co Cavan, Irish Republic* Tel (00353) (49) 854 9960 Mobile 86-832 9911

JOHNSTON, William Francis (Frank). b 30. CB83. TCD BA55 MA69. **d** 55 **p** 56. C Orangefield *D & D* 55-59; CF 59-77; Asst Chapl Gen 77-80; Chapl Gen 80-87; P-in-c Winslow *Ox* 87-91; RD Claydon 89-94; R Winslow w Gt Horwood and Addington 91-95; rtd 95; Perm to Offic *Ex* from 95. *Lower Axehill, Chard Road, Axminster EX13 5ED* Tel (01297) 33259

JOHNSTON, Canon William John. b 35. Lon Univ DipTh72 BA85 MA90 PhD. CITC 67. **d** 70 **p** 71. C Belfast St Donard *D & D* 70-72; C Derg *D & R* 72-78; I Drumclamph w Lower and Upper Langfield 78-91; I Kilskeery w Trillick *Clogh* from 91; Preb Clogh Cathl from 04. *The Rectory, 130 Kilskeery Road, Trillick, Omagh BT78 3RJ* Tel (028) 8956 1228

JOHNSTON, William Malcolm. b 48. St Alb and Ox Min Course 92. **d** 95 **p** 96. NSM Banbury *Ox* 95-01; P-in-c Netherton *Carl* 01-03; C Flimby 01-03. *2 Clough Mill, Slack Lane, Little Hayfield, High Peak SK22 2NJ* Tel (01663) 741900 E-mail kaybees@supanet.com

JOHNSTON, William McConnell. b 33. TCD BA57. **d** 58 **p** 59. C Ballymena w Ballyclug *Conn* 58-61; C Belfast St Thos 61-63; C Finaghy 63-66; S Africa 66-99; R Kambula 66-74; Dean Eshowe 74-86; R Mtubatuba 86-99; rtd 00. *Honeysuckle Cottage, Redford, Midhurst GU29 0QG* Tel (01428) 741131

JOHNSTON-HUBBOLD, Clifford Johnston. b 19. Lon Univ BA76 BD80. St Aid Birkenhead 49. **d** 52 **p** 53. C Stanwix *Carl* 52-55; V Gt Broughton 55-59; R Sedgeberrow *Worc* 59-73; P-in-c Hinton-on-the-Green 72-73; R Sedgeberrow w Hinton-on-the-Green 73-92; rtd 92; Perm to Offic *Worc* from 92. *2 Mills Close, Broadway WR12 7RB* Tel (01386) 852199

JOHNSTONE, William Henry Green. b 26. **d** 92 **p** 94. Belize 92-98; Hon C Tollard Royal w Farnham, Gussage St Michael etc *Sarum* 98-01; Hon C Chase from 01; OCF 94-98 and from 01. *Church Cottage, Chettle, Blandford Forum DT11 8DB* Tel (01258) 830396 E-mail padrewmchettle@aol.com

JOINT, Canon Michael John. b 39. Sarum & Wells Th Coll 79. **d** 79 **p** 79. CA from 61; Hon C Chandler's Ford *Win* 79-83; Youth Chapl 79-83; V Lymington 83-95; Co-ord Chapl R Bournemouth and Christchurch Hosps NHS Trust 96-03; Hon Can Win Cathl 00-03; rtd 03; Perm to Offic *Win* from 03. *21 Wycliffe Road, Winton, Bournemouth BH9 1JP* Tel (01202) 528677

JOLLEY, Andrew John. b 61. Nottm Univ BSc83 Warwick Univ MBA88 CEng88 MIMechE88. St Jo Coll Nottm BTh97. **d** 98 **p** 99. C Sparkhill w Greet and Sparkbrook *Birm* 98-02; V Aston SS Pet and Paul from 02. *The Vicarage, Sycamore Road, Aston, Birmingham B6 5UH* Tel 0121-327 5856 E-mail andy@astonparishchurch.org.uk

JOLLY, Leslie Alfred Walter. b 16. AKC40. **d** 40 **p** 41. C Bow w Bromley St Leon *Lon* 40-42; C Cheam Common St Phil *S'wark* 42-50; C Mottingham St Andr 50-52; V Newington St Matt 52-57; R Chaldon 57-85; rtd 85; Perm to Offic *S'ward* 85-94 and *York* 85-04. *12 Roseneath Court, Greenwood Gardens, Caterham CR3 6RX* Tel (01883) 332463

JONAS, Alan Charles. b 56. Leeds Univ BA79 Univ of Wales (Abth) PGCE80. Wycliffe Hall Ox DipMin94. **d** 94 **p** 95. C Hersham *Guildf* 94-98; P-in-c Westcott from 98; Chapl Priory Sch from 01. *The Vicarage, Guildford Road, Westcott, Dorking RH4 3QB* Tel (01306) 885309

JONAS, Ian Robert. b 54. St Jo Coll Nottm BTh80. **d** 80 **p** 81. C Portadown St Mark *Arm* 80-82; C Cregagh *D & D* 82-85; BCMS Sec *D & G* 85-90; V Langley Mill *Derby* 90-97; I Kilgariffe Union *C, C & R* from 97. *The Rectory, Gallanes, Clonakilty, Co Cork, Irish Republic* Tel and fax (00353) (23) 33357 E-mail ianjonas@oceanfree.net *or* kilgariffe@ross.anglican.org

JONES, Alan. b 28. Man Univ LLB48 LLM50. Coll of Resurr Mirfield 53. **d** 56 **p** 57. C Streatham St Pet *S'wark* 56-59; C Hornsey St Luke *Lon* 59-60; Miss to Seamen 60-61; Chapl RN 61-65; rtd 94. *73 Mousehole Lane, Southampton SO18 4FB* Tel (023) 8055 0008

JONES, Alan David. b 32. Lon Coll of Div ALCD58. **d** 58 **p** 59. C Ipswich All SS *St E* 58-60; C Southend St Jo *Chelmsf* 60-64; CF (TA) 60-62; CF (TA - R of O) 62-67; V Leyton St Cath *Chelmsf* 64-70; V Hatfield Broad Oak 70-77; P-in-c Bush End 77-79; V Theydon Bois 77-88; P-in-c Finchingfield and Cornish Hall End 88-93; rtd 94; Perm to Offic *Chelmsf* and *St E* from 94. *3 Grammar School Place, Sudbury CO10 2GE* Tel (01787) 370864

JONES, Alan John. b 47. Nottm Univ BA71. Coll of Resurr Mirfield 71. **d** 73 **p** 74. C Sedgley St Mary *Lich* 73-76; C Cov St Jo *Cov* 76-78; V W Bromwich St Fran *Lich* 78-94; V Ettingshall from 94; AD Wolverhampton from 03. *The Vicarage, Farrington Road, Wolverhampton WV4 6QH* Tel (01902) 884616

JONES, Alan Pierce. *See* PIERCE-JONES, Alan

JONES, Albert. b 13. K Coll Lon 37. **d** 41 **p** 42. C Farnworth and Kearsley *Man* 41-46; P-in-c 45-46; C Felixstowe St Jo *St E* 46-47; C Headstone St Geo *Lon* 47-49; R Stretford All SS *Man* 49-52; Trinidad and Tobago 52-56; V Farnworth St Pet *Man* 56-58; Area Sec USPG *York* 58-63; V Tillingham *Chelmsf* 63-66; R Dengie w Asheldham 63-66; R Stifford 66-72; P-in-c Stondon Massey 72-79; R Doddinghurst 72-79; rtd 79; Perm to Offic *Chelmsf* from 79. *29 Seaview Road, Brightlingsea, Colchester CO7 0PP* Tel (01206) 303994

JONES, Alison. *See* JONES, Helen Alison

JONES, Alison. *See* WAGSTAFF, Ms Alison

JONES, Alun. b 52. Leeds Univ BA96. Cuddesdon Coll 94. **d** 96 **p** 97. C Newc St Geo *Newc* 96-98; C Cowgate 98-99; C Fenham St Jas and St Basil 99-04; P-in-c Carl St Herbert w St Steph *Carl* from 04. *St Herbert's Vicarage, Blackwell Road, Carlisle CA2 4RA* Tel (01228) 523375 E-mail alun52@btinternet.com

JONES, Alwyn Humphrey Griffith. b 30. Leeds Univ BSc51. Coll of Resurr Mirfield 53. **d** 55 **p** 56. C W Hackney St Barn *Lon* 55-58; C-in-c Dacca St Thos E Pakistan 58-64; Ox Miss to Calcutta India 65-68; Chapl R Bombay Seamen's Soc 68-73; P-in-c Bedminster St Fran *Bris* 73-75; TR Bedminster 75-83; TV Langport Area Chs *B & W* 83-85; Dep Chapl HM Pris Nor 85; Chapl HM Pris Preston 85-89; Chapl HM Pris Ashwell 89-91; C Acton Green *Lon* 91-93; rtd 93; NSM Langport Area Chs *B & W* 93-98; Perm to Offic *B & W* and *Bris* from 98. *4 All Saints House, 1 Upper York Street, Bristol BS2 8NT* Tel 0117-923 2331 E-mail alwyn@fish.co.uk

✠**JONES, The Rt Revd Alwyn Rice.** b 34. Univ of Wales (Lamp) BA55 Fitzw Ho Cam BA57 MA61. St Mich Coll Llan 57. **d** 58 **p** 59 **c** 82. C Llanfairisgaer *Ban* 58-62; N Wales Sec SCM 60-62; Staff Sec SCM 62-65; Chapl St Winifred's Sch Llanfairfechan 65-68; Dir RE *Ban* 65-75; Dioc Youth Officer 66-72; Dir of Ords 70-75; Asst Tutor Univ of Wales (Ban) 73-76; V Porthmadog *Ban* 75-79; Hon Can Ban Cathl 75-78; Preb 78-79; Dean Brecon *S & B* 79-82; V Brecon w Battle 79-82; Bp St As 82-99; Abp Wales 91-99; rtd 99. *Curig, 7 Llwyn Onn, St Asaph LL17 0SQ* Tel (01745) 584621

JONES, Alyson Elizabeth. *See* DAVIE, Mrs Alyson Elizabeth

JONES, Mrs Andrea Margaret. b 46. Qu Coll Birm 88. **d** 90 **p** 94. Par Dn Kidderminster St Geo *Worc* 90-94; TV 94-95; C Penn Fields *Lich* 95-00; C Gt Wyrley from 00. *46 Gorsey Lane, Great Wyrley, Walsall WS6 6EX* Tel (01922) 418271

JONES, Andrew. *See* JONES, Ian Andrew

JONES, Canon Andrew. b 61. Univ of Wales (Ban) BD82 PGCE82 TCD BTh85 MA91 Univ of Wales MPhil93. CITC 82 St Geo Coll Jerusalem 84. **d** 85 **p** 86. Min Can Ban Cathl *Ban* 85-88; R Dolgellau 88-92; Dir Past Studies St Mich Coll Llan 92-96; Lect Th Univ of Wales (Cardiff) 92-96; Research Fell from 96; R Llanbedrog w Llannor w Llanfihangel etc *Ban* 96-01; R Llanbedrog w Llannor and Llangian from 01; Dioc CME Officer from 96; RD Llyn and Eifionydd from 99; Hon Can Ban Cathl from 04. *Tyn-Llan Rectory, Llanbedrog, Pwllheli LL53 7TU* Tel and fax (01758) 740919

JONES, Andrew. b 64. York Univ BA85. Westmr Th Sem (USA) MDiv91 St Jo Coll Nottm 92. **d** 94 **p** 95. C Win Ch Ch *Win* 94-98; C St Helen Bishopsgate w St Andr Undershaft etc *Lon* from 98. *15 Morgan Street, London E3 5AB* Tel (020) 8983 1463 *or* 7283 2231 E-mail a.jones@st-helens.org.uk

JONES, Andrew Christopher. b 47. Southn Univ BA69 PhD75. Ridley Hall Cam 78. **d** 80 **p** 81. C Wareham *Sarum* 80-83; P-in-c Symondsbury 83; P-in-c Chideock 83; R Symondsbury and Chideock 84-91; V Shottermill *Guildf* 91-99; P-in-c Bishopsnympton, Rose Ash, Mariansleigh etc *Ex* from 99. *The Rectory, Bishops Nympton, South Molton EX36 4NY* Tel (01769) 550427 E-mail a.c.jones@bnrec.f9.co.uk

JONES, Andrew Collins. b 62. Univ Coll Dur BA83 MA84 MLitt92. St Steph Ho Ox 88. **d** 90 **p** 91. C Llangefni w Tregaean and Llangristiolus etc *Ban* 90-94; C Hartlepool St Aid *Dur* 94-98; Chapl Hartlepool Gen Hosp 94-98; R Hendon *Dur* from 98. *St Ignatius' Rectory, Bramwell Road, Sunderland SR2 8BY* Tel 0191-567 5575

JONES, Anne. *See* JONES, Christine Anne

JONES, Anthony. b 43. WEMTC 99. **d** 01 **p** 02. OLM Lydney *Glouc* from 01. *12 Almond Walk, Lydney GL15 5LP* Tel (01594) 843192 Mobile 07860-331755

JONES, Canon Anthony Spacie. b 34. AKC58. **d** 59 **p** 60. C Bedford St Martin *St Alb* 59-63; Br Guiana 63-66; Guyana 66-71; V Ipswich All Hallows *St E* 72-80; RD Ipswich 78-86; Bp's Dom Chapl 80-82; V Rushmere 82-91; Hon Can St E Cathl 83-99; R Brantham w Stutton 91-99; P-in-c Bentley w Tattingstone 95-99; rtd 99; Perm to Offic *St E* from 99. *6 Fritillary Close, Pinewood, Ipswich IP8 3QT* Tel (01473) 601848 E-mail tonyjones.pinewood@btinternet.com

JONES, Barbara Christine. b 48. St Hugh's Coll Ox BA71 MA74 Lady Spencer Chu Coll of Educn PGCE74. Carl and Blackb Dioc Tr Inst 97. **d** 00 **p** 01. NSM Bolton-le-Sands *Blackb* from 00. *11 Sandown Road, Lancaster LA1 4LN* Tel (01524) 65598 E-mail jones@barbara.bbfree.co.uk

JONES, Barry Mervyn. b 46. St Chad's Coll Dur BA68 DipTh69. **d** 70 **p** 71. C Bloxwich *Lich* 70-72; C Norwood All SS *Cant* 72-76; C New Addington 76-78; Chapl Mayday Univ Hosp Thornton Heath 78-86; Chapl Qu and St Mary's Hosps Croydon 78-86; Chapl Bromsgrove and Redditch DHA 86-94; Chapl Alexandra Hosp Redditch 86-94; Chapl Alexandra Healthcare NHS Trust Redditch 94-00; Chapl Worcs Acute Hosps NHS Trust from 00. *The Alexandra Hospital, Woodrow Drive, Redditch B98 7UB* Tel (01527) 503030 Fax 517432 E-mail barry.jones@worcsacute.wmids.nhs.uk

JONES, Canon Basil Henry. b 26. Bps' Coll Cheshunt 63. **d** 64 **p** 65. C Gt Berkhamsted *St Alb* 64-67; V Leagrave 68-74; RD Luton 71-74; P-in-c Bedford St Paul 74-75; V Wigginton 75-93; Hon Can St Alb 82-93; rtd 93; Perm to Offic *St Alb* from 00. *17 Lochnell Road, Northchurch, Berkhamsted HP4 3QD* Tel (01442) 864485 E-mail bazilhjones@aol.com

JONES, The Ven Benjamin Jenkin Hywel. b 39. Univ of Wales BA61. St Mich Coll Llan 61. **d** 64 **p** 65. C Carmarthen St Pet *St D* 64-70; V Cynwyl Gaeo w Llansawel and Talley 70-79; R Llanbadarn Fawr 79-82; V Llanbadarn Fawr w Capel Bangor and Goginan 82-92; V Llanychaearn w Llanddeiniol 92-05; Warden of Readers from 82; Can St D Cathl 86-90; RD Llanbadarn Fawr 89-90; Adn Cardigan from 90. *Dowerdd, Waun Fawr, Aberystwyth SY23 3QF* Tel (01970) 617100

JONES, Benjamin Tecwyn. b 17. Univ of Wales BA38. K Coll Lon 38. **d** 40 **p** 41. C Hawarden *St As* 40-45; C Pleasley *Derby* 45-46; C Ormskirk *Liv* 46-49; R Rufford *Blackb* 49-55; V S Shore St Pet 55-65; C Oldham St Mary w St Pet *Man* 65-69; Hd Master and Chapl St Mary's Sch Bexhill-on-Sea 69-71; V Blackb St Luke *Blackb* 71-72; P-in-c Griffin 71-72; V Blackb St Luke w St Phil 72-83; rtd 83; Perm to Offic *Blackb* from 83. *527A Livesey Branch Road, Blackburn BB2 5DB* Tel (01254) 209206

JONES, Bernard. *See* JONES, Robert Bernard

JONES, Bernard Lewis. b 48. Llan Dioc Tr Scheme 89. **d** 93 **p** 94. NSM Aberaman and Abercwmboi w Cwmaman *Llan* 93-99; V Hirwaun from 99. *The Vicarage, High Steet, Hirwaun, Aberdare CF44 9SL* Tel (01685) 811316

JONES, Brenda. b 50. Cranmer Hall Dur 02. **d** 04 **p** 05. C Jarrow *Dur* from 04. *St Mark's Vicarage, Randolph Street, Jarrow NE32 3AQ* Tel 0191-483 2092

JONES, Brian. BSc. **d** 94 **p** 96. Lic to Offic *D & D* from 94. *16 Massey Avenue, Belfast BT4 2JS*

JONES, Canon Brian Howell. b 35. Univ of Wales MPhil96. St Mich Coll Llan DipTh61. **d** 61 **p** 62. C Llangiwg *S & B* 61-63; C Swansea St Mary and H Trin 63-70; R New Radnor w Llanfihangel Nantmelan etc 70-75; V Llansamlet 75-89; Dioc Dir of Stewardship 82-89; P-in-c Capel Coelbren 89-95; Dioc Missr 89-95; Can Res Brecon Cathl 89-00; Can Treas 98-00; Chan 99-00; RD Cwmtawe 89-93; V Killay 95-00; rtd 00. *12 Harlech Crescent, Sketty, Swansea SA2 9LP* Tel (01792) 207159 E-mail canonbrian@compuserve.com

JONES, Canon Brian Michael. b 34. Trin Coll Bris DipHE81 Oak Hill Th Coll BA82. **d** 84 **p** 84. CMS 82-93; Sierra Leone 84-93; Can Bo from 91; C Frimley *Guildf* 93-99; rtd 99; Perm to Offic *Newc* 00-01; Hon C N Tyne and Redesdale from 01. *7 Redesmouth Court, Bellingham, Hexham NE48 2ES* Tel (01434) 220430 E-mail bmj.retired@btopenworld.com

JONES, Canon Brian Noel. b 32. Edin Th Coll 59. **d** 62 **p** 63. C Monkseaton St Mary *Newc* 62-65; C Saffron Walden *Chelmsf* 65-69; P-in-c Swaffham Bulbeck *Ely* 69-75; Dioc Youth Officer 69-75; RD St Ives 75-83 and 87-89; V Ramsey 75-89; V Upwood w Gt and Lt Raveley 75-89; P-in-c Ramsey St Mary's 82-89; Hon Can Ely Cathl 85-97; V Cherry Hinton St Jo 89-97; RD Cambridge 94-97; rtd 97; Perm to Offic *Nor* from 97. *11 Winns Close, Holt NR25 6NQ* Tel (01263) 713645

JONES, Canon Bryan Maldwyn. b 32. St Mich Coll Llan DipTh62. **d** 62 **p** 63. C Swansea St Barn *S & B* 62-69; V Trallwng and Betws Penpont 69-75; V Trallwng, Bettws Penpont w Aberyskir etc 75-00; RD Brecon II 80-91; RD Brecon 91-99; Hon Can Brecon Cathl 92-00; rtd 00. *Plas Newydd, 8 Camden Crescent, Brecon LD3 7BY* Tel (01874) 625063

JONES, Bryan William. b 30. Selw Coll Cam BA53 MA57. Linc Th Coll 53. **d** 55 **p** 56. C Bedminster Down *Bris* 55-58; C Filton 58-62; P-in-c Bedminster St Mich 62-65; V 65-72; P-in-c Moorfields 72-75; TV E Bris 75-95; rtd 95; Perm to Offic *Bris* from 95. *89 Canterbury Close, Yate, Bristol BS37 5TU* Tel (01454) 316795

JONES, Bryon. b 34. Open Univ BA84. St D Coll Lamp 61. **d** 64 **p** 65. C Port Talbot St Theodore *Llan* 64-67; C Aberdare 68-69; C Up Hatherley *Glouc* 69-71; C Oystermouth *S & B* 71-74; V Camrose *St D* 74-77; V Camrose and St Lawrence w Ford and Haycastle 77-04; rtd 04. *31 New Road, Haverfordwest SA61 1TU* Tel (01639) 766176

JONES, Mrs Carol. b 45. **d** 04. OLM Shirley St Geo *S'wark* from 04. *50 Belgrave Court, Sloane Walk, Croydon CR0 7NW* Tel (020) 8777 6247 E-mail caroljonesolm@yahoo.co.uk

JONES, Miss Celia Lynn. b 54. Trin Coll Bris. **d** 01. C Bris St Paul's *Bris* from 01. *15 St Werburghs Park, Bristol BS2 9YT* Tel 0117-955 6258 E-mail celialynn@supanet.com

JONES, Charles Derek. b 37. K Coll Lon BD60 AKC60. **d** 61 **p** 62. C Stockton St Chad *Dur* 61-64; C Becontree St Elisabeth *Chelmsf* 64-66; C S Beddington St Mich *S'wark* 66-73; Lic to Offic *Ex* 73-77; Perm to Offic *Liv* 77-99; rtd 02. *4 Bryn Glas, Graigfechan, Ruthin LL15 2EX* Tel (01824) 705015

JONES, Charles Eurwyn. b 27. Univ of Wales BSc48 DipEd51. St Mich Coll Llan 53. **d** 55 **p** 56. C Brecon St Dav *S & B* 55-57; C Carmarthen St Dav *St D* 57-61; Tutor Old Cath Sem Bonn 61-64; Tutor Bps' Coll Cheshunt 64-67; V Carlton *S'well* 67-75; P-in-c Colwick 69-75; V Bunny w Bradmore 75-95; rtd 95; Perm to Offic *S'well* from 95. *9 Wentworth Way, Edwalton, Nottingham NG12 4DJ* Tel 0115-923 4119

JONES, Christine Anne. b 51. Leic Coll of Educn CertEd73 Open Univ BA76 Man Univ DASE79 MEd84 PhD91 Chester Coll of HE MTh02. N Ord Course 99. **d** 02 **p** 03. C Offerton *Ches* from 02. *11 Martham Drive, Stockport SK2 5XZ* Tel 0161-487 1067 Mobile 07771-601615 E-mail c-anne@fish.co.uk

JONES, Christopher Howell. b 50. BA FCCA. Oak Hill Th Coll 80. **d** 83 **p** 84. C Leyton St Mary w St Edw *Chelmsf* 83-86; C Becontree St Mary 86-90; P-in-c Bootle St Matt *Liv* 90-93; V 93-99; AD Bootle 97-99; V Ormskirk from 99; Chapl W Lancashire NHS Trust from 99. *The Vicarage, Park Road, Ormskirk L39 3AJ* Tel (01695) 572143

JONES, Christopher John Stark. b 39. Lon Univ BA60 AKC60. Wells Th Coll 63. **d** 65 **p** 66. C Stanmore *Win* 65-67; C Bournemouth St Pet 67-71; C W Wycombe *Ox* 71-75; TV High Wycombe 75-77; V Wokingham St Sebastian 77-84; R Didsbury Ch Ch *Man* 84-00; rtd 00; Perm to Offic *Ches* from 01. *5 Trueman Close, Prenton CH43 7YR* Tel 0151-513 3436

JONES, Christopher Mark. b 54. St Pet Coll Ox BA75 MA79 Selw Coll Cam MPhil80. Ridley Hall Cam 77. **d** 80 **p** 81. C Putney St Marg *S'wark* 80-83; C Ham St Andr 83-86; Chapl HM Rem Cen Latchmere Ho 83-86; Chapl St Jo Coll Dur 87-93; Tutor Cranmer Hall Dur 87-93; Chapl and Fell St Pet Coll Ox 93-04; Home Affairs Policy Adv Abps' Coun Bd for Soc Resp from 04. *Archbishops' Council, Church House, Great Smith Street, London SW1P 3NZ* Tel (020) 7898 1531 Fax 7898 1536 E-mail christopher.jones@c-of-e.org.uk

JONES, Christopher Mark. b 56. St Jo Coll Cam BA78 MA82 Wycliffe Hall Ox BA81 MA85. **d** 82 **p** 83. C Walsall *Lich* 82-84; Chapl St Jo Coll Cam 84-89; Chapl Eton Coll from 89; Ho Master from 97. *The Hopgarden, Eton College, Windsor SL4 6EQ* Tel (01753) 671065 Fax 671067 E-mail c.m.jones@etoncollege.org.uk

JONES, Christopher Yeates. b 51. STETS 97. **d** 00 **p** 01. NSM Yeovil St Mich *B & W* from 00. *20 Bedford Road, Yeovil BA21 5UQ* Tel (01935) 420886 Mobile 07803-371617 E-mail cyjones@care4free.net

JONES, Clifford Albert. b 20. Edin Th Coll 54. **d** 56 **p** 57. C Dundee St Salvador *Bre* 56-58; C Linc St Swithin *Linc* 58-59; C Grantham St Wulfram 59-60; R Dundee St Salvador *Bre* 60-69; V Bradford *B & W* 69-74; V Bridgwater St Jo 74-78; RD Bridgwater 76-80; R Bridgwater St Jo w Chedzoy 78-80; P-in-c Timsbury 80-85; R Timsbury and Priston 85; rtd 85; P-in-c Nor St Geo Tombland *Nor* 85-90; Hon C St Marylebone All SS *Lon* 90-94; Perm to Offic *Nor* 94-99 and *Lon* from 97. *188 John Aird Court, London W2 1UX* Tel (020) 7262 9295

JONES, Clive. b 51. BA82. Oak Hill Th Coll 79. **d** 82 **p** 83. C Brunswick *Man* 82-85; V Pendlebury St Jo 85-96; V Attleborough *Cov* from 96. *Attleborough Vicarage, 5 Fifield Close, Nuneaton CV11 4TS* Tel (024) 7635 4114 E-mail clivej@hta1.freeserve.co.uk

JONES, Clive Morlais Peter. b 40. LTCL71 Univ of Wales (Cardiff) BA63 CertEd64. Chich Th Coll 64. **d** 66 **p** 67. C Llanfabon *Llan* 66-70; PV Llan Cathl 70-75; R Gelligaer 75-85; Prec and Can Llan Cathl 84-85; R Tilehurst St Mich *Ox* 85-94; Chapl Costa Blanca *Eur* 94-97; V Newton St Pet *S & B* from 97. *The Vicarage, Mary Twill Lane, Newton, Swansea SA3 4RB* Tel (01792) 368348

JONES, Clive Wesley. b 68. SSC. St Steph Ho Ox 95. **d** 98 **p** 99. C Swanley St Mary *Roch* 98-02; P-in-c Belvedere St Aug from 02; Chapl Trin Sch Belvedere 02-04. *The Vicarage, St Augustine's*

Road, Belvedere DA17 5HH Tel (020) 8311 6307 *or* (01322) 441371 E-mail frclive@tiscali.co.uk

JONES, Colin Stuart. b 56. Southn Univ LLB77. Coll of Resurr Mirfield 81. **d** 84 **p** 85. C Mountain Ash *Llan* 84-86; C Castle Bromwich SS Mary and Marg *Birm* 86-89; V Kingshurst 89-94; V Perry Barr from 94. *Perry Barr Vicarage, Church Road, Birmingham B42 2LB* Tel 0121-356 7998

JONES, Cyril Ernest. b 29. St D Coll Lamp BA54. **d** 56 **p** 57. C Llanedy *St D* 56-60; C Llanelli 60-63; V Mydroilyn w Dihewyd 63-66; V Llanybydder 66-73; V Llanybydder and Llanwenog w Llanwnnen 73-78; V Betws w Ammanford 78-81; V Cynwyl Gaeo w Llansawel and Talley 81-94; rtd 94. *21 Pontardulais Road, Tycroes, Ammanford SA18 3QD* Tel (01269) 596421

JONES, David. *See* JONES, Preb Wilfred David

JONES, David. *See* JONES, Canon William David

JONES, David. b 55. CA Tr Coll 74 St Steph Ho Ox 83. **d** 85 **p** 86. C Fleur-de-Lis *Mon* 85-87; V Ynysddu 87-93; V Blackwood from 93. *The Vicarage, South View Road, Blackwood NP12 1HR* Tel (01495) 224214

JONES, David Arthur. b 44. Liv Univ BA66 Sussex Univ MA68. St D Coll Lamp LTh74. **d** 74 **p** 75. C Tenby *St D* 74-76; C Chepstow *Mon* 76-78; P-in-c Teversal *S'well* 78-81; R 81-91; Chapl Sutton Cen 78-89; V Radford All So w Ch Ch and St Mich 91-04; Adv to Urban Priority Par 96-01; Officer for Urban Life and Miss from 04. *13 Rolleston Drive, Nottingham NG7 1JS* Tel 0115-958 7883 E-mail urban.officer@southwell.anglican.org

JONES, David Emrys. b 21. Lon Univ BD69 Univ of Wales MA74. St D Coll Lamp BA42. **d** 47 **p** 48. C Llandinorwig *Ban* 47-50; C Conwy w Gyffin 50-57; V Beddgelert 57-72; R Llangystennin *St As* 72-91; rtd 91. *The Rectory, Llanfor, Bala LL23 7YA* Tel (01678) 520080

JONES, Chan David Frederick Donald. b 19. Univ of Wales (Abth) BA41. Westcott Ho Cam 41. **d** 43 **p** 44. C Henfynyw w Aberaeron *St D* 43-46; C Carmarthen St Pet 46-53; V Pencarreg 53-64; Lect Bp Burgess Th Hall Lamp 59-72; V Betws w Ammanford 64-78; RD Dyffryn Aman 72-78; Can St D Cathl 75-88; Chan St D Cathl 83-88; V Felin-foel 78-88; rtd 88. *93 Nun Street, St Davids, Haverfordwest SA62 6NU* Tel (01437) 720359

JONES, David Gornal. b 47. **d** 74 **p** 75. S Africa 75-94; Miss to Seafarers from 95; Port Chapl Walvis Bay Namibia 95-00; Port Chapl Vlissingen (Flushing) *Eur* 00-02; R Ayr *Glas* from 02; R Girvan from 02; R Maybole from 02. *12 Barnes Terrace, Ayr KA7 2DB* Tel and fax (01292) 269141 E-mail dgjones@clara.co.uk

JONES, David Hugh. b 34. St D Coll Lamp BA56. St Mich Coll Llan 58. **d** 58 **p** 59. C Swansea St Mary and H Trin *S & B* 58-61; Inter-Colleg Sec SCM (Liv) 61-63; Hon Chapl Liv Univ 61-63; C Swansea St Pet *S & B* 63-69; V Llanddewi Ystradenni and Abbey Cwmhir 69-75; R Port Eynon w Rhosili and Llanddewi and Knelston 75-83; V Swansea St Barn 83-92; rtd 92. *16 Lon Ger-y-Coed, Cockett, Swansea SA2 0YH*

✠**JONES, The Rt Revd David <u>Huw</u>.** b 34. Univ of Wales (Ban) BA55 Univ Coll Ox BA58 MA62. St Mich Coll Llan 58. **d** 59 **p** 60 **c** 93. C Aberdare *Llan* 59-61; C Neath w Llantwit 61-65; V Crynant 65-69; V Cwmavon 69-74; Lect Th Univ of Wales (Cardiff) 74-78; Sub-Warden St Mich Coll Llan 74-78; V Prestatyn *St As* 78-82; Dioc Ecum Officer 78-82; Dean Brecon *S & B* 82-93; V Brecon w Battle 82-83; V Brecon St Mary and Battle w Llanddew 83-93; Asst Bp St As 93-96; Bp St D 96-01; rtd 02. *31 The Cathedral Green, Llandaff, Cardiff CF5 2EB*

JONES, David <u>Huw</u>. b 49. Univ of Wales MB, BCh72 Chelsea Coll Lon MSc78 Univ of Wales MD79 FRCR83 FRCP96. EAMTC 95. **d** 98 **p** 99. NSM Trumpington *Ely* 98-02; Perm to Offic from 02. *17 Barrow Road, Cambridge CB2 2AP* Tel and fax (01223) 358458 E-mail drhuw@btopenworld.com

JONES, David Ian Stewart. b 34. Selw Coll Cam BA57 MA61. Westcott Ho Cam 57. **d** 59 **p** 60. C Oldham *Man* 59-63; V Elton All SS 63-66; Chapl Eton Coll 66-70; Sen Chapl 70-74; Hd Master Bryanston Sch 74-82; P-in-c Bris Ch Ch w St Ewen and All SS *Bris* 82-84; P-in-c Bris St Steph w St Nic and St Leon 82-84; Soc Resp Adv 84-85; Dir Lambeth Endowed Charities 85-94; Hon PV S'wark Cathl *S'wark* 85-94; rtd 94. *4 Kensington Park, Milford-on-Sea, Lymington SO41 0WD* Tel (01590) 641107

JONES, David James Hammond. b 45. Kelham Th Coll 65. **d** 70 **p** 70. C Cheadle *Lich* 70-73; Hon C W Bromwich All SS 78-83; Hon C Primrose Hill St Mary w Avenue Road St Paul *Lon* 91-03; Hon C Regent's Park St Mark from 03. *9 Elliott Square, London NW3 3SU* Tel (020) 7483 3363 Fax 7483 1133 E-mail david@colourwash.co.uk

JONES, David <u>Michael</u>. b 48. Chich Th Coll 75. **d** 78 **p** 79. C Yeovil *B & W* 78-84; C Barwick 81-84; V Cleeve w Chelvey and Brockley 84-92; V Heigham St Barn w St Bart *Nor* 92-00; V Writtle w Highwood *Chelmsf* from 00. *The Vicarage, 19 Lodge Road, Writtle, Chelmsford CM1 3HY* Tel (01245) 421282 E-mail revmjoneswrittle@aol.com

JONES, David <u>Ormond</u>. b 46. Llan Dioc Tr Scheme 90. **d** 94 **p** 95. NSM Resolven w Tonna *Llan* 94-01; C Skewen from 01. *30 Henfaes Road, Tonna, Neath SA11 3EX* Tel (01639) 770930 E-mail ormond.jones@ntlworld.com

JONES, David Raymond (<u>Ray</u>). b 34. Univ of Wales (Lamp) BA54 St Cath Coll Ox BA57 MA61. Wycliffe Hall Ox 58. **d** 58 **p** 59. C Ex St Dav *Ex* 58-60; C Bideford 60-63; Chapl Grenville Coll Bideford 63-66; Chapl RN 66-89; QHC 84-89; Warden and Dir Ch Min of Healing Crowhurst 89-97; rtd 97; Perm to Offic *Chich* from 97. *Mill View, North Fields Lane, Westergate, Chichester PO20 3UH* Tel (01243) 543179

JONES, David Robert. b 37. Dur Univ BA59 QUB MA83 MBIM83. Cranmer Hall Dur. **d** 69 **p** 70. C Middleton *Man* 69-72; CF 72-92; V Staindrop *Dur* 92-04; rtd 04. *8 Heugh Wynd, Craster, Alnwick NE66 3TL* Tel (01665) 576313

JONES, David Robert Deverell. b 50. Sarum & Wells Th Coll 72. **d** 75 **p** 78. C Altrincham St Geo *Ches* 75-76; C Clayton *Lich* 77-80; Carriacou 80-81; P-in-c Baschurch *Lich* 81-83; R Baschurch and Weston Lullingfield w Hordley 83-96; RD Ellesmere 85-95; P-in-c Criftins 94-96; P-in-c Dudleston 94-96; P-in-c Jersey St Luke *Win* 96-99; V from 99; P-in-c Jersey St Jas 96-99; V from 99; R Jersey St Mary from 02. *The Vicarage, Longueville Farm, Longueville Road, St Saviour, Jersey JE2 7WG* Tel (01534) 251445

JONES, David Roy. b 47. CQSW76 Hull Univ BA74 Man Univ DipAdEd76 Bradf Univ MA85 Leic Univ Dip Ind Relns 91. Bernard Gilpin Soc Dur 69 N Ord Course 77. **d** 80 **p** 81. C New Bury *Man* 80-83; NSM Ringley w Prestolee 92-97; NSM Belmont 97-01; TV Turton Moorland Min from 01. *The Vicarage, High Street, Bemont, Bolton BL7 8AP* Tel (01204) 811221

JONES, David <u>Sebastian</u>. b 43. St Cath Coll Cam BA67 MA73. Linc Th Coll 66. **d** 68 **p** 69. C Baguley *Man* 68-71; C Bray and Braywood *Ox* 71-73; V S Ascot from 73; Chapl Heatherwood Hosp E Berks 81-94; Chapl Heatherwood and Wexham Park Hosp NHS Trust from 94; AD Bracknell *Ox* 96-04. *The Vicarage, Vicarage Gardens, South Ascot, Ascot SL5 9DX* Tel and fax (01344) 622388 E-mail sebjones@aol.com

JONES, David Victor. b 37. St Jo Coll Dur BA59. Cranmer Hall Dur DipTh60 Bossey Ecum Inst Geneva 61. **d** 62 **p** 63. C Farnworth *Liv* 62-65; CF 65-68; Asst Master Hutton Gr Sch Preston 68-97; rtd 02. *10 Houghton Close, Penwortham, Preston PR1 9HT* Tel (01772) 745306 E-mail d.v.jones@btinternet.com

JONES, David William. b 42. St Mark & St Jo Coll Lon CertEd64 Open Univ BA79. SEITE 97. **d** 00 **p** 01. NSM Coxheath, E Farleigh, Hunton, Linton etc *Roch* from 00; Perm to Offic *Cant* from 04. *13 Woodlands, Coxheath, Maidstone ME17 4EE* Tel (01622) 741474 E-mail david_w_jones@talk21.com

JONES, Denise Gloria. b 56. Cov Univ BA93. WMMTC 95. **d** 98 **p** 99. C Hobs Moat *Birm* 98-02; C Olton 02-05; Chapl S Birm Mental Health NHS Trust from 02. *St Margaret's Vicarage, 5 Old Warwick Road, Solihull B92 7JU* Tel 0121-706 2318 E-mail revddee@aol.com

JONES, Miss Diana. b 46. Qu Coll Birm 89. **d** 91 **p** 94. Par Dn Harnham *Sarum* 91-94; C 94-95; C Tidworth, Ludgershall and Faberstown 95-00; P-in-c Hazelbury Bryan and the Hillside Par from 00. *The Rectory, Hazelbury Bryan, Sturminster Newton DT10 2ED* Tel (01258) 818287

JONES, Canon Dick Heath Remi. b 32. Jes Coll Cam BA56. Linc Th Coll 56. **d** 58 **p** 59. C Ipswich St Thos *St E* 58-61; C Putney St Mary *S'wark* 61-65; P-in-c Dawley Parva *Lich* 65-75; P-in-c Lawley 65-75; RD Wrockwardine 70-72; P-in-c Malins Lee 72-75; RD Telford 72-80; P-in-c Stirchley 74-75; TR Cen Telford 75-80; Preb Lich Cathl 76-80; TR Bournemouth St Pet w St Swithun, H Trin etc *Win* 80-96; RD Bournemouth 90-95; Hon Can Win Cathl 91-96; rtd 96; Perm to Offic *Sarum* from 96. *Maltings, Church Street, Fontmell Magna, Shaftesbury SP7 0NY* Tel (01747) 812071 E-mail dick.jones@talk21.com

JONES, Donald. b 50. BA BSc. St Jo Coll Nottm 79. **d** 82 **p** 83. C Hutton *Chelmsf* 82-86; C E Ham w Upton Park St Alb 86-88; TV 88-96; V Nuneaton St Nic *Cov* from 96; RD Nuneaton from 01. *61 Ambleside Way, Nuneaton CV11 6AU* Tel (024) 7634 6900

JONES, Douglas. *See* JONES, John Douglas Mathias

JONES, Canon Douglas Rawlinson. b 19. St Edm Hall Ox BA41 MA45. Lambeth DD Wycliffe Hall Ox 41. **d** 42 **p** 43. C Windmill Hill *Bris* 42-45; Lect Wycliffe Hall Ox 45-50; Chapl Wadh Coll Ox 45-50; Lect Th Dur Univ 51-64; Prof Div 64-85; Can Res Dur Cathl *Dur* 64-85; rtd 85; Lic to Offic *Edin* from 85. *Whitefriars, King's Road, Longniddry EH32 0NN* Tel (01875) 52149

JONES, Edgar John. b 32. Univ of Wales (Lamp) BA53 Univ of Wales (Ban) PGCE74. St Mich Coll Llan 53. **d** 55 **p** 56. C Holyhead w Rhoscolyn w Llanfair-yn-Neubwll *Ban* 55-61; R Bodedern and Llechcynfarwy 61-70; V Bodedern w Llechgynfarwy and Llechylched etc 70-73; Perm to Offic 73-96 and from 98; P-in-c Llangefni w Tregaean and Llangristiolus etc 96-98; rtd 98. *5 Glan Llyn, Llanfachraeth, Holyhead LL65 4UW* Tel (01407) 742322

JONES, Edward. b 36. Dur Univ BA60. Ely Th Coll 60. **d** 62 **p** 63. C S Shields St Hilda w St Thos *Dur* 62-65; C Cleadon Park 65-68; V Hebburn St Cuth 68-79; R Winlaton 79-00; rtd 00;

Perm to Offic *Dur* from 00 and *Newc* from 01. *10 Melkridge Gardens, Benton, Newcastle upon Tyne NE7 7GQ* Tel 0191-266 4388

JONES, Edward Harries. b 16. St D Coll Lamp BA38. Ely Th Coll 38. **d** 39 **p** 40. C Rhyl *St As* 39-52; V Ffynnongroew 52-81; rtd 81. *Queen Elizabeth Court, Clarence Drive, Llandudno LL30 1TR*

JONES, Miss Elaine Edith. b 58. St Jo Coll Nottm BA99. **d** 99 **p** 00. C Gainsborough and Morton *Linc* 99-02; C Netherton *Carl* 02-04; TV Maryport, Netherton and Flimby 04-05; Lay Tr Officer 02-05; V Binley *Cov* from 05. *The Vicarage, 68 Brandon Road, Binley, Coventry CV3 2JF* Tel (024) 7663 6334

JONES, Canon Elaine Joan. b 50. Oak Hill Th Coll. **d** 87 **p** 94. Par Dn Tottenham H Trin *Lon* 87-92; Par Dn Clay Hill St Jo and St Luke 92-94; C St Botolph Aldgate w H Trin Minories 94-96; V Hackney Wick St Mary of Eton w St Aug 96-04; AD Hackney 99-04; Can Res Derby Cathl *Derby* from 04. *22 Kedleston Road, Derby DE22 1GU* Tel (01332) 208995 E-mail pastor@derbycathedral.org

JONES, Mrs Elizabeth Mary. b 48. QUB BA69. N Ord Course 88. **d** 91 **p** 94. Par Dn Kippax w Allerton Bywater *Ripon* 91-94; C 94-95; R Swillington 95-00; TV Wordsley *Worc* 00-02; rtd 02. *Le Bourg, 47410 Segalas, France*

JONES, Mrs Elizabeth Somerset. b 49. St Jo Coll Nottm. **d** 88 **p** 94. NSM Duns *Edin* 88-99; NSM Selkirk 89-90; Dioc Dir of Ords from 95; NSM Dalkeith from 02; NSM Lasswade from 02. *255 Carnethie Street, Rosewell EH24 9DR* Tel 0131-653 6767 Fax 653 3646 E-mail esjones@eihc.org

JONES, Emile Conrad Modupe Kojo. b 50. Univ of Sierra Leone BA74 MA BD. Trin Coll Bris 74. **d** 77 **p** 78. C Kissy St Patr Sierra Leone 77-78; C Freetown H Trin 78-81; Asst Chapl and Lect OT Studies Fourah Bay Coll 81-85; Chapl Heidelberg *Eur* 86-97; Miss Partner CMS 97-03; C Holloway St Mary Magd *Lon* 97-04; Asst Chapl Whittington Hosp NHS Trust from 04; Hon C Walthamstow St Pet *Chelmsf* from 05. *1 Beech Court, 28 Bisterne Avenue, London E17 3QX* Tel (020) 8521 1213

JONES, Emmanuel Thomas (Tom). b 19. S Dios Minl Tr Scheme 79. **d** 81 **p** 82. NSM Fareham H Trin *Portsm* 81-89; rtd 89; Perm to Offic *Portsm* from 89. *24 Maylings Farm Road, Fareham PO16 7QU* Tel (01329) 310137

JONES, Eric Alexander. b 19. TCD BA40 MA45 BD45. **d** 42 **p** 43. C Belfast St Matt *Conn* 42-45 and 48-51; C Belfast St Jas 45-47; C Belfast St Nic 47-48; I Larne and Inver 51-59; I Jordanstown 59-68; I Carnmoney 68-76; V Hensall *Sheff* 76-84; RD Snaith and Hatfield 79-84; rtd 84. *222 Cowper Downs, Rathmines, Dublin 6, Irish Republic* Tel (00353) (1) 498 3233

JONES, Canon Eric Vernon. b 26. Ely Th Coll 57. **d** 59 **p** 60. C S Shore H Trin *Blackb* 59-63; V Preston St Matt 64-77; R Chorley St Laur 77-91; Hon Can Blackb Cathl 81-91; rtd 91; Perm to Offic *Blackb* from 91. *8 Glamis Drive, Chorley PR7 1LX* Tel (01257) 230660

JONES, Canon Eric Wilfred. b 22. Linc Coll Ox BA48 MA53. Cuddesdon Coll 48. **d** 50 **p** 51. C E Dulwich St Jo *S'wark* 50-56; V Cov St Pet *Cov* 56-65; Fiji 65-68; Solomon Is 69-74; V Binley *Cov* 74-82; Hon Can Cov Cathl 80-87; RD Cov E 80-82; V Hatton w Haseley and Rowington w Lowsonford 82-87; P-in-c Honiley 85-87; R Hatton w Haseley, Rowington w Lowsonford etc 87; rtd 87; Perm to Offic *Bradf* from 87. *31 Hall Croft, Skipton BD23 1PG* Tel (01756) 793302

JONES, Ernest Edward Stephen. b 39. Lon Univ BD76. St D Coll Lamp. **d** 66 **p** 67. C N Meols *Liv* 66-69; C Kirkby 69-71; V Farnworth All SS *Man* 71-75; P-in-c Bempton *York* 75-78; R Rufford *Blackb* 78-84; V Cropredy w Gt Bourton and Wardington *Ox* 84-90; R York St Clem w St Mary Bishophill Senior *York* 90-98; P-in-c York All SS N Street 90-98; V Northampton St Benedict *Pet* 98-05; rtd 05; P-in-c Wootton w Glympton and Kiddington *Ox* from 05. *The Rectory, 22 Castle Road, Wootton, Woodstock OX20 1EG* Tel (01993) 812543 E-mail stephen@samarnic.wanadoo.co.uk

JONES, Evan Hopkins. b 38. St Mich Coll Llan 65. **d** 67 **p** 68. C Churston Ferrers w Goodrington *Ex* 67-70; C Tavistock and Gulworthy 70-73; R Ashprington 73-78; V Cornworthy 73-78; R S Hackney St Jo w Ch Ch *Lon* 78-92; AD Hackney 84-89; V Islington St Jas w St Pet from 92. *St James's Vicarage, 1 Arlington Square, London N1 7DS* Tel (020) 7226 4108 E-mail fr.evan@virgin.net

JONES, Evan Merfyn. b 40. **d** 97 **p** 98. NSM Ystradyfodwg *Llan* 97-04; Lic to Offic from 04. *71 Tyntyla Road, Llwynypia, Tonypandy CF40 2SR* Tel (01443) 436763

JONES, Evan Trefor. b 32. Univ of Wales (Ban) BA54 Cert Hosp Chapl 82. Coll of Resurr Mirfield 54. **d** 56 **p** 57. C Ban St Mary *Ban* 56-62; V Llandinorwig 62-71; TV Llanbeblig w Caernarfon and Betws Garmon etc 71-84; Ed dioc magazine *The Link* 79-89; R Llanfairfechan w Aber 84-97; Can Ban Cathl 95-97; rtd 97. *Flat 19, Marlborough Place, Vaughan Street, Llandudno LL30 1AE* Tel (01492) 878411

JONES, Frederick Morgan. b 19. Univ of Wales (Lamp) BA40 BD49. St Mich Coll Llan 42. **d** 42 **p** 43. C Llanelli St Paul *St D* 42-50; Org Sec (Wales) Ind Chr Fellowship 50-53; C-in-c Llwynhendy CD *St D* 52-56; C Llanelli 56-57; V Penrhyncoch and Elerch 57-61; R Llanbedrog and Penrhos *Ban* 61-74; R Llanbedrog w Llannor w Llanfihangel etc 74-84; C Llangefni w Tregaean and Llangristiolus etc 84-85; rtd 85; Perm to Offic *Ban* from 85. *15 Ponc-y-Fron, Llangefni LL77 7NY* Tel (01248) 722850

JONES, Gareth. b 35. St Aid Birkenhead 58. **d** 61 **p** 62. C Doncaster Ch Ch *Sheff* 61-65; Min Can Ripon Cathl *Ripon* 65-68; Chapl RAF 68-85; St Jo Cathl Hong Kong 85-89; R Spofforth w Kirk Deighton *Ripon* 89-00; rtd 00; Perm to Offic *Ripon* from 00 and *Dur* from 02. *36 Whitcliffe Lane, Ripon HG4 2JL* Tel (01765) 601745

JONES, Gareth Lewis. b 42. K Coll Lon BD64 AKC64. **d** 65 **p** 66. C Risca *Mon* 65-70; Perm to Offic *Win* 70-74; *Newc* 74-75; *Sarum* 75; C Pontesbury I and II *Heref* 75-77; P-in-c Presteigne w Discoed 77-79; TV Hemel Hempstead *St Alb* 79-86; R Longden and Annscroft w Pulverbatch *Heref* 86-93; TV Leominster from 93. *118 Buckfield Road, Leominster HR6 8SQ* Tel (01568) 612124

JONES, Prof Gareth Lloyd. b 38. Univ of Wales BA61 Selw Coll Cam BA63 MA67 Yale Univ STM69 TCD BD70 Lon Univ PhD75. Episc Sem Austin Texas Hon DD90 Westcott Ho Cam 62. **d** 65 **p** 66. C Holyhead w Rhoscolyn *Ban* 65-68; USA 68-70; P-in-c Merton *Ox* 70-72; Tutor Ripon Hall Ox 72; Sen Tutor 73-75; Lect Ex Coll Ox 73-77; Tutor and Lib Ripon Coll Cuddesdon 75-77; Lect Th Univ of Wales (Ban) 77-89; Sen Lect 89-95; Reader and Hd of Sch from 95; Prof from 98; Sub-Dean Faculty of Th 80-89; Dean 89-92; Chan Ban Cathl *Ban* from 90; Select Preacher Ox Univ 89. *22 Bron-y-Felin, Llandegfan, Menai Bridge LL59 5UY*

JONES, Glyn Evan. b 44. Lon Coll of Div ALCD67 LTh. **d** 67 **p** 68. C Gt Horton *Bradf* 67-70; SAMS 71-78; Argentina 71-78; V Idle H Trin *Bradf* 78-84; V Hyson Green *S'well* 84-87; V Nottingham St Steph 84-87; V Hyson Green St Paul w St Steph 87-89; V Hyson Green 89-91; V Basford w Hyson Green 91-92; V Worksop St Jo 92-99; RD Worksop 93-99; V Nottingham St Sav from 99. *St Saviour's Vicarage, Arkwright Walk, The Meadows, Nottingham NG2 2JU* Tel and fax 0115-986 4046 Mobile 07885-816697 E-mail chezjones@ntlworld.com

JONES, Canon Glyndwr. b 35. St Mich Coll Llan DipTh62. **d** 62 **p** 63. C Clydach *S & B* 62-64; C Llangyfelach 64-67; C Sketty 67-70; V Bryngwyn and Newchurch and Llanbedr etc 70-72; Miss to Seafarers 72-00; Swansea 72-76; Port of Lon 76-81; Aux Min Sec 81-85; Asst Gen Sec 85-90; Sec Gen 90-00; V St Mich Paternoster Royal *Lon* 91-00; rtd 01; Hon Can Kobe Japan from 88; Chapl to The Queen 90-05; Perm to Offic *Chelmsf* from 91 and *Lon* from 01. *5 The Close, Grays RM16 2XU*

JONES, Glynn. b 56. NEOC 91. **d** 94 **p** 95. NSM Glendale Gp *Newc* 94-97; Sen Chapl HM Pris Leeds 97-99; Chapl HM Pris Dur 99-00; Chapl HM YOI Wetherby from 00. *HM Young Offender Institution, York Road, Wetherby LS22 5ED* Tel (01937) 544325 *or* 544200 E-mail glynnwe@hmps@gsi.gov.uk

JONES, Godfrey Caine. b 36. Dur Univ BA59 Lon Univ CertEd60 Birm Univ MEd71. St Deiniol's Hawarden 76. **d** 78 **p** 79. Hd Humanities Denbigh High Sch 75-81; NSM Ruthin w Llanrhydd *St As* 78-81; C 83-84; Sen Lect Matlock Coll 81-83; P-in-c Llanfwrog and Clocaenog and Gyffylliog 84-85; R 85-93; V Ruabon 93-02; RD Llangollen 93-02; rtd 02; Min Pradoe *Lich* from 02. *Idoma, Penylan, Ruabon, Wrexham LL14 6HP* Tel (01978) 812102 E-mail dorothy.e.jones@btopenworld.com

JONES, Gordon Howlett. b 26. G&C Coll Cam BA47 MA51. Westcott Ho Cam 49. **d** 51 **p** 52. C Milton *Win* 51-54; Study Sec SCM and C St Helen Bishopsgate w St Martin Outwich *Lon* 54-58; V Claremont H Angels *Man* 58-63; R Northenden 63-79; P-in-c Hilmarton and Highway *Sarum* 79-83; V Bremhill w Foxham and Hilmarton 83-92; RD Calne 84-88; rtd 92; Perm to Offic *Sarum* from 92. *63 New Park Street, Devizes SN11 8SB* Tel (01380) 720950

JONES, Gordon Michael Campbell. b 33. St D Coll Lamp BA56 St Jo Coll Dur 56. **d** 58 **p** 59. C Maindee *Mon* 58-60; C Penhow, St Brides Netherwent w Llandavenny etc 60-63; V Magor w Redwick 63-68; R Southern Cross Australia 68-71; R Kirkby Thore w Temple Sowerby *Carl* 72-73; R Kirkby Thore w Temple Sowerby and Newbiggin 73-79; P-in-c Accrington St Jas *Blackb* 79-81; P-in-c Accrington St Andr 81-83; Chapl Ahmadi Kuwait 83-91; R Swardeston w E Carleton, Intwood, Keswick etc *Nor* 91-96; Chapl Limassol St Barn and Miss to Seafarers 96-03; rtd 03; Perm to Offic *Blackb* from 03. *29 Fell Brow, Longridge, Preston PR3 3NT* Tel and fax (01772) 780668

JONES, Graham Frederick. b 37. Leeds Univ BA60 GradIPM63. ALCD66. **d** 66 **p** 67. C Chesterfield H Trin *Derby* 66-70; C Leeds St Geo *Ripon* 70-73; P-in-c Newcastle St Geo *Lich* 73-83; New Zealand 83-87; P-in-c Westcote w Icomb and Bledington *Glouc* 89-94; rtd 94. *7 Keynsham Bank, Cheltenham GL52 6ER* Tel (01242) 238680

JONES, Griffith Bernard. b 20. Univ of Wales (Lamp) BA42. St Mich Coll Llan 42. **d** 44 **p** 45. C Ynyshir *Llan* 44-51; C Handsworth St Jas *Birm* 51-56; V Smethwick St Matt 56-60; V Swalcliffe w E Shutford *Ox* 60-64; Perm to Offic *Pet* 64-82; Perm to Offic *St Alb* 74-82; R Llanfallteg w Clunderwen and Castell Dwyran etc *St D* 82-88; rtd 88. *17 Heol Ceirios, Llandybie, Ammanford SA18 2SR* Tel (01269) 851803

JONES, Griffith Trevor. b 56. BSc MPS Univ of Wales BD. **d** 87 **p** 88. C Llandrygarn w Bodwrog and Heneglwys etc *Ban* 87-89; R Llangefni w Tregaean and Llangristiolus etc 89-91; TV Bangor 91-94; Chapl Ysbyty Gwynedd 91-94; Lic to Offic 94-00. *8 Carreg-y-Gad, Llanfairpwllgwyngyll LL61 5QF* Tel (01248) 713094

JONES, Preb Griffith Walter Hywyn. b 24. St Mich Coll Llan 47. **d** 50 **p** 51. C Llanaber *Ban* 50-52; Chapl RAF 52-67; V Betws y Coed *Ban* 67-69; V Betws y Coed and Capel Curig 70-78; R Holyhead w Rhoscolyn w Llanfair-yn-Neubwll 78-87; Can and Preb Ban Cathl 78-90; RD Llifon and Talybolion 80-85; Spiritual Dir Cursillo Cymru 81-90; V Ynyscynhaearn w Penmorfa and Porthmadog *Ban* 87-90; rtd 90; Lic to Offic *St As* from 90 and *Ban* 90-96. *Cysgod y Coed, 12 Church View, Ruabon, Wrexham LL14 6TD* Tel (01978) 822206

JONES, Canon Griffith William. b 31. St D Coll Lamp BA53 LTh55. **d** 55 **p** 56. C Llanycil w Bala and Frongoch *St As* 55-58; V Llandrillo 58-66; V Llandrillo and Llandderfel 66-96; RD Penllyn 83-96; Can Cursal St As Cathl from 87; rtd 96. *45 Yr Hafan, Bala LL23 7AU* Tel (01678) 520217

JONES, Gwyn Harris. b 19. Univ of Wales (Lamp) BA42. K Coll Lon 42. **d** 43 **p** 44. C Pembroke Dock *St D* 43-44; C Letterston 44-46; Uganda 46-53; C Llanelli *St D* 53-54; V Wolverhampton St Paul *Lich* 54-56; V Burton St Chad 56-79; V Shrewsbury St Geo 79-87; rtd 87; Perm to Offic *Lich* from 87. *18 Kenwood Gardens, Shrewsbury SY3 8AQ* Tel (01743) 351057

JONES, Gwynfryn Lloyd. b 35. Univ of Wales (Lamp) BA59. St Mich Coll Llan 59. **d** 61 **p** 62. C Rhyl w St Ann *St As* 61-64; C Prestatyn 64-67; V Whitford 67-75; V Llay 75-83; V Northop 83-98; rtd 98. *Tryfan, 41 Snowdon Avenue, Bryn-y-Baal, Mold CH7 6SZ* Tel (01352) 751036

JONES, Gwynn Rees. b 32. St D Coll Lamp BA55. **d** 57 **p** 58. C Llangystennin *St As* 57-59; C Llanrhos 59-64; R Cefn 64-68; R Llanfyllin 68-80; V Bistre 80-89; R Flint 89-97; rtd 97. *Tan y Coed, 68 Bryn Aber, Bryn Twr, Abergele LL22 8DD* Tel (01745) 825188

JONES, Canon Harold Desmond. b 22. Sarum Th Coll 52. **d** 55 **p** 56. C Bushey Heath *St Alb* 55-58; C Stevenage 58-64; V Milton Ernest and Thurleigh 64-80; RD Sharnbrook 70-81; Hon Can St Alb 78-90; V Sharnbrook 80-82; P-in-c Knotting w Souldrop 80-82; R Sharnbrook and Knotting w Souldrop 82-90; P-in-c Felmersham 82-87; RD Sharnbrook 86-90; rtd 90; Perm to Offic *St Alb* 00-04. *8 Capel Court, The Burgage, Prestbury, Cheltenham GL52 3EL* Tel (01242) 576510

JONES, Harold Philip. b 49. Leeds Univ BA72 St Jo Coll Dur BA84. Cranmer Hall Dur 82. **d** 85 **p** 86. C Scartho *Linc* 85-88; V Dodworth *Wakef* 88-91; C Penistone and Thurlstone 91-95; C Scunthorpe All SS *Linc* 95-96; TV Brumby 96-02; Chapl S Derbyshire Acute Hosps NHS Trust from 02. *Derby City General Hospital, Uttoxeter Road, Derby DE22 3NE* Tel (01332) 340131 Fax 290559 E-mail harold.jones@sdah-tr.trent.nhs.uk

JONES, Haydn Llewellyn. b 42. Edin Th Coll 63. **d** 65 **p** 66. C Towcester w Easton Neston *Pet* 65-68; C Northampton St Matt 68-72; CF 72-97; Perm to Offic *Roch* 97-98; *Ex* from 98; rtd 99. *11 Lady Park Road, Livermead, Torquay TQ2 6UA* Tel (01803) 690483

JONES, Helen Alison. b 59. St Andr Univ BSc81. EMMTC 93. **d** 96 **p** 97. C Limber Magna w Brocklesby *Linc* 96-97; C Brocklesby Park 97-98. *Address temp unknown*

JONES, Hilary Christine. b 55. Ch Ch Coll Cant CertEd76 Lon Univ BEd77. SEITE. **d** 99 **p** 00. C Kennington *Cant* 99-02; R Cheriton from 02; Bp's Adv for Women's Min from 04. *St Martin's Rectory, Horn Street, Folkestone CT20 3JJ* Tel (01303) 238509 E-mail hilarycjones@lycos.co.uk

JONES, Howard. *See* JONES, John Howard

JONES, Hugh Owen. b 14. Coates Hall Edin 45. **d** 47 **p** 48. C Dundee St Mary Magd *Bre* 47-50; P-in-c Airdrie *Glas* 50-52; CF 52-58; R Hope w Shelve *Heref* 58-63; V Bodenham w Hope-under-Dinmore 63-78; R Bodenham w Hope-under-Dinmore, Felton etc 78-80; rtd 80; Perm to Offic *Ban* 96-99. *32 Dulverton Hall, Esplanade, Scarborough YO11 2AR*

JONES, Hughie. *See* JONES, The Ven Thomas Hughie

JONES, Huw. *See* JONES, David Huw

JONES, Hywyn. *See* JONES, Preb Griffith Walter Hywyn

JONES, Ian. b 63. Trin Coll Carmarthen BEd88. St Mich Coll Llan 95. **d** 97 **p** 98. NSM Tycoch *S & B* 97-01; NSM Swansea St Nic 01-04; Chapl Wymondham Coll from 04. *Staff House 8, Wymondham College, Golf Links Road, Wymondham NR18 9SX* Tel (01953) 607120 E-mail ianjones99@yahoo.com

JONES, Ian Andrew. b 65. Lanc Univ BA87. St Mich Coll Llan DPS90. **d** 90 **p** 91. C Caerphilly *Llan* 90-96; Chapl RAF from 96. *Chaplaincy Services (RAF), HQ, Personnel and Training Command, RAF Innsworth, Gloucester GL3 1EZ* Tel (01452) 712612 ext 5164 Fax 510828

JONES, Idris. b 31. **d** 88 **p** 94. NSM Llanfihangel Ysgeifiog and Llanffinan etc *Ban* 88-97; NSM Llangefni w Tregaean and Llangristiolus etc 98-01; NSM Llanfihangel Ysgeifiog w Llangristiolus etc 01-02. *Rhoslyn, Gaerwen LL60 6HQ* Tel (01248) 421797

✠**JONES, The Rt Revd Idris.** b 43. Univ of Wales (Lamp) BA64 NY Th Sem DMin86. Edin Th Coll 64. **d** 67 **p** 68 **c** 98. C Stafford St Mary *Lich* 67-70; Prec St Paul's Cathl Dundee *Bre* 70-73; P-in-c Gosforth All SS *Newc* 73-80; R Montrose and Inverbervie *Bre* 80-89; Can St Paul's Cathl Dundee 84-92; Chapl Angl Students Dundee Univ 89-92; P-in-c Invergowrie 89-92; TR S Ayrshire TM 92-98; Bp Glas from 98. *Diocesan Centre, 5 St Vincent Place, Glasgow G1 2DH* Tel 0141-221 6911 *or* tel and fax 633 5877 Fax 221 6490
E-mail bishop@glasgow.anglican.org

JONES, Ivor Wyn. b 56. Trin Coll Bris 92. **d** 94 **p** 95. C Gabalfa *Llan* 94-97; TV Daventry, Ashby St Ledgers, Braunston etc *Pet* 97-01; P-in-c Dawley St Jerome *Lon* from 01; C-in-c Harlington Ch Ch CD from 03. *St Jerome's Lodge, 42 Corwell Lane, Uxbridge UB8 3DE* Tel (020) 8561 7393 *or* 8573 1895
E-mail wynjones@blueyonder.co.uk

JONES, James Richard. b 65. SS Hild & Bede Coll Dur BA87 Open Univ MBA95. Wycliffe Hall Ox 02. **d** 04 **p** 05. C Ashtead *Guildf* from 04. *17 Loraine Gardens, Ashtead KT21 1PD*

✠**JONES, The Rt Revd James Stuart.** b 48. Ex Univ BA70 PGCE71 Hull Univ Hon DD99 Lincs & Humberside Univ Hon DLitt01. Wycliffe Hall Ox 81. **d** 82 **p** 83 **c** 94. C Clifton Ch Ch w Em *Bris* 82-90; V S Croydon Em *S'wark* 90-94; Suff Bp Hull *York* 94-98; Bp Liv from 98. *Bishop's Lodge, Woolton Park, Liverpool L25 6DT* Tel 0151-421 0831 Fax 428 3055
E-mail bishopslodge@liverpool.anglican.org

JONES, Canon Jaqueline Dorian. b 58. K Coll Lon BD80 AKC80 MTh81. Westcott Ho Cam 84. **dss** 86 **d** 87 **p** 94. Epsom St Martin *Guildf* 86-87; C 87-91; Chapl Chelmsf Cathl *Chelmsf* 91-97; V Bridgemary *Portsm* 97-03; Can Res S'well Minster *S'well* from 03. *2 Vicars Court, Southwell NG25 0HP* Tel (01636) 813188

JONES, Jeffrey Lloyd. b 66. Univ of Wales (Abth) BD87 PGCE90. Wycliffe Hall Ox DipMin95. **d** 97 **p** 98. C Lampeter Pont Steffan w Silian *St D* 97; C Carmarthen St Dav 97-00; TV Llantwit Major *Llan* from 00. *The Vicarage, Trepit Road, Wick, Cowbridge CF71 7QL* Tel (01656) 890471

JONES, Jennifer Margaret. b 49. Lon Univ CertEd. Cranmer Hall Dur 87. **d** 89 **p** 94. C Musselburgh *Edin* 89-93; Dn-in-c 93-94; P-in-c 94-95; R 95-02; C Prestonpans 89-93; Dn-in-c 93-94; P-in-c 94-95; R 95-02. *Meadowbank, Main Street, Newtonmore PH20 1DD* Tel (01540) 673532
E-mail jennifer.jones@lineone.net

JONES, John Bernard. b 49. Qu Coll Birm 86. **d** 88 **p** 89. C Mold *St As* 88-91; P-in-c Treuddyn and Nercwys and Eryrys 91-92; V Treuddyn w Nercwys from 92; RD Mold 95-00. *The Vicarage, Ffordd y Llan, Treuddyn, Mold CH7 4LN* Tel (01352) 770919
E-mail revjbj@hotmail.com

JONES, John Brian. St Mich Coll Llan. **d** 05. NSM Gors-las *St D* from 05. *Penpentre, 79 Carmarthen Road, Cross Hands, Lanelli SA14 6SU* Tel (01269) 842236

JONES, John David Emrys. b 36. Univ of Wales (Abth). Trin Coll Carmarthen. **d** 96 **p** 97. NSM Llanfihangel Ystrad and Cilcennin w Trefilan etc *St D* 96-97; P-in-c Llangeitho and Blaenpennal w Betws Leucu etc from 97. *Dolfor, Ciliau Aeron, Lampeter SA48 8DE* Tel (01570) 470569

JONES, John Douglas Mathias. b 24. Clare Coll Cam BA49 MA51. Chich Th Coll 49. **d** 51 **p** 52. C Battersea Park All SS *S'wark* 51-54; C Caversham *Ox* 54-59; Chapl RAF 59-66; C Harrogate St Wilfrid *Ripon* 66-67; V Cross Stone *Wakef* 67-76; V Hepworth 76-89; Chapl Storthes Hall Hosp Wakef 81-89; rtd 89; Perm to Offic *Wakef* from 89. *59 Luke Lane, Holmfirth, Huddersfield HD7 2SZ* Tel (01484) 681036

JONES, Canon John Francis Williams. b 26. St D Coll Lamp 48. **d** 52 **p** 53. C Glanadda *Ban* 52-55; C Porthmadog 55-57; V Llandrygarn w Bodwrog 57-62; V Llandrygarn and Bodwrog w Heneglwys 62-74; V Llandrygarn w Bodwrog and Heneglwys etc 74-96; RD Menai and Malltraeth 75-97; Hon Can Ban Cathl 81-83; Can from 83; Preb from 90; rtd 96. *The Vicarage, Tynlon, Holyhead LL65 3AZ* Tel (01407) 720234

JONES, John Hellyer. b 20. Birm Univ LDS43. Westcott Ho Cam 65. **d** 67 **p** 68. C Haddenham *Ely* 67-70; P-in-c Lolworth 70-79 and 81-85; P-in-c Conington 75-79 and 81-85; R Houghton w Wyton 79; rtd 85; Perm to Offic *Ely* 85-02. *13 High Street, Haddenham, Ely CB6 3XA* Tel (01353) 740530
E-mail jonhadnam@ntlworld.com

JONES, John Howard. b 48. New Coll Ox BA69 MA73 K Coll Cam CertEd70. Sarum & Wells Th Coll 76. **d** 77 **p** 78. C Salisbury St Mark *Sarum* 77-78; C Morriston *S & B* 78-80; Dir of Ords 80-83; V Gowerton 80-83; V Swansea St Jas 85-89; Chapl Alleyn's Sch Dulwich from 89; Hon C Dulwich St Barn *S'wark* from 90. *53 Gilkes Crescent, London SE21 7BP* Tel (020) 8299 4826

JONES, The Ven John Samuel. b 16. Univ of Wales (Lamp) BA37 BD42. St Mich Coll Llan 38. **d** 39 **p** 40. C Llandysul *St D* 39-42; C Llandybie 42-49; V Llanllwni 49-86; RD Lampeter 64-68; RD

Lampeter and Ultra-Aeron 68-82; Can St D Cathl 72-82; Chan 78-82; Adn Cardigan 82-86; rtd 86. *Brynheulwen, Bryn Road, Lampeter SA48 7EE* Tel (01570) 423278

JONES, John Trevor. b 14. St D Coll Lamp BA42. **d** 43 **p** 44. C Rhosddu *St As* 43-52; C Timperley *Ches* 52-53; V Barnton 53-60; V Poulton 60-81; rtd 81; Perm to Offic *Ches* from 82. *21 Sandy Lane, Wallasey CH45 3JY* Tel 0151-639 4794

JONES, Joyce Rosemary. b 54. Newnham Coll Cam BA76 MA82 Coll of Ripon & York St Jo MA97 Solicitor 79. N Ord Course 94. **d** 97 **p** 98. C Pontefract All SS *Wakef* 97-00; NSM Cumberworth, Denby and Denby Dale 00-01; Dioc Voc Adv 00-01; Asst Chapl Kirkwood Hospice Huddersfield 00-01; P-in-c Shelley and Shepley *Wakef* from 01. *Oakfield, 206 Barnsley Road, Denby Dale, Huddersfield HD8 8TS* Tel and fax (01484) 862350 E-mail joycerjones@aol.com

JONES, Judith Frances. *See* HUBBARD-JONES, Ms Judith Frances

JONES, Kathryn Mary. *See* BUCK, Mrs Kathryn Mary

JONES (née SANDELLS-REES), Ms Kathy Louise. b 68. Abth Coll of FE DipBBSS87 Univ of Wales (Cardiff) DipTh90 Univ of Wales (Ban) BTh96 Univ Coll Ches Dip Counselling 99. Qu Coll Birm DipTh92. **d** 92 **p** 97. C Holyhead w Rhoscolyn w Llanfair-yn-Neubwll *Ban* 92-94; C Bangor 94-95; Chapl Gwynedd Hosp Ban 94-99; P-in-c Bangor *Ban* 95-99; P-in-c Betws-y-Coed and Capel Curig w Penmachno etc from 99. *The Vicarage, Betws-y-Coed LL24 0AD* Tel (01690) 710313 Fax as telephone

JONES, Mrs Katie Ann. d 99 **p** 00. NSM Sutton Courtenay w Appleford *Ox* 99-04; Perm to Offic *Cant* from 04. *The Headmaster's House, Dover College, Effingham Crescent, Dover CT17 9RH* Tel (01304) 205969

JONES, The Very Revd Keith Brynmor. b 44. Selw Coll Cam BA65 MA69. Cuddesdon Coll 67. **d** 69 **p** 70. C Limpsfield and Titsey *S'wark* 69-72; Dean's V St Alb Abbey *St Alb* 72-76; P-in-c Boreham Wood St Mich 76-79; TV Borehamwood 79-82; V Ipswich St Mary-le-Tower *St E* 82-96; RD Ipswich 92-96; Hon Can St E Cathl 93-96; Dean Ex 96-04; Dean York from 04. *The Deanery, York YO1 7JQ* Tel (01904) 557202 *or* 623618 Fax 557204 E-mail dean@yorkminster.org

JONES, Keith Bythell. b 35. ACP BA DipHE CertEd. Trin Coll Bris. **d** 83 **p** 84. C Bris St Mary Redcliffe w Temple etc *Bris* 83-86; C Filton 86-88; TV Yate New Town 88-95; rtd 95; Perm to Offic *Mon* from 95. *3 Woodlands Close, St Arvans, Chepstow NP16 6EF* Tel (01291) 622377

JONES, Keith Ellison. b 47. Wycliffe Hall Ox 72. **d** 75 **p** 76. C Everton St Chrys *Liv* 75-79; C Buckhurst Hill *Chelmsf* 79-81; TV 81-88; TR Leek and Meerbrook *Lich* 88-99; V Formby H Trin *Liv* from 99. *Holy Trinity Vicarage, 2A Brows Lane, Liverpool L37 3HZ* Tel and fax (01704) 386464
E-mail kejones@classicfm.net

JONES, Kenneth Elwyn. b 32. Nottm Univ BA54 Sheff Univ CertEd55 DipEd55. Linc Th Coll 80. **d** 82 **p** 83. C Rotherham *Sheff* 82-85; R Harthill and Thorpe Salvin 85-93; V Millhouses H Trin 93-97; RD Ecclesall 94-97; rtd 97; Perm to Offic *Sheff* from 97. *27 Hawthorne Avenue, Sheffield S25 5GR* Tel (01909) 560065

JONES, Kingsley Charles. b 45. Birm Univ BSc66 Open Univ BA75. Sarum Th Coll 66. **d** 69 **p** 70. C Penwortham St Mary *Blackb* 69-72; C Broughton 72-74; P-in-c Gt Wollaston *Heref* 74-77; Chapl RAF 77-83; V Colwich w Gt Haywood *Lich* 83-94; V Winshill *Derby* 94-01; P-in-c Glouc St Aldate *Glouc* from 01. *St Aldate's Vicarage, Finlay Road, Gloucester GL4 6TN* Tel (01452) 523906

JONES, Lesley Anne. b 46. Luton Coll of HE CertEd77. St Alb and Ox Min Course 01. **d** 04. NSM Gravenhurst, Shillington and Stondon *St Alb* from 04. *91 Manton Drive, Luton LU2 7DL* Tel (01582) 616888 E-mail lesleyjones31647@aol.com

JONES, Leslie Joseph. b 23. Linc Th Coll. **d** 57 **p** 58. C Penhill *Bris* 57-60; C-in-c Lockleaze St Mary CD 60-62; V Bris Lockleaze St Mary Magd w St Fran 62-69; V Bedminster St Aldhelm 69-75; TV Bedminster 75-80; V Abbots Leigh w Leigh Woods 80-88; rtd 88; Perm to Offic *Bris* from 88. *4 Summerleaze, Bristol BS16 4ER* Tel 0117-965 3597

JONES, Lloyd. *See* JONES, Jeffrey Lloyd

JONES, Lloyd. *See* JONES, Prof Gareth Lloyd

JONES, Miss Mair. b 41. Cartrefle Coll of Educn TCert61 Dip Special Educn 73. St Mich Coll Llan 91. **d** 93 **p** 97. C Llangollen w Trevor and Llantysilio *St As* 93-97; V Llandrillo and Llandderfel 97-00; R Llanelian w Betws-yn-Rhos w Trofarth 00-03; V Llanelian w Trofarth from 03; P-in-c Colwyn Bay w Brynymaen from 04. *The Rectory, 1 Rhodfa Sant Elian, Colwyn Bay LL29 8PY* Tel (01492) 517866
E-mail mair@jones6527.fsnet.co.uk

JONES, Malcolm. *See* JONES, Philip Malcolm

JONES, Malcolm Francis. b 44. Open Univ BA88 Hull Univ MA96 Univ of Wales (Cardiff) LLM05. Chich Th Coll 67. **d** 70 **p** 71. C Prestbury *Ches* 70-73; Chapl RAF 73-81; R Heaton Reddish *Man* 81-84; CF (ACF) 82-84 and from 98; CF (TA) 83-84; CF 84-93; CF (R of O) 93-99; TV Cleethorpes *Linc* 93-97; V Ryde H Trin *Portsm* from 97; V Swanmore St Mich from 97. *The Vicarage, 11 Wray Street, Swanmore, Ryde PO33 3ED* Tel and fax (01983) 562984 Mobile 07710-543155
E-mail frmalcolmjones@hotmail.com

JONES, Malcolm Stuart. b 41. Sheff Univ BA62. Linc Th Coll 64. **d** 66 **p** 67. C Monkseaton St Mary *Newc* 66-69; C Ponteland 69-72; Venezuela 73-75; C Hexham *Newc* 75-77; P-in-c Killingworth 77-92; V Delaval 92-01; TV Ch the King from 01. *The Vicarage, 2 East Acres, Dinnington, Newcastle upon Tyne NE13 7NA* Tel (01661) 871377

JONES, Maldwyn Lloyd. b 17. St D Coll Lamp BA39. **d** 40 **p** 41. C Gorseinon *S & B* 40-43; Lic to Offic *Ox* 43-46; Brazil 46-50; Falkland Is 50-51; Chapl RN 52-68; USA 68-70; Chapl Lon Nautical Sch 71-72; Lic to Offic *Ban* 72-82; rtd 82; Perm to Offic *Ban* from 82. *Clover Cottage, Ledbury Road, Tirley, Gloucester GL19 4ES*

JONES, Ms Margaret. b 28. TCD BA53 Man Univ PGCE54 Lon Univ BD66. **d** 87 **p** 94. NSM Stanstead Abbots *St Alb* 87-88; NSM Grappenhall *Ches* 89-98; rtd 98; Perm to Offic *Ches* from 98. *19 Hill Top Road, Grappenhall, Warrington WA4 2ED* Tel (01925) 261992

JONES, Mrs Margaret Angela. b 53. Wolv Univ CertEd91. Qu Coll Birm BA99. **d** 99 **p** 00. C Pershore w Pinvin, Wick and Birlingham *Worc* 99-03; TV Solihull *Birm* from 03. *St Helen's House, 6 St Helen's Road, Solihull B91 2DA* Tel 0121-704 2878
E-mail margaret@mccnjones.fsnet.co.uk

JONES, Mrs Margaret Anne. b 47. Lon Univ TCert68 Ches Coll of HE BTh04. N Ord Course 01. **d** 04 **p** 05. NSM Altrincham St Geo *Ches* from 04. *12 Moorland Avenue, Sale M33 3FH* Tel 0161-973 8020 Mobile 07748-645596
E-mail margaret_jones@talk21.com

JONES, Margaret Mary. b 47. Oak Hill Th Coll 92. **d** 95 **p** 96. C Sydenham H Trin *S'wark* 95-98; V Anerley St Paul *Roch* from 98. *St Paul's Vicarage, Hamlet Road, London SE19 2AW* Tel (020) 8653 0978

JONES, Mark. *See* JONES, Christopher Mark

JONES, Mark Andrew. b 60. Southn Univ BSc82 Sussex Univ PGCE83. Oak Hill Th Coll BA91. **d** 91 **p** 92. C Wolverhampton St Luke *Lich* 91-96; I Inishmacsaint *Clogh* 96-01; V Padiham w Hapton and Padiham Green *Blackb* from 01. *The Vicarage, 1 Arbory Drive, Padiham, Burnley BB12 8JS* Tel (01282) 772442
E-mail jones.rectory@care4free.net

JONES, Mark Vincent. b 60. Univ of Wales (Cardiff) DipTh84. St Mich Coll Llan 81. **d** 84 **p** 85. C Whitchurch *Llan* 84-89; V Pwllgwaun w Llanddewi Rhondda 89-90; CF from 90. *c/o MOD Chaplains (Army)* Tel (01980) 615804 Fax 615800

JONES, Martin Patrick. b 62. K Coll Lon BDS85. Dioc OLM tr scheme 02. **d** 05. NSM Kingsnorth and Shadoxhurst *Cant* from 05. *3 Hewitts Place, Willesborough, Ashford TN24 0AH* Tel (01233) 613271 E-mail martin.os@ntlworld.com

JONES, Mrs Mary Catherine Theresa Bridget. b 41. Westhill Coll Birm CertEd77 Birm Univ BA80. Qu Coll Birm 04. **d** 05. NSM Bromsgrove St Jo *Worc* from 05. *15 Greyfriars Drive, Bromsgrove B61 7LF* Tel (01527) 837018
E-mail theresa@supalife.com

JONES, Canon Mary Nerissa Anna. b 41. MBE02. Qu Mary Coll Lon BA86 FRSA91. Ripon Coll Cuddesdon 86. **d** 88 **p** 94. Par Dn St Botolph Aldgate w H Trin Minories *Lon* 88-93; P-in-c Wood End *Cov* 93-95; V 95-01; Hon Can Cov Cathl 01; rtd 01; P-in-c Askerswell, Loders and Powerstock *Sarum* from 01. *The Vicarage, Loders, Bridport DT6 3SA* Tel (01308) 425419
E-mail nerissa@surfaid.org

JONES, Canon Mary Valerie. b 37. Univ of Wales (Ban) BD84. St Deiniol's Hawarden 84. **d** 85 **p** 97. C Holyhead w Rhoscolyn w Llanfair-yn-Neubwll *Ban* 85-87; C Ynyscynhaearn w Penmorfa and Porthmadog 87-90; Dn-in-c Llansantffraid Glyn Ceirog and Llanarmon etc *St As* 90-97; V 97-98; R Overton and Erbistock and Penley 98-04; RD Bangor Isycoed 98-04; Can Cursal St As Cathl 01-04; rtd 04. *Cysgod y Coed, 12 Church View, Ruabon, Wrexham LL14 6TD* Tel (01978) 822206
E-mail valerie@hywyn.freeserve.co.uk

JONES, Matthew Christopher Howell. b 74. Leeds Univ BSc95 Cam Univ BTh01. Westcott Ho Cam 98. **d** 01 **p** 02. C Cheshunt *St Alb* from 01. *156 Churchgate, Cheshunt, Waltham Cross EN8 9DX* Tel (01992) 620659 E-mail mchjones@lineone.net

JONES, Maurice Maxwell Hughes. b 32. Lon Univ DipTh58 Univ of Wales (Cardiff) DPS72. Clifton Th Coll 56. **d** 60 **p** 61. C Islington St Andr w St Thos and St Matthias *Lon* 60-63; Argentina 63-71; C Whitchurch *Llan* 72-73; Area Sec (NW England) SAMS 73-77; V Haydock St Mark *Liv* 78-87; V Paddington Em Harrow Road *Lon* 87-97; rtd 98. *Glyn Orig, Cemmaes, Machynlleth SY20 9PR* Tel (01650) 511632 Fax as telephone

JONES, Canon Melville Kenneth. b 40. Open Univ BA82. St D Coll Lamp DipTh66. **d** 66 **p** 67. C Aberdare *Llan* 66-71; C Caerau w Ely 71-72; Chapl Pontypridd Hosps 72-89; V Graig *Llan* 72-89; P-in-c Cilfynydd 86-89; V Llantwit Fardre from 89; Chapl E Glam Hosp 89-99; RD Pontypridd from 99; Hon Can Llan Cathl from 04; Chapl Pontypridd and Rhondda NHS Trust

99-01. *The Vicarage, Upper Church Village, Pontypridd CF38 1EP* Tel (01443) 202538 Mobile 07974-120268 Fax (01443) 207278 E-mail melville_k.jones@virgin.net

JONES, Michael. *See* JONES, David Michael

JONES, Michael. *See* JONES, Gordon Michael Campbell

JONES, Michael. b 49. Leeds Univ BA71 Man Univ MA73. Qu Coll Birm 83. **d** 85 **p** 86. C Leigh St Mary *Man* 85-88; C-in-c Holts CD 88-93; V Hamer 93-05. *Address temp unknown*

JONES, Michael Christopher. b 67. Southn Univ BSc88. St Jo Coll Nottm MTh03 MA04. **d** 04 **p** 05. C Aldridge *Lich* from 04. *5 Whetsone Lane, Aldridge, Walsall WS9 8NH* Tel (01922) 745738

JONES, Michael Denis Dyson. b 39. CCC Cam BA62 MA66 Lon Univ MSc73. Wycliffe Hall Ox. **d** 76 **p** 77. C Plymouth St Andr w St Paul and St Geo *Ex* 76-81; V Devonport St Budeaux 81-00; RD Plymouth Devonport 93-95; TV Barnstaple from 00; RD Barnstaple from 03. *Holy Trinity Vicarage, Victoria Road, Barnstaple EX32 9HP* Tel (01271) 344321 E-mail mddjamj@onetel.com

JONES, Michael Emlyn. b 47. Aber Univ MB, ChB72 MRCP75 FRCP95 Nottm Univ Dip Past Counselling 93. **d** 79 **p** 79. Asst P Moshi St Marg Tanzania 79-82; NSM Duns *Edin* 83-99; NSM Dalkeith from 02; NSM Lasswade from 02. *255 Carnethie Street, Rosewell EH24 9DR* Tel 0131-440 2602 *or* 653 6767 Mobile 07710-276208 Fax 0131-653 3646 E-mail michaelejones@doctors.org.uk

JONES, Michael Kevin. b 57. Llan Ord Course 94. **d** 98 **p** 99. NSM Caerau w Ely *Llan* 98-00; NSM Cen Cardiff 01; P-in-c Tremorfa St Phil CD from 02; Area Fundraising Manager Children's Soc *Llan* and *Mon* 98-00; Ch Strategy Manager Wales 01-02. *4 Glas Canol, Whitchurch, Cardiff CF14 1LA* Tel (029) 2061 1669 Fax as telephone

JONES, Morgan. *See* JONES, Frederick Morgan

JONES, Canon Neil Crawford. b 42. Univ of Wales BA63 K Coll Lon BD66 AKC66. **d** 67 **p** 68. C Holywell *St As* 67-69; C Rhyl w St Ann 69-73; C Christchurch *Win* 73-77; V Stanmore 77-84; RD Win 82-84; V Romsey from 84; RD Romsey 89-94; Hon Can Win Cathl from 93. *The Vicarage, Church Lane, Romsey SO51 8EP* Tel (01794) 513125

JONES, Nerissa. *See* JONES, Canon Mary Nerissa Anna

JONES, Canon Neville George. b 36. Univ of Wales (Ban) BA59. St Mich Coll Llan 59. **d** 61 **p** 62. C Broughton *St As* 61-65; C Newcastle *Llan* 65-68; V Laleston w Tythegston 68-84; V Llanishen and Lisvane 84-93; V Llanishen 93-02; Hon Can Llan Cathl 96-02; rtd 02. *21 Cwm Gwynlais, Tongwynlais, Cardiff CF15 7HU* Tel (029) 2081 1150

JONES, Nicholas Godwin. b 58. St Jo Coll Cam BA81 MA84 Hughes Hall Cam PGCE90. Ridley Hall Cam CTM93. **d** 93 **p** 94. C Cambridge H Trin *Ely* 93-97; Chapl St Bede's Sch Cam 97-00; C Fulbourn w Gt and Lt Wilbraham 97-00; V Harston w Hauxton and Newton 00-03; V Gt Horton *Bradf* from 03. *The Vicarage, 30 Bartle Close, Bradford BD7 4QH* Tel (01274) 521456 *or* 572002 Mobile 07957-387698 E-mail nandjjones@aol.com

JONES, Canon Nicholas Newman. b 51. K Coll Lon 71 St Aug Coll Cant 74. **d** 75 **p** 76. C Derringham Bank *York* 75-78; C Stokesley 78-81; P-in-c Kirby Misperton 81-85; R Normanby w Edston and Salton 83-85; R Kirby Misperton w Normanby, Edston and Salton 85-87; V Eskdaleside w Ugglebarnby and Sneaton 87-98; RD Whitby 92-98; P-in-c Wykeham and Hutton Buscel 98-99; P-in-c New Malton 99-02; V from 02; RD S Ryedale from 02; Can and Preb York Minster from 05. *The Vicarage, 17 The Mount, Malton YO17 7ND* Tel and fax (01653) 692089 E-mail vicarage17@hotmail.com

JONES, Nicholas Peter. b 55. St Mich Coll Llan DipTh82. **d** 82 **p** 83. C St Andrews Major w Michaelston-le-Pit *Llan* 82-84; C Aberdare 84-88; Youth Chapl 85-89; V Abercynon 88-96; R Llanilid w Pencoed from 96. *The Rectory, 60 Coychurch Road, Pencoed, Bridgend CF35 5NA* Tel (01656) 860337

JONES, Nigel David. b 69. Qu Coll Cam MA95. Westcott Ho Cam 97. **d** 00 **p** 01. C Abbots Langley *St Alb* 00-03; TV Dunstable from 03. *St Augustine's Vicarage, 83 Half Moon Lane, Dunstable LU5 4AE* Tel (01582) 703919 E-mail nigel.david.jones@ukgateway.net

JONES, Nigel Ivor. b 54. Sheff Univ MMin04. WMMTC 91. **d** 94 **p** 95. C Shirley *Birm* 94-99; TV Salter Street and Shirley 99-01; V Olton from 01. *St Margaret's Vicarage, 5 Old Warwick Road, Solihull B92 7JU* Tel 0121-706 2318 Mobile 07719-951856 E-mail revnigel@aol.com

JONES, Norman. b 50. Oak Hill Th Coll BA83. **d** 83 **p** 84. C Ulverston St Mary w H Trin *Carl* 83-87; Hong Kong 88-92; TR Eccles *Man* 92-01; AD Eccles 95-00; R Haslemere and Grayswood *Guildf* from 01; RD Godalming from 02; Chapl Wispers Sch Haslemere from 01. *The Rectory, 7 Derby Road, Haslemere GU27 1BS* Tel (01428) 658107 *or* tel and fax 644578 E-mail revnjones@aol.com

✠**JONES, The Rt Revd Noël Debroy.** b 32. CB86. Univ of Wales (Lamp) BA53. Wells Th Coll 53. **d** 55 **p** 56 **c** 89. C Tredegar St Jas *Mon* 55-57; C Newport St Mark 57-60; V Kano Nigeria 60-62; Chapl RN 62-84; Chapl of the Fleet and Adn for the RN 84-89; QHC from 83; Hon Can Gib Cathl *Eur* from 86; Bp S & M 89-03; rtd 03; Hon Asst Bp York from 03. *The Sudreys, Pickering Road, Thornton Dale, Pickering YO18 7LH* E-mail holy.noellee@sagainternet.co.uk

JONES, Ormond. *See* JONES, David Ormond

JONES, Mrs Patricia Ann. b 43. **d** 97 **p** 98. OLM Bincombe w Broadwey, Upwey and Buckland Ripers *Sarum* 97-05. *23 Camedown Close, Weymouth DT3 5RB* Tel (01305) 813056

JONES, Mrs Patricia Anne. b 55. NNEB75 CSS81. Oak Hill Th Coll 92. **d** 95. NSM Mill Hill Jo Keble Ch *Lon* 95-01; NSM Queensbury All SS from 01. *The Flat, St Paul's School, The Ridgeway, London NW7 1QU* Tel (020) 8201 1583

JONES, Canon Patrick Geoffrey Dickson. b 28. Ch Ch Ox BA51 MA55 Aber Univ MLitt98. St Deiniol's Hawarden 79. **d** 82 **p** 83. NSM Sandbach *Ches* 82-84; R Aboyne *Ab* 84-96; R Ballater 84-96; P-in-c Braemar 84-96; rtd 96; Hon Can St Andr Cathl *Ab* from 01. *Byebush of Fedderate, New Deer, Turriff AB53 6UL* Tel (01771) 644110 E-mail pg.dj@tiscali.co.uk

JONES, Patrick George. b 42. Cant Ch Ch Univ Coll MA99. Lich Th Coll 69. **d** 72 **p** 73. C Chesterton St Geo *Ely* 72-75; P-in-c Waterbeach 75-78; P-in-c Landbeach 76-78; R Charlton-in-Dover *Cant* 78-90; Cautley Trust from 90. *Cautley House, 95 Seabrook Road, Seabrook, Hythe CT21 5QY* Tel (01303) 230762 E-mail cautleyhouse@compuserve.com

JONES, Paul Anthony. b 72. Cov Univ BSc95. Ripon Coll Cuddesdon BTh99. **d** 99 **p** 00. C Dolgellau w Llanfachreth and Brithdir etc *Ban* 99-02; P-in-c Ffestiniog w Blaenau Ffestiniog 02-04. *The Vicarage, Betws-y-Coed LL24 0AD* Tel and fax (01690) 710313 *or* (01766) 832142 E-mail monty@classicfm.net

JONES, Paul Evan. b 62. York Univ BA84. SEITE 02. **d** 05. C Kingstanding St Luke *Birm* from 05. *45 Epwell Road, Birmingham B44 8DH* E-mail liberty.hall@tiscali.co.uk

JONES, Paul Terence. b 35. Dur Univ BA60. Qu Coll Birm 60. **d** 62 **p** 63. C Rainford *Liv* 62-65; C Skelmersdale St Paul 65-68; V Huyton Quarry 68-78; V Widnes St Ambrose 78-00; rtd 00; Perm to Offic *Liv* from 00. *9 Hunter Court, Prescot L34 2UH* Tel 0151-430 6057

JONES, Penelope Howson. b 58. Girton Coll Cam BA80 MA83 LGSM79. Ripon Coll Cuddesdon BA85 MA88. **dss** 86 **d** 87 **p** 94. Hackney *Lon* 86-87; Par Dn 87-88; Tutor Ripon Coll Cuddesdon 88-90; Par Dn Cuddesdon *Ox* 88-90; Perm to Offic *Dur* 92-95; Dir Practical Th NEOC *Newc* 93-97; Hon C Eastgate w Rookhope *Dur* 93-97; Hon C Stanhope w Frosterley 93-97; Perm to Offic *York* 93-97; P-in-c Stanhope w Frosterley *Dur* 97-01; P-in-c Eastgate w Rookhope 97-01; Woman Adv in Min 97-01; Hon Can Dur Cathl 98-01; Sen Assoc P Gosford Australia from 01. *78 Henry Parry Drive, PO Box 4255, Gosford East, NSW, Australia 2250* Tel (0061) (2) 4324 2630 E-mail redimp@bigpong.com

JONES, Canon Peter Anthony Watson. b 53. AKC75. Sarum & Wells Th Coll 76. **d** 77 **p** 78. C Hessle *York* 77-81; C Stainton-in-Cleveland 81-82; P-in-c Weston Mill *Ex* 82-84; Chapl Plymouth Poly 82-90; V Gt Ayton w Easby and Newton in Cleveland *York* 90-92; C Devonport St Aubyn *Ex* 92-98; P-in-c Yealmpton and Brixton 98-01; Team Chapl Portsm Hosps NHS Trust 01-05; Chapl Portsm Univ *Portsm* from 05; Can Res Portsm Cathl from 05. *Chaplaincy, Nuffield Centre, St Michael's Road, Portsmouth PO1 2ED* Tel (023) 9284 3157 E-mail peter.jones383@ntlworld.com

JONES, Peter Charles. b 57. Univ of Wales BA81 MA82 PGCE97. St Mich Coll Llan 80. **d** 83 **p** 84. C Pontnewynydd *Mon* 83-85; C Bassaleg 85-87; TV Cwmbran 87-94; V Blaenavon w Capel Newydd 94-01; Chapl CME 00-01; Chapl and Fell Trin Coll Carmarthen 01-05; V Llangennech and Hendy *St D* from 05. *The Vicarage, 2A Mwrwg Road, Llangennech, Llanelli SA14 8UA* Tel (01554) 820324

JONES, Peter David. b 48. S'wark Ord Course 89. **d** 92 **p** 93. NSM Coulsdon St Andr *S'wark* 92-04. *79 Beverley Road, Whyteleafe CR3 0DU* Tel (020) 8668 6398

JONES, Peter Gordon Lewis. b 31. Llan Dioc Tr Scheme. **d** 82 **p** 83. NSM Llangynwyd w Maesteg *Llan* 82-84; Deputation Appeals Org (S & M Glam) CECS 84-87; Appeals Manager (Wales and Glouc) Children's Soc 87-97; NSM Pyle w Kenfig *Llan* 89-97; rtd 97. *18 Fulmar Road, Porthcawl CF36 3UL* Tel (01656) 785455 Mobile 07785-755399

JONES, Peter Henry. b 50. Qu Coll Cam MA72 Ex Univ CertEd73 Bradf Univ MSc81 Nottm Univ MA05. EMMTC 02. **d** 05. NSM Annesley w Newstead *S'well* from 05. *3 Roland Avenue, Nuthall, Nottingham NG16 1BB* Tel 0115-975 1868 E-mail jones@ng161bb.fsnet.co.uk

JONES, Peter Robin. b 42. Open Univ BA75 Bp Otter Coll Chich CertEd68. EMMTC 79. **d** 82 **p** 83. NSM Doveridge *Derby* 82-97; NSM Doveridge, Scropton, Sudbury etc from 98; Bp's Inspector of Th Colls and Courses from 98; Chapl Derby Gr Sch for Boys from 03; Perm to Offic *Lich* from 93. *4 Cross Road, Uttoxeter ST14 7BN* Tel (01889) 565123

JONES, Canon Peter Russell. b 48. St Jo Coll Cam BA71 MA75 Univ of Wales MTh86. Wycliffe Hall Ox DipTh72. **d** 75 **p** 76. C

Northampton All SS w St Kath *Pet* 75-79; C Ban Cathl Par *Ban* 79-81; Min Can Ban Cathl 79-81; R Pentraeth and Llanddyfnan 81-85; V Conwy w Gyffin from 85; Lect Univ of Wales (Ban) 89-95; RD Arllechwedd *Ban* 96-01; AD from 01; Can and Treas Ban Cathl from 99. *The Vicarage, Rose Hill Street, Conwy LL32 8LD* Tel (01492) 593402

JONES, The Ven Philip Hugh. b 51. Solicitor. Chich Th Coll 92. **d** 94 **p** 95. C Horsham *Chich* 94-97; V Southwater 97-05; RD Horsham 02-04; Adn Lewes and Hastings from 05. *27 The Avenue, Lewes BN7 1QT* Tel (01273) 479530 E-mail archlandh@diochi.org.uk

JONES, Philip Malcolm. b 43. Qu Coll Birm. **d** 04 **p** 05. NSM Birm St Paul *Birm* from 04. *73 Oxford Road, Moseley, Birmingham B13 9SG* Tel 0121-449 7139

JONES, Philip Thomas Henry. b 34. Qu Coll Birm 58. **d** 60 **p** 61. C Castle Bromwich SS Mary and Marg *Birm* 60-67; C Reading St Mary V *Ox* 67-72; C-in-c Reading All SS CD 72-75; V Reading All SS 75-95; Perm to Offic *Portsm* from 97; Hon Chapl Portsm Cathl from 97. *13 Oyster Street, Portsmouth PO1 2HZ* Tel (023) 9275 6676

JONES, Canon Phillip Bryan. b 34. St Mich Coll Llan DipTh61. **d** 61 **p** 62. C Hope *St As* 61-64; C Llanrhos 64-67; V Kerry 67-74; R Newtown w Llanllwchaiarn w Aberhafesp 74-97; RD Cedewain 76-97; Sec Ch in Wales Prov Evang Cttee 80-83; Hon Can St As Cathl *St As* 86-93; Can 93-97; rtd 97. *7 Dalton Drive, Shrewsbury SY3 8DA* Tel (01743) 351426

JONES, Phillip Edmund. b 56. Man Poly BA78 Fitzw Coll Cam BA84 MA88. Westcott Ho Cam 82. **d** 85 **p** 86. C Stafford St Jo and Tixall w Ingestre *Lich* 85-89; TV Redditch, The Ridge *Worc* 89-95; TV Worc SE from 95; Ind Chapl from 89; Team Ldr Worcs Ind Miss from 01. *The Vicarage, Walkers Lane, Whittington, Worcester WR5 2RE* Tel and fax (01905) 355989 E-mail phillip@wimworcester.fsnet.co.uk

JONES, Ray. *See* JONES, David Raymond

JONES, Raymond. b 43. N Ord Course 99. **d** 02 **p** 03. NSM Ashton-in-Makerfield St Thos *Liv* 02-03; C Widnes St Mary w St Paul from 03. *The Vicarage, 24 Dock Street, Widnes WA8 0QX* Tel 0151-424 2221

JONES, Raymond Blake. b 29. K Coll Lon BD54 AKC54. **d** 55 **p** 56. C Fenny Stratford *Ox* 55-58; C Lt Brickhill 55-58; C Wooburn 58-60; C Southbourne St Kath *Win* 60-66; R Braiseworth *St E* 66-76; V Eye 66-76; P-in-c Yaxley 74-77; RD Hartismere 76-77; V Eye w Braiseworth and Yaxley 77; R Ufford 77-82; Chapl St Audry's Hosp Melton 77-82; V Southbourne St Kath *Win* 82-95; rtd 95; Perm to Offic *Win* from 95. *4 Russell Drive, Riverslea, Christchurch BH23 3PA* Tel (01202) 473205

JONES, Raymond Sydney. b 35. MSERT71. Glouc Th Course 85. **d** 87 **p** 88. NSM Madley *Heref* 87-89; NSM Preston-on-Wye w Blakemere 87-89; NSM Madley w Tyberton, Preston-on-Wye and Blakemere 89; Chapl St Mich Hospice Bartestree 90-00; Perm to Offic from 00. *The Old Cedars, Much Birch, Hereford HR2 8HR* Tel (01981) 540851

JONES, Canon Raymond Trevor. b 35. Linc Th Coll. **d** 82 **p** 83. C Rushmere *St E* 82-85; Bp's Dom Chapl 85-86; CF 86-91; TV Ridgeway *Sarum* 91-97; Relig Programmes Producer BBC Wiltshire Sound 91-97; Chapl Fuengirola St Andr *Eur* 97-00; P-in-c Ypres from 00; Can Gib Cathl from 04. *MLK Haiglaan 12, B 8900, Ypres, Belgium* Tel (0032) (5) 721 5685 Fax 721 5927 E-mail raymondstg@hotmail.com

JONES, Ms Rhiannon Elizabeth. b 72. Ex Univ BA93 Brunel Univ MA95 Anglia Poly Univ MA05. Ridley Hall Cam 98. **d** 00 **p** 01. C Huntingdon *Ely* 00-04; R Fulbourn from 04; V Gt Wilbraham from 04; R Lt Wilbraham from 04. *The Rectory, 2 Apthorpe Street, Fulbourn, Cambridge CB1 5EY* Tel (01223) 880337 E-mail rhiannon.jones@ely.anglican.org

JONES, Richard. *See* JONES, James Richard

JONES, Richard. b 23. BEM. St Deiniol's Hawarden 74. **d** 76 **p** 77. NSM Welshpool w Castle Caereinion *St As* 76-94; rtd 94. *Sherwood, Rhos Common, Llandrinio, Llanymynech SY22 6RN* Tel (01691) 830534

JONES, Canon Richard. b 28. St D Coll Lamp 54. **d** 56 **p** 57. C Llanaber w Caerdeon *Ban* 56-61; R Aberffraw w Llangwyfan 61-74; CF (TA) 61-71; V Llanfairisgaer *Ban* 74-79; Bp's Private Chapl 78-82; V Llanfair-is-gaer and Llanddeiniolen 79-89; RD Arfon 82-89; Can Ban Cathl from 86; V Llandegfan w Llandysilio 89-96; Chapl ATC from 90; rtd 96; Perm to Offic *Ban* from 96. *Bryn Hedydd, Cildwrn Road, Llangefni LL77 7NN* Tel (01248) 724609

JONES, Canon Richard. b 36. Ely Th Coll 61. **d** 64 **p** 65. C Blyth St Mary *Newc* 64-67; C Wallsend St Pet 67-69; R Paisley H Trin *Glas* 69-78; R Monifieth *Bre* 78-99; Can St Paul's Cathl Dundee 93-99; Hon Can from 00; rtd 99; Hon C Kelso *Edin* from 99. *12 Hendersyde Avenue, Kelso TD5 7TZ* Tel (01573) 228644 E-mail skypilot111@hotmail.com

JONES, Richard Eifion. b 23. St D Dioc Tr Course 80 St Mich Coll Llan 84. **d** 82 **p** 83. NSM Llangennech and Hendy *St D* 82-84; C Llanbadarn Fawr w Capel Bangor and Goginan 84-86; V Llangadog and Gwynfe w Llanddeusant 86-91; rtd 91. *Gercoed, 186 St Teilo Street, Pontarddulais, Swansea SA4 8LH* Tel (01792) 882234

JONES, Richard Keith. b 40. Jes Coll Ox BA63. Wycliffe Hall Ox 61. **d** 63 **p** 64. C Blaenavon w Capel Newydd *Mon* 63-67; C Mynyddislwyn 67-71; C Pontypool 71; V Abercarn 71-81; V Penhow, St Brides Netherwent w Llandavenny etc 81-88. *32 Quantock Court, South Esplanade, Burnham-on-Sea TA8 1DL* Tel (01278) 458123

JONES, Robert. b 26. Lon Univ BA52 K Coll Lon BD65 Hull Univ MA82. St Deiniol's Hawarden 79. **d** 80 **p** 81. NSM Doncaster St Mary *Sheff* 80-81; C Halifax St Jo Bapt *Wakef* 81-82; C Halifax 83; P-in-c Dewsbury St Mark 83-84; TV Dewsbury 84-92; rtd 92; NSM Halifax St Jo *Wakef* 92-95; Perm to Offic 95-04. *14 Fosbrooke House, Clifton Drive, Ansdell, Lytham St Annes FY8 5RQ* Tel (01253) 667052

JONES, Robert. b 40. **d** 80 **p** 81. C St Laur in Thanet *Cant* 80-83. *Erbacher Strasse 72, 64287 Darmstadt, Germany*

JONES, Robert. b 45. Culham Coll Ox CertEd67. St Steph Ho Ox. **d** 85 **p** 86. C High Wycombe *Ox* 85-89; V Beckenham St Barn *Roch* 89-90; C Swanley St Mary 90-91; C Edenbridge from 91; C Crockham Hill H Trin from 91. *The Vicarage, Oakdale Lane, Crockham Hill, Edenbridge TN8 6RL* Tel (01732) 866515 Fax 864352

JONES, Robert Bernard. b 24. St Jo Coll Dur BA48. Wycliffe Hall Ox. **d** 50 **p** 51. C Ecclesall *Sheff* 50-53; C Apsley End *St Alb* 53-58; C Christchurch *Win* 58-61; V Ringwood 61-75; R N Stoneham 75-89; rtd 89; Perm to Offic *Win* from 89. *4 Rowden Close, West Wellow, Romsey SO51 6RF* Tel (01794) 22966

JONES, Robert Cecil. b 32. Univ of Wales (Abth) BA54 DipEd55. Qu Coll Birm 84. **d** 86 **p** 87. C Llanbadarn Fawr w Capel Bangor and Goginan *St D* 86-88; R Llanllwchaearn and Llanina 88-91; R Newport w Cilgwyn and Dinas w Llanllawer 91-98; rtd 98. *Old Craigstead Works, High Street, Stoney Middleton, Hope Valley S32 4TL* Tel (01433) 631857

JONES, Robert George. b 42. Univ of Wales (Lamp) 87. St Mich Coll Llan DipMin93. **d** 95 **p** 96. NSM Treboeth *S & B* 95-02; P-in-c Treboeth from 02; P-in-c Landore from 03. *Green Gables, 42 Heol Fach, Treboeth, Swansea SA5 9DE* Tel (01792) 774229

JONES, Canon Robert George. b 55. Hatf Coll Dur BA77 Ox Univ BA79 MA87. Ripon Coll Cuddesdon 77. **d** 80 **p** 81. C Foley Park *Worc* 80-84; V Dudley St Fran 84-92; TR Worc St Barn w Ch Ch from 92; RD Worc E from 99; Hon Can Worc Cathl from 03. *St Barnabas' Vicarage, Church Road, Worcester WR3 8NX* Tel and fax (01905) 23785 E-mail rob.gjones@lineone.net

JONES, Robert Ivan. b 33. Bede Coll Dur CertEd57. Westcott Ho Cam 85. **d** 85 **p** 86. NSM Wymondham *Nor* 85-86; C Epsom St Martin *Guildf* 87-89; V Hutton Cranswick w Skerne, Watton and Beswick *York* 89-94; RD Harthill 92-97; V Wetwang and Garton-on-the-Wolds w Kirkburn 94-98; V Waggoners 98-00; rtd 00; P-in-c Newbald *York* 00-04; Perm to Offic from 04. *North Wing, Saxby Hall, 72 Main Street, Saxby-All-Saints, Brigg DN20 0QB* Tel (01652) 618036 E-mail beemajo@onetel.com

JONES, The Very Revd Robert William. b 55. Open Univ BA85 MA88. Ian Ramsey Coll 75 Chich Th Coll 76 TCD Div Sch 77. **d** 79 **p** 80. C Seapatrick *D & D* 79; C Bangor Abbey 81-83; I Drumgath w Drumgooland and Clonduff 83-89; I Finaghy *Conn* 89-93; I Kilwaughter w Cairncastle and Craigy Hill 94-98; I Athlone w Benown, Kiltoom and Forgney *M & K* 98-02; Dean Clonmacnoise from 02; I Trim and Athboy Gp from 02. *St Patrick's Deanery, Loman Street, Trim, Co Meath, Irish Republic* Tel (00353) (46) 943 6698 Mobile 87-290 8344

JONES, Robert William Aplin. b 32. Univ of Wales (Cardiff) BSc52 MSc65 FRSC71 CChem72. St Deiniol's Hawarden 72. **d** 73 **p** 74. C Bassaleg *Mon* 73-77; V Nantyglo 77-82; Perm to Offic 82-86; R Colwinston w Llandow and Llysworney *Llan* 86-95; rtd 95; Perm to Offic *St D* from 99. *Golwg-y-Lan, Feidr Ganol, Newport SA42 0RR* Tel (01239) 820297 Mobile 07968-173759

JONES, Robin Dominic Edwin. b 78. St Chad's Coll Dur BA00 K Coll Lon MA01. St Steph Ho Ox 02. **d** 04 **p** 05. C Ealing Ch the Sav *Lon* from 04. *The Clergy House, The Grove, London W5 5DX* Tel (020) 8810 7740 Mobile 07779-299924 E-mail rdejones@dunelm.org.uk

JONES, Roderick. b 48. Leeds Univ BA70 PGCE72. Westmr Th Sem (USA) 73 Oak Hill Th Coll 74. **d** 76 **p** 77. C Beckenham Ch Ch *Roch* 76-80; C Uphill *B & W* 80-84; R Springfield All SS *Chelmsf* 84-90; Selection Sec ABM 91-96; V Horsell *Guildf* from 96. *The Vicarage, Wilson Way, Horsell, Woking GU21 4QJ* Tel (01483) 772134 E-mail rjones2558@aol.com

JONES, Roger. b 49. St Mich Coll Llan 84. **d** 86 **p** 87. C Llangynwyd w Maesteg *Llan* 86-90; V Wiston w Walton E and Clarbeston *St D* 90-01; V Pembroke Gp 01-04; TV Monkton from 04. *The Vicarage, Lower Lamphey Road, Pembroke SA71 4AF* Tel and fax (01646) 682710 Mobile 07971-528933 E-mail roger@revjones.fsnet.co.uk

JONES, Russell Frederick. b 55. Man Univ BA77 Edin Univ BD84. Edin Th Coll 81. **d** 84 **p** 85. C Croxteth *Liv* 84-87; V Edgehill St Dunstan 87-98; R Glas St Bride *Glas* from 98; Hon

Chapl Glas Univ from 00. *St Bride's Rectory, Flat 1/1, 25 Queensborough Gardens, Glasgow G12 9QP* Tel 0141-334 1401 E-mail howisonandjones@btopenworld.com

JONES, Samuel. b 44. CITC. **d** 86 **p** 87. C Agherton *Conn* 86-88; I Connor w Antrim St Patr 88-97; I Whitehead and Islandmagee 97-01; Bp's C Kilbroney *D & D* from 01. *The Vicarage, 15 Kilbroney Road, Rostrevor, Newry BT34 3BH* Tel (028) 4173 8293

JONES, Sarah. d 04 **p** 05. NSM Ramsden, Finstock and Fawler, Leafield etc *Ox* from 04. *4 Tower Hill, Witney OX28 5ER*

JONES, Ms Sarah Jane. b 61. St Hugh's Coll Ox BA95 MA03 Northumbria Univ MSc02. Westcott Ho Cam 02. **d** 04. C Ross *Heref* from 04. *3 Redwood Close, Ross-on-Wye HR9 5UD* Tel (01989) 564412 Mobile 07973-143950 E-mail sarah@sarahj.demon.co.uk

JONES, Sebastian. *See* JONES, David Sebastian

JONES, Mrs Sharon Ann. b 60. Liv Univ BA82. Cranmer Hall Dur 83. **dss** 85 **d** 87 **p** 94. Rubery *Birm* 85-87; Par Dn 87-89; C-in-c Chelmsley Wood St Aug CD 89-92; Perm to Offic *Newc* 92-93; Chapl HM Pris Acklington 93-97; Chapl HM YOI Castington 97-00; Chapl HM Pris Forest Bank from 00; AD Salford *Man* from 03. *HM Prison, Forest Bank, Swinton, Manchester M27 8FB* Tel 0161-925 7000 ext 2066 Fax 925 7001

JONES, Mrs Shelagh Deirdre. b 46. St Mary's Coll Dur BA68. NEOC 01. **d** 04 **p** 05. NSM Burnby *York* from 04; NSM Londesborough from 04; NSM Nunburnholme and Warter and Huggate from 04; NSM Shiptonthorpe and Hayton from 04; Chapl HM YOI Wetherby from 04. *HM Young Offender Institution, York Road, Wetherby LS22 5ED* Tel (01937) 544325 Fax 544201 Mobile 07971-054674 E-mail revd-shelagh@amserve.com

JONES, Miss Sian Eira. b 63. Univ of Wales (Lamp) BA84 Southn Univ BTh88. Sarum & Wells Th Coll 85. **d** 88 **p** 97. C Llan-llwch w Llangain and Llangynog *St D* 88-93; Dn-in-c Llansteffan and Llan-y-bri etc 93-97; V from 97; RD Carmarthen from 00. *The Vicarage, Llanstephan, Carmarthen SA33 5JT* Tel (01267) 241807

JONES, Sian Hilary. *See* WIGHT, Mrs Sian Hilary

JONES, Simon. b 63. Trin Coll Bris BA89. **d** 89 **p** 90. C Hildenborough *Roch* 89-93; C Crofton *Portsm* 93-96; C Northwood Em *Lon* 96-01; Min in charge Ignite from 01. *44A Azalea Walk, Eastcote, Pinner HA5 2EH* Tel (020) 8868 4185 E-mail sijones@ignitetrust.org.uk

JONES, Simon Matthew. b 72. SS Hild & Bede Coll Dur BA93 MA94 Selw Coll Cam PhD00 Ox Univ MA02 DPhil03. Westcott Ho Cam 95. **d** 99 **p** 00. C Tewkesbury w Walton Cardiff and Twyning *Glouc* 99-02; Chapl and Fell Mert Coll Ox from 02. *Merton College, Oxford OX1 4JD* Tel (01865) 276365 *or* 281793 Fax 276361 E-mail simon.jones@merton.ox.ac.uk

JONES, Stephen. *See* JONES, Ernest Edward Stephen

JONES, Stephen Frederick. b 53. Magd Coll Ox BA75 MA79 Lon Univ BD89 Leeds Univ MA96. Linc Th Coll BCombStuds84. **d** 84 **p** 85. C Kingswinford St Mary *Lich* 84-87; Min Can, Succ and Dean's V Windsor 87-94; C Howden *York* 94-96; Chapl St Elphin's Sch Matlock 96-01; C Worksop Priory *S'well* 01-03; R Longton *Lich* from 03. *The Rectory, Rutland Road, Stoke-on-Trent ST3 1EH* Tel (01782) 595098

JONES, Stephen Leslie. b 59. Hull Univ BA80. Sarum & Wells Th Coll 82. **d** 85 **p** 86. C Perry Barr *Birm* 85-88; C Blackpool St Steph *Blackb* 88-90; V Greenlands 90-95; V Carnforth from 95. *The Vicarage, North Road, Carnforth LA5 9LJ* Tel (01524) 732948 E-mail stephenjones17@hotmail.com

JONES, Stephen Richard. b 49. Heythrop Coll Lon MA01. Oak Hill Th Coll 72. **d** 75 **p** 76. C Welling *Roch* 75-79; C Cheltenham St Mark *Glouc* 79-82; V Shiregreen St Jas and St Chris *Sheff* 82-86; P-in-c Harold Hill St Geo *Chelmsf* 86-88; V 88-97; P-in-c Harold Hill St Paul 94-95; V Kippington *Roch* from 97; RD Sevenoaks 00-05. *The Vicarage, 59 Kippington Road, Sevenoaks TN13 2LL* Tel (01732) 452112 E-mail srjones49@hotmail.com

JONES, Stephen William. b 46. K Coll Lon BD70 AKC70. **d** 71 **p** 72. C Streatham St Pet *S'wark* 71-76; C Leeds St Pet *Ripon* 76-79; C Leeds Richmond Hill 79-85; R Gourock *Glas* 85-88; V Porthleven w Sithney *Truro* 88-94; Miss to Seamen 88-94; P-in-c Portsea Ascension *Portsm* 96-00; V Grimsby St Aug *Linc* from 00. *St Augustine's Vicarage, 145 Legsby Avenue, Grimsby DN32 0LA* Tel (01472) 877109

JONES, Canon Stewart William. b 57. Heriot-Watt Univ BA79 Bris Univ BA88 DipHE87. Trin Coll Bris 86. **d** 88 **p** 89. C Stoke Bishop *Bris* 88-92; P-in-c Brislington St Luke 92-97; Abp's Chapl and Dioc Missr *Cant* 97-03; P-in-c Cant All SS from 01; AD Cant from 02; Hon Prov Can Cant Cathl from 02. *All Saints' Vicarage, Military Road, Canterbury CT1 1PA* Tel (01227) 463505 E-mail sjones@canterbury.clara.net *or* stewart@perkin-jones.com

JONES, Mrs Susan. b 55. Liv Hope BA03. Cranmer Hall Dur 03. **d** 05. C Skelmersdale St Paul *Liv* from 05. *6 Wilcove, Skelmersdale WN8 8NF* Tel (01695) 726491 E-mail 27harris@supanet.com

JONES, Susan Helen. b 60. Trin Coll Carmarthen BEd92 MPhil94 Univ of Wales (Ban) PhD. Ripon Coll Cuddesdon DipMin95. **d** 95 **p** 97. Chapl Univ of Wales (Swansea) *S & B* 95-98; Hon C Sketty 95-98; Dir Past Studies St Mich Coll Llan 98-00; TV Bangor *Ban* from 00. *Deiniol, 31 Trefonwys, Bangor LL57 2HU* Tel (01248) 355530 E-mail suejone@netscapeonline.co.uk

JONES, Mrs Susan Jean. b 47. Bp Grosseteste Coll CertEd69. St Alb and Ox Min Course 93. **d** 96 **p** 97. C S Ascot *Ox* 96-01; NSM from 01. *The Vicarage, Vicarage Gardens, South Ascot, Ascot SL5 9DX* Tel and fax (01344) 622388

JONES, Tegid Owen. b 27. Univ of Wales (Abth) LLB47. St Deiniol's Hawarden. **d** 68 **p** 69. C Rhosddu *St As* 68-71; C Wrexham 71-75; R Marchwiel 75-83; R Marchwiel and Isycoed 83-92; RD Bangor Isycoed 86-92; rtd 92. *Teglys, 2 Bungalow, Pentre, Chirk, Wrexham LL14 5AW*

JONES, Theresa. *See* JONES, Mrs Mary Catherine Theresa Bridget

JONES, Thomas. *See* JONES, Emmanuel Thomas

JONES, Thomas Glyndwr. b 41. Clifton Th Coll 65. **d** 65 **p** 66. C Islington St Mary *Lon* 65-69; USA from 69. *4425 Colchester Court, Columbus, GA 31907, USA*

JONES, Canon Thomas Graham. b 33. St D Coll Lamp BA57. **d** 59 **p** 60. C Llanelli *St D* 59-64; V Ysbyty Cynfyn 64-69; V Ysbyty Cynfyn w Llantrisant 69-72; V Llanelli Ch Ch 72-94; RD Cydweli 89-93; V Carmarthen St Dav 94-00; Hon Can St D Cathl 93-99; Can from 99; RD Carmarthen 98-00; rtd 00. *32 Pen y Morfa, Llangunnor, Carmarthen SA31 2NP* Tel (01267) 231846

JONES, The Ven Thomas Hughie. b 27. Univ of Wales BA49 LLM94 Lon Univ BD53 Leic Univ MA72 FRSA. St Deiniol's Hawarden. **d** 66 **p** 67. Hon C Evington *Leic* 66-76; Hon C Kirby Muxloe 76-81; Dioc Adult Educn Officer 81-85; R Church Langton w Thorpe Langton and Tur Langton 81-85; Hon Can Leic Cathl 83-86; R Church Langton w Tur Langton, Thorpe Langton etc 85-86; Adn Loughborough 86-92; rtd 92; Perm to Offic *Leic* from 92. *Four Trees, 68 Main Street, Thorpe Satchville, Melton Mowbray LE14 2DQ* Tel (01664) 840262 E-mail thj@connectfree.co.uk

JONES, Thomas Percy Norman Devonshire. b 34. St Jo Coll Ox BA58 MA61 Lambeth MLitt02. Cuddesdon Coll 58. **d** 60 **p** 61. C Portsea St Cuth *Portsm* 60-61; C Portsea N End St Mark 61-67; Asst Chapl Portsm Tech Coll 67-70; Chapl Portsm Poly *Portsm* 70-73; USA 73-74; V Folkestone St Sav *Cant* 75-81; V Regent's Park St Mark *Lon* 81-00; rtd 00; Dir Art and Chr Enquiry Trust from 94; Perm to Offic *Lon* from 00. *ACE, 107 Crundale Avenue, London NW9 9PS* Tel and fax (020) 8206 2253 E-mail tom@devonshirejones.fsnet.co.uk

JONES, Canon Thomas Peter. b 20. Ex Coll Ox BA43 MA46. St Mich Coll Llan 43. **d** 45 **p** 46. C Wrexham *St As* 45-48; C Llandrillo-yn-Rhos 48-57; R Erbistock and Overton 57-83; Can St As Cathl 78-84; Preb and Prec St As Cathl 84-86; RD Bangor Isycoed 80-86; R Overton and Erbistock and Penley 83-86; rtd 86; Perm to Offic *Cov* 86-98; *St As* from 98. *18 All Hallows Close, Retford DN22 7UP* Tel (01777) 700481

JONES, Timothy Llewellyn. b 67. York Univ BA90. Ripon Coll Cuddesdon BA94. **d** 94 **p** 95. C Middlesbrough St Martin *York* 94-96; Chapl HM YOI Northallerton 96-99; P-in-c Rounton w Welbury *York* 96-02; Adv for Young Adults and Voc (Cleveland) 99-02; R Corinth St Paul USA from 02. *St Paul's Episcopal Church, PO Box 1225, Corinth, Mississippi, MS 38834, USA* Tel (001) (662) 286 2922

JONES, Timothy Richard Nigel. b 54. Collingwood Coll Dur BSc75 Birm Univ MSc76 FGS. Trin Coll Bris DipHE86. **d** 86 **p** 87. C Hailsham *Chich* 86-91; V Madley w Tyberton, Preston-on-Wye and Blakemere *Heref* 91-00; R Madley w Tyberton, Peterchurch, Vowchurch etc from 00. *The Vicarage, Madley, Hereford HR2 9LP* Tel (01981) 250245

JONES, Trevor Blandon. b 43. Oak Hill Th Coll 77. **d** 80 **p** 81. NSM Homerton St Barn w St Paul *Lon* 80-83; NSM Harlow New Town w Lt Parndon *Chelmsf* 83-90; C 90-92; V Leyton Em 92-01; rtd 02; Perm to Offic *Chelmsf* from 03. *5 Wheatley Close, Sawbridgeworth CM21 0HS* Tel (01279) 600248 E-mail rev.trev@lineone.net

JONES, Trevor Charles. b 50. Oak Hill Th Coll DipHE91. **d** 91 **p** 92. C Goodmayes All SS *Chelmsf* 91-93; C Widford 93-96; V Stowmarket *St E* 96-01. *Address temp unknown*

JONES, Trevor Edwin. b 49. SSC79. Ripon Coll Cuddesdon 74. **d** 76 **p** 77. C Cannock *Lich* 76-79; C Middlesbrough Ascension *York* 79-81; V Oldham St Steph and All Martyrs *Man* 81-84; V Perry Beeches *Birm* 84-90; P-in-c Saltley 90-93; P-in-c Shaw Hill 90-93; V Saltley and Shaw Hill 93-97; R Lon Docks St Pet w Wapping St Jo *Lon* from 97. *St Peter's Clergy House, Wapping Lane, London E1W 2RW* Tel (020) 7481 2985 Fax 7265 1100 E-mail fatherjones@stpeterslondondocks.org.uk *or* frtejones@aol.com

JONES, The Ven Trevor Pryce. b 48. Southn Univ BEd76 BTh79 Univ of Wales (Cardiff) LLM04. Sarum & Wells Th Coll 73. **d** 76 **p** 77. C Glouc St Geo *Glouc* 76-79; Warden Bp Mascall Cen

Heref 79-84; Dioc Communications Officer 81-86; TR Heref S Wye 84-97; Preb Heref Cathl 93-97; OCF 85-97; Adn Hertford and Hon Can St Alb from 97. *St Mary's House, Church Lane, Stapleford, Hertford SG14 3NB* Tel (01992) 581629 Fax 558745 E-mail archdhert@stalbans.anglican.org

JONES, Canon Tudor Howell. b 39. Univ of Wales (Cardiff) BD91. St Mich Coll Llan DipTh67 DPS68. **d** 68 **p** 69. C Clydach *S & B* 68-72; C Swansea St Pet 72-75; V Ystradfellte 75-79; V Llangiwg 79-91; V Manselton from 91; RD Penderi from 98; Can Res Brecon Cathl from 00. *The Vicarage, Manor Road, Manselton, Swansea SA5 9PA* Tel (01792) 654848

JONES, Victor Harvey. b 25. St D Coll Lamp BA53 Coll of Resurr Mirfield. **d** 55 **p** 56. C Canton St Luke *Llan* 55-57; C Caerau w Ely 57-61; Chapl RN 62-76; Perm to Offic *Truro* 77-80; C Portishead *B & W* 80-83; rtd 83; Perm to Offic *Ex* 92-98. *17 Beech Road, Findon, Worthing BN14 0UR* Tel (01903) 873461

JONES, Preb Wilfred David. b 22. Keble Coll Ox BA47 MA48. St Mich Coll Llan 47. **d** 48 **p** 49. C Aberaman *Llan* 48-50; C Cardiff St Jo 50-55; Chapl Kelly Coll Tavistock 55-62; V St Decumans *B & W* 62-76; V Ilminster w Whitelackington 76-92; RD Ilminster 78-87; Preb Wells Cathl from 81; rtd 92; Perm to Offic *B & W* from 92. *Dragons, Lambrook Road, Shepton Beauchamp, Ilminster TA19 0NA* Tel (01460) 240967

JONES, Wilfred Lovell. b 39. Lon Univ BD71 Cam Univ CertEd. St D Coll Lamp. **d** 63 **p** 64. C Llanllyfni *Ban* 63-65; C Llanbeblig w Caernarfon 65-68; V Llanwnog w Penstrowed 68-73; V Llanwnnog and Caersws w Carno 73-75; Asst Chapl Dover Coll 77-90; Chapl Wrekin Coll Telford 91-94; V Llangollen w Trevor and Llantysilio *St As* 94-04; AD Llangollen 03-04; rtd 04. *7 Beech Hollows, Lavister, Rossett LL12 0DA* E-mail vicar@stcollen.freeserve.co.uk

JONES, Canon William. b 30. Univ of Wales (Ban) DipTh54. St Mich Coll Llan 54 BTh92. **d** 55 **p** 56. C Denio w Abererch *Ban* 55-60; V Aberdaron and Bodferin 60-66; R Llandwrog 66-71; R Llanstumdwy, Llangybi w Llanarmon 71-74; R Dolbenmaen w Llanystymdwy w Llangybi etc 74-99; RD Eifionydd 75-99; Can Ban Cathl 84-93; Can and Treas Ban Cathl 93-99; rtd 99; Perm to Offic *Ban* from 99. *Y Fachwen, Rhoshirwaun, Pwllheli LL53 8LB* Tel (01758) 760262

JONES, Canon William David. b 28. St D Coll Lamp BA48 Lon Univ BD57 Leeds Univ MA73. St Mich Coll Llan 48. **d** 51 **p** 52. C Risca *Mon* 51-54; C Chepstow St Arvan's w Penterry 54-55; C St Geo-in-the-East w Ch Ch w St Jo *Lon* 55-59; C Farnham Royal *Ox* 59-64; Lect Div Culham Coll 65-67; Hd of Relig Studies Doncaster Coll of Educn 67-74; Lic to Offic *Sheff* 67-74; Vice-Prin St Bede Coll Dur 74; Vice-Prin SS Hild and Bede Coll Dur 75-89; Lect Th Dur Univ 75-89; Lic to Offic *Dur* 80-85; Dir of Miss Ch in Wales 89-93; Metropolitical and Hon Can St D Cathl *St D* 90-93; rtd 93; Perm to Offic *Glouc* from 93. *Hatfield Cottage, 14 Bath Road, Tetbury GL8 8EF* Tel (01666) 504050 E-mail wdjones@talk21.com

JONES, William Douglas. b 28. St Fran Coll Brisbane ThL56. **d** 56 **p** 58. Australia 56-58; Papua New Guinea 58-72; C Manston *Ripon* 72-75; V Middleton St Mary 75-87; V Ireland Wood 87-94; rtd 94; Perm to Offic *Ripon* from 94. *6 Willow Court, Pool in Wharfedale, Otley LS21 1RX* Tel 0113-284 2028

JONES, William Edward Benjamin. b 19. TCD BA43 MA53. TCD Div Sch Div Test44. **d** 44 **p** 45. C Belfast St Thos *Conn* 44-47; C Sudbury St Andr *Lon* 47-50; CF 50-54; V Edmonton St Pet w St Martin *Lon* 54-59; V N Wembley St Cuth 59-81; V Ripley *Guildf* 81-87; Chapl HM Pris Send 81-87; rtd 87; Perm to Offic *Nor* from 87. *37 Bircham Road, Reepham, Norwich NR10 4NG* Tel (01603) 870738

JONES, William John. b 59. St Mich Coll Llan Dip Minl Studies 93. **d** 93 **p** 94. C Pembroke Dock w Cosheston w Nash and Upton *St D* 93-96; C Tenby 96; TV 96-99; V Llanrhian w Llanhywel and Carnhedryn etc 99-00; rtd 00. *13 George Street, Milford Haven SA73 2AY* Tel (01646) 697094

JONES, William Lincoln. b 19. St D Coll Lamp BA41 St Mich Coll Llan 41. **d** 43 **p** 44. C Roath *Llan* 43-47; C Wooburn *Ox* 47-50; C Bridgwater w Chilton *B & W* 50-55; V Langford Budville w Runnington 55-60; V Winscombe 60-71; V Bishops Lydeard 71-73; V Bishops Lydeard w Cothelstone 73-80; P-in-c Bagborough 78-80; R Bishops Lydeard w Bagborough and Cothelstone 80-84; rtd 84; Perm to Offic *Ex* from 86. *Holme Lea, Well Mead, Kilmington, Axminster EX13 7SQ* Tel (01297) 32744

JONES, Mrs Wyn. **d** 01 **p** 02. OLM Linslade *Ox* from 01. *2 Woodside Way, Linslade, Leighton Buzzard LU7 7PN* Tel (01525) 373638

JONES, Wyn. *See* JONES, Ivor Wyn

JONES-BLACKETT, Enid Olive. b 40. Reading Univ BA61. LNSM course 95. **d** 97 **p** 98. OLM Hellesdon *Nor* from 97. *8 Fastolf Close, Hellesdon, Norwich NR6 5RE* Tel (01603) 414895

JONES-CRABTREE, Stephen. b 56. Nottm Univ BTh80. Linc Th Coll 76. **d** 80 **p** 81. C Chorley St Pet *Blackb* 80-83; C Blackpool St Steph 83-84; C Penwortham St Mary 84-88; R Mareham-le-Fen and Revesby *Linc* 88-02; R Hameringham w Scrafield and Winceby 98-02; V Mareham on the Hill 98-02; R Washingborough w Heighington and Canwick from 02. *The Rectory, Church Hill, Washingborough, Lincoln LN4 1EJ* Tel (01522) 800240 E-mail stephen.jones-crabtree@ukonline.co.uk

JONGMAN, Kären Anngel Irene. b 43. EMMTC 97. **d** 01 **p** 02. NSM Northampton St Mary *Pet* 01-03; NSM Guilsborough w Hollowell and Cold Ashby 03-04; P-in-c Walgrave w Hannington and Wold and Scaldwell from 04; Chapl Northants Fire and Rescue Service from 03. *The Rectory, Lower Green, Walgrave, Northampton NN6 9QF* Tel (01604) 781974 Mobile 07980-881252 E-mail jongman@nccnet.co.uk

JORDAN, Anne. b 42. RGN66 DipN77. Dioc OLM tr scheme 00. **d** 02 **p** 03. OLM Crofton *Wakef* from 02. *95 Ashdene Avenue, Crofton, Wakefield WF4 1LY* Tel (01924) 865527 Mobile 07450-475184

JORDAN, Anthony John. b 50. Birm Univ BEd73. LNSM course. **d** 83 **p** 84. Asst Chapl Uppingham Sch 83-86; Hon C Uppingham w Ayston and Wardley w Belton *Pet* 83-86; Asst Chapl Sherborne Sch 86-87; NSM Bournemouth St Fran *Win* 88-03. *Address temp unknown* E-mail anthonyjordan1@aol.com

JORDAN, Darryl Mark. b 62. Univ of Texas at Dallas BSc85 S Methodist Univ Dallas MDiv05. Perkins Sch of Th (USA) 01. **d** 04 **p** 04. C Dallas Ch Ch USA 04-05; C Bishop's Stortford St Mich *St Alb* from 05. *Cowell House, 24 Apton Road, Bishop's Stortford CM23 3SN* Tel (01279) 654414 E-mail darryljordan@btinternet.com

JORDAN, Mrs Elizabeth Ann. b 58. New Hall Cam MA82. St Jo Coll Nottm DipTh84. **d** 87 **p** 94. Par Dn Blackpool St Jo *Blackb* 87-90; Par Dn Ewood 90-94; C 94-95; Asst Dir of Ords 90-95; Min Shelfield St Mark CD *Lich* 95-00; Local Min Adv (Wolverhampton) from 95; OLM Course Ldr and Team Ldr Min Division from 03. *17 Blackberry Lane, Shire Oak, Walsall WS9 9RQ* Tel (01543) 820352 E-mail elizabeth.jordan@lichfield.anglican.org

JORDAN, John Charles. b 37. CQSW81. N Ord Course 84. **d** 87 **p** 88. C Southport Em *Liv* 87-90; V Abram and Bickershaw 90-95; V Bempton w Flamborough, Reighton w Speeton *York* 95-00; rtd 01; Perm to Offic *York* from 05. *35 Hollycroft, Barnston, Driffield YO25 8PP* Tel (01262) 468925 E-mail john@jordan55.freeserve.co.uk

JORDAN, Kenneth John. b 31. K Coll Lon. **d** 69 **p** 70. Guyana 69-74; C Roath *Llan* 74-76; V Nantymoel w Wyndham 76-81; V Cardiff St Mary w St Steph 81-83; V Cardiff St Mary and St Steph w St Dyfrig etc 83-01; Miss to Seafarers 83-01; rtd 01. *45 Kimberley Road, Cardiff CF23 5DL*

JORDAN, Miss Pamela Mary. b 43. Univ of Wales (Cardiff) BSc64 Ox Univ DipEd65. WEMTC 02. **d** 05. NSM Coalbrookdale, Iron-Bridge and Lt Wenlock *Heref* from 05. *2 Madeley Wood View, Madeley, Telford TF7 5TF* Tel (01952) 583254

JORDAN, Patrick Glen. b 69. SEITE 01. **d** 04. C Charlton *S'wark* from 04. *73 Elliscombe Road, London SE7 7PF* Tel (020) 8858 4336 *or* 8769 3256

JORDAN, Peter Harry. b 42. Leeds Univ BA64. Cranmer Hall Dur 70. **d** 73 **p** 74. C Nottingham St Ann w Em *S'well* 73-77; C Edgware *Lon* 77-82; V Everton St Chrys *Liv* 82-94; Dioc Ev and V Bootle St Mary w St Paul 94-02; Chapl Barcelona *Eur* from 02. *St George's Church, C/ Horacio 38, 08022 Barcelona, Spain* Tel (0034) (93) 417 8867 E-mail stgeorges@wanadoo.es

JORDAN, Richard William. b 56. Lanchester Poly BSc78. St Jo Coll Nottm DipTh84 St Jo Coll Nottm DPS87. **d** 87 **p** 88. C Blackpool St Jo *Blackb* 87-90; V Ewood 90-95; Perm to Offic *Lich* 95-97; Co-ord Walsall Town Cen Min from 97; Asst Min Walsall St Paul from 97. *17 Blackberry Lane, Walsall Wood, Walsall WS9 9RQ* Tel (01922) 614159 Mobile 07773-340207 E-mail richard@church-links.org.uk *or* wbcclp@beep.net

JORDAN, Robert Brian. b 43. Qu Coll Birm 68. **d** 69 **p** 70. C Norton St Mich *Dur* 69-73; C Hastings St Clem and All SS *Chich* 73-74; C Carshalton *S'wark* 74-81; V Catford St Andr from 81. *The Vicarage, 135 Wellmeadow Road, London SE6 1HP* Tel (020) 8697 2600

JORDAN, Ronald Henry. b 30. K Coll Lon. **d** 57 **p** 58. C Clerkenwell H Redeemer w St Phil *Lon* 57-58; C Southgate Ch Ch 58-59; C Edmonton St Mary w St Jo 62-69; Hon C 86-94; V Wood Green St Mich 69-73; Hon C Finchley H Trin 80-86; Perm to Offic from 94; rtd 95. *120 Church Lane, London N2 0TB* Tel (020) 8883 7828

JORDAN, Thomas. b 36. Man Univ DSPT91. NW Ord Course 76. **d** 79 **p** 80. NSM Prenton *Ches* 79-84; NSM Egremont St Jo 84-91; C 91-96; Ind Chapl 91-96; TV Birkenhead Priory 96-01; rtd 01; Perm to Offic *Ches* from 02. *31 Willowbank Road, Birkenhead CH42 7JU* Tel 0151-652 4212 E-mail jordan@farndene.freeserve.co.uk

JORDAN, Trevor. b 44. Lon Hosp MB, BS67 LRCP68 MRCS68. St Jo Coll Nottm MA99. **d** 03 **p** 04. NSM Seamer *York* from 03. *The Vicarage, 3 Stockshill, Seamer, Scarborough YO12 4QG* Tel (01723) 863102 Mobile 07887-537244 E-mail trevor@trevorsweb.net

JORDINSON, Vera (Sister Hilary). b 37. Liv Univ BA60 CertEd61. Westcott Ho Cam 88. **d** 89 **p** 94. CSF from 74; Prov Sec 90-01; Gen Sec 96-02; Sec for Miss SSF 96-99; Gift Aid Sec from 01; Lic to Offic *Heref* 89-92; Perm to Offic *Lich* 90-92; *Birm* 92-94 and from 97; NSM Birchfield *Birm* 94-96. *St Francis House, 113 Gillott Road, Birmingham B16 0ET* Tel 0121-454 8302 Fax 455 9784 E-mail hilcsf@fish.co.uk

JORYSZ, Ian Herbert. b 62. Van Mildert Coll Dur BSc84 MA95 Liv Univ PhD87. Ripon Coll Cuddesdon BA89 MA95. **d** 90 **p** 91. C Houghton le Spring *Dur* 90-93; C Ferryhill 93-95; Research Officer to Bp of Bradwell from 95; P-in-c S Weald *Chelmsf* 95-00; V from 00. *The Vicarage, Wigley Bush Lane, South Weald, Brentwood CM14 5QP* Tel (01277) 212054 Fax 262388 E-mail ian@jorysz.com

JOSS, Martin James Torquil. b 60. Univ of Wales (Lamp) BA79. EAMTC 03. **d** 03 **p** 04. C Harlow Town Cen w Lt Parndon *Chelmsf* from 03. *92 Ram Gorse, Harlow CM20 1PZ* Tel (01279) 863074 Mobile 07816-042476 E-mail martin@thejosses.co.uk

JOUSTRA, Jan Tjeerd. b 57. Univ of Tasmania BA83 La Trobe Univ Vic MA97. Melbourne Coll of Div BTh91. **d** 89 **p** 91. Australia 89-97; C Melbourne E 90-91; C Wangaratta Cathl 91-93; R Rutherglen w Chiltern 93-97; P-in-c St Steph Chpl Hong Kong 97-03; Sen Chapl St Jo Cathl 00-03; Chapl Monte Carlo *Eur* from 04. *22 avenue de Grande-Bretagne, MC 98000 Monte Carlo, Monaco* Tel (00377) 9330 7106 Fax 9330 5039 E-mail stpauls@monaco.mc

JOWETT, Ms Hilary Anne. b 54. Hull Univ BA75. Cranmer Hall Dur IDC80. **dss** 82 **d** 87 **p** 94. Sheff St Jo *Sheff* 80-83; Brampton Bierlow 83-87; Par Dn 87-89; Hon Par Dn Sharrow St Andr 89-95; Chapl Nether Edge Hosp Sheff 89-95; C Sheff St Mark Broomhill *Sheff* 95-97; C Mosbrough 97-00; TR Gleadless from 00. *The Rectory, 243 Hollinsend Road, Sheffield S12 2EE* Tel 0114-239 0757 E-mail hjowett@fish.co.uk

JOWETT, Nicholas Peter Alfred. b 44. St Cath Coll Cam BA66 MA Bris Univ CertEd67. Qu Coll Birm 72. **d** 75 **p** 76. C Wales *Sheff* 75-78; TV Sheff Manor 78-83; V Brampton Bierlow 83-89; V Psalter Lane St Andr from 89; Dioc Ecum Adv from 01. *The Rectory, 243 Hollinsend Road, Sheffield S12 2EE* Tel 0114-239 0757 *or* 258 6550 E-mail njowett@fish.co.uk

JOWITT, Andrew Robert Benson. b 56. Down Coll Cam BA78 PGCE79 MA81. Wycliffe Hall Ox 88. **d** 90 **p** 91. C Northampton Em *Pet* 90-94; C Barking St Marg w St Patr *Chelmsf* 94-98; TV 98-00; TV Stantonbury and Willen *Ox* from 00; Bp's Officer for Evang from 00. *Church House, 1A Atterbrook, Bradwell, Milton Keynes MK13 9EY* Tel (01908) 320850

JOWITT, David Arthur Benson. b 25. St Jo Coll Ox BA49 MA53. Sarum Th Coll 49. **d** 51 **p** 52. C Heckmondwike *Wakef* 51-56; C Harrogate St Wilfrid *Ripon* 56-59; V Kirkby Fleetham 60-69; R Langton on Swale 60-69; OGS from 65; Superior 75-81; P-in-c Edin St Ninian *Edin* 69-77; Dioc Supernumerary 77-80; Chapl Edin R Infirmary 77-80; Syn Clerk *Edin* 77-90; Can St Mary's Cathl 77-90; Vice-Provost 81-86; P-in-c S Queensferry 86-90; rtd 90; Hon C Edin Old St Paul *Edin* 91-99; Perm to Offic *S'wark* from 01. *16 The Quadrangle, Morden College, 19 St German's Place, London SE3 0PW* Tel (020) 8305 0811

JOWITT, John Frederick Benson. b 23. Oak Hill Th Coll 57. **d** 59 **p** 59. Uganda 59-63; CF 63-73; R Thrandeston, Stuston and Brome w Oakley *St E* 73-82; V Docking *Nor* 82-83; P-in-c Gt Bircham 82-83; R Docking w the Birchams 83-88; P-in-c Stanhoe w Barwick 85-88; R Docking w The Birchams and Stanhoe w Barwick 88; rtd 88; Perm to Offic *Nor* from 88 and *St E* from 90. *White Lodge, The Street, North Cove, Beccles NR34 7PN* Tel (01502) 476404

JOY, Bernard David. b 50. Sarum & Wells Th Coll 90. **d** 92 **p** 93. C Shortlands *Roch* 92-94; C Henbury *Bris* 94-96; V Bristol St Aid w St Geo 96-03; P-in-c Bridgwater St Fran *B & W* from 03. *The Vicarage, Saxon Green, Bridgwater TA6 4JA* Tel (01278) 422744 Mobile 07796-678478 E-mail rev.obejoyful@btopenworld.com

JOY, Canon Matthew Osmund Clifton. b 40. St Edm Hall Ox BA62 MA66. St Steph Ho Ox 62. **d** 64 **p** 65. C Brinksway *Ches* 64-66; C Southwick St Columba *Dur* 66-69; V Hartlepool H Trin 69-85; V Rotherham St Paul, St Mich and St Jo Ferham Park *Sheff* 85-88; V Masbrough 88-95; RD Rotherham 88-93; P-in-c Bordesley St Benedict *Birm* 95-01; V 01-05; Bp's Adv on Chr/Muslim Relns 95-05; rtd 05. *Lindisfarne, Eddyfield Road, Oxspring, Sheffield S36 8YH* Tel (01226) 762276 E-mail matthewjoy@fish.co.uk

JOYCE, Alison Jane. b 59. Univ of Wales (Swansea) BA81 Bris Univ MLitt87 Birm Univ PhD00 SS Coll Cam PGCE84. Ripon Coll Cuddesdon BA87 MA94. **d** 88 **p** 94. Par Dn Chalgrove w Berrick Salome *Ox* 88-90; Tutor WMMTC 90-95; Tutor Qu Coll Birm 95-96; NSM Moseley St Anne *Birm* 96-05; NSM Birm Cathl from 05; Dean NSMs 00-03. *88 Willows Road, Balsall Heath, Birmingham B12 9QD* Tel 0121-440 5171 E-mail ajjoyce@grinners.demon.co.uk

JOYCE, Anthony Owen. b 35. Selw Coll Cam BA60 MA64. Wycliffe Hall Ox 60. **d** 62 **p** 63. C Birm St Martin *Birm* 62-67; Rhodesia 67-70; V Birm St Luke *Birm* 70-79; V Downend *Bris* 79-01; RD Stapleton 83-89; rtd 01; Perm to Offic *Bris* from 02. *116 Jellicoe Avenue, Stapleton, Bristol BS16 1WJ* Tel 0117-956 2510 E-mail tony@joycet.freeserve.co.uk

JOYCE, Ernest Thomas Chancellor. b 16. Lon Univ LLB67. Chich Th Coll 68. **d** 70 **p** 71. C Southsea H Spirit *Portsm* 70-75; V New Southgate St Paul *Lon* 75-77; Chantry P Chpl St Mich and H So Walsingham 77-81; Perm to Offic *Nor* 77-04; rtd 81. *St Benedict, 16 Cleaves Drive, Walsingham NR22 6EQ* Tel (01328) 820612

JOYCE, Gordon Franklin. b 51. Birm Univ BA72. St Jo Coll Nottm 86. **d** 88 **p** 89. C Didsbury St Jas and Em *Man* 88-92; V Tonge w Alkrington from 92. *St Michael's Vicarage, 184 Kirkway, Middleton, Manchester M24 1LN* Tel 0161-643 2891

JOYCE, Graham Leslie. b 49. Lon Univ CertEd71. Trin Coll Bris DipHE89. **d** 89 **p** 90. C Heald Green St Cath *Ches* 89-93; R Church Lawton from 93. *The Rectory, 1 Liverpool Road West, Church Lawton, Stoke-on-Trent ST7 3DE* Tel (01270) 882103 Fax as telephone E-mail grahamljoyce@aol.com

JOYCE, John Barnabas Altham. b 47. St Chad's Coll Dur BA69 Lon Univ DipEd86. St Steph Ho Ox 72. **d** 74 **p** 75. C Reading St Giles *Ox* 74-77; C Cowley St Jo 77-80; Dioc Youth and Community Officer 80-87; V Hangleton *Chich* 87-94; Dioc Adv for Schs and Dir Educn 94-99; R Hurstpierpoint from 99. *The Rectory, 21 Cuckfield Road, Hurstpierpoint, Hassocks BN6 9RP* Tel (01273) 832203 E-mail rectorhurst@aol.com

JOYCE, Kingsley Reginald. b 49. MBE00 TD91. Man Univ BSc70. Cuddesdon Coll 70. **d** 73 **p** 74. C High Wycombe *Ox* 73-76; C Fingest 76-79; C Hambleden 76-79; C Medmenham 76-79; C Fawley (Bucks) 76-79; C Turville 76-79; P-in-c Hambleden Valley 79-80; R 80-87; R Friern Barnet St Jas *Lon* 87-91; CF from 91. *c/o MOD Chaplains (Army)* Tel (01980) 615804 Fax 615800

JOYCE, Margaret. b 47. Oak Hill NSM Course 86. **d** 89 **p** 94. NSM Chadwell Heath *Chelmsf* 89-92; NSM Bath Odd Down w Combe Hay *B & W* from 92; Chapl Bath and West Community NHS Trust from 95. *69 Bloomfield Rise, Bath BA2 2BN* Tel (01225) 840864 E-mail margaretjoyce@stphilipstjames.org

JOYCE, Canon Norman. b 14. St Jo Coll Dur BA35 MA38 DipTh38. **d** 37 **p** 38. C Monkwearmouth All SS *Dur* 37-40; C W Hartlepool St Paul 40-43; V Monkwearmouth All SS 43-53; R Bowness *Carl* 53-57; R N Wingfield *Derby* 57-73; TR N Wingfield, Pilsley and Tupton 73-80; Hon Can Derby Cathl 77-80; rtd 80; Perm to Offic *Carl* from 80. *c/o I S Sutcliffe Esq, Mulcaster House, Brampton Road, Carlisle CA3 9AN* Tel (01228) 526314

JOYCE, Paul David. b 70. Qu Coll Birm 00. **d** 02 **p** 03. C Perry Beeches *Birm* 02-05; V Eastwood St Dav *Chelmsf* from 05. *St David's Vicarage, 400 Rayleigh Road, Leigh-on-Sea SS9 5PT* Tel (01702) 523126 E-mail joycefamily400@btinternet.com

JOYCE, Miss Penelope Anne. b 53. St Mary's Coll Chelt CertEd74. Wycliffe Hall Ox. **d** 00 **p** 01. C Ox St Clem *Ox* 00-03; C Cogges and S Leigh from 03. *Discovery, 7 Barleyfield Way, Witney OX28 1AA* Tel 07808-181885 (mobile) E-mail pennyre.joyce@virgin.net

JOYCE, Philip Rupert. b 38. Selw Coll Cam BA68 MA72. Cranmer Hall Dur 68. **d** 70 **p** 71. C Newland St Jo *York* 70-73; C Woolwich St Mary w H Trin *S'wark* 73-77; Chapl Thames Poly 73-77; Chapl S Bank Poly 77-79; rtd 03. *49 Ashton Gardens, Chadwell Heath, Romford RM6 6RT* Tel (020) 8491 5427 E-mail philipjoyce@ntlworld.com

JOYCE, Raymond. b 37. Keele Univ BA60 MA67 Linc Coll Ox BA62 MA68 Leic Univ MA97. St Steph Ho Ox 78. **d** 80 **p** 81. NSM Normanton *Derby* 80-83; NSM Derby St Alkmund and St Werburgh 83-87; Lic to Offic 87-97; NSM Mickleover All SS 97-00; Perm to Offic from 01. *23 Hindscarth Crescent, Mickleover, Derby DE3 9NN* Tel (01332) 519001

JOYCE, Sister. *See* CROSSLAND, Sister Joyce

JOYCE, Canon Terence Alan. b 57. St Jo Coll Nottm BTh84. **d** 84 **p** 85. C Mansfield SS Pet and Paul *S'well* 84-88; V Greasley 88-00; Dioc Dir of Ords from 99; Dir Post-Ord Support and Tr from 01; Hon Can S'well Minster from 02. *86 Main Road, Ravenshead, Nottingham NG15 9GW* Tel (01623) 489819 E-mail tjoyce@southwell.anglican.org

JUBA, Bishop of. *See* MARONA, The Most Revd Joseph Biringi Hassan

JUCKES, Jonathan Sydney. b 61. St Andr Univ MA83. Ridley Hall Cam BA87. **d** 88 **p** 89. C Sevenoaks St Nic *Roch* 88-92; Proclamation Trust 92-95; C St Helen Bishopsgate w St Andr Undershaft etc *Lon* 95-98; TR Kirk Ella and Willerby *York* from 98. *The Rectory, 2 School Lane, Kirk Ella, Hull HU10 7NR* Tel (01482) 653040 E-mail juckes@juckes.karoo.co.uk

JUDD, Adrian Timothy. b 67. Lanc Univ BA88. Cranmer Hall Dur BA92 Trin Coll Singapore 92 St Jo Coll Dur Dip Minl Studies 93. **d** 93 **p** 94. C Dudley St Aug Holly Hall *Worc* 93-97; V Stockbridge Village *Liv* 97-99; V Went Valley *Wakef* from 00. *The Vicarage, Marlpit Lane, Darrington, Pontefract WF8 3AB* Tel (01977) 704744

JUDD, Colin Ivor. b 35. Dur Univ BA61. Ridley Hall Cam 61. **d** 63 **p** 64. C Stratford St Jo w Ch Ch *Chelmsf* 63-66; C

Kimberworth *Sheff* 66-68; Area Sec CMS *Bradf* and *Wakef* 68-80; V Bradf St Columba w St Andr *Bradf* 80-00; rtd 00; Perm to Offic *Bradf* from 01. *57 Grosvenor Road, Shipley BD18 4RB* Tel (01274) 584775

JUDD, Mrs Nicola Jane. b 51. Birm Coll of Educn CertEd72. S Dios Minl Tr Scheme 87. **d** 90 **p** 94. NSM Abbotts Ann and Upper and Goodworth Clatford *Win* from 90; Adv for NSM from 01. *13 Belmont Close, Andover SP10 2DE* Tel (01264) 363364 E-mail nicola.judd@ukonline.co.uk

JUDD, The Very Revd Peter Somerset Margesson. b 49. Trin Hall Cam BA71. Cuddesdon Coll 71. **d** 74 **p** 75. C Salford St Phil w St Steph *Man* 74-76; Chapl Clare Coll Cam 76-81; C Burnham *Ox* 81-82; TV Burnham w Dropmore, Hitcham and Taplow 82-88; V Iffley 88-97; RD Cowley 94-97; Provost Chelmsf 97-00; Dean Chelmsf from 00. *The Deanery, 3 Harlings Grove, Chelmsford CM1 1YQ* Tel (01245) 354318 *or* 294480 E-mail dean@chelmsfordcathedral.org.uk

JUDGE, Andrew Duncan. b 50. Cape Town Univ BCom72 Keble Coll Ox MA81. Pietermaritzburg Th Sem 82. **d** 83 **p** 84. S Africa 83-01; C Westville 84-87; R Prestbury 88-94; R Westville 94-01; TV Keynsham *B & W* from 01. *St Francis's Vicarage, Warwick Road, Keynsham, Bristol BS31 2PW* Tel 0117-373 7478 E-mail revjudge@blueyonder.co.uk

JUDGE, Mark Rollo. b 60. Chich Th Coll BTh92. **d** 92 **p** 93. C Forest Gate St Edm *Chelmsf* 92-96; V Gt Ilford St Luke 96-01; Asst Chapl Barking Havering and Redbridge Hosps NHS Trust from 01. *Harold Wood Hospital, Gubbins Lane, Harold Wood, Romford RM3 0BE* Tel (01708) 345533 *or* 746090 ext 2633 E-mail markjudge_new.uk@excite.co.uk

JUDSON, Mrs Mary Ruth. b 47. Bretton Hall Coll DipEd68. NEOC 89. **d** 92 **p** 94. Par Dn Chester le Street *Dur* 92-94; C 94-96; V Millfield St Mark and Pallion St Luke 96-04; V Hartlepool St Luke from 04. *St Luke's Vicarage, 5 Tunstall Avenue, Hartlepool TS26 8NF* Tel (01429) 272893 E-mail mary.judson@durham.anglican.org

JUDSON, Paul Wesley. b 46. Leic Poly DipAD69 ATD71. Cranmer Hall Dur 87. **d** 89 **p** 90. C Lobley Hill *Dur* 89-92; C Chester le Street 92-96; Ed Dioc Publications and Sec Dioc Bd of Soc Resp 96-98; C Millfield St Mark and Pallion St Luke 96-04; C Hartlepool St Luke from 04; Dioc Publications Officer from 98; Dioc Dir of Communications from 02. *St Luke's Vicarage, 5 Tunstall Avenue, Hartlepool TS26 8NF* Tel (01429) 272893 E-mail director.of.communications@durham.anglican.org

JUDSON, Peter. b 39. Lon Univ BSc61 Plymouth Univ PGCE87. SW Minl Tr Course 99. **d** 02 **p** 03. OLM Bude Haven and Marhamchurch *Truro* from 02. *Meadowcroft, Bagbury Road, Bude EX23 8QJ* Tel and fax (01288) 356597 Mobile 07970-115538

JUKES, Keith Michael. b 54. Leeds Univ BA76. Linc Th Coll 77. **d** 78 **p** 79. C Wordsley *Lich* 78-81; C Wolverhampton 81-83; C-in-c Stoneydelph St Martin CD 83-90; TR Glascote and Stonydelph 90-91; RD Tamworth 90-91; TR Cannock 91-97; V Hatherton 91-97; Preb Lich Cathl 96-97; P-in-c Selby Abbey *York* 97-99; V from 99. *The Abbey Vicarage, 32A Leeds Road, Selby YO8 4HX* Tel (01757) 709218 *or* 703123 E-mail kmjukes@aol.com

JUKES (née WEATHERHOGG), Mrs Susanne. b 56. Leeds Univ BA77 Coll of Ripon & York St Jo PGCE78. NEOC 98. **d** 01 **p** 02. C Monk Fryston and S Milford *York* 01-05; P-in-c from 05. *The Rectory, Main Street, Hillam, Leeds LS25 5HH* Tel (01977) 682357 Mobile 07764-375430 E-mail susanne_jukes@hotmail.com

JUMP, Elizabeth Anne. b 63. Liv Inst of Educn BA95. N Ord Course 97. **d** 00 **p** 01. C Walkden and Lt Hulton *Man* 00-03; P-in-c Elton St Steph 03-05; C Ashton Ch Ch from 05. *St Peter's Vicarage, Chester Square, Ashton under Lyne OL7 0LB* Tel 0161-343 3770 E-mail revlizjump@hotmail.com

JUNG, Mrs Jennifer Margaret. b 61. STETS 95. **d** 98 **p** 99. NSM Fareham H Trin *Portsm* 98-02. *Address temp unknown*

JUPE, Canon Derek Robert. b 26. TCD BA53 Div Test54 MA67. **d** 54 **p** 55. C Lurgan Ch the Redeemer *D & D* 54-57; C Dublin Harold's Cross *D & G* 57-60; I Easkey w Kilglass *T, K & A* 60-65; Deputation Sec (Ireland) BCMS 65-72; R Man St Jerome w Ardwick St Silas *Man* 72-78; V Ardsley *Sheff* 78-83; I Tempo and Clabby *Clogh* 83-92; Can Clogh Cathl 89-92; rtd 92; Perm to Offic *Cov* 92-05. *4 Leithen Mills, Innerleithen EH44 6JJ* Tel (01896) 831701

JUPE, Martin Roy. b 27. Lon Univ BD63. St Deiniol's Hawarden. **d** 61 **p** 62. C Camborne *Truro* 61-64; V Penzance St Jo 64-92; RD Penwith 73-76; rtd 92; Perm to Offic *Truro* from 92. *25 Nancherrow Terrace, St Just, Penzance TR19 7LA* Tel (01736) 788320

✠**JUPP, The Rt Revd Roger Alan.** b 56. St Edm Hall Ox BA78 MA82 Surrey Univ PGCE96. Chich Th Coll 79. **d** 80 **p** 81 **c** 03. C Newbold w Dunston *Derby* 80-83; C Cowley St Jo *Ox* 83-85; C Islington St Jas w St Phil *Lon* 85-86; V Lower Beeding *Chich* 86-90; Dom Chapl to Bp Horsham 86-91; V Burgess Hill St Jo 90-93; TR Burgess Hill St Jo w St Edw 93-94; Perm to Offic 97-98; C Aldwick 98-00; Prin Newton Th Coll Papua New Guinea 00-03; Bp Popondota 03-05; P-in-c St Leonards Ch Ch and St Mary *Chich* from 05; Hon Asst Bp Chich from 05. *Christ Church Rectory, 3 Silchester Road, St Leonards-on-Sea TN38 0JB* Tel (01424) 444052 E-mail rajupp1@hotmail.com

JUPP, Vincent John. b 64. Leic Poly BTEC HNC87. St Jo Coll Nottm Dip Th & Min 00. **d** 00 **p** 01. C Evington *Leic* 00-03; TV Ascension TM from 03. *Christ Church Vicarage, 73 Nursery Road, Leicester LE5 2HQ* Tel 0116-241 3848 E-mail vjupp@leicester.anglican.org

JUSTICE, Keith Leonard. b 42. Wolv Univ BSc68 CEng83 MIMechE83. Wycliffe Hall Ox 91. **d** 93 **p** 94. C Penwortham St Mary *Blackb* 93-96; C Dovercourt and Parkeston w Harwich *Chelmsf* 96-98; V Wentworth *Sheff* 98-01; Chapl Rotherham Gen Hosps NHS Trust 98-01; Chapl Rotherham Priority Health Services NHS Trust 98-01; R Melrose *Edin* 01-04; P-in-c Royton St Anne *Man* from 04. *St Anne's Vicarage, St Anne's Avenue, Royton, Oldham OL2 5AD* Tel and fax 0161-624 2249 E-mail keith.justice@ntlworld.com

JUSTICE, Peter John Michael. b 37. Bernard Gilpin Soc Dur 59 Chich Th Coll 60. **d** 63 **p** 64. C Digswell *St Alb* 63-67; C Guildf St Nic *Guildf* 67-68; C Mill End *St Alb* 68-70; V Eaton Bray 70-73; Hon C Prestwood *Ox* 73-84; Chapl to the Deaf 84-90; rtd 90; Perm to Offic *Ox* 90-93; *Ex* 94-95; *St E* from 95. *8 Theatre Street, Woodbridge IP12 4NE* Tel (01394) 380899

JUSTICE, Simon Charles. b 66. Univ of Wales (Lamp) BD88 Edin Univ MTh90. Cranmer Hall Dur 90. **d** 92 **p** 93. C Tilehurst St Mich *Ox* 92-95; USA 95-04; R Troy St Paul 95-98; R Tigard St Jas 01-04; Can All SS Cathl Albany 98-04; R Edin Ch Ch *Edin* from 04. *4 Morningside Road, Edinburgh EH10 4DD* Tel 0131-229 6556 E-mail justicemm@aol.com *or* rector@6a.org.uk

JUTSUM, Linda Mary. *See* ELLIOTT, Mrs Linda Mary

K

KABOLEH, David Reardon. b 64. Westmr Coll Ox MTh00. Trin Coll Nairobi 88. **d** 90 **p** 91. Kenya 90-95; C-in-c Nairobi St Phil 90-92; TV Nairobi St Luke and Immanuel 93-95; Hon C Hoddesdon *St Alb* 95-97; Hon C Ox St Matt *Ox* 97-99; Hon C Blackbird Leys 99-02; NSM Ox St Aldate 03-04; NSM Akeman from 04. *The Rectory, Troy Lane, Kirtlington, Kidlington OX5 3HA* Tel and fax (01869) 350224 E-mail kaboleh@aol.com

✠**KAFITY, The Rt Revd Samir.** b 33. Beirut Univ BA57. Near E Sch of Th 57. **d** 57 **p** 58 **c** 86. Israel 57-64 and 77-98; Lebanon 64-77; Adn Jerusalem 77-82; Bp Jerusalem 84-98; Pres Bp Episc Ch Jerusalem and Middle E 86-96; rtd 98. *11964 Callado Road, San Diego, CA 92128, USA*

KAGGWA, Nelson Sonny. b 58. E Lon Univ BA91. Bible Tr Inst Tennessee DipTh84 Bp Tucker Coll Mukono 77. **d** 80 **p** 80. Kenya 80-83; USA 83; Hon C Ox SS Phil and Jas w St Marg *Ox* 84-85; C W Ham *Chelmsf* 86-87; TV Walthamstow St Mary w St Steph 87-92; Perm to Offic *Sheff* 92-95; V Sheff St Paul 96-97; rtd 98. *Al-Salam, 36 Standish Gardens, Sheffield S5 8YD* Tel 0114-273 1428 Mobile 07989-261278 Fax 0114-273 1348 E-mail kaggwanelsonibrahim@msn.com

KAJUMBA, The Ven Daniel Steven Kimbugwe. b 52. S'wark Ord Course. **d** 85 **p** 86. C Goldington *St Alb* 85-87; Uganda 87-99; TV Horley *S'wark* 99-01; Adn Reigate from 01. *84 Higher Drive, Purley CR8 2HJ* Tel (020) 8660 9276 E-mail daniel@kajumba.freeserve.co.uk

KALUS, Rupert. b 61. St Jo Coll Dur BA85 MA93 BA01 W Sussex Inst of HE PGCE87. Cranmer Hall Dur 99. **d** 02 **p** 03. C Dur St Cuth *Dur* 02; C Dur N from 02. *112 Moor Crescent, Durham DH1 1DL* Tel 0191-386 3644

KAMBLE, Anupama. b 76. Pune Univ India BSc97. Qu Coll Birm BD03. **d** 02 **p** 04. Perm to Offic *Nor* 03; C Birm St Martin w Bordesley St Andr *Birm* from 04. *4 Woodrough Drive, Birmingham B13 9EP* Tel 0121-449 5950 Mobile 07787-920905 E-mail revdanupama@hotmail.com

KAMEGERI, Stephen. *See* NSHIMYE, Stephen Kamegeri

KAMPALA, Bishop of. *See* OROMBI, The Most Revd Henry Luke

KANERIA, Rajni. b 57. Bath Univ BPharm82. Wycliffe Hall Ox 83. **d** 86 **p** 87. C Hyson Green *S'well* 86-87; C Hyson Green St Paul w St Steph 87-89; C Harold Hill St Geo *Chelmsf* 89-91; TV Oadby *Leic* 91-97. *32 Rendall Road, Leicester LE4 6LE* Tel 0116-266 6613

KARAMURA, Grace Patrick. b 62. Nat Teachers' Coll Uganda DipEd89 Rob Coll Cam MPhil95 Leeds Univ PhD98. Bp Tucker Coll Mukono BD92. **d** 92 **p** 93. C All SS Cathl Kampala Uganda 92-93; C Ebbw Vale *Mon* 98-01; TV 01-03; V Pontyclun w Talygarn *Llan* from 03. *The Vicarage, Heol Miskin, Pontyclun CF72 9AJ* Tel (01443) 225477 Fax as telephone E-mail gracekaramu@hotmail.com

KARRACH, Herbert Adolf. b 24. TCD BA46 MB48 BCh48 BAO48 LSHTM DTM&H55. EAMTC 85. **d** 88 **p** 89. Hon C Snettisham w Ingoldisthorpe and Fring *Nor* 88-95; Perm to Offic from 95. *Narnia, 5 Docking Road, Fring, King's Lynn PE31 6SQ* Tel (01485) 518346

KASHOURIS, Peter Zacharias. b 66. Peterho Cam BA89 MA93. St Steph Ho Ox 92. **d** 94 **p** 95. C Hampstead St Jo *Lon* 94-97; R Hartlepool St Hilda *Dur* 97-03; P-in-c Dur St Oswald from 03; Dioc Ecum Officer from 03. *St Mary's Vicarage, 89 Front Street, Sherburn, Durham DH6 1HD* Tel 0191-372 0374 E-mail p.j.kashouris@durham.anglican.org

KASIBANTE, Amos Sebadduka. b 54. Trin Coll Cam BA83 MA87 Yale Univ STM89. Bp Tucker Coll Mukono DipTh80 Berkeley Div Sch 88. **d** 79 **p** 80. Uganda 79-92; C Lyantonde 79-80; Tutor Bp Tucker Coll Mukono 83-92; Tutor Coll of Ascension Selly Oak 93-95; Prin Simon of Cyrene Th Inst 95-97; Vice-Prin St Mich Coll Llan 97-02; Chapl Leic Univ *Leic* from 02. *290 Victoria Park Road, Leicester LE2 1XE* Tel 0116-270 1900 Fax 255 6318 E-mail amos.kasibante@virgin.net *or* ask11@le.ac.uk

KASOZI NSAMBA, Jackson. b 50. Bp Tucker Coll Mukono BD91 Birm Univ MPhil94 All Nations Chr Coll MA00. **d** 83 **p** 84. Uganda 84-92 and 96-99; V St Andr Cathl Mityana 84-88; Adn 86-88; Chapl to Bp W Buganda 91-92; Perm to Offic *Cov* 93-94; Adn W Buganda 95-98; Acting Dean St Paul's Cathl 98-99; NSM Limehouse *Lon* 00-02; NSM Old Ford St Paul and St Mark 02-03; C Harold Hill St Geo *Chelmsf* from 04. *18 Petersfield Avenue, Romford RM3 9PA* Tel (01708) 374388 Mobile 07743-011220

KASSELL, Colin George Henry. b 42. DCC90. Valladolid Spain 63 Ripon Coll Cuddesdon 76. **d** 68 **p** 69. In RC Ch 69-75; Perm to Offic *Ox* 76-77; C Denham 77-80; V Brotherton *Wakef* 80-84; Chapl and Past Ldr St Cath Hospice Crawley 84-91; R Rogate w Terwick and Trotton w Chithurst *Chich* 91-94; C Heene from 94; Chapl Worthing Hosp from 94. *Park House, 3 Madeira Avenue, Worthing BN11 2AT* Tel (01903) 526571 Mobile 07802-259310

KATE, Sister. *See* BURGESS, Kate Lamorna

KAUNHOVEN, Anthony Peter. b 55. Leeds Univ BA78 Coll of Ripon & York St Jo PGCE79 Edin Univ DipMin80. Edin Th Coll 79. **d** 81 **p** 82. C Leeds St Aid *Ripon* 81-84; C Hawksworth Wood 84-89; V Upper Nidderdale 89-91; Hon C Rawdon *Bradf* 96-99; P-in-c Old Brampton *Derby* from 99; P-in-c Gt Barlow from 04; Dioc Ecum Officer from 01. *The Rectory, 25 Oldridge Close, Chesterfield S40 4UF* Tel (01246) 558112 E-mail jazzyrector@aol.com

KAVANAGH, Michael Lowther. b 58. York Univ BA80 Newc Univ MSc82 Leeds Univ BA86 MBPsS90. Coll of Resurr Mirfield 84. **d** 87 **p** 88. C Boston Spa *York* 87-91; V Beverley St Nic 91-97; RD Beverley 95-97; Abp's Dom Chapl from 97; Dioc Dir of Ords from 97; Chapl HM Pris Full Sutton from 05. *The Chaplaincy, HM Prison Full Sutton, York YO41 1PS* Tel (01759) 475100

KAY, Dennis. b 57. St As Minl Tr Course 96. **d** 99 **p** 00. NSM Llangystennin *St As* 99-03; NSM Llanelian w Trofarth from 04. *3 Ty Ucha, Abergele Road, Llanddulas, Abergele LL22 8EN*

KAY, George Ronald. b 24. Sarum & Wells Th Coll 74. **d** 77 **p** 78. NSM Bemerton *Sarum* 77-87; rtd 87; Perm to Offic *Sarum* 89-00. *The Lodge, 157 Wilton Road, Salisbury SP2 7JH* Tel (01722) 338326

KAY, Ian Geoffrey. N Ord Course. **d** 89 **p** 90. NSM Rochdale *Man* 89-91 and from 95; NSM Heywood St Luke w All So 91-95. *161 Norden Road, Rochdale OL11 5PT* Tel (01706) 639497

KAY, Marjory Marianne Kate. b 61. **d** 97. NSM Godshill *Portsm* from 97. *3 Wootton Lodge, Church Road, Wootton Bridge, Ryde PO33 4PU*

KAY, Ronald William. b 28. Liv Univ BEng49 MEng51. Tyndale Hall Bris 59. **d** 61 **p** 62. C Sparkbrook Ch Ch *Birm* 61-65; V Westcombe Park St Geo *S'wark* 65-76; V Skellingthorpe *Linc* 76-78; R Doddington 76-78; R Skellingthorpe w Doddington 78-91; rtd 91; Perm to Offic *Linc* 91-00. *18 Abingdon Avenue, Lincoln LN6 3LE* Tel (01522) 696275

KAYE, Alistair Geoffrey. b 62. Reading Univ BSc85. St Jo Coll Nottm DPS90 Dip Th Studies 90. **d** 90 **p** 91. C Gt Horton *Bradf* 90-94; C Rushden w Newton Bromswold *Pet* 94-98; V Upper Armley *Ripon* from 98; Asst AD Armley from 02. *22 Hill End Crescent, Leeds LS12 3PW* Tel 0113-263 8788 Mobile 07881-804104 E-mail alistair@armley.freeserve.co.uk

KAYE, Bruce Norman. b 39. Lon Univ BD64 Sydney Univ BA66 Basel Univ DrTheol75. Moore Th Coll Sydney ThL64. **d** 64 **p** 65. Australia 64-66 and from 83; Perm to Offic *Dur* 67-69; Tutor St Jo Coll Dur 68-75; Sen Tutor 75-83; Vice Prin 79-83; rtd 04. *217 Hopetown Avenue, Watsons Bay, NSW, Australia 2030* Tel (0061) (2) 9337 6795

KAYE, Canon Gerald Trevor. b 32. Man Univ BSc54. Oak Hill Th Coll. **d** 56 **p** 57. C Widnes St Ambrose *Liv* 56-58; C St Helens St Mark 58-62; V Brixton Hill St Sav *S'wark* 62-65; Canada 65-85; Hon Can Keewatin 70-75; Adn Patricia 75-78; V Slough *Ox* 85-97; rtd 97. *Craiguanach, Torlundy, Fort William PH33 6SW* Tel (01397) 705395

KAYE, Peter Alan. b 47. K Coll Lon BD71 AKC71 Birm Univ DPS80 Leic Univ MA82 CQSW82. St Aug Coll Cant 71. **d** 72 **p** 73. C Fulham All SS *Lon* 72-74; Chapl Jo Conolly Hosp Birm 74-80; Rubery Hill and Jos Sheldon Hosps 74-80; Hon C Northfield *Birm* 80-83; Perm to Offic from 00. *Hildegarden, 99 Bunbury Road, Northfield, Birmingham B31 2ND* Tel 0121-624 8399 E-mail peter@alankaye.totalserve.co.uk

KAYE, Timothy Henry. b 52. Linc Th Coll 77. **d** 80 **p** 81. C Warsop *S'well* 80-83; C Far Headingley St Chad *Ripon* 83-86; P-in-c Birkby *Wakef* 86; TV N Huddersfield 86-91; R Stone St Mich w Aston St Sav *Lich* 91-95; V S Kirkby *Wakef* from 95. *The Vicarage, Bull Lane, South Kirkby, Pontefract WF9 3QD* Tel and fax (01977) 642795 E-mail mail@kaye5.fsworld.co.uk

KAYE-BESLEY, Mrs Lesley Kathleen. b 47. Cam Inst of Educn CertEd69 Kingston Univ MA94 FRSA85. **d** 04 **p** 05. OLM Walton-on-Thames *Guildf* from 04. *Minggay, 1 Park Road, Esher KT10 8NP* Tel (01372) 465185

KAZIRO, Godfrey Sam. b 48. BDSc Lon Univ MSc FDSRCPSGlas FFDRCSI. **d** 02 **p** 03. OLM Waterloo St Jo w St Andr *S'wark* from 02. *19 Hampshire Road, Hornchurch RM11 3EU* Tel (01708) 441609

KEARLEY-HEYWOOD, Deiniol John Owen. b 73. K Coll Lon BA95 Peterho Cam MPhil03. Westcott Ho Cam 02. **d** 04 **p** 05. C Paddington St Jo w St Mich *Lon* from 04. *23 Archery Close, London W2 2BE* Tel (020) 7706 4984 E-mail deiniol@postmaster.co.uk

KEARNEY, Mrs Sandra. b 55. Bolton Inst of HE BSc89 Univ Coll Ches BTh04. N Ord Course 01. **d** 04 **p** 05. C Blackpool Ch Ch w All SS *Blackb* from 04. *122 Park Road, Blackpool FY1 4ES* Tel (01253) 626313

KEARNS, Mrs Mary Leah. b 38. **d** 87 **p** 94. Par Dn Morden *S'wark* 87-88; Asst Chapl HM Pris Holloway 88-98; rtd 99; Perm to Offic *Guildf* from 01. *48 The Orchard, North Holmwood, Dorking RH5 4JT* Tel (01306) 886858

KEARNS, Philip Gillin. b 59. Ripon Coll Cuddesdon 90. **d** 92 **p** 93. C Winchmore Hill St Paul *Lon* 92-97; V N Shoebury *Chelmsf* 97-02; TR Wickford and Runwell from 02. *The Rectory, 120 Southend Road, Wickford SS11 8EB* Tel (01268) 733147 Mobile 07747-826066 E-mail philip@pkearns.fsnet.co.uk

KEARON, Canon Kenneth Arthur. b 53. TCD BA76 MA79 MPhil91. CITC 78. **d** 81 **p** 82. C Raheny w Coolock *D & G* 81-84; Lect TCD 82-90; Dean of Res TCD 84-90; I Tullow *D & G* 91-99; Can Ch Ch Cathl Dublin from 95; Dir Irish Sch Ecum 99-05; Sec Gen ACC from 05. *Anglican Communion Office, 16 Tavistock Crescent, London W11 1AX* Tel (020) 7313 3900 Fax 7313 3999

KEARTON, Janet Elizabeth. b 54. Univ Coll Lon BSc78 Birkbeck Coll Lon MSc81. NEOC 01. **d** 04 **p** 05. C Richmond w Hudswell *Ripon* 04-05; C Richmond w Hudswell and Downholme and Marske from 05. *1 Wathcote Place, Richmond DL10 7SR* Tel (01748) 826260 E-mail sewmadly01@btinternet.com

KEAST, William. b 43. Univ Coll Ox BA65 DipEd66. LNSM course 86. **d** 88 **p** 89. OLM Scotton w Northorpe *Linc* from 88. *4 Crapple Lane, Scotton, Gainsborough DN21 3QT* Tel (01724) 763190 E-mail wkeast@hotmail.com

KEATING, Christopher Robin. b 39. K Coll Lon BD AKC84. Sarum Th Coll 62. **d** 65 **p** 66. C Baildon *Bradf* 65-67; CF 67-72; V Thornton Heath St Paul *Cant* 72-79; C Harold Hill St Geo *Chelmsf* 85-89; V Goodmayes All SS from 89. *All Saints' Vicarage, Broomhill Road, Ilford IG3 9SJ* Tel (020) 8590 1476

KEATING, Geoffrey John. b 52. Liv Poly HND79 Open Univ BA94. St Steph Ho Ox 81. **d** 84 **p** 85. C Lancaster Ch Ch w St Jo and St Anne *Blackb* 84-85; C Rotherham *Sheff* 85-87; C Mexborough 87; V Bentley 87-91; V Penponds *Truro* 91-96; V Pet St Jude *Pet* from 96. *St Jude's Vicarage, 49 Atherstone Avenue, Peterborough PE3 9TZ* Tel (01733) 264169 *or* 268816 Fax as telephone E-mail geoffkeatg@aol.com

KEAY, Alfred David. b 26. Aston Univ MSc72. Qu Coll Birm 76. **d** 79 **p** 80. Hon C Penkridge w Stretton *Lich* 79-82; C Rugeley 82-85; V Cheswardine 85-95; V Hales 85-95; rtd 95. *2 The Coppice, Farcroft Gardens, Market Drayton TF9 3UA* Tel (01630) 657924

KEAY, Charles Edward. b 70. Glos Univ BA94. St Steph Ho Ox 01. **d** 03 **p** 04. C Havant *Portsm* from 03. *1 Churchfields, South Street, Havant PO9 1BY* Tel (023) 9247 0817

KEDDIE, Canon Tony. b 37. Qu Coll Birm 63. **d** 66 **p** 67. C Barnoldswick w Bracewell *Bradf* 66-69; C New Bentley *Sheff* 69-71; TV Seacroft *Ripon* 71-79; V Kippax 79-85; TR Kippax w Allerton Bywater 85-92; R Fountains Gp 92-02; Hon Can Ripon

Cathl 94-02; rtd 02. *2 Westcroft, Station Road, Otley LS21 3HX* Tel (01943) 464146 E-mail keddie@fish.co.uk

KEEBLE, Dorothy Deborah. b 20. **d** 87. NSM Glas H Cross *Glas* from 87. *12 Housel Avenue, Glasgow G13 3UR* Tel 0141-959 3102

KEEBLE, Stephen Robert. b 56. K Coll Lon BD84 AKC84 MA98 Selw Coll Cam DipTh86. Westcott Ho Cam 85. **d** 87 **p** 88. C Lt Stanmore St Lawr *Lon* 87-90; C Headstone St Geo 90-93; P-in-c 93-98; V from 98. *St George's Vicarage, 96 Pinner View, Harrow HA1 4RJ* Tel and fax (020) 8427 1253 E-mail megpointer@supanet.com

KEECH, Canon April Irene. b 52. Penn State Univ BA76. Trin Coll Bris BA89. **d** 89 **p** 92. C Walthamstow St Luke *Chelmsf* 89-92; USA 92-95; V Deptford St Jo w H Trin *S'wark* 95-02; Asst Dioc Dir of Ords 96-00; Hon Can S'wark Cathl from 99; V Hoxton St Jo w Ch Ch *Lon* from 02. *St John's Vicarage, Crondall Street, London N1 6PT* Tel (020) 7739 9823 *or* 7739 9302 E-mail akeech@fish.co.uk

KEEGAN, Donald Leslie. b 37. ACII. CITC 65. **d** 68 **p** 69. C Drumragh w Mountfield *D & R* 68-72; I Birr w Lorrha, Dorrha and Lockeen *L & K* 72-02; Can Killaloe Cathl 80-82; Treas Killaloe Cathl 82-87; Prec Limerick and Killaloe Cathls 87-89; Adn Killaloe, Kilfenora, Clonfert etc 89-02; rtd 02. *279 Redford Park, Greystones, Co Wicklow, Irish Republic* Tel (00353) (1) 201 7259 E-mail donkee@eircom.net

KEEGAN, Frances Ann (Sister Isabel). b 44. SEN74. Franciscan Study Cen 87. **d** 99 **p** 00. NSM Sherborne w Castleton and Lillington *Sarum* 99-01; NSM Golden Cap Team from 01. *The Vicarage, 5 Georges Close, Charmouth, Bridport DT6 6RU* Tel (01297) 560409

KEEGAN, Graham Brownell. b 40. Nottm Univ CertEd68. N Ord Course 81. **d** 84 **p** 85. C Highfield *Liv* 84-87; V Ince St Mary 87-95; V Newton in Makerfield St Pet 95-05; rtd 05. *5 Scott Road, Lowton, Warrington WA3 2HD* Tel (01942) 713809

KEELER, Alan. b 58. City Univ BSc81. St Jo Coll Nottm MA01. **d** 90 **p** 91. C Paddock Wood *Roch* 90-94; V Blendon from 94. *The Vicarage, 37 Bladindon Drive, Bexley DA5 3BS* Tel (020) 8301 5387 E-mail agkeeler@talk21.com

KEELEY, John Robin. b 38. G&C Coll Cam BA62. Clifton Th Coll 62. **d** 64 **p** 65. C Onslow Square St Paul *Lon* 64-66; C Hove Bp Hannington Memorial Ch *Chich* 66-69; C Harborne Heath *Birm* 69-72; V Leic H Trin *Leic* 72-74; V Leic H Trin w St Jo 74-80; Perm to Offic *St Alb* 81-86; NSM Carterton *Ox* 89-95; Tutor EAMTC *Ely* 95-99; TV Bishopsnympton, Rose Ash, Mariansleigh etc *Ex* 99-03; RD S Molton 01-03; rtd 03. *Lamb Cottage, 11 Townsend, Little Downham, Ely CB6 2TA* Tel (01769) 550551 E-mail rkeeley@spck.co.uk

KEELEY, Keith Morgan. b 12. Man Univ BA33 MA36. **d** 49 **p** 50. C Shipley St Paul *Bradf* 49-52; C Gt Barr *Lich* 52-53; C Blakenall Heath 53-55; V Tipton St Jo 55-59; R Hinstock 59-64; rtd 77. *22A Kingsley Avenue, Whitley Bay NE25 8RX*

KEELING, Peter Frank. b 34. Kelham Th Coll. **d** 58 **p** 59. C S Elmsall *Wakef* 58-63; C Barnsley St Mary 63-67; V Ravensthorpe 67-73; V Cudworth 73-83; R Downham Market w Bexwell *Ely* 83-00; RD Fincham 83-94; V Crimplesham w Stradsett 85-00; rtd 00; P-in-c Hempton and Pudding Norton *Nor* 00-04; Perm to Offic from 04. *23 Cleaves Drive, Walsingham NR22 6EQ* Tel (01328) 820310

KEEN, David Mark. b 69. Oriel Coll Ox BA91. St Jo Coll Nottm BTh96 MPhil98. **d** 98 **p** 99. C Yeovil w Kingston Pitney *B & W* 98-02; C Haughton le Skerne *Dur* from 02. *57 Rivergarth, Darlington DL1 3SJ* Tel (01325) 243381 E-mail david.keen@ukonline.co.uk

KEEN, Michael Spencer. b 41. St Pet Coll Ox BA68 MA72 GRSM62 ARCM Reading Univ CertEd. Westcott Ho Cam 68. **d** 73 **p** 74. NSM W Derby St Jo *Liv* 73-74; NSM Stanley 74-76; Chs Youth and Community Officer Telford *Lich* 77-82; Dioc Unemployment Officer *Sheff* 82-89; NSM Brixton Road Ch Ch *S'wark* 89-92; Employment Development Officer 89-92; Perm to Offic 92-99; NSM Camberwell St Giles w St Matt 99-01. *12 Grovelands Close, London SE5 8JN* Tel (020) 7787 6872

KEEN, Miriam Frances. b 65. Ex Univ BSc87 Westmr Coll of Educn PGCE89. Wycliffe Hall Ox 03. **d** 05. C Cogges and S Leigh *Ox* from 05. *17 Meadow View, Witney OX28 3TY* Tel (01993) 773844 E-mail miri@coggesparish.com

KEENAN, Leslie Herbert (Bertie). b 32. Cranmer Hall Dur. **d** 66 **p** 67. C Anston *Sheff* 66-70; C Woodsetts 66-70; Chapl HM Borstal Pollington 70-78; V Balne *Sheff* 70-78; V Poughill *Truro* 78-99; rtd 99; Perm to Offic *Chich* from 01. *177 Lyndhurst Road, Worthing BN11 2DG* Tel (01903) 200387

KEENE, Canon David Peter. b 32. Trin Hall Cam BA56 MA60. Westcott Ho Cam. **d** 58 **p** 59. C Radcliffe-on-Trent *S'well* 58-61; C Mansfield SS Pet and Paul 61-64; V Nottingham St Cath 64-71; R Bingham 71-81; Dioc Dir of Ords 81-90; Can Res S'well Minster 81-97; rtd 97; Perm to Offic *S'well* from 02. *Averham Cottage, Church Lane, Averham, Newark NG23 5RB* Tel (01636) 708601 E-mail keene@averham.fsnet.co.uk

KEENE, Mrs Muriel Ada. b 35. **dss** 83 **d** 87 **p** 94. Dioc Lay Min Adv *S'well* 87-88; Asst Dir of Ords 88-90; Dn-in-c Oxton 90-93; Dn-in-c Epperstone 90-94; Dn-in-c Gonalston 90-94; NSM Lowdham w Caythorpe, and Gunthorpe 94-00; rtd 95; Perm to Offic *S'well* from 05. *Averham Cottage, Church Lane, Averham, Newark NG23 5RB* Tel (01636) 708601

KEEP, Andrew James. b 55. Collingwood Coll Dur BA77 Yale Univ STM84. Sarum & Wells Th Coll 78. **d** 80 **p** 81. C Banstead *Guildf* 80-83; Chapl Qu Eliz Hosp Banstead 80-83; USA 83-84; Chapl Cranleigh Sch Surrey 84-98; Chapl Wells Cathl Sch from 98; PV Wells Cathl *B & W* from 01. *18 Vicars Close, Wells BA5 2UJ* Tel (01749) 834207 E-mail andrew.keep@lineone.net

KEEP, Hugh Charles John Martin. b 45. Qu Coll Birm 90. **d** 92 **p** 93. C Aston Cantlow and Wilmcote w Billesley *Cov* 92-95; P-in-c Hampton Lucy w Charlecote and Loxley 95-02; Chapl Rainsbrook Secure Tr Cen from 02. *4 Old Town, Stratford-upon-Avon CV37 6BG* Tel (01789) 414142 E-mail hrkeepnet@aol.com

KEETON, Barry. b 40. Dur Univ BA61 MA69 MLitt78 K Coll Lon BD63 AKC63. **d** 64 **p** 65. C S Bank *York* 64-67; C Middlesbrough St Cuth 67-69; C Kingston upon Hull St Alb 70-71; V Appleton-le-Street w Amotherby 71-74; Dioc Ecum Adv 74-81; R Ampleforth w Oswaldkirk 74-78; V Howden 78-79; P-in-c Barmby on the Marsh 78-79; P-in-c Laxton w Blacktoft 78-79; P-in-c Wressell 78-79; TR Howden 80-91; Can and Preb York Minster 85-91; RD Howden 86-91; TR Lewes All SS, St Anne, St Mich and St Thos *Chich* 91-96; R Cov St Jo *Cov* 96-01; RD Cov N 97-01; rtd 01; Perm to Offic *Sheff* from 01 and *York* from 05. *19 Shardlow Gardens, Bessacarr, Doncaster DN4 6UB* Tel (01302) 532045 E-mail barry.k3@ukonline.co.uk

KEFFORD, Canon Peter Charles. b 44. Nottm Univ BTh74. Linc Th Coll 70. **d** 74 **p** 75. C W Wimbledon Ch Ch *S'wark* 74-77; C All Hallows by the Tower etc *Lon* 77-81; C-in-c Pound Hill CD *Chich* 81; TV Worth 82-83; TR 83-92; V Henfield w Shermanbury and Woodmancote 92-01; Can Res and Treas Chich Cathl from 01; Adv for Ord Min and Dioc Dir of Ords from 01. *12 St Martin's Square, Chichester PO19 1NR* Tel (01243) 783509 E-mail peter_kefford@hotmail.com

KEGG, Mrs Georgina. b 47. Oak Hill Th Coll BA99. EAMTC 02. **d** 05. NSM Mattishall w Mattishall Burgh, Welborne etc *Nor* from 05. *The Vicarage, Back Lane, Mattishall, Dereham NR20 3PU* Tel (01362) 850243

KEGG, Gordon Rutherford. b 45. Reading Univ BSc66 Imp Coll Lon PhD71 DIC71 Lon Univ CertEd74. Oak Hill Th Coll DipHE90. **d** 90 **p** 91. C Luton Lewsey St Hugh *St Alb* 90-94; TV Hemel Hempstead 94-01; P-in-c Mattishall w Mattishall Burgh, Welborne etc *Nor* from 01; P-in-c Hockering, Honingham, E and N Tuddenham from 04. *The Vicarage, Back Lane, Mattishall, Dereham NR20 3PU* Tel (01362) 850243

KEIGHLEY, Andrew Kenneth. b 62. Nottm Univ LLB84 Solicitor 85. Wycliffe Hall Ox 94. **d** 97 **p** 98. C Westminster St Jas the Less *Lon* 97-00; NSM 00-04; C Brompton H Trin w Onslow Square St Paul from 04. *90 Abercrombie Street, London SW11 2JD* Tel and fax (020) 7924 5951 Mobile 07747-611577 E-mail andy.keighley@htb.org.uk

KEIGHLEY, David John. b 48. CertEd Open Univ BA88. Sarum & Wells Th Coll 82. **d** 83 **p** 84. C Sawbridgeworth *St Alb* 83-86; TV Saltash *Truro* 86-89; V Lanlivery w Luxulyan 89-00; P-in-c The Candover Valley *Win* from 00; P-in-c Wield from 03. *The Rectory, Alresford Road, Preston Candover, Basingstoke RG25 2EE* Tel and fax (01256) 389245 Mobile 07736-799262 E-mail davidkeighley@hotmail.com

KEIGHLEY, Martin Philip. b 61. Edin Univ MA83. Westcott Ho Cam 86. **d** 88 **p** 89. C Lytham St Cuth *Blackb* 88-91; C Lancaster St Mary 91-93; R Halton w Aughton 93-00; V Poulton-le-Fylde 00-04; V Poulton Carleton and Singleton from 04. *The Vicarage, 7 Vicarage Road, Poulton-le-Fylde FY6 7BE* Tel (01253) 883086 E-mail martinkeighley@btconnect.com

KEIGHLEY, Thomas Christopher. b 51. DipN81 Open Univ BA85. NEOC 00. **d** 03 **p** 04. NSM Upper Nidderdale *Ripon* from 03. *The Old Chapel, Middlesmoor, Harrogate HG3 5ST* Tel and fax (01423) 755344 Mobile 07740-721032 E-mail nurprc@nursing.u-net.com

KEIGHTLEY, Canon Peter Edward. b 17. Leeds Univ BA41. Coll of Resurr Mirfield 41. **d** 43 **p** 44. C Wellingborough All Hallows *Pet* 43-45; C Solihull *Birm* 45-49; C Cirencester *Glouc* 50-53; V Glouc St Paul 53-59; V Widley w Wymering *Portsm* 59-67; V Southsea H Spirit 67-76; Chapl St Mary's Hosp Portsm 76-82; Hon Can Portsm Cathl *Portsm* 81-82; rtd 82; Perm to Offic *Portsm* from 83. *11 Dolphin Court, St Helen's Parade, Southsea PO4 0QL* Tel (023) 9281 6697

KEIGHTLEY, Canon Thomas. b 44. CITC 79. **d** 79 **p** 80. C Seagoe *D & D* 79-83; I Belvoir from 83; Can Down Cathl from 95; Treas 00-01; Prec from 01. *The Rectory, 86B Beechill Road, Belfast BT8 6QN* Tel (028) 9064 3777 *or* 9049 1436

KEIGHTLEY, Trevor Charles. b 54. St Jo Coll Nottm. **d** 03 **p** 04. C Wombwell *Sheff* from 03. *202 Summer Lane, Wombwell, Barnsley S73 8QH* Tel (01226) 211102 E-mail trevorkeightley@aol.com

KEILLER, Canon Jane Elizabeth. b 52. Westmr Coll Ox BEd74. Cranmer Hall Dur 76. **dss** 80 **d** 87 **p** 94. Cambridge H Trin w

St Andr Gt *Ely* 80-86; NSM Cambridge St Barn 86-88 and 90-94; NSM Cambridge H Cross 95-02; Chapl and Tutor Ridley Hall Cam from 96; Hon Can Ely Cathl *Ely* from 05. *68 Pierce Lane, Cambridge CB1 5DL* Tel (01223) 575776 *or* tel and fax 741076 E-mail jk271@cam.ac.uk

KEIR, Mrs Gillian Irene. b 44. Westf Coll Lon BA66 Somerville Coll Ox BLitt70 Lon Univ MA95. St Alb and Ox Min Course 95. **d** 98 **p** 99. NSM St Alb St Steph *St Alb* from 98. *17 Battlefield Road, St Albans AL1 4DA* Tel (01727) 839392

KEIRLE, Michael Robert. b 62. Trin Coll Bris BA89. **d** 89 **p** 90. C Orpington Ch Ch *Roch* 89-92; Zimbabwe 92-95; R Keston *Roch* 95-03; R Guernsey St Martin *Win* from 03. *St Martin's Rectory, La Grande Rue, St Martin, Guernsey GY4 6RR* Tel (01481) 238303 Fax 237710 E-mail mrkeirle@cwgsy.net

KEITH, Andrew James Buchanan. b 47. Qu Coll Cam BA69 MA73. Wycliffe Hall Ox 71. **d** 74 **p** 75. C Warrington St Elphin *Liv* 74-77; C Southgate *Chich* 77-80; C-in-c Broadfield CD 80-82; P-in-c Walberton w Binsted 82-85; P-in-c Aldingbourne 83-85; Chapl Oswestry Sch 85-95; Chapl HM Pris Liv 95-96; Chapl HM Pris Preston 96-01; Chapl HM Pris Garth from 01. *HM Prison Garth, Ulnes Walton Lane, Leyland PR26 8NE* Tel (01772) 622722 E-mail andrewandjudi@keith20.freeserve.co.uk

KEITH, Gary Mark Wayne. b 71. Ripon Coll Cuddesdon 01. **d** 03 **p** 04. C Botley *Portsm* from 03; C Curdridge from 03; C Durley from 03; Chapl RNR from 05. *1 Rectory Court, Botley, Southampton SO30 2SJ* Tel (01489) 787715 Mobile 07971-448049 E-mail gazzaloulou@tiscali.co.uk

KEITH, John. b 25. LRAM50 LGSM50 AGSM51. Cuddesdon Coll 60. **d** 62 **p** 63. C Lee-on-the-Solent *Portsm* 62-65; C Raynes Park St Sav *S'wark* 65-68; rtd 90. *7 Torr An Eas, Glenfinnan PH37 4LS* Tel (01397) 722314

KELHAM, Adèle. b 46. St Andr Univ BSc69. Cranmer Hall Dur. **d** 98 **p** 99. Asst Chapl Zürich *Eur* 98-01; P-in-c Bishop Middleham *Dur* 01-05; AD Sedgefield 03-05; P-in-c Lausanne *Eur* from 05. *Rue des Terreaux 13, 1003 Lausanne, Switzerland*

KELK, Michael Anthony. b 48. Sarum & Wells Th Coll. **d** 83 **p** 84. C Ross w Brampton Abbotts, Bridstow and Peterstow *Heref* 83-86; P-in-c Burghill 86-97; P-in-c Stretton Sugwas 86-97; P-in-c Walford and St John w Bishopswood, Goodrich etc 97-02; P-in-c Llangarron w Llangrove, Whitchurch and Ganarew from 02. *The Vicarage, Llangrove, Ross-on-Wye HR9 6EZ* Tel (01989) 770341 E-mail tonykelk@fish.co.uk

KELLAND, Kenneth William Jerome. b 16. S'wark Ord Course 63. **d** 66 **p** 67. C Addlestone *Guildf* 66-69; C Sholing *Win* 69-74; V Weston 74-82; rtd 82; Hon C Odiham w S Warnborough and Long Sutton *Win* 82-85; Hon C Herriard w Winslade and Long Sutton etc 85-86. *50 Wooteys Way, Alton GU34 2JZ* Tel (01420) 85325

KELLEHER, Mrs Cheryl. b 56. Sheff Univ BA97. N Ord Course 98. **d** 01 **p** 02. NSM Worsbrough *Sheff* from 01. *10 Fieldsend, Oxspring, Sheffield S36 8WH* Tel (01226) 763236

KELLEN, David. b 52. Univ of Wales (Cardiff) DipTh73. St Mich Coll Llan 70. **d** 75 **p** 76. C Mynyddislwyn *Mon* 75-77; C Risca 77-78; C Malpas 78-81; V Newport All SS 81-88; V St Mellons from 88; R Michaelston-y-Fedw 89-96. *The Vicarage, Ty'r Winch Road, St Mellons, Cardiff CF3 5UP* Tel (029) 2079 6560

KELLETT, Garth. *See* KELLETT, Ronald Garth

KELLETT, Neil. b 41. Bps' Coll Cheshunt 64. **d** 66 **p** 67. C Ex St Thos *Ex* 66-72; C Win H Trin *Win* 72-74; P-in-c Redditch St Geo *Worc* 74-77; Canada from 77. *39 Fox Avenue, St John's NF, Canada, A1B 2H8* Tel (001) (709) 726 2883

KELLETT, Richard. b 64. Leeds Univ BSc85 PhD89. St Jo Coll Nottm BTh95 MA96. **d** 96 **p** 97. C Nottingham St Jude *S'well* 96-00; P-in-c Skegby 00-02; P-in-c Teversal 00-02; R Skegby w Teversal from 02. *The Vicarage, Mansfield Road, Skegby, Sutton-in-Ashfield NG17 3ED* Tel and fax (01623) 558800 E-mail richard@kellett.com

KELLETT, Ronald Garth. b 41. N Ord Course 04. **d** 05. NSM Ilkley St Marg *Bradf* from 05. *2 Westville Avenue, Ilkley LS29 9AH* Tel (01943) 601906 E-mail garthandmaggie@gmkellett.freeserve.co.uk

KELLEY, Neil George. b 64. ARCM85 DipRCM87. Westcott Ho Cam 88. **d** 91 **p** 92. C E Bedfont *Lon* 91-93; C Chiswick St Nic w St Mary 93-97; C Kirkby *Liv* 97-99; V Gt Crosby St Faith and Waterloo Park St Mary from 99. *The Vicarage, Milton Road, Waterloo, Liverpool L22 4RE* Tel and fax 0151-928 3342 Mobile 07980-872203 E-mail frneilkelley@tiscali.co.uk

KELLY, Canon Albert Norman. b 21. TCD BA43 MA63. **d** 44 **p** 45. C Donaghcloney *D & D* 44-46; C Belfast Malone St Jo *Conn* 46-55; I Billy 55-63; C Dorking w Ranmore *Guildf* 63-66; C-in-c New Haw CD 66-72; V New Haw 72-78; RD Chertsey 73-75; RD Runnymede 75-78; V Egham Hythe 78-86; Hon Can Guildf Cathl 80-86; rtd 86; USPG Area Sec 88-93. *21 Rosetta Road, Belfast BT6 0LQ* Tel (028) 9069 3921 E-mail knorman@fish.co.uk

KELLY, Brian Eugene. b 56. Otago Univ BA77 Dunedin Coll PGCE79 Bris Univ PhD93. Trin Coll Bris BA89. **d** 90 **p** 91. NSM Redland *Bris* 90-93; C Scarborough St Mary w Ch Ch and H Apostles *York* 93-96; Dean Chpl Cant Ch Ch Univ Coll 96-03. *2 Riverside Close, Bridge, Canterbury CT4 5BN* E-mail bek1@cant.ac.uk

KELLY, Canon Brian Horace. b 34. St Jo Coll Dur BA57 MA69 DipTh58. **d** 58 **p** 59. C Douglas St Geo and St Barn *S & M* 58-61; V Foxdale 61-64; V Bolton All So w St Jas *Man* 64-73; V Maughold *S & M* 73-77; Dir of Ords 76-93; V German from 77; Can and Prec St German's Cathl from 80; RD Castletown and Peel 97-04. *The Cathedral Vicarage, Albany Road, Peel, Isle of Man IM5 1JS* Tel (01624) 842608

KELLY, Christopher Augustine (Kit). b 15. 45 TD65. Keble Coll Ox BA37. Ripon Hall Ox 37. **d** 45 **p** 46. C Aston SS Pet and Paul *Birm* 45-51; V Habergham Eaves H Trin *Blackb* 51-57; V Knuzden 57-67; V Bolton Breightmet St Jas *Man* 67-76; V Nelson in Lt Marsden *Blackb* 76-83; rtd 83; Perm to Offic *Bradf* from 83. *Steeton Court Nursing Home, Steeton Hall Gardens, Steeton, Keighley BD20 6SW* Tel (01535) 656124

KELLY, Canon Dennis Charles. b 31. Liv Univ BA52. Lich Th Coll 54. **d** 56 **p** 57. C Tranmere St Paul *Ches* 56-59; C-in-c Grange St Andr CD 59-63; P-in-c Grange St Andr 63-65; V 65-67; R Coppenhall 67-82; V W Kirby St Andr 82-01; Hon Can Ches Cathl 86-01; rtd 01; Perm to Offic *Ches* from 01. *26 Lyndhurst Road, Hoylake, Wirral CH47 7BP* Tel 0151-632 0335

KELLY, Desmond Norman. b 42. Oak Hill Th Coll DipHE90. **d** 90 **p** 91. C Braintree *Chelmsf* 90-94; P-in-c Castle Hedingham 94-95; P-in-c Sible Hedingham 94-95; R Sible Hedingham w Castle Hedingham from 95. *The Vicarage, Queen Street, Castle Hedingham, Halstead CO9 3EZ* Tel (01787) 460274 E-mail des.kelly@virgin.net

KELLY, Canon Edward William Moncrieff. b 28. AKC57. **d** 57 **p** 58. C Petersfield w Sheet *Portsm* 57-60; Papua New Guinea 60-65; Dioc Sec Samarai and Hon Chapl Miss to Seamen 61; V Gosport Ch Ch *Portsm* 65-69; Hon C Eltham St Jo *S'wark* 69-87; Org Sec New Guinea Miss 69-77; Org Sec Papua New Guinea Ch Partnership 77-87; Hon Can Papua New Guinea from 78; TR Trowbridge H Trin *Sarum* 87-94; Chapl St Jo Hosp Trowbridge 87-94; Acting RD Bradford 91-92; rtd 94; Perm to Offic *Portsm* from 94. *133 Borough Road, Petersfield GU32 3LP* Tel (01730) 260399

KELLY, John Adrian. b 49. Qu Coll Birm 70. **d** 73 **p** 74. C Formby St Pet *Liv* 73-77; Org Sec CECS *Liv*, *Blackb* and *S & M* 77-92; Deputation Appeals Org (Lancs and Is of Man) 88-92; Perm to Offic *Liv* from 77; *Bradf* 77-00; *Man* 88-97. *39 Cornwall Way, Southport PR8 3SG*

KELLY, Canon John Dickinson. b 42. Nottm Univ BA63. Ripon Hall Ox 63. **d** 65 **p** 66. C Egremont *Carl* 65-67; C Upperby St Jo 67-70; V Arlecdon 70-73; V Barrow St Aid 73-79; V Milnthorpe 79-83; V Beetham and Milnthorpe 83-85; V Camerton St Pet 85-88; P-in-c Camerton H Trin W Seaton 86-88; V Camerton, Seaton and W Seaton 88-01; P-in-c Kells from 01; Hon Can Carl Cathl from 00; Chapl N Cumbria Acute Hosps NHS Trust from 03. *St Peter's Vicarage, Cliff Road, Whitehaven CA28 9ET* Tel (01946) 692496

KELLY, John Graham. b 60. Lanc Univ LLB82 Man Poly Solicitor 84. St Jo Coll Nottm BTh91. **d** 94 **p** 95. C Normanton *Derby* 94-97; P-in-c Ockbrook 97-01; Tutor St Jo Coll Nottm from 01. *St John's College, Chilwell Lane, Bramcote, Nottingham NG9 3DS* Tel 0115-925 1114

KELLY, John Rowe. b 32. Edin Th Coll. **d** 85 **p** 86. C Blyth St Mary *Newc* 85-88; C Slaley and Healey 88-91; TV Alston Team 91-96; P-in-c 96-00; R Alston Moor 00-02; Chapl Alston Cottage Hosp 91-02; rtd 02; Perm to Offic *Carl* and *Newc* from 03. *The Nook, Brampton Road, Alston CA9 3AA* Tel (01434) 382952 E-mail alstonvicar@aol.com

KELLY, Malcolm Bernard. b 46. St Mich Coll Llan 72. **d** 74 **p** 75. C Tranmere St Paul w St Luke *Ches* 74-77; Chapl Bebington Hosp from 76; C Barnston *Ches* 77-80; R Thurstaston 80-92; R Grappenhall from 92. *The Rectory, 17 Hill Top Road, Stockton Heath, Warrington WA4 2ED* Tel (01925) 261546

KELLY, Martin Herbert. b 55. Selw Coll Cam MA90. Aston Tr Scheme 78 Ripon Coll Cuddesdon 80. **d** 83 **p** 84. C Clapham Old Town *S'wark* 83-87; Chapl and Fell Selw Coll Cam 87-92; Chapl Newnham Coll Cam 87-92; Chapl St Piers Hosp Sch Lingfield *S'wark* 95-01; C Limpsfield and Titsey 95-01; Chapl Basildon and Thurrock Gen Hosps NHS Trust from 03. *Basildon Hospital, Nethermayne, Basildon SS16 5NL* Tel (01268) 533911 *or* 593242 Fax 593757

KELLY, Nigel James (Ned). b 60. N Staffs Poly BSc83. Ripon Coll Cuddesdon 83. **d** 86 **p** 87. C Cen Telford *Lich* 86-90; TV 90-92; Chapl RN from 92. *Royal Naval Chaplaincy Service, Room 203, Victory Building, HM Naval Base, Portsmouth PO1 3LS* Tel (023) 9272 7903 Fax 9272 7111

KELLY, Paul. b 60. Qu Coll Birm 02. **d** 04 **p** 05. C Ogley Hay *Lich* from 04. *50 Lichfield Road, Brownhills, Walsall WS8 6HT* Tel (01543) 371170 Mobile 07815-452616

KELLY, Paul Maitland Hillyard. b 24. Ball Coll Ox BA50 MA54. Wells Th Coll 50. **d** 52 **p** 53. C Epsom St Martin *Guildf* 52-57; C-in-c New Cathl CD 57-61; R Abinger cum Coldharbour

61-67; P-in-c Preston St Pet *Blackb* 67-70; V Ottershaw *Guildf* 70-77; R Ickenham *Lon* 77-94; rtd 94; Perm to Offic *B & W* from 94. *37 Dodd Avenue, Wells BA5 3JU* Tel (01749) 673334

KELLY, Peter Hugh. b 46. Sarum & Wells Th Coll 81. **d** 84 **p** 85. C Fareham H Trin *Portsm* 84-87; Chapl and Prec Portsm Cathl 87-90; V Eastney 90-97; P-in-c Swanmore St Barn from 97; RD Bishop's Waltham from 03. *The Vicarage, Church Road, Swanmore, Southampton SO32 2PA* Tel (01489) 892105 E-mail peterkelly@swanmore.net

KELLY, Stephen Alexander. b 61. Man Univ BSc84. Ridley Hall Cam 03. **d** 05. C Meole Brace *Lich* from 05. *7 Dargate Close, Shrewsbury SY3 9QE* Tel (01743) 340709 E-mail steve.kelly7@virgin.net

KELLY, Stephen Paul. b 55. Keble Coll Ox BA77. Linc Th Coll 77. **d** 79 **p** 80. C Illingworth *Wakef* 79-82; C Knottingley 82-84; V Alverthorpe 84-93; Dioc Ecum Officer 88-93; TR Bingley All SS *Bradf* 93-03; P-in-c Woolley *Wakef* from 03; Dioc CME Officer from 03. *The Vicarage, Church Street, Woolley, Wakefield WF4 2JU* Tel (01226) 382550 E-mail stephen@kellys4.freeserve.co.uk

KELLY, Canon William. b 35. Dur Univ BA58 St Cath Coll Ox DipTh59. Lambeth STh75 Wycliffe Hall Ox 58. **d** 60 **p** 61. C Walney Is *Carl* 60-66; R Distington 66-71; V Barrow St Matt 71-81; RD Furness 77-81; Hon Can Carl Cathl 79-00; Dir of Ords 81-97; V Dalston 81-92; RD Carl 83-88; P-in-c Raughton Head w Gatesgill 86-92; P-in-c Maryport 92-97; P-in-c Flimby 93-96; P-in-c Arthuret and Nicholforest and Kirkandrews on Esk 97-00; rtd 00; Perm to Offic *Carl* from 00. *73 Upperby Road, Carlisle CA2 4JE* Tel (01228) 511535

KELLY, William Norman. b 21. St Aid Birkenhead. **d** 64 **p** 65. Miss to Seamen 64-66; C Douglas St Geo and St Barn *S & M* 66-69; V Wingates *Man* 69-75; Perm to Offic 76-84; Chapl HM Pris Liv 77-78; Chapl HM Borstal Stoke Heath 78-84; V Castletown *S & M* 84-92; rtd 92; Perm to Offic *S & M* from 92. *Crossag Villa, St Mark's Road, Ballasalla, Isle of Man IM9 3EF* Tel (01624) 825582

KELLY, Canon William Robert. b 28. QUB BSc57. CITC 62. **d** 62 **p** 63. C Lurgan Ch the Redeemer *D & D* 62-66; I Clondehorkey *D & R* 66-70; I Raheny w Coolock *D & G* 70-75; Peru 75-83; Hon Can Peru 83; I Ballinderry *Conn* 83-89; I Belfast St Aid 89-96; Can Belf Cathl 94-96; rtd 96. *17 College Avenue, Bangor BT20 5HJ* Tel (028) 9147 3679

KELSEY, George Robert. b 61. Imp Coll Lon BSc83 Newc Univ MSc84 PhD92. Cranmer Hall Dur 95. **d** 97 **p** 98. C Denton *Newc* 97-01; TV Glendale Gp from 01. *Eglingham Vicarage, The Village, Eglingham, Alnwick NE66 2TX* Tel (01665) 578250 E-mail robert@josephkelsey.fsnet.co.uk

KELSEY, Michael Ray. b 22. FEPA57. Wycliffe Hall Ox 60. **d** 62 **p** 63. C Lower Broughton St Clem *Man* 62-64; V Ingleby Greenhow *York* 64-68; V Scarborough St Jas 68-71; Asst to the Gen Sec USCL 71-74; V Blackheath St Jo *S'wark* 74-87; rtd 87; Perm to Offic *St E* 88-05. *20 Sweet Briar, Marcham, Abingdon OX13 6PD* Tel (01865) 391835

✠KELSHAW, The Rt Revd Terence. b 36. Lon Univ DipTh67 Pittsburgh Th Sem DMin86. Oak Hill Th Coll. **d** 67 **p** 68 **c** 89. C Clifton Ch Ch w Em *Bris* 67-71; C Woking St Jo *Guildf* 71-73; V Bris H Trin *Bris* 73-75; P-in-c Easton St Gabr w St Laur 73-75; V Easton H Trin w St Gabr and St Lawr 75-80; P-in-c Barton Hill St Luke w Ch Ch 76-80; USA from 80; Bp Rio Grande from 89. *4304 Carlisle Boulevard NE, Albuquerque, NM 87107-4811, USA* Tel (001) (505) 881 0636 Fax 883 9048 E-mail tkelshaw@aol.com

KELSO, Andrew John. b 47. LRAM73 Lon Univ BA70. St Jo Coll Nottm 83. **d** 85 **p** 86. C Gorleston St Mary *Nor* 85-87; C Hellesdon 87-90; TV Ipsley *Worc* from 90. *Matchborough Vicarage, Winward Road, Redditch B98 0SX* Tel (01527) 529098 Fax 450177 Mobile 07795-431382 E-mail andykelso@blueyonder.co.uk

KEMM, William St John. b 39. Birm Univ BA62 MA65. Ridley Hall Cam 62. **d** 64 **p** 65. C Kingswinford H Trin *Lich* 64-68; C Hednesford 68-71; V Hanbury 71-76; R Berrow and Breane *B & W* 76-92; V Hertford All SS *St Alb* from 92. *All Saints' Vicarage, Churchfields, Hertford SG13 8AE* Tel (01992) 582096

KEMP, Canon Allan. b 43. Bps' Coll Cheshunt 65 Oak Hill Th Coll 67. **d** 68 **p** 69. C Tunbridge Wells St Jas *Roch* 68-76; V Becontree St Mary *Chelmsf* 76-90; RD Barking and Dagenham 81-86; V Gt w Lt Chesterford from 90; Hon Can Chelmsf Cathl from 99. *The Vicarage, Church Street, Great Chesterford, Saffron Walden CB10 1NP* Tel (01799) 530317

KEMP, Prof Anthony Eric. b 34. St Mark & St Jo Coll Lon CertEd57 LTCL63 FTCL63 Lon Inst of Educn DipEd70 Sussex Univ MA71 DPhil79 Hon FLCM83 CPsychol89 FBPsS97 Helsinki Univ MusDoc03. St Alb and Ox Min Course 96. **d** 98 **p** 99. NSM Wokingham All SS *Ox* from 98. *18 Blagrove Lane, Wokingham RG41 4BA* Tel 0118-978 2586 Fax as telephone E-mail a.e.kemp@blagrovelane.freeserve.co.uk

KEMP, Ms Audrey. b 26. MSR49. Gilmore Ho 62. **dss** 69 **d** 87 **p** 94. Cranford *Lon* 67-70; S Ockendon Hosp 70-71; N Greenford All Hallows *Lon* 71-72; Feltham 72-80; Brentford St Faith 80-83; Hanworth All SS 83-85; Hanworth St Geo 85-87; Par Dn 87-88; rtd 88; Perm to Offic *B & W* 88-89 and from 99; Hon Par Dn Ditcheat w E Pennard and Pylle 89-94; P-in-c 94-95; Perm to Offic *Win* 95-98. *28 Queen Elizabeth Court, Blake Place, Bridgwater TA6 5QN* Tel (01278) 451348

KEMP, Barry. b 48. St Edm Hall Ox BA70 MA75 Newc Univ CertEd82. Linc Th Coll 71. **d** 74 **p** 75. C Ashton Ch Ch *Man* 74-77; CF 77-81; C Dunston *Dur* 81-83; Perm to Offic *Newc* 83-87; C Monkseaton St Mary 88; Chapl Ld Wandsworth Coll Basingstoke 92-02. *Address temp unknown*

KEMP, Christopher Michael. b 48. K Coll Lon BD71 AKC71. St Aug Coll Cant 75. **d** 76 **p** 77. C Weaverham *Ches* 76-79; C Latchford St Jas 79-82; P-in-c Sandbach Heath 82-88; V Macclesfield St Paul 88-89; C Cheadle Hulme All SS 89-93; C Oxton 93-98; P-in-c Seacombe 98-02; P-in-c Brereton w Swettenham from 02. *The Rectory, Brereton Park, Brereton, Sandbach CW11 1RY* Tel (01477) 533263

✠KEMP, The Rt Revd Eric Waldram. b 15. Ex Coll Ox BA36 MA40 BD44 DD61 Sussex Univ Hon DLitt FRHistS51 DLitt01. St Steph Ho Ox 36. **d** 39 **p** 40 **c** 74. C Newtown St Luke *Win* 39-41; Lib Pusey Ho 41-46; Chapl Ch Ch Ox 43-46; Tutor and Chapl Ex Coll Ox 46-69; Can and Preb Linc Cathl *Linc* 52-01; Chapl to The Queen 67-69; Dean Worc 69-74; Bp Chich 74-01; rtd 01. *5 Alexandra Road, Chichester PO19 7LX* Tel (01243) 780647

KEMP, Geoffrey Bernard. b 20. Lon Univ BD43. ALCD42. **d** 43 **p** 44. C Leyton All SS *Chelmsf* 43-46; C Woodford St Mary 46-49; V Barkingside St Laur 49-60; V Hadleigh St Barn 60-79; R Kelvedon Hatch 79-86; V Navestock 79-86; rtd 86; Perm to Offic *Chelmsf* and *St E* from 86. *24 Roman Way, Felixstowe IP11 9NJ* Tel (01394) 276691

KEMP, John Graham Edwin. b 29. Bris Univ BA51 PGCE52 Lon Univ BD65. Wells Th Coll 63. **d** 65 **p** 66. C Maidenhead St Luke *Ox* 65-70; R Rotherfield Greys 70-78; V Highmore 70-78; Dep Dir Tr Scheme for NSM 78-84; P-in-c Taplow 78-82; TV Burnham w Dropmore, Hitcham and Taplow 82-84; Prin EAMTC 84-92; rtd 92; Perm to Offic *St E* from 92. *Lea Cottage, The Street, Middleton, Saxmundham IP17 3NJ* Tel (01728) 648324

KEMP, John Robert Deverall. b 42. City Univ BSc65 BD69. Oak Hill Th Coll 66. **d** 70 **p** 71. C Fulham Ch Ch *Lon* 70-73; C Widford *Chelmsf* 73-79; P-in-c New Thundersley 79-84; V 84-98; Chapl HM Pris Bullwood Hall 79-98; R S Shoebury *Chelmsf* from 98. *The Rectory, 42 Church Road, Shoeburyness, Southend-on-Sea SS3 9EU* Tel (01702) 292778

KEMP, Mrs Pamela Ann. b 52. Coll of St Matthias Bris CertEd73 RMN98. Ripon Coll Cuddesdon 00. **d** 02 **p** 03. C Portland All SS w St Pet *Sarum* 02-04; C Verwood from 04. *23 Bridport Road, Verwood BH31 6UP* Tel (01202) 825966 Mobile 07989-604543 E-mail pam.kemp@cuddesdon47.fsnet.co.uk

KEMP, Ralph John. b 71. Wye Coll Lon BSc93 Trin Hall Cam BTh04. Ridley Hall Cam 01. **d** 04 **p** 05. C Astbury and Smallwood *Ches* from 04. *2 Astbury Marsh, Astbury, Congleton CW12 4HP* Tel (01260) 271954 Mobile 07762-847211 E-mail rjk30@cam.ac.uk

KEMP, Trevor George. b 62. Trin Coll Bris 98. **d** 00 **p** 01. C Old Catton *Nor* 00-03; V S Nutfield w Outwood *S'wark* from 03. *The Vicarage, 136 Mid Street, South Nutfield, Redhill RH1 5RP* Tel (01737) 822211 E-mail sixkemps@tiscali.co.uk

KEMP, William. b 67. St Anne's Coll Ox BA91 Brunel Univ PGCE92. Ridley Hall Cam BTh99. **d** 99 **p** 00. C Kensington St Barn *Lon* 99-04; P-in-c Mid Sussex Network Ch *Chich* from 04. *12 Western Road, Hurstpierpoint BN6 9TA* Tel (01273) 835829

KEMPSTER, Miss Helen Edith. b 49. Guildf Dioc Min Course 98. **d** 00 **p** 01. OLM Weybridge *Guildf* from 00. *28 Dorchester Road, Weybridge KT13 8PE* Tel (01932) 845861

KEMPSTER, Robert Alec. b 29. Selw Coll Cam MA53. Coll of Resurr Mirfield 53. **d** 55 **p** 56. C W Hackney St Barn *Lon* 55-57; C-in-c S'wark All Hallows CD *S'wark* 57-70; PV S'wark Cathl 57-60; Chapl Evelina Children's Hosp 57-70; Chapl Guy's Hosp Lon 70-81; Chapl Nat Hosp for Nervous Diseases Lon 81-89; Chapl Convent Companions Jes Gd Shep W Ogwell 89; rtd 90; Perm to Offic *Ex* from 90. *15A Seymour Road, Newton Abbot TQ12 2PT*

KEMPTHORNE, Renatus. b 39. Wadh Coll Ox BA60 MA64. Wycliffe Hall Ox 60. **d** 62 **p** 63. C Stoke *Cov* 62-65; Lect St Jo Coll Auckland New Zealand 65-68; R Wytham *Ox* 68-75; Chapl Bp Grosseteste Coll Linc 75-83; V Waimea New Zealand 83-90; Th Consultant 90-96; Researcher and Educator from 97; rtd 04. *140 Nile Street, Nelson, New Zealand 7001* Tel (0064) (3) 546 7447 E-mail kempthorne@xtra.co.nz

KENCHINGTON (née BALLANTYNE), Mrs Jane Elizabeth Ballantyne. b 58. Hull Univ BSc79 Cam Univ PGCE83. Westcott Ho Cam 88. **d** 90 **p** 94. C Winchcombe, Gretton, Sudeley Manor etc *Glouc* 90-96; Perm to Offic 96-99; NSM Dursley 99-02; Dir Reader Tr from 01. *7 Warren Croft, North Nibley, Dursley GL11 6EN* Tel (01453) 546509 E-mail janeeb.kenchington@virgin.net

KENCHINGTON, Paul Henry. b 54. Worc Coll Ox MA76. St Jo Coll Nottm BA81. **d** 82 **p** 83. C Scarborough St Mary w Ch Ch and H Apostles *York* 82-85; C Caversham St Pet and Mapledurham etc *Ox* 85-89; V Hucclecote *Glouc* 89-00; V Kowloon St Andr Hong Kong 00-05; Chapl Versailles w Chevry *Eur* from 05. *31 rue du pont Colbert, 78000 Versailles, France* Tel (0033) (1) 39 02 79 45 E-mail office@stmarksversailles.org

KENDAL, Gordon McGregor. b 46. Dundee Univ MA70 Mansf Coll Ox BA72 MA76 Lon Univ BA73 PhD79. Edin Th Coll 72. **d** 74 **p** 75. C Bracknell *Ox* 74-77; C Wokingham All SS 77-79; Chapl and Fell Linc Coll Ox 79-83; R Edin St Pet *Edin* 83-87; Man Gr Sch 88-92; Gen Sec Fellowship of St Alb and St Sergius 92-96; V S Lambeth St Anne and All SS *S'wark* 96-00. *10 Bamff Road, Alyth, Blairgowrie PH11 8DT* Tel (01828) 633400

KENDAL, Henry David. b 59. ASVA83. Lon Bible Coll 90 Oak Hill NSM Course 92. **d** 94 **p** 95. C Roxeth *Lon* 94-99; C Woodside Park St Barn from 99. *78 Woodside Avenue, London N12 8TB* Tel (020) 8343 7776 *or* 8343 5775 Mobile 07977-521656 Fax (020) 8446 7492 *or* 8343 5771 E-mail henrykendal@compuserve.com *or* henrykendal@stbarnabas.co.uk

KENDAL, Canon Stephen. b 35. Leeds Univ BA59. Coll of Resurr Mirfield 59. **d** 61 **p** 62. C Seaton Hirst *Newc* 61-63; C Newc St Geo 63-66; C Gosforth All SS 66-70; Ind Chapl *Llan* 70-78; Ind Chapl *Dur* 78-91; Hon C Houghton le Spring 78-90; Ind Chapl *Worc* 91-00; Hon Can Worc Cathl 98-00; rtd 00; Perm to Offic *Heref* from 00. *15 Coneybury View, Broseley TF12 5AX* Tel (01952) 882447 E-mail wimkiddy@aol.com

KENDALL, Alastair Geoffrey. b 55. BSc DipTh. St Jo Coll Nottm DPS. **d** 84 **p** 85. C Glouc St Aldate *Glouc* 84-87; C Sheff St Jo *Sheff* 87-92; V Bream *Glouc* from 92. *The Vicarage, Bream, Lydney GL15 6ES* Tel (01594) 562376 E-mail breamchurch@btinternet.com

KENDALL, Edward Oliver Vaughan. b 33. Dur Univ BA59. Ridley Hall Cam 59. **d** 61 **p** 62. C Corsham *Bris* 61-64; C Portsea St Mary *Portsm* 64-67; Asst Chapl HM Pris Pentonville 67-68; Chapl HM Borstal Portland 68-71; Lic to Offic *Bradf* from 71; rtd 94. *10 Halsteads Cottages, Settle BD24 9QJ* Tel and fax (01729) 822207

KENDALL, Frank. b 40. CCC Cam BA62 MA68 FRSA90. S'wark Ord Course 74. **d** 74 **p** 75. NSM Lingfield *S'wark* 74-75 and 78-82; NSM Sketty *S & B* 75-78; NSM Limpsfield and Titsey *S'wark* 82-84; Lic to Offic *Man* 84-89 and *Liv* 89-96; NSM Adnry St Helens *Liv* 96-00; Perm to Offic from 01; NSM Farington Moss *Blackb* from 03; NSM Lostock Hall from 03. *52 Kingsway, Penwortham, Preston PR1 0ED* Tel (01772) 748021

KENDALL, Giles. b 57. Lon Univ BA80 Univ Coll Lon BSc86 Lon Univ PhD90. STETS BTh98. **d** 98 **p** 99. C Wareham *Sarum* 98-01; V Sawston *Ely* from 01; P-in-c Babraham from 01. *The Vicarage, Church Lane, Sawston, Cambridge CB2 4JR* Tel (01223) 832248 E-mail stm_stp@fish.co.uk

KENDALL, Gordon Sydney. b 41. **d** 72 **p** 74. Hon C Old Ford St Paul w St Steph and St Mark *Lon* 72-82; Hon C Homerton St Luke 86-92; Asst Chapl Hackney and Homerton Hosp Lon 87-92; Chapl S Devon Healthcare NHS Trust from 92; Lic to Offic *Ex* from 92. *Torbay Hospital, Lawes Bridge, Newton Road, Torquay TQ2 7AA* Tel (01803) 614567 *or* 814054

KENDRA, Kenneth Ernest. b 13. OBE66. Leeds Univ BA41 MA48. Linc Th Coll 40. **d** 42 **p** 43. C Pocklington and Kilnwick Percy *York* 42-46; CF 46-71; QHC 70-71; V Lee-on-the-Solent *Portsm* 71-80; RD Alverstoke 77-79; rtd 80. *Bookers Barn, Bolney, Haywards Heath RH17 5NB* Tel (01444) 881064

KENDRA, Neil Stuart. b 46. JP96. FCIPD84 Leeds Univ BA67 Univ of Wales (Swansea) DipAD72 Bradf Univ MSc80 PhD84. Linc Th Coll 67. **d** 69 **p** 70. C Allerton *Liv* 69-72; Ldr Leeds City Cen Detached Youth Work Project 73-75; Dioc Youth Officer *Ripon* 75-77; Lect Ilkley Coll 77-78; Sen Lect Bradf and Ilkley Community Coll 78-88; Hd Community and Youth Studies St Martin's Coll 88-94; Hd Applied Soc Sciences from 94. *St Martin's College, Lancaster LA1 3JD* Tel (01524) 384350

KENDREW, Geoffrey David. b 42. K Coll Lon BD66 AKC66. **d** 67 **p** 68. C Bourne *Guildf* 67-70; C Haslemere 70-76; V Derby St Barn *Derby* 76-95; R Deal St Leon w St Rich and Sholden etc *Cant* from 95; Chapl E Kent NHS and Soc Care Partnership Trust from 00. *St Leonard's Rectory, Addelam Road, Deal CT14 9BZ* Tel (01304) 374076

KENDRICK, Dale Evans. b 62. Ch Ch Coll Cant BA86 Nottm Univ MA87 Leeds Univ MA95. Coll of Resurr Mirfield 94. **d** 95 **p** 96. C Tividale *Lich* 95-96; C Blakenall Heath 96-97; C Stafford 97-98; Dep Chapl HM Pris Birm 98-01; Chapl HM Pris Drake Hall 01-03; Chapl RAF 03-04; Chapl HM YOI Werrington Ho from 04. *HM Youth Custody Centre, Werrington, Stoke-On-Trent ST9 0DX* Tel (01782) 463300 Fax 463301

KENDRICK, Canon Desmond Max. b 22. Leeds Univ BA47. Wycliffe Hall Ox 50. **d** 52 **p** 53. C Glodwick St Mark *Man* 52-54; Chapl Leeds Road Hosp Bradf 54-77; V Bradf St Clem *Bradf* 54-77; RD Bradf 63-73; Hon Can Bradf Cathl 64-89; V Otley 77-89; Chapl Wharfdale Gen Hosp 77-90; rtd 89; Perm to Offic *Bradf* from 89. *26 Ashtofts Mount, Guiseley LS20 9DB* Tel (01943) 870430

KENDRICK, Mrs Helen Grace. b 66. Bris Univ BA88. St Alb and Ox Min Course 96. **d** 99 **p** 00. C Icknield *Ox* 99-03; P-in-c Sutton Courtenay w Appleford from 03. *The Vicarage, 3 Tullis Close, Sutton Courtenay, Abingdon OX14 4BD* Tel (01235) 848297 E-mail helen@kendricks.fsnet.co.uk

KENDRICK, Ronald Horace. b 35. Univ of Wales (Ban) BD78 DPS79. **d** 82 **p** 83. C Wrexham *St As* 82-85; R Llanelian and Betws-yn-Rhos 85-99; rtd 99. *2 Chapelfield, Marl Lane, Deganwy, Conwy LL31 9BF* Tel (01492) 582522

KENNAR, Thomas Philip. b 66. STETS 02. **d** 05. C Warblington w Emsworth *Portsm* from 05. *1 Godwin Close, Emsworth PO10 7XT* Tel (01243) 432429 Mobile 07899-952318

KENNARD, Ms Alice Marina. b 36. **d** 00. NSM Mynyddislwyn *Mon* 00-02. *21 Trostrey, Hollybush, Cwmbran NP44 7JD* Tel (01633) 482812

KENNARD, Mark Philip Donald. b 60. Man Univ BSc82. Cranmer Hall Dur 85. **d** 88 **p** 89. C Newark w Hawton, Cotham and Shelton *S'well* 88-89; C Newark 89-91; C Cropwell Bishop w Colston Bassett, Granby etc 91-93; P-in-c Shireoaks 93-99; Chapl Bassetlaw Hosp and Community Services NHS Trust 93-96; Chapl RAF from 99. *Chaplaincy Services (RAF), HQ, Personnel and Training Command, RAF Innsworth, Gloucester GL3 1EZ* Tel (01452) 712612 ext 5164 Fax 510828

KENNEDY, Alan. b 52. Liv Univ BSc95. N Ord Course 01. **d** 03. C Westbrook St Phil *Liv* from 03. *16 Ridgebourne Close, Callands, Warrington WA5 9YB* Tel (01925) 657881

KENNEDY, Ms Alison Mary. b 66. K Coll Lon BMus87 Roehampton Inst 88 LTCL90 Heythrop Coll Lon MA95. NTMTC DipTh99. **d** 99 **p** 00. C De Beauvoir Town St Pet *Lon* 99-02; TV Walthamstow *Chelmsf* from 02. *St Gabriel's Vicarage, 17 Shernhall Street, London E17 3EU* Tel (020) 8509 1135 E-mail alison_m_kennedy@hotmail.com

KENNEDY, Anthony Reeves. b 32. Lon Univ DipTh67. Roch Th Coll 64. **d** 67 **p** 68. C Ross *Heref* 67-69; C Marfleet *York* 69-71; TV 72-76; V Lightwater *Guildf* 76-83; V W Ham *Chelmsf* 83-89; V Lutton w Gedney Drove End, Dawsmere *Linc* 89-94; Perm to Offic *Chich* from 94 and *Win* from 01; rtd 97. *40 Haydock Close, Alton GU34 2TL* Tel (01420) 549860 E-mail anthreev.kennedy@virgin.net

KENNEDY, Miss Carolyn Ruth. b 59. Univ of Wales (Ban) BA81 GradCertEd(FE)85. Ripon Coll Cuddesdon BA90. **d** 91 **p** 94. C Frodingham *Linc* 91-95; Chapl Cov Univ *Cov* 95-00; R Uffington Gp *Linc* from 00. *The Rectory, 67 Main Road, Uffington, Stamford PE9 4SN* Tel (01780) 481786 E-mail crkennedy@clara.co.uk

KENNEDY, David George. b 46. Hull Univ BEd71 MA76. Linc Th Coll 77. **d** 79 **p** 80. C Linc St Faith and St Martin w St Pet *Linc* 79-82; V Bilton St Pet *York* 82-90; V New Seaham *Dur* 90-92; Chapl Lincs and Humberside Univ *York* 92-97; P-in-c Barrow St Matt *Carl* 97-99; TR 99-03; Chapl Furness Coll 97-03; P-in-c Blackb St Aid *Blackb* 03-04; V Blackb St Fran and St Aid from 04. *St Aidan's Vicarage, St Aidan's Avenue, Blackburn BB2 4EA* Tel (01254) 610570

KENNEDY, Canon David John. b 57. St Jo Coll Dur BA78 Nottm Univ MTh81 Birm Univ PhD96. St Jo Coll Nottm 79. **d** 81 **p** 82. C Tudhoe Grange *Dur* 81-87; C Merrington 84-87; Tutor Qu Coll Birm 88-96; R Haughton le Skerne *Dur* 96-01; Can Res Dur Cathl from 01; Chapl Grey Coll Dur from 01. *7 The College, Durham DH1 3EQ* Tel 0191-375 0242 Fax 386 4267 E-mail canon.precentor@durhamcathedral.co.uk

KENNEDY, Gary. b 63. Qu Coll Birm BA02. **d** 03 **p** 04. C New Bury *Man* from 03. *The Vicarage, 15 Lowick Avenue, Bolton BL3 2DS* E-mail garynbogusia@screaming.net

KENNEDY, Ian Duncan. b 53. **d** 04 **p** 05. OLM Whitnash *Cov* from 04. *128 Coppice Road, Whitnash, Leamington Spa CV31 2LU* Tel (01926) 313275

KENNEDY, James Ernest. b 20. TCD BA46 MA51. CITC 46. **d** 46 **p** 47. C Kilnamanagh w Kilcormack, Castle Ellis etc *C & O* 46-48; C Ahoghill *Conn* 48; P-in-c Portglenone 48-51; I 51-60; I Agherton 60-67; I Errigal w Desertoghill *D & R* 67-81; rtd 81. *38 Prospect Road, Portstewart BT55 7LQ* Tel (028) 7083 2052

KENNEDY, Jason Grant. b 68. Oak Hill Th Coll BA95. **d** 98 **p** 99. C Beccles St Mich *St E* 98-01; R Hollington St Leon *Chich* from 01. *The Rectory, Tile Barn Road, St Leonards-on-Sea TN38 9PA* Tel (01424) 852257 Fax 853896 E-mail jason.kennedy@hollingtonpc.org.uk

KENNEDY, Joseph. b 69. Edin Univ BSc91 BD94 Moray Ho Coll of Educn PGCE97 St Hugh's Coll Ox MSt00. St Steph Ho Ox 98. **d** 02 **p** 03. C Stratfield Mortimer and Mortimer W End etc *Ox* 02-03; C Abingdon 03-05; Dean of Chpl, Chapl and Fell Selw Coll Cam from 05; Chapl Newnham Coll Cam from 05. *10 Croft Lodge, Barton Road, Cambridge CB3 9LA* Tel (01223) 335875 E-mail jk385@cam.ac.uk

KENNEDY, Canon Michael Charles. b 39. TCD BA63 MA79 BD79 Open Univ PhD87. TCD Div Sch 61. **d** 63 **p** 64. C Drumglass *Arm* 63-66; I Lisnadill w Kildarton from 66; Warden Dioc Guild of Lay Readers from 74; Hon V Choral Arm Cathl from 75; Tutor for Aux Min (Arm) from 82; Preb Yagoe St Patr Cathl Dublin from 92. *Lisnadill Rectory, 60 Newtownhamilton Road, Armagh BT60 2PW* Tel (028) 3752 3630 E-mail lisnadill@armagh.anglican.org

KENNEDY, Paul Alan. b 67. ACA92 Brighton Poly. St Steph Ho Ox BA95. **d** 95 **p** 96. C Romford St Andr *Chelmsf* 95-98; C Cheam *S'wark* 98-01; V Steep and Froxfield w Privett *Portsm* from 01; Bp's Adv on Healing from 04. *The Vicarage, 77 Church Road, Steep, Petersfield GU32 2DF* Tel (01730) 264282 Mobile 07989-255864 E-mail paulak@madasafish.com

KENNEDY, Paul Joseph Alan. b 57. Newc Univ MA93. Sarum & Wells Th Coll 81. **d** 84 **p** 85. C Shildon w Eldon *Dur* 84-86; C Shotton *St As* 86-88; V Waterhouses *Dur* 88-93; V Denton *Newc* 93-95; CF 95-98; P-in-c Leam Lane *Dur* 98-99; V 99-05; P-in-c S Westoe from 05. *St Michael's Vicarage, Westoe Road, South Shields NE33 3PJ* Tel 0191-455 2132

KENNEDY, Brother Philip Bartholomew. b 47. STETS 95. **d** 98 **p** 99. SSF from 77. *The Friary, Hilfield, Dorchester DT2 7BE* Tel (01300) 341345/6 Fax 341293

KENNEDY, Ross Kenneth. b 40. Edin Th Coll 83. **d** 85 **p** 86. C Hexham *Newc* 85-89; TV Glendale Gp 89-93; TR Ch the King from 93. *North Gosforth Vicarage, Wideopen, Newcastle upon Tyne NE13 6NH* Tel 0191-236 2280

KENNEDY, Wendy Patricia. b 58. STETS 00. **d** 03 **p** 04. NSM Warren Park and Leigh Park *Portsm* from 03. *13 Ashcroft Lane, Waterlooville PO8 0AX* Tel (023) 9241 3190 E-mail teamkennedy@lineone.net

KENNEDY, William Edmund. b 20. QUB BA43 TCD BA45 MA48. **d** 45 **p** 46. C Seagoe *D & D* 45-48; C Ballynafeigh St Jude 48-57; I Ballyculter w Kilclief 57-85; rtd 85. *Shalom, 8 Dunnanew Road, Seaforde, Downpatrick BT30 8PJ* Tel (028) 4481 1706

KENNERLEY, Canon Katherine Virginia (Ginnie). Somerville Coll Ox BA58 MA65 TCD BA86 Princeton Th Sem DMin98. CITC 86. **d** 88 **p** 90. Lect Applied Th CITC 88-93; NSM Bray *D & G* 88-93; I Narraghmore and Timolin w Castledermot etc from 93; Can Ch Ch Cathl Dublin from 96. *4 Seafield Terrace, Dalkey, Co Dublin, Irish Republic* Tel (00353) (1) 275 0737 Mobile 87-647 5092 E-mail kennerley@eircom.net

KENNETT-ORPWOOD, Jason Robert. b 55. St Mich Coll Llan DipTh77 DPS78. **d** 78 **p** 79. Chapl St Woolos Cathl *Mon* 78-82; Chapl St Woolos Hosp Newport 79-82; Dioc Youth Chapl *Mon* 82-85; V Cwmcarn 82-85; TV Wrexham *St As* 85-89; Dioc Ecum Officer 94-99; Chapl Wrexham Maelor Hosp 86-89; V Bistre 89-99. *94 Erddig Road, Wrexham LL13 7DR*

KENNEY, Canon Peter. b 50. Edin Univ BD75. Edin Th Coll 73. **d** 76 **p** 77. C Cullercoats St Geo *Newc* 76-81; TV Whorlton 81-88; TR Ch the King 88-93; P-in-c Newc St Jo 93-02; P-in-c Gosforth St Hugh from 02; Dioc Adv in Past Care and Counselling from 02; Hon Can Newc Cathl from 04. *The Vicarage, Wansbeck Road, Newcastle upon Tyne NE3 2LR* Tel 0191-285 8792 E-mail kenney@globalnet.co.uk

KENNING, Michael Stephen. b 47. St Chad's Coll Dur BA68. Westcott Ho Cam 69. **d** 71 **p** 72. C Hythe *Cant* 71-75; TV Bow w Bromley St Leon *Lon* 75-77; C-in-c W Leigh CD *Portsm* 77-81; V Lee-on-the-Solent 81-92; R N Waltham and Steventon, Ashe and Deane *Win* from 92; RD Whitchurch from 03. *The Rectory, North Waltham, Basingstoke RG25 2BQ* Tel and fax (01256) 397256 E-mail michael.kenning@ukgateway.net

KENNINGTON, John Paul. b 61. Collingwood Coll Dur BA85. St Steph Ho Ox BA87 MA92. **d** 88 **p** 89. C Headington *Ox* 88-91; C Dulwich St Clem w St Pet *S'wark* 91-94; TV Mortlake w E Sheen 94-01; V Battersea St Mary from 01. *St Mary's Vicarage, 32 Vicarage Crescent, London SW11 3LD* Tel (020) 7585 3986 E-mail pkennington@clara.net

KENNY, Canon Charles John. b 39. LGSM74 QUB BA61 MEd78. CITC 69. **d** 69 **p** 70. C Belfast St Paul *Conn* 69-71; Hd of RE Grosvenor High Sch 71-94; V Choral Belf Cathl 94-00; Can Treas 95-00; rtd 00; Lic to Offic *Conn* from 84. *45 Deramore Drive, Belfast BT9 5JS* Tel (028) 9066 9632 *or* 9032 8332 Fax 9023 8855 E-mail charlesjoankenny@utvinternet.com

KENNY, Frederick William Bouvier. b 28. TCD BA53 DipEd54 MA56 LTh. **d** 56 **p** 57. C Ballymacarrett St Patr *D & D* 56-58; C Blackpool St Jo *Blackb* 58-61; Chapl Preston R Infirmary 61-66; V Preston St Paul *Blackb* 61-66; Youth Adv CMS (Lon) 66-70; Youth Sec (Ireland) CMS 70-75; I Belfast St Clem *D & D* 75-80; V Preston St Cuth *Blackb* 80-86; TV Bushbury *Lich* 86-90; P-in-c Stambridge *Chelmsf* 90-97; Chapl Southend Community Care Services NHS Trust 90-97; rtd 97; Perm to Offic *Pet* from 97; Perm to Offic *Chelmsf* from 99. *89 Cavendish Gardens, Westcliff-on-Sea SS0 9XP* Tel (01702) 344791 E-mail c-jkenny@dial.pipex.com

KENNY, Mark Anthony. b 74. Leeds Univ BA97 PGCE98. NTMTC 02. **d** 04 **p** 05. NSM Covent Garden St Paul *Lon* from 04. *110 Perth Road, Ilford IG2 6AS* Tel (020) 8554 2492 Mobile 07974-572074 E-mail mark.kenny@btinternet.com

KENRICK, Kenneth David Norman. b 44. Liv Univ RMN. Ripon Hall Ox 70 NW Ord Course 77. **d** 77 **p** 78. C Stockport St Geo *Ches* 77-83; R Stockport St Thos 83-85; R Stockport St Thos w St Pet from 86; Chapl St Thos and Cheadle Royal Hospitals from 88. *St Thomas's Rectory, 25 Heath Road, Stockport SK2 6JJ* Tel 0161-483 2483 E-mail truefaith_@hotmail.com

KENSINGTON, Area Bishop of. *See* COLCLOUGH, The Rt Revd Michael John

KENT, Barry James. b 41. CPC78. Dioc OLM tr scheme. **d** 02 **p** 03. OLM Kinson *Sarum* from 02. *15 Summers Avenue, Bournemouth BH11 9DQ* Tel (01202) 582484 E-mail barry@kentb60.freeserve.co.uk

KENT, Christopher Alfred. b 48. CEng77 MIChemE77 Birm Univ BSc69 PhD72 Nottm Univ DipTh83. St Jo Coll Nottm 82. **d** 84 **p** 85. C Bucknall and Bagnall *Lich* 84-86; Hon C Halesowen *Worc* 86-96; NSM Reddal Hill St Luke 96-01; NSM The Lye and Stambermill from 01. *40 County Park Avenue, Halesowen B62 8SP* Tel 0121-550 3132 E-mail c.a.kent@bham.ac.uk

KENT, David. b 44. CEng MIMechE. N Ord Course. **d** 83 **p** 84. NSM Huddersfield St Pet and All SS *Wakef* 83-98; NSM Newsome and Armitage Bridge 98-03; NSM Em TM from 03. *2 Hillside Crescent, Huddersfield HD4 6LY* Tel (01484) 324049 Mobile 07949-762186 E-mail david.kent3@ntlworld.com

KENT, Frank. b 44. Open Univ BA82 ARCM76. Ridley Hall Cam. **d** 86 **p** 87. C Faversham *Cant* 86-89; R Lyminge w Paddlesworth, Stanford w Postling etc 89-99; P-in-c Sittingbourne St Mich 99-00; V Sittingbourne St Mary and St Mich 01-04; R Eastry and Northbourne w Tilmanstone etc from 04. *The Vicarage, Brook Street, Eastry, Sandwich CT13 0HR* Tel (01304) 611323 E-mail revkent@francikent.freeserve.co.uk

KENT, Hugh. *See* KENT, Richard Hugh

KENT, Keith Meredith. b 32. St Aid Birkenhead 55. **d** 58 **p** 59. C Fulwood Ch Ch *Blackb* 58-60; C Everton St Chrys *Liv* 60-62; C Litherland St Phil 64-68; P-in-c Everton St Polycarp 68-74; V Liv All So Springwood 74-78; V Carr Mill 78-86; V Beddgelert *Ban* 86-91; rtd 91; Perm to Offic *Blackb* from 91. *14 Crow Hills Road, Penwortham, Preston PR1 0JE* Tel (01772) 746831

KENT, Canon Michael Patrick. b 27. St Edm Hall Ox BA50 MA52. Cuddesdon Coll 50. **d** 52 **p** 53. C W Hartlepool St Aid *Dur* 52-57; C-in-c Pennywell St Thos and Grindon St Oswald CD 57-70; V Cockerton 70-93; RD Darlington 79-84; Hon Can Dur Cathl 83-98; rtd 93; Chapl St Chad's Coll *Dur* 94-95. *5 Ferens Close, Durham DH1 1JX* Tel 0191-386 2835

KENT, Preb Neville. b 40. Sarum & Wells Th Coll 70. **d** 72 **p** 73. C Taunton St Andr *B & W* 72-77; R Bradford w Oake, Hillfarrance and Heathfield 77-89; Adv on Soc Concerns 80-87; RD Tone 87-89; V Worle 89-93; TR from 93; Preb Wells Cathl from 94; Perm to Offic *Bris* from 97. *The Vicarage, 93 Church Road, Worle, Weston-super-Mare BS22 9EA* Tel (01934) 510694 *or* 515922 E-mail worlepo@aol.com

KENT, Richard Hugh. b 38. Worc Coll Ox BA61 MA63. Chich Th Coll 61. **d** 63 **p** 64. C Emscote *Cov* 63-66; C Finham 66-70; V Parkend *Glouc* 70-75; V Glouc St Aldate 75-86; Chapl and Warden Harnhill Healing Cen 86-96; R N Buckingham *Ox* 96-04; AD Buckingham 00-04; rtd 04. *10 Booth Close, Pattishall, Towcester NN12 8JP* Tel (01327) 836231 E-mail hugh.k@talk21.com

KENT, Roger Anthony Edward. b 56. Kent Univ BA78. St Steph Ho Ox 79. **d** 81 **p** 82. C Ipswich All Hallows *St E* 81-84; C Poplar *Lon* 84-88; V Newington w Hartlip and Stockbury *Cant* 88-95; Chapl Prague *Eur* 95-98; Perm to Offic *Nor* 99; TV Cullercoats St Geo *Newc* 99-04; R Somerleyton, Ashby, Fritton, Herringfleet etc *Nor* from 04. *The Rectory, The Street, Somerleyton, Lowestoft NR32 5PT* Tel (01502) 731885

KENT, Ms Susan Elizabeth. b 52. St Aid Coll Dur BA74 St Mary's Coll Newc PGCE77. Ripon Coll Cuddesdon 98. **d** 00 **p** 01. C Westgate Common *Wakef* 00-03; P-in-c Oxclose *Dur* from 03. *37 Brancepeth Road, Washington NE38 0LA* Tel 0191-415 9468 Mobile 07884-024202 E-mail revsusan@arken.freeserve.co.uk

KENTIGERN-FOX, Canon William Poyntere Kentigern. b 38. AKC63. **d** 64 **p** 65. C S Mimms St Mary and Potters Bar *Lon* 64-67; C S Tottenham 67-70; P-in-c Duddington w Tixover *Pet* 70-76; R Barrowden and Wakerley 70-76; P-in-c Morcott w S Luffenham 75-77; R Barrowden and Wakerley w S Luffenham 77-79; R Byfield w Boddington 79-86; V Northampton St Mich w St Edm 86-95; V Raunds 95-03; Can Pet Cathl 94-03; RD Higham 97-02; rtd 03. *41 Parkfield Road, Ruskington, Sleaford NG34 9HT* Tel (01526) 830944

KENWARD, Roger Nelson. b 34. Selw Coll Cam BA58 MA62. Ripon Hall Ox 58. **d** 60 **p** 61. C Paddington St Jas *Lon* 60-63; Chapl RAF 64-82; Asst Chapl-in-Chief RAF 82-89; P-in-c Lyneham w Bradenstoke *Sarum* 72-76; QHC 85-89; R Laughton w Ripe and Chalvington *Chich* 90-95; Chapl Laughton Lodge Hosp 90-95; rtd 95; NSM Chiddingly w E Hoathly *Chich* 96; Perm to Offic from 96. *The Coach House, School Hill, Old Heathfield, Heathfield TN21 9AE* Tel (01435) 862618

KENWAY, Ian Michael. b 52. Leeds Univ BA74 Bris Univ PhD86. Coll of Resurr Mirfield 74. **d** 76 **p** 77. C Cov E *Cov* 76-79; C Southmead *Bris* 79-81; P-in-c Shaw Hill *Birm* 82-88;

Asst Sec Gen Syn Bd for Soc Resp 88-93; Chapl Essex Univ *Chelmsf* 93-99; Dir Studies Cen for Study of Th 93-99; Perm to Offic *S & B* from 01. *6 Kings Court, Presteigne LD8 2AJ* Tel (01544) 260547 Mobile 07748-223090 Fax 07092-315825 E-mail iank@cischr.org

KENWAY, Robert Andrew. b 56. Bris Univ BA78. Westcott Ho Cam 80. **d** 82 **p** 83. C Birchfield *Birm* 82-85; C Queensbury All SS *Lon* 87-89; R Birm St Geo *Birm* 89-97; V Calne and Blackland *Sarum* from 97. *The Vicarage, Vicarage Close, Calne SN11 8DD* Tel (01249) 812340 E-mail bobandsadie.kenway@btopenworld.com

KENYA, Archbishop of. *See* NZIMBI, The Most Revd Benjamin

KENYON, Lee Stuart. b 78. Lanc Univ BA01 Leeds Univ BA04. Coll of Resurr Mirfield 02. **d** 05. C Darwen St Cuth w Tockholes St Steph *Blackb* from 05. *St Chad's House, 14 The Meadows, Darwen BB3 0PF* Tel (01254) 701180 E-mail leekenyon@fsmail.net

KENYON, Stanley Robert. b 31. Kelham Th Coll 51. **d** 55 **p** 56. C Eckington *Derby* 55-57; C Derby St Andr 57-59; C Lullington 59-61; C Nether and Over Seale 59-61; P-in-c Grimsby St Steph *Linc* 61-71; V Habrough 71-82; V E Halton 73-82; V Killingholme 73-82; V Barnetby le Wold Gp 82-94; rtd 94; Perm to Offic *Linc* from 94. *Machindor, 47 Highfields, Crowle, Scunthorpe DN17 4NP* Tel (01724) 711435

KEOGH, Anthony. b 35. St Mich Coll Llan 63. **d** 66 **p** 67. C Aberaman and Abercwmboi *Llan* 66-70; Hon C Penarth All SS 70-76; R Jersey H Trin *Win* from 76. *Holy Trinity Rectory, La rue du Presbytere, Jersey JE3 5JB* Tel (01534) 861110 E-mail jill.keogh@virgin.net

KEOGH, Henry James. b 39. TCD BA61 NUI BMus65. **d** 62 **p** 63. C Cork St Fin Barre's Cathl *C, C & R* 62-65; C Belfast St Luke *Conn* 65-66; C Dromore Cathl *D & D* 66-68; I Castlecomer *C & O* 68-85; I Kilscoran w Killinick and Mulrankin 85-02; Hon Chapl Miss to Seafarers 85-02; Preb Ferns Cathl *C & O* 96-02; rtd 02. *5 Ard na Gréine, Dark Road, Midleton, Co Cork, Irish Republic* Tel (00353) (21) 463 0841

KEOGH, Paul Anthony. b 37. Order of Friars Minor 55. **d** 62 **p** 63. In RC Ch 62-66; Hon C Eltham Park St Luke *S'wark* from 00. *78 Greenvale Road, London SE9 1PD* Tel (020) 8850 9958 *or* 8303 4786

KEOGH, Robert Gordon. b 56. TCD DipTh84. **d** 84 **p** 85. C Mossley *Conn* 84-87; I Taunagh w Kilmactranny, Ballysumaghan etc *K, E & A* 87-90; I Swanlinbar w Tomregan, Kinawley, Drumlane etc 90-02; Preb Kilmore Cathl 98-02; I Drumclamph w Lower and Upper Langfield *D & R* from 02. *Drumclamph Rectory, 70 Greenville Road, Castlederg BT81 7NU* Tel (028) 8167 1433 E-mail rgkeogh@utvinternet.com

KEOWN, Paul. b 58. Univ of Wales (Swansea) BA95 PGCE98 AGSM76. Ripon Coll Cuddesdon BTh02. **d** 02 **p** 03. C Llansamlet *S & B* 02-04; P-in-c Swansea St Nic from 04. *St Nicholas' Vicarage, 58A Dyfed Avenue, Townhill, Swansea SA1 6NG* Tel (01792) 547703 E-mail frpaulkeown@mac.com

KER, Desmond Agar-Ellis. b 15. Wells Th Coll 58. **d** 58 **p** 60. C Wyken *Cov* 58-59; C Dawlish *Ex* 60-61; C Cockington 61-69; V Bovey Tracey St Jo 69-80; rtd 80; Perm to Offic *S'wark* 84-92; Perm to Offic *Chich* 92-97. *Flat 36, St Clements Court, Wear Bay Crescent, Folkestone CT19 5AU*

KER, Robert Andrew. d 05. Aux Min Larne and Inver *Conn* from 05. *24 Ravensdale, Newtownabbey BT36 6FA* Tel (028) 9083 6901 E-mail a.ker@btinternet.com

KERLEY, Brian Edwin. b 36. St Jo Coll Cam BA57 MA61. Linc Th Coll 59. **d** 61 **p** 62. C Sheerness H Trin w St Paul *Cant* 61-64; C St Laur in Thanet 64-69; C Coulsdon St Andr *S'wark* 69-76; P-in-c Fulbourn *Ely* 76-77; R 77-03; P-in-c Gt and Lt Wilbraham 86-03; RD Quy 83-93 and 97-00; rtd 03; Perm to Offic *Ely* from 03. *11 Dalton Way, Ely CB6 1DS* Tel (01353) 665641 E-mail brian.kerley@ely.anglican.org

KERLEY, Patrick Thomas Stewart. b 42. Linc Th Coll. **d** 85 **p** 86. Hon C Thorpe *Nor* 85-90; C Wymondham 90-94; C Gt Yarmouth 94-95; TV 95-00; TV Wilford Peninsula *St E* from 00. *The Rectory, Eyke, Woodbridge IP12 2QW* Tel (01394) 460289 Mobile 07940-739769

KERNER, Vivienne Jane. b 49. Liv Univ CertEd71 BEd72. WEMTC 91. **d** 94 **p** 95. NSM Glouc St Jas and All SS *Glouc* 94-01; NSM Glouc St Mark and St Mary de Crypt w St Jo etc 01-02; Perm to Offic 02-04; NSM Hardwicke and Elmore w Longney from 04; Hon Chapl Leckhampton Court Hospice from 03. *Cornerstone, 10 Arkendale Drive, Hardwicke, Gloucester GL4 2JA* Tel (01452) 883126 E-mail wsm.kerner@tesco.net

KERNEY, Barbara. *See* SHERLOCK, Mrs Barbara Lee Kerney

KERR, Andrew Harry Mayne. b 41. TCD BA63 Birm Univ DPS72. Melbourne Coll of Div MMin98. **d** 65 **p** 66. C Belfast St Luke *Conn* 65-68; SCM Sec (Ireland) 68-72; C Clooney *D & R* 72-74; Australia from 74; C Swinburne 74-80; I Dallas 80-88; I Mont Albert 88-94; P-in-c W Geelong from 96. *101 Katrina Street, Blackburn North, Vic, Australia 3130* Tel (0061) (3) 5221 6694 *or* 9893 4946 Fax 9893 4946 E-mail ahmkerr@hotmail.com

KERR, Anthony. b 43. Sheff Univ BA64 Man Univ CertEd65. N Ord Course. **d** 85 **p** 86. NSM Greenfield *Man* 85-87; NSM Leesfield 87-97; P-in-c Oldham St Steph and All Martyrs 97-02; NSM Lydgate w Friezland 02-03; NSM Saddleworth from 03. *16 Netherlees, Spring Lane, Oldham OL4 5BA* Tel 0161-620 6512

KERR, Arthur Henry. LRAM47 TCD BA48 DA65. **d** 49 **p** 50. C Templemore *D & R* 49-50; C Dublin Harold's Cross *D & G* 50-57; ICM 57-60; Chapl Rotunda Hosp 60-75; Lic to Offic *Conn* 88-94; P-in-c Clondevaddock w Portsalon and Leatbeg *D & R* 94-01; rtd 01. *Halothane, 172 Mountsandel Road, Coleraine BT52 1JE* Tel (028) 7034 4940

KERR, Bryan Thomas. b 70. QUB BD91 TCD MPhil96. CITC 94. **d** 96 **p** 97. C Enniskillen *Clogh* 96-99; I Garrison w Slavin and Belleek from 99; Dioc Communications Officer from 00. *The Rectory, Knockarevan, Enniskillen BT93 4AE* Tel (028) 6865 8372 Fax 07092-073480 E-mail rector@belleek.org *or* dco@clogher.anglican.org

KERR, Charles. *See* KERR, Ewan Charles

KERR, Charles Alexander Gray. b 33. Open Univ BA75 Birm Univ MA83 MA88. Edin Th Coll 63. **d** 67 **p** 68. C Hawick *Edin* 67-70; C Edgbaston St Geo *Birm* 70-72; Chapl Birm Skin Hosp 70-75; P-in-c Quinton Road W St Boniface *Birm* 72-79; V 79-84; R Musselburgh *Edin* 84-86; P-in-c Prestonpans 84-86; NSM Reighton w Speeton *York* 89-91; P-in-c Burton Pidsea and Humbleton w Elsternwick 91-95; V Anlaby Common St Mark 95; rtd 96; Perm to Offic *York* 96-02. *6A Glebeland Close, West Stafford, Dorchester DT2 8AE*

KERR, David James. b 36. TCD BA58 MA61 BD61 HDipEd66. TCD Div Sch Div Test 59. **d** 60 **p** 61. C Belfast Trin Coll Miss *Conn* 60-63; Dean's V St Patr Cathl Dublin 63-66; Chapl Beechwood Park Sch St Alb 66-01; Hon C Flamstead *St Alb* 74-00; Perm to Offic from 00; rtd 01. *Trumpton Cottage, 12A Pickford Road, Markyate, St Albans AL3 8RU* Tel (01582) 841191 E-mail kerr_david@hotmail.com

KERR, Derek Preston. b 64. TCD BTh90. Oak Hill Th Coll 85. **d** 90 **p** 91. C Belfast St Donard *D & D* 90-93; C Carrickfergus *Conn* 93-96; I Devenish w Boho *Clogh* from 96. *Monea Rectory, Monea, Enniskillen BT74 8GE* Tel (028) 6634 1228

KERR, Miss Dora Elizabeth. b 41. QUB BA65 Southn Univ DipEd66 Nottm Univ DipTh83. St Jo Coll Nottm 82. **dss** 84 **d** 87 **p** 94. Becontree St Mary *Chelmsf* 84-88; Par Dn 87-88; Par Dn Rushden w Newton Bromswold *Pet* 88-93; C Finham *Cov* 94-00; Chapl Walsgrave Hosps NHS Trust 94-00; C Belper *Derby* from 00. *St Mark's House, Openwoodgate, Belper DE56 0SD* Tel (01773) 825727 E-mail elizabeth@ekerr.freeserve.co.uk

KERR, Ewan Charles. b 74. Fitzw Coll Cam BA96 MA00. Ripon Coll Cuddesdon MTh01. **d** 01 **p** 02. C Nor St Pet Mancroft w St Jo Maddermarket *Nor* 01-04; Chapl Glenalmond Coll *St And* from 04. *The Chaplain's House, Glenalmond College, Glenalmond, Perth PH1 3RY* Tel (01738) 880268 *or* 842064 E-mail charliekerr@glenalmondcollege.co.uk

KERR, Frank George. b 52. **d** 05. OLM Levenshulme St Andr and St Pet *Man* from 05. *4 Limefield Terrace, Levenshulme, Manchester M19 2EP* Tel 0161-225 4200 E-mail frankkerr@btinternet.com

KERR, George Cecil. b 36. TCD BA60 MA65. CITC 60. **d** 60 **p** 61. C Coleraine *Conn* 60-63; Div Master Annandale Gr Sch Belf 63-65; Dean of Res QUB 65-74; Lic to Offic *D & D* 75-00; rtd 00. *12 Berkeley Grove, Warrenpoint BT34 3TS*

KERR, Canon Jean. b 46. Man Univ MA93 SS Hild & Bede Coll Dur CertEd69. N Ord Course 84. **d** 87 **p** 94. NSM Peel *Man* 87-93; Par Dn Dixon Green 88-89; Par Dn New Bury 89-93; Par Dn Gillingham St Mark *Roch* 93-94; C 94-98; Chapl Medway Secure Tr Cen 98-01; Warden of Ev 98-05; NSM Roch St Justus 01-05; Hon Can Roch Cathl 03-05; Can Missr from 05; Tr Officer for Lay Minl Educn 03-05; Bp's Officer for Miss and Unity from 05; Dioc Lay Tr Adv from 05. *St Justus's Vicarage, 1 Binnacle Road, Rochester ME1 2XR* Tel and fax (01634) 841183 *or* 400673 E-mail jean.kerr@rochester.anglican.org

KERR, John Maxwell. b 43. MSOSc88 Toronto Univ BASc66 Leeds Univ MSc70. Linc Th Coll 75. **d** 77 **p** 78. C New Windsor *Ox* 77-80; Asst Chapl Cheltenham Coll 80-81; Chapl 81-82; NSM Win St Lawr and St Maurice w St Swithun *Win* 82-94; Chapl Win Coll 82-92; Hd RS 86-97; Visiting Lect Dept of Continuing Educn Ox Univ 92-04; rtd 02; Perm to Offic *Portsm* 03-04; USA from 05. *820 Grey Avenue, Evanston, IL 60202, USA* E-mail jmk@kerr.newnet.co.uk

KERR, Canon Nicholas Ian. b 46. Em Coll Cam BA68 MA72. Westcott Ho Cam 74. **d** 77 **p** 78. C Merton St Mary *S'wark* 77-80; C Rainham *Roch* 80-84; Chapl Joyce Green Hosp Dartford 84-90; V Dartford St Edm *Roch* 84-90; V Lamorbey H Redeemer from 90; RD Sidcup 98-03; Hon Can Roch Cathl from 02. *The Vicarage, 64 Day's Lane, Sidcup DA15 8JR* Tel (020) 8300 1508 E-mail nik@dircon.co.uk

KERR, Paul Turner. b 47. Man Univ MA92. Cranmer Hall Dur 68. **d** 71 **p** 72. C Kingston upon Hull St Martin *York* 71-72; C Linthorpe 72-76; C Cherry Hinton St Jo *Ely* 76-78; Chapl

Addenbrooke's Hosp Cam 76-78; TV Rochdale *Man* 78-84; Chapl Birch Hill Hosp Rochdale 78-84; V New Bury 84-87; TR 87-93; C Gillingham St Mark *Roch* 93-98; RD Gillingham 96-98; V Roch St Justus from 98; RD Roch from 02. *St Justus's Vicarage, 1 Binnacle Road, Rochester ME1 2XR* Tel (01634) 841183 Fax 818353 E-mail kerrevan@global.net *or* office@stjustuschurch.freeserve.co.uk

KERR, Canon Stephen Peter. b 46. TCD BA68 Edin Univ BD71 MPhil80. **d** 71 **p** 72. C Belfast H Trin *Conn* 72-76; C Ballywillan 76-78; Lect Linc Th Coll 78-87; Dioc Officer for Adult Educn and Minl Tr *Worc* 87-99; P-in-c Ombersley w Doverdale from 87; Hon Can Worc Cathl from 93; Bp's Th Adv from 99. *The Rectory, Ombersley, Droitwich WR9 0EW* Tel (01905) 620950 E-mail peter.kerr@cofe-worcester.org.uk

KERR, Terence Philip. b 54. QUB BD97. CITC 97. **d** 99 **p** 00. C Antrim All SS *Conn* 99-01; I Drummaul w Duneane and Ballyscullion from 01. *The Vicarage, 1A Glenkeen, Randalstown, Antrim BT41 3JX* Tel (028) 9447 2561 E-mail terry@revkerr99.freeserve.co.uk

KERRIDGE, Donald George. b 32. Bede Coll Dur CertEd72 Hull Univ BA84. Wesley Coll Leeds 57 Bps' Coll Cheshunt 61. **d** 62 **p** 63. C Manston *Ripon* 62-66; C Hawksworth Wood 66-71; Asst Chapl Brentwood Sch Essex 72-74; Lic to Offic *Linc* 81-89; R Tetney, Marshchapel and N Coates 89-91; P-in-c Linc St Swithin 91-95; P-in-c Linc St Swithin w All SS 95-99; Asst Chapl Linc Co Hosp 91-94; rtd 99. *28 Caverleigh Way, Worcester Park KT4 8DG* Tel (020) 8337 3171

KERRIN, Albert Eric. b 26. Aber Univ MA51. Edin Th Coll 51. **d** 53 **p** 54. C Dumfries *Glas* 53-55; P-in-c Cambuslang w Newton Cathl Miss 55-57; I Alford *Ab* 57-69; P-in-c Portpatrick *Glas* 69-98; P-in-c Stranraer 69-98; rtd 91; Perm to Offic *Glas* from 98. *15 London Road, Stranraer DG9 8AF* Tel (01776) 702822

KERRISON, Mrs Anne Edmonstone. b 23. Cranmer Hall Dur 69. **dss** 77 **d** 87 **p** 94. Hellesdon *Nor* 76-78; Ind Miss 78-79; Lic to Offic 79-88; Perm to Offic 88-94; NSM Hevingham w Hainford and Stratton Strawless 94-96; Perm to Offic from 96. *Sloley Lodge, Sloley, Norwich NR12 8HE* Tel (01692) 538253

KERRY, Martin John. b 55. Ox Univ MA78. St Jo Coll Nottm BA81 MTh83. **d** 82 **p** 83. C Everton St Geo *Liv* 82-85; Lic to Offic *S'well* 85-04; Chapl Asst Nottm City Hosp 85-89; Chapl 89-94; Hd Chapl Nottm City Hosp NHS Trust 94-04; Lead Chapl (NE) *Caring for the Spirit* NHS Project from 04. *Mobility Centre, Nottingham City Hospital, Hucknall Road, Nottingham NG5 1PB* Tel 0115-969 1169 *or* 962 7616

KERSHAW, John Harvey. b 51. Coll of Resurr Mirfield 84. **d** 86 **p** 87. C Hollinwood *Man* 86-89; V Audenshaw St Hilda from 89; Chapl Tameside Gen Hosp 90-94; Chapl Tameside and Glossop NHS Trust 94-95. *St Hilda's Vicarage, Denton Road, Audenshaw, Manchester M34 5BL* Tel 0161-336 2310

KERSHAW, Savile. b 37. Bernard Gilpin Soc Dur 60 Chich Th Coll 61. **d** 64 **p** 65. C Staincliffe *Wakef* 64-66; C Saltley *Birm* 66-68; C Birm St Aid Small Heath 68-72; Perm to Offic from 88; rtd 02. *74 Longmore Road, Shirley, Solihull B90 3EE* Tel 0121-744 3470

KERSLAKE, Mrs Mary. **d** 05. OLM Hethersett w Canteloff w Lt and Gt Melton *Nor* from 05. *Melton Vista, Green Lane, Little Melton, Norwich NR9 3LE* Tel (01603) 811228

KERSLEY, Stuart Casburn. b 40. CEng MIEE. Trin Coll Bris. **d** 82 **p** 83. C Lancing w Coombes *Chich* 82-87; TV Littlehampton and Wick 87-90; R Kingston Buci 90-98; V Kirdford from 98. *The Vicarage, Kirdford, Billingshurst RH14 0LU* Tel (01403) 820605

KERSWILL, Canon Anthony John. b 39. Lambeth STh85. Linc Th Coll 72. **d** 73 **p** 73. C Boultham *Linc* 73-76; P-in-c N Kelsey and Cadney 76-83; V Gainsborough St Geo 83-91; V Bracebridge 91-00; P-in-c Linc St Swithin 00-01; V Linc All SS 01-05; RD Christianity 96-02; Can and Preb Linc Cathl 02-05; rtd 05; Chapl Trin Hosp Retford from 05. *The Rectory Farm, Rectory Road, Retford DN22 7AY* Tel (01777) 862533 E-mail anthokers@aol.com

KERTON-JOHNSON, Peter. b 41. St Paul's Coll Grahamstown. **d** 81 **p** 82. S Africa 81-99; Perm to Offic *Sarum* 99-00; P-in-c Stoke sub Hamdon *B & W* from 00. *The Vicarage, 1 Castle Street, Stoke-sub-Hamdon TA14 6RE* Tel (01935) 822529 Fax 818289 E-mail kertonjohnson@btopenworld.com

KESLAKE, Peter Ralegh. b 33. Sarum & Wells Th Coll. **d** 83 **p** 84. C Glouc St Geo w Whaddon *Glouc* 83-86; P-in-c France Lynch 86-91; V Chalford and France Lynch 91-03; rtd 03; Perm to Offic *Glouc* from 04. *4 Farmcote Close, Eastcombe, Stroud GL6 7EG*

KESTER, Jonathan George Frederick. b 66. Ex Univ BA90. Coll of Resurr Mirfield Cert Past Th93. **d** 93 **p** 94. C Cheshunt *St Alb* 93-96; Chapl to Bp Edmonton *Lon* 96-00; Hon C Munster Square Ch Ch and St Mary Magd 96-00; V Gt Ilford St Mary *Chelmsf* from 00. *St Mary's Vicarage, 26 South Park Road, Ilford IG1 1SS* Tel (020) 8478 0546 *or* 8478 0768 E-mail frjonathan.kester@ntlworld.com

KESTON, Marion. b 44. Glas Univ MB, ChB68 Edin Univ MTh95. St And Dioc Tr Course 87 Edin Th Coll 92. **d** 90 **p** 94. NSM W Fife Team Min *St And* 90-93; C Dunfermline 93-96; Priest Livingston LEP *Edin* 96-04; P-in-c Kinross *St And* from 04. *Hattonburn Lodge, Milnathort, Kinross KY13 0SA* Tel (01577) 866834 E-mail marionkeston@lineone.net

KETLEY, Christopher Glen. b 62. Aston Tr Scheme 91 Coll of Resurr Mirfield 93. **d** 95 **p** 96. C Gt Crosby St Faith *Liv* 95-98; C Swinton and Pendlebury *Man* 98-00; V Belfield from 00. *St Ann's Vicarage, 310 Milnrow Road, Rochdale OL16 5BT* Tel (01706) 646173

KETLEY, Michael James. b 39. DipHE81. Oak Hill Th Coll 79. **d** 81 **p** 82. C Bedhampton *Portsm* 81-85; R St Ive w Quethiock *Truro* 85-86; NSM Basildon St Andr w H Cross *Chelmsf* 89-90; C Barkingside St Cedd 90-92; P-in-c 92-95; R Hadleigh St Jas from 95. *The Rectory, 50 Rectory Road, Hadleigh, Benfleet SS7 2ND* Tel (01702) 558992 E-mail revmike@stjamesless.freeserve.co.uk

KETTLE, Alan Marshall. b 51. Leeds Univ BA72. Wycliffe Hall Ox MA78. **d** 78 **p** 79. C Llantwit Fardre *Llan* 78-81; Prov RE Adv Ch in Wales 81-84; Chapl Llandovery Coll 84-92; P-in-c Cil-y-Cwm and Ystrad-ffin w Rhandir-mwyn etc *St D* 85-92; Chapl W Buckland Sch Barnstaple from 92; Lic to Offic *Ex* from 92. *2 West Close, West Buckland, Barnstaple EX32 0ST* Tel (01598) 760542

KETTLE, David John. b 47. Bris Univ BSc69 MLitt86 Fitzw Coll Cam BA75 MA79. Westcott Ho Cam 73. **d** 76 **p** 77. C Bris St Andr Hartcliffe *Bris* 76-79; C Fishponds All SS 79-80; P-in-c 81-83; Perm to Offic *St E* 83-91; New Zealand 91-97; NSM Anglesey Gp *Ely* from 99. *11 Redgate Road, Girton, Cambridge CB3 0PP* Tel (01223) 277505 E-mail djk@kettle.force9.co.uk

KETTLE, Martin Drew. b 52. New Coll Ox BA74 Selw Coll Cam BA76 Cam Univ MA85. Ridley Hall Cam 74. **d** 77 **p** 78. C Enfield St Andr *Lon* 77-80; Chapl Ridley Hall Cam 80-84; V Hendon St Paul Mill Hill *Lon* 85-98; AD W Barnet 90-95; Perm to Offic *Ely* 03-04; Hon C Huntingdon from 04. *83 Wertheim Way, Huntingdon PE29 6UH* Tel (01480) 434075 Mobile 07968-909492 E-mail mdkettle@msn.com

KETTLE, Mrs Patricia Mary Carole. b 41. Worc Coll of Educn CertEd61 Lon Univ DipTh68. Dalton Ho Bris 66. **d** 87 **p** 94. C Wonersh *Guildf* 87-98; C Wonersh w Blackheath 98-01; rtd 01; Perm to Offic *Guildf* from 02. *Wakehurst Cottage, Links Road, Bramley GU5 0AL* Tel (01483) 898856

KETTLE, Peter. b 51. K Coll Lon BD74 AKC74. St Aug Coll Cant 74. **d** 75 **p** 76. C Angell Town St Jo *S'wark* 75-78; C Putney St Mary 78-80; V Raynes Park St Sav 80-85; Perm to Offic *S'wark* from 85 and *Lon* from 03. *46 Allenswood, Albert Drive, London SW19 6JX* Tel (020) 8785 3797

KEULEMANS, Andrew Francis Charles. b 68. Univ of Wales (Abth) BSc90. St Jo Coll Nottm BTh93. **d** 94 **p** 95. C Mold *St As* 94-97; TV Wrexham 97-02; Chapl Loretto Sch Musselburgh from 02. *The Manse, 4 Eskside East, Musselburgh EH21 7RS* Tel 0131-653 4429

KEVILL-DAVIES, Christopher Charles. b 44. AKC69. St Aug Coll Cant 70. **d** 70 **p** 71. C Folkestone St Sav *Cant* 70-75; V Yaxley *Ely* 75-78; R Chevington w Hargrave and Whepstead w Brockley *St E* 78-86; Perm to Offic *St Alb* 86-89; NSM Stansted Mountfitchet *Chelmsf* 87-89; R Barkway, Reed and Buckland w Barley *St Alb* 89-97; R Chelsea St Luke and Ch Ch *Lon* from 97; rtd 06. *35 Clapham Common South Side, London SW4 9BS*

KEVIS, Lionel William Graham. b 55. York Univ BA. Wycliffe Hall Ox 83. **d** 86 **p** 87. C Plaistow St Mary *Roch* 86-90; R Ash and Ridley 90-00; P-in-c Bidborough 00-02; P-in-c Leigh from 00; RD Tonbridge from 03. *The Vicarage, The Green, Leigh, Tonbridge TN11 8QJ* Tel (01732) 833022

KEW, William Richard. b 45. Lon Univ BD69. Lon Coll of Div LTh68. **d** 69 **p** 70. C Finchley St Paul Long Lane *Lon* 69-72; C Stoke Bishop *Bris* 72-76; USA from 76. *1015 Old Lascassas Road, Murfreesboro, TN 37130, USA* E-mail richardkew@aol.com

KEY, Christopher Halstead. b 56. St Jo Coll Dur BA77 K Coll Lon MTh78. Ridley Hall Cam 79. **d** 81 **p** 82. C Balderstone *Man* 81-84; C Wandsworth All SS *S'wark* 84-88; C-in-c W Dulwich Em CD 88-93; V W Dulwich Em 93-95; R Ore *Chich* from 95; RD Hastings from 03. *St Helen's Rectory, 266 Elphinstone Road, Hastings TN34 2AG* Tel (01424) 425172 E-mail chriskey@st-helens-ore.freeserve.co.uk

KEY, The Very Revd Robert Frederick. b 52. Bris Univ BA73. Oak Hill Th Coll 74. **d** 76 **p** 77. C Ox St Ebbe w St Pet *Ox* 76-80; C Wallington H Trin *S'wark* 80-85; P-in-c Eynsham *Ox* 85; V Eynsham and Cassington 85-91; V Ox St Andr 91-01; Gen Dir CPAS 01-05; Dean Jersey *Win* from 05; P-in-c Jersey St Helier from 05. *The Deanery, David Place, St Helier, Jersey JE2 4TE* Tel (01534) 720001 E-mail bob@familykey.fsnet.co.uk *or* deanofjersey@jerseymail.co.uk

KEY, Roderick Charles Halstead. b 57. MTh. **d** 84 **p** 85. C Up Hatherley *Glouc* 84-87; V Glouc St Paul 87-04; TR Trunch *Nor* from 04. *The Rectory, Knapton Road, Trunch, North Walsham NR28 0QE* Tel (01263) 722725 *or* 834603

KEY, Roger Astley. b 49. Coll of Resurr Mirfield 72. **d** 74 **p** 75. Perm to Offic *Wakef* 74-75; P-in-c Khomasdal Grace Ch

Namibia 75-77; R Luderitz 77-81; Adn The South 77-80; R Walvis Bay 81-85; Personal Asst to Bp Windhoek 85-86; Dean Windhoek 86-00; V Hopton w Corton *Nor* from 00. *The Vicarage, 51 The Street, Corton, Lowestoft NR32 5HT* Tel (01502) 730977 Mobile 07733-028048
E-mail thekeybunch@aol.com *or* rogerkey30@hotmail.com

KEYES, Graham George. b 44. St Cath Coll Cam BA65 MA68 Lanc Univ MA74 Nottm Univ MTh85 MPhil92. EMMTC 82. **d** 84 **p** 85. C Evington *Leic* 84-86; Vice-Prin NEOC 86-89; C Monkseaton St Mary *Newc* 86-89; P-in-c Newc St Hilda 89-94; TV Ch the King 94-99; rtd 99. *1 East Avenue, Newcastle upon Tyne NE12 9PH* Tel 0191-259 9024
E-mail simeon.and.anna@talk21.com

KEYES, Mrs Iris Doreen. b 28. SRN. Gilmore Ho 69. **dss** 76 **d** 87 **p** 94. Egham Hythe *Guildf* 76-78; Chapl Asst St Pet Hosp Chertsey 78-82; Addlestone 83-86; Walton-on-Thames 86-87; C 87-89; rtd 89; NSM Addlestone *Guildf* 94-95; Perm to Offic from 95. *36 Finlay Gardens, Addlestone KT15 2XN* Tel (01932) 846912

KEYMER, Philip John. b 72. Bris Univ BSc93. Oak Hill Th Coll 96. **d** 99 **p** 00. C Partington and Carrington *Ches* 99-02; C Cheadle 02-04. *10 Central Avenue, Levenshulme, Manchester M19 2EN* Tel 0161-224 2384
E-mail phil.keymer@ntlworld.com

KEYS, Christopher David. b 56. Southn Univ BTh95. Trin Coll Bris. **d** 02 **p** 03. C Fressingfield, Mendham etc *St E* 02-04; C Ipswich St Helen, H Trin, and St Luke from 04. *6 Collinsons, Hadleigh Road, Ipswich IP2 0DS* Tel (01473) 281364 Mobile 07887-797361 E-mail chris.keys@new-wine.net

KEYT, Fitzroy John. b 34. Linc Th Coll. **d** 67 **p** 68. C Highters Heath *Birm* 67-70; Hon C Sheldon 70-73; Australia from 73; V Miles 73-76; R Rayton 76-86; R Coolangatta 86-98; P-in-c Clayfield 98-01. *58 Thompson Street, Zillmere, Qld, Australia 4034* Tel (0061) (7) 3314 3011 E-mail dskeyt@optusnet.com.au

KEYTE, Douglas Joseph Henry. b 18. St Jo Coll Cam BA40 MA46. Wycliffe Hall Ox 46. **d** 48 **p** 49. C Kersal Moor *Man* 48-51; C Newall Green St Fran 51-54; Chapl K Wm's Coll Is of Man 55-57; Ghana 57-61; Asst Master Co Gr Sch for Girls Sale 61-75; Hon C Charlestown *Man* 75-89; rtd 83; Hon C Pendleton St Thos w Charlestown *Man* 89-95; Hon C Pendleton from 95. *26 Heathfield Close, Sale M33 2PQ* Tel 0161-973 2844

KHAKHRIA, Rohitkumar Prabhulal (Roy). b 60. Sheff Univ BSc82 PGCE83. Oak Hill Th Coll 94. **d** 96 **p** 97. C Muswell Hill St Jas w St Matt *Lon* 96-01; C Stoughton *Guildf* 01-04; V Boscombe St Jo *Win* from 04. *St John's Vicarage, 17 Browning Avenue, Bournemouth BH5 1NR* Tel (01202) 396667 *or* tel and fax 301916 E-mail roy.khakhria@lycosmax.co.uk

KHAMBATTA, Neville Holbery. b 48. St Chad's Coll Dur BA74. S'wark Ord Course 81. **d** 84 **p** 85. Asst Chapl Em Sch Wandsworth 84-87; Hon C Thornton Heath St Jude w St Aid *S'wark* 84-87; Asst Warden Horstead Cen 87-01; Hon C Coltishall w Gt Hautbois and Horstead *Nor* 87-01; V Ludham, Potter Heigham, Hickling and Catfield from 01. *The Vicarage, Norwich Road, Ludham, Great Yarmouth NR29 5QA* Tel (01692) 678282 E-mail khambatta@lineone.net

KHOO, Boon-Hor. b 31. FBCO. Llan Dioc Tr Scheme. **d** 87 **p** 88. NSM Llandaff w Capel Llanilltern *Llan* 87-96; Perm to Offic from 96. *38 The Cathedral Green, Llandaff, Cardiff CF5 2EB* Tel (029) 2056 1478

KICHENSIDE, Mark Gregory. b 53. Nottm Univ BTh83. St Jo Coll Nottm 80. **d** 83 **p** 84. C Orpington Ch Ch *Roch* 83-86; C Bexley St Jo 86-90; V Blendon 90-93; V Welling 93-00; R Flegg Coastal Benefice *Nor* from 00; RD Gt Yarmouth from 02. *The Rectory, Somerton Road, Winterton-on-Sea, Great Yarmouth NR29 4AW* Tel and fax (01493) 393227
E-mail mark@kiche.enterprise-plc.com

KIDD, Anthony John Eric. b 38. Solicitor. Oak Hill NSM Course. **d** 89 **p** 90. NSM Rawdon *Bradf* 89-91; C Ilkley All SS 91-93; Perm to Offic *Bradf* 93-95; Perm to Offic *York* 95-96 and 98-04; Hon C Gt and Lt Driffield 96-98; P-in-c Burton Agnes w Harpham and Lowthorpe etc from 04. *The Rectory, Burton Agnes, Driffield YO25 4NE* Tel (01262) 490217

KIDD, Canon Carol Ivy. b 47. Trent Park Coll of Educn CertEd69. Oak Hill Th Coll 92. **d** 95 **p** 96. C Bootle St Mary w St Paul *Liv* 95-99; TV Speke St Aid 99-05; TR from 05; Hon Can Liv Cathl from 03. *All Saints' Vicarage, Speke Church Road, Liverpool L24 3TA* Tel 0151-486 0292

KIDD, John Alan. b 32. Pemb Coll Cam BA58 MA61. Ridley Hall Cam 57. **d** 61 **p** 62. C Onslow Square St Paul *Lon* 61-65; S Africa 65-67; Uganda 67-69; P-in-c Mayfair Ch Ch *Lon* 69-75; V 75-79; V Virginia Water *Guildf* 79-88; Lic to Offic 88-94; rtd 94. *Flat 1, Blayds House, Spring Street, Easingwold, York YO61 3BL* Tel (01347) 823201

KIDD, Maurice Edward. b 26. LTh. **d** 55 **p** 56. C Wembley St Jo *Lon* 55-58; C Middleton *Man* 58-61; Chapl Pastures Hosp Derby 61-69; Chapl Guild of Health Lon 69-72; R Hanworth St Geo *Lon* 72-82; R Chartham *Cant* 82-91; rtd 91; Perm to Offic *Cant* from 91. *Harvest View, The Mint, Harbledown, Canterbury CT2 9AA* Tel (01227) 761655

KIDD, Timothy. b 24. St Chad's Coll Dur BA48 DipTh50 MA53 Nottm Univ MA57 MPhil71 MEd80. Lambeth STh74. **d** 50 **p** 51. C Mexborough *Sheff* 50-52; Lect Boston 52-56; C Boston *Linc* 52-56; Offg Chapl RAF 56-65; V Grantham St Anne *Linc* 56-65; Asst Dioc Youth Chapl 59-65; Prin Lect Kesteven Coll of Educn 65-79; Hon C Harlaxton, Lt Ponton and Stroxton 66-72; Gen Preacher from 73; Visiting Lect Univ Evansville (USA) 79-86; Teacher K Sch Grantham 80-90; Perm to Offic *Leic* from 89; rtd 90. *14 Woodlands Drive, Grantham NG31 9DJ* Tel (01476) 563273

KIDDLE, Canon John. b 58. Qu Coll Cam BA80 MA83 Heythrop Coll Lon MTh02. Ridley Hall Cam 79. **d** 82 **p** 83. C Ormskirk *Liv* 82-86; V Huyton Quarry 86-91; V Watford St Luke *St Alb* from 91; RD Watford 99-04; Hon Can St Alb from 05. *St Luke's Vicarage, Devereux Drive, Watford WD17 3DD* Tel (01923) 242208 Fax 246161
E-mail j.kiddle@btopenworld.com

KIDDLE, Mark Brydges. b 34. ACP61. Wycliffe Hall Ox. **d** 63 **p** 64. C Scarborough St Luke *York* 63-66; C Walthamstow St Sav *Chelmsf* 66-71; V Nelson St Bede *Blackb* 71-76; V Perry Common *Birm* 76-79; R Grayingham *Linc* 79-84; V Kirton in Lindsey 79-84; R Manton 79-84; Hon C St Botolph Aldgate w H Trin Minories *Lon* 85-91; Hon C St Clem Eastcheap w St Martin Orgar from 91. *4 Mandela House, 79 Virginia Road, London E2 7NE* Tel (020) 7613 1113
E-mail markinlondon@aol.com

KIDDLE, Martin John. b 42. Lon Univ DipTh75 Open Univ BA80. St Jo Coll Nottm 74. **d** 76 **p** 77. C Gt Parndon *Chelmsf* 76-80; Asst Chapl HM Pris Wakef 80-81; Asst Chapl HM Youth Cust Cen Portland 81-88; Chapl HM Pris Cardiff 88-97; Chapl HM Pris Channings Wood 97-02; rtd 02; Perm to Offic *Ex* from 02. *2 Cricketfield Close, Chudleigh, Newton Abbot TQ13 0GA* Tel (01626) 853980 E-mail mkiddle@btopenworld.com

KIDDLE, Canon Peter. b 22. Fitzw Ho Cam BA50 MA54. Clifton Th Coll 57. **d** 57 **p** 58. Kenya 57-72; Hon Can Nairobi Cathl 72; V Worthing St Paul *Chich* 73-87; rtd 87; Perm to Offic *Sarum* from 87; P-in-c Milton Lilbourne w Easton Royal 87-90. *64 Damask Way, Warminster BA12 9PP* Tel (01985) 214572

KIDDLE, Miss Susan Elizabeth. b 44. Birm Univ BSc66 Nottm Univ CertEd67. LNSM course 86. **d** 89 **p** 95. OLM Waddington *Linc* 89-97; OLM Bracebridge from 98. *16 Sycamore Drive, Waddington, Lincoln LN5 9DR* Tel (01522) 722010

KIDNER, Frank Derek. b 13. ARCM33 Ch Coll Cam BA40 MA44. Ridley Hall Cam 40. **d** 41 **p** 42. C Sevenoaks St Nic *Roch* 41-47; V Felsted *Chelmsf* 47-51; Sen Tutor Oak Hill Th Coll 51-64; Warden Tyndale Ho Cam 64-78; rtd 78; Perm to Offic *Ely* from 79. *56 Manor Park, Histon, Cambridge CB4 9JT* Tel (01223) 232579

KIGALI, Bishop of. *See* KOLINI, The Most Revd Emmanuel Musaba

KIGGELL, Mrs Anne. b 36. Liv Univ BA57. St Alb and Ox Min Course 99. **d** 02 **p** 03. OLM Basildon w Aldworth and Ashampstead *Ox* from 02. *Straight Ash, Ashampstead Common, Reading RG8 8QT* Tel (01635) 201385
E-mail anne.kiggell@virgin.net

KIGHTLEY, Canon David John. b 39. AKC67. **d** 68 **p** 69. C Plymouth St Andr *Ex* 68-70; C Ex St Dav 70-73; Chapl Greenwich Distr Hosp & Brook Gen Hosp Lon 73-76; P-in-c Chippenham *Ely* 76-96; P-in-c Snailwell 76-96; P-in-c Isleham 76-96; RD Fordham 95-96; P-in-c Feltwell 96-98; P-in-c Methwold 96-98; R Feltwell and Methwold from 98; RD Feltwell 96-04; RD Fincham 98-04; RD Fincham and Feltwell from 04; Hon Can Ely Cathl from 00. *The Rectory, 7 Oak Street, Feltwell, Thetford IP26 4DD* Tel (01842) 828104
E-mail davidkightley@aol.com

KILBEY, Mrs Sarah. b 39. MBE98. Edin Univ MA75 Man Poly CETD82. Bp Otter Coll TDip59 Edin Dioc NSM Course 84. **d** 93 **p** 97. NSM Edin St Columba *Edin* 93-96; NSM Edin St Martin from 96. *77 Morningside Park, Edinburgh EH10 5EZ* Tel 0131-447 2378

KILBOURN-MACKIE, Canon Mary Elizabeth. b 26. Toronto Univ BA48 Harvard Univ MA49. Trin Coll Toronto MDiv77. **d** 77 **p** 78. Canada 77-00; Hon Can Toronto from 96; Perm to Offic *Sarum* from 00 and *B W* from 02. *14 Chatham Court, Station Road, Warminster BA12 9LS* Tel (01985) 211049

KILDARE, Archdeacon of. *See* LAWRENCE, The Ven Patrick Henry Andrew

KILDARE, Dean of. *See* TOWNLEY, The Very Revd Robert Keith

KILFORD, John Douglas. b 38. Oak Hill Th Coll 73. **d** 75 **p** 76. C Beckenham St Jo *Roch* 75-80; P-in-c Sinfin Moor *Derby* 80-83; V Penge St Jo *Roch* 83-92; Staff Member Ellel Min 92-03; rtd 03; Perm to Offic *Truro* from 03. *Trelowarren Christian Fellowship, Mawgan, Helston TR12 6AF* Tel (01326) 221366
E-mail trelowarren@fellowshipt.freeserve.co.uk

KILFORD, William Roy. b 38. Bris Univ BA60. Sarum & Wells Th Coll 82. **d** 84 **p** 85. C Herne *Cant* 84-87; Chapl Wm Harvey Hosp Ashford 87-93; R Mersham w Hinxhill *Cant* 87-93; P-in-c

Sevington 87-93; V Reculver and Herne Bay St Bart 93-95; Chapl Paphos Cyprus 95-98; P-in-c Doddington, Newnham and Wychling *Cant* 98-02; P-in-c Lynsted w Kingsdown 98-02; P-in-c Norton 98-02; AD Ospringe 01-02; rtd 02; Chapl Nord Pas de Calais *Eur* 02-04; Hon C Burton Fleming w Fordon, Grindale etc *York* from 04. *The Vicarage, Back Street, Burton Fleming, Driffield YO25 3PD* Tel (01262) 470873

KILGOUR, The Very Revd Richard Eifl. b 57. Edin Univ BD85. Edin Th Coll 81. **d** 85 **p** 86. C Wrexham *St As* 85-88; V Whitford 88-97; Ind Chapl 89-97; R Newtown w Llanllwchaiarn w Aberhafesp 97-03; RD Cedewain 01-03; Provost St Andr Cathl *Ab* from 03; R Aberdeen St Andr from 03; P-in-c Aberdeen St Ninian from 03. *St Andrew's Cathedral, King Street, Aberdeen AB24 5AX* Tel (01224) 640119 E-mail provost@aberdeen.anglican.org *or* newrect@hotmail.com

KILLALA AND ACHONRY, Archdeacon of. *See* DADSWELL, The Ven Richard Edward

KILLALA, Dean of. *See* PATTERSON, The Very Revd Susan Margaret

KILLALOE, KILFENORA AND CLONFERT, Dean of. *See* WHITE, The Very Revd Stephen Ross

KILLALOE, KILFENORA, CLONFERT AND KILMACDUAGH, Archdeacon of. *See* CARNEY, The Ven Richard Wayne

KILLE, Canon Vivian Edwy. b 30. Tyndale Hall Bris 60. **d** 62 **p** 63. C Dublin Miss Ch *D & G* 62-66; I Emlaghfad *T, K & A* 66-74; I Aghadrumsee w Clogh and Drumsnatt *Clogh* from 74; Can Clogh Cathl from 93. *Sunshine Rectory, 16 Dernawilt Road, Rosslea, Enniskillen BT92 7QY* Tel (028) 6775 1206 E-mail vek@hallelujah.demon.co.uk

KILLOCK, Alfred Kenneth. b 26. Cranmer Hall Dur 72. **d** 74 **p** 75. C Moor Allerton *Ripon* 74-79; Hon C Bolton St Jas w St Chrys *Bradf* 79-83; P-in-c Oakenshaw cum Woodlands 84-90; P-in-c Allerton 90-91; rtd 91; Perm to Offic *Bradf* from 91. *15 Warwick Road, Bradford BD4 7RA* Tel (01274) 394462

KILLWICK, Canon Simon David Andrew. b 56. K Coll Lon BD80 AKC80. St Steph Ho Ox 80. **d** 81 **p** 82. C Worsley *Man* 81-84; TV 84-97; P-in-c Moss Side Ch Ch from 97; Hon Can Man Cathl from 04. *Christ Church Rectory, Monton Street, Manchester M14 4LT* Tel 0161-226 2476

KILMORE, Archdeacon of. *See* DAVISON, The Ven George Thomas William

KILMORE, Dean of. *Vacant*

KILMORE, ELPHIN AND ARDAGH, Bishop of. *See* CLARKE, The Rt Revd Kenneth Herbert

KILNER, Canon Frederick James. b 43. Qu Coll Cam BA65 MA69. Ridley Hall Cam 67. **d** 70 **p** 71. C Harlow New Town w Lt Parndon *Chelmsf* 70-74; C Cambridge St Andr Less *Ely* 74-79; P-in-c Milton 79-88; R 88-94; Hon Can Ely Cathl from 88; P-in-c Ely 94-96; P-in-c Chettisham 94-96; P-in-c Prickwillow 94-96; P-in-c Stretham w Thetford 94-96; P-in-c Stuntney 95-96; TR Ely from 96. *St Mary's Vicarage, St Mary's Street, Ely CB7 4ER* Tel (01353) 662308 E-mail kilner@btinternet.com

KILNER, Mrs Valerie June. b 42. MICFM91 Univ of Wales (Abth) BSc64 Hughes Hall Cam PGCE65. EAMTC 98. **d** 98 **p** 99. NSM Ely from 98. *St Mary's Vicarage, St Mary's Street, Ely CB7 4ER* Tel (01353) 662308 Fax as telephone E-mail kilner@btinternet.com

KILPATRICK, Alan William. b 64. Oak Hill Th Coll BA96 Birm Bible Inst 91. **d** 96 **p** 97. C Ealing St Paul *Lon* 96-01; Assoc R Mt Pleasant USA 01-04; P-in-c Prestonville St Luke *Chich* from 04. *St Luke's Vicarage, 64A Old Shoreham Road, Brighton BN1 5DD* Tel (01273) 552267

KILSBY, Miss Joyce (Jocelyn). b 40. Univ Coll Lon BSc62 Ox Univ DipEd63. N Ord Course 98. **d** 01 **p** 02. NSM Stanley *Wakef* from 01. *18 Hazelwood Court, Outwood, Wakefield WF1 3HP* Tel (01924) 824396 E-mail hilkil.hazco@virgin.net

KIMBALL, Melodie Irene. b 49. **d** 99. USA 99-01; Chapl Asst S Man Univ Hosps NHS Trust 01-02; Asst Chapl Qu Medical Cen Nottm Univ Hosp NHS Trust 02-03; Asst Chapl Leeds Mental Health Teaching NHS Trust from 03. *Meanwood Park, Tongue Lane, Leeds LS6 4QB* Tel 0113-295 2800

KIMBER, Geoffrey Francis. b 46. Univ Coll Lon BA67 PGCE70 DipTh74. St Jo Coll Nottm 86. **d** 88 **p** 89. C Buckhurst Hill *Chelmsf* 88-92; R Arley *Cov* 92-02; P-in-c Ansley 97-02; CMS Romania from 02. *Cross of Nails Reconciliation Centre, Ascensium, Str Ion Slavici nr 7, Sibiu 2400, Romania* Tel (0040) (69) 215181 Fax as telephone E-mail geoff.kimber@btinternet.com

KIMBER, Mrs Gillian Margaret. b 48. Bedf Coll Lon BA70. Oak Hill Th Coll 89. **d** 91. NSM Buckhurst Hill *Chelmsf* 91-92; C Arley *Cov* 92-97; C Ansley 97-02; CMS Romania from 02. *Cross of Nails Reconciliation Centre, Ascensium, Str Ion Slavici nr 7, Sibiu 2400, Romania* Tel (0040) (69) 215181 Fax as telephone E-mail gill.kimber@btinternet.com

KIMBER, Mrs Hazel Olive. b 33. Lon Univ CertEd73. LNSM course 92. **d** 95 **p** 96. OLM W Dulwich Em *S'wark* from 95. *18 Michaelson House, Kingswood Estate, London SE21 8PX* Tel (020) 8670 5298

KIMBER, John Keith. b 45. Bris Univ BSc66. St Mich Coll Llan. **d** 69 **p** 70. C Caerphilly *Llan* 69-72; Chapl Birm Univ *Birm* 72-75; TR Bris St Agnes and St Simon w St Werburgh *Bris* 75-82; P-in-c Bris St Paul w St Barn 80-82; Hon C Westbury-on-Trym H Trin 82-83; Area Sec (Wales) USPG 83-89; TR Halesowen *Worc* 89-92; Chapl Geneva *Eur* 92-01; Chapl Monte Carlo 01-02; TR Cen Cardiff *Llan* from 02. *The Vicarage, 16 Queen Anne Square, Cardiff CF10 3ED* Tel (029) 2022 0375 E-mail jkk@ntlworld.com

KIMBER, Jonathan Richard. b 69. K Coll Cam BA91 MA95 St Jo Coll Dur MA02. Cranmer Hall Dur 99. **d** 02 **p** 03. C Weston Favell *Pet* from 02. *5 Kestrel Close, Northampton NN3 3JG* Tel (01604) 403213 E-mail jrkimber@yahoo.co.uk

KIMBER, Stuart Francis. b 53. Qu Eliz Coll Lon BSc74 Fitzw Coll Cam BA79 MA83. Ridley Hall Cam 77. **d** 80 **p** 81. C Edgware *Lon* 80-83; C Cheltenham St Mark *Glouc* 83-84; TV 84-92; C Hawkwell *Chelmsf* 92-01; V Westcliff St Andr from 01. *St Andrew's Vicarage, 65 Electric Avenue, Westcliff-on-Sea SS0 9NN* Tel (01702) 302255 E-mail revskimber@compuserve.com

KIMBERLEY, Countess of (Carol Lylie Wodehouse). b 51. St Hugh's Coll Ox BA73 CertEd74 MA77. Ripon Coll Cuddesdon 87. **d** 89 **p** 94. NSM Hambleden Valley *Ox* 89-02; P-in-c Hormead, Wyddial, Anstey, Brent Pelham etc *St Alb* from 02. *The Vicarage, Great Hormead, Buntingford SG9 0NT* Tel (01763) 289258

KIMBERLEY, John Harry. b 49. Brasted Th Coll 72 St Steph Ho Ox 74. **d** 76 **p** 77. C W Tarring *Chich* 76-79; C Portslade St Nic 79-82; C-in-c Findon Valley CD 82-89; V Findon Valley 89-90; V E Preston w Kingston 90-95; Chapl Eastbourne Hosps NHS Trust from 95. *Eastbourne District General Hospital, King's Drive, Eastbourne BN21 2UD* Tel (01323) 417400 ext 4145

KIMBERLEY, The Ven Owen Charles Lawrence. b 27. Univ of NZ BCom53. Tyndale Hall Bris 57. **d** 59 **p** 60. C Higher Openshaw *Man* 59-62; New Zealand 62-94; C Nelson All SS 62-64; V Motupiko 64-69; V Kaikoura 69-76; V Tahunanui 76-85 76-85; Can Nelson Cathl 77-78; Adn Waimea 78-92; V Richmond 85-92; Egypt 94-98; Chapl Port Said 94-98; Adn Egypt 96-98. *11B Gilbert Street, Richmond, Nelson, New Zealand* Tel (0064) (3) 544 2115 Fax as telephone

KIMBERLEY, Canon Wilfred Harry. b 19. St Steph Ho Ox 51. **d** 53 **p** 54. C Wallingford St Mary w All Hallows and St Leon *Ox* 53-55; C Newbury St Jo 55-57; V Highters Heath *Birm* 57-65; V Marsworth *Ox* 65-72; P-in-c Slapton 65-72; P-in-c Cheddington w Mentmore 68-72; V Buckingham 72-78; RD Buckingham 76-78; TR High Wycombe 78-84; Hon Can Ch Ch 79-84; rtd 84; Perm to Offic *Glouc* 85-97; *Ox* 86-98. *Tangle Trees, Springfield, Bourton-on-the-Water, Cheltenham GL54 2DF* Tel (01451) 820779

KIME, Thomas Frederick. b 28. Linc Coll Ox BA50 MA53. Cuddesdon Coll 54. **d** 56 **p** 57. C Forest Gate St Edm *Chelmsf* 56-58; S Africa 58-74; R Ellisfield w Farleigh Wallop and Dummer *Win* 74-83; P-in-c Cliddesden 82-83; R Cliddesden and Ellisfield w Farleigh Wallop etc 83-94; rtd 94; Perm to Offic *Win* from 94. *7 Sparkford Close, Winchester SO22 4NH* Tel (01962) 870240

KINAHAN, Canon Timothy Charles. b 53. Jes Coll Cam BA75. CITC 77. **d** 78 **p** 79. C Carrickfergus *Conn* 78-81; Papua New Guinea 81-84; I Belfast Whiterock *Conn* 84-90; I Gilnahirk *D & D* from 90; Can Belf Cathl from 04. *237 Lower Braniel Road, Belfast BT5 7NQ* Tel (028) 9079 1748 Fax 9079 2413

KINCH, Christopher David. b 81. K Alfred's Coll Win BTh02. St Steph Ho Ox 03. **d** 05. C Long Eaton St Laur *Derby* from 05. *10 Brecon Close, Long Eaton, Nottingham NG10 4JW* Tel 0115-972 4762 E-mail christopherkinch@hotmail.com

KINCHIN-SMITH, John Michael. b 52. Fitzw Coll Cam MA. Ridley Hall Cam 79. **d** 82 **p** 83. C Sanderstead All SS *S'wark* 82-87; TV Halesworth w Linstead, Chediston, Holton etc *St E* 87-92; R Mursley w Swanbourne and Lt Horwood *Ox* 92-02; R Newton Longville and Mursley w Swanbourne etc from 03. *The Rectory, Main Street, Mursley, Milton Keynes MK17 0RT* Tel (01296) 720056

KINDER, David James. b 55. EAMTC 01. **d** 04 **p** 05. NSM Warboys w Broughton and Bury w Wistow *Ely* from 04. *6 Queens Close, St Ives PE27 5QD* Tel (01480) 392500 Mobile 07880-713583 E-mail d.kinder@ntlworld.com

KINDER, Mark Russell. b 66. Univ of Wales (Swansea) BA(Econ)88. St Jo Coll Nottm 91. **d** 94 **p** 95. C Pheasey *Lich* 94-98; TV Tettenhall Regis from 98. *St Paul's Vicarage, 1 Talaton Close, Pendeford, Wolverhampton WV9 5LS* Tel (01902) 787199

KINDER, Mrs Sylvia Patricia. b 61. Ridley Hall Cam 03. **d** 05. C Warboys w Broughton and Bury w Wistow *Ely* from 05. *41 Pathfinder Way, Warboys, Huntingdon PE28 2RD* Tel 07876-204624 (mobile) E-mail sylvia.kinder@ntlworld.com

KING, Mrs Angela Margaret. b 45. Bedf Coll Lon BA67 Lon Inst of Educn PGCE68. SEITE 00. **d** 03 **p** 04. NSM Bromley

St Andr *Roch* from 03. *4 Avondale Road, Bromley BR1 4EP* Tel and fax (020) 8402 0847 E-mail angelaking45@hotmail.com

KING, Anthony Richard. b 34. Trin Hall Cam BA58. Ely Th Coll 58 Linc Th Coll 61. **d** 62 **p** 63. C Benwell St Jas *Newc* 62-64; C Thirsk w S Kilvington *York* 64-67; V Halifax St Aug *Wakef* 67-74; R Upton on Severn *Worc* 74-99; RD Upton 86-92; rtd 99; Perm to Offic *Ex* from 99. *4 The Elms, Colyford, Colyton EX24 6QU* Tel (01297) 552666

KING, Benjamin John. b 74. Down Coll Cam BA96 MA00 Peterho Cam 97 Harvard Univ MTh03. Westcott Ho Cam 97. **d** 00 **p** 00. NSM Eastbourne St Mary *Chich* from 00; C Boston the Advent USA from 00. *30 Brimmer Street, Boston, MA 02108, USA* Tel (001) (617) 523 2377 ext 33 Fax 523 0302 E-mail curate@theadvent.org

✠**KING, The Rt Revd Brian Franklin Vernon.** b 38. ACA59 Univ of NSW BComm61 Lon Univ BD64 Fuller Th Sem California DMin85. Moore Th Coll Sydney. **d** 64 **p** 65 **c** 93. C Manly Australia 64-67; R Dural 67-73; R Wahroonga 73-87; R Manly 87-93; Can Sydney 89-93; Bp W Sydney 93-03; Bp Aus Defence Force 94-01; rtd 03. *Address temp unknown*

KING, Brian Henry. b 39. Chich Th Coll 63. **d** 65 **p** 66. C Castle Bromwich SS Mary and Marg *Birm* 65-67; C Southwick St Mich *Chich* 68-70; V Southwater 70-73; C Brighton St Alb Preston 73-74; TV Brighton Resurr 74-75; V Eastbourne St Eliz 75-96; rtd 96; Perm to Offic *Chich* from 96. *7 Bracken Road, Eastbourne BN20 8SH* Tel (01323) 431118

KING, Caroline Naomi. b 62. New Coll Edin BD94. Ripon Coll Cuddesdon 94. **d** 97 **p** 98. C Wheatley *Ox* from 97. *The Vicarage, Holton, Oxford OX33 1PR* Tel (01865) 873451 E-mail caroline.king1@ntlworld.com

KING, Christopher John. b 56. Chelsea Coll Lon BSc78 CertEd79. St Jo Coll Nottm LTh87. **d** 88 **p** 89. C Wandsworth All SS *S'wark* 88-92; Canada from 92; R Geraldton w Jellicoe, Longlac, Collins etc 92-97; R Toronto Lt Trin Ch from 97. *425 King Street East, Toronto ON, Canada, M5A 1L3* Tel (001) (416) 367 0272 Fax 367 2074 E-mail chrisking@sympatico.ca

KING, Clare Maria. b 68. St Andr Univ BD91 K Coll Lon MPhil98. Westcott Ho Cam 91. **d** 94. Hon C Norbury St Phil *S'wark* 94-96; Chapl Croydon Coll 95-96; Asst Chapl Cen Sheff Univ Hosps NHS Trust 96-01; C Leic Presentation *Leic* from 02. *The Vicarage, 12 Saddington Road, Fleckney, Leicester LE8 8AW* Tel 0116-240 2215

KING, Mrs Daphne Eileen. b 37. EMMTC 78. **dss** 81 **d** 87 **p** 94. Theddlethorpe *Linc* 84-89; Dn-in-c 87-89; Saltfleetby 84-89; Dn-in-c 87-89; Dn-in-c Healing and Stallingborough 89-94; P-in-c 94-97; rtd 97; Perm to Offic *Linc* 99-02. *28 Charles Street, Louth LN11 0LE* Tel (01507) 606062 E-mail daphneking@lud28.freeserve.co.uk

KING, David Charles. b 52. K Coll Lon 73 Coll of Resurr Mirfield 77. **d** 78 **p** 79. C Saltburn-by-the-Sea *York* 78-81; Youth Officer 81-85; P-in-c Crathorne 81-85; Par Educn Adv *Wakef* 85-91; Min Coulby Newham LEP *York* 91-94; P-in-c Egton w Grosmont 94-00; P-in-c Goathland and Glaisdale 99-00; V Middle Esk Moor from 00. *St Hilda's Vicarage, Egton, Whitby YO21 1UT* Tel (01947) 895315

KING, David Frederick. b 32. Southn Coll of Tech DMA70. Sarum Th Coll 59. **d** 61 **p** 72. C Hanworth All SS *Lon* 61-62; Hon C Andover St Mich *Win* 71-83; P-in-c 83-88; V 88-90; Chapl R S Hants Hosp 90-92; Chapl Countess Mountbatten Hospice 90-92; Chapl Andover District Community Health Care NHS Trust from 92; Perm to Offic *Win* 92-97; rtd 97; P-in-c Smannell w Enham Alamein *Win* 97-04. *158 Weyhill Road, Andover SP10 3BG* Tel (01264) 365694

KING, David John. b 67. W Sussex Inst of HE BEd91. St Steph Ho Ox 98. **d** 00 **p** 01. C Bexhill St Pet *Chich* 00-03; TV from 03. *The Vicarage, 20 Glassenbury Drive, Bexhill-on-Sea TN40 2NY* Tel (01424) 219937

KING, David Michael. b 73. St Jo Coll Dur BA95 PGCE96 Cam Univ BA02. Ridley Hall Cam 00. **d** 03 **p** 04. C Claygate *Guildf* from 03. *4 Denman Drive, Claygate, Esher KT10 0EA* Tel (01372) 464918 *or* 470703 Fax 464894 E-mail rev.d.king@btinternet.com

KING, Canon David Russell. b 42. Univ of Wales (Lamp) BA67. St D Coll Lamp DipTh68. **d** 68 **p** 69. C Barrow St Geo w St Luke *Carl* 68-72; P-in-c Kirkland 72-74; V Edenhall w Langwathby 72-73; P-in-c Culgaith 72-73; V Edenhall w Langwathby and Culgaith 73-74; V Flookburgh 75-79; V Barrow St Jas 79-82; P-in-c Bolton w Ireby and Uldale 82-83; R 83-90; R Burgh-by-Sands and Kirkbampton w Kirkandrews etc 90-00; P-in-c Aikton 95-00; P-in-c Orton St Giles 95-00; R Barony of Burgh 00-02; Hon Can Carl Cathl from 01; P-in-c Gt Broughton and Broughton Moor from 02. *The Vicarage, Little Broughton, Cockermouth CA13 0YG* Tel (01900) 825317

KING, David William Anthony. b 42. Ch Ch Ox BA63 MA68. Westcott Ho Cam 63. **d** 65 **p** 66. C Cayton w Eastfield *York* 65-68; C Southbroom *Sarum* 68-71; R Hinton Parva 71-72; V Holt St Jas 71-72; V Holt St Jas and Hinton Parva 72-75; P-in-c Horton and Chalbury 73-75; R Holt St Jas, Hinton Parva, Horton and Chalbury 75-79; TV Melton Mowbray w Thorpe Arnold *Leic* 79-83; V Foxton w Gumley and Laughton and Lubenham 83-90; P-in-c Boreham *Chelmsf* 90-00; R Tendring and Lt Bentley w Beaumont cum Moze from 00. *The Rectory, The Street, Tendring, Clacton-on-Sea CO16 0BW* Tel (01255) 830586

KING, Dennis. b 31. ACA53 FCA64. EMMTC 73. **d** 76 **p** 77. NSM Chesterfield St Mary and All SS *Derby* 76-00; Perm to Offic from 00. *Hillcrest, Stubben Edge, Ashover, Chesterfield S45 0EU* Tel (01246) 590279

KING, Dennis Charles. b 27. Chich Th Coll 53. **d** 55 **p** 56. C Luton Ch Ch *St Alb* 55-58 and 59-63; USA 58-59; Bahamas 63-66; Jamaica 66-77; V Bromham w Oakley *St Alb* 77-84; TR St Marylebone Ch Ch *Lon* 84-89; V Flamstead *St Alb* 89-93; rtd 93; Perm to Offic *St Alb* from 93. *Te Deum, 36 Manor Road, Toddington, Dunstable LU5 6AH* Tel (01525) 873557

KING, Dennis Keppel. b 33. Lich Th Coll 63. **d** 65 **p** 66. C Eccleston St Thos *Liv* 65-68; C W Derby St Mary 68-71; V Aintree St Giles 71-96; rtd 96; Perm to Offic *York* from 96 and *Liv* from 00. *8 Whiteoak Avenue, Easingwold, York YO61 3GB* Tel (01347) 822625 E-mail dennis.k.king@btinternet.com

KING, Derek Edwin Noel. b 31. Qu Mary Coll Lon BSc54 Birkbeck Coll Lon PhD60. LNSM course 91. **d** 93 **p** 94. OLM Nacton and Levington w Bucklesham and Foxhall *St E* from 93. *Vindelis, 1 Eastcliff, Felixstowe IP11 9TA* Tel and fax (01394) 270815

KING, Donald. b 32. ISM82. Chich Th Coll. **d** 86. NSM Forton *Portsm* 86-98; Perm to Offic from 98. *8 Burnett Road, Gosport PO12 3AH* Tel (023) 9252 3440

KING, Fergus John. b 62. St Andr Univ MA Edin Univ BD89. Edin Th Coll 86. **d** 89 **p** 90. Chapl St Jo Cathl Oban *Arg* 89-92; C Oban St Jo 89-92; Tanzania 92-98; Perm to Offic *S'wark* 99-03; Hon C Thamesmead from 03. *27 Felixstowe Road, London SE2 9QW* Tel (020) 7928 8681 E-mail fergusk@uspg.org.uk

KING, George Henry. b 24. MRHS55 NDH55. St Alb Minl Tr Scheme. **d** 79 **p** 80. Hon C Flamstead *St Alb* 79-98; Dioc Agric Chapl 90-98; Perm to Offic from 98. *Chad Lane Farm, Chad Lane, Flamstead, St Albans AL3 8HW* Tel (01582) 841648

KING, Mrs Gillian Daphne. b 38. EMMTC 79. **dss** 83 **d** 87 **p** 94. Knighton St Jo *Leic* 83-85; Clarendon Park St Jo w Knighton St Mich 86-89; Par Dn 87-89; Chapl Kingston and Esher Mental Health Services 89-93; Chapl Kingston and Esher Community Health Unit 93-97; Chapl Long Grove Hosp Epsom 90-92; Chapl Tolworth Hosp Surbiton 91-97; Chapl Kingston and Distr Community NHS Trust 94-97; TV Hale w Badshot Lea *Guildf* 97-99; V Egham Hythe from 99. *St Paul's Vicarage, 214 Wendover Road, Staines TW18 3DF* Tel (01784) 453625 Mobile 07775-724090 E-mail gking.st_pauls-egham-hythe@btinternet.com

KING, James Anthony. b 46. CBE76. K Coll Lon BA69 AKC69 Lon Inst of Educn AcDipEd77. St Alb and Ox Min Course 99. **d** 01 **p** 02. NSM Gerrards Cross and Fulmer *Ox* 01-03; NSM S Tottenham St Ann *Lon* from 03. *16 Linden Road, London N15 3QB* Tel (020) 8374 0905 E-mail jim.king@gs.com

KING, Canon Jeffrey Douglas Wallace. b 43. AKC67. **d** 68 **p** 69. C S Harrow St Paul *Lon* 68-71; C Garforth *Ripon* 71-74; V Potternewton 74-83; TR Moor Allerton 83-99; RD Allerton 85-89; Hon Can Ripon Cathl from 90; R Thorner from 99; Dioc Ecum Officer from 99. *The Vicarage, Church View, Thorner, Leeds LS14 3ED* Tel 0113-289 2437 E-mail jeffking@thinkdifferent.co.uk

KING, Jennifer Mary. b 41. Lon Univ BDS65 MSc75 PhD Ox Univ DipTh97. Ripon Coll Cuddesdon 86. **d** 88 **p** 94. NSM S Hackney St Mich w Haggerston St Paul *Lon* 88-99; Chapl St Bart's and RLSMD Qu Mary and Westf Coll from 98; NSM St John-at-Hackney from 99. *83 Victoria Park Road, London E9 7NA* Tel (020) 7377 7000 ext 3069 *or* 7377 7167 E-mail jenny.king@qmul.ac.uk

KING, Jeremy Norman. *See* CLARK-KING, Jeremy Norman

KING, John. **d** 05. NSM Buckingham *Ox* from 05. *Wood End Farm, 2 Wood End, Nash, Milton Keynes MK17 0EL* Tel (01908) 501860 E-mail john@kingsfold100.freeserve.co.uk

KING, John. b 38. S'wark Ord Course DipRS77. **d** 80 **p** 81. C S Gillingham *Roch* 80-85; Min Joydens Wood St Barn CD 85-90; V Borstal 90-98; Chapl HM Pris Cookham Wood 90-98; Chapl The Foord Almshouses 90-98; rtd 98; Perm to Offic *Cant* from 99. *14 Lamberhurst Way, Cliftonville, Margate CT9 3HH* Tel (01843) 229405 Mobile 07889-277195

KING, John Andrew. b 50. Qu Coll Birm 72. **d** 75 **p** 76. C Halesowen *Worc* 75-77; C Belper Ch Ch and Milford *Derby* 78-81; Perm to Offic from 87. *11 Well Lane, Milford, Belper DE56 0QQ* Tel (01332) 841810

KING, John Charles. b 27. St Pet Hall Ox BA51 MA55. Oak Hill Th Coll 51. **d** 53 **p** 54. C Slough *Ox* 53-57; V Ware Ch Ch *St Alb* 57-60; Ed *C of E Newspaper* 60-68; Lic to Offic *St Alb* 60-70; Teacher St Fran Bacon Sch St Alb 68-71; Boston Gr Sch 71-88; Lic to Offic *Linc* 74-92; rtd 92. *6 Somersby Way, Boston PE21 9PQ* Tel (01205) 363061

KING, John Colin. b 39. Cuddesdon Coll 69. **d** 71 **p** 72. C Cookham *Ox* 71-75; Youth Chapl *B & W* 75-80; P-in-c Merriott

76-80; P-in-c Hinton w Dinnington 79-80; R Merriott w Hinton, Dinnington and Lopen 80-04; rtd 04. *Les Chênes, Les Arquies, St Henri, Cahors 46000, France*

KING, Joseph Stephen. b 39. St Chad's Coll Dur BA62 MPhil83. **d** 64 **p** 65. C Lewisham St Mary *S'wark* 64-69; Hon C Milton next Gravesend Ch Ch *Roch* 70-85; V from 85. *The Vicarage, 48 Old Road East, Gravesend DA12 1NR* Tel (01474) 352643

KING, Mrs Katharine Mary. b 63. St Hugh's Coll Ox BA85 MA89 SS Coll Cam BA88. Ridley Hall Cam 86. **d** 89 **p** 94. C Ipswich St Aug *St E* 89-91; NSM Bures 92-02; NSM Bures w Assington and Lt Cornard from 02. *The Vicarage, Church Square, Bures CO8 5AA* Tel (01787) 227315 Mobile 07885-863687 E-mail katharine@kmking.fsnet.co.uk

KING, Malcolm Charles. b 37. Chich Th Coll 67. **d** 70 **p** 71. C Mill End *St Alb* 70-72; Chapl RAF 72-76; R W Lynn *Nor* 76-81; V Croxley Green All SS *St Alb* 81-90; V Grimsby St Aug *Linc* 90-99; V Bury w Houghton and Coldwaltham and Hardham *Chich* 99-02; OGS from 90; Asst Local Min Officer *Linc* 90-95; rtd 02; Warden Community of St Pet Woking 02-03; Perm to Offic *Chich* from 02. *9 Riverside Court, Station Road, Pulborough RH20 1RG* Tel (01798) 875213

KING, Malcolm Stewart. b 56. Sarum & Wells Th Coll 77. **d** 80 **p** 81. C Farnham *Guildf* 80-83; C Chertsey 83-86; Chapl St Pet Hosp Chertsey 83-86; V Egham Hythe *Guildf* 86-91; TR Cove St Jo 91-98; RD Aldershot 93-98; V Dorking w Ranmore 98-04; Hon Can Guildf Cathl 99-04; RD Dorking 01-04; P-in-c Portsea N End St Mark *Portsm* from 04. *The Vicarage, 3A Wadham Road, Portsmouth PO2 9ED* Tel (023) 9266 2500 *or* 9266 5753 E-mail malcolm.king3@btinternet.com

KING (née COWIE), Mrs Margaret Harriet. b 53. Glas Univ BSc76 AMA85 FMA97. TISEC 95. **d** 98 **p** 99. NSM Montrose and Inverbervie *Bre* 98-05; Dioc Dir of Ord 00-05; TV N Hinckford *Chelmsf* from 05. *The Vicarage, Great Henny, Sudbury CO10 7NW* Tel (01787) 269385 Mobile 07855-558056 E-mail mandgking39@hotmail.com

KING, Marie. b 40. CertEd78. **d** 03 **p** 04. OLM Addiscombe St Mildred *S'wark* from 03. *8 Annandale Road, Croydon CR0 7HP* Tel (020) 8654 2651 E-mail marieking@8annan.fsnet.co.uk

KING, Martin Harry. b 42. St Jo Coll Cam MA68 MBCS85. St Alb and Ox Min Course 03. **d** 05. NSM Wheathampstead *St Alb* from 05. *29 Parkfields, Welwyn Garden City AL8 6EE* Tel (01707) 328905 E-mail martin@king-priestley.freeserve.co.uk

KING, Martin Peter James. b 73. Bris Univ BEng95. Oak Hill Th Coll BA05. **d** 05. C Leamington Priors St Paul *Cov* from 05. *49 Wathen Road, Leamington Spa CV32 5UY* Tel (01926) 451439 E-mail msssking@hotmail.com

KING, Martin Quartermain. b 39. Reading Univ BA61. Cuddesdon Coll 62. **d** 64 **p** 65. C S Shields St Hilda w St Thos *Dur* 64-66; C Newton Aycliffe 66-71; V Chilton Moor 71-78; R Middleton St Geo 78-91; R Sedgefield 91-04; RD Sedgefield 91-96; Chapl Co Dur & Darlington Priority Services NHS Trust 91-04; rtd 04. *22 South View, Bishop Middleham, Ferryhill DL17 9BA* E-mail martin.king@durham.anglican.org

KING, Maurice Charles Francis. b 32. ACP58 Em Coll Cam BA55 MA59. Chich Th Coll 78. **d** 79 **p** 80. C Burnley St Cath *Blackb* 79-81; C Burnley St Cath w St Alb and St Paul 81-83; C Sheff St Cecilia Parson Cross *Sheff* 83-88; V New Bentley 88-94; rtd 94; Perm to Offic *Carl* from 94. *204 Wordsworth Court, Cockermouth CA13 0EB* Tel (01900) 827503

KING, Michael Charles. Worc Coll Ox BA56 MA60. Coll of Resurr Mirfield. **d** 62 **p** 63. Hon C Hampstead All So *Lon* 62-65; Ed Asst SCM Press 62-65; C Thorpe *Nor* 66-69; Ed Sec BRF 69-90; Hon C Queensbury All SS *Lon* 69-79; Hon C Lt Stanmore St Lawr 80-90; R Cawston w Haveringland, Booton and Brandiston *Nor* 91-96; P-in-c Heydon 94-96; R Cawston w Booton and Brandiston etc 96-01; rtd 01; Perm to Offic *Leic* from 01. *84 Beacon Road, Loughborough LE11 2BH* Tel (01509) 563103

KING, Nathan Richard. b 68. Whitelands Coll Lon BA89 Univ of Wales (Cardiff) BTh94 Man Univ MA00. St Mich Coll Llan 91. **d** 94 **p** 95. C Hawarden *St As* 94-99; P-in-c 99-00; P-in-c Coreley and Doddington *Heref* 00-02; P-in-c Knowbury w Clee Hill 00-02; TV Ellesmere Port *Ches* from 02. *4 Deeside Close, Whitby, Ellesmere Port CH65 6TH* Tel 0151-355 3571 E-mail nathanking@onetel.com

KING, Nicholas Bernard Paul. b 46. Wycliffe Hall Ox 72. **d** 75 **p** 76. C Pitsmoor w Wicker *Sheff* 75-78; C Erdington St Barn *Birm* 78-80; C Sutton Coldfield H Trin 80-84; V Lynesack *Dur* 84-92; rtd 93. *16 Chatsworth Avenue, Bishop Auckland DL14 6AX* Tel (01388) 605614

KING, Peter Duncan. b 48. TD. K Coll Lon LLB70 AKC70 Fitzw Coll Cam BA72 MA77. Westcott Ho Cam 70. **d** 80 **p** 81. Hon C Notting Hill *Lon* 80-84; Hon C Mortlake w E Sheen *S'wark* from 84; Dean MSE from 99. *49 Leinster Avenue, London SW14 7JW* Tel (020) 8876 8997 Fax 8287 9329

KING, Peter William Stephen. b 65. St Steph Ho Ox BTh01. **d** 01 **p** 02. C Abertillery w Cwmtillery w Six Bells *Mon* from 01. *St Paul's Vicarage, Church Lane, Cwmtillery, Abertillery NP13 1LS* Tel (01495) 212364 Fax as telephone

KING, Canon Philip David. b 35. Keble Coll Ox BA57 MA61. Tyndale Hall Bris 58. **d** 60 **p** 61. C Redhill H Trin *S'wark* 60-63; C Wallington H Trin 63-68; V Fulham Ch Ch *Lon* 68-74; Lic to Offic *S'wark* 74-86; Gen Sec SAMS 74-86; V Roxeth Ch Ch and Harrow St Pet *Lon* 86-89; Gen Sec Gen Syn Bd for Miss 89-00; Perm to Offic *Lon* from 89; Lic to Offic *Cant* and *York* from 98; rtd 00. *31 Myrtle Avenue, Ruislip HA4 8SA* Tel and fax (020) 8429 0636 *or* tel 7898 1468 E-mail philip.king5@virgin.net

KING, Miss Philipa Ann. b 65. Heythrop Coll Lon. Westcott Ho Cam CTM95. **d** 95 **p** 96. C Cambridge Ascension *Ely* 95-00; TV 00-02; TR from 02. *Ascension Rectory, 95 Richmond Road, Cambridge CB4 3PS* Tel (01223) 361919 Mobile 07816-833363 E-mail pipking@btinternet.com

KING, Richard Andrew. b 51. Linc Th Coll. **d** 84 **p** 85. C Bramhall *Ches* 84-87; V Heald Green St Cath 87-92; P-in-c Ashprington, Cornworthy and Dittisham *Ex* 92-99; RD Totnes 97-99; P-in-c Torquay St Jo and Ellacombe 99-02; P-in-c Stoneleigh *Guildf* from 02; Dioc Spirituality Adv from 02. *The Vicarage, 59 Stoneleigh Park Road, Epsom KT19 0QU* Tel and fax (020) 8393 3738 E-mail rking11@hotmail.com

KING, Richard David. b 63. Oak Hill Th Coll 87. **d** 90 **p** 91. C Foord St Jo *Cant* 90-94; P-in-c Orlestone w Snave and Ruckinge w Warehorne 94-02; R Orlestone w Snave and Ruckinge w Warehorne etc 02; Dioc Ecum Officer 97-02; CA Field Officer *Cant, Lon, Roch* and *S'wark* from 02. *38 Rosewood Drive, Ashford TN25 4QF* Tel (01233) 731280 E-mail richard.d.king@tesco.net

KING, Robert Dan. b 57. Sarum & Wells Th Coll 92. **d** 94 **p** 95. C Heref H Trin *Heref* 94-97; TV W Heref 97-00; V Weobley w Sarnesfield and Norton Canon from 00; P-in-c Letton w Staunton, Byford, Mansel Gamage etc 00-04; R from 04. *The Vicarage, Church Road, Weobley, Hereford HR4 8SD* Tel (01544) 318415 E-mail bobking@wbsnet.co.uk

KING, Robin Lucas Colin. b 59. Dundee Univ MA81. Ridley Hall Cam 87. **d** 89 **p** 90. C Ipswich St Aug *St E* 89-92; V Bures 92-02; C Assington w Newton Green and Lt Cornard 00-02; V Bures w Assington and Lt Cornard from 02. *The Vicarage, Church Square, Bures CO8 5AA* Tel (01787) 227315 Mobile 07885-863687 E-mail robin@rlcking.freeserve.co.uk

KING, Canon Stuart John Langley. b 33. Selw Coll Cam BA57 MA61. Linc Th Coll 57. **d** 59 **p** 60. C Plymouth Crownhill Ascension *Ex* 59-62; C Horsham *Chich* 62-67; V Devonport St Mark Ford *Ex* 67-77; RD Plymouth 74-77; Can Res Cov Cathl *Cov* 77-84; V Tooting All SS *S'wark* 84-96; rtd 96; Perm to Offic *Ex* from 96. *12 Lowertown Close, Landrake, Saltash PL12 5DG* Tel (01752) 851512

KING, Timothy William. b 52. CertEd. Ripon Coll Cuddesdon. **d** 81 **p** 82. C Ludlow *Heref* 81-83; C Walton-on-Thames *Guildf* 83-86; C Hammersmith St Paul *Lon* 86-88; V Send *Guildf* 88-95; R Farncombe 95-00. *Address temp unknown*

KING, Tony Christopher. b 62. Lanc Univ BA83. Coll of Resurr Mirfield 83. **d** 86 **p** 87. C Stansted Mountfitchet *Chelmsf* 86-89; USPG 89-92; Botswana 90-92; C Chingford SS Pet and Paul *Chelmsf* 92-93. *252 Brettenham Road, London E17 5AY*

KING, Canon Walter Raleigh. b 45. New Coll Ox BA67 MA74. Cuddesdon Coll 71. **d** 74 **p** 75. C Wisbech SS Pet and Paul *Ely* 74-77; C Barrow St Geo w St Luke *Carl* 77-79; P-in-c Clifford *Heref* 79-83; P-in-c Cusop 79-83; P-in-c Hardwick 79-83; P-in-c Whitney w Winforton 81-84; R Cusop w Clifford, Hardwicke, Bredwardine etc 83-86; R Heref St Nic 86-92; Dir of Ords 86-92; Preb Heref Cathl 86-92; TR Huntingdon *Ely* 92-01; RD Huntingdon 94-99; Hon Can Ely Cathl 99-01; Vice Dean and Can Res Chelmsf Cathl *Chelmsf* from 01. *115 Rainsford Road, Chelmsford CM1 2PF* Tel (01245) 267773 *or* 294493 E-mail vicedean@chelmsfordcathedral.org.uk

KING-SMITH, Giles Anthony Beaumont. b 53. Univ Coll Ox BA75. Trin Coll Bris DipHE88. **d** 88 **p** 89. C Gtr Corsham *Bris* 88-92; V Two Mile Hill St Mich 92-96; TV Ilfracombe, Lee, Woolacombe, Bittadon etc *Ex* from 96. *The Vicarage, Springfield Road, Woolacombe EX34 7BX* Tel (01271) 870467

KING-SMITH, Philip Hugh (Brother Robert Hugh). b 28. CCC Cam BA52 MA56. Cuddesdon Coll 52. **d** 54 **p** 55. C Stockton St Pet *Dur* 54-59; V Bishopwearmouth Gd Shep 59-64; SSF from 64; USA from 66; rtd 98. *San Damiano, 573 Dolores, San Francisco, CA 94110, USA* Tel (001) (415) 861 1372 Fax 861 7952

KINGCOME, John Parken. b 18. CEng50 MIMechE50. Sarum Th Coll 65. **d** 67 **p** 68. C Melksham *Sarum* 67-70; P-in-c Woodborough w Manningford Bohun etc 70-72; R Swanborough 72-75; TR Swanborough 75-79; RD Pewsey 75-84; Custos St Jo Hosp Heytesbury 79-84; rtd 84; Perm to Offic *B & W* from 85-95 and *Bris* from 92. *Stonecrop, The Butts, Biddestone, Chippenham SN14 7DY* Tel (01249) 713412

KINGDON, Mrs Margaret Victoria. b 44. NNEB. St Alb and Ox Min Course 95. **d** 98 **p** 99. OLM Wokingham St Sebastian *Ox* 98-03. *60 Pinewood Avenue, Crowthorne RG45 6RP* Tel (01344) 774625

KINGHAM, Derek Henry. b 29. Oak Hill Th Coll 56. **d** 58 **p** 59. C Deptford St Jo *S'wark* 58-60; C Normanton *Derby* 60-63; R Gaulby w Kings Norton and Stretton Parva *Leic* 63-73; V Bacup St Sav *Man* 73-95; rtd 95; Perm to Offic *Carl* from 95. *12 Castle Green Close, Kendal LA9 6AT* Tel (01539) 727008

KINGHAM, Mair Josephine. *See* TALBOT, Canon Mair Josephine

KINGMAN, Paul Henry Charles. b 64. Reading Univ BSc86. Wycliffe Hall Ox BTh95. **d** 95 **p** 96. C Whitton *Sarum* 95-99; C Harold Wood *Chelmsf* 99-03; V Stone Ch Ch and Oulton *Lich* from 03. *Christ Church Vicarage, Bromfield Court, Stone ST15 8ED* Tel (01785) 812669

KINGS, Mrs Frances Bridget (Biddi). b 48. City Univ BSc70 Birm Univ MSc77. WEMTC 00. **d** 03 **p** 04. NSM Defford w Besford *Worc* from 03; NSM Eckington from 03. *Merebrook Farm, Hanley Swan, Worcester WR8 0DX* Tel (01684) 310950 E-mail biddi@merebrook.clara.co.uk

KINGS, Canon Graham Ralph. b 53. Hertf Coll Ox BA77 MA80 Selw Coll Cam DipTh80 Utrecht Univ PhD02. Ridley Hall Cam 78. **d** 80 **p** 81. C Harlesden St Mark *Lon* 80-84; CMS 85-91; Kenya 85-91; Dir Studies St Andr Inst Kabare 85-88; Vice Prin 89-91; Lect Miss Studies Cam Th Federation 92-00; Overseas Adv Henry Martyn Trust 92-95; Dir Henry Martyn Cen Westmr Coll Cam 95-00; Hon C Cambridge H Trin *Ely* 92-96; Hon C Chesterton St Andr 96-00; V Islington St Mary *Lon* from 00. *St Mary's Vicarage, Upper Street, London N1 2TX* Tel (020) 7226 8981 *or* tel and fax 7226 3400 E-mail vicar@stmaryislington.org

KINGS, Mrs Jean Alison. *See* THORN, Mrs Jean Alison

KINGSBURY, Canon Richard John. b 41. Lon Univ BA63. Linc Th Coll 65. **d** 67 **p** 68. C Wallsend St Luke *Newc* 67-69; C Monkseaton St Mary 69-70; Chapl K Coll Lon 70-75; V Hungerford and Denford *Ox* 75-83; R Caversham and Mapledurham from 83; Hon Can Ch Ch from 92. *The Rectory, 20 Church Road, Reading RG4 7AD* Tel 0118-947 9130 *or* 947 1703

KINGSLAND, Desmond George. b 23. Sarum Th Coll 75. **d** 78 **p** 79. Hon C Bournemouth H Epiphany *Win* 78-95; rtd 95. *Windy Ridge, 23 Granby Road, Bournemouth BH9 3NZ* Tel (01202) 526011

KINGSLEY, Brian St Clair. b 26. St Steph Ho Ox 56. **d** 59 **p** 60. C Tilehurst St Mich *Ox* 59-63; CSWG from 63; Prior from 85; Lic to Offic *Chich* 66-00; rtd 96; Perm to Offic *Chich* from 01. *The Monastery of the Holy Trinity, Cuttinglye Lane, Crawley Down, Crawley RH10 4LH* Tel (01342) 712074

KINGSLEY-SMITH, John Sydney. b 45. ARCM. Ridley Hall Cam 78. **d** 80 **p** 81. C Nailsea H Trin *B & W* 80-84; TV Whitton *Sarum* 84-91; V Chorleywood Ch Ch *St Alb* 91-01; RD Rickmansworth 98-01; rtd 01; Perm to Offic *St Alb* from 01. *29 Lewes Way, Croxley Green, Rickmansworth WD3 3SW* Tel (01923) 249949

KINGSTON, Canon Albert William. b 47. Bernard Gilpin Soc Dur 68 Oak Hill Th Coll 69. **d** 72 **p** 73. C Walton Breck *Liv* 72-74; C Templemore *D & R* 74-76; I Kildallan w Newtowngore and Corrawallen *K, E & A* 76-82; Bp's C Ardagh w Tashinny, Shrule and Kilcommick from 82; Can and Preb Elphin Cathl from 95. *Oakhill Lodge, Rathmore, Ballymahon, Co Longford, Irish Republic* Tel (00353) (90) 643 8945 Mobile 87-919 5473

KINGSTON, Mrs Avril Dawson. b 34. Local Minl Tr Course 91. **d** 94 **p** 95. Aux Min Douglas Union w Frankfield *C, C & R* 94-02; rtd 02. *Ballymartin House, Glencairn, Co Waterford, Irish Republic* Tel (00353) (58) 56227 E-mail akingston@esatclear.ie

KINGSTON, Desmond. *See* KINGSTON, John Desmond George

KINGSTON, Canon Eric. b 24. **d** 69 **p** 70. C Ballymacarrett St Patr *D & D* 69-72; C Knock 72-76; I Annahilt w Magherahamlet 76-93; rtd 93; Can and Prec Dromore Cathl *D & D* 93. *38 Kinedale Park, Ballynahinch BT24 8YS* Tel (028) 9756 5715

KINGSTON, George Mervyn. b 47. CITC 70. **d** 73 **p** 74. C Comber *D & D* 73-77; C Belfast St Donard 77-80; Min Can Down Cathl 80-84; Bp's C Lecale Gp 82-84; Bp's C Belfast St Andr *Conn* 84-90; I Ballymascanlan w Creggan and Rathcor *Arm* 90-03; V Choral Arm Cathl from 03. *The Cloisters, 36 Seahill Road, Holywood BT18 0DJ* Tel and fax (028) 9042 5016 Mobile 07816-462107 E-mail creggan@iolfree.ie

KINGSTON, John Desmond George. b 40. TCD BA63 MA66. CITC 64. **d** 64 **p** 65. C Arm St Mark *Arm* 64-70; Hon V Choral Arm Cathl 69-70; Chapl Portora R Sch Enniskillen 70-01; Lic to Offic *Clogh* 70-01; Can Clogh Cathl 96-01; rtd 01. *Ambleside, 45 Old Rossory Road, Enniskillen BT74 7LF* Tel (028) 6632 4493

KINGSTON, Canon Kenneth Robert. b 42. TCD BA65 MA69. **d** 66 **p** 67. C Enniscorthy *C & O* 66-69; C Ballymena *Conn* 70-72; C Drumragh w Mountfield *D & R* 72-78; I Badoney Lower w Greenan and Badoney Upper 78-84; I Desertmartin w Termoneeny from 84; Can Derry Cathl from 97. *25 Dromore Road, Desertmartin, Magherafelt BT45 5JZ* Tel (028) 7963 2455

KINGSTON, Malcolm Trevor. b 75. QUB BSc97 MSc98 TCD BTh04. CITC 01. **d** 04. C Portadown St Mark *Arm* from 04. *4 Killycomain Drive, Portadown, Craigavon BT63 5JJ* Tel (028) 3833 5813 E-mail malcolm.kingston@btinternet.com

KINGSTON, Michael Joseph. b 51. K Coll Lon BD73 AKC73. St Aug Coll Cant 73. **d** 74 **p** 75. C Reading H Trin *Ox* 74-77; C New Eltham All SS *S'wark* 77-83; V Plumstead Ascension 83-94; Sub-Dean Greenwich N 92-94; V Sydenham St Bart from 94; RD W Lewisham from 04. *St Bartholomew's Vicarage, 4 Westwood Hill, London SE26 6QR* Tel (020) 8778 5290 E-mail michaelkingston@lineone.net

KINGSTON, Michael Marshall. b 54. St Jo Coll Nottm MA94. **d** 96 **p** 97. C Drayton w Felthorpe *Nor* 96-99; R Gt and Lt Plumstead w Thorpe End and Witton from 99; Chapl Norwich Primary Care Trust from 01. *The Rectory, 9 Lawn Crescent, Thorpe End, Norwich NR13 5BP* Tel (01603) 434778

KINGSTON, Robert George. b 46. TCD BA68 Div Test69. **d** 69 **p** 72. C Belfast St Thos *Conn* 69-72; C Kilkenny St Canice Cathl *C & O* 72-75; I Ballinasloe w Taughmaconnell *L & K* 77-79; I Maryborough w Dysart Enos and Ballyfin *C & O* 79-85; I Lurgan w Billis, Killinkere and Munterconnaught *K, E & A* 85-88; Registrar Kilmore 87-92; I Lurgan etc w Ballymachugh, Kildrumferton etc 88-92; I Tallaght *D & G* 92-98; Warden of Readers 93-98; I Mallow Union *C, C & R* from 98. *The Rectory, Lower Bearforest, Mallow, Co Cork, Irish Republic* Tel (00353) (22) 21473

KINGSTON, Roy William Henry. b 31. Chich Th Coll 60. **d** 62 **p** 63. C Leeds St Aid *Ripon* 62-66; S Africa 66-73; V Bramley *Ripon* 74-81; TR Hemel Hempstead *St Alb* 81-85; TR Fareham H Trin *Portsm* 85-93; RD Alverstoke 89-90; RD Fareham 90-93; P-in-c Hambledon 93-97; rtd 97; Perm to Offic *Guildf, Portsm* and *Win* from 97. *8 Pengilly Road, Farnham GU9 7XQ* Tel (01252) 711371 Mobile 07855-457670 E-mail roy@roykingston.plus.com

KINGSTON, Mrs Shirley Alexandra. b 42. Ch of Ireland Tr Coll Dip Primary Educn 61 TCD BA68 HDipEd70. CITC 90. **d** 93 **p** 94. NSM Castlemacadam w Ballinaclash, Aughrim etc *D & G* 93-95; NSM Rathdrum w Glenealy, Derralossary and Laragh 95-97; NSM Bray from 97. *Kilpatrick House, Redcross, Co Wicklow, Irish Republic* Tel (00353) (404) 47137

KINGSTON-UPON-THAMES, Area Bishop of. *See* CHEETHAM, The Rt Revd Richard Ian

KINGTON, Canon David Bruce. b 45. Trin Coll Bris 72. **d** 72 **p** 73. C Wellington w Eyton *Lich* 72-77; C Boscombe St Jo *Win* 77-81; R Michelmersh, Timsbury, Farley Chamberlayne etc 81-98; R Michelmersh and Awbridge and Braishfield etc from 98; RD Romsey from 95; Hon Can Win Cathl from 02. *The Rectory, Braishfield Road, Braishfield, Romsey SO51 0PR* Tel (01794) 368335 E-mail dbkington@dbkington.worldonline.co.uk

KINNA, Michael Andrew. b 46. Chich Th Coll 84. **d** 86 **p** 87. C Leominster *Heref* 86-90; TV Wenlock 90-93; R Broseley w Benthall, Jackfield, Linley etc from 94; RD Telford Severn Gorge from 03. *The Rectory, Church Street, Broseley TF12 5DA* Tel and fax (01952) 882647 E-mail mak@ridewise.fsnet.co.uk

KINNAIRD, Jennifer. b 41. Hull Univ BA62 Ex Univ PGCE63. NEOC DipHE94. **d** 97 **p** 98. NSM Corbridge w Halton and Newton Hall *Newc* from 97. *17 Glebelands, Corbridge NE45 5DS* Tel (01434) 632695 E-mail j.kinnaird@btopenworld.com

KINNAIRD, Keith. b 42. Chich Th Coll 72. **d** 75 **p** 76. C Didcot St Pet *Ox* 75-78; C Abingdon w Shippon 78-82; Chapl Abingdon Hosp 79-92; P-in-c Sunningwell *Ox* 82-90; P-in-c Radley 88-90; R Radley and Sunningwell 90-95; V Old Shoreham *Chich* 95-00; V New Shoreham 95-00; V Caversham St Andr *Ox* from 00; Voc Adv from 00; Adv for Min of Healing from 00. *St Andrew's Vicarage, Harrogate Road, Reading RG4 7PW* Tel 0118-947 2788 Fax as telephone E-mail kinnaird@waitrose.com

KINSELLA, Nigel Paul. b 66. Wolv Univ LLB95. Westcott Ho Cam 00. **d** 02 **p** 03. C Attleborough w Besthorpe *Nor* 02-03; C Quidenham Gp from 03. *The Vicarage, Mill Road, Old Buckenham, Attleborough NR17 1SG* Tel (01953) 861181 E-mail kinsella@fish.co.uk

KINSEY, Bruce Richard Lawrence. b 59. K Coll Lon BD81 AKC81 MTh86 MA94. Wycliffe Hall Ox. **d** 84 **p** 85. C Gt Stanmore *Lon* 84-88; C Shepherd's Bush St Steph w St Thos 88-91; Chapl and Fell Down Coll Cam 91-01; Hd Philolosophy and RS Perse Sch Cam from 01. *The Perse School, Hills Road, Cambridge CB2 2QF* Tel (01223) 3568266 E-mail br@perse.co.uk

KINSEY, Paul. b 56. Nottm Univ BTh89. Linc Th Coll 86. **d** 89 **p** 90. C Connah's Quay *St As* 89-91; Min Can St As Cathl 91-94; Asst Chapl Univ Coll Lon Hosps NHS Trust 94-00; R S Lynn *Nor* from 00; Ind Chapl from 00. *All Saints' Rectory, 33 Goodwins Road, King's Lynn PE30 5QX* Tel (01553) 771779 E-mail therector.allsaints@btinternet.com

KINSEY, Russell Frederick David. b 34. Sarum Th Coll 59. **d** 62 **p** 63. C Twerton *B & W* 62-66; C N Cadbury 66-76; C Yarlington 66-76; P-in-c Compton Pauncefoot w Blackford 66-76; P-in-c Maperton 66-76; P-in-c N Cheriton 66-76; TV Camelot Par 76-79; V Pill 79-82; P-in-c Easton-in-Gordano w Portbury and

Clapton 80-82; V Pill w Easton in Gordano and Portbury 82-92; rtd 94. *25 Newbourne Road, Weston-super-Mare BS22 8NF*

KINSMEN, Barry William. b 40. Chan Sch Truro. **d** 74 **p** 75. NSM Padstow *Truro* 74-78; Dioc Adv in RE 79-95; P-in-c St Issey 80-81; P-in-c Lt Petherick 80-81; R St Issey w St Petroc Minor 81-95; rtd 95; Perm to Offic *Truro* from 95. *14 Old School Court, School Hill, Padstow PL28 8ED* Tel (01841) 532507

KIPPAX, Michael John. b 48. Open Univ BA82. SW Minl Tr Course 89. **d** 92 **p** 93. C Camborne *Truro* 92-95; C Woughton *Ox* 95-96; TV 96-98; R St Illogan *Truro* from 98. *The Rectory, Robartes Terrace, Illogan, Redruth TR16 4RX* Tel (01209) 842233 Fax (08707) 051466 E-mail mike@illogan.plus.com

KIRBY, Bernard William Alexander (Alex). b 39. Keble Coll Ox BA62. Coll of Resurr Mirfield 62. **d** 65 **p** 72. C Is of Dogs Ch Ch and St Jo w St Luke *Lon* 65-66; Hon C Battersea St Phil *S'wark* 72; Hon C Battersea St Phil w St Bart 73-76; Perm to Offic 76-78 and 83-95. *28 Prince Edward Road, Lewes BN7 1BE* Tel (01273) 474935 Fax 486685

KIRBY, David Anthony. b 42. Dur Univ BA64 PhD68 Huddersfield Univ Hon DLitt98. N Ord Course 84. **d** 87 **p** 88. NSM Crosland Moor *Wakef* 87-00; Asst Chapl Algarve *Eur* 00-05. *4 North Mead, Bramhope, Leeds LS16 9DT* E-mail revdakirby@hotmail.com

KIRBY, David Graham. b 58. Univ of Wales (Cardiff) BA80. Wycliffe Hall Ox BA85 MA92. **d** 86 **p** 87. C Northallerton w Kirby Sigston *York* 86-89; C Southport Ch Ch *Liv* 89-92; R Bishop Burton w Walkington *York* from 92. *The Rectory, Walkington, Beverley HU17 8SP* Tel (01482) 868379

KIRBY, Mrs Joan Florence. b 32. St Hugh's Coll Ox MA57 Lon Univ BA66. St Alb Minl Tr Scheme 79. **d** 87 **p** 94. NSM Hemel Hempstead *St Alb* 87-90; C Blisland w St Breward *Truro* 90-94; NSM Cardynham 94-96; rtd 96; Perm to Offic *Truro* 96-04. *Penrose, Tresarrett, Blisland, Bodmin PL30 4QY* Tel (01208) 851003

KIRBY, Mary Elizabeth. BEd. **d** 04 **p** 05. OLM Worplesdon *Guildf* from 04. *Liddington Hall East, Liddington Hall Drive, Guildford GU3 3AD* Tel (01483) 237131 E-mail mary.kirby@fish.co.uk

KIRBY, Maurice William Herbert. b 31. K Coll Lon CertEd AKC. **d** 55 **p** 56. C Eltham Park St Luke *S'wark* 55-56; C Horley 56-59; C Westbury *Sarum* 59-62; R Poulshot w Worton 62-66; P-in-c Gt Cheverell 65; P-in-c Burcombe 66-68; V 68-70; V Salisbury St Mich 70-73; Chapl SS Helen and Kath Sch Abingdon 73-79; Chapl and Hd RS Wrekin Coll Telford 79-84; V Frensham *Guildf* 84-93; Dir of Reader Tr 84-93; rtd 93; Perm to Offic *Ex* 93-94; *Chich* 94-97; *York* 01-03 and from 04. *41 Eglinton Avenue, Guisborough TS14 7BN* Tel (01287) 631160 Mobile 07866-338314

KIRBY, Paul Michael. b 51. Wycliffe Hall Ox 74 Seabury-Western Th Sem DMin99. **d** 76 **p** 77. C Gateacre *Liv* 76-79; C Barton Seagrave w Warkton *Pet* 79-83; V Bidston *Ches* 83-93; V Ormskirk *Liv* 93-99; Team Ldr Chapl E Kent Hosps NHS Trust 99-00; Sen Team Ldr Chapl from 00; Bp's Adv for Hosp Chapl *Cant* from 02. *Buckland Hospital, Coombe Valley Road, Dover CT17 0HD* Tel (01304) 201624 ext 43334 Mobile 07811-134383 E-mail paul.kirby@ekht.nhs.uk

KIRBY, Richard Arthur. b 48. Lon Univ BSc69. **d** 05. OLM Wellington, All SS w Eyton *Lich* from 05. *4 Donnerville Gardens, Admaston, Telford TF5 0DE* Tel (01952) 411358 E-mail richard.kirby@lichfield.anglican.org

KIRBY, Simon Thomas. b 67. Lon Bible Coll BA92. NTMTC 00. **d** 03 **p** 04. C Woodside Park St Barn *Lon* from 03. *48 Bawtry Road, London N20 0ST* Tel (020) 8361 1545 Mobile 07967-838272 E-mail simonkirby@stbarnabas.co.uk

KIRBY, Stennett Roger. b 54. St Pet Coll Ox BA75 MA79. Sarum & Wells Th Coll 75. **d** 77 **p** 78. C Belsize Park *Lon* 77-79; NSM Plumstead St Nic *S'wark* 88; C Leic Ch Sav *Leic* 90-91; TV Hanley H Ev *Lich* 91-95; P-in-c Walsall St Pet 95-01; V from 01. *St Peter's Vicarage, 22 Bloxwich Road, Walsall WS2 8DB* Tel (01922) 623995 E-mail sgable@blueyonder.co.uk

KIRK, Andrew. *See* KIRK, John Andrew

KIRK, Clive John Charles. b 37. TD81. FIBMS66. Guildf Dioc Min Course 95. **d** 98 **p** 99. OLM E Molesey St Paul *Guildf* from 98. *9 Fleet Close, West Molesey KT8 2NS* Tel (020) 8979 1227 E-mail candakirk@lineone.net

KIRK, Miss Erika Cottam. b 55. Nottm Univ LLB76 Solicitor 81. St Jo Coll Nottm MA98. **d** 98 **p** 99. NSM Epperstone, Gonalston, Oxton etc *S'well* 98-03; NSM Burton Joyce w Bulcote and Stoke Bardolph *S'well* from 03. *24 St Helen's Crescent, Burton Joyce, Nottingham NG14 5DW* Tel 0115-931 4125 E-mail erika.kirk@ntu.ac.uk

KIRK, Canon Gavin John. b 61. Southn Univ BTh. Chich Th Coll 83. **d** 86 **p** 87. C Seaford w Sutton *Chich* 86-89; Chapl and Succ Roch Cath *Roch* 89-91; Min Can 89-91; Hon PV 91-98; Asst Chapl K Sch Roch 91-98; Can Res Portsm Cathl *Portsm* 98-03; Can Res and Prec Linc Cathl *Linc* from 03. *The Precentory, 16 Minster Yard, Lincoln LN2 1PX* Tel (01522) 523644 E-mail precentor@lincolncathedral.com

KIRK, Geoffrey. b 45. Keble Coll Ox BA67. Coll of Resurr Mirfield 71. **d** 72 **p** 73. C Leeds St Aid *Ripon* 72-74; C St Marylebone St Mark w St Luke *Lon* 74-76; C Kennington St Jo *S'wark* 77-79; C Kennington St Jo w St Jas 79-81; P-in-c Lewisham St Steph and St Mark 81-87; V from 87. *St Stephen's Vicarage, Cressingham Road, London SE13 5AG* Tel (020) 8318 1295 Fax 8318 1446

KIRK, George. b 14. Kelham Th Coll 32. **d** 38 **p** 39. C Norbury St Oswald *Cant* 38-41; C Sheff St Cuth *Sheff* 41-43; Chapl City Gen Hosp 41-43; P-in-c Brightside St Thos 43-44; V 44-48; V Bentley 48-56; R Aston cum Aughton 56-80; P-in-c Ulley 57-65; V 65-80; RD Laughton 72-79; rtd 80; Chapl to Rtd Clergy and Clergy Widows Officer *Sheff* 80-86; Lic to Offic 86-93; Perm to Offic from 93. *3 Borrowdale Crescent, North Anston, Sheffield S25 4JW* Tel (01909) 566774

KIRK, Miss Geraldine Mercedes. b 49. Hull Univ MA89. **d** 87 **p** 94. Ind Chapl *Linc* 87-99; P-in-c Bridgwater St Jo *B & W* from 99; Chapl Taunton and Somerset NHS Trust from 99. *St John's Vicarage, Blake Place, Bridgwater TA6 5AU* Tel (01278) 422540 E-mail geraldine@kirk50.freeserve.co.uk

KIRK, Henry Logan. b 52. Adelaide Univ BA74 New Coll Edin BD77 K Coll Lon MA96. **d** 80 **p** 81. Chapl Dioc Coll Cape Prov S Africa 80-85; Asst Master Haileybury Coll 86; Asst Chapl Rugby Sch 86-93; Dep Hd Dulwich Coll Prep Sch 93-94; NSM S Dulwich St Steph *S'wark* 93-94; C Linslade *Ox* 94-96; Chapl Birkenhead Sch Merseyside 96-03; Chapl Abingdon Sch from 04. *Abingdon School, Park Road, Abingdon OX14 1DA* Tel (01235) 849112 *or* 534674 E-mail henry.kirk@abingdon.org.uk

KIRK, John Andrew. b 37. Lon Univ BD61 AKC61 MPhil75 Fitzw Ho Cam BA63. Ridley Hall Cam 61. **d** 63 **p** 64. C Finchley Ch Ch *Lon* 63-66; Argentina 66-79; SAMS 79-81; CMS 82-90; Dean of Miss Selly Oak Coll Birm 90-99; Dept of Th Birm Univ *Birm* 99-02; Perm to Offic *Glouc* from 99; rtd 02. *The Old Stable, Market Square, Lechlade GL7 3AB* Tel (01367) 253254

KIRK, Ms Natalie Roberta. b 71. Leeds Univ BA93. Wycliffe Hall Ox 03. **d** 05. C Gipsy Hill Ch Ch *S'wark* from 05. *1A Highland Road, London SE19 1DP* Tel (020) 8761 5927

KIRK, Peter Fenwick. b 30. Leeds Univ 50. **d** 83 **p** 84. NSM Bathgate *Edin* 83-91; NSM Linlithgow 83-91; NSM Bathgate from 92. *18 Inch Crescent, Bathgate EH48 1EU* Tel (01506) 655369

KIRK, Steven Paul. b 59. Ex Univ LLB80 Univ of Wales (Cardiff) BD87 LLM94. St Mich Coll Llan 84. **d** 87 **p** 88. C Ebbw Vale *Mon* 87-89; PV Llan Cathl *Llan* 89-91; PV and Succ 91-94; V Port Talbot St Agnes w Oakwood 94-01; TR Aberavon from 01. *The Rectory, 29 Ynys Street, Port Talbot SA13 1YW* Tel (01639) 883630

KIRK-DUNCAN, The Ven Brian Andrew Campbell. b 15. Pemb Coll Ox BA46 MA47 TCD MA59 DPhil64. Cuddesdon Coll 39. **d** 41 **p** 42. C Summertown *Ox* 41-43; Asst Master Dragon Sch Ox 41-43; C Headington Quarry *Ox* 43-44; V Sevenhampton w Charlton Abbots *Glouc* 44-47; P-in-c Hawling w Cold Salperton 46-47; R Bredon w Bredon's Norton *Worc* 47-62; R St Mary at Hill w St Andr Hubbard etc *Lon* from 62; Prin Becket Coll Lon 63-67; Dep Min Can St Paul's Cathl *Lon* from 69; Hon Adn Guinea from 87; Perm to Offic *St E* from 91 and *Chelmsf* from 92. *The Rectory, St Mary-at-Hill, London EC3R 8EE* Tel (020) 7626 4184 Fax 7283 4421

KIRKBRIDE, Martin Lea. b 51. Oak Hill Th Coll BA94. **d** 97 **p** 98. C Lancaster St Thos *Blackb* 97-00; TV Hampreston *Sarum* 00-05; V Lenton *S'well* from 05. *The Vicarage, 35A Church Street, Nottingham NG7 2FF* Tel 0115-970 1059 E-mail martinkirkbride@aol.com

KIRKBY, John Victor Michael. b 39. Lon Univ BScEng62 DipMaths64 BD73. Ridley Hall Cam 65. **d** 67 **p** 68. C Muswell Hill St Jas *Lon* 67-70; Chapl Hatf Poly *St Alb* 71-75; V Wootton 75-86; RD Elstow 82-86; R Byfleet *Guildf* 86-92; P-in-c Potten End w Nettleden *St Alb* 92-97; V from 97; Chapl Ashridge Management Coll from 92. *The Vicarage, Church Road, Potten End, Berkhamsted HP4 2QY* Tel (01442) 865217

KIRKBY, Reginald Gresham. b 16. Leeds Univ BA40. Coll of Resurr Mirfield 40. **d** 42 **p** 43. C Gorton St Mary and St Thos *Man* 42-44; C Middlesbrough All SS *York* 44-46; C Becontree St Pet *Chelmsf* 46-48; C Notting Hill St Mich and Ch Ch *Lon* 48-51; V Bow Common 51-94; rtd 94. *7 St James's Court, Bishop Street, London N1 8PH* Tel (020) 7226 5714

KIRKE, Clive Henry. b 51. Ridley Hall Cam. **d** 83 **p** 84. C Ainsdale *Liv* 83-86; Gen Asst Bootle Deanery 86-89; P-in-c Litherland St Andr 89-98; V Ingrow cum Hainworth *Bradf* from 98. *St John's Vicarage, Oakfield Road, Keighley BD21 1BT* Tel (01535) 604069

KIRKER, Richard Ennis. b 51. Sarum & Wells Th Coll 72. **d** 77. C Hitchin *St Alb* 77-78; Gen Sec LGCM from 79. *Oxford House, Derbyshire Street, London E2 6HG* Tel and fax (020) 7739 1249 *or* tel 7791 1802 E-mail lgcm@aol.com

KIRKHAM, Alan. b 46. **d** 01 **p** 02. OLM Parr *Liv* from 01. *21 Avondale Road, Haydock, St Helens WA11 0HJ* Tel (01744) 28046

KIRKHAM, Clifford Gerald Frank. b 34. Open Univ BA91. Sarum & Wells Th Coll 72. **d** 74 **p** 75. C Worle *B & W* 74-76; C E

Preston w Kingston *Chich* 76-78; C Goring-by-Sea 78-80; C-in-c Maybridge CD 80-82; V Maybridge 82-88; R N Chapel w Ebernoe 88-99; Chapl for Rural Affairs 89-99; rtd 99; Perm to Offic *Nor* from 99. *5 Meadow Way, Rollesby, Great Yarmouth NR29 5HA* Tel (01493) 749036 E-mail kirkham@fish.co.uk

✠**KIRKHAM, The Rt Revd John Dudley Galtrey.** b 35. Trin Coll Cam BA59 MA63. Westcott Ho Cam 60. **d** 62 **p** 63 **c** 76. C Ipswich St Mary le Tower *St E* 62-65; Bp's Chapl *Nor* 65-69; P-in-c Rockland St Mary w Hellington 67-69; Papua New Guinea 69-70; C St Martin-in-the-Fields *Lon* 70-72; C Westmr St Marg 70-72; Abp's Dom Chapl *Cant* 72-76; Suff Bp Sherborne *Sarum* 76-81; Area Bp Sherborne 81-01; Can and Preb Sarum Cathl 77-01; Abp's Adv to the Headmasters' Conf from 90; Bp HM Forces 92-01; rtd 01; Hon Asst Bp Sarum from 01; Can and Preb Sarum Cathl from 02. *Flamstone House, Flamstone Street, Bishopstone, Salisbury SP5 4BZ* Tel (01722) 780221 E-mail jsherborne@salisbury.anglican.org

KIRKHAM, June Margaret. b 54. EMMTC 99. **d** 02 **p** 03. C Nottingham St Jude *S'well* from 02. *19 Kent Road, Nottingham NG3 6BE* Tel 0115-960 9899
E-mail june@kirkham7260.fsnet.co.uk

KIRKHAM, Stephen Gawin. b 51. MC74. Ridley Hall Cam 96. **d** 98 **p** 99. C Histon and Impington *Ely* 98-02; P-in-c N Leigh *Ox* from 02. *The Vicarage, New Yatt Road, North Leigh, Witney OX29 6TT* Tel (01993) 881136
E-mail sg.kirkham@btinternet.com

KIRKLAND, Richard John. b 53. Leic Univ BA75. St Jo Coll Dur 76. **d** 79 **p** 80. C Knutsford St Jo and Toft *Ches* 79-82; C Bebington 82-89; V Poulton Lancelyn H Trin 89-95; V Hoole from 95. *All Saints' Vicarage, 2 Vicarage Road, Chester CH2 3HZ* Tel (01244) 322056 E-mail j.kirkland@clara.net

KIRKMAN, Richard Marsden. b 55. Cranmer Hall Dur. **d** 87 **p** 88. C Bridlington Priory *York* 87-90; TV Thirsk 90-96; R Escrick and Stillingfleet w Naburn from 96; RD Derwent from 01. *The Rectory, York Road, Escrick, York YO19 6EY* Tel (01904) 728406 E-mail rmkquanta@telco4u.net

KIRKMAN, Trevor Harwood. b 51. Trin Hall Cam BA73 MA77. EMMTC 94. **d** 96 **p** 97. NSM Hickling w Kinoulton and Broughton Sulney *S'well* 96-01; NSM Keyworth and Stanton-on-the-Wolds and Bunny etc from 01; Dioc Registrar and Bp's Legal Adv *Leic* from 02. *The Old Vicarage, 43 Church Lane, Long Clawson, Melton Mowbray LE14 4ND* Tel (01664) 822270 Fax (01509) 238833 E-mail trevorkirkman@lathamlawyers.co.uk

KIRKPATRICK, Errol Francis. b 28. TCD MA HDipEd. **d** 52 **p** 53. C Enniscorthy *C & O* 52-55; Dioc C (Ferns) 55-56; C Wexford St Iberius 55-56; C Bridgwater St Mary w Chilton Trinity *B & W* 56-59; R Bromley All Hallows *Lon* 59-66; R Kentchurch w Llangua *Heref* 66-77; V Rowlestone w Llancillo 66-77; V Walterstone 66-77; RD Abbeydore 72-77; R Porlock w Stoke Pero *B & W* 77-83; R Lapworth *Birm* 83-89; R Baddesley Clinton 83-89; rtd 89; Perm to Offic *B & W* from 89. *51 Runnymede Road, Yeovil BA21 5RY*

KIRKPATRICK, The Very Revd Jonathan Richard. b 58. CA81 Goldsmiths' Coll Lon BA85 Otago Univ MBA02. Wilson Carlile Coll 78 S'wark Ord Course 83. **d** 85 **p** 85. C Lewisham St Mary *S'wark* 85-87; Chapl Lewisham Hosp 85-87; Selection Sec ACCM 88-91; Sec Aston Tr Scheme 89-91; Hon C Noel Park St Mark *Lon* 88-91; V Christchurch St Mich New Zealand 91-96; Dean Dunedin 96-01; V Gen 97-01; Lic to Offic Auckland from 02. *33 Haycock Avenue, Mount Roskill, Auckland, New Zealand 1004* Tel (0064) (9) 627 7225 E-mail jonrk@xtra.co.nz

KIRKPATRICK, Nigel David Joseph. b 68. CITC BTh96. **d** 96 **p** 97. C Portadown St Columba *Arm* 96-99; C Lecale Gp *D & D* 99-01; I Killinchy w Kilmood and Tullynakill from 01. *Killinchy Rectory, 11 Whiterock Road, Killinchy, Newtownards BT23 6PR* Tel and fax (028) 9754 1249
E-mail killinchy@down.anglican.org

KIRKPATRICK, Roger James (Brother Damian). b 41. FCA. **d** 86 **p** 87. SSF from 66; Guardian Belf Friary 80-88; Birm 89-93; Prov Min 91-02; NSM Belfast St Pet *Conn* 86-88; Chapl R Victoria Hosp Belf 86-88; Lic to Offic *Linc* 94-96; *Lon* 97-01; *Sarum* 01-03; V Holy Is *Newc* from 03. *The Vicarage, Holy Island, Berwick-upon-Tweed TD15 2RX* Tel (01289) 389216
E-mail damianssf@aol.com *or* damianssf@franciscans.org.uk

KIRKPATRICK, William John Ashley. b 27. SEN SRN RMN. Sarum Th Coll 63. **d** 68 **p** 70. NSM St Mary le Bow w St Pancras Soper Lane etc *Lon* 68-70; NSM Soho St Anne w St Thos and St Pet 70-75; SSF 76-79; NSM S Kensington St Aug *Lon* 79-80; NSM Earl's Court St Cuth w St Matthias 80-98; rtd 98; Perm to Offic *Lon* from 98. *15 Child's Street, London SW5 9RY* Tel and fax (020) 7373 1330 E-mail fr.bill@lineone.net

KIRKUP, Nigel Norman. b 54. K Coll Lon BD79 AKC79. **d** 80 **p** 80. Hon C Catford (Southend) and Downham *S'wark* 80-83; Hon C Surbiton St Andr and St Mark 83-85; Hon C Shirley St Geo 85-93; Perm to Offic *Lon* from 96. *29 Peartree Lane, London E1 9SR* Tel (020) 7488 4217

KIRKWOOD, David Christopher. b 40. Pemb Coll Ox BA63. Clifton Th Coll 63. **d** 65 **p** 66. C Wilmington *Roch* 65-68; C Green Street Green 68-72; Youth and Area Sec BCMS 72-73; Educn and Youth Sec 73-80; Hon C Sidcup Ch Ch *Roch* 74-80; V Rothley *Leic* 80-92; RD Goscote II 84-88; RD Goscote 88-90; P-in-c Toxteth St Philemon w St Gabr and St Cleopas *Liv* 92-95; TR 95-01; AD Toxteth and Wavertree 96-01; TR Harlow Town Cen w Lt Parndon *Chelmsf* from 01; AD Harlow from 04. *The Rectory, 43 Upper Park, Harlow CM20 1TW* Tel (01279) 444292
E-mail davidk@minternet.org

KIRKWOOD, Jack. b 21. Worc Ord Coll 62. **d** 63 **p** 64. C Penwerris *Truro* 63-66; V Torpoint 66-73; V Turton *Man* 73-81; P-in-c Castleton All So 81-82; Hon C Heywood St Luke 82-84; rtd 86; Perm to Offic *Blackb* from 86 and *York* 89-94. *2 Westover Grove, Warton, Carnforth LA5 9QR* Tel (01524) 732552

KIRLEW, John Richard Francis. b 52. STETS 92. **d** 05. NSM Castle Cary w Ansford *B & W* from 05. *Weavers Cottage, Torbay Road, Castle Cary BA7 7DS*

KIRTLEY, Georgina. b 44. St Jo Coll Dur BA94. Cranmer Hall Dur. **d** 95 **p** 96. NSM Barnard Castle w Whorlton *Dur* 95-00; Chapl HM YOI Deerbolt from 00; Asst Adv to Self Supporting Ministers from 00. *Ryelands, Stainton, Barnard Castle DL12 8RB* Tel (01833) 630871

KIRTON, Canon Richard Arthur. b 43. Dur Univ BA67 MA73 DipTh68. Wycliffe Hall Ox 68. **d** 69 **p** 70. C Warsop *S'well* 69-72; C Newark St Mary 72-75; Malaysia 75-83; Dean of Studies Th Sem Kuala Lumpur 79-82; P-in-c Bleasby w Halloughton *S'well* 83-89; V Thurgarton w Hoveringham 83-89; V Thurgarton w Hoveringham and Bleasby etc 89-91; Bp's Adv on Overseas Relns 85-91; Hon Can Kuala Lumpur from 88; Tutor Wilson Carlile Coll of Evang 91-98; P-in-c Ollerton w Boughton *S'well* from 98. *St Paulinus Vicarage, 65 Larch Road, New Ollerton, Newark NG22 9SX* Tel (01623) 860323

KISH, Paul Alexander. b 68. K Coll Lon BD92 AKC92 Leeds Univ MA96. St Steph Ho Ox 96. **d** 98 **p** 99. C Prestbury *Glouc* 98-01; Chapl Sutton Valence Sch Kent from 01. *1 Holdgate House, South Lane, Sutton Valence, Maidstone ME17 3BG* Tel (01622) 842814 E-mail chaplain@svs.org.uk

KISSELL, Barrington John. b 38. Lon Coll of Div 64. **d** 67 **p** 68. C Camborne *Truro* 67-71; C Chorleywood St Andr *St Alb* 71-00; Dir Faith Sharing Min from 74; C Bryanston Square St Mary w St Marylebone St Mark *Lon* from 00. *19 Lena Gardens, London W6 7PY*

KISSELL, Jonathan Mark Barrington. b 66. Trin Coll Bris 99. **d** 01 **p** 02. C Stevenage St Pet Broadwater *St Alb* 01-05; C Dublin St Patr Cathl Gp *D & G* from 05. *3 Beechpark Close, Castleknock, Dublin 8, Irish Republic* Tel (00353) (1) 473 5100
E-mail jonathankissell@hotmail.com

KITA KANTO, Bishop of. *See* UNO, The Most Revd James Toru

KITCHEN, Ian Brian. b 60. Worc Coll Ox BA81 Southn Univ PGCE82. Wycliffe Hall Ox 98. **d** 00 **p** 01. C Brandesburton and Leven w Catwick *York* 00-03; P-in-c Coxwold and Husthwaite from 03; P-in-c Crayke w Brandsby and Yearsley from 03. *The Rectory, Church Hill, Crayke, York YO61 4TA* Tel (01347) 821876 E-mail luddite@fish.co.uk

KITCHEN, The Very Revd Martin. b 47. N Lon Poly BA71 K Coll Lon BD76 AKC77 Man Univ PhD88. S'wark Ord Course 77. **d** 79 **p** 80. Lect CA Tr Coll Blackheath 79-83; Hon C Kidbrooke St Jas *S'wark* 79-83; Chapl Man Poly *Man* 83-88; TV Man Whitworth 83-86; TR 86-88; Adv In-Service Tr *S'wark* 88-95; Dioc Co-ord of Tr 95-97; Can Res S'wark Cathl 88-97; Can Res Dur Cathl *Dur* 97-05; Sub-Dean 99-05; Dean Derby from 05. *The Deanery, 9 Highfield Road, Derby DE22 1GX* Tel and fax (01332) 342971 E-mail dean@derbycathedral.org

KITCHENER, Christopher William. b 46. Open Univ BA. Sarum & Wells Th Coll 82. **d** 84 **p** 85. C Bexleyheath Ch Ch *Roch* 84-88; V Gravesend St Mary 88-97; V Biggin Hill from 97. *St Mark's Vicarage, 10 Church Road, Biggin Hill, Westerham TN16 3LB* Tel (01959) 540482 E-mail chris@chriskitchener.freeserve.co.uk

KITCHENER, Mrs Evarina Carol. b 51. Stockwell Coll of Educn CertEd70 Heythrop Coll Lon MA00. Cant Sch of Min 89. **d** 92 **p** 94. NSM Gravesend St Mary *Roch* 92-97; NSM Biggin Hill from 97; Asst Chapl Bromley Hosps NHS Trust 98-99; Distr Evang Miss Enabler S Prov URC 99-01; Par Development Officer *Roch* from 01. *St Mark's Vicarage, 10 Church Road, Biggin Hill, Westerham TN16 3LB* Tel (01959) 540482 *or* tel and fax 571607 Mobile 07947-674775
E-mail carol@eckitchener.freeserve.co.uk

KITCHENER, Canon Michael Anthony. b 45. Trin Coll Cam BA67 MA70 PhD71. Cuddesdon Coll 70. **d** 71 **p** 72. C Aldwick *Chich* 71-74; C Caversham *Ox* 74-77; Tutor Coll of Resurr Mirfield 77-83; Prin NEOC *Dur* 83-90; Hon Can Newc Cathl *Newc* 84-90; Can Res and Chan Blackb Cathl *Blackb* 90-95; P-in-c Rydal *Carl* 95-99; Warden Rydal Hall 95-99; Ldr Rydal Hall Community 95-99; Can Res Nor Cathl *Nor* from 99; Dioc Dir of Ords 99-04; Bp's Officer for Ord and Initial Tr from 04. *55 The Close, Norwich NR1 4EG* Tel (01603) 630934
E-mail michaelkitchener@norwich.anglican.org

KITCHIN, Kenneth. b 46. Trin Coll Bris. **d** 89 **p** 90. C Barrow St Mark *Carl* 89-93; C Dalton-in-Furness 93-95; P-in-c

Dearham 95-01; P-in-c Clifton, Dean and Mosser from 01. *The Vicarage, 1 Clifton Gardens, Great Clifton, Workington CA14 1TT* Tel (01900) 603886 E-mail kenkitchin@uk2k.com

KITCHING, David Monro. b 26. New Coll Ox BA49. Ridley Hall Cam 80. **d** 82 **p** 83. C Hornchurch St Andr *Chelmsf* 82-86; P-in-c Graveley w Papworth St Agnes w Yelling etc *Ely* 86-90; rtd 91; Perm to Offic *Ely* from 91. *20 Victoria Park, Cambridge CB4 3EL* Tel (01223) 365687

KITCHING, Miss Elizabeth. b 49. Trent Park Coll of Educn CertEd74. St Jo Coll Nottm. **d** 01 **p** 02. C Northallerton w Kirby Sigston *York* 01-05; P-in-c Cloughton and Burniston w Ravenscar etc from 05. *The Vicarage, Mill Lane, Cloughton, Scarborough YO13 0AB* Tel (01723) 870270 Mobile 07889-425025

KITCHING, Paul. b 53. GTCL LTCL. Coll of Resurr Mirfield 80. **d** 83 **p** 84. C Hessle *York* 83-86; P-in-c Crathorne 86-98; Youth Officer 86-98; rtd 98; P-in-c Crathorne *York* from 98. *The Rectory, Crathorne, Yarm TS15 0BB* Tel (01642) 701158 Fax 700806 E-mail paulkitching@btinternet.com

KITELEY, Robert John. b 51. Hull Univ BSc73 Univ of Wales (Abth) MSc75 Lon Univ PhD82. Trin Coll Bris DipTh83. **d** 83 **p** 84. C Bebington *Ches* 83-88; C Hoole 88-91; V Plas Newton 91-99; R Ashtead *Guildf* from 99. *The Rectory, Ashdene, Dene Road, Ashtead KT21 1EE* Tel and fax (01372) 805182 E-mail bobkiteley@ntlworld.com

KITLEY, Canon David Buchan. b 53. St Jo Coll Dur BA. Trin Coll Bris 78. **d** 81 **p** 82. C Tonbridge St Steph *Roch* 81-84; C-in-c Southall Em CD *Lon* 84-91; V Dartford Ch Ch *Roch* from 91; RD Dartford from 98; Hon Can Roch Cathl from 05; Hon Can Mpwampwa from 05. *The Vicarage, 67 Shepherds Lane, Dartford DA1 2NS* Tel (01322) 220036 E-mail kitley@clara.net

KITNEY, Miss Joan Olive Lily. b 22. Gilmore Ho 50. **dss** 60 **d** 87. Horsell *Guildf* 59-63; Chapl Asst Reading Hosps 63-79; Hermitage and Hampstead Norreys, Cold Ash etc *Ox* 80-84; NSM Staines St Mary and St Pet *Lon* 87-89; rtd 89; Perm to Offic *Ox* from 90. *54 Newtown Road, Newbury RG14 7BT* Tel (01635) 36416

KITTERINGHAM, Canon Ian. b 35. CCC Cam BA59 MA63. Westcott Ho Cam 59. **d** 61 **p** 62. C Rotherham *Sheff* 61-64; C Eltham H Trin *S'wark* 64-66; V Battersea St Mary-le-Park 66-73; V Reigate St Mark 73-80; V Caterham Valley 80-85; RD Caterham 84-85; V Wandsworth Common St Mary 85-00; RD Tooting 88-93; Hon Can S'wark Cathl 95-00; rtd 00; Perm to Offic *Cov* from 02. *17 Sandfield Road, Stratford-upon-Avon CV37 9AG* Tel (01789) 266384

KITTS, Joseph. b 27. Tyndale Hall Bris 59. **d** 60 **p** 61. C Parr *Liv* 60-63; C Bootle St Leon 63-66; V Southport SS Simon and Jude 66-74; USA 74-94; rtd 92. *Windyridge, Cottage Lane, St Martin's, Oswestry SY11 3BL* Tel (01691) 777090

KIVETT, Michael Stephen. b 50. Bethany Coll W Virginia BA72. Chr Th Sem Indiana MDiv76 Sarum & Wells Th Coll 76. **d** 77 **p** 78. C Harnham *Sarum* 77-80; C E Dereham *Nor* 80-83; R S Walsham and V Upton 83-88; Chapl Lt Plumstead Hosp 84-88; V Chard St Mary *B & W* 88-99; TR Chard and Distr 99-04; RD Crewkerne and Ilminster 93-98; R Staplegrove w Norton Fitzwarren from 04. *The Rectory, Rectory Drive, Staplegrove, Taunton TA2 6AP* Tel (01823) 272787 E-mail msk@fish.co.uk *or* skivett@fish.co.uk

KLIMAS, Miss Lynda. b 58. Jes Coll Cam BA89 MA93. Cranmer Hall Dur 89. **d** 90 **p** 94. Par Dn Sandy *St Alb* 90-93; Par Dn Bishop's Stortford St Mich 93-94; C 94-98; P-in-c Weston and C Baldock w Bygrave 98-03; TV Baldock w Bygrave and Weston 03-04; V Cople, Moggerhanger and Willington from 04. *The Vicarage, 3 Grange Lane, Cople, Bedford MK44 3TT* Tel (01234) 838431

KNAPP, Antony Blair. b 48. Imp Coll Lon BSc68. N Ord Course 86. **d** 89 **p** 90. C Bolton St Jas w St Chrys *Bradf* 89-92; V Kettlewell w Conistone, Hubberholme etc 92-00; TR Swindon Dorcan *Bris* from 00. *23 Sedgebrook, Swindon SN3 6EY* Tel (01793) 525130 E-mail tonybknapp@aol.com

KNAPP, Bryan Thomas. b 61. Trin Coll Bris DipHE90 BA91. **d** 91 **p** 92. C S Gillingham *Roch* 91-95; V Chatham St Paul w All SS from 95. *The Vicarage, 2A Waghorn Street, Chatham ME4 5LT* Tel (01634) 845419

KNAPP, Jeremy Michael. b 67. Westhill Coll Birm BEd91. Ripon Coll Cuddesdon BTh99. **d** 99 **p** 00. C Hill *Birm* 99-02; TV Salter Street and Shirley from 02. *68 Tythe Barn Lane, Solihull B90 1RW* Tel 0121-733 6658 E-mail toposcope@fish.co.uk

KNAPP (née STOCKER), Mrs Rachael Ann. b 64. Bris Univ BA86. Trin Coll Bris DipHE90 BA91. **d** 91 **p** 94. C Ditton *Roch* 91-95; C Chatham St Paul w All SS from 95. *The Vicarage, 2A Waghorn Street, Chatham ME4 5LT* Tel (01634) 845419

KNAPPER, Peter Charles. b 39. Lon Univ BA61. St Steph Ho Ox 61. **d** 63 **p** 64. C Carl H Trin *Carl* 63-68; V Westfield St Mary 68-76; V Bridekirk 76-83; P-in-c Blackheath Ascension *S'wark* 83-96; P-in-c Holmwood *Guildf* 96-03; TV Surrey Weald 03-04; rtd 04. *20 Boyne Road, London SE13 5AL* Tel (020) 8473 1501 E-mail peter/pat@pknapper.fsnet.co.uk

KNARESBOROUGH, Suffragan Bishop of. *See* BELL, The Rt Revd James Harold

KNEE, Geoffrey. b 31. Whitelands Coll Lon CertEd71. CA Tr Coll 56 Glouc Sch of Min 91. **d** 92 **p** 93. NSM Hampton *Worc* 92-97; Chapl St Richard's Hospice Worc 95-97; NSM Badsey w Aldington and Offenham and Bretforton *Worc* 97; rtd 97; Perm to Offic *Worc* from 98. *8 Mayfair, Fairfield, Evesham WR11 1JJ* Tel (01386) 443574 E-mail geoff@kneehome.freeserve.co.uk

KNEE, Jacob Samuel. b 66. LSE BSc(Econ)87 MSc(Econ)88 Ox Univ BA92. Ripon Coll Cuddesdon 90. **d** 93 **p** 94. C Ashby-de-la-Zouch St Helen w Coleorton *Leic* 93-96; C Boston *Linc* 96-00; Chapl Boston Coll of FE 96-00; V Cam w Stinchcombe *Glouc* from 00. *The Vicarage, Church Road, Cam, Dursley GL11 5PQ* Tel (01453) 542084 E-mail jknee@globalnet.co.uk

KNEE-ROBINSON, Keith Frederick. b 40. Thames Poly BSc75 MICE76. St Alb and Ox Min Course 99. **d** 01 **p** 02. OLM Caversham and Mapledurham *Ox* from 01. *Mill Cottage, Church Road, Bradfield, Reading RG7 6BX* Tel 0118-974 4526 E-mail kkrmill@globalnet.co.uk

KNEEN, Michael John. b 55. Univ Coll Lon BSc76 MSc77 St Jo Coll Dur BA85. Cranmer Hall Dur 83. **d** 86 **p** 87. C Bishop's Castle w Mainstone *Heref* 86-90; TV Bridgnorth, Tasley, Astley Abbotts, etc from 90. *41 Innage Lane, Bridgnorth WV16 4HS* Tel (01746) 766418 *or* 767174 E-mail mkneen@btopenworld.com

KNELL, John George. b 35. Cant Sch of Min 79. **d** 82 **p** 83. Hd Master St Geo C of E Middle Sch Sheerness 80-87; NSM Sheerness H Trin w St Paul *Cant* 82-87; NSM Minster-in-Sheppey from 87. *11 Uplands Way, Queenborough Road, Sheerness ME12 3EF* Tel (01795) 665945

KNELL, Canon Raymond John. b 27. Qu Coll Cam BA48 MA52. Ridley Hall Cam 50. **d** 52 **p** 53. C Bishopwearmouth St Gabr *Dur* 52-57; C S Shields St Hilda 57-58; P-in-c Hebburn St Oswald 58-67; V Castleside 67-76; V Heworth St Mary 76-93; RD Gateshead 83-87; Hon Can Dur Cathl 87-93; rtd 93. *40 St Andrew's Drive, Low Fell, Gateshead NE9 6JU* Tel 0191-442 1069

KNICKERBOCKER, Driss Richard. b 39. Univ of Michigan BA63 MDiv68 Ox Univ DPhil81. **d** 68 **p** 69. USA 68-76 and from 85; C St Marylebone w H Trin *Lon* 78-81; C Chelsea St Luke 81-83; P-in-c Isleworth St Fran 83-85; rtd 04. *985 Pierpont Street, Rahway, NJ 07065, USA*

KNIFTON, Gladys Elizabeth. b 52. SRN73 SCM75 FE TCert84 Kingston Univ DipHE94 BSc95. NTMTC 95. **d** 98 **p** 99. NSM Churt *Guildf* 98-01; Chapl Surrey Hants Borders NHS Trust from 01. *Bryanston, Boundary Road, Grayshott, Hindhead GU26 6TX* Tel and fax (01428) 604977 E-mail elizabeth@knifton.com

KNIGHT, The Very Revd Alexander Francis (Alec). b 39. St Cath Coll Cam BA61 MA65. Wells Th Coll. **d** 63 **p** 64. C Hemel Hempstead *St Alb* 63-68; Chapl Taunton Sch 68-75; Dir Bloxham Project 75-81; Dir of Studies Aston Tr Scheme 81-83; P-in-c Easton and Martyr Worthy *Win* 83-91; Adn Basingstoke 90-98; Can Res Win Cathl 91-98; Dean Linc from 98. *The Deanery, 12 Eastgate, Lincoln LN2 1QG* Tel (01522) 523608 E-mail dean@lincolncathedral.com

KNIGHT, Canon Andrew James. b 50. Grey Coll Dur BA72 Ox Univ BA74 MA81. Wycliffe Hall Ox 72. **d** 75 **p** 76. Min Can Brecon Cathl *S & B* 75-78; C Brecon w Battle 75-78; C Morriston 78-82; V 89-00; V Llanwrtyd w Llanddulas in Tir Abad etc 82-89; RD Cwmtawe 97-00; Can Res Brecon Cathl 98-04; Treas from 04; V Sketty from 00. *The Vicarage, De La Beche Road, Sketty, Swansea SA2 9AR* Tel (01792) 202767

KNIGHT, Mrs Ann. b 54. Lanc Univ CertEd75. Trin Coll Bris DipHE83 DPS84. **dss** 84 **d** 87 **p** 94. Wigan St Jas w St Thos *Liv* 84-87; Par Dn 87-90; C Costessey *Nor* 90-96; R Gt and Lt Ellingham, Rockland and Shropham etc 96-03; Chapl Norwich Primary Care Trust 96-02; P-in-c Worthen *Heref* from 03; P-in-c Hope w Shelve from 03. *The Rectory, Worthen, Shrewsbury SY5 9HN* Tel (01743) 891930

KNIGHT, Arthur Clifford Edwin. b 42. Univ of Wales BSc64. Wells Th Coll 64. **d** 66 **p** 67. C Llangyfelach and Morriston *S & B* 66-68; C Oystermouth 68-73; Chapl RAF 73-95; Perm to Offic *Heref* 95-97; P-in-c Brant Broughton and Beckingham *Linc* 97-99; P-in-c Credenhill w Brinsop and Wormsley etc *Heref* from 99. *26 Meadow Drive, Credenhill, Hereford HR4 7EE* Tel (01432) 760530

KNIGHT, Mrs Barbara. b 46. St Alb Minl Tr Scheme 86. **d** 90 **p** 94. NSM Weston and Ardeley *St Alb* 90-95; C Norton 95-97; R Barkway, Reed and Buckland w Barley 97-05; rtd 05. *c/o Lucinda Jobson, 156A Sinclair Road, London W14 0NL*

KNIGHT, Mrs Barbara Mary. b 43. SRN64 SCM70. EMMTC 94. **d** 97 **p** 98. NSM Market Harborough and The Transfiguration etc *Leic* 97-99; C Church Langton cum Tur Langton etc 99-02; P-in-c Billesdon and Skeffington 02; R Church Langton cum Tur Langton etc from 02. *The Vicarage, Gaulby Road, Billesdon, Leicester LE7 9AG* Tel 0116-259 6321 E-mail revbarbarak@btopenworld.com

KNIGHT, Brenda Evelyn. b 27. St Alb and Ox Min Course 96. **d** 98 **p** 99. OLM Wheatley *Ox* from 98. *22 Middle Road, Stanton St John, Oxford OX33 1HD* Tel (01865) 351227

KNIGHT, Christopher. b 61. Wycliffe Hall Ox 94. **d** 96 **p** 97. C Banbury *Ox* 96-98; C Banbury St Paul 98-01; Chapl HM Pris Lowdham Grange from 01. *HM Prison Lowdham Grange, Nottingham NG14 7DQ* Tel 0115-966 9308 E-mail 2cv@clara.net

KNIGHT, Christopher Colson. b 52. Ex Univ BSc73 Man Univ PhD77 SS Coll Cam MA90. Sarum & Wells Th Coll BTh83. **d** 81 **p** 82. Chapl St Mary's Cathl *Edin* 81-84; V Chesterton *Cov* 84-87; R Lighthorne 84-87; V Newbold Pacey w Moreton Morrell 84-87; Chapl and Fell SS Coll Cam 87-92; Sen Research Assoc St Edm Coll Cam from 92. *Hope Cottage, Hindringham Road, Walsingham NR22 6DR* Tel (01328) 820108

KNIGHT, Clifford. *See* KNIGHT, Arthur Clifford Edwin

KNIGHT, David Alan. b 59. Lanc Univ BA81. Ripon Coll Cuddesdon 82. **d** 85 **p** 86. C Stretford All SS *Man* 85-88; C Charlestown 88-89; TV Pendleton St Thos w Charlestown 89-94; V Tysoe w Oxhill and Whatcote *Cov* from 94; RD Shipston from 04. *The Vicarage, Peacock Lane, Tysoe, Warwick CV35 0SG* Tel and fax (01295) 680201 E-mail david.knight20@virgin.net

KNIGHT, David Charles. b 32. Clare Coll Cam BA55 MA59. Tyndale Hall Bris 55. **d** 57 **p** 58. C Cambridge St Paul *Ely* 57-58; C St Alb Ch Ch *St Alb* 58-61; C-in-c Wimbledon Em Ridgway Prop Chpl *S'wark* 61-67; Publications Sec BCMS 67-68; Ed Asst *The Christian* 68-69; V Lannarth *Truro* 69-75; RD Carnmarth N 72-75; V Fremington *Ex* 75-83; C Edmonton All SS w St Mich *Lon* 83; Chapl N Middx Hosp 83; rtd 94; Perm to Offic *Chelmsf* from 94. *Tudor Court, High Street, Hatfield Broad Oak, Bishop's Stortford CM22 7HF* Tel (01279) 718650

KNIGHT, Canon David Charles. b 45. ATCL63 Lon Univ BA66 St Edm Hall Ox BA68 MA73. St Steph Ho Ox 68. **d** 70 **p** 71. C Northwood H Trin *Lon* 70-73; C Stevenage All SS Pin Green *St Alb* 73-77; C Cippenham CD *Ox* 77-78; TV W Slough 78-83; Dep Min Can Windsor from 81; Ecum Officer to Bp Willesden 83-91; R Lt Stanmore St Lawr *Lon* 83-91; Prec and Can Res Chelmsf Cathl *Chelmsf* 91-01; V Ranmoor *Sheff* from 01. *The Vicarage, 389A Fulwood Road, Sheffield S10 3GA* Tel 0114-230 1671 *or* 230 1199 Fax 0114-263 0158 E-mail dknight@fish.co.uk

KNIGHT, Canon David Lansley. b 33. Em Coll Cam BA58 MA61 PGCE76. Ridley Hall Cam 57. **d** 59 **p** 60. C Chatham St Steph *Roch* 59-63; C Plymouth St Andr *Ex* 63-65; V Gravesend St Aid *Roch* 65-71; V Bexley St Mary 71-98; RD Sidcup 93-97; Hon Can Roch Cathl 97; rtd 98; Perm to Offic *Chich* from 98. *1 Newlands Avenue, Bexhill-on-Sea TN39 4HA* Tel (01424) 212120

KNIGHT, Eric Frank Walter. b 19. St Paul's Coll Grahamstown. **d** 51 **p** 52. S Africa 51-59; C Knysna 51-55; R Victoria W w Carnarvon 55-57; R Beaconsfield 57-59; R Wick *Mor* 61-63; R Girvan *Glas* 63-68; V Charlton All Saints *Sarum* 68-89; rtd 89. *c/o Ms Gail Grainger, Receivership Office, Greenlane Hospital, Devizes SN10 5DS* Tel (01380) 731317

KNIGHT (née SMITH), Frances Mary. b 48. St Jo Coll York CertEd69. EMMTC 98. **d** 03 **p** 04. NSM Braunstone *Leic* from 03. *32 Aster Way, Burbage, Hinckley LE10 2UG* Tel (01455) 618218

KNIGHT, Gavin Rees. b 65. St Andr Univ MTheol94. Ripon Coll Cuddesdon MTh96. **d** 98 **p** 99. C Solihull *Birm* 98-02; P-in-c Fulham St Andr Fulham Fields *Lon* from 02; P-in-c Fulham St Alb w St Aug from 04; Chapl Mon Sch from 05. *Monmouth School, Almshouse Street, Monmouth NP25 3XP* Tel (01600) 713143 Fax 772701 E-mail grk@fish.co.uk

KNIGHT, Henry Christian. b 34. Fitzw Ho Cam BA62 MA66. Ridley Hall Cam 62. **d** 63 **p** 64. Succ Bradf Cathl *Bradf* 63-64; Chapl 64-66; Israel 67-79; CMJ 79-86; V Allithwaite *Carl* 86-93; rtd 93; Perm to Offic *Leic* from 93. *20 Saxon Way, Ashby-de-la-Zouch LE65 2JR* Tel (01530) 460709

KNIGHT, Canon John Bernard. b 34. Fuller Th Sem California DMin91 ACIS60. Oak Hill Th Coll 61. **d** 65 **p** 66. C Morden *S'wark* 65-69; USA 69-71; V Summerfield *Birm* from 71; Hon Can Birm Cathl from 01. *Christ Church Vicarage, 64 Selwyn Road, Birmingham B16 0SW* Tel 0121-454 2689 E-mail lollard@lineone.net

KNIGHT, Canon John Francis Alan Macdonald. b 36. Coll of Resurr Mirfield 59. **d** 61 **p** 62. S Rhodesia 61-65; Rhodesia 65-80; Zimbabwe 80-87; Dean Mutare 81-87; TR Northampton Em *Pet* 87-97; RD Northn 88-92; P-in-c Greens Norton w Bradden and Lichborough from 97; Bp's Adv for Min of Healing from 99; Can Pet Cathl from 01. *The Rectory, Towcester Road, Greens Norton, Towcester NN12 8BL* Tel (01327) 359508 E-mail jfam@knight40.freeserve.co.uk

KNIGHT, Jonathan Morshead. b 59. Fitzw Coll Cam BA81 MA85 W Lon Inst of HE PGCE82 Jes Coll Cam PhD91 Jes Coll Ox MA87 Worc Coll Ox DPhil02 Sheff Univ PGCE00 SNTS99. Wycliffe Hall Ox 86. **d** 88 **p** 89. C Hillingdon St Jo *Lon* 88-91; NSM Baslow *Derby* 91-92; NSM Curbar and Stoney Middleton 91-92; Lect Bibl Studies Sheff Univ *Sheff* 91-92; Research Fell 92-94; NSM Sheff St Paul 92-94; Bp's Research Asst *Ely* 94-98; Min Whittlesford LEP 95-96; Bp's Dom Chapl 96; Sec Doctrine Commn 96-98; P-in-c Holywell w Needingworth *Ely* 98-01; Tutor Westcott Ho Cam 98-99; Dir Studies Focus Chr Inst Cambridge 99-02; OCF from 99; CF (TAVR) from 00; Hon Lect Th Kent Univ from 00; Chapl Worc Coll Ox 02-03. *Address temp unknown* E-mail jonathanknight5@hotmail.com

KNIGHT, Mrs June. b 28. Glouc Sch of Min 85. **d** 87 **p** 94. NSM Leckhampton SS Phil and Jas w Cheltenham St Jas *Glouc* 87-96; rtd 96; Perm to Offic *Glouc* from 96. *31 St Michael's Road, Woodlands, Cheltenham GL51 5RP* Tel (01242) 517911

KNIGHT, Mrs June Elizabeth. b 42. St Alb Minl Tr Scheme 90. **d** 93 **p** 94. NSM Stanstead Abbots *St Alb* 93-96; NSM Gt Amwell w St Margaret's and Stanstead Abbots 96-97; NSM Lt Hadham w Albury 97-98; NSM Bishop's Stortford St Mich from 98. *The White Cottage, Albury Hall Park, Albury, Ware SG11 2HX* Tel (01279) 771756 E-mail june.e.knight@btopenworld.com

KNIGHT, Keith Kenneth. b 36. Southn Univ BSc58. Wycliffe Hall Ox 59. **d** 62 **p** 63. C Lower Darwen St Jas *Blackb* 62-64; C Leyland St Andr 64-68; P-in-c Blackb All SS 68-71; Dioc Youth Chapl 71-88; Hon C Burnley St Pet 71-74; Warden Scargill Ho 88-01; rtd 01; Perm to Offic *Bradf* from 01. *4 The Hawthorns, Sutton-in-Craven, Keighley BD20 8BP* Tel (01535) 632920

KNIGHT, Kenneth William. b 15. TD50. Wycliffe Hall Ox. **d** 61 **p** 62. C Paignton Ch Ch *Ex* 61-63; V Holbeton 63-91; rtd 91; Perm to Offic *Ex* from 91. *West Heanton, Buckland Filleigh, Beaworthy EX21 5PJ* Tel (01409) 281754

KNIGHT, Mrs Margaret Owen. b 34. Oak Hill Th Coll 78. **dss** 80 **d** 87 **p** 94. Chorleywood St Andr *St Alb* 80-04; Par Dn 87-94; C 94-04; rtd 94; Perm to Offic *St Alb* from 04. *15A Blacketts Wood Drive, Chorleywood, Rickmansworth WD3 5PY* Tel (01923) 283832 E-mail moknight@waitrose.com

KNIGHT, Michael Richard. b 47. St Jo Coll Dur BA69 MA79 Fitzw Coll Cam BA73 MA78 St Cross Coll Ox MA92. Westcott Ho Cam 71. **d** 74 **p** 75. C Bishop's Stortford St Mich *St Alb* 74-75; C Bedford St Andr 75-79; Chapl Angl Students Glas 79-86; V Riddings and Ironville *Derby* 86-91; Lib Pusey Ho 91-94; Fell St Cross Coll Ox 92-94; V Chesterfield St Mary and All SS *Derby* from 94. *28 Cromwell Road, Chesterfield S40 4TH* Tel (01246) 232937 *or* 206506 E-mail vicar.chesterfield@virgin.net

KNIGHT, Paul James Joseph. b 50. Oak Hill Th Coll. **d** 84 **p** 85. C Broadwater St Mary *Chich* 84-87; R Itchingfield w Slinfold 87-92; Chapl Highgate Sch Lon from 92. *15A Bishopswood Road, London N6 4PB* Tel (020) 8348 9211 *or* 8340 1524 E-mail paul.knight@highgateschool.org.uk

KNIGHT, Paul Jeremy. b 53. **d** 94 **p** 95. CA 77-04; C Moreton Say *Lich* 94-97; V Birstall *Wakef* from 97. *St Peter's Vicarage, King's Drive, Birstall, Batley WF17 9JJ* Tel and fax (01924) 473715 E-mail rev.paul@ntlworld.com *or* vicar@stpetersbirstall.org.uk

KNIGHT, Peter John. b 51. Lon Univ AKC73 CertEd77. Sarum & Wells Th Coll 79. **d** 80 **p** 81. C Greenford H Cross *Lon* 80-83; C Langley Marish *Ox* 83; NSM W Acton St Martin *Lon* 89-90; C E Acton St Dunstan w St Thos 90-92; V Malden St Jo *S'wark* 92-02; Chapl HM Pris Long Lartin from 02. *HM Prison Long Lartin, South Littleton, Evesham WR11 5TZ* Tel (01386) 835100 E-mail peter.knight01@hmps.gsi.gov.uk

KNIGHT, Peter Malcolm. b 55. DA81 DRCOG83 MRCGP85 DTM&H86 Cam Univ BA76 Lon Hosp MB, BS76. Trin Coll Bris BA94. **d** 94 **p** 95. C Quidenham *Nor* 94-97; C Quidenham Gp 97; R Thurton from 97; RD Loddon from 99. *The Rectory, 29 Ashby Road, Thurton, Norwich NR14 6AX* Tel (01508) 480738

KNIGHT, Peter Michael. b 47. St Luke's Coll Ex BEd71. Trin Coll Bris DipHE92. **d** 92 **p** 93. C Bris Ch the Servant Stockwood *Bris* 92-95; Chapl St Brendan's Sixth Form Coll 92-94; C W Swindon and the Lydiards *Bris* 95-96; TV from 96. *The Vicarage, The Butts, Lydiard Millicent, Swindon SN5 3LR* Tel (01793) 772417 Fax as telephone E-mail peter@knight15.freeserve.co.uk

KNIGHT, Philip Stephen. b 46. Ian Ramsey Coll 74. **d** 77 **p** 78. C Pennycross *Ex* 77-80; C Epsom St Martin *Guildf* 80-83; V Clay Hill St Jo *Lon* 83-86; TV Washfield, Stoodleigh, Withleigh etc *Ex* 86-90; Chapl ATC from 86; Chapl S Warks Hosps 90-94; Chapl S Warks Health Care NHS Trust from 94. *37 Lodge Crescent, Warwick CV34 6BB,* or *Warwick Hospital, Lakin Road, Warwick CV34 5BW* Tel (01926) 403053 *or* 495321 ext 4121 Fax 482603 E-mail stephen.knight@swh.nhs.uk

KNIGHT, Canon Roger George. b 41. Culham Coll Ox CertEd63. Linc Th Coll 65. **d** 67 **p** 68. C Bris St Andr Hartcliffe *Bris* 67-69; Hd Master Twywell Sch Kettering 69-74; V Naseby *Pet* 74-79; P-in-c Haselbeech 74-79; R Clipston w Naseby and Haselbech 79-82; P-in-c Kelmarsh 79-82; TR Corby SS Pet and Andr w Gt and Lt Oakley 82-88; R Irthlingborough 88-99; RD Higham 89-94; R Burton Latimer 99-03; Can Pet Cathl 92-03; rtd 03; Perm to Offic *Pet* from 03. *37 School Lane, Higham Ferrers, Rushden NN10 8NQ* Tel (01933) 319001

KNIGHT, Roger Ivan. b 54. K Coll Lon BD79 AKC79. Ripon Coll Cuddesdon 79. **d** 80 **p** 81. C Orpington All SS *Roch* 80-84; C St Laur in Thanet *Cant* 84-87; R Cuxton and Halling *Roch* from 87. *The Rectory, 6 Rochester Road, Cuxton, Rochester ME2 1AF* Tel (01634) 717134 E-mail rogerknight@aol.com

KNIGHT, Stephen. *See* KNIGHT, Philip Stephen

KNIGHT, Ms Sue Elizabeth. b 47. Southlands Coll Lon CertEd68. SEITE 01. **d** 03 **p** 04. NSM Lee St Mildred *S'wark* from 03. *101 Lyme Farm Road, London SE12 8JH* Tel (020) 8852 1781

KNIGHT, Mrs Susan Margaret. d 02 **p** 03. C Clydach *S & B* 02-03; C Cen Swansea from 04. *The Vicarage, 27 Bowen Street, Swansea SA1 2NA* Tel (01792) 473047

KNIGHT, Suzanne. d 00 **p** 01. NSM Reading St Jo *Ox* from 00. *9 Victoria Way, Reading RG1 3HD* Tel 0118-967 5645 E-mail suz-knight@yahoo.co.uk

KNIGHT, William Lawrence. b 39. Univ Coll Lon BSc61 PhD65. Coll of Resurr Mirfield 75. **d** 77 **p** 78. C Bp's Hatfield *St Alb* 77-81; Asst Chapl Brussels Cathl *Eur* 81-84; V Pet H Spirit Bretton *Pet* 84-89; P-in-c Marholm 84-89; TR Riverside *Ox* 89-04; rtd 04. *7 Sunnydown Court, Hendon Avenue, Rustington, Littlehampton BN16 2NB* Tel (01903) 716750 E-mail knightsmvd@dial.pipex.com

KNIGHTS, Christopher Hammond. b 61. St Jo Coll Dur BA83 PhD88. Linc Th Coll 87. **d** 89 **p** 90. C Stockton St Pet *Dur* 89-92; C Chich St Paul and St Pet *Chich* 92-94; Tutor Chich Th Coll 92-94; V Ashington *Newc* 94-00; V Monkseaton St Mary 00-04; Dioc Moderator Reader Tr from 03; P-in-c Scotswood from 04. *St Margaret's Vicarage, 14 Heighley Street, Newcastle upon Tyne NE15 6AR* Tel 0191-274 6322 E-mail the.knights@tiscali.co.uk *or* stmarymkstn@waitrose.com

KNIGHTS, James William. b 34. AKC66. **d** 67 **p** 68. C Kettering St Andr *Pet* 67-71; V Braunston w Brooke 71-81; V Dudley St Jo *Worc* 81-97; rtd 97; Perm to Offic *Worc* from 98. *192 Brook Farm Road, Malvern WR14 3SL* Tel (01684) 561358

KNIGHTS JOHNSON, Nigel Anthony. b 52. Ealing Tech Coll BA74 Westmr Coll Ox MTh99. Wycliffe Hall Ox 78. **d** 80 **p** 81. C Beckenham Ch Ch *Roch* 80-84; CF from 84. *c/o MOD Chaplains (Army)* Tel (01980) 615804 Fax 615800

KNILL-JONES, Jonathan Waring (Jack). b 58. Univ Coll Lon BSc79. St Jo Coll Nottm Dip Th Studies 90. **d** 90 **p** 91. C Northolt W End St Jos *Lon* 90-94; C Hayes St Nic CD 94-99; V Airedale w Fryston *Wakef* from 99. *The Vicarage, The Mount, Castleford WF10 3JL* Tel (01977) 553157 E-mail jackknill@aol.com

KNOPP, Alexander Edward Robert. b 09. St Jo Coll Cam BA33 MA37. Ridley Hall Cam 32. **d** 34 **p** 35. C Loughton St Mary *Chelmsf* 34-38; C Prittlewell St Mary 38-40; R Nevendon 40; R N Benfleet w Nevendon 41-48; V Walthamstow St Jo 48-50; V Pampisford *Ely* 50-59; V Babraham 50-59; R Quendon w Rickling *Chelmsf* 59-68; R Gt Yeldham 68-73; R Gt w Lt Snoring *Nor* 73-76; rtd 76; Perm to Offic *Ely* 77-00. *6 Rose Lane, Melbourn, Royston SG8 6AD* Tel (01763) 262143

KNOTT, Graham Keith. b 53. Oak Hill Th Coll BA80. **d** 80 **p** 81. C Normanton *Derby* 80-83; C Ripley 83-87; TV Newark w Hawton, Cotham and Shelton *S'well* 87-89; TV Newark 89-97; P-in-c Mansfield St Jo from 97; AD Mansfield from 03. *The Vicarage, St John Street, Mansfield NG18 1QH* Tel (01623) 625999 E-mail st.johnchurch@ukgateway.net

KNOTT, Janet Patricia. b 50. Avery Hill Coll CertEd71. S Dios Minl Tr Scheme MTS91. **d** 92 **p** 94. NSM Clutton w Cameley *B & W* 92-99; Chapl R Sch Bath 94-98; Chapl R High Sch Bath 98-99; R Farmborough, Marksbury and Stanton Prior *B & W* from 99; Chapl Bath Spa Univ Coll from 99; RD Chew Magna *B & W* from 04. *The Rectory, Church Lane, Farmborough, Bath BA3 1AN* Tel (01761) 479311 E-mail jan@knott111.fsnet.co.uk

KNOTT, John Wensley. b 51. FIA84 Fitzw Coll Cam MA75. S Dios Minl Tr Scheme 87. **d** 90 **p** 91. NSM Canford Magna *Sarum* 90-94; Perm to Offic *St Alb* 94-03; Germany from 03. *Stern Strasse 19, 80538 Munich, Germany* Tel (0049) (89) 488298

KNOTT, Montague Hardwick. b 05. Oak Hill Th Coll 54. **d** 55 **p** 56. C Walthamstow St Mary *Chelmsf* 55-57; V Blackmore 57-80; P-in-c Stondon Massey 80; V Blackmore and Stondon Massey 80-85; rtd 85; Perm to Offic *Chelmsf* from 85. *1 Wadham Close, Ingatestone CM4 0DL* Tel (01277) 352024

KNOTT, Pamela Frances. *See* IVE, Mrs Pamela Frances

KNOWD, George Alexander. b 31. St Deiniol's Hawarden. **d** 88 **p** 89. NSM Aghalurcher w Tattykeeran, Cooneen etc *Clogh* 88-91; Dioc Communications Officer 89-90 and 92-97; NSM Ballybay w Mucknoe and Clontibret 91-92; C 92-94; I 94-97; I Clonmel w Innislounagh, Tullaghmelan etc *C & O* from 97. *The Rectory, 7 Linden Lea, Silversprings, Clonmel, Co Tipperary, Irish Republic* Tel and fax (00353) (52) 26643 *or* tel 72975 Mobile 87-284 2350 Fax (52) 80847 E-mail gknowd@eircom.net

KNOWERS, Stephen John. b 49. K Coll Lon BD72 AKC72. **d** 73 **p** 74. C Bp's Hatfield *St Alb* 73-77; C Cheshunt 77-81; P-in-c Barnet Vale St Mark 81-83; V 83-85; Chapl S Bank Poly *S'wark* 85-92; Chapl S Bank Univ 92-94; V Croydon St Pet from 94; P-in-c Croydon St Aug from 04. *20 Haling Park Road, South Croydon CR2 6NE* Tel (020) 8688 4715 E-mail ulbo@appleonline.net

KNOWLES, Canon Andrew William Allen. b 46. St Cath Coll Cam BA68 MA72. St Jo Coll Nottm 69. **d** 71 **p** 72. C Leic H Trin *Leic* 71-74; C Cambridge H Trin *Ely* 74-77; C Woking St Jo *Guildf* 77-81; V Goldsworth Park 81-93; V Wyke 93-98; Dioc Officer Educn and Development of Lay People 93-98; Can Res Chelmsf Cathl *Chelmsf* from 98. *2 Harlings Grove, Chelmsford CM1 1YQ* Tel (01245) 355041 *or* 294484 E-mail andrew.knowles@btinternet.com

KNOWLES, Charles Howard. b 43. Sheff Univ BSc65 Fitzw Coll Cam BA69 MA73. Westcott Ho Cam 67. **d** 69 **p** 70. C Bilborough St Jo *S'well* 69-72; V Choral S'well Minster 72-82; V Cinderhill 82-94; AD Nottingham W 91-94; V Cov St Mary *Cov* from 94; AD Cov S 96-02. *St Mary Magdalen's Vicarage, Craven Street, Coventry CV5 8DT* Tel (024) 7667 5838 E-mail charles.h.knowles@dial.pipex.com

KNOWLES, Clay. *See* KNOWLES, Melvin Clay

KNOWLES, Clifford. b 35. Open Univ BA82. NW Ord Course 74. **d** 77 **p** 78. C Urmston *Man* 77-80; V Chadderton St Luke 80-87; V Heywood St Luke w All So 87-95; AD Heywood and Middleton 92-95; Perm to Offic *Linc* 95-98; rtd 00; Perm to Offic *Linc* from 02. *12B Far Lane, Coleby, Lincoln LN5 0AH* Tel (01522) 810720

KNOWLES, Dorothy Joy. b 20. Gilmore Ho 64. **dss** 69 **d** 89. Finham *Cov* 69-72; Canley 72-76; Styvechale 76-84; rtd 84; Asst Chapl Harnhill Cen for Chr Healing 88-93; Perm to Offic *Ex* from 95. *8 Station Road, Topsham, Exeter EX3 0DT* Tel (01392) 874708

KNOWLES, Canon Eric Gordon. b 44. WMMTC 79. **d** 82 **p** 83. NSM Gt Malvern St Mary *Worc* 82-83; NSM Malvern H Trin and St Jas 83-90; NSM Lt Malvern, Malvern Wells and Wyche 90-99; NSM Lt Malvern 99-00; P-in-c from 00; Hon Can Worc Cathl from 05. *45 Wykewane, Malvern WR14 2XD* Tel (01684) 567439

KNOWLES, George. b 37. **d** 95 **p** 96. NSM Hucknall Torkard *S'well* 95-02; rtd 02; Perm to Offic *S'well* from 02. *8 North Hill Avenue, Hucknall, Nottingham NG15 7FE* Tel 0115-955 9822

KNOWLES, The Ven George Woods Atkin. b 21. TCD BA44 MA47. **d** 44 **p** 45. C Ardoyne *C & O* 44-46; C Knockbreda *D & D* 46-49; I Ballyscullion *D & R* 49-63; I Drumachose 63-89; Can Derry Cathl 75-86; Adn Derry 86-89; rtd 89. *22 Shanreagh Park, Limavady BT49 0SF* Tel (028) 7772 2298

✠**KNOWLES, The Rt Revd Graeme Paul.** b 51. AKC73. St Aug Coll Cant 73. **d** 74 **p** 75 **c** 03. C St Peter-in-Thanet *Cant* 74-79; C Leeds St Pet *Ripon* 79-81; Chapl and Prec Portsm Cathl *Portsm* 81-87; Chapter Clerk 85-87; V Leigh Park 87-93; RD Havant 90-93; Adn Portsm 93-99; Dean Carl 99-03; Bp S & M from 03. *Thie yn Aspick, The Falls, Tromode Road, Cronkbourne, Douglas, Isle of Man IM4 4PZ* Tel (01624) 622108 Fax 672890 E-mail bishop-sodor@mcb.net

KNOWLES, Irene. *See* KNOWLES, Margaret Irene

KNOWLES, Mrs Jane Frances. b 44. GGSM66 Lon Inst of Educn TCert67. Ox Min Course CBTS93. **d** 93 **p** 94. NSM Sandhurst *Ox* 93-97; C Wargrave 97-99; P-in-c Ramsden, Finstock and Fawler, Leafield etc 99-01; V from 01. *The Vicarage, Mount Skippett, Ramsden, Chipping Norton OX7 3AP* Tel (01993) 868687 Fax 868534 E-mail jane.knowles@telinco.co.uk

KNOWLES, John Geoffrey. b 48. Man Univ BSc69 Ox Univ PGCE70 Lon Univ MSc75 FRSA. WMMTC 95. **d** 98 **p** 99. NSM The Lickey *Birm* 98-99; R Hutcheson's Gr Sch 99-04; P-in-c Woodford *Ches* from 05; Dioc Warden of Readers from 05. *The Vicarage, Wilmslow Road, Woodford, Stockport SK7 1RH* Tel 0161-439 2286 E-mail john.knowles2@virgin.net

KNOWLES, Margaret Irene. b 48. EAMTC 96. **d** 99 **p** 00. C Gt Yarmouth *Nor* 99-03; TV from 03; Chapl Norfolk Mental Health Care NHS Trust from 00. *18 Royal Avenue, Great Yarmouth NR30 4EB* Tel and fax (01493) 857292 Mobile 07713-30382 E-mail revmik@btinternet.com

KNOWLES, Melvin Clay. b 43. Stetson Univ (USA) BA66 Ex Univ MA73 Ox Univ DipTh76. Ripon Coll Cuddesdon 75. **d** 77 **p** 78. C Minchinhampton *Glouc* 77-80; St Helena 80-82; TV Haywards Heath St Wilfrid *Chich* 82-88; Adult Educn Adv 88-94; TR Burgess Hill St Jo w St Edw 94-00; V Burgess Hill St Jo from 00. *St John's Vicarage, Park Road, Burgess Hill RH15 8HG* Tel (01444) 232582

KNOWLES, The Very Revd Philip John. b 48. MA PhD BTh LTCL ALCM LLAM. CITC 76. **d** 76 **p** 77. C Lisburn St Paul *Conn* 76-79; I Clooncläre w Killasnett and Lurganboy *K, E & A* 79-87; I Gorey w Kilnahue *C & O* 87-89; I Gorey w Kilnahue, Leskinfere and Ballycanew 89-95; Preb Ferns Cathl 91-95; Dean Cashel from 95; I Cashel w Magorban, Tipperary, Clonbeg etc from 95; Chan Waterford Cathl from 95; Chan Lismore Cathl from 95; Can Ossory and Leighlin Cathls from 96. *The Deanery, Cashel, Co Tipperary, Irish Republic* Tel (00353) (62) 61232 *or* 61944

KNOWLES, Richard John. b 47. EAMTC 00. **d** 01 **p** 02. C Burlingham St Edmund w Lingwood, Strumpshaw etc *Nor* 01-04; TV Gt Yarmouth from 04. *18 Royal Avenue, Great Yarmouth NR30 4EB* Tel (01493) 308711 Mobile 07855-165008 E-mail revrjk@btinternet.com

KNOWLES-BROWN, Canon John Henry. b 30. AKC53. **d** 54 **p** 55. C Hertford St Andr *St Alb* 54-58; C Bushey 58-61; Chapl RAF 61-65; C-in-c Farley Hill St Jo CD *St Alb* 65-69; V Farley Hill St Jo 69-72; V Totteridge 72-95; RD Barnet 79-89; Hon Can St Alb 85-95; rtd 95; Perm to Offic *Ex* from 97. *1 Ascerton Close, Sidmouth EX10 9BS* Tel (01395) 579286

KNOWLING, Richard Charles. b 46. K Coll Lon BSc67 St Edm Hall Ox BA70 MA89. St Steph Ho Ox 69. **d** 71 **p** 72. C Hobs Moat *Birm* 71-75; C Shrewsbury St Mary w All SS and St Mich *Lich* 75-77; V Rough Hills 77-83; Dir Past Th Coll of Resurr Mirfield 83-90; V Palmers Green St Jo *Lon* 90-05; AD Enfield 96-01; V Edmonton St Alphege from 05; P-in-c Ponders End St Matt from 05. *St Alphege's Vicarage, Rossdale Drive, London N9 7LG* Tel (020) 8245 3588
E-mail richard.knowling@london.anglican.org

KNOX, Anthony. *See* KNOX, Thomas Anthony

KNOX, Geoffrey Martin. b 44. Dur Univ BA66 DipTh67 Sheff City Coll of Educn DipEd73. St Chad's Coll Dur 63. **d** 67 **p** 68. C Newark St Mary *S'well* 67-72; Perm to Offic *Derby* 72-74; V Woodville 74-81; RD Repton 79-81; V Long Eaton St Laur 81-00; V Somercotes from 00; RD Alfreton from 04. *The Vicarage, 114 Nottingham Road, Somercotes, Alfreton DE55 4LY* Tel (01773) 602840

KNOX, Iain John Edward. b 46. TCD BA70 MA74 Hull Univ BPhil76. Irish Sch of Ecum 74 CITC 71. **d** 71 **p** 72. C Belfast Malone St Jo *Conn* 71-74; Bp's Dom Chapl 72-74; Perm to Offic *D & R* 74-76; I Gweedore Union 76-80; I Clonmel w Innislounagh, Tullaghmelan etc *C & O* 80-96; Bp's Dom Chapl 82-97; Press & Radio Officer (Cashel) 90-95; Dioc Info Officer (Cashel and Waterford) 92-95; Lic to Offic from 96. *Rossnowlagh, Heywood Road, Clonmel, Co Tipperary, Irish Republic* Tel (00353) (52) 27107 Mobile 87-236 8186

KNOX, Thomas Anthony. b 31. BA. Ely Th Coll. **d** 56 **p** 57. C Poplar All SS w St Frideswide *Lon* 56-59; C Eastbourne St Andr *Chich* 59-61; C Welwyn *St Alb* 61-66; V Boreham Wood St Mich 66-71; R Puttenham w Long Marston 71-79; R Toddington 79-96; rtd 96. *Croft Cottage, Little Blenheim, Yarnton, Oxford OX5 1LX* Tel (01865) 378672

KOBE, Bishop of. *See* FURUMOTO, The Rt Revd John Junichiro

KOHNER, Canon Jeno George. b 31. K Coll Lon BD56 AKC56 Concordia Univ Montreal MA82. Westcott Ho Cam 56. **d** 57 **p** 58. C Eccleston St Thos *Liv* 57-60; Canada from 60; Hon Can Montreal from 75. *850 Lakeshore Drive, Apt H3, Dorval PQ, Canada, H9S 5T9* Tel (001) (514) 631 0066

✠**KOLINI, The Most Revd Emmanuel Musaba.** b 44. Balya Bible Coll Uganda 67 Can Werner Coll Burundi 68 Bp Tucker Coll Mukono 75. **d** 69 **c** 80. Uganda 69-79; Kyangwali 69-74; Bulinda 77-79; Zaïre 80-97; Adn Bukavu 80; Asst Bp Bukavu 81-85; Bp Shaba 86-97; Bp Kigali from 97; Abp Rwanda from 98. *PO Box 61, Kigali, Rwanda* Tel (00250) 576340 Fax 573213 *or* 576504 E-mail ek@rwanda1.com

KOLOGARAS, Mrs Linda Audrey. b 48. Humberside Univ BA97. EMMTC 89. **d** 95 **p** 96. NSM Gt and Lt Coates w Bradley *Linc* 95-98; C Immingham 98-02; R Rosewood Australia from 03. *The Rectory, 28 Delvene Crescent, Rosewood, Qld, Australia 4300* Tel (0061) (7) 5464 1430

KOMOR, Michael. b 60. Univ of Wales BSc83. Chich Th Coll 83. **d** 86 **p** 87. C Mountain Ash *Llan* 86-89; C Llantwit Major 89-91; TV 91-00; V Ewenny w St Brides Major 00-05; R Coity w Nolton from 05; AD Bridgend from 04. *Nolton Rectory, Merthyr Mawr Road North, Bridgend CF31 3NH* Tel (01656) 652247 E-mail mkomor@talk21.com

KONIG, Peter Montgomery. b 44. Westcott Ho Cam 80. **d** 82 **p** 83. C Oundle *Pet* 82-86; Chapl Westwood Ho Sch Pet 86-92; Chapl Pet High Sch 92-95; Chapl Worksop Coll Notts 95-99; Chapl Glenalmond Coll *St And* 99-04; rtd 04; Perm to Offic *Pet* from 04. *27 Main Street, Yarwell, Peterborough PE8 6PR* Tel (01780) 782873

KOPSCH, Hartmut. b 41. Sheff Univ BA63 Univ of BC MA66 Lon Univ PhD70 DipHE. Trin Coll Bris 78. **d** 80 **p** 81. C Cranham Park *Chelmsf* 80-85; V Springfield *Birm* 85-92; V Dover St Martin *Cant* 92-96; R Bath Walcot *B & W* from 96. *The Rectory, 6 River Street, Bath BA1 2PZ* Tel (01225) 425570 E-mail kopsch@lineone.net

KOREA, Presiding Bishop of. *See* CHUNG, The Most Revd Matthew Chul Bum

KORNAHRENS, Wallace Douglas. b 43. The Citadel Charleston BA66 Gen Th Sem (NY) STB69. **d** 69 **p** 70. USA 69-72; C Potters Green *Cov* 72-75; Chapl Community of Celebration Wargrave Oxon 75-76; P-in-c Cumbrae (or Millport) *Arg* 76-78; R Grantown-on-Spey *Mor* 78-83; R Rothiemurchus 78-83; R Edin H Cross *Edin* from 83. *Holy Cross Rectory, 18 Barnton Gardens, Edinburgh EH4 6AF* Tel 0131-336 2311

KOSLA, Mrs Ann Louise. b 56. Middx Univ BA04. NTMTC 01. **d** 04 **p** 05. NSM Thorley *St Alb* from 04. *18 Broadleaf Avenue, Bishop's Stortford CM23 4JY* Tel (01279) 412772 *or* 506753 E-mail ann.kosla@ntlworld.com

KOSLA, Charles Antoni. b 58. Ridley Hall Cam 97. **d** 99 **p** 00. C Widford *Chelmsf* 99-03; C Thorley *St Alb* from 03. *18 Broadleaf Avenue, Bishop's Stortford CM23 4JY* Tel (01279) 412772 *or* 506753 E-mail charlie@kosla.freeserve.co.uk

KOSONEN, Ulla. p 99. Finland 99-02; Chapl Finnish Ch in Lon from 02. *The Finnish Church in London, 33 Albion Street, London SE16 7JG* Tel (020) 7237 1261

KOTHARE, Jayant Sunderrao. b 41. Bombay Univ BA Heidelberg Univ MDiv. **d** 86 **p** 87. C Handsworth St Mich *Birm* 86-89; C Southall St Geo *Lon* 89-92; TV Thamesmead *S'wark* 92-97; Dioc Community Relns Officer *Man* 97-00; P-in-c Moston St Chad 97-02; rtd 02. *c/o Mrs Cavanagh, 3 Evesham Road, Manchester M9 7DS*

KOVOOR, George Iype. b 57. Delhi Univ BA77 Serampore Univ BD80. Union Bibl Sem Yavatmal 78. **d** 80 **p** 80. India 80-90; Dean St Paul's Cathl Ambala 84-88; C Derby St Aug *Derby* 90-94; Min Derby Asian Chr Min Project 90-94; Tutor Crowther Hall CMS Tr Coll Selly Oak 94-97; Prin 97-05; Hon Can Worc Cathl *Worc* 01-05; Prin Trin Coll Bris from 05; Chapl to The Queen from 03. *Trinity College, Stoke Hill, Bristol BS9 1JP* Tel 0117-968 2803 *or* 968 2646 Fax 968 7470
E-mail principal@trinity-bris.ac.uk

KRAFT (née STEVENS), Mrs Jane. b 45. SRN66 SCM68. NTMTC 01. **d** 03 **p** 04. NSM Finchley St Mary *Lon* from 03. *9 The Fairway, New Barnet, Barnet EN5 1HH* Tel and fax (020) 8440 3434 Mobile 07803-868482
E-mail jane@kraft09.fsnet.co.uk

KRAMER, Beaman Kristopher (Kris). b 67. Mars Hill Coll (USA) BS88 Duke Univ (USA) MTS95. Wycliffe Hall Ox MTh98. **d** 98 **p** 99. C Hersham *Guildf* 98-99; C Paddington St Jo w St Mich *Lon* 99-00; R Radford Grace USA from 00. *Grace Rectory, 212 Fourth Street, Radford, VA 24141, USA*
E-mail frkris@i-plus.net

KRAMER, Mrs Caroline Anne. b 70. Wycliffe Hall Ox BTh98. **d** 98. C Oatlands *Guildf* 98-99; USA from 00. *Grace Rectory, 212 Fourth Street, Radford, VA 24141, USA*
E-mail revkramer@cwcom.net

KROLL,Una Margaret Patricia. b 25. Girton Coll Cam MB51 BChir51. S'wark Ord Course 68. **d** 88 **p** 97. NSM Monmouth *Mon* 88-97; Lic to Offic 97-04. *6 Hamilton House, 57 Hanson Street, Bury BL9 6LR* Tel 0161-797 7877

KRONBERGS, Paul Mark. b 55. NEOC 02. **d** 05. NSM Middlesbrough St Columba w St Paul *York* from 05. *39 Northumberland Grove, Stockton-on-Tees TS20 1PB* Tel (01642) 890571 E-mail paul.kronbergs@ntlworld.com

KRONENBERG, John Simon. b 59. Greenwich Univ BSc85 Open Univ BA00 MRICS87 MBEng94. Ripon Coll Cuddesdon 02. **d** 02 **p** 03. C Chandler's Ford *Win* from 02. *St Martin's House, 50 Randall Road, Chandler's Ford, Eastleigh SO53 5AL* Tel and fax (023) 8025 4469 Mobile 07956-517065
E-mail j.kronenberg@btinternet.com

KRONENBERG, Selwyn Thomas Denzil. b 32. Univ of Wales (Swansea) BA54 St Cath Soc Ox BA57 MA60 Leic Univ MA72 California Univ MA82. Wycliffe Hall Ox 54. **d** 57 **p** 58. C Surbiton St Matt *S'wark* 57-59; C Luton St Mary *St Alb* 59-61; P-in-c Loscoe *Derby* 61-65; Lect RE Bulmershe Coll 65-67; Whitelands Coll from 67; Perm to Offic *Guildf* from 77; rtd 97. *58 Woodfield Lane, Ashtead KT21 2BS* Tel (01372) 272505

KRZEMINSKI, Stefan. b 51. Nottm Univ BTh77. Linc Th Coll 74. **d** 77 **p** 78. C Sawley *Derby* 77-79; Asst Chapl Bluecoat Sch Nottm 79-86; Hon C W Hallam and Mapperley *Derby* 84-96; Hd of RE Nottm High Sch from 86; Perm to Offic *Derby* from 96. *12 Newbridge Close, West Hallam, Ilkeston DE7 6LY* Tel 0115-930 5052

KUHRT, The Ven Gordon Wilfred. b 41. Lon Univ BD63 Middx Univ DProf01. Oak Hill Th Coll 65. **d** 67 **p** 68. C Illogan *Truro* 67-70; C Wallington H Trin *S'wark* 70-73; V Shenstone *Lich* 73-79; P-in-c S Croydon Em *Cant* 79-81; V S Croydon Em *S'wark* 81-89; RD Croydon Cen *Cant* 81-86; Hon Can S'wark Cathl *S'wark* 87-89; Adn Lewisham 89-96; Chief Sec ABM 96-98; Dir Min Division Abps' Coun from 99. *6 Layzell Walk, London SE9 4QD* Tel (020) 8857 3476

KUHRT, Martin Gordon. b 66. Nottm Univ LLB88. Trin Coll Bris 93. **d** 96 **p** 97. C Morden *S'wark* 96-00; Chapl Lee Abbey 00-02; TV Melksham *Sarum* from 02. *St Andrew's Vicarage, 33 Church Street, Melksham SN12 7EF* Tel (01225) 704056 E-mail martinannakuhrt@classicfm.net

KUHRT, Stephen John. b 69. Man Univ BA91 Lon Inst of Educn PGCE93. Wycliffe Hall Ox BA03. **d** 03 **p** 04. C New Malden and Coombe *S'wark* from 03. *12 Rosebery Avenue, New Malden KT3 4JS* Tel (020) 8942 2523

KURK, Pamela Ann (Annie). b 56. **d** 04. OLM Wandsworth St Steph *S'wark* from 04; OLM Wandsworth St Mich from 04. *64 Pulborough Road, London SW18 5UJ* Tel (020) 8265 8985 Mobile 07774-437471 E-mail thekurks@aol.com

KURRLE, Canon Stanley Wynton. b 22. OBE82. Melbourne Univ BA47 St Cath Soc Ox BA50 MA54. Wycliffe Hall Ox 49. **d** 52 **p** 53. C Sutton *Liv* 52-54; Australia from 54; Fell St Paul's Coll Univ of Sydney from 69; Can Sydney 81-95; Can Emer 95. *25 Marieba Road, PO Box 53, Kenthurst, NSW, Australia 2156* Tel (0061) (2) 9654 1334 Mobile 427-277919 Fax 9654 1368 E-mail mathourastation@bigpond.com

KURTI, Peter Walter. b 60. Qu Mary Coll Lon LLB82 K Coll Lon MTh89. Ch Div Sch of Pacific 82 Ripon Coll Cuddesdon 83. **d** 86 **p** 87. C Prittlewell *Chelmsf* 86-90; Chapl Derby Coll of HE *Derby* 90-92; Chapl Derby Univ 92-94; Dep Hd Relig Resource and Research Cen 90-94; Australia from 94; Prec St Geo Cathl Perth 94-97; R Scarborough 97-01; R Sydney St Jas from 01. *Level 1, 169-171 Phillip Street, Sydney, NSW, Australia 2000* Tel (0061) (2) 9363 3335 *or* 9232 3022 Mobile 412-049271 Fax 9232 4182 E-mail peter.kurti@bigpond.com

KUSTNER, Ms Jane Lesley. b 54. Lanchester Poly BA76 FCA79. St Steph Ho Ox 03. **d** 05. C Waterloo St Jo w St Andr *S'wark* from 05. *1 Cranfield Row, Gerridge Street, London SE1 7QN* Tel (020) 7928 2259 *or* 7633 9819 Mobile 07734-1137 E-mail jane.kustner@btopenworld.com

✠KWONG KONG KIT, The Most Revd Peter. b 36. Kenyon Coll Ohio BD65 DD86 Hong Kong Univ DD00. Bexley Hall Div Sch Ohio MTh71 DD98. **d** 65 **p** 66 **c** 81. P-in-c Hong Kong Crown of Thorns 65-66; C Hong Kong St Paul 71-72; Bp Hong Kong and Macao 81-98; Bp Hong Kong Is from 98; Abp Hong Kong Sheng Kung Hui from 98. *Bishop's House, 1 Lower Albert Road, Hong Kong, China* Tel (00852) 2526 5355 Fax 2525 2537 E-mail office1@hkskh.org

KYLE, Miss Sharon Patricia Culvinor. b 55. Open Univ BA90 Edin Univ BD94 MTh96. Coates Hall Edin 91. **d** 94 **p** 95. C Edin SS Phil and Jas *Edin* 94-96; C Neston *Ches* 96-99; TV Kirkby *Liv* 99-01. *c/o The Revd J Morrell, 1 Sandycroft Road, Liverpool L12 0LX* E-mail mother.shaz@btinternet.com

KYRIACOU, Brian George. b 42. Lon Univ LLB64. Oak Hill Th Coll 79. **d** 81 **p** 82. C Becontree St Mary *Chelmsf* 81-83; C Becontree St Cedd 83-85; C Becontree W 85; TV 85-87; V Shiregreen St Jas and St Chris *Sheff* 87-92; TV Schorne *Ox* 92-98; V Edmonton All SS w St Mich *Lon* from 98. *All Saints' Vicarage, 43 All Saints' Close, London N9 9AT* Tel (020) 8803 9199 Mobile 07970-719094 Fax (020) 8884 4348 E-mail bgk@alls.freeserve.co.uk

KYRIAKIDES-YELDHAM, Anthony Paul Richard. b 48. CPsychol91 Birkbeck Coll Lon BSc82 Goldsmiths' Coll Lon DASS83 CQSW83 Warwick Univ MSc90. K Coll Lon BD73 AKC73. **d** 74 **p** 75. C Dalston H Trin w St Phil *Lon* 74-78; NSM Lon Docks St Pet w Wapping St Jo 79-81; NSM Hackney Wick St Mary of Eton w St Aug 81-85; NSM Wandsworth Common St Mary *S'wark* 85-87; Chapl Wandsworth HA Mental Health Unit 87-93; Chapl Springfield Univ Hosp Lon 87-93; Perm to Offic *Ex* 94-98; Lic to Offic from 98; Sen Chapl Plymouth Hosps NHS Trust from 98. *The Chaplaincy, Derriford Hospital, Derriford Road, Plymouth PL6 8DH* Tel (01752) 777111 *or* 792313 Fax 768976 E-mail tony.yeldham@phnt.swest.nhs.uk

KYTE, Eric Anthony. b 62. Leeds Univ BSc84 PGCE85. Trin Coll Bris BA98. **d** 98 **p** 99. C Pudsey St Lawr and St Paul *Bradf* 98-01; P-in-c Gisburn from 01; P-in-c Hellifield from 01. *St Mary's Vicarage, Gisburn, Clitheroe BB7 4HR* Tel (01200) 415935

KYUMU MOTUKO, Norbert. *See* CHUMU MUTUKU, Norbert

L

LA TOUCHE, Francis William Reginald. b 51. Linc Th Coll 73. **d** 76 **p** 77. C Yate *Bris* 76-77; C Yate New Town 77-79; Chapl Vlissingen (Flushing) Miss to Seamen *Eur* 79-83; Port Chapl Hull Miss to Seamen 83-91; V Burstwick w Thorngumbald *York* 91-02. *Address temp unknown* E-mail frank@latouche.fsnet.co.uk

LABDON, John. b 32. Oak Hill Th Coll. **d** 84 **p** 85. C Formby H Trin *Liv* 84-87; P-in-c St Helens St Mark 87-97; rtd 97; Perm to Offic *Ches* from 97. *28 Burton Road, Little Neston, Neston CH64 9RA* Tel 0151 336 7039

LABOUREL, Elaine Odette. b 58. St Jo Coll Nottm 03. **d** 05. C Paris St Mich *Eur* from 05. *4 avenue de Savigny, 91700 Ste Geneviève des Bois, France* Tel (0033) (1) 69 04 09 91 Mobile 660-596598 E-mail elaine.labourel@wanadoo.fr

LACEY, Allan John. b 48. Wycliffe Hall Ox. **d** 82 **p** 83. C Greasbrough *Sheff* 82-85; R Treeton 85-92; V Thorpe Hesley 92-00; R Rossington from 00. *The Rectory, Sheep Bridge Lane, Rossington, Doncaster DN11 0EZ* Tel (01302) 867597 E-mail laceys@easynet.co.uk

LACEY, Eric. b 33. Cranmer Hall Dur 69. **d** 71 **p** 72. C Blackpool St Jo *Blackb* 71-75; V Whittle-le-Woods 75-88; R Heysham 88-98; rtd 98; Perm to Offic *Blackb* from 98. *143 Bredon Avenue, Chorley PR7 6NS* Tel (01257) 273040

LACEY, Canon Frank Gordon. b 26. Magd Coll Cam BA47 MA51. Ely Th Coll 48. **d** 50 **p** 51. C Nottingham St Cath *S'well* 50-53; C Mansfield Woodhouse 53-56; V Rubery *Birm* 56-64; PC Dethick, Lea and Holloway *Derby* 64-69; V Ockbrook 69-73; Dir Past Studies N Ord Course 73-81; V Birtles *Ches* 73-82; Can Res Sheff Cathl *Sheff* 82-91; rtd 91; Perm to Offic *Sheff* and *Derby* from 91. *6 Barnes Avenue, Dronfield Woodhouse, Dronfield S18 8YG* Tel (01246) 416589

LACEY, Nigel Jeremy. b 59. St Jo Coll Nottm BTh94. **d** 94 **p** 95. C Mildenhall *St E* 94-97; C Selly Park St Steph and St Wulstan *Birm* 97-01; P-in-c W Wycombe w Bledlow Ridge, Bradenham and Radnage *Ox* from 01. *The Rectory, Church Lane, West Wycombe, High Wycombe HP14 3AH* Tel (01494) 529988 E-mail nigel.lacey@whsmithnet.co.uk

LACK, Catherine Mary. b 59. Clare Coll Cam BA81 Ox Univ MTh00 ARCM. Qu Coll Birm 90. **d** 92 **p** 94. Par Dn Leiston *St E* 92-94; C 94-95; TV Ipswich St Mary at Stoke w St Pet 95-97; TV Ipswich St Mary at Stoke w St Pet and St Fran 97-98; Chapl Keele Univ *Lich* from 98. *Berachah House, 51 Quarry Bank Road, Keele, Newcastle ST5 5AG* Tel (01782) 627385 *or* 583393 Fax 627385 E-mail cpa02@keele.ac.uk

LACK, Martin Paul. b 57. St Jo Coll Ox MA79 MSc80. Linc Th Coll 83. **d** 86 **p** 87. C E Bowbrook and W Bowbrook *Worc* 86-89; C Bowbrook S and Bowbrook N 89-90; R Teme Valley S 90-01; rtd 01. *Colbridge Cottage, Bottom Lane, Whitbourne, Worcester WR6 5RT* Tel (01886) 821978

LACKEY, Michael Geoffrey Herbert. b 42. Oak Hill Th Coll 73. **d** 75 **p** 76. C Hatcham St Jas *S'wark* 75-81; V New Barnet St Jas *St Alb* 81-91; V Hollington St Jo *Chich* 91-02; Dir Crowhurst Chr Healing Cen 02-05; Hon C Gt Amwell w St Margaret's and Stanstead Abbots *St Alb* from 05. *30 South Street, Stanstead Abbotts, Ware SG12 8AJ* Tel (01920) 872077 E-mail assistant@3churches.net

LACKEY, William Terence Charles. b 32. St Mich Coll Llan 80. **d** 82 **p** 83. C Wrexham *St As* 82-85; V Gwersyllt 85-93; R Trefnant 93-98; rtd 98. *24 Old Farm Road, Rhostyllen, Wrexham LL14 4DX* Tel (01978) 311969

LACY, Melanie June. b 75. TCD BA98 All Hallows Coll Dublin MA00. CITC 98. **d** 00. C Bangor St Comgall *D & D* 00-02; N Ireland Regional Co-ord Crosslinks from 02. *Crosslinks, 60A Castlereagh Street, Belfast BT5 4NH* Tel and fax (028) 9046 6489 E-mail crosslinks@belfast.region.crosslinks.org

LACY, Sarah Frances. b 49. Sarum Th Coll 93. **d** 96 **p** 97. C Weston Zoyland w Chedzoy *B & W* 96-00; C Middlezoy and Othery and Moorlinch 00-01; R Berrow and Breane from 01. *The Rectory, 1 Manor Way, Berrow, Burnham-on-Sea TA8 2RG* Tel (01278) 751057 E-mail sally@lacys.freeserve.co.uk

LADD, Mrs Anne de Chair. b 56. Nottm Univ BA78 Birm Univ CQSW80. St Jo Coll Nottm LTh. **dss** 86 **d** 87 **p** 94. Bucknall and Bagnall *Lich* 86-91; Par Dn 87-91; NSM Bricket Wood *St Alb* 91-01; Chapl Garden Ho Hospice Letchworth from 98; Perm to Offic *Ely* from 01. *57 St Barnabas Road, Cambridge CB1 2BX* Tel (01223) 316228

LADD, John George Morgan. b 36. Univ of Wales (Ban) BA58 MA65. Trin Coll Carmarthen St Mich Coll Llan. **d** 90 **p** 91. NSM Nevern and Y Beifil w Eglwyswrw and Meline etc *St D* 90-92; NSM Llandysilio w Egremont and Llanglydwen etc 92-93; V Gwaun-cae-Gurwen 93-04; rtd 04. *Penybanc, Rhiw Road, Swansea SA9 2RE*

LADD, Nicholas Mark. b 57. Ex Univ BA78 Selw Coll Cam BA81. Ridley Hall Cam 79. **d** 82 **p** 83. C Aston SS Pet and Paul *Birm* 82-86; TV Bucknall and Bagnall *Lich* 86-91; V Bricket Wood *St Alb* 91-01; V Cambridge St Barn *Ely* from 01. *The Vicarage, 57 St Barnabas Road, Cambridge CB1 2BX* Tel (01223) 316228 *or* 519526 E-mail vicar@stbs.org.uk

✠LADDS, The Rt Revd Robert Sidney. b 41. LRSC72 Lon Univ BEd71. Cant Sch of Min 79. **d** 80 **p** 81 **c** 99. C Hythe *Cant* 80-83; R Bretherton *Blackb* 83-91; Chapl Bp Rawstorne Sch Preston 83-87; Bp's Chapl for Min and Adv Coun for Min *Blackb* 86-91; P-in-c Preston St Jo 91-96; R Preston St Jo and St Geo 96-97; Hon Can Blackb Cathl 93-97; Adn Lancaster 97-99; Suff Bp Whitby *York* from 99. *60 West Green, Stokesley, Middlesbrough TS9 5BD* Tel (01642) 714475 E-mail bishopofwhitby@episcopus.co.uk

LADIPO, Canon Adeyemi Olalekan. b 37. Trin Coll Bris 63. **d** 66 **p** 76. C Bilston St Leon *Lich* 66-68; Nigeria 68-84; V Canonbury St Steph *Lon* 85-87; Sec for Internat Miss BCMS 87-90; Hon C Bromley SS Pet and Paul *Roch* 89-90; V Herne Hill *S'wark* 90-99; Hon Can Jos from 95; V S Malling *Chich* 99-02; rtd 02. *1 The Martletts, Ringmer, Lewes BN8 5PX* Tel (01273) 813057

LAFFORD, Sylvia June. b 46. Middx Univ BA04. NTMTC 01. **d** 04 **p** 05. NSM Hayes St Edm *Lon* from 04. *17 Audley Court, Pinner HA5 3TQ* Tel (020) 8868 2574 E-mail sylvialafford@aol.com

LAIDLAW, Juliet. *See* MONTAGUE, Mrs Juliet

LAIN-PRIESTLEY, Ms Rosemary Jane. b 67. Kent Univ BA89 K Coll Lon MA02. Carl Dioc Tr Course 92. **d** 96 **p** 97. C Scotforth *Blackb* 96-98; C St Martin-in-the-Fields *Lon* from 98. *5 St Martin's Place, London WC2N 4JH* Tel (020) 7766 1103 Fax 7839 5163 E-mail clergy@smitf.org

LAING, Canon Alexander Burns. b 34. RD90. Edin Th Coll 57. **d** 60 **p** 61. C Falkirk *Edin* 60-62; C Edin Ch Ch 62-70; Chapl RNR 64-91; P-in-c Edin St Fillan *Edin* 70-74; Chapl Edin R Infirmary 74-77; Dioc Supernumerary *Edin* from 77; R Helensburgh *Glas* 77-03; Can St Mary's Cathl 87-03; rtd 03. *13 Drumadoon Drive, Helensburgh G84 9SF* Tel (01436) 675705

LAING, William Sydney. b 32. TCD BA54 MA62. **d** 55 **p** 56. C Dublin Crumlin *D & G* 55-59; C Dublin St Ann 59-65; I Carbury *M & K* 65-68; I Dublin Finglas *D & G* 68-80; I Tallaght 80-91; Can Ch Ch Cathl Dublin 90-94; Preb 94-97; I Dublin Crumlin w Chapelizod 91-97; rtd 97. *42 Hazelwood Crescent, Clondalkin, Dublin 22, Irish Republic* Tel (00353) (1) 459 3893 Mobile 87-760 1210

LAIRD, Alisdair Mark. b 60. Auckland Univ BA84. Trin Coll Bris BA92. **d** 92 **p** 93. C Linthorpe *York* 92-98; V Hull St Cuth from 98. *The Vicarage, 112 Marlborough Avenue, Hull HU5 3JX* Tel (01482) 342848 E-mail laird@onetel.com

LAIRD, Canon John Charles. b 32. Sheff Univ BA53 MA54 St Cath Coll Ox BA58 MA62 Lon Univ DipEd70. Ripon Hall Ox 56. **d** 58 **p** 59. C Cheshunt *St Alb* 58-62; Chapl Bps' Coll Cheshunt 62-64; Vice-Prin 64-67; Prin 67-69; V Keysoe w Bolnhurst and Lt Staughton *St Alb* 69-01; Hon Can St Alb 87-02; Lic to Offic from 01. *The Chaplaincy, Fore Street Lodge, Hatfield Park, Hatfield AL9 5NQ* Tel (01707) 274941

LAIRD, Robert George (Robin). b 40. TCD Div Sch 58 Edin Th Coll 63. **d** 65 **p** 66. C Drumragh *D & R* 65-68; CF 68-93; QHC 91-93; Sen Chapl Sedbergh Sch 93-98; Lic to Offic *Bradf* 93-98; rtd 98; Perm to Offic *Ex* and *Sarum* from 98. *Barrule, Hillside Road, Sidmouth EX10 8JD* Tel (01395) 513948

LAIRD, Stephen Charles Edward. b 66. Oriel Coll Ox BA88 MA92 MSt93 K Coll Lon MTh91 FRSA00. Wycliffe Hall Ox MPhil96. **d** 94 **p** 95. C Ilfracombe, Lee, Woolacombe, Bittadon etc *Ex* 94-98; Chapl Kent Univ *Cant* 98-03; Dean of Chapl from 03; Hon Lect from 98; Hon C Hackington from 03; Chapl Kent Inst of Art and Design 98-02. *Landon, Giles Lane, Canterbury CT2 7LR* Tel (01227) 827491 *or* 787476 Mobile 07970-438840 E-mail s.c.e.laird@kent.ac.uk

LAKE, Canon David Eurwyn. b 17. TD60. St D Coll Lamp BA39. **d** 40 **p** 41. C Miskin *Llan* 40-43; C Cardiff St Jo 43-50; CF (TA) 48-67; P-in-c Llansawel *Llan* 50-56; V 56-62; V Skewen 62-84; RD Neath 76-84; rtd 84; Perm to Offic *Llan* from 84. *Fairwell, 42 Brecon Road, Ystradgynlais, Swansea SA9 1HF* Tel (01639) 849541

LAKE, David Michael. b 57. St Mary's Sem Oscott 76. St Jo Coll Nottm BA01. **d** 01 **p** 02. C Lilleshall, Muxton and Sheriffhales *Lich* 01-05; P-in-c Crick and Yelvertoft w Clay Coton and Lilbourne *Pet* from 05. *The Rectory, Main Road, Crick, Northampton NN6 7TU* Tel (01788) 822147 E-mail davidlake@mailserver97.freeserve.co.uk

LAKE, Eileen Veronica. *See* CREMIN, Mrs Eileen Veronica

LAKE, Kevin William. b 57. St Mich Coll Llan 97. **d** 99 **p** 00. C Penarth w Lavernock *Llan* 99-02; Chapl Marie Curie Cen Holme Tower 02-04; P-in-c Cwm Ogwr *Llan* from 04. *The Vicarage, Coronation Street, Ogmore Vale, Bridgend CF32 7HE* Tel (01656) 840248

LAKE, Canon Stephen David. b 63. Southn Univ BTh. Chich Th Coll 85. **d** 88 **p** 89. C Sherborne w Castleton and Lillington *Sarum* 88-92; P-in-c Branksome St Aldhelm 92-96; V 96-01; RD Poole 00-01; Can Res and Sub-Dean St Alb from 01. *The Old Rectory, Sumpter Yard, St Albans AL1 1BY* Tel (01727) 890201 Fax 850944 E-mail subdean@stalbanscathedral.org.uk

LAKE, Vivienne Elizabeth. b 38. Lon Univ DHistA78. Westcott Ho Cam 84. **dss** 86 **d** 87 **p** 94. Chesterton Gd Shep *Ely* 86-90; C 87-90; Ecum Min K Hedges Ch Cen 87-90; NSM Bourn Deanery 90-01; NSM Papworth Everard 94-96; Perm to Offic from 01. *15 Storey's House, Mount Pleasant, Cambridge CB3 0BZ* Tel (01223) 369523

LAKE, Wynne Vaughan. b 34. St D Coll Lamp BA55. St Mich Coll Llan 55. **d** 57 **p** 58. C Cadoxton-juxta-Barry *Llan* 57-61; C Roath St Sav 61-64; V Oakwood 64-67; V Oakwood w Bryn 67-72; R Shirenewton and Newchurch *Mon* 72-77; rtd 99. *32 Belvedere Close, Kittle, Swansea SA3 3LA*

LAKER, Clive Sheridan. b 59. Greenwich Univ BSc92 RGN82 DipNursing87. Aston Tr Scheme 93 SEITE 95. **d** 98 **p** 99. C Bridlington Quay Ch Ch *York* 98-00; C Bridlington Em 00-01; TV Bucknall *Lich* 01-04; C Surbiton St Matt *S'wark* from 04. *127 Hamilton Avenue, Surbiton KT6 7QA* Tel (020) 8397 4294 E-mail lakerfamily@ntlworld.com

LAKER, Grace. *See* SWIFT, Mrs Grace

LAKEY, Elizabeth Flora. b 46. DipOT69 Open Univ BA81. St Alb and Ox Min Course 98. **d** 01 **p** 02. OLM Nettlebed w Bix, Highmoor, Pishill etc *Ox* from 01. *Bank Farm, Pishill, Henley-on-Thames RG9 6HJ* Tel and fax (01491) 638601 Mobile 07799-752933 E-mail bankfarm@btinternet.com

LAMB, Mrs Alison. b 60. Ches Coll of HE BTh04. N Ord Course 01. **d** 04 **p** 05. C Rossington *Sheff* from 04. *18 Farringdon Drive, Rossington, Doncaster DN11 0SH* Tel (01302) 865707

LAMB, Miss Alyson Margaret. b 55. LMH Ox BA77 MA80. Ridley Hall Cam 03. **d** 05. C York St Mich-le-Belfrey *York* from 05. *157 Haxby Road, York YO31 8JL* Tel (01904) 624190 E-mail alyson@st-michael-le-belfrey.org

LAMB, Bruce. b 47. Keble Coll Ox BA69 MA73 Leeds Univ DipTh72. Coll of Resurr Mirfield 70. **d** 73 **p** 74. C Romford St Edw *Chelmsf* 73-76; C Canning Town St Cedd 76-79; V New Brompton St Luke *Roch* 79-83; Chapl RN 83-87; C Rugeley *Lich* 87-88; V Trent Vale 88-92; Bereavement Cllr Cruse 94-99; Hon C Chorlton-cum-Hardy St Clem *Man* 98-99; Asst Chapl N Man Health Care NHS Trust 99-02; P-in-c Barton w Peel Green *Man* from 02. *St Michael's Vicarage, 684 Liverpool Road, Eccles, Manchester M30 7LP* Tel 0161-789 3751

LAMB, Bryan John Harry. b 35. Leeds Univ BA60 Aston Univ Dip Counselling 72. Coll of Resurr Mirfield 60. **d** 62 **p** 63. C Solihull *Birm* 62-65 and 88-89; Asst Master Malvern Hall Sch Solihull 65-74; Alderbrook Sch and Hd of Light Hall Adult Educn Cen 74-88; V Wragby *Linc* 89; Dioc Dir of Readers 89; Perm to Offic *Birm* from 89; rtd 95. *27 Ladbrook Road, Solihull B91 3RN* Tel 0121-705 2489

LAMB, Canon Christopher Avon. b 39. Qu Coll Ox BA61 MA65 Birm Univ MA78 PhD87. Wycliffe Hall Ox BA63. **d** 63 **p** 64. C Enfield St Andr *Lon* 63-69; Pakistan 69-75; Tutor Crowther Hall CMS Tr Coll Selly Oak 75-78; Co-ord BCMS/CMS Other Faiths Th Project 78-87; Dioc Community Relns Officer *Cov* 87-92; Can Th Cov Cathl from 92; Sec Inter-Faith Relns Bd of Miss 92-99; R Warmington w Shotteswell and Radway w Ratley *Cov* from 99. *The Rectory, Warmington, Banbury OX17 1BT* Tel (01295) 690213 E-mail lamb@easynet.co.uk

LAMB, David Andrew. b 60. Liv Inst of HE BA94 Man Univ MA01. N Ord Course 90. **d** 94 **p** 95. C Formby H Trin *Liv* 94-97; C St Helens St Matt Thatto Heath 97-98; C Halewood 98-01; Lect Liv Hope 99-00; V Birkenhead St Jas w St Bede *Ches* from 01. *St James's Vicarage, 56 Tollemache Road, Prenton CH43 8SZ* Tel 0151-652 1016

LAMB, Graeme William. b 68. Trin Coll Bris 99. **d** 01 **p** 02. C Heald Green St Cath *Ches* from 01. *103 Baslow Drive, Heald Green, Cheadle SK8 3HW* Tel 0161-437 2395 *or* 437 0228 E-mail graeme@graemelamb.com

LAMB, Mrs Jean Evelyn. b 57. Reading Univ BA79 Nottm Univ MA88. St Steph Ho Ox 81. **dss** 84 **d** 88 **p** 01. Leic H Spirit *Leic* 84-87; Asst Chapl Leic Poly 84-87; Par Dn Beeston *S'well* 88-91; Hon C and Artist in Res Nottingham St Mary and St Cath 92-95; Hon Par Dn Sneinton St Steph w St Alb 97-01; NSM Rolleston w Fiskerton, Morton and Upton 01-02; Perm to Offic 02-04; C Bilborough St Jo from 04; C Bilborough w Strelley from 04. *St Alban's House, 4 Dale Street, Nottingham NG2 4JX* Tel 0115-958 5892 Mobile 07851-792552 E-mail stalbanshouse@supanet.com

LAMB, John Romney. b 21. Ch Ch Ox BA48 MA53. Wells Th Coll 49. **d** 50 **p** 51. C Tenterden St Mildred w Smallhythe *Cant* 50-53; C Hythe 53-55; CF 55-70; V Horsell *Guildf* 70-76; V Dorking w Ranmore 76-82; P-in-c Charing Heath w Egerton *Cant* 82-83; P-in-c Pluckley w Pevington 82-83; R Egerton w Pluckley 84-87; rtd 87; Perm to Offic *Chich* 87-04 and *Cant* from 04. *16 Provender Walk, Belvedere Road, Faversham ME13 7NF* Tel (01795) 534378

LAMB, Nicholas Henry. b 52. St Jo Coll Dur BA74. St Jo Coll Nottm 76. **d** 79 **p** 80. C Luton Lewsey St Hugh *St Alb* 79-84; Bethany Fellowship 84-86; In Bapt Min 86-94; Perm to Offic *Chich* 97-99; C E Grinstead St Swithun 99-04; V Forest Row from 04. *The Vicarage, Ashdown Road, Forest Row RH18 5BW* Tel (01342) 822595 E-mail revnicklamb@hotmail.com

LAMB, Peter Francis Charles. b 15. St Cath Coll Cam BA37 MA41. Wells Th Coll 37. **d** 38 **p** 39. C Wellingborough All Hallows *Pet* 38-42; C Somersham w Pidley and Colne *Ely* 42-48; Chapl RNVR 46-48; C Sherborne w Castleton and Lillington *Sarum* 48-51; The Gambia 51-57; V Winkleigh *Ex* 57-70; RD Chulmleigh 62-63; R Mells w Vobster, Whatley and Chantry *B & W* 70-77; rtd 77; Perm to Offic *B & W* from 77. *6 Parsons Close, Long Sutton, Langport TA10 9LN* Tel (01458) 241481

LAMB, Philip Richard James. b 42. Sarum & Wells Th Coll. **d** 83 **p** 84. C Wotton-under-Edge w Ozleworth and N Nibley *Glouc* 83-86; TV Worc SE *Worc* 86-91; R Billingsley w Sidbury, Middleton Scriven etc *Heref* 91-96; R St Dominic, Landulph and St Mellion w Pillaton *Truro* from 96. *The Rectory, St Mellion, Saltash PL12 6RN* Tel (01579) 350061 E-mail frlamb@stmellion141.freeserve.co.uk

LAMB, Phillip. b 68. NEOC 00. **d** 03 **p** 04. C Bridlington Priory *York* from 03. *20 The Lawns, Bridlington YO16 6FL* Tel (01262) 401353 Mobile 07803-239611 E-mail phil_lamb2002@yahoo.co.uk

LAMB, Scott Innes. b 64. Edin Univ BSc86. Aston Tr Scheme 88 Ridley Hall Cam BA92. **d** 93 **p** 94. C E Ham w Upton Park St Alb *Chelmsf* 93-97; V W Holloway St Luke *Lon* 97-00; P-in-c Hammersmith H Innocents 00-03; Chapl RN from 03. *Royal Naval Chaplaincy Service, Room 203, Victory Building, HM Naval Base, Portsmouth PO1 3LS* Tel (01705) 727903 Fax 727112 E-mail scott@hamleylamb.fsnet.co.uk

LAMB, William Robert Stuart. b 70. Ball Coll Ox BA91 MA95 Peterho Cam MPhil94. Westcott Ho Cam 92. **d** 95 **p** 96. C Halifax *Wakef* 95-98; TV Penistone and Thurlstone 98-01; Chapl Sheff Univ *Sheff* from 01. *119 Ashdell Road, Sheffield S10 3DB* Tel 0114-266 9243 *or* 222 8923 E-mail w.lamb@shef.ac.uk

LAMBERT, Antony. *See* LAMBERT, John Clement Antony

LAMBERT, David Francis. b 40. Oak Hill Th Coll 72. **d** 74 **p** 75. C Paignton St Paul Preston *Ex* 74-77; C Woking Ch Ch *Guildf* 77-84; P-in-c Willesden Green St Gabr *Lon* 84-91; P-in-c Cricklewood St Mich 85-91; V Cricklewood St Gabr and St Mich 92-93; R Chenies and Lt Chalfont, Latimer and Flaunden *Ox* 93-01; Chapl Izmir (Smyrna) w Bornova *Eur* 01-03; TV Brixham w Churston Ferrers and Kingswear *Ex* from 03. *54 Brunel Road, Broadsands, Paignton TQ4 6HW* Tel (01803) 842076 E-mail churston@fstmail.fm

LAMBERT, David Hardy. b 44. AKC66. **d** 67 **p** 68. C Marske in Cleveland *York* 67-72; V from 85; V N Ormesby 73-85; RD Guisborough 86-91. *The Vicarage, 6 Windy Hill Lane, Marske-by-the-Sea, Redcar TS11 7BN* Tel (01642) 482896

LAMBERT, David Joseph. b 66. Coll of Resurr Mirfield 99. **d** 01 **p** 02. C Camberwell St Geo *S'wark* 01-04; C Walworth St Jo from 04. *St John's Vicarage Flat, 18A Larcom Street, London SE17 1NQ* Tel (020) 7703 3633

LAMBERT, David Nathaniel. b 34. Headingley Meth Coll 58 Linc Th Coll 66. **d** 66 **p** 67. In Methodist Ch 58-66; C Canwick *Linc* 66-68; C-in-c Bracebridge Heath CD 68-69; R Saltfleetby All SS w St Pet 69-73; R Saltfleetby St Clem 70-73; V Skidbrooke 70-73; V Saltfleetby 73-80; R Theddlethorpe 74-80; RD Louthesk 76-82; R N Ormsby w Wyham 80; R Fotherby 81-94; rtd 94; Perm to Offic *Linc* 94-97; *York* and *Ripon* from 03. *32 Brookside Avenue, Bedale DL8 2DP* Tel (01677) 422699

LAMBERT, Gordon. b 32. Univ of Wales (Lamp) BA56. Wycliffe Hall Ox 56. **d** 58 **p** 59. C Newbarns w Hawcoat *Carl* 58-63; C-in-c Barrow St Aid CD 63-67; V Barrow St Aid 67-68; R Ousby w Melmerby 68-71; V Farlam 71-76; TV Thirsk w S Kilvington and Carlton Miniott etc *York* 76-77; TV Thirsk 77-89; RD Thirsk 81-89; V Belvedere All SS *Roch* 89-96; rtd 96; Perm to Offic *Chich* from 98. *19 The Barnhams, Bexhill-on-Sea TN39 3RE* Tel (01424) 844443

LAMBERT, Ian Anderson. b 43. Lon Univ BA72 Nottm Univ MTh87. Ridley Hall Cam 66. **d** 67 **p** 68. C Bermondsey St Mary w St Olave, St Jo etc *S'wark* 67-70; Jamaica 71-75; Chapl RAF 75-98; rtd 98; P-in-c N and S Muskham *S'well* 01-03; P-in-c Averham w Kelham 01-03; Bp's Adv for Past Care and Counselling from 04. *34 Hayside Avenue, Balderton, Newark NG24 3GB* Tel (01636) 702655

LAMBERT, John Clement Antony. b 28. St Cath Coll Cam BA48 MA52. Cuddesdon Coll 50. **d** 52 **p** 53. C Hornsea and Goxhill *York* 52-55; C Leeds St Pet *Ripon* 55-59; R Carlton in Lindrick *S'well* 59-93; rtd 93; Perm to Offic *Derby* from 93 and *S'well* 93-00. *139 Longedge Lane, Wingerworth, Chesterfield S42 6PR* Tel (01246) 551774

LAMBERT, John Connolly. b 61. Univ of Wales (Ban) BTh04. EAMTC 01. **d** 05. C Paris St Mich *Eur* from 05. *8 allée des Cerfs, 78480 Verneuil-sur-Seine, France* Tel (0033) (1) 47 42 70 88 Fax 47 42 74 75 E-mail john@saintmichaelsparis.org

LAMBERT, Malcolm Eric. b 58. Leic Univ BSc80 Fitzw Coll Cam BA89 Nottm Univ MPhil02 RMN84. Ridley Hall Cam 87. **d** 90 **p** 91. C Humberstone *Leic* 90-94; R S Croxton Gp 94-99; V Birstall and Wanlip 99-05; TR Leic Resurr from 05; RD Christianity N from 05; Warden of Readers from 97. *St Gabriel's House, 20 Kerrysdale Avenue, Leicester LE4 7GH* Tel 0116-220 2625 E-mail me.lambert@ntlworld.com

LAMBERT, Michael Roy. b 25. Univ Coll Dur BSc49. Cuddesdon Coll 52. **d** 52 **p** 53. C Middlesbrough St Oswald *York* 52-56; C Romsey *Win* 56-59; C Cottingham *York* 59-64; Chapl Hull Univ 59-64; V Saltburn-by-the-Sea 64-72; P-in-c Shaftesbury H Trin *Sarum* 72-73; R Shaston 74-78; R Corfe Mullen 78-91; rtd 91; Perm to Offic *Glouc* from 91. *16 Pheasant Way, Cirencester GL7 1BL* Tel (01285) 654657

LAMBERT, Neil James. b 58. Goldsmiths' Coll Lon BA81. Ridley Hall Cam 02. **d** 04 **p** 05. C Wisley w Pyrford *Guildf* from 04. *Church House, Coldharbour Road, Woking GU22 8SP* Tel (01932) 336278 Mobile 07812-989313 E-mail curate@wisleywithpyrford.org

LAMBERT, Miss Olivia Jane. b 48. Matlock Coll of Educn BEd70. Trin Coll Bris DipHE86. **dss** 86 **d** 87 **p** 94. York St Luke *York* 86-90; Par Dn 87-90; Chapl York Distr Hosp 86-90; Par Dn Huntington *York* 90-94; C 94-95; TV 95-00; TV Marfleet from 00. *St Philip's House, 107 Amethyst Road, Hull HU9 4JG* Tel (01482) 376208 E-mail oliviajlambert@aol.com

LAMBERT, Peter George. b 29. Coll of Resurr Mirfield 86. **d** 87 **p** 88. NSM Rothwell w Orton, Rushton w Glendon and Pipewell *Pet* 87-93; P-in-c Corby Epiphany w St Jo 93-96; rtd 96; Perm to Offic *Pet* from 96. *4 Cogan Crescent, Rothwell, Kettering NN14 6AS* Tel (01536) 710692

LAMBERT, Philip Charles. b 54. St Jo Coll Dur BA75 Fitzw Coll Cam BA77 MA81. Ridley Hall Cam 75. **d** 78 **p** 79. C Upper Tooting H Trin *S'wark* 78-81; C Whorlton *Newc* 81-84; P-in-c Alston cum Garrigill w Nenthead and Kirkhaugh 84-87; TV Alston Team 87-89; R Curry Rivel w Fivehead and Swell *B & W* 89-01; RD Crewkerne and Ilminster 98-01; TR Dorchester *Sarum* from 01; RD Dorchester from 02. *The Rectory, 17A Edward Road, Dorchester DT1 2HL* Tel and fax (01305) 268434 Fax 849667 E-mail philiplambert@dsl.pipex.com

LAMBERT (née JOHNSON), Mrs Ruth Alice. b 59. Leic Univ BA80 PGCE93 Nottm Univ MA01 RGN85. **d** 01 **p** 02. C Mountsorrel Ch Ch and St Pet *Leic* 01-04; Chapl Univ Hosps Leic NHS Trust from 04. *St Gabriel's House, 20 Kerrysdale Avenue, Leicester LE4 7GH* Tel 0116-220 2625 Mobile 07808-321695 E-mail ruth.lambert@uhl-tr.nhs.uk

LAMBERT, Sydney Thomas. b 17. Keble Coll Ox BA39 MA44 CertEd71. Wells Th Coll 40. **d** 41 **p** 42. C Poplar *Lon* 41-44; C Ox St Barn *Ox* 44-45; Asst Master Bp Cotton Sch Bangalore India 45-49; Asst R Cincinnati the Advent USA 49-50; CF 50-67; R Rendcomb *Glouc* 67-74; V Colesborne 67-74; P-in-c Cheltenham St Pet 74-78; P-in-c Todenham w Lower Lemington 78-83; P-in-c Bourton on the Hill 78-83; rtd 83; Perm to Offic *Worc* from 83. *97 Elm Road, Evesham WR11 3DR* Tel and fax (01386) 446725

LAMBETH, Archdeacon of. *See* SKILTON, The Ven Christopher John

LAMBOURN, David Malcolm. b 37. Lanc Univ BEd76 Man Univ MEd78 Warwick Univ PhD01. Linc Th Coll 63. **d** 65 **p** 66. C Camberwell St Geo *S'wark* 65-67; C Mottingham St Andr 67-70; rtd 03. *28 Frederick Road, Birmingham B15 1JN* Tel 0121-242 3953 E-mail david.lambourn@blueyonder.co.uk

LAMBOURNE, John Brian. b 36. Chich Th Coll 62. **d** 65 **p** 66. C Cant St Greg *Cant* 65-67; C St Mary in the Marsh 67-68; C E Grinstead St Swithun *Chich* 68-70; C Storrington and Sullington 70-76; CF (TA) 87-96; V Salehurst *Chich* from 76; Bp's Adv on Rural Affairs from 89; Agric Chapl from 89. *St Mary's Vicarage, Fair Lane, Robertsbridge TN32 5AR* Tel (01580) 880408

LAMDIN, Canon Keith Hamilton. b 47. Bris Univ BA69. Ripon Coll Cuddesdon 86. **d** 86 **p** 87. Adult Educn Officer *Ox* 86-98; Team Ldr Par Resources Dept from 88; Dioc Dir Tr from 94; Hon Can Ch Ch from 97; NSM Cowley St Jo from 98. *41 Stapleton Road, Headington, Oxford OX3 7LX* Tel (01865) 767160 E-mail training@oxford.anglican.org

LAMEY, Richard John. b 77. Keble Coll Ox BA98 MA02 Em Coll Cam BA01 MA05. Westcott Ho Cam 99. **d** 02 **p** 03. C Stockport SW *Ches* from 02; P-in-c Newton in Mottram from 05. *39 Bradley Green Road, Hyde SK14 4NA* Tel 0161-368 1489 E-mail lamey@surefish.co.uk

LAMMAS, Miss Diane Beverley. b 47. Trin Coll Bris 76. **dss** 79 **d** 87 **p** 94. Lenton Abbey *S'well* 79-84; Wollaton Park 79-84; E Regional Co-ord and Sec for Voc and Min CPAS 84-89; Hon C Cambridge St Paul *Ely* 87-90; Voc and Min Adv CPAS 89-92; Sen Voc and Min Adv CPAS 92-95; R Hethersett w Canteloff w Lt and Gt Melton *Nor* from 95; RD Humbleyard 98-03. *The Rectory, 27 Norwich Road, Hethersett, Norwich NR9 3AR* Tel (01603) 810273 E-mail di.lammas@freeuk.com

LAMMENS, Erwin Bernard Eddy. b 62. Catholic Univ Leuven BA86 Gregorian Univ Rome MDiv90. Grootseminarie Gent 84. **d** 87 **p** 88. In RC Ch 87-96; Asst Chapl Antwerp St Boniface *Eur* 98-05; TV Harwich Peninsula *Chelmsf* from 05. *The Vicarage, Church Hill, Ramsey, Harwich CO12 5EU* Tel (01255) 880291 E-mail erwinlammens@btinternet.com

LAMOND, Stephen Paul. b 64. Trin Coll Bris BA99. **d** 99 **p** 00. C Weston-super-Mare Ch Ch *B & W* 99-02; C Congresbury w Puxton and Hewish St Ann 02-03; Chapl RAF from 03. *Chaplaincy Services (RAF), HQ, Personnel and Training Command, RAF Innsworth, Gloucester GL3 1EZ* Tel (01452) 712612 ext 5164 Fax 510828

LAMONT, Euphemia Margaret (Fay). b 53. N Coll of Educn BA98. TISEC 00. **d** 00 **p** 00. C Monifieth *Bre* from 00; C Carnoustie from 00. *St Ninian's Church House, Kingsway East, Dundee DD4 7RW* Tel (01382) 453818 Mobile 07931-222092 E-mail faylamont@hotmail.com

LAMONT, Roger. b 37. Jes Coll Ox BA60 MA62. St Steph Ho Ox 59. **d** 61 **p** 62. C Northampton St Alb *Pet* 61-66; V Mitcham St Olave *S'wark* 66-73; V N Sheen St Phil and All SS 73-85; P-in-c Richmond St Luke 82-85; Chapl St Lawr Hosp Caterham 85-94; Chapl Lifecare NHS Trust 92-99; Surrey Oaklands NHS Trust 99-01; rtd 01; Perm to Offic *S'wark* from 01. *8 Montague Drive, Caterham CR3 5BY* Tel (01883) 340803

LAMONT, Ms Veronica Jane (Ronni). b 56. Bp Grosseteste Coll CertEd77 Anglia Poly Univ MA05. St Jo Coll Nottm 90. **d** 92 **p** 94. Par Dn St Alb St Pet *St Alb* 92-94; C 94-96; TV Hemel Hempstead 96-01; V Bexley St Jo *Roch* from 01. *St John's*

Vicarage, 29 Park Hill Road, Bexley DA5 1HX Tel (01322) 521786 Mobile 07802-793910 E-mail ronni@fish.co.uk *or* ronni@dsl.pipex.com

LAMPARD, Ms Ruth Margaret. b 65. St Jo Coll Dur BA87 Jes Coll Cam BA99 MA04 Heythrop Coll Lon MA04. Westcott Ho Cam 97 Berkeley Div Sch 99. **d** 00 **p** 01. C Ealing St Pet Mt Park *Lon* 00-01; C Eastcote St Lawr 01-05; Hon C Norton *St Alb* from 05. *The Vicarage, Stevenage Road, St Ippolyts, Hitchin SG4 7PE* Tel (01462) 457552 E-mail lampard@fish.co.uk

LANCASTER, Mrs Jennifer. b 48. NEOC 00. **d** 03 **p** 04. C Walker *Newc* from 03. *2 Heathdale Gardens, Newcastle upon Tyne NE7 7QR* Tel 0191-240 1652 *or* 295 4253 E-mail jenny@lancaster7206.fsnet.co.uk

LANCASTER, The Ven John. b 38. Univ of BC BA60 St Andr Univ BPhil78. Angl Th Coll (BC) STB66 Princeton Th Sem ThM69 San Francisco Th Sem DMin92. **d** 63 **p** 64. Canada 63-03; C Sooke 63-64; V 64-68; C Ch Ch Cathl Victoria 69-81; Hon Can from 79; Adn Quatsino and R Courtenay St Jo 81-03; P-in-c Venice w Trieste *Eur* 03. *253 Dorsoduro, 30123 Venice, Italy* Tel (0039) (41) 520 0571 Fax as telephone

LANCASTER, John Rawson. b 47. BSc. N Ord Course. **d** 82 **p** 83. C Bolton St Jas w St Chrys *Bradf* 82-86; V Barnoldswick w Bracewell from 86. *The Vicarage, 131 Gisburn Road, Barnoldswick BB18 5JU* Tel (01282) 812028 Fax 850346

LANCASTER, Norman. b 13. Leeds Univ BA36. Coll of Resurr Mirfield 36. **d** 38 **p** 39. C Skegness *Linc* 38-41; C New Cleethorpes 41-42; C Gt Grimsby St Jas 42-47; V Caistor w Holton le Moor and Clixby 47-52; PC Louth H Trin 52-57; V Keddington 52-57; V Hogsthorpe 57-62; Chapl Butlin's Holiday Camps 59-62; R Panton w Wragby 62-71; V Langton by Wragby 62-71; R Gt Coates 71-77; PC Aylesby 71-77; rtd 77; Perm to Offic *Linc* 77-95. *6 Dulverton Hall, Esplanade, Scarborough YO11 2AR* Tel (01723) 340106

LANCASTER, Ronald. b 31. MBE93. FRSC83 CChem83 St Jo Coll Dur BA53 MA56. Cuddesdon Coll 55. **d** 57 **p** 58. C Morley St Pet w Churwell *Wakef* 57-60; C High Harrogate St Pet *Ripon* 60-63; Lic to Offic *Ely* 63-88; Chapl Kimbolton Sch Cambs 63-88; Asst Chapl 88-91; Perm to Offic *Ely* from 88; rtd 96. *7 High Street, Kimbolton, Huntingdon PE28 0HB* Tel (01480) 860498 Fax 861277

LANCASTER, Mrs Susan Louise. b 47. Leic Univ BA79 CPES81. EMMTC 88. **d** 93 **p** 94. NSM Clarendon Park St Jo w Knighton St Mich *Leic* 93-97; Perm to Offic 97-01; NSM Roundhay St Edm *Ripon* from 01. *38 Talbot Avenue, Leeds LS17 6SB* Tel 0113-288 0145

LANCASTER, Archdeacon of. *See* WILLIAMS, The Ven Colin Henry

LANCASTER, Suffragan Bishop of. *See* PEDLEY, The Rt Revd Geoffrey Stephen

LAND, Michael Robert John. b 43. Ripon Hall Ox 70. **d** 72 **p** 73. C Newbury St Nic *Ox* 72-75; TV Chigwell *Chelmsf* 75-80; V Walthamstow St Andr from 80. *St Andrew's Vicarage, 37 Sutton Road, London E17 5QA* Tel (020) 8527 3969 E-mail michael@land7249.fslife.co.uk

LANDALL, Capt Allan Roy. b 55. Qu Coll Birm BA98. **d** 98 **p** 99. C Thurnby w Stoughton *Leic* 98-02; R Walsoken *Ely* from 02. *The Vicarage, Church Road, Wisbech PE13 3RA* Tel (01945) 583740 E-mail arlandall@btinternet.com

LANDALL, Richard. b 57. St Jo Coll Dur 85. **d** 88 **p** 89. C Nailsea H Trin *B & W* 88-92; CF 92-99; TV Westborough *Guildf* 99-01; R Armthorpe *Sheff* from 01. *The Rectory, Church Street, Armthorpe, Doncaster DN3 3AD* Tel (01302) 831231 Fax as telephone E-mail rlandall@lineone.net

LANDEN, Edgar Sydney. b 23. ARCM46 FRCO46 St Jo Coll Dur BA54 BMus55. **d** 55 **p** 56. Succ Leeds *Ripon* 55-58; Prec Chelmsf Cathl *Chelmsf* 58-60; V Bathampton *B & W* 60-65; Perm to Offic *Glouc* 65-69; C Cirencester 69-76; Min Can Ch Ch *Ox* 76-88; R Wytham 76-88; rtd 88; Perm to Offic *B & W* 88-98. *The Old Vicarage, Bakers Hill, Tiverton EX16 5NE* Tel (01884) 256815

LANDER, Mrs Elizabeth Anne. b 69. St Andr Univ BSc93 Ox Univ PGCE94. Wycliffe Hall Ox 00. **d** 02 **p** 03. C Glascote and Stonydelph *Lich* from 02. *87 Belgrave Road, Wilnecote, Tamworth B77 2LS* Tel 07790-212302 (mobile) E-mail landerliz@yahoo.co.uk

LANDER, John Stanley. b 55. **d** 04 **p** 05. OLM Uttoxeter Area *Lich* from 04. *Bidston, Bramshall, Uttoxeter ST14 5BG* Tel (01889) 565228

LANDMAN, Denis Cooper. b 21. MBE60 OM(Ger)80. Lon Univ BA41 DipEd52. St Deiniol's Hawarden 79. **d** 82 **p** 83. Hon C Tranmere St Paul w St Luke *Ches* 82-86; Australia from 86; C Southport St Pet 86-88; P-in-c Biggera Waters 88-92; rtd 92. *1/24 Stretton Drive, Helensvale, Qld, Australia 4212* Tel (0061) (7) 5573 4660 Mobile 407-758376

LANDRETH, Mrs Mavis Isabella (Isabel). b 32. SEN81. Gilmore Ho 67. **dss** 74 **d** 87. Walthamstow St Sav *Chelmsf* 70-75; Sanderstead All SS *S'wark* 76-79; Sheff St Cuth *Sheff* 84-85; N Gen Hosp Sheff 84-85; Icklesham *Chich* 86-87; Hon Par Dn 87-89; Perm to Offic from 89. *Gossamer Cottage, Slindon, Arundel BN18 0QT* Tel (01243) 814224

LANE, Alexander John. b 71. Leeds Univ BA02. Coll of Resurr Mirfield 99. **d** 02 **p** 03. C Eastbourne St Andr *Chich* from 02. *75 Churchdale Road, Eastbourne BN22 8RX* Tel (01323) 732741 E-mail thecurate@hotmail.com

LANE, Andrew Harry John. b 49. MBE92. Lanc Univ BA71. Cuddesdon Coll 71. **d** 73 **p** 74. C Abingdon w Shippon *Ox* 73-78; Chapl Abingdon Sch 75-78; Chapl RAF 78-94; rtd 94; Perm to Offic *Nor* 94-01; Public Preacher from 01; RD Repps from 02. *Society of St Luke, 32B Beeston Common, Sheringham NR26 8ES* Tel (01263) 825623 Fax 820334 E-mail superior@ssluke.org.uk

LANE, Anthony James. b 29. Leeds Univ BA53. Coll of Resurr Mirfield 53. **d** 55 **p** 56. C Tilehurst St Mich *Ox* 55-60; Min Can Win Cathl *Win* 60-63; R Handley w Pentridge *Sarum* 64-80; V Thurmaston *Leic* 80-85; TV Bournemouth St Pet w St Swithun, H Trin etc *Win* 85-93; rtd 93. *5 Richards Way, Salisbury SP2 8NT* Tel (01722) 332163

LANE, Antony Kenneth. b 58. Ripon Coll Cuddesdon 84. **d** 87 **p** 88. C Crediton and Shobrooke *Ex* 87-90; C Amblecote *Worc* 90-94; C Sedgley All SS 94-95; TV 95-00; R Crayford *Roch* from 00. *The Rectory, 1 Claremont Crescent, Crayford, Dartford DA1 4RJ* Tel (01322) 522078 Mobile 07931-603470 E-mail ak.lane@btinternet.com

LANE, Bernard Charles. b 59. Cam Coll of Art & Tech BA81 Bris Univ BA91 Anglia Poly Univ MA01. Trin Coll Bris 88 Ridley Hall Cam 99. **d** 01 **p** 02. C Sittingbourne St Mary and St Mich *Cant* from 01. *88 Albany Road, Sittingbourne ME10 1EL* Tel (01795) 426947 E-mail lane@train66.fsnet.co.uk

LANE, Christopher George. b 48. NDH. Sarum & Wells Th Coll 84. **d** 86 **p** 87. C Petersfield *Portsm* 86-90; P-in-c Barton 90-95; Perm to Offic from 95. *Carisbrooke Priory, 39 Whitcombe Road, Carisbrooke, Newport PO30 1YS* Tel (01983) 523354

LANE, Denis John Victor. b 29. Lon Univ LLB49 BD55. Oak Hill Th Coll 50. **d** 53 **p** 54. C Deptford St Jo *S'wark* 53-56; C Cam St Steph CD *Ely* 56-59; OMF 60-94; Malaysia 60-66; Singapore 66-94; Lic to Offic *Chich* 91-94; rtd 94; Perm to Offic *Chich* from 94. *2 Parry Drive, Rustington, Littlehampton BN16 2QY* Tel (01903) 785430 Fax as telephone

LANE, Ms Elizabeth Jane Holden. b 66. St Pet Coll Ox BA89 MA93. Cranmer Hall Dur 91. **d** 93 **p** 94. C Blackb St Jas *Blackb* 93-96; Perm to Offic *York* 96-99; Family Life Educn Officer *Ches* 00-02; TV Stockport SW from 02; Asst Dir of Ords from 05. *The Vicarage, 217 Outwood Road, Heald Green, Cheadle SK8 3JS* Tel 0161-437 4614

LANE, George David Christopher. b 68. St Pet Coll Ox BA89 MA93. Cranmer Hall Dur DMS93. **d** 93 **p** 94. C Blackb St Jas *Blackb* 93-96; C Beverley Minster *York* 96-99; V Heald Green St Cath *Ches* from 99. *The Vicarage, 217 Outwood Road, Heald Green, Cheadle SK8 3JS* Tel 0161-437 4614 *or* 3685 E-mail george.lane@ntlworld.com

LANE, Canon Gerald. b 29. Bede Coll Dur BA52 MA96. Sarum Th Coll 52. **d** 54 **p** 55. C Camberwell St Giles *S'wark* 54-58; C Gillingham St Aug *Roch* 58-59; V Camberwell St Phil and St Mark *S'wark* 59-67; V Plumstead St Nic 67-73; V Gillingham St Aug *Roch* 73-78; V Hadlow 78-94; Hon Can Roch Cathl 87-94; rtd 94; Perm to Offic *Roch* 94-97; Perm to Offic *St Alb* 97-03. *14 Park House Drive, Dewsbury WF12 0DQ* Tel (01924) 485680

LANE, Canon Iain Robert. b 61. CCC Ox BA83. Ripon Coll Cuddesdon BA86 MA88. **d** 87 **p** 88. C Rotherhithe St Mary w All SS *S'wark* 87-91; V Bierley *Bradf* 91-00; Can Res St Alb from 00. *2 Sumpter Yard, St Albans AL1 1BY* Tel (01727) 890205 E-mail edcanon@stalbanscathedral.org.uk

LANE, John Ernest. b 39. OBE94. MBIM76 Cranfield Info Tech Inst MSc80. Handsworth Coll Birm 58. **d** 80 **p** 80. In Meth Ch 62-80; Hon C Peckham St Jo w St Andr *S'wark* 80-95; Hon C Greenwich St Alfege 98-99; Dir St Mungo Housing Assn 80-94; Dir Corporate Affairs from 94; Perm to Offic 95-98. *2 Tregony Rise, Lichfield WS14 9SN* Tel (01543) 415078

LANE, Mrs Lilian June. b 37. Stockwell Coll Lon TCert59. **d** 02 **p** 03. OLM E Knoyle, Semley and Sedgehill *Sarum* from 02. *Ashmede, Watery Lane, Donhead St Mary, Shaftesbury SP7 9DP* Tel (01747) 828427

LANE, Mrs Linda Mary. b 41. ACIB66 Lon Univ BD87. Gilmore Ho DipRK67. **dss** 82 **d** 87 **p** 94. Hadlow *Roch* 82-94; Hon Par Dn 87-94; Perm to Offic 94-96; C Dartford H Trin 96-97; V Kensworth, Studham and Whipsnade *St Alb* 97-03; rtd 03. *14 Park House Drive, Dewsbury WF12 0DQ* Tel (01924) 485680

LANE, Malcolm Clifford George. b 48. JP. ACIB. St D Coll Lamp. **d** 02. Par Dn Abergavenny St Mary w Llanwenarth Citra *Mon* from 02; Asst Chapl Gwent Healthcare NHS Trust from 02. *33 Sarno Square, Abergavenny NP7 5JT* E-mail st8711@msn.com

LANE, Martin John. b 69. Open Univ BSc03. Coll of Resurr Mirfield 92. **d** 95 **p** 96. C Liss *Portsm* 95-98; C Warren Park and Leigh Park 98-00; TV Littlehampton and Wick *Chich* 00-04; P-in-c Harting w Elsted and Treyford cum Didling from 04. *The Rectory, The Street, South Harting, Petersfield GU31 5QB* Tel (01730) 825234

LANE, Mrs Pamela. b 44. **d** 00 **p** 01. OLM Betley *Lich* from 00. *Brandon, Main Road, Betley, Crewe CW3 9BH* Tel (01270) 820258

LANE, Richard Peter. b 60. Linc Th Coll 85. **d** 88 **p** 89. C Towcester w Easton Neston *Pet* 88-91; Asst Chapl Oslo w Bergen, Trondheim, Stavanger etc *Eur* 91-93; V Writtle w Highwood *Chelmsf* 93-99; Chapl Whitelands Coll Roehampton Inst *S'wark* 99-03; P-in-c W Wimbledon Ch Ch 03-04; V from 04. *The Vicarage, 16 Copse Hill, London SW20 0HG* Tel (020) 8946 4491

LANE, Ms Rosalind Anne. b 69. Trevelyan Coll Dur BA91 Heythrop Coll Lon MTh93 Man Univ MA01. Westcott Ho Cam. **d** 95 **p** 96. C Huddersfield St Pet and All SS *Wakef* 95-99; Sub Chapl HM Pris and YOI New Hall 97-99; Asst Chapl HM Pris and YOI Doncaster 99-01; Chapl 01; Chapl HM Pris Wymott 01-05; Chapl HM Pris Kirkham from 05. *HM Prison, Freckleton Road, Kirkham, Preston PR4 2RN* Tel (01772) 675400 E-mail rosalind.lane@hmps.gsi.gov.uk

LANE, Roy Albert. b 42. Bris Sch of Min 82. **d** 85 **p** 86. NSM Bedminster *Bris* 85-97; Perm to Offic 97-02; NSM Bishopsworth and Bedminster Down from 02. *20 Ashton Drive, Bristol BS3 2PW* Tel 0117-983 0747 Mobile 07747-808972 E-mail roypeg@blueyonder.co.uk

LANE, Simon. *See* DOUGLAS LANE, Charles Simon Pellew

LANE, Stuart Alexander Rhys. *See* LANE, Alexander John

LANE, Terry. b 50. STETS 94. **d** 97 **p** 98. NSM Freemantle *Win* 97-99; Chapl HM Pris Kingston (Portsm) 99-01; Chapl HM Pris Parkhurst from 01. *HM Prison Parkhurst, Newport PO30 5NX* Tel (01983) 523855 ext 416 Fax 524861

LANE, William Henry Howard. b 63. Bris Poly BA85. Trin Coll Bris 00. **d** 02 **p** 03. C Frome H Trin *B & W* from 02. *54 Oakfield Road, Frome BA11 4JE* Tel (01373) 474334 E-mail lane@fish.co.uk

LANG, Geoffrey Wilfrid Francis. b 33. St Jo Coll Ox BA56 MA61. Cuddesdon Coll 56. **d** 58 **p** 59. C Spalding *Linc* 58-61; Asst Chapl Leeds Univ *Ripon* 61-62; C Chesterton St Luke *Ely* 62-63; C-in-c Chesterton Gd Shep CD 63-69; V Chesterton Gd Shep 69-72; V Willian *St Alb* 72-76; Dioc Dir of Educn 72-76; R N Lynn w St Marg and St Nic *Nor* 77-86; V Hammersmith St Pet *Lon* 86-00; rtd 00. *54 Old Oak Road, London W3 7HQ* Tel (020) 8746 1371

LANG, The Very Revd John Harley. b 27. LRAM Em Coll Cam MA60 K Coll Lon AKC49 BD60 Keele Univ Hon DLitt88. St Boniface Warminster 49. **d** 52 **p** 53. C Portsea St Mary *Portsm* 52-57; PV and Sacr S'wark Cathl *S'wark* 57-60; Chapl Em Coll Cam 60-64; Asst Hd Relig Broadcasting BBC 64-67; Hd Relig Progr BBC Radio 67-71; Hd Relig Broadcasting BBC 71-80; C Sacombe *St Alb* 73-80; Chapl to The Queen 77-80; Dean Lich 80-93; rtd 93; Perm to Offic *Glouc* 93-96. *1 Abbotsdene, 6 Cudnall Street, Charlton Kings, Cheltenham GL53 8HT* Tel (01242) 577742 Fax as telephone E-mail jhlang@email.com

LANG, Nicholas. b 45. DipTh97. SEITE 94. **d** 97 **p** 98. NSM Beckenham St Jo *Roch* 97-98; NSM Penge Lane H Trin 98-01; Chapl St Chris Hospice Lon 00; V Beckenham St Jo *Roch* from 01. *St John's Vicarage, 249 Eden Park Avenue, Beckenham BR3 3JN* Tel and fax (020) 8650 6110 Mobile 07968-985051 E-mail niklang@ntlworld.com

LANG, William David. b 51. K Coll Lon BD74 MA94 AKC74. St Aug Coll Cant 74. **d** 75 **p** 76. C Fleet *Guildf* 75-79; C Ewell St Fran 79-82; C W Ewell 79-82; V Holmwood 82-92; R Elstead from 92; V Thursley from 92. *The Rectory, Thursley Road, Elstead, Godalming GU8 6DG* Tel (01252) 703251 E-mail william@lang.net

LANGAN, Mrs Eleanor Susan. b 56. Homerton Coll Cam BEd78. Ripon Coll Cuddesdon 84. **d** 87 **p** 94. Hon Par Dn Grays Thurrock *Chelmsf* 87-89; Lic to Offic 89-94; NSM Creeksea w Althorne, Latchingdon and N Fambridge 94-95; NSM S Woodham Ferrers 95-99; NSM Overstrand, Northrepps, Sidestrand etc *Nor* 99-03; Chapl Norfolk and Nor Univ Hosp NHS Trust from 00. *The Rectory, 22A Harbord Road, Overstrand, Cromer NR27 0PN* Tel (01263) 579350

LANGAN, Michael Leslie. b 54. Cam Univ BA PGCE. Cranmer Hall Dur. **d** 84 **p** 85. C Grays Thurrock *Chelmsf* 84-89; V Creeksea w Althorne, Latchingdon and N Fambridge 89-95; RD Maldon and Dengie 92-95; P-in-c S Woodham Ferrers 95-99; R Overstrand, Northrepps, Sidestrand etc *Nor* from 99. *The Rectory, 22A Harbord Road, Overstrand, Cromer NR27 0PN* Tel (01263) 579350 E-mail mlangan@tiscali.co.uk

LANGDON, John Bonsall. b 21. Linc Coll Ox BA51 MA55. Ripon Hall Ox 52. **d** 54 **p** 55. C Erith St Jo *Roch* 54-57; C Christchurch *Win* 57-60; Min Can Ripon Cathl *Ripon* 60-63; R Swillington 63-75; P-in-c Wrangthorn 75-76; V Leeds All Hallows w St Simon 75-76; V Leeds All Hallows w Wrangthorn 76-87; P-in-c Woodhouse St Mark 85-87; V Woodhouse and Wrangthorn 87-92; rtd 92; Perm to Offic *Ripon* from 92; Hon Min Can Ripon Cathl from 02. *32 Magdalen's Road, Ripon HG4 1HT* Tel (01765) 606814

LANGDON, Ms Susan Mary. b 48. RN69. Ripon Coll Cuddesdon 01. **d** 03 **p** 04. C Amesbury *Sarum* from 03. *1 Devereux Road, Amesbury, Salisbury SP4 7NR* Tel (01980) 625733 E-mail slangdon@ripon-cuddeson.ac.uk *or* suelangdon@btopenworld.com

LANGDON-DAVIES, Mrs Stella Mary. b 44. Bris Univ BSc85 Nottm Univ MBA97. St Jo Coll Nottm MTh01. **d** 01 **p** 02. C Stamford All SS w St Jo *Linc* 01-04; V Herne *Cant* from 04. *The New Vicarage, Herne Street, Herne Bay CT6 7HE* Tel (01227) 374328 Mobile 07976-380659 E-mail stellald@onetel.com

LANGDOWN, Jennifer May. b 48. STETS 95. **d** 98 **p** 99. C S Petherton w the Seavingtons *B & W* 98-02; R Curry Rivel w Fivehead and Swell from 02. *The Rectory, Curry Rivel, Langport TA10 0HQ* Tel (01458) 251375 E-mail ubcrfhsw@beeb.net

LANGE-SMITH, Michael Leslie. b 56. Bris Univ BSc83 Lon Bible Coll MA90. Trin Coll Bris 87. **d** 90 **p** 91. Zimbabwe 90-02; C Greendale 91-92; R Melfort 93-98; Dir Th Educn by Ext Coll of Zimbabwe 99-02; R Chinnor, Sydenham, Aston Rowant and Crowell *Ox* from 03. *The Rectory, High Street, Chinnor OX39 4DH* Tel (01844) 351309

LANGFORD, David Laurence. b 51. LNSM course 86. **d** 88 **p** 89. OLM Scotton w Northorpe *Linc* from 88. *1 Westgate, Scotton, Gainsborough DN21 3QX* Tel (01724) 763139

LANGFORD, Prof Michael John. b 31. New Coll Ox BA54 MA58 Cam Univ MA59 Lon Univ PhD66. Westcott Ho Cam 55. **d** 56 **p** 57. C Bris St Nath w St Kath *Bris* 56-59; Chapl Qu Coll Cam 59-63; C Hampstead St Jo *Lon* 63-67; Canada 67-96; Prof Philosophy Newfoundland Univ 82-96; Prof Medical Ethics 87-96; rtd 96; Perm to Offic *Ely* from 96. *90 Field View, Bar Hill, Cambridge CB3 8SY* Tel (01954) 789593

LANGFORD, Peter Francis. b 54. Sarum & Wells Th Coll 76. **d** 79 **p** 80. C N Ormesby *York* 79-82; Ind Chapl 83-91; V Middlesbrough St Chad 91-96; R Easington w Liverton from 96. *The Rectory, Grinkle Lane, Easington, Saltburn-by-the-Sea TS13 4NT* Tel (01287) 641348 E-mail peterlan2@aol.com

LANGFORD, Peter Julian. b 33. Selw Coll Cam BA58. Westcott Ho Cam 59. **d** 60 **p** 61. C E Ham St Mary *Chelmsf* 60-67; Hon C 67-71; Hon C Beccles St Mich *St E* 71-76; Warden Ringsfield Hall Suffolk 71-87; P-in-c Ringsfield w Redisham *St E* 76-80; TV Seacroft *Ripon* 87-98; rtd 98; Perm to Offic *St E* from 99. *36 Ringsfield Road, Beccles NR34 9PF* Tel (01502) 710034

LANGHAM, Paul Jonathan. b 60. Ex Univ BA81 DipTh83 Fitzw Coll Cam BA86 MA91. Ridley Hall Cam 84. **d** 87 **p** 88. C Bath Weston All SS w N Stoke *B & W* 87-91; Chapl and Fell St Cath Coll Cam 91-96; V Combe Down w Monkton Combe and S Stoke *B & W* from 96; Examining Chapl from 04. *Church Office, Avenue Place, Combe Down, Bath BA2 5EE* Tel (01225) 835835 *or* 833152 E-mail vicar@htcd.co.uk

LANGILLE, Melvin Owen. b 58. St Mary's Univ Halifax NS BA79. Atlantic Sch of Th MDiv82. **d** 82 **p** 83. Dn-in-c Falkland Canada 82; R Lockeport and Barrington 83-86; R French Village 87-90; R Cole Harbour St Andr 90-96; R Yarmouth H Trin 97-03; P-in-c Brora *Mor* from 03; P-in-c Dornoch from 03. *An t-Errain Beag, 42 Ross Street, Golspie, Sutherland KW10 6SA* Tel (01408) 633341 Mobile 07780-512990 E-mail mel@langille.freeserve.co.uk

LANGLEY, Emma Louise. *See* BAUGHAN, Mrs Emma Louise Langley

LANGLEY, Canon Myrtle Sarah. b 39. FRAI TCD BA61 HDipEd62 MA67 Bris Univ PhD76 Lon Univ BD66. Dalton Ho Bris 64. **d** 88 **p** 94. Dir Chr Development for Miss *Liv* 87-89; Dir Dioc Tr Inst *Carl* 90-98; Dioc Dir of Tr 90-98; Hon Can Carl Cathl 91-98; P-in-c Long Marton w Dufton and w Milburn from 98. *The Rectory, Long Marton, Appleby-in-Westmorland CA16 6BN* Tel (01768) 361269 Fax 361196 E-mail canonmlangley@hotmail.com

LANGLEY, The Ven Robert. b 37. St Cath Soc Ox BA61. St Steph Ho Ox. **d** 63 **p** 64. C Aston cum Aughton *Sheff* 63-68; Midl Area Sec Chr Educn Movement 68-71; HQ Sec Chr Educn Movement 71-74; Prin Ian Ramsey Coll Brasted 74-77; Dir St Alb Minl Tr Scheme 77-85; Can Res St Alb 77-85; Dioc Missr *Newc* 85-98; Can Res Newc Cathl 85-01; Dioc Dir of Min and Tr 98-01; Adn Lindisfarne from 01; Local Min Development Officer from 01. *4 Acomb Close, Stobhill, Morpeth NE61 2YH* Tel (01670) 503810 Fax 503469 E-mail b.langley@newcastle.anglican.org *or* kca85@dial.pipex.com

LANGMAN, Barry Edward. b 46. Master Mariner 73. Cant Sch of Min 87. **d** 90 **p** 91. NSM St Margarets-at-Cliffe w Westcliffe etc *Cant* 90-92; C Sandgate St Paul 92; C Sandgate St Paul w Folkestone St Geo 92-95; P-in-c Headcorn 95-01; V from 01. *The Vicarage, 64 Oak Lane, Headcorn, Ashford TN27 9TB* Tel (01622) 890342

LANGRELL, Gordon John. b 35. Cant Univ (NZ) BA58. Ridley Hall Cam 65. **d** 67 **p** 68. C Tonbridge SS Pet and Paul *Roch* 67-71; New Zealand from 71; rtd 05. *11A Henry Wigram Drive, Upper Riccarton, Christchurch 8004, New Zealand* Tel (0064) (3) 348 9554 Fax 348 9805 E-mail gorlang@paradise.net.nz

LANGRIDGE, Molly Deirdre. b 48. Bris Poly CQSW88. LNSM course 96. **d** 98 **p** 99. OLM King's Lynn St Marg w St Nic *Nor* 98-03. *Address temp unknown* E-mail langa@tesco.net

✠**LANGRISH, The Rt Revd Michael Laurence.** b 46. Birm Univ BSocSc67 Fitzw Coll Cam BA73 MA77. Ridley Hall Cam 71. **d** 73 **p** 74 **c** 93. C Stratford-on-Avon w Bishopton *Cov* 73-76; Chapl Rugby Sch 76-81; P-in-c Offchurch *Cov* 81-87; Dioc Dir of Ords 81-87; P-in-c Rugby St Andr 87-91; Hon Can Cov Cathl 90-93; TR Rugby St Andr 91-93; Suff Bp Birkenhead *Ches* 93-00; Bp Ex from 00. *The Palace, Exeter EX1 1HY* Tel (01392) 272362 Fax 430923
E-mail bishop.of.exeter@exeter.anglican.org

✠**LANGSTAFF, The Rt Revd James Henry.** b 56. St Cath Coll Ox BA77 MA81 Nottm Univ BA80. St Jo Coll Nottm 78. **d** 81 **p** 82 **c** 04. C Farnborough *Guildf* 81-84 and 85-86; P-in-c 84-85; P-in-c Duddeston w Nechells *Birm* 86; V 87-96; RD Birm City 95-96; Bp's Dom Chapl 96-00; P-in-c Short Heath 98-00; R Sutton Coldfield H Trin 00-04; AD Sutton Coldfield 02-04; Suff Bp Lynn *Nor* from 04. *The Old Vicarage, Castle Acre, King's Lynn PE32 2AA* Tel (01760) 755553 Fax 755085 Mobile 07989-330582 E-mail bishoplynn@norwich.anglican.org

LANGSTON, Clinton Matthew. b 62. Derby Coll of Educn BCombStuds86. Qu Coll Birm 87. **d** 90 **p** 91. C Shirley *Birm* 90-94; CF from 94. *c/o MOD Chaplains (Army)* Tel (01980) 615804 Fax 615800

LANGTON, Canon Kenneth. b 26. Open Univ BA76. St Aid Birkenhead 52. **d** 55 **p** 56. C Oldham St Paul *Man* 55-57; C Ashton Ch Ch 57-58; P-in-c 58; V Stalybridge New St Geo 58-69; P-in-c Stalybridge Old St Geo 67-69; V Stalybridge 69-71; R Radcliffe St Mary 71-83; Hon Can Man Cathl 80-91; V Tyldesley w Shakerley 83-91; rtd 91; Perm to Offic *Man* from 91. *889 Walmersley Road, Bury BL9 5LE* Tel 0161-764 1552

LANGTON, Robert. b 45. St Alb and Ox Min Course 97. **d** 00 **p** 01. C Boyne Hill *Ox* 00-03; Chapl St Mich Hospice from 03. *St Michael's Hospice, 25 Upper Maze Hill, St Leonards-on-Sea TN38 0LB* Tel (01424) 445177 *or* 420889

LANHAM, Geoffrey Peter. b 62. Cam Univ MA84 Ox Univ MPhil86. Wycliffe Hall Ox 86. **d** 89 **p** 90. C Southborough St Pet w Ch Ch and St Matt *Roch* 89-92; C Harborne Heath *Birm* 92-00; C Birm St Paul from 00; Deanery Missr from 00. *117 Metchley Lane, Harborne, Birmingham B17 0JH* Tel 0121-427 6907 *or* 427 4601 E-mail geoff@b1church.net

LANHAM, Richard Paul White. b 42. Dur Univ BA64. Wycliffe Hall Ox 65. **d** 67 **p** 68. C Gerrards Cross *Ox* 67-69; C Horwich H Trin *Man* 69-72; C Worsley 72-74; V Accrington St Andr *Blackb* 74-80; V Shillington *St Alb* 80-85; V Upper w Lower Gravenhurst 80-85; rtd 85; Perm to Offic *St Alb* from 85. *10 Alexander Close, Clifton, Shefford SG17 5RB* Tel (01462) 813520

LANKEY, David. b 41. MBCS68 CEng88 Southn Univ BSc62. S'wark Ord Course 79. **d** 82 **p** 83. NSM W Wimbledon Ch Ch *S'wark* 82-92; C Tooting All SS 92-95; R Long Ditton *S'wark* 95-00; R Long Ditton *Guildf* 00-02; rtd 02; Perm to Offic *Guildf* from 03. *15B Heathfield Road, Seaford BN25 1TH* Tel (01323) 894452

LANKSHEAR, Jane Frances. *See* MAINWARING, Jane Frances

LANSDALE, Canon Charles Roderick. b 38. Leeds Univ BA59. Coll of Resurr Mirfield 59. **d** 61 **p** 62. C Nunhead St Antony *S'wark* 61-65; Swaziland 65-71; V Benhilton *S'wark* 72-78; TR Catford (Southend) and Downham 78-87; TR Moulsecoomb *Chich* 87-97; V Eastbourne St Mary from 97; Can and Preb Chich Cathl from 98. *The Vicarage, 2 Glebe Close, Eastbourne BN20 8AW* Tel (01323) 720420

LANYON-HOGG, Mrs Anne Chester. b 49. St Anne's Coll Ox BA71 MA75 Worc Coll of Educn PGCE92. WEMTC 01. **d** 04. NSM Colwall w Upper Colwall and Coddington *Heref* from 04. *13 Lower Road, Malvern WR14 4BX* Tel (01684) 573995 Mobile 07890-995297 E-mail annelh@fish.co.uk

LANYON JONES, Keith. b 49. Southn Univ BTh79. Sarum & Wells Th Coll 74. **d** 77 **p** 78. C Charlton Kings St Mary *Glouc* 77-81; Sen Chapl Rugby Sch 81-99; Lic to Offic *Truro* 83-00; P-in-c St Cleer from 00; C St Ive and Pensilva w Quethiock from 02. *The Vicarage, St Cleer, Liskeard PL14 5DN* Tel (01579) 343240 E-mail lanyon67@hotmail.com

LAPAGE, Michael Clement. b 23. Selw Coll Cam BA47 MA73. Clifton Th Coll 60. **d** 61 **p** 62. Kenya 61-72; Chapl Bedford Sch 73-75; Chapl Lyon w Grenoble *Eur* 76-79; V Walford w Bishopswood *Heref* 79-88; P-in-c Goodrich w Welsh Bicknor and Marstow 83-88; rtd 88; Perm to Offic *Ex* from 88. *Moorlands, 20 Watts Road, Tavistock PL19 8LG* Tel (01822) 615901

LAPHAM, Canon Fred. b 31. Univ of Wales (Lamp) BA53 PhD00. Vancouver Sch of Th LTh55 BD58. **d** 55 **p** 55. Canada 55-59; C Wallasey St Hilary *Ches* 59-62; V Over St Jo 62-70; V Upton Ascension 70-82; R Grappenhall 82-91; RD Gt Budworth 85-91; Hon Can Ches Cathl 88-91; rtd 91; Perm to Offic *Ches* and *Heref* from 91. *1 Coppice Gate, Lyth Hill, Shrewsbury SY3 0BT* Tel (01743) 872284

LAPWOOD, Robin Rowland John. b 57. Selw Coll Cam MA. Ridley Hall Cam 80. **d** 82 **p** 83. C Bury St Edmunds St Mary *St E* 82-86; P-in-c Bentley w Tattingstone 86-93; P-in-c Copdock w Washbrook and Belstead 86-93; TV High Wycombe *Ox* 93-96; P-in-c Marcham w Garford 96-02; Asst Master Summer Fields Sch Ox from 02. *Summer Fields School, Mayfield Road, Oxford OX2 7EN* Tel (01865) 454433
E-mail robin.lapwood@bigfoot.com

LARCOMBE, Paul Richard. b 57. Portsm Poly BSc79 CEng MIEE. Trin Coll Bris 94. **d** 96 **p** 97. C Werrington *Pet* 96-98; C Longthorpe 98-00; V Pet St Paul from 00. *St Paul's Vicarage, Lincoln Road, Peterborough PE1 2PA* Tel (01733) 343746
E-mail paul@peterborough-stpauls.org.uk

LARGE, William Roy. b 40. Dur Univ BA DipEd. Edin Th Coll 82. **d** 84 **p** 85. C Leamington Priors All SS *Cov* 84-88; V Bishop's Tachbrook 88-99; Warden of Readers and Sen Tutor 88-99; TV N Tyne and Redesdale *Newc* 99-01; TR from 01. *The Rectory, Bellingham, Hexham NE48 2JS* Tel (01434) 220019

LARK, William Donald Starling. b 35. Keble Coll Ox BA59 MA63. Wells Th Coll 59. **d** 61 **p** 62. C Wyken *Cov* 61-64; C Christchurch *Win* 64-66; V Yeovil St Mich *B & W* 66-75; V Earley St Pet *Ox* 75-85; V Prittlewell *Chelmsf* 85-88; V Dawlish *Ex* 88-00; rtd 00; P-in-c Lanzarote *Eur* 00-05. *Calle Los Sabandenos 37, 35510 Puerto del Carmen, Lanzarote, Canary Islands, Spain* Tel (0034) (928) 514241

LARKEY, Mrs Deborah Frances. b 63. Univ of Wales (Abth) BA85 Liv Inst of Educn PGCE90. LNSM course 95. **d** 98 **p** 99. OLM Toxteth St Cypr w Ch Ch *Liv* 98-01; OLM Edge Hill St Cypr w St Mary 01-04; C Netherton from 04. *57 Park Lane West, Bootle L30 3SX* Tel 0151-521 5977
E-mail deborah@larkey.fsworld.co.uk

LARKIN, Canon Peter John. b 39. ALCD62. **d** 62 **p** 63. C Liskeard w St Keyne *Truro* 62-65; C Rugby St Andr *Cov* 65-67; Sec Bp Cov Call to Miss 67-68; V Kea *Truro* 68-78; P-in-c Bromsgrove St Jo *Worc* 78-81; R Torquay St Matthias, St Mark and H Trin *Ex* 81-97; Can Sokoto Nigeria 91-98; Can Kaduna from 98; TR Plymouth Em, St Paul Efford and St Aug *Ex* 97-00; rtd 00; Perm to Offic *Ex* from 00. *Picklecombe, 57 Babbacombe Downs Road, Torquay TQ1 3LP* Tel (01803) 326888
E-mail larkin@petermolly.freeserve.co.uk

LARLEE, David Alexander. b 78. Univ of W Ontario MA01. Wycliffe Hall Ox BTh04. **d** 04. NSM Battersea Rise St Mark *S'wark* from 04. *24 Parma Crescent, London SW11 1LT*
E-mail david_larlee@yahoo.com

LARNER, Gordon Edward Stanley. b 30. Brasted Th Coll 54 Oak Hill Th Coll 55. **d** 59 **p** 60. C Peckham St Mary Magd *S'wark* 59-62; C Luton w E Hyde *St Alb* 62-68; V Lower Sydenham St Mich *S'wark* 68-73; Ind Chapl 73-84; Chapl HM Pris Ranby 84-92; rtd 92. *Glen Rosa, Meshaw, South Molton EX36 4NE*

LARSEN, Clive Erik. b 55. St Jo Coll Nottm 88. **d** 90 **p** 91. C Weaverham *Ches* 90-92; C Alvanley and Helsby and Dunham-on-the-Hill 92-95; P-in-c Cheadle Heath 95-02; P-in-c N Reddish *Man* from 05. *The Rectory, 551 Gorton Road, Stockport SK5 6NX* Tel 0161-223 0692 Mobile 07789-915263
E-mail clive.larsen@ntlworld.com

LASHBROOKE, David. b 60. Ex Univ BA87. Ripon Coll Cuddesdon 90. **d** 92 **p** 93. C Sherborne w Castleton and Lillington *Sarum* 92-95; P-in-c Weymouth St Paul 95-99; V 99-02; V St Marychurch *Ex* from 02. *The Vicarage, Hampton Avenue, Torquay TQ1 3LA* Tel (01803) 329054 *or* 327661
E-mail frdavid@wdi.co.uk

LASKEY, Cyril Edward. b 44. RMN71 RGN74. Llan Dioc Tr Scheme 85. **d** 88 **p** 89. NSM Troedrhiwgarth *Llan* 88-93; NSM Caerau St Cynfelin 94-01; P-in-c Glyncorrwg and Upper Afan Valley from 01. *207 Bridgend Road, Maesteg CF34 0NL* Tel (01656) 734639

LASKEY, Stephen Allan. b 56. Manitoba Univ BA85. St Jo Coll Winnipeg MDiv88. **d** 89 **p** 89. Canada 89-01; C Labrador W 89; C Battle Harbour 89-91; R 91-96; R Goulds St Paul 96-99; Assoc P Foxtrap All SS 00-01; C Paddington St Jo w St Mich *Lon* 01-02; P-in-c Sydenham H Trin *S'wark* from 02; P-in-c Forest Hill St Aug from 03. *Holy Trinity Vicarage, 1 Sydenham Park Road, London SE26 4DY* Tel (020) 8699 5303
E-mail stephenlaskey@onetel.com

LAST, Eric Cyril. b 30. Oak Hill Th Coll 77. **d** 79 **p** 80. C Wandsworth All SS *S'wark* 79-83; V Earlsfield St Andr 83-88; V S Merstham 88-96; Asst RD Reigate 92-96; rtd 96; Hon C Upper Tean *Lich* from 96. *29 Vicarage Road, Tean, Stoke-on-Trent ST10 4LE* Tel (01538) 723551 Fax as telephone
E-mail eric.last1@btopenworld.com

LAST, Harold Wilfred. b 17. ARCM52 ARCO53 CCC Cam BA38 MA42. Linc Th Coll 39. **d** 40 **p** 41. C Bolton St Jas *Bradf* 40-44; C Woodbridge St Mary *St E* 44-45; Lect K Coll Lon 45-53; Dir of Music St Bees, St Olave's & Felstead Schs 53-73; rtd 73. *Flat 1, Knapton House, North Walsham Road, Knapton, North Walsham NR28 0RT* Tel (01263) 720084

LAST, Michael Leonard Eric. b 60. St Jo Coll Nottm Dip Th & Min 94. **d** 94 **p** 95. C Tettenhall Wood *Lich* 94-98; V Pelsall 98-02; V Alton w Bradley-le-Moors and Oakamoor w Cotton from 02. *The New Vicarage, Limekiln Lane, Alton, Stoke-on-Trent ST10 4AR* Tel (01538) 702469
E-mail michael.l.e.last@btinternet.com

LAST, Norman Percy George. b 31. BA CertEd ATPL. Sarum & Wells Th Coll 77 Wycliffe Hall Ox 80. **d** 81 **p** 82. C Walton-on-Thames *Guildf* 81-83; C Farnham 83-87; R Monks Eleigh w Chelsworth and Brent Eleigh etc *St E* 87-90; P-in-c Bradworthy *Ex* 91-97; rtd 97; Perm to Offic *Ex* from 98; C Stansted *Chich* 00-02. *9 Wensley Gardens, Emsworth PO10 7RA* Tel (01243) 374174

LATHAM, Christine Elizabeth. b 46. S'wark Ord Course 87. **d** 90 **p** 94. Par Dn Battersea St Pet and St Paul *S'wark* 90-94; Par Dn S'wark Ch Ch 94; C 94-97; C Merstham and Gatton from 97; Chapl E Surrey Learning Disability NHS Trust from 97. *Epiphany House, Mansfield Drive, Merstham, Redhill RH1 3JP* Tel (01737) 642628

LATHAM, Henry Nicholas Lomax. b 64. Reading Univ BA86. Wycliffe Hall Ox BTh93. **d** 93 **p** 94. C Aberystwyth *St D* 93-99; P-in-c Stoke Poges *Ox* from 99. *The Vicarage, Park Road, Stoke Poges, Slough SL2 4PE* Tel (01753) 642261 E-mail harryandtracy@isaiah61.freeserve.co.uk

LATHAM, John Montgomery. b 37. Univ of NZ BA Cam Univ MA Cant Univ (NZ) MEd. Westcott Ho Cam 60. **d** 62 **p** 63. C Camberwell St Geo *S'wark* 62-65; Chapl Trin Coll Cam 65-70; New Zealand from 71; Chapl Wanganui Colleg Sch 71-79; Min Enabler N New Brighton 96-01; V Christchurch St Luke 98-02; rtd 02. *43 Rugby Street, Christchurch, New Zealand 8001* Tel (0064) (3) 355 6654 Fax 355 6658 E-mail latham@xtra.co.nz

LATHAM, John Westwood. b 31. Ely Th Coll 57. **d** 60 **p** 61. C Cleckheaton St Jo *Wakef* 60-63; C Hemel Hempstead *St Alb* 63-65; C Wakef Cathl *Wakef* 65-67; V Outwood 67-72; TV Daventry w Norton *Pet* 72-79; V Flore w Dodford and Brockhall 79-96; rtd 96; Perm to Offic *Leic* from 97. *53 Lubenham Hill, Market Harborough LE16 9DG* Tel (01858) 469023

LATHAM, Robert Norman. b 53. Qu Coll Birm 82. **d** 85 **p** 86. C Tamworth *Lich* 85-89; TV Wordsley 89-96; P-in-c Hallow *Worc* 96-97; R Hallow and Grimley w Holt from 97. *Hallow Vicarage, 26 Baveney Road, Worcester WR2 6DS* Tel (01905) 748711 E-mail robert@hallowvicarage.freeserve.co.uk

LATHAM, Roger Allonby. b 69. Leic Univ BA90 Warwick Univ MA92 Leeds Univ PGCE93. St Jo Coll Nottm BTh98. **d** 99 **p** 00. C Paston *Pet* 99-02; TV Cartmel Peninsula *Carl* from 02. *The Vicarage, Boarbank Lane, Allithwaite, Grange-over-Sands LA11 7QR* Tel (01539) 532437 E-mail lathams@home71.swinternet.co.uk

LATHAM, Ms Rosamond Mary. b 54. Coll of Ripon & York St Jo BEd90 MA00. Westcott Ho Cam 00. **d** 02 **p** 03. C Frodingham *Linc* from 02. *66 Church Lane, Scunthorpe DN15 7AF* Tel (01724) 848171 Mobile 07779-784320 E-mail ros@peterandros.freeserve.co.uk

LATHAM, Trevor Martin. b 56. BD84. Ripon Coll Cuddesdon 84. **d** 86 **p** 87. C Cantril Farm *Liv* 86-89; TV Croxteth Park 89-98; V 98-99; TR Walton-on-the-Hill from 99. *The Rectory, Walton Village, Liverpool L4 6TJ* Tel and fax 0151-525 3130 E-mail trevor.latham@virgin.net

LATHE, Canon Anthony Charles Hudson. b 36. Jes Coll Ox BA59 MA64 UEA Dip Sociology 68. Lich Th Coll 59. **d** 61 **p** 62. C Selby Abbey *York* 61-63; V Hempnall *Nor* 63-72; R Woodton w Bedingham 63-72; R Fritton w Morningthorpe w Shelton and Hardwick 63-72; R Topcroft 63-72; R Banham 72-76; TR Quidenham 76-83; P-in-c New Buckenham 78-79; V Heigham St Thos 83-94; Hon Can Nor Cathl 87-99; RD Nor S 90-94; P-in-c Sheringham 94-99; rtd 99; Perm to Offic *Nor* from 99. *38 Chestnut Hill, Norwich NR4 6NL* Tel (01603) 455846

LATIFA, Andrew Murdoch. b 73. Univ of Wales (Abth) BTh96 Univ of Wales (Cardiff) MTh00. St Mich Coll Llan 99. **d** 01 **p** 02. C Betws w Ammanford *St D* 01-03; C Llangynwyd w Maesteg *Llan* 03-05; CF from 05. *c/o MOD Chaplains (Army)* Tel (01980) 615804 Fax 615800

LATIMER, Clifford James. b 45. City Univ BSc68. OLM course 97. **d** 99 **p** 00. OLM Burntwood *Lich* from 99. *24 Dove Close, Burntwood WS7 9JL* Tel (01543) 671471 E-mail cliff.latimer@virgin.net

LATTIMORE, Anthony Leigh. b 35. Dur Univ BA57. Lich Th Coll 60. **d** 62 **p** 63. C Aylestone *Leic* 62-66; C-in-c Eyres Monsell CD 66-69; V Eyres Monsell 69-73; V Somerby, Burrough on the Hill and Pickwell 73-86; RD Goscote I 80-86; R Glenfield 86-95; rtd 95; Perm to Offic *Leic* and *Pet* from 95. *28 Elizabeth Way, Uppingham, Oakham LE15 9PQ* Tel (01572) 823193

LATTY, Howard James. b 54. SRCh71. WEMTC 98. **d** 01 **p** 02. NSM Bath St Mich w St Paul *B & W* from 01. *68 Cedric Road, Bath BA1 3PB* Tel (01225) 319403

LAU, Paul Chow Sing. b 49. Nat Chengchi Univ BA74 Chinese Univ of Hong Kong MDiv80. **d** 80 **p** 81. Hong Kong 80-82 and 83-94; C Hong Kong H Trin 80-82; Macao 82-83; V Macao St Mark 82-83; P-in-c Hong Kong Ch of Our Sav 83-94; New Zealand 94-01; V Ang Chinese Miss Ch *Wellington* 94-01; Chapl Chinese Congregation *Lon* from 01. *3 Strutton Court, 54 Great Peter Street, London SW1P 2HH* Tel (020) 7233 4027 *or* 7766 1206 E-mail paul.lau@smitf.org

LAUCKNER, Averil Ann. b 55. Lanc Univ BSc76. Ripon Coll Cuddesdon 03. **d** 04. C Royston *St Alb* from 04. *12 Prince Andrews Close, Royston SG8 9DZ* Tel (01763) 243265 E-mail averil.lauckner@btinternet.com

LAUGHTON, Derek Basil. b 24. Worc Coll Ox BA49 MA52. Westcott Ho Cam 49. **d** 51 **p** 52. C Wareham w Arne *Sarum* 51-53; CF 53-56; C Hemel Hempstead St Mary *St Alb* 56-59; V Stretton cum Wetmoor *Lich* 59-64; Chapl Wellington Sch Somerset 64-73; Chapl Ardingly Coll 73-77; R Plumpton w E Chiltington *Chich* 77-88; Perm to Offic *B & W* from 88; rtd 89. *13 Pyles Thorne Road, Wellington TA21 8DX* Tel (01823) 667386

LAURENCE, Brother. *See* EYERS, Frederick Thomas Laurence

LAURENCE, The Ven John Harvard Christopher. b 29. Trin Hall Cam BA53 MA57. Westcott Ho Cam 53. **d** 55 **p** 56. C Linc St Nic w St Jo Newport *Linc* 55-59; V Crosby 59-74; Can and Preb Linc Cathl 74-79 and 85-94; Dioc Missr 74-79; Bp's Dir of Clergy Tr *Lon* 80-85; Adn Lindsey *Linc* 85-94; rtd 94; Perm to Offic *Linc* 94-97. *5 Haffenden Road, Lincoln LN2 1RP* Tel (01522) 531444

LAURENCE, Julian Bernard Vere. b 60. Kent Univ BA82. St Steph Ho Ox 86. **d** 88 **p** 89. C Yeovil St Mich *B & W* 88-91; Chapl Yeovil Coll 90-91; Chapl Yeovil Distr Gen Hosp 91; P-in-c Barwick *B & W* 91-94; V Taunton H Trin from 94. *Holy Trinity Vicarage, 18 Holway Avenue, Taunton TA1 3AR* Tel (01823) 337890 E-mail jlaurence@htvicarage.fsnet.co.uk

LAURENCE, Vere Deacon. b 11. Ex Coll Ox BA33 BSc34 MA37. Sarum Th Coll 34. **d** 36 **p** 37. C Horfield St Greg *Bris* 36-42; Sec Dioc Reorganization Cttee 42-43; C Fishponds St Jo 42-43; C Knowle St Barn 43-47; Chapl HM Pris Stafford 47-52; V Upper Sunbury St Sav *Lon* 53-74; R Jacobstow w Warbstow and Treneglos *Truro* 74-83; RD Stratton 77-83; rtd 83; Perm to Offic *B & W* 85-97. *The Manor Nursing Home, Haydon Close, Bishops Hull, Taunton TA1 5HF* Tel (01823) 336633

LAURIE, Canon Donovan Hugh. b 40. Man Univ MSc. Oak Hill NSM Course. **d** 82 **p** 83. NSM Cudham and Downe *Roch* 82-84; C Tunbridge Wells St Jas 84-88; P-in-c Ventnor St Cath *Portsm* 88-99; V 99-04; P-in-c Ventnor H Trin 88-99; V 99-04; P-in-c Bonchurch 00-03; R 03-04; Hon Chapl St Cath Sch Ventnor 88-04; Hon Can Portsm Cathl *Portsm* from 01; rtd 04. *24 Cleveland, Tunbridge Wells TN2 3NF* Tel (01892) 539951 E-mail don@dlaurie.fsbusiness.co.uk

LAUT, Graham Peter. b 37. Chich Th Coll 63. **d** 67 **p** 68. C Corringham *Chelmsf* 67-68; C Leytonstone St Marg w St Columba 68-71; P-in-c Leytonstone St Andr 71-75; V 75-80; V Romford Ascension Collier Row from 80. *The Ascension Vicarage, 68 Collier Row Road, Romford RM5 2BA* Tel (01708) 741658 E-mail glaut10497@aol.com

LAUTENBACH, Edward Wayne. b 59. Univ Coll Ches BTh04. St Paul's Coll Grahamstown DipTh87. **d** 88 **p** 88. S Africa 88-99; C Weltevredenpark St Mich 88-89; Asst P Florida St Gabr 89-91; Sen Asst P Bryanston St Mich 91-94; R Brakpan St Pet 94-99; P-in-c Grange St Andr *Ches* 99-04; P-in-c Runcorn H Trin 99-04; V Prenton from 04. *The Vicarage, 1 Vicarage Close, Birkenhead CH42 8QX* Tel 0151-608 1808 E-mail wayne.lautenbach@btopenworld.com

LAVERACK, John Justin. b 51. Keele Univ BA CertEd Bris Univ BA. Bris Bapt Coll 76 Ex & Truro NSM Scheme 81. **d** 82 **p** 83. In Bapt Ch 79-81; C Braunton *Ex* 82-84; V Ex St Mark 84-92; Perm to Offic 92-98. *Tynewydd, Cwm Rhyd, Blaenwaun, Whitland SA34 0DB* Tel (01994) 419731 E-mail laverack@connect-wales.co.uk

LAVERTY, Canon Walter Joseph Robert. b 49. CITC 70 Glouc Th Course 73. **d** 73 **p** 74. C Belfast St Donard *D & D* 73-77; C Ballymacarrett St Patr 77-82; I Kilwarlin Upper w Kilwarlin Lower 82-86; I Orangefield w Moneyreagh from 86; Warden of Readers from 96; Can Down Cathl 97-00; Preb 97-00; Treas from 01. *The Rectory, 397 Castlereagh Road, Belfast BT5 6AB* Tel and fax (028) 9070 4493

LAVERY, Canon Edward Robinson. Lon Univ BA DipTh. St Aid Birkenhead 65. **d** 67 **p** 68. C Belfast Trin Coll Miss *Conn* 67-69; C Belfast St Mary Magd 69-71; CF (TA) 70-95; OCF from 75; I Belfast St Phil *Conn* 71-74; I Craigs w Dunaghy and Killagan 74-83; I Ballymoney w Finvoy and Rasharkin from 83; Dioc Info Officer from 83; Can Conn Cathl 96-98; Treas 98-01; Chan from 01. *The Rectory, Queen Street, Ballymoney BT53 6JA* Tel (028) 2766 2149

LAW, Andrew Philip. b 61. BNC Ox BA83 MA93 G&C Coll Cam PGCE86 Leic Univ MBA04. WEMTC 90. **d** 93 **p** 94. C Tupsley w Hampton Bishop *Heref* 93-95; Chapl Heref Sixth Form Coll 94-95; Chapl City of Lon Freemen's Sch Ashtead Park 95-97; Lic to Offic *Guildf* 95-97; Chapl and Hd RS Heref Cathl Sch 97-02; Chapl Malvern Coll from 02; Perm to Offic *Heref* from 02. *The Chaplain's House, College Road, Malvern WR14 3DD* Tel (01684) 581540 Fax 581617 E-mail apl@malcol.org.uk

LAW, Bryan. b 36. Leeds Univ BA59 Lon Univ BD76. Coll of Resurr Mirfield 59. **d** 61 **p** 62. C Winshill *Derby* 61-64; R Gorton St Phil *Man* 64-70; Lic to Offic 70-71; Perm to Offic *Ox* from 71; Hd Master Page Hill Co Middle Sch Buckingham 81-95; rtd 95.

35 Little Meadow, Loughton, Milton Keynes MK5 8EH Tel (01908) 661333

LAW, David Richard. b 60. **d** 01 **p** 02. NSM Ashton-upon-Mersey St Martin *Ches* from 01. *2 Winston Close, Sale M33 6UG* Tel 0161-962 0297

LAW, Canon Donald Edward Boughton. b 22. Lon Coll of Div 67. **d** 69 **p** 70. C Leic H Apostles *Leic* 69-73; V Cosby 73-81; RD Guthlaxton I 75-81; V Melton Mowbray w Thorpe Arnold 81-86; Hon Can Leic Cathl 81-88; RD Framland II 84-88; TR Melton Gt Framland 86-88; rtd 88; Perm to Offic *Leic* and *Pet* from 88. *36 Mill Grove, Whissendine, Oakham LE15 7EY* Tel (01664) 474411

LAW, Mrs Elizabeth Ann. b 49. Doncaster Coll of Educn CertEd70 Loughb Univ MA01. EAMTC 99. **d** 01 **p** 02. C Wickham Bishops w Lt Braxted *Chelmsf* from 01. *27 Dengie Close, Witham CM8 1DJ* Tel (01376) 514622 E-mail lizz@messages.co.uk

LAW, Gordon James. b 19. Worc Ord Coll 67. **d** 69 **p** 70. C Hillingdon St Jo *Lon* 69-72; C Brixham *Ex* 72-76; R Drewsteignton 76-79; V Hittisleigh 76-79; V Spreyton 76-79; C Aldershot St Mich *Guildf* 79-82; rtd 82; Perm to Offic *Ex* 83-89; *Ab* from 83; *Bris* 93-99. *69 Maunsell Way, Wroughton, Swindon SN4 9JF* Tel (01793) 812948

LAW, Gordon Peter. b 35. Bernard Gilpin Soc Dur 59 Chich Th Coll 60. **d** 64 **p** 65. C Walthamstow St Barn and St Jas Gt *Chelmsf* 64-67; C Southchurch H Trin 67-68; C Plaistow St Andr 68-69; Chapl Aldersbrook Medical Unit 69-83; P-in-c Forest Gate All SS 69-74; V 74-83; V Romford St Jo 83-97; rtd 97; Perm to Offic *Chelmsf* from 97. *40 Molram's Lane, Great Baddow, Chelmsford CM2 7AH* Tel (01245) 477272

LAW, Jeremy Stuart Alan. b 67. RMN93 Man Metrop Univ BSc96. Westcott Ho Cam. **d** 00 **p** 01. C Newton Heath *Man* 00-01; C Wythenshawe 01-04; P-in-c Lawton Moor from 04. *The Vicarage, Orton Road, Manchester M23 0LH* Tel 0161-998 2461 E-mail jeremylaw@ntlworld.com

LAW, Jeremy Thomson. b 61. Univ of Wales (Abth) BSc82 Southn Univ BTh89 Ox Univ DPhil00. Sarum & Wells Th Coll 84. **d** 87 **p** 88. C Wimborne Minster and Holt *Sarum* 87-90; C Highfield *Ox* 90-94; Chapl Ex Univ *Ex* 94-03; Dean of Chpl Cant Ch Ch Univ Coll from 03. *Canterbury Christ Church University College, North Holmes Road, Canterbury CT1 1QU* Tel (01227) 767700 E-mail jl89@cant.ac.uk

LAW, John Francis. b 35. Bps' Coll Cheshunt 65. **d** 67 **p** 68. C Styvechale *Cov* 67-71; P-in-c Cov St Anne and All SS 71-73; TV Cov E 73-77; P-in-c Fillongley 77-82; P-in-c Corley 77-82; V Fillongley and Corley 82-00; RD Nuneaton 90-95; rtd 00; Perm to Offic *Cov* from 00. *10 Brodick Way, Nuneaton CV10 7LH* Tel (024) 7632 5582

LAW, Canon John Michael. b 43. Open Univ BA79. Westcott Ho Cam 65. **d** 68 **p** 69. C Chapel Allerton *Ripon* 68-72; C Ryhope *Dur* 72-73; Chapl Fulbourn Hosp Cam 74-94; Chapl Ida Darwin Hosp Cam 74-98; Mental Health Chapl Cam Univ Hosps NHS Foundn Trust 94-04; Mental Health Fell Bethlem R and Maudsley Hosps 82; Hon Can Ely Cathl *Ely* from 04; rtd 04. *2 Suffolk Close, Ely CB6 3EW*

LAW, Nicholas Charles. b 58. Trin Coll Bris BA89. **d** 89 **p** 90. C Goldington *St Alb* 89-92; C Teignmouth, Ideford w Luton, Ashcombe etc *Ex* 92-97; R Bere Ferrers from 97. *The Rectory, Bere Alston, Yelverton PL20 7HH* Tel (01822) 840229 E-mail nicklaw@breathemail.net

LAW, Peter James. b 46. Ridley Hall Cam 85. **d** 87 **p** 88. C Bournemouth St Jo w St Mich *Win* 87-91; V Chineham 91-96; V Luton Lewsey St Hugh *St Alb* from 96. *St Hugh's Vicarage, 367 Leagrave High Street, Luton LU4 0ND* Tel (01582) 605297 *or* 664433 Fax 696332 E-mail peterlaw@sthughslewsey.fsnet.co.uk

LAW, Peter Leslie. b 25. Bede Coll Dur BA48 DipEd49. Qu Coll Birm 53. **d** 55 **p** 56. C Tooting All SS *S'wark* 55-57; C Frome St Jo *B & W* 57-59; V Battersea St Mary-le-Park *S'wark* 59-65; R Brampton Ash w Dingley *Pet* 65-69; Chapl St Luke's Sch Southsea 69-79; Chapl Portsm Cathl *Portsm* 69-79; V Eastney 79-90; rtd 90; Perm to Offic *Portsm* from 90. *123 Hayling Avenue, Portsmouth PO3 6DY* Tel (023) 9261 9913

LAW, Richard Anthony Kelway. b 57. UWIST BEng79. St Jo Coll Nottm MA(TS)01 99. **d** 01 **p** 02. C Brundall w Braydeston and Postwick *Nor* 01-04; V Hollingworth w Tintwistle *Ches* from 04. *The Vicarage, 10 Church Street, Tintwistle, Glossop SK13 1JR* Tel (01457) 852575 E-mail richardaklaw@tiscali.co.uk

LAW, Richard Lindsey. b 34. Univ Coll Ox BA58 MA63 St Pet Coll Birm GradDipEd70. Cuddesdon Coll 58. **d** 60 **p** 61. C Leighton Buzzard *St Alb* 60-63; Trinidad and Tobago 63-67; V Stottesdon *Heref* 67-72; P-in-c Farlow 67-72; Chapl Framlingham Coll 72-83; V Leigh-on-Sea St Marg *Chelmsf* 83-91; Warden Framlingham Ho of Prayer and Retreat 91-94; rtd 96. *20 Singleton Road, Broadbridge Heath, Horsham RH12 3NP* Tel (01403) 754737

LAW, Canon Robert Frederick. b 43. St Aid Birkenhead 67. **d** 69 **p** 70. C Bengeo *St Alb* 69-72; C Sandy 72-76; P-in-c St Ippolyts 76-81; Chapl Jersey Gp of Hosps 81-84; V Crowan w Godolphin *Truro* 84-92; RD Kerrier 90-91; R St Columb Major w St Wenn 92-02; RD Pydar 95-02; P-in-c St Minver from 02; Hon Can Truro Cathl from 98. *The Vicarage, Churchtown, St Minver, Wadebridge PL27 6QH* Tel and fax (01208) 862398 Mobile 078819-33024 E-mail robeva-2@tiscali.co.uk

LAW, Robert James. b 31. Lon Univ MB, BS55. Ridley Hall Cam 62. **d** 64 **p** 65. C Barnehurst *Roch* 64-66; C Edgware *Lon* 66-72; V Halwell w Moreleigh *Ex* 72-94; P-in-c Woodleigh and Loddiswell 76-79; R 79-94; rtd 96. *38 Wheatlands Road, Paignton TQ4 5HU* Tel (01803) 559450

LAW, Simon Anthony. b 55. Middx Univ BA93 DipHE79. NTMTC 94. **d** 96 **p** 97. NSM Forest Gate St Mark *Chelmsf* 96-98; C Becontree W 98-99; TV 99-02; TR from 02. *St Cedd's Vicarage, 185 Lodge Avenue, Dagenham RM8 2HQ* Tel (020) 8592 5900 E-mail law@fish.co.uk

LAW-JONES, Peter Deniston. b 55. Newc Univ BA77 Man Univ PGCE81 Nottm Univ BTh87. Linc Th Coll 84. **d** 87 **p** 88. C Chorley St Laur *Blackb* 87-91; V Feniscliffe 91-96; V St Annes St Thos from 96; Chapl Blackpool, Wyre and Fylde Community NHS Trust from 97. *The Vicarage, St Thomas Road, Lytham St Annes FY8 1JL* Tel (01253) 723750 E-mail peter@law-jones.fsnet.co.uk

LAWAL, Miss Basirat Adebanke Amope (Ade). b 67. Lon Bible Coll BTh02. St Alb and Ox Min Course 03. **d** 05. C Blurton *Lich* from 05. *St Alban's House, 51 Ripon Road, Stoke-on-Trent ST3 3BS* Tel (01782) 315029 E-mail ps25.bal@fsmail.net

LAWES, David Alan. b 33. Lon Bible Coll BD57 PGCE58 AcDipEd66 Lon Inst of Educn MA70. Cranmer Hall Dur 90. **d** 91 **p** 92. NSM Shaston *Sarum* 91-94; Hon C Diptford, N Huish, Harberton and Harbertonford *Ex* 94-98; rtd 98; Perm to Offic *Sarum* from 98. *47 Grosvenor Road, Shaftesbury SP7 8DP* Tel (01747) 855621

LAWES, Geoffrey Hyland. b 37. St Jo Coll Dur BA58 DipTh62 Hertf Coll Ox BA60 MA64 Newc Univ PGCE76 MEd79. Cranmer Hall Dur 61. **d** 63 **p** 64. C Millfield St Mark *Dur* 63-66; C Jarrow Grange 66-69; Hon C 69-86; Lic to Offic 86-90; V Collierley w Annfield Plain from 90. *Collierley Vicarage, Annfield Plain, Stanley DH9 8QS* Tel (01207) 236254

LAWES, Stephen George. b 40. Nottm Univ PGCE75. St Jo Coll Nottm BTh74. **d** 82 **p** 83. NSM Hillmorton *Cov* 82-86; NSM Daventry Deanery from 87. *Oak Tree Cottage, 34 Stowe Nine Churches, Northampton NN7 4SG* Tel (01327) 349167

LAWES, Timothy Stanley. b 57. Nottm Univ BTh88. Linc Th Coll 85. **d** 88 **p** 89. C Wymondham *Nor* 88-92; R Felmingham, Skeyton, Colby, Banningham etc 92-96; Sweden from 96; Asst V Byske from 98. *Bankgatan 5, 93047 Byske, Sweden* Tel (0046) (912) 10137

LAWLESS, Mrs Patricia Elizabeth. b 36. Bris Univ BA58 PGCE59 Lon Univ DipSocSc77. S Dios Minl Tr Scheme 91. **d** 93 **p** 94. NSM Frome Ch Ch *B & W* 93-95; NSM Mells w Buckland Dinham, Elm, Whatley etc 96; NSM Frome St Jo and St Mary 96-00; Chapl Victoria Hosp Frome 96-98; rtd 00; Perm to Offic *B & W* from 00. *22 Braithwaite Way, Frome BA11 2XG* Tel (01373) 466106

LAWLEY, Peter Gerald Fitch. b 52. Chich Th Coll 77. **d** 80 **p** 81. C Pet St Jo *Pet* 80-83; C Daventry 83-87; P-in-c Syresham w Whitfield 87-90; TV Cen Telford *Lich* 90-98; V Priors Lee and St Georges from 98. *The Vicarage, Ashley Road, Telford TF2 9LF* Tel and fax (01952) 612923 E-mail peterlawley@onetel.com

LAWLEY, Rosemary Ann. b 47. WMMTC 00. **d** 03 **p** 04. NSM Kinver and Enville *Lich* from 03. *White Hill Farm Cottage, White Hill, Kinver, Stourbridge DY7 6AS* Tel (01384) 873389 Mobile 07940-426399 E-mail rosemarylawley@tiscali.co.uk

LAWLOR, Colin Robert. b 63. Lanc Univ BA89 MPhil97 St Martin's Coll Lanc PGCE90. Chich Th Coll Dip Minl Th93. **d** 93 **p** 94. C Moulsecoomb *Chich* 93-97; TV 97-99; Chapl Brighton Univ from 99. *204 Bevendean Crescent, Brighton BN2 4RD* Tel 07802-580946 (mobile) E-mail cla4251245@aol.com

LAWRANCE, Hugh Norcliffe. b 49. N Riding Coll of Educn BEd79. Linc Th Coll 83. **d** 85 **p** 86. C Lindley *Wakef* 85-87; C Barkisland w W Scammonden 87-92; C Ripponden 87-92; V Knottingley 92-98; C Thorp Arch w Walton *York* 98-00; C Boston Spa 98-00; C Clifford 98-00; P-in-c Bramham from 00; P-in-c Clifford from 00. *The Vicarage, 19 Chapel Lane, Clifford, Wetherby LS23 6HU* Tel (01937) 849792 E-mail stmary's@bostonspa2.freeserve.co.uk

LAWRANCE, Robert William. b 63. Jes Coll Ox BA85 MA89. Ripon Coll Cuddesdon BA87. **d** 88 **p** 89. C Astley *Man* 88-91; Lect Bolton St Pet 91-94; V Bury St Jo w St Mark 94-00; Chapl Bury Healthcare NHS Trust 95-00; Dir of Ords *Dur* from 00; Chapl Hatf Coll Dur from 00. *20 Dickens Wynd, Durham DH1 3QR* Tel 0191-383 2035

LAWRENCE, Charles Anthony Edwin. b 53. AKC75. St Aug Coll Cant 75. **d** 76 **p** 77. C Mitcham St Mark *S'wark* 76-80; C Haslemere *Guildf* 80-82; P-in-c Ashton H Trin *Man* 82-84; V 84-93; V Saddleworth 93-97; AD Ashton-under-Lyne 91-97; V Effingham w Lt Bookham *Guildf* 97-05; Chapl Manor Ho Sch

97-05; R Shere, Albury and Chilworth *Guildf* from 05. *The Rectory, The Spinning Walk, Shere, Guildford GU5 9HN* Tel and fax (01483) 202394 E-mail sally@apostle.fsnet.co.uk

LAWRENCE, Christopher David. b 55. Wycliffe Hall Ox 01. **d** 03 **p** 04. C Wadhurst *Chich* from 03; C Tidebrook from 03; C Stonegate from 03. *The Vicarage, Bardown Road, Stonegate, Wadhurst TN5 7EJ* Tel (01580) 201855 Mobile 07941-557537 E-mail chris_d_lawrence@hotmail.com

LAWRENCE, Christopher David. b 73. Liv Jo Moores Univ BEd98. Ridley Hall Cam 03. **d** 05. C Letchworth St Paul w Willian *St Alb* from 05. *89 Howard Drive, Letchworth SG6 2BX* E-mail sclawrence@yahoo.co.uk

LAWRENCE, David Ian. b 48. AIMLS71 MIBiol76 Univ Coll Lon BSc74. Glouc Sch of Min 84 Sarum & Wells Th Coll 87. **d** 88 **p** 89. C Wotton St Mary *Glouc* 88-91; P-in-c Cheltenham St Mich 91-93; V from 93. *St Michael's Vicarage, 1 Severn Road, Cheltenham GL52 5QA* Tel (01242) 222644 E-mail dlawr15948@aol.com

LAWRENCE, Miss Helen. b 30. St Mich Ho Ox 62. **dss** 74 **d** 87 **p** 94. Braintree *Chelmsf* 74-87; Par Dn 87-90; rtd 90; Perm to Offic *Chelmsf* from 90. *6 Reynards Close, Kirby Cross, Frinton-on-Sea CO13 0RA* Tel (01255) 673837

LAWRENCE, Miss Ida Eugenia Laura. b 14. Open Univ BA81. Gilmore Ho 45. **dss** 78 **d** 87 **p** 94. Rayleigh *Chelmsf* 78-87; NSM 87-90; Perm to Offic from 90. *Dilkusha, Hardwick Close, Rayleigh SS6 7QP* Tel (01268) 773059

LAWRENCE, James Conrad. b 62. St Jo Coll Dur BA85. Ridley Hall Cam 85. **d** 87 **p** 88. Min Bar Hill LEP *Ely* 87-93; Deanery Adv in Evang 90-93; CPAS Evang 93-98; Perm to Offic *Cov* from 93; Springboard Missr from 97; CPAS Dir Evang Projects from 99. *236 Cubbington Road, Leamington Spa CV32 7AY* Tel (01926) 316368 *or* 334242 Fax 337613

LAWRENCE, Mrs Janet Maureen. b 43. Hockerill Teacher Tr Coll TCert64. Ox Min Course 89. **d** 92 **p** 94. Hon Par Dn Bletchley *Ox* 92-94; NSM N Bletchley CD 94-05; rtd 05. *20 The Elms, Bletchley, Milton Keynes MK3 6DB* Tel (01908) 377660

LAWRENCE, John Graham Clive. b 47. ACIB. Trin Coll Bris. **d** 78 **p** 79. C Chatham St Phil and St Jas *Roch* 78-83; V Roch St Justus 83-97; Asst Chapl HM Pris Roch 83-97; UK Dir CMJ 97-00; Internat Co-ord Light to the Nations UK from 00; Chapl Maidstone and Tunbridge Wells NHS Trust 03-04; Chapl W Kent NHS and Soc Care Trust from 05. *George Villa, Maidstone Hospital, Hermitage Lane, Maidstone ME16 9PH* Tel (01622) 723819 Mobile 07770-735698 E-mail john@lttn.fsnet.co.uk

LAWRENCE, John Shaw. b 27. WMMTC. **d** 81. NSM Birm St Martin *Birm* 81-85; Chapl Coun for Soc Aid 84-89; NSM Birm St Martin w Bordesley St Andr 85-89; rtd 89. *309 Grosvenor Court, 58 The Green, Kings Norton, Birmingham B38 8RU* Tel 0121-458 3853

LAWRENCE, Mrs Judith Patricia. b 53. DCR74 DMU80. WEMTC 01. **d** 04 **p** 05. C Glastonbury w Meare *B & W* from 04. *11 Higher Actis, Glastonbury BA6 8DR* Tel (01458) 834975 Mobile 07969-381488 E-mail lawrence@wedmore100.fsnet.co.uk

LAWRENCE, Canon Leonard Roy. b 31. Keble Coll Ox BA56 MA59. Westcott Ho Cam 56. **d** 58 **p** 59. C Stockport St Geo *Ches* 58-62; V Thelwall 62-68; V Hyde St Geo 68-75; V Prenton 75-96; Hon Can Ches Cathl 86-96; rtd 96; Perm to Offic *Ches* from 96; Acorn Chr Foundn from 97. *39 Mockbeggar Drive, Wallasey CH45 3NN* Tel 0151-346 9438

LAWRENCE, Leslie. b 44. Lon Univ DipRS84. S'wark Ord Course 86. **d** 88 **p** 89. NSM Stanwell *Lon* 88-92; C Hounslow H Trin w St Paul 92-97; P-in-c Norwood St Mary from 97. *The Rectory, 26 Tentelow Lane, Norwood Green, Southall UB2 4LE* Tel (020) 8574 1362 Fax 8606 9647 E-mail leslie.lawrence@tesco.net

LAWRENCE, Martin Kenneth. b 59. Univ Coll Dur BA82. St Steph Ho Ox 94. **d** 96 **p** 97. C Wanstead St Mary w Ch Ch *Chelmsf* 96-00; PV Westmr Abbey 99-00; Chapl Malta and Gozo *Eur* 00-01; C Becontree S *Chelmsf* 02; C Romford St Edw from 02. *54 Parkside Avenue, Romford RM1 4ND* Tel (01708) 727960 Mobile 07905-290849 E-mail martin@lawrence.net

LAWRENCE, Norman. b 45. Lon Univ BEd75. S'wark Ord Course 77. **d** 80 **p** 81. NSM Hounslow H Trin *Lon* 80-88; NSM Hounslow H Trin w St Paul from 88. *89 Bulstrode Avenue, Hounslow TW3 3AE* Tel (020) 8572 6292 E-mail nlawrence@lampton.hounslow.sch.uk

LAWRENCE, The Ven Patrick Henry Andrew. b 51. TCD Div Test 79 BA81. **d** 81 **p** 82. C Templemore *D & R* 81-84; C Kilkenny St Canice Cathl *C & O* 84-85; I Templebreedy w Tracton and Nohoval *C, C & R* 85-92; I Geashill w Killeigh and Ballycommon *M & K* 92-98; Can Kildare Cathl from 92; Adn Kildare from 93; Adn Meath from 97; Warden of Readers from 97; I Julianstown and Colpe w Drogheda and Duleek from 98; Preb Monmohenock St Patr Cathl Dublin from 00. *The Rectory, Julianstown, Co Meath, Irish Republic* Tel and fax (00353) (41) 982 9883 E-mail archdeacon@meath.anglican.org

LAWRENCE, Canon Peter Anthony. b 36. Lich Th Coll 67. **d** 69 **p** 70. C Oadby *Leic* 69-74; P-in-c Northmarston and Granborough *Ox* 74-81; P-in-c Hardwick St Mary 74-81; P-in-c Quainton 76-81; P-in-c Oving w Pitchcott 76-81; TR Schorne 81-91; RD Claydon 84-88; V Ivinghoe w Pitstone and Slapton 91-97; Hon Can Ch Ch 97; rtd 97; Perm to Offic *Ox* from 99 and *Worc* from 01. *Hill House, Back Lane, Malvern WR14 2HJ* Tel (01684) 564075

LAWRENCE, Peter Halliday. b 47. ALCM K Alfred's Coll Win CertEd69 Nottm Univ BTh76. St Jo Coll Nottm 72. **d** 76 **p** 77. C Birm St Luke *Birm* 76-79; V Burney Lane 79-93; TV Canford Magna *Sarum* 93-95; TR from 95; RD Wimborne 00-04. *The Rectory, Canford Magna, Wimborne BH21 3AF* Tel (01202) 883382 E-mail pandclawrence@clara.co.uk

LAWRENCE, Ralph Guy. b 55. Trin Coll Bris DipHE89. **d** 89 **p** 90. C Cotmanhay *Derby* 89-93; P-in-c Tansley, Dethick, Lea and Holloway 93-04; R Ashover and Brackenfield w Wessington from 04. *The Rectory, Narrowleys Lane, Ashover, Chesterfield S45 0AU* Tel (01246) 590246 E-mail ralph.lawrence@lineone.net

LAWRENCE, Roy. *See* LAWRENCE, Canon Leonard Roy

LAWRENCE, Simon Peter. b 60. TD VRSM. Nottm Univ BTh88 MA97 Indiana State Univ DMin01. St Jo Coll Nottm 85. **d** 88 **p** 89. C Holbeach *Linc* 88-90; C Alford w Rigsby 90-91; R Rattlesden w Thorpe Morieux and Brettenham *St E* 91-93; V Churchdown *Glouc* 93; V Maenclochog w Henry's Moat and Mynachlogddu etc *St D* 93-94; R Overstrand, Northrepps, Sidestrand etc *Nor* 95-98; CF (TA) 89-05; CF (ACF) 90-05; rtd 98; Perm to Offic *Nor* from 02. *14 Broadgate, Taverham, Norwich NR8 6GH* Tel (01603) 864775 E-mail silvpug@aol.com

LAWRENCE, Timothy Hervey. b 25. Ripon Hall Ox 58. **d** 60 **p** 61. C Newmarket All SS *St E* 60-62; V Kentford w Higham Green 62-84; P-in-c Herringswell 78-84; rtd 84. *13 South Street, Risby, Bury St Edmunds IP28 6QU* Tel (01284) 810083

LAWRENCE (née FOREMAN), Mrs Vanessa Jane. b 73. Ch Ch Coll Cant BA95. Westcott Ho Cam. **d** 00 **p** 01. C N Stoneham *Win* 00-04; NSM Swaythling from 04. *17 St Denys Road, Southampton SO17 2GN* Tel (023) 8058 3655 E-mail vanessalawrence@waitrose.com

LAWRENCE, Victor John. b 43. ACII. Oak Hill Th Coll. **d** 83 **p** 84. C Paddock Wood *Roch* 83-87; R Milton next Gravesend w Denton from 87; RD Gravesend from 05. *The Rectory, Church Walk, Milton Road, Gravesend DA12 2QU* Tel (01474) 533434

LAWRENCE-MARCH, David Lawrence. b 61. Univ of Wales (Lamp) BA83. Coll of Resurr Mirfield 83. **d** 85 **p** 86. C Pet St Jude *Pet* 85-89; Chapl St Aug Sch Kilburn 89-92; C Kilburn St Aug w St Jo *Lon* 89-90; C Paddington St Mary 90-92; Chapl Bearwood Coll Wokingham 92-96; R Holt w High Kelling *Nor* 96-98; Sen Chapl Bedford Sch from 98; Perm to Offic *Pet* from 98. *Bedford School, De Parys Avenue, Bedford MK40 2TU* Tel (01234) 326488 E-mail dl-march@bedfordschool.beds.sch.uk

LAWRENSON, Michael. b 35. Leeds Univ BA60 Liv Univ CertSS65 Newc Univ DASS69. Coll of Resurr Mirfield 60. **d** 74 **p** 74. NSM Glenrothes *St And* 74-90; Dioc Supernumerary 90-95; Chapl HM Pris Perth 91-95; NSM Glenrothes *St And* 95-00; NSM Leven 95-00; NSM Lochgelly 95-00; NSM St Andrews St Andr 95-00; rtd 00. *Hollyburn, West Port, Falkland, Cupar KY15 7BW* Tel (01337) 857311 E-mail mlawrenson@compuserve.com *or* michaellawrenson@aol.com

LAWRENSON, Ronald David. b 41. CITC 68. **d** 71 **p** 72. C Seapatrick *D & D* 71-78; Min Can Down Cathl 78-79; V Choral Belf Cathl 79-86; Bp's C Tynan w Middletown *Arm* 86-93; Hon V Choral Arm Cathl 87-02; Bp's C Tynan w Middletown 92-93; I Donaghmore w Upper Donaghmore 93-98; rtd 02. *Riverbrook Apartments, 9A Brooklands Drive, Whitehead, Carrickfergus BT38 9SL* Tel (028) 9337 3625

LAWRIE, Paul Edward. b 12. Freiburg Univ LLD35 St Cath Soc Ox BA48 MA53. Wycliffe Hall Ox 46. **d** 48 **p** 49. C Walkley *Sheff* 48-51; C Thrybergh 51-54; V Drax 54-64; R Todwick 64-78; rtd 78; Chapl Rotherham Distr Gen Hosp 78-85; Hon C Handsworth Woodhouse *Sheff* 85-88; Hon C Aston cum Aughton w Swallownest, Todwick etc 88-92; Perm to Offic from 92. *15 Haddon Way, Aston, Sheffield S26 2EH* Tel 0114-287 4864

LAWRIE, Peter Sinclair. b 39. Clifton Th Coll 62. **d** 65 **p** 66. C Derby St Chad *Derby* 65-68; C Toxteth Park St Philemon w St Silas *Liv* 68-71; V Ramsey St Mary's w Ponds Bridge *Ely* 71-81; V Whitwick St Jo the Bapt *Leic* 81-96; P-in-c Felixstowe SS Pet and Paul *St E* 96-03; rtd 03. *71 Lincroft, Oakley, Bedford MK43 7SS* E-mail p.lawrie@talk21.com

LAWRINSON, Leslie Norman. b 35. IEng MIPD90 MCMI84. **d** 99 **p** 00. OLM Onchan *S & M* 99-05; NSM Scarisbrick *Liv* from 05. *Address temp unknown* Tel 07624-491980 (mobile) E-mail leslaw@mcb.net

LAWRY, Mrs Fianach Alice Moir. b 35. St And Dioc Tr Course 85. **d** 88 **p** 94. NSM Dollar *St And* from 88; Chapl HM Pris Glenochil from 91. *Sunnybank, Muckhart, Dollar FK14 7JN* Tel (01259) 781426

LAWRY, Richard Henry. b 57. Bris Univ BA79 Wolfs Coll Cam PGCE81. St Jo Coll Nottm MA01. **d** 99 **p** 00. C Macclesfield

Team Par *Ches* 99-02; P-in-c Stalybridge St Paul from 02. *St Paul's Vicarage, Huddersfield Road, Stalybridge SK15 2PT* Tel 0161-338 2514 E-mail richardlawry@talk21.com

LAWS, Clive Loudon. b 54. UEA BEd76 Leeds Univ CertEd75. Wycliffe Hall Ox 79. **d** 82 **p** 83. C Newcastle w Butterton *Lich* 82-85; C Gabalfa *Llan* 85-88; R Pendine w Llanmiloe and Eglwys Gymyn w Marros *St D* 89-94; CF 89-94; Perm to Offic *B & W* 95-96; C Portishead 96-02; TV from 02. *24 St Mary's Park Road, Portishead, Bristol BS20 6SL* Tel (01275) 848934

LAWS, Edwin Kingsley. b 06. LVO53 KPM39. Bps' Coll Cheshunt 56. **d** 57 **p** 58. C Shaftesbury H Trin w St Pet *Sarum* 57-60; R Winterborne Whitechurch w Clenston 60-72; R Milton Abbas w Winterborne Whitechurch etc 72-74; RD Milton 66-73; Custos St Jo Hosp Heytesbury 74-79; rtd 79; Perm to Offic *B & W* 79-97. *6 Abbeyfield, 58 Bath Road, Wells BA5 3LQ* Tel (01749) 679949

LAWSON, Canon Alma Felicity. b 51. St Hugh's Coll Ox BA73 MA78. St Jo Coll Nottm DPS74. **d** 98 **p** 99. Dean of Min and Dir of Ords *Wakef* 93-00; Hon C Wakef Cathl 98-00; V Gildersome from 00; Hon Can Wakef Cathl from 01. *St Peter's House, 2A Church Street, Gildersome, Morley, Leeds LS27 7AF* Tel and fax 0113-253 3339 E-mail felicity@lawson99.fsnet.co.uk

LAWSON, Anne. *See* LAWSON, Miss Sarah Anne

LAWSON, David McKenzie. b 47. Glas Univ MA69 Edin Univ BD76. Edin Th Coll 73. **d** 76 **p** 77. C Glas St Mary *Glas* 76-82; V Keighley All SS *Bradf* 82-85; Chapl Asst Univ Coll Hosp Lon 85-91; Hon C St Pancras w St Jas and Ch Ch *Lon* 86-91; R Smithfield St Bart Gt 91-93; Hon C Paddington St Jas 94-00; TV Chambersbury *St Alb* 00-03; TR from 03. *St Mary's Vicarage, 7 Belswains Lane, Hemel Hempstead HP3 9PN* Tel (01442) 261610 Mobile 07939-473717 E-mail davidmlawson@lineone.net

LAWSON, David William. b 50. ACA. Linc Th Coll. **d** 82 **p** 83. C Stafford *Lich* 82-85; TV Redruth w Lanner *Truro* 85-87; P-in-c Whitley *Cov* 87-93; Chapl Whitley Hosp Cov 87-94; Chapl Gulson Road Hosp Cov 87-94; Chapl Cov and Warks Hosp 87-94; V S Leamington St Jo *Cov* from 93. *St John's Vicarage, Tachbrook Street, Leamington Spa CV31 3BN* Tel (01926) 422208

LAWSON, Felicity. *See* LAWSON, Canon Alma Felicity

LAWSON, The Very Revd Frederick Quinney (Rick). b 45. Leic Univ BA. St Steph Ho Ox. **d** 83 **p** 84. Hon C Loughborough Em *Leic* 83-86; NSM Somerby, Burrough on the Hill and Pickwell 86-87; NSM Burrough Hill Pars 87; USA from 87; Hon Can Salt Lake City 87-02; Dean from 02. *4294 Adonis Drive, Salt Lake City, UT 84124, USA* Tel (001) (801) 595 5380 *or* 277 9623 Fax 278 5903 E-mail rql@xmission.com

LAWSON, Gary Austin. b 53. Man Univ BA80. Ripon Coll Cuddesdon 80. **d** 82 **p** 83. C Nunhead St Antony *S'wark* 82-86; Hon C Reddish *Man* 86-87; Hon C Longsight St Jo w St Cypr 87-88; V Wythenshawe St Rich 88-98; Chapl Bolton Inst of F&HE 98-03; C Bolton St Pet 98-03; TR Westhoughton and Wingates from 03. *The Rectory, Market Street, Westhoughton, Bolton BL5 3AZ* Tel (01942) 859251

LAWSON, James Barry. b 68. Edin Univ MA91 New Coll Ox DPhil96. Coll of Resurr Mirfield 98. **d** 99 **p** 00. C Poplar *Lon* 99-02; Chapl CCC Cam from 02. *Corpus Christi College, Trumpington Street, Cambridge CB2 1RH* Tel and fax (01223) 338002 E-mail jbl24@cam.ac.uk

LAWSON, John Alexander. b 62. Sheff Univ BA84 Nottm Univ MA97. St Jo Coll Nottm DPS87. **d** 87 **p** 88. C Wellington, All SS w Eyton *Lich* 87-92; TV Dewsbury *Wakef* 92-98; P-in-c Birchencliffe from 98; Dioc Vocations Adv and Asst Dir of Ords from 02. *St Philip's Vicarage, 38 Holly Grove, Lindley, Huddersfield HD3 3NS* Tel (01484) 531667 Fax 518482 E-mail jal@bh-cc.co.uk

LAWSON, Jonathan Halford. b 68. St Chad's Coll Dur BA90 Heythrop Coll Lon MA04. Westcott Ho Cam 91. **d** 93 **p** 94. C Sedgefield *Dur* 93-96; C Usworth 96-97; TV 97-00; TV Epping Distr *Chelmsf* 00-04; Chapl St Hild and St Bede Coll *Dur* from 04. *The College of St Hild and St Bede, St Hild's Lane, Durham DH1 1SZ* Tel 0191-334 8522 Fax 334 8501 E-mail j.h.lawson@durham.ac.uk

LAWSON, June Margaret. b 62. Birm Univ BA83 Didsbury Coll of Educn PGCE84 St Jo Coll York MA02. N Ord Course 00. **d** 02 **p** 03. C Huddersfield H Trin *Wakef* from 02. *St Philip's Vicarage, 38 Holly Grove, Lindley, Huddersfield HD3 3NS* Tel (01484) 531667 Fax 518482 E-mail jml@bh-cc.co.uk

LAWSON, Matthew James. b 67. St Andr Univ MTheol91 FRSA02. Ripon Coll Cuddesdon MTh94. **d** 94 **p** 95. C Bedford St Andr *St Alb* 94-97; Chapl and Hd RS St Jo Sch Leatherhead from 97; Tutor Dioc Min Course *Guildf* from 98. *The Chaplain's House, 4 Linden Pit Path, Leatherhead KT22 7JD* Tel (01372) 361665 Mobile 07768-515950 Fax (01372) 386606 E-mail frlawson@aol.com

LAWSON, The Ven Michael Charles. b 52. Sussex Univ BA75. Trin Coll Bris 75. **d** 78 **p** 79. C Horsham *Chich* 78-81; C St Marylebone All So w SS Pet and Jo *Lon* 81-87; V Bromley Ch Ch *Roch* 87-99; Adn Hampstead *Lon* from 99. *London Diocesan House, 36 Causton Street, London SW1P 4AU* Tel (020) 7932 1190 Fax 7932 1192 E-mail archdeacon.hampstead@london.anglican.org

LAWSON, Rick. *See* LAWSON, The Very Revd Frederick Quinney

LAWSON, Russell Thomas. b 70. Leeds Univ BA92 Ox Univ BTh98. St Steph Ho Ox 98. **d** 98 **p** 99. C Cheshunt *St Alb* 98-02; C Cheam *S'wark* from 02. *4 Tudor Close, Cheam, Sutton SM3 8QS* Tel (020) 8641 7911

LAWSON, Miss Sarah Anne. b 66. Ches Coll of HE BA87. Ridley Hall Cam. **d** 00 **p** 01. C Hollingworth w Tintwistle *Ches* 00-05; V Haslington w Crewe Green from 05. *The Vicarage, 163 Crewe Road, Haslington, Crewe CW1 5RL* Tel (01270) 582388 E-mail revanne@lawson66.fsnet.co.uk

LAWSON-JONES, Christopher Mark. b 68. Open Univ BA98. St Mich Coll Llan 98. **d** 00 **p** 01. C Risca *Mon* 00-03; Chapl Cross Keys Campus Coleg Gwent 00-03; TV Cyncoed from 03. *40 Felbrigg Crescent, Pontprennau, Cardiff CF23 8SE* Tel (029) 2054 9795 E-mail mark@lawson-jones.freeserve.co.uk

LAWTON, David Andrew. b 62. Man Univ BA83. Cranmer Hall Dur. **d** 00 **p** 01. C Deptford St Jo w H Trin *S'wark* 00-04; TV Walton H Trin *Ox* from 04. *60 Grenville Road, Aylesbury HP21 8EY* Tel (01296) 424175 Mobile 07799-713358 E-mail revdave15@aol.com

LAXON, Colin John. b 44. Cant Sch of Min 86. **d** 89 **p** 90. C Folkestone St Mary and St Eanswythe *Cant* 89-94; P-in-c Barrow St Jas *Carl* 94-01; Soc Resp Officer from 01; C Brampton and Farlam and Castle Carrock w Cumrew 01-02; TV Eden, Gelt and Irthing from 02. *The Rectory, Castle Carrock, Brampton CA8 9LZ* Tel (01228) 670745 E-mail sro@carlislediocese.org.uk

LAY, Brian Robert. b 37. Bernard Gilpin Soc Dur 59 Chich Th Coll 60. **d** 63 **p** 64. C Battyeford *Wakef* 63-66; C Belhus Park *Chelmsf* 66-73; P-in-c Sutton on Plym *Ex* 73-80; V from 80. *St John's Vicarage, 3 Alma Street, Plymouth PL4 0NL* Tel (01752) 664191

LAY, Geoffrey Arthur. b 54. Leic Poly BA77 Man Univ MA83 Lon Univ BD88. Ridley Hall Cam CTM92. **d** 92 **p** 93. C St Neots *Ely* 92-95; P-in-c Long Stanton w St Mich 95-01; P-in-c Dry Drayton 95-97; R Chailey *Chich* from 01; Chapl Chailey Heritage Hosp Lewes from 01. *Chailey Rectory, Chailey Green, Lewes BN8 4DA* Tel (01825) 722286 E-mail geofflay@ntlworld.com

LAYBOURNE, Michael Frederick. b 37. Qu Coll Birm 81. **d** 83 **p** 84. C High Elswick St Phil *Newc* 83-85; C High Elswick St Phil and Newc St Aug 86; C Cramlington 86-87; TV 87-95; C Killingworth 95-02; rtd 02; Perm to Offic *Newc* from 02. *16 Rockcliffe Gardens, Whitley Bay NE26 2NL* Tel 0191-251 0115 E-mail mikelaybourne@waitrose.com

LAYCOCK, Charles. b 37. Open Univ BA88. N Ord Course 80. **d** 83 **p** 84. C Astley Bridge *Man* 83-86; R Crumpsall 86-94; V Ashton Ch Ch 94-00; rtd 00. *23 The Mere, Ashton-under-Lyne OL6 9NH* Tel 0161-330 2824

LAYCOCK, Lawrence. b 42. St Deiniol's Hawarden 86. **d** 89 **p** 90. C Blackpool St Mich *Blackb* 89-94; P-in-c Worsthorne 94-99; P-in-c Holme 96-99; V Holme-in-Cliviger w Worsthorne from 99; AD Burnley from 04. *The Vicarage, Gorple Road, Worsthorne, Burnley BB10 3NN* Tel (01282) 428478 *or* 453728

LAYNESMITH, Mark David. b 74. York Univ BA97 MA99. Ripon Coll Cuddesdon BA01. **d** 02 **p** 03. C Tadcaster w Newton Kyme *York* from 02. *3 Heatherdene, Tadcaster LS24 8EZ* Tel (01937) 830041 E-mail marklaynesmith@fish.co.uk

LAYTON, Miss Norene. b 39. Trin Coll Bris 84. **dss** 86 **d** 87 **p** 94. Lindfield *Chich* 86-92; Par Dn 87-92; Par Dn Loughborough Em *Leic* 92-94; C Loughborough Em and St Mary in Charnwood 94-96; V Hengrove *Bris* 96-04; rtd 04. *104 Outwoods Drive, Loughborough LE11 3LU* Tel (01509) 218127

LE BAS, Ms Jennifer Anne. b 60. Hull Univ BSc81. S Dios Minl Tr Scheme 90. **d** 93 **p** 94. C Alverstoke *Portsm* 93-96; C Elson 97-01; P-in-c Gosport Ch Ch and Dioc FE Officer 01-04; Perm to Offic *Roch* from 05. *2 Little Wood, Sevenoaks TN13 3RL* Tel (01732) 457469 E-mail annelebas@dsl.pipex.com

LE BILLON, Mrs Janet. b 42. STETS 99. **d** 02 **p** 03. NSM Guernsey St Jo *Win* from 02; Chapl States of Guernsey Bd of Health from 02. *Tranquillité, Clos des Quatre Vents, St Martin, Guernsey GY4 6SU* Tel (01481) 234283

LE CRAS, Allan. b 20. Linc Th Coll LTh84. **d** 84 **p** 85. Hon C Toynton All Saints w Toynton St Peter *Linc* 84-88; Hon C Marden Hill Gp 88-90; Perm to Offic 90-01. *Snipe Dales Cottage, Lusby, Spilsby PE23 4JB* Tel (01507) 588636

LE DIEU, Miss Heather Muriel. b 41. Birm Univ BA62 MA67 DipTh. St Jo Coll Dur 77. **dss** 79 **d** 87. Birchfield *Birm* 79-82; Kings Heath 82-84; Walsall Pleck and Bescot *Lich* 84-88; Par Dn 87-88; rtd 88. *159 Swarthmore Road, Selly Oak, Birmingham B29 4NW* Tel 0121-475 1236

LE GRICE, Elizabeth Margaret. b 53. Man Univ BA75 MA(Theol)78. Nor Bapt Coll 75 Westcott Ho Cam 87. **d** 88 **p** 97. In Bapt Ch 78-82; C Whitchurch *Llan* 88-95; Chapl among the Deaf SE Wales *Mon* from 95; Lic to Offic from 95. *9 Hawarden Road, Newport NP19 8JP*

LE GRYS, Alan Arthur. b 51. K Coll Lon BD73 AKC73 MTh90. St Aug Coll Cant 73. **d** 74 **p** 75. C Harpenden St Jo *St Alb* 74-77; C Hampstead St Jo *Lon* 77-81; Chapl Westf Coll and Bedf Coll 81-84; V Stoneleigh *Guildf* 84-91; Lect Ripon Coll Cuddesdon 91-96; Prin SEITE from 96; Hon PV Roch Cathl *Roch* from 96. *21 Grizedale Close, Rochester ME1 2UX* Tel (01634) 402678 *or* 832299 Fax 819347 Mobile 07958-547053 E-mail principal@seite.fsnet.co.uk

LE ROSSIGNOL, Richard Lewis. b 52. Aston Univ BSc75. Oak Hill Th Coll BA79. **d** 79 **p** 80. C E Ham St Paul *Chelmsf* 79-81; C Willesborough w Hinxhill *Cant* 81-85; Perm to Offic 85-94; NSM Brabourne w Smeeth 94-01; NSM Mersham w Hinxhill and Sellindge from 01. *64 Osborne Road, Willesborough, Ashford TN24 0EF* Tel (01233) 625193 E-mail richard@lerossi.fsnet.co.uk

LE SÈVE, Mrs Jane Hilary. b 63. SS Hild & Bede Coll Dur BA86. EAMTC 01. **d** 04 **p** 05. NSM Brightlingsea *Chelmsf* from 04. *4 Deal Way, Colchester CO7 0RR* Tel (01206) 305787 E-mail johnhilarylesève@yahoo.co.uk

LE SUEUR, Paul John. b 38. Lon Univ BSc59. Wycliffe Hall Ox 60. **d** 62 **p** 63. C Mortlake w E Sheen *S'wark* 62-65; C Witney *Ox* 65-69; R Sarsden w Churchill 69-74; P-in-c Clifton Hampden 74-77; P-in-c Rotherfield Greys H Trin 77-82; V 82-90; V Blacklands Hastings Ch Ch and St Andr *Chich* 90-97; V Ticehurst and Flimwell 97-00; rtd 00; Perm to Offic *Chich* from 01. *80 Barnhorn Road, Bexhill-on-Sea TN39 4QA* Tel (01424) 844747 E-mail halomanpaul@talk21.com

LE VASSEUR, Mrs Linda Susan. b 48. Shenstone Coll of Educn CertEd70. S Dios Minl Tr Scheme 92. **d** 95 **p** 96. NSM Guernsey Ste Marie du Castel *Win* 95-01; NSM Guernsey St Matt 95-01; NSM Guernsey St Sav from 01; NSM Guernsey St Marguerite de la Foret from 01. *Coin des Arquets, Les Arquets, St Pierre du Bois, Guernsey GY7 9HE* Tel (01481) 264047

LE VAY, Clare Forbes Agard Bramhall Joanna. b 41. St Anne's Coll Ox BA64 MA66 Univ of Wales (Abth) MSc72 PhD86. Westcott Ho Cam 86. **d** 88 **p** 94. C Stamford Hill St Thos *Lon* 88-89; C Hackney 89-92; Asst Chapl Brook Gen Hosp Lon 92-95; Asst Chapl Greenwich Distr Hosp Lon 92-95; Chapl Greenwich Healthcare NHS Trust 95-01; Perm to Offic *S'wark* from 02. *91 Mildenhall Road, London E5 0RY* Tel (020) 8985 3150 E-mail clarelevay@yahoo.com

LE-WORTHY, Michael Raymond. b 50. LNSM course 97. **d** 98 **p** 99. OLM Glascote and Stonydelph *Lich* from 98. *15 Abbey Road, Glascote, Tamworth B77 2QE* Tel (01827) 55762

LEA, Carolyn Jane. *See* COOKE, Mrs Carolyn Jane

LEA, His Honour Christopher Gerald. b 17. MC. RMC Called to the Bar (Inner Temple) 48. Ox Min Course 91. **d** 92 **p** 93. NSM Stratfield Mortimer *Ox* 92-99; NSM Stratfield Mortimer and Mortimer W End etc from 99. *Simms Farm House, Simms Lane, Mortimer, Reading RG7 2JP* Tel 0118-933 2360

LEA, Canon Montague Brian. b 34. OBE00. St Jo Coll Cam BA55 Lon Univ BD71. St Jo Coll Nottm 68. **d** 71 **p** 72. C Northwood Em *Lon* 71-74; Chapl Barcelona *Eur* 74-79; V Hove Bp Hannington Memorial Ch *Chich* 79-86; Adn N France *Eur* 86-94; Chapl Paris St Mich 86-94; Hon Can Gib Cathl from 95; R Chiddingly w E Hoathly *Chich* 94-96; Chapl The Hague *Eur* 96-00; rtd 01; Perm to Offic *Chich* from 01. *35 Summerdown Lane, East Dean, Eastbourne BN20 0LE* Tel (01323) 423226 E-mail brian.lea@freedom255.co.uk

LEA, Norman. b 42. JP89. Univ of Wales (Lamp) BA67. Coll of Resurr Mirfield 66. **d** 68 **p** 69. C Newton St Pet *S & B* 68-71; C Oystermouth 71-73; C Brecon w Battle 73-74; TV Cwmbran *Mon* 74-77; V Talgarth and Llanelieu *S & B* 77-84; V Port Talbot St Theodore *Llan* 84-95; Hon Chapl Miss to Seafarers from 84; V Cadoxton-juxta-Neath *Llan* from 95; P-in-c Tonna from 04. *St Cattwg's Vicarage, Main Road, Cadoxton, Neath SA10 8AS* Tel (01639) 795199

LEA, Canon Richard John Rutland. b 40. Trin Hall Cam BA63 MA67. Westcott Ho Cam 63. **d** 65 **p** 66. C Edenbridge *Roch* 65-68; C Hayes 68-71; V Larkfield 71-86; P-in-c Leybourne 76-86; RD Malling 79-84; V Chatham St Steph 86-88; Can Res and Prec Roch Cathl 88-98; V Iffley *Ox* from 98. *The Rectory, Mill Lane, Iffley, Oxford OX4 4EJ* Tel (01865) 773516 E-mail richard.lea@lineone.net

LEACH, Alan Charles Graham. b 46. Univ Coll Ches BTh04 Master Mariner 73. N Ord Course 04. **d** 05. NSM Neston *Ches* from 05. *8 Hill Top Lane, Ness, Neston CH64 4EL* Tel 0151-336 5046 Mobile 07802-622143 E-mail alan.leach5@btinternet.com

LEACH, Alan William Brickett. b 28. MSc CEng FIStructE FASI FICE. S'wark Ord Course. **d** 89 **p** 90. NSM Forest Row *Chich* 89-98; Perm to Offic from 98. *Hathaway, Ashdown Road, Forest Row RH18 5BN* Tel (01342) 823778

LEACH, Miss Bethia Morag. b 62. Sheff Univ BA84 Liv Inst of Educn PGCE85. Ripon Coll Cuddesdon 95. **d** 97 **p** 98. C Stafford *Lich* 97-00; TV Bilston from 00. *St Mary's Vicarage, 43 Willenhall Road, Bilston, Wolverhampton WV14 6NW* Tel (01902) 490255

LEACH, Gerald. b 27. Sarum & Wells Th Coll 85. **d** 73 **p** 74. NSM Cyncoed *Mon* 73-86; C 86-87; V Dingestow and Llangovan w Penyclawdd etc 87-94; rtd 94; Perm to Offic *Heref* from 95; Lic to Offic *Mon* from 98. *19 Grange Park, Whitchurch, Ross-on-Wye HR9 6EA* Tel (01600) 890397

LEACH, James Roger. b 66. Ball Coll Ox BA89 MA99. Wycliffe Hall Ox BA98. **d** 99 **p** 00. C Knowle *Birm* from 99. *49 Newton Road, Knowle, Solihull B93 9HN* Tel (01564) 779783 E-mail james@jrleach.freeserve.co.uk

LEACH, John. b 52. K Coll Lon BD79 AKC79 St Jo Coll Dur MA. **d** 81 **p** 82. C N Walsham w Antingham *Nor* 81-85; C Crookes St Thos *Sheff* 85-89; V Styvechale *Cov* 89-97; Dir Angl Renewal Min 97-04; Par Development Adv *Mon* from 04. *44 Oakfield Road, Newport NP20 4LP*

LEACH, Robert Neville. b 54. Trin Coll Bris DipHE93. **d** 93 **p** 94. C Towcester w Easton Neston *Pet* 93-96; P-in-c Cowley *Lon* 96-01; P-in-c Brandon and Santon Downham w Elveden *St E* 01-04; P-in-c Lakenheath 02-04; R Brandon and Santon Downham w Elveden etc from 04. *The Rectory, 40 London Road, Brandon IP27 0HY* Tel (01842) 811907

LEACH, Stephen Lance. b 42. St Steph Ho Ox 66. **d** 69 **p** 70. C Higham Ferrers w Chelveston *Pet* 69-72; TV Ilfracombe H Trin *Ex* 72-74; V Barnstaple St Mary 74-77; R Goodleigh 74-77; P-in-c Barnstaple St Pet w H Trin 76-77; P-in-c Landkey 77-79; TR Barnstaple and Goodleigh 77-79; TR Barnstaple, Goodleigh and Landkey 79-82; V Paignton St Jo 82-95; Gen Sec ACS from 95; Public Preacher *Birm* from 95. *Gordon Browning House, 8 Spitfire Road, Birmingham B24 9PB* Tel 0121-382 5533 *or* 354 9885 Fax 382 6999 E-mail acsb24@aol.com

LEACH, Stephen Windsor. b 47. St Chad's Coll Dur BSc70 Linacre Coll Ox BA72 MA76. Ripon Hall Ox 70. **d** 73 **p** 74. C Swinton St Pet *Man* 73-77; C Oldham St Chad Limeside 77-79; V Shaw 79-87; V St Just in Penwith *Truro* from 87; V Sancreed from 87. *The Vicarage, St Just, Penzance TR19 7UB* Tel (01736) 788672

LEACH, Timothy Edmund. b 41. Dur Univ BA63. Ridley Hall Cam 63. **d** 65 **p** 66. C Ecclesfield *Sheff* 65-68; C Stocksbridge 68-71; C-in-c W Bessacarr CD 71-80; V Goole 80-95; Hon Chapl Miss to Seamen 80-95; V Wath-upon-Dearne *Sheff* from 95. *The Vicarage, Church Street, Wath-upon-Dearne, Rotherham S63 7RD* Tel (01709) 872299 E-mail comedy@tinyonline.co.uk

LEADBEATER, Canon Nicolas James. b 20. Univ of Wales BA43 LLM95. St Steph Ho Ox 43. **d** 45 **p** 46. C Abergavenny H Trin *Mon* 45-47; C Coleford w Staunton *Glouc* 47-55; PC Moreton Valence and V Whitminster 55-67; V Westcote 67-72; P-in-c Icomb 67-72; V Westcote w Icomb 72-79; V Westcote w Icomb and Bledington 79-88; Hon Can Glouc Cathl 83-88; rtd 88; Perm to Offic *Glouc* from 88. *39 Park Farm, Bourton-on-the-Water, Cheltenham GL54 2HF* Tel (01451) 810192

LEADER, Miss Janette Patricia. b 46. Cam Coll of Art and Tech DipHCM66. EAMTC 94. **d** 97 **p** 98. C Desborough, Brampton Ash, Dingley and Braybrooke *Pet* 97-01; V Wellingborough St Barn from 01. *St Barnabas' Vicarage, St Barnabas Street, Wellingborough NN8 3HB* Tel (01933) 226337 Fax as telephone E-mail revdjan@aol.com

LEADER, Stephen. b 64. City Univ DipN97. Ripon Coll Cuddesdon 99. **d** 01 **p** 02. C Battersea St Luke *S'wark* 01-04; V Enfield St Jas *Lon* from 04. *St James's Vicarage, 144 Hertford Road, Enfield EN3 5AY* Tel (020) 7640 9932 E-mail therevstelea@waitrose.com

LEAF, Edward David Hugh. b 65. Oak Hill Th Coll BA97. **d** 98 **p** 99. C Bath St Bart *B & W* 98-01; C Minehead from 01. *75 Summerland Avenue, Minehead TA24 5BW* Tel (01643) 706882 E-mail dave@dleaf.fslife.co.uk

LEAH, William Albert. b 34. K Coll Lon BA56 AKC57 K Coll Cam MA63. Ripon Hall Ox 60. **d** 62 **p** 63. C Falmouth K Chas *Truro* 62-63; Chapl K Coll Cam 63-67; Min Can Westmr Abbey 67-74; V Hawkhurst *Cant* 74-83; Hon Min Can Cant Cathl 78-83; V St Ives *Truro* 83-94; rtd 98. *Trerice Cottage, Sancreed Newbridge, Penzance TR20 8QR* Tel (01736) 810987

LEAHY, David Adrian. b 56. Open Univ BA90. Qu Coll Birm. **d** 85 **p** 86. C Tile Cross *Birm* 85-88; C Warley Woods 88-91; V Hobs Moat from 91; AD Solihull 97-04. *St Mary's House, 30 Hobs Meadow, Solihull B92 8PN* Tel 0121-743 4955 E-mail a.leahy@virgin.net

LEAK, Adrian Scudamore. b 38. Ch Ch Ox BA60 MA65 BD89. Cuddesdon Coll 64. **d** 66 **p** 67. C Cov St Mark *Cov* 66-69; C Dorchester *Ox* 69-73; V Badsey *Worc* 73-80; V Wickhamford 73-80; P-in-c Monkwearmouth St Pet *Dur* 80-81; V Choral and Archivist York Minster *York* 81-86; Can Res and Prec Guildf Cathl *Guildf* 86-90; Hon C Guildf H Trin w St Mary 96-00; Hon C Worplesdon from 00. *St Alban's House, 96 Oak Hill, Wood Street Village, Guildford GU3 3ES* Tel (01483) 235136 E-mail adrianleak@8kingsroad.fsnet.co.uk

LEAK, Harry Duncan. b 30. St Cath Coll Cam BA53 MA57. Ely Th Coll 53. **d** 54 **p** 55. S Africa 54-57; Portuguese E Africa 57-61; C Eccleshall *Lich* 62-64; V Normacot 64-66; C Stoke upon Trent 66-68; V Hanley All SS 68-71; R Swynnerton 71-80; Perm to Offic 80-03; rtd 92. *15 Sutherland Road, Tittensor, Stoke-on-Trent ST12 9JQ* Tel (01782) 351024 *or* 351036

LEAK, John Michael. b 42. St Jo Coll Nottm. **d** 84 **p** 85. NSM Beeston *Ripon* 84-87; C Far Headingley St Chad 87-88; Hon C 88-90; C Headingley 90-95; TV Bramley 95-98; rtd 98. *23 Arthington Close, Tingley, Wakefield WF3 1BT* Tel 0113-253 3763

✠**LEAKE, The Rt Revd David.** b 35. CBE03. ALCD59. **d** 59 **p** 60 **c** 69. C Watford *St Alb* 59-61; Lect 61-63; SAMS Argentina 63-69; Asst Bp Paraguay 69-73; Asst Bp N Argentina 69-80; Bp 80-90; Bp Argentina 90-02; rtd 02; Hon Asst Bp Nor from 03. *The Anchorage, Lower Common, East Runton, Cromer NR27 9PG* Tel (01263) 513536
E-mail david@leake8.wanadoo.co.uk

LEAKE, Duncan Burton. b 49. Leeds Univ BA71 Leeds and Carnegie Coll PGCE72 Birm Univ Ad Dip RE78 Keele Univ MA85. Oak Hill Th Coll 90. **d** 92 **p** 93. C Stanwix *Carl* 92-97; C Chasetown *Lich* 97-00; V Chase Terrace from 00. *The Vicarage, 3 Chapel Street, Burntwood WS7 1NL* Tel (01543) 306649 *or* 304611 Fax 304642 E-mail duncan.leake@ntlworld.com

LEAKEY, Ian Raymond Arundell. b 24. K Coll Cam BA47 MA49. Ridley Hall Cam 48. **d** 50 **p** 51. C Litherland St Jo and St Jas *Liv* 50-53; Rwanda Miss 53-73; Can Burundi 66; V Cudham *Roch* 73-76; P-in-c Downe 76; V Cudham and Downe 76-89; rtd 89; Perm to Offic *Sarum* from 89. *5 Shelley Drive, Salisbury SP1 3JZ* Tel (01722) 329243

LEAKEY, Peter Wippell. b 39. Lon Univ BSc60. Trin Coll Bris 73. **d** 75 **p** 76. C Colne St Bart *Blackb* 75-79; V Copp 79-85; V Pennington *Man* 85-05; AD Leigh 93-00; Hon Can Man Cathl 02-05; rtd 05. *28 Gilda Road, Worsley, Manchester M28 1BP* Tel 0161-703 8076

LEAL, Malcolm Colin. b 33. Chich Th Coll 72. **d** 75 **p** 76. Hon C Shoreham St Giles CD *Chich* 75-87; Chapl NE Surrey Coll Ewell 87-95; Hon C Arundel w Tortington and S Stoke *Chich* 88-95; Perm to Offic from 95. *8 West Park Lane, Goring-by-Sea, Worthing BN12 4EK* Tel (01903) 244160

LEALMAN, Helen. b 46. N Ord Course 03. **d** 05. NSM Ben Rhydding *Bradf* from 05. *8 Parkfield Road, Shipley BD18 4EA* Tel (01274) 584569 E-mail gthl@gotadsl.co.uk

LEAMING, Ralph Desmond. b 21. Ripon Coll Cuddesdon 79. **d** 81 **p** 82. C Darlington H Trin *Dur* 81-84; V Hamsterley 84-92; rtd 92. *The Gables, 5 Tower Mews, Wolsingham, Bishop Auckland DL13 3DA* Tel (01388) 526610

LEAMY, Stuart Nigel. b 46. Pemb Coll Ox BA68 MA73 ACA76 FCA81. Sarum Th Coll 68. **d** 70 **p** 71. C Upholland *Liv* 70-78; Lic to Offic *Lon* 78-83 and 94-97; NSM Pimlico St Mary Bourne Street from 97. *92 Gloucester Road, Hampton TW12 2UJ* Tel (020) 8979 9068 Fax 8255 1112 E-mail leamy@globalnet.co.uk

LEAN, Canon David Jonathan Rees. b 52. Univ of Wales (Lamp) DipTh74. Coll of Resurr Mirfield 74. **d** 75 **p** 76. C Tenby *St D* 75-81; V Llanrhian w Llanhywel and Carnhedryn etc 81-88; V Haverfordwest St Martin w Lambston 88-00; RD Roose 99-00; Can St D Cathl from 00; TV Dewisland from 01. *The Archdeaconry, The Close, St Davids, Haverfordwest SA62 6PE* Tel (01437) 720456

LEANING, The Very Revd David. b 36. Lambeth MA01 Nottm Trent Univ Hon MA03. Lich Th Coll 58. **d** 60 **p** 61. C Gainsborough All SS *Linc* 60-65; R Warsop *S'well* 65-76; RD Kington and Weobley *Heref* 76-80; R Kington w Huntington 76-80; Adn Newark *S'well* 80-91; Provost S'well 91-00; Dean S'well from 00; P-in-c Rolleston w Fiskerton, Morton and Upton 91-93; P-in-c Edingley w Halam from 02. *The Residence, Southwell NG25 0HP* Tel (01636) 812593 *or* 812649 Fax 812782 E-mail dean@southwellminster.org.uk

LEAR, Peter Malcolm. b 45. FCMA Kent Univ DipTh98. SEITE 95. **d** 98 **p** 99. NSM Ham St Andr *S'wark* 98-03; NSM Wandsworth St Anne 03-04; NSM Upper Coquetdale *Newc* from 04. *The Rectory, High Street, Rothbury, Morpeth NE65 7TL* Tel (01669) 620482
E-mail peter@learpm.demon.co.uk

LEARMOUTH, Michael Walter. b 50. FCA. Oak Hill Th Coll 84. **d** 84 **p** 85. C Harlow St Mary and St Hugh w St Jo the Bapt *Chelmsf* 84-89; V Hainault 89-97; TR Harlow Town Cen w Lt Parndon 97-00; TR Barnsbury *Lon* from 00. *The Rectory, 10 Thornhill Square, London N1 1BQ* Tel (020) 7607 9039 *or* 7607 4552 E-mail michael@learmouth.fsworld.co.uk

LEARY, Thomas Glasbrook. b 42. AKC66. **d** 67 **p** 68. C W Bromwich All SS *Lich* 67-70; TV Croydon St Jo *Cant* 70-75; C Limpsfield and Titsey *S'wark* 75-83; V Sutton New Town St Barn 83-92; V Merton St Mary from 92; RD Merton 98-01. *The Vicarage, 3 Church Path, London SW19 3HJ* Tel (020) 8543 6192

LEATHARD, Preb Brian. b 56. Sussex Univ BA Cam Univ MA Loughb Univ PhD91. Westcott Ho Cam 79. **d** 82 **p** 83. C Seaford w Sutton *Chich* 82-85; Chapl Loughb Univ *Leic* 85-89; V Hampton Hill *Lon* from 89; Dir of Ords from 99; Preb St Paul's Cathl from 05. *The Vicarage, 46 St James's Road, Hampton TW12 1DQ* Tel and fax (020) 8979 2069 Fax 8255 8095
E-mail bleathard@blueyonder.co.uk

LEATHERBARROW, Ronald. b 35. Chester Coll TCert59. NW Ord Course 71. **d** 75 **p** 76. C Eccleston Ch Ch *Liv* 75-80; C Eccleston St Thos 80-83; R Kirklinton w Hethersgill and Scaleby *Carl* 83-86; R Blackley St Mark White Moss *Man* 86-99; rtd 99. *1 Chapel Street, St Helens WA10 2BG* Tel (01744) 614426

LEATHERS, Brian Stanley Peter. b 61. Nottm Univ BSc83. Oak Hill Th Coll BA89. **d** 89 **p** 90. C Watford *St Alb* 89-92; C Welwyn w Ayot St Peter 92-96; V Heacham *Nor* 96-99; P-in-c Stapenhill Immanuel *Derby* 99-00; V from 00. *Immanuel Vicarage, 150 Hawthorn Crescent, Burton-on-Trent DE15 9QW* Tel (01283) 563959 E-mail brian@topsey.worldonline.co.uk

LEATHES, David Burlton de Mussenden. b 49. R Agric Coll Cirencester Dip Estate Mgt 70. St Jo Coll Nottm DCM92. **d** 92 **p** 93. C Kirkby Stephen w Mallerstang etc *Carl* 92-00; C Brough w Stainmore, Musgrave and Warcop 94-00. *Low Beck House, Rookby, Kirkby Stephen CA17 4HX* Tel (01768) 371713

LEATHLEY, Susan Mary. b 57. Bath Univ BPharm78 MRPharmS. Oak Hill Th Coll DTPS94 Trin Coll Bris MA98. **d** 94 **p** 98. C Weston-super-Mare Ch Ch *B & W* 94-95; C Toxteth St Philemon w St Gabr and St Cleopas *Liv* 97-01; TV Maghull from 01. *23 Green Link, Maghull, Liverpool L31 8DW* Tel 0151-526 6626

LEATHLEY, Terence Michael. b 63. Coll of Resurr Mirfield 99. **d** 01 **p** 02. C Whitby w Aislaby and Ruswarp *York* 01-04; TV from 04. *The Vicarage, 26 Egton Road, Aislaby, Whitby YO21 1SU* Tel (01947) 811527 Mobile 07678-986916

LEATON, Martin John. b 46. Clifton Th Coll 68. **d** 71 **p** 72. C Kenilworth St Jo *Cov* 71-74; C Stratford-on-Avon w Bishopton 74-77; P-in-c Meriden 77-81; R Meriden and Packington 82-84; R Heanton Punchardon w Marwood *Ex* 84-87; Perm to Offic 95-97; P-in-c Rampton w Laneham, Treswell, Cottam and Stokeham *S'well* from 97; P-in-c N and S Leverton from 03. *The Rectory, Main Street, Rampton, Retford DN22 0HR* Tel (01777) 248143 E-mail martinleaton@yahoo.co.uk

LEAVER, David Noel. b 63. Hatf Coll Dur BA85. Wycliffe Hall Ox 89. **d** 91 **p** 92. C Blackheath Park St Mich *S'wark* 91-95; C Upton (Overchurch) *Ches* 95-98; C Wilmslow 98-99; Perm to Offic from 99. *42 Hill Top Avenue, Cheadle Hulme, Cheadle SK8 7HY* Tel 0161-485 4302
E-mail davidleaver@btconnect.com

LEAVER (née SMYTH), Mrs Lucinda Elizabeth Jane (Liz). b 67. New Hall Cam BA88 MA92. Wycliffe Hall Ox BTh93. **d** 93 **p** 94. C Cambridge St Barn *Ely* 93-97; Chapl St Kath Hall Liv Inst of HE 97-98; TV Stockport SW *Ches* 99-01; Chapl Stockport Gr Sch from 99. *42 Hill Top Avenue, Cheadle Hulme, Cheadle SK8 7HY* Tel 0161-485 4302 E-mail liz.leaver@boltblue.net

LEAVER, Prof Robin Alan. b 39. Groningen Univ DTh87. Clifton Th Coll 62. **d** 64 **p** 65. C Gipsy Hill Ch Ch *S'wark* 64-67; C Gt Baddow *Chelmsf* 67-71; P-in-c Reading St Mary Castle Street Prop Chpl *Ox* 71-77; P-in-c Cogges 77-84; Chapl Luckley-Oakfield Sch Wokingham 73-75; Lect Wycliffe Hall Ox 84-85; USA from 84; Prof Ch Music Westmr Choir Coll from 84; Visiting Liturgy Lect Drew Univ 88-00; Visiting Prof Guilliard Sch from 04. *32 Summerall Road, Somerset, NJ 08873, USA* Tel (001) (732) 745 9207 Fax (609) 921 8829
E-mail leaver@rider.edu

LEAVES (née CRAIG), Julie Elizabeth. b 63. Southn Univ BTh87. Sarum & Wells Th Coll 82. **dss** 86 **d** 87 **p** 92. Thatcham *Ox* 86-87; Par Dn 87-88; Hong Kong 88-92; Australia from 92; Assoc P Fremantle 92-95; Chapl St Mary's Angl Girls' Sch Karrinyup from 96. *Wollaston College, Wollaston Road, Mount Claremont, W Australia 6010* Tel (0061) (8) 9341 9111 *or* tel and fax 9402 0998 Fax 9341 9222 E-mail leaves@iinet.net.au

LEAVES, Nigel. b 58. Keble Coll Ox BA80 MA83 K Coll Lon PGCE81 MA86. Sarum & Wells Th Coll 84. **d** 86 **p** 87. C Boyne Hill *Ox* 86-88; Chapl Hong Kong Cathl 88-92; Australia from 92; Abp's Chapl and R W Perth *Perth* 92-98; Tutor and Research Fell Murdoch Univ 98-00; Warden Wollaston Coll & Dir Cen for Belief, Spirituality and Aus Culture from 00. *Wollaston College, Wollaston Road, Mount Claremont, W Australia 6010* Tel (0061) (8) 9384 5511 *or* tel and fax 9383 2774 Fax 9385 3364
E-mail leaves@iinet.net.au

LEAWORTHY, John Owen. b 40. Univ of Wales (Swansea) BSc62. Oak Hill Th Coll 80. **d** 82 **p** 83. C Compton Gifford *Ex* 82-85; C Plymouth Em w Efford 85-86; P-in-c Marks Tey w Aldham and Lt Tey *Chelmsf* 86-88; R 88-89; Chapl HM Pris Full Sutton 89-91; NSM Portree *Arg* 96-04; rtd 05; Perm to Offic *Chelmsf* from 05. *46 Wilkin Drive, Tiptree, Colchester CO5 0QP* Tel (01621) 810905 E-mail jleaworthy@tesco.net

LECKEY, The Very Revd Hamilton. b 29. TCD BA51 MA58. **d** 51 **p** 52. C Ballymacarrett St Martin *D & D* 51-55; C Bangor St Comgall 55-60; I Drumgooland w Kilcoo 60-62; I Comber 62-79; Private Chapl Bp Down 62-73; Dir of Ords 62-87; I Bangor Abbey 79-96; Can Down Cathl 74-87; Dean Down 87-96; rtd 96. *34 Beechfield Drive, Bangor BT19 7ZW* Tel (028) 9146 9370

LECKEY, Paul Robert. b 61. QUB. Ripon Coll Cuddesdon Aston Tr Scheme. **d** 96 **p** 97. C Eastleigh *Win* 96-01; P-in-c Upton St Leonards *Glouc* from 01. *The Rectory, Bond End Road, Upton St Leonards, Gloucester GL4 8AG* Tel (01452) 617443
E-mail paul@pleckey.abel.co.uk

LEDBETTER, Shannon Carroll. b 64. Louisville Univ (USA) BA85 Liv Univ PhD00. Virginia Th Sem MTS96. **d** 03 **p** 04. NSM Knowsley *Liv* from 03. *7 Cathedral Close, Liverpool L1 7BR* Tel 07720-072787 (mobile) E-mail scledbetter2008@yahoo.co.uk

LEDGARD, Canon Frank William Armitage. b 24. Wells Th Coll 49. **d** 52 **p** 53. C Ipswich St Mary le Tower *St E* 52-55; V Tottington *Man* 55-62; V Kirkby Malzeard w Dallow Gill *Ripon* 62-66; R Bedale 66-87; RD Wensley 79-85; Hon Can Ripon Cathl 80-89; Bp's Adv on Chr Healing 87-89; rtd 89; Perm to Offic *Ripon* from 89. *c/o Wrigleys Solicitors, 19 Cookridge Street, Leeds LS2 3AG* Tel 0113-244 6100 Fax 244 6101

LEDGER, James Henry. b 23. Oak Hill Th Coll 68. **d** 70 **p** 71. C Spitalfields Ch Ch w All SS *Lon* 70-75; V Chitts Hill St Cuth 75-91; rtd 91; Perm to Offic *Lon* 93-96; *St Alb* from 93. *6 Acorn Street, Hunsdon, Ware SG12 8PB* Tel (01279) 842878

LEDGER, Mrs Margaret Phyllis. b 47. **d** 04 **p** 05. OLM Newburn *Newc* from 04. *14 Woodside Avenue, Throckley, Newcastle upon Tyne NE15 9BE* Tel 0191-267 2953 E-mail margaret.p.ledger@btinternet.com

LEDWARD, John Archibald. b 30. FRSA85 Lon Univ BD58 Man Univ DSPT78 MA81 ThD. ALCD57. **d** 58 **p** 59. C St Helens St Helen *Liv* 58-62; V Dearham *Carl* 62-66; V Mirehouse 66-71; V Daubhill *Man* 71-77; R Newcastle w Butterton *Lich* 77-88; R Rockland St Mary w Hellington, Bramerton etc *Nor* 88-94; P-in-c Kirby Bedon w Bixley and Whitlingham 92-94; R Rockland St Mary w Hellington, Bramerton etc 94-95; RD Loddon 92-95; rtd 95; Perm to Offic *Nor* from 95. *41 Lackford Close, Brundall, Norwich NR13 5NL* Tel (01603) 714745

LEE, Agnes Elizabeth. b 31. Open Univ BA87 Whitelands Coll Lon TCert51 ACP76. N Ord Course 97. **d** 98 **p** 99. NSM Dewsbury *Wakef* 98-02; rtd 02; Perm to Offic *Wakef* from 02. *1 Moor Park Court, Dewsbury WF12 7AU* Tel (01924) 467319

LEE, Alan Charles. b 32. S'wark Ord Course 77. **d** 79 **p** 80. NSM Acton Green St Pet *Lon* 79-82; Chapl RADD 82-83; P-in-c St Magnus the Martyr w St Marg New Fish Street *Lon* 83-84; NSM Barnes St Mich *S'wark* 84-90; Perm to Offic *Lon* 89-91; C Brighton St Pet and St Nic w Chpl Royal *Chich* 90-92; C Brighton St Bart 92-94; rtd 92; Hon C Holborn St Alb w Saffron Hill St Pet *Lon* from 02. *27 Leigh Court, Avonmore Road, London W14 8RJ*

LEE, Mrs Anne Louise. b 65. St Jo Coll Nottm BTh90 Wycliffe Hall Ox 94. **d** 95 **p** 96. C Wembley St Jo *Lon* 95-98; NSM S Gillingham *Roch* from 98. *26 Pear Tree Lane, Hempstead, Gillingham ME7 3PT* Tel (01634) 387892 E-mail annerichard@blueyonder.co.uk

LEE, Anthony Maurice. b 35. Bps' Coll Cheshunt 62. **d** 65 **p** 66. C Pinner *Lon* 65-71; Asst Youth Chapl *Glouc* 71-72; V Childswyckham 72-73; R Aston Somerville 72-73; V Childswyckham w Aston Somerville 73-91; P-in-c Buckland 88-91; P-in-c Stanton w Snowshill 88-91; R Childswyckham w Aston Somerville, Buckland etc 91-94; RD Winchcombe 86-94; rtd 94. *11 Holly Close, Broadclyst, Exeter EX5 3JB*

LEE, Canon Arthur Gordon. b 32. Univ of Wales (Swansea) BA52 DipSocSc53. St Mich Coll Llan 53. **d** 55 **p** 56. C Brynmawr *S & B* 55-57; C Llangyfelach and Morriston 57-60; V Llanddewi Ystradenni and Abbey Cwmhir 60-69; V Swansea St Pet 69-98; RD Penderi 90-98; Hon Can Brecon Cathl 91-95; Can Res Brecon Cathl 95-98; rtd 98. *51 Dunvant Road, Killay, Swansea SA2 7NL* Tel (01792) 207715

LEE, Canon Brian. b 37. Linc Th Coll 78. **d** 80 **p** 81. C Duston *Pet* 80-84; P-in-c Spratton 84-89; V from 89; Jt P-in-c Maidwell w Draughton, Lamport w Faxton 89-01; Jt P-in-c Cottesbrooke w Gt Creaton and Thornby from 89; RD Brixworth 94-01; Can Pet Cathl from 98. *The Vicarage, 2 Church Road, Spratton, Northampton NN6 8HR* Tel (01604) 847212

LEE, Canon Brian Ernest. b 32. ACA59 FCA70. Linc Th Coll 60. **d** 62 **p** 63. C Birch St Jas *Man* 62-65; C Withington St Paul 65-66; R Abbey Hey 66-70; Hon C Gatley *Ches* 86-88; V Egremont St Jo 88-97; RD Wallasey 91-96; OGS from 92; Hon Can Ches Cathl *Ches* 96-97; rtd 97; Perm to Offic *Nor* from 97. *St Fursey's House, Convent of All Hallows, Ditchingham, Bungay NR35 2DZ* Tel and fax (01986) 892308

LEE, Brian John. b 51. K Coll Lon BD78 AKC78. Coll of Resurr Mirfield 78. **d** 79 **p** 80. C Ham St Rich *S'wark* 79-82; C Surbiton St Andr and St Mark 82-85; V Shirley St Geo 85-93; V St Botolph Aldgate w H Trin Minories *Lon* from 93. *St Botolph's Vestry, Aldgate, London EC3N 1AB* Tel (020) 7283 1670 *or* 7283 1950 Fax 7283 9302 E-mail brian.stbotolphsaldgate@eggconnect.net

LEE, Christopher Garfield. b 41. St Deiniol's Hawarden 80. **d** 80 **p** 81. C Swansea St Pet *S & B* 80-81; C Oystermouth 81-83; R Cromhall w Tortworth and Tytherington *Glouc* 83-93; R Bishopston *S & B* 93-05; UK Field Dir Educn for Min Progr 93-05; R Windsor Mill USA from 05. *Episcopal Church of Christ the King, 1930 Brookdale Road, Windsor Mill, MD 21244, USA* Tel (001) (410) 944 6683

LEE, Clifford Samuel (Sam). b 53. **d** 95 **p** 96. NSM S Elmham and Ilketshall *St E* from 95. *Packway Lodge, Flixton, Bungay NR35 1NR* Tel (01986) 782300

LEE, Clive Warwick. b 34. St Pet Coll Ox BA58 MA62 Ox Univ PGCE73. Coll of Resurr Mirfield 58. **d** 60 **p** 61. C W End *Win* 60-64; C Upper Norwood St Jo *Cant* 65-69; Chapl Vinehall Sch E Sussex 69-94; rtd 94; Perm to Offic *Cant* from 04. *28 St Radigund's Street, Canterbury CT1 2AA* Tel (01227) 780624

LEE, Colin John Willmot. b 21. Wycliffe Hall Ox 57. **d** 59 **p** 59. C Gravesend St Jas *Roch* 59-62; V Dartford St Edm 62-67; Bp's Ind Adv *Derby* 67-91; C-in-c Ilkeston St Bart CD 67-69; P-in-c Stanton by Dale 69-76; V Ilkeston St Jo 76-91; rtd 91; Perm to Offic *Derby* and *S'well* from 91. *3 Buttermead Close, Trowell, Nottingham NG9 3QT* Tel 0115-949 0100

LEE, The Ven David John. b 46. Bris Univ BSc67 Fitzw Coll Cam BA76 MA79 Birm Univ PhD96. Ridley Hall Cam 74. **d** 77 **p** 78. C Putney St Marg *S'wark* 77-80; Tutor Bp Tucker Th Coll Uganda 80-86; Tutor Crowther Hall CMS Tr Coll Selly Oak 86-91; P-in-c Wishaw and Middleton *Birm* 91-96; Can Res Birm Cathl 96-04; Dir Dioc Bd for Miss 96-04; Adn Bradf from 04. *14 Park Cliffe Road, Bradford BD2 4NS* Tel (01274) 200698 *or* tel and fax 730196 Mobile 07711-671351 E-mail david.lee@bradford.anglican.org

LEE, The Ven David Stanley. b 30. Univ of Wales (Cardiff) BSc51. St Mich Coll Llan 56. **d** 57 **p** 58. C Caerau w Ely *Llan* 57-60; C Port Talbot St Agnes 60-70; Ind Chapl 60-70; R Merthyr Tydfil 70-72; Chapl Merthyr Tydfil Hosp 70-91; R Merthyr Tydfil and Cyfarthfa *Llan* 72-91; RD Merthyr Tydfil 82-91; Can Llan Cathl 84-97; Adn Llan 91-97; R Llanfabon 91-97; rtd 97; Perm to Offic *Llan* from 97; *Mon* from 98. *2 Old Vicarage Close, Llanishen, Cardiff CF14 5UZ* Tel (029) 2075 2431

LEE, David Wight Dunsmore. b 39. Wells Th Coll 61. **d** 63 **p** 64. C Middlesbrough St Oswald *York* 63-67; C Northallerton w Kirby Sigston 67-69; R Limbe w Thyolo and Mulanje Malawi 69-71; R S Highlands 71-75; V Newington Transfiguration 76-81; P-in-c Sheriff Hutton 81-85; P-in-c Sheriff Hutton and Farlington 85-97; V Sheriff Hutton, Farlington, Stillington etc 97-04; rtd 04; Perm to Offic *York* from 04. *Kirkstone Cottage, Main Street, Oswaldkirk, York YO62 5XT* Tel (01439) 788283 E-mail dwdlee@talk21.com

LEE, Derek Alfred. **d** 00. Hon Par Dn Llantilio Pertholey w Bettws Chpl etc *Mon* from 00. *94 Croesonen Parc, Abergavenny NP7 6PF* Tel (01873) 855042

LEE, Edmund Hugh. b 53. Trin Coll Ox BA75 MA79 Goldsmiths' Coll Lon BMus83 K Coll Lon MA98. Ripon Coll Cuddesdon 93. **d** 95 **p** 96. C Malden St Jas *S'wark* 95-99; TV Mortlake w E Sheen from 99. *17 Sheen Gate Gardens, London SW14 7PD* Tel (020) 8876 5002 Fax as telephone E-mail edknife@aol.com

LEE, Elizabeth. *See* LEE, Agnes Elizabeth

LEE, Gilbert (Sai Kuen). b 51. Hong Kong Univ BD80 Kent Univ MA98. Chung Chi Coll Hong Kong 77. **d** 80 **p** 81. Hong Kong 80-88; C Angl Ch Hong Kong 80-81; V 81-88; NSM St Martin-in-the-Fields *Lon* 88-00; Chapl to Chinese in London 88-00; Canada from 00; I St Jo Chinese Ch Toronto from 00. *135 First Avenue, Toronto ON, Canada, M4M 1W9* Tel (001) (416) 461 0692

LEE, Gordon. *See* LEE, Canon Arthur Gordon

LEE, Henry. b 31. St Chad's Coll Dur BA53 DipTh55 Bede Coll Dur PGCE71. **d** 55 **p** 56. C Hendon St Ignatius *Dur* 55-60; C Dur St Marg 60-65; V Medomsley 65-75; Chapl Darlington Memorial Hosp 75-79; V Darlington H Trin *Dur* 75-82; V Brompton w Deighton *York* 82-90; rtd 90; Perm to Offic *York* from 90. *103 Benfieldside Road, Consett DH8 0RS* Tel (01207) 592170

LEE, Hugh. *See* LEE, John Charles Hugh Mellanby

LEE, Hugh Gordon Cassels. b 41. St Andr Univ BSc64. Edin Th Coll 64. **d** 67 **p** 68. C Dumfries *Glas* 67-70; C Totteridge *St Alb* 70-73; R Glas St Jas *Glas* 73-80; R Bishopbriggs 80-86; R St Fillans *St And* 86-89; R Crieff and Comrie 86-01; P-in-c Muthill 86-01; P-in-c Lochearnhead 89-01; R Dunoon *Arg* from 01. *Holy Trinity Rectory, Kilbride Road, Dunoon PA23 7LN* Tel (01369) 702444

LEE, Miss Iris Audrey Olive. b 26. St Andr Coll Southsea 54 Gilmore Ho 76. **dss** 76 **d** 87. N Weald Bassett *Chelmsf* 76-87; rtd 87; NSM Clacton St Jas *Chelmsf* 87-00; Chapl Clacton Hosp 90-95; Perm to Offic from 00. *30 Marine Court, Marine Parade West, Clacton-on-Sea CO15 1ND* Tel (01255) 423719

LEE, Mrs Jennifer. b 42. Westf Coll Lon BA64 CQSW78. N Ord Course 01. **d** 03 **p** 04. NSM Millhouses H Trin *Sheff* from 03. *Whirlow Croft, Whirlow Lane, Sheffield S11 9QF* Tel 0114-236 7938 E-mail leejandm@aol.com

LEE, John. b 47. Univ of Wales (Swansea) BSc70 MSc73 MInstGA87. Ripon Hall Ox 73. **d** 75 **p** 76. C Swansea St Pet *S & B* 75-78; C St Botolph Aldgate w H Trin Minories *Lon* 79-84; P-in-c Chiddingstone w Chiddingstone Causeway *Roch* 84-89; R 89-98; Clergy Appts Adv from 98. *Cowley House, 9 Little College Street, London SW1P 3SH* Tel (020) 7898 1898 Fax 7898 1899 E-mail sue.manners@caa.c-of-e.org.uk

LEE, John Charles Hugh Mellanby. b 44. Trin Hall Cam BA66 MA69 Brunel Univ MTech71. Ox NSM Course 78. **d** 81 **p** 82. NSM Amersham on the Hill *Ox* 81-88; NSM Ox St Aldate w St Matt 88-93; NSM Wheatley 93-95; Dioc Development Officer for Miss in Work and Economic Life 95-02; P-in-c Ox St Mich w St Martin and All SS from 02. *12 Walton Street, Oxford OX1 2HG* Tel and fax (01865) 316245
E-mail hugh.lee@btinternet.com

LEE, John Michael Andrew. b 62. Leeds Univ BA84. Trin Coll Bris 88. **d** 90 **p** 91. C Norbiton *S'wark* 90-94; C Leic H Trin w St Jo *Leic* 94-02; R York St Paul *York* from 02. *St Paul's Rectory, 100 Acomb Road, York YO24 4ER* Tel (01904) 792304
E-mail john_lee@lineone.net

LEE, John Samuel. b 47. Chich Th Coll 74. **d** 77 **p** 78. C Bramley *Ripon* 77-80; C Bideford *Ex* 81-84; TV Littleham w Exmouth 84-90; P-in-c Sidbury 90-91; TV Sidmouth, Woolbrook, Salcombe Regis, Sidbury etc 91-04; rtd 04. *Westward Ho!, Torpark Road, Torquay TQ2 5BQ* Tel (01803) 293086
E-mail johnslee@glensidf.freeserve.co.uk

LEE, Joseph Patrick. b 53. St Jos Coll Upholland 72 Ushaw Coll Dur 75. **d** 78 **p** 79. In RC Ch 78-99; Hon C Charlton *S'wark* from 99. *45 Chestnut Rise, London SE18 1RJ* Tel (020) 8316 4674 Mobile 07956-294429 Fax 8317 7304
E-mail joe_lee@lineone.net

LEE, Canon Kenneth Peter. b 45. Em Coll Cam BA67 MA71. Cuddesdon Coll 67. **d** 69 **p** 70. C Stoke Poges *Ox* 69-72; C Witton *Ches* 72-74; V Frankby w Greasby 74-92; R Christleton from 92; Hon Can Ches Cathl from 05. *The Rectory, Birch Heath Lane, Christleton, Chester CH3 7AP* Tel (01244) 335663
E-mail kpeter.lee@btinternet.com

LEE, Luke Gun-Hong. b 37. Univ of Yon Sei BTh62. St Jo Coll Morpeth 64. **d** 67 **p** 68. Korea 67-79; C Bloxwich *Lich* 79-83; TV Dunstable *St Alb* 83-90; V Croxley Green All SS from 90. *All Saints' Vicarage, Croxley Green, Rickmansworth WD3 3HJ* Tel (01923) 772109 E-mail luke.lee@ntlworld.com

LEE, Miss Lynley Hoe. b 52. Trin Coll Bris DipHE81. St Jo Coll Nottm BTh89 K Coll Lon MA93. **d** 90 **p** 94. Par Dn Pitsea *Chelmsf* 90-95; Singapore 95-98; C Gt Ilford St Andr *Chelmsf* 99-02; TV Grays Thurrock from 02. *Wendover, College Avenue, Grays RM17 5UW* Tel (01375) 373468 *or* 371566
E-mail lynleyhoe@aol.com

LEE, Martin Paul. b 66. Aston Tr Scheme 91 Linc Th Coll 93 St Steph Ho Ox 94. **d** 96 **p** 97. C Wells St Thos w Horrington *B & W* 96-00; P-in-c Brent Knoll, E Brent and Lympsham 00-01; R from 01; RD Axbridge from 03. *The Rectory, 3 Ash Trees, East Brent, Highbridge TA9 4DQ* Tel (01278) 760874
E-mail frmlee@aol.com

LEE, Nicholas Knyvett. b 54. Trin Coll Cam BA76 MA77. Cranmer Hall Dur 82. **d** 85 **p** 86. C Brompton H Trin w Onslow Square St Paul *Lon* from 85; Chapl R Brompton and Harefield NHS Trust 86-90 and from 94. *St Paul's Church House, Onslow Square, London SW7 3NX* Tel 08456-447533
E-mail nicky.lee@htb.org.uk

LEE, Peter. *See* LEE, Canon Kenneth Peter

LEE, Peter Alexander. b 44. Hull Univ BSc(Econ)65. Ex & Truro NSM Scheme 80. **d** 83 **p** 84. NSM Ex St Sidwell and St Matt *Ex* 83-89; NSM Ex St Dav 90-98; C Paignton St Jo 98-01; Perm to Offic 01-03; Hon C Ex St Dav from 03. *Windyridge, Beech Avenue, Exeter EX4 6HF* Tel (01392) 254118

✠**LEE, The Rt Revd Peter John.** b 47. St Jo Coll Cam BA69 CertEd70 MA73. Ridley Hall Cam 70 St Jo Coll Nottm 72. **d** 73 **p** 74 **c** 90. C Onslow Square St Paul *Lon* 73-76; S Africa from 76; V-Gen and Bp Ch the K from 90. *PO Box 1653, Rosettenville, 2130 South Africa* Tel (0027) (11) 435 0097 *or* 942 1179 Fax 435 2868 E-mail dckpeter@netactive.co.za

LEE, Peter Kenneth. b 44. Selw Coll Cam BA66 MA69. Cuddesdon Coll 67. **d** 69 **p** 70. C Manston *Ripon* 69-72; C Bingley All SS *Bradf* 72-77; Chapl Bingley Coll of Educn 72-77; V Cross Roads cum Lees *Bradf* 77-90; V Auckland St Pet *Dur* from 90; Tutor NEOC from 91; Tutor N of England Inst for Chr Educn from 03. *St Peter's Vicarage, 39 Etherley Lane, Bishop Auckland DL14 7QZ* Tel (01388) 661856

LEE, Canon Raymond John. b 30. St Edm Hall Ox BA53 MA57. Tyndale Hall Bris 54. **d** 56 **p** 57. C Tooting Graveney St Nic *S'wark* 56-59; C Muswell Hill St Jas *Lon* 59-62; V Woking St Mary *Guildf* 62-70; V Gt Crosby St Luke *Liv* 70-82; Dioc Adv NSM 79-95; V Allerton 82-94; P-in-c Altcar 94-98; Hon Can Liv Cathl 89-95; rtd 95; Perm to Offic *Liv* from 98. *15 Barkfield Lane, Liverpool L37 1LY* Tel (01704) 872670

LEE, Richard Alexander. b 63. St Jo Coll Nottm BTh91. **d** 91 **p** 92. C Gt Stanmore *Lon* 91-95; C Edgware 95-98; TV S Gillingham *Roch* from 98. *26 Pear Tree Lane, Hempstead, Gillingham ME7 3PT* Tel (01634) 387892
E-mail annerichard@blueyonder.co.uk

LEE, Robert David. b 53. QUB BD75. CITC 77. **d** 77 **p** 78. C Comber *D & D* 77-83; I Mt Merrion 83-87; CMS 89-92; Egypt 89-97; R Peebles *Edin* from 97; P-in-c Innerleithen from 97. *The Rectory, 45 Edderston Road, Peebles EH45 9DT* Tel and fax (01721) 720571 E-mail robert.l@virgin.net

LEE, Robert William. b 31. Keele Univ BA54 St Cath Soc Ox BA58 MA63. Ripon Hall Ox 56. **d** 59 **p** 60. C Dawley St Jerome *Lon* 59-62; C Bromley H Trin *Roch* 62-65; R Clayton *Man* 65-70; P-in-c Man St Paul 65-70; TV Hemel Hempstead *St Alb* 70-72; TV Corby SS Pet and Andr w Gt and Lt Oakley *Pet* 72-80; V Weedon Lois w Plumpton and Moreton Pinkney etc 80-88; R Thornhams Magna and Parva, Gislingham and Mellis *St E* 88-96; rtd 96; Perm to Offic *Bradf* and *Carl* from 96. *2 Guldrey Fold, Sedbergh LA10 5DY* Tel (01539) 621907

LEE, Roderick James. b 50. Linc Th Coll 88. **d** 90 **p** 91. C Rushden w Newton Bromswold *Pet* 90-93; C Kingsthorpe w Northampton St Dav 93-94; TV 94-99; R Mears Ashby and Hardwick and Sywell etc 99-04; P-in-c Corby St Columba from 04. *St Columba's Vicarage, 157 Studfall Avenue, Corby NN17 1LG* Tel (01536) 204158 *or* 261436
E-mail rlee103400@aol.com

LEE, Sai Kuen. *See* LEE, Gilbert

LEE, Sam. *See* LEE, Clifford Samuel

LEE, Steven Michael. b 56. Dur Univ BA. Trin Coll Bris 80. **d** 83 **p** 84. C Beckenham St Jo *Roch* 83-86; C Leic Martyrs *Leic* 86-90; V Coalville and Bardon Hill 90-95; P-in-c Kibworth and Smeeton Westerby and Saddington 95-00; P-in-c Foxton w Gumley and Laughton and Lubenham 96-97; P-in-c Foxton w Gumley and Laughton 97-00; R Kibworth and Smeeton Westerby and Saddington from 00. *The Rectory, 25 Church Road, Kibworth, Leicester LE8 0NB* Tel 0116-279 2294
E-mail lee.fam@btinternet.com

LEE, Stuart Graham. b 73. Roehampton Inst BA94. St Steph Ho Ox BTh00. **d** 00 **p** 01. C Eltham H Trin *S'wark* 00-03; TV Wimbledon from 03. *St Matthew's House, 10 Coombe Gardens, London SW20 0QU* Tel (020) 8944 1010

LEE, Thomas Richard. b 52. AKC73. St Aug Coll Cant 74. **d** 75 **p** 76. C Leam Lane CD *Dur* 75-80; Chapl RAF from 80. *Chaplaincy Services (RAF), HQ, Personnel and Training Command, RAF Innsworth, Gloucester GL3 1EZ* Tel (01452) 712612 ext 5164 Fax 510828

LEE, Veronica. b 47. Redland Coll of Educn TCert68 Open Univ BA84 Bris Poly MEd89. STETS 02. **d** 05. NSM Bishopston and St Andrews *Bris* from 05. *48 Chesterfield Road, Bristol BS6 5DL* Tel 0117-949 8325 E-mail vronlee@hotmail.com

LEE, William George. b 11. TCD BA33 MA48. **d** 34 **p** 35. C Southport St Andr *Liv* 34-37; C Cambridge St Paul *Ely* 37-44; V Matlock Bath *Derby* 44-49; V Deptford St Jo *S'wark* 49-61; RD Greenwich and Deptford 60; V Chislehurst Ch Ch *Roch* 61-76; rtd 76. *Dale Garth, Harmby, Leyburn DL8 5PD* Tel (01969) 622649

LEE WARNER, Canon Theodore John. b 22. Univ Coll Ox BA49 MA54. Wells Th Coll 50. **d** 51 **p** 52. C S Westoe *Dur* 51-55; P-in-c Cassop cum Quarrington 55-59; V Peterlee 59-63; V Darlington H Trin 63-74; Chapl Darlington Memorial Hosp 63-74; V Norton St Mary *Dur* 74-80; RD Barnard Castle 80-87; V Gainford 80-87; R Winston 80-87; Hon Can Dur Cathl 83-87; rtd 87. *112 Cleveland Terrace, Darlington DL3 8JA* Tel (01325) 467585

LEECE, Roderick Neil Stephen. b 59. ARCM85 Wadh Coll Ox BA81 MA85 Leeds Univ BA84. Coll of Resurr Mirfield 82. **d** 85 **p** 86. C Portsea St Mary *Portsm* 85-91; V Stamford Hill St Bart *Lon* from 91. *St Bartholomew's Vicarage, Craven Park Road, London N15 6AA* Tel (020) 8800 1554
E-mail rleece@lineone.net

LEECH, Kenneth. b 39. Lon Univ BA61 AKC61 Trin Coll Ox BA63 MA71 Lambeth DD98. St Steph Ho Ox 62. **d** 64 **p** 65. C Hoxton H Trin w St Mary *Lon* 64-67; C Soho St Anne w St Thos and St Pet 67-71; Tutor St Aug Coll Cant 71-74; R Bethnal Green St Matt *Lon* 74-79; Field Officer Community & Race Relns Unit BCC 80; Race Relns Officer Gen Syn Bd for Soc Resp 81-87; Hon C Notting Hill St Clem and St Mark *Lon* 82-85; Hon C Notting Dale St Clem w St Mark and St Jas 85-88; Dir Runnymede Trust 87-90; Hon C St Botolph Aldgate w H Trin Minories *Lon* 91-04; rtd 04. *89 Manchester Road, Mossley, Ashton-under-Lyne OL5 9LZ* Tel (01457) 835119
E-mail kenleech@aol.com

LEEDS, Archdeacon of. *See* OLIVER, The Ven John Michael

LEEFIELD, Michael John. b 37. Liv Univ BA60 K Coll Lon BD65 AKC65. St Boniface Warminster 62. **d** 66 **p** 67. C Gt Yarmouth *Nor* 66-70; V Trowse 70-75; V Arminghall 70-75; R Caistor w Markshall 70-75; Chapl Norfolk and Nor Hosp 70-75; V Lydney w Aylburton *Glouc* 75-84; RD Forest S 82-84; Lic to Offic from 85; rtd 01. *Brays Court, Awre, Newnham GL14 1EP* Tel (01594) 510483

LEEKE, Charles Browne. b 39. TCD DipTh83 Stranmillis Coll CertEd62. CITC 80. **d** 83 **p** 84. C Ballymoney w Finvoy and Rasharkin *Conn* 83-86; I Faughanvale *D & R* 86-97; Chapl Port Londonderry Miss to Seamen 92-97; Bp's Dom Chapl *D & R* 92-96; Can Derry Cathl 96-00; I Drumragh w Mountfield 97-00; Reconciliation Development Officer *D & D* from 00. *41 Beechfield Lodge, Aghalee, Craigavon BT67 0GA* Tel (028) 9265 2838 *or* 9032 3188 Fax 9265 0178 *or* 9032 1635
E-mail charlie@reconcile-think.fsnet.co.uk

LEEKE, Canon Stephen Owen. b 50. EAMTC 82 Ridley Hall Cam 83. **d** 84 **p** 85. C Cherry Hinton St Andr *Ely* 84-87; P-in-c Warboys 87-91; P-in-c Bury 87-91; P-in-c Wistow 87-91; R Warboys w Broughton and Bury w Wistow 91-01; RD St Ives 92-01; V Cambridge St Martin from 01; Hon Can Ely Cathl from 05. *St Martin's Vicarage, 127 Suez Road, Cambridge CB1 3QD* Tel (01223) 214203
E-mail stephen.leeke@ely.anglican.org

LEEMAN, John Graham. b 41. N Ord Course 78. **d** 80 **p** 81. NSM Hull St Mary Sculcoates *York* 80-96; Perm to Offic 96-99; Hon C Hull St Mary Sculcoates 99-04; P-in-c from 04; Hon C Hull St Steph Sculcoates 99-04; Hon C Sculcoates St Paul w Ch Ch and St Silas 99-04. *1 Snuff Mill Lane, Cottingham HU16 4RY* Tel (01482) 840355

LEEMING, Jack. b 34. Kelham Th Coll 56. **d** 61 **p** 62. C Sydenham St Phil *S'wark* 61-64; Chapl RAF 64-84; Chapl Salisbury Gen Infirmary 84-89; R Barford St Martin, Dinton, Baverstock etc *Sarum* 89-99; rtd 99; Perm to Offic *Sarum* from 01. *8 Bower Gardens, Salisbury SP1 2RL* Tel (01722) 416800

LEEMING, Mrs Janice Doreen. b 45. EMMTC 97. **d** 00 **p** 01. NSM Lenton *S'well* from 00. *5 Hollinwell Avenue, Wollaton, Nottingham NG8 1JY* Tel 0115-928 2145

LEEMING, John Maurice. b 24. CEng MIMechE MIProdE FIED. NW Ord Course 72. **d** 75 **p** 76. NSM Endcliffe *Sheff* 75-78; C Norton 78-80; V Bolsterstone 80-89; Jt Min Stocksbridge Chr Cen LEP 80-89; Ind Chapl 81-89; rtd 89; Perm to Offic *S'well* from 89; *Sheff* from 93; *Derby* from 98. *Beck House, Toftdyke Lane, Clayworth, Retford DN22 9AH* Tel (01777) 817795 E-mail maurice@leeming02.freeserve.co.uk

LEES, Allan Garside. b 39. OLM course 96. **d** 99 **p** 00. OLM Hurst *Man* from 99. *1 Exeter Drive, Ashton-under-Lyne OL6 8BZ* Tel 0161-339 3105

LEES, Charles Alan. b 38. RGN OND FE TCert. WMMTC 78. **d** 81 **p** 82. NSM Yardley St Cypr Hay Mill *Birm* 81-84 and 86-87; Hon C Dorridge 84-86; Chapl E Birm Hosp 85-87; Hon C Leamington Spa H Trin and Old Milverton *Cov* 89-90; Perm to Offic *Birm* 95-96 and from 98. *49 Gordon Street, Leamington Spa CV31 1HR*

LEES, Christopher John. b 58. Fitzw Coll Cam BA80 Birkbeck Coll Lon MA86 FCIPD. N Ord Course 01. **d** 04 **p** 05. NSM Wilmslow *Ches* from 04. *110 Grove Park, Knutsford WA16 8QB* Tel (01565) 631625 E-mail info@johnleescareers.com

LEES, John Raymond. b 57. Selw Coll Cam BA78 MA82. St Steph Ho Ox 89. **d** 91 **p** 92. C Eastbourne St Mary *Chich* 91-93; Min Can and Succ St Paul's Cathl *Lon* 93-98; TR Swindon New Town *Bris* 98-01; Asst to AD Swindon and C Highworth w Sevenhampton and Inglesham etc 01-02; Perm to Offic *Lon* from 02 and *Pet* and *Ely* from 04. *27 St Margaret's Road, Peterborough PE2 9EA* Tel (01733) 312404 Mobile 07769-606947 E-mail johnlees@onetel.com

LEES, Mrs Kathleen Marion. b 30. Birkbeck Coll Lon BA60. S'wark Ord Course 77. **dss** 80 **d** 87 **p** 94. Epping St Jo *Chelmsf* 80-86; Hon C Hunstanton St Mary w Ringstead Parva, Holme etc *Nor* 87-88; Perm to Offic 88-94; Chapl King's Lynn and Wisbech Hosps NHS Trust 94-00; NSM Gaywood *Nor* 94-00; rtd 00; Perm to Offic *Nor* from 00. *20 North Hirne Court, St Anns Street, King's Lynn PE31 1LT* Tel (01553) 661294

LEES, Peter John. b 39. **d** 95 **p** 96. NSM Buckie *Ab* 95-00; NSM Turriff 95-00; P-in-c Fraserburgh 00-01; R from 01. *6 Crimond Court, Fraserburgh AB43 9QW* Tel (01346) 518158 *or* (01542) 835261

LEES, Peter John William. b 37. **d** 02. NSM Walsall St Paul *Lich* from 02. *66 Cresswell Crescent, Bloxwich, Walsall WS3 2UH* Tel (01922) 497869

LEES, Stephen. b 55. St Jo Coll York CertEd77 BEd78 Nottm Univ MA96. St Jo Coll Nottm 88. **d** 90 **p** 91. C Mansfield St Jo *S'well* 90-93; TV Bestwood 93-98; V Baxenden *Blackb* from 98. *The Vicarage, Langford Street, Baxenden, Accrington BB5 2RF* Tel (01254) 232471 E-mail steve.lees@stjohnsbaxenden.org.uk

LEES, Stuart Charles Roderick. b 62. Trin Coll Bris BA. **d** 89 **p** 90. C Woodford Wells *Chelmsf* 89-93; C Brompton H Trin w Onslow Square St Paul *Lon* 93-97; Chapl Stewards Trust 93-97; P-in-c Fulham Ch Ch 97-03; V from 03. *Christ Church Vicarage, 40 Clancarty Road, London SW6 3AA* Tel (020) 7736 4261
E-mail stuart@ccfulham.com

LEES-SMITH, Christopher John (Brother Edward). b 21. CCC Ox BA49 MA65. Cuddesdon Coll 48. **d** 50 **p** 51. C Pallion *Dur* 50-54; SSF from 54; Lic to Offic *Sarum* 57-62; Perm to Offic *Newc* 62-74; Guardian Alnmouth Friary 65-74; Chapl Third Order SSF 74-91; rtd 91. *The Friary, Alnmouth, Alnwick NE66 6NJ* Tel (01665) 830213

LEESE, Arthur Selwyn Mountford. b 09. K Coll Lon BD31 AKC31 St Cath Soc Ox BA33 MA44. Ripon Hall Ox 31. **d** 33 **p** 34. C Bexleyheath Ch Ch *Roch* 33-37; C Cockington *Ex* 37-39; C Langley Mill *Derby* 39-51; V Hawkhurst *Cant* 51-74; rtd 74; Perm to Offic *Cant* from 74; *Chich* from 75. *84 Wickham Avenue, Bexhill-on-Sea TN39 3ER* Tel (01424) 213137

LEESE, Frederick Henry Brooke. b 24. AKC47. **d** 47 **p** 48. C Mitcham St Mark *S'wark* 47-50; C Bourne *Guildf* 50-54; V Croydon St Martin *Cant* 54-60; V Pagham *Chich* 60-70; V Chorley *Ches* 70-82; R Rogate w Terwick and Trotton w Chithurst *Chich* 82-90; RD Midhurst 85-90; rtd 90; Perm to Offic *B & W* from 90. *Treetops, Furnham Crescent, Chard TA20 1AZ* Tel (01460) 65524

LEESE, Mrs Jane Elizabeth. b 50. Man Univ BA(Econ)72 Avery Hill Coll PGCE73. Sarum Th Coll 93. **d** 96 **p** 97. NSM Kempshott *Win* 96-01; NSM Herriard w Winslade and Long Sutton etc from 01. *The Parsonage, Gaston Lane, South Warnborough, Hook RG29 1RH* Tel (01256) 862843
E-mail jane.leese@ukgateway.net

LEESON, Bernard Alan. b 47. FCollP92 FRSA92 Bris Univ CertEd68 Open Univ BA75 Southn Univ MA78 Sheff Univ PhD97. EMMTC 84. **d** 87 **p** 88. Dep Hd Master Ripley Mill Hill Sch 80-91; NSM Breadsall *Derby* 87-91; Hd St Aid CE High Sch Lancs from 91; Perm to Offic *Blackb* 91-92; Lic to Offic from 92; NSM Officer 92-96. *The Lodge, Daggers Lane, Preesall, Poulton-le-Fylde FY6 0QN* Tel (01253) 811020 *or* 810504 Fax 810244
E-mail alan-leeson@st-aidans.lancs.sch.uk

LEESON, David Harry Stanley. b 45. Glouc Th Course 82. **d** 85 **p** 86. NSM Stratton w Baunton *Glouc* 85-94; NSM N Cerney w Bagendon 91-94; NSM Stratton, N Cerney, Baunton and Bagendon from 95. *83 Cheltenham Road, Stratton, Cirencester GL7 2JB* Tel (01285) 651186

LEESON, Mrs Sally Elizabeth. b 57. Sussex Univ BA79. Westcott Ho Cam 83. **dss** 85 **d** 87 **p** 94. Battersea St Pet and St Paul *S'wark* 85-87; Par Dn 87-90; Par Dn Limpsfield and Titsey 90-94; C 94; Perm to Offic from 94; Chapl Bp Wand Sch Sunbury-on-Thames from 05. *32 Albany Road, New Malden KT3 3NY*

LEFFLER, Christopher. b 33. Em Coll Cam BA57 MA61. Linc Th Coll. **d** 59 **p** 60. C Bermondsey St Mary w St Olave and St Jo *S'wark* 59-60; C Herne Hill St Paul 60-63; C-in-c Canley CD *Cov* 63-67; R Gt and Lt Glemham *St E* 67-72; R Badwell Ash w Gt Ashfield, Stowlangtoft etc 72-82; R Trimley 82-99; rtd 99; Perm to Offic *St E* from 99. *308 High Street, Felixstowe IP11 9QJ* Tel (01394) 672279 E-mail chrisleffler@quista.net

LEFFLER, Jeremy Paul (Jem). b 62. Westmr Coll Ox BEd88. Wycliffe Hall Ox BTh94. **d** 94 **p** 95. C Ormskirk *Liv* 94-97; C Much Woolton 97-00; P-in-c Widnes St Ambrose 00-03; V from 03. *St Ambrose Vicarage, 45 Hargreaves Court, Widnes WA8 0QA* Tel and fax 0151-420 8044
E-mail info@stambrose.fsnet.co.uk

LEFROY, John Perceval. b 40. Trin Coll Cam BA62. Cuddesdon Coll 64. **d** 66 **p** 67. C Maidstone St Martin *Cant* 66-69; C St Peter-in-Thanet 69-74; V Barming Heath 74-82; V Upchurch w Lower Halstow from 82; P-in-c Iwade from 95; rtd 05. *23 Heather Avenue, Melksham SN12 6FX*
E-mail jclefroy@tiscali.co.uk

LEFROY, Kathleen Christine. *See* ENGLAND, Mrs Kathleen Christine

LEFROY, Matthew William. b 62. Trin Coll Cam BA84 Keele Univ PGCE91. St Jo Coll Nottm MTh02. **d** 02 **p** 03. C Portswood Ch Ch *Win* from 02. *6 Royston Close, Southampton SO17 1TB* Tel (023) 8055 5883 *or* 8059 5015
E-mail matthew@mjlefroy.freeserve.co.uk

LEFROY-OWEN, Neal. b 62. Bradf Univ BA99. N Ord Course 00. **d** 03 **p** 04. C Sandal St Cath *Wakef* from 03. *The Vicarage, Johnston Street, Wakefield WF1 4DZ* Tel (01924) 380964
E-mail neal@owen21.fslife.co.uk

LEGG, Adrian James. b 52. St Jo Coll Nottm LTh82 BTh82. **d** 82 **p** 83. C Haughton le Skerne *Dur* 82-85; C Llanishen and Lisvane *Llan* 85-89; V Llanwddyn and Llanfihangel-yng-Nghwynfa etc *St As* 89-93; V Llansadwrn w Llanwrda and Manordeilo *St D* from 93. *The Vicarage, Llanwrda SA19 8HD* Tel (01550) 777343
E-mail alegg94523@aol.com

LEGG, Joanna Susan Penberthy. *See* PENBERTHY, Ms Joanna Susan

LEGG, John Andrew Douglas. b 32. Selw Coll Cam BA55 MA57. Wells Th Coll 57. **d** 59 **p** 59. Australia 59-63; Chapl Rugby Sch 63-64; P-in-c Ashford w Sheldon *Derby* 64-67; Kuwait 67-69; Solomon Is 70-71; Asst Master Lt Ilford Comp Sch 72-83; P-in-c Stapleford Tawney w Theydon Mt *Chelmsf* 78-83; R Hemingby *Linc* 83-88; Greece from 88; rtd 92. *Prastos, Kynorias, Arkadia, Greece 22-006* Tel (0030) (755) 051693

LEGG, Peter Ellis. b 51. STETS 02. **d** 05. NSM Radipole and Melcombe Regis *Sarum* from 05. *449 Dorchester Road, Weymouth DT3 5BW* Tel (01305) 815342 Mobile 07779-334520
E-mail pleggwey@aol.com

LEGG, Richard. b 37. Selw Coll Cam BA62 MA66 Brunel Univ MPhil77 NY Th Sem DMin85. Coll of Resurr Mirfield 63. **d** 65 **p** 66. C Ealing St Pet Mt Park *Lon* 65-68; Chapl Brunel Univ 68-78; Wychcroft Ho (Dioc Retreat Cen) *S'wark* 78-81; C Chipping Barnet w Arkley *St Alb* 81-83; TV 83-85; R St Buryan, St Levan and Sennen *Truro* 85-93; Subwarden St Deiniol's Lib Hawarden 93; Perm to Offic *Ches* 93; TV Beaminster Area

Sarum 93-97; P-in-c Veryan w Ruan Lanihorne *Truro* 97-00; rtd 01; Perm to Offic *Truro* from 03. *Sans Bruit, Plain-an-Gwarry, Marazion TR17 0DR* Tel (01736) 710712 E-mail richard.legg@tesco.net

LEGG, Robert Richard. b 16. MBE45. Open Univ BA78. St Aug Coll Cant 36. **d** 59 **p** 60. C Andover w Foxcott *Win* 59-62; V W w E Tytherley 62-71; V Kingsclere 71-83; rtd 83; Perm to Offic *Win* from 83. *The Furrow, Evingar Road, Whitchurch RG28 7EU* Tel (01256) 892126

LEGG, Roger Keith. b 35. Lich Th Coll 61. **d** 63 **p** 64. C Petersfield w Sheet *Portsm* 63-66; C Portsea St Mary 66-70; Rhodesia 70-75; V Clayton *Lich* 75-00; rtd 01; Perm to Offic *Lich* from 01. *High Crest, Chapel Lane, Hookgate, Market Drayton TF9 4QP* Tel (01630) 672766 E-mail rogjud@aol.com

LEGG, Miss Ruth Helen Margaret. b 52. Hull Univ BA74 Homerton Coll Cam CertEd75. Trin Coll Bris DipHE88. **d** 88 **p** 94. C Clevedon St Andr and Ch Ch *B & W* 88-92; C Nailsea Ch Ch 92-96; C Nailsea Ch Ch w Tickenham 96-97; V Pill, Portbury and Easton-in-Gordano from 97. *The Rectory, 17 Church Road, Easton-in-Gordano, Bristol BS20 0PQ* Tel (01275) 372804

LEGGATE, Colin Archibald Gunson. b 44. Bris Sch of Min 86. **d** 88 **p** 89. NSM Brislington St Luke *Bris* 88-97; Asst Chapl Frenchay Healthcare NHS Trust Bris 97-99; Asst Chapl N Bris NHS Trust from 99. *Frenchay Hospital, Frenchay Park Road, Bristol BS16 1LE* Tel 0117-970 1212 *or* 965 1434

LEGGETT, James Henry Aufrere. b 61. Oak Hill Th Coll DipHE93. **d** 93 **p** 94. C Hensingham *Carl* 93-97; C-in-c Ryde St Jas Prop Chpl *Portsm* from 97. *84 Pellhurst Road, Ryde PO33 3BS* Tel (01983) 565621 *or* 566381 E-mail jleggett@onetel.com

LEGGETT, Nicholas William Michael. b 62. St Steph Ho Ox 00. **d** 02 **p** 04. C Clevedon St Jo *B & W* from 02. *103 Cannons Gate, Clevedon BS21 5HZ* Tel (01275) 342043 Mobile 07762-156380 E-mail leggett1uwe@yahoo.co.uk

LEGGETT, Vanessa Gisela. *See* CATO, Ms Vanessa Gisela

LEGOOD, Giles Leslie. b 67. K Coll Lon BD88 AKC88 Heythrop Coll Lon MTh98 Derby Univ DMin04. Ripon Coll Cuddesdon 90. **d** 92 **p** 93. C N Mymms *St Alb* 92-95; Chapl R Veterinary Coll *Lon* from 95; Chapl R Free and Univ Coll Medical Sch from 95; Chapl RAuxAF from 04. *15 Ormonde Mansions, 106 Southampton Row, London WC1B 4BP* Tel (020) 7242 2574 *or* 7468 5145 E-mail glegood@rvc.ac.uk

LEGRAND, Nigel Stuart. b 51. STETS 96. **d** 99 **p** 00. NSM Boscombe St Jo *Win* 99-03; NSM Southbourne St Chris from 03; NSM Pokesdown All SS from 03. *50 Meon Road, Bournemouth BH7 6PP* Tel (01202) 428603 Fax 300400 E-mail nlegrandfamily@aol.com

LEHANEY, Frank George. b 44. City of Lon Poly 64 MCIT75 MILT99 MIAM78. Dioc OLM tr scheme 96. **d** 99 **p** 00. OLM Brockham Green *S'wark* from 99; OLM Leigh from 99. *Twelve Trees, Small's Hill Road, Leigh, Reigate RH2 8PE* Tel (01306) 611201

LEICESTER, Archdeacon of. *See* ATKINSON, The Ven Richard William Bryant

LEICESTER, Bishop of. *See* STEVENS, The Rt Revd Timothy John

LEICESTER, Dean of. *See* FAULL, The Very Revd Vivienne Frances

LEIGH, Mrs Alison Margaret. b 40. CertEd63 Goldsmiths' Coll Lon BEd75. Sarum & Wells Th Coll 85. **d** 87 **p** 94. C Chessington *Guildf* 87-90; C Green Street Green *Roch* 90-92; Dn-in-c E Peckham and Nettlestead 92-94; P-in-c 94-95; R 95-01; rtd 01; Perm to Offic *Heref* from 02. *17 Orchard Green, Marden, Hereford HR1 3ED* Tel (01432) 882032 E-mail alison.leigh@which.net

LEIGH, Arnold Robert. b 36. AKC60. **d** 61 **p** 62. C Lewisham St Mary *S'wark* 61-66; C Stockwell Green St Andr 66-69; V 69-72; TV Withycombe Raleigh *Ex* 72-74; TR 74-80; V Devonport St Bart 80-93; P-in-c Moretonhampstead, N Bovey and Manaton 93-96; R Moretonhampstead, Manaton, N Bovey and Lustleigh 96-00; rtd 00; Perm to Offic *Win* from 03. *1 Southwick Road, Bournemouth BH6 5PR* Tel (01202) 420135

LEIGH, Dennis Herbert. b 34. Lon Univ BSc56 DipTh68. Chich Th Coll 58. **d** 60 **p** 61. C Roehampton H Trin *S'wark* 60-62; C E Wickham 62-67; C Plumstead St Mark and St Marg 67-73; C Corby Epiphany w St Jo *Pet* 73-74; C Paston 84-86; C Aylestone St Andr w St Jas *Leic* 86-95; rtd 95; Perm to Offic *Pet* from 95 and *Leic* from 00. *14 Willowbrook Road, Corby NN17 2EB* Tel (01536) 263405

LEIGH, Canon James Ronald. b 32. S'wark Ord Course 63. **d** 67 **p** 68. C Purley St Barn *S'wark* 67-71; Prec St Ninian's Cathl Perth *St And* 71-73; R Leven 73-79; R Kirkcaldy 79-98; R Kinghorn 81-98; Can St Ninian's Cathl Perth from 90; rtd 98. *8 Pan Ha', Dysart, Kirkcaldy KY1 2TL* Tel (01592) 653113

LEIGH, Martin Francis. b 40. Sheff Univ BSc63. Cuddesdon Coll 65. **d** 67 **p** 68. C St Mary-at-Lambeth *S'wark* 67-70; C Bakewell *Derby* 70-74; V Ockbrook 74-82; RD Ilkeston 78-82; V Baslow 82-92; Bp's Ecum Officer 82-92; TR Kings Norton *Birm* 92-99; V Cheddleton *Lich* from 99; RD Leek from 01. *The Vicarage, Hollow Lane, Cheddleton, Leek ST13 7HP* Tel (01538) 360226 Mobile 07751-984122 Fax (07092) 330994 E-mail revmleigh@btopenworld.com *or* martin.f.leigh@stud.man.ac.uk

LEIGH, Mary Elizabeth. b 42. K Coll Lon BA64. Westcott Ho Cam 89. **d** 91 **p** 94. NSM Chesterfield St Mary and All SS *Derby* 91-92; C Hall Green Ascension *Birm* 92-94; Asst P Yardley St Edburgha 94-97; Chapl and Tutor N Ord Course from 97; Lic Preacher *Man* from 97; Perm to Offic *Lich* from 99. *The Vicarage, Hollow Lane, Cheddleton, Leek ST13 7HP* Tel (01538) 360226 E-mail mary@thenoc.co.uk

LEIGH, Michael John. b 69. Leeds Univ BA02 LWCMD93. Coll of Resurr Mirfield 00. **d** 02 **p** 03. C N Hull St Mich *York* from 02. *1 Clergy Houses, Orchard Park Road, Hull HU6 9BX* Tel (01482) 802206 E-mail mach@fish.co.uk

LEIGH, Raymond. b 37. Lon Univ BEd81. Clifton Th Coll 65. **d** 68 **p** 69. C Chadwell *Chelmsf* 68-71; Chapl RAF 71-77; Asst Master Swakeleys Sch Hillingdon 81-88; NSM Hillingdon St Jo *Lon* 87-88; C Rowley Regis *Birm* 88-90; V Londonderry 90-95; R Westbury w Turweston, Shalstone and Biddlesden *Ox* 95-99; CF (ACF) 95-02; rtd 99; Perm to Offic *Chich* from 99. *39 Pryors Lane, Bognor Regis PO21 4LH* Tel and fax (01243) 263076 Mobile 07745-493014 E-mail rayleigh306@aol.com

LEIGH, Richenda Mary Celia. b 71. St Mary's Coll Strawberry Hill BA93. Ripon Coll Cuddesdon BTh98. **d** 99 **p** 00. C Dalston H Trin w St Phil and Haggerston All SS *Lon* 99-02; Asst Chapl R Free Hampstead NHS Trust 02-05; Chapl Lon Metrop Univ *Lon* from 05. *St Luke's Church House, 21 Roscoe Street, London EC1Y 8PT* Tel (020) 7320 2379 Mobile 07971-659534

LEIGH, Roy Stephen. b 28. Imp Coll Lon BSc49. S'wark Ord Course 87. **d** 90 **p** 92. NSM Green Street Green *Roch* 90-92; NSM E Peckham and Nettlestead 92-00; Perm to Offic *Roch* 01 and *Heref* from 02. *17 Orchard Green, Marden, Hereford HR1 3ED* Tel (01432) 882032 E-mail r.s.leigh@reading.ac.uk

LEIGH-HUNT, Edward Christopher. b 22. Univ Coll Dur BA47. Ely Th Coll 48. **d** 50 **p** 51. C Wandsworth St Anne *S'wark* 50-54; C Bethnal Green St Matt *Lon* 54-56; C Lewisham St Jo Southend *S'wark* 56-57; C Ealing St Barn *Lon* 57-66; C St Bart Less 66-73; Chapl Asst St Bart Hosp Lon 66-73; Chapl Middx Hosp 73-86; rtd 87; Perm to Offic *Lon* 95-02. *College of St Barnabas, Blackberry Lane, Lingfield RH7 6NJ* Tel (01342) 870834

LEIGH-HUNT, Nicolas Adrian. b 46. MIEx70. Qu Coll Birm 85. **d** 87 **p** 88. C Tilehurst St Geo *Ox* 87-91; TV Wexcombe *Sarum* 91-99; TR 99-02; TR Savernake from 02; RD Pewsey from 97. *The Vicarage, 5 Eastcourt, Burbage, Marlborough SN8 3AG* Tel and fax (01672) 810258 E-mail leighhunt@aol.com

LEIGH-WILLIAMS, Owen Charles. b 32. BNC Ox BA56 MA60. Wycliffe Hall Ox 56. **d** 58 **p** 59. C Southgate *Chich* 64-62; C Gt Warley Ch Ch *Chelmsf* 64-68; Asst Chapl Warley Hosp Brentwood 64-68; C Dagenham *Chelmsf* 68-72; P-in-c Basildon St Andr 72-86; rtd 96. *309A Church Road, Basildon SS14 2NE* Tel (01268) 521628

LEIGHLIN, Dean of. *See* WYNNE, The Very Revd Frederick John Gordon

LEIGHTON, Adrian Barry. b 44. LTh. Lon Coll of Div 65. **d** 69 **p** 70. C Erith St Paul *Roch* 69-72; C Ipswich St Marg *St E* 72-75; P-in-c Ipswich St Helen 75-82; R 82-88; P-in-c Holbrook w Freston and Woolverstone 88-97; P-in-c Wherstead 94-97; R Holbrook, Freston, Woolverstone and Wherstead 97-98; RD Samford 90-93; P-in-c Woore and Norton in Hales *Lich* from 98; Local Min Adv (Shrewsbury) from 99. *The Vicarage, Nantwich Road, Woore, Crewe CW3 9SA* Tel (01630) 647316 E-mail adrian.leighton@lichfield.anglican.org

LEIGHTON, Alan Granville Clyde. b 37. MInstM AMIDHE Lon Univ DipRS. S'wark Ord Course 73. **d** 76 **p** 77. C Silverhill St Matt *Chich* 76-79; C Eston *York* 79-82; V 82-84; TR Eston w Normanby 84-02; rtd 02; Perm to Offic *York* from 02. *Priory Lodge, 86B Church Lane, Eston, Middlesbrough TS6 9QR* Tel (01642) 504798 Fax 283016 E-mail aleighton@argonet.co.uk

LEIGHTON, Anthony Robert. b 56. Trin Coll Bris BA88. **d** 88 **p** 89. C Harrow Trin St Mich *Lon* 88-92; TV Ratby cum Groby *Leic* 92-94; TR Bradgate Team 94-00; P-in-c Newtown Linford 95-98; V Thorpe Acre w Dishley from 00. *The Vicarage, Thorpe Acre Road, Loughborough LE11 4LF* Tel (01509) 214553 *or* 236789 E-mail tony_leighton@uk2.net

LEIGHTON, Mrs Susan. Bretton Hall Coll BEd80. Trin Coll Bris BA89. **d** 89 **p** 94. Par Dn Harrow Weald All SS *Lon* 89-92; NSM Ratby cum Groby *Leic* 92-96; C Bradgate Team 96-00; NSM Thorpe Acre w Dishley from 00. *The Vicarage, Thorpe Acre Road, Loughborough LE11 4LF* Tel 0116-231 3090 *or* (01509) 214553 E-mail susan@astad.org

LEIPER, Nicholas Keith. b 34. SS Coll Cam BA55 MB58 BChir58 MA65. St Jo Coll Nottm LTh82. **d** 84 **p** 85. C Bidston *Ches* 84-87; TV Gateacre *Liv* 87-92; P-in-c Bickerstaffe 92-94; P-in-c Melling 92-94; V Bickerstaffe and Melling 94-00; rtd 00; Perm to Offic *Liv* from 00. *31 Weldale House, Chase Close, Southport PR8 2DX* Tel (01704) 566393

LEITCH, Peter William. b 36. FCA58 ATII59. Coll of Resurr Mirfield 83. **d** 85 **p** 86. C Newsome and Armitage Bridge *Wakef* 85-88; P-in-c Upper Hopton 88-91; P-in-c Mirfield Eastthorpe St Paul 88-91; Chapl Rouen Miss to Seamen *Eur* 92-94; Sen Chapl Rotterdam Miss to Seamen 94-97; Chapl Felixstowe Miss to Seafarers *St E* 97-01; rtd 01; Perm to Offic *St E* from 01. *104 St Andrew's Road, Felixstowe IP11 7ED* Tel (01394) 285320

LEMMEY, William Henry Michael. b 59. Jes Coll Cam BA81 Jes Coll Ox PGCE82. Westcott Ho Cam 03. **d** 05. C Milton *Win* from 05. *10 Spinacre, Barton-on-Sea, New Milton BH25 7DF* Tel (01425) 621930

LEMPRIERE, Norman Everard. b 28. Liv Univ BEng54. Ridley Hall Cam 55. **d** 57 **p** 58. C Ware Ch Ch *St Alb* 57-61; R Lt Munden 61-64; R Sacombe 61-64; Lee Abbey 64-66; Perm to Offic *Ex* 64-66; C Witheridge 66-69; R Nymet Rowland w Coldridge 69-75; R Denton w S Heighton and Tarring Neville *Chich* 75-81; R Sullington and Thakeham w Warminghurst 81-92; rtd 92; Perm to Offic *B & W* from 92. *38 Woodbury Avenue, Wells BA5 2XP* Tel (01749) 673368

LENDRUM, William Henry. b 24. TCD BA50 MA62. CITC 50. **d** 50 **p** 51. C Belfast St Mich *Conn* 50-53; C Lisburn Ch Ch Cathl 53-61; P-in-c Belfast Whiterock 61-69; I Belfast St Mary Magd 69-91; Can Conn Cathl 87-91; rtd 91. *38 Lancefield Road, Belfast BT9 6LL* Tel (028) 9028 0635 Mobile 07808-749599

LENG, Bruce Edgar. b 38. St Aid Birkenhead 68. **d** 69 **p** 70. C Sheff St Swithun *Sheff* 69-74; TV Speke St Aid *Liv* 74-78; TV Yate New Town *Bris* 78-82; R Handsworth *Sheff* 82-95; R Thrybergh 95-05; Warden for Past Workers 96-05; rtd 05. *41 Hall Close Avenue, Whiston, Rotherham S60 4AH*
E-mail bruce@faith.f9.co.uk

LENNARD, Mrs Elizabeth Jemima Mary Patricia (Mary Pat). b 21. Edin Dioc NSM Course 78. **dss** 82 **d** 86 **p** 94. Falkirk *Edin* 82-86; Hon C 86-91; Asst Dioc Supernumerary 91-96; rtd 92; Hon C Grangemouth *Edin* from 96; Hon C Bo'ness from 96. *36 Heugh Street, Falkirk FK1 5QR* Tel (01324) 623240

LENNON, Alfred Dennis. b 32. Oak Hill Th Coll 72. **d** 74 **p** 74. C Cambridge H Sepulchre w All SS *Ely* 74-77; P-in-c Cambridge St Barn 77-83; R Edin St Thos *Edin* 83-90; P-in-c Burghwallis *Sheff* 90-97; Dioc Adv for Evang 90-97; rtd 97; Perm to Offic *Pet* from 98. *5 Stockerston Crescent, Uppingham, Oakham LE15 9UA* Tel (01572) 822452

LENNOX, James. b 12. TCD BA36 MA40. Div Test 37. **d** 38 **p** 39. C Houghton le Spring *Dur* 38-43; C Darlington St Cuth 43-47; V Woodhouse *Wakef* 47-63; V Bingley All SS *Bradf* 63-77; rtd 77; Perm to Offic *Bradf* from 77. *30 Hazel Beck, Cottingley Bridge, Bingley BD16 1LZ* Tel (01274) 560189

LENNOX, Joan Baxter. b 50. Strathclyde Univ BA70 Dip Counselling 94. St Jo Coll Nottm 90. **d** 96. C Baillieston *Glas* 96-97. *Address temp unknown*

LENNOX, William Ernest Michael. b 28. Selw Coll Cam BA52 MA63 Leeds Univ CertEd55. K Coll Lon 62. **d** 63 **p** 64. C Bramley *Ripon* 63-66; C Margate St Jo *Cant* 66-71; R Kingsnorth 71-73; R Shadoxhurst 71-73; R Kingsnorth w Shadoxhurst 73-93; rtd 93. *6 rue Aux Savons, Le Boisle, 80150 Crecy en Ponthieu, France*

LENON, Philip John FitzMaurice. b 24. ARIBA52 Lon Univ BD60. Wycliffe Hall Ox 55. **d** 57 **p** 58. C Hornsey Ch Ch *Lon* 57-60; C-in-c Sidcup St Andr CD *Roch* 60-67; V Crowborough *Chich* 67-89; rtd 89; Perm to Offic *Sarum* from 89. *Snowhill Cottage, Dinton, Salisbury SP3 5HN* Tel (01722) 716754

LENOX-CONYNGHAM, Andrew George. b 44. Magd Coll Ox BA65 MA73 CCC Cam PhD73. Westcott Ho Cam 72. **d** 74 **p** 75. C Poplar *Lon* 74-77; TV 77-80; Chapl Heidelberg *Eur* 80-82 and 91-96; Chapl Ch Coll Cam 82-86; Chapl and Fell St Cath Coll Cam 86-91; V Birm St Luke *Birm* from 96; AD Birm City Cen from 04. *St Luke's Vicarage, 10 St Luke's Road, Birmingham B5 7DA* Tel 0121-666 6089 *or* 622 2435 Fax 622 4532
E-mail andrew@stlukesbirm.freeserve.co.uk

LENS VAN RIJN, Robert Adriaan. b 47. St Jo Coll Nottm 78. **d** 80 **p** 81. C Gt Baddow *Chelmsf* 80-83; C Edgware *Lon* 83-86; C Derby St Pet and Ch Ch w H Trin *Derby* 86-90; Chapl Eindhoven *Eur* 91-00. *Pinkelbergen 21, 5683 LN Best, The Netherlands* Tel (0031) (499) 330222 Fax 330224
E-mail rlvr@iae.nl

LENTHALL, Mrs Nicola Yvonne. b 73. Southn Univ BA95. Westcott Ho Cam. **d** 99 **p** 00. C Leighton Buzzard w Eggington, Hockliffe etc *St Alb* 99-03; V Kensworth, Studham and Whipsnade from 03. *The Vicarage, Clay Hall Road, Kensworth, Dunstable LU6 3RF* Tel (01582) 872223
E-mail nicolal@fish.co.uk

LENTON, Colin William. b 23. CertEd. Cuddesdon Coll 80. **d** 81 **p** 81. NSM Cowley St Jo *Ox* 81-82; NSM Oakley 82-85; V Langtoft w Foxholes, Butterwick, Cottam etc *York* 85-89; rtd 89; Perm to Offic *Ripon* and *York* from 89. *Flat 3, 24 South Drive, Harrogate HG2 8AU* Tel (01423) 564751

LENTON, John Robert. b 46. Ex Coll Ox BA69 Harvard Univ MBA74. Oak Hill Th Coll. **d** 00. NSM Muswell Hill St Jas w St Matt *Lon* from 00. *St James's Vicarage, St James's Lane, London N10 3DB* Tel (020) 8444 2579 Mobile 07714-237235
E-mail johnlenton@iname.com

LEONARD, Ms Ann Cressey. b 50. Open Univ BA90. S Dios Minl Tr Scheme 90. **d** 94 **p** 95. C Portsea St Cuth *Portsm* 94-96; C Farlington 96-00; Asst to RD Petersfield 00-03; Deanery Co-ord for Educn and Tr 00-03; V Hayling Is St Andr from 03; V N Hayling St Pet from 03; Dioc Ecum Officer from 02. *29 Selsmore Road, Hayling Island PO11 9JZ*
E-mail ann.leonard@ukgateway.net

LEONARD, John Francis. b 48. Lich Th Coll 69. **d** 72 **p** 73. C Chorley St Geo *Blackb* 72-75; C S Shore H Trin 75-80; V Marton Moss 81-89; V Kingskerswell w Coffinswell *Ex* from 89. *The Vicarage, Pound Lane, Kingskerswell, Newton Abbot TQ12 5DW* Tel (01803) 407217 *or* 873006
E-mail kingskerswell.parish.church@tinyworld.co.uk

LEONARD, Canon John James. b 41. Southn Univ BSc62. Sarum Th Coll 63. **d** 65 **p** 66. C Loughborough Em *Leic* 65-70; V New Humberstone 70-78; C-in-c Rushey Mead CD 78-85; V Leic St Theodore from 85; Hon Can Leic Cathl from 96; RD Christianity N 97-05. *St Theodore's House, 4 Sandfield Close, Leicester LE4 7RE* Tel 0116-266 9956
E-mail jleonard@leicester.anglican.org

LEONARD, Peter Michael. b 47. MRTPI Portsm Poly BSc Trent Poly Dip Town Planning. Sarum & Wells Th Coll 82. **d** 84 **p** 85. C Llantwit Major *Llan* 84-88; V Cymmer and Porth 88-96; R Colwinston w Llandow and Llysworney from 96; AD Llantwit Major and Cowbridge from 02. *The Rectory, Llandow, Cowbridge CF71 7NT* Tel (01656) 890205 Fax as telephone
E-mail leonards@fdn.co.uk

LEONARD, Peter Philip. b 70. Trin Coll Bris BA94. **d** 97 **p** 98. C Haslemere *Guildf* 97-00; C Haslemere and Grayswood 00-01; C Woodham from 01. *St Michael's House, 288 Albert Drive, Woking GU21 5TX* Tel (01932) 341694 *or* tel and fax 340166 Mobile 07730-311830 E-mail rev.peter@btopenworld.com

LEONARD, Vaughan Thomas. b 51. Coll of Resurr Mirfield 94. **d** 96 **p** 97. C Broadstone *Sarum* 96-99; C Worth *Chich* 99-00; TV from 00. *St Barnabas' Vicarage, 2 Crawley Lane, Crawley RH10 7EB* Tel (01293) 513398

LEONARD-JOHNSON, Canon Philip Anthony. b 35. Selw Coll Cam BA58 MA60. Linc Th Coll 63. **d** 65 **p** 66. C Wymondham *Nor* 65-68; Zimbabwe 69-82; V Drayton in Hales *Lich* 82-92; R Adderley 82-92; P-in-c Moreton Say 88-92; S Africa 92-98; rtd 97; Hon Can Grahamstown from 97; Perm to Offic *Lich* from 99. *Hillside, Mount Lane, Market Drayton TF9 1AG* Tel (01630) 655480

LEONARDI, Jeffrey. b 49. Warwick Univ BA71 Aston Univ Dip Counselling 79. Carl Dioc Tr Course 85. **d** 88 **p** 89. C Netherton *Carl* 88-91; V Cross Canonby 91-97; V Allonby 91-97; Bp's Adv for Past Care and Counselling *Lich* from 97; Asst Min Colton, Colwich and Gt Haywood from 97. *The New Rectory, Bellamour Way, Colton, Rugeley WS15 3JW* Tel (01889) 570897 Fax as telephone E-mail jeff.leonardi@btinternet.com

LEPINE, Jeremy John. b 56. BA. St Jo Coll Nottm 82. **d** 84 **p** 85. C Harrow Trin St Mich *Lon* 84-88; TV Horley *S'wark* 88-95; Evang Adv Croydon Area Miss Team 95-02; Dioc Evang Adv and Hon Chapl S'wark Cathl 97-02; R Wollaton *S'well* from 02. *St Leonard's Rectory, 143 Russell Drive, Nottingham NG8 2BD* Tel 0115-928 1798 E-mail jerry.lepine@btopenworld.com

LEPPINGTON, Dian Marjorie. b 46. Leeds Univ BA85. Cranmer Hall Dur 81. **dss** 83 **d** 87 **p** 94. Potternewton *Ripon* 83-85; Ind Chapl 85-97; Chapl Teesside Univ *York* 97-04; Can and Preb York Minster 03-04. *3 Booth-Clibborn Court, Salford M7 4PJ*

LERRY, Keith Doyle. b 49. Univ of Wales (Cardiff) DipTh72. St Mich Coll Llan 69. **d** 72 **p** 73. C Caerau w Ely *Llan* 72-75; C Roath St Martin 75-84; V Glyntaff from 84. *The Vicarage, Glyntaff Road, Pontypridd CF37 4AS* Tel (01443) 402535

LERVY, Hugh Martin. b 68. Univ of Wales (Lamp) BA89. Qu Coll Birm 89. **d** 91 **p** 92. C Brecon St Mary and Battle w Llanddew *S & B* 91-93; C Oystermouth 93-95; V Glantawe 95-00; V Morriston from 00. *The Vicarage, Vicarage Road, Morriston, Swansea SA6 6DR* Tel (01792) 771329 Mobile 07976-725644 E-mail hugh@lervy.freeserve.co.uk

LESITER, The Ven Malcolm Leslie. b 37. Selw Coll Cam BA61 MA65. Cuddesdon Coll 61. **d** 63 **p** 64. C Eastney *Portsm* 63-66; C Hemel Hempstead *St Alb* 66-71; TV 71-73; V Leavesden All SS 73-88; RD Watford 81-88; V Radlett 88-93; Hon Can St Alb Abbey 90-93; Adn Bedford 93-03; rtd 03; Perm to Offic *Ely* from 03. *349 Ipswich Road, Colchester CO4 0HN*

LESLIE, Christopher James. b 42. Open Univ BA75. Wycliffe Hall Ox 97. **d** 05. NSM Loddon Reach *Ox* from 05. *68 Northcourt Avenue, Reading RG2 7HQ* Tel 0118-987 4540 Fax 986 1256 E-mail chris_leslie@compuserve.com

LESLIE, David Rodney. b 43. AKC67 Liv Univ MEd94 Birm Univ PhD01. **d** 68 **p** 69. C Belmont *Lon* 68-71; C St Giles Cripplegate w St Bart Moor Lane etc 71-75; TV Kirkby *Liv* 76-84; TR Ditton St Mich 84-98; V Ditton St Mich w St Thos

98-03; V Croxteth Park from 03. *The Vicarage, 1 Sandicroft Road, Liverpool L12 0LX* Tel and fax 0151-549 2202 E-mail david_leslie@lineone.net

LESLIE, Richard Charles Alan. b 46. ACIB71. St Alb Minl Tr Scheme 76. **d** 79 **p** 91. NSM Redbourn *St Alb* 79-88; NSM Newport Pagnell w Lathbury and Moulsoe *Ox* 88-94; Stewardship Adv St Alb Adnry *St Alb* 94-97; TV Borehamwood 97-05; TV Elstree and Borehamwood from 05. *St Michael's Vicarage, 142 Brook Road, Borehamwood WD6 5EQ* Tel (020) 8953 2362 *or* 8905 1365 E-mail rcaleslie@idreamtime.com

LESTER, David Charles. b 46. BSc. **d** 99 **p** 00. NSM Trowell *S'well* 99-02; NSM Trowell, Awsworth and Cossall from 02. *The Vicarage, The Lane, Awsworth, Nottingham NG16 2QP* Tel 0115-944 0473 E-mail d.lester@ntlworld.com

LESTER, The Very Revd Trevor Rashleigh. b 50. CITC 83 St Deiniol's Hawarden 92. **d** 89 **p** 90. NSM Douglas Union w Frankfield *C, C & R* 89-93; C Kilkenny w Aghour and Kilmanagh *C & O* 93-95; Bp's V Ossory Cathl 93-95; Dioc Registrar (Ossory, Ferns and Leighlin) 93-95; Dioc Lib St Canice's Lib 93-95; I Abbeystrewry Union *C, C & R* 95-03; Dean Waterford *C & O* from 03; I Waterford w Killea, Drumcannon and Dunhill from 03. *The Deanery, 41 Grange Park Road, Waterford, Irish Republic* Tel (00353) (51) 874119 E-mail dean@waterford.anglican.org

L'ESTRANGE, Timothy John Nicholas. b 67. Surrey Univ BA90. St Steph Ho Ox BA92 MA96. **d** 93 **p** 94. C Halesworth w Linstead, Chediston, Holton etc *St E* 93-96; Dom Chapl to Bp Horsham *Chich* 96-98; R Beeding and Bramber w Botolphs from 98. *The Rectory, Sele Priory Church, Church Lane, Upper Beeding, Steyning BN44 3HP* Tel (01903) 815474 *or* 815850 E-mail rector@upper-beeding.fsnet.co.uk

LETALL, Ronald Richard. b 29. ACII76 SSC. Linc Th Coll 82. **d** 84 **p** 85. C Scarborough St Martin *York* 84-86; C Middlesbrough St Thos 86-88; R Kirby Misperton w Normanby, Edston and Salton 88-90; TV Louth *Linc* 90-94; rtd 94; Perm to Offic *Sheff* from 95; *Wakef* 95-97; *Chich* 97-99; and from 01. *20 Greenwood Drive, Angmering, Littlehampton BN16 4ND* Tel (01903) 859469 E-mail ronald@letall.fsnet.co.uk

LETCHER, Canon David John. b 34. K Coll Lon 54. Chich Th Coll 56. **d** 58 **p** 59. C St Austell *Truro* 58-62; C Southbroom *Sarum* 62-64; R Odstock w Nunton and Bodenham 64-72; RD Alderbury 68-73 and 77-82; V Downton 72-85; Can and Preb Sarum Cathl 79-99; TV Dorchester 85-97; RD Dorchester 89-95; rtd 97; Perm to Offic *Sarum* from 97; CF (ACF) 97-00. *6 Longmoor Street, Poundbury, Dorchester DT1 3GN* Tel (01305) 257764

LETHBRIDGE, Christopher David. b 43. N Ord Course 90. **d** 93 **p** 94. NSM S Elmsall *Wakef* 93-95; C Knottingley 95-97; R Badsworth 97-01; P-in-c Bilham *Sheff* from 01; Chapl HM YOI Hatfield from 01. *Bilham Vicarage, Churchfield Road, Clayton, Doncaster DN5 7DH* Tel (01977) 643756

LETHEREN, William Neils. b 37. St Aid Birkenhead 61. **d** 64 **p** 65. C Liv St Mich *Liv* 64-67; V 71-75; C Kirkdale St Athanasius 67-69; C Walsall Wood *Lich* 69-71; V W Derby St Jas *Liv* 75-84; R Newton in Makerfield Em 84-88; V Garston 88-04; rtd 04. *24 Pitville Avenue, Liverpool L18 7JG* Tel 0151-724 5543

LETSON, Barry. b 55. Univ of Wales (Lamp) BA77. St Deiniol's Hawarden 82. **d** 83 **p** 84. C Flint *St As* 83-86; V Llansantffraid Glyn Ceirog and Llanarmon etc 86-89; R Montgomery and Forden and Llandyssil 89-96; RD Pool 92-96; V Mountain Ash *Llan* 96-97; V Mountain Ash and Miskin 97-02; V Crickhowell w Cwmdu and Tretower *S & B* from 02. *The Rectory, Rectory Road, Crickhowell NP8 1DW* Tel (01873) 810017

LETTERS, Mark Ian. b 68. Keble Coll Ox BA89 MA93 Magd Coll Cam PGCE90. St Alb and Ox Min Course 03. **d** 05. NSM Ox St Barn and St Paul *Ox* from 05. *84 Islip Road, Oxford OX2 7SW* Tel 07791-974727 (mobile)

LETTS, Gerald Vincent. b 33. Univ of Wales BA63. Qu Coll Birm DipTh65 NY Th Sem DMin. **d** 65 **p** 66. C Birstall *Leic* 65-68; V Belgrave St Mich 68-75; P-in-c Brightside All SS *Sheff* 75-78; V Sheff St Cuth 75-91; R Bradfield 91-00; rtd 00; Perm to Offic *Ely* from 01. *12 Norico Bay, March PE15 9HJ* Tel (01354) 650820

LETTS, Canon Kenneth John. b 42. Melbourne Univ BA65 DipEd67. Coll of Resurr Mirfield 68. **d** 71 **p** 72. Australia 71-94; C Mt Waverley St Steph 71-74; Chapl Melbourne C of E Gr Sch 74-81; P-in-c Albert Park 81-94; Sen Chapl St Mich Sch 82-94; Chapl Nice w Vence *Eur* from 94; Can Gib Cathl from 04. *11 rue de la Buffa, 06000 Nice, France* Tel (0033) (4) 93 87 19 83 E-mail anglican@free.fr

LEUNG, Peter. b 36. Trin Coll Singapore BTh60 St Andr Univ PhD73. SE Asia Sch of Th MTh69. **d** 60 **p** 61. Singapore 60-62 and 65-76; Br N Borneo 62-63; Malaysia 63-65; Lect Congr Coll Man 76-77; USPG 77-83; Perm to Offic *Roch* 83-89; BCC 83-90; CTBI from 90; Perm to Offic *S'wark* 88-94; Hon C Shortlands *Roch* 90-01; Regional Sec (S and E Asia) CMS 91-99; rtd 99. *35 Tufton Gardens, West Molesey KT8 1TD* Tel (020) 8650 4157

LEVELL, Peter John. b 40. Bris Univ BA62 CertEd63. STETS 99. **d** 02 **p** 03. NSM Guildf St Sav *Guildf* from 02. *23 Mountside, Guildford GU2 4JD* Tel (01483) 871656 E-mail plevell@ntlworld.com

LEVER, Julian Lawrence Gerrard. b 36. Fitzw Coll Cam BA60 MA64. Sarum Th Coll 60. **d** 62 **p** 63. C Amesbury *Sarum* 62-66; R Corfe Mullen 66-78; RD Wimborne 73-75; P-in-c Wilton w Netherhampton and Fugglestone 78-82; R 82-86; R Salisbury St Martin 86-94; Perm to Offic *Win* from 96; rtd 98. *6 St John's Close, Wimborne BH21 1LY* Tel (01202) 848249

LEVERTON, James. *See* LEVERTON, Peter James Austin

LEVERTON, Mrs Judith. b 55. Eaton Hall Coll of Educn CertEd76. St Jo Coll Nottm 02. **d** 04 **p** 05. C Doncaster St Jas *Sheff* from 04. *61A Balby Road, Doncaster DN4 0RD* Tel (01302) 342558 Mobile 07960-573529 E-mail leverton@lineone.net

LEVERTON, Michael John. b 52. K Coll Lon BD76 AKC76 MTh77. Cant Sch of Min 84. **d** 87 **p** 88. NSM Elham w Denton and Wootton *Cant* 87-92; C Yelverton, Meavy, Sheepstor and Walkhampton *Ex* 92-93; TV 93-98; C Tavistock and Gulworthy 98-00; P-in-c Stevenage All SS Pin Green *St Alb* from 00. *All Saints' Vicarage, 100 Derby Way, Stevenage SG1 5TJ* Tel (01438) 318706 E-mail michael.leverton@btinternet.com

LEVERTON, Peter James Austin. b 33. Nottm Univ BA55. Ripon Coll Cuddesdon 79. **d** 81 **p** 82. C St Jo in Bedwardine *Worc* 81-84; V Worc St Mich 84-88; TR Worc St Barn w Ch Ch 88-92; V Riddings and Ironville *Derby* 92-00; rtd 00; Perm to Offic *Derby* from 00. *2 George Street, Langley Mill, Nottingham NG16 4DJ* Tel (01773) 710243 E-mail jim@rev-levs.freeserve.co.uk

LEVERTON, Peter Robert. b 25. Lich Th Coll 59. **d** 60 **p** 61. C Shepshed *Leic* 60-64; Australia 64-69; V Marshchapel *Linc* 70-73; V Grainthorpe w Conisholme 70-73; R N Coates 70-73; Miss to Seamen 73-77; P-in-c Brislington St Luke *Bris* 77-84; V Avonmouth St Andr 84-87; Ind Chapl 84-87; P-in-c Ugborough *Ex* 87-91; P-in-c Ermington 88-91; rtd 91; Perm to Offic *Ex* from 91. *4 Drakes Avenue, Sidford, Sidmouth EX10 9QY* Tel (01395) 579835

LEVETT, The Ven Howard. b 44. K Coll Lon AKC67. **d** 68 **p** 69. C Rotherhithe St Mary w All SS *S'wark* 68-72; P-in-c Walworth St Jo 72-77; V Walworth St Jo 77-80; P-in-c Walworth Lady Marg w St Mary 78; RD S'wark and Newington 78-80; Adn Egypt 80-94; Miss to Seafarers from 80; JMECA from 80; V Holborn St Alb w Saffron Hill St Pet *Lon* from 94. *St Alban's Clergy House, 18 Brooke Street, London EC1N 7RD* Tel (020) 7405 1831 Mobile 07815-111429 Fax (020) 7430 2551 E-mail secretary@saintalbanthemartyr.org.uk

LEVICK, Brian William. b 30. Solicitor 51. Westcott Ho Cam 63. **d** 64 **p** 65. C Bourne *Linc* 64-69; C Deeping St James 69-70; C Hemel Hempstead *St Alb* 70-71; TV 71-77; Hon C Sedbergh, Cautley and Garsdale *Bradf* 77-83; V Firbank, Howgill and Killington 77-83; V Cononley w Bradley 83-90; Methodist Min 83-90; rtd 90; C Kettlewell w Conistone, Hubberholme etc *Bradf* 90-93; Hon C New Sleaford *Linc* 93-97; Dioc Ecum Officer 93-97; Ecum Officer Chs Together Lincs and S Humberside 93-97; Perm to Offic *Bradf* from 99. *42 Robin Lane, Bentham, Lancaster LA2 7AG* Tel (01524) 261473

LEVICK, Canon Frank Hemsley. b 29. Kelham Th Coll 49. **d** 54 **p** 55. C Anfield St Marg *Liv* 54-58; V 58-67; V Ribbleton *Blackb* 67-80; TR 80-85; Hon Can Blackb Cathl 75-90; R Ribchester w Stidd 85-90; rtd 90; Perm to Offic *S'well* from 90; *Linc* 96-99. *The Old Nurseries, Low Street, Beckingham, Doncaster DN10 4PS* Tel (01427) 848668 E-mail frank.canon@virgin.net

LEVISEUR, Nicholas Templer. b 56. Magd Coll Ox MA82 Barrister 79. STETS 97 Ven English Coll Rome 00. **d** 00 **p** 01. NSM Hartfield w Coleman's Hatch *Chich* from 00. *Tye House East, Edenbridge Road, Hartfield TN7 4JR* Tel (01892) 770451

LEVY, Christopher Charles. b 51. Southn Univ BTh82. Sarum & Wells Th Coll 79. **d** 82 **p** 83. C Rubery *Birm* 82-85; C Stratford-on-Avon w Bishopton *Cov* 85-87; TV Clifton *S'well* 87-95; V Egmanton from 95; R Kirton from 95; V Walesby from 95; Chapl Center Parcs Holiday Village from 01. *St Edmund's Vicarage, Walesby, Newark NG22 9PA* Tel (01623) 860522 E-mail chris@walesbyvic.fsnet.co.uk

LEW, Henry. b 39. **d** 96 **p** 97. NSM Dublin Whitechurch *D & G* 96-99; Manager Brabazon Trust Sheltered Housing 96-00; Lic to Offic from 99; NSM Powerscourt w Kilbride from 00. *51 Butterfield Park, Rathfarnham, Dublin 14, Irish Republic* Tel (00353) (1) 493 1483 *or* 269 1677 Mobile 87-628 8049 Fax (1) 283 9508 E-mail healew@iol.ie

LEWER ALLEN, Mrs Patricia (Paddy). b 47. SRN70 UNISA BA79 HDipEd85 Cape Town Univ BA86. Th Ext Educn Coll 94. **d** 97 **p** 98. P-in-c Dunbar *Edin* from 98. *St Anne's House, 1 Westgate, Dunbar EH42 1JL* Tel and fax (01368) 865711 E-mail paddyallen@aol.com

LEWERS, The Very Revd Benjamin Hugh. b 32. Selw Coll Cam BA60 MA64. Linc Th Coll. **d** 62 **p** 63. C Northampton St Mary *Pet* 62-65; C Hounslow Heath St Paul *Lon* 65-68; C-in-c Hounslow Gd Shep Beavers Lane CD 65-68; Chapl Heathrow

Airport 68-75; V Newark St Mary *S'well* 75-80; TR Newark w Hawton, Cotham and Shelton 80-81; P-in-c Averham w Kelham 79-81; Provost Derby 81-97; rtd 98; Perm to Offic *Sarum* from 98 and *B & W* from 00. *Thimble Cottage, Marshwood, Bridport DT6 5QF* Tel (01297) 678515

LEWES AND HASTINGS, Archdeacon of. *See* JONES, The Ven Philip Hugh

LEWES, Area Bishop of. *See* BENN, The Rt Revd Wallace Parke

LEWIS, The Ven Albert John Francis. b 21. Univ Coll of S Wales BA(Econ)45. St Mich Coll Llan 46. **d** 48 **p** 49. C Cardiff St Jo *Llan* 48-61; Dioc Dir RE 60-91; V Pendoylan 61-73; P-in-c Welsh St Donats 70-73; V Pendoylan w Welsh St Donats 73-81; RD Llan 69-81; Can Llan Cathl 76-81; Treas 81-88; Adn Margam 81-88; Adn Llan 88-91; rtd 91; Chapl to Rtd Clerics and Widows of Clergy *Llan* from 91; Perm to Offic from 91. *11 Downs View Close, Aberthin, Cowbridge CF71 7HG* Tel (01446) 773320

LEWIS, Ann Theodora Rachel. b 33. Univ of Wales (Ban) BA55. Qu Coll Birm 78. **d** 80 **p** 97. C Swansea St Mary w H Trin *S & B* 80-96; Chapl St Mary's Coll 90-96; rtd 96; Public Preacher *St D* from 96. *Fisherywish, Maes yr Eglwys, Llansaint, Kidwelly SA17 5JE* Tel (01267) 267386

LEWIS, Canon Arthur Griffith. b 15. Univ of Wales (Lamp) BA40. **d** 47 **p** 48. C Clydach *S & B* 47-55; R Aberyscir and Llanfihangel Nantbran 55-63; V Ystalyfera 63-87; RD Cwmtawe 79-85; Hon Can Brecon Cathl 80-89; Can 81-85; P-in-c Capel Coelbren 85-89; rtd 89. *14 Pontwillim, Brecon LD3 9BT* Tel (01874) 622869

LEWIS, Arthur Jenkin Llewellyn. b 42. Univ of Wales (Cardiff) MPS67 BPharm. Coll of Resurr Mirfield 71. **d** 73 **p** 74. C Cardiff St Jo *Llan* 73-78; C Christchurch *Win* 78-82; R Lightbowne *Man* 82-04. *25 Dene Street Gardens, Dorking RH4 2DN*

LEWIS, Arthur Roland. b 20. St Edm Hall Ox BA41 MA45. St Steph Ho Ox 41. **d** 43 **p** 44. C Sutton in Ashfield St Mich *S'well* 43-45; C Stirchley *Birm* 45-47; Zanzibar and Tanganyika 47-58; S Rhodesia 58-65; Rhodesia 65-80; Adn Inyanga 66-69; S Africa 80-87; rtd 87; Perm to Offic *Birm* 88-99. *The College of St Barnabas, Blackberry Lane, Lingfield RH7 6NJ* Tel (01342) 870028 Fax 870731 E-mail arthur_r_lewis@compuserve.com

LEWIS, The Very Revd Bertie. b 31. Univ of Wales (Lamp) BA54 St Cath Soc Ox BA57 MA60. Wycliffe Hall Ox 54. **d** 57 **p** 58. C Cwmaman *St D* 57-60; C Aberystwyth St Mich 60-62; V Llanddewi Brefi w Llanbadarn Odwyn 62-65; V Henfynyw w Aberaeron and Llanddewi Aberarth 65-75; V Lampeter 75-80; Can St D Cathl 78-86; Chapl Abth Hosps 80-88; R Aberystwyth *St D* 80-88; Adn Cardigan 86-90; V Nevern and Y Beifil w Eglwyswrw and Meline etc 88-90 and 94-96; Dean St D 90-94; V St D Cathl 90-94; Hon Can St D Cathl 94-97; rtd 96. *Bryn Golau, Llanfarian, Aberystwyth SY23 4BT* Tel (01970) 612492

LEWIS, Brian James. b 52. Cant Univ (NZ) BA75. St Jo Coll Auckland 76. **d** 78 **p** 79. C Ashburton New Zealand 78-80; C Shrub End *Chelmsf* 80-82; P-in-c Colchester St Barn 82-84; V 84-88; P-in-c Romford St Andr 88-90; R 90-99; RD Havering 93-97; R Lt Ilford St Mich from 99. *The Rectory, Church Road, London E12 6HA* Tel (020) 8478 2182 E-mail brian@littleilford.fsnet.co.uk

LEWIS, The Very Revd Christopher Andrew. b 44. Bris Univ BA69 CCC Cam PhD74. Westcott Ho Cam 71. **d** 73 **p** 74. C Barnard Castle *Dur* 73-76; Dir Ox Inst for Ch and Soc 76-79; Tutor Ripon Coll Cuddesdon 76-79; Sen Tutor 79-81; Vice-Prin 81-82; P-in-c Aston Rowant w Crowell *Ox* 78-81; V Spalding *Linc* 82-87; Can Res Cant Cathl *Cant* 87-94; Dir of Minl Tr 89-94; Dean St Alb 94-03; Dean Ch Ch *Ox* from 03. *The Deanery, Christ Church, Oxford OX1 1DP* Tel (01865) 276161 Fax 276238 E-mail jan.bolongaro@christ-church.ox.ac.uk

LEWIS, Christopher Gouldson. b 42. K Coll Cam BA64 MA68. Cuddesdon Coll 65. **d** 67 **p** 68. C Gosforth All SS *Newc* 67-71; Sarawak 71-74; V Luton St Chris Round Green *St Alb* 74-80; RD Reculver *Cant* 80-86 and 92-93; V Whitstable All SS w St Pet 80-84; TR Whitstable 84-93; Dir Post-Ord Tr 88-93; Hon Can Cant Cathl 91-93; Can Res Bradf Cathl *Bradf* 93-01; Bp's Officer for Min and Tr 93-01; P-in-c Riding Mill *Newc* from 01; Chapl Shepherd's Dene Retreat Ho from 01; Adv for Spirituality and Spiritual Direction from 02. *The Vicarage, Riding Mill NE44 6AT* Tel (01434) 682811

LEWIS, David Antony. b 48. Dur Univ BA69 Nottm Univ MTh84. St Jo Coll Nottm 81. **d** 83 **p** 84. C Gateacre *Liv* 83-86; V Toxteth St Cypr w Ch Ch 86-01; V Edge Hill St Cypr w St Mary from 01; AD Liv N 94-03. *The Vicarage, 48 John Lennon Drive, Liverpool L6 9HT* Tel 0151-260 3262 E-mail stcyps@boltblue.com

LEWIS, David Hugh. b 45. Oak Hill Th Coll 88. **d** 90 **p** 91. C Oakham, Hambleton, Egleton, Braunston and Brooke *Pet* 90-94; R Ewhurst *Guildf* 94-99; V Southway *Ex* 99-03; RD Plymouth Moorside 01-03; P-in-c Anglesey Gp *Ely* 03-04; V from 04. *The Vicarage, 86 High Street, Bottisham, Cambridge CB5 9BA* Tel (01223) 812367 E-mail david.hlewis@tinyworld.co.uk

LEWIS, David Tudor. b 61. Jes Coll Cam BA83. Trin Coll Bris BA88. **d** 88 **p** 89. C Tile Cross *Birm* 88-91; C Woking St Jo *Guildf* 91-95; TV Carl H Trin and St Barn *Carl* 95-97; Chapl Carl Hosps NHS Trust 95-97; Asst Chapl Oslo w Bergen, Trondheim and Stavanger *Eur* 97-04; TV E Richmond *Ripon* from 04. *The Rectory, Great Smeaton, Northallerton DL6 2EP* Tel (01609) 881205

LEWIS, David Tudor Bowes. b 63. Keele Univ BA85 Univ of Wales (Cardiff) BTh90. St Mich Coll Llan 87. **d** 90 **p** 91. C Llangollen w Trevor and Llantysilio *St As* 90-93; C Bistre 93-97; V Berse and Southsea 97-02; V Bwlchgwyn w Berse w Southsea 02-04; R Overton and Erbistock and Penley from 04. *The Rectory, 4 Sundorne, Overton, Wrexham LL13 0EB* Tel (01978) 710229

LEWIS, Canon David Vaughan. b 36. Trin Coll Cam BA60 MA64. Ridley Hall Cam 60. **d** 62 **p** 63. C Rugby St Matt *Cov* 62-65; Asst Chapl K Edw Sch Witley 65-71; Hon C Rainham *Chelmsf* 71-76; V Stoke Hill *Guildf* 76-87; V Wallington H Trin *S'wark* 87-03; Hon Can S'wark Cathl 95-03; RD Sutton 97-00; rtd 03; Perm to Offic *Ely* from 03. *11 The Meadows, Haslingfield, Cambridge CB3 7JD* Tel (01223) 874029

LEWIS, Canon David Watkin. b 40. Univ of Wales (Lamp) BA61 Univ of Wales (Swansea) DipYL65. Wycliffe Hall Ox 61. **d** 63 **p** 64. C Skewen *Llan* 63-66; Field Tr Officer Prov Youth Coun Ch in Wales 66-68; C Gabalfa 68-71; P-in-c Marcross w Monknash and Wick 71-73; R 73-83; RD Llantwit Major and Cowbridge 81-83; V Baglan from 83; Can Llan Cathl from 00; Treas Llan Cathl from 04. *The Vicarage, 29 Church Road, Port Talbot SA12 8ST* Tel (01639) 812199

LEWIS, Edward John. b 58. JP93. Univ of Wales BEd80 BA82 FRSA97 MInstD01. Chich Th Coll 82. **d** 83 **p** 84. C Llangiwg *S & B* 83-85; C Morriston 85-87; Asst Chapl Morriston Hosp 85-87; V Tregaron w Ystrad Meurig and Strata Florida *St D* 87-89; Chapl Tregaron Hosp 87-89; Chapl Manor Hosp Walsall 89-92; Distr Co-ord Chapl Walsall Hosps 90-92; Sen Chapl Walsall Hosps NHS Trust 92-00; Chapl Walsall Community Health Trust 92-00; Chief Exec and Dir Tr Gen Syn Hosp Chapl Coun from 00; Perm to Offic *Lich* from 00 and *St Alb* from 02; Visiting Lect St Mary's Univ Coll Twickenham *Lon* from 04. *Hospital Chaplaincies Council, Church House, Great Smith Street, London SW1P 3NZ* Tel (020) 7898 1892 Fax 7898 1891 E-mail edward.lewis@c-of-e.org.uk *or* fr.edward@ntlworld.com

LEWIS, Ella Pauline. b 41. SW Minl Tr Course 94. **d** 98. NSM Paignton St Paul Preston *Ex* 98-02; NSM Paignton Ch Ch and Preston St Paul from 03. *Roselands, 5 Great Headland Road, Paignton TQ3 2DY* Tel (01803) 555171 E-mail paulinelewis@eclipse.co.uk

LEWIS, Elsie Leonora. b 26. Cranmer Hall Dur 72. **dss** 78 **d** 87 **p** 94. S Westoe *Dur* 78-80; Ryton 80-86; rtd 86. *53 Cushy Cow Lane, Ryton NE40 3NL* Tel 0191-413 5845

LEWIS, Eric. b 36. Sarum & Wells Th Coll 74. **d** 77 **p** 78. NSM Oldbury *Sarum* 77-92; C Weymouth St Paul 92-94; P-in-c Portland St Jo 94-99; Chapl Weymouth Coll 94-97; Asst Chapl Dorset Community NHS Trust 95-99; rtd 99; Chapl Costa Blanca *Eur* from 01. *Buzon T765, Tabaira 03724, Moraira, Alicante, Spain* Tel (0034) (965) 744493 Mobile 696-754439 E-mail fatherlewis@wanadoo.es

LEWIS, Frederick Norman. b 23. Leeds Univ BA47. Coll of Resurr Mirfield 47. **d** 49 **p** 50. C Haydock St Jas *Liv* 49-51; C Dresden *Lich* 51-55; C Stafford St Mary 55-56; V Wednesfield St Thos 56-65; V Shrewsbury St Chad 65-69; V Kingswinford St Mary 69-88; rtd 88; Perm to Offic *Lich* from 88. *27 Bramblewood Drive, Wolverhampton WV3 9DB* Tel (01902) 334934

LEWIS, Gary. b 61. Lanc Univ BA85. Ripon Coll Cuddesdon 86. **d** 89 **p** 90. C Blackb St Mich w St Jo and H Trin *Blackb* 89-92; C Altham w Clayton le Moors 92-95; V Lea 95-01; V Skerton St Luke from 01. *St Luke's Vicarage, Slyne Road, Lancaster LA1 2HU* Tel (01524) 63249

LEWIS, Graham Rhys. b 54. Loughb Univ BTech76 Cranfield Inst of Tech MBA89. SEITE 95. **d** 98 **p** 99. NSM S Gillingham *Roch* from 98. *53 Oastview, Gillingham ME8 8JG* Tel (01634) 373036 E-mail graham@53oastview.fsnet.co.uk

LEWIS, Gwynne. *See* LEWIS, Hywel Gwynne

LEWIS, Ms Hannah Margaret. b 71. CCC Cam BA93 MA96. Qu Coll Birm 95. **d** 97 **p** 98. C Cannock *Lich* 97-00; Perm to Offic from 00. *53 Derwent Drive, Priorslee, Telford TF2 9QN*

LEWIS, Hubert Godfrey. b 33. Univ of Wales (Lamp) BA59 DipTh60. **d** 60 **p** 61. C Merthyr Tydfil *Llan* 60-64; C Caerphilly 64-66; Perm to Offic *S'wark* 66-76; Perm to Offic *Cant* 76-82; Hon C Shirley St Jo *S'wark* 82-93; Hon C Whitchurch *Llan* from 94. *2 Heol Wernlas, Cardiff CF14 1RY* Tel (029) 2061 3079

LEWIS, Hywel Gwynne. b 37. FCA75. St D Dioc Tr Course 94. **d** 97 **p** 98. NSM Henfynyw w Aberaeron and Llanddewi Aberarth etc *St D* from 97. *Danycoed, Lampeter Road, Aberaeron SA46 0ED* Tel (01545) 570577

LEWIS, Ian. b 33. Lon Univ MB, BS57. Oak Hill Th Coll 61. **d** 63 **p** 64. C Heatherlands St Jo *Sarum* 63-66; Ethiopia 66-73; Hon C Bath Walcot *B & W* 75-77; Lic to Offic 78-98; rtd 98. *22C Ashley Road, Bathford, Bath BA1 7TT* Tel (01225) 859818 E-mail i.lewis@btinvemev.com

LEWIS, Ian Richard. b 54. Sheff Univ BA76 Ox Univ BA83 MA87. Wycliffe Hall Ox 81. **d** 84 **p** 85. C Rusholme H Trin *Man* 84-88; C Sandal St Helen *Wakef* 88-91; V Bath St Bart *B & W* from 91. *St Bartholomew's Vicarage, 5 Oldfield Road, Bath BA2 3ND* Tel (01225) 422070 Fax as telephone E-mail ianlewis@stbartsbath.org

LEWIS, James Edward. b 22. St D Coll Lamp BA50. **d** 51 **p** 52. C Gorseinon *S & B* 51-52; C Defynnog 52-56; R Llangynllo w Troed-yr-aur *St D* 56-61; V Brynamman 61-72; R Llangathen w Llanfihangel Cilfargen 72-82; V Llangathen w Llanfihangel Cilfargen etc 82-90; RD Llangadog and Llandeilo 85-89; rtd 90. *The Flat, 3 St Mary's Street, Carmarthen SA31 1TN* Tel (01267) 221660

LEWIS, James Michael. b 51. Trin Coll Carmarthen CertEd73 Open Univ BA86 MA91. St Mich Coll Llan 98. **d** 02 **p** 03. NSM Laleston w Tythegston and Merthyr Mawr *Llan* from 02. *19 Austin Avenue, Laleston, Bridgend CF32 0LG* Tel (01656) 660648 Mobile 07951-300206 E-mail mike.lewis11@virgin.net

LEWIS, Jean Anwyl. Surrey Univ BA05 CertEd. **d** 05. OLM Windlesham *Guildf* from 05. *2 Hillside Cottages, Broadway Road, Windlesham GU20 6BY* Tel (01276) 472681 E-mail jean.lewis1@btopenworld.com

LEWIS, Jocelyn Vivien. b 49. Trevelyan Coll Dur BSc70 Sheff Univ PhD75. EMMTC DTPS94. **d** 94 **p** 95. NSM Brimington *Derby* 94-99; P-in-c Whittington from 99; Dioc Dir Reader Tr from 99; P-in-c New Whittington from 04. *Whittington Rectory, Church Street North, Old Whittington, Chesterfield S41 9QP* Tel (01246) 450651 E-mail bart@jocelyn.fsbusiness.co.uk

LEWIS, The Ven John Arthur. b 34. Jes Coll Ox BA56 MA60. Cuddesdon Coll 58. **d** 60 **p** 61. C Prestbury *Glouc* 60-63; C Wimborne Minster *Sarum* 63-66; R Eastington and Frocester *Glouc* 66-70; V Nailsworth 70-78; Chapl Memorial and Querns Hosp Cirencester 78-88; V Cirencester *Glouc* 78-88; RD Cirencester 84-88; Hon Can Glouc Cathl 85-98; Adn Cheltenham 88-98; rtd 98; Perm to Offic *Glouc* from 98. *5 Vilverie Mead, Bishop's Cleeve, Cheltenham GL52 7YY* Tel (01242) 678425

LEWIS, John Edward. b 31. SS Mark & Jo Coll Chelsea CertEd53. Qu Coll Birm 83. **d** 85 **p** 86. C Leominster *Heref* 85-87; TV 87-95; rtd 95; Perm to Offic *Heref* from 97. *The Holms, 253 Godiva Road, Leominster HR6 8TB* Tel (01568) 612280

LEWIS, John Goddard. b 52. Houston Bapt Univ (USA) BA74 JD77 Ox Univ 98. Virginia Th Sem MDiv97. **d** 97. USA 97-98 and from 01; Hon C Bladon w Woodstock *Ox* 98-01; Min Cen for Faith in the Work Place San Antonio from 01. *c/o The Lord Bishop of West Texas DD, PO Box 6885, San Antonio, TX 78209, USA* E-mail lewbrid@aol.com

LEWIS, John Herbert. b 42. Selw Coll Cam BA64 MA68. Westcott Ho Cam 64. **d** 66 **p** 67. C Wyken *Cov* 66-70; C Bedford St Andr *St Alb* 70-73; Lib Pusey Ho 73-77; Bp's Chapl for Graduates *Ox* 73-77; TV Woughton 78-82; TV Gt Chesham 82-88; P-in-c Newport Pagnell w Lathbury and Moulsoe 88-91; R from 91. *New Rectory, 81 High Street, Newport Pagnell MK16 8AB* Tel (01908) 611145

LEWIS, John Horatio George. b 47. Southn Univ BEd72 MA85. Ox NSM Course 86. **d** 89 **p** 90. NSM Newbury *Ox* 89-04; Perm to Offic *Win* 94-04; P-in-c Borden *Cant* from 05. *The Vicarage, School Lane, Borden, Sittingbourne ME9 8JS* Tel (01795) 472986 Mobile 07973-406622 E-mail fr.johnlewis@tiscali.co.uk

✠**LEWIS, The Rt Revd John Hubert Richard.** b 43. AKC66. **d** 67 **p** 68 **c** 92. C Hexham *Newc* 67-70; Ind Chapl 70-77; Communications Officer *Dur* 77-82; Chapl for Agric *Heref* 82-87; Adn Ludlow 87-92; Suff Bp Taunton *B & W* 92-97; Bp St E from 97. *The Bishop's House, 4 Park Road, Ipswich IP1 3ST* Tel (01473) 252829 Fax 232552 E-mail bishop.richard@stedmundsbury.anglican.org

LEWIS, John Malcolm. b 41. Reading Univ BEd. Trin Coll Bris. **d** 82 **p** 83. C Kingswood *Bris* 82-85; TV Weston-super-Mare Cen Par *B & W* 85-91; Dioc Children's Adv *Nor* 91-97; TV Bishopsworth and Bedminster Down *Bris* from 97; Hon Min Can Bris Cathl from 04. *St Oswald's Vicarage, Cheddar Grove, Bedminster Down, Bristol BS13 7EN* Tel and fax 0117-964 2649 E-mail john@stoswalds.freeserve.co.uk

LEWIS, John Percival. b 19. TCD BA44. CITC 47. **d** 47 **p** 48. C Galway *T, K & A* 47-51; I Knappagh 51-74; Can Tuam Cathl from 70; I Omey w Ballynakill, Errislannan and Roundstone 73-91; Provost Tuam 73-91; rtd 91. *McBride Home, Westport, Co Mayo, Irish Republic*

LEWIS, John Pryce. b 65. Trin Coll Carmarthen BA87. Wycliffe Hall Ox 92. **d** 94 **p** 95. C Carmarthen St Pet *St D* 94-97; V Nevern and Y Beifil w Eglwyswrw and Meline etc from 97. *The Vicarage, Nevern, Newport SA42 0NF* Tel (01239) 820427

LEWIS, The Very Revd John Thomas. b 47. Jes Coll Ox BA69 MA73 St Jo Coll Cam BA72 MA92. Westcott Ho Cam 71. **d** 73 **p** 74. C Whitchurch *Llan* 73-77; C Llanishen and Lisvane 77-80; Asst Chapl Univ of Wales (Cardiff) 80-85; Warden of Ords 81-85; V Brecon St David w Llanspyddid and Llanilltyd *S & B* 85-91; Sec Prov Selection Panel and Bd Ch in Wales 87-94; V Bassaleg *Mon* 91-96; TR 96-00; Bp's Chapl for CME 98-00; Dean Llan from 00; V Llandaff from 00. *The Deanery, The Cathedral Green, Llandaff, Cardiff CF5 2YF* Tel (029) 2056 1545

LEWIS, Kenneth Lionel. b 22. Univ of Wales (Swansea) 42 Keble Coll Ox BA50 MA54 Ch Coll Cam CertEd52. Wycliffe Hall Ox 52. **d** 52 **p** 53. C Bromley St Jo *Roch* 52-55; C Streatham Hill St Marg *S'wark* 55-57; R Tatsfield 57-72; Lic to Offic 72-78 and from 89; Perm to Offic *Roch* 75-78 and 83-93; Perm to Offic *Cant* 75-78. *3 Towerfields, Westerham Road, Keston BR2 6HF* Tel (01689) 851125

LEWIS, Kevin James. b 76. Nottm Univ BA98. St Jo Coll Nottm MTh04 MA(MM)05. **d** 05. C Southgate *Chich* from 05. *54 Dovedale Crescent, Crawley RH11 8SG* Tel (01293) 517075

LEWIS, Leslie. b 28. LRAM56. St Aid Birkenhead 61. **d** 63 **p** 64. C Eastham *Ches* 63-66; C W Kirby St Bridget 66-72; V Rainow w Saltersford 72-73; V Rainow w Saltersford and Forest 73-02; Dioc Clergy Widows and Retirement Officer 88-93; rtd 02; Perm to Offic *Ches* from 02. *25 Appleby Close, Macclesfield SK11 8XB* Tel (01625) 616395

LEWIS, Mrs Mary Carola Melton. b 51. LRAM72 S Glam Inst HE CertEd76 Lon Univ BD93. St Mich Coll Llan 97. **d** 98 **p** 99. NSM Aberedw w Llandeilo Graban and Llanbadarn etc *S & B* 98-03. *Brynglocsen, Dolanog, Welshpool SY21 0LJ* Tel (01938) 811202 E-mail marylewis@btinternet.com

LEWIS, Maureen. b 50. Chester Coll BA92. St Jo Coll Nottm DipMM94. **d** 94 **p** 95. C Ellesmere Port *Ches* 94-98; C Prenton 98-00; C New Brighton St Jas w Em from 00. *32 Magazine Brow, Wallasey CH45 1HP* Tel 0151-630 7203

LEWIS, Melville. *See* LEWIS, William George Melville

LEWIS, Michael. *See* LEWIS, James Michael

✠**LEWIS, The Rt Revd Michael Augustine Owen.** b 53. Mert Coll Ox BA75 MA79. Cuddesdon Coll 75. **d** 78 **p** 79 **c** 99. C Salfords *S'wark* 78-80; Chapl Thames Poly 80-84; V Welling 84-91; TR Worc SE *Worc* 91-99; RD Worc E 93-99; Hon Can Worc Cathl 98-99; Suff Bp Middleton *Man* from 99. *The Hollies, Manchester Road, Rochdale OL11 3QY* Tel (01706) 358550 Fax 354851 E-mail maolewis_2000@yahoo.com

LEWIS, Michael David Bennett. b 41. Univ of Wales DipTh68 Portsm Univ MA01. St Mich Coll Llan 65. **d** 68 **p** 69. C Penarth w Lavernock *Llan* 68-72; Chapl RAF 72-74; C Llanishen and Lisvane *Llan* 74-77; V Penyfai w Tondu 77-82; Chapl Ardingly Coll 82-90; R Merrow *Guildf* 90-95; RD Guildf 94-95; V Southsea H Spirit *Portsm* from 95. *The Vicarage, 26 Victoria Grove, Southsea PO5 1NY* Tel (023) 9287 3535 Mobile 07808-609912

LEWIS, Michael John. b 37. LLAM86. St Aid Birkenhead 64. **d** 66 **p** 67. C Whitnash *Cov* 66-69; C Nuneaton St Nic 69-73; TV Basildon St Martin w H Cross and Laindon *Chelmsf* 73-79; V W Bromwich St Jas *Lich* 79-85; TV Buxton w Burbage and King Sterndale *Derby* 85-95; P-in-c Brampton St Mark 95-02; rtd 02. *15 Langley Street, Basford, Stoke-on-Trent ST4 6DX* Tel (01782) 622762

LEWIS, Norman Eric. b 34. SRN55 Open Univ BA77. Roch Th Coll 59 Lich Th Coll 60. **d** 63 **p** 64. C Hope St Jas *Man* 63-67; V Hindsford 67-77; V Bolton SS Simon and Jude 77-90; rtd 90; Perm to Offic *York* from 90. *Millbank Cottage, Kirby Misperton, Malton YO17 6XZ* Tel (01653) 668526 E-mail normanl@btinternet.com

LEWIS, Patrick Mansel. *See* MANSEL LEWIS, Patrick Charles Archibald

LEWIS, Paul Wilfred. b 37. Ch Ch Ox BA60 DipEd61 MA64 DipTh72. Chich Th Coll 62. **d** 64 **p** 65. C St Pancras H Cross w St Jude and St Pet *Lon* 64-66; C Tottenham St Jo 66-68; Barbados 68-71; Lect Sarum & Wells Th Coll 72-74; Chapl 73-74; Chapl LSE *Lon* 74-80; Chapl St Chris Hospice Lon 80-86; C St Giles Cripplegate w St Bart Moor Lane etc *Lon* 86-89; Chapl Nat Hosp for Neurology and Neurosurgery Lon 89-99; Chapl Univ Coll Lon Hosps NHS Trust 96-99; P-in-c St Pancras H Cross w St Jude and St Pet *Lon* from 99. *Holy Cross Vicarage, 47 Argyle Square, London WC1H 8AL* Tel (020) 7278 3706 E-mail wilfredpaul@email.com

LEWIS, Peter. *See* LEWIS, Thomas Peter

LEWIS, Peter Andrew. b 67. Pemb Coll Ox MA PhD Univ of Wales (Abth) Bris Univ BA. Trin Coll Bris. **d** 96 **p** 97. C Cardigan w Mwnt and Y Ferwig *St D* 96-98; C Gabalfa *Llan* 98-01; V Aberpergwm and Blaengwrach 01-04; V Vale of Neath from 04. *The Vicarage, 11 Roberts Close, Glynneath, Neath SA11 5HR* Tel (01639) 721964 E-mail peterlewis@net.ntl.com

LEWIS, Peter Richard. b 40. Dur Univ BA62 Birm Univ DipTh64. Qu Coll Birm 62. **d** 64 **p** 65. C Moseley St Mary *Birm* 64-67; C Sherborne w Castleton and Lillington *Sarum* 67-71; P-in-c Bishopstone w Stratford Tony 72-80; V Amesbury 80-02; Offg Chapl RAF from 80; rtd 02; Perm to Offic *Sarum* from 02. *Rose Cottage, Silton Road, Bourton, Gillingham SP8 5DE*

LEWIS, Miss Rachel Veronica Clare. b 59. St Jo Coll Dur BA80 Man Univ PGCE81 Univ of Wales (Cardiff) MSc. Sarum & Wells Th Coll 86. **d** 86 **p** 94. C Caereithin *S & B* 86-88; Par Dn Bolton St Pet *Man* 88-91; Chapl Bolton Colls of H&FE 88-91; Chapl Trin Coll Carmarthen 91-94; C Yatton Keynell *Bris* 94-97; P-in-c 97-99; C Biddestone w Slaughterford 94-97; P-in-c 97-99;

C Castle Combe 94-97; P-in-c 97-99; C W Kington 94-97; P-in-c 97-99; C Nettleton w Littleton Drew 94-97; P-in-c 97-99; P-in-c Grittleton and Leigh Delamere 94-99; TR By Brook 99-02; I Adare and Kilmallock w Kilpeacon, Croom etc *L & K* from 02. *The Rectory, Adare, Co Limerick, Irish Republic* Tel and fax (00353) (61) 396227 E-mail revlewis@eircom.net

LEWIS, Ray Arthur. b 63. Oak Hill Th Coll 87. **d** 90 **p** 91. C Holloway St Mary Magd *Lon* 90-93; TV Forest Gate St Sav w W Ham St Matt *Chelmsf* 93-97; St Vincent 97-98; Grenada 98-99. *45 Avenue Road, London E7 0LA*

LEWIS, Raymond James. b 34. Univ of Wales (Cardiff) BA Open Univ BSc. St Mich Coll Llan. **d** 91 **p** 92. C Llanelli *St D* 91-94; rtd 99. *36 Yorath Road, Whitchurch, Cardiff CF14 1QD*

LEWIS, Richard. *See* LEWIS, The Rt Revd John Hubert Richard

LEWIS, The Very Revd Richard. b 35. Fitzw Ho Cam BA78 MA63. Ripon Hall Ox 58. **d** 60 **p** 61. C Hinckley St Mary *Leic* 60-63; C Sanderstead All SS *S'wark* 63-66; V S Merstham 67-72; V S Wimbledon H Trin 72-74; P-in-c S Wimbledon St Pet 72-74; V S Wimbledon H Trin and St Pet 74-79; V Dulwich St Barn 79-90; Chapl Alleyn's Foundn Dulwich 79-90; RD Dulwich *S'wark* 83-90; Hon Can S'wark Cathl 87-90; Dean Wells *B & W* 90-03; Warden of Readers 91-03; rtd 03; Perm to Offic *Worc* from 03. *Wells House, 152 Lower Howsell Road, Malvern WR14 1DL* Tel (01886) 833820
E-mail dean.richard@btopenworld.com

LEWIS, Canon Richard Charles. b 44. Lon Univ DipSocSc78 Univ of Wales (Lamp) MA94 Sheff Univ MEd96. ALCD69. **d** 69 **p** 70. C Kendal H Trin *Carl* 69-72; C Chipping Barnet *St Alb* 72-76; V Watford Ch Ch from 76; Chapl Abbots Hill Sch Hemel Hempstead 81-96; Hon Can St Alb Abbey from 90. *Christ Church Vicarage, Leggatts Way, Watford WD24 5NQ* Tel (01923) 672240 Fax 279919 E-mail vicar@ccwatford.u-net.com *or* rts@ccwatford.u-net.com

LEWIS, Robert. b 38. St Pet Coll Ox BA62 MA66. Cuddesdon Coll 62. **d** 64 **p** 65. C Kirkby *Liv* 64-67 and 70-71; TV 71-75; Chapl St Boniface Coll Warminster 68-69; Tutor St Aug Coll Cant 69-70; Abp's Dom Chapl and Dir of Ords *York* 76-79; TR Thirsk 79-92; Chapl Oslo w Bergen, Trondheim, Stavanger etc *Eur* 93-96; P-in-c Danby *York* 96-98; V 98-04; RD Whitby 98-04; rtd 04; Perm to Offic *York* from 04. *19 Long Street, Thirsk YO7 1AW* Tel (01845) 523256

LEWIS, Canon Robert George. b 53. Lanc Univ BEd76. Ripon Coll Cuddesdon. **d** 78 **p** 79. C Liv Our Lady and St Nic w St Anne *Liv* 78-81; Asst Dir of Educn 81-88; P-in-c Newchurch 88-89; P-in-c Glazebury 88-89; R Newchurch and Glazebury 89-94; R Winwick from 94; R Glazebury w Hollinfare from 04; AD Winwick from 01; Hon Can Liv Cathl from 01. *The Rectory, Golborne Road, Winwick, Warrington WA2 8SZ* Tel (01925) 632760 E-mail thelewises@hotmail.com

LEWIS, Roger Edward. b 24. Qu Coll Cam BA45 MA49. Ridley Hall Cam 47. **d** 49 **p** 50. C Handsworth St Mary *Birm* 49-52; R Hadleigh St Jas *Chelmsf* 52-58; V Clacton St Paul 58-71; V Surbiton St Matt *S'wark* 71-89; rtd 89; Perm to Offic *S'wark* from 89. *Rose Cottage, 40 Grove Road, Horley RH6 8EL* Tel (01293) 771197

LEWIS, Roger Gilbert. b 49. St Jo Coll Dur BA70. Ripon Hall Ox 70. **d** 72 **p** 73. C Boldmere *Birm* 72-76; C Birm St Pet 76-77; TV Tettenhall Regis *Lich* 77-81; V Ward End *Birm* 81-91; rtd 91; Perm to Offic *Birm* from 91. *8 Tudor Terrace, Ravenhurst Road, Birmingham B17 9SB* Tel 0121-427 4915

LEWIS, Stuart William. b 54. Newc Univ BA79 Newc Poly PGCE80. Edin Th Coll 86. **d** 86 **p** 87. C Ledbury w Eastnor *Heref* 86-89; Chapl Malvern Coll 89-96; Chapl and Prec Portsm Cathl *Portsm* 96-97; TV Ross *Heref* 97-01; P-in-c Lower Wharfedale *Ripon* 01-03; R from 03; Chapl St Aid Sch Harrogate 01-05. *The Rectory, Main Street, Kirkby Overblow, Harrogate HG3 1HD* Tel (01423) 872314

LEWIS, Thomas Peter. b 45. Selw Coll Cam BA67 MA. Ripon Hall Ox 68. **d** 70 **p** 71. C Bp's Hatfield *St Alb* 70-74; C Boreham Wood All SS 74-78; Chapl Haileybury Coll 78-85; Chapl Abingdon Sch 86-03; R Narberth w Mounton w Robeston Wathen and Crinow *St D* from 03. *The Rectory, Adams Drive, Narberth SA67 7AE* Tel (01834) 860370

LEWIS, Timothy John. b 56. Univ of Wales (Swansea) BA76. Sarum & Wells Th Coll 83. **d** 86 **p** 87. C Taunton St Mary *B & W* 86-89; Chapl RN 89-02. *Address temp unknown*

LEWIS, Vera Elizabeth. b 45. Lon Univ BA66 Univ of Wales (Abth) DipEd67 Dip Librarianship 73. St As Minl Tr Course 82. **d** 85 **p** 97. NSM Garthbeibio and Llanerfyl and Llangadfan *St As* 85-86; C 87-88; NSM Llanfair Caereinion w Llanllugan 85-86; C 87-88; Dn-in-c Llanrhaeadr-ym-Mochnant etc 88-96; Dn-in-c Llanddulas and Llysfaen 96-97; R 97-03; rtd 03. *Heulwen, Bronwylfa Square, St Asaph LL17 0BU*

LEWIS, Canon Walter Arnold. b 45. NUI BA68 TCD MPhil91. TCD Div Sch 71. **d** 71 **p** 72. C Belfast Whiterock *Conn* 71-73; C Belfast St Mark 73-80; Bp's C Belfast St Andr 80-84; I Belfast St Thos from 84; Can Belf Cathl from 97. *St Thomas's Rectory, 1A Eglantine Avenue, Belfast BT9 6DW* Tel and fax (028) 9080 8343 E-mail walter.lewis@ntlworld.com

LEWIS, William George Melville. b 31. Open Univ BA. S'wark Ord Course. **d** 69 **p** 70. C Coulsdon St Jo *S'wark* 69-71; C Perry Hill St Geo 71-74; V Eltham St Barn 74-80; V Reigate St Mark 80-89; V Ham St Rich 89-97; rtd 97; Hon C Kew *S'wark* 97-00. *20 Avenue Court, The Avenue, Tadworth KT20 5BG* Tel (01737) 819748

LEWIS, William George Rees. b 35. Hertf Coll Ox BA59 MA63. Tyndale Hall Bris 61. **d** 63 **p** 64. C Tenby w Gumfreston *St D* 63-66; C Llanelli St Paul 66-69; R Letterston 69-84; R Jordanston w Llanstinan 73-78; R Punchestown and Lt Newc 78-84; R Hubberston w Herbrandston and Hasguard etc 84-90; Prov Officer for Evang and Adult Educn 90-94; V Gabalfa *Llan* 94-00; rtd 00. *5 Westaway Drive, Hakin, Milford Haven SA73 3EG* Tel (01646) 692280

LEWIS, William Rhys. b 20. St Mich Coll Llan 53. **d** 55 **p** 56. C Ystrad Mynach *Llan* 55-58; C Bassaleg *Mon* 58-59; V Cwmtillery 59-62; V Newport St Andr 62-64; TR Ebbw Vale 64-73; R Llangattock and Llangyndir *S & B* 73-78; V Swansea St Luke 78-85; rtd 85; Perm to Offic *Llan* from 85. *6 Beech Avenue, Llantwit Major CF61 1RT* Tel (01446) 796741

LEWIS-ANTHONY, Justin Griffith. b 64. LSE BA86. Ripon Coll Cuddesdon BA91 MA97. **d** 92 **p** 93. C Cirencester *Glouc* 92-98; Prec Ch Ch *Ox* 98-03; R Hackington *Cant* from 03. *The Rectory, St Stephen's Green, Canterbury CT2 7JU* Tel (01227) 765391 E-mail rector@ststephenscanterbury.net

LEWIS-JENKINS, Christopher Robin. b 50. St Mich Coll Llan Dip Past Th 96. **d** 96 **p** 97. C Barry All SS *Llan* 96-01; V Dinas and Penygraig w Williamstown from 01. *The Vicarage, 1 Llanfair Road, Penygraig, Tonypandy CF40 1TA* Tel (01443) 422677

LEWIS LLOYD, Canon Timothy David. b 37. Clare Coll Cam BA58 MA62. Cuddesdon Coll 58. **d** 60 **p** 61. C Stepney St Dunstan and All SS *Lon* 60-64; C St Alb Abbey *St Alb* 64-67; Prec St Alb Abbey 67-69; V St Paul's Walden 69-78; V Braughing w Furneux Pelham and Stocking Pelham 78-79; P-in-c Lt Hadham 78-79; V Braughing, Lt Hadham, Albury, Furneux Pelham etc 79-82; V Cheshunt 82-95; RD Cheshunt 89-94; Hon Can St Alb 94-01; V Sawbridgeworth 95-01; rtd 01. *c/o M Lewis Lloyd Esq, 42F Forest Lane, London E15 1HA* Tel (020) 8534 1693

LEWIS-NICHOLSON, Russell John. b 45. Caulfield Inst of Tech Dip Civil Engineering 68. Oak Hill Th Coll DipTh81. **d** 81 **p** 82. C Clayton *Bradf* 81-84; Australia from 84. *14 Cedar Grove, Highton, Vic, Australia 3216* Tel (0061) (3) 5241 2408 Mobile 429-358490

LEWISHAM, Archdeacon of. *See* HARDMAN, The Ven Christine Elizabeth

LEWORTHY, Graham Llewelyn. b 47. Reading Univ BA69. S Dios Minl Tr Scheme 91. **d** 94 **p** 95. NSM Sark *Win* 94-96; C from 96. *Baleine Studio, La Collenette, Sark, Guernsey GY9 0SB* Tel (01481) 832140

LEYLAND, Derek James. b 34. Lon Univ BSc55. Qu Coll Birm 58. **d** 60 **p** 61. C Ashton-on-Ribble St Andr *Blackb* 60-63; V 80-87; C Salesbury 63-65; V Preston St Oswald 65-67; V Pendleton 67-74; Dioc Youth Chapl 67-69; Ind Youth Chapl 70-74; R Brindle 74-80; V Garstang St Helen Churchtown 87-94; Sec SOSc 90-94; rtd 94; Perm to Offic *Blackb* from 94. *Greystocks, Goosnargh Lane, Goosnargh, Preston PR3 2BP* Tel (01772) 865682

LEYLAND, Tyrone John. b 49. Aston Univ BSc68. St Jo Coll Nottm 89. **d** 91 **p** 92. C Lich St Mary w St Mich *Lich* 91-94; TV Willenhall H Trin 94-99; P-in-c The Ridwares and Kings Bromley from 99. *The Rectory, Alrewas Road, Kings Bromley, Burton-on-Trent DE13 7HP* Tel (01543) 472932 Fax as telephone

LEYSHON, Philip Alan. b 76. Glam Univ BA. Ripon Coll Cuddesdon BTh03. **d** 03 **p** 04. C Newton Nottage *Llan* from 03. *79 Meadow Lane, Porthcawl CF36 5EY* Tel (01656) 788176

LEYSHON, Simon. b 63. Trin Coll Carmarthen BA86 Southn Univ BTh89 Glam Univ CertMS96. Sarum & Wells Th Coll. **d** 89 **p** 90. C Tenby *St D* 89-92; TV 92-96; Chapl and Hd RS Llandovery Coll 96-02; Chapl Ld Wandsworth Coll Basingstoke from 02. *Kimbers, Lord Wandsworth College, Long Sutton, Hook, Basingstoke RG29 1TB* Tel (01256) 862206
E-mail simonleyshon@hotmail.com

LIBBY, John Ralph. b 55. Trin Coll Cam BA83. Ridley Hall Cam 89. **d** 91 **p** 92. C Enfield St Andr *Lon* 91-93; C Northwood Em 93-96; V Denton Holme *Carl* from 96; RD Carl from 04. *St James's Vicarage, Goschen Road, Carlisle CA2 5PF* Tel (01228) 515639 *or* 810616 Fax 524569
E-mail john.libby@btinternet.com

LICHFIELD, Archdeacon of. *See* LILEY, The Ven Christopher Frank

LICHFIELD, Bishop of. *See* GLEDHILL, The Rt Revd Jonathan Michael

LICHFIELD, Dean of. *See* DORBER, The Very Revd Adrian John

LICHTENBERGER, Miss Ruth Eileen. b 34. NY Th Sem 64 N Ord Course 95. **d** 96 **p** 97. NSM Warrington H Trin *Liv* 96-05; rtd 05. *Address temp unknown*

LICKESS, Canon David Frederick. b 37. St Chad's Coll Dur BA63. **d** 65 **p** 66. C Howden *York* 65-70; V Rudby in Cleveland w Middleton from 70; Can and Preb York Minster from 90; RD Stokesley 93-00. *The Vicarage, Hutton Rudby, Yarm TS15 0HY* Tel and fax (01642) 700223
E-mail david.lickess@btinternet.com

LIDDELL, Mark. b 55. Birm Univ BA00. Coll of Resurr Mirfield 96. **d** 98 **p** 99. C Wednesbury St Jas and St Jo *Lich* 98-00; C Walsall St Andr 00-01; P-in-c from 01. *St Andrew's Vicarage, 119 Hollyhedge Lane, Birchills, Walsall WS2 8PZ* Tel (01922) 721658

LIDDELL, Canon Peter Gregory. b 40. St Andr Univ MA63 Linacre Ho Ox BA65 MA70 Andover Newton Th Sch DMin75. Ripon Hall Ox 63. **d** 65 **p** 66. C Bp's Hatfield *St Alb* 65-71; USA 71-76; P-in-c Kimpton w Ayot St Lawrence *St Alb* 77-83; Dir of Past Counselling 80-05; Hon Can St Alb 99-05; rtd 05. *The Coach House, Hitchin Road, Kimpton, Hitchin SG4 8EF* Tel (01438) 832266 E-mail petermary.liddell@btinternet.com

LIDDELOW, Peter William. b 33. Oak Hill NSM Course. **d** 82 **p** 83. NSM Finchley Ch Ch *Lon* 82-84; NSM S Mimms Ch Ch from 84; Perm to Offic *St Alb* from 95. *23 King's Road, Barnet EN5 4EF* Tel (020) 8441 2968
E-mail peterliddelow@talk21.com

LIDDLE, George. b 48. NEOC 88. **d** 90 **p** 91. C Auckland St Andr and St Anne *Dur* 90-92; C Crook 92-94; C Stanley 92-94; P-in-c Evenwood 94-96; V 96-03; R Blackhall, Castle Eden and Monkhesleden from 03. *The Rectory, The Crescent, Blackhall Colliery, Hartlepool TS27 4LE* Tel 0191-586 4202

LIDDLE, Harry. b 36. Wadh Coll Ox BA57 MA61. Wycliffe Hall Ox 62. **d** 64 **p** 65. C Withington St Paul *Man* 64-68; R Broughton St Jo 68-73; V Balby *Sheff* 73-82; R Firbeck w Letwell 82-94; V Woodsetts 82-94; TV Aston cum Aughton w Swallownest, Todwick etc 94-01; rtd 01; Perm to Offic *Sheff* from 01. *30 Meadow Grove Road, Totley, Sheffield S17 4FF* Tel 0114-236 4941

LIDDLE, Stephen John. b 60. St Jo Coll Ox BA81 PGCE82. Linc Th Coll 88. **d** 91 **p** 92. C Morpeth *Newc* 91-95; P-in-c Byker St Mich w St Lawr 95-98; R Bothal and Pegswood w Longhirst 98-05; P-in-c Billingham St Aid *Dur* from 05. *The Rectory, 12A Tintern Avenue, Billingham TS23 2DE* Tel (01642) 397108

LIDSTONE, Vernon Henry. b 43. SW Minl Tr Course 89. **d** 92 **p** 93. NSM Bovey Tracey SS Pet, Paul and Thos w Hennock *Ex* 92-94; Sub-Chapl HM Pris Channings Wood 92-96; Asst Dioc Chr Stewardship Adv 92-93; Dioc Chr Stewardship Adv 93-96; Dioc Officer for Par Development *Glouc* 96-97; Chapl HM Pris Leyhill 97-03; rtd 03. *The Pike House, Saul, Gloucester GL2 7JD* Tel (01452) 741410 E-mail vernon@lidstone.net

LIDWILL, Canon Mark Robert. b 57. TCD DipTh87. **d** 87 **p** 88. C Annagh w Drumgoon, Ashfield etc *K, E & A* 87-90; I Urney w Denn and Derryheen from 90; Dioc Youth Adv from 92; Preb Kilmore Cathl from 98. *The Rectory, Keadue Lane, Cavan, Co Cavan, Irish Republic* Tel (00353) (49) 436 1016

LIEVESLEY, Mrs Joy Margaret. b 48. Lady Mabel Coll CertEd69. Guildf Dioc Min Course 98. **d** 00 **p** 01. NSM Farnham *Guildf* from 00. *3 Kingfisher Close, Church Crookham, Fleet GU52 6JP* Tel (01252) 690223
E-mail joy.lievesley@ntlworld.com

LIGHT, Mrs Madeline Margaret. b 54. Girton Coll Cam BA77 MA80 Lon Inst of Educn PGCE78. EAMTC 96. **d** 99 **p** 00. C Eaton *Nor* 99-02; P-in-c Nor St Helen from 02; Chapl Gt Hosp Nor from 02. *Calthorpe Lodge, Bishopgate, Norwich NR1 4EJ* Tel (01603) 219894 E-mail madelinelight@fish.co.uk

LIGHTFOOT, The Very Revd Vernon Keith. b 34. St Jo Coll Dur BA58. Ripon Hall Ox 58. **d** 60 **p** 61. C Rainhill *Liv* 60-62; C Liv Our Lady and St Nic 62-65; V Stanley 65-75; Chapl St Edm Coll Liv 66-68; Chapl Rathbone Hosp Liv 70-75; New Zealand from 75; V Mt Albert St Luke 75-85; Dean Waikato 85-97; rtd 98. *16C Acacia Crescent, Hamilton, New Zealand* Tel and fax (0064) (7) 843 5538 E-mail keith.jennie@xtra.co.nz

LIGHTOWLER, Joseph Trevor. b 33. **d** 79 **p** 80. Hon C Leverstock Green *St Alb* 79-80; Hon C Chambersbury 80-84; C Woodmansterne *S'wark* 84-88; R Odell and Pavenham *St Alb* 88-97; rtd 97; Perm to Offic *St Alb* from 97. *41 Oakwood Drive, St Albans AL4 0UL* Tel (01727) 833422

LIKEMAN, Canon Martin Kaye. b 34. St Mich Coll Llan 55. **d** 57 **p** 58. C Llanwnog w Penstrowed *Ban* 57-60; C Llandudno 60-64; V Llanrhian w Llanhywel and Carnhedryn *St D* 64-73; RD Dewisland and Fishguard 71-73; V Llanstadwel 73-99; Can St D Cathl 88-99; rtd 99. *10 Lawrenny Street, Neyland, Milford Haven SA73 1TB* Tel (01646) 600983

LILES, Malcolm David. b 48. Nottm Univ BA69. St Steph Ho Ox 69. **d** 71 **p** 72. C Corby Epiphany w St Jo *Pet* 71-74; C New Cleethorpes *Linc* 74-76; TV Lt Coates 76-77; TV Gt and Lt Coates w Bradley 78-82; Soc Resp Sec 82-93; Hon C Gt Grimsby St Mary and St Jas 82-93; P-in-c Grimsby All SS 88-93; TV Dronfield w Holmesfield *Derby* 93-98; TR Crawley *Chich* from 98. *The Rectory, 1 Southgate Road, Crawley RH10 6BL* Tel (01293) 535856 *or* 520421
E-mail rectorcrawley@btinternet.com

LILEY, The Ven Christopher Frank. b 47. Nottm Univ BEd70. Linc Th Coll 72. **d** 74 **p** 75. C Kingswinford H Trin *Lich* 74-79; TV Stafford 79-84; V Norton *St Alb* 84-96; RD Hitchin 89-94; V Shrewsbury St Chad w St Mary *Lich* 96-01; P-in-c Shrewsbury St Alkmund 96-01; Adn Lich from 01; Can Res and Treas Lich Cathl from 01. *24 The Close, Lichfield WS13 7LD* Tel (01543) 306145 Fax 306147
E-mail archdeacon.lichfield@lichfield.anglican.org

LILEY, Peter James. b 60. Liv Univ BA82 Westmr Coll Ox PGCE83. Oak Hill Th Coll 91. **d** 93 **p** 94. C Exning St Martin w Landwade *St E* 93-96; V Acton w Gt Waldingfield 96-00; TV Bottesford w Ashby *Linc* 00-05; TR from 05. *The Vicarage, 10 Old School Lane, Bottesford, Scunthorpe DN16 3RD* Tel and fax (01724) 867256 *or* 842732 E-mail peter.liley@ntlworld.com

LILEY, Stephen John. b 65. Liv Univ BA87 MMus88 ARCM93. Wycliffe Hall Ox 97. **d** 99 **p** 00. C Throop *Win* 99-03; V Clapham *St Alb* from 03. *The Vicarage, Green Lane, Clapham, Bedford MK41 6ER* Tel (01234) 352814
E-mail the.lileys@ukgateway.net

LILLEY, Christopher Howard. b 51. FCA75 FTII83. St Jo Coll Nottm DCM93 LNSM course 83. **d** 85 **p** 86. OLM Skegness and Winthorpe *Linc* 85-93; C Limber Magna w Brocklesby 93-96; Perm to Offic *S'well* 93-96; P-in-c Middle Rasen Gp *Linc* 96-97; R 97-02; V Scawby, Redbourne and Hibaldstow from 02; RD Yarborough from 02. *St Hybald's Vicarage, Vicarage Lane, Scawby, Brigg DN20 9LX* Tel (01652) 652725
E-mail lilley@btinternet.com

LILLEY, Ivan Ray. b 32. Bps' Coll Cheshunt 58. **d** 61 **p** 62. C Kettering SS Pet and Paul *Pet* 61-64; C Gt Yarmouth *Nor* 64-75; P-in-c Tottenhill w Wormegay *Ely* 76-83; P-in-c Watlington 76-83; P-in-c Holme Runcton w S Runcton and Wallington 76-83; V Tysoe w Oxhill and Whatcote *Cov* 83-86; C Langold *S'well* 87-91; P-in-c 91-98; rtd 98; Perm to Offic *Nor* from 98. *Linden Lea, 41 Cedar Drive, Attleborough NR17 2EY* Tel and fax (01953) 452710

LILLIAN, Mother. *See* MORRIS, Lillian Rosina

LILLICRAP, Peter Andrew. b 65. Hatf Poly BEng87 CEng93 MIMechE93. Trin Coll Bris 00. **d** 02 **p** 03. C Kineton *Cov* 02-04; C Napton-on-the-Hill, Lower Shuckburgh etc from 04. *16 Priors Meadow, Southam CV47 1GE* Tel (01926) 812762 Mobile 07762-230189 E-mail peterlillicrap@tiscali.co.uk

LILLICRAP, Stephen Hunter. b 58. Newc Univ MB, BS81 DRCOG84 MRCGP85. SEITE 00. **d** 03 **p** 04. C Wye w Brook *Cant* from 03. *The Vicarage, Pilgrims Way, Hastingleigh, Ashford TN25 5HP* Tel (01233) 750140 Mobile 07971-224094
E-mail steve.lillicrap@btopenworld.com

LILLIE, Judith Virginia. *See* THOMPSON, Mrs Judith Virginia

LILLIE, Mrs Shona Lorimer. b 49. St Jo Coll Nottm BA03. **d** 03. C Bishopbriggs *Glas* from 03. *7 Meadowburn, Bishopbriggs, Glasgow G64 3HA* Tel 0141-772 7421 Mobile 07773-501706
E-mail shonalillie@hotmail.com

LILLINGTON, Brian Ray. b 36. RMN60 FRSH84. S Dios Minl Tr Scheme 87. **d** 90 **p** 91. NSM Yateley *Win* 90-98; NSM Eversley 98-02; rtd 03. *Kaos, Little Vigo, Yateley GU46 6ES* Tel and fax (01252) 872760 E-mail ardnagrask@aol.com

LILLINGTON (née POLLIT), Mrs Ruth Mary. b 65. SS Paul & Mary Coll Cheltenham BA88. St Jo Coll Nottm DPS90. **d** 90 **p** 94. Par Dn Caverswall *Lich* 90-92; Par Dn Caverswall and Weston Coyney w Dilhorne 92-93; Par Dn Luton St Mary *St Alb* 93-94; C 94-97; Chapl Luton Univ 93-97. *20 Harcourt Road, Bracknell RG12 7JD* Tel (01344) 423025

LILLISTONE, Canon Brian David. b 38. SS Coll Cam BA61 MA65. St Steph Ho Ox 61. **d** 63 **p** 64. C Ipswich All Hallows *St E* 63-66; C Stokesay *Heref* 66-71; P-in-c Lyonshall w Titley 71-76; R Martlesham w Brightwell *St E* 76-03; Hon Can St E Cathl 98-03; rtd 03; Perm to Offic *St E* from 03. *23 Woodland Close, Risby, Bury St Edmunds IP28 6QN* Tel (01284) 811330
E-mail brian@lillistone.freeserve.co.uk

LIMBERT, Kenneth Edward. b 25. CEng69 MIMechE. S'wark Ord Course 72. **d** 75 **p** 76. NSM Northwood Hills St Edm *Lon* 75-90; Perm to Offic from 90. *55 York Road, Northwood HA6 1JJ* Tel (01923) 825791

LIMBRICK, Gordon. b 36. Open Univ BA88. St Jo Coll Nottm. **d** 87 **p** 91. Hon C Troon *Glas* 87-90; Hon C Yaxley *Ely* 90-97; Hon C Yaxley and Holme w Conington 97-04; rtd 04; Perm to Offic *Pet* from 98 and *Ely* from 04. *271 Broadway, Yaxley, Peterborough PE7 3NR* Tel (01733) 243170
E-mail moandgol@tesco.net

LIMERICK AND ARDFERT, Dean of. *See* SIRR, The Very Revd John Maurice Glover

LIMERICK, Archdeacon of. *See* SHANNON, The Ven Malcolm James Douglas

LIMERICK, ARDFERT, AGHADOE, KILLALOE, KILFENORA, CLONFERT, KILMACDUAGH AND EMLY, Bishop of. *See* MAYES, The Rt Revd Michael

LINAKER, David Julian John Ramage. b 65. Ripon Coll Cuddesdon BTh95. **d** 95 **p** 96. C Colehill *Sarum* 95-99; V Mere w

W Knoyle and Maiden Bradley from 99. *The Vicarage, Angel Lane, Mere, Warminster BA12 6DH* Tel (01747) 860292 E-mail david.linaker@virgin.net

LINCOLN, Archdeacon of. *See* HAWES, The Ven Arthur John

LINCOLN, Bishop of. *See* SAXBEE, The Rt Revd John Charles

LINCOLN, Dean of. *See* KNIGHT, The Very Revd Alexander Francis

LIND-JACKSON, Peter Wilfrid. b 35. Leeds Univ BA67. Linc Th Coll 67. **d** 68 **p** 69. C Heref St Martin *Heref* 68-71; P-in-c Burghill 71-78; V 78-82; V Barnard Castle *Dur* 82-83; P-in-c Whorlton 82-83; V Barnard Castle w Whorlton 83-00; rtd 00; Perm to Offic *Ripon* from 03. *15 Greenbank, Eggleston, Barnard Castle DL12 0BQ* Tel (01833) 650014

LINDARS, Frank. b 23. Wycliffe Hall Ox 54. **d** 56 **p** 57. C Beeston Hill St Luke *Ripon* 56-59; C Harrogate St Wilfrid 59-61; V Shadwell 61-80; RD Allerton 73-78; V Masham and Healey 80-88; rtd 88; Perm to Offic *Ripon* from 88. *Hope Cottage, Reeth, Richmond DL11 6SF* Tel (01748) 884685

LINDECK, Peter Stephen. b 31. Oak Hill Th Coll 57. **d** 59 **p** 60. C Homerton St Luke *Lon* 59-62; C Salterhebble All SS *Wakef* 62-63; C Islington St Andr w St Thos and St Matthias *Lon* 64-67; V Toxteth Park St Bede *Liv* 68-74; Nigeria 74-76; C Netherton *Liv* 76-77; C Ollerton *S'well* 77-80; C Boughton 77-80; V Whitgift w Adlingfleet and Eastoft *Sheff* 80-86; P-in-c Swinefleet 81-86; V Kilnhurst 86-94; Chapl Montagu Hosp Mexborough 86-94; rtd 94; Perm to Offic *Sheff* from 94. *41 Church Lane, Doncaster DN4 0XB* Tel (01302) 855957 E-mail peter@lindeck.freeserve.co.uk

LINDEN, Gregory. b 25. Roch Th Coll. **d** 65 **p** 66. C Roundhay St Edm *Ripon* 65-68; C Highweek *Ex* 68-72; V Brampford Speke 72-82; R Upton Pyne 72-82; R Middleton-in-Teesdale *Dur* 82-85; V Eggleston 85-95; R Middleton-in-Teesdale w Forest and Frith 85-95; rtd 95; Perm to Offic *Ripon* from 96. *Ashlind, 15 Ashdown Court, Little Crakehall, Bedale DL8 1LQ* Tel (01677) 426380

LINDISFARNE, Archdeacon of. *See* LANGLEY, The Ven Robert

LINDLAR, Christopher Max Dierichs. b 55. Leeds Univ BA00. Coll of Resurr Mirfield 98. **d** 00 **p** 01. C Lancing w Coombes *Chich* 00-04; P-in-c Deal St Andr *Cant* from 04. *St Andrew's Rectory, St Andrew's Road, Deal CT14 6AS* Tel (01304) 374354 Mobile 07710-090195 E-mail c.lindlar@btinternet.com

LINDLEY, Geoffrey. b 22. St Jo Coll Ox BA45 MA47. Westcott Ho Cam 47. **d** 47 **p** 48. C E Wickham *S'wark* 47-51; C Welling 51-52; V Lambeth St Phil 52-56; V Ox St Marg *Ox* 56-72; P-in-c Pyrton w Shirburn 72-79; P-in-c Lewknor 72-79; P-in-c Shipton-under-Wychwood 79-80; P-in-c Milton-under-Wychwood 79-80; V Shipton-under-Wychwood w Milton, Fifield etc 80-85; Perm to Offic from 86; rtd 87. *St John's Home, St Mary's Road, Oxford OX4 1QE* Tel (01865) 247725

LINDLEY, Graham William. b 47. Man Poly CIPFA77. LNSM course 94. **d** 97 **p** 98. OLM E Crompton *Man* 97-02; NSM Newhey from 02. *37 Jordan Avenue, Shaw, Oldham OL2 8DQ* Tel (01706) 845677

LINDLEY, Harold Thomas. b 28. St Jo Coll Ox BA51 MA73. Wells Th Coll 51. **d** 53 **p** 54. C Normanton *Wakef* 53-57; C-in-c Rawthorpe CD 57-63; P-in-c Longstone *Derby* 63-67; V 68-74; P-in-c Barrow w Twyford 74-84; V Barrow-on-Trent w Twyford and Swarkestone 84-93; rtd 93. *Gorwel, 35 Nant Bychan, Moelfre LL72 8HE* Tel (01248) 410484

LINDLEY, The Ven Ralph Adrian. b 20. CBE75. St Jo Coll Dur BA51 DipTh53. **d** 53 **p** 54. C Burnley St Steph *Blackb* 53-55; Chapl RAF 55-70; UAE 70-78; Adn Gulf 70-78; Gen Sec JMECA 78-85; rtd 86; Perm to Offic *Glouc* from 86. *Taffrail, Lower Road, St Briavels, Lydney GL15 6SA* Tel (01594) 530230

LINDLEY, Canon Richard Adrian. b 44. Hull Univ BA65 Man Univ MA79 Birm Univ DPS68 Birm Poly DMS91. Cuddesdon Coll 66. **d** 68 **p** 69. C Ingrow cum Hainworth *Bradf* 68-70; Perm to Offic *Birm* 70-74; TV Ellesmere Port *Ches* 74-79; V Westborough *Guildf* 79-80; TR 80-84; Dir of Educn *Birm* 84-96; Hon Can Birm Cathl 96; Dir of Educn *Win* 96-04; Hon Can Win Cathl 03-04. *28 Denham Close, Winchester SO23 7BL* Tel (01962) 621851 E-mail randslindley@care4free.net

LINDO, Leithland Oscar. b 29. St Aug Coll Cant 57 St Pet Coll Jamaica 53. **d** 56 **p** 57. Jamaica 56-58; C Edmonton St Mary w St Jo *Lon* 58-62; C Heston 62-66; V Staines Ch Ch 66-04; rtd 04. *7 Windmill Close, Waterlooville PO8 0NA* Tel (023) 9259 6675

LINDOP, Andrew John. b 57. Cam Univ MA. Cranmer Hall Dur 80. **d** 82 **p** 83. C Brinsworth w Catcliffe *Sheff* 82-85; C S Shoebury *Chelmsf* 85-89; V Mosley Common *Man* 89-99; V Astley Bridge from 99; AD Walmsley from 02. *St Paul's Vicarage, Sweetloves Lane, Bolton BL1 7ET* Tel (01204) 304119 Fax as telephone E-mail andy.lindop@tesco.net

LINDOP, Canon Kenneth. b 45. Linc Th Coll 71. **d** 74 **p** 75. C Leic St Phil *Leic* 74-77; C Cov H Trin *Cov* 77-80; P-in-c Cubbington 80-82; V from 82; RD Warwick and Leamington 91-96; Jt P-in-c Leamington Spa H Trin and Old Milverton from 03; Hon Can Cov Cathl from 04. *St Mary's Vicarage, 15 Pinehurst, Cubbington, Leamington Spa CV32 7XA* Tel (01926) 423056

LINDSAY, Alan. *See* LINDSAY, Canon Richard John Alan

LINDSAY, Alexandra Jane (Sandra). b 43. CITC 90. **d** 93 **p** 94. Lic to Offic *K, E & A* 93-94; NSM Bailieborough w Knockbride, Shercock and Mullagh from 94. *Clementstown House, Cootehill, Co Cavan, Irish Republic* Tel and fax (00353) (49) 555 2207

LINDSAY, Anne. *See* LINDSAY, Mrs Mary Jane Anne

LINDSAY, Anthony. b 38. Trin Coll Bris DipHE93 St Jo Coll Nottm CertCS88. **d** 89 **p** 90. CMS 76-92; Sierra Leone 88-92; C Rainham w Wennington *Chelmsf* 93-96; R Quendon w Rickling and Wicken Bonhunt etc 96-03; rtd 03; Perm to Offic *York* from 03. *17 Hall Garth, Pickering YO18 7AW* Tel (01751) 476849

LINDSAY, Ashley. *See* LINDSAY, Robert Ashley Charles

LINDSAY, Cecil. b 43. Iona Coll (NY) BBA68. CITC 85. **d** 88 **p** 88. NSM Kilmore w Ballintemple, Kildallan etc *K, E & A* 88-90; Lic to Offic 90-91; NSM Roscommon w Donamon, Rathcline, Kilkeevin etc 91-96; NSM Killeshandra w Killegar and Derrylane 96-02; NSM Mohill w Farnaught, Aughavas, Oughteragh etc from 02; Dioc Registrar from 97. *Clementstown House, Cootehill, Co Cavan, Irish Republic* Tel and fax (00353) (49) 555 2207

LINDSAY, David Macintyre. b 46. Trin Hall Cam BA68 MA72. Cuddesdon Coll 68. **d** 71 **p** 72. C Gosforth All SS *Newc* 71-74; C Keele *Lich* 74-78; Perm to Offic *St E* 79-80; Chapl Haberdashers' Aske's Sch Elstree from 80. *St Stephen's Vicarage, 1 Spring Close, Barnet EN5 2UR* Tel (020) 8275 0858

LINDSAY, Eric Graham. b 30. Witwatersrand Univ BA51 Lon Univ DipAdEd78 MA80 Heythrop Coll Lon DipTh82. Coll of Resurr Mirfield 55. **d** 57 **p** 59. C Stella *Dur* 57-58; C W Hartlepool St Aid 58-60; C St Geo Grenada 60-61; Perm to Offic *Win* 61-65; *Roch* 65-72; and *Chelmsf* 72-84; C Stepney St Dunstan and All SS *Lon* 84-85; P-in-c Stepney St Dunstan LEP 84-85; R Bridge of Weir *Glas* 85-98; R Kilmacolm 85-98. *1 Woodrow Court, 26-32 Port Glasgow Road, Kilmacolm PA13 4QA* Tel (01505) 874668

LINDSAY, Canon John Carruthers. b 50. Edin Univ MA72 BD82. Edin Th Coll 79. **d** 82 **p** 83. C Broughty Ferry *Bre* 82-84; C Edin St Hilda *Edin* 84-85; TP 85-88; C Edin St Fillan 84-85; TP 85-88; R N Berwick from 88; R Gullane from 88; Can St Mary's Cathl from 00. *The Rectory, 2 May Terrace, North Berwick EH39 4BA* Tel (01620) 892154 Mobile 07977-520277 E-mail jclscot@aol.com

LINDSAY, Keith Malcolm. b 18. Adelaide Univ BA39. ACT ThL41. **d** 41 **p** 42. Australia 41-49 and from 53; C N Adelaide Ch Ch 41-42; Chapl Kensington Miss 42-44; Brotherhood of St Jo 44-47; P-in-c Tailem Bend 47-49; C W Derby St Jo *Liv* 50-53; R Yorketown 53-57; RD Yorke Peninsula 54-57; R Adelaide St Mary Magd 57-67; Chapl R Adelaide Hosp 58-65; Chapl Magill Reform Inst 66-67; R Ararat 67-71; R Port Fairy 71-74; P-in-c Maylands w Firle 74-79; R Toorak Gardens 79-83; rtd 83; Lic to Offic *Adelaide* from 83; Chapl Glenside Hosp 87-90. *2 Canterbury Avenue, Trinity Gardens, S Australia 5068* Tel (0061) (8) 8332 9228 E-mail kml@bns.com.au

LINDSAY (née CLEALL), Mrs Mary Jane Anne. b 54. Keele Univ BA77 Herts Univ PGCE92. St Alb and Ox Min Course 00. **d** 03 **p** 04. NSM Chipping Barnet *St Alb* 03-04; C from 04. *St Stephen's Vicarage, 1 Spring Close, Barnet EN5 2UR* Tel (020) 8275 0858 E-mail annelindsay54@hotmail.com

LINDSAY, Richard John. b 46. Sarum & Wells Th Coll 74. **d** 78 **p** 79. C Aldwick *Chich* 78-81; C Almondbury w Farnley Tyas *Wakef* 81-84; V Mossley *Man* from 84. *The Vicarage, Stamford Street, Mossley, Ashton-under-Lyne OL5 0LP* Tel (01457) 832219

LINDSAY, Canon Richard John Alan. b 24. TCD BA46 BD52. **d** 49 **p** 50. C Denton Holme *Carl* 49-52; CMS Burundi 52-64; Chapl and Tutor CMS Tr Coll Chislehurst 65-68; R Chich St Pancras and St Jo *Chich* 68-74; Chapl Maisons-Laffitte *Eur* 74-82; Can Brussels Cathl 81-88; Chapl The Hague w Leiden and Voorschoten 82-89; rtd 89; Perm to Offic *Heref 88-01; Portsm* from 01; *Guildf* from 03. *The Bothy, Hewshott Lane, Liphook GU30 7SU* Tel (01428) 723645

LINDSAY, Canon Robert. b 16. St Jo Coll Dur BA37 DipTh38 MA40. **d** 39 **p** 40. C Gateshead St Mary *Dur* 39-43; P-in-c Sacriston 43-45; P-in-c Benfieldside 45-46; V Lanercost w Kirkcambeck *Carl* 46-55; V Hawkshead and Low Wray 55-70; R Dean 70-74; RD Derwent 70-81; Hon Can Carl Cathl 72-81; V Loweswater w Buttermere 74-81; rtd 81; Perm to Offic *Ex* from 81. *58 Primley Road, Sidmouth EX10 9LF* Tel (01395) 577882

LINDSAY, Robert Ashley Charles. b 43. Leeds Univ BA66 Ex Univ BPhil81. Coll of Resurr Mirfield 66. **d** 68 **p** 69. C Mill Hill Jo Keble Ch *Lon* 68-72; C Sherborne w Castleton and Lillington *Sarum* 73-78; Chapl Coldharbour Hosp Dorset 73-78; Perm to Offic *Leic* 87-92. *79 Castledine Street, Loughborough LE11 2DX* Tel (01509) 264360

LINDSAY, Sandra. *See* LINDSAY, Alexandra Jane

LINDSAY-PARKINSON, Michael. b 28. Edin Th Coll 66. **d** 67 **p** 68. C Edin Ch Ch *Edin* 67-70; C Helensburgh *Glas* 70-72; R Lockerbie 72-83; R Annan 72-83; S Africa 83-88; V Alsager

St Mary *Ches* 88-93; rtd 93; Perm to Offic *Ches* 93-98. *10 Cherry Tree Avenue, Church Lawton, Stoke-on-Trent ST7 3EL* Tel (01270) 875574

LINDSAY-SMITH, Kevin Roy. b 55. **d** 05. OLM Glascote and Stonydelph *Lich* from 05. *34 Castlehall, Tamworth B77 2EJ* Tel (01827) 251557 E-mail lindsay-smith@supanet.com

LINDSEY, Archdeacon of. *Vacant*

LINES, Canon Andrew John. b 60. Univ Coll Dur BA82. All Nations Chr Coll DipMM90. **d** 97 **p** 98. Paraguay 91-99; Dir Caleb Bible Cen 91-99; SAMS 97-00; Hon Can Paraguay from 00; Gen Sec Crosslinks from 00. *59 Woodside Road, New Malden KT3 3AW* Tel (020) 8942 2179 E-mail gensec@crosslinks.org

LINES, Graham Martin. b 55. St Jo Coll Nottm 97. **d** 99 **p** 00. C Crosby *Linc* 99-02; C Bottesford w Ashby 02-03; TV from 03. *The Rectory, St Paul's Road, Ashby, Scunthorpe DN16 3DL* Tel (01724) 842083 E-mail graham@ml47.sflife.co.uk

LINES, Nicholas David John. b 64. St Jo Coll Nottm 94. **d** 96 **p** 97. C Burton All SS w Ch Ch *Lich* 96-01; P-in-c Rodbourne Cheney *Bris* 01-02; R from 02. *St Mary's Rectory, 298 Cheney Manor Road, Swindon SN2 2PF* Tel (01793) 522379 E-mail nick.lines@lineone.net

LINFORD, Preb John Kenneth. b 31. Liv Univ BA52. Chich Th Coll 54. **d** 56 **p** 57. C Stoke upon Trent *Lich* 56-61; V Tunstall Ch Ch 61-70; V Sedgley All SS 70-78; Chapl Chase Hosp Cannock 78-91; TR Cannock *Lich* 78-91; V Hatherton 80-91; Preb Lich Cathl 88-98; rtd 91; Perm to Offic *Lich* 91-00. *16 School Lane, Hill Ridware, Rugeley WS15 3QN* Tel (01543) 492831

LING, Adrian Roger. b 66. Goldsmiths' Coll Lon BA89 Leeds Univ BA02. Coll of Resurr Mirfield 00. **d** 02 **p** 03. C Mill End and Heronsgate w W Hyde *St Alb* from 02. *St Thomas's House, 46 Chalfont Road, Rickmansworth WD3 9TB* Tel (01923) 771022 E-mail adrianling@btinternet.com

LING, Andrew Joyner. b 35. ACP69 St Luke's Coll Ex TCert63 Open Univ BA80. SW Minl Tr Course 83. **d** 86 **p** 87. NSM St Dominic, Landulph and St Mellion w Pillaton *Truro* 86-90; C Saltash 90-94; TV 94-97; Chapl Montreux w Gstaad *Eur* 98-03; rtd 03. *Martinets, Chemin des Martinets 7, 1872 Troistorrents, Switzerland* Tel (0041) (24) 477 2408

LING, Timothy Charles. b 61. Ex Univ BA85 Selw Coll Cam BA91. Ridley Hall Cam 89. **d** 92 **p** 93. C Gerrards Cross and Fulmer *Ox* 92-96; C Woking St Pet *Guildf* 96-00; V Bathford *B & W* from 00. *The Vicarage, 27 Church Street, Bathford, Bath BA1 7RS* Tel (01225) 858325 E-mail tim.ling@whsmithnet.co.uk

LINGARD, Colin. b 36. Kelham Th Coll 58. **d** 63 **p** 64. C Middlesbrough St Martin *York* 63-66; C Stainton-in-Cleveland 66-71; V Eskdaleside w Ugglebarnby 71-77; P-in-c Redcar w Kirkleatham 77; V Kirkleatham 78-86; RD Guisborough 83-86; V Linc St Botolph *Linc* 86-89; Dioc Dir of Readers 86-89; R Washington *Dur* 89-93; P-in-c Middleton St Geo 93-97; R 97-01; Chapl Teesside Airport from 97; rtd 01. *29 Belgrave Terrace, Hurworth Place, Darlington DL2 2DW* Tel 07752-179418 (mobile)

LINGARD, Keith Patrick. b 30. AKC53. **d** 54 **p** 55. C Bedford Park *Lon* 54-56; C Ruislip St Martin 56-58; C Kempston All SS *St Alb* 58-63; Metrop Area Sec UMCA 63-65; V S Farnborough *Guildf* 65-75; R Glaston w Bisbrooke *Pet* 75-76; R Morcott w Glaston and Bisbrooke 77-95; rtd 95; Perm to Offic *Linc* from 95. *13 Woodside East, Thurlby, Bourne PE10 0HT* Tel (01778) 425572

LINGS, George William. b 49. Nottm Univ BTh74 Ox Univ PGCE75. Lambeth Hon MLitt93 St Jo Coll Nottm 70. **d** 75 **p** 76. C Harold Wood *Chelmsf* 75-78; C Reigate St Mary *S'wark* 78-85; V Deal St Geo *Cant* 85-97; First Dir CA Sheff Cen for Ch Planting and Evang from 97; NSM Norfolk Park St Leonard CD *Sheff* from 97. *The Sheffield Centre, 50 Cavendish Street, Sheffield S3 7RZ* Tel 0114-272 7451 E-mail g.lings@sheffieldcentre.org.uk

LINGWOOD, Preb David Peter. b 51. Lon Univ BEd73 Southn Univ BTh80. Sarum & Wells Th Coll 75. **d** 78 **p** 79. C Ashford St Hilda *Lon* 78-81; C Astwood Bank w Crabbs Cross *Worc* 81; TV Redditch, The Ridge 81-86; TR Blakenall Heath *Lich* 86-96; V Rushall 96-04; RD Walsall 98-03; TR Stoke-upon-Trent from 04; Preb Lich Cathl from 02. *Trent Vale Vicarage, Crosby Road, Stoke-on-Trent ST4 6JY1* Tel (01782) 747737 E-mail david@dplingwood.freeserve.co.uk

LINKENS, Timothy Martin. b 67. Strathclyde Univ MEng90. Wycliffe Hall Ox BTh99. **d** 99 **p** 00. C Blackheath St Jo *S'wark* 99-03; V Kidbrooke St Nic from 03. *66A Whetstone Road, London SE3 8PZ* Tel (020) 8856 6317

LINN, Frederick Hugh. b 37. Em Coll Cam BA61 MA65. Ripon Hall Ox 61. **d** 63 **p** 64. C Bramhall *Ches* 63-68; V Liscard St Mary 68-71; V Liscard St Mary w St Columba 71-74; V Wybunbury 74-82; R Eccleston and Pulford 82-98; rtd 98; Perm to Offic *Ches* from 98. *4 Stonewalls, Rossett, Wrexham LL12 0LG* Tel (01244) 571942 *or* (01407) 810372

LINNEGAR, George Leonard. b 33. CGA. Kelham Th Coll 63. **d** 62 **p** 63. C Wellingborough St Mary *Pet* 62-65; Lic to Offic *Lich* 65-69; Lic to Offic *B & W* 69-80; Hon C Lewes All SS, St Anne, St Mich and St Thos *Chich* 80-86; C 87-99; rtd 99; Perm to Offic *Chich* from 99. *20 Morris Road, Lewes BN7 2AT* Tel (01273) 478145

LINNEY, Barry James. b 64. Spurgeon's Coll BD97 Anglia Poly Univ MA02. Westcott Ho Cam 99. **d** 01 **p** 02. C Chingford SS Pet and Paul *Chelmsf* 01-04; V Cherry Hinton St Andr *Ely* from 04. *The Vicarage, 2 Fulbourn Old Drift, Cherry Hinton, Cambridge CB1 9NE* Tel (01223) 247740 E-mail standrews.cherryhinton@btinternet.com

LINNEY, Gordon Charles Scott. b 39. CITC 66. **d** 69 **p** 70. C Agherton *Conn* 69-72; Min Can Down Cathl *D & D* 72-75; V Dublin St Cath w St Jas *D & G* 75-80; Preb Tipperkevin St Patr Cathl Dublin 77-80; I Glenageary *D & G* 80-04; Adn Dublin 88-04; Lect CITC 89-93; rtd 04. *208 Upper Glenageary Road, Glenageary, Co Dublin, Irish Republic* Tel (00353) (1) 284 8503 Mobile 87-254 1775 E-mail glinney@eircom.net

LINNING, Alexander. b 19. Birm Univ BA40 Lon Univ BD42. **d** 61 **p** 62. Hon C W Bridgford *S'well* 61-80; Lic to Offic 80-95. *7 Kingston Road, Nottingham NG2 7AQ* Tel 0115-981 2959

LINTERN, John. b 61. Linc Th Coll BTh93. **d** 93 **p** 94. C Preston on Tees *Dur* 93-96; P-in-c W Pelton from 96; P-in-c Pelton from 99; Asst Dioc Youth Adv 96-99. *The Vicarage, West Pelton, Stanley DH9 6RT* Tel 0191-370 2146 Fax 0797-111 4359 E-mail john.lintern@durham.anglican.org

LINTHICUM, James Douglas. b 58. Towson State Univ (USA) BSc81 Leeds Univ MA00. Wesley Th Sem Washington MDiv86. **d** 01 **p** 02. Chapl Barnet and Chase Farm Hosps NHS Trust from 01; NSM Monken Hadley *Lon* from 01. *St Mark's Vicarage, 56 Potters Road, Barnet EN5 5HY* Tel (020) 8449 4265 *or* 8216 4355 Mobile 07931-562189 E-mail jlinth5481@aol.com

LINTON, Alan Ross. b 28. St Aid Birkenhead 57. **d** 60 **p** 61. C Blundellsands St Nic *Liv* 60-62; C Southport St Phil 62-63; C Aigburth 63-66; V Glazebury 66-67; C Formby St Pet 67-69; C Douglas *Blackb* 69-71; P-in-c Appley Bridge All SS CD 71-76; P-in-c Scorton and Calder Vale w Admarsh 76-85; R Hoole 85-93; rtd 93; Perm to Offic *Blackb* from 93. *12 Clive Road, Penwortham, Preston PR1 0AT* Tel (01772) 747813

LINTON, Mrs Angela Margaret. b 45. St Alb and Ox Min Course 97. **d** 00 **p** 01. NSM Langtree *Ox* from 00. *10 Yew Tree Court, Goring, Reading RG8 9HF* Tel and fax (01491) 874236 Mobile 07884-346552

LINTON, Barry Ian. b 76. Glas Univ BSc98 TCD BTh04 MCIBS01. CITC 01. **d** 04. C Enniskillen *Clogh* from 04. *2 Halls Lane, Enniskillen BT74 7DR* Tel (028) 6632 5882

LINTON, Joseph Edmund. b 19. St Andr Univ MA46. Sarum Th Coll 46. **d** 48 **p** 49. C Monkseaton St Mary *Newc* 48-53; CF (TA) 50-54; C-in-c Lynemouth St Aid CD *Newc* 53-59; V Beltingham w Henshaw 59-93; rtd 93; Perm to Offic *Newc* from 93. *4 Dipton Close, Eastwood Grange, Hexham NE46 1UG* Tel (01434) 601457

LINTOTT, William Ince. b 36. St Cath Coll Cam BA58. Ely Th Coll 58. **d** 60 **p** 61. C Brighton St Wilfrid *Chich* 60-62; C Chingford SS Pet and Paul *Chelmsf* 62-66; Chapl Fulbourn Hosp Cam 66-73; Lic to Offic *Ely* 66-97; rtd 01. *7 Haverhill Road, Stapleford, Cambridge CB2 5BX* Tel (01223) 842008

LINZEY, Prof Andrew. b 52. K Coll Lon BD73 PhD86 AKC73 Lambeth DD01 Univ of Wales (Cardiff) DPS74. St Aug Coll Cant 75. **d** 75 **p** 76. C Charlton-by-Dover SS Pet and Paul *Cant* 75-77; Chapl and Lect Th NE Surrey Coll of Tech 77-81; Chapl Essex Univ *Chelmsf* 81-92; Dir of Studies Cen for Study of Th 87-92; Sen Research Fell Mansf Coll Ox 92-00; Tutor Chr Ethics 93-00; Special Prof Th Nottm Univ 92-96; Special Prof St Xavier Univ Chicago from 96; Hon Prof Birm Univ from 97; Sen Research Fell Blackfriars Hall Ox from 00. *91 Iffley Road, Oxford OX4 1EG* Tel (01865) 201565 E-mail andrewlinzey@aol.com

LIONEL, Brother. *See* PEIRIS, Lionel James Harold

LIPP-NATHANIEL, Julie Christiane. b 41. Melbourne Univ BA63 MA72. **d** 95 **p** 95. Tutor United Coll of Ascension Selly Oak 96-99; Lic to Offic *Birm* 96-99; Regional Desk Officer S Asia & Middle East USPG 99-05; Perm to Offic *S'wark* 00-05; rtd 05. *Frankentobel Strasse 4, 73079 Suessen, Germany* Tel (0049) (71) 625846 E-mail julinath@aol.com

LIPPIATT, Michael Charles. b 39. Oak Hill Th Coll BD71. **d** 71 **p** 72. C Ardsley *Sheff* 71-74; C Lenton *S'well* 74-78; V Jesmond H Trin *Newc* 78-96; rtd 96. *69 Lansdowne Crescent, Stanwix, Carlisle CA3 9ES* Tel (01228) 537080

LIPPIETT, Peter Vernon. b 47. Lon Univ MB, BS73 DRCOG79 MRCGP80. Ripon Coll Cuddesdon 86. **d** 88 **p** 89. C Pinner *Lon* 88-91; V Twyford and Owslebury and Morestead *Win* 91-99; Warden Rydal Hall *Carl* 99-03; P-in-c Rydal 99-03; Dioc Spirituality Adv *Portsm* from 03. *50 Penny Street, Portsmouth PO1 2NL* Tel (023) 9282 6120

LIPSCOMB, Ian Craig. b 30. ACT ThL67 Wells Th Coll 61. **d** 63 **p** 64. C Feltham *Lon* 63-65; Australia from 65; rtd 94. *South Hill, Garroorigang Road, PO Box 118, Goulburn, NSW, Australia 2580* Tel (0061) (2) 4821 9591 Fax as telephone

LIPSCOMB, Timothy William. b 52. Chich Th Coll 82. **d** 85 **p** 86. C Sevenoaks St Jo *Roch* 85-89; C Stanningley St Thos *Ripon*

89-92; V Armley w New Wortley from 92; AD Armley from 98. *Armley Vicarage, Wesley Road, Leeds LS12 1SR* Tel 0113-263 8620 E-mail lavish@ermine2.fsnet.co.uk

LIPSCOMBE, Brian. b 37. Bris Univ BA62. Tyndale Hall Bris 62. **d** 64 **p** 65. C Eccleston Ch Ch *Liv* 64-66; C Halliwell St Pet *Man* 66-69; C Frogmore *St Alb* 69-72; V Richmond Ch Ch *S'wark* 72-75; TV Mortlake w E Sheen 76-80; P-in-c Streatham Vale H Redeemer 80-85; V 85-91; R Norris Bank *Man* 91-96; V Droylsden St Martin 96-02; rtd 02. *15 St Anne's Drive, Leeds LS4 2SA* Tel 0113-275 1893 Mobile 07743-168641 E-mail yvonne@ylipscombe.freeserve.co.uk

LISK, Stewart. b 62. Regent's Park Coll Ox BA84 MA88. St Mich Coll Llan 86. **d** 88 **p** 89. C Glan Ely *Llan* 88-92; Chapl Cardiff Inst of HE 92-96; Chapl Welsh Coll of Music and Drama 92-96; Asst Chapl Univ of Wales (Cardiff) 92-96; V Glan Ely from 96; AD Llan from 04. *Church House, Grand Avenue, Ely, Cardiff CF5 4HX* Tel (029) 2059 1633

LISMORE, Dean of. *See* BEARE, The Very Revd William

LISTER, Anthony Galen. b 27. Hull Univ DipArch53 RIBA54. NEOC 80. **d** 83 **p** 84. Hon C Anlaby St Pet *York* 83-87. *Hunter's Colt, Glenborrodale, Ardnamurchan PH36 4JP* Tel (01972) 500219

LISTER, David Ian. b 26. Roch Th Coll 61. **d** 62 **p** 64. C Scarborough St Mary w Ch Ch, St Paul and St Thos *York* 62-66; C Buttershaw St Aid *Bradf* 66-68; V Tufnell Park St Geo *Lon* 68-83; V Tufnell Park St Geo and All SS 83-92; rtd 92; Perm to Offic *York* from 92. *8 Stonethwaite, Woodthorpe, York YO24 2SY* Tel (01904) 704586

LISTER, Mrs Jennifer Grace. b 44. Totley Hall Coll CertEd65. N Ord Course 87. **d** 92 **p** 94. C Cowgate *Newc* 92-95; C Lich St Mary w St Mich *Lich* 95-96; C Wall 95-96; P-in-c Yoxall from 96; Asst P The Ridwares and Kings Bromley from 96. *The Rectory, Savey Lane, Yoxall, Burton-on-Trent DE13 8PD* Tel (01543) 472528 E-mail jenny.lister@talk21.com

LISTER (née AISBITT), Mrs Joanne. b 69. St Jo Coll Dur BA91. St Steph Ho Ox 91. **d** 93. NSM Mill End and Heronsgate w W Hyde *St Alb* 93-96. *Address temp unknown* E-mail listerwilliam@hotmail.com

LISTER, The Very Revd John Field. b 16. Keble Coll Ox BA38 MA42. Cuddesdon Coll 38. **d** 39 **p** 41. C Radford *Cov* 39-44; C Cov St Jo 44-45; V Huddersfield St Jo *Wakef* 45-54; V Brighouse 54-71; Adn Halifax 61-72; Chapl to The Queen 66-72; RD Wakef 72-80; Provost Wakef 72-82; rtd 82; Perm to Offic *Cant* 82-03. *The College of St Barnabas, Blackberry Lane, Lingfield RH7 6NJ* Tel (01342) 870260

LISTER, Joseph Hugh. b 38. Tyndale Hall Bris 61. **d** 64 **p** 65. C Pemberton St Mark Newtown *Liv* 64-68; Hon C Braintree *Chelmsf* 68-71; C Darfield *Sheff* 71-73; P-in-c Sheff St Swithun 73-76; TV Sheff Manor 76-80; TR Winfarthing w Shelfanger *Nor* 80-81; P-in-c Burston 80-81; P-in-c Gissing 80-81; P-in-c Tivetshall 80-81; R Winfarthing w Shelfanger w Burston w Gissing etc 81-88; P-in-c Sandon, Wallington and Rushden w Clothall *St Alb* 88-89; R 89-93; R Nether and Over Seale *Derby* 93-96; V Lullington 93-96; R Seale and Lullington 96-98; RD Repton 96-98; Dean Ndola Zambia 99-02; rtd 02; Hon C Hartington, Biggin and Earl Sterndale *Derby* 02-04; C Stoke Canon, Poltimore w Huxham and Rewe etc *Ex* from 05. *Brooksong, Longmeadow Road, Lympstone, Exmouth EX8 5LF* Tel (01395) 266784 E-mail jandglister@tesco.net

LISTER, Miss Mary Phyllis. b 28. St Andr Ho Portsm 52. **dss** 80 **d** 87. Inkberrow w Cookhill and Kington w Dormston *Worc* 80-82; Ancaster *Linc* 82-87; C 87-88; rtd 88; Perm to Offic *Worc* 88-00 and *Leic* from 00. *6 Stuart Court, High Street, Kibworth, Leicester LE8 0LR* Tel 0116-279 3763

LISTER, Peter. b 42. Leeds Univ BA64 Newc Univ PGCE75. Coll of Resurr Mirfield 63. **d** 65 **p** 66. C Monkseaton St Pet *Newc* 65-68; C Cramlington 68-70; Hon C 71-78; C Morpeth 79-83; V Shilbottle 83-88; Asst Dioc Dir of Educn 83-88; Dir of Educn 88-95; Hon Can Newc Cathl 88-95; Dioc Dir of Educn *Lich* from 95. *The Rectory, Savey Lane, Yoxall, Burton-on-Trent DE13 8PD* Tel (01543) 472528 *or* 306030 Fax 306039 E-mail peter.lister@lichfield.anglican.org

LISTER, William Bernard. b 67. Keble Coll Ox BA88 MA92. St Steph Ho Ox BA91. **d** 92 **p** 93. C Mill End and Heronsgate w W Hyde *St Alb* 92-96; CF from 96. *c/o MOD Chaplains (Army)* Tel (01980) 615804 Fax 615800 E-mail listerwilliam@hotmail.com

LISTON, Scott Carnie. b 62. Edin Univ BD87. Edin Th Coll. **d** 88 **p** 88. C Edin St Martin *Edin* 88-91; C Edin St Luke 88-91; C Edin St Dav 91-92; Chapl HM YOI Guys Marsh 92-97; Perm to Offic *B & W* 92-97; Chapl HM YOI Onley 97-03; Chapl HM Pris Woodhill from 03. *The Chaplain's Office, HM Prison Woodhill, Wisewood Road, Milton Keynes MK4 4DA* Tel (01908) 722000

LITHERLAND, Norman Richard. b 30. Lon Univ BA51 BA52 Man Univ MEd72. N Ord Course 78. **d** 81 **p** 82. NSM Flixton St Mich *Man* 81-94; rtd 94; Perm to Offic *Man* from 94. *1 Overdale Crescent, Urmston, Manchester M41 5GR* Tel 0161-748 4243

LITHERLAND, Terence. b 46. LNSM course 90. **d** 93 **p** 94. OLM Horwich and Rivington *Man* from 93. *61 Tomlinson Street, Horwich, Bolton BL6 5QR* Tel (01204) 692201

LITJENS, Shan Elizabeth. b 55. **d** 95. C Fareham SS Pet and Paul *Portsm* 95-96; C Fareham H Trin 96-99; NSM Hedge End St Jo *Win* from 00. *11 Abraham Close, Botley, Southampton SO30 2RQ* Tel (01489) 796321 E-mail shanlitjens@aol.com

LITTLE, Andrew. b 27. Open Univ BA83 UEA BA03. AKC51. **d** 52 **p** 53. C Fulham All SS *Lon* 52-54; C Epsom St Barn *Guildf* 54-61; V Northwood *Lich* 61-72; P-in-c Hixon 72-86; V Stowe 72-86; V Hixon w Stowe-by-Chartley 86-89; rtd 89; Perm to Offic *Nor* from 89; Hon PV Nor Cathl from 93. *5 Damocles Court, Norwich NR2 1HN* Tel (01603) 662241

LITTLE, Ms Christine. b 60. Lanc Univ BA83. St Jo Coll Nottm 88. **d** 91 **p** 94. Par Dn Meltham *Wakef* 91-94; C Hatcham St Jas *S'wark* 94-99; P-in-c 99-04; C Nottingham St Pet and All SS *S'well* from 04. *15 Hamilton Drive, Nottingham NG7 1DF* Tel 0115-924 3354

LITTLE, David John. b 65. Oak Hill Th Coll BA94. **d** 94 **p** 95. C Chislehurst Ch Ch *Roch* 94-98; TV Bath Twerton-on-Avon *B & W* 98; Dep Chapl HM Pris Bris 98-99; Chapl HM Pris Reading from 99. *The Chaplain's Office, HM Prison, Forbury Road, Reading RG1 3HY* Tel 0118-908 5000

LITTLE, Derek Peter. b 50. St Jo Coll Dur BA72 DipTh75. Trin Coll Bris. **d** 75 **p** 76. C Bradley *Wakef* 75-78; C Kidderminster St Geo *Worc* 78-82; V Lepton *Wakef* 82-85; E Regional Sec CPAS 85-88; Lic to Offic *Ely* 86-88; V Canonbury St Steph *Lon* 88-96; R Bedhampton *Portsm* 96-99. *61 Hart Plain Lane, Waterlooville PO8 8RG*

LITTLE, George Nelson. b 39. CITC 70. **d** 72 **p** 73. C Portadown St Mark *Arm* 72-76; I Newtownhamilton w Ballymoyer and Belleek 76-80; I Aghaderg w Donaghmore *D & D* 80-82; I Aghaderg w Donaghmore and Scarva 82-05; Can Dromore Cathl 93-05; Treas 93-05; Chan 03-05; rtd 05. *22 Willow Dean, Markethill, Armagh BT60 1QG* Tel (028) 3755 2848

LITTLE, Herbert Edwin Samuel. b 21. Lon Univ BA54 BD68. NEOC 79. **d** 80 **p** 81. NSM Dur St Cuth *Dur* 80-88; rtd 88. *3 Whitesmocks Avenue, Durham DH1 4HP* Tel 0191-384 2897

LITTLE, Ian Dawtry Torrance. b 49. Keele Univ BEd72. SW Minl Tr Course 81. **d** 85 **p** 86. NSM St Stythians w Perranarworthal and Gwennap *Truro* 85-97; NSM Chacewater w St Day and Carharrack from 97. *Kernyk, Crellow Fields, Stithians, Truro TR3 7RE*

LITTLE, James Harry. b 57. York Univ BA79 Birm Univ DipTh86. Qu Coll Birm 84. **d** 87 **p** 88. C Wollaton *S'well* 87-90; C N Wheatley, W Burton, Bole, Saundby, Sturton etc 90-93; R E Markham w Askham, Headon w Upton and Grove from 93; P-in-c Dunham w Darlton, Ragnall, Fledborough etc from 04. *The Rectory, Lincoln Road, East Markham, Newark NG22 0SH* Tel (01777) 871731 E-mail revjlittle@aol.com

LITTLE, Nigel James. b 73. Middx Univ BA93. Oak Hill Th Coll 98. **d** 01 **p** 02. C Highgate St Mich *Lon* from 01. *17 Bisham Gardens, London N6 6DJ* Tel (020) 8340 7676 E-mail nigel_little@yahoo.com

LITTLE, Rebekah Mary. b 70. Oak Hill Th Coll. **d** 97 **p** 03. NSM Chislehurst Ch Ch *Roch* 97-98; NSM Bath Twerton-on-Avon *B & W* 98; Perm to Offic *Ox* 00-04; NSM Reading St Mary w St Laur from 04. *Address withheld by request*

LITTLE, Stephen Clifford. b 47. Man Univ MEd81. AKC72. **d** 72 **p** 73. C Grange St Andr *Ches* 72-73; C E Runcorn w Halton 73-75; P-in-c Newbold *Man* 75-77; P-in-c Broughton and Milton Keynes *Ox* 77-82; Sector Min Milton Keynes Chr Coun 77-84; TR Warwick *Cov* 84-93; R Harvington and Norton and Lenchwick *Worc* 93-96; R Harvington 96-98; Exec Officer Dioc Bd for Ch and Soc *Man* 98-05; Exec Officer Dioc Bd for Min and Soc 01-05; Hon Can Man Cathl 00-05; Perm to Offic from 05. *12 Redwood, Westhoughton, Bolton BL5 2RU* Tel 0161-832 5253

LITTLEFAIR, David. b 38. ACCA71 FCCA85 Lon Univ BD79. Trin Coll Bris 76. **d** 79 **p** 80. C Bursledon *Win* 79-82; V Charles w Plymouth St Matthias *Ex* 82-89; Warden Lee Abbey Internat Students' Club Kensington 89-94; V Malmesbury w Westport and Brokenborough *Bris* 94-03; rtd 03. *6 Matford Mews, Matford, Exeter EX2 8XP* Tel (01392) 218784

LITTLEFORD, Peter John. b 40. St Mark & St Jo Coll Lon CertEd63 ACP65 Birkbeck Coll Lon BSc70 Lon Inst of Educn DipEd73 MA76. St Alb and Ox Min Course 96. **d** 99 **p** 00. NSM Bedf St Mark *St Alb* from 99; Chapl De Montfort Univ *Leic* from 99. *15 Harrington Drive, Putnoe, Bedford MK41 8DB* Tel (01234) 356645 E-mail plittlef@dmu.ac.uk

LITTLEJOHN, Keith Douglas. b 59. Ripon Coll Cuddesdon BTh03. **d** 03 **p** 04. C Horsham *Chich* from 03. *18 Queensway, Horsham RH13 5AY* Tel (01403) 250329 Mobile 07905-595041 E-mail keithdlj@aol.com

LITTLER, Eric Raymond. b 36. Lon Univ DipTh67 AMIC93. Roch Th Coll 65. **d** 68 **p** 69. C Hatfield Hyde *St Alb* 68-73; Chapl Welwyn Garden City Hosp 70-73; TV Pemberton St Jo *Liv* 73-78; Chapl Billinge Hosp Wigan 76-81; V Pemberton St Fran Kitt Green *Liv* 78-81; V White Notley, Faulkbourne and Cressing *Chelmsf* 81-88; V Westcliff St Andr 88-96; Chapl

Westcliff Hosp 88-96; Chapl Southend HA 89-96; R E and W Tilbury and Linford *Chelmsf* 96-98; Chapl Orsett Hosp 96-98; RD Thurrock *Chelmsf* 96-98; R Gt Oakley w Wix and Wrabness 98-02; Chapl Essex Rivers Healthcare NHS Trust 98-02; rtd 02; Perm to Offic *Sarum* from 98; *Chelmsf* and *B & W* from 02; Chapl St Jo Hosp Heytesbury from 03. *Minster Hall, 1 Pound Row, Warminster BA12 8NQ* Tel (01985) 218818

LITTLER, Keith Trevor. b 35. Lon Univ BSc(Soc)63 TCert64 York Univ MA82 Hull Univ PhD89 Westmr Coll Ox MTh98. St D Dioc Tr Course 89 St Mich Coll Llan 94. **d** 92 **p** 93. NSM Betws w Ammanford *St D* 92-94; C 94; R Pendine w Llanmiloe and Eglwys Gymyn w Marros 94-03; RD St Clears 98-03; rtd 03. *Myrtle Hill Cottage, Broadway, Laugharne, Carmarthen SA33 4NS* Tel (01994) 427779

LITTLER, Malcolm Kenneth. b 34. Univ of Wales (Lamp) BA55. **d** 57 **p** 58. C Llanelli *St D* 57-60; C Llandeilo Fawr 60-61; R Puncheston, Lt Newcastle and Castle Bythe 61-64; R Lamp Velfrey 64-68; V Llanwnda w Goodwick and Manorowen 68-74; V Llanfynydd 74-78; V The Suttons w Tydd *Linc* 87-90; V Graffoe 90-94; rtd 94; Perm to Offic *Linc* 94-97. *Ivy Cottage, 11 Chapel Lane, Lincoln LN1 3BA*

LITTLEWOOD, Alan James. b 51. Man Poly BEd77. LNSM course 91. **d** 95 **p** 96. OLM Gosberton *Linc* 95-97; OLM Gosberton, Gosberton Clough and Quadring 97-01; C Bourne 01-03; P-in-c Leasingham from 03; P-in-c Cranwell from 03. *The Rectory, 3 Moor Lane, Leasingham, Sleaford NG34 8JN* Tel (01529) 309239 E-mail alan@littlewood35.freeserve.co.uk

LITTLEWOOD, Alistair David. b 68. St Cath Coll Ox BA89. Qu Coll Birm 93. **d** 96 **p** 97. C Keyworth and Stanton-on-the-Wolds *S'well* 96-00; Chapl Birm Univ *Birm* 00-05; P-in-c Edwinstowe *S'well* from 05; P-in-c Perlethorpe from 05. *5 West Lane, Edwinstowe, Mansfield NG21 9QT* Tel (01623) 822430 E-mail vicarofeandp@yahoo.co.uk

LITTLEWOOD, Miss Jacqueline Patricia. b 52. Linc Th Coll 77. **dss** 80 **d** 87 **p** 94. Crayford *Roch* 80-84; Gravesend H Family w Ifield 84-87; Par Dn 87-93; rtd 93; NSM Gravesend St Aid *Roch* from 93. *25 Beltana Drive, Gravesend DA12 4BT* Tel (01474) 560106

LITTLEWOOD, John Richard. b 37. Ridley Hall Cam 69. **d** 72 **p** 73. C Rushden w Newton Bromswold *Pet* 72-75; Chapl Scargill Ho 75-77; V Werrington *Pet* 77-91; V Highbury Ch Ch w St Jo and St Sav *Lon* 91-02; rtd 02; Perm to Offic *York* from 03. *8 Aldersyde Court, York YO24 1QN* Tel (01904) 778879

LITTLEWOOD, Philip Nigel. b 59. Sarum & Wells Th Coll 87. **d** 90 **p** 91. C Frome St Jo and St Mary *B & W* 90-95; P-in-c Keinton Mandeville w Lydford-on-Fosse etc 95-00; R Wheathill Priory Gp from 00. *Wheathill Priory Rectory, Church Street, Keinton Mandeville, Somerton TA11 6ER* Tel (01458) 223216 E-mail philiplittlewood@keinton.fsbusiness.co.uk

LITTON, Alan. b 42. Ridley Hall Cam 66. **d** 69 **p** 70. C Bolton St Bede *Man* 69-71; C Ashton St Mich 71-73; V Haslingden St Jo Stonefold *Blackb* 73-77; Ind Chapl *York* 77-81; V Crewe All SS and St Paul *Ches* 81-84; Ind Chapl *Liv* 84-89; V Spotland *Man* 89-94; R Newchurch *Liv* 94-02; P-in-c Croft w Southworth 99-02; R Newchurch w Croft 02; rtd 02; Perm to Offic *Liv* from 03. *3 Rosemary Close, Great Sankey, Warrington WA5 1TL* Tel (01925) 453264

LIVERPOOL, Archdeacon of. *See* PANTER, The Ven Richard James Graham

LIVERPOOL, Bishop of. *See* JONES, The Rt Revd James Stuart

LIVERPOOL, Dean of. *See* HOARE, The Rt Revd Rupert William Noel

LIVERSIDGE, Mrs Linda Sheila. b 48. Oak Hill Th Coll BA98. **d** 98 **p** 99. C Kensal Rise St Mark and St Martin *Lon* 98-01; TV N Wingfield, Clay Cross and Pilsley *Derby* from 01. *The New Vicarage, Morton Road, Pilsley, Chesterfield S45 8EF* Tel and fax (01773) 590529 Mobile 07941-667616 E-mail linda@lindalan.free-online.co.uk

LIVERSUCH, Ian Martin. b 56. St Jo Coll Dur BA79 Univ of Wales (Cardiff) DPS84. Wycliffe Hall Ox 79. **d** 83 **p** 84. C Newport St Mark *Mon* 83-85; C Risca 85-88; P-in-c Newport All SS 88-91; Canada from 91; R Hemmingford w Clarenceville 92-98; R La Salle St Lawr from 98. *350 12th Avenue, La Salle QC, Canada, LI8P 3P7* Tel (001) (514) 364 5718 E-mail islwyn@total.net

LIVESEY, Kenneth. b 29. Codrington Coll Barbados 57. **d** 59 **p** 60. C Georgetown St Phil Br Guiana 59-62; R Canje 62-73; P-in-c Royton St Paul *Man* 72-73; V 73-81; P-in-c Bury H Trin 81-82; TR Bury Ch King w H Trin 82-84; Guyana 84-89; V Oldham St Steph and All Martyrs *Man* 89-91; rtd 91; Perm to Offic *Man* 91-97. *2 Malvern Close, Royton, Oldham OL2 5HH* Tel 0161-628 8617

LIVINGSTON, Bertram. TCD BA56. **d** 57 **p** 58. C Enniscorthy *C & O* 57-59; I Carrickmacross *Clogh* 59-61; I Carrickmacross w Magheracloone 61-63; C-in-c Derryvolgie *Conn* 63-78; I 78-79; I Monaghan *Clogh* 79-86; I Desertlyn w Ballyeglish *Arm* 86-94; rtd 94. *6 The Green, Portadown, Craigavon BT63 5LH* Tel (028) 3835 1859

LIVINGSTON, Richard. b 46. Qu Coll Birm. **d** 83 **p** 84. C Hobs Moat *Birm* 83-87; V Droylsden St Martin *Man* 87-95; P-in-c Wolverton w Norton Lindsey and Langley *Cov* from 95; Chapl to the Deaf 95-03; P-in-c Snitterfield w Bearley from 03. *The Rectory, Wolverton, Stratford-upon-Avon CV37 0HF* Tel (01789) 731278 E-mail richard@livingstonr.freeserve.co.uk

LIVINGSTONE, Canon Francis Kenneth. b 26. TCD BA48 MA64. TCD Div Sch Div Test49. **d** 49 **p** 50. C Dublin Santry Union w Coolock *D & G* 49-52; C Dublin St Geo 52-57; I Castledermot Union 57-62; C Arm St Mark *Arm* 62-66; Hon V Choral Arm Cathl 63-92; I Portadown St Sav 66-78; I Kilmore St Aid w St Sav 78-83; I Donaghmore w Upper Donaghmore 83-92; Preb Yagoe St Patr Cathl Dublin 85-92; rtd 92. *9 Castle Parade, Richhill, Armagh BT61 9QQ* Tel (028) 3887 1574

LIVINGSTONE, Canon John Morris. b 28. Peterho Cam BA53 MA56. Cuddesdon Coll 53. **d** 55 **p** 56. C Hunslet St Mary and Stourton *Ripon* 55-60; Chapl Liddon Ho Lon 60-63; V Notting Hill St Jo *Lon* 63-74; P-in-c Notting Hill St Mark 66-73; P-in-c Notting Hill All SS w St Columb 67-74; P-in-c Notting Hill St Clem 68-74; TR Notting Hill 74-75; Chapl Paris St Geo *Eur* 75-84; Adn N France 79-84; Adn Riviera 84-93; Chapl Nice w Vence 84-93; Chapl Biarritz 93-05; rtd 93. *47 Côte des Basques, 64200 Biarritz, France* Tel and fax (0033) (5) 59 24 71 18 E-mail biarritz.cofe@infonie.fr

LIVINGSTONE, John Philip. b 51. Univ of Wales (Abth) BA PGCE. St D Dioc Tr Course. **d** 96 **p** 97. NSM Maenclochog and New Moat etc *St D* 96-02; V Elerch w Penrhyncoch w Capel Bangor and Goginan from 02. *The Vicarage, 78 Ger y Llan, Penrhyncoch, Aberystwyth SY23 3HQ* Tel (01970) 820988

LIVINGSTONE, Kenneth. *See* LIVINGSTONE, Canon Francis Kenneth

LLANDAFF, Archdeacon of. *See* THOMAS, The Ven William Phillip

LLANDAFF, Bishop of. *See* MORGAN, The Most Revd Barry Cennydd

LLANDAFF, Dean of. *See* LEWIS, The Very Revd John Thomas

✠**LLEWELLIN, The Rt Revd John Richard Allan.** b 38. Fitzw Ho Cam BA64 MA78. Westcott Ho Cam 61. **d** 64 **p** 65 **c** 85. C Radlett *St Alb* 64-68; C Johannesburg Cathl S Africa 68-71; V Waltham Cross *St Alb* 71-79; R Harpenden St Nic 79-85; Hon Can Truro Cathl *Truro* 85-92; Suff Bp St Germans 85-92; Suff Bp Dover *Cant* 92-99; Bp at Lambeth (Hd of Staff) 99-03; rtd 03; Perm to Offic *Truro* from 04. *The Cottage, Housel Bay, The Lizard, Helston TR12 7PG* Tel (01326) 290354 E-mail rllewellin@clara.co.uk

LLEWELLYN, Brian Michael. b 47. Univ of Wales (Cardiff) LLM99 MRICS73. Sarum & Wells Th Coll 78. **d** 80 **p** 81. C Farncombe *Guildf* 80-83; Chapl RAF 83-87; R Hethersett w Canteloff w Lt and Gt Melton *Nor* 87-95; RD Humbleyard 94-95; P-in-c Smallburgh w Dilham w Honing and Crostwight 95-98; R 98-00; P-in-c Folkestone St Sav *Cant* from 00. *St Saviour's Vicarage, 134 Canterbury Road, Folkestone CT19 5PH* Tel (01303) 254686 Fax as telephone E-mail brianllewellyn@ricsonline.org

LLEWELLYN, Canon Christine Ann. b 46. Univ of Wales (Ban) BA69 DipEd70. **d** 89 **p** 97. NSM Arthog w Fairbourne w Llangelynnin w Rhoslefain *Ban* 90-93; NSM Holyhead w Rhoscolyn w Llanfair-yn-Neubwll 93-94; C 94-95; C Holyhead 95-97; TV 97-04; R from 04; Hon Can Ban Cathl from 03. *The Old School, Rhoscolyn, Holyhead LL65 2RQ* Tel (01407) 763001

LLEWELLYN, David John Patrick. b 16. AKC40. Wells Th Coll. **d** 46 **p** 47. C Dorking *Guildf* 46-49; C Dudley St Fran *Worc* 49-50; C Redditch St Steph 50-52; V Bretforton 52-59; V Wolverley 59-60; S Africa 60-65; Rhodesia 65-69; I Kinneigh Union *C, C & R* 76-83; rtd 83. *c/o Mr and Mrs Lehane, Desert, Enniskean, Co Cork, Irish Republic* Tel (00353) (23) 22763

LLEWELLYN, Neil Alexander. b 55. LWCMD78. Westcott Ho Cam 79 Sarum & Wells Th Coll 83. **d** 84 **p** 85. C Heref St Martin *Heref* 84-86; Chapl Rotterdam Miss to Seamen *Eur* 86-89; R Docking w The Birchams and Stanhoe w Barwick *Nor* 89-92; Chapl Ypres *Eur* 92-95; Toc H 92-95; CF from 95; Perm to Offic *Newc* from 01. *c/o MOD Chaplains (Army)* Tel (01980) 615804 Fax 615800

LLEWELLYN, Richard Morgan. b 37. CB91 OBE79 MBE76. FCMI81. Sarum & Wells Th Coll 91. **d** 93 **p** 94. C Brecon St Mary and Battle w Llanddew *S & B* 93-95; Min Can Brecon Cathl 93-95; Chapl Ch Coll Brecon from 95. *Llangattock Court, Llangattock, Crickhowell NP8 1PH* Tel (01873) 810116

LLEWELLYN, William David. b 22. Univ of Wales (Lamp) BA43. **d** 48 **p** 49. C Llanishen and Lisvane *Llan* 48-51; C Whitchurch 51-63; V Treharris 63-70; V Penmaen *Mon* 70-77; V St Mellons 77-87; rtd 87. *262 Cardiff Road, Newport NP20 3AH* Tel (01633) 817278

LLEWELLYN-MACDUFF, Ms Lindsay. b 75. Kent Univ BA97. St Mich Coll Llan 97. **d** 99 **p** 00. C Milton next Sittingbourne *Cant* 99-01; C Barham w Bishopsbourne and Kingston 01-03; C Margate All SS 03-05; P-in-c Gt Finborough w Onehouse, Harleston, Buxhall etc *St E* from 05. *The Rectory, Woodlands Close, Onehouse, Stowmarket IP14 3HL* Tel (01449) 616010 E-mail lindsay@hercomputer.fsworld.co.uk

LLEWELYN, Robert Charles. b 09. Pemb Coll Cam BA32 MA36. **d** 36 **p** 37. Asst Master Westmr Sch 32-47; Chapl 46-47; C Westmr St Steph w St Mary *Lon* 36-40; India 41-45; Bahamas 47-51; India 51-71; Adn Poona 69-71; Warden Bede Ho Staplehurst 72-75; rtd 74; Chapl Shrine of St Julian 76-90. *80A King Street, Norwich NR1 1PG* Tel (01603) 662600

LLEWELYN, Canon Robert John. b 32. Keble Coll Ox BA54 MA58 Cheltenham & Glouc Coll of HE PhD01. Cuddesdon Coll 65. **d** 66 **p** 67. C Bedford St Andr *St Alb* 66-69; C Cheltenham St Luke and St Jo *Glouc* 69-75; V S Cerney w Cerney Wick 75-80; V Glouc St Cath 80-99; P-in-c Glouc St Mark 87-89; Hon Can Glouc Cathl 94-99; rtd 99; Perm to Offic *Glouc* from 99. *10 Beaufort Court, Chesterton Lane, Cirencester GL7 1WJ* Tel (01285) 650526 E-mail robert@llewe4.freeserve.co.uk

LLEWELYN-EVANS, Catherine Ruth. b 55. St Mary's Coll Dur BA76 Southlands Coll Lon PGCE78. STETS 99. **d** 02 **p** 03. NSM Yatton Moor *B & W* from 02. *The Court House, The Triangle, Wrington, Bristol BS40 5LB* Tel (01934) 863269 E-mail cthlle@aol.com

LLOYD, Canon Bernard James. b 29. AKC56. **d** 57 **p** 58. C Laindon w Basildon *Chelmsf* 57-65; V E Ham St Geo 65-82; RD Newham 76-82; Hon Can Chelmsf Cathl 82-94; R Danbury 82-94; P-in-c Woodham Ferrers 87-90; rtd 94; Perm to Offic *Chelmsf* from 94. *Chanterelle, 47 Seaview Avenue, West Mersea, Colchester CO5 8HE* Tel (01206) 383892

LLOYD, Bertram John. b 26. St Mich Coll Llan 81. **d** 83 **p** 84. C Malpas *Mon* 83-85; V Blaenavon w Capel Newydd 85-93; rtd 93; Lic to Offic *Mon* 93-96; St Vincent 96-02. *91 Hillside Avenue, Blaenavon, Pontypool NP4 9JL* Tel (01495) 792616 E-mail llwydunion@caribsurf.com

LLOYD, The Ven Bertram Trevor. b 38. Hertf Coll Ox BA60 MA64. Clifton Th Coll 62. **d** 64 **p** 65. C S Mimms Ch Ch *Lon* 64-70; V Wealdstone H Trin 70-84; RD Harrow 77-82; P-in-c Harrow Weald St Mich 80-84; V Harrow Trin St Mich 84-89; Adn Barnstaple *Ex* 89-02; Preb Ex Cathl 91-02; rtd 02. *8 Pebbleridge Road, Westward Ho!, Bideford EX39 1HN* Tel (01237) 424701 E-mail trevor@stagex.fsnet.co.uk

LLOYD, Mrs Carole Barbara. b 53. Sheff Univ BA74 Leeds Metrop Univ PGCE93 Coll of Ripon & York St Jo MA03. N Ord Course 00. **d** 03 **p** 04. C Bolton St Jas w St Chrys *Bradf* from 03. *29 Park Cliffe Road, Bradford BD2 4NS* Tel (01274) 640948 E-mail carolelloyd@cricketers.fsnet.co.uk

LLOYD, David Edgar Charles. b 59. Univ of Wales (Cardiff) Dip Past Th 99. St Mich Coll Llan DMS98. **d** 99 **p** 00. C Newton Nottage *Llan* 99-03; V Newcastle from 03. *The Vicarage, 1 Walters Road, Bridgend CF31 4HE* Tel (01656) 655999 E-mail revd.lloyd@virgin.net

LLOYD, David Hanbury. b 28. Univ of Wales (Abth) BSc49 Reading Univ PhD70. LNSM course 97. **d** 97 **p** 98. NSM Swanage and Studland *Sarum* 97-98; Perm to Offic from 98. *Scar Bank House, Russell Avenue, Swanage BH19 2ED* Tel (01929) 426015

LLOYD, David John. b 52. Lon Univ BD82. St D Coll Lamp DipTh76. **d** 76 **p** 77. C Pembroke St Mary w St Mich *St D* 76-77; C Llanelli 77-80; V Cil-y-Cwm and Ystrad-ffin w Rhandir-mwyn etc 80-82; Oman 82-84; R Llanllwchaearn and Llanina *St D* 84-88; V Llangennech and Hendy 88-90; Perm to Offic *St Alb* 91-95; P-in-c Bampton w Clanfield *Ox* 96-97; V from 97; AD Witney 02-03. *5 Deanery Court, Broad Street, Bampton OX18 2LY* Tel (01993) 851222 E-mail revdjlloyd@aol.com

LLOYD, David John Silk. b 37. Univ of Wales (Lamp) BA62. St Steph Ho Ox 71. **d** 73 **p** 74. C Brentwood St Thos *Chelmsf* 73-77; C Hockley 77-80; C Wickford 80-81; C Wickford and Runwell 81-83; TV 83-88; Chapl Runwell Hosp Wickford 81-88; S Africa from 88; Perm to Offic *Chelmsf* from 88; rtd 97. *D4 Argyll House, Seaforth Road, Westcliff-on-Sea SS0 7SJ*

LLOYD, Dennis John. b 46. BSc70 MSc74 PhD81. S Dios Minl Tr Scheme. **d** 90 **p** 91. C Hamworthy *Sarum* 90-92; Chapl UEA *Nor* 92-97; P-in-c Malvern St Andr *Worc* 97-99; V 99-01; Chapl Defence Evaluation Research Agency 97-01; RD Malvern 98-01; P-in-c Rowlands Castle *Portsm* from 01; Warden of Readers from 01. *The Rectory, 9 College Close, Rowland's Castle PO9 6AJ* Tel (023) 9241 2605 E-mail djlloyd@btinternet.com

LLOYD, Derek James. b 78. Birm Univ BA00 Leeds Univ BA03. Coll of Resurr Mirfield 02. **d** 04 **p** 05. C Burnley St Andr w St Marg and St Jas *Blackb* from 04. *18 Lower Manor Lane, Burnley BB12 0EB* Tel (01282) 411162

LLOYD, Dyfrig Cennydd. b 80. K Coll Lon BA01. Ripon Coll Cuddesdon 01. **d** 04 **p** 05. C Llandysul w Bangor Teifi w Henllan etc *St D* from 04. *Dolawelon, Seion Hill, Llandysul SA44 4BX* Tel (01559) 363159 E-mail dyfriglloyd@hotmail.com

LLOYD, Edward Gareth. b 60. K Coll Cam BA81 MA85 Dur Univ PhD98. Ridley Hall Cam 85. **d** 88 **p** 89. C Jarrow *Dur* 88-91; C Monkwearmouth St Pet 91-92; P-in-c 92-96; TV Monkwearmouth 97-99; V Birtley from 99. *6 Ruskin Road, Birtley, Chester le Street DH3 1AD* Tel 0191-410 2115 E-mail gareth@dunelm.org.uk

LLOYD, Eileen. *See* TAVERNOR, Mrs Eileen

LLOYD, Canon Elizabeth Jane. b 52. GRIC74 CChem MRIC77. Linc Th Coll 77. **dss** 80 **d** 87 **p** 94. Linc St Nic w St Jo Newport *Linc* 80-81; Lic to Offic *Sarum* 81-87; Hon Par Dn Lytchett Matravers 87-92; Chapl Poole Gen Hosp 85-94; Chapl Poole Hosp NHS Trust from 94; Can and Preb Sarum Cathl *Sarum* from 03; Pres Coll of Health Care Chapl 02-04. *The Rectory, 19 Springfield Road, Poole BH14 0LG* Tel (01202) 748860 *or* 442167 E-mail jane.lloyd@poole.nhs.uk *or* jane@jalloyd.fsnet.co.uk

LLOYD, Gareth. *See* LLOYD, Edward Gareth

LLOYD, Geoffrey. *See* LLOYD, William Geoffrey

LLOYD, Graham. b 36. Brasted Th Coll 62 St Aid Birkenhead 64 Glouc Sch of Min 86. **d** 89 **p** 90. NSM Churchstoke w Hyssington and Sarn *Heref* 89-97; NSM Lydbury N w Hopesay and Edgton 97-01; rtd 01; Perm to Offic *Heref* from 01. *The Pullets Cottage, Church Stoke, Montgomery SY15 6TL* Tel (01588) 620285

LLOYD, Gwilym Wyn. b 50. Leic Univ BA72 Birm Univ MSc73 Lon Univ LLB78. Trin Coll Bris DipHE85. **d** 87 **p** 88. C Bexleyheath Ch Ch *Roch* 87-91; R Darlaston St Lawr *Lich* 91-98. *24 Grosvenor Avenue, Streetly, Sutton Coldfield B74 3PB*

LLOYD, Hamilton William John Marteine. b 19. Jes Coll Ox BA41 MA45. Ripon Hall Ox. **d** 43 **p** 44. C Falmouth K Chas *Truro* 43-47; R Gerrans w St Anthony in Roseland 47-51; Min Bournemouth H Epiphany CD 51-53; V Bournemouth H Epiphany *Win* 53-60; V Whitchurch w Tufton 60-68; V Whitchurch w Tufton and Litchfield 68-71; V Lyndhurst 71-73; V Lyndhurst and Emery Down 73-84; rtd 84; Perm to Offic *Win* from 86. *Post Office House, Litchfield, Whitchurch RG28 7PT* Tel (01256) 893507

LLOYD, Harry James. b 22. Univ of Wales (Lamp) BA50. **d** 51 **p** 52. C Hay *S & B* 51-55; C Llanigon 51-55; C Hillingdon St Jo *Lon* 55-56; C Marlborough *Sarum* 56-60; V Kingston and Worth Matravers 60-83; C Milton Abbas, Hilton w Cheselbourne etc 83-87; rtd 87; Perm to Offic *Sarum* 87-00. *Riverside Cottage, 35 Rockbridge Park, Presteigne LD8 2NF* Tel (01547) 560115

LLOYD, Canon Herbert James. b 31. TD. St D Coll Lamp BA57. **d** 58 **p** 59. C Wrexham *St As* 58-65; TV 71-74; R Llanferres 65-67; R Llanferres, Nercwys and Eryrys 67-71; V Rhyl w St Ann 74-96; CF (TA) from 74; Can St As Cathl *St As* from 81; Prec St As Cathl from 89. *The Orchard, 8 Stoneby Drive, Prestatyn LL19 9PE* Tel (01745) 851185

LLOYD, Jane. *See* LLOYD, Canon Elizabeth Jane

LLOYD, John. **d** 01. OLM Tettenhall Regis *Lich* from 01. *The Barn, West Trescott Farm, Bridgnorth Road, Trescott, Wolverhampton WV6 7EU* Tel (01902) 765612

LLOYD, John Everard. b 27. LSE BSc50 FCMA60. St Alb Minl Tr Scheme 84. **d** 87 **p** 88. NSM Harpenden St Nic *St Alb* 87-90; Hon C Addingham *Bradf* 90-92; rtd 92; Perm to Offic *Bradf* 92-99. *2 High Springs, Owler Park Road, Ilkley LS29 0BG* Tel (01943) 609267

LLOYD, Jonathan Wilford. b 56. Surrey Univ & City of Lon Poly BSc80 Goldsmiths' Coll Lon CQSW82 DASS82 N Lon Poly MA86. S'wark Ord Course 87. **d** 90 **p** 91. NSM Sydenham St Bart *S'wark* 90-93; P-in-c 93-94; Dir of Soc Resp 91-95; Bp's Officer for Ch in Soc 95-97; Hon PV S'wark Cathl 91-97; Chapl Team Ldr Bath Univ *B & W* 97-04; P-in-c Charlcombe w Bath St Steph from 04. *St Stephen's Rectory, Richmond Place, Bath BA1 5PZ* Tel (01225) 466114 Fax 314099 E-mail jonathan.lloyd@bathwells.anglican.org

LLOYD, Michael Francis. b 57. Down Coll Cam BA79 MA82 St Jo Coll Dur BA83 Worc Coll Ox DPhil97. Cranmer Hall Dur 81. **d** 84 **p** 85. C Locks Heath *Portsm* 84-87; Asst Chapl Worc Coll Ox 89-90; Chapl Ch Coll Cam 90-94; Chapl Fitzw Coll Cam 95-96; Hon C Westminster St Jas the Less *Lon* 96-03; Tutor St Steph Ho Ox from 03. *St Stephen's House, 16 Marston Street, Oxford OX4 1JX* Tel (01865) 247874

LLOYD, Canon Nigel James Clifford. b 51. Nottm Univ BTh81 Lambeth STh90. Linc Th Coll 77. **d** 81 **p** 82. C Sherborne w Castleton and Lillington *Sarum* 81-84; R Lytchett Matravers 84-92; TR Parkstone St Pet w Branksea and St Osmund 92-02; R Parkstone St Pet and St Osmund w Branksea from 02; Ecum Officer (Sherborne Episc Area) from 92; Dioc Ecum Officer 00-01; RD Poole from 01; Can and Preb Sarum Cathl from 02. *The Rectory, 19 Springfield Road, Poole BH14 0LG* Tel (01202) 748860 *or* 749085 Fax 08700-558534 E-mail nigel@branksea.co.uk

LLOYD, Mrs Pamela Valpy. b 25. Gilmore Ho 48 St Aug Coll Cant 76. **dss** 76 **d** 87 **p** 94. Chartham *Cant* 76-78; Cant All SS 78-85; rtd 85; Chapl Asst Kent and Cant Hosp 87; Chapl Chaucer Hosp Cant 87-90; NSM Elham w Denton and Wootton *Cant* 87-93; Sub-Chapl HM Pris Cant 88-96; Perm to Offic *Cant* from 96; Hon C Cant St Martin and St Paul 93-95. *Cavendish House, 9 North Holmes Road, Canterbury CT1 1QJ* Tel (01227) 457782

LLOYD (née WALMSLEY), Patricia Jane. b 62. Bris Univ BSc83 PhD87 Trin Coll Cam BTh01. Ridley Hall Cam 99. **d** 01 **p** 02. C Bowdon *Ches* 01-05; V Over Peover w Lower Peover

from 05. *The Vicarage, The Cobbles, Lower Peover, Knutsford WA16 9PZ* Tel (01565) 812304
E-mail jane@walmsley92.freeserve.co.uk

LLOYD, Canon Peter John. b 32. TD78. Leic Univ DipSocSc53. Wells Th Coll 59. **d** 61 **p** 62. C Walmer *Cant* 61-63; CF (TA) 62-73 and 77-87; C Maidstone All SS w St Phil *Cant* 63-66; V Milton next Sittingbourne 66-69; R Brinkley, Burrough Green and Carlton *Ely* 69-73; CF 73-77; V Chessington *Guildf* 77-85; RD Epsom 82-87; V Epsom St Martin 85-92; rtd 92; Perm to Offic *B & W* from 92. *74 Southover, Wells BA5 1UH* Tel (01749) 672213

LLOYD, Peter Vernon James. b 36. St Jo Coll Cam BA61 MA. Ridley Hall Cam 60. **d** 62 **p** 63. C Keynsham w Queen Charlton *B & W* 62-65; Perm to Offic *Sarum* from 65; NSM Bournemouth St Jo w St Mich *Win* 87-90; NSM Bournemouth St Pet w St Swithun, H Trin etc 90-93; Perm to Offic *Win* 93-95; rtd 01. *18 Cornelia Crescent, Branksome, Poole BH12 1LU* Tel and fax (01202) 741422

LLOYD, Richard Gary. b 75. Ex Coll Ox BA98 St Jo Coll Dur MA00. Cranmer Hall Dur 98. **d** 00 **p** 01. C Dibden *Win* 00-03; Asst Chapl Charterhouse Sch Godalming from 04. *Northway Cottage, Northway, Godalming GU7 2EU* Tel (01483) 425501 Mobile 07753-835744 E-mail r.g.lloyd@lineone.net

LLOYD, Robert Graham. b 42. St Jo Coll Nottm 82. **d** 84 **p** 85. C Tonyrefail *Llan* 84-87; V Martletwy w Lawrenny and Minwear and Yerbeston *St D* 87-91; V Monkton 91-96; V Cymmer and Porth *Llan* from 96; AD Rhondda from 04. *The Vicarage, Maesgwyn, Cymmer, Porth CF39 9HW* Tel (01443) 682219

LLOYD, Robert James Clifford. b 18. Selw Coll Cam BA41 MA49. Linc Th Coll 46. **d** 47 **p** 48. C Clapham H Trin *S'wark* 47-50; C High Wycombe All SS *Ox* 50-53; CF (TA) 50-53; C Hampstead St Jo *Lon* 53-55; V Wellington w W Buckland *B & W* 55-66; P-in-c Nynehead 56-57; V 57-66; RD Wellington 59-66; R Chartham *Cant* 66-81; RD W Bridge 75-81; Hon C Elham w Denton and Wootton 81-92; rtd 92; Perm to Offic *Cant* from 83. *Cavendish House, 9 North Holmes Road, Canterbury CT1 1QJ* Tel (01227) 457782

LLOYD, Roger Bernard. b 58. K Coll Lon BA. Cranmer Hall Dur. **d** 84 **p** 85. C Hornchurch St Andr *Chelmsf* 84-87; C Gt Parndon 87-94; V Elm Park St Nic Hornchurch 94-99. *494 Heathway, Dagenham RM10 7SH* Tel (020) 8984 9887 Mobile 07703-383176

LLOYD, Ronald. b 37. St Mich Coll Llan. **d** 83 **p** 84. C Penarth All SS *Llan* 83-85; V Cwmbach 85-91; Perm to Offic from 91. *23 Teilo Street, Cardiff CF11 9JN*

LLOYD, Canon Ronald Henry. b 32. Univ of Wales (Lamp) BA52 LTh54. **d** 54 **p** 56. C Manselton *S & B* 54-56; C Sketty 56-59; C Swansea St Mary 59-63; CF (TA) 59-65; V Elmley Castle w Netherton and Bricklehampton *Worc* 63-69; Chapl Dragon Sch Ox 69-82; Chapl St Hugh's Coll Ox 75-80; P-in-c Ox St Marg *Ox* 75-76; Chapl Magd Coll Ox 75-82; Prec and Chapl Ch Ch *Ox* 82-87; R Alvescot w Black Bourton, Shilton, Holwell etc 87-95; P-in-c Broughton Poggs w Filkins, Broadwell etc 94-95; R Shill Valley and Broadshire 95-01; rtd 01; Perm to Offic *Glouc* and *Ox* from 02. *2 The Farriers, Southrop, Lechlade GL7 3RL* Tel (01367) 850071

LLOYD, Mrs Sandra Edith. b 48. Sarum & Wells Th Coll 83. **dss** 86 **d** 87 **p** 94. Freshwater *Portsm* 86-87; C 87-89; C Whitwell 89-95; V from 95; C Niton 89-95; P-in-c 95-96; R from 96; R St Lawrence 96-04. *The Rectory, Pan Lane, Niton, Ventnor PO38 2BT* Tel and fax (01983) 730595
E-mail rhadegunde@aol.com

LLOYD, Simon David. b 58. Portsm Poly BA79 RGN91 RSCN95. Wycliffe Hall Ox 80. **d** 83 **p** 84. C Cotmanhay *Derby* 83-85; Chapl Asst Nottm City Hosp 85-87; Chapl Basford Hosp Nottm 85-87; Perm to Offic *Birm* 91-97; TV Solihull 97-04; V Minehead *B & W* from 04. *The Vicarage, 7 Paganel Road, Minehead TA24 5ET* Tel (01643) 703530
E-mail fathersi@fish.co.uk

LLOYD, Stephen Russell. b 47. Worc Coll Ox BA69 MA77 CertEd DipTh. Oak Hill Th Coll 76. **d** 77 **p** 78. C Canonbury St Steph *Lon* 77-80; C Braintree *Chelmsf* 80-92; V Braintree St Paul 92-01; V Ipswich St Andr *St E* from 01. *The Vicarage, 286 Britannia Road, Ipswich IP4 5HF* Tel (01473) 714341
E-mail rev.lloyd@tiscali.co.uk

LLOYD, Canon Stuart George Errington. b 49. TCD BA72. **d** 75 **p** 76. C Cloughfern *Conn* 75-79; C Cregagh *D & D* 79-82; I Eglantine *Conn* 82-89; I Ballymena w Ballyclug from 89; Can Conn Cathl from 97; Preb 97-01; Prec from 01. *St Patrick's Rectory, 102 Galgorm Road, Ballymena BT42 1AE* Tel and fax (028) 2565 2253 *or* tel 2563 0741
E-mail ballymena@connor.anglican.org

LLOYD, Timothy David Lewis. *See* LEWIS LLOYD, Canon Timothy David

LLOYD, Trevor. *See* LLOYD, The Ven Bertram Trevor

LLOYD, William Geoffrey. b 48. Man Univ BA70. Oak Hill Th Coll 92. **d** 95 **p** 96. C Plaistow St Mary *Roch* 95-99; TV Ottery St Mary, Alfington, W Hill, Tipton etc *Ex* 99-04; P-in-c Sampford Spiney w Horrabridge from 04. *The Rectory, Tor View, Horrabridge, Yelverton PL20 7RE* Tel (01822) 855198
E-mail geoffllloyd@ukgateway.net

LLOYD-DAVIES, Arthur (Lloyd). b 31. Univ of Wales BA55. Cuddesdon Coll 55. **d** 57 **p** 58. C Tonypandy w Clydach Vale *Llan* 57-59; C Merthyr Dyfan 59-62; C Amersham *Ox* 62-65; V Tilehurst St Geo 65-73; R Wokingham St Paul 73-84; R Nuthurst *Chich* 84-90; I Fiddown w Clonegam, Guilcagh and Kilmeaden *C & O* 90-96; rtd 96; Hon C Bratton, Edington and Imber, Erlestoke etc *Sarum* 96-99. *The Gatehouse Lodge, Terrys Cross House, Brighton Road, Woodmancote, Henfield BN5 9SX* Tel (01273) 491210

LLOYD HUGHES, Gwilym. *See* HUGHES, Gwilym Lloyd

LLOYD-JAMES, Duncan Geraint. b 66. St Steph Ho Ox BTh94. **d** 94 **p** 96. C St Leonards Ch Ch and St Mary *Chich* 94-96; C Rottingdean 96-99; R Brede w Udimore from 99. *Forge House, Udimore Road, Udimore, Rye TN31 6AY* Tel (01424) 882457
E-mail djlj@btinternet.com

LLOYD-JAMES, Canon John Eifion. b 39. Brasted Th Coll 60 Clifton Th Coll 63. **d** 65 **p** 66. C Burgess Hill St Andr *Chich* 65-68; C-in-c Portslade Gd Shep CD 68-74; V Lancing St Mich 74-88; V Billingshurst 88-93; Chapl St Mary's Hall Brighton 93-96; V Kemp Town St Mary *Chich* 93-99; P-in-c Bishopstone 99-01; V 01-04; Can and Preb Chich Cathl from 00; rtd 04. *32 Sutton Avenue, Seaford BN25 4LH* Tel (01323) 890598

LLOYD JONES, Ieuan. b 31. St Cath Coll Cam BA51 MA54 FBIM. Sarum & Wells Th Coll 80. **d** 83 **p** 84. NSM Claygate *Guildf* 83-89; Perm to Offic *Ox* from 89. *11 Southcroft, Marston, Oxford OX3 0PF* Tel (01865) 793098

LLOYD MORGAN, Richard Edward. b 48. Trin Coll Cam MA70 Ox Univ DipEd71. SEITE 95. **d** 98 **p** 99. NSM Clapham St Paul *S'wark* 98-03; Chapl K Coll Cam from 03. *King's College, Cambridge CB2 1ST* Tel (01223) 331100

LLOYD-RICHARDS, David Robert. b 48. Open Univ BA84 Hull Univ MA87. St D Coll Lamp DipTh70. **d** 71 **p** 72. C Skewen *Llan* 71-73; C Neath w Llantwit 73-76; Miss to Seamen 76-77; V Pontlottyn w Fochriw *Llan* 77-84; R Merthyr Dyfan 84-90; Chapl Barry Neale-Kent Hosp 84-90; Tutor Open Univ from 85; Sen Chapl Univ Hosp of Wales Cardiff 90-95; Sen Chapl Univ Hosp of Wales and Llandough NHS Trust 95-00; Sen Chapl Cardiff and Vale NHS Trust from 00. *University Hospital of Wales, Heath Park, Cardiff CF14 4XW* Tel (029) 2074 7747 ext 4854 E-mail lloyd-richards@cf.co.uk

LLOYD WILLIAMS, Martin Clifford. b 65. Westmr Coll Lon BEd87. Trin Coll Bris BA93. **d** 93 **p** 94. C Bath Walcot *B & W* 93-97; R Bath St Mich w St Paul from 97. *71 Priory Close, Combe Down, Bath BA2 5AP* Tel (01225) 835490

LO, Peter Kwan Ho. b 54. Chinese Univ of Hong Kong BD84 Stirling Univ MBA92 K Coll Lon LLB99. **d** 84 **p** 85. Hong Kong 84-91; Perm to Offic *Chich* 02-03; C Uckfield from 03. *7 Park View Road, Uckfield TN22 1JP* Tel (01825) 762304 Mobile 07759-013791 E-mail peterkwanholo@hotmail.com

lo POLITO, Nicola. b 59. Catholic Th Union Chicago MDiv85 MA(Theol)87. Comboni Miss. **d** 85 **p** 86. In RC Ch 85-94; Egypt 86-88; Sudan 88-91; Italy 91-94; Asst Chapl Malta and Gozo *Eur* 94-98; C Castle Bromwich SS Mary and Marg *Birm* 98-01; TV Salter Street and Shirley from 01. *18 Widney Lane, Solihull, Birmingham B91 3LS* Tel 0121-705 6586
E-mail nlopolito@hotmail.com

LOAT, Canon Andrew Graham. b 61. Aber Univ BD83 Univ of Wales (Ban) MTh00. St Jo Coll Nottm DPS87. **d** 87 **p** 88. C Llangynwyd w Maesteg *Llan* 87-90; C Llansamlet *S & B* 90-91; R Whitton and Pilleth and Cascob etc 91-98; R Llandrindod w Cefnllys and Disserth from 98; Warden of Readers from 02; Can Res Brecon Cathl from 03. *The Rectory, Broadway, Llandrindod Wells LD1 5HT* Tel (01597) 822043
E-mail aloat@cactus90.freeserve.co.uk

LOBB, Edward Eric. b 51. Magd Coll Ox BA74 MA76. Wycliffe Hall Ox 73. **d** 76 **p** 77. C Haughton St Mary *Man* 76-80; C Rusholme H Trin 80-84; P-in-c Whitfield *Derby* 84-90; V 90-92; V Stapenhill w Cauldwell 92-03; rtd 03; Perm to Offic *Derby* from 03. *6 Clay Street, Stapenhill, Burton-on-Trent DE15 9BB* Tel (01283) 561437

LOBB, Miss Josephine Mary. b 57. SRN83 Plymouth Univ Dip Nursing89. LNSM course 94. **d** 96 **p** 97. OLM St Germans *Truro* from 96. *19 Lowertown Close, Landrake, Saltash PL12 5DG* Tel (01752) 851488

LOBLEY, Mrs Shirley Bruce Fenwick. b 44. Moray Ho Coll of Educn TCert64. TISEC 98. **d** 01. C Alloa *St And* from 01. *20 Parkdyke, Stirling FK7 9LR* Tel (01786) 462799 *or* (01259) 724550 E-mail shirley.lobley@btopenworld.com

LOCK, Mrs Beverley. b 59. Loughb Univ BA81 Bris Univ PGCE82. Carl and Blackb Dioc Tr Inst 01. **d** 04 **p** 05. C Kendal St Geo *Carl* from 04. *Cedar Lodge, Mealbank, Kendal LA8 9DP* Tel (01539) 726050

LOCK, David Stephen. b 28. **d** 63 **p** 64. C Streatham Vale H Redeemer *S'wark* 63-66; C Hatcham St Jas 66-75; V Leyton All SS *Chelmsf* 75-95; rtd 95; Perm to Offic *Roch* from 95. *26 Eldred Drive, Orpington BR5 4PF* Tel (01689) 601726

LOCK, Graham Robert. b 39. Hertf Coll Ox BA63 MA67. Ridley Hall Cam 62. **d** 64 **p** 65. C Bexleyheath St Pet *Roch* 64-66; C Roch St Justus 66-71; C St Mary Cray and St Paul's Cray 71-75; V Chatham St Paul w All SS 75-83; R Lambourne w Abridge and Stapleford Abbotts *Chelmsf* 83-92; V Barkingside St Laur 92-03; rtd 04. *107 Spencer Road, Benfleet SS7 3HS* Tel (01268) 750882

LOCK, Paul Alan. b 65. St Chad's Coll Dur BA86. Coll of Resurr Mirfield 87. **d** 89 **p** 90. C Upholland *Liv* 89-92; C Teddington SS Pet and Paul and Fulwell *Lon* 92-95; V 95-99; V Wigan St Anne *Liv* 99-04. *151 Mossy Lea Road, Wrightington, Wigan WN6 9RE* Tel (01257) 424817 E-mail paul.a_lock@virgin.net

LOCK, The Ven Peter Harcourt D'Arcy. b 44. AKC67. **d** 68 **p** 69. C Meopham *Roch* 68-72; C Wigmore w Hempstead 72; C S Gillingham 72-77; R Hartley 77-83; R Fawkham and Hartley 83-84; V Dartford H Trin 84-93; Hon Can Roch Cathl 90-01; V Bromley SS Pet and Paul 93-01; RD Bromley 96-01; Adn Roch from 01; Can Res Roch Cathl from 01. *The Archdeaconry, King's Orchard, Rochester ME1 1TG* Tel (01634) 843366 ext 111 E-mail phdlock@ukonline.co.uk

LOCKE, Nigel Richard. *See* HESFORD-LOCKE, Richard Nigel

LOCKE, Robert Andrew. b 62. St Steph Ho Ox 89. **d** 92 **p** 93. C Colchester St Jas, All SS, St Nic and St Runwald *Chelmsf* 92-95; CF 95-00; V Burnham *Chelmsf* 00-04. *331 Broomfield Road, Chelmsford CM1 4DU* Tel (01245) 440745 Mobile 07949-862867 E-mail robert@robertlocke.wanadoo.co.uk

LOCKE, Stephen John. b 60. St Chad's Coll Dur BA82. Sarum & Wells Th Coll 84. **d** 86 **p** 87. C Blackb St Mich w St Jo and H Trin *Blackb* 86-89; C Oswaldtwistle Immanuel and All SS 89-92; V Blackb St Mich w St Jo and H Trin 92-98; Chapl to the Deaf 98-04; V Owton Manor *Dur* from 04. *The Vicarage, 18 Rossmere Way, Hartlepool TS25 5EF* Tel (01429) 290278

LOCKETT, Preb Paul. b 48. Sarum & Wells Th Coll 73. **d** 76 **p** 77. C Horninglow *Lich* 76-78; C Tewkesbury w Walton Cardiff *Glouc* 78-81; P-in-c W Bromwich St Pet *Lich* 81-90; R Norton Canes 90-95; V Longton St Mary and St Chad from 95; Dean's V Lich Cathl from 91; Preb Lich Cathl from 04. *St Mary and St Chad's Presbytery, 269 Anchor Road, Stoke-on-Trent ST3 5DH* Tel (01782) 313142

LOCKETT, Simon David. b 66. Stirling Univ BA96. Wycliffe Hall Ox 00. **d** 02 **p** 03. C Ray Valley *Ox* from 02. *3 The Rise, Islip, Kidlington OX5 2TG* Tel (01865) 849497 E-mail simonlizlockett@hotmail.com

LOCKEY, Malcolm. b 45. Sunderland Poly BA67 Newc Univ DipEd68 FRSA75 SSC. NEOC 87. **d** 90 **p** 91. NSM Yarm *York* 90-97; C 97-98; TV Whitby w Aislaby and Ruswarp 98-03; Hon Chapl Miss to Seafarers 98-03; Chapl RNLI 00-03; P-in-c Coldstream *Edin* from 04. *Crooks House, The Hirsel, Coldstream TD12 4LR* Tel (01890) 882833 E-mail macbrac@hotmail.com

LOCKHART, Clare Patricia Anne (Sister Clare). b 44. Bris Univ BA74 Newc Univ MLitt96. Cranmer Hall Dur 84. **d** 87 **p** 94. Sisters of Charity from 63; Chapl Asst Sunderland Distr Gen Hosp 84-89; Chapl 89-95; NSM N Hylton St Marg Castletown *Dur* 87-95; P-in-c 95-99; NSM Eorropaidh *Arg* from 99; Perm to Offic *Dur* from 02. *The Sisters of Charity, Carmel, 7A Gress, Isle of Lewis HS2 0NB* Tel (01851) 820734 E-mail carmelsc7@netscapeonline.co.uk

LOCKHART, David. b 68. QUB BSc90 TCD BTh93. CITC 90. **d** 93 **p** 94. C Belfast St Mary w H Redeemer *Conn* 93-96; I Belfast St Steph w St Luke 96-03; I Cloughfern from 03. *Cloughfern Rectory, 126 Doagh Road, Newtownabbey BT37 9QR* Tel (028) 9086 2437 E-mail dlockh1010@aol.com

LOCKHART, Eileen Ann. b 52. ACII74 Open Univ BA93. EAMTC 95. **d** 98 **p** 99. NSM Shenfield *Chelmsf* from 98. *6 Granary Meadow, Wyatts Green, Brentwood CM15 0QD* Tel and fax (01277) 822537

LOCKHART, Ms Michelle. *See* THOMPSON, Ms Michelle

LOCKHART, Raymond William. b 37. Qu Coll Cam BA58 MA61 LLB60. St Jo Coll Nottm 72. **d** 74 **p** 75. C Aspley *S'well* 74-76; V 81-88; R Knebworth *St Alb* 76-81; Warden Stella Carmel Haifa (CMJ) 88-91; R Jerusalem Ch Ch 91-99; Dir CMJ Israel 99-02; rtd 02. *2 Paddock Woods, Combe Down, Bath BA2 7AD* Tel (01225) 840432 Mobile 07817-330831 E-mail lockhart@xalt.co.uk

LOCKHART, The Very Revd Robert Joseph Norman. b 24. TCD BA46 MA53. **d** 46 **p** 48. C Belfast St Mary Magd *Conn* 46-49; C Knockbreda *D & D* 49-54; P-in-c Killaney w Carryduff 54-60; I Comber 60-62; I Belfast St Donard 62-70; I Lurgan Ch the Redeemer 70-89; Prec Dromore Cathl 71-75; Dean Dromore 75-89; rtd 89; Lic to Offic *D & D* from 90. *30 Church Road, Belfast BT8 7AQ* Tel (028) 9049 1588

LOCKLEY, Miss Pauline Margaret. b 41. **d** 02. OLM Stoke-upon-Trent *Lich* from 02. *Highfields, 89 Tolkien Way, Stoke-on-Trent ST4 7SJ* Tel (01782) 849806

LOCKWOOD, Richard. **d** 01. OLM Glascote and Stonydelph *Lich* from 01. *26 Mossdale, Wilnecote, Tamworth B77 4PJ* Tel (01827) 738105 *or* 330306

LOCKWOOD, Mrs Thelma. b 42. WEMTC 01. **d** 03 **p** 04. OLM Bourton-on-the-Water w Clapton etc *Glouc* from 03. *Keilder, Letch Hill Drive, Bourton-on-the-Water, Cheltenham GL54 2DQ* Tel (01451) 810974 E-mail thelin@surfaid.org

LOCKWOOD, Wilfred Eric. b 18. Leeds Univ BA49. Coll of Resurr Mirfield 49. **d** 51 **p** 52. C Tettenhall Regis *Lich* 51-53; C Bournemouth St Fran *Win* 53-57; V Wardleworth St Mary *Man* 57-62; V Leeds Ch Ch and St Jo and St Barn Holbeck *Ripon* 62-71; R Ducklington *Ox* 71-83; CF (ACF) 62-83; rtd 83; Perm to Offic *Nor* 83-04. *15A Wells Road, Walsingham NR22 6DL* Tel (01328) 820723

LOCKYER, David Ralph George. b 41. Wells Th Coll 65. **d** 67 **p** 68. C Bottesford *Linc* 67-69; C Eling *Win* 69-73; TV Eling, Testwood and Marchwood 73-77; TR Speke St Aid *Liv* 77-84; V Halifax St Jude *Wakef* 84-96; Chapl Halifax R Infirmary 84-96; V Banwell *B & W* from 96. *The Vicarage, 3 East Street, Banwell, Weston-super-Mare BS29 6BN* Tel (01934) 822320

LOCKYER, Desmond Edward Weston. b 18. AKC49. **d** 50 **p** 51. C Norwood St Luke *S'wark* 50-52; C Surbiton St Matt 52-54; Chapl Asst United Sheff Hosps 54-56; C Sheff St Anne and St Phil *Sheff* 54-56; C Eastbourne St Mary *Chich* 56-59; V Hellingly 59-68; V Upper Dicker 62-68; V Eastbourne St Mich 68-75; V Preston 75-87; rtd 87; Perm to Offic *Chich* from 87. *Pilgrims, Nep Town Road, Henfield BN5 9DY* Tel (01273) 493681

LOCKYER, Peter Weston. b 60. Linc Coll Ox BA80 MA83 PGCE98. St Jo Coll Nottm 84. **d** 87 **p** 88. C Rowner *Portsm* 87-90; C Beaconsfield *Ox* 90-91; TV 91-95; Dep Chapl HM YOI Glen Parva 95; Chapl Wellingborough Sch 96-00; R Ewhurst *Guildf* 00-03; Hd Schs & Youth Chr Aid from 03. *38 Rushes Road, Petersfield GU32 3BW* Tel (01730) 269661 E-mail peterlockyer@btinternet.com

LOCOCK (née MILES), Mrs Jillian Maud. b 33. Lon Univ BSc55 Man Univ Cert Counselling 89. N Ord Course 81. **dss** 84 **d** 87 **p** 95. Didsbury Ch Ch *Man* 84-86; Chapl Asst Man R Infirmary 85-87; Chapl Asst Withington Hosp 86-88; Chapl Asst RN 88-93; NSM Dumbarton *Glas* 93-96; Perm to Offic *Ex* from 02. *Glebe Cottage, Dousland, Yelverton PL20 6LU* Tel (01822) 854098 E-mail rjbirtles@aol.com

LODER, Sister Helen. b 43. Goldsmiths' Coll Lon 65. S'wark Ord Course 91. **d** 94 **p** 95. Soc of St Marg from 70; Hon C S Hackney St Mich w Haggerston St Paul *Lon* 94-01; Hon C Bethnal Green St Matt w St Jas the Gt from 02. *St Saviour's Priory, 18 Queensbridge Road, London E2 8NS* Tel (020) 7613 1464 E-mail helenloder@aol.com

LODGE, Anthony William Rayner. b 26. Wadh Coll Ox BA51 MA55. Cuddesdon Coll 65. **d** 66 **p** 67. Asst Chapl Forest Sch Snaresbrook 66-68; C Walthamstow St Pet *Chelmsf* 66-68; Chapl Ripon Gr Sch 68-91; rtd 91; Perm to Offic *Heref* from 92. *Church Cottage, Diddlebury, Craven Arms SY7 9DH* Tel (01584) 841340

LODGE, Canon John Alfred Ainley. b 29. Wells Th Coll 54. **d** 57 **p** 58. C Huddersfield St Jo *Wakef* 57-60; V Shepley 60-64; V Salterhebble St Jude 64-69; C-in-c Mixenden CD 69-75; V Mixenden 75-76; V Almondbury 76-79; RD Almondbury 76-79; V Warmfield 79-88; Bp's Dom Chapl 79-87; Hon Can Wakef Cathl 85-92; RD Kirkburton 88-92; P-in-c Emley 88-92; R 92; rtd 92; Perm to Offic *Ripon* and *Wakef* from 92. *Bygate, 2 Station Court, Morton on Swale, Northallerton DL7 9TQ* Tel (01609) 778551

LODGE, Michael John. b 53. Wycliffe Hall Ox 87. **d** 89 **p** 90. C Highworth w Sevenhampton and Inglesham etc *Bris* 89-93; P-in-c Cheltenham St Luke and St Jo *Glouc* 93-05; TR Rayleigh *Chelmsf* from 05. *The Rectory, 3 Hockley Road, Rayleigh SS6 8BA* Tel (01268) 742151 E-mail mike.lodge@btinternet.com

LODGE, Robin Paul. b 60. Bris Univ BA82 Ch Ch Coll Cant PGCE83. Chich Th Coll 88. **d** 90 **p** 91. C Calne and Blackland *Sarum* 90-94; Asst Chapl St Mary's Sch Calne 90-94; TV Wellington and Distr *B & W* 94-03; V Highbridge from 03. *The Vicarage, 81A Church Street, Highbridge TA9 3HS* Tel (01278) 783671 E-mail rp.lodge@btinternet.com

LODGE, Roy Frederick. b 38. MBE97. BTh Dip Sociology 62 DPhil93. Tyndale Hall Bris 63. **d** 66 **p** 67. C Tardebigge *Worc* 66-67; Chapl and Warden Probation Hostel Redditch 67-69; Chapl RAF 69-75; C Kinson *Sarum* 76; Lic to Offic *Pet* 76-77; Asst Chapl HM Pris Stafford 77-78; Chapl HM Pris Ranby 78-84; Chapl HM Pris Long Lartin 84-93; Chapl HM Pris Service Coll 87-93; Chapl HM Pris Hewell Grange 93-98; Chapl HM Pris Brockhill 93-98; rtd 98; Perm to Offic *Cov* from 98 and *Glouc* from 99. *44 Eton Road, Stratford-upon-Avon CV37 7ER*

LODWICK, Canon Brian Martin. b 40. Leeds Univ BA61 MPhil76 Linacre Coll Ox BA63 MA67 Univ of Wales PhD87. St Steph Ho Ox 61. **d** 64 **p** 65. C Aberaman *Llan* 64-66; C Newton Nottage 66-73; R Llansannor and Llanfrynach w Penllyn etc 73-94; R Llandough w Leckwith 94-04; RD Llantwit Major and Cowbridge 83-94; Warden of Readers 92-03; Chan Llan Cathl 92-02; Treas 02-04; Chapl Llandough Hosp 94-99; Chapl Univ Hosp of Wales and Llandough NHS Trust 99-01; rtd 04. *26 New Road, Neath Abbey, Neath SA10 7NH*

LODWICK, Stephen Huw. b 64. Plymouth Poly BSc85. St Mich Coll Llan DipTh94. **d** 94 **p** 95. C Clydach *S & B* 94-95; Chapl

St Woolos Cathl *Mon* 95-98; R Grosmont and Skenfrith and Llangattock etc 98-01; CF from 01. *c/o MOD Chaplains (Army)* Tel (01980) 615804 Fax 615800

LOEWE, Jost Andreas. b 73. St Pet Coll Ox BA95 MA99 MPhil97 Selw Coll Cam PhD01. Westcott Ho Cam 97. **d** 01 **p** 02. C Upton cum Chalvey *Ox* 01-04; C Cambridge Gt St Mary w St Mich *Ely* from 04. *Great St Mary's Church, St Mary's Passage, Cambridge CB2 3PQ* Tel (01223) 741718 E-mail jal33@cam.ac.uk

LOEWENDAHL, David Jacob (Jake). b 50. SS Coll Cam BA74 MA77. Ripon Coll Cuddesdon 75. **d** 77 **p** 78. C Walworth *S'wark* 77-80; Chapl St Alb Abbey *St Alb* 80-83; Chapl St Alb Sch 80-83; Team Ldr Community Service Volunteers 84-90; Perm to Offic *Lon* 83-90; R E and W Tilbury and Linford *Chelmsf* 90-95; V Menheniot *Truro* 95-98; RD W Wivelshire 97-98; rtd 98; Perm to Offic *Truro* from 98. *Ashpark House, Ash Park Terrace, Liskeard PL14 4DN* Tel (01579) 348205

LOFGREN, Ms Claire. b 54. Univ of California BA76 Ch Div Sch of the Pacific (USA) MDiv89. Cranmer Hall Dur 88. **d** 90 **p** 94. Par Dn Usworth *Dur* 90-91; C Heworth St Mary 91-93; USA from 93. *PO Box 426, Vails Gate, NY 12584, USA* E-mail clofgren@osh.org

LOFT, Edmund Martin Boswell. b 25. St Jo Coll Cam BA49 MA55. Ely Th Coll 49. **d** 51 **p** 52. C Carl H Trin *Carl* 51-54; C Barrow St Geo 54-56; V Allonby w W Newton 56-62; V Fillongley *Cov* 62-77; V Earlsdon 77-90; rtd 90; Perm to Offic *Sheff* from 90. *10 Quarry Road, Sheffield S17 4DA* Tel 0114-236 0759

LOFTHOUSE, Canon Alexander Francis Joseph. b 30. Keble Coll Ox BA54 MA58. St Steph Ho Ox 54. **d** 56 **p** 57. C Barrow St Jas *Carl* 56-59; C Castleford All SS *Wakef* 59-60; V Airedale w Fryston 60-70; V Maryport *Carl* 70-78; V Helsington 78-95; V Underbarrow 78-95; V Levens 78-95; Hon Can Carl Cathl 85-95; rtd 95; Perm to Offic *Blackb* and *Carl* from 95. *Hazel Grove House, Yealand Redmayne, Carnforth LA5 9RW* Tel (01524) 782405

LOFTHOUSE, Canon Brenda. b 33. RGN60 RM62 RNT69. N Ord Course 84. **d** 87 **p** 94. Hon Par Dn Greengates *Bradf* 87-89; Par Dn Farsley 89-94; V Bolton St Jas w St Chrys 94-00; Hon Can Bradf Cathl 98-00; rtd 00; Perm to Offic *Bradf* from 00. *22 Heaton Drive, Baildon, Shipley BD17 5PH* Tel (01274) 584030

LOFTUS, Francis. b 52. Newc Univ BA73 St Andr Univ BPhil76 Coll of Ripon & York St Jo PGCE76 FRSA94. NEOC 93. **d** 96 **p** 97. Hd Master Barlby High Sch from 90; NSM Barlby w Riccall *York* from 96. *19 Green Lane, North Duffield, Selby YO8 5RR* Tel (01757) 288030 *or* 706161 Fax 213699 E-mail francis-loftus2@supanet.com

LOFTUS, John Michael. b 52. Sheff Univ BSc74 Solicitor 77. Dioc OLM tr scheme 97. **d** 00 **p** 01. OLM Hundred River *St E* from 00. *Keld House, Hulver Street, Henstead, Beccles NR34 7UE* Tel (01502) 476257 Fax 533001 E-mail jloftus@nortonpeskett.co.uk

LOGAN, Ms Alexandra Jane. b 73. Trin Coll Carmarthen BA94 St Martin's Coll Lanc CYCW97. Ridley Hall Cam 99. **d** 02 **p** 03. C Penwortham St Mary *Blackb* from 02. *4 Hill Road, Penwortham, Preston PR1 9XH* Tel (01772) 750060 E-mail alexandra.logan@btopenworld.com

LOGAN, Ms Joanne. b 64. Ch Coll Cam BA87 St Jo Coll Dur BA04. Cranmer Hall Dur 02. **d** 05. C Harrogate St Mark *Ripon* from 05. *30 Halstead Road, Harrogate HG2 8BP* Tel (01423) 870593

LOGAN, Kevin. b 43. Oak Hill Th Coll 73. **d** 75 **p** 76. C Blackb Sav *Blackb* 75-78; C Leyland St Andr 78-82; V Gt Harwood St Jo 82-91; V Accrington Ch Ch from 91. *Christ Church Vicarage, 3 Bentcliff Gardens, Accrington BB5 2NX* Tel (01254) 235089 E-mail kevinlogan@fish.co.uk

LOGAN, Samuel Desmond. b 39. TEng. CITC. **d** 78 **p** 79. NSM Belvoir *D & D* 78-85; NSM Knock 85-87; NSM Belfast St Brendan 87-91; Lic to Offic 91-95; C Bangor Abbey 95-97; I Belfast St Clem from 97. *8 Casaeldona Crescent, Belfast BT6 9RE* Tel (028) 9079 5473

LOGUE, Mrs Rosemary Christine. TCD BTh93. CITC 90. **d** 93 **p** 94. C Clooney w Strathfoyle *D & R* 93-96; I Londonderry St Aug 96-03; I Tullyaughnish w Kilmacrennan and Killygarvan 03-05; I Sixmilecross w Termonmaguirke *Arm* from 05. *St Michael's Rectory, 104 Cooley Road, Sixmilecross, Omagh BT79 9DH* Tel (028) 8075 8218 E-mail r.logue@btinternet.com

LOMAS, David Xavier. b 39. St Jo Coll Dur BA78. Cranmer Hall Dur 75. **d** 78 **p** 79. C Chester le Street *Dur* 78-81; C-in-c Newton Hall LEP 81-85; Chapl Scunthorpe Distr HA 85-93; Sen Chapl Linc and Louth NHS Trust 93-01; Sen Chapl Chapl Manager United Lincs Hosps NHS Trust 01-04; rtd 04. *9 Hazel Grove, Welton, Lincoln LN2 3JZ* Tel (01673) 861409 E-mail xavlomas@aol.com

LOMAS, John Derrick Percy. b 58. St Mich Coll Llan 94. **d** 94 **p** 95. C Rhyl w St Ann *St As* 94-00; Chapl RN 00-01; V Holywell *St As* from 01. *The Vicarage, Fron Park Road, Holywell CH8 7UT* Tel (01352) 710010

LOMAX, Canon Barry Walter John. b 39. Lambeth STh Lon Coll of Div 63. **d** 66 **p** 67. C Sevenoaks St Nic *Roch* 66-71; C Southport Ch Ch *Liv* 71-73; V Bootle St Matt 73-78; P-in-c Litherland St Andr 76-78; V New Borough and Leigh *Sarum* 78-94; Can and Preb Sarum Cathl 91-02; R Blandford Forum and Langton Long 94-02; rtd 02; Perm to Offic *Sarum* from 03. *Shiloh, 2 Colborne Avenue, Wimborne BH21 2PZ* Tel (01202) 856104 E-mail barry.lomax@virgin.net

LOMAX, Eric John. b 64. St Jo Coll Dur BA93. Wilson Carlile Coll Dip Evang88 Cranmer Hall Dur 90. **d** 96 **p** 97. C Goodshaw and Crawshawbooth *Man* 96-00; V Copmanthorpe *York* 00-01. *Address withheld by request*

LOMAX, Canon Frank. b 20. Leeds Univ BA42. Coll of Resurr Mirfield 42. **d** 44 **p** 45. C Byker St Ant *Newc* 44-50; Borneo 50-63; P-in-c Sandakan 50-63; Can Borneo 60-62; Can Jesselton 62-63; V Prudhoe *Newc* 64-74; Singapore from 75; Hon Can and V St Andr Cathl from 75; rtd 87. *100 Clemenceau Avenue North, #03-103 Cavenagh House, Singapore 229491*

LOMAX, Mrs Katie Jane. b 73. RGN96. St Jo Coll Nottm BA02. **d** 02 **p** 03. C Luton St Mary *St Alb* 02-04; Asst Chapl Cam Univ Hosps NHS Foundn Trust from 04. *The Chaplaincy Centre, Box 105, Addenbrooke's NHS Trust, Hills Road, Cambridge CB2 2QQ* Tel (01223) 217769 *or* 245151 E-mail kate.lomax@addenbrookes.nhs.uk

LONDON (St Paul's), Dean of. *See* MOSES, The Very Revd John Henry

LONDON, Archdeacon of. *See* DELANEY, The Ven Peter Anthony

LONDON, Bishop of. *See* CHARTRES, The Rt Revd and Rt Hon Richard John Carew

LONEY, Mark William James. b 72. Cen Lancs Univ BSc94 MA97 TCD BTh03. CITC 00. **d** 03 **p** 04. C Larne and Inver *Conn* from 03. *23 Glenburn Avenue, Glynn, Larne BT40 3DJ* E-mail rev.loney@btopenworld.com

LONG, Canon Anne Christine. b 33. Leic Univ BA56 Ox Univ DipEd57 Lon Univ BD65 ALBC. **dss** 80 **d** 87 **p** 94. Lect St Jo Coll Nottm 73-84; Acorn Chr Healing Trust 85-98; Stanstead Abbots *St Alb* 85-92; Hon Par Dn 87-92; Hon Par Dn Camberley St Paul *Guildf* 92-94; Hon C 94-03; Hon Can Guildf Cathl 96-03. *3 Chiselbury Grove, Salisbury SP2 8EP* Tel (01722) 341488

LONG, Anthony Auguste. b 45. Linc Th Coll 79. **d** 81 **p** 82. C Kingswinford St Mary *Lich* 81-84; TV Ellesmere Port *Ches* 84-87; V Witton 87-97; P-in-c Wybunbury w Doddington 97-02; V from 02. *The Vicarage, Main Road, Wybunbury, Nantwich CW5 7LS* Tel (01270) 841178

LONG, Anthony Robert. b 48. SS Mark & Jo Coll Chelsea CertEd70 Southn Univ BTh93 UEA MA96 Lambeth MA04. Chich Th Coll 74. **d** 77 **p** 78. C Chiswick St Nic w St Mary *Lon* 77-80; C Earley St Pet *Ox* 80-85; P-in-c Worstead w Westwick and Sloley *Nor* 85-92; R Worstead, Westwick, Sloley, Swanton Abbot etc from 92; P-in-c Tunstead w Sco' Ruston from 85; Chapl Nor Cathl from 85. *The Vicarage, Withergate Road, Worstead, North Walsham NR28 9SE* Tel (01692) 536800

LONG, Bill. *See* LONG, Edward Percy Eades

LONG, Christopher William. b 47. OBE94. Nottm Univ BTh78 Open Univ BA80. Linc Th Coll 75. **d** 78 **p** 79. C Shiregreen St Jas and St Chris *Sheff* 78-81; V 81-82; Chapl RAF 82-05; I Enniscorthy w Clone, Clonmore, Monart etc *C & O* from 05. *The Rectory, 3 Madeira Grove, The Moyne, Enniscorthy, Co Wexford, Irish Republic* Tel (00353) (54) 39009 E-mail enniscorthy@ferns.anglican.org

LONG, Canon David William. b 47. St Aug Coll Cant 70. **d** 72 **p** 73. C Stanley *Liv* 72-73; C W Derby St Luke 73-76; C Cantril Farm 76-79; V Warrington St Barn 79-81; V Westbrook St Jas 82-96; V Ince St Mary from 96; AD Wigan E from 03; Hon Can Liv Cathl from 03. *St Mary's Vicarage, 240A Warrington Road, Ince, Wigan WN3 4NH* Tel (01942) 864383 E-mail david@scars.org.uk

LONG, Edward Percy Eades (Bill). b 14. Liv Univ BA36 MA38. Linc Th Coll 73. **d** 73 **p** 74. C Sedbergh, Cautley and Garsdale *Bradf* 73-84; rtd 85; Perm to Offic *Bradf* from 85. *4 Derry Cottages, Sedbergh LA10 5SN* Tel (01539) 620577

LONG, Mrs Frances Mary. b 58. SEITE 98. **d** 01 **p** 02. NSM Caterham *S'wark* 01-05; Chapl Surrey and Sussex Healthcare NHS Trust 01-03; C Riddlesdown *S'wark* from 05. *56 Roffes Lane, Caterham CR3 5PT* Tel (01883) 342273 E-mail franyb8@hotmail.com

LONG, Frederick Hugh. b 43. EMMTC 90. **d** 90 **p** 91. NSM Grantham *Linc* 90-00; C 00-01; TV 01-02; V Grantham St Anne New Somerby and Spitalgate from 02. *St Anne's Vicarage, Harrowby Road, Grantham NG31 9ED* Tel (01476) 562822

LONG, Geoffrey Lawrence. b 47. La Sainte Union Coll BTh93 PGCE94. Portsm Dioc Tr Course 88. **d** 89 **p** 98. NSM Whippingham w E Cowes *Portsm* 89-01; Chapl HM Pris Maidstone from 01. *HM Prison, County Road, Maidstone ME14 1UZ* Tel (01622) 755611

LONG, The Ven John Sanderson. b 13. Qu Coll Cam BA35 MA39. Cuddesdon Coll 35. **d** 36 **p** 37. C Folkestone St Mary and St Eanswythe *Cant* 36-41; Chapl RNVR 41-46; C St Peter-in-Thanet *Cant* 46; Abp's Dom Chapl 46-53; V Bearsted 53-59; V Petersfield w Sheet *Portsm* 59-70; RD Petersfield 62-70; Hon Can Portsm Cathl 67-70; Adn Ely 70-81; R Cambridge St Botolph 70-81; Hon Can Ely Cathl 70-81; rtd 81; Perm to Offic *Ely* from 81. *23 Thornton Road, Girton, Cambridge CB3 0NP* Tel (01223) 276421

LONG, Canon John Sydney. b 25. Lon Univ BSc49. Wycliffe Hall Ox 50. **d** 51 **p** 52. C Plaistow St Andr *Chelmsf* 51-54; C Keighley *Bradf* 54-57; C-in-c Horton Bank Top CD 57-59; V Buttershaw St Aid 59-64; V Barnoldswick w Bracewell 64-85; Hon Can Bradf Cathl 77-91; RD Skipton 83-90; R Broughton, Marton and Thornton 85-91; rtd 91; Perm to Offic *Bradf* from 91. *1 Church Villa, Carleton, Skipton BD23 3DQ* Tel (01756) 799095

LONG, Kingsley Edward. b 41. CITC 90. **d** 93 **p** 94. NSM Swords w Donabate and Kilsallaghan *D & G* 93-94 and 96-99; NSM Howth 94-96; NSM Holmpatrick w Balbriggan and Kenure 99-01; NSM Dublin Clontarf 02-03; NSM Swords w Donabate and Kilsallaghan from 03. *Crimond, 125 Seapark, Malahide, Co Dublin, Irish Republic* Tel (00353) (1) 845 3179

LONG, Canon Michael David Barnby. b 32. AKC55. **d** 56 **p** 57. C Whitby *York* 56-59; C Cottingham 59-61; V Elloughton 61-66; P-in-c Brantingham 61-66; V Sheff St Cecilia Parson Cross *Sheff* 66-68; V Flamborough *York* 68-73; R Litcham w Kempston w E and W Lexham *Nor* 73-75; P-in-c York St Luke *York* 75-77; V 77-80; V Hatton w Haseley and Rowington w Lowsonford *Cov* 80-82; V Derringham Bank *York* 82-85; R Castleacre w Newton, Rougham and Southacre *Nor* 85-86; TV Grantham *Linc* 86-89; V Cayton w Eastfield *York* 89-98; RD Scarborough 94-98; Can and Preb York Minster 97-03; rtd 98; P-in-c York St Clem w St Mary Bishophill Senior *York* 98-03; P-in-c Trowse *Nor* from 03. *19 Ipswich Grove, Norwich NR2 2LU* Tel (01603) 613224 E-mail michael-long@amserve.com

LONG, Peter Ronald. b 48. Nottm Univ BA69 Man Univ CertEd70. Cuddesdon Coll 71. **d** 73 **p** 74. Chapl RAFVR 74-99; C Bodmin *Truro* 73-75; C Newquay 75-76; Asst Youth Chapl 75-76; Dioc Youth Chapl 76-79; Perm to Offic *Eur* 76, 78-85 and 87-98; Public Preacher *Truro* 77; P-in-c Mawgan w St Martin-in-Meneage 79-82; Chapl Helston-Meneage Community and Geriatric Hosp 80-95; Miss to Seamen 80-98; P-in-c Cury w Gunwalloe *Truro* 80-82; R Cury and Gunwalloe w Mawgan 83-98; Perm to Offic *Ex* 82-93; Personal Asst to Ecum Th in UK Rail Ind from 97. *26 Jubilee Street, Newquay TR7 1LA* Tel 07780-976113 (mobile) Fax (01637) 877060 E-mail peterronaldlong@alumni.nottingham.ac.uk

LONG, Richard John William. b 59. Cranmer Hall Dur. **d** 05. C Beverley St Nic *York* from 05. *7 St Nicholas Drive, Beverley HU17 0QY* Tel (01482) 862770 E-mail richard@long6426.freeserve.co.uk

LONG, Roger Eric. b 36. Univ Coll Dur BSc59 PhD62. NEOC 90. **d** 93 **p** 94. C Street *York* 93-97; P-in-c Coxwold and Husthwaite 97-02; rtd 02. *Ivy House, Coxwold, York YO61 4AD* Tel (01347) 868301

LONG, Samuel Allen. b 48. EAMTC 03. **d** 05. NSM Barrow *St E* from 05. *16 Drury Close, Rougham, Bury St Edmunds IP30 9JE* Tel (01359) 270972 Mobile 07732-971925 E-mail valerielong16@aol.com

LONG, Canon Samuel Ernest. b 18. JP68. ALCD50 LTh MTh ThD. **d** 49 **p** 50. C Belfast St Clem *D & D* 49-52; C Willowfield 52-56; I Dromara w Garvaghy 56-85; Can Dromore Cathl 81-85; Treas 82-85; rtd 85. *9 Cairnshill Court, Saintfield Road, Belfast BT8 4TX* Tel (028) 9079 3401

LONG, Simon Richard. b 40. Birm Univ DPS69. Bernard Gilpin Soc Dur 61 Ely Th Coll 62 Coll of Resurr Mirfield 64. **d** 65 **p** 66. C Bournemouth St Fran *Win* 65-68; Belgium 68; USA 69-88; P-in-c Medbourne cum Holt w Stockerston and Blaston *Leic* 88-89; P-in-c Bringhurst w Gt Easton 88-89; R Six Saints circa Holt 90-99; RD Gartree I 93-97; rtd 99. *17C Craft Village, Balnakeil, Durness, Lairg IV27 4PT* Tel (01971) 511777

LONG, William Thomas. b 53. Dur Univ MA88 QUB PhD99. **d** 81 **p** 82. C Orangefield *D & D* 81-84; C Portadown St Mark *Arm* 84-86; I Dromara w Garvaghy *D & D* 86-91; I Aghalurcher w Tattykeeran, Cooneen etc *Clogh* 91-96; I Annalong *D & D* 96-03; I Belfast St Simon w St Phil *Conn* from 03. *106 Upper Lisburn Road, Belfast BT10 0BB* Tel (028) 9061 7562 Mobile 07715-773979 E-mail wlhudhud@bushinternet.com

LONGBOTTOM, Canon Frank. b 41. Lon Univ DipTh68 Birm Univ DPS74. Ripon Hall Ox 65. **d** 68 **p** 69. C Epsom St Martin *Guildf* 68-72; Asst Chapl St Ebbas Hosp Epsom 68-72; Asst Chapl Qu Mary's Hosp Carshalton 68-72; Asst Chapl Henderson Hosp Sutton 68-72; Chapl Highcroft Hosp Birm 72-94; Chapl Northcroft Hosp Birm 74-94; Dioc Adv for Past Care of Clergy & Families from 89; Bp's Adv from 94; Hon Can Birm Cathl *Birm* from 91; P-in-c Middleton 99-00; Bp's Adv on Health and Soc Care from 01. *46 Sunnybank Road, Sutton Coldfield B73 5RE* Tel and fax 0121-350 5823 *or* tel 378 2211 E-mail frank@pascare.fsnet.co.uk

LONGBOTTOM, Canon Paul Edward. b 44. AKC67. **d** 68 **p** 69. C Rainham *Roch* 68-71; C Riverhead 71-75; C Dunton Green 71-75; V Penge Lane H Trin 75-84; V Chatham St Wm 84-94; V Shorne from 94; Dioc Dir of Ords from 94; Hon Can Roch Cathl from 96. *The Vicarage, Butcher's Hill, Shorne, Gravesend DA12 3EB* Tel (01474) 822239 Fax 824502 E-mail paul.longbottom@rochester.anglican.org

LONGDEN, Lee Paul. b 70. Peterho Cam BA91 MA95 Ches Coll of HE MTh03 FRCO91 LLCM93 ARCM93 LRSM96. Qu Coll Birm 03. **d** 05. C Langley and Parkfield *Man* from 05. *The Vicarage, 316 Windermere Road, Middleton, Manchester M24 4LA* Tel 0161-654 8562

LONGDON, Anthony Robert James. b 44. STETS 00. **d** 03 **p** 04. OLM N Bradley, Southwick and Heywood *Sarum* from 03. *1A Holbrook Lane, Trowbridge BA14 0PP* Tel and fax (01225) 754771 E-mail longdon@tesco.net

LONGE, James Robert. b 46. EAMTC 02. **d** 04 **p** 05. NSM Pakenham w Norton and Tostock *St E* from 04. *Bush House, Bradfield St Clare, Bury St Edmunds IP30 0EQ* Tel (01284) 386209 E-mail lonjar@doves.freeserve.co.uk

LONGFELLOW, Erica Denise. b 74. Duke Univ (USA) BA97 Linc Coll Ox MSt98 DPhil01. SEITE 02. **d** 05. NSM Kew St Phil and All SS w St Luke *S'wark* from 05. *3 Mortlake Terrace, Richmond TW9 3DT* Tel (020) 8948 4112 E-mail e.longfellow@kingston.ac.uk

LONGFOOT, Canon Richard. b 46. Oak Hill Th Coll 76. **d** 78 **p** 79. C Chaddesden St Mary *Derby* 78-81; C Cambridge St Martin *Ely* 81-83; R Folksworth w Morborne 83-89; R Stilton w Denton and Caldecote 83-89; R Stilton w Denton and Caldecote etc from 90; RD Yaxley from 02; Hon Can Ely Cathl from 04. *The Rectory, Stilton, Peterborough PE7 3RF* Tel (01733) 240282 E-mail richard.lfoot@lineone.net

LONGFORD, Canon Edward de Toesny Wingfield. b 25. Ch Ch Ox BA48 MA53. Wells Th Coll 49. **d** 51 **p** 52. C Stevenage *St Alb* 51-54; PC Chettisham 55-68; Min Can, Prec and Sacr Ely Cathl *Ely* 55-68; P-in-c Everton w Tetworth 68-71; V 71-73; R Gamlingay 68-80; P-in-c Hatley 78-80; Hon Can Ely Cathl 79-90; R Gamlingay w Hatley St Geo and E Hatley 80-90; RD St Neots 82-90; rtd 90; Perm to Offic *Ely* from 90. *9 Philippa Close, Ely CB6 1BT* Tel (01353) 667495

LONGMAN, Edward. b 37. Hatf Coll Dur BSc62 Fitzw Coll Cam BA66 MA70. Clifton Th Coll 62. **d** 66 **p** 67. C Lower Homerton St Paul *Lon* 66-72; C Parr *Liv* 72-73; TV 74-85; Perm to Offic *Liv* 87-02 and *Ches* from 96. *21 Canadian Avenue, Hoole, Chester CH2 3HG* Tel (01244) 317544 Mobile 07779-650791 Fax (01244) 400450 E-mail elongman@onetel.com

LONGMAN, Edward George. b 35. St Pet Hall Ox BA58 MA62. Westcott Ho Cam 59. **d** 61 **p** 62. C Sheff St Mark Broomhall *Sheff* 61-65; V Brightside St Thos 65-74; V Yardley St Edburgha *Birm* 74-84; RD Yardley 77-84; Hon Can Birm Cathl 81-96; R Sutton Coldfield H Trin 84-96; RD Sutton Coldfield 94-96; Chapl Gd Hope Distr Gen Hosp Sutton Coldfield 84-90; P-in-c Cerne Abbas w Godmanstone and Minterne Magna *Sarum* 96-02; RD Dorchester 00-02; rtd 02. *5 Old Wells Road, Shepton Mallet BA4 5XN* Tel (01749) 343699 E-mail ted@roseted.co.uk

LONGRIDGE, Richard Nevile. b 15. Sarum Th Coll 46. **d** 48 **p** 49. C Portsea N End St Mark *Portsm* 48-51; R Bourton w Silton *Sarum* 51-63; R Okeford Fitzpaine 63-67; R Spetisbury w Charlton Marshall 67-77; rtd 77; Perm to Offic *Ex* from 78. *The Lodge, 22 Spicer Road, Exeter EX1 1SY* Tel (01392) 493848

LONGUET-HIGGINS, John. b 62. Leeds Univ BA85. St Jo Coll Nottm Dip Th Studies 90 DPS91. **d** 91 **p** 92. C Kidlington w Hampton Poyle *Ox* 91-95; TV N Huddersfield *Wakef* 95-01; V Painswick, Sheepscombe, Cranham, The Edge etc *Glouc* from 02. *The Vicarage, Orchard Mead, Painswick, Stroud GL6 6YD* Tel (01452) 812334

LONSDALE, Mrs Gillian. b 36. Qu Mary Coll Lon BA57 MA59 Ex Univ MPhil81 Bedf Coll Lon DipSocSc60 AIMSW61. SW Minl Tr Course 96. **d** 99 **p** 00. NSM Duloe, Herodsfoot, Morval and St Pinnock *Truro* from 99; NSM Lansallos and Talland 01-03; RD W Wivelshire from 03. *Woodhill Manor, Liskeard PL14 6RD* Tel (01579) 340697 Mobile 07801-301031 E-mail gill@glonsdale.freeserve.co.uk

LOOKER, Miss Clare Margaret. b 55. Liv Univ CertEd. Westcott Ho Cam 85. **d** 87 **p** 02. Par Dn Prestwood and Gt Hampden *Ox* 87-90; Hon C Olney w Emberton 90-92; Hon C Blunham, Gt Barford, Roxton and Tempsford etc *St Alb* 01-03; P-in-c Welford w Sibbertoft and Marston Trussell *Pet* 03-04; Hon C Wilden w Colmworth and Ravensden *St Alb* from 05. *24 Towns End Road, Sharnbrook, Bedford MK44 1HY*

LOOMES, Gaenor Mary. *See* HOCKEY, Gaenor Mary

LOONE, Sean Joseph Patrick. b 60. Cov Poly BA83 Wolv Poly CertEd84 Leeds Univ BA88 Birm Univ MEd94. Coll of Resurr Mirfield 86. **d** 89 **p** 90. C Solihull *Birm* 89-92; Hd RE Bromsgrove Jun Sch from 93. *9 Broomfield Road, Solihull B91 2ND* Tel 0121-705 5117

✠**LÓPEZ LOZANO, The Rt Revd Carlos.** b 62. Madrid Univ BA89 Pontifical Univ Salamanca PhD93. United Th Sem Madrid MTh91. **d** 90 **p** 90 **c** 95. Spain from 90; Bp's Chapl 90-91; R Espiritu Santo 92-95; Adn Cen and N Spain 94-95; Bp in Madrid from 95; Hon Asst Bp Eur from 95. *Calle Beneficencia*

18, 28004 Madrid, Spain Tel (0034) (91) 445 2560 Fax 594 4572 E-mail eclesiae@arrakis.es

LORAINE, Kenneth. b 34. Cranmer Hall Dur 63. **d** 66 **p** 67. C Hartlepool All SS Stranton *Dur* 66-69; C Darlington St Cuth 69-72; V Preston on Tees 72-79; V Staindrop 79-87; P-in-c Haynes *St Alb* 87-96; Dioc Stewardship Adv 87-96; rtd 96; Perm to Offic *York* from 96. *116 Turker Lane, Northallerton DL6 1QD* Tel (01609) 771277

LORD, Alexander. b 13. ALCD43. **d** 43 **p** 44. C Wakef St Mary *Wakef* 43-45; P-in-c Thornham St Jas *Man* 45-47; R Clitheroe St Jas *Blackb* 47-55; V Madeley *Heref* 55-69; R Illogan *Truro* 70-81; rtd 81; C Letton w Staunton, Byford, Mansel Gamage etc *Heref* 81-84. *43 Narrow Lane, Llandudno Junction LL31 9SZ* Tel (01492) 584647

LORD, Andrew Michael. b 66. Warwick Univ BSc87 Birm Univ MA99 Fitzw Coll Cam BA02. Ridley Hall Cam 00. **d** 03 **p** 04. C Long Buckby w Watford *Pet* from 03; C W Haddon w Winwick and Ravensthorpe from 03. *The Vicarage, 4 West Road, West Haddon, Northampton NN6 7AY* Tel (01788) 510535 E-mail andylord@freenet.co.uk

LORD, Clive Gavin. b 69. St Martin's Coll Lanc BA. St Steph Ho Ox BTh. **d** 96 **p** 97. C Penwortham St Leon *Blackb* 96-98; C Blackpool St Mary 98-01; P-in-c 01-04; V from 04. *St Mary's Vicarage, 59 Stony Hill Avenue, Blackpool FY4 1PR* Tel (01253) 342713 E-mail livecg@aol.com

LORD, Canon John Fairbourne. b 19. Kelham Th Coll 38. **d** 43 **p** 44. C Dallington *Pet* 43-45; C Langley Marish *Ox* 47-51; R Thornage w Brinton w Hunworth and Stody *Nor* 64-84; RD Holt 64-79; Hon Can Nor Cathl 77-84; rtd 84; Perm to Offic *Nor* 84-01. *Holly Cottage, 32 The Street, Hindolveston, Dereham NR20 5BU* Tel (01263) 860501

LORD, Stuart James. b 59. K Coll Lon BD81 AKC81. Sarum & Wells Th Coll 83. **d** 85 **p** 86. C Darwen St Pet w Hoddlesden *Blackb* 85-88; C Otley *Bradf* 88-93; P-in-c Low Moor St Mark 93-02; TV Brighouse and Clifton *Wakef* from 02. *31 Robin Hood Way, Clifton, Brighouse HD6 4LA* Tel (01484) 713290 E-mail kuriosmba@hotmail.com

LORDING, Miss Claire Ann. b 75. Roehampton Inst BA96. Ripon Coll Cuddesdon BTh96. **d** 99 **p** 00. C Ledbury *Heref* 99-02; TV Tenbury from 02. *The Vicarage, Church Street, Tenbury Wells WR15 8BP* Tel (01584) 810811 E-mail claire.lording@virgin.net

LORIMER, Eileen Jean. b 35. CertEd56. Dalton Ho Bris 62. **dss** 84 **d** 89 **p** 94. Chiddingstone w Chiddingstone Causeway *Roch* 84-04; NSM 89-04. *3 Causeway Cottages, Chiddingstone Causeway, Tonbridge TN11 8JR* Tel (01892) 871393

LORT-PHILLIPS, Mrs Elizabeth Priscilla. b 47. STETS 02. **d** 05. NSM Redhorn *Sarum* from 05. *The Cottage on the Green, 1 Manor Farm Lane, Patney, Devizes SN10 3RB* Tel (01380) 84071 E-mail e.lortphillips@btinternet.com

LOSACK, Marcus Charles. b 53. Ch Coll Cam BA76 MA78 MPhil. Sarum & Wells Th Coll 78. **d** 80 **p** 81. C Hattersley *Ches* 80-82; C Dublin Zion Ch *D & G* 83-86; Libya 86-89; CMS Jerusalem 89-92; I Newcastle w Newtownmountkennedy and Calary *D & G* 93-95; Exec Dir Céile Dé from 95. *Céile Dé, Castlekevin, Annamoe, Bray, Co Wicklow, Irish Republic* Tel and fax (00353) (404) 45595

LOSEBY, Everitt James Carnall. b 22. Launde Abbey. **d** 66 **p** 67. C Thurmaston *Leic* 66-70; R Seagrave w Walton le Wolds 70-75; V Thurnby Lodge 75-84; V Swinford w Catthorpe, Shawell and Stanford 84-87; rtd 87; Perm to Offic *Leic* from 87. *13 Stuart Court, High Street, Kibworth, Leicester LE8 0LR* Tel 0116-279 1169

LOTHIAN, Iain Nigel Cunningham. b 59. Aber Univ MA84 Bath Univ PGCE86 Leeds Univ MA05. N Ord Course 02. **d** 05. C Sheff St Pet Abbeydale *Sheff* from 05. *33 Gatefield Road, Sheffield S7 1RD* Tel 0114-250 9736 E-mail i.lothian@btopenworld.com

LOTT, Eric John. b 34. Lon Univ BA65 Lanc Univ MLitt70 PhD77. Richmond Th Coll BD59. **d** 60 **p** 61. India 60-88; Prof United Th Coll Bangalore 77-88; Wesley Hall Ch and Community Project Leics 88-94; rtd 94; Perm to Offic *Leic* from 94. *16 Main Road, Old Dalby, Melton Mowbray LE14 3LR* Tel (01664) 822405 E-mail eric.lott@breathemail.net

LOUDEN, Canon Terence Edmund. b 48. Ch Coll Cam BA70 MA74. Sarum & Wells Th Coll 72. **d** 75 **p** 76. C Portsea N End St Mark *Portsm* 75-78; C-in-c Leigh Park St Clare CD 78-81; R Chale 81-88; R Niton 81-88; P-in-c Whitwell 82-84; V Cosham 88-96; Hon Can Portsm Cathl from 92; V E Meon from 96; V Langrish from 96; CME Officer 96-03. *The Vicarage, Church Street, East Meon, Petersfield GU32 1NH* Tel (01730) 823221 Mobile 07711-319752 E-mail telouden@cwcom.net

LOUGHBOROUGH, Archdeacon of. *See* STANES, The Ven Ian Thomas

LOUGHEED, Brian Frederick Britain. b 38. TCD BA60. CITC 61. **d** 61 **p** 62. C Dublin St Pet w St Audoen *D & G* 61-63; C Glenageary 63-66; I Rathmolyon Union *M & K* 66-79; I Killarney w Aghadoe and Muckross *L & K* 79-04; Can Limerick and Killaloe Cathls 87-95; Preb Taney St Patr Cathl Dublin 89-04; Dioc Info Officer (Limerick) *L & K* 90-91; Radio Officer 91-04; rtd 04. *2 Arlington Heights, Park Road, Killarney, Co Kerry, Irish Republic* E-mail brianfbl@iolfree.ie

LOUGHLIN, Canon Alfred. b 10. Clifton Th Coll 37. **d** 39 **p** 40. C Preston St Mark *Blackb* 39-44; Chapl RAFVR 41-43; Org Sec (SE Area) CPAS 44-48; V Sneinton St Chris *S'well* 48-54; R Kinson *Sarum* 54-81; Can and Preb Sarum Cathl 75-81; rtd 81. *2 Friars Close, Wilmslow SK9 5PP* Tel (01625) 530403

LOUGHLIN, George Alfred Graham. b 43. Lon Univ DipTh68. Clifton Th Coll 65. **d** 69 **p** 70. C Plumstead All SS *S'wark* 69-73; C Bromley Ch Ch *Roch* 73-76; P-in-c Bothenhampton w Walditch *Sarum* 76-79; TV Bridport 79-83; V Heatherlands St Jo from 83. *St John's Vicarage, 72 Alexandra Road, Poole BH14 9EW* Tel (01202) 741276 E-mail vicar@gagl.co.uk

LOUGHTON, Michael. b 34. K Coll Lon BD58 AKC58. **d** 59 **p** 60. C Chingford SS Pet and Paul *Chelmsf* 59-62; C Eastbourne St Eliz *Chich* 62-65; R Lewes St Jo sub Castro 65-74; Perm to Offic from 87; rtd 99. *Green Woodpecker, 1 Kammond Avenue, Seaford BN25 3JL* Tel (01323) 893506

LOUIS, Ms Emma Christine. b 69. Coll of Ripon & York St Jo BA92 St Jo Coll Dur BA96. Cranmer Hall Dur 94. **d** 97 **p** 98. C Birm St Martin w Bordesley St Andr *Birm* 97-00; Arts Development Officer 97-00; Asst Chapl Harrogate Health Care NHS Trust 00-02; C Bilton *Ripon* 01; Chapl Co-ord St Mich Hospice Harrogate 01-02; Asst Chapl Birm Heartlands and Solihull NHS Trust 02-04; Lead Chapl Sandwell Mental Health NHS and Social Care Trust from 04. *Scott House, Heath Lane Hospital, Heath Lane, West Bromwich B71 2BG* Tel 0121-553 7676 ext 6255 *or* 773 7158 Mobile 07946-451954 E-mail emma.louis@smhsct.nhs.uk

LOUIS, Canon Peter Anthony. b 41. St Cath Coll Ox BA63 MA77 Jes Coll Cam CertEd64 Man Univ MPhil85. Wells Th Coll 66. **d** 68 **p** 70. C E Grinstead St Mary *Chich* 68-75; C Radcliffe-on-Trent *S'well* 75-80; Hd Master Blue Coat Comp Sch Cov 80-85; V Welwyn Garden City *St Alb* from 85; Chapl Oaklands Coll 93-95; Hon Can St Alb from 04. *The Vicarage, 48 Parkway, Welwyn Garden City AL8 6HH* Tel (01707) 323316 Fax 694188 E-mail plouis@ntlworld.com

LOVATT, Bernard James. b 31. Lich Th Coll 64. **d** 65 **p** 66. C Burford III w Lt Heref 65-67; C Cleobury Mortimer w Hopton Wafers 67-68; C Bradford-on-Avon *Sarum* 68-69; C Wootton Bassett 69-72; C Broad Town 69-72; R Bishopstrow and Boreham 72-79; P-in-c Brighton St Geo *Chich* 79-83; V Brighton St Anne 79-83; V Brighton St Geo and St Anne 83-86; P-in-c Kemp Town St Mark and St Matt 85-86; V Brighton St Geo w St Anne and St Mark 86-95; rtd 95; Perm to Offic *Ex* from 95. *7 Cambridge Terrace, Salcombe Road, Sidmouth EX10 8PL* Tel (01395) 514154

LOVATT, Mrs Pamela. b 50. LNSM course 95. **d** 98 **p** 99. OLM Warrington St Ann *Liv* from 98; Chapl Warrington Community Health Care NHS Trust from 99. *59 Amelia Street, Warrington WA2 7QD* Tel (01925) 650849 *or* 655221

LOVATT, William Robert. b 54. SS Coll Cam MA75 K Coll Lon PGCE77 MA78. Oak Hill Th Coll 85. **d** 87 **p** 88. C Devonport St Budeaux *Ex* 87-90; Asst Chapl Paris St Mich *Eur* 90-94; P-in-c Lenton *S'well* 94-00; V 00-04; V Eastbourne All SS *Chich* from 04. *All Saints' Vicarage, Grange Road, Eastbourne BN21 4HE* Tel (01323) 410033 E-mail wrlovatt@msn.com

LOVE, Ms Anette. b 53. Matlock Coll of Educn CertEd74 Nottm Univ BEd75. St Jo Coll Dur 88. **d** 90 **p** 94. Par Dn Gresley *Derby* 90-92; C Heanor 92-94; C Loscoe 94-02; V Heath from 02. *The Vicarage, Main Road, Heath, Chesterfield S44 5RX* Tel (01246) 850339 E-mail anette@fish.co.uk

LOVE, Richard Angus. b 45. AKC67. **d** 68 **p** 69. C Balham Hill Ascension *S'wark* 68-71; C Amersham *Ox* 71-73; R Scotter w E Ferry *Linc* 73-79; P-in-c Petham w Waltham and Lower Hardres w Nackington *Cant* 79-85; R Petham and Waltham w Lower Hardres etc 85-90; V Sittingbourne H Trin w Bobbing 90-02; P-in-c Aldington w Bonnington and Bilsington etc from 02. *The Rectory, Roman Road, Aldington, Ashford TN25 7EF* Tel (01233) 720898 E-mail revralove@msn.com

LOVE, Robert. b 45. Bradf Univ BSc68 PhD74 NE Lon Poly PGCE89. Trin Coll Bris DipTh75. **d** 75 **p** 76. C Bowling St Jo *Bradf* 75-79; TV Forest Gate St Sav w W Ham St Matt *Chelmsf* 79-85; P-in-c Becontree St Elisabeth 85-96; V S Hornchurch St Jo and St Matt from 96. *St John's Vicarage, South End Road, Rainham RM13 7XT* Tel (01708) 555260 E-mail stjohns-centre@tiscali.co.uk

LOVEDAY, Joseph Michael. b 54. AKC75. St Aug Coll Cant 75. **d** 78 **p** 79. C Kettering SS Pet and Paul *Pet* 78-81; C Upper Teddington SS Pet and Paul *Lon* 81-84; CF from 84. *c/o MOD Chaplains (Army)* Tel (01980) 615804 Fax 615800

LOVEDAY, Susan Mary. b 49. Sussex Univ BA70 Surrey Univ MSc81. STETS 94. **d** 97 **p** 98. NSM New Haw *Guildf* 97-03; NSM Egham Hythe from 03; Ecum Co-ord Churches Together in Surrey from 00. *10 Abbey Gardens, Chertsey KT16 8RQ* Tel (01932) 566920 E-mail sue.loveday.ctsurrey@lineone.net

LOVEGROVE, Mrs Anne Maureen. b 44. DipHE90. Oak Hill Th Coll 88. **d** 90 **p** 94. Par Dn Thorley *St Alb* 90-94; C 94-95; V

Croxley Green St Oswald 95-02; V Letchworth St Paul w Willian from 02. *St Paul's Vicarage, 177 Pixmore Way, Letchworth Garden City SG6 1QT* Tel (01462) 637373 E-mail ann.lovegrove1@ntlworld.com

LOVEGROVE, Michael John Bennett. b 42. FCII FCIPD ACIArb. SEITE. **d** 00 **p** 01. NSM Saffron Walden w Wendens Ambo, Littlebury etc *Chelmsf* from 00; TV from 05. *Craigside, 8 Beck Road, Saffron Walden CB11 4EH* Tel (01799) 528232 Mobile 07980-103541 E-mail lovegrove8_@hotmail.com

LOVELESS, Christopher Hugh. b 61. Trin Coll Ox BA84 MA91. Linc Th Coll 89. **d** 91 **p** 92. C Willingdon *Chich* 91-95; C Goring-by-Sea 95-99; V Warnham from 99. *The Vicarage, Church Street, Warnham, Horsham RH12 3QW* Tel (01403) 265041

LOVELESS, Martin Frank. b 46. Wycliffe Hall Ox 72. **d** 75 **p** 76. C Caversham *Ox* 75-81; V Carterton 81-86; Chapl RAF 86-02; Chapl K Coll Taunton 02-04; Perm to Offic *Heref* 04-05; P-in-c Glossop *Derby* from 05. *The Vicarage, Church Street South, Glossop SK13 7RU* Tel (01457) 852146

LOVELESS, Robert Alfred. b 43. Birm Univ BA66. Westcott Ho Cam 66. **d** 68 **p** 69. C Kenilworth St Nic *Cov* 68-72; C Costessey *Nor* 73-75; R Colney 75-80; R Lt w Gt Melton, Marlingford and Bawburgh 75-80; V Lt and Gt Melton w Bawburgh 80-82; P-in-c Westwood *Sarum* 82-83; Chapl Stonar Sch Melksham 82-87; P-in-c Wingfield w Rowley *Sarum* 82-83; R Westwood and Wingfield 83-87; R Paston *Pet* 87-93; V Nassington w Yarwell and Woodnewton from 93. *The Vicarage, 34 Station Road, Nassington, Peterborough PE8 6QB* Tel (01780) 782271

LOVELESS, Canon William Harry. b 21. Lon Univ BSc60. Ridley Hall Cam 61. **d** 63 **p** 64. C Danbury *Chelmsf* 63-65; C Cambridge Gt St Mary w St Mich *Ely* 65-67; V Cambridge St Mark 67-87; RD Cambridge 81-84; Hon Can Ely Cathl 81-87; rtd 87; Perm to Offic *Ely* from 87. *103 High Street, Swaffham Bulbeck, Cambridge CB5 0LX* Tel (01223) 812307

LOVELL, Charles Nelson. b 34. Oriel Coll Ox BA57 MA61. Wycliffe Hall Ox. **d** 59 **p** 60. C Walsall St Matt *Lich* 59-63; C St Giles-in-the-Fields *Lon* 63; Argentina 64-67; C Cambridge H Trin *Ely* 64; V Esh *Dur* 67-75; V Hamsteels 67-75; Chapl Winterton Hosp Sedgefield 75-83; R Stanhope *Dur* 83-86; Chapl Horn Hall Hosp Weardale 83-97; R Stanhope w Frosterley *Dur* 86-97; V Eastgate w Rookhope 86-97; RD Stanhope 87-97; rtd 97. *10 Riverside, Wolsingham, Bishop Auckland DL13 3BP* Tel (01388) 527038 E-mail charles@thefreeinternet.co.uk

LOVELL, David John. b 38. JP89. Univ of Tasmania BEcon86. Qu Coll Birm 60. **d** 60 **p** 62. C Glouc St Steph *Glouc* 60-64; C Lower Tuffley St Geo CD 64-67; V Lydbrook 67-73; Australia from 73; rtd 98. *26 Lynden Road, Bonnet Hill, Tas, Australia 7053*

LOVELL, Mrs Gillian Jayne. b 58. Univ of Wales (Ban) BA79 PGCE80. Qu Coll Birm MA04. **d** 04 **p** 05. C Burnham w Dropmore, Hitcham and Taplow *Ox* from 04. *12 Hatchgate Gardens, Burnham, Slough SL1 8DD* Tel (01628) 559992 E-mail gill.lovell@lineone.net

LOVELL, Helen Sarah. *See* HOUSTON, Helen Sarah

LOVELL, Keith Michael Beard. b 43. K Coll Lon 67. **d** 68 **p** 69. C Romford St Edw *Chelmsf* 68-73; P-in-c Elmstead 73-79; V Tollesbury w Salcot Virley from 79. *The Vicarage, 12 King's Walk, Tollesbury, Maldon CM9 8XH* Tel (01621) 869393 *or* 868441 E-mail keith@mary.freewire.co.uk

LOVELL, Laurence John. b 31. St D Coll Lamp BA54 Tyndale Hall Bris 54. **d** 56 **p** 57. C Penge Ch Ch w H Trin *Roch* 56-61; C Illogan *Truro* 61-63; V St Keverne 63-68; Australia from 68; rtd 95. *1/64 Cambridge Street, Penshurst, NSW, Australia 2222* Tel (0061) (2) 9580 7554 Fax as telephone E-mail laurence@acon.net.au

LOVELUCK, Canon Allan (Illtyd). b 30. Univ of Qld BSW74 MSocWork79. St D Coll Lamp BA52 St Mich Coll Llan 54. **d** 55 **p** 56. C Dowlais *Llan* 55-58; SSF 58-79; Lic to Offic *Chelmsf* 62-64; Australia from 64; Hon Can Brisbane 92-00; rtd 95. *5/48 Dunmore Terrace, Auchenflower, Qld, Australia 4066* Tel (0061) (7) 3719 5342 *or* 3870 2566 Mobile 414-500837

LOVELUCK, Canon Graham David. b 34. Univ of Wales (Abth) BSc55 PhD58 CChem FRSC. St Deiniol's Hawarden 77. **d** 78 **p** 79. NSM Llanfair Mathafarn Eithaf w Llanbedrgoch *Ban* 78-87; NSM Llaneugrad w Llanallgo and Penrhosllugwy etc 87-96; P-in-c 96-03; R 03-04; Dioc Dir of Educn 92-03; Can Cursal Ban Cathl 00-04; rtd 04. *Gwenallt, Marianglas LL73 8PE* Tel (01248) 853741

LOVEMAN, Mrs Ruth. b 45. STETS 01. **d** 04 **p** 05. NSM Portsea N End St Mark *Portsm* from 04. *3 Cotwell Avenue, Waterlooville PO8 9AP* Tel (023) 9259 1933

LOVERIDGE, Douglas Henry. b 52. Sarum & Wells Th Coll. **d** 84 **p** 85. C Earley St Pet *Ox* 84-88; V Hurst 88-03; Asst Chapl R Berks and Battle Hosps NHS Trust from 03. *The Rectory, Hollybush Lane, Burghfield Common, Reading RG7 3JL* Tel 0118-983 4433 E-mail dhloveridge@hotmail.com

LOVERIDGE, Emma Warren. b 65. St Jo Coll Cam BA87 MA90 PhD01. **d** 99 **p** 00. NSM Highbury Ch Ch w St Jo and St Sav *Lon* 99-02; Hon C Islington St Mary from 03. *Rafan House, 6 Tyndale Terrace, London N1 2AT* Tel 07000-777977 (mobile) E-mail eloveridge@windsandstars.co.uk

LOVERIDGE (née RODEN), Ms Joan Margaretha Holland (Jo). b 57. K Coll Lon BD78 AKC78 Regent's Park Coll Ox MTh98. St Alb and Ox Min Course 95. **d** 97 **p** 98. NSM Caversham St Jo *Ox* 97-98; C Earley St Pet 98-03; P-in-c Burghfield from 03; AD Bradfield from 04. *The Rectory, Hollybush Lane, Burghfield Common, Reading RG7 3JL* Tel 0118-983 4433 E-mail jonloveridge@hotmail.com

LOVERING, Mrs Jennifer Mary. b 39. Eastbourne Tr Coll CertEd59. Wycliffe Hall Ox 81. **dss** 84 **d** 87 **p** 94. Abingdon w Shippon *Ox* 84-87; Par Dn Abingdon 87-94; C 94-97; rtd 98. *5 Monksmead, Brightwell-cum-Sotwell, Wallingford OX10 0RL* Tel (01491) 825329

LOVERING, Martin. b 35. Imp Coll Lon BScEng57 DMS66. Wycliffe Hall Ox 82. **d** 84 **p** 85. NSM Abingdon w Shippon *Ox* 84-88; C Abingdon 88-89; TV 89-00; rtd 01. *5 Monks Mead, Brightwell-cum-Sotwell, Wallingford OX10 0RL* Tel (01491) 825329

LOVESEY, Katharine Patience Beresford. b 62. Trin Coll Bris 01. **d** 03 **p** 04. C Nor Lakenham St Jo and All SS and Tuckswood *Nor* from 03. *St Paul's Vicarage, 22 Little John Road, Norwich NR4 6BH* E-mail katelovesey@aol.com

LOVETT, Mrs Frances Mary Anderson. b 46. Plymouth Univ BA92. N Ord Course 00. **d** 03 **p** 04. Ind Chapl *Liv* from 03; NSM Newton in Makerfield St Pet from 03. *8 The Parchments, Newton-le-Willows WA12 0DY* Tel and fax (01925) 220586 E-mail franian.lovett@virgin.net

LOVETT, Francis Roland. b 25. Glouc Th Course. **d** 85 **p** 86. NSM Ludlow *Heref* 85-91; rtd 92; Perm to Offic *Heref* from 96. *7 Poyner Road, Ludlow SY8 1QT* Tel (01584) 872470

LOVETT, Ian Arthur. b 43. NE Lon Poly BSc74. Linc Th Coll 85. **d** 87 **p** 88. C Uppingham w Ayston and Wardley w Belton *Pet* 87-91; R Polebrook and Lutton w Hemington and Luddington 91-04; Asst to RD Corby from 05. *The Rectory, 13 School Lane, Weldon, Corby NN17 3JN* Tel (01536) 268735

LOVETT, Ian James. b 49. JP99. CertEd72 BTh89 MA92. S'wark Ord Course 73. **d** 76 **p** 77. NSM Gravesend St Geo *Roch* 76-77; NSM Willesborough w Hinxhill *Cant* 77-83; NSM Landcross, Littleham, Monkleigh etc *Ex* 83-85; C Compton Gifford 85-86; TV Plymouth Em w Efford 86-92; TV Plymouth Em, St Paul Efford and St Aug 93-97; Chapl Aintree Hosps NHS Trust Liv from 97; Bp's Adv for Hosp Chapl *Liv* from 03. *University Hospital Aintree, Lower Lane, Fazakerley, Liverpool L9 7AL* Tel 0151-525 5980 *or* 529 2203

LOVITT, Gerald Elliott. b 25. St Mich Coll Llan 59. **d** 61 **p** 62. C Aberdare *Llan* 61-66; C Whitchurch 66-71; V Grangetown 71-76; V Rockfield and Llangattock w St Maughan's *Mon* 76-83; V Rockfield and St Maughen's w Llangattock etc 83-93; rtd 93; Perm to Offic *Llan* from 93; Lic to Offic *Mon* from 93. *78 Ninian Road, Penylan, Cardiff CF23 5EN*

LOW, Alastair Graham. b 43. Brunel Univ BSc68 Reading Univ PhD74. Ripon Coll Cuddesdon 90. **d** 92 **p** 93. C Brighton Gd Shep Preston *Chich* 92-96; TV Ifield 96-99; TV Horsham from 99; Chapl Surrey and Sussex Healthcare NHS Trust from 02. *Trinity House, Blunts Way, Horsham RH12 2BL* Tel (01403) 265401 *or* 227000 ext 7338 E-mail graham@glowpigs.freeserve.co.uk

LOW, Mrs Christine Mabel. b 48. Southlands Coll Lon CertEd69 SS Mark & Jo Coll Plymouth BEd87. SW Minl Tr Course. **d** 99 **p** 00. NSM Bideford, Northam, Westward Ho, Appledore etc *Ex* 99-03; P-in-c Thornton in Lonsdale w Burton in Lonsdale *Bradf* from 03. *The Vicarage, Low Street, Burton in Lonsdale, Carnforth LA6 3LF* Tel (01524) 261579 Mobile 07870-766634 E-mail jandclow@jlow.freeserve.co.uk

LOW, Canon David Anthony. b 42. AKC66. **d** 67 **p** 68. C Gillingham St Barn *Roch* 67-70; V 82-88; C Wallingford *Ox* 70-73; V Spencer's Wood 73-82; P-in-c Grazeley and Beech Hill 77-82; Chapl Medway Hosp Gillingham 86-88; V Hoo St Werburgh *Roch* 88-02; RD Strood 97-02; Hon Can Roch Cathl 01-02; rtd 02. *12 Stonecrop Close, St Mary's Island, Chatham ME4 3HA*

LOW, Canon David Michael. b 39. Cape Town Univ BA60. Cuddesdon Coll 61. **d** 63 **p** 64. C Portsea St Cuth *Portsm* 63-65; S Africa 65-69; C Havant *Portsm* 69-72; V St Helens 72-88; V Sea View 81-88; V Sandown Ch Ch 88-95; V Lower Sandown St Jo 88-95; R Brading w Yaverland 95-01; Hon Can Portsm Cathl 00-01; rtd 01. *Copeland, Lane End Close, Bembridge PO35 5UF* Tel (01983) 874306

LOW, Mrs Jennifer Anne. b 49. St Anne's Coll Ox MA70 Nottm Univ PGCE71. Trin Coll Bris 01. **d** 03 **p** 04. C Bris St Andr Hartcliffe *Bris* from 03. *404 Bishport Avenue, Bristol BS13 0HX* Tel 0117-978 4052

LOW, Peter James. b 52. Nottm Univ BTh89. Linc Th Coll 86. **d** 89 **p** 90. C Dartford H Trin *Roch* 89-92; C Plympton St Mary *Ex* 92-94; TR Devonport St Boniface and St Phil from 94. *St Boniface Vicarage, 1 Normandy Way, Plymouth PL5 1SW* Tel (01752) 361137

LOW, Robbie. *See* LOW, William Roberson

LOW, Stafford. b 42. N Lon Poly BSc65. Trin Coll Bris 82. **d** 85 **p** 86. C Yeovil *B & W* 85-88; C Glastonbury w Meare, W

Pennard and Godney 88-92; R Berrow and Breane 92-00; R Wincanton from 00; R Pen Selwood from 00; Chapl Voc and Min from 97; RD Bruton from 03; RD Cary from 03. *The Rectory, Bayford Hill, Wincanton BA9 9LQ* Tel (01963) 33367 E-mail lowandco@aol.com

LOW, Terence John Gordon. b 37. Oak Hill Th Coll 75. **d** 77 **p** 78. C Kensal Rise St Martin *Lon* 77-79; C Longfleet *Sarum* 79-83; P-in-c Maiden Newton and Valleys 83-84; TV Melbury 84-88; TV Buckhurst Hill *Chelmsf* 88-92; R Gt Hallingbury and Lt Hallingbury 92-01; rtd 01; Perm to Offic *Sarum* from 02. *37 Vicarage Lane, Charminster, Dorchester DT2 9QF* Tel (01305) 260180

LOW, William Roberson (Robbie). b 50. Pemb Coll Cam BA73 MA77. Westcott Ho Cam 76. **d** 79 **p** 80. C Poplar *Lon* 79-83; Chapl St Alb Abbey *St Alb* 83-88; V Bushey Heath 88-03. *3 Trewince Lane, Bodmin Hill, Lostwithiel PL22 0AJ* Tel (01208) 871517

LOWATER, Canon Jennifer Blanche. b 34. Eastbourne Tr Coll TCert54. Sarum & Wells Th Coll 82. **dss** 85 **d** 87 **p** 94. Locks Heath *Portsm* 85-88; Hon C 87-88; NSM Southsea St Pet 88-94; NSM Hook w Warsash 94-01; Asst Dir of Ords 91-99; Hon Can Portsm Cathl 95-97; rtd 97. *Lower Gubbles, Hook Lane, Warsash, Southampton SO31 9HH* Tel (01489) 572156 Fax 572252 E-mail jenny.lowater@care4free.net

LOWE, Anthony Richard. b 45. York Univ BA66. Qu Coll Birm 66. **d** 69 **p** 70. C Greasbrough *Sheff* 69-71; C Thrybergh 71-75; P-in-c Sheff St Mary w St Simon w St Matthias 75-78; V Shiregreen St Hilda 78-85; V Hoxne w Denham St Jo and Syleham *St E* 85-89; P-in-c Wingfield 86-89; R Hoxne w Denham, Syleham and Wingfield from 90. *The Vicarage, Church Hill, Hoxne, Eye IP21 5AT* Tel (01379) 668246

LOWE, Mrs Brenda June. b 53. Cranmer Hall Dur 75. **d** 88 **p** 94. Chapl to Families Trin Coll and Mortimer Ho Bris 86-91; NSM Clifton Ch Ch w Em *Bris* 88-91; Asst Chapl Southmead Health Services NHS Trust 86-91; NSM Marple All SS *Ches* from 91; Perm to Offic *Man* 91-97; Asst Chapl Wythenshawe Hosp Man 94-96; Chapl Stockport Acute Services NHS Trust 96-98; Sen Chapl Stockport NHS Trust from 98. *4 Greenway Road, Heald Green, Cheadle SK8 3NR* Tel 0161-282 3850 *or* 419 5889 E-mail malowe@mail.com

LOWE, Canon David Charles. b 43. Kelham Th Coll 62. **d** 67 **p** 68. C Wingerworth *Derby* 67-70; C Greenhill St Pet 70-73; TV Eckington 73-74; TV Eckington w Handley and Ridgeway 74-78; V Bury St Edmunds St Geo *St E* 78-86; V Leiston 86-98; RD Saxmundham 88-96; P-in-c Felixstowe St Jo from 98; Hon Can St E Cathl from 98. *The New Vicarage, 54 Princes Road, Felixstowe IP11 7PL* Tel (01394) 284226 E-mail david_lowechurch@lineone.net

LOWE, David Reginald. b 42. K Coll Lon BD65 AKC65. St Boniface Warminster 65. **d** 66 **p** 67. C Tupsley *Heref* 66-69; C Lewes St Anne *Chich* 69-73; C Heref H Trin *Heref* 73-77; P-in-c Lyonshall w Titley 77-88; V Lyonshall w Titley, Almeley and Kinnersley 88-96; Perm to Offic 97-00; rtd 00. *26 Chapel Street, Penzance TR18 4AP* Tel (01736) 331068

LOWE, Donald. b 33. Lich Th Coll 57. **d** 60 **p** 61. C Horwich H Trin *Man* 60; C Wythenshawe St Martin CD 60-62; C Bury St Paul 62-65; S Africa 65-69 and 73-81; V Gannow *Blackb* 70-73; V Colne H Trin 81-89; TV Melbury *Sarum* 89-94; RD Beaminster 93-94; rtd 94; Perm to Offic *Bradf* from 94. *28 High Bank, Threshfield, Skipton BD23 5BU* Tel (01756) 752344

LOWE, Mrs Elaine Mary. b 55. LNSM course 95. **d** 98 **p** 99. OLM Bardsley *Man* from 98. *5 Danisher Lane, Bardsley, Oldham OL8 3HU* Tel 0161-633 4535

LOWE, The Ven Frank McLean Rhodes. b 26. ACT 59. **d** 61 **p** 63. Australia 61-86 and from 87; Hon Can Gippsland 73-81; Adn Latrobe Valley 81-86; Adn Gippsland 81-86; P-in-c Kirkby in Ashfield St Thos *S'well* 86-87; C Mansfield Woodhouse 87; rtd 91. *Unit 2, 3 Berg Street, Morwell, Vic, Australia 3840* Tel (0061) (3) 5134 1338

LOWE, Mrs Janet Eleanor. b 56. Univ Coll Lon BSc77. NTMTC 98. **d** 01 **p** 02. C Hendon St Paul Mill Hill *Lon* from 01. *12 Frobisher Road, London N8 0QS* Tel (020) 8340 8764 E-mail janlowe@btinternet.com

LOWE, Canon John Bethel. b 30. TCD BA52 BD65. Ridley Hall Cam 55. **d** 55 **p** 56. C Belfast St Mary Magd *Conn* 55-57; Sudan 59-64; Uganda 64-74; Warden CMS Fellowship Ho Foxbury 74-76; V Kippington *Roch* 76-96; Dioc Dir of Ords 82-96; Hon Can Roch Cathl 85-96; rtd 96; Perm to Offic *Ely* from 96. *228 Cambridge Road, Great Shelford, Cambridge CB2 5JU* Tel (01223) 840019

LOWE, John Forrester. b 39. Nottm Univ BA61. Lich Th Coll 61. **d** 64 **p** 65. C N Woolwich *Chelmsf* 64-70; V Marks Gate 70-74; V Moulsham St Jo 74-79; V N Woolwich w Silvertown 79-82; V Birm St Pet *Birm* 82-86; Gen Sec SOMA UK 86-91; V Heckmondwike *Wakef* 92-98; rtd 98; Perm to Offic *Heref* from 99. *37 Jubilee Close, Ledbury HR8 2XA* Tel (01531) 631890

LOWE, Keith Gregory. b 50. Sarum & Wells Th Coll 91. **d** 93 **p** 94. C Wallasey St Hilary *Ches* 93-94; C W Kirby St Bridget 94-98; V Sandbach Heath w Wheelock 98-01; V High Lane 01-04; Chapl Stockport NHS Trust 01-04; Asst Chapl Sheff Teaching Hosps NHS Trust from 04. *169 Mortomley Lane, High Green, Sheffield S35 3HT* Tel 0114-284 4076 E-mail keithglowe@mail.com

LOWE, Canon Michael Arthur. b 46. Lon Univ BD67 Hull Univ MA85. Cranmer Hall Dur DipTh75. **d** 76 **p** 77. C Thorpe Edge *Bradf* 76-79; C N Ferriby *York* 79-84; TV 84-86; Dir Past Studies Trin Coll Bris 86-91; V Marple All SS *Ches* 91-00; RD Chadkirk 95-00; Dir of Miss and Unity from 00; Hon Can Ches Cathl from 00; C Delamere 00-02. *4 Greenway Road, Heald Green, Cheadle SK8 3NR* Tel 0161-282 3850 *or* (01244) 620444 E-mail malowe@mail.com

LOWE, Samuel. b 35. St D Coll Lamp. **d** 65 **p** 66. C Tenby w Gumfreston *St D* 65-67; C Lower Mitton *Worc* 67-69; C Halesowen 69-72; R Droitwich St Nic w St Pet 72-73; TV Droitwich 73-77; P-in-c Claines St Geo 77-78; P-in-c Worc St Mary the Tything 77-78; P-in-c Worc St Geo w St Mary Magd 78-84; V 84-00; rtd 00. *57 Camp Hill Road, Worcester WR5 2HG* Tel (01905) 357807

LOWE, Stephen Arthur. b 49. Nottm Univ BSc71 DipTh. Cuddesdon Coll 71. **d** 74 **p** 75. C Mansfield St Mark *S'well* 74-77; Papua New Guinea 77-79; V Kirkby Woodhouse *S'well* 80-86; V Beeston 86-99; TR Wenlock *Heref* from 99. *The Rectory, New Road, Much Wenlock TF13 6EQ* Tel (01952) 727396 E-mail wenlockchurches@proweb.co.uk

✠**LOWE, The Rt Revd Stephen Richard.** b 44. Lon Univ BSc66. Ripon Hall Ox 68. **d** 68 **p** 69 **c** 99. C Gospel Lane St Mich *Birm* 68-72; C-in-c Woodgate Valley CD 72-75; V E Ham w Upton Park *Chelmsf* 75-76; TR E Ham w Upton Park St Alb 76-88; Hon Can Chelmsf Cathl 85-88; Adn Sheff 88-99; Can Res Sheff Cathl 88-99; Suff Bp Hulme *Man* from 99. *14 Moorgate Avenue, Withington, Manchester M20 1HE* Tel 0161-445 5922 Mobile 07801-505277 Fax 0161-448 9687 E-mail lowehulme@btinternet.com

LOWELL, Ian Russell. b 53. AKC75. St Aug Coll Cant 75. **d** 76 **p** 77. C Llwynderw *S & B* 76-79; C Swansea St Mary w H Trin and St Mark 79-81; Chapl Ox Hosps 81-83; TV Gt and Lt Coates w Bradley *Linc* 83-88; V Wellingborough St Mark *Pet* 88-02; V Northampton St Alb from 02; Chapl Northants Ambulance Service from 92. *St Alban's Vicarage, Broadmead Avenue, Northampton NN3 2RA* Tel (01604) 407074 E-mail irlowell@aol.com

LOWEN, David John. b 42. Sussex Univ BSc74 Univ of Wales (Lamp) MA84. Llan Dioc Tr Scheme 86. **d** 88 **p** 89. C Carmarthen St Pet *St D* 88-90; P-in-c Walwyn's Castle w Robeston W 90-92; R from 92. *The Rectory, Walwyn's Castle, Haverfordwest SA62 3ED* Tel (01437) 781257

LOWEN, John Michael. b 47. Nottm Univ BTh77. Linc Th Coll 73. **d** 77 **p** 78. C Beeston *S'well* 77-80; C Stratford-on-Avon w Bishopton *Cov* 80-82; V Monkseaton St Mary *Newc* 82-90; V Ponteland 90-95; Chapl HM Pris Leeds 95; P-in-c Sutton St Mary *Linc* 95-00; R Dunvegan Canada from 00. *10900, Box 787, 103 Avenue, Fairview AB, Canada, T0H 1L0* Tel (001) (780) 835 2580

LOWERSON, John Ridley. b 41. FRHistS83 Leeds Univ BA62 MA65. S Dios Minl Tr Scheme 85. **d** 88 **p** 89. NSM Ringmer *Chich* 88-00; NSM Lewes St Anne from 00. *9 Bradford Road, Lewes BN7 9RB* Tel (01273) 473413

LOWLES, Martin John. b 48. Thames Poly BSc72. St Jo Coll Dur DipTh78. **d** 78 **p** 79. C Leyton St Mary w St Edw *Chelmsf* 78-81; C Waltham Abbey 81-85; V E Ham St Paul 85-95; Asst AD Newham 91-95; TR N Huddersfield *Wakef* from 95. *The Rectory, 10 The Dell, Fixby, Huddersfield HD2 2FD* Tel (01484) 534564 E-mail martinlowles@northhudds.fsnet.co.uk

LOWMAN, The Ven David Walter. b 48. K Coll Lon BD73 AKC73. St Aug Coll Cant 73. **d** 75 **p** 76. C Notting Hill *Lon* 75-78; C Kilburn St Aug w St Jo 78-81; Selection Sec and Voc Adv ACCM 81-86; TR Wickford and Runwell *Chelmsf* 86-93; Dioc Dir of Ords 93-01; C Chelmsf All SS 93-01; C Chelmsf Ascension 93-01; Hon Can Chelmsf Cathl from 93; Adn Southend from 01. *The Archdeacon's Lodge, 136 Broomfield Road, Chelmsford CM1 1RN* Tel (01245) 258257 Fax 250845 E-mail a.southend@chelmsford.anglican.org

LOWNDES, Charles. b 22. MISW57 CQSW72 Rotherham Poly Dip Deaf Welfare 57. **d** 87 **p** 88. NSM Hanley H Ev *Lich* 87-97; rtd 97. *7 Beacon Rise, Stone ST15 0AL* Tel (01785) 812698

LOWNDES, Harold John (Nobby). b 31. St Alb and Ox Min Course 96. **d** 99 **p** 00. OLM Lamp *Ox* from 99. *98 Wolverton Road, Haversham, Milton Keynes MK19 7AB* Tel (01908) 319939 E-mail hlowndes@vivao.net

LOWNDES, Richard Owen Lewis. b 63. Univ of Wales (Ban) BD86. Coll of Resurr Mirfield 87. **d** 89 **p** 90. C Milford Haven *St D* 89-91; C Roath St German *Llan* 91-94; Chapl Cardiff Royal Infirmary 91-94; V Tylorstown w Ynyshir *Llan* 94-96; Asst Chapl St Helier NHS Trust 96-98; Chapl Team Ldr W Middx Univ Hosp NHS Trust 98-03; Chapl Team Ldr Ealing Hosp NHS Trust 01-03; Chapl Team Ldr Southn Univ Hosps NHS Trust from 03. *Trust Management Offices, Southampton General Hospital, Tremona Road, Southampton SO16 6TD* Tel (023) 8077 7222 Fax 8079 4153

LOWRIE, Ronald Malcolm. b 48. Ripon Hall Ox 70. **d** 72 **p** 73. C Knowle *Birm* 72-75; C Bourton-on-the-Water w Clapton *Glouc* 75-79; R Broadwell, Evenlode, Oddington and Adlestrop 79-81; TV Trowbridge H Trin *Sarum* 81-88; P-in-c Westwood and Wingfield 88-90; R from 90; P-in-c Bradford-on-Avon Ch Ch from 03; Chapl Wilts and Swindon Healthcare NHS Trust from 88. *The Rectory, Westwood, Bradford-on-Avon BA15 2AF* Tel and fax (01225) 863109 *or* tel and fax 867040 E-mail parishoffice@christchurchboa.fsnet.co.uk

LOWRY, Robert Harold. b 19. TCD BA44 MA49. CITC 44. **d** 44 **p** 45. C Belfast St Mary Magd *Conn* 44-48; C Belfast St Donard *D & D* 48-52; I Drumgooland w Kilcoo 52-59; I Aghalee 59-62; I Willowfield 62-75; I Lambeg *Conn* 75-89; Can Conn Cathl 82-89; rtd 90; Lic to Offic *D & D* from 90. *9 Innisfayle Park, Bangor BT19 1DP* Tel (028) 9147 2423

LOWRY, The Very Revd Stephen Harold. b 58. QUB BSc79 CertEd80. CITC DipTh85. **d** 85 **p** 86. C Coleraine *Conn* 85-88; I Greenisland 88-98; I Dromore Cathl *D & D* from 98; Dean Dromore from 02. *Dromore Cathedral Rectory, 28 Church Street, Dromore BT25 1AA* Tel (028) 9269 2275 *or* 3968 Mobile 07960-840321 E-mail cathedral@dromore.anglican.org

LOWSON, The Ven Christopher. b 53. AKC75 Heythrop Coll Lon MTh96 Univ of Wales (Cardiff) LLM03. Pacific Sch of Religion Berkeley STM78 St Aug Coll Cant 76. **d** 77 **p** 78. C Richmond St Mary *S'wark* 77-79; C Richmond St Mary w St Matthias and St Jo 79-82; P-in-c Eltham H Trin 82-83; V 83-91; R Buriton *Portsm* 91-99; V Petersfield 91-99; RD Petersfield 95-99; Adn Portsdown from 99; Bp's Liaison Officer for Pris 00-03; Bp's Adv to Hosp Chapl from 03. *5 Brading Avenue, Southsea PO4 9QJ* Tel (023) 9243 2693 Mobile 07957-657312 Fax (023) 9229 8788 E-mail lowson@surfaid.org

LOWSON, Geoffrey Addison. b 47. Bede Coll Dur BEd70 DipHE98. NEOC 95. **d** 98 **p** 99. NSM Sherburn in Elmet w Saxton *York* 98-04; Fieldworker (NE England) USPG from 98; Perm to Offic *Dur* from 98; Lic to Offic *York* from 04. *25 Mill Lane, Acaster Malbis, York YO23 2UJ* Tel and fax (01904) 702304 E-mail geofflowson@compuserve.com

LOWTHER, Ms Kareen Anne. b 59. Loughb Univ BSc81. WMMTC 98. **d** 01. C Lich St Mich w St Mary and Wall *Lich* 01-04; TV Bloxwich from 04. *9 Sanstone Road, Walsall WS3 3SJ* Tel (01922) 711225 Mobile 07940-936033

LOWTON, Nicholas Gerard. b 53. St Jo Coll Ox BA76 FRSA94. Glouc Sch of Min 86. **d** 89 **p** 90. NSM Prestbury *Glouc* 89-94. *Hazelwell, College Road, Cheltenham GL53 7JD* Tel (01242) 265609 *or* 513540 ext 209 Fax 265688 E-mail ngl@cheltcoll.gloucs.sch.uk

LOXHAM, Edward. **d** 04. OLM Birkdale St Pet *Liv* from 04. *34 Alma Road, Southport PR8 4AN* Tel (01704) 568141

LOXHAM, Geoffrey Richard. b 40. Hull Univ BA62. Cranmer Hall Dur. **d** 65 **p** 66. C Darwen St Barn *Blackb* 65-68; C Leyland St Andr 68-72; V Preston St Mark 72-79; V Edgeside *Man* 79-91; P-in-c Heapey St Barnabas and Withnell St Paul *Blackb* 91-92; V 92-99; V Grimsargh from 99. *St Michael's Vicarage, 46 Preston Road, Preston PR2 5SD* Tel (01772) 653283

LOXLEY, Mrs Deirdre. b 41. **d** 96 **p** 97. OLM Heacham *Nor* 96-05; NSM Knaresborough *Ripon* from 05. *39 Birkdale Avenue, Knaresborough HG5 0LS* Tel (01423) 864484 E-mail banddloxley@btinternet.com

LOXLEY, Harold. b 43. N Ord Course 79. **d** 82 **p** 83. NSM Sheff St Cecilia Parson Cross *Sheff* 82-87; C Gleadless 87-90; V Sheff St Cath Richmond Road from 90. *St Catherine's Vicarage, 300 Hastilar Road South, Sheffield S13 8EJ* Tel 0114-239 9598 Fax as telephone

LOXLEY, Ronald Alan Keith. b 26. St Jo Coll Ox BA51 MA55. Wm Temple Coll Rugby 66 Cuddesdon Coll 67. **d** 68 **p** 69. C Swindon Ch Ch *Bris* 68-71; Ind Chapl *Lon* 71-83; Ind Chapl *Chelmsf* 83-92; P-in-c Theydon Garnon 83-92; rtd 92; Perm to Offic *Linc* from 92. *15 Wainwell Mews, Winnowsty Lane, Lincoln LN2 4BF* Tel (01522) 511738

LOXTON, John Sherwood. b 29. Bris Univ BSc50 Birm Univ BA53. Handsworth Coll Birm 50 Chich Th Coll 80. **d** 80 **p** 81. In Meth Ch 50-80; C Haywards Heath St Wilfrid *Chich* 80-82; TV 82-89; V Turners Hill 89-96; rtd 96; Perm to Offic *Chich* from 96. *3 Ashurst Drive, Worth, Crawley RH10 7FS* Tel (01293) 887762

LOXTON, Mrs Susan Ann. b 57. EAMTC. **d** 05. NSM Colchester, New Town and The Hythe *Chelmsf* from 05. *2 Barrington Road, Colchester CO2 7SE* Tel (01206) 366345 E-mail susanloxton@btinternet.com

LOZADA-UZURIAGA, Ernesto. b 61. Wycliffe Hall Ox. **d** 02 **p** 03. C Henley w Remenham *Ox* from 02. *1 Bell Street Mews, Henley-on-Thames RG9 2BF* Tel (01491) 575608 E-mail leon-juda@hotmail.com

LUBBOCK, David John. b 34. S'wark Ord Course. **d** 87 **p** 88. NSM Tulse Hill H Trin and St Matthias *S'wark* 87-04; rtd 04; Perm to Offic *S'wark* from 04. *The Old Vicarage, 107 Upper Tulse Hill, London SW2 2RD* Tel (020) 8674 6146

LUBKOWSKI, Richard Jan. b 51. Westmr Coll Ox BEd75 Warw Univ MA79. St Jo Coll Dur 86. **d** 88 **p** 89. C Duston *Pet* 88-90; C Hellesdon *Nor* 90-91; Perm to Offic *Sheff* 91-94; In RC Ch 94-00; Chapl HM Pris Ashwell from 00. *HM Prison Ashwell, Oakham LE15 7LS* Tel (01572) 774100 Mobile 07449-122406

LUCAS, Anthony Stanley. b 41. Man Univ BA62 K Coll Lon MA99. Qu Coll Birm 63. **d** 65 **p** 66. C N Hammersmith St Kath *Lon* 65-69; C W Wimbledon Ch Ch *S'wark* 69-74; C Caterham 74-78; P-in-c Stockwell St Mich 78-86; V 86-91; P-in-c S'wark St Geo 91; R S'wark St Geo the Martyr w St Jude 91-94; P-in-c S'wark St Alphege 92-94; R S'wark St Geo w St Alphege and St Jude from 95. *St George's Rectory, Manciple Street, London SE1 4LW* Tel (020) 7407 2796 Fax as telephone E-mail tonyslucas@btinternet.com

LUCAS, Arthur Edgar. b 24. Clifton Th Coll 60. **d** 62 **p** 63. C Hyson Green *S'well* 62-66; V Willoughby-on-the-Wolds w Wysall 66-74; P-in-c Widmerpool 71-74; R Collyhurst *Man* 75-80; V Heapey *Blackb* 80-91; rtd 91; Perm to Offic *Blackb* and *Liv* 91-00. *18 Parkway, Standish, Wigan WN6 0SJ*

LUCAS, The Ven Brian Humphrey. b 40. CB93. FRSA93 Univ of Wales (Lamp) BA62. St Steph Ho Ox 62. **d** 64 **p** 65. C Llandaff w Capel Llanilltern *Llan* 64-67; C Neath w Llantwit 67-70; Chapl RAF 70-87; Asst Chapl-in-Chief RAF 87-91; Chapl-in-Chief RAF 91-95; QHC from 88; Perm to Offic *Llan* from 88; Can and Preb Linc Cathl *Linc* 91-95; P-in-c Caythorpe 96-00; R 00-03. *Pen-y-Coed, 6 Arnhem Drive, Caythorpe, Grantham NG32 3DQ* Tel (01400) 272085 E-mail brian.lucas@savageclub.com

LUCAS, Mrs Jane Eleanor. b 49. SW Minl Tr Course 99. **d** 03 **p** 04. NSM N Creedy *Ex* from 03. *Lakehead Farm, Chulmleigh EX18 7AG* Tel (01769) 580339 E-mail j.e.lucas@btinternet.com

LUCAS, John Arthur. b 07. Keble Coll Ox BA29 MA45. Cuddesdon Coll 29. **d** 33 **p** 34. C Ox St Thos *Ox* 33-35; C Brighton St Wilfrid *Chich* 35-37; C London Docks St Pet *Lon* 37-39; V Swanley St Mary *Roch* 39-47; V Ox St Thos *Ox* 47-74; P-in-c 74-79; Hon Can Ch Ch 70-85; rtd 74; Hon C Ox St Mary V w St Cross and St Pet *Ox* 78-85; Perm to Offic 85-96. *7 McMaster House, Latimer Road, Headington, Oxford OX3 7PX* Tel (01865) 742531

LUCAS, John Kenneth. b 32. LNSM course 92. **d** 95 **p** 96. NSM Deptford St Nic and St Luke *S'wark* 95-97; Perm to Offic 97-00. *4 The Colonnade, Grove Street, London SE8 3AY* Tel (020) 8691 3161

LUCAS, John Maxwell. b 34. TD85. Cranmer Hall Dur 59. **d** 62 **p** 63. C Lancaster St Mary *Blackb* 62-65; C Lytham St Cuth 65-68; V Blackb St Aid 68-72; V Sparkhill St Jo *Birm* 72-78; CF (TAVR) from 73; V Edgbaston St Aug *Birm* 78-85; V Slyne w Hest *Blackb* 85-89; Chapl HM YOI Stoke Heath 89-93; rtd 93. *2 Glendon Close, Market Drayton TF9 1NX* Tel (01630) 652977

LUCAS, Lorna Yvonne. b 48. Bp Lonsdale Coll TCert69. EMMTC 95. **d** 98 **p** 99. NSM Haxey *Linc* 98-00; NSM Owston 98-00; NSM Scawby, Redbourne and Hibaldstow 00-04; NSM Lea Gp from 05. *4 Willingham Road, Lea, Gainsborough DN21 5EH* E-mail ly.l@virgin.net

LUCAS, Mark Wesley. b 62. Man Univ BSc83. Oak Hill Th Coll BA94. **d** 94 **p** 95. C Harold Wood *Chelmsf* 94-98; Dir Oast Ho Retreat Cen *Chich* 98-00; Co-ord for Adult Educn (E Sussex Area) 98-00; V Polegate from 00. *St John's Vicarage, 1 Church Road, Polegate BN26 5BX* Tel (01323) 483259 Mobile 07788-100757 Fax (01323) 483305 E-mail vicar@polegate.org.uk

LUCAS, Maxwell. *See* LUCAS, John Maxwell

LUCAS, Ms Pamela Turnbull. b 68. Westmr Coll Ox BA91 Glas Univ MSW98 Edin Univ MTh99 UNISA MTh05. TISEC 98. **d** 00 **p** 01. C Easington, Easington Colliery and S Hetton *Dur* 00-04; Perm to Offic *S'wark* from 04. *St Michael's Convent, 56 Ham Common, Richmond TW10 7JH* Tel (020) 8940 8711 *or* 8948 2502 E-mail revd_ptlucas@yahoo.co.uk

LUCAS, Paul de Neufville. b 33. Ch Ch Ox BA59 MA59 Cam Univ MA63. Cuddesdon Coll 57. **d** 59 **p** 60. C Westmr St Steph w St Jo *Lon* 59-63; Chapl Trin Hall Cam 63-69; V Greenside *Dur* 69-73; Chapl Shrewsbury Sch 73-77; V Batheaston w St Cath *B & W* 78-88; Preb Wells Cathl 87-88; Can Res and Prec 88-99; rtd 99; Perm to Offic *Sarum* from 01. *11 Fisherton Island, Salisbury SP2 7TG* Tel and fax (01722) 325266

LUCAS, Peter Stanley. b 21. Sarum Th Coll 48. **d** 50 **p** 51. C Gillingham *Sarum* 50-53; Min Heald Green St Cath CD *Ches* 53-58; V Heald Green St Cath 58-62; V Egremont St Jo 62-65; Canada from 66. *404 - 1241 Fairfield Road, Victoria BC, Canada, V8V 3B3* E-mail pmlucas@smartt.com

LUCAS, Preb Richard Charles. b 25. Trin Coll Cam BA49 MA57. Ridley Hall Cam. **d** 51 **p** 52. C Sevenoaks St Nic *Roch* 51-55; Cand Sec CPAS 55-61; Asst Sec 61-67; R St Helen Bishopsgate w St Martin Outwich *Lon* 61-80; P-in-c St Andr Undershaft w St Mary Axe 77-80; R St Helen Bishopsgate w St Andr Undershaft etc 80-98; Preb St Paul's Cathl 85-98; rtd 98. *16 Merrick Square, London SE1 4JB* Tel (020) 7407 4164

LUCAS, Ronald James. b 38. St Aid Birkenhead 64. **d** 67 **p** 68. C Swindon Ch Ch *Bris* 67-71; C Knowle St Martin 71-74; V Swindon St Jo 74-77; TR Swindon St Jo and St Andr 77-81; V Wroughton 81-83; TV Liskeard w St Keyne, St Pinnock and Morval *Truro* 83-87; R St Ive w Quethiock 87-91; R St Ive and

Pensilva w Quethiock 91-01; rtd 01; Perm to Offic *Truro* from 01. *Ough's Folly, Castle Lane, Liskeard PL14 3AH* Tel (01579) 345611 E-mail ronjulialucas@hotmail.com

LUCAS, Ms Susan Catherine. b 59. City of Lon Poly BSc90. STETS 97. **d** 00 **p** 01. C Streetly *Lich* 00-02; C Pheasey 02-04; Chapl HM Pris Albany from 04. *HM Prison Albany, 55 Parkhurst Road, Newport PO30 5RS* Tel (01983) 524055

LUCAS, Mrs Vivienne Kathleen. b 44. Sarum & Wells Th Coll 84. **d** 87 **p** 94. Chapl Asst W Middx Univ Hosp Isleworth 87-92; Par Dn Whitton St Aug *Lon* 87-94; C Isleworth St Jo 94-97; P-in-c Isleworth St Mary 97-01; P-in-c Pirbright *Guildf* from 01. *The Vicarage, The Green, Pirbright, Woking GU24 0JE* Tel (01483) 473332 E-mail viviennelucas@beeb.net

LUCAS, William Wallace. b 29. Sarum Th Coll 56. **d** 59 **p** 60. C Stockton St Jo *Dur* 59-63; V Norton St Mich 63-81; R Broseley w Benthall *Heref* 81-93; P-in-c Jackfield 81-93; P-in-c Linley w Willey and Barrow 81-93; rtd 93; Perm to Offic *Dur* from 93. *105 Side Cliff Road, Sunderland SR6 9JR* Tel 0191-549 1573

LUCK, Benjamin Paul. b 53. BD. St Mich Coll Llan 80. **d** 83 **p** 84. C Blakenall Heath *Lich* 83-87; C Torpoint *Truro* 87-89; V Tuckingmill 89-96; C Knowle St Barn and H Cross Inns Court *Bris* 96-02; V Inns Court H Cross 02-05; C Washfield, Stoodleigh, Withleigh etc *Ex* from 05. *The Rectory, Withleigh, Tiverton EX16 8JQ* Tel (01884) 250509

LUCKCUCK, Anthony Michael. b 47. Lon Univ BA70. Wycliffe Hall Ox 70. **d** 77 **p** 78. C Mansfield Woodhouse *S'well* 77-79; C Beeston 79-82; V Harworth 82-85; V Carlton from 85. *St John's Vicarage, 261 Oakdale Road, Nottingham NG4 1BP* Tel 07734-032900 (mobile) E-mail amleclerc@btinternet.com

LUCKETT, Nicholas Frank. b 43. Ch Ch Ox BA65 DipEd66 MA69. OLM course 95. **d** 98 **p** 99. Hd Master St Edw C of E Middle Sch Leek 94-00; OLM Ipstones w Berkhamsytch and Onecote w Bradnop *Lich* 98-02; NSM Siddington w Preston *Glouc* from 02. *The Rectory, Preston, Cirencester GL7 5PR* Tel (01285) 654187

LUCKMAN, David Thomas William. b 71. Oak Hill Th Coll BA95 K Coll Lon PGCE96. CITC 98. **d** 00 **p** 01. C Portadown St Mark *Arm* 00-02; C Enniskillen *Clogh* 02-03; I Galloon w Drummully and Sallaghy 03-04. *5 Olde Forge, New Forge Road, Magheralin, Craigavon BT67 0RS* Tel (028) 9167 7376 E-mail daveluckman@hotmail.com

LUCKRAFT, Christopher John. b 50. K Coll Lon BD80 AKC80. Ripon Coll Cuddesdon 80. **d** 81 **p** 82. C Sherborne w Castleton and Lillington *Sarum* 81-84; Bermuda 84-87; Chapl RN from 87. *Royal Naval Chaplaincy Service, Room 203, Victory Building, HM Naval Base, Portsmouth PO1 3LS* Tel (01705) 727903 Fax 727112

LUCY CLARE, Sister. *See* WALKER, Margaret

LUDKIN, Miss Linda Elaine. b 50. NEOC 02. **d** 05. NSM Dunnington *York* from 05. *27A Lavender Grove, York YO26 5RX* Tel (01904) 784651 E-mail l.e.ludkin@btinternet.com

LUDLOW, Brian Peter. b 55. Lon Univ MB, BS78 Birm Univ MMedSc90 LRCP90 MRCS90 MRAeS87 AFOM90 MFOM92 FFOM01. WEMTC 01. **d** 04 **p** 05. NSM Winchcombe *Glouc* from 04. *38 Riverside, Winchcombe, Cheltenham GL54 5JP* Tel (01242) 602585 Mobile 07836-667530 E-mail brian.ludlow2@btopenworld.com

LUDLOW, Lady Margaret Maude. b 56. WEMTC 98. **d** 01 **p** 02. C Winchcombe *Glouc* from 01. *38 Riverside, Winchcombe, Cheltenham GL54 5JP* Tel (01242) 602585

LUDLOW, Archdeacon of. *See* HOOPER, The Rt Revd Michael Wrenford

LUDLOW, Suffragan Bishop of. *See* HOOPER, The Rt Revd Michael Wrenford

LUFF, Canon Alan Harold Frank. b 28. Univ Coll Ox MA54 ARCM77 Hon FGCM93. Westcott Ho Cam 54. **d** 56 **p** 57. C Stretford St Matt *Man* 56-59; C Swinton St Pet 59-61; Prec Man Cathl 61-68; V Dwygyfylchi *Ban* 68-79; Prec and Sacr Westmr Abbey 79-86; Prec 86-92; Can Res Birm Cathl *Birm* 92-96; rtd 96; Perm to Offic *Llan* from 96. *12 Heol Ty'n-y-Cae, Cardiff CF14 6DJ* Tel and fax (029) 2061 6023 E-mail alanluff@fish.co.uk

LUFF, Mrs Caroline Margaret Synia. b 44. St Hild Coll Dur BA65 Bris Univ CertEd66. SW Minl Tr Course 87. **d** 90 **p** 94. Par Dn Teignmouth, Ideford w Luton, Ashcombe etc *Ex* 90-94; C from 94; Chapl Trin Sch Teignmouth from 97. *The Rectory, 30 Dawlish Road, Teignmouth TQ14 8TG* Tel (01626) 774495 E-mail luff@fish.co.uk

LUFF, Preb Philip Garth. b 42. St Chad's Coll Dur BA63. **d** 65 **p** 66. C Sidmouth St Nic *Ex* 65-69; C Plymstock 69-71; Asst Chapl Worksop Coll Notts 71-74; V Gainsborough St Jo *Linc* 74-80; V E Teignmouth *Ex* 80-89; P-in-c W Teignmouth 85-89; TR Teignmouth, Ideford w Luton, Ashcombe etc from 90; RD Kenn 01-05; Preb Ex Cathl from 02; Chapl S Devon Healthcare NHS Trust from 85; Chapl Trin Sch Teignmouth 88-97. *The Rectory, 30 Dawlish Road, Teignmouth TQ14 8TG* Tel (01626) 774495 E-mail luff@fish.co.uk

LUGG, Donald Arthur. b 31. St Aid Birkenhead 56. **d** 59 **p** 60. C Folkestone H Trin w Ch Ch *Cant* 59-62; V Seasalter 62-66; Iran 67-73; V Cliftonville *Cant* 74-94; rtd 94; Perm to Offic *Cant* from 94. *Redcroft, Vulcan Close, Whitstable CT9 1DF* Tel (01227) 770434

LUGG, Stuart John. b 26. Glouc Th Course 74. **d** 76 **p** 77. NSM Fairford *Glouc* 76-79; P-in-c Kempsford w Welford 80-88; Perm to Offic from 88. *Content, Station Road, South Cerney, Cirencester GL7 5UB* Tel (01285) 860498

LUKE, Anthony. b 58. Down Coll Cam BA81 MA85 Geneva Univ Cert Ecum Studies 84. Ridley Hall Cam 82. **d** 84 **p** 85. C Allestree *Derby* 84-87; C Oakham, Hambleton, Egleton, Braunston and Brooke *Pet* 87-88; V Allenton and Shelton Lock *Derby* 88-02; Dir Reader Tr 95-97; Warden of Readers 97-00; R Aston on Trent, Elvaston, Weston on Trent etc from 02. *The Rectory, Rectory Gardens, Aston-on-Trent, Derby DE72 2AZ* Tel (01332) 792658 E-mail tonyluke@lineone.net

LUMB, David Leslie. b 28. Jes Coll Cam BA52 MA56. Oak Hill Th Coll 52. **d** 54 **p** 55. C Walcot *B & W* 54-58; C Lenton *S'well* 58-60; V Handforth *Ches* 60-71; V Plymouth St Jude *Ex* 71-87; V Southminster *Chelmsf* 87-93; rtd 93; Perm to Offic *Worc* from 93. *13 Glebe Close, Redditch B98 0AW* Tel (01527) 528623 E-mail lumb@fish.co.uk

LUMBY, Jonathan Bertram. b 39. Em Coll Cam BA62 MA66 Lon Univ PGCE66. Ripon Hall Ox 62. **d** 64 **p** 65. C Moseley St Mary *Birm* 64-65; Asst Master Enfield Gr Sch 66-67; C Hall Green Ascension 67-70; V Melling *Liv* 70-81; P-in-c Milverton w Halse and Fitzhead *B & W* 81-82; R 82-86; P-in-c Gisburn and Dioc Rural Adv *Bradf* 90-93; P-in-c Easton w Colton and Marlingford *Nor* 95-98; Dioc Missr 95-98; R Eccleston and Pulford *Ches* 98-05; rtd 05; Hon C Redmarley D'Abitot, Bromesberrow, Pauntley etc *Glouc* from 05. *The Vicarage, St Mary's Close, Dymock GL18 2AX* Tel (01531) 892967

LUMBY, Simon. b 70. Coll of Resurr Mirfield 99. **d** 02 **p** 03. C Worksop Priory *S'well* from 02. *18 Cheapside, Worksop S80 2HU* Tel (01909) 480128 Mobile 07951-762385 E-mail fathersimon@lumby1970.fsnet.co.uk

LUMBY, Simon John. b 56. Hull Univ BSc80 Open Univ MTh01. St Jo Coll Nottm 99. **d** 01. C Wirksworth *Derby* from 01. *57 Yokecliffe Drive, Wirksworth, Matlock DE4 4PF* Tel (01629) 820049 Fax 820235 E-mail revd.s.j.lumby@ntlworld.com

LUMGAIR, Michael Hugh Crawford. b 43. Lon Univ BD71. Oak Hill Th Coll 66. **d** 71 **p** 72. C Chorleywood Ch Ch *St Alb* 71-74; C Prestonville St Luke *Chich* 74-75; C Attenborough *S'well* 75-80; R Tollerton 80-91; V Bexleyheath St Pet *Roch* from 91. *St Peter's Vicarage, 50 Bristow Road, Bexleyheath DA7 4QA* Tel (020) 8303 8713 E-mail michael@mlumgair.co.uk

LUMLEY, William. b 22. TCD BA44 MA49 BD49 QUB PhD77. Edgehill Th Coll Belf 49. **d** 50 **p** 51. C Dublin Drumcondra w N Strand *D & G* 50-52; Clerical V Ch Ch Cathl Dublin 52-53; C Clooney *D & R* 55-59; I Aghabog *Clogh* 59-63; V Newhey *Man* 63-66; I Ballybay *Clogh* 66-73; I Derryvullen S w Garvary 73-82; I Killucan w Clonard and Castlelost *M & K* 82-88; rtd 88. *15 Roe Fold, Main Street, Limavady BT49 0EL* Tel (028) 7776 6174

LUMMIS, Elizabeth Howieson. *See* McNAB, Mrs Elizabeth Howieson

LUMSDEN, Frank. b 20. Edin Th Coll 51. **d** 53 **p** 54. C Usworth *Dur* 53-56; V Lynesack 56-76; R Castle Eden w Monkhesleden 76-86; rtd 86; Perm to Offic *Dur* 86-04 and *Ripon* 90-04. *Linnhe House, Port Appin, Argyll PA38 4DE* Tel (01631) 730245

LUMSDON, Keith. b 45. Linc Th Coll 68. **d** 71 **p** 72. C S Westoe *Dur* 71-74; C Jarrow St Paul 74-77; TV Jarrow 77-88; V Ferryhill from 88; P-in-c Cornforth from 03; AD Sedgefield from 05. *St Luke's Vicarage, Church Lane, Ferryhill DL17 8LT* Tel (01740) 651438

LUND, David Peter. b 46. N Ord Course 88. **d** 91 **p** 92. C Maghull *Liv* 91-94; V Hindley All SS 94-01; V Teddington St Mark and Hampton Wick St Jo *Lon* from 01. *The Vicarage, 23 St Mark's Road, Teddington TW11 9DE* Tel (020) 8977 4067 Mobile 07813-493761 E-mail saintseddington@aol.com

LUND, John Edward. b 48. St Jo Coll Dur 78. **d** 80 **p** 81. C Peterlee *Dur* 80-83; C Bishopton w Gt Stainton 83-85; C Redmarshall 83-85; C Grindon and Stillington 83-85; V Hart w Elwick Hall from 85; Hon Chapl Miss to Seamen 85-99; Chapl Hartlepool and E Durham NHS Trust 94-99; Chapl N Tees and Hartlepool NHS Trust 99-04. *The Vicarage, Hart, Hartlepool TS27 3AP* Tel and fax (01429) 262340 E-mail lund@telco4u.net

LUNGA, Cleophus. b 66. UNISA BTh00. Bp Gaul Th Coll Harare 91. **d** 93 **p** 94. Zimbabwe 94-03; TV Coventry Caludon *Cov* from 03. *7 St Catherine's Close, Coventry CV3 1EH* Tel (024) 7663 5737 Mobile 07717-672929 E-mail cleophaslunga@hotmail.com

LUNGLEY, Canon John Sydney. b 41. St Pet Coll Ox BA64 MA70. St Steph Ho Ox 64. **d** 66 **p** 67. C Burslem St Werburgh *Lich* 66-70; C Codsall 70-73; V Ocker Hill 73-88; RD Wednesbury 84-88; V Kingswinford St Mary 88-93; V Kingswinford St Mary *Worc* 93-96; TR from 96; Hon Can Worc Cathl from 94. *The Vicarage, 17 Penzer Street, Kingswinford DY6 7AA* Tel (01384) 273716

LUNN, Preb Brooke Kingsmill. b 32. TCD BA62 MA66. Chich Th Coll 62. **d** 64 **p** 65. C Northolt Park St Barn *Lon* 64-66; C N St Pancras All Hallows 66-68; P-in-c Hornsey St Luke 68-79; V Stroud Green H Trin 79-02; AD W Haringey 90-95; Preb St Paul's Cathl 96-02; rtd 02; Perm to Offic *Lon* from 02. *The Charterhouse, Charterhouse Square, London EC1M 6AN* Tel (020) 7251 5143

LUNN, Christopher James Edward. b 34. AKC58. **d** 59 **p** 60. C Clapham H Trin *S'wark* 59-62; C Cranleigh *Guildf* 63-64; C Ham St Andr *S'wark* 64-66; V Ham St Rich 66-75; V Coulsdon St Andr 75-96; rtd 96. *24 Penally Heights, Penally, Tenby SA70 7QP* Tel (01834) 845277

LUNN, David. b 47. Bris Univ BSc69. St Jo Coll Dur BA73. **d** 74 **p** 75. C Aigburth *Liv* 74-77; C Slough *Ox* 77-81; P-in-c Haversham w Lt Linford 81-84; R Haversham w Lt Linford, Tyringham w Filgrave 84-93; RD Newport 86-92; TR Walton Milton Keynes from 93; Dioc Ecum Officer from 00. *The Rectory, Walton Road, Wavendon, Milton Keynes MK17 8LW* Tel (01908) 582839

✠**LUNN, The Rt Revd David Ramsay.** b 30. K Coll Cam BA53 MA57. Cuddesdon Coll 53. **d** 55 **p** 56 **c** 80. C Sugley *Newc* 55-59; C N Gosforth 59-63; Chapl Linc Th Coll 63-66; Sub-Warden 66-70; V Cullercoats St Geo *Newc* 71-72; TR 72-80; RD Tynemouth 75-80; Bp Sheff 80-97; rtd 97; Perm to Offic *York* 97-99; Hon Asst Bp York from 99. *Rivendell, 28 Southfield Road, Wetwang, Driffield YO25 9XX* Tel (01377) 236657

LUNN, Leonard Arthur. b 42. Trin Coll Bris 69. **d** 72 **p** 73. C Walthamstow St Mary w St Steph *Chelmsf* 72-75; V Collier Row St Jas 75-85; V Collier Row St Jas and Havering-atte-Bower 86-87; Sen Chapl St Chris Hospice Sydenham *S'wark* 87-03; Hon Chapl S'wark Cathl 97-03; Hon C Redlynch and Morgan's Vale *Sarum* from 03. *The Vicarage, Vicarage Road, Lover, Salisbury SP5 2PE* Tel (01725) 510439

LUNN, Mrs Rosemary Christine. b 51. Bris Univ BA72. Trin Coll Bris 98. **d** 00 **p** 01. NSM Stoke Bishop *Bris* 00-01; C Chippenham St Pet 01-04; Hon Min Can Bris Cathl 02-04; P-in-c Wraxall *B & W* from 04. *The Rectory, 8 School View, Wraxall, Bristol BS48 1HG* Tel (01275) 857086 Mobile 07799-497533

LUNN, Sarah Anne. b 63. Lanc Univ BMus84 Man Metrop Univ MA93. Cranmer Hall Dur 00. **d** 02 **p** 03. C Kirkby Lonsdale *Carl* from 02. *6 Mill Brow, Kirkby Lonsdale, Carnforth LA6 2AT* Tel (015242) 71928 E-mail sarahlunn@care4free.net

LUNNEY, Canon Henry. b 31. ACIB57. Wycliffe Hall Ox 73. **d** 74 **p** 75. C Ipswich St Aug *St E* 74-77; P-in-c Westerfield w Tuddenham St Martin 77-83; R Westerfield and Tuddenham w Witnesham 83-97; Asst Dioc Chr Stewardship Adv 78-83; Hon Can St E Cathl 92-97; rtd 97; Perm to Offic *St E* from 98. *6 Karen Close, Ipswich IP1 4LP* Tel (01473) 252876

LUNNON, Canon Robert Reginald. b 31. K Coll Lon BD55 AKC55 Kent Univ MA99. St Boniface Warminster 55. **d** 56 **p** 57. C Maidstone St Mich *Cant* 56-58; C Deal St Leon 58-62; V Sturry 63-68; V Norbury St Steph 68-77; V Orpington All SS *Roch* 77-96; RD Orpington 79-95; Hon Can Roch Cathl 96; rtd 96; Perm to Offic *Cant* from 96. *10 King Edward Road, Deal CT14 6QL* Tel (01304) 364898

LUNT, Colin Peter. b 54. York Univ BA75 Bris Univ MA02. Trin Coll Bris 95. **d** 97 **p** 98. C Westbury-on-Trym H Trin *Bris* 97-00; V Coalpit Heath from 00. *The Vicarage, Beesmoor Road, Coalpit Heath, Bristol BS36 2RP* Tel and fax (01454) 775129 E-mail colin@lunt.co.uk

LUNT, Derek. b 32. St Jo Coll Dur 51. St Aid Birkenhead 55. **d** 57 **p** 58. C Toxteth Park Ch Ch *Liv* 57-59; C Prescot 59-61; V Much Dewchurch w Llanwarne and Llandinabo *Heref* 61-67; R Pembridge 67-74; Chapl Lucton Sch 71-74; rtd 91; Perm to Offic *Worc* from 93. *Olcote, 5 Mansfield Road, Malvern WR14 2WE* Tel (01684) 573932

LUNT, Margaret Joan. b 44. Leeds Univ MB, ChB68. Cranmer Hall Dur 91. **d** 94 **p** 95. C Stanford-le-Hope w Mucking *Chelmsf* 94-97; C Rayleigh 97-00; TV 00-03; TV Rivers Team *Sheff* from 03. *24 Highgate, Tinsley, Sheffield S9 1WL* Tel 0114-244 1740 E-mail robertlunt@luntrfreeserve.co.uk

LURIE, Miss Gillian Ruth. b 42. LRAM62 GNSM63 ACertCM80. Gilmore Ho 68. **dss** 74 **d** 87 **p** 94. Camberwell St Phil and St Mark *S'wark* 74-76; Haddenham *Ely* 76-79; Dioc Lay Min Adv 79-86; Longthorpe *Pet* 79-81; Pet H Spirit Bretton 81-86; Bramley *Ripon* 86-93; C 87-88; TD 88-93; P-in-c Methley w Mickletown 93-98; R 98-01; rtd 02; Perm to Offic *Cant* from 02. *42A Cuthbert Road, Westgate-on-Sea CT8 8NR* Tel (01843) 831698 Fax as telephone E-mail gillandjean@hotmail.com

LURY, Anthony Patrick. b 49. K Coll Lon BD71 AKC71. St Aug Coll Cant 71. **d** 72 **p** 73. C Richmond St Mary *S'wark* 72-76; P-in-c Streatham Hill St Marg 76-81; V Salfords 81-90; V Emscote *Cov* 90-01; P-in-c Ascot Heath *Ox* from 01. *All Saints' Rectory, London Road, Ascot SL5 8DQ* Tel (01344) 621200 E-mail anthony@all-saints-ascot.org

LUSBY, Dennis John. b 27. Brentwood Coll of Educn CertEd70. **d** 93 **p** 94. NSM Grayshott *Guildf* 93-99; Perm to Offic from 99. *Squirrels Drey, Waggoners Way, Grayshott, Hindhead GU26 6DX* Tel (01428) 604419

LUSCOMBE, John Nickels. b 45. St Jo Coll Nottm Dip Past Counselling 97 Birm Univ BA99. AKC68. **d** 69 **p** 70. C Stoke Newington St Faith, St Matthias and All SS *Lon* 69-74; V Tottenham St Phil 74-81; Zimbabwe 82-86; V Queensbury All SS *Lon* 86-99; V Estover *Ex* 99-01; Dioc Ecum Officer 99-01; V Norton *St Alb* from 01; RD Hitchin from 02. *Norton Vicarage, 17 Norton Way North, Letchworth Garden City SG6 1BY* Tel (01462) 685059 *or* 678133 E-mail jluscombe@callnetuk.com

✠**LUSCOMBE, The Rt Revd Lawrence Edward (Ted).** b 24. Dundee Univ LLD87 MPhil91 PhD93 ACA52 FSA80 FRSA87. K Coll Lon 63. **d** 63 **p** 64 **c** 75. C Glas St Marg *Glas* 63-66; R Paisley St Barn 66-71; Provost St Paul's Cathl Dundee *Bre* 71-75; R Dundee St Paul 71-75; Bp Bre 75-90; Primus 85-90; rtd 90; Perm to Offic *Bre* from 90. *Woodville, Kirkton of Tealing, Dundee DD4 0RD* Tel (01382) 380331

LUSITANIAN CHURCH, Bishop of the. *See* SOARES, The Rt Revd Fernando da Luz

LUSTED, Jack Andrew. b 58. Sussex Univ BSc79 PGCE81. St Steph Ho Ox 88. **d** 90 **p** 91. C Moulsecoomb *Chich* 90-93; C Southwick St Mich 93-97; R Lurgashall, Lodsworth and Selham from 97. *The Rectory, Lodsworth, Petworth GU28 9DE* Tel (01798) 861274 E-mail jack.lusted@btinternet.com

LUSTY, Tom Peter. b 71. Glas Univ BD94 Leeds Univ MA99. Coll of Resurr Mirfield 97. **d** 99 **p** 00. C Billingshurst *Chich* 99-02; Asst Chapl Leeds Teaching Hosps NHS Trust from 02. *Chaplaincy Services, St James's University Hospital, Beckett Street, Leeds LS9 7TF* Tel 0113-206 5935 E-mail tom.lusty@leedsth.nhs.uk

LUTHER, Canon Richard Grenville Litton. b 42. Lon Univ BD64. Tyndale Hall Bris 66. **d** 68 **p** 69. C Preston St Mary *Blackb* 68-70; C Bishopsworth *Bris* 70-71; C Radipole *Sarum* 72-76; TV Radipole and Melcombe Regis 77-90; TR Hampreston from 90; Can and Preb Sarum Cathl from 00. *The Rectory, 9 Pinewood Road, Ferndown, Wimborne BH22 9RW* Tel (01202) 872084

LUTHER THOMAS, The Ven Ilar Roy. b 30. St D Coll Lamp BA51. St Mich Coll Llan 51. **d** 53 **p** 54. C Oystermouth *S & B* 53-56; C Gorseinon 56-59; R Llanbadarn Fawr and Llandegley 59-60; R Llanbadarn Fawr, Llandegley and Llanfihangel etc 60-65; CF (ACF) 62-90; Children's Adv *S & B* 63-77; V Knighton and Norton 65-79; RD Knighton 66-79; V Sketty 79-89; Can Brecon Cathl from 75; Treas 87-88; Chan 88-90; Adn Gower 90-95; rtd 95. *2 Druids Close, Mumbles, Swansea SA3 5TY* Tel (01792) 419455

LUTTON, Percy Theodore Bell Boyce. b 24. TCD BA45 MA48. **d** 46 **p** 48. C Whitehouse *Conn* 47-49; C Dudley St Jo *Worc* 49-52; V Stambermill 52-61; V Wribbenhall 61-80; R Castlemorton, Hollybush and Birtsmorton 80-89; rtd 89; Perm to Offic *Lich* from 90. *23 Bridgeman Road, Oswestry SY11 2JP* Tel (01691) 656425

✠**LUXMOORE, The Rt Revd Christopher Charles.** b 26. Trin Coll Cam BA50 MA54. Chich Th Coll 50. **d** 52 **p** 53 **c** 84. C Newc St Jo *Newc* 52-55; C-in-c Newsham St Bede CD 55-57; V Newsham 57-58; Trinidad and Tobago 58-66; V Headingley *Ripon* 67-81; Hon Can Ripon Cathl 80-81; Can Res and Prec Chich Cathl *Chich* 81-84; Bp Bermuda 84-89; Adn Lewes and Hastings *Chich* 89-91; rtd 91; Provost Woodard Corp (S Division) 89-96; Asst Bp Chich from 91. *42 Willowbed Drive, Chichester PO19 8JB* Tel (01243) 784680

LYALL, Canon Graham. b 37. Univ of Wales (Lamp) BA61. Qu Coll Birm 61. **d** 63 **p** 64. C Middlesbrough Ascension *York* 63-67; C Kidderminster St Mary *Worc* 67-72; V Dudley St Aug Holly Hall 72-79; P-in-c Barbourne 79-81; V 81-93; RD Worc E 83-89; TR Malvern Link w Cowleigh 93-04; Hon Can Worc Cathl 85-04; rtd 04; Perm to Offic *Worc* from 04. *44 Victoria Street, Worcester WR3 7BD* Tel (01905) 20511

LYALL, Richard Keith. b 70. Glas Univ BSc92 MSc95 Strathclyde Univ MSc97. Trin Coll Bris BA02. **d** 02 **p** 03. C Gateacre *Liv* from 02. *24 Lee Vale Road, Gateacre, Liverpool L25 3RW* Tel 0151-487 9391 E-mail rklyall@yahoo.com

LYDDON, David Andrew. b 47. LDSRCSEng70 Lon Univ BDS70. SW Minl Tr Course 90. **d** 93 **p** 94. NSM Tiverton St Pet *Ex* 93-95; NSM Tiverton St Pet w Chevithorne 95-96; NSM W Exe 96-01; NSM Tiverton St Geo and St Paul from 01. *Hightrees, 19 Patches Road, Tiverton EX16 5AH* Tel (01884) 257250 E-mail dlyddon597@aol.uk

LYDON, Mrs Barbara. b 34. Gilmore Ho 64. **dss** 72 **d** 87 **p** 94. Rastrick St Matt *Wakef* 72-85; Upper Hopton 85-87; Par Dn 87; Dn-in-c Kellington w Whitley 87-94; P-in-c 94-95; rtd 95; Perm to Offic *Wakef* from 95. *17 Garlick Street, Brighouse HD6 3PW* Tel (01484) 722704

LYES-WILSDON, Canon Patricia Mary. b 45. Open Univ BA87 ALA65. Glouc Sch of Min 84 Qu Coll Birm 86. **d** 87 **p** 94. C Thornbury *Glouc* 87-94; P-in-c Cromhall w Tortworth and Tytherington 94-03; Asst Dioc Dir of Ords 90-98; Dioc Voc Officer 94-01; RD Hawkesbury 98-04; Dioc Adv for Women's

Min from 01; Hon Can Glouc Cathl from 02; R Cromhall, Tortworth, Tytherington, Falfield etc from 02. *The New Rectory, Rectory Lane, Cromhall, Wotton-under-Edge GL12 8AN* Tel (01454) 294767 E-mail revd.pat@virgin.net

LYMBERY, Peter. b 32. JP73. St Alb and Ox Min Course 95. **d** 98 **p** 99. OLM Stewkley w Soulbury and Drayton Parslow *Ox* from 98; Dep Chapl Guild of Servants of the Sanctuary from 00; P Assoc Shrine of Our Lady of Walsingham from 00. *17 Hartwell Crescent, Leighton Buzzard LU7 1NP* Tel (01525) 371235

LYNAS, Mrs Judith. b 53. S Dios Minl Tr Scheme 89. **d** 92 **p** 94. Par Dn Lytchett Minster *Sarum* 92-94; C 94-96; Hon C Longfleet 97-99. *Address temp unknown*

LYNAS, The Very Revd Norman Noel. b 55. St Andr Univ MTheol78. CITC 78. **d** 79 **p** 80. C Knockbreda *D & D* 79-81; C Holywood 81-85; I Portadown St Columba *Arm* 85-91; Dioc Communications Officer 86-89; Tutor for Aux Min (Arm) 88-91; Radio Officer (Arm) 90-91; I Kilkenny w Aghour and Kilmanagh *C & O* from 91; Dean Ossory from 91; Can Leighlin Cathl from 91. *The Deanery, Kilkenny, Irish Republic* Tel (00353) (56) 772 1516 Fax 775 1817 E-mail lynas@gofree.indigo.ie

LYNAS, Stephen Brian. b 52. MBE00. St Jo Coll Nottm BTh77. **d** 78 **p** 79. C Penn *Lich* 78-81; Relig Progr Org BBC Radio Stoke-on-Trent 81-84; C Hanley H Ev 81-82; C Edensor 82-84; Relig Progr Producer BBC Bris 85-88; Relig Progr Sen Producer BBC S & W England 88-91; Hd Relig Progr TV South 91-92; Community (and Relig) Affairs Ed Westcountry TV from 92; Abps' Officer for Millennium 96-01; Dioc Resources Adv *B & W* from 01. *Old Honeygar Cottage, Honeygar Lane, Westhay, Glastonbury BA6 9TS* Tel (01458) 860763 *or* (01749) 670777 E-mail stephen.lynas@bathwells.anglican.org

LYNCH, Eithne Elizabeth Mary. b 45. CITC BTh94. **d** 97 **p** 98. C Douglas Union w Frankfield *C, C & R* 97-01; Min Can Cork Cathl from 99; Bp's Dom Chapl from 99; I Kilmoe Union from 01. *Altar Rectory, Toormore, Skibbereen, Co Cork, Irish Republic* Tel (00353) (28) 28249 Mobile 86-253 5002 E-mail kilmoe@cork.anglican.org *or* eithnel@eircom.net

LYNCH, James. EAMTC 93. **d** 96 **p** 97. NSM High Oak *Nor* 96-97; NSM High Oak, Hingham and Scoulton w Wood Rising 97-99; Asst Chapl Norfolk Mental Health Care NHS Trust 99-03; P-in-c Nor St Steph 99-03; NSM Blanchland w Hunstanworth and Edmundbyers etc *Newc* from 03; NSM Slaley from 03; NSM Healey from 03; NSM Whittonstall from 03. *The Vicarage, Blanchland, Consett DH8 9ST* Tel (01434) 675141 E-mail jcrescent@fish.co.uk

LYNCH-WATSON, Graham Leslie. b 30. AKC55. **d** 56 **p** 57. C New Eltham All SS *S'wark* 56-60; C W Brompton St Mary *Lon* 60-62; V Camberwell St Bart *S'wark* 62-66; V Purley St Barn 67-77; C Caversham *Ox* 77-81; C Caversham St Pet and Mapledurham etc 81-85; P-in-c Warwick St Paul *Cov* 85-86; V 86-92; rtd 92; Perm to Offic *Ox* 96-00. *11 Crouch Street, Banbury OX16 9PP* Tel (01295) 263172

LYNE, Peter. b 27. Sheff Univ BA51. Qu Coll Birm 51. **d** 53 **p** 54. C Newland St Aug *York* 53-55; C Harworth *S'well* 55-56; C Burbage *Derby* 56-58; V Horsley Woodhouse 58-62; V Rawcliffe *Sheff* 62-69; V Elvaston and Shardlow *Derby* 69-74; P-in-c Ashbourne St Jo 74-80; P-in-c Kniveton w Hognaston 75-80; P-in-c Fenny Bentley, Thorpe and Tissington 77-78; P-in-c Osmaston w Edlaston 78-80; P-in-c Lt Eaton 80-84; P-in-c Holbrooke 80-84; V Holbrook and Lt Eaton 84-91; rtd 91; Perm to Offic *Derby* from 91. *3 Vicarage Close, High Street, Belper DE56 1TB* Tel (01773) 829188

LYNE, Roger Howard. b 28. Mert Coll Ox BA52 MA56. Oak Hill Th Coll 52. **d** 54 **p** 55. C Rugby St Matt *Cov* 54-58; C Weymouth St Jo *Sarum* 58-61; V Newchapel *Lich* 61-65; C Bucknall and Bagnall 76-81; Perm to Offic *Win* from 82; rtd 88. *21 Copse Road, Burley, Ringwood BH24 4EG* Tel (01425) 402232

LYNESS, Nicholas Jonathan. b 55. Oak Hill Th Coll BA97. **d** 97. C Reading Greyfriars *Ox* 97-98. *3 Roe Green Cottages, Roe Green, Sandon, Buntingford SG9 0QE* Tel (01763) 288172 Mobile 07802-730485

LYNETT, Anthony Martin. b 54. K Coll Lon BD75 AKC75 Darw Coll Cam PGCE76. Sarum & Wells Th Coll 77. **d** 78 **p** 79. C Swindon Ch Ch *Bris* 78-81; C Leckhampton SS Phil and Jas w Cheltenham St Jas *Glouc* 81-83; Asst Chapl HM Pris Glouc 83-88; Chapl 91-98; V Coney Hill *Glouc* 83-88; Chapl HM YOI Deerbolt 88-91; P-in-c Glouc St Mark *Glouc* 91-99; P-in-c Glouc St Mary de Crypt w St Jo, Ch Ch etc 98-99; Chapl HM Pris Wellingborough 99-01; V Wellingborough All SS *Pet* from 01. *The Vicarage, 154 Midland Road, Wellingborough NN8 1NF* Tel (01933) 227101 E-mail tony.lynett@cableinet.co.uk

LYNN, Anthony Hilton. b 44. Golds Coll Lon TCert66 Open Univ BA80. St Alb and Ox Min Course 95. **d** 98 **p** 99. NSM Stanford in the Vale w Goosey and Hatford *Ox* 98-00; NSM Cherbury w Gainfield 00-03; TV Hermitage from 03. *The Rectory, Yattendon, Thatcham RG18 0UR* Tel (01635) 201203 E-mail tony@hlynn.fsnet.co.uk

LYNN, Mrs Antonia Jane. b 59. Girton Coll Cam BA80 MA84. St Steph Ho Ox 82. **dss** 84 **d** 87. Portsm Cathl *Portsm* 84-87; Dn-in-c Camberwell St Mich w All So w Em *S'wark* 87-91; Par Dn Newington St Mary 87-91; Perm to Offic 91-94; Chapl Horton Hosp Epsom 91-94; Gen Sec Guild of Health from 94; Hon Par Dn Ewell *Guildf* 94-99; Perm to Offic *Lon* from 94. *7 Kingsmead Close, West Ewell, Epsom KT19 9RD* Tel (020) 8786 8983

LYNN, Frank Trevor. b 36. Keble Coll Ox BA61 MA63. St Steph Ho Ox 61. **d** 63 **p** 64. C W Derby St Mary *Liv* 63-65; C Chorley *Ches* 65-68; V Altrincham St Jo 68-72; Chapl RN 72-88; Hon C Walworth St Jo *S'wark* 88-90; C Cheam 90-96; rtd 99. *7 Kingsmead Close, West Ewell, Epsom KT19 9RD* Tel (020) 8786 8983

LYNN, Jeffrey. b 39. Moore Th Coll Sydney 67 EMMTC 76. **d** 79 **p** 80. C Littleover *Derby* 79-80; Hon C Allestree 80-85; Chapl HM Pris Man 85-86; Chapl HM Pris Kirkham 86-93; Chapl HM Pris Wakef 93-95; Chapl HM Pris Sudbury 95-96; Chapl HM Pris Foston Hall 95-96; rtd 96; Perm to Offic *Blackb* from 98. *48 South Park, Lytham St Annes FY8 4QQ* Tel (01253) 730490

LYNN, Peter Anthony. b 38. Keele Univ BA62 St Jo Coll Cam BA64 MA68 PhD72. Westcott Ho Cam 67. **d** 68 **p** 69. C Soham *Ely* 68-72; Min Can St Paul's Cathl *Lon* 72-78; Perm to Offic *St Alb* 78-86; Min Can and Sacr St Paul's Cathl *Lon* 86-88; C Westmr St Matt 89-91; V Glynde, W Firle and Beddingham *Chich* 91-03; rtd 03. *119 Stanford Avenue, Brighton BN1 6FA* Tel (01273) 553361

LYNN, Trevor. *See* LYNN, Frank Trevor

LYNN, Archdeacon of. *See* GRAY, The Ven Martin Clifford

LYNN, Suffragan Bishop of. *See* LANGSTAFF, The Rt Revd James Henry

LYON, Adrian David. b 55. Coll of Resurr Mirfield 84. **d** 87 **p** 88. C Crewe St Andr *Ches* 87-90; C Altrincham St Geo 90-91; TV Accrington *Blackb* 91-00; TR Accrington Ch the King from 00. *St Peter's Vicarage, 151 Willows Lane, Accrington BB5 0LR* Tel and fax (01254) 382173 E-mail lyons@ddens.freeserve.co.uk

LYON, Christopher David. b 55. Strathclyde Univ LLB75 Edin Univ BD81. Edin Th Coll 78. **d** 81 **p** 82. C Dumfries *Glas* 81-84; P-in-c Alexandria 84-88; R Greenock 88-00; R Ayr, Girvan and Maybole 00-02; Chapl Luxembourg *Eur* from 02. *98 rue de Mühlenbach, L-2168 Luxembourg* Tel and fax (00352) 439593

LYON, Dennis. b 36. Wycliffe Hall Ox 64. **d** 67 **p** 68. C Woodthorpe *S'well* 67-70; Warden Walton Cen 70-72; V W Derby Gd Shep *Liv* 72-81; V Billinge 81-00; AD Wigan W 89-00; rtd 00; Perm to Offic *Liv* from 01. *10 Arniam Road, Rainford, St Helens WA11 8BU* Tel (01744) 885623

LYON, Canon Donald Robert. b 20. Trin Coll Cam BA41 PhD44 MA45. Linc Th Coll 46. **d** 47 **p** 48. C Dursley *Glouc* 47-51; C Brislington St Luke *Bris* 51-52; V Glouc St Mark *Glouc* 52-85; Hon Can Glouc Cathl 74-90; RD Glouc City 77-83; rtd 85; Perm to Offic *Glouc* 86-97. *12 Doverdale Drive, Longlevens, Gloucester GL2 0NN* Tel (01452) 524070

LYON, Joan Baxter. b 50. Strathclyde Univ BA70. TISEC 94. **d** 96 **p** 00. NSM Glas E End *Glas* 96-00; Luxembourg *Eur* from 02. *98 rue de Mühlenbach, L-2168 Luxembourg* Tel and fax (00352) 439593 E-mail joanblyon@hotmail.com

LYON, John Forrester. b 39. Edin Th Coll CertEd95. **d** 95 **p** 96. C Greenock *Glas* 95-98; C Gourock 95-98; Chapl Ardgowan Hospice 95-98; P-in-c Glas Gd Shep and Ascension *Glas* from 98. *31 Westfield Drive, Glasgow G52 2SG* Tel 0141-882 4996 E-mail revjohnlyon@goodshepherd31.freeserve.co.uk

LYON, John Harry. b 51. S Dios Minl Tr Scheme 86. **d** 89 **p** 90. NSM S Patcham *Chich* 89-91; C Chich St Paul and St Pet 91-94; R Earnley and E Wittering 94-04; V E Preston w Kingston from 04. *The Vicarage, 33 Vicarage Lane, East Preston, Littlehampton BN16 2SP* Tel (01903) 783318

LYONS, Bruce Twyford. b 37. K Alfred's Coll Win CertEd61. Tyndale Hall Bris DipTh69. **d** 70 **p** 71. C Virginia Water *Guildf* 70-73; Chapl Ostend w Knokke and Bruges *Eur* 73-78; V E Ham St Paul *Chelmsf* 78-85; V St Alb Ch Ch *St Alb* 85-91; Chapl Wellingborough Sch 92-95; P-in-c Stogumber w Nettlecombe and Monksilver *B & W* 96-98; P-in-c Ostend w Knokke and Bruges *Eur* 98-00; NSM Newbury Deanery *Ox* 01; Chapl Milton Abbey Sch Dorset 01-02; Perm to Offic *Sarum* from 01; rtd 02. *Tudor Barn, Spring Street, Wool, Wareham BH20 6DB* Tel (01929) 462901 E-mail blyons@fish.co.uk

LYONS, Edward Charles. b 44. Nottm Univ BTh75 LTh. St Jo Coll Nottm 71. **d** 75 **p** 76. C Cambridge St Martin *Ely* 75-78; P-in-c Bestwood Park *S'well* 78-85; R W Hallam and Mapperley *Derby* 85-98; P-in-c Brownsover CD *Cov* 98-02; V Brownsover from 02; AD Rugby from 99; Dioc Ecum Officer from 03. *43 Bowfell, Brownsover, Rugby CV21 1JF* Tel (01788) 573696 E-mail ted.lyons@btinternet.com

LYONS, Graham Selby. b 29. MBE84. Open Univ BA79. LNSM course 94. **d** 97 **p** 98. OLM New Eltham All SS *S'wark* from 97. *56 Cadwallon Road, London SE9 3PY* Tel (020) 8850 6576 E-mail holyons2@aol.com

LYONS, Margaret Rose Marie. b 47. LNSM course 89. **d** 89. OLM Gainsborough All SS *Linc* 89-91. *1C Common Road, Low Moor, Bradford BD12 0NT*

LYONS, Paul. b 67. Ulster Univ BA91. TCD Div Sch BTh98. **d** 98 **p** 99. C Seapatrick *D & D* 98-03; I Greenisland *Conn* from 03.

4 Tinamara, Upper Station Road, Greenisland, Carrickfergus BT38 8FE Tel (028) 9086 3421 *or* 9085 9676 Mobile 07791-472225 E-mail greenisland@connor.anglican.org

LYONS, Paul Benson. b 44. Qu Coll Birm 68. **d** 69 **p** 70. C Rugby St Andr *Cov* 69-70; C Moston St Jo *Man* 70-72; PV Llan Cathl *Llan* 73-74; C Brookfield St Anne, Highgate Rise *Lon* 74-75; Perm to Offic 76-82; C Westmr St Sav and St Jas Less 82-86; V Gt Cambridge Road St Jo and St Jas from 86. *St John's Vicarage, 113 Creighton Road, London N17 8JS* Tel (020) 8808 4077 E-mail stjohnstjames@hotmail.com

LYONS, William. b 22. LNSM course 78. **d** 80 **p** 81. NSM Glenrothes *St And* 80-81; NSM Kirkcaldy 81-91; NSM Kinghorn 81-91; rtd 91. *24 Auchmithie Place, Glenrothes KY7 4TY* Tel (01592) 630757

LYTLE, Canon John Deaville. b 23. Wadh Coll Ox BA50 MA52. Wycliffe Hall Ox 50. **d** 51 **p** 52. C Ilkeston St Mary *Derby* 51-56; P-in-c Brassington 56-59; V Bradbourne and Brassington 59-89; RD Wirksworth 78-88; Hon Can Derby Cathl 82-89; rtd 89; Perm to Offic *Derby* from 89. *14 Manor Road, Ashbourne DE6 1EH* Tel (01335) 346588

LYTTLE, Norma Irene. b 47. CITC. **d** 01 **p** 02. Aux Min Drumachose *D & R* 01-04; Aux Min Dungiven w Bovevagh from 04. *121 Castlerock Road, Coleraine BT51 3NW* Tel and fax (028) 7035 5911 Mobile 07742-836688 E-mail irenenlyttle@btopenworld.com

M

MABBS, Miss Margaret Joyce. b 24. St Hilda's Coll Ox BA45 MA47 DipEd46. S'wark Ord Course 79. **dss** 82 **d** 87 **p** 94. Eltham Park St Luke *S'wark* 82-05; NSM 87-05; Perm to Offic from 05. *70 Westmount Road, London SE9 1JE* Tel (020) 8850 4621

McADAM, Gordon Paul. b 66. QUB BSc88 TCD BTh93. CITC 90. **d** 93 **p** 94. C Drumglass w Moygashel *Arm* 93-96; I Dungiven w Bovevagh *D & R* 96-02; I Loughgall w Grange *Arm* from 02. *The Rectory, 2 Main Street, Loughgall, Armagh BT61 8HZ* Tel (028) 3889 1587 E-mail loughgall@armagh.anglican.org

McADAM, Canon Michael Anthony. b 30. K Coll Cam BA52 MA56. Westcott Ho Cam 54. **d** 56 **p** 57. C Towcester w Easton Neston *Pet* 56-59; Chapl Hurstpierpoint Coll 60-68; Bp's Chapl *Lon* 69-73; R Much Hadham *St Alb* 73-95; Hon Can St Alb 89-95; rtd 95; RD Oundle *Pet* 96-97; Perm to Offic *Pet* from 98 and *St Alb* from 03. *Parkers Patch, 55 Barnwell, Peterborough PE8 5PG* Tel (01832) 273451

McALISTER, Canon David. b 39. St Jo Coll Nottm 83. **d** 87 **p** 88. NSM Arpafeelie *Mor* 87-93; NSM Cromarty 87-93; NSM Fortrose 87-93; C Broughty Ferry *Bre* 93-95; P-in-c Nairn *Mor* from 95; Chapl Inverness Airport from 98; Can St Andr Cathl Inverness from 01. *1 Clova Crescent, Nairn IV12 4TE* Tel (01667) 452458 E-mail revdavidmca@yahoo.co.uk

McALISTER, Kenneth Bloomer. b 25. TCD BA51. **d** 51 **p** 53. C Cregagh *D & D* 51-54; C Monaghan *Clogh* 54-57; C Portadown St Mark *Arm* 57-62; R Ripley *Ripon* 62-91; rtd 91; Perm to Offic *Ripon* from 91. *31 Wetherby Road, Knaresborough HG5 8LH* Tel (01423) 860705

McALISTER, Margaret Elizabeth Anne (Sister Margaret Anne). b 55. St Mary's Coll Dur BA78 Ex Univ PGCE79. Wycliffe Hall Ox 83 St Alb and Ox Min Course 99. **d** 01 **p** 02. ASSP from 91; NSM Cowley St Jas *Ox* 01-04; NSM Cowley St Jo from 04. *All Saints Convent, St Mary's Road, Oxford OX4 1RU* Tel (01865) 200479 Fax 726547

MacALISTER, The Very Revd Randal George Leslie. b 41. TCD BA63 Div Test 64 MA66. **d** 64 **p** 66. C Portadown St Mark *Arm* 64-67; I Keady w Armaghbreague and Derrynoose 67-74; R Kirriemuir *St And* 74-81; R Greenock *Glas* 81-87; R Forfar *St And* 87-95; R Lunan Head 87-95; Chapl Sophia Antipolis *Eur* 95-98; R Auchterarder *St And* from 98; R Muthill from 98; Dean St Andr from 98. *St Kessog's Rectory, High Street, Auchterarder PH3 1AD* Tel and fax (01764) 662525

McALISTER, Thomas George. b 20. TCD BA42 MA47. **d** 43 **p** 44. C Aghalee *D & D* 43-45; C Belfast St Pet *Conn* 45-53; V Southport St Andr *Liv* 53-59; V Spring Grove St Mary *Lon* 59-69; Chapl Wispers Sch Surrey 69-79; R Haslemere *Guildf* 69-79; V Slyne w Hest *Blackb* 79-85; rtd 85; Perm to Offic *Guildf* 86-96; *Portsm* 86-98; P-in-c Linchmere *Chich* 92-93. *4 Rosemary Court, Church Road, Haslemere GU27 1BH* Tel (01428) 643516

McALLEN, James. b 38. Lon Univ BD71. Oak Hill Th Coll 63. **d** 66 **p** 67. C Blackheath St Jo *S'wark* 66-69; C Edin St Thos *Edin* 69-73; V Selby St Jas *York* 73-80; V Wistow 75-80; V Houghton *Carl* 80-91; Gen Sec Lon City Miss 92-03; Hon C Blackheath St Jo *S'wark* 94-04; rtd 04; Perm to Offic *Carl* from 04. *205 Brampton Road, Carlisle CA3 9AX* Tel (01228) 540505

McALLEN, Robert Roy. b 41. Bps' Coll Cheshunt 62. **d** 65 **p** 66. C Seagoe *D & D* 65-67; C Knockbreda 67-70; CF 70-96; Chapl R Memorial Chpl Sandhurst 87-92; Chapl Guards Chpl Lon 92-96; Perm to Offic *Guildf* 96-98; R Ockley, Okewood and Forest Green from 98. *The Rectory, Stane Street, Ockley, Dorking RH5 5SY* Tel (01306) 711550 E-mail roy-gill@mcallenr.freeserve.co.uk

MACAN, Peter John Erdley. b 36. Bp Gray Coll Cape Town 58 LTh60. **d** 60 **p** 61. S Africa 60-67; C S Lambeth St Ann *S'wark* 68-71; V Nunhead St Silas 72-81; P-in-c Clapham H Spirit 81-87; TV Clapham Team 87-90; V Dulwich St Clem w St Pet 90-02; rtd 02. *19 The Windings, South Croydon CR2 0HW* Tel (020) 8657 1398 E-mail peter.macan@virgin.net

McARTHUR, Duncan Walker. b 50. Strathclyde Univ BSc73 Moore Th Coll Sydney ThL80 Melbourne Univ BD82 Newc Univ MA94. **d** 82 **p** 82. Australia 82-90 and from 93; C Hornsby 82-85; Asst Min 88-89; Asst Chapl Barker Coll Hornsby 86-88; P-in-c Harraby *Carl* 90-93; R Hurstville 93-95; Hon Asst P Wauchope St Matt from 99. *43 Narran River Road, Wauchope, NSW, Australia 2446* Tel (0061) (2) 6585 1147 *or* 6583 6999 Mobile 412-828341 Fax (2) 6583 6982 E-mail duncanmcarthur@tsn.cc

McARTHUR-EDWARDS, Mrs Judith Sarah. b 71. Westmr Coll Ox BTh94. Cranmer Hall Dur 97. **d** 99 **p** 00. C Cradley *Worc* 99-02; C Quarry Bank 02-03; Asst Chapl Frimley Park Hosp NHS Trust from 04; Chapl R Surrey Co Hosp NHS Trust from 04. *The Vicarage, 37 Sturt Road, Frimley Green, Camberley GU16 6HY* Tel (01252) 835179

MACARTNEY, Prof Fergus James. b 40. MRCP68 FACC76 FRCP77 Qu Coll Cam BA62 MA84 St Thos Hosp Cam BCh66 MB67. EAMTC 86 SW Minl Tr Course 88. **d** 90 **p** 91. Chapl Lee Abbey 90-91; NSM Shirwell, Loxhore, Kentisbury, Arlington, etc *Ex* 90-91; Asst Chapl Amsterdam w Den Helder and Heiloo *Eur* 91-98; Perm to Offic *Ely* from 99. *6 Cook Close, Cambridge CB4 1PH* Tel (01223) 423902

MACARTNEY, Gerald William. b 52. TCD BTh03. CITC. **d** 03 **p** 04. C Drumglass w Moygashel *Arm* 03-05; I Milltown from 05. *10 Derrylileagh Road, Portadown, Craigavon BT62 1TQ* Tel (028) 3885 2626 Mobile 07850-040027 E-mail milltown@armagh.anglican.org

MACAULAY (née BRAYBROOKS), Mrs Bridget Ann. b 63. Trin Coll Bris BA92 DipCOT84. TISEC 96. **d** 98 **p** 99. C Edin Old St Paul *Edin* 98-01; C Edin St Pet from 01. *5 Lutton Place, Edinburgh EH8 9PD* Tel 0131-667 6856 E-mail kbmac@gmx.net

MACAULAY, John Roland. b 39. Man Univ BSc61 Liv Inst of Educn PGCE80. Wells Th Coll 61. **d** 63 **p** 64. C Padgate Ch Ch *Liv* 63-66; C Upholland 66-73; TV 73-75; V Hindley St Pet 75-81; Chapl Liv Coll 81-96; Sub-Chapl HM Pris Risley 85-96; R Lowton St Luke *Liv* 96-05; rtd 05. *58 Rectory Road, Ashton-in-Makerfield, Wigan WN4 0QD* Tel (01942) 711336

MACAULAY, Kenneth Lionel. b 55. Edin Univ BD78. Edin Th Coll 74. **d** 78 **p** 79. C Glas St Ninian *Glas* 78-80; Dioc Youth Chapl 80-87; P-in-c Glas St Matt 80-87; R Glenrothes *St And* 87-89; Chapl St Mary's Cathl *Glas* 89-92; Min Glas St Mary 89-92; Min Glas St Serf 92-94; Perm to Offic 94-96; NSM Glas St Oswald 96-98; P-in-c 98-01; Chapl HM Pris Glas (Barlinnie) 99-00; P-in-c Dumbarton *Glas* from 01. *The Rectory, 45 St Andrew's Crescent, Dumbarton G82 3ES* Tel (01389) 602261 *or* 734514 Mobile 07904-974272 E-mail frkenny@blueyonder.co.uk

MACAULAY, Kenneth Russell. b 63. Strathclyde Univ BSc85. TISEC 95. **d** 98 **p** 99. C Edin Old St Paul *Edin* 98-01; C Edin St Pet from 01. *5 Lutton Place, Edinburgh EH8 9PD* Tel 0131-667 6856 E-mail kbmac@gmx.net

McAULAY, Mark John Simon. b 71. Lanc Univ LLB92 Leeds Univ BA04 Barrister-at-Law (Inner Temple) 93. Coll of Resurr Mirfield 02. **d** 04 **p** 05. C Ruislip St Martin *Lon* from 04. *5 Wyteleaf Close, Ruislip HA4 7SP* Tel (01895) 633370 E-mail frmarkmcaulay@hotmail.com

McAUSLAND, Canon William James. b 36. Edin Th Coll 56. **d** 59 **p** 60. C Dundee St Mary Magd *Bre* 59-64; R 71-79; R Glas H Cross *Glas* 64-71; Chapl St Marg Old People's Home 79-85; R Dundee St Marg *Bre* 79-01; Chapl St Mary's Sisterhood 82-87; Chapl Ninewells Hosp 85-01; Can St Paul's Cathl Dundee 93-01; Hon Can St Paul's Cathl Dundee from 01; rtd 01. *18 Broadford Terrace, Broughty Ferry DD5 3EF* Tel (01382) 737721 E-mail williammcausland@care4free.net

McAVOY, George Brian. b 41. MBE78. TCD BA61 MA72. Div Test 63. **d** 63 **p** 65. C Cork St Luke w St Ann *C, C & R* 63-66; I Timoleague w Abbeymahon 66-68; Chapl RAF 68-88; Asst Chapl-in-Chief RAF 88-95; QHC 91-95; Chapl Fosse Health NHS Trust 95-98; Chapl Oakham Sch 98-03; rtd 03. *1 The Leas, Cottesmore, Oakham LE15 7DG* Tel (01572) 812404 E-mail gbm@oakham.rutland.sch.uk

McAVOY, Philip George. b 63. Imp Coll Lon BSc85 SS Coll Cam BA90. Westcott Ho Cam 88. **d** 91 **p** 92. C W End *Win* 91-95; TV Swanage and Studland *Sarum* 95-00; P-in-c Littleton *Lon* from 00. *Littleton Rectory, Squires Bridge Road, Shepperton TW17 0QE* Tel (01932) 562249
E-mail philmac@littletonrectory.fsnet.co.uk

McBRIDE, Murray. b 61. Wilson Carlile Coll Trin Coll Bris BA00. **d** 00 **p** 01. C S Lawres Gp *Linc* 00-04; V Aspatria w Hayton and Gilcrux *Carl* from 04. *St Kentigern's Vicarage, King Street, Aspatria, Carlisle CA7 3AL* Tel (016973) 20398
E-mail k.e.mcbride@bgc.ac.uk

McBRIDE, The Ven Stephen Richard. b 61. QUB BSc84 TCD DipTh87 BTh89 MA92 QUB PhD96. CITC 84. **d** 87 **p** 88. C Antrim All SS *Conn* 87-90; I Belfast St Pet 90-95; Bp's Dom Chapl 94-02; I Antrim All SS from 95; Adn Conn from 02; Prec Belfast St Anne from 02. *The Vicarage, 10 Vicarage Gardens, Antrim BT41 4JP* Tel and fax (028) 9446 2186 Mobile 07718-588191 E-mail archdeacon@connor.anglican.org

McCABE, Alan. b 37. Lon Univ BScEng61. Ridley Hall Cam 61. **d** 63 **p** 64. C Bromley SS Pet and Paul *Roch* 63-67; PV Roch Cathl 67-70; V Bromley H Trin 70-77; V Westerham 77-88; V Eastbourne St Jo *Chich* 88-99; rtd 00; Perm to Offic *Chich* from 00. *94 Baldwin Avenue, Eastbourne BN21 1UP* Tel (01323) 643731 Fax as telephone E-mail alanmcc37@hotmail.com

McCABE, Carol. b 49. **d** 03 **p** 04. OLM Blackrod *Man* from 03. *27 Lymbridge Drive, Blackrod, Bolton BL6 5TH* Tel (01204) 669775

McCABE, John Hamilton. b 59. St Edm Hall Ox MA82 PGCE84 Bris Univ MA01. Trin Coll Bris 99. **d** 01 **p** 02. C Burpham *Guildf* from 01. *8 Selbourne Road, Burpham, Guildford GU4 7PJ* Tel and fax (01483) 456602 Mobile 07710-094357
E-mail jh.mccabe@ntlworld.com

McCABE, The Ven John Trevor. b 33. RD78. Nottm Univ BA55 St Cath Soc Ox DipTh59. Wycliffe Hall Ox 57. **d** 59 **p** 60. C Compton Gifford *Ex* 59-63; P-in-c Ex St Martin, St Steph, St Laur etc 63-66; Chapl RNR from 63; Chapl Ex Sch 64-66; V Capel *Guildf* 66-71; V Scilly Is *Truro* 71-74; TR Is of Scilly 74-81; Can Res Bris Cathl *Bris* 81-83; V Manaccan w St Anthony-in-Meneage and St Martin *Truro* 83-96; RD Kerrier 87-90 and 94-96; Chmn Cornwall NHS Trust for Mental Handicap 91-00; Hon Can Truro Cathl from 93; Adn Cornwall 96-99; rtd 00; Non Exec Dir Cornwall Healthcare NHS Trust from 99; Perm to Offic *Truro* from 99. *Sunhill, Budock Water, Falmouth TR11 5DG* Tel (01326) 378095

McCABE, Terence John. b 46. Sarum Th Coll 71. **d** 74 **p** 75. C Radford *Cov* 74-77; P-in-c Bris St Paul w St Barn *Bris* 77-80; TV E Bris 80-84; USA 84-90; R Eynesbury *Ely* from 90. *The Rectory, 7 Howitt's Lane, Eynesbury, St Neots PE19 2JA* Tel (01480) 403884 *or* 385364 E-mail mccabe@nildram.co.uk

McCABE, William Alexander Beck. b 27. QUB BA50 PhD65. **d** 74 **p** 74. Sec Sheff Coun of Chs 74-80; Hon C Millhouses H Trin *Sheff* 74-80; TV Sheff Manor 80-83; C Mosbrough 83; C Portsea St Cuth *Portsm* 83-86; C S w N Hayling 86-87; V Mickleover St Jo *Derby* 87-91; rtd 91; Perm to Offic *Derby* from 91. *Tawelfan, Ruthin Road, Cadole, Mold CH7 5LL* Tel (01352) 810435

McCAFFERTY, Andrew. *See* McCAFFERTY, William Andrew

McCAFFERTY, Canon Christine Ann. b 43. FCA76. Gilmore Course 76. **dss** 79 **d** 87 **p** 94. Writtle *Chelmsf* 79-81; Writtle w Highwood 81-94; C 87-94; NSM Officer 88-94; Dom Chapl to Bp Bradwell 88-93; Hon Can Chelmsf Cathl from 91; TR Wickford and Runwell 94-00; rtd 00; Hon C Lt Baddow *Chelmsf* from 00. *3 Hanlee Brook, Great Baddow, Chelmsford CM2 8GB* Tel (01245) 476371 E-mail mccafferty@jcmcc.freeserve.co.uk

McCAFFERTY (née BACK), Mrs Esther Elaine. b 52. Saffron Walden Coll CertEd74. Trin Coll Bris 79 Oak Hill Th Coll BA81. **dss** 81 **d** 87 **p** 94. Collyhurst *Man* 81-84; Upton (Overchurch) *Ches* 84-88; Par Dn 87-88; Par Dn Upper Holloway St Pet w St Jo *Lon* 88-90; Min in charge 90-97; P-in-c Pitsea w Nevendon *Chelmsf* 97-02; R Basildon St Martin from 02; RD Basildon 99-04. *The Rectory, St Martin's Square, Basildon SS14 1DX* Tel and fax (01268) 522455
E-mail emccafferty@talk21.com

McCAFFERTY, Keith Alexander. *See* DUCKETT, Keith Alexander

McCAFFERTY, William Andrew (Andy). b 49. Open Univ BA93. SW Minl Tr Course 94. **d** 97 **p** 98. NSM Lapford, Nymet Rowland and Coldridge *Ex* 97-00; CF 00-04; TR Crosslacon *Carl* from 04. *The Vicarage, Trumpet Road, Cleator CA23 3EF* Tel (01946) 810510 Mobile 07891-119684
E-mail andrew.mccafferty@care4free.net

McCAGHREY, Mark Allan. b 66. Warwick Univ BSc87. St Jo Coll Nottm BTh93. **d** 94 **p** 95. C Byfleet *Guildf* 94-97; V Lowestoft St Andr *Nor* from 97. *The Vicarage, 51 Beresford Road, Lowestoft NR32 2NQ* Tel (01502) 511521 Fax 08701-377567 E-mail mark@romanhill.org.uk

McCALLA, Robert Ian. b 31. AKC55. St Boniface Warminster 56. **d** 56 **p** 57. C Barrow St Jo *Carl* 56-58; C Penrith St Andr 58-61; R Greenheys St Clem *Man* 61-64; V Glodwick 64-71; R Distington *Carl* 71-73; V Howe Bridge *Man* 73-87; Chapl Atherleigh Hosp 75-98; R Heaton Mersey *Man* 87-92; V Tyldesley w Shakerley 92-98; rtd 98; Perm to Offic *Carl* from 98. *17 Brunswick Square, Penrith CA11 7LW* Tel (01768) 895212

McCALLIG, Darren. **d** 05. C Monkstown *D & G* from 05. *2 Grange Crescent, Kill o' the Grange, Co Dublin, Irish Republic* Tel (00353) 87-286 6637 (mobile) E-mail mcallid@tcd.ie

MacCALLUM, The Very Revd Norman Donald. b 47. Edin Univ LTh70. Edin Th Coll 67. **d** 71 **p** 72. TV Livingston LEP *Edin* 71-82; P-in-c Bo'ness and R Grangemouth 82-00; Syn Clerk 96-00; Can St Mary's Cathl 96-00; Provost St Jo Cathl Oban *Arg* from 00; R Oban St Jo from 00; R Ardchattan from 00; R Ardbrecknish from 00. *The Rectory, Ardconnel Terrace, Oban PA34 5DJ* Tel and fax (01631) 562323
E-mail provostoban@argyll.anglican.org

McCAMLEY, The Ven Gregor Alexander. b 42. TCD BA64 MA67. CITC 65. **d** 65 **p** 66. C Holywood *D & D* 65-68; C Bangor St Comgall 68-72; I Carnalea 72-80; I Knock from 80; Stewardship Adv from 89; Can Down Cathl from 90; Dioc Registrar 90-95; Adn Down from 95; Chan Belf Cathl from 95. *The Rectory, 29 King's Road, Belfast BT5 6JG* Tel (028) 9047 1514 E-mail archdeacon@down.anglican.org

McCAMMON, John Taylor. b 42. QUB BSc65 Lon Univ BD70. Clifton Th Coll 67. **d** 71 **p** 72. C Lurgan Ch the Redeemer *D & D* 71-75; I Kilkeel 75-82; I Lisburn Ch Ch Cathl *Conn* 82-98; Treas 94-96; Prec 96; Chan 96-98; Can Conn Cathl 85-98; CMS Kenya from 98. *CMS, Partnership House, 157 Waterloo Road, London SE1 8UU* Tel (020) 7928 8681

McCANDLESS, John Hamilton Moore. b 24. QUB BA Ulster Poly BEd. **d** 63 **p** 64. C Belfast St Matt *Conn* 63-66; I Termonmaguirke *Arm* 66-69; C Jordanstown *Conn* 69-70; I Ballinderry, Tamlaght and Arboe *Arm* 70-74; I Kilbarron w Rossnowlagh and Drumholm *D & R* 84-87; rtd 87. *4 Greenhill Drive, Ballymoney BT53 6DE* Tel (028) 2766 2078
E-mail jack@theloughan.fsnet.co.uk

McCANN, Alan. *See* McCANN, Thomas Alan George

McCANN, Hilda. b 36. N Ord Course. **d** 03. OLM Parr *Liv* from 03. *25 Newton Road, St Helens WA9 2HZ* Tel (01744) 758759

McCANN, Michael Joseph. b 61. Man Univ BSc82 TCD BTh91 FCA. **d** 91 **p** 92. C Derryloran *Arm* 91-94; I Dunmurry *Conn* 94-99; I Kilroot and Templecorran from 99. *Kilroot Rectory, 29 Downshire Gardens, Carrickfergus BT38 7LW* Tel (028) 9336 2387

McCANN, Roland Neil. b 39. Serampore Coll BD73. Bp's Coll Calcutta DipTh70. **d** 70 **p** 73. India 70-74; C Earley St Bart *Ox* 74-77; C-in-c Harlington Ch Ch CD *Lon* 77-99; rtd 99; Perm to Offic *Lon* from 02. *195 Park Road, Uxbridge UB8 1NP* Tel (01895) 259265

McCANN, Thomas Alan George. b 66. Ulster Univ BA90 TCD BTh93 QUB MPhil99. CITC 90. **d** 93 **p** 94. C Carrickfergus *Conn* 93-00; I Woodburn H Trin from 00. *20 Meadow Hill Close, Carrickfergus BT38 9RQ* Tel (028) 9336 2126
E-mail alan@thehobbit.fsnet.co.uk

McCARRAHER, Seymour. b 26. Magd Coll Cam BA48 MA55. St Steph Ho Ox. **d** 55 **p** 56. C Southwick St Columba *Dur* 55-59; Chapl RN 59-75; C Christchurch *Win* 75-81; V Darton *Wakef* 81-92; rtd 92; Perm to Offic *York* from 93. *34 Moorside, Boston Spa, Wetherby LS23 6PN* Tel (01937) 843948

McCARTAN, Mrs Audrey Doris. b 50. Keele Univ CertEd71 BEd72 Lanc Univ MA75 Northumbria Univ MSc99. NEOC 01. **d** 04 **p** 05. NSM Gosforth St Hugh *Newc* from 04. *10 Meadowvale, Ponteland, Newcastle upon Tyne NE20 9NF* Tel (01661) 871056

McCARTHY, David William. b 63. Edin Th Coll BD88. **d** 88 **p** 89. C Edin St Paul and St Geo *Edin* 88-91; P-in-c S Queensferry 91-95; R Glas St Silas *Glas* from 95. *77 Southbrae Drive, Glasgow G13 1PU* Tel 0141-954 9368
E-mail dwmccarthy@ntworld.com

McCARTHY, The Very Revd John Francis. b 38. TCD BA61 MA72. **d** 62 **p** 63. C Seapatrick *D & D* 62-66; C Seagoe 66-71; I Moira 71-75; I Dundalk *Arm* 75-86; I Enniskillen *Clogh* 86-94; Dean Clogh 89-94; USA from 94. *St John's Anglican Church, 7th and Hampshire Street, Quincy, IL 62301, USA*

McCARTHY, Peter James. b 25. OBE. Cranmer Hall Dur. **d** 85 **p** 86. Hon C Farnham w Scotton, Staveley, Copgrove etc *Ripon* 85-87; V Startforth w Bowes 87-92; rtd 92; C Dufftown *Ab* 92-95; Perm to Offic *Ripon* from 95 and *Newc* from 99. *Manderley, Farnham Lane, Ferrensby, Knaresborough HG5 9JG* Tel (01423) 340503

MacCARTHY, The Very Revd Robert Brian. b 40. TCD BA63 MA66 PhD83 NUI MA65 Ox Univ MA82. Cuddesdon Coll 77. **d** 79 **p** 80. C Carlow w Urglin and Staplestown *C & O* 79-81; Lic to Offic (Cashel, Waterford and Lismore) 81-86; Lib Pusey Ho 81-82; Fell St Cross Coll Ox 81-82; C Bracknell *Ox* 82-83; TV 83-86; C Kilkenny w Aghour and Kilmanagh *C & O* 86-88; Bp's V and Lib Kilkenny Cathl 86-88; Chapl Kilkenny Coll 86-88; Bp's Dom Chapl 86-89; I Castlecomer w Colliery Ch, Mothel and Bilbo 88-95; Dioc Info Officer (Ossory and Leighlin) 88-90; Glebes Sec (Ossory and Leighlin) 92-94; Preb Monmohenock

St Patr Cathl Dublin 94-99; Provost Tuam *T, K & A* 95-99; I Galway w Kilcummin 95-99; Chapl Univ Coll Galway 95-99; Dean St Patr Cathl Dublin from 99. *The Deanery, Upper Kevin Street, Dublin 8, Irish Republic* Tel (00353) (1) 475 5449 *or* 453 9472

McCARTHY, Sandra Ellen. *See* MANLEY, Mrs Sandra Ellen

MacCARTHY, Stephen Samuel. b 49. ACII81 Univ Coll Chich BA02. **d** 01. NSM Burgess Hill St Edw *Chich* from 01. *St Edward's House, 9 Coopers Close, Burgess Hill RH15 8AN* Tel (01444) 248520 Mobile 07802-734903 E-mail ssmaccarthy@aol.com

McCARTHY, Terence Arthur. b 46. Open Univ BA90. Kelham Th Coll 66. **d** 70 **p** 71. C Gt Burstead *Chelmsf* 70-74; C Wickford 74-76; TV E Runcorn w Halton *Ches* 76-80; V Runcorn H Trin 80-84; Chapl HM Pris Liv 84; Chapl HM Pris Acklington 84-92; Chapl HM Pris Holme Ho from 92. *The Chaplaincy, HM Prison Holme House, Stockton-on-Tees TS18 2QU* Tel (01642) 744115

McCARTNEY, Adrian Alexander. b 57. Stranmillis Coll BEd79 TCD BTh88. St Jo Coll Nottm LTh86. **d** 88 **p** 89. C Jordanstown w Monkstown *Conn* 88-91; Bp's C Monkstown 91-94; I 94-96; C Belvoir *D & D* from 02. *73 Dunlady Manor, Dundonald, Belfast BT16 1YR* Tel (028) 9048 1197 *or* 9067 3379 E-mail adrian@summermadness.co.uk

McCARTNEY, Ellis. b 47. Univ Coll Lon BSc73 Goldsmiths' Coll Lon DipRE80 Lon Inst of Educn MA82 Cert Counselling 94. NTMTC 94. **d** 97 **p** 98. NSM Tollington *Lon* from 97. *6 Elfort Road, London N5 1AZ* Tel (020) 7226 1533 E-mail macfour@btinternet.com

McCARTNEY, Robert Charles. CITC. **d** 85 **p** 85. C Portadown St Mark *Arm* 85-88; I Errigle Keerogue w Ballygawley and Killeshil 88-89; CF 89-04; I Belfast St Donard *D & D* from 04. *St Donard's Rectory, 421 Beersbridge Road, Belfast BT5 5DU* Tel (028) 9065 2321

McCARTY, Colin Terence. b 46. Loughb Univ BTech68 PhD71 Lon Univ PGCE73 FRSA89. EAMTC 91. **d** 94 **p** 95. NSM Exning St Martin w Landwade *St E* from 94; Perm to Offic *Ely* from 96. *1 Seymour Close, Newmarket CB8 8EL* Tel (01638) 669400 *or* (01223) 552716 Mobile 07711-825157 Fax (01223) 553537 E-mail mccarty.c@ucles.org.uk *or* gjy02@dial.pipex.com

MacCARTY, Paul Andrew. b 34. Sarum & Wells Th Coll 73. **d** 75 **p** 76. Ind Chapl *Win* 75-80; C Bournemouth St Andr 75-84; Hon C Christchurch 80-91; C 91-99; rtd 99; Perm to Offic *Win* from 01. *3 Douglas Avenue, Christchurch BH23 1JT* Tel (01202) 483807 E-mail paulmaccarty@aol.com

McCASKILL, James Calvin. b 73. Wheaton Coll Illinois BA95. Coll of Resurr Mirfield MA02. **d** 02 **p** 03. C Mt Lebanon St Paul USA 02-04; P-in-c Lundwood *Wakef* from 04. *4 Parkland View, Barnsley S71 5LL* Tel (01226) 711365 E-mail james@mccaskill.info

McCATHIE, Neil. b 62. N Staffs Poly BA84 De Montfort Univ MA00 Huddersfield Univ PGCE93 MAAT96. St Jo Coll Nottm 03. **d** 05. C Shipley St Pet *Bradf* from 05. *2B Nab Lane, Shipley BD18 4HB*

McCAUGHEY, Canon Robert Morley. b 07. MA35. **d** 35 **p** 36. C Walker *Newc* 35-38; C Ponteland 38-41; C Benwell St Jas 41-43; V Wallsend St Luke 43-52; V Berwick H Trin 52-61; V Wisbech SS Pet and Paul *Ely* 61-74; RD Wisbech 62-72; Hon Can Ely Cathl 72-74; rtd 74; Perm to Offic *D & R* from 76. *51 Ballinahone House, Knockcloughrim, Magherafelt BT45 8PT* Tel (028) 7964 2110

McCAULAY, Stephen Thomas John. b 61. Coll of Resurr Mirfield BA98. **d** 98 **p** 99. C Chaddesden St Phil *Derby* 98-02; V Mackworth St Fran 02-04; CF from 04. *c/o MOD Chaplains (Army)* Tel (01980) 615804 Fax 615800 E-mail mccaulay@ntlworld.com

McCAULEY, Craig William Leslie. b 72. Glam Univ BA95 DipHum96 TCD BTh99. CITC 96. **d** 99 **p** 00. C Seapatrick *D & D* 99-02; C Kill *D & G* 02-04; I Lurgan w Billis, Killinkere and Munterconnaught *K, E & A* from 04. *The Rectory, Virginia, Co Cavan, Irish Republic* Tel (00353) (49) 854 8465

McCAUSLAND, Norman. b 58. TCD BTh89. CITC 89. **d** 89 **p** 90. C Portadown St Columba *Arm* 89-91; P-in-c Clonmel Union *C, C & R* 91-94; Miss to Seamen 91-94; CMS 94-95; Bp's V and Lib Ossory Cathl *C & O* 96; Chapl and Tutor CITC 96-00; PV Ch Ch Cathl Dublin *D & G* 96-00; CMS 00-01; Lic to Offic *D & G* from 01. *17 Congress Gardens, Glasthule, Dun Laoghaire, Co Dublin, Irish Republic* E-mail mccausln@tcd.ie

M'CAW, Stephen Aragorn. b 61. Magd Coll Cam BA83 Lon Univ MB, BS86 FRCS90 MRCGP92. Cranmer Hall Dur 97. **d** 99 **p** 00. C Thetford *Nor* 99-02; R Steeple Aston w N Aston and Tackley *Ox* from 02. *The Rectory, Fir Lane, Steeple Aston, Bicester OX25 4SF* Tel (01869) 347793 E-mail samcaw@talk21.com

McCLAY, Canon David Alexander. b 59. TCD MA87. **d** 87 **p** 88. C Magheralin w Dollingstown *D & D* 87-90; I Kilkeel 90-01; I Willowfield from 01; Can Belf Cathl from 05. *Willowfield Rectory, 149 My Lady's Road, Belfast BT6 8FE* Tel and fax (028) 9046 0105 *or* 9045 7654 E-mail david.mcclay1@btinternet.com

McCLEAN, Lydia Margaret Sheelagh. *See* COOK, Mrs Lydia Margaret Sheelagh

McCLEAN, Robert Mervyn. b 38. Greenwich Univ BTh91. Edgehill Th Coll Belf 57. **d** 85 **p** 88. NSM Seapatrick *D & D* 85-99. *2 Kiloanin Crescent, Banbridge BT32 4NU* Tel (028) 4062 7419 E-mail r.m.mcclean@btinternet.com

McCLELLAN, Andrew David. b 71. St Jo Coll Cam BA93 MA96. Oak Hill Th Coll BA05. **d** 05. C Sevenoaks St Nic *Roch* from 05. *40 South Park, Sevenoaks TN13 1TJ* Tel 07931-731062 (mobile) E-mail aj_mcc@btinternet.com

McCLENAGHAN, John. **d** 05. C Portadown St Columba *Arm* from 05. *8 Ardmore Close, Portadown, Craigavon BT62 4DX*

MACCLESFIELD, Archdeacon of. *See* GILLINGS, The Ven Richard John

McCLINTOCK, Darren John. b 77. Hull Univ BA98 Open Univ MA(TS)00. St Jo Coll Nottm 98. **d** 01 **p** 02. C Drypool *York* 01-04; C Bilton *Ripon* from 04; Asst Dir of Ords from 02. *8 Pecketts Way, Harrogate HG1 3EW* Tel (01423) 560863 E-mail daren@djmcclintock@freeserve.co.uk

McCLOSKEY, Robert Johnson. b 42. Stetson Univ (USA) AB63. Gen Th Sem NY STB67. **d** 67 **p** 68. USA from 67; C Gt Medford 67-69; R Somerville W St Jas and Chapl Tufts Univ 69-72; Dioc Adv for Liturgy and Music Massachusetts 71-76; R Westford St Mark 72-76; R Blowing Rock St Mary 76-82; Liturg and Musical Adv and Ecum Officer Dio W N Carolina 76-81; Dio SE Florida 90-93; Ecum Officer Dio Long Is 81-89; R Bay Shore St Pet and St Pet Sch 82-89; R Miami St Steph and St Steph Sch 89-01; Staff Officer Lambeth Conf 98; rtd 01; Perm to Offic *Glouc* from 00. *PO Box 530125, Miami Shores, FL 33153, USA* Tel (001) (305) 759 0970

McCLURE, Mrs Catherine Abigail. b 63. Birm Univ BA84 SS Hild & Bede Coll Dur PGCE85. Ripon Coll Cuddesdon 01. **d** 03 **p** 04. C Cirencester *Glouc* from 03. *15 Partridge Way, Cirencester GL7 1BH* Tel (01285) 654779 Mobile 07711-476749 E-mail mcclure.staverton@virgin.net

McCLURE, Robert (Roy). b 30. Open Univ BA92. TCD Div Sch 68. **d** 70 **p** 71. C Monaghan *Clogh* 70-72; C Belfast St Matt *Conn* 72-76; Chapl HM Pris Liv 76-77; Chapl HM Pris Preston 77-82; V Foulridge *Blackb* 82-88; rtd 88; Perm to Offic *Liv* from 89. *4 Mill Lane Crescent, Southport PR9 7PF* Tel (01704) 27476

McCLURE, The Ven Timothy Elston. b 46. St Jo Coll Dur BA68. Ridley Hall Cam 68. **d** 70 **p** 71. C Kirkheaton *Wakef* 70-73; C Chorlton upon Medlock *Man* 74-79; Chapl Man Poly 74-82; TR Man Whitworth 79-82; Gen Sec SCM 82-92; Bp's Soc and Ind Adv and Dir Chs' Coun for Ind and Soc Resp LEP *Bris* 92-99; Hon Can Bris Cathl from 92; Hon C Cotham St Sav w St Mary 96; Chapl Lord Mayor's Chpl 96-99; Adn Bris from 99. *Church House, 23 Great George Street, Bristol BS1 5QZ* Tel 0117-906 0102 Fax 925 0460 E-mail tim.mcclure@bristoldiocese.org

McCLUSKEY, Coralie Christine. b 52. Univ of Wales (Cardiff) BEd74. St Alb and Ox Min Course 98. **d** 01 **p** 02. C Welwyn w Ayot St Peter *St Alb* 01-04; P-in-c Datchworth from 04. *The Rectory, Brookbridge Lane, Datchworth, Knebworth SG3 6SU* Tel (01438) 813067 *or* 817183 E-mail coralie_mccluskey@yahoo.co.uk

McCLUSKEY, James Terence. b 65. Coll of Resurr Mirfield 01. **d** 03 **p** 04. C Swanley St Mary *Roch* from 03. *77 Pinks Hill, Swanley BR8 8NN* Tel (01322) 406860 Mobile 07761-632734 E-mail mccluskey@katy-james.freeserve.co.uk

McCLUSKEY, Miss Lesley. b 45. Hull Univ LLB72 Bolton Coll of Educn PGCE77. N Ord Course 89. **d** 92 **p** 94. C Bootle St Mary w St Paul *Liv* 92-94; C Wigan St Anne 94-98; P-in-c Newton in Makerfield Em from 98; Chapl St Helens and Knowsley Hosps NHS Trust from 98. *The Rectory, Wargrave Road, Newton-le-Willows WA12 8RR* Tel (01925) 224920 E-mail lesley-mccluskey@yahoo.co.uk

McCOACH, Jennifer Sara. b 69. Leeds Univ BSc94. Ripon Coll Cuddesdon 99. **d** 01 **p** 02. C Lillington *Cov* from 01; Chapl amongst Deaf People from 03. *34 Lime Avenue, Lillington, Leamington Spa CV32 7DF* Tel (01926) 339030 E-mail jmccoach@fish.co.uk

McCOLLUM, Alastair Colston. b 69. Whitelands Coll Lon BA91. Westcott Ho Cam 95. **d** 96 **p** 97. C Hampton All SS *Lon* 96-98; C S Kensington St Aug 98-00; Chapl Imp Coll 98-00; TV Papworth *Ely* from 00. *The Rectory, The Green, Eltisley, St Neots PE19 6TG* Tel (01480) 880152 E-mail alastair.mccollum@ely.anglican.org

McCOLLUM, Charles James. b 41. TCD BTh89. CITC 85. **d** 89 **p** 90. C Larne and Inver *Conn* 89-91; Bp's C Belfast Whiterock 91-96; I Belfast St Pet and St Jas from 96. *St Peter's Rectory, 17 Waterloo Park South, Belfast BT15 5HX* Tel and fax (028) 9077 7053

McCOMB, Samuel. b 33. CITC 70. **d** 71 **p** 72. C Belfast St Mich *Conn* 71-74; C Lisburn Ch Ch 74-79; I Ballinderry *Arm* 79-83; I Lisburn Ch Ch *Conn* 83-04; Can Conn Cathl 98-04; Treas 01-04; rtd 04. *209 Hillsborough Old Road, Lisburn BT27 5QE*

McCONACHIE, Robert Noel. b 40. Goldsmiths' Coll Lon BA86. Oak Hill Th Coll 86. **d** 88 **p** 89. C Larkfield *Roch* 88-93; R

Mereworth w W Peckham from 93. *The Rectory, The Street, Mereworth, Maidstone ME18 5NA* Tel (01622) 812214

McCONKEY, Brian Robert. b 62. Carl Dioc Tr Inst 92. **d** 95 **p** 96. C Blackb St Gabr *Blackb* 95-98; Dioc Youth Officer 99-04; V Fulwood Ch Ch from 04. *Christ Church Vicarage, 19 Vicarage Close, Fulwood, Preston PR2 8EG* Tel (01772) 719210 E-mail christchurchfulwood@btinternet.com

McCONKEY, David Benton. b 53. Kansas Wesleyan Univ (USA) BA75 Yale Univ MusM77 SSC. Yale Div Sch MDiv79. **d** 83 **p** 84. Dn Ch Cathl Salina USA 83-84; C S Lake Anchorage 84-85; P-in-c Louisville St Luke 85-86; R Warrensburgh H Cross 86-94; Can Capitular All SS Cath Albany 88-93; R Belvedere St Eliz Zimbabwe 94-03; P-in-c Norton St Fran and St Jas 94-99; Lect Bp Gaul Coll 94-01; TR Swindon New Town *Bris* from 03. *St Mark's Rectory, 5 Gold View, Swindon SN5 8ZG* Tel (01793) 873140 *or* 538220 Fax 491065 E-mail frdbmcconkey@yahoo.co.uk

McCONNELL, Canon Brian Roy. b 46. St Paul's Coll Grahamstown DipTh71. **d** 71 **p** 72. S Africa 71-77 and 79-85; C Plumstead 71-74; C St Geo Cathl Cape Town 74-77; C Prestwich St Marg *Man* 77-79; V Liscard St Mary w St Columba *Ches* 85-90; V Altrincham St Geo from 90; RD Bowdon 95-03; Hon Can Ches Cathl from 97. *St George's Vicarage, Townfield Road, Altrincham WA14 4DS* Tel 0161-928 1279 Fax 929 8826

McCONNELL, Peter Stuart. b 54. Linc Th Coll 89. **d** 91 **p** 92. C N Shields *Newc* 91-95; V Balkwell 95-03; Sen Chapl Northumbria Police from 98; C Killingworth from 03. *27 Mount Close, Killingworth, Newcastle upon Tyne NE12 6GE* Tel 0191-268 8788 E-mail mcconnell@balkwell.freeserve.co.uk

McCONNELL, Robert Mark. b 60. Oak Hill Th Coll BA88. **d** 89 **p** 90. C Bedford Ch Ch *St Alb* 89-92; C Bangor St Comgall *D & D* 92-94; I Killyleagh 94-99; I Ballynure and Ballyeaston *Conn* from 99. *The Rectory, 11 Church Road, Ballyclare BT39 9UF* Tel (028) 9332 2350 E-mail coiballynure@excite.co.uk

McCORMACK, Alan William. b 68. Jes Coll Ox BA90 MA94 DPhil94. CITC 93. **d** 96 **p** 97. C Knock *D & D* 96-98; Dean of Res and Chapl TCD from 98; Succ St Patr Cathl Dublin *D & G* from 98; Abp's Dom Chapl from 03. *House 27, Trinity College, Dublin 2, Irish Republic* Tel (00353) (1) 608 1402 Fax 679 0335 E-mail mccorma@tcd.ie

McCORMACK, Colin. b 47. QUB BSc70 DipEd71 Nottm Univ BA77. St Jo Coll Nottm 75. **d** 78 **p** 79. C Carl St Jo *Carl* 78-81; C Ballynafeigh St Jude *D & D* 81-84; V Harraby *Carl* 84-89; NSM Carl H Trin and St Barn 95-99; Asst Chapl Costa Blanca *Eur* 00-04; Chapl Torrevieja from 04. *Edificio Torre del More 1B, 03180 Torrevieja, Alicante, Spain* Tel (0034) (96) 692 5205 Fax as telephone E-mail cormack@euroseek.com

McCORMACK, Canon David Eugene. b 34. Wells Th Coll 66. **d** 68 **p** 69. C Lillington *Cov* 68-71; C The Lickey *Birm* 71-75; V Highters Heath 75-82; V Four Oaks 82-00; Hon Can Birm Cathl 95-00; rtd 00; Perm to Offic *Linc* and *Pet* from 00. *27 Rockingham Close, Market Deeping, Peterborough PE6 8BY* Tel (01778) 347569

McCORMACK, George Brash. b 32. ACIS65 FCIS75 Lon Univ DipRS85. S'wark Ord Course 82. **d** 85 **p** 86. Hon C Crofton St Paul *Roch* 85-89; C Crayford 89-91; R Fawkham and Hartley 91-97; rtd 97; Perm to Offic *Roch* from 98. *11 Turnpike Drive, Pratts Bottom, Orpington BR6 7SJ*

McCORMACK, John Heddon. b 58. Chich Th Coll 85. **d** 88 **p** 89. C Cleobury Mortimer w Hopton Wafers *Heref* 88-90; C Lymington *Win* 90-92; C Portsea N End St Mark *Portsm* 92-95; Chapl St Barn Hospice Worthing from 95. *St Barnabas Hospice, Columbia Drive, Worthing BN13 2QF* Tel (01903) 264222 ext 205 *or* 534035 E-mail john.mccormack@stbarnabas-hospice.org.uk

McCORMACK, Kevan Sean. b 50. Chich Th Coll 77. **d** 80 **p** 81. C Ross *Heref* 80-81; C Ross w Brampton Abbotts, Bridstow and Peterstow 81-83; C Leominster 83; TV 84-87; Chapl R Hosp Sch Holbrook 87-00; P-in-c Woodbridge St Mary *St E* 00; R from 00. *St Mary's Rectory, Church Street, Woodbridge IP12 1DS* Tel (01394) 610424 Fax as telephone

McCORMACK, Canon Lesley Sharman. b 50. EAMTC. **d** 88 **p** 94. Hon Par Dn Chevington w Hargrave and Whepstead w Brockley *St E* 88-95; Asst Chapl W Suffolk Hosp Bury St Edm 88-95; Chapl Kettering Gen Hosp NHS Trust from 95; Bp's Hosp Chapl Adv *Pet* from 00; Can Pet Cathl from 03. *Kettering General Hospital, Rothwell Road, Kettering NN16 8UZ* Tel (01536) 492170 Fax 493767 E-mail lesley.mccormack@kgh.nhs.uk

MacCORMACK, Michael Ian. b 54. Kent Univ BA77 Bris Univ PGCE78 Ch Ch Coll Cant MA87. STETS 02. **d** 05. NSM Martock w Ash *B & W* from 05. *35 North Street, Martock TA12 6DH* Tel (01935) 824456 Mobile 07717-878736 E-mail mike.maccormack@btinternet.com

McCORMACK, Mrs Susan. b 60. NEOC 00. **d** 03 **p** 04. C Newburn *Newc* from 03. *St Mary's Parsonage, Newburn Road, Newcastle upon Tyne NE15 9AB* Tel 0191-267 4553

McCORMICK, Mrs Anne Irene. b 67. Sheff Univ BA89 Hull Univ PGCE90. Ripon Coll Cuddesdon 90. **d** 92 **p** 94. C Spalding *Linc* 92-96; C Gt Grimsby St Mary and St Jas 96-01; C Gt and Lt Coates w Bradley 98-03. *The Glebe House, 11 Church Lane, Limber, Grimsby DN37 8JN* Tel (01469) 561068 E-mail dmc@fish.co.uk

McCORMICK, David Mark. b 68. Univ of Wales (Ban) BD89. Ripon Coll Cuddesdon 90. **d** 92 **p** 93. C Holbeach *Linc* 92-96; TV Gt Grimsby St Mary and St Jas 96-01; Prin Linc Min Tr Scheme from 01. *The Glebe House, 11 Church Lane, Limber, Grimsby DN37 8JN* Tel (01469) 561068 E-mail dmc@fish.co.uk

McCOSH, Duncan Ian. b 50. Edin Dioc NSM Course 82. **d** 91 **p** 92. C Dalkeith *Edin* 91-96; C Lasswade 91-96; P-in-c Falkirk 96-97; R 97-03; R Galashiels from 03. *The Rectory, 6 Parsonage Road, Galashiels TD1 3HS* Tel (01896) 753118 E-mail christchurch@blueyonder.co.uk

McCOUBREY, William Arthur. b 36. CEng MIMechE. Sarum & Wells Th Coll 86. **d** 89 **p** 90. C Bedhampton *Portsm* 89-92; V Stokenham w Sherford *Ex* 92-96; R Stokenham w Sherford and Beesands, and Slapton 96-02; rtd 02; Perm to Offic *Chich* and *Portsm* from 02. *19 Warblington Road, Emsworth PO10 7HE* Tel (01243) 374011

McCOULOUGH, David. b 61. Man Univ BA84 St Jo Coll Dur BA88. Cranmer Hall Dur 86. **d** 89 **p** 90. C Man Apostles w Miles Platting *Man* 89-92; C Elton All SS 92-94; V Halliwell St Marg 94-98; Min Can Ripon Cathl *Ripon* 98-01; Chapl Univ Coll of Ripon and York St Jo 98-01; Ind Chapl *S'well* from 01; Chapl Boots PLC from 01; C Nottingham St Pet and St Jas 01-02; C Nottingham St Pet and All SS from 02. *3 Cromdale Close, Arnold, Nottingham NG5 8DF* Tel 0115-920 0630 E-mail office@stpetersnottingham.org

McCOULOUGH, Thomas Alexander. b 32. AKC59. **d** 60 **p** 61. C Norton St Mich *Dur* 60-63; India 63-67; P-in-c Derby St Jas *Derby* 67-72; Ind Chapl *York* 72-82; P-in-c Sutton on the Forest 82-96; Dioc Sec for Local Min 82-89; Lay Tr Officer 89-96; rtd 96; Perm to Offic *Newc* from 96. *1 Horsley Gardens, Holywell, Whitley Bay NE25 0TU* Tel 0191-298 0332

McCREA, Basil Wolfe. b 21. QUB BA49. Wycliffe Hall Ox 51. **d** 53 **p** 54. C Kingston upon Hull H Trin *York* 53-56; C Dundela St Mark *D & D* 56-59; C Cork H Trin w St Paul, St Pet and St Mary *C, C & R* 59-61; I Tullyaughnish *D & R* 61-65; I Rathkeale *L & K* 65-68; I Cork H Trin *C, C & R* 68-72; I Carrigaline Union 72-90; rtd 90. *30 Somerville, Carrigaline, Co Cork, Irish Republic* Tel (00353) (21) 437 1538

McCREA, Francis. b 53. BTh. **d** 91 **p** 92. C Dundonald *D & D* 91-94; I Belfast St Brendan from 94. *St Brendan's Rectory, 36 Circular Road, Belfast BT4 2GA* Tel (028) 9076 3458

McCREADY, Kennedy Lemar. b 26. Woolwich Poly CEng56 FIEE56 Garnett Coll Lon TCert54 Birkbeck Coll Lon BSc59 Sussex Univ Dip Bibl Studies 92 MA94. Chich Th Coll 91. **d** 92 **p** 99. NSM Mayfield *Chich* 92-97; Perm to Offic 97-00; NSM New Groombridge 99-01; Perm to Offic from 01. *Quarry House, Groombridge, Tunbridge Wells TN3 9PS* Tel (01892) 864297

McCREADY, Marcus Diarmuid Julian. b 63. NUU BA85 TCD BTh88 MPhil93. CITC 82. **d** 88 **p** 89. C Seagoe *D & D* 88-91; I Clonallon w Warrenpoint 91-96; Chapl Liv Coll 96-97; Chapl HM Pris Lindholme from 97. *HMP Lindholme, Bawtry Road, Hatfield, Doncaster DN7 6EE* Tel (01302) 848829 *or* 848700 Fax 843352 E-mail julian@mccready.u-net.com

McCREADY, Maurice Shaun. b 55. Fitzw Coll Cam BA77 MA81 PGCE95. Ripon Coll Cuddesdon 80. **d** 83 **p** 84. C Bridgwater St Fran *B & W* 83-86; C Walton-on-Thames *Guildf* 86-88; C Elm Park St Nic Hornchurch *Chelmsf* 88-97; NSM 93-01; P-in-c Bridgwater H Trin *B & W* 02-04. *Address temp unknown*

McCREERY, William Robert Desmond. b 35. QUB BD MA03. Oak Hill Th Coll 59. **d** 62 **p** 63. C Dundonald *D & D* 62-66; C Belfast St Donard 66-69; I Annalong 69-78; I Knockbreda 78-89; I Bangor St Comgall 89-03; Can Belf Cathl 88-03; rtd 03. *3 Glenbeigh Drive, Belfast BT8 6NE* Tel (028) 9079 4509

McCRORY, Canon Peter. b 34. Chich Th Coll 63. **d** 67 **p** 68. C St Marychurch *Ex* 67-72; R Kenn w Mamhead 72-76; R Kenn 76-78; Bp's Dom Chapl *S'wark* 78-81; V Kew 81-00; RD Richmond and Barnes 84-89; Hon Can S'wark Cathl 90-00; rtd 00; Perm to Offic *Nor* from 00. *Dane House, The Street, Kettlestone, Fakenham NR21 0AU* Tel (01328) 878455

McCROSKERY, Andrew. b 74. Glas Univ BD97 TCD MPhil99. CITC 98. **d** 99 **p** 00. C Newtownards *D & D* 99-02; Dean's V Cork Cathl *C, C & R* 02-04; Bp's Dom Chapl from 03; I Youghal Union from 04; Chapl Univ Coll Cork from 04; Min Can Cork Cathl from 04. *The Rectory, Old Rectory Road, Upper Strand, Youghal, Co Cork, Irish Republic* Tel (00353) (24) 92350

McCRUM, Michael Scott. b 35. Glas Univ BSc57 UNISA BTh85. **d** 85 **p** 85. S Africa 85-89; Asst P Lynnwood 86-87; P-in-c Mamelodi 87; P-in-c Villieria 87-88; Kerygma Internat Chr Min 89-92; Perm to Offic *Nor* 93-94; NSM Chesham Bois *Ox* 94-95; Perm to Offic *St Alb* 95-98; Hon C Chorleywood St Andr from 98. *Cranbrook, 31 South Road, Chorleywood, Rickmansworth WD3 5AS* Tel and fax (01923) 336897 Mobile 07971-393721 E-mail misamccrum@ntlworld.com

McCULLAGH, Elspeth Jane Alexandra. *See* SAVILLE, Mrs Elspeth Jane Alexandra

McCULLAGH, Canon John Eric. b 46. TCD BA68 BTh88 QUB DipEd70. **d** 88 **p** 89. C Stillorgan w Blackrock *D & G* 88-91; Chapl and Hd of RE Newpark Sch Dub 90-99; I Clondalkin w Rathcoole 91-99; Sec Gen Syn Bd of Educn 99-02; Can Ch Ch Cathl Dublin *D & G* from 99. *Harcourt Villa, Kimberley Road, Greystones, Co Wicklow, Irish Republic* Tel (00353) (1) 497 8422

McCULLAGH, Canon Mervyn Alexander. b 44. TCD BA BAI68. CITC 79. **d** 79 **p** 80. C Larne and Inver *Conn* 79-83; C Ballymacash 83-85; C Dublin St Ann w St Mark and St Steph *D & G* 85-88; I Baltinglass w Ballynure etc *C & O* from 88; Warden of Readers from 90; Can Ossory and Leighlin Cathls 92-96; Treas from 96; P-in-c Kiltegan w Hacketstown, Clonmore and Moyne 00-03. *The Rectory, Baltinglass, Co Wicklow, Irish Republic* Tel (00353) (59) 648 1321

McCULLOCH, Alistair John. b 59. Univ of Wales (Lamp) BA81 Leeds Univ BA86. Coll of Resurr Mirfield 84. **d** 87 **p** 88. C Portsm Cathl *Portsm* 87-90; C Portsea St Mary 90-94; V Reading St Matt *Ox* 94-95; Perm to Offic *S'wark* 99; Chapl King's Coll Hosp NHS Trust 00-04; Chapl R Marsden NHS Trust from 04. *The Royal Marsden Hospital, Fulham Road, London SW3 6JJ* Tel (020) 7808 2818 E-mail alistair.mcculloch@rmh.nhs.uk

MacCULLOCH, Prof Diarmaid Ninian John. b 51. Chu Coll Cam BA72 MA76 PhD77 Liv Univ DAA73 FSA78 FRHistS81. Ripon Coll Cuddesdon DipTh87. **d** 87. NSM Clifton All SS w St Jo *Bris* 87-88. *St Cross College, St Giles, Oxford OX1 3LZ* Tel (01865) 270794 Fax 270795
E-mail diarmaid.macculloch@theology.ox.ac.uk

✠**McCULLOCH, The Rt Revd Nigel Simeon.** b 42. Selw Coll Cam BA64 MA69. Cuddesdon Coll 64. **d** 66 **p** 67 **c** 86. C Ellesmere Port *Ches* 66-70; Dir Th Studies Ch Coll Cam 70-75; Chapl 70-73; Dioc Missr *Nor* 73-78; P-in-c Salisbury St Thos and St Edm *Sarum* 78-81; R 81-86; Adn Sarum 79-86; Can and Preb Sarum Cathl 79-86; Suff Bp Taunton *B & W* 86-92; Preb Wells Cathl 86-92; Bp Wakef 92-03; Bp Man from 03; High Almoner from 97. *Bishopscourt, Bury New Road, Salford, Manchester M7 4LE* Tel 0161-792 2096 Fax 792 6826
E-mail bishop@bishopscourt.manchester.anglican.org

McCULLOCK, Mrs Patricia Ann. b 46. CertEd72. EMMTC 87. **d** 90 **p** 94. C Bottesford w Ashby *Linc* 90-95; P-in-c Wragby 95-98; Chapl N Lincs Coll of FE 95-98; Ind Chapl 98-01; rtd 01; Perm to Offic *Linc* from 01. *36 Deepdale Lane, Nettleham, Lincoln LN2 2LT* Tel (01522) 595470
E-mail patricia.mccullock@virgin.net

McCULLOUGH, Mrs Aphrodite Maria. b 47. Derby Univ MSc95. EMMTC 97. **d** 00 **p** 01. NSM Kirby Muxloe *Leic* 00-04; TV from 04. *106 Hinckley Road, Leicester Forest East, Leicester LE3 3JS* Tel 0116-238 6344 E-mail dibley@care4free.net

McCULLOUGH, Canon Roy. b 46. Linc Th Coll 70. **d** 73 **p** 74. Chapl Highfield Priory Sch Lancs 73-77; C Ashton-on-Ribble St Andr *Blackb* 73-77; V Rishton 77-86; V Burnley St Matt w H Trin 86-97; RD Burnley 91-97; Chapl Victoria Hosp Blackpool 91-97; V Walton-le-Dale St Leon w Samlesbury St Leon *Blackb* from 97; Hon Can Blackb Cathl from 97. *The Vicarage, Church Brow, Preston PR5 4BH* Tel (01772) 880233 Fax 880289

McCURDY, The Ven Hugh Kyle. b 58. Portsm Poly BA Univ of Wales (Cardiff) PGCE. Trin Coll Bris. **d** 85 **p** 86. C Egham *Guildf* 85-88; C Woking St Jo 88-91; V Histon *Ely* 91-05; P-in-c Impington 98-05; RD N Stowe 94-05; Hon Can Ely Cathl 04-05; Adn Huntingdon and Wisbech from 05. *12 Boadicea Court, Chatteris PE16 6BN* Tel (01354) 692142
E-mail archdeacon@chatteris.plus.com

McDERMID, The Ven Norman George Lloyd Roberts. b 27. St Edm Hall Ox BA49 MA52. Wells Th Coll 49. **d** 51 **p** 52. C Leeds St Pet *Ripon* 51-56; V Bramley 56-64; Dioc Stewardship Adv 64-76; R Kirkby Overblow 64-80; Hon Can Ripon Cathl 72-93; Dioc Stewardship Adv *Wakef* 73-76; Dioc Stewardship Adv *Bradf* 73-76; RD Harrogate *Ripon* 77-83; V Knaresborough 80-83; Adn Richmond 83-93; rtd 93; Perm to Offic *Ripon* from 93. *Greystones, 10 North End, Bedale DL8 1AB* Tel (01677) 422210 Mobile 07761-572758
E-mail norman@gmcdermid.fsbusiness.co.uk

McDERMOTT, Christopher Francis Patrick. b 54. Southeastern Coll USA BA84 Wheaton Coll Illinois MA87. EAMTC. **d** 95 **p** 96. C Gt Ilford St Clem and St Marg *Chelmsf* 95-99. *17 Benton Road, Ilford IG1 4AT*

McDERMOTT, Fraser Graeme. b 65. NTMTC 97. **d** 98 **p** 00. NSM Oak Tree Angl Fellowship *Lon* 98-02; V N Wembley St Cuth from 02. *St Cuthbert's Vicarage, 214 Carlton Avenue West, Wembley HA0 3QY* Tel (020) 8904 7657 *or* 8904 8599
E-mail fraser@stcuths.org

MACDONALD, Alan Hendry. b 49. St Steph Ho Ox 86. **d** 88 **p** 89. C Heavitree w Ex St Paul *Ex* 88-91; C Withycombe Raleigh 91-92; TV 92-95; R Silverton, Butterleigh, Bickleigh and Cadeleigh from 95; RD Tiverton 00-02. *The Rectory, 21A King Street, Silverton, Exeter EX5 4JG* Tel (01392) 860350
E-mail almac01@tinyonline.co.uk

MacDONALD, Alastair Douglas. b 48. Cranmer Hall Dur 71. **d** 74 **p** 75. C Mottingham St Andr *S'wark* 74-78; C Woolwich St Mary w St Mich 78-81; V S Wimbledon St Andr 81-89; V Brighton St Matthias *Chich* 89-94; Chapl Southn Community Services NHS Trust 94-01; Mental Health Chapl Hants Partnerships NHS Trust 01-04. *Address temp unknown*

MacDONALD, Alastair Robert. b 72. Edin Univ MA94. TISEC. **d** 02 **p** 03. C Edin St Thos *Edin* from 02. *81 Glasgow Road, Edinburgh EH12 8LJ* Tel 0131-334 8109
E-mail asmacdonald@hotmail.com

MACDONALD, Cameron. b 51. Open Univ BA89. Wilson Carlile Coll 76 NEOC 89. **d** 90 **p** 91. CA from 76; C Nairn *Mor* 90-92; P-in-c 92-95; CF from 95; Perm to Offic *Ely* from 00. *c/o MOD Chaplains (Army)* Tel (01980) 615804 Fax 615800

MACDONALD, Christopher Kenneth. b 57. Ex Univ BA79 PGCE80. Trin Coll Bris DipHE93. **d** 93 **p** 94. C Eastbourne All SS *Chich* 93-96; C Polegate 96-99; Chapl Eastbourne Coll from 99. *14A Grange Road, Eastbourne BN21 4HJ* Tel (01323) 452317

MACDONALD, Colin. b 47. St Jo Coll Nottm 87. **d** 89 **p** 90. C Limber Magna w Brocklesby *Linc* 89-92; P-in-c Barrow and Goxhill 92-97; V 97-99; R Hemingby 99-02; V Fulletby 99-02; R Belchford 99-02; TV Wilford Peninsula *St E* from 02. *33 Fountains Road, Watersfield Park, Rendlesham, Woodbridge IP12 2UF* Tel (01394) 460547
E-mail cmacdonald4@compuserve.com

MACDONALD, Canon Donald Courtenay. b 45. Nottm Univ BTh74 St Martin's Coll Lanc CertEd75. Kelham Th Coll 70. **d** 75 **p** 76. C Clifton All SS w Tyndalls Park *Bris* 75-78; C Clifton All SS w St Jo 78-79; Chapl Derby Lonsdale Coll *Derby* 79-84; V Derby St Andr w St Osmund from 84; RD Derby S 89-99; Dioc Communications Officer 89-93; Hon Can Derby Cathl from 95. *St Osmund's Vicarage, London Road, Derby DE24 8UW* Tel (01332) 571329 E-mail donald.c.macdonald@btinternet.com

McDONALD, Douglas Mark. b 28. Linc Coll Ox BA54 MA59. Wells Th Coll 68. **d** 69 **p** 70. C Horsham *Chich* 69-76; TV Kirkby Lonsdale *Carl* 76-79; P-in-c Tidmarsh w Sulham *Ox* 79-83; Chapl St Audries Sch W Quantoxhead 83-91; rtd 91; Perm to Offic *B & W* 91-97. *18 Lower Park, Minehead TA24 8AX* Tel (01643) 703104

MACDONALD, Helen Maria. *See* BARTON, Helen Maria

McDONALD, Ian Henry. b 40. TD. St Aid Birkenhead 65. **d** 68 **p** 69. C Kingston upon Hull H Trin *York* 68-70; C Drumglass *Arm* 70-73; I Eglish w Killylea 73-80; I Maghera w Killelagh *D & R* 80-91; I Killowen 91-98; I Errigal w Garvagh 98-05; Can Derry Cathl 94-00; Preb 00-05; CF (TAVR) 91-05; rtd 05. *4 Ballylagan Lane, Aghadowey, Coleraine BT51 4DD* Tel (028) 7086 9150 Mobile 07740-708402

McDONALD, James Damian (Jack). b 66. Pemb Coll Cam BA87 MA91 SS Hild & Bede Coll Dur PGCE88 K Coll Lon MA96. Qu Coll Birm 90. **d** 92 **p** 93. C Camberwell St Geo *S'wark* 92-95; Chapl G&C Coll Cam 95-99; Fell and Dean from 99; Lic to Offic *Ely* from 95. *Gonville and Caius College, Cambridge CB2 1TA* Tel (01223) 332408 *or* 332482 Mobile 07779-719763 Fax (01223) 332336 E-mail jdm39@cam.ac.uk

MacDONALD, John. b 16. St Cath Soc Ox BA38 MA42 BLitt58. St Steph Ho Ox 39. **d** 41 **p** 42. C Birkdale St Jo *Liv* 41-44; C Walton St Mary 44-49; Chapl St Steph Ho Ox 49-54; Chapl Ch Ch Ox 51-60; Chapl New Coll Ox 52-60; Lib Pusey Ho 54-60; Chapl Burgess Hall Lamp 60-76; Sub-Warden 62-76; V Edstaston *Lich* 76-82; V Whixall 76-82; Chapl Choral Ches Cathl *Ches* 82-85; rtd 85; Perm to Offic *Ches* from 85. *47 The Links, Gwernaffield, Mold CH7 5DZ* Tel (01352) 740015

McDONALD, John Richard Burleigh. b 17. TCD BA40 BD41. **d** 41 **p** 42. C Belfast St Pet *Conn* 41-45; Uganda 46-61; Educn Officer Ch of Ireland 61-64; Hd RE Stranmills Coll of Educn Belf 66-86; Dir Post-Ord Tr *Conn* 86-94; rtd 94. *76 Osborne Drive, Belfast BT9 6LJ* Tel (028) 9066 6737

McDONALD, Lawrence Ronald. b 32. St Alb Minl Tr Scheme 84. **d** 87 **p** 88. NSM Sharnbrook and Knotting w Souldrop *St Alb* 87-90; C Bromham w Oakley and Stagsden 90-93; P-in-c Renhold 93-98; rtd 99; P-in-c Stevington *St Alb* 99-02; Perm to Offic from 02. *16 Townsend Road, Sharnbrook, Bedford MK44 1HY* Tel (01234) 782849
E-mail fathermac@ukgateway.net

MACDONALD, Malcolm Crawford. b 75. St Andr Univ MA97 MLitt98. Wycliffe Hall Ox BTh05. **d** 05. C Kensington St Barn *Lon* from 05. *87 Blythe Road, London W14 0HP* Tel 07821-011435 (mobile) E-mail malco9lm@stbk.org.uk

MACDONALD, Malcolm James. b 42. Sarum Th Coll 70. **d** 71 **p** 73. C Hounslow St Steph *Lon* 71-72; C Hammersmith St Sav 72-76; P-in-c Hammersmith St Luke 76-79; V 79-87; V Kirkby Woodhouse *S'well* from 87. *The Vicarage, 57 Skegby Road, Kirkby-in-Ashfield, Nottingham NG17 9JE* Tel (01623) 759094

MACDONALD, Martin Stanley Harrison. b 51. Dur Univ BSc72 ACA75 FCA82. St Alb and Ox Min Course. **d** 01 **p** 02. NSM Tring *St Alb* from 01. *9 Hall Park, Berkhamsted HP4 2NU* Tel (01442) 384953 Mobile 07710-390115
E-mail mshmacdonald@ntlworld.com

MACDONALD, Canon Murray Somerled. b 23. Pemb Coll Cam BA46 MA49. Ely Th Coll 47. **d** 48 **p** 49. C Hendon St Mary *Lon* 48-51; C Hanover Square St Geo 51-53; P-in-c Upton and Copmanford *Ely* 53-54; R Sawtry 53-54; R Sawtry, Upton and Copmanford 54-57; V Upwood w Gt and Lt Raveley 57-62; R Wood Walton 57-62; V Fenstanton 62-70; V Hilton 62-70; RD Huntingdon 69-76; R Huntingdon All SS w St Jo 70-82; R Huntingdon St Mary w St Benedict 71-82; Hon Can Ely Cathl 72-82; Can Res 82-88; rtd 89; Perm to Offic *Linc* 89-01 and *Ely* 89-97. *4 Hacconby Lane, Morton, Bourne PE10 0NT* Tel (01778) 570711

MACDONALD, Stephen Calliss. b 35. Selw Coll Cam BA58. Westcott Ho Cam 58. **d** 60 **p** 61. C Norwood All SS *Cant* 60-64; Chapl Cov Cathl *Cov* 64-68; Chr Aid 68-70; rtd 96. *c/o Mrs G M Macdonald, Linden House, Meadow Lane, Huntingdon PE28 2BP* Tel (01480) 492807

MacDONALD, Trevor John. b 33. Hertf Coll Ox BA55 MA59. Chich Th Coll 92. **d** 93 **p** 94. NSM Hove St Barn and St Agnes *Chich* from 93. *31 Orchard Gardens, Hove BN3 7BH* Tel (01273) 771228

MACDONALD, Warren. Monash Univ Aus BEng Leeds Univ MPhil Gothenburg Univ PhD00 CEng CPEng MIEAust. Trin Coll Bris DipHE95. **d** 95 **p** 96. NSM Iford *Win* 95-98; Perm to Offic from 98. *5 St James's Square, Bournemouth BH5 2BX* Tel (01202) 422131 Fax 422101
E-mail warren.macdonald@dial.pipex.com

MACDONALD-MILNE, Brian James. b 35. CCC Cam BA58 MA62 St Pet Coll Ox MA81. Cuddesdon Coll 58. **d** 60 **p** 61. C Fleetwood St Pet *Blackb* 60-63; Solomon Is 64-78; New Hebrides 78-80; Acting Chapl Trin Coll Ox 81; Acting Chapl St Pet Coll Ox 81-82; Relief Chapl HM Pris Grendon and Spring Hill 81-82; Research Fell Qu Coll Birm 82-83; Hon Asst P Bordesley SS Alb and Patr *Birm* 82-83; R Landbeach *Ely* 83-88; V Waterbeach 83-88; OCF 83-88; R Radwinter w Hempstead *Chelmsf* 88-97; RD Saffron Walden 91-97; P-in-c The Sampfords 95-97; rtd 97; Perm to Offic *Ely* from 97 and *Chelmsf* from 02; Dioc Rep Melanesian Miss and Papua New Guinea Ch Partnership from 99; Chapl Ely Chapter Guild of Servants of the Sanctuary from 00. *39 Way Lane, Waterbeach, Cambridge CB5 9NQ* Tel (01223) 861631
E-mail macdonaldmilne@talk21.com

McDONNELL, Mrs Mavis Marian. b 42. LNSM course 95. **d** 98 **p** 99. OLM Warrington St Ann *Liv* from 98. *32 Shaws Avenue, Warrington WA2 8AX* Tel (01925) 634408

McDONOUGH, David Sean. b 55. **d** 89 **p** 90. C Moseley St Mary *Birm* 89-92; TV Glascote and Stonydelph *Lich* from 92. *90 Briar, Tamworth B77 4DZ* Tel (01827) 52754 *or* 330306
E-mail david@dmcdonough.freeserve.co.uk

McDONOUGH, Terence. b 57. St Jo Coll Nottm LTh86. **d** 89 **p** 90. C Linthorpe *York* 89-94; TV Heworth H Trin 94-98; V Heworth Ch Ch from 98. *95 Stockton Lane, York YO31 1JA* Tel (01904) 425678

McDOUGAL, John Anthony Phelps Standen. *See* STANDEN McDOUGAL, Canon John Anthony Phelps

McDOUGALL, David Robin. b 61. Avery Hill Coll CertEd BEd84. Ridley Hall Cam 85. **d** 87 **p** 88. C Bletchley *Ox* 87-91; C High Wycombe 91-93; C E Twickenham St Steph *Lon* 93-02; P-in-c Upper Sunbury St Sav from 02. *St Saviour's Vicarage, 205 Vicarage Road, Sunbury-on-Thames TW16 7TP* Tel (01932) 782800 E-mail david@st-saviours-sunbury.org.uk

McDOUGALL, Mrs Denise Alma. b 48. Ban Coll TCert69. N Ord Course 00. **d** 03. NSM Waterloo Ch Ch and St Jo *Liv* from 03. *27 Mayfair Avenue, Crosby, Liverpool L23 2TL* Tel 0151-924 8870 E-mail denisemcdougall@yahoo.co.uk

MacDOUGALL, Canon Iain William. b 20. TCD BA43 MA59. CITC 43. **d** 43 **p** 44. C Belfast St Steph *Conn* 43-45; C Enniskillen and Trory *Clogh* 45-48; I Drumlane *K, E & A* 48-50; I Ballinaclash *D & G* 51-54; I Moate *M & K* 54-58; I Ballyloughloe 54-58; I Ferbane 54-58; I Mullingar, Portnashangan, Moyliscar, Kilbixy etc 58-85; Can Meath 81-85; rtd 85. *18 Denville Court, Killiney, Co Dublin, Irish Republic* Tel (00353) (1) 285 4751

McDOUGALL, Sally-Anne. b 64. Glas Univ BMus86 Edin Univ BD04. TISEC 01. **d** 04. C Glas St Marg *Glas* from 04. *Flat 2/1, 266 Camphill Avenue, Glasgow G41 3AS* Tel 0141-636 8577
E-mail sal@mcdougall.gg

McDOUGALL, Stuart Ronald. b 28. Leeds Univ DipAdEd MEd84. Roch Th Coll 64. **d** 66 **p** 67. C Gravesend St Aid *Roch* 66-69; C Wells St Thos w Horrington *B & W* 69-70; TV Tong *Bradf* 70-73; V Cononley w Bradley 73-82; C Thornthwaite w Thruscross and Darley *Ripon* 82-83; P-in-c Dacre w Hartwith 83-86; rtd 86; Perm to Offic *Sarum* from 90. *Portman Chase Lodge, Chalbury, Wimborne BH21 7EU* Tel (01258) 840558

MacDOUGALL, William Duncan. b 47. Nottm Univ BTh74 LTh74. St Jo Coll Nottm 69. **d** 74 **p** 75. C Highbury New Park St Aug *Lon* 74-77; SAMS 77-82; Argentina 78-82; V Rashcliffe and Lockwood *Wakef* 83-87; V Tonbridge St Steph *Roch* 87-03; RD Tonbridge 01-03; Dir Past and Evang Studies Trin Coll Bris from 03. *15 Cranleigh Gardens, Bristol BS9 1HD* Tel 0117-968 2028 E-mail billmacdougall@clara.net

McDOWALL, Julian Thomas. b 39. CCC Cam BA62 MA67 Barrister 61. Linc Th Coll 62. **d** 64 **p** 65. C Rugby St Andr *Cov* 64-70; C-in-c Stoke Hill CD *Guildf* 70-72; V Stoke Hill 72-76; R Elstead 76-91; V Thursley 82-91; TV Wellington and Distr *B & W* 91-93; C Lymington *Win* 93-04; rtd 04; Perm to Offic *Win* from 04. *Juniper Cottage, 20 Solent Avenue, Lymington SO41 3SD* Tel (01590) 676750

McDOWALL, Robert Angus (Robin). b 39. AKC66. **d** 67 **p** 68. C Bishopwearmouth St Mich w St Hilda *Dur* 67-69; CF 69-05; Sen CF 80-91; Asst Chapl Gen 91-94; QHC 93-05; rtd 04; Perm to Offic *York* from 05. *c/o Crockford, Church House, Great Smith Street, London SW1P 3NZ* Tel (01482) 862504

McDOWALL, Roger Ian. b 40. AKC64. **d** 65 **p** 66. C Peterlee *Dur* 65-68; C Weaste *Man* 68-70; C Tonge Moor 70-73; V Whitworth St Bart 73-80; TV Torre *Ex* 80-88; V Torre All SS 88-00; Chapl S Devon Tech Coll Torbay 80-00; rtd 04. *1 Dunanellerich, Dunvegan, Isle of Skye IV55 8ZH* Tel (01470) 521271
E-mail mcdowall@lineone.net

McDOWELL, Francis John. b 56. QUB BA78 LSE DipBS84. CITC BTh93. **d** 96 **p** 97. C Antrim *Conn* 96-99; I Ballyrashane w Kildollagh 99-02; I Dundela St Mark *D & D* from 02. *St Mark's Rectory, 4 Sydenham Avenue, Belfast BT4 2DR* Tel (028) 9065 9047 *or* 4090

McDOWELL, Ian. b 67. Ch Coll Cam MA88 BA92. Westcott Ho Cam CTM93. **d** 93 **p** 94. C Hackney *Lon* 93-96; Asst Chapl Homerton Hosp NHS Trust Lon 96-98; Chapl Newham Healthcare NHS Trust Lon 98-03. *37 Hemsworth Street, London N1 5LF* Tel (020) 7363 8053 E-mail mcdow@dircon.co.uk

McDOWELL, Ian James. b 37. St Jo Coll Morpeth ACT ThL60 St Aug Coll Cant. **d** 61 **p** 62. Australia 61-66; C Naracoorte 61-63; P-in-c Elliston Miss 63-66; C S Harrow St Paul *Lon* 66; C Southgate Ch Ch 67; V Ganton *York* 67-71; P-in-c Foxholes and Butterwick 67-68; R 68-71; Australia from 71; R Angaston 71-76; R Colonel Light Gardens 76-94; R Gawler 94-98; R Merriwa from 98. *20 Gooch Street, PO Box 58, Merriwa, NSW, Australia 2329* Tel (0061) (2) 6548 2218 *or* 4930 9051

McDOWELL, John. *See* McDOWELL, Francis John

McDOWELL, Peter Kerr. b 69. QUB BA91. CITC BTh94. **d** 94 **p** 95. C Lisburn St Paul *Conn* 94-98; C Arm St Mark *Arm* 98-99; I Belfast Upper Malone (Epiphany) *Conn* from 99. *The Rectory, 74 Locksley Park, Upper Lisburn Road, Belfast BT10 0AS* Tel (028) 9060 1588 E-mail peter.mcdowell1@ntlworld.com

McDOWELL, Sheilah Rosamond Girgis. b 72. **d** 05. NSM Hammersmith H Innocents and St Jo *Lon* from 05. *36 Avenue Gardens, Teddington TW11 0BH* Tel (020) 8943 9259
E-mail rosamond.mcdowell@collyerbristow.com

MACE, Alan Herbert. b 28. Lon Univ BA49 Ex Inst of Educn TCert50. Wycliffe Hall Ox 59. **d** 60 **p** 61. C Disley *Ches* 60-63; C Folkestone H Trin w Ch Ch *Cant* 63-67; Lic to Offic *Win* 67-93; rtd 93; Perm to Offic *Win* 93-97. *15 Bassett Heath Avenue, Southampton SO16 7GP* Tel (023) 8076 8161

MACE, David Sinclair. b 37. Cam Univ BA61. **d** 95 **p** 96. OLM Godalming *Guildf* from 95. *Torridon, Grosvenor Road, Godalming GU7 1NZ* Tel (01483) 414646
E-mail dmace@fish.co.uk

MACE, Mrs Helen Elizabeth. b 31. Ox Univ MA52 Solicitor 56. Coll of Ascension 62. **dss** 74 **d** 87 **p** 94. Tadcaster *York* 77-84; Asst Chapl Leeds Gen Infirmary 84-94; C Woodhouse and Wrangthorn *Ripon* 94-96; Perm to Offic from 96. *Hobthrush, Wath, Harrogate HG3 5PL* E-mail hppriest@cstone.net

MACE, Robert Alfred Beasley. b 16. Leeds Univ BA49. Coll of Resurr Mirfield 48. **d** 50 **p** 51. C Callander *St And* 50-53; C Newc St Mary *Newc* 53-54; C Penton Street St Silas w All SS *Lon* 54-56; C Aylesbury *Ox* 56-59; P-in-c Glas St Gabr *Glas* 59-61; R Campbeltown *Arg* 61-65; V Barnsley St Pet *Wakef* 65-72; V Barnsley St Pet and St Jo 72-84; rtd 85; Perm to Offic *Wakef* from 85. *18 Chestnut Court, Barnsley S70 4HW* Tel (01226) 280729

McELHINNEY, Canon Mary Elizabeth Ellen (Liz). b 45. TCD BSSc67 BA67. CITC BTh94. **d** 97 **p** 98. C Magheralin w Dollingstown *D & D* 97-01; I Calry *K, E & A* from 01; Preb Elphin Cathl from 04. *Calry Rectory, The Mall, Co Sligo, Irish Republic* Tel and fax (00353) (71) 914 6513
E-mail lizmcelhinney@hotmail.com

McELHINNEY, Robert Stephen. b 70. Aston Univ BSc91. CITC BTh05. **d** 05. C Kill *D & G* from 05. *31 Foxrock Green, Foxrock, Dublin 18, Irish Republic* Tel (00353) (1) 289 1249
E-mail scrap5@eircom.net

McENDOO, Canon Neil Gilbert. b 50. TCD BA72. CITC 75. **d** 75 **p** 76. C Cregagh *D & D* 75-79; C Dublin St Ann *D & G* 79-82; I Dublin Rathmines w Harold's Cross from 82; Can Ch Ch Cathl Dublin 92-02; Preb from 02; Chan from 05. *The Rectory, Purser Gardens, Church Avenue, Rathmines, Dublin 6, Irish Republic* Tel (00353) (1) 497 1797

McEUNE, Patrick John. b 55. **d** 04. NSM White Horse *Sarum* from 04. *82 Danvers Way, Westbury BA13 3UF* Tel 07770-695794 (mobile)

McEVITT, Peter Benedict. b 58. Coll of Resurr Mirfield 91. **d** 93 **p** 94. C Swinton and Pendlebury *Man* 93-96; TV 96-97; V Darwen St Cuth w Tockholes St Steph *Blackb* 97-02; P-in-c Failsworth H Family *Man* from 02; AD Oldham from 02. *The Rectory, 190 Lord Lane, Failsworth, Manchester M35 0PG* Tel 0161-681 3644

MACEY, Preb Anthony Keith Frank. b 46. St Steph Ho Ox 69. **d** 71 **p** 72. C Ex St Thos *Ex* 71-76; V Wembury 76-88; RD Ivybridge 83-91; V Cockington from 88; RD Torbay 98-03; Preb Ex Cathl from 05. *The Vicarage, 22 Monterey Close, Torquay TQ2 6QW* Tel (01803) 607957 Fax 690338 E-mail smacey@lineone.net *or* cockington@lineone.net

MACEY, Michael David. b 81. Ex Univ BA03. Cranmer Hall Dur 03. **d** 05. C Dartmouth and Dittisham *Ex* from 05. *22 Church Road, Dartmouth TQ6 9HQ* Tel (01803) 839687 E-mail frmacey@hotmail.com

McFADDEN, Canon Ronald Bayle. b 30. TCD BA53 MA55. **d** 54 **p** 55. C Drumglass *Arm* 54-58; S Africa 58-62; Bp's Dom Chapl *D & D* 62-64; C Dundela St Mark 62-64; V Pateley Bridge and Greenhow Hill *Ripon* 64-73; V Knaresborough St Jo 73-79; P-in-c Knaresborough H Trin 78-79; Can Res Ripon Cathl 79-90; rtd 90; Chapl Qu Mary's Sch Baldersby Park 90-00; Perm to Offic *Ripon* from 90 and *York* from 97. *12 Ure Bank Terrace, Ripon HG4 1JG* Tel (01765) 604043

McFADYEN, Donald Colin Ross. b 63. Wolfs Coll Cam BTh00 Peterho Cam MPhil02. Ridley Hall Cam 97. **d** 01 **p** 02. NSM Haslingfield w Harlton and Gt and Lt Eversden *Ely* 01-05; P-in-c Bassingbourn from 05; P-in-c Whaddon from 05. *The Vicarage, 21 North End, Bassingbourn, Royston SG8 5NZ* Tel (01763) 244836 Mobile 07763-401567

McFADYEN, Canon Phillip. b 44. K Coll Lon BD69 AKC69 MTh70 ATD. St Aug Coll Cant 69. **d** 71 **p** 72. C Sheff St Mark Broomhall *Sheff* 71-74; Chapl Keswick Hall Coll of Educn 74-79; V Swardeston *Nor* 79-81; P-in-c E Carleton 79-81; P-in-c Intwood w Keswick 79-81; R Swardeston w E Carleton, Intwood, Keswick etc 81-90; R Ranworth w Panxworth, Woodbastwick etc from 90; Dioc Clergy Tr Officer 90-98; P-in-c Nor St Geo Colegate from 05; Hon Can Nor Cathl from 97; Bp's Officer for Visual Arts from 01; Relig Adv Anglia TV from 01. *12 The Crescent, Norwich NR2 1SA* E-mail phillipmcfadyen@aol.com

McFARLAND, Alan Malcolm. b 24. Lon Univ BA53. Bris Sch of Min 82. **d** 85 **p** 86. NSM Westbury-on-Trym H Trin *Bris* 85-88; Asst Lect Bris Sch of Min 85-88; Perm to Offic *Glouc* 88-89; NSM Lechlade 89-93; Perm to Offic *Lon* from 92 and *Sarum* from 93. *11 The Seahorse, Higher Sea Lane, Charmouth, Bridport DT6 6BB* Tel (01297) 560414

McFARLAND, Darren William. b 71. QUB BA93. CITC BTh96. **d** 96 **p** 97. C Greystones *D & G* 96-98; PV Ch Ch Cathl Dublin 97-99; P-in-c Clydebank *Glas* 99-02; Asst Dioc Miss 21 Co-ord 99-02; R Paisley St Barn from 02; R Paisley H Trin from 02. *The Rectory, 11 Tantallon Drive, Paisley PA2 9JT* Tel (01505) 812359 Mobile 07773-772610 E-mail rector@paisley.freeserve.co.uk

MACFARLANE, Miss Elizabeth Clare. b 71. St Hugh's Coll Ox BA92. Ripon Coll Cuddesdon BA02. **d** 03 **p** 04. C Watford St Mich *St Alb* from 03. *57 Whippendell Road, Watford WD18 7LY* Tel (01923) 248739

MACFARLANE, Iain Philip. b 64. Essex Univ BSc85 W Sussex Inst of HE PGCE88. Trin Coll Bris BA99. **d** 99 **p** 00. C Fishponds St Jo *Bris* 99-03; TV Yate New Town from 03. *The Vicarage, 57 Brockworth, Bristol BS37 8SJ* Tel (01454) 322921 E-mail imacfarlane@ukonline.co.uk

McFARLANE, Iain Scott. b 70. St Jo Coll Nottm 02. **d** 04 **p** 05. C Malvern St Andr and Malvern Wells and Wyche *Worc* from 04. *96 Fruitlands, Malvern WR14 4XB* Tel (01684) 575013 *or* 893146 Mobile 07834-191507 E-mail revmac@tiscali.co.uk

McFARLANE, Janet Elizabeth. b 64. Sheff Univ BMedSci87 St Jo Coll Dur BA92. Cranmer Hall Dur 93. **d** 93 **p** 94. Par Dn Stafford *Lich* 93-94; C 94-96; Chapl and Min Can Ely Cathl *Ely* 96-99; Dioc Communications Officer *Nor* from 99; Hon PV Nor Cathl from 00; Bp's Chapl from 01. *Bishop's House, Norwich NR3 1SB* Tel and fax (01603) 614172 *or* tel 880853 E-mail bishopschaplain@bishopofnorwich.org

MACFARLANE, William Angus. b 17. Worc Coll Ox BA39 MA43. Wycliffe Hall Ox 39. **d** 40 **p** 41. C Charles w Plymouth St Luke *Ex* 40-45; C Reading St Jo *Ox* 45-47; CMS Tr Coll Blackheath 47-48; C Brompton H Trin *Lon* 48-49; R Bighton *Win* 49-52; V Bishop's Sutton 49-52; V Southwold *St E* 52-59; V Plaistow St Mary *Roch* 59-71; V Bexleyheath Ch Ch 71-79; Perm to Offic *B & W* 79-95; Chapl Sandhill Park Hosp Taunton 80-87; rtd 82. *Moorlands, Blue Anchor, Minehead TA24 6JZ* Tel (01643) 821564

McFIE, Canon James Ian. b 28. Open Univ BA99. Lich Th Coll 59. **d** 61 **p** 62. C Salford St Phil w St Steph *Man* 61-65; V Hey 65-75; V Elton All SS 75-85; V Walmsley 85-95; AD Walmsley 85-95; Hon Can Man Cathl 90-95; rtd 95; Perm to Offic *Carl* from 95. *4 Devonshire Road, Millom LA18 4JF* Tel (01229) 775192

McGANITY, Steven. b 61. Nottm Univ BTh93. St Jo Coll Nottm 90. **d** 93 **p** 94. C Gateacre *Liv* 93-97; V Clubmoor from 97. *St Andrew's Vicarage, 176 Queen's Drive, West Derby, Liverpool L13 0AL* Tel 0151-226 1977 E-mail smcganity@bigfoot.com

McGARAHAN, Kevin Francis. b 51. Oak Hill Th Coll BA84 MA90. **d** 84 **p** 85. C Balderstone *Man* 84-87; C Stoughton *Guildf* 87-89; Par Lect Ashton St Mich *Man* 89-92; TV Madeley *Heref* 92-96; CF 96-99; TV Woughton *Ox* from 99. *The Vicarage, 5 Newport Road, Woolstones, Milton Keynes MK15 0AR* Tel (01908) 667611

McGEARY, Peter. b 59. K Coll Lon BD AKC. Chich Th Coll 84. **d** 86 **p** 87. C Brighton St Pet and St Nic w Chpl Royal *Chich* 86-90; C St Marylebone All SS *Lon* 90-95; P-in-c Hayes St Anselm 95-97; V 97-98; V St Geo-in-the-East St Mary from 98; PV Westmr Abbey from 00. *The Clergy House, All Saints Court, 68 Johnson Street, London E1 0BQ* Tel and fax (020) 7790 0973 E-mail mcgeary@pmcg.demon.co.uk

McGEE, Preb Peter John. b 36. Trin Coll Cam BA60 MA. Chich Th Coll 60. **d** 62 **p** 63. C N Keyham *Ex* 62-63; C St Marychurch 63-65; C Townstall w Dartmouth 65-68; C Cockington 68-71; V Exminster 71-78; V Alfington 78-82; V Ottery St Mary 78-82; RD Ottery 82-90; Preb Ex Cathl 82-97; TR Ottery St Mary, Alfington and W Hill 82-87; TR Ottery St Mary, Alfington, W Hill, Tipton etc 87-96; P-in-c Woodbury 96-97; rtd 97; Perm to Offic *Ex* from 97. *177 Exeter Road, Exmouth EX8 3DX* Tel (01395) 272279

McGEE, The Very Revd Stuart Irwin. b 30. TCD BA53 MA68. **d** 53 **p** 54. C Belfast St Simon *Conn* 53-55; Singapore 55-58; I Drumholm and Rossnowlagh *D & R* 58-65; CF 65-77; Dep Asst Chapl Gen 77-88; Can Achonry Cathl *T, K & A* 89-92; I Achonry w Tubbercurry and Killoran 89-92; Dean Elphin and Ardagh *K, E & A* 92-99; I Sligo w Knocknarea and Rosses Pt 92-99; rtd 99. *Teach na Mara, Strandhill, Sligo, Irish Republic* Tel (00353) (71) 916 8910

MacGEOCH, David John Lamont. b 64. Bath Univ BSc90 CQSW90. Westcott Ho Cam 97. **d** 99 **p** 00. C Midsomer Norton w Clandown *B & W* 99-03; V Puriton and Pawlett from 03. *The Vicarage, 1 The Rye, Puriton, Bridgwater TA7 8BZ* Tel (01278) 683500 E-mail all@macgeoch.fsnet.co.uk

McGHIE, Clinton Adolphus. b 44. Univ of W Indies. CA Tr Coll. **d** 78 **p** 79. Jamaica 78-96; Perm to Offic *Chelmsf* 96-97; P-in-c Highams Park All SS 97-02; V from 02. *All Saints' Vicarage, 12A Castle Avenue, London E4 9QD* Tel (020) 8527 3269

McGILL, Francis Leonard. b 31. **d** 93 **p** 94. NSM Howell Hill *Guildf* 93-01; Perm to Offic from 02. *27 Hampton Grove, Ewell, Epsom KT17 1LA* Tel (020) 8393 2226

MacGILLIVRAY, Canon Alexander Buchan. b 33. Edin Univ MA55 Aber Univ DipEd67. Edin Th Coll 55. **d** 57 **p** 58. Chapl St Ninian's Cathl Perth *St And* 57-59; Chapl Aberlour Orphanage 59-62; C Aberlour *Mor* 59-62; R Oldmeldrum *Ab* from 62; R Whiterashes from 62; R Fyvie and Insch 74-81; Can St Andr Cathl from 78. *The Rectory, Oldmeldrum, Inverurie AB51 0AD* Tel (01651) 872208

MacGILLIVRAY, Jonathan Martin. b 53. Aber Univ MA75. Coll of Resurr Mirfield. **d** 80 **p** 81. C Hulme Ascension *Man* 80-84; P-in-c Birch St Agnes 84-85; R 85-91; V Hurst 91-96; Chapl Tameside Gen Hosp 92-96; Dir of Ords and OLM Officer *Man* 96-02; V Carrington *S'well* from 02. *Carrington Vicarage, 6 Watcombe Circus, Nottingham NG5 2DT* Tel 0115-962 1291 E-mail j.macg@virgin.net

McGINLEY, Canon Jack Francis. b 36. ALCD65. **d** 65 **p** 66. C Erith St Paul *Roch* 65-70; C Morden *S'wark* 70-74; V New Catton Ch Ch *Nor* 74-94; RD Nor N 84-89; Hon Can Nor Cathl 90-94; R Carlton-in-the-Willows *S'well* 94-02; R Colwick 96-02; rtd 02; Perm to Offic *Nor* from 03. *14 Clovelly Drive, Norwich NR6 5EY* Tel (01603) 788848 E-mail jack.mcginley@talk21.com

McGINLEY, John Charles. b 69. Birm Univ BSocSc90. Trin Coll Bris BA96. **d** 96 **p** 97. C Hounslow H Trin w St Paul *Lon* 96-00; TV Hinckley H Trin *Leic* 00-04; TR from 04. *7 Rosemary Way, Hinckley LE10 0LN* Tel (01455) 446088 E-mail mcginley@globalnet.co.uk

McGIRR, Canon William Eric. b 43. CITC 68. **d** 71 **p** 72. C Carrickfergus *Conn* 71-74; C Mt Merrion *D & D* 74-77; I Donacavey w Barr *Clogh* 77-88; I Ballybeen *D & D* 88-94; I Magheraculmoney *Clogh* from 94; Can Clogh Cathl from 95. *The Rectory, Kesh, Enniskillen BT93 1TF* Tel (028) 6863 2221

McGLADDERY, David John. b 62. Homerton Coll Cam BEd85 Univ of Wales (Cardiff) MA93. St Mich Coll Llan 02. **d** 05. NSM Monmouth w Overmonnow etc *Mon* from 05; Asst Chapl Mon Sch from 05. *2 Kingswood Road, Monmouth NP25 5BX* Tel (01600) 715924

McGLASHAN, Alastair Robin. b 33. SAP90 Ch Ch Ox BA57 MA58 St Jo Coll Cam BA59 MA63. Ridley Hall Cam 58. **d** 60 **p** 61. C St Helens St Helen *Liv* 60; C Ormskirk 60-62; India 63-74; USA 74-75; C Lamorbey H Redeemer *Roch* 75-77; Chapl W Park Hosp Epsom 77-85; Chapl Maudsley Hosp Lon 85-87; Perm to Offic *S'wark* 86-04; rtd 98. *102 Westway, London SW20 9LS* Tel (020) 8542 2125

McGLINCHEY, Patrick Gerard. b 59. NUU BA82 Nottm Univ BTh95. St Jo Coll Nottm 93. **d** 95 **p** 96. C Kettering Ch the King *Pet* 95-97; C Gorleston St Andr *Nor* 97-02; Assoc Min Cliff Park Community Ch 99-02; Chapl and Dean of Res QUB from 03. *20 Elmwood Avenue, Belfast BT9 6AY* Tel (028) 9066 7754

McGONIGLE, Martin Leo Thomas. b 64. Univ of Greenwich BA94 Anglia Poly Univ MA99. EAMTC 96. **d** 98 **p** 99. C Forest Gate All SS and St Edm *Chelmsf* 98-01; Perm to Offic *Lon* 01-02; Chapl Asst Cen Man/Man Children's Univ Hosp NHS Trust 02-03; Lead Chapl from 03. *Chaplain's Office, Manchester Royal Infirmary, Oxford Road, Manchester M13 9WL* Tel 0161-276 8792 *or* 276 1234
E-mail martin.mcgonigle@cmmc.nhs.uk

McGONIGLE, Thomas. b 22. TCD BA45 MA65. TCD Div Sch 43. **d** 46 **p** 47. C Drumglass *Arm* 46-50; I Clogherny 50-53; I Magherafelt 53-61 and 74-88; I Portadown St Mark 61-74; Can Arm Cathl 72-88; Treas 79-83; Chan 83-88; Prec 88; rtd 88; Lic to Offic *Arm* from 88. *91 Kernan Gardens, Portadown, Craigavon BT63 5RA* Tel (028) 3833 0892

McGOWAN, Anthony Charles. b 57. Jes Coll Cam BA79 MA83. Coll of Resurr Mirfield 80. **d** 82 **p** 83. C Milford Haven *St D* 82-85; C Penistone and Thurlstone *Wakef* 85-88; CR 88-91; Asst Chapl Radcliffe Infirmary Ox 91-94; Chapl Ox Radcliffe Hosps NHS Trust 94-04; V Northampton H Trin and St Paul *Pet* from 05. *The Vicarage, 24 Edinburgh Road, Northampton NN2 6PH* Tel (01604) 711468

McGOWAN, Daniel Richard Hugh. b 71. Oak Hill Th Coll. **d** 03 **p** 04. C Peterlee *Dur* from 03. *59 O'Neill Drive, Peterlee SR8 5UD* Tel 0191-527 0287

McGOWN, Robert Jackson. b 20. Keble Coll Ox BA42 MA46. Linc Th Coll 42. **d** 45 **p** 46. C Ipswich St Mary le Tower *St E* 45-47; Chapl Brockhurst Sch 47-49; Perm to Offic *Ox* 49-50; C Astbury *Ches* 50-51; C Glouc St Mary de Lode and St Nic *Glouc* 51-54; Min Can Glouc Cathl 51-54; C W Kirby St Bridget *Ches* 64-71; Perm to Offic from 76; rtd 85. *16 Church Road, West Kirby, Wirral CH48 0RW* Tel 0151-625 9481

McGRANAGHAN, Patrick Joseph Colum. b 46. Glas Univ BSc68 Lanc Univ MA72. St Alb Minl Tr Scheme 82. **d** 85 **p** 86. NSM Markyate Street *St Alb* 85-91; NSM Johnstone *Glas* 91-99; NSM Renfrew 97-99; P-in-c Kilmacolm from 99; P-in-c Bridge of Weir from 99. *The Rectory, 4 Balmore Court, Kilmacolm PA13 4LX* Tel (01505) 872733 *or* tel and fax 872961 Mobile 07932-643893 E-mail colum.mcgranaghan@talk21.com

McGRATH, Prof Alister Edgar. b 53. Wadh Coll Ox BA75 Mert Coll Ox MA78 DPhil78 BD83 DD01. Westcott Ho Cam 78. **d** 80 **p** 81. C Wollaton *S'well* 80-83; Chapl St Hilda's Coll Ox 83-87; Tutor Wycliffe Hall Ox from 83; Prin 95-04; Prof Systematic Th Regent Coll Vancouver 93-97; Research Lect in Th Ox Univ 93-99; Prof Hist Th from 99; Dir Ox Cen for Evang and Apologetics from 04. *Wycliffe Hall, 54 Banbury Road, Oxford OX2 6PW* Tel (01865) 274200 Fax 274215

McGRATH, Gavin John. b 53. Marietta Coll (USA) BA76 Trin Episc Sch for Min MDiv81 Dur Univ PhD90. **d** 81 **p** 82. USA 81-87 and from 99; Assoc Th Prof Trin Episc Sch for Min Ambridge from 99; C Fulwood *Sheff* 87-95. *412 Little Street, Sewickley, PA 15143, USA* Tel (001) (412) 259 6446 *or* (724) 266 3838 ext 203 E-mail gavinmcgrath@tesm.edu

McGRATH, Ian Denver. b 47. Leeds Univ CertEd72. LNSM course 85. **d** 87 **p** 88. OLM Ancaster *Linc* 87-89; OLM Ancaster Wilsford Gp 89-92; C Spilsby w Hundleby 92-95; P-in-c Asterby Gp 95-99; R from 99. *The Rectory, 6 Simons Close, Donington-on-Bain, Louth LN11 9TX* Tel and fax (01507) 343345
E-mail ian@idmcgrath.fsnet.co.uk

McGRATH, John. b 49. Salford Univ BSc78 Man Poly CertEd79. N Ord Course 82. **d** 85 **p** 86. C Horwich *Man* 85-88; P-in-c Hillock 88-89; V 89-94; V York St Luke *York* 94-97; V Hollinwood *Man* 97-02; P-in-c Oldham St Chad Limeside 97-02; V Hollinwood and Limeside 02-03; TV Turton Moorland Min from 03. *Walmsley Vicarage, Blackburn Road, Bolton BL7 9RZ* Tel (01204) 304283

McGRATH, Kenneth David. b 59. Surrey Univ BSc82 QUB PGCE83 TCD BTh03. CITC 00. **d** 03 **p** 04. C Lisburn Ch Ch Cathl *Conn* from 03. *82 Thornleigh Drive, Lisburn BT28 2DS* Tel (028) 9267 6499 E-mail revken.mcgrath@btopenworld.com

McGRATH, Patrick Desmond. b 64. Liv Univ LLB86. Wycliffe Hall Ox 92. **d** 96 **p** 97. C Netherton *Liv* 96-98; C Ravenhead 98-02; P-in-c Ightham *Roch* from 02. *The Rectory, Bates Hill, Ightham, Sevenoaks TN15 9BG* Tel (01732) 884176

MacGREGOR, Alan John. b 31. Jes Coll Ox MA57 Lon Univ DBRS61 Lon Inst of Educn DipRE71. S Tr Scheme 94. **d** 97 **p** 98. NSM Worting *Win* 97-00; Perm to Offic *Lon* 01 and *Sarum* from 03. *7 Sterte Avenue, Poole BH15 2AJ* Tel (01202) 667267

McGREGOR, Alistair Darrant. b 45. ALCD69. **d** 69 **p** 70. C Streatham Immanuel w St Anselm *S'wark* 69-73; Bermuda 73-76; Warden St Mich Cen New Cross 76-80; C Hatcham St Jas *S'wark* 76-80; V Nor Heartsease St Fran *Nor* 80-87; TR Thetford 87-96; P-in-c Kilverstone 87-90; P-in-c Croxton 87-90; RD Thetford and Rockland 90-95; TR Gt Baddow *Chelmsf* from 96. *The Rectory, 12 Church Street, Great Baddow, Chelmsford CM2 7HZ* Tel (01245) 471740
E-mail amcgregor@care4free.net

MacGREGOR, Colin Highmoor. b 19. Lon Univ BSc45 Magd Coll Cam BA47 MA50. Wells Th Coll 54. **d** 56 **p** 57. C Camberwell St Giles *S'wark* 56-60; V Clapham St Pet 60-73; V Riddlesdown 73-87; rtd 87. *Flat 3, Longacre Court, 21 Mayfield Road, South Croydon CR2 0BG* Tel (020) 8651 2615

MacGREGOR, Donald Alexander Thomson. b 52. Loughb Univ BSc75 Nottm Univ MA97 Leic Univ CertEd78. St Jo Coll Nottm 91. **d** 93 **p** 94. C Walmley *Birm* 93-96; C Braunstone *Leic* 96-97; TV 97-99; Chapl Loughb Univ 99-04; V Fishguard w Llanychar and Pontfaen w Morfil etc *St D* from 04. *The Vicarage, High Street, Fishguard SA65 9AU* Tel (01348) 872895
E-mail don@macgregors.wanadoo.co.uk

McGREGOR, Mrs Lynn. b 61. Chester Coll of HE BTh00. N Ord Course 97. **d** 00 **p** 01. C Colne and Villages *Blackb* 00-03; C Gt Harwood St Bart from 03; C Gt Harwood St Jo from 03. *3 Bostons, Great Harwood, Blackburn BB6 7HJ* Tel (01254) 889284 Mobile 07944-801952
E-mail ian.mcgregor@homecall.co.uk

MacGREGOR, Preb Neil. b 35. Keble Coll Ox BA60 MA80. Wells Th Coll. **d** 65 **p** 66. C Bath Bathwick St Mary w Woolley *B & W* 65-70; R Oare w Culbone 70-74; C Lynton, Brendon, Countisbury and Lynmouth *Ex* 70-74; P-in-c Kenn w Kingston Seymour *B & W* 74-76; R 76-80; R Wem and V Lee Brockhurst *Lich* 80-01; P-in-c Loppington w Newtown 95-01; RD Wem and Whitchurch 95-01; Preb Lich Cathl 97-01; rtd 01; Perm to Offic *Heref* from 01. *19 Castle View Terrace, Ludlow SY8 2NG* Tel (01584) 872671 E-mail juvenal@martial.fsnet.co.uk

McGREGOR, Nigel Selwyn. b 47. FCA69. Sarum & Wells Th Coll 87. **d** 89 **p** 90. C Charlton Kings St Mary *Glouc* 89-92; P-in-c Seale *Guildf* 92-95; P-in-c Puttenham and Wanborough 92-95; R Seale, Puttenham and Wanborough 95-04; R Barming *Roch* from 04. *The Rectory, Church Lane, Barming, Maidstone ME16 9HA* Tel (01622) 726263 E-mail mcgregorn@aol.com

McGREGOR, Stephen Paul. b 55. **d** 03 **p** 04. OLM Tonge Fold *Man* from 03. *32 Rawcliffe Avenue, Bolton BL2 6JX* Tel (01204) 391205 E-mail steve.mcgregor2@ntlworld.com

McGUFFIE, Duncan Stuart. b 45. Man Univ MA70 Regent's Park Coll Ox DPhil80. S Dios Minl Tr Scheme 84. **d** 85 **p** 85. C Sholing *Win* 85-89; V Clavering and Langley w Arkesden etc *Chelmsf* from 89. *The Vicarage, 54 Pelham Road, Clavering, Saffron Walden CB11 4PQ* Tel (01799) 550703

McGUINNESS, Gordon Baxter. b 57. St Andr Univ BSc79 BNC Ox MSc80. Oak Hill NSM Course 86. **d** 89 **p** 90. NSM Loudwater *Ox* 89-92; C Chilwell *S'well* 92-01; TR Ellesmere Port *Ches* from 01. *The Rectory, Vale Road, Whitby, Ellesmere Port CH65 9AY* Tel 0151-355 2516 *or* 356 8351
E-mail rev@gordon239.freeserve.co.uk

McGUIRE, Alec John. b 51. K Coll Cam BA73 MA76 Societas Liturgica 85 MRSH86 FRSH90. Westcott Ho Cam 74. **d** 78 **p** 79. C Hungerford and Denford *Ox* 78-81; Prec Leeds St Pet *Ripon* 81-86; Perm to Offic from 86; rtd 01. *34 Gledhow Wood Road, Leeds LS8 4BZ* Tel 0113-240 0336

McGUIRE, John. b 31. Oak Hill Th Coll 59. **d** 62 **p** 65. C Tooting Graveney St Nic *S'wark* 62-64; C Normanton *Derby* 64-67; N Area Sec ICM 67-71; Chapl RNR 67-81; R Biddulph Moor *Lich* 71-00; rtd 00; Perm to Offic *Blackb* from 00. *25 Victoria Road, Fulwood, Preston PR2 8NE* Tel (01772) 719549
E-mail jmcguire@argonet.co.uk

MACHA, David. b 65. Keele Univ BA88 CertEd88 St Jo Coll Dur BA97. **d** 97 **p** 98. C Loughborough Em and St Mary in Charnwood *Leic* 97-01; CMS from 01; Tanzania from 02. *St Margaret's Church, PO Box 306, Moshi, Tanzania*
E-mail david@dmacha.idps.co.uk

McHAFFIE, Alistair. b 57. Oak Hill Th Coll DipHE94. **d** 94 **p** 95. C Braintree *Chelmsf* 94-98; R Falkland Is 98-03; V Leyland St Jo *Blackb* from 03. *St John's Vicarage, Leyland Lane, Leyland PR25 1XB* Tel (01772) 621646 E-mail alistair@mchaffie.com

MACHAM, Miss Anna. b 77. Trin Coll Ox BA98 Cam Univ BA02. Ridley Hall Cam 00. **d** 04 **p** 05. C Cheshunt *St Alb* from 04. *2 Barley Court, 44 Bury Green Road, Cheshunt, Waltham Cross EN7 5AG* Tel (01992) 633872
E-mail annamacham@hotmail.com

McHARDY, David William. b 61. Aber Coll of Educn DCE82 Edin Univ BD88 BD90 Strathclyde Univ Additional Teaching Qualification94 Edin Univ PhD97. Ab Dioc Tr Course 82 Edin Th Coll 85. **d** 88. C Dumfries *Glas* 88-89; Lect in World Religions Open Univ from 97; Hon C Oldmeldrum *Ab* from 99. *17 Kirkhill View, Blackburn, Aberdeen AB21 0XX* Tel (01224) 791758 *or* (01467) 621655 Mobile 07855-581714 Fax (01467) 624425
E-mail cincture@aol.com

MACHELL, Leigh Douglas. b 64. Leic Poly BSc85. St Jo Coll Nottm MTh03. **d** 03 **p** 04. C Beoley *Worc* from 03. *4 Marshfield Close, Redditch B98 8RW* Tel (01527) 60457 Mobile 07939-203787 E-mail rev.leigh@ntlworld.com

MACHIN, Roy Anthony. b 38. BA79. Oak Hill Th Coll 76. **d** 79 **p** 80. C Halliwell St Pet *Man* 79-83; V Eccleston St Luke *Liv*

83-91; V Kendal St Thos and Crook *Carl* 91-99; V Wigan St Barn Marsh Green *Liv* 99-03; rtd 03. *56 Ferndown Road, Harwood, Bolton BL2 3NN* Tel (01204) 362220 Fax as telephone E-mail roy.machin@btinternet.com

McHUGH, Brian Robert. b 50. York Univ BA72 Keele Univ CertEd73 Southn Univ Cert Eur Studies 78 Portsm Poly Cert Computing 84 DPSE90 IEng92 MIMA98 CMath98. S Dios Minl Tr Scheme 79. **d** 82 **p** 83. NSM Sarisbury *Portsm* 82-86; NSM Shedfield from 86. *28 Siskin Close, Bishops Waltham, Southampton SO32 1RQ* Tel (01489) 896658 E-mail brian.mchugh@bcs.org.uk *or* mchughb@tauntons.ac.uk

McILROY, Sister Honor Margaret. b 24. LRAM44 GRSM45. **d** 98 **p** 99. CSMV from 98. *St Mary's Convent, Challow Road, Wantage OX12 9DJ* Tel (01235) 763141 E-mail sisterscsmv@btinternet.com

MACINNES, Canon David Rennie. b 32. Jes Coll Cam BA55 MA59. Ridley Hall Cam 55. **d** 57 **p** 58. C Gillingham St Mark *Roch* 57-61; C St Helen Bishopsgate w St Martin Outwich *Lon* 61-67; Prec Birm Cathl *Birm* 67-78; Angl Adv ATV 67-82; Angl Adv Cen TV 82-93; Dioc Missr *Birm* 79-87; Hon Can Birm Cathl 81-87; R Ox St Aldate w St Matt *Ox* 87-94; R Ox St Aldate 95-02; Hon Can Ch Ch 98-02; rtd 02. *Pear Tree Cottage, Milcombe, Banbury OX15 4RS* Tel (01295) 721119

MacINNES, Harry Campbell. b 67. Nottm Poly BA89. Wycliffe Hall Ox BTh94. **d** 97 **p** 98. C E Twickenham St Steph *Lon* 97-00; P-in-c St Margaret's-on-Thames 00-04; R Shill Valley and Broadshire *Ox* from 04. *The Rectory, Church Lane, Shilton, Burford OX18 4AE* Tel (01993) 845954

MACINTOSH, Andrew Alexander. b 36. St Jo Coll Cam BA59 MA63 BD80 DD97. Ridley Hall Cam 60. **d** 62 **p** 63. C S Ormsby Gp *Linc* 62-64; Lect St D Coll Lamp 64-67; Lic to Offic *Ely* from 67; Chapl St Jo Coll Cam 67-69; Asst Dean 69-79; Dean 79-02; Lect Th from 70; Pres 95-99. *St John's College, Cambridge CB2 1TP* Tel (01223) 338709 E-mail aam1003@cus.cam.ac.uk

McINTOSH, Andrew Malcolm Ashwell. b 43. Chich Th Coll 67. **d** 70 **p** 71. C Brentwood St Thos *Chelmsf* 70-74; C Chingford SS Pet and Paul 74-79; P-in-c Maldon St Mary w Mundon 79-83; R from 83. *St Mary's Rectory, Park Drive, Maldon CM9 7JG* Tel (01621) 857191

MacINTOSH, Canon George Grant. b 41. St Jo Coll Dur BA75. **d** 76 **p** 77. C Ecclesall *Sheff* 76-79; Hon C Sheff St Oswald 79-81; Research Fell Sheff Univ 79-81; Dioc Adult Educn Officer 81-88; V Crookes St Tim 81-88; V Abbeydale St Jo 88-97; RD Ecclesall 89-94; P-in-c Turriff *Ab* from 97; P-in-c Cuminestown from 97; Can St Andr Cathl from 01. *The Rectory, 9 Deveron Road, Turriff AB53 4BB* Tel and fax (01888) 563238 Mobile 07974-748080 E-mail gmacintosh@onetel.com

McINTOSH, Ian MacDonald. b 64. Jes Coll Cam BA86. Trin Coll Bris BA90. **d** 90 **p** 91. C Belmont *Lon* 90-92; C Pinner 92-95; Chapl Leic Univ *Leic* 96-02; TV Leic H Spirit 96-02; Co-ord Reader Tr 00-02; Dir Cen for Ecum Studies Westcott Ho Cam 02-04; C Milton Ernest, Pavenham and Thurleigh *St Alb* from 02; RD Sharnbrook from 04. *The Vicarage, Thurleigh Road, Milton Ernest, Bedford MK44 1RF* Tel (01234) 822885 E-mail vicarage@fish.co.uk

McINTOSH, Mrs Nicola Ann. b 60. Trin Coll Bris DipHE89. **d** 90 **p** 94. Par Dn Queensbury All SS *Lon* 90-93; Par Dn Ruislip Manor St Paul 93-94; C 94-95; NSM Clarendon Park St Jo w Knighton St Mich *Leic* 96-02; Asst Dioc Dir of Ords 00-02; V Milton Ernest, Pavenham and Thurleigh *St Alb* from 02. *The Vicarage, Thurleigh Road, Milton Ernest, Bedford MK44 1RF* Tel (01234) 822885 E-mail vicarage@fish.co.uk

McINTYRE, Robert Mark. b 69. Nottm Univ BA91. Coll of Resurr Mirfield 92. **d** 94 **p** 95. C Wednesbury St Jas and St Jo *Lich* 94-97; TV Wolstanton from 97. *14 Dorrington Grove, Porthill, Newcastle ST5 0HY* Tel (01782) 715001 E-mail m-mcintyre@netlineuk.net

McINTYRE DE ROMERO, Ms Iris Evelyn. b 60. Worc Coll Ox BA82 MA90. St Steph Ho Ox 82. **dss** 84 **d** 87 **p** 97. Southbroom *Sarum* 84-86; Oakdale 86-88; Par Dn 87-88; Par Dn Ireland Wood *Ripon* 88-89; Area Co-ord (NW) Chr Aid 92-94; Hon C W Derby St Mary *Liv* 94-98; R Bangor Monachorum and Worthenbury *St As* 98-03; Chapl HM Pris Brockhill from 03. *HM Prison and YOI, Brockhill, Redditch B97 6RD* Tel (01527) 552650 E-mail iris.marco@virgin.net

MACK, Mrs Gillian Frances. b 50. SCM72. Cant Sch of Min 84. **d** 87 **p** 94. NSM Deal St Geo *Cant* 87-88; NSM Deal St Leon and St Rich and Sholden 88-92; Par Dn 93-94; C 94-97; rtd 97; Perm to Offic *Cant* from 97; Hon Chapl Cautley Trust from 98. *4 Palmbeach Avenue, Hythe CT21 6NH* Tel (01303) 268523 E-mail gill.mack@tesco.net

McKAE, William John. b 42. Liv Univ BSc63 St Mark & St Jo Coll Lon PGCE64 Bris Univ DipTh70. Wells Th Coll 68. **d** 71 **p** 72. C Tranmere St Paul w St Luke *Ches* 71-74; C Midsomer Norton *B & W* 74-75; TV Birkenhead Priory *Ches* 75-80; R Oughtrington 80-91; Chapl Asst Hope, Salford R and Ladywell Hosps Man 91-92; Lic Preacher *Man* 91-92; R Heaton Reddish from 92. *The Rectory, 8 St Mary's Drive, Stockport SK5 7AX* Tel 0161-477 6702

MACKARILL, Ian David. b 54. FIBMS86. NEOC 01. **d** 04 **p** 05. NSM Waggoners *York* from 04. *The Old Farmhouse, Fridaythorpe, Driffield YO25 9RT* Tel (01377) 288369 Fax 288459 Mobile 07730-314093 E-mail ianmackarill@btconnect.com

McKAVANAGH, Dermot James. b 51. TCD BA75 MA78 K Coll Lon BD78 AKC78. **d** 78 **p** 79. C Croydon H Sav *Cant* 78-82; Asst Chapl Wellington Coll Berks 82-87; Chapl RAF 87-00; rtd 02. *42 Freshfields, Lea, Preston PR2 1TJ*

McKAY, Brian Andrew. b 39. Sarum Th Coll 69. **d** 71 **p** 72. C Walker *Newc* 71-74; C Wooler Gp 74-77; TV 77-81; V Long Benton St Mary 81-89; TV Bellingham/Otterburn Gp 89-91; TV N Tyne and Redesdale 91-02; rtd 02. *26 Punchards Down, Totnes TQ9 5FB* Tel (01803) 840675

MACKAY, Canon Douglas Brysson. b 27. Edin Th Coll 56. **d** 58 **p** 59. Prec St Andr Cathl Inverness *Mor* 58-61; P-in-c Fochabers 61-70; R 70-72; Chapl Aberlour Orphanage 64-67; P-in-c Aberlour 64-72; Syn Clerk 65-72; Can St Andr Cathl Inverness 65-72; Hon Can 72; R Carnoustie *Bre* 72-98; Can St Paul's Cathl Dundee 81-97; Hon Can from 98; Syn Clerk 81-97; rtd 97; Tutor Dundee Univ *Bre* from 97; Chapl St Paul's Cathl Dundee from 99. *24 Philip Street, Carnoustie DD7 6ED*

MACKAY, Hedley Neill. b 27. St Aid Birkenhead 53. **d** 56 **p** 57. C Beverley St Mary *York* 56-59; C Scarborough St Mary 59-60; Nigeria 61-70; C Wawne *York* 70-71; TV Sutton St Jas and Wawne 72-76; V Huntington 76-82; TR 82-93; rtd 93; Perm to Offic *York* from 93; Rtd Clergy and Widows Officer (York Adnry) 94-98. *2 Elmfield Terrace, Heworth, York YO31 1EH* Tel (01904) 412971

McKAY, John Andrew. b 38. HDipEd. Chich Th Coll. **d** 74 **p** 75. C Primrose Hill St Mary w Avenue Road St Paul *Lon* 74-77; V Battersea Ch Ch and St Steph *S'wark* 77-82; I Rathkeale w Askeaton and Kilcornan *L & K* 82-85; I Dublin St Bart w Leeson Park *D & G* 85-00; Chapl Venice w Trieste *Eur* 00-03; rtd 03; Chapl Dublin Sandymount *D & G* from 05. *5 St Peter's Place, Drogheda, Co Louth, Irish Republic* Tel (00353) (41) 987 3277

McKAY, Margaret McLeish. *See* HALE, Mrs Margaret McLeish

MACKAY, Neill. *See* MACKAY, Hedley Neill

MACKAY, Paul Douglas. b 60. Trin Coll Bris. **d** 00 **p** 01. C Becontree St Mary *Chelmsf* 00-03; V Mile Cross *Nor* from 03. *St Catherine's Vicarage, Aylsham Road, Norwich NR3 2RJ* Tel (01603) 426767 E-mail mackay@fish.co.uk

MACKAY, Rupert. b 61. Oak Hill Th Coll BA00. **d** 00 **p** 01. C Knutsford St Jo and Toft *Ches* 00-04; Min Hadley Wood St Paul Prop Chpl *Lon* from 04. *34 Crescent East, Barnet EN4 0EN* Tel and fax (020) 8449 2572 E-mail rupmac@mac.com

McKEACHIE, The Very Revd William Noble. b 43. Univ of the South (USA) BA66. Trin Coll Toronto STB70. **d** 70 **p** 70. Asst Chapl St Jo Coll Ox 70-72; Dioc Th Toronto Canada 73-78; USA from 78; Dir Ch Relns and Tutor Univ of the South 78-80; R Baltimore St Paul 81-95; Dean S Carolina and R Charleston Cathl from 95. *126 Coming Street, Charleston, SC 29403, USA* Tel (001) (843) 722 7345 Fax 722 2105 E-mail cathchlp@dycon.com

McKEARNEY, Andrew Richard. b 57. Selw Coll Cam MA. Edin Th Coll 81. **d** 82 **p** 83. Prec St Ninian's Cathl Perth *St And* 82-84; Chapl St Mary's Cathl *Edin* 84-88; R Hardwick *Ely* 88-94; R Toft w Caldecote and Childerley 88-94; V Chesterton Gd Shep from 94. *The Good Shepherd Vicarage, 51 Highworth Avenue, Cambridge CB4 2BQ* Tel (01223) 351844 *or* 312933 E-mail theophan@surfaid.org

McKECHNIE, John Gregg. b 30. Em Coll Cam BA54 MA57. Ridley Hall Cam 54. **d** 55 **p** 56. C Morden *S'wark* 55-57; Tutor Clifton Th Coll 57-62; R Chich St Pancras and St Jo *Chich* 62-68; V Reading St Jo *Ox* 68-85; RD Reading 83-85; V Lindfield *Chich* 85-95; rtd 95; Perm to Offic *Chich* from 95. *3 The Courtyard, Stockbridge Road, Chichester PO19 8GP* Tel (01243) 531703

McKEE, Douglas John Dunstan. b 34. Univ of W Aus BA65. St Mich Th Coll Crafers 54. **d** 57 **p** 58. Australia 57-72 and from 85; SSM from 58; Lic to Offic *S'well* 73-85. *St John's Priory, 14 St John Street, Adelaide, South Australia 5000* Tel (0061) (8) 8223 1014 *or* 8416 8445 Fax (0061) (8) 8223 2764 *or* 8416 8450 E-mail dunstan.mckee@flinders.edu.au

McKEE, Patrick Joseph. b 49. Ripon Coll Cuddesdon DipMin94. **d** 94 **p** 95. C Oakham, Hambleton, Egleton, Braunston and Brooke *Pet* 94-97; V Ryhall w Essendine and Carlby from 97. *The Vicarage, Church Street, Ryhall, Stamford PE9 4HR* Tel (01780) 762398 E-mail pmkee@ryhall.clara.co.uk

McKEEMAN, David Christopher. b 36. AKC58 DipEd76. **d** 60 **p** 61. C Catford St Andr *S'wark* 60-64; P-in-c W Dulwich Em 64-69; Lic to Offic *Win* 70-82; R Silchester 82-01; rtd 01; Perm to Offic *Heref* from 01. *The Maltings, Woodend Lane, Stoke Lacy, Bromyard HR7 4HQ* Tel (01885) 490705 E-mail david.mckeeman@ntlworld.com

McKEGNEY, Canon John Wade. b 47. TCD BA70 MA81. CITC 70. **d** 72 **p** 73. C Ballynafeigh St Jude *D & D* 72-75; C Bangor St Comgall 75-80; I Drumgath w Drumgooland and Clonduff

80-83; I Gilnahirk 83-90; I Arm St Mark *Arm* from 90; Can Arm Cathl from 01. *St Mark's Rectory, 14 Portadown Road, Armagh BT61 9EE* Tel and fax (028) 3752 2970 *or* 3197 E-mail john.mckegney@virgin.net *or* armagh@armagh.anglican.org

MacKEITH (née GODFREY), Mrs Ann Veronica. b 35. Bris Univ BSc57 CertEd. Gilmore Course 78. **dss** 79 **d** 87 **p** 94. Bishopwearmouth Ch Ch *Dur* 79-83; Bishopwearmouth St Gabr 83-86; Ryhope 86-88; Par Dn 87-88; Par Dn Darlington H Trin 88-94; C 94-95; Family Life Officer 95-97; rtd 98. *135 Hummersknott Avenue, Darlington DL3 8RR* Tel (01325) 463481 E-mail annmackeith@webportal.co.uk

McKELLAR, John Lorne. b 19. Sarum Th Coll 70. **d** 72 **p** 73. C Warminster St Denys *Sarum* 72-75; USA 75-79 and 81-84; P-in-c Colchester St Barn *Chelmsf* 79-81; rtd 84; Perm to Offic *Sarum* from 84. *Corrie, 105A Clay Street, Crockerton, Warminster BA12 8AG* Tel (01985) 213161

McKELLEN, Pamela Joyce. b 47. Homerton Coll Cam TCert69 BEd70. Cranmer Hall Dur 01. **d** 02 **p** 03. C Ox St Matt *Ox* 02-04; P-in-c Radley and Sunningwell from 04. *The Vicarage, Kennington Road, Radley, Abingdon OX14 2JN* Tel (01235) 554739 E-mail pjmck@compuserve.com

McKELVEY, Mrs Jane Lilian. b 48. Liv Inst of Educn BA94. Nor Bapt Coll 94. **d** 97 **p** 98. C Aughton St Mich *Liv* 97-01; TV Gateacre from 01. *St Mark's Vicarage, Cranwell Road, Liverpool L25 1NZ* Tel 0151-487 9634

McKELVEY, The Very Revd Robert Samuel James Houston. b 42. QVRM00 TD. QUB BA65 MA(Ed)88 Garrett-Evang Th Sem DMin93. CITC 67. **d** 67 **p** 68. C Dunmurry *Conn* 67-70; CF (TAVR) 70-99; P-in-c Kilmakee *Conn* 70-77; I 77-81; Sec Gen Syn Bd of Educn (N Ireland) 81-01; Preb Newcastle St Patr Cathl Dublin 89-01; Dean Belf from 01. *Belfast Cathedral, Donegal Street, Belfast BT1 2HB* Tel (028) 9032 8332 *or* 9066 0980 Fax 9023 8855 E-mail dean@belfastcathedral.org

McKEMEY, Canon Robert. b 15. St Aid Birkenhead 50. **d** 52 **p** 53. C Blackb Ch Ch *Blackb* 52-53; PC Blackb St Barn 53-57; Schs Supervisor Kenya 57-64; Adn Nakuru 64-69; I Kilrea *D & R* 69-73; R Meysey Hampton w Marston Meysey *Glouc* 73-81; RD Fairford 77-81; I Clondevaddock *D & R* 81-85; rtd 85. *c/o Dr K McKemey, 14 Andrews Road, Earley, Reading RG6 7PJ* Tel 0118-9264 4281

McKENDREY, Susan. b 55. **d** 02 **p** 03. NSM Allonby *Carl* 02-03; NSM Cross Canonby 02-03; NSM Dearham 02-03; NSM Allonby, Cross Canonby and Dearham from 03. *14 Ghyll Bank, Little Broughton, Cockermouth CA13 0LJ* E-mail revdsusan.mckendrey@virgin.net

MACKENNA, Christopher. *See* MACKENNA, Robert Christopher Douglass

McKENNA, Dermot William. b 41. TCD BA63 MA66. CITC 64. **d** 64 **p** 65. C Enniscorthy *C & O* 64-66; I Killeshin 66-84; rtd 84. *20 Sherwood, Pollerton, Carlow, Irish Republic* Tel (00353) (59) 913 0915 E-mail mckenna@itcarlow.ie

McKENNA, Lindsay Taylor. b 62. Glas Univ MA83 Aber Univ BD86. Edin Th Coll 87. **d** 87 **p** 88. C Broughty Ferry *Bre* 87-90; C Wantage *Ox* 90-93; V Illingworth *Wakef* 93-99; Dir CARA 99-02; V Hanworth All SS *Lon* from 02. *All Saints' Vicarage, Uxbridge Road, Feltham TW13 5EE* Tel (020) 8894 9330 E-mail macdolly@blueyonder.co.uk

MACKENNA, Richard William. b 49. Pemb Coll Cam BA71 MA75. Ripon Coll Cuddesdon BA77 MA81. **d** 78 **p** 79. C Fulham St Dionis Parson's Green *Lon* 78-81; C Paddington St Jas 81-85; Tutor Westcott Ho Cam 85-89; V Kingston All SS w St Jo *S'wark* 90-91; Perm to Offic *S'wark* 94-01 and *Nor* 99-04. *Flat 5, 11 Grassington Road, Eastbourne BN20 7BJ* Tel (01323) 730477

MACKENNA, Robert Christopher Douglass. b 44. Oriel Coll Ox BA72 MA75 MBAP85. Cuddesdon Coll 71. **d** 73 **p** 74. C Farncombe *Guildf* 73-77; C Tattenham Corner and Burgh Heath 77-80; P-in-c Hascombe 80-90; R 90-00; RD Godalming 91-96; Hon Can Guildf Cathl 99-00; Dir St Marylebone Healing and Counselling Cen from 00; NSM St Marylebone w H Trin *Lon* from 00. *Flat 5, 38 Nottingham Place, London W1U 5NU* Tel (020) 7486 9363 *or* 7935 5066 Fax 7486 5493 E-mail cmackenna@stmarylebone.org

MACKENZIE, Alfred Arthur. b 25. Bps' Coll Cheshunt 61. **d** 61 **p** 62. C Waltham Abbey *Chelmsf* 61-64; V Barking St Erkenwald 64-72; V Broomfield 72-83; P-in-c Willerby w Ganton and Folkton *York* 83-91; R 91-95; rtd 95; Perm to Offic *Linc* 96-99. *7 Lovett Street, Cleethorpes DN35 7BJ* Tel 07791-864393 (mobile)

MACKENZIE, Andrew John Kett. b 46. Southn Univ BA68. LNSM course 88 Guildf Dioc Min Course 98. **d** 91 **p** 92. Fullbrook Sch New Haw 76-99; OLM Woodham *Guildf* 91-99; C Aldershot St Mich from 99. *Ascension House, Ayling Hill, Aldershot GU11 3LL* Tel and fax (01252) 330224 Mobile 07703-983312 E-mail andrew.mackenzie1@ntlworld.com

MACKENZIE, Miss Ann. b 54. CertEd76 DipHE82 DPS86. Trin Coll Bris 82. **dss** 85 **d** 87 **p** 94. Normanton *Wakef* 85-90; Par Dn 87-90; Par Dn Bletchley *Ox* 90-94; C 94-98; TV W Swindon and the Lydiards *Bris* 98-04; P-in-c E Springfield *Chelmsf* from 04. *The Vicarage, Ashton Place, Chelmsford CM2 6ST* Tel (01245) 462387 E-mail annmackenzie@tregoze.fsnet.co.uk

McKENZIE, Mrs Ann Elizabeth. b 45. Leic Univ BA67 PGCE68. STETS 95. **d** 98 **p** 99. NSM Appleshaw, Kimpton, Thruxton, Fyfield etc *Win* from 98. *The Post House, Thruxton, Andover SP11 8LZ* Tel (01264) 772788 E-mail ann.mckenzie@tinyonline.co.uk

McKENZIE, Cilla. *See* McKENZIE, Mrs Priscilla Ann

MACKENZIE, David Stuart. b 45. Open Univ BA95 FRSA00. Linc Th Coll 66. **d** 69 **p** 70. C Bishopwearmouth St Mary V w St Pet CD *Dur* 69-72; C Pontefract St Giles *Wakef* 72-74; Chapl RAF 74-02; Chapl OHP from 02; QHC from 00; RD Whitby *York* from 04. *St Hilda's Priory, Sneaton Castle, Whitby YO21 3QN* Tel (01947) 602079 Fax 820854 E-mail ohppriorywhitby@btinternet.com

MACKENZIE, Duncan. *See* MACKENZIE, Preb Lawrence Duncan

McKENZIE, Ian Colin. b 31. CA56. EMMTC 89. **d** 93. NSM Edin St Mark and Edin St Andr and St Aid *Edin* 93-94; Perm to Offic *S'well* from 01. *21 Crafts Way, Southwell NG25 0BL* Tel (01636) 815755

MACKENZIE, Ian William (Bill). b 46. Trin Coll Bris DipHE95. **d** 95 **p** 96. C Bideford *Ex* 95-96; C Bideford, Northam, Westward Ho!, Appledore etc 96-99; TV Littleham w Exmouth from 99. *The Vicarage, 96 Littleham Road, Littleham, Exmouth EX8 2RD* Tel (01395) 275085

McKENZIE, Jack Llewellyn. b 29. FRSH AMIEHO MAMIT. S'wark Ord Course. **d** 79 **p** 80. Hon C Stonebridge St Mich *Lon* 79-88; Hon C Willesden St Mary 88-91; Perm to Offic *St Alb* from 00. *2 Beckets Square, Berkhamsted HP4 1BZ* Tel (01442) 874265

MacKENZIE, John Christopher Newman. b 67. Trin Coll Bris 02. **d** 04 **p** 05. C Staplehurst *Cant* from 04. *12 Watkins Close, Staplehurst, Tonbridge TN12 0PT* Tel (01580) 892324 E-mail john@jjsmack.me.uk

MACKENZIE, Preb Lawrence Duncan. b 30. St Aid Birkenhead 52. **d** 55 **p** 56. C Blackb St Gabr *Blackb* 55-58; C Burnley St Pet 58-60; C St Giles-in-the-Fields *Lon* 60-63; V Queensbury All SS 63-85; V Hillingdon St Jo 85-96; Preb St Paul's Cathl 89-96; rtd 96; NSM Gt Stanmore *Lon* 96-99; Perm to Offic *Lon* and *Ely* from 99. *1 Walnut Tree Close, Little Downham, Ely CB6 2SQ* Tel (01353) 698793 E-mail kathmac@fish.co.uk

MACKENZIE, Peter Sterling. b 65. Univ Coll Lon BSc88. Oak Hill Th Coll BA95. **d** 95 **p** 96. C Roxeth *Lon* 95-99; Assoc V 99-00; TV from 00. *65 Butler Road, Harrow HA1 4DS* Tel (020) 8537 7332 E-mail peter@mackenziep.fsnet.co.uk

MACKENZIE, Canon Peter Thomas. b 44. Lon Univ LLB67 Nottm Univ DipTh68 Westmr Coll Ox MTh97 Univ of E Lon MA01. Cuddesdon Coll 68. **d** 70 **p** 71. C Leigh Park *Portsm* 70-75; P-in-c Sittingbourne St Mary *Cant* 75-82; V Folkestone St Sav 82-90; RD Elham 89-90; R Cant St Martin and St Paul 90-99; RD Cant 95-99; Hon Can Cant Cathl from 97; V Goudhurst w Kilndown from 99; AD Cranbrook from 01. *The Vicarage, Back Lane, Goudhurst, Cranbrook TN17 1AN* Tel (01580) 211332 E-mail canonmack@talk21.com

McKENZIE, Mrs Priscilla Ann. b 47. St Jo Coll Nottm 87. **d** 93 **p** 94. NSM Ellon *Ab* 93-96; NSM Cruden Bay 93-96; Perm to Offic *Roch* 96-99; Chapl Medway NHS Trust from 99. *Iona, Linton Hill, Linton, Maidstone ME17 4AW* Tel (01622) 741318

MACKENZIE, Richard Graham. b 49. St Aug Coll Cant 72. **d** 73 **p** 74. C Deal St Leon *Cant* 73-75; C Deal St Leon w Sholden 75-78; C Herne 78-81; Canada from 81; I Pakenham 81-88; I Richmond 88-90; I Petawawa from 90. *46 Victoria Street, Petawawa ON, Canada, K8H 2E6* Tel (001) (613) 687 2218

McKENZIE, Robin Peter. b 61. Sheff Univ BEng82 Birm Univ MSc(Eng)87 Dur Univ BA02 Warwick Univ EngD02 MIEE. Cranmer Hall Dur 00. **d** 03 **p** 04. C Shrewsbury St Chad w St Mary *Lich* from 03. *1 St Chad's Terrace, Shrewsbury SY1 1JL* Tel (01743) 235834 E-mail mckenzie_robin@hotmail.com

MACKENZIE, Simon Peter Munro. b 52. Univ Coll Ox BA74. Coll of Resurr Mirfield 82. **d** 85 **p** 86. C Tipton St Jo *Lich* 85-91; V Perry Beeches *Birm* from 91. *St Matthew's Vicarage, 313 Beeches Road, Birmingham B42 2QR* Tel 0121-360 2100

McKENZIE, Stephen George. b 58. Leeds Univ BSc80 Imp Coll Lon PhD85. Oak Hill Th Coll 03. **d** 05. C Barton Seagrave w Warkton *Pet* from 05. *5 Lavendon Court, Barton Seagrave, Kettering NN15 6QH* Tel (01536) 723472 Mobile 07986-558861

MACKENZIE, William. *See* MACKENZIE, Ian William

MACKENZIE MILLS, David Graham. b 75. Bris Univ BA96 St Jo Coll Dur BA01. Cranmer Hall Dur. **d** 01 **p** 02. C Glas St Marg *Glas* 01-04; Chapl Trin Coll Cam from 04. *12 Bridge Street, Cambridge CB2 1UF* Tel (01223) 741112

McKEON, James Ernest. b 22. TCD BA45 HDipEd49 Div Test. TCD Div Sch. **d** 46 **p** 47. C Dundalk *Arm* 46-48; C Dublin St Geo *D & G* 48-52; I Kilsaran w Drumcar, Dunleer and Dunany *Arm* 52-59; I Drogheda 59-64; P-in-c Termonfeckin and

Beaulieu 62-64; Warden Wilson's Hosp Sch Multyfarnham 64-83; Can Kildare Cathl *M & K* 83-88; Prec 87-88; P-in-c Geashill w Killeigh and Ballycommon 83-88; rtd 88; Dioc Info Officer (Meath) *M & K* 90-91; Radio Officer 91-96. *Araucaria, 200 Bassaleg Road, Newport NP20 3PX* Tel (01633) 661974 E-mail j.mckeon@ntlworld.com

McKEON, Canon Victor Edward Samuel. b 39. FCA65 Lon Univ BD. CITC. **d** 68 **p** 69. C Enniskillen *Clogh* 68-72; Accountant to Conn & D & D 72-79; P-in-c Magherahamlet *D & D* 77-79; I Derryvullen N w Castlearchdale *Clogh* 79-91; Dioc Treas from 83; Can Clogh Cathl 86-89; Preb 89-95; Chan from 95; I Monaghan w Tydavnet and Kilmore 91-95; I Trory w Killadeas from 95. *Trory Rectory, Rossfad, Ballinamallard BT94 2LS* Tel and fax (028) 6638 8477

McKEOWN, Trevor James. **d** 04. Aux Min Dromore Cathl *D & D* from 04. *39 Cedar Park, Portadown, Craigavon BT63 5LL* Tel (028) 3832 1217

MACKERACHER, Alasdair John. b 22. Linc Th Coll 69. **d** 71 **p** 72. C Oakdale St Geo *Sarum* 71-73; C Swanage 73-78; V W Alvington w S Milton *Ex* 78-81; R Ashreigney 81-85; R Broadwoodkelly 81-85; V Brushford 81-85; V Winkleigh 81-85; V Swimbridge and W Buckland 85-88; rtd 88; Perm to Offic *Ex* from 98. *3 Gracey Court, Woodland Road, Exeter EX5 3LP* Tel (01392) 468163

McKERRELL, Euan Harvey. b 45. Aber Univ BSc69 CChem78 MRSC78. St Jo Coll Nottm MTh01. **d** 01 **p** 02. C Ness Gp *Linc* 01-03. *Address temp unkown* Tel 07718-140239 (mobile)

MACKEY, John. b 34. Lich Th Coll. **d** 64 **p** 65. C Kells *Carl* 64-67; C Barrow St Matt 67-70; R Clayton *Man* 70-75; V Low Marple *Ches* 75-83; R Coppenhall 83-00; rtd 00; Perm to Offic *Ches* from 00. *361 Hungerford Road, Crewe CW1 5EZ* Tel (01270) 254951

McKIBBIN, Gordon. b 29. St Aid Birkenhead 55. **d** 58 **p** 59. C Dundela St Mark *D & D* 58-60; C Knotty Ash St Jo *Liv* 61-64; V Gt Sankey 64-97; rtd 97; Perm to Offic *Liv* from 97. *6 Penmark Close, Warrington WA5 5TG* Tel (01925) 445125

MacKICHAN, Gillian Margaret. b 34. Bedf Teacher Tr Coll DipPE56 Cam Univ CertEd56 Lon Univ DSS76 CQSW80. S Dios Minl Tr Scheme 90. **d** 93 **p** 94. NSM Upper Kennet *Sarum* 93-04; TV 95-04; RD Marlborough 02-04; rtd 04; Perm to Offic *Sarum* from 04. *West Bailey, Lockeridge, Marlborough SN8 4ED* Tel (01672) 861629 E-mail lalmack@globalnet.co.uk

MACKIE, Andrew. b 53. Glas Univ BSc74 CEng MIEE. St Alb and Ox Min Course 00. **d** 00 **p** 01. OLM Purley *Ox* from 00. *12 Church Mews, Purley-on-Thames, Pangbourne, Reading RG8 8AG* Tel 0118-941 7170
E-mail mackie.family@btinternet.com

MACKIE, Ian William. b 31. Lon Univ BSc53 Ex Univ PGCE54. Linc Th Coll 81. **d** 83 **p** 84. C Market Rasen *Linc* 83-87; V Bracebridge Heath 87-96; RD Christianity 92-96; rtd 96; Perm to Offic *Sheff* 96-02. *57 Bridle Crescent, Chapeltown, Sheffield S35 2QX* Tel 0114-284 4073

MACKIE, Kenneth Johnston. b 20. Univ of NZ BA45 MA46 La Trobe Univ Vic BEd77. St Jo Coll Auckland 46. **d** 47 **p** 48. New Zealand 46-66; C Whangarei 47-51; P-in-c S Hokianga 51-53; V Opotiki 53-56; V Napier St Aug 56-61; Gen Sec NZ Coun for Chr Educn 62-66; Australia 66-72 and 74-94; Chapl Traralgon and Macleod High Schs 66-70; Chapl Univ of Papua New Guinea 72-75; Perm to Offic Melbourne and Gippsland 75-89; Hon P-in-c Nerang 91-94; Perm to Offic *Roch* from 97. *Flat 1, 21 Lime Hill Road, Tunbridge Wells TN1 1LJ* Tel (01892) 540624

McKIE, The Very Revd Kenyon Vincent. b 60. Aus Nat Univ BA83 ACT BTh88 K Coll Lon MTh92 Canberra Coll DipEd84 ACT DipMin89. **d** 86 **p** 87. Australia 86-89 and from 91; Dn Queanbeyan 86; C 87; Lucas-Tooth Scholar K Coll Lon 89-91; Hon C Coulsdon St Andr *S'wark* 89-91; R Monaro S 91-94; R Bega 94-99; Adn S Coast and Monaro 96-99; Dean Goulburn from 99. *PO Box 205, Goulburn, NSW, Australia 2580* Tel (0061) (2) 4821 9192 *or* 4821 2206 Fax 4822 2639
E-mail mesacgbn@tpgi.com.au *or* deanery@tpgi.com.au

McKILLOP, Mrs Caroline Annis. b 47. Glas Univ MB, ChB72 PhD77. TISEC 95. **d** 98 **p** 99. NSM Glas St Matt *Glas* 98-01; Chapl Stobhill NHS Trust 99-00; NSM Glas St Mary *Glas* from 02. *18 Beaumont Gate, Glasgow G12 9ED* Tel 0141-339 7000 Mobile 07967-649149 Fax 0141-334 6636
E-mail carolinemckillop@yahoo.co.uk

McKINLEY, Canon Arthur Horace Nelson. b 46. TCD BA69 MA79. CITC 70. **d** 70 **p** 71. C Taney Ch Ch *D & G* 71-76; I Dublin Whitechurch from 76; Preb Dunlavin St Patr Cathl Dublin from 91. *Whitechurch Vicarage, Whitechurch Road, Rathfarnham, Dublin 16, Irish Republic* Tel (00353) (1) 493 3953 *or* 4972 E-mail whitechurchparish@ireland.com

McKINLEY, George Henry. b 23. TCD BA44 MA51. **d** 46 **p** 47. C Waterford Ch Ch *C & O* 46-49; I Fiddown 49-51; I Fiddown w Kilmacow 51-54; C S Harrow St Paul *Lon* 54-58; V Stonebridge St Mich 58-65; R Hackney St Jo 65-72; TR Hackney 72-77; V Painswick w Sheepscombe *Glouc* 77-83; Bp's Chapl 83-87; C Sandhurst 83-85; C Twigworth, Down Hatherley, Norton, The Leigh etc 85-87; rtd 88; Perm to Offic *Heref* and *Worc* from 96. *Middlemarch, 2 Old Barn Court, Bircher, Leominster HR6 0AU* Tel (01568) 780795

McKINNEL, Preb Nicholas Howard Paul. b 54. Qu Coll Cam BA75 MA79. Wycliffe Hall Ox BA79 MA86. **d** 80 **p** 81. C Fulham St Mary N End *Lon* 80-83; Chapl Liv Univ *Liv* 83-87; P-in-c Hatherleigh *Ex* 87-88; R Hatherleigh, Meeth, Exbourne and Jacobstowe 88-94; P-in-c Plymouth St Andr w St Paul and St Geo 94-95; TR Plymouth St Andr and St Paul Stonehouse from 95; RD Plymouth Sutton from 01; Preb Ex Cathl from 02. *St Andrew's Vicarage, 13 Bainbridge Avenue, Plymouth PL3 5QZ* Tel (01752) 772139 *or* 661414
E-mail nick@standrewschurch.org.uk

McKINNEY, James Alexander. b 52. Ex Univ BA74 Hull Univ MA87. Ripon Coll Cuddesdon 75. **d** 78 **p** 79. C Wath-upon-Dearne w Adwick-upon-Dearne *Sheff* 78-82; V Doncaster Intake 82-87; Ind Chapl 84-87; Chapl Bramshill Police Coll *Win* 87-92; V Cleator Moor w Cleator *Carl* 92-96; Chapl Cumbria Constabulary 93-96; P-in-c Frizington and Arlecdon 94-96; V Roehampton H Trin *S'wark* from 96. *The Vicarage, 7 Ponsonby Road, London SW15 4LA* Tel (020) 8788 9460
E-mail jim.mckinney@dswark.org

McKINNEY, Canon Mervyn Roy. b 48. St Jo Coll Nottm. **d** 81 **p** 82. C Tile Cross *Birm* 81-84; C Bickenhill w Elmdon 84-89; V Addiscombe St Mary *S'wark* 89-93; V Addiscombe St Mary Magd w St Martin 93-99; P-in-c W Wickham St Fran 99-02; V W Wickham St Fran and St Mary from 02; Hon Can S'wark Cathl from 05. *7 Woodland Way, West Wickham BR4 9LL* Tel (020) 8777 5034

MacKINNON, Mrs Karen Audrey. b 64. Ex Univ BA85. Linc Th Coll 92. **d** 92 **p** 94. Par Dn Filton *Bris* 92-93; Par Dn Bris Lockleaze St Mary Magd w St Fran 93-94; C 94-96; P-in-c 96-98; V 98-00; Asst Chapl Southn Univ Hosps NHS Trust 00-03; Chapl 03-04; Dep Team Ldr from 04. *Chaplaincy Department, Southampton General Hospital, Tremona Road, Southampton SO16 6YD* Tel (023) 8079 8517

McKINNON, Neil Alexander. b 46. Wycliffe Hall Ox 71. **d** 74 **p** 75. C Deptford St Nic w Ch Ch *S'wark* 74-76; C St Helier 76-79; Min W Dulwich All SS and Em 79-81; TV Thamesmead 87-95; R S'wark H Trin w St Matt from 95. *The Rectory, Meadow Row, London SE1 6RG* Tel (020) 7407 1707 *or* 7357 8532 Fax 7357 8531 E-mail neilatelephant@aol.com

MACKINTOSH, Robin Geoffrey James. b 46. Rhodes Univ BCom71 Cranfield Inst of Tech MBA78 Ox Univ BA85 MA91. Ripon Coll Cuddesdon 83. **d** 86 **p** 87. C Cuddesdon *Ox* 86; C Cannock *Lich* 86-89; R Girton *Ely* 89-01; Exec Dir The Leadership Inst from 01; Perm to Offic *Cant* from 03. *42 Queens Avenue, Canterbury CT2 8BA* Tel (01227) 479706
E-mail rob.mackintosh@ntlworld.com

McKINTY, Norman Alexander (Fionn). b 63. St D Coll Lamp BA86. Westcott Ho Cam 97. **d** 99 **p** 00. C Yeovil St Mich *B & W* 99-03; C Gillingham and Milton-on-Stour *Sarum* 03-05; P-in-c Portland All SS w St Pet from 05. *The Rectory, Straits, Portland DT5 1HG* Tel (01305) 861285
E-mail fionn@mckinty.fsworld.co.uk

McKITTRICK, The Ven Douglas Henry. b 53. St Steph Ho Ox 74. **d** 77 **p** 78. C Deptford St Paul *S'wark* 77-80; C W Derby St Jo *Liv* 80-81; TV St Luke in the City 81-89; V Toxteth Park St Agnes and St Pancras 89-97; V Brighton St Pet w Chpl Royal *Chich* 97-02; RD Brighton 98-02; Can and Preb Chich Cathl 98-02; Adn Chich from 02. *2 Yorklands, Dyke Road Avenue, Hove BN3 6RW* Tel (01273) 505330 *or* 421021
E-mail archchichester@diochi.org.uk
or fr.douglas@btinternet.com

McKITTRICK, Noel Thomas Llewellyn. b 28. TCD BA50 MA57 BD71. **d** 51 **p** 53. C Londonderry Ch Ch *D & R* 51-52; C Belfast St Aid *Conn* 52-54; C Knockbreda *D & D* 54-58; C Keynsham w Queen Charlton *B & W* 58-59; V Glastonbury St Benedict 59-82; V Weston-super-Mare St Paul 82-92; rtd 93; Perm to Offic *Ex* from 94. *Priory Lodge, Latimer Road, Exeter EX4 7JP* Tel (01392) 496744

MACKLEY, Robert Michael. b 78. Ch Coll Cam BA99 MA03. Westcott Ho Cam 00. **d** 03 **p** 04. C Clerkenwell H Redeemer *Lon* from 03; C Clerkenwell St Mark from 03. *The Clergy House, 24 Exmouth Market, London EC1R 4QE* Tel (020) 7837 1861 *or* 7278 0516 E-mail father_mackley@oratorium.zzn.com
or rob_mackley@hotmail.com

MACKLIN, Reginald John. b 29. Bris Univ BA52. Ely Th Coll 54. **d** 55 **p** 56. C W Hackney St Barn *Lon* 55-58; C E Ham St Mary *Chelmsf* 58-61; C Northolt St Mary *Lon* 61-64; Jordan 64-68; Palma de Mallorca and Balearic Is *Eur* 68-69; P-in-c Hammersmith St Matt *Lon* 69-70; V Stanwell 70-82; V Kimbolton *Ely* 82-88; V Stow Longa 82-88; RD Leightonstone 82-88; P-in-c Keyston and Bythorn 85-88; P-in-c Catworth Magna 85-88; P-in-c Tilbrook 85-88; P-in-c Covington 85-88; R Coveney 88-96; R Downham 88-96; RD Ely 89-96; rtd 96; Perm to Offic *Ely* from 96. *11 Castelhythe, Ely CB7 4BU* Tel (01353) 662205 Fax as telephone E-mail macklinrj@aol.com

MACKNESS, Paul Robert. b 73. Univ of Wales (Lamp) BA96 Univ of Wales (Cardiff) BA01. St Mich Coll Llan 98. **d** 01 **p** 02. C Llanelli *St D* 01-04; P-in-c Maenordeifi and Capel Colman w Llanfihangel etc from 04. *The Rectory, Manordeifi, Llechryd, Cardigan SA43 2PJ* Tel (01239) 682830 E-mail paulr@pmackness.fsnet.co.uk

MACKNEY, John Pearson. b 17. Univ of Wales BA39 Lon Univ MA81 PGCE73. St D Coll Lamp 39. **d** 41 **p** 42. C Gelligaer *Llan* 41-44; CF 44-47; C Llangeinor *Llan* 47-49; P-in-c Cardiff All SS 49-58; Chapl HM Pris Cardiff 49-58; V Mountain Ash *Llan* 58-69; Hon C Streatley *Ox* from 81. *Merlebank, Reading Road, Moulsford, Wallingford OX10 9JG* Tel (01491) 651347

McKNIGHT, Thomas Raymond. b 48. QUB BEd71. CITC 74. **d** 77 **p** 78. C Lisburn Ch Ch Cathl *Conn* 77-80; C Carrickfergus 80-82; I Kilcronaghan w Draperstown and Sixtowns *D & R* 82-86; I Magheragall *Conn* 86-91; CF from 91; Perm to Offic *Bris* from 99 and *Ripon* from 03. *c/o MOD Chaplains (Army)* Tel (01980) 615804 Fax 615800

MACKRIELL, Peter John. b 64. Mansf Coll Ox BA85 MA93 Man Univ PGCE87. St Jo Coll Nottm BTh93 MA94. **d** 94 **p** 95. C Hale and Ashley *Ches* 94-96; C Marple All SS 96-98; V Brandwood *Birm* 98-01; V Pontblyddyn *St As* from 01; Chapl to Deaf People from 01. *The Vicarage, Wrexham Road, Pontblyddyn, Mold CH7 4HG* Tel (01352) 771489 Fax 779093 E-mail peter@jmackriell.freeserve.co.uk

MACKRILL, Robert John. b 51. RIBA79 Univ Coll Lon BSc73 DipArch76. EMMTC 92. **d** 93 **p** 94. NSM Stamford All SS w St Jo *Linc* 93-97; P-in-c Stamford Ch Ch from 97. *110 Lonsdale Road, Stamford PE9 2SF* Tel (01780) 754490 Fax 756212 E-mail bob@mackrill.freeserve.co.uk

MacLACHLAN (née GRIFFITHS), Mrs Margaret. b 44. SRN67 Birm Poly CertEd81 Open Univ BA82. WMMTC 92. **d** 95 **p** 96. NSM Tile Cross *Birm* from 95. *Wayside, 17 Chester Road, Birmingham B36 9DA* Tel 0121-747 2340

MacLACHLAN, Michael Ronald Frederic. b 39. Wycliffe Hall Ox 75. **d** 75 **p** 76. C Mansfield SS Pet and Paul *S'well* 75-78; P-in-c Newark Ch Ch 78-80; TV Newark w Hawton, Cotham and Shelton 80-86; P-in-c Sparkhill St Jo *Birm* 86-90; P-in-c Sparkbrook Em 86-90; V Sparkhill w Greet and Sparkbrook 90-92; RD Bordesley 90-92; P-in-c Kugluktuk Canada 92-97; R Stoke-next-Guildf 97-05; rtd 05; Hon C Drayton Bassett *Lich* from 05. *35 Moat Drive, Drayton Bassett, Tamworth B78 3UG* Tel (01827) 259730 E-mail mkanddmaclachlan@btinternet.com

McLACHLAN, Ms Sheila Elizabeth. b 52. SRN73 Kent Univ MA89. Wycliffe Hall Ox 80. **dss** 83 **d** 87 **p** 94. Chapl Kent Univ *Cant* 83-94; Dep Master Rutherford Coll 87-94; Dn-in-c Kingsnorth w Shadoxhurst 94; P-in-c Kingsnorth and Shadoxhurst from 94; AD Ashford from 03. *The Rectory, Church Hill, Kingsnorth, Ashford TN23 3EG* Tel (01233) 620433 E-mail sheila.mclachlan@tesco.net

MacLAREN, Ms Clare. b 67. Edin Univ LLB88. Linc Th Coll BTh95. **d** 95 **p** 96. C Benchill *Man* 95-98; C Bilton *Ripon* 98-03; TV Seacroft from 03. *St Paul's Vicarage, 58 Whinmoor Crescent, Leeds LS14 1EW* Tel 0113-265 5649 E-mail claremac@bigfoot.com

MacLAREN, Duncan Arthur Spencer. b 69. Oriel Coll Ox BA90 MA96 K Coll Lon MA97 PhD03. Oak Hill Th Coll 92. **d** 94 **p** 95. C Ox St Clem *Ox* 94-97; Chapl St Edm Hall Ox 97-04; C Edin St Paul and St Geo *Edin* from 04. *53 Balgreen Road, Edinburgh EH12 5TY*

MacLAREN (née ALEXANDER), Mrs Jane Louise. b 69. LMH Ox BA90 MA96. Oak Hill Th Coll BA95. **d** 95 **p** 96. C Ox St Clem *Ox* 95-98; Chapl St Aug Sch 98-02; Chapl Ox Brookes Univ 02-04; C Edin St Paul and St Geo *Edin* from 04. *53 Balgreen Road, Edinburgh EH12 5TY*

McLAREN, Mrs Jeanette Moira. b 59. **d** 95 **p** 96. C Dulwich St Clem w St Pet *S'wark* 95-99; P-in-c Brixton St Paul from 99. *73 Baytree Road, London SW2 5RR* Tel (020) 7274 6907

McLAREN, Richard Francis. b 46. Mansf Coll Ox DSS69. S'wark Ord Course 72. **d** 75 **p** 76. C Charlton St Luke w H Trin *S'wark* 75-78; C Kensington St Mary Abbots w St Geo *Lon* 78-81; Hon C St Marylebone w H Trin 82-96; P-in-c 96-97; Development Officer CUF 97; Chmn Art and Christianity Enquiry Trust from 97; Hon C Regent's Park St Mark from 97. *8 Gray's Court, 51-53 Gray's Inn Road, London WC1X 8PP* Tel and fax (020) 7404 5642 E-mail richard@mclaren7.fsnet.co.uk

McLAREN, Robert Ian. b 62. Bris Univ BSc84 St Jo Coll Dur BA87. Cranmer Hall Dur 85. **d** 88 **p** 89. C Birkenhead Ch Ch *Ches* 88-90; C Bebington 90-95; V Cheadle All Hallows 95-05; V Poynton from 05. *The Vicarage, 41 London Road North, Poynton, Stockport SK12 1AF* Tel (01625) 850524 *or* 872711 E-mail vicar@orange.net

McLAREN, Ronald. b 31. Kelham Th Coll. **d** 59 **p** 60. C Redcar *York* 59-62; C Hornsea and Goxhill 62-65; V Middlesbrough St Thos 65-70; Chapl RN 70-73; Australia from 73; rtd 96. *16 Moselle Drive, Thornlands, Qld, Australia 4164* Tel (0061) (7) 3821 2069 Mobile 409-039768 E-mail ronanne@ozemail.com.au

McLAREN, William Henry. b 27. OBE94. Edin Th Coll 55. **d** 56 **p** 57. C Skipton H Trin *Bradf* 56-60; V Bingley H Trin 60-65; V Allerton 65-68; R Aberdeen St Mary *Ab* 68-73; P-in-c Newland St Aug *York* 73-74; V 74-75; V Hull St Cuth 75-81; V Hedon w Paull 81-94; RD S Holderness 84-94; rtd 94; Perm to Offic *York* from 94. *Kirklea, Ottringham Road, Keyingham, Hull HU12 9RX* Tel (01964) 624159

McLAREN-COOK, Paul Raymond. b 43. LTh66. **d** 66 **p** 67. Australia 66-72 and 76-00; C Mt Lawley 66-67; C Perth Cathl 67-69; R Carnarvon 69-72; Malaysia 72-76; V Seremban 72-75; Warden Coll of Th 75-76; R Kensington 76-79; R Narrogin 79-84; P-in-c Wellington 84-85; R Eugowra 85-86; P-in-c Berrigan 86-87; P-in-c Hay 87-88; P-in-c Yass 88; R Moruya 88-90; R Heywood 90-92; R Warracknabeal 92-95; Chapl Ballarat Base and St Jo of God Hosps 95-00; R Kansas City St Mary USA 00-03; R Stanway *Chelmsf* from 03. *The Rectory, Church Lane, Stanway, Colchester CO3 5LR* Tel (01206) 210407 E-mail mclarencook@uksprite.com

McLARNON, Mrs Sylvia Caroline Millicent. b 45. S Dios Minl Tr Scheme 92. **d** 95 **p** 96. NSM Burgess Hill St Andr *Chich* 95-99; C from 99. *75 Cants Lane, Burgess Hill RH15 0LX* Tel (01444) 233902

McLAUGHLIN, Hubert James Kenneth. b 45. Belf Coll of Tech HNC70 Greenwich Univ BTh93. CITC 85 97. **d** 88 **p** 89. NSM Donagheady *D & R* 88-89; NSM Glendermott 89-98; P-in-c Inver, Mountcharles and Killaghtee 98-02; I from 02. *The Rectory, Inver, Co Donegal, Irish Republic* Tel (00353) (74) 973 6013 Mobile 802-549380 E-mail inver@raphoe.anglican.org

McLAUGHLIN, Capt Michael Anthony. b 48. **d** 97 **p** 98. C Gt Chart *Cant* 97-01; C-in-c Parkwood CD from 01. *The Vicarage, Wallis Avenue, Maidstone ME15 9JJ* Tel (01622) 764170 E-mail mmcl@btinternet.com

MACLAURIN, Ms Anne Fiona. b 62. St Andr Univ MA84. Ridley Hall Cam. **d** 99 **p** 00. C Crookes St Thos *Sheff* 99-04; TV from 04; Miss P Philadelphia St Thos from 05. *St Thomas's Church, Philadelphia Campus, 6 Gilpin Street, Sheffield S6 3BL* Tel 0114-241 9560 Fax 278 9600 E-mail anne.maclaurin@stthomaschurch.org.uk

MACLAY, Christopher Willis. b 64. Stirling Univ BA88 Reading Univ MA92 Bris Univ BA01. Trin Coll Bris 99. **d** 01 **p** 02. C Bedhampton *Portsm* from 01. *2 Lester Avenue, Havant PO9 3HE* Tel (023) 9247 0200

McLAY, Canon Robert James. b 49. Cant Univ (NZ) BA71. St Jo Coll Auckland. **d** 73 **p** 74. New Zealand 73-75 and from 77; C Fendalton 73-75; Hon C Yardley St Edburgha *Birm* 75-77; V Banks Peninsular 77-80; V Marchwiel 80-83; V Huntly 83-89; Lect St Jo Coll 86-88; V Stokes Valley 89-93; V Pauatahanui from 93; Can Wellington Cathl from 96. *4 Livet Place, Papakowhai, Porirua, New Zealand* Tel (0064) (4) 233 1211 *or* 233 9781 E-mail el.mclay@xtra.co.nz

MACLEAN, Canon Allan Murray. b 50. Edin Univ MA72. Cuddesdon Coll 72. **d** 76 **p** 77. Chapl St Mary's Cathl *Edin* 76-81; Tutor Edin Univ 77-80; R Dunoon *Arg* 81-86; R Tighnabruaich 84-86; Provost St Jo Cathl Oban 86-99; R Oban St Jo 86-99; R Ardbrecknish 86-99; R Ardchattan 89-99; Hon Can St Jo Cathl Oban from 99; Perm to Offic *Mor* from 00. *5 North Charlotte Street, Edinburgh EH2 4HR* Tel 0131-225 8609

McLEAN, Bradley Halstead. b 57. McMaster Univ Ontario BSc Toronto Univ MDiv MTh PhD. **d** 83 **p** 84. C Dur St Giles *Dur* 83-84; Canada from 84. *38 Tweedsmuir Road, Winnipeg MB, Canada, R3P 1Z2*

McLEAN, The Ven Donald Stewart. b 48. TCD BA70. CITC 70. **d** 72 **p** 73. C Glendermott *D & R* 72-75; I Castledawson 75-87 and from 03; Dioc Dir of Ords 79-96; I Londonderry Ch Ch 87-03; Can Derry Cathl from 91; Adn Derry from 96. *12 Station Road, Castledawson, Magherafelt BT45 8AZ* Tel (028) 7946 8235 E-mail archdeacon@derry.anglican.org *or* dsmclean@iol.ie

MACLEAN, Mrs Dorothy. b 31. Dundee Coll DipEd70. St And Dioc Tr Course 79. **d** 86. NSM Kirriemuir *St And* 82-93; Asst Min from 99. *84 Slade Gardens, Kirriemuir DD8 5AG* Tel (01575) 572396

McLEAN, Mrs Eileen Mary. b 44. City Univ BSc67. N Ord Course 85. **d** 88 **p** 94. Par Dn Burley in Wharfedale *Bradf* 88-92; Par Dn Nottingham St Pet and St Jas *S'well* 92-94; C 94-02; AD Nottingham Cen 98-02; V Bamburgh *Newc* from 02; V Ellingham from 02. *The Vicarage, 7 The Wynding, Bamburgh NE69 7DB* Tel (01668) 214748

McLEAN, Miss Frances Ellen. b 21. RGN44 SCM45. Edin Dioc NSM Course 85. **d** 88 **p** 94. NSM Penicuik *Edin* 88-00; NSM W Linton 88-00. *56 Cuikenburn, Penicuik EH26 0JQ* Tel (01968) 675029

MACLEAN, Kenneth John Forbes. b 31. St Deiniol's Hawarden 80. **d** 81 **p** 82. C Sedgley All SS *Lich* 81-85; V Shareshill 85-90; R Bicton, Montford w Shrawardine and Fitz 90-96; rtd 96; Perm to Offic *Lich* from 99. *7 The Armoury, Wenlock Road, Shrewsbury SY2 6PA* Tel (01743) 243308

MacLEAN, Lawrence Alexander Charles. b 61. K Coll Lon BD84 AKC84. Chich Th Coll 86. **d** 88 **p** 89. C Cirencester *Glouc* 88-91; C Prestbury 91-96; Perm to Offic 01-02; Chapl Florence w Siena *Eur* from 02. *The English Church of St Mark, Via Maggio 16/18, 50125 Firenze, Italy* Tel (0039) (055) 294764

McLEAN, Ms Margaret Anne. b 62. Birm Univ BA91 Heythrop Coll Lon MA99. Qu Coll Birm 88. **d** 91 **p** 94. Par Dn Bedford All SS *St Alb* 91-94; C 94; Chapl St Alb High Sch for Girls 94-98; Asst Soc Resp Officer *Derby* 98-99; Chapl Huddersfield Univ *Wakef* 99-02; P-in-c Scholes from 02; P-in-c Cleckheaton St Luke and Whitechapel from 02. *The Vicarage, Scholes Lane, Scholes, Cleckheaton BD19 6PA* Tel (01274) 873024 Mobile 07974-125494 Fax (01274) 303374
E-mail m.a.mclean@btinternet.com

McLEAN, Canon Michael Stuart. b 32. Dur Univ BA57. Cuddesdon Coll 57. **d** 59 **p** 60. C Camberwell St Giles *S'wark* 59-61; Lic to Offic *Nor* 61-68; R Marsham 68-74; R Burgh 68-74; RD Ingworth 70-74; P-in-c Nor St Pet Parmentergate w St Jo 74-75; TV 75-78; TR 78-86; Hon Can Nor Cathl 82-86; Can Res Nor Cathl 86-94; P-in-c Nor St Mary in the Marsh 87-94; Perm to Offic from 94; rtd 97. *30 Friars Quay, Norwich NR3 1ES* Tel (01603) 630398

McLEAN, Peter. b 50. **d** 94 **p** 95. NSM Mold *St As* 94-02; Perm to Offic 02-03; P-in-c Bodedern w Llanfaethlu *Ban* 03-05; R Llangefni w Tregaean from 05. *Llety'r Llan, 50 Bro Ednyfed, Llangefni LL77 7WB* Tel (01248) 722667

McLEAN, Robert Hedley. b 47. St Jo Coll Dur BA69. Ripon Hall Ox 69. **d** 71 **p** 72. C Redhill St Jo *S'wark* 71-74; C S Beddington St Mich 74-77; C-in-c Raynes Park H Cross CD 77; P-in-c Motspur Park 77-80; V 80-84; V Tadworth 84-00; Asst RD Reigate 92-93; RD Reigate 93-00; R Morpeth *Newc* from 00; Chapl Northd Mental Health NHS Trust from 00; Chapl Northumbria Healthcare NHS Trust from 00. *The Rectory, Cottingwood Lane, Morpeth NE61 1ED* Tel (01670) 513517
E-mail robert@morpeth-rectory.fsnet.co.uk

McLEAN-REID, Robert. b 43. Oak Hill Th Coll DipHE83. **d** 83 **p** 84. C Rainham *Chelmsf* 83-86; R Challoch w Newton Stewart *Glas* 86-87; R Aberdeen St Pet *Ab* 87-90; P-in-c Aberdeen St Clem 89-90; V Easington Colliery *Dur* 90-95; rtd 95. *37 Middleton Close, Seaton, Seaham SR7 0PQ* Tel 0191-581 1729

MacLEAY, Angus Murdo. b 59. Univ Coll Ox BA81 MA86 Man Univ MPhil92 Solicitor 83. Wycliffe Hall Ox 85. **d** 88 **p** 89. C Rusholme H Trin *Man* 88-92; V Houghton *Carl* 92-01; R Sevenoaks St Nic *Roch* from 01. *The Rectory, Rectory Lane, Sevenoaks TN13 1JA* Tel (01732) 740340 Fax 742810
E-mail macleay@ukonline.co.uk

McLELLAN, Eric Macpherson Thompson. b 16. St Jo Coll Dur BA38 DipTh39 MA41. **d** 39 **p** 40. C Byker St Mark *Newc* 39-44; C Fazakerley Em *Liv* 44-45; V Everton Em 45-54; R Sevenoaks St Nic *Roch* 54-70; Hon Can Roch Cathl 68-70; Chapl Br Embassy Ch Paris *Eur* 70-80; RD France 75-79; Adn N France 79-80; Perm to Offic *Chich* 80-99; Perm to Offic *Roch* from 80; rtd 81. *7 Stainer Road, Tonbridge TN10 4DS* Tel (01732) 356491

MacLEOD, Alan Roderick Hugh (Roddie). b 33. St Edm Hall Ox BA56 MA61 Ox Univ DipEd62 Lon Univ Dip Ch Development 69. Wycliffe Hall Ox 56. **d** 58 **p** 59. C Bognor St Jo *Chich* 58-61; Chapl Wadh Coll Ox 62; Hd of RE Picardy Boys' Sch Erith 62-68; C Erith St Jo *Roch* 63-69; Dean Lonsdale Coll Lanc Univ 70-72; Hd of RE K Edw VI Sch Totnes 72-73; Dir of Resources St Helier Boys' Sch Jersey 73-84; V Shipton Bellinger *Win* 84-02; rtd 02; Perm to Offic *Win* from 02. *Pippins Toft, Lashmar's Corner, East Preston, Littlehampton BN16 1EZ* Tel (01903) 783523

McLEOD, Everton William. b 57. DCR78. Oak Hill Th Coll DipHE91. **d** 91 **p** 92. C New Ferry *Ches* 91-93; C Moreton 93-98; Chapl R Liv Univ Hosp NHS Trust 98-01; TR Uphill *B & W* from 01. *Uphill Rectory, 3 Old Church Road, Uphill, Weston-super-Mare BS23 4UH* Tel (01934) 620156
E-mail mcleod@xalt.co.uk

MacLEOD, John Malcolm (Jay). b 61. Harvard Univ AB84 Pemb Coll Ox BA87 MA91. Linc Th Coll MDiv93. **d** 93 **p** 94. C Chesterfield St Aug *Derby* 93-96; C Stalybridge St Paul *Ches* 96-98; P-in-c Micklehurst 98-03; P-in-c Bedford All SS *St Alb* from 03; Dioc Interfaith Adv from 03. *All Saints' Vicarage, 1 Cutcliffe Place, Bedford MK40 4DF* Tel (01234) 266945
E-mail macasher@dial.pipex.com

McLEOD, Paul Douglas. b 66. Cuddesdon Coll BTh95. **d** 98 **p** 99. C Morpeth *Newc* 98-02; V Newbiggin Hall from 02. *St Wilfrid's House, Trevelyan Drive, Newcastle upon Tyne NE5 4DA* Tel 0191-271 4005 E-mail revpaulmcleod@aol.com

MacLEOD, Roderick. *See* MacLEOD, Alan Roderick Hugh

McLEOD, Canon Ronald. b 17. Lon Univ BA39 BA50 BD71 Ex Univ BA56 Man Univ MA59 Ex Univ MPhil01. Bps' Coll Cheshunt 39. **d** 41 **p** 42. C Plymouth St Pet *Ex* 41-44; Chapl RAF 44-69; Prin RAF Chapl Sch and Asst Chapl-in-Chief RAF 69-73; QHC 72-73; R Itchen Abbas cum Avington *Win* 73-91; Hon Can Win Cathl 84-91; rtd 91; Perm to Offic *Ex* from 92. *Melfort, High Wall, Barnstaple EX31 2DP* Tel (01271) 343636

McLEOD, Ms Susan Margaret. b 48. SEN69 Sheff Poly CQSW89 Liv Univ DATh97. N Ord Course 92. **d** 95 **p** 96. NSM Charlesworth and Dinting Vale *Derby* from 95; Chapl Asst S Man Univ Hosps NHS Trust from 97. *Withington Hospital, Nell Lane, Manchester M20 8LR* Tel 0161-291 4800 *or* 445 8111

MacLEOD-MILLER, Peter Norman. b 66. **d** 91 **p** 91. C Cardiff Australia 91-92; C Hillston 92-94; C Fitzroy 95-97; Perm to Offic Melbourne 97-01; P-in-c Risby w Gt and Lt Saxham *St E* 02-04; V Barrow from 05. *The Rectory, Barrow, Bury St Edmunds IP29 5BA* Tel (01284) 810929

McLOUGHLIN, Ian Livingstone. b 38. CEng MICE64. Carl Dioc Tr Course 78. **d** 83 **p** 84. NSM Stanwix *Carl* 83-88; C Barrow St Geo w St Luke 88-90; R Kirkby Thore w Temple Sowerby and Newbiggin 90-01; rtd 01; Perm to Offic *Bradf* and *Carl* from 01. *20 Long Lane, Sedbergh LA10 5AH* Tel (01539) 620496

McLUCKIE, John Mark. b 67. St Andr Univ BD89. Edin Th Coll MTh91. **d** 91 **p** 92. C Perth St Ninian *St And* 91-94; Chapl K Coll Cam 94-96; TV Glas E End *Glas* 96-00; Assoc R Edin St Jo *Edin* 00-03. *2 Deuchrie Cottages, Dunbar EH42 1TG* Tel (01368) 850645 E-mail johnmark.mcluckie@virgin.net *or* johnmcluckie@btconnect.com

MACLUSKIE, Mrs Linda. b 55. Lanc Univ MA99. Carl and Blackb Dioc Tr Inst 95. **d** 98 **p** 99. NSM Halton w Aughton *Blackb* 98-02; NSM Bolton-le-Sands from 02. *15 Whitendale Drive, Bolton le Sands, Carnforth LA5 8LY* Tel (01524) 822769
E-mail ian@macluskie.freeserve.co.uk

McMAHON, Brian Richard. b 39. ACII. Oak Hill NSM Course 84. **d** 87 **p** 88. NSM Colney Heath St Mark *St Alb* 87-03. *Address temp unknown*

McMAHON, George Ian Robertson. b 23. Monmouth Coll Illinois BA44 Univ of N Carolina BA44 MA49 Ox Univ MLitt61 Birm Univ PhD73. Gen Th Sem NY STB52. **d** 52 **p** 53. P-in-c Roxboro, Yanceyville and Milton USA 52-57; Perm to Offic *Ox* 57-64; Prin Lect Homerton Coll Cam 65-88; P-in-c Cambridge St Clem *Ely* 89-04. *44 Grantchester Road, Cambridge CB3 9ED* Tel (01223) 350988

McMAHON, Stephen. b 66. Newc Univ BSc87 MSc89 Leeds Univ BA03 CEng97 MBES97. Coll of Resurr Mirfield 01. **d** 03 **p** 04. C Lancaster St Mary w St John and St Anne *Blackb* from 03. *Chauntry Cottage, 1 Priory Close, Lancaster LA1 1YZ* Tel (01524) 849123 E-mail steve1345.mcmahon@virgin.net

McMANN, Duncan. b 34. Jes Coll Ox BA55 MA60. Clifton Th Coll 55. **d** 58 **p** 59. C Newburn *Newc* 58-60; C Bishopwearmouth St Gabr *Dur* 60-62; N Area Sec BCMS 62-66; Midl and E Anglia Area Sec 66-92; Support Co-ord 84-92; Lic to Offic *Man* 62-66 and *Cov* 66-92; P-in-c Awsworth w Cossall *S'well* 92-99; Chapl Notts Constabulary 93-99; rtd 99; Perm to Offic *Nor* from 00. *7 Evans Drive, Lowestoft NR32 2RX* Tel (01502) 568724

McMANN, Mrs Judith. b 46. Hull Univ BTh96. EMMTC MA98. **d** 98 **p** 99. NSM Gt Grimsby St Mary and St Jas *Linc* from 98. *23 Grasby Crescent, Grimsby DN37 9HE* Tel (01472) 887523
E-mail jmcmann@btopenworld.com

McMANNERS, Prof John. b 16. CBE00. St Edm Hall Ox BA39 MA45 DLitt77 St Chad's Coll Dur DipTh47 Hon DLitt84 FBA78 FRHistS73 FAHA70. **d** 47 **p** 48. C Leeds St Pet *Ripon* 47-48; Chapl St Edm Hall Ox 48-56; Fell 49-56; Dean 51-56; Australia 56-67; Prof Th Tas Univ 56-59; Prof Th Sydney Univ 59-66; Prof Fell All So Coll Ox 65-66; Fell and Chapl 85-01; Prof Hist Leic Univ *Leic* 67-72; Regius Prof Ecclesiastical Hist Ox Univ 72-84; Can Res Ch Ch *Ox* 72-84; rtd 84. *71 Cunliffe Close, Oxford OX2 7BJ,* or *All Souls College, Oxford OX1 4AL* Tel (01865) 279368

McMANNERS, John Roland. b 46. Liv Univ LLB68. Cranmer Hall Dur 99. **d** 01 **p** 02. C Monkwearmouth *Dur* from 01. *6 Lonsdale Road, Sunderland SR6 9TB* Tel 0191-384 1353

McMANUS, James Robert. b 33. Man Univ Dip Soc & Past Th 82. Wycliffe Hall Ox 56. **d** 58 **p** 59. C Leic H Trin *Leic* 58-60; C Aylestone 60-63; India 66-79; V Oldham St Barn *Man* 79-83; Asst Regional Sec CMS 83-85; V Wolverhampton St Matt *Lich* 85-93; V Lapley w Wheaton Aston 93-99; P-in-c Blymhill w Weston-under-Lizard 93-99; rtd 99; Perm to Offic *Lich* from 99. *Delamere, McBean Road, Wolverhampton WV6 0JQ* Tel (01902) 833436 Fax 834170 E-mail jimvicar@aol.com

McMASTER, James Alexander. b 43. **d** 69 **p** 70. C Dundonald *D & D* 69-73; C Antrim All SS *Conn* 73-78; I Tempo and Clabby *Clogh* 78-83; I Knocknamuckley *D & D* 83-95; I Carrickfergus *Conn* from 95. *The Rectory, 12 Harwood Gardens, Carrickfergus BT38 7US* Tel (028) 9336 3244 *or* 9336 0061

MACMASTER, Mrs Norma. **d** 04. Aux Min Dublin St Geo and St Thos *D & G* from 04. *1 The Orchard, Tennis Court Lane, Skerries, Co Dublin, Irish Republic* Tel (00353) (1) 849 1387
E-mail nmacmaster@eircom.net

McMASTER, Richard Ian. b 32. Edin Th Coll 57. **d** 60 **p** 61. C Carl H Trin *Carl* 60-63; Tanganyika 63-64; Tanzania 64-66; V Broughton Moor *Carl* 66-69; V Burnley St Steph *Blackb* 69-77; V New Longton 77-89; P-in-c Woodhall Spa and Kirkstead *Linc* 89-91; P-in-c Langton w Woodhall 89-91; P-in-c Bucknall w Tupholme 89-91; P-in-c Horsington w Stixwould 89-91; R

Woodhall Spa Gp 92-97; rtd 97; Perm to Offic *Birm* from 97. *18 Marsden Close, Solihull B92 7JR* Tel 0121-707 6208 E-mail bettyandianmc@aol.com

McMASTER, William Keith. b 45. TCD. **d** 82 **p** 84. C Portadown St Columba *Arm* 82-84; C Erdington St Barn *Birm* 84-87; TV Shirley 87-00; TV Salter Street and Shirley 00-02; rtd 02. *38 Lambscote Close, Shirley, Solihull B90 1NS*

MACMATH, Terence Handley. *See* HANDLEY MACMATH, Terence

McMICHAEL, Andrew Hamilton. b 48. Univ of Wales (Ban) BA77. Chich Th Coll 87. **d** 89 **p** 90. C Chorley St Geo *Blackb* 89-92; C Burnley St Andr w St Marg 92-94; Chapl Burnley Health Care NHS Trust 92-94; R Eccleston *Blackb* 94-99; V Lt Marsden w Nelson St Mary 99-04; P-in-c Tain *Mor* from 04; P-in-c Invergordon St Ninian from 04; P-in-c Lochinver from 04. *St Andrew's Rectory, Manse Street, Tain IV19 1HE* Tel (01862) 892193

MacMILLAN, Douglas Middleton. b 41. St Thos Hosp Lon MB, BS66 FRCS70 FTCL82 AMusLCM80 FLCM83. Guildf Dioc Min Course 96. **d** 00. NSM Guildf Cathl *Guildf* 00-02; Perm to Offic 02-04; NSM E and W Clandon from 04. *Rivendell, 50 Speedwell Close, Guildford GU4 7HE* Tel (01483) 533019

McMONAGLE, William Archibald. b 36. CITC 65. **d** 68 **p** 69. C Magheralin *D & D* 68-71; C Bangor Abbey 71-81; I Grey Abbey w Kircubbin 81-00; rtd 00. *50 Ashfield Court, Donaghadee BT21 0BF* Tel (028) 9188 4306

✠**McMULLAN, The Rt Revd Gordon.** b 34. ACIS57 QUB BSc61 PhD71 Cam Univ DipRS78 Irish Sch of Ecum TCD MPhil90 Univ of the South (USA) DMin95. Ridley Hall Cam 61. **d** 62 **p** 63 **c** 80. C Ballymacarrett St Patr *D & D* 62-67; Cen Adv on Chr Stewardship to Ch of Ireland 67-70; C Knock 70-71; I 76-80; I Belfast St Brendan 71-76; Offg Chapl RAF 71-78; Bp's Dom Chapl *D & D* 73-78; Adn Down 79-80; Bp Clogh 80-86; Bp D & D 86-97; rtd 97. *26 Wellington Park, Bangor BT20 4PJ* Tel (028) 9146 0821

McMULLEN, Philip Kenneth. b 55. RMN80 Glam Univ DMS92. St Mich Coll Llan DipTh95. **d** 95 **p** 96. C Coity w Nolton *Llan* 95-98; V Fleur-de-Lis *Mon* 98-04. *29 Clos Coed Bach, Blackwood NP12 1GT* Tel (01495) 220210

McMULLEN, Ronald Norman. b 36. TCD BA61 MA66 Liv Univ DSS73 York Univ Dip Community Work 74 California Inst of Integral Studies MA92. Ridley Hall Cam 61. **d** 63 **p** 64. C Fulham St Mary N End *Lon* 63-67; C Cambridge St Sepulchre *Ely* 67-70; C Everton St Ambrose w St Tim *Liv* 70-73; Community Work Course & Research Asst York Univ 73-75; P-in-c Heanor *Derby* 75-79; V 79-88; RD Heanor 76-83; USA 88-93; rtd 98. *Apple Tree Cottage, 38A Main Street, Lowick, Berwick-upon-Tweed TD15 2UA* Tel and fax (01289) 388301

McMULLON, Andrew Brian. b 56. Sheff Univ BSc DipTh. St Jo Coll Nottm. **d** 83 **p** 84. C Stainforth *Sheff* 83-86; V Blackb Redeemer *Blackb* 86-90; Chapl RAF from 90. *Chaplaincy Services (RAF), HQ, Personnel and Training Command, RAF Innsworth, Gloucester GL3 1EZ* Tel (01452) 712612 ext 5164 Fax 510828

McMUNN, Lee James. b 78. LSE BSc99. Wycliffe Hall Ox BA04. **d** 05. C Hull St Jo Newland *York* from 05. *17 Minton Street, Hull HU5 1QP* Tel (01482) 472969 Mobile 07957-898884 E-mail lee@stjohnnewland.org.uk

McNAB (née LUMMIS), Mrs Elizabeth Howieson. b 44. Lon Univ LDSRCSEng68 BDS68. St Jo Coll Nottm CertCS88. **d** 88 **p** 95. NSM Lerwick *Ab* from 88; NSM Burravoe from 88. *Waters Edge, Bridge of Walls, Shetland ZE2 9NP* Tel (01595) 809441

MACNAB, Kenneth Edward. b 65. LMH Ox BA87 MA91. Coll of Resurr Mirfield 89. **d** 91 **p** 92. C Northampton All SS w St Kath *Pet* 91-93; Lib Pusey Ho 93-98; P-in-c Tunbridge Wells St Barn *Roch* 98-01; V from 01. *St Barnabas' Parochial House, 114 Upper Grosvenor Road, Tunbridge Wells TN1 2EX* Tel and fax (01892) 533826 E-mail father.macnab@btopenworld.com

McNAMARA, Barbara. *See* SMITH, Mrs Barbara Mary

McNAMARA, Michael Ian. b 59. Van Mildert Coll Dur BA81. Ridley Hall Cam 83. **d** 85 **p** 86. C Bedford Ch Ch *St Alb* 85-89; BCMS Tanzania 89-92; TV Bolton St Paul w Em *Man* 93-97; C Galleywood Common *Chelmsf* 97-03; R Elmswell *St E* from 03. *The Rectory, Church Road, Elmswell, Bury St Edmunds IP30 9DY* Tel (01359) 240512 E-mail mwanza@lineone.net

McNAMEE, William Graham. b 38. Birm Univ BSocSc59. Cranmer Hall Dur BA74 DipTh. **d** 75 **p** 76. C Tonbridge St Steph *Roch* 75-78; C Fazeley *Lich* 78-87; Chapl Staffs Poly 87-92; Chapl Staffs Univ 92-97; P-in-c Lt Malvern, Malvern Wells and Wyche *Worc* 97-00; P-in-c Malvern Wells and Wyche 00-01; rtd 01. *22 Leadon Road, Malvern WR14 2XF* Tel (01684) 562771

McNAUGHTAN-OWEN, James Thomas (Tom). b 48. Liv Univ MA00. Linc Th Coll 77. **d** 80 **p** 81. C Palmers Green St Jo *Lon* 80-84; C Timperley *Ches* 84-87; C Bramhall 87-92; V Latchford St Jas from 92; RD Gt Budworth 96-03. *St James's Vicarage, Manx Road, Warrington WA4 6AJ* Tel (01925) 631893

MACNAUGHTON, Mrs Diana. b 54. St Hugh's Coll Ox BA76 MA90 Dur Univ PGCE78. NEOC 95. **d** 98 **p** 99. NSM Gosforth All SS *Newc* 98-01; C Willington 01-04; Chapl Team Ldr Northumbria Healthcare NHS Trust from 04. *33 Twyford Close, Cramlington NE23 1PH* Tel (01670) 712259 Mobile 07950-627799 E-mail dmacnaughton@btinternet.com

MACNAUGHTON, James Alastair. b 54. St Jo Coll Ox BA78 MA82 Fitzw Coll Cam BA80. Ridley Hall Cam 78. **d** 81 **p** 82. C Rounds Green *Birm* 81-85; TV Bestwood Park *S'well* 85-86; TV Bestwood 86-90; V Amble *Newc* 90-97; TR Cramlington from 97. *33 Twyford Close, Cramlington NE23 1PH* Tel (01670) 736064 E-mail macnaughton@btinternet.com

McNAUGHTON, John. b 29. St Chad's Coll Dur DipTh54. **d** 54 **p** 55. C Thorney Close CD *Dur* 54-58; C-in-c E Herrington St Chad CD 58-62; PC E Herrington 62-66; CF 66-94; V Hutton Cranswick w Skerne, Watton and Beswick *York* 94-99; rtd 99; Perm to Offic *York* from 99. *47 Southgate, Cranswick, Driffield YO25 9QX* Tel (01377) 270869

MACNAUGHTON, William Malcolm. b 57. Qu Coll Cam BA80. Ridley Hall Cam 79. **d** 81 **p** 82. C Haughton le Skerne *Dur* 81-85; P-in-c Newton Hall 85-90; TV Shoreditch St Leon and Hoxton St Jo *Lon* 90-00; AD Hackney 94-99; V Hoxton St Jo w Ch Ch 00-02; R Hambleden Valley *Ox* from 02. *The Rectory, Hambledon, Henley-on-Thames RG9 6RP* Tel (01491) 571231 Fax as telephone

McNEE, Canon William Creighton. FCIPD TCD DipTh Univ of Wales (Cardiff) Dip Personnel Mgt Ulster Univ MA NUU MA. **d** 82 **p** 83. C Larne and Inver *Conn* 82-84; I Donagheady *D & R* 84-91; I Kilwaughter w Cairncastle and Craigy Hill *Conn* 91-93; I Ardstraw w Baronscourt, Badoney Lower etc *D & R* 93-04; P-in-c Londonderry Ch Ch from 04; Bp's Dom Chapl from 96; Can Derry Cathl from 00. *2 Bunderg Road, Newtownstewart, Omagh BT78 4NQ* Tel and fax (028) 8166 1342 E-mail billmcnee@usa.net

MACNEICE, Alan Donor. b 34. TCD Div Sch 62. **d** 64 **p** 65. C Ballymoney w Finvoy and Rasharkin *Conn* 64-67; Jamaica 67-70; C Winchmore Hill H Trin *Lon* 71-76; C Harringay St Paul 76-77; C Kensington St Barn 77-78; P-in-c 78-79; USA from 83; rtd 99. *PO Box 293, Kilauea, Kauai, HI 96754, USA* Tel (001) (808) 826 4510 Fax 826 4444 E-mail donor@aloha.net

McNEIL, Mrs Ann. b 41. **d** 89 **p** 94. NSM Henfield w Shermanbury and Woodmancote *Chich* 89-99; Perm to Offic from 00. *6 The Daisycroft, Henfield BN5 9LH* Tel (01273) 492606

McNEILE, Donald Hugh. b 30. Trin Coll Cam BA53. Coll of Resurr Mirfield 53. **d** 55 **p** 56. C Wigan All SS *Liv* 55-57; C W Derby Gd Shep 57-61; rtd 95. *Manor Farm Household, North Hinksey, Oxford OX2 0NA* Tel (01865) 245473

MACNEILL, Nicholas Terence. b 62. St Steph Ho Ox BTh93. **d** 93 **p** 94. C Ex St Thos and Em *Ex* 93-97; TV 97-98; V Cople, Moggerhanger and Willington *St Alb* 98-03; R Toddington and Chalgrave from 03. *The Rectory, 41 Leighton Road, Toddington, Dunstable LU5 6AL* Tel (01525) 872298 E-mail nicm@tesco.net

McNEISH, Canon John. b 34. Edin Th Coll 58. **d** 61 **p** 62. C Kirkcaldy *St And* 61-64; Prec St Andr Cathl *Ab* 64-66; Chapl RAF 66-72; C Wootton Bassett *Sarum* 72-75; P-in-c Stour Provost w Todbere 75-79; TR Gillingham 79-99; RD Blackmore Vale 81-86; Can and Preb Sarum Cathl 92-99; rtd 99; Perm to Offic *Sarum* from 01. *2B Holbrook Lane, Trowbridge BA14 0PR* Tel (01225) 719029 E-mail mcneishjd@yahoo.co.uk

McNICOL, Andrew Keith. b 45. Westmr Coll of Educn CertEd69 Westmr Coll Ox DipApTh89 MA90 Open Univ BA79. Westmr Coll Cam 70 Westcott Ho Cam 92. **d** 92 **p** 93. C Whitstable *Cant* 92-95; V Ferring *Chich* 95-00; P-in-c Willesborough *Cant* from 00. *The Rectory, 66 Church Road, Willesborough, Ashford TN24 0JG* Tel (01233) 624064 E-mail akmcnicol@tesco.net

McNIVEN, Mrs Betty. b 47. Lanc Univ BA68. N Ord Course 83. **dss** 86 **d** 87 **p** 94. Baguley *Man* 86-87; Hon Par Dn 87-88; Par Dn Newton Heath All SS 88-91; Par Dn E Farnworth and Kearsley 91-94; TV 94-95; P-in-c Spotland 95-02; Hon Can Man Cathl 00-02; TV Cwm Gwendraeth *St D* from 02. *The Vicarage, 1 Heol Mansant, Pontyates, Llanelli SA15 5SB* Tel (01269) 860451 E-mail betty.mcniven@talk21.com

MACONACHIE, Charles Leslie. b 27. TCD BA71 MA74 MDiv85 PhD90. Em Coll Saskatoon 47. **d** 50 **p** 51. C Clooney *D & R* 50-54; P-in-c Lower Tamlaght O'Crilly 54-61; Chapl Newsham Gen Hosp Liv 61-63; Chapl RAF 63-67; C Londonderry Ch Ch *D & R* 69-75; I Belmont 75-78; Warden for Min of Healing 75-96; I Culmore w Muff and Belmont 78-96; Warden Irish Internat Order of St Luke Physician 82-96; Can Derry Cathl 85-96; rtd 96; Chmn Ch's Min of Healing from 96. *3 Broomhill Court, Waterside, Londonderry BT47 6WP* Tel (028) 7134 8942

MACOURT, William Albany. b 19. TCD BA40 MA46. CITC 41. **d** 42 **p** 43. C Ballymena *Conn* 42-46; C Belf Cathl 46-48; I Duneane w Ballyscullion *Conn* 48-51; I Belfast St Mark 51-64; I Ballymacarrett St Patr *D & D* 64-89; Preb Swords St Patr Cathl Dublin 75-89; Adn Down *D & D* 80-89; Chan Belf Cathl 85-89; rtd 89; Dioc Info Officer *D & D* 89-97. *19 Abbey Court, Abbey Gardens, Belfast BT5 7JE* Tel (028) 9048 2041

McPHATE, The Very Revd Gordon Ferguson. b 50. Aber Univ MB, ChB74 Fitzw Coll Cam BA77 MA81 MD88 Surrey Univ MSc86 Edin Univ MTh94 FRCPEd98. Westcott Ho Cam 75. **d** 78 **p** 79. NSM Sanderstead All SS *S'wark* 78-81; Hon PV S'wark Cathl 81-86; Lect Lon Univ 81-86; Chapl St Andr Univ *St And* 86-02; Lect 86-93; Sen Lect 93-02; Dean Ches from 02. *The Deanery, 7 Abbey Street, Chester CH1 2JF* Tel (01244) 500956 *or* 500971 Fax 341110 E-mail dean@chestercathedral.com

MacPHEE, Canon Roger Hunter. b 43. Leeds Univ BSc65. EAMTC. **d** 86 **p** 87. NSM Trunch *Nor* from 86; Dioc NSM Officer from 97; Hon Can Nor Cathl from 03. *8 Lawn Close, Knapton, North Walsham NR28 0SD* Tel (01263) 720045

McPHERSON, Andrew Lindsay. b 58. MCIPD84 St Jo Coll Dur BA79. St Jo Coll Nottm DPS88. **d** 88 **p** 89. C Bitterne *Win* 88-92; V Weston 92-99; V Holdenhurst and Iford from 99. *The Vicarage, 53A Holdenhurst Avenue, Bournemouth BH7 6RB* Tel (01202) 425978 E-mail andy.mcpherson@ukgateway.net

MACPHERSON, Anthony Stuart. b 56. Qu Coll Birm 77. **d** 80 **p** 81. C Morley St Pet w Churwell *Wakef* 80-84; C Penistone 84-85; P-in-c Thurlstone 85-86; TV Penistone and Thurlstone 86-88; V Grimethorpe 88-95; P-in-c Westgate Common 95-96; V from 96; P-in-c Horbury Junction from 02; RD Wakef from 99. *The Vicarage, Millfield Road, Horbury, Wakefield WF4 5DU* Tel (01924) 275274 Mobile 07780-990354 Fax (01924) 275311 E-mail frtony.mac@ntlworld.com

MACPHERSON, Archibald McQuarrie. b 27. Edin Th Coll 50. **d** 52 **p** 53. Asst Chapl St Andr Cathl *Ab* 52-55; Prec 55-56; P-in-c Airdrie *Glas* 56-63; R Dumbarton 63-92; rtd 92. *29 Bramblehedge Path, Alexandria G83 8PH* Tel (01389) 753981

MacPHERSON, David Alan John. b 42. Lon Univ DipTh71 BD75 Open Univ BA83 Hatf Poly MSc89. Clifton Th Coll 69 Trin Coll Bris 72. **d** 72 **p** 73. C Drypool St Columba w St Andr and St Pet *York* 72-76; Asst Chapl HM Pris Hull 72-76; P-in-c Bessingby *York* 76-78; P-in-c Carnaby 76-78; Chapl RAF 78-83; P-in-c Chedgrave w Hardley and Langley *Nor* 83-87; R 87-97; Chapl Langley Sch Nor 83-97; P-in-c Brington w Whilton and Norton *Pet* 97-98; R Brington w Whilton and Norton etc 98-02; rtd 02. *24 Coldstream Close, Daventry NN11 9HL* Tel (01327) 704500 E-mail dmacp@compuserve.com

MACPHERSON, Ewan Alexander. b 43. Toronto Univ BA74. Wycliffe Coll Toronto MDiv78. **d** 78 **p** 79. Canada 78-86; V Westbury sub Mendip w Easton *B & W* from 86; V Priddy from 86. *The Vicarage, Crow Lane, Westbury sub Mendip, Wells BA5 1HB* Tel (01749) 870293

MACPHERSON, John. b 28. Lon Univ BSc50 Ex Univ DipEd51 Univ of W Indies HDipEd65. St Alb Minl Tr Scheme 82. **d** 89 **p** 90. NSM Gt Berkhamsted *St Alb* 89-95; Perm to Offic from 00. *Little Tanglewood, Luton Road, Markyate, St Albans AL3 8PZ* Tel (01582) 841219

MACPHERSON, Peter Sinclair. b 44. Lich Th Coll 68. **d** 71 **p** 72. C Honiton, Gittisham and Combe Raleigh *Ex* 71-72; C Bideford 72-74; C Devonport St Mark Ford 74-75; V Thorncombe *Sarum* 75-79; TV Dorchester 79-85; Chapl Jersey Gp of Hosps 85-90; Chapl Derriford Hosp Plymouth 90-98; rtd 98. *Pump Cottage, 1 Rosemary Lane, Musbury, Axminster EX13 6AT* Tel (01297) 552524

MACQUARRIE, Canon John. b 19. TD62. Glas Univ MA40 BD43 PhD54 DLitt64 Hon DD69 Univ of the South (USA) Hon STD67 Gen Th Sem NY Hon STD68 Ox Univ MA70 DD81 Episc Sem Austin Texas Hon DD81 Nashotah Ho Wisconsin Hon DCnL86 Dayton Univ Hon DD94 FBA84. **d** 65 **p** 65. USA 62-70; Prof Systematic Th Union Th Sem NY 62-70; Lady Marg Prof Div Ox Univ 70-86; Can Res Ch Ch *Ox* 70-86; rtd 86. *206 Headley Way, Oxford OX3 7TA* Tel (01865) 761889

MACQUIBAN, Gordon Alexander. b 24. Univ of Wales (Lamp) BA49 Crewe Coll of Educn CertEd72. Ely Th Coll 49. **d** 51 **p** 52. C Christleton *Ches* 51-53; C Disley 53-55; C Heswall and Chapl R Liv Children's Hosp 55-58; V Norley *Ches* 58-64; V Ches Ch Ch 64-71; Hon C Ches H Trin 71-85; Hon C Runcorn All SS 85-87; Hon C Frodsham 87-88; rtd 88; Perm to Offic *B & W* 88-01. *Westlands Residential Home, Reed Vale, Teignmouth TQ14 9EH* Tel (01626) 775843

McQUILLAN, Miss Martha. b 33. St Mich Ho Ox 66. **dss** 70 **d** 87 **p** 94. Barnsbury St Andr *Lon* 70-72; Nottingham St Ann w Em *S'well* 72-79; Chapl Asst Univ Hosp Nottm 79-90; Chapl Asst Nottm Gen Hosp 79-90; rtd 90; Perm to Offic *S'well* from 90. *27 Penarth Rise, Nottingham NG5 4EE* Tel 0115-969 2249 E-mail matty.mcquillan@linby.ndo.co.uk

McQUILLEN, Brian Anthony. b 45. Ripon Hall Ox 73. **d** 75 **p** 76. C Northfield *Birm* 75-78; C Sutton Coldfield H Trin 78-80; V Bearwood 80-89; V Glouc St Geo w Whaddon *Glouc* 89-96; R St Martin w Looe *Truro* from 96; RD W Wivelshire 98-03. *St Martin's Rectory, Barbican Road, Looe PL13 1NX* Tel (01503) 263070 Fax 265550 E-mail revmcq.looe@btopenworld.com

McQUILLEN-WRIGHT, Christopher Charles. b 71. Kent Univ BA92. Westcott Ho Cam CTM95. **d** 95 **p** 96. C Hayle, St Erth and Phillack w Gwithian and Gwinear *Truro* 95-96; C Godrevy 96-99; TV Bodmin w Lanhydrock and Lanivet 99-02; P-in-c St Columb Minor and St Colan from 02. *The Vicarage, Parkenbutts, Newquay TR7 3HE* Tel (01637) 873496 *or* 877165

MACRAE, Charles. b 27. RD71. Edin Univ BDS62 OGS96. S Dios Minl Tr Scheme 88. **d** 91 **p** 92. NSM Heene *Chich* 91-94; NSM Portsea St Alb *Portsm* 94-96; Perm to Offic *Chich* from 96. *64 Stone Lane, Worthing BN13 2BQ* Tel (01903) 691660

McRAE, Keith Alban. b 44. S'wark Ord Course 68. **d** 73 **p** 74. NSM Crawley *Chich* 73-78; NSM Ifield 78-90. *52 Downsview, Small Dole, Henfield BN5 9YB*

MacRAE, Mrs Rosalind Phyllis. b 41. Sarum & Wells Th Coll 81. **dss** 84 **d** 87 **p** 94. Feltham *Lon* 84-87; Par Dn 87; Asst Chapl R Cornwall Hosps Trust 87-88; Chapl Mt Edgcumbe Hospice 88-92; Chapl St Austell Hosp 88-92; Chapl Penrice Hosp St Austell 88-92; NSM St Austell *Truro* 88-92; Chapl R Cornwall Hosps Trust 92-95; rtd 95. *Nairnside Cottage, Nairnside, Inverness IV1 2BU* Tel (01463) 793804

McREYNOLDS, Kenneth Anthony. b 48. TCD DipTh83. **d** 83 **p** 84. C Ballymena w Ballyclug *Conn* 83-86; I Rathcoole 86-90; I Lambeg from 90. *Lambeg Rectory, 58 Belfast Road, Lisburn BT27 4AT* Tel and fax (028) 9266 3872 E-mail kenmcreynolds@btinternet.com

MacROBERT, Iain. b 49. Wolv Univ BA80 PGCE81 Aston Univ CertPSC83 Birm Univ MA85 PhD89. **d** 00 **p** 00. NSM S Queensferry *Edin* from 00. *21 Long Crook, South Queensferry EH30 9XR* Tel and fax 0131-319 1558 *or* tel 244 0651 E-mail iain.macrobert@talk21.com

McROSTIE, Ms Lyn. b 50. Canberra Univ BA77 Portsm Univ MA03 MIInfSc81. STETS 95. **d** 98 **p** 99. C Portsea St Cuth *Portsm* 98-02; P-in-c Shadwell St Paul w Ratcliffe St Jas *Lon* 02-04; Course Ldr NTMTC from 04. *North Thames Ministerial Training Course, Chase Side, London N14 4PS* Tel (020) 8364 9442 Mobile 07718-300732 E-mail lyn.mcrostie@mcrostie.info

MACROW-WOOD, Antony Charles. b 60. York Univ BA82 Jes Coll Cam BA91 ACA86. Westcott Ho Cam 89. **d** 92 **p** 93. C Swindon St Jo and St Andr *Bris* 92-96; TV Preston w Sutton Poyntz and Osmington w Poxwell *Sarum* 96-04; P-in-c Oakdale from 04. *St George's Vicarage, 99 Darbys Lane, Poole BH15 3EU* Tel (01202) 675419 Mobile 07775-574971 E-mail amacrowwood@mac.com

McSPARRON, Cecil. b 35. Regent Coll Vancouver MCS87 Bible Tr Inst Glas DipMin63 Trin Th Coll Singapore DipMin68 MMin77 MDiv86. **d** 68 **p** 69. C Glendermott *D & R* 68-70; Singapore 70-77 and 83-89; C Portadown St Mark *Arm* 78-80; UK Regional Dir OMF 80-82; Tutor Miss Studies Lon Bible Coll 90-93. *1 Tutors House, Green Lane, Northwood HA6 2UZ*

McTEER, Robert Ian. b 56. Chich Th Coll 90. **d** 92 **p** 93. C S Shields All SS *Dur* 92-95; P-in-c Auckland St Helen 95-97; V from 97; Chapl Bishop Auckland Hospitals NHS Trust 95-98; Chapl S Durham Healthcare NHS Trust from 98. *The Vicarage, 8 Manor Road, St Helen Auckland, Bishop Auckland DL14 9EN* Tel (01388) 604152 E-mail fr.r.mcteer@btinternet.com

MacVANE, Sara. **d** 05. C Rome *Eur* from 05. *Address temp unknown*

McVEAGH, Paul Stuart. b 56. Southn Univ BA78. Oak Hill Th Coll BA88. **d** 88 **p** 89. C Bebington *Ches* 88-92; Crosslinks Portugal 92-95; R High Halstow w All Hallows and Hoo St Mary *Roch* 95-02; V Westerham from 02. *The Vicarage, Borde Hill, Vicarage Hill, Westerham TN16 1TL* Tel (01959) 563127 E-mail pmcveagh@aol.com

McVEETY, Ian. b 46. N Ord Course 82. **d** 85 **p** 86. NSM Langley and Parkfield *Man* 85-86; C 87-89; V Castleton Moor 89-99; AD Heywood and Middleton 95-99; V Baguley from 99. *St John's Vicarage, 186 Brooklands Road, Sale M33 3PB* Tel 0161-973 5947

McVEIGH, Miss Dorothy Sarah. b 67. QUB BA89 TCD BTh93. CITC 90. **d** 93 **p** 94. C Belfast St Matt *Conn* 93-96; C Carrickfergus 96-99; C Lurgan Ch the Redeemer *D & D* 99-04; I Annaghmore *Arm* from 04. *54 Moss Road, Portadown, Craigavon BT62 1NB* Tel (028) 3885 1555 Mobile 07786-454346

McVEIGH, Canon Samuel. b 49. CITC 77. **d** 79 **p** 80. C Drumragh w Mountfield *D & R* 79-82; I Dromore *Clogh* 82-90; I Drumachose *D & R* from 90; Can Derry Cathl from 01. *49 Killane Road, Limavady BT49 0DJ* Tel (028) 7776 2680

McVEIGH, Sandra. *See* BUTLER, Mrs Sandra

MACVICAR, Miss Mary. b 23. Edin Univ MA44 Ox Univ DipEd45. Ripon Coll Cuddesdon 85. **dss** 86 **d** 87 **p** 94. Bishop's Waltham *Portsm* 86-89; Hon C 87-89; Perm to Offic 89-94; Hon C Portsm Cathl 94-95; Hon Chapl from 94; rtd 95; Perm to Offic *Portsm* from 95. *15 Roman Row, Bank Street, Bishops Waltham, Southampton SO32 1RW* Tel (01489) 895955

McWATT, Glenn Ellsworth. b 48. Birkbeck Coll Lon DipRS92. Lon Bible Coll 70 S'wark Ord Course 89. **d** 92 **p** 93. NSM Tulse Hill H Trin and St Matthias *S'wark* 92-99; C New Malden and Coombe 99-03; C Reigate St Mary from 03. *63 Chart Lane, Reigate RH2 7EA* Tel (01737) 243085 E-mail mcwatt@ic24.net

McWHIRTER, James Angus. b 58. Portsm Poly BA91 Trin Coll Carmarthen PGCE93. St Steph Ho Ox 00. **d** 02 **p** 03. C Shifnal

Lich from 02. *Noost, 38 Maple Close, Shifnal TF11 8HA* Tel (01952) 461548 E-mail revdjames.mcwh@btopenworld.com

MacWILLIAM, The Very Revd Alexander Gordon. b 23. Univ of Wales BA43 Lon Univ BD47 PhD52. St Mich Coll Llan 43. **d** 45 **p** 46. C Llanllyfni *Ban* 46-49; Min Can Ban Cathl 49-55; C Ban St Mary 50-53; C Ban St Jas 53-55; R Llanfaethlu w Llanfwrog 55-56; R Llanfaethlu w Llanfwrog and Llanrhuddlad etc 56-58; Hd of RE Dept Lic to Offic *St D* 60-78; Trin Coll Carmarthen 60-70; Hd Sch of Soc Studies 70-84; Visiting Prof Th Cen Univ Iowa USA 83-84; Can St D Cathl *St D* 78-84; Prec, V, and Dean 84-90; rtd 90. *Pen Parc, Smyrna Road, Llangain, Carmarthen SA33 5AD* Tel (01267) 241333

McWILLIAMS, Mrs Laura Jane. b 67. Cranmer Hall Dur 01. **d** 03 **p** 04. C Kingston upon Hull St Aid Southcoates *York* from 03. *9 Lorenzo Way, Hull HU9 3HS* Tel (01482) 704517 Mobile 07984-003660 E-mail mcwilliams@lmcwilliams.freeserve.co.uk

MADDERN, James Thomas. b 76. Edin Univ BD99. Wycliffe Hall Ox 00. **d** 02 **p** 03. C Stratford St Jo w Ch Ch and St Jas *Chelmsf* from 02. *29 Maryland Park, London E15 1HB* Tel (020) 8534 7503 E-mail james_maddern@hotmail.com

MADDEX, Patrick John. b 31. Edin Univ BSc54. Bps' Coll Cheshunt 55. **d** 57 **p** 58. C Baldock w Bygrave and Clothall *St Alb* 57-61; C Oxhey All SS 61-64; V Codicote 64-82; R Gt and Lt Wymondley w Graveley and Chivesfield 82-96; rtd 96. *19 Bramber Road, Seaford BN25 1AG*

MADDOCK, Mrs Audrey. b 27. Lon Univ CertEd79 Open Univ BA80 MBPsS80. Bris Sch of Min 81. **dss** 84 **d** 87 **p** 94. Stanton St Quintin, Hullavington, Grittleton etc *Bris* 84-94; Par Dn 87-94; C 94; P-in-c Littleton Drew 95-97; rtd 97; Perm to Offic *Bris* from 97. *1 Brookside, Hullavington, Chippenham SN14 6HD* Tel (01666) 837275

MADDOCK (née FARLEY), Ms Claire Louise. b 69. Man Univ BA91 Heythrop Coll Lon MTh99. Westcott Ho Cam 96. **d** 99 **p** 00. C Sherborne w Castleton and Lillington *Sarum* 99-00; C Weymouth H Trin 00-02; Chapl Barts and The Lon NHS Trust 02-03; Chapl Ealing Hosp NHS Trust from 03; Chapl W Middx Univ Hosp NHS Trust from 03. *The Chaplaincy, Ealing Hospital, Uxbridge Road, Southall UB1 3HW* Tel (020) 8967 5130 *or* 8321 5447 E-mail claire.maddock@eht.nhs.uk

MADDOCK, David John Newcomb. b 36. Qu Coll Cam BA60 MA64. Oak Hill Th Coll 60. **d** 62 **p** 63. C Bispham *Blackb* 62-65; R 82-93; RD Blackpool 90-93; Miss Payne Bay Canada 65-69; R Frobisher Bay 70; R Walsoken *Ely* 70-77; V Ore Ch Ch *Chich* 77-82; V Fowey *Truro* 93-02; Chapl Cornwall Healthcare NHS Trust 94-02; rtd 02; Perm to Offic *Truro* from 02. *Orchards, Biscovey Road, Par PL24 2HW* Tel (01726) 813288

MADDOCK, Francis James Wilson. b 14. Bris Univ BA36 Wadh Coll Ox BA38 MA42. Cuddesdon Coll 39. **d** 40 **p** 41. C Southfields St Barn *S'wark* 40-44; C Horfield H Trin *Bris* 44-49; PC Brislington St Anne 49-56; V Newlyn St Pet *Truro* 56-60; Perm to Offic 60-64; R Forrabury w Minster and Trevalga 64-74; P-in-c Davidstow w Otterham 64-74; RD Trigg Minor 66-69; TR Boscastle w Davidstow 74-78; P-in-c Port Isaac 78-79; rtd 79; Perm to Offic *Ex* from 87. *8 Sylvan Close, Exmouth EX8 3BQ*

MADDOCK, Nicholas Rokeby. b 47. ABSM72 Birm Coll of Educn CertEd73. Linc Th Coll 82. **d** 82 **p** 83. C Romford St Edw *Chelmsf* 82-87; V Sway *Win* 87-94; V Taunton St Mary *B & W* 94-04; R Wrington w Butcombe from 04. *The Rectory, 3 Alburys, Wrington, Bristol BS40 5NZ* Tel (01934) 862201

MADDOCK, Philip Arthur Louis. b 47. Open Univ BA82 Lanc Univ MPhil02. Oak Hill Th Coll 75. **d** 78 **p** 79. C New Ferry *Ches* 78-81; C Barnston 81-82; V Over St Jo 82-85; V Norley and Chapl to the Deaf 85-88; P-in-c Treales and Chapl to the Deaf *Blackb* 88-96; Chapl to the Deaf *Lich* 96-02; C Yoxall and The Ridwares and Kings Bromley 98-02; Adv for Deaf and Disabled People Min Div from 03; NSM Alrewas *Lich* from 03; NSM Wychnor from 03. *Ministry Division, Church House, Great Smith Street, London SW1P 3NZ* Tel (020) 7898 1439 E-mail philip.maddock@c-of-e.org.uk *or* palm@clara.net

MADDOCK, Canon Philip Lawrence. b 20. Bris Univ BA42. Cuddesdon Coll 42. **d** 43 **p** 44. C Kilburn St Aug *Lon* 43-48; C Weston-super-Mare All SS *B & W* 48-57; Chapl Community of the Epiphany Truro 57-60; Sub-Warden 60-63; Chapl HM Pris Wandsworth 63-64; HM Pris Birm 64-67; Ex 67-69; Chapl St Lawr Hosp Bodmin 69-76; Can Res and Treas Truro Cathl *Truro* 76-88; rtd 88; Perm to Offic *Truro* from 88. *31 Trenethick Avenue, Helston TR13 8LU* Tel (01326) 564909

MADDOCKS, Alison Julie. b 63. Birm Univ BSc84 Loughb Univ MBA92. St Jo Coll Nottm MTh03. **d** 03 **p** 04. C Wollaton *S'well* from 03. *73 Torvill Drive, Nottingham NG8 2BR* Tel 0115-928 3009 E-mail alison.maddocks@handbag.com

✠**MADDOCKS, The Rt Revd Morris Henry St John.** b 28. Trin Coll Cam BA52 MA56. Chich Th Coll 52. **d** 54 **p** 55 **c** 72. C Ealing St Pet Mt Park *Lon* 54-55; C Uxbridge St Andr w St Jo 55-58; V Weaverthorpe w Helperthorpe and Luttons *York* 58-61; V Scarborough St Martin 61-71; Suff Bp Selby 72-83; Adv Min Health and Healing to Abps Cant and York 83-95; Asst Bp B & W 83-87; Asst Bp Chich from 87; Jt Founding Dir Acorn Chr Healing Trust from 91; Can and Preb Chich Cathl from 92; rtd 95; Perm to Offic *Guildf* 95-96. *3 The Chantry, Canon Lane, Chichester PO19 1PZ* Tel (01243) 788888

MADDOX, David John. b 34. AIMLS58. Sarum & Wells Th Coll 92. **d** 81 **p** 93. In RC Ch 81-91; NSM Wimborne Minster and Holt *Sarum* 93-95; NSM Broadstone 95-01; Perm to Offic *Sarum* and *Win* from 00. *298 Wimborne Road, Poole BH15 3EG* Tel (01202) 672597

MADDOX, Derek Adrian James. b 64. Kingston Poly BA88. Trin Coll Bris 02. **d** 04 **p** 05. C Mitcham St Mark *S'wark* from 04. *7 Graham Road, Mitcham CR4 2HB* Tel (020) 8665 2547 E-mail maddoxmob@aol.com

MADDOX, Goronwy Owen. b 23. Univ of Wales (Swansea) BA52 DipEd53. Sarum Th Coll 67. **d** 70 **p** 71. Hd Master H Trin Sch Calne 57-82; Hon C Calne and Blackland *Sarum* 70-82; C 82-83; V Llywel and Traean-glas w Llanulid *S & B* 83-92; rtd 92; Perm to Offic *Sarum* from 92. *4 St Matthew's Close, Rowde, Devizes SN10 2PG* Tel (01380) 728965

MADDOX, Hugh Inglis Monteath. b 37. CCC Cam BA60. Westcott Ho Cam 61. **d** 63 **p** 64. C Attercliffe *Sheff* 63-66; C Maidstone All SS w St Phil *Cant* 66-67; C Folkestone St Mary and St Eanswythe 67-69; C St Martin-in-the-Fields *Lon* 69-73; R Sandwich *Cant* 73-81; V St Peter-in-Thanet 81-84; V Red Post *Sarum* 84-03; rtd 03; Perm to Offic *Sarum* from 03. *36 Corfe Road, Stoborough, Wareham BH20 5AD* Tel (01929) 550872

MADDY, Kevin. b 58. GRNCM79 Selw Coll Cam BA83 FRSA96. Westcott Ho Cam 81. **d** 85 **p** 86. C St Peter-in-Thanet *Cant* 85-88; Perm to Offic *Nor* 88-91; Chapl RAF 88-02; CF from 02. *c/o MOD Chaplains (Army)* Tel (01980) 615804 Fax 615800

MADELEY, Mark Keith. b 68. DipHE92 AVCM96. Oak Hill Th Coll BA93. **d** 93 **p** 94. C Mickleover All SS *Derby* 93-96; C Charlesworth and Dinting Vale 96-99; Chapl Chr Tours (UK) Ltd 99-00; NSM Moldgreen and Rawthorpe *Wakef* 99-00; V Coley from 00. *Coley Vicarage, 41 Ing Head Terrace, Shelf, Halifax HX3 7LB* Tel and fax (01422) 202292 Mobile 07050-021860 E-mail mark@mibtravel.co.uk

MADGE, Francis Sidney. b 35. AKC58. **d** 59 **p** 60. C York St Mary Bishophill Senior *York* 59-62; C Sutton St Mich 62-64; C Ex St Jas *Ex* 64-69; R Sutton by Dover w Waldershare *Cant* 69-78; P-in-c W Wickham St Mary 78-81; V 81-02; rtd 02. *1 Callums Walk, Bexhill-on-Sea TN40 2JF* Tel (01424) 222756

MADRID, Bishop in. *See* LÓPEZ LOZANO, The Rt Revd Carlos

MADZIMURE, Dominic Makusha. b 52. Middx Univ MA03. **d** 77 **p** 78. Zimbabwe 77-99; Perm to Offic *Cant* 01-03; P-in-c Woodchurch from 03. *The Rectory, 6 Rectory Close, Woodchurch, Ashford TN26 3QJ* Tel (01233) 860257 E-mail dominic@madzimure.fsnet.co.uk

MAGAHY, Gerald Samuel. b 23. TCD BA45 MA61 LLD80 Univ Coll Galway HDipEd55. **d** 53 **p** 54. Dioc Chapl and Hd Master Villiers Sch Limerick 53-61; Chapl and Hd Master K Hosp Sch Dub 61-83; Treas St Patr Cathl Dublin 80-89; Chan 89-91; Prec 91-95; rtd 95. *2 Maryland, Beechfield Manor, Shankill, Co Dublin, Irish Republic*

MAGEE, Frederick Hugh. b 33. Yale Univ BA56. Westcott Ho Cam 58. **d** 59 **p** 60. C Bury St Mark *Man* 59-62; USA 63-64 and 87-05; Chapl St Paul's Cathl Dundee *Bre* 74-79; P-in-c Invergowrie 76-79; R St Andrews St Andr *St And* 79-83; R Forfar 83-87; rtd 05. *9 Craigmore, 39 Wellington Road, Bournemouth BH8 8JH* Tel (01202) 559246 E-mail hugh@twomagees.plus.com

MAGEE, Keith Robert. b 60. Bris Univ BA95 PGCE96. Trin Coll Bris 92 Westcott Ho Cam 99. **d** 01 **p** 02. C S Woodham Ferrers *Chelmsf* 01-05; V Moulsham St Jo from 05. *St John's Vicarage, Vicarage Road, Chelmsford CM2 9PH* Tel (01245) 352344 E-mail keith.magee@btinternet.com

MAGEE, Canon Patrick Connor. b 15. K Coll Cam BA37 MA41. Westcott Ho Cam 38. **d** 39 **p** 40. C King Cross *Wakef* 39-42; Chapl RNVR 43-46; Chapl K Coll Cam 46-52; V Kingston All SS *S'wark* 52-60; Chapl Bryanston Sch 60-70; V Ryde All SS *Portsm* 70-72; Chapl Tiffin Sch Kingston 72-73; V Salisbury St Mich *Sarum* 73-75; TR Bemerton 75-84; rtd 84; Perm to Offic *Sarum* from 84. *16A Donaldson Road, Salisbury SP1 3AD* Tel (01722) 324278

MAGILL, Robert James Henderson. b 59. Paisley Coll of Tech BSc81. Sarum & Wells Th Coll Dip Th & Min 94. **d** 94 **p** 95. C W Moors *Sarum* 94-98; P-in-c Hilperton w Whaddon and Staverton etc from 98; Community Affairs Chapl from 02. *The Rectory, Hilperton, Trowbridge BA14 7RL* Tel (01225) 752804

MAGILL, Waller Brian Brendan. b 20. TCD BA42 BD45. **d** 44 **p** 45. C Knock *D & D* 44-47; C Holywood 47-50; Vice-Prin Qu Coll Birm 50-55; Chapl Rugby Sch 55-62; Lect Div Nottm Coll of Educn 62-75; Hd of Dept Trent Poly 75-85; Lic to Offic *S'well* from 66; rtd 85. *16 Parkcroft Road, Nottingham NG2 6FN* Tel 0115-923 3293

MAGNESS, Anthony William John. b 37. New Coll Ox BA62 MA65. Coll of Resurr Mirfield 78. **d** 80 **p** 81. C Gt Crosby St Faith *Liv* 80-83; C Newc St Jo *Newc* 83-85; P-in-c Newc St Luke 85-88; P-in-c Newc St Andr 88; V Newc St Andr and St Luke 89-99; Chapl Hunter's Moor Hosp 89-95; P-in-c

Cambois *Newc* 99-00; P-in-c Sleekburn 99-00; V Cambois and Sleekburn 00-03; rtd 03; Perm to Offic *Newc* from 03. *59 Firtree Crescent, Newcastle upon Tyne NE12 7JU* Tel and fax 0191-268 4596

MAGNUSSON, Lisbet Maria. b 50. Mid-Sweden Univ BSc85 Uppsala Univ MDiv93 ML98. Past Inst Uppsala 93. **p** 94. In Ch of Sweden 94-98; C Crosby *Linc* 98-99; TV Gainsborough and Morton 99-04; P-in-c Swallow from 04; Chapl Doncaster and S Humber Healthcare NHS Trust from 04. *The Rectory, Beelsby Road, Swallow, Market Rasen LN7 6DG* Tel (01472) 371957 E-mail swallowrectory@hotmail.com

MAGOR, Robert Jolyon. b 47. Wilson Carlile Coll IDC82 Sarum & Wells Th Coll 93. **d** 93 **p** 94. C Plaistow *Chelmsf* 93-96; TV Plaistow and N Canning Town 96-99; V Leigh-on-Sea St Aid 99-01; C Thorpe Bay from 01. *254 Woodgrange Drive, Southend-on-Sea SS1 2SH* Tel (01702) 616192

MAGORRIAN, Brian Geoffrey. b 64. St Aid Coll Dur BSc85 York Univ DPhil89. St Jo Coll Nottm. **d** 01 **p** 02. C Bishopwearmouth St Gabr *Dur* 01-04; P-in-c Brough w Stainmore, Musgrave and Warcop *Carl* from 04. *The Rectory, Church Brough, Kirkby Stephen CA17 4EJ* Tel (01768) 341238 E-mail brian.magorrian@btinternet.com

MAGOWAN, The Ven Alistair James. b 55. Leeds Univ BSc77 DipHE. Trin Coll Bris 78. **d** 81 **p** 82. C Owlerton *Sheff* 81-84; C Dur St Nic *Dur* 84-89; Chapl St Aid Coll 85-89; V Egham *Guildf* 89-00; RD Runnymede 93-98; Adn Dorset *Sarum* from 00; Can and Preb Sarum Cathl from 00. *Little Bailie, Dullar Lane, Sturminster Marshall, Wimborne BH21 4AD* Tel (01258) 859110 Fax 859118 E-mail addorset@salisbury.anglican.org

MAGOWAN, Harold Victor. b 34. ACII69 FCII73 Chartered Insurance Practitioner 89 QUB BA55 BSc(Econ)66 DipEd69. TCD Div Sch Div Test57. **d** 57 **p** 58. C Antrim All SS w Muckamore *Conn* 57-59. *6 Fold Mews, 22 Ballyholme Road, Bangor BT20 5JS* Tel (028) 9146 5091

MAGUIRE, Canon Brian William. b 33. Hull Univ BTh84 MA88. Coll of Resurr Mirfield 70. **d** 72 **p** 73. C Guisborough *York* 72-76; TV Haxby w Wigginton 76-77; TR 78-89; V Huddersfield St Pet and All SS *Wakef* 89-00; Hon Can Wakef Cathl 94-00; rtd 00; Perm to Offic *Wakef* from 00; Bp's Dom Chapl 03-04. *Lupset Vicarage, Broadway, Wakefield WF2 8AA* Tel (01924) 373088

MAGUIRE, Michael Timothy Gale (Tim). b 34. Ox Univ Inst of Educn DipEd61. Wycliffe Hall Ox 58. **d** 61 **p** 62. C Southampton St Mary Extra *Win* 61-63; Bp's Youth Chapl 63-66; Perm to Offic *Win* from 97 and *Truro* from 02; rtd 99. *Mordros, Mullion, Helston TR12 7EP* Tel (01326) 241063

MAGUIRE (formerly GRATTON), Mrs Patricia Margaret. b 46. Leeds Univ BTh94 MA96 SRN67 TCert84 CertEd88. EMMTC 89 N Ord Course 96. **d** 97 **p** 98. NSM Shipley St Pet *Bradf* 97-99; C Brighouse and Clifton *Wakef* 99-00; Chapl Wakef Cathl Sch 00-05; P-in-c Thornes St Jas w Ch Ch *Wakef* from 00; P-in-c Lupset from 05. *Lupset Vicarage, Broadway, Wakefield WF2 8AA* Tel (01924) 373088 E-mail pat@revmaguire.freeserve.co.uk

MAGUMBA, Patrick John. b 53. Bp Tucker Coll Mukono BD85 Makerere Univ Kampala PGDE88 Birm Univ MA92 Leeds Univ PhD03. **d** 79 **p** 80. Uganda 79-90 and 93-04; C Kamuli 79-81; V Kaliro 86-90; Sub-Dean Busoga 90; Hon C Harborne Heath *Birm* 91-93; Sen Lect Uganda Chr Univ Mukono 93-04; TV S Rochdale *Man* from 04. *St Luke's Vicarage, 9 Deeplish Road, Rochdale OL11 1NY* Tel (01706) 354623 Mobile 07901-782329 E-mail jmagumba@hotmail.com

MAHER, David James. b 70. St Jo Coll Dur BA01. Cranmer Hall Dur 98. **d** 01 **p** 02. C Hounslow H Trin w St Paul *Lon* 01-04; C Staines Ch Ch from 04; Chapl to Bp Kensington from 04. *Christ Church Vicarage, Kenilworth Gardens, Staines TW18 1DR* Tel (01784) 455457 E-mail david.maher@london.anglican.org

MAHONEY, William Denis. b 35. Sem of the Immaculate Conception (NY) 77. **d** 79 **p** 95. In RC Ch USA 79-87; NSM Egremont and Haile *Carl* 92-93; NSM Kells 93-96; USA 96-98; P-in-c Beckermet St Jo and St Bridget w Ponsonby *Carl* 98-05; rtd 05. *2 Bowden Drive, Huntington Statton, NY 11746, USA* E-mail vlwd17@aol.com

MAHONY, Conal Martin. b 38. Pontificio Ateneo Antoniano Rome Lic in Sacred Th 64 Lateran Univ Rome ThD66. Franciscan Ho of Studies 57. **d** 62 **p** 63. In RC Ch 62-89; Dir Folkestone Family Care Cen 86-92; Lic to Offic *Cant* 89-92; C Hempnall *Nor* 92-94; TV 94-97; TR from 97. *The Rectory, The Street, Hempnall, Norwich NR15 2AD* Tel (01508) 498157

MAIDEN, Charles Alistair Kingsley. b 60. Trent Poly BSc84. St Jo Coll Nottm LTh88. **d** 89 **p** 90. C Porchester *S'well* 89-93; C Selston 93-96; P-in-c Huthwaite from 96. *The Vicarage, Blackwell Road, Huthwaite, Sutton-in-Ashfield NG17 2QT* Tel (01623) 555053 E-mail charlie@maiden02.fsnet.co.uk

MAIDMENT, Thomas John Louis. b 43. Lon Univ BSc65. St Steph Ho Ox. **d** 67 **p** 68. C Westmr St Steph w St Jo *Lon* 67-73; P-in-c Twickenham Common H Trin 73-77; V 77-80; V Heston 80-98; V Bolton-le-Sands *Blackb* from 98; P-in-c Tunstall w Melling and Leck 02-03; AD Tunstall from 99. *The Vicarage, 5 Ancliffe Lane, Bolton-le-Sands, Carnforth LA5 8DS* Tel (01524) 822335 E-mail t.j.l.m@btinternet.com

MAIDSTONE, Archdeacon of. *See* DOWN, The Ven Philip Roy

MAIDSTONE, Suffragan Bishop. *See* CRAY, The Rt Revd Graham Alan

MAIN, Mrs Brigid Mary Harvey. b 49. EAMTC 96. **d** 99 **p** 00. NSM Tillingham *Chelmsf* 99-03; NSM Pleshey from 03. *Parsonage Cottage, The Street, Pleshey CM3 1HA* Tel (01245) 237012 E-mail lmm@globalnet.co.uk

MAIN, Clive Timothy. b 53. St Andr Univ MA75 Cam Univ PGCE76. Oak Hill Th Coll BA94. **d** 96 **p** 97. C Alperton *Lon* 96-00; V Highbury New Park St Aug from 00. *St Augustine's Vicarage, 108 Highbury New Park, London N5 2DR* Tel (020) 7226 6870 E-mail clivemain@blueyonder.co.uk

MAIN, Canon David Murray. b 28. Univ Coll Ox BA52 MA56. St Deiniol's Hawarden 73. **d** 73 **p** 74. C Glas St Marg *Glas* 73-75; R Challoch w Newton Stewart 75-79; R Kilmarnock 79-93; Can St Mary's Cathl 85-93; rtd 93; Hon Can St Mary's Cathl *Glas* from 93. *Sunnybrae, 50 Abercromby Road, Castle Douglas DG7 1BA* Tel (01556) 504669

MAINA, Simon Mwangi. b 52. Nairobi Univ 85. **d** 80 **p** 81. Kenya 80-95; C Acton St Mary *Lon* 95-97; Worthing Churches Homeless Project from 98. *18 Cambourne Court, Shelley Road, Worthing BN11 4BQ* Tel (01903) 600507

MAINES, Canon Trevor. b 40. Leeds Univ BSc63. Ripon Hall Ox 63. **d** 65 **p** 66. C Speke All SS *Liv* 65-70; C Stevenage St Geo *St Alb* 70-73; V Dorridge *Birm* 73-78; Org Sec CECS *Ex* 79-80; Hon C Tiverton St Pet *Ex* 79-80; Org Sec (Wales) CECS 80-87; Hon C Newton Nottage *Llan* 81-83; Perm to Offic *Mon* 83-87; V Arlesey w Astwick *St Alb* 87-95; RD Shefford 91-95; V Goldington 95-05; RD Bedford 98-05; Hon Can St Alb 04-05; rtd 05; Hon C Beedon and Peasemore w W Ilsley and Farnborough *Ox* from 05; Hon C Brightwalton w Catmore, Leckhampstead etc from 05. *The Rectory, 3 Drakes Farm, Peasemore, Newbury RG20 7DF* Tel (01635) 248925 E-mail trevor.maines@tesco.net

MAINEY, Ian George. b 51. CertEd73. Oak Hill Th Coll DipHE86 BA87. **d** 87 **p** 88. C Denton Holme *Carl* 87-91; V Hensingham 91-02; RD Calder 01-02; TR Deane *Man* from 02. *Deane Rectory, 234 Wigan Road, Bolton BL3 5QE* Tel (01204) 61819 E-mail ian.mainey@lineone.net

MAINWARING, Islwyn Paul. b 52. Univ of Wales (Swansea) BD75 DPS79. St Mich Coll Llan 77. **d** 79 **p** 80. C Llanilid w Pencoed *Llan* 79-82; C Llanishen and Lisvane 82-85; TV Cwmbran *Mon* 85-88; V Troedyrhiw w Merthyr Vale *Llan* 88-91. *Pennant, 109 Penygroes Road, Blaenau, Ammanford SA18 3BZ* Tel (01269) 850350

MAINWARING (née LANKSHEAR), Jane Frances. b 70. Leeds Univ BA92 Trin Coll Carmarthen MPhil97 PhD99. EAMTC 98. **d** 00 **p** 01. C Sudbury and Chilton *St E* 00-03; TV Hitchin *St Alb* from 03. *St Mark's Vicarage, St Mark's Close, Hitchin SG5 1UR* Tel (01462) 422862 *or* 434686 E-mail jane@stmarks-hitchin.org.uk

MAINWARING, Simon James. b 74. St Anne's Coll Ox BA96 MA03 Em Coll Cam BA02 Harvard Div Sch ThM04. Westcott Ho Cam 00. **d** 03. C Pensnett *Worc* 03 and from 04; USA 03-04. *35 Primrose Park, Pensnett DY5 4EF* Tel (01384) 70156 Mobile 07789-657174 E-mail simonmainwaring74@hotmail.com

MAIRS, Canon Adrian Samuel. b 43. DipHE. Oak Hill Th Coll 76. **d** 78 **p** 79. C Rugby St Matt *Cov* 78-82; P-in-c Mancetter 82-84; V from 84; P-in-c Hartshill 97-01; Hon Can Cov Cathl from 03. *The Vicarage, Quarry Lane, Mancetter, Atherstone CV9 1NL* Tel (01827) 713266

MAIS, Jeremy Hugh. b 47. **d** 00 **p** 01. NSM Bibury w Winson and Barnsley *Glouc* 00-02; P-in-c from 04; NSM Stratton, N Cerney, Baunton and Bagendon 02-04. *The Vicarage, Bibury, Cirencester GL7 5NT* Tel (01285) 740387

MAITIN, Ito. b 36. Lon Univ DipTh67 BA. Kelham Th Coll 63. **d** 68 **p** 69. C Longton St Jo *Lich* 68-69; C Leek St Edw 69-71; C Lich St Chad 71-74; C Tamworth 74-81; V Penkhull from 81. *The Vicarage, 214 Queen's Road, Stoke-on-Trent ST4 7LG* Tel (01782) 414092

MAITLAND, The Hon Sydney Milivoge Patrick. b 51. Edin Univ BSc Strathclyde Univ Dip Town Planning MRTPI. St Jo Coll Nottm. **d** 86 **p** 87. Hon C Glas St Geo *Glas* from 86. *14 Kersland Street, Glasgow G12 8BL* Tel 0141-339 4573

MAJOR, Richard James Edward. b 54. DipTh. Trin Coll Bris 78. **d** 81 **p** 82. C Parr *Liv* 81-84; V Burton Fleming w Fordon *York* 84-85; V Grindale and Ergham 84-85; P-in-c Wold Newton 84-85; V Burton Fleming w Fordon, Grindale etc 85-91; V Bilton St Pet from 91. *The Vicarage, 14 Cherrytree Close, Bilton, Hull HU11 4EZ* Tel (01482) 811441

MAJOR, Richard John Charles. b 63. Massey Univ (NZ) BA85 Ex Coll Ox BA91 MA93 Magd Coll Ox DPhil91. St Steph Ho Ox 92. **d** 94 **p** 95. C Truro Cathl *Truro* 94-97; C Putney St Mary *S'wark* 97-98; Chapl Florence w Siena *Eur* 98-01; USA from 01. *Nansough Manor, Ladock, Truro TR2 4PB* Tel (01726) 883315 *or* (001) (718) 442 1589 Fax (001) (718) 442 4555 E-mail email@richardmajor.com

MAKAMBWE, Canon Francis James. b 40. St Jo Sem Lusaka. **d** 65 **p** 67. Zambia 65-91; Miss Partner CMS from 91; C Waterloo St Jo w St Andr *S'wark* 91-96; V Hatcham St Cath from 96; Hon Can S'wark Cathl from 03. *St Catherine's Vicarage, 102A Pepys Road, London SE14 5SG* Tel (020) 7639 1050 Fax 7401 3215 E-mail fmakam@aol.com

MAKEL, Arthur. b 39. AKC63. **d** 64 **p** 65. C Beamish *Dur* 64-68; Ind Chapl *York* 68-72; Ind Chapl and P-in-c Scotton w Northorpe *Linc* 72-81; R Epworth 81-89; P-in-c Wroot 81-89; R Epworth and Wroot 89-92; R Sigglesthorne and Rise w Nunkeeling and Bewholme *York* 92-04; P-in-c Aldbrough, Mappleton w Goxhill and Withernwick 98-04; rtd 04; Perm to Offic *York* from 04. *43 Lowfield Road, Beverley HU17 9RF* Tel (01482) 865798

MAKEPEACE, David Norman Harry. b 51. Magd Coll Ox BA74. Trin Coll Bris 83. **d** 85 **p** 86. C Romford Gd Shep Collier Row *Chelmsf* 85-88; Tanzania 88-89; C York St Paul *York* 89-91; TV Radipole and Melcombe Regis *Sarum* 91-98; V Sandgate St Paul w Folkestone St Geo *Cant* 98-00; rtd 00; Perm to Offic *Cant* from 01. *10 Limes Road, Folkestone CT19 4AU* Tel (01303) 274011 E-mail dnhm@talk21.com

MAKEPEACE, Preb James Dugard. b 40. Keble Coll Ox BA63 MA67. Cuddesdon Coll 63. **d** 65 **p** 66. C Cullercoats St Geo *Newc* 65-68; Chapl Wadh Coll Ox 68-72; Lib Pusey Ho 68-72; V Romford St Edw *Chelmsf* 72-79; V Tettenhall Regis *Lich* 79-80; TR 80-99; RD Trysull 87-97; Preb Lich Cathl 96-99; rtd 00; Perm to Offic *Lich* from 00. *The Retreat, 9 Clive Road, Pattingham, Wolverhampton WV6 7BU* Tel (01902) 710713

✠**MAKHULU, The Most Revd Walter Paul Khotso.** b 35. CMG00. Kent Univ Hon DD88 Gen Th Sem NY Hon DD99. St Pet Rosettenville Selly Oak Coll. **d** 57 **p** 58 **c** 79. S Africa 57-61; Bechuanaland 61-63; C Poplar All SS w St Frideswide *Lon* 64-66; C Pentonville St Silas w Barnsbury St Clem 66-68; V Battersea St Phil *S'wark* 68-73; V Battersea St Phil w St Bart 73-75; Bp Botswana 79-00; Abp Cen Africa 80-00; rtd 00. *Cheyne House, 10 Crondace Road, London SW6 4BB* Tel (020) 7371 9419 E-mail makhulu@btinternet.com

MAKIN, Hubert. b 18. ACP66 Open Univ BA74. NW Ord Course 75. **d** 78 **p** 79. Hon C Mount Pellon *Wakef* 78-91; Hon C King Cross 91-94; Perm to Offic from 94. *46 Upper Highfield, Gibb Lane, Mount Tabor, Halifax HX2 0UG* Tel (01422) 244642

MAKIN, Miss Pauline. b 45. Cranmer Hall Dur 75. **dss** 78 **d** 87 **p** 94. Ashton-in-Makerfield St Thos *Liv* 78-89; Par Dn 87-89; Par Dn Rainford 89-94; C 94-95; C Farnworth from 95; Asst Dioc Chapl to the Deaf from 89. *43 Hampton Drive, Widnes WA8 5DA* Tel and fax and text 0151-423 3900

MAKIN, Valerie Diana. Lon Univ DipRS83. S'wark Ord Course 86. **d** 88 **p** 94. Hon Par Dn Bryanston Square St Mary w St Marylebone St Mark *Lon* 88-95; Chapl St Marylebone Healing and Counselling Cen 88-94; NSM Godalming *Guildf* 94-95; Perm to Offic *Lon* 95-97 and *Guildf* from 95. *Crowts, Tuesley, Godalming GU7 1UD* Tel (01483) 416613

MAKOWER, Canon Malory. b 38. TCD BA61 MA68 St Jo Coll Ox MA64 DPhil64. Ridley Hall Cam 64. **d** 66 **p** 67. C Onslow Square St Paul *Lon* 66-69; Tutor Ridley Hall Cam 69-71; Sen Tutor 71-76; P-in-c Lode and Longmeadow *Ely* 76-84; Warden EAMTC 77-79; Prin 79-84; Dir of Post-Ord Tr for NSM *Nor* 84-90; C Gt Yarmouth 84-89; TV 89-95; Dioc NSM Officer 88-95; Hon Can Nor Cathl 94-97; Prin LNSM Tr Scheme 94-97; rtd 97; Perm to Offic *Nor* from 98. *114 Yarmouth Road, Lowestoft NR32 4AQ* Tel (01502) 574769

MALAN, Victor Christian de Roubaix. b 39. Cape Town Univ BA60 Linacre Coll Ox BA63 MA68. Wycliffe Hall Ox 61. **d** 63 **p** 64. C Springfield *Birm* 63-66; P-in-c 66-67; C New Windsor *Ox* 67-69; Chapl St Jo Coll Cam 69-74; V Northampton All SS w St Kath *Pet* 74-86; V Stockport St Geo *Ches* 86-89; R N Mundham w Hunston and Merston *Chich* from 89. *The Rectory, Church Lane, Hunston, Chichester PO20 1AJ* Tel (01243) 782003

✠**MALANGO, The Most Revd Bernard Amos.** b 43. TCD MPhil84. St Jo Sem Lusaka DipTh71. **d** 71 **p** 72 **c** 88. Malawi 71-88 and from 02; Bp N Zambia 88-02; Bp Upper Shire from 02; Abp Cen Africa from 00. *Private Bag 1, Chilema, Zomba, Malawi* Tel and fax (00265) (1) 539203 E-mail angus@malawinet *or* bernardmalango@hotmail.com

MALBON, Canon John Allin. b 36. Oak Hill Th Coll 62. **d** 65 **p** 66. C Wolverhampton St Jude *Lich* 65-68; C Hoole *Ches* 68-71; P-in-c Crewe Ch Ch 71-75; V 75-79; V Plemstall w Guilden Sutton 79-01; Hon Can Ches Cathl 96-01; rtd 01; Perm to Offic *Ches* from 02. *22 Hawksey Drive, Nantwich CW5 7GF* Tel (01270) 611584

MALCOLM, Brother. *See* FOUNTAIN, David Roy

MALCOLM, Miss Mercia Alana. b 54. St Andr Univ MA77 Lon Univ DipRS87. S'wark Ord Course 84. **d** 87 **p** 94. C Dartford Ch Ch *Roch* 87-91; Par Dn Stockport St Geo *Ches* 91-94; C Jordanstown *Conn* 95-99; Chapl Ulster Univ 95-03; I Carnmoney *Conn* from 03. *Coole Glebe, 20 Glebe Road, Newtownabbey BT36 6UW* Tel (028) 9083 6337 E-mail carnmoney@connor.anglican.org

MALDOOM, Ms Julie Marilyn. b 65. Jes Coll Ox BA88 PGCE89. Cuddesdon Coll BTh93. **d** 96 **p** 97. C Chinnor w Emmington and Sydenham etc *Ox* 96-99. *Address temp unknown*

MALE, David Edward. b 62. Southn Univ BA83. St Jo Coll Dur BA90 Cranmer Hall Dur 88. **d** 91 **p** 92. C Leic St Chris *Leic* 91-94; C Kirkheaton *Wakef* 94-98; P Missr Huddersfield from 99. *50 Longcroft, Almondbury, Huddersfield HD5 8XW* Tel (01484) 315511 E-mail david.male@ntlworld.com

MALEK, Mark Mayool. b 44. Khartoum Univ BSc69 Salford Univ BSc76 Bradf Coll of Educn PGCE93. **d** 03 **p** 04. NSM Horton *Bradf* 03-04; NSM Bradf St Oswald Chapel Green 03-04; NSM Lt Horton from 04. *26 Martlett Drive, Bradford BD5 8QG* Tel (01274) 732712

MALES, Jeanne Margaret. b 49. Reading Univ BA71 Lon Univ MPhil73 Surrey Univ PhD86 AFBPsS75 CPsychol88. S'wark Ord Course 93. **d** 96 **p** 97. NSM Caterham *S'wark* 96-00; C Addington 00-03; V from 03. *Addington Vicarage, Spout Hill, Croydon CR0 5AN* Tel (01689) 841839 *or* 842167 E-mail jeanne@u.genie.co.uk

MALINS, Mrs Judith. b 47. Bris Univ BA69. STETS 97. **d** 00 **p** 01. NSM Wilton w Netherhampton and Fugglestone *Sarum* 00-04; P-in-c Kingston, Langton Matravers and Worth Matravers from 04. *The Rectory, St George's Close, Langton Matravers, Swanage BH19 3HZ* Tel (01929) 422559 E-mail judith.malins@tesco.net

MALINS, Peter. b 18. Down Coll Cam BA40 MA47. Ridley Hall Cam 40. **d** 42 **p** 43. C Earlsdon *Cov* 42-44; CF (EC) 44-47; CF 47-73; QHC 72-73; V Greenwich St Alfege w St Pet and St Paul *S'wark* 73-87; P-in-c Greenwich H Trin and St Paul 76-84; Sub-Dean Greenwich 79-81; rtd 87; Perm to Offic *Guildf* from 87. *12 Ridgeway Drive, Dorking RH4 3AN* Tel (01306) 882035

MALKIN, Thomas Ross. b 64. Hertf Coll Ox BA86. Trin Coll Bris BA98. **d** 99 **p** 00. C Old Trafford St Bride *Man* 99-03; P-in-c Firswood and Gorse Hill from 03. *The Vicarage, 24 Canute Road, Stretford, Manchester M32 0RJ* Tel 0161-865 1802 Mobile 07973-240023 E-mail trm@fish.co.uk

MALKINSON, Christopher Mark. b 47. Chich Th Coll 84. **d** 86 **p** 87. C Stroud and Uplands w Slad *Glouc* 86-89; V Cam w Stinchcombe 89-00; P-in-c Tywardreath w Tregaminion *Truro* 00-02; P-in-c St Sampson 00-02; V Padstow from 02; RD Pydar from 03; Chapl Miss to Seafarers from 00. *The Vicarage, 46 Treverbyn Road, Padstow PL28 8DN* Tel (01841) 533776 E-mail chrismalk@hotmail.com

MALKINSON, Michael Stephen. b 43. St Steph Ho Ox 65. **d** 68 **p** 69. C New Addington *Cant* 68-71; C Blackpool St Steph *Blackb* 71-74; V Wainfleet St Mary *Linc* 74-81; R Wainfleet All SS w St Thos 74-81; P-in-c Croft 80-81; V Lund *Blackb* 81-93; V Heyhouses on Sea 93-00; R Balcombe *Chich* from 00; P-in-c Staplefield Common 00-03. *The Rectory, Balcombe, Haywards Heath RH17 6PA* Tel (01444) 811249 Fax 811346 E-mail stephen@malkinson.co.uk

MALLAS, Mrs Wendy Norris. b 42. Cov Coll of Educn CertEd63 Reading Univ MA91 Dip Counselling 99. STETS 00. **d** 03 **p** 04. NSM Liss *Portsm* from 03. *Mayfield, 45 Hogmoor Road, Whitehill, Bordon GU35 9ET* Tel (01420) 478883

MALLESON, Michael Lawson. b 42. Univ of Wales (Swansea) BA64 Nottm Univ DipTh68 MA92. Linc Th Coll 67. **d** 70 **p** 71. C Wakef St Jo *Wakef* 70-73; C-in-c Holmfield St Andr CD 73-75; V Holmfield 75-80; V Heworth St Alb *Dur* 80-93; V Killingworth *Newc* from 93. *The Vicarage, West Lane, Killingworth Village, Newcastle upon Tyne NE12 6BL* Tel 0191-268 3242 E-mail michaellmallesson@aol.com

MALLETT, John Christopher. b 44. EAMTC. **d** 82 **p** 83. NSM Hethersett w Canteloff *Nor* 82-85; NSM Hethersett w Canteloff w Lt and Gt Melton 85-90; Chapl Wayland Hosp Norfolk 88-94; Chapl Norwich Community Health Partnership NHS Trust 94-00; Perm to Offic *Nor* 00-03; NSM Hethersett w Canteloff w Lt and Gt Melton from 03. *2 Bailey Close, Hethersett, Norwich NR9 3EU* Tel (01603) 811010

MALLETT, Marlene Rosemarie. b 59. Sussex Univ BA81 Warwick Univ PhD94. SEITE 01. **d** 04. C Brixton Road Ch Ch *S'wark* from 04. *96 Canterbury Grove, London SE27 0PA* Tel (020) 8766 7068 E-mail mrmallett@btopenworld.com

MALLINSON, Canon Ralph Edward. b 40. Oriel Coll Ox BA63 MA66. St Steph Ho Ox 63. **d** 66 **p** 67. C Bolton St Pet *Man* 66-68; C Elton All SS 68-72; V Bury St Thos 72-76; V Bury Ch King 76-81; P-in-c Goodshaw 81-82; V 82-84; V Goodshaw and Crawshawbooth 84-93; AD Rossendale 83-93; Hon Can Man Cathl from 92; V Unsworth from 93; Vice Prin Dioc OLM Scheme from 98. *St George's Vicarage, Hollins Lane, Bury BL9 8JJ* Tel 0161-766 2429 E-mail ralphandhelen@rmallinson.fsnet.co.uk

MALLON, Allister. b 61. Sheff Univ BA83 TCD DipTh87 BTh89 MA. CITC. **d** 87 **p** 88. C Ballymoney w Finvoy and Rasharkin *Conn* 87-90; C Belfast St Mary w H Redeemer 90-92; Bp's C Belfast St Mary Magd 92-00; Bp's C Stoneyford from 00; Chapl R Group of Hosps Health and Soc Services Trust from 00. *St John's Rectory, 62 Stoneyford Road, Lisburn BT28 3SP* Tel (028) 9264 8300 E-mail bigal@talk21.com

MALLORY, George Henry. b 14. JP. Lon Univ BSc63. St Deiniol's Hawarden. **d** 80 **p** 81. NSM Oaks in Charnwood and Copt Oak *Leic* 80-88; rtd 88; Perm to Offic *Leic* 88-91; Perm to Offic *Worc* from 91. *Claudina, Bewdley Road North, Stourport-on-Severn DY13 8PX* Tel (01299) 827969

MALMESBURY, Archdeacon of. *See* HAWKER, The Ven Alan Fort

MALONE, Richard Patrick. b 66. Wycliffe Hall Ox BTh03. **d** 03 **p** 04. C Fulham Ch Ch *Lon* from 03. *76 Rylston Road, London SW6 7HR* Tel 07973-104941 (mobile) E-mail rpmalone@yahoo.com

MALONEY, Ms Fiona Elizabeth. b 60. Bradf Univ BSc82. Cranmer Hall Dur BA91 N Ord Course 91. **d** 92 **p** 94. Par Dn Castleton Moor *Man* 92-94; C 94-96; C Pendlebury St Jo 96-99; C Fatfield *Dur* 99-03; NSM Harrow Trin St Mich *Lon* 03-05; NSM Wealdstone H Trin from 05. *The Vicarage, 39 Rusland Park Road, Harrow HA1 1UN* Tel (020) 8863 5844 E-mail fiona@cofe.org.uk

MALONEY, Terence Mark. b 63. York Univ BSc84. Cranmer Hall Dur 88. **d** 91 **p** 92. C Blackley St Andr *Man* 91-96; P-in-c Pendlebury St Jo 96-99; P-in-c Fatfield *Dur* 99-03; P-in-c Harrow Trin St Mich *Lon* 03-05; V Wealdstone H Trin from 05. *The Vicarage, 39 Rusland Park Road, Harrow HA1 1UN* Tel (020) 8863 5844 *or* 8863 6131 Mobile 07967-659666 E-mail mark@cofe.org.uk

MALPASS, Clive William. b 36. AKC60. **d** 61 **p** 62. C Malden St Jo *S'wark* 61-64; C Horley 64-69; Youth Chapl *Dur* 69-72; Adv in Lay Tr 72-76; V Wyther Ven Bede *Ripon* 76-82; V Askrigg w Stallingbusk 82-01; RD Wensley 94-98; rtd 01; Perm to Offic *Ripon* from 02. *2 Hargill Drive, Redmire, Leyburn DL8 4DZ* Tel (01969) 625680

MALTBY, Canon Geoffrey. b 38. Leeds Univ BA62 Nottm Univ DipRE72 Glas Coll of Ed Cert Special Past Catechesis 92. Wells Th Coll 68. **d** 70 **p** 71. C Mansfield St Mark *S'well* 70-73; V Skegby 73-78; V Carrington 78-87; C Rainworth 87-90; Chapl for People w Learning Disability (Mental Handicap) 90-03; Hon Can S'well Minster 99-03; rtd 03; Perm to Offic *S'well* from 03. *18 Beverley Close, Rainworth, Mansfield NG21 0LW* Tel (01623) 474452

MALTBY, Canon Judith Diane. b 57. Illinois Univ BA79 Newnham Coll Cam PhD92 FRHistS99. S Dios Minl Tr Scheme 89. **d** 92 **p** 94. Tutor Sarum & Wells Th Coll 87-93; Hon Par Dn Wilton w Netherhampton and Fugglestone *Sarum* 92-93; Chapl and Fell CCC Ox from 93; Lic to Offic *Ox* from 93; Can Th Leic Cathl *Leic* from 04. *Corpus Christi College, Oxford OX1 4JF* Tel (01865) 276722 E-mail judith.maltby@ccc.ox.ac.uk

MALTIN, Basil St Clair Aston. b 24. Qu Coll Cam BA49 MA54. Westcott Ho Cam 50. **d** 51 **p** 52. C Dursley *Glouc* 51-53; C Bathwick w Woolley *B & W* 53-57; V Frome Ch Ch 57-63; P-in-c Marston Bigot 57-59; V Bishops Lydeard 63-71; R Pulborough *Chich* 71-90; RD Storrington 84-89; rtd 90; Perm to Offic *Chich* from 90. *13 Somerstown, Chichester PO19 6AG* Tel (01243) 786740

MALTON, William Peter Antony. b 33. K Coll Lon AKC56. **d** 57 **p** 58. C N Hammersmith St Kath *Lon* 57-60; C-in-c Blackbird Leys CD *Ox* 60-65; R Pitsford *Pet* 65-66; Canada from 66; rtd 93. *106 Hughes Road, Port Sydney ON, Canada, P0B 1L0*

MAN, Archdeacon of. *See* SMITH, The Ven Brian

MANCHESTER, Canon John Charles. b 45. Lon Univ BD69. ALCD68. **d** 69 **p** 70. C Scarborough St Martin *York* 69-73; C Selby Abbey 73-76; P-in-c Old Malton 76-79; V from 79; RD Bulmer and Malton 85-91; Can and Preb York Minster from 05. *The Gannock House, Old Malton, Malton YO17 7HB* Tel (01653) 692121

MANCHESTER, Simon Lorimer. b 53. Univ of NSW BA. Moore Th Coll Sydney ThL79 Melbourne Coll of Div BD80. **d** 80 **p** 80. Australia 80-82 and from 84; C Wollongong Pro-Cathl 80-82; C St Helen Bishopsgate w St Andr Undershaft etc *Lon* 82-84; R Lalor Park 84-89; R N Sydney St Thos from 90. *17 Kitchener Street, PO Box 132, Artarmon, NSW, Australia 2059* Tel (0061) (2) 9420 3661 *or* 9929 4807 Fax 9955 5180 E-mail st-thomas@st-thomas.org.au

MANCHESTER, Archdeacon of. *Vacant*

MANCHESTER, Bishop of. *See* McCULLOCH, The Rt Revd Nigel Simeon

MANCHESTER, Dean of. *Vacant*

MANCO, Gwenda Diane. b 54. N Ord Course 97. **d** 99 **p** 00. NSM Rochdale *Man* 99-02; NSM Dearnley 02-04; NSM Spotland from 04; Asst Chapl HM Pris Buckley Hall 99-03; Chapl HM Pris Styal 03. *5 Stansfield Hall, Littleborough OL15 9RH* Tel (01706) 370264 Mobile 07966-217252 E-mail gwenda.manco@tesco.net

MANCOR, Neil McKay. Univ of BC MA Reading Univ PhD. Wycliffe Hall Ox. **d** 99 **p** 00. C Llandeilo Fawr and Taliaris *St D* 99-02; Canada from 02. *1575 West 59th Avenue, Vancouver BC, Canada, V6P 1Z1* E-mail neilmancor@hotmail.com

MANDER, Peter John. b 52. Liv Univ BA85. Sarum & Wells Th Coll 85. **d** 87 **p** 88. C Hale and Ashley *Ches* 87-90; TV Grantham *Linc* 90-00; P-in-c Quarrington w Old Sleaford from 00; P-in-c Silk Willoughby from 00; RD Lafford from 03. *The Rectory, 5 Spire View, Northfield Road, Quarrington, Sleaford NG34 7RN* Tel (01529) 306776 E-mail peter@mander52.freeserve.co.uk

MANDER, Canon Thomas Leonard Frederick. b 33. Ely Th Coll 60. **d** 62 **p** 63. C Cov St Mary *Cov* 62-66; V Bishop's Tachbrook 66-70; V Earlsdon 70-76; V Chesterton 76-83; R Lighthorne 76-83; V Newbold Pacey w Moreton Morrell 76-83; Hon Can Cov Cathl 80-92; P-in-c S Leamington St Jo 83-84; V 84-92; rtd 92; Perm to Offic *Cov* from 92. *59 Murcott Road East, Whitnash, Leamington Spa CV31 2JJ* Tel (01926) 339950

MANDERSON, Robert Dunlop (Leslie). b 35. LDS59 FDS65. Ox Min Course 92. **d** 94 **p** 95. NSM Maidenhead St Andr and St Mary *Ox* 94-00; Perm to Offic 00-02 and from 03; NSM Chipping Norton 02-03; rtd 03. *67 Park Street, Dry Drayton, Cambridge CB3 8DA* Tel (01954) 782388 E-mail lpmanderson@aol.com

MANHIRE, Ashley Lewin. b 31. AKC55. **d** 56 **p** 57. C Plymouth St Gabr *Ex* 56-59; C Cockington 59-66; V Torquay St Martin Barton 66-83; RD Ipplepen 82-87; V Shaldon 83-01; rtd 01; Perm to Offic *Ex* from 01. *15 Friars Gate, Exeter EX2 4AZ*

MANHOOD, Phyllis. *See* DELVES, Canon Phyllis

✠MANKTELOW, The Rt Revd Michael Richard John. b 27. Ch Coll Cam BA48 MA52. Chich Th Coll 51. **d** 53 **p** 54 **c** 77. C Boston *Linc* 53-56; Chapl Ch Coll Cam 57-61; Chapl Linc Th Coll 61-63; Sub-Warden 64-66; V Knaresborough St Jo *Ripon* 66-73; RD Harrogate 72-77; V Harrogate St Wilfrid 73-77; P-in-c Harrogate St Luke 75-77; Hon Can Ripon Cathl 75-77; Suff Bp Basingstoke *Win* 77-93; Can Res Win Cathl 77-91; Hon Can 91-93; Vice-Dean 87-93; rtd 93; Hon Asst Bp Chich from 94; Hon Asst Bp Eur from 94; Wiccamical Preb Chich Cathl *Chich* 97-02. *14 Little London, Chichester PO19 1NZ* Tel (01243) 531096

MANLEY, Mrs Gillian. b 59. St Martin's Coll Lanc BEd80. St Jo Coll Nottm MA00. **d** 00 **p** 01. C Eckington and Ridgeway *Derby* 00-04; TV Wirksworth from 04. *58 Yokecliffe Drive, Wirksworth, Matlock DE4 4EX* Tel (01629) 822896 *or* 826202 Mobile 07949-458383 E-mail gill-manley@supanet.com

MANLEY, Canon Gordon Russell Delpratt. b 33. Ch Coll Cam BA56 MA60. Linc Th Coll 57. **d** 59 **p** 60. C Westbury-on-Trym St Alb *Bris* 59-61; Chapl Ch Coll Cam 61-66; V Radlett *St Alb* 66-75; V Faversham *Cant* 75-99; RD Ospringe 84-90; Hon Can Cant Cathl 90-99; rtd 99; Perm to Offic *Cant* from 99; Retirement Officer (Cant Adnry) from 01. *170 Old Dover Road, Canterbury CT1 3EX* Tel (01227) 784016

MANLEY, Michael Alan. b 60. SS Hild & Bede Coll Dur BA82. Trin Coll Bris DipTh86. **d** 86 **p** 87. C Accrington St Jo *Blackb* 86-89; C Huncoat 88-89; C Accrington St Jo w Huncoat 89-90; V Preston St Luke and St Oswald 90-96; V Blackpool St Jo from 96. *St John's Vicarage, 19 Leamington Road, Blackpool FY1 4HD* Tel (01253) 620626 *or* 294451 E-mail manleyrev@hotmail.com

MANLEY (née McCARTHY), Mrs Sandra Ellen. b 56. Man Univ MusB77 Goldsmiths' Coll Lon PGCE79 ARCM75 FRCO77 GRNCM78. S'wark Ord Course 92. **d** 95 **p** 96. C Beckenham St Geo *Roch* 95-99; V Heybridge w Langford *Chelmsf* from 99. *The Vicarage, 1A Crescent Road, Heybridge, Maldon CM9 4SJ* Tel and fax (01621) 841274 Mobile 07904-292036 E-mail sandra@revdsmcc.fsnet.co.uk

MANLEY-COOPER, Simon James. b 46. S Dios Minl Tr Scheme 91. **d** 94 **p** 95. NSM Soho St Anne w St Thos and St Pet *Lon* 94-96; Ind Chapl 94-96; P-in-c Bedford St Mich *St Alb* 96-01; Ind Chapl 96-01; R Bramfield, Stapleford, Waterford etc 01-02; Chapl E and N Herts NHS Trust from 03. *Queen Elizabeth II Hospital, Howlands, Welwyn Garden City AL7 4HQ* Tel (01707) 328111 *or* 365331 E-mail manley-c@fish.co.uk

MANN, Alexandrina Elizabeth. b 67. Westmr Coll Ox BA92 PGCE93 Birm Univ MA95. Trin Coll Bris 01. **d** 03 **p** 04. C Austrey and Warton *Birm* from 03. *20 Austrey Road, Warton, Tamworth B79 0HW* Tel (01827) 899664 Mobile 07761-263849 E-mail alexandrina.shalom@virgin.net

MANN, Ms Angela. b 58. Bath Univ BA80 Bris Univ PGCE83. Trin Coll Bris DipHE94. **d** 94 **p** 95. C Marlborough *Sarum* 94-97; Perm to Offic 97-99. *Address temp unknown*

MANN, Lt Comdr Anthony James. b 34. Open Univ BA76. St Jo Coll Nottm 85. **d** 88 **p** 89. NSM Helensburgh *Glas* 88-01; rtd 01. *Loughrigg, 13 Rossway Road, Kirkcudbright DG6 4BS* Tel (01557) 330286 E-mail didnpud@aol.com

MANN, Canon Charmion Anne Montgomery. b 36. Liv Univ BA57 CertEd62 AdDipEd79. Trin Coll Bris 80. **dss** 82 **d** 87 **p** 94. Bris St Nath w St Kath *Bris* 82-84; Bris St Matt and St Nath 84-85; Asst Chapl City Cen Hosps Bris 85-88; Chapl Bris Maternity Hosp 88-94; Chapl Bris R Hosp for Sick Children 88-94; Chapl Bris R Infirmary 88-94; Hon Can Bris Cathl *Bris* 93-00; P-in-c Lacock w Bowden Hill 94-00; C Gtr Corsham 97-00; rtd 00; Perm to Offic *Bris* from 00 and *Sarum* from 01. *1 Kingsbury Street, Calne SN11 8DF* Tel and fax (01249) 811228 E-mail charmion@mann7747.fsnet.co.uk

MANN, Christopher John. b 57. Glas Univ BSc79. Westcott Ho Cam 83. **d** 86 **p** 87. C Worc SE *Worc* 86-89; Min Can and Sacr St Paul's Cathl *Lon* 89-96; R Upminster *Chelmsf* from 96. *The Rectory, 89 Park Drive, Upminster RM14 3AT* Tel (01708) 220174 E-mail rector@saintlaurence.com

MANN, David. b 57. BA. Ridley Hall Cam. **d** 82 **p** 83. C Monkwearmouth St Andr *Dur* 82-86; Chapl Sheff Cathl *Sheff* 86-87; C Leeds St Geo *Ripon* 87-94; V Ripon H Trin from 94. *Holy Trinity Vicarage, 3 College Road, Ripon HG4 2AE* Tel (01765) 605865 *or* tel and fax 690930 E-mail dave@htripon.freeserve.co.uk

MANN, Donald Leonard. b 22. Westcott Ho Cam. **d** 47 **p** 48. C S'well Minster *S'well* 47-49; C Edwinstowe 49-51; C St Alb St Paul *St Alb* 51-54; C Baldock w Bygrave and Clothall 54-56; V Guilden Morden *Ely* 56-59; V Rocester *Lich* 59-63; V Gnosall w Knightley 63-69; V Sheen 69-76; P-in-c Calton 72-76; P-in-c Ellastone 76; rtd 76; Perm to Offic *Ches* from 93. *Bungalow 24, Lyme Green Settlement, Macclesfield SK11 0LD* Tel (01260) 252209

MANN (née WELLS), Ms Gillian Mary. b 46. Bedf Coll Lon BA67 Goldsmiths' Coll Lon TCert68 MCIPD89. EMMTC 99. **d** 01 **p** 02. NSM Wirksworth *Derby* 01-05; P-in-c The Sampfords and Radwinter w Hempstead *Chelmsf* from 05. *The Rectory, Walden Road, Radwinter, Saffron Walden CB10 2SW* Tel (01799) 599332 Mobile 07719-470363 E-mail gillianmann@eidosnet.co.uk

MANN, Canon Ivan John. b 52. Brunel Univ BTech74 Southn Univ BTh80. Sarum & Wells Th Coll 75. **d** 78 **p** 79. C Hadleigh w Layham and Shelley *St E* 78-81; C Whitton and Thurleston w Akenham 81-83; V Leiston 83-86; Perm to Offic 86-89; R Aldringham w Thorpe, Knodishall w Buxlow etc 89-93; V Ipswich St Jo 93-96; Chapl St Mary's Convent Wantage 96-00; Asst Chapl R Berks and Battle Hosps NHS Trust 00; TV Gt Yarmouth *Nor* 00-03; Team Member Loyola Hall Jesuit Spirituality Cen Prescot 03-05; Prec and Hon Can St Jo Cathl Oban *Arg* from 05. *The College, College Street, Millport, Isle of Cumbrae KA28 0HE* Tel (01475) 530353 E-mail ivanmann@f2s.com

MANN, Joan. d 98. NSM Eastbourne St Mary *Chich* 98-02; NSM The Hydneye from 02. *39 Cherry Garden Road, Eastbourne BN20 8HF* Tel (01323) 728259

MANN, John. b 35. ISO91. Lon Univ Dip Economics 66. Oak Hill NSM Course 89. **d** 92 **p** 93. NSM Springfield All SS *Chelmsf* from 92; RD Chelmsf N 99-04. *18 Humber Road, Chelmsford CM1 7PE* Tel (01245) 259596

MANN, Canon John Owen. b 55. QUB BD77 MTh86 MPhil98. CITC 79. **d** 79 **p** 81. C Cloughfern *Conn* 79-82; C Knock *D & D* 82-85; I Ballyrashane w Kildollagh *Conn* 85-89; R Bentworth and Shalden and Lasham *Win* 89-93; RD Alton 92-93; I Cloughfern *Conn* 93-02; I Belfast Malone St Jo from 02; Preb Clonmethan St Patr Cathl Dublin from 99. *St John's Rectory, 86 Maryville Park, Belfast BT9 6LQ* Tel (028) 9066 6644 *or* 9066 7861 E-mail mann86@tiscali.co.uk

MANN, Julian Farrer Edgar. b 64. Peterho Cam MA90. Oak Hill Th Coll BA93. **d** 96 **p** 97. C Hoole *Ches* 96-00; V Oughtibridge *Sheff* from 00. *The Vicarage, Church Street, Oughtibridge, Sheffield S35 0FU* Tel 0114-286 2317 E-mail julianlisa@oughtimann.freeserve.co.uk

✠**MANN, The Rt Revd Michael Ashley.** b 24. KCVO89. CBIM RMA 42 Harvard Univ Ad Mgt Progr 73. Wells Th Coll 55. **d** 57 **p** 58 **c** 74. C Wolborough w Newton Abbot *Ex* 57-59; V Sparkwell 59-62; Nigeria 62-67; Home Sec Miss to Seamen 67-69; Can Res Nor Cathl *Nor* 69-74; Vice-Dean 73-74; Dioc Ind Adv 69-74; Suff Bp Dudley *Worc* 74-76; Dean Windsor and Dom Chapl to The Queen 76-89; rtd 89; Hon Asst Bp Glouc from 89. *Lower End Farm Cottage, Eastington, Northleach, Cheltenham GL54 3PN* Tel (01451) 860767

MANN, Paul William. b 63. Leeds Univ BSc84 CEng MIEE. EAMTC 01. **d** 04 **p** 05. NSM Lawford *Chelmsf* from 04. *8 Cherrywoods, Great Bentley, Colchester CO7 8QF* Tel (01206) 252420 E-mail riffhams@btopenworld.com

MANN, Canon Peter Eric. b 51. St Jo Coll Dur BA73. Westcott Ho Cam 73. **d** 75 **p** 76. C Barrow St Jo *Carl* 75-78; C Egremont 78-80; V Carl St Luke Morton 80-86; TR Egremont and Haile 86-93; P-in-c Barrow St Geo w St Luke 93-99; TR S Barrow from 99; P-in-c Barrow St Jo 95-96; RD Furness 94-01; RD Barrow from 01; Hon Can Carl Cathl from 95. *The Rectory, 98 Roose Road, Barrow-in-Furness LA13 9RL* Tel (01229) 821641 Fax as telephone E-mail cookbird@u.genie.co.uk

MANN, Ms Rachel. b 70. Lanc Univ BA91 MA93. Qu Coll Birm 03. **d** 05. C Stretford St Matt *Man* from 05. *2 Trafford Grove, Stretford, Manchester M32 8LW* Tel 0161-865 5273 Mobile 07834-403195 E-mail rachelmann@hotmail.co.uk

MANN, Ralph Norman. b 27. BNC Ox BA51 MA55 DipEd52. Ox NSM Course 79. **d** 82 **p** 83. NSM Kingham w Churchill, Daylesford and Sarsden *Ox* 82-85; S Area Sec BCMS 82-89; P-in-c Broadwell, Evenlode, Oddington and Adlestrop *Glouc* 89-97; rtd 97; P-in-c Upton St Leonards *Glouc* 97-00. *2 Whittons Close, Hook Norton, Banbury OX15 5QG* Tel (01608) 730327

MANN, Robin. b 45. Fitzw Coll Cam BA76 MA80 MRTPI73. Ridley Hall Cam 73. **d** 77 **p** 78. C Wetherby *Ripon* 77-80; V Hipswell 80-86; V Mamble w Bayton, Rock w Heightington etc *Worc* 86-96; V Avon Valley *Sarum* 96-02; R Selworthy, Timberscombe, Wootton Courtenay etc *B & W* from 02. *The Rectory, Great House Street, Timberscombe, Minehead TA24 7TQ* Tel (01643) 841544 E-mail robinmann@sourceuk.net

MANN, Stephen Paul. b 52. Staffs Univ BA76 Keele Univ PGCE78. Cranmer Hall Dur 96. **d** 98 **p** 99. C Spennymoor, Whitworth and Merrington *Dur* 98-03; Chapl Dur Constabulary 99-03; TV Madeley *Heref* 03-04; rtd 05. *The Vicarage, Vicarage Lane, Weston Rhyn, Oswestry SY10 7RE* E-mail steve.mann99@telco4u.net

MANN, Terence John. b 47. GGSM68 LRSM79 FTCL79 Miami Univ MA80 Lon Univ PGCE69. Ox Min Course CBTS94. **d** 94 **p** 95. NSM Kingham w Churchill, Daylesford and Sarsden *Ox* 94-00; Chapl HM Pris Camp Hill from 00. *HM Prison, Camp Hill, Newport PO30 5PB* Tel (01983) 527661 Fax 520505

MANNALL, Michael John Frederick. b 37. St Mich Coll Llan 61. **d** 63 **p** 64. C Clapham H Spirit *S'wark* 63-66; C Brighton St Bart *Chich* 66-68; C Willesden St Matt *Lon* 68-69; C-in-c Cricklewood St Pet CD 69-73; R Broughton *Pet* 73-75; Hon C Kingston St Luke *S'wark* 76-94; rtd 84; Perm to Offic *Nor* from 95. *The Blessings, 55 Sculthorpe Road, Fakenham NR21 9ET* Tel (01328) 863496 E-mail michael.mannall@btinternet.com

MANNERS, Kenneth. b 29. N Ord Course. **d** 84 **p** 85. NSM Brayton *York* 84-00; rtd 00; Perm to Offic *York* from 00. *16 Wistow Road, Selby YO8 3LY* Tel (01757) 702129

MANNING, Adrian Peter. b 63. St Cath Coll Cam MA88 K Coll Lon PGCE88 St Cath Coll Cam BA84. Ridley Hall Cam 92. **d** 95 **p** 96. C Oxhey All SS *St Alb* 95-97; Asst Chapl Bedford Sch 97-02; Chapl St Geo Sch Harpenden from 02. *2 Bramley Cottages, Sun Lane, Harpenden AL5 4SZ* Tel (01582) 765477 *or* 716231 E-mail amanning@fish.co.uk

MANNING, Mrs Ann. b 42. Liv Univ CertEd75. St Jo Coll Nottm 93 N Ord Course 94. **d** 95 **p** 96. NSM Grasmere *Carl* 95-96; NSM Delamere *Ches* 96-99; C Middlewich w Byley 99-02; Chapl Mid Cheshire Hosps Trust 99-02; P-in-c Dunton w Wrestlingworth and Eyeworth *St Alb* 02-05; R from 05. *The Rectory, 7 Braggs Lane, Wrestlingworth, Sandy SG19 2ER* Tel (01767) 631596

MANNING, David Godfrey. b 47. Trin Coll Bris 73. **d** 76 **p** 77. C Richmond H Trin and Ch Ch *S'wark* 76-79; C Anston *Sheff* 79-83; V Blackpool St Mark *Blackb* 83-91; V Creech St Michael *B & W* from 91. *The Vicarage, Creech St Michael, Taunton TA3 5PP* Tel (01823) 442237

MANNING, Neville Alexander. b 41. Lon Univ BD68. ALCD68. **d** 68 **p** 69. C Belvedere All SS *Roch* 68-71; C Hollington St Leon *Chich* 71-73; C Hersham *Guildf* 73-77; V Dawley St Jerome *Lon* 77-94; R Denton w S Heighton and Tarring Neville *Chich* from 94. *The Rectory, 6 Heighton Road, Newhaven BN9 0RB* Tel (01273) 514319 E-mail nmanning@dentonrectory.fsnet.co.uk

MANNINGS, Andrew James. b 52. Trent Park Coll of Educn CertEd73. St Jo Coll Nottm DCM92. **d** 92 **p** 94. C Over St Chad *Ches* 92-93; C Sale St Anne 93-96; C Timperley 96-98; P-in-c Egremont St Jo 98-04; P-in-c Liscard St Mary w St Columba 03-04; V Liscard Resurr from 04; RD Wallasey from 02. *The Vicarage, 107 Manor Road, Wallasey CH45 7LU* Tel 0151-639 1553 E-mail andrew.mannings4@ntlworld.com

MANNS, Edwin Ernest. b 30. Portsm Dioc Tr Course 84. **d** 85. C Paulsgrove *Portsm* 85-95; Chapl St Mary's Hosp Portsm 90-91; Team Chapl Portsm Hosp 91-95; rtd 95. *17 Kelvin Grove, Portchester, Fareham PO16 8LQ* Tel (023) 9232 4818

MANSBRIDGE, The Ven Michael Winstanley. b 32. Southn Univ BA54. Ridley Hall Cam 56. **d** 58 **p** 59. C Ware St Mary *St Alb* 58-60; C Claverdon w Preston Bagot *Cov* 60-62; Kenya 62-65; Asst P Nairobi Cathl and Chapl Nairobi Univ 62-65; V Chilvers Coton w Astley *Cov* 65-75; RD Nuneaton 66-73; V Leamington Priors H Trin 75-83; Chapl Abu Dhabi St Andr UAE 83-97; Adn the Gulf 83-91; Adn Cyprus and the Gulf 91-99; Can Nicosia 86-99; Provost 97-99; Can Bahrain 87 99; rtd 97; Hon Can Nicosia and Bahrain from 99. *Blue Skies, 7 Norman Way, Wootton Bridge, Ryde PO33 4NJ* Tel (01983) 882394 E-mail fiona_mansbridge@compuserve.com

MANSEL LEWIS, Patrick Charles Archibald. b 53. Solicitor 79. St Mich Coll Llan 01. **d** 04 **p** 05. NSM Llandeilo Fawr and Taliaris *St D* from 04. *Capel Isaf, Manordeilo, Llandeilo SA19 7BS* Tel (01558) 822273

MANSELL, Cary Stuart. b 61. St Jo Coll Morpeth LTh DipMin80 DipTh83. **d** 83 **p** 84. Australia 83-97 and from 99; C Warrnambool Australia 83-86; V Edenhope 86-91; R Camperdown 91-97; C Addlestone *Guildf* 97-99; Lic to Offic *Cant* from 97; Asst Chapl St Mich Gr Sch and Assoc P E St Kilda from 99. *St Michael's Grammar School, 20 Redan Street, St Kilda, Vic, Australia 3182* Tel (0061) (3) 8530 3200 Fax 9510 9392 E-mail cmansell@stmichaels.vic.edu.au

MANSELL, The Ven Clive Neville Ross. b 53. Leic Univ LLB74 Solicitor 77. Trin Coll Bris DipHE81. **d** 82 **p** 83. C Gt Malvern

St Mary *Worc* 82-85; Min Can Ripon Cathl *Ripon* 85-89; R Kirklington w Burneston and Wath and Pickhill 89-02; AD Wensley 98-02; Adn Tonbridge *Roch* from 02. *3 The Ridings, Blackhurst Lane, Tunbridge Wells TN2 4RU* Tel (01892) 520660 E-mail archdeacon.tonbridge@rochester.anglican.org

MANSFIELD, Alastair John Fraser. b 60. Ex Univ BA82 Ch Coll Cam PGCE84 City Univ MSc92. SEITE. **d** 99 **p** 00. C Palmers Green St Jo *Lon* 99-02; P-in-c Enfield St Mich from 02. *The Vicarage, 2 Gordon Hill, Enfield EN2 0QP* Tel (020) 8363 1063 E-mail ajstrawber@aol.com

MANSFIELD, Gordon Reginald. b 35. Lon Univ BA CertEd. Clifton Th Coll 58. **d** 63 **p** 64. C Carl St Jo *Carl* 63-65; C Westcombe Park St Geo *S'wark* 65-68; C Rashcliffe *Wakef* 68-70; V Woodlands *Sheff* 70-80; V Steeple Bumpstead and Helions Bumpstead *Chelmsf* 80-02; Perm to Offic *Ely* 03-04. *18 Caefelyn, Norton, Presteigne LD8 2UB* Tel (01544) 260380

MANSFIELD, Julian Nicolas (Nick). b 59. K Coll Lon BD AKC. Edin Th Coll 83. **d** 85 **p** 86. C Kirkby *Liv* 85-89; TV Ditton St Mich 89-96; P-in-c Preston St Oswald *Blackb* 96-01; V Penwortham St Leon from 01. *St Leonard's Vicarage, Marshall's Brow, Penwortham, Preston PR1 9HY* Tel (01772) 742367 E-mail nick-vic@fish.co.uk

MANSFIELD, Robert William. b 45. Nottm Trent Univ DipHE95. LNSM course 89. **d** 88 **p** 89. OLM Louth *Linc* from 88. *The Old Railway House, Stewton, Louth LN11 8SD* Tel (01507) 327533 E-mail mansfieldstewton@hotmail.com

MANSFIELD, Simon David. b 55. Brunel Univ BSc81 Lon Univ MA94. Ripon Coll Cuddesdon 88. **d** 90 **p** 91. C N Harrow St Alb *Lon* 90-93; C Birchington w Acol and Minnis Bay *Cant* 93-97; TV Accrington *Blackb* 97-00; TV Accrington Ch the King from 00. *The Vicarage, Barnfield Street, Accrington BB5 2AQ* Tel (01254) 399322 E-mail simon@simonmansfield.freeserve.co.uk

MANSFIELD, Stephen McLaren. b 59. FGA Dip Retail Jewellery Gemmology Dip. Cranmer Hall Dur 86. **d** 89 **p** 90. C Poynton *Ches* 89-92; C Bromborough 92-94; V Bidston 94-02; C Heswall from 02. *15 Castle Drive, Heswall, Wirral CH60 4RJ* Tel 0151-342 4841 E-mail smfield@fish.co.uk

MANSHIP, Charmain Margaret. b 45. RCM BMus68 ARCM65 GRSM67 FRCO68. St Alb and Ox Min Course 95. **d** 98 **p** 99. NSM Abingdon *Ox* 98-04; Succ and Min Can Worc Cathl *Worc* from 04. *22 Stanmore Road, Worcester WR2 4PW* Tel (01905) 421147

MANSHIP, Canon David. b 27. ARCO Keble Coll Ox BA52 MA58. Qu Coll Birm 52. **d** 54 **p** 55. C Hackney St Jo *Lon* 54-58; C Preston Ascension 58-61; C St Andr Holborn 61-65; Members' Tr Officer C of E Youth Coun 65-68; Clergy Tr Officer 68-70; Dir of Educn *Win* 70-79; Hon Can Win Cathl 74-79; R Old Alresford 76-79; V Abingdon w Shippon *Ox* 79-89; TR Abingdon 89-93; V Shippon 89; RD Abingdon 87-90; rtd 93; Perm to Offic *Ox* 93-03 and *Worc* from 04. *22 Stanmore Road, Worcester WR2 4PW* Tel (01905) 421147

MANSLEY, Colin Edward. b 56. Edin Univ MA80 BA85. Ripon Coll Cuddesdon 83. **d** 86 **p** 87. C Worle *B & W* 86-89; C Baguley *Man* 89-91; C Radcliffe St Mary 91; TV Radcliffe 91-96; V Bartley Green *Birm* from 96. *The Vicarage, 96 Romsley Road, Birmingham B32 3PS* Tel 0121-475 1508 Fax 475 6880 E-mail colin@archangel.clara.co.uk

MANSON-BRAILSFORD, Andrew Henry. b 64. NUU BA86 Liv Univ MPhil98. Ripon Coll Cuddesdon 87. **d** 90 **p** 91. C Warrington St Elphin *Liv* 90-93; C Torrisholme *Blackb* 93-96; V Brighton St Geo w St Anne and St Mark *Chich* from 96; Chapl St Mary's Hall Brighton from 97. *22 Seymour Square, Kemp Town, Brighton BN2 1DW* Tel (01273) 699779 *or* 279448 E-mail stgeochuch@aol.com

MANT, Frances Joy. b 61. Jes Coll Cam BA82 MA86 Lon Univ MB, BS85 Ex Univ BPhil88. Qu Coll Birm BA05. **d** 05. NSM Bromsgrove All SS *Worc* from 05. *107 New Road, Bromsgrove B60 2LJ* Tel (01527) 872040

✠**MANTLE, The Rt Revd John Ambrose Cyril.** b 46. St Andr Univ MTheol74 Kent Univ MA90 Leeds Univ PhD98 FRHistS01. Edin Th Coll 66. **d** 69 **p** 70 **c** 05. C Broughty Ferry *Bre* 69-71; C St Andrews All SS *St And* 71-75; C Edin SS Phil and Jas *Edin* 75-77; Teacher Royal High Sch Edin 75-77; Chapl and Tutor in Th St Andr Univ *St And* 77-80; P-in-c Pittenweem 78-80; P-in-c Elie and Earlsferry 78-80; Chapl and Fell Fitzw Coll Cam 80-86; Tutor Wesley Ho Cam 80-86; Hon C Cambridge Ascension *Ely* 80-86; Tutor and Vice-Prin Cant Sch of Min 86-91; Visiting Lect Th Kent Univ *Cant* 91-93; C Boxley w Detling 86-93; Dioc Adv for Educn and Tr of Adults *Chich* 94-99; Visiting Lect Th Sussex Univ 95-98; Abps' Adv for Bps' Min *Cant* 99-05; Bp Bre from 05. *5 Glamis Drive, Dundee DD2 1QG* Tel (01382) 641586 Fax 220888 E-mail bishop@brechin.anglican.org

MANTON, Paul Arthur. b 45. Oak Hill Th Coll BD77. **d** 77 **p** 78. C Wolverhampton *Lich* 77-80; Ind Chapl *Lon* 80-87; Hon C St Marylebone All So w SS Pet and Jo 80-87; Perm to Offic from 03. *1 Wickliffe Avenue, London N3 3EL* Tel (020) 8346 1787

MANUEL, Paul. b 55. Univ of Wales (Ban) BA76 ACIS79 FCIS88. St Alb and Ox Min Course 97. **d** 00 **p** 01. NSM Luton St Paul *St Alb* 00-03; C Chorleywood Ch Ch from 03. *4 Berry Way, Rickmansworth WD3 7EY* Tel (01923) 447185 E-mail pmfrompetham@aol.com

MAPLE, David Charles. b 34. Sarum Th Coll 64. **d** 66 **p** 66. C Buckland in Dover *Cant* 66-67; C St Laur in Thanet 67-71; Chapl RAF 71-75; P-in-c Ivychurch 75-76; P-in-c Newchurch *Cant* 75-78; P-in-c Burmarsh 75-78; P-in-c St Mary in the Marsh 75-76; R Dymchurch 76-78; R Dymchurch w Burmarsh and Newchurch 78-81; Hon Min Can Cant Cathl from 79; Abp's Dioc Chapl 81-91; Chapl St Jo Hosp Cant 91-95; rtd 95; Perm to Offic *Cant* from 98. *1 Mount Pleasant, Blean, Canterbury CT2 9EU* Tel (01227) 459044

MAPLE, John Philip. b 50. Chich Th Coll 71. **d** 74 **p** 79. C Notting Hill St Mich and Ch Ch *Lon* 74-75; Lic to Offic 78-79; C Barnsbury St Dav w St Clem 79-80; C Cotham St Sav w St Mary *Bris* 80-83; TV St Marylebone Ch Ch *Lon* 83-91; R St Marylebone St Paul 91-99; P-in-c Fulham St Alb w St Aug 99-04; P-in-c Fulham St Pet 99-02; Community Min Adv from 04. *London Diocesan House, 36 Causton Street, London SW1P 4AU* Tel (020) 7932 1122 E-mail jack.maple@london.anglican.org

MAPLEY, Mrs Barbara Jean. b 46. Guy's Hosp Medical Sch MCSP69. Oak Hill NSM Course 86. **d** 89 **p** 94. NSM Kelvedon *Chelmsf* 89-93; C Witham 93-94; TV 94-01; R Belbroughton w Fairfield and Clent *Worc* from 01. *The Rectory, Bradford Lane, Belbroughton, Stourbridge DY9 9TF* Tel (01562) 730531 E-mail barbaramapley@waitrose.com

MAPPLEBECKPALMER, Richard Warwick. b 32. CCC Cam BA56 MA60. Cuddesdon Coll 56. **d** 58 **p** 59. C Redcar *York* 58-60; C Drypool St Jo 61-63; V Pendleton St Ambrose *Man* 63-77; P-in-c Piddington *Ox* 77; P-in-c Ambrosden w Arncot and Blackthorn 77; P-in-c Merton 77; V Ambrosden w Merton and Piddington 77-88; USA from 88; rtd 97. *472 Dale Road, Martinez, CA 94553-4829, USA* Tel (001) (510) 228 5252

MAPSON, Preb John Victor. b 31. Lon Univ BA60. Oak Hill Th Coll 55. **d** 60 **p** 61. C Littleover *Derby* 60-62; C Wandsworth St Mich *S'wark* 62-65; R Willand *Ex* 65-71; P-in-c Axmouth 71-72; V 72-75; V Axmouth w Musbury 75-77; RD Honiton 76-77; V Cullompton 77-89; R Kentisbeare w Blackborough 77-89; RD Cullompton 81-89; P-in-c Sidmouth All SS 89-96; Preb Ex Cathl 91-01; RD Ottery 94-96; rtd 96; Ed *Exeter Diocesan Directory Ex* from 00. *47 Head Weir Road, Cullompton EX15 1NN* Tel (01884) 38037 E-mail jmapson@care4free.net *or* diocesan.news@exeter.anglican.org

MAPSTONE, Trevor Anthony. b 63. Lanc Univ BSc84 MA96. St Jo Coll Nottm LTh88 DPS89. **d** 89 **p** 90. C Hoole *Ches* 89-92; C Lancaster St Thos *Blackb* 92-96; V Harrow Trin St Mich *Lon* 96-03; Dir of Ords Willesden Area 98-03; V S Croydon Em *S'wark* from 03. *Emmanuel Vicarage, 38 Croham Manor Road, South Croydon CR2 7BE* Tel (020) 8688 2478 *or* 8688 6676 E-mail tmapstone@blueyonder.co.uk

MARAIS, Rudolph James. b 41. St Bede's Coll Umtata BTh. **d** 81 **p** 82. S Africa 81-85 and from 87; C Belmont *S'wark* 85-87. *PO Box 1087, Humansdorp, 6300 South Africa* Tel (0027) (42) 291 1659 Mobile 82-578 7522

MARAJH, Brian Melvin. BA. **d** 86 **p** 87. S Africa 86-94 and from 99; Perm to Offic *Glas* 94-99; Lect Coll of Transfiguration Grahamstown 99-04. *Address temp unknown*

MARBUS, Alida Janny. *See* WHITTOCK, Alida Janny

MARCER, Graham John. b 52. Ripon Coll Cuddesdon 75. **d** 78 **p** 79. C Sherborne w Castleton and Lillington *Sarum* 78-81; C Christchurch *Win* 81-84; V Southampton St Jude 84-90; P-in-c Moordown 90-91; C Sheff St Cecilia Parson Cross *Sheff* 91-93; V Balby 93-00; RD W Doncaster 97-00; V Radford *Cov* from 00; AD Cov N 01-04. *The Vicarage, 21 Tulliver Street, Coventry CV6 3BY* Tel (024) 7659 8449 E-mail graham.marcer@btinternet.com

MARCETTI, Alvin Julian. b 41. San Jose State Univ BA66 Santa Clara Univ MA76. Cranmer Hall Dur 85. **d** 87 **p** 88. C Stepney St Dunstan and All SS *Lon* 87-91; Chapl City of Lon Poly 91-92; Chapl Lon Guildhall Univ 92-96; Chapl Homerton Univ Hosp NHS Trust Lon 96-03; Chapl City and Hackney Community Services NHS Trust 96-03; rtd 03. *38 Becquerel Court, West Parkside, London SE1 0QQ* E-mail almarcetti@yahoo.co.uk

MARCH, Alan Mervyn. b 48. CPFA73 Open Univ BA91. EAMTC 00. **d** 03 **p** 04. NSM Northampton St Alb *Pet* from 03. *236 Beech Avenue, Northampton NN3 2LE* Tel (01604) 405722

MARCH, Charles Anthony Maclea (Tony). b 32. CCC Cam BA55 MA70. Oak Hill Th Coll 55. **d** 57 **p** 58. C S Croydon Em *Cant* 57-60; C Eastbourne H Trin *Chich* 60-63; V Whitehall Park St Andr Hornsey Lane *Lon* 63-67; V Tunbridge Wells H Trin w Ch Ch *Roch* 67-82; V Prestonville St Luke *Chich* 82-97; rtd 97; Perm to Offic *Roch* from 99. *The Barn, 2 Town Farm Dairy, Brenchley Road, Brenchley, Tonbridge TN12 7PA* Tel (01892) 722802

MARCH, Gerald. b 44. Nottm Univ BA75. Oak Hill Th Coll 92. **d** 95 **p** 96. C Sandgate St Paul w Folkestone St Geo *Cant* 95-99;

P-in-c Southampton St Mark *Win* 99-03; V from 03. *St Mark's Vicarage, 54 Archers Road, Southampton SO15 2LU* Tel (023) 8063 6425 E-mail gerald.march@lineone.net

MARCH, Jonathan. b 79. Wycliffe Hall Ox. **d** 05. C Brompton H Trin w Onslow Square St Paul *Lon* from 05. *Basement Flat, 2 Victoria Rise, London SW4 0NY*

MARCHAND, Canon Rex Anthony Victor (Toby). b 47. K Coll Lon BD69 AKC69. St Aug Coll Cant 69. **d** 70 **p** 71. C Leigh Park *Portsm* 70-73; C Bp's Hatfield *St Alb* 73-80; R Deal St Leon and St Rich and Sholden *Cant* 80-95; RD Sandwich 91-94; Hon Can Cant Cathl 94-95; V Bishop's Stortford St Mich *St Alb* from 95. *St Michael's Vicarage, 8 Larkspur Road, Bishop's Stortford CM23 4LL* Tel (01279) 651415 E-mail tandmmarchand@ntlworld.com

MARCHANT, The Ven George John Charles. b 16. St Jo Coll Dur LTh38 BA39 MA42 BD64. Tyndale Hall Bris 35. **d** 39 **p** 40. C Whitehall Park St Andr Hornsey Lane *Lon* 39-41; Lic to Offic 41-44; C Cambridge St Andr Less *Ely* 44-48; V Skirbeck H Trin *Linc* 48-54; V Dur St Nic *Dur* 54-74; RD Dur 64-74; Hon Can Dur Cathl 72-74; Adn Auckland 74-83; Can Res Dur Cathl 74-83; rtd 83; Perm to Offic *Nor* 83-01. *28 Greenways, Eaton, Norwich NR4 6PE* Tel (01603) 58295

MARCHANT, Canon Iain William. b 26. Wells Th Coll 59. **d** 60 **p** 61. C Dalston *Carl* 60-63; V Hawkesbury *Glouc* 63-76; R Newent 76-85; Hon Can Glouc Cathl 84-92; R Newent and Gorsley w Cliffords Mesne 85-92; rtd 92; Perm to Offic *Glouc* from 92. *Daisy Green, Daisy Lane, Howley, Wotton-under-Edge GL12 7PF* Tel (01453) 844779

MARCHANT, Canon Ronald Albert. b 26. Em Coll Cam BA50 MA52 PhD57 BD64. Ridley Hall Cam 50. **d** 54 **p** 55. C Acomb St Steph *York* 54-57; C Willian *St Alb* 57-59; V Laxfield *St E* 59-92; RD Hoxne 73-78; Hon Can St E Cathl 75-92; P-in-c Wilby w Brundish 86-92; rtd 92; Perm to Offic *York* from 98. *34 The Paddock, Boroughbridge Road, York YO26 6AW* Tel (01904) 798446

MARCUSSEN, Mrs Yolande Roberta. b 47. SEITE 98. **d** 01 **p** 02. NSM Bromley Common St Aug *Roch* 01-03; NSM Orpington All SS from 03; Asst Chapl HM Pris Roch from 01. *Charis, 24 Lucerne Road, Orpington BR6 0EP* Tel (01689) 833599 Mobile 07790-915697 E-mail yolande.marcussen@ntlworld.com

MARGAM, Archdeacon of. *See* MORRIS, The Ven Philip Gregory

MARGARET ANNE, Sister. *See* McALISTER, Margaret Elizabeth Anne

MARGARET JOY, Sister. *See* HARRIS, Margaret Claire

MARINER, Aris. b 43. Alexandria Univ BSc65. St Alb Minl Tr Scheme 84. **d** 87. NSM Stevenage H Trin *St Alb* from 87. *13 Church Lane, Stevenage SG1 3QS* Tel (01438) 365596

MARION EVA, Sister. *See* RECORD, Sister Marion Eva

MARK, Timothy John. b 34. Bris Univ BA57 PGCE58 MLitt68 MEd71 Leeds Univ PhD79. Didsbury Methodist Coll 54. **d** 59 **p** 61. India 59-64 and 65-69; Perm to Offic *Sheff* from 73. *15 Fieldhouse Road, Sprotborough, Doncaster DN5 7RN* Tel (01302) 853022 E-mail timothy.mark@eggconnect.net

MARKBY, Archibald Campbell. b 15. Em Coll Cam BA37 MA41. Ridley Hall Cam 37. **d** 39 **p** 39. C Bradf St Clem *Bradf* 39-42; C Ox St Aldate *Ox* 42-46; V Kilburn St Mary *Lon* 46-53; V Hornsey Ch Ch 53-64; R Ickenham 64-68; V Crowfield w Stonham Aspal *St E* 68-71; V Damerham *Sarum* 71-80; V Martin 71-80; rtd 80; Perm to Offic *Sarum* 80-00. *8 Timbermill Court, Church Sreet, Fordingbridge SP6 1RG* Tel (01425) 656141

MARKBY, Ms Jane Elizabeth. b 67. Em Coll Cam BA88 Homerton Coll Cam PGCE89. Ridley Hall Cam 00. **d** 02 **p** 03. NSM Edmonton All SS w St Mich *Lon* from 02. *1A Uvedale Road, Enfield EN2 6HA* Tel (020) 8482 0452 E-mail janemarkby@blueyonder.co.uk

MARKBY, Peter John Jenner. b 38. Em Coll Cam BA60. Clifton Th Coll 62. **d** 64 **p** 65. C Tufnell Park St Geo *Lon* 64-68; C Crowborough *Chich* 68-73; C Polegate 73-77; R Southover 77-02; rtd 02. *66 Leylands Road, Burgess Hill RH15 8AJ* Tel (01444) 870831 E-mail petermarkby@onetel.com

MARKEY, Andrew John. b 73. Univ of Wales (Swansea) BSc96. Westcott Ho Cam BTh02. **d** 02 **p** 03. C Wotton-under-Edge w Ozleworth, N Nibley etc *Glouc* from 02. *39 Parklands, Wotton-under-Edge GL12 7LT* Tel (07814) 654495

MARKHAM, Deryck O'Leary. b 28. Oak Hill Th Coll 66. **d** 68 **p** 69. C Purley Ch Ch *S'wark* 68-72; V E Budleigh and Bicton *Ex* 72-93; RD Aylesbeare 89-93; rtd 93; Perm to Offic *Ex* 93-03 and *Win* from 03. *8 Milford House, Milford on Sea, Lymington SO41 0QJ* Tel (01590) 643515 E-mail dolm@onetel.com

MARKHAM, Canon Gervase William. b 10. MBE00. Trin Coll Cam BA32 MA36. Westcott Ho Cam 34. **d** 36 **p** 37. C Bishopwearmouth St Mich *Dur* 36-39; Bp's Dom Chapl 39-40; CF (EC) 40-46; V Burnley St Steph *Blackb* 46-52; CF (TA) 50-52; CF (TA - R of O) from 52; V Gt Grimsby St Jas *Linc* 52-65; Can and Preb Linc Cathl 56-65; RD Grimsby and Cleethorpes 62-64; V Morland w Thrimby and Gt Strickland *Carl* 65-84; RD Lowther 65-69; Hon Can Carl Cathl 72-84; rtd 84; Perm to Offic *Carl* from 84. *The Garden Flat, Morland House, Penrith CA10 3AZ* Tel (01931) 714654

MARKS, Allan Willi. b 56. Cranmer Hall Dur 92. **d** 94 **p** 95. C Barnoldswick w Bracewell *Bradf* 94-96; C Willington *Newc* 96-98; TV 98-02; V Newc H Cross from 02. *Holy Cross Vicarage, 16 Whittington Grove, Newcastle upon Tyne NE5 2QP* Tel 0191-274 4476 *or* 275 3916 E-mail fatherallan@blueyonder.co.uk

MARKS, Anthony Alfred. b 28. AKC53. **d** 54 **p** 55. C Fleetwood St Pet *Blackb* 54-58; V Burnley St Cuth 58-63; Chapl RN 63-83; QHC from 81; P-in-c Bradninch *Ex* 83-88; R Bradninch and Clyst Hydon 88-90; rtd 90; Perm to Offic *B & W* from 90. *Bryony Cottage, The Combe, Compton Martin, Bristol BS40 6JD*

MARKS, Anthony Wendt. b 43. G&C Coll Cam BA63 MA67 PhD70 BNC Ox DPhil72. St Steph Ho Ox 70. **d** 72 **p** 73. C Withington St Crispin *Man* 72-75; Chapl Lon Univ Medical Students *Lon* 75-80; Warden Liddon Ho Lon 80-92; C-in-c Grosvenor Chpl *Lon* 80-92; V Shrewsbury All SS w St Mich *Lich* 92-99; V Fareham SS Pet and Paul *Portsm* from 99. *St Peter and St Paul's Vicarage, 22 Harrison Road, Fareham PO16 7EJ* Tel (01329) 280256 *or* 236003

MARKS, Robert Wesley. b 58. Guelph Univ (Canada) BSc81. Cranmer Hall Dur 03. **d** 05. C Baxenden *Blackb* from 05. *50 Southwood Drive, Accrington BB5 2PZ* Tel (01254) 391760 Mobile 07906-175379 E-mail wesmarks@supanet.com

MARKS, Timothy John. b 45. Man Univ BA76 Cert Counselling 94 Anglia Poly Univ MA97. **d** 88 **p** 89. NSM Burton and Sopley *Win* 88-91; R Croxton and Eltisley *Ely* 91-96; R Graveley w Papworth St Agnes w Yelling etc 91-96; Dir Network Counselling and Tr 96-97; Perm to Offic *B & W* 97-00. *8 Arundell Road, Weston-super-Mare BS23 2QQ* Tel (01934) 415807

MARKWELL, Donald Stanley. b 30. Victoria Univ Wellington MA53. **d** 79 **p** 80. NSM Kingston Hill St Paul *S'wark* 79-82; NSM Ham St Andr 82-04. *12 Albany Mews, Albany Park Road, Kingston upon Thames KT2 5SL* Tel (020) 8546 0740

MARL, David John. b 42. ARCA67. **d** 01 **p** 02. OLM Okeford *Sarum* from 01. *Gothic Cottage, Upper Street, Child Okeford, Blandford Forum DT11 8EF* Tel (01258) 860249 E-mail gothic.cottage@ukgateway.net

MARLEY, The Very Revd Alan Gordon. b 59. Birm Univ BA89. Qu Coll Birm 87. **d** 89 **p** 90. C Blandford Forum and Langton Long *Sarum* 89-93; Chapl HM YOI Aylesbury 93-97; I Fermoy Union *C, C & R* 97-03; Bp's Dom Chapl 99-03; Dean Cloyne from 03; I Cloyne Union from 03; Dioc Dir of Ords from 05. *The Deanery, Deanery Road, Midleton, Co Cork, Irish Republic* Tel (00353) (21) 463 1449 E-mail dean@cloyne.anglican.org

MARLOW (née SIBBALD), Mrs Olwyn Eileen. b 57. Aston Tr Scheme 85 Linc Th Coll 87. **d** 89 **p** 94. Par Dn Wythenshawe St Martin *Man* 89-93; Par Dn Baguley 93-94; C 94-95; Asst Chapl Cen Man Healthcare NHS Trust 95-00; NSM Newall Green St Fran *Man* 97-98; rtd 01; NSM Wythenshawe *Man* from 01. *28 Arcadia Avenue, Sale M33 3SA* Tel 0161-962 9292

MARLOW, Walter Geoffrey. b 29. AKC57. **d** 57 **p** 58. C Long Eaton St Laur *Derby* 57-61; C Mackworth St Fran 61-63; R Stoke Albany w Wilbarston *Pet* 63-68; PC Calow *Derby* 68-73; R Wingerworth 73-82; P-in-c Islington St Jas w St Phil *Lon* 82-87; P-in-c Islington St Pet 82-87; V Islington St Jas w St Pet 87-92; AD Islington 84-90; Preb St Paul's Cathl 87-92; Bp's Dom Chapl *B & W* 92-96; Preb Wells Cathl 92-96; rtd 96; Perm to Offic *Nor* 96-04. *Taverners Cottage, Park Road, Wells-next-the-Sea NR23 1DQ* Tel (01328) 710432

MARNHAM, Charles Christopher. b 51. Jes Coll Cam BA73 MA77. Cranmer Hall Dur DipTh76. **d** 77 **p** 78. C Brompton H Trin *Lon* 77-78; C Brompton H Trin w Onslow Square St Paul 78-80; C Linthorpe *York* 80-84; R Haughton le Skerne *Dur* 84-95; V Ches Square St Mich w St Phil *Lon* from 95. *St Michael's Vicarage, 4 Chester Square, London SW1W 9HH* Tel (020) 7730 8889 Fax 7730 0043 E-mail charles@stmichaelschurch.org.uk

MARNS, Nigel Geoffrey. b 63. Univ of Wales (Abth) BSc(Econ)85 Birm Univ BD92. Qu Coll Birm 90. **d** 93 **p** 94. C Addington *S'wark* 93-96; P-in-c W Bromwich Gd Shep w St Jo *Lich* 96-01; V Bromsgrove St Jo *Worc* from 01. *The Vicarage, 12 Kidderminster Road, Bromsgrove B61 7JW* Tel (01527) 876517 Fax 878801 E-mail parishoffice@fish.co.uk

✠**MARONA, The Most Revd Joseph Biringi Hassan.** b 41. Bp Gwynne Th Coll 78. **d** 81 **p** 82 **c** 84. Chapl Rumbek State Secondary Sch Sudan 81-82; Chapl Maridi Teachers' Tr Coll 82-83; Area Bp Maridi 85-89; Bp Maridi 89-00; Dean of Prov from 98; Abp Sudan and Bp Juba from 00. *ECS Liaison Office, PO Box 604, Khartoum, Sudan* Tel (00249) (811) 20040 *or* (11) 485720 Fax (811) 20065 *or* (11) 485717 E-mail ecsprovince@hotmail.com

MARQUEZ, Edilberto. b 57. Bible Sem Alliance Peru BA80 Westmr Coll Ox PGDTheol92 MTh93 St Steph Ho Ox PGCTh94. **d** 94 **p** 95. C Reading St Jo *Ox* 94-98; C New Malden and Coombe *S'wark* 98-01; P-in-c Bucklebury w Marlston *Ox* from 01; P-in-c Bradfield and Stanford Dingley from 04.

Bucklebury Vicarage, Burdens Heath, Upper Bucklebury, Reading RG7 6SX Tel (01635) 866731 E-mail emarquez@tiscali.co.uk

MARQUIS-FAULKES, Edmund. b 62. Hatf Coll Dur BA85. Ridley Hall Cam 87 Coates Hall Edin 90. **d** 91 **p** 92. C Broughty Ferry *Bre* 91-93; P-in-c Dundee St Ninian 93-02; R Bieldside *Ab* from 02. *St Devenick's Rectory, Baillieswell Road, Bieldside, Aberdeen AB15 9AP* Tel (01224) 861552 *or* 863574 Fax 869463 E-mail marquisfaulkes@yahoo.com *or* rector@stdevenicks.org.uk

MARR (née PARKER), Mrs Anne Elizabeth. b 46. Hull Univ BSc67 CertEd68. NEOC 91. **d** 96. NSM Whorlton *Newc* 96-97; NSM Chapel House from 97; Chapl Newc City Health NHS Trust 96-01; Chapl Newc Mental Health Unit from 01. *26 The Chesters, Newcastle upon Tyne NE5 1AF* Tel 0191-267 4808

MARR, Derek Paul. b 33. Dur Univ TCert69. Dioc OLM tr scheme 97. **d** 00 **p** 01. OLM Chapel House *Newc* from 00. *26 The Chesters, West Denton, Newcastle upon Tyne NE5 1AF* Tel 0191-267 4808

MARR, Canon Donald Radley. b 37. K Coll Lon 57. St Aid Birkenhead 61. **d** 64 **p** 65. C Macclesfield St Mich *Ches* 64-66; C Sale St Anne 66-67; V Marthall 67-72; C W Kirby St Bridget 72-76; R Waverton 76-83; R Nantwich 83-87; RD Nantwich 86-87; RD Malpas 87-91; V Bunbury 87-91; rtd 91; Dioc Rural Officer *Ches* from 91; Hon Can Ches Cathl 91-92; Perm to Offic *Truro* from 94. *St Boniface, 5 Hockenhull Crescent, Tarvin, Chester CH3 8LJ,* or *The Parsonage, Tresco TR24 0QQ* Tel (01829) 741302 *or* (01720) 423176

MARR, Mrs Joan Mary. b 36. SRN58 SCM75 HVCert78 NDN79. St Jo Coll Nottm CertCS91. **d** 91. Hon Par Dn Moffat *Glas* 91-97; Hon Par Dn Dumfries 98-03; rtd 03; Perm to Offic *Glas* from 03. *Auburn Cottage, Templand, Lockerbie DG11 1TG* Tel (01387) 810734 Mobile 07802-823658 Fax (01387) 810994

MARR, Mrs Margaret Rose. b 36. JP81. St Mary's Coll Ban TCert56 Open Univ BA00. Ripon Coll Cuddesdon 02. **d** 02 **p** 03. NSM Tarvin *Ches* from 02; Perm to Offic *Truro* from 02. *St Boniface, 5 Hockenhull Crescent, Tarvin, Chester CH3 8LJ,* or *The Parsonage, Tresco TR24 0QQ* Tel (01829) 741302 *or* (01720) 423176 E-mail therevs@marr4321.fsnet.co.uk

MARR, Peter. b 36. Reading Univ PhD78. Ox NSM Course 84. **d** 87 **p** 88. NSM Reading St Giles *Ox* 87-89; C Beverley Minster *York* 90-92; P-in-c Beckenham St Barn *Roch* 92-96; V 96-03; rtd 03. *31 Kingsley Road, Mutley, Plymouth PL4 6QP* Tel (01752) 228426 E-mail pbmarr@dircon.co.uk

MARRIOTT (née REID), Mrs Amanda Joy. b 63. Nottm Univ BTh92. Linc Th Coll 89. **d** 92 **p** 96. Par Dn Rothwell *Ripon* 92-94; C 94-95; C Manston 95-97; C Wetherby 97-01; P-in-c Water Eaton *Ox* from 01; AD Milton Keynes from 05. *The Vicarage, 38 Mill Road, Bletchley, Milton Keynes MK2 2LD* Tel (01908) 374585 E-mail mandy@marriott-wetherby.freeserve.co.uk

MARRIOTT, Frank Lewis. b 29. Lich Th Coll 57. **d** 60 **p** 61. C Earlsdon *Cov* 60-64; R Tysoe w Compton Winyates and Oxhill 64-70; P-in-c Cov St Marg 70-77; R Ufton 77-83; V Long Itchington 77-83; RD Southam 82-89; V Long Itchington and Marton 83-95; rtd 95; Perm to Offic *Heref* from 95. *12 Traherne Close, Ledbury HR8 2JF* Tel (01531) 634576

MARRIOTT, Stanley Richard. b 36. AKC60 Warwick Univ MA92. **d** 61 **p** 62. C Coleshill *Birm* 61-64; C Maxstoke 61-64; V Ansley *Cov* 64-78; Org Sec (E Midl) CECS 79-83; P-in-c Baxterley w Hurley and Wood End and Merevale etc *Birm* 83-84; R 84-87; R Newton Regis w Seckington and Shuttington 87-97; rtd 97; Perm to Offic *B & W* from 97. *Dunkery Pleck, Wootton Courtenay, Minehead TA24 8RH* Tel (01643) 841058

MARRISON, Geoffrey Edward. b 23. Lon Univ BA48 PhD67. Bps' Coll Cheshunt 49 Kirchliche Hochschule Berlin 50. **d** 51 **p** 52. C Wormley *St Alb* 51-52; Malaya 52-55; Singapore 55-56; C Radlett *St Alb* 56-57; C St Botolph Aldgate w H Trin Minories *Lon* 57-58; V Crookes St Tim *Sheff* 58-61; India 62-64; Perm to Offic *Cant* 64-69; Lic to Offic 69-82; Perm to Offic *Carl* from 83; Tutor Carl Dioc Tr Course from 83. *1 Ainsworth Street, Ulverston LA12 7EU* Tel (01229) 586874

MARROW, David Edward Armfield. b 42. Nottm Univ BA65 MA. Tyndale Hall Bris 65. **d** 67 **p** 68. C Clifton Ch Ch w Em *Bris* 67-70; BCMS Ethiopia 70-75; N Area Sec BCMS 75-77; C-in-c Ryde St Jas Prop Chpl *Portsm* 77-84; V Worthing St Geo *Chich* from 84. *The Vicarage, 20 Seldon Road, Worthing BN11 2LN* Tel (01903) 203309

MARSBURG, John Edward. b 53. Oak Hill Th Coll DipHE94 BA96. Coll of Resurr Mirfield 98. **d** 99 **p** 00. NSM Selby Abbey *York* 99-02; R Lenzie *Glas* from 02. *The Rectory, 1A Beech Road, Lenzie, Kirkintilloch, Glasgow G66 4HN* Tel 0141-776 4149 E-mail rev.jem@marsburg.org

MARSDEN, Andrew Philip. b 63. Keble Coll Ox BA85 MA90 Birm Univ MA86. Wycliffe Hall Ox BA90. **d** 91 **p** 92. C Newport St Jo *Portsm* 91-94; C Cowplain 94-97; V Wokingham St Sebastian *Ox* from 97. *St Sebastian's Vicarage, Nine Mile Ride, Wokingham RG40 3AT* Tel (01344) 761050

MARSDEN, Andrew Robert. b 49. AKC71. St Aug Coll Cant 68. **d** 72 **p** 73. C New Addington *Cant* 72-75; C Prudhoe *Newc* 75-77; Asst Chapl HM Pris Wakef 77; Chapl HM Borstal Portland 77-82; Chapl HM YOI Onley 82-89; V Ulceby Gp *Linc* 89-98; Chapl Calderdale Healthcare NHS Trust 98-01; Chapl Calderdale and Huddersfield NHS Trust 01; Chapl St Andr Hospice Grimsby from 01; Community Chapl *Linc* 01-05; Chapl Hull and E Yorks Hosps NHS Trust from 05; Gen Preacher *Linc* from 01. *St Andrew's Hospice, Peaks Lane, Grimsby DN32 9RP* Tel (01472) 350908 *or* (01482) 676422 E-mail chaplain.standrewshospice@nelpct.nhs.uk

MARSDEN, Mrs Carole. b 44. Avery Hill Coll TCert65 Sheff Poly DipEd87. N Ord Course 88. **d** 91 **p** 94. NSM Saddleworth *Man* 91-92; Par Dn 92-94; C 94-95; P-in-c Oldham St Paul 95-02; C Werneth 98-02; P-in-c Shap w Swindale and Bampton w Mardale *Carl* from 02. *The Vicarage, Shap, Penrith CA10 3LB* Tel and fax (01931) 716232 E-mail revmothershap@hotmail.com

MARSDEN, Mrs Diana Marion (Dodie). b 53. Deakin Univ Australia BEd88. STETS 00. **d** 03 **p** 04. NSM Hurstbourne Priors, Longparish etc *Win* from 03. *Little Brook House, Church Street, St Mary Bourne, Andover SP11 6BG* Tel (01264) 738211 E-mail dodie.marsden@ukgateway.net

MARSDEN, John Joseph. b 53. York Univ BA74 Nottm Univ DipTh78 MTh81 Kent Univ PhD88. St Jo Coll Nottm 77. **d** 80 **p** 81. C Leigh St Mary *Man* 80-83; Hon C Chatham St Steph *Roch* 83-91; Ind Chapl 83-91; Lect Systematic Th CITC and TCD from 91; I Newbridge w Carnalway and Kilcullen *M & K* from 97. *The Rectory, Morristown, Newbridge, Co Kildare, Irish Republic* Tel (00353) (45) 438185

MARSDEN, John Robert. b 22. Linc Coll Ox BA48 MA49. Ripon Hall Ox 57. **d** 58 **p** 59. C Dur St Cuth *Dur* 58-61; Chapl Dur Sch 61-85; rtd 85. *Prebends, High Kilburn, York YO61 4AJ* Tel (01347) 868597

MARSDEN, Canon Joyce. b 47. Eliz Gaskell Coll Man TCert68. Trin Coll Bris 78. **dss** 83 **d** 87 **p** 94. Wavertree H Trin *Liv* 83-85; Much Woolton 85-97; Par Dn 87-94; C 94-97; TV Parr from 97; Hon Can Liv Cathl from 03. *459 Fleet Lane, St Helens WA9 2NQ* Tel (01744) 21213 E-mail jmarsden@stphilips22.fsnet.co.uk

MARSDEN, Michael John. b 59. St Mich Coll Llan 78. **d** 82 **p** 83. C Neath w Llantwit *Llan* 82-85; Asst Chapl Univ Hosp of Wales Cardiff 85-89; V Graig *Llan* 89-93; P-in-c Cilfynydd 89-93; R Merthyr Tydfil St Dav 93-01; Chapl Gwent Healthcare NHS Trust from 01. *Nevill Hall Hospital, Brecon Road, Abergavenny NP7 7EG* Tel (01873) 732112 E-mail michael.marsden@gwent.wales.nhs.uk

MARSDEN, Robert. b 59. Ch Ch Ox BA81 PGCE82. Oak Hill Th Coll BA92. **d** 92 **p** 93. C Sevenoaks St Nic *Roch* 92-95; Chapl Fettes Coll Edin 95-99; C-in-c Buxton Trin Prop Chpl *Derby* from 99. *37 Temple Road, Buxton SK17 9BA* Tel (01298) 73656

MARSDEN, Robert James. b 56. Ch Ch Coll Cant BEd79. Oak Hill Th Coll DipHE92. **d** 94 **p** 95. C Margate H Trin *Cant* 94-98; P-in-c Brinton, Briningham, Hunworth, Stody etc *Nor* from 98. *The Rectory, The Street, Brinton, Melton Constable NR24 2QF* Tel (01263) 860295 E-mail rbmarsden@skynow.net

MARSDEN, Robert William. b 24. TCD BA49 MA52. CITC 50. **d** 50 **p** 51. C Dublin St Jas *D & G* 50-54; Asst Chapl Miss to Seamen 54-58; I Currin w Drum *Clogh* 58-66; I Clones w Killeevan 66-94; Prec Clogh Cathl 86-94; rtd 94. *30 Claremont Park, Sandymount, Dublin 4, Irish Republic* Tel (00353) (1) 668 0210

MARSDEN, Samuel Edward. b 44. Keble Coll Ox BA66 MA85. Linc Th Coll 66. **d** 68 **p** 69. C Liskeard w St Keyne *Truro* 68-72; R Gerrans w St Anthony in Roseland 72-77; Hong Kong 77-81; P-in-c Ingrave *Chelmsf* 81-82; P-in-c Gt Warley w Childerditch 81-82; R Gt Warley w Childerditch and Ingrave 82-89; Australia from 89. *12 Hill Street, PO Box 86, Parkes, NSW, Australia 2870* Tel (0061) (2) 6862 2083 *or* 6862 1868 Fax 6862 1547 E-mail samuelmarsden@hotmail.com

MARSDEN-JONES, Watkin David. b 22. St D Coll Lamp BA48. **d** 49 **p** 50. C Flint *St As* 49-54; C Forest Row *Chich* 54-56; V Copthorne 56-70; RD E Grinstead 66-70; V Bosham 70-86; rtd 86; Perm to Offic *Chich* from 86. *10 Fairfield Road, Bosham, Chichester PO18 8JH* Tel (01243) 575053 E-mail dmj@wdmarjon.go-plus.net

MARSH, Anthony David. b 29. Roch Th Coll 64. **d** 66 **p** 67. C Liskeard w St Keyne *Truro* 66-69; R Wrentham w Benacre and Covehithe *St E* 69-75; R Wrentham w Benacre, Covehithe, Frostenden etc 75-80; P-in-c Beyton and Hessett 80-86; C Felixstowe St Jo 86-88; rtd 88; Perm to Offic *St E* 88-03 and *B & W* 01-03. *15 Martello Place, Golf Road, Felixstowe IP11 7NB*

MARSH, Carol Ann. *See* HATHORNE, Mrs Carol Ann

MARSH, Colin Arthur. b 54. Edin Univ PhD02. St Jo Coll Nottm 79. **d** 82 **p** 83. C Kirkby *Liv* 82-86; TV St Luke in the City 86-91; P-in-c Chingola St Barn Zambia 91-95; Perm to Offic *Edin* 95-03; Tutor United Coll of Ascension Selly Oak from 03. *4 Huddleston Way, Selly Oak, Birmingham B29 5AJ* Tel 0121-472 8448 E-mail c.marsh@bham.ac.uk

MARSH, David. b 32. St Jo Coll Dur BA54 DipTh57. **d** 57 **p** 58. C Bilston St Leon *Lich* 57-62; Kenya 63-66 and 70-72; Chapl Scargill Ho 67-69; Adn S Maseno 70-72; V Meole Brace *Lich*

72-77; V Westlands St Andr 77-86; V Trentham 86-96; P-in-c Alstonfield, Butterton, Warslow w Elkstone etc 96-99; rtd 99; Perm to Offic *Ches* from 99. *31 Spring Gardens, Nantwich CW5 5SH* Tel (01270) 610079

MARSH, Donald. b 35. WMMTC. **d** 90 **p** 91. NSM Wednesbury St Bart *Lich* 90-03; Lic to Offic from 03. *Holly Rise, 19 Trouse Lane, Wednesbury WS10 7HR* Tel and fax 0121-556 0095 *or* tel (01902) 723310

MARSH, Francis John. b 47. York Univ BA69 DPhil76 ATCL65 ARCM66 ARCO71. Oak Hill Th Coll 72 Selw Coll Cam 73. **d** 75 **p** 76. C Cambridge St Matt *Ely* 75-78; C Pitsmoor w Wicker *Sheff* 79; C Pitsmoor w Ellesmere 79-81; C Crookes St Thos 81-85; V S Ossett *Wakef* 85-96; RD Dewsbury 93-96; Adn Blackb 96-01; Bp's Adv on Hosp Chapls 96-01. *137 Edge Lane, Dewsbury WF12 0HB* Tel (01924) 451233 E-mail vendocjon@aol.com

MARSH, Gordon Bloxham. b 25. Cant Sch of Min 82. **d** 85 **p** 86. NSM Loose *Cant* 85-86; NSM New Romney w Old Romney and Midley 86-90; NSM Asst to RD S Lympne 90-94; rtd 94; Perm to Offic *Cant* from 94. *Westleton, St John's Road, New Romney TN28 8EN* Tel (01797) 366506

MARSH, Lawrence Allan. b 36. Sarum Th Coll 66. **d** 67 **p** 68. C Waterlooville *Portsm* 67-70; V Shedfield 70-76; R Fen Ditton *Ely* 76-01; P-in-c Horningsea 83-01; rtd 01; Perm to Offic *Ely* from 01. *The Old Bakery, 22 High Street, Bottisham, Cambridge CB5 9DA* Tel (01223) 811314 E-mail landjmarsh@aol.com

MARSH, Leonard Stuart Alexander. b 55. Hull Univ BA77 SOAS Lon MA00. Linc Th Coll 77. **d** 79 **p** 80. C Eltham St Barn *S'wark* 79-81; C Camberwell St Giles 81-83; Hon C Clifton St Paul *Bris* 83-86; Asst Chapl Bris Univ 83-86; Area Sec (Dio S'wark) USPG 86-91; Chapl Guildhall Sch of Music and Drama *Lon* 91-97; Chapl City Univ 91-98; NSM Clerkenwell H Redeemer and St Mark 94-95; P-in-c Finsbury St Clem w St Barn and St Matt 95-01; P-in-c Upper Norwood All SS *S'wark* from 01. *All Saints' Vicarage, 12 Beulah Hill, London SE19 3LS* Tel (020) 8653 2820

MARSH, Mrs Margaret Ann. b 37. Nottm Univ BSc59 Ox Univ DipEd60 Lambeth STh87 Newc Univ MA93 Man Univ MPhil95. Carl Dioc Tr Course 86. **d** 87. Asst Chapl Garlands Hosp 87-92; Dn Carl Cathl *Carl* 87-93; NSM Carl St Luke Morton 93-94; Hon Chapl Carl Hosps NHS Trust 94-00; rtd 00; Perm to Offic *Carl* 00-02 and *St Alb* from 02. *1 The Maltings, Leighton Buzzard LU7 4BS* Tel (01525) 384655

MARSH, Mrs Margaret Evaline. b 47. STETS 96. **d** 99 **p** 00. NSM Tattenham Corner and Burgh Heath *Guildf* 99-03; NSM Epsom St Martin 03-04; P-in-c Walton-on-the-Hill from 04. *The Rectory, Breech Lane, Tadworth KT20 7SD* Tel (01737) 812105 Fax 814333 E-mail margaret.marsh@talk21.com

MARSH, Miss Maxine Dorothy. b 49. Bretton Hall Coll TCert72. Westcott Ho Cam 90. **d** 92 **p** 94. C Kings Norton *Birm* 92-95; P-in-c Kingsbury 95-96; V 96-02; P-in-c Middleton 99; AD Polesworth 99-02; P-in-c Glastonbury w Meare *B & W* from 02. *The Vicarage, 24 Wells Road, Glastonbury BA6 9DJ* Tel (01458) 834281 E-mail maxinemarsh@glastonbury666.fsnet.co.uk

MARSH, Phillip Edward. b 73. Univ of Wales (Abth) BSc94 Ch Ch Coll Cant PGCE96. Wycliffe Hall Ox BTh02. **d** 02 **p** 03. C Hubberston *St D* 02-05; C Werrington *Pet* from 05. *44 Woodhall Rise, Peterborough PE4 5BU* Tel (01773) 323146 E-mail snuzzgrot@aol.com

MARSH, Ralph. b 42. ACP65 Chester Coll CertEd63 Birm Univ BPhil77 Liv Univ MA00. St Deiniol's Hawarden 86. **d** 88 **p** 89. NSM Tranmere St Paul w St Luke *Ches* 88-90; C Guiseley w Esholt *Bradf* 90-92; V Broughton *St As* 92-94; Hon C W Derby St Jo *Liv* 94; C Ribbleton *Blackb* 94-97; NSM Man Victoria Park *Man* 98-00; NSM Croxteth *Liv* 00-03. *47 Rolleston Drive, Wallasey CH45 6XE*

MARSH, Canon Richard St John Jeremy. b 60. Keble Coll Ox BA82 MA86 Dur Univ PhD91. Coll of Resurr Mirfield 83. **d** 85 **p** 86. C Grange St Andr *Ches* 85-87; Solway Fell and Chapl Univ Coll Dur 87-92; Abp's Asst Sec for Ecum Affairs *Cant* 92-95; Abp's Sec for Ecum Affairs 95-01; Hon C Westmr St Steph w St Jo *Lon* 94-96; Assoc P Westmr St Matt 96-01; Can Gib Cathl *Eur* 95-01; Hon Prov Can Cant Cathl *Cant* 98-01; Can Res Cant Cathl from 01; Dir of Educn from 01. *15 The Precincts, Canterbury CT1 2EL* Tel (01227) 865232 Fax 865222 E-mail directorofeducation@canterbury-cathedral.org

MARSH, Robert Christopher. b 53. Ex Univ BEd76. St Steph Ho Ox 86. **d** 88 **p** 89. C St Leonards Ch Ch and St Mary *Chich* 88-91; TV Crawley 91-00; V Maybridge 00-02. *67 Hythe Crescent, Seaford BN25 3TZ* E-mail rmarsh6204@aol.com

MARSH, Roger Philip. b 44. K Coll Lon BD72 AKC72 Sussex Univ MA95. St Aug Coll Cant 73. **d** 73 **p** 74. C Leagrave *St Alb* 73-76; Asst Youth Officer 76-77; Resources Officer 77-80; Chapl Marlborough Coll 80-86; Master Ardingly Coll Jun Sch Haywards Heath 86-95; Hd Master St Geo Sch Windsor 95-99; Chapl Lancing Coll from 99. *Lancing College, Lancing BN15 0RW* Tel (01273) 465960 E-mail frrogermarsh@hotmail.com

MARSH, Mrs Shelley Ann. b 54. SRN75 SCM76. St Jo Coll Nottm CertCS87 TISEC 96. **d** 89 **p** 94. Hon C Glas Gd Shep and Ascension *Glas* 89-96; P-in-c Johnstone from 96; P-in-c Renfrew from 96; Chapl Paisley Univ 98-00. *44 Atholl Crescent, Ralston, Paisley PA1 3AW* Tel 0141-883 8668 E-mail revshelleymarsh@ntlworld.com

MARSH, Simon Robert. b 59. Sarum & Wells Th Coll 79. **d** 82 **p** 83. C Mottram in Longdendale w Woodhead *Ches* 82-85; Bp's Dom Chapl *Bradf* 85-87; V Ashton Hayes *Ches* 87-90; V Macclesfield St Paul 90-96; V Ringway 96-01; V Bollington St Jo from 01. *The Vicarage, Shrigley Road, Bollington, Macclesfield SK10 5RD* Tel (01625) 573162 Fax 571146 E-mail frsimon@btinternet.com

MARSH, Susan Edith. b 42. Southn Univ BA63 CertEd64. St Alb and Ox Min Course 01. **d** 01 **p** 02. NSM Bp's Hatfield *St Alb* from 01. *141 Handside Lane, Welwyn Garden City AL8 6TA* Tel (01707) 329744 E-mail susanianmarsh@ntlworld.com

MARSHALL, Alexander John. Leeds Univ BSc. **d** 95 **p** 96. OLM Holbrook, Stutton, Freston, Woolverstone etc *St E* 95-05; Perm to Offic from 05. *Well Cottage, 1 The Street, Freston, Ipswich IP9 1AF* Tel (01473) 780738

MARSHALL, Alexander Robert. b 43. Glouc Sch of Min 84. **d** 87 **p** 88. NSM Newtown w Llanllwchaiarn w Aberhafesp *St As* 87-00; P-in-c Mochdre from 00. *The Vicarage, Bettws Cedewen, Newtown SY16 3DS* Tel (01686) 650345 E-mail marshall@rhayapow.kc3ltd.co.uk

MARSHALL, Mrs Alison Mary. b 54. Middx Hosp MB, BS79 MRCGP84. St Alb and Ox Min Course 98. **d** 01 **p** 02. NSM Reading St Jo *Ox* from 01. *36 Bulmershe Road, Reading RG1 5RJ* Tel 0118-966 8794 Mobile 07740-944102 E-mail ali.marshall@ntlworld.com

MARSHALL, Ms Alison Rose Marie. b 60. Leic Univ BA83 Birkbeck Coll Lon MA86 UEA PGCE87. Ridley Hall Cam. **d** 95 **p** 96. C Whittlesey, Pondersbridge and Coates *Ely* 95-98; Dep Chapl HM Pris Nor 98-99; Chapl HM Pris Northallerton 99-03; TV Sunderland and Chapl Sunderland Univ *Dur* 03-04; rtd 04. *2 Thornhill Terrace, Sunderland SR2 7JL* Tel 0191-510 8267 Mobile 07905-173171 E-mail amarshal@fish.co.uk

MARSHALL, Andrew Stephen. b 74. UNISA BTh00. Coll of Resurr Mirfield 02. **d** 99 **p** 00. C Port Elizabeth St Hugh S Africa 00-02; C Port Elizabeth St Jo 02; C Easthampstead *Ox* from 03. *4 Qualitas, Bracknell RG12 7QG* Tel (01344) 426741 E-mail andyroo@ananzi.co.za

MARSHALL, Mrs Angela. b 48. Trin Coll Bris 74. **d** 88 **p** 96. Hon Par Dn Newcastle St Geo *Lich* 88-92; Lic to Offic *Eur* 92-94; Dn Versailles 94-96; Asst Chapl 96-04; Perm to Offic *St E* from 04. *Southgate Church House, 65A Home Farm Lane, Bury St Edmunds IP33 2QL* Tel (01284) 767693

MARSHALL, Basil Eustace Edwin. b 21. OBE69. Westcott Ho Cam 71. **d** 73 **p** 74. C Edenbridge *Roch* 73-78; P-in-c Matfield 78-85; P-in-c Lamberhurst 78-85; C Farnborough 85-86; rtd 86; Perm to Offic *Roch* from 86; *Chich* from 01. *7 Boyne Park, Tunbridge Wells TN4 8EL* Tel (01892) 521664

MARSHALL, Canon Bryan John. b 40. Chich Th Coll 63. **d** 65 **p** 66. C Poulton-le-Fylde *Blackb* 65-68; C S Shore H Trin 68-70; V Wesham 70-74; PV Chich Cathl *Chich* 74-82; V Boxgrove 82-91; P-in-c Tangmere 82-84; R 84-91; R Westbourne 91-95; V E Preston w Kingston 95-03; Can and Preb Chich Cathl 94-03; rtd 03. *11 Priory Close, Boxgrove, Chichester PO18 0EA* Tel (01243) 536337

MARSHALL, Christine. *See* MARSHALL, Melinda Christine

MARSHALL, Mrs Christine Anne. b 40. Leeds Univ BSc64. **d** 95 **p** 96. OLM Holbrook, Stutton, Freston, Woolverstone etc *St E* 95-05; Perm to Offic from 05. *Well Cottage, 1 The Street, Freston, Ipswich IP9 1AF* Tel (01473) 780738 E-mail marshall@freston40.freeserve.co.uk

MARSHALL, Christopher John. b 56. Edge Hill Coll of HE BEd79. St Alb Minl Tr Scheme 83. **d** 86 **p** 87. C Biggleswade *St Alb* 86-89; Chapl Asst S Beds Area HA 89-91; Chapl St Helier Hosp Carshalton 91-93; Sen Chapl St Helier NHS Trust 93-98; Gen Office and Bereavement Manager Newham Healthcare NHS Trust from 98; Gen Services Manager from 99. *Newham General Hospital, Glen Road, London E13 8SL* Tel (020) 7363 8462

MARSHALL, Preb Christopher John Bickford. b 32. TD78. AKC56. **d** 57 **p** 58. C Leatherhead *Guildf* 57-60; C Crewkerne *B & W* 60-63; V Long Sutton 63-72; V Long Sutton w Long Load 72-76; V Wiveliscombe 76-93; RD Tone 78-87; Preb Wells Cathl 88-96; P-in-c Chipstable w Huish Champflower and Clatworthy 93; R Wiveliscombe w Chipstable, Huish Champflower etc 93-96; rtd 96; Perm to Offic *B & W* from 96. *Tap Cottage, High Street, Milverton, Taunton TA4 1LL* Tel (01823) 400419

MARSHALL, Christopher Robert. b 49. St Chad's Coll Dur BA71. Sarum & Wells Th Coll 72. **d** 74 **p** 75. C Sheff St Cecilia Parson Cross *Sheff* 74-77; C Walsall St Gabr Fulbrook *Lich* 77-78; C Upper Gornal 78-80; V Walsall St Andr 80-86; V Willenhall St Giles 86-00; V Tividale from 00. *26 View Point, Tividale, Oldbury B69 1UU* Tel (01384) 243309

MARSHALL, Craig Laurence. b 64. Southn Univ BEd87 Open Univ MA93 Nottm Univ MTh01. St Jo Coll Nottm 99. **d** 01 **p** 02. C Staplegrove w Norton Fitzwarren *B & W* 01-04; Chapl K Coll Taunton from 04. *Chilton Lodge, 81 South Road, Taunton TA1 3EA* Tel (01823) 274348

MARSHALL, David. b 66. St Kath Coll Liv CertRS88 Liv Univ BA88. Ripon Coll Cuddesdon 89. **d** 92 **p** 93. C Dovecot *Liv* 92-96; P-in-c Westbrook St Jas 96-98; Dioc Communications Officer 95-98; Dioc Communications Officer *Ches* from 98. *Church House, Lower Lane, Aldford, Chester CH3 6HP* Tel and fax (01925) 419201 *or* (01244) 620444 Fax (01244) 620456 E-mail dco@chester.anglican.org

MARSHALL, David Charles. b 52. St Chad's Coll Dur BA73. Trin Coll Bris 74. **d** 76 **p** 77. C Meole Brace *Lich* 76-78; C W Teignmouth *Ex* 78-80; C Broadwater St Mary *Chich* 80-84; V Newcastle St Geo *Lich* 84-92; Chapl Versailles w Chevry *Eur* 92-04; Min Southgate LEP *St E* from 04. *Southgate Church House, 65A Home Farm Lane, Bury St Edmunds IP33 2QL* Tel (01284) 767693

MARSHALL, Canon David Evelyn. b 63. New Coll Ox BA85 Birm Univ MA88 PhD96. Ridley Hall Cam 88. **d** 90 **p** 91. C Roundhay St Edm *Ripon* 90-92; Chapl Ex Coll Ox 95-98; Lect St Paul's United Th Coll Limuru Kenya 98-99; P-in-c Buckden and Hail Weston *Ely* 99-00; Abp's Dom Chapl *Cant* 00-05; Hon Can All SS Cathl Cairo from 02; Perm to Offic *S'wark* from 05. *St Mildred's Parish Office, Sefton Road, Croydon CR0 7HR* Tel (020) 8655 1434

MARSHALL, Eric. b 20. EMMTC. **d** 82 **p** 83. Chapl Grimsby Distr Hosps 82-98; Hon C Gt Grimsby St Mary and St Jas *Linc* 85-98; rtd 98; Perm to Offic *Linc* from 99. *Morn Tide, Waithe Lane, Grimsby DN37 0RJ* Tel (01472) 823681

MARSHALL, Geoffrey Osborne. b 48. St Jo Coll Dur BA71. Coll of Resurr Mirfield 71. **d** 73 **p** 74. C Waltham Cross *St Alb* 73-76; C Digswell 76-78; P-in-c Belper Ch Ch and Milford *Derby* 78-86; V Spondon 86-93; Chapl Derby High Sch 87-01; RD Derby N *Derby* 90-95; Can Res Derby Cathl 93-02; Dioc Dir of Ords 95-00; R Wrexham *St As* from 02; RD Wrexham from 02. *The Rectory, 7 Westminster Drive, Wrexham LL12 7AT* Tel (01978) 263905 E-mail geoffrey@canonry.demon.co.uk

MARSHALL, Mrs Gillian Kathryn. b 54. Glouc Sch of Min 84. **d** 87 **p** 97. NSM Newtown w Llanllwchaiarn w Aberhafesp *St As* 87-98; P-in-c Betws Cedewain and Tregynon and Llanwyddelan 98-02; V from 02. *The Vicarage, Bettws Cedewen, Newtown SY16 3DS* Tel (01686) 650345

MARSHALL, Graham George. b 38. Dur Univ BA60 St Chad's Coll Dur DipTh65. **d** 65 **p** 66. C Ashton-on-Ribble St Mich *Blackb* 65-67; C Lancaster St Mary 67-71; R Church Eaton *Lich* 71-75; Prec Man Cathl *Man* 75-78; R Reddish 78-85; V Chadderton St Luke 87-02; rtd 02; Perm to Offic *Man* from 02. *7 The Woods, Rochdale OL11 3NT* Tel (01706) 642139 E-mail ggm@manutd.com

MARSHALL (née CHADWICK), Mrs Helen Jane. b 63. UEA BA84. St Jo Coll Nottm MTh91. **d** 91 **p** 94. Par Dn Easton H Trin w St Gabr and St Lawr and St Jude *Bris* 91-94; C 94-95; Perm to Offic *Ox* 95-98; Lect St Paul's Th Coll Limuru Kenya 98-99; Perm to Offic *Ely* 99-00; Chapl K Coll Lon 01-05; P-in-c Addiscombe St Mildred *S'wark* from 05. *St Mildred's Parish Office, Sefton Road, Croydon CR0 7HR* Tel (020) 8655 1434

MARSHALL, Canon Hugh Phillips. b 34. SS Coll Cam BA57 MA61. Linc Th Coll 57. **d** 59 **p** 60. C Westmr St Steph w St Jo *Lon* 59-65; V Tupsley *Heref* 65-74; V Wimbledon *S'wark* 74-78; TR 78-87; RD Merton 79-86; V Mitcham SS Pet and Paul 87-90; Hon Can S'wark Cathl 89-90; Perm to Offic 90-96; Chief Sec ABM 90-96; V Wendover *Ox* 96-01; P-in-c Halton 96-01; Hon Can Bulawayo from 96; rtd 01. *7 The Daedings, Deddington, Banbury OX15 0RT* Tel (01869) 337761 E-mail hughm@fish.co.uk

MARSHALL, Mrs Jean. b 36. SW Minl Tr Course 84. **d** 87 **p** 94. NSM Stratton *Truro* 87-89; NSM Bodmin w Lanhydrock and Lanivet 89-94; P-in-c Lawhitton and S Petherwin w Trewen 94-98; rtd 98; Hon C Bodmin w Lanhydrock and Lanivet *Truro* from 00. *10 Springwell View, Love Lane, Bodmin PL31 2QP* Tel (01208) 79891

MARSHALL, John. b 37. Kelham Th Coll 53. **d** 62 **p** 63. C Winshill *Derby* 62-64; C Chaddesden St Phil 64-65; Chapl HM Borstal Morton Hall 65-75; V Swinderby *Linc* 66-77; R Church Aston *Lich* 77-84; V Auckland St Andr and St Anne *Dur* 84-02; P-in-c Hunwick 88-90; Chapl Bishop Auckland Gen Hosp 84-94; Chapl Bishop Auckland Hospitals NHS Trust 94-98; Chapl S Durham Healthcare NHS Trust 98-00; rtd 02; Perm to Offic *Derby* from 02. *Croft House, West Bank, Winster, Matlock DE4 2DQ* Tel (01629) 650310

MARSHALL, John. b 50. St Luke's Coll Ex CertEd74 W Lon Inst of HE DEHC79. S'wark Ord Course 88. **d** 91 **p** 92. Hon C Brixton Hill St Sav *S'wark* 91-95; Hon C Clapham St Jas from 95. *57A Kingscourt Road, London SW16 1JA* Tel (020) 8769 3665

MARSHALL, John Douglas. b 23. Univ of Wales (Cardiff) BA43. St Alb Minl Tr Scheme 76. **d** 79 **p** 80. Hon C Radlett *St Alb* 79-86; Lic to Offic *Llan* from 86. *Meiros, 3 River Walk, Cowbridge CF71 7DW* Tel (01446) 773930

MARSHALL, John Linton. b 42. Worc Coll Ox BA64 MA68 Bris Univ MLitt75. Wells Th Coll 66. **d** 68 **p** 69. C Bris St Mary Redcliffe w Temple etc *Bris* 68-71; Tutor Sarum & Wells Th Coll 71-73; Perm to Offic *Pet* 74-77; Lic to Offic *S'well* 77-81; V Choral S'well Minster 79-81; R Ordsall 81-88; P-in-c Grove 84-88; RD Retford 84-88; V Northowram *Wakef* 88-99; P-in-c Glouc St Mark and St Mary de Crypt w St Jo etc *Glouc* 99-00; R from 00. *The Rectory, 38 St Mary's Square, Gloucester GL1 2QT* Tel (01452) 412679 E-mail cyprian@tesco.net

MARSHALL, Kirstin Heather. b 64. St Jo Coll Nottm 90 TISEC 95. **d** 93 **p** 95. NSM Glas St Marg *Glas* 93-96; Hon Asst P Glas St Mary 96-99; P-in-c E Kilbride from 99. *St Mark's Rectory, Telford Road, East Kilbride, Glasgow G75 0HN* Tel (01355) 244042 E-mail kirstinhm@hotmail.com

MARSHALL, Canon Lionel Alan. b 41. TEng. St Deiniol's Hawarden 84 Qu Coll Birm 86. **d** 87 **p** 88. C Llandudno *Ban* 87-90; V Rhayader and Nantmel *S & B* 90-01; P-in-c Llanbister w Llanbadarn Fynydd w Llananno etc from 01; RD Maelienydd from 98; Hon Can Brecon Cathl 00-04; Can Res from 04. *The Vicarage, Llanbister, Llandrindod Wells LD1 6TN* Tel (01597) 840333

MARSHALL, Mrs Margaret Elizabeth. b 60. New Hall Cam BA81 MA84. EAMTC 01. **d** 04 **p** 05. C St Neots *Ely* from 04. *80 Hardwick Road, Eynesbury, St Neots PE19 2SD* Tel (01480) 473920 E-mail m.e.marshall@ntlworld.com

MARSHALL, Canon Maurice Peter. b 23. Oak Hill Th Coll 59. **d** 61 **p** 62. C Haydock St Mark *Liv* 61-64; V New Ferry *Ches* 64-79; V Hartford 79-89; Hon Can Ches Cathl 87-89; rtd 89; Perm to Offic *Ches* from 89. *27 East Lane, Sandiway, Northwich CW8 2QQ* Tel (01606) 888591

MARSHALL, Melinda Christine. b 54. Cov Coll of Educn CertEd76. Ridley Hall Cam. **d** 01 **p** 02. C Exning St Martin w Landwade *St E* 01-05; TV Heatons *Man* from 05. *6 Glenfield Road, Stockport SK4 2QP* Tel 0161-432 1227

MARSHALL, Michael David. b 51. BSc. Trin Coll Bris. **d** 84 **p** 85. C Kennington St Mark *S'wark* 84-88; V Streatham Park St Alb 88-96; RD Tooting 93-96; V Blackheath St Jo from 96; RD Charlton from 01. *146 Langton Way, London SE3 7JS* Tel (020) 8293 1248

✠**MARSHALL, The Rt Revd Michael Eric.** b 36. Ch Coll Cam BA58 MA60. Cuddesdon Coll 58. **d** 60 **p** 61 **c** 75. C Birm St Pet *Birm* 60-62; Tutor Ely Th Coll 62-64; Min Can Ely Cathl *Ely* 62-64; Chapl Lon Univ *Lon* 64-69; V St Marylebone All SS 69-75; Suff Bp Woolwich *S'wark* 75-84; Episc Dir Angl Inst Missouri 84-92; Abps' Adv Springboard for Decade of Evang 92-97; Hon Asst Bp Lon from 84; Hon Asst Bp Chich from 92; Can and Preb Chich Cathl 90-99; P-in-c Upper Chelsea H Trin w St Jude *Lon* 97-02; R from 02. *Upper Chelsea Rectory, 97A Cadogan Lane, London SW1X 9DU* Tel (020) 7235 3383 *or* 7730 7270 Mobile 07710-215131 E-mail bishop@holytrinitysloanestreet.org

MARSHALL (formerly WEBB), Pauline Nikola. b 49. WMMTC 84. **d** 87 **p** 94. C Walsgrave on Sowe *Cov* 87-91; TD Grantham *Linc* 91-94; Ind Chapl 91-96; TV Grantham 94-96; Perm to Offic 01-02; C Boston from 02; Mental Health Chapl Lincs Partnership NHS Trust from 05. *St Christopher's Vicarage, Fenside Road, Boston PE21 8HY* Tel (01205) 352110 *or* tel and fax 366892 Mobile 07815-438831 E-mail nikola.marshall@btopenworld.com

MARSHALL, Canon Peter Arthur. b 31. AKC58. **d** 59 **p** 60. C Hutton *Chelmsf* 59-61; C Rickmansworth *St Alb* 61-66; Chapl Orchard View and Kingsmead Court Hosps 66-94; R Lexden *Chelmsf* 66-94; RD Colchester 88-93; Hon Can Chelmsf Cathl 90-94; rtd 94; Perm to Offic *Win* from 94. *21 Manor Close, Wickham, Fareham PO17 5BZ* Tel (01329) 832988

MARSHALL, Peter James. b 48. Qu Coll Birm 78. **d** 80 **p** 81. C Ormskirk *Liv* 80-83; V Dallam from 83. *St Mark's Vicarage, Longshaw Street, Warrington WA5 0DY* Tel (01925) 631193 E-mail pjorm.marshall@btinternet.com

MARSHALL, The Very Revd Peter Jerome. b 40. McGill Univ Montreal. Westcott Ho Cam 61. **d** 63 **p** 64. C E Ham St Mary *Chelmsf* 63-66; C Woodford St Mary 66-71; C-in-c S Woodford 66-71; V Walthamstow St Pet 71-81; Dep Dir of Tr 81-84; Can Res Chelmsf Cathl 81-85; Dioc Dir of Tr *Ripon* 85-97; Can Res Ripon Cathl 85-97; Dean Worc from 97. *The Deanery, 10 College Green, Worcester WR1 2LH* Tel (01905) 27821 Fax 611139 E-mail petermarshall@worcestercathedral.org.uk

MARSHALL, Peter John Charles. b 35. Bris Univ BA60. Ridley Hall Cam 60. **d** 62 **p** 63. C Lindfield *Chich* 62-65; Travelling Sec Scripture Union 65-83; Hon C Nottingham St Nic *S'well* 65-67; Hon C Cheadle Hulme St Andr *Ches* 67-83; V Ilkley All SS *Bradf* 83-98; RD Otley 92-97; rtd 98; Perm to Offic *Ches* from 00 and *St As* from 03. *Creuddyn Barn, Glanwydden, Llandudno Junction LL31 9JL* Tel (01492) 547352 E-mail revmarsh@tiscali.co.uk

MARSHALL, Richard Arthur Howard. b 66. Regent's Park Coll Ox BA88 MA92 SS Coll Cam PGCE89. Wycliffe Hall Ox

BTh99. **d** 98 **p** 99. C Broughton *Man* 98-02; Asst Chapl Sedbergh Sch 02-03; Sub Chapl HM Pris Man from 02; Perm to Offic *Man* from 02; V Blackb Redeemer *Blackb* from 04. *2 Kendall Close, Blackburn BB2 4FB* Tel (01254) 51206

MARSHALL, Robert David. b 52. TCD BA75 MA00 Solicitor 77. CITC 99. **d** 02 **p** 03. NSM Stillorgan w Blackrock *D & G* from 02. *The Tontine, 84 The Rise, Mount Merrion, Co Dublin, Irish Republic* Tel (00353) (1) 288 6170 *or* 649 2137 Fax 649 2649 E-mail curate@stillorgan.dublin.anglican.org

MARSHALL, Robert Paul. b 60. Sheff Univ BA81 St Jo Coll Dur MA85. Cranmer Hall Dur 81. **d** 83 **p** 84. C Kirkstall *Ripon* 83-85; C Otley *Bradf* 85-87; Dioc Communications Officer 87-91; P-in-c Embsay w Eastby 87-91; Dioc Communications Officer *Lon* 91-95; P-in-c S Kensington St Aug 95-00; Media Adv to Abp *York* 95-05; Communications Adv *Sheff* from 04; Public Relns Adv Fresh Expressions from 05; Hd of Marketing St Mary's Univ Coll Twickenham *Lon* from 05. *11 Polychrome Court, 261 Waterloo Road, London SE1 8XH* Tel 07785-767594 (mobile) E-mail robmarshall@aol.com

MARSHALL, Rodney Henry. b 46. Bernard Gilpin Soc Dur 71 St Steph Ho Ox 72. **d** 75 **p** 76. C Gorton St Mary and St Thos *Man* 75-78; C Bedford Leigh 78-82; V Goldthorpe w Hickleton *Sheff* 82-90; Dioc Dir of In-Service Tr 88-90; NSM Hemsworth *Wakef* 96-97; P-in-c Athersley 97-04; V from 04; P-in-c Monk Bretton from 04. *St Helen's Vicarage, 27 Laithes Lane, Barnsley S71 3AF* Tel (01226) 245361

MARSHALL, Simon. b 54. Kingston Poly BSc77 Leeds Univ PGCE78 MA(Ed)79. Qu Coll Birm DipTh93. **d** 93 **p** 94. C Gt Clacton *Chelmsf* 93-97; TV Chigwell and Chigwell Row 97-02; C Woodford Wells from 02. *107 Monkhams Avenue, Woodford Green IG8 0ER* Tel (020) 8220 5143
E-mail simon.marshall17@ntlworld.com

MARSHALL, Simon Hardy. b 69. Bp Grosseteste Coll BA92. St Jo Coll Nottm 00. **d** 02 **p** 03. C Bartley Green *Birm* from 02. *19 Elmcroft Avenue, Birmingham B32 4LZ* Tel 0121-422 1436
E-mail themarshalls@fish.co.uk

MARSHALL, Mrs Sonia Margaret Cecilia. b 49. Westf Coll Lon BA71. EMMTC 01. **d** 03 **p** 04. NSM Deeping St James *Linc* from 03. *135C Eastgate, Deeping St James, Peterborough PE6 8RB* Tel (01778) 346420 E-mail curate@dsj.org.uk

MARSHALL, Susan. *See* PANTER MARSHALL, Mrs Susan Lesley

MARSHALL, Canon Timothy James. b 26. Barrister-at-Law (Middle Temple) 50 BNC Ox BA48 BCL49 MA53. St Steph Ho Ox DipTh51. **d** 52 **p** 53. C Staveley *Derby* 52-60; V Shirebrook 60-92; Hon Can Derby Cathl 86-92; rtd 92. *43 Charleston Road, Penrhyn Bay, Llandudno LL30 3HB* Tel (01492) 543541

MARSHALL, Timothy John. b 53. GRSM74. Oak Hill Th Coll BA79. **d** 79 **p** 80. C Muswell Hill St Jas w St Matt *Lon* 79-85; V Hammersmith St Simon 85-92; V Bovingdon *St Alb* from 92; RD Rickmansworth from 01. *The Vicarage, Vicarage Lane, Bovingdon, Hemel Hempstead HP3 0LP* Tel and fax (01442) 833298 E-mail vicartim@btopenworld.com

MARSHALL, William John. b 35. TCD BA57 BD61 PhD75. TCD Div Sch 59. **d** 59 **p** 60. C Ballyholme *D & D* 59-61; India 62-72; Asst Dean of Residence TCD 73-76; I Rathmichael *D & G* 76-92; Can Ch Ch Cathl Dublin 90-02; Chan 91-02; Vice-Prin CITC 92-02; rtd 02. *115 The Elms, Abberley, Killiney, Co Dublin, Irish Republic* Tel (00353) (1) 239 0832

MARSHALL, William Michael. b 30. Pemb Coll Ox BA53 MA57 DipEd65 Bris Univ MLitt72 PhD79. Wells Th Coll 63 Sarum & Wells Th Coll 79. **d** 80 **p** 81. Asst Chapl Millfield Sch Somerset 80-96; Hon C Glastonbury St Jo w Godney *B & W* 80-84; Hon C Glastonbury w Meare, W Pennard and Godney 84-96; rtd 96; Perm to Offic *Portsm* and *Win* from 96; *Ely* from 01. *7 The Paddock, Ely CB6 1TP* Tel (01353) 612287 Fax as telephone E-mail william.m@ukonline.co.uk

MARSTON, David Howarth. b 48. St Jo Coll Dur BA69. Edin Th Coll 69. **d** 71 **p** 72. C Kendal H Trin *Carl* 71-75; Perm to Offic *Glas* 75-78; NSM Barrow St Matt *Carl* 79-86; Perm to Offic *York* 86-91; *Liv* 91-93 and 99-00; NSM Southport All SS and All So *Liv* 93-99; NSM Southport St Luke from 00. *33 Sandringham Road, Ainsdale, Southport PR8 2NY* Tel (01704) 578303

MARSTON, Neville Charles. b 37. Univ of Wales (Cardiff) DipSocSc62 BA65 Waterloo Univ (Canada) MA67. Ox Cen for Miss Studies 95. **d** 97 **p** 99. Dioc Dir Tr Seychelles 92-00; C Coven *Lich* 00-02; rtd 02. *88 Mill Rise, Swanland, North Ferriby HU14 3PW* Tel 07866-935844 (mobile)
E-mail nevillemarston@aol.com

MARSTON, William Thornton. b 59. Worc Coll Ox BA81 MA85 Cam Univ CertEd83. St Steph Ho Ox BA87. **d** 88 **p** 89. C Beckenham St Geo *Roch* 88-92; TV Ifield *Chich* 92-97; C-in-c Middleton-on-Sea CD 97-99; V Middleton from 99. *The Vicarage, 106 Elmer Road, Middleton-on-Sea, Bognor Regis PO22 6LJ* Tel (01243) 586348
E-mail w.marston@btopenworld.com

MART, Terence Eugene. b 47. CertEd76 BA82. St Jo Coll Nottm LTh87. **d** 87 **p** 88. C Prestatyn *St As* 87-91; Chapl Theatr Clwyd Mold 87-91; R Llangystennin 91-01; RD Llanrwst 96-00; V Llanfair DC, Derwen, Llanelidan and Efenechtyd from 01. *The Vicarage, Llanfair Dyffryn Clwyd, Ruthin LL15 2SA* Tel (01824) 704551

MARTIN, Alexander Lewendon. b 26. Em Coll Cam BA47 MA51. Ridley Hall Cam 56. **d** 57 **p** 58. C Ashtead *Guildf* 57-59; Asst Chapl Tonbridge Sch 59-64; Chapl Felsted Sch 64-74; Chapl Sedbergh Sch 74-84; R Askerswell, Loders and Powerstock *Sarum* 84-89; RD Lyme Bay 86-89; rtd 89; Perm to Offic *Ex* from 89. *Thirtover, 7 Alexandra Way, Crediton EX17 2EA* Tel (01363) 776206
E-mail alexmartin777@hotmail.com

MARTIN, Angela Lee. EMMTC 00. **d** 03 **p** 04. NSM Derby St Barn *Derby* from 03. *The Joiners' Arms, 60 Church Road, Quarndon, Derby DE22 5JA* Tel (01332) 552876 Mobile 07967-180531 E-mail trevor@joinersarms.com

MARTIN, Canon Anthony Bluett. b 29. St Jo Coll Cam BA52 MA56. Ridley Hall Cam 52. **d** 54 **p** 55. C Rushden *Pet* 54-57; C Worthing St Geo *Chich* 57-59; CSSM 59-63; Lic to Offic *Man* 59-63; V Hoole *Ches* 63-84; Hon Can Ches Cathl 83-94; V Bowdon 84-94; rtd 94; Perm to Offic *Ches* from 94. *8 Eaton Mews, Chester CH4 7EJ* Tel (01244) 680307

MARTIN, Ms Briony June. b 71. St Cath Coll Cam BA92 MA96. Trin Coll Bris BA96 MA97. **d** 02 **p** 03. C Leatherhead and Mickleham *Guildf* from 02. *58 Kingscroft Road, Leatherhead KT22 7BU* Tel (01372) 379954 E-mail pmbm@fish.co.uk

MARTIN, Brother. *See* COOMBE, John Morrell

MARTIN, Bryan Robert. b 71. TCD BTh01. CITC 98. **d** 01 **p** 02. C Magheralin w Dollingstown *D & D* 01-04; C Knockbreda from 04. *28 Church Road, Newtownbreda, Belfast BT8 7AQ* Tel and fax (028) 9064 1339 E-mail brymrtn@aol.com

MARTIN, Christopher John. b 45. Ball Coll Ox BA67 MA87. Wycliffe Hall Ox 86. **d** 88 **p** 89. C Edin St Thos *Edin* 88-90; R Duns 90-00; Chapl Lyon *Eur* from 00. *38 Chemin de Taffignon, 69110 Ste-Foy-lès-Lyon, France* Tel (0033) (4) 78 59 67 06
E-mail lyonchurch@aol.com

MARTIN, Prof David Alfred. b 29. LSE BSc PhD. Westcott Ho Cam. **d** 83 **p** 84. Hon C Guildf Cathl *Guildf* 83-99; Perm to Offic from 99. *174 St John's Road, Woking GU21 7PQ* Tel (01483) 762134

MARTIN, David Howard. b 47. Worc Coll Ox BEd79. AKC70 St Aug Coll Cant 70. **d** 71 **p** 72. C Sedgley All SS *Lich* 71-75; Dioc Youth Chapl *Worc* 75-81; P-in-c Worc St Andr and All SS w St Helen 75-81; R Newland, Guarlford and Madresfield 81-91; R Alvechurch from 91. *The Rectory, Alvechurch, Birmingham B48 7SB* Tel 0121-445 1087 E-mail davidmartin@lynkserve.net

MARTIN, Donald Philip (Ralph). b 30. Trin Coll Toronto MA55 STB55. **d** 54 **p** 55. Canada 54-57; C Toronto St Simon 55-57; Tutor Kelham Th Coll 57-73; SSM from 60; P-in-c Willen *Ox* 73-81; Japan 81-82; Ghana 83-89; Dir Cleveland Lay Tr Course 89-91; C Middlesbrough All SS *York* 89-91; Kuwait 92-93; Italy 93-94; Canada 94-95; Tutor St Alb and Ox Min Course *Ox* 95-96; Chapl OHP 96; Lesotho from 97; rtd 98. *PO Box 1579, Maseru, Lesotho*

MARTIN, Edward Eldred William. b 37. Cranfield Inst of Tech MSc84 Herts Univ MA88. S'wark Ord Course 65. **d** 68 **p** 69. C Greenwich St Alfege w St Pet *S'wark* 68-71; C Kidbrooke St Jas 71-75; V Peckham St Jo 75-78; P-in-c Peckham St Andr w All SS 76-78; V Peckham St Jo w St Andr 78-81; Hon Chapl S'wark Cathl 81-02; Chapl Guy's Hosp Lon 81-88; rtd 02; Perm to Offic *S'wark* 02-03; Hon C Lee St Marg from 03. *17 Honor Oak Rise, London SE23 3QY* Tel (020) 8699 2303 Fax 8291 9237 Mobile 07956-204869 E-mail emartin@horise.fsnet.co.uk

MARTIN, Edward James Russell. b 76. Hull Univ BA98 Leeds Univ BA02. Coll of Resurr Mirfield 00. **d** 03 **p** 04. C Carrington *S'well* from 03. *St John's House, 65 Osborne Grove, Nottingham NG5 2HE* Tel 0115-844 9805 Mobile 07736-711360
E-mail father.edward.martin@ntlworld.com

MARTIN, Mrs Eileen. b 43. City of Portsm Coll of Educn TCert65. OLM course 00. **d** 03. OLM Queen Thorne *Sarum* from 03. *School House, Trent, Sherborne DT9 4SW* Tel (01935) 851078 E-mail martin@queenthorne.freeserve.co.uk

MARTIN, Miss Eileen Susan Kirkland. b 45. LCST66. Lon Bible Coll DipTh71 Cranmer Hall Dur 77. **dss** 83 **d** 86. Kilmarnock *Glas* 84-86; Par Dn Heanor *Derby* 87-92; Perm to Offic 92-95. *303 Cressex Road, High Wycombe HP12 4QF*

MARTIN, George Cobain. b 34. TCD BA57 MA65. **d** 57 **p** 58. C Bangor St Comgall *D & D* 57-64; I Kircubbin 64-74; R Ashby by Partney *Linc* 75-78; R Partney w Dalby 75-78; V Skendleby 75-78; P-in-c Candlesby w Scremby 77-78; R Partney 78-95; rtd 95; Perm to Offic *Linc* 95-98. *Hapstead Cottage, 26 Mill Leat, Baltonsborough, Glastonbury BA6 8HX* Tel (01458) 850590

MARTIN, Glenn. b 52. Qu Coll Birm 84. **d** 86 **p** 87. C Chatham St Wm *Roch* 86-89; Chapl Pastures Hosp Derby 89-94; Chapl Kingsway Hosp Derby 89-94; Sen Chapl S Derbys Mental Health NHS Trust 94-97; Sen Chapl Community Health Sheff NHS Trust 97-01; Professional Development Officer for Chapl and Spiritual Healthcare from 01; NSM Gilmorton, Peatling Parva, Kimcote etc *Leic* from 04. *The Rectory, Dag Lane, North*

Kilworth, Lutterworth LE17 6HA Tel (01858) 881299 *or* 0116-246 2435 Fax 0116-246 1222
E-mail glenn.martin@leicspart.nhs.uk

MARTIN, Canon Gordon Albion John. b 30. AKC54. **d** 55 **p** 56. C Enfield Chase St Mary *Lon* 55-59; C Palmers Green St Jo 59-61; V Edmonton St Martin 61-64; V Culham *Ox* 64-67; Bp's Youth Chapl *St Alb* 67-73; P-in-c Wareside 69-73; V Harpenden St Jo 73-96; RD Wheathampstead 76-87; Hon Can St Alb 85-96; rtd 96; Perm to Offic *Ex* from 96. *2 Pottery Court, Church Road, Dartmouth TQ6 9SN* Tel (01803) 835628

MARTIN, Graham Rowland. b 39. Liv Univ CertEd58 Lon Univ BD70 Bris Univ BEd73 FRSA LCP. Wells Th Coll 71. **d** 71 **p** 72. Hon C Glouc St Cath *Glouc* 71-76; P-in-c Brookthorpe w Whaddon 76-78; Perm to Offic 78-80; Hon C Hucclecote 80-82; Hon C Tuffley 82-88; NSM Hardwicke, Quedgeley and Elmore w Longney 88-89; V Kemble, Poole Keynes, Somerford Keynes etc 89-96; P-in-c Bibury w Winson and Barnsley 96-04; Dioc Ecum Officer 96-04; rtd 04; Perm to Offic *Glouc* from 04. *Wharf Cottage, Wharf Lane, Lechlade GL7 3AU* Tel (01367) 252825

MARTIN, Henry Rowland Felix. b 67. Leeds Univ BA89 SS Coll Cam BA95. Ridley Hall Cam CTM96. **d** 96 **p** 97. C Becontree St Mary *Chelmsf* 96-00; C Broughton *Man* 00-02; TR from 02. *St James's Vicarage, 396 Great Cheetham Street East, Salford M7 4UH* Tel 0161-792 1208
E-mail felixmartin@ukonline.co.uk

MARTIN, James Alwyn. b 47. St Paul's Coll Grahamstown 76. **d** 78 **p** 79. Zimbabwe 78-04; C Highlands St Mary 78-80; P-in-c Lowveld 80-84; R Masvingo St Mich 84-87; Adn Victoria 82-87; R Borrowdale Ch Ch 87-98; Adn Harare S 96-98; Dean Bulawayo 98-04; V Aldershot St Mich *Guildf* from 05. *St Michael's Vicarage, 120 Church Lane East, Aldershot GU11 3SS* Tel (01252) 320108 Mobile 07749-770035
E-mail burchapas@yahoo.com

MARTIN, James Smiley. b 32. MBE98. TCD 65. **d** 67 **p** 68. C Glenavy *Conn* 67-70; C Belfast St Mary 70-73; I Carnmoney 73-74; I Mallusk 74-94; rtd 94. *21 Dundesert Road, Nutts Corner, Crumlin BT29 4SL* Tel (028) 9082 5636

MARTIN, Jessica Heloise. b 63. Trin Hall Cam BA86 PhD93. EAMTC 00. **d** 03 **p** 04. NSM Trin Coll Cam from 03. *82 Ditton Walk, Cambridge CB5 8QE* Tel (01223) 411196 Mobile 07780-704006 E-mail jhm28@cam.ac.uk

MARTIN, John Henry. b 42. St Jo Coll Cam BA63 MA67. St Jo Coll Nottm BA73. **d** 73 **p** 74. C Ecclesall *Sheff* 73-77; C Hednesford *Lich* 77-82; V Walsall Pleck and Bescot 82-92; V Whittington w Weeford from 92; V Hints from 05. *5 Bramley Way, Lichfield WS14 9SB* Tel (01543) 432233

MARTIN, John Hunter. b 42. AKC64. **d** 65 **p** 66. C Mortlake w E Sheen *S'wark* 65-69; C-in-c Bermondsey St Hugh CD 69-72; V Bermondsey St Anne 72-78; P-in-c Lt Ouse *Ely* 78; V Littleport 78-89; V Attercliffe *Sheff* 89-90; P-in-c Darnall 89-90; TR Darnall-cum-Attercliffe 90-96; TR Attercliffe, Darnall and Tinsley 96; R Kirk Sandall and Edenthorpe from 96. *The Rectory, 31 Doncaster Road, Kirk Sandall, Doncaster DN3 1HP* Tel (01302) 882861

MARTIN, Canon John Pringle. b 24. Bris Univ BA50. Clifton Th Coll 50. **d** 52 **p** 53. C Braintree *Chelmsf* 52-56; C St Alb St Paul *St Alb* 56-59; V Congleton St Pet *Ches* 59-81; RD Congleton 74-85; Hon Can Ches Cathl 80-90; R Brereton w Swettenham 81-90; rtd 90; Perm to Offic *B & W* from 90. *49 Parkhouse Road, Minehead TA24 8AD* Tel (01643) 706769

MARTIN, John Stuart. b 11. St Jo Coll Dur BA34. Wycliffe Hall Ox. **d** 35 **p** 36. C Mansfield SS Pet and Paul *S'well* 35-37; C Newhaven *Chich* 37-39; C Barcombe 39-43; V Ox H Trin *Ox* 43-46; V Leafield w Wychwood 46-51; R Rotherfield Greys 51-63; V Highmore 55-63; R Bow w Broad Nymet *Ex* 63-65; V Upottery 65-72; TV Farway w Northleigh and Southleigh 72-73; rtd 73. *Church Villa, 8 Church Road, Bawdrip, Bridgwater TA7 8PU* Tel (01278) 684092

MARTIN, Canon John Tidswell. b 24. Em Coll Cam BA48 MA52. Kelham Th Coll 48. **d** 53 **p** 54. C Yardley Wood *Birm* 53-55; Asst Gen Sec and Sec Th Colls Dept SCM 55-58; Gen Sec 58-62; R Withington St Chris *Man* 62-68; V Kingston All SS *S'wark* 68-76; V Kingston All SS w St Jo 76-89; Hon Can S'wark Cathl 87-89; rtd 89; Hon C Twickenham St Mary *Lon* from 89; Perm to Offic *S'wark* from 89 and *Lon* from 93. *175 Lincoln Avenue, Twickenham TW2 6NL*

MARTIN, Jonathan Patrick McLeod. b 55. Leic Univ BA81. Sarum & Wells Th Coll 84. **d** 86 **p** 87. C Southampton Thornhill St Chris *Win* 86-89; Perm to Offic 89-92; C Heatherlands St Jo *Sarum* 92-97; Dioc Link Officer for ACUPA 95-97; Chief Exec Dame Agnes Weston's R Sailors' Rests from 97; Perm to Offic 98-01; NSM Parkstone St Pet and St Osmund w Branksea from 01. *5 Jennings Road, Poole BH14 8RY* Tel (01202) 748566 *or* 733580 E-mail purc@fish.co.uk

MARTIN, Joseph Edward. b 35. NDD55. Bps' Coll Cheshunt 58. **d** 60 **p** 61. C Short Heath *Birm* 60-62; C Caterham Valley *S'wark* 63-66; R W Hallam and Mapperley *Derby* 66-70; P-in-c Mapperley 66-67; V Wykeham and Hutton Buscel *York* 71-78; Chapl HM Pris Askham Grange 78-82; V Askham Bryan w Askham Richard *York* 78-82; R Amotherby w Appleton and Barton-le-Street 82-84; C Banbury *Ox* 85-88; C Warsop *S'well* 88-90; V Tuxford w Weston and Markham Clinton 90-00; rtd 00; Perm to Offic *Carl* from 03. *Windsmead, Allithwaite Road, Cartmel, Grange-over-Sands LA11 7SB* Tel (01539) 532693

MARTIN, Kenneth. b 20. Univ of Wales (Lamp) BA47. Bp Burgess Hall Lamp. **d** 48 **p** 49. C Rumney *Mon* 48-49; C Griffithstown 49-51; CF (TA) from 52; Perm to Offic *Llan* from 51. *21 Earls Court Road, Penylan, Cardiff CF23 9DE* Tel (029) 2049 3796

MARTIN, Lee. *See* MARTIN, Angela Lee

MARTIN, Miss Marion. b 47. Oak Hill Th Coll DipHE85. **dss** 86 **d** 87. Ditton *Roch* 86-88; C 87-88; rtd 88; Perm to Offic *Glouc* 89-01. *Address temp unknown*

MARTIN, Nicholas Roger. b 53. St Jo Coll Dur BA74. Ripon Coll Cuddesdon 75. **d** 77 **p** 78. C Wolvercote w Summertown *Ox* 77-80; C Kidlington 80-82; TV 82-84; V Happisburgh w Walcot *Nor* 84-85; P-in-c Hempstead w Lessingham and Eccles 84-85; R Happisburgh w Walcot, Hempstead, Lessingham etc 85-89; R Blakeney w Cley, Wiveton, Glandford etc 89-97; TR Totnes w Bridgetown, Berry Pomeroy etc *Ex* 97-05; RD Totnes 99-03; Co-ord Chapl HM Pris Channings Wood from 05. *HM Prison, Channings Wood, Denbury, Newton Abbot TQ12 6DW* Tel (01803) 814647 E-mail nick.martin@hmps.gsi.gov.uk

MARTIN, Norman George. b 22. Sarum & Wells Th Coll 74. **d** 77 **p** 78. NSM Long Ashton *B & W* 77-81; NSM Walton in Gordano 81-82; NSM E Clevedon and Walton w Weston w Clapton 82-87; Chapl Barrow Hosp Bris 87-91; Chapl United Bris Healthcare NHS Trust 91-00; Chapl Farleigh Hosp 87-00; Perm to Offic *B & W* 87-00; Perm to Offic *Mon* from 00. *27 Fairview, High Beech, Chepstow NP16 5BX*

MARTIN, Paul Dexter. b 50. Wabash Coll (USA) BA72 Univ of the South (USA) MDiv75. **d** 75 **p** 76. Educn Tutor Cov Cathl 75-76; C Norbury St Phil *Cant* 76-80; USA from 80. *275 Southfield Road, Shreveport, LA 71105, USA*
E-mail pdmartin@iamerica.net

MARTIN, Canon Penelope Elizabeth. b 44. Cranmer Hall Dur 83. **dss** 86 **d** 87 **p** 94. Seaham w Seaham Harbour *Dur* 86-89; Par Dn 87-89; Par Dn Cassop cum Quarrington 89-93; Par Dn Sherburn w Pittington 93-94; C 94-95; V 95-02; R Shadforth 95-02; R Pittington, Shadforth and Sherburn 02-03; Hon Can Dur Cathl 01-03; rtd 03. *34A Rosemount, Durham DH1 5GA* Tel 0191-386 1742 E-mail penny.martin@charis.co.uk

MARTIN, Peter. b 50. MCIH75. Linc Th Coll 82. **d** 84 **p** 85. C Taunton H Trin *B & W* 84-86; C Bath Bathwick 86-88; R Cannington, Otterhampton, Combwich and Stockland from 88; RD Sedgemoor from 00; Chapl Cannington Coll from 89. *The Rectory, 27 Brook Street, Cannington, Bridgwater TA5 2HP* Tel (01278) 652953 E-mail petermartin@petermmartin.fsnet.co.uk

MARTIN, Peter. b 66. Univ of Wales (Ban) BD89. Qu Coll Birm 90. **d** 92 **p** 93. C Kingswinford St Mary *Lich* 92-93; C Kingswinford St Mary *Worc* 93-95; Sen Chapl Redbridge Health Care NHS Trust 95-01; Sen Chapl Barking Havering and Redbridge Hosps NHS Trust from 01. *The Chaplain's Office, King George Hospital, Barley Lane, Goodmayes, Ilford IG3 8YB* Tel (020) 8983 8000 ext 8841 *or* (01708) 746090 ext 3299
E-mail pete.martin@bhrhospitals.nhs.uk

MARTIN, Philip James. b 58. Cam Univ BA. Coll of Resurr Mirfield. **d** 84 **p** 85. C Pontefract St Giles *Wakef* 84-88; C Wantage *Ox* 88-90; C Didcot All SS 90; V Alderholt *Sarum* from 90; Dioc USPG Rep from 90. *The Vicarage, Daggons Road, Alderholt, Fordingbridge SP6 3DN* Tel (01425) 653179
E-mail vicar@stjamesalderholt.org.uk

MARTIN, Ralph. *See* MARTIN, Donald Philip

MARTIN, Raymond William. b 32. MBIM Lon Univ BSc66 DMA. Glouc Th Course 73. **d** 76 **p** 76. Hon C Glouc St Mary de Lode and St Nic *Glouc* 76-77; Hon C Redmarley D'Abitot, Bromesberrow w Pauntley etc 77-84; R 84-91; P-in-c Falfield w Rockhampton 91-98; P-in-c Oldbury-on-Severn 91-98; Chapl HM YOI Eastwood Park 91-92; rtd 98; Perm to Offic *Glouc* 98-00 and from 02; Clergy Widows' Officer (Glouc Adnry) from 99; P-in-c Shipton Moyne w Westonbirt and Lasborough 00-02; Perm to Offic *Heref* and *Worc* from 03. *Tree Tops, 35 Thirlstane Road, Malvern WR14 3PL* Tel (01684) 562714

MARTIN, Rhys Jonathan. b 68. Heythrop Coll Lon BD98. EAMTC 98. **d** 00 **p** 01. C Stansted Mountfitchet w Birchanger and Farnham *Chelmsf* 00-02; C Dovercourt and Parkeston w Harwich 02-04; R Fingringhoe w E Donyland and Abberton etc from 04. *St Lawrence House, Rectory Road, Rowhedge, Colchester CO5 7HR* Tel (01206) 728640
E-mail rhys.martin@zetnet.co.uk

MARTIN, Richard. b 34. Rhodes Univ BA54 Em Coll Cam BA57 MA58. Wells Th Coll 57. **d** 59 **p** 60. C Portsea St Mary *Portsm* 59-60; S Africa 60-87; C Bloemfontein Cathl 60-62; R Wepener 62-64; R Odendaalsrus 64-67; R Newton Park St Hugh 67-76; Chapl St Bede's Coll Umtata 77-79; R Hillcrest 79-87; C Aldershot St Mich *Guildf* 87-94; R Wick *Mor* 94-99; P-in-c Thurso 94-99; rtd 99; Hon C Diptford, N Huish, Harberton,

Harbertonford etc *Ex* 99-01; Perm to Offic 01-03. *10 Royal Oak Drive, Invergordon IV18 0RP* Tel (01349) 853787 E-mail martin@chilledthames.com

MARTIN, Richard Charles de Villeval. b 41. St Jo Coll Ox BA63 MA67. Ox Ord Course. **d** 84 **p** 85. NSM Ox St Thos w St Frideswide and Binsey *Ox* 84-04; Asst Chapl Highgate Sch Lon 86-92; Magd Coll Sch Ox 92-02; Chapl 94-02; rtd 04. *11 Benson Place, Oxford OX2 6QH* Tel (01865) 510694 E-mail richardmartin@sabrehost.net

MARTIN, Richard Hugh. b 55. Van Mildert Coll Dur BA78 St Jo Coll Nottm BA81 Leeds Univ MA01. Cranmer Hall Dur 79. **d** 82 **p** 83. C Gateshead *Dur* 82-85; C Redmarshall 85-88; V Scarborough St Jas w H Trin *York* 88-96; Chapl R Wolv Hosps NHS Trust 96-02; V Bris St Andr Hartcliffe *Bris* from 02. *St Andrew's Vicarage, Peterson Square, Bristol BS13 0EE* Tel 0117-964 3554 Mobile 07870-147355 E-mail richardtherev@blueyonder.co.uk

MARTIN, Robert David Markland. b 49. FCA80 Trin Coll Cam BA71 MA74. Trin Coll Bris BA91. **d** 91 **p** 92. C Kingswood *Bris* 91-95; V Frome H Trin *B & W* from 95; RD Frome from 03. *Holy Trinity Vicarage, Orchard Street, Frome BA11 3BX* Tel (01373) 462586 E-mail rob@holytrinityfrome.info

MARTIN, Robert Paul Peter. b 58. Chich Th Coll. **d** 83 **p** 84. C Anfield St Columba *Liv* 83-86; C Orford St Marg 86-87; R Blackley H Trin *Man* 87-90; C Oseney Crescent St Luke *Lon* 90-93; C Kentish Town 93-96; V Harringay St Paul from 96; P-in-c W Green Ch Ch w St Pet from 04. *St Paul's Vicarage, Wightman Road, London N4 1RW* Tel and fax (020) 8340 5299 E-mail fr.robert@btinternet.com

MARTIN, Robin. *See* MARTIN, Thomas Robin

MARTIN, Robin Hugh. b 35. Rhodes Univ BA56 Birm Univ DipTh57. **d** 58 **p** 59. C Darnall *Sheff* 58-62; C-in-c Kimberworth Park 62-65; Lic to Offic *Sheff* 65-66 and *Newc* 67-71; Perm to Offic *Man* 79-93; *Lich* 97-99; *Heref* from 97; P-in-c Maesbury *Lich* from 99. *Offa House, Treflach, Oswestry SY10 9HQ* Tel (01691) 657090

MARTIN, Roger Allen. b 38. Westmr Coll Lon CertEd59 Birkbeck Coll Lon BA64 FRMetS79. St Alb and Ox Min Course 97. **d** 99 **p** 00. NSM Bramfield, Stapleford, Waterford etc *St Alb* from 99. *41 The Avenue, Bengeo, Hertford SG14 3DS* Tel (01992) 422441 E-mail roger.martin@ntlworld.com

MARTIN, Roger Ivor. b 42. DMS76 MCMI. Cant Sch of Min. **d** 85 **p** 86. NSM Saltwood *Cant* 85-90; P-in-c Crundale w Godmersham 90-01; Dioc Exec Officer for Adult Educn and Lay Tr 90-96; CME Officer 94-96; Chapl to Bp Maidstone 96-01; R Saltwood from 01. *The Rectory, Rectory Lane, Saltwood, Hythe CT21 4QA* Tel (01303) 266932 Fax 266998 E-mail rogmartin@clara.co.uk

MARTIN, Mrs Rosanna Stuart. b 60. Bris Univ BA81. Wycliffe Hall Ox 89. **d** 92 **p** 94. Par Dn Stanford in the Vale w Goosey and Hatford *Ox* 92-94; C 94-96; C Abingdon 96-00; Perm to Offic 00-04; P-in-c Uffington, Shellingford, Woolstone and Baulking from 04. *St Mary's Vicarage, Broad Street, Uffington, Faringdon SN7 7RA* Tel (01367) 820633

MARTIN, Rupert Gresley. b 57. Worc Coll Ox BA78 Ox Univ MA95. Trin Coll Bris DipHE91. **d** 91 **p** 92. C Yateley *Win* 91-95; V Sandal St Helen *Wakef* from 95. *The Vicarage, 333 Barnsley Road, Wakefield WF2 6EJ* Tel (01924) 255441 E-mail srsth@netscapeonline.co.uk

MARTIN, Russell Derek. b 47. St Jo Coll Dur 71. **d** 74 **p** 75. C Hartlepool H Trin *Dur* 74-78; C Swindon St Jo and St Andr *Bris* 78-79; V Penhill 79-91; V Haselbury Plucknett, Misterton and N Perrott *B & W* 91-99. *59 North Street, Martock TA12 6EH* Tel (01935) 829266 Mobile 07770-783893

MARTIN, Scott. b 73. Herts Univ BA99 Leeds Univ BA04. Coll of Resurr Mirfield 02. **d** 05. C Leagrave *St Alb* from 05. *St Luke's House, 39 Butely Road, Luton LU4 9EW* Tel (01582) 572054 Mobile 07766-295678 E-mail scottmar73@hotmail.com

MARTIN, Miss Susan. b 56. Nottm Univ BA77. Edin Th Coll 86. **d** 88 **p** 94. C Leigh Park *Portsm* 88-91; C Sandown Ch Ch 91-94; C Portsea St Cuth 94-95; rtd 95; Perm to Offic *Portsm* 95-01 and from 04; NSM Portsea St Geo 01-04. *7 Farthingdale Terrace, Peacock Lane, Portsmouth PO1 2TL* Tel (023) 9229 7994

MARTIN, Sylvia. b 24. **dss** 75 **d** 87 **p** 94. NSM Selsdon St Jo w St Fran *S'wark* 87-99; Perm to Offic from 99. *17 Frobisher Court, Sydenham Rise, London SE23 3XH* Tel (020) 8699 6247

MARTIN, Sylvia. b 43. Dip Counselling 93. Sarum Th Coll 94. **d** 97 **p** 98. NSM Locks Heath *Portsm* 97-02; Perm to Offic 02-04; NSM Fareham H Trin from 04; Chapl Fareham Coll of F&HE from 04. *9 Harvester Drive, Fareham PO15 5NR* Tel (01329) 312269 E-mail revd_syliamartin@hotmail.com

MARTIN, Thomas Robin. b 40. Bps' Coll Cheshunt 64. **d** 67 **p** 68. C Ripley *Derby* 67-70; C Ilkeston St Mary 70-74; V Chinley w Buxworth 74-83; V Knighton St Mich *Leic* 83-85; V Thurmaston from 85. *The Vicarage, 828 Melton Road, Thurmaston, Leicester LE4 8BE* Tel 0116-269 2555

MARTIN, William Harrison. b 38. Sarum & Wells Th Coll 91. **d** 87 **p** 88. NSM Rushen *S & M* 87-92; C German 92-97; V Lonan from 97; V Laxey from 97. *The Vicarage, 56 Ard Reayrt, Ramsey Road, Laxey, Isle of Man IM4 7QQ* Tel (01624) 862050

MARTIN, William Matthew. b 28. Ch Coll Cam BA52 MA56 FE TCert81. Ridley Hall Cam 52. **d** 54 **p** 55. C Weaste *Man* 54-56; V 56-61; CF (TA) 58-61; CF 61-82; Dep Asst Chapl Gen 73-82; Asst Master St Jo Southworth RC High Sch Preston 82-88; Lic to Offic *Blackb* 82-93; rtd 93; Perm to Offic *Blackb* from 93. *2B The Farthings, Chorley PR7 1TP* Tel (01257) 262772

MARTIN-DOYLE, Mrs Audrey Brenda. b 35. Cranmer Hall Dur 80. **dss** 82 **d** 87 **p** 95. The Lye and Stambermill *Worc* 82-86; Chapl Lee Abbey 86-88; Ldr Aston Cottage Community 88-93; C Cheltenham St Mary, St Matt, St Paul and H Trin *Glouc* 94-97; rtd 97; Perm to Offic *Glouc* from 97. *39 Moorend Street, Cheltenham GL53 0EH* Tel (01242) 510352 E-mail audrey@martin-doyle.freeserve.co.uk

MARTIN PHILIP, Brother. *See* FREEMAN, Philip Martin

MARTIN-SMITH, Paul. b 38. TCD BA64 Lon Univ MSc67 FIPEM88. WMMTC 94. **d** 97 **p** 98. NSM Tile Hill *Cov* 97-99; Perm to Offic *Ex* from 00. *12 Emmasfield, Exmouth EX8 2LS* Tel (01395) 269505

MARTINDALE, Mrs Patricia Ann. b 24. Qu Coll Birm. **dss** 84 **d** 87 **p** 94. Rugby St Andr *Cov* 84-94; NSM 87-94; Perm to Offic from 95. *54 Hillmorton Road, Rugby CV22 5AD* Tel (01788) 543038

MARTINEAU, Canon Christopher Lee. b 16. Trin Hall Cam BA38 MA70. Linc Th Coll 39. **d** 41 **p** 42. C Hinckley St Mary *Leic* 41-43; Chapl RNVR 43-46; C St Alb Abbey *St Alb* 46-48; V Balsall Heath St Paul *Birm* 48-54; P-in-c Shard End 54-58; V 58-65; R Skipton H Trin *Bradf* 65-83; Hon Can Bradf Cathl 72-83; rtd 83; Perm to Offic *Bradf* 83-02. *70 New Street, Ledbury HR8 2EE* Tel (01531) 635479

MARTINEAU, Canon David Richards Durani. b 36. AKC59. **d** 60 **p** 61. C Ches St Jo *Ches* 60-64; S Africa 64-69; C St Mark's Cathl George 64; C Riversdale 64-66; R Beaufort W and Victoria W 66-69; C Jarrow St Paul *Dur* 69-72; TV 72-75; TR Jarrow 76-85; V Gildersome *Wakef* 85-00; Hon Can Wakef Cathl 94-00; rtd 00; Perm to Offic *Linc* from 00; Hon Asst Chapl Voorschoten *Eur* 02-03. *Harlough, St Chad, Barrow-upon-Humber DN19 7AU* Tel (01469) 531475 E-mail david-martineau@harlough.freeserve.co.uk

MARTINEAU, Canon Jeremy Fletcher. b 40. OBE03. K Coll Lon BD65 AKC65. **d** 66 **p** 67. C Jarrow St Paul *Dur* 66-73; Bp's Ind Adv 69-73; P-in-c Raughton Head w Gatesgill *Carl* 73-80; Chapl to Agric 73-80; Ind Chapl *Bris* 80-90; Sec Abps' Commission on Rural Affairs 88-90; Nat Rural Officer Gen Syn Bd of Miss 90-03; Hon Can Cov Cathl *Cov* 01-03; rtd 04; Lic to Offic *St D* from 05. *11 New Hill Villas, Goodwick SA64 0DT* Tel (01348) 874886 E-mail jeremy.m@tiscali.co.uk

MARTLEW, Andrew Charles. b 50. Nottm Univ BTh76 Lanc Univ MA80. Linc Th Coll 72. **d** 76 **p** 77. C Poulton-le-Fylde *Blackb* 76-79; Hon C Lancaster Ch Ch 79-80; Malaysia 81-83; V Golcar *Wakef* 83-89; Dioc Schs Officer 89-95; V Warmfield 89-95; Dioc Dir of Educn *York* 95-02; CF from 02. *c/o MOD Chaplains (Army),* Tel (01980) 615804 Fax 615800 E-mail andrew@elk.demon.co.uk

MARVELL, John. b 32. Lon Univ BD63 Leic Univ MEd73 PhD85. Oak Hill Th Coll 79. **d** 80 **p** 81. NSM Colchester Ch Ch w St Mary V *Chelmsf* 80-85; Perm to Offic 85-87; P-in-c Stisted w Bradwell and Pattiswick 87-98; rtd 98. *3 Impasse de Genets, Vicomte, 35800 Dinard, France* Tel (0033) (2) 9916 5674 E-mail jmarvell@ctacom.fr

MARVIN, David Arthur. b 51. HND73. St Jo Coll Nottm 96. **d** 97 **p** 98. C Mansfield St Jo *S'well* 97-01; P-in-c Greasley from 01. *The Vicarage, 36 Moorgreen, Newthorpe, Nottingham NG16 2FB* Tel (01773) 712509 E-mail dave.marvin1@ntlworld.com

MARWOOD, Timothy John Edmonds. b 51. Whitelands Coll Lon CertEd72 Open Univ BA89 Lon Inst of Educn MA91. S'wark Ord Course 92. **d** 95 **p** 96. NSM Putney St Mary *S'wark* from 95; Perm to Offic *Ex* from 00. *172 Elborough Street, London SW18 5DL* Tel (020) 8875 0284 *or* 8788 9591 E-mail timmarwood@yahoo.co.uk

MARY CLARE, Sister. *See* FOGG, Cynthia Mary

MASCALL, Mrs Margaret Ann. b 43. LRAM64 Bris Univ CertEd65 St Jo Coll Dur BA71 MA79. Cranmer Hall Dur 69. **dss** 76 **d** 87 **p** 94. Hertford St Andr *St Alb* 75-79; Herne Bay Ch Ch *Cant* 79-82; Seasalter 82-84; Whitstable 84-90; Par Dn 87-90; Perm to Offic 91-94; Hon C Hackington 94-95; V Newington w Hartlip and Stockbury 95-03; rtd 03; Perm to Offic *Cant* from 03. *48 Holmside Avenue, Minster on Sea, Sheerness ME12 3EY* Tel (01795) 663095

MASCARENHAS, Felix Pedro Antonio. b 55. Bombay Univ BA80 Pontifical Univ Rome JCD88. Pilar Major Th Sem Goa BTh81. **d** 82 **p** 82. In RC Ch 82-02; C Chich St Paul and Westhampnett *Chich* from 02. *The Vicarage, 11 Old Arundel Road, Westhampnett, Chichester PO18 0TH* Tel (01243) 783010 Mobile 07814-739312 E-mail felixmas@hotmail.com

MASDING, John William. b 39. Magd Coll Ox BA61 DipEd63 MA65 Univ of Wales (Cardiff) LLM94 FRSA96. Ridley Hall Cam 63. **d** 65 **p** 66. C Boldmere *Birm* 65-71; V Hamstead St Paul

71-97; rtd 97; Perm to Offic *B & W* from 97 and *Bris* from 00. *The Old School House, Norton Hawkfield, Pensford, Bristol BS39 4HB* Tel (01275) 830017 Fax as telephone E-mail masding@breathe.co.uk

MASH, William Edward John. b 54. ARCS Imp Coll Lon BSc75 Open Univ MA00. St Jo Coll Nottm 87. **d** 89 **p** 90. C Beverley Minster *York* 89-93; V Elloughton and Brough w Brantingham 93-01; P-in-c Newcastle St Geo *Lich* from 01; Chapl Town Cen and Newcastle Coll of H&FE from 01. *St George's Vicarage, 28 Hempstalls Lane, Newcastle ST5 0SS* Tel (01782) 710056 E-mail billmash@tiscali.co.uk

MASHEDER, Peter Timothy Charles. b 49. AKC71. St Aug Coll Cant 71. **d** 72 **p** 73. C Barkingside St Fran *Chelmsf* 72-75; C Chingford SS Pet and Paul 75-91; P-in-c High Laver w Magdalen Laver and Lt Laver etc 91-98; R from 98; RD Ongar 98-04. *The Lavers Rectory, Magdalen Laver, Ongar CM5 0ES* Tel (01279) 426774 E-mail chasmash@ic24.net

MASHEDER, Richard. b 36. AKC59. **d** 60 **p** 61. C Preston St Matt *Blackb* 60-62; C Padiham 62-65; P-in-c Worsthorne 65; V 65-74; CF (TA) 65-67; P-in-c Blackb St Jude *Blackb* 74-78; V Blackb St Thos 76-78; V Blackb St Thos w St Jude 78-82; V Silverdale 82-01; rtd 01; Perm to Offic *Blackb* from 01. *59 Twemlow Parade, Heysham, Morecambe LA3 2AL* Tel and fax (01524) 851151 E-mail revakela@talk21.com

MASHITER, Mrs Marion. b 48. Carl and Blackb Dioc Tr Inst 01. **d** 04 **p** 05. NSM Burneside *Carl* from 04. *The Maples, 5 Esthwaite Avenue, Kendal LA9 7NN* Tel (01539) 731957 Mobile 07748-771836

MASKELL, John Michael. b 45. Sarum & Wells Th Coll 86. **d** 88 **p** 89. C Swanborough *Sarum* 88-91; Chapl RAF 91-95; P-in-c Ollerton w Boughton *S'well* 95-97; P-in-c Capel *Guildf* 97-02; TV Walton H Trin *Ox* 02-03; Healing Co-ord Acorn Chr Foundn 03-04; rtd 04. *37 Great College Street, Brighton BN2 1HJ* Tel (01273) 692722 Mobile 07929-134962 E-mail john@maskell.freeserve.co.uk

MASKELL, Miss Rosemary Helen. b 58. Ripon Coll Cuddesdon. **d** 00 **p** 01. C Goodrington *Ex* 00-04; V Littleport *Ely* from 04. *St George's Vicarage, 30 Church Lane, Littleport, Ely CB6 1PS* Tel (01353) 860207 Mobile 07803-499755 E-mail revrose@goodevon.fsnet.co.uk

MASKREY, Mrs Susan Elizabeth. b 43. Cranmer Hall Dur IDC70. **dss** 76 **d** 92 **p** 94. Littleover *Derby* 76-77; Sec to Publicity Manager CMS Lon 77-78; Stantonbury and Willen *Ox* 78-88; Billingham St Aid *Dur* 88-95; C 92-95; Asst Chapl HM Pris Holme Ho 94-95; Asst Chapl HM Pris Preston 95-01; Chapl HM Pris Kirkham 01-05; rtd 05; Perm to Offic *Blackb* from 05. *c/o the Bishop of Blackburn, Bishop's House, Ribchester Road, Blackburn BB1 9EF*

MASLEN, Darren Robert Dunstan. b 71. St Martin's Coll Lanc BA93 Open Univ MA97 Leeds Univ BA99. Coll of Resurr Mirfield 97. **d** 00 **p** 01. C Shaston *Sarum* 00-04; C S Shields All SS *Dur* 04-05; TV from 05. *4 Mitford Road, South Shields NE34 0EQ* Tel 0191-456 1300

MASLEN (formerly CHILD), Mrs Margaret Mary. b 44. ALA76 Open Univ BA79. S Dios Minl Tr Scheme 89. **d** 92 **p** 94. C Portishead *B & W* 92-93; C Ilminster w Whitelackington 93-94; C Ilminster and Distr 94-96; C Tatworth 96-00; TV Chard and Distr 00-05; Chapl Taunton and Somerset NHS Trust 97-05; rtd 05. *2 Woods Close, Sherston, Malmesbury SN16 0LF* Tel (01666) 840387

MASLEN, Richard Ernest. b 34. S Dios Minl Tr Scheme 89. **d** 92 **p** 93. NSM Sherston Magna, Easton Grey, Luckington etc *Bris* 92-93; NSM Ilminster w Whitelackington *B & W* 93-94; NSM Ilminster and Distr 94-96; P-in-c Tatworth 96-99; TV Chard and Distr 99-00; rtd 00; Perm to Offic *B & W* 00-05. *2 Woods Close, Sherston, Malmesbury SN16 0LF* Tel (01666) 840387

MASLEN, Canon Stephen Henry. b 37. CCC Ox BA62 MA65. Ridley Hall Cam 62. **d** 64 **p** 65. C Keynsham w Queen Charlton *B & W* 64-67; C Cheltenham St Mary *Glouc* 67-71; P-in-c St Mary-at-Lambeth *S'wark* 72-74; TV N Lambeth 74-79; V Horley 79-84; TR 84-94; RD Reigate 86-91; R Coulsdon St Jo 94-02; Hon Can S'wark Cathl 95-02; rtd 02; Perm to Offic *Worc* from 02. *The Red House, Back Lane, Bredon, Tewkesbury GL20 7LH* Tel (01684) 772575

MASON, Adrian Stanley. b 54. Hatf Poly BSc77. Ripon Coll Cuddesdon 77. **d** 80 **p** 81. C Mill End and Heronsgate w W Hyde *St Alb* 80-83; TV Axminster, Chardstock, Combe Pyne and Rousdon *Ex* 83-87; TV Halesworth w Linstead, Chediston, Holton etc *St E* 87-88; R Brandon and Santon Downham 88-91; R Glemsford, Hartest w Boxted, Somerton etc 91-95; Min Can St E Cathl 95-97. *42 Duddery Road, Haverhill CB9 8EA* Tel (01440) 703581

MASON, Alan Hambleton. b 27. Lon Univ BD59. Wycliffe Hall Ox 56. **d** 59 **p** 60. C Norbiton *S'wark* 59-63; V 73-84; V Thornton St Jas *Bradf* 63-73; V Wavertree St Thos *Liv* 84-92; rtd 92; Perm to Offic *Liv* from 92. *17 Lovelace Road, Liverpool L19 1QE* Tel 0151-427 5678

MASON, Ambrose. *See* MASON, Thomas Henry Ambrose

MASON, Miss Beverley Anne. Trin Coll Bris BA00. **d** 01 **p** 03. C Rusthall *Roch* 01-02; C Rainham 02-05; P-in-c Upper Norwood St Jo *S'wark* from 05. *St John's Vicarage, 2 Sylvan Road, London SE19 2RX* Tel (020) 8653 0378 E-mail revd@bamason.fsnet.co.uk

MASON, Charles Oliver. b 51. Jes Coll Cam BA73 MA99 St Jo Coll Dur BA79. **d** 80 **p** 81. C Cheltenham St Mary, St Matt, St Paul and H Trin *Glouc* 80-84; C Enfield Ch Ch Trent Park *Lon* 84-88; P-in-c W Hampstead St Cuth 88-93; V 93-01; AD N Camden 98-01; V Braintree *Chelmsf* from 01. *St Michael's Vicarage, 10A Marshalls Road, Braintree CM7 2LL* Tel (01376) 322840 E-mail comason@beeb.net

MASON, Mrs Christine Mary. b 43. Sarum & Wells Th Coll 91. **d** 93 **p** 94. Par Dn Blakenall Heath *Lich* 93-94; C 94-97; TV Rugeley from 97. *The Vicarage, 14 Peakes Road, Rugeley WS15 2LY* Tel (01889) 582809

MASON, Christopher David. b 51. Lanc Univ BA72 Leic Univ MEd82 Pet Regional Coll ACertC98. EAMTC 91. **d** 94 **p** 95. NSM Pet St Mary Boongate *Pet* 94-00 and from 03; P-in-c Newborough 00-02. *74 Derby Drive, Peterborough PE1 4NQ* Tel (01733) 700000 E-mail mason.cd@virgin.net

MASON, Clive Ray. b 34. St Chad's Coll Dur BA57. Qu Coll Birm 57. **d** 59 **p** 60. C Gateshead St Mary *Dur* 59-62; C Bishopwearmouth Ch Ch 62-64; V Darlington St Jo 64-74; P-in-c Southwick H Trin 75-84; R 84-89; V Bearpark 89-95; rtd 95; Perm to Offic *Dur* from 95. *41 Harbour View, Littlehaven, South Shields NE33 1LS* Tel 0191-454 0234

MASON, David Gray. b 37. MPhil LDS RCS. St Alb Minl Tr Scheme 83. **d** 95 **p** 95. NSM Biddenham *St Alb* 95-98; NSM Felmersham from 98; P-in-c 98-05; NSM Sharnbrook and Knotting w Souldrop from 05. *2A Devon Road, Bedford MK40 3DF* Tel and fax (01234) 309737 E-mail david@devon.powernet.co.uk

MASON, Dawn Lavinia. b 53. Ripon Coll Cuddesdon 95. **d** 97 **p** 98. C Wisbech St Aug *Ely* 97-00; V Emneth and Marshland St James from 00; P-in-c Elm and Friday Bridge w Coldham from 04. *The Vicarage, 72 Church Road, Emneth, Wisbech PE14 8AF* Tel (01945) 583089 E-mail dawnmason@augustine12.freeserve.co.uk

MASON, Dennis Wardell. b 28. Ox NSM Course 83. **d** 86 **p** 87. NSM Ox St Barn and St Paul *Ox* from 86. *26 John Lopes Road, Eynsham, Witney OX29 4JR* Tel (01865) 880440

MASON, Edward. *See* MASON, Preb Thomas Edward

MASON, Mrs Elizabeth Ann. b 42. Homerton Coll Cam TCert64 Open Univ BA90. Ox Min Course 91. **d** 94 **p** 95. NSM Worminghall w Ickford, Oakley and Shabbington *Ox* 94-95; NSM Swan 95-98; TV 98-05; rtd 05. *35 Common Road, North Leigh, Witney OX29 6RD* Tel (01993) 883966

MASON, Francis Robert Anthony. b 56. Trin Coll Bris BA90. **d** 90 **p** 91. C Denham *Ox* 90-94; P-in-c Jersey Grouville *Win* 94-98; R 98-04. *Address temp unknown* E-mail francismason@jerseymail.co.uk

MASON, Geoffrey Charles. b 48. K Coll Lon BD74 AKC74. St Aug Coll Cant 74. **d** 75 **p** 76. C Hatcham Park All SS *S'wark* 75-78; V Bellingham St Dunstan 78-87; RD E Lewisham 82-87; C Catford (Southend) and Downham 87-88; Bp's Adv for Min Development from 88. *32 King's Orchard, London SE9 5TJ* Tel (020) 8859 7614 *or* 7378 7506 Fax 7403 6497

✠**MASON, The Rt Revd James Philip.** b 54. Solomon Is Coll of HE TCert73 St Jo Coll Auckland STh86. Bp Patteson Th Coll (Solomon Is) 78. **d** 81 **p** 82 **c** 91. Solomon Is 81-04; Dean Honiara 88-91; Bp Hanuato'o 91-04; P-in-c Plympton St Maurice *Ex* from 05. *St Maurice's Rectory, 31 Wain Park, Plymouth PL7 2HX* Tel (01752) 346114 E-mail jamesphilipmason@gmail.com

MASON, John Evans. b 32. RD. Linc Th Coll 57. **d** 59 **p** 60. C Putney St Mary *S'wark* 59-62; C Berry Pomeroy *Ex* 62-64; Chapl RN 64-68; V Hopton *Nor* 68-72; Chapl RNR 69-82; P-in-c Roydon St Remigius *Nor* 72-76; R Diss 72-80; Dir YMCA Cam 80-85; Prin YMCA Dunford Coll 85-88; Perm to Offic *Glouc* 88-97 and *Ox* 89-99; rtd 96; Perm to Offic *Nor* 98-02 and *Sarum* 02-04. *Barretts House Farm, Yeovil Road, Halstock, Yeovil BA22 9RP* Tel (01935) 891400

MASON, John Martin. b 41. UMIST BSc63. Glouc Sch of Min 80 Qu Coll Birm 82. **d** 84 **p** 85. C Tuffley *Glouc* 84-87; P-in-c Willersey, Saintbury, Weston-sub-Edge etc 87-92; R 92-96; P-in-c Selling w Throwley, Sheldwich w Badlesmere etc *Cant* from 96; Dioc Rural Officer from 96. *The Rectory, Vicarage Lane, Selling, Faversham ME13 9RD* Tel (01227) 752221 Fax 752658 E-mail ruraljoe@aol.com

MASON, Jonathan Patrick. b 55. Edin Th Coll 90. **d** 92 **p** 93. C Edin Ch Ch *Edin* 92-94; C Edin Old St Paul 94-96; R St Andrews All SS *St And* from 96; Chapl St Andr Univ from 97. *All Saints' Rectory, North Street, St Andrews KY16 9AQ* Tel and fax (01334) 473193 E-mail jpm2@st-and.ac.uk

MASON, Ms Josephine Margaret. b 41. Edin Univ BMus64. WMMTC 88. **d** 93 **p** 94. Chapl Asst S Birm Mental Health NHS Trust from 91; C Birm St Jo Ladywood *Birm* 93-01; C Ladywood

St Jo and St Pet from 01. *340 Selly Oak Road, Birmingham B30 1HP* Tel 0121-451 1412

MASON, Julia Ann. b 43. St Jo Coll Nottm 89. **d** 91 **p** 95. NSM Troon *Glas* 91-93; NSM Ayr from 93; NSM Maybole from 93; NSM Girvan from 93. *27A Bellevue Crescent, Ayr KA7 2DP* Tel (01292) 263673 E-mail revdjuliamason@btinternet.com

MASON, Canon Kenneth Staveley. b 31. ARCS53 Lon Univ BSc53 BD64. Wells Th Coll 56. **d** 58 **p** 59. C Kingston upon Hull St Martin *York* 58-61; C Pocklington w Yapham-cum-Meltonby, Owsthorpe etc 61-63; C Millington w Gt Givendale 61-63; V Thornton w Allerthorpe 63-69; Sub-Warden St Aug Coll Cant 69-76; Abp's Adv in Past Min 76-77; Dir Cant Sch of Min 77-81; Prin 81-89; Sec to Dioc Bd of Min *Cant* 77-87; Six Preacher Cant Cathl 79-84; Hon Can Cant Cathl 84-89; Prin Edin Th Coll 89-95; Can St Mary's Cathl *Edin* 89-96; rtd 95; Perm to Offic *Ripon* from 96. *2 Williamson Close, Ripon HG4 1AZ* Tel (01765) 607041

MASON, Matthew. Man Univ MusB. Oak Hill Th Coll MTh. **d** 05. C Tunbridge Wells St Jo *Roch* from 05. *112 Stephen's Road, Tunbridge Wells TN4 9QA*
E-mail matthewwmason@gmail.com

MASON, Nigel Frederick. b 60. Wycliffe Hall Ox DipMin95. **d** 95 **p** 96. C Highbury Ch Ch w St Jo and St Sav *Lon* 95-98; C Seaford w Sutton *Chich* 98-01; R Rotherfield w Mark Cross from 01. *The Rectory, Mayfield Road, Rotherfield, Crowborough TN6 3LU* Tel (01892) 852536

MASON, Nigel James. b 56. Culham Coll of Educn BEd78 Dip Law84. St Steph Ho Ox 95. **d** 97 **p** 98. C Hove *Chich* 97-00; V Kemp Town St Mary from 00. *St Mary's Vicarage, 11 West Drive, Brighton BN2 0GD* Tel (01273) 698601

MASON, Paul. b 51. Cranmer Hall Dur 93. **d** 93 **p** 94. C Handforth *Ches* 93-97; V Partington and Carrington 97-04; V Church Hulme from 04. *The Vicarage, 74 London Road, Holmes Chapel, Crewe CW4 7BD* Tel and fax (01477) 533124

MASON, Peter Charles. b 45. K Coll Lon BD72 AKC72 Birm Univ PGCE89. St Aug Coll Cant 72. **d** 73 **p** 74. C Ilkeston St Mary *Derby* 73-76; C Bridgnorth St Mary *Heref* 76-78; TV Bridgnorth, Tasley, Astley Abbotts, etc 78-88; RE Teacher from 89; Perm to Offic *Heref* 89-04 and *St D* from 04. *63 Nun Street, St Davids, Haverfordwest SA62 6NU* Tel (01437) 721715

MASON, Canon Peter Joseph. b 34. Lon Univ BA58. Coll of Resurr Mirfield 58. **d** 60 **p** 61. C Belhus Park CD *Chelmsf* 60-63; Lic to Offic *Eur* 63-64; Asst Chapl Lon Univ *Lon* 64-70; Chapl City Univ 66-70; R Stoke Newington St Mary 70-78; V Writtle *Chelmsf* 78-81; P-in-c Highwood 78-81; V Writtle w Highwood 81-86; R Shenfield 86-93; Hon Can Chelmsf Cathl 89-00; P-in-c Maldon All SS w St Pet 93-95; V 95-00; RD Maldon and Dengie 95-00; rtd 00; Perm to Offic *Chelmsf* from 00. *32 Providence, Burnham-on-Crouch CM0 8JU* Tel (01621) 785921
E-mail peter@franknox.demon.co.uk

MASON, Robert Herbert George. b 48. ACII. Oak Hill Th Coll 82. **d** 84 **p** 85. C Ware Ch Ch *St Alb* 84-88; V Eastbourne All So *Chich* 88-98; P-in-c Poole *Sarum* 98-01; R from 01; Chapl Miss to Seafarers from 98. *The Rectory, 10 Poplar Close, Poole BH15 1LP* Tel (01202) 672694 Fax 677117
E-mail revbobmelmason@hotmail.com

MASON, Canon Roger Arthur. b 41. Lon Univ BSc65 K Coll Lon BD68 AKC68. **d** 69 **p** 70. C Enfield St Andr *Lon* 69-72; P-in-c Westbury *Heref* 72-78; P-in-c Yockleton 72-78; P-in-c Gt Wollaston 77-78; V Willesden St Mary *Lon* 78-88; V Prittlewell *Chelmsf* from 88; P-in-c Prittlewell St Steph 92-04; Hon Can Chelmsf Cathl from 01. *Prittlewell Vicarage, 489 Victoria Avenue, Southend-on-Sea SS2 6NL* Tel (01702) 343470
E-mail rogeramason@lineone.net

MASON (formerly FOALE), Sheila Rosemary. b 40. Saffron Walden Coll CertEd61 ARCM62. SW Minl Tr Course 98. **d** 01 **p** 02. NSM Shebbear, Buckland Filleigh, Sheepwash etc *Ex* 01-04; C Cobham and Stoke D'Abernon *Guildf* from 04. *The Rectory, Blundel Lane, Stoke D'Abernon KT11 2SE* Tel (01932) 862502 Mobile 07712-086540
E-mail rosemary@foale16.fsworld.co.uk

MASON, Simon Ion Vincent. b 60. Birm Univ BA82. Trin Coll Bris BA00. **d** 00 **p** 01. C Nottingham St Nic *S'well* from 00. *99 Seymour Road, West Bridgford, Nottingham NG2 5EE* Tel 0115-914 8946 *or* 952 4600 E-mail mason.simon@ntlworld.com

MASON, Stephen David. b 65. Univ of Wales (Lamp) BA87. Ripon Coll Cuddesdon 89. **d** 92 **p** 93. C Gt Grimsby St Mary and St Jas *Linc* 92-97; V Southborough St Thos *Roch* 97-02; V Paddington St Jo w St Mich *Lon* from 02. *18 Somers Crescent, London W2 2PN* Tel (020) 7706 8101 *or* 7262 1732 Fax 7706 4475 E-mail stjohnhp@netcomuk.co.uk

MASON, Terry Mathew. b 56. Trin Coll Bris 94. **d** 96 **p** 97. C Bexleyheath Ch Ch *Roch* 96-99; P-in-c Stone 99-03; V Broadway w Wickhamford *Worc* from 03. *The Vicarage, 4 Lifford Gardens, Broadway WR12 7DA* Tel (01386) 852352
E-mail broadwayvicarage@tesco.net

MASON, Preb Thomas Edward. b 52. Bris Univ MEd80. Trin Coll Bris BA91. **d** 91 **p** 92. C Glouc St Jas and All SS *Glouc* 91-94; V Churchdown 94-04; RD Glouc N 99-04; R Bath Abbey w St Jas *B & W* from 04; Preb Wells Cathl from 05. *The Rectory, 12 Cleveland Walk, Bath BA2 6JX* Tel (01225) 464171 *or* 422462
E-mail temason@cableinet.co.uk

MASON, Thomas Henry Ambrose. b 51. BA86. **d** 86 **p** 87. C W Drayton *Lon* 86-89; Field Officer Oak Hill Ext Coll 89-94; Eur Sec ICS 94-95; Dir of Tr *Eur* 95-03; Dir Min and Dir of Ords 01-03; Can Brussels Cathl 00-03; R Grosmont and Skenfrith and Llangattock etc *Mon* from 03. *The Rectory, Grosmont, Abergavenny NP7 8LW* Tel (01981) 240587
E-mail ambrose@rectorygrosmont.fsnet.co.uk

MASON, William Frederick. b 48. Linc Th Coll 75. **d** 78 **p** 79. C Ipswich St Aug *St E* 78-81; TV Dronfield *Derby* 81-88; V Ellesmere St Pet *Sheff* 88-91; V Bedgrove *Ox* 91-00; C Hazlemere from 00. *17 Southcote Way, Penn, High Wycombe HP10 8JG* Tel (01494) 812648

MASSEY, George Douglas. b 44. St Jo Coll Nottm DCM93. **d** 93 **p** 94. C Higher Bebington *Ches* 93-98; V Messingham *Linc* from 98. *The Vicarage, 12 Holme Lane, Messingham, Scunthorpe DN17 3SG* Tel (01724) 762823
E-mail george.massey@ntlworld.com

MASSEY, Keith John. b 46. Oak Hill Th Coll 69. **d** 72 **p** 73. C Bermondsey St Jas w Ch Ch *S'wark* 72-76; C Benchill *Man* 76-82; V Clifton Green 82-97; V Flixton St Jo from 97. *St John's Vicarage, Irlam Road, Urmston, Manchester M41 6AP* Tel 0161-748 6754

MASSEY, Michelle Elaine (Shellie). Plymouth Univ BA00. Trin Coll Bris BA04. **d** 04 **p** 05. C Barrowby and Gt Gonerby *Linc* from 04. *25 Hedgefield Road, Barrowby, Grantham NG32 1TA* Tel (01476) 577008 Mobile 07876-645786
E-mail revdmichellem@aol.com

MASSEY, Nigel John. b 60. Birm Univ BA81 MA82. Wycliffe Hall Ox. **d** 87 **p** 88. C Bearwood *Birm* 87-90; C Warley Woods 90; C Tottenham St Paul *Lon* 91-94; USA from 94. *French Church du St Spirit, 111 East 60th Street #4, NY 10022, USA* Tel (001) (212) 838 5680

MASSEY, Paul Daniel Shaw. b 70. Nottm Univ BA93. Westcott Ho Cam 94. **d** 96 **p** 97. C Ashby-de-la-Zouch St Helen w Coleorton *Leic* 96-01; R Cotgrave *S'well* from 01; P-in-c Owthorpe from 01. *The Rectory, 2 Thurman Drive, Cotgrave, Nottingham NG12 3LG* Tel and fax 0115-989 2223
E-mail pmassey@supanet.com

MASSEY, Peter William. b 45. St Mark & St Jo Coll Lon TCert66 Open Univ BA75. WMMTC 96. **d** 99 **p** 00. NSM Holmer w Huntington *Heref* 99-03; NSM Heref St Pet w St Owen and St Jas from 03. *5 Nursery Drive, Moreton-on-Lugg, Hereford HR4 8DJ* Tel and fax (01432) 761794 Mobile 07803-826728 E-mail petermassey@surefish.co.uk

MASSEY, Shellie. *See* MASSEY, Michelle Elaine

MASSEY, Preb William Cyril. b 32. Lich Th Coll 58. **d** 61 **p** 62. C Heref St Martin *Heref* 61-66; V Kimbolton w Middleton-on-the-Hill 66-75; V Alveley 75-83; P-in-c Quatt 81-83; R Alveley and Quatt 84-85; R Llangarron w Llangrove, Whitchurch and Ganarew 85-97; Preb Heref Cathl 92-97; rtd 97; Perm to Offic *Heref* from 97. *Hollybush Cottage, Pencombe, Bromyard HR7 4RW* Tel (01885) 400713

MASSEY, William Peter. b 50. CITC 96. **d** 99 **p** 00. C Fermoy Union *C, C & R* 99-00; C Carrigrohane Union and Kinsale Union 00-03; Perm to Offic *Eur* from 04. *1801 Chemin des Pailles, Lorgues, 83510 France* E-mail petermassey@wanadoo.fr

MASSHEDAR, John Frederick. b 50. Dur Univ BEd74. Linc Th Coll 76. **d** 78 **p** 79. C Pocklington w Yapham-cum-Meltonby, Owsthorpe etc *York* 78-81; C Middlesbrough Ascension 81-82; V 82-85; V Eskdaleside w Ugglebarnby and Sneaton 85-87; V Shotton *Dur* 87-99; V Haswell, Shotton and Thornley 99-04. *9 Stewart Drive, Wingate TS28 5PS* Tel (01429) 836397

MASSHEDAR, Richard Eric. b 57. Nottm Univ BTh86. Linc Th Coll 83. **d** 86 **p** 87. C Cassop cum Quarrington *Dur* 86-89; C Ferryhill 89-91; V Leam Lane 91-94; P-in-c Hartlepool St Paul 94-96; V from 96. *St Paul's Vicarage, 6 Hutton Avenue, Hartlepool TS26 9PN* Tel (01429) 272934
E-mail r.masshedar@ntlworld.com

MASSINGBERD-MUNDY, John. b 07. Pemb Coll Cam BA30 MA46. Cuddesdon Coll 31. **d** 32 **p** 33. C Dagenham St Martin *Chelmsf* 32-34; C Sheff St Cuth *Sheff* 34-37; C Linthorpe *York* 37-40; V Sewerby cum Marton and Grindale 40-43; V Market Weighton 43-50; R Goodmanham 46-50; P-in-c Bedale *Ripon* 50-59; R 59-65; V Limber Magna w Brocklesby *Linc* 65-72; V Kirmington 65-72; rtd 72. *Norwood, 14 Park Road, Ipswich IP1 3ST* Tel (01473) 225622

MASSINGBERD-MUNDY, Roger William Burrell. b 36. TD. Univ of Wales (Lamp) BA59. Ridley Hall Cam 59. **d** 61 **p** 62. C Benwell St Jas *Newc* 61-64; C Whorlton 64-72; TV 73; P-in-c Healey 73-85; Dioc Stewardship Adv 73-85; Hon Can Newc Cathl 82-85; CF (TA) 63-68; CF (TAVR) 71-83; R S Ormsby w Ketsby, Calceby and Driby *Linc* 85-86; P-in-c Harrington w Brinkhill 85-86; P-in-c Haugh 85-86; P-in-c Oxcombe 85-86; P-in-c Ruckland w Farforth and Maidenwell 85-86; P-in-c Somersby w Bag Enderby 85-86; P-in-c Tetford and Salmonby

85-86; R S Ormsby Gp 86-96; RD Bolingbroke 88-96; rtd 96; Chapl Taverham Hall Sch from 03. *The Old Post Office, West Raynham, Fakenham NR21 7AD* Tel (01328) 838611 Fax 838698 E-mail rogermundy@markeaton.co.uk

MASSON, Canon Philip Roy. b 52. Hertf Coll Ox BA75 Leeds Univ BA77. Coll of Resurr Mirfield 75. **d** 78 **p** 79. C Port Talbot St Theodore *Llan* 78-82; V Penyfai w Tondu 82-92; Dioc Dir Post-Ord Tr 85-88; Warden of Ords 88-01; R Newton Nottage from 92; RD Margam from 01; Can Llan Cathl from 02. *The Rectory, 64 Victoria Avenue, Porthcawl CF36 3HE* Tel (01656) 782042 *or* 786899 Fax as telephone E-mail philipmasson@hotmail.com

MASTERMAN, Malcolm. b 49. K Coll Lon 73 City Univ MSc00. Chich Th Coll 76. **d** 77 **p** 78. C Peterlee *Dur* 77-80; Chapl Basingstoke Distr Hosp 80-85; Chapl Freeman Hosp Newc 85-95; Tr and Development Officer Hosp Chapl Coun 96-00; Sen Chapl N Dur Healthcare NHS Trust from 00. *Chaplain's Office, University Hospital of North Durham, Durham DH1 5TW* Tel 0191-333 2183

MASTERMAN, Miss Patricia Hope. b 28. St Mich Ho Ox 59. **dss** 79 **d** 87. Asst CF 79-90; rtd 90; Perm to Offic *Chich* from 90. *33 Sea Lane Gardens, Ferring, Worthing BN12 5EQ* Tel (01903) 245231

MASTERS, Kenneth Leslie. b 44. Leeds Univ BA68. Cuddesdon Coll 68. **d** 70 **p** 71. C Wednesbury St Paul Wood Green *Lich* 70-71; C Tettenhall Regis 71-75; TV Chelmsley Wood *Birm* 75-79; R Harting *Chich* 79-87; V Rustington 87-00; TR Beaminster Area *Sarum* from 00. *The Rectory, 3 Clay Lane, Beaminster DT8 3BU* Tel (01308) 862150 E-mail kmasters@ukonline.co.uk

MASTERS, Leslie. b 31. Ripon Hall Ox 73. **d** 75 **p** 76. C Hanham *Bris* 75-78; TV Bris St Agnes and St Simon w St Werburgh 78-84; Asst Chapl HM Pris Man 84; Chapl HM Pris Northeye 84-88; Chapl HM Pris Littlehey 88-94; rtd 94; P-in-c St Goran w Caerhays *Truro* 94-00; Perm to Offic *Chich* from 01. *46 Manor Road, Bexhill-on-Sea TN40 1SN* Tel (01424) 218294

MASTERS, Stephen Michael. b 52. **d** 87 **p** 88. C Primrose Hill St Mary w Avenue Road St Paul *Lon* 87-90; C Hornsey St Mary w St Geo 90-91; Bp's Dom Chapl *Chich* 91-96; V Brighton St Mich 96-99; C Eastbourne St Andr 00-01; Chapl to Bp Lewes 00-01; Asst to Adn Lewes and Hastings 00-01; P-in-c Alderney *Win* 01-03; V from 03. *The New Vicarage, La Vallee, Alderney, Guernsey GY9 3XA* Tel (01481) 824866

MASTIN, Brian Arthur. b 38. Peterho Cam BA60 MA63 BD80 Mert Coll Ox MA63. Ripon Hall Ox 62. **d** 63 **p** 64. Asst Lect Hebrew Univ Coll of N Wales (Ban) 63-65; Lect Hebrew 65-82; Sen Lect 82-98; Chapl Ban Cathl *Ban* 63-65; Lic to Offic 65-98; rtd 98; Perm to Offic *Ely* from 98. *2A Gurney Way, Cambridge CB4 2ED* Tel (01223) 355078

MATABELELAND, Bishop of. *See* SITSHEBO, The Rt Revd Wilson Timothy

MATANA, Bishop of. *See* NTAHOTURI, The Most Revd Bernard

MATCHETT, Alan William. b 70. TCD BTh01. CITC 98. **d** 01 **p** 02. C Limerick City *L & K* 01-03; C Stillorgan w Blackrock *D & G* from 03. *Canon Taylor Lodge, St Brigid's, Church Road, Stillorgan, Co Dublin, Irish Republic* Tel (00353) 87-964 2054 (mobile) E-mail alanmatc@mac.com

MATCHETT, Christopher Jonathan. b 65. QUB BSSc TCD BTh98. **d** 98 **p** 99. C Ballynafeigh St Jude *D & D* 98-01; C Holywood 01-04; I Magheracross *Clogh* from 04. *The Rectory, 27 Craghan Road, Ballinamallard, Enniskillen BT94 2BT* Tel and fax (028) 6638 8238 E-mail magheracross@clogher.anglican.org

MATCHETT, Miss Diane Margaret. b 71. Open Univ BA98. TCD Div Sch BTh05. **d** 05. C Lisburn Ch Ch *Conn* from 05. *74 Woodland Park, Lisburn BT28 1LD* Tel (028) 9260 1618 Mobile 07810-048367 E-mail dianematchett@hotmail.com

MATCHETT, Edward James Boyd. b 19. TCD BA43 MA60. **d** 43 **p** 44. C Belfast St Mary *Conn* 43-45; Miss to Seamen 45-86; Chapl Basrah Iraq 47-50; Chapl Sunderland 50-52; Chapl Belfast 52-64; Chapl RNR 60-65; Chapl Wellington New Zealand 64-69; Area Sec Miss to Seamen E England 69-74; Chapl Hong Kong 74-83; Chapl Cornish Ports 83-86; Perm to Offic *Nor* 86-00. *10 Southern Reach, Mulbarton, Norwich NR14 8BU* Tel (01508) 570337

MATHER, Cuthbert. b 15. Tyndale Hall Bris 36. **d** 40 **p** 41. C Bebington *Ches* 40-42; C Stapenhill w Cauldwell *Derby* 43-51; C Cambridge St Andr Less *Ely* 51-52; C Dagenham *Chelmsf* 53-57; V Needham w Rushall *Nor* 57-80; rtd 80; Perm to Offic *Nor* from 80. *2 Church Close, Hunstanton PE36 6BE* Tel (01485) 533084

MATHER, David Jonathan. b 65. New Coll Ox BA88 MA95. St Steph Ho Ox BTh95. **d** 95 **p** 96. C Pickering w Lockton and Levisham *York* 95-98; P-in-c Bridlington H Trin and Sewerby w Marton 98-99; V from 99. *Sewerby Vicarage, Cloverley Road, Bridlington YO16 5TX* Tel (01262) 675725

MATHER, Mrs Elizabeth Ann. b 45. CertEd66. Dalton Ho Bris IDC70 St Jo Coll Nottm 92. **d** 94 **p** 95. NSM Littleover *Derby* 94-02; Lic to Offic *St Alb* from 02. *13 Heath Park Drive, Leighton Buzzard LU7 3BF* Tel (01525) 377128 E-mail revlib@libbymather.freeserve.co.uk

MATHER, James William. b 63. Sheff Univ BA86. St Steph Ho Ox 88. **d** 91 **p** 92. C Doncaster St Leon and St Jude *Sheff* 91-94; C Cantley 94-95; V Lakenheath *St E* 95-01; P-in-c Downham Market w Bexwell *Ely* 01-02; P-in-c Crimplesham w Stradsett 01-02; R Downham Market and Crimplesham w Stradsett from 02. *The Rectory, King's Walk, Downham Market PE38 9LF* Tel (01366) 382187

MATHER, Stephen Albert. b 54. Qu Coll Birm 85. **d** 87 **p** 88. C Sutton *Liv* 87-90; TV 90-96; V Abram 96-99; V Bickershaw 96-99; V Hindley St Pet from 99. *St Peter's Vicarage, 122 Wigan Road, Hindley, Wigan WN2 3DF* Tel (01942) 55505

MATHER, William Bernard George. b 45. St Jo Coll Nottm 77. **d** 79 **p** 80. C St Leonards St Leon *Chich* 79-82; TR Netherthorpe *Sheff* 82-90; V Littleover *Derby* 90-02; Assoc Dir SOMA UK 02-05; TR Drypool *York* from 05. *The Vicarage, 139 Laburnum Avenue, Garden Village, Hull HU8 8PA* Tel (01482) 374257

MATHERS, Alan Edward. b 36. FPhS Lon Univ BA BTh. Oak Hill Th Coll 61. **d** 64 **p** 65. C Ox St Matt *Ox* 64-66; C Bootle St Leon *Liv* 66-68; C Hampreston *Sarum* 68-70; P-in-c Damerham 70-71; V Queniborough *Leic* 71-76; USA 76-77; P-in-c Tipton St Paul *Lich* 77-84; V 85-86; V Tipton St Matt 77-86; V Sutton Ch Ch *S'wark* 86-95; Chapl Cannes *Eur* 95-98; rtd 98; Perm to Offic *S'wark* and *Chich* from 98. *52 The Meadow, Copthorne, Crawley RH10 3RQ* Tel (01342) 713325

MATHERS, David Michael Brownlow. b 43. Em Coll Cam BA65 MA69. Clifton Th Coll 65. **d** 67 **p** 68. C Branksome St Clem *Sarum* 67-70; C Bromley Ch Ch *Roch* 70-73; V Bures *St E* 73-80; Brazil 80-82; P-in-c Old Newton w Stowupland *St E* 82-86; V 87-90; V Thurston from 90; RD Ixworth 94-03. *The Vicarage, Church Road, Thurston, Bury St Edmunds IP31 3RU* Tel (01359) 230301

MATHERS, Derek. b 48. N Ord Course 82. **d** 85 **p** 86. C Huddersfield St Jo *Wakef* 85-86; C N Huddersfield 86-88; TV Almondbury w Farnley Tyas 88-92; V Marsden 92-02; R Badsworth from 02. *The Rectory, Main Street, Badsworth, Pontefract WF9 1AF* Tel (01977) 643642

MATHERS, Kenneth Ernest William. b 56. Trin Coll Bris 93. **d** 95 **p** 96. C Bournemouth St Jo w St Mich *Win* 95-99; NSM Darenth *Roch* 99-04; Chapl Dartford and Gravesham NHS Trust 01-04; Chapl N Devon Healthcare NHS Trust from 05. *The Rectory, Newton Tracey, Barnstaple EX31 3PL* Tel (01271) 858292 E-mail revkmathers@yahoo.com

MATHERS, Mrs Kim Deborah. b 61. Southn Univ LLB82. Trin Coll Bris 86. **d** 89 **p** 94. Par Dn Bitterne *Win* 89-93; NSM Stoke Bishop *Bris* 93-95; NSM Bournemouth St Jo w St Mich *Win* 95-99; P-in-c Darenth *Roch* 99-04; TR Newton Tracey, Horwood, Alverdiscott etc *Ex* from 04. *The Rectory, Newton Tracey, Barnstaple EX31 3PL* Tel (01271) 858292 E-mail revkmathers@btinternet.com

MATHESON, Alexander John. b 59. Lon Bible Coll BA84 S Tr Scheme 94. **d** 97 **p** 98. NSM Cowplain *Portsm* 97-01; C Portchester 01-04; V Sarisbury from 04. *The Vicarage, 149 Bridge Road, Sarisbury Green, Southampton SO31 7EN* Tel (01489) 572207 E-mail sandy@mathesonuk.com

MATHEW, Laurence Allen Stanfield. b 47. Sarum Th Coll 99. **d** 02 **p** 03. OLM Warminster Ch Ch *Sarum* from 02. *Chalvedune, 25 King Street, Warminster BA12 8DG* Tel (01985) 217282 Mobile 07768-006245 E-mail laurence01@blueyonder.co.uk

MATHEWS, Richard Twitchell. b 27. Bps' Coll Cheshunt 57. **d** 59 **p** 60. C Leic St Phil *Leic* 59-62; Chapl Beirut 62-63; Qatar 63-67; V Riddlesden *Bradf* 67-74; Australia 74-78; P-in-c Medbourne cum Holt w Stockerston and Blaston *Leic* 78-82; Chapl Alassio *Eur* 82-83; Chapl San Remo 82-83; Chapl Palma and Balearic Is w Ibiza etc 83-87; P-in-c Witchford w Wentworth *Ely* 87-91; rtd 91; Perm to Offic *Cant* from 96. *Rosecroft, Church Lane, Ringwould, Deal CT14 8HR* Tel (01304) 367554

MATHEWS, Trevor John. b 50. Anglia Poly Univ CertPSC94 Goldsmiths' Coll Lon DipCACP95 MSc98 DipREBT95. St Steph Ho Ox 87. **d** 89 **p** 90. C Cheltenham St Steph *Glouc* 89-91; C Up Hatherley 89-91. *11 Arundel Mews, Billericay CM12 0FW* Tel (01277) 634817 E-mail mathews@conflict.co.uk

MATHIAS, John Maelgwyn. b 15. St D Coll Lamp BA38 St Mich Coll Llan 40. **d** 40 **p** 41. C Ban St Mary *Ban* 40-44; C Swansea St Pet *S & B* 44-49; V Mydroilyn w Dihewyd *St D* 49-54; R Cellan w Llanfair Clydogau 54-83; Lect St Jo Ch Coll Ystrad Meurig 67-77; rtd 83. *Bronallt, Capel Seion Road, Drefach, Llanelli SA14 7BN* Tel (01269) 844350

MATHIAS, Ms Lesley. b 49. Portsm Poly BA72 Nottm Univ MTh90. EMMTC 93. **d** 96 **p** 97. C Oadby *Leic* 96-98; Asst Chapl United Bris Healthcare NHS Trust 98-99; C Pet St Mary Boongate *Pet* 99-01; V Kings Heath from 01; TV Bp's Interfaith Adv from 01; Perm to Offic *B & W* 99-01. *1 Nene Drive, Northampton NN5 7NQ* Tel (01604) 756809 E-mail lesley@lmathias.freeserve.co.uk

MATHIAS-JONES, Edward Lloyd. b 71. SSC98 Univ of Wales (Lamp) BA93. St Mich Coll Llan BD96 Dip Past Counselling 97. **d** 97 **p** 98. C Llanelli *St D* 97-00; C Milford Haven 00-04; V Newport St Steph and H Trin *Mon* from 04. *St Stephen's Vicarage, Adeline Street, Newport NP20 2HA* Tel (01633) 265192 E-mail frmathias-jones@aol.com

MATHIE, Patricia Jean (Sister Donella). b 22. Worc Coll of Educn CertEd49. CertRK74. **dss** 79 **d** 87. CSA from 74; Asst Superior 82-94; Mother Superior 94-00; Notting Hill St Jo *Lon* 79-80; Abbey Ho Malmesbury 81-82; Notting Hill St Clem and St Mark 82-84; Kensal Town St Thos w St Andr and St Phil 85-87; Hon C 87-96; Perm to Offic from 00. *8/9 Verona Court, London W4 2JD* Tel (020) 8987 2799

MATLOOB, Nazir Ahmad Barnabas. b 48. Punjab Univ BA79. Gujranwala Th Sem 74 BD81 MDiv85 NTMTC 95. **d** 78 **p** 78. Pakistan 78-93; Perm to Offic *Chelmsf* 94-97; C Forest Gate All SS and St Edm from 98. *64 Henderson Road, London E7 8EF* Tel (020) 8552 4280

MATON, Oswald. b 24. St Aug Coll Cant 75. **d** 77 **p** 78. NSM Chatham St Steph *Roch* 77-94; Perm to Offic from 94. *304 Maidstone Road, Chatham ME4 6JJ* Tel (01634) 843568

MATSON de LAURIER, Mrs Sarah Kennerley. b 46. EMMTC 00. **d** 02 **p** 03. NSM Hilton w Marston-on-Dove *Derby* from 02. *1 Park Way, Etwall, Derby DE65 6HU* Tel (01283) 732859 E-mail pskmdl@aol.com

MATTAPALLY, Sebastian. b 57. N Bengal Univ BA77 Pontifical Salesian Univ BTh84 Pontifical Gregorian Univ MA98. **d** 83 **p** 83. In RC Ch 83-00; Perm to Offic *Eur* 01-04; C Patcham *Chich* from 05. *78A Mackie Avenue, Brighton BN1 8RB* Tel (01273) 554791 E-mail smattapally@tiscali.co.uk

MATTEN, Derek Norman William. b 30. Man Univ BA51. Wycliffe Hall Ox 54. **d** 56 **p** 57. C Farnworth *Liv* 56-59; C Walton H Trin *Ox* 59-62; Uganda 62-69; Lic to Offic *Eur* 69-93; W Germany 69-90; Germany 90-93; Perm to Offic *Ex* 90-93; rtd 93; Hon C Modbury, Bigbury, Ringmore w Kingston etc *Ex* 95-00; Perm to Offic from 01. *1 Bramley Meadow, Landkey, Barnstaple EX32 0PB* Tel (01271) 830952 E-mail dnwm@supanet.com

MATTHEWS, Adrian James. b 51. Edge Hill Coll of HE CertEd73. N Ord Course. **d** 87 **p** 88. C Blackley St Andr *Man* 87-90; NSM Tonge w Alkrington 96-01; R Failsworth St Jo from 01. *St John's Rectory, Pole Lane, Manchester M35 9PB* Tel 0161-681 2734 Fax as telephone

MATTHEWS, The Rt Revd Alan Montague (Dom Basil). b 37. Ex Univ BA86. **d** 02 **p** 02. OSB from 65; Abbot Elmore Abbey from 88. *Elmore Abbey, Church Lane, Speen, Newbury RG14 1SA* Tel (01635) 33080 Fax 580729

MATTHEWS, Anita Kathryn. b 70. Dur Univ BTh91. Ripon Coll Cuddesdon 93. **d** 97 **p** 98. C E Barnet *St Alb* 97-01; Chapl Derby High Sch 01-05; Nat Adv for Children's Work CMS from 05. *5 Bamford Avenue, Derby DE23 8DT* Tel (01332) 270917

MATTHEWS, Mrs Anna Ruth. b 78. Rob Coll Cam BA99 MPhil03. Westcott Ho Cam 01. **d** 03 **p** 04. C Abbots Langley *St Alb* from 03. *40 Kindersley Way, Abbots Langley WD5 0DQ* Tel (01923) 265729 Mobile 07974-647226 E-mail annamatthews@fish.co.uk

MATTHEWS, Barry Alan. b 46. AKC68. St Boniface Warminster 68 St Paul's Coll Grahamstown 69. **d** 69 **p** 70. S Africa 69-74, 77-83 and 01-04; C De Aar 69-72; C Kimberley St Aug 72-74; P-in-c Kimberley St Matt 74-75; C Leeds St Aid *Ripon* 75-77; R Vryburg St Steph 77-81; Dioc Missr 81-82; R Kimberley St Aug 82-83; C Shotton *St As* 83-84; R Hwange St Jas Zimbabwe 84-89; R Bulawayo N St Marg 89-95; R Nkulumane H Family 95-97; Adn N Matabeleland 89-97; Sen P St Mary's Cathl Harare 97-00; rtd 01. *23 Clovelly Drive, Newburgh, Wigan WN8 7LY* Tel (01257) 462149

MATTHEWS, Basil. *See* MATTHEWS, The Rt Revd Alan Montague

MATTHEWS, Brian. *See* MATTHEWS, Gilbert Brian Reeves

MATTHEWS, Canon Campbell Thurlow. b 33. Lon Univ BA56 Dur Univ DipEd57. St Jo Coll Nottm 70. **d** 71 **p** 72. C Ryton *Dur* 71-74; Chapl R Victoria Infirmary Newc 74-82; V Greenside *Dur* 74-82; R Wetheral w Warwick *Carl* 82-93; RD Brampton 83-91; P-in-c Farlam and Nether Denton 87-93; P-in-c Gilsland 87-93; Hon Can Carl Cathl 87-00; P-in-c Thornthwaite cum Braithwaite and Newlands 93-00; P-in-c Borrowdale 97-00; rtd 00; Perm to Offic *Carl* from 00 and *Newc* from 01. *The Hayes, Newcastle Road, Corbridge NE45 5LP* Tel (01434) 632010

MATTHEWS, Celia Inger. b 30. St Chris Coll Blackheath 50. **d** 86 **p** 94. Dioc Missr *St And* from 86; rtd 95. *24 Barossa Place, Perth PH1 5HH* Tel (01738) 623578 E-mail celiamatt@talk21.com

MATTHEWS, Cilla. *See* MATTHEWS, Mrs Francilla Lacey

MATTHEWS, Canon Colin John. b 44. Jes Coll Ox BA67 MA71 Fitzw Coll Cam BA70 MA74. Ridley Hall Cam 68. **d** 71 **p** 72. C Onslow Square St Paul *Lon* 71-74; C Leic H Apostles *Leic* 74-78; Bible Use Sec Scripture Union 78-89; Dir Ch Cen Guildf St Sav *Guildf* 89-95; V Burpham from 95; RD Guildf from 01; Hon Can Guildf Cathl from 02. *The Vicarage, 5 Orchard Road, Burpham, Guildford GU4 7JH* Tel (01483) 853023 Mobile 07787-575923 Fax (01483) 855645 E-mail vicarage@dial.pipex.com

MATTHEWS, David Charles. b 61. TCD BA84 HDipEd86 MA87 BTh95 Lille Univ LèsL85 QUB Cert Counselling 97. CITC 95. **d** 95 **p** 96. C Arm St Mark *Arm* 95-97; Hon V Choral Arm Cathl 96-97; Min Can and Chapl St Woolos Cathl *Mon* 97-01; V Marshfield and Peterstone Wentloog etc from 01. *The Vicarage, Church Lane, Marshfield, Cardiff CF3 2UF* Tel (01633) 680257 E-mail david@hebron97.freeserve.co.uk

MATTHEWS, David William. b 49. St Paul's Coll Grahamstown 88. **d** 90 **p** 91. S Africa 90-03; C Port Eliz St Sav 90-91; C Port Eliz St Paul 91-94; R Zwartkops River Valley Par 94-00; Chapl Miss to Seafarers 00-03; R Boxford, Edwardstone, Groton etc *St E* from 03. *The Rectory, School Hill, Boxford, Sudbury CO10 5JT* Tel and fax (01787) 210752 E-mail david.matthews@stedmundsbury.anglican.org

MATTHEWS, David William Grover. b 73. Acadia Univ (NS) BA93 Toronto Univ MDiv98. Trin Coll Toronto 95. **d** 98 **p** 99. C Newport St Teilo *Mon* 98-00; NSM Cobbold Road St Sav w St Mary *Lon* 00-03; P-in-c Hammersmith H Innocents 03-05; P-in-c Hammersmith H Innocents and St Jo from 05. *35 Paddenswick Road, London W6 0UA* Tel (020) 8741 6480 E-mail holyinnocentsw6@yahoo.com

MATTHEWS, Mrs Deborah Lynne. b 57. Southn Univ BTh98 MIPD92. Ripon Coll Cuddesdon MTh01. **d** 00 **p** 01. C Southampton (City Cen) *Win* 00-04; V Clapham St Paul *S'wark* from 04. *St Paul's Vicarage, Rectory Grove, London SW4 0DX* Tel (020) 7622 2128 E-mail revdebmatthews@waitrose.com

MATTHEWS, Mrs Diana Elizabeth Charlotte. b 43. MCSP65. LNSM course 92. **d** 93 **p** 96. OLM Merrow *Guildf* from 93. *Avila, 13 Wells Road, Guildford GU4 7XQ* Tel (01483) 839738 E-mail diana.matthews@ntlworld.com

MATTHEWS, Mrs Francilla Lacey. b 37. S'wark Ord Course 83. **dss** 86 **d** 87 **p** 94. Bromley St Mark *Roch* 86-90; Hon Par Dn 87-90; Par Dn Hayes 90-94; C 94-02; rtd 02. *71 Hayes Road, Bromley BR2 9AE* Tel (020) 8464 4083

MATTHEWS, Frederick Peter. b 45. Grey Coll Dur BA66 MA68 K Coll Lon PGCE68 Lon Univ BSc(Econ)75. Sarum & Wells Th Coll 70. **d** 72 **p** 73. C W Wickham St Jo *Cant* 72-74; C Sholing *Win* 74-77; Lic to Offic 78-79; V Woolston 79-03; P-in-c Over Wallop w Nether Wallop from 03; Dioc Ecum Officer from 03. *The Rectory, Over Wallop, Stockbridge SO20 8HT* Tel (01264) 781345 E-mail peter.matthews1@telinco.co.uk

MATTHEWS, George Charles Wallace. b 27. Sarum Th Coll 58. **d** 60 **p** 61. C Coppenhall St Paul *Ches* 60-63; C Lewes St Anne *Chich* 63-67; V Wheelock *Ches* 67-76; V Mossley 76-93; rtd 93; Perm to Offic *Ches* from 93. *145 Primrose Avenue, Haslington, Crewe CW1 5QB* Tel (01270) 587463

MATTHEWS, Gerald Lancelot. b 31. Bris Univ LLB50. Ripon Hall Ox 55. **d** 57 **p** 58. C The Quinton *Birm* 57-60; C Olton 60-63; V Brent Tor *Ex* 63-72; P-in-c Lydford w Bridestowe and Sourton 70-72; TR Lydford, Brent Tor, Bridestowe and Sourton 72-78; P-in-c Black Torrington, Bradf w Cookbury etc 78-90; Perm to Offic from 90; rtd 94. *The Larches, Black Torrington, Beaworthy EX21 5PU* Tel (01409) 231228

MATTHEWS, Gilbert Brian Reeves. b 19. Keble Coll Ox BA42 MA48. St Steph Ho Ox 42. **d** 44 **p** 45. C Brighton St Wilfrid *Chich* 45-49; C St Leonards Ch Ch 49-55; Org Sec Fellowship of St Nic 49-55; C Finedon *Pet* 55-58; Youth Chapl 58-64; R Rushton and Glendon 58-79; P-in-c Thorpe Malsor 76-79; R Rushton and Glendon w Thorpe Malsor 79-81; Chapl Bp Stopford Sch Kettering 77-81; C Spondon *Derby* 81-87; rtd 87; Hon C Walsall St Gabr Fulbrook *Lich* 88-90; Hon C Glen Parva and S Wigston *Leic* 90-93; Asst Chapl HM YOI Glen Parva 88-93; Hon C Wrington w Butcombe *B & W* 93-97; Perm to Offic *Chelmsf* 97-98; Hon C Thorpe Bay 98-01. *2 Faversham Lodge, 203 Eastern Esplanade, Southend-on-Sea SS1 3AD* Tel (01702) 584251

MATTHEWS, Harold James. b 46. Leeds Univ BSc68 Fitzw Coll Cam BA70 MA74. Westcott Ho Cam 68. **d** 71 **p** 72. C Mossley Hill St Matt and St Jas *Liv* 71-74; C Stanley 74-76; TV Hackney *Lon* 76-78; Chapl Forest Sch Snaresbrook 78-83; Hd Master Vernon Holme Sch Cant 83-88; Perm to Offic *Cant* 83-88; Hd Master Heath Mt Sch Hertf from 88. *Heath Mount School, Woodhall Park, Watton at Stone, Hertford SG14 3NG* Tel (01920) 830230 *or* 830541 E-mail hmatth1568@aol.com

MATTHEWS, Mrs Heather Ann. b 49. Bris Univ BA71 Lon Univ CertEd72. Trin Coll Bris 87. **d** 89 **p** 94. C Blagdon w Compton Martin and Ubley *B & W* 89-93; Dn-in-c 93-94; R 94-01; R Hodnet w Weston under Redcastle *Lich* 01-03; C Skipton Ch Ch *Bradf* 03-04; rtd 04. *The Sett, Yate Lane, Oxenhope, Keighley BD22 9HL* Tel (01535) 649095

MATTHEWS, Canon Joan Muriel. b 53. N Ord Course 89. **d** 92 **p** 94. C Aughton St Mich *Liv* 92-97; R Wavertree St Mary from 97; AD Toxteth and Wavertree from 04; Hon Can Liv Cathl from 04. *St Mary's Rectory, 1 South Drive, Wavertree, Liverpool L15 8JJ* Tel 0151-734 3103 E-mail revjoan@hotmail.com

MATTHEWS, Canon John. b 22. TD66. Trin Coll Cam BA48 MA51. Bps' Coll Cheshunt 49. **d** 51 **p** 52. C Woodlands *Sheff*

51-54; CF (TA) from 53; C Sharrow St Andr *Sheff* 54-57; V Sheff St Barn 57-62; P-in-c Lt Canfield *Chelmsf* 62-70; V Gt Dunmow 62-88; P-in-c Gt Easton 70-83; RD Dunmow 75-88; Hon Can Chelmsf Cathl 85-88; rtd 88; Perm to Offic *St E* from 88 and *Ely* from 99. *Moorside Cottage, Palmers Lane, Walberswick, Southwold IP18 6TE* Tel (01502) 722783

MATTHEWS, John Goodman. b 77. Univ of Wales BTh99. St Mich Coll Llan 99. **d** 02 **p** 03. C Lampeter and Llanddewibrefi Gp *St D* from 02. *Dwyfor, Maes-y-Llan, Lampeter SA48 7EN* Tel (01570) 422706

MATTHEWS, Lewis William (Bill). b 29. St Jo Coll Dur BA53 DipTh55 MSc76. **d** 55 **p** 56. C Eston *York* 55-57; C Wicker w Neepsend *Sheff* 57; Ind Chapl 57-61; V Copt Oak *Leic* 61-64; R Braunstone 64-70; V Thornaby on Tees St Paul *York* 70-72; TR Thornaby on Tees 72-78; Dir Dioc Bd for Soc Resp *Lon* 79-84; Perm to Offic 84-94; Warden Durning Hall Chr Community Cen Forest Gate 84-94; rtd 94; Hon C Jersey Gouray St Martin *Win* from 94. *Gouray Vicarage, La grande route de Faldouet, St Martin, Jersey JE3 6UA* Tel (01534) 853255

MATTHEWS, Liam. *See* MATTHEWS, William Temple Atkinson

MATTHEWS, Canon Melvyn William. b 40. St Edm Hall Ox BA63 MA68. K Coll Lon BD66 AKC67. **d** 67 **p** 68. C Enfield St Andr *Lon* 67-70; Asst Chapl Southn Univ *Win* 70-73; Lect Univ of Nairobi Kenya 73-76; V Highgate All SS *Lon* 76-79; P-in-c Clifton St Paul *Bris* 79-87; Sen Chapl Bris Univ 79-87; Dir Ammerdown Cen for Study and Renewal 87-93; V Chew Magna w Dundry *B & W* 93-97; Can and Chan Wells Cathl 97-05; rtd 05. *Yew Tree House, 22 Beaufort Avenue, Midsomer Norton, Radstock BA3 2TG* Tel (01761) 413630 E-mail mwmatthews@firenet.ws

MATTHEWS, Michael Raymond. b 55. JP96. Cov Univ CQSW82 Huddersfield Univ MBA96 Leeds Univ BA04. Coll of Resurr Mirfield 02. **d** 04 **p** 05. C Featherstone *Wakef* from 04; C Purston cum S Featherstone from 04. *St Thomas's House, Victoria Street, Featherstone, Pontefract WF7 5EZ* Tel and fax (01977) 792288 E-mail frmichael@yahoo.co.uk

MATTHEWS, Oswald John. b 13. St Edm Hall Ox BA37 MA40. Ripon Hall Ox 35. **d** 37 **p** 38. C Beverley Minster *York* 37-41; V Drypool St Andr and St Pet 41-48; Offg Chapl RAF 42-45; Chapl Hull Hosps 42-48; V Fridaythorpe w Fimber and Thixendale *York* 48-52; Miss to Seamen 52-64; Buenos Aires Argentina 53-54; Wellington New Zealand 55-64; V Taita 64-69; V Wanganui E 69-77; rtd 77. *12/107 Walker Road, Point Chevalier, Auckland 2, New Zealand* Tel (0064) (9) 815 3846

MATTHEWS, Paul. b 47. Brunel Univ BTech70 S Bank Poly DipEED72. S Dios Minl Tr Scheme 89. **d** 92 **p** 93. NSM Goring-by-Sea *Chich* from 92. *19 Angus Road, Goring-by-Sea, Worthing BN12 4NY* Tel (01903) 505859

MATTHEWS, Peter. *See* MATTHEWS, Frederick Peter

MATTHEWS, Peter Henry. b 22. Sarum Th Coll 62. **d** 64 **p** 65. C Wareham w Arne *Sarum* 64-67; P-in-c Houghton 67; C Sholing *Win* 67-69; R Hilperton w Whaddon *Sarum* 70-78; P-in-c Staverton 71-72; V 72-78; P-in-c Milborne St Andrew w Dewlish 78-87; rtd 87; Perm to Offic *B & W* from 87. *Holmlands, Lambrook Road, Shepton Beauchamp, Ilminster TA19 0LZ* Tel (01460) 40938

MATTHEWS, Canon Rodney Charles. b 36. Sarum Th Coll 62. **d** 64 **p** 65. C Gt Clacton *Chelmsf* 64-68; C Loughton St Mary 68-74; TV 74-76; V Goodmayes All SS 76-87; V Woodford Bridge 87-02; Hon Chapl Sail Tr Assn from 89; P-in-c Barkingside St Cedd 90-92; Hon Can Chelmsf Cathl 99-02; rtd 02; Perm to Offic *Chelmsf* from 03. *93 King's Head Hill, London E4 7JG* Tel (020) 8529 4372

MATTHEWS, Canon Roger Charles. b 54. MBCS82 CEng90 Man Univ BSc75 CDipAF78 Nottm Univ MA02. Trin Coll Bris 87. **d** 89 **p** 90. C Gt Baddow *Chelmsf* 89-93; P-in-c Chigwell Row 93-94; TV Chigwell and Chigwell Row 94-96; Dioc Miss Officer 96-00; Millenium Ecum Officer 98-00; Bp's Adv for Miss and Min from 01; Hon C Gt Baddow from 01; Hon Can Chelmsf Cathl from 00. *62 Longmead Avenue, Great Baddow, Chelmsford CM2 7EY* Tel (01245) 478959 *or* 294455 Fax 294477 E-mail rmatthews@chelmsford.anglican.org

MATTHEWS, Canon Roy Ian John. b 27. TD71. St Cath Soc Ox BA52 MA56. St Steph Ho Ox 52. **d** 54 **p** 55. C Barnsley St Mary *Wakef* 54-58; V Staincliffe 58-65; CF (TA) 58-92; V Penistone w Midhope *Wakef* 65-72; V Brighouse 72-84; Hon Can Wakef Cathl 76-92; V Darrington 84-92; Dioc Schs Officer 84-89; Dep Dir of Educn 85-89; rtd 92; Perm to Offic *Wakef* and *York* from 92; P-in-c Selby Abbey *York* 96-97. *14 Spring Walk, Brayton, Selby YO8 9DS* Tel (01757) 707259

MATTHEWS, Canon Royston Peter. b 39. Univ of Wales (Lamp) BA61. St Mich Coll Llan 61. **d** 64 **p** 65. C Fairwater CD *Llan* 64-67; C Cadoxton-juxta-Barry 67-71; V Bettws *Mon* 71-84; V Abergavenny H Trin 84-05; Hon Can St Woolos Cathl 05; rtd 05. *Address temp unknown*

MATTHEWS, Canon Stuart James. b 37. St Jo Coll Dur BA60. Bps' Coll Cheshunt 60. **d** 62 **p** 63. C Horsham *Chich* 62-65; C Rednal *Birm* 65-67; Min Brandwood St Bede CD 67-68; C Northfield 68-73; V Thurcroft *Sheff* 73-82; RD Laughton 79-82; R Sprotbrough 82-00; RD Adwick 84-89; Hon Can Sheff Cathl 92-00; rtd 00; Perm to Offic *Sheff* from 00. *43 Dinnington Road, Woodsetts, Worksop S81 8RL* Tel (01909) 560160

MATTHEWS, Terence Leslie. b 35. Handsworth Coll Birm 55. **d** 61 **p** 62. C W Acklam *York* 61-64; V Horden *Dur* 64-72; R Witton Gilbert 72-77; P-in-c Grangetown 77-85; V Cleadon 85-86; V Hebburn St Cuth 86-88; rtd 88. *7 Holmlands Park South, Sunderland SR2 7SG* Tel 0191-522 6466

MATTHEWS, Thomas Bartholomew Hall. *See* HALL, Thomas Bartholomew Berners

MATTHEWS, William. *See* MATTHEWS, Lewis William

MATTHEWS, Canon William Andrew. b 44. Reading Univ BA65 MA94. St Steph Ho Ox 65. **d** 67 **p** 68. C Westbury-on-Trym St Alb *Bris* 67-70; C Marlborough *Sarum* 70-73; P-in-c Winsley 73-75; V 75-81; V Bradford-on-Avon from 81; RD Bradford 84-94; Can and Preb Sarum Cathl from 88; Chapl to The Queen from 01. *Holy Trinity Vicarage, 18A Woolley Street, Bradford-on-Avon BA15 1AF* Tel (01225) 864444 Fax 863623 E-mail w.a.matthews@btinternet.com

MATTHEWS, William Temple Atkinson (Liam). b 47. DipApTh98. EMMTC 86. **d** 83 **p** 83. SSF 83-86; C Brinsley w Underwood *S'well* 86-89; TV Hitchin *St Alb* 89-97; R Toddington and Chalgrave 97-03; R N Albury Australia from 03. *St Mark's Rectory, 328 Gulpha Street, North Albury, NSW, Australia 2640* Tel (0061) (2) 5794 2443

MATTHEWS-LOYDALL, Mrs Elaine. b 63. Bp Otter Coll BA85. St Jo Coll Nottm 87. **d** 90 **p** 94. Par Dn Nottingham All SS *S'well* 90-94; C 94-95; Asst Chapl to the Deaf 91-93; Chapl to the Deaf 93-99; Chapl for Deaf People *Leic* from 99; TV Leic H Spirit from 99. *Pumpkin Cottage, 54 Wilne Road, Long Eaton, Nottingham NG10 3AN* Tel 0115-972 8943 E-mail chaplaincy@cfdpleicester.org.uk

MATTHEWS-PAYNE, James. b 19. St D Coll Lamp BA41. Lich Th Coll 41 St Mich Coll Llan 46. **d** 46 **p** 47. C Barry All SS *Llan* 46-51; C Canton St Cath 51-53; P-in-c Aberavon 53-55; Bermuda 55-60; V Woolston *Win* 60-65; Australia from 65; R Bridgetown 65-68; R Narrogin 68-70; R Morley 70-79; rtd 80. *12/11 Freedman Road, Mount Lawley, W Australia 6050* Tel (0061) (8) 9272 5253

MATTHIAE, Canon David. b 40. Fitzw Ho Cam BA63 MA69. Linc Th Coll 63. **d** 65 **p** 66. C New Addington *Cant* 65-70; C Charlton-by-Dover SS Pet and Paul 70-75; V Cant All SS 75-84; P-in-c Tunstall 84-87; R Tunstall w Rodmersham from 87; RD Sittingbourne 88-94; Hon Can Cant Cathl from 99. *The Rectory, Tunstall, Sittingbourne ME9 8DU* Tel (01795) 423907 E-mail david@matthiae.demon.co.uk

MATTHIAS, George Ronald. b 30. CertEd51. St Deiniol's Hawarden 76. **d** 78 **p** 79. NSM Broughton *St As* 78-83; NSM Wrexham 83-85; C 85-87; V Brymbo 87-95; rtd 95. *Bryn Adref, Pisgah Hill, Pentre Hill, Wrexham LL11 5DB* Tel (01978) 750757

MATTHIAS, John Rex. b 61. St Mich Coll Llan DMS94. **d** 94 **p** 95. C Llandrillo-yn-Rhos *St As* 94-98; R Llanfair Talhaearn and Llansannan etc 98-03; R Betws-yn-Rhos w Petryal from 03. *The Rectory, Llanfairtalhaiarn, Abergele LL22 8ST* Tel (01745) 720273 E-mail r.matthias@tesco.net

MATTHIAS, Paul. b 47. Philippa Fawcett Coll CertEd75 Kent Univ DipEd84. Cant Sch of Min 92. **d** 94 **p** 95. Head RE Hever Sch Maidstone 80-94; Chapl Ch Ch High Sch Ashford from 94; NSM Gillingham St Aug *Roch* from 94. *33 Malvern Road, Gillingham ME7 4BA* Tel (01634) 576197 E-mail matthias01@surfaid.org

MATTOCK, Colin Graham. b 38. Chich Th Coll. **d** 84 **p** 85. C Hove All SS *Chich* 84-87; C Bexhill St Pet 87-90; V Henlow *St Alb* 90-96; V Linslade *Ox* 96-00; P-in-c Pebworth w Dorsington and Honeybourne *Glouc* 00-02; R Pebworth, Dorsington, Honeybourne etc from 02. *The Vicarage, Stratford Road, Honeybourne, Evesham WR11 7PP* Tel (01386) 830302

MATTY, Horace Anthony (Tony). b 36. Ely Th Coll 61. **d** 63 **p** 64. C Minchinhampton *Glouc* 63-66; C Hunslet St Mary and Stourton *Ripon* 66-69; TV Wendy w Shingay *Ely* 69-71; V Parson Drove 71-74; V Southea cum Murrow 71-74; V Coven *Lich* 74-82; TV Hednesford 82-85; TV Basildon St Martin w Nevendon *Chelmsf* 85-92; P-in-c Basildon St Andr w H Cross 85-92; P-in-c Sandon 92-98; P-in-c E Hanningfield 92-98; rtd 98; Perm to Offic *Truro* 00-01 and 03-04. *7 Calvin Close, Fordhouses, Wolverhampton WV10 6LN* Tel (01902) 781789

MAUCHAN, Andrew. b 44. Hertf Coll Ox BA65 MA69 Man Univ CertEd66. Oak Hill Th Coll DipHE90. **d** 90 **p** 91. C Bridlington Priory *York* 90-94; V Alverthorpe *Wakef* 94-01; R Wombwell *Sheff* from 01. *The Rectory, 1 Rectory Close, Wombwell, Barnsley S73 8EY* Tel (01226) 211100

MAUDE, Canon Alan. b 41. Lon Univ DipTh67 BD69 Newc Univ MSc90. Lambeth STh74 Oak Hill Th Coll 66. **d** 69 **p** 70. C Balderstone *Man* 69-73; Asst Chapl Crumpsall and Springfield Hosps 73-75; C Crumpsall St Matt 73-75; Chapl R Victoria Infirmary Newc 75-94; Chapl R Victoria Infirmary and Assoc Hosps NHS Trust 94-98; Chapl Newcastle upon Tyne Hosps

NHS Trust from 98; Hon Can Newc Cathl *Newc* from 88. *Royal Victoria Infirmary, Queen Victoria Road, Newcastle upon Tyne NE1 4LP* Tel 0191-284 4966 *or* 232 5131
E-mail alan.maude@trvi.nuth.northy.nhs.uk

MAUDE, Alexander. b 53. Bingley Coll of Educn TCert74. N Ord Course. **d** 02 **p** 03. NSM Erringden *Wakef* from 02; Chapl Ravenscliffe High Sch from 02. *47 Vicar Park Drive, Norton Tower, Halifax HX2 0NN* Tel (01422) 355856 Mobile 07816-597074 E-mail sandie@maude47.fsnet.co.uk

MAUDE, Gillian Hamer. b 53. St Anne's Coll Ox BA75 MA79 Edin Univ MSc77. St Steph Ho Ox 99. **d** 01 **p** 02. C Hackney Wick St Mary of Eton w St Aug *Lon* 01-05; P-in-c Goodrington *Ex* from 05. *Goodrington Vicarage, 16 Cliff Park Avenue, Paignton TQ4 6LT* Tel (01803) 558949 Mobile 07932-056071

MAUDLIN, David. b 39. EAMTC 92. **d** 95 **p** 96. NSM Bury St Edmunds St Jo *St E* 95-97; NSM Haverhill w Withersfield 97-98; P-in-c The Sampfords and Radwinter w Hempstead *Chelmsf* 98-04; RD Saffron Walden 00-04; rtd 04; Perm to Offic *Leic, Pet* and *Eur* from 04. *3 Goldfinch Road, Uppingham LE15 9UJ* Tel (01572) 820181

MAUDSLEY, Canon George Lambert. b 27. St Jo Coll Nottm 74. **d** 75 **p** 76. C Binley *Cov* 75-77; Chapl Barn Fellowship Winterborne Whitechurch 77-83; V Salford Priors *Cov* 83-94; RD Alcester 87-92; Hon Can Cov Cathl 91-94; rtd 94; Perm to Offic *Cov* and *Worc* from 94. *7 Flax Piece, Upton Snodsbury, Worcester WR7 4PA* Tel (01905) 381034

MAUDSLEY, Keith. b 51. York Univ BA72. Ripon Hall Ox 72. **d** 75 **p** 76. C Rugby St Andr *Cov* 75-79; C Cambridge Gt St Mary w St Mich *Ely* 79-82; Chapl Girton Coll 79-82; P-in-c Binley *Cov* 82-89; RD Cov E 87-89; P-in-c Leek Wootton 89-91; Dioc Policy Development Adv 89-91; Dioc Adv on UPA *Liv* 91-97; Soc Resp Officer 91-97; R Lymm *Ches* from 97. *The Rectory, 46 Rectory Lane, Lymm WA13 0AL* Tel (01925) 752164
E-mail keith@maudsleykms.freeserve.co.uk

MAUDSLEY, Canon Michael Peter. b 38. St Andr Univ BSc61. Oak Hill Th Coll 65. **d** 67 **p** 68. C Blackpool St Mark *Blackb* 67-70; C Hartford *Ches* 70-72; R Balerno *Edin* 72-82; V Stapenhill w Cauldwell *Derby* 82-91; Assoc R Edin St Paul and St Geo *Edin* 91-95 and 00-03; R 95-00; rtd 03. *36 Forbes Road, Edinburgh EH10 4ED*

MAUGHAN, Angela. b 54. Newc Univ BA93. NEOC 94. **d** 97 **p** 98. C Willington *Newc* 97-01; V Weetslade from 01. *Weetslade Vicarage, 59 Kirklands, Burradon, Cramlington NE23 7LE* Tel 0191-268 9366

MAUGHAN, Geoffrey Nigel. b 48. CCC Cam BA69 MA73. Oak Hill Th Coll 75. **d** 77 **p** 78. C New Malden and Coombe *S'wark* 77-81; C Abingdon w Shippon *Ox* 81-89; TV Abingdon 89-98; Dir of Min and Chapl Wycliffe Hall Ox from 98. *Wycliffe Hall, 54 Banbury Road, Oxford OX2 6PW* Tel (01865) 274207
E-mail geoffrey.maughan@wycliffe.ox.ac.uk

MAUGHAN, John. b 28. Keble Coll Ox BA51 MA55. Linc Th Coll 51. **d** 53 **p** 54. C Heworth St Mary *Dur* 53-56; C Winlaton 56-59; R Penshaw 59-72; V Cleadon Park 72-93; rtd 93. *2 Struddar's Farm Court, Bates Lane, Blaydon-on-Tyne NE21 5TF* Tel 0191-414 8350

MAUND, Mrs Margaret Jennifer. b 42. RGN64 RM65 DTM66 Midwife Teacher's Dip 72. Llan Dioc Tr Scheme 89. **d** 94 **p** 97. NSM Cymmer and Porth *Llan* 94-97; NSM Pwllgwaun w Llanddewi Rhondda 97-04. *27 Mill Street, Tonyrefail, Porth CF39 8AB* Tel (01443) 670085

MAUNDER, Alan John. b 52. UWIST BSc74. Oak Hill Th Coll 88. **d** 90 **p** 91. C Birkenhead Ch Ch *Ches* 90-95; P-in-c Poulton from 95. *St Luke's Vicarage, Mill Lane, Wallasey CH44 3BP* Tel 0151-638 4663 E-mail ajmaunder@lineone.net

MAUNDER, Miss Vicky Alexandra. b 73. Leeds Univ BA95. Ripon Coll Cuddesdon BA01. **d** 02 **p** 03. C Swaythling *Win* from 02. *12 Willis Road, Southampton SO16 2NT* Tel (023) 8058 6002
E-mail vmaunder@fish.co.uk

MAUNDRELL, Canon Wolseley David. b 20. New Coll Ox BA41 MA45. **d** 43 **p** 44. C Haslemere *Guildf* 43-49; Bp's Dom Chapl *Chich* 49-50; V Sparsholt w Lainston *Win* 50-56; R Weeke 56-61; Can Res and Treas Win Cathl 61-70; Vice-Dean Win 66-70; Asst Chapl Brussels *Eur* 70-71; V Icklesham *Chich* 72-82; RD Rye 78-84; Can and Preb Chich Cathl 81-89; TR Rye 82-89; rtd 89; P-in-c Stonegate *Chich* 89-95; Perm to Offic from 95. *c/o J W Maundrell Esq, Box Cottage, High Street, Hempstead, Saffron Walden CB10 2PD* Tel (01799) 599268

MAUNSELL, Colin Wray Dymock. b 33. Pemb Coll Cam BA56 MA59 Lon Univ DipTh58. Tyndale Hall Bris 56. **d** 58 **p** 59. C Virginia Water *Guildf* 58-60; BCMS 60-93; Ethiopia 61-79 and from 91; Portugal 81-91; Crosslinks 93-94; rtd 94. *PO Box 18984, Addis Ababa, Ethiopia*

MAURICE, David Pierce. b 50. Pemb Coll Cam BA72 MA76 BChir76. Dioc OLM tr scheme. **d** 01 **p** 02. OLM Marlborough *Sarum* from 01. *Isbury House, Kingsbury Street, Marlborough SN8 1JA* Tel (01672) 514119
E-mail david.maurice2000@yahoo.com

MAURICE, The Ven Peter David. b 51. St Chad's Coll Dur BA72. Coll of Resurr Mirfield. **d** 75 **p** 76. C Wandsworth St Paul *S'wark* 75-79; TV Mortlake w E Sheen 79-85; V Rotherhithe H Trin 85-96; RD Bermondsey 91-96; V Tooting All SS 96-03; Adn Wells, Can Res and Preb Wells Cathl *B & W* from 03. *6 The Liberty, Wells BA5 2SU* Tel (01749) 685147
E-mail pmaurice@aol.com *or* adwells@bathwells.anglican.org

MAWBEY, Miss Diane. b 55. Birm Univ MMedSc97. Cranmer Hall Dur. **d** 89 **p** 94. Par Dn Menston w Woodhead *Bradf* 89-92; C Barnoldswick w Bracewell 92-93; Chapl Asst Birm Children's Hosp 93-96; Chapl Asst Birm Maternity Hosp 93-96; Chapl Birm Women's Healthcare NHS Trust 96-98; R The Whitacres and Shustoke *Birm* from 98. *The Rectory, Dog Lane, Coleshill, Birmingham B46 2DU* Tel (01675) 481252 Mobile 07710-281648

MAWDITT, Stephen Donald Harvey. b 56. **d** 96 **p** 97. OLM Ashill w Saham Toney *Nor* 96-05; OLM Watton w Carbrooke and Ovington 00-05; Min Fountain of Life from 05. *43 Cressingham Road, Ashill, Thetford IP25 7DG* Tel (01760) 440363
E-mail themawditts@tiscali.co.uk

MAWER, Canon David Ronald. b 32. Keble Coll Ox BA55 MA58 Dur Univ BA57 McGill Univ Montreal PhD77. Wells Th Coll 58. **d** 59 **p** 60. C Cullercoats St Geo *Newc* 59-61; Canada 61-92; Co-ord Angl Studies St Paul Univ Ottawa 81-92; Can Ottawa from 85; rtd 92; Perm to Offic *Newc* from 93. *Moorside, Church Lane, Thropton, Morpeth NE65 7JA* Tel (01669) 620597

MAWSON, Canon Arthur Cyril. b 35. St Pet Coll Ox BA56 MA61. Wycliffe Hall Ox 61. **d** 62 **p** 63. C Walsall *Lich* 62-66; V Millhouses H Trin *Sheff* 66-73; Selection Sec ACCM 73-79; Can Res and Treas Ex Cathl *Ex* 79-98; Dioc Dir of Ords 81-87; rtd 99. *4 Woodlands Close, Headington, Oxford OX3 7RY* Tel (01865) 764099

MAWSON, David Frank. b 44. Selw Coll Cam BA65 MA69. Linc Th Coll 79 SSC. **d** 80 **p** 81. C Tunstall *Lich* 80-83; C Blakenall Heath 83-84; TV 84-90; Chapl Goscote Hosp Walsall 87-90; V Pelsall *Lich* 90-94; V Tividale 94-99; V Shrewsbury All SS w St Mich from 99. *All Saints' Vicarage, 5 Lingen Close, Shrewsbury SY1 2UN* Tel (01743) 358820 Fax 243409
E-mail df.mawson@btinternet.com

MAXTED, Neil Andrew. b 58. Aston Tr Scheme 88 Sarum & Wells Th Coll 92. **d** 92 **p** 93. C Folkestone St Sav *Cant* 92-96; CF 96-05; P-in-c Frome Ch Ch *B & W* from 05. *The Vicarage, 73 Weymouth Road, Frome BA11 1HJ* Tel (01373) 473249

MAXWELL, Christopher John Moore (Bill). b 31. MRCS59 LRCP59 Qu Coll Cam MA75. Trin Coll Bris 74. **d** 75 **p** 76. Chile 75-81; C Clevedon Ch Ch *B & W* 75; Hon C Homerton St Luke *Lon* 81-94; Chapl Ibiza *Eur* 94-99; rtd 99; Perm to Offic *Chich* from 99. *Boscobel, Brightling Road, Robertsbridge TN32 5EJ* Tel (01580) 880475

MAXWELL, Marcus Howard. b 54. Liv Univ BSc76 Man Univ MPhil89. St Jo Coll Nottm BA79. **d** 80 **p** 81. C Chadderton St Matt *Man* 80-84; V Bircle 84-93; P-in-c Heaton Mersey 93-02; TR Heatons from 02; AD Heaton 98-04. *St John's Rectory, 15 Priestnall Road, Stockport SK4 3HR* Tel 0161-432 2165

MAXWELL, Ralph. b 21. CEng MIMechE. **d** 86 **p** 87. NSM Belfast St Mich *Conn* 86-87; Lic to Offic 87-89; NSM Belfast St Jas w St Silas 89-97; NSM Belfast St Pet 97-02; rtd 02. *69 Woodvale Road, Belfast BT13 3BN* Tel (028) 9074 2421

MAY, Charles Henry. b 29. Lon Coll of Div ALCD58 LTh74. **d** 58 **p** 59. C Bethnal Green St Jas Less *Lon* 58-61; C Woking St Pet *Guildf* 61-64; Area Sec (W Midl) CPAS 64-67; V Homerton St Luke *Lon* 67-80; Home Sec SAMS 80-84; V Fulham Ch Ch *Lon* 84-94; rtd 94; Perm to Offic *Ely* and *Pet* from 94; *Linc* from 95. *16 Kilverstone, Werrington, Peterborough PE4 5DX* Tel (01733) 328108 E-mail cclergyman@aol.com

MAY, Mrs Deborah Kim. b 60. Trin Coll Bris DipTh01. **d** 01 **p** 02. C Haughley w Wetherden and Stowupland *St E* 01-04; R Ashwater, Halwill, Beaworthy, Clawton etc *Ex* from 04. *The Rectory, Ashwater, Beaworthy EX21 5EZ* Tel (01409) 211205
E-mail debbie.may@btinternet.com

MAY, Donald Charles Leonard. b 25. Chich Th Coll 72. **d** 73 **p** 74. C Barkingside H Trin *Chelmsf* 73-77; V Aldersbrook 77-91; rtd 92; Perm to Offic *Chelmsf* from 92. *236 Prospect Road, Woodford Green IG8 7NQ* Tel (020) 8504 6119

MAY, George Louis. b 27. Selw Coll Cam BA52 MA55 Cam Univ PGCE67 AdDipEd78. Ridley Hall Cam 52. **d** 54 **p** 55. C St Mary Cray and St Paul's Cray *Roch* 54-56; C St Paul's Cray St Barn CD 56-57; C-in-c Elburton CD *Ex* 57-66; Asst Master Guthlaxton Sch Wigston 67-70; Ixworth Sch 70-72; Thurston Upper Sch 73-74; Perias Sch New Alresford 75-85; Hon C Ropley w W Tisted *Win* 78-79; Perm to Offic 79-96; rtd 92. *Oven House, Water Lane, Eyam, Hope Valley S32 5RG* Tel (01433) 630599

MAY, Janet Isabel. b 51. Lon Univ CertEd72. Dioc OLM tr scheme 99. **d** 00 **p** 01. OLM Attleborough w Besthorpe *Nor* from 00. *The Mill House, Church Street, Great Ellingham, Attleborough NR17 1LE* Tel (01953) 452198

MAY, John Alexander Cyril. b 52. K Coll Lon BD77 PhD98 Ch Ch Ox PGCE78. Linc Th Coll 79. **d** 80 **p** 81. C Tynemouth Ch Ch *Newc* 80-82; C Tynemouth Ch Ch w H Trin 82-85; C Tynemouth St Aug 82-85; TV Glendale Gp 85-90; V Wotton-under-Edge w Ozleworth, N Nibley etc *Glouc* from 90. *The Vicarage, Culverhay, Wotton-under-Edge GL12 7LS* Tel (01453) 842175 E-mail may187@hotmail.com

MAY, Peter Richard. b 43. St Jo Coll Cam BA64 MA68 MICE70. Trin Coll Bris 77. **d** 79 **p** 80. C Lancaster St Thos *Blackb* 79-85; V Darwen St Barn 85-91; Chapl Lyon w Grenoble *Eur* 91-92; Chapl Lyon 92-94; Perm to Offic *S'wark* 94-95; TR Horley 95-02; rtd 03. *14 Acorn Way, Hurst Green, Etchingham TN19 7QG* Tel (01580) 860441 E-mail rev@petermay.fsnet.co.uk

MAY, Simon George. b 47. FCA77 Ex Univ BA69 Univ of Wales (Ban) CertEd72. Sarum & Wells Th Coll 86. **d** 88 **p** 89. C Tamworth *Lich* 88-92; V Whitchurch *Ex* from 92; Warden of Readers (Plymouth Adnry) from 00; RD Tavistock from 02. *The Vicarage, 204 Whitchurch Road, Tavistock PL19 9DQ* Tel (01822) 610364

MAY, Stephen Charles Arthur. b 52. Mert Coll Ox BA73 Edin Univ BD78 Aber Univ PhD86. Ridley Hall Cam 84. **d** 86 **p** 87. C Sawley *Derby* 86-88; Lect St Jo Coll Auckland New Zealand 88-01; V Norden w Ashworth *Man* from 01. *St Paul's Vicarage, Heap Road, Rochdale OL12 7SN* Tel (01706) 641001 E-mail smaysfiction@hotmail.com

MAY, Toby Sebstian. b 67. Bris Univ BEng89. St Jo Coll Nottm MTh02. **d** 02 **p** 03. C Kendal St Thos *Carl* from 02. *79 High Garth, Kendal LA9 5NR* Tel (01539) 732602 E-mail toby@mays-in-grace.co.uk

MAYBEE, Christine. *See* DALE, Ms Christine

MAYBURY, David Kaines. b 32. G&C Coll Cam BA55 MA59. Ridley Hall Cam 55. **d** 57 **p** 58. C Sydenham H Trin *S'wark* 57-60; C Rainham *Chelmsf* 60-63; R Edin St Jas *Edin* 63-75; R Jedburgh 75-84; NSM Duns 84-91; Warden Whitchester Conf Cen 84-91; NSM Hawick *Edin* 91-97; Warden Whitchester Chr Guest Ho and Retreat Cen 91-97; rtd 97. *DaDo Heights, Borthaugh, Hawick TD9 7LN* Tel and fax (01450) 370809 Mobile 07941-448402 E-mail dado@maybud.fsnet.co.uk

MAYBURY, Doreen Lorna. b 33. RGN54 SCM56. Edin Th Coll 76. **dss** 81 **d** 95 **p** 95. Jedburgh *Edin* 81-84; Warden Whitchester Conf Cen 84-91; Duns 84-91; Hawick 91-97; NSM 95-97; rtd 97; Chapl Borders Gen Hosp NHS Trust from 98. *DaDo Heights, Borthaugh, Hawick TD9 7LN* Tel and fax (01450) 370809 Mobile 07801-354134 E-mail dado@maybud.fsnet.co.uk

MAYBURY, Canon John Montague. b 30. G&C Coll Cam BA53 MA57. Ridley Hall Cam 53. **d** 55 **p** 56. C Allerton *Liv* 55-59; C Rowner *Portsm* 59-62; V Wroxall 62-67; V Southsea St Simon 67-78; V Crofton 78-91; Hon Can Portsm Cathl 81-95; C Locks Heath 91-95; rtd 95; Perm to Offic *Portsm* from 95. *19 Netley Road, Titchfield Common, Fareham PO14 4PE* Tel (01489) 584168

MAYBURY, Paul. b 31. St Deiniol's Hawarden 87. **d** 88 **p** 90. NSM Sutton St Geo *Ches* 88-94; Perm to Offic 94-98 and from 01; P-in-c Towednack *Truro* 98-00. *43 Flowerscroft, Nantwich CW5 7GN* Tel (01270) 620639

MAYBURY, Paul Dorian. b 58. Trin Coll Bris 93. **d** 95 **p** 96. C Spondon *Derby* 95-99; V Gawthorpe and Chickenley Heath *Wakef* 99-02; P-in-c Ossett cum Gawthorpe 01-02; V Ossett and Gawthorpe from 02. *The Vicarage, 12 Fearnley Avenue, Ossett WF5 9ET* Tel (01924) 217379 *or* 263497 Fax 08701-375994 E-mail paul@htossett.org.uk

MAYCOCK, Ms Jane Ellen. b 66. Somerville Coll Ox BA90 MA95 Glas Univ MPhil98. Cranmer Hall Dur 90. **d** 92 **p** 94. Par Dn Harrow Trin St Mich *Lon* 92-94; C 94-95; C Kendal H Trin *Carl* 95-99; Dir of Ords from 01. *The Rectory, Longlands Road, Bowness-on-Windermere, Windermere LA23 3AS* Tel (01539) 443063 E-mail jemaycock@lineone.net

MAYELL, Howard John. b 50. Bris Sch of Min 81. **d** 84 **p** 88. NSM Patchway *Bris* 84-86; NSM Weston-super-Mare Cen Par *B & W* 87-88; C N Stoneham *Win* 88-91; P-in-c Black Torrington, Bradf w Cookbury etc *Ex* 91-97; C Ledbury w Eastnor *Heref* 97-98; TV Ledbury from 98. *27 Hazle Close, Ledbury HR8 2XX* Tel (01531) 631530

MAYER, Alan John. b 46. AKC70. St Aug Coll Cant 70. **d** 71 **p** 72. C Stanningley St Thos *Ripon* 71-74; C St Helier *S'wark* 74-79; TV Wimbledon 79-85; V Reigate St Luke S Park 85-00; R Oxted and Tandridge from 00. *The Rectory, 29 Chichele Road, Oxted RH8 0AE* Tel (01883) 712955 *or* 0771-4661911 E-mail alanmayer1@compuserve.com

MAYER, Graham Keith. b 46. St Cath Coll Ox BA68 Nottm Univ PGCE69 Ex Univ MA93 Plymouth Univ Dip Counselling 95. Linc Th Coll 78. **d** 80 **p** 81. C Paignton St Jo *Ex* 80-93; Perm to Offic 93-96; P-in-c Christow, Ashton and Bridford from 96; P-in-c Dunchideock and Shillingford St George w Ide from 97; RD Kenn from 05. *The Rectory, Dry Lane, Christow, Exeter EX6 7PE* Tel (01647) 252845

MAYER, Mrs Paula Denise. b 45. St Hilda's Coll Ox BA68 Nottm Univ CertEd69. SW Minl Tr Course 84. **d** 88. Hon Par Dn Paignton St Jo *Ex* 88-90; Par Dn 90-93; Perm to Offic from 93. *The Haven, 1 Parkside Road, Paignton TQ4 6AE* Tel (01803) 558727

MAYERSON, Paul Strom. b 28. PhD MEd MusBac. Ridley Hall Cam 80. **d** 82 **p** 83. C New Romney w Old Romney and Midley *Cant* 82-85; P-in-c Ospringe 85; P-in-c Eastling 85; R Eastling w Ospringe and Stalisfield w Otterden 85-90; rtd 90; Perm to Offic *Cant* 90-95. *360 Piper Hill Road, Center Harbour, NH 03226, USA*

MAYES, Canon Andrew Dennis. b 56. Dartmouth Coll (USA) 78 K Coll Lon BD79 AKC79 Armenian Orthodox Sem Jerusalem 79 Man Univ MA97. St Steph Ho Ox 80. **d** 81 **p** 82. C Hendon St Alphage *Lon* 81-84; C Hockley *Chelmsf* 84-87; V Kingstanding St Mark *Birm* 87-92; V Saltdean *Chich* 92-01; CME Officer from 01; P-in-c Ovingdean from 01; Hon Can Niger Delta from 96. *St Wulfran's Rectory, 43 Ainsworth Avenue, Brighton BN2 7BG* Tel (01273) 303633

MAYES, Anthony Bernard Duncan. b 29. Down Coll Cam BA53 MA57. Coll of Resurr Mirfield 56. **d** 58 **p** 59. C Leeds Halton St Wilfrid *Ripon* 58-60; USA from 61; V Fairfax St Aug California 61-63; Dir The Parsonage Center San Francisco 72-82; Fell Brown Coll Univ of Virginia from 86; Asst Dean Charlottesville 86-91; Asst Dean Coll of Arts and Sciences 91-99; rtd 99. *217 South, Sausalito, CA 94965, USA* E-mail bdm3g@gateway.net

MAYES, Aonghus. d 05. C Cregagh *D & D* from 05. *54 Rochester Avenue, Belfast BT6 9JW* Tel (028) 9079 6193

MAYES, The Very Revd Gilbert. b 15. TCD BA43 MA61. CITC 44. **d** 44 **p** 45. C Arm St Mark *Arm* 44-47; Hd Master Cathl Sch Arm 47-48; Dioc C 47-48; I Upper Donaghmore w Pomeroy 48-52; I Dundalk 52-61; Dean Lismore *C & O* 61-87; I Lismore w Cappoquin, Kilwatermoy, Dungarvan etc 61-87; Prec Waterford Cathl 84-87; Preb Stagonil St Patr Cathl Dublin 85-87; rtd 87. *Woodford, Ballybride Road, Rathmichael, Shankill, Co Dublin, Irish Republic* Tel (00353) (1) 282 4089

MAYES, Canon John Charles Dougan. b 44. Bps' Coll Cheshunt 63. **d** 67 **p** 68. C Portadown St Mark *Arm* 67-74; I Aghadowey w Kilrea *D & R* 74-86; USPG Area Sec 77-94; I Clooney w Strathfoyle from 86; Can Derry Cathl 92-96; Preb from 96. *All Saints' Rectory, 20 Limavady Road, Londonderry BT47 6JD* Tel (028) 7134 4306

✠**MAYES, The Rt Revd Michael Hugh Gunton.** b 41. TCD BA62 Lon Univ BD85. TCD Div Sch Div Test64. **d** 64 **p** 65 **c** 93. C Portadown St Columba *Arm* 64-68; Japan 68-74; Area Sec (Dios Cashel, Cork, Lim and Tuam) USPG 75-93; I Cork St Mich Union *C, C & R* 75-86; Adn Cork, Cloyne and Ross 86-93; I Moviddy Union 86-88; I Rathcooney Union 88-93; Bp K, E & A 93-00; Can Elphin Cathl 93-00; Bp L & K from 00. *Bishop's House, North Circular Road, Limerick, Irish Republic* Tel (00353) (61) 451532 Fax 451100 E-mail bishop@limerick.anglican.org

MAYES, Stephen Thomas. b 47. St Jo Coll Nottm 67. **d** 71 **p** 72. C Cullompton *Ex* 71-75; C Cheltenham St Mark *Glouc* 76-84; P-in-c Water Orton *Birm* 84-91; V from 91; AD Coleshill from 99. *The Vicarage, Water Orton, Birmingham B46 1RX* Tel 0121-747 2751 Fax 749 7294 E-mail stmayes@yahoo.co.uk

MAYES, Suzanne Janette. b 55. NTMTC 95. **d** 98 **p** 99. NSM E Ham w Upton Park St Alb *Chelmsf* 98-02; Chapl HM Pris Wellingborough 02-04. *Address temp unknown*

✠**MAYFIELD, The Rt Revd Christopher John.** b 35. G&C Coll Cam BA57 MA61 Linacre Ho Ox DipTh63 Cranfield Inst of Tech MSc83. Wycliffe Hall Ox 61. **d** 63 **p** 64 **c** 85. C Birm St Martin *Birm* 63-67; Lect 67-71; V Luton St Mary *St Alb* 71-80; RD Luton 74-80; Adn Bedford 80-85; Suff Bp Wolverhampton *Lich* 85-92; Area Bp Wolverhampton 92-93; Bp Man 93-02; rtd 02; Hon Asst Bp Worc from 02. *Harewood House, 54 Primrose Crescent, Worcester WR5 3HT* Tel (01905) 764822

MAYFIELD, Timothy James Edward. b 60. LMH Ox BA82. Trin Coll Bris BA88. **d** 88 **p** 89. C Ovenden *Wakef* 88-92; V Mount Pellon 92-03; V Cheltenham Ch Ch *Glouc* from 03. *Christ Church Vicarage, Malvern Road, Cheltenham GL50 2NU* Tel (01242) 515983

MAYFIELD, Timothy John Joseph. b 59. BA MA. **d** 99 **p** 00. C Battersea Rise St Mark *S'wark* from 99. *93A Bolingbroke Grove, London SW11 6HA* Tel (020) 7924 6833 *or* 7223 6188

MAYHEW, Canon Charles. b 40. K Coll Lon BD64 AKC64. **d** 65 **p** 66. C Nottingham St Mary *S'well* 65-69; R Cawston *Nor* 69-74; P-in-c Felthorpe w Haveringland 69-74; R Barnack w Ufford and Bainton *Pet* 74-86; RD Barnack 77-86; Can Pet Cathl 83-94; V Oakham, Hambleton, Egleton, Braunston and Brooke 86-94; Chapl Catmose Vale & Rutland Memorial Hosps 86-94; rtd 94; Perm to Offic *Pet* from 94. *Thorndon Green, Church Road, Lyndon, Oakham LE15 8TU* Tel (01572) 737594

MAYHEW, David Francis. b 51. Ch Ch Ox BA72 MA76 Newc Poly DCG76. Wycliffe Hall Ox BA75 NEOC 89. **d** 91 **p** 92. NSM High Elswick St Paul *Newc* 91-94; Toc H 91-94; V Mitford *Newc* from 94; Chapl Northgate and Prudhoe NHS Trust from 94. *The Vicarage, Stable Green, Mitford, Morpeth NE61 3PZ* Tel (01670) 511468 E-mail dfmayhew@aol.com

MAYHEW (née GURNEY), Jean Elizabeth. b 39. OBE97. New Hall Cam BA61 MA85 K Coll Lon BD84 AKC84 PGCE85 Ulster Univ Hon DUniv98 FKC00. SEITE 02. **d** 05. NSM

Maidstone St Paul *Cant* from 05. *Twysden, Riseden Lane, Kilndown, Cranbrook TN17 2SG* Tel (01580) 211820 Fax 212232 Mobile 07773-404554 E-mail jean@jmayhew.free-online.co.uk

MAYLAND, Mrs Jean Mary. b 36. JP77. LMH Ox BA58 MA61 TCert60. St Deiniol's Hawarden 91. **d** 91 **p** 94. NSM York Minster *York* 91-93; Lect and Tutor N Ord Course 91-93; Lect NEOC 93-96; Dioc Ecum Officer *Dur* 93-96; Local Unity Officer Dur Ecum Relns Gp 93-96; Assoc Sec CCBI 96-99; Co-ord Sec for Ch Life CTBI 99-03; Asst Gen Sec 99-03; rtd 03; Perm to Offic *York* from 03 and *Newc* from 04. *Minster Cottage, 51 Sands Lane, Barmston, Driffield YO25 8PQ* Tel (01262) 468709 E-mail jean.mayland@fish.co.uk

MAYLAND, Canon Ralph. b 27. VRD63. Ripon Hall Ox 57. **d** 59 **p** 60. C Lambeth St Andr w St Thos *S'wark* 59-62; Chapl RNR 61-94; C-in-c Worksop St Paul CD *S'well* 62-68; V Brightside St Marg *Sheff* 68-72; Ind Chapl 68-81; V Ecclesfield 72-81; Can Res and Treas York Minster *York* 82-94; rtd 94; Hon C Brancepeth *Dur* 94-96; Perm to Offic *York* from 96 and *Chelmsf* 01-03. *Minster Cottage, 51 Sands Lane, Barmston, Driffield YO25 8PQ* Tel (01262) 468709

MAYLOR, David Charles. b 59. Lanc Univ BSc80 Edge Hill Coll of HE PGCE81. St Jo Coll Nottm 89. **d** 91 **p** 92. C Hindley All SS *Liv* 91-94; P-in-c Spalding St Paul *Linc* from 94; Chapl United Lincs Hosps NHS Trust from 99. *St Paul's Vicarage, 65 Holbeach Road, Spalding PE11 2HY* Tel (01775) 722532 E-mail dave@stpauls-spalding.co.uk

MAYLOR, Miles. St Mich Coll Llan. **d** 05. NSM Mountain Ash and Miskin *Llan* from 05. *20 Wingfield Close, Pontypridd CF37 4AB*

MAYNARD, John William. b 37. Lon Univ BSc58. Ripon Hall Ox 60. **d** 62 **p** 63. C St Laur in Thanet *Cant* 62-67; C S Ashford Ch Ch 67-70; V Pagham *Chich* 70-00; rtd 00. *Two Hedges, Lower Budleigh, East Budleigh, Budleigh Salterton EX9 7DL* Tel (01395) 443869

MAYNARD, Raymond. b 30. S'wark Ord Course 75 Ox Ord Course 76. **d** 77 **p** 78. NSM Hedsor and Bourne End *Ox* 77-80; C Newport Pagnell w Lathbury 80-83; P-in-c Lacey Green 83-89; V 89; Perm to Offic *Guildf* 90-01. *Hardore, Ven Ottery, Ottery St Mary EX11 1RY* Tel (01404) 814307

MAYNARD, Canon Richard Edward Buller. b 42. AKC66. **d** 67 **p** 68. C St Ives *Truro* 67-71; C Falmouth K Chas 71-74; V St Germans 74-85; RD E Wivelshire 81-85; TR Saltash from 85; Hon Can Truro Cathl from 82; Chapl St Barn Hosp Saltash 90-93; Chapl Cornwall Healthcare NHS Trust 93-02; Chapl N and E Cornwall Primary Care Trust from 02. *The Vicarage, 11 Higher Port View, Saltash PL12 4BU* Tel (01752) 843142

MAYNE, Brian John. b 52. Univ of Wales (Cardiff) BA73 LTCL75 MRICS81. NEOC 82 Coll of Resurr Mirfield 84. **d** 85 **p** 86. C Stainton-in-Cleveland *York* 85-89; P-in-c Rounton w Welbury 89-96; Chapl HM YOI Northallerton 89-96; Chapl HM YOI Lanc Farms from 96. *HM Young Offender Institution, Lancaster Farms, Stone Row Head, Lancaster LA1 3QZ* Tel (01524) 848745 E-mail brianmayne@tiscali.co.uk *or* brianmayne@lycos.co.uk

MAYNE, John Andrew Brian. b 34. QUB BA55 Lon Univ BD62. TCD Div Sch Div Test 57. **d** 57 **p** 58. C Ballymoney *Conn* 57-60; C Knock *D & D* 60-62; P-in-c Knocknagoney 62-68; P-in-c Belvoir 68-71; I 71-80; Dean Waterford *C & O* 80-84; I Lecale Gp *D & D* 84-01; Can Down Cathl 87-01; Prec 91-00; Chan 00-01; Sec Gen Syn Liturg Cttee 89-99; rtd 01. *114 Ballydugan Road, Downpatrick BT30 8HF* Tel (028) 4461 2521 Mobile 07092-207229 E-mail jab@brianmayne.co.uk *or* editor.bcp@ireland.anglican.org

MAYNE, The Very Revd Michael Clement Otway. b 29. KCVO96. CCC Cam BA55 MA56. Cuddesdon Coll 55. **d** 57 **p** 58. C Harpenden St Jo *St Alb* 57-59; Bp's Dom Chapl *S'wark* 59-65; V Norton *St Alb* 65-72; Hd of Relig Progr BBC Radio 72-79; Hon Can S'wark Cathl *S'wark* 75-79; V Cambridge Gt St Mary w St Mich *Ely* 79-86; Dean Westmr 86-96; rtd 96; Perm to Offic *Sarum* from 97. *37 St Mark's Road, Salisbury SP1 3AY* Tel (01722) 331069

MAYO, Christopher Paul. b 68. Heythrop Coll Lon BD91 Birm Univ PGCE96. Qu Coll Birm 91. **d** 93 **p** 94. C Wednesfield *Lich* 93-94; C Bilston 94-95. *73 Gorse Road, Wednesfield, Wolverhampton WV11 2PY* Tel (01902) 733163

MAYO, Deborah Ann. *See* MURPHY, Deborah Ann

MAYO, Inglis John. b 46. FCA. Ripon Coll Cuddesdon 74. **d** 77 **p** 78. C Bitterne Park *Win* 77-81; C Christchurch 81-86; P-in-c Sturminster Marshall *Sarum* 86-89; P-in-c Kingston Lacy and Shapwick 86-89; V Sturminster Marshall, Kingston Lacy and Shapwick 89-00; P-in-c Lilliput from 00. *The Vicarage, 55 Lilliput Road, Parkstone, Poole BH14 8JX* Tel (01202) 708567 E-mail holyangelschurchlilliput@fish.co.uk

MAYO, Robert William. b 61. Keble Coll Ox BA83. Cranmer Hall Dur 85. **d** 87 **p** 88. C Luton Lewsey St Hugh *St Alb* 87-90; Hd Cam Univ Miss 90-95; Hon C Bermondsey St Jas w Ch Ch *S'wark* 90-95; Chapl S Bank Univ 95-98; Dir of Youth Work Tr Ridley Hall Cam from 98. *Ridley Hall, Cambridge CB3 9HG* Tel (01223) 741067 E-mail bm231@cam.ac.uk

MAYOH, Margaret Evelyn. b 38. Open Univ BA87 Matlock Coll of Educn TCert87. Trin Coll Bris DipHE82. **dss** 82 **d** 87 **p** 94. Halliwell St Paul *Man* 82-87; Hon Par Dn 87-91; Hon Par Dn Walmersley 91-94; Hon C 94-97; NSM Heaton Ch Ch from 97. *40 Hillside Avenue, Bromley Cross, Bolton BL7 9NJ* Tel (01204) 305423

MAYOR, Henry William. b 39. Oriel Coll Ox BA62 Birm Univ DPS67. Westcott Ho Cam 62. **d** 64 **p** 65. C The Quinton *Birm* 64-66; C Dudley St Thos *Worc* 67-71; R Birch St Agnes *Man* 71-83; Community Chapl Aylesbury *Ox* 83-89; Community Chapl Aylesbury w Bierton and Hulcott 89; R Cheetham St Luke and Lower Crumpsall St Thos *Man* 89-96; R Cheetham and Lower Crumpsall 97-01; rtd 01. *57 Hill Street, Manchester M20 3FY* Tel (07960) 767155 E-mail henrywmayor@hotmail.com

MAYOSS, Anthony (Aidan). b 31. Leeds Univ BA55. Coll of Resurr Mirfield 55. **d** 57 **p** 58. C Meir *Lich* 57-62; Lic to Offic *Wakef* 62-72 and from 78; CR from 64; S Africa 73-75; Asst Chapl Lon Univ *Lon* 76-78; Bursar CR 84-90; rtd 98; Perm to Offic *Lon* from 98. *St Michael's Priory, 14 Burleigh Street, London WC2E 7PX* Tel (020) 7379 6669 E-mail amayoss@mirfield.org.uk

MAYOSS-HURD, Canon Susan Patricia. b 59. Lanc Univ BA81. Cranmer Hall Dur 82. **dss** 84 **d** 87 **p** 94. Ribbesford w Bewdley and Dowles *Worc* 84-88; Par Dn 87-88; Chapl W Heath Hosp 88-96; C W Heath *Birm* 88-96; V 96-03; V Peachland St Marg Canada from 03. *6146 Turner Avenue, Peachland BC, Canada, V0H 1X4* Tel (001) (250) 767 9682 E-mail revsuemh@shaw.ca

MAZUR, Mrs Ann Carol. b 47. St Mich Coll Sarum CertEd69. TISEC 01. **d** 04 **p** 05. NSM Perth St Ninian *St And* from 04; Chapl Craigclowan Sch Perth from 04. *Finlaggan House, Logiealmond, Perth PH1 3TH* Tel (01738) 880374 E-mail ann.mazur@tesco.net

MBALI, Escourt Zolile. b 40. Fort Hare Univ BA68 Ox Univ BA71. St Bede's Coll Umtata 62. **d** 71 **p** 72. S Africa 71-74 and from 93; Botswana 74-81; V Preston on Tees *Dur* 81-83; C Knighton St Mary Magd *Leic* 84-88; P-in-c Church Langton w Tur Langton, Thorpe Langton etc 88-92; Community Relns Officer 88-93; Hon Can Leic Cathl 92-93; rtd 02. *1 Halford Road, Berea, Durban, 4001 South Africa* Tel (0027) (31) 201 6195

MDUMULLA, Jonas Habel. b 50. Nairobi Univ Hull Univ BTh87 MA89. St Phil Coll Kongwa DipTh74. **d** 74 **p** 75. Tanzania 74-82; C Sutton St Jas and Wawne *York* 82-96; P-in-c Carlton and Drax from 96; Ind Chapl from 96. *The Vicarage, 2 Church Dike Lane, Drax, Selby YO8 8NZ* Tel (01757) 618313

MEACHAM, John David. b 24. AKC51 Open Univ MPhil90 Lambeth STh77. **d** 52 **p** 53. C Maidenhead St Luke *Ox* 52-55; Asst Master Linton Ho Maidenhead 52-55; C Croydon St Jo *Cant* 55-58; V Sittingbourne St Mich 58-74; V Brenchley *Roch* 74-83; Teacher Tunbridge Wells Girls' Gr Sch 78-83; P-in-c Gt Wishford and S Newton *Sarum* 83-88; Bp's Chapl and Research Asst 83-86; Sec C of E Doctrine Commn 84-89; rtd 88; Perm to Offic *Sarum* 88-98. *Trewinnard, Grams Road, Walmer, Deal CT14 7NT* Tel (01304) 239613

MEAD, Arthur Hugh. b 39. K Coll Cam BA60 MA64 New Coll Ox BLitt66. St Steph Ho Ox 61. **d** 80 **p** 80. NSM Hammersmith St Jo *Lon* 80-05; NSM Hammersmith H Innocents and St Jo from 05; Chapl St Paul's Sch Barnes 82-97; rtd 97; Dep P in O 85-90 and from 95; P in O 90-95; Reader of The Temple from 95. *11 Dungarvan Avenue, London SW15 5QU* Tel (020) 8876 5833

MEAD, Colin Harvey. b 26. FCA. S Dios Minl Tr Scheme 81. **d** 84 **p** 85. NSM Talbot Village *Sarum* 84-96; rtd 96; Perm to Offic *Sarum* from 96. *59 Alyth Road, Bournemouth BH3 7HB* Tel (01202) 763647

MEAD, Canon John Harold. b 37. Wells Th Coll 69. **d** 71 **p** 72. C Charlton Kings St Mary *Glouc* 71-75; R Stratton w Baunton 75-82; R Bishop's Cleeve 82-00; RD Tewkesbury 88-97; Hon Can Glouc Cathl 90-00; rtd 00; Perm to Offic *Glouc* from 00. *13 Cleevemount Close, Cheltenham GL52 3HW* Tel (01242) 241050

MEAD, Mrs Lynda Roberta. b 44. Open Univ BA91. STETS DipTh99. **d** 99 **p** 00. NSM Hythe *Win* 99-04. *22 Furzedale Park, Hythe, Southampton SO45 3HW* Tel (023) 8084 8901

MEAD, Nicholas Charles. b 50. Newc Univ BEd73 Reading Univ MA76. Ridley Hall Cam 83. **d** 85 **p** 86. C Bilton *Cov* 85-88; C Whittlesey *Ely* 88-89; Hd of Relig Studies Neale-Wade Community Coll March 89-97; Fell Farmington Inst for Chr Studies Ox from 96; Sen Lect RE Westmr Coll Ox 97-00; Sen Lect RE Ox Brookes Univ *Ox* from 00. *Westminster Institute of Education, Oxford Brookes University, Harcourt Hill, Oxford OX2 9AT* Tel (01865) 488294 E-mail nmead@brookes.ac.uk

MEADEN, Philip George William. b 40. Open Univ BA75. Lich Th Coll 63. **d** 66 **p** 67. C Aston SS Pet and Paul *Birm* 66-70; V Lozells St Paul 70-76; Asst Chapl HM Pris Brixton 76-77; Chapl HM Pris Lewes 77-84; Chapl HM Pris Aylesbury 84-88; Chapl HM Pris Wandsworth 88-01; rtd 01; Perm to Offic *St E* 01-05. *2 Waterloo Lane, Fairford GL7 4BP* Tel (01285) 713917

MEADER, Jennifer Lindsay. b 68. UEA BA89. Westcott Ho Cam. **d** 01 **p** 02. C Cherry Hinton St Andr *Ely* from 01; C

Teversham from 01. *39 Eland Way, Cherry Hinton, Cambridge CB1 9XQ* Tel (01223) 474542 E-mail revlindsay@ntlworld.com

MEADER, Philip John. b 44. Oak Hill Th Coll 73. **d** 75 **p** 76. C E Ham St Paul *Chelmsf* 75-77; CMJ 77-90; TV Lowestoft and Kirkley *Nor* 90-94; V Lowestoft St Andr 94-96; R Panfield and Rayne *Chelmsf* from 96. *The Rectory, Shalford Road, Rayne, Braintree CM77 6BT* Tel (01376) 320517

MEADOWS, Mrs Freda Angela. b 46. CertEd68. Oak Hill Th Coll 93. **d** 96 **p** 97. NSM N Wembley St Cuth *Lon* 96-01; NSM Roxeth from 01. *48 Torrington Drive, Harrow HA2 8NF* Tel (020) 8248 3523 E-mail fam@revfredmead.freeserve.co.uk

MEADOWS, John Michael. b 27. St Jo Coll Cam BA50. Ridley Hall Cam 51. **d** 53 **p** 54. C Daubhill *Man* 53-55; Overseas Miss Fellowship 56-87; Malaya 57-61; Vietnam 62-75; Refugee Reception Cen Sopley *Win* 79-82; NSM Canford Magna *Sarum* 86-88; C Radipole and Melcombe Regis 89-94; rtd 94; Perm to Offic *Win* from 94. *c/o Dr A J Meadows, 28 Strawberry Fields, Hedge End, Southampton SO30 4QY*

MEADOWS, Philip Michael. b 71. Univ of Wales (Lamp) BA95. St Steph Ho Ox BTh01. **d** 01 **p** 03. C W Bromwich St Fran *Lich* 01; C Leeds Belle Is St Jo and St Barn *Ripon* from 02. *St Barnabas' House, 28 Low Grange View, Leeds LS10 3DT* Tel 0113-271 8346 E-mail frpmeadows@btinternet.com

MEADOWS, Canon Stanley Percival. b 14. TD61. St D Coll Lamp BA46. **d** 47 **p** 48. C Worsley *Man* 47-49; C Littleborough 49-51; V Charlestown 51-61; R Man St Geo w St Barn 61-72; R Man Miles Platting 72-82; RD Ardwick 77-82; rtd 82; Perm to Offic *Man* from 82. *20 Dantall Avenue, Manchester M9 7BH* Tel 0161-795 9478

MEADS, William Ivan. b 35. ACIS67 ACMA75 Qu Mary Coll Lon BA56. Linc Th Coll 75. **d** 77 **p** 78. C Cheltenham St Luke and St Jo *Glouc* 77-81; Chapl HM Pris Pentonville 81-82; Preston 82-85; Wakef 85-88; P-in-c Wroxton w Balscote and Shenington w Alkerton *Ox* 88-90; R Broughton w N Newington and Shutford etc 90-95; P-in-c Week St Mary w Poundstock and Whitstone *Truro* 95-97; rtd 97; Perm to Offic *B & W* 97-00. *15 Southlands, St Daniels Hill, Pembroke SA71 5QY* E-mail nanmeads@whsmithnet.co.uk

MEADWAY, Jeanette Valerie. b 47. FRCP87 FRCPEd87 Edin Univ MB, ChB69. Oak Hill NSM Course 89. **d** 93 **p** 94. NSM Stratford St Jo w Ch Ch and St Jas *Chelmsf* from 93. *4 Glebe Avenue, Woodford Green IG8 9HB* Tel and fax (020) 8491 6040 E-mail meadwayj@dial.pipex.com

MEAKIN, Canon Anthony John. b 28. TD76. Down Coll Cam BA52 MA56. Westcott Ho Cam 52. **d** 54 **p** 55. C Gosforth All SS *Newc* 54-60; V Alnwick St Paul 60-71; V Edlingham 62-71; CF (TA) 63-83; R Whickham *Dur* 71-88; RD Gateshead W 78-88; Hon Can Dur Cathl 83-93; Bp's Sen Chapl and Exec Officer for Dioc Affairs 88-93; rtd 93. *73 Oakfields, Burnopfield, Newcastle upon Tyne NE16 6PQ* Tel (01207) 270429

MEAKIN, David John. b 61. Hull Univ BA82 Hughes Hall Cam PGCE83 Lambeth STh88. Westcott Ho Cam 86. **d** 88 **p** 89. C Upminster *Chelmsf* 88-92; Prec and Sacr Dur Cathl *Dur* 92-97; V Ryhope 97-04; P-in-c Schorne *Ox* from 04. *The Rectory, 1 Green Acres Close, Whitchurch, Aylesbury HP22 4JP* Tel (01296) 641606 E-mail d.meakin@btinternet.com

MEARA, Canon David Gwynne. b 47. Oriel Coll Ox BA70 MA73. Lambeth STh76 Cuddesdon Coll 71. **d** 73 **p** 74. C Whitley Ch Ch *Ox* 73-77; Chapl Reading Univ 77-82; V Basildon 82-87; P-in-c Aldworth and Ashampstead 85-87; V Basildon w Aldworth and Ashampstead 87-94; RD Bradfield 90-94; V Buckingham w Radclive cum Chackmore 94-97; P-in-c Nash w Thornton, Beachampton and Thornborough 96-97; R Buckingham 97-00; RD Buckingham 95-00; Hon Can Ch Ch 98-00; R St Bride Fleet Street w Bridewell etc *Lon* from 00. *St Bride's Rectory, Fleet Street, London EC4Y 8AU* Tel (020) 7353 7999 *or* 7427 0133 Fax 7583 4867 E-mail info@stbrides.com

MEARDON, Canon Brian Henry. b 44. Reading Univ BSc66 PhD71. Oak Hill Th Coll DipHE79 MPhil84. **d** 79 **p** 80. C Reading St Jo *Ox* 79-82; V Warfield from 82; Hon Can Ch Ch from 03. *The Vicarage, Church Lane, Warfield, Bracknell RG42 6EE* Tel (01344) 882228 E-mail brian.h.meardon@btinternet.com

MEARNS, Christopher Lee. b 30. Worc Coll Ox BA54 MA58. Ripon Hall Ox BTh56. **d** 57 **p** 58. C Greenhill St Jo *Lon* 57-60; Canada 60-62; Lect Ripon Coll of Educn 63-75; Sen Lect Coll of Ripon and York St Jo 75-85; USA 87 and 89; Tutor Ridley Hall Cam 88; Seychelles 88 and 89-90; Perm to Offic *Ripon* from 90. *14 Primrose Drive, Ripon HG4 1EY* Tel (01765) 602695

✠**MEARS, The Rt Revd John Cledan.** b 22. Univ of Wales (Abth) BA43 Univ of Wales MA48. Wycliffe Hall Ox 43. **d** 47 **p** 48 **c** 82. C Mostyn *St As* 47-49; C Rhosllannerchrugog 49-56; V Cwm 56-59; Lic to Offic *Llan* 59-73; Chapl St Mich Coll Llan 59-67; Lect Th Univ of Wales (Cardiff) 59-73; Sub-Warden St Mich Coll Llan 67-73; V Gabalfa *Llan* 73-82; Hon Can Llan Cathl 81-82; Bp Ban 82-92; rtd 92; Perm to Offic *Llan* from 92. *Isfryn, 23 Avonridge, Cardiff CF14 9AU* Tel (029) 2061 5505

MEARS, Phillip David. b 40. Dur Univ BA62. **d** 65 **p** 66. C Sandylands *Blackb* 65-68; C Chorley St Geo 68-71; V Leyland St Ambrose 71-81; Perm to Offic *Ches* from 81; Chapl Warrington Distr Gen Hosp 81-00. *20 Kingsley Drive, Appleton, Warrington WA4 5AE* Tel (01925) 264082 *or* 662146

MEATH AND KILDARE, Bishop of. *See* CLARKE, The Most Revd Richard Lionel

MEATH, Archdeacon of. *See* LAWRENCE, The Ven Patrick Henry Andrew

MEATS, Canon Alan John. b 41. Univ of Wales (Cardiff) BA62 DipEd63 Lon Univ BD70. St Mich Coll Llan 68. **d** 70 **p** 71. C Pontypridd St Cath *Llan* 70-73; TV Ystradyfodwg 73-75; Dioc Insp of Schs 73-75 and 83-89; V Llandeilo Tal-y-bont *S & B* 75-83; RD Llwchwr 81-83; V Aberdare St Fagan *Llan* 83-89; V Felin-foel *St D* 89-01; Asst Dioc Dir of Educn 89-92; Dioc Dir of Educn 92-97; Can St D Cathl from 94; V Pen-bre from 01. *The Vicarage, Ar y Bryn, Pembrey, Burry Port SA16 0AJ* Tel (01554) 832403

MEATYARD, Mrs Christina. b 51. SRN74. STETS 96. **d** 99 **p** 01. NSM S Hayling *Portsm* from 99. *38 Staunton Avenue, Hayling Island PO11 0EW* Tel (023) 9234 8886 *or* 9263 7649 Mobile 07979-096779 E-mail parishoffice@haylinganglicans.freeserve.com.uk

MECHANIC, Rodney Ian (Roni). b 48. Man Univ MA(Theol)00. **d** 78 **p** 78. S Africa 78-98; P-in-c Shebbear, Buckland Filleigh, Sheepwash etc *Ex* 98-01; Australia 01-02; TV Heatons *Man* from 02. *The Rectory, 110 Crescent Park, Stockport SK4 2JE* Tel 0161-432 3537 E-mail ronimecahnic@ntlworld.com *or* roni@mechanic777.fsnet.co.uk

MEDCALF, James Gordon. b 31. CB. Solicitor 63. S'wark Ord Course 87. **d** 90 **p** 91. NSM Shortlands *Roch* 90-00. *15 Losecoat Close, Stamford PE9 1DU* Tel (01780) 482583

MEDCALF, John Edward. b 19. Oak Hill Th Coll 47. **d** 50 **p** 51. C Rugby St Matt *Cov* 50-53; TR Chell *Lich* 53-61; V Wednesfield Heath 61-85; rtd 85; Perm to Offic *Heref* from 86. *9 Richmond Care Village, St Joseph's Way, Nantwich CW5 6TD* Tel (01270) 623244

MEDCALF, William Henry. b 15. TCD BA45 MA49. CITC 46. **d** 46 **p** 47. C Belfast St Mich *Conn* 46-48; C Bedford St Pet *St Alb* 48-50; SE Sec CMJ 50-63; Dir Exhibitions CMJ 63-80; rtd 80; Perm to Offic *Lon* from 80. *185 Dibdin House, Maida Vale, London W9 1QQ* Tel (020) 7328 3133

MEDFORTH, Allan Hargreaves. b 27. Qu Coll Cam BA48 MA52. Westcott Ho Cam 50. **d** 51 **p** 52. C Hexham *Newc* 51-55; PV S'well Minster *S'well* 55-59; V Farnsfield 59-72; RD S'well 66-72; V St Alb St Pet *St Alb* 72-95; RD St Alb 74-84; rtd 95; Perm to Offic *St Alb* from 95. *62 Cuckman's Drive, St Albans AL2 3AF* Tel (01727) 836437

MEDHURST, Mrs June. b 44. St Hild Coll Dur TCert66. N Ord Course 99. **d** 02 **p** 03. C Silsden *Bradf* from 02. *12 Westerley Crescent, Silsden, Keighley BD20 0BW* Tel (01535) 658465 E-mail medjune@btinternet.com

MEDHURST, Prof Kenneth Noel. b 38. Edin Univ MA61 Man Univ PhD69. **d** 91 **p** 93. NSM Baildon *Bradf* from 91; Can Th Bradf Cathl from 00. *12 Westerley Crescent, Silsden, Keighley BD20 0BW* Tel (01535) 658465 E-mail kenmed@btinternet.com

MEDHURST, Leslie John. b 56. TCD DipTh85 BTh90 MA93 Open Univ BA91. **d** 85 **p** 86. C Seapatrick *D & D* 85-90; I Belfast St Mark *Conn* 90-97; I Helen's Bay *D & D* from 97. *The Rectory, 2 Woodland Avenue, Helen's Bay, Bangor BT19 1TX* Tel (028) 9185 3601

MEDLEY, Canon Philip Roger. b 46. Birm Univ CertEd73 Sheff Univ MA00 FCollP96. SW Minl Tr Course. **d** 85 **p** 86. NSM Ottery St Mary, Alfington and W Hill *Ex* 85-86; C S Hill w Callington *Truro* 86-89; C Linkinhorne 86-89; V 89-03; Dioc Officer for Evang 93-99; Warden Cornwall Preachers' Coll 93-99; Hon Can Truro Cathl 01-03; Dioc Missr *B & W* from 03. *The Old Deanery, Wells BA5 2UG* Tel (01749) 670777 E-mail roger.medley@bathwells.anglican.org

MEDWAY, Mrs Christine Jean. b 57. Qu Coll Birm 93. **d** 95 **p** 98. C Milton *Win* 95-97; C Southampton St Mary Extra 97-01; P-in-c Haselbury Plucknett, Misterton and N Perrott *B & W* 01-03; rtd 03. *40 Lime Avenue, Southampton SO19 8NZ* Tel (023) 8044 5105 E-mail cjmx2@fish.co.uk

MEDWAY, Daron. b 72. Univ of N Lon BA98. Wycliffe Hall Ox BTh04. **d** 04 **p** 05. C Crofton *Portsm* from 04. *7 Darren Close, Fareham PO14 2LU* Tel (01329) 663896 Mobile 07900-574691 E-mail d.medway@mac.com

MEE, Colin Henry. b 36. Reading Univ BSc58. Bris Sch of Min 83. **d** 85 **p** 86. NSM Stanton St Quintin, Hullavington, Grittleton etc *Bris* 85-87; C Swindon Ch Ch 88-90; TV Washfield, Stoodleigh, Withleigh etc *Ex* 90-95; TR 95-99; Chapl Marie Curie Foundn (Tidcombe Hall) 95-99; rtd 99; Perm to Offic *B & W* from 02. *Rickstones, Burgundy Road, Minehead TA24 5QJ* Tel (01643) 706048

MEEHAN, Cyril Frederick. b 52. St Jo Coll Nottm BTh80. **d** 80 **p** 81. C Keresley and Coundon *Cov* 80-83; P-in-c Linton and Castle Gresley *Derby* 83-90; P-in-c Alvaston 90-00; V 00; Chapl Asst Freeman Gp of Hosps NHS Trust 00-03; Chapl Northumbria Healthcare NHS Trust from 03. *North Tyneside*

General Hospital, Rake Lane, North Shields NE29 8NH Tel 0191-259 6660 *or* 237 3416

MEEK, Anthony William. b 45. ACIB. Ox NSM Course 80. **d** 83 **p** 84. NSM Gt Chesham *Ox* 83-01; Perm to Offic *Ex* from 01; Clergy Widow(er)s Officer from 02. *The Willows, Orley Road, Ipplepen, Newton Abbot TQ12 5SA* Tel (01803) 814370 E-mail frtonymeek@aol.com

MEERE, Mrs Alison Elizabeth. b 44. SRN65 HVCert67. Ripon Coll Cuddesdon 85. **d** 87 **p** 94. Par Dn Hengrove *Bris* 87-88; Par Dn Winterbourne 88-91; Par Dn Southmead 91-93; Par Dn Hackney *Lon* 93-94; TV 94-95; Asst Chapl R Berks Hosp Reading 95-96; Asst Chapl Battle Hosp Reading 95-96; Indonesia 02-03; rtd 03. *19 St Elmos Road, London SE16 1SA* Tel 07754-808579 (mobile)

MEERING, Laurence Piers Ralph. b 48. Man Univ BSc70. Trin Coll Bris 79. **d** 81 **p** 82. C Downend *Bris* 81-84; C Crofton *Portsm* 84-87; V Witheridge, Thelbridge, Creacombe, Meshaw etc *Ex* 87-94; TV Southgate *Chich* 94-02; TV Walton H Trin *Ox* from 02; P-in-c Bedgrove from 02. *252 Wendover Road, Aylesbury HP2 9PD* Tel (01296) 394759 E-mail lawrence.meering@btinternet.com

MEESE, Dudley Noel. b 63. Leic Univ BA86 Nottm Univ PGCE87. Ridley Hall Cam 99. **d** 01 **p** 02. C Sheff St Jo *Sheff* 01-05; Chapl Lee Abbey from 05. *Lee Abbey Fellowship, Lee Abbey, Lynton EX35 6JJ* Tel (01598) 752621

MEGAHEY, Alan John. b 44. Selw Coll Cam BA65 MA69 QUB PhD69. Westcott Ho Cam 69. **d** 70 **p** 71. Asst Chapl Wrekin Coll Telford 70-73; Ho Master Cranleigh Sch Surrey 73-83; Zimbabwe 84-93; Chapl Uppingham Sch 93-01; R Brant Broughton and Beckingham *Linc* from 01; R Leadenham from 01; R Welbourn from 01; RD Loveden from 03. *The Rectory, Church End, Leadenham, Lincoln LN5 0PX* Tel (01400) 273987 E-mail rector.leadenham@btopenworld.com

MEGARRELL, Miss Joanne Myrtle. b 70. QUB BA93 PGCE94. CITC BTh03. **d** 03 **p** 04. C Moira *D & D* from 03. *27 Danesfoot, Moira, Craigavon BT67 0SG* Tel (028) 9261 7346 E-mail jmegarrell@talk21.com

✠**MEHAFFEY, The Rt Revd James.** b 31. TCD BA52 MA56 BD56 QUB PhD75 Ulster Univ Hon DLitt99. **d** 54 **p** 55 **c** 80. C Ballymacarrett St Patr *D & D* 54-56; C Deptford St Jo *S'wark* 56-58; C Down Cathl *D & D* 58-60; C-in-c Ballymacarrett St Chris 60-62; I Kilkeel 62-66; I Cregagh 66-80; Bp's Private Chapl 72-76; Preb Down Cathl 76-80; Dioc Missr 76-80; Bp D & R 80-02; rtd 02. *10 Clearwater, Londonderry BT47 6BE* Tel and fax (028) 7134 2624 E-mail james.mehaffey@btinternet.com

MEHEN, Donald Wilfrid. b 44. Birkbeck Coll Lon BSc72 CertEd66. Dioc OLM tr scheme 97. **d** 00 **p** 01. OLM Sproughton w Burstall, Copdock w Washbrook etc *St E* from 00. *19 The Link, Bentley, Ipswich IP9 2DJ* Tel (01473) 310383 E-mail don@mehen.freeserve.co.uk

MEIER, Paul. b 64. St Jo Coll Nottm BA98. **d** 98 **p** 99. C Highley w Billingsley, Glazeley etc *Heref* 98-01; C Hildenborough *Roch* from 01. *12 Fellows Way, Hildenborough, Tonbridge TN11 9DG* Tel (01732) 838674 E-mail paul-meier@virgin.net

MEIKLE, Canon David Skene. b 39. St Cath Coll Cam BA60 MA89. Westcott Ho Cam. **d** 63 **p** 64. C Hawick *Edin* 63-67; C Edin SS Phil and Jas 67-72; C Banbury *Ox* 72-73; TV 74-78; R Ipswich St Matt *St E* 78-91; Hon Can St E Cathl 90-01; TR Mildenhall 91-01; rtd 01; Perm to Offic *St E* from 01. *172 Nacton Road, Ipswich IP3 9JN* Tel (01473) 439113 E-mail dandrmeikle@ntlworld.com

MEIN, The Very Revd James Adlington. b 38. Nottm Univ BA60. Westcott Ho Cam 61. **d** 63 **p** 64. C Edin St Columba *Edin* 63-67; Bp's Dom Chapl 65-67; Malawi 67-72; R Grangemouth *Edin* 72-82; P-in-c Bo'ness 76-82; TV Livingston LEP 82-90; R Edin Ch Ch 90-04; Can St Mary's Cathl 90-01; Syn Clerk 00-01; Dean Edin 01-04; rtd 04. *Cardhu, Bridgend, Linlithgow EH49 6NH* Tel (01506) 834317

MEIN, Canon Peter Simon. b 27. Nottm Univ BA55 MA59. Kelham Th Coll 48. **d** 55 **p** 56. SSM 54-70; Chapl Kelham Th Coll 55-61; Warden 62-70; Prior 64-70; USA from 71; Chapl St Andr Sch Delaware 71-92; Hon Can Delaware 89; rtd 92; Assoc Member S Delaware TM 92. *215 Bay Avenue, Lewes, DE 19958, USA* E-mail nsmein@earthlink.net

MEIRION-JONES, Dafydd Padrig ap Geraint. b 70. Magd Coll Cam BA91 PGCE92 Oak Hill Th Coll BA01. **d** 01 **p** 02. C Ex St Leon w H Trin *Ex* from 01. *27 Barnardo Road, Exeter EX2 4ND* Tel (01392) 277540 Mobile 07989-390028 E-mail dafandboo@hotmail.com

MEIRION-JONES, Canon Huw Geraint (Gary). b 39. MRAC61 K Coll Lon AKC69 BD71 MA84. St Aug Coll Cant 69. **d** 70 **p** 71. C Harlescott *Lich* 70-73; C Worplesdon *Guildf* 73-77; V Ash Vale 77-85; TR Westborough 85-96; Dioc Press Officer 85-94; P-in-c Shere 96-98; P-in-c Albury 97-98; R Shere, Albury and Chilworth 98-04; Hon Can Guildf Cathl 99-04; Dioc Rural Adv 99-03; RD Cranleigh 00-04; rtd 04; Perm to Offic *Guildf* and *Ban* from 04. *Parc Newydd, Rhosgadfan, Caernarfon LL54 7LF* Tel (01286) 831195 Mobile 07880-707414 Fax (01286) 830141

MEIRIONNYDD, Archdeacon of. *See* ROWLANDS, The Ven Emyr Wyn

MELANESIA, Archbishop of. *See* POGO, The Most Revd Sir Ellison Leslie

MELANIPHY, Miss Angela Ellen. b 55. SRN79. Cranmer Hall Dur 87. **d** 90 **p** 94. Par Dn Leytonstone St Jo *Chelmsf* 90-94; C 94-95; TV Harlow Town Cen w Lt Parndon from 95. *4A The Drive, Harlow CM20 3QD* Tel (01279) 439721 E-mail angie@melaniphy.freeserve.co.uk

MELBOURNE, Brian Kenneth. b 45. York Univ Toronto 77. Trin Coll Toronto LTh82. **d** 82 **p** 82. Canada 82-87; Bermuda 88-94; P-in-c Biddenden and Smarden *Cant* 94-97; Hon C Isfield *Chich* from 01. *The Parsonage, Station Road, Isfield, Uckfield TN22 5EY* Tel (01825) 750247

MELBOURNE, Dean of. *See* RICHARDSON, The Very Revd David John Leyburn

MELDRUM, Andrew John Bruce. b 66. Univ of Wales (Abth) LLB89 Lon Univ MA98. Westcott Ho Cam CTM94. **d** 94 **p** 95. C Paddington St Jas *Lon* 94-99; P-in-c Brookfield St Anne, Highgate Rise 99-02; V from 02; Communications Adv to Bp Edmonton from 00. *St Anne's Vicarage, 106 Highgate West Hill, London N6 6AP* Tel and fax (020) 8340 5190 E-mail javintner@aol.com

MELDRUM, David Peter John. b 73. St Andr Univ MA95. Oak Hill Th Coll BA01. **d** 01 **p** 02. C Leyton St Mary w St Edw and St Luke *Chelmsf* 01-03; C Cranham Park 03-05; C Wandsworth St Steph *S'wark* from 05. *St Stephen's Vicarage, 2A Oakhill Road, London SW15 2QU* Tel (020) 8870 0561 E-mail davidpjmeldrum@yahoo.com

MELINSKY, Canon Michael Arthur Hugh. b 24. Ch Coll Cam BA47 MA49. Ripon Hall Ox 57. **d** 57 **p** 59. C Wimborne Minster *Sarum* 57-59; C Wareham w Arne 59-61; V Nor St Steph *Nor* 61-68; Chapl Norfolk and Nor Hosp 61-68; Hon Can Nor Cathl and Can Missr *Nor* 68-73; Chief Sec ACCM 73-78; Prin N Ord Course 78-88; rtd 88; Perm to Offic *Nor* from 88. *15 Parson's Mead, Norwich NR4 6PG* Tel (01603) 455042

MELLERUP, Miss Eiler Mary. b 37. Saffron Walden Coll CertEd58. LNSM course 94. **d** 96 **p** 97. OLM Happisburgh, Walcott, Hempstead w Eccles etc *Nor* from 96. *Channings, The Crescent, Walcott, Norwich NR12 0NH* Tel (01692) 651393

MELLING, Canon Leonard Richard. b 13. St Aid Birkenhead 38. **d** 41 **p** 42. C W Acklam *York* 41-45; C Scarborough St Mary 45-48; V Newby 48-54; Borneo 54-59; Area Sec USPG *Ox* and *Cov* 59-64; *York* 64-67; V Osbaldwick w Murton *York* 67-78; RD Bulmer 72-78; Malaysia 78-81; Dean Kuching 78-81; rtd 81; Perm to Offic *York* from 81. *82 Tranby Avenue, Osbaldwick, York YO10 3NN* Tel (01904) 413796

MELLISH, John. b 26. Cranmer Hall Dur 67. **d** 69 **p** 70. C Ulverston St Mary w H Trin *Carl* 69-72; V Bromfield 72-73; V Bromfield w Waverton 73-79; P-in-c Allonby w W Newton 77-79; V Shap w Swindale 79-86; RD Appleby 82-86; V Bassenthwaite, Isel and Setmurthy 86-90; rtd 90; Perm to Offic *Carl* from 90. *Wyndham, 3 Old Road, Longtown, Carlisle CA6 5TH* Tel (01228) 791441

MELLISS, Laurence John Albert. b 21. DSM45 RD69. AKC52. **d** 53 **p** 54. C Norbury St Steph *Cant* 53-56; C Folkestone St Mary and St Eanswythe 56-60; Chapl RNVR 56-59; Chapl RNR 59-76; R Upper St Leonards St Jo *Chich* 60-64; V Littlehampton St Mary 64-76; RD Arundel 75-76; V Findon 76-81; R Catsfield and Crowhurst 81-86; rtd 86; Perm to Offic *Sarum* from 95. *4 St Osmond Close, Yetminster, Sherborne DT9 6LU* Tel (01935) 872536

MELLOR, Frederick Charles Walter (Tony). b 24. Oak Hill NSM Course 80. **d** 83 **p** 84. NSM Loughton St Jo *Chelmsf* 83-93; Chapl Asst Whipps Cross Hosp Lon from 87; Perm to Offic from 93. *4 Scotland Road, Buckhurst Hill IG9 5NR* Tel (020) 8504 6203

MELLOR, The Very Revd Kenneth Paul. b 49. Southn Univ BA71 Leeds Univ MA72. Cuddesdon Coll 72. **d** 73 **p** 74. C Cottingham *York* 73-76; C Ascot Heath *Ox* 76-80; V Tilehurst St Mary 80-85; V Menheniot *Truro* 85-94; Hon Can Truro Cathl 90-94 and from 03; Can Res and Treas 94-03; RD W Wivelshire 88-96; R Guernsey St Peter Port *Win* from 03; P-in-c Sark from 03; Dean Guernsey from 03. *The Deanery, Cornet Street, St Peter Port, Guernsey GY1 1BZ* Tel (01481) 720036 Fax 722948 E-mail kpmellor@aol.com

MELLOR, Roy. b 52. Lanc Univ BA92. Cuddesdon Coll 94. **d** 96 **p** 97. C Oakdale *Sarum* 96-00; TV Kingsthorpe w Northampton St Dav *Pet* 00-03; R Blisworth and Stoke Bruerne w Grafton Regis etc from 03. *The Rectory, High Street, Blisworth, Northampton NN7 3BJ* Tel (01604) 879112 E-mail roy_mellor2002@yahoo.co.uk

MELLOR, Tony. *See* MELLOR, Frederick Charles Walter

MELLORS, Derek George. b 38. Bris Univ CertEd60 Lon Univ BSc71 Nottm Univ DipEd74 Liv Univ MEd83. N Ord Course 81. **d** 84 **p** 85. NSM Eccleston Ch Ch *Liv* 84-92; C Lowton St Mary 92-93; V Ashton-in-Makerfield St Thos 93-99; rtd 99; Perm to Offic *Liv* from 00. *20 Millbrook Lane, Eccleston, St Helens WA10 4QU* Tel (01744) 28424

MELLORS, James. b 32. Kelham Th Coll 52. **d** 56 **p** 57. C Horbury *Wakef* 56-61; V Scholes 61-72; V Mirfield 72-88; Hon Can Wakef Cathl 83-88; V Leyburn w Bellerby *Ripon* 88-93; rtd 93; Perm to Offic *Ripon* from 93. *Broomhill, 22 The Shawl, Leyburn DL8 5DG* Tel (01969) 622452 E-mail jjwestwitton@btinternet.com

MELLOWS, Canon Alan Frank. b 23. Qu Coll Cam BA45 MA49. Tyndale Hall Bris 47. **d** 49 **p** 50. C Morden *S'wark* 49-54; V Brimscombe *Glouc* 54-62; R Mileham *Nor* 62-74; P-in-c Beeston next Mileham 62-66; R 66-74; P-in-c Stanfield 62-74; P-in-c Gt w Lt Dunham 70-73; R Ashill 74-79; P-in-c Saham Toney 78-79; R Ashill w Saham Toney 79-88; Hon Can Nor Cathl 82-88; rtd 88; Perm to Offic *Nor* from 88. *8 Smugglers Close, Hunstanton PE36 6JU* Tel (01485) 534271

MELLOWSHIP, Robert John. b 52. St Mich Coll Llan BD92. **d** 92 **p** 93. C Brecon St Mary and Battle w Llanddew *S & B* 92-94; Min Can Brecon Cathl 92-94; C Pontypool *Mon* 94-95; TV 95-97; P-in-c Bressingham w N and S Lopham and Fersfield *Nor* from 97; P-in-c Roydon St Remigius from 04. *The Rectory, High Road, Bressingham, Diss IP22 2AT* Tel and fax (01379) 688267 E-mail robmellowship@msn.com

MELLUISH, Mark Peter. b 59. Oak Hill Th Coll. **d** 89 **p** 90. C Ashtead *Guildf* 89-93; V Ealing St Paul *Lon* from 93. *St Paul's Vicarage, 102 Elers Road, London W13 9QE* Tel and fax (020) 8567 4628 *or* tel 8799 3779 E-mail mark.melluish@stpauls-ealing.org

MELLUISH, Stephen. b 60. Trin Coll Bris DipHE93. **d** 93 **p** 94. C Gipsy Hill Ch Ch *S'wark* 93-96; V Wandsworth St Steph from 96; P-in-c Wandsworth St Mich from 01. *St Stephen's Vicarage, 2A Oakhill Road, London SW15 2QU* Tel (020) 8874 5610 E-mail smelluish@aol.com

MELLY, Aleck Emerson. b 24. Oak Hill Th Coll 50. **d** 53 **p** 54. C Chadderton Ch Ch *Man* 53-56; C Cheltenham St Mark *Glouc* 56-59; V Tipton St Paul *Lich* 59-68; R Kemberton w Sutton Maddock 68-80; P-in-c Stockton 74-80; R Kemberton, Sutton Maddock and Stockton 81-89; rtd 89; Perm to Offic *Lich* 89-03 and *Heref* from 90. *Bethany, 47 Greenfields Road, Bridgnorth WV16 4JG* Tel (01746) 762711

MELROSE, Kenneth Mark Cecil. b 15. Ex Coll Ox BA37 DipTh38 MA41. Ripon Hall Ox 37. **d** 39 **p** 40. C Clifton St Jo *Bris* 39-41; Lic to Offic *Glouc* 41-42; Chapl RNVR 42-46; Lic to Offic *St Alb* 47-49; V Bedminster St Aldhelm *Bris* 49-55; V Hurstbourne Tarrant *Win* 55-63; V Portswood St Denys 63-71; V Bovey Tracey SS Pet and Paul *Ex* 71-85; rtd 85; Perm to Offic *Cant* 87-03. *23 Ramsay Hall, 11-13 Byron Road, Worthing BN11 3HN* Tel (01903) 235422

MELROSE, Michael James Gervase. b 47. St Chad's Coll Dur BA69 DipTh70. **d** 71 **p** 72. C Chelmsf All SS *Chelmsf* 71-74; C Pimlico St Pet w Westmr Ch Ch *Lon* 74-80; R Man Victoria Park *Man* 80-94; P-in-c Cheetwood St Alb 85-91; R Reading St Giles *Ox* from 94. *St Giles's Rectory, Church Street, Reading RG1 2SB* Tel 0118-957 2831

MELTON, Mrs Anne. b 44. N Riding Coll of Educn CertEd65. St Jo Coll Dur 80. **dss** 83 **d** 87 **p** 94. Newton Aycliffe *Dur* 83-87; Par Dn 87-88; Par Dn Shildon w Eldon 88-94; Asst Dir of Ords 88-94; C Shildon w Eldon 94; P-in-c Usworth 94-96; TR from 96. *4 Highbury Close, Springwell, Gateshead NE9 7PU* Tel 0191-416 3533

MELVILLE, Dominic. b 63. Sussex Univ BA84 Southn Univ BTh90. Sarum & Wells Th Coll 87. **d** 90 **p** 91. C Willenhall H Trin *Lich* 90-94; V Wednesfield St Greg 94-99; V Worc St Wulstan *Worc* from 99. *The Vicarage, Cranham Drive, Worcester WR4 9PA* Tel (01905) 456944

MELVIN, Gordon Thomas. b 55. BA86. Sarum & Wells Th Coll 86. **d** 88 **p** 89. C Linc St Faith and St Martin w St Pet *Linc* 88-91; TV Horsham *Chich* 91-94; Chapl Horsham Gen Hosp 91-94; Chapl Ipswich Hosp NHS Trust 94-00; Sen Chapl from 00; Chapl Local Health Partnerships NHS Trust 94-00; Sen Chapl from 00; Perm to Offic *St E* from 04. *The Ipswich Hospital NHS Trust, Heath Road, Ipswich IP4 5PD* Tel (01473) 704100 *or* 712233

MEMBERY, Donald Percy. b 20. K Coll Lon BSc50 DipEd51 AKC51. Ox NSM Course. **d** 79 **p** 80. NSM Aston Rowant w Crowell *Ox* 79-81; P-in-c Swyncombe 81-85; R Swyncombe w Britwell Salome 85-88; rtd 88; Perm to Offic *Ripon* from 88. *11 Carr Manor Gardens, Leeds LS17 5DQ* Tel 0113-269 1578 Mobile 07779-432061 E-mail donald@heretics.demon.co.uk

MENDEL, Canon Thomas Oliver. b 57. Down Coll Cam BA79 MA82. Cranmer Hall Dur 79. **d** 81 **p** 82. Chapl Down Coll Cam 81-86; Fell 84-86; Hon C Cambridge St Mary Less *Ely* 81-86; V Minsterley *Heref* 86-92; R Habberley 86-92; Chapl Shrewsbury Sch 93-95; Chapl Milan w Genoa and Varese *Eur* 95-96; Chapl Copenhagen w Aarhus 96-04; Sen Chapl Malta and Gozo from 04; Can and Chan Malta Cathl from 04. *St Paul's Anglican Pro-Cathedral, Independence Square, Valetta VLT 12, Malta GC* Tel (00356) 2122 5714 Fax 2122 5867 E-mail anglican@onvol.net

✠**MENIN, The Rt Revd Malcolm James.** b 32. Univ Coll Ox BA55 MA59. Cuddesdon Coll 55. **d** 57 **p** 58 **c** 86. C Southsea H Spirit *Portsm* 57-59; C Fareham SS Pet and Paul 59-62; V Nor St Jas w Pockthorpe *Nor* 62-72; P-in-c Nor St Martin 62-74; P-in-c Nor St Mary Magd 68-72; V Nor St Mary Magd w St Jas 72-86; RD Nor E 81-86; Hon Can Nor Cathl 82-86; Suff Bp Knaresborough *Ripon* 86-97; rtd 97; Perm to Offic *Nor* 97-04; Hon Asst Bp Nor from 00. *32C Bracondale, Norwich NR1 2AN* Tel (01603) 627987

MENNISS, Andrew Philip. b 49. Univ of Wales (Swansea) BSc73. Sarum & Wells Th Coll 83. **d** 85 **p** 86. C Horsell *Guildf* 85-89; V Bembridge *Portsm* from 89; RD E Wight 95-00. *The Vicarage, Church Road, Bembridge PO35 5NA* Tel (01983) 872175 Fax 875255 E-mail apmenniss@aol.com

MENON, Nicholas Anthony Thotekat. b 39. Mert Coll Ox BA61 MA65. St Steph Ho Ox 61. **d** 63 **p** 64. C Paddington Ch Ch *Lon* 63-66; Hon C 66-70; V Thorpe *Guildf* 70-76; V Ox SS Phil and Jas w St Marg *Ox* 76-79; Chapl Surrey Univ *Guildf* 79-82; Chapl and Ho Master Cranleigh Sch Surrey 82-00; Asst Chapl Malvern Coll 00-04; rtd 04; Perm to Offic *Worc* from 00. *Pilgrim Cottage, 187 West Malvern Road, Malvern WR14 4BB* Tel (01684) 577189 E-mail nicholas.menon@ukonline.co.uk

MENSAH, Isaac Kingsley. b 48. St Jo Coll Nottm BA03. **d** 01 **p** 02. C Brussels *Eur* from 01. *Rue de l'Intendant 152, B-1080 Brussels, Belgium* Tel (0032) (2) 420 0604 *or* 512 4796 Fax 511 1028 Mobile 476-970442 E-mail isaac.mensah@htbrussels.com

MENSINGH, Gregg Richard. b 69. Portsm Univ BSc94. Westcott Ho Cam 95. **d** 97 **p** 98. C Birchfield *Birm* 97-01; V Gravelly Hill from 01. *All Saints' Vicarage, Broomfield Road, Birmingham B23 7QA* Tel 0121-373 0730 E-mail greggm@onetel.com

MENTZEL, Kevin David. b 60. Reading Univ BSc82 Down Coll Cam BA87 MA91 QUB MTh04. Ridley Hall Cam 85. **d** 88 **p** 89. C Ditton *Roch* 88-91; Asst Chapl Eton Coll 91-93; Asst Chapl R Hosp Sch Holbrook 93-94; Sen C Fulham St Dionis Parson's Green *Lon* 94-97; CF from 97. *c/o MOD Chaplains (Army)* Tel (01980) 615804 Fax 615800

MENZIES, Stanley Hay. b 33. Edin Univ MA55 BD58. New Coll Edin 55. **d** 02 **p** 03. NSM Boston Spa *York* from 02. *Cairn Croft, 2 Crag Gardens, Bramham, Wetherby LS23 6RP* Tel and fax (01937) 541047

MEON, Archdeacon of the. *See* HANCOCK, The Ven Peter

MEPHAM, Stephen Richard. b 64. K Coll Lon BD85 AKC85. Linc Th Coll 87. **d** 89 **p** 90. C Newark *S'well* 89-92; C Cheshunt *St Alb* 92-95; C-in-c Turnford St Clem CD 95-98; V Rickmansworth from 98. *The Vicarage, Bury Lane, Rickmansworth WD3 1ED* Tel (01923) 772627 E-mail srmepham@aol.com

MERCER, James John. b 56. Bp Otter Coll Chich BEd79 Lon Inst of Educn MA85. Ridley Hall Cam 00. **d** 02 **p** 03. C Heref St Pet w St Owen and St Jas *Heref* from 02. *15 Belgravia Gardens, Hereford HR1 1RB* Tel (01432) 267287 Mobile 07940-506188 E-mail jjmercer@fish.co.uk

MERCER, Canon John James Glendinning. b 20. TCD BA49 MA55. **d** 50 **p** 51. C Newtownards *D & D* 50-53; C Bangor St Comgall 53-55; I Ballyholme 55-90; Can Belf Cathl 76-88; Preb Wicklow St Patr Cathl Dublin 88-90; rtd 90. *6 Hillfoot, Groomsport, Bangor BT19 6JJ* Tel (028) 9147 2979

MERCER, Nicholas Stanley. b 49. Selw Coll Cam BA72 MA76 PGCE73 Spurgeon's Coll BA78 Lon Bible Coll MPhil86. Cranmer Hall Dur 95. **d** 95 **p** 95. C Northwood Hills St Edm *Lon* 95-98; C Pimlico St Mary Bourne Street 98-03; Dir of Min from 03. *20 Collingham Road, London SW5 0LX* Tel (020) 7373 1693 *or* 7932 1100 Mobile 07973-226153 E-mail nick.mercer@london.anglican.org

✠**MERCER, The Rt Revd Robert William Stanley.** b 35. St Paul's Coll Grahamstown LTh59. **d** 59 **p** 60 **c** 77. S Rhodesia 59-63; Lic to Offic *Wakef* 64-66; CR from 65; Perm to Offic *Llan* 66-68; S Africa 68-70; Rhodesia 70-80; Zimbabwe 80-87; Bp Matabeleland 77-87; Canada 87-05; rtd 05. *Flat 4, 48 Manor Road, Worthing BN11 4SH*

MERCER, Timothy James. b 54. Fitzw Coll Cam BA76 MA80. Westcott Ho Cam 78. **d** 81 **p** 82. C Bromley SS Pet and Paul *Roch* 81-85; R Swanscombe 85-96; Chapl Bromley Hosps NHS Trust from 96. *Farnborough Hospital, Farnborough Common, Orpington BR6 8ND* Tel (01689) 814000 *or* 821171

MERCERON, Daniel John. b 58. Lon Univ BA81. Westcott Ho Cam 88. **d** 90 **p** 91. C Clevedon St Jo *B & W* 90-94; CF from 94. *c/o MOD Chaplains (Army)* Tel (01980) 615804 Fax 615800

MERCHANT, Robert Ian. b 73. Keele Univ BA98. Wycliffe Hall Ox BA00. **d** 01 **p** 02. C Harborne Heath *Birm* 01-04; NSM Cheltenham St Mark *Glouc* from 05. *17 Arthur Bliss Gardens, Cheltenham GL50 2LN* Tel (01242) 220190 Mobile 07957-519699 E-mail rob@uk.com

MERCHANT, Mrs Tamsin Laetitia Rachel. b 70. Wycliffe Hall Ox BTh01. **d** 01 **p** 02. C Harborne Heath *Birm* 01-04; Chapl Glos Univ from 04. *17 Arthur Bliss Gardens, Cheltenham GL50 2LN* Tel (01242) 220190 Mobile 07957-519699

MERCURIO, Frank James Charles. b 46. Webster Univ (USA) BA73 MA75. St Alb Minl Tr Scheme 87. **d** 89 **p** 90. C Cheshunt *St Alb* 89-93; TV Hitchin 93-00; RD Hitchin 94-00; TR Tring

from 00. *The Rectory, Church Yard, Tring HP23 5AE* Tel (01442) 822170 Fax 07092-177459
E-mail frankmercurio@dialstart.net

MEREDITH, Andrew James MacPherson. b 59. St Jo Coll Nottm DCM93. **d** 93 **p** 94. C Killay *S & B* 93-97; V Waunarllwydd 97-00; V Swansea St Thos and Kilvey from 00. *The Vicarage, Lewis Street, St Thomas, Swansea SA1 8BP* Tel (01792) 652891

MEREDITH, Ian. b 53. Univ of Wales BA85 Lon Univ MTh89 Edin Univ MTh96. K Coll Lon 86. **d** 02 **p** 03. Assoc Min Dumfries *Glas* from 02. *Skedholm, Greenhill, Lockerbie DG11 1JB* Tel (01387) 810843 E-mail imeredith2001@aol.com

MEREDITH, Robert. b 21. Bps' Coll Cheshunt 56. **d** 58 **p** 59. C Bedford St Andr *St Alb* 58-61; V Luton All SS 61-67; V Kimpton 67-75; RD Wheathampstead 72-76; R Kimpton w Ayot St Lawrence 75-76; R Hunsdon 76-80; R Widford 76-80; R Hunsdon w Widford and Wareside 80-84; P-in-c Braughing, Lt Hadham, Albury, Furneux Pelham etc 84-88; R Braughing w Furneux Pelham and Stocking Pelham 88-90; rtd 90; Perm to Offic *St Alb* 90-97; *Worc* from 98. *57 Ledwych Road, Droitwich WR9 9LA* Tel (01905) 797568

MEREDITH, Canon Roland Evan. b 32. Trin Coll Cam BA55 MA59. Cuddesdon Coll 55. **d** 57 **p** 58. C Bishopwearmouth St Mich *Dur* 57-59; Dioc Chapl *Birm* 59-60; C Kirkby *Liv* 60-63; V Hitchin St Mary *St Alb* 63-72; V Preston St Jo *Blackb* 72-76; TR 76-79; RD Preston 72-79; Hon Can Blackb Cathl 77-79; TR Witney *Ox* 79-94; P-in-c Hailey w Crawley 79-82; RD Witney 89-97; Hon Can Ch Ch 92-97; rtd 94; Perm to Offic *Ox* from 97; *Eur* from 98; *Glouc* from 03. *12 Clover Place, Eynsham, Witney OX29 4QL* Tel (01865) 880210

MEREDITH-JONES, Richard. b 26. JP79. K Coll Lon 50. **d** 54 **p** 55. C Perry Hill St Geo *S'wark* 54-56; P-in-c New Charlton H Trin 56-58; V Cinderford St Jo *Glouc* 58-62; Chapl Dilke Hosp Cinderford 58-62; V Richmond St Jo *S'wark* 62-66; Chapl Royal Hosp Richmond 62-66; Ind Chapl *Wakef* 66-70; Chapl Glenside Hosp Bris from 70; Perm to Offic *Glouc* 70-88; CF (TAVR) 78-91; Perm to Offic *Ban* 88-93; rtd 91; Perm to Offic *St D* and *B & W* from 91. *18 Wetlands Lane, Portishead, Bristol BS20 6RA* Tel (01275) 817217

MERIVALE, Charles Christian Robert. b 44. Cranmer Hall Dur 76. **d** 78 **p** 79. C Highbury Ch Ch w St Jo *Lon* 78-81; P-in-c Hawes *Ripon* 81-82; P-in-c Hardrow and St Jo w Lunds 81-82; V Hawes and Hardraw 82-84; Chapl R Cornwall Hosps Trust 85-92; Perm to Offic *B & W* 92-00; *Ex* 00-02; TV Shebbear, Buckland Filleigh, Sheepwash etc *Ex* from 02. *The Rectory, Petrockstowe, Okehampton EX20 3HQ* Tel (01837) 810499 *or* 08454-589942 E-mail christian@phonebox50.co.uk

MERRICK, Canon John. b 51. New Univ of Ulster BA72 DipAdEd75 TCD HDipEd73. CITC 89. **d** 92 **p** 93. Hd Master Sligo Gr Sch from 86; Lic to Offic *K, E & A* from 92; Preb Elphin Cathl from 01. *Pier Lodge, Dunfanaghy PO, Letterkenny, Co Donegal, Irish Republic* Tel and fax (00353) (74) 913 6971 Mobile 87-227 4978

MERRIMAN, Stephen Richard. b 74. Leeds Univ BA02. Coll of Resurr Mirfield 99. **d** 02 **p** 03. C Littlehampton and Wick *Chich* from 02. *95 The Winter Knoll, Littlehampton BN17 6NQ* Tel (01903) 733618

MERRINGTON, Canon Bill. b 55. Sheff Hallam Univ BSc78 Birm Univ MPhil95 Warwick Univ PhD03. Cranmer Hall Dur 80. **d** 83 **p** 84. C Harborne Heath *Birm* 83-88; V Leamington Priors St Paul *Cov* 88-99; RD Warwick and Leamington 97-99; R Ilmington w Stretton-on-Fosse etc from 99; RD Shipston 99-03; Hon Can Cov Cathl from 01. *The Rectory, Valenders Lane, Ilmington, Shipston-on-Stour CV36 4LB* Tel and fax (01608) 682210 E-mail billmerri@aol.com

MERRY, David Thomas (Tom). b 48. St Chad's Coll Dur BA70. AKC73. **d** 74 **p** 75. C Cirencester *Glouc* 74-78; TV Bridgnorth, Tasley, Astley Abbotts and Oldbury *Heref* 78-83; P-in-c Quatford 81-83; P-in-c Stroud H Trin *Glouc* 83-87; V 87-01; Chapl Stroud Gen Hosp 83-93; Chapl Severn NHS Trust 93-01; Chapl Cheltenham Ladies' Coll from 01. *The Cheltenham Ladies' College, Bayshill Road, Cheltenham GL50 3EP* Tel (01242) 520691

MERRY, Ivor John. b 28. WMMTC 84. **d** 87 **p** 88. NSM Redditch, The Ridge *Worc* 87-94; NSM Astwood Bank 94-98; Perm to Offic from 98. *186 Moorcroft Gardens, Redditch B97 5WQ*

MERRY, Rex Edwin. b 38. AKC67. **d** 68 **p** 69. C Spalding St Jo *Linc* 68-73; C Boxmoor St Jo *St Alb* 73-83; TV Hemel Hempstead 83-95; V Farley Hill St Jo from 95. *The Vicarage, 47 Rotherham Avenue, Luton LU1 5PP* Tel (01582) 729466

MERRY, Thomas. *See* MERRY, David Thomas

MERRYWEATHER, Mrs Rosalynd. b 50. Hull Coll of Educn CertEd72. NEOC. **d** 00 **p** 01. NSM Beverley St Nic *York* from 00. *10 West Close, Beverley HU17 7JJ* Tel (01482) 867958

MESLEY, Mark Terence. b 59. Plymouth Poly BSc88. St Steph Ho Ox 98. **d** 00 **p** 01. C Bickleigh and Shaugh Prior *Ex* 00-03; P-in-c Llanhilleth *Mon* from 03. *The Rectory, Pendarren Road, Aberbeeg, Abertillery NP13 2DA* Tel (01495) 214236
E-mail mesleyrev@eurobell.co.uk

MESSAM, Paul James. b 65. Lon Coll of Printing BA87. Cranmer Hall Dur 01. **d** 03 **p** 04. C Market Harborough and The Transfiguration etc *Leic* from 03. *69 Tymecrosse Gardens, Market Harborough LE16 7US* Tel (01858) 463062 Mobile 07711-098209 E-mail paul.messam@virgin.net

MESSENGER, Paul. b 38. Univ of Wales (Lamp) BA63. Coll of Resurr Mirfield 63. **d** 65 **p** 66. C Battersea St Luke *S'wark* 65-69; C Ainsdale *Liv* 69-71; V Wigan St Steph 71-74; Asst Chapl St Marg Convent E Grinstead 74-76; Chapl Kingsley St Mich Sch W Sussex 74-76; P-in-c Southwater *Chich* 76-81; V 81-97; R Sullington and Thakeham w Warminghurst from 97. *The Rectory, Thakeham, Pulborough RH20 3EP* Tel (01798) 813121

MESSENGER, Canon Reginald James. b 13. Univ Coll Dur LTh38 BA39 MA57. St Aug Coll Cant 35. **d** 39 **p** 40. C E Dulwich St Jo *S'wark* 39-42; Miss India 43-64; V Sturminster Newton and Hinton St Mary *Sarum* 65-68; Miss India 68-80; rtd 80; Perm to Offic *Chich* from 80. *Flat 3, 46 Norfolk Road, Littlehampton BN17 5HE* Tel (01903) 714113

MESSER, David Harry. b 61. MCIH93. EAMTC 01. **d** 04 **p** 05. C Stanton, Hopton, Market Weston, Barningham etc *St E* from 04. *5 St Andrews Close, Barningham, Bury St Edmunds IP31 1EQ* Tel (01359) 242041
E-mail david@dmesser.freeserve.co.uk

MESSHAM, Mrs Barbara Lynn. b 52. Bretton Hall Coll CertEd75. STETS DipTh99. **d** 99 **p** 00. C The Bourne and Tilford *Guildf* 99-03; V Guildf All SS from 03. *All Saints' Vicarage, 18 Vicarage Gate, Guildford GU2 7QJ* Tel (01483) 572006 Mobile 07932-615132
E-mail barbara@messhams.co.uk

METCALF, Preb Michael Ralph. b 37. Clare Coll Cam BA61 MA65 Birm Univ MA80. Ridley Hall Cam 63. **d** 64 **p** 65. C Downend *Bris* 64-67; Perm to Offic *Birm* 68-78; Perm to Offic *Lich* 72-81; Dioc Dir of Educn 83-94; Perm to Offic *Heref* from 87; Preb Lich Cathl *Lich* from 91; V Stafford St Paul Forebridge from 94; RD Stafford from 00. *St Paul's Vicarage, 31 The Oval, Stafford ST17 4LQ* Tel (01785) 251683 Fax 600260
E-mail prebmetcalf@hotmail.com *or* berylm@ntlworld.com

METCALF, The Ven Robert Laurence. b 35. Dur Univ BA60. Cranmer Hall Dur. **d** 62 **p** 63. C Bootle Ch Ch *Liv* 62-65; C Farnworth 65-67; V Wigan St Cath 67-75; R Wavertree H Trin 75-94; Chapl Blue Coat Sch Liv 75-94; Dir of Ords *Liv* 82-94; Hon Can Liv Cathl 87-02; Adn Liv 94-02; rtd 02; P-in-c Garston *Liv* from 04. *32 Storrsdale Road, Liverpool L18 7JZ* Tel 0151-724 3956 Fax 729 0587 E-mail bobmetcalf@ukgateway.net

METCALFE, Alan. b 22. St Aid Birkenhead 49. **d** 52 **p** 53. C Cleckheaton St Jo *Wakef* 52-55; C Todmorden 55-56; C Thornhill Lees 56-58; V Middlestown 58-60; V S Crosland 60-64; V Upwood w Gt and Lt Raveley *Ely* 64-69; Chapl RAF 64-68; V Dewsbury St Matt and St Jo *Wakef* 69-71; Warden Bridgehead Hostel Cardiff 71-73; Field View Hostel Stoke Prior 73-75; McIntyre Ho Nuneaton 75-79; C Southam w Stockton *Cov* 79-84; P-in-c Kinwarton w Gt Alne and Haselor 84-87; rtd 87; Hon C Yarcombe w Membury and Upottery *Ex* 89-92; Perm to Offic *St E* from 92. *3 Mays Court, Garrison Road, Felixstowe IP11 7ST* Tel (01394) 271665

METCALFE, Bernard. *See* METCALFE, William Bernard

METCALFE, James. b 17. St Pet Hall Ox BA39 MA44. Wycliffe Hall Ox 39. **d** 41 **p** 42. C Dartford Ch Ch *Roch* 41-43; CF (EC) 43-47; C Goole *Sheff* 47-49; V Batley St Thos *Wakef* 49-55; V Mexborough *Sheff* 55-71; R Wickersley 71-82; rtd 82; Perm to Offic *Bradf* 83-99 and from 03. *Scar Fields, The Mains, Giggleswick, Settle BD24 0AX* Tel (01729) 823983

METCALFE, Reginald Herbert. b 38. **d** 79. Hon C Aspley Guise *St Alb* 79; Hon C Aspley Guise w Husborne Crawley and Ridgmont 80-84; Hon C Bovingdon 84-03; Perm to Offic from 03. *30 Manorville Road, Hemel Hempstead HP3 0AP* Tel (01442) 242952 Fax 213137

METCALFE, Canon Ronald. b 41. BA. Edin Th Coll 67. **d** 69 **p** 70. C Saltburn-by-the-Sea *York* 69-72; P-in-c Crathorne 73-77; Youth Officer 73-77; Dioc Adult Tr Officer 78-88; Can Res York Minster 88-00; Sec for Miss and Min 88-00; V Kendal H Trin *Carl* from 00. *Holy Trinity Vicarage, 2 Lynngarth Drive, Kendal LA9 4JA* Tel (01539) 721541 *or* 721248 Fax 737506
E-mail ronald.metcalfe@ukonline.co.uk

METCALFE, William Bernard. b 47. St Jo Coll Cam BA69 MA73 Ball Coll Ox BA71. Ripon Hall Ox 70. **d** 72 **p** 73. C Caversham *Ox* 72-75; C Aylesbury 75-79; Ind Chapl 75-79; TV Thamesmead *S'wark* 79-84; TR Totton *Win* 84-94; R Gt Bentley and Frating w Thorrington *Chelmsf* from 94; RD St Osyth from 00. *The Rectory, Moors Close, Great Bentley, Colchester CO7 8QL* Tel (01206) 250476
E-mail wellmet@netcomuk.co.uk

METHUEN, Charlotte Mary. b 64. Girton Coll Cam BA85 MA89 New Coll Edin BD91 PhD95. Edin Th Coll 87. **d** 98 **p** 99. C E Netherlands *Eur* 98-01; C Bonn w Cologne 01-03; Hon Asst

Chapl from 03; Dioc Dir of Tr 03-05. *Lotharstrasse 8, 45131 Essen, Germany* Tel (0049) (201) 425660 Fax 423834 E-mail charlotte.methuen@ruhr-uni-bochum.de

METHUEN, The Very Revd John Alan Robert. b 47. BNC Ox BA69 MA74. Cuddesdon Coll 69. **d** 71 **p** 72. C Fenny Stratford *Ox* 71-73; C Fenny Stratford and Water Eaton 74; Asst Chapl Eton Coll 74-77; P-in-c Dorney *Ox* 74-77; Warden Dorney/Eton Coll Conf Cen 74-77; V Reading St Mark 77-83; R Hulme Ascension *Man* 83-95; Dean Ripon from 95. *The Minster House, Ripon HG4 1PE* Tel (01765) 603615 *or* 603462 Fax 690530 E-mail deanjohn@riponcathedral.org.uk

METHVEN, Alexander George. b 26. Lon Univ BD52 Em Coll Cam BA54 MA58. ACT ThL47 Lon Coll of Div 50. **d** 52 **p** 53. C Cambridge St Andr Less *Ely* 52-54; Chapl RAF 55-60; V Lower Sydenham St Mich *S'wark* 60-67; Australia from 68; rtd 91. *PO Box 494, Belgrave, Vic, Australia 3160* Tel (0061) (3) 9754 8056 E-mail agmethven@hotmail.com

METIVIER, Canon Robert John. b 31. Lon Univ BA68. Lambeth STh61 Ch Div Sch of the Pacific (USA) BD66 MDiv69 Codrington Coll Barbados 56. **d** 60 **p** 61. Trinidad and Tobago 61-64 and 68-78; USPG 66-67; C Gt Berkhamsted *St Alb* 78-82; V Goff's Oak St Jas 82-90; V Tokyngton St Mich *Lon* 90-01; Hon Can Trinidad from 98; rtd 01; Perm to Offic *Lon* from 02. *17 Willowcourt Avenue, Kenton, Harrow HA3 8ET* Tel (020) 8909 1371

METTERS, Anthony John Francis. b 43. AKC65. **d** 68 **p** 69. C Heavitree *Ex* 68-74; V Plymouth Crownhill Ascension 74-79; RD Plymouth 77-79; Chapl RN 79-99; rtd 99. *Knightshayes, 1 De Port Heights, Corhampton, Southampton SO32 3DA*

METZNER (née JEFFREY), Mrs Katrina. b 73. St Jo Coll Ox BA96 MA01. St Steph Ho Ox 97. **d** 99 **p** 00. C Glouc St Geo w Whaddon *Glouc* 99-00; C Parkstone St Pet and St Osmund w Branksea *Sarum* 00-04. *All Saints' Vicarage, 84 Franciscan Road, London SW17 8DQ* Tel (020) 8672 3706

METZNER, Simon David. b 64. Magd Coll Ox BA85 K Coll Lon MA95 St Luke's Coll Ex PGCE93. St Steph Ho Ox. **d** 00 **p** 01. C Branksome St Aldhelm *Sarum* 00-04; V Tooting All SS *S'wark* from 04. *All Saints' Vicarage, 84 Franciscan Road, London SW17 8DQ* Tel (020) 8672 3706 E-mail simon.metzner@ntlworld.com

MEWIS, Canon David William. b 47. Leeds Inst of Educn CertEd68 Leeds Poly BEd83. N Ord Course 87. **d** 90 **p** 91. C Skipton Ch Ch *Bradf* 90-92; R Bolton by Bowland w Grindleton from 92; RD Bowland from 99; Hon Can Bradf Cathl from 00. *The Rectory, Sawley Road, Grindleton, Clitheroe BB7 4QS* Tel (01200) 441154 E-mail dwm@dmewis.freeserve.co.uk

MEWS, Stuart Paul. b 44. Leeds Univ BA64 MA67 Trin Hall Cam PhD74 FRHistS75. Westcott Ho Cam 86. **d** 87 **p** 88. Lect Lanc Univ 68-92; NSM Caton w Littledale *Blackb* 87-90; Hon C Lancaster St Mary 88-92; Reader RS Cheltenham and Glouc Coll of HE 92-00; Acting P-in-c Croxton and Eltisley *Ely* 97-98; P-in-c Tilbrook 00-03; P-in-c Covington 00-03; P-in-c Catworth Magna 00-03; P-in-c Keyston and Bythorn 00-03; P-in-c Tilbrook from 00; P-in-c Keyston and Bythorn from 00; P-in-c Catworth Magna from 00; P-in-c Covington from 00. *The Rectory, Church Lane, Tilbrook, Huntingdon PE28 0JS* Tel (01480) 860147

MEYER, Donovan Candido. b 60. **d** 91 **p** 91. S Africa 91-03; TV Oldham *Man* from 03. *Holy Trinity Vicarage, 46 Godson Street, Oldham OL1 2DB* Tel 0161-627 1640 E-mail donnymeyer15@hotmail.com

MEYER, Stuart Thomas. b 45. Open Univ BA85 GLCM69. Trin Coll Bris 76. **d** 78 **p** 79. C Heref St Pet w St Owen *Heref* 78-79; C Heref St Pet w St Owen and St Jas 79-80; Chapl K Coll Cam 80-84; Chapl Lon Univ Medical Schs *S'wark* 84-87; Hon C Streatham St Pet from 87; Chapl Dulwich Hosp 87-93; Chapl Camberwell Distr HA 90-93; Chapl K Coll Hosp Lon 90-93; Sen Chapl King's Coll Hosp NHS Trust from 93. *The Chaplain's Office, King's College Hospital, Denmark Hill, London SE5 9RS* Tel (020) 7346 3522 E-mail stuart.meyer@kingsch.nhs.uk

MEYER, William John. b 46. ACIB. Cranmer Hall Dur 83. **d** 85 **p** 86. C Merrow *Guildf* 85-89; V Grayshott 89-98; R Binfield *Ox* from 98. *The Rectory, Terrace Road North, Bracknell RG12 5JG* Tel and fax (01344) 454406 E-mail bill@bmeyer.freeserve.co.uk

MEYNELL, Canon Andrew Francis. b 43. Westcott Ho Cam 70. **d** 73 **p** 74. C Cowley St Jas *Ox* 73-79; TV 79-81; P-in-c Halton 81-95; V Wendover 81-95; P-in-c Monks Risborough 95-98; TV Risborough from 98; Dir Ords Bucks Adnry from 95; Hon Can Ch Ch from 01. *The Rectory, Mill Lane, Monks Risborough, Princes Risborough HP27 9JE* Tel and fax (01844) 342556 E-mail andrew.meynell@oxford.anglican.org

MEYNELL, Mrs Honor Mary. b 37. EMMTC 84. **d** 87 **p** 94. NSM Kirk Langley *Derby* 87-03; NSM Mackworth All SS 87-03; NSM Mugginton and Kedleston 87-03; rtd 04. *The Coachman's Cottage, Meynell Langley, Kirk Langley, Ashbourne DE6 4NT* Tel (01332) 824207

MEYNELL, Canon Mark. b 14. Ch Ch Ox BA37 MA44. Cuddesdon Coll. **d** 40 **p** 41. C St Alb Abbey *St Alb* 40-46; R Folkington *Chich* 46-49; R Marlesford *St E* 49-56; R Campsey Ashe 51-56; R Cogenhoe *Pet* 56-63; V Leamington Hastings *Cov* 65-79; R Birdingbury 74-79; Can Th Cov Cathl 73-78; rtd 79; Perm to Offic *St E* 80-98. *2 Double Street, Framlingham, Woodbridge IP13 9BN* Tel (01728) 723898

MEYNELL, Mark John Henrik. b 70. New Coll Ox MA93. Ridley Hall Cam MA95. **d** 97 **p** 98. C Fulwood *Sheff* 97-01; Kampala Evang Sch of Th Uganda 01-05; C Langham Place All So *Lon* from 05. *2 St Paul's Court, 56 Manchester Street, London W1U 3AF* Tel (020) 7486 0006 E-mail mark.meynell@allsouls.org

MEYRICK, The Very Revd Cyril Jonathan. b 52. St Jo Coll Ox BA73 MA77. Sarum & Wells Th Coll 74. **d** 76 **p** 77. C Bicester *Ox* 76-78; Bp's Dom Chapl 78-81; Barbados 81-84; TV Burnham w Dropmore, Hitcham and Taplow *Ox* 84-90; TR Tisbury *Sarum* 90-98; Link Officer Black Anglican Concerns 90-98; RD Chalke 97-98; Can Res Roch Cathl *Roch* 98-05; Dean Ex from 05. *The Deanery, Cathedral Close, Exeter EX1 1HT* Tel (01392) 272697 E-mail dean@exeter-cathedral.org.uk

MEYRICK, Thomas Henry Corfe. b 67. Magd Coll Ox BA88 MA92. St Steph Ho Ox BA94. **d** 95 **p** 96. C Bierley *Bradf* 95-99; Chapl Oriel Coll Ox 99-04; P-in-c Ox St Thos w St Frideswide and Binsey *Ox* from 04. *Oriel College, Oxford OX1 4EW* Tel (01865) 276582 *or* 276555 E-mail tom.meyrick@oriel.ox.ac.uk

MIALL, Peter Brian. b 30. Scawsby Coll of Educn TCert69. **d** 89 **p** 89. Hon C Bolsterstone *Sheff* 89-98; Perm to Offic from 98. *Waldershaigh Cottage, Heads Lane, Bolsterstone, Sheffield S36 3ZH* Tel 0114-288 5558

MICHAEL, Canon Ian MacRae. b 40. Aber Univ MA62 Hertf Coll Ox DPhil66. Westcott Ho Cam 77. **d** 79 **p** 80. C Kings Heath *Birm* 79-82; Vice-Provost St Paul's Cathl Dundee *Bre* 82-88; V Harborne St Faith and St Laur *Birm* 88-03; RD Edgbaston 91-98; Hon Can Birm Cathl 00-03; rtd 03. *46 Argyle Court, St Andrews KY16 9BW* Tel (01334) 473901

MICHAEL, Stephen David. b 71. Ripon Coll Cuddesdon 01. **d** 03 **p** 04. C St Blazey *Truro* from 03; C Tywardreath w Tregaminion from 03; C Lanlivery w Luxulyan from 03. *4 Churchfield Place, Fore Street, St Blazey PL24 2NT* Tel (01726) 815669 E-mail sd.michael@tiscali.co.uk

MICHAELS, David Albert Emmanuel. b 49. Bede Coll Dur BA72 Barrister-at-Law (Inner Temple) 73. Westcott Ho Cam 86. **d** 88 **p** 89. C Hampstead St Jo *Lon* 88-91; TV Wolvercote w Summertown *Ox* 91-04; P-in-c Launceston *Truro* from 04. *The Rectory, Dunheved Road, Launceston PL15 9JE* Tel (01566) 772101 E-mail david.michaels@dunelm.org.uk

MICHELL, Canon Douglas Reginald. b 19. St Jo Coll Dur BA41 MA44. Westcott Ho Cam 41. **d** 43 **p** 44. C Wanstead H Trin Hermon Hill *Chelmsf* 43-45; Chapl St Jo Coll Dur 45-48; Lic to Offic *Dur* 45-48; R Moss Side St Jas *Man* 48-53; V Horwich H Trin 53-61; V Evington *Leic* 61-80; Hon Can Leic Cathl 67-84; RD Christianity N 74-79; V Billesdon w Goadby and Rolleston 80-82; RD Gartree I 81-84; V Billesdon and Skeffington 82-84; rtd 85; Perm to Offic *St Alb* 85-97 and *Chich* from 97. *9 Ramsay Hall, 11-13 Byron Road, Worthing BN11 3HN* Tel (01903) 207294

MICHELL, Francis Richard Noel. b 42. St Cath Coll Cam BA64 MA68. Tyndale Hall Bris 64. **d** 66 **p** 67. C Northampton St Giles *Pet* 66-69; C Gateacre *Liv* 69-72; V Litherland St Paul Hatton Hill 72-79; V Rainhill 79-88; V Rainford from 88. *The Vicarage, Church Road, Rainford, St Helens WA11 8HD* Tel (01744) 882200

MICKLETHWAITE, Andrew Quentin. b 67. Univ Coll Dur BA89. Trin Coll Bris BA94. **d** 94 **p** 95. C Abington *Pet* 94-97; TV Duston Team 97-04; V Castle Donington and Lockington cum Hemington *Leic* from 04. *The Vicarage, 6 Delven Lane, Castle Donington, Derby DE74 2LJ* Tel (01332) 810364 E-mail andrew@duston.org.uk

MICKLETHWAITE, Mrs Dorothy Eileen. b 41. St Alb and Ox Min Course 98. **d** 01 **p** 02. NSM Helmdon w Stuchbury and Radstone etc *Pet* 01-03; NSM Astwell Gp from 03; Asst Chapl Ox Radcliffe Hosps NHS Trust from 02; Perm to Offic *Ox* from 02. *54 Stuart Road, Brackley NN13 6HZ* Tel (01280) 703697 E-mail dorothymick@aol.com

MICKLETHWAITE, Jane Catherine. b 56. Lanc Univ BSc78. Trin Coll Bris 92. **d** 95 **p** 96. C Kings Heath *Pet* 95-98; Chapl Nene Coll of HE Northn 97-98; Perm to Offic *Pet* 98-01; NSM Kings Heath 01-04. *The Vicarage, 6 Delven Lane, Castle Donington, Derby DE74 2LJ* Tel (01332) 810364 E-mail j.micklethwaite@talk21.com

MICKLETHWAITE, Peter William. b 62. Peterho Cam BA84 MA88. St Jo Coll Nottm DipTh89 DPS90. **d** 90 **p** 91. C Leatherhead *Guildf* 90-93; C Wisley w Pyrford 93-97; R Windlesham from 97. *The Rectory, Kennel Lane, Windlesham GU20 6AA* Tel and fax (01276) 472363 E-mail rector@windleshamchurch.org.uk

MIDDLEBROOK, Bryan. b 33. Dur Univ BA55 DipEd58 Newc Univ MEd74. NEOC 85. **d** 88 **p** 88. NSM Dur St Cuth *Dur* 88-99; NSM Witton Gilbert 97-99. *5 Fieldhouse Terrace, Durham DH1 4NA* Tel 0191-386 6665

MIDDLEBROOK, David John. b 61. Newc Univ BSc83 Cranfield Inst of Tech MSc85. Trin Coll Bris BA98. **d** 98 **p** 99. C

Chorleywood Ch Ch *St Alb* 98-02; TV Hemel Hempstead from 02. *St Barnabas Vicarage, Everest Way, Hemel Hempstead HP2 4HY* Tel (01442) 253681
E-mail dave.middlebrook@btinternet.com

MIDDLEDITCH, Terry Gordon. b 30. Univ of Wales (Lamp) BA62 St Martin's Coll Lanc PGCE68. St D Coll Lamp 59. **d** 63 **p** 64. C Poulton-le-Fylde *Blackb* 63-65; C-in-c Heysham 65-67; Sch Master 68-88; Hon C Cheltenham St Pet *Glouc* 75-87; Hon C Badgeworth w Shurdington 75-87; Hon C Up Hatherley 75-87; C Poulton-le-Sands w Morecambe St Laur *Blackb* 88-91; V Stalmine 91-00; rtd 00; Perm to Offic *Blackb* from 00. *93 Thornton Road, Morecambe LA4 5PG* Tel (01524) 413378 Mobile 07879-426173

MIDDLEMISS, Fritha Leonora. b 47. Man Univ BA68 CertEd69. Glouc Sch of Min 86. **d** 89 **p** 94. NSM Bengeworth *Worc* 89-94; NSM Stoulton w Drake's Broughton and Pirton etc 94-96; Chapl Malvern Girls' Coll 96-03; Asst Chapl HM Pris Long Lartin from 03. *HM Prison Long Lartin, South Littleton, Evesham WR11 8TZ* Tel (01386) 835100

MIDDLEMISS, Jeffrey Thomas. b 50. Padgate Coll of Educn BEd79 Edge Hill Coll of HE DASE85. N Ord Course 87. **d** 90 **p** 91. C Gateacre *Liv* 90-93; V W Derby Gd Shep 93-94; V Wigan St Cath 94-00; TV Leominster *Heref* from 01. *The New Vicarage, Kimbolton, Leominster HR6 0EJ* Tel (01568) 615295
E-mail jeff_middlemiss@lineone.net

MIDDLEMISS, Mrs Justine. b 68. Aston Univ BSc90. Ripon Coll Cuddesdon 00. **d** 02 **p** 03. C Lee St Marg *S'wark* from 02. *55 Longhurst Road, London SE13 5NA* Tel (020) 8318 6875
E-mail gandj@fish.co.uk

MIDDLESEX, Archdeacon of. *Vacant*

MIDDLETON, Alan Derek. b 46. St Jo Coll Dur BA68 MA85 Bris Univ PGCE70 Sheff Univ MMin00. Qu Coll Birm. **d** 72 **p** 73. C Cannock *Lich* 72-76; Warden St Helen's Youth & Community Cen Bp Auckd 76-79; V Darlington St Jo *Dur* 79-89; TR E Darlington 89-90; V Upper Norwood All SS *S'wark* 90-99; TR Warlingham w Chelsham and Farleigh from 99; Bp's Ecum Adv from 96; AD Caterham from 05. *The Rectory, 35 Dane Road, Warlingham CR6 9NP* Tel (01883) 624125 Fax 624490 E-mail alan.middleton@southwark.anglican.org

MIDDLETON, Arthur. *See* MIDDLETON, Canon Thomas Arthur

MIDDLETON, Barry Glen. b 41. Lich Th Coll 68. **d** 70 **p** 71. C Westhoughton *Man* 70-73; C Prestwich St Marg 73-74; TV Buxton w Burbage and King Sterndale *Derby* 74-77; Chapl Worc R Infirmary 77-83; Chapl Fairfield Hosp Hitchin 83-85; P-in-c Erpingham w Calthorpe *Nor* 85-86; R Erpingham w Calthorpe, Ingworth, Aldborough etc 86-92; R Badingham w Bruisyard, Cransford and Dennington *St E* 92-96; V Sidcup St Jo *Roch* 96-98; V Gt and Lt Bardfield w Gt and Lt Saling *Chelmsf* 98-00; rtd 00; Perm to Offic *St E* from 00. *20 Lynwood Avenue, Felixstowe IP11 9HS* Tel (01394) 286506

MIDDLETON, David Jeremy. b 68. Ex Univ BSc90. Wycliffe Hall Ox 01. **d** 03 **p** 04. C Ipswich St Jo *St E* from 03. *2A Norbury Road, Ipswich IP4 4RQ* Tel (01473) 710025

MIDDLETON, Hugh Charles. b 50. Nottm Univ BTh77. Linc Th Coll 73. **d** 77 **p** 78. C New Sleaford *Linc* 77-81; C Grantham 81; TV 81-83; R Caythorpe 83-95; P-in-c Bracebridge Heath 97-00; V from 00. *The Vicarage, 11 Salisbury Drive, Bracebridge Heath, Lincoln LN4 2SW* Tel (01522) 540460

MIDDLETON, Canon Kenneth Frank. b 28. Keble Coll Ox BA52 MA64. St Steph Ho Ox 52. **d** 55 **p** 56. C Leic St Matt *Leic* 55-58; C W Hackney St Barn *Lon* 58-60; V Leic St Matt and St Geo *Leic* 60-82; RD Christianity N 79-82; P-in-c Leic St Alb 80-82; Hon Can Leic Cathl 80-82; P-in-c Belgrave St Mich 81-82; TR Bridgnorth, Tasley, Astley Abbotts, etc *Heref* 82-87; P-in-c Quatford 83; RD Bridgnorth 83-87; TR Littleham w Exmouth *Ex* 87-99; Chapl Ex and Distr Community Health Service NHS Trust 87-99; rtd 99; Perm to Offic *Ex* from 99. *15 Strawberry Hill, Lympstone, Exmouth EX8 5JZ* Tel (01395) 263804

MIDDLETON, Canon Michael John. b 40. Dur Univ BSc62 Fitzw Ho Cam BA66 MA70. Westcott Ho Cam 63. **d** 66 **p** 67. C Newc St Geo *Newc* 66-69; V 77-85; Chapl St Geo Gr Sch Cape Town 69-72; Chapl K Sch Tynemouth 72-77; R Hexham *Newc* 85-92; Hon Can Newc Cathl 90-92; Adn Swindon *Bris* 92-97; Can and Treas Westmr Abbey 97-04; rtd 04. *37 High Fellside, Kendal LA9 4JG* Tel (01539) 729320

MIDDLETON, Rodney. b 54. St Andr Univ BD80. St Steph Ho Ox 80. **d** 82 **p** 83. C Walton St Mary *Liv* 82-87; C-in-c Kew St Fran CD 87-94; V Kew 94-95; Chapl Southport and Formby Distr Gen Hosp 87-95; V Haydock St Jas from 95. *The Vicarage, 169 Church Road, Haydock, St Helens WA11 0NJ* Tel (01942) 727956 E-mail rodmid@blueyonder.co.uk

MIDDLETON, Canon Thomas Arthur. b 36. Dur Univ MLitt95 FRHistS04. K Coll Lon AKC61 St Boniface Warminster 61. **d** 62 **p** 63. C Sunderland *Dur* 62-63; C Auckland St Helen 63-67; C Winlaton 67-70; C-in-c Pennywell St Thos and Grindon St Oswald CD 70-79; Chapl Grindon Hall Hosp 73-79; R Boldon 79-03; Adv in Stewardship Dur Adnry 87-92; Acting Prin St Chad's Coll Dur 97; Hon Can Dur Cathl *Dur* 98-03; rtd 03. *1 St Mary's Drive, Sherburn, Durham DH6 1RL* Tel 0191-372 3436
E-mail thomas@thomas.middleton.wanadoo.co.uk

MIDDLETON-DANSKY, Serge Wladimir. b 45. Cuddesdon Coll 74. **d** 77 **p** 78. C Wisbech SS Pet and Paul *Ely* 77-79; Lic to Offic Adnry Riviera *Eur* from 80; C Ox St Giles and SS Phil and Jas w St Marg *Ox* 83-86; Perm to Offic *Ox* 86-88 and *Truro* 88-90; P-in-c Zennor and Towednack *Truro* 90-96; Perm to Offic 97-99; Lic to Offic from 99. *The Old Vicarage, Zennor, St Ives TR26 3BY* Tel (01736) 796955

MIDDLETON, Suffragan Bishop of. *See* LEWIS, The Rt Revd Michael Augustine Owen

MIDDLEWICK, Robert James. b 44. K Alfred's Coll Win CertEd67 Lon Univ BD76. Ripon Coll Cuddesdon 75. **d** 77 **p** 78. C Bromley SS Pet and Paul *Roch* 77-81; C Belvedere All SS 81-84; P-in-c Lamberhurst 85-88; P-in-c Matfield 85-88; V Lamberhurst and Matfield 88-99. *12 Mill Stream Place, Tonbridge TN9 1QJ* Tel (01580) 212054

MIDGLEY, George William. b 38. N Ord Course. **d** 83 **p** 84. C Penistone and Thurlstone *Wakef* 88-89; TV 89-94; TR 94-04; rtd 04. *20 Smithies Moor Lane, Batley WF17 9AR* Tel (01924) 472289

MIDGLEY, Stephen Nicholas. b 60. Jes Coll Cam BA83 MA86 Lon Hosp MB, BS86. Wycliffe Hall Ox. **d** 97 **p** 98. C Hove Bp Hannington Memorial Ch *Chich* 97-01; C Cambridge H Sepulchre *Ely* 01-04; P-in-c Cambridge St Andr Less from 04. *St Andrew the Less Vicarage, Parsonage Street, Cambridge CB5 8DN* Tel (01223) 353794 E-mail steve.midgley@stag.org

MIDLANE, Colin John. b 50. Qu Mary Coll Lon BA72. Westcott Ho Cam 73 Sarum & Wells Th Coll 77. **d** 78 **p** 79. C Bethnal Green St Pet w St Thos *Lon* 78-82; P-in-c Haggerston All SS 82-88; Chapl Hengrave Hall Ecum Cen 88-89; P Cllr St Botolph Aldgate *Lon* 89-94; C St Botolph Aldgate w H Trin Minories 93-94; TV Haywards Heath St Wilfrid *Chich* 94-97; C Brighton St Geo w St Anne and St Mark 97-01; Chapl Brighton and Sussex Univ Hosps NHS Trust 01-03; rtd 03. *30 Damien Court, Damien Street, London E1 2HL* Tel (020) 7791 0001

MIDWINTER, Sister Josie Isabel. b 46. Open Univ BA84 Univ of Wales (Lamp) MA98. CA Tr Coll IDC71. **d** 87 **p** 99. CA from 71; CMS 84-93; Uganda 85-91; Kenya 92-96; C Didcot All SS *Ox* 98-05; P-in-c Drayton St Pet (Berks) from 05. *The Vicarage, Gravel Lane, Drayton, Abingdon OX14 4HY* Tel (01235) 531374

MIDWOOD, Peter Stanley. b 47. CertEd69. Linc Th Coll 80. **d** 82 **p** 83. C Garforth *Ripon* 82-85; C-in-c Grinton w Arkengarthdale, Downholme and Marske 85-86; C-in-c Melbecks and Muker 85-86; V Swaledale 86-97; AD Richmond from 97; R Romaldkirk w Laithkirk from 97. *The Rectory, Romaldkirk, Barnard Castle DL12 9EE* Tel (01833) 650202
E-mail ps.midwood@virgin.net

MIELL, David Keith. b 57. BSc PhD BA. Westcott Ho Cam 83. **d** 86 **p** 87. C Blackbird Leys CD *Ox* 86-89; C Walton 89-90; TV Walton Milton Keynes 90-96; RD Milton Keynes 93-95; TR Upton cum Chalvey from 96; AD Burnham and Slough from 02. *The Rectory, 18 Albert Street, Slough SL1 2BU* Tel (01753) 529988 E-mail drdmiell@surfaid.org

MIER, Ms Catherine Elizabeth. b 60. Bris Univ BSc81 Chelsea Coll Lon MSc84 Dur Univ BA95. Cranmer Hall Dur 93. **d** 96 **p** 97. C Royston *St Alb* 96-00; C Bilton *Cov* 00-04; P-in-c Wellesbourne from 04; P-in-c Walton d'Eiville from 04. *The Vicarage, Church Street, Wellesbourne, Warwick CV35 9LS* Tel (01789) 840262 E-mail kate.mier@virgin.net

MIGHALL, Robert. b 33. St Pet Coll Ox BA57 MA61. Wycliffe Hall Ox 57. **d** 58 **p** 59. C Stoke *Cov* 58-62; C Rugby St Andr 62-64; V Newbold on Avon 64-76; V Combroke w Compton Verney 76-96; V Kineton 76-96; rtd 96; Perm to Offic *Glouc* from 97. *The Dairy House, Quarleston Farm, Clenston Road, Winterborne Stickland, Blandford Forum DT11 0NP* Tel (01258) 881467 E-mail robert@rmighall.fsnet.co.uk

MIHILL, Dennis George. b 31. St Alb Minl Tr Scheme 78. **d** 81 **p** 82. NSM Harpenden St Nic *St Alb* 81-86; C Sawbridgeworth 86-89; V Motspur Park *S'wark* 89-96; rtd 96; Perm to Offic *St Alb* 96-98 and from 01; Hon C Biddenham 98-01. *5 Regents Mews, Biddenham, Bedford MK40 4DL* Tel (01234) 269903

MIKHAIL, Stella Frances. TCD BTh02. CITC. **d** 02 **p** 03. C Bandon Union *C, C & R* 02-05; I Clonenagh w Offerlane, Borris-in-Ossory etc *C & O* from 05. *St Peter's Rectory, Portlaoise Road, Mountrath, Co Laois, Irish Republic* Tel (00353) (502) 32146 E-mail clonenagh@ossory.anglican.org

MILBURN, John Frederick. b 56. Westmr Coll Ox BA84. Sarum & Wells Th Coll 84. **d** 86 **p** 87. C Leavesden All SS *St Alb* 86-89; C Broxbourne w Wormley 89-93; CF (TA) 90-93; Australia from 93; R Inglewood St Jo w Texas Qld 93-98; P-in-c Holland Park St Matt from 98. *PO Box 248, Holland Park, Qld, Australia 4121* Tel and fax (0061) (7) 3397 0390 *or* Tel 3397 2300
E-mail john.milburn@optushome.com.au

MILES, Damian Stewart. b 76. Fitzw Coll Cam BTh02. Westcott Ho Cam 99. **d** 02 **p** 03. C Willingdon *Chich* from 02. *11 Winchester Way, Eastbourne BN22 0JP* Tel (01323) 520928 Mobile 07815-848735 E-mail damomiles@hotmail.com

MILES, Gerald Christopher Morgan. b 36. Peterho Cam BA57 MA72 Cranfield Inst of Tech MSc72 CEng MIEE. Wycliffe Hall Ox 74. **d** 76 **p** 77. C Tunbridge Wells St Jas *Roch* 76-80; V Leigh 80-90; R Addington w Trottiscliffe 90-91; P-in-c Ryarsh w Birling 90-91; R Birling, Addington, Ryarsh and Trottiscliffe 91-00; Hon Chapl London and SE Region ATC from 96; rtd 00; Perm to Offic *Roch* from 00. *2 Spa Close, Hadlow, Tonbridge TN11 0JX* Tel and fax (01732) 852323 E-mail cmiles@supanet.com

MILES (née HOARE), Ms Janet Francis Mary. b 48. St Aid Coll Dur BA70 Bris Univ MEd84. Sarum & Wells Th Coll 91. **d** 93 **p** 94. C Bruton and Distr *B & W* 93-98; P-in-c Llangarron w Llangrove, Whitchurch and Ganarew *Heref* 98-02; P-in-c Dixton 02-04; P-in-c Chewton Mendip w Ston Easton, Litton etc *B & W* from 04. *The Rectory, Lower Street, Chewton Mendip, Radstock BA3 4GP* Tel (01761) 241644 E-mail jfm2@fish.co.uk

MILES, Malcolm Robert. b 36. AKC60. **d** 61 **p** 62. C Northampton St Mary *Pet* 61-63; C E Haddon 63-67; R Broughton 67-73; Asst Chapl Nottm Univ *S'well* 73-74; V Northampton H Trin *Pet* 75-84; V Painswick w Sheepscombe *Glouc* 84-97; V Painswick w Sheepscombe and Cranham 97-01; RD Bisley 90-94; rtd 01; P-in-c Wensley and W Witton *Ripon* 01-05. *32 Turker Lane, Northallerton DL6 1PZ* Tel (01609) 773133 E-mail rachel@milesr.freeserve.co.uk

MILES, Mrs Marion Claire. b 41. S Dios Minl Tr Scheme 86. **d** 88 **p** 94. Hon Par Dn Blandford Forum and Langton Long *Sarum* 88-94; Hon C 94-01; Chapl Blandford Community Hosp from 88; NSM The Winterbournes and Compton Valence from 01. *153 Salisbury Road, Blandford Forum DT11 7SW* Tel (01258) 452010 E-mail marion_miles@onetel.com

MILES, Ms Patricia Ellen. b 56. RGN79. STETS 00. **d** 03 **p** 04. NSM Verwood *Sarum* from 03. *4 Firs Glen Road, Verwood BH31 6JB* Tel (01202) 824211 E-mail pat.miles@rbch-tr.swest.nhs.uk *or* patmiles@oz.co.uk

MILES, Robert. *See* MILES, Malcolm Robert

MILES, Canon Robert William. b 27. Magd Coll Cam BA50 MA55. Westcott Ho Cam 50. **d** 52 **p** 53. C Bury St Mary *Man* 52-55; Bp's Dom Chapl *Chich* 55-58; Kenya 58-63; Provost Mombasa 58-63; R Dalmahoy *Edin* 65-70; R Batsford w Moreton-in-Marsh *Glouc* 70-77; rtd 77; Perm to Offic *Glouc* from 79. *Boilingwell, Winchcombe, Cheltenham GL54 5JB* Tel (01242) 603337

MILES, Miss Sharon Elizabeth Ann. b 66. Westcott Ho Cam 00. **d** 02 **p** 03. C Shrub End *Chelmsf* from 02. *St Cedd's House, 47 Eldred Avenue, Colchester CO2 9AR* Tel (01206) 572017 E-mail revdsmiles@hotmail.com

MILES, Stephen John. b 44. Monash Univ Aus BA66 Worc Coll Ox DipEd68 Univ Coll Lon MA75 California Univ PhD80. Melbourne Coll of Div BTheol86. **d** 87 **p** 88. Australia 87-97 and from 03; C E Malvern St Jo 87; C Clifton Hill St Andr 87-89; Chapl Co-ord and Angl Chapl Monash Medical Cen 89-97; Asst Chapl Bonn w Cologne *Eur* 97-00; Chapl 00-03; rtd 03. *67 Caroline Street, South Yarra, Vic, Australia 3141* Tel (0061) (3) 9866 1463

MILFORD, Canon Catherine Helena. b 39. LMH Ox BA61 MA65 FRSA92. Gilmore Course 81. **dss** 82 **d** 87 **p** 94. Heaton St Barn *Bradf* 82-88; Par Dn 87-88; Adult Educn Adv *Win* 88-96; TR Barnham Broom *Nor* 96-00; P-in-c Reymerston w Cranworth, Letton, Southburgh etc 96-00; TR Barnham Broom and Upper Yare 00-04; Hon Can Nor Cathl 00-04; rtd 04. *6 Leylands Grove, Bradford BD9 5QP*

MILFORD, Graham Alan. b 57. Trin Coll Bris 00. **d** 02 **p** 03. C Wolborough and Ogwell *Ex* from 02. *5 Gothic Road, Newton Abbot TQ12 1LD* Tel (01626) 368412 E-mail gram57@supanet.com

MILFORD, Mrs Nicola Claire. b 75. Univ Coll Ches BTh03. Trin Coll Bris 00 N Ord Course 02. **d** 04 **p** 05. C Alphington *Ex* from 04. *5 Gothic Road, Newton Abbot TQ12 1LD* Tel (01626) 368412 *or* (01392) 858662

MILLAM, Peter John. b 36. Univ of Wales (Lamp) BA58. Ridley Hall Cam 58. **d** 63 **p** 64. C Cheltenham Ch Ch *Glouc* 63-66; Falkland Is 66-70; V Pulloxhill w Flitton *St Alb* 70-79; V Luton St Paul 79-89; V Chipping Campden w Ebrington *Glouc* 89-94; rtd 94; Perm to Offic *Chich* from 94. *22 Willowhale Avenue, Aldwick, Bognor Regis PO21 4AY* Tel (01243) 268316

MILLAR, Alan Askwith. b 26. Qu Coll Birm 59. **d** 60 **p** 61. C Redcar *York* 60-64; C Kirkleatham 60-64; V Middlesbrough St Aid 64-72; V Cayton w Eastfield 72-88; Chapl to RD of Scarborough 88-89; rtd 89; Perm to Offic *Bradf* from 89. *20 Guardian Court, Wells Promenade, Ilkley LS29 9JT* Tel (01943) 602081

MILLAR, Alan William. b 46. Toronto Univ MDiv. **d** 00 **p** 01. C Drumglass w Moygashel *Arm* 00-02; I Dromara w Garvaghy *D & D* from 02. *58 Banbridge Road, Dromara, Dromore BT25 2NE* Tel (028) 9753 3063 E-mail mimwam17@aol.com

MILLAR, Alexander. *See* MILLAR, Preb John Alexander Kirkpatrick

MILLAR, Andrew Charles. b 48. Hull Univ BSc69. Cuddesdon Coll 71. **d** 73 **p** 74. C Rushmere *St E* 73-76; C Ipswich All Hallows 76-79; Dioc Youth Chapl *Sheff* 79-83; Youth Chapl *Win* 83-92; V Colden from 92. *The Vicarage, Colden Common, Winchester SO21 1TL* Tel and fax (01962) 712505

MILLAR, Christine. *See* WHEELER, Mrs Christine

MILLAR, Gary. b 67. St Mich Coll Llan 88. **d** 91 **p** 92. C Tonyrefail w Gilfach Goch *Llan* 91-93; C Barry All SS 93-95; TV Cowbridge 95-97; I Dromara w Garvaghy *D & D* 97-01; I Kilkeel from 01. *The Rectory, 44 Manse Road, Kilkeel, Newry BT34 4BN* Tel (028) 4176 2300 *or* 4176 5994 E-mail g.millar@btinternet.com

MILLAR, Preb John Alexander Kirkpatrick (Sandy). b 39. Trin Coll Cam BA62 MA66. St Jo Coll Dur 74. **d** 76 **p** 77. C Brompton H Trin *Lon* 76-78; C Brompton H Trin w Onslow Square St Paul 78-85; V 85-05; Hon C from 05; P-in-c Tollington from 03; AD Chelsea 89-94; Preb St Paul's Cathl from 97. *1 Moray Road, London N4 3LD* E-mail catherine.tye@htb.org.uk

MILLAR, Mrs Julie Ann. b 65. Bris Poly BA87 ACA. SW Minl Tr Course 02. **d** 05. NSM Penzance St Mary w St Paul and St Jo *Truro* from 05. *14 Tolver Place, Penzance TR18 2AD* Tel (01736) 333682 Mobile 07719-823600 E-mail revdjulie.pz@btopenworld.com

MILLAR, Sandra Doreen. b 57. Univ of Wales (Cardiff) BA79 Warwick Univ MA94 PhD99. Ripon Coll Cuddesdon 98. **d** 00 **p** 01. C Chipping Barnet w Arkley *St Alb* 00-03; TV Dorchester *Ox* from 03. *The Vicarage, Cherwell Drive, Berinsfield, Wallingford OX10 7PB* Tel 07787-842674 (mobile) E-mail revdocsand@aol.com

MILLARD, Canon Jane Mary. b 43. Open Univ BA80. Edin Dioc NSM Course 81. **d** 90 **p** 94. NSM Edin St Mary *Edin* 90-94; Chapl HIV/AIDS 90-94; Can St Mary's Cathl from 95; Vice Provost from 98. *Honeybrae, Ninemileburn, Penicuik EH26 9NB* Tel (01968) 660253 Mobile 07889-468932 E-mail vice.provost@cathedral.net

MILLARD, Jonathan Neil. b 62. Aston Univ BSc83 Barrister-at-Law (Gray's Inn) 84. Wycliffe Hall Ox 89. **d** 92 **p** 93. C Haddenham w Cuddington, Kingsey etc *Ox* 92-94; USA 94-00 and from 04; R Church Stretton *Heref* 00-03; R Pittsburgh Ascension from 04. *Church of the Ascension, 4729 Ellsworth Avenue, Pittsburgh, PA 15213-2888, USA* Tel (001) (412) 621 4361 Fax 621 5746 E-mail jonathan.millard@comcast.net

MILLARD, Malcolm Edoric. b 38. Lon Univ BA60 AKC60 Lon Inst of Educn PGCE61. St Jo Coll Nottm 80. **d** 77 **p** 81. The Gambia 77-95; Deacon Banjul Cathl 77-79; Deacon Lamin St Andr 79-81; P-in-c 81-82; P-in-c Fajara St Paul 82-88; V Gen 86-88; P-in-c Farafenni Ch of African Martyrs 89-95; C S Shoebury *Chelmsf* 95-97; C Rainham w Wennington 97-02; P-in-c N Ockendon from 02. *52 Birch Crescent, South Ockendon RM15 6TZ* Tel (01708) 857859

MILLARD, Canon Murray Clinton. b 29. Ex Coll Ox BA50 MA58. St Steph Ho Ox 51. **d** 53 **p** 54. C Horfield St Greg *Bris* 53-55; C Guernsey St Steph *Win* 55-61; V 82-04; R Jersey St Mary 61-71; R Guernsey St Sampson 71-82; Hon Can Win Cathl 83-04; rtd 04. *St Stephen's House, Belmont Estate, King's Road, St Peter Port, Guernsey GY1 1QA* Tel (01481) 725660

MILLARD, Richard Stuart Marsh. b 33. St Pet Coll Ox BA57 MA. Oak Hill NSM Course 90. **d** 93 **p** 94. NSM Laleham *Lon* 93-94; NSM Neatishead, Barton Turf and Irstead *Nor* 94-95; NSM Ashmanhaugh, Barton Turf etc 95-99; rtd 99; Perm to Offic *Nor* from 99. *Semaphore Lodge, 30 Weybourne Road, Sheringham NR25 8HF*

MILLER, Andrew. *See* MILLER, Ronald Andrew John

MILLER, Anthony. *See* MILLER, Ronald Anthony Tony

MILLER, Anthony Talbot. b 37. Univ of Wales (Lamp) BA59. Coll of Resurr Mirfield. **d** 61 **p** 62. C Panteg w Llanddewi Fach and Llandegfeth *Mon* 61-63; C Monmouth 63-65; V Holme Cultram St Mary *Carl* 65-76; Lic to Offic *Lich* 76-78; P-in-c Wrockwardine Wood 78-80; R 80-94; OCF 92-94; rtd 94. *Smallhythe, 26 Rosemary Lane, Whitchurch SY13 1EG* Tel (01948) 662120

MILLER, Barry. b 42. Bede Coll Dur TCert63 Open Univ BA79 Leic Univ MEd86. Linc Th Coll 63. **d** 65 **p** 66. C Greenside *Dur* 65-68; C Auckland St Andr and St Anne 68-71; Adv in Educn *Leic* 71-77; C Leic St Nic 77-80; Asst Chapl Leic Univ 77-80; Lect RS Leic Poly 77-80; Children's Officer Gen Syn Bd of Educn 80-84; Hd RS W Midl Coll of HE 84-89; Hd Initial Teacher Educn Wolv Poly 89-92; Wolv Univ 92-93; Hd Teacher Educn Bradf Coll from 94. *Bradford College, Great Horton Road, Bradford BD7 1AY* Tel (01274) 433472 E-mail b.miller@bilk.ac.uk

MILLER, Charles. *See* MILLER, Ernest Charles

MILLER, Charles Irvine. b 35. Nottm Univ BEd76. Bps' Coll Cheshunt 61. **d** 63 **p** 64. C Anlaby Common St Mark *York* 63-66; C Whitby 66-68; R Ingoldmells w Addlethorpe *Linc* 68-72; P-in-c Bishop Norton 72-76; V Scunthorpe St Jo 76-83; Chapl Manor Hosp Walsall 83-89; rtd 89; Perm to Offic *Ely* 89-98 and from 99; P-in-c Isleham 98-99. *The Old Studio, 6 Chapel Street, Duxford, Cambridge CB2 4RJ*

MILLER, Darren Noel. b 67. Birm Univ BSocSc89. Chich Th Coll BTh95 Coll of Resurr Mirfield 94. **d** 95 **p** 96. C Weoley Castle *Birm* 95-98; C Shard End 98-00; V Castle Vale St Cuth from 00; AD Sutton Coldfield from 04. *St Cuthbert's Vicarage, St Cuthbert's Place, Birmingham B35 7PL* Tel 0121-747 4041 Mobile 07747-858697 E-mail vicar@stcuthbertsb35.org.uk

MILLER, David George. b 54. Oriel Coll Ox BA76 MA80. Ripon Coll Cuddesdon 78. **d** 81 **p** 82. C Henfield w Shermanbury and Woodmancote *Chich* 81-84; C Monk Bretton *Wakef* 84-87; V Rastrick St Jo 87-93; TR Helston and Wendron *Truro* from 93; Chapl R Cornwall Hosps Trust 95-01; Chapl W of Cornwall Primary Care Trust from 01. *St Michael's Rectory, Church Lane, Helston TR13 8PF* Tel (01326) 572516

MILLER, David James Tringham. b 45. AKC70. Sarum & Wells Th Coll 76. **d** 77 **p** 78. C Abington *Pet* 77-80; TV Corby SS Pet and Andr w Gt and Lt Oakley 80-83; V Kettering All SS 83-94; RD Kettering 87-94; V Pet All SS from 94. *All Saints' Vicarage, 208 Park Road, Peterborough PE1 2UJ* Tel (01733) 554130 E-mail 208prp@totalise.co.uk

MILLER, David John. b 37. Louvain Univ Belgium Lic en Sciences Catéchétiques 68. Chich Th Coll 60. **d** 62 **p** 63. C Southsea H Spirit *Portsm* 62-65; C Roehampton H Trin *S'wark* 67-68; Chapl Luxembourg *Eur* 68-72; Chapl Lausanne 72-91; Asst Chapl 91-93; Chapl Le Rosey Sch Switzerland 72-02; Perm to Offic from 94; rtd 02. *1 bis avenue de l'Eglise Anglaise, 1006 Lausanne, Switzerland* Tel (0041) (21) 616 2636

MILLER, David Samuel. b 31. Lich Th Coll 62. **d** 63 **p** 64. C Leek St Edw *Lich* 63-66; C Blurton 66; C Southbourne St Kath *Win* 66-71; V E and W Worldham, Hartley Mauditt w Kingsley etc 71-76; TV Buckhurst Hill *Chelmsf* 76-80; V Elm Park St Nic Hornchurch 80-93; rtd 93; Chapl Torrevieja *Eur* 95-97. *8 Church Road, Lowestoft NR32 1TQ*

MILLER, Ernest Charles. b 56. Franklin & Marshall Coll (USA) BA78 Univ of Michigan MA79 Keble Coll Ox DPhil90. Nashotah Ho MDiv82. **d** 82 **p** 83. USA 82-84 and from 96; Asst Chapl Keble Coll Ox 84-88; Warden Ho of SS Greg and Macrina 84-90; P-in-c New Marston *Ox* 91-96; Prof Th Nashotah Ho Wisconsin 96-00; R New York Transfiguration from 00. *1 East 29th Street, New York, NY 10016, USA* Tel (001) (212) 684 6770 E-mail ecmiller@littlechurch.org

MILLER, Francis Rogers. b 54. Ex Univ BA86. St Steph Ho Ox 86. **d** 88 **p** 89. C Wednesfield *Lich* 88-93; P-in-c Caldmore 93-99; V 99-02; C Walsall St Mary and All SS Palfrey 93-97; P-in-c 97-02; V Caldmore w Palfrey from 02. *St Michael's Vicarage, 12 St Michael's Street, Walsall WS1 3RQ* Tel (01922) 623445

MILLER, Gareth. See MILLER, John Gareth

MILLER, The Ven Geoffrey Vincent. b 56. Dur Univ BEd78 Newc Univ MA94. St Jo Coll Nottm 81. **d** 83 **p** 84. C Jarrow *Dur* 83-86; TV Billingham St Aid 86-92; Dioc Urban Development Officer 91-97; Community Chapl Stockton-on-Tees 92-94; P-in-c Darlington St Cuth 94-96; V 96-99; Soc Resp Officer 97-99; Can Res Newc Cathl *Newc* 99-05; Dioc Urban Officer 99-05; Adn Northd and Can Res Newc Cathl from 05. *80 Moorside North, Newcastle upon Tyne NE4 9DU* Tel 0191-273 8245 Fax 226 0286 E-mail geoff.miller@btinternet.com

MILLER, The Ven George Charles Alexander. b 20. TCD BA45. CITC Div Test 46. **d** 46 **p** 47. C Wexford w Rathaspeck *C & O* 46-49; Asst Chapl Miss to Seamen Belf 49; Chapl Miss to Seamen Immingham 49-51; Chapl Pernis Miss to Seamen *Eur* 51-55; I Billis w Ballyjamesduff *K, E & A* 55-57; I Knockbride w Shercock 57-65; I Urney w Denn and Derryheen 65-89; Preb Kilmore Cathl 77-87; Adn Kilmore 87-89; rtd 89. *Wavecrest, Blenacup, Cavan, Irish Republic* Tel (00353) (49) 436 1270

MILLER, Graham William. b 71. St Andr Univ BD94 Dur Univ MA98. Westcott Ho Cam 99. **d** 01 **p** 02. C Ex St Dav *Ex* 01-03; C Sunderland St Mary and St Pet *Dur* from 03; C Sunderland Pennywell St Thos from 03. *72 Sevenoaks Drive, Sunderland SR4 9NU* Tel 0191-534 3009 E-mail grahamwmiller@aol.com

✠**MILLER, The Rt Revd Harold Creeth.** b 50. TCD BA73 MA78 Nottm Univ BA75. St Jo Coll Nottm 73. **d** 76 **p** 77 **c** 97. C Carrickfergus *Conn* 76-79; Dir Ext Studies St Jo Coll Nottm 79-84; Chapl QUB 84-89; I Carrigrohane Union *C, C & R* 89-97; Bp's Dom Chapl 91-97; Can Cork and Cloyne Cathls 94-96; Treas Cork Cathl 96-97; Can Cork Cathl 96-97; Preb Tymothan St Patr Cathl Dublin from 96; Bp D & D from 97. *The See House, 32 Knockdene Park South, Belfast BT5 7AB* Tel (028) 9047 1973 Fax 9065 0584 E-mail bishop@down.anglican.org

MILLER (née BLUNDEN), Mrs Jacqueline Ann. b 63. Leic Univ BA86 SS Coll Cam BA90. Ridley Hall Cam 88. **d** 91. Par Dn Bedford St Paul *St Alb* 91-94; C 94-95. *St Mary's Vicarage, Lansdowne Road, London N17 9XE* Tel (020) 8808 6644

MILLER, James Ivimey. b 33. Trin Hall Cam BA55 MA59. Ridley Hall Cam 56. **d** 61 **p** 62. C Beccles St Mich *St E* 61-63; C Blackpool St Jo *Blackb* 63-67; C Kirk Ella *York* 67-73; R Cockfield *St E* 73-78; rtd 78; Perm to Offic *St E* from 78. *3 Grosvenor Gardens, Bury St Edmunds IP33 2JS* Tel (01284) 762839

MILLER, Canon John David. b 50. Nottm Univ BTh73 Lanc Univ GradCertEd74 Newc Univ MA93. Kelham Th Coll 68. **d** 74 **p** 75. C Horden *Dur* 74-79; C Billingham St Aid 79-80; TV 80-84; TR S Shields All SS from 84; Hon Can Dur Cathl from 04. *The Rectory, Tyne Terrace, South Shields NE34 0NF* Tel 0191-456 1851

MILLER, John Douglas. b 24. FCA60. N Ord Course 74. **d** 77 **p** 78. C Prestbury *Ches* 77-80; V Ashton Hayes 80-87; rtd 87; Perm to Offic *Ex* from 87. *35 Branscombe Close, Colyford, Colyton EX24 6RF* Tel (01297) 553581

MILLER, John Forster. b 32. Ox NSM Course. **d** 83 **p** 84. NSM Patcham *Chich* 83-86; NSM Radlett *St Alb* 86-93; Perm to Offic *St Alb* 93-00 and *Sarum* from 00. *Wedgwood, 29 Lansdowne Crescent, Derry Hill, Calne SN11 9NT* Tel (01249) 819252

MILLER, John Gareth. b 57. St Jo Coll Dur BA78. Ridley Hall Cam 79 Ven English Coll Rome 80. **d** 81 **p** 82. C Addiscombe St Mary *Cant* 81-84; TV Melbury *Sarum* 84-88; TR 88-91; V Leamington Priors All SS *Cov* 91-94. *Chelwood, Market Street, Charlbury, Chipping Norton OX7 3PL* Tel (01608) 811410 E-mail garethmiller@tiscali.co.uk

MILLER, John Selborne. b 32. RMN70. S'wark Ord Course 64. **d** 71 **p** 72. C Kenton *Lon* 71-74; C Fulham St Etheldreda w St Clem 74-78; Asst at Convent of the Epiphany Truro 79-80; Hon C Pimlico St Sav 80-84; C Shirley *Birm* 84-86; rtd 86; Perm to Offic *Nor* 86-01. *28 Knight Street, Walsingham NR22 6DA* Tel (01328) 820824

MILLER, Kenneth Leslie. b 50. Lanc Univ BEd74 Liv Univ BPhil94 FRSA. N Ord Course 78. **d** 80 **p** 81. NSM Formby St Pet *Liv* 80-87; NSM Anfield St Columba from 87; Chapl St Marg C of E High Sch Aigburth Liv from 86. *9 Hampton Road, Liverpool L37 6EJ* Tel (01704) 831256

MILLER, Kim Hurst. b 49. Ex Univ PhD89. Canberra Coll of Min BTh82 DipMin82. **d** 82 **p** 83. Australia 82-85 and from 89; C Goulburn Cathl 83-84; P-in-c Koorawatha 84-85; Perm to Offic *Ex* 85-89; R Wagga Wagga St Alb 89-98; Chapl Bathurst Gaol from 98. *3 Oates Place, Eglinton, NSW, Australia 2795* Tel (0061) (2) 6337 1841 *or* 6338 3282 E-mail kkmiller@globalfreeway.com.au

MILLER, Luke Jonathan. b 66. SS Coll Cam BA87 MA91. St Steph Ho Ox BA90. **d** 91 **p** 92. C Oxhey St Matt *St Alb* 91-94; C Tottenham St Mary *Lon* 94-95; V from 95; AD E Haringey from 05. *St Mary's Vicarage, Lansdowne Road, London N17 9XE* Tel (020) 8808 6644 E-mail frmiller@stmarystottenham.org

MILLER, Martin Michael. b 55. St Jo Coll Dur BSc78. Trin Coll Bris 94. **d** 96 **p** 97. C Leamington Priors St Paul *Cov* 96-99; C Bermondsey St Anne and St Aug *S'wark* 99-05; R Newhaven *Chich* from 05. *The Rectory, 36 Second Avenue, Newhaven BN9 9HN* Tel (01273) 515251 E-mail martinmrev@aol.com

MILLER, Michael Andrew. b 58. Ripon Coll Cuddesdon 03. **d** 05. C Hockerill *St Alb* from 05. *17 Legions Way, Bishop's Stortford CM23 2AU* Tel (01279) 657261 Mobile 07778-617482 E-mail mmiller363@aol.com

MILLER, Michael Daukes. b 46. MRCGP74 DRCOG Qu Coll Cam MA71 Lon Univ BCh70 MB71 DCH. Glouc Th Course 82. **d** 85 **p** 94. NSM Lydney w Aylburton *Glouc* 85-95; NSM Lydney from 95. *Highmead House, Blakeney GL15 4DY* Tel (01594) 516668

MILLER, Patrick Figgis. b 33. Ch Coll Cam BA56 MA60 Surrey Univ PhD95. Cuddesdon Coll 56. **d** 58 **p** 59. C Portsea St Cuth *Portsm* 58-61; C Cambridge Gt St Mary w St Mich *Ely* 61-63; Chapl SCM 61-63; Hd RS Man Gr Sch 63-69; Can Res and Lib S'wark Cathl *S'wark* 69-72; Dir of Soc Studies Qu Mary's Coll Basingstoke 72-79; Prin Sunbury Coll 79-80; Prin Esher Coll 81-98; Project Dir Learning for Living from 00; Chapl London Flotilla from 00; Perm to Offic *Guildf* from 01. *9 Fairfax Avenue, Epsom KT17 2QN* Tel (020) 8394 0593 Mobile 07740-503259 E-mail patrickmiller@ewell3.freeserve.co.uk

MILLER, Canon Paul. b 49. Oak Hill Th Coll 71. **d** 74 **p** 75. C Upton *Ex* 74-77; C Farnborough *Guildf* 77-78; P-in-c Torquay St Luke *Ex* 78-81; V 81-86; V Green Street Green *Roch* 86-94; V Green Street Green and Pratts Bottom 94-01; RD Orpington 96-01; Hon Can Roch Cathl from 00; V Shortlands from 01. *The Vicarage, 37 Kingswood Road, Bromley BR2 0HG* Tel (020) 8460 4989 Fax 8289 7577 Mobile 07940-582040 E-mail pmiller@amserve.net

MILLER, Paul Richard. b 37. K Coll Lon BSc60 AKC60. Linc Th Coll 60. **d** 62 **p** 63. C Sheff St Geo *Sheff* 62-65; C Bottesford *Linc* 65-67; Bp's Youth Chapl 67-69; C Corringham 67-69; Dioc Youth Officer *Ripon* 69-74; Sec Nat Coun for Voluntary Youth Services 74-79; Hd Youth Nat Coun of Soc Services 74-79; P-in-c Battlesden and Pottesgrove *St Alb* 79-80; P-in-c Eversholt w Milton Bryan 79-80; P-in-c Woburn 79-80; V Woburn w Eversholt, Milton Bryan, Battlesden etc 80-98; rtd 98; Perm to Offic *Heref* from 98 and *Lich* from 03. *6 Elms Paddock, Little Stretton, Church Stretton SY6 6RD* Tel (01694) 724596 E-mail paulmiller@macunlimited.net

MILLER, Peter Tennant. b 21. Keble Coll Ox BA47 MA63. Ripon Hall Ox 62. **d** 63 **p** 64. C Wigmore w Hempstead *Roch* 63-68; V Worksop St Paul *S'well* 68-73; P-in-c Nottingham St Cath 74-75; C Nottingham St Mary 75-77; R Edith Weston w N Luffenham and Lyndon w Manton *Pet* 77-86; rtd 86; Perm to

Offic *Cov* from 86. *Regency Cottage, 9 Cross Road, Leamington Spa CV32 5PD* Tel (01926) 314236

MILLER, Philip Harry. b 58. Leeds Univ BA79. Chich Th Coll 80. **d** 82 **p** 83. C Reddish *Man* 82-86; R Lower Broughton Ascension 86-94; P-in-c Cheetwood St Alb 91-94; P-in-c Langley and Parkfield 95-00; TR from 00. *The Rectory, Wood Street, Middleton, Manchester M24 5GL* Tel 0161-643 5013

MILLER, Philip Howard. b 40. Tyndale Hall Bris 67. **d** 72 **p** 73. Argentina 72-73; C Rusholme H Trin *Man* 73-74; Paraguay 74-77; C Toxteth St Cypr w Ch Ch *Liv* 78-80; V Burscough Bridge 80-85; V Woodbridge St Jo *St E* 85-91; P-in-c Combs 91-92 and 93-96; Chapl Burrswood Cen for Divine Healing 92-93; V Yoxford and Peasenhall w Sibton *St E* 96-01; rtd 01. *Salta, 54 Orchard Close, Melton, Woodbridge IP12 1LD* Tel (01394) 388615 E-mail phm914@lineone.net

MILLER, Richard Bracebridge. b 45. Wycliffe Hall Ox 68. **d** 70 **p** 71. C Lee Gd Shep w St Pet *S'wark* 70-74; C Roehampton H Trin 74-77; C Earley St Pet *Ox* 77-80; V Aldermaston w Wasing and Brimpton 80-96; C Newbury 96-01; Perm to Offic from 03. *14 Burcot Park, Burcot, Abingdon OX14 3DH* Tel (01865) 407521 E-mail rbmoxford@hotmail.com

MILLER, Robert Stephen. b 71. QUB BSc92. CITC BTh95. **d** 95 **p** 96. C Lurgan Ch the Redeemer *D & D* 95-99; I Tullylish 99-03; I Maghera w Killelagh *D & R* from 03. *The Rectory, 20 Church Street, Maghera BT46 5EA* Tel (028) 7964 2252 E-mail robsmiller@aol.com *or* maghera@derry.anglican.org

MILLER, Ronald Andrew John. b 46. LNSM course 96. **d** 96 **p** 97. OLM Heywood *Man* from 96. *153 Rochdale Road East, Heywood OL10 1QU* Tel (01706) 624326 Fax as telephone E-mail andrew.miller1@virgin.net

MILLER, Ronald Anthony (Tony). b 41. CEng CPA MRAeS City Univ BSc63. S'wark Ord Course 69. **d** 72 **p** 80. NSM Crookham *Guildf* 72-73 and 80-85; NSM New Haw 85-95; NSM Effingham w Lt Bookham 95-04. *Glen Anton, Horsley Road, Downside, Cobham KT11 3JZ* Tel and fax (01932) 863394 Mobile 07710-294786 E-mail ramiller@fish.co.uk

MILLER, Rosamund Joy. *See* SEAL, Mrs Rosamund Joy

MILLER, Mrs Rosslyn Leslie. b 43. St Andr Univ MA65 Ox Univ DipEd66. **dss** 72 **d** 87. Dir of Studies Inst of Chr Studies 72; St Marylebone All SS *Lon* 72; Adult Educn Officer 73-78; Alford w Rigsby *Linc* 86-87; C 87-90; Dioc Dir of Readers 90-03; rtd 03. *59 Malham Drive, Lincoln LN6 0XD* Tel (01522) 831294 E-mail rosslyn.miller@aol.com

MILLER, Roy. b 29. **d** 88 **p** 93. NSM Leic Cathl *Leic* 88-91; NSM Leic H Apostles 91-97; Perm to Offic 97-99. *5 Bratmyr, Fleckney, Leicester LE8 8BJ* Tel 0116-240 2004

MILLER, Miss Sarah Lydia. b 65. St Andr Univ BD90 Hughes Hall Cam PGCE91. EAMTC 98. **d** 01 **p** 02. NSM Nor St Pet Mancroft w St Jo Maddermarket *Nor* 01-03; C Wythenshawe *Man* from 03. *St Luke's House, Brownley Road, Manchester M22 4PT* Tel 0161-945 7399

MILLER, Stephen Michael. b 63. NE Lon Poly BSc86 Nottm Univ BTh91. Linc Th Coll 88. **d** 91 **p** 92. C Dudley St Fran *Worc* 91-94; V Sedgley St Mary 94-99; Miss to Seafarers from 99; Chapl Rotterdam w Schiedam Miss to Seafarers *Eur* 99-03. *Address temp unknown* E-mail vichill@aol.com

MILLER, Stuart William. b 71. Univ of Wales (Cardiff) BA92. Trin Coll Bris BA97. **d** 97 **p** 98. C Fordingbridge *Win* 97-98; C Bursledon 98-02; V W Moors *Sarum* 02-05; Chapl Bournemouth and Poole Coll of FE *Win* from 05. *Bournemouth and Poole College, North Road, Poole BH14 0LS* Tel (01202) 205205 E-mail stu@fish.co.uk

MILLER, William David. b 45. Man Univ BA66. Linc Th Coll 69. **d** 71 **p** 72. C Newc St Geo *Newc* 71-74; C Corbridge w Halton 74-77; C N Gosforth 77-81; TV Whorlton 81-90; Chapl K Sch Tynemouth from 90. *7 Strawberry Terrace, Hazelrigg, Newcastle upon Tyne NE13 7AR* Tel 0191-236 5024 *or* 258 5995

MILLETT, Maxwell Roy. b 45. Clare Coll Cam BA67. S Dios Minl Tr Scheme 92. **d** 95 **p** 96. NSM Southsea St Pet *Portsm* 95-03; Perm to Offic from 03. *32 Belmont Street, Southsea PO5 1ND* Tel (023) 9281 7216

MILLETT, William Hugh. b 21. AKC49. **d** 50 **p** 51. C Barbourne *Worc* 50-53; V Catshill 53-58; R Richard's Castle *Heref* 58-78; P-in-c Stoke Lacy, Moreton Jeffries w Much Cowarne etc 78-82; Perm to Offic *Worc* from 83; rtd 86; Perm to Offic *Heref* from 93. *18 Shirley Close, Malvern WR14 2NH* Tel (01684) 567056

MILLGATE, Victor Frederick. b 44. St Mich Coll Llan 81. **d** 83 **p** 84. C Pembroke St Mary w St Mich *St D* 83-85; V Manorbier and St Florence w Redberth 85-04; TR Carew from 04; AD Castlemartin from 03. *The Vicarage, Manorbier, Tenby SA70 7TN* Tel (01834) 871617 E-mail esmillgate@yahoo.co.uk

MILLICHAMP, Mrs Penelope Mary. b 39. CertEd60. WMMTC 82. **dss** 85 **d** 87 **p** 94. Wednesfield *Lich* 85-94; Par Dn 87-90; TD 90-94; Perm to Offic 94-95; NSM Wrockwardine Deanery 95-99; rtd 99; Perm to Offic *Lich* 99-00. *3 Mathon Lodge, 16 Stockwell Road, Wolverhampton WV6 9PQ* Tel (01902) 741996 Mobile 07971-421562 E-mail penny@millichamp.com

MILLIER, Gordon. b 28. St Aid Birkenhead 63. **d** 65 **p** 66. C Congresbury *B & W* 65-69; P-in-c Badgworth w Biddisham 69-76; R Weare w Badgworth and Biddisham 76-84; R Pilton w Croscombe, N Wootton and Dinder 84-93; rtd 93; Perm to Offic *Ex* from 93. *28 Withy Close, Canal Hill, Tiverton EX16 4HZ* Tel (01884) 253128

MILLIGAN, Peter John. **d** 01 **p** 02. NSM Putney St Marg *S'wark* from 01. *39 Stapleton Road, London SW17 8BA* Tel (020) 8767 3497

MILLIGAN, Canon William John (Barney). b 28. OBE95. Em Coll Cam BA49. Cuddesdon Coll 53. **d** 55 **p** 56. C Portsea N End St Mark *Portsm* 55-62; V New Eltham All SS *S'wark* 62-71; V Roehampton H Trin 71-79; Can Res St Alb 79-86; Chapl Strasbourg *Eur* 86-95; Angl Rep Eur Insts 90-95; rtd 95; Perm to Offic *S'wark* 95-00 and *Sarum* from 98. *3 East Street, Beaminster DT8 3DS* Tel (01308) 862806

MILLINER, Llewelyn Douglas. b 14. Univ of Wales BSc35. **d** 38 **p** 39. C Aberdare St Fagan *Llan* 38-41; C Wellingborough St Mary *Pet* 41-43; CF 43-63; Asst Master K Sch Worc 63-66; C-in-c Chelmsf St Luke CD *Chelmsf* 66-69; Dep Hd Master Widford Lodge Sch Chelmsf 69-80; Perm to Offic *Chelmsf* 69-80 and *Ex* from 80; rtd 80. *Fordings, Weare Giffard, Bideford EX39 4QS* Tel (01237) 473729

MILLING, David Horace. b 29. Oriel Coll Ox BA51 MA54 Cam Univ PhD73. Cuddesdon Coll 54. **d** 56 **p** 57. C Bris St Mary Redcliffe w Temple *Bris* 56-59; C Fishponds St Jo 59-62; India 62-69; Lect St D Coll Lamp 73-75; C Caversham *Ox* 77-81; C Mapledurham 77-81; C Caversham St Andr 81-86; TV Upper Kennet *Sarum* 86-88; rtd 88; Perm to Offic *Glouc* 90-99 and *Ex* from 00. *14 Matford Mews, Matford, Alphington, Exeter EX2 8XP* Tel (01392) 219718

MILLINGTON, Robert William Ernest. b 51. Sheff Univ BA73 St Jo Coll Dur DipTh75. **d** 76 **p** 77. C Ormskirk *Liv* 76-79; C Litherland St Paul Hatton Hill 79-81; V Bootle Ch Ch 81-88; Chapl K Edw Sch Witley from 88. *1 South Lodge, Petworth Road, Wormley, Godalming GU8 5SQ* Tel (01428) 685163 *or* 686700 E-mail rwe.millington@virgin.net

MILLINGTON, Stuart. b 45. Lich Th Coll 67. **d** 70 **p** 71. C Boulton *Derby* 70-73; C Moseley St Mary *Birm* 73-76; TV Staveley and Barrow Hill *Derby* 76-82; R Wingerworth 82-99; RD Chesterfield 91-97; P-in-c Elton All SS *Man* from 99. *All Saints' Vicarage, 10 Kirkburn View, Bury BL8 1DL* Tel 0161-797 1595

MILLS, Alan Francis. b 29. Ch Coll Cam BA52 MA91. Linc Th Coll 52. **d** 54 **p** 55. C Hucknall Torkard *S'well* 54-58; C Bath Bathwick St Jo *B & W* 58-70; V Drayton 70-76; V Muchelney 70-76; V Alcombe 76-99; rtd 99; Perm to Offic *B & W* from 00. *194 Locking Road, Weston-super-Mare BS23 3LU* Tel (01934) 622679

MILLS, Alexandra. b 56. Univ of Wales (Abth) BMus78 CertEd79. Ripon Coll Cuddesdon 88. **d** 90 **p** 94. Par Dn Earlsfield St Andr *S'wark* 90-94; C Kingston All SS w St Jo 94-99; C Brixton Road Ch Ch 99-00; Perm to Offic from 05. *121A Transmere Road, London SW18 3QP* Tel (020) 8944 1641 Mobile 07900-543068

MILLS, Anne. *See* MILLS, Mrs Leslie Anne

MILLS, Anthony James. b 55. Nottm Univ BA. Linc Th Coll. **d** 84 **p** 85. C Mexborough *Sheff* 84-86; C Howden *York* 86-89; V Fylingdales and Hawsker cum Stainsacre 89-95; V Scarborough St Sav w All SS from 95; P-in-c Scarborough St Martin 02-05; V from 05. *St Martin's Vicarage, Craven Street, Scarborough YO11 2BY* Tel (01723) 360437

MILLS, David Bryn. b 49. Ox NSM Course. **d** 83 **p** 84. NSM Stantonbury *Ox* 83-87; NSM Deanery of Milton Keynes 87-00; NSM Brampton and Farlam and Castle Carrock w Cumrew *Carl* 00-02; NSM Eden, Gelt and Irthing from 02. *The Barn, Far Long Park, Scaleby, Carlisle CA6 4JP*

MILLS, David Francis. b 51. Oak Hill Th Coll 76. **d** 79 **p** 80. C Rodbourne Cheney *Bris* 79-82; C Wolverhampton St Matt *Lich* 82-85; CF 85-88; TV Braunstone *Leic* 88-95; Past Asst to Adn Leic 95-97; C Barkestone w Plungar, Redmile and Stathern 97-99; C Bottesford and Muston 97-99; C Harby, Long Clawson and Hose 97-99; C Vale of Belvoir Par 00-02; R Winfarthing w Shelfanger w Burston w Gissing etc *Nor* from 02. *The Rectory, Church Lane, Winfarthing, Diss IP22 2EA* Tel (01379) 642543 E-mail dmills@leicester.anglican.org

MILLS, David Graham Mackenzie. *See* MACKENZIE MILLS, David Graham

MILLS, Canon Geoffrey Charles Malcolm. b 33. Wycliffe Hall Ox 59. **d** 61 **p** 62. C Buckhurst Hill *Chelmsf* 61-65; C Ecclesall *Sheff* 65-69; V Endcliffe 69-78; R Whiston 78-99; Hon Can Sheff Cathl 96-99; rtd 99; Perm to Offic *Sheff* from 99. *8 Hall Road, Rotherham S60 2BP* Tel (01709) 373863

MILLS, Miss Glenys Christine. b 38. Open Univ BA81. Dalton Ho Bris 64. **d** 87 **p** 94. Par Dn Clifton Ch Ch w Em *Bris* 87-94; C 94-95; P-in-c Gt w Lt Abington *Ely* 95-00; Chapl Arthur Rank Hospice Cam 95-00; Perm to Offic *Bris* from 00. *14 St Bartholomew's Road, Bristol BS7 9BJ* Tel 0117-909 8859

MILLS, Gordon Derek. b 35. Lich Th Coll 60. **d** 63 **p** 64. C W Derby St Mary *Liv* 63-65; C Clifton w Glapton *S'well* 65-67; V N Wilford St Faith 67-72; V Farnsfield and P-in-c Kirklington w

Hockerton 77-82; P-in-c Brindle and Asst Dir of Educn *Blackb* 82-86; V Gt Budworth *Ches* 86-88; P-in-c Antrobus 87-88; V Gt Budworth and Antrobus 88-92; V Gt Budworth 92-00; rtd 00; Perm to Offic *Blackb* 01-04 and *York* from 04. *Holmelands House, Raby Lane, East Cowton, Northallerton DL7 0BW* Tel (01325) 378798

MILLS, Canon Hubert Cecil. b 44. TCD BA66 MA71 HDipEd73. CITC 67. **d** 67 **p** 68. C Dublin Rathfarnham *D & G* 67-72; Min Can St Patr Cathl Dublin 69-92; Succ 77-92; Preb Rathmichael St Patr Cathl Dublin 92-02; Treas from 02; C Dublin St Steph and St Ann *D & G* 72-77; I Holmpatrick w Balbriggan and Kenure 77-86; I Killiney H Trin from 86. *Holy Trinity Rectory, Killiney Road, Killiney, Co Dublin, Irish Republic* Tel (00353) (1) 285 2695 Fax 235 4811 E-mail revcecilmills@club.ie

MILLS, Ian Anderson. b 35. Coll of Resurr Mirfield 60 K Coll Lon AKC65. **d** 65 **p** 70. C S'wark St Alphege *S'wark* 65-67; C Hartlepool St Paul *Dur* 69-72; NSM Hartlepool St Hilda 90-95; Perm to Offic from 95. *7 Claypool Farm Close, Hutton Henry, Hartlepool TS27 4QZ* Tel (01429) 836204

MILLS, Jack Herbert. b 14. Selw Coll Cam BA38 MA42. Cuddesdon Coll 39. **d** 40 **p** 41. C Camberwell St Geo *S'wark* 40-42; C Southfields St Barn 42-46; USPG 46-47; Chapl Hurstpierpoint Coll 47-52; New Zealand 52-56, 59-61 and from 87; Australia 57-59 and 62-73; Hd Master St Wilfrid's Sch Ex 74-79; Chapl Community of St Wilfrid 74-79; Hon C Ewhurst *Chich* 79-81; Hon C Bodiam 79-81; Perm to Offic *Ex* 81-85; Perm to Offic *Chich* 85-87; rtd 87. *14/28 Maranui Avenue, Point Chevalier 1002, Auckland, New Zealand* Tel (0064) (9) 849 2243

MILLS, Jennifer Clare. *See* TOMLINSON, Mrs Jennifer Clare

MILLS, John Kettlewell. b 53. BA. Cranmer Hall Dur. **d** 84 **p** 85. C Ashton-upon-Mersey St Mary *Ches* 84-87; TV Didsbury St Jas and Em *Man* 87-98; V Styvechale *Cov* from 98. *Styvechale Vicarage, 16 Armorial Road, Coventry CV3 6GJ* Tel (024) 7641 6074 *or* 7669 2299 E-mail jkm@stivichall.freeserve.co.uk

MILLS, Mrs Leslie Anne. b 44. K Alfred's Coll Win CertEd65. SW Minl Tr Course 99. **d** 02 **p** 03. NSM Kilmington, Stockland, Dalwood, Yarcombe etc *Ex* from 02. *Gorse Bungalow, Cotleigh, Honiton EX14 9JB* Tel (01404) 861430 E-mail anne@stockland.cx

MILLS, Michael Henry. b 51. AKC73. St Aug Coll Cant. **d** 74 **p** 75. C Newton Aycliffe *Dur* 74-78; C Padgate *Liv* 78-79; TV 79-95; V Frodsham *Ches* from 95. *The Vicarage, Vicarage Lane, Frodsham, Warrington WA6 7DU* Tel (01928) 733378 E-mail michael.mills3@virgin.net

MILLS, Michael John. b 52. St Andr Univ BSc75 Cam Univ PGCE76. Cranmer Hall Dur 97. **d** 99 **p** 00. C Brockmoor *Worc* 99-03; P-in-c St Leonards St Leon *Chich* from 04; P-in-c St Leonards St Ethelburga from 04. *The Rectory, 81A Filsham Road, St Leonards-on-Sea TN38 0PE* Tel and fax (01424) 203639 Mobile 07789-913013 E-mail michael.mills1@ntlworld.com

MILLS, Michael Shane. b 68. Nashotah Ho Wisconsin MDiv. **d** 95 **p** 96. C Dallas Incarnation USA 95-98 and from 00; NSM Pelton *Dur* 98-99. *6006 Penrose Avenue, Dallas, TX 75206, USA* E-mail father.michael.mills@worldnet.att.net

MILLS, Pamela Ann. b 44. Southn Univ DAES82. S Tr Scheme 94. **d** 97 **p** 98. NSM Hurstbourne Tarrant, Faccombe, Vernham Dean etc *Win* from 97. *Sunnyside, The Dene, Hurstbourne Tarrant, Andover SP11 0AS* Tel (01264) 736286

MILLS, Peter James. b 32. Univ Coll Lon LLB58. **d** 99 **p** 00. NSM Woodchurch *Ches* 99-03; rtd 03; Perm to Offic *Ches* from 03. *6 West Heath Court, Gerard Road, West Kirby, Wirral CH48 4ES* Tel 0151-625 4459 Mobile 07989-374499

MILLS, Peter John. b 52. Sarum & Wells Th Coll 87. **d** 89 **p** 90. C Chatham St Wm *Roch* 89-92; V Perry Street 92-95; V E Malling 95-00; CF from 00. *c/o MOD Chaplains (Army)* Tel (01980) 615804 Fax 615800

MILLS, Roger Conrad. b 58. Selw Coll Cam BA79 MA83. St Jo Coll Nottm DPS85. **d** 85 **p** 86. C Jesmond H Trin *Newc* 85-88; C Alnwick 88-91; Chapl Newc Univ 91-00; P-in-c Newc St Barn and St Jude 95-97; V Kingston Park from 00. *12 Shannon Court, Newcastle upon Tyne NE3 2XF* Tel 0191-286 4050 Fax as telephone E-mail rogermills123@yahoo.co.uk

MILLS, Timothy John. b 57. Wye Coll Lon BSc79. Trin Coll Bris 01. **d** 03 **p** 04. C Chislehurst Ch Ch *Roch* from 03. *56 Walden Road, Chislehurst BR7 5JX* Tel (020) 8467 6669 Mobile 07786-540819 E-mail hoppy@tmills33.fsnet.co.uk

MILLS-POWELL, Mark Oliver McLay. b 55. Edin Th Sem Virginia. **d** 83 **p** 84. C Huyton St Mich *Liv* 83-86; USA 86-95; P-in-c Basildon w Aldworth and Ashampstead *Ox* 95-02; TR Linton *Ely* from 02. *The Rectory, Church Lane, Linton, Cambridge CB1 6JX* Tel (01223) 891291 E-mail mark.mills-powell@ely.anglican.org

MILLSON, Brian Douglas. b 53. Univ of W Ontario BA76 Huron Coll MDiv84. Westcott Ho Cam 82. **d** 83 **p** 84. C Walton-on-Thames *Guildf* 83-86; Canada 86-98; R Par of the Six Nations 86-89; Canadian Forces Chapl 89-98; CF from 98. *c/o MOD Chaplains (Army)* Tel (01980) 615804 Fax 615800 E-mail brian.millson@btinternet.com

MILLSON, Mrs Margaret Lily. b 41. CertEd61. EMMTC 83. **dss** 86 **d** 87 **p** 94. NSM Bottesford w Ashby *Linc* 86-01; P-in-c St Tudy w St Mabyn and Michaelstow *Truro* from 01. *The Rectory, Glebe Parc, St Tudy, Bodmin PL30 3AS* Tel and fax (01208) 851691 E-mail mlmillson@aol.com

MILLWARD, Miss Pauline Freda. b 50. AMA74. N Ord Course 89. **d** 92 **p** 94. NSM Warley *Wakef* 92-95; P-in-c Halifax St Hilda from 95; Missr for Halifax Town Cen from 95. *8 Hill Park Mount, Sowerby Bridge HX6 3JB* Tel (01422) 823576 Pager 07666-750242 Fax (01422) 354448 E-mail paulinemillward@beeb.net

MILLWOOD, Stephen Grant. b 44. Sheff Tech Coll HNC66 Sheff City Coll of Educn CertEd77 Open Univ BA92. St Jo Coll Nottm Dip Th & Min 92. **d** 94 **p** 95. C Anston *Sheff* 94-98; V Kimberworth Park from 98. *The Vicarage, 21 Birks Road, Rotherham S61 3JX* Tel (01709) 552268 E-mail restegram@lineone.net

MILLYARD, Alexander John. b 29. St Jo Coll Dur BA53. Qu Coll Birm 53. **d** 54 **p** 55. C Middlesbrough St Aid *York* 54-56; C Pocklington w Yapham-cum-Meltonby, Owsthorpe etc 56-58; C Millington w Gt Givendale 56-58; C Rickmansworth *St Alb* 58-61; R Wormley 61-65; Asst Chapl HM Pris Pentonville 65-67; Chapl HM Pris Leeds 67-69; Chapl HM Pris Ex 69-71; Chapl HM Pris Wandsworth 72-73; V Snibston *Leic* 73-75; V Leic All So 75-79; V Blakesley and Adstone *Pet* 79-89; R Blakesley w Adstone and Maidford etc 89-91; rtd 91; Perm to Offic *Chich* from 91. *6 Gainsborough House, Eaton Gardens, Hove BN3 3UA* Tel (01273) 728722

✠**MILMINE, The Rt Revd Douglas.** b 21. CBE83. St Pet Hall Ox BA46 MA46. Clifton Th Coll 47. **d** 47 **p** 48 **c** 73. C Ilfracombe SS Phil and Jas *Ex* 47-50; C Slough *Ox* 50-53; Chile 54-69; Adn N Chile, Bolivia and Peru 63-69; Hon Can Chile from 69; Area Sec SAMS 69-72; Bp Paraguay 73-85; rtd 86. *1C Clive Court, 24 Grand Parade, Eastbourne BN21 3DD* Tel (01323) 734159

MILMINE, Canon Neil Edward Douglas. b 46. Kent Univ BSc70. Wycliffe Hall Ox 80. **d** 82 **p** 83. C Hailsham *Chich* 82-86; C Horsham 86; TV 86-93; V Patcham from 93; Can and Preb Chich Cathl from 00; RD Brighton from 02. *The Vicarage, 12 Church Hill, Brighton BN1 8YE* Tel (01273) 552157 E-mail neil@milmine.freeserve.co.uk

MILNE, Alan. b 54. RMN SRN FE TCert. Cranmer Hall Dur 89. **d** 91 **p** 92. C Hartlepool St Luke *Dur* 91-94; P-in-c Dalton le Dale 94-00; V 00-05; P-in-c Hawthorn 94-00; R 00-05; R Hawthorn and Murton from 05; AD Easington from 03. *The Vicarage, Church Lane, Murton, Seaham SR7 9RD* Tel 0191-526 2410

MILNE, Miss Christine Helen. b 48. LTCL71 Lon Univ DipRS86. S'wark Ord Course 83. **dss** 86 **d** 87 **p** 90. S Lambeth St Steph *S'wark* 86-89; Par Dn 87-89; New Zealand from 89. *NGA Tawa School, Private Bag 1101, Marton, New Zealand* Tel (0064) (6) 327 7955 *or* 327 6429 Fax 327 7954

MILNE, James Harley. b 73. Univ of Wales (Lamp) BD94 New Coll Edin MTh96. TISEC 95. **d** 98 **p** 99. C Dundee St Mary Magd *Bre* 98-01; Chapl St Marg Res Home Dundee 98-01; R Dundee St Marg from 01; Episc Chapl Ninewells Hosp Dundee from 01. *St Margaret's Rectory, 19 Ancrum Road, Dundee DD2 2JL* Tel (01382) 667227 E-mail rector@stmargaret.freeserve.co.uk

MILNER, Catherine Mary (Kitty). *See* WILLIAMS, Ms Catherine Mary

MILNER, Darryl Vickers. b 43. Natal Univ BA63 DipTh66. St Chad's Coll Dur 64. **d** 66 **p** 67. C Oswestry H Trin *Lich* 66-69; S Africa 69-76; New Zealand from 76. *The Vicarage, 47 Church Street, Northcote, North Shore 1309, New Zealand* Tel (0064) (9) 480 7568 Fax 419 7459 E-mail dvmilner@clear.net.nz

MILNER, David. *See* MILNER, William David

MILNER, David. b 38. St Aid Birkenhead 63. **d** 66 **p** 67. C Ulverston H Trin *Carl* 66-68; C Mickleover All SS *Derby* 68-71; C Mickleover St Jo 68-71; V 71-82; P-in-c Sandiacre 82-86; P-in-c Doveridge 86-97; P-in-c Sudbury and Somersal Herbert 92-97; R Doveridge, Scropton, Sudbury etc 98-03; RD Longford 86-96 and 01-03; rtd 03; Perm to Offic *Lich* from 04. *21 Greenwood Park, Hednesford WS12 4DQ* Tel (01543) 428972

✠**MILNER, The Rt Revd Ronald James.** b 27. Pemb Coll Cam BA49 MA52. Wycliffe Hall Ox 51. **d** 53 **p** 54 **c** 88. Succ Sheff Cathl *Sheff* 53-58; V Westwood *Cov* 58-64; V Fletchamstead 64-70; R Southampton St Mary w H Trin *Win* 70-72; P-in-c Southampton St Matt 70-72; Lic to Offic 72-73; TR Southampton (City Cen) 73-83; Hon Can Win Cathl 75-83; Adn Linc 83-88; Can and Preb Linc Cathl 83-88; Suff Bp Burnley *Blackb* 88-93; rtd 93; Asst Bp S'well from 94. *7 Crafts Way, Southwell NG25 0BL* Tel (01636) 816256

MILNER, William David. b 52. St Jo Coll Nottm. **d** 93 **p** 94. C Wollaton *S'well* 93-97; P-in-c Daybrook 97; C W Bridgford 98-99; TV Clifton 99-04; P-in-c Collingham w S Scarle and

Besthorpe and Girton from 04. *The Rectory, 1 Vicarage Close, Collingham, Newark NG23 7PQ* Tel (01636) 892317

MILNES, David Ian. b 45. Chich Th Coll 74. **d** 76 **p** 77. C Walthamstow St Sav *Chelmsf* 76-80; C Chingford SS Pet and Paul 80-83; P-in-c Gt Ilford St Alb 83-87; V from 87. *The Vicarage, 99 Albert Road, Ilford IG1 1HS* Tel (020) 8478 2428 E-mail frmilnes@aol.com

MILNES, James Clark. b 79. St Chad's Coll Dur BA00 MA01. Westcott Ho Cam 03. **d** 05. C Newbold w Dunston *Derby* from 05. *29 Bank Wood Close, Chesterfield S41 8XQ* Tel (01246) 238342 E-mail jamesclarkmilnes@yahoo.co.uk

MILROY, Mrs Ethel Doreen. b 33. Bedf Coll Lon BSc54 Bris Univ PGCE69 Nottm Univ MEd79. N Ord Course 88. **d** 91 **p** 94. NSM Tideswell *Derby* 91-95; P-in-c Rowsley 95-02; rtd 02; Perm to Offic *Derby* from 02. *40 Eccles Close, Hope Valley S33 6RG* Tel (01433) 623582

MILSON, Julian James. b 70. De Montfort Univ BEd96. Oak Hill Th Coll BA04. **d** 04 **p** 05. C Bramcote *S'well* from 04. *46 Rufford Avenue, Beeston, Nottingham NG9 3JH* Tel 0115-939 1372 E-mail jmilson@bigfoot.com

MILTON, Andrew John. b 54. BD. St Steph Ho Ox. **d** 83 **p** 84. C Highfield *Ox* 83-87; TV Banbury 87-95; P-in-c Thorney Abbey *Ely* 95-02; TR Huntingdon from 02; P-in-c Gt w Lt Stukeley from 04. *The Rectory, 1 The Walks East, Huntingdon PE29 3AP* Tel (01480) 412674 E-mail miltons@walkseast.fsnet.co.uk

MILTON, Miss Angela Daphne. b 50. FILEx79. Oak Hill Th Coll 84. **d** 87 **p** 94. NSM Watford *St Alb* 87-95; NSM St Alb St Mary Marshalswick 95-97; C Stevenage St Mary Shephall w Aston 97-02; P-in-c E Molesey St Paul *Guildf* from 02. *St Paul's Vicarage, 101 Palace Road, East Molesey KT8 9DU* Tel (020) 8979 1580 E-mail angelamilton@msn.com

MILTON, Claudius James Barton. b 29. K Coll Lon BD52 AKC53. **d** 53 **p** 54. C Sudbury St Andr *Lon* 53-56; Asst Chapl Bedford Sch 57-65; Asst Master 57-65; Chapl Cranbrook Sch Kent 65-74; Asst Master and Housemaster 65-74; Chapl & Asst Master Clayesmore Sch Blandford 74-89; Clayesmore Prep Sch 74-89; rtd 89. *28 Oakwood Drive, Iwerne Minster, Blandford Forum DT11 8QT* Tel (01747) 811792

MILTON, Derek Rees. b 45. Open Univ BA76 Lon Univ BD80 Ex Univ MA95 Bris Univ CertEd81. St Jo Sem Wonersh 63. **d** 68 **p** 69. In RC Ch 68-84; Hon C Luton Lewsey St Hugh *St Alb* 84-85; Hon C Houghton Regis 85-86; C 86-89; TV Brixham w Churston Ferrers and Kingswear *Ex* 89-99; V Newport St Teilo *Mon* 99-02; C Chepstow from 02. *St Christopher's House, Bulwark Road, Bulwark, Chepstow NP16 5JW* Tel (01291) 622207 E-mail derek.milton@tesco.net

MILTON-THOMPSON, David Gerald. b 17. OBE76. Em Coll Cam BA39 MA MB BChir49 MRCS LRCP42. Lon Coll of Div 62. **d** 63 **p** 64. CMS 49-81 and 85-88; Kenya 52-81; C Chadwell *Chelmsf* 81-82; Hon C 82-85; Uganda 85-88; rtd 88; Hon C Sevenoaks St Nic *Roch* from 88. *Room 26, Rockdale House, Rockdale Road, Sevenoaks TN13 1JT* Tel (01732) 462977

MILTON-THOMPSON, Jonathan Patrick. b 51. Nottm Univ BA76. Oak Hill Th Coll 86. **d** 88 **p** 89. C Bispham *Blackb* 88-92; C Darfield *Sheff* 92; C-in-c Gt Houghton CD 92-03; P-in-c Livesey *Blackb* from 03. *St Andrew's Vicarage, 112 Full View, Blackburn BB2 4QB* Tel (01254) 259422

MILVERTON, The Revd and Rt Hon Lord (Fraser Arthur Richard Richards). b 30. Bps' Coll Cheshunt. **d** 57 **p** 58. C Beckenham St Geo *Roch* 57-59; C Sevenoaks St Jo 59-60; C Gt Bookham *Guildf* 60-63; V Okewood 63-67; R Christian Malford w Sutton Benger etc *Bris* 67-93; Public Preacher 93-95; rtd 95; Perm to Offic *Sarum* from 96. *7 Betjeman Road, Marlborough SN8 1TL* Tel (01672) 514068

MILVERTON, Frederic Jack. b 15. Lon Univ BSc37 Leeds Univ MEd40. Ripon Hall Ox 56. **d** 57 **p** 58. C Ecclesall *Sheff* 57-60; V Thurcroft 60-61; Lect Nottm Coll of Educn 61-67; Lect Weymouth Coll of Educn 67-76; Hd of Educn 70-76; Dean Educn Dorset Inst of HE 76-79; TV Oakdale St Geo *Sarum* 79-82; rtd 82; Perm to Offic *Sarum* from 82. *4 Compass South, Rodwell Road, Weymouth DT4 8QT* Tel (01305) 788930 E-mail rev.milv.compass@care4free.net

MILVERTON, Mrs Ruth Erica. b 32. Open Univ BA78 Southn Univ MA82. Sarum Th Coll 83. **dss** 86 **d** 87 **p** 95. Weymouth H Trin *Sarum* 86-87; Hon Par Dn 87-95; NSM 95-02; Dioc NSM Officer 89-97; rtd 02; Perm to Offic *Sarum* from 02. *4 Compass South, Rodwell Road, Weymouth DT4 8QT* Tel (01305) 788930 E-mail rev.milv.compass@care4free.net

MILWARD, Terence George. b 23. Ripon Hall Ox 66. **d** 68 **p** 69. C Selly Oak St Mary *Birm* 68-70; C Edgbaston St Bart 70-75; TV Bournemouth St Pet w St Swithun, H Trin etc *Win* 75-81; R Smannell w Enham Alamein 81-88; rtd 88; Perm to Offic *Guildf* from 88. *Church House Flat, Church Lane, Witley, Godalming GU8 5PN* Tel (01428) 685308

MINALL, Peter. b 26. Lon Univ BSc47. Bps' Coll Cheshunt 51. **d** 53 **p** 54. C Bishop's Stortford St Mich *St Alb* 53-57; C Luton w E Hyde 57-63; C Tuffley *Glouc* 63-65; Asst Youth Chapl 65-69; V Stroud 69-84; RD Bisley 78-84; P-in-c Barnwood 84-91; rtd 91; Lic to Offic *Glouc* from 91; Chapl Coney Hill Hosp Glouc 86-95; Chapl Severn NHS Trust from 95. *Amberwood, Knapp Lane, Painswick, Stroud GL6 6YE* Tel (01452) 813730 E-mail peter.minall@btinternet.com

MINAY, Francis Arthur Rodney. b 44. Edin Coll of Art DA65. Westcott Ho Cam 66. **d** 68 **p** 69. C Edenbridge *Roch* 68-73; C Bromley St Mark 73-75; V Tudeley w Capel 75-79; TV Littleham w Exmouth *Ex* 79-82; P-in-c Bolton Percy *York* from 82; Asst Chapl to Arts and Recreation in the NE from 82. *The Rectory, Bolton Percy, York YO23 7AL* Tel (01904) 744213

MINCHER, John Derek Bernard. b 31. **d** 60 **p** 61. OSB 54-80; Lic to Offic *Ox* 60-80; Perm to Offic *St E* 81-87; C Halesworth w Linstead, Chediston, Holton etc 87-90; P-in-c Worlingworth, Southolt, Tannington, Bedfield etc 90-91; R 91-96; rtd 96; Perm to Offic *St E* from 96. *3 Bracken Row, Thurston, Bury St Edmunds IP31 3AT* Tel (01359) 231976

MINCHEW, Donald Patrick. b 48. Univ of Wales (Cardiff) BD76. St Mich Coll Llan 72. **d** 76 **p** 77. C Glouc St Aldate *Glouc* 76-80; P-in-c Sharpness CD 80-81; V Sharpness w Purton and Brookend 81-95; Miss to Seafarers from 81; V Croydon St Mich w St Jas *S'wark* from 95. *St Michael's Vicarage, 39 Oakfield Road, Croydon CR0 2UX* Tel (020) 8680 8413

MINCHIN, Anthony John. b 35. St Cath Coll Cam BA59 MA. Wells Th Coll 59. **d** 61 **p** 62. C Cheltenham St Pet *Glouc* 61-64; C Bushey *St Alb* 64-67; V Cheltenham St Mich *Glouc* 67-74; V Lower Cam 74-82; V Tuffley 82-92; R Huntley and Longhope 92-00; rtd 00; Perm to Offic *Glouc* from 00. *2 Melbourne Drive, Stonehouse GL10 2PJ* Tel (01453) 828899

MINCHIN, Charles Scott. b 51. Trin Coll Cam BA72 MA75. Linc Th Coll 73. **d** 75 **p** 76. C Gt Wyrley *Lich* 75-78; TV Wilnecote 78-82; C Tamworth 82-84; C-in-c Glascote CD 84-88; R Brierley Hill 88-93; R Brierley Hill *Worc* 93-03; P-in-c Stonehouse *Glouc* from 03. *The Vicarage, Elms Road, Stonehouse GL10 2NP* Tel (01453) 822332 E-mail cminchin@lineone.net

MINGINS, Canon Marion Elizabeth. b 52. Birm Univ BSocSc73 CQSW75. **d** 87 **p** 94. CA 79-89; NSM Battersea Park All SS *S'wark* 87-88; Sen Selection Sec ACCM 87-88; OHP 89-91; Asst Dioc Dir of Ords *St E* 91-92; Dioc Dir of Ords 92-99; Min Can St E Cathl 91-92; Hon Can 92-93; Can Res 93-02; Can Pastor 99-02; Chapl to The Queen from 96; rtd 02; Perm to Offic *St E* from 02. *54 College Street, Bury St Edmunds IP33 1NH* Tel (01284) 753396 E-mail marionmingins@freezone.co.uk

MINHINNICK, Leslie. b 18. Jes Coll Ox BA39 MA43. Wycliffe Hall Ox 40. **d** 41 **p** 42. C Briton Ferry *Llan* 41-43; C Canton St Jo 43-45; Tutor St Aid Birkenhead 45-50; Vice-Prin 50-51; V Over St Jo *Ches* 51-54; V Birkenhead St Mark 54-60; V Preston St Jo *Blackb* 60-61; V Chipping 61-66; V Lytham St Jo 66-81; rtd 81; Perm to Offic *Ban* from 81. *The Old School House, Cemaes Bay LL67 0NG* Tel (01407) 710601

MINICH, Mason Faulconer. b 38. **d** 66 **p** 67. USA 66-71 and from 81; C Alverstoke *Portsm* 80; C Romford Ascension Collier Row *Chelmsf* 80-81. *5055 Seminary Road, Apartment 1319, Alexandria, VA 22311, USA*

MINION, Arthur. b 65. TCD BTh92. CITC 89. **d** 92 **p** 93. C Bandon Union *C, C & R* 92-95; I Taunagh w Kilmactranny, Ballysumaghan etc *K, E & A* 95-99; I Shinrone w Aghancon etc *L & K* from 99. *St Mary's Rectory, Shinrone, Birr, Co Offaly, Irish Republic* Tel and fax (00353) (505) 47164

MINION, Hazel Elizabeth Alice. b 47. TCD BA68 HDipEd69. CITC 00. **d** 03 **p** 04. Aux Min Templebreedy w Tracton and Nohoval *C, C & R* from 03; Chapl Ashton Sch Cork from 03. *22 Inchvale Drive, Shamrock Lawn, Douglas, Cork, Irish Republic* Tel (00353) (21) 496 6044 *or* 436 1924 Fax 496 6321 E-mail hminion22@hotmail.com

MINNS, David Andrew. b 59. St Jo Coll Nottm 95. **d** 97 **p** 98. C Burpham *Guildf* 97-00; C Knaphill w Brookwood 00-04; R Ewhurst from 04. *The Rectory, The Street, Ewhurst, Cranleigh GU6 7PX* Tel (01483) 277584 E-mail dlkminns@tinyworld.co.uk

MINNS, John Alfred. b 38. Oak Hill Th Coll 63. **d** 68 **p** 69. C Cheadle Hulme St Andr *Ches* 68-72; C Hartford 72-74; V Wharton 74-85; V Halliwell St Paul *Man* 85-87; C Halliwell St Pet 87-91; rtd 91; Perm to Offic *Glouc* 91-97. *39 Hambidge Lane, Lechlade GL7 3BJ* Tel (01367) 253549

MINNS, Canon John Charles. b 42. EAMTC. **d** 85 **p** 86. NSM Heigham St Barn w St Bart *Nor* 85-91; P-in-c Nor St Geo Tombland from 91; Asst Chapl Norfolk and Nor Hosp 92-95; Chapl Nor Sch of Art and Design 99-04; Hon Can Nor Cathl *Nor* from 05. *18 Thunder Lane, Thorpe St Andrew, Norwich NR7 0PX* Tel (01603) 437000 E-mail stgeorge.tombland@virgin.net

MINORS, Graham Glyndwr Cavil. b 44. Glouc Sch of Min. **d** 79 **p** 79. Hon C Lower Cam *Glouc* 79-83; C Leckhampton SS Phil and Jas w Cheltenham St Jas 83-89; V Cainscross w Selsley 89-99; RD Stonehouse 97-99; TR Bodmin w Lanhydrock and Lanivet *Truro* from 99; Chapl N and E Cornwall Primary Care Trust from 02. *The Rectory, Priory Road, Bodmin PL31 2AB* Tel (01208) 73867 E-mail revgminors@hotmail.com

MINSON, Roger Graham. b 41. Leeds Univ BA64. Coll of Resurr Mirfield 64. **d** 66 **p** 67. C Horfield St Greg *Bris* 66-70; C

Southmead 70-73; V Lawrence Weston 74-81; TV Knowle 81-93; V Knowle St Martin 93-95; V Fishponds St Mary from 95. *St Mary's Vicarage, Vicar's Close, Bristol BS16 3TH* Tel 0117-965 4462 *or* 958 6412
E-mail stmarys.fishponds@virgin.net

MINTON, Bernard John. b 68. St Chad's Coll Dur BA89 MRICS00. Coll of Resurr Mirfield 00. **d** 04 **p** 05. C Lancing w Coombes *Chich* from 04. *30 Greenoaks, Lancing BN15 0HE* Tel (01903) 767077 E-mail bernardminton@aol.com

MINTY, Kenneth Desmond. b 25. Ch Ch Ox BA48 MA51. Lich Th Coll 71 Qu Coll Birm 72. **d** 73 **p** 74. Asst Chapl Wrekin Coll Telford 73-84; Chapl 84-86; Hon C Lawley *Lich* 74-75; Hon C Cen Telford 75-81; Hon C Longdon-upon-Tern, Rodington, Uppington etc 81-89; V Ercall Magna 89-95; V Rowton 89-95; rtd 95; Perm to Offic *Lich* from 95. *9 Shawbirch Road, Telford TF5 0AD* Tel (01952) 244218

MINTY, Selwyn Francis. b 34. St D Coll Lamp 58. **d** 61 **p** 62. C Tonyrefail *Llan* 61-66; C Pontypridd St Cath 66-69; V Cilfynydd 69-84; V Crynant 84-00; rtd 00. *24 Derwen Fawr, Cilfrew, Neath SA10 8NX*

MIR, Amene Rahman. b 58. Man Univ BA81 PhD93. Coll of Resurr Mirfield 81. **d** 83 **p** 84. C Walton St Mary *Liv* 83-87; Chapl Walton Hosp Liv 83-87; Perm to Offic *Man* 87-90; Asst Chapl Salford Mental Health Unit 90-94; Chapl Salford Mental Health Services NHS Trust 94-96; Chapl R Marsden NHS Trust from 96. *The Chaplain's Office, Royal Marsden Hospital, Fulham Road, London SW3 6JJ* Tel (020) 7808 2818 *or* 7352 8171
E-mail mir.amene@rmh.nthames.nhs.uk

MITCHAM, Andrew Mark. b 66. Kent Univ BA87 Leeds Univ BA90. Coll of Resurr Mirfield 88. **d** 91 **p** 92. C Downham Market w Bexwell *Ely* 91-94; P Shrine of Our Lady of Walsingham 94-96; V W Worthing St Jo *Chich* 96-04; R Eye *St E* from 04. *The Vicarage, 41 Castle Street, Eye IP23 7AW* Tel (01379) 870277 E-mail andrew@redmail.co.uk

MITCHELL, Albert George. b 25. TCD MA. **d** 88 **p** 89. Bp's C Skreen w Kilmacshalgan and Dromard *T, K & A* 88-00; Can Killala Cathl 96-00; rtd 00. *The Glebe, Kilglass, Enniscrone, Co Sligo, Irish Republic* Tel (00353) (96) 36258

MITCHELL, Alec Silas. b 52. Man Univ BA75 MPhil95. Nor Bapt Coll 77 Coll of Resurr Mirfield 98. **d** 99 **p** 99. C Ashton *Man* 99-05; TV from 05; Dioc Officer for Racial Justice from 02. *Holy Trinity Vicarage, Dean Street, Ashton-under-Lyne OL6 7HD* Tel 0161-344 0075

MITCHELL, Allan. b 52. Kelham Th Coll 74 Linc Th Coll 78. **d** 78 **p** 79. C Kells *Carl* 78-81; C Upperby St Jo 81-83; V Pennington w Lindal and Marton 83-88; V Westfield St Mary 88-98; P-in-c Dalton-in-Furness 98-02; V Dalton-in-Furness and Ireleth-with-Askam from 02. *The Vicarage, Market Place, Dalton-in-Furness LA15 8AZ* Tel (01229) 462526

MITCHELL, Andrew Patrick (Paddy). b 37. English Coll Valladolid 59 Ripon Coll Cuddesdon 84. **d** 64 **p** 65. In RC Ch 64-85; C Woolwich St Mary w St Mich *S'wark* 85-87; V E Wickham 87-94; P-in-c Walsall St Andr *Lich* 94-00; TV Sedgley All SS *Worc* 00-03; rtd 03; Perm to Offic *Birm* 03-04. *714 Pershore Road, Selly Oak, Birmingham B29 7NR* Tel 0121-258 1776

MITCHELL, Christopher Allan. b 51. Newc Univ BA72. Oak Hill Th Coll 82. **d** 84 **p** 85. C Guisborough *York* 84-87; C Thornaby on Tees 87-88; TV 88-92; V Dent w Cowgill *Bradf* 92-98; R Barney, Fulmodeston w Croxton, Hindringham etc *Nor* 98-03; R Hulland, Atlow, Kniveton, Bradley and Hognaston *Derby* from 03. *The Rectory, 16 Eaton Close, Hulland Ward, Ashbourne DE6 3EX* Tel (01335) 372138
E-mail revchris8@aol.com

MITCHELL, Christopher Ashley. b 69. Leeds Univ BA(Econ)91. Ridley Hall Cam CTM92. **d** 95 **p** 96. Min Can St As Cathl *St As* 95-98; CF 98-02; Chapl RAF from 02; Perm to Offic *Ely* from 01. *Chaplaincy Services (RAF), HQ, Personnel and Training Command, RAF Innsworth, Gloucester GL3 1EZ* Tel (01452) 712612 ext 5164 Fax 615800

MITCHELL, Christopher Derek. b 61. Univ of Wales (Lamp) BA85 Leic Univ MA86 Qu Coll Cam BA88 MA92. Westcott Ho Cam 87. **d** 89 **p** 90. C Streetly *Lich* 89-92; C Brookfield St Mary *Lon* 92-96. *Address temp unknown*

MITCHELL, Clare. *See* GRIFFITHS, Mrs Clare

MITCHELL, Canon David George. b 35. QUB BA56. Sarum Th Coll 59. **d** 61 **p** 62. C Westbury-on-Trym H Trin *Bris* 61-64; C Cricklade w Latton 64-68; V Fishponds St Jo 68-77; RD Stapleton 76-77; TR E Bris 77-87; R Syston 87-94; V Warmley 87-94; P-in-c Bitton 87-94; R Warmley, Syston and Bitton 94-01; RD Bitton 87-93; Hon Can Bris Cathl 87-01; rtd 01; P-in-c Chedworth, Yanworth and Stowell, Coln Rogers etc *Glouc* from 01; Perm to Offic *Bris* from 01. *The Vicarage, Cheap Street, Chedworth, Cheltenham GL54 4AA* Tel (01285) 720392
E-mail canongeorgemitchell@btinternet.com

MITCHELL, Preb David Norman. b 35. Tyndale Hall Bris 64. **d** 67 **p** 68. C Marple All SS *Ches* 67-70; C St Helens St Helen *Liv* 70-72; V S Lambeth St Steph *S'wark* 72-78; P-in-c Brixton Road Ch Ch 73-75; SE Area Sec CPAS 78-81; R Uphill *B & W* 81-92; TR 92-01; Chapl Weston Area Health Trust 86-01; Preb Wells Cathl *B & W* from 90; rtd 01; Perm to Offic *B & W* from 02. *3 Pizey Close, Clevedon BS21 7TP* Tel (01275) 349176

MITCHELL, Edwin. b 44. St Jo Coll Nottm BTh74. **d** 74 **p** 75. C Worksop St Jo *S'well* 74-77; C Waltham Abbey *Chelmsf* 77-80; V Whiston *Liv* 80-91; R Wombwell *Sheff* 91-99; V Mortomley St Sav High Green from 99; AD Ecclesfield from 01. *The Vicarage, Mortomley Lane, High Green, Sheffield S35 3HS* Tel 0114-284 8231 E-mail mitchell5@supanet.com

MITCHELL, Eric Sidney. b 24. S Dios Minl Tr Scheme 77. **d** 80 **p** 81. NSM Portland All SS w St Pet *Sarum* 80-83; C 88-92; Bermuda 83-88; Chapl HM Pris The Verne 91-92; rtd 92; Perm to Offic *Sarum* from 92. *10 Underhedge Gardens, Portland DT5 2DX* Tel (01305) 821059

MITCHELL, Geoffrey. b 36. SS Coll Cam BA60 MA64 Nottm Univ BA97 CEng66 FIMechE76 FCIT92. EMMTC 88. **d** 91 **p** 92. NSM Oaks in Charnwood and Copt Oak *Leic* 91-94; NSM Loughborough All SS w H Trin 94-00; P-in-c Oaks in Charnwood and Copt Oak 00-03; NSM Shepshed and Oaks in Charnwood 03-04; Dioc NSM Officer 98-02; rtd 04; Perm to Offic *Leic* from 04. *36 Brick Kiln Lane, Shepshed, Loughborough LE12 9EL* Tel (01509) 502280
E-mail mitchell.household@talk21.com

MITCHELL, Geoffrey Peter. b 30. Liv Univ BEng57 Man Univ MSc68. Wells Th Coll 57. **d** 59 **p** 60. C Bradford cum Beswick *Man* 59-61; R Man St Pet Oldham Road w St Jas 61-64; Lic to Offic 64-68; Hon C Unsworth 68-86; V Woolfold 86-95; rtd 95; Perm to Offic *Man* from 95. *14 Redfearn Wood, Rochdale OL12 7GA* Tel (01706) 638180

MITCHELL, George. *See* MITCHELL, Canon David George

MITCHELL, George Alfred. b 23. TCD BA45 MA56. **d** 46 **p** 47. C Belfast St Matt *Conn* 46-48; C Ballymoney 48-51; C Belf Cathl Miss 51-52; I Broomhedge 52-58; I Carrickfergus 59-70; I Bangor St Comgall *D & D* 70-88; Can Belf Cathl 78-88; rtd 88. *2 Glendun Park, Bangor BT20 4UX* Tel (028) 9146 0882

MITCHELL, Geraint Owain. b 71. Lincs & Humberside Univ BA96 Leeds Univ BA99. Coll of Resurr Mirfield 99. **d** 02 **p** 03. C Bridlington Em *York* from 02. *40 Georgian Way, Bridlington YO15 3TB* Tel (01262) 678560

MITCHELL, Gordon Frank Henry. b 26. QFSM. FIFireE. Sarum & Wells Th Coll 74. **d** 77 **p** 78. NSM Alderbury and W Grimstead *Sarum* 77-91; NSM Alderbury Team 91-96; Perm to Offic from 96. *Seefeld, Southampton Road, Whaddon, Salisbury SP5 3EB* Tel (01722) 710516

MITCHELL, Graham Bell. b 40. Otago Univ BA64 MA65 Worc Coll Ox BA73 MA76. St Chad's Coll Dur 66. **d** 68 **p** 69. C Bris St Agnes w St Simon *Bris* 68-71; C Bedminster St Mich 73-76; V Auckland St Pet *Dur* 76-78; Vice-Prin Chich Th Coll 78-83; C Brighton St Pet w Chpl Royal and St Jo *Chich* 83-86; P-in-c Scaynes Hill 86-96; V 96-04; rtd 04. *32 Wynyard Street, Mount Eden, Auckland, New Zealand* Tel (0064) (9) 630 7186

MITCHELL, Ian. *See* MITCHELL, Stuart Ian

MITCHELL, Jolyon Peter. b 64. Selw Coll Cam BA88 MA90 Edin Univ PhD97. St Jo Coll Dur MA93. **d** 93 **p** 94. NSM St Mary's Cathl *Edin* 93-97; NSM Edin Ch Ch 97-01; NSM Edin St Jas from 01; Lect Edin Univ 93-01; Sen Lect from 01; Visiting Fell Clare Hall Cam 02. *11 Eildon Street, Edinburgh EH3 5JU* Tel 0131-226 1092 *or* 650 8900 E-mail jolyon.mitchell@ed.ac.uk

MITCHELL, Kevin. b 49. Newc Univ BSc71 Ox Univ BA83. Ripon Coll Cuddesdon 81. **d** 83 **p** 84. C Cantril Farm *Liv* 83-86; Chapl N Middx Hosp 86-90; C Gt Cambridge Road St Jo and St Jas *Lon* 86-90; P-in-c Cricklewood St Pet 90-96; V Whetstone St Jo from 96. *St John's Vicarage, 1163 High Road, London N20 0PG* Tel (020) 8445 4569
E-mail kevinmitchell@onetel.com

MITCHELL, Owain. *See* MITCHELL, Geraint Owain

MITCHELL, Paddy. *See* MITCHELL, Andrew Patrick

MITCHELL, The Very Revd Patrick Reynolds. b 30. FSA81 Mert Coll Ox BA52 MA56. Wells Th Coll 52. **d** 54 **p** 55. C Mansfield St Mark *S'well* 54-57; Chapl Wells Th Coll and PV Wells Cathl *B & W* 57-61; V Milton *Portsm* 61-67; V Frome St Jo and P-in-c Woodlands *B & W* 67-73; Dir of Ords 70-74; Dean Wells 73-89; Dean Windsor and Dom Chapl to The Queen 89-98; rtd 98; Perm to Offic *Ex* from 98 and *Sarum* from 00. *Wolford Lodge, Dunkeswell, Honiton EX14 4SQ* Tel (01404) 841244

MITCHELL, Peter Derek. b 30. Roch Th Coll 67. **d** 69 **p** 70. C Wargrave *Ox* 69-72; V Lund *Blackb* 72-80; V Badsey w Aldington and Wickhamford *Worc* 80-96; rtd 96. *Althaea, 29 Lavender Walk, Evesham WR11 2LN*

MITCHELL, Richard John Anthony. b 64. St Martin's Coll Lanc BA85 PGCE86. Sarum & Wells Th Coll 88. **d** 91 **p** 92. C Kendal H Trin *Carl* 91-95; TV Kirkby Lonsdale 95-04; P-in-c Badgeworth, Shurdington and Witcombe w Bentham *Glouc* from 04; RD Glouc N from 04. *The Vicarage, School Lane, Shurdington, Cheltenham GL51 4TF* Tel (01242) 702911
E-mail richard.mitchell@talk21.com

MITCHELL, Robert Hugh. b 53. Ripon Coll Cuddesdon. **d** 82 **p** 83. C E Dulwich St Jo *S'wark* 82-86; C Cambridge Gt St Mary w St Mich *Ely* 86-90; Chapl Girton Coll Cam 86-90; Asst Chapl

Win Coll 90-91; Assoc Chapl Addenbrooke's Hosp Cam 91-93; Chapl Portsm Hosps NHS Trust 93-95; Chapl St Mary's Hosp Portsm 93-95; Chapl R Free Hampstead NHS Trust from 95. *The Chaplains' Office, The Royal Free Hospital, Pond Street, London NW3 2QG* Tel (020) 7794 0500 ext 3096 *or* 7830 2742 E-mail robert.mitchell@royalfree.nhs.uk

MITCHELL, Robert McFarlane. b 50. Man Univ BA72. Wycliffe Hall Ox 73. **d** 75 **p** 76. C Tonbridge SS Pet and Paul *Roch* 75-80; CF from 80. *c/o MOD Chaplains (Army)* Tel (01980) 615804 Fax 615800

MITCHELL, Roger Sulway. b 36. Chich Th Coll 70. **d** 71 **p** 71. C Sidcup St Jo *Roch* 71-74; C Pembury 74-76; Chapl St Lawr Hosp Bodmin 76-96; Chapl Cornwall and Is of Scilly Mental Health Unit 88-96; Chapl Cornwall Healthcare NHS Trust 96-00; TV Bodmin w Lanhydrock and Lanivet *Truro* 97-00; rtd 00. *12 Beacon Road, Bodmin PL31 1AS* Tel (01208) 76357 Mobile 07771-881258

MITCHELL, Miss Sarah Rachel. b 79. Birm Univ BA00 Anglia Poly Univ BA04. Westcott Ho Cam 02. **d** 05. C Reddal Hill St Luke *Worc* from 05. *15 Morgan Close, Cradley Heath B64 6DH* Tel (01384) 411132 E-mail s.r.mitchell.02@cantab.net

MITCHELL, Sheila Rosemary. b 53. Univ Coll Ches CertEd74 AdDipEd80 PGDPT98. N Ord Course 93. **d** 96 **p** 97. NSM Plemstall w Guilden Sutton *Ches* 96-98; C New Brighton St Jas w Em 98-00; C New Brighton All SS 98-00; P-in-c Weston 00-02; V from 02. *All Saints' Vicarage, 13 Cemetery Road, Weston, Crewe CW2 5LQ* Tel (01270) 582585

MITCHELL, Stephen Andrew John. b 56. Ch Ch Coll Cant CertEd78 K Coll Lon AKC77 BD80 MA02 Lambeth STh90. Coll of Resurr Mirfield 80. **d** 82 **p** 83. C Chatham St Steph *Roch* 82-87; C Edenbridge 87-91; V from 91; P-in-c Crockham Hill H Trin from 91; Chapl Invicta Community Care NHS Trust from 91. *The Vicarage, Mill Hill, Edenbridge TN8 5DA* Tel (01732) 862258 Fax 864335

MITCHELL, Stephen John. b 51. Ex Univ BA73 Fitzw Coll Cam BA78 MA. Ridley Hall Cam 76. **d** 79 **p** 80. C Gt Malvern St Mary *Worc* 79-81; Prec Leic Cathl *Leic* 82-85; R Barrow upon Soar w Walton le Wolds 85-02; P-in-c Gazeley w Dalham, Moulton and Kentford *St E* 02-04; V Dalham, Gazeley, Higham, Kentford and Moulton from 05. *All Saints' Vicarage, The Street, Gazeley, Newmarket CB8 8RB* Tel (01638) 552630 E-mail smitch4517@aol.com

MITCHELL, Steven. b 58. Nottm Univ BTh83. St Jo Coll Nottm. **d** 83 **p** 84. C Ovenden *Wakef* 83-87; V Gawthorpe and Chickenley Heath 87-98; V Birkenshaw w Hunsworth from 98. *The Vicarage, 6 Vicarage Gardens, Birkenshaw, Bradford BD11 2EF* Tel (01274) 683776

MITCHELL, Stuart. b 53. Cranmer Hall Dur 01. **d** 03 **p** 04. C Pocklington and Owsthorpe and Kilnwick Percy etc *York* from 03. *110 Wold Road, Pocklington, York YO42 2QG* Tel (01759) 306966

MITCHELL, Stuart Ian. b 50. Wadh Coll Ox BA71 DPhil74. S'wark Ord Course DipRS84. **d** 85 **p** 87. NSM Charlton St Luke w H Trin *S'wark* 85-86; NSM Kidbrooke St Jas 86-88; NSM Newbold w Dunston *Derby* 88-94; C 94-96; C Newbold and Gt Barlow 96-97; P-in-c Matlock Bank 97-03; RD Wirksworth 98-03; P-in-c Mackworth All SS from 03; P-in-c Mugginton and Kedleston from 03; P-in-c Kirk Langley from 03. *The Vicarage, 4 Church Lane, Kirk Langley, Ashbourne DE6 4NG* Tel (01332) 824729

MITCHELL, Tim. b 63. Trin Coll Bris 95. **d** 97 **p** 98. C Cromer *Nor* 97-01; P-in-c Selston *S'well* 01-05; P-in-c Sutton in Ashfield St Mich from 05. *The Vicarage, 11A Deepdale Gardens, Sutton-in-Ashfield NG17 4ER* Tel (01623) 476358 E-mail t.mitchell58@ntlworld.com

MITCHELL, Wendy Mary. b 47. Glas Univ MA70 Callendar Park Coll of Educn Falkirk PGCE71. Trin Coll Bris 99. **d** 01 **p** 02. C Yatton Moor *B & W* from 01. *129 High Street, Yatton, Bristol BS49 4DH* Tel (01934) 876676

MITCHELL, William Blanchard. b 26. Lon Univ DipTh54. St Aid Birkenhead 53. **d** 55 **p** 56. C Kendal H Trin *Carl* 55-59; C Dalton-in-Furness 59-60; V Nichol Forest 60-61; CF 61-77; V Nicholforest and Kirkandrews on Esk *Carl* 77-84; R Kirkby Thore w Temple Sowerby and Newbiggin 84-89; rtd 89; Perm to Offic *Carl* from 89. *Koi Hai, 23 Longlands Road, Carlisle CA3 9AD* Tel (01228) 546230

MITCHELL-INNES, Charles William. b 47. Pemb Coll Cam BA69 MA73. Sarum Th Coll 83. **d** 86 **p** 87. Asst Chapl Sherborne Sch 86-89; Chapl Milton Abbey Sch Dorset 90-96; Conduct Eton Coll from 96. *3 Savile House, Eton College, Windsor SL4 6DT* Tel (01753) 671004

MITCHELL-INNES, James Alexander. b 39. Ch Ch Ox BA64 MA66. Lon Coll of Div 65. **d** 67 **p** 68. C Cullompton *Ex* 67-71; Nigeria 71-75; P-in-c Puddletown w Athelhampton and Burleston *Sarum* 75-78; R Puddletown and Tolpuddle 78-82; V Win Ch Ch *Win* 82-92; V Titchfield *Portsm* 92-98; rtd 98; Perm to Offic *Win* from 99. *The Cherries, 14 Test Rise, Chilbolton, Stockbridge SO20 6AF* Tel (01264) 860815 E-mail jamesmi@tiscali.co.uk

MITCHINSON, Frank. b 37. AKC60. **d** 61 **p** 62. C Cross Heath *Lich* 61-64; C Forrabury w Minster and Trevalga *Truro* 64-68; C Harpenden St Nic *St Alb* 68-70; R Southwick St Mich *Chich* 70-83; V Billingshurst 83-88; V Preston 88-02; rtd 02; P-in-c Bolney *Chich* 02-05. *7 St Cyr, 26 Douglas Avenue, Exmouth EX8 2HA*

MITCHINSON, Canon Ronald. b 35. Westmr Coll Ox MA91. Linc Th Coll 66. **d** 68 **p** 69. C Heworth St Mary *Dur* 68-72; C Banbury *Ox* 72-73; TV 73-76; New Zealand 76-82; TR Banbury *Ox* 82-86; RD Deddington 84-86; Ind Chapl 86-92; Hon Can Ch Ch 90-92; TV Brayton *York* 92-96; Sen Chapl Selby Coalfield Ind Chapl 92-96; rtd 96; Perm to Offic *York* from 04. *6 St John's Crescent, York YO31 7QP* Tel (01904) 642382 E-mail rmitchinson@freire.org

MITFORD, Bertram William Jeremy (Bill). b 27. Wells Th Coll 62. **d** 64 **p** 65. C Hollinwood *Man* 64-67; C Atherton 67-68; C Frome St Jo *B & W* 68-71; V Cleeve 72-74; V Cleeve w Chelvey and Brockley 74-79; Chapl HM Pris Shepton Mallet 79-92; C Shepton Mallet *B & W* 79-84; C Shepton Mallet w Doulting 84-92; rtd 92. *2 Charlton Road, Shepton Mallet BA4 5NY* Tel (01749) 342825

MITRA, Avijit (Munna). b 53. Keble Coll Ox BA76. Ox NSM Course 84. **d** 88 **p** 89. NSM Abingdon *Ox* 88-96; Asst Chapl Abingdon Sch 88-96; Sen Chapl Ch Hosp Horsham from 96. *Cornerways, Christ's Hospital, Horsham RH13 0LD* Tel (01403) 258348 E-mail munna@amitra.fsnet.co.uk

MITRA, Mrs Nicola Jane. b 54. St Hugh's Coll Ox BA76 PGCE77 MA81. Ox Min Course 92. **d** 94 **p** 95. NSM Abingdon *Ox* 94-96; Asst Chapl Ch Hosp Horsham from 96. *Cornerways, Christ's Hospital, Horsham RH13 0LD* Tel (01403) 258348

MITSON, Mrs Carol Mae. b 46. SRN SCM HVCert. Oak Hill NSM Course 89. **d** 93 **p** 94. NSM Lawford *Chelmsf* 93-96; NSM Elmstead 96-98; NSM Harwich 96-98; NSM Dedham 98-00; Perm to Offic from 01. *Drift Cottage, The Drift, Dedham, Colchester CO7 6AH* Tel and fax (01206) 323116

MITSON, John Dane. b 29. Solicitor 56 SS Coll Cam MA53 LLM54. Oak Hill Th Coll 91 EAMTC 93. **d** 94 **p** 95. Dioc Registrar and Legal Sec to Bp St E 75-97; NSM Greenstead *Chelmsf* 94-96; NSM Elmstead 96-98; NSM Dedham 98-00; Perm to Offic from 00. *Drift Cottage, The Drift, Dedham, Colchester CO7 6AH* Tel and fax (01206) 323116

MITSON, Miss Joyce. b 37. Man Univ CertEd64. Trin Coll Bris DipHE79. **dss** 79 **d** 87 **p** 94. Wellington w Eyton *Lich* 79-85; Farnworth *Liv* 85-91; Par Dn 87-91; TD Bilston *Lich* 91-94; TV 94; Lich Local Min Adv 91-94; C W Bromwich St Jas 94-97; C W Bromwich St Jas w St Paul 97-98; rtd 98. *13 Birkenhills Drive, Bolton BL3 4TX* Tel (01204) 655081

MITTON, Michael Simon. b 53. Ex Univ BA75. St Jo Coll Nottm 76. **d** 78 **p** 79. C High Wycombe *Ox* 78-82; C Kidderminster St Geo *Worc* 82; TV 82-89; Dir Angl Renewal Min 89-97; Dep Dir Acorn Chr Foundn 97-03; Renewing Min Project Officer *Derby* from 03. *50 Kedleston Road, Derby DE22 1GW* Tel (01332) 340088 *or* 370955 E-mail mmitton@fish.co.uk

MLEMETA, Kedmon Hezron. b 60. CertEd78. CA Tr Coll Nairobi 86. **d** 89 **p** 90. Tanzania 89-96 and from 99; P-in-c Loughb Gd Shep *Leic* 96-99. *The Diocese of Mount Kilimanjaro, PO Box 1057, Arusha, Tanzania*

MNGOMEZULU, Sipho Percy. **d** 78 **p** 78. Swaziland 78-96 and from 03; NSM Cricklewood St Gabr and St Mich *Lon* 96-03. *Address temp unknown*

MOAT, Terry. b 61. Nottm Univ BTh92. Aston Tr Scheme 86 Linc Th Coll 88. **d** 92 **p** 93. C Caterham *S'wark* 92-96; Hon C Tynemouth Priory *Newc* from 04. *171 Queen Alexandra Road, North Shields NE29 9BE* Tel 0191-291 2302

MOATE, Gerard Grigglestone. b 54. BA FRSA01. Oak Hill Th Coll 79. **d** 82 **p** 83. C Mildmay Grove St Jude and St Paul *Lon* 82-85; C Hampstead St Jo 85-88; P-in-c Pinxton *Derby* 88; V Charlesworth and Dinting Vale 88-95; V Dedham *Chelmsf* from 95; RD Dedham and Tey 98-03. *The Vicarage, High Street, Dedham, Colchester CO7 6DE* Tel (01206) 322136 E-mail gerard@moate.org *or* vicar@dedham-parishchurch.org.uk

MOATE, Phillip. b 47. RGN70 Lon Univ DN73 RNT75 Leeds Univ Cert Counselling 94. N Ord Course 87. **d** 90 **p** 91. NSM Upper Holme Valley *Wakef* 90-92; NSM Almondbury Deanery 92-94; NSM Honley 94-95; P-in-c Roos and Garton w Tunstall, Grimston and Hilston *York* 95-02; R Lockington and Lund and Scorborough w Leconfield from 02. *Rectory House, Church Lane, Lockington, Driffield YO25 9SU* Tel (01430) 810604 E-mail pmoate@tiscali.co.uk

MOATT, Richard Albert. b 54. K Coll Lon BD76 AKC76. Linc Th Coll 80. **d** 81 **p** 82. C Egremont and Haile *Carl* 81-85; V Addingham, Edenhall, Langwathby and Culgaith 85-04; P-in-c Skirwith, Ousby and Melmerby w Kirkland 98-04; V Cross Fell Gp from 04. *The Vicarage, Langwathby, Penrith CA10 1LW* Tel (01768) 881212 E-mail moatt@btinternet.com

MOBBERLEY, Keith John. b 56. BA. Westcott Ho Cam. **d** 84 **p** 85. C Coventry Caludon *Cov* 84-87; C Kenilworth St Nic 87-92; V Keresley and Coundon 92-98; P-in-c Hatton w Haseley,

Rowington w Lowsonford etc 98-00; R from 00. *North Ferncumbe Rectory, Hatton Green, Hatton, Warwick CV35 7LA* Tel (01926) 484332

MOBBERLEY, Mrs Susan. b 57. Kent Univ BA79. Westcott Ho Cam 81. **dss** 84 **d** 90 **p** 94. Coventry Caludon *Cov* 84-87; Lic to Offic 87-92; NSM Keresley and Coundon 92-98; NSM Hatton w Haseley, Rowington w Lowsonford etc from 98. *North Ferncumbe Rectory, Hatton Green, Hatton, Warwick CV35 7LA* Tel (01926) 484332

MOBBS, Bernard Frederick. b 26. S'wark Ord Course 71. **d** 72 **p** 73. C Purley St Barn *S'wark* 72-74; Vice-Prin S'wark Ord Course 74-80; P-in-c Sydenham St Bart *S'wark* 80-87; V Dormansland 87-92; rtd 92; Perm to Offic *Chich* from 92. *Fair Havens, Fletching Street, Mayfield TN20 6TH* Tel (01435) 872910

MOBERLY (née McCLURE), Mrs Jennifer Lynne. b 62. Ball State Univ (USA) BSc84. Cranmer Hall Dur 98. **d** 01 **p** 02. C Belmont *Dur* from 01. *8 Princes Street, Durham DH1 4RP* Tel 0191-386 4255

MOBERLY, Richard Hamilton. b 30. Trin Hall Cam BA53 MA57. Cuddesdon Coll 53. **d** 55 **p** 56. C Walton St Mary *Liv* 55-59; C Kensington St Mary Abbots w St Geo *Lon* 59-63; R Chingola 63-66; N Rhodesia 63-64; Zambia 64-66; V Kennington Cross St Anselm *S'wark* 67-73; TV N Lambeth 74-80; Ind Chapl 80-95; rtd 95; Perm to Offic *S'wark* from 95. *24 Wincott Street, London SE11 4NT* Tel (020) 7735 2233 Fax 7793 9021 E-mail richard@richardmoberly.org.uk

MOBERLY, Robert Walter Lambert. b 52. New Coll Ox MA77 Selw Coll Cam MA80 Trin Coll Cam PhD81. Ridley Hall Cam 74. **d** 81 **p** 82. C Knowle *Birm* 81-85; Lect Dur Univ from 85; Perm to Offic *Dur* from 85. *8 Princes Street, Durham DH1 4RP* Tel 0191-386 4255 *or* 374 2067 E-mail r.w.l.moberly@durham.ac.uk

MOBSBY, Ian Jonathan. b 68. Leeds Univ BHSc93 SROT93. EAMTC 01. **d** 04 **p** 05. NSM Westmr St Matt *Lon* from 04. *71 Osprey Heights, Bramlands Close, London SW11 2NP* Tel (020) 7924 7898 Mobile 07787-158868 E-mail ian.mobsby@ukonline.co.uk

MOCK, David Lawrence. b 64. Whitman Coll Washington BA86 Heythrop Coll Lon MTh01. Trin Coll Bris BA98. **d** 98 **p** 99. C Tadworth *S'wark* 98-01; P-in-c Sutton St Geo *Ches* 01-02; C Macclesfield Team Par 01-02; TV from 02. *St George's Vicarage, 88 Byrons Lane, Macclesfield SK11 7JS* Tel (01625) 432919 E-mail dave@mockcrew.freeserve.co.uk

MOCKFORD (née WATKINS), Mrs Betty Anne. b 45. Leeds Univ BA66 Nottm Univ CertEd67 UEA DipHE98. EAMTC 94. **d** 97 **p** 98. C Ipswich St Aug *St E* 97-00; P-in-c Charsfield w Debach, Monewden, Hoo etc from 01. *Mirembe, 10 Castle Brooks, Framlingham, Woodbridge IP13 9SF* Tel (01728) 724193 Mobile 07890-110741

MOCKFORD, Canon John Frederick. b 28. Em Coll Cam BA52 MA56. Ridley Hall Cam 52. **d** 54 **p** 55. C Ardwick St Silas *Man* 54; C Harpurhey Ch Ch 54-57; V Bootle St Leon *Liv* 57-64; CMS 65-73; Uganda 66-73; Can Missr Kampala 72-73; V Bushbury *Lich* 73-77; TR 77-84; Preb Lich Cathl 81-84; Dir Miss and Past Studies Ridley Hall Cam 84-88; V Ipswich St Marg *St E* 88-93; rtd 93; Perm to Offic *St E* from 93. *Mirembe, 10 Castle Brooks, Framlingham, Woodbridge IP13 9SF* Tel (01728) 724193

MOCKFORD, Peter John. b 57. Nottm Univ BSc79 St Jo Coll Dur BA88. Cranmer Hall Dur 86. **d** 89 **p** 90. C Tamworth *Lich* 89-94; V Blurton from 94; P-in-c Dresden from 04. *The Vicarage, School Lane, Stoke-on-Trent ST3 3DU* Tel (01782) 312163 E-mail p.mockford@ukgateway.net

MODY, Rohintan Keki. b 63. New Coll Ox BA85 MA88. Oak Hill Th Coll BA00. **d** 00 **p** 01. C Wolverhampton St Luke *Lich* 00-03. *74 Brenda Gautrey Way, Cottenham, Cambridge CB4 8XW* E-mail romody@hotmail.com

MOESEL, Joseph Sams. b 65. Villanova Univ USA BA90 Harris Man Coll Ox BTh93 Regent's Park Coll Ox MTh03. Ripon Coll Cuddesdon DipMin95. **d** 95 **p** 96. C Twigworth, Down Hatherley, Norton, The Leigh etc *Glouc* 95-98; CF from 98; Perm to Offic *Cant* 98-01. *c/o MOD Chaplains (Army)* Tel (01980) 615804 Fax 615800

MOFFAT, Canon George. b 46. Edin Univ BD77 Open Univ BA87 Bradf Univ MA04. Edin Th Coll 67. **d** 72 **p** 73. C Falkirk *Edin* 73-76; C Edin St Pet 76-81; Chapl Edin Univ 77-81; C Heston *Lon* 81-84; V S Elmsall *Wakef* 84-93; TR Manningham *Bradf* from 93; Chapl to The Queen from 00; Hon Can Bradf Cathl *Bradf* from 02. *1 Selborne Grove, Bradford BD9 4NL* Tel (01274) 498566

MOFFATT, Joseph Barnaby. b 72. Fitzw Coll Cam BA96 MA99. Ripon Coll Cuddesdon 97. **d** 99 **p** 00. C Cen Wolverhampton *Lich* 99-03; C Chelsea St Luke and Ch Ch *Lon* from 03. *29 Burnsall Street, London SW3 3SR* Tel (020) 7352 5608 E-mail joemoffatt@supanet.com

MOFFATT, Neil Thomas. b 46. Fitzw Coll Cam BA68 MA72. Qu Coll Birm 69. **d** 71 **p** 72. C Charlton St Luke w St Paul *S'wark* 71-74; C Walworth St Pet 74-75; C Walworth 75-77; V Dormansland 77-86; TR Padgate *Liv* 86-96; V Padgate 96-98; TR Thatcham *Ox* from 98; AD Newbury from 02. *The Rectory, 17 Church Gate, Thatcham RG19 3PN* Tel (01635) 862616 E-mail tom@moffatt20.freeserve.co.uk

MOFFETT, Mrs Marie-Louise. b 25. St Andr Univ MA46 Cam Univ DipRS76. **d** 87 **p** 94. St Andr Univ Angl Chapl Team 87-91; C St Andrews All SS *St And* from 91. *10 Queen's Gardens, St Andrews KY16 9TA* Tel (01334) 473678

MOFFITT, Mrs Vivien Louisa. b 37. LSE BSc59 Dip Personnel Mgt 60. Sarum & Wells Th Coll 90. **d** 91 **p** 94. NSM Chandler's Ford *Win* 91-99; NSM Twyford and Owslebury and Morestead 99-01; rtd 01. *13 Velmore Road, Eastleigh SO53 3HD* Tel (023) 8026 5327

MOGER, Peter John. b 64. Mert Coll Ox BA85 BMus86 MA89 St Jo Coll Dur BA93. Cranmer Hall Dur 89. **d** 93 **p** 94. C Whitby *York* 93-95; Prec, Sacr and Min Can Ely Cathl *Ely* 95-01; V Godmanchester 01-05; Nat Worship Development Officer Abps' Coun from 05; Perm to Offic *Ely* from 05. *Church House, Great Smith Street, London SW1P 3NZ* Tel (020) 7898 1365 Mobile 07970-694021 E-mail peter.moger@c-of-e.org.uk *or* peter.moger@ntlworld.com

MOGFORD, Canon Stanley Howard. b 13. St Pet Hall Ox BA35 DipTh36 MA39. Westcott Ho Cam 36. **d** 37 **p** 38. C Aberdare *Llan* 37-41; C Llan Cathl 41-48; V Cyfarthfa 48-54; V Pontypridd St Cath 54-63; V Llanblethian w Cowbridge 63-66; V Llanblethian w Cowbridge and Llandough etc 66-80; RD Llantwit Major and Cowbridge 69-80; Can Llan Cathl 71-80; rtd 80; Perm to Offic *Llan* from 80. *Fortis Green, 19 Plas Treoda, Cardiff CF14 1PT* Tel (029) 2061 8839

MOGRIDGE, Christopher James. b 31. Culham Coll of Educn CertEd62 LCP70 FCollP86. St Steph Ho Ox 93. **d** 94 **p** 95. NSM Wellingborough St Andr *Pet* 94-98; NSM Ecton 98-02; rtd 02; Perm to Offic *Pet* from 02. *April Cottage, Little Harrowden, Wellingborough NN9 5BB* Tel (01933) 678412

MOIR, Canon David William. b 38. St Aid Birkenhead 64. **d** 67 **p** 68. C Danbury *Chelmsf* 67-70; C Bollington St Jo *Ches* 70-72; V Sutton St Jas 72-81; V Prestbury 81-95; RD Macclesfield 88-98; P-in-c Bosley and N Rode w Wincle and Wildboarclough 95-98; V 98-03; Hon Can Ches Cathl 96-03; Chapl E Cheshire NHS Trust 96-03; rtd 04; Perm to Offic *Heref* from 04. *Dove Top, Bentlawnt, Minsterley, Shrewsbury SY5 0HE* Tel (01743) 891209 E-mail moirdl@compuserve.com

MOIR, Nicholas Ian. b 61. G&C Coll Cam BA82 MA86 Ox Univ BA86 MA91 Lon Univ MTh92. Wycliffe Hall Ox 84. **d** 87 **p** 88. C Enfield St Andr *Lon* 87-91; Bp's Dom Chapl *St Alb* 91-94; Chapl St Jo Coll Cam 94-98; V Waterbeach *Ely* from 98; R Landbeach from 98; RD N Stowe from 05. *The Vicarage, 8 Chapel Street, Waterbeach, Cambridge CB5 9HR* Tel (01223) 860353 E-mail nicholas.moir@ntlworld.com

MOLD, Peter John. b 33. **d** 63 **p** 64. C Boston *Linc* 63-66; C Scarborough St Mary w Ch Ch, St Paul and St Thos *York* 67-68; Australia from 68; rtd 91. *Stone Grange, 29 Newcastle Street, York, PO Box 355, W Australia 6302* Tel (0061) (8) 9641 1965

MOLE, Arthur Penton. b 10. Witwatersrand Univ BA30. Bps' Coll Cheshunt 33. **d** 35 **p** 36. C Pokesdown All SS *Win* 35-37; C Wolborough w Newton Abbot *Ex* 37-44; R Goldsborough *Ripon* 44-49; Dioc Dir of Educn *St Alb* 49-51; V Barnet Vale St Mark 51-59; RD Barnet 55-59; V Southbourne St Kath *Win* 59-71; R Old Alresford 71-76; P-in-c Brown and Chilton Candover w Northington etc 72-74; R 74-76; rtd 76; Perm to Offic *Worc* 76-01. *15 Garden Styles, Pershore WR10 1JW* Tel (01386) 554167

MOLE, David Eric Harton. b 33. Em Coll Cam BA54 MA58 PhD62. Ridley Hall Cam 55. **d** 59 **p** 59. C Selly Hill St Steph *Birm* 59-62; Tutor St Aid Birkenhead 62-63; Chapl Peterho Cam 63-69; Ghana 69-72; Lect Qu Coll Birm 72-76; Tutor USPG Coll of the Ascension Selly Oak 76-87; C Burton *Lich* 87-93; Chapl Burton Gen Hosp 90-93; Chapl Ostend w Knokke and Bruges *Eur* 93-98; rtd 98; Perm to Offic *Birm* from 99. *48 Green Meadow Road, Selly Oak, Birmingham B29 4DE* Tel 0121-475 1589 E-mail susananddavidmole@yahoo.co.uk

MOLE, Jennifer Vera. b 49. CertEd70. Qu Coll Birm 82. **d** 84 **p** 97. C Pontypool *Mon* 84-87; C Cyncoed 87-88; TV 88-96; C Caerleon 96-99; V Maesglas and Duffryn from 99. *The Vicarage, Old Cardiff Road, Newport NP20 3AT* Tel (01633) 815738

MOLESWORTH, Canon Anthony Edward Nassau. b 23. Pemb Coll Cam BA45 MA48. Coll of Resurr Mirfield 45. **d** 46 **p** 47. C Blyth St Mary *Newc* 46-51; C High Elswick St Phil 51-52; Swaziland 52-68; Can 68-71; Can Zululand 63-68; R Huish Episcopi w Pitney *B & W* 71-78; P-in-c High Ham 76-78; TR Langport Area Chs 78-84; R Charlton Musgrove, Cucklington and Stoke Trister 84-90; RD Bruton 86-90; rtd 90; Perm to Offic *B & W* and *Sarum* from 90. *3 Barrow Hill, Stourton Caundle, Sturminster Newton DT10 2LD* Tel (01963) 362337

MOLL, Christopher David Edward. b 67. St Cath Coll Cam BA89 MA93. Ridley Hall Cam CTM97. **d** 98 **p** 99. C Byker St Mark and Walkergate St Oswald *Newc* 98-02; C Eastrop *Win* from 02. *15 Camwood Close, Basingstoke RG21 3BL* Tel (01256) 332454 E-mail ed.moll@stmarys-basingstoke.org.uk

MOLL, Nicola. b 47. Bedf Coll Lon BA69. TISEC 99. **d** 03 **p** 04. C Edin Gd Shep *Edin* from 03; C Edin St Salvador from 03. *9/3 Forth Street, Edinburgh EH1 3JX* Tel 0131-558 3729 E-mail mollnicola@hotmail.com

MOLL, Randell Tabrum. b 41. Lon Univ BD65. Wycliffe Hall Ox 62. **d** 66 **p** 67. C Drypool St Columba w St Andr and St Pet *York* 66-70; Asst Chapl HM Pris Hull 66-70; Asst Master Hull Gr Sch 66-70; C Netherton *Liv* 70-74; C Sefton 70-72; Ind Chapl 70-74 and 92-99; Belgium 75-76; P-in-c Brockmoor *Lich* 76-81; Team Ldr Black Country Urban Ind Miss 76-81; Dir Chilworth Home Services 81-84; Asst Master Bp Reindorp Sch Guildf 84-90; France and Iraq 91; Chapl Sedbergh Sch 92; Sen Chapl Miss in the Economy (Merseyside) 92-99; Hon Can Liv Cathl *Liv* 97-99; Chapl Campsfield Ho Immigration and Detention Cen 00-02; Sen Chapl Immigration Detention Services 01-02; Team Ldr Workplace Min *St Alb* from 03. *Penn Cottage, Green End, Granborough, Buckingham MK18 3NT* Tel and fax (01296) 670970 E-mail rmoll@stalbans.anglican.org

MOLLAN, Patricia Ann Fairbanks. b 44. QUB BSc67 PhD70 BD97. **d** 97 **p** 98. Aux Min *D & D* from 97; Aux Min Lecale Gp 02-04; Dep Dir Ch's Min of Healing from 04. *Echo Sound, 69 Killyleagh Road, Downpatrick BT30 9BN* Tel (028) 4482 1620 Fax 9073 8665 E-mail pat@mollan.net *or* cmhbel@btconnect.com

MOLLAN, Prof Raymond Alexander Boyce. b 43. QUB MB, BCh69 BAO69 MD84 FRCS. CITC 97. **d** 97 **p** 98. Aux Min *D & D* from 97; Aux Min Comber from 02. *Echo Sound, 69 Killyleagh Road, Downpatrick BT30 9BN* Tel (028) 4482 1620 E-mail rab@mollan.net

MOLLER, The Very Revd George Brian. b 35. TCD BA60 MA64 Div Test 61 Lon Univ BD84. **d** 61 **p** 62. C Belfast St Pet *Conn* 61-64; C Larne and Inver 64-68; P-in-c Rathcoole 68-69; I 69-86; Dioc Dir Ords 82-92; I Belfast St Bart 86-01; Chapl Stranmillis Univ Coll Belf 88-01; Preb Conn Cathl *Conn* 90-96; Treas 96; Prec 96-98; Dean 98-01; rtd 01. *7 Sunningdale Park, Bangor BT20 4UU* Tel (028) 9145 5903 E-mail gb@moller2.freeserve.co.uk

MOLLOY, Mrs Heather. b 54. Bradf Univ BTech76. LNSM course 92. **d** 95 **p** 96. OLM Harwood *Man* from 95. *7 Fellside, Bolton BL2 4HB* Tel (01204) 520395

MOLLOY, Terence Harold. b 36. St Jo Coll Auckland 68 LTh76. **d** 71 **p** 72. New Zealand 71-81 and from 82; C Auckland St Paul 71-76; V Mount Roskill 76-81; C Skegness and Winthorpe *Linc* 81-82; V Eastbourne 82-89; V Tuakau 89-95; Asst P Clendon from 95. *190B Finlayson Avenue, Manurewa, Auckland 1702, New Zealand* Tel (0064) (9) 267 1455 Fax as telephone

MOLONY, Nicholas John. b 43. St Jo Coll Dur BA67 Birm Univ DipTh70 MA78. Qu Coll Birm 67. **d** 70 **p** 71. C Beaconsfield *Ox* 70-75; P-in-c Chesham Ch Ch 75-80; TV Gt Chesham 80-81; P-in-c Weston Turville 81-90; P-in-c Stoke Mandeville 87-89; P-in-c Gt Marlow 90-93; P-in-c Bisham 90-93; TR Gt Marlow w Marlow Bottom, Lt Marlow and Bisham from 93. *The Rectory, The Causeway, Marlow SL7 2AA* Tel (01628) 482660 *or* 481806 E-mail nick.molony@btinternet.com

MONBERG, Ms Ulla Stefan. b 52. Copenhagen Univ BA79. Westcott Ho Cam 88. **d** 90 **p** 94. C Westmr St Jas *Lon* 90-94; Dean Women's Min and Area Dir of Ords Cen Lon 94-99; Dean Women's Min Kensington 94-99; C Paddington St Jo w St Mich 96-98; P-in-c S Kensington H Trin w All SS 98-02; Dir of Ords Two Cities Area 99-02; Denmark from 02; Dioc Adv for Women's Min *Eur* from 04. *Borgmester Jensens Alle 9, 2th, DK-2100 Copenhagen, Denmark* Tel (0045) 3526 0660

✠MONDAL, The Rt Revd Barnabas Dwijen. b 37. Dhaka Univ BA61 Serampore Univ BD64. Bp's Coll Calcutta 61. **d** 64 **p** 65 **c** 75. Barisal 64-67; Khulna 67-69; Rhode Is USA 69-70; Bollorepur 70-71; Thakurpukur 71-72; Prin Coll of Chr Th 72-74; Dhaka St Thos 74-75; Asst Bp Dhaka 75; Bp Dhaka and Moderator Ch of Bangladesh 75-03; rtd 03. *Merlin Apartment, 59/A-1 Barobagh, Dhaka 1216, Bangladesh* Tel (00880) (2) 805 1656 Mobile 172-031350

MONDON, Simon Charles. b 57. WEMTC. **d** 02 **p** 03. OLM Worfield *Heref* from 02. *Duken Lane Cottage, Duken Lane, Wootton, Bridgnorth WV15 6EA* Tel (01746) 780265

MONDS, Anthony John Beatty. b 53. Solicitor 77. **d** 97 **p** 00. OLM Queen Thorne *Sarum* 97-04; C Sherborne w Castleton and Lillington from 04. *32 Abbots Way, Sherborne DT9 6DT* Tel and fax (01935) 389910 E-mail tonymonds@tmonds.freeserve.co.uk

MONEY, John Charles. b 69. Wycliffe Hall Ox 01. **d** 03 **p** 04. C Porchester *S'well* from 03. *127A Digby Avenue, Nottingham NG3 6DT* Tel 0115-952 4610 Mobile 07711-285217 E-mail john.stjames@ntlworld.com

MONGER, John Dennis. b 26. Univ of Wales (Cardiff) DipTh51. **d** 99 **p** 99. NSM Ewyas Harold w Dulas, Kenderchurch etc *Heref* 99-04; RD Abbeydore 00-02; rtd 04; Perm to Offic *Heref* from 04. *Chapel Cottage, Longtown, Hereford HR2 0LE* Tel (01873) 860306

MONK, Mrs Mary. b 38. CertEd58. S'wark Ord Course 85. **d** 88 **p** 94. NSM Lee Gd Shep w St Pet *S'wark* 88-99; NSM Harpenden St Jo *St Alb* from 99. *3 Hawthorn Close, Harpenden AL5 1HN* Tel (01582) 462057

MONK, Nicholas John. b 32. Westcott Ho Cam 61. **d** 63 **p** 64. C Bris H Cross Inns Court *Bris* 63-67; C Stoke Bishop 67-69; V Swindon All SS 69-75; V Ashton Keynes w Leigh 75-87; P-in-c Minety w Oaksey 82-87; RD Malmesbury 85-88; V Ashton Keynes, Leigh and Minety 87-91; TR Swindon St Jo and St Andr 91-97; rtd 97; Perm to Offic *Heref* from 97. *The Riddings Cottage, Newcastle on Clun, Craven Arms SY7 8QT* Tel (01686) 670929

MONKHOUSE, Henry Alistair. b 34. **d** 99 **p** 00. OLM Quidenham Gp *Nor* 99-05; Perm to Offic from 05. *Wildwood, Mill Road, Old Buckenham, Attleborough NR17 1SG* Tel (01953) 860845

MONKS, Ian Kay. b 36. K Coll Lon BA60 Lon Inst of Educn PGCE61. Oak Hill NSM Course 90. **d** 93 **p** 94. NSM Woodford Bridge *Chelmsf* from 93. *46 Summit Drive, Woodford Green IG8 8QP* Tel (020) 8550 2390

MONMOUTH, Archdeacon of. *See* HACKETT, The Ven Ronald Glyndwr

MONMOUTH, Bishop of. *See* WALKER, The Rt Revd Edward William Murray

MONMOUTH, Dean of. *See* FENWICK, The Very Revd Richard David

MONTAGUE (née LAIDLAW), Mrs Juliet. b 52. Nottm Univ BTh82. Linc Th Coll 78. **dss** 82 **d** 87 **p** 94. Gainsborough All SS *Linc* 82-86; Chapl Linc Cathl and Linc Colls of FE 86-92; Dn-in-c Gedney Hill and Whaplode Drove 92-94; P-in-c 94-99; P-in-c Crawley and Littleton and Sparsholt w Lainston *Win* 99-03; R from 03. *The Rectory, Church Lane, Littleton, Winchester SO22 6QY* Tel (01962) 881898 E-mail revdjulietmontague@surefish.co.uk

MONTAGUE-YOUENS, Canon Hubert Edward. b 30. Ripon Hall Ox 55. **d** 58 **p** 59. C Redditch St Steph *Worc* 58-59; C Halesowen 59-62; V Kempsey 62-69; V Kidderminster St Geo 69-72; R Ribbesford w Bewdley and Dowles 72-81; RD Kidderminster 74-81; Hon Can Worc Cathl 78-81; TR Bridport *Sarum* 81-86; RD Lyme Bay 82-86; V Easebourne *Chich* 86-89; Chapl K Edw VII Hosp Midhurst 86-89; rtd 89; Perm to Offic *Worc* from 89; Perm to Offic *Glouc* 89-95 and from 98; P-in-c Twyning 96-98. *6 Harbour View, Bredon Road, Tewkesbury GL20 5AZ* Tel (01684) 292363

MONTEITH, David Robert Malvern. b 68. St Jo Coll Dur BSc89 Nottm Univ BTh92 MA93. St Jo Coll Nottm 90. **d** 93 **p** 94. C Kings Heath *Birm* 93-97; C St Martin-in-the-Fields *Lon* 97-02; P-in-c S Wimbledon H Trin and St Pet *S'wark* from 02; RD Merton from 04. *The Vicarage, 1 Trinity Road, London SW19 8QT* Tel (020) 8543 2838 *or* 8542 1388 E-mail david.monteith1@btinternet.com

MONTGOMERIE, Alexander (Sandy). b 47. St Jo Coll Nottm CertCS94. **d** 94 **p** 96. NSM Irvine St Andr LEP *Glas* from 94; NSM Ardrossan from 94. *105 Sharphill Road, Saltcoats KA21 5QU* Tel and fax (01294) 465193 E-mail sandy.montgomerie@btinternet.com

MONTGOMERIE, Andrew Simon. b 60. Keble Coll Ox BA82. Ridley Hall Cam 83. **d** 85 **p** 86. C Childwall All SS *Liv* 85-87; C Yardley St Edburgha *Birm* 87-90; TV Solihull 90-96; V Balsall Common 96-05; P-in-c Eyam *Derby* from 05. *The Rectory, Church Street, Eyam, Hope Valley S32 5QH* Tel (01433) 630821

MONTGOMERY, Canon Anthony Alan. b 33. Trin Hall Cam BA56. Edin Th Coll 56. **d** 58 **p** 59. C Dumfries *Glas* 58-63; P-in-c Airdrie 63-66; R 66-68; Asst Chapl Gordonstoun Sch 68-93; Can St Andr Cathl Inverness *Mor* from 81; rtd 93. *Easter Hillside, Mosstowie, Elgin IV30 8XE* Tel and fax (01343) 850282 E-mail anthony_montgomery@compuserve.com

MONTGOMERY, Ian David. b 44. St Andr Univ LLB66 Univ of the South (USA) DMin02 FCA69. Wycliffe Hall Ox 71. **d** 75 **p** 76. C Fulham St Dionis Parson's Green *Lon* 75-78; Chapl Amherst Coll USA 78-83; R New Orleans St Phil 83-92; R Nashville St Bart 92-97; R Menasha St Thos from 97. *335 East Wisconsin Avenue, Neenah, WI 54956, USA* Tel (001) (920) 725 5601 E-mail frianm@aol.com

MONTGOMERY (née YOUATT), Mrs Jennifer Alison. b 49. St Aid Coll Dur BSc70 Homerton Coll Cam PGCE71. N Ord Course 89. **d** 92 **p** 94. NSM Ripon H Trin *Ripon* from 92; Warden of Readers from 99. *Washington House, Littlethorpe, Ripon HG4 3LJ* Tel (01765) 605276 *or* tel and fax 690930 E-mail montgomery@littlethorpe97.freeserve.co.uk

MONTGOMERY, Jennifer Susan. b 54. QUB MB, BCh77 DRCOG80. N Ord Course 02. **d** 05. NSM Ackworth *Wakef* from 05. *37 Highfield Road, Pontefract WF8 4LL* Tel (01977) 702726 Mobile 07780-764233 E-mail jsm1954@hotmail.com

MONTGOMERY, Pembroke John Charles. b 24. Codrington Coll Barbados. **d** 53 **p** 55. St Vincent 55-73; Can Kingstown Cathl 63-73; P-in-c Derby St Jas *Derby* 73-74; V 74-90; rtd 90. *37 Church Street, Tetbury GL8 8JG* Tel (01666) 504817

MONTGOMERY, Miss Rachel. b 63. Reading Univ BA85. Wycliffe Hall Ox BTh94. **d** 94 **p** 95. C Tufnell Park St Geo and All SS *Lon* 94-99; V Bethnal Green St Jas Less from 99; CME

Officer from 99. *St James the Less Vicarage, St James's Avenue, London E2 9JD* Tel and fax (020) 8980 1612
E-mail rachel.montgomery@london.anglican.org

MONTGOMERY, Stanley. b 18. Lich Th Coll. **d** 52 **p** 53. P-in-c Hitcham w Lt Finborough, Kettlebaston etc 93-95; Perm to Offic *St E* from 95. *34 Drovers Rise, Stanton, Bury St Edmunds IP31 2BW* Tel (01359) 250359
E-mail freddie@fmontgomery.fslife.co.uk

MONTGOMERY, Canon Thomas Charles Osborne. b 59. Edin Univ BD81. Edin Th Coll 77. **d** 82 **p** 83. C Glas St Mary *Glas* 82-85; C Dumfries 85-88; R Hamilton 88-96; Can St Mary's Cathl from 94; R Glas St Marg from 96. *St Margaret's Rectory, 22 Monreith Road, Glasgow G43 2NY* Tel and fax 0141-632 3292 *or* 636 1131 E-mail stmargarets@gm.apc.org

MONTGOMERY, Timothy Robert. b 59. Hull Univ BA82 Cam Univ PGCE83. EAMTC 90. **d** 93 **p** 94. Dir Romsey Mill Community Cen *Ely* 93-94; NSM Cambridge St Phil 93-96; Warden Kepplewray Cen Broughton-in-Furness 96-00; NSM Kendal St Thos *Carl* 96-00; V from 00. *St Thomas's Vicarage, South View Lane, Kendal LA9 4QN* Tel (01539) 729617 *or* 730683 Fax 729010 E-mail vicar@saintthomaskendal.net

MONTGOMERY, Archdeacon of. *See* THELWELL, The Ven John Berry

MOODY, Canon Christopher John Everard. b 51. New Coll Ox BA72 Lon Univ MSc90. Cuddesdon Coll BA74. **d** 75 **p** 76. C Fulham All SS *Lon* 75-79; C Surbiton St Andr and St Mark *S'wark* 79-82; Chapl K Coll Lon 82-87; V S Lambeth St Anne and All SS *S'wark* 87-95; RD Lambeth 90-95; P-in-c Market Harborough *Leic* 95-97; P-in-c Market Harborough Transfiguration 95-97; V Market Harborough and The Transfiguration etc from 97; Hon Can Leic Cathl from 04. *The Rectory, Rectory Lane, Market Harborough LE16 8AS* Tel (01858) 462926
E-mail chris.moody@harborough-anglican.org.uk

MOODY, Colin John. b 36. Bris Univ CASS71. Chich Th Coll 61. **d** 63 **p** 64. C Hove All SS *Chich* 63-69; C Dulwich St Barn *S'wark* 69-70; Perm to Offic *Bris* 70-71; *Chich* 72-78 and from 90; Lic to Offic *Ely* 78-89; rtd 01. *11 Hewitts, Henfield BN5 9DT* Tel and fax (01273) 495062

MOODY, Ms Elizabeth Jane. b 61. Hull Univ BA82 Westmr Coll Ox PGCE84. Ridley Hall Cam 00. **d** 02 **p** 03. C Uxbridge *Lon* 02-05; C Hanwell St Mary w St Chris from 05. *St Christopher's Vicarage, 4 Hillyard Road, London W7 1BH* Tel (020) 8578 2796 Mobile 07796-988302 E-mail lizmoody@blueyonder.co.uk

MOODY, Preb George Henry. b 27. ACIS56 ARCA68. Cranmer Hall Dur 69. **d** 71 **p** 72. C Marske in Cleveland *York* 71-74; Chapl to the Deaf *Lich* 74-89; Preb Lich Cathl 83-89; rtd 89; Perm to Offic *York* from 90. *21 Priestcrofts, Marske-by-the-Sea, Redcar TS11 7HW* Tel (01642) 489660

MOODY, Ivor Robert. b 57. K Coll Lon BD AKC. Coll of Resurr Mirfield. **d** 82 **p** 83. C Leytonstone St Marg w St Columba *Chelmsf* 82-85; C Leigh-on-Sea St Marg 85-88; V Tilbury Docks 88-96; Chapl Anglia Poly Univ from 96. *4 Bishops Court Gardens, Chelmsford CM2 6AZ* Tel (01245) 261700 *or* 493131
E-mail i.r.moody@apu.ac.uk

MOODY, Canon John Kelvin. b 30. St Fran Coll Brisbane ThL55. **d** 56 **p** 57. Australia 56-61; C Earl's Court St Cuth w St Matthias *Lon* 61-64; Chapl Ankara *Eur* 64-69; Chapl Istanbul 64-66; Chapl Palma 69-75; Chapl Tangier 75-79; Can Gib Cathl 74-79; Hon Can from 79; Australia from 79; rtd 95. *1 Short Street, Watson's Bay, NSW, Australia 2030* Tel (0061) (2) 9337 2871

MOOKERJI, Michael Manoje. b 45. Baring Union Coll Punjab BSc69. Ridley Hall Cam 83. **d** 85 **p** 86. C Heanor *Derby* 85-92; V Codnor and Loscoe 92-93; V Codnor 93-02; V Winshill from 02. *The Vicarage, 54 Mill Hill Lane, Burton-on-Trent DE15 0BB* Tel (01283) 545043

MOON, Arthur Thomas. b 22. ACP53 LCP56. Sarum Th Coll 65. **d** 66 **p** 67. C Fulwood Ch Ch *Blackb* 66-71; Hon C Bispham 71-80; C 80-87; rtd 87; Perm to Offic *Blackb* from 87. *15 Kirkstone Drive, Thornton-Cleveleys FY5 1QQ* Tel (01253) 853521

MOON, Sister Catherine Joy. b 48. LRAM68 ARCM69. Gen Th Sem NY 84. **d** 84 **p** 85. USA 84-02; CSF from 87; Chapl Ashworth Hosp Maghull from 04. *Liverpool Parish Church, Old Churchyard, Liverpool L2 8TZ* Tel 07906-365962 (mobile)

MOON, John Charles. b 23. Sarum Th Coll 49. **d** 51 **p** 52. C Bottesford *Linc* 51-54; C Habrough 54-55; V Immingham 55-61; V Weaste *Man* 61-67; V Spalding St Jo *Linc* 67-82; V Spalding St Jo w Deeping St Nicholas 82-86; rtd 86; Perm to Offic *Linc* 87-02. *14 Harrox Road, Moulton, Spalding PE12 6PR* Tel (01406) 370111

MOON, Philip. b 59. CCC Ox BA80 Warwick Univ PhD92. Wycliffe Hall Ox BTh01. **d** 01 **p** 02. C Otley *Bradf* 01-05; V Lt Aston *Lich* from 05. *The Vicarage, 3 Walsall Road, Little Aston, Sutton Coldfield B74 3BD* Tel 0121-353 0798
E-mail familyofmoon@aol.com

MOON, Philip Russell. b 56. Em Coll Cam BA78 MA81 Reading Univ PGCE79. Wycliffe Hall Ox BA82. **d** 85 **p** 86. C Crowborough *Chich* 85-87; Hd of CYFA (CPAS) 87-94; V Lowestoft Ch Ch *Nor* 94-04; P-in-c Hove Bp Hannington Memorial Ch *Chich* from 04. *82 Holmes Avenue, Hove BN3 7LD* Tel (01273) 732821

MOON, Thomas Arnold. b 24. Lon Univ BA51. Oak Hill Th Coll 49. **d** 52 **p** 53. C Fazakerley Em *Liv* 52-56; V Everton St Benedict 56-70; V Formby St Luke 70-95; rtd 95; Perm to Offic *Liv* from 95. *8 Harington Road, Formby, Liverpool L37 1NU* Tel (01704) 872249

MOONEY, The Ven Paul Gerard. b 58. St Patr Coll Maynooth BD84 Asian Cen for Th Studies and Miss Seoul ThM92. **d** 84 **p** 85. In RC Ch 84-90; Chapl Miss to Seamen Korea 90-94; Hon Can Pusan from 94; Chapl Antwerp Miss to Seamen 94-97; Asst Chapl Antwerp St Boniface *Eur* 94-97; C Galway w Kilcummin *T, K & A* 97-98; I New w Old Ross, Whitechurch, Fethard etc *C & O* from 98; Hon Chapl New Ross and Waterford Miss to Seamen from 98; Prec Ferns Cathl from 01; Adn Ferns from 02. *The Rectory, College Road, New Ross, Co Wexford, Irish Republic* Tel (00353) (51) 425004 E-mail archdeacon@ferns.anglican.org

MOOR, David Drury. b 18. St Edm Hall Ox BA39 MA44. Wells Th Coll 46. **d** 48 **p** 49. C Tuffley *Glouc* 48-52; P-in-c Symondsbury *Sarum* 52-53; R 53-61; V Bournemouth St Andr *Win* 61-69; V Bournemouth St Mich 69-83; rtd 83; Perm to Offic *Sarum* and *Win* from 83. *c/o J Moor Esq, 8 Mynchen End, Beaconsfield HP9 2AT* Tel (01494) 673548

MOOR, Simon Alan. b 65. Nottm Univ BTh93. Linc Th Coll 90. **d** 93 **p** 94. C Skegness and Winthorpe *Linc* 93-96; C Airedale w Fryston *Wakef* 96-98; V Hoylandswaine and Silkstone w Stainborough from 98. *The Vicarage, 12 High Street, Silkstone, Barnsley S75 4JN* Tel and fax (01226) 790232

MOORE, Albert William (Bill). b 47. Birm Poly FTC72. WMMTC 91. **d** 94 **p** 95. C Hobs Moat *Birm* 94-98; V Dosthill from 98. *The Vicarage, Dosthill, Tamworth B77 1LU* Tel (01827) 281349

MOORE, Andrew Jonathan. b 57. York Univ BA82 Wycliffe Hall Ox BA84 MA89 Worc Coll Ox DPhil99. **d** 86 **p** 86. C Camberwell St Jo Australia 86-87; Assoc P S Yarra Ch Ch 87-90; Asst/Acting Chapl Worc Coll Ox 91-94; Chapl Jes Coll Ox 94-99; Voc Adv *Ox* 98-04; Dir of Ords from 04; Hon Chapl Cen for Mediaeval and Renaissance Studies Ox 99-04; Research Fell Regent's Park Coll Ox 01-04; Chapl St Pet Coll Ox from 04. *St Peter's College, New Inn Hall Street, Oxford OX1 2DL* Tel (01865) 278903 E-mail andrew.moore@spc.ox.ac.uk

MOORE, Anthony Harry. b 34. Westcott Ho Cam 88. **d** 90 **p** 91. C Eyke w Bromeswell, Rendlesham, Tunstall etc *St E* 90-93; V Aldeburgh w Hazlewood 93-02; rtd 02; Perm to Offic *St E* and *Chelmsf* from 02. *5 Kings Meadow, Great Cornard, Sudbury CO10 0HP* Tel (01787) 377967

MOORE, Anthony Michael. b 71. Ex Univ BA94 Leeds Univ BA98 MA99. Coll of Resurr Mirfield 96. **d** 99 **p** 00. C Carnforth *Blackb* 99-03; Fell and Past Tutor Coll of Resurr Mirfield 03-04; C Wilton Place St Paul *Lon* from 04. *Flat 7, 32 Wilton Place, London SW1X 8SH* Tel (020) 7201 9996 *or* 7201 9999
E-mail anthony@stpaulsknightsbridge.org

MOORE, Anthony Richmond. b 36. Clare Coll Cam BA59 MA63. Linc Th Coll 59. **d** 61 **p** 62. C Roehampton H Trin *S'wark* 61-66; C New Eltham All SS 66-70; P Missr Blackbird Leys CD *Ox* 70-81; Dioc Ecum Officer 80-00; TV Dorchester 81-93; V Enstone and Heythrop 93-01; rtd 01. *13 Cobden Crescent, Oxford OX1 4LJ* Tel (01865) 244673
E-mail moore.t@which.net

MOORE, Arlene. b 64. Dundee Univ BSc87 N Coll of Educn PGCE90 TCD BTh95. CITC 92. **d** 95 **p** 96. C Portadown St Mark *Arm* 95-99; Perm to Offic *Sheff* 99-02 and from 03; C Crookes St Thos 02-03. *183 Brookhouse Hill, Sheffield S10 3TE* Tel 0114-230 8878

MOORE, Arthur Lewis. b 33. Dur Univ BA58 PhD64. Cranmer Hall Dur DipTh59. **d** 62 **p** 63. C Stone *Roch* 62-66; C Clevedon St Andr *B & W* 66-68; Chapl Wycliffe Hall Ox 68-70; Vice-Prin 70-83; P-in-c Ampfield *Win* 83-84; V Hursley and Ampfield 84-92; TV Ewyas Harold w Dulas, Kenderchurch etc *Heref* 92-94; P-in-c 94-98; rtd 98. *2 Tollstone Way, Grosmont, Abergavenny NP7 8ER*

MOORE, Arthur Robert (Bob). b 15. MBE98. Sarum Th Coll 62. **d** 63 **p** 64. C Calne and Blackland *Sarum* 63-67; V Steeple Ashton w Semington 67-79; V Keevil 72-79; Chapl Southwick w Boarhunt *Portsm* 79-91; rtd 84; Perm to Offic *Portsm* from 91. *1 High Street, Southwick, Fareham PO17 6EB* Tel (023) 9238 2113 Fax 9237 0991

MOORE, Canon Bernard Geoffrey. b 27. New Coll Ox BA47 MA52. Ely Th Coll 49. **d** 51 **p** 52. C Chorley St Pet *Blackb* 51-54; Bp's Dom Chapl 54-55; C-in-c Blackpool St Mich CD 55-67; Chapl Victoria Hosp Blackpool 58-67; V Morecambe St Barn *Blackb* 67-81; R Standish 81-88; Hon Can Blackb Cathl 86-92; RD Chorley 86-92; V Charnock Richard 88-92; rtd 92; Perm to Offic *Ex* from 92; *Carl* from 01; *Win* from 00. *29 Wiltshire Close, Exeter EX4 1LU* Tel (01392) 58686

MOORE, Bernard George. b 32. Imp Coll Lon DIC54. Qu Coll Birm 57. **d** 60 **p** 62. C Middlesbrough St Columba *York* 60-62; S

Africa 62-70; Chapl RN 70-74; C Milton *Portsm* 74-76; New Zealand from 76; rtd 97. *45 Feasegate Street, Manurewa, South Auckland 1702, New Zealand* Tel (0064) (9) 267 6924

MOORE, Brian Philip. b 51. AKC72. St Aug Coll Cant 72. **d** 74 **p** 75. C Bp's Hatfield *St Alb* 74-78; C Radlett 78-81; V Eaton Bray w Edlesborough 81-92; RD Dunstable 85-90; V St Alb St Sav 92-03; V St Peter-in-Thanet *Cant* from 03. *The Vicarage, 14 Vicarage Street, St Peters, Broadstairs CT10 2SG* Tel (01843) 869169 *or* 866061 E-mail brian.moore90@ntlworld.com

✠**MOORE, The Rt Revd Bruce Macgregor.** b 31. Univ of NZ BA55. Coll of Resurr Mirfield. **d** 57 **p** 58 **c** 92. C Blackpool St Steph *Blackb* 57-61; New Zealand from 61; Hon Can Auckland 78-96; Adn Manukau 81-90; Asst Bp Auckland 92-97. *5 Pokaka Crescent, Wharewaka, Taupo, New Zealand* Tel (0064) (7) 378 4849 E-mail brucemoore@xtra.co.nz

MOORE, Charles David. b 59. Dundee Univ BSc82 BArch85 Open Univ MA96 RIBA86. St Jo Coll Nottm Dip Th Studies 93. **d** 93 **p** 94. C Deane *Man* 93-97; Crosslinks 98-02; R and Sub Dean Mutare Zimbabwe 98-02; R Bermondsey St Mary w St Olave, St Jo etc *S'wark* from 02. *The Rectory, 193 Bermondsey Street, London SE1 3UW* Tel (020) 7357 0984

MOORE, Canon Colin Frederick. b 49. CITC 69. **d** 72 **p** 73. C Drumglass w Moygashel *Arm* 72-80; I Newtownhamilton w Ballymoyer and Belleek from 80; Hon V Choral Arm Cathl 85-96; Can and Preb from 97. *71 Ballymoyer Road, Whitecross, Armagh BT60 2LA* Tel (028) 3750 7256

MOORE, Darren Lee. b 73. Kingston Univ BEng95. Oak Hill Th Coll BA01. **d** 01 **p** 02. C Camberwell All SS *S'wark* 01-04; P-in-c Tranmere St Cath *Ches* from 04. *39 Westbank Road, Birkenhead CH42 7JP* E-mail rev.darren.moore@whsmithnet.co.uk

MOORE, Darren Richard. b 70. Univ of Wales (Abth) BD91 Hull Univ PGCE97 St Jo Coll York MA(Ed)03 Leeds Univ MA04. Coll of Resurr Mirfield 02. **d** 04 **p** 05. C Scarborough St Martin *York* from 04. *St Michael's House, 136 Filey Road, Scarborough YO11 3AA* Tel (01723) 378105 Mobile 07745-296406 E-mail frdarren.moore@tiscali.co.uk

MOORE, David. b 36. Univ of Wales (Lamp) BA61 Magd Coll Cam BA63 MA68. Linc Th Coll 63. **d** 65 **p** 66. C Saltburn-by-the-Sea *York* 65-69; C Northallerton w Kirby Sigston 69-72; V Kirklevington 72-02; V High and Low Worsall 73-02; Chapl HM Det Cen Kirklevington 72-89; Chapl HM YOI Kirklevington Grange 89-02; rtd 02. *15 King's Drive, Eastbourne BN21 2NX* Tel (01325) 726947

MOORE, David James Paton. b 60. Sheff Univ BEng82. Cranmer Hall Dur 88. **d** 91 **p** 92. C Pemberton St Mark Newtown *Liv* 91-94; C St Helens St Helen 94-97; V Canonbury St Steph *Lon* from 97. *St Stephen's Vicarage, 9 River Place, London N1 2DE* Tel (020) 7354 9118 *or* tel and fax 7226 7526 E-mail ststephen.canonbury@london.anglican.org

MOORE, David Leonard. b 51. **d** 80 **p** 82. Hon C Brixton St Matt *S'wark* 80-82; C 82-84; TV Bris St Agnes and St Simon w St Werburgh *Bris* 84-86; Perm to Offic *Bris* 86-88 and *Blackb* from 88. *154 Victoria Road, Fulwood, Preston PR2 8NQ*

MOORE, David Metcalfe. b 41. Hull Univ BA64 PhD69. Trin Coll Bris 76. **d** 78 **p** 79. C Marple All SS *Ches* 78-82; V Loudwater *Ox* 82-90; V Chilwell *S'well* 90-93; rtd 93. *12 Rhugarve Gardens, Linton, Cambridge CB1 6LX* Tel (01223) 894315

MOORE, David Roy. b 39. Clare Coll Cam BA61. Ripon Hall Ox 61. **d** 63 **p** 64. C Melton Mowbray w Thorpe Arnold *Leic* 63-66; C St Steph Walbrook and St Swithun etc *Lon* 66-72; Dep Dir The Samaritans 66-72; Public Preacher *S'well* 72-77; C Daybrook 77-80; V 80-87; V Ham St Andr *S'wark* 87-99; P-in-c Rothbury *Newc* 99-04; rtd 04; P-in-c Kneesall w Laxton and Wellow *S'well* from 04. *The Vicarage, 19 Baulk Lane, Kneesall, Newark NG22 0AA* Tel (01623) 860579

MOORE, Canon Dennis Charles. b 19. Lon Univ BD46. Tyndale Hall Bris 39. **d** 43 **p** 44. C Broadwater St Mary *Chich* 43-47; Org Sec (E England) CPAS 47-51; V Eccleston St Luke *Liv* 51-55; V New Catton St Luke *Nor* 55-62; V Wellington w Eyton *Lich* 62-70; RD Wrockwardine 66-70; V Watford St Mary *St Alb* 70-73; P-in-c Watford St Jas 70-73; V Watford 73-84; RD Watford 75-81; Hon Can St Alb 80-84; rtd 84; Perm to Offic *Nor* from 84. *82 Greenways, Eaton, Norwich NR4 6HF* Tel (01603) 502492

MOORE, Donald John. b 31. Chich Th Coll 86. **d** 87 **p** 88. C Uckfield *Chich* 87-88; C Southwick St Mich 88-90; Bermuda from 90; Asst P St Geo 90-97; P-in-c St Dav 90-97; Chapl St Brendan's Psychiatric Hosp 92-97; rtd 97. *PO Box FL 239, Flatts FL BX, Bermuda* Tel (001) (441) 236 8360

MOORE, Douglas Gregory. b 49. Bris Univ BA71 CertEd72. Coll of Resurr Mirfield 87. **d** 89 **p** 90. C Hessle *York* 89-93; P-in-c Micklefield w Aberford 93-95; V Aberford w Micklefield 95-04; P-in-c Darwen St Cuth w Tockholes St Steph *Blackb* from 04. *21 The Meadows, Darwen BB3 0PF* Tel (01254) 771196

MOORE, Edward James. b 32. TD85. TCD BA56 MA59. **d** 56 **p** 57. C Belfast St Luke *Conn* 56-59; CF 59-62; C Dunmurry *Conn* 62-64; P-in-c Kilmakee 64-70; I Belfast H Trin 70-80; I Jordanstown w Monkstown 80-91; I Jordanstown 91-97; Chapl Ulster Poly 80-84; Chapl Ulster Univ 84-88; CF (ACF) 66-70 and 88-97; CF (TAVR) 70-88; Can Belf Cathl 89-97; rtd 97. *16 Langford Close, Carrickfergus BT38 8HG* Tel (028) 9336 7209 E-mail ejmh@onetel.com

MOORE, Canon Henry James William. b 33. TCD BA55 MA70. **d** 56 **p** 57. C Mullabrack *Arm* 56-61; C Drumglass 61-63; I Clogherny 63-81; I Ballinderry, Tamlaght and Arboe from 81; Can Arm Cathl from 90; Chan 98-01; Prec from 01. *Ballinderry Rectory, 10 Brookmount Road, Coagh, Cookstown BT80 0BB* Tel (028) 7941 8255

✠**MOORE, The Rt Revd Henry Wylie.** b 23. Liv Univ BCom50 Leeds Univ MA72. Wycliffe Hall Ox 50. **d** 52 **p** 53 **c** 83. C Farnworth *Liv* 52-54; C Middleton *Man* 54-56; CMS 56-60; Iran 57-60; R Burnage St Marg *Man* 60-63; R Middleton 60-74; Home Sec CMS 74-80; Exec Sec CMS 80-83; Bp Cyprus and the Gulf 83-86; Gen Sec CMS 86-90; rtd 90; Asst Bp Dur 90-94; Perm to Offic *Heref* from 94. *Fern Hill Cottage, Hopesay, Craven Arms SY7 8HD* Tel (01588) 660248

MOORE, Preb Hugh Desmond. b 37. St Cath Soc Ox BA58 MA64. St Steph Ho Ox 58. **d** 61 **p** 62. C Kingston St Luke *S'wark* 61-68; Asst Chapl Lon Univ *Lon* 68-70; Chapl Edgware Community Hosp 70-92; Chapl Wellhouse NHS Trust 92-99; V Hendon St Alphage *Lon* from 70; AD W Barnet 85-90; Preb St Paul's Cathl from 95. *The Vicarage, Montrose Avenue, Edgware HA8 0DN* Tel (020) 8952 4611 E-mail hugh.moore@tesco.net

MOORE, Ivan. MA BTh. **d** 90 **p** 91. C Knock *D & D* 90-93; I Taney *D & G* 97-99; Chapl Bancroft's Sch Woodford Green from 99. *Bancroft's School, 611-627 High Road, Woodford Green IG8 0RF* Tel (020) 8505 4821 Fax 8559 0032

MOORE, James. *See* MOORE, Edward James

MOORE, Canon James Kenneth. b 37. AKC62. St Boniface Warminster 62. **d** 63 **p** 64. C W Hartlepool St Oswald *Dur* 63-66; C-in-c Manor Park CD *Sheff* 66-76; TV Sheff Manor 76-78; R Frecheville and Hackenthorpe 78-87; V Bilham 87-91; V Sheff St Oswald 91-02; Hon Can Sheff Cathl 93-02; rtd 02; Perm to Offic *Sheff* from 02. *115 Greenhill Main Road, Sheffield S8 7RG* Tel 0114-283 9634

MOORE (formerly BEVAN), Ms Janet Mary. b 46. Bris Poly CertEd86. WMMTC DipApTh98. **d** 98 **p** 99. C Bishop's Cleeve *Glouc* 98-02; V Overbury w Teddington, Alstone etc *Worc* from 02. *The Vicarage, Station Road, Beckford, Tewkesbury GL20 7AD* Tel (01386) 881349

MOORE, John. b 26. Univ of Wales (Lamp) BA51. Oak Hill Th Coll 51. **d** 53 **p** 54. C Illogan *Truro* 53-57; C Margate H Trin *Cant* 57-58; C Abingdon w Shippon *Ox* 58-67; V Retford St Sav *S'well* 67-73; R Aspenden and Layston w Buntingford *St Alb* 73-86; V Stanstead Abbots 86-91; rtd 91; Perm to Offic *Ox* from 95. *20 Radley Road, Abingdon OX14 3PQ* Tel (01235) 532518

MOORE, John Arthur. b 33. Cuddesdon Coll 70. **d** 71 **p** 72. Hon C Gt Burstead *Chelmsf* 71-74; Chapl Barnard Castle Sch 74-97; rtd 97; Perm to Offic *Dur* from 97 and *Ripon* from 02. *39 Woodside, Barnard Castle DL12 8DY* Tel (01833) 690947

MOORE, John Cecil. b 37. TCD BA61 MA67 BD69. CITC 62. **d** 62 **p** 63. C Belfast St Matt *Conn* 62-65; C Holywood *D & D* 65-70; I Ballyphilip w Ardquin 70-77; I Mt Merrion 77-79; I Donaghcloney w Waringstown 79-02; Treas Dromore Cathl 90-93; Chan 93-02; rtd 02. *22 Kensington Court, Dollingstown, Craigavon BT66 7HU* Tel (028) 3832 1606 E-mail johnmoore_@btinternet.com

MOORE, John David. b 30. St Chad's Coll Dur BA54 DipTh55 DipEd56. **d** 56 **p** 57. C Wallsend St Pet *Newc* 56-60; C Leamington Priors All SS *Cov* 60-62; V Longford 62-75; P-in-c Nuneaton St Mary 75-77; V 77-83; V St Ives *Ely* 83-00; rtd 00; Perm to Offic *Chelmsf* from 01. *25 Felmongers, Harlow CM20 3DH* Tel (01279) 436496

MOORE, John Ernest. b 24. Oak Hill NSM Course. **d** 84 **p** 85. NSM Hornchurch H Cross *Chelmsf* 84-86; NSM S Woodham Ferrers 86-91; NSM Canvey Is 91-95; Perm to Offic from 95. *7 Butterbur Chase, South Woodham Ferrers, Chelmsford CM3 7AG* Tel (01245) 325092

MOORE, John Henry. b 35. Nottm Univ BMus56 CertEd57 MA61. EMMTC 87. **d** 90 **p** 91. NSM Gotham *S'well* 90-95; NSM Kingston and Ratcliffe-on-Soar 90-95; NSM Bunny w Bradmore 95-00; P-in-c 97-00; rtd 00. *19 Hall Drive, Gotham, Nottingham NG11 0JT* Tel 0115-983 0670 E-mail john@moorerev.freeserve.co.uk

MOORE, John Jack. b 22. St Aid Birkenhead 54. **d** 57 **p** 58. C Glenavy w Tunny and Crumlin *Conn* 57-59; I Kingscourt w Syddan *M & K* 60-63; C Carnmoney *Conn* 63-65; P-in-c Templepatrick w Donegore 65-68; I Templepatrick 68-85; rtd 85. *Cuthona, 67 Prospect Road, Portstewart BT55 7NQ* Tel (028) 7083 3905 E-mail jack@cuthona.fsnet.co.uk

MOORE, John Keith. b 26. Sarum & Wells Th Coll 78. **d** 81 **p** 82. NSM Guildf All SS *Guildf* 81-86; NSM Guildf H Trin w St Mary 86-94; Dean of Chapter 90-94; Perm to Offic *Chich* and *Guildf* from 94. *6 Oakhurst, Crossways Road, Grayshott, Hindhead GU26 6JW* Tel (01428) 605871

MOORE, John Michael. b 48. Em Coll Cam BA70 MA73. Cuddesdon Coll 72. **d** 74 **p** 75. C Almondbury *Wakef* 74-78; TV Basingstoke *Win* 78-88; P-in-c Southampton St Alb 88-91; V Swaythling 91-99; rtd 99; Chapl St Jo Win Charity from 99. *13 Priors Way, Winchester SO22 4HQ* Tel (01962) 862341 *or* 854226 Fax 840602 E-mail office@stjohnswinchester.co.uk

MOORE, Canon John Richard. b 35. Nottm Univ LTh59 Lambeth MA01. St Jo Coll Nottm 56. **d** 59 **p** 60. C Northwood Em *Lon* 59-63; V Burton Dassett *Cov* 63-66; Dioc Youth Chapl 63-71; Dir Lindley Lodge Educn Trust Nuneaton 71-82; TR Kinson *Sarum* 82-88; Gen Dir CPAS 88-96; Hon Can Cov Cathl *Cov* 95-01; Internat Dir ICS 96-01; rtd 01; Perm to Offic *Cov* from 01. *26 Jourdain Park, Heathcote, Warwick CV34 6FJ* Tel (01926) 429299

MOORE, John Richard. b 45. Linc Th Coll 80. **d** 82 **p** 83. C Gt Grimsby St Mary and St Jas *Linc* 82-86; V Skirbeck Quarter 86-95; Miss to Seafarers from 86; P-in-c Coningsby w Tattershall *Linc* 95-99; R from 99. *The Rectory, 22 High Street, Coningsby, Lincoln LN4 4RA* Tel (01526) 342223

MOORE, Mrs Joyce. b 48. TCD BA70 HDipEd71 ARIAM68. CITC 98. **d** 01 **p** 02. NSM Camlough w Mullaglass *Arm* from 01. *Dundalk Road, Dunleer, Co Louth, Irish Republic* Tel (00353) (41) 685 1327 E-mail am.camlough@armagh.anglican.org

MOORE, Leonard Richard. b 22. Leeds Univ BA47. Coll of Resurr Mirfield 47. **d** 49 **p** 50. C Hendon St Mary *Lon* 49-54; C Stevenage *St Alb* 54-60; V Bedford All SS 60-68; Lic to Offic 68-70; P-in-c Bedford H Trin 70-74; rtd 87; Hon C Cardington *St Alb* 87-91; Perm to Offic from 92. *22 Dart Road, Bedford MK41 7BT* Tel (01234) 357536

MOORE, Mrs Margaret Doreen. b 37. Westf Coll Lon BA58 CertEd59 BD63 Lambeth STh91. Dalton Ho Bris 61. **dss** 85 **d** 87 **p** 94. Harold Hill St Paul *Chelmsf* 85-87; Hon Par Dn S Woodham Ferrers 87-91; C Canvey Is 91-95; TV Gt Baddow 95-99; P-in-c Woodham Mortimer w Hazeleigh 99-04; P-in-c Woodham Walter 99-04; rtd 04. *7 Butterbur Chase, South Woodham Ferrers, Chelmsford CM3 7AG* Tel (01245) 325092

MOORE, Canon Matthew Edward George. b 38. Oak Hill Th Coll 77. **d** 77 **p** 78. C Larne and Inver *Conn* 77-80; I Desertmartin w Termoneeny *D & R* 80-84; I Milltown *Arm* 84-96; I Culmore w Muff and Belmont *D & R* from 96; Dioc Warden for Min of Healing from 97; Can Derry Cathl from 04. *The Rectory, Heathfield, Culmore Road, Londonderry BT48 8JD* Tel and fax (028) 7135 2396 E-mail matthew.moore3@btopenworld.com

MOORE, Canon Michael Mervlyn Hamond. b 35. LVO99. Pemb Coll Ox BA60 MA63. Wells Th Coll 60. **d** 62 **p** 63. C Bethnal Green St Matt *Lon* 62-66; Chapl Bucharest w Sofia and Belgrade *Eur* 66-67; Asst Gen Sec C of E Coun on Foreign Relns 67-70; Gen Sec 70-72; Abp's Chapl on Foreign Relns *Cant* 72-82; Hon C Walworth St Pet *S'wark* 67-80; Hon Can Cant Cathl *Cant* 74-90; Chapl Chpl Royal Hampton Court Palace 82-99; Dep P in O 92-99; rtd 99. *College of St Barnabas, Blackberry Lane, Lingfield RH7 6NJ* Tel (01342) 870717

MOORE, Norman Butler. b 25. St Jo Coll Dur BA50. Cranmer Hall Dur. **d** 52 **p** 53. C Aston St Jas *Birm* 52-55; V 57-59; C Gravesend St Jas *Roch* 55-57; PC Warley Woods *Birm* 59-64; Bp's Youth Chapl and Asst Dir of Educn *Worc* 65-66; V Lucton w Eyton *Heref* 66-69; V Hazelwell *Birm* 69-75; V Watford St Andr *St Alb* 75-94; rtd 94; Perm to Offic *St Alb* from 94. *5 Vicarage Close, St Albans AL1 2PU* Tel (01727) 863219

MOORE, Paul Henry. b 59. Ball Coll Ox BA82 DPhil86. Wycliffe Hall Ox DipTh87. **d** 89 **p** 90. C Ox St Andr *Ox* 89-93; V Kildwick *Bradf* 93-01; V Cowplain *Portsm* from 01; RD Havant from 04. *The Vicarage, Padnell Road, Cowplain, Waterlooville PO8 8DZ* Tel (023) 9226 2295
E-mail p.h.moore@btinternet.com

MOORE, Philip. b 49. York Univ MA71 Leeds Univ MA05 PGCE72. N Ord Course 02. **d** 05. NSM Heworth Ch Ch *York* from 05. *14 Whitby Avenue, York YO31 1ET* Tel (01904) 425250
E-mail philip.moore@britishlibrary.net

MOORE, Raymond. b 47. QUB BSc70. **d** 87 **p** 88. NSM Belfast All SS *Conn* 87-95; NSM 95-96; NSM Kilmakee from 96. *17 Royal Lodge Avenue, Purdysburn, Belfast BT8 4YR* Tel (028) 9070 5481 *or* 9026 3960 Fax 9031 4055 *or* 9026 3744
E-mail raymond@rmoore.uklinux.net

MOORE, Richard William Robert. b 39. UCD BA70 TCD HDipEd71. CITC 98. **d** 01 **p** 02. Aux Min Drogheda w Ardee, Collon and Termonfeckin *Arm* 01-05; Aux Min Dundalk w Heynestown from 05; Aux Min Ballymascanlan w Creggan and Rathcor from 05. *Dundalk Road, Dunleer, Co Louth, Irish Republic* Tel (00353) (41) 685 1327
E-mail richardmoore@eircom.ie

MOORE, Richard Noel. b 34. TCD BA56 MA60. **d** 57 **p** 58. C Derry Cathl *D & R* 57-60; I Clondehorkey 60-66; I Stranorlar w Meenglas and Kilteevogue 66-76; I Glendermott 76-00; Can Derry Cathl 89-00; rtd 00. *Evergreen House, 37 Mullanahoe Road, Dungannon BT71 5AT* Tel (028) 8673 7112

MOORE, Richard Norman Theobald. b 39. St Andr Univ BSc62 Lon Univ BD66. Clifton Th Coll. **d** 66 **p** 67. C Stowmarket *St E* 66-69; C New Humberstone *Leic* 69-72; P-in-c Leic Martyrs 73; V 73-84; Chapl Manor Hosp Epsom 84-94; Chapl Surrey Oaklands NHS Trust 94-00; rtd 00; Perm to Offic *Guildf* from 02. *72 Newton Wood Road, Ashtead KT19 8NL* Tel (01372) 813999

MOORE, Robert. *See* MOORE, Arthur Robert

MOORE, Robert Allen. b 32. Univ of the Pacific BA54 Boston Univ STB58 STM59. **d** 63 **p** 63. USA 63-80; V Farington *Blackb* 80-83; TV Preston St Jo 83-85; P-in-c Fleetwood St Pet 85-87; V Leyland St Jas 87-97; rtd 97; Perm to Offic *Blackb* from 97. *19 Lea Road, Whittle-le-Woods, Chorley PR6 7PF* Tel (01257) 265701 E-mail rmoore1980@aol.com

MOORE, Robert Denholm. b 23. TCD BA45 Div Test46. **d** 46 **p** 47. C Londonderry Ch Ch *D & R* 46-49; C Dublin Clontarf *D & G* 49-53; I Clondehorkey *D & R* 53-60; I Clonleigh w Donaghmore 60-65; I Tamlaghtfinlagan w Myroe 65-92; Chapl HM Pris Magilligan 72-92; Can Derry Cathl *D & R* 80-92; rtd 92. *22 Tyler Road, Limavady BT49 0DP* Tel (028) 7776 8597

MOORE, Robin Alan. b 42. Portsm Coll of Tech DipBS65 Lon Univ BA71 Garnett Coll Lon CertEd75 Open Univ Ad Dip Educn Mgt 87 Brighton Univ Dip Counselling 95. S Dios Minl Tr Scheme 91. **d** 94 **p** 95. NSM Barcombe *Chich* from 94; Chapl St Pet and St Jas Hospice N Chailey from 99. *Yew Tree House, School Path, Barcombe, Lewes BN8 5DN* Tel (01273) 400747

MOORE, Robin Hugh. b 52. CertEd BEd QUB BD TCD DipTh. **d** 84 **p** 85. C Derryloran *Arm* 84-86; C Knock *D & D* 86-89; Bp's C Belfast St Steph w St Luke *Conn* 89-94; I 94-96; I Whitehouse 96-03; Bp's C Belfast St Mary Magd from 03. *9 Sycamore Park, Newtownabbey BT37 0NR* Tel (028) 9086 9569

MOORE, Simon Quentin. b 61. Sheff Univ BA83 PGCE84. St Jo Coll Nottm MA99. **d** 00 **p** 01. C St Alb St Paul *St Alb* 00-03; TV Digswell and Panshanger from 03. *69 Hardings, Welwyn Garden City AL7 2HA* Tel (01707) 375333
E-mail simon@qmoore.freeserve.co.uk

MOORE, Thomas Robert. b 38. TCD 65. Lambeth MA84. **d** 68 **p** 69. C Dublin Drumcondra w N Strand *D & G* 68-70; C Portadown St Columba *Arm* 70-72; I Kilskeery w Trillick *Clogh* 72-85; Dioc Sec 83-04; I Trory w Killadeas 85-95; Can Clogh Cathl 86-89; Preb 89-91; Preb Donaghmore St Patr Cathl Dublin 91-95; Dean Clogh 95-04; I Clogh w Errigal Portclare 95-04; rtd 04. *Daintree Drumbane, 209 Kesh Road, Kesh, Enniskillen BT93 1SQ* Tel (028) 6863 3177
E-mail deantrmoore@sagainternet.co.uk

MOORE, Thomas Sydney. b 50. St Paul's Coll Grahamstown 77. **d** 79 **p** 80. S Africa 79-96; C Rondebosch St Thos 79-82 and 83-84; C Bredasdorp 82-83; R Green Point 84-88; C Bushey *St Alb* from 97. *Trinity House, 466 Bushey Mill Lane, Bushey, Watford WD23 2AS* Tel (01923) 220565
E-mail ts.moore@virgin.net

MOORE, Mrs Wendy. b 44. Westcott Ho Cam CTM94. **d** 94 **p** 95. C Rotherham *Sheff* 94-97; V Laughton w Throapham 97-01; V Bromsgrove All SS *Worc* from 01. *All Saints' Vicarage, 20 Burcot Lane, Bromsgrove B60 1AE* Tel (01527) 576515

MOORE, William. *See* MOORE, Albert William

MOORE, William Henry. b 14. K Coll Lon 34. **d** 38 **p** 39. C Mill End *St Alb* 38-41; C Tring 41-44; C Gt Yarmouth *Nor* 44-46; New Zealand 46-52; R Houghton Conquest *St Alb* 52-56; Canada 56-59; R Filby w Thrigby *Nor* 60-62; P-in-c Mautby 60-62; Perm to Offic 62-71; Asst Master Mildenhall Sec Sch 68-73; Heartsease Sch Nor 73-75; C Mildenhall *St E* 71-73; rtd 79; Perm to Offic *Nor* from 88. *21 Green Court, Avenue Green, Norwich NR7 0DN* Tel (01603) 432758

MOORE, William Morris. b 33. QUB BSc55 TCD. **d** 61 **p** 62. C Belfast St Mich *Conn* 61-64; I 70-80; C Belfast All SS 64-70; I Ballynafeigh St Jude *D & D* 80-03; Can Belf Cathl 95-03; rtd 03. *10 Hollygate Park, Carryduff, Belfast BT8 8DZ* Tel (028) 9081 4896

MOORE-BICK, Miss Elizabeth Mary. b 77. Qu Coll Cam BA99 MA03 Anglia Poly Univ BA04. Westcott Ho Cam 02. **d** 05. C Hillingdon St Jo *Lon* from 05. *155 Pield Heath Road, Uxbridge UB8 3NL* Tel (01895) 252119 Mobile 07803-044217
E-mail lizmoore_bick@yahoo.co.uk *or* emm25@cam.ac.uk

MOORE BROOKS, Dorothy Anne. b 66. York Univ BA87 Hughes Hall Cam PGCE88. Ridley Hall Cam 96. **d** 98 **p** 99. C S Kensington St Jude *Lon* 98-01; NSM Hoddesdon *St Alb* from 01; Chapl Gt Ormond Street Hosp for Children NHS Trust from 02; Perm to Offic *Lon* from 02. *11 Oxenden Drive, Hoddesdon EN11 8QF* Tel (01992) 464335
E-mail moorebrooks@ntlworld.com

MOORGAS, Geoffrey Gordon. b 30. Sarum & Wells Th Coll 80. **d** 81 **p** 82. C Brixton St Matt *S'wark* 81-84; C Clapham Old Town 84-87; Namibia 87-94; rtd 95; NSM Limpsfield and Titsey *S'wark* 95-05; Perm to Offic from 05. *St Silvan's House, Red Lane, Oxted RH8 0RS* Tel (01883) 723452

MOORHEAD, Michael David. b 52. BSc BA. St Steph Ho Ox. **d** 83 **p** 84. C Kilburn St Aug w St Jo *Lon* 83-87; C Kenton 87-89; Chapl Cen Middx Hosp NHS Trust from 89; V Harlesden All So *Lon* from 89; P-in-c Willesden St Matt 92-02. *All Souls' Vicarage, 3 Station Road, London NW10 4UJ* Tel and fax (020) 8965 4988
E-mail michael@allsoulschurch.fsnet.co.uk

MOORHOUSE, Christine Susan. b 49. K Coll Lon BD71 AKC71. WMMTC. **dss** 86 **d** 87 **p** 94. NSM Stourbridge St Thos *Worc* 86-99; Perm to Offic from 02. *20 High Street, Wollaston, Stourbridge DY8 4NJ* Tel (01384) 395381

MOORHOUSE, Humphrey John. b 18. Oak Hill Th Coll 37. **d** 41 **p** 42. C Dalston St Mark w St Bart *Lon* 41-42; C Chadwell Heath *Chelmsf* 42-45; R Vange 45-83; rtd 83; Perm to Offic *Chelmsf* from 83. *12 Waverley Road, Benfleet SS7 4AZ* Tel (01268) 754952

MOORHOUSE, Peter. b 42. Liv Univ BSc64 Hull Univ CertEd. Linc Th Coll 79. **d** 81 **p** 82. C Horsforth *Ripon* 81-85; R Ackworth *Wakef* 85-96; Dep Chapl HM Pris Leeds 96-97; Chapl HM Pris Stocken 97-98; Chapl HM Pris Everthorpe from 98. *HM Prison Everthorpe, Everthorpe, Brough HU15 1RB* Tel (01430) 422471 Fax 421351

MOORSE, Michael William. b 36. Culham Coll of Educn TCert63. Guildf Dioc Min Course 96. **d** 98 **p** 99. OLM Woking St Pet *Guildf* from 98. *4 Bonners Close, Woking GU22 9RA* Tel (01483) 767460

MOORSOM, Christopher Arthur Robert. b 55. Ox Univ BA. Sarum & Wells Th Coll 79. **d** 82 **p** 83. C Bradford-on-Avon *Sarum* 82-85; R Broad Town, Clyffe Pypard and Tockenham 85-89; V Banwell *B & W* 89-96; R Upper Stour *Sarum* from 96. *The Rectory, Portnells Lane, Zeals, Warminster BA12 6PG* Tel (01747) 840221 E-mail chrisliz.moorsom@btopenworld.com

MORALEE, Thomas Edward (Tony). b 33. S'wark Ord Course. **d** 82 **p** 83. NSM Wandsworth All SS *S'wark* 82-90; NSM Gt Bookham *Guildf* 91-92; Perm to Offic from 92. *71 Eastwick Park Avenue, Bookham, Leatherhead KT23 3NH* Tel (01372) 454433

MORAY, ROSS AND CAITHNESS, Bishop of. *See* CROOK, The Rt Revd John Michael

MORAY, ROSS AND CAITHNESS, Dean of. *See* BLACK, The Very Revd Leonard Albert

MORBY, Mrs Helen Mary. b 62. Wolv Univ BA99. Ripon Coll Cuddesdon 99. **d** 01 **p** 02. C Lich St Chad *Lich* 01-04; V Farnworth *Liv* from 04. *The Vicarage, Coroners Lane, Widnes WA8 9HY* Tel 0151-424 2735 E-mail helen@morby.freeserve.co.uk

MORDECAI, Mrs Betty. b 27. Birm Univ BA48 Cam Univ CertEd49. Wycliffe Hall Ox 85. **dss** 86 **d** 87 **p** 94. Leamington Priors All SS *Cov* 86-89; Hon Par Dn 87-89; C Worc City St Paul and Old St Martin etc *Worc* 89-94; rtd 94; Perm to Offic *Cov* from 00. *8 Swains Crofts, Leamington Spa CV31 1YW* Tel (01926) 882001 E-mail bettyhoward@darwen23.freeserve.co.uk

MORDECAI, Thomas Huw. b 59. Bris Univ BA81 St Jo Coll Dur BA85 MA92. Cranmer Hall Dur 83. **d** 87 **p** 88. C Gillingham St Mary *Roch* 87-90; Chapl Warw Sch 90-96; Chapl Giggleswick Sch 96-98; Chapl Westmr Sch and PV Westmr Abbey 98-01. *Address temp unknown*

MORE, Canon Richard David Antrobus. b 48. St Jo Coll Dur BA70 DipTh71. Cranmer Hall Dur 70. **d** 72 **p** 73. C Macclesfield St Mich *Ches* 72-77; Chapl Lee Abbey 77-82; V Porchester *S'well* 82-96; RD Gedling 90-96; Bp's Dom Chapl *Chelmsf* 96-01; Dioc Dir of Ords from 01; Dioc NSM Officer from 01; Hon Can Chelmsf Cathl from 96. *25 Roxwell Road, Chelmsford CM1 2LY* Tel (01245) 264187 Fax 348789 E-mail ddo@chelmsford.anglican.org

MORECROFT, Michael William. b 40. MIBiol Man Univ MEd. WMMTC. **d** 86 **p** 87. Hd Master Polesworth Sch Warks 86-91; Educn Inspector/Consultant 92-02; Hon C Wylde Green *Birm* 86-89; Hon C Castle Bromwich St Clem 89-98; Perm to Offic from 98. *St Clement's Croft, 11 Wood Green Road, Wednesbury WS10 9AX* Tel 0121-505 5954 E-mail mwm@fort34.freeserve.co.uk

MORETON, Ann Louise. b 32. **d** 02 **p** 03. OLM Whitstable *Cant* 02-04; Perm to Offic from 04. *Church House, 24 Freemans Close, Seasalter, Whitstable CT5 4BB* Tel (01227) 277140 E-mail annmoreton@hotmail.com

MORETON, Preb Mark. b 39. Jes Coll Cam BA64 MA68. Westcott Ho Cam 63. **d** 65 **p** 66. C Portsea All SS *Portsm* 65-70; C St Martin-in-the-Fields *Lon* 70-72; Chapl Jes Coll Cam 72-77; R Stafford St Mary and St Chad *Lich* 77-79; P-in-c Stafford Ch Ch 77-79; TR Stafford 79-91; P-in-c Marston w Whitgreave 77-79; V W Bromwich All SS 91-04; Preb Lich Cathl 99-04; rtd 04. *Rosemont, Dry Mill Lane, Bewdley DY12 2BL* Tel (01299) 401965

MORETON, Michael Bernard. b 44. St Jo Coll Cam BA66 MA70 Ch Ch Ox BA66 MA69 DPhil69. St Steph Ho Ox 66. **d** 68 **p** 69. C Banstead *Guildf* 68-74; R Alburgh *Nor* 74-75; R Denton 74-75; R Middleton Cheney w Chacombe *Pet* 75-87; Perm to Offic *Cant* from 00. *Waterloo House, 56-58 High Street, Rolvenden, Cranbrook TN17 4LN* Tel (01580) 241287

MORETON, Preb Michael Joseph. b 17. Univ Coll Lon BA40 Ch Ch Ox BA47 MA53. Wells Th Coll 47. **d** 48 **p** 49. C Rowbarton *B & W* 48-52; C Ilfracombe H Trin *Ex* 52-59; Lect Th Ex Univ 57-86; R Ex St Mary Steps *Ex* 59-86; P-in-c 86-92; RD Christianity 83-89; Preb Ex Cathl 85-86; rtd 86; Perm to Offic *Ex* from 86. *3 Glenthorne Road, Duryard, Exeter EX4 4QU* Tel (01392) 438083

MORETON, Philip Norman Harley. b 28. Linc Th Coll. **d** 57 **p** 58. C Howden *York* 57-60; C Bottesford *Linc* 60-65; V Linc St Giles 65-70; V Bracebridge Heath 71-77; V Seasalter *Cant* 77-84; TV Whitstable 84-88; rtd 88; Perm to Offic *York* from 96. *The Cottage, 2 Broad Lane, Treeton Road, Howden, Goole DN14 7DN* Tel (01430) 430552

MORETON, Rupert Robert James. b 66. TCD BA89. CITC BTh92. **d** 92 **p** 93. C Dublin Ch Ch Cathl Gp *D & G* 92-96; Asst Chapl Costa Blanca *Eur* 96-98; Chapl Helsinki from 98. *Mannerheimintie 19 A7, 00250 Helsinki, Finland* Tel (00358) (9) 490424 *or* 680 1515 Fax 698 6302 E-mail rupert.moreton@icon.fi

MORFILL, Mrs Mary Joanna. b 46. Seaford Coll of Educn TCert67. STETS 01. **d** 04. NSM Swanmore St Barn *Portsm* from 04. *Meonstoke Post Office, Warnford Road, Corhampton, Southampton SO32 3ND* Tel (01489) 878227 Mobile 07906-755145 E-mail mary@meonstoke.fslife.co.uk

✠**MORGAN, The Rt Revd Alan Wyndham.** b 40. OBE05. Univ of Wales (Lamp) BA62. St Mich Coll Llan 62. **d** 64 **p** 65 **c** 89. C Llangyfelach and Morriston *S & B* 64-69; C Swansea St Pet 69-72; C Cov E *Cov* 72-73; TV 73-83; Bp's Officer for Soc Resp 78-83; Adn Cov 83-89; Suff Bp Sherwood *S'well* 89-04; rtd 04. *10 Station Road, Alcester B49 5ET* Tel (01789) 762486

MORGAN, Alison Jean. b 59. Girton Coll Cam BA82 MA85 Darw Coll Cam PhD86. EMMTC 93. **d** 96 **p** 97. NSM Oadby *Leic* 96; NSM Leic H Trin w St Jo from 98. *29 Holmfield Road, Leicester LE2 1SE* Tel 0116-270 4986

MORGAN, Anthony Hogarth. b 42. St Josef Missiehuis Holland 60 St Jos RC Coll Lon 62. **d** 65 **p** 66. In RC Ch 66-93; NSM Handsworth Woodhouse *Sheff* 93-94; C Sheff St Leon Norwood 94-97; P-in-c Shiregreen St Hilda 97-05; C Shiregreen St Jas and St Chris from 05. *St Hilda's House, 2 Firth Park Crescent, Sheffield S5 6HE* Tel 0114-243 6308

MORGAN, Anthony Paul George. b 57. Sarum & Wells Th Coll 89. **d** 91 **p** 92. C Plymstock *Ex* 91-95; P-in-c Wolborough w Newton Abbot 95-00; V York St Hilda *York* from 01. *St Hilda's Vicarage, 155 Tang Hall Lane, York YO10 3SD* Tel (01904) 413150 E-mail tony@thefms.fsnet.co.uk

✠**MORGAN, The Most Revd Barry Cennydd.** b 47. Lon Univ BA69 Selw Coll Cam BA72 MA74 Univ of Wales PhD86. Westcott Ho Cam 70. **d** 72 **p** 73 **c** 93. Chapl Bryn-y-Don Community Sch 72-75; C St Andrews Major w Michaelston-le-Pit *Llan* 72-75; Ed *Welsh Churchman* 75-82; Lect Th Univ of Wales (Cardiff) 75-77; Chapl and Lect St Mich Coll Llan 75-77; Warden Ch Hostel Ban 77-84; Chapl and Lect Th Univ of Wales (Ban) 77-84; In-Service Tr Adv *Ban* 78-84; Dir of Ords 82-84; Can Ban Cathl 83-84; R Wrexham *St As* 84-86; Adn Meirionnydd *Ban* 86-93; R Criccieth w Treflys 86-93; Bp Ban 93-99; Bp Llan from 99; Abp Wales from 03. *Llys Esgob, The Cathedral Green, Llandaff, Cardiff CF5 2YE* Tel (029) 2056 2400 Fax 2057 7129 E-mail archbishop@churchinwales.org.uk

MORGAN, Miss Beryl. b 30. **dss** 63 **d** 87 **p** 94. Rickerscote *Lich* 63-69; Hd Dss 70-87; Dioc Lay Min Adv 70-93; Willenhall H Trin 80-87; Par Dn 87-93; rtd 93; Hon C Penn *Lich* 94-01; Perm to Offic 01-04. *12 Stuart Court, Kibworth, Leicester LE8 0LR* Tel 0116-279 6345

✠**MORGAN, The Rt Revd Christopher Heudebourck.** b 47. Lon Univ DipTh70 Lanc Univ BA73 Heythrop Coll Lon MTh91. Kelham Th Coll 66. **d** 73 **p** 74 **c** 01. C Birstall *Leic* 73-76; Asst Chapl Brussels *Eur* 76-80; P-in-c Redditch St Geo *Worc* 80-81; TV Redditch, The Ridge 81-85; V Sonning *Ox* 85-96; Prin Berks Chr Tr Scheme 85-89; Dir Past Studies Ox Min Course 92-96; Dioc Can Res Glouc Cathl and Officer for Min *Glouc* 96-01; Area Bp Colchester *Chelmsf* from 01. *1 Fitzwalter Road, Colchester CO3 3SS* Tel (01206) 576648 Fax 763868 E-mail b.colchester@chelmsford.anglican.org

MORGAN, Christopher John. b 46. Brasted Th Coll 68 Linc Th Coll 70. **d** 72 **p** 73. C Earley St Pet *Ox* 72-76; C Epsom St Martin *Guildf* 76-79; V Stoneleigh 79-83; Ind Chapl *York* 83-92; NACRO 87-91; V York St Hilda *York* 92-96; TV E Greenwich *S'wark* 96-03; P-in-c Norbury St Oswald from 03; V from 05. *The Vicarage, 2B St Oswald's Road, London SW16 3SB* Tel (020) 8764 2853

MORGAN, Clive. b 41. **d** 02. Par Dn Blaina and Nantyglo *Mon* from 02. *26 Victoria Street, Blaina, Abertillery NP13 3BG* Tel (01495) 291637

MORGAN, David Farnon Charles. b 43. Leeds Univ BA68. Coll of Resurr Mirfield 68. **d** 70 **p** 71. C Swinton St Pet *Man* 70-73; C Langley All SS and Martyrs 73-75; R Salford St Clem w St Cypr Ordsall 75-76; R Salford Ordsall St Clem 76-86; V Adlington *Blackb* from 86; AD Chorley 98-04. *St Paul's Vicarage, Railway Road, Adlington, Chorley PR6 9QZ* Tel (01257) 480253 E-mail morgyvic@tinyworld.co.uk

MORGAN, David Joseph (Joe). b 47. Bp Burgess Hall Lamp 66 St Deiniol's Hawarden 74. **d** 74 **p** 75. C Pembroke Dock *St D* 74-77; C Burry Port and Pwll 77-80; Miss to Seafarers from 80; Sen Chapl and Sec Welsh Coun from 85. *25 Glanmor Park Road, Sketty, Swansea SA2 0QG* Tel (01792) 206637

MORGAN, Deiniol Tudur. d 02 p 03. Min Can Ban Cathl *Ban* 02-04; P-in-c Llanberis w Llanrug 04-05; Prec and Min Can Westmr Abbey from 05. *7 Little Cloister, London SW1P 3PL* Tel (020) 7654 4855 E-mail deiniol.morgan@westminster-abbey.org *or* deiniol@fish.co.uk

MORGAN, Denis. b 36. Cuddesdon Coll 67. **d** 69 **p** 70. C Bush Hill Park St Steph *Lon* 69-72; C Stevenage St Nic *St Alb* 72-75; V Croxley Green St Oswald 75-85; V Shillington 85-95; rtd 95; Perm to Offic *Roch* from 95. *7 Fromandez Drive, Horsmonden, Tonbridge TN12 8LN* Tel (01892) 722388

MORGAN, Canon Enid Morris Roberts. b 40. St Anne's Coll Ox BA61 Univ of Wales (Ban) MA73. United Th Coll Abth BD81. **d** 84 **p** 97. C Llanfihangel w Llanafan and Llanwnnws etc *St D* 84-86; Dn-in-c 86-93; Dir Bd of Miss Ch in Wales 93-00; V Llangynwyd w Maesteg *Llan* 00-05; Hon Can Llan Cathl 02-05; rtd 05. *Rhiwlas, Cliff Terrace, Aberystwyth SY23 2DN* Tel (01970) 624648

MORGAN, Gareth Morison Kilby. b 33. Bris Univ BA56. Cuddesdon Coll 57 Bangalore Th Coll. **d** 61 **p** 62. C St Helier *S'wark* 61-65; Chapl Scargill Ho 65-70; Dir RE *Linc* 71-74; Dioc Dir of Educn *St E* 74-81; TR Hanley H Ev *Lich* 81-89; TR Cen Telford 89-92; Warden Glenfall Ho *Glouc* 92-98; rtd 98; Perm to Offic *Win* from 00. *St Neots, Kanes Hill, Southampton SO19 6AH* Tel (023) 8046 6509 E-mail geejaymo@aol.com

MORGAN, Geoffrey. *See* MORGAN, James Geoffrey Selwyn

MORGAN, Gerwyn. *See* MORGAN, William Charles Gerwyn

MORGAN, Glyn. b 21. Oak Hill Th Coll 73. **d** 76 **p** 77. Hon C Barton Seagrave w Warkton *Pet* 76-00; Perm to Offic from 00. *St Edmund's House, Warkton, Kettering NN15 5AB* Tel (01536) 520610

MORGAN, Glyn. b 33. Univ of Wales (Ban) BA55 MA69. Coll of Resurr Mirfield 55. **d** 57 **p** 58. C Dolgellau *Ban* 57-60; C Conway 60-63; V Corris 63-68; Hd of RE Friars' Sch Ban 69-70; Lic to Offic 70-71; Hd of RE Oswestry Boys' Modern Sch 70-74; Hd of RE Oswestry High Sch for Girls 74-79; Hon C Oswestry H Trin *Lich* 71-79; Hd of RE Fitzalan Sch Oswestry 79-88; V Meifod and Llangynyw *St As* 88-01; RD Caereinion 89-01; rtd 01. *Crib y Gwynt Annexe, Trefnanney, Meifod SY22 6XX* Tel (01938) 500066

MORGAN, Graham. b 47. KBE00. S'wark Ord Course. **d** 83 **p** 84. NSM S Kensington St Steph *Lon* 83-90; NSM Hammersmith H Innocents 90-02; NSM Bedford Park from 02. *24 Charleville Court, Charleville Road, London W14 9JG* Tel (020) 7381 3211 E-mail graham.morgan@nwlh.nhs.uk

MORGAN, Harold Evan. b 17. St D Coll Lamp BA38. **d** 40 **p** 41. C Oldbury *Birm* 40-42; C Northleach and Hampnett w Stowell and Yanworth *Glouc* 42-43; CF 43-47; PC Milford *Derby* 47-50; R Yerbeston w Loveston *St D* 50-52; V Uzmaston and Boulston 52-53; R Llanilid w Pencoed *Llan* 53-68; V Newcastle 68-83; rtd 83; Perm to Offic *Llan* from 83. *Greystones, 28 Seaview Drive, Ogmore-by-Sea, Bridgend CF32 0PB* Tel (01656) 880467

MORGAN, Henry. b 45. Hertf Coll Ox BA68. Westcott Ho Cam 68. **d** 70 **p** 71. C Lee St Marg *S'wark* 70-73; C Newington St Paul 73-76; V Camberwell St Mich w All So w Em 76-84; V Kingswood 84-93; Perm to Offic *S'wark* 93-03 and *Sheff* from 03. *St Helen's, Grange Lane, Burghwallis, Doncaster DN6 9JL* Tel (01302) 700227 E-mail henry.morgan1@virgin.net

MORGAN, Hogarth. *See* MORGAN, Anthony Hogarth

MORGAN, Ian David John. b 57. LTCL75 Hull Univ BA78. Ripon Coll Cuddesdon 80. **d** 83 **p** 84. C Heref H Trin *Heref* 83-86; C New Shoreham *Chich* 86-88; Researcher, Producer & Presenter BBC Local Radio 88-92; V Ipswich All Hallows *St E* 92-95; TR Ipswich St Mary at Stoke w St Pet 95-97; TR Ipswich St Mary at Stoke w St Pet and St Fran from 97. *The Rectory, 74 Ancaster Road, Ipswich IP2 9AJ* Tel (01473) 601895 Fax 683303 E-mail ianmorgan@aol.com

MORGAN, Ian Stephen. b 50. Open Univ BA88. Sarum & Wells Th Coll 86. **d** 88 **p** 89. C Baldock w Bygrave *St Alb* 88-91; C S Elmham and Ilketshall *St E* 91-95; V Bungay H Trin w St Mary from 95. *The Vicarage, 3 Trinity Gardens, Bungay NR35 1HH* Tel (01986) 892553 Fax 895369 Mobile 07808-451350 E-mail sm01020158@aol.com

MORGAN, James Geoffrey Selwyn. b 59. Ex Univ BA81 PGCE82 St Jo Coll Dur CCSk91 Open Univ MPhil97. Cranmer Hall Dur 88. **d** 91 **p** 92. C Reading St Agnes w St Paul *Ox* 91-93; C Bromham w Oakley and Stagsden *St Alb* 94-95; Perm to Offic *Pet* 96-98; C Epsom St Martin *Guildf* 98-01; Ox Cen for Miss Studies from 01. *Oxford Centre for Mission Studies, PO Box 70, Oxford OX2 6HB* Tel (01865) 556071 Fax 510823 E-mail jgs_morgan@tiscali.co.uk

MORGAN, Joe. *See* MORGAN, David Joseph

MORGAN, John. *See* MORGAN, William John

MORGAN, John Geoffrey Basil. b 21. Wells Th Coll 59. **d** 60 **p** 61. C Oakdale St Geo *Sarum* 60-64; C Talbot Village 64-67; C-in-c Ensbury St Thos CD 67-69; V Ensbury 69-82; C W Parley 82-86; rtd 86; Perm to Offic *Sarum* from 01. *57 Selwood Caravan Park, Weymans Avenue, Bournemouth BH10 7JX* Tel (01202) 582327

MORGAN, John Laurence. b 41. Melbourne Univ BA62 Oriel Coll Ox BA69 MA73 DPhil76. **d** 68 **p** 69. Acting Chapl Oriel Coll Ox 69 and 70-76; USA 77-78; Australia from 78. *St John's College, College Road, St Lucia, Qld, Australia 4067* Tel (0062) (7) 3371 3741 *or* 3842 6600 Fax 3870 5124 E-mail john.morgan@mailbox.uq.edu.au

MORGAN, John Roland. b 31. Birm Univ BA54. Bps' Coll Cheshunt 54. **d** 55 **p** 56. C Selly Oak St Mary *Birm* 55-57; C Yardley Wood 57-58; C Hamstead St Paul 58-61; V Smethwick St Chad 61-68; V Balsall Common 68-82; V N Leigh *Ox* 82-95; RD Woodstock 87-92; rtd 95; Perm to Offic *Ely* from 95. *Dyn Caryn, 2 Hayling Close, Godmanchester, Huntingdon PE29 2XB* Tel (01480) 459522

MORGAN, John William Miller. b 34. Lon Univ BSc56. Wycliffe Hall Ox 61. **d** 63 **p** 64. C St Alb Ch Ch *St Alb* 63-68; V Luton St Matt High Town 68-79; V Mangotsfield *Bris* 79-90; P-in-c Stanton St Quintin, Hullavington, Grittleton etc 90-95; R Hullavington, Norton and Stanton St Quintin 95-99; rtd 99; Perm to Offic *Bris* from 00. *3 Bouverie Park, Stanton St Quintin, Chippenham SN14 6EE* Tel (01666) 837670 E-mail johnwmmorgan@compuserve.com

MORGAN, Mrs Judith. b 62. Carl and Blackb Dioc Tr Inst 96. **d** 99 **p** 00. C Brigham and Broughton and Broughton Moor *Carl* 99-04; P-in-c Doxford St Wilfrid *Dur* from 04. *2 Whitebark, Sunderland SR3 2NX* Tel 0191-522 7639 E-mail morgjud@aol.com

MORGAN, Katharine. b 41. **d** 91 **p** 97. NSM Loughor *S & B* from 91. *68 Borough Road, Lougher, Swansea SA4 6RT*

MORGAN, Kathleen Irene. b 52. St Martin's Coll Lanc CertEd74. WEMTC 93. **d** 96 **p** 97. NSM Barnwood *Glouc* 96-99; C Coney Hill 99-02; V Churchdown St Jo and Innsworth from 02. *The Vicarage, St John's Avenue, Churchdown, Gloucester GL3 2DA* Tel (01452) 713421 E-mail revkaty@aol.com

MORGAN, Kenneth James. b 14. Selw Coll Cam BA36 MA43. Wells Th Coll 36. **d** 38 **p** 39. C Moulsecoomb *Chich* 38-40; C Preston 40-41; Chapl RAFVR 41-47; Chapl Miss to Seamen 47; Lic to Offic *Dur* 47; Chapl Oslo Norway 47-51; V Blacklands Ch Ch *Chich* 51-58; V Weston St Jo *B & W* 58-66; V Shalford *Guildf* 66-84; rtd 84; Perm to Offic *Guildf* from 85. *Greenwood, The Close, Wonersh, Guildford GU5 0PA* Tel (01483) 898791

MORGAN, Linda Marianne. b 48. Bris Univ BSc69 Surrey Univ MSc72 Lon Univ PhD77 FRCPath01. STETS 99. **d** 02 **p** 03. NSM Claygate *Guildf* from 02. *8 Melbury Close, Claygate KT10 0EX* Tel (01372) 462911 E-mail l.morgan@surrey.ac.uk

MORGAN, Mrs Marian Kathleen Eleanor. b 38. Birm Univ MA94 FCMI82. WEMTC. **d** 00 **p** 01. NSM Cusop w Blakemere, Bredwardine w Brobury etc *Heref* 00-03; P-in-c New Radnor and Llanfihangel Nantmelan etc *S & B* from 03. *The Rectory, School Lane, New Radnor, Presteigne LD8 2SS* Tel (01544) 350258 Mobile 07977-477212

MORGAN, Mark Anthony. b 58. LLB. Chich Th Coll. **d** 84 **p** 85. C Thorpe *Nor* 84-87; C Eaton 87-90; V Southtown 90-92; Perm to Offic from 92. *Nethergate End, The Street, Saxlingham, Nethergate, Norwich NR15 1AJ* Tel (01603) 762850

MORGAN, Mark Steven Glyn. b 60. Essex Univ BSc83 RGN86. Ridley Hall Cam 95. **d** 97 **p** 99. C Herne Bay Ch Ch *Cant* 97-02; TV Ipswich St Mary at Stoke w St Pet and St Fran *St E* from 02. *St Peter's Church House, Stoke Park Drive, Ipswich IP2 9TH* Tel (01473) 601438 E-mail hama.morgan-@tinyworld.co.uk

MORGAN, Martin Paul. b 46. St Steph Ho Ox 71. **d** 73 **p** 74. C Kettering St Mary *Pet* 73-76; C Fareham SS Pet and Paul *Portsm* 76-80; V Portsea Ascension 80-94; V Rottingdean *Chich* from 94. *The Vicarage, Steyning Road, Rottingdean, Brighton BN2 7GA* Tel (01273) 309216

MORGAN, Mrs Melanie Jane. b 54. RMN. Qu Coll Birm 98. **d** 02 **p** 03. NSM Derby St Andr w St Osmund *Derby* from 02. *16 Brading Close, Alvaston, Derby DE24 0UW* Tel (01332) 754419 E-mail clifden@btinternet.com

MORGAN, Michael. b 32. Lon Univ BSc57 MSc67 PhD63. **d** 74 **p** 75. NSM Portsdown *Portsm* 74-98; Perm to Offic from 98. *12 East Cosham Road, Cosham, Portsmouth PO6 2JS* Tel (023) 9237 7442

MORGAN, Michael John. b 45. Nottm Univ BA66 MEd71. Linc Th Coll 80. **d** 82 **p** 83. C Bulkington *Cov* 82-83; C Bulkington w Shilton and Ansty 83-85; V Longford 85-89; R Norton *Sheff* 89-99; R Lapworth *Birm* from 99; R Baddesley Clinton from 99. *The Rectory, Church Lane, Lapworth, Solihull B94 5NX* Tel (01564) 782098

MORGAN, Morley Roland. b 47. Univ of Wales (Lamp) BA76. St Steph Ho Ox 76. **d** 77 **p** 78. C Merthyr Dyfan *Llan* 77-78; C Llantrisant 78-80; TV Coventry Caludon *Cov* 80-86; Chapl N Man Gen Hosp 86-93; Chapl N Man Health Care NHS Trust 93-02; Chapl Pennine Acute Hosps NHS Trust from 02. *North Manchester General Hospital, Delaunays Road, Crumpsall, Manchester M8 6RL* Tel 0161-720 2990 *or* 795 4567 ext 2990 Fax 720 2748

MORGAN, Canon Nicholas John. b 50. K Coll Lon BD71 AKC71 CertEd. St Aug Coll Cant 72. **d** 73 **p** 74. C Wythenshawe Wm Temple Ch *Man* 73-76; C Southam w Stockton *Cov* 76-79; V Brailes from 79; R Sutton under Brailes from 79; RD Shipston 90-98; Hon Can Cov Cathl from 03. *The Vicarage, Brailes, Banbury OX15 5HT* Tel (01608) 685230

MORGAN, Nicola. b 64. Nottm Univ BA86. Linc Th Coll BTh95. **d** 95 **p** 96. C Lillington *Cov* 95-98; C Gospel Lane St Mich *Birm* 98-01; P-in-c Gt Paxton *Ely* 01-05; P-in-c Lt Paxton 01-05; P-in-c Diddington 01-05; V The Paxtons w Diddington 05. *The Vicarage, 24 St James's Road, Little Paxton, St Neots PE19 6QW* Tel (01480) 214280 *or* 475085 E-mail revnickmorg@stmicks.freeserve.co.uk

MORGAN, Peter Neville. b 36. Univ of Wales (Cardiff) BSc60 BD63 PGCE80. **d** 98 **p** 99. NSM Ardingly *Chich* from 98. *12 Victoria Close, Burgess Hill RH15 9QS* Tel (01444) 247647 E-mail revpnm98@aol.com

MORGAN, Philip. b 51. Lon Univ BSc75 Univ of Wales (Cardiff) BD78. St Mich Coll Llan 75. **d** 78 **p** 79. C Swansea St Nic *S & B* 78-81; C Morriston 81-83; C Swansea St Mary w H Trin 83-84; USA from 84. *17476 Hawthorne Avenue, Culpeper, VA 22701, USA* E-mail padre4u@hotmail.com

MORGAN, Canon Philip Brendan. b 35. G&C Coll Cam BA59 MA63. Wells Th Coll 59. **d** 61 **p** 62. C Paddington Ch Ch *Lon* 61-66; C Trunch w Swafield *Nor* 66-68; P-in-c Nor St Steph 68-72; Sacr Nor Cathl 72-74; Can Res and Sub-Dean St Alb 74-81; Hon Can St Alb 81-94; R Bushey 81-94; RD Aldenham 91-94; Can Res and Treas Win Cathl *Win* 94-01; rtd 01; Perm to Offic *Win* from 01. *9 Clifton Hill, Winchester SO22 5BL* Tel (01962) 867549

MORGAN, Canon Philip Reginald Strange. b 27. St D Coll Lamp BA51 Keble Coll Ox BA53 MA57. Wells Th Coll 57. **d** 57 **p** 58. C Fleur-de-Lis *Mon* 57-59; C Bassaleg 59-62; CF (TA) 62-74; V Dingestow and Wanastow *Mon* 62-65; V Dingestow and Penrhos 65-66; R Machen and Rudry 66-75; R Machen 75-76; V Caerleon 76-95; Can St Woolos Cathl 84-95; rtd 95; Lic to Offic *Mon* from 95. *4 Anthony Drive, Caerleon, Newport NP18 3DS* Tel (01633) 422238

MORGAN, Philip Richard Llewelyn. b 27. Wadh Coll Ox BA50 MA52. St Steph Ho Ox 53. **d** 55 **p** 56. C Warlingham w Chelsham and Farleigh *S'wark* 55-58; Chapl Haileybury Coll 58-73; Hd Master Haileybury Jun Sch Berks 73-87; R The Deverills *Sarum* 87-94; rtd 94; Perm to Offic *Guildf* and *Win* from 95. *6 Phillips Close, Headley, Bordon GU35 8LY* Tel and fax (01428) 712194 E-mail philipmorgan@msn.com

MORGAN, Canon Reginald Graham. b 25. St D Coll Lamp BA46 LTh48. **d** 48 **p** 49. C Chirk *St As* 48-50; C Llangollen and Trevor 50-55; R Llanwyddelan w Manafon 55-66; V Rhuddlan 66-94; RD St As 78-94; Hon Can St As Cathl 83-89; Can from 89; rtd 94. *Manafon, 49 Ffordd Ffynnon, Rhuddlan, Rhyl LL18 2SP* Tel (01745) 591036

MORGAN, The Ven Reginald Graham Tharle. b 46. St Jo Coll Nottm LTh75. **d** 75 **p** 76. C Oadby *Leic* 75-78; S Africa from 79; R Greytown St Jas from 88; Adn Estcourt from 95. *PO Box 112, Greytown, Natal, 3250 South Africa* Tel and fax (0027) (334) 71240 *or* tel 71241 E-mail beehive@cybertrade.co.za

MORGAN, Rhys Bryn. b 65. E Lon Univ BA94. St Mich Coll Llan 00. **d** 02 **p** 03. C Carmarthen St Pet *St D* 02-05; P-in-c Cil-y-Cwm and Ystrad-ffin w Rhandir-mwyn etc from 05. *The Vicarage, Cilycwm, Llandovery SA20 0SP* Tel (01550) 721109 Mobile 07973-254062 E-mail rhys.morgan1@btinternet.com

MORGAN, Richard Mervyn. b 50. Wadh Coll Ox BA73 MA75 K Alfred's Coll Win PGCE74. **d** 92 **p** 93. CMS 85-94; Kenya 88-94; Perm to Offic *S'wark* 95-96; R Therfield w Kelshall *St Alb* from 96; Tutor EAMTC *Ely* from 99. *The Rectory, Church Lane, Therfield, Royston SG8 9QD* Tel (01763) 287364 E-mail rm@therfieldrectory.freeserve.co.uk

MORGAN, Richard Thomas. b 70. Peterho Cam BA91 MA95. Wycliffe Hall Ox 94. **d** 96 **p** 97. C Bath Twerton-on-Avon *B & W* 96-99; Chapl Lee Abbey 99-01; R Marks Tey and Aldham *Chelmsf* from 01. *The Rectory, Church Lane, Marks Tey, Colchester CO6 1LW* Tel (01206) 210396 *or* 213231 E-mail richardtmorgan@ic24.net *or* rector@marksteychurch.org

MORGAN, Robert Chowen. b 40. St Cath Coll Cam BA63 MA67. St Chad's Coll Dur 64. **d** 66 **p** 67. C Lancaster St Mary *Blackb* 66-76; Lect Th Lanc Univ 67-76; Fell Linacre Coll Ox from 76; Lect Th Ox Univ 76-97; Reader from 97; P-in-c Sandford-on-Thames *Ox* from 87. *Lower Farm, Sandford-on-Thames, Oxford OX4 4YR* Tel (01865) 748848 E-mail robert.morgan@theology.oxford.ac.uk

MORGAN, Canon Robert Harman. b 28. OBE94. Univ of Wales (Cardiff) BA55. Coll of Resurr Mirfield 55. **d** 57 **p** 58. C Penarth w Lavernock *Llan* 57-61; C Caerau w Ely 61-67; V Glan Ely 67-95; Hon Can Llan Cathl 94-95; rtd 95; Perm to Offic *St D* and *Llan* from 95. *Y Felin Wynt, St Davids, Haverfordwest SA62 6QS* Tel (01437) 720130

MORGAN, Roger William. b 40. Mert Coll Ox BA62 Cam Univ MA67. Ridley Hall Cam 80. **d** 81 **p** 82. NSM Cambridge St Paul *Ely* 81-84; V Corby St Columba *Pet* 84-90; V Leic H Trin w St Jo *Leic* from 90; C-in-c Leic St Leon CD from 01. *29 Holmfield Road, Leicester LE2 1SE* Tel 0116-270 4986

MORGAN, Canon Samuel. b 07. St D Coll Lamp BA32. **d** 32 **p** 33. C Llandysul *St D* 32-35; Argentina 35-42; V Llanwenog w Llanwnen *St D* 42-64; RD Lampeter 54-64; V Felin-foel 64-77; RD Kidwelly 72-77; Can St D Cathl 72-79; rtd 77. *10 Ty'r Fran Avenue, Llanelli SA15 3LP* Tel (01554) 772977

MORGAN, Simon John. b 58. Univ of Wales (Swansea) BA81 Univ of Wales (Cardiff) BD86 MA94 FRGS03. St Mich Coll Llan 83. **d** 86 **p** 87. C Penarth All SS *Llan* 86-87; C Port Talbot St Theodore 87-89; C Gelligaer 89-91; R Dowlais 91-96; Asst P Peacehaven and Telscombe w Piddinghoe and Southease *Chich* 96; P-in-c E Dean w Friston and Jevington 96-99; NSM Hellingly and Upper Dicker 99-05; NSM Fairwarp from 05; Chapl St Bede's Sch Upper Dicker from 99. *The Vicarage, Back Lane, Fairwarp, Uckfield TN22 3BL* Tel (01825) 712277

MORGAN, Stephen. *See* MORGAN, Ian Stephen

MORGAN, Stephen John. b 67. UEA BA89 SS Coll Cam BA02. Westcott Ho Cam 99. **d** 02 **p** 03. NSM Pitlochry and Kilmaveonaig *St And* 02-04; NSM Hook w Warsash *Portsm* from 05. *3 Romford Road, Warsash, Southampton SO31 9GZ* Tel (01489) 481964 E-mail stevejemma@waitrose.com

MORGAN, Canon Steve Shelley. b 48. Univ of Wales DipTh70. St Mich Coll Llan 67. **d** 71 **p** 72. C Llanharan w Peterston-super-Montem *Llan* 71; C Llandaff w Capel Llanilltern 71-74; C Neath w Llantwit 74-77; TV Merthyr Tydfil and Cyfarthfa 77-91; V Merthyr Tydfil Ch Ch from 91; RD Merthyr Tydfil 93-04; Can Llan Cathl from 98. *24 Pen y Bryn View, Incline Top, Merthyr Tydfil CF47 0GB* Tel (01685) 723272

MORGAN, Mrs Susan Dianne. b 53. Univ of Wales (Lamp) BA74 Westmr Coll Ox PGCE75. N Ord Course 03. **d** 05. C Cheetham *Man* from 05. *14 Rectory Road, Manchester M8 5EA* Tel 0161-740 9925 Mobile 07967-908033 E-mail sue_morgan14@hotmail.com

MORGAN, Teresa Jean. b 68. Clare Coll Cam BA90 MA94 PhD95 Oriel Coll Ox MA98 BA01 LRAM91. St Alb and Ox Min Course 00. **d** 02 **p** 03. NSM Littlemore *Ox* from 02. *Oriel College, Oxford OX1 4EW* Tel (01865) 276579 E-mail teresa.morgan@classics.ox.ac.uk

MORGAN, Thomas John Walford. b 16. Univ of Wales BA37. St D Coll Lamp 37. **d** 39 **p** 40. C Roath *Llan* 39-42; C Heavitree *Ex* 42-45; C Merton St Mary *S'wark* 45-50; CF 50-71; V Swallowfield *Ox* 71-81; rtd 81. *57 Felinfoel Road, Llanelli SA15 3JQ* Tel (01554) 752303

MORGAN, Trevor. b 45. **d** 01. NSM Fleur-de-Lis *Mon* 01-04; C from 04. *The Tidings, Woodfieldside, Blackwood NP12 0PJ* Tel and fax (01495) 222198 E-mail tmo1036014@aol.com

MORGAN, Verna Ireta. b 42. NEOC. **d** 89 **p** 94. NSM Potternewton *Ripon* 89-92; Par Dn Longsight St Luke *Man* 92-94; C 94-95; P-in-c Gorton St Phil 95-02; rtd 02. *Butler's Village, St James's Parish, Nevis, West Indies*

MORGAN, William Charles <u>Gerwyn</u>. b 30. Univ of Wales (Lamp) BA52. St Mich Coll Llan 52. **d** 56 **p** 57. C Hubberston *St D* 56-62; V Ambleston w St Dogwells 62-68; Miss to Seamen 68-93; V Fishguard w Llanychar *St D* 68-85; V Fishguard w Llanychar and Pontfaen w Morfil etc 85-93; Can St D Cathl 85-93; Chan 91-93; rtd 93. *Wrth y Llan, Pontycleifion, Cardigan SA43 1DW* Tel (01239) 613943

MORGAN, William <u>John</u>. b 38. Selw Coll Cam BA62 MA66. Cuddesdon Coll 62. **d** 65 **p** 66. C Cardiff St Jo *Llan* 65-68; Asst Chapl Univ of Wales (Cardiff) 68-70; Perm to Offic *Lon* 70-73; C Albany Street Ch Ch 73-78; P-in-c E Acton St Dunstan 78-80; V E Acton St Dunstan w St Thos 80-95; V Isleworth All SS 95-04; P-in-c St Margaret's-on-Thames 95-00; rtd 04. *Marvol la Rivière, 24310 Bourdeilles, France* Tel (0033) (5) 53 54 18 90

MORGAN, William Stanley Timothy. b 41. Univ of Wales (Lamp) BA63. Wycliffe Hall Ox 63. **d** 66 **p** 67. C Aberystwyth St Mich *St D* 66-69; V Ambleston w St Dogwells 69-70; V Ambleston, St Dogwells, Walton E and Llysyfran 70-74; V Llannon 74-80; V Lampeter 80-87; V Lampeter Pont Steffan w Silian 87-01; V Llanbadarn Fawr from 01. *The Vicarage, Llanbadarn Fawr, Aberystwyth SY23 3TT* Tel (01970) 623368

MORGAN-CROMAR, Christopher. b 66. Wycliffe Hall Ox 02. **d** 04 **p** 05. C Brackley St Pet w St Jas *Pet* from 04. *36 Prices Way, Brackley NN13 6NR* Tel (01280) 701839 Mobile 07986-069831 E-mail morgancromar@btinternet.com

MORGAN-GUY, John Richard. b 44. St D Coll Lamp BA65 Univ of Wales PhD85 ARHistS80 FRHistS05 FRSM81. St Steph Ho Ox 65. **d** 67 **p** 68. C Canton St Cath *Llan* 67-68; C Roath St Sav 68-70; Chapl Llandough Hosp 70-71; C Machen and Rudry *Mon* 71-74; R Wolvesnewton w Kilgwrrwg and Devauden 74-80; Perm to Offic *B & W* 80-93; V Betws Cedewain and Tregynon and Llanwyddelan *St As* 93-97; RD Cedewain 97; Lect Univ of Wales (Lamp) 98-03; Research Fell from 04; Research Fell Cen for Adv Welsh & Celtic Studies 99-04; Tutor Welsh Nat Cen for Ecum Studies Carmarthen from 00. *Tyngors, Silian, Lampeter SA48 8AS* Tel (01570) 422710

MORGAN-JONES, Canon Christopher John. b 43. Bris Univ BA66 Chicago Univ MBA68 McMaster Univ Ontario MA69. Cuddesdon Coll 70. **d** 73 **p** 74. C Folkestone St Sav *Cant* 73-76; P-in-c Swalecliffe 76-82; V Addington 82-84; V Addington *S'wark* 85-92; RD Croydon Addington 85-90; V Maidstone All SS and St Phil w Tovil *Cant* from 92; Hon Can Cant Cathl from

99. *The Vicarage, Priory Road, Maidstone ME15 6NL* Tel (01622) 756002 Fax 692320 E-mail ramj@allsaints.u-net.com

MORGANNWG, Archdeacon of. *See* YEOMAN, The Rt Revd David

MORGANS, Paul Hywel. b 61. LWCMD83. Chich Th Coll 86. **d** 90 **p** 91. C Johnston w Steynton *St D* 90-92; C Caerau w Ely *Llan* 92-95; V Pentre 95-99; Hon C Roath St German 99-00. *129 Bishopston Road, Caerau, Cardiff CF5 5DX*

MORIARTY, Mrs Susan Margaret. b 43. Cartrefle Coll of Educn TCert65. St As Minl Tr Course. **d** 02. Par Dn Gorsedd w Brynford, Ysgeifiog and Whitford *St As* from 02. *7 St Michael's Drive, Caerwys, Mold CH7 5BS* Tel (01352) 720874

MORISON, John Donald. b 34. ALCD60. **d** 61 **p** 62. C Rayleigh *Chelmsf* 61-64; C St Austell *Truro* 64-67; V Meltham Mills *Wakef* 67-71; Youth Chapl *Cov* 71-76; S Africa 76-82; Can Port Elizabeth 80-82; Bardsley Missr 82-86; Lic to Offic *S'wark* 82-86; Dioc Missr *Derby* 86-99; V Quarndon 86-99; rtd 99; Perm to Offic *Sarum* from 01. *Flat 1, Canford Place, 59 Cliff Drive, Canford Cliffs, Poole BH13 7JX* Tel (01202) 709377

MORLEY, Athelstan John. b 29. Linc Coll Ox BA52 MA56. Ridley Hall Cam. **d** 54 **p** 55. C Surbiton St Matt *S'wark* 54-57; Succ Chelmsf Cathl *Chelmsf* 57-60; R Mistley w Manningtree 60-69; R Hadleigh St Jas 69-94; rtd 94; Hon C Prittlewell *Chelmsf* 94-97; Perm to Offic from 94; P-in-c St Martin Ludgate *Lon* from 01. *38 Bridgwater Drive, Westcliff-on-Sea SS0 0DH* Tel (01702) 339335

MORLEY, Georgina Laura (George). b 63. Dur Univ BA84 Nottm Univ MTh95 DPhil99. Cranmer Hall Dur. **d** 03 **p** 03. Dir Studies NEOC from 99; NSM Osmotherley w Harlsey and Ingleby Arncliffe *York* from 03. *Moorstones, Ruebury Lane, Osmotherley, Northallerton DL6 3BG* Tel (01609) 883787 E-mail gmorley@fish.co.uk

MORLEY, Miss Gillian Dorothy. b 21. Greyladies Coll 49. **dss** 70 **d** 87. Lewisham St Swithun *S'wark* 70-82; Sturry w Fordwich and Westbere w Hersden *Cant* 82-87; Perm to Offic from 87. *28 Glen Iris Avenue, Canterbury CT2 8HP* Tel (01227) 459992

MORLEY, John. *See* MORLEY, Athelstan John

MORLEY, John. b 43. K Coll Lon AKC67 St Deiniol's Hawarden 67. **d** 68 **p** 69. C Newbold on Avon *Cov* 69-73; C Solihull *Birm* 73-77; C-in-c Elmdon Heath CD 76-77; Chapl RAF 77-93; TR Wallingford w Crowmarsh Gifford etc *Ox* 93-98; TR Wallingford 98-99; RD Wallingford 95-99; Provost Nicosia 99-02; V Henlow and Langford *St Alb* from 02. *The Vicarage, 65 Church Street, Langford, Biggleswade SG18 9QT* Tel (01462) 700248 Mobile 07900-892566 E-mail revjmorley@ntlworld.com

MORLEY, Keith. b 44. St Chad's Coll Dur BA66 DipTh67 Open Univ BSc93. **d** 67 **p** 68. C S Yardley St Mich *Birm* 67-70; C Solihull 70-73; V Shaw Hill 73-77; P-in-c Burton Coggles *Linc* 77-79; P-in-c Boothby Pagnell 77-79; V Lenton w Ingoldsby 77-79; P-in-c Bassingthorpe w Bitchfield 77-79; R Ingoldsby 79-87; RD Beltisloe 84-87; P-in-c Old Dalby and Nether Broughton *Leic* 87-94; RD Framland 88-90; Perm to Offic *Linc* from 03; rtd 04. *11 Swallow Close, Quarrington, Sleaford NG34 7UU*

MORLEY, Canon Leslie James. b 45. K Coll Lon BD67 AKC67 MTh68. St Boniface Warminster 68. **d** 69 **p** 70. C Birm St Pet *Birm* 69-72; C W Brompton St Mary *Lon* 72; C W Brompton St Mary w St Pet 73-74; Chapl Nottm Univ *S'well* 74-80; Dir Post-Ord Tr 80-85; Can Res and Vice-Provost S'well Minster 80-85; Hon Can 85-99; Chapl Bluecoat Sch Nottm 85-90; R Nottingham St Pet and St Jas *S'well* 85-99; AD Nottingham Cen 90-93; Dioc Rural Officer *Ripon* from 99; Perm to Offic *York* from 00. *Moorstones, Ruebury Lane, Osmotherley, Northallerton DL6 3BG* Tel (01609) 883787 Fax 780760 E-mail leslie.morley@virgin.net

MORLEY, Peter. b 36. St Jo Coll Nottm 81. **d** 83 **p** 84. C Sheff St Jo *Sheff* 83-87; Chapl The Shrewsbury Hosp Sheff 85-87; V Worsbrough Common *Sheff* 87-93; Chapl Mt Vernon Hosp Barnsley 87-93; R Harthill and Thorpe Salvin *Sheff* 93-99; rtd 99. *39 Hallcroft Road, Retford DN22 7LE* Tel (01777) 719081

MORLEY, Terence Martin Simon. b 49. SS Hild & Bede Coll Dur CertEd78. St Steph Ho Ox 71. **d** 74 **p** 75. C Kingston upon Hull St Alb *York* 74-76; C Middlesbrough All SS 76-77; Perm to Offic *Dur* 77-78; Hon C Worthing St Andr *Chich* 78-80; C Brighton Ch Ch 80-82; C Hove St Patr 80-82; C Ayr *Glas* 83-86; C Maybole 83-84; P-in-c Coatbridge 86-88; R 88-92; P-in-c 92; V Plymouth St Jas Ham *Ex* from 93; Chapl Plymouth Community Services NHS Trust 96-98. *St James's Presbytery, Ham Drive, Plymouth PL2 2NJ* Tel (01752) 362485

MORLEY, Trevor. b 39. Man Univ BSc62 MPS62 MRSH84. Ripon Hall Ox 65. **d** 67 **p** 68. C Compton Gifford *Ex* 67-70; Chapl Hammersmith Hosp Lon 70-83; Hon C N Hammersmith St Kath *Lon* 70-83; Chapl Univ Coll Hosp Lon 83-94; Chapl Univ Coll Lon Hosps NHS Trust 94-99; Hon Chapl St Luke's Hosp for the Clergy 89-99; V Linthwaite *Wakef* from 99. *The Vicarage, Church Lane, Linthwaite, Huddersfield HD7 5TA* Tel (01484) 842591 E-mail linthwaitevicarage@tinyworld.co.uk

MORLEY-BUNKER, John Arthur. b 27. Wells Th Coll 67. **d** 68 **p** 69. C Horfield H Trin *Bris* 68-71; P-in-c Easton All Hallows 71-75; V 75-82; RD Bris City 74-79; V Horfield St Greg 82-93; rtd 93; Perm to Offic *Bris* from 93. *1 Knoll Court, Knoll Hill, Bristol BS9 1QX* Tel 0117-968 5837

MORLEY-JONES, Anthony Roger. St Mich Coll Llan. **d** 04 **p** 05. NSM Cydweli and Llandyfaelog *St D* from 04. *11 Westhill Crescent, Cydweli SA17 4US*

MORLING, David Arthur. b 45. Saltley Tr Coll Birm CertEd66 Open Univ BA78. S Dios Minl Tr Scheme 83 Linc Th Coll. **d** 85 **p** 86. NSM Chich 85-97; P-in-c Doncaster Intake *Sheff* 97-02; P-in-c Doncaster H Trin 97-02; rtd 02; Perm to Offic *Bradf* from 02. *Lorindell, 61 Layton Lane, Rawdon, Leeds LS19 6RA* Tel 0113-250 3488

MORONEY, Kevin John. b 61. Valley Forge Chr Coll Pennsylvania BS86. Gen Th Sem NY MDiv92. **d** 92 **p** 93. USA 92-00; Asst Pastor Metuchen St Luke New Jersey 92-94; R Metuchen All SS 94-98; Chapl St James Sch St James Maryland 98-00; Chapl and Tutor CITC from 00; P-in-c Dublin Sandymount *D & G* from 01. *CITC, Braemor Park, Dublin 14, Irish Republic* Tel (00353) (1) 492 3506 Fax 492 3082 E-mail kjmcoi@yahoo.com

MORPHY, George David. b 49. Birm Univ BEd71 Lon Univ BA75 Warwick Univ MA90. WMMTC. **d** 89 **p** 90. Hon C Ribbesford w Bewdley and Dowles *Worc* from 89; Dioc Dir of Educn from 99. *41 Hallow Road, Worcester WR2 6BX* Tel (01905) 422007 *or* 732825 Mobile 07867-525779 E-mail dmorphy@cofe-worcester.org

MORPHY, Michael John. b 43. Newc Univ BSc65 Dur Univ MSc66 QUB PhD73. Ripon Coll Cuddesdon 82. **d** 84 **p** 85. C Halifax *Wakef* 84-86; V Luddenden w Luddenden Foot 86-97; V Corbridge w Halton and Newton Hall *Newc* from 97. *The Vicarage, Greencroft Avenue, Corbridge NE45 5DW* Tel (01434) 632128 E-mail mj.morphy@btinternet.com

MORRELL, Geoffrey Bernard. b 45. AKC68. **d** 69 **p** 71. C W Leigh CD *Portsm* 69-76; V Shedfield 76-02; RD Bishop's Waltham 82-88; rtd 02. *28 Chase Farm Close, Waltham Chase, Southampton SO32 2UD* Tel (01489) 896880 E-mail revgeoffmorrell@aol.com

MORRELL, Mrs Jennifer Mary. b 49. N Ord Course 84. **d** 87 **p** 94. Par Dn Crewe All SS and St Paul *Ches* 87-90; Par Dn Padgate *Liv* 90-94; C 94-95; TV Kirkby 95-00; V Croxteth Park 00-02. *24 Oak Tree Close, Kingsbury, Tamworth B78 2JF* Tel (01827) 874445

MORRELL, Canon Nigel Paul. b 38. S'wark Ord Course 73. **d** 76 **p** 77. C Letchworth St Paul w Willian *St Alb* 76-85; V Farley Hill St Jo 85-95; RD Luton 90-94; V Cardington 95-03; Hon Can St Alb 01-03; RD Elstow from 03; rtd 03. *22 Sunderland Place, Shortstown, Bedford MK42 0FD* Tel and fax (01234) 743202 E-mail nigel.morrell@btopenworld.com

MORRELL, Paul Rodney. b 49. SRN70. SW Minl Tr Course 91. **d** 93 **p** 94. NSM Heavitree w Ex St Paul *Ex* 93-00; C 00-02; C Heavitree and St Mary Steps from 02. *65 Quarry Park Road, Exeter EX2 5PD* Tel (01392) 431367

MORRELL, Robin Mark George. b 29. Cuddesdon Coll 58. **d** 60 **p** 61. C Petersfield w Sheet *Portsm* 60-63; C-in-c Stockwood CD *Bris* 63-71; Lic to Offic 71-72; R Honiton, Gittisham and Combe Raleigh *Ex* 72-78; Lay Tr Officer *S'wark* 78-81; Asst Chapl HM Pris Brixton 81-85; Past Cllr from 85; Hon C Hatcham St Cath *S'wark* 91-97; rtd 94; Perm to Offic *Chich* from 96. *46 Erlanger Road, London SE14 5TG* Tel (020) 7252 9346

MORRELL, Mrs Susan Marjorie. b 46. Open Univ BA94. SEITE 93. **d** 96 **p** 97. NSM E Peckham and Nettlestead *Roch* from 96; Chapl Kent Coll Pembury from 99. *7 Pippin Road, East Peckham, Tonbridge TN12 5BT* Tel (01622) 871150

MORRIS, Alan Ralph Oakden. b 29. Roch Th Coll 59. **d** 61 **p** 62. C Riverhead *Roch* 61-62; C Roch St Pet w St Marg 62-66; C Wrotham 66-74; V Biggin Hill 74-82; R Kingsdown 82-88; V Seal St Pet 88-92; rtd 92; P-in-c Renhold *St Alb* 92-93; Perm to Offic *Roch* 93-02. *268 Woolwich Road, London SE2 0DW* Tel (020) 8310 7860

MORRIS, Canon Alexander Dorner. b 23. Jes Coll Cam BA48 MA53. Linc Th Coll 49. **d** 51 **p** 52. C Wincobank *Sheff* 51-53; C Rotherham 53-54; C-in-c Manor Park CD 54-59; India 59-63; V Bexley St Mary *Roch* 63-71; V Leatherhead *Guildf* 71-89; RD Leatherhead 72-77; Hon Can Guildf Cathl 86-89; rtd 89; Perm to Offic *Guildf* from 89. *9 Roses Cottages, West Street, Dorking RH4 1QL* Tel (01306) 882485

MORRIS, Andy. *See* MORRIS, Edward Andrew

MORRIS, Mrs Ann. b 52. N Co Coll Newc CertEd73. WEMTC 00. **d** 03 **p** 04. C Churchdown St Jo and Innsworth *Glouc* from 03. *24 Sandycroft Road, Churchdown, Gloucester GL3 1JH* Tel (01452) 712608

MORRIS, Mrs Ann Veronica Marsham. b 46. Open Univ BA83. WEMTC 99. **d** 01 **p** 02. NSM Amberley *Glouc* from 01. *Cotswold, Amberley, Stroud GL5 5AB* Tel (01453) 872587 E-mail annmorris@hcliffe.powernet.co.uk

MORRIS, Anne. *See* MORRIS, Ms Margaret Anne

MORRIS (née SHAW), Mrs Anne. b 47. LMH Ox BA69 MA72 Lon Univ BD82. N Ord Course 01. **d** 03. NSM Leamington

Priors All SS *Cov* from 03; NSM Leamington Spa H Trin and Old Milverton from 03. *The Vicarage, Vicarage Lane, Priors Marston, Southam CV47 7RT* Tel (01327) 260053

MORRIS, Bernard Lyn. b 28. St Aid Birkenhead 55. **d** 58 **p** 59. C-in-c Hartcliffe St Andr CD *Bris* 58-61; C Bishopston 61-63; R Ardwick St Thos *Man* 63-69; R Aylton w Pixley, Munsley and Putley *Heref* 69-79; P-in-c Tarrington w Stoke Edith 72-77; R 77-79; P-in-c Queen Camel, Marston Magna, W Camel, Rimpton etc *B & W* 79-80; R 80-87; R Queen Camel w W Camel, Corton Denham etc 87-95; rtd 95; Perm to Offic *B & W* 95-97 and *Ex* from 01. *Canterbury Bells, Ansford Hill, Castle Cary BA7 7JL* Tel (01963) 351154 E-mail revblmorris@supanet.com

MORRIS, Beti Elin. b 36. CertEd57. Sarum & Wells Th Coll 87. **d** 89 **p** 97. C Llangeitho and Blaenpennal w Betws Leucu etc *St D* 89-92; C-in-c Pencarreg and Llanycrwys 92-97; V from 97. *The Vicarage, Cwmann, Lampeter SA48 8DU* Tel (01570) 422385

MORRIS, Brian Michael Charles. b 32. S Dios Minl Tr Scheme 82. **d** 85 **p** 86. NSM Denmead *Portsm* 85-89; C S w N Hayling 89-96; P-in-c Shalfleet 96-97; rtd 97; Perm to Offic *Portsm* from 97. *Ashleigh, 5 Ashwood Close, Hayling Island PO11 9AX* Tel (023) 9246 7292 E-mail rev_b_morris@talk21.com

MORRIS, Ms Catharine Mary. b 75. Regent's Park Coll Ox BA96 MA00. Ridley Hall Cam 99. **d** 01 **p** 02. C Malpas *Mon* from 01. *4 Aspen Way, Malpas, Newport NP20 6LB* Tel (01633) 821362 E-mail catharine@stmarysmalpas.freeserve.co.uk

MORRIS, Canon Christopher John. b 45. K Coll Lon AKC67 BD68. **d** 68 **p** 69. C W Bromwich All SS *Lich* 68-72; C Porthill 72-74; Min Can Carl Cathl *Carl* 74-77; Ecum Liaison Officer BBC Radio Carl 74-77; Dioc Communications Officer *Carl* 77-83; V Thursby 77-83; Angl Adv Border TV from 82; V Upperby St Jo *Carl* 83-91; P-in-c Lanercost w Kirkcambeck and Walton 91-99; P-in-c Gilsland w Nether Denton 96-99; R Lanercost, Walton, Gilsland and Nether Denton from 99; RD Brampton from 98; Hon Can Carl Cathl from 98. *The Vicarage, Lanercost, Brampton CA8 2HQ* Tel (01697) 72478 E-mail chris@ca8morris.fsnet.co.uk

MORRIS, Christopher Mangan. b 47. Chich Th Coll 71. **d** 73 **p** 74. C Athersley *Wakef* 73-76; C Kippax *Ripon* 76-78; TV Seacroft 78-81; V Oulton w Woodlesford 81-86; V Hawksworth Wood 86-93; V Rawdon *Bradf* from 93. *The Vicarage, Layton Avenue, Rawdon, Leeds LS19 6QQ* Tel 0113-250 3263

MORRIS, Prof Colin. b 28. Qu Coll Ox BA48 BA51 MA53 FRHistS71. Linc Th Coll 51. **d** 53 **p** 54. Fell and Chapl Pemb Coll Ox 53-69; Lic to Offic *Ox* 53-69; Prof Medieval Hist Southn Univ 69-92; Lic to Offic *Win* from 69; rtd 92. *12 Bassett Crescent East, Southampton SO16 7PB* Tel (023) 8076 8176

MORRIS, Canon David Edmond. b 27. Univ of Wales (Cardiff) BA55. St D Coll Lamp 55. **d** 57 **p** 58. C Llanfihangel-ar-arth *St D* 57-59; C Ysbyty Ystwyth w Ystradmeurig 59-61; Asst Master St Jo Coll 59-61; CF 61-81; QHC 78-93; V Penllergaer *S & B* 81-93; RD Llwchwr 86-93; Warden of Readers 87-92; Can Brecon Cathl 90-93; Hon Can from 93; rtd 93; Perm to Offic *St D* from 93. *Crud y Môr, 17 Danlan Park, Pembrey, Burry Port SA16 0UG* Tel (01554) 830099

MORRIS, Preb David Meeson. b 35. Trin Coll Ox BA56 MA60. Chich Th Coll 57. **d** 60 **p** 61. C Westmr St Steph w St Jo *Lon* 60-65; Lib Pusey Ho 65-68; Chapl Wadh Coll Ox 67-68; C Sheff St Leon Norwood *Sheff* 68-69; Ind Chapl 68-72; C Brightside St Marg 69-72; R Adderley *Lich* 72-82; V Drayton in Hales 72-82; RD Tutbury 82-95; Chapl Burton Gen Hosp 82-90; P-in-c Burton St Modwen *Lich* 82; V Burton 82-99; Preb Lich Cathl 93-99; P-in-c Shobnall 94-99; rtd 99; Perm to Offic *Heref* and *Lich* from 99. *Watling House, All Stretton, Church Stretton SY6 6HH* Tel (01694) 722243

MORRIS, David Michael. b 59. Ox Univ MA84 Cam Univ PGCE91. Sarum & Wells Th Coll 82. **d** 84 **p** 85. C Angell Town St Jo *S'wark* 84-87; C Mitcham SS Pet and Paul 87-90; V Llandygwydd and Cenarth w Cilrhedyn etc *St D* 90-98; Lect Th St D Coll Lamp from 90; Hd RE Lampeter Comp Sch from 98. *Bronant, Rhydargaeau, Carmarthen SA32 7DR*

MORRIS, Canon David Pryce. b 39. Univ of Wales (Ban) DipTh62. Kelham Th Coll 55 St Mich Coll Llan 62. **d** 63 **p** 64. C Colwyn Bay *St As* 63-70; R St George 70-76; Dioc Children's Adv 75-87; V Bodelwyddan and St George 76-79; V Connah's Quay 79-95; St As Dioc Adult Lay Tr Team from 88; Ed St As Dioc News from 89; Dioc Communications Officer from 90; V Shotton from 95; Hon Can St As Cathl 96-00; Can Cursal St As Cathl from 00. *The Vicarage, Chester Road East, Shotton, Deeside CH5 1QD* Tel and fax (01244) 812183 Mobile 07711-519752 E-mail dprycemorris@care4free.net

MORRIS, Dennis Gordon. b 41. ALCM58. St D Coll Lamp DipTh67. **d** 67 **p** 68. C Neath w Llantwit *Llan* 67-92; V Troedrhiwgarth from 92. *Garth Vicarage, 72 Bridgend Road, Maesteg CF34 0NL* Tel (01656) 732441

MORRIS, Edward. b 42. **d** 72 **p** 73. C Darlington H Trin *Dur* 72-75; Tutor St Steph Ho Ox 75-82; Sen Tutor 79-82; R Shadforth *Dur* 82-86; Chapl Hammersmith Hosp Lon 86-94; Chapl Qu Charlotte's Hosp Lon 86-94; Hd Chapl Hammersmith Hosps NHS Trust from 94. *The Chaplain's Office, Hammersmith Hospital, Du Cane Road, London W12 0HS* Tel and fax (020) 8383 4574 *or* 8383 1701 E-mail chaplain@hhnt.org *or* morristed@hotmail.com

MORRIS, Edward Andrew (Andy). b 57. St Jo Coll Nottm BTh93. **d** 96 **p** 97. C Conisbrough *Sheff* 96-01; Perm to Offic *S'well* 01-04; V Bestwood St Matt w St Phil from 04. *42 Henrietta Street, Nottingham NG6 9JD* Tel 0115-877 2469 Mobile 07775-925297 E-mail andy-morris@ntlworld.com

MORRIS, Canon Edwin Alfred. b 32. Wells Th Coll 62. **d** 64 **p** 65. C Wood End *Cov* 64-66; Lic to Offic 66-68; Ind Chapl 68-85; P-in-c Churchover w Willey 74-85; RD Rugby 78-85; R City of Bris 85-97; Hon Can Bris Cathl 89-97; RD Bris City 91-94; rtd 97; Perm to Offic *Cov* 97-00. *117 Lower Hillmorton Road, Rugby CV21 3TN* Tel (01788) 546980

MORRIS, Mrs Elizabeth Anne. b 59. **d** 00 **p** 01. OLM Darsham and Westleton w Dunwich *St E* 00-04; C Hadleigh, Layham and Shelley from 04. *74 Ann Beaumont Way, Hadleigh, Ipswich IP7 6SB* Tel (01473) 823235 E-mail elizabethannes@talk21.com

MORRIS, Canon Frank Leo. b 20. St Steph Ho Ox 50. **d** 53 **p** 54. C Bickley *Roch* 53-55; C Letchworth *St Alb* 55-61; V Wareside 61-65; R Wyddial 65-79; P-in-c 79-82; V Gt w Lt Hormead 65-79; RD Buntingford 68-75; V Gt w Lt Hormead, Anstey, Brent Pelham etc 79-82; V Hormead, Wyddial, Anstey, Brent Pelham etc 82-89; Hon Can St Alb 85-89; rtd 89; Perm to Offic *St Alb* from 00. *9 Manland Avenue, Harpenden AL5 4RG* Tel (01582) 462348 E-mail leo@harpenden9.freeserve.co.uk

MORRIS, Geoffrey. *See* MORRIS, Canon Martin Geoffrey Roger

MORRIS, Geoffrey David. b 43. Fitzw Coll Cam BA65 MA69 Westmr Coll Ox DipEd67. N Ord Course. **d** 82 **p** 83. C Man Clayton St Cross w St Paul *Man* 82-85; V Lower Kersal 85-03; P-in-c Priors Hardwick, Priors Marston and Wormleighton *Cov* from 03; Asst Chapl HM Pris Rye Hill from 03. *The Vicarage, Vicarage Lane, Priors Marston, Southam CV47 7RT* Tel (01327) 260053

MORRIS, Graham Edwin. b 60. Sarum & Wells Th Coll 83. **d** 86 **p** 87. C Coalbrookdale, Iron-Bridge and Lt Wenlock *Heref* 86-90; TV Bilston *Lich* 90-99; R Northwood *Portsm* from 99; V Gurnard from 99. *The Rectory, Chawton Lane, Cowes PO31 8PR* Tel (01983) 292050 E-mail graham.morris@btinternet.com

MORRIS, Henry James. b 47. Lon Univ BSc69. Wycliffe Hall Ox MA. **d** 79 **p** 80. C Woodford Wells *Chelmsf* 79-82; C Gt Baddow 82-87; R Siddington w Preston *Glouc* 87-01; RD Cirencester 97-01; TR Madeley *Heref* from 01. *St Michael's Vicarage, Church Street, Madeley, Telford TF7 5BN* Tel and fax (01952) 586645 *or* tel 585718 E-mail henrym@dircon.co.uk

MORRIS, Ian Henry. b 42. Sarum & Wells Th Coll 73. **d** 75 **p** 76. C Lawrence Weston *Bris* 75-78; C St Buryan, St Levan and Sennen *Truro* 78-81; P-in-c Lanteglos by Fowey 81-84; V 84-85; R Lanteglos by Camelford w Advent 85-95; RD Trigg Minor and Bodmin 93-95; TR Probus, Ladock and Grampound w Creed and St Erme from 95; RD Powder from 01. *The Sanctuary, Wagg Lane, Probus, Truro TR2 4JX* Tel (01726) 882746

MORRIS, Ivor Leslie. b 50. Chich Th Coll 82. **d** 84 **p** 85. C Southend *Chelmsf* 84-87; C Somers Town *Lon* 87-90; P-in-c Chelmsf Ascension *Chelmsf* 90-96; V from 96; P-in-c Chelmsf All SS 92-96. *The Vicarage, 57 Maltese Road, Chelmsford CM1 2PB* Tel (01245) 353914 E-mail il.morris@virgin.net

MORRIS, Miss Jane Elizabeth. b 50. York Univ BA71 CertEd72 MSc80. NEOC 92. **d** 92 **p** 94. NSM York St Mich-le-Belfrey *York* 92-95; C Leeds St Geo *Ripon* 95-05; V Cricklewood St Gabr and St Mich *Lon* from 05. *St Gabriel's Vicarage, 156 Anson Road, London NW2 6BH* Tel (020) 8452 6305 E-mail janemorris@ntlworld.com

MORRIS, Jeremy Nigel. b 60. Ball Coll Ox MA81 DPhil86 Clare Coll Cam BA92. Westcott Ho Cam CTM93. **d** 93 **p** 94. C Battersea St Mary *S'wark* 93-96; Dir Studies Westcott Ho Cam 96-01; Vice-Prin 97-01; Dean and Chapl Trin Hall Cam from 01. *Trinity Hall, Cambridge CB2 1TJ* Tel (01223) 332500 E-mail jnm20@cam.ac.uk

MORRIS, Canon John. b 25. Westcott Ho Cam. **d** 65 **p** 66. C St Alb St Mich *St Alb* 65-68; V Leverstock Green 68-80; TR Chambersbury 80-82; V N Mymms 82-90; RD Hatfield 83-88; Hon Can St Alb 89-90; rtd 90; Perm to Offic *St Alb* from 90; *Nor* 92-94 and from 95; P-in-c Barney, Fulmodeston w Croxton, Hindringham etc *Nor* 94-95. *Elba, Croxton Road, Fulmodeston, Fakenham NR21 0NJ* Tel (01328) 878685

MORRIS, John Derrick. b 18. MRCS43 LRCP43. Lon Coll of Div 62. **d** 64 **p** 65. C Cromer *Nor* 64-67; V Broadway *Worc* 67-71; Hon C St Leonards St Leon *Chich* 71-83; rtd 83; Perm to Offic *Chich* from 84. *17 Bourne Way, Midhurst GU29 9HZ* Tel (01730) 814084

MORRIS, John Douglas. b 37. Cam Univ BA58 Lon Inst of Educn PGCE60 Univ of E Africa MEd67 Ex Univ PhD87. S Dios Minl Tr Scheme 94. **d** 95 **p** 96. NSM Twyford and Owslebury and Morestead *Win* 95-98; Perm to Offic from 01; Chapl Twyford Sch Win from 96. *Gifford House, St Giles Hill, Winchester SO23 0JH* Tel (01962) 869720 E-mail johnmarymorris@btopenworld.com

MORRIS, John Dudley. b 33. Ball Coll Ox BA57 DipTh59 MA61. Wycliffe Hall Ox 58. **d** 60 **p** 61. C Tonbridge SS Pet and Paul *Roch* 60-65; C Enfield Ch Ch Trent Park *Lon* 65-69; Chapl Elstree Sch Woolhampton 70-74; Hd Master Handcross Park Sch W Sussex 74-89; V Rudgwick *Chich* 89-98; RD Horsham 93-98; rtd 98; Perm to Offic *Chich* from 98. *13 Hoadlands, Handcross, Haywards Heath RH17 6HB* Tel (01444) 400184

MORRIS, John Edgar. b 20. Keble Coll Ox BA42 MA50. Wycliffe Hall Ox 42. **d** 44 **p** 45. C Eccleston St Thos *Liv* 44-48; C Warrington H Trin 48-50; V Newton-le-Willows 50-57; R Wavertree H Trin 57-66; V Ainsdale 66-82; R Broadwell, Evenlode, Oddington and Adlestrop *Glouc* 82-88; rtd 89; Perm to Offic *Glouc* 89-97 and from 01. *29 Letch Hill Drive, Bourton-on-the-Water, Cheltenham GL54 2DQ* Tel (01451) 820571

MORRIS, John Owen. b 56. Nottm Univ BCom82. Linc Th Coll 79. **d** 82 **p** 83. C Morriston *S & B* 82-84; C Kingstone w Clehonger and Eaton Bishop *Heref* 84-87; P-in-c Lugwardine w Bartestree and Weston Beggard 87-92; Chapl RN from 92. *Royal Naval Chaplaincy Service, Room 203, Victory Building, HM Naval Base, Portsmouth PO1 3LS* Tel (023) 9272 7903 Fax 9272 7112

MORRIS, Jonathan Richard. b 57. Lanc Univ BA78 Trin Coll Ox MSc84. WEMTC 99. **d** 02 **p** 03. C Taunton St Andr *B & W* from 02. *1 Peter Street, Taunton TA2 7BZ* Tel (01823) 337668 E-mail jonbea@supanet.com

MORRIS, Kevin John. b 63. Univ of Wales (Ban) BMus84. Westcott Ho Cam 85. **d** 88 **p** 89. C Roath *Llan* 88-91; C Holborn St Alb w Saffron Hill St Pet *Lon* 91-96; V Bedford Park from 96; Dir Post-Ord Tr from 99. *The Vicarage, Priory Gardens, London W4 1TT* Tel (020) 8994 0139 *or* 8994 1380 E-mail kevin.john.morris@ukgateway.net

MORRIS, Kirsteen Helen Grace. b 44. STETS 99. **d** 02 **p** 03. NSM Cowes H Trin and St Mary *Portsm* from 02. *35 Granville Road, Cowes PO31 7JF* Tel (01983) 289585 Fax 292919 E-mail morris.scawfell@virgin.net

MORRIS, Leo. *See* MORRIS, Canon Frank Leo

MORRIS, Leslie Heber. b 26. Ox Univ MA47. Qu Coll Birm 83. **d** 84 **p** 93. NSM W Leigh *Portsm* 84-85; NSM Warblington w Emsworth 86-96. *Mermaid Cottage, 7 Slipper Road, Emsworth PO10 8BS* Tel (01243) 373389

MORRIS, Lillian Rosina (Mother Lillian). b 29. **dss** 70 **d** 87. CSA 68-97; Mother Superior 82-94 and from 00; Sherston Magna w Easton Grey *Bris* 71-73; Notting Hill All SS w St Columb *Lon* 74-82; Perm to Offic from 00. *8/9 Verona Court, London W4 2JD* Tel (020) 8987 2799

MORRIS, Lyn. *See* MORRIS, Bernard Lyn

MORRIS, Mrs Lynne Margaret. b 53. SEN. WMMTC 95. **d** 98 **p** 99. NSM Wrockwardine Wood *Lich* 98-01; Chapl Birm Specialist Community Health NHS Trust from 01; Perm to Offic *Lich* from 01. *5 Kingston Road, Trench, Telford TF2 7HT* Tel (01952) 618158

MORRIS, Ms Margaret Anne. b 61. Man Univ BA82 MA91. N Ord Course 94. **d** 96 **p** 97. C Bury St Pet *Man* 96-98; C Accrington St Jo w Huncoat *Blackb* 98-01; V Knuzden from 01. *St Oswald's Vicarage, 68 Bank Lane, Blackburn BB1 2AP* Tel (01254) 698321 E-mail anne_morris@ntlworld.com

MORRIS, Canon Margaret Jane. Ox Univ MTh96 Leic Univ Hon LLM96. EMMTC 86. **d** 89 **p** 94. NSM Quorndon *Leic* 89-96; Chapl for People affected by HIV 94-05; NSM Loughborough All SS w H Trin 96-98; Hon Can Leic Cathl from 97; Chapl Asst Leic R Infirmary NHS Trust 98-00; Chapl Asst Univ Hosps Leic NHS Trust from 00. *10 Toller Road, Quorn, Loughborough LE12 8AH* Tel and fax (01509) 412092 E-mail morris@rog15.freeserve.co.uk

MORRIS, Canon Martin Geoffrey Roger. b 41. Trin Coll Cam BA63 MA67. St D Coll Lamp 63. **d** 66 **p** 67. C Newport St Paul *Mon* 66-72; R Lamp Velfrey *St D* 72-74; R Lamp Velfrey and Llanddewi Velfrey from 74; RD St Clears 83-98; Can St D Cathl from 92; Chan from 03. *The Rectory, Lampeter Velfrey, Narberth SA67 8UH* Tel (01834) 831241

MORRIS, Ms Mary. b 27. Birm Univ BA49 CertEd50 MA56. **dss** 68 **d** 87 **p** 94. Kinver *Lich* 83-87; Hon Par Dn Kinver and Enville 87-94; Hon C from 94. *12 Pavilion End, Prestwood, Stourbridge DY7 5PF* Tel (01384) 877245

MORRIS, Michael Alan. b 46. Jes Coll Cam BA70 MA74. Coll of Resurr Mirfield 79. **d** 81 **p** 82. C Leamington Priors All SS *Cov* 81-83; C Milton *Portsm* 83-88; R Petworth *Chich* 88-90; R Egdean 88-90; Chapl St Pet Hosp Chertsey 90-95; Hon C Thorpe *Guildf* 90-95; P-in-c Harbledown *Cant* 95-97; R from 97; Chapl St Nic Hosp Cant from 95. *The Rectory, Summer Hill, Harbledown, Canterbury CT2 8NW* Tel (01227) 464117 Fax 760530 E-mail michael@summer-hill.freeserve.co.uk

MORRIS, Michael James. b 70. Univ of Wales (Abth) BScEcon92. Qu Coll Birm BA. **d** 00 **p** 01. C Tupsley w Hampton Bishop *Heref* 00-04; TV Watling Valley *Ox* from 04. *21 Edzell Crescent, Westcroft, Milton Keynes MK4 4EU* Tel (01908) 507123 E-mail mike.morris@wvep.org

MORRIS, Norman Foster Maxwell. b 46. Ex Univ BA68 MA71 Leic Univ PGCE69 K Coll Lon MTh85 Univ of Wales (Cardiff) MA91 Cheltenham & Glouc Coll of HE MA98. S'wark Ord Course 75. **d** 78 **p** 79. C Hackbridge and N Beddington *S'wark* 78-81; Chapl Tonbridge Sch 81-85; Chapl Mon Sch 85-00; Asst Warden Jones Almshouses Mon 89-00; R Wentnor w Ratlinghope, Myndtown, Norbury etc *Heref* from 00; P-in-c Churchstoke w Hyssington from 04; CF (ACF) from 02. *The Rectory, Wentnor, Bishops Castle SY9 5EE* Tel (01588) 650244 Mobile 07974-771069 E-mail revnorm@btinternet.com

MORRIS, Paul David. b 56. St Jo Coll Nottm BTh79. **d** 80 **p** 81. C Billericay and Lt Burstead *Chelmsf* 80-84; C Luton Lewsey St Hugh *St Alb* 84-89; Dioc Adv on Evang *S'well* 89-00; Dioc Millennium Officer 97-01; Min Tommy's (ch for the unchurched) 96-01; C Barton in Fabis 01-02; C Gotham 01-02; C Thrumpton 01-02; C Kingston and Ratcliffe-on-Soar 01-02; C Sutton Bonington w Normanton-on-Soar 01-02; Dir Evang Chr Associates Internat from 02. *39 Davies Road, Nottingham NG2 5JE* Tel 0115-981 1311 E-mail pmorris@christianassociates.org

MORRIS, Peter. b 45. Leeds Univ CertEd66. Tyndale Hall Bris 68. **d** 71 **p** 72. C Southport SS Simon and Jude *Liv* 71-74; Min-in-c Ch Ch Netherley LEP 74-76; V Bryn 76-91; R Redenhall, Harleston, Wortwell and Needham *Nor* from 91. *The Rectory, 10 Swan Lane, Harleston IP20 9AN* Tel (01379) 852068

MORRIS, Canon Peter Arthur William. b 23. Bps' Coll Cheshunt 57. **d** 58 **p** 59. C Croxley Green All SS *St Alb* 58-62; V Sawbridgeworth 62-74; V S Gillingham *Roch* 74-79; Warden Pleshey Retreat Ho 79-85; P-in-c Pleshey *Chelmsf* 79-85; Hon Can Chelmsf Cathl 81-85; P-in-c Rumburgh w S Elmham w the Ilketshalls *St E* 85-89; rtd 89; Perm to Offic *St E* from 90. *The Cottage on the Common, Bakers Lane, Westleton, Saxmundham IP17 3AZ* Tel (01728) 648788

MORRIS, Canon Peter Michael Keighley. b 27. St Jo Coll Ox BA49 MA56. Westcott Ho Cam 51. **d** 54 **p** 55. C Bedwellty *Mon* 54-55; Lic to Offic *St D* 55-85; Lect Univ of Wales (Lamp) 55-69; Sen Lect 69-90; Dean Faculty of Th 77-81; Can St D Cathl 85-90; rtd 90; Can and Treas St D Cathl *St D* 92-97. *The Vicarage, Cwmann, Lampeter SA48 8DU* Tel (01570) 422385

MORRIS, The Ven Philip Gregory. b 50. Leeds Univ BA71 MPhil74. Coll of Resurr Mirfield 71. **d** 73 **p** 74. C Aberdare *Llan* 74-77; C Neath w Llantwit 77-80; V Cymmer and Porth 80-88; TV Llantwit Major 88-01; Dioc Missr 88-99; Can Res Llan Cathl 00-01; Adn Margam from 02; TV Aberavon 02; P-in-c Kenfig Hill from 02. *60 Ham Lane South, Llantwit Major CF61 1RN* Tel (01446) 793770 Fax as telephone E-mail pmorri@globalnet.co.uk

MORRIS, Philip John. b 50. FCIPD96. St Mich Coll Llan 97. **d** 99 **p** 00. NSM Builth and Llanddewi'r Cwm w Llangynog etc *S & B* 99-04; NSM Aberedw w Llandeilo Graban and Llanbadarn etc from 04. *Lochaber, 22 North Road, Builth Wells LD2 3BU* Tel (01982) 552390

MORRIS, Raymond. b 48. Open Univ HND70 BA88. N Ord Course 80. **d** 83 **p** 84. C Tonge w Alkrington *Man* 83-86; R Blackley St Paul 86-91; V Heyside from 91; AD Tandle from 02. *St Mark's Vicarage, Perth Street, Royton, Oldham OL2 6LY* Tel (01706) 847177

MORRIS, Raymond Arthur. b 42. Trin Coll Ox BA64 MA66 Lon Univ LLB71 CQSW72. Clifton Th Coll 66. **d** 67 **p** 91. C Greenstead *Chelmsf* 67-68; Perm to Offic *York* 69-91; NSM Linthorpe from 91. *3 Medina Gardens, Middlesbrough TS5 8BN* Tel (01642) 593726 E-mail raykate@themorrises.freeserve.co.uk

MORRIS, Raymond John Walton. b 08. OBE69. Em Coll Cam BA33 MA37. Lon Coll of Div 33. **d** 34 **p** 35. C E Twickenham St Steph *Lon* 34-37; C Bradf Cathl *Bradf* 37-40; V Plymouth Em *Ex* 40-45; V E Twickenham St Steph *Lon* 45-56; Chapl Br Embassy Ch Paris *Eur* 56-69; RD France 56-69; V Brompton H Trin *Lon* 69-75; rtd 75; Perm to Offic *Sarum* 75-99. *The Malt House, Bay Road, Gillingham SP8 4EN* Tel (01747) 821973

MORRIS, Reginald Brian. b 31. St Mich Coll Llan 56. **d** 59 **p** 60. C St Jo in Bedwardine *Worc* 59-61; P-in-c Tolladine 61-62; CF 62-78; V Cheswardine *Lich* 78-84; V Hales 78-84; Perm to Offic 84-86; C Cen Telford 86-89; rtd 89; Perm to Offic *Heref* from 90. *Woodside Cottage, School Lane, Prees, Whitchurch SY13 2BU* Tel (01948) 840090

MORRIS, Canon Robert John. b 45. Leeds Univ BA67. Coll of Resurr Mirfield 74. **d** 76 **p** 77. C Beeston Hill St Luke *Ripon* 76; C Holbeck 76-78; C Moseley St Mary *Birm* 78-83; P-in-c Handsworth St Jas 83-88; V 88-99; P-in-c Handsworth St Mich 86-87; AD Handsworth 92-99; TR Kings Norton from 99; Hon Can Birm Cathl from 97. *The Rectory, 273 Pershore Road South, Kings Norton, Birmingham B30 3EX* Tel 0121-459 0560 *or* 458 3289 Mobile 07973-389427 Fax 0121-486 2825

MORRIS, Robert Lee. b 47. W Virginia Univ BA69. Gen Th Sem (NY) MDiv73. **d** 73 **p** 74. USA 73-74 and from 84; Community of Celebration 74-94; P-in-c Cumbrae (or Millport) *Arg* 75-76 and 79-84. *All Saints Church, 3577 McClure Avenue, Pittsburgh, PA 15212, USA*

MORRIS, Canon Robin Edward. b 32. St Jo Coll Ox BA55 MA60. Westcott Ho Cam 55. **d** 57 **p** 58. C Halliwell St Thos *Man* 57-61; V Castleton Moor 61-71; V Stalybridge 71-80; R Heswall *Ches* 80-97; Hon Can Ches Cathl 91-97; RD Wirral N 93-97; rtd 97; Perm to Offic *Man* from 97. *122 Kiln Lane, Milnrow, Rochdale OL16 3HA* Tel (01706) 642846

MORRIS, Roger Anthony Brett. b 68. Imp Coll Lon BSc89 Trin Coll Cam BA92 ARCS89. Ridley Hall Cam CTM93. **d** 93 **p** 94. C Northleach w Hampnett and Farmington *Glouc* 93-96; C Cold Aston w Notgrove and Turkdean 93-96; P-in-c Sevenhampton w Charlton Abbotts and Hawling etc 96-00; P-in-c Dowdeswell and Andoversford w the Shiptons etc 96-00; R Sevenhampton w Charlton Abbots, Hawling etc 00-03; Dioc Dir Par Development and Evang *Cov* from 03. *The Vicarage, Church Road, Snitterfield, Stratford-upon-Avon CV37 0LN* Tel (01789) 751263 *or* (024) 7652 1200 E-mail roger.morris@virgin.net *or* roger.morris@covcofe.org

MORRIS, Stanley James. b 35. Keble Coll Ox BA58 MA63. Chich Th Coll 59. **d** 61 **p** 62. C Tunstall Ch Ch *Lich* 61-64; C W Bromwich All SS 64-67; V Wilnecote 67-88; V Alrewas and Wychnor 88-00; rtd 01; Perm to Offic *Derby* from 01. *44 Pinfold Close, Repton, Derby DE65 6FR* Tel (01283) 703453

MORRIS, Stephen Bryan. b 54. Linc Th Coll 88. **d** 90 **p** 91. C Glouc St Geo w Whaddon *Glouc* 90-94; Chapl for the Deaf from 94; C Glouc St Mary de Crypt w St Jo, Ch Ch etc 94-99; C Glouc St Mark and St Mary de Crypt w St Jo etc 00-02; C Barnwood 02-03. *24 Sandycroft Road, Churchdown, Gloucester GL3 1JH* Tel (01452) 712608

MORRIS, Stephen Francis. b 52. St Jo Coll Nottm BTh79. **d** 79 **p** 80. C N Hinksey *Ox* 79-82; C Leic H Apostles *Leic* 82-85; TV Shenley and Loughton *Ox* 85-88; TV Watling Valley 88-95; V Chatham St Wm *Roch* 95-98; TR S Chatham H Trin 98-00; Lect Nottingham St Mary and St Cath *S'well* from 00; AD Nottingham Cen from 02. *6 Boyce Gardens, Mapperley, Nottingham NG3 3FB* Tel 0115-958 2996 E-mail parishoffice@stmarysnottingham.org

MORRIS, Canon Stuart Collard. b 43. AKC66. St Boniface Warminster 66. **d** 67 **p** 68. C Hanham *Bris* 67-71; C Whitchurch 71-74; P-in-c Wapley w Codrington and Dodington 74-77; P-in-c Westerleigh 74-77; P-in-c Holdgate w Tugford *Heref* 77-82; P-in-c Abdon w Clee St Margaret 77-82; R Diddlebury w Bouldon and Munslow 77-82; P-in-c Sotterley, Willingham, Shadingfield, Ellough etc *St E* 82-87; RD Beccles and S Elmham 83-94; P-in-c Westhall w Brampton and Stoven 86-88; P-in-c Flixton w Homersfield and S Elmham 86-92; Hon Can St E Cathl 87-99; V Bungay H Trin w St Mary 87-94; P-in-c Hadleigh w Layham and Shelley 94-96; R Hadleigh 96-99; Dean Bocking 94-99; RD Hadleigh 94-98; rtd 99. *Ty'r Gelliffynonau, Cwm Cadlan, Penderyn, Aberdare CF44 0YJ* Tel (01685) 813196

MORRIS, Canon Timothy David. b 48. Lon Univ BSc69. Trin Coll Bris DipTh75. **d** 75 **p** 76. C Edin St Thos *Edin* 75-77; R Edin St Jas 77-83; R Troon *Glas* 83-85; R Galashiels *Edin* 85-02; Dean Edin 92-01; Hon Can St Mary's Cathl from 01; R Edin Gd Shep from 02. *The Rectory, 9 Upper Coltbridge Terrace, Edinburgh EH12 6AD* Tel and fax 0131-337 2698 E-mail tim@parsonage.scotborders.co.uk

MORRIS, Mrs Valerie Ruth. b 46. St Hugh's Coll Ox BA68 MA72. Qu Coll Birm 76. **dss** 78 **d** 87. Drayton in Hales *Lich* 78-82; Burton 82-90; Par Dn 87-90; Hon Par Dn 90-91; Perm to Offic *Heref* from 04. *Watling House, All Stretton, Church Stretton SY6 6HH* Tel (01694) 722243

MORRIS, William Humphrey Francis. b 29. Univ of Wales BA54 MA72 Birm Univ DipTh58 Trin Coll Cam BA62 MA66 PhD75 Man Univ MEd76 PhD80 Ox Univ DPhil85 DD88 FRAS84 FInstP92. Qu Coll Birm 56. **d** 58 **p** 59. C Prestbury *Ches* 58-60; C Neston 60-65; V Sandbach Heath 65-68; Lic to Offic 69-93; rtd 84; Lic to Offic *Lich* from 93; Perm to Offic *Ches* from 93. *Stonyflats Farm, Smallwood, Sandbach CW11 2XH* Tel (01477) 500354

MORRIS, William James. b 23. St Deiniol's Hawarden 72. **d** 73 **p** 74. NSM Brecon Adnry 73-78; NSM Crickhowell w Cwmdu and Tretower *S & B* 78-98; rtd 98. *The School House, Cwmdu, Crickhowell NP8 1RU* Tel (01874) 730355

MORRIS, William Richard Price. b 23. FCollP82. Glouc Sch of Min 86. **d** 88 **p** 89. Hon C Bussage *Glouc* 88-90; Perm to Offic 90-91; Hon C France Lynch 91; Hon C Chalford and France Lynch 91-93; rtd 93; Perm to Offic *Glouc* from 93. *Langendun House, Manor Close, Michinhampton, Stroud GL6 9DG* Tel (01453) 886382

MORRISH, James William. b 65. Plymouth Univ BSc92 St Steph Ho Ox BTh05. 99. **d** 01 **p** 02. C Porlock w Stoke Pero *B & W* 01-04; P-in-c Kingstone w Clehonger, Eaton Bishop etc *Heref* from 04. *The Rectory, Kingstone, Hereford HR2 9EY* Tel (01981) 250350 E-mail jamesmorrish@kingrec.wanadoo.co.uk

MORRISON, Alexander Grant. b 37. St Fran Coll Brisbane ThL ACT St Columb's Hall Wangaratta. **d** 66 **p** 67. Australia 66-82; C Hayes St Mary *Lon* 83-84; R Black Notley *Chelmsf* from 84. *The Rectory, 71 Witham Road, Black Notley, Braintree CM77 7LJ* Tel (01376) 349619

MORRISON, Andrew Leslie. b 11. TD53. Pemb Coll Ox BA33 MA37. Westcott Ho Cam 33. **d** 35 **p** 36. C S Westoe *Dur* 35-38; V Castleside 38-42; CF (TA) 39-56; R Branston *Linc* 46-49; V Gateshead Ch Ch *Dur* 49-55; Chapl Bensham Hosp Gateshead 50-55; R Fenny Compton and Wormleighton *Cov* 55-64; RD Dassett Magna 59-64; V Bury and Houghton *Chich* 64-76; rtd 76; Perm to Offic *Chich* from 76. *14 Guildford Place, Chichester PO19 5DU* Tel (01243) 784310

MORRISON, Barbara Anne. b 29. St Andr Univ BSc50. **d** 95 **p** 96. NSM Eorropaidh *Arg* 95-00; P-in-c from 00. *46 Upper Coll, Back, Isle of Lewis HS2 0LT* Tel and fax (01851) 820559 E-mail barbara.stmoluag@care4free.net

MORRISON, Barry John. b 44. Pemb Coll Cam BA66 MA70. ALCD69. **d** 69 **p** 70. C Stoke Bishop *Bris* 69-72; C Edgware *Lon* 72-76; Chapl Poly Cen Lon 76-83; Hon C Langham Place All So 76-83; P-in-c W Hampstead St Luke 83-88; V 88-98; Chapl Westf Coll 84-92; R Rushden St Mary w Newton Bromswold *Pet* from 98. *The Rectory, Rectory Road, Rushden NN10 0HA* Tel (01933) 312554 E-mail morrison@barryandgill.freeserve.co.uk

MORRISON, Bryony Clare. b 47. Lon Univ CertEd77 Brentwood Coll of Educn BEd86. NTMTC 96. **d** 99 **p** 00. C Epping Distr *Chelmsf* from 99; TV from 05; Chapl Epping Forest Primary Care Trust from 02. *Theydon Garnon Vicarage, Fiddlers Hamlet, Epping CM16 7PQ* Tel (01992) 573672 Mobile 07850-876304 E-mail revbry@dibleyhouse.com

MORRISON, Diana Mary (Sister Diana). b 43. St Kath Coll Liv CertEd64. EAMTC 02. **d** 05. NSM Breadsall *Derby* from 05. *The Convent of the Holy Name, Morley Road, Chaddesden, Derby DE21 4QZ* Tel (01332) 671716 Fax 669712 E-mail dianachn@care4free.net

MORRISON, Iain Edward. b 36. St Steph Ho Ox 76. **d** 78 **p** 79. C Brighton St Aug and St Sav *Chich* 78-81; C Felpham w Middleton 81-83; P-in-c Barnham and Eastergate 83-85; R Aldingbourne, Barnham and Eastergate 85-91; V Jarvis Brook 91-98; R Hastings St Clem and All SS 98-03; rtd 03; P-in-c Arlington, Folkington and Wilmington *Chich* from 03. *The Vicarage, The Street, Wilmington, Polegate BN26 5SL* Tel (01323) 870268 E-mail iain@hafodty.demon.uk

MORRISON, James Wilson Rennie. b 42. Aber Univ MA65. Linc Th Coll 76. **d** 78 **p** 79. C Whitley Ch Ch *Ox* 78-81; R Burghfield 81-87; CF 87-97; P-in-c Burghill *Heref* 97-03; V from 03; P-in-c Stretton Sugwas 97-03; R from 03; P-in-c Pipe-cum-Lyde 97-03; P-in-c Pipe-cum-Lyde and Moreton-on-Lugg from 03. *The Vicarage, Burghill, Hereford HR4 7SG* Tel (01432) 760246

MORRISON, The Ven John Anthony. b 38. Jes Coll Cam BA60 MA64 Linc Coll Ox MA68. Chich Th Coll 61. **d** 64 **p** 65. C Birm St Pet *Birm* 64-68; C Ox St Mich *Ox* 68-71; Chapl Linc Coll Ox 68-74; C Ox St Mich w St Martin and All SS *Ox* 71-74; V Basildon 74-82; RD Bradfield 78-82; V Aylesbury 82-89; RD Aylesbury 85-89; TR Aylesbury w Bierton and Hulcott 89-90; Adn Buckingham 90-98; P-in-c Princes Risborough w Ilmer 96-97; Adn Ox and Can Res Ch Ch 98-05; rtd 05; Perm to Offic *Ox* from 05. *39 Crown Road, Wheatley, Oxford OX33 1UJ* Tel (01865) 876625 E-mail johnmorrison@christchurch.oxford.ac.uk

MORRISON, Keith Charles. b 63. Wycliffe Hall Ox. **d** 01 **p** 02. C Ipswich St Aug *St E* 01-04; Asst Chapl Cam Univ Hosps NHS Foundn Trust from 04. *Addenbrooke's Hospital, Hills Road, Cambridge CB2 2QQ* Tel (01223) 245151 Mobile 07798-965651 E-mail keithmorrisonk@hotmail.com

MORRISON, Raymond. *See* MORRISON, Walter John Raymond

MORRISON, Richard James. b 55. Sarum & Wells Th Coll 87. **d** 89 **p** 90. C Boston *Linc* 89-93; P-in-c Digby 93-99; V Whaplode Drove from 99; V Gedney Hill from 99. *The Vicarage, 1 Broadgate, Whaplode Drove, Spalding PE12 0TN* Tel (01406) 330392

MORRISON, Robin Victor Adair. b 45. Nottm Univ BA67. Bucharest Th Inst 67 Ripon Hall Ox 68. **d** 70 **p** 71. C Hackney St Jo *Lon* 70-73; Chapl Newc Univ *Newc* 73-76; P-in-c Teversal *S'well* 76-78; Chapl Sutton Cen 76-78; Asst Hd Deans Community Sch Livingston *Edin* 78-80; R Edin St Columba 80-81; Chapl Birm Univ *Birm* 81-88; Prin Soc Resp Officer *Derby* 88-96; TV Southampton (City Cen) *Win* 96-01; Ind Chapl 96-01; Non Exec Dir Southampton and SW Hants HA 00-01; Officer for Ch and Soc Ch in Wales Prov Coun from 01. *1 Dannog y Coed, Barry CF63 1HF* Tel (01446) 741900 E-mail robin@sparticus.net

MORRISON, Walter John Raymond (Ray). b 30. Jes Coll Cam BA55 MA58. Westcott Ho Cam 55. **d** 57 **p** 58. C Dalston St Mark w St Bart *Lon* 57-60; C Totteridge *St Alb* 60-63; V Letchworth St Paul 63-71; RD Hitchin 70-71; R Ludlow *Heref* 72-83; RD Ludlow 78-83; Preb Heref Cathl 78-83; P-in-c

Ludlow, Ludford, Ashford Carbonell etc 80-83; Chapl St Thos Hosp Lon 83-86; Chapl Eastbourne Distr Gen Hosp 86-95; rtd 95; Perm to Offic *Worc* from 95. *190 Farleigh Road, Pershore WR10 1LY* Tel (01386) 556542 E-mail ray@mossnet.co.uk

MORROW, David. b 63. NUU BSc86 TCD BTh89. CITC 86. **d** 89 **p** 90. C Portadown St Mark *Arm* 89-91; C Ballymena w Ballyclug *Conn* 91-94; I Tempo and Clabby *Clogh* 94-01; I Kilcronaghan w Draperstown and Sixtowns *D & R* from 01. *Kilcronaghan Rectory, 12 Rectory Road, Tobermore, Magherafelt BT45 5QP* Tel (028) 7962 8823
E-mail morrowdavid@hotmail.com

MORROW, Canon Henry Hugh. b 26. TCD BA49 MA67 Flinders Univ Aus BSocAdmin76. TCD Div Sch Div Test49. **d** 49 **p** 50. C Dublin St Thos *D & G* 49-53; I Rathmolyon *M & K* 53-58; I Killoughter *K, E & A* 58-63; C Portadown St Columba *Arm* 63-65; I Ballinderry w Tamlaght 65-70; Australia from 70; Hon Can Adelaide from 84. *5 Allendale Grove, Stonyfell, S Australia 5066* Tel (0061) (8) 8332 5890

MORROW, Canon Joseph John. b 54. JP87. Edin Univ BD79 Dundee Univ LLB92 DLLP93 NY Th Sem DMin87. Edin Th Coll 76. **d** 79 **p** 80. Chapl St Paul's Cathl Dundee *Bre* 79-82; P-in-c Dundee St Martin 82-85; R 85-90; P-in-c Dundee St Jo from 85; P-in-c Dundee St Ninian from 02; Can St Paul's Cathl Dundee from 00. *St Ninian's Rectory, Kingsway East, Dundee DD4 7RW* Tel (01382) 453818 E-mail jjmidt@glamis.sol.co.uk

MORROW, Nigel Patrick. b 68. Dur Univ BA94 TCD MPhil02. Westcott Ho Cam 03. **d** 05. C Linc St Pet-at-Gowts and St Andr *Linc* from 05; C Linc St Botolph from 05. *69 Western Crescent, Lincoln LN6 7TA* Tel (01522) 514506 Mobile 07764-608433
E-mail paddymorrow@hotmail.com

MORSE, Mrs Elisabeth Ann. b 51. New Hall Cam MA73 Qu Eliz Coll Lon MSc74 Heythrop Coll Lon MA97. S'wark Ord Course 91. **d** 94 **p** 95. C Wimbledon *S'wark* 94-99; C Fulham All SS *Lon* from 99. *70A Fulham High Street, London SW6 3LG* Tel (020) 7371 7540 E-mail emorse@fish.co.uk *or* morse@wilko31.freeserve.co.uk

MORSHEAD, Ivo Francis Trelawny. b 27. ACA52 FCA63. Cuddesdon Coll 61. **d** 63 **p** 64. C Bris St Mary Redcliffe w Temple etc *Bris* 63-68; C Wimbledon *S'wark* 68-73; V Elham *Cant* 73-78; V Whitchurch *Ex* 78-91; rtd 91; Perm to Offic *Lon* from 91. *28 Edge Street, London W8 7PN* Tel (020) 7727 5975

MORSON, Mrs Dorothy Mary. b 29. Linc Th Coll 71. **d** 87. Par Dn Cen Telford *Lich* 87-89; rtd 89; Perm to Offic *Lich* 89-00. *Ashleigh, Hunter Street, Shrewsbury SY3 8QN* Tel (01743) 369225

MORSON, Mrs Eleanor. b 42. CA Tr Coll 63 TISEC 95. **d** 96 **p** 96. NSM Kirkwall *Ab* 96-01; R Edin St Mark *Edin* 01-05. *Tammy-norie, 2 Royal Oak Court, Kirkwall KW15 1US*

MORSON, John. b 41. CA Tr Coll 62. **d** 88 **p** 92. NSM Duns *Edin* 88-89; CF 89-92; R Kirkwall *Ab* 92-01; R Stromness 92-01; NSM Edin St Mark *Edin* 01-05. *Tammy-norie, 2 Royal Oak Court, Kirkwall KW15 1US*

MORT, Alister. b 52. BSc BA. Oak Hill Th Coll. **d** 82 **p** 83. C Cheadle Hulme St Andr *Ches* 82-85; C Rodbourne Cheney *Bris* 86-87; TV 87-90; V New Milverton *Cov* from 90. *2 St Mark's Road, Leamington Spa CV32 6DL* Tel (01926) 421004
E-mail office@stmarkslspa.freeserve.co.uk

MORT, Ivan Laurence (Laurie). b 61. Nottm Univ BTh87. Linc Th Coll 84. **d** 87 **p** 88. C Aston cum Aughton and Ulley *Sheff* 87-90; C Greenstead *Chelmsf* 90-94; Chapl Toulouse *Eur* from 94. *19 rue Bel Soulhel, Cornebarrieu 31700, Toulouse, France* Tel (0033) (5) 61 85 17 67

MORT, Canon Margaret Marion. b 38. Edin Univ MA. S Tr Scheme 94. **d** 97 **p** 98. NSM Swanmore St Barn *Portsm* from 97; Hon Can Portsm Cathl from 01. *Rivendell, High Street, Shirrell Heath, Southampton SO32 2JN* Tel and fax (01329) 832178 Mobile 07761-225222 E-mail marion@holyharp.co.uk

MORTER, Ian Charles. b 54. AKC77. Coll of Resurr Mirfield 77. **d** 78 **p** 79. C Colchester St Jas, All SS, St Nic and St Runwald *Chelmsf* 78-82; C Brixham w Churston Ferrers *Ex* 82-83; TV 84-86; TV Sidmouth, Woolbrook and Salcombe Regis 86-91; TV Sidmouth, Woolbrook, Salcombe Regis, Sidbury etc 91-95; P-in-c Exminster and Kenn 95-00; TR Littleham w Exmouth from 00. *The Rectory, 1 Maer Road, Exmouth EX8 2DA* Tel (01395) 272227

MORTIBOYS, John William. b 45. K Coll Lon BD69 AKC69. Sarum Th Coll 71. **d** 71 **p** 72. C Reading All SS *Ox* 71-95; Perm to Offic *Portsm* from 97. *13 Oyster Street, Portsmouth PO1 2HZ* Tel (023) 9275 6676 Fax 9266 2626

MORTIMER, Anthony John. b 42. Sarum & Wells Th Coll 68. **d** 71 **p** 72. C Heref St Martin *Heref* 71-79; V Kingstone 79-85; P-in-c Clehonger 80-85; P-in-c Eaton Bishop 80-85; TR Pinhoe and Broadclyst *Ex* from 85. *The Rectory, 9 Church Hill, Pinhoe, Exeter EX4 9ER* Tel (01392) 467541

MORTIMER, Charles Philip. b 38. Linc Th Coll 68. **d** 70 **p** 71. C Penistone w Midhope *Wakef* 70-74; V Luddenden 74-77; P-in-c Luddenden Foot 74-77; Chapl RAF 77-91; Asst Chapl-in-Chief RAF 91-93; V Staincliffe *Wakef* 93-99; rtd 99; Perm to Offic *Wakef* from 99. *15 Park Avenue, Liversedge Hall Lane, Liversedge WF15 7EQ* Tel (01924) 510051

MORTIMER, The Very Revd Hugh Sterling. b 23. TCD BA44 MA53. **d** 46 **p** 47. C Finaghy *Conn* 46-49; Dean's V Belf Cathl 49-53; V Choral Belf Cathl 53-55; I Tartaraghan *Arm* 55-61; Hon VC 57-85; I Magherafelt 61-66; I Arm St Mark 66-83; Can Arm Cathl 67-72; Treas 72-73; Chan 73-75; Prec 75-83; Dean Elphin and Ardagh *K, E & A* 83-91; I Sligo w Knocknarea and Rosses Pt 83-91; rtd 91; Perm to Offic *Conn* from 91. *95 Sharman Road, Belfast BT9 5HE* Tel (028) 9066 9184

MORTIMER, Jonathan Michael. b 60. Bris Univ BA83. Oak Hill Th Coll BA92. **d** 92 **p** 93. C Rugby St Matt *Cov* 92-96; C Southgate *Chich* 96-98; TR from 98. *The Rectory, Forester Road, Crawley RH10 6EH* Tel (01293) 523463

MORTIMER, Canon Lawrence George. b 45. St Edm Hall Ox BA67 MA71 St Chad's Coll Dur DipTh68. **d** 70 **p** 71. C Rugby St Andr *Cov* 70-75; V Styvechale 75-89; Dioc Broadcasting Officer 80-89; Dioc Communications Officer 89-03; P-in-c Wootton Wawen from 95; P-in-c Claverdon w Preston Bagot from 03; Hon Can Cov Cathl from 98. *The Vicarage, Stratford Road, Wootton Wawen, Henley-in-Arden B95 6BD* Tel and fax (01564) 792659 *or* tel 795545
E-mail l.mortimer@btinternet.com

MORTIMER, Peter Jackson. b 41. MBE95 TD73. St Jo Coll York CertEd63 RTC63 Essex Univ MA71 FRSA97. EAMTC 97. **d** 98 **p** 99. NSM Needham Market w Badley *St E* 98-02; NSM Ringshall w Battisford, Barking w Darmsden etc 98-02; Bp's Ecum Adv from 02; Chapl to Suffolk Fire Service from 03. *20 Leggatt Drive, Bramford, Ipswich IP8 4ET* Tel (01473) 747419

MORTIMER, Philip. *See* MORTIMER, Charles Philip

MORTIMER, Richard James. b 63. Ex Univ BSc85 Lon Bible Coll BA97. Oak Hill Th Coll. **d** 01 **p** 02. C Ore *Chich* 01-05; Chapl Hastings Univ from 05; C Hastings H Trin from 05. *4 Gresham Way, St Leonards-on-Sea TN38 0UE*
E-mail richard@rmortimer.freeserve.co.uk

MORTIMER, William Raymond. b 31. GradIEE58 AMIEE66. St Deiniol's Hawarden 68. **d** 69 **p** 70. C Flint *St As* 69-71; Lic to Offic 72-73; V Llanwddyn and Llanfihangel-yng-Nghwynfa etc 73-85; RD Llanfyllin 83-84; R Llanrwst and Llanddoget and Capel Garmon 85-96; rtd 96. *1 Coed Masarn, Woodlands Estate, Abergele LL22 7EE* Tel (01745) 822306

MORTIMORE, David Jack. b 42. Master Mariner 69. St Mich Coll Llan 90. **d** 91 **p** 92. C Pembroke St Mary w St Mich *St D* 91-92; C Bargoed and Deri w Brithdir *Llan* 92-97; Perm to Offic 98-02; P-in-c Llangeinor 02-04; P-in-c Llangeinor and the Garw Valley from 04. *The Vicarage, St Davids Street, Pontycymer, Bridgend CF32 8LT* Tel (01656) 870280
E-mail cleddau@tesco.net

MORTIMORE, Robert Edward. b 39. Kelham Th Coll 61 Wells Th Coll 66. **d** 69 **p** 70. C Byfleet *Guildf* 69-72; New Zealand from 72. *10 Otakau Road, Milford, Auckland 1309, New Zealand* Tel (0064) (9) 486 1010 Fax as telephone

MORTIS, Lorna Anne. b 54. Moray Ho Coll of Educn DipEd76 Open Univ BA88 Heriot-Watt Univ 92. TISEC CMM95. **d** 98 **p** 99. C N Berwick *Edin* from 98; C Gullane from 98. *Rosebank, 2 Main Street, Athelstaneford, North Berwick EH39 5BE* Tel (01620) 880505 Mobile 07779-553807 E-mail anrola@aol.com

MORTON, Adrian Ian. b 65. Brighton Poly BSc87 Brunel Univ MSc93. Ridley Hall Cam 98. **d** 00 **p** 01. C Kettering Ch the King *Pet* 00-04; P-in-c Bozeat w Easton Maudit from 04; P-in-c Wollaston and Strixton from 04. *The Vicarage, 81 Irchester Road, Wollaston, Wellingborough NN29 7RW* Tel (01933) 664256 E-mail adrian-morton@supanet.com

MORTON, Albert George. b 34. Saskatchewan Univ BA61 McGill Univ Montreal MA73. Em Coll Saskatoon 56. **d** 61 **p** 61. Canada 61-65; C Stanford-le-Hope *Chelmsf* 66-69; V Linc St Geo Swallowbeck *Linc* 69-82; R Lt Munden w Sacombe *St Alb* 82-89; R The Mundens w Sacombe 89-96; rtd 96; Perm to Offic *Sarum* from 00. *10 Church Green, Bishop's Caundle, Sherborne DT9 5NN* Tel (01963) 23383

MORTON, Andrew Edward. b 51. Lon Univ BA72 BD74 AKC74 Univ of Wales (Cardiff) MPhil93 Dip Counselling 98. St Aug Coll Cant 75. **d** 76 **p** 77. C Feltham *Lon* 76-79; C Pontlottyn w Fochriw *Llan* 79-81; V Ferndale w Maerdy 81-88; V Tylorstown w Ynyshir 88-93; Dir of Studies Llan Ord Course 91-93; R Llangybi and Coedypaen w Llanbadoc *Mon* from 93; Chapl Coleg Gwent from 93; Dioc FE Officer from 93; Prov HE Officer from 01; Dioc Dir NSM Studies from 00. *The Rectory, Parc Road, Llangybi, Usk NP15 1NL* Tel (01633) 450214

MORTON, Mrs Christine Mary. b 39. Linc Th Coll 78. **dss** 80 **d** 87 **p** 94. Ore *Chich* 80-84; Southwick St Mich 84-85; Winchmore Hill St Paul *Lon* 85-87; Par Dn 87-94; C 94-99; Hon C from 00; rtd 00. *122 Bourne Hill, London N13 4BD* Tel (020) 8886 3157

MORTON, Clive Frederick. b 47. Lon Univ BA70 Birm Univ MA98. Cranmer Hall Dur 78. **d** 80 **p** 81. C Countesthorpe w Foston *Leic* 80-83; C Glen Parva and S Wigston 83-86; Asst Chapl HM Youth Cust Cen Glen Parva 83-86; V Birm St Pet

Birm 86-98; Miss Partner CMS 99-02; Chapl St Petersburg *Eur* 99-02; Lect St Petersburg Th Academy and Sem 99-02; V Kingsbury H Innocents *Lon* from 02. *Kingsbury Vicarage, 54 Roe Green, London NW9 0PJ* Tel (020) 8204 7531 Mobile 07947-883559 E-mail holyinnocents.kingsbury@virgin.net

MORTON, Derek. *See* MORTON, Canon William Derek

MORTON, Howard Knyvett. b 30. St Jo Coll Cam BA51 MA67. Linc Th Coll 55. **d** 57 **p** 58. C Hatfield Hyde *St Alb* 57-60; Hd RE Heaton Gr Sch Newc 60-66 and 72-75; CMS 66-72; Heworth Grange Sch Dur 75-83; Regional Org Oxfam 88-91; Grainger Gr Sch Newc 91-94; Lic to Offic *Newc* 73-93; Dioc World Development Officer 94-95; rtd 95; Perm to Offic *Dur* 95-98; Perm to Offic *Newc* from 96. *Daisy Cottage, Hawthorn Lane, Rothbury, Morpeth NE65 7TL* Tel (01665) 577958

MORTON, Mrs Jacqueline Mavis. b 46. UEA BSc67 York Univ BSc82. EMMTC 97. **d** 00 **p** 01. NSM Sibsey w Frithville *Linc* from 00. *8 Lucan Close, Sibsey, Boston PE22 0SH* Tel (01205) 751378 E-mail jacqui.morton@care4free.net

MORTON, Jennifer. b 50. Bedf Coll Lon BA72 Leic Univ PGCE73. EMMTC 87. **d** 90 **p** 94. C New Mills *Derby* 90-94; Chapl Asst Nottm City Hosp NHS Trust 94-98; Chapl Basford Hosp Nottm 94-98; Chapl S Derbyshire Acute Hosps NHS Trust 98-02; Vice Prin EMMTC *S'well* from 02. *56 Marshall Drive, Beeston, Nottingham NG9 3LD* Tel 0115-939 5784 *or* 951 4852 Fax 951 4817 E-mail jenny.morton@nottingham.ac.uk

MORTON, Mark Paul. b 58. Univ of Wales (Swansea) BA79 Univ of Wales (Lamp) MA99. Ridley Hall Cam CTM92. **d** 92 **p** 93. C Daventry, Ashby St Ledgers, Braunston etc *Pet* 92-95; CF (TA) 93-95; CF from 95. *c/o MOD Chaplains (Army)* Tel (01980) 615804 Fax 615800

MORTON, Michael James. **d** 04. OLM Westerfield and Tuddenham w Witnesham *St E* from 04. *Fynndale House, Upper Street, Witnesham, Ipswich IP6 9EW* Tel (01473) 785487 E-mail morton@ritamike.freeserve.co.uk

MORTON, Michelle. b 67. Ripon Coll Cuddesdon 00. **d** 02 **p** 03. C Buckingham *Ox* 02-05; P-in-c Stewkley w Soulbury and Drayton Parslow from 05. *The Vicarage, High Street North, Stewkley, Leighton Buzzard LU7 0HH* Tel (01525) 240287 E-mail squarenalo@hotmail.com

MORTON, Rex Gerald. b 61. St Jo Coll Nottm DipTh98. **d** 98 **p** 99. C Bury St Edmunds All SS *St E* 98-01; C Woodside Park St Barn *Lon* from 01. *12 Courthouse Road, London N12 7PJ* Tel (020) 8446 7506 *or* 8343 5778 Mobile 07968-088714 Fax (020) 8343 5771 E-mail sj@morton4.swinternet.co.uk *or* rexmorton@stbarnabas.co.uk

MORTON, Sister Rita. b 34. Wilson Carlile Coll. **dss** 85 **d** 87 **p** 94. CA from 76; Par Dn Harlow New Town w Lt Parndon *Chelmsf* 87-89; C Harold Hill St Geo 89-94; rtd 94; NSM Elm Park St Nic Hornchurch *Chelmsf* from 94. *16 Cheviot Road, Hornchurch RH11 1LP* Tel (01708) 709842

MORTON, Robert Hart. b 28. Moray Ord Course 91. **d** 94. Hon C St Andr Cathl Inverness *Mor* from 94. *75 Fairfield Road, Inverness IV3 5LJ* Tel (01463) 223525

MORTON, Miss Rosemary Grania. b 65. Qu Coll Birm BA05. **d** 05. C Kings Heath *Birm* from 05. *14 All Saints Road, Kings Heath, Birmingham B14 7LL* Tel 0121-444 2491 E-mail rosie_morton@yahoo.co.uk

MORTON, Rupert Neville. b 25. St Steph Ho Ox 51. **d** 54 **p** 55. C Aldershot St Mich *Guildf* 54-57; Prec Guildf Cathl 57-58; V Middlesbrough St Chad *York* 58-62; Chapl Carter Bequest Hosp 58-62; V Bramley *Guildf* 62-79; V Grafham 62-79; RD Cranleigh 71-76; R Haslemere 79-91; rtd 91; Perm to Offic *Guildf* and *Chich* from 91. *Rock House, Wormley, Godalming GU8 5SN* Tel (01428) 682614

MORTON, Mrs Sheila. b 44. Leeds Univ. Sarum & Wells Th Coll 79. **dss** 84 **d** 87 **p** 94. HM Forces Düsseldorf 84-86; Cov St Mary *Cov* 86-89; Par Dn 87-89; Par Dn Boston Spa *York* 89-92; C Flitwick *St Alb* 93-00; R Wilden w Colmworth and Ravensden from 00. *The New Rectory, High Street, Wilden, Bedford MK44 2PB* Tel (01234) 772895 E-mail revsheila@vicarage727freeserve.co.uk

MORTON, Canon William Derek. b 28. Wells Th Coll 67. **d** 69 **p** 70. C Kibworth Beauchamp *Leic* 69-72; Ind Chapl *Nor* 72-93; Hon Can Nor Cathl 90-93; RD Nor E 90-93; rtd 93; Perm to Offic *Nor* from 93. *55 Cameron Green, Taverham, Norwich NR8 6UA* Tel (01603) 861240

MORTON, The Very Revd William Wright. b 56. ALAM TCD BTh88 MA95 QUB PhD96. CITC. **d** 88 **p** 89. C Drumachose *D & R* 88-91; I Conwal Union w Gartan 91-97; Bp's Dom Chapl 92-97; Can Raphoe Cathl 94-97; Dean Derry from 97; I Templemore from 97. *The Deanery, 30 Bishop Street, Londonderry BT48 6PP* Tel (028) 7126 2746 E-mail dean@derry.anglican.org

MOSDOL, Hallvard. **p** 00. C Norwegian Ch and Seamen's Miss Lon from 02; NSM Bermondsey Deanery *S'wark* from 02. *St Olav's Church, 1 St Olav's Square, Albion Street, London SE16 1JB* Tel (020) 8852 3264

MOSELEY, David John Reading. b 30. Univ Coll Ox BA54 MA58. Wells Th Coll 54. **d** 56 **p** 57. C Farnworth and Kearsley *Man* 56-59; Trinidad and Tobago 59-63; V Bedminster St Paul *Bris* 63-75; TV Bedminster 75-78; V Kilmington w Shute *Ex* 78-95; P-in-c Stockland w Dalwood 90; rtd 95; Perm to Offic *Ex* from 95. *1B Seaton Down Road, Seaton EX12 2RZ* Tel (01297) 24174

MOSELEY, Hugh Martin. b 47. St Jo Coll Dur BA70. Westcott Ho Cam 71. **d** 73 **p** 74. C Hythe *Cant* 73-77; P-in-c Eythorne w Waldershare 77-83; V Ringmer *Chich* 83-99; RD Lewes and Seaford 93-97; P-in-c E Dean w Friston and Jevington 99-00; R 00-03; TR Rye from 03; RD Rye from 03. *St Mary's Rectory, Gungarden, Rye TN31 7HH* Tel (01797) 222430

MOSELEY, Michael. b 45. Oak Hill Th Coll 02. **d** 04 **p** 05. NSM Forty Hill Jes Ch *Lon* from 04. *107 Old Park Avenue, Enfield EN2 6PP* Tel (020) 8363 2475 E-mail michael_m@fsmail.net

MOSELEY, Roger Henry. b 38. Edin Th Coll 60. **d** 63 **p** 64. C Friern Barnet All SS *Lon* 63-66; C Grantham St Wulfram *Linc* 66-69; P-in-c Swaton w Spanby 69-73; P-in-c Horbling 69-73; V Soberton w Newtown *Portsm* 73-80; V Sarisbury 80-03; rtd 03; Perm to Offic *Portsm* from 03. *53B St Michael's Road, St Helens, Ryde PO33 1YJ* Tel (01983) 875203 E-mail rhmoseley@talk21.com

MOSELING, Peter. b 48. WMMTC 92. **d** 95 **p** 96. C Daventry, Ashby St Ledgers, Braunston etc *Pet* 95-97; P-in-c Northampton H Trin 97-99; P-in-c Northampton St Paul 98-99; V Northampton H Trin and St Paul 99-05; Chapl Northampton Univ Coll 99-05; P-in-c Bletchingley *S'wark* from 05. *The Rectory, Outwood Lane, Bletchingley, Redhill RH1 4LR* Tel (01883) 743252 E-mail p.moseling@tiscali.co.uk

MOSES, The Very Revd John Henry. b 38. Nottm Univ BA59 PhD65. Linc Th Coll 62. **d** 64 **p** 65. C Bedford St Andr *St Alb* 64-70; P-in-c Cov St Pet *Cov* 70-73; P-in-c Cov St Mark 71-73; TR Cov E 73-77; RD Cov E 73-77; Adn Southend *Chelmsf* 77-82; Provost Chelmsf 82-96; Chmn Coun of Cen for Th Study Essex Univ 87-96; Dean St Paul's *Lon* from 96. *The Deanery, 9 Amen Court, London EC4M 7BU* Tel (020) 7236 2827 Fax 7332 0298 E-mail thedean@stpaulscathedral.org.uk

MOSES, Leslie Alan. b 49. Hull Univ BA71 Edin Univ BD76. Edin Th Coll 73. **d** 76 **p** 77. C Edin Old St Paul *Edin* 76-79; R Leven *St And* 79-85; R Edin Old St Paul *Edin* 85-95; P-in-c Edin St Marg 86-92; V St Marylebone All SS *Lon* from 95; AD Westmr St Marylebone from 01. *All Saints' Vicarage, 7 Margaret Street, London W1W 8JG* Tel (020) 7636 1788 *or* 7636 9961 Fax 7436 4470 E-mail alan@moses.org.uk

MOSFORD, Canon Denzil Huw Erasmus. b 56. Florida State Univ MTh04 AKC78. Sarum & Wells Th Coll 77. **d** 79 **p** 80. C Clydach *S & B* 79-82; V 87-97; Jamaica 82-85; V Ystalyfera *S & B* 85-87; Dioc World Miss Officer from 91; RD Cwmtawe 93-97; V Gorseinon from 97; RD Llwchwr from 00; Hon Can Brecon Cathl 01-04; Can Res from 04. *The Vicarage, 42 Princess Street, Gorseinon, Swansea SA4 4US* Tel (01792) 892849 E-mail huw.mosford@ntlworld.com

MOSLEY, Edward Peter. b 38. Clifton Th Coll 62. **d** 67 **p** 68. C Mirehouse *Carl* 67-69; C Newbarns w Hawcoat 69-72; R Aikton 72-77; R Orton St Giles 72-77; V Silloth 77-78; CF 78-94; Hon C Grantown-on-Spey *Mor* 94-95; Hon C Rothiemurchus 94-95; rtd 98; P-in-c Strathnairn St Paul *Mor* from 03. *St Paul's Parsonage, Croachy, Inverness IV2 6UB* Tel (01808) 521397 E-mail epmos@onetel.com

MOSS, Barbara Penelope. b 46. St Anne's Coll Ox BA66 MA70 Lon Univ BD97 Middx Univ MA00. EAMTC 95. **d** 97 **p** 98. NSM Leytonstone H Trin Harrow Green *Chelmsf* 97-00; C Cambridge Gt St Mary w St Mich *Ely* 00-05; P-in-c Gothenburg w Halmstad, Jönköping etc *Eur* from 05; Chapl Gothenburg Univ and Chalmers Univ of Tech from 05. *St Andrew's Church Flat, Norra Liden 15, 411-18 Gothenburg, Sweden* E-mail bar@barmoss.demon.co.uk *or* bpm23@cam.ac.uk

MOSS, The Very Revd Basil Stanley. b 18. Qu Coll Ox BA41 MA45. Linc Th Coll 42. **d** 43 **p** 44. C Leigh St Mary *Man* 43-45; Tutor Linc Th Coll 45-46; Sub-Warden 46-51; Tutor St Cath Cumberland Lodge 51-53; V Bris St Nath w St Kath *Bris* 53-60; Dioc Dir of Ords 56-66; Hon Can Bris Cathl 59-60 and 66-73; Can Res Bris Cathl 60-66; Chief Sec ACCM 66-73; Provost Birm 73-85; rtd 85; Perm to Offic *Worc* from 85 and *Birm* from 86. *c/o Mrs Margaret Manson, 92 Sefton Park Road, St Andrews, Bristol BS7 9AL*

MOSS (née BELL), Mrs Catherine Ann. b 63. Trin Coll Bris BA88. **d** 89 **p** 94. Par Dn Southsea St Jude *Portsm* 89-94; C 94-97; C Luton St Mary *St Alb* from 97; Chapl Luton Univ 97-02. *2 Saxtead Close, Luton LU2 9SQ* Tel (01582) 391125

MOSS, Christopher Ashley. b 52. Ex Univ BA73 Southn Univ DASS78 CQSW78. Wycliffe Hall Ox 89. **d** 91 **p** 92. C Malvern H Trin and St Jas *Worc* 91-96; V Longdon, Castlemorton, Bushley, Queenhill etc from 96. *The Vicarage, Longdon, Tewkesbury GL20 6AT* Tel and fax (01684) 833256 E-mail cmoss@holyplace.feeserve.co.uk

MOSS, David Glyn. b 62. St Anne's Coll Ox BA83 Em Coll Cam BA89. Westcott Ho Cam 87. **d** 90 **p** 91. C Halesowen *Worc* 90-93; Tutor St Steph Ho Ox 93-03; Vice-Prin 00-03; Dioc Tr Officer *Ex* 03-04; Prin SWMTC from 04. *South West Ministry*

Training Course, Haighton Building, St Luke's Campus, Heavitree Road, Exeter EX1 2LU Tel (01392) 264737 E-mail principal@swmtc.org.uk

MOSS, David Sefton. b 59. Sunderland Poly BSc80 Anglia Poly Univ MA05 MRPharmS81. Ridley Hall Cam 91. **d** 93 **p** 94. C Highworth w Sevenhampton and Inglesham etc *Bris* 93-97; V Bedminster St Mich from 97. *St Michael's Vicarage, 153 St John's Lane, Bedminster, Bristol BS3 5AE* Tel and fax 0117-977 6132 E-mail david.moss@iname.com

MOSS, Canon Denis. b 32. St Jo Coll Auckland LTh83. **d** 74 **p** 75. New Zealand 74-92; Chapl Budapest *Eur* from 92; Hon Can Malta Cathl from 01. *The Rectory, 2092 Budakeszi, Pf 25, Hungary* Tel (0036) (23) 452023

MOSS, James Wilfred. b 15. Oak Hill Th Coll 75. **d** 76 **p** 77. Hon C Frogmore *St Alb* 76-78 and 81-93; Hon C Watford St Luke 78-81; Perm to Offic from 93. *8A The Rise, Park Street, St Albans AL2 2NT* Tel (01727) 872467

MOSS, Preb Kenneth Charles. b 37. Imp Coll Lon BSc59 PhD62 DIC62 ARCS59. **d** 66 **p** 67. Canada 66-73; Chapl Ex Univ *Ex* 73-83; V St Marychurch 83-02; RD Ipplepen 87-93; Preb Ex Cathl from 92; rtd 02. *3 Mondeville Way, Northam, Bideford EX39 1DQ* Tel (01237) 422251

MOSS, The Ven Leonard Godfrey. b 32. K Coll Lon BD59 AKC59. **d** 60 **p** 61. C Putney St Marg *S'wark* 60-63; C Cheam 63-67; V Much Dewchurch w Llanwarne and Llandinabo *Heref* 67-72; Dioc Ecum Officer 69-83; V Marden w Amberley 72-80; V Marden w Amberley and Wisteston 80-84; P-in-c 92-94; Preb Heref Cathl 79-97; Can Heref Cathl 84-91; Dioc Soc Resp Officer 84-91; Adn Heref 91-97; rtd 97; Perm to Offic *Heref* from 97. *10 Saxon Way, Ledbury HR8 2QY* Tel (01531) 631195

MOSS, Leslie. **d** 02 **p** 03. OLM Ditton St Mich w St Thos *Liv* from 02. *105 Heath Road, Widnes WA8 7NU* Tel 0151-423 1100

MOSS, Mrs Nelva Elizabeth. b 44. Bp Grosseteste Coll TCert66 Sussex Univ BEd73. S Dios Minl Tr Scheme 90. **d** 93 **p** 94. NSM Bincombe w Broadwey, Upwey and Buckland Ripers *Sarum* 93-96; NSM Langtree *Ox* 96-98; TV from 98. *The Vicarage, Reading Road, Woodcote, Reading RG8 0QX* Tel (01491) 680979

MOSS, Peter Hextall. b 34. Clare Coll Cam BA59 MA62. Linc Th Coll 59. **d** 61 **p** 62. C Easington Colliery *Dur* 61-63; C Whickham 63-65; C-in-c Town End Farm CD 65-72; TV Mattishall *Nor* 72-75; P-in-c Welborne 75-84; P-in-c Mattishall w Mattishall Burgh 75-84; P-in-c Yaxham 80-84; TR Hempnall 84-89. *High House Cottage, Gunn Street, Foulsham, Dereham NR20 5RN* Tel (01362) 683823

MOSS, Peter John. b 41. K Coll Cam BA64 MA67. Westcott Ho Cam 63. **d** 84 **p** 85. Hon C Leighton Buzzard w Eggington, Hockliffe etc *St Alb* 84-93; NSM Luton St Sav 93-98; Hon C Houghton Regis 03-05; P-in-c Devizes St Pet *Sarum* from 05. *St Peter's Vicarage, Bath Road, Devizes SN10 2AP* Tel (01380) 722621

MOSS, Victor Charles. b 25. Oak Hill Th Coll BD65. **d** 66 **p** 67. C Macclesfield St Mich *Ches* 66-68; C Belper *Derby* 69-71; V Chesterfield Ch Ch 71-93; rtd 93; Perm to Offic *Derby* from 93. *16 Nether Croft Road, Brimington, Chesterfield S43 1QD* Tel (01246) 206260

MOSSE, Mrs Barbara Ann. b 51. CertEd73 Open Univ BA77 Univ of Wales (Lamp) MA99. CA Tr Coll IDC81 Lambeth STh83. **d** 90 **p** 95. CA 81-91; NSM Southbourne w W Thorney *Chich* 90-93; Community Mental Health Chapl Fareham/Gosport 94-97; NSM Purbrook *Portsm* 95-03; Team Chapl Portsm Hosps NHS Trust from 01; Asst Dioc Spirituality Adv *Portsm* from 05. *Drogo, 1 Grenfield Court, Emsworth PO10 7SA* Tel (01243) 376155 E-mail bamosse@aol.com

MOSSLEY, Iain Stephen. b 72. Univ of Wales (Ban) DipTh93 BTh94. St Steph Ho Ox 95. **d** 98 **p** 99. C Ribbleton *Blackb* 98-01; C Marton Moss 01-03; V Burnley St Matt w H Trin from 03. *St Matthew's Vicarage, Harriet Street, Burnley BB11 4JH* Tel (01282) 424839 E-mail father.iain@btinternet.com

MOSSMAN, Mrs Margaret. b 46. N Ord Course 97. **d** 00 **p** 01. NSM Beighton *Sheff* 00-02; C 02-04; V Owston from 04. *The Vicarage, 11 Crabgate Lane, Skellow, Doncaster DN6 8LE* Tel (01302) 337101

MOSSOP, Patrick John. b 48. Solicitor St Jo Coll Cam MA LLB. Linc Th Coll BTh93. **d** 93 **p** 94. C Halstead St Andr w H Trin and Greenstead Green *Chelmsf* 93-97; Assoc Chapl Essex Univ 97-99; Chapl 99-04; V Forest Gate Em w Upton Cross from 04. *Emmanuel Vicarage, 2B Margery Park Road, London E7 9JY* Tel (020) 8534 8780 *or* 8522 1900 E-mail pat.mos@btinternet.com

MOTE, Gregory Justin. b 60. Oak Hill Th Coll BA83. **d** 86 **p** 87. C W Ealing St Jo w St Jas *Lon* 86-90; C St Helen Bishopsgate w St Andr Undershaft etc 90-95; V Poulton Lancelyn H Trin *Ches* 96-04; Perm to Offic *Blackb* from 04. *1 Dunham Drive, Chorley PR6 7DN* Tel (01772) 423337 E-mail gjmote@aol.com

MOTH, Miss Susan. b 44. Leic Univ BA65 K Coll Lon CertEd66. Linc Th Coll 83. **dss** 85 **d** 87 **p** 94. Churchdown St Jo *Glouc* 85-93; C 87-93; Dn-in-c The Rissingtons 93-94; P-in-c 94-05; rtd 05. *19 Cunliffe Close, Oxford OX2 7BJ*

MOTHERSDALE, Paul John. b 52. N Ord Course 94. **d** 97 **p** 98. C Kirkleatham *York* 97-00; V Middlesbrough St Agnes from 00. *St Agnes' Vicarage, 1 Broughton Avenue, Middlesbrough TS4 3PX* Tel (01642) 323804 E-mail paulmothersdale@bigfoot.com

MOTHERSOLE, John Robert. b 25. Lon Univ MA99. Chich Th Coll. **d** 84 **p** 85. NSM Hayes St Anselm *Lon* 84-93; NSM Hayes St Edm 93-98; P-in-c St Mary Aldermary from 98. *116 Nestles Avenue, Hayes UB3 4QD* Tel (020) 8848 0626 E-mail john@stmaryaldermary.co.uk

MOTT, Julian Ward. b 52. Loughb Univ BSc77. Ripon Coll Cuddesdon 78. **d** 81 **p** 82. C Aylestone *Leic* 81-84; C Gt Ilford St Mary *Chelmsf* 84-88; R Chevington w Hargrave and Whepstead w Brockley *St E* 88-99; V Lower Gornal *Worc* from 99. *The Vicarage, Church Street, Lower Gornal, Dudley DY3 2PF* Tel (01902) 882023

MOTT, Peter John. b 49. Ch Coll Cam BA70 MA75 Dundee Univ PhD73 Nottm Univ BA79. St Jo Coll Nottm 77. **d** 80 **p** 81. C Hull St Jo Newland *York* 80-83; C Selly Park St Steph and St Wulstan *Birm* 83-87; C Mosbrough *Sheff* 87-92; R Colne St Bart *Blackb* 92-98; TV Colne and Villages 98-01; P-in-c Keighley St Andr *Bradf* from 01. *The Rectory, 13 Westview Grove, Keighley BD20 6JJ* Tel (01535) 601499 E-mail peter@mottp.freeserve.co.uk

✠**MOTTAHEDEH, The Rt Revd Iraj Kalimi.** b 32. United Th Coll Bangalore 56. **d** 59 **p** 60 **c** 86. C Isfahan St Luke Iran 59-62; V Shiraz St Simon 62-66; V Tehran St Paul 67-75; V Isfahan St Luke 75-83; Adn Iran 83-86; Asst Bp Iran 86-90; Bp Iran 90-02; Pres Bp Episc Ch Jerusalem and Middle E 00-02; rtd 02; Interim Bp Iran 02-04; Hon Asst Bp Birm from 05. *United College of the Ascension, Weoley Park Road, Birmingham B29 6RD* Tel 0121-415 6818 Fax 472 4320

MOTTERSHEAD, Derek. b 39. Open Univ BA74 BEd. Chich Th Coll 65. **d** 69 **p** 70. C Walthamstow St Barn and St Jas Gt *Chelmsf* 69-72; C Chelmsf All SS 72-77; P-in-c Cold Norton w Stow Maries 77-80; V Leytonstone St Andr 80-92; V Eastbourne St Sav and St Pet *Chich* 92-04; Miss to Seafarers 92-04; rtd 04; Perm to Offic *Cant* from 05. *Sherwood, 25B The Paddock, Spring Lane, Canterbury CT1 1SX* Tel (01227) 453118 E-mail de@dmotters.fsnet.co.uk

MOTTRAM, Andrew Peter. b 53. AKC77. Ripon Coll Cuddesdon 77. **d** 78 **p** 79. C E Bedfont *Lon* 78-81; C Bp's Hatfield *St Alb* 81-84; V Milton Ernest 84-91; V Thurleigh 84-91; P-in-c Heref All SS *Heref* from 91; RD Heref City 02-03. *10 St Barnabas Close, Hereford HR1 1EY* Tel (01432) 266588 Fax 344428 E-mail andrew.mottram@btinternet.com

MOTYER, John Alexander. b 24. TCD BA46 MA51 BD51 Lambeth DD97. Wycliffe Hall Ox 47. **d** 47 **p** 48. C Penn Fields *Lich* 47-50; C Bris H Trin *Bris* 51-54; Tutor Clifton Th Coll 51-54; Vice-Prin 54-65; Tutor Tyndale Hall Bris 52-54; V W Hampstead St Luke *Lon* 65-70; Dep Prin Tyndale Hall Bris 70-71; Prin and Dean Trin Coll Bris 71-81; Min Westbourne Ch Ch Prop Chpl *Win* 81-89; rtd 89; Perm to Offic *Ex* from 90. *10 Littlefield, Bishopsteignton, Teignmouth TQ14 9SG* Tel (01626) 770986

MOTYER, Stephen. b 50. Pemb Coll Cam BA73 MA77 Bris Univ MLitt79 K Coll Lon PhD93. Trin Coll Bris 73. **d** 76 **p** 77. Lect Oak Hill Th Coll 76-83; C Braughing, Lt Hadham, Albury, Furneux Pelham etc *St Alb* 83-87; Lect Lon Bible Coll from 87; Perm to Offic *Lon* and *St Alb* from 87. *7 Hangar Ruding, Watford WD19 5BH* Tel (020) 8386 6829 *or* (01923) 826061 E-mail s.motyer@londonbiblecollege.ac.uk

MOUGHTIN, Ross. b 48. St Cath Coll Cam BA70 St Jo Coll Dur BA75. **d** 76 **p** 77. C Litherland St Paul Hatton Hill *Liv* 76-79; C Heswall *Ches* 79-84; Chapl Edw Unit Rochdale Infirmary 83-92; V Thornham w Gravel Hole *Man* 84-92; V Aughton Ch Ch *Liv* from 92; Chapl W Lancashire NHS Trust from 94. *Christ Church Vicarage, 22 Long Lane, Aughton, Ormskirk L39 5AT* Tel (01695) 422175 E-mail ross.moughtin@lineone.net

MOUL, Russell Derek. b 56. Reading Univ BA83. Oak Hill Th Coll DipTh99. **d** 99 **p** 00. C Harold Wood *Chelmsf* 99-02; C Harold Hill St Paul 02-03; V from 03. *St Paul's Vicarage, Redcar Road, Romford RM3 9PT* Tel (01708) 341225 E-mail russell@themouls.fslife.co.uk

MOULAND, Norman Francis. b 38. OLM course 98. **d** 99 **p** 00. OLM Verwood *Sarum* from 99. *13 Park Drive, Verwood BH31 7PE* Tel (01202) 825320

MOULD, Mrs Jacqueline. b 66. QUB BD88. CITC BTh91. **d** 91 **p** 92. C Belfast St Aid *Conn* 91-94; C Drumragh w Mountfield *D & R* 94-96; NSM Kinson *Sarum* 97-00; C Belvoir *D & D* from 03. *10A Ballyclough Road, Lisburn BT28 3UY* Tel (028) 9264 7912

MOULD, James Michael. b 46. SEITE 95. **d** 98 **p** 99. NSM Wallington H Trin *S'wark* 98-03; NSM W Wittering and Birdham w Itchenor *Chich* from 03. *Quinneys, Itchenor Road, Itchenor, Chichester PO20 7DD* Tel (01243) 513600 E-mail james_pauline@btinternet.com

MOULD, Jeremy James. b 63. Nottm Univ BA85 TCD BTh91. CITC 88. **d** 91 **p** 92. C Mossley *Conn* 91-94; C Drumragh w

Mountfield *D & R* 94-96; C Kinson *Sarum* 97-00. *10A Ballyclough Road, Lisburn BT28 3UY* Tel (028) 9264 7912

MOULDER, John William Michael Cornock. b 39. City of Lon Poly ACIB67. Glouc Sch of Min 82. **d** 86 **p** 86. C Broken Hill Australia 86-88; P-in-c Berrigan 88-94; P-in-c Edenhope 94-98; C Tividale *Lich* 98-01; P-in-c W Bromwich St Pet 01-04; rtd 04; Hon Asst P Cobram Australia from 04. *Goldwick, 130 Jerilderie Street, Berrigan, NSW, Australia 2712* Tel and fax (0061) (3) 5885 2913 E-mail fatherm@dragnet.com.au

MOULDER, Kenneth. b 53. Lon Univ BEd75. Ridley Hall Cam 78. **d** 81 **p** 82. C Harold Wood *Chelmsf* 81-84; C Darfield *Sheff* 84-88; V Walkergate *Newc* 88-92; P-in-c Byker St Mark 90-92; V Byker St Mark and Walkergate St Oswald from 92. *St Oswald's Parsonage, Woodhead Road, Newcastle upon Tyne NE6 4RX* Tel 0191-263 6249

MOULE, Prof Charles Francis Digby. b 08. CBE85. FBA66 Em Coll Cam BA31 MA34 St Andr Univ Hon DD58 Cam Univ Hon DD88. Ridley Hall Cam 31. **d** 33 **p** 34. C Cambridge St Mark *Ely* 33-34; Tutor Ridley Hall Cam 33-34; C Rugby St Andr *Cov* 34-36; C Cambridge Gt St Mary w St Mich *Ely* 36-40; Vice-Prin Ridley Hall Cam 36-44; Dean Clare Coll Cam 44-51; Fell from 44; Select Preacher Cam Univ 42, 48 and 53; Select Preacher Ox Univ 54 and 73; Lect Div Cam Univ 47-51; Lady Marg Prof Div Cam Univ 51-76; Can Th Leic Cathl *Leic* 55-76; rtd 76; Perm to Offic *Chich* from 81. *The Old Vicarage, Leigh, Sherborne DT9 6HL*

MOULT, Jane Elizabeth Kate. b 61. Trin Coll Bris 91. **d** 94 **p** 95. C St Jo in Bedwardine *Worc* 94-97; NSM Bilton *Cov* 97-99; Chapl Staunton Harold Hosp 00; Chapl Leics Partnership NHS Trust 01-05. *Address temp unknown*

MOULT, Simon Paul. b 66. Trin Coll Bris BA94. **d** 94 **p** 95. C St Jo in Bedwardine *Worc* 94-97; C Bilton *Cov* 97-99; P-in-c Thringstone St Andr *Leic* 99-05; RD Akeley S 03-05; Chapl N Warks NHS Trust from 05; Chapl Geo Eliot Hosp NHS Trust Nuneaton from 05. *The Chaplaincy, George Eliot Hospital, College Street, Nuneaton CV10 7DJ* Tel (024) 7686 5046 *or* 7635 1351

MOULTON, Paul Oliver. b 43. BSc. N Ord Course 77. **d** 80 **p** 81. C Wilmslow *Ches* 80-85; V Knutsford St Cross 85-92; Chapl Mary Dendy Hosp Knutsford 86-92; V Gatley *Ches* 92-01; Chapl Cen Man Healthcare NHS Trust 92-01; P-in-c Capesthorne w Siddington and Marton *Ches* from 01. *The Vicarage, School Lane, Marton, Macclesfield SK11 9HD* Tel (01260) 224447

MOUNCER, David Peter. b 65. Univ of Wales (Abth) BA86. Oak Hill Th Coll BA94. **d** 94 **p** 95. C Foord St Jo *Cant* 94-98; Min Grove Green LEP 98-03; P-in-c Brampton St Thos *Derby* from 03. *674 Chatsworth Road, Chesterfield S40 3NU* Tel (01246) 567634

MOUNSEY, William Lawrence Fraser. b 51. St Andr Univ BD75. Edin Th Coll 76. **d** 78 **p** 79. C Edin St Mark *Edin* 78-81; Chapl RAF 81-90 and from 02; R Dalmahoy and Chapl Heriot-Watt Univ *Edin* 90-96; Perm to Offic *Edin* and *St And* from 02. *Chaplaincy Services (RAF), HQ, Personnel and Training Command, RAF Innsworth, Gloucester GL3 1EZ* Tel (01452) 712612 ext 5164 Fax 510828

MOUNSTEPHEN, Philip Ian. b 59. Southn Univ BA80 Magd Coll Ox MA87 PGCE. Wycliffe Hall Ox 85. **d** 88 **p** 89. C Gerrards Cross and Fulmer *Ox* 88-92; V W Streatham St Jas *S'wark* 92-98; Hd Pathfinders CPAS 98-02; Dir CY Network 01-02; Hd Min from 02; Dep Gen Dir from 04; Perm to Offic *Cov* and *Glouc* from 99. *CPAS, Athena Drive, Tachbrook Park, Warwick CV34 6NG* Tel (01926) 458446 E-mail philip@cpas.org.uk

MOUNT, Canon Judith Mary. b 35. Bedf Coll Lon BA56 Lon Univ CertEd57. Ripon Coll Cuddesdon 81. **dss** 83 **d** 87 **p** 94. Carterton *Ox* 83-85; Charlton on Otmoor and Oddington 85-87; Dioc Lay Min Adv and Asst Dir of Ords 86-89; Par Dn Islip w Charlton on Otmoor, Oddington, Noke etc 87-94; C 94-95; Assoc Dioc Dir Ords and Adv for Women in Ord Min 89-95; Hon Can Ch Ch 92-95; rtd 95; Hon C Shill Valley and Broadshire *Ox* from 95; Perm to Offic *Glouc* from 99. *The Owl House, Bell Lane, Poulton, Cirencester GL7 5JF* Tel (01285) 850242

MOUNTFORD, Canon Brian Wakling. b 45. Newc Univ BA66 Cam Univ MA73 Ox Univ MA90. Westcott Ho Cam 66. **d** 68 **p** 69. C Westmr St Steph w St Jo *Lon* 68-69; C Paddington Ch Ch 69-73; Chapl SS Coll Cam 73-78; V Southgate Ch Ch *Lon* 78-86; V Ox St Mary V w St Cross and St Pet *Ox* from 86; Chapl St Hilda's Coll Ox from 89; Hon Can Ch Ch *Ox* from 98. *9A Norham Gardens, Oxford OX2 6PS* Tel (01865) 515778 *or* 279111 E-mail brian.mountford@oriel.ox.ac.uk

MOUNTFORD, Ian David. b 65. St Jo Coll Nottm BTh93. **d** 96 **p** 97. C Chilwell *S'well* 96-00; TV Thame *Ox* from 00. *22 Stuart Way, Thame OX9 3WP* Tel (01844) 216508 E-mail mounty@fish.co.uk

MOUNTNEY, Frederick Hugh. b 14. St Chad's Coll Dur BA36 MA39. Lich Th Coll 36. **d** 37 **p** 38. C Beighton *Derby* 37-39; C Spondon 39-40; C Byker St Laur *Newc* 40-44; Backworth St Jo 44-48; V N Gosforth 48-51; R Lillingstone Dayrell w Lillingstone Lovell *Ox* 51-56; V Heref All SS *Heref* 56-75; Chapl Victoria Eye Hosp Heref 56-75; Dioc Ecum Officer 63-69; Chapl Bonn w Cologne *Eur* 75-79; rtd 79; Perm to Offic *Heref* 79-90; *Nor* 82-00; *St E* 82-02; *Eur* 90-02. *19 Woodsteads, Embleton, Alnwick NE66 3XY* Tel (01655) 576075

MOUNTNEY, John Michael. b 47. St Chad's Coll Dur BA69 MA84. Cuddesdon Coll 69. **d** 71 **p** 72. C Morpeth *Newc* 71-75; C Longbenton St Bart 75-77; Sub-Warden Community of All Hallows Ditchingham 77-83; R Blundeston w Flixton and Lound *Nor* 83-87; TR Nor St Pet Parmentergate w St Jo 87-93; Warden Julian Shrine 87-93; V Embleton w Rennington and Rock *Newc* from 93. *The Vicarage, Embleton, Alnwick NE66 3UW* Tel (01665) 576660

MOURANT, Julia Caroline. b 58. Sheff Univ BA79. St Jo Coll Nottm DPS84. **dss** 84 **d** 92 **p** 94. Cropwell Bishop w Colston Bassett, Granby etc *S'well* 84-86; Marple All SS *Ches* 86-89; Harlow St Mary and St Hugh w St Jo the Bapt *Chelmsf* 89-92; NSM from 92; Asst Dir of Min 98-04; CME Officer 00-02. *The Vicarage, 2 Bursledon Road, Southampton SO19 7LW* Tel (023) 8043 7949

MOURANT, Sidney Eric. b 39. Lon Univ BD73. Oak Hill Th Coll. **d** 89 **p** 90. C Oxton *Ches* 89-92; V Douglas All SS and St Thos *S & M* 92-96; I Rathkeale w Askeaton, Kilcornan and Kilnaughtin *L & K* 96-00; I Nenagh 00-04; rtd 04. *12 Breezemount, Hamiltonsbawn, Armagh BT61 9SB* Tel (00353) (48) 3887 2203 Mobile 87-239 9785 E-mail sid@sidneymourant.wanadoo.co.uk

MOURANT, Stephen Philip Edward. b 54. Nottm Univ BTh83. St Jo Coll Nottm. **d** 83 **p** 84. C Cropwell Bishop w Colston Bassett, Granby etc *S'well* 83-86; C Marple All SS *Ches* 86-89; P-in-c Harlow St Mary and St Hugh w St Jo the Bapt *Chelmsf* 89-90; V 90-04; P-in-c Bitterne *Win* from 04. *The Vicarage, 2 Bursledon Road, Southampton SO19 7LW* Tel (023) 8043 7949 *or* 8044 6488

MOUSIR-HARRISON, Stuart Nicholas. b 68. SW Poly Plymouth BSc89 Nottm Univ MSc92 St Martin's Coll Lanc PhD99 St Jo Coll Dur BA99. Cranmer Hall Dur. **d** 00 **p** 01. C Oadby *Leic* 00-03; C W Malling w Offham *Roch* from 03; C Mereworth w W Peckham from 03. *19 Worcester Avenue, Kings Hill, West Malling ME19 4FL* Tel (01732) 870785 E-mail rev.moose@mousir.org

MOVERLEY, Ruth Elaine. b 55. K Alfred's Coll Win CertEd76. St Mich Coll Llan. **d** 90 **p** 97. C Llangynwyd w Maesteg *Llan* 90-95; C Glan Ely 95-97; V Llanharan w Peterston-super-Montem 97-05; V Tonyrefail w Gilfach Goch from 05. *The Vicarage, High Street, Tonyrefail, Porth CF39 8PL* Tel (01443) 670330

MOWAT, Robert Alexander Laird (Sandy). b 50. CD80 and Bar 90. Univ Coll of Em and St Chad Saskatoon BTh96. **d** 96 **p** 96. C Saskatchewan Gateway Canada 96-01; P-in-c Kinnerley w Melverley and Knockin w Maesbrook *Lich* from 01. *The Rectory, Vicarage Lane, Kinnerley, Oswestry SY10 8DE* Tel (01691) 682233 E-mail smowat@sk.sympatico.ca

MOWBRAY, David. b 38. Fitzw Ho Cam BA60 MA64 Lon Univ BD62. Clifton Th Coll. **d** 63 **p** 64. C Northampton St Giles *Pet* 63-66; Lect Watford St Mary *St Alb* 66-70; V Broxbourne 70-77; R Broxbourne w Wormley 77-84; V Hertford All SS 84-91; V Darley Abbey *Derby* 91-03; Asst Chapl Derby R Infirmary 91-94; Chapl S Derbyshire Community and Mental Health Trust 99-03; rtd 03. *Blackbird Cottage, 169 Newport, Lincoln LN1 3DZ* Tel (01522) 546753

MOWBRAY, James Edward. b 78. Univ of Wales (Abth) BTh00 Leeds Univ BA03. Coll of Resurr Mirfield 01. **d** 03 **p** 04. C Perry Street *Roch* from 03. *6 Dene Holm Road, Northfleet, Gravesend DA11 8LE* Tel (01474) 332652

MOWBRAY, Ms Jill Valerie. b 54. Sussex Univ BEd76 Lon Inst of Educn MA86 Anglia Poly Univ MA01. Ridley Hall Cam 99. **d** 01 **p** 02. C Tufnell Park St Geo and All SS *Lon* 01-04; V Whitton SS Phil and Jas from 04. *The Vicarage, 205 Kneller Road, Twickenham TW2 7DY* Tel (020) 8894 1932 Mobile 07761-236910 E-mail jill.mowbray@virgin.net

MOWER, Miss Marguerite Mary. b 36. Bris Univ BA57. Cant Sch of Min 90. **d** 93 **p** 94. NSM Eythorne and Elvington w Waldershare etc *Cant* 93-03; NSM Harden and Wilsden *Bradf* from 04; NSM Denholme from 04. *3 Burnholme, Regency Gardens, Denholme, Bradford BD13 4NJ*

MOWFORTH, Mark. b 64. Reading Univ BSc86. Trin Coll Bris 93. **d** 96 **p** 97. C Buckingham *Ox* 96-98; C High Wycombe 98-03; P-in-c Prestwood and Gt Hampden from 03. *The Rectory, 140 Wycombe Road, Prestwood, Great Missenden HP16 0HJ* Tel (01494) 862130

MOWLL, John William Rutley. b 42. Sarum Th Coll 63. **d** 66 **p** 67. C Oughtibridge *Sheff* 66-69; C Hill *Birm* 69-73; Ind Chapl and V Upper Arley *Worc* 73-78; P-in-c Upton Snodsbury and Broughton Hackett etc 78-81; R 81-83; V Boughton under Blean w Dunkirk *Cant* 83-89; V Boughton under Blean w Dunkirk and Hernhill from 89; RD Ospringe 95-01; Hon Min Can Cant Cathl from 96; Chapl to The Queen from 00. *The Vicarage, 101 The*

Street, Boughton-under-Blean, Faversham ME13 9BG Tel (01227) 751410

MOXLEY, Mrs Elizabeth Jane. b 52. St Jo Coll Nottm. **d** 05. C Aston Clinton w Buckland and Drayton Beauchamp *Ox* from 05. *21 Dean Way, Aston Clinton, Aylesbury HP22 5GB* E-mail elizabethmoxley@hotmail.com

MOXON, John. **d** 02 **p** 03. NSM Birm St Luke *Birm* 02-04. *41 Mariner Avenue, Birmingham B16 9DF* Tel 0121-456 1628 *or* 472 0726 Mobile 07887-573122 E-mail john.moxon@birminghamchristiancollege.ac.uk

MOXON, Michael Anthony. b 42. LVO98. Lon Univ BD78 MA96. Sarum Th Coll 67. **d** 70 **p** 71. C Kirkley *Nor* 70-74; Min Can St Paul's Cathl *Lon* 74-81; Sacr 77-81; Warden Coll of Min Canons 79-81; V Tewkesbury w Walton Cardiff *Glouc* 81-90; Chapl to The Queen 86-98; Can Windsor 90-98; Chapl in Windsor Gt Park 90-98; Dean Truro 98-04; R Truro St Mary 98-04; Chapl Cornwall Fire Brigade HQ 98-04; rtd 05. *c/o Crockford, Church House, Great Smith Street, London SW1P 3NZ* Tel 07745-120453 (mobile)

MOY, Mrs Joy Patricia. b 35. Cant Sch of Min 87. **d** 90 **p** 94. NSM Cranbrook *Cant* 90-96; Perm to Offic *Win* 96-02. *16 Hillside Avenue, Purley CR8 2DP*

MOY, Richard John. b 78. St Cath Coll Cam BA99. Trin Coll Bris MA03. **d** 04 **p** 05. C Wolverhampton St Jude *Lich* from 04. *21 St Jude's Road, Wolverhampton WV6 0EB* Tel 07811-336910 (mobile) E-mail notintheratrace@yahoo.co.uk

MOYES (née WATSON), Mrs Stephanie Abigail. b 61. Heriot-Watt Univ BA84 Dur Univ CCSk90. Cranmer Hall Dur 86. **d** 90 **p** 94. C Bishop's Castle w Mainstone *Heref* 90-93; Dep Chapl HM Pris Dur 93-95; Chapl HM Rem Cen Low Newton 95-98; V Chilton and Cornforth *Dur* 98-02; Chapl Wrekin Coll Telford 02-04; Perm to Offic *Worc* from 04. *7 Birchanger Green, Worcester WR4 0DW* Tel (01905) 619181

MOYNAGH, David Kenneth. b 46. LRCP70 MRCS70 MRCGP76 Lon Univ MB, BS70. S Dios Minl Tr Scheme 88. **d** 91 **p** 92. NSM Ore *Chich* 91-99; Perm to Offic *Win* from 01. *White Cottage, Jordan's Lane, Sway, Lymington SO41 6AR* Tel (01590) 682475

MOYNAGH, Michael Digby. b 50. Southn Univ BA73 Lon Univ MA74 Aus Nat Univ PhD78 Bris Univ MA85. Trin Coll Bris. **d** 85 **p** 86. C Northwood Em *Lon* 85-89; P-in-c Wilton *B & W* 89-90; TR 90-96; Dir Cen for Futures Studies St Jo Coll Nottm 96-04; Co-Dir Tomorrow Project from 04. *Templeton College, Oxford OX1 5NY* Tel (01865) 422713 E-mail michael.moynagh@templeton.ox.ac.uk

MOYNAN, Canon David George. b 53. DipTh. **d** 86 **p** 87. C Seagoe *D & D* 86-88; C Taney *D & G* 88-89; I Arklow w Inch and Kilbride 89-94; Dioc Stewardship Adv from 92; Dioc Ch of Ireland Bps' Appeal Rep from 92; I Kilternan from 94; Dioc Dir for Decade of Evang from 96; Can Ch Ch Cathl Dublin from 97. *The Rectory, Kilternan, Co Dublin, Irish Republic* Tel and fax (00353) (1) 295 5603 *or* tel 295 2643 E-mail moynandg@iol.ie

MOYNAN, William John. b 20. TCD BA44. **d** 44 **p** 45. C Chapelizod *D & G* 44-49; C Dublin Drumcondra w N Strand 49-56; Clerical V Ch Ch Cathl Dublin 52-56; I Portarlington w Cloneyhurke, Ballykeane and Lea *M & K* 56-63; I Donabate w Lusk *D & G* 63-68; I Swords w Donabate and Kilsallaghan 68-90; Can Ch Ch Cathl Dublin 83-90; rtd 90. *Briarwood, Ballycarnane, Tramore, Waterford, Irish Republic* Tel (00353) (51) 390199

MOYSE, Mrs Pauline Patricia. b 42. Ex Univ CertEd62. S Dios Minl Tr Scheme 88. **d** 91 **p** 94. Hon C Fleet *Guildf* 91-92; C 93-97; Chapl Farnborough Coll of Tech 96-97; P-in-c Stoneleigh *Guildf* 97-02; Warden of Readers from 97; Dioc Adv Lay Min from 01. *Beechend, 2 Hillcrest, Fleet GU51 4PZ* Tel (01252) 671382 E-mail moyseadpp@aol.com

✠MPALANYI-NKOYOYO, The Rt Revd Livingstone. b 37. **d** 69 **p** 70 **c** 80. Kasubi 69-75; Nsangi 75-77; Adn Namirembe 77-79; Suff Bp 80-81; Suff Bp Mukono 81-94; Abp Uganda and Bp Kampala 94-02; rtd 02. *Address temp unknown* E-mail couab@uol.co.ug

MPUNZI, Nduna Ananias. b 46. Federal Th Coll S Africa 69. **d** 71 **p** 72. C Galeshewe St Jas S Africa 71-74; C Taung 74-75; C Vaal Hartz 75-77; R Vryburg St Phil 77-78; Lic to Offic *Glas* 82-84; C Bilston *Lich* 84-86; TV 86-90; P-in-c Walsall St Mary and All SS Palfrey 90-97; P-in-c Caldmore 90-93; P-in-c Shobnall 02-04; TV Worc St Barn w Ch Ch *Worc* from 04. *214 Tolladine Road, Worcester WR4 9AU* Tel (01905) 734614

✠MTETEMELA, The Most Revd Donald Leo. b 47. St Phil Th Coll Kongwa Wycliffe Hall Ox 75. **p** 71 **c** 82. Asst Bp Cen Tanganyika 82-90; Bp Ruaha from 90; Abp Tanzania from 98. *Box 1028, Iringa, Tanzania* Tel (00255) (262) 270 1211 Fax 702479 E-mail ruaha@maf.or.tz

MUDD, Mrs Linda Anne. b 59. WMMTC 00. **d** 03 **p** 04. C Exhall *Cov* from 03. *St Giles House, 222 Coventry Road, Exhall, Coventry CV7 9BH* Tel (024) 7631 1582 E-mail muddie@mudda.freeserve.co.uk

MUDDIMAN, John Bernard. b 47. Keble Coll Ox BA67 MA72 DPhil76 Selw Coll Cam BA71 MA75. Westcott Ho Cam 69. **d** 72 **p** 73. Hon C Ox St Giles *Ox* 72-83; Chapl New Coll Ox 72-76; Tutor St Steph Ho Ox 76-83; Vice-Prin 80-83; Lect Th Nottm Univ 83-90; Fell Mansf Coll Ox from 90; Chapl from 97; Lic to Offic *Ox* 90-02; NSM Littlemore from 97. *Mansfield College, Oxford OX1 3TF* Tel (01865) 270999 E-mail john.muddiman@mansfield.ox.ac.uk

MUDGE, Frederick Alfred George. b 31. Leeds Univ BSc58 Univ of Wales BD67. St Mich Coll Llan 58. **d** 61 **p** 62. C Cwmavon *Llan* 61-64; PV Llan Cathl 64-70; R Llandough w Leckwith 70-88; V Penarth All SS 88-96; rtd 96. *Pathways, 6 Fairwater Road, Llandaff, Cardiff CF5 2LD*

MUDIE, Martin Bruce. b 54. Goldsmiths' Coll Lon BA76. Sarum & Wells Th Coll 92. **d** 92 **p** 93. C Bromley St Mark *Roch* 92-95; rtd 95; Perm to Offic *B & W* 02-03; Hon C Glastonbury w Meare from 03. *20 Oriel Road, Street BA16 0JL* Tel (01458) 448034

MUELLER-SCHNURR, Mrs Jutta. b 71. Bayreuth Th Sem 97. **d** 97 **p** 02. In Lutheran Ch Germany 97-02; Chapl (Asst) Bris Univ *Bris* from 02. *12 St Paul's Road, Clifton, Bristol BS8 1LR* Tel 0117-973 3963 Fax 954 6602 E-mail jutta.mueller-schnurr@bris.ac.uk

MUFFETT, Mrs Sarah Susan. b 53. STETS 02. **d** 05. NSM Okeford *Sarum* from 05. *Prides Cottage, High Street, Child Okeford, Blandford Forum DT11 8EH* Tel (01258) 860010 E-mail sarahmuffett@btopenworld.com

MUGAN, Miriam Ruth. b 56. RNMH77. Oak Hill Th Coll 93. **d** 96 **p** 97. NSM St Alb St Sav *St Alb* from 96. *137 Kings Road, London Colney, St Albans AL2 1ER* Tel (01727) 825971 E-mail miriam.mugan@btopenworld.com

MUGGLETON, James. b 55. Bris Univ BA80. Chich Th Coll 81 EAMTC 99. **d** 01 **p** 02. NSM E Leightonstone *Ely* 01-03; C 03-04; C Buckworth and Alconbury w Alconbury Weston 04; R Barney, Fulmodeston w Croxton, Hindringham etc *Nor* from 04. *The Rectory, The Street, Hindringham, Fakenham NR21 0AA* Tel (01328) 878159

MUGGLETON, Major George. b 25. Chich Th Coll 55. **d** 57 **p** 58. C Oldham St Mary *Man* 57-59; C Ashton St Mich 59-61; V Croydon H Trin *Cant* 61-68; R Stisted *Chelmsf* 68-69; P-in-c Pattiswick 68-69; P-in-c Bradwell 68-69; R Stisted w Bradwell and Pattiswick 69-87; rtd 87. *Curvalion House, Creech St Michael, Taunton TA3 5QF* Tel (01823) 443842

MUGRIDGE, Mrs Gloria Janet. b 45. R Holloway Coll Lon BA66 Bedf Coll Lon DipSS67. S Dios Minl Tr Scheme 92. **d** 95 **p** 96. NSM Dorchester *Sarum* 95-97; Asst Chapl Weymouth Coll 95-97; Chapl 97-04; NSM Melbury *Sarum* 97-02; NSM Stour Vale from 04. *63 Syward Close, Dorchester DT1 2AN* Tel (01305) 269203 E-mail janetmug@aol.com

MUIR, David Murray. b 49. Glas Univ MA70 Nottm Univ BA72. St Jo Coll Nottm 70. **d** 76 **p** 77. C Fulham St Mary N End *Lon* 76-80; C Aspley *S'well* 80; India 81-85; Dir Ext Studies St Jo Coll Nottm 85-02; C Upton (Overchurch) *Ches* 02-04; Adult Educn and Par Development Adv *Ex* from 04. *25 Southernhay East, Exeter EX1 1QP* Tel (01392) 685041 E-mail david.muir@exeter.anglican.org

MUIR, David Trevor. b 49. TCD MA MLitt93. CITC 75. **d** 78 **p** 79. C Dublin Clontarf *D & G* 78-80; C Monkstown St Mary 80-83; I Kilternan 83-94; I Delgany 94-97; Can Ch Ch Cathl Dublin 95-97; Chapl to Ch of Ireland Assn of Deaf People from 97. *Luogh North, Doolin, Co Clare, Irish Republic* Tel (00353) (65) 707 4778 Fax 707 4871

MUIR, John William. b 38. Dur Univ BA59 Mansf Coll Ox MA65. Chich Th Coll 78. **d** 78 **p** 79. In Congr Ch 62-70; United Ch of Zambia 70-78; C Brighouse *Wakef* 78-80; V Northowram 80-87; V Sowerby 87-01; rtd 01; Perm to Offic *Wakef* from 02. *8 Whitley Drive, Holmfield, Halifax HX2 9SJ* Tel (01422) 244163 Mobile 07733-152089 E-mail jmuir@msn.com

MUKHERJEE (or MUKHOPADHYAY), Supriyo. b 42. Calcutta Univ BA70 Serampore Th Coll BD76 Derby Univ MA97. Bp's Coll Calcutta 70. **d** 75 **p** 76. India 75-91; C Crook *Dur* 91-92; V Nelson in Lt Marsden *Blackb* 92-95; Dioc Community Relns Officer *Cov* 95-02; TV Cov E 95-02; rtd 02; Perm to Offic *Cov* from 02. *16 Nunts Lane, Coventry CV6 4HB* Tel (024) 7636 3064 E-mail samukh@lineone.net

MUKHOLI, Eshuchi Patrick. b 60. Nairobi Univ BSc86. Nairobi Evang Graduate Sch of Th MDiv98. **d** 98 **p** 99. Dioc Youth Adv Mombasa Kenya 98-02; Dioc Miss and Communications Officer 99-02; Chapl St Aug Prep Sch 99-02; NSM Blackbird Leys *Ox* from 02. *88 Blackbird Leys Road, Oxford OX4 6HS* Tel (01865) 748284 Mobile 07781-489070 E-mail pmukholi@yahoo.com

MULCAHY, Richard Patrick. b 67. SW Poly Plymouth BSc90. St Mich Coll Llan 02. **d** 05. NSM Bassaleg *Mon* from 05. *9 High Cross Drive, Rogerstone, Newport NP10 9AB* Tel (01633) 894641 E-mail richard-mulcahy@ntlworld.com

MULHOLLAND, Nicholas Christopher John. b 44. Chich Th Coll 77. **d** 79 **p** 80. C Thornbury *Glouc* 79-83; R Boxwell, Leighterton, Didmarton, Oldbury etc from 83; RD Tetbury 00-03. *The Vicarage, Badminton GL9 1ET* Tel (01454) 218427

MULKERN, Richard Neville. b 39. S'wark Ord Course 88. **d** 91 **p** 92. NSM Leytonstone St Andr *Chelmsf* 91-93; Min Sec and Welfare Officer Miss to Seamen 91-93; Welfare Sec 93-94; Dir N

Region 94-00; Perm to Offic *Wakef* from 93; NSM Oulton w Woodlesford *Ripon* 96-99; rtd 00. *120 Norwood Road, Birkby, Huddersfield HD2 2XX* Tel (01484) 480864

MULLALLY, Dame Sarah Elisabeth. b 62. DBE05. S Bank Univ BSc84 MSc92 Bournemouth Univ Hon DSc01 RGN84. SEITE 98. **d** 01 **p** 02. C Battersea Fields *S'wark* from 01. *11 Cupar Road, London SW11 4JW* Tel (020) 7622 4925

MULLANEY, Mrs Jane Megan. b 48. Kingston Poly BA72. **d** 04 **p** 05. OLM Kenilworth St Jo *Cov* from 04. *5 Knightlow Close, Kenilworth CV8 2PX* Tel (01926) 850723 E-mail jane_m_mullaney@tiscali.co.uk

MULLARD, George Edward. b 14. St D Coll Lamp BA38 Sarum Th Coll 38. **d** 39 **p** 40. C Hartland and Welcombe *Ex* 39-42; C Plymouth St Gabr 42-45; C Northam 45-48; V E Coker *B & W* 48-69; V E Coker w Sutton Bingham 69-79; rtd 79; Perm to Offic *B & W* from 79. *Alvington Cottage, Brympton, Yeovil BA22 8TH* Tel (01935) 471752

MULLEN, Charles William. b 64. CITC BTh92. **d** 92 **p** 93. C Lecale Gp *D & D* 92-95; I Gorey w Kilnahue, Leskinfere and Ballycanew *C & O* 95-00; Dean's V St Patr Cathl Dublin from 00. *St Kevin's Rectory, 258 South Circular Road, Dublin 8, Irish Republic* Tel (00353) (1) 453 9472 Mobile 87-261 8878 E-mail deansvicar@stpatrickscathedral.ie

MULLEN, Peter John. b 42. Liv Univ BA70 Middx Univ PhD00. St Aid Birkenhead 66. **d** 70 **p** 71. C Manston *Ripon* 70-72; C Stretford All SS *Man* 72-73; C Oldham St Mary w St Pet 73-74; Lic to Offic 74-77; V Tockwith and Bilton w Bickerton *York* 77-89; Perm to Offic 97-98; P-in-c St Mich Cornhill w St Pet le Poer etc *Lon* from 98; P-in-c St Sepulchre w Ch Ch Greyfriars etc from 98; Chapl City Inst Stock Exchange from 98. *The Watch House, Giltspur Street, London EC1A 9DE* Tel and fax (020) 7248 3826 E-mail citychurches@pmullen.freeserve.co.uk

MULLENGER, William. b 44. Linc Th Coll 68. **d** 69 **p** 70. C Clapham St Jo *S'wark* 69-73; C Hook 73-81; P-in-c Camberwell St Phil and St Mark 81-85; V Hackbridge and N Beddington 85-93; rtd 93; Perm to Offic *Roch* from 93. *30 Constance Crescent, Bromley BR2 7QJ*

MULLER, Anton Michael. b 61. **d** 99 **p** 00. C Sandgate St Paul w Folkestone St Geo *Cant* 99-03; TV Penrith w Newton Reigny and Plumpton Wall *Carl* 03-04; P-in-c Dacre 03-04; Chapl N Cumbria Mental Health NHS Trust 03-04. *Address temp unknown* E-mail amulleruk@aol.com

MULLER, Vernon. b 40. Natal Univ BA61 Birm Univ MPhil93. St Chad's Coll Dur. **d** 64 **p** 65. S Africa 64-76; C Durban N St Martin 64-68; R Queensburgh 68-76; Chapl Friern Hosp Lon 77-91; Chapl R Berks Hosp Reading 91-95; Chapl Battle Hosp Reading 91-95; Perm to Offic *Chelmsf* from 95. *8 Ruskin Road, Chelmsford CM2 6HN* Tel (01245) 345865

MULLER, Wolfgang Wilhelm Bernard Heinrich Paul. b 28. ALCD54. **d** 55 **p** 56. C Tonbridge SS Pet and Paul *Roch* 55-56; C Chatham St Steph 56-59; C-in-c Wigmore w Hempstead CD 59-65; V Wigmore w Hempstead 65-72; V S Gillingham 72-73; W Germany 73-90; Germany from 90; rtd 93. *Auf der Mauer 7, 34431 Marsberg, Germany*

MULLETT, John St Hilary. b 25. St Cath Coll Cam BA47 MA49. Linc Th Coll. **d** 50 **p** 51. C Tottenham All Hallows *Lon* 50-52; R Que Que S Rhodesia 52-61; V Bollington St Jo *Ches* 61-69; V Oxton 69-77; R Ashwell *St Alb* 77-90; RD Buntingford 82-88; rtd 90; Fell St Cath Coll Cam from 90; Perm to Offic *Ely* from 90. *13 Church Lane, Madingley, Cambridge CB3 8AF* Tel (01954) 211670

MULLIGAN, Colin Arthur. b 42. Llan Ord Course 96. **d** 96 **p** 97. NSM Neath w Llantwit *Llan* 96-01; NSM Neath from 01. *12 Chestnut Road, Cimla, Neath SA11 3PB* Tel (01639) 630409

MULLIN, Horace Boies (Dan). b 44. Dioc OLM tr scheme. **d** 00 **p** 01. OLM Mildenhall *St E* from 00. *47 Oak Drive, Beck Row, Bury St Edmunds IP28 8UA* Tel (01638) 718200 E-mail dan-martha@mullin47.freeserve.co.uk

MULLINER, Denis Ratliffe. b 40. BNC Ox BA62 MA66. Linc Th Coll 70. **d** 72 **p** 73. C Sandhurst *Ox* 72-76; Chapl Bradfield Coll Berks 76-99; Chapl Chpl Royal Hampton Court Palace from 00; Dep P in O from 00. *Chapel Royal, Hampton Court Palace, East Molesey KT8 9AU* Tel (020) 8781 9598

MULLINS, Mrs Christine Ann. b 60. Regents Th Coll BA98. N Ord Course 03. **d** 05. C Brunswick *Man* from 05. *18 Polygon Avenue, Manchester M13 9FX* Tel 0161-273 1236 Mobile 07952-623750 E-mail christineannmullins@hotmail.com

MULLINS, Joe. b 20. MC45. Trin Coll Ox BA49 MA59. Ridley Hall Cam 48. **d** 50 **p** 51. C Portman Square St Paul *Lon* 50-52; India 52-74; Australia from 74; rtd 86. *33/31 Cockcroft Avenue, Monash, ACT, Australia 2904* Tel (0061) (2) 6291 0345 E-mail emullins@autarmetro.com.au

MULLINS, Malcolm David. b 42. St Edm Hall Ox BA63. St Steph Ho Ox 63. **d** 65 **p** 66. C Kirkby *Liv* 65-69; C Lamorbey H Redeemer *Roch* 69-75; C Solihull *Birm* 75-77. *16 Juniper Court, Neal Close, Northwood HA6 1TJ* Tel (01923) 829923

MULLINS, Mrs Margaret. b 49. Southn Univ CertEd70 K Alfred's Coll Win Dip Special Educn 87. Sarum & Wells Th Coll 94. **d** 94 **p** 95. C Bishopstoke *Win* 94-98; TV Bicester w Bucknell, Caversfield and Launton *Ox* from 98. *The Vicarage, The Spinney, Launton, Bicester OX25 6EP* Tel and fax (01869) 252377

MULLINS, Canon Peter Matthew. b 60. Ch Ch Ox BA82 MA86 Irish Sch of Ecum MPhil90. Qu Coll Birm 82. **d** 84 **p** 85. C Caversham St Pet and Mapledurham etc *Ox* 84-88; Perm to Offic *D & G* 88-89; TV Old Brumby *Linc* 89-94; Clergy Tr Adv 94-99; TR Gt and Lt Coates w Bradley from 99; Can and Preb Linc Cathl from 02; RD Grimsby and Cleethorpes from 05. *The Rectory, 23 Littlecoates Road, Grimsby DN34 4NG* Tel (01472) 329548 E-mail peter.mullins2@ntlworld.com

MULLINS, Timothy Dougal. b 59. Dur Univ. Wycliffe Hall Ox 83. **d** 85 **p** 86. C Reading Greyfriars *Ox* 85-89; C Haughton le Skerne *Dur* 89-95; Chapl Eton Coll 95-05; Chapl Radley Coll from 05. *Radley College, Radley, Abingdon OX14 2HR* Tel (01235) 543080

MULLIS, Robert Owen. b 49. Bris Univ BA71 CertEd71 Birm Univ AdCertEd91. St Mich Coll Llan 93. **d** 93 **p** 94. NSM Llangenni and Llanbedr Ystrad Yw w Patricio *S & B* from 93. *16 Chestnut Drive, Abergavenny NP7 5JZ* Tel (01873) 851613

MULRAINE, Miss Margaret Haskell. b 24. Birm Univ BA45 DipEd46. Sarum Th Coll 83. **dss** 86 **d** 87 **p** 94. Wareham *Sarum* 86-87; Hon Par Dn 87-93; Perm to Offic from 93. *9 Turnworth Close, Broadstone BH18 8LS* Tel (01202) 640292

MULRYNE, Thomas Mark. b 70. St Cath Coll Cam BA91 MA95 Lon Inst of Educn PGCE93. Oak Hill Th Coll BA02. **d** 02 **p** 03. C W Streatham St Jas *S'wark* from 02. *171 Mitcham Lane, London SW16 6NA* Tel (020) 8769 0695 *or* 8677 3947 E-mail mark_and_caroline_mulryne@hotmail.com

MUMFORD, David. *See* MUMFORD, Michael David

MUMFORD, David Bardwell. b 49. MRCPsych86 St Cath Coll Cam BA71 MA75 Bris Univ MB, ChB81 MD92 Edin Univ MPhil89. Bp's Coll Calcutta 71 Cuddesdon Coll 73. **d** 75. C Bris St Mary Redcliffe w Temple etc *Bris* 75-76; NSM 76-82; NSM Edin St Columba *Edin* 82-86; NSM Calverley *Bradf* 86-92; Perm to Offic *B & W* from 92. *14 Clifton Vale, Clifton, Bristol BS8 4PT* Tel 0117-927 2221 E-mail david.mumford@bristol.ac.uk

MUMFORD, David Christopher. b 47. Mert Coll Ox BA68 MA74 York Univ MSW CQSW81. Linc Th Coll 84. **d** 86 **p** 87. C Shiremoor *Newc* 86-89; C N Shields 89-91; V Byker St Ant 91-97; RD Newc E 96-97; V Cowgate 97-02; Internat Co-ord Internat Fellowship of Reconciliation from 02. *Spoorstraat 40, 1815 BK Alkmaar, The Netherlands* Tel (0031) (72) 512 3014

MUMFORD, Geoffrey Robert. b 70. York Univ BSc92 St Jo Coll Nottm MA00. **d** 00 **p** 01. C Rowley Regis *Birm* 00-03; TV Darwen St Pet w Hoddlesden *Blackb* from 03. *St Paul's Vicarage, Johnson New Road, Hoddlesden, Darwen BB3 3NN* Tel (01254) 702598 E-mail gmumford@fish.co.uk

MUMFORD, Grenville Alan. b 34. Richmond Th Coll DipTh. **d** 78 **p** 78. C Witham *Chelmsf* 78-81; C-in-c Gt Ilford St Marg CD 81-85; V Gt Ilford St Marg 85-87; P-in-c Everton and Mattersey w Clayworth *S'well* 87-89; R 89-96; RD Bawtry 93-96; rtd 96; Perm to Offic *Ches* from 96. *146 Audlem Road, Nantwich CW5 7EB* Tel (01270) 610221

MUMFORD, Canon Hugh Raymond. b 24. Oak Hill Th Coll 50. **d** 53 **p** 54. C Bethnal Green St Jas Less *Lon* 53-57; C Watford St Mary *St Alb* 57-59; R Thetford St Pet w St Nic *Nor* 59-69; RD Thetford 68-69; V Nether Cerne *Sarum* 69-71; R Godmanstone 69-71; R Cerne Abbas w Upcerne 69-71; R Minterne Magna 69-71; V Cerne Abbas w Godmanstone and Minterne Magna 71-89; RD Dorchester 75-79; Can and Preb Sarum Cathl 77-89; rtd 89; Perm to Offic *Sarum* from 89. *10 South Walks Road, Dorchester DT1 1ED* Tel (01305) 264971

MUMFORD, Michael David. b 29. **d** 79 **p** 80. Chapl Lister Hosp Stevenage 79-83; C Royston *St Alb* 83-87; P-in-c Kelshall 83-88; P-in-c Therfield 83-88; C Barkway, Reed and Buckland w Barley 87-88; R Ewhurst *Chich* 88-94; V Bodiam 88-94; RD Rye 90-91; rtd 94; Perm to Offic *Chich* from 94. *6 Whydown Place, Bexhill-on-Sea TN39 4RA* Tel (01424) 845278

MUNBY, Canon David Philip James. b 52. Pemb Coll Ox BA75 MA80. St Jo Coll Nottm 76. **d** 78 **p** 79. C Gipsy Hill Ch Ch *S'wark* 78-82; C-in-c W Dulwich Em CD 82-88; V Barnsley St Geo *Wakef* from 88; Asst Dioc Ecum Officer 99-01; Can Bungoma from 04. *St George's Vicarage, 100 Dodworth Road, Barnsley S70 6HL* Tel (01226) 203870 E-mail david.munby@bigfoot.com

MUNCEY, William. b 49. Oak Hill Th Coll BA80. **d** 80 **p** 81. C Wandsworth St Mich *S'wark* 80-84; C Morden 84-88; TV 88-01; RD Merton 00-01; P-in-c Croydon Ch Ch 01-04; V from 04. *Christ Church Vicarage, 34 Longley Road, Croydon CR0 3LH* Tel (020) 8665 9664

MUNCH, Philip Douglas. b 55. Witwatersrand Univ BMus. Cranmer Hall Dur. **d** 88 **p** 89. C Walvis Bay Namibia 88-89; P-in-c 89-92; Warden Ho of Prayer Luderitz 92-99; Prec Port Elizabeth S Africa 99-02; Warden Emmaus Ho of Prayer Northampton from 02; NSM Northampton St Mich w St Edm *Pet* from 02. *Emmaus House of Prayer, St Michael's Church, Perry Street, Northampton NN1 4HL* Tel (01604) 627669 Fax 230316

MUNCHIN, David Leighfield. b 67. Imp Coll Lon BSc88 K Coll Lon MA00. Ripon Coll Cuddesdon 89. **d** 92 **p** 93. C Golders Green *Lon* 92-96; Prec and Min Can St Alb Abbey *St Alb* 96-02; P-in-c Hatfield Hyde from 02. *St Mary Magdalene Vicarage, Hollybush Lane, Welwyn Garden City AL7 4JS* Tel and fax (01707) 322313 Mobile 07787-567747
E-mail munchin@waitrose.com

MUNCHIN, Ysmena Rachael. *See* PENTELOW, Mrs Ysmena Rachael

MUNDAY, Mrs Sandra Anne. b 61. St Jo Sem Wonersh BTh89 Ripon Coll Cuddesdon 97. **d** 99 **p** 00. C Esher *Guildf* 99-02; Team Chapl R United Hosp Bath NHS Trust 02-03. *Address temp unknown*

MUNDELL, Mrs Christine Elizabeth. b 49. WEMTC 01. **d** 04. C Ledbury *Heref* from 04. *21 Biddulph Way, Ledbury HR8 2HP* Tel (01531) 637210 *or* 631697

MUNDEN, Alan Frederick. b 43. Nottm Univ BTh74 Birm Univ MLitt80 Dur Univ PhD87. St Jo Coll Nottm. **d** 74 **p** 75. C Cheltenham St Mary *Glouc* 74-76; C Cheltenham St Mary, St Matt, St Paul and H Trin 76; Hon C Jesmond Clayton Memorial *Newc* 76-80; C 80-83; V Cheylesmore *Cov* 83-01; R Weddington and Caldecote 01-03; rtd 03; Hon C Jesmond Clayton Memorial *Newc* from 03. *11 The Crescent, Benton, Newcastle upon Tyne NE7 7ST* Tel 0191-266 1227

MUNGAVIN, David Stewart. b 60. Stirling Univ BA80. Edin Th Coll 87. **d** 90 **p** 91. C Glas St Marg *Glas* 90-92; P-in-c Airdrie 92-96; R 96-99; P-in-c Coatbridge 92-96; R 96-99; P-in-c Gartcosh 92-96; R 96-99; R Troon from 99. *70 Bentinck Drive, Troon KA10 6HZ* Tel (01292) 313731
E-mail david@mumgavin.freeserve.co.uk

MUNGAVIN, Canon Gerald Clarence. b 27. Edin Th Coll 51. **d** 54 **p** 55. C Dunfermline *St And* 54-55; C Glas Gd Shep *Glas* 55-57; CF 57-60; C Stanwix *Carl* 60-62; Chapl RAF 62-75; R Turriff *Ab* 75-81; R Cuminestown 75-81; R Banff 75-81; R Banchory 81-92; R Kincardine O'Neil 81-92; Can St Andr Cathl 89-92; Hon Can from 92; rtd 92. *5 Lade Court, Lochwinnoch PA12 4BT* Tel (01505) 843972

MUNN, Carole Christine. b 45. EMMTC 83. **d** 90 **p** 94. NSM Long Bennington w Foston *Linc* 90-95; NSM Saxonwell 95-98; Asst Chapl HM Pris Linc 94-01; Chapl HM Pris Morton Hall from 01; NSM Claypole *Linc* from 98; Gen Preacher from 01. *HM Prison, Morton Hall, Swinderby, Lincoln LN6 9PT* Tel (01522) 866700

MUNN, George. b 44. Master Mariner 72. Linc Th Coll 85. **d** 87 **p** 88. C Boston *Linc* 87-90; R Claypole from 90. *The Rectory, 6 Rectory Lane, Claypole, Newark NG23 5BH* Tel (01636) 626224 E-mail g.munn@tiscali.co.uk

MUNN, Richard Probyn. b 45. Selw Coll Cam BA67 MA69. Cuddesdon Coll 67. **d** 69 **p** 70. C Cirencester *Glouc* 69-71; USPG 71-79; Zambia 71-79; Adn S Zambia 79; P-in-c Kings Stanley *Glouc* 80-83; R Lezant w Lawhitton and S Petherwin w Trewen *Truro* 84-92; Lesotho from 93; rtd 01. *PO Box 249, Leribe, Lesotho* Tel (00266) 877 8553

MUNNS, John Millington. b 76. Univ Coll Dur BA99 MA00 FRSA04. Westcott Ho Cam 01. **d** 03 **p** 04. C Bridgwater St Mary, Chilton Trinity and Durleigh *B & W* from 03. *11 Alexandra Road, Bridgwater TA6 3HE* Tel (01278) 429565
E-mail j.m.munns@dunelm.org.uk

MUNNS, Stuart Millington. b 36. OBE77. St Cath Coll Cam BA58 MA62 MCIPD91. Cuddesdon Coll 58. **d** 60 **p** 61. C Allenton and Shelton Lock *Derby* 60-63; C Brampton St Thos 63-65; C-in-c Loundsley Green Ascension CD 65-66; Bp's Youth Chapl 66-72; Nat Dir of Community Industry 72-77; Hon C Hornsey Ch Ch *Lon* 72-77; Dioc Missr *Liv* 77-82; V Knowsley 77-82; P-in-c Stramshall *Lich* 82-88; V Uttoxeter w Bramshall 82-88; RD Uttoxeter 82-87; P-in-c Kingstone w Gratwich 84-88; P-in-c Marchington w Marchington Woodlands 84-88; P-in-c Checkley 86-88; Perm to Offic *B & W* 88-90; NSM Wells St Thos w Horrington 90-94; P-in-c Fosse Trinity 94-02; rtd 02; Dioc Pre-Th Educn Co-ord *B & W* from 02. *Applewood House, Ham Street, Baltonsborough, Glastonbury BA6 8PX* Tel (01458) 851443 E-mail munns@ukonline.co.uk

MUNOZ-TRIVINO, Daniel. b 75. Hatf Coll Dur BA99. Wycliffe Hall Ox MTh01. **d** 01 **p** 02. C Hazlemere *Ox* 01-04; TV Gt Marlow w Marlow Bottom, Lt Marlow and Bisham from 04. *165 Marlow Bottom, Marlow SL7 3PL* Tel (01628) 472816 Mobile 07866-678766 E-mail dani-munoz-2000@yahoo.co.uk

MUNRO, Basil Henry. b 40. Ripon Hall Ox 73. **d** 75 **p** 76. C N Mymms *St Alb* 75-78; C St Alb St Steph 78-80; V 80-87; R Aston-on-Trent and Weston-on-Trent *Derby* 87-99; P-in-c Elvaston and Shardlow 98-99; R Aston on Trent, Elvaston, Weston on Trent etc 99-01; Chapl Aston Hall Hosp Derby 87-93; Chapl S Derbyshire Community Health Services NHS Trust 93-01; rtd 01; Perm to Offic *Derby* from 01. *40 Brisbane Road, Mickleover, Derby DE3 9JZ*

MUNRO, Duncan John Studd. b 50. Magd Coll Ox BA72 MA76 Warwick Univ MBA96. Wycliffe Hall Ox 73. **d** 76 **p** 77. C Ecclesall *Sheff* 76-77; C Sheff St Barn and St Mary 78-80; Lic to Offic 80-86 and 97-98; Perm to Offic from 04. *23 Canterbury Crescent, Sheffield S10 3RW* Tel 0114-230 4930 *or* 261 4338

MUNRO, Ingrid Phyllis. b 51. Herts Univ BEd80. St Jo Coll Nottm MA96 St Alb Minl Tr Scheme 83. **d** 98 **p** 99. NSM Walbrook Epiphany *Derby* 98-01. *40 Brisbane Road, Mickleover, Derby DE3 9JZ*

MUNRO, Robert. b 40. Leeds Univ BA62 Bris Univ PGCE63. SW Minl Tr Course 95. **d** 98 **p** 99. NSM Saltash *Truro* 98-03; NSM Calstock from 03. *15 Valley Road, Saltash PL12 4BT* Tel (01752) 844731 E-mail bobmu@valley151.fsnet.co.uk

MUNRO, Robert Speight. b 63. Bris Univ BSc84 Man Univ PGCE87. All So Coll of Applied Th DipApTh86 Oak Hill Th Coll BA93. **d** 93 **p** 94. C Hartford *Ches* 93-97; R Davenham 97-03; R Cheadle from 03. *The Rectory, 1 Depleach Road, Cheadle SK8 1DZ* Tel 0161-428 3440 *or* 428 8050
E-mail rob@munro.org.uk

MUNRO, Canon Terence George. b 34. Jes Coll Cam BA56 MA60. Linc Th Coll 59. **d** 61 **p** 62. C Far Headingley St Chad *Ripon* 61-64; Jamaica 64-70; R Methley w Mickletown *Ripon* 70-79; V Hunslet Moor St Pet and St Cuth 79-85; R Barwick in Elmet 85-93; V Woodhouse and Wrangthorn 93-99; Dioc Ecum Officer 93-99; Hon Can Ripon Cathl 94-99; rtd 99; Perm to Offic *York* from 00. *45 Laburnum Drive, Beverley HU17 9UQ* Tel (01482) 861237

MUNRO-SMITH, Alison Jean. b 73. Regent's Park Coll Ox MA94. Wycliffe Hall Ox 02. **d** 04 **p** 05. C Lostwithiel, St Winnow w St Nectan's Chpl etc *Truro* from 04. *32 Pendour Park, Lostwithiel PL22 0PQ* Tel (01208) 873805
E-mail alisonmunrosmith@hotmail.com

MUNT, Cyril. b 27. AKC52. **d** 53 **p** 54. C Ashford *Cant* 53-56; C Dorking w Ranmore *Guildf* 56-60; R Cheriton w Newington *Cant* 60-68; R Harbledown 68-83; R Porlock w Stoke Pero *B & W* 83-92; rtd 92; Perm to Offic *B & W* from 92. *Applegarth, 26 Hood Close, Glastonbury BA6 8ES* Tel (01458) 831842

MUNT, Canon Donald James. b 20. ALCD53 St Jo Coll Nottm LTh74. **d** 53 **p** 54. C Purley Ch Ch *S'wark* 53-56; C Hatcham St Jas 56-61; V Oulton Broad *Nor* 61-69; V Deptford St Pet *S'wark* 69-76; R Litcham w Kempston w E and W Lexham *Nor* 76-83; P-in-c Mileham 81-83; P-in-c Beeston next Mileham 81-83; P-in-c Stanfield 81-83; R Litcham, Kempston, Lexham, Mileham, Beeston etc 84-87; RD Brisley and Elmham 85-87; Hon Can Nor Cathl 87-88; rtd 88; Perm to Offic *Nor* 88-02. *c/o A Munt Esq, 5 The Shires, Drayton, Norwich NR8 6EX* Tel (01603) 867316

MUNT, Mrs Linda Christine. b 55. NEOC 92. **d** 95 **p** 96. C Beverley St Nic *York* 95-98; Chapl E Yorkshire Hosps NHS Trust 98-99; V Bridlington Em *York* 99-03; P-in-c Skipsea w Ulrome and Barmston w Fraisthorpe 02-03; Chapl Martin House Hospice for Children Boston Spa 03-05; Hon C Boston Spa, Thorp Arch w Walton etc 03-05; V Market Weighton *York* from 05; V Sancton from 05; R Goodmanham from 05. *The Vicarage, 38 Cliffe Road, Market Weighton, York YO43 3BN* Tel (01430) 873230

MUNYANGAJU, Canon Jerome Cassian. b 53. Serampore Univ BD85 Open Univ MA97. St Phil Coll Kongwa 73. **d** 75 **p** 76. Tanzania 75-80 and 85-95; India 80-85; Hon Can Kagera from 91; Overseas Resource Person *D & D* 95-97; C Bangor Abbey *D & D* 98-00; I Killyleagh from 00. *The Rectory, 34 Inishbeg, Killyleagh, Downpatrick BT80 9TR* Tel and fax (028) 4482 8231
E-mail jerome@surefish.co.uk

MURCH, Canon Robin Norman. b 37. Wells Th Coll. **d** 67 **p** 68. C Wisbech St Aug *Ely* 67-70; C Basingstoke *Win* 70-73; C Whitstable All SS *Cant* 73-76; V Queenborough 76-99; Hon Can Cant Cathl 96-99; rtd 99; Perm to Offic *Ex* from 00. *Flat 3, Narenta, 2 Barton Crescent, Dawlish EX7 9QL* Tel (01626) 863532 Mobile 07836-514528

MURDIN, Frank Laurence. b 11. Leeds Univ BA34. Coll of Resurr Mirfield 34. **d** 36 **p** 37. C Pet St Paul *Pet* 36-41; R Culworth 41-58; RD Culworth 50-58; V Moreton Pinkney 55-58; R Brampton Ash w Dingley 58-65; RD Weldon 64-65; V Greetham w Stretton and Clipsham 65-76; rtd 76. *c/o R L Murdin Esq, 20 Roman Way, Brackley NN13 7JA* Tel (01280) 700352

MURDOCH, Alexander Edward Duncan. b 37. Oak Hill Th Coll 68. **d** 71 **p** 72. C Kensington St Helen w H Trin *Lon* 71-72; C Kensington St Barn 73-74; CF 74-78; C W Kirby St Bridget *Ches* 78-84; V N Shoebury *Chelmsf* 84-87; V W Poldens *B & W* 87-96; R Gayhurst w Ravenstone, Stoke Goldington etc *Ox* from 96. *The Rectory, Mount Pleasant, Stoke Goldington, Newport Pagnell MK16 8LL* Tel (01908) 551221

MURDOCH, David John. b 58. Birm Univ BSocSc81 Leeds Univ MA03. Ripon Coll Cuddesdon 81. **d** 84 **p** 85. C Penwortham St Leon *Blackb* 84-87; C Wirksworth w Alderwasley, Carsington etc *Derby* 87-89; R Shirland 89-97; Dioc World Development Officer 96-00; P-in-c New Mills 97-01; V from 01; RD Glossop from 04. *St George's Vicarage, Church Lane, New Mills, Stockport SK22 4NP* Tel and fax (01663) 743225
E-mail murdochs@btopenworld.com

MURDOCH, Mrs Lucy Eleanor. b 41. STETS BTh99. **d** 99 **p** 00. NSM Warbleton and Bodle Street Green *Chich* 99-02; NSM Rye from 02; TV from 03. *The Vicarage, 39 Lydd Road, Camber, Rye TN31 7RN* Tel (01797) 225386 E-mail lucy@murdoch26.fsnet.co.uk

MURFET, Edward David. b 36. Qu Coll Cam BA59 MA63. Chich Th Coll 59. **d** 61 **p** 62. C Croydon St Mich *Cant* 61-64; C Hunslet St Mary and Stourton *Ripon* 64-65; C Hackney Wick St Mary of Eton w St Aug *Lon* 65-69; Chapl Berne *Eur* 69-71; Chapl Naples 71-74; Chapl Rome 74-77; Lic to Offic *Bris* 78-81; Gen Sec CEMS 81-86; C Leeds St Pet *Ripon* 87-89; P-in-c 89-90; C Leeds City 91-93; Min Can Ripon Cathl 93-03; rtd 03. *3 Old Deanery Close, St Marygate, Ripon HG4 1LZ* Tel (01765) 608422 E-mail edmurfet@bronco.co.uk

MURFET, Gwyn. b 44. Linc Th Coll 71. **d** 74 **p** 75. C Scalby w Ravenscar and Staintondale *York* 74-77; P-in-c S Milford 77-83; R 83-84; V Kirkby Ireleth *Carl* from 84. *The Vicarage, School Road, Kirkby-in-Furness LA17 7UQ* Tel (01229) 889256 Fax as telephone

MURIEL, Sister. *See* ARTHINGTON, Sister Muriel

MURPHIE, Andrew Graham. b 65. Reading Univ BA86. St Jo Coll Nottm BTh91 MA92. **d** 92 **p** 93. C Boulton *Derby* 92-96; C Marston on Dove w Scropton 96-97; V Hilton w Marston-on-Dove from 98; RD Longford from 04. *The Vicarage, 28 Back Lane, Hilton, Derby DE65 5GJ* Tel (01283) 733433 E-mail andymurphie@fish.co.uk

MURPHY, Alexander Charles. b 28. St Edm Coll Ware 50. **d** 55 **p** 56. NSM Edin St Jas *Edin* 88-90; TV Edin St Mark 90-93; TV Edin St Andr and St Aid 90-93; TV Edin St Marg 93-96; rtd 96. *29 Shadepark Drive, Dalkeith EH22 1DA* Tel 0131-660 1574

MURPHY, Andrew John. b 46. Edin Univ LLB67 MA68. **d** 95. NSM Aberdeen St Marg *Ab* 95-98; NSM Fraserburgh 98-01; Hon Asst C Bridge of Don St Luke's Miss from 01. *Old Schoolhouse, Logie, Crimond AB43 8QN* Tel (01346) 532711

MURPHY, Deborah Ann. b 67. Newc Univ BA89 Birm Univ BD92. Qu Coll Birm 90. **d** 93 **p** 94. Par Dn Bloxwich *Lich* 93-94; C 94-97; TV Gt Grimsby St Mary and St Jas *Linc* 97-00; Perm to Offic *St Alb* from 01. *77 School Lane, Bushey WD23 1BY* Tel (020) 8386 0926 E-mail john@murphy14.freeserve.co.uk

MURPHY, Gerry. *See* MURPHY, Canon John Gervase Maurice Walker

MURPHY, Ms Hilary Elizabeth. b 57. St Martin's Coll Lanc BSc00. St Jo Coll Nottm MTh05. **d** 05. C Blackpool H Cross *Blackb* from 05. *38 Dean Street, Blackpool FY4 1BP*

MURPHY, Jack. b 27. N Ord Course 83. **d** 86 **p** 87. C Armley w New Wortley *Ripon* 86-90; C Hawksworth Wood 90-94; rtd 94; Perm to Offic *York* from 96. *70 Avocet Way, Bridlington YO15 3NT* Tel (01262) 609477

MURPHY, James Royse. b 54. Bris Univ MB, ChB77 DRCOG80 MRCGP81. Glouc Sch of Min 89. **d** 92 **p** 94. NSM Glouc St Cath *Glouc* 92-98; NSM Glouc St Paul from 98. *52 Lansdown Road, Gloucester GL1 3JD* Tel (01452) 505080

MURPHY, Canon John Gervase Maurice Walker (Gerry). b 26. LVO87. TCD BA52 MA55. **d** 52 **p** 53. C Lurgan Ch the Redeemer *D & D* 52-55; CF 55-73; Asst Chapl Gen 73-77; V Ranworth w Panxworth *Nor* 77-79; RD Blofield 79; Dom Chapl to The Queen 79-87; Chapl to The Queen 87-96; R Sandringham w W Newton *Nor* 79-87; RD Heacham and Rising 85-87; Hon Can Nor Cathl 86-87; Chapl ICS 87-91; Falkland Is 87-91; Miss to Seamen 87-91; rtd 91; Chapl St Pet-ad-Vincula at HM Tower of Lon 91-96; Dep P in O 92-96; Extra Chapl to The Queen from 96; Perm to Offic *Nor* from 98. *Saffron Close, 17 Ringstead Road, Heacham, King's Lynn PE31 7JA* Tel (01485) 572351

MURPHY, Owen. b 52. Open Univ BA85. Chich Th Coll 92. **d** 94 **p** 95. C Oxhey St Matt *St Alb* 94-96; C Watford St Mich 96-98; P-in-c Shinfield *Ox* 98-05; V Barnehurst *Roch* from 05. *The Vicarage, 93 Pelham Road, Bexleyheath DA7 4LY* Tel (01322) 523344 E-mail omurphy@globalnet.co.uk

MURPHY, Peter Frederick. b 40. AKC65. **d** 67 **p** 68. C Paddington St Jo w St Mich *Lon* 67-72; P-in-c Basingstoke *Win* 72-76; TV 76-81; V Hythe 81-92; V Lyndhurst and Emery Down 92-99; P-in-c Minstead 95-99; V Lyndhurst and Emery Down and Minstead 99-05; rtd 05; Hon C Fordingbridge and Breamore and Hale etc *Win* from 05. *Smuggler's Cottage, 20 Shaftesbury Street, Fordingbridge SP6 1JF* Tel (01425) 650209 Mobile 07815-050096 E-mail petermurf@gmail.com

MURPHY, Philip John Warwick. b 65. Kent Univ BA87 Southn Univ BTh93 SSC. Chich Th Coll 88. **d** 91 **p** 92. C Broadstone *Sarum* 91-94; C Teddington SS Pet and Paul and Fulwell *Lon* 94-96; V Leytonstone St Marg w St Columba *Chelmsf* 96-01; P-in-c Leytonstone St Andr 96-97; Australia from 01; R Benalla 01-04; V Fitzroy from 04. *268 George Street, PO Box 124, Fitzroy, Vic, Australia 3065* Tel (0061) (3) 9419 4587 E-mail pjwm@bigpond.net.au

MURPHY, Ronald Frederick. b 38. **d** 84 **p** 85. NSM Swindon Dorcan *Bris* 84-87; P-in-c N Cerney w Bagendon *Glouc* 87-90. *Flat 2, 7 Hulham Road, Exmouth EX8 3HR* Tel (01395) 224375

MURPHY, Rosalyn Frances Thomas. b 55. Marquette Univ (USA) BA85 Ustinov Coll Dur MTh00 Union Th Sem Virginia MDiv99 St Jo Coll Dur PhD05. Cranmer Hall Dur 04. **d** 05. C Dur St Nic *Dur* from 05. *Glebe Cottage, Sunderland Bridge, Durham DH6 5HB* Tel 0191-378 9332 Mobile 07730-466782 E-mail murphyfamuk@aol.com

MURPHY, Royse. *See* MURPHY, James Royse

MURPHY, Canon William Albert. b 43. MBE98. Lon Univ BD73 QUB MTh78. **d** 73 **p** 74. C Lisburn Ch Ch *Conn* 73-79; Supt & Chapl Ulster Inst for the Deaf 79-98; Chapl HM Pris Maze from 82; Dioc Dir Ords *Conn* from 92; Chapl Ch of Ireland Min to Deaf people from 98; Can Belf Cathl from 04. *2 Maghaberry Manor, Moira, Craigavon BT67 0JZ* Tel (028) 9261 9140 E-mail ddo@connor.anglican.org

MURPHY, Mrs Yvonne Letita. b 52. Brunel Univ BA90 PGCE91. SEITE 95. **d** 98 **p** 99. NSM Hampton St Mary *Lon* 98-01; NSM Staines St Mary and St Pet 01-04; Chapl Bp Wand Sch 98-04; P-in-c Kennington *Cant* from 04. *The Vicarage, 212 Faversham Road, Kennington, Ashford TN24 9AF* Tel (01233) 620500 E-mail ylm.bwm@virgin.net

MURRAY, Alan. b 61. St Jo Coll Nottm BTh92. **d** 92 **p** 93. C Wombwell *Sheff* 92-95; C Mortomley St Sav High Green 95-99; P-in-c Doncaster St Jas 99-01; V from 01. *The Vicarage, 54 Littlemoor Lane, Doncaster DN4 0LB* Tel (01302) 365544

MURRAY, Christine Jean. *See* MEDWAY, Mrs Christine Jean

MURRAY, Christopher James. b 49. Open Univ BA78. St Jo Coll Nottm 79. **d** 81 **p** 82. C Heatherlands St Jo *Sarum* 81-84; C Hamworthy 84-90; R Passenham *Pet* from 90. *The Rectory, Wicken Road, Deanshanger, Milton Keynes MK19 6JP* Tel (01908) 262371

MURRAY, David McIlveen. b 36. ALCD61. **d** 61 **p** 62. C Mortlake w E Sheen *S'wark* 61-64; C Lyncombe *B & W* 64-67; C Horsham *Chich* 67-73; V Devonport St Bart *Ex* 73-79; R Chalfont St Peter *Ox* 79-95; RD Amersham 86-89; R Lower Windrush 95-03; rtd 03; Perm to Offic *Glouc* from 03. *Collum End Farm, 88 Church Road, Leckhampton, Cheltenham GL53 0PD* Tel (01242) 528008

MURRAY, Elaine Mary Edel. b 58. TCD BTh05 MICS97. CITC 02. **d** 05. Bp's V and C Kilkenny w Aghour and Kilmanagh *C & O* from 05. *The Vicar's Residence, St Canice's Library, Cathedral Close, Kilkenny, Irish Republic* Tel (00353) (56) 777 1998 E-mail vicar.cathedral@ossory.anglican.org

MURRAY, Elizabeth Ruth. d 03 **p** 04. C Antrim All SS *Conn* from 03. *17 Birch Hill Avenue, Antrim BT41 1BT* Tel (028) 9448 8316

MURRAY, Gordon John. b 33. St Cath Coll Cam BA57 MA61. Clifton Th Coll 57. **d** 59 **p** 60. C Heref St Jas *Heref* 59-61; C Uphill *B & W* 62-65; C-in-c Reading St Mary Castle Street Prop Chpl *Ox* 65-68; Ed *English Churchman* 65-71; Prin Kensit Coll Finchley 68-75; Hd of RE Sandown High Sch 76-78; rtd 98. *18 Longcroft, Felixstowe IP11 9QH* Tel (01394) 273372

MURRAY, Gordon Stewart. b 33. Birkbeck Coll Lon BSc72. Ripon Coll Cuddesdon 76. **d** 78 **p** 79. C Kenilworth St Nic *Cov* 78-81; V Potterspury w Furtho and Yardley Gobion *Pet* 81-83; V Potterspury, Furtho, Yardley Gobion and Cosgrove 84; TV Wolvercote w Summertown *Ox* 84-90; P-in-c Walworth *S'wark* 90-95; TR Walworth St Pet 95-98; rtd 98; P-in-c Tillington *Chich* 98-01; P-in-c Duncton 98-01; P-in-c Up Waltham 98-01. *26 Burton Stone Lane, York YO30 6BU* Tel (01904) 330401 E-mail gordon.murray11@ntlworld.com

MURRAY, Ian Hargraves. b 48. Man Univ BSc71. St Jo Coll Nottm 79. **d** 81 **p** 82. C Erith St Paul *Roch* 81-84; C Willenhall H Trin *Lich* 84-87; TV 87-92; P-in-c Moxley 92-00; C Darlaston St Lawr 99-00; TR Glascote and Stonydelph from 00; RD Tamworth from 04. *20 Melmerby, Wilnecote, Tamworth B77 4LP* Tel (01827) 737326 *or* 330306 E-mail rockin.rev@ntlworld.com

MURRAY, Ian William. b 32. Lon Univ BA53 PGCE54. Oak Hill NSM Course 80. **d** 83 **p** 84. NSM Pinner *Lon* 83-03; Perm to Offic from 03. *4 Mansard Close, Pinner HA5 3FQ* Tel (020) 8866 2984 E-mail bimurray@talk21.com

MURRAY, James Beattie. b 67. Goldsmiths' Coll Lon BMus87 Southlands Coll Lon PGCE89. Oak Hill Th Coll 01. **d** 03 **p** 04. C Upper Holloway *Lon* from 03. *6 Zoffany Street, London N19 3ER* Tel (020) 7263 4217 *or* 7281 6198 E-mail jamiebmurray@hotmail.com

MURRAY, John Desmond. b 16. TCD BA38 MA46. CITC 39. **d** 39 **p** 40. C Dublin St Werburgh *D & G* 39-41; C Dublin Ch Ch Leeson Park 41-43; C Dublin Rathmines 43-49; Min Can St Patr Cathl Dublin 43-53; I Powerscourt *D & G* 49-53; Chapl RN 53-55; I Dalkey St Patr *D & G* 55-70; I Milltown 70-82; Hon Chapl to Abp Dublin 73-82; Can Ch Ch Cathl Dublin 79-82; rtd 82. *3 Adare Close, Killincarrig, Greystones, Co Wicklow, Irish Republic* Tel (00353) (1) 287 6359

MURRAY, The Ven John Grainger. b 45. CITC 67. **d** 70 **p** 71. C Carlow *C & O* 70-72; C Limerick St Mary *L & K* 72-77; I Rathdowney w Castlefleming, Donaghmore etc *C & O* from 77; Can Leighlin Cathl 83-88; Treas 88-89; Chan 89-90; Prec 90-92; Preb Ossory Cathl 83-88; Treas 88-89; Chan 89-90; Prec 90-92; Adn Ossory and Leighlin from 92; Adn Cashel, Waterford and Lismore from 94. *The Rectory, Rathdowney, Portlaoise, Co Laois, Irish Republic* Tel (00353) (505) 46311 Fax 46540 E-mail venjgm@iol.ie *or* archdeacon@cashel.anglican.org

MURRAY, John Louis. b 47. Keble Coll Ox BA67 MA69. **d** 82 **p** 83. Asst Chapl Strasbourg *Eur* from 82. *11 rue des Juifs, 67000 Strasbourg, France* Tel (0033) (3) 88 36 12 25 Fax 88 41 27 31

MURRAY, Mrs Margaret Janice. b 46. Carl Dioc Tr Course. **dss** 86 **d** 87 **p** 94. Walney Is *Carl* 86-87; Hon Par Dn 87-89; Par Dn Carl H Trin and St Barn 89-94; Chapl Cumberland Infirmary 90-94; C Harraby *Carl* 94-97; P-in-c 97-00; V 00-02; Chapl to the Deaf and Hard of Hearing 94-02; rtd 02; Perm to Offic *Carl* from 02. *6 Follyskye Cottages, Tindale Fell, Brampton CA8 2QB* Tel (01697) 746400

MURRAY, Paul Ridsdale. b 55. BEd. St Steph Ho Ox. **d** 83 **p** 84. C Hartlepool St Oswald *Dur* 83-86; C S Shields All SS 86-88; V Sacriston and Kimblesworth 88-94; P-in-c Waterhouses 94-98; P-in-c Chopwell from 98; Perm to Offic *Newc* from 99. *St John's Vicarage, Derwent View, Chopwell, Newcastle upon Tyne NE17 7AN* Tel (01207) 561248 Mobile 07803-906727 Fax 563850 E-mail p.r.murray@durham.anglican.org

MURRAY, Robert Blake. b 49. EMMTC. **d** 00 **p** 01. NSM Annesley w Newstead *S'well* 00-03; P-in-c Brinsley w Underwood from 03. *The Vicarage, 102A Church Lane, Brinsley, Nottingham NG16 5AB* Tel and fax (01773) 713978 E-mail rb.murray@ntlworld.com

MURRAY, Roy John. b 47. Open Univ BA92 Wolv Poly CertEd89 RGN75 RMN77. WMMTC 01. **d** 04 **p** 05. NSM Solihull *Birm* from 04. *23 Farlow Road, Birmingham B31 3AH* Tel 0121-478 1618 Mobile 07768-436363 E-mail roy.j.murray@btinternet.com

MURRAY, Ruth. *See* MURRAY, Elizabeth Ruth

MURRAY, Mrs Ruth Elizabeth. b 55. Dur Univ BA77 Man Coll of Educn CertEd78. BA. **d** 94 **p** 95. NSM Alloa *St And* 94-98; Chapl Stirling Univ 94-99. *2 Wallace Street, Alloa FK10 3RZ* Tel (01259) 217432 E-mail ruthemurray@lineone.net

MURRAY (née GOULD), Mrs Susan Judith. b 61. Poly of Wales BSc83 Open Univ MA95. St Jo Coll Nottm 90. **d** 91 **p** 94. Par Dn Stokesley *York* 91-94; CMS 94-95; Argentina 95-03; P-in-c Haddlesey w Hambleton and Birkin *York* from 03. *The Rectory, Chapel Haddlesey, Selby YO8 8QF* Tel (01757) 270245

MURRAY, Canon William Robert Craufurd. b 44. St Chad's Coll Dur BA66 DipTh68. **d** 68 **p** 69. C Workington St Mich *Carl* 68-71; C Harrogate St Wilfrid *Ripon* 71-74; P-in-c Sawley 74; V Winksley cum Grantley and Aldfield w Studley 74; R Fountains 75-81; New Zealand from 81; V Hutt 81-87; V Fendalton from 87; Can Christchurch Cathl from 91. *St Barnabas's Vicarage, 7 Makora Street, Christchurch 8004, New Zealand* Tel (0064) (3) 351 7064 *or* 351 7392 Fax 351 6374 E-mail craufurd@clear.net.nz

MURRAY-LESLIE, Adrian John Gervase. b 46. Lich Th Coll 67. **d** 69 **p** 70. C Sheff St Cuth *Sheff* 69-73; C Mosbrough 73-75; C-in-c Mosborough CD 75-80; P-in-c Edale *Derby* from 80; Warden The Peak Cen from 80. *The Vicarage, Edale, Hope Valley S33 7ZA* Tel (01433) 670254

MURRAY, THE, Bishop of. *See* DAVIES, The Rt Revd Ross Owen

MURRELL, Canon John Edmund. b 28. Westcott Ho Cam. **d** 66 **p** 67. C Ivychurch w Old Romney and Midley *Cant* 66-70; R Bardwell *St E* 70-75; Perm to Offic *Ely* 75-77; V Wenhaston w Thorington and Bramfield w Walpole *St E* 77-86; V Thorington w Wenhaston and Bramfield 86-92; P-in-c Walberswick w Blythburgh 86-92; V Thorington w Wenhaston, Bramfield etc 92-93; RD Halesworth 85-90; Hon Can St E Cathl 89-93; rtd 93; Perm to Offic *St E* from 93. *Strickland Cottage, 12 Lorne Road, Southwold IP18 6EP* Tel (01502) 722074

MURRIE, Clive Robert. b 44. Ripon Coll Cuddesdon 77. **d** 79 **p** 80. C Kenton Ascension *Newc* 79-80; C Prudhoe 80-83; V Burnopfield *Dur* 83-87; R Stella 87-91; V Coalpit Heath *Bris* 91-95; P-in-c Sittingbourne St Mich *Cant* 95-98; Chapl HM Pris Stocken 98-03; Chapl HM YOI Castington from 03. *HM YOI, Castington, Morpeth NE65 9XG* Tel (01670) 762100

MURRIN, Robert Staddon. b 42. RMA 62 Reading Univ BA68 Birm Univ DPS93 Open Univ MA96. WMMTC 90 Birm Bible Inst DipRS92. **d** 93 **p** 95. NSM Peterchurch w Vowchurch, Turnastone and Dorstone *Heref* 93-95; NSM Tupsley w Hampton Bishop 95-97; Chapl Kemp Hospice Kidderminster from 97. *Albion Cottage, Peterchurch, Hereford HR2 0RP* Tel (01981) 550656 *or* 550467 Fax 550432

✠**MURSELL, The Rt Revd Alfred Gordon.** b 49. BNC Ox BA70 MA73 BD87 Birm Univ Hon DD05 ARCM74. Cuddesdon Coll 71. **d** 73 **p** 74 **c** 05. C Walton St Mary *Liv* 73-77; V E Dulwich St Jo *S'wark* 77-86; Tutor Sarum Th Coll 87-91; TR Stafford *Lich* 91-99; Provost Birm 99-02; Dean Birm 02-05; Area Bp Stafford *Lich* from 05. *Ash Garth, Broughton Crescent, Barlaston, Stoke-on-Trent ST12 9DD* Tel (01782) 373308 Fax 373705 E-mail bishop.stafford@lichfield.anglican.org

MUSGRAVE, James Robert Lord. b 20. MBE97. TCD BA43 MA51. **d** 44 **p** 45. C Belfast St Andr *Conn* 44-46; C Derriaghy 46-51; R Duneane w Ballyscullion 51-54; I Belfast St Steph 54-64; I Magheragall 64-85; Can Conn Cathl 82-85; Bp's C Killead w Gartree 87-95; rtd 95. *14 Earlsfort, Moira, Craigavon BT67 0LY* Tel (028) 9261 2047

MUSHEN, Canon Francis John. b 34. Birm Univ BA60. Ripon Hall Ox 60. **d** 62 **p** 63. C Foleshill St Laur *Cov* 62-65; C Halesowen *Worc* 65-69; V Stourbridge St Mich Norton 69-81; Hon Can Worc Cathl 81-99; P-in-c Bromsgrove St Jo 81-87; V 87-92; R Kempsey and Severn Stoke w Croome d'Abitot 92-99; rtd 99; Perm to Offic *Worc* from 99. *16 Longheadland, Ombersley, Droitwich WR9 0JB* Tel (01905) 621461

MUSINDI, Mrs Beatrice Nambuya Balibali. b 64. Birm Univ MA94. Bp Tucker Coll Mukono BD90. **d** 03 **p** 04. C Caerleon w Llanhennock *Mon* from 03. *The Vicarage, 1 Brookfield Close, Llyswerry, Newport NP19 4LA* Tel (01633) 783912 Mobile 07989-469938

MUSINDI, Philip. b 63. Bp Tucker Coll Mukono BD91 Univ of Wales (Cardiff) MTh94. Bp Tucker Coll Mukono DipTh87 St Mich Coll Llan 91. **d** 87 **p** 90. Uganda 87-92; C Builth and Llanddewi'r Cwm w Llangynog etc *S & B* 92-94; C Newport St Teilo *Mon* 94-97; P-in-c Newport St Matt 97-04; V Newport St Andr from 04. *The Vicarage, 1 Brookfield Close, Llyswerry, Newport NP19 4LA* Tel (01633) 783912

MUSK, Bill Andrew. b 49. Ox Univ BA70 MA75 Univ of S Africa D Litt et Phil84 Lon Univ DipTh73. Fuller Th Sem California ThM80 Trin Coll Bris DipTh81. **d** 81 **p** 82. Egypt 81-86; CMS 88-89; TV Maghull *Liv* 89-97; V Tulse Hill H Trin and St Matthias *S'wark* from 97. *The Vicarage, 49 Trinity Rise, London SW2 2QP* Tel (020) 8674 6721 E-mail billamusk@aol.com

MUSKETT, David John. b 63. Southn Univ BA85. Ripon Coll Cuddesdon 87. **d** 90 **p** 91. C Kempston Transfiguration *St Alb* 90-93; C Ampthill w Millbrook and Steppingley 93-96; V Milford *Guildf* from 96. *The Vicarage, Milford Heath Road, Godalming GU8 5BX* Tel (01483) 414710 E-mail stjohn_milford@hotmail.com

MUSSER, Ms Christine. b 55. Ex Univ 96. **d** 00 **p** 01. C Torpoint *Truro* 00-03; P-in-c Boscastle w Davidstow from 03. *The Rectory, Forrabury, Boscastle PL35 0DJ* Tel (01840) 250359 E-mail revdchrismusser@aol.com

MUSSON, David John. b 46. Open Univ BA86 Univ of Wales (Lamp) MPhil96 Univ of Wales (Ban) PhD00. Linc Th Coll 70. **d** 73 **p** 74. C New Sleaford *Linc* 73-76; C Morton 76-80; P-in-c Thurlby 80-86; R Quarrington w Old Sleaford 86-99; P-in-c Silk Willoughby 86-87; R 87-99; Perm to Offic *Chich* from 01. *Flat A, 6 Chatsworth Gardens, Eastbourne BN20 7JP* Tel (01323) 738776 E-mail david@davidmusson.fsnet.co.uk

MUSSON, John Keith. b 39. Nottm Univ BSc61 PhD66 CEng MIMechE. St As Minl Tr Course 85. **d** 88 **p** 89. Assoc Prin NE Wales Inst of HE 80-93; NSM Holywell *St As* 88-93; C 93-95; R Caerwys and Bodfari 95-02; rtd 02. *4 Hayes View, Oswestry SY11 1TP* Tel (01691) 656212

MUSSON, William John. b 58. UMIST BSc80 Open Univ MA02. St Jo Coll Nottm 88. **d** 91 **p** 92. C Nantwich *Ches* 91-94; C Finchley Ch Ch *Lon* 94-97; V Lynchmere and Camelsdale *Chich* from 97. *The Vicarage, School Road, Camelsdale, Haslemere GU27 3RN* Tel (01428) 642983 E-mail stpandp@btinternet.com

MUST, Albert Henry. b 27. Clifton Th Coll 61. **d** 63 **p** 64. C Becontree St Mary *Chelmsf* 63-68; V Highbury Vale St Jo *Lon* 68-78; V Highbury New Park St Aug 78-84; V Walthamstow St Jo *Chelmsf* 84-93; rtd 93; Perm to Offic *Cant* from 93. *24 Nightingale Avenue, Whitstable CT5 4TR* Tel (01227) 772160

MUST, Mrs Shirley Ann. b 35. St Mich Ho Ox 61. **dss** 82 **d** 87 **p** 94. Highbury New Park St Aug *Lon* 82-84; Walthamstow St Jo *Chelmsf* 84-93; Hon Par Dn 87-93; Perm to Offic *Cant* 93-94; Hon C Herne Bay Ch Ch 94-05; Perm to Offic from 05. *24 Nightingale Avenue, Whitstable CT5 4TR* Tel (01227) 772160

MUSTARD, James Edmond Alexander. b 74. Ex Univ BA95 Clare Coll Cam BA04. Westcott Ho Cam 02 Berkeley Div Sch 04. **d** 05. C Nor St Pet Mancroft w St Jo Maddermarket *Nor* from 05. *63 Recreation Road, Norwich NR2 3PA* Tel (01603) 451878

MUSTOE, Alan Andrew. b 52. Man Univ BA74. Qu Coll Birm. **d** 78 **p** 79. C Chatham St Wm *Roch* 78-82; R Burham and Wouldham 82-88; Dioc Info Officer 83-88; V Strood St Nic w St Mary 88-99; V Orpington All SS from 99; AD Orpington from 05. *The Vicarage, 1A Keswick Road, Orpington BR6 0EU* Tel and fax (01689) 824624 E-mail akmustoe@btopenworld.com

MUSTON, David Alan. b 33. Nottm Univ BA60. Ridley Hall Cam 62. **d** 64 **p** 65. C Tankersley *Sheff* 64-67; C Goole 67-70; Sec Ind Cttee of Gen Syn Bd for Soc Resp 70-76; Asst Gen Sec Bd for Soc Resp 74-76; Ind Chapl *Win* 77-79; V Leigh St Mary *Man* 79-83; R Otham w Langley *Cant* 83-97; rtd 97; Perm to Offic *Ox* from 01. *7 The Homestead, Bladon, Woodstock OX20 1XA* Tel (01993) 812650 E-mail musto33@tiscali.co.uk

MUSTON, James Arthur. b 48. Open Univ BA92 Derby Univ MA. EMMTC 89. **d** 91 **p** 92. NSM Chaddesden St Mary *Derby*

91-95; Community Min E Marsh Grimsby *Linc* 95-99; V Gresley *Derby* 99-04; rtd 04. *20 Whitmore Road, Chaddesden, Derby DE21 6HR* Tel (01332) 678073 Mobile 07946-575563

MUTCH, Canon Sylvia Edna. b 36. St Mich Ho Ox 57. **dss** 79 **d** 87 **p** 94. Clifton *York* 79-95; Par Dn 87-94; C 94-95; Chapl Clifton Hosp York 81-94; R Elvington w Sutton on Derwent and E Cottingwith *York* 95-01; Can and Preb York Minster 98-01; rtd 01; Perm to Offic *York* from 01. *18 Waite Close, Pocklington, York YO42 2YU* Tel (01759) 307894

MUTETE, Lameck. b 61. Bp Gaul Th Coll Harare 94. **d** 96 **p** 97. C Harare St Luke Zimbabwe 96-97; Asst P Harare Cathl 97-01; P-in-c 01; Adn Harare E 01; Can Harare 01-04; Perm to Offic *Bradf* 04; P-in-c Tattenhall and Handley *Ches* from 04. *The Rectory, 4 Rean Meadow, Tattenhall, Chester CH3 9PU* Tel (01829) 770245 Mobile 07940-512748 E-mail lameckmutete@yahoo.co.uk

MUXLOW, Judy Ann. b 47. Univ of Wales (Cardiff) BSc69 St Luke's Coll Ex CertEd73. SEITE. **d** 00 **p** 01. NSM Biddenden and Smarden *Cant* from 00; Chapl Ch Ch High Sch Ashford 00-03; Perm to Offic *Roch* from 00; Bp's Officer for NSM *Cant* from 03. *29 The Meadows, Biddenden, Ashford TN27 8AW* Tel (01580) 291016 E-mail mucat@fish.co.uk

MUYAMBI, Canon Lazarus Tashaya. b 33. St Jo Sem Lusaka 64. **d** 66 **p** 68. Zimbabwe 66-03; Perm to Offic *Birm* from 03. *32 Pennyroyal Close, Walsall WS5 4SJ* Tel (01922) 647312

MWANGI, Capt Joel Waweru. b 59. CA Tr Coll Nairobi 81. **d** 93 **p** 94. Kenya 93-96 and from 00; C Sheff St Mary Bramall Lane *Sheff* 96-99. *PO Box 57227, Nairobi, Kenya*

MWAURA, Nicholas Chege. b 65. DipTh90. **d** 90 **p** 91. Nairobi 91-95; NSM Limehouse *Lon* 99-00. *Flat C, 53 Hanbury Street, London E1 5JP*

MYANMAR, Archbishop of. *See* SAN SI HTAY, The Most Revd Samuel

MYATT, Edwin Henry. b 54. MA. Ripon Coll Cuddesdon. **d** 84 **p** 85. C W Bromwich St Fran *Lich* 84-88; C Sedgley All SS 88-93; V Trent Vale 93-94. *The Conifers, 5 Prestwick Road, Kingswinford ST4 6JY*

MYATT, Francis Eric. b 60. St Jo Coll Nottm LTh92. **d** 92 **p** 93. C W Derby St Luke *Liv* 92-95; TV Sutton 95-98; V Liv St Chris Norris Green 98-01; CF from 01. *c/o MOD Chaplains (Army)* Tel (01980) 615804 Fax 615800

MYATT, Philip Bryan. b 29. Wycliffe Hall Ox 54. **d** 57 **p** 58. C Fareham St Jo *Portsm* 57-61; C Westgate St Jas *Cant* 61-64; R Woodchester *Glouc* 64-70; R Bath Walcot *B & W* 70-91; R The Edge, Pitchcombe, Harescombe and Brookthorpe *Glouc* 91-94; rtd 94; Perm to Offic *Glouc* from 94. *West Cottage, Littleworth, Amberley, Stroud GL5 5AL*

MYCOCK, Geoffrey John Arthur. b 22. Open Univ BA76. St Deiniol's Hawarden 76. **d** 77 **p** 78. Hon C Ches H Trin *Ches* 77-79; Bp's Dom Chapl 79-80; P-in-c Hargrave 79-80; V Sandbach Heath 80-82; Chapl and Lect St Deiniol's Lib Hawarden 82-85; V Holt *St As* 85-90; rtd 90; Perm to Offic *St A* from 90 and *Ches* from 91. *20 Eaton Close, Broughton, Chester CH4 0RF* Tel (01244) 531214

MYERS, Andrew Thomas Christopher. b 57. Leeds Univ BA81. N Ord Course 02. **d** 04 **p** 05. C Leeds St Aid *Ripon* from 04. *84 Copgrove Road, Leeds LS8 2ST* Tel 0113-248 0050 Mobile 07876-431183 E-mail andymyers@elm664.freeserve.co.uk

MYERS, Duncan Frank. b 57. Warwick Univ BSc. St Jo Coll Nottm 81. **d** 84 **p** 85. C Upton cum Chalvey *Ox* 84-86; C Farnborough *Guildf* 86-90; Chapl Nottm Poly *S'well* 90-92; Chapl Nottm Trent Univ 92-95; Sen Past Adv 95-02; Hon Min Can Dur Cathl *Dur* from 04. *6A The College, Durham DH1 3EQ* Tel 0191-384 2481 E-mail duncan@myers.uk.net

MYERS, Ms Gillian Mary. b 57. Warwick Univ BSc78 Nottm Univ MA96. St Jo Coll Nottm 83. **d** 95 **p** 97. NSM Nottingham St Jude *S'well* 95-97; NSM Gedling 97-00; P-in-c Nottingham All SS 00-02; Succ, Sacr and Min Can Dur Cathl *Dur* from 02. *6A The College, Durham DH1 3EQ* Tel 0191-384 2481 E-mail gilly@myers.uk.net

MYERS, John Bulmer. b 19. Worc Ord Coll 64. **d** 66 **p** 67. C Linthorpe *York* 66-68; NSM Huddersfield St Jo *Wakef* 74-76; C 76-79; V Cornholme 79-88; rtd 88; Perm to Offic *Wakef* from 88. *284 Burnley Road, Todmorden OL14 8EW* Tel (01706) 812224

MYERS, Paul Henry. b 49. ALA72. Qu Coll Birm 74. **d** 77 **p** 78. C Baildon *Bradf* 77-80; C W Bromwich All SS *Lich* 80-83; Chapl RAF 83-86; V Milton *Lich* 87-92; C Baswich 96-99; C Hixon w Stowe-by-Chartley 99-02; TV Mid Trent from 02. *2 Vicarage Way, Hixon, Stafford ST18 0FT* Tel (01889) 270418

MYERS, Peter John. b 60. St Jo Coll Dur BA81. Linc Th Coll 84. **d** 84 **p** 85. C Bulwell St Mary *S'well* 84-88; C Shrewsbury H Cross *Lich* 88-92; rtd 92. *15 Winchelsea Street, Dover CT17 9ST* Tel (01304) 204354

MYERS, Robert William John. b 57. Aus Nat Univ BSc80 Newc Univ Aus DipEd82. Trin Coll Bris DipHE95. **d** 95 **p** 96. C Addiscombe St Mary Magd w St Martin *S'wark* 95-98; C Surbiton St Matt 98-03; Australia from 03. *88 Adelaide Street, PO Box125, Blayney, NSW, Australia 2799* Tel (0061) (2) 6368 2065 Fax 6368 4185 E-mail rwjmyers@netscape.net

MYERSCOUGH, Robin Nigel. b 44. K Coll Lon BD69 Nottm Univ PGCE70. Coll of Resurr Mirfield 66. **d** 81 **p** 82. Hon C Diss *Nor* 81-84; Chapl Nor Sch 81-84; Hd RS Sedbergh Sch 84-85; Chapl and Hd RS Dur Sch 85-92; Chapl Gresham's Sch Holt 92-01; Asst Chapl 01-04; rtd 04; Perm to Offic *Nor* from 04. *Hamer, The Street, Bodham, Holt NR25 6NW* Tel (01263) 588859

MYLNE, Mrs Christine. b 44. Open Univ BA76 Univ of Wales (Lamp) MA03. St Alb Minl Tr Scheme 89 NEOC 04. **d** 04. NSM Norham and Duddo *Newc* from 04; NSM Cornhill w Carham from 04; NSM Branxton from 04. *Gracegarth, Norham, Berwick-upon-Tweed TD15 2JZ* Tel (01289) 382187

MYLNE, Denis Colin. b 31. Jordan Hill Coll Glas CYCW75. Kelham Th Coll 69. **d** 71. Perm to Offic *Glas* 74-84 and *Ab* 84-88; C Bedford All SS *St Alb* 88-91; C Harpenden St Jo 91-96; rtd 96; Perm to Offic *Newc* from 96; Hon C Kelso *Edin* from 99. *Gracegarth, Ubbanford, Norham, Berwick-upon-Tweed TD15 2JZ* Tel (01289) 382187

MYNETT, Colin. b 25. Roch Th Coll 61. **d** 63 **p** 64. C Liskeard w St Keyne *Truro* 63-66; R Lifton *Ex* 66-71; R Kelly w Bradstone 66-71; TV Devonport St Aubyn 71-75; V Cinderford St Jo *Glouc* 75-84; P-in-c Pittville All SS 84-89; rtd 89. *5 Heron Close, Cheltenham GL51 6HA* Tel (01242) 523341

MYNETT, John Alan. b 37. CEng MIMechE67 Bris Univ BSc59 MSc61. N Ord Course 82. **d** 85 **p** 86. NSM Poynton *Ches* 85-90; NSM Macclesfield Team Par 90-01; P-in-c Sutton St Geo 98-01; Perm to Offic from 01. *1 Landseer Drive, Marple Bridge, Stockport SK6 5BL* Tel 0161-285 8558 E-mail johanne@mynett46.freeserve.co.uk

MYNORS, James Baskerville. b 49. Peterho Cam BA70 MA74. Ridley Hall Cam 70 St Jo Coll Nottm 77. **d** 78 **p** 80. Hon C Leic H Apostles *Leic* 78-79; C Virginia Water *Guildf* 79-83; C Patcham *Chich* 83-88; P-in-c Fowlmere and Thriplow *Ely* 88-01; Sen Tutor EAMTC 88-90; Vice-Prin 90-97; P-in-c Gt w Lt Abington from 01; P-in-c Hildersham from 01; Dioc Rural Miss Officer from 04. *The Vicarage, 35 Church Lane, Little Abington, Cambridge CB1 6BQ* Tel (01223) 891350 E-mail jim@mynors.me.uk

N

NADEN, Anthony Joshua. b 38. Jes Coll Ox BA62 MA64 SOAS Lon PhD73. Wycliffe Hall Ox 60. **d** 62 **p** 63. C Rowner *Portsm* 62-66; C Fisherton Anger *Sarum* 69-72; Ghana from 72. *PO Box TM524, Techiman, B-A/R, Ghana* E-mail tanddbusiness@yahoo.com

NADIN, Dennis Lloyd. b 37. St D Coll Lamp BA60 Man Univ MEd81. Ridley Hall Cam 60. **d** 64 **p** 65. C Childwall All SS *Liv* 64-67; P-in-c Seacroft *Ripon* 67-69; Project Officer Grubb Inst 69-70; Lect CA Tr Coll Blackheath 70-72; Community Educn Essex Co Coun 73-80; Public Preacher *Chelmsf* from 73; Perm to Offic *St Alb* from 01; rtd 02. *The Hermitage, 201 Willowfield, Harlow CM18 6RZ* Tel (01279) 325904

NAGEL, Canon Lawson Chase Joseph. b 49. Univ of Michigan BA71 K Coll Lon PhD82 ARHistS75. Sarum & Wells Th Coll 81. **d** 83 **p** 84. C Chiswick St Nic w St Mary *Lon* 83-86; Sec Gen Confraternity of the Blessed Sacrament from 85; C Horsham *Chich* 86; TV 86-91; V Aldwick from 91; Hon Can Popondota from 05. *The Vicarage, 25 Gossamer Lane, Aldwick, Bognor Regis PO21 3AT* Tel (01243) 262049 E-mail nagel@aldwick.demon.co.uk

NAIDU, Michael Sriram. b 28. Univ of the South (USA) 81. Ridley Hall Cam 86. **d** 80 **p** 85. Acting Chapl Stuttgart *Eur* 85-91; Chapl 91-00; rtd 00. *Kloster Kinchberg, 72172 Sulz am Neckar, Stuttgart, Germany* Tel (0049) (7454) 883136 *or* 87418 Fax 883250

NAIRN, Frederick William. b 43. TCD 64. Luther NW Th Sem DMin88. **d** 67 **p** 68. C Larne and Inver *Conn* 67-70; Chapl RAF 70-74; P-in-c Harmston *Linc* 75-77; V 77-84; V Coleby 78-84; USA from 84; rtd 04. *5895 Stoneybrook Drive, Minnetonka, MN 55345, USA*

NAIRN, Canon Stuart Robert. b 51. K Coll Lon BD75 AKC75 Univ of Wales (Lamp) MTh04. St Aug Coll Cant 75. **d** 76 **p** 77. C E Dereham *Nor* 76-80; TV Hempnall 80-88; V Narborough w Narford 88-99; R Pentney St Mary Magd w W Bilney 88-99; R Narborough w Narford and Pentney from 99; P-in-c Castleacre, Newton, Westacre and Southacre from 97; RD Lynn 91-99; Hon Can Nor Cathl from 03. *The Rectory, Main Road, Narborough, King's Lynn PE32 1TE* Tel (01760) 338552 *or* tel and fax 338562 E-mail nairn@narvalleygroup.freeserve.co.uk

NAIRN-BRIGGS, The Very Revd George Peter. b 45. AKC69. St Aug Coll Cant 69. **d** 70 **p** 71. C Catford St Laur *S'wark* 70-73; C Raynes Park St Sav 73-75; V Salfords 75-81; V St Helier 81-87; Dioc Soc Resp Adv *Wakef* 87-97; Can Res Wakef Cathl 92-97; Provost Wakef 97-00; Dean Wakef from 00. *The Deanery, 1 Cathedral Close, Margaret Street, Wakefield WF1 2DP* Tel (01924) 210005 Mobile 07770-636840 Fax (01924) 210009 E-mail thedeanofwakefield@hotmail.com

NAISH, Miss Ann. b 65. St Jo Coll Dur BA04. Cranmer Hall Dur. **d** 05. C Gorleston St Andr *Nor* from 05. *2 Elmgrove Road, Gorleston, Great Yarmouth NR31 7PP* Tel 07800-866494 (mobile) E-mail annien@fish.co.uk

NAISH, Timothy James Neville. b 57. St Jo Coll Ox BA80 MA88. WMMTC 86. **d** 87 **p** 88. CMS from 81; C Cov H Trin *Cov* 87; Dir Th Formation (Shaba) Zaïre 88-91; Research Fell, Tutor, and Lect Qu Coll Birm 92-93; Perm to Offic *Birm* 92-93; Tutor and Lect Bp Tucker Th Coll Uganda 93-00; R Hanborough and Freeland *Ox* from 00. *The Rectory, Swan Lane, Long Hanborough, Witney OX29 8BT* Tel (01993) 881270 E-mail naish@beeb.net

NAISMITH, Mrs Carol. b 37. St Andr Univ MA59 Edin Univ MTh98. Edin Dioc NSM Course 85. **d** 90 **p** 94. NSM Edin St Marg *Edin* 90-94; NSM Edin Old St Paul 90-00; C Edin St Salvador from 00. *38 Castle Avenue, Edinburgh EH12 7LB* Tel 0131-334 4486 E-mail carol@naismith.freeserve.co.uk

✠**NALEDI, The Rt Revd Theophilus Tswere.** b 36. UNISA BTh82 K Coll Lon MTh84. St Bede's Coll Umtata LTh59. **d** 59 **p** 60 **c** 87. S Africa 59-70; R Kimberley St Jas 67-70; Botswana 71-83 and 85-87; R Gaborone 71-73; Adn and R Lobatse 74-83; C Wimbledon *S'wark* 83-85; Prov Sec Ch of the Prov of Cen Africa 86-87; Bp Matabeleland Zimbabwe 87-01; Bp Botswana 01-04; rtd 04. *PO Box 237, Gaborone, Botswana*

NALL, Sheila Ann. b 48. Univ of Wales (Ban) BA69. WMMTC 00. **d** 03 **p** 04. NSM Worc St Wulstan *Worc* from 03. *108 Ombersley Road, Worcester WR3 7EZ* Tel and fax (01905) 26284 E-mail nall@simplesurveys.freeserve.co.uk

NANCARROW, Mrs Rachel Mary. b 38. Cam Inst of Educn TCert59. EAMTC 87. **d** 90 **p** 94. NSM Girton *Ely* 90-95; P-in-c Foxton 95-01; P-in-c Shepreth 98-01; C Fulbourn and Gt and Lt Wilbraham 01-03; rtd 03. *Thimble Cottage, 11 Geeston, Ketton, Stamford PE9 3RH* Tel (01780) 729382 E-mail r.m.nancarrow@skogen.co.uk

NANKIVELL, Christopher Robert Trevelyan. b 33. Jes Coll Ox BA55 MA63 Birm Univ MSocSc79. Linc Th Coll 56. **d** 58 **p** 59. C Bloxwich *Lich* 58-60; C Stafford St Mary 60-64; P-in-c Malins Lee 64-72; Soc Welfare Sector Min to Milton Keynes Chr Coun 73-76; Tutor Qu Coll Birm 76-81; rtd 96. *77 Pereira Road, Birmingham B17 9JA* Tel 0121-427 1197

NAPIER, Graeme Stewart Patrick Columbanus. b 66. Magd Coll Ox BA MA MPhil LRSM. St Steph Ho Ox. **d** 95 **p** 96. C Inverness St Andr *Mor* 95-98; Asst P St Laurence Ch Ch Australia 98-02; Min Can and Succ Westmr Abbey from 02. *4B Little Cloister, Westminster Abbey, London SW1P 3PL* Tel (020) 7654 4850 E-mail graeme.napier@westminster-abbey.org

NAPIER, Lady (Jennifer Beryl). *See* BLACK, Jennifer Beryl

NARUSAWA, Masaki Alec. b 53. K Coll Lon BD77 AKC77. Linc Th Coll 77. **d** 78 **p** 79. C Hendon St Alphage *Lon* 78-81; C Eastcote St Lawr 81-84; V Glodwick *Man* 84-99; P-in-c Withington St Crispin 99-03; Perm to Offic *Blackb* from 03. *7 Clevedon Road, Blackpool FY1 2NX* Tel (01253) 625404 Fax 625354 E-mail masaki.narusawa@lineone.net

NASCIMENTO COOK, Mrs Anesia. b 62. Mogidas Cruces Univ BA86. Porto Allegre Th Sem BTh91. **d** 91 **p** 93. Brazil 91-94; Lic to Offic *St Alb* 96-97; C Dinnington *Sheff* 97-99; P-in-c Shiregreen St Jas and St Chris from 99; P-in-c Shiregreen St Hilda from 05. *The Vicarage, 510 Bellhouse Road, Sheffield S5 0RG* Tel 0114-245 6526

NASH, Alan Frederick. b 46. Sarum & Wells Th Coll 72. **d** 75 **p** 76. C Foley Park *Worc* 75-79; P-in-c Mildenhall *Sarum* 79-82; Wilts Adnry Youth Officer 79-82; TV N Wingfield, Pilsley and Tupton *Derby* 82-85. *33 Manvers Road, Sheffield S6 2PJ*

NASH, David. b 25. K Coll Lon BD51 AKC51. **d** 52 **p** 53. C Buckhurst Hill *Chelmsf* 52-58; Min St Cedd CD Westcliff 58-66; R Rivenhall 66-83; P-in-c Boscastle w Davidstow *Truro* 83-85; TR 85-90; rtd 90; Perm to Offic *Truro* from 90. *9 Boscundle Avenue, Falmouth TR11 5BU*

NASH, Preb David John. b 41. Pemb Coll Ox BA64 MA70. Wells Th Coll 65. **d** 67 **p** 68. C Preston Ascension *Lon* 67-70; TV Hackney 70-75; TV Clifton *S'well* 76-82; V Winchmore Hill St Paul *Lon* 82-98; AD Enfield 87-91; R Monken Hadley from 98; AD Cen Barnet 00-04; Preb St Paul's Cathl from 96. *The Rectory, Hadley Common, Barnet EN5 5QD* Tel (020) 8449 2414 E-mail prebdjnash@yahoo.co.uk

NASH, Mrs Ingrid. b 36. SRN57 RNT80 BEd78 Cert Counselling 89. S'wark Ord Course 91. **d** 94 **p** 95. NSM Eltham Park St Luke *S'wark* from 94; Perm to Offic *Roch* from 97. *13 Crookston Road, London SE9 1YH* Tel (020) 8850 0750

NASH, James Alexander. b 56. Seale-Hayne Agric Coll HND79. St Jo Coll Nottm BA94. **d** 97 **p** 98. C Trunch *Nor* 97-01; R Stratton St Mary w Stratton St Michael etc from 01. *The Rectory, Flowerpot Lane, Long Stratton, Norwich NR15 2TS* Tel (01508) 530238 E-mail james.nash8@btopenworld.com

NASH, James David Gifford. b 76. New Coll Ox MEng98. Wycliffe Hall Ox BTh03. **d** 03 **p** 04. C Plymouth St Andr and St Paul Stonehouse *Ex* from 03. *117 Lipson Road, Plymouth PL4 7NQ* Tel (01752) 661334 E-mail james.nash@wycliffe.ox.ac.uk

NASH, Paul. *See* NASH, William Paul

NASH, Paul. b 59. WMMTC 94. **d** 97 **p** 98. C Aston SS Pet and Paul *Birm* 97-02; Asst Chapl Birm Children's Hosp NHS Trust from 02; Tutor St Jo Coll Nottm from 02. *13 Jaffray Road, Birmingham B24 8AZ* Tel 0121-384 6034 E-mail paulandsal@msn.com

NASH, Paul Alexander. b 20. Glouc Th Course 73. **d** 76 **p** 76. NSM Coleford w Staunton *Glouc* 76-88; Perm to Offic from 98. *16 Orchard Road, Coleford GL16 8AU* Tel (01594) 832758

NASH, Reginald Frank. b 15. **d** 66 **p** 67. C Glouc St Jas *Glouc* 66-69; P-in-c Sharpness 69-75; V Dymock w Donnington 75-77; R Dymock w Donnington and Kempley 77-80; rtd 80; Perm to Offic *Glouc* 80-94. *Holcombe Glen Cottage, Minchinhampton, Stroud GL6 9AJ* Tel (01453) 835635

NASH, Robin Louis. b 51. Open Univ BA87. Aston Tr Scheme 80 Chich Th Coll 82. **d** 84 **p** 85. C Lymington *Win* 84-86; C Andover w Foxcott 86-90; R Kegworth *Leic* 90-01; P-in-c Bournemouth St Alb *Win* from 01. *St Alban's Vicarage, 17 Linwood Road, Bournemouth BH9 1DW* Tel (01202) 534193 E-mail vicar@saintalban.org.uk

NASH, The Ven Trevor Gifford. b 30. Clare Coll Cam BA53 MA57. Cuddesdon Coll 53. **d** 55 **p** 56. C Cheshunt *St Alb* 55-57; CF (TA) 56-61; C Kingston All SS *S'wark* 57-61; C Stevenage *St Alb* 61-63; V Leagrave 63-67; Dir Luton Samaritans 66-67; Chapl St Geo Hosp Lon 67-73; R Win St Lawr and St Maurice w St Swithun *Win* 73-82; Bp's Adv Min of Healing 73-98; P-in-c Win H Trin 77-82; RD Win 75-82; Hon Can Win Cathl 80-90; Adn Basingstoke 82-90; Exec Co-ord Acorn Chr Healing Trust 90-97; Pres Guild of Health 92-97; Warden Guild of St Raphael 95-98; Perm to Offic *Win* from 95; rtd 97; Hon Chapl Win Cathl *Win* from 98. *The Corner Stone, 50B Hyde Street, Winchester SO23 7DY* Tel (01962) 861759

NASH, William Henry. b 31. Oak Hill Th Coll 58. **d** 61 **p** 62. C New Milverton *Cov* 61-64; C Toxteth Park St Philemon w St Silas *Liv* 64-67; V Bryn 67-76; NW Area Sec CPAS 76-82; V Penn Fields *Lich* 82-99; rtd 99; Perm to Offic *Lich* from 01. *29 Peterdale Drive, Penn, Wolverhampton WV4 5NY* Tel (01902) 344745

NASH, William Paul. b 48. St Mich Coll Llan 86. **d** 87 **p** 88. C Pembroke Dock *St D* 87-89; P-in-c Llawhaden w Bletherston and Llanycefn 89-90; V 90-92; P-in-c E Brixton St Jude *S'wark* 92-96; V 96-99; V Cwmaman *St D* 99-04; R Pendine w Llanmiloe and Eglwys Gymyn w Marros from 04. *The Rectory, Pendine, Carmarthen SA33 4PD* Tel (01994) 453405

NASH-WILLIAMS, Barbara Ruth. b 66. Lanc Univ BA88. EAMTC 96. **d** 99 **p** 00. C Tettenhall Wood and Perton *Lich* 99-02; NSM Cheswardine, Childs Ercall, Hales, Hinstock etc from 04. *The Rectory, Tibberton, Newport TF10 8NL* Tel (01952) 551063 E-mail barnw@fish.co.uk

NASH-WILLIAMS, Mark Christian Victor. b 64. Trin Hall Cam BA86 MA90 PGCE87. Qu Coll Birm BD01. **d** 02 **p** 03. C Edgmond w Kynnersley and Preston Wealdmoors *Lich* from 02. *The Rectory, Tibberton, Newport TF10 8NN* Tel (01952) 551063 E-mail mnw@fish.co.uk

NASH-WILLIAMS, Canon Piers le Sor Victor. b 35. Trin Hall Cam BA57 MA61. Cuddesdon Coll 59. **d** 61 **p** 62. C Milton *Win* 61-64; Asst Chapl Eton Coll 64-66; Perm to Offic *Chich* 66-68; C Furze Platt *Ox* 69-72; V Newbury St Geo Wash Common 72-73; TV Newbury 73-91; R Ascot Heath 91-01; Hon Can Ch Ch 01; rtd 01; Perm to Offic *Ox* from 02. *18 Chiltern Close, Newbury RG14 6SZ* Tel (01635) 31762 E-mail pnashwilliams@tesco.net

NASON, David. b 44. Open Univ BA92 ACA68 FCA78. Ripon Coll Cuddesdon 84. **d** 86 **p** 87. C Banstead *Guildf* 86-89; PV Chich Cathl *Chich* from 89; Chapl Prebendal Sch Chich from 89. *1 St Richard's Walk, Canon Lane, Chichester PO19 1QA* Tel (01243) 775615

NASSAR, Nadim. b 64. Near E Sch of Th BTh88. **d** 03 **p** 04. Prin Trin Inst for Christianity and Culture 03-05; Dir from 05. *Holy Trinity Church, Sloane Street, London SW1X 9DF* Tel (020) 7730 8830 Mobile 07961-968193 E-mail principal@theticc.com

NATERS, Charles James Reginald. b 20. Selw Coll Cam BA45 MA47. Coll of Resurr Mirfield 46. **d** 47 **p** 48. C Ardwick St Benedict *Man* 47-52; SSJE from 54; S Africa 59-68; Lic to Offic *Ox* 69-76; *Lon* 76-85 and 88-02; *Leic* 85-88; Superior SSJE 91-00. *College of St Barnabas, Blackberry Lane, Lingfield RH7 6NJ*

NATHANAEL, Brother. *See* THOMPSON, Kenneth

NATHANAEL, Martin Moses. b 43. Lon Univ BEd73 K Coll Lon MTh77. Ripon Coll Cuddesdon 77. **d** 79 **p** 80. C Hampton All SS *Lon* 79-82; P-in-c Kensal Town St Thos w St Andr and St Phil 82-83; Hd Div Bp Stopford Sch Lon 83-91; TV Tring

St Alb 91-00; rtd 00. *6 Ryelands, Welwyn Garden City AL7 4LQ* Tel (01707) 390323 E-mail martinascend@aol.com

NATHANIEL, Garth Edwin Peter. b 61. Brunel Univ BTh99. Lon Bible Coll 96. **d** 98 **p** 99. NSM Hanwell St Mary w St Chris *Lon* 98-99; C Lt Stanmore St Lawr 99-01; P-in-c Brockmoor *Worc* from 02. *5 Leys Road, Brockmoor, Brierley Hill DY5 3UR* Tel (01384) 263327 Mobile 07949-490265 Fax (01384) 573382 E-mail gn004d6359@blueyonder.co.uk

NATHANIEL, Ivan Wasim. Punjab Univ MA65. Bp's Coll Calcutta 59. **d** 62 **p** 64. India 62-68; C Newland St Aug *York* 68-70; Hon C Crawley *Chich* 70-98; Chapl H Trin Sch Crawley 76-97; Hd of Relig Studies 76-97; Perm to Offic *Chich* from 97. *13 Haywards, Crawley RH10 3TR* Tel (01293) 882932

NATTRASS, Elizabeth Jane. b 59. Carl and Blackb Dioc Tr Inst 97. **d** 00 **p** 01. C Dalston w Cumdivock, Raughton Head and Wreay *Carl* 00-03; TV S Barrow from 03. *St Aidan's Vicarage, 31 Middle Hill, Barrow-in-Furness LA13 9HD* Tel (01229) 830445 E-mail nattrassjane@aol.com

NATTRASS, Michael Stuart. b 41. CBE98. Man Univ BA62. Cuddesdon Coll 62. **d** 64 **p** 65. C Easington Colliery *Dur* 64-65; C Silksworth 65-68; Perm to Offic *S'well* 68-72; Lic to Offic *Dur* 72-76; Perm to Offic *Lon* 76-78; Hon C Pinner from 78. *81 Cecil Park, Pinner HA5 5HL* Tel (020) 8866 0217 Fax 8930 0622 E-mail msnattrass@onetel.com

NAUDÉ, John Donald. b 62. Ridley Hall Cam 95. **d** 97 **p** 98. C Kettering Ch the King *Pet* 97-00; C Wellingborough All Hallows from 00; Dioc Disability Adv from 05. *20 Ribble Close, Wellingborough NN8 5XJ* Tel (01933) 679688 E-mail johnnaude@tinyworld.co.uk

NAUMANN, Canon David Sydney. b 26. Ripon Hall Ox 54. **d** 55 **p** 56. C Herne Bay Ch Ch *Cant* 55-58; Asst Chapl United Sheff Hosps 58-60; V Reculver *Cant* 60-64; Dioc Youth Chapl 63-70; R Eastwell w Boughton Aluph 65-67; V Westwell 65-67; Warden St Gabr Retreat Ho Westgate 68-70; V Littlebourne 70-82; RD E Bridge 78-82; Hon Can Cant Cathl 81-00; R Sandwich 82-91; RD Sandwich 85-90; rtd 91; Perm to Offic *Cant* from 91. *2 The Forrens, The Precincts, Canterbury CT1 2ER* Tel (01227) 458939

NAUNTON, Hugh Raymond. b 38. Whitelands Coll Lon CertEd69 Open Univ BA75. Bernard Gilpin Soc Dur 59 Chich Th Coll 60. **d** 63 **p** 64. C Stanground *Ely* 63-66; NSM Woolwich St Mary w H Trin *S'wark* 66-67; NSM Wandsworth St Anne 67-69 and 71-73; NSM Paddington St Sav *Lon* 69-71; NSM Cuddington *Guildf* 73-78; Hd RE Raynes Park High Sch 69-76; Hd RE Paddington Sch 76-78; Sen Teacher and Hd RE Christ's Sch Richmond 79-93; Hon C Cheam Common St Phil *S'wark* 79-95; C Cheam 95-02; Perm to Offic *Guildf* 97-02; TV Selsdon St Jo w St Fran *S'wark* 02-03; rtd 03; Perm to Offic *S'wark* from 04. *35 Farm Way, Worcester Park KT4 8RZ* Tel (020) 8395 1748 E-mail hugh.naunton@ukgateway.net

NAYLOR, Alison Louise. *See* CHESWORTH, Mrs Alison Louise

NAYLOR, Barry. *See* NAYLOR, Canon James Barry

NAYLOR, Fiona. b 68. CQSW93. St Jo Coll Nottm 02. **d** 05. C Len Valley *Cant* from 05. *The Vicarage, Old Ashford Road, Lenham, Maidstone ME17 2PX* Tel (01622) 853919 E-mail fionanaylor@btinternet.com

NAYLOR, Canon Frank. b 36. Lon Univ BA58 Liv Univ MA63. NW Ord Course 75. **d** 75 **p** 76. NSM Eccleston Ch Ch *Liv* 75-92; Asst Dioc Chapl to the Deaf 92-94; Sen Chapl from 94; Hon Can Liv Cathl from 01. *27 Daresbury Road, Eccleston, St Helens WA10 5DR* Tel (01744) 757034

NAYLOR, Ian Frederick. b 47. AKC70 Open Univ BA92 Heythrop Coll Lon MA00. St Aug Coll Cant 70. **d** 71 **p** 72. C Camberwell St Giles *S'wark* 71-74; OSB 74-86; Chapl RN 86-04; rtd 04. *35 Carlton House, Western Parade, Southsea PO5 3ED* Tel (023) 9282 6264 E-mail if.naylor@ntlworld.com

NAYLOR, Ian Stuart. b 63. Wycliffe Hall Ox. **d** 01 **p** 02. C Ipswich St Marg *St E* 01-04; P-in-c Martlesham w Brightwell from 04. *The Rectory, 17 Lark Rise, Martlesham Heath, Ipswich IP5 3SA* Tel (01473) 622424 Mobile 07712-309848 E-mail inaylor17@aol.com

NAYLOR, Canon James Barry. b 50. Lon Univ BSc71 St Benet's Hall Ox BA75. Wycliffe Hall Ox 72. **d** 76 **p** 76. C Catford (Southend) and Downham *S'wark* 76-79; TV 79-82; P-in-c Lewisham St Swithun 82-87; V E Dulwich St Jo 87-97; RD Dulwich 90-97; P-in-c Blythburgh w Reydon *St E* 97-99; P-in-c Frostenden, Henastead, Covehithe etc 97-99; P-in-c Southwold 97-99; P-in-c Uggeshall w Sotherton, Wangford and Henham 97-99; TR Sole Bay 99-02; Chapl Supervisor St Felix Sch Southwold 99-02; Can Res Leic Cathl *Leic* from 02; C The Abbey Leic from 02; C Leic H Spirit from 02. *1 Kirby Road, Leicester LE3 6BD* Tel 0116-262 0788 E-mail barry.cathedral@leicester.anglican.org

NAYLOR, Miss Jean. b 29. Linc Th Coll 77. **dss** 79 **d** 87. Charlton St Luke w H Trin *S'wark* 79-84; Crofton Park St Hilda w St Cypr 84-89; Par Dn 87-89; rtd 89; Perm to Offic *Wakef* from 89. *12 Winter Terrace, Barnsley S75 2ES* Tel (01226) 204767

NAYLOR, John Watson. b 26. Trin Hall Cam BA52 MA56. Ripon Hall Ox 64. **d** 66 **p** 67. C Newc St Andr *Newc* 66-69; C Otterburn w Elsdon and Horsley w Byrness 69-72; R Husborne Crawley w Ridgmont *St Alb* 72-76; Chapl Caldicott Sch Farnham Royal 76-80; P-in-c Chollerton w Thockrington *Newc* 80-82; R Chollerton w Birtley and Thockrington 82-91; rtd 91; Perm to Offic *Newc* from 91. *Abbeyfield House, Bellingham, Hexham NE48 2BS* Tel (01434) 220106

NAYLOR, Canon Peter Aubrey. b 33. Kelham Th Coll 54 Ely Th Coll 57. **d** 58 **p** 59. C Shepherd's Bush St Steph *Lon* 58-62; C Portsea N End St Mark *Portsm* 62-66; Chapl HM Borstal Portsm 64-66; V Foley Park *Worc* 66-74; V Maidstone All SS w St Phil and H Trin *Cant* 74-81; P-in-c Tovil 79-81; V Maidstone All SS and St Phil w Tovil 81-91; Hon Can Cant Cathl 79-93; RD Sutton 80-86; R Biddenden and Smarden 91-93; P-in-c Leic St Marg and All SS *Leic* 93-96; P-in-c Leic St Aug 93-96; TR The Abbey Leic 96; rtd 98; Perm to Offic *Chich* 98-02; P-in-c Crowborough St Jo from 02. *St John's Vicarage, St John's Road, Crowborough TN6 1RZ* Tel and fax (01892) 654660

NAYLOR, Peter Edward. b 30. Linc Th Coll 58. **d** 61 **p** 62. C S Beddington St Mich *S'wark* 61-64; V S Lambeth St Ann 64-77; V Nork *Guildf* 77-90; R Ecton *Pet* 90-97; Warden Ecton Ho 90-97; rtd 97; Perm to Offic *Ely* 97-01; Perm to Offic *Eur* from 03. *51 avenue du Bezet, 64000 Pau, France* Tel (0033) (5) 59 62 41 68 E-mail peternaylor30@hotmail.com

NAYLOR, Peter Henry. b 41. MIMechE. Chich Th Coll 64. **d** 67 **p** 68. C Filton *Bris* 67-70; C Brixham *Ex* 70-72; C Leckhampton St Pet *Glouc* 72-76; V Brockworth 76-94; P-in-c Gt Witcombe 91-94; RD Glouc N 91-94; P-in-c The Ampneys w Driffield and Poulton 94-95; R 95-99; P-in-c Cheltenham Em w St Steph from 99. *The Vicarage, 25 Hatherley Court Road, Cheltenham GL51 5AG* Tel (01242) 523240

NAYLOR, Robert James. b 42. Liv Univ CQSW66. N Ord Course 74. **d** 77 **p** 78. C Aigburth *Liv* 77-80; Soc Resp Officer *Glouc* 80-85; Leonard Cheshire Foundn (Lon) 85-91; Dir The Stable Family Home Trust (Hants) from 91; NSM The Lulworths, Winfrith Newburgh and Chaldon *Sarum* 98-00; P-in-c from 00; RD Purbeck from 02. *The Rectory, West Road, West Lulworth, Wareham BH20 5RY* Tel (01929) 400550 E-mail robertnaylor@westlulworthrectory.org.uk

NAYLOR, Russell Stephen. b 45. Leeds Univ BA70. St Chad's Coll Dur 70. **d** 72 **p** 73. C Chapel Allerton *Ripon* 72-75; Ind Chapl *Liv* 75-81; P-in-c Burtonwood 81-83; V from 83. *The Vicarage, Chapel Lane, Burtonwood, Warrington WA5 4PT* Tel (01925) 225371 E-mail russ.naylor@btinternet.com

NAYLOR, Vivien Frances Damaris. *See* BRADLEY, Ms Vivien Frances Damaris

✠NAZIR-ALI, The Rt Revd Michael James. b 49. Karachi Univ BA70 St Edm Hall Ox BLitt74 MLitt81 Fitzw Coll Cam PGCTh72 MLitt77 ACT ThD85 Bath Univ Hon DLitt03 Greenwich Univ Hon DLitt03 Kent Univ Hon DD04 Westmr Coll Penn (USA) DHumLit04 Lambeth DD05. Ridley Hall Cam 70. **d** 74 **p** 76 **c** 84. C Cambridge H Sepulchre w All SS *Ely* 74-76; Tutorial Supervisor Th Cam Univ 74-76; Pakistan 76-86; Sen Tutor Karachi Th Coll 76-81; Provost Lahore 81-84; Bp Raiwind 84-86; Asst to Abp Cant 86-89; Co-ord of Studies and Ed Lambeth Conf 86-89; Hon C Ox St Giles and SS Phil and Jas w St Marg *Ox* 86-89; Gen Sec CMS 89-94; Asst Bp S'wark 89-94; Hon C Limpsfield and Titsey 89-94; Can Th Leic Cathl *Leic* 92-94; Bp Roch from 94; Visiting Prof Th and RS Univ of Greenwich from 96; Hon Fell St Edm Hall Ox from 99. *Bishopscourt, Rochester ME1 1TS* Tel (01634) 842721 Fax 831136 E-mail bishops.secretary@rochester.anglican.org

✠NDUNGANE, The Most Revd Winston Hugh Njongonkulu. b 41. K Coll Lon BD78 AKC78 MTh. St Pet Coll Alice 71. **d** 73 **p** 74 **c** 91. C Atholone S Africa 73-75; C Mitcham St Mark *S'wark* 75-76; C Hammersmith St Pet *Lon* 76-77; C Primrose Hill St Mary w Avenue Road St Paul 77-79; Asst Chapl Paris St Geo *Eur* 79; R Elsies River S Africa 80-81; Prov Liaison Officer 81-84; Prin St Bede's Th Coll Umtata 85-86; Prov Exec Officer 87-91; Bp Kimberley and Kuruman 91-96; Abp Cape Town from 96. *Bishopscourt, 16-20 Bishopscourt Drive, Claremont, 7708 South Africa* Tel (0027) (21) 761 2531 Fax 797 1298 *or* 761 4193 E-mail archbish@bishopscourt-cpsa.org.za

NEAL, Alan. b 27. Trin Coll Bris DipTh84. **d** 84 **p** 85. Hon C Broughty Ferry *Bre* 84-85; P-in-c Dundee St Ninian 85-86; R Annan *Glas* 86-94; R Lockerbie 86-94; rtd 94. *c/o Mr and Mrs Graham Rew, 3 Vallance Drive, Lockerbie DG11 2DU*

NEAL, Canon Anthony Terrence. b 42. BA CertEd. Chich Th Coll 65. **d** 68 **p** 69. C Cross Green St Sav and St Hilda *Ripon* 68-73; NSM Hawksworth Wood 73-78; Asst Chapl and Hd RE Abbey Grange High Sch Leeds 73-81; NSM Farnley *Ripon* 78-81; Dioc Adv in RE *Truro* 81-85; Children's Officer 85-87; Stewardship Adv 87-88; P-in-c St Erth 81-84; V 84-96; P-in-c Phillack w Gwithian and Gwinear 94-96; P-in-c Hayle 94-96; TR Godrevy from 96; Hon Can Truro Cathl from 94. *The Rectory, Forth an Tewennow, Phillack, Hayle TR27 4QE* Tel (01736) 753541 *or* 754866 Fax 755235 E-mail steamerneal@tiscali.co.uk

NEAL, Canon Christopher Charles. b 47. St Pet Coll Ox BA69. Ridley Hall Cam 69. **d** 72 **p** 73. C Addiscombe St Mary *Cant* 72-76; C Camberley St Paul *Guildf* 76-83; TV 83-86; V Thame w Towersey *Ox* 86-98; TR Thame 98-03; Hon Can Ch Ch 98-03;

Dir Miss Movement CMS from 03. *CMS, Partnership House, 157 Waterloo Road, London SE1 8XA* Tel (020) 7928 8681 E-mail katrina@stmarys.psa-online.com

NEAL, Miss Frances Mary. b 37. BEd76. S'wark Ord Course 94. **d** 96 **p** 97. NSM Catford (Southend) and Downham *S'wark* from 96. *29 Ballamore Road, Downham, Bromley BR1 5LN* Tel (020) 8698 6616

NEAL, Gary Roy. b 57. St Jo Coll Nottm 03. **d** 05. C Kinson *Sarum* from 05. *13 Greaves Close, Bournemouth BH10 5EG* Tel (01202) 521480 E-mail gary@cofekinson.org.uk

NEAL, Canon Geoffrey Martin. b 40. AKC63. **d** 64 **p** 65. C Wandsworth St Paul *S'wark* 64-66; USA 66-68; C Reigate St Mark *S'wark* 68-70; P-in-c Wandsworth St Faith 70-72; V 72-75; V Houghton Regis *St Alb* 75-95; Hon Can St Alb 93-95; rtd 00; Perm to Offic *St Alb* from 00. *63 The Moor, Carlton, Bedford MK43 7JS* Tel (01234) 720938

NEAL, John Edward. b 44. Nottm Univ BTh74. Linc Th Coll 70. **d** 74 **p** 75. C Lee St Marg *S'wark* 74-77; C Clapham St Jo 77; C Clapham Ch Ch and St Jo 77-81; P-in-c Eltham St Barn 81-83; V 83-98; Sub-Dean Eltham 89-91; Sub-Dean Greenwich S 91-97; RD Greenwich S from 97; V Eltham St Jo from 98. *The Vicarage, Sowerby Close, London SE9 6HB* Tel (020) 8850 2731 *or* 8859 1242

NEAL, Mrs Stephanie Kae. b 34. Girton Coll Cam BA56 MA60. Dioc OLM tr scheme 97. **d** 00 **p** 01. OLM Hundred River *St E* from 00. *12 Chartres Piece, Willingham, Beccles NR34 8DA* Tel (01502) 575208

NEAL, Stephen Charles. b 44. K Coll Lon BSc66 MCMI76. N Ord Course 90. **d** 93 **p** 94. C Walmsley *Man* 93-96; P-in-c Bolton St Matt w St Barn 96-98; TV Halliwell 98-02; Chapl Bolton Hospice from 02. *47 The Woodlands, Lostock, Bolton BL6 4JD* Tel (01204) 496070 *or* 364375 E-mail steveneal@themutual.net

NEALE, Alan James Robert. b 52. LSE BSc(Econ)73. Wycliffe Hall Ox BA76 MA81. **d** 77 **p** 78. C Plymouth St Andr w St Paul and St Geo *Ex* 77-80; C Portswood Ch Ch *Win* 80-82; V Stanstead Abbots *St Alb* 82-85; Asst Master Chelmsf Hall Sch Eastbourne 85-88; USA from 88. *390 Indian Avenue, Middletown, RI 02842, USA*

NEALE, Andrew Jackson. b 58. Oak Hill Th Coll 97. **d** 99 **p** 00. C Harold Hill St Geo *Chelmsf* 99-02; C Bentley Common, Kelvedon Hatch and Navestock 02-03; TV Chigwell and Chigwell Row from 03. *The Vicarage, Romford Road, Chigwell IG7 4QD* Tel (020) 8501 5150 E-mail andy@neale2pray.freeserve.co.uk

NEALE, David. b 50. Lanchester Poly BSc72. St Mich Coll Llan BD83. **d** 83 **p** 84. Min Can St Woolos Cathl *Mon* 83-87; Chapl St Woolos Hosp Newport 85-87; R Blaina and Nantyglo *Mon* 87-91; Video and Tech Officer Bd of Miss 91-01; TV Cyncoed 99-01; Creative Resources Officer 01-03; V Maindee from 03. *St John's Vicarage, 25 St John's Road, Newport NP19 8GR* Tel (01633) 674155 E-mail dneale@ntlworld.com

NEALE, Edward. *See* NEALE, Canon James Edward McKenzie

NEALE, Geoffrey Arthur. b 41. Brasted Th Coll 61 St Aid Birkenhead 63. **d** 65 **p** 66. C Stoke *Cov* 65-68; C Fareham H Trin *Portsm* 68-71; TV 71-72; R Binstead 72-77; TR Bottesford w Ashby *Linc* 77-80; V Horncastle w Low Toynton 80-90; V Brigg 90-95; V Blockley w Aston Magna and Bourton on the Hill *Glouc* 95-01; Local Min Officer 95-01; V Heath and Reach *St Alb* from 01; RD Dunstable 02-04. *The Vicarage, 2 Reach Lane, Heath and Reach, Leighton Buzzard LU7 0AL* Tel (01525) 237633 Mobile 07703-174761 E-mail geoffneale@msn.com

NEALE, Hannah. b 40. SEITE. **d** 99 **p** 00. NSM Mitcham St Mark *S'wark* from 99. *3D Grenfell Road, Mitcham CR4 2BZ* Tel (020) 8646 4752

NEALE, Canon James Edward McKenzie (Eddie). b 38. MBE04. Selw Coll Cam BA61 Nottm Trent Univ Hon DLitt00 Nottm Univ Hon DD03. Clifton Th Coll 61. **d** 63 **p** 64. C Everton St Ambrose w St Tim *Liv* 63-72; Relig Adv BBC Radio Merseyside 72-76; V Bestwood St Matt *S'well* 76-86; Dioc Urban Officer 86-91; V Nottingham St Mary and St Cath 91-03; Hon Can S'well Minster 91-03; rtd 03; Perm to Offic *S'well* from 03. *Church Cottage, Church Lane, Maplebeck, Nottingham NG22 0BS* Tel (01636) 636559 E-mail eddie@neale007.freeserve.co.uk

NEALE, Mrs Jan Celia. b 42. EMMTC 92. **d** 92 **p** 94. C Gt and Lt Coates w Bradley *Linc* 92-96; TV 96-01; TV Chambersbury *St Alb* from 01. *St Benedict's Vicarage, Peascroft Road, Hemel Hempstead HP3 8EP* Tel (01442) 243934

✠**NEALE, The Rt Revd John Robert Geoffrey.** b 26. AKC54 St Boniface Warminster 54. **d** 55 **p** 56 **c** 74. C St Helier *S'wark* 55-58; Chapl Ardingly Coll 58-62; Recruitment Sec CACTM 63-66; ACCM 66-68; R Hascombe *Guildf* 68-74; Can Missr and Dir Post-Ord Tr 68-74; Hon Can Guildf Cathl 68-74; Adn Wilts *Sarum* 74-80; Suff Bp Ramsbury 74-81; Area Bp Ramsbury 81-88; Can and Preb Sarum Cathl 74-88; Sec Partnership for World Miss 89-91; Asst Bp S'wark 89-91; Asst Bp Lon 89-91; rtd 91; Asst Bp B & W from 91; Hon Asst Bp Bris from 92; Hon Asst Bp Glouc from 94. *26 Prospect, Corsham SN13 9AF* Tel (01249) 712557

NEALE, Martyn William. b 57. G&C Coll Cam BA78 MA82. Ripon Coll Cuddesdon 78. **d** 81 **p** 82. C Perry Hill St Geo *S'wark* 81-83; C Purley St Mark 83-85; V Abbey Wood 85-97; V Hawley H Trin *Guildf* from 97; V Minley from 97. *The Vicarage, Hawley, Blackwater, Camberley GU17 9BN* Tel (01276) 35287 E-mail frmartyn@aol.com

NEAUM, Canon David. b 12. Lich Th Coll 34. **d** 37 **p** 38. C Burton All SS *Lich* 37-39; C Cannock 39-43; R Kingstone w Gratwich 43-46; R Leigh 46-52; Tristan da Cunha 52-56; S Rhodesia 56-65; Rhodesia 65-80; Zimbabwe 80-81; St Helena 81-84; rtd 84; Australia from 84. *St John's Rectory, 225 Beechworth, Wodonga, Vic, Australia 3690* Tel (0061) (2) 6024 2053

NEAVE, Garry Reginald. b 51. Leic Univ BA72 MA73 PGCE74 MCMI. S'wark Ord Course. **d** 82 **p** 83. NSM Harlow St Mary Magd *Chelmsf* 82-87 and 92-99; Chapl Harlow Tertiary Coll 84-99; NSM St Mary-at-Latton *Chelmsf* 87-92; Dir Student Services and Admin W Herts Coll from 99. *West Hertfordshire College, Hempstead Road, Watford WD17 3EZ* Tel (01923) 812575 *or* (01279) 411775 E-mail garryn@westherts.ac.uk

NEECH, Canon Alan Summons. b 15. Dur Univ LTh37. Tyndale Hall Bris 34. **d** 39 **p** 40. BCMS 39-81; India 39-66; Can Lucknow 64-66; Overseas Sec BCMS 64-66; Gen Sec 66-81; Hon Can Cen Tanganyika from 72; Hon C Slough *Ox* 75-81; rtd 80; RD Loddon *Nor* 85-90; Perm to Offic from 90. *The Gardens Cottage, Rockland St Mary, Norwich NR14 7HQ* Tel (01508) 538519

NEED, The Very Revd Philip Alan. b 54. AKC75. Chich Th Coll 76. **d** 77 **p** 78. C Clapham Ch Ch and St Jo *S'wark* 77-79; C Luton All SS w St Pet *St Alb* 80-83; V Harlow St Mary Magd *Chelmsf* 83-89; P-in-c Chaddesden St Phil *Derby* 89-91; Bp's Dom Chapl *Chelmsf* 91-96; R Bocking St Mary from 96; Dean Bocking from 96; RD Braintree from 00. *The Deanery, Deanery Hill, Braintree CM7 5SR* Tel (01376) 324887 *or* 553092 E-mail philipneed@bocking81.freeserve.co.uk

NEEDHAM, Miss Patricia. b 32. **d** 87 **p** 94. Par Dn Warmsworth *Sheff* 87-89; Par Dn Norton Woodseats St Chad 89-92; Chapl Beauchief Abbey from 89; rtd 92; Perm to Offic *Sheff* 01-02. *14 Dalewood Drive, Sheffield S8 0EA* Tel 0114-236 2688

NEEDHAM, Brother Peter Douglas. b 56. Chich Th Coll 86. **d** 88 **p** 88. SSF from 80; C S Moor *Dur* 88-90; Chapl RN 91-93; Lic to Offic *Newc* 91-96 and *Lon* 97-99; C Ealing Ch the Sav *Lon* 99-02; P-in-c Grimethorpe *Wakef* 02-05; V Grimethorpe w Brierley from 05. *St Luke's Vicarage, High Street, Grimethorpe, Barnsley S72 7JA* Tel (01226) 717561 E-mail neddyneedham@mcmail.com

NEEDLE, Mrs Jill Mary. b 56. Matlock Coll of Educn TCert77 BEd78. St Jo Coll Nottm 03. **d** 05. NSM Allestree St Nic *Derby* from 05. *117 Hazelwood Road, Duffield, Belper DE56 4AA* Tel (01332) 840746 E-mail jill.needle@btinternet.com

NEEDLE, Paul Robert. b 45. Lon Univ DipTh70. Oak Hill Th Coll 67. **d** 70 **p** 71. C Gt Horton *Bradf* 70-74; C Pudsey St Lawr 74-77; Chapl St Luke's Hosp Bradf 78-80; Hon C Horton *Bradf* 78-80; NSM Irthlingborough *Pet* 87-90; NSM Gt w Lt Addington 90-94; NSM Gt w Lt Addington and Woodford 94-98; Bp's Media Adv from 97; NSM Higham Ferrers w Chelveston from 02. *106 Wharf Road, Higham Ferrers, Rushden NN10 8BH* Tel and fax (01933) 312800 Mobile 07802-731751 E-mail paulneedle@aol.com

NEEDS, Michael John. b 42. Open Univ BA82 Univ of Wales (Swansea) MSc84 PhD87. Wycliffe Hall Ox 91. **d** 93 **p** 94. C Aberystwyth *St D* 93-96; R Llanllwchaearn and Llanina from 96. *The Rectory, Llandysul Road, New Quay SA45 9RE* Tel and fax (01545) 560059 E-mail michael@mneeds.freeserve.co.uk

NEELY, Canon William George. b 32. Lon Univ BD62 QUB PhD. **d** 56 **p** 57. C Cregagh *D & D* 56-62; C-in-c Mt Merrion 62-68; I 68-76; Dioc Missr (Down) 70-76; Can Down Cathl 74-76; I Kilcooley w Littleton, Crohane and Killenaule *C & O* 76-84; P-in-c Fertagh 79-84; I Keady w Armaghbreague and Derrynoose *Arm* from 84; Tutor for Aux Min (Arm) from 86; Dir Post-Ord Tr from 86; Preb Swords St Patr Cathl Dublin from 97. *The Rectory, 31 Crossmore Road, Keady, Armagh BT60 3RH* Tel (028) 3753 1230

NEILAND, Paul Andrew. b 62. Dip Counselling & Psychotherapy 96 Wm Glasser Inst Dub RTCert96. St Pet Coll Wexford 80 CITC 00. **d** 01 **p** 02. NSM Enniscorthy w Clone, Clonmore, Monart etc *C & O* from 01. *Butlerstown, Killinick, Co Wexford, Irish Republic* Tel (00353) (53) 35701 *or* tel and fax 41784 Mobile 87-242 2842

NEILL, Barbara June. b 39. St Jo Coll Nottm. **d** 00 **p** 01. NSM Bestwood Park w Rise Park *S'well* from 00. *17 Harvest Close, Nottingham NG5 9BW* Tel 0115-975 3378 E-mail barbjn@btopenworld.com

NEILL, James Purdon. b 41. Lon Univ DipTh63. Oak Hill Th Coll 60. **d** 64 **p** 65. C Kendal St Thos *Carl* 64-68; Chapl Park Hill Flats Sheff 68-71; P-in-c Mansfield St Jo *S'well* 71-77; V

Nottingham St Ann w Em from 77. *St Ann's Vicarage, 17 Robin Hood Chase, Nottingham NG3 4EY* Tel 0115-950 5471 E-mail revd.jim.neill@talk21.com

✠**NEILL, The Most Revd John Robert Winder.** b 45. TCD BA66 MA69 Jes Coll Cam BA68 MA72 NUI Hon LLD03. Ridley Hall Cam 67. **d** 69 **p** 70 **c** 86. C Glenageary *D & G* 69-71; Lect CITC 70-71 and 82-84; Dioc Registrar (Ossory, Ferns and Leighlin) *C & O* 71-74; Bp's V, Lib and Chapter Registrar Kilkenny Cathl 71-74; I Abbeystrewry *C, C & R* 74-78; I Dublin St Bart w Leeson Park *D & G* 78-84; Chapl Community of St Jo the Ev 78-84; Dean Waterford *C & O* 84-86; Prec Lismore Cathl 84-86; Adn Waterford 84-86; I Waterford w Killea, Drumcannon and Dunhill 84-86; Bp T, K & A 86-97; Bp C & O 97-02; Abp Dublin *D & G* from 02. *The See House, 17 Temple Road, Dartry, Dublin 6, Irish Republic* Tel (00353) (1) 497 7849 Fax 497 6355 E-mail archbishop@dublin.anglican.org

NEILL, Richard Walter. b 67. Wadh Coll Ox BA89 Em Coll Cam BA92. Westcott Ho Cam CTM93. **d** 93 **p** 94. C Abbots Langley *St Alb* 93-97; C Wisley w Pyrford *Guildf* 97-00; V Winkfield and Cranbourne *Ox* from 00. *The Vicarage, Winkfield Street, Winkfield, Windsor SL4 4SW* Tel (01344) 882322 E-mail neill.hall@care4free.net

NEILL, Robert Chapman. b 51. Lon Univ BD82. CITC 77. **d** 77 **p** 78. C Lurgan Ch the Redeemer *D & D* 77-82; I Tullylish 82-88; I Mt Merrion 88-98; I Drumbo from 98. *Drumbo Rectory, 5 Pinehill Road, Ballylesson, Belfast BT8 8LA* Tel (028) 9082 6225 E-mail rc.neill@btinternet.com

NEILL, Canon Stephen Mahon. b 69. TCD BA91. CITC 91. **d** 93 **p** 94. C Monkstown *D & G* 93-95; Dom Chapl to Bp of Killaloe and Clonfert *L & K* from 95; C Limerick City 95-98; I Cloughjordan w Borrisokane etc from 98; Can Limerick Cathl from 04. *Modreeny Rectory, Cloughjordan, Co Tipperary, Irish Republic* Tel and fax (00353) (505) 42183 Mobile 87-232 8172 E-mail smneillmodreeny@eircom.net

NEILL, The Ven William Barnet. b 30. TCD BA61. **d** 63 **p** 64. C Belfast St Clem *D & D* 63-66; C Dundonald 66-72; I Drumgath 72-80; I Drumgooland 76-80; I Mt Merrion 80-83; I Dromore Cathl 83-97; Adn Dromore 85-97; rtd 97. *10 Cairnshill Court, Saintfield Road, Belfast BT8 4TX* Tel (028) 9079 2969

NEILL, Canon William Benjamin Alan. b 46. Open Univ BA76. CITC 68. **d** 71 **p** 72. C Dunmurry *Conn* 71-74; C Coleraine 75-77; C Dublin St Ann w St Steph *D & G* 77-78; I Convoy w Monellan and Donaghmore *D & R* 78-81; I Faughanvale 81-86; I Waterford w Killea, Drumcannon and Dunhill *C & O* 86-97; Dean Waterford 86-97; Prec Lismore Cathl 86-97; Prec Cashel Cathl 87-97; Can Ossory and Leighlin Cathls 96-97; I Dalkey St Patr *D & G* from 97; Can Ch Ch Cathl Dublin from 04. *The Rectory, Dalkey, Dun Laoghaire, Co Dublin, Irish Republic* Tel (00353) (1) 280 3369

NELLIST, Canon Valerie Ann. b 48. SRN69 SCM71. St And Dioc Tr Course 87. **d** 90 **p** 94. NSM W Fife Team Min *St And* 90-99; Hon Can St Ninian's Cathl Perth from 97; R Aberdour from 99; R Burntisland from 99; R Inverkeithing from 99. *28 Glamis Gardens, Dalgety Bay, Dunfermline KY11 9TD* Tel (01383) 824066 Fax 824668 E-mail rnellist44@aol.com

NELMES, Mrs Christine. b 41. St Mary's Coll Chelt Dip Teaching63 UWE BA97. S Dios Minl Tr Scheme 92. **d** 95 **p** 96. NSM Winscombe *B & W* 95-99; Perm to Offic 00-03; P-in-c Mark w Allerton from 03. *Yarrow Farm, Yarrow Road, Mark, Highbridge TA9 4LW* Tel (01278) 641650

NELSON, Canon Allen James. b 29. CITC 53. **d** 55 **p** 56. C Glenageary *D & G* 55-57; C Dublin Clontarf 57-60; I Bailieborough w Mullagh *K, E & A* 60-75; P-in-c Knockbride 66-72; P-in-c Knockbride w Shercock 72-75; I Julianstown w Colpe *M & K* 75-81; I Julianstown and Colpe w Drogheda and Duleek 81-98; Dioc Glebes Sec 81-98; Can Meath 84-98; rtd 98. *21 Seaview Park, Mornington, Co Meath, Irish Republic* Tel (00353) (41) 982 7044 E-mail jimnelson@eircom.net

NELSON, Bishop of. *See* EATON, The Rt Revd Derek Lionel

NELSON, Christopher James. b 57. Lanc Univ MA91. Aston Tr Scheme 83 St Jo Coll Nottm BTh88. **d** 88 **p** 89. C Blackpool St Thos *Blackb* 88-90; C Altham w Clayton le Moors 90-92; V Knuzden 92-01; V Penwortham St Mary from 01; AD Leyland from 04. *St Mary's Vicarage, 14 Cop Lane, Penwortham, Preston PR1 0SR* Tel (01772) 743143 E-mail kitnel@btinternet.com

NELSON, Gibson. *See* NELSON, Robert Gibson

NELSON, Graham William. b 61. Birm Univ CYCW85. St Jo Coll Nottm BA91. **d** 91 **p** 92. C Pype Hayes *Birm* 91-93; C Lancaster St Mary *Blackb* 94-97; Chapl HM Pris Lanc Castle 94-97; P-in-c Preston St Jude w St Paul *Blackb* from 97; P-in-c Preston St Oswald from 01. *St Jude's Vicarage, 97 Garstang Road, Preston PR1 1LD* Tel (01772) 252987

NELSON, Jane. b 42. **d** 94 **p** 99. Par Dn Muchalls *Bre* 94-99; C 99-04; Asst Chapl Grampian Healthcare NHS Trust 93-97; NSM Brechin *Bre* from 04. *4 St Michael's Road, Newtonhill, Stonehaven AB39 3RW* Tel (01569) 730967 E-mail nelson.jane1@btopenworld.com

NELSON, Mrs Julie. b 52. St Aid Coll Dur BA73 Ex Univ MA95. SW Minl Tr Course 92. **d** 95 **p** 96. NSM Tavistock and Gulworthy *Ex* 95-01; Germany 01-04; P-in-c Kirklington w Burneston and Wath and Pickhill *Ripon* from 04. *The Rectory, Kirklington, Bedale DL8 2NJ* Tel (01845) 567429 E-mail revjulie@tesco.net

NELSON, Michael. b 44. Newc Univ Aus BSc68 BA72 St Jo Coll Cam BA74 Cam Univ MA78. Westcott Ho Cam 74. **d** 75 **p** 76. Perm to Offic *Newc* 75; Australia from 77. *185 Bourbong Street, Chapel Hill, Qld, Australia 4069* Tel (0061) (7) 3720 1283 Fax 3720 1620 E-mail mnelson@hradvantage.com.au

NELSON, Canon Michael. b 44. Lon Univ BD66. Coll of Resurr Mirfield 66. **d** 68 **p** 69. C Newbold w Dunston *Derby* 68-72; C N Gosforth *Newc* 72-77; V Seaton Hirst 77-83; V Blyth St Mary 83-93; P-in-c Horton 86-87; RD Bedlington 88-93; R Hexham 93-03; Hon Can Newc Cathl from 94; P-in-c Ovingham from 03; RD Corbridge from 03. *St Mary's Vicarage, 2 Burnside Close, Ovingham, Prudhoe NE42 6BS* Tel (01661) 832273 E-mail canon.michael.nelson@care4free.net

NELSON, Sister Norma Margaret. b 34. Liv Univ DASS77 CQSW77. CA Tr Coll IDC60. **d** 93 **p** 94. TD Kirkby *Liv* 93-94; TV 94-95; rtd 95; Perm to Offic *Liv* from 95. *15 Pateley Close, Kirkby, Liverpool L32 4UT* Tel 0151-292 0255

NELSON, Paul John. b 52. Nottm Univ BCombStuds84. Linc Th Coll 81. **d** 84 **p** 85. C Waltham Cross *St Alb* 84-87; C Sandridge 87-90; V 90-98; R Hundred River *St E* from 98; RD Beccles and S Elmham from 03. *The Rectory, Moll's Lane, Brampton, Beccles NR34 8DB* Tel (01502) 575859

NELSON, Peter Joseph. b 46. Nottm Poly BSc73. Nor Bapt Coll 82 NEOC 99. **d** 99 **p** 99. In Bapt Min 85-99; Chapl R Hull Hosps NHS Trust 94-99; Chapl Hull and E Yorks Hosps NHS Trust 99-02; Sen Chapl from 02; NSM Sutton St Mich *York* from 99. *19 Swallowfield Drive, Hull HU4 6UG* Tel (01482) 568364 Pager 01399-113732115

NELSON, Ralph Archbold. b 27. St Cuth Soc Dur BA50. Bps' Coll Cheshunt 50. **d** 52 **p** 53. C Penwortham St Mary *Blackb* 52-57; C Eglingham *Newc* 57-58; V Featherstone *Wakef* 58-80; V Kirkham *Blackb* 80-92; RD Kirkham 88-91; rtd 92; Perm to Offic *Blackb* from 92. *6 Blundell Lane, Penwortham, Preston PR1 0EA* Tel (01772) 742573

NELSON, Robert Gibson. b 34. ALCD61. **d** 61 **p** 62. C Isleworth St Mary *Lon* 61-64; C-in-c Reading St Barn CD *Ox* 64-69; Australia 69-72; V Guernsey St Jo *Win* 72-78; R Guernsey Ste Marie du Castel 78-86; V Guernsey St Matt 84-86; rtd 86; Perm to Offic *Win* from 86. *Le Petit Feugre, Clos des Mielles, Castel, Guernsey GY5 7XV* Tel (01481) 52726

NELSON, Robert Towers. b 43. MSOSc Liv Coll of Tech BSc65. NW Ord Course 76. **d** 79 **p** 80. NSM Liv Our Lady and St Nic w St Anne *Liv* 79-83; NSM Liscard St Thos *Ches* 83-87; P-in-c from 87; Ind Missr from 87; Asst Sec SOSc from 89; Perm to Offic *Liv* 89-98; Chapl Wirral and W Cheshire Community NHS Trust 98-03. *5 Sedbergh Road, Wallasey CH44 2BR* Tel 0151-630 2830

NELSON, Roger Charles. b 44. ATII74 Newc Univ LLB66 Solicitor 69. Cant Sch of Min 88. **d** 91 **p** 92. NSM Deal St Leon and St Rich and Sholden *Cant* 91-96; NSM Northbourne and Gt Mongeham w Ripple and Sutton by Dover 96-97; Perm to Offic *Cant* 97-00; *Wakef* from 01. *26 Meal Hill Road, Holme, Holmfirth HD9 2QQ* Tel (01484) 680309 E-mail nelsontrap@aol.com

NELSON, Warren David. b 38. TCD BA67. **d** 68 **p** 69. C Belfast St Mich *Conn* 68-70; I Kilcooley w Littleton, Crohane, Killenaule etc *C & O* 70-76; Chapl Coalbrook Fellowship Hosp Ho Thurles 76-94; Perm to Offic (Cashel, Waterford and Lismore) 93-94; I Lurgan w Billis, Killinkere and Munterconnaught *K, E & A* 94-98; rtd 98. *6 Mucklagh, Tullamore, Co Offaly, Irish Republic* Tel (00353) (506) 24218 E-mail wnelson@eircom.net

NELSON, William. b 38. Oak Hill Th Coll 74. **d** 76 **p** 77. C Hensingham *Carl* 76-81; V Widnes St Paul *Liv* 81-89; R Higher Openshaw *Man* 89-03; AD Ardwick 96-00; rtd 03; Perm to Offic *S'well* from 03. *215 Stapleford Road, Trowell, Nottingham NG9 3QE* Tel 0115-932 2910

NENER, Canon Thomas Paul Edgar. b 42. Liv Univ MB, ChB FRCSEd71 FRCS71. Coll of Resurr Mirfield 78. **d** 80 **p** 81. C Warrington St Elphin *Liv* 80-83; V Haydock St Jas 83-95; V W Derby St Jo from 95; Hon Can Liv Cathl from 95. *St John's Vicarage, Green Lane, Stoneycroft, Liverpool L13 7EA* Tel 0151-228 2023

NENO, David Edward. b 62. SS Mark & Jo Coll Plymouth BA85. Ripon Coll Cuddesdon 85. **d** 88 **p** 89. C Chapel Allerton *Ripon* 88-91; C Acton St Mary *Lon* 91-94; V Kingsbury H Innocents 94-02; R Brondesbury Ch Ch and St Laur from 02. *The Rectory, Chevening Road, London NW6 6DU* Tel (020) 8969 5961 Mobile 07976-905294 E-mail d.s.neno@dial.pipex.com

NERY, Ms Caroline Chalmers. b 55. Wycliffe Hall Ox 02. **d** 04 **p** 05. C Melksham *Sarum* from 04. *The Vicarage, 5 Brampton Court, Bowerhill, Melksham SN12 6TH* Tel (01225) 345225 E-mail caroline@fulham.fsworld.co.uk

NESBITT, Heather Hastings. b 48. S'wark Ord Course 88. **d** 90 **p** 94. Par Dn Camberwell St Luke *S'wark* 90-94; C Addiscombe

St Mary Magd w St Martin 94-01; TV Sutton St Jas and Wawne *York* from 01. *Sutton Rectory, 25 Church Street, Sutton-on-Hull, Hull HU7 4TL* Tel (01482) 782154 E-mail h.nesbitt@tinyworld.co.uk

NESBITT, Patrick Joseph. b 72. St Martin's Coll Lanc BA96. St Jo Coll Nottm 00. **d** 03 **p** 04. C Blackpool St Thos *Blackb* from 03. *8 Collingwood Avenue, Blackpool FY3 8BZ* Tel (01253) 302679 Mobile 07879-660100 E-mail patricknesbitt72@hotmail.com

NESBITT, Canon Ronald. b 58. Sheff Univ LLB TCD DipTh85. CITC 82. **d** 85 **p** 86. C Ballymena w Ballyclug *Conn* 85-88; C Holywood *D & D* 88-90; I Helen's Bay 90-96; I Bangor Abbey from 96; Can Belf Cathl from 04. *The Abbey Rectory, 5 Downshire Road, Bangor BT20 3TW* Tel (028) 9146 0173 E-mail ronnienesbitt@aol.co.uk

NESBITT, Miss Wilhelmina. b 65. Qu Coll Birm 98. **d** 00 **p** 01. C Bridgnorth, Tasley, Astley Abbotts, etc *Heref* 00-04; TV Saddleworth *Man* from 04. *The Vicarage, Station Road, Uppermill, Oldham OL3 6HQ* Tel (01457) 872412 E-mail weatherwax01@aol.com

NESHAM, George Dove. b 20. ALCD50. Lon Coll of Div. **d** 50 **p** 51. C Harrington *Carl* 50-52; C Ferryhill *Dur* 52-55; V Stanley 55-62; V W Ardsley *Wakef* 62-77; V Ripponden 77-80; V Satley *Dur* 80-87; RD Stanhope 81-87; Chapl Dur Constabulary 81-87; rtd 87. *29 Ettrick Road, Jarrow NE32 5SL* Tel 0191-489 8071

NETHERWAY, Diana Margaret. b 47. Bp Otter Coll 94. **d** 96. NSM Northwood *Portsm* from 96; NSM Gurnard from 96. *138 Bellevue Road, Cowes PO31 7LD* Tel (01983) 298505 E-mail revbob@netherway1.freeserve.co.uk

NETHERWAY, Robert Sydney. b 37. Bp Otter Coll 94. **d** 96. NSM Cowes St Faith *Portsm* from 96. *138 Bellevue Road, Cowes PO31 7LD* Tel (01983) 298505 E-mail revbob@netherway1.freeserve.co.uk

NETHERWOOD, Mrs Anne Christine. b 43. ARIBA68 Liv Univ BArch66 Lon Univ BD92. St Deiniol's Hawarden 88. **d** 91 **p** 94. NSM Ellesmere and Welsh Frankton *Lich* 91-94; C Dudleston 94-97; C Criftins 94-97; C Criftins w Dudleston and Welsh Frankton 97; P-in-c from 97. *The Vicarage, Criftins, Ellesmere SY12 9LN* Tel (01691) 690401 Fax 690778 E-mail anne_netherwood@talk21.com

NEUDEGG, Mrs Joan Mary. b 36. Cant Sch of Min 81. **dss** 84 **d** 87 **p** 94. Chalk *Roch* 84-86; Hon C Dean Forest H Trin *Glouc* 87-90; Hon C Woolaston w Alvington 90-95; Hon C Woolaston w Alvington and Aylburton 95-96; rtd 96; Perm to Offic *Ex* from 96. *48 Marker Way, Honiton EX14 2EN* Tel (01404) 43957

NEUPERT, Douglas Alan. b 46. Chris Newport Univ (USA) BA78. Dioc OLM tr scheme 97. **d** 99 **p** 00. OLM Blackbourne *St E* from 99. *Hall Farm, Troston, Bury St Edmunds IP31 1EZ* Tel (01359) 269614 Mobile 07944-214417 E-mail doug_neupert@eu.odedodea.edu

NEVILL, James Michael. b 50. Cranmer Hall Dur 84. **d** 86 **p** 87. C Sowerby Bridge w Norland *Wakef* 86-91; CF 91-94; TV Broadwater St Mary *Chich* 94-99; Chapl St Mich Hospice Hereford 99-05; Spiritual Care Co-ord St Cath Hospice from 05. *St Catherine's Hospice, Malthouse Road, Crawley RH10 6BH* Tel (01293) 447333 Fax 611977

NEVILL, Mavis Hetty. b 45. Westhill Coll Birm CertYS68 Sheff Poly Dip Educn Mgt 85 Bradf and Ilkley Coll DipPSE85 Bradf Univ BEd95 Univ Coll Ches CertRE96. N Ord Course 92. **d** 95 **p** 96. NSM Mount Pellon *Wakef* 95-99; P-in-c Mixenden 99-04; rtd 04. *1 Willow Bank Close, Allerton, Bradford BD15 7YL* Tel (01274) 813191 E-mail gordon.nevill@btinternet.com

NEVILLE, Alfred John. b 21. K Coll Lon BA40. Sarum & Wells Th Coll 80. **d** 83 **p** 84. NSM Weston-super-Mare St Paul *B & W* 83-93; Perm to Offic from 93. *10 Clarence House, 17 Clarence Road North, Weston-super-Mare BS23 4AS* Tel (01934) 631176

NEVILLE, David Bruce. b 61. Ravensbourne Coll of Art & Design BA83. St Jo Coll Nottm LTh89 St Jo Coll Nottm DPS91. **d** 91 **p** 92. C Broxtowe *S'well* 91-94; C Attenborough 94-95; Perm to Offic 95-97; C Carrington 97-99; C Bulwell St Mary 99-02; Perm to Offic from 02. *3 Inham Road, Beeston, Nottingham NG9 4FL* Tel 0115-854 5648 E-mail rev.dnev@virgin.net

NEVILLE, Canon Graham. b 22. CCC Cam BA47 MA49 CertEd Cam Univ BD94 PhD02. Chich Th Coll 48. **d** 50 **p** 51. C Sutton in Ashfield St Mary *S'well* 50-53; Chapl Sheff Univ *Sheff* 53-58; R Culworth *Pet* 58-63; R Eydon 58-63; RD Culworth 62-63; Chapl Ch Ch Coll of HE Cant 63-68; Chapl Sutton Valence Sch Kent 68-73; Six Preacher Cant Cathl *Cant* 69-78; Prin Lect Relig Studies Eastbourne Coll of Educn 73-80; Dir of Educn *Linc* 80-87; Can and Preb Linc Cathl 82-88; rtd 87; Perm to Offic *Linc* 88-00 and *Worc* from 95. *16 Silverdale Avenue, Worcester WR5 1PY* Tel (01905) 360319

NEVILLE, Michael Robert John. b 56. Hatf Coll Dur BA80 Hughes Hall Cam PGCE81. Wycliffe Hall Ox 82. **d** 85 **p** 86. C E Twickenham St Steph *Lon* 85-88; Asst Dir Proclamation Trust 88-93; R Fordham *Chelmsf* from 93. *Fordham Hall, Church Road, Fordham, Colchester CO6 3NL* Tel (01206) 240221 E-mail mike.neville@fordhamchurch.org.uk

NEVILLE, Paul Stewart David. b 61. Wycliffe Hall Ox 98. **d** 00 **p** 01. C Chester le Street *Dur* 00-03; R Middleton St Geo from 03; R Sadberge from 03. *10 The Crescent, Middleton St George, Darlington DL2 1HL* Tel (01325) 332017

NEVIN, Alan Joseph. b 51. MCIPD80 Univ Coll Galway BA72. Aux Course 92 St Deiniol's Hawarden CertRS94. **d** 92 **p** 93. Aux Min Youghal Union *C, C & R* 92-94; Aux Min Waterford w Killea, Drumcannon and Dunhill *C & O* 94-95; C 95-98; I Bunclody w Kildavin, Clonegal and Kilrush 98-04; I Clonfert Gp *L & K* from 04. *The Rectory, Banagher, Birr, Co Offaly, Irish Republic* Tel and fax (00353) (509) 51269 Mobile 87-285 8251

NEVIN, Ronald. b 32. DMin88. Wesley Coll Leeds Linc Th Coll 63. **d** 64 **p** 65. C Norton St Mary *Dur* 64-66; R Cockfield 66-70; USA from 70; rtd 95. *20940 Rivers Ford, Estero, FL 33928, USA* Tel (001) (941) 495 8696 E-mail ronnevin@naplesnet.com

NEW, David John. b 37. Lon Univ BScEng58. Chich Th Coll 65. **d** 67 **p** 68. C Folkestone St Mary and St Eanswythe *Cant* 67-72; C Kings Heath *Birm* 72-74; V S Yardley St Mich 74-83; V Moseley St Agnes 83-00; rtd 00; Perm to Offic *Birm* and *Worc* from 00. *6 Falmouth, Worcester WR4 0TE* Tel (01905) 458084 E-mail david@revnew.freeserve.co.uk

NEW, Derek. b 30. **d** 86 **p** 87. NSM Brondesbury St Anne w Kilburn H Trin *Lon* 86-98; NSM Willesden St Matt 99-02; Perm to Offic from 02. *20 Lynton Road, London NW6 6BL* Tel (020) 7912 0640

NEW, Canon Thomas Stephen. b 30. K Coll Cam BA52 MA56. Cuddesdon Coll 52. **d** 54 **p** 55. C Greenford H Cross *Lon* 54-55; C Old St Pancras w Bedford New Town St Matt 55-58; C Woodham *Guildf* 58-64; V Guildf All SS 64-72; V Banstead 72-93; RD Epsom 76-80; Hon Can Guildf Cathl 79-93; Sub-Chapl HM Pris Downview 88-93; rtd 93; Perm to Offic *Ex* from 94. *St Katharine's, North Street, Denbury, Newton Abbot TQ12 6DJ* Tel (01803) 813775

NEW ZEALAND, Archbishop of. *See* VERCOE, The Most Revd Whakahuihui

NEWALL, Arthur William. b 24. Univ of Wales (Lamp) BA49. Chich Th Coll 49. **d** 51 **p** 52. C Hulme St Phil *Man* 51-53; C Fallowfield 53-55; V Oldham St Barn 55-60; V Aspull *Liv* 60-68; R Foots Cray *Roch* 68-78; V Henlow *St Alb* 78-89; rtd 89; Perm to Offic *Liv* from 89. *38 Fairhaven Road, Southport PR9 9UH* Tel (01704) 26045

NEWALL, Richard Lucas. b 43. K Coll Lon AKC66. **d** 66 **p** 67. C Roby *Liv* 66-69; C Douglas St Geo and St Barn *S & M* 69-71; Lic to Offic *Man* 72-75; C Ban St Mary *Ban* 75-77; R Newborough w Llangeinwen w Llangaffo etc 77-97; R Newborough w Llanidan and Llangeinwen etc from 98; AD Tindaethwy from 03. *Newborough Rectory, Dwyran, Llanfairpwllgwyngyll LL61 6RP* Tel (01248) 440285

NEWARK, Archdeacon of. *See* PEYTON, The Ven Nigel

NEWBOLD, Stephen Mark. b 60. Trin Coll Bris 01. **d** 03 **p** 04. C Roxeth *Lon* from 03. *69 Southdown Crescent, Harrow HA2 0QT* Tel (020) 8864 5392 E-mail steve.newbold@roxethteam.org

NEWBON, Eric. b 23. Fitzw Ho Cam BA51 MA55. Ridley Hall Cam 51. **d** 53 **p** 54. C Garston *Liv* 53-57; V Bickershaw 57-65; V Southport All So 65-85; rtd 85; Perm to Offic *Ches* from 86. *33 Haymakers Way, Saughall, Chester CH1 6AR* Tel (01244) 880123

NEWBON, Kenneth. b 29. Wells Th Coll 67. **d** 69 **p** 70. C Church Stretton *Heref* 69-72; P-in-c Cressage w Sheinton 72-75; R Braunstone *Leic* 75-81; TR 81-84; P-in-c Eardisley w Bollingham and Willersley *Heref* 84-88; P-in-c Brilley w Michaelchurch on Arrow 84-88; P-in-c Whitney w Winforton 84-88; RD Kington and Weobley 87-95; R Eardisley w Bollingham, Willersley, Brilley etc 88-96; rtd 96; Perm to Offic *Heref* from 96. *Grace Dieu House, Staunton-on-Wye, Hereford HR4 7LT* Tel (01981) 500188

NEWBON, Michael Charles. b 59. Oak Hill Th Coll DipHE94. **d** 94 **p** 95. C Bedford St Jo and St Leon *St Alb* 94-99; V Luton St Fran from 99. *The Vicarage, 145 Hollybush Road, Luton LU2 9HQ* Tel (01582) 753919 E-mail lutonstfrancis@aol.com

NEWBORN, Carol Margaret. b 45. **d** 05. OLM Styvechale *Cov* from 05. *76 The Park Paling, Coventry CV3 5LL* Tel (024) 7650 3707

NEWBURY, Canon Robert. b 22. St D Coll Lamp BA46. **d** 48 **p** 49. C Killay *S & B* 48-55; V Glascombe w Rhulen and Gregrina 55-63; V Manselton 63-84; V Manselton w Hafod 84-90; Hon Can Brecon Cathl from 85; rtd 90. *4 Cobham Close, Gorseinon, Swansea SA4 4FA* Tel (01792) 896438

NEWBY, Mrs Ailsa Ballantyne. b 56. Collingwood Coll Dur BA78. St Steph Ho Ox 98. **d** 98 **p** 99. C Streatham Ch Ch *S'wark* 98-01; V S Lambeth St Anne and All SS from 01. *The Vicarage, 179 Fentiman Road, London SW8 1JY* Tel (020) 7735 3191 E-mail ailsanewby@f2s.com

NEWBY, Peter Gordon. b 23. **d** 64 **p** 65. C Leic St Phil *Leic* 64-69; R Lt Bowden St Nic 69-72; V Jersey Gouray St Martin *Win* 72-77; Chapl Jersey Gp of Hosps 78-80; R Much Birch w Lt Birch, Much Dewchurch etc *Heref* 80-88; rtd 89; Perm to Offic *Ex* from 90. *18 Woodfields, Seaton EX12 2UX* Tel (01297) 24562

NEWBY, Susan. d 04 **p** 05. OLM Adderbury w Milton *Ox* from 04. *Master's House, 190 Warwick Road, Alkerton, Banbury OX16 2AP*

NEWCASTLE, Bishop of. *See* WHARTON, The Rt Revd John Martin

NEWCASTLE, Dean of. *See* DALLISTON, The Very Revd Christopher Charles

NEWCOMBE, Andrew Charles. b 70. Melbourne Univ BA92 BMus93 Monash Univ Aus DipEd96 LTCL93. St Steph Ho Ox 03. **d** 05. C Tottenham St Mary *Lon* from 05. *Kemble Cottage, 1 St Mary's Close, London N17 9UD* Tel 07931-700675 (mobile) E-mail andrewnewcombe@yahoo.co.uk

NEWCOMBE, John Adrian. b 61. Univ of Wales (Lamp) BA83 SS Paul & Mary Coll Cheltenham PGCE85. Ripon Coll Cuddesdon 90. **d** 92 **p** 93. C Stroud and Uplands w Slad *Glouc* 92-96; C Nailsworth 96-01; P-in-c Childswyckham w Aston Somerville, Buckland etc 01-05; TV Winchcombe from 05. *New Vicarage, Buckland Road, Childswickham, Broadway WR12 7HH* Tel (01386) 853824

NEWCOMBE, Timothy James Grahame. b 47. AKC75. St Aug Coll Cant 75. **d** 76 **p** 77. C Heref St Martin *Heref* 76-79; C Hitchin *St Alb* 79-85; R Croft and Stoney Stanton *Leic* 85-91; P-in-c Launceston *Truro* 91-92; V Launceston 92-97; TR Launceston 97-03; Hon Can Truro Cathl 01-03; Chapl Cornwall Healthcare NHS Trust 96-03; V Wotton St Mary *Glouc* from 03. *Holy Trinity Vicarage, Church Road, Longlevens, Gloucester GL2 0AJ* Tel (01452) 524129 E-mail canontim@silvermead.net

✠**NEWCOME, The Rt Revd James William Scobie.** b 53. Trin Coll Ox BA74 MA78 Selw Coll Cam BA77 MA81. Ridley Hall Cam 75. **d** 78 **p** 79 **c** 02. C Leavesden All SS *St Alb* 78-82; P-in-c Bar Hill LEP *Ely* 82-92; V Bar Hill 92-94; Tutor Ridley Hall Cam 83-88; P-in-c Dry Drayton *Ely* 89-94; RD N Stowe 93-94; Can Res Ches Cathl and Dioc Dir of Ords *Ches* 94-02; Dir of Educn and Tr 96-02; Suff Bp Penrith *Carl* from 02. *Holm Croft, 13 Castle Road, Kendal LA9 7AU* Tel (01539) 727836 Fax 734380 E-mail bishop.penrith@carlislediocese.org.uk

NEWELL, Aubrey Francis Thomas. b 20. St D Coll Lamp BA43. **d** 45 **p** 46. C Rhosddu *St As* 45-49; C Llanwnog *Ban* 49-50; C Gabalfa *Llan* 50-53; C Gt Marlow *Ox* 53-57; R Lavendon w Cold Brayfield 57-62; V Gawcott and Hillesden 62-77; P-in-c Radclive 69-72; RD Buckingham 70-76 and 82-84; P-in-c Padbury w Adstock 72-77; V Lenborough 77-87; rtd 87; Perm to Offic *Ox* 89-00. *5 Church View, Steeple Claydon, Buckingham MK18 2QR* Tel (01296) 738271

NEWELL, Christopher David. b 53. Cert Counselling 92 Ex Univ MA03. S'wark Ord Course 84. **d** 87 **p** 88. C Stockwell St Mich *S'wark* 87-90; Asst Chapl R Lon Hosp (Whitechapel) 90-92; Asst Chapl R Lon Hosp (Mile End) 90-92; R Birch St Agnes *Man* 92-96; P-in-c Longsight St Jo w St Cypr 94-96; R Birch St Agnes w Longsight St Jo w St Cypr 97; R Lansallos and V Talland *Truro* 97-98; Asst P Liskeard and St Keyne 00-02; C Duloe, Herodsfoot, Morval and St Pinnock 02-03; P-in-c 03-05; C Lansallos and Talland 02-03; Chapl Cornwall Partnership NHS Trust from 02. *4 Russell Street, Liskeard PL14 4BP* Tel (01579) 349617 E-mail christopher.newell@cpt.cornwall.nhs.uk

NEWELL, David Walter. b 37. Nottm Univ BSc57. WEMTC 01. **d** 03 **p** 04. OLM Painswick, Sheepscombe, Cranham, The Edge etc *Glouc* from 03. *Woodside, Kingsmill Lane, Painswick, Stroud GL6 6SA* Tel (01452) 812083 E-mail davidjean@painswick41.freeserve.co.uk

NEWELL, Canon Edmund John. b 61. Univ Coll Lon BSc83 Nuff Coll Ox DPhil88 MA89 FRHistS98. Ox Min Course 89 Ripon Coll Cuddesdon 92. **d** 94 **p** 95. C Deddington w Barford, Clifton and Hempton *Ox* 94-98; Bp's Dom Chapl 98-01; Chapl Headington Sch 98-01; Can Res St Paul's Cathl *Lon* from 01; Chan from 03. *6 Amen Court, London EC4M 7BU* Tel (020) 7248 8572 E-mail newell@amencourt.freeserve.co.uk

NEWELL, Jack Ernest. b 26. CEng FIChemE ARCS BSc. Glouc Th Course 80. **d** 83 **p** 84. NSM Hempsted *Glouc* 83-96; Perm to Offic from 96. *Hempsted House, Rectory Lane, Hempsted, Gloucester GL2 5LW* Tel (01452) 523320

NEWELL, Kenneth Ernest. b 22. S Dios Minl Tr Scheme 77. **d** 79 **p** 80. NSM Lynton, Brendon, Countisbury, Lynmouth etc *Ex* 79-85; TR 85-89; RD Shirwell 84-89; rtd 89; Perm to Offic *Ex* from 89. *Mole End, Lydiate Lane, Lynton EX35 6HE*

NEWELL, Samuel James (Jim). b 28. TCD BA53 MA63. TCD Div Sch Div Test54. **d** 54 **p** 55. C Belfast St Mary *Conn* 54-57; C Derriaghy 57-60; C Reading St Mary V *Ox* 60-63; V Chesham Ch Ch 63-74; P-in-c Wraysbury 74-78; TV Riverside 78-94; rtd 94; Perm to Offic *Ox* from 97. *41 Redford Road, Windsor SL4 5ST* Tel (01753) 862300

NEWELL OF STAFFA, Gerald Frederick Watson. b 34. Sarum Th Coll 56. **d** 59 **p** 61. C Southampton SS Pet and Paul w All SS *Win* 59-61; C Overton w Laverstoke and Freefolk 61-63; CF (TA) 61-63; CF 63-66; R Spennithorne *Ripon* 66-68; R Finghall 66-68; R Hauxwell 66-68; Hon C Steyning *Chich* 74-78; Perm to Offic *Ex* 93-95 and 99-00; P-in-c Breamore *Win* 95-98; rtd 99; P-in-c Palermo w Taormina *Eur* 99-00; R Glencarse *Bre* 00-03; Perm to Offic *Ox* from 04. *Church Cottage, 62 Church Lane, Compton Beauchamp, Swindon SN6 8NN* Tel (01738) 710334

NEWELL PRICE, John Charles. b 29. SS Coll Cam BA50 MA MB, BChir MRCGP. LNSM course 88. **d** 91 **p** 94. OLM Frensham *Guildf* 91-99; rtd 99; Perm to Offic *Guildf* from 99. *7 Collards Gate, High Street, Haslemere GU27 2HE* Tel (01428) 661336

NEWEY, Edmund James. b 71. Linc Coll Ox BA95 MA97 Em Coll Cam BA99. Westcott Ho Cam 97. **d** 00 **p** 01. C Birch w Fallowfield *Man* 00-03; R Newmarket St Mary w Exning St Agnes *St E* from 03. *The Rectory, 21 Hamilton Road, Newmarket CB8 0NY* Tel (01638) 662448 Mobile 07986-530511 E-mail ejnewey@fish.co.uk

NEWHAM, Simon Frank Eric. b 65. Sheff Univ BSc87 MSc89 Bris Univ BA00. Trin Coll Bris 98. **d** 00 **p** 01. C Horsham *Chich* 00-04; P-in-c Wisborough Green from 04. *The Vicarage, Glebe Way, Wisborough Green, Billingshurst RH14 0DZ* Tel (01403) 700339

✠**NEWING, The Rt Revd Dom Kenneth Albert.** b 23. Selw Coll Cam BA53 MA57. Coll of Resurr Mirfield 53. **d** 55 **p** 56 **c** 82. C Plymstock *Ex* 55-63; R Plympton St Maurice 63-82; RD Plympton 71-76; Preb Ex Cathl 75-82; Adn Plymouth 78-82; Suff Bp Plymouth 82-88; Lic to Offic *Ox* 88-93; OSB from 89; rtd 93. *Elmore Abbey, Church Lane, Newbury RG14 1SA* Tel (01635) 33080

NEWING, Peter. b 33. Birm Univ CertEd55 Dur Univ BA63 Bris Univ BEd76 State Univ NY BSc85 EdD88 FRSA60 FSAScot59 ACP67 MCollP86 FCollP95 APhS63. Cranmer Hall Dur 63. **d** 65 **p** 66. C Blockley w Aston Magna *Glouc* 65-69; P-in-c Taynton 69-75; P-in-c Tibberton 69-75; R Brimpsfield w Elkstone and Syde 75-83; R Brimpsfield, Cranham, Elkstone and Syde 83-97; P-in-c Daglingworth w the Duntisbournes and Winstone 95-97; R Brimpsfield w Birdlip, Syde, Daglingworth etc 97-01; C Redmarley D'Abitot, Bromesberrow, Pauntley etc 01-02; NSM from 02; rtd 02; Perm to Offic *Heref* from 02. *The Rectory, Albright Lane, Bromesberrow, Ledbury HR8 1RU* Tel (01531) 650898

NEWITT, Mark Julian. b 76. Bradf Univ BSc97 St Jo Coll Dur BA02. Cranmer Hall Dur 00. **d** 03 **p** 04. C Billing *Pet* from 03. *80 Worcester Close, Northampton NN3 9GD* Tel (01604) 787163

NEWLAND, Mrs Patricia Frances. b 35. Edin Univ MA56 Dip Sociology 57. EAMTC 96. **d** 97 **p** 98. NSM Duxford *Ely* 97-02; NSM Hinxton 97-02; NSM Ickleton 97-02; rtd 02; Perm to Offic *Ely* from 02. *Ickelton Lodge, 14 Frogge Street, Ickleton, Saffron Walden CB10 1SH* Tel (01799) 530268 Fax 531146 E-mail tricia.newland@ukgateway.net

NEWLANDS, Christopher William. b 57. Bris Univ BA79. Westcott Ho Cam 81. **d** 84 **p** 85. C Bishop's Waltham *Portsm* 84-87; Hon C Upham 85-87; Prec, Sacr and Min Can Dur Cathl *Dur* 87-92; Chapl Bucharest w Sofia *Eur* 92-95; V Shrub End *Chelmsf* 96-04; Bp's Chapl from 04. *The Vicarage, Penny's Lane, Margaretting, Ingatestone CM4 0HA* Tel (01277) 356277 E-mail cnewlands@chelmsford.anglican.org

NEWLANDS, Prof George McLeod. b 41. Edin Univ MA63 Heidelberg Univ BD66 PhD70 Ch Coll Cam MA73. **d** 82 **p** 82. Lect Cam Univ 73-86; Fell and Dean Trin Hall Cam 82-86; Prof Div Glas Univ from 86; Perm to Offic *Glas* from 86. *2/19 Succoth Court, Edinburgh EH12 6BZ,* or *The University, Glasgow G12 8QQ* Tel 0131-337 4941 *or* 0141-330 5297 Mobile 07979-691966 Fax 0141-330 4943 E-mail g.newlands@arts.gla.ac.uk

NEWLYN, Canon Edwin. b 39. AKC64. **d** 65 **p** 66. C Belgrave St Mich *Leic* 65-68; Miss to Seamen 68-81; Chapl Santos Brazil 68-69; Asst Chapl Glas and C Glas St Gabr *Glas* 69-73; Chapl E Lon S Africa 73-76; R W Bank St Pet 75-76; V Fylingdales *York* 81; P-in-c Hawsker 81; V Fylingdales and Hawsker cum Stainsacre 81-88; RD Whitby 85-92; Sec Dioc Adv Cttee for Care of Chs 87-01; P-in-c Goathland 88-99; Can and Preb York Minster from 90; rtd 01; Perm to Offic *York* from 01. *8 Metropole Towers, Argyle Road, Whitby YO21 3HU* Tel (01947) 604533 E-mail edwin.newlyn@btinternet.com

NEWMAN, The Very Revd Adrian. b 58. Bris Univ BSc80 MPhil89. Trin Coll Bris 82. **d** 85 **p** 86. C Forest Gate St Mark *Chelmsf* 85-89; V Hillsborough and Wadsley Bridge *Sheff* 89-96; RD Hallam 94-96; R Birm St Martin w Bordesley St Andr *Birm* 96-05; Hon Can Birm Cathl 01-05; Dean Roch from 05. *The Deanery, Priors Gate House, The Precinct, Rochester ME1 1SR* Tel (01634) 843366 *or* 857330 Fax 410410 E-mail deanspa@rochestercathedraluk.org

NEWMAN, Alan George. b 18. Lich Th Coll 41. **d** 44 **p** 45. C Twerton *B & W* 44-52; V Clandown 52-56; V Bradford-on-Avon Ch Ch *Sarum* 56-76; R Monkton Farleigh w S Wraxall 76-84; rtd 84; Perm to Offic *Sarum* and *B & W* from 00. *14 White Horse Road, Winsley, Bradford-on-Avon BA15 2JZ* Tel (01225) 854119

NEWMAN, Alfred John Gordon. b 19. Qu Coll Birm 71. **d** 74 **p** 74. Hon C Hall Green St Pet *Birm* 74-84; Perm to Offic *St E* 84-96 and *Chich* from 96. *Flat 5, Southdown Court, Bell Banks Road, Hailsham BN27 2AT* Tel (01323) 441378

NEWMAN, Mrs Alison Myra. b 55. K Coll Lon BD77. SEITE 99. **d** 02 **p** 03. C Bromley SS Pet and Paul *Roch* from 02. *13 Rochester Avenue, Bromley BR1 3DB* Tel (020) 8464 9532 E-mail newmans8@btopenworld.com

NEWMAN, Cecil Ernest. b 21. Bris Univ BA58 DipTh58. Roch Th Coll 61. **d** 62 **p** 63. C Tiverton St Pet *Ex* 62-64; C Wolborough w Newton Abbot 64-67; Lic to Offic *Roch* 67-86; Chapl Darenth Park Hosp Dartford 67-86; rtd 86; Perm to Offic *Roch* 86-98. *27 Nursery Road, Meopham, Gravesend DA13 0LR* Tel (01474) 812955

NEWMAN, David. *See* NEWMAN, Richard David

NEWMAN, David Malcolm. b 54. FSAScot81 Aber Univ LTh BTh. St Steph Ho Ox 89. **d** 91 **p** 92. C St Mary-at-Latton *Chelmsf* 91-94; R Weeley and Lt Clacton from 94. *The Vicarage, 2 Holland Road, Little Clacton, Clacton-on-Sea CO16 9RS* Tel (01255) 860241

NEWMAN, David Maurice Frederick. b 54. Hertf Coll Ox BA75 MA79. St Jo Coll Nottm. **d** 79 **p** 80. C Orpington Ch Ch *Roch* 79-83; C Bushbury *Lich* 83-86; V Ockbrook *Derby* 86-97; TR Loughborough Em and St Mary in Charnwood *Leic* from 97; RD Akeley E from 99. *Emmanuel Rectory, 47 Forest Road, Loughborough LE11 3NW* Tel and fax (01509) 263264 *or* tel 261773 E-mail davidnewman@emmanuel.fsnet.co.uk

NEWMAN, Mrs Diana Joan. b 43. Sarum Th Coll 81. **dss** 84 **d** 87 **p** 94. Parkstone St Pet w Branksea and St Osmund *Sarum* 84-87; NSM from 87; TV 96-02. *62 Vale Road, Poole BH14 9AU* Tel and fax (01202) 745136 E-mail diana.n@ntlworld.com

NEWMAN, Geoffrey Maurice. b 22. Ox NSM Course 77. **d** 80 **p** 81. NSM Binfield *Ox* 80-84; Chapl St Geo Sch Ascot 82-84; V Teynham *Cant* 84-87; rtd 87; Perm to Offic *Cant* 87-05. *55 St Mildred's Road, Westgate-on-Sea CT8 8RJ* Tel (01843) 833837

NEWMAN, Graham Anthony. b 44. Ripon Coll Cuddesdon 79. **d** 81 **p** 82. C Walker *Newc* 81-84; C Whorlton 84-87; V Warkworth and Acklington 87-94; V Haltwhistle and Greenhead 94-99; Chapl Northd HA 94-99; TV N Shields *Newc* 99-00; rtd 00; Perm to Offic *Newc* from 01. *49 Burnbank Avenue, Wellfield, Whitley Bay NE25 9HG* Tel 0191-253 5914

NEWMAN, Mrs Helen Margaret. b 58. York Univ BA80 Nottm Univ MA02. EMMTC 99. **d** 02 **p** 03. NSM Thorpe Acre w Dishley *Leic* 02-05; NSM Loughborough Em and St Mary in Charnwood from 05. *Emmanuel Rectory, 47 Forest Road, Loughborough LE11 3NW* Tel (01509) 216652 E-mail helen@astad.org

NEWMAN, James Edwin Michael. b 59. Nottm Univ BA80 Ox Univ BA90. Wycliffe Hall Ox 88. **d** 91 **p** 92. C Bidston *Ches* 91-95; C Cheadle from 95. *4 Cuthbert Road, Cheadle SK8 2DT* Tel 0161-428 3983 E-mail mike@stcuthberts.org

NEWMAN, John Humphrey. b 17. ALCD49. **d** 49 **p** 50. C Hove Bp Hannington Memorial Ch *Chich* 49-52; V Welling *Roch* 52-64; V Penge St Jo 64-74; R Knockholt 74-82; rtd 82; Perm to Offic *Chich* from 82. *Stonegarth, Pett Level Road, Fairlight, Hastings TN35 4EA* Tel (01424) 812518

NEWMAN, Michael Alan. b 40. Chich Th Coll 67. **d** 70 **p** 71. C Kilburn St Aug *Lon* 70-73; C St Geo-in-the-East St Mary 75-78; rtd 78. *April Cottage, Georges Lane, Storrington, Pulborough RH20 3JH* Tel (01903) 744354 E-mail tcepriest@tiscali.co.uk

NEWMAN, Preb Michael John. b 50. Leic Univ BA72 MA75 Ex Coll Ox DipTh74. Cuddesdon Coll 73. **d** 75 **p** 76. C Tettenhall Regis *Lich* 75-79; C Uttoxeter w Bramshall 79-82; R Norton Canes 82-89; TR Rugeley from 89; Preb Lich Cathl from 02. *The Rectory, 20 Church Street, Rugeley WS15 2AB* Tel (01889) 582149

NEWMAN, Canon Michael Robert. b 30. K Coll Lon BD61 Massey Univ (NZ) DSS91. St Jo Coll Auckland LTh53. **d** 54 **p** 55. New Zealand 54-58; C Hampstead St Jo *Lon* 58-61; New Zealand from 61; Can Auckland 81-93. *2/26 Alfriston Road, Manurewa 1702, New Zealand* Tel (0064) (9) 267 4357

NEWMAN, Paul. b 65. St Martin's Coll Lanc BA90. Oak Hill Th Coll. **d** 00 **p** 01. C Poynton *Ches* 00-04; V Barnton from 04. *The Vicarage, Church Road, Barnton, Northwich CW8 4JH* Tel (01606) 74358 E-mail scallyvic@yahoo.com

NEWMAN, Paul Anthony. b 48. Lon Univ BSc70 Leeds Univ DipTh75. Coll of Resurr Mirfield 73. **d** 76 **p** 77. C Catford St Laur *S'wark* 76-81; TV Grays All SS *Chelmsf* 81-83; TV Lt Thurrock St Mary 81-83; W Ham Adnry Youth Chapl 83-87; P-in-c Forest Gate All SS 83-89; V 89-91; Dep Chapl HM Pris Wormwood Scrubs 91-92; Chapl HM Pris Downview 92-02; Chapl HM Pris Win from 02. *HM Prison Winchester, Romsey Road, Winchester SO22 5DF* Tel (01962) 723055 E-mail paul.anthony.newman@hmps.gsi.gov.uk

NEWMAN, Richard David. b 38. BNC Ox BA60 MA63. Lich Th Coll 60. **d** 62 **p** 63. C E Grinstead St Swithun *Chich* 62-66; C Gt Grimsby St Jas *Linc* 66-69; C Gt Grimsby St Mary and St Jas 69-73; TV 73-74; V St Nicholas at Wade w Sarre *Cant* 74-75; P-in-c Chislet w Hoath 74-75; V St Nicholas at Wade w Sarre and Chislet w Hoath 75-81; V S Norwood H Innocents 81-84; V S Norwood H Innocents *S'wark* 85-04; rtd 04. *10 Hardy Court, Lang Road, Crewkerne TA18 8JE* Tel (01460) 271496

NEWMAN, William Nigel Edward. b 61. St Jo Coll Dur BA83 Bris Univ PGCE86. Westcott Ho Cam 99. **d** 01 **p** 02. C Halstead Area *Chelmsf* 01-04; Chapl St Jo Cathl Hong Kong from 04; P-in-c Stanley St Steph from 04. *Bungalow 5, St Stephen's College, 22 Tung Tau Wan Road, Stanley, Hong Kong, China* E-mail willanddot@netvigator.org

NEWNHAM, Eric Robert. b 43. FCA. Sarum & Wells Th Coll 70. **d** 75 **p** 76. NSM Blackheath Ascension *S'wark* from 75. *27 Morden Hill, London SE13 7NN* Tel (020) 8692 6507 *or* 8691 6559

NEWPORT, Derek James. b 39. Acadia Univ (NS) BA82 MEd84. Sarum & Wells Th Coll 74. **d** 76 **p** 77. C Tavistock and Gulworthy *Ex* 76-78; Canada 78-86; V Malborough w S Huish, W Alvington and Churchstow *Ex* 86-95; TR Widecombe-in-the-Moor, Leusdon, Princetown etc 95-04; rtd 04. *Woodland Cottage, Southdown Woods, Yarnscombe, Barnstaple EX31 3LZ* Tel (01271) 858685 E-mail dereknewport@dnewport.fsnet.co.uk

NEWPORT, Prof Kenneth George Charles. b 57. Columbia Union Coll (USA) BA83 Andrews Univ (USA) MA84 Linacre Coll Ox MSt85 St Hugh's Coll Ox DPhil88. N Ord Course 98. **d** 00 **p** 01. Reader Chr Thought Liv Hope 99-01; Prof Th and RS Liv Hope Univ Coll from 01; Hon Research Fell Man Univ *Man* from 98; NSM Bolton St Pet from 00; Perm to Offic *Liv* from 00. *Theology and Religious Studies, Liverpool Hope, Hope Park, Taggart Avenue, Liverpool L16 9JD* Tel 0151-291 3510 Fax 291 3772 E-mail knewport@hope.ac.uk

NEWPORT, Archdeacon of. *See* SHARPE, The Ven Kenneth William

NEWSOME, David Ellis. b 55. St Jo Coll Dur BA77. Westcott Ho Cam 80. **d** 82 **p** 83. C Finchley St Mary *Lon* 82-85; C Fulham All SS 85-87; Bp's Dom Chapl *Birm* 87-91; V Gravelly Hill 91-00; P-in-c Stockland Green 93-96; AD Aston 95-00; TR Tettenhall Regis *Lich* from 00. *The Vicarage, 2 Lloyd Road, Tettenhall, Wolverhampton WV6 9AU* Tel (01902) 742801

NEWSOME, Canon John Keith. b 49. Mert Coll Ox BA73 MA76. Ripon Coll Cuddesdon 73. **d** 76 **p** 77. C Bywell *Newc* 76-78; C Berwick H Trin 78-82; Chapl Bonn w Cologne *Eur* 86-93; Chapl Hamburg 93-00; Chapl Zürich from 00; Can Brussels Cathl from 98. *Promenadengasse 9, 8001 Zürich, Switzerland* Tel (0041) (44) 252 6024 Fax 252 6042 E-mail jknewsome@anglican.ch

NEWSOME, Monica Jane. b 55. WMMTC 96. **d** 99 **p** 00. NSM Kingshurst *Birm* 99-00; Asst Chapl HM YOI Stoke Heath from 00. *HM Young Offender Institution, Stoke Heath, Market Drayton TF9 2LJ* Tel (01630) 636000

NEWSON, Julie. b 60. Southn Univ BA97. Bp Otter Coll 00. **d** 03. NSM Brighton St Pet w Chpl Royal *Chich* from 03. *77 Wilson Avenue, Brighton BN2 5PA* Tel (01273) 570978 Mobile 07803-750147 E-mail julie.newson@btinternet.com

NEWSTEAD, Dominic Gerald. b 65. Wycliffe Hall Ox BTh95. **d** 95 **p** 96. C Windlesham *Guildf* 95-00; Asst Chapl Fontainebleau *Eur* from 00. *29 rue de Chailly, 77930 Perthes-en-Gâtinais, France* Tel (0033) (1) 60 66 26 47 E-mail newsteadinfrance@aol.com *or* fontainebleau.church@free.fr

NEWSUM, Alfred Turner Paul. b 28. Coll of Resurr Mirfield 52. **d** 53 **p** 54. C Roath St German *Llan* 53-59; C Westmr St Matt *Lon* 59-60; C Washwood Heath *Birm* 60-68; P-in-c Small Heath St Greg 68-78; V Birm St Aid Small Heath 72-80; V Stockland Green 80-93; rtd 93; Perm to Offic *Llan* and *Mon* from 93. *Ty'r Offeiriad, 18 Almond Drive, Cardiff CF23 8HD*

NEWTH, Barry Wilfred. b 33. Bris Univ BA56. ALCD58. **d** 58 **p** 59. C Upton (Overchurch) *Ches* 58-62; C Kimberworth *Sheff* 62-63; V Clifton *Man* 63-72; V Radcliffe St Thos 72-74; V Radcliffe St Thos and St Jo 74-81; R Heaton Mersey 81-86; V Kirkby Malham *Bradf* 86-87; P-in-c Coniston Cold 86-87; V Kirkby-in-Malhamdale w Coniston Cold 87-97; rtd 97; Perm to Offic *Man* from 00. *1 Higher Ridings, Bromley Cross, Bolton BL7 9HP* Tel (01204) 451927

NEWTON, Miss Ann. b 46. Trin Coll Bris 75. **d** 87 **p** 94. Par Dn Rothley *Leic* 87-91; Par Dn Becontree St Mary *Chelmsf* 91-94; C 94-01; V Canley *Cov* from 01. *St Stephen's Vicarage, 47 Glebe Close, Coventry CV4 8DJ* Tel (024) 7642 1721

NEWTON, Barrie Arthur. b 38. Dur Univ BA61. Wells Th Coll 61. **d** 63 **p** 64. C Walton St Mary *Liv* 63-67; C N Lynn w St Marg and St Nic *Nor* 67-69; Chapl Asst The Lon Hosp (Whitechapel) 69-71; Chapl K Coll Hosp Lon 72-77; P-in-c Bishops Sutton w Stowey *B & W* 77-81; P-in-c Compton Martin w Ubley 79-81; P-in-c Bridgwater St Jo w Chedzoy 81-83; Chapl St Mary's Hosp Praed Street Lon 83-94; Chapl St Mary's NHS Trust Paddington 94-99; rtd 00. *10 Brondesbury Park Mansions, 132 Salusbury Road, London NW6 6PD* Tel (020) 7328 0397 Fax as telephone

NEWTON, Brian Karl. b 30. Keble Coll Ox BA55 MA59. Wells Th Coll 56. **d** 58 **p** 59. C Barrow St Geo *Carl* 58-61; Trinidad and Tobago 61-69 and 71-77; Gen Ed USPG 69-71; P-in-c Gt Coates *Linc* 77; TV Gt and Lt Coates w Bradley 78-88; V Burgh le Marsh 88-94; R Bratoft w Irby-in-the-Marsh 88-94; V Orby

88-94; R Welton-le-Marsh w Gunby 88-94; rtd 94; Perm to Offic *Linc* 94-97. *27 Somersby Way, Boston PE21 9PQ* Tel (01205) 362433

NEWTON, Canon Christopher Wynne. b 25. Trin Hall Cam BA46. Westcott Ho Cam 48. **d** 50 **p** 51. C Gateshead Ch Ch *Dur* 50-52; Canada 52-55; C Harrow Weald All SS *Lon* 55-58; V Radlett *St Alb* 58-66; RD St Alb 63-66; TR Hemel Hempstead 66-72; RD Milton Keynes *Ox* 72-77; TV Swan 78-84; RD Claydon 78-84; Dioc Ecum Officer 79-84; Hon Can Ch Ch 80-83; P-in-c Lt Gaddesden *St Alb* 84-86; rtd 86; Perm to Offic *St Alb* from 86. *24 Slade Court, Watling Street, Radlett WD7 7BT* Tel (01923) 859131

NEWTON, David Ernest. b 42. Sarum & Wells Th Coll 72. **d** 74 **p** 75. C Wigan All SS *Liv* 74-80; V Choral York Minster *York* 80-85; R Ampleforth w Oswaldkirk 85-86; P-in-c E Gilling 85-86; R Ampleforth and Oswaldkirk and Gilling E 86-97; V Ampleforth w Oswaldkirk, Gilling E etc 98-01; RD Helmsley 94-99; P-in-c Overton *Blackb* from 01. *St Helen's Vicarage, Chapel Lane, Overton, Morecambe LA3 3HU* Tel (01524) 858234 E-mail davidnoot@aol.com

NEWTON, Derek. b 50. Sunderland Poly HND72 Dur Univ ACertC95. NEOC 89. **d** 92 **p** 93. NSM Houghton le Spring *Dur* 92-96; NSM Deanery of Houghton from 97. *Pinelodge, Warwick Drive, Houghton le Spring DH5 8JR* Tel 0191-584 9169

NEWTON, Mrs Fiona Olive. b 46. GTCL67. WMMTC 96. **d** 99 **p** 00. C Southam and Ufton *Cov* 99-03; P-in-c Laxfield, Cratfield, Wilby and Brundish *St E* 03-04; R from 04. *The Vicarage, 15 Noyes Avenue, Laxfield, Woodbridge IP13 8EB* Tel (01986) 798998 E-mail fionanewton@rmplc.co.uk

NEWTON, George Peter Howgill. b 62. Pemb Coll Cam BA84 MA88. Oak Hill Th Coll BA93. **d** 93 **p** 94. C Blackpool St Thos *Blackb* 93-99; P-in-c Aldershot H Trin *Guildf* 99-03; V from 03. *2 Cranmore Lane, Aldershot GU11 3AS* Tel (01252) 320618 E-mail g@gjsk.prestel.co.uk

NEWTON, Gerald Blamire. b 30. Lich Th Coll. **d** 69 **p** 70. C Leeds Halton St Wilfrid *Ripon* 69-73; C Gt Yarmouth *Nor* 73-74; P-in-c Cattistock w Chilfrome and Rampisham w Wraxall *Sarum* 74-77; V Coney Hill *Glouc* 77-79; V Bryneglwys and Llandegla *St As* 79-80; R Llandegla and Bryneglwys and Llanarmon-yn-Ial 80-86; P-in-c Burythorpe, Acklam and Leavening w Westow *York* 86-95; rtd 95; Perm to Offic *York* from 95. *9 Ropery Walk, Malton YO17 7JS* Tel (01653) 698980

NEWTON, Graham Hayden. b 47. AKC69. St Aug Coll Cant 70. **d** 70 **p** 71. C St Mary-at-Lambeth *S'wark* 70-73; TV Catford (Southend) and Downham 73-78; P-in-c Porthill *Lich* 78-79; TV Wolstanton 79-86; V Stevenage H Trin *St Alb* 86-96; TR Dunstable 96-04; RD Dunstable 96-02; R Barton-le-Cley w Higham Gobion and Hexton from 04. *The Rectory, 2 Manor Farm Close, Barton-le-Clay, Bedford MK45 4TB* Tel (01582) 881873 E-mail revghnewton@hotmail.com

NEWTON, Ian. b 66. Westmr Coll Ox BEd89 Leeds Univ BA03. Coll of Resurr Mirfield 01. **d** 03 **p** 04. C Horninglow *Lich* from 03. *10 Field Rise, Burton-on-Trent DE13 0NR* Tel (01283) 540933 E-mail fatheriannewton@yahoo.co.uk

NEWTON, John. b 39. AKC65. **d** 66 **p** 67. C Whipton *Ex* 66-68; C Plympton St Mary 68-74; V Broadwoodwidger 74-81; R Kelly w Bradstone 74-81; R Lifton 74-81; Chapl All Hallows Sch Rousdon 81-94; Lic to Offic *Ex* 81-94; rtd 99. *Flat 2, 5 Eyewell Green, Seaton EX12 2BN* Tel (01297) 625887

NEWTON, John Richard. b 25. FBIM. St Jo Coll Dur 76 Cranmer Hall Dur. **d** 78 **p** 79. C Cottingham *York* 78-80; R Beeford w Frodingham and Foston 80-86; R Todwick *Sheff* 86-92; rtd 92; Perm to Offic *Linc* from 92. *Quiet Corner, 12 Pelham Close, Sudbrooke, Lincoln LN2 2SQ* Tel (01522) 595123

✠**NEWTON, The Rt Revd Keith.** b 52. K Coll Lon BD73 AKC73 Ch Ch Coll Cant PGCE75. St Aug Coll Cant 74. **d** 75 **p** 76 **c** 02. C Gt Ilford St Mary *Chelmsf* 75-78; TV Wimbledon *S'wark* 78-85; Malawi 85-91; Dean Blantyre 86-91; Can S Malawi from 86; P-in-c Knowle *Bris* 91-93; V Knowle H Nativity 93-02; P-in-c Easton All Hallows 97-02; RD Brislington 95-99; AD Bris S 99-01; Hon Can Bris Cathl 00-02; Suff Bp Richborough (PEV) *Cant* from 02. *Richborough House, 6 Mellish Gardens, Woodford Green IG8 0BH* Tel (020) 8505 7259 E-mail pev@btinternet.com

NEWTON, Louis Kalbfield. b 44. N Texas State Univ BA73. Westcott Ho Cam CTM93. **d** 93 **p** 94. C Walthamstow St Pet *Chelmsf* 93-97; USA from 97. *573 Dolores Street, San Francisco, CA 94110, USA* Tel (001) (415) 861 1372 E-mail louisknewton@hotmail.com

NEWTON, Miles Julius Albert. b 69. K Alfred's Coll Win BA91. Qu Coll Birm BTh96. **d** 97 **p** 98. C Sholing *Win* 97-01; C Bitterne Park 01-03; V Woolston from 03. *St Mark's Vicarage, 117 Swift Road, Southampton SO19 9ER* Tel (023) 8044 1124 *or* 8032 6908

NEWTON, Canon Nigel Ernest Hartley. b 38. St Jo Coll Nottm CertCS87. **d** 89 **p** 90. C Largs *Glas* 89-92; Angl Chapl Ashbourne Home Largs 89-92; P-in-c Eyemouth *Edin* 92-95; Chapl Miss to Seamen 92-95; P-in-c Challoch *Glas* from 95; Can St Mary's Cathl *Edin* from 04. *All Saints' Rectory, Challoch, Newton Stewart DG8 6RB* Tel (01671) 402101 Mobile 07885-436892 Fax (01671) 401462 E-mail challoch@btinternet.com

NEWTON, Miss Pauline Dorothy. b 48. Southn Univ BA70 PGCE71 MPhil79. Sarum Th Coll 79. **dss** 82 **d** 87 **p** 94. Bemerton *Sarum* 82-87; NSM from 87; Dep Hd Malvern Girls' Coll from 86; Perm to Offic *Worc* from 86. *13 Highbury Avenue, Salisbury SP2 7EX* Tel (01722) 325707 E-mail pnewton48@hotmail.com

NEWTON, Peter. b 39. St Jo Coll Nottm 73. **d** 75 **p** 76. C Porchester *S'well* 75-79; R Wilford 79-99; rtd 99; Perm to Offic *Leic* from 99 and *S'well* from 04. *Appletree Cottage, 20 Main Street, Eaton, Grantham NG32 1SE* Tel (01476) 870024

NEWTON, Richard. b 47. Lon Univ DipTh72. Trin Coll Bris 72. **d** 73 **p** 74. C Fareham St Jo *Portsm* 73-76; C Cheltenham St Mark *Glouc* 76-83; P-in-c Malvern St Andr *Worc* 83-95; TR Kingswood *Bris* 95-99; Master St Jo Hosp Bath from 00. *The Master's Lodge, Chapel Court, Bath BA1 1SL* Tel (01225) 486411 Fax 481291 E-mail richard.newton@stjohnsbath.org.uk

NEWTON, Richard John Christopher. b 60. Bris Univ BSc81 Birm Univ DipTh87. Qu Coll Birm 85. **d** 88 **p** 89. C Bris Ch the Servant Stockwood *Bris* 88-92; C Dorking w Ranmore *Guildf* 92-96; P-in-c Hagley *Worc* 96-00; R from 00. *The Rectory, 6 Middlefield Lane, Hagley, Stourbridge DY9 0PX* Tel (01562) 882442 *or* 886363 Fax 887833 E-mail richard.kathy@yescomputers.co.uk *or* hagley.pcc@freeuk.com

NEWTON, Canon William Ronald. b 12. Birm Univ BA43. Westcott Ho Cam 41. **d** 43 **p** 44. C Truro St Paul *Truro* 43-48; PV Truro Cathl 45-46; V Treslothan 48-52; V Moulsecoomb *Chich* 52-56; V Stanmer w Falmer and Moulsecoomb 56-63; V Truro St Paul *Truro* 63-73; Hon Can Truro Cathl 71-83; V Penzance St Mary w St Paul 73-82; rtd 82; Perm to Offic *Chich* and *Truro* from 83. *52 Rutland Court, New Church Road, Hove BN3 4AF* Tel (01273) 773422

NIASSA, Bishop of. *See* VAN KOEVERING, The Rt Revd Mark Allan

NIBLETT, David John Morton. b 24. Wells Th Coll 51. **d** 54 **p** 55. C Stepney St Dunstan and All SS *Lon* 54-59; V Syston *Leic* 59-65; V Barnstaple St Pet w H Trin *Ex* 65-75; V S Brent 75-90; rtd 90; Perm to Offic *B & W* from 90. *2 Beretun Orchard, Glastonbury BA6 8AX* Tel (01458) 833101

NICE, Canon John Edmund. b 51. Univ of Wales (Ban) BA73. Coll of Resurr Mirfield 74. **d** 76 **p** 77. C Oxton *Ches* 76-79; C Liscard St Mary w St Columba 79-82; V Latchford St Jas 82-92; R Holyhead w Rhoscolyn w Llanfair-yn-Neubwll *Ban* 92-95; R Holyhead 95-04; RD Llifon and Talybolion 97-01; AD 01-04; R Llandudno from 04; Can Cursal Ban Cathl 02-04; Can and Preb Ban Cathl from 04. *The Rectory, Church Walks, Llandudno LL30 2HL* Tel (01492) 876624 E-mail john.nice2@btopenworld.com

NICHOL, William David. b 58. Hull Univ BA84. Ridley Hall Cam 84. **d** 87 **p** 88. C Hull St Jo Newland *York* 87-90; C Kirk Ella 90-92; TV 92-98; P-in-c Powick *Worc* 98-99; R Powick and Guarlford and Madresfield w Newland 99-05; V Malvern H Trin and St Jas from 05. *Holy Trinity Vicarage, 2 North Malvern Road, Malvern WR14 4LR* Tel (01684) 561126 E-mail david@trinityandthewest.wanadoo.co.uk

NICHOLAS, Canon Arnold Frederick. b 34. Jes Coll Cam BA58 MA62. Ely Th Coll 58. **d** 60 **p** 61. C Wisbech St Aug *Ely* 60-63; P-in-c Lt Massingham *Nor* 63-65; Youth Chapl 63-67; Chapl Bp Otter Coll Chich 67-70; R Westbourne *Chich* 70-76; V Stansted 70-76; Can and Preb Chich Cathl 76-82; RD Chich 76-80; P-in-c Chich St Pet 76-81; V Chich St Paul and St Bart 80-81; V Chich St Paul and St Pet 81-82; V Wisbech SS Pet and Paul *Ely* 82-90; RD Wisbech 82-90; V Fordham St Pet 90-95; P-in-c Kennett 90-95; Perm to Offic *Chich* from 97; rtd 99. *19 Roman Way, Chichester PO19 3QN* Tel (01243) 781388

NICHOLAS, Brian Arthur. b 19. St Edm Hall Ox BA47 MA53. Wycliffe Hall Ox 62. **d** 64 **p** 65. C Gerrards Cross *Ox* 64-66; C Whitley Ch Ch 66-69; V Chudleigh Knighton *Ex* 69-76; V Ex St Mark 76-84; rtd 84; Perm to Offic *Ex* from 84. *Windyridge, 4 Little John's Cross Hill, Exeter EX2 9PJ* Tel (01392) 219222

NICHOLAS, Ernest Milton. b 25. ACP50 Newc Univ DipAdEd69 Lanc Univ MA78. NEOC 85. **d** 86 **p** 87. NSM Hexham *Newc* 86-96; Perm to Offic from 96. *Hillside, Eilansgate, Hexham NE46 3EW* Tel (01434) 603609

NICHOLAS, Herbert Llewellyn. b 19. St D Coll Lamp 51. **d** 53 **p** 54. C Merthyr Tydfil *Llan* 53-65; V Pontypridd St Matt and Cilfynydd 65-89; rtd 89; Perm to Offic *Llan* from 89. *47 Meadow Crescent, Tonteg, Pontypridd CF38 1NL* Tel (01443) 206156

NICHOLAS, Malcolm Keith. b 46. FIBMS71 Open Univ BA79. S Dios Minl Tr Scheme 81. **d** 84 **p** 85. NSM Gatcombe *Portsm* 84-92; NSM Shorwell w Kingston 88-92; C Hartley Wintney, Elvetham, Winchfield etc *Win* 92-96; TV Grantham *Linc* 96-02; V Grantham, Harrowby w Londonthorpe 02-03; V Carr Dyke Gp from 03. *The Vicarage, 6 Walcott Road, Billinghay, Lincoln LN4 4EH* Tel (01526) 861746 E-mail revmalc@vicarage14.freeserve.co.uk

NICHOLAS, Maurice Lloyd. b 30. Kelham Th Coll 54. **d** 58 **p** 59. C Stepney St Dunstan and All SS *Lon* 58-60; C Sevenoaks St Jo *Roch* 60-65; Chapl RADD 65-75; C Northolt St Mary *Lon* 75-85; rtd 85; Hon C Upper Teddington SS Pet and Paul *Lon* 85-90; Perm to Offic from 91. *58 Elton Close, Hampton Wick, Kingston upon Thames KT1 4EE* Tel (020) 8977 9340

NICHOLAS, Milton. *See* NICHOLAS, Ernest Milton

NICHOLAS, Patrick. b 37. Selw Coll Cam BA60 MA65. Wells Th Coll 60. **d** 62 **p** 63. C Camberwell St Giles *S'wark* 62-63; C Warlingham w Chelsham and Farleigh 63-65; C Oxted 65-68; Hong Kong 68-74; C Portsea St Mary *Portsm* 75; Hd of Ho St Chris Fellowship Chiswick 76-79; Dept of Soc Services Glos Co Coun 79-92; Probation Officer Glouc Probation Service 92-97; rtd 97; Chapl St Jo Coll Hong Kong 97-00; Perm to Offic *Glouc* from 02. *35 Norwich Drive, Cheltenham GL51 3HD* Tel (01242) 510007 E-mail patnic@btinternet.com

NICHOLAS, Paul James. b 51. Univ of Wales (Lamp) DipTh73 BA. Coll of Resurr Mirfield 73. **d** 74 **p** 75. C Llanelli *St D* 74-78; C Roath *Llan* 78-84; P-in-c Leic St Pet *Leic* 84-87; V Shard End *Birm* 87-96; rtd 96; Perm to Offic *Birm* from 96. *50 Delrene Road, Shirley, Solihull B90 2HJ* Tel 0121-745 7339
E-mail frpaul@oikos.screaming.net

NICHOLLS, Alan Fryer. b 26. Univ Coll Ex BA50. Sarum Th Coll 50. **d** 52 **p** 53. C Wootton Bassett *Sarum* 52-55; C Chesterfield St Mary and All SS *Derby* 55-56; V Ringley *Man* 56-60; Chapl Prebendal Sch Chich 60-63; PV Chich Cathl *Chich* 60-63; V Selmeston w Alciston 63-65; Chapl Woodbridge Sch 65-66; Asst Chapl and Ho Master 66-86; TV Bruton and Distr *B & W* 86-92; rtd 92; Perm to Offic *B & W* 92-99 and *St Alb* from 00. *36 Turpins Close, Hertford SG14 2EH* Tel (01992) 535749

NICHOLLS, Brian Albert. b 39. LBIPP LMPA. St Jo Coll Nottm 82 WMMTC 90. **d** 93 **p** 94. NSM Oakham, Hambleton, Egleton, Braunston and Brooke *Pet* 93-96; R Edith Weston w N Luffenham and Lyndon w Manton 96-05; P-in-c Empingham w Whitwell 02-05; rtd 05. *28 Heron Road, Oakham LE15 6BN* Tel (01572) 759657 E-mail whollynich@ewrut.fsnet.co.uk

NICHOLLS (née HUMPHRIES), Mrs Catherine Elizabeth. b 53. Anglia Poly Univ MA97. Trin Coll Bris BA87. **d** 87 **p** 94. C Bath Twerton-on-Avon *B & W* 87-90; Personnel Manager and Tr Officer TEAR Fund 90-95; Hon C Norbiton *S'wark* 91-95; Perm to Offic *Ely* 95-97; Dir Past Studies EAMTC 97-03; Vice Prin 01-03; Hon Min Can Pet Cathl *Pet* 97-03; Perm to Offic *Nor* 03-05; Dioc Dir CME from 05. *North Cottage, Church Lane, Hethel, Norwich NR14 8HE* Tel (01508) 570557
E-mail cathynicholls@norwich.anglican.org

✠**NICHOLLS, The Rt Revd John.** b 43. AKC66. **d** 67 **p** 68 **c** 90. C Salford St Clem Ordsall *Man* 67-69; C Langley All SS and Martyrs 69-72; V 72-78; Dir Past Th Coll of Resurr Mirfield 78-83; Lic to Offic *Wakef* 79-83; Can Res Man Cathl *Man* 83-90; Suff Bp Lancaster *Blackb* 90-97; Bp Sheff from 97. *Bishopscroft, Snaithing Lane, Sheffield S10 3LG* Tel 0114-230 2170 Fax 263 0110 E-mail bishop.jack@bishopscroft.idps.co.uk

NICHOLLS, Keith Barclay. b 57. Nottm Univ BA78. Wycliffe Hall Ox 03. **d** 05. C Bisley and W End *Guildf* from 05. *2 Prunus Close, West End, Woking GU24 9NU* Tel (01483) 832200
E-mail keithpam@fish.co.uk

NICHOLLS, Mark Richard. b 60. LSE BSc(Econ)82 Leeds Univ BA88. Coll of Resurr Mirfield 86. **d** 89 **p** 90. C Warrington St Elphin *Liv* 89-92; V Wigan St Andr 92-96; R North End St Marg Zimbabwe 96-00; Shrine P Shrine of Our Lady of Walsingham 00-02; V Mill End and Heronsgate w W Hyde *St Alb* from 02. *St Peter's Vicarage, Berry Lane, Rickmansworth WD3 7HQ* Tel (01923) 770369 *or* 772785 Mobile 07909-546659
E-mail mmarini2001@aol.com

NICHOLLS, Mark Simon. b 57. Down Coll Cam MA79. Ripon Coll Cuddesdon 92. **d** 94 **p** 95. C Farnham *Guildf* 94-98; P-in-c Crookham 98-03; V from 03. *The Vicarage, 14 Gally Hill Road, Church Crookham, Fleet GU52 6LH* Tel (01252) 617130

NICHOLLS, Michael Stanley. b 34. AKC59. St Boniface Warminster 59. **d** 60 **p** 61. C Torquay St Martin Barton CD *Ex* 60-63; C E Grinstead St Mary *Chich* 63-66; C-in-c Salfords CD *S'wark* 66-68; V Salfords 68-75; V Tunbridge Wells St Barn *Roch* 75-97; rtd 97; Perm to Offic *Cant* 98-99; *Chich* from 99. *30 St Itha Road, Selsey, Chichester PO20 0AA* Tel (01243) 603837

NICHOLLS, Neil David Raymond. b 65. Univ Coll Lon BA86. Wycliffe Hall Ox BA90. **d** 91 **p** 92. C Westmr St Steph w St Jo *Lon* 91-94; C Islington St Mary 94-96; Chapl LSE 96-00; C St Bride Fleet Street w Bridewell etc 99-00; V Ealing St Barn from 00. *St Barnabas' Vicarage, 66 Woodfield Road, London W5 1SH* Tel (020) 8998 0826 E-mail rev.neil@tiscali.co.uk

NICHOLLS, Rachel. BA MPhil. **d** 00 **p** 01. NSM Chesterton St Geo *Ely* from 00. *5 Eachard Road, Cambridge CB3 0HZ* Tel (01223) 359167

NICHOLLS, Roger. Ox Univ MA Cam Univ DipEd. **d** 01 **p** 02. OLM Kenwyn w St Allen *Truro* 01-04; NSM Truro St Paul and St Clem from 04; NSM Truro St Geo and St Jo from 04. *8 Truro Vean Terrace, Truro TR1 1HA* Tel (01872) 275753
E-mail rognicholls@tesco.net

NICHOLLS, Simon James. b 53. Trent Park Coll of Educn CertEd76. Ridley Hall Cam. **d** 00 **p** 01. C Nuneaton St Nic *Cov* 00-04; R Markfield, Thornton, Bagworth and Stanton etc *Leic* from 04. *The Rectory, 3A The Nook, Markfield LE67 9WE* Tel (01530) 242844

NICHOLS, Barry Edward. b 40. ACA63 FCA73. S'wark Ord Course 66. **d** 69 **p** 70. NSM Surbiton St Andr and St Mark *S'wark* 69-92; Dean for MSE Kingston 90-92; Hon Can S'wark Cathl 90-92; Perm to Offic 99-01; NSM Upper Tooting H Trin 01-04; NSM Upper Tooting H Trin w St Aug from 04. *19 Arterberry Road, London SW20 8AF* Tel and fax (020) 8879 0154 E-mail barrynichols@btinternet.com

NICHOLS, Dennis Harry. b 25. Kelham Th Coll 47. **d** 52 **p** 53. C Oakham *Pet* 52-55; C Kettering St Mary 55-57; P-in-c Spalding St Paul *Linc* 57-61; V Bury H Trin *Man* 61-81; V St Gluvias *Truro* 81-90; RD Carnmarth S 85-90; rtd 90; Perm to Offic *Truro* from 90. *Westwood House, 8 Tremorvah Crescent, Truro TR1 1NL* Tel (01872) 225630

NICHOLS, Mrs Elizabeth Margaret. b 45. WEMTC 00. **d** 02 **p** 03. NSM Ledbury *Heref* 02-05; NSM Boxwell, Leighterton, Didmarton, Oldbury etc *Glouc* from 05. *The Rectory, The Meads, Leighterton, Tetbury GL8 8UW* Tel (01666) 890283
E-mail elizabeth@nichols.fsworld.co.uk

NICHOLS, Howard Keith. b 41. CCC Ox BA64 MA68 CEng86 FIEE92 EurIng94. WEMTC 98. **d** 01 **p** 02. NSM Ledbury *Heref* 01-04; NSM Boxwell, Leighterton, Didmarton, Oldbury etc *Glouc* from 04. *The Rectory, The Meads, Leighterton, Tetbury GL8 8UW* Tel (01666) 890283
E-mail hkn@extra-galactic.freeserve.co.uk

NICHOLS, Mark Steven. b 68. Lon Bible Coll BA94 Ridley Hall Cam 95. **d** 97. C Balham Hill Ascension *S'wark* 97-99. *37 Harrier Court, Fenton Street, Lancaster LA1 1AE*
E-mail markn1968uk@yahoo.co.uk

NICHOLS, Canon Raymond Maurice. b 22. ALCD53. **d** 53 **p** 54. C Childwall All SS *Liv* 53-56; Kenya 56-64; Home Sec SPCK 64-71; Overseas Sec 67-73; Publisher 73-74; P-in-c Dorchester *Ox* 74-78; P-in-c Newington 77-78; TR Dorchester 78-87; V Warborough 78-87; Hon Can Ch Ch 84-87; rtd 87; Perm to Offic *Sarum* from 91. *12 Abbey Court, Cerne Abbas, Dorchester DT2 7JH* Tel (01300) 341456

NICHOLS, Robert Warren. b 54. Biola Univ (USA) BA77. Fuller Th Sem California MA81 St Alb and Ox Min Course 93. **d** 96 **p** 97. NSM Headington Quarry *Ox* 96-97; C 97-00; Chapl Ox Radcliffe Hosps NHS Trust 00; Sen Asst P Wymondham *Nor* from 00; Lect from 01. *76A Norwich Road, Wymondham NR18 0SZ* Tel (01953) 604342
E-mail bob.nichols@bigfoot.com

NICHOLSON, Andrew John. b 69. Leeds Univ BA93 MA00. St Jo Coll Nottm MTh04. **d** 05. C E Richmond *Ripon* from 05. *The Vicarage, East Cowton, Northallerton DL7 0BN* Tel (01325) 378689 Mobile 07723-345917
E-mail andydebbie80@hotmail.com

NICHOLSON, Mrs Barbara Ruth. b 39. Nor City Coll TCert59. Dioc OLM tr scheme 99. **d** 02 **p** 03. OLM Reculver and Herne Bay St Bart *Cant* from 02. *34 Cliff Avenue, Herne Bay CT6 6LZ* Tel (01227) 364606

NICHOLSON, Brian Warburton. b 44. St Jo Coll Nottm 70 Lon Coll of Div ALCD73 LTh74. **d** 73 **p** 74. C Canford Magna *Sarum* 73-77; C E Twickenham St Steph *Lon* 77-80; V Colchester St Jo *Chelmsf* 80-96; R Oakley w Wootton St Lawrence *Win* from 96. *The Rectory, 9 The Drive, Oakley, Basingstoke RG23 7DA* Tel (01256) 780825
E-mail rectory@oakley.ndirect.co.uk

NICHOLSON, Miss Clare. b 46. RMN80 Keele Univ BA70 CertEd70 Lon Univ DN80. St Jo Coll Nottm DPS85. **dss** 85 **d** 87 **p** 94. Bletchley *Ox* 85-89; Par Dn 87-89; Par Dn Milton Keynes 89-90; Par Dn Prestwood and Gt Hampden 90-94; C 94-99; P-in-c E Springfield *Chelmsf* 99-03; V Aldborough Hatch from 03. *The Vicarage, 89 St Peter's Close, Ilford IG2 7QN* Tel (020) 8599 0524 E-mail revclare46@aol.com

NICHOLSON, David. b 57. Sarum & Wells Th Coll 80. **d** 83 **p** 84. C Trevethin *Mon* 83-85; C Ebbw Vale 85-87; V Newport St Steph and H Trin 87-95; V Abertillery w Cwmtillery w Six Bells 95-97; Hon Chapl Miss to Seamen 87-97; P-in-c Cudworth *Wakef* 97-98; V from 98; P-in-c Lundwood 01-04. *The Vicarage, St John's Road, Cudworth, Barnsley S72 8DE* Tel (01226) 710279
E-mail fr_d_pp_cudworth@hotmail.com

NICHOLSON, Mrs Diane Maureen. b 45. Birm Coll of Educn CertEd68. LNSM course 95. **d** 97 **p** 98. OLM Ludham, Potter Heigham, Hickling and Catfield *Nor* from 97. *25 Latchmoor Park, Ludham, Great Yarmouth NR29 5RA* Tel (01692) 678683

NICHOLSON, Dorothy Ann. b 40. Surrey Univ Roehampton MSc04. S'wark Ord Course 81. **dss** 84 **d** 87 **p** 94. Carshalton Beeches *S'wark* 84-88; Par Dn 87-88; Par Dn Brixton Road Ch Ch 88-89; C Malden St Jo 89-95; V Balham St Mary and St Jo from 95. *St Mary's Vicarage, 35 Elmfield Road, London SW17 8AG* Tel and fax (020) 8673 1188
E-mail nicholsonda@btopenworld.com

NICHOLSON, Eric. d 01 **p** 02. OLM W Wycombe w Bledlow Ridge, Bradenham and Radnage *Ox* from 01. *3 Cherry Tree Walk, Chesham HP5 3JN* Tel (01494) 785500

NICHOLSON, Prof Ernest Wilson. b 38. Comdr OM (Italy)90. TCD BA60 MA64 Glas Univ PhD64 Cam Univ MA67 BD71 DD78 Ox Univ DD79 FBA87. Westcott Ho Cam 69. **d** 69 **p** 70. Lect Div Cam Univ 67-79; Fell, Chapl and Dir of Th Studies Pemb Coll Cam 69-79; Dean 73-79; Prof of Interpr of H Scripture Oriel Coll Ox 79-90; Provost from 90; Pro-Vice-Chan Ox Univ from 93; Lic to Offic *Ox* from 84. *The Provost's Lodgings, Oriel College, Oxford OX1 4EW* Tel (01865) 276533

NICHOLSON, Gary. b 62. Open Univ BA89. Cranmer Hall Dur 91 NEOC DipHE95. **d** 95 **p** 96. NSM Whitworth w Spennymoor *Dur* 95-97; NSM Spennymoor, Whitworth and Merrington 97-00; C Coundon and Eldon 00-02; P-in-c from 02. *St James's Vicarage, 2A Collingwood Street, Coundon, Bishop Auckland DL14 8LG* Tel (01388) 603312 E-mail frgary@hotmail.com

NICHOLSON, Harold Sydney Leonard. b 35. Garnett Coll Lon PGCE67 Open Univ BA77. Oak Hill NSM Course 92. **d** 94 **p** 95. NSM Stanwell *Lon* 94-00; NSM Sunbury 98-00; NSM Shepperton from 00. *7 Academy Court, Fordbridge Road, Sunbury-on-Thames TW16 6AN* Tel (01932) 787690 E-mail hslnicholson@onetel.com

NICHOLSON, John Paul. b 57. Sarum Th Coll. **d** 82 **p** 83. C Kirkby *Liv* 82-85; TV Speke St Aid 85-95; Ind Chapl *Ox* 95-04; Chapl Cambs & Pet Mental Health Partnerships NHS Trust from 04. *Chaplaincy Office, Kent House, Fulbourn Hospital, Cambridge CB1 5EF* Tel (01223) 218598 E-mail john.nicholson@cambsmh.nhs.uk

NICHOLSON, Mrs Julie Karina. b 53. UWE BA97. Trin Coll Bris. **d** 00 **p** 01. C Henbury *Bris* 00-04; P-in-c Bristol St Aid w St Geo from 04. *St Aidan's Vicarage, 2 Jockey Lane, Bristol BS5 8NZ* Tel 0117-967 7812 E-mail julie.nicholson@fish.co.uk

NICHOLSON, Kevin Smith. b 47. CQSW76. Edin Th Coll 89. **d** 91 **p** 92. C W Fife Team Min *St And* 91-94; P-in-c 94-95; R Kinross 95-03; rtd 03. *Oldshoremore, 3A West Huntingtower, Perth PH1 3NU* Tel (01738) 583555

NICHOLSON, Canon Nigel Patrick. b 46. Sarum & Wells Th Coll 72. **d** 75 **p** 76. C Farnham *Guildf* 75-78; C Worplesdon 78-81; CF (ACF) from 80; P-in-c Compton *Guildf* 81-85; R Compton w Shackleford and Peper Harow 85-89; R Cranleigh from 89; RD Cranleigh 95-00; Hon Can Guildf Cathl from 01. *The Rectory, High Street, Cranleigh GU6 8AS* Tel (01483) 273620 E-mail stnicoloff@aol.com

NICHOLSON, Miss Pamela Elizabeth. b 47. Ripon Coll Cuddesdon. **d** 92 **p** 94. C Balsall Heath St Paul *Birm* 92-95; V Smethwick St Matt w St Chad from 95. *1 St Matthew's Road, Smethwick, Warley B66 3TN* Tel 0121-558 1653

NICHOLSON, Paul Shannon. b 52. York Univ BA74 Middx Univ BA02 ARCO74 ARCM75. NTMTC 99. **d** 02 **p** 03. C Primrose Hill St Mary w Avenue Road St Paul *Lon* from 02. *30A Hadley Street, London NW1 8SS* Tel (020) 7482 1170 Mobile 07971-223764 E-mail nicholsongarrison@hotmail.com

NICHOLSON, Canon Peter Charles. b 25. OBE92. Lambeth Hon MA89 Chich Th Coll 57. **d** 59 **p** 60. C Sawbridgeworth *St Alb* 59-62; Min Can, Prec and Sacr Pet Cathl *Pet* 62-67; V Wroxham w Hoveton *Nor* 67-74; V Lyme Regis *Sarum* 74-80; Gen Sec St Luke's Hosp for the Clergy 80-93; NSM Harlington *Lon* 80-87; Hon Chapl S'wark Cathl *S'wark* from 87; Can and Preb Chich Cathl *Chich* 89-93; rtd 93. *St Luke's Cottage, 13 Brearley Close, Uxbridge UB8 1JJ* Tel (01895) 233522

NICHOLSON, Peter Charles. b 44. Oak Hill Th Coll 74. **d** 76 **p** 77. C Croydon Ch Ch Broad Green *Cant* 76-80; C Gt Baddow *Chelmsf* 80-88; TV 88-96; V Westcliff St Mich from 96. *St Michael's Vicarage, 5 Mount Avenue, Westcliff-on-Sea SS0 8PS* Tel (01702) 478462 E-mail pedinic@talk21.com

NICHOLSON, Rodney. b 45. Mert Coll Ox BA68 MA71. Ridley Hall Cam 69. **d** 72 **p** 73. C Colne St Bart *Blackb* 72-75; C Blackpool St Jo 75-78; V Ewood 78-90; V Clitheroe St Paul Low Moor from 90; P-in-c Chatburn and Downham from 03. *The Vicarage, St Paul's Street, Clitheroe BB7 2LS* Tel and fax (01200) 458019 E-mail rodnic@btopenworld.com

NICHOLSON, Roland. b 40. Sarum & Wells Th Coll 72. **d** 74 **p** 75. C Morecambe St Barn *Blackb* 74-78; V Feniscliffe 78-90; V Sabden and Pendleton 90-02; C Poulton-le-Fylde 02-04; C Poulton Carleton and Singleton from 04. *29 Moss Bourne Road, Poulton-le-Fylde FY6 7DU* Tel (01253) 884298

NICHOLSON, Mrs Samantha. b 69. St Jo Coll York BA92. St Jo Coll Nottm MA95 LTh93. **d** 96 **p** 97. C Toxteth St Cypr w Ch Ch *Liv* 96-01; P-in-c W Derby St Luke from 01. *St Luke's Vicarage, Princess Drive, West Derby, Liverpool L14 8XG* Tel 0151-228 6025

NICHOLSON, Stephen Lee. b 65. St Jo Coll Cam BA87 MA91 PhD94. St Steph Ho Ox 98. **d** 00 **p** 01. C Middlesbrough All SS *York* from 00; Asst Chapl HM Pris Holme Ho from 00. *14 Chipchase Road, Linthorpe, Middlesbrough TS5 6EY* Tel (01642) 827196 Mobile 07788-781560

NICHOLSON, Trevor Parry. b 35. St Edm Hall Ox BA58 MA. Wycliffe Hall Ox 58. **d** 60 **p** 61. C Eastbourne Ch Ch *Chich* 60-63; C Ifield 63-67; Asst Youth Chapl *Win* 67-73; Chapl Shoreham Gr Sch 73-78; P-in-c Capel *Guildf* 78-85; V 85-90; Chapl Qu Anne's Sch Caversham 90-00; rtd 00; P-in-c N Chapel w Ebernoe *Chich* 00-05. *Lexham, Dodsley Lane, Easebourne, Midhurst GU29 9BB* Tel (01730) 810452

NICHOLSON, Miss Velda Christine. b 44. Charlotte Mason Coll of Educn TCert65. Birm Bible Inst DipTh69 Cranmer Hall Dur 81. **dss** 82 **d** 87 **p** 94. Gt and Lt Driffield *York* 82-86; Newby 86-88; Par Dn 87-88; TD Cramlington *Newc* 88-94; TV 94-96; Perm to Offic from 96; rtd 04. *24 Glendale, Amble, Morpeth NE65 0RG* Tel (01665) 713796

NICHOLSON, Veronica Mary. *See* WILSON, Mrs Veronica Mary

NICKLAS-CARTER, Derath May. *See* CARTER, Miss Derath May

NICKLESS, Christopher John. b 58. Univ of Wales BA79. Coll of Resurr Mirfield 79. **d** 81 **p** 82. C Bassaleg *Mon* 81-85; TV Ebbw Vale 85-93; V Newport St Teilo 93-99. *Address temp unknown*

NICKLIN, Ivor. b 41. FRSA68 BEd MTh73 PhD76 MA84. Wycliffe Hall Ox. **d** 84 **p** 85. NSM Weaverham *Ches* 84-89; P-in-c Kings Walden *St Alb* 89-91; P-in-c Offley w Lilley 89-91; V King's Walden and Offley w Lilley 91-93; V Basford *Lich* 93-98; rtd 98; Perm to Offic *Ches* from 99 and *Lich* from 00. *232 Manor Way, Crewe CW2 6PH* Tel (01270) 669080

NICKOLS, James Alexander. b 75. Regent's Park Coll Ox BA96. Ridley Hall Cam 98. **d** 00 **p** 01. C Plymouth St Jude *Ex* 00-04; C Camberwell All SS *S'wark* from 04. *2A Barforth Road, London SE15 3PS* Tel 07968-062339 (mobile) E-mail jamesnkls@aol.com

NICKOLS-RAWLE, Peter John. b 44. St Luke's Coll Ex CertEd73. Sarum & Wells Th Coll 76. **d** 78 **p** 79. C Ex St Thos *Ex* 78-80; C Old Shoreham *Chich* 80-86; C New Shoreham 80-86; P-in-c Donnington 86-90; Chapl RAF 90-92; TV Ottery St Mary, Alfington, W Hill, Tipton etc *Ex* 92-97; V Breage w Germoe and Godolphin *Truro* 98-01; rtd 01; Perm to Offic *Truro* from 01. *2 Kroonstadt Villas, Godolphin Road, Helston TR13 8QR* Tel (01326) 569664

NICKSON, Ann Louise. b 58. New Hall Cam BA80 Fitzw Coll Cam BA95 Solicitor 81. Ridley Hall Cam PhD98. **d** 98 **p** 99. C Sanderstead All SS *S'wark* 98-01; P-in-c Norbury St Steph and Thornton Heath 01-05; V from 05. *St Stephen's Vicarage, 9 Warwick Road, Thornton Heath CR7 7NH* Tel (020) 8684 3820 E-mail annnickson@aol.com

NICKSON, Patricia Jane. b 44. CBE05. RN66 RM68 Liv Univ MCommH81 PhD89. St Jo Coll Nottm 03. **d** 04 **p** 05. NSM Upton (Overchurch) *Ches* from 04. *14 Aughton Court, Church Road, Wirral CH49 6JY* Tel 0151-678 6682 E-mail patricia@pnickson@fslife.co.uk

NICOL, David Christopher. b 56. Westmr Coll Ox BEd84 Ox Univ Inst of Educn 91. St Alb and Ox Min Course 95. **d** 98 **p** 99. NSM Deddington w Barford, Clifton and Hempton *Ox* 98-01; V Longnor, Quarnford and Sheen *Lich* from 01. *The Vicarage, Gauledge Lane, Longnor, Buxton SK17 0PA* Tel (01298) 83742 Fax as telephone E-mail fr.david@tinyworld.co.uk

NICOL, Ernest. b 25. S'wark Ord Course 71. **d** 74 **p** 75. NSM Hornsey Ch Ch *Lon* 74-75; NSM Hornsey St Geo 76-84; C Hendon Ch Ch 85-90; rtd 90; C Steeton *Bradf* 90-96; Asst Chapl Airedale Hosp Bradf 90-96; Perm to Offic *Lon* 96-01; Hon C Hornsey St Mary w St Geo from 01. *75 Nightingale Lane, London N8 7RA* Tel (020) 8341 5496

NICOL, Harvie Thomas. b 61. Aston Tr Scheme DipHE97 St Jo Coll Nottm DipTh99. **d** 99 **p** 00. C Balderstone *Man* 99; C S Rochdale 00-03; P-in-c Ashton St Pet from 03; TV Ashton from 03. *The Rectory, 2A Hutton Avenue, Ashton-under-Lyne OL6 6DY* Tel 0161-330 8251

NICOLE, Bruce. b 54. K Coll Lon MA96 ACIB. Wycliffe Hall Ox 89. **d** 91 **p** 92. C Headley All SS *Guildf* 91-95; V Camberley St Mich Yorktown from 95; RD Surrey Heath from 02. *The Vicarage, 286 London Road, Camberley GU15 3JP* Tel (01276) 23602 E-mail revbrucenicole@aol.com

NICOLL, Alexander Charles Fiennes Jack. b 34. Lon Univ DipTh66. Lon Coll of Div 66. **d** 68 **p** 69. C Trentham *Lich* 68-71; C Hednesford 72-74; P-in-c Quarnford 74-84; V Longnor 74-84; P-in-c Sheen 80-84; V Longnor, Quarnford and Sheen 85-00; RD Alstonfield 96-00; Perm to Offic from 00; rtd 00. *110 Stone Road, Uttoxeter ST14 7QW* Tel (01889) 569361

NICOLL, Miss Angela Olive. b 50. Linc Th Coll 77. **dss** 79 **d** 87 **p** 94. Catford St Laur *S'wark* 79-83; Peckham St Jo w St Andr 83-87; Par Dn 87-88; Par Dn New Addington 88-94; C 94-02; S Africa from 02. *St Monica's House of Prayer, 46 Green Street, Kimberley, South Africa*

NICOLLS, Andrew John. b 67. Regents Th Coll BA03 RN. Trin Coll Bris 03. **d** 05. C Higher Bebington *Ches* from 05. *3 Beech Road, Bebington, Wirral CH63 8PE* Tel 0151-645 9074

NICOLSON, Paul Roderick. b 32. Cuddesdon Coll 65. **d** 67 **p** 68. C Farnham Royal *Ox* 67-70; Lic to Offic *St Alb* 70-82; C Hambleden Valley *Ox* 82-99; rtd 99; Perm to Offic *Lon* from 02. *93 Campbell Road, London N17 0AX* Tel (020) 8376 5455 Mobile 07961-177889 Fax (020) 8376 5319 E-mail paul@nicolson.com

NIE, Miss Muriel Rose. b 29. St Mich Ho Ox IDC57. **d** 87 **p** 94. NSM Leyton All SS *Chelmsf* 87-99; Perm to Offic from 99. *2 Queens Court, Manor Road, London E10 7HP* Tel (020) 8556 0457

NIEMIEC, Paul Kevin. b 56. EAMTC 03. **d** 05. Youth Officer *Pet* from 97; NSM Thrapston from 05. *142 St John's Road, Kettering NN15 5AT* Tel (01536) 391064 E-mail youth@peterborough-diocese.org.uk

NIGER, Bishop on the. *See* OKEKE, The Rt Revd Ken Sandy Edozie

NIGERIA, Archbishop of. *See* AKINOLA, The Most Revd Peter Jasper

NIGHTINGALE, Catherine. b 72. **d** 01 **p** 02. C Birchencliffe *Wakef* 01-04; C to Dioc Chapl among Deaf People 01-04; TV E Farnworth and Kearsley *Man* from 04; Chapl among Deaf People from 04. *The Rectory, 55 Church Street, Farnworth, Bolton BL4 8AQ* Tel (01204) 572819 E-mail c.nightingale@tiscali.co.uk

NIGHTINGALE, Mrs Jennifer. b 66. Wolv Univ BA99. Qu Coll Birm. **d** 04 **p** 05. C Walsall St Paul *Lich* from 04. *11 The Cloisters, Walsall WS4 2AJ* Tel (01922) 721144 *or* 613558 Mobile 07703-558668

NIGHTINGALE, Canon John Brodie. b 42. Pemb Coll Ox BA64 Bris Univ DSS65 Qu Coll Cam BA67. Westcott Ho Cam 65. **d** 67 **p** 68. C Wythenshawe St Martin *Man* 67-70; Nigeria 70-76; P-in-c Amberley w N Stoke *Chich* 76-79; Adult Educn Adv 76-79; Asst Home Sec Gen Syn Bd for Miss and Unity 80-84; Miss Sec 84-87; P-in-c Wolverton w Norton Lindsey and Langley *Cov* 87-95; Dioc Miss Adv 87-95; V Rowley Regis *Birm* from 95; Hon Can Birm Cathl from 01; Warden of Readers from 03. *St Giles' Vicarage, 192 Hanover Road, Rowley Regis, Warley B65 9EQ* Tel 0121-559 1251 Fax 559 1553 E-mail john.nightingale@which.net

NIGHTINGALE, Susan Kay. b 44. Keele Univ BA66 DipSocSc66 Seabury-Western Th Sem DMin99 Coll of Ripon & York St Jo CertCS85. S'wark Ord Course 90. **d** 93 **p** 94. NSM St Giles Cripplegate w St Bart Moor Lane etc *Lon* 93-99; Perm to Offic *York* 93-99; Asst Chapl H Trin Geneva *Eur* 99-02; P-in-c Sutton on the Forest *York* from 03. *Westfield Farm, Sheriff Hutton, York YO60 6QQ* Tel (01347) 878423

NIMMO, Canon Alexander Emsley. b 53. Aber Univ BD76 PhD97 Edin Univ MPhil83 FSAScot93. Edin Th Coll 76. **d** 78 **p** 79. Prec St Andr Cathl Inverness *Mor* 78-81; P-in-c Stornoway *Arg* 81-83; R 84; R Edin St Mich and All SS *Edin* 84-90; Chapl HM Pris Saughton 87-90; R Aberdeen St Marg *Ab* from 90; Can St Andr Cathl from 96; Syn Clerk from 01. *St Margaret's Rectory, Gallowgate, Aberdeen AB25 1EA* Tel (01224) 644969 Fax 630767 E-mail emsley@aberdeengallowgate.fsnet.co.uk

NIND, Robert William Hampden. b 31. Ball Coll Ox BA54 MA60. Cuddesdon Coll 54. **d** 56 **p** 57. C Spalding *Linc* 56-60; Jamaica 60-67; P-in-c Battersea St Bart *S'wark* 67-70; V Brixton St Matt 70-82; Lic to Offic 82-84; Ind Chapl 84-89; Ind Chapl *Ox* 89-95; rtd 95. *19 Binswood Avenue, Headington, Oxford OX3 8NY* Tel (01865) 66604 E-mail bawalker@rwhnind.freeserve.co.uk

NINEHAM, Prof Dennis Eric. b 21. Qu Coll Ox BA43 MA46 Cam Univ BD64 Birm Univ Hon DD72. Linc Th Coll 44. **d** 44 **p** 45. Asst Chapl Qu Coll Ox 44-46; Chapl 46-54; Prof Bibl and Hist Th K Coll Lon 54-58; Prof Div Lon Univ 58-64; Regius Prof Div Cam Univ 64-69; Warden Keble Coll Ox 69-79; Hon Can Bris Cathl *Bris* 80-86; Prof Th Bris Univ 80-86; rtd 86; Perm to Offic *Ox* from 87. *9 Fitzherbert Close, Iffley, Oxford OX4 4EN* Tel (01865) 715941

NINIS, The Ven Richard Betts. b 31. Linc Coll Ox BA53 MA62 Derby Univ. Linc Th Coll 53. **d** 55 **p** 56. C Poplar All SS w St Frideswide *Lon* 55-62; V Heref St Martin *Heref* 62-71; V Upper and Lower Bullinghope w Grafton 68-71; R Dewsall w Callow 68-71; Dioc Missr 69-74; Preb Heref Cathl 70-74; Telford Planning Officer *Lich* 70-74; Can Res and Treas Lich Cathl 74-98; Adn Stafford 74-80; Adn Lich 80-98; rtd 98; Perm to Offic *B & W* from 00. *Hill View, 32 Robert Street, Williton, Taunton TA4 4QL* Tel (01984) 634987 Fax as telephone

NISBET, Gillian Ruth. b 65. N Ord Course 00. **d** 03. NSM Childwall St Dav *Liv* from 03. *20 Stuart Avenue, Liverpool L25 0NJ* Tel 0151-486 0608 E-mail nessies@nisbet20.freeserve.co.uk

NISBETT, Canon Thomas Norman. b 25. OBE91. Codrington Coll Barbados. **d** 62 **p** 63. Barbados 62-64; Bermuda from 65; Hon Can Bermuda Cathl from 81; rtd 97. *2 Shelton Road, Pembroke HM 20, Bermuda* Tel (001441) 236 0537 Fax as telephone

NIXON, David John. b 59. St Chad's Coll Dur BA81 Ex Univ PhD02. St Steph Ho Ox 88. **d** 91 **p** 92. C Plymouth St Pet *Ex* 91-94; Chapl Ex Univ 94-03; P-in-c Stoke Damerel from 03; P-in-c Devonport St Aubyn from 03. *The Rectory, 6 Underhill Road, Plymouth PL3 4BP* Tel (01752) 562348 E-mail rev.dave@virgin.net

NIXON, Frances (Isobel). b 34. TCD BA62. **d** 94 **p** 95. NSM Rossory *Clogh* from 94. *Honiara, 61 Granshagh Road, Enniskillen BT92 2BL* Tel (028) 6634 8723 Mobile 07710-307263 E-mail isobel@honiara.fsnet.co.uk

NIXON, John David. b 38. Leeds Univ BSc60 CEng70 MICE. Linc Th Coll 76. **d** 78 **p** 79. C Rugby St Andr *Cov* 78-83; TV 83-86; TV Bicester w Bucknell, Caversfield and Launton *Ox* 86-98; USA from 98; rtd 03. *1209 W 21st Street, Lawrence, KS 66044, USA* E-mail frjdn@hotmail.com *or* allsaintskcrector@juno.com

NIXON, Ms Naomi Jane. b 75. Keele Univ BA97. St Jo Coll Nottm MA00. **d** 01 **p** 02. C Ludlow, Ludford, Ashford Carbonell etc *Heref* 01-04; Chapl N Warks and Hinckley Coll of FE from 04. *St Philip's Vicarage, Ringwood Highway, Coventry CV2 2GF* Tel (024) 7661 7706 E-mail nnixon@fish.co.uk

NIXON, Pauline Margaret. b 49. **d** 05. NSM Perranzabuloe *Truro* from 05. *3 Dorrington House, Grannys Lane, Perranporth TR6 0HB* Tel (01872) 571697 E-mail pmnixon2004-hjv@yahoo.co.uk

NIXON, Canon Phillip Edward. b 48. Ch Ch Ox MA73 DPhil73 Trin Coll Cam BA80 K Coll Lon MA00. Westcott Ho Cam 78. **d** 81 **p** 82. C Leeds Halton St Wilfrid *Ripon* 81-84; V Goring *Ox* 84; V Goring w S Stoke 84-03; RD Henley 94-02; Hon Can Ch Ch 00-03; P-in-c Northampton St Jas *Pet* from 03; Warden of Readers from 05. *St James's Vicarage, Vicarage Road, Northampton NN5 7AX* Tel (01604) 751164 E-mail phillipn@btopenworld.com

NIXON, Miss Rosemary Ann. b 45. Bp Grosseteste Coll CertEd66 Dur Univ MA83 Edin Univ MTh95. Dalton Ho Bris IDC72 DipTh72 BD73. **d** 87 **p** 94. Tutor St Jo Coll w Cranmer Hall Dur 75-89; Dir St Jo Coll Ext Progr 82-89; NSM Chester le Street *Dur* 87-89; TD Gateshead 89-92; Dir Cranmer Hall Urban Studies Unit 89-92; TISEC 92-99; Prin 95-99; Can St Mary's Cathl *Edin* 96-99; V Cleadon *Dur* from 99. *The Vicarage, 5 Sunderland Road, Cleadon, Sunderland SR6 7UR* Tel and fax 0191-536 7147

NIXON, William Samuel. BSc BTh. **d** 00 **p** 01. C Lisburn St Paul *Conn* 00-02; C Hillsborough *D & D* from 02. *11 Ashvale Drive, Hillsborough BT26 6DN* Tel (028) 9268 9099

NIXSON, Peter. b 27. Ball Coll Ox BA51 MA59 Ex Univ PGCE67 DipEd72. Coll of Resurr Mirfield 51. **d** 53 **p** 54. C Babbacombe *Ex* 53-56; C Swindon New Town *Bris* 56-57; C Boyne Hill *Ox* 57-60; C-in-c Bayswater St Mary CD 60-66; Perm to Offic *Ex* 66-67 and 70-85; Perm to Offic *Lich* 67-69; Hd RE Oswestry Boys' High Sch 67-69; Hon C Oswestry H Trin 69-70; Sch Coun Tiverton 70-75; Newton Abbot 75-85; V Winkleigh *Ex* 85-92; R Ashreigney 85-92; R Broadwoodkelly 85-92; V Brushford 85-92; RD Chulmleigh 87-93; rtd 93; Perm to Offic *Ex* from 93. *40 Lidford Tor Avenue, Paignton TQ4 7ED* Tel (01803) 522698

NIXSON, Rosemary Clare. *See* WARD, Mrs Rosemary Clare

NJENGA, Kennedy Samuel. b 60. Oak Hill Th Coll Qu Coll Birm. **d** 01 **p** 02. C Old Trafford St Jo *Man* 01-04; P-in-c Pheasey *Lich* from 04. *St Chad's Vicarage, 88 Hillingford Avenue, Birmingham B43 7HN* Tel 0121-360 6098 E-mail njambinjenga@aol.com

✠**NJOJO, The Rt Revd Patrice Byankya.** b 38. BA76. Montreal Dioc Th Coll 79. **d** 70 **p** 80 **c** 80. Bp Boga from 80; Abp Congo 92-02. *PO Box 25586, Kampala, Uganda* Tel (00256) 77-647495 E-mail eac-mags@infocom.co.uk

NJUGUNA, Daniel Cahira. b 73. St Jo Coll Nottm BA04. **d** 00 **p** 01. Kenya 00-03; C Balderton and Barnby-in-the-Willows *S'well* from 04. *8 Alvey Road, Balderton, Newark NG24 3PE* Tel (01636) 701128 Mobile 07817-577436 E-mail dcahira@yahoo.co.uk

NJUGUNA, Timothy. b 49. St Paul's Coll Limuru BD84 Presbyterian Th Coll Seoul ThM89 San Francisco Th Sem DMin03. **d** 83 **p** 84. V Nairobi St Mary Kenya 84-86; V Karura 86-87; V Kirangari 89-90; Dioc Sec Mt Kenya S 91-93; P-in-c San Bruno USA 99-03; Perm to Offic *S'wark* from 05. *95 Gonville Road, Thornton Heath CR7 6DF* Tel (020) 8240 9741 Mobile 07950-536215 E-mail tegssa@hotmail.com

NOAH, Michael John. b 44. WEMTC 00. **d** 02 **p** 03. NSM Hucclecote *Glouc* 02-05; NSM Malmesbury w Westport and Brokenborough *Bris* from 05. *10 Old Railway Close, Malmesbury SN16 9TU* Tel (01666) 826564 E-mail mikenoah@supanet.com

NOAKES, Mrs Dorothy. b 35. Derby Coll of Educn CertEd55 Ex Univ BEd85 BPhil(Ed)92. LNSM course 94. **d** 96 **p** 97. OLM Helston and Wendron *Truro* from 96. *6 Tenderah Road, Helston TR13 8NT* Tel (01326) 573239 E-mail poppyno@tinyworld.co.uk

✠**NOAKES, The Rt Revd George.** b 24. Univ of Wales (Abth) BA48 Univ of Wales Hon DD90. Wycliffe Hall Ox 49. **d** 50 **p** 52 **c** 82. C Lampeter *St D* 50-56; V Eglwyswrw and Meline 56-59; V Tregaron 59-67; V Cardiff Dewi Sant *Llan* 67-76; R

Aberystwyth *St D* 76-80; Can St D Cathl 77-79; Adn Cardigan 79-82; V Llanychaearn w Llanddeiniol 80-82; Bp St D 82-91; Abp Wales 87-91; rtd 91. *1 Ger-y-Llan, The Parade, Carmarthen SA31 1LY* Tel (01267) 235284

NOBBS, Charles Henry ffrench. b 67. Hatf Coll Dur BSc89 St Jo Coll Dur BA99 CEng96. Cranmer Hall Dur 97. **d** 99 **p** 00. C Northampton St Giles *Pet* 99-02; C Collingtree w Courteenhall and Milton Malsor from 02. *10 Foxglove Close, Grange Park, Northampton NN4 5DD* Tel (01604) 875188 E-mail charlie@dunelm.org.uk

NOBBS, John Ernest. b 35. Tyndale Hall Bris 60. **d** 63 **p** 64. C Walthamstow St Mary *Chelmsf* 63-66; C Braintree 66-69; C Wakef St Andr and St Mary *Wakef* 69-71; C Tooting Graveney St Nic *S'wark* 71-74; C Woking St Pet *Guildf* 74-78; C Worthing St Geo *Chich* 78-88; C Rayleigh *Chelmsf* 88-94; rtd 94; Perm to Offic *Chelmsf* from 00. *89 Panfield Lane, Braintree CM7 5RP* Tel (01376) 322901

NOBLE, Alexander Frederick Innes (Sandy). b 30. Selw Coll Cam BA53 MA58. Lon Coll of Div ALCD55. **d** 55 **p** 56. C Stratton St Margaret *Bris* 55-57; C Brislington St Luke 57-59; Chapl Pierrepont Sch Frensham 59-61; Asst Chapl Repton Sch Derby 61-63; Chapl 63-66; Chapl Blundell's Sch Tiverton 66-72; St Jo C of E Sch Cowley 73-77; Chapl Cranbrook Sch Kent 77-81; Chapl St Geo Sch Harpenden 81-90; Hon C Herriard w Winslade and Long Sutton etc *Win* 90-94; rtd 95; P-in-c Oare w Culbone *B & W* 95-99; Perm to Offic from 00. *Upway, Church Street, Minehead TA24 5JU* Tel (01643) 708976

NOBLE, Christopher John Lancelot. b 58. Aston Tr Scheme 88 Oak Hill Th Coll DipHE90. **d** 90 **p** 91. C Tonbridge SS Pet and Paul *Roch* 90-95; P-in-c Stansted w Fairseat and Vigo 95-98; R from 98. *The Rectory, 9 The Coach Drive, Meopham, Gravesend DA13 0SZ* Tel (01732) 822494

NOBLE, David. b 37. S Dios Minl Tr Scheme 84. **d** 87 **p** 88. C Alverstoke *Portsm* 87-89; Australia from 90; rtd 02. *Quill Studio, 9 Chaparral Crescent, Willetton, W Australia 6155* Tel 417-172542 (mobile) E-mail thenobles@surak.com.au

NOBLE, Mrs Eileen Joan. b 45. NEOC 90. **d** 93 **p** 94. C Gosforth All SS *Newc* 93-96; C Cramlington 96-97; TV 97-01; V Ashington from 01. *Holy Sepulchre Vicarage, Wansbeck Road, Ashington NE63 8HZ* Tel (01670) 813358 E-mail revnoble2000@yahoo.com

NOBLE, Canon Graham Edward. b 49. SS Paul & Mary Coll Cheltenham CertEd71 Open Univ BA74. EAMTC 85. **d** 88 **p** 89. C Kesgrave *St E* 88-90; P-in-c Gt and Lt Blakenham w Baylham and Nettlestead 90-95; P-in-c Debenham w Aspall and Kenton 95-04; P-in-c Helmingham w Framsden and Pettaugh w Winston 99-04; R Debenham and Helmingham from 04; RD Loes 99-05; Hon Can St E Cathl from 03. *The Vicarage, 34 Gracechurch Street, Debenham, Stowmarket IP14 6RE* Tel (01728) 860265 E-mail graham@noblefamily.fsnet.co.uk

NOBLE, Paul Vincent. b 54. Leeds Univ BA75 PGCE76 Ox Univ BA81 MA85. St Steph Ho Ox 79. **d** 82 **p** 83. C Prestbury *Glouc* 82-85; P-in-c Avening w Cherington 85-90; V The Suttons w Tydd *Linc* 90-98; R Skirbeck St Nic from 98. *The Rectory, Fishtoft Road, Skirbeck, Boston PE21 0DJ* Tel (01205) 362734 E-mail frpnoble@skirbeckrectory.freeserve.co.uk

NOBLE, Peter Hirst. b 37. Lon Univ BD68 Leeds Univ MPhil72. Cranmer Hall Dur 65. **d** 68 **p** 69. C Honley *Wakef* 68-72; P-in-c Moss *Sheff* 72-81; V Askern 72-92; rtd 92. *40 Broome Close, Huntington, York YO32 9RH* Tel (01904) 766203

NOBLE, Canon Philip David. b 46. Glas Univ BSc67 Edin Univ BD70. Edin Th Coll 67. **d** 70 **p** 71. C Edin Ch Ch *Edin* 70-72; Papua New Guinea 72-75; R Cambuslang *Glas* 76-83; R Uddingston 76-83; Ev Prestwick 83-85; R Prestwick from 85; Can St Mary's Cathl from 99. *56 Ayr Road, Prestwick KA9 1RR* Tel (01292) 477108

NOBLE, Robert. b 43. TCD BA66 BD73. **d** 68 **p** 69. C Holywood *D & D* 68-71; Chapl RAF 71-98; Chapl Holmewood Ho Sch Tunbridge Wells from 98; Perm to Offic *Chich* from 01. *The Little House, Holmewood House School, Langton Green, Tunbridge Wells TN3 0EB* Tel (01892) 860030

NOBLES, Mrs Mary. b 37. **d** 05. NSM Malvern Link w Cowleigh *Worc* from 05. *4 Hamilton Close, Powick, Worcester WR2 4NH* Tel (01905) 831925

NOBLET, David. b 62. Cen Lancs Univ HND95. Cranmer Hall Dur DTM99. **d** 99 **p** 00. C Carnforth *Blackb* 99; C Standish 00-03; P-in-c Langho Billington from 03. *The Vicarage, 11 Whalley New Road, Billington, Blackburn BB7 9NA* Tel (01254) 822246

NOBLETT, The Ven William Alexander. b 53. Southn Univ BTh78 Westmr Coll Ox MTh99. Sarum & Wells Th Coll 74. **d** 78 **p** 79. C Sholing *Win* 78-80; I Ardamine w Kiltennel, Glascarrig etc *C & O* 80-82; Chapl RAF 82-84; V Middlesbrough St Thos *York* 84-87; Asst Chapl HM Pris Wakef 87-89; Chapl 89-92; Chapl HM Pris Nor 92-97; Chapl HM Pris Full Sutton 97-01; Chapl Gen of Pris and Adn to HM Pris from 01; Can and Preb York Minster *York* from 01; Lic to Offic from 01; Chapl to The Queen from 05. *HM Prison Service Chaplaincy, Room 620, Horseferry House, Dean Ryle Street, London SW1P 2AW* Tel (020) 7217 8201 *or* 7217 8844 E-mail wnoblett@fish.co.uk

NOCK, Peter Arthur. b 15. Keble Coll Ox BA36 MA42. Bps' Coll Cheshunt 37. **d** 39 **p** 40. C Gt Harwood St Bart *Blackb* 39-40; C Lancaster Priory Ch 40-45; V Over Wyresdale 45-50; V Darwen St Cuth 50-64; V Sparkhill St Jo *Birm* 64-71; RD Bordesley 67-71; V Maney 71-81; rtd 81; Perm to Offic *Carl* from 81. *Westlands, Linden Fold, Grange-over-Sands LA11 7AY* Tel (01539) 535139

NOCK, Roland George William. b 62. St Andr Univ BSc84 BD89. Edin Th Coll 91. **d** 91 **p** 92. C Dunfermline *St And* 91-93; C W Fife Team Min 91-93; R Cupar 93-96; CF 96-99. *46 Heol Y Parc, Cefneithin, Llanelli SA14 7DL* Tel (01269) 845847 E-mail roland@nock.screaming.net

NOCKELS, John Martin. b 46. Lich Th Coll Qu Coll Birm 73. **d** 73 **p** 74. C Eccleshill *Bradf* 73-76; C Fawley *Win* 76-78; V Southampton St Jude 78-84; R Tadley St Pet 84-98; P-in-c South Raynham, E w W Raynham, Helhoughton, etc *Nor* 98-99; P-in-c Gt and Lt Massingham and Harpley 98-99; R Gt w Lt Massingham, Harpley, Rougham etc from 99. *The Rectory, 68 Station Road, Great Massingham, King's Lynn PE32 2HW* Tel (01485) 520211

NODDER, Marcus Charles Colmore. b 67. Pemb Coll Cam BA89 PGCE90. Oak Hill Th Coll BA01. **d** 01 **p** 02. C Denton Holme *Carl* 01-04; C Limehouse *Lon* from 04. *49 Three Colts Street, London E14 8HH* Tel (020) 7515 2844 E-mail mnodder@hotmail.com *or* marcus@nodder.fsbusiness.co.uk

NODDER, Thomas Arthur (Brother Arnold). b 20. K Coll Lon 58. **d** 60 **p** 61. Brotherhood of the H Cross from 49; C Rotherhithe St Mary w All SS *S'wark* 60-63; SSF from 63; Lic to Offic *Chelmsf* 63-66; C Plaistow St Andr 66-68; Lic to Offic *Newc* 69-70; Lic to Offic *Birm* 70-83; Perm to Offic 90-98; Lic to Offic *Sarum* 83-89; rtd 90; Perm to Offic *Chelmsf* from 98. *Society of St Francis, 42 Balaam Street, London E13 8AQ* Tel (020) 7476 5189

NODDINGS, John Henry. b 39. Chich Th Coll 80. **d** 81 **p** 82. C Southborough St Pet w Ch Ch and St Matt *Roch* 81-83; C Prittlewell *Chelmsf* 83-86; V Clay Hill St Jo *Lon* 86-88; V Clay Hill St Jo and St Luke 88-02; Chapl Chase Farm Hosp Enfield 88-94; Chapl Chase Farm Hosps NHS Trust 94-95; rtd 03; P-in-c Gt Coxwell w Buscot, Coleshill etc *Ox* from 03. *The Vicarage, Great Coxwell, Faringdon SN7 7NG* Tel (01367) 240665

NOEL, Brother. *See* ALLEN, Noel Stephen

NOKES, Michael David Patrick. b 44. CA MCMI. **d** 02 **p** 03. NSM Heworth Ch Ch *York* from 02; Perm to Offic *Bradf* from 02 and *Ripon* from 03. *5 Fox Covert, York YO31 9EN* Tel (01904) 620411 *or* 674879 Mobile 07776-252440 E-mail michaelanddi@talktalk.net *or* mnokes@cpas.org.uk

NOKES, Peter Warwick. b 48. Leic Univ BA71. Westcott Ho Cam 79. **d** 81 **p** 82. C Northfield *Birm* 81-84; C Ludlow *Heref* 84-87; P-in-c Writtle w Highwood *Chelmsf* 87-91; V 91-92; P-in-c Epping St Jo 92-95; P-in-c Coopersale 93-95; TR Epping Distr 95-99; R Nor St Pet Mancroft w St Jo Maddermarket *Nor* from 99. *37 Unthank Road, Norwich NR2 2PB* Tel (01603) 627816 *or* 610443 Fax 766652 Mobile 07711-384009 E-mail vicar@petermancroft.org.uk

NOKES, Robert Harvey. b 39. Keble Coll Ox BA61 MA65 Birm Univ DipTh63. Qu Coll Birm 61. **d** 63 **p** 64. C Totteridge *St Alb* 63-67; C Dunstable 67-73; V Langford 73-90; R Braughing w Furneux Pelham and Stocking Pelham 90-04; Perm to Offic *Ox* from 04. *92 Western Drive, Hanslope, Milton Keynes MK19 7LE* Tel (01908) 337939 E-mail nokes@easykey.com

NOLAN, James Charles William. b 44. Chich Th Coll 75. **d** 77 **p** 78. C Crewe St Andr *Ches* 77-79; C Sale St Anne 79-83; R Holme Runcton w S Runcton and Wallington *Ely* from 83; V Tottenhill w Wormegay from 83; R Watlington from 83. *The Rectory, Downham Road, Watlington, King's Lynn PE33 0HS* Tel (01553) 810305

NOLAN, Marcus. b 54. Bris Univ BEd. Ridley Hall Cam. **d** 83 **p** 84. C Dagenham *Chelmsf* 83-86; C Finchley St Paul and St Luke *Lon* 86-90; V W Hampstead Trin 90-98; rtd 99; Perm to Offic *Derby* from 00. *55 Blanch Croft, Melbourne, Derby DE73 8GG*

NOLES, Jeremy Andrew. b 67. St Jo Coll Nottm 02. **d** 04 **p** 05. C Southchurch Ch Ch *Chelmsf* from 04. *201 Ambleside Drive, Southend-on-Sea SS1 2UE* Tel 07719-652333 (mobile)

NOLLAND, John Leslie. b 47. New England Univ (NSW) BSc67 Clare Coll Cam PhD78. Moore Th Coll Sydney ThL70 BD71. **d** 71 **p** 72. Australia 71-78; Canada 78-86; Asst Prof NT Studies Regent Coll Vancouver 78-86; Tutor Trin Coll Bris from 86; Vice Prin 91-97. *Trinity College, Stoke Hill, Bristol BS9 1JP* Tel 0117-968 2083 *or* 968 4053 Fax 968 7470 E-mail john.nolland@trinity-bris.ac.uk

NOLLER, Hilda Elizabeth Mary (Sister Elizabeth Mary). b 26. MSR47 FSR53. **d** 95 **p** 96. Lic to Offic *Chelmsf* from 96; Sister Superior CSD from 00. *7 Regal Court, Weymouth Street, Warminster BA12 9NH* Tel (01985) 220453

NOON, Canon Edward Arthur. b 16. Selw Coll Cam BA38 MA42. Bps' Coll Cheshunt 38. **d** 40 **p** 41. C Kingston St Jo *S'wark* 40-43; C Dulwich St Barn 43-48; P-in-c S Wimbledon St Pet 48-50; V 50-55; V Mitcham St Mark 55-65; V Horley 65-77; RD Reigate 72-76; Hon Can S'wark Cathl 72-83; P-in-c Purley St Barn 77-83; rtd 83; Hon C Overbury w Teddington, Alstone etc *Worc* 83-86; Perm to Offic *Glouc* 86-95. *40 Shepherds Leaze, Wotton-under-Edge GL12 7LQ* Tel (01453) 844978

NOORDANUS, Francis Peter. b 61. Cant Univ (NZ) BA82 ACT BTh90. **d** 92 **p** 93. New Zealand 92-02; C Ashburton 92-94; V Masterton St Matt 94-02; Chapl Eindhoven *Eur* from 02. *Paradijslaan 76, 5611 KR Eindhoven, The Netherlands* Tel (0031) (40) 246 5219 E-mail f.p.noordanus@planet.nl

NORBURN, Christopher Richard. b 62. Cov Poly BSc85. Aston Tr Scheme 92 Ridley Hall Cam 94. **d** 96 **p** 97. C Exning St Martin w Landwade *St E* 96-99; P-in-c Redgrave cum Botesdale w Rickinghall 99-01; R from 01. *The Rectory, Bury Road, Rickinghall, Diss IP22 1HA* Tel (01379) 898685

NORBURN, The Very Revd Richard Evelyn Walter. b 21. Witwatersrand Univ BA44 TDip44. St Paul's Coll Grahamstown 49. **d** 51 **p** 53. Vice-Prin Dioc Tr Coll Pretoria S Africa 51-56; Dioc Dir RE and R Potgietersrus 56-62; C Croydon St Sav *Cant* 63-64; V Norbury St Phil 65-75; V Addington 75-81; Hon Can Cant Cathl 79-81; RD Croydon Addington 81; Dean Botswana 81-88; rtd 89; Perm to Offic *Cant* 98-05. *The College of St Barnabas, Blackberry Lane, Lingfield RH7 6NJ* Tel (01342) 870460

NORBURN, Canon Richard Henry. b 32. MBE97. St Edm Hall Ox BA57 DipTh58. Wycliffe Hall Ox 57. **d** 59 **p** 59. C Sudbury St Greg and St Pet *St E* 59-65; Dioc Youth Officer 65-74; P-in-c Gt Livermere 74-81; R Ampton w Lt Livermere and Ingham 74-81; RD Thingoe 78-88; Hon Can St E Cathl 81-97; R Ingham w Ampton and Gt and Lt Livermere 81-92; TV Blackbourne 92-97; rtd 97; Perm to Offic *St E* from 97. *69 Churchgate Street, Bury St Edmunds IP33 1RL* Tel (01284) 702644 E-mail richardhnorburn@btopenworld.com

NORBURY, Robert John. b 60. Southn Univ BA83. **d** 04. OLM Eltham Park St Luke *S'wark* from 04. *69 Greenvale Road, London SE9 1PB* Tel (020) 8850 7631 E-mail thenorburys@aol.com

NORFIELD, David Jonathan. b 67. Humberside Univ BA89. Linc Th Coll MA94 Westcott Ho Cam 95. **d** 97 **p** 98. C Halstead St Andr w H Trin and Greenstead Green *Chelmsf* 97-01; V Moulsham St Jo 01-04; Chapl RAF from 04. *Chaplaincy Services (RAF), HQ, Personnel and Training Command, RAF Innsworth, Gloucester GL3 1EZ* Tel (01452) 712612 ext 5164 Fax 510828 E-mail davidnorfield@hotmail.com

NORFOLK, The Ven Edward Matheson. b 21. Leeds Univ BA44. Coll of Resurr Mirfield 41. **d** 46 **p** 47. C Greenford H Cross *Lon* 46-47; C S Mymms K Chas 47-50; C Bushey *St Alb* 50-53; PC Waltham Cross 53-59; V Welwyn Garden City 59-69; R Gt Berkhamsted 69-81; Hon Can St Alb 72-82; V Kings Langley 81-82; Adn St Alb 82-87; rtd 87; Perm to Offic *Ex* from 87. *5 Fairlawn Court, Sidmouth EX10 8UR* Tel (01395) 514222

NORFOLK, Archdeacon of. *See* HAYDEN, The Ven David Frank

✠**NORGATE, The Rt Revd Cecil Richard.** b 21. St Chad's Coll Dur BA47 DipTh49. **d** 49 **p** 50 **c** 84. C Wallsend St Pet *Newc* 49-54; Tanganyika 54-64; Tanzania from 64; UMCA 54-57; V-Gen Masasi 77-84; Bp Masasi 84-92; rtd 92. *St Cyprian's College, Rondo, PO Box 212, Lindi, Tanzania*

NORGATE, Norman George. b 32. Qu Coll Cam BA55 MA58. Ridley Hall Cam. **d** 57 **p** 58. C Erith St Paul *Roch* 57-60; C E Twickenham St Steph *Lon* 60-63; V Bexleyheath St Pet *Roch* 63-71; V Woking St Mary *Guildf* 71-83; V Tunbridge Wells St Jas *Roch* 83-92; TR Tunbridge Wells St Jas w St Phil 92-97; rtd 97; Perm to Offic *St E* from 97. *Crathie, 58 Sexton Meadows, Bury St Edmunds IP33 2SB* Tel (01284) 767363

NORKETT, Alan. b 45. Sarum & Wells Th Coll 85. **d** 87 **p** 88. C Shrewsbury St Giles w Sutton and Atcham *Lich* 87-90; V Mow Cop 90-94; NSM Astbury and Smallwood *Ches* 96-97; NSM Sandbach Heath w Wheelock 97-98; C Castleford All SS and Whitwood *Wakef* 98-01; C Glass Houghton 98-01; R Shrawley, Witley, Astley and Abberley *Worc* from 01. *The Rectory, Shrawley, Worcester WR6 6TS* Tel (01905) 620489 E-mail vicaralan@aol.com

NORMAN, Andrew Herbert. b 54. K Coll Lon BD77 AKC77 Lon Univ PhD88. St Steph Ho Ox 77. **d** 78 **p** 79. C Deal St Leon w Sholden *Cant* 78-81; C Maidstone All SS and St Phil w Tovil 81-84; V Tenterden St Mich 84-93; Chapl Benenden Hosp 86-91; Dir Post-Ord Tr *Cant* 91-93; R Guildf St Nic *Guildf* from 93. *The Rectory, 3 Flower Walk, Guildford GU2 4EP* Tel (01483) 504895 E-mail fr-andrew@st-nicholas.freeserve.co.uk

NORMAN, Andrew Robert. b 63. Univ Coll Ox BA84 MA99 Newc Poly DMS90 AIL89 Selw Coll Cam BA94 MA99. Ridley Hall Cam CTM95 BA94. **d** 95 **p** 96. Asst Chapl Paris St Mich *Eur* 95-00; C Clifton Ch Ch w Em *Bris* 00-02; Abp's Asst Sec for Ecum and Angl Affairs *Cant* from 02. *Cottage 2, Lambeth Palace, Lambeth Palace Road, London SE1 7JU* Tel (020) 7620 0636 *or* 7898 1200

NORMAN, Catherine. b 51. Nottm Univ BSc73 N Counties Coll Newc CertEd74. Linc Th Coll 95. **d** 95 **p** 96. C Scartho *Linc* 95-99; V Ulceby Gp 99-02; TV Guiseley w Esholt *Bradf* from 02. *The Vicarage, 1 Tranfield Close, Guiseley, Leeds LS20 8LT* Tel (01943) 879787

NORMAN, Canon Edward Robert. b 38. Selw Coll Cam BA61 PhD64 MA65 BD67 DD78 FRHistS72 FRSA88. Linc Th Coll 65. **d** 65 **p** 71. Fell Jes Coll Cam 64-71; Lect Cam Univ 65-88; Dean Peterho Cam 71-88; Dean of Chpl Ch Ch Coll of HE Cant 88-95; Six Preacher Cant Cathl *Cant* 84-90; Can Res York Minster *York* 95-04; Treas 95-99; Chan 99-04; Hon Prof York Univ from 96; Hon C St Andr-by-the-Wardrobe w St Ann, Blackfriars *Lon* from 05; Hon C St Jas Garlickhythe w St Mich Queenhithe etc from 05. *2 St Anne's Court, Brighton BN2 1AA* Tel (01273) 679952

NORMAN, Mrs Elizabeth Ann. b 43. St Alb and Ox Min Course 95. **d** 98 **p** 99. OLM Amersham *Ox* 98-04. *Lamorna, Main Road, Bickington, Barnstaple EX31 2NA* Tel (01271) 859314

NORMAN, The Ven Garth. b 38. St Chad's Coll Dur BA62 MA68 UEA MEd84 Cam Inst of Educn PGCE68. **d** 63 **p** 64. C Wandsworth St Anne *S'wark* 63-66; C Trunch w Swafield *Nor* 66-71; R Gimingham 71-77; TR Trunch 77-83; RD Repps 75-83; Prin Chiltern Chr Tr Course *Ox* 83-87; C W Wycombe w Bledlow Ridge, Bradenham and Radnage 83-87; Dir of Tr *Roch* 88-94; Adn Bromley and Bexley 94-03; Hon Can Roch Cathl 91-03; rtd 03; Perm to Offic *S'well* from 03; Chapl to Retired Clergy from 04. *5 Riverside, Southwell NG25 0HA* Tel (01636) 815209 E-mail gnorman@southwell.anglican.org

NORMAN, Gary. b 64. Newc Univ BA87. Ripon Coll Cuddesdon 02. **d** 04 **p** 05. C Spennymoor, Whitworth and Merrington *Dur* from 04. *34 Bluebell Drive, Spennymoor DL16 7YF* Tel (01388) 811108

NORMAN, Jillianne Elizabeth. b 59. DCR80. Ridley Hall Cam 85. **d** 88 **p** 94. Par Dn Fishponds St Jo *Bris* 88-92; Perm to Offic 92-94; Hon C Warmley, Syston and Bitton from 94; Chapl United Bris Healthcare NHS Trust from 02. *74 Blackhorse Road, Mangotsfield, Bristol BS16 9AY* Tel 0117-956 1551 Fax 904 6894 E-mail jilliannenorman@blueyonder.co.uk

NORMAN, Canon John Ronald. b 15. GradInstT Lon Univ BA40. Linc Th Coll 40. **d** 42 **p** 43. C Yarm *York* 42-43; C Stokesley 43-46; R Muchalls *Bre* 46-50; V Kirkby Ireleth *Carl* 50-55; R Greystoke 55-60; P-in-c Matterdale 56-60; Warden Greystoke Coll Carl 56-60; Chapl St Hilda's Priory and Sch Whitby 60-61; R Dunnington *York* 61-72; RD Bulmer 65-72; R Bolton Percy 72-82; Dioc Worship Adv 72-82; Can and Preb York Minster 77-92; rtd 82; Perm to Offic *York* from 98. *Iona, 5 Northfield Close, Pocklington, York YO42 2EG* Tel (01759) 303170

NORMAN, Linda Mary. b 48. Man Univ BSc69 CertEd70 St Jo Coll Dur BA82. **dss** 83 **d** 87. York St Mich-le-Belfrey *York* 83-88; Par Dn 87-88; rtd 88. *23 Ainsty Avenue, Dringhouses, York YO24 1HH* Tel (01904) 706152

NORMAN, Lynette Dianne. b 52. Sussex Univ CertEd73 Univ of Wales (Ban) BEd89. Ripon Coll Cuddesdon 00. **d** 02 **p** 03. C Welshpool w Castle Caereinion *St As* 02-04; R Llanrwst and Llanddoget and Capel Garmon from 04. *The Rectory, Llanddoged Road, Llanrwst LL26 0DW* Tel (01492) 640223 Mobile 07889-184517

NORMAN, Canon Michael Heugh. b 18. Qu Coll Cam BA48 Kent Univ MA. Westcott Ho Cam 48. **d** 50 **p** 51. C St Peter-in-Thanet *Cant* 50-52; S Africa from 52; rtd 86; Hon Can Cape Town from 86. *5 Rosedale Cottage, Lower Nursery Road, Rosebank, 7700 South Africa* Tel (0027) (21) 685 3622

NORMAN, Michael John. b 59. Southn Univ LLB82. Wycliffe Hall Ox 82. **d** 85 **p** 86. C Woodley St Jo the Ev *Ox* 85-89; C Uphill *B & W* 89-92; TV 92-98; R Bath St Sav w Swainswick and Woolley from 98. *St Saviour's Rectory, Claremont Road, Bath BA1 6LX* Tel (01225) 311637 E-mail michael@stsaviours.org.uk

NORMAN, Michael John. b 61. St Jo Coll Ox BSc83 Univ Coll Lon MSc84. Aston Tr Scheme 89 St Jo Coll Nottm 91. **d** 93 **p** 94. C Haughton le Skerne *Dur* 93-97; R Sapcote and Sharnford w Wigston Parva *Leic* from 97; RD Sparkenhoe W from 02. *The Rectory, 4 Sharnford Road, Sapcote, Leicester LE9 4JN* Tel (01455) 272215 E-mail micknorman@msn.com

NORMAN, Peter John. b 42. Culham Coll of Educn TCert66 Lon Inst of Educn DipEd83 MA86. STETS DipTh98. **d** 98 **p** 99. NSM Bath Weston All SS w N Stoke and Langridge *B & W* from 98. *5 Rockliffe Avenue, Bathwick, Bath BA2 6QP* Tel (01225) 463348

NORMAN, Peter John. b 59. Chich Th Coll 84. **d** 87 **p** 88. C Farncombe *Guildf* 87-91; C Cockington *Ex* 91-94; V Winkleigh from 94; R Ashreigney from 94; R Broadwoodkelly from 94; V Brushford from 94. *The Vicarage, Torrington Road, Winkleigh EX19 8HR* Tel (01837) 83719

NORMAN, Richard Hudson. b 58. Louisiana State Univ BS84 MA88. Gen Th Sem NY MDiv93 STM93. **d** 92 **p** 93. C

Southgate St Andr *Lon* 92 and 97-98; USA 92-97 and from 02; Assoc New York City St Matt and St Tim 92-93; R Abbeville St Paul 93-95; Assoc R Chevy Chase All SS 95-97; V Mill Hill St Mich *Lon* 98-02; R Greenville Redeemer from 02. *101 Taniere Court, Simpsonville, SC 29680, USA* Tel (001) (864) 962 2370 *or* 277 4562 Fax 277 6330
E-mail rnorman@churchoftheredeemer.com

NORMAN, Timothy. b 68. Jes Coll Cam BA91 Univ Coll Lon PhD95. Spurgeon's Coll 95 Wycliffe Hall Ox BA00. **d** 01 **p** 02. C Chipping Norton *Ox* 01-04; Asst Chapl Paris St Mich *Eur* from 04. *St Michael's Church, 5 rue d'Aguesseau, 7500 Paris, France* Tel (0033) (1) 47 42 70 88 E-mail tim.norman@bigfoot.com

NORMAN, Canon William Beadon. b 26. Trin Coll Cam BA49 MA55. Ridley Hall Cam 52. **d** 52 **p** 53. C Beckenham St Jo *Roch* 52-54; Uganda 55-65; V Alne *York* 65-74; RD Warley *Birm* 74-79; V Blackheath 74-79; Hon Can Birm Cathl 78-91; TR Kings Norton 79-91; RD Kings Norton 82-87; Warden Dioc Readers Bd 84-91; rtd 91; Perm to Offic *S'wark* from 91 and *Lon* from 94; Preacher Lincoln's Inn from 94. *37 Cloudesdale Road, London SW17 8ET* Tel (020) 8673 9134 Fax 8675 6890

NORMAN-WALKER, Mrs Anna Elizabeth. b 67. RGN89. St Jo Coll Nottm BA03. **d** 03 **p** 04. C Cullompton, Willand, Uffculme, Kentisbeare etc *Ex* from 03. *16 Gravel Walk, Cullompton EX15 1DA* Tel (01884) 35480 *or* 33249 Mobile 07986-450330 Fax 08701-645107 E-mail anna@norman-walker.fsnet.co.uk

NORMAND, Stephen Joseph William. b 48. N Texas State Univ BSEd80. Sarum & Wells Th Coll 90. **d** 92 **p** 93. C Norton *St Alb* 92-94; C St Alb St Pet 95-97; Chapl Oaklands Coll 95-97; TV Horsham *Chich* 97-01; R Wimbotsham w Stow Bardolph and Stow Bridge etc *Ely* 01-04; rtd 04. *3 Fincham Road, Stow Bardolph, King's Lynn PE34 3HX* Tel (01366) 387037

NORMINGTON, Eric. b 16. S'wark Ord Course. **d** 63 **p** 64. C Coulsdon St Jo *S'wark* 63-66; C Bath Abbey w St Jas *B & W* 66-71; V Bath Weston All SS 71-78; P-in-c N Stoke 76-78; R Bath Weston All SS w N Stoke 78-81; RD Keynsham 75-76; rtd 81; Perm to Offic *Ex* 81-98. *Flat 16, Manormead, Tilford Road, Hindhead GU26 6RA* Tel (01428) 604780

NORRINGTON, Paul Richard. b 57. Brighton Poly BSc80 Thurrock Coll Essex DMS90. Trin Coll Bris DipTh98. **d** 98 **p** 99. C Prittlewell w Westcliff *Chelmsf* 98-02; R Colchester Ch Ch w St Mary V from 02. *The Rectory, 21 Cambridge Road, Colchester CO3 3NS* Tel (01206) 563478 E-mail pnozzer@tesco.net

NORRIS, Mrs Alison. b 55. St Andr Univ MTheol77 Dur Univ PGCE78. Cant Sch of Min 80. **dss** 82 **d** 87 **p** 94. Warlingham w Chelsham and Farleigh *S'wark* 82-85; Willingham *Ely* 85-87; Hon Par Dn 87-90; Hon Par Dn Worle *B & W* 90-94; NSM Milverton w Halse and Fitzhead 94-02; P-in-c Bradford w Oake, Hillfarrance and Heathfield from 02. *The Vicarage, Parsonage Lane, Milverton, Taunton TA4 1LR* Tel (01823) 401407 Fax 400739

NORRIS, Allan Edward. b 43. St Jo Coll Dur BA72 DipTh73. Cranmer Hall Dur 69. **d** 73 **p** 74. C Plumstead St Jo w St Jas and St Paul *S'wark* 73-78; C Battersea Park St Sav 78-82; C Battersea St Geo w St Andr 78-82; V Grain w Stoke *Roch* 82-92; V Sissinghurst w Frittenden *Cant* from 92. *The Rectory, Oakleaves, Frittenden, Cranbrook TN17 2DD* Tel (01580) 852275
E-mail revco@amserve.com

NORRIS, Andrew David. b 54. CPsychol St Andr Univ BSc78 Lon Univ MPhil80. EAMTC 87. **d** 90 **p** 91. C Worle *B & W* 90-94; R Milverton w Halse and Fitzhead from 94; RD Tone from 01. *The Vicarage, Parsonage Lane, Milverton, Taunton TA4 1LR* Tel (01823) 400305 E-mail revnog@tinyonline.co.uk

NORRIS, Andrew Peter. b 62. Aston Univ BSc83. St Jo Coll Nottm BA86 DPS87. **d** 87 **p** 88. C Mountsorrel Ch Ch and St Pet *Leic* 87-90; C Harborne Heath *Birm* 90-91; P-in-c Edgbaston St Germain 91-92; V 92-99; P-in-c Hook w Warsash *Portsm* 99-00; V from 00. *The Vicarage, 113 Church Road, Warsash, Southampton SO31 9GF* Tel (01489) 572324 Fax as telephone

NORRIS, Barry John. b 46. Nottm Univ CQSW75 MTh86 Open Univ BA80 K Coll Lon PhD95. St Jo Sem Wonersh. **d** 70 **p** 71. In RC Ch 70-72; C Wisbech SS Pet and Paul *Ely* 76-78; TV E Ham w Upton Park St Alb *Chelmsf* 78-81; Chapl RAF 81-87; V N Tadley St Mary *Win* from 87. *St Mary's Vicarage, Bishopswood Road, Tadley, Basingstoke RG26 4HQ* Tel 0118-981 4435 E-mail baz.norris@btinternet.com

NORRIS, Canon Clifford Joseph. b 29. Codrington Coll Barbados. **d** 61 **p** 68. Antigua 61-62; C Penton Street St Silas w All SS *Lon* 68-70; C Stepney St Dunstan and All SS 70-73; P-in-c Bethnal Green St Jas the Gt w St Jude 73-82; V Aveley and Purfleet *Chelmsf* 82-98; Hon Can NE Caribbean from 95; rtd 98; Perm to Offic *Chelmsf* from 98. *20 Hayhouse Road, Earls Colne, Colchester CO6 2PD* Tel (01787) 222015

NORRIS, Eric Richard. b 43. MICFM86. Bernard Gilpin Soc Dur 65 Ripon Hall Ox 66. **d** 69 **p** 70. C Huyton St Mich *Liv* 69-72; C Mexborough *Sheff* 72-74; V Dalton 74-78; Org Sec CECS *Carl* 78-89; Area Appeals Manager N Co 89-93; TR Thirsk *York* 93-02; RD Mowbray 00-02; V Boosbeck w Moorsholm from 02; Abp's Adv in Tourism from 02. *The Vicarage, Church Drive, Boosbeck, Saltburn-by-the-Sea TS12 3AY* Tel (01287) 651728

NORRIS, Mrs Helen. b 53. Univ of Wales (Abth) LLB74 Univ Coll Lon LLM76 Solicitor 78. **d** 04. OLM Coddenham w Gosbeck and Hemingstone w Henley *St E* from 04; OLM Crowfield w Stonham Aspal and Mickfield from 04. *The Villa, The Street, Stonham Aspal, Stowmarket IP14 6AQ* Tel (01449) 711395 E-mail helen.norris@btinternet.com

NORRIS, Keith David. b 47. E Lon Univ BA89 MIAM76 MBIM80. NTMTC AdDipTh98 ADPS98. **d** 98 **p** 02. NSM Cranham Park *Chelmsf* 98-99; NSM S Hornchurch St Jo and St Matt from 01. *Still Waters, 8 Hesselyn Drive, Rainham RM13 7EJ* Tel (01708) 780767

NORRIS, Mark. b 68. Brunel Univ BEng90. Oak Hill Th Coll BA93. **d** 93 **p** 94. C Roby *Liv* 93-97; C St Helens St Helen 97-00; TV Gateacre from 00; Asst Dioc Dir of Ords from 05. *Christchurch House, 44 Brownbill Bank, Liverpool L27 7AE* Tel 0151-487 7759 E-mail vicar@netherley.org.uk

NORRIS, Michael Charles Latham. b 69. Reading Univ LLB. Wycliffe Hall Ox 99. **d** 01 **p** 02. C Bryanston Square St Mary w St Marylebone St Mark *Lon* 01-03; New Zealand from 04. *38 Carlton Gore Road, Newmarket, Auckland, New Zealand*
E-mail mikenorris1@hotmail.com

NORTH, Barry Albert. b 46. **d** 82 **p** 83. C Brampton St Thos *Derby* 82-84; C Chesterfield St Aug 84-88; P-in-c Derby St Mark 88-91; R Coalbrookdale, Iron-Bridge and Lt Wenlock *Heref* 91-97; Ch and Community Worker (Manlake Deanery) *Linc* 97-00; Soc Resp Adv *Chich* from 00; C Brighton St Mich from 00. *2 Windlesham Road, Brighton BN1 3AG* Tel (01273) 778083

NORTH, Christopher David. b 69. Trin Coll Bris BA01. **d** 01 **p** 02. C Bathampton w Claverton *B & W* 01-05; P-in-c Chilcompton w Downside and Stratton on the Fosse from 05. *The Rectory, The Street, Chilcompton, Radstock BA3 4HN* Tel (01761) 232219
E-mail chris.north1@tesco.net

NORTH, David Roland. b 45. Lich Th Coll 70 Qu Coll Birm 72. **d** 73 **p** 74. C Salesbury *Blackb* 73-76; C Marton 76-79; V Penwortham St Leon 79-87; R Whittington St Jo *Lich* from 87; P-in-c W Felton from 96; RD Oswestry from 02; Chapl Robert Jones/Agnes Hunt Orthopaedic NHS Trust 00-01. *The Rectory, Castle Street, Whittington, Oswestry SY11 4DF* Tel (01691) 652222 E-mail davidnorth@micro-plus-web.net

NORTH, Lyndon Percival. b 55. Lon Bible Coll BA77. NTMTC. **d** 00 **p** 01. NSM Sudbury St Andr *Lon* 00-04 and from 05; C Roxbourne St Andr 04-05. *143 Abbotts Drive, Wembley HA0 3SH* Tel (020) 8904 2408 Mobile 07774-685906
E-mail lyndonnorth@hotmail.com

NORTH, Mark Richard. b 71. St Steph Ho Ox 03. **d** 05. C Sevenoaks St Jo *Roch* from 05. *14 Quakers Hall Lane, Sevenoaks TN13 3TR* Tel (01732) 741691 Mobile 07776-231681
E-mail mark.north@ssho.ox.ac.uk

NORTH, Philip John. b 66. York Univ BA88. St Steph Ho Ox BA91 MA01. **d** 92 **p** 93. C Sunderland Springwell w Thorney Close *Dur* 92-95; C Sunderland St Mary and St Pet 95-96; V Hartlepool H Trin 96-02; AD Hartlepool 00-02; P Admin Shrine of Our Lady of Walsingham from 02; P-in-c Hempton and Pudding Norton *Nor* from 04. *The Shrine of Our Lady of Walsingham, The College, Knight Street, Walsingham NR22 6EF* Tel (01328) 824204 *or* 820323 Fax 824208
E-mail pr.adm@olw-shrine.org.uk

NORTH, Preb Robert. b 54. Lon Univ BSc77. Ripon Coll Cuddesdon 78. **d** 81 **p** 82. C Leominster *Heref* 81-86; TV Heref St Martin w St Fran 86-92; TV Dewsall w Callow 86-92; TV Holme Lacy w Dinedor 86-92; TV Lt Dewchurch, Aconbury w Ballingham and Bolstone 86-92; TV Upper and Lower Bullinghope w Grafton 86-92; P-in-c Heref St Nic 92-97; Dir of Ords 92-00; Preb Heref Cathl from 94; TR W Heref from 97; V Heref H Trin from 97; V Breinton from 97. *St Nicholas's Rectory, 76 Breinton Road, Hereford HR4 0JY* Tel (01432) 273810 Pager 07623-476523 E-mail robnorth@fish.co.uk

NORTH, Canon Vernon Leslie. b 26. Bps' Coll Cheshunt 61. **d** 63 **p** 64. C N Holmwood *Guildf* 63-65; C Dunstable *St Alb* 65-68; V Stotfold 68-91; V Stotfold and Radwell 91-92; RD Shefford 79-91; Hon Can St Alb 89-92; rtd 92; Perm to Offic *St Alb* from 92 and *Ely* from 00. *Hunters Moon, 10 High Street, Little Paxton, St Neots PE19 6HA* Tel (01480) 471146

NORTH INDIA, Moderator of the Church of. *See* TEROM, The Rt Revd Zechariah James

NORTH SYDNEY, Bishop of. *See* DAVIES, The Rt Revd Glenn Naunton

NORTH WEST EUROPE, Archdeacon of. *See* VAN LEEUWEN, The Ven Dirk Willem

NORTHALL, Malcolm Walter. b 26. Cheshunt Coll Cam 59 Ely Th Coll 63. **d** 64 **p** 65. C Bromsgrove St Jo *Worc* 64-67; V Blockley w Aston Magna *Glouc* 67-82; P-in-c Churchdown 82; V 82-92; rtd 92; Perm to Offic *Ban* from 92. *5 Maethlon Close, Tywyn LL36 0BN* Tel (01654) 710123

NORTHAM, Cavell Herbert James Cavell. *See* CAVELL-NORTHAM, Canon Cavell Herbert James

NORTHAM, Mrs Susan Jillian. b 36. Oak Hill Th Coll DipHE87. **d** 89. NSM Enfield Ch Ch Trent Park *Lon* 89-91; Par Dn 91-94; C 94-97; rtd 97; Perm to Offic *Lon* from 02. *5 Beech Hill Avenue, Barnet EN4 0LW* Tel and fax (020) 8440 2723 E-mail jillandjohn.northam@btinternet.com

NORTHAMPTON, Archdeacon of. *See* ALLSOPP, The Ven Christine

NORTHCOTT, Canon Michael Stafford. b 55. St Chad's Coll Dur BA76 MA77 Sunderland Univ PhD81. St Jo Coll Dur 80. **d** 81 **p** 82. C Chorlton-cum-Hardy St Clem *Man* 81-84; USPG 84-89; Malaysia 84-89; Sen Lect Chr Ethics New Coll Edin Univ 89-91; NSM Edin Old St Paul *Edin* 89-91; NSM Edin St Jas from 91; TV Edin St Marg 93-96; Can Th Liv Cathl *Liv* from 05. *8 Dudley Gardens, Edinburgh EH6 4PY* Tel 0131-554 1651 E-mail m.northcott@ed.ac.uk

NORTHCOTT, William Mark. b 36. Clifton Th Coll 61. **d** 64 **p** 65. C Walthamstow St Luke *Chelmsf* 64-68; C Idle H Trin *Bradf* 68-70; N Sec CMJ 70-79; V Withnell *Blackb* 79-90; P-in-c Glenrothes *St And* 90-91; Asst Dioc Supernumerary 90-91; Perm to Offic *Blackb* and *Liv* from 91. *30 The Laund, Leyland, Preston PR5 3XX* Tel (01772) 493932

NORTHERN, Mrs Elaine Joy. b 54. Leic Univ BSc75 Dip Counselling 97. SEITE 00. **d** 03 **p** 04. C Snodland All SS w Ch Ch *Roch* from 03. *20 Lewis Mews, Snodland ME6 5LN* Tel (01634) 241014 E-mail thenortherns@btinternet.com

NORTHERN LUZON, Bishop of. *See* SOLIBA, The Most Revd Ignacio Capuyan

NORTHERN MALAWI, Bishop of. *See* BOYLE, The Rt Revd Christopher John

NORTHFIELD, Stephen Richmond. b 55. Lon Univ BSc77 Southn Univ BTh84. Sarum & Wells Th Coll 79. **d** 82 **p** 83. C Colchester St Jas, All SS, St Nic and St Runwald *Chelmsf* 82-85; C Chelmsf All SS 85-89; V Ramsey w Lt Oakley and Wrabness 89-95; V Hatfield Peverel w Ulting from 95. *The Vicarage, Church Road, Hatfield Peverel, Chelmsford CM3 2LE* Tel (01245) 380958

NORTHING, Ross. b 58. Wilson Carlile Coll Dip Evang87 St Steph Ho Ox DipMin94 SSC99. **d** 94 **p** 95. CA from 87; C Up Hatherley *Glouc* 94-98; C Cheltenham St Steph 94-95; C Cheltenham Em w St Steph 95-98; V Stony Stratford *Ox* from 98; R Calverton from 98. *St Mary and St Giles Vicarage, 14 Willow Lane, Stony Stratford, Milton Keynes MK11 1FG* Tel (01908) 562148 Fax 565132 E-mail r.northing@btinternet.com

NORTHOLT, Archdeacon of. *Vacant*

NORTHOVER, Kevin Charles. b 57. Coll of Resurr Mirfield 89. **d** 91 **p** 92. C Kingston upon Hull St Alb *York* 91-94; V Moorends *Sheff* 94-00; R Guernsey St Michel du Valle *Win* from 00. *The Rectory, L'Abbaye, Vale, Guernsey GY3 5SF* Tel (01481) 244088 Fax 249985 E-mail frkevin@cwgsy.net

NORTHRIDGE, Herbert Aubrey Hamilton. b 16. TCD BA40 MA43. **d** 41 **p** 42. C Londonderry Ch Ch *D & R* 41-45; P-in-c Convoy 45-47; I 47-50; I Derg 50-70; I Derg w Termonamongan 70-81; Can Derry Cathl 72-81; rtd 81. *Goblusk, Ballinamallard BT94 2LW* Tel (028) 6638 8676

NORTHUMBERLAND, Archdeacon of. *See* MILLER, The Ven Geoffrey Vincent

NORTHWOOD, Michael Alan. b 36. Lon Univ BSc60 MInstP69. Wells Th Coll 62. **d** 64 **p** 65. C Eastbourne St Mary *Chich* 64-66; C Sanderstead All SS *S'wark* 66-68; P-in-c Alton Barnes w Alton Priors etc *Sarum* 69-75; Lic to Offic 76-86; Perm to Offic *Ox* from 86; rtd 01. *The Garth, 31 Mill Road, Marlow SL7 1QB* Tel (01628) 488646 Mobile 07836-372021 Fax (01628) 488649 E-mail michael@mmsolutions.com

NORTON, Andrew. *See* NORTON, John Colin

NORTON, Anthony Bernard. b 40. Man Univ BA62. Linc Th Coll 63. **d** 65 **p** 66. C Westbury-on-Trym H Trin *Bris* 65-68; C Bris St Agnes w St Simon 68-70; P-in-c Bris St Werburgh 70-72; TV Bris St Agnes and St Simon w St Werburgh 72-77; V Lakenham St Alb *Nor* 77-85; TV Trunch 85-93; TV Halesworth w Linstead, Chediston, Holton etc *St E* 93-99; TV Blyth Valley from 99; RD Halesworth 98-01. *The Vicarage, Church Road, Spexhall, Halesworth IP19 0RQ* Tel (01986) 875453 Fax as telephone

NORTON, Howard John. b 41. Fitzw Coll Cam BA64 MA68. S'wark Ord Course 78 St Jo Coll Nottm 79. **d** 80 **p** 81. C Sutton Ch Ch *S'wark* 80-82; C Morden 82-84; V Motspur Park 84-88; Perm to Offic *Chich* from 03. *Chellwood, Upper Clarence Road, St Leonards-on-Sea TN37 6PG* Tel (01424) 715780

NORTON, James Herbert Kitchener. b 37. Qu Coll Birm 78. **d** 81 **p** 82. NSM Donnington Wood *Lich* 81-83; C Matson *Glouc* 83-86; V New Mills *Derby* 86-96; RD Glossop 93-96; TR Buxton w Burbage and King Sterndale 96-02; RD Buxton 99-02; rtd 02; Perm to Offic *Derby* from 02; P-in-c Lt Drayton *Lich* from 04. *Heather Glen, 11 Ellis Peter's Drive, Telford TF3 1AW* Tel (01952) 595343 Mobile 07879-470172 E-mail jhknorton@lineone.net

NORTON, John Colin (Andrew). b 25. Magd Coll Ox BA50 MA54. Cuddesdon Coll 50. **d** 52 **p** 53. C Bris St Mary Redcliffe w Temple *Bris* 52-57; C Bitterne Park *Win* 57-61; C-in-c Bishopwearmouth St Mary V w St Pet CD *Dur* 63-68; V Clifton All SS w Tyndalls Park *Bris* 68-78; Hon Can Bris Cathl 77-80; V Clifton All SS w St Jo 78-80; V Penistone *Wakef* 80-83; CR from 85; rtd 95. *House of the Resurrection, Stocks Bank Road, Mirfield WF14 0BN* Tel (01924) 494318

NORTON, Mrs Lesley Gillian. b 47. STETS 99. **d** 02 **p** 03. NSM Kinson *Sarum* from 02. *3 Viscount Walk, Bournemouth BH11 9TA* Tel (01202) 590205 E-mail norton@fish.co.uk

NORTON (or HARCOURT-NORTON), Michael Clive Harcourt. b 34. Selw Coll Cam BA58 MA60 Union Th Sem (NY) STM69 Univ of NSW MCom81 MACE84. Wells Th Coll 56 Bossey Ecum Inst Geneva 57. **d** 58 **p** 59. C Gt Ilford St Jo *Chelmsf* 58-62; Australia 62-68 and from 69; NSW Sec Aus Coun Chs 62-68; C Manhattan St Steph USA 68-69; C-in-c Mortdale 69-77; R 77-79; Assoc Chapl and Hd RS Cranbrook Sch Sydney 79-85; R Hunter's Hill 85-00; rtd 00. *7 Dulwich Road, Chatswood, NSW, Australia 2067* Tel (0061) (2) 9411 8606 Mobile 417-041779 Fax (2) 9410 2069 E-mail chnorton@bigpond.com

NORTON, Michael James Murfin. b 42. Lich Th Coll 66. **d** 67 **p** 68. C W Bromwich St Fran *Lich* 67-70; C Wellington Ch Ch 70-72; C Norwood All SS *Cant* 72-76; V Elstow *St Alb* 76-82; Asst Chapl HM Pris Wakef 82-83; Chapl HM Pris Camp Hill 83-86; Chapl HM Pris Parkhurst 86-88; Chapl HM Pris Win 88-93; V Somborne w Ashley *Win* 93-03; rtd 03. *Bryneirian, Penparc, Cardigan SA43 1RG* Tel (01239) 623512 E-mail revmnorton@aol.com

NORTON, Neville. *See* MORTON, Rupert Neville

NORTON, Paul James. b 55. Oak Hill Th Coll BA86. **d** 86 **p** 87. C Luton St Fran *St Alb* 86-89; C Bedworth *Cov* 89-95; TV Hitchin *St Alb* 95-02; V Portsdown *Portsm* from 03. *Portsdown Vicarage, 1A London Road, Widley, Waterlooville PO7 5AT* Tel (023) 9237 5360

NORTON, Canon Peter Eric Pepler. b 38. TCD BA61 G&C Coll Cam PhD64. Cranmer Hall Dur 78. **d** 80 **p** 81. C Ulverston St Mary w H Trin *Carl* 80-83; P-in-c Warcop, Musgrave, Soulby and Crosby Garrett 83-84; R 84-90; OCF 83-90; V Appleby and R Ormside *Carl* 90-04; P-in-c Kirkby Thore w Temple Sowerby and Newbiggin 01-04; RD Appleby 00-04; Hon Can Carl Cathl 00-04; rtd 04. *Street Farmhouse, High Street, Shipdham, Thetford IP25 7PA* Tel (01362) 822171 Mobile 07802-334575 E-mail peter_norton@mac.com

NORTON, Sam Charles. b 70. Trin Coll Ox BA92 MA99 Heythrop Coll Lon MA00. Westcott Ho Cam 97. **d** 99 **p** 00. C Stepney St Dunstan and All SS *Lon* 99-02; R W w E Mersea *Chelmsf* from 03; P-in-c Peldon w Gt and Lt Wigborough from 03. *93 Kingsland Road, West Mersea, Colchester CO5 8AG* Tel (01206) 385635 E-mail elizaphanian@hotmail.com

NORTON (née FISHER), Mrs Susan Alexandra. b 54. Man Univ BA75 Hughes Hall Cam PGCE76. NEOC 01. **d** 04 **p** 05. NSM York St Olave w St Giles *York* from 04; NSM York St Helen w St Martin from 04. *21 Wentworth Road, York YO24 1DG* Tel (01904) 634911 E-mail e.norton@tinyworld.co.uk

NORTON, William Fullerton. b 23. Selw Coll Cam BA46 MA52. Wycliffe Hall Ox 46. **d** 48 **p** 49. C Leic H Apostles *Leic* 48-52; C Singapore St Matt 52-54; Miss Selangor Malaya 54-56; Miss Kampong Tawas 56-60; V Ipoh St Pet 60-63; R Manila St Steph Philippines 63-66; C Homerton St Luke *Lon* 67; C Tooting Graveney St Nic *S'wark* 68-71; V Hanley Road St Sav w St Paul *Lon* 71-89; rtd 89. *21 Peel Road, Brighton BN2 5ND* Tel (01273) 677332

NORWICH, Archdeacon of. *See* OFFER, The Ven Clifford Jocelyn

NORWICH, Bishop of. *See* JAMES, The Rt Revd Graham Richard

NORWICH, Dean of. *See* SMITH, The Very Revd Graham Charles Morell

NORWOOD, Andrew David. b 65. Lon Bible Coll BA91. Cranmer Hall Dur 92. **d** 94 **p** 95. C Headingley *Ripon* 94-97; C Handsworth St Mary *Birm* 97-00; Perm to Offic *Lon* 01-02; Chapl Chelsea Coll from 02. *11 Ormonde Mansions, 106 Southampton Row, London WC1B 4BP* Tel (020) 7242 7533 *or* 7514 8458 E-mail a.norwood@arts.ac.uk *or* a.norwood@csm.linst.ac.uk

NORWOOD, David John. b 40. SS Paul & Mary Coll Cheltenham BEd82. Linc Th Coll 65. **d** 68 **p** 69. C Hitchin St Mary *St Alb* 68-71; P-in-c Luanshya Zambia 72-76; C Littlehampton St Jas *Chich* 76-77; P-in-c Chacewater *Truro* 77-79; Chapl R Cornwall Hosp Treliske 77-79; Hd RE Red Maids Sch Bris 82-85; Appeals Organiser Children's Soc 86-94; P-in-c Clarkston *Glas* 94-97; R 97-99; R Dalbeattie 99-05; rtd 05. *Dove Cottage, Wellfield Terrace, Ferryside SA17 5SD* Tel (01267) 267125 E-mail norwoods@supanet.com

NORWOOD, Canon Philip Geoffrey Frank. b 39. Em Coll Cam BA62 MA66. Cuddesdon Coll 63. **d** 65 **p** 66. C New Addington *Cant* 65-69; Abp's Dom Chapl 69-72; V Hollingbourne 72-78; P-in-c Wormshill 74-78; P-in-c Huckinge 74-78; V St Laur in Thanet 78-88; RD Thanet 86-88; V Spalding *Linc* 88-98; RD Elloe W 96-98; R Blakeney w Cley, Wiveton, Glandford etc *Nor* from 98; RD Holt 02-05; Hon Can Nor Cathl 03-05; rtd 05.

9 Home Close Road, Houghton-on-the-Hill, Leicester LE7 9GT Tel 0116-243 4685

NORWOOD, Robert William. b 38. Lon Univ TCert64 Keble Coll Ox BA71 MA71 Lambeth STh83. **d** 01 **p** 03. NSM St Pancras H Cross w St Jude and St Pet *Lon* from 01. *Carlton Court, 11A Hermon Hill, London E11 2AR* Tel (020) 8530 2493

NORWOOD, Timothy. b 70. Aber Univ BD94. Westcott Ho Cam 95. **d** 97 **p** 98. C Upton cum Chalvey *Ox* 97-00; TV Watling Valley from 00. *3 Daubeney Gate, Shenley Church End, Milton Keynes MK5 6EH* Tel (01908) 505812 E-mail tim@thenorwoods.fsnet.co.uk

NOTLEY, Michael James. b 41. St Edm Hall Ox BA63 MA68 DipEd64. EMMTC 84. **d** 87 **p** 88. Hon C Oadby *Leic* 87-96; P-in-c Holbeach Marsh *Linc* from 96; P-in-c Lutton w Gedney Drove End, Dawsmere from 96. *The Vicarage, Marsh Road, Holbeach Hurn, Holbeach, Spalding PE12 8JX* Tel (01406) 425816

NOTT, Canon George Thomas Michael. b 34. Ex Coll Ox BA58 MA62 Birm Univ MEd88 Cov Univ PhD95. Coll of Resurr Mirfield. **d** 60 **p** 61. C Solihull *Birm* 60-69; Chapl K Sch Worc and Min Can Worc Cathl *Worc* 69-77; P-in-c Worc St Nic and Children's Officer 77-87; P-in-c Worc St Andr and All SS w St Helen 82-84; Droitwich Spa 87-89; V Broadheath, Crown East and Rushwick 89-04; Chapl Worc Coll of HE 89-96; RD Martley and Worc W *Worc* 95-03; Hon Can Worc Cathl 99-04; P-in-c Worc St Mich 00-01; rtd 04. *17 Wirlpiece Avenue, Worcester WR4 0NF* E-mail michael.nott39@mgownersclub.net

✠**NOTT, The Rt Revd Peter John.** b 33. Fitzw Ho Cam BA61 MA65. Westcott Ho Cam 58. **d** 61 **p** 62 **c** 77. C Harpenden St Nic *St Alb* 61-64; Chapl Fitzw Coll Cam 64-69; Fell 66-69; Chapl New Hall Cam 66-69; R Beaconsfield *Ox* 69-76; TR 76-77; Preb Wells Cathl *B & W* 77-85; Suff Bp Taunton 77-85; Bp Nor 85-99; rtd 99; Hon Asst Bp Ox from 99. *16 St Joseph's Mews, Candlemas Lane, Beaconsfield HP9 1GA1* Tel (01494) 678007

NOTT, Philip James. b 69. Nottm Trent Univ BA92. Ridley Hall Cam 95. **d** 98 **p** 99. C Kersal Moor *Man* 98-01; C Ealing St Mary *Lon* 01-04; Chapl Thames Valley Univ 01-04; P-in-c Broxtowe *S'well* from 04. *St Martha's Vicarage, 135 Frinton Road, Nottingham NG8 6GR* Tel 0115-927 8837 E-mail nottfamily@fish.co.uk

NOTTAGE, Preb Terence John. b 36. Oak Hill Th Coll 62. **d** 65 **p** 66. C Finchley St Paul Long Lane *Lon* 65-68; C Edgware 68-72; V Harlesden St Mark 72-86; V Kensal Rise St Mark and St Martin 86; TR Plymouth Em w Efford *Ex* 86-92; P-in-c Laira 88-92; TR Plymouth Em, St Paul Efford and St Aug 93-96; Preb Ex Cathl from 96; Adv for Voc and Dioc Dir of Ords 96-01; rtd 01. *4 Keyberry Close, Newton Abbot TQ12 1DA* Tel (01626) 332277 E-mail terry.nottage@tesco.net

NOTTINGHAM, Archdeacon of. *See* OGILVIE, The Ven Gordon

NOURSE, John. b 22. St Jo Coll Cam BA43 MA47 ACertCM90. Wells Th Coll 48. **d** 49 **p** 51. C Bournemouth St Aug *Win* 49-51; Asst Master Hurstpierpoint Coll 51-52; C Shere *Guildf* 52-57; C Eton w Boveney *Ox* 57-62; Min Can Windsor and Asst Master St Geo Choir Sch 57-67; Succ 61-67; V Amesbury *Sarum* 67-69; Offg Chapl RAF 67-69; Prec Cant Cathl *Cant* 69-73; V Charing w Lt Chart 73-83; V Charing w Charing Heath and Lt Chart 84-88; rtd 88; Perm to Offic *Ex* from 90. *High Meadow, Greenhill Avenue, Lympstone, Exmouth EX8 5HW* Tel (01395) 264480

NOVELL, Jill. b 49. Bris Univ BA72 Open Univ MA89 St Martin's Coll Lanc PGCE77. Carl and Blackb Dioc Tr Inst 01. **d** 04 **p** 05. NSM Silverdale *Blackb* from 04. *29 Hall Park, Lancaster LA1 4SH* Tel (01524) 381046

NOWELL, Canon John David. b 44. AKC67. **d** 68 **p** 69. C Lindley *Wakef* 68-70; C Lightcliffe 70-72; V Wyke *Bradf* 72-80; V Silsden 80-92; V Baildon from 92; Hon Can Bradf Cathl from 00. *The Vicarage, Baildon, Shipley BD17 6BY* Tel (01274) 594941 Fax as telephone

NOWÉN, Lars Fredrik. b 71. Summit Pacific Coll BC BTh93 Regent Coll Vancouver MCS98. **d** 98 **p** 99. Dn Halifax St Geo Canada 98-99; P-in-c Meadow Lake and Loon Lake 99-04; C Pelton *Dur* from 04; C W Pelton from 04. *The Vicarage, Church Road, Pelton, Chester le Street DH2 1XB* Tel 0191-370 2204 E-mail lars_nowen@hotmail.com

NOY, Frederick William Vernon. b 47. Sarum Th Coll 67. **d** 71 **p** 72. C Swindon St Jo *Bris* 71-75; Chapl to the Deaf *Sarum* 75-80; P-in-c Stinsford, Winterborne Came w Whitcombe etc 76-80; Perm to Offic from 80. *54 Casterbridge Road, Dorchester DT1 2AG* Tel (01305) 264269

NOYCE, Colin Martley. b 45. Brasted Th Coll 73 Ridley Hall Cam 74. **d** 76 **p** 77. C Cambridge St Jas *Ely* 76-78; Chapl RN 78-82; R Mistley w Manningtree *Chelmsf* 82-86; Miss to Seamen 86-90; Kenya 86-89; Trinidad and Tobago 89-90; V Four Marks *Win* 90-99; Chapl Pilgrim's Hospices E Kent 99-01; Chapl and Dir Ch Ch and Ras Morbat Clinics Yemen 01-03; Chapl Limassol St Barn and Miss to Seafarers from 03. *St Barnabas' Church, PO Box 1494, 3506 Limassol, Cyprus* Tel (00357) (5) 362713 Fax 747211 E-mail colinnoyce@aol.com

NOYCE, Graham Peter. b 62. Bedf Coll Lon BSc84. Trin Coll Bris BA92. **d** 92 **p** 93. C Sketty *S & B* 92-94; C Swansea St Jas 94-96; C Kensal Rise St Mark and St Martin *Lon* 96-04; TV from 04. *26 Ashburnham Road, London NW10 5SD* Tel (020) 8960 6211 E-mail graham@noycefamily.co.uk

NOYES, Roger. b 39. Linc Th Coll 65. **d** 67 **p** 68. C Adel *Ripon* 67-70; Chapl Aldenham Sch Herts 70-74; V Aldborough w Boroughbridge and Roecliffe *Ripon* 74-89; Rural Min Adv 89-90; Perm to Offic from 91; rtd 04. *Rose Cottage, Moor End, Nun Monkton, York YO26 8EN* Tel (01423) 330846

NSHIMYE, Stephen Kamegeri. b 60. Bp Lutaya Th Coll Uganda 88. **d** 90 **p** 91. Uganda 90-93; Rwanda 94-99; Perm to Offic *S'wark* from 02. *58 Hickin Close, London SE7 8SH* Tel (020) 8305 0934 Mobile 07950-346477

NSUBUGA, Eridard Kironde. b 58. Birm Univ DipRE96. Bp Tucker Coll Mukono. **d** 84 **p** 85. Uganda 85-88 and 92-00; C St Andr Cathl Mityana 85-88; V 92-95; R Kadoma Zimbabwe 88-91; V St Mark's Cathl Luwero 96-00; Perm to Offic *Glouc* 02-03. *Address temp unknown* Tel 07979-904397 (mobile) E-mail nsubuga@bigfoot.com *or* jeridard@yahoo.com

✠**NTAHOTURI, The Most Revd Bernard.** b 48. St Jo Coll Cam MA. Bp Tucker Coll Mukono 68. **d** 73 **c** 97. Burundi from 73; Bp Matana from 97; Abp Burundi from 05. *BP 447, Bujumbura, Burundi* Tel (00257) (2) 70361 Fax 29129 E-mail ntahober@cbinf.com

NTEGE, Nathan Kasolo. b 59. **d** 87 **p** 89. St Paul's Cathl Namirembe 87-91; Bp Tucker Coll Mukono 91-94; V Luzira and Kabowa 94-96; Perm to Offic *S'wark* 97-02; P-in-c Thornton Heath St Jude w St Aid from 02. *St Jude's Vicarage, 11 Dunheved Road North, Thornton Heath CR7 6AH* Tel (01342) 832021 Mobile 07951-673589

NUDDS, Douglas John. b 24. St Aid Birkenhead 48. **d** 51 **p** 52. C E Dereham w Hoe *Nor* 51-55; C Birstall *Leic* 55-58; V Bardon Hill 58-62; V Belgrave St Mich 62-68; Chapl Leic R Infirmary 68-72; High Royds Hosp Menston 72-79; V Bradf St Wilfrid Lidget Green *Bradf* 79-84; Lic to Offic *St Alb* 84-93; Chapl Shenley Hosp Radlett Herts 84-89; rtd 89; Perm to Offic *Nor* from 89. *Longview, Southgate Close, Wells-next-the-Sea NR23 1HG* Tel (01328) 711926

NUGENT, Canon Alan Hubert. b 42. Dur Univ BA65 MA78. Wycliffe Hall Ox 65 United Th Coll Bangalore DipTh66. **d** 67 **p** 68. C Mossley Hill St Matt and St Jas *Liv* 67-71; C Bridgnorth St Mary *Heref* 71-72; Chapl Dur Univ *Dur* 72-78; P-in-c Bishopwearmouth Ch Ch 78-85; P-in-c Brancepeth 85-94; Dioc Dir of Educn 85-97; Hon Can Dur Cathl 86-97; Dir of Miss and Tr Development Forum *Linc* 97-03; Can and Preb Linc Cathl 98-03; Can Res and Subdean Linc Cathl from 03. *The Subdeanery, 18 Minster Yard, Lincoln LN2 1RU* Tel (01522) 521932 *or* 523113 E-mail subdean@lincolncathedral.com

NUGENT, David Richard. b 54. MInstPS84 Liv Poly BA87. Oak Hill Th Coll BA95. **d** 95 **p** 96. C Birkenhead St Jas w St Bede *Ches* 95-99; V Blundellsands St Mich *Liv* 99-02; Asst Chapl Wirral and W Cheshire Community NHS Trust 02-03; Asst Chapl Cheshire and Wirral Partnership NHS Trust from 03. *Chaplains' Office, Clatterbridge Hospital, Clatterbridge Road, Wirral CH63 4JY* Tel 0151-334 4000 E-mail dave.nugent@whnt.nhs.uk

NUGENT, Eric William. b 26. Bps' Coll Cheshunt 56. **d** 58 **p** 59. C Rochford *Chelmsf* 58-61; C Eastwood 61-62; C-in-c Eastwood St Dav CD 62-66; V Eastwood St Dav 66-79; P-in-c Weeley 79-81; V Lt Clacton 80-81; R Weeley and Lt Clacton 81-93; rtd 93; Perm to Offic *Chelmsf* from 93. *1 King's Court, King's Road, Dovercourt, Harwich CO12 4DS* Tel (01255) 552640

NUNN, Ms Alice Candida. b 52. Ripon Coll Cuddesdon 95. **d** 97 **p** 98. C Margate St Jo *Cant* 97-01; V Winterton Gp *Linc* from 01. *The Vicarage, High Street, Winterton, Scunthorpe DN15 9PU* Tel (01724) 732262

NUNN, Canon Andrew Peter. b 57. Leic Poly BA79 Leeds Univ BA82. Coll of Resurr Mirfield 80. **d** 83 **p** 84. C Manston *Ripon* 83-87; C Leeds Richmond Hill 87-91; Chapl Agnes Stewart C of E High Sch Leeds 87-95; V Leeds Richmond Hill *Ripon* 91-95; Personal Asst to Bp S'wark 95-99; Hon PV S'wark Cathl 95-99; Sub-Dean, Prec and Can Res S'wark Cathl from 99; Warden Dioc Readers Assn from 01. *73 St George's Road, London SE1 6ER* Tel (020) 7735 8322 *or* 7367 6727 Mobile 07961-332051 Fax 7367 6725 E-mail andrew.nunn@southwark.anglican.org

NUNN, Peter. b 32. Kelham Th Coll 53. **d** 57 **p** 58. C Wigan St Geo *Liv* 57-60; C Warrington St Elphin 60-62; V Warrington St Pet 62-65; Chapl Winwick Hosp Warrington 65-90; rtd 90; Perm to Offic *Liv* from 90. *9 Derby House, Scholes, Wigan WN1 3RN* Tel (01942) 235407

NUNN, Canon Peter Michael. b 38. MBE98. Sarum Th Coll 64. **d** 66 **p** 67. C Hornsey St Geo *Lon* 66-71; C Cleator Moor w Cleator *Carl* 71-72; V Carl St Luke Morton 72-79; V Wotton St Mary *Glouc* 79-02; Offg Chapl RAF 80-97; RD Glouc City *Glouc* 88-94; Hon Can Glouc Cathl 90-02; rtd 02; Perm to Offic

Chich from 02. *87 South Street, Tarring, Worthing BN14 7ND* Tel (01903) 233748

NUNN, Peter Rawling. b 51. Ox Univ BA73 Sheff Univ MSc74 BA85. Oak Hill Th Coll 82. **d** 85 **p** 86. C Bispham *Blackb* 85-87; C-in-c Anchorsholme 87-89; V from 89. *The Vicarage, 36 Valeway Avenue, Thornton-Cleveleys FY5 3RN* Tel (01253) 823904 E-mail anchorsholme@ukonline.co.uk

NUNN, Richard Ernest. b 38. St Alb and Ox Min Course 96. **d** 99 **p** 00. NSM Maidenhead St Luke *Ox* 99-02; NSM Waltham St Lawrence from 02. *The Parsonage, School Road, Waltham St Lawrence, Reading RG10 0NU* Tel 0118-934 5082 Mobile 07887-930983 E-mail richard@rjnunn.fsnet.co.uk

NUNN, Stephen Robert. b 64. St Jo Coll Nottm BTh92. **d** 92 **p** 93. C Hailsham *Chich* 92-95; C Hollington St Leon 95-97; R Clymping and Yapton w Ford 97-01; Chapl HM Pris Kingston (Portsm) 01-03. *Address temp unknown*

NUNNERLEY, William John Arthur. b 27. Univ of Wales (Lamp) BA54 St Chad's Coll Dur DipTh56. **d** 56 **p** 57. C Tredegar St Geo *Mon* 56-60; Chapl RN 60-81; QHC from 79; R Barnoldby le Beck *Linc* 81-92; R Waltham 81-92; rtd 92; Perm to Offic *B & W* from 00. *Juniper Cottage, 82B Lower Street, Merriott TA16 5NW* Tel (01460) 76049

NUNNEY, Miss Sheila Frances. b 49. NNEB69 SRN74 RSCN74 SCM75 RCN Sister-Tutor's Dip 81. Oak Hill Th Coll BA92. **d** 92 **p** 94. C Swaffham *Nor* 92-96; Chapl Asst Norfolk and Nor Health Care NHS Trust 96-00; Chapl 00-01; Chapl Norwich Primary Care Trust from 01; Chapl Norfolk Mental Health Care NHS Trust from 03. *Priscilla Bacon Lodge, Colman Hospital, Unthank Road, Norwich NR2 2PJ* Tel (01603) 255728 *or* 421203 E-mail sfnunney@chestnut43a.freeserve.co.uk

NURSER, Canon John Shelley. b 29. Peterho Cam BA50 MA54 PhD58. Wells Th Coll 58. **d** 58 **p** 59. C Tankersley *Sheff* 58-61; Dean Trin Hall Cam 61-68; Australia 68-74; R Freckenham w Worlington *St E* 74-76; Can Res and Chan Linc Cathl *Linc* 76-92; Can and Preb Linc Cathl 92-94; P-in-c Shudy Camps *Ely* 92-94; rtd 94; Perm to Offic *St E* from 94 and *Ely* from 00. *68 Friars Street, Sudbury CO10 2AG* Tel (01787) 378595

NURTON, Robert. b 44. Univ of Wales (Lamp) BA67. Ridley Hall Cam 67. **d** 69 **p** 70. C Bris St Andr Hartcliffe *Bris* 69-73; C Ipswich St Mary at Stoke w St Pet & St Mary Quay *St E* 73-77; Chapl RN 77-99; Chapl Morden Coll Blackheath from 99. *Morden College, 19 St Germans Place, London SE3 0PW* Tel (020) 8858 3365

NUTH, Stephen William. b 55. Nazarene Th Coll Man CertRS87 St Jo Coll Nottm LTh95. **d** 95 **p** 96. C Wadhurst and Stonegate *Chich* 95-99; R Marks Tey and Aldham *Chelmsf* 99-01; Perm to Offic *St E* 01-04; P-in-c Woburn w Eversholt, Milton Bryan, Battlesden etc *St Alb* from 04. *The Vicarage, Park Street, Woburn, Milton Keynes MK17 9PG* Tel (01525) 290225 E-mail nuthman@arsenalfc.net

NUTT, Susan Mary. b 45. **d** 99 **p** 00. OLM Blackbourne *St E* from 99. *Portelet, Blacksmith Lane, Barnham, Thetford IP24 2NE* Tel (01842) 890409 E-mail revdsuenutt@hotmail.com

NUTTALL, George Herman. b 31. St Jo Coll Dur BA59 DipTh61. Cranmer Hall Dur 59. **d** 61 **p** 62. C Eccleshill *Bradf* 61-65; V Oldham St Barn *Man* 65-70; Area Sec CMS *Derby* and *Lich* 70-81; V Derby St Aug *Derby* 81-84; Chapl Bournemouth and Poole Coll of FE *Sarum* 85-97; Chapl Dorset Inst of HE 85-90; Chapl Bournemouth Poly *Win* 90-92; Chapl Bournemouth Univ 92-97; rtd 97; Perm to Offic *Sarum* 97-03 and *Carl* from 03. *Orchard End, 91 Silverdale Road, Arnside, Carnforth LA5 0EH* Tel (01524) 760001

NUTTALL, Michael John Berkeley. b 36. K Coll Lon AKC60. St Boniface Warminster 61. **d** 61 **p** 62. C Chapel Allerton *Ripon* 61-64; C Stanningley St Thos 64-68; V Leeds Gipton Epiphany 68-76; P-in-c Stainby w Gunby *Linc* 76-83; R N Witham 76-83; R S Witham 76-83; TV Bottesford w Ashby 83-88; I Adare w Kilpeacon and Croom *L & K* 88-94; I Adare and Kilmallock w Kilpeacon, Croom etc 94-01; Chapl Limerick Univ 88-95; Adn Limerick 92-01; rtd 01. *11 Cluaindara, Anglesborough, Kilmallock, Co Limerick, Irish Republic* Tel (00353) (62) 46280 Mobile 87-904 5738 E-mail adnmichaelnuttall@yahoo.com

NUZUM, Daniel Robert. b 73. RGN94 TCD BTh99. **d** 99 **p** 00. C Bandon Union *C, C & R* 99-01; I Templebreedy w Tracton and Nohoval from 02. *The Rectory, Crosshaven, Co Cork, Irish Repubic* Tel and fax (00353) (21) 483 1236 E-mail templebreedy@cork.anglican.org

NYATSANZA, Petros. b 69. Redcliffe Coll Glouc BA04. Bp Gaul Th Coll Harare 95. **d** 95 **p** 96. Zimbabwe 95-01; C Greendale St Luke 95-96; C Highfields St Paul 96-97; R Mufakose St Luke 97-01; Perm to Offic *Glouc* 02-04; P-in-c Rounds Green *Birm* from 04. *The Vicarage, Shelsley Avenue, Oldbury B69 1BG* Tel 0121-552 2822 Mobile 07721-726201 E-mail petrosnyatsanza@yahoo.co.uk

NYE, Canon David Charles. b 39. K Coll Lon BD65 Glos Univ MA01. **d** 63 **p** 64. C Charlton Kings St Mary *Glouc* 63-67; C Yeovil St Jo w Preston Plucknett *B & W* 67-70; V Lower Cam *Glouc* 70-74; Min Can Glouc Cathl 74-79; Dir of Ords 74-79; Prin Glouc Th Course 74-79; V Glouc St Mary de Lode and St Nic *Glouc* 74-76; V Maisemore 76-79; Chapl Grenville Coll Bideford 79-81; V Leckhampton SS Phil and Jas w Cheltenham St Jas *Glouc* 81-95; Hon Can Glouc Cathl 88-04; RD Cheltenham 89-95; P-in-c Northleach w Hampnett and Farmington 95-00; P-in-c Cold Aston w Notgrove and Turkdean 95-00; R Northleach w Hampnett and Farmington etc 00-04; RD Northleach 99-04; rtd 04. *2 Old Burford Road, Bledington, Chipping Norton OX7 6US* Tel (01608) 659140 E-mail tisnyes@tiscali.co.uk

✠**NZIMBI, The Most Revd Benjamin.** Bp All SS Cathl Dio from 02; Abp Kenya from 02. *PO Box 40502, Nairobi 00100, Kenya* Tel (00254) (2) 714753 Fax 718442 E-mail archoffice@swiftkenya.com

O

OADES, Michael Anthony John. b 45. Brasted Th Coll 69 Sarum & Wells Th Coll 71. **d** 73 **p** 74. C Eltham Park St Luke *S'wark* 73-78; C Coulsdon St Andr 78-81; P-in-c Merton St Jas 81-86; V 86-87; V Benhilton from 87. *All Saints' Vicarage, All Saints' Road, Sutton SM1 3DA* Tel (020) 8644 9070

OADES, Canon Peter Robert. b 24. Fitzw Ho Cam BA47 CertEd48 MA53. **d** 67 **p** 67. C Warblington w Emsworth *Portsm* 67-68; V Choral Sarum Cathl *Sarum* 68-74; Chapl Salisbury Cathl Sch 68-74; P-in-c Sturminster Newton and Hinton St Mary *Sarum* 74-75; V 75-81; R Stock and Lydlinch 75-81; RD Blackmore Vale 78-81; V Woodford Valley 81-89; Can and Preb Sarum Cathl 85-89; rtd 89; Hon Chapl to the Deaf *Sarum* 82-92; Perm to Offic *Sarum* and *Win* from 89. *28 Mulberry Gardens, Fordingbridge SP6 1BP* Tel (01425) 657113

OAKE, Barry Richard. b 47. MRICS71. Ripon Coll Cuddesdon 83. **d** 85 **p** 86. C Wantage *Ox* 85-88; C Warlingham w Chelsham and Farleigh *S'wark* 88-91; R N w S Wootton *Nor* from 91; Asst Chapl among Deaf and Hearing-Impaired People from 01. *The Rectory, 47 Castle Rising Road, South Wootton, King's Lynn PE30 3JA* Tel (01553) 671381

OAKES, Graham. b 42. Leeds Univ DipTh68. Chich Th Coll 68. **d** 70 **p** 71. C Hulme Ascension *Man* 70-74; C Clifton All SS w Tyndalls Park *Bris* 74-76; P-in-c Chadderton St Mark *Man* 76-78; V 78-82; V King Cross *Wakef* 82-95; R Bath H Trin *B & W* from 95; Chapl R United Hosp Bath NHS Trust from 99. *Holy Trinity Rectory, 9 Marlborough Lane, Bath BA1 2NQ* Tel (01225) 422311 E-mail revd@goakes.fsbusiness.co.uk

OAKES, Miss Jennifer May. b 43. Trin Coll Bris 78. **dss** 82 **d** 87 **p** 94. Wilnecote *Lich* 82-85; Stoneydelph St Martin CD 82-85; Bentley 85-89; Par Dn 87-89; Par Dn Hixon w Stowe-by-Chartley 89-94; C 94-98; Par Dn Fradswell, Gayton, Milwich and Weston 93-94; C 94-98; P-in-c Standon and Cotes Heath 98-00; rtd 03; Hon C Alfrick, Lulsley, Suckley, Leigh and Bransford *Worc* 03-04; Perm to Offic *Lich* from 05. *Willow Rise, Ashbourne Road, Whiston, Stoke-on-Trent ST10 2JE* Tel (01538) 260013 E-mail oaklud@supanet.com

OAKES, Canon Jeremy Charles. b 51. ACA75 FCA81. Westcott Ho Cam 75. **d** 78 **p** 79. C Evington *Leic* 78-81; C Ringwood *Win* 81-84; P-in-c Thurnby Lodge *Leic* 84-89; TV Oakdale *Sarum* 89-95; P-in-c Canford Cliffs and Sandbanks 95-03; V from 03; Can and Preb Sarum Cathl from 03. *The Vicarage, 14 Flaghead Road, Canford Cliffs, Poole BH13 7JW* Tel and fax (01202) 700341 E-mail jeremy.oakes@virgin.net

OAKES, John Cyril. b 49. AKC71. St Aug Coll Cant 71. **d** 72 **p** 73. C Broseley w Benthall *Heref* 72-76; C Cannock *Lich* 76-79; TV 79-83; V Rough Hills from 83; P-in-c Wolverhampton St Steph from 94. *St Martin's Vicarage, Dixon Street, Wolverhampton WV2 2BG* Tel (01902) 341030

OAKES, Canon Leslie John. b 28. AKC53. **d** 54 **p** 55. C Bedford Leigh *Man* 54-58; C Walsall St Matt *Lich* 58-60; Chapl Selly Oak Hosp Birm 60-64; V Longbridge *Birm* 64-93; Hon Can Birm Cathl 84-93; rtd 93; Perm to Offic *Birm* from 93. *108 Hole Lane, Birmingham B31 2DF* Tel 0121-476 8514

OAKES, Melvin. b 36. Linc Th Coll 77. **d** 79 **p** 80. C Lt Ilford St Mich *Chelmsf* 79-82; V Highams Park All SS 82-96; rtd 96; Perm to Offic *Chelmsf* from 99. *115 Richmond Avenue, London E4 9RR* Tel (020) 8527 0457

OAKES, Robert. b 47. Ex & Truro NSM Scheme. **d** 82 **p** 83. NSM Probus, Ladock and Grampound w Creed and St Erme *Truro* 82-84; TV Bodmin w Lanhydrock and Lanivet 85-88; R S Hill w Callington 88-03; P-in-c Linkinhorne 88-03; RD E Wivelshire 95-00; Hon Can Truro Cathl 01-03. *Address temp unknown* E-mail rector@revrobert.freeserve.co.uk

OAKHAM, Archdeacon of. *See* PAINTER, The Ven David Scott
OAKLAND, Mrs Sarah Marie. b 54. UEA BEd85. EAMTC 99. **d** 02 **p** 03. C Diss *Nor* from 02. *7 de Lucy Close, Diss IP22 4YL* Tel (01379) 644955 E-mail saraho@hotmail.com
OAKLEY, Barry Wyndham. b 32. TD72. SS Coll Cam BA53 MA57. Ridley Hall Cam 56. **d** 58 **p** 59. C Alverstoke *Portsm* 58-61; C Bermondsey St Mary w St Olave and St Jo *S'wark* 61-63; V Crofton *Portsm* 63-78; V Edmonton All SS *Lon* 78-82; P-in-c Edmonton St Mich 80-82; V Edmonton All SS w St Mich 82-97; rtd 97; Perm to Offic *Lon* from 98. *25 Queen's Road, Enfield EN1 1NF* Tel (020) 8363 3199
OAKLEY, Hilary Robert Mark. b 53. Univ of Wales (Ban) BSc75 Ox Univ BA78 MA81 MIPD91. Ripon Coll Cuddesdon 76. **d** 79 **p** 80. C Birm St Pet *Birm* 79-82; C Cambridge Gt St Mary w St Mich *Ely* 82-86; Chapl Girton Coll Cam 82-86; Chapl Zürich w St Gallen and Winterthur *Eur* 86-88; NSM Lon 88-92; Perm to Offic *St Alb* from 92. *55 Southdown Road, Harpenden AL5 1PQ* Tel (01582) 761514 E-mail hilary.oakley@talk21.com
OAKLEY, James Robert. b 75. St Edm Hall Ox BA96. Oak Hill Th Coll BA05. **d** 05. C Audley *Lich* from 05. *St John's Vicarage, High Street, Alsagers Bank, Stoke-on-Trent ST7 8BQ* Tel (01782) 720808 Mobile 07963-655941 E-mail james@oakleys.org.uk
OAKLEY, Jeremy Steven. b 52. Birm Univ BA99. Trin Coll Bris 95. **d** 97 **p** 98. C Walsall *Lich* 97-02; V Penn Fields from 02. *St Philip's Vicarage, Church Road, Bradmore, Wolverhampton WV3 7EJ* Tel (01902) 332749 E-mail jeremy@pennfieldsparish.co.uk
OAKLEY, The Ven Mark David. b 68. K Coll Lon BD90 AKC90 FRSA96. St Steph Ho Ox 90. **d** 93 **p** 94. C St John's Wood *Lon* 93-96; Bp's Chapl 96-00; P-in-c Covent Garden St Paul 00-03; R 03-05; AD Westmr St Marg 04-05; Chapl RADA 03-05; Dep P in O 96-05; Adn Germany *Eur* from 05; Chapl Copenhagen from 05. *St Alban's House, Tuborgvej 82, DK 2900, Hellerup, Denmark* Tel (0045) 3962 7736 Fax 3962 7735 E-mail md.oakley1@virgin.net
OAKLEY, Richard John. b 46. AKC69 St Aug Coll Cant 69. **d** 70 **p** 71. C Wythenshawe Wm Temple Ch *Man* 70-75; V Ashton H Trin 75-80; CR 80-93; Lic to Offic *Lon* 88-93; V Cantley *Sheff* 93-99; V Carl St Aid and Ch Ch *Carl* from 99. *St Aidan's Vicarage, 6 Lismore Place, Carlisle CA1 1LX* Tel (01228) 522942 E-mail fr.oakley.staidan@virgin.net
OAKLEY, Robert Paul. b 51. Sheff Univ BScTech72 PGCE74. St Jo Coll Nottm DipTh89. **d** 89 **p** 90. C Heatherlands St Jo *Sarum* 89-92; V Burton All SS w Ch Ch *Lich* 92-99; V Gt Wyrley from 99. *St Mark's Vicarage, 1 Cleves Crescent, Cheslyn Hay, Walsall WS6 7LR* Tel (01922) 414309
OAKLEY, Robin Ian. b 37. Ripon Hall Ox 68. **d** 70 **p** 71. C Leighton Buzzard *St Alb* 70-73; C Watford St Mich 73-76; R Ickleford 76-80; R Ickleford w Holwell 80-02; rtd 02; Perm to Offic *St Alb* from 02 and *Win* from 03. *13 Anders Road, South Wonston, Winchester SO21 3EL* Tel (01962) 880613
OAKLEY, Susan Mary. *See* HENWOOD, Mrs Susan Mary
OAKLEY, Timothy Crispin. b 45. Qu Coll Cam BA66 MA70 Bris Univ PGCE69. St Jo Coll Nottm DipTh74 DPS76. **d** 76 **p** 77. C Bromley Common St Aug *Roch* 76-79; C Fairfield *Liv* 79-81; CMS Kenya 82-90; P-in-c Beaford, Roborough and St Giles in the Wood *Ex* 91-96; Chapl St Andr Sch Turi Kenya 96-98; V Woodford Halse w Eydon *Pet* from 99; RD Brackley from 03. *The New Vicarage, Parsons Street, Woodford Halse, Daventry NN11 3RE* Tel (01327) 261477 E-mail tim@revoakley.freeserve.co.uk
OATES, Alan. b 32. S'wark Ord Course 79. **d** 80 **p** 81. NSM Rayleigh *Chelmsf* 80-87; TV Jarrow *Dur* 87-92; P-in-c Stella 92-95; R 95-97; rtd 97; Perm to Offic *Dur* from 98 and *Newc* from 00. *1 The Haven, North Shields NE29 6YH* Tel 0191-258 6984
OATES, Alexander John. b 38. Clifton Th Coll 63. **d** 67 **p** 68. C Brixton Hill St Sav *S'wark* 67-68; C Westcombe Park St Geo 68-71; C Stechford *Birm* 71-74; R Greenhithe St Mary *Roch* 74-77; Soc worker 77-02; rtd 03. *1 Fairlight Villas, North Road, Havering-atte-Bower, Romford RM4 1PP* Tel (01708) 760252
OATES, Douglas. b 39. Bolton Coll of Educn CertEd74 Chester Coll of HE BTh97. N Ord Course 94. **d** 97 **p** 98. NSM Balderstone *Man* 97-99; NSM S Rochdale 00-01; NSM Oldham St Barn 01-03; P-in-c from 03. *St Barnabas' Vicarage, 1 Arundel Street, Oldham OL4 1NL* Tel 0161-624 7708 E-mail dco@surfaid.org
OATES, Canon John. b 30. Kelham Th Coll 53. **d** 57 **p** 58. C Hackney Wick St Mary of Eton w St Aug *Lon* 57-60; Development Officer C of E Youth Coun 60-64; Sec C of E Coun Commonwealth Settlement 64-65; Gen Sec 65-72; Sec C of E Cttee on Migration & Internat Affairs 68-72; Hon Can Bunbury from 69; V Richmond St Mary *S'wark* 70-79; P-in-c Richmond St Jo 76-79; V Richmond St Mary w St Matthias and St Jo 79-84; RD Richmond and Barnes 79-84; R St Bride Fleet Street w Bridewell etc *Lon* 84-00; AD The City 97-00; Preb St Paul's Cathl 97-00; rtd 00. *27 York Court, Albany Park Road, Kingston upon Thames KT2 5ST* Tel (020) 8974 8821 E-mail john@joates.co.uk
OATES, Michael Graham. b 62. Leic Poly BSc84. Aston Tr Scheme 87 Cranmer Hall Dur 89. **d** 92 **p** 93. C Enfield St Andr *Lon* 92-96; TV Oakdale *Sarum* from 96. *The Vicarage, 16 Rowbarrow Close, Canford Heath, Poole BH17 9EA* Tel (01202) 699807 E-mail oates@fish.co.uk
OATES (née ADAMS), Mrs Ruth. b 47. Bris Univ BSc69. SEITE 97. **d** 00 **p** 01. C Rainham *Roch* 00-03; V Gravesend St Mary from 03. *The Vicarage, 57 New House Lane, Gravesend DA11 7HJ* Tel (01474) 740565 E-mail ruthoates@fish.co.uk
OBAN, Provost of. *See* MacCALLUM, The Very Revd Norman Donald
OBEE, Douglas Walter. b 18. Roch Th Coll 65. **d** 67 **p** 68. C Beckenham St Geo *Roch* 67-71; R Whitestone *Ex* 71-75; V Oldridge 72-75; P-in-c Harford 76-87; V Ivybridge 76-87; V Ivybridge w Harford 87; rtd 87; Perm to Offic *Ex* from 88. *16 Kerswill Road, Exeter EX4 1NY* Tel (01392) 439405
O'BENEY, Robin Mervyn. b 35. Ely Th Coll 61. **d** 64 **p** 65. C Liss *Portsm* 64-65; C Portsea St Cuth 65-68; Hon C Wymondham *Nor* 74-76; R Swainsthorpe w Newton Flotman 76-80; NSM Sparkenhoe Deanery *Leic* 87-90; V Billesdon and Skeffington 90-91; rtd 95. *19 Bridge Street, Kington HR5 3DL* Tel (01544) 230416
OBIN, Raymond Clive. b 63. Girton Coll Cam BA85 MA89. Wycliffe Hall Ox BTh. **d** 04 **p** 05. NSM Bucklebury w Marlston *Ox* from 04; NSM Bradfield and Stanford Dingley from 04. *Solfonn, Enborne Row, Wash Water, Newbury RG20 0LY* Tel (01635) 38212 E-mail raymond@2bsd.org.uk
OBIORA, Arthur Cuenyem. b 42. JP91. DipSM68. LNSM course 92. **d** 95 **p** 95. OLM Hatcham St Cath *S'wark* from 95. *3 Lanchester Way, London SE14 5HQ* Tel (020) 7732 1065
O'BOYLE, Liam Patrick Butler. b 66. Nottm Univ BA90 MA98. EMMTC 98. **d** 01 **p** 02. C Cinderhill *S'well* from 01. *24 Coventry Road, Beeston, Nottingham NG9 2EG* Tel 0115-943 1032
O'BRIEN, Andrew David. b 61. Nottm Univ BTh88. Linc Th Coll 85. **d** 88 **p** 89. C Clare w Poslingford *St E* 88-89; C Clare w Poslingford, Cavendish etc 89-91; V Belton *Linc* 91-97; P-in-c Melbourn *Ely* 97-99; V from 99; P-in-c Meldreth 97-99; V from 99. *The Vicarage, Vicarage Close, Melbourn, Royston SG8 6DY* Tel (01763) 260295 E-mail revobrien@tesco.net
O'BRIEN, David. b 62. Moorlands Th Coll BA99 Carl and Blackb Dioc Tr Inst 01. **d** 04 **p** 05. C Bispham *Blackb* from 04. *1 Prenton Gardens, Thornton-Cleveleys FY5 3RR* Tel (01253) 828041
O'BRIEN, Donogh Smith. b 34. St Pet Hall Ox BA56 MA60. Ripon Hall Ox 56. **d** 57 **p** 58. C Gt Sankey *Liv* 57-63; C Farnworth 63-66; Lic to Offic 66-03; Asst Master Wade Deacon Gr Sch Widnes 66-99; rtd 99; Perm to Offic *Liv* from 03. *Fourways, 178 Lunts Heath Road, Widnes WA8 5AZ* Tel 0151-424 0147
O'BRIEN, Mrs Elaine. b 55. CITC 94. **d** 97 **p** 98. Aux Min Killyman *Arm* 97-00; Aux Min Gilnahirk *D & D* from 00. *9 Moorfield Gardens, Comber, Newtownards BT23 5WF* Tel (028) 9187 1055 E-mail curate.gilnahirk@down.anglican.org
O'BRIEN, George Edward. b 32. Clifton Th Coll 61. **d** 64 **p** 65. C Denton Holme *Carl* 64-68; V Castle Town *Lich* 68-88; Chapl St Geo Hosp Stafford 88-94; Chapl Kingsmead Hosp Stafford 88-94; Chapl Foundation NHS Trust Stafford 94-99; rtd 99; Perm to Offic *Lich* from 99. *Abily, 185 Tixall Road, Stafford ST16 3XJ* Tel (01785) 244261
O'BRIEN, Kevin Michael. b 60. Herts Univ BA82. St Steph Ho Ox 99. **d** 01 **p** 02. C Uppingham w Ayston and Wardley w Belton *Pet* 01-04; Asst Chapl Wellington Coll Berks from 04. *Rose Cottage, Wellington College, Crowthorne RG45 7QG* Tel (01344) 777139 E-mail kevin.obrien@rutnet.co.uk
O'BRIEN, Mary. *See* GUBBINS, Mrs Mary
O'BRIEN, Peter Thomas. b 35. Lon Univ BD61 Man Univ PhD71. Moore Th Coll Sydney ThL60. **d** 61 **p** 62. Australia 61-63 and from 74; India 64-68 and 71-73; C Cheadle *Ches* 68-71. *Moore Theological College, 1 King Street, Newtown, NSW, Australia 2042* Tel (0061) (2) 9577 9999 *or* 9557 3072 Fax 9577 9988
O'BRIEN, Shelagh Ann. *See* STACEY, Mrs Shelagh Ann
OCKFORD, Paul Philip. b 46. St Chad's Coll Dur BA67. St Steph Ho Ox 68. **d** 70 **p** 71. C Streatham St Pet *S'wark* 70-74; C Cheam 74-77; P-in-c Eastrington *York* 77-79; TV Howden 80-83; R Sherburn and W and E Heslerton w Yedingham 83-92; V Bampton, Morebath, Clayhanger and Petton *Ex* 92-98; R Goodmanham *York* 98-04; V Market Weighton 98-04; V Sancton 98-04; rtd 04. *78 Wold Road, Pocklington, York YO42 2QG*
OCKWELL, Canon Herbert Grant. b 12. Kelham Th Coll 30. **d** 36 **p** 37. C Newington St Matt *S'wark* 36-40; CF (EC) 40-46; V Lambeth St Phil *S'wark* 46-52; V Surbiton St Andr 52-62; V Balham Hill Ascension 62-70; Hon Can S'wark Cathl 64-70; R Blendworth, Chalton and Idsworth *Portsm* 70-81; rtd 81; Perm to Offic *Portsm* from 81; *Chich* from 82. *Abbeyfield House, 30 Crockford Road, Westbourne, Emsworth PO10 8TN* Tel (01243) 374686
O'CONNELL, Miss Mary Joy. b 49. York Univ BA71 Leeds Univ CertEd74. Chich Th Coll 84. **dss** 86 **d** 87 **p** 94. Cinderhill

S'well 86-87; Par Dn 87-94; C 94; P-in-c 94-98; V Linc St Giles *Linc* from 98. *The Vicarage, 25 Shelley Drive, Lincoln LN2 4BY* Tel (01522) 527655 E-mail mjoconnell@lineone.net

O'CONNOR, Alfred Stanley. b 20. TCD BA43 MA60. **d** 43 **p** 44. C Belfast St Mich *Conn* 43-45; C Urney Union *K, E & A* 45-49; I Killesher 49-54; I Roscrea *L & K* 54-62; I Camlough w Killeavy *Arm* 62-65; I Drumglass 65-85; Can Arm Cathl 83-85; rtd 85. *25 West Street, Stewartstown, Dungannon BT71 5HT* Tel (028) 8773 8784

O'CONNOR, Canon Brian Michael McDougal. b 42. St Cath Coll Cam BA67 MA69. Cuddesdon Coll 67. **d** 69 **p** 70. C Headington *Ox* 69-71; Sec Dioc Past and Redundant Chs Uses Cttees 72-79; P-in-c Merton 72-76; V Rainham *Roch* 79-97; RD Gillingham 81-88; Hon Can Roch Cathl 89-97; Dean Auckland 97-00; Hon Can from 00; Perm to Offic *Ox* 00-02; P-in-c Lt Missenden 02-04; rtd 04. *1 Steadys Lane, Stanton Harcourt, Witney OX29 5RL* Tel (01865) 882776 Mobile 07740-702161 E-mail canonmichaeloc@aol.com

O'CONNOR, Canon Daniel. b 33. Univ Coll Dur BA54 MA67 St Andr Univ PhD81. Cuddesdon Coll 56. **d** 58 **p** 59. C Stockton St Pet *Dur* 58-62; C W Hartlepool St Aid 62-63; Cam Miss to Delhi 63-70; USPG India 70-72; Chapl St Andr Univ *St And* 72-77; R Edin Gd Shep *Edin* 77-82; Prin Coll of Ascension Selly Oak 82-90; Dir Scottish Chs Ho (Chs Together in Scotland) 90-93; Can Res Wakef Cathl *Wakef* 93-96; Bp's Adv on Inter-Faith Issues 93-96; rtd 96. *15 School Road, Balmullo, St Andrews KY16 0BA* Tel (01334) 871326 E-mail danoconnor@btinternet.com

O'CONNOR, Edward Howard. b 32. AIMLS59 FRSH65. Linc Th Coll 81 Immanuel Coll Ibadan 76. **d** 77 **p** 79. Nigeria 77-81; P-in-c Newchurch *Portsm* 81-83; V 83-91; P-in-c Arreton 82-83; V 83-91; Chapl HM Pris Kingston (Portsm) 91-97; rtd 92. *23 Arundel Road, Ryde PO33 1BW* Tel (01983) 617062

O'CONNOR, John Goodrich. b 34. Keble Coll Ox BA58 MA60. Lich Th Coll. **d** 61 **p** 62. C Blackpool St Steph *Blackb* 61-66; C Holbeck *Ripon* 66-68; C Hendon St Mary *Lon* 68-73; TV Thornaby on Tees *York* 73-79; TR 79-89; V Blyth St Cuth *Newc* 89-96; Chapl Wellesley Nautical Sch 89-96; V Feniscliffe *Blackb* 96-04; rtd 04; Hon C Lightbowne *Man* from 04. *The Rectory, 173 Kenyon Lane, Manchester M40 5HS* Tel 0161-681 1308 E-mail johnoak@fish.co.uk

O'CONNOR, Michael. *See* O'CONNOR, Canon Brian Michael McDougal

O'CONNOR, Nigel George. b 25. TD66. Linc Th Coll 53. **d** 55 **p** 56. C S Ormsby w Ketsby, Calceby and Driby *Linc* 55-58; R Partney w Dalby 58-65; V Skendleby 59-65; R Ashby by Partney 59-65; CF (TA) 62-71; R Ivychurch w Old Romney and Midley *Cant* 65-74; V Brenzett w Snargate and Snave 65-74; R Newchurch 65-74; R St Mary in the Marsh 65-74; R Burmarsh 65-74; V Brookland w Fairfield 65-74; CF (R of O) 71-91; V S w N Hayling *Portsm* 74-85; V Corby Glen *Linc* 85-91; rtd 91; Perm to Offic *Sarum* from 91 and *Win* from 01. *Winterbourne House, Newton Toney Road, Allington, Salisbury SP4 0BZ* Tel (01980) 611453

O'CONNOR, Rosemary Irene. b 43. St Gabr Coll Lon TCert65. WMMTC 96. **d** 99 **p** 00. NSM Cannock *Lich* 99-01; TV from 01. *St Aidan's Vicarage, Albert Street, Cannock WS11 5JD* Tel (01543) 500015 *or* 502131

ODA-BURNS, John Macdonald. b 31. AKC56. **d** 57 **p** 58. C St Marychurch *Ex* 57-59; S Africa 59-64; Bahamas 64-67; USA from 67; rtd 96. *611 La Mesa Drive, Portola Valley, CA 94028, USA* Tel (001) (650) 854 2831 Fax as telephone E-mail bussels@batnet.com

ODDY, Canon Frederick Brian. b 29. Univ of Wales (Lamp) BA50. Linc Th Coll 50. **d** 52 **p** 53. C Preston Em *Blackb* 52-55; C St Annes St Thos 55-57; V Chorley St Jas 57-64; V Warton St Oswald 64-76; P-in-c Yealand Conyers 74-76; V Warton St Oswald w Yealand Conyers 76-98; RD Tunstall 84-90; Hon Can Blackb Cathl 89-98; rtd 98; Perm to Offic *Blackb* from 98. *9 Main Road, Nether Kellet, Carnforth LA6 1HG*

ODDY, Joan Winifred. b 34. **d** 97 **p** 98. OLM Kessingland w Gisleham *Nor* 97-99; OLM Kessingland, Gisleham and Rushmere 99-04; rtd 04; Perm to Offic *Nor* from 04. *Rose Cottage, Wash Lane, Kessingland, Lowestoft NR33 7QY* Tel (01502) 742001

ODLING-SMEE, George William. b 35. K Coll Dur MB, BS59 FRCS68 FRCSI86. **d** 77 **p** 78. NSM Belfast St Thos *Conn* 77-90; NSM Belfast St Geo 90-02. *The Boathouse, 24 Rossglass Road South, Killough, Downpatrick BT30 7RA* Tel (028) 4484 1868 Fax 4484 1143 E-mail wodlingsmee@aol.com

O'DONNELL, Kevin George. b 57. Man Univ BA78 Didsbury Coll Man PGCE79. St Steph Ho Ox 86. **d** 88 **p** 89. C Tokyngton St Mich *Lon* 88-90; C Ascot Heath *Ox* 90-92; Perm to Offic 94-96; Chapl Heathfield Sch Ascot 96-99; R W Chiltington *Chich* from 99. *The Rectory, East Street, West Chiltington, Pulborough RH20 2JY* Tel (01798) 813117 Mobile 07957-880404 E-mail kevino'donnell@lastlaugh.demon.co.uk

O'DONNELL, Mrs Mollie. b 39. Portsm Poly BA91. STETS 97. **d** 00 **p** 03. NSM Calbourne w Newtown *Portsm* from 00; NSM Shalfleet from 00. *1 Mill Green Cottages, Newbridge, Yarmouth PO41 0TZ* Tel (01983) 531320

O'DONOGHUE, Mark Ronald. b 69. St Aid Coll Dur BA91 Solicitor 93. Oak Hill Th Coll 01. **d** 04 **p** 05. C St Helen Bishopsgate w St Andr Undershaft etc *Lon* from 04. *22 Chisenhale Road, London E3 5QZ* Tel (020) 8980 9150 E-mail odonoghue_maru@hotmail.com

O'DONOVAN, Canon Oliver Michael Timothy. b 45. Ball Coll Ox BA68 MA71 DPhil75. Wycliffe Hall Ox 68. **d** 72 **p** 73. Tutor Wycliffe Hall Ox 72-77; Canada 77-82; Regius Prof Moral and Past Th Ox Univ from 82; Can Res Ch Ch *Ox* from 82. *Christ Church, Oxford OX1 1DP* Tel (01865) 276219 E-mail oliver.odonovan@chch.ox.ac.uk

O'DWYER, John Francis Joseph. b 61. N Ord Course 00. **d** 03 **p** 04. C Bury St Jo w St Mark *Man* from 03. *14 Mather Road, Bury BL9 6QU* Tel 0161-764 3943 E-mail johntricia2000@yahoo.co.uk

OEHRING, Anthony Charles. b 56. Sheff City Poly BA79 CQSW79 Kent Univ MA02. Ridley Hall Cam 86. **d** 88 **p** 89. C Gillingham *Sarum* 88-91; TV S Gillingham *Roch* 91-00; P-in-c Faversham *Cant* from 00; AD Ospringe from 02; C Preston next Faversham, Goodnestone and Graveney from 02; P-in-c The Brents and Davington w Oare and Luddenham from 03. *The Vicarage, 16 Newton Road, Faversham ME13 8DY* Tel (01795) 532592 E-mail anthonyoehring@aol.com

OEPPEN, Canon John Gerard David. b 44. St D Coll Lamp DipTh67. **d** 67 **p** 68. C-in-c Cwmmer w Abercregan CD *Llan* 67-70; TV Glyncorrwg w Afan Vale and Cymmer Afan 70-71; C Whitchurch 71-74; V Aberavon H Trin 74-78; V Bargoed and Deri w Brithdir 78-86; R Barry All SS from 86; Can Llan Cathl from 04. *The Rectory, 3 Park Road, Barry CF62 6NU* Tel (01446) 734629

OESTREICHER, Canon Paul. b 31. OM(Ger)95. Univ of NZ BA53 MA56 Cov Poly Hon DLitt91 Sussex Univ Hon LLD05. Linc Th Coll 56. **d** 59 **p** 60. C Dalston H Trin w St Phil *Lon* 59-61; C S Mymms K Chas 61-68; Asst in Relig Broadcasting BBC 61-64; Assoc Sec Internat Affairs Dept BCC 64-69; V Blackheath Ascension *S'wark* 68-81; Dir of Tr 69-72; Hon Can S'wark Cathl 78-81; Asst Gen Sec BCC 81-86; Can Res Cov Cathl *Cov* 86-97; Dir of Internat Min 86-97; Humboldt Fell Inst of Th Free Univ of Berlin 92-93; rtd 98; Perm to Offic *Cov* from 98 and *Chich* from 03; Hon Chapl Sussex Univ *Chich* from 04. *97 Furze Croft, Furze Hill, Hove BN3 1PE* Tel (01273) 728033 E-mail paulo@reconcile.org.uk

O'FERRALL, The Very Revd Basil Arthur. b 24. CB79. TCD BA48 MA65. TCD Div Sch Div Test48. **d** 48 **p** 49. C Coleraine *Conn* 48-51; Chapl RN 51-75; Chapl of the Fleet and Adn for the RN 75-80; QHC 75-80; Hon Can Gib Cathl *Eur* 77-80; Chapl to The Queen 80-85; V Ranworth w Panxworth and Woodbastwick *Nor* 80-85; Bp's Chapl Norfolk Broads 80-85; Hon Can Win Cathl *Win* 85-93; R Jersey St Helier 85-93; Dean Jersey 85-93; Pres Jersey Miss to Seamen 85-93; Angl Adv Channel TV 85-93; rtd 93; Perm to Offic *Chich* from 93. *The Stone House, Barrack Square, Winchelsea TN36 4EG* Tel (01797) 223458

O'FERRALL, Patrick Charles Kenneth. b 34. New Coll Ox BA58 MA60. Guildf Dioc Min Course 99. **d** 00 **p** 01. OLM Godalming *Guildf* 00-04; Perm to Offic from 04. *Catteshall Grange, Catteshall Road, Godalming GU7 1LZ* Tel (01483) 410134 Fax 414161 E-mail pof59@hotmail.com

OFFER, The Ven Clifford Jocelyn. b 43. Ex Univ BA67 FRSA97. Westcott Ho Cam 67. **d** 69 **p** 70. C Bromley SS Pet and Paul *Roch* 69-74; TV Southampton (City Cen) *Win* 74-83; TR Hitchin *St Alb* 83-94; Adn Nor from 94; Can Res Nor Cathl from 94. *26 The Close, Norwich NR1 4DZ* Tel (01603) 620375 Fax 661104 E-mail archdeacon.norwich@4frontmedia.co.uk

OFFER, Mrs Jill Patricia. b 44. CertEd65. **d** 03 **p** 04. OLM Salisbury St Mark *Sarum* from 03. *11 Netheravon Road, Salisbury SP1 3BJ* Tel (01722) 334455 E-mail j.p.offer@talk21.com

OGADA, John Ochieng. b 56. Nairobi Univ LLB83 Univ of Wales (Cardiff) LLM89. **d** 01. Perm to Offic *York* 01-02; NSM Hull St Martin w Transfiguration 02-03. *44 Kingston Road, Willerby, Hull HU10 6BH* Tel (01482) 653592

O'GARRO, Henry Roland Furlonge. b 30. Leeward Is TCert52. St Steph Ho Ox 00. **d** 00. NSM Kilburn St Aug w St Jo *Lon* 00-05; NSM Willesden St Mary from 05. *32 Cedar Road, London NW2 6SR* Tel (020) 8452 4530

OGDEN, Eric. b 34. NW Ord Course 73. **d** 76 **p** 77. NSM Lydgate St Anne *Man* 76-92; NSM Lydgate w Friezland 92-01; rtd 01; Perm to Offic *Man* from 01. *40 Burnedge Lane, Grasscroft, Oldham OL4 4EA* Tel (01457) 873661

OGDEN, Harry. b 30. AKC57. **d** 58 **p** 59. C Hollinwood *Man* 58-60; C Langley St Aid CD 60-61; R Lightbowne 61-69; V Farnworth and Kearsley 69-72; V Oldham St Steph and All Martyrs 72-79; R Moss Side Ch Ch 79-95; rtd 95; Perm to Offic *Man* 95-98 and *Worc* 01-05. *29 Fosbrooke House, 8 Clifton Drive, Lytham St Annes FY8 5RQ*

OGILVIE, The Ven Gordon. b 42. Glas Univ MA64 Lon Univ BD67. ALCD66. **d** 67 **p** 68. C Ashtead *Guildf* 67-72; V New

Barnet St Jas *St Alb* 72-80; Dir Past Studies Wycliffe Hall Ox 80-87; P-in-c Harlow New Town w Lt Parndon *Chelmsf* 87-89; R 89-94; TR Harlow Town Cen w Lt Parndon 94-96; Hon Can Chelmsf Cathl 94-96; Chapl Princess Alexandra Hosp Harlow 88-96; Adn Nottingham *S'well* from 96. *2B Spencer Avenue, Mapperley, Nottingham NG3 5SP* Tel 0115-967 0875 *or* (01636) 817206 Fax 0115-967 1014 *or* (01636) 815882 E-mail gogilvie@southwell.anglican.org

OGILVIE, Ian Douglas. b 37. Em Coll Cam BA59 MA63. Linc Th Coll 59. **d** 61 **p** 62. C Clapham H Trin *S'wark* 61-63; C Cambridge Gt St Mary w St Mich *Ely* 63-66; Chapl Sevenoaks Sch 66-77; Hon C Sevenoaks St Nic *Roch* 67-77; Chapl Malvern Coll 77-84; Hd Master St Geo Sch Harpenden 84-87; Lic to Offic *St Alb* 84-87; Bp's Dom Chapl 87-89; P-in-c Aldenham 87-91; Appeals Dir Mind 89-91; Fund Raising Dir Br Deaf Assn 91-94; NSM Tring *St Alb* 92-94; Perm to Offic from 94; Fund Raising Dir R Nat Miss to Deep Sea Fishermen from 94. *The White House, 19 Lower Icknield Way, Marsworth, Tring HP23 4LN* Tel (01296) 661479

OGILVIE, Pamela. b 56. N Lon Poly CQSW82 Brunel Univ MA89. Qu Coll Birm 01. **d** 03 **p** 04. C Hill *Birm* from 03. *3 Dower Road, Sutton Coldfield B75 6UA* Tel 0121-308 0759 Mobile 07789-911576 E-mail pogilvie@fish.co.uk

OGLE, Ms Catherine. b 61. Leeds Univ BA82 MPhil85 MA91 Fitzw Coll Cam BA87. Westcott Ho Cam 85. **d** 88 **p** 94. C Middleton St Mary *Ripon* 88-91; Relig Progr Ed BBC Radio Leeds 91-95; NSM Leeds St Marg and All Hallows 91-95; P-in-c Woolley *Wakef* 95-01; P-in-c Huddersfield St Pet and All SS 01-03; V Huddersfield St Pet from 03. *59 Lightridge Road, Fixby, Huddersfield HD2 2HF* Tel (01484) 544558 Fax 427964 E-mail ogle@woolleyvic.freeserve.co.uk

OGLESBY, Ms Elizabeth Jane. b 73. Roehampton Inst BA95 Man Univ BPhil98. Westcott Ho Cam 00. **d** 03 **p** 04. C S Dulwich St Steph *S'wark* from 03. *161 Westwood Park, London SE23 3QL* Tel (020) 8766 7281 Mobile 07790-219725 E-mail curate@ststephensdulwich.org

OGLESBY, Canon Leslie Ellis. b 46. Univ Coll Ox BA69 MA73 City Univ MPhil73 Fitzw Coll Cam BA73 MA77. Ripon Coll Cuddesdon 77. **d** 78 **p** 79. C Stevenage St Mary Shephall *St Alb* 78-80; Dir St Alb Minl Tr Scheme 80-87; V Markyate Street *St Alb* 80-87; Dir CME 87-94; Hon Can St Alb 93-01; TR Hitchin 94-01; Adult Educn and Tr Officer *Ely* from 01; Hon Can Ely Cathl from 04. *8 Hertford Close, Ely CB6 3QS* Tel (01353) 666628 *or* 652713 Fax 652700 E-mail les.oglesby@ely.anglican.org

OGLEY, John. b 40. Oak Hill Th Coll 62. **d** 65 **p** 66. C Ardsley *Sheff* 65-68; C Carlton-in-the-Willows *S'well* 68-71; P-in-c Tollerton 71-79; V Skegby 79-93; R Carlton in Lindrick 93-01; P-in-c Langold 98-01; rtd 01; Perm to Offic *S'well* from 01. *Shalom, 39 Sparken Dale, Worksop S80 1BL* Tel (01909) 479462

O'GORMAN, Paul Anthony. b 46. Portsm Poly BSc79. Oak Hill Th Coll DipHE81. **d** 81 **p** 82. C Leyton St Mary w St Edw *Chelmsf* 81-83; C Rayleigh 83-84; CF 84-87; R Northiam *Chich* 87-93; V Hastings Em and St Mary in the Castle 93-99; rtd 99; NSM Southsea St Simon *Portsm* from 99. *281 Fawcett Road, Southsea PO4 0LB* Tel (023) 9283 9323

OGSTON, Russell James. b 71. La Sainte Union Coll BA94. Qu Coll Birm BD97. **d** 98 **p** 99. C Andover w Foxcott *Win* 98-01; C Southampton Maybush St Pet 01-03; Asst Chapl Homerton Univ Hosp NHS Trust Lon 03-05; Chapl from 05. *Homerton Hospital, Homerton Row, London E9 6SR* Tel (020) 8510 7385 E-mail russell.ogston@homerton.nhs.uk

OGUGUO, Barnabas Ahuna. b 47. Rome Univ BA70 BD74 Glas Univ MTh84 PhD90 Strathclyde Univ PGCE93. **d** 73 **p** 74. Nigeria 73-93; RE Teacher Lenzie Academy *Glas* 93-96; Bearsden Academy from 96; Hon C Lenzie from 95. *32 Carron Crescent, Lenzie, Glasgow G66 5PJ* Tel 0141-776 1321 *or* 942 2297 Fax 578 9802 E-mail boguguo@lycos.co.uk

O'HANLON, Canon William Douglas. b 11. Peterho Cam BA32 MA37. Clifton Th Coll 32. **d** 37 **p** 38. C Heatherlands St Jo *Sarum* 37-39; Chapl RAFVR 39-46; R Langton Matravers *Sarum* 46-51; V Calne 51-62; P-in-c Heddington 53-62; V Calne and Blackland 62-69; Can and Preb Sarum Cathl 61-82; V Coombe Bissett w Homington 69-72; R Studland 72-82; rtd 82; Perm to Offic *Sarum* from 82. *Crown Hill, 14 Bon Accord Road, Swanage BH19 2DT* Tel (01929) 425416

OHS, Lt Comdr Douglas Fredrick. b 49. Saskatchewan Univ BA74. Em Coll Saskatoon LTh75. **d** 74 **p** 75. C Bridgwater St Mary w Chilton Trinity *B & W* 75-77; Canada from 77. *Chaplain (P), 17 Wing Winnipeg, PO Box 17000 STN Forces, Winnipeg MB, Canada, R3J 3Y5* Tel (001) (204) 833 2500 ext 5417 Fax 833 2565

OJI, Erasmus Oluchukwu. b 43. Lon Univ BSc66 LRCP70 MRCS70 FRCS76. Oak Hill Th Coll 75. **d** 78 **p** 79. C Ealing Dean St Jo *Lon* 78-80; Nigeria 80-90; Asst Chapl Rotherham Distr Gen Hosp 90-91; Perm to Offic *Sheff* 92-04. *369 Fulwood Road, Sheffield S10 3BS* Tel and fax (07092) 147747 E-mail crasmus@doctors.org.uk

OKE, Mrs Elizabeth Mary. b 43. St Alb and Ox Min Course 96. **d** 99 **p** 00. NSM Woolhampton w Midgham and Beenham Valance *Ox* from 99; NSM Aldermaston w Wasing and Brimpton from 05. *Gladstone Cottage, 18 Windmill Road, Mortimer, Reading RG7 3RN* Tel 0118-933 2829

OKE, Michael John. b 42. Ox Min Course 89. **d** 92 **p** 93. NSM Stratfield Mortimer *Ox* 92-99; NSM Stratfield Mortimer and Mortimer W End etc 99-03; NSM Tilehurst St Geo from 03; NSM Tilehurst St Mary from 03. *Gladstone Cottage, 18 Windmill Road, Mortimer, Reading RG7 3RN* Tel 0118-933 2829

OKECHI, Patrick Otosio. b 62. Chas Univ Prague MTh94. **d** 95 **p** 98. Perm to Offic *Eur* 95-02; Asst P Angl Episc Congregation Czech Republic 02; V W Bromwich Gd Shep w St Jo *Lich* from 02. *The Vicarage, 4 Bromford Lane, West Bromwich B70 7HP* Tel 0121-525 5530 E-mail pokechi@btopenworld.com

✠**OKEKE, The Rt Revd Ken Sandy Edozie.** b 41. Nigeria Univ BSc67 Man Univ MA94. Igbaja Sem Nigeria. **d** 76 **p** 76 **c** 00. Nigeria 76-80 and 87-89; Chapl to Nigerians in UK and Irish Republic 80-87; Hon Can Kwara from 85; Hon Adn from 98; C Man Whitworth *Man* 89-95; Chapl Inst of Higher Learning Man 89-95; CMS 95-01; Perm to Offic *S'wark* 96-02; Bp on the Niger from 00. *PO Box 42, Onitsha, Nigeria* Tel (00234) (46) 411282 *or* 410337

OKELLO, Modicum. b 53. Nairobi Sch of Miss Dip Miss82 Haggaih Inst of Chr Leadership Dip Chr Leadership 86 Wycliffe Hall Ox 86 Trin Coll Bris BA90 St Paul's Coll Limuru DipTh78. **d** 78 **p** 79. Kenya 78-80; Uganda 80-86; NSM Goodmayes All SS *Chelmsf* 91-92; C Barking St Marg w St Patr 92-96; C Stratford St Jo and Ch Ch w Forest Gate St Jas 96-99; TV Forest Gate St Sav w W Ham St Matt from 99. *St Matthew's Vicarage, Dyson Road, Stratford E15 4JX* Tel (020) 8519 2524 E-mail modicumokello@okello8726modicum.freeserve.co.uk

✠**OKINE, The Rt Revd Robert Garshong Allotey.** b 37. Huron Coll Ontario BMin73 Hon DD82 Vanderbilt Univ (USA) MA75. Kelham Th Coll 58. **d** 64 **p** 65 **c** 81. C Sekondi St Andr 64-66; Chapl Adisadel Coll 66-68; R Agona-Swedru St Jas 68-69; R Bp Aglionby Memorial Par Tamale 69-71; Asst P Byron and London Canada 71-73; Asst P Nashville H Trin USA 73-75; Asst P Cape Coast Ch Ch 75-81; Hd Master Ch K Academy and Prin St Nic Th Coll 76-81; Adn Koforidua and R Koforidua St Pet 81; Hon Can Accra 79-81; Bp Koforidua 81-02; Abp W Africa 93-02; rtd 02. *Address temp unknown* E-mail robokine@yahoo.com

OKWUOSA, Canon Amaechi Chukwudube. b 64. Anambra State Univ LLB89 Nigerian Law Sch Lagos BL90. Faith Th Sem 94. **d** 96 **p** 97. Nigeria 96-98; Hon Can Nnewi from 01; Perm to Offic *Lon* 98-01; NSM Gt Ilford St Jo *Chelmsf* from 01. *97 Beehive Lane, Ilford IG1 3RN* Tel (020) 8554 4540 E-mail dubem@okwuosa.com

OLADUJI, Christopher Temitayo. b 57. Awosika Th Coll Nigeria 84. **d** 87 **p** 88. Nigeria 87-89; C Ilutitun Ebenezer 87; Asst P Ondo Cathl 88; NSM W Ham *Chelmsf* 89-93; NSM Peckham St Jo w St Andr *S'wark* 97-98; NSM E Ham St Geo *Chelmsf* 99-01; NSM Hackney Wick St Mary of Eton w St Aug *Lon* 02-04; NSM Smithfield St Bart Gt from 04. *Church House, Cloth Fair, London EC1A 7JQ* Tel (020) 7606 1575 Mobile 07985-465401 E-mail coladuji@yahoo.com

OLANCZUK, Jonathan Paul Tadeusz. b 49. EAMTC 94. **d** 96 **p** 97. C Haverhill w Withersfield *St E* 96-00; P-in-c Badingham w Bruisyard, Cransford and Dennington 00-04; P-in-c Rendham w Sweffling 00-04; R Badingham w Bruisyard, Cransford etc from 04. *The Rectory, 5 Orchard Rise, Badingham, Woodbridge IP13 8LN* Tel and fax (01728) 638823 Mobile 07766-953558 *or* 07944-186526 E-mail olanczuk@suffolkonline.net *or* jolanczuk@aol.com

OLD, Arthur Anthony George (Tony). b 36. Clifton Th Coll 69. **d** 71 **p** 72. C Clitheroe St Jas *Blackb* 71-73; C Bispham 73-77; V Haslingden St Jo Stonefold 77-81; TV Lowestoft and Kirkley *Nor* 81-83; Chapl to the Deaf *Cant* 83-01; P-in-c Hernhill 83-85; C Preston next Faversham, Goodnestone and Graveney 85-01; rtd 01; Perm to Offic *Cant* from 01. *62 Knaves Acre, Headcorn, Ashford TN27 9TJ* Tel (01227) 749196

OLDFIELD, Canon Roger Fielden. b 45. Qu Coll Cam BA67 MA71 City of Lon Poly DMS69 Lon Univ BD75. Trin Coll Bris 75. **d** 75 **p** 76. C Halliwell St Pet *Man* 75-80 and from 03; V 80-03; AD Bolton 93-02; Hon Can Man Cathl from 00. *505 Church Road, Bolton BL1 5RE* Tel (01204) 849412 E-mail rogerandruth@3strands.net

OLDHAM, Dale Raymond. b 40. NZ Coll of Pharmacy MPS63 Cant Univ (NZ) MA87. Ridley Hall Cam 64. **d** 67 **p** 68. C Woking St Mary *Guildf* 67-70; New Zealand 71-73 and from 81; CMS Tanzania 74-81. *PO Box 27016, Christchurch 8030, New Zealand* Tel (0064) (3) 385 6282 *or* 385 2027 Fax 385 6283 E-mail oldham@clear.net.nz

OLDNALL, Frederick Herbert. b 16. Ripon Hall Ox 56. **d** 57 **p** 58. C Radford *Cov* 57-59; C Stratford-on-Avon 59-62; V Rosliston w Coton in the Elms *Derby* 62-83; rtd 83; Perm to Offic *Cov* from 93. *4 Margetts Close, Kenilworth CV8 1EN* Tel (01926) 852417

OLDROYD, Preb Colin Mitchell. b 30. Down Coll Cam BA54 MA60. Wells Th Coll 60. **d** 61 **p** 62. C Elton All SS *Man* 61-63; C Ex St Dav *Ex* 63-66; P-in-c Neen Sollars w Milson *Heref* 66-78; P-in-c Coreley and Doddington 66-78; R Cleobury Mortimer w Hopton Wafers 66-78; RD Ludlow 75-78; P-in-c Eastnor 78-81; R Ledbury 78-81; RD Ledbury 78-81; Chapl Ledbury Cottage Hosp Heref 79-95; R Ledbury w Eastnor *Heref* 81-95; Preb Heref Cathl 84-95; P-in-c Lt Marcle 85-95; rtd 95; Perm to Offic *Heref* from 96. *2 Hampton Manor Close, Hereford HR1 1TG* Tel (01432) 340569

OLDROYD, David Christopher Leslie. b 42. FRICS. S Dios Minl Tr Scheme. **d** 85 **p** 86. NSM Four Marks *Win* 85-90; rtd 90. *Hill House, Spring Lane, Farnham GU9 0JD* Tel (01252) 737586

OLDROYD, Mrs Sheila Margaret. b 40. Liv Univ BSc63. St Steph Ho Ox 98. **d** 99 **p** 00. NSM Cotgrave *S'well* 99-03; NSM Keyworth and Stanton-on-the-Wolds and Bunny etc from 03. *8 Taunton Road, West Bridgford, Nottingham NG2 6EW* Tel 0115-923 5121 Mobile 07974-785242 E-mail margaretoldroyd@aol.com

OLDROYD, Trevor. b 33. Hatf Coll Dur BA55 Lon Univ BD60. Wycliffe Hall Ox 60. **d** 61 **p** 62. C Barnes St Mary *S'wark* 61-65; C Wimbledon 65-68; W Germany 68-73; Chapl Dudley Sch 73-80; Asst Chapl Wellington Coll Berks 80-82; P-in-c Rendcomb *Glouc* 82-86; Chapl Rendcomb Coll 82-86; Chapl Wrekin Coll Telford 86-90; V Deptford St Jo w H Trin *S'wark* 91-94; rtd 94; Perm to Offic *Sarum* 94-00 and *Guildf* from 02. *4 The Larches, Woking GU21 4RE* Tel (01483) 720398

OLHAUSEN, William Paul. b 67. Wycliffe Hall Ox BA97. **d** 98 **p** 99. C Reading Greyfriars *Ox* 98-01; Sub Chapl HM YOI Reading 98-01; C Cambridge H Trin *Ely* 01-04; I Carrigrohane Union *C, C & R* from 04. *The Rectory, Church Hill, Carrigrohane, Cork, Irish Republic* Tel (00353) (21) 487 1106 E-mail wpo@oceanfree.net

OLIVE, Dan. b 29. ARIBA54. Sarum & Wells Th Coll 79. **d** 82 **p** 83. NSM Wells St Cuth w Wookey Hole *B & W* 82-85; C Yatton Moor 86-88; R Mells w Buckland Dinham, Elm, Whatley etc 88-97; RD Frome 93-97; rtd 97; Perm to Offic *B & W* from 97. *Roseleigh, Woodcombe, Minehead TA24 8SA* Tel (01643) 702218

OLIVER, Bernard John. b 31. CEng65 MIMechE. S'wark Ord Course 75. **d** 78 **p** 79. NSM Chipping Ongar *Chelmsf* 78-81; C Waltham Abbey 81-85; C High Ongar w Norton Mandeville 85-87; C Somerton w Compton Dundon, the Charltons etc *B & W* 87-88; rtd 96; Perm to Offic *Sarum* from 01. *1 Orchard Way, Mosterton, Beaminster DT8 3LT* Tel (01308) 868037

OLIVER, Canon Beverley Stephen. b 29. Lich Th Coll 58. **d** 60 **p** 61. S Africa 61-96; C Goodwood 61; R Paarl H Trin 61-69; R Camps Bay 69-78; R Cape Town St Paul 74-78; R Milnerton 78-80; R Newlands and Adn Cape Town 80-96; Warden, Lect and Preacher Newland Almshouses 96-03. *Jubilee Cottage, Staunton, Coleford GL16 8NX* Tel (01594) 838450

OLIVER, Canon David Ryland. b 34. Univ of Wales (Lamp) BA56 St Cath Coll Ox BA58 MA62. Wycliffe Hall Ox 56. **d** 58 **p** 59. C Carmarthen St Pet *St D* 58-61; C Llangyfelach and Morriston *S & B* 61-63; R Aberedw w Llandeilo Graban etc 63-66; R Llanbadarn Fawr, Llandegley and Llanfihangel etc 66-67; Lic to Offic *Llan* 68-70; *Ban* 70-73; V Nefyn w Pistyll w Tudweiliog w Llandudwen etc 73-74; V Abercraf and Callwen *S & B* 74-77; V Llangyfelach 77-79; R Llanllwchaearn and Llanina *St D* 79-83; V Cwmaman 83-94; Can St D Cathl from 90; RD Dyffryn Aman 93-94; V Cynwyl Gaeo w Llansawel and Talley 94-99; rtd 99. *Maes y Gelynen, 40 Heol Bryngwili, Cross Hands, Llanelli SA14 6LR*

OLIVER, Gordon. *See* OLIVER, Canon Thomas Gordon

OLIVER, Graham Frank. b 42. St Barn Coll Adelaide. **d** 68 **p** 69. Australia 68-86; C Ealing Ch the Sav *Lon* 86-93; Perm to Offic 94-97 and from 00; Asst Chapl Ypres *Eur* 97-99; P-in-c 99-00. *Flat 1, 4 High Street, London NW10 4LY* Tel (020) 8963 0477

OLIVER, John Andrew George. b 28. OBE83. St Jo Coll Dur BA53 DipTh55. **d** 55 **p** 56. C Bermondsey St Mary w St Olave and St Jo *S'wark* 55-58; C Dulwich St Barn 58-61; Chapl RN 61-83; QHC 79-83; R Guisborough *York* 83-89; Tutor and Chapl Whittington Coll Felbridge 89-93; rtd 93; Perm to Offic *Carl* from 93. *Allandale, Thacka Lane, Penrith CA11 9HX* Tel (01768) 892096

OLIVER, The Ven John Graham Wyand. b 47. Ridley Hall Cam 76. **d** 78 **p** 79. C Shortlands *Roch* 78-81; C Hammersmith St Paul *Lon* 81-85; Zambia from 85; Adn S Zambia from 89. *USPG, Partnership House, 157 Waterloo Road, London SE1 8XA* Tel (020) 7928 8681 Fax 7928 2371

✠**OLIVER, The Rt Revd John Keith.** b 35. G&C Coll Cam BA59 MA63 MLitt65. Westcott Ho Cam 59. **d** 64 **p** 65 **c** 90. C Hilborough w Bodney *Nor* 64-68; Chapl Eton Coll 68-72; R S Molton w Nymet St George *Ex* 73-75; P-in-c Filleigh w E Buckland 73-75; P-in-c Warkleigh w Satterleigh and Chittlehamholt 73-75; P-in-c High Bray w Charles 73-75; TR S Molton, Nymet St George, High Bray etc 75-82; P-in-c N Molton w Twitchen 77-79; RD S Molton 74-80; TR Cen Ex 82-85; Adn Sherborne *Sarum* 85-90; P-in-c W Stafford w Frome Billet 85-90; Can Res Sarum Cathl 85-90; Bp Heref 90-03; rtd 03; Hon Asst Bp S & B from 04. *The Old Vicarage, Glascwm, Llandrindod Wells LD1 5SE* Tel and fax (01982) 570771

OLIVER, John Kenneth. b 47. Brunel Univ MA92 ALBC70. EAMTC 98. **d** 00 **p** 01. C E Ham St Paul *Chelmsf* 00-03; V Stratford New Town St Paul 03-05; TV Totton *Win* from 05. *Calmore Vicarage, Cooks Lane, Calmore, Southampton SO40 2RU* Tel (023) 8081 2702 E-mail j.k.oliver@tesco.net

OLIVER, The Ven John Michael. b 39. Univ of Wales (Lamp) BA62. Ripon Hall Ox 62. **d** 64 **p** 65. C High Harrogate St Pet *Ripon* 64-67; C Bramley 67-72; V Low Harrogate St Mary 72-78; V Beeston 78-92; RD Armley 86-92; Hon Can Ripon Cathl from 87; Adn Leeds from 92. *Archdeacon's Lodge, 3 West Park Grove, Leeds LS8 2HQ* Tel and fax 0113-269 0594 E-mail archdeacon.leeds@riponleeds.anglican.org

OLIVER, The Ven John Rodney. b 31. Melbourne Univ BA53 Lon Univ MTh73. Bps' Coll Cheshunt 54 ACT ThSchol68. **d** 56 **p** 57. C Much Hadham *St Alb* 56-57; Australia 58-69; Chapl Ballarat GS 58-69; C Thorley *St Alb* 70-73; C Bishop's Stortford H Trin 70-73; Australia from 73; I Aberfeldie 74-77; Chapl Trin Coll Melbourne 77-81; I Dandenong 81-91; Adn Box Hill 87-00; I East Kew St Paul 91-00; rtd 00. *27 Asquith Street, Box Hill South, Vic, Australia 3128* Tel (0061) (3) 9888 7517 Fax 9888 7598 E-mail rodley@smartchat.net.au

OLIVER, Mrs Josephine May. b 48. Cranmer Hall Dur. **d** 01 **p** 02. C Buckrose Carrs *York* 01-04; P-in-c Bubwith w Skipwith from 04. *The Vicarage, The Green, North Duffield, Selby YO8 5RR* Tel (01757) 288613 Mobile 07885-448331 E-mail jo@j-oliver.freeserve.co.uk

OLIVER, Mrs Judith Anne. b 54. WMMTC. **d** 96 **p** 97. C Old Swinford Stourbridge *Worc* 96-99; C Pensnett 99-01; Asst to Suff Bp Dudley 99-01; P-in-c Dudley Wood from 01. *The Vicarage, 57 Lantern Road, Dudley DY2 0DL* Tel (01384) 832164 Mobile 07885-088301 E-mail revjao@aol.com

OLIVER, Canon Paul Robert. b 41. Lon Univ DipTh65. Tyndale Hall Bris 63. **d** 66 **p** 67. C Virginia Water *Guildf* 66-70; Scripture Union (E Region) 70-74; TV Thetford *Nor* 75-83; V Earlham St Anne 83-98; RD Nor S 94-98; Hon Can Nor Cathl 96-98; rtd 98; Perm to Offic *Nor* from 98. *Cherry Tree Cottage, 91 High Road, Needham, Harleston IP20 9LF* Tel (01379) 852892

OLIVER, Canon Philip Maule. b 38. Birm Univ LLB59. Wells Th Coll 62. **d** 64 **p** 65. C Chesterton *Lich* 64-67; C Tettenhall Wood 67-71; V Milton 71-78; V Ixworth and Bardwell *St E* 78-92; P-in-c Honington w Sapiston and Troston 81-92; TR Blackbourne from 92; RD Ixworth 85-94; Hon Can St E Cathl from 00. *The Vicarage, Ixworth, Bury St Edmunds IP31 2HE* Tel (01359) 230311

OLIVER, Rodney. *See* OLIVER, The Ven John Rodney

OLIVER, Ryland. *See* OLIVER, Canon David Ryland

OLIVER, Simon Andrew. b 71. Mansf Coll Ox BA93 MA98 Peterho Cam BA97 MA00 PhD03. Westcott Ho Cam 95. **d** 98 **p** 99. NSM Teversham *Ely* 98-01; NSM Cherry Hinton St Andr 98-01; Chapl Hertf Coll Ox 01-05; Lect Univ of Wales (Lamp) *St D* from 05. *Department of Theology, University of Wales Lampeter, College Street, Lampeter SA48 7ED* Tel (01570) 424959 E-mail s.oliver@lamp.ac.uk

✠**OLIVER, The Rt Revd Stephen John.** b 48. AKC69. St Aug Coll Cant 70. **d** 71 **p** 72 **c** 03. C Clifton w Glapton *S'well* 71-75; P-in-c Newark Ch Ch 75-79; R Plumtree 79-85; Sen Producer BBC Relig Broadcasting Dept Lon 85-87; Chief Producer 87-91; TR Leeds City *Ripon* 91-97; Can Res and Prec St Paul's Cathl *Lon* 97-03; Area Bp Stepney from 03. *63 Coborn Road, London E3 2DB* Tel (020) 8981 2323 Fax 8981 8015 E-mail bishop.stepney@london.anglican.org

OLIVER, Mrs Susan Jacqueline. b 54. Univ Coll Lon LLB78 Birm Poly CQSW86. Qu Coll Birm 03. **d** 05. C Fladbury w Wyre Piddle and Moor etc *Worc* from 05. *19 Gibbs Close, Lower Moor, Pershore WR10 2NQ* Tel (01386) 860695 Mobile 07740-460313 E-mail suejoliver@tiscali.co.uk

OLIVER, Suzanne Marie. *See* PATTLE, Mrs Suzanne Marie

OLIVER, Canon Thomas Gordon. b 48. Nottm Univ BTh72 LTh74 DipAdEd80. St Jo Coll Nottm 68 ALCD72. **d** 72 **p** 73. C Thorpe Edge *Bradf* 72-76; C Woodthorpe *S'well* 76-80; V Huthwaite 80-85; Dir Past Studies St Jo Coll Nottm 85-94; Dir of Min and Tr *Roch* from 94; Hon Can Roch Cathl from 95. *18 King's Avenue, Rochester ME1 3DS* Tel (01634) 841232 *or* 830333 Fax 829463 E-mail gordon.oliver@rochdiooff.co.uk

OLIVER, Ms Wendy Louise. b 54. Aston Tr Scheme 93 Oak Hill Th Coll DipHE94. **d** 96 **p** 97. C Walmsley *Man* 96-99; P-in-c Goodshaw and Crawshawbooth from 99; AD Rossendale from 04. *Goodshaw Vicarage, Goodshawfold Road, Rossendale BB4 8QN* Tel and fax (01706) 213969 E-mail wendyloliver@hotmail.com

OLIVEY, Hugh Charles Tony. b 35. St Mich Coll Llan 77. **d** 79 **p** 80. C St Winnow *Truro* 79-81; C Lanhydrock 81-82; C Lostwithiel 81-82; C Lanivet 81-82; P-in-c 82-83; TV Bodmin w Lanhydrock and Lanivet 84-89; P-in-c St Neot 89-90; P-in-c Warleggan 89-90; R St Neot and Warleggan 90-99; P-in-c Cardynham 97-99; rtd 99; Perm to Offic *Truro* from 99; Hon

Chapl Duchy Hosp Truro from 04. *The Bungalow, 2 Lower Hugus Road, Threemilestone, Truro TR3 6BD* Tel (01872) 223103

OLIVIER, Bertrand Maurice Daniel. b 62. BA84. S'wark Ord Course 93. **d** 96 **p** 97. C Walworth St Jo *S'wark* 96-00; V Southfields St Barn 00-05; RD Wandsworth 03-05; V All Hallows by the Tower etc *Lon* from 05. *The Residence, 43 Trinity Square, London EC3N 4DJ* Tel (020) 7488 4772 Mobile 07958-411529 E-mail bertrand@allhallowsbythetower.org.uk *or* bob@bob.org.uk

OLLIER, Mrs Jane Sarah. b 60. Leeds Univ BA81. SW Minl Tr Course 02. **d** 05. NSM Seaton and Beer *Ex* from 05. *7 Celandine Close, Seaton EX12 2XA* Tel (01297) 24213

OLLIER, Canon Timothy John Douglas. b 44. Trin Hall Cam BA66 MA69. Cuddesdon Coll 66. **d** 68 **p** 69. C Silksworth *Dur* 68-71; C St Marylebone w H Trin *Lon* 71-74; C Winlaton *Dur* 74-77; V Bishopton w Gt Stainton 77-88; R Redmarshall 77-88; P-in-c Grindon and Stillington 83-88; V Gainford 88-00; R Winston 88-00; AD Barnard Castle 88-00; P-in-c Egglescliffe 00-03; R from 03; AD Stockton from 01; Hon Can Dur Cathl from 94. *The Rectory, 10 Butts Lane, Egglescliffe, Stockton-on-Tees TS16 9BT* Tel (01642) 780185 Fax 791886 E-mail timollier@onyxnet.co.uk

OLLIFF, Roland. b 61. Coll of Resurr Mirfield CPS95. **d** 95 **p** 96. C Bickleigh and Shaugh Prior *Ex* 95-98; CF from 98. *c/o MOD Chaplains (Army)* Tel (01980) 615804 Fax 615800 E-mail olliff@btinternet.com

OLLIVE, Mrs Patricia Ann. b 55. St Luke's Coll Ex BA91. Ripon Coll Cuddesdon BTh05. **d** 05. C Backwell w Chelvey and Brockley *B & W* from 05. *30 Rodney Road, Backwell, Bristol BS48 3HB* Tel (01275) 463510 Mobile 07840-387121 E-mail trishollive@hotmail.com

OLNEY, Dorian Frederick (Fred). b 50. Kingston Poly BA71 MIL88 MIPD88 Anglia Poly Univ MA03. All Nations Chr Coll 75 Ridley Hall Cam CTM98. **d** 98 **p** 99. C Glenfield *Leic* 98-02; Chapl ATC 99-01; TV Newark *S'well* from 02. *Christ Church Vicarage, Boundary Road, Newark NG24 4AJ* Tel (01636) 704969 E-mail fred.olney@webleicester.co.uk

O'LOUGHLIN, Mrs Kathryn. b 60. Man Univ BSc81. STETS 96. **d** 99 **p** 00. NSM Basing *Win* 99-03; Perm to Offic from 03. *45 Pyotts Copse, Old Basing, Basingstoke RG24 8WE* Tel (01256) 354248 *or* 476323

OLSEN, Arthur Barry. b 37. Univ of NZ BA61 Melbourne Coll of Div BD73. ACT ThL64. **d** 64 **p** 64. New Zealand 64-81; C Nelson All SS 64-67; V Ahuara 67-69; V Motupiko 69-70; V Amuri 70-73; Maori Miss and C Dunedin St Matt 73-76; V Brooklyn 77-81; C Hersham *Guildf* 81-84; P-in-c Botleys and Lyne 84-95; V 95-03; P-in-c Long Cross 84-95; V 95-03; Chapl NW Surrey Mental Health NHS Trust 85-03; rtd 03; Hon C Rotherfield Peppard and Kidmore End etc *Ox* from 03. *2 Priory Copse, Peppard Common, Henley-on-Thames RG9 5LH* Tel 0118-924 2812 E-mail abandmolsen@tinyworld.co.uk

OLSSON, Elinor. b 72. Gothenburg Univ MDiv98. Lund Inst Past Th 98. **p** 98. P Harlanda Sweden 98-04; Chapl Swedish Seamen's Ch from 04; Lic to Offic *S'wark* from 05. *120 Lower Road, London SE16 2UB* Tel (020) 7252 2139 Mobile 07887-751452 E-mail prast@swedish-church.org.uk

OLSWORTH-PETER, Edward James. b 77. UWE BA99. Wycliffe Hall Ox BTh04. **d** 04 **p** 05. C Guildf Ch Ch w St Martha-on-the-Hill *Guildf* from 04. *2 Ivor Close, Guildford GU1 2ET* Tel (01483) 546577 E-mail ed_olsworth@hotmail.com

OLUKANMI, Miss Stella Grace Oluwafunmilayo Olanrewaju. b 57. St Jo Coll Nottm BTh95 LTh92. **d** 96 **p** 97. C Gt Ilford St Jo *Chelmsf* 96-01; V Barkingside St Cedd from 01. *The Vicarage, 10 Marston Road, Ilford IG5 0LY* Tel (020) 8551 3406 E-mail olukanmi@fish.co.uk

OLUMIDE, The Ven Oluseye Abiola Abisogun Okikiade ('Seye). b 42. Westhill Coll Birm CLCE66 Bradf Univ BA89 MSc92. Clifton Th Coll 68. **d** 71 **p** 72. C Halliwell St Pet *Man* 71-72; C Salford St Phil w St Steph 72; P-in-c Wood Green St Mich *Lon* 73; C Stanmer w Falmer and Moulsecoomb *Chich* 73-76; C Hulme Ascension *Man* 76-77; Chapl Asst N Man Gen Hosp 77-80; Chapl St Bernard's and Ealing Hosps 80-86; Chapl Bradf R Infirmary 86-91; Chapl Lynfield Mt Hosp Bradf 86-91; Chapl St Luke's Hosp Bradf 86-91; Chapl Bradf Hosps NHS Trust 91-96; Chapl Co-ord Parkside Community NHS Trust Lon 96-01; rtd 01; Can Lagos Cathl from 98; Adn in Egba from 00. *11 Walters Road, Cwmllynfell, Swansea SA9 2FH* Tel 07768-753874 (mobile)

O'MALLEY, Canon Brian Denis Brendan. b 40. Birm Univ LicTh77 Gwent Coll of HE Dip Counselling 94 Univ of Wales (Lamp) MA97 MHCIMA60. Nunraw Abbey (RC) 60 Oscott Coll (RC) 74 Coll of Resurr Mirfield 82. **d** 77 **p** 83. In RC Ch 77-81; Warden St Greg Retreat Rhandirmwyn *St D* 80-83; Lic to Offic 82-83; Chapl and Min Can St D Cathl 83-85; V Wiston w Ambleston, St Dogwells, Walton E etc 85-89; V Wiston w Clarbeston and Walton E 89; R Walton W w Talbenny and Haroldston W 89-98; Chapl Pembrokeshire Coll of FE 93-98; Chapl St D Coll Lamp from 98; Can St D Cathl *St D* from 01. *Fairfield, North Road, Lampeter SA48 7HZ* Tel (01570) 422148 E-mail b.o.malley@lamp.ac.uk

OMAN, Brian Malcolm. b 14. Qu Coll Cam BA36 MA46. Chich Th Coll 36. **d** 37 **p** 38. C Gorton St Mary and St Thos *Man* 37-40; OGS from 39; Perm to Offic *Ox* 40-42; Chapl St Mary's Abbey W Malling 42-46; C Tunbridge Wells St Barn *Roch* 46-55; V Cardiff St Mary *Llan* 55-62; R Greenford H Cross *Lon* 62-74; V Kings Sutton *Pet* 74-88; rtd 88; Perm to Offic *Pet* from 88. *The Old Post Office, Church Street, Sulgrave, Banbury OX17 2RP* Tel (01295) 768317

O'MEARA, Colette Margaret Mary. *See* THORNBOROUGH, Ms Colette Margaret Mary

OMOLE, Oluremi Richard. b 63. **d** 05. NSM Dur N *Dur* from 05. *7 Frensham Way, Meadowfield, Durham DH7 8UR* Tel 0191-378 9756

OMOYAJOWO, Justus Akinwale. b 65. Obafemi Awolowo Univ BA87 Ibadan Univ Nigeria MA90 Bayreuth Univ PhD99. Vining Coll of Th 90. **d** 92 **p** 93. Nigeria 92-94; C Akure St Andr 92; Chapl Ondo-State Pris 93; Chapl Ondo-State Univ 94; Asst Lect Bayreuth Univ Germany 95-97; Perm to Offic *S'wark* 98-99 and 00-01; C Hatcham St Jas 99-00; Chapl Goldsmiths' Coll Lon 99-00; P-in-c Sutton New Town St Barn 01-03; P-in-c Yardley St Edburgha *Birm* from 03. *The Vicarage, 541 Church Road, Yardley, Birmingham B33 8PG* Tel 0121-784 6556 E-mail justus-omoyajowo1@tiscali.co.uk

O'NEILL, Mrs Caroline Lois. b 55. CQSW DASS. Trin Coll Bris BA00. **d** 00 **p** 01. C Bath St Sav w Swainswick and Woolley *B & W* 00-03; C Charlcombe w Bath St Steph from 03. *40 Fairfield Avenue, Bath BA1 6NH* Tel (01225) 311796

O'NEILL, Christopher John. b 53. Worc Coll Ox BA75 MA80 Surrey Univ PhD03 CertEd91 ALAM LGSM Dip Th & Min 91 Cert Counselling 91 DCH98. Ripon Coll Cuddesdon 77. **d** 78 **p** 79. Asst Chapl Rugby Sch 78-80; Chapl Charterhouse Sch Godalming 81-98; Hd of Counselling from 98. *14 Chapelfields, Charterhouse Road, Godalming GU7 2BF* Tel (01483) 414437 E-mail cbenedictoneill@hotmail.com

O'NEILL, Edward Daniel. b 42. Man Univ BA62 Bradf Univ MSc76. N Ord Course 89. **d** 92 **p** 93. NSM Prenton *Ches* 92-94; NSM Newton 94-95; Perm to Offic *Liv* 97-98; NSM W Derby Gd Shep 98-99; C 99-02; V Stockbridge Village from 02. *1 The Cross, Stanley Road, Huyton, Liverpool L36 9XL* Tel 0151-449 3800 E-mail eddieoneill@blueyonder.co.uk

O'NEILL, Canon Gary. b 57. K Coll Lon BD79 AKC79. Westcott Ho Cam 80. **d** 81 **p** 82. C Oldham *Man* 81-84; C Birch w Fallowfield 84-87; R Moston St Chad 87-97; Can Res Birm Cathl *Birm* from 97. *119 Selly Park Road, Birmingham B29 7HY* Tel 0121-472 0146 *or* 262 1843 Fax 212 0868 E-mail garyoneill@fish.co.uk

O'NEILL, Irene. *See* CARTER, Mrs Irene

ONIONS, Mrs Angela Ann. b 33. STETS 01. **d** 02. NSM Bradford-on-Avon *Sarum* from 02. *27 Berryfield Road, Bradford-on-Avon BA15 1SX* Tel (01225) 309001 Mobile 07719-726461

ONIONS, Martin Giles. b 63. TC Bp Otter Coll Chich BA99 Univ Coll Chich MA02. Chich Th Coll 85. **d** 88 **p** 89. C Eastbourne St Mary *Chich* 88-91; C-in-c The Hydneye CD 91-96; V The Hydneye 96-97; V Findon Valley 97-01; V Willingdon from 01. *The Vicarage, 35A Church Street, Willingdon, Eastbourne BN20 9HR* Tel (01323) 502079 Fax as telephone E-mail martin.onions@btinternet.com

ONSLOW, Sister Denzil Octavia. b 19. CertRK58. **dss** 61 **d** 87 **p** 94. CSA from 56; Novice Guardian 68-73 and 90-94; R Foundn of St Kath in Ratcliffe 73-79; Notting Hill St Jo and St Pet *Lon* 80-87; Hon Par Dn 87-94; Hon C 94-01; Perm to Offic from 01. *8/9 Verona Court, London W4 2JD* Tel (020) 8987 2799

ONUNWA, The Ven Udobata Rufus. b 47. Univ of Nigeria BA78 MA81 PhD85. Trin Coll Umuahia 72. **d** 74 **p** 75. C Owo Nigeria 74-95; Hon Adn Calabar from 95; Tutor Crowther Hall CMS Tr Coll Selly Oak 96-03; NW Regional Co-ord Crosslinks 03-05; P-in-c Grange St Andr *Ches* from 05. *The Vicarage, 37 Lime Grove, Runcorn WA7 5JZ* Tel (01928) 574411

OOSTERHOF, Ms Liesbeth. b 61. Ripon Coll Cuddesdon 02. **d** 04 **p** 05. C E Bergholt and Brantham *St E* from 04. *2 Fern Cottages, East End, East Bergholt, Colchester CO7 6XE* Tel (01206) 393520

OOSTRA, Catharina Henriët. b 60. Uppsala Univ MDiv92. **p** 92. Sweden 92-04; C Linköping Cathl 92-93; V Simrishamn 93-96; V Lund Cathl 96-99; V Stora Köpinge 99-01; V Brösarp - Tranås 01-04; C Upton cum Chalvey *Ox* from 04. *16 Victoria Street, Slough SL1 1PR* Tel (01753) 531267

OPPERMAN, Graham William. b 40. Th Ext Educn Coll 98. **d** 00 **p** 03. C Linden St Thos S Africa 00-04; NSM Aberdour *St And* 04; NSM Burntisland 04; NSM Inverkeithing 04; TV Jarrow *Dur* from 05. *St John the Baptist House, Iona Road, Jarrow NE32 4HY* Tel 0191-489 2043 Mobile 07792-451622 E-mail graham.opperman@btinternet.com

ORAM, Canon Geoffrey William James. b 14. Em Coll Cam BA37 MA40. Ridley Hall Cam 36. **d** 38 **p** 39. C Tooting

Graveney St Nic *S'wark* 38-40; C Rugby St Andr *Cov* 40-41; V Ipswich St Thos *St E* 41-49; R E Bergholt 49-64; Bp's Chapl 54-67; Hon Can St E Cathl 59-80; RD Samford 59-64; V Aldeburgh w Hazlewood 64-80; rtd 80; Perm to Offic *St E* 80-81 and from 86; P-in-c Ipswich St Mich 81-86. *Pantiles, Spring Meadow, Playford, Ipswich IP6 9ED* Tel (01473) 622566

ORAM, John Ernest Donald. b 34. Open Univ BA74. Tyndale Hall Bris. **d** 61 **p** 62. C Cheetham Hill *Man* 61-64; C Gt Baddow *Chelmsf* 64-67; V Blackb St Barn *Blackb* 67-72; Bp's Chapl for Soc Resp *Sheff* 72-86; Chapl Psychotherapist 79-86; Perm to Offic from 86; rtd 99. *12 Montgomery Road, Sheffield S7 1LQ* Tel 0114-221 4982

ORAM, Roland Martin David. b 45. Trin Coll Cam BA68 ARCM70. Cranmer Hall Dur DipTh78. **d** 78 **p** 79. C Aspley *S'well* 78-81; Chapl Alleyn's Sch Dulwich 81-88; Chapl Versailles w Grandchamp and Chevry *Eur* 88-92; Chapl Denstone Coll Uttoxeter 92-01; Assoc V Hanford *Lich* from 01; Assoc V Trentham from 02. *Hanford Vicarage, 76 Church Lane, Stoke-on-Trent ST4 4QD* Tel (01782) 657848

ORAM, Stephen John. b 58. **d** 84 **p** 85. C Kidderminster St Jo *Worc* 84-88; Chapl RAF 88-92; P-in-c Brislington St Anne *Bris* 92-97; V Cricklade w Latton 97-04; Co-ord Chapl N Bris NHS Trust from 04. *North Bristol NHS Trust, Frenchay Park Road, Bristol BS16 1LE* Tel 0117-970 1212
E-mail stephen.oram@ntlworld.com

ORAM, Vincent Charles. b 55. Rhodes Univ BA78 Fort Hare Univ BTh84. St Paul's Coll Grahamstown. **d** 81 **p** 82. S Africa 81-99; C King Williams Town H Trin 81-85; R Barkly East St Steph 85-90; Can Grahamstown Cathl 96; Adn East London South 97-99; P-in-c Shenley *St Alb* 00-05; TV Aldenham, Radlett and Shenley from 05. *The Rectory, 63 London Road, Shenley, Radlett WD7 9BW* Tel (01923) 855383
E-mail vincent.oram@ntlworld.com

O'RAW, Neal John. **d** 02 **p** 03. C Killala w Dunfeeny, Crossmolina, Kilmoremoy etc *T, K & A* 02-05; Bp's C from 05. *The Rectory, Ballina Road, Crossmolina, Co Mayo, Irish Republic* Tel (00353) (96) 31384 E-mail revdoraw@hotmail.com

ORCHARD, Canon George Richard. b 41. Ex Coll Ox BA62 BA64 MA66. Ripon Hall Ox 62. **d** 65 **p** 66. C Greenhill St Pet *Derby* 65-70; Member Ecum Team Min Sinfin Moor 70-78; V Sinfin Moor 76-78; TR Dronfield 78-86; Can Res Derby Cathl 86-92; Hon Can Derby Cathl from 92; P-in-c Baslow 92-93; P-in-c Curbar and Stoney Middleton 92-93; V Baslow w Curbar and Stoney Middleton from 93. *The Vicarage, Curbar Lane, Calver, Hope Valley S32 3YF* Tel (01433) 630387 Fax as telephone

ORCHARD, Harry Frank. b 23. Roch Th Coll. **d** 63 **p** 64. C Sturminster Newton *Sarum* 63-65; Argentina 65-67; V Preston *Sarum* 67-71; R Teffont Evias and Teffont Magna 71-73; V Dinton 71-73; C Fovant w Compton Chamberlayne etc 76-78; Lic to Offic 78-02; RD Chalke 80-82; rtd 88. *49 Highfields, Ashby Meadows, Ashby Road, Spilsby PE23 5DN* Tel (01790) 753044

ORCHARD, Helen Claire. b 65. Sheff Univ BA87 PhD96 Em Coll Cam MPhil02. Westcott Ho Cam 01. **d** 03 **p** 04. C Merrow *Guildf* from 03. *5 Gilliat Drive, Guildford GU4 7EN* Tel (01483) 506294 Mobile 07879-622920
E-mail hco@hcorchard.freeserve.co.uk

ORCHARD, Nigel John. b 56. CertEd78. St Steph Ho Ox 82. **d** 85 **p** 86. C Tottenham St Paul *Lon* 85-89; C Is of Dogs Ch Ch and St Jo w St Luke 89-90; TV 90-92; P-in-c Southall Ch Redeemer 92-99; V from 99. *Christ The Redeemer Vicarage, 299 Allenby Road, Southall UB1 2HE* Tel (020) 8578 2711
E-mail nigel.orchard@virgin.net

ORCHARD, Mrs Tryphena Jane. b 35. Westf Coll Lon BA57. S'wark Ord Course 87. **d** 92 **p** 94. NSM Shaston *Sarum* 92-01; rtd 01; Perm to Offic *Sarum* from 01. *Dunscar Fold, Hawkesdene Lane, Shaftesbury SP7 8NU* Tel (01747) 855228

ORCHIN, Robert Andrew. b 71. K Coll Lon BD92. Ripon Coll Cuddesdon 93. **d** 95 **p** 96. C Leigh Park *Portsm* 95-98; C Warren Park 96-98; Perm to Offic *Portsm* 98-99; *S'wark* 99-00; P-in-c Portsea St Geo 00-02. *Address temp unknown*

O'REILLY, Clare Maria. *See* KING, Clare Maria

O'REILLY, Ms Eileen Catherine. b 47. TCD BTh95. **d** 96 **p** 97. C Annagh w Drumgoon, Ashfield etc *K, E & A* 96-98; Bp's C 98-00; Dioc Communications Officer 98-00; Dioc Sec (Kilmore) 98-00; USA from 00. *Address temp unknown*

O'REILLY, Philip Jonathon. b 66. Portsm Poly BSc87 Kent Univ MA97 MRICS. Westcott Ho Cam 93. **d** 93 **p** 94. C Selsdon St Jo w St Fran *S'wark* 93-96; TV Staveley and Barrow Hill *Derby* 96-01; V Wistow *Leic* from 01. *The Vicarage, 12 Saddington Road, Fleckney, Leicester LE8 8AW* Tel 0116-240 2215
E-mail philiporeilly@leicester.anglican.org

ORFORD, Barry Antony. b 49. Univ of Wales (Ban) BA71 MTh97 PhD01. St Steph Ho Ox 71. **d** 73 **p** 74. C Monmouth *Mon* 73-77; V Choral St As Cathl *St As* 77-81; CR 83-96; Perm to Offic *St As* from 97; Hon Asst Chapl Univ of Wales (Ban) *Ban* 99-01; P Lib Pusey Ho Ox from 01. *Pusey House, St Giles, Oxford OX1 3LZ* Tel (01865) 278415

ORFORD, Canon Keith John. b 40. FCIT. EMMTC 76. **d** 79 **p** 80. NSM Matlock Bank *Derby* 79-99; NSM Wirksworth from 99; Hon Can Derby Cathl from 00. *27 Lums Hill Rise, Matlock DE4 3FX* Tel and fax (01629) 55349
E-mail keith.orford@btinternet.com

ORGAN, Peter. b 73. K Coll Lon BA97 Birm Univ MA01. Qu Coll Birm 99. **d** 01 **p** 02. C E Wickham *S'wark* 01-05; TV Thamesmead from 05. *5 Finchale Road, London SE2 9PG* Tel (020) 8310 5614 E-mail revpeterorgan@yahoo.co.uk

ORLAND, Canon Ernest George. b 28. Lich Th Coll 61. **d** 62 **p** 63. C Northampton St Mich *Pet* 62-65; R Gayton w Tiffield 65-69; R Corby SS Pet and Andr 69-72; TR Corby SS Pet and Andr w Gt and Lt Oakley 72-81; RD Corby 79-81; Can Pet Cathl 79-93; V Pet All SS 81-93; rtd 93; Perm to Offic *Pet* from 93; *Linc* 95-02. *43 Godsey Lane, Market Deeping, Peterborough PE6 8HY* Tel (01778) 380724

ORME, Christopher Malcolm. b 60. City Univ BSc83. Wycliffe Hall Ox 03. **d** 05. C Shrewsbury H Cross *Lich* from 05. *14 Langholm Drive, Shrewsbury SY2 5UN* Tel (01743) 357404

ORME, John. b 29. Sarum Th Coll 58. **d** 60 **p** 61. C Heald Green St Cath *Ches* 60-64; C Ellesmere Port 64-67; Chapl Harperbury Hosp Radlett 67-73; P-in-c Luton All SS w St Pet *St Alb* 73-79; V 79-87; V Oxhey St Matt 87-96; rtd 97; Perm to Offic *St Alb* from 97. *1 Alzey Gardens, Harpenden AL5 5SZ* Tel (01582) 761931 E-mail john@orme117.freeserve.co.uk

ORME, Sydney. b 27. Oak Hill Th Coll 54. **d** 58 **p** 59. C Halliwell St Pet *Man* 58-61; V Friarmere 61-73; V Knypersley *Lich* 73-92; rtd 92; Perm to Offic *Ches* from 92. *10 Elworth Road, Sandbach CW11 9HQ* Tel (01270) 759233

ORMEROD, Henry Lawrence. b 35. Pemb Coll Cam BA58 MA63. Qu Coll Birm DipTh59. **d** 60 **p** 61. C Chigwell *Chelmsf* 60-64; C Thundersley 64-68; C Canvey Is 68-72; V Stanground *Ely* 72-77; TR Stanground and Farcet 77-81; TR Swindon St Jo and St Andr *Bris* 81-90; TR N Wingfield, Clay Cross and Pilsley *Derby* 90-97; rtd 97; Hon C Ironstone *Ox* 98-03; Perm to Offic from 03. *5 Waterloo Drive, Banbury OX16 3QN* Tel (01295) 278483 E-mail henryormerod@aol.com

ORMESHER, David Rodney. **d** 05. OLM Delaval *Newc* from 05. *14 The Crest, Seaton Sluice, Whitley Bay NE26 4BG* Tel 0191-237 1104

ORMISTON, Albert Edward. b 26. AMCT46. Oak Hill Th Coll 53. **d** 56 **p** 57. C Worksop St Jo *S'well* 56-58; P-in-c Everton St Polycarp *Liv* 58-59; V 59-63; Org Sec SAMS 63-67; R Gateacre *Liv* 67-73; V Tonbridge St Steph *Roch* 73-86; V Dent w Cowgill *Bradf* 86-91; rtd 91; Perm to Offic *Ches* 91-00; *Glouc* from 02. *30 Capel Court, The Burgage, Prestbury, Cheltenham GL52 3EL* Tel (01242) 518625

ORMROD, Paul William. b 57. Liv Univ BA80. Westcott Ho Cam 80. **d** 83 **p** 84. C Prescot *Liv* 83-86; TV Padgate 86-95; V Formby St Pet from 95. *St Peter's Vicarage, Cricket Path, Formby, Liverpool L37 7DP* Tel (01704) 873369

ORMSBY, Diana Clare. b 21. CertEd41. Sarum & Wells Th Coll 77 Gilmore Course 78. **dss** 80 **d** 87 **p** 94. Lydford, Brent Tor, Bridestowe and Sourton *Ex* 80-87; Hon C Lydford and Brent Tor 87-96; Perm to Offic from 96. *Lipscliffe, Coryton, Okehampton EX20 4AB* Tel (01822) 860344

ORMSBY, Robert Daly. b 22. CCC Ox BA42 MA48. Sarum & Wells Th Coll 77. **d** 78 **p** 79. Hon C Lydford and Brent Tor *Ex* 78-96; Hon C Peter Tavy, Mary Tavy, Lydford and Brent Tor from 96. *Lipscliffe, Coryton, Okehampton EX20 4AB* Tel (01822) 860344

ORMSTON, Derek. b 43. Univ of Wales (Lamp) DipTh67. **d** 67 **p** 68. C Ogley Hay *Lich* 67-70; C Tettenhall Regis 70-74; P-in-c Leek All SS 74-79; TV Leek and Meerbrook 79-83; Youth Chapl *Bris* 83-87; R Brinkworth w Dauntsey from 87; Chapl New Coll Swindon from 87. *The Rectory, Brinkworth, Chippenham SN15 5AF* Tel (01666) 510207

ORMSTON, Canon Richard Jeremy. b 61. Southlands Coll Lon BA83 Brunel Univ MTh98. Oak Hill Th Coll BA87. **d** 87 **p** 88. C Rodbourne Cheney *Bris* 87-91; R Collingtree w Courteenhall and Milton Malsor *Pet* 91-01; RD Wootton 96-01; R Oundle w Ashton and Benefield w Glapthorn from 01; Can Pet Cathl from 03; RD Oundle from 03. *The Vicarage, 12 New Street, Oundle, Peterborough PE8 4EA* Tel (01832) 273595
E-mail rjo@talk21.com

✠**OROMBI, The Most Revd Henry Luke.** b 49. Bp Tucker Coll Mukono 75 St Jo Coll Nottm BTh83. **d** 79 **p** 79 **c** 93. Dioc Youth Officer Madi/W Nile Uganda 79-86; Adn Goli 87-93; Bp Nebbi 93-03; Abp Uganda and Bp Kampala from 03. *PO Box 14123, Kampala, Uganda* Tel (00256) (41) 270218, 270219 *or* 271138 Mobile 77-476476 Fax (41) 251925 *or* 245597
E-mail orombih@yahoo.com *or* couab@uol.co.ug

O'ROURKE, Brian Joseph Gerard. b 58. TCD BA82 HDipEd83. CITC 89. **d** 92 **p** 93. Chapl Glendalough Sch 90-96; C Newcastle w Newtownmountkennedy and Calary *D & G* 92-96; Bp's C 96-98; I 98-00; I Cork St Ann's Union *C, C & R* from 00. *The Rectory, 49 Ard na Laoi, Montenotte, Co Cork, Irish Republic* Tel and fax (00353) (21) 450456 Mobile 87-686 8260
E-mail stanneshandon@cork.anglican.org

O'ROURKE, Shaun. b 58. N Ord Course 02. **d** 05. C Gorton St Phil *Man* from 05; C Abbey Hey from 05. *5 Old Oak Drive, Denton, Manchester M34 6FJ* Tel 0161-320 0043 E-mail sorourke@freezone.co.uk

ORPIN, Mrs Gillian. b 32. SRN53. Oak Hill Th Coll 82. **d** 87 **p** 95. Par Dn Passenham *Pet* 87-92; rtd 92; NSM Oban St Jo *Arg* 92-95; Dioc Chapl 95-98; Perm to Offic *St Alb* from 98. *11 Berwick Way, Sandy SG19 1TR* Tel (01767) 680629

ORR, Andrew Dermot Harman. b 66. Sheff Univ BSc89. CITC BTh92. **d** 92 **p** 93. C Ballymacash *Conn* 92-95; I Castlecomer w Colliery Ch, Mothel and Bilbo *C & O* 95-00; Dioc Registrar 95-00; I Castleknock and Mulhuddart, w Clonsilla *D & G* from 00. *Castleknock Rectory, 12 Hawthorn Lawn, Castleknock, Dublin 15, Irish Republic* Tel (00353) (1) 821 3083 *or* 820 0040 Fax 820 4505 E-mail greenorr@esatclear.ie

ORR, David Cecil. b 33. TCD BA56 MA68. **d** 57 **p** 58. C Drumragh *D & R* 57-60; I Convoy 60-70; I Maghera 70-80; I Drumragh w Mountfield 80-84; Dean Derry 84-97; I Templemore 84-97; Miss to Seamen 84-97; rtd 97. *Kilrory, 11 Broomhill Court, Londonderry BT47 6WP* Tel (028) 7134 8183 E-mail dcecilorr@btopenworld.com

ORR, Donald Macrae. b 50. Humberside Poly BA73 Glas Univ BD02 MTh04. TISEC 02. **d** 04. C Greenock *Glas* from 04. *16 Neilston Road, Barrhead, Glasgow G78 1TY* Tel 0141-881 1372

ORR, Robert Vernon. b 50. Westmr Univ 80 MIQA89. Wycliffe Hall Ox 96. **d** 98 **p** 99. C Cowley St Jo *Ox* 98-01; P-in-c Reading St Agnes w St Paul 01-02; R Reading St Agnes w St Paul and St Barn from 02. *The Vicarage, 290 Northumberland Avenue, Reading RG2 8DD* Tel 0118-987 4448 E-mail vernon.orr@lineone.net

ORR, William James Craig. TCD BTh01. CITC 98. **d** 01 **p** 02. C Lurgan Ch the Redeemer *D & D* from 01. *14 Sandhill Park, Lurgan, Craigavon BT66 7AX* Tel (028) 3832 6040 E-mail worrshankill@hotmail.com *or* willy.orr@btinternet.com

ORR-EWING, Francis Ian Lance (Frog). b 75. Regent's Park Coll Ox BA97. Wycliffe Hall Ox MTh00. **d** 00 **p** 01. C Ox St Aldate *Ox* 00-03; V Camberwell All SS *S'wark* from 03. *All Saints' Church, Blenheim Grove, London SE15 4QS* Tel (020) 7639 3052 Mobile 07979-594762 E-mail vicar@allsaintspeckham.co.uk

ORTON, Peter Joseph. b 57. **d** 03 **p** 04. OLM Burton St Chad *Lich* from 03. *237 Wetmore Road, Burton-on-Trent DE14 1RB* Tel (01283) 537574 E-mail lightcommunity@yahoo.co.uk

ORTON, Canon Richard. b 33. Keble Coll Ox BA56 MA60 Leeds Univ. Lich Th Coll 60. **d** 61 **p** 64. C Penistone w Midhope *Wakef* 61-62; Hon C Meltham 62-69; Hon C Horsforth *Ripon* 69-72; C Far Headingley St Chad 72-75; V Hellifield *Bradf* 75-80; RD Bowland 78-80; R Hutton *Chelmsf* 80-87; R Wallasey St Hilary *Ches* 87-00; Dioc Ecum Officer 92-99; RD Wallasey 96-99; Hon Can Ches Cathl 97-00; rtd 00; C Gt Sutton *Ches* 01-05. *137 Brimstage Road, Barnston, Wirral CH60 1XF* Tel 0151-348 4911

OSBORN, Miss Anne. b 40. Reading Univ BA62 MA64 Lon Univ PGCE67. Oak Hill NSM Course 87. **d** 92. Chapl Lon Univ *Lon* 92-94; Chapl Lon Guildhall Univ 94-96; Chapl Univ of Westmr 94-95; Assoc Tutor NTMTC from 97. *8 Beaufort House, Talbot Road, London N15 4DR* Tel (020) 8801 0115

OSBORN, David Ronald. b 42. Bris Univ BA66 Leeds Univ CertEd77 Bath Univ MEd80. Clifton Th Coll 62. **d** 66 **p** 67. C Farndon *S'well* 66-69; P-in-c W Bridgford 69-72; Asst Dioc Dir Educn *Carl* 72-77; P-in-c Kirkandrews-on-Eden w Beaumont and Grinsdale 72-77; Hd RE and Chapl Dauntsey's Sch Devizes 77-83; USA 83; V Southbroom *Sarum* 83-86; Consultant to Lay Tr Schemes *Ox* 86; Hd RE Bexhill High Sch 86-93; TV Langtree 93-95; TR 95-97; TR Bracknell from 97. *The Rectory, 26 Park Road, Bracknell RG12 2LU* Tel and fax (01344) 445090 Mobile 07803-618464 E-mail davidsosborn@ntlworld.com

OSBORN, David Thomas. b 58. PGCE80 K Coll Lon BD79 AKC79. Linc Th Coll 82. **d** 83 **p** 84. C Bearsted w Thurnham *Cant* 83-86; Chapl RAF 86-90; R Bassingham *Linc* 90-91; V Aubourn w Haddington 90-91; V Carlton-le-Moorland w Stapleford 90-91; R Thurlby w Norton Disney 90-91; Chapl RAF from 91. *Chaplaincy Services (RAF), HQ, Personnel and Training Command, RAF Innsworth, Gloucester GL3 1EZ* Tel (01452) 712612 ext 5164 Fax 510828

OSBORN, Mrs Diana Marian. b 52. R Holloway Coll Lon BSc74 Birm Univ PGCE75. NEOC 81. **dss** 84 **d** 87 **p** 94. Malden St Jo *S'wark* 84-89; Par Dn 87-89; Par Dn Brampton *Ely* 89-92; Par Dn Richmond H Trin and Ch Ch *S'wark* 92-93; Chapl Ridley Hall Cam 94-96; Chapl Milton Children's Hospice 96-98; Chapl E Anglia's Children's Hospices from 98. *70 Thrapston Road, Brampton, Huntingdon PE28 4TD* Tel (01480) 353701 *or* (01223) 860306

OSBORN, Preb John Geoffrey Rowland. b 33. Jes Coll Cam BA55 MA59. Wells Th Coll 63. **d** 65 **p** 66. C Easthampstead *Ox* 65-68; Lic to Offic *Blackb* 68-70; Brunei 70-75; Asst Dir RE *Blackb* 75-77; V Tockholes 75-77; Dir RE *B & W* 77-83; Dir and Sec Lon Dioc Bd for Schs *Lon* 83-95; Preb St Paul's Cathl 86-95; rtd 96. *4 Musson Close, Abingdon OX14 5RE* Tel (01235) 528701

OSBORN, Maurice. b 25. Univ of Wales BA50. Wycliffe Hall Ox 55. **d** 55 **p** 56. C E Wickham *S'wark* 55-57; Chapl Dauntsey's Sch Devizes 57-72; Asst Master 58-78; P-in-c Bishop's Lavington *Sarum* 79-83; P-in-c Lt Cheverell 82-83; P-in-c W Lavington and the Cheverells 83-90; rtd 90; Perm to Offic *Sarum* from 90. *Greensand Cottage, West Lavington, Devizes SN10 4LB* Tel (01380) 813244

OSBORNE, Alexander Deas. b 34. Liv Univ BSc54 PhD57. Oak Hill NSM Course 78. **d** 81 **p** 82. NSM Redbourn *St Alb* 81-98; rtd 98; Perm to Offic *Ely* and *St Alb* from 00. *6 Cam Farm, North End, Meldreth, Royston SG8 6NT* Tel (01763) 260456

OSBORNE, Anthony Russell. b 47. Sarum & Wells Th Coll 77. **d** 79 **p** 80. C Heref St Martin *Heref* 79-81; TV 82-86; TV Hanley H Ev *Lich* 86-92; Dioc Soc Resp Officer *Heref* 92-97; Can Heref Cathl 92-97; TR Cannock *Lich* from 97; V Hatherton from 97. *The Rectory, 11 Sherbrook Road, Cannock WS11 1HJ* Tel (01543) 578381 *or* 502131 E-mail aandb.osborne@cwcom.net

OSBORNE, Canon Brian Charles. b 38. St Andr Univ MA61 Lon Univ DipTh80. Clifton Th Coll 61. **d** 63 **p** 64. C Skirbeck H Trin *Linc* 63-68; V 80-03; P-in-c New Clee 68-71; V 71-75; V Derby St Aug *Derby* 75-80; Chapl Pilgrim Hosp Boston 84-88; RD Holland E *Linc* 85-95; Can and Preb Linc Cathl 92-03; Chapl to The Queen from 97; rtd 03. *3 Newlands Road, Haconby, Bourne PE10 0UT* Tel (01778) 570818 E-mail revbrianosborne@ukonline.co.uk

OSBORNE, Christopher Hazell. b 60. Aston Tr Scheme 89 Sarum & Wells Th Coll DCM93. **d** 93 **p** 94. C Paignton St Jo *Ex* 93-96; C Hooe 96-97; TV Plymstock and Hooe 97-01; V Ivybridge w Harford from 01. *The Vicarage, Blachford Road, Ivybridge PL21 0AD* Tel (01752) 690193 E-mail osborne2001@btinternet.com

OSBORNE, David Robert. b 50. Birm Univ BSc71 MEd86 Nottm Univ DipTh72 Bris Univ PGCE73. St Jo Coll Dur 78. **d** 80 **p** 81. C Penkridge w Stretton *Lich* 80-85; R Longdon-upon-Tern, Rodington, Uppington etc 85-94; R Pilton w Croscombe, N Wootton and Dinder *B & W* from 94; RD Shepton Mallet from 01. *The Rectory, Pilton, Shepton Mallet BA4 4DX* Tel (01749) 890423 E-mail osbornepilton@ukonline.co.uk

OSBORNE, David Victor. b 36. Dur Univ BA59 Univ of Wales MA99. Cranmer Hall Dur DipTh62. **d** 62 **p** 63. C Kennington Cross St Anselm *S'wark* 62-66; C Sandal St Helen *Wakef* 66-67; R Ancoats *Man* 67-73; V Claremont H Angels 73-80; R Breedon cum Isley Walton and Worthington *Leic* 80-87; V Beaumont Leys 87-92; V Billesdon and Skeffington 92-01; rtd 01; Perm to Offic *Leic* and *Pet* from 02. *Rose Cottage, 12 Barlows Lane, Wilbarston, Market Harborough LE16 8QB* Tel (01536) 770400

OSBORNE, Canon Derek James. b 32. Tyndale Hall Bris 53. **d** 57 **p** 58. C Weymouth St Mary *Sarum* 57-60; C Southgate *Chich* 60-63; V Croydon Ch Ch Broad Green *Cant* 63-71; V Cromer *Nor* 71-83; P-in-c Gresham w Bessingham 71-83; Hon Can Nor Cathl 77-83; V Northwood Em *Lon* 83-94; Chapl Lee Abbey 94-97; rtd 97; Perm to Offic *Nor* from 97. *50 Clifton Park, Cromer NR27 9BG* Tel (01263) 511272

OSBORNE, Gerald Edward Richard. b 63. Ch Ch Ox MA85 Wye Coll Lon MSc86. LNSM course 98. **d** 99 **p** 00. OLM Pewsey and Swanborough *Sarum* from 99. *Lawn Farm, Milton Lilbourne, Pewsey SN9 5LQ* Tel (01672) 563459 Mobile 07798-942118 Fax (01672) 564271 E-mail gerald.osborne@farmline.com

OSBORNE, Graham Daking. b 51. City Univ ACII74 FCII77. Cuddesdon Coll 94. **d** 96 **p** 97. C Cirencester *Glouc* 96-00; V Glouc St Cath from 00; RD Glouc City from 03. *St Catharine's Vicarage, 29 Denmark Road, Gloucester GL1 3JQ* Tel and fax (01452) 524497 E-mail gdosborne@bigfoot.com

OSBORNE, The Ven Hayward John. b 48. New Coll Ox BA70 MA73. Westcott Ho Cam 71. **d** 73 **p** 74. C Bromley SS Pet and Paul *Roch* 73-77; C Halesowen *Worc* 77-80; TV 80-83; TR Worc St Barn w Ch Ch 83-88; V Moseley St Mary *Birm* 88-01; AD Moseley 94-01; Hon Can Birm Cathl 00-01; Adn Birm from 01. *23 Carisbrooke Road, Birmingham B17 8NN* Tel 0121-420 3299 *or* 426 0441 Fax 428 1114 E-mail archdeacon_of_bham@birmingham.anglican.org

OSBORNE, Jonathan Lloyd. b 62. Ripon Coll Cuddesdon 95. **d** 97 **p** 98. C Mill End and Heronsgate w W Hyde *St Alb* 97-00; Asst Chapl Ealing Hosp NHS Trust 00-03; Chapl Team Ldr from 03; Asst Chapl W Middx Univ Hosp NHS Trust 00-03; Chapl Team Ldr from 03; Chapl Team Ldr Meadow House Hospice from 03; Chapl Team Ldr W Lon Mental Health NHS Trust from 03; Hon Chapl S'wark Cathl *S'wark* from 03. *3 Teignmouth Gardens, Greenford UB6 8BX* Tel (020) 8997 7371 *or* 8321 5447 E-mail jonathan.osborne@wmuh-tr.nthames.nhs.uk

OSBORNE, The Very Revd June. b 53. Man Univ BA74. St Jo Coll Nottm. **dss** 80 **d** 87 **p** 94. Birm St Martin *Birm* 80-84; Old Ford St Paul and St Mark *Lon* 84-95; Par Dn Old Ford St Paul w St Steph and St Mark 87-94; P-in-c Old Ford St Paul and St Mark 94-95; Can Res and Treas Sarum Cathl *Sarum* 95-04; Bp's Dom Chapl 95-97; Dean Sarum from 04. *The Deanery, 7 The Close, Salisbury SP1 2EF* Tel (01722) 555176 Fax 555177 E-mail dean@salcath.co.uk

OSBORNE, Malcolm Eric (Max). b 64. EN(G)87 RMN92. St Jo Coll Nottm 94. **d** 96 **p** 97. C Walton *St E* 96-99; C Ipswich St Matt 99-02; Soc Resp Adv 99-02; V Newmarket All SS from 02. *All Saints' Vicarage, 32 Warrington Street, Newmarket CB8 8BA* Tel (01638) 662514 E-mail max.osborne@stedmundsbury.anglican.org

OSBORNE, Mark William. b 67. Univ of Wales BA89. Coll of Resurr Mirfield 94. **d** 94 **p** 95. C Goldthorpe w Hickleton *Sheff* 94-97; C-in-c Southey Green St Bernard CD 97-01; P-in-c Walham Green St Jo w St Jas *Lon* from 01. *The Vicarage, 40 Racton Road, London SW6 1LP* Tel and fax (020) 7385 3676 *or* 7385 7634 E-mail mark.osborne5@btopenworld.com

OSBORNE, Ralph. b 38. Kent Univ DipTh80. Bernard Gilpin Soc Dur 62 Clifton Th Coll 63. **d** 66 **p** 67. C Harpurhey Ch Ch *Man* 66-68; C Chorlton on Medlock St Sav 68-71; C Wilmington *Roch* 71-74; V St Mary Cray and St Paul's Cray 74-85; P-in-c Bath St Steph *B & W* 85-88; P-in-c Charlcombe 86-88; R Charlcombe w Bath St Steph 88-03; rtd 03. *406 Bath Road, Saltford, Bristol BS31 3DH* Tel (01225) 872536 E-mail ralph.osborne@ic24.net

OSBORNE, Canon Robin Orbell. b 29. Leeds Univ BA54. Coll of Resurr Mirfield 52. **d** 54 **p** 55. C Wellingborough All Hallows *Pet* 54-58; C Oxhey St Matt *St Alb* 60-61; V Woburn 61-65; V Battlesden and Pottesgrove 61-65; V Cheshunt 65-82; RD Cheshunt 70-81; Hon Can St Alb 76-82; V Penzance St Mary w St Paul *Truro* 82-88; Can Res and Treas Truro Cathl 88-94; rtd 94; Perm to Offic *B & W* from 94. *College of St Barnabas, Blackberry Lane, Lingfield RH7 6NJ* Tel (01342) 871615 Mobile 07776-081564 E-mail r.osborne@ukonline.co.uk

OSBOURNE, David John. b 56. Linc Th Coll 78. **d** 79 **p** 80. C Houghton le Spring *Dur* 79-82; C Spalding St Jo *Linc* 82-83; C Spalding St Jo w Deeping St Nicholas 83-84; V Swineshead 84-94; RD Holland W 86-92; P-in-c Boultham 94-01; R from 01. *The Rectory, 2A St Helen's Avenue, Lincoln LN6 7RA* Tel (01522) 682026 *or* tel and fax 686527 E-mail daosbourne@supanet.com

OSBOURNE, Steven John. b 59. St Jo Coll Nottm 92. **d** 94 **p** 95. C Bushbury *Lich* 94-98; C Tamworth 98-03; V Caverswall and Weston Coyney w Dilhorne from 03. *8 Vicarage Crescent, Caverswall, Stoke-on-Trent ST11 9EW* Tel (01782) 388037 *or* 312570 E-mail steve.osbourne@btopenworld.com

OSEI, Robert Emmanuel. b 56. **d** 76 **p** 77. Kumasi 76-83; C Hangleton *Chich* 83-84; Perm to Offic *S'wark* 00-02. *8 Plummer Court, London SE13 6RA*

OSGERBY, John Martin. b 34. Sheff Univ BSc56 PhD59. Linc Th Coll 75. **d** 77 **p** 78. C Rotherham *Sheff* 77-80; C-in-c W Bessacarr CD 80-84; V W Bessacarr 84-87; Warden of Readers 86-99; R Fishlake w Sykehouse and Kirk Bramwith etc 87-99; RD Snaith and Hatfield 93-99; rtd 99; Perm to Offic *Sheff* from 99 and *Linc* 00-02. *4 Marlborough Avenue, Haxey, Doncaster DN9 2HL* Tel (01427) 754815 E-mail jmosgerby.hax@virgin.net

OSGOOD, Graham Dean. b 39. Lon Univ BSc62 ALCD71. St Jo Coll Nottm 71. **d** 71 **p** 72. C Bebington *Ches* 71-76; V Gee Cross from 76. *The Vicarage, 16 Higham Lane, Hyde SK14 5LX* Tel 0161-368 2337 E-mail graham.htgx@btinternet.com

OSGOOD, Sylvia Joy. b 47. QUB BSc68 Lon Univ BD78 Man Univ PhD92. St Jo Coll Nottm MA98. **d** 97 **p** 98. NSM Bredbury St Mark *Ches* 97-01; Chapl Spurgeon's Coll from 01. *The Vicarage, 16 Higham Lane, Hyde SK14 5LX* Tel 0161-368 2337 E-mail j.osgood@spurgeons.ac.uk

O'SHAUGHNESSY, Mrs Janice Florence. b 51. STETS 95. **d** 98 **p** 99. NSM Bembridge *Portsm* 98-02; Asst Chapl Isle of Wight Healthcare NHS Trust 99-02; C Catherington and Clanfield *Portsm* from 02. *23 Pipers Mead, Clanfield, Waterlooville PO8 0ST* Tel (023) 9259 1357

O'SHEA, Mrs Helen Mary. b 55. Univ of Wales (Abth) BA77 SRN79. Llan Ord Course 94. **d** 98 **p** 99. NSM Skewen *Llan* 98-01; C Llangynwyd w Maesteg 01-02; P-in-c Cwmafan from 02. *Y Berth, 11 Tabernacle Terrace, Cwmavon, Port Talbot SA12 9HS*

OSLER, Philip. b 55. SEITE 99. **d** 02 **p** 03. NSM Staplehurst *Cant* from 02. *39 Marden Road, Staplehurst, Tonbridge TN12 0NE* Tel (01580) 892626 E-mail phil.osler@ukgateway.net

OSMAN, David Thomas. b 49. Bradf Univ BTech72 Newc Univ MA93. Trin Coll Bris 75. **d** 78 **p** 79. C Stranton *Dur* 78-81; C Denton Holme *Carl* 81-84; V Preston on Tees *Dur* 84-97; P-in-c Hebburn St Jo from 97; P-in-c Jarrow Grange from 00. *St John's Vicarage, 23 St John's Avenue, Hebburn NE31 2TZ* Tel 0191-422 7505

OSMAN, Ernest. b 35. St Aid Birkenhead 61. **d** 64 **p** 65. C Heaton Ch Ch *Man* 64-68; V Farnworth St Pet 68-77; V St Martin's *Lich* 77-85; V Endon w Stanley 85-00; rtd 01; Hon C Llanyblodwel and Trefonen *Lich* from 01. *The Paddock, Silverdale Drive, Trefonen, Oswestry SY10 9DW* Tel (01691) 654184 E-mail paddock6@btinternet.com

OSMAN, Stephen William. b 53. Matlock Coll of Educn CertEd74 Teesside Poly CQSW80. St Jo Coll Dur 88. **d** 90 **p** 91. C Newbarns w Hawcoat *Carl* 90-93; TV Marfleet *York* 93-00; P-in-c Gotham *S'well* from 00; P-in-c Barton in Fabis from 02; P-in-c Thrumpton from 02; P-in-c Kingston and Ratcliffe-on-Soar from 02. *The New Rectory, 39 Leake Road, Gotham, Nottingham NG11 0JL* Tel 0115-983 0608 E-mail steveosman500@aol.com

OSMASTON, Canon Amiel Mary Ellinor. b 51. Ex Univ BA73 St Jo Coll Dur BA84. St Jo Coll Nottm DPS77 Cranmer Hall Dur 82. **dss** 84 **d** 87 **p** 94. Chester le Street *Dur* 84-88; Par Dn 87-88; Dir Miss and Past Studies Ridley Hall Cam 89-96; Min Development Officer *Ches* 96-03; C Lache cum Saltney 00-03; Min Development Officer *Carl* from 03; C Penrith w Newton Reigny and Plumpton Wall from 03; Hon Can Carl Cathl from 05. *The New Vicarage, Plumpton, Penrith CA11 9PA* Tel (01758) 885756 *or* (01228) 522573 Fax (01758) 885773 E-mail ministry.dev@carlislediocese.org.uk

✠**OSMERS, The Rt Revd John Robert.** b 35. Cant Univ (NZ) MA58. Coll of Resurr Mirfield 59. **d** 61 **p** 62 **c** 95. C Rawmarsh w Parkgate *Sheff* 61-65; Lesotho 65-81; Par P Quthing 65-73; R Masite Miss 73-81; Botswana 81-88; Asst P H Cross Cathl 82-87; R Molepolole 82-88; Zambia from 88; Chapl ANC 88-91; Dioc Tr Chapl Lusaka 90-95; Bp E Zambia 95-03; Asst Bp Lusaka from 03. *PO Box 30477, Lusaka, Zambia* Tel and fax (00260) (1) 227385 E-mail josmers@zamnet.zm

OSMOND, David Methuen. b 38. Qu Coll Birm 75. **d** 77 **p** 78. C Yardley St Edburgha *Birm* 77-80; V Withall 80-89; R W Coker w Hardington Mandeville, E Chinnock etc *B & W* 89-95; Perm to Offic 96-98; rtd 98; Hon C Castle Town *Lich* 01-03; Perm to Offic *Blackb* from 05. *2 George Street, Clitheroe BB7 1BU* Tel (01200) 426208

OSMOND, Mrs Heather Christine. b 44. ABSM64 ARCM65 Birm Poly CertEd65. Qu Coll Birm 83. **dss** 84 **d** 87 **p** 97. Brandwood *Birm* 84-85; Withall 85-89; Par Dn 87-89; Perm to Offic *B & W* 89-01; P-in-c Castle Town *Lich* 01-03; rtd 04; Perm to Offic *Blackb* from 05. *2 George Street, Clitheroe BB7 1BU* Tel (01200) 426208

OSMOND, Oliver Robert. b 44. Ch Coll Cam BA66 MA70. Cuddesdon Coll 66 Trin Coll Toronto STB69. **d** 69 **p** 70. Canada 69-81; V Mill Hill Jo Keble Ch *Lon* from 81. *John Keble Vicarage, 142 Deans Lane, Edgware HA8 9NT* Tel (020) 8959 1312 Fax 8931 2433 E-mail oro@johnkeble.org.uk

OSMOND, Tobias Charles. b 74. Plymouth Univ BSc96. Ripon Coll Cuddesdon BTh99. **d** 99 **p** 00. C Wilton *B & W* 99-02; C Bath Abbey w St Jas from 02. *48 Devonshire Buildings, Bath BA2 4SU* Tel (01225) 422506 Mobile 07808-695732 E-mail tob@fish.co.uk

OSSORY AND LEIGHLIN, Archdeacon of. *See* MURRAY, The Ven John Grainger

OSSORY, Dean of. *See* LYNAS, The Very Revd Norman Noel

O'SULLIVAN, Mrs Hazel. b 50. S Dios Minl Tr Scheme 91. **d** 94 **p** 95. C Cove St Jo *Guildf* 94-98; TV Headley All SS 98-02; V Bordon 02-04; Chapl Whiteley Village from 04; Perm to Offic *Portsm* from 02. *West Lodge, West Avenue, Whiteley Village, Walton-on-Thames KT12 4DQ* Tel (01932) 827428 E-mail hazel@revd.fsnet.co.uk

O'SULLIVAN, Richard Norton. b 59. Glas Coll of Tech BSc80. Gregorian Univ Rome PhB85 STB88 STL90. **d** 89 **p** 90. In RC Ch 89-96; NSM Clarkston *Glas* 00-02; P-in-c Glas St Oswald from 02. *36 Kingsbridge Crescent, Glasgow G44 4JU* Tel 0141-583 7207 *or* 616 6446 E-mail dick@osullivan53.fsnet.co.uk

OSWALD, John Edward Guy. b 39. Qu Coll Cam BA63 MA67. Ridley Hall Cam. **d** 68 **p** 69. C Chippenham St Paul w Langley Burrell *Bris* 68-72; C Hengrove 72-75; P-in-c Hardenhuish 75-79; P-in-c Kington St Michael 75-79; TV Chippenham St Paul w Hardenhuish etc 79-82; P-in-c Gt w Lt Somerford and Seagry 82-86; P-in-c Corston w Rodbourne 84-86; R Gt Somerford, Lt Somerford, Seagry, Corston etc from 86. *The Rectory, Frog Lane, Great Somerford, Chippenham SN15 5JA* Tel (01249) 720220

OSWIN, Frank Anthony (Tony). b 43. Chich Th Coll 69. **d** 71 **p** 72. C Radford *Cov* 71-74; C Shrub End *Chelmsf* 74-76; V Layer de la Haye 76-80; V Eastwood St Dav 80-93; TR Withycombe Raleigh *Ex* from 93. *The Rectory, 74 Withycombe Village Road, Exmouth EX8 3AE* Tel (01395) 264182

OTTAWAY, Michael John. b 17. Mert Coll Ox BA40 MA44. Cuddesdon Coll 40. **d** 41 **p** 42. C Leytonstone St Marg *Chelmsf* 41-45; C Kettering SS Pet and Paul *Pet* 45-48; C Kibworth Beauchamp *Leic* 48-49; V Wolvercote *Ox* 49-76; TV Wolvercote w Summertown 76-83; rtd 83; Perm to Offic *Chich* from 84. *3 Lower Drive, Seaford BN25 3AR* Tel (01323) 899179

OTTER, Anthony Frank. b 32. Kelham Th Coll 54. **d** 59 **p** 60. C Bethnal Green St Jo w St Simon *Lon* 59-63; C Aylesbury *Ox* 63-68; V Hanslope w Castlethorpe 68-77; P-in-c N w S Moreton 77-79; P-in-c Aston Tirrold w Aston Upthorpe 77-79; R S w N Moreton, Aston Tirrold and Aston Upthorpe 79-97; rtd 97; Perm to Offic *Ox* from 97. *4 Emden House, Barton Lane, Headington, Oxford OX3 9JU* Tel (01865) 765447

OTTEWELL, David. b 42. Sheff Univ BSc65 Leic Univ PhD69. N Ord Course 90. **d** 93 **p** 94. NSM Barnby Dun *Sheff* 93-97; P-in-c Finningley w Auckley *S'well* from 97. *The Rectory,*

Rectory Lane, Finningley, Doncaster DN9 3DA Tel (01302) 770240 E-mail d.ottewell@virgin.net

OTTEY, Canon John Leonard. b 34. AKC60 Nottm Univ BA70. **d** 61 **p** 62. C Grantham St Wulfram *Linc* 61-64; R Keyworth *S'well* 70-85; P-in-c Stanton-on-the-Wolds 71-85; P-in-c E Retford 85-87; V 87-99; P-in-c W Retford 85-87; R 87-99; Hon Can S'well Minster 93-99; rtd 99; Perm to Offic *Linc* from 00 and *S'well* from 04. *1 The Orchards, Grantham NG31 9GW* Tel (01476) 578762

OTTLEY, David Ronald. b 57. Lanc Univ BA78. Sarum & Wells Th Coll 79. **d** 81 **p** 82. C Urmston *Man* 81-85; Lect Bolton St Pet 85-87; P-in-c Halliwell St Thos 87-88; V Bolton St Thos 88-98; TR Halliwell 98-03; P-in-c Goostrey *Ches* from 03. *The Vicarage, Blackden Lane, Goostrey, Crewe CW4 8PG* Tel (01477) 532109

OTTLEY, Ronald. b 28. St Deiniol's Hawarden 81. **d** 83 **p** 84. Hon C Prestbury *Ches* 83-95; rtd 95; Perm to Offic *Ches* from 95. *2 Brocklehurst Court, Tytherington Drive, Macclesfield SK10 2HD* Tel (01625) 432649

OTTO, Andrew James. b 63. St Pet Coll Ox BA86 MA90 Bris Univ BA01. Trin Coll Bris 99. **d** 01 **p** 02. C Trowbridge H Trin *Sarum* 01-05. *Address temp unknown* E-mail otto@fish.co.uk

OTTO, Francis James Reeve. b 42. New Coll Ox BA64 BA68 Ex Univ 82. St Steph Ho Ox 66 Wells Th Coll 68. **d** 69 **p** 70. C St Stephen by Saltash *Truro* 69-72; C Newquay 72-73; V Lanteglos by Fowey 73-79; V St Goran w Caerhays 79-82; Chapl St Mary's Hall Brighton 82-88; Chapl Reading Sch 88-90; Teacher The Abbey Sch Reading 91-93; Chapl Lic Victuallers' Sch Ascot 93-94; Lic to Offic *Ox* 89-95; C Boyne Hill 95; P-in-c Cocking, Bepton and W Lavington *Chich* 95-99; Chapl Heathfield Sch Ascot 99-04; Perm to Offic *Ox* from 04. *Address temp unknown* E-mail fjrotto@lincon.net

OUGH, John Christopher. b 51. Lon Univ CertEd74 Open Univ BA82. SW Minl Tr Course 91. **d** 94 **p** 95. C Plymouth Em, St Paul Efford and St Aug *Ex* 94-97; P-in-c Diptford, N Huish, Harberton and Harbertonford 97-01; P-in-c Halwell w Moreleigh 97-01; R Diptford, N Huish, Harberton, Harbertonford etc from 01. *The Rectory, Diptford, Totnes TQ9 7NY* Tel (01548) 821148
E-mail john@diptfordough.freeserve.co.uk

OULD, Julian Charles. b 57. MHCIMA77. Coll of Resurr Mirfield 80. **d** 83 **p** 84. C Hebburn St Cuth *Dur* 83-86; C Pet H Spirit Bretton *Pet* 86-90; R Peakirk w Glinton 90-95; R Peakirk w Glinton and Northborough 95-96; TR Is of Scilly *Truro* 96-98; R from 98. *The Chaplaincy, Church Road, St Mary's TR21 0NA* Tel and fax (01720) 423128 E-mail ypj69@dial.pipex.com

OULESS, John Michael. b 22. AKC49. Ridley Hall Cam 49. **d** 50 **p** 51. C Dallington *Pet* 50-55; C Evesham *Worc* 55-56; R Halewood *Liv* 56-62; V Southwick w Glapthorn *Pet* 62-71; Chapl Glapthorn Road Hosp Oundle 63-71; R Cogenhoe *Pet* 71-89; R Whiston 71-89; rtd 89; Perm to Offic *Win* from 92. *2 Clos du Roncherez, St Brelade, Jersey JE3 8FG* Tel (01534) 44916

OUTEN (née BAILEY), Mrs Joyce Mary Josephine. b 33. St Gabr Coll Lon CertEd69 DipRS83. S'wark Ord Course 80. **dss** 83 **d** 87 **p** 94. Par Dn Woolwich St Mary w St Mich *S'wark* 87-89; Par Dn Rusthall *Roch* 89-94; C 94-97; rtd 97; Asst Chapl Kent and Cant Hosps NHS Trust 97-99; Asst Chapl E Kent Hosps NHS Trust 99-00; Hon C Whitstable *Cant* from 00. *10 Foxgrove Road, Whitstable CT5 1PB* Tel (01227) 273643
E-mail outen@foxgrove.fsnet.co.uk

OUTHWAITE, Stephen Anthony (Tony). b 35. Wells Th Coll 62. **d** 64 **p** 65. C Bitterne Park *Win* 64-67; C-in-c N Tadley CD 67-71; R Milton 71-93; RD Christchurch 82-90; V Win St Cross w St Faith 93-04; Master St Cross Hosp 93-04; rtd 04. *Wason House, Upper High Street, Castle Cary BA7 7AT* Tel (01963) 350302 Mobile 07940-389946

OUTRAM, David Michael. b 42. Univ of Wales (Ban) BA77 BD79. Coll of Resurr Mirfield 79. **d** 80 **p** 81. C Llandegfan and Beaumaris w Llanfaes w Penmon etc *Ban* 80-82; Chapl Prebendal Sch Chich 82-86; PV Chich Cathl *Chich* 82-86; Asst Chapl Wellington Coll Berks 86-89; Hd Div 87-03; Chapl 89-03; V Dwygyfylchi *Ban* from 03. *The Vicarage, Church Road, Penmaenmawr LL34 6BN* Tel (01492) 621276

OVENDEN, Canon John Anthony. b 45. Open Univ BA80 BA93 K Coll Lon MA96. Sarum & Wells Th Coll 71. **d** 74 **p** 75. C Handsworth *Sheff* 74-77; C Isfield *Chich* 77-80; C Uckfield 77-80; P-in-c Stuntney *Ely* 80-85; Min Can, Prec and Sacr Ely Cathl 80-85; V Primrose Hill St Mary w Avenue Road St Paul *Lon* 85-98; Dir English Hymnal Co from 93; Can Windsor and Chapl in Windsor Gt Park from 98; Chapl to The Queen from 02. *Chaplain's Lodge, Windsor Great Park, Windsor SL4 2HP* Tel (01784) 432434

OVEREND, Alan. b 53. Sheff Univ BA75. Oak Hill Th Coll 84. **d** 86 **p** 87. C Aughton St Mich *Liv* 86-89; P-in-c Eccleston Park 89-92; V 92-99; V Ainsdale from 99. *St John's Vicarage, 708 Liverpool Road, Ainsdale, Southport PR8 3QE* Tel (01704) 577760

OVEREND, Barry Malcolm. b 49. K Coll Lon BD71 AKC71 DipMin88. St Aug Coll Cant 71. **d** 72 **p** 73. C Nailsworth *Glouc* 72-74; C High Harrogate Ch Ch *Ripon* 75-78; V Collingham w Harewood 78-87; V Far Headingley St Chad from 87. *St Chad's Vicarage, Otley Road, Leeds LS16 5JT* Tel 0113-275 2224 *or* 274 4322 E-mail bmchad@aol.com

OVEREND, Paul. b 66. Coll of Ripon & York St Jo BA88 Hull Univ MA97 Univ of Wales (Cardiff) PhD04. Coll of Resurr Mirfield 88. **d** 93 **p** 94. C Cayton w Eastfield *York* 93-96; Asst Chapl Univ of Wales (Cardiff) *Llan* 96; Sen Chapl 97-03; Tutor 03-04; Tutor St Mich Coll Llan 03-04; Teaching Fell Liv Hope Univ Coll 04-05; Dir Initial Minl Formation *Sarum* from 05. *Russell House, Stratford Road, Stratford sub Castle, Salisbury SP1 3LG* Tel (01722) 411944
E-mail paul.overend@salisbury.anglican.org

OVERINGTON, Canon David Vernon. b 34. ALCD60. **d** 60 **p** 61. C Penge Ch Ch w H Trin *Roch* 60-62; C Lenton *S'well* 62-65; PC Brackenfield w Wessington *Derby* 65-71; P-in-c Cubley w Marston Montgomery 71-76; R Bridgetown Australia 76-79; Par P Denmark 79-85; Can Bunbury 84-85; R E Fremantle w Palmyra 85-90; Field Officer Angl Dept of Educn 90-93; R Wembley 93-99; Hon Can Perth from 96; rtd 99; P-in-c Longside *Ab* 99-03; P-in-c New Pitsligo 99-03; P-in-c Old Deer 99-03; P-in-c Strichen 99-03. *223 Ralph Perring Court, Stone Park Avenue, Beckenham BR3 3LX* Tel (020) 8650 5291
E-mail djoverington@onetel.com

OVERTHROW, Royston John. b 45. Southn Univ BTh94. Portsm Dioc Tr Course 84. **d** 85. NSM Portsm Cathl *Portsm* 85-91; Perm to Offic 91-94; Bp's Dom Chapl *Sarum* 94-02; NSM Marlborough 02-04; rtd 04. *19 Bratton Avenue, Devizes SN10 5BA* Tel (01380) 722404 E-mail liznroyuk@supanet.com

OVERTON, Charles Henry. b 51. CCC Ox BA74 MA77 Fitzw Coll Cam PGCE75 BA79 MA85. Ridley Hall Cam 77. **d** 80 **p** 81. C Tonbridge SS Pet and Paul *Roch* 80-84; Asst Chapl St Lawr Coll Ramsgate 84-87; P-in-c Aythorpe w High and Leaden Roding *Chelmsf* 88-95; P-in-c Hughenden *Ox* 95-01; P-in-c Chalfont St Peter from 05. *The Vicarage, 4 Austenway, Chalfont St Peter, Gerrards Cross SL9 8NW* Tel (01753) 882389
E-mail charlesoverton@hotmail.com

OVERTON, David Malcolm. b 52. Surrey Univ BA97. Chich Th Coll. **d** 84 **p** 85. C Ches H Trin *Ches* 84-86; C Woodchurch 86-88; C Coppenhall 88-91; C Croydon St Jo *S'wark* 91-94; Perm to Offic *Lon* 97-00; C Selsey *Chich* 98-02; Miss P Ribbleton *Blackb* from 02. *140 Teil Green, Fulwood, Preston PR2 9PE* Tel (01772) 468009

OVERTON, Keith Charles. b 28. EAMTC 78. **d** 81 **p** 82. NSM Duxford *Ely* 81-84; NSM Whittlesford 84-88; P-in-c 88-94; P-in-c Pampisford 88-90; Perm to Offic *Bris* from 94. *86 Pittsfield, Cricklade, Swindon SN6 6AW* Tel (01793) 750321

OVERTON, Thomas Vincent Edersheim. b 34. New Coll Ox BA58 DipTh59 MA61. Wycliffe Hall Ox 58. **d** 60 **p** 61. C W Hampstead Trin *Lon* 60-63; C Leeds St Geo *Ripon* 63-67; Perm to Offic *Lon* 68-71; Thailand 71-78; R Knossington and Cold Overton *Leic* 78-81; V Owston and Withcote 78-81; R Bedford St Jo and St Leon *St Alb* 81-90; V Leigh *Roch* 91-99; rtd 99; Perm to Offic *B & W* 90-91 and *Lon* from 99. *14 The Broadwalk, Northwood HA6 2XD* Tel (01923) 829612

OVERTON-BENGE, Mrs Angela Margaret. b 46. UEA BA99. EAMTC 94. **d** 97 **p** 98. NSM Moulsham St Jo *Chelmsf* 97-01; Ind Chapl 01-04; C Aveley and Purfleet 01-04; Bp's Soc and Ind Adv *Bris* from 04; C Swindon All SS w St Barn from 04; C Swindon St Aug from 04. *St Augustine's Vicarage, Morris Street, Swindon SN2 2HT* Tel (01793) 618986
E-mail oangela@fish.co.uk

OVERY, Arthur William. b 19. JP. Nor Ord Course 73. **d** 76 **p** 77. NSM Lowestoft St Marg *Nor* 76-78; NSM Lowestoft and Kirkley 79-89; Perm to Offic from 89. *The Hollies, Warren Road, Lowestoft NR32 4QD* Tel (01502) 561289

OVEY, Michael John. b 58. Ball Coll Ox BA81 BCL82 ACT MTh00. Ridley Hall Cam 88. **d** 91 **p** 92. C Crowborough *Chich* 91-95; Australia 95-98; Kingham Hill Fell Oak Hill Th Coll from 98. *Oak Hill Theological College, Chase Side, London N14 4PS* Tel (020) 8449 0467 ext 248 E-mail mikeo@oakhill.ac.uk

OWEN, Bryan Philip. b 47. Keswick Hall Coll CertEd70 Coll of Ripon & York St Jo Cert Counselling 82. Cant Sch of Min 83. **d** 86 **p** 87. NSM Deal St Geo *Cant* 86-87; C Herne 87-89; R Clarkston *Glas* 89-93; Warden Scottish Chs Ho (Chs Together in Scotland) 93-96; V Cuddington *Guildf* 96-01; rtd 01; Perm to Offic *Glas* from 01. *Columcille, 10 Waverley Park, Kirkintilloch, Glasgow G66 2BP* Tel 0141-776 0407 Mobile 07796-155560
E-mail owen@clara.co.uk

OWEN, Mrs Carole Janice. b 55. **d** 01 **p** 02. NSM Cley Hill Warminster *Sarum* from 01. *11 Stuart Green, Warminster BA12 9NU* Tel (01985) 214849

OWEN, Caroline Ann. b 59. Univ of Wales (Abth) BA80 PGCE81. St Mich Coll Llan 03. **d** 05. NSM Bangor *Ban* from 05. *Ty'r Esgob, Upper Garth Road, Ffordd Garth, Bangor LL57 2SS* Tel (01248) 370847

OWEN, Christine Rose. b 62. Univ of Wales (Ban) BA83 PGCE84. Qu Coll Birm 86. **d** 88 **p** 94. C Ynyscynhaearn w Penmorfa and Porthmadog *Ban* 88-90; Chapl Lon Univ *Lon*

90-96; Hon C St Marylebone w H Trin 94-96; Min Can and Prec Worc Cathl *Worc* 96-00; R Llansantffraid Glan Conwy and Eglwysbach *St As* from 00. *The Rectory, 16 Y Bryn, Glan Conwy, Colwyn Bay LL28 5NJ* Tel (01492) 583099

OWEN, Clifford. *See* OWEN, Phillip Clifford

OWEN, Dafydd Gwyn. b 62. St Steph Ho Ox 95. **d** 97 **p** 98. C Whitchurch *Bris* 97-01; V Bris Ch the Servant Stockwood from 01; Hon Min Can Bris Cathl from 04. *The Vicarage, Goslet Road, Stockwood, Bristol BS14 8SP* Tel (01275) 831138 E-mail christheservant@blueyonder.co.uk

OWEN, Daniel James. b 71. Anglia Poly Univ BSc94 TCD BTh00. CITC 97. **d** 00 **p** 01. C Belfast St Donard *D & D* 00-03; I Rathcooney Union *C, C & R* from 03. *The Rectory, Fota View, Glounthaune, Cork, Irish Republic* Tel (00353) (21) 435 5208 E-mail danielsonja@eircom.net

OWEN, David Cadwaladr. b 56. Grey Coll Dur BSc77 Univ Coll Worc PGCE99. WEMTC 00. **d** 03 **p** 04. NSM Pershore w Pinvin, Wick and Birlingham *Worc* from 03. *Caedmon, Main Street, Pinvin, Pershore WR10 2ER* Tel (01386) 554249 Mobile 07837-800009 E-mail dc.owen@dunelm.org.uk

OWEN, Canon David William. b 31. Down Coll Cam BA55 MA58. Linc Th Coll 55. **d** 57 **p** 58. C Salford St Phil w St Steph *Man* 57-61; C Grantham St Wulfram *Linc* 61-65; V Messingham 65-70; V Spilsby w Hundleby 70-77; R Aswardby w Sausthorpe 71-77; R Langton w Sutterby 71-77; R Halton Holgate 73-77; P-in-c Firsby w Gt Steeping 75-77; P-in-c Lt Steeping 75-77; TR Louth 77-92; Chapl Louth Co Hosp 77-92; RD Louthesk *Linc* 82-89; Can and Preb Linc Cathl 85-92; TR Swan *Ox* 92-97; RD Claydon 94-96; rtd 97. *19 Stephen Road, Headington, Oxford OX3 9AY* Tel (01865) 766585

OWEN, Derek Malden. b 29. Oak Hill Th Coll 74. **d** 76 **p** 77. C Eastbourne H Trin *Chich* 76-78; C Walthamstow St Mary w St Steph *Chelmsf* 78-81; R Ditcheat w E Pennard and Pylle *B & W* 81-83; Warden Shaftesbury Housing Assn 86-94; rtd 94; Hon C Fairlight, Guestling and Pett *Chich* 94-97; P-in-c Llanishen w Trellech Grange and Llanfihangel etc *Mon* from 00. *The Vicarage, Llanishen, Chepstow NP16 6QL* Tel (01600) 860845

OWEN, Edgar. b 26. WMMTC. **d** 82 **p** 83. NSM Garretts Green *Birm* 82-88; NSM Stechford 88-94; rtd 94; Perm to Offic *Birm* from 94. *36 Colbourne Court, 116 Frederick Road, Stechford, Birmingham B33 8AE* Tel 0121-783 5603

OWEN, Emyr. b 69. Lancs Poly BSc91. Westcott Ho Cam BA94 CTM95. **d** 95 **p** 96. C Llanbeblig w Caernarfon and Betws Garmon etc *Ban* 95-96; C Llanberis w Llanrug 96-98; TV Bangor 98-02; P-in-c Llandygai and Maes y Groes 98-02; V Nefyn w Tudweiliog w Llandudwen w Edern from 02. *The Vicarage, Lon Isaf, Morfa Nefyn, Pwllheli LL53 6BS* Tel (01758) 720494 E-mail emyr_owen@hotmail.com

OWEN, Eric Cyril Hammersley. b 46. Liv Univ LLB68 Barrister 69. St As Minl Tr Course 95. **d** 97 **p** 98. NSM Gresford *St As* 97-03; NSM Rhosymedre w Penycae 03-04. *Thistle Patch, 28 Wynnstay Lane, Marford, Wrexham LL12 8LG* Tel (01978) 856495 E-mail eowen@lineone.net

OWEN, Gary John. b 72. City Univ BSc93. Ridley Hall Cam BA97 CTM98. **d** 98 **p** 99. C Welshpool w Castle Caereinion *St As* 98-01; TV Wrexham from 01. *The Vicarage, 160 Borras Road, Wrexham LL13 9ER* Tel (01978) 350202

OWEN, Geoffrey Neill. b 55. Chich Th Coll. **d** 85 **p** 86. C Streatham St Pet *S'wark* 85-89; C Battersea Ch Ch and St Steph 89-91; TV Surbiton St Andr and St Mark 91-97; V Merton St Jas from 97. *St James's Vicarage, Beaford Grove, London SW20 9LB* Tel (020) 8540 3122

OWEN, Glyn John. b 56. Open Univ BA91 Nottm Univ MSc93. Cranmer Hall Dur 01. **d** 03 **p** 04. C Whiston *Sheff* from 03. *40 Flat Lane, Whiston, Rotherham S60 4EF* Tel (01709) 837388 E-mail revglynowen@blueyonder.co.uk

OWEN, Gordon Campbell. b 41. FRMetS65 MRAeS66 Univ of Wales (Ban) BD76 PGCE77 Ox Univ DipApTh97. Ban Ord Course 79. **d** 81 **p** 82. Hd RE Eirias High Sch Colwyn Bay 77-88; Chapl RAFVR from 81; Asst P Ban Cathl *Ban* 82-88; Chapl St Kath Coll and Liv Inst of HE 88-91; Dioc Liaison Officer for RE *Liv* 88-91; V Llanfair-is-gaer and Llanddeiniolen *Ban* 91-97; Educn Officer 91-97; Lic to Offic 97-00. *The Shieling, Penrhosgarnedd, Bangor LL57 2NH* Tel (01248) 352841

OWEN, Graham Anthony. b 54. Birm Univ BA77. Trin Coll Bris DipHE94. **d** 94 **p** 95. C Wiveliscombe w Chipstable, Huish Champflower etc *B & W* 94-98; R from 98. *The Vicarage, South Street, Wiveliscombe, Taunton TA4 2LZ* Tel (01984) 623309 E-mail graham@owen31.freeserve.co.uk

OWEN, Graham Wynne. b 46. Lon Inst of Educn MA81 GTCL67 FTCL70. Cant Sch of Min 90. **d** 93 **p** 94. C Eltham H Trin *S'wark* 93-97; P-in-c Shooters Hill Ch Ch 97-00; V 00-01; TV Sole Bay *St E* 01-04; P-in-c Framlingham w Saxtead from 04; RD Loes from 05. *The Rectory, St Michael's Close, Framlingham, Woodbridge IP13 9BJ* Tel and fax (01728) 621082 E-mail gowen.mowen@btinternet.com

OWEN, Gwyn. *See* OWEN, Dafydd Gwyn

OWEN, Harry Dennis. b 47. Oak Hill Th Coll 73. **d** 76 **p** 77. C Fulham Ch Ch *Lon* 76-81; V Byker St Mark *Newc* 81-89; V Plumstead All SS *S'wark* from 89; RD Plumstead from 03. *All Saints' Vicarage, 106 Herbert Road, London SE18 3PU* Tel (020) 8854 2995 E-mail h.d.owen@talk21.com

OWEN, James Thomas. *See* McNAUGHTAN-OWEN, James Thomas

OWEN, John Edward. b 52. Middx Poly BA75. Sarum & Wells Th Coll BTh81. **d** 81 **p** 82. C S Ashford Ch Ch *Cant* 81-85; TV Bemerton *Sarum* 85-91; V St Leonards and St Ives *Win* 91-95; R N Stoneham from 95. *The Rectory, 62 Glen Eyre Road, Southampton SO16 3NL* Tel (023) 8076 8123 E-mail jeowen@fish.co.uk

OWEN, Keith Robert. b 57. Warwick Univ BA Ox Univ BA MA85 Hull Univ MA(Ed)89. St Steph Ho Ox 79. **d** 82 **p** 83. C Headingley *Ripon* 82-85; Chapl Grimsby Colls of H&FE 85-90; Chapl for Educn *Linc* 85-90; P-in-c Linc St Botolph 90-95; Chapl to Caring Agencies Linc City Cen 90-95; V Steeton *Bradf* 95-01; Chapl Airedale NHS Trust 95-01; P-in-c Penzance St Mary w St Paul *Truro* 01-02; P-in-c Penzance St Jo 01-02; TR Penzance St Mary w St Paul and St Jo from 02. *St Mary's Vicarage, Chapel Street, Penzance TR18 4AP* Tel (01736) 363079 E-mail keith@gresley.f9.co.uk

OWEN, Kenneth Phillip. b 56. Liv Univ BA77 PGCE78. N Ord Course 92. **d** 95 **p** 96. C Heswall *Ches* 95-01; V Frankby w Greasby from 01. *The Vicarage, 14 Arrowe Road, Greasby, Wirral CH49 1RA* Tel 0151-678 6155 E-mail greasby@office.fsworld.co.uk

OWEN, Lionel Edward Joseph. b 19. S'wark Ord Course 66. **d** 69 **p** 70. C Hythe *Cant* 69-73; C Deal St Leon 73-75; V Teynham 75-84; RD Ospringe 80-84; rtd 84; Perm to Offic *Cant* 84-02. *5 The Dene, Hillside Street, Hythe CT21 5DH* Tel (01303) 267642

OWEN, Mark. St Mich Coll Llan. **d** 05. C Tredegar *Mon* from 05. *St James's Vicarage, Poplar Road, Tredegar NP22 4LH* Tel (01495) 722510

OWEN, Paul Jonathan. b 59. S Bank Poly BSc81. Ridley Hall Cam 00. **d** 02 **p** 03. C Seaford w Sutton *Chich* from 02. *2 Benenden Close, Seaford BN25 3PG* Tel (01323) 891831 E-mail paulowen@freenet.co.uk

OWEN, Peter Russell. b 35. St Mich Coll Llan DipTh63. **d** 63 **p** 64. C Wrexham *St As* 63-64; C Connah's Quay 64-65; Asst Chapl Miss to Seamen 66-69; P-in-c Upper Norwood All SS w St Marg *Cant* 69-72; C Hawarden *St As* 72-75; V Cilcain and Nannerch 75-79; R Cilcain and Nannerch and Rhydymwyn 79-83; V Brymbo and Bwlchgwyn 83-87; R Llangynhafal and Llanbedr Dyffryn Clwyd 87-99; P-in-c Llanychan 87-99; rtd 00. *Telpyn Forge, Rhewl, Ruthin LL15 1TP* Tel (01824) 704051

OWEN, Ms Petra Davine. b 65. Liv Univ BA87 Lanc Univ PGCE88. St Jo Coll Nottm MA97 and 98. **d** 98 **p** 99. C Brampton St Thos *Derby* 98-01; USA from 01. *The Church of the Good Shepherd, 345 South 312th, Federal Way, WA 95003, USA*

OWEN, Phillip Clifford. b 42. G&C Coll Cam BA65 MA69. Ridley Hall Cam 71. **d** 73 **p** 74. C Stowmarket *St E* 73-76; C Headley All SS *Guildf* 76-81; TV 81-89; P-in-c Clifton-on-Teme, Lower Sapey and the Shelsleys *Worc* 89-97; R 97-02; Dioc Ecum Officer 89-02; P-in-c Corfu *Eur* from 03. *Holy Trinity Anglican Church, 21 L Mavili St, Kerkira TK 49131, Corfu, Greece* Tel and fax (0661) 031467 E-mail clavis@hotmail.com *or* holytrin@otenet.gr

OWEN, Mrs Phyllis Elizabeth. NTMTC. **d** 05. NSM Southend *Chelmsf* from 05. *42 Harcourt Avenue, Southend-on-Sea SS2 6HU* Tel (01702) 313312

OWEN, Raymond Philip. b 37. Man Univ BScTech60 AMCST60 Teesside Poly DMS83. Chich Th Coll 65. **d** 67 **p** 68. C Elland *Wakef* 67-70; C Lindley 70-73; V Bradshaw 73-80; Ind Chapl *Dur* 80-91; TR Hanley H Ev *Lich* 91-99; Bp Stafford's Past Aux 03-04; rtd 04; Perm to Offic *Lich* from 04. *Hall Lodge, Wootton Road, Ellastone, Ashbourne DE6 2GU* Tel (01335) 324653 Mobile 07747-601379 Fax (01782) 201390 E-mail revrayowen@hotmail.com

OWEN, Richard Ellis. b 12. Clifton Th Coll 48. **d** 50 **p** 51. C Littleover *Derby* 50-53; C Whitchurch *Lich* 53-55; R Elkstone w Syde and Winstone *Glouc* 55-61; V Badminton w Acton Turville 61-71; V Kemble w Poole Keynes 71-73; R Pebworth w Dorsington 73-83; rtd 83; Perm to Offic *Glouc* 83-94. *40 Ballards Close, Mickleton, Chipping Camden GL55 6TN* Tel (01386) 438755

OWEN, Canon Richard Llewelyn. b 27. Univ of Wales (Lamp) BA51. St Mich Coll Llan 51. **d** 53 **p** 54. C Holyhead w Rhoscolyn w Llanfair-yn-Neubwll *Ban* 53-57; C Porthmadog 57-59; R Llanfechell w Bodewryd, Rhosbeirio etc 59-67; Youth Chapl 66-67; V Penrhyndeudraeth and Llanfrothen 67-77; R Llangefni w Tregaean and Llangristiolus etc 77-89; Can Ban Cathl 82-93; Hon Can from 93; Treas 86-93; Can Missr and V Bangor Cathl Par 89-93; RD Arfon 92-93; rtd 93; Perm to Offic *Ban* from 93. *Bodowen, Great Orme's Road, Llandudno LL30 2BF* Tel (01492) 872765

OWEN, Richard Matthew. b 49. Sheff Univ BA70 Leeds Univ CertEd73. N Ord Course 84. **d** 87 **p** 88. NSM Chorlton-cum-

Hardy St Werburgh *Man* 87-89; C N Reddish 89-91; Perm to Offic *York* 91-96; NSM York St Olave w St Giles 96-97; Perm to Offic 97-03. *The Old Mill, High Street, Lamberhurst, Tunbridge Wells TN3 8EQ*

OWEN, Robert Glynne. b 33. St Mich Coll Llan 56. **d** 58 **p** 59. C Machynlleth and Llanwrin *Ban* 58-62; C Llanbeblig w Caernarfon 62-65; V Carno and Trefeglwys 65-69; Hon C Dorking w Ranmore *Guildf* 69-75; Perm to Offic *St As* 75-94; V Broughton 94-99; rtd 99. *Briarcroft, Minera Road, Cefn y Bedd, Wrexham LL12 9TR* Tel (01978) 752864

OWEN, Robert Lee. b 56. Univ of Wales (Cardiff) BD79. Qu Coll Birm 79. **d** 81 **p** 82. C Holywell *St As* 81-84; Perm to Offic *Birm* 85-87; Chapl Blue Coat Sch Birm 85-87; Chapl St Elphin's Sch Matlock 87-94; Chapl Qu Marg Sch York from 94. *Queen Margaret's School, Escrick Park, Escrick, York YO19 6EU* Tel (01904) 728261

OWEN, Ronald Alfred. b 44. Wilson Carlile Coll 73 Sarum & Wells Th Coll 80. **d** 81 **p** 82. C Wotton St Mary *Glouc* 81-83; CF 83-97; P-in-c Salcombe *Ex* 97-02; V Salcombe and Malborough w S Huish from 02; RD Woodleigh 00-03. *The Vicarage, Devon Road, Salcombe TQ8 8HJ* Tel and fax (01548) 842626 Mobile 07970-727229 Fax (01548) 770361
E-mail revraowen@hotmail.com

OWEN, Roy Meredith. b 21. Univ of Wales BA43. St Mich Coll Llan 43. **d** 45 **p** 46. C Roath St Martin *Llan* 45-47; C Penarth w Lavernock 47-51; C Merthyr Dyfan 51-56; V Llangeinor 56-62; V Pontyclun w Talygarn 62-75; C Cadoxton-juxta-Barry 82-85; rtd 85; Perm to Offic *Llan* 86-88. *20 Mary Street, Llandaff North, Cardiff CF14 2JQ* Tel (029) 2021 4555

OWEN, Canon Stanley Alfred George. b 17. Worc Ord Coll 57. **d** 59 **p** 60. C Bickenhill w Elmdon *Birm* 59-60; R 60-86; rtd 86; Perm to Offic *Birm* from 86; Chmn and Sec Assn Ch Fellowships from 88. *Bickenhill House, 154 Lode Lane, Solihull B91 2HP* Tel 0121-704 9281

OWEN, Stuart James. b 68. Sunderland Poly BA91. Ripon Coll Cuddesdon BTh00. **d** 00 **p** 01. C Hendon St Mary *Lon* 00-01; C Hendon St Mary and Ch Ch 01-04; P Missr Edmonton St Mary w St Jo from 04. *St John's Vicarage, Dysons Road, London N18 2DS* Tel (020) 8807 2767 E-mail fr_stuart@hotmail.com

OWEN, Mrs Susan Margaret. b 38. St Andr Univ MA61 Univ of Wales (Swansea) MPhil91 Univ of Wales (Ban) BD93. Qu Coll Birm 94. **d** 95 **p** 96. NSM Shrewsbury St Geo *Lich* 95-98; P-in-c Penrhyndeudraeth w Llanfrothen w Beddgelert *Ban* 98-99; V from 99. *The Vicarage, Penrhyndeudraeth LL48 6LG* Tel (01766) 770021 E-mail sowen@vicarage.fsnet.co.uk

OWEN-JONES, Peter Charles. b 57. Ridley Hall Cam 92. **d** 94 **p** 95. C Leverington and Wisbech St Mary *Ely* 94-97; R Haslingfield w Harlton and Gt and Lt Eversden 97-05; P-in-c Glynde, W Firle and Beddingham *Chich* from 05. *The Vicarage, The Street, Firle, Lewes BN8 6NP* Tel (01273) 858227
E-mail poj@lineone.net

OWEN-JONES, Peter John. b 47. RMCS BScEng68 CEng84 MIMechE84 MBIM87. EMMTC 85. **d** 88 **p** 89. NSM Holbrook and Lt Eaton *Derby* 88-00; NSM W Hallam and Mapperley w Stanley from 01. *Bridge Cottage, 63 Derby Road, Stanley, Ilkeston DE7 6EX* Tel 0115-932 0764 Fax as telephone
E-mail jowenjones@aol.com

OWENS, Mrs Ann Lindsay. b 47. St Hild Coll Dur CertEd68 Man Univ BA94. N Ord Course 92. **d** 95 **p** 96. Chapl St Jas Sch Farnworth 94-97; NSM New Bury *Man* 95-97; C Heywood St Luke w All So 97-98; C Heywood 98-99; P-in-c Chadderton St Matt 99-04; P-in-c Chadderton St Luke 03-04; V Chadderton St Matt w St Luke 04-05; V Hurst from 05. *St John's Vicarage, 155 Kings Road, Ashton-under-Lyne OL6 8EZ* Tel 0161-330 1935 E-mail ann-lindsay.owens@virgin.net

OWENS, Christopher Lee. b 42. SS Mark & Jo Coll Chelsea 61 Lon Inst of Educn TCert. Linc Th Coll 66. **d** 69 **p** 70. C Dalston H Trin w St Phil *Lon* 69-72; C Portsea N End St Mark *Portsm* 72-81; TV E Ham w Upton Park St Alb *Chelmsf* 81-92; C Is of Dogs Ch Ch and St Jo w St Luke *Lon* 92-98; P-in-c Chingford St Edm *Chelmsf* 98-02; V from 02. *St Edmund's Vicarage, Larkswood Road, London E4 9DS* Tel (020) 8529 5226
E-mail christopher@owenseaster.freeserve.co.uk

OWENS, Mrs Margaret Jean. b 49. Man Univ BSc70 Birm Univ MSc72. St Jo Coll Nottm 99. **d** 01 **p** 02. NSM Hurdsfield *Ches* from 01. *44 Ryles Park Road, Macclesfield SK11 8AH* Tel (01625) 262335 Mobile 07775-801613 Fax (01625) 430284
E-mail mowens44@hotmail.com

OWENS, Philip Roger. b 47. Univ of Wales (Ban) DipTh70. Wells Th Coll 71. **d** 71 **p** 72. C Colwyn Bay *St As* 71-74; C Wrexham 74-77; TV 77-80; P-in-c Yoxford *St E* 80-85; Asst Stewardship and Resources Adv 80-85; R Bangor Monachorum and Worthenbury *St As* 85-98; Sec Dioc Stewardship Cttee 89-98; RD Bangor Isycoed 92-98; R Flint 98-03; RD Holywell 02-03. *3 Turnberry Avenue, Wrexham LL13 9GG* Tel 07808-167147 (mobile)

OWENS, Stephen Graham Frank. b 49. Ch Coll Cam BA71 MA75 CertEd72. Qu Coll Birm 73. **d** 75 **p** 76. C Stourbridge St Mich Norton *Worc* 75-80; Tanzania 80-88; V Dudley Wood *Worc* 88-99; P-in-c Mamble w Bayton, Rock w Heightington etc 99-02; V from 02. *The Vicarage, Church Lane, Rock, Kidderminster DY14 9TT* Tel (01299) 266580
E-mail stephen.owens@ffvicarage.fsnet.co.uk

OWERS, Ian Humphrey. b 46. Em Coll Cam BA68 MA72. Westcott Ho Cam 71. **d** 73 **p** 74. C Champion Hill St Sav *S'wark* 73-77; V Peckham St Sav 77-82; P-in-c E Greenwich Ch Ch w St Andr and St Mich 82-83; V 83-94; P-in-c Westcombe Park St Geo 85-94; RD Greenwich 92-94; Perm to Offic *St E* from 01 and *Bradf* from 03. *St Margaret's Vicarage, Newlay Lane, Leeds LS13 2AJ* Tel 0113-527 4811 Mobile 07808-613252
E-mail ianhowers@beeb.net

OXBROW, Canon Mark. b 51. Reading Univ BSc72 Fitzw Ho Cam BA75 MA79. Ridley Hall Cam 73. **d** 76 **p** 77. C Luton Ch Ch *Roch* 76-80; TV Newc Epiphany *Newc* 80-88; Chapl Newc Mental Health Unit 80-88; Regional Sec Eur CMS from 88; Communication Resources Sec from 94; Internat Miss Dir from 01; Hon Can Brussels Cathl *Eur* from 98; Perm to Offic *Lon* from 02. *10 Nettleden Avenue, Wembley HA9 6DP,* or *CMS, Partnership House, 157 Waterloo Road, London SE1 8UU* Tel (020) 8900 2485 *or* 7928 8681 Fax 7401 3215
E-mail markoxbrow@aol.com

OXENFORTH, Colin Bryan. b 45. St Chad's Coll Dur BA67. **d** 69 **p** 70. C Bromley St Andr *Roch* 69-72; C Nunhead St Antony *S'wark* 72-76; V Toxteth St Marg *Liv* 76-89; V Brixton St Matt *S'wark* 89-00; V Pemberton St Jo *Liv* from 00. *2 Shelley Drive, Orrell, Wigan WN5 8HW* Tel and fax (01942) 222237 E-mail oxenforth@3tc4u.net

OXFORD (Christ Church), Dean of. *See* LEWIS, The Very Revd Christopher Andrew

OXFORD, Archdeacon of. *See* HUBBARD, The Ven Julian Richard Hawes

OXFORD, Bishop of. *See* HARRIES, The Rt Revd Richard Douglas

OXLEY, Christopher Robert. b 51. Sheff Univ BA73 PGCE74 Ox Univ BA78 MA83. Wycliffe Hall Ox 76. **d** 79 **p** 80. C Greasbrough *Sheff* 79-82; C Doncaster St Leon and St Jude 82-84; Asst Chapl Brussels *Eur* 84-87; V Humberstone *Leic* 87-93; V Beaumont Leys 93-05; P-in-c Leic St Anne from 05; RD Christianity S 98-01; Dioc Dir Post-Ord Tr from 04. *St Anne's Vicarage, 76 Letchworth Road, Leicester LE3 6FH* Tel 0116-285 8452 E-mail oxley@leicester.anglican.org

OXLEY, David William. b 63. TCD BA85 BTh89. CITC 85. **d** 89 **p** 90. C Dublin Ch Ch Cathl Gp *D & G* 89-92; Clerical V Ch Ch Cathl Dublin 90-92; I Templebreedy w Tracton and Nohoval *C, C & R* 92-96; Min Can Cork Cathl 95-96; I Tullow w Shillelagh, Aghold and Mullinacuff *C & O* 96-02; I Dublin Santry w Glasnevin and Finglas *D & G* from 02. *The Rectory, Church Street, Finglass, Dublin 11, Irish Republic* Tel (00353) (1) 834 1015 Mobile 86-881 6486 E-mail revdwo@hotmail.com

OXLEY, Martin Neil. b 65. Birm Univ BA86 Edin Univ BD95. Edin Th Coll CECM95. **d** 95 **p** 96. C Glas St Mary *Glas* 95-97; C Glas St Matt 95-97; C Clydebank 95-97; P-in-c Glas St Matt 97-00; Dir Studies Edin Th Coll 97-00; R Lerwick *Ab* from 00; P-in-c Burravoe from 00; Warden Soc of Our Lady of the Is from 00. *St Magnus Rectory, Greenfield Place, Lerwick, Shetland ZE1 0AQ* Tel (01595) 693862 Mobile 07970-266578
E-mail frmartin@globalnet.co.uk

OXLEY, Mrs Paula Jane. b 51. Sheff Univ BA74 Nottm Univ MA00 PGCE75. EMMTC 93. **d** 93 **p** 94. NSM Birstall and Wanlip *Leic* 93-95; NSM Beaumont Leys 95-96; C 96-05; NSM Leic St Anne from 05. *St Anne's Vicarage, 76 Letchworth Road, Leicester LE3 6FH* Tel 0116-285 8452
E-mail oxleyp@btopenworld.com

OYET, Canon Julius Isotuk. b 34. Concordia Coll (USA) MA79. Immanuel Coll Ibadan DipTh70. **d** 70 **p** 72. Nigeria 70-90 and from 96; Hon Can Ondo from 88; Miss Partner CMS from 91; C Warblington w Emsworth *Portsm* 91-95; C Kirkby *Liv* 95-96; V Port Harcourt St Cyprian and Dioc Dir Tr 97-99; rtd 00. *c/o U J Oyet Esq, 34 White Horse Drive, Poole BH15 3BD*
E-mail ugbanaoyet@poole.hoarelea.com

P

PACEY, Edgar Prentice. b 29. Edin Univ MA50. Edin Th Coll 52. **d** 54 **p** 55. C Motherwell *Glas* 54-56; C Glas St Mary 56-61; R Coatbridge 61-70; Perm to Offic 70-77; Hon C Glas St Martin 77-83; Hon C Glas St Ninian 83-87; R Rothesay *Arg* 86-89; P-in-c 89-94; P-in-c Tighnabruaich 90-94; Perm to Offic *Glas* from 91 and *Arg* from 93; rtd 94; NSM Dunoon *Arg* 94-98; New

Zealand from 00. *Dunstan, 16 Broomfield Drive, Dunoon PA23 7LJ* Tel (01369) 702972 E-mail epp@dunstan16.fsnet.co.uk

PACEY, Graham John. b 52. Leeds Univ CertEd74 Open Univ BA81 Teesside Poly AdDipEd85. NEOC 90. **d** 93 **p** 94. C Kirkleatham *York* 93-96; V Middlesbrough St Agnes 96-00; R Skelton w Upleatham from 00. *The Rectory, North Terrace, Skelton-in-Cleveland, Saltburn-by-the-Sea TS12 2ES* Tel (01287) 650329 E-mail graham.pacey@ntlworld.com

PACEY, Michael John. d 96 **p** 97. NSM Tamworth *Lich* from 96. *1 Benson View, Tamworth B79 8TD* Tel (01827) 700410

PACKER, Catherine Ruth. *See* PICKFORD, Mrs Catherine Ruth

PACKER, Prof James Innell. b 26. CCC Ox BA48 MA52 DPhil55. Wycliffe Hall Ox 49. **d** 52 **p** 53. C Harborne Heath *Birm* 52-54; Lect Tyndale Hall Bris 55-61; Lib Latimer Ho Ox 61-62; Warden 62-69; Prin Tyndale Hall Bris 70-72; Assoc Prin Trin Coll Bris 72-79; Prof Hist Th Regent Coll Vancouver 79-89; Prof Th from 89; rtd 91. *6017 Holland Street, Vancouver BC, Canada, V6N 2B2*

✠**PACKER, The Rt Revd John Richard.** b 46. Keble Coll Ox BA67 MA. Ripon Hall Ox 67. **d** 70 **p** 71 **c** 96. C St Helier *S'wark* 70-73; Chapl Abingdon St Nic *Ox* 73-77; Tutor Ripon Hall Ox 73-75; Tutor Ripon Coll Cuddesdon 75-77; V Wath-upon-Dearne w Adwick-upon-Dearne *Sheff* 77-86; RD Wath 83-86; TR Sheff Manor 86-91; RD Attercliffe 90-91; Adn W Cumberland *Carl* 91-96; P-in-c Bridekirk 95-96; Suff Bp Warrington *Liv* 96-00; Bp Ripon and Leeds *Ripon* from 00. *Bishop Mount, Hutton Bank, Ripon HG4 5DP* Tel (01765) 602045 *or* 604148 Fax 600758 E-mail bishop.riponleeds@virgin.net

PACKER, Canon John William. b 18. K Coll Lon BA40 AKC40 BD41 MTh48. **d** 41 **p** 42. C Attenborough w Bramcote *S'well* 41-44; Asst Master Lanc Gr Sch 44-49; Lect RE Leeds Univ 50-53; Hd Master Canon Slade Gr Sch Bolton 53-77; Lic to Offic *Man* 53-77; Hon Can Man Cathl 75-78; rtd 77; Perm to Offic *Cant* from 78. *Netherbury, Meadow Close, Bridge, Canterbury CT4 5AT* Tel (01227) 830364

PACKER, Peter Aelred. b 48. St Jo Coll Dur BA70 St Chad's Coll Dur PhD79 Warwick Univ PGC Gp Psychotherapy 94 Strathclyde Univ MBA00. Ven English Coll Rome 95. **d** 96 **p** 97. SSM 93-99; Hon C S Lambeth St Anne and All SS *S'wark* 96-98; Lic to Offic *Ox* 97-99; Bp's Adv in Miss and Resources *Glas* 99-00. *133 Metro Central Heights, 119 Newington Causeway, London SE1 6BB* Tel (020) 7450 6554 E-mail p.packer@btinternet.com

PACKER, Preb Roger Ernest John. b 37. ARCO59 Pemb Coll Cam BA60 MA64. Cuddesdon Coll 60. **d** 62 **p** 63. C Chippenham St Andr w Tytherton Lucas *Bris* 62-65; C Caversham *Ox* 65-70; R Sandhurst 70-91; V Bridgwater St Mary, Chilton Trinity and Durleigh *B & W* 91-00; RD Bridgwater 94-00; Preb Wells Cathl 96-00; rtd 00; Perm to Offic *Chelmsf* from 00. *3 Kreswell Grove, Harwich CO12 3SZ* Tel (01255) 502239

PACKHAM, Ms Elizabeth Daisy. b 33. Goldsmiths' Coll Lon BSc54 CertEd55. N Ord Course. **dss** 83 **d** 87 **p** 94. Fairfield *Derby* 83-84; Buxton w Burbage and King Sterndale 84-95; Par Dn 87-94; C 94-95; P-in-c Chinley w Buxworth 95-98; Perm to Offic from 98; rtd 98. *100 Manchester Road, Chapel-en-le-Frith, Stockport SK23 9TP* Tel (01298) 812921

PACKMAN, James Morley. b 76. SS Hild & Bede Coll Dur MSci99. Oak Hill Th Coll BA04. **d** 04 **p** 05. C Eastbourne All SS *Chich* from 04. *1F Grassington Road, Eastbourne BN20 7BP* Tel (01323) 721231

PADDICK, Graham. b 47. S'wark Ord Course. **d** 89 **p** 90. C St Helier *S'wark* 89-93; P-in-c Thornton Heath St Paul 93-96; V 96-98; V Dormansland from 98. *St John's Vicarage, The Platt, Dormansland, Lingfield RH7 6QU* Tel (01342) 832391 E-mail stjohndor@supanet.com

PADDISON, Canon Michael David William. b 41. Oak Hill Th Coll 75. **d** 77 **p** 78. C Gt Warley Ch Ch *Chelmsf* 77-80; C Rayleigh 80-83; R Scole, Brockdish, Billingford, Thorpe Abbots etc *Nor* 83-95; RD Redenhall 89-94; R Reepham, Hackford w Whitwell, Kerdiston etc from 95; RD Sparham from 00; Hon Can Nor Cathl from 02. *The Rectory, Station Road, Reepham, Norwich NR10 4LJ* Tel (01603) 870220

PADDOCK, John Allan Barnes. b 51. Liv Univ BA74 MA91 Ox Univ BA77 MA81 Glas Univ PhD05 Man Univ PGCE75 FRSA94. St Steph Ho Ox 75. **d** 80 **p** 81. C Matson *Glouc* 80-82; Asst Chapl Madrid *Eur* 82-83; Chapl R Gr Sch Lanc 83-86; Hon C Blackb Ch Ch w St Matt *Blackb* 83-86; Chapl RAF 86-91; Offg Chapl RAF 92-94; Chapl St Olave's Gr Sch Orpington 91-94; Perm to Offic *Blackb* 94-97; Chapl R Russell Sch Croydon 97-00; Hon C Bickley *Roch* 97-00; V Folkestone St Pet *Cant* 00-03; Hon Min Can Cant Cathl 01-03; V Glouc St Geo w Whaddon *Glouc* from 03. *St George's Vicarage, Grange Road, Tuffley, Gloucester GL4 0PE* Tel and fax (01452) 520851

PADFIELD, Stephen James. b 68. Ex Univ BA90 Univ Coll Dur PGCE92. Trin Coll Bris BA00 MA01. **d** 01 **p** 02. C Luton Ch Ch *Roch* 01-05; Chapl R Russell Sch Croydon from 05. *The Royal Russell School, Coombe Lane, Croydon CR9 5BX* Tel (020) 8657 4433 Mobile 07747-775385 E-mail stevepadfield@tiscali.co.uk

PADGET, William Thomas. b 19. **d** 77 **p** 78. NSM Rodbourne Cheney *Bris* 77-90; rtd 90; Perm to Offic *Bris* from 90. *39 George Tweed Gardens, Ramleaze Drive, Swindon SN5 8WB* Tel (01793) 723789

PADLEY, Miss Karen. b 68. RGN89. St Jo Coll Nottm MA00. **d** 00 **p** 01. C Broxtowe *S'well* 00-04; V Marlpool *Derby* from 04. *All Saints' Vicarage, 85 Ilkeston Road, Heanor DE75 7BP* Tel (01773) 712097 E-mail karen@hpadley.fsnet.co.uk

PADLEY, Kenneth Peter Joseph. b 78. Ex Coll Ox BA00 MA04. Ripon Coll Cuddesdon BA03. **d** 04 **p** 05. C Cen Swansea *S & B* from 04. *32 Fernhill Close, Blackpill, Swansea SA3 5BX* Tel (01792) 402437 E-mail kenneth_padley@hotmail.com

PAGAN, Canon Keith Vivian. b 37. St Jo Coll Dur BA60 MA66. Chich Th Coll 60. **d** 62 **p** 63. C Clacton St Jas *Chelmsf* 62-64; C Wymondham *Nor* 64-70; P-in-c Guestwick 70-80; P-in-c Kettlestone 70-79; V Hindolveston 70-80; R Islay *Arg* 80-98; R Campbeltown 80-98; Miss to Seamen 80-98; Can St Jo Cathl Oban *Arg* 85-98; Can Cumbrae 85-98; Hon Can from 99; rtd 98. *Mariefield, Southend, Campbeltown PA28 6RW* Tel (01586) 830310

PAGE, Canon Alan George. b 24. Em Coll Cam BA48 MA52. Wycliffe Hall Ox 49. **d** 51 **p** 52. C Islington St Andr w St Thos and St Matthias *Lon* 51-53; Kenya 53-71; Hon Can Mt Kenya 71-75; Hon Can Mt Kenya S 75-84; C S Lyncombe *B & W* 71-72; R Freshford w Limpley Stoke 72-76; R Freshford, Limpley Stoke and Hinton Charterhouse 76-84; Can Mt Kenya Cen from 84; C Fulham St Mary N End *Lon* 87-89; rtd 89; Perm to Offic *B & W* from 89. *45 Ashley Avenue, Bath BA1 3DS* Tel (01225) 310532 E-mail ag.page@ukonline.co.uk

PAGE, Alan Richard Benjamin. b 38. Univ of Wales (Lamp) BA60 BSc. St Mich Coll Llan 60. **d** 62 **p** 63. C Cardiff St Andr and St Teilo *Llan* 62-64; C Newport St Julian *Mon* 64-67; C Hoxton H Trin w St Mary *Lon* 67-69; C Winchmore Hill H Trin 69-71; V Camden Town St Mich w All SS and St Thos 71-98; Public Preacher 98-02; rtd 02. *7 Four Ash Street, Usk NP15 1BW*

PAGE, David. b 48. Bris Univ BA70 Leic Univ MA74 Southn Univ PGCE74 Nottm Univ DipTh82. St Jo Coll Nottm 81. **d** 83 **p** 84. C Morden *S'wark* 83-86; V Wimbledon St Luke 86-91; P-in-c Clapham Common St Barn 91-92; V from 92. *St Barnabas' Vicarage, 12 Lavender Gardens, London SW11 1DL* Tel (020) 7223 5953 E-mail dp@fish.co.uk

PAGE, David James. b 62. Liv Univ BSc83 Qu Coll Ox DPhil87. Trin Coll Bris BA93 MA95. **d** 96 **p** 97. C Knutsford St Jo and Toft *Ches* 96-99; R Elworth and Warmingham from 99. *The Rectory, 38 Roman Way, Sandbach CW11 9EW* Tel (01270) 762415 E-mail page.stpeter@tinyworld.co.uk

✠**PAGE, The Rt Revd Dennis Fountain.** b 19. G&C Coll Cam BA41 MA45 Open Univ BSc96. Linc Th Coll 41. **d** 43 **p** 44 **c** 75. C Rugby St Andr *Cov* 43-49; R Weeting *Ely* 49-65; R Hockwold w Wilton 49-65; RD Feltwell 53-65; Hon Can Ely Cathl 63-65 and 68-75; V Yaxley 65-75; Adn Huntingdon 65-75; Suff Bp Lancaster *Blackb* 75-85; rtd 85; Perm to Offic *St E* from 85. *Larkrise, Hartest, Bury St Edmunds IP29 4ES* Tel (01284) 830694

PAGE, Mrs Dorothy Jean. b 29. Portsm Poly CertEd50. Ox NSM Course 84. **d** 87 **p** 94. NSM Wantage Downs *Ox* from 87. *11 North Street, Marcham, Abingdon OX13 6NG* Tel (01865) 391462

PAGE, The Ven Gilbert Alfred Derek. b 35. **d** 93 **p** 94. Australia from 79; Dir Miss Tas 89-94; Asst P Launceston St Jo 94-95; P-in-c George Town 95-98; Chapl Miss to Seamen Bell Bay 95-98; Adn Burnie 97-00; R Devonport 98-01; Miss Support Officer from 01. *17 Hoskin Street, North Nowra, NSW, Australia 2541* Tel (0061) (2) 4422 3403 Mobile 419-241950 E-mail gandrpage@shoal.net.au

PAGE, Mrs Irene May. b 38. Birm Univ BA58. NEOC 85. **d** 87 **p** 94. Par Dn Cockfield *Dur* 87-90; Par Dn Waterloo St Jo w St Andr *S'wark* 90-94; C 94-95; R Old Charlton St Thos 95-02; C Charlton 02-03; rtd 03. *40 Wolverton Road, Rednal, Birmingham B45 8RN* Tel 0121-460 1745

PAGE, Jacqueline Anne. b 57. St Alb and Ox Min Course 96. **d** 99 **p** 00. NSM Stevenage H Trin *St Alb* 99-03; NSM Benington w Walkern from 03. *5 Sinfield Close, Stevenage SG1 1LQ* Tel (01438) 368502

PAGE, Jean. *See* PAGE, Mrs Dorothy Jean

PAGE, John Jeremy. b 56. Keble Coll Ox BA79 MA82 New Coll Edin BD86. Edin Th Coll 83. **d** 86 **p** 87. C Wetherby *Ripon* 86-89; TV Wrexham *St As* 89-92; Chapl Hymers Coll Hull 92-98; Chapl Charterhouse Sch Godalming 98-03; TR Hale w Badshot Lea *Guildf* from 03. *The Rectory, 25 Upper Hale Road, Farnham GU9 0NX* Tel (01252) 716469 Fax 713862 E-mail john@padblack.co.uk

PAGE, John Laurance Howard. b 40. ALCD. **d** 65 **p** 66. C Spitalfields Ch Ch w All SS *Lon* 65-69; C Win Ch Ch *Win* 69-72; C Ringwood 72-76; V Lockerley and E Dean w E and W Tytherley 76-89; V Lord's Hill 89-97; P-in-c Darby Green 97-02;

V 02-05; RD Romsey 85-89; rtd 05. *2 Champions Close, Fowlmere, Royston SG8 7TR* Tel (01763) 208214 E-mail page@web-hq.com

PAGE, Jonathan Michael. b 58. Ripon Coll Cuddesdon 97. **d** 99 **p** 00. C Littlemore *Ox* 99-02; V Chaddesden St Phil *Derby* from 02. *St Philip's Vicarage, Taddington Road, Chaddesden, Derby DE21 4JU* Tel (01332) 660072 E-mail chadphil@fish.co.uk

PAGE, Canon Michael John. b 42. K Coll Lon BD66 AKC66. **d** 67 **p** 68. C Rawmarsh w Parkgate *Sheff* 67-72; C-in-c Gleadless Valley CD 72-74; TR Gleadless Valley 74-77; V Lechlade *Glouc* 77-86; RD Fairford 81-86; V Winchcombe, Gretton, Sudeley Manor etc 86-02; Hon Can Glouc Cathl 91-02; RD Winchcombe 94-99; Chapl E Glos NHS Trust 94-02; rtd 02; Perm to Offic *Sheff* from 03. *18 Brocco Bank, Sheffield S11 8RR* Tel 0114-266 3798 E-mail michael_j_page@hotmail.com

PAGE, Owen Richard. b 53. FIBMS83. Linc Th Coll 89. **d** 91 **p** 92. C Gt Bookham *Guildf* 91-94; V Kings Heath *Pet* 94-99; TR Daventry, Ashby St Ledgers, Braunston etc from 99; RD Daventry from 00; ACUPA Link Officer from 00; CUF Project Officer 00-05. *31 Newbury Drive, Daventry NN11 0WQ* Tel (01327) 702638 E-mail owen@opage.freeserve.co.uk

PAGE, Canon Richard Dennis. b 23. G&C Coll Cam BA48 MA50. Ridley Hall Cam 48. **d** 50 **p** 51. C Ecclesfield *Sheff* 50-52; Chapl St Lawr Coll Ramsgate 52-58; Chapl Dean Close Sch Cheltenham 58-60 and 62-64; Chapl Netherton Tr Sch Morpeth 60-62; V Ecclesfield *Sheff* 64-71; RD Ecclesfield 66-71; P-in-c Holkham w Egmere and Waterden *Nor* 71-78; R Wells next the Sea 71-78; RD Burnham and Walsingham 72-78; V Hemsby 78-83; P-in-c Brooke w Kirstead 83-85; P-in-c Mundham w Seething 83-85; P-in-c Thwaite 83-85; R Brooke, Kirstead, Mundham w Seething and Thwaite 85-89; Hon Can Nor Cathl 87-89; rtd 90; Perm to Offic *Nor* from 90. *39 Bircham Road, Reepham, Norwich NR10 4NG* Tel (01603) 870886

PAGE, Robert William Charles. b 67. St Steph Ho Ox 90. **d** 93 **p** 94. C Hockerill *St Alb* 93-95; C Kilburn St Aug w St Jo *Lon* 95-02; V Leytonstone St Marg w St Columba *Chelmsf* from 02. *St Margaret's Vicarage, 15 Woodhouse Road, London E11 3NG* Tel (020) 8519 0813 E-mail rob@stmandstc.fsnet.co.uk

PAGE, Teehan Dawson. b 61. Ch Ch Ox BA83 MA87 K Coll Lon MA96. St Steph Ho Ox 91. **d** 93 **p** 94. C Surbiton St Andr and St Mark *S'wark* 93-96; Chapl Reed's Sch Cobham 96-99; Asst Chapl Tonbridge Sch 99-00; Sen Chapl from 00. *1 Dry Hill Road, Tonbridge TN9 1LT* Tel (01732) 353468 E-mail tdp@tonbschl.demon.co.uk

PAGE, Thomas William. b 57. Sarum & Wells Th Coll 84. **d** 87 **p** 88. C Caterham *S'wark* 87-91; C Cheam 91-95; P-in-c Cranham *Chelmsf* 95-04; Dioc NSM Officer from 99; R Chingford SS Pet and Paul from 04. *The Rectory, 2 The Green Walk, London E4 7ER* Tel (020) 8529 1291 E-mail frtompage@priest.com

PAGE, Canon Trevor Melvyn. b 41. Dur Univ BA63 Fitzw Coll Cam BA67 MA72. Westcott Ho Cam 64. **d** 67 **p** 68. C Millhouses H Trin *Sheff* 67-69; Chapl Sheff Univ 69-74; V Doncaster Intake 74-82; Can Res Sheff Cathl 82-00; Dioc Dir of In-Service Tr 82-95; Dioc Dir of Ords and Post-Ord Tr 82-00; R Bradfield from 00; Hon Can Sheff Cathl from 01. *The Rectory, High Bradfield, Bradfield, Sheffield S6 6LG* Tel 0114-285 1225

PAGE, William George. b 42. Linc Th Coll 83. **d** 85 **p** 86. C Boston *Linc* 85-89; V Sibsey w Frithville from 89; RD Holland E 95-97. *The Vicarage, Vicarage Lane, Sibsey, Boston PE22 0RT* Tel and fax (01205) 750305 E-mail pageatsibseyvicarage@care4free.net

PAGE-CHESTNEY, Michael William. b 47. Linc Th Coll 80. **d** 82 **p** 83. C Barton upon Humber *Linc* 82-85; TV Gt Grimsby St Mary and St Jas 85-91; V E Stockwith 91-96; V Blyton w Pilham and Laughton w Wildsworth 91-93; V Corringham and Blyton Gp 93-03; P-in-c Immingham from 03; P-in-c Habrough Gp from 03. *The Vicarage, 344 Pelham Road, Immingham DN40 1PU* Tel (01469) 572560 E-mail mike@page-chestney.co.uk

PAGE-CHESTNEY, Mrs Susan Valerie. b 49. EMMTC DipTh86. **dss** 86 **d** 87 **p** 94. NSM Gt Grimsby St Mary and St Jas *Linc* 86-91; NSM Blyton w Pilham and Laughton w Wildsworth 91-93; NSM Corringham and Blyton Gp 93-03; Chapl W Lindsey NHS Trust 94-99; Chapl Linc and Louth NHS Trust 99-01; Chapl United Lincs Hosps NHS Trust 01-03; NSM Immingham *Linc* from 03; NSM Habrough Gp from 03. *The Vicarage, 344 Pelham Road, Immingham DN40 1PU* Tel (01469) 572560 E-mail sue@heavenlyhugs.com

PAGE-CLARK, Howard David. b 53. Fitzw Coll Cam MA77. LNSM course 96. **d** 97 **p** 98. OLM Lytchett Minster *Sarum* from 97. *37 Gorse Lane, Poole BH16 5RR* Tel (01202) 620239 E-mail howard.pageclark@btopenworld.com

PAGE DAVIES, David John. b 36. St Cath Soc Ox BA58 MA62. St D Coll Lamp 58. **d** 60 **p** 61. C Rhosddu *St As* 60-68; Chr Aid Area Sec (Glos, Herefords and Worcs) 68-85; Midl Regional Co-ord 78-85; Area Co-ord (Devon and Cornwall) 86-01; Lic to Offic *Truro* 86-01; Perm to Offic from 01; rtd 01. *3 Chyenhal Cottages, Buryas Bridge, Penzance TR19 6AN* Tel (01736) 732466 E-mail jpagedavies@aol.com

PAGE-TURNER, Canon Edward Gregory Ambrose Wilford. b 31. Qu Coll Birm 57. **d** 60 **p** 61. C Helmsley *York* 60-64; C Kensington St Phil Earl's Court *Lon* 64-67; C Walton-on-Thames *Guildf* 67-70; V Seend *Sarum* 70-71; V Seend and Bulkington 71-79; R Bladon w Woodstock *Ox* 79-87; P-in-c Begbroke 80-86; P-in-c Shipton-on-Cherwell 80-86; P-in-c Hampton Gay 80-85; RD Woodstock 84-87; P-in-c Wootton by Woodstock 85-87; R Patterdale *Carl* 87-89; R Askerswell, Loders and Powerstock *Sarum* 89-01; RD Lyme Bay 92-98; RD Beaminster 94-98; Can and Preb Sarum Cathl 99-01; rtd 01; Perm to Offic *B & W* from 02 and *Sarum* from 01. *The Old School House, 9 School House Close, Beaminster DT8 3AH* Tel and fax (01308) 861410

PAGET, Alfred Ivor. b 24. St Aid Birkenhead 56. **d** 59 **p** 60. C Hoylake *Ches* 59-62; Chapl Miss to Seamen Hong Kong 62-63; Melbourne Australia 63-64; C Hyde St Geo *Ches* 64-66; R Gt and Lt Henny w Middleton *Chelmsf* 66-74; C Gt Holland 74-79; V Holland-on-Sea 79-92; rtd 92; Perm to Offic *S'wark* 92-98; *Lon* 96-02; *Chelmsf* 99-05. *6 Bary Close, Cheriton Fitzpaine, Crediton EX17 4JY* Tel (01363) 860069

PAGET, Richard Campbell. b 54. Collingwood Coll Dur BA76 Rob Coll Cam BA87. Ridley Hall Cam 85. **d** 88 **p** 89. C Gipsy Hill Ch Ch *S'wark* 88-92; R Chatham St Mary w St Jo *Roch* 92-98; P-in-c Brenchley 99-00; V from 00. *The Vicarage, 8 Broadoak, Brenchley, Tonbridge TN12 7NN* Tel (01892) 722140

PAGET, Robert James Innes. b 35. AKC59. **d** 60 **p** 61. C Attenborough w Bramcote *S'well* 60-63; C Cheltenham St Mark *Glouc* 63-72; P-in-c Pilsley *Derby* 72-73; TV N Wingfield, Pilsley and Tupton 73-89; R Pinxton 89-97; P-in-c Ambergate and Heage from 97. *The Vicarage, 65 Derby Road, Ambergate, Belper DE56 2GD* Tel (01773) 852072

PAGET-WILKES, The Ven Michael Jocelyn James. b 41. NDA64 ALCD69. **d** 69 **p** 70. C Wandsworth All SS *S'wark* 69-74; V Hatcham St Jas 74-82; V Rugby St Matt *Cov* 82-90; Adn Warwick from 90. *10 Northumberland Road, Leamington Spa CV32 6HA* Tel (01926) 313337 *or* 674328 E-mail archdeacon.michael@covdioc.org

PAGETT, Andrew Stephen. b 45. Bris & Glouc Tr Course. **d** 82 **p** 83. NSM Swindon New Town *Bris* 82-01; C Paignton St Jo *Ex* 01-04; V Lifton, Broadwoodwidger, Stowford etc from 04. *The Rectory, Parsonage Court, Lifton PL16 0BJ* Tel (01566) 784008

PAICE, Alan. b 26. AKC53. **d** 55 **p** 56. C Leek St Edw *Lich* 55-59; C Haslemere *Guildf* 59-63; C Eton w Boveney *Ox* 63-74; P-in-c Hawridge w Cholesbury 74-83; P-in-c The Lee 74-83; V 83-86; P-in-c Aston Clinton St Leon 79-83; R Hawridge w Cholesbury and St Leonard 83-86; rtd 86. *2 The Poplars, Park Lane, Pinhoe, Exeter EX4 9HH* Tel (01392) 464741

PAICE, Michael Antony. b 35. Kelham Th Coll 55. **d** 60 **p** 61. C Skegby *S'well* 60-62; C Carlton 62-66; V Misterton and W Stockwith 66-81; V Olveston and P-in-c Littleton on Severn w Elberton *Bris* 81-83; Deputation Appeals Org CECS 83-89; R Sutton St Nicholas w Sutton St Michael *Heref* 89-96; R Withington w Westhide 89-96; rtd 96. *Frankhurst, Sutton St Nicholas, Hereford HR1 3BN* Tel (01432) 880279

PAICE, Richard James Rowland. b 72. Ch Ch Ox BA94 MA99. Oak Hill Th Coll BA00. **d** 00 **p** 01. C Eastbourne All So *Chich* 00-03; Chapl Bp Bell Sch 00-03; P-in-c Warbleton and Bodle Street Green *Chich* from 03. *Warbleton Rectory, Rushlake Green, Heathfield TN21 9QJ* Tel (01435) 830421 E-mail rjrpaice@yahoo.com

PAILING, Crispin Alexander. b 75. Qu Coll Ox BA98 MA01. Ripon Coll Cuddesdon BA02. **d** 03 **p** 04. C Four Oaks *Birm* from 03. *12 Clarence Gardens, Sutton Coldfield B74 4AP* Tel 0121-308 6279 E-mail pailing@fish.co.uk

PAILING, Rowena Fay. b 77. Qu Coll Ox BA99 MA02. Ripon Coll Cuddesdon BA02. **d** 03 **p** 04. C Four Oaks *Birm* 03-04; C Gravelly Hill from 04. *12 Clarence Gardens, Sutton Coldfield B74 4AP* Tel 0121-308 6730 E-mail pailing@fish.co.uk

PAIN, Canon David Clinton. b 36. K Coll Lon 56. **d** 64 **p** 64. Benin 64-67; Ghana 67-86; Hon Can Accra 80-86; V Kemp Town St Mary *Chich* 86-93; Chapl St Mary's Hall Brighton 88-93; V Billingshurst *Chich* 93-05; RD Horsham 98-02; rtd 05; P-in-c Chidham *Chich* from 05. *The Vicarage, Cot Lane, Chidham, Chichester PO18 8TA* Tel (01243) 573147

PAIN, Michael Broughton George. b 37. Dur Univ BA61. Wycliffe Hall Ox 61. **d** 63 **p** 64. C Downend *Bris* 63-67; C Swindon Ch Ch 67-70; V Alveston 70-78; V Guildf Ch Ch *Guildf* 78-90; TR Melksham *Sarum* 90-98; Chapl Melksham Hosp 90-98; TR Redhorn *Sarum* 98-03; rtd 03; Perm to Offic *Sarum* from 03. *Rickety Cottage, 70 Bradenstoke, Chippenham SN15 4EL* Tel (01249) 890727

PAIN, Canon Richard Edward. b 56. Bris Univ BA79 Univ of Wales (Cardiff) BD84. St Mich Coll Llan 81. **d** 84 **p** 85. C Caldicot *Mon* 84-86; P-in-c Cwmtillery 86-88; V 88-91; V Six Bells 88-91; V Risca 91-98; V Overmonnow w Wonastow and Michel Troy 98-03; V Monmouth w Overmonnow etc from 03; Dioc Warden of Ord from 01; Can St Woolos Cathl from 03. *The Vicarage, The Parade, Monmouth NP25 3PA* Tel (01600) 714454

PAINE, Alasdair David MacConnell. b 60. Trin Coll Cam BA82 MA86 MSc84. Wycliffe Hall Ox 94. **d** 96 **p** 97. C Ex St Leon w H Trin *Ex* 96-01; V Westbourne Ch Ch Prop Chpl *Win* from 02. *134 Alumhurst Road, Bournemouth BH4 8HU* Tel (01202) 762164 E-mail alasdair@claranet.co.uk

PAINE, Peter Stanley. b 46. K Coll Lon BD69 AKC69. Cuddesdon Coll 69. **d** 71 **p** 72. C Leeds St Aid *Ripon* 71-74; C Harrogate St Wilfrid 74-78; V Beeston Hill H Spirit 78-82; TV Seacroft 82-90; V Martham w Repps w Bastwick *Nor* 90-94; V Martham and Repps with Bastwick, Thurne etc 94-04; P-in-c Foremark and Repton w Newton Solney *Derby* from 04. *St Wystan's Vicarage, Willington Road, Repton, Derby DE65 6FH* Tel (01283) 703317
E-mail peterspaine@surefish.co.uk

PAINE, William Barry. b 58. TCD DipTh84. CITC. **d** 84 **p** 85. C Glendermott *D & R* 84-86; C Lurgan St Jo *D & D* 86-88; I Kilbarron w Rossnowlagh and Drumholm *D & R* 88-91; CF 91-00; I Tynan w Middletown and Aghavilly *Arm* from 00. *The Rectory, 16 Derryhaw Road, Tynan BT60 4SS* Tel (028) 3756 8619

PAINE DAVEY, Nathan Paul. b 64. Barrister-at-Law 88 Birm Poly LLB86. St Steph Ho Ox 89. **d** 92 **p** 93. C Palmers Green St Jo *Lon* 92-95; C Kentish Town St Silas 95-98; C Haverstock Hill H Trin w Kentish Town St Barn 95-98; C Kentish Town St Silas and H Trin w St Barn 98-01; Perm to Offic from 01. *30A Hadley Street, London NW1 8SS* Tel (020) 7482 1170

PAINTER, Christopher Mark. b 65. Cranmer Hall Dur. **d** 00 **p** 01. C Melksham *Sarum* 00-03; Chapl Wilts and Swindon Healthcare NHS Trust 02-03; TV Eccles *Man* from 03. *St Andrew's Vicarage, 11 Abbey Grove, Eccles, Manchester M30 9QN* Tel 0161-707 1742 E-mail ckpainter@blueyonder.co.uk

PAINTER, The Ven David Scott. b 44. Worc Coll Ox BA68 MA72 LTCL65. Cuddesdon Coll 68. **d** 70 **p** 71. C Plymouth St Andr *Ex* 70-73; Chapl Plymouth Poly 71-73; C St Marylebone All SS *Lon* 73-76; Abp's Dom Chapl *Cant* 76-80; Dir of Ords 76-80; V Roehampton H Trin *S'wark* 80-91; PV Westmr Abbey 81-91; RD Wandsworth *S'wark* 85-90; Perm to Offic 91; Can Res and Treas S'wark Cathl 91-00; Dioc Dir of Ords 91-00; Adn Oakham *Pet* from 00. *7 Minster Precincts, Peterborough PE1 1XS* Tel (01733) 891360 Fax 554524
E-mail david.painter@peterborough-cathedral.org.uk

PAINTER, John. b 25. Selw Coll Cam BA48 MA53. Ripon Hall Ox 48. **d** 50 **p** 51. C Stoke Newington St Mary *Lon* 50-55; C Woodside Park St Barn 55-56; C Llangiwg *S & B* 56-59; C-in-c Swansea St Jo 59-60; R Chipstable w Raddington *B & W* 61-64; V Audenshaw St Steph *Man* 64-66; V Sandown Ch Ch *Portsm* 66-72; R Keinton Mandeville *B & W* 72-77; P-in-c Lydford-on-Fosse 76-77; R Keinton Mandeville w Lydford on Fosse 77-90; RD Cary 81-90; RD Bruton 82-85; rtd 90; Perm to Offic *B & W* from 90; Perm to Offic *Sarum* from 96. *2 Juniper Gardens, Gillingham SP8 4RF* Tel (01747) 823818

PAINTING, Stephen Nigel. b 60. Trin Coll Bris 01. **d** 03 **p** 04. C Heanton Punchardon w Marwood *Ex* from 03. *Fig Tree House, 58A Poyers, Wrafton, Braunton EX33 2DN* Tel (01271) 812112
E-mail painting@fish.co.uk

PAIRMAN, David Drummond. b 47. GGSM CertEd. Chich Th Coll 82. **d** 84 **p** 85. C Cowes St Mary *Portsm* 84-87; C Marshwood Vale *Sarum* 87-90; C Hawkchurch 87-90; C Marshwood Vale 90-95; rtd 95. *Achilles, Old Pinn Lane, Exeter EX1 3RF* Tel (01392) 464488

PAISEY, Gerald Herbert John. b 31. Wm Booth Memorial Coll 51 Lon Univ CertRS60 Leic Univ CertEd62 Nottm Univ DipRE68 DipAdEd70 MPhil77 Lanc Univ MA78 K Coll Lon PhD91. St Alb Minl Tr Scheme 80. **d** 88 **p** 90. NSM Montrose *Bre* 88-90; NSM Inverbervie 88-90; Lect Robert Gordon Univ *Ab* 89-97; P-in-c Stonehaven and Catterline *Bre* 90-01; rtd 01; Tutor Open Univ from 90; Perm to Offic *Bre* from 01. *20 St Michael's Way, Newtonhill, Stonehaven AB39 2GS* Tel (01569) 730338

PAISEY, Jeremy Mark. b 58. Aber Univ LLB81 Solicitor 83. Coates Hall Edin 92. **d** 94 **p** 95. C Turriff *Ab* 94-97; C Buckie 94-97; C Banff 94-97; C Cuminestown 94-97; C Portsoy 94-97; P-in-c Buckie from 97; P-in-c Portsoy from 97; P-in-c Banff from 98. *All Saints House, 14 Cluny Square, Buckie AB56 1HA* Tel (01542) 832312 Mobile 07887-893582 Fax (01542) 832299
E-mail jpaisey@compuserve.com

PAISLEY, Samuel Robinson (Robin). b 51. Man Univ BSc72. Edin Th Coll BD91. **d** 91 **p** 92. C St Mary's Cathl *Glas* 91-95; P-in-c Bishopbriggs from 95; Chapl Stobhill NHS Trust 95-99; Teaching Consultant Glas Univ *Glas* 95-99; Bp's Adv in Min from 99. *St James's Rectory, 9 Meadowburn, Bishopbriggs, Glasgow G64 3HA* Tel 0141-772 4514 Fax 569 7508
E-mail rector@stjamesbishopbriggs.org.uk

PAJUNEN, Mika Kari Tapani. b 76. Helsinki Univ MTh00. **p** 01. C Helsinki *Eur* 02-04; Asst Chapl from 05. *Kivikarintie 3, 21570 Sauvo, Finland* E-mail mika.pajunen@helsinki.fi

PAKENHAM, Charles Wilfrid. b 18. Trin Coll Ox BA40 MA52. Wycliffe Hall Ox 40. **d** 41 **p** 42. C Sutton *Liv* 41-44; CMS 44-49; Nigeria 44-49; C Cheltenham St Mary *Glouc* 49-52; V Litherland Ch Ch *Liv* 52-84; rtd 84; Perm to Offic *Sarum* from 90; P-in-c W Woodhay w Enborne, Hampstead Marshall etc *Ox* 91-92; Perm to Offic 92-00. *15 Cook Road, Marlborough SN8 2EG* Tel (01672) 540531

PAKENHAM, Stephen Walter. b 29. Qu Coll Cam BA57 MA61. Linc Th Coll 57. **d** 59 **p** 60. C Handsworth St Jas *Birm* 59-61; C Handsworth St Andr 61-64; V Donnington *Chich* 64-75; V Appledram 64-75; V Durrington 75-81; V St Mary Bourne and Woodcott *Win* 81-88; rtd 88; Perm to Offic *Ex* 88-98 and *Win* from 98. *9 Chattis Hill Stables, Spitfire Lane, Stockbridge SO20 6JS* Tel (01264) 810225

PALIN, John Edward. b 47. Open Univ BA83 Leeds Univ MA89. St Mich Coll Llan 67. **d** 71 **p** 72. C Staveley *Derby* 71-74; C Nottingham St Mary *S'well* 75-77; P-in-c Thistleton 77-79; V Greetham w Stretton and Clipsham *Pet* 77-79; V Greetham and Thistleton w Stretton and Clipsham 79-83; TR Staveley and Barrow Hill *Derby* 83-87; Chapl R Hallamshire Hosp Sheff 87-88; Perm to Offic *Sheff* 88-90; C Bramley *Ripon* 90-91; TV 91-93; Chapl Doncaster and S Humber Healthcare NHS Trust from 93. *St Catherine's Hospital, Tickhill Road, Doncaster DN4 8QN* Tel (01302) 796018

PALIN, Roy. b 34. Man Univ BA56. Ripon Hall Ox 65. **d** 67 **p** 68. C Ilkeston St Mary *Derby* 67-70; C Wollaton *S'well* 70-71; V Harby w Swinethorpe 71-79; V Thorney w Wigsley and Broadholme 71-79; P-in-c N Clifton 75-79; R Harby w Thorney and N and S Clifton 79-80; V Tuxford 80-81; P-in-c Laxton 80-81; P-in-c Markham Clinton 80-81; P-in-c Weston 80-81; V Tuxford w Weston and Markham Clinton 81-90; R Nuthall 90-99; rtd 99; Perm to Offic *Nor* from 00. *31 Pine Walk, Weybourne, Holt NR25 7HJ* Tel (01263) 588146

PALK, Mrs Deirdre Elizabeth Pauline. b 41. Reading Univ BA63 Lon Univ MA94 AIL77 FIOSH96. S'wark Ord Course 81. **dss** 84 **d** 87. Wanstead H Trin Hermon Hill *Chelmsf* 84-87; Hon Par Dn 87-88; Hon Par Dn Walthamstow St Pet 88-93; Hon Chapl UPA Projects 93-97; Tutor NTMTC from 97. *North Thames Ministerial Training Course, Oak Hill, Chase Side, London N14 4PS* Tel (020) 8364 9442 Fax 8364 8889

PALLANT, Canon Roger Frank. b 35. Trin Coll Cam BA57 MA61. Wells Th Coll 57. **d** 59 **p** 60. C Stafford St Mary *Lich* 59-62; C Ipswich St Mary le Tower *St E* 62-65; Dioc Youth Chapl 62-65; Development Officer C of E Youth Coun 65-70; Hon C Putney St Mary *S'wark* 66-71; Org Sec New Syn Gp 70-71; R Hintlesham w Chattisham *St E* 71-80; V Ipswich All Hallows 80-88; Hon Can St E Cathl 85-00; P-in-c Sproughton w Burstall 88-00; Dioc Officer for OLM 88-00; RD Samford 93-99; rtd 00; Perm to Offic *St E* from 00. *163 Fircroft Road, Ipswich IP1 6PT* Tel (01473) 461148

PALLETT, Ian Nigel. b 59. Leeds Univ BA80. Linc Th Coll 81. **d** 84 **p** 85. C Halesowen *Worc* 84-88; C Mansfield Woodhouse *S'well* 88-91; R Morton and Stonebroom *Derby* 91-98; P-in-c Heanor 98-01; V 01-03; P-in-c Dingwall *Mor* from 03; P-in-c Strathpeffer from 03. *The Parsonage, 4 Castle Street, Dingwall IV15 9HU* Tel (01349) 862204

PALLIS, Mrs Maria. b 60. N Ord Course 96. **d** 99 **p** 00. C Chapel Allerton *Ripon* 99-03; P-in-c Collingham w Harewood from 03. *The Vicarage, Church Lane, Collingham, Wetherby LS22 5AU* Tel (01937) 573975 E-mail revdmp@aol.com

PALMER, Alister Gordon. b 46. Univ of Tasmania BA73 DipEd74. Trin Coll Bris 76 Ridley Hall Cam 78. **d** 80 **p** 81. C Patchway *Bris* 80-83; C Bushbury *Lich* 83-86; V Wednesfield Heath 86-93; NSM Independent Ch Community Work 93-98; Dioc Officer for Min Tas Australia 98-02; Dir Angl Miss 99-02; C Smestow Vale *Lich* 02-03; V Knowle St Barn *Bris* from 03. *St Barnabas' Vicarage, Daventry Road, Bristol BS4 1DQ* Tel 0117-966 4139 E-mail agpal46@btopenworld.com

PALMER, Angus Douglas. b 40. St Chad's Coll Dur BA62 DipTh63. **d** 63 **p** 64. C Wallsend St Pet *Newc* 63-66; C Newc H Cross 66-69; C Bottesford *Linc* 69-70; R Penicuik *Edin* 70-84; R W Linton 77-84. *6 Hackworth Gardens, Wylam NE41 8EJ* Tel (01661) 853786

PALMER, Christopher. b 71. **d** 98 **p** 99. C Emscote *Cov* 98-02; TV Mortlake w E Sheen *S'wark* from 02; AD Richmond and Barnes from 05. *86 East Sheen Avenue, London SW14 8AU* Tel (020) 8487 8208 E-mail christopherpalmer@talk21.com

PALMER, David Michael. b 53. QUB BA95 MSc. CITC 95. **d** 97 **p** 98. C Glenageary *D & G* 97-99; C Agherton *Conn* 99-00; I Ramoan w Ballycastle and Culfeightrin from 00. *Ramoan Rectory, 12 Novally Road, Ballycastle BT54 6HB* Tel (028) 2076 2461 E-mail ramoan@connor.anglican.org

PALMER, David Philip. b 50. Sarum & Wells Th Coll. **d** 84 **p** 85. C St Ives *Ely* 84-86; C Luton All SS w St Pet *St Alb* 86-88; V Stocksbridge *Sheff* 88-97; P-in-c Seaton Hirst *Newc* 97-98; TR from 98; Chapl Northd Coll from 99. *The Vicarage, Newbiggin Road, Ashington NE63 0TQ* Tel (01670) 813218
E-mail davidseahirst@aol.com

PALMER, David Roderick. b 34. St Jo Coll Dur BA56 Birm Univ DipTh58 Trin Coll Ox. Qu Coll Birm 56. **d** 60 **p** 61. C Loughton St Jo *Chelmsf* 60-63; C Pimlico St Gabr *Lon* 63-64; Miss to Seamen 64-67; CF 67-74; Chapl Luxembourg *Eur* 74-80; P-in-c

Exton and Winsford and Cutcombe w Luxborough *B & W* 80-82; P-in-c Wrington w Butcombe 82-84; Dep Dir of Tr Inst Wednesbury St Jas *Lich* 84-86; C Gt Wyrley 86-89; V Wilshamstead and Houghton Conquest *St Alb* 90-00; rtd 01. *14B Place du Marché, Céaucé, 61330 Normandie, France*

PALMER, Derek James. b 54. Man Univ BA77. Qu Coll Birm 77. **d** 79 **p** 80. C Leek *Lich* 79-83; CF 83-92; USA 92-95; C S Ockendon and Belhus Park *Chelmsf* 95-98; V Walthamstow St Mich 98-00; Chapl Salford Univ *Man* from 00; AD Salford 02-03; Bp's Adv on New Relig Movements from 02. *The Chaplaincy, University of Salford, The Crescent, Salford M5 4WT* Tel 0161-295 4660 Mobile 07702-384945 E-mail father.derek@ntlworld.com *or* salfordunichaps@yahoo.co.uk

PALMER, Elizabeth. *See* BLATCHLEY, Ms Elizabeth

PALMER, Miss Elizabeth Anne. b 46. Reading Univ BA68 Nottm Univ PGCE69 MEd78 MA97. St Jo Coll Nottm 91. **d** 91 **p** 94. C Scartho *Linc* 91-96; P-in-c Ilkeston St Jo *Derby* 96-01; V 01-05. *3 Collins Close, Nottingham NG6 7AH*

PALMER, Preb Francis Harvey. b 30. Jes Coll Cam BA52 MA56. Wycliffe Hall Ox 53. **d** 55 **p** 56. C Knotty Ash St Jo *Liv* 55-57; C Southgate *Chich* 58-60; Chapl Fitzw Ho Cam 60-64; V Cambridge H Trin *Ely* 64-71; Chapl to Cam Pastorate 64-71; Prin Ridley Hall Cam 71-72; R Worplesdon *Guildf* 72-80; Bp's Ecum Officer 74-80; P-in-c Blymhill w Weston-under-Lizard *Lich* 80-82; Dioc Missr and Sec to Bd for Miss and Unity 80-90; Preb Lich Cathl 86-89; TV Walsall 87-90; rtd 90; Perm to Offic *Lich* 90-99, *Heref* and *Glouc* from 93. *The Old Vicarage, Claverley, Wolverhampton WV5 7DT* Tel (01746) 710746 E-mail francis@palmerfh.freeserve.co.uk

PALMER, Graham. b 31. Em Coll Cam BA53 MA57. Qu Coll Birm 56. **d** 58 **p** 59. C Camberwell St Giles *S'wark* 58-61; C Kilburn St Aug *Lon* 61-67; P-in-c Fulham St Alb 67-73; V 73-92; V Fulham St Alb w St Aug 92-97; rtd 97; Perm to Offic *Lon* from 97. *7 Wellington Court, 116 Knightsbridge, London SW1X 7PL* Tel (020) 7584 4036

PALMER, Hugh. b 50. Pemb Coll Cam BA72 MA76. Ridley Hall Cam 73. **d** 76 **p** 77. C Heigham H Trin *Nor* 76-80; Bp's Chapl for Tr and Miss 80-84; C St Helen Bishopsgate w St Andr Undershaft etc *Lon* 85-95; C Fulwood *Sheff* 95-97; V 97-05; Hon Can Sheff Cathl 01-05; R Langham Place All So *Lon* from 05. *12 Weymouth Street, London W1W 5BY* Tel (020) 7580 6029 E-mail hugh.palmer@allsouls.org

PALMER, Hugh Maurice Webber. b 28. Magd Coll Cam BA51 MA55. Cuddesdon Coll 51. **d** 53 **p** 54. C Bitterne Park *Win* 53-57; N Rhodesia 57-62; V Owslebury w Morestead *Win* 62-65; Rhodesia 65-70; C Headbourne Worthy *Win* 70-71; P-in-c Stratton Strawless *Nor* 72-77; R Hainford 72-77; R Haynford w Stratton Strawless 77-80; Chapl HM Pris Stafford 80-82; Chapl HM Pris Standford Hill 82-89; Sub-Chapl HM Pris Nor 89-91; rtd 91. *29 Mayfield Way, North Walsham NR28 0DQ* Tel (01692) 403664

PALMER, The Ven Ian Stanley. b 50. K Coll Lon BD71. Cranmer Hall Dur 73. **d** 75 **p** 76. C Huyton St Mich *Liv* 75-78; Chapl Dur Univ *Dur* 78-83; V Collierley w Annfield Plain 83-90; Australia from 90; Adn Upper Hunter from 00; R Muswellbrook from 00. *19 Brook Street, PO Box 125, Muswellbrook, NSW, Australia 2333* Tel (0061) (2) 6541 2713 Mobile 411-242596 Fax 6541 2306 E-mail palmeris@hunterlink.net.au

PALMER, John Richard Henry. b 29. AKC52. **d** 53 **p** 54. C Englefield Green *Guildf* 53-57; P-in-c Brewarrina Australia 57-62; C Wareham w Arne *Sarum* 62-63; PC Derby St Jo *Derby* 63-66; Chapl Holloway Sanatorium Virginia Water 66-70; Chapl Brookwood Hosp Woking 70-94; rtd 94; Perm to Offic *Truro* from 94. *Lightning Ridge, Pentreath Road, The Lizard, Helston TR12 7NY* Tel (01326) 290654 E-mail vsp@oldlizardhead.freeserve.co.uk

PALMER, Judith Angela. b 47. Bris Univ MB, ChB71. N Ord Course 02. **d** 05. NSM Strensall *York* from 05. *20 Bedern, York YO1 7LP* Tel (01904) 637629 E-mail j.palmer@britishlibrary.net

PALMER, Mrs Julia Elizabeth. b 57. Hull Univ BA80. St Jo Coll Nottm MA98. **d** 99 **p** 00. C Snodland All SS w Ch Ch *Roch* 99-03; P-in-c Sutton Bonington w Normanton-on-Soar *S'well* from 03. *The Rectory, 19A Park Lane, Sutton Bonington, Loughborough LE12 5NQ* Tel (01509) 670757 E-mail revjuliap@msn.com

PALMER, Kevin Anthony. b 59. St Steph Ho Ox. **d** 01 **p** 02. C Tunstall *Lich* 01-04; R Wednesbury St Jas and St Jo from 04. *The Rectory, 1 Hollies Drive, Wednesbury WS10 9EQ* Tel 0121-505 1188 *or* 505 1568

PALMER, Malcolm Leonard. b 46. Sarum & Wells Th Coll 80. **d** 82 **p** 83. C Cannock *Lich* 82-85; Chapl RAF 85-89; Asst Chapl HM Pris Dur 89-90; Chapl HM YOI Hewell Grange 90-93; Chapl HM Rem Cen Brockhill 90-93; Chapl HM Pris Blakenhurst 93-01; Miss P Kugluktuk Canada from 01. *Address temp unknown*

PALMER, Marc Richard. b 72. St Jo Coll Dur BA96. Cranmer Hall Dur 93. **d** 98 **p** 99. C Chester le Street *Dur* 98-03; TV Bensham from 03. *12 Red Admiral Court, Gateshead NE11 9TW* Tel 0191-460 1932 E-mail marc.plamer@virgin.net

PALMER, Marion Denise. b 42. Open Univ BA82 SRN64 SCM66. Linc Th Coll 84. **dss** 86 **d** 87 **p** 94. Poplar *Lon* 86-90; Par Dn 87-90; Par Dn Gillingham St Mary *Roch* 90-94; C 94-96; C Farnborough 96-02; rtd 02; Perm to Offic *St E* from 04. *14 Prestwick Avenue, Felixstowe IP11 9LF* Tel (01394) 671588

PALMER, Canon Maureen Florence. b 38. Qu Eliz Coll Lon BSc60 PhD64 DipRS79. Ripon Coll Cuddesdon DipTh84. **dss** 85 **d** 87 **p** 94. Par Dss Tupsley *Heref* 85-87; C 87-88; Par Dn Talbot Village *Sarum* 88-91; Chapl Birm Cathl *Birm* 91-96; Can Pastor and Can Res Guildf Cathl *Guildf* from 96; Sub-Dean from 99. *2 Cathedral Close, Guildford GU2 7TL* Tel (01483) 560329 *or* 565287 E-mail maureen@guildford-cathedral.org

PALMER, Michael Christopher. b 43. MBE00. AKC67 S Bank Poly CQSW76. **d** 68 **p** 69. C Easthampstead *Ox* 68-71; Miss to Seamen 71-73; Hong Kong 73; Lic to Offic *Ox* 76-79; Lic to Offic *Truro* 79-83; Dioc Soc Resp Adv 83-98; Bp's Dom Chapl 85-87; V Devoran 87-98; rtd 98; Perm to Offic *Truro* from 98. *Vine Cottages, 13 High Steet, Cuddesdon, Oxford OX44 9HP* Tel (01865) 875284

PALMER, Norman Ernest. b 28. Lon Univ BD59. Roch Th Coll 66. **d** 67 **p** 67. C Chipping Norton *Ox* 67-69; V Bozeat w Easton Maudit *Pet* 69-90; rtd 90; Perm to Offic *Chich* 90-94. *6 Abbeyfield House, 22 Falmouth Road, Truro TR1 2HX* Tel (01872) 273846

PALMER, Canon Peter Malcolm. b 31. Chich Th Coll 56. **d** 59 **p** 60. C Leighton Buzzard *St Alb* 59-63; C Apsley End 63-65; C Hitchin H Sav 65-69; R Ickleford 69-76; V Oxhey St Matt 76-86; V Kensworth, Studham and Whipsnade 86-96; Hon Can St Alb 94-96; rtd 97; Perm to Offic *St Alb* from 97; Bishop's Retirement Officer from 97. *4 Sefton Close, St Albans AL1 4PF* Tel (01727) 763196

PALMER, Peter Parsons. b 27. **d** 59 **p** 61. SSJE from 59; Canada 59-79; Perm to Offic *Leic* 80-86 and *Lon* 86-94; Lic to Offic *Lon* 94-02. *College of St Barnabas, Blackberry Lane, Lingfield RH7 6NJ*

PALMER, Philip Edward Hitchen. b 35. St Jo Coll Cam MA61 DipAdEd74. Ridley Hall Cam 61 EAMTC 87. **d** 90 **p** 91. NSM Gt Oakley w Wix *Chelmsf* 90-96; NSM Gt Oakley w Wix and Wrabness 96-00; Perm to Offic from 00. *Glebe House, Wix Road, Great Oakley, Harwich CO12 5BJ* Tel (01255) 880737

PALMER, Robert William. b 28. DMS. Wells Th Coll 63. **d** 65 **p** 66. C Earlsdon *Cov* 65-69; P-in-c Cov St Mark 69-71; Chapl Cov and Warks Hosp 69-71; Hon C Binley *Cov* 72-76; V Sheff St Paul *Sheff* 76-84; V Deepcar 84-93; rtd 93; Perm to Offic *Sheff* from 93. *Moorlands, 26 Coal Pit Lane, Stocksbridge, Sheffield S36 1AW*

PALMER, Canon Stephen Charles. b 47. FRGS98 FLS01 Portsm Univ PhD04. Oak Hill Th Coll 71. **d** 74 **p** 75. C Crofton *Portsm* 74-77; Bp's Dom Chapl 77-80; Chapl RNR 78-91; R Brighstone and Brooke w Mottistone *Portsm* 80-91; P-in-c Shorwell w Kingston 82-86; RD W Wight 87-91; Hon Can Portsm Cathl from 91; Falkland Is 91-96; V Portsdown *Portsm* 96-02; V Newport St Jo from 02; V Newport St Thos from 02; Bp's Ecological Adv from 00. *The Vicarage, 72A Medina Avenue, Newport PO30 1HF* Tel (01983) 539580 *or* tel and fax 821961 E-mail newport@fish.co.uk *or* stephen.palmer@fish.co.uk

PALMER, Steven Roy. b 51. Birm Univ BSc71. WMMTC 91. **d** 94 **p** 95. C Sheldon *Birm* 94-97; P-in-c Duddeston w Nechells 97-99; V Nechells 99-03; R Billing *Pet* from 03. *The Rectory, 25 Church Walk, Great Billing, Northampton NN3 4ED* Tel (01604) 784870 Fax 401641

PALMER, Canon Terence Henry James. b 34. Univ of Wales (Lamp) BA55 LTh57 St Edm Hall Ox BA65 MA69. **d** 57 **p** 58. C Griffithstown *Mon* 57-60; Min Can and C St D Cathl *St D* 60-63; Perm to Offic *B & W* and *Ox* 63-65; C Monmouth *Mon* 65-69; C-in-c St Hilary Greenway CD 69-72; R Roggiett w Llanfihangel Roggiet 72-80; R Portskewett and Rogiet w Llanfihangel Rogiet 80-00; RD Netherwent 89-00; Dir NSM Studies 91-99; Can St Woolos Cathl 96-00; rtd 00; Perm to Offic *Eur* from 99; Lic to Offic *Mon* from 00; P-in-c Newport St Teilo from 03. *Terleen, 12 Windsor Park, Magor, Caldicot NP26 3NJ* Tel (01633) 881927

PALMER-PALMER-FFYNCHE, Barry Marshall. b 23. Hertf Coll Ox BA47 MA48. Westcott Ho Cam 47. **d** 49 **p** 50. C Alrewas *Lich* 49-52; C Wychnor 49-52; C Birchington w Acol *Cant* 52-56; R Harrietsham 56-66; Chapl Westmr Hosp Lon 66-73; V Chipping Sodbury and Old Sodbury *Glouc* 73-88; rtd 88; Perm to Offic *Glouc* and *Bris* from 90; *Lon* 90-00. *Finch's Folly, 45 Hay Street, Marshfield, Chippenham SN14 8PF* Tel (01225) 891096

PAMMENT, Gordon Charles. b 31. TCD BA54. Linc Th Coll 56. **d** 58 **p** 60. C Hemel Hempstead *St Alb* 58-63; C Gedney Drove End *Linc* 63-65; I Macroom Union *C, C & R* 65-72; I Rathcormac Union 72-78; I Fermoy Union 78-91; Can Ross Cathl 89-91; Can Cork Cathl 89-91; rtd 91. *Derry, Berrings, Co Cork, Irish Republic* Tel (00353) (21) 743 7020

PAMPLIN, Canon Richard Lawrence. b 46. Lon Univ BScEng68 Dur Univ BA75. NY Th Sem DMin85 Wycliffe Hall Ox 75. **d** 77

p 78. C Greenside *Dur* 77-80; C Sheff St Barn and St Mary *Sheff* 80-84; R Wombwell 84-90; P-in-c Madeley *Heref* 90-91; TR 91-01; Chapl Berne w Neuchâtel *Eur* from 01; Can Gib Cathl from 04. *St Ursula's, Jubiläumsplatz 2, CH 3005 Bern, Switzerland* Tel (0041) (31) 351 0343 *or* 352 8567 Fax 351 0548 E-mail chaplain@bluewin.ch

PANG, Wing-On. b 43. BA67 Lon Univ MA70. Oak Hill Th Coll DipHE87. **d** 87 **p** 88. C Pennycross *Ex* 87-91; TV Mildenhall *St E* 91-96; Hong Kong from 96. *St Andrew's Church, 138 Nathan Road, Tsim Sha Tsui, Kowloon, Hong Kong* Tel (00852) 2367 1478 Fax 2367 6562 E-mail standrew@hk.super.net

PANGBOURNE, John Godfrey. b 36. Ridley Hall Cam 82. **d** 84 **p** 85. C Ashtead *Guildf* 84-88; V Ore Ch Ch *Chich* 88-03; rtd 03. *Meon Croft, Toadpit Lane, West Hill, Ottery St Mary EX11 1TR* Tel (01404) 812393

PANKHURST, Donald Araunah. b 28. Qu Coll Birm. **d** 64 **p** 65. C Pemberton St Jo *Liv* 64-68; V Aspull 68-76; R Newchurch 76-88; R Winwick 88-94; rtd 94; Perm to Offic *Carl* from 94. *Hunters Hill, Spooner Vale, Windermere LA23 1AU* Tel (01539) 446390

PANKHURST, Ian Charles. b 50. Trin Coll Cam BA72 Lon Inst of Educn PGCE88. St Alb and Ox Min Course 01. **d** 04. NSM Watford St Luke *St Alb* from 04. *2 Albert Road North, Watford WD17 1QE* Tel (01923) 249139 E-mail sueandian.pankhurst@virgin.net

PANNETT, Philip Anthony. b 36. Brighton Poly MPS59 MRPharmS59. K Coll Lon AKC63 St Boniface Warminster 63. **d** 64 **p** 65. C Stanmer w Falmer and Moulsecoomb *Chich* 64-68; C Hangleton 68-72; Teacher Finchden Manor Sch Tenterden 72-74; Teacher Bodiam Manor Sch 74-76; Perm to Offic from 76; rtd 01. *1 Fitzjohns Road, Lewes BN7 1PP* Tel (01273) 472804

PANTER, The Ven Richard James Graham. b 48. Oak Hill Th Coll 73. **d** 76 **p** 77. C Rusholme H Trin *Man* 76-80; C Toxteth St Cypr w Ch Ch *Liv* 80-85; V Clubmoor 85-96; P-in-c Litherland St Jo and St Jas 96-02; AD Bootle 99-02; Adn Liv from 02; V Orrell Hey St Jo and St Jas from 02. *St John and St James Vicarage, 2A Monfa Road, Bootle L20 6BQ* Tel and fax 0151-922 3758 E-mail archdeaconricky@blueyonder.co.uk

PANTER MARSHALL, Mrs Susan Lesley. b 49. Portsm Poly BSc72 Grad LI84. S Dios Minl Tr Scheme 88. **d** 91 **p** 94. NSM Southover *Chich* 91-95; C Iford w Kingston and Rodmell 95-98; C Hollington St Jo 98-02; P-in-c Herstmonceux and Wartling from 02. *The Rectory, West End, Herstmonceux, Hailsham BN27 4NY* Tel (01323) 833124 E-mail supm@fish.co.uk

PANTLING, Mrs Rosemary Caroline. b 60. Ex Coll Ox BA83 MA Birm Univ PGCE84. EAMTC 98. **d** 01 **p** 02. NSM Bishop's Tachbrook *Cov* from 01. *22 Touchstone Road, Heathcote, Warwick CV34 6EE* Tel (01926) 316597 E-mail krpantling@waitrose.com

PANTON, Alan Edward. b 45. K Coll Lon BD67 AKC67. **d** 68 **p** 69. C Eltham St Jo *S'wark* 68-73; C Horley 73-78; V Dallington *Pet* from 78. *The Vicarage, The Barton's Close, Dallington, Northampton NN5 7HQ* Tel (01604) 751478

PANTRY, John Richard. b 46. Oak Hill NSM Course 90. **d** 93 **p** 94. NSM Alresford *Chelmsf* 93-04; NSM W w E Mersea from 04. *48 Empress Avenue, West Mersea, Colchester CO5 8EX* Tel and fax (01206) 386910 E-mail johnpantry@fsmail.net

PAPADOPULOS, Nicholas Charles. b 66. G&C Coll Cam BA88 MA92 Barrister-at-Law (Middle Temple) 90. Ripon Coll Cuddesdon. **d** 99 **p** 00. C Portsea N End St Mark *Portsm* 99-02; Bp's Dom Chapl *Sarum* from 02. *11 Albany Road, Salisbury SP1 3YQ* Tel (01722) 415925 *or* 334031 E-mail senior.chaplain@salisbury.anglican.org

PAPANTONIOU, Ms Frances Caroline. b 52. S Dios Minl Tr Scheme 89. **d** 92 **p** 94. Par Dn Harrow Weald All SS *Lon* 92-94; C 94-95; C Preston Ascension 95-98; Assoc V Wembley Park 98-99; TV 99-04; V Horton Kirby and Sutton-at-Hone *Roch* from 04. *The Vicarage, 51A Main Road, Sutton at Hone, Dartford DA4 9HQ* Tel (01322) 862253 E-mail fpapantoniou@aol.com

PAPE, David. b 54. LNSM course 95. **d** 98 **p** 99. OLM S'wark St Geo w St Alphege and St Jude *S'wark* from 98; OLM Waterloo St Jo w St Andr from 98. *10 Stopher House, Webber Street, London SE1 0RE* Tel (020) 7928 3503

PAPE, Timothy Vernon Francis. b 39. OBE. Lon Univ BSc63. Wells Th Coll 63. **d** 65 **p** 66. C Pershore w Wick *Worc* 65-69; Perm to Offic *Bris* 69-73; NSM Southbroom *Sarum* from 75; Hd Master Chirton Primary Sch Wilts from 81; Dir Gen Shaw Trust from 90. *Mallards, Chirton, Devizes SN10 3QX* Tel (01380) 840593

PAPUA NEW GUINEA, Archbishop of. *See* AYONG, The Most Revd James Simon

PAPWORTH, Daniel John. b 69. Plymouth Poly BSc90. Trin Coll Bris BA98 MA00. **d** 99 **p** 00. C Gabalfa *Llan* 99-02; Perm to Offic *B & W* 03-04; Asst Chapl Dudley Gp of Hosps NHS Trust from 04. *Russells Hall Hospital, Pensnett Road, Dudley DY1 2HQ* Tel (01384) 456111 ext 2352 E-mail dan.papworth@dgoh.nhs.uk

PAPWORTH, John. b 21. Lon Univ BSc(Econ). **d** 75 **p** 76. Zambia 76-81; Hon C Paddington St Sav *Lon* 81-83; Hon C St Marylebone St Mark Hamilton Terrace 85-97; Perm to Offic *Bris* from 01. *The Fourth World, The Close, 26 High Street, Purton, Swindon SN5 4AE* Tel (01793) 772214 Fax 772521

PAPWORTH, Miss Shirley Marjorie. b 33. CA Tr Coll. **d** 88 **p** 94. Par Dn Hornchurch H Cross *Chelmsf* 88-93; rtd 93; NSM Hornchurch St Andr *Chelmsf* from 94. *4 Gosport Drive, Hornchurch RM12 6NU* Tel (01708) 524348

PARADISE, Bryan John. b 49. Southn Univ BSc Lon Bible Coll BA. Cranmer Hall Dur. **d** 82 **p** 83. C High Harrogate Ch Ch *Ripon* 82-86; Dioc Adult Educn Officer *Guildf* from 86; P-in-c Dunsfold 86-90; R 90-93; R E Horsley 93-01; RD Leatherhead 98-03; R E Horsley and Ockham w Hatchford and Downside from 02. *The Rectory, Ockham Road South, East Horsley, Leatherhead KT24 6RL* Tel (01483) 282359 E-mail revbjp@mwfree.net

PARAGUAY, Bishop of. *See* ELLISON, The Rt Revd John Alexander

PARBURY, Heather Christina Winifred. b 56. **d** 01 **p** 02. C Long Compton, Whichford and Barton-on-the-Heath *Cov* from 01; C Barcheston from 01; C Cherington w Stourton from 01; C Wolford w Burmington from 01. *The Vicarage, Great Wolford, Shipton-on-Stour CV36 5NQ* Tel (01608) 674361 E-mail heather@parbury.co.uk

PARE, Stephen Charles. b 53. Sussex Univ BEd75. St Mich Coll Llan DipTh80. **d** 80 **p** 81. C Cardiff St Jo *Llan* 80-83; P-in-c Marcross w Monknash and Wick 83; TV Llantwit Major 83-91; V Penmark w Porthkerry from 91; Chapl Cardiff Wales Airport from 91. *The Vicarage, 6 Milburn Close, Rhoose, Barry CF62 3EJ* Tel (01446) 711713 E-mail penmarkporthceri@orngenet.co.uk

PARFFETT, Allan John. b 51. Keele Univ CQSW76 Spurgeon's Coll CertRS90 Open Univ DASSc95 BA97 Birm Univ MA00. Qu Coll Birm 97. **d** 98 **p** 99. C Hall Green Ascension *Birm* 98-00; Soc Worker from 00. *20 Kiln Close, Corfe Mullen, Wimbourne BH21 3UR*

PARFITT, Anthony Colin. b 44. Ox Univ Inst of Educn CertEd66 Open Univ BA71 Plymouth Poly MPhil84. SW Minl Tr Course 93. **d** 96 **p** 97. NSM Langport Area Chs *B & W* 96-00; NSM Bruton and Distr from 01. *Tile Hill Cottage, North Brewham, Bruton BA10 0JT* Tel (01749) 850188 Fax 850189 E-mail tony.parfitt@ukonline.co.uk

PARFITT, Brian John. b 49. Ex Coll Ox BA71 MA76. Wycliffe Hall Ox 71. **d** 74 **p** 75. C Newport St Mark *Mon* 74-78; R Blaina 78-83; R Blaina and Nantyglo 83-86; Chapl Blaina and Distr Hosp Gwent 83-86; Consultant W Midlands and Wales CPAS 86-95; V Magor w Redwick and Undy *Mon* 95-98; TR Magor from 98. *The Rectory, Redwick Road, Magor, Caldicot NP26 3HU* Tel (01633) 880266

PARFITT, David George. b 65. De Montfort Univ Leic BA87 DipArch90. Wycliffe Hall Ox BTh92. **d** 95 **p** 96. C Malpas *Mon* 95-98; C Bassaleg 98-00; TV 00-01; V Malpas from 01. *The Vicarage, Malpas Road, Newport NP20 6GQ* Tel (01633) 852047

PARFITT, George Rudolf William. b 54. WMMTC 96. **d** 99 **p** 00. OLM Highnam, Lassington, Rudford, Tibberton etc *Glouc* from 99. *8 Hillcrest, Highnam, Gloucester GL2 8LS* Tel (01452) 301635 E-mail george.parfitt@btinternet.com

PARFITT, Graeme Stanley. b 36. Qu Coll Birm 77. **d** 79 **p** 80. C Fishponds St Jo *Bris* 79-82; V Southmead 82-91; V Stockwell St Mich *S'wark* 91-01; rtd 01; Perm to Offic *Bris* from 02. *Garden Cottage, The Old House, Rectory Gardens, Henbury, Bristol BS10 7AQ* Tel 0117-959 0293

PARFITT, Preb John Hubert. b 29. Southn Univ MA72 BPhil. Qu Coll Birm 78. **d** 80 **p** 81. C Fladbury, Wyre Piddle and Moor *Worc* 80-82; C Malvern Link w Cowleigh 82; V Hanley Castle, Hanley Swan and Welland 82-83; Dir RE *B & W* 84-93; Preb Wells Cathl from 85; rtd 93; Perm to Offic *B & W* 93-05; Master Hugh Sexey's Hosp Bruton 95-05. *3 Willow Farm Cottages, Brister End, Yetminster, Sherborne DT9 6NH* Tel (01935) 873260 E-mail passitatwillow@btinternet.com

PARFITT, Canon Keith John. b 44. K Coll Lon BD68 AKC68. St Aug Coll Cant 69. **d** 70 **p** 71. C Kettering St Andr *Pet* 70-74; Asst Soc and Ind Adv *Portsm* 74-89; RD Alverstoke 79-86; C-in-c Bridgemary CD 81-82; V Bridgemary 82-89; Dioc UPA Officer *Blackb* 89-97; Can Res Blackb Cathl 94-97; Dir Is of Wight Rural Community Coun from 97. *Downsview, Farriers Way, Shorwell, Newport PO30 3JP* Tel (01983) 740434

PARFITT, Neil. **d** 99 **p** 00. C Caerleon *Mon* 99-01; C Ebbw Vale 01-02; P-in-c Ferndale w Maerdy *Llan* 02-03; V 03-04. *Address temp unknown*

PARFITT, Susan Mary. b 42. Bris Univ BA63 CertEd68 Univ of Wales DASS70. Bris Minl Tr Scheme 82 Ripon Coll Cuddesdon. **dss** 84 **d** 87 **p** 94. Assoc Dir of Ords *Bris* 84-86; CME Officer 87-91; Dir Past Care and Counselling *S'wark* 91-01; rtd 01; Perm to Offic *Bris* from 02. *Garden Cottage, The Old House, Rectory Gardens, Bristol BS10 7AQ* Tel 0117-959 0293

PARGETER, Canon Muriel Elizabeth. b 28. St Mich Ho Ox 53. **dss** 82 **d** 87 **p** 95. Hd Dss *Roch* 82-87; Dioc Dir of Ords 87-90; Hon Can Roch Cathl 87-90; rtd 90; NSM Worthing Ch the King *Chich* from 95. *63 Pavilion Road, Worthing BN45 7EE* Tel (01903) 214476

PARISH, Mrs Mary Eileen. b 48. Nottm Univ BA70 Southn Univ BTh98. All Nations Chr Coll 73 STETS 95. **d** 98 **p** 99. NSM Worthing Ch the King *Chich* from 98. *The Heritage, 10 Winchester Road, Worthing BN11 4DJ* Tel (01903) 236909 E-mail frmary@theheritage.freeserve.co.uk

PARISH, Nicholas Anthony. b 58. Oak Hill Th Coll BA84 Kingston Univ MA97. Ridley Hall Cam 84. **d** 86 **p** 87. C Eltham H Trin *S'wark* 86-89; C Barnes St Mary 89-91; V Streatham St Paul 91-96; Ind Chapl *Ox* from 96; AD Bracknell from 04. *1 Old Lands Hill, Bracknell RG12 2QX* Tel and fax (01344) 641498 E-mail nick.parish@ntlworld.com

PARISH, Stephen Richard. b 49. Oak Hill Th Coll. **d** 77 **p** 78. C Chadderton Ch Ch *Man* 77-81; C Chell *Lich* 81-82; TV 82-88; V Warrington St Ann *Liv* from 88. *St Ann's Vicarage, 1A Fitzherbert Street, Warrington WA2 7QG* Tel (01925) 631781 E-mail bloovee@ntlworld.com

PARK, Christopher John. b 62. Sheff Poly BA83. Cranmer Hall Dur 00. **d** 02 **p** 03. C Didsbury St Jas and Em *Man* from 02. *99 Mellington Avenue, East Didsbury, Manchester M20 5WF* Tel 0161-445 9758 E-mail pasta@cjparko.freeserve.co.uk

PARK, John Charles. b 55. St Pet Coll Ox BA77 St Mary's Coll Newc PGCE81. Cranmer Hall Dur 00. **d** 02 **p** 03. C Morpeth *Newc* from 02. *23 Green Acres, Morpeth NE61 2AD* Tel (01670) 511662

PARK, Tarjei Erling Alan. b 64. W Lon Inst of HE BA88 Lanc Univ MA89 Pemb Coll Ox DPhil96. Ripon Coll Cuddesdon DipMin94. **d** 94 **p** 95. C Lancaster St Mary *Blackb* 94-98; V Enfield St Mich *Lon* 98-01; Asst Dir Post-Ord Tr from 98; V Golders Green from 01. *The Vicarage, 3 St Alban's Close, London NW11 7RA* Tel (020) 8455 4525 E-mail tarjei.park@london.anglican.org

PARK, Trevor. b 38. MBE05. Lon Univ BA64 Open Univ PhD90 Lambeth STh81. Linc Th Coll 64. **d** 66 **p** 67. C Crosthwaite Kendal *Carl* 66-68; Asst Chapl Solihull Sch 69-71; Chapl St Bees Sch and V St Bees *Carl* 71-77; V Dalton-in-Furness 77-84; V Natland 84-97; Hon Can Carl Cathl 86-97; RD Kendal 89-94; Chapl Oslo w Bergen, Trondheim and Stavanger *Eur* 97-05; rtd 05. *1 The Willows, Egremont CA22 2HT*

PARKE, Simon Frederick Fenning. b 57. MA. Wycliffe Hall Ox. **d** 84 **p** 85. C Isleworth St Jo *Lon* 84-87; C St Marylebone All So w SS Pet and Jo 87-88; C Langham Place All So 88-93; V Tufnell Park St Geo and All SS 93-03; P-in-c W Holloway St Luke 96-97. *Address temp unknown*

PARKER, Alfred. b 20. Man Univ BA47. Wycliffe Hall Ox 47. **d** 49 **p** 50. C Droylsden St Mary *Man* 49-53; C New Bury 53-54; P-in-c Bolton St Bart 54-56; V 56-61; P-in-c Gt Lever 59-61; R 61-65; V Belmont 65-87; rtd 87. *21 Edgeley Road, Whitchurch SY13 1EU*

PARKER, Angus Michael Macdonald. b 53. Bris Univ BSc74. St Jo Coll Nottm DipTh81 DPS83. **d** 83 **p** 84. C Northampton St Giles *Pet* 83-86; C Attenborough *S'well* 86-96; V Pennycross *Ex* from 96. *St Pancras' Vicarage, 66 Glentor Road, Plymouth PL3 5TR* Tel (01752) 774332 E-mail angus.julie@btinternet.com

PARKER, Mrs Ann Jacqueline. b 41. Dur Inst of Educn TCert63 Sunderland Poly TCert65 Open Univ BA82. WEMTC 91. **d** 95 **p** 96. NSM Pilning w Compton Greenfield *Bris* 95-98; NSM Almondsbury and Olveston 98-03; Asst Chapl N Bris NHS Trust from 98. *Wyngarth, Easter Compton, Bristol BS35 5RA* Tel (01454) 632329 E-mail annatdibley@aol.com

PARKER, Mrs Anne Margaret. b 57. Leeds Univ BSc78. EAMTC 96. **d** 99 **p** 00. NSM Greenstead w Colchester St Anne *Chelmsf* 99-02; C 02-04; TV from 04. *1 Blackwater Avenue, Roach Vale, Colchester CO4 3UY* Tel (01206) 861525 Mobile 07703-571879 E-mail amparker20@hotmail.com

PARKER, Mrs Brenda. b 36. Dioc OLM tr scheme 97. **d** 00 **p** 01. OLM Eccleston Ch Ch *Liv* from 00. *22 Selkirk Drive, Eccleston, St Helens WA10 5PE* Tel (01744) 757495

PARKER, Brian William. b 39. Ulster Univ BA88. CITC 99. **d** 01 **p** 02. NSM Knock *D & D* 01-02; NSM Glencraig from 02. *7 Cairnsville Park, Bangor BT19 6EW* Tel (028) 9145 4549 Fax 9147 1804 E-mail bwparker@ukgateway.net

PARKER, Carole Maureen. *See* PROUSE, Ms Carole Maureen

PARKER, David Anthony. b 38. St Chad's Coll Dur BA62 DipTh64. **d** 64 **p** 65. C Palmers Green St Jo *Lon* 64-65; C Kenton 65-71; C W Hyde St Thos *St Alb* 71-75; P-in-c Brinksway *Ches* 76-80; V 80-83; V Weston 83-92; NSM Cheadle Hulme All SS 97-98; C Offerton 98-00; TV Crosslacon *Carl* 00-02; rtd 02; C Cheadle Hulme All SS *Ches* from 02; Perm to Offic *Man* from 02. *77 Station Road, Cheadle Hulme, Cheadle SK8 7BG* Tel 0161-485 4451

PARKER, David Arthur. b 48. Lon Univ DipTh71. Kelham Th Coll. **d** 71 **p** 72. C Newc Ch Ch *Newc* 71-74; C Hendon *Dur* 74-79; C-in-c Southwick St Cuth CD 79-84; V Sunderland Red Ho 84-88; rtd 88; Perm to Offic *Ex* 88-99; Chapl Sisters of Charity from 95. *7 Woodside Court, Plympton, Plymouth PL7 1HL* Tel (01752) 330467

PARKER, David Charles. b 53. St Andr Univ MTh75 Em Coll Cam DipTh76 Univ of Leiden DTh90. Ridley Hall Cam 75. **d** 77 **p** 78. C Hendon St Paul Mill Hill *Lon* 77-80; C Bladon w Woodstock *Ox* 80-85; C-in-c Shipton-on-Cherwell 80-85; C-in-c Begbroke 80-85; C-in-c Hampton Gay 80-85; Lect Qu Coll Birm 85-93 and 89-93; Lect Birm Univ *Birm* 93-96; Sen Lect 96-98; Reader in NT Textual Criticism and Palaeography from 98. *Dumbleton Cottage, 24 Church Street, Bromyard HR7 4DP* Tel 0121-415 2415 E-mail d.c.parker@bham.ac.uk

PARKER, Canon David John. b 33. St Chad's Coll Dur BA55 Hull Univ MA85. Linc Th Coll 57. **d** 59 **p** 60. C Tynemouth Ch Ch *Newc* 59-60; C Ponteland 60-63; C Byker St Mich 63-64; C-in-c Byker St Martin CD 64-69; V Whorlton 69-73; TR 73-80; Ind Chapl *Linc* 80-84; Master Newc St Thos Prop Chpl *Newc* 84-89; Exec Officer Dioc Bd for Ch and Soc *Man* 90-98; Lic Preacher 90-98; Hon Can Man Cathl 97-98; rtd 98; Perm to Offic *Newc* from 98. *4 The Kylins, Morpeth NE61 2DJ* Tel (01670) 516218 E-mail d.j.parker@tesco.net

PARKER, Canon David Louis. b 47. Lon Univ LLB70 Ox Univ MA82. Wycliffe Hall Ox BA79. **d** 80 **p** 81. C Broadwater St Mary *Chich* 80-84; TR Ifield 84-97; R Lavant from 97; RD Chich from 01; Can and Preb Chich Cathl from 03. *The Rectory, Pook Lane, Lavant, Chichester PO18 0AH* Tel (01243) 527313

PARKER, David William. b 21. SEN CQSW MBASW. Glouc Th Course 77 Sarum & Wells Th Coll 81. **d** 81 **p** 81. Chapl HM Pris Leyhill 81-84; NSM Cromhall w Tortworth *Glouc* 81-83; NSM Wickwar w Rangeworthy 83-87; Perm to Offic from 88. *22 Durham Road, Charfield, Wotton-under-Edge GL12 8TH* Tel (01454) 260253

PARKER, Dennis. b 22. Tyndale Hall Bris 63. **d** 64 **p** 65. C Polegate *Chich* 64-68; C-in-c Reading St Mary Castle Street Prop Chpl *Ox* 68-70; R Newdigate *Guildf* 70-87; rtd 87; Perm to Offic *Guildf* from 87. *7 Harrow Close, Dorking RH4 3BB* Tel (01306) 889458

PARKER, George William. b 29. BS53 BD57 Lon Univ PGCE67. K Coll (NS) 49. **d** 53 **p** 54. Canada 53-59 and 68-71 and 78-93; C W Hackney St Barn *Lon* 59-61; V Haggerston St Mary w St Chad 61-68; C Portsea N End St Mark *Portsm* 72-75; V Darlington St Jo *Dur* 75-78; rtd 91. *Spider Cottage, RR3 Newport NS, Canada, B0N 2A0*

PARKER, Hugh James. b 30. ACP55 TCD MA57 Ulster Univ DASE74. **d** 63 **p** 64. Lic to Offic *Conn* 63-70 and 96-01; Dioc C 70-96; Hd Master Larne High Sch 71-92; rtd 96. *25 Ballykillaire Terrace, Bangor BT19 1GS* Tel (028) 9185 7142

PARKER, John. *See* PARKER, Linsey John Owen

PARKER, John Bristo. b 26. Edin Th Coll 61. **d** 64 **p** 65. C Barrow St Jo *Carl* 64-68; V Sledmere *York* 68-74; V Sledmere and Wetwang w Cowlan 74-79; R Cowlam 68-74; P-in-c Wetwang 69-74; V Kirkby Ireleth *Carl* 79-83; V Rillington w Scampston, Wintringham etc *York* 83-87; R Bishop Wilton w Full Sutton, Kirby Underdale etc 87-91; rtd 91; Perm to Offic *York* from 91. *East Lodge, Sledmere, Driffield YO25 3XQ* Tel (01377) 86325

PARKER, John David. b 61. Ridley Hall Cam 00. **d** 02 **p** 03. C Aston cum Aughton w Swallownest and Ulley *Sheff* from 02. *14 Cradley Drive, Aston, Sheffield S26 2FF* Tel 0114-287 9473 E-mail jdparkeruk@aol.com

PARKER, Preb Joseph French. b 09. St Chad's Coll Dur BA37 DipTh38 MA40. **d** 38 **p** 39. C Warrington St Elphin *Liv* 38-40; C Shrewsbury St Mary *Lich* 40-42; C Wolverhampton St Pet 42-46; V Kingswinford St Mary 46-51; V Toxteth Park St Agnes *Liv* 51-60; RD W Bromwich *Lich* 61-76; V W Bromwich All SS 61-76; RD W Bromwich 61-76; Preb Lich Cathl 67-76; rtd 76; Perm to Offic *Carl* 77-93. *c/o J Parker Esq, 25 Butleigh Avenue, Cardiff CF5 1BX* Tel (029) 2025 6161

PARKER, Julian Roderick. b 57. Essex Univ BA80. Sarum & Wells Th Coll DipMin93. **d** 93 **p** 94. C Gillingham *Sarum* 93-97; V N Bradley, Southwick and Heywood from 97. *The Vicarage, 62 Church Lane, North Bradley, Trowbridge BA14 0TA* Tel (01225) 752635 E-mail julian@roderick17.freeserve.co.uk

PARKER, Linsey John Owen. b 70. Oriel Coll Ox BA91 Lon Univ PGCE94. Oak Hill Th Coll 02. **d** 05. C Arborfield w Barkham *Ox* from 05. *7 Sheerlands Road, Arborfield, Reading RG2 9ND* Tel 0118-976 0245 E-mail johnandmim@bigfoot.com

PARKER, Miss Margaret. b 27. Lightfoot Ho Dur 54. **dss** 60 **d** 87 **p** 94. Ryhope *Dur* 56-61; Monkwearmouth St Andr 61-79; Adv for Accredited Lay Min 74-87; Adv for Accredited Lay Min *Newc* 79-87; Newc St Geo 79-87; C 87; rtd 87; Perm to Offic *Dur* and *Newc* from 87; Tutor Cranmer Hall Dur 87-92; Hon C Dur Cathl *Dur* 87-94; Min Can Dur Cathl 94-97; Chapl St Mary's Coll Dur 95-98. *53 Devonshire Road, Durham DH1 2BJ* Tel 0191-386 3233

PARKER, Margaret Grace. *See* TORDOFF, Mrs Margaret Grace

PARKER, Matthew John. b 63. Man Univ BA85 SS Coll Cam BA88. Ridley Hall Cam 85. **d** 88 **p** 89. C Twickenham St Mary *Lon* 88-91; Chapl Stockport Gr Sch 91-94; C Stockport St Geo *Ches* 91-93; P-in-c Stockport St Mark 93-94; TV Stockport SW 94-00; TR Leek and Meerbrook *Lich* from 00. *The Vicarage, 6 Church Street, Leek ST13 6AB* Tel (01538) 382515 *or* 388134 E-mail matpark01@aol.com

PARKER, Michael Alan. b 70. St Jo Coll Dur BA91. CITC BTh93. **d** 96 **p** 97. C Dundela St Mark *D & D* 96-00; I Carnalea from 00. *St Gall's Rectory, 171 Crawfordsburn Road, Bangor BT19 1BT* Tel (028) 9185 3366 *or* 9185 3810 E-mail carnalea@down.anglican.org *or* stgall@fish.co.uk

PARKER, Michael John. b 54. Cam Coll of Art and Tech BA76 Lon Univ BD85. Trin Coll Bris 82. **d** 85 **p** 86. C Leic H Trin w St Jo *Leic* 85-88; P-in-c Edin Clermiston Em *Edin* 88-90; Chapl Edin St Thos 90-03; Can St Mary's Cathl 94-03; NSM Edin St Paul and St Geo from 03; Gen Sec Evang Alliance from 03. *4 Liberton Place, Edinburgh EH16 6NA* Tel 0131-666 1119 *or* 0141-332 8700 E-mail m.parker@eauk.org *or* mikepedinb@aol.com

PARKER, Canon Michael John. b 57. BSc Nottm Univ MA04. Wycliffe Hall Ox 80. **d** 83 **p** 84. C Heigham H Trin *Nor* 83-86; C Muswell Hill St Jas w St Matt *Lon* 86-90; R Bedford St Jo and St Leon *St Alb* 90-98; V Knowle *Birm* from 98; AD Solihull from 04; Hon Can Birm Cathl from 05. *The Vicarage, 1811 Warwick Road, Knowle, Solihull B93 0DS* Tel and fax (01564) 773666 *or* tel 778802 Fax 779123 E-mail vicar@knowleparishchurch.org.uk

PARKER, Nigel Howard. b 69. St Jo Coll Dur BSc90. CITC BTh97. **d** 97 **p** 98. C Holywood *D & D* 97-00; Outreach Development Officer Think Again 00-04; I Bangor St Comgall from 04. *The Rectory, 2 Raglan Road, Bangor BT20 3TL* Tel (028) 9146 0712 E-mail nigelparker@revparker.freeserve.co.uk

PARKER, Peter Edward. b 32. Edin Univ MA55 Lon Univ PGCE56 FRSA. Sarum & Wells Th Coll 73. **d** 74 **p** 75. C Kirkby Lonsdale w Mansergh *Carl* 74-76; C Kingston All SS w St Jo *S'wark* 76-80; Chapl S Bank Poly 80-85; Ind Chapl *Chelmsf* 85-90; Chapl Chelmsf Cathl 85-90; R Mistley w Manningtree and Bradfield 90-97; rtd 97; Perm to Offic *Ely* from 97. *2 Waterside, Ely CB7 4AZ* Tel (01353) 614103

PARKER, Philip Vernon. b 60. Birm Univ BSc82 PGCE83. Wycliffe Hall Ox BA89. **d** 90 **p** 91. C Walkergate *Newc* 90-93; Chapl Shiplake Coll Henley 93-96; C Lindfield *Chich* 97-99; Scripture Union 99-04; Chapl Cranleigh Sch Surrey from 04; CF (TA) from 97. *Cranleigh School, Horseshoe Lane, Cranleigh GU6 8QQ* Tel (01483) 273666

PARKER, Ramon Lewis (Brother Raphael). b 36. Kelham Th Coll 56. **d** 61 **p** 62. C Tonge Moor *Man* 61-64; C Clerkenwell H Redeemer w St Phil *Lon* 64-65; V Prestwich St Hilda *Man* 65-71; SSF from 71; Chapl Univ of Wales (Lamp) *St D* 81-86; Lic to Offic *Sarum* from 87; rtd 97. *c/o Brother Samuel SSF, The Friary, Hilfield, Dorchester DT2 7BE* Tel (01300) 341345 Fax 341293

PARKER, Richard Bryan. b 64. Sheff Poly BA87. Coll of Resurr Mirfield 92. **d** 95 **p** 96. C Norton *Sheff* 95-98; C Hoyland 98-00; V Moorends from 00. *The Vicarage, West Road, Moorends, Doncaster DN8 4LH* Tel (01405) 741758 Fax as telephone E-mail richardparker@ukgateway.net

PARKER, Richard Frederick. b 36. Oak Hill Th Coll 72. **d** 74 **p** 75. C Wootton *St Alb* 74-76; C Hove Bp Hannington Memorial Ch *Chich* 76-81; R Northwood *Portsm* 81-88; V W Cowes H Trin 81-88; V Aldershot H Trin *Guildf* 88-98; R Spaxton w Charlynch, Goathurst, Enmore etc *B & W* 98-03; rtd 03. *47 Banneson Road, Nether Stowey, Bridgwater TA5 1NS* Tel (01278) 671265

PARKER, Robert. b 43. Lon Univ BSc65. Cuddesdon Coll. **d** 67 **p** 68. C Sheff St Cuth *Sheff* 67-70; Asst Chapl Cheltenham Coll 70-74; R Yate *Glouc* 74-76; R Yate *Bris* 76-77; TR Yate New Town 77-80; C of E Development Officer 80-83; P-in-c Pool Quay *St As* 99-04; NSM from 05. *Pool Grange, Pool Quay, Welshpool SY21 9JU* Tel (01938) 590496

PARKER, Robert Lawrence. b 34. ALCD59. **d** 59 **p** 60. C Chippenham St Paul *Bris* 59-61; C Swindon Ch Ch 61-63; New Zealand 63-71; P-in-c Over Stowey w Aisholt *B & W* 71-73; V Nether Stowey 71-73; V Nether Stowey w Over Stowey 73-93; RD Quantock 87-93; V Pitminster w Corfe 93-99; rtd 99; Perm to Offic *B & W* from 00. *Oratia, 9 Brookfield Way, Street BA16 0UE* Tel (01458) 442906

PARKER, Robert Nicolas. b 71. Nottm Univ BA93 PGCE95. Ridley Hall Cam 95. **d** 98 **p** 99. C Yardley St Edburgha *Birm* 98-02; Asst P Eugene St Mary USA 02-05; P-in-c Coleshill *Birm* from 05; P-in-c Maxstoke from 05. *The Vicarage, High Street, Coleshill, Birmingham B46 3BP* Tel (01675) 462188 E-mail nickthevicparker@btinernet.com

PARKER, Roger Thomas Donaldson. b 55. Simon Fraser Univ BC BA80 Univ of Wales (Cardiff) LLB84 Univ Coll Lon LLM85. Coll of Resurr Mirfield 95. **d** 95 **p** 96. C Swinton and Pendlebury *Man* 95-02; V Burnley St Cath w St Alb and St Paul *Blackb* from 02. *St Catherine's Parsonage, 156 Todmorden Road, Burnley BB11 3ER* Tel (01282) 424587 Mobile 07977-291166 E-mail frrogerparker@aol.com

PARKER, Roland John Graham. b 48. AKC72 Hull Univ BA(Ed)83. St Aug Coll Cant 71. **d** 74 **p** 75. C Linc St Faith and St Martin w St Pet *Linc* 74-78; V Appleby 78-84; Ind Chapl 78-84; V N Kelsey 84-92; V Cadney 84-92; P-in-c Waddington 92-97; R from 97. *The Rectory, Rectory Lane, Waddington, Lincoln LN5 9RS* Tel (01522) 720323 E-mail rolapark2@btinternet.com

PARKER, Russell Edward. b 48. Man Univ BA80. St Jo Coll Nottm MTh82. **d** 81 **p** 82. C Walmsley *Man* 81-85; V Coalville and Bardon Hill *Leic* 85-90; Dir Acorn Chr Foundn from 90. *Ravensdale, Old Lane, Dockenfield, Farnham GU10 4HQ* Tel (01420) 477675 E-mail rparker@acornchristian.org

PARKER, Stephen George. b 65. Birm Univ BEd89 MA97 PhD03. Qu Coll Birm 96. **d** 98. Teaching Asst Westhill Coll of HE Birm 98-01; Sen Lect Th Univ Coll Ches 01-04; Hd RS Cadbury Sixth Form Coll from 04. *Cadbury Sixth Form College, Downland Close, Birmingham B38 8QT* Tel 0121-458 3898 *or* 249 3417 Fax 433 2619 E-mail spk@cadcol.ac.uk

PARKER, Thomas Henry Louis. b 16. Em Coll Cam BA38 MA42 BD50 DD61. Lon Coll of Div 38. **d** 39 **p** 40. C Chesham St Mary *Ox* 39-42; C Cambridge St Phil *Ely* 42-43; C Cambridge St Andr Less 43-45; C Luddesdowne *Roch* 45-48; V Brothertoft *Linc* 48-55; R Lt Ponton w Stroxton 55-59; R Lt Ponton 59-61; R Gt Ponton 58-61; V Oakington *Ely* 61-71; Lect Dur Univ 71-81; rtd 81; Perm to Offic *Ely* 97-00. *Ceriogh, Flaggoners Green, Bromyard HR7 4QR* Tel (01885) 489307

PARKER, Thomas Richard. b 52. Imp Coll Lon BScEng73 Keele Univ MEd83. Cranmer Hall Dur. **d** 94 **p** 95. C Chadkirk *Ches* from 94; RD Chadkirk from 04. *The Vicarage, 18 Chadkirk Road, Romiley, Stockport SK6 3JY* Tel 0161-430 8709 E-mail tom_parker@ntlworld.com

PARKER, Timothy Percy. b 58. Man Univ BA. St Jo Coll Nottm DipTh. **d** 85 **p** 86. C Pitsmoor Ch Ch *Sheff* 85-87; C Kimberworth 87-89; C Brightside w Wincobank 89-91; C Upper Armley *Ripon* 91-95; TV Billingham St Aid *Dur* 95-97; V Billingham St Luke from 97. *17 Shadforth Drive, Billingham TS23 3PW* Tel (01642) 561870 E-mail timparker@ntlworld.com

PARKES, Kevin. b 62. Trent Poly BA84. Sarum & Wells Th Coll BTh90. **d** 88 **p** 89. C Wandsworth St Anne *S'wark* 88-92; USPG 92-95; Trinidad and Tobago 93-95; Kingston Area Miss Team *S'wark* 95-01; V Wandsworth Common St Mary from 01. *The Vicarage, 291 Burntwood Lane, London SW17 0AP* Tel (020) 8874 4804

PARKHILL, Alan John. b 43. TCD BA66. CITC 68. **d** 67 **p** 68. C Knockbreda *D & D* 67-70; Asst Warden Elswick Lodge Newc 71-72; C Bangor St Comgall 73-78; Bp's C Kilmore 78-82; I Kilmore and Inch 82-86; I Clonfeacle w Derrygortreavy *Arm* from 86. *4 Clonfeacle Road, Benburb, Dungannon BT71 7LQ* Tel and fax (028) 3754 8239

PARKIN, George David. b 37. Cranmer Hall Dur BA60 DipTh62. **d** 62 **p** 63. C Balderstone *Man* 62-65; C Tunstead 65-67; C Gateshead Fell *Dur* 69-73; Nigeria 74-76; V Walton Breck *Liv* 80-92; V Rawtenstall St Mary *Man* from 92; P-in-c Constable Lee from 02. *2 Melia Close, Rawtenstal, Rossendale BB4 6RQ* Tel (01706) 215585

PARKIN, Mrs Jennifer Anne. b 47. Nene Coll Northampton BEd85. WMMTC 95. **d** 98 **p** 99. C Northampton St Alb *Pet* 98-02; P-in-c Ecton from 02; Chapl Northants Healthcare NHS Trust from 02; Warden of Past Assts *Pet* from 06. *The Rectory, 32 West Street, Ecton, Northampton NN6 0QF* Tel (01604) 416326 E-mail parkinjen@aol.com

PARKIN, John Edmund. b 44. Open Univ BA73. St Jo Coll Nottm 83. **d** 85 **p** 86. C Aberavon *Llan* 85-90; R Eglwysilan 90-01; P Missr Merthyr Tydfil Ch Ch from 01. *12 Heol Scwrfa, Merthyr Tydfil CF48 1HE*

PARKIN, John Francis. b 40. Linc Th Coll 65. **d** 68 **p** 69. C Cullercoats St Geo *Newc* 68-72; C Stony Stratford *Ox* 72-73; TV Lt Coates *Linc* 73-76; Perm to Offic 88-93; NSM Horncastle w Low Toynton from 93; NSM High Toynton from 93. *The Firs, 68 Louth Road, Horncastle LN9 5LJ* Tel (01507) 523208

PARKIN, Jonathan Samuel. b 73. La Sainte Union Coll BTh95 Birm Univ MA97. Qu Coll Birm 98. **d** 98 **p** 99. C Skegness and Winthorpe *Linc* 98-01; Chapl Leic Coll of FE *Leic* 01-03; Chapl De Montfort Univ from 04; Chapl Leic Cathl from 01. *1 Finchway, Narborough, Leicester LE19 2TP*

PARKIN, Melvyn Christopher. b 57. NEOC 99. **d** 02 **p** 03. NSM Boston Spa *York* 02-03; C Elvington w Sutton on Derwent and E Cottingwith from 03. *The Rectory, Church Lane, Elvington, York YO41 4AD* Tel (01904) 608462

PARKIN, Canon Trevor Kinross. b 37. MCMI. Cranmer Hall Dur 63. **d** 66 **p** 67. C Kingston upon Hull St Martin *York* 66-69; C Reading St Jo *Ox* 69-73; Ind Chapl *Lon* 73-80; Hon C Langham Place All So 73-80; Ind Chapl *Ely* 80-82; V Maidenhead St Andr and St Mary *Ox* 82-02; Hon Can Butare from 00; rtd 02; Perm to Offic *Guildf* from 03. *2 High Meadow Place, Chertsey KT16 9HD* Tel (01932) 560322

PARKINSON, Alan. *See* PARKINSON, Thomas Alan

PARKINSON, Andrew. b 56. Keble Coll Ox BA77 MA80. Westcott Ho Cam 78. **d** 80 **p** 81. C S Shore H Trin *Blackb* 80-85; V Lea 85-94; V Longton from 94. *Longton Vicarage, Birchwood Avenue, Hutton, Preston PR4 5EE* Tel (01772) 612179 E-mail aparkinson@longtonvicarage.freeserve.co.uk

PARKINSON, Andrew. b 74. St Steph Ho Ox. **d** 01 **p** 02. C Lancaster Ch Ch *Blackb* 01-04; P-in-c Yarnton w Begbroke and Shipton on Cherwell *Ox* 04-05; TV Blenheim from 05. *The Rectory, 26 Church Lane, Yarnton, Kidlington OX5 1PY* Tel (01865) 375749

PARKINSON, Miss Brenda. b 40. Lancs Poly CQSW. Dalton Ho Bris 65. **dss** 74 **d** 87 **p** 94. Ribbleton *Blackb* 75-80; Ingol 82-88; Par Dn 87-88; Par Dn Ashton-on-Ribble St Mich 88-91; Par Dn Ashton-on-Ribble St Mich w Preston St Mark 91-92; Par Dn Gt Marsden 92-94; C 94-98; C Gt Marsden w Nelson St Phil 99-00; rtd 00; Perm to Offic *Blackb* from 01. *18 Thorn Hill Close, Blackburn BB1 1YE* Tel (01254) 678367

PARKINSON, David Thomas. b 42. Linc Th Coll 77. **d** 79 **p** 80. C Yate New Town *Bris* 79-82; TV Keynsham *B & W* 82-88; R Bleadon from 88. *The Rectory, 17 Coronation Road, Bleadon, Weston-super-Mare BS24 0PG* Tel (01934) 812297

PARKINSON, Derek Leslie. b 29. Ripon Hall Ox 64. **d** 66 **p** 67. C Guildf Ch Ch *Guildf* 66-69; P-in-c Preston St Sav *Blackb* 69-74; P-in-c Preston St Jas 69-74; P-in-c Fontmell Magna *Sarum* 74-81; P-in-c Ashmore 74-81; P-in-c Kingswood w Alderley and Hillesley *Glouc* 81-82; R 82-94; rtd 94. *25 Fountain Crescent, Wotton-under-Edge GL12 7LD*

PARKINSON, Francis Wilson. b 37. Lon Univ DipTh62 Open Univ BA80. St Aid Birkenhead 59. **d** 62 **p** 63. C Monkwearmouth St Andr *Dur* 62-64; C Speke All SS *Liv* 64-67; CF 67-92; Perm to Offic *Ox* from 92; rtd 02. *9 Priory Mead, Longcot, Faringdon SN7 7TJ* Tel (01793) 784406

PARKINSON, George Stanley. b 20. St Jo Coll Dur BA47 DipTh48. **d** 48 **p** 49. C Widnes St Paul *Liv* 48-51; C Bradf Cathl Par *Bradf* 51-55; V Greengates 55-58; V Pennington *Man* 58-71; V Eccles St Mary 71-80; V Churt *Guildf* 80-90; RD Farnham 82-88; rtd 90; Perm to Offic *Worc* from 90. *12 Bevere Court, Bevere, Worcester WR3 7RE* Tel (01905) 457106 E-mail revgsp@yahoo.co.uk

PARKINSON, Ian Richard. b 58. Dur Univ BA79 Lon Univ BD84. Wycliffe Hall Ox 80. **d** 83 **p** 84. C Hull St Jo Newland *York* 83-86; C Linthorpe 86-92; V Saltburn-by-the-Sea 92-01; V Marple All SS *Ches* from 01. *The Vicarage, 155 Church Lane, Marple, Stockport SK6 7LD* Tel and fax 0161-449 0950 *or* tel 427 2378 E-mail ian.parkinson7@ntlworld.com

PARKINSON, John Reginald. b 32. Qu Coll Birm 79. **d** 81 **p** 82. NSM Catshill *Worc* 81-85; C Knightwick w Doddenham, Broadwas and Cotheridge 85-88; C Martley and Wichenford 85-88; P-in-c Berrow w Pendock and Eldersfield 88-89; R Berrow w Pendock, Eldersfield, Hollybush etc 89-97; RD Upton 95-97; rtd 97; Perm to Offic *Glouc* and *Worc* from 97. *8 Glebe Close, Stow on the Wold, Cheltenham GL54 1DJ* Tel (01451) 830822

PARKINSON, Leslie. *See* PARKINSON, Derek Leslie

PARKINSON, Nicholas John. b 46. FCCA75 Cranfield Inst of Tech MBA85. St Alb Minl Tr Scheme 92. **d** 95 **p** 96. NSM Woburn Sands *St Alb* 95-98; NSM Westoning w Tingrith 98-01; NSM Woburn Sands from 01. *Thornbank House, 7 Church Road, Woburn Sands, Milton Keynes MK17 8TE* Tel (01908) 583397

PARKINSON, Peter. b 23. Roch Th Coll 61. **d** 63 **p** 64. C Linc St Mary-le-Wigford w St Martin *Linc* 63-65; C Skegness 65-68; R Kettlethorpe 68-73; V Newton-on-Trent 68-73; V Grainthorpe w Conisholme 74-83; V Marshchapel 74-83; R N Coates 74-83; V Bicker 83-88; rtd 88. *11 Waltham Road, Lincoln LN6 0SD* Tel (01522) 680604

PARKINSON, Raymond Neville. b 21. Bris Univ BA53. Tyndale Hall Bris 50. **d** 54 **p** 55. C Hove Bp Hannington Memorial Ch *Chich* 54-57; C Reading St Jo *Ox* 57-59; R Folke w Long Burton, N Wootton and Haydon *Sarum* 59-69; V Ashby-de-la-Zouch H Trin *Leic* 69-79; V Swannington St Geo and Coleorton 79-87; rtd 87; Perm to Offic *Leic* 87-88; *Linc* 88-00. *31 Chestnut Crescent, Chedburgh, Bury St Edmunds IP29 4UJ* Tel (01284) 850993

PARKINSON, Simon George Denis. b 39. Univ of Wales (Lamp) BA66. Westcott Ho Cam 65. **d** 67 **p** 68. C Rothwell *Ripon* 67-70; Chapl RAF 70-73; C Leeds St Pet *Ripon* 74-75; V Horbury Junction *Wakef* 76-83; V Hanging Heaton 83-92; P-in-c Upper Hopton 92; V Eastthorpe and Upper Hopton 92-02; rtd 02. *126 Edge Lane, Dewsbury WF12 0HB* Tel (01924) 508885

PARKINSON, Thomas Alan. b 40. St Jo Coll York CertEd61. NW Ord Course 75. **d** 78 **p** 79. NSM Sheff St Cecilia Parson Cross *Sheff* 78-82; NSM Goldthorpe w Hickleton 82-90; C Cantley 90-01; Dioc RE and Worship Adv 93-04; V Ryecroft St Nic from 02. *St Nicolas' Presbytery, Kilnhurst Road, Rawmarsh, Rotherham S62 5NG* Tel (01709) 522596

PARKINSON, Vivian Leslie. b 54. St Luke's Coll Ex CertEd76 Brighton Poly BEd87. St Jo Coll Nottm Dip Th Studies. **d** 94 **p** 95. C Cowbridge *Llan* 94-97; V Llantrisant from 97. *The Vicarage, Coed yr Esgob, Llantrisant, Pontyclun CF72 8EL* Tel (01443) 223356 *or* 237983 Fax 230631

PARKS, Paul. b 59. K Coll Lon BA96. St Jo Coll Nottm MA97. **d** 98 **p** 99. C S Molton w Nymet St George, High Bray etc *Ex* 98-04; P-in-c Hurst *Ox* 04-05; C Wokingham St Sebastian from 05. *50 Lupin Ride, Crowthorne RG45 6UR* Tel (01344) 772201 E-mail revpaulparks@tiscali.co.uk

PARMENTER, Canon Deirdre Joy. b 45. EAMTC 91. **d** 94 **p** 95. C Ipswich St Aug *St E* 94-97; P-in-c Haughley w Wetherden 97-00; V Haughley w Wetherden and Stowupland from 00; RD Stowmarket 99-05; Hon Can St E Cathl from 03. *The Vicarage, The Folly, Haughley, Stowmarket IP14 3NS* Tel and fax (01449) 771647 Mobile 07721-587634 E-mail parmenter@ed-ip.freeserve.co.uk

PARNELL, Bryan Donald. b 38. JP. DipEd88. Chich Th Coll 66. **d** 69 **p** 70. C Lewisham St Jo Southend *S'wark* 69-72; Australia from 72; Asst Chapl Colleg Sch of St Pet 72-76; R Angaston 76-78; Chapl RAN 78-88; R Edwardstown 89-02; rtd 02. *PO Box 6619, Halifax Street, Adelaide, S Australia 5000* Tel (0061) (8) 4100337 Mobile 414-692340 E-mail trinitas@senet.com.au

PARNELL-HOPKINSON, Clive. b 46. SSC93 DipM75 FRSA01. Sarum & Wells Th Coll 75. **d** 78 **p** 79. C Maldon All SS w St Pet *Chelmsf* 78-81; C Chandler's Ford *Win* 81-84; Chapl RAF 84-01; P-in-c Cliddesden and Ellisfield w Farleigh Wallop etc *Win* from 01; Dioc Adv in Tourism from 01. *The Rectory, Church Lane, Ellisfield, Basingstoke RG25 2QR* Tel (01256) 381217 E-mail halo.cph@ukonline.co.uk

PARR, Clive William. b 41. FCIS. WEMTC 02. **d** 03 **p** 04. NSM Evesham w Norton and Lenchwick *Worc* from 03. *Grace Cottage, Mill Lane, Elmley Castle, Pershore WR10 3HP* Tel (01386) 710700 Mobile 07801-820006 Fax (01386) 761214

PARR, David Jonathan. b 77. Chelt & Glouc Coll of HE BA98. Trin Coll Bris BA04. **d** 04 **p** 05. C Whitchurch *Ex* from 04. *1 St Andrew's Road, Tavistock PL19 9BY* Tel (01822) 611167 Mobile 07816-752990 E-mail davejparr@yahoo.co.uk

PARR, Frank. b 35. Nottm Univ BCombStuds82 Lanc Univ MA86. Linc Th Coll 79. **d** 82 **p** 83. C Padiham *Blackb* 82-85; P-in-c Accrington St Andr 85-88; V Oswaldtwistle Immanuel and All SS 88-96; V Tunstall w Melling and Leck 96-01; rtd 01; Perm to Offic *Blackb* from 01. *1 Bank View, Burton Road, Lower Bentham, Lancaster LA2 7DZ* Tel (015242) 61159 E-mail frank_parr@lineone.net

PARR, John. b 53. St Edm Hall Ox BA74 MA87 Lon Univ BD79 Sheff Univ PhD90. Trin Coll Bris 75. **d** 79 **p** 80. C Gt Crosby St Luke *Liv* 79-82; C Walton St Mary 82-84; V Ince St Mary 84-87; Tutor and Lect Ridley Hall Cam 87-95; Chapl 87-93; Dir Studies 93-95; CME Officer *Ely* 95-99; P-in-c Harston w Hauxton 95-99; P-in-c Newton 97-99; CME Officer *St E* 99-00; Can Res St E Cathl 99-00. *7A College Lane, Bury St Edmunds IP33 1NN* Tel (01284) 754247 E-mail jpl@talk21.com

PARRATT, Dennis. b 53. St Steph Ho Ox. **d** 84 **p** 85. C Cainscross w Selsley *Glouc* 84-88; C Old Shoreham *Chich* 88-91; C New Shoreham 88-91; Perm to Offic *Glouc* from 02. *The Basement Flat, 17 Montpellier Terrace, Cheltenham GL50 1UX* Tel (01242) 255812

PARRETT, Mrs Mary Margaret. b 42. Shenstone Coll of Educn DipEd63. St Alb Minl Tr Scheme 86. **d** 98 **p** 99. NSM Barton-le-Cley w Higham Gobion and Hexton *St Alb* from 98. *49 Manor Road, Barton-le-Clay, Bedford MK45 4NP* Tel (01582) 833089

PARRETT, Mrs Rosalind Virginia. b 43. Ox Brookes Univ MTh02. Cant Sch of Min 84. **d** 87 **p** 94. NSM Selling w Throwley, Sheldwich w Badlesmere etc *Cant* 87-91; Asst Chapl Cant Hosp 87-91; Par Dn Stantonbury and Willen *Ox* 91-94; TV 94-96; P-in-c Owlsmoor 96-98; V 98-03; rtd 03; Perm to Offic *Cant* 03-04; Hon C Faversham from 04. *16 Hilton Close, Faversham ME13 8NN* Tel (01795) 530380 Mobile 07881-788155 E-mail parrett.rosalind@virgin.net

PARRETT, Simon Christopher. b 60. Sarum & Wells Th Coll. **d** 87 **p** 88. C Ifield *Chich* 87-91; Chapl to the Deaf *Sarum* 91-94; NSM Bournemouth H Epiphany *Win* 94-96; Asst Chapl Poole Hosp NHS Trust 96-03; Chapl Dorothy House Hospice Winsley 01-04. *90 Wareham Road, Lytchett Matravers, Poole BH16 6DT*

PARRETT, Stanley Frederick Donald. b 24. **d** 78 **p** 79. NSM Whitchurch w Ganarew *Heref* 78-83; C Goodrich w Welsh Bicknor and Marstow 83-86; C Walford w Bishopswood 83-86; R Pembridge w Moorcourt, Shobdon, Staunton etc 86-89; rtd 89. *4 Manley Lane, Pembridge, Leominster HR6 9EE*

PARRI, Emyr. Univ of Wales BA96 FRAS. Ban & St As Minl Tr Course 98. **d** 98 **p** 99. NSM Tregarth *Ban* from 98. *The Rectory, Llanllechid, Bangor LL57 3SD* Tel (01248) 602176

PARRISH, Robert Carey. b 57. St Steph Ho Ox 89. **d** 91 **p** 92. C Abington *Pet* 91-94; C Leckhampton SS Phil and Jas w Cheltenham St Jas *Glouc* 94-97; PV Llan Cathl *Llan* 97-02; R Merthyr Dyfan from 02. *Merthyr Dyfan Rectory, 10 Buttrills Road, Barry CF62 8EF* Tel (01446) 735943

PARROTT, David Wesley. b 58. Univ of Wales (Cardiff) LLM01. Oak Hill Th Coll BA. **d** 84 **p** 85. C Thundersley *Chelmsf* 84-87; C Rainham 87-89; P-in-c Heydon w Gt and Lt Chishill 89-90; P-in-c Chrishall 89-90; P-in-c Elmdon w Wendon Lofts and Strethall 89-90; R Heydon, Gt and Lt Chishill, Chrishall etc 91-96; R Rayleigh 96-00; TR 00-04; RD Rochford 02-04; Barking Area CME Adv from 04; C Hornchurch St Andr from 05. *5 Poole Road, Hornchurch RM11 3AS* Tel (01708) 464591 E-mail dwparrott@chelmsford.anglican.org

PARROTT, George. b 37. Leeds Univ BA61. Bps' Coll Cheshunt 61. **d** 63 **p** 64. C Lower Mitton *Worc* 63-65; C-in-c Fairfield St Rich CD 65-68; Zambia 68-70; C Cleethorpes *Linc* 70-75; R Withern 75-80; P-in-c Gayton le Marsh 76-80; P-in-c Strubby 76-80; P-in-c Authorpe 76-80; P-in-c Belleau w Aby and Claythorpe 76-80; P-in-c N and S Reston 76-80; P-in-c Swaby w S Thoresby 76-80; R Withern 80-90; V Reston 80-90; V Messingham 90-93; P-in-c Fincham *Ely* 95-02; P-in-c Marham 95-02; P-in-c Shouldham 95-02; P-in-c Shouldham Thorpe 95-02; rtd 02; Perm to Offic *Linc* from 03. *8 Anson Close, Skellingthorpe, Lincoln LN6 5TH* Tel (01522) 694417

PARROTT, Canon Gerald Arthur. b 32. St Cath Coll Cam BA56 MA60. Chich Th Coll. **d** 58 **p** 59. C Ashington *Newc* 58-61; C Brighton St Pet *Chich* 61-63; V Leeds St Wilfrid *Ripon* 63-68; R Lewisham St Jo Southend *S'wark* 69-73; TR Catford (Southend) and Downham 73-77; RD E Lewisham 75-77; Can Res and Prec S'wark Cathl 77-88; TR Wimbledon 88-95; rtd 95; Perm to Offic *Chich* from 95. *10 Palings Way, Fernhurst, Haslemere GU27 3HJ*

PARROTT, Martin William. b 57. Keele Univ BA79 Lon Univ PGCE80. Ripon Coll Cuddesdon 82. **d** 85 **p** 86. C Birchfield *Birm* 85-88; Chapl Lon Univ *Lon* 88-93; P-in-c Univ Ch Ch the K Lon 90-93; V Hebden Bridge *Wakef* 93-01; Asst Chapl Pinderfields and Pontefract Hosps NHS Trust 01-02; Chapl Calderdale and Huddersfield NHS Trust from 02. *The Royal Infirmary, Acre Street, Lindley, Huddersfield HD3 3EA* Tel (01484) 342000 E-mail martin.parrott@cht.nhs.uk

PARRY, Canon Alfred Charles Ascough. b 37. Natal Univ BA58. Westcott Ho Cam 59. **d** 61 **p** 62. C E Ham w Upton Park *Chelmsf* 61-63; S Africa 63-98; C Durban N St Martin 63-64; R Newcastle H Trin 64-70; Dir Chr Educn Kloof 70-76; Sub Dean Pietermaritzburg 76-81; R Estcourt 81; Adn N Natal 81-85; R Kloof 86-93; R Berea 93-98; Hon Can Pietermaritzburg from 86; Sen Asst Min Hornchurch St Andr *Chelmsf* 99-04; C Furze Platt *Ox* 04-05; Hon C from 05; rtd 05. *St John's House, Spring Lane, Cookham, Maidenhead SL6 9PN* Tel (01628) 483342 E-mail burnway49@supanet.com

PARRY, Canon Bryan Horace. b 33. St Mich Coll Llan 65. **d** 67 **p** 68. C Holyhead w Rhoscolyn w Llanfair-yn-Neubwll *Ban* 67-71; TV 71-73; P-in-c Small Heath St Greg *Birm* 73-78; V 78-80; V Perry Barr 80-94; RD Handsworth 83-91; P-in-c Kingstanding St Luke 86-92; Hon Can Birm Cathl 87-94; rtd 94; Perm to Offic *Nor* from 94. *St Seiriol, Old Crown Yard, Walsingham NR22 6BU* Tel (01328) 820019

PARRY, Charles. *See* PARRY, Canon Alfred Charles Ascough

PARRY, David Allan. b 62. Bris Univ BSc83 Univ of Wales (Cardiff) CQSW88 DASS88. Trin Coll Bris. **d** 94 **p** 95. C Withywood *Bris* 94-98; P-in-c Litherland St Phil *Liv* 98-02; V from 02; Hon Chapl to the Deaf 00-05; AD Bootle 02-05; Hon Can Liv Cathl 03-05; Dioc Dir of Ords from 05. *The Vicarage, St Michael's Church Road, Liverpool L17 7BD* Tel and fax 0151-727 2601

PARRY, David Thomas Newton. b 45. Selw Coll Cam BA67 MA71. Lambeth STh76 Cuddesdon Coll 67. **d** 69 **p** 70. C Oldham St Mary w St Pet *Man* 69-73; C Baguley 73-74; Tutor Sarum & Wells Th Coll 74-78; V Westleigh St Pet *Man* 78-88; TR E Farnworth and Kearsley 88-97; TR Chambersbury *St Alb* 97-03; V Blackbird Leys *Ox* from 03. *Church House, 5 Cuddesdon Way, Oxford OX4 6JH* Tel (01865) 778728 E-mail dtnparry@parsonage.u-net.com

PARRY, Denis. b 34. Sarum & Wells Th Coll 83. **d** 85 **p** 86. C Hubberston w Herbrandston and Hasguard etc *St D* 85-89; P-in-c Herbrandston and Hasguard w St Ishmael's 89-90; R 90-99; Dioc RE Adv 89-99; rtd 99; Perm to Offic *Heref* from 99. *Mayfield, Mill Street, Kington HR5 3AL* Tel (01544) 230550

PARRY, Canon Dennis John. b 38. Univ of Wales (Lamp) BA60. St Mich Coll Llan 60. **d** 62 **p** 63. C Caerphilly *Llan* 62-64; C Aberdare St Fagan 64-67; Miss at Povungnituk Canada 67-69; R Gelligaer *Llan* 69-75; V Llanwnnog and Caersws w Carno *Ban* 75-89; V Llanidloes w Llangurig 89-01; RD Arwystli 89-01; Hon Can Ban Cathl 90-01; Can Cursal 97-01; rtd 02; Perm to Offic *Ban* from 02. *Lock Cottage, Groesfford, Brecon LD3 7UY* Tel (01874) 665400 E-mail dennis@stidloes.freeserve.co.uk

PARRY, Derek Nugent Goulding. b 32. Ely Th Coll 60. **d** 63 **p** 64. C Fareham SS Pet and Paul *Portsm* 63-67; C Portsea N End St Mark 67-74; P-in-c Piddletrenthide w Plush, Alton Pancras etc *Sarum* 74-92; rtd 92; Perm to Offic *Sarum* from 92. *Farthing Cottage, 12 Fordington Green, Dorchester DT1 1LU* Tel (01305) 269794

PARRY, Gordon Martyn Winn. b 47. Down Coll Cam BA68 MA70 Univ Coll Chich MA02. **d** 04 **p** 05. NSM Turners Hill *Chich* from 04. *8 Hoathly Hill, West Hoathly, East Grinstead RH19 4SJ* Tel and fax (01342) 810618 Mobile 07802-432398 E-mail gordonmwparry@btinternet.com

PARRY, Jane. *See* PARRY, Mrs Patricia Jane

PARRY, John Gareth. b 61. Univ of Wales (Abth) BA83 Univ of Wales (Ban) PGCE84. Westcott Ho Cam CTM96. **d** 96 **p** 97. C Holyhead *Ban* 96-99; C-in-c Llandinorwig w Penisa'r-waen 99-00; Perm to Offic from 00; Asst Master Bodedern Secondary Sch 00-01; Hd RE Pensby High Sch for Boys Wirral 02; Chapl and Hd RE Tettenhall Coll Wolv from 03. *34 Merton Park, Penmaenmawr LL34 6DH,* or *Tettenhall College, Wood Road, Wolverhampton WV6 8QX* Tel (01492) 622671 *or* (01902) 793010

PARRY, Keith Melville. b 31. MRICS65. S'wark Ord Course 80. **d** 83 **p** 84. NSM Bexley St Jo *Roch* 83-88; C Orpington All SS 88-96; rtd 96; Perm to Offic *Roch* from 96. *5 Greenside, Bexley DA5 3PA*

PARRY, Canon Kenneth Charles. b 34. Ripon Hall Ox 56. **d** 58 **p** 59. C Stoke *Cov* 58-61; Chapl RN 61-65; V Cradley *Worc* 65-70; V Gt Malvern H Trin 70-83; RD Malvern 74-83; Hon Can Worc Cathl 80-83; V Budleigh Salterton *Ex* 83-91; Can Res and Prec Ex Cathl 91-00; rtd 00. *Brook Cottage, Pye Corner, Kennford, Exeter EX6 7TB* Tel (01392) 832767 E-mail kcparry@ic24.net

PARRY, Ms Manon Ceridwen. b 69. Poly of Wales BA90 Selw Coll Cam BA93 MA97. Ridley Hall Cam. **d** 94 **p** 97. C Llandudno *Ban* 94-98; P-in-c Glanogwen w St Ann's w Llanllechid 98-99; V 99-05; V Pentir 04-05; C Llanrhos *St As* from 05. *The Vicarage, Llanrwst Road, Bryn-y-Maen, Colwyn Bay LL28 5EW* Tel (01492) 533692 E-mail manon@ogwen.demon.co.uk

PARRY, Canon Marilyn Marie. b 46. W Coll Ohio BA68 Man Univ MA77 PhD00. Episc Th Sch Cam Mass 68 Gilmore Ho 76. **dss** 79 **d** 87 **p** 94. Westleigh St Pet *Man* 78-85; Chapl Asst N Man Gen Hosp 85-90; Tutor N Ord Course 90-97; Dir Studies 91-97; Lic Preacher *Man* 90-94; Hon C E Farnworth and Kearsley 94-97; Nat Adv for Pre-Th Educn and Selection Sec Min Division Abps' Coun 97-01; Public Preacher *St Alb* 98-01; Can Res Ch Ch *Ox* from 01; Dioc Dir of Ords from 01. *Diocesan Church House, North Hinksey, Oxford OX2 0NB* Tel (01865) 276215 *or* 208289 Mobile 07712-834973 Fax (01865) 790470 *or* 208246 E-mail marilyn.parry@oxford.anglican.org

PARRY, Nicholas John Sinclair. b 56. Sarum & Wells Th Coll 82. **d** 85 **p** 86. C Hendon St Mary *Lon* 85-87; C Verwood *Sarum* 87-90; TV Witney *Ox* 90-96; V Costessey *Nor* from 96. *The Vicarage, Folgate Lane, Costessey, Norwich NR8 5DP* Tel (01603) 742818 E-mail nicholas.parry@btinternet.com

PARRY, Mrs Olwen Margaret. b 45. Cardiff Coll of Educn CertEd67. Llan Dioc Tr Scheme 88. **d** 92 **p** 97. NSM Newcastle *Llan* 92-04; NSM Llansantffraid, Bettws and Aberkenfig from 04. *17 Wernlys Road, Bridgend CF31 4NS* Tel (01656) 721860

PARRY, Owen Benjamin. b 42. St As Minl Tr Course 99. **d** 01 **p** 02. NSM Llangollen w Trevor and Llantysilio *St As* 01-03; C from 03. *Fairways, Halton, Chirk, Wrexham LL14 5BD* Tel (01691) 778484

PARRY, Mrs Patricia Jane. b 54. Liv Univ BTh99. N Ord Course 97. **d** 99 **p** 00. C Wilmslow *Ches* 99-03; V Baddiley and Wrenbury w Burleydam from 03. *The Vicarage, The Green, Wrenbury, Nantwich CW5 8EY* Tel (01270) 780398 E-mail formidocornicarum@hotmail.com

PARRY, Peter John. b 42. Westmr Coll Ox BTh99. EAMTC 99. **d** 01 **p** 02. NSM Montreux w Gstaad *Eur* from 01. *Les Muscaris, Route de Brent 25, CH-1807 Blonay, Switzerland* Tel and fax (0041) (21) 943 4991 E-mail pparry@compuserve.com

PARRY, Richard Neil. **d** 98 **p** 99. C Glan Ely *Llan* 98-00; C Merthyr Dyfan 00-02; TV Canton Cardiff from 02. *Canton Vicarage, 3A Romilly Road, Cardiff CF5 1FH* Tel (029) 2022 9683

PARRY, Miss Violet Margaret. b 30. Selly Oak Coll 53. **dss** 82 **d** 87. W Kilburn St Luke w St Simon and St Jude *Lon* 82-83; St Marylebone St Mary 83-86; Stamford All SS w St Jo *Linc* 86-87; C 87-90; rtd 90; Perm to Offic *Linc* 90-01. *2 Stuart Court, High Street, Kibworth, Leicester LE8 0LR* Tel 0116-279 6858

PARRY, William Daniel. b 09. St Chad's Coll Dur BA31 DipTh32 MA34. **d** 32 **p** 33. C Tywyn *Ban* 32-36; C Dwygyfylchi 36-38; C Llanaber 38-45; V Arthog 45-48; V Llandinam 48-72; V Llandinam w Trefeglwys w Penstrowed 72-78; RD Arwystli 53-73; Can Ban Cathl 60-70; Chan 70-78; rtd 78; Lic to Offic *Ban* 78-96; Perm to Offic *St D* from 78. *14 Cae Mawr, Penrhyncoch, Aberystwyth SY23 3EJ* Tel (01970) 828118

PARRY-JENNINGS, Christopher William. b 34. Lon Coll of Div 57. **d** 60 **p** 62. C Claughton cum Grange *Ches* 60-63; C Folkestone H Trin w Ch Ch *Cant* 63-67; New Zealand from 67; V Lincoln 67-72; Chapl Cant Univ 68-72; V Riccarton St Jas 72-88; V Heathcote Mt Pleasant 88-96; First Gen Sec SPCK (NZ) 89-90; P Asst Upper Riccarton St Pet from 96. *22 Ambleside Drive, Burnside, Christchurch 8005, New Zealand* Tel (0064) (3) 358 9304 Fax as telephone

PARRY JONES, Leonard. b 29. Univ of Wales (Ban) BA52. St Mich Coll Llan 52. **d** 54 **p** 55. C Newtown w Llanllwchaiarn w Aberhafesp *St As* 54-58; C Abergele 58-60; V Pennant, Hirnant and Llangynog 60-65; V Llanynys w Llanychan 65-71; V Brynymaen w Trofarth 71-94; RD Rhos 77-94; rtd 94. *The Cottage, Kerry, Newtown SY16 4NU* Tel (01686) 670822

PARSELL, Howard Vivian. b 60. Univ of Wales (Lamp) BA87 Univ of Wales (Swansea) PGCE88. St Mich Coll Llan 93. **d** 94 **p** 95. C Builth and Llanddewi'r Cwm w Llangynog etc *S & B* 94-96; C Swansea St Thos and Kilvey 96-98; P-in-c Swansea

St Jude from 98; Chapl to the Deaf from 98; AD Swansea from 04. *St Jude's Vicarage, Hillside Crescent, Uplands, Swansea SA2 0RD* Tel (01792) 473154

PARSELLE, Stephen Paul. b 53. LTh. St Jo Coll Nottm. **d** 82 **p** 83. C Boscombe St Jo *Win* 82-86; CF 86-05; Dir of Ords 02-05; Chapl RN from 05. *Royal Naval Chaplaincy Service, Room 203, Victory Building, HM Naval Base PO1 3LS* Tel (01705) 727903 Fax 727112 E-mail parselle@aol.com

PARSONAGE, Robert Hugh. b 55. Nottm Trent Univ BSc78. Trin Coll Bris BA97. **d** 97 **p** 98. C Chell *Lich* 97-01; R Poringland *Nor* from 01. *The Rectory, Rectory Lane, Poringland, Norwich NR14 7SL* Tel (01508) 492215 E-mail robert@hparsonage.freeserve.co.uk

PARSONAGE, Robert Leslie. b 20. St Aid Birkenhead 43. **d** 46 **p** 47. C Farnworth *Liv* 46-47; C Bowdon *Ches* 47-51; V Everton St Geo *Liv* 51-52; CF 52-74; V Bayswater *Lon* 74-83; Perm to Offic 83-88; Preacher Newland Almshouses Glos 88-96; rtd 83; Perm to Offic *Glouc* from 96. *36 St Mary's Square, Gloucester GL1 2QT* Tel (01452) 309459

PARSONS, Andrew David. b 53. UEA BA74 Fitzw Coll Cam BA77 MA81. Westcott Ho Cam 75. **d** 78 **p** 79. C Hellesdon *Nor* 78-82; C Eaton 82-85; P-in-c Burnham Thorpe w Burnham Overy 85-87; R Burnham Sutton w Burnham Ulph etc 85-87; R Burnham Gp of Par 87-93; P-in-c Wroxham w Hoveton and Belaugh 93; R from 93; RD St Benet from 99. *The Vicarage, 11 Church Lane, Wroxham, Norwich NR12 8SH* Tel (01603) 782678 E-mail 2andrew@andrewparsons.fsnet.co.uk

PARSONS, Arthur. b 45. St Jo Coll Nottm LTh. **d** 75 **p** 76. C Cuddington *Guildf* 75-78; C Liskeard w St Keyne and St Pinnock *Truro* 78-81; P-in-c Ludgvan 81-83; R 83-99; Chapl Falmouth Fire Brigade 91-99; P-in-c Perranuthnoe 93-99; RD Penwith 93-98; TR Newton Tracey, Horwood, Alverdiscott etc *Ex* 99-02; C Chudleigh w Chudleigh Knighton and Trusham 02-03; C Okehampton w Inwardleigh, Bratton Clovelly etc from 03. *St Bridget's House, Bridestowe, Okehampton EX20 4ER* Tel (01837) 861612 E-mail arthur.parsons@btinternet.com

PARSONS, Arthur Gordon Boyd (Father Bob). b 20. TD50. SSC FCIPD47. Ripon Hall Ox BA54. **d** 56 **p** 57. C Doncaster St Mary *Sheff* 56-58; V N Wilford St Faith *S'well* 58-60; R W w E Allington and Sedgebrook *Linc* 60-66; P-in-c Woolsthorpe 60-64; R 64-66; V Grantham St Anne 66-69; Offg Chapl RAF 65-74; V Friskney *Linc* 69-74; R Tansor w Cotterstock and Fotheringhay *Pet* 74-76; V Forest Town *S'well* 76-78; V Sutton cum Lound 78-85; rtd 85; P-in-c Sampford Courtenay w Honeychurch *Ex* 85-87; P-in-c Exbourne w Jacobstowe 85-87; Hon C Holsworthy w Hollacombe and Milton Damerel 87-88; Hon C Bude Haven *Truro* 88-89; Hon C Stratton and Launcells 89-95; Perm to Offic *Linc* 95-96; *B & W* 96-99 and from 00; *Derby* from 01. *30 Penn Lane, Melbourne, Derby DE73 8EQ* Tel (01332) 694375

PARSONS, Bernard. b 26. Ely Th Coll 60. **d** 62 **p** 63. C Bourne *Linc* 62-64; V W Pinchbeck 64-71; V Sutton Bridge 71-83; R Coningsby w Tattershall 83-93; rtd 93; Perm to Offic *Linc* from 93. *12 St Peter's Drive, Woodhall Spa LN10 6SY* Tel (01526) 353027

PARSONS, Chrisopher Paul. b 58. EAMTC 01. **d** 04 **p** 05. C Pakefield *Nor* from 04. *9 Ryedale, Lowestoft NR33 8TB* Tel (01502) 512864 E-mail chris@cpp1.freeserve.co.uk

PARSONS, Christopher James Hutton. b 54. Univ of Wales (Ban) BA75 Birm Univ DipTh78. Qu Coll Birm. **d** 79 **p** 80. C Crowthorne *Ox* 79-83; V Tilehurst St Cath 83-88; P-in-c Wrentham w Benacre, Covehithe, Frostenden etc *St E* 89-91; R 91-94. *35 Tufton Gardens, West Molesey KT8 1TD*

PARSONS, David. b 37. SOAS Lon 57 Qu Coll Cam BA61 MA98 ARCO75. Ridley Hall Cam 61. **d** 62 **p** 63. C Ormskirk *Liv* 62-65; C Beccles St Mich *St E* 65-68; V Woodbridge St Jo 68-73; Chapl Edgarley Hall Sch Glastonbury 73-78; Asst Master Bruton Sch for Girls 78-98; Chapl 86-98; C Downend *Bris* 98-02; rtd 02. *13 Ivythorn Road, Street BA16 0TE* Tel (01458) 446110 Mobile 07966-367099 E-mail david.parsons@ndirect.co.uk

PARSONS, David Norman. b 39. FCIB83. Trin Coll Bris 92. **d** 94 **p** 95. NSM Swindon Dorcan *Bris* 94-03; Perm to Offic *Glouc* from 03. *31 Couzens Close, Chipping Sodbury, Bristol BS37 6BT* Tel (01454) 323070 E-mail david.parsons39@virgin.net

PARSONS, Desmond John. b 25. Coll of Resurr Mirfield 65. **d** 66 **p** 67. C Purley St Mark *S'wark* 66-70; V W Dulwich All SS and Em 71-83; R Limpsfield and Titsey 83-95; rtd 95; Perm to Offic *Guildf* and *S'wark* from 96. *Priors House, The Court, Croft Lane, Crondall, Farnham GU10 5QF* Tel (01252) 851137

PARSONS, Geoffrey Fairbanks. b 35. Trin Coll Cam BA58 MA68. Ridley Hall Cam 59. **d** 61 **p** 62. C Over St Chad *Ches* 61-64; C Heswall 64-69; V Congleton St Steph 69-75; V Weaverham 75-94; P-in-c Backford and Capenhurst 94-00; R 00-01; rtd 01; Perm to Offic *Ches* from 02. *28 Springcroft, Parkgate, South Wirral CH64 6SE* Tel 0151-336 3354

PARSONS, George Edward. b 35. St D Coll Lamp BA60 Ripon Hall Ox 60. **d** 62 **p** 63. C Leominster *Heref* 62-66; NSM Bromfield 67-72; NSM Culmington w Onibury 67-72; NSM Stanton Lacy 67-72; NSM Ludlow 72-77; P-in-c Caynham 77-79; NSM Bishop's Cleeve *Glouc* 79-91; Sub-Chapl HM Pris Glouc 88-91; P-in-c Hasfield w Tirley and Ashleworth 91-00; P-in-c Maisemore 91-00; rtd 00; Perm to Offic *Glouc 00-02 and Blackb* from 02. *Ballalona, 2 The Meadows, Hollins Lane, Forton, Preston PR3 0AF* Tel (01524) 792656

PARSONS, George Horace Norman. b 19. S'wark Ord Course 65. **d** 68 **p** 69. C Hatcham St Cath *S'wark* 68-72; C Horley 72-76; P-in-c S Wimbledon All SS 76-78; P-in-c Caterham 78-81; C Caterham and Chapl St Lawr Hosp 82-84; RAChD 72-84; rtd 85; Perm to Offic *S'wark* from 85. *8 Whitgift House, 76 Brighton Road, Croydon CR2 6AB* Tel (020) 8680 0028

PARSONS, Gilbert Harvey. b 20. St Pet Hall Ox BA46 MA46. Cuddesdon Coll 48. **d** 50 **p** 51. C Clapham St Pet *S'wark* 50-51; C Charlton St Luke w St Paul 51-56; V Stokenchurch and PC Cadmore End 56-61; V Stokenchurch and Cadmore End *Ox* 61-72; P-in-c Radnage 65-68; P-in-c Ibstone w Fingest 65-72; RD Aston 66-72; V Burford w Fulbrook 72-74; V Burford w Fulbrook and Taynton 74-85; rtd 85; Perm to Offic *Sarum* from 85. *Windrush, 23 Highlands Way, Whiteparish, Salisbury SP5 2SZ* Tel (01794) 884832

PARSONS, Jennifer Anne (Jeni). b 53. Univ of Wales (Lamp) BA76 MA78 Jes Coll Cam PhD90. Westcott Ho Cam CTM94. **d** 94 **p** 95. C Halesowen *Worc* 94-97; TV Worc St Barn w Ch Ch 97-04; R Matson *Glouc* from 04. *The Rectory, Matson Lane, Gloucester GL4 6DX* Tel (01452) 522598 E-mail jeni@hencity.fsnet.co.uk

PARSONS, Canon John Banham. b 43. Selw Coll Cam BA65 MA68. Ridley Hall Cam 65. **d** 67 **p** 68. C Downend *Bris* 67-71; Public Preacher Withywood LEP 71-77; P-in-c Hengrove 77-78; V 78-85; V Letchworth St Paul w Willian *St Alb* 85-94; P-in-c Barking St Marg w St Patr *Chelmsf* 94-98; TR 98-04; RD Barking and Dagenham 00-04; P-in-c Hornchurch H Cross from 04; RD Havering from 04; Hon Can Chelmsf Cathl from 01. *Holy Cross Vicarage, 260 Hornchurch Road, Hornchurch RM11 1PX* Tel (01708) 447976

PARSONS, Laurie. b 19. Keble Coll Ox BA41. Wells Th Coll 41. **d** 43 **p** 44. C Westwood *Cov* 43-49; C-in-c Galley Common Stockingford CD 49-57; V Priors Marston 57-69; V Radford Semele 70-83; V Radford Semele and Ufton 83-84; rtd 84; Perm to Offic *Cov* 84-92; Perm to Offic *Pet* from 84. *86 Bull Baulk, Middleton Cheney, Banbury OX17 2SR* Tel (01295) 711829

PARSONS, Mrs Margaret Anne. b 31. Sheff Poly CQSW77. EMMTC 73. **dss** 77 **d** 87 **p** 94. Dronfield *Derby* 77-89; Par Dn 87-89; Par Dn Tidworth, Ludgershall and Faberstown *Sarum* 89-94; C 94-95; P-in-c Wold-Marsh Gp *Linc* 95-99; P-in-c Perlethorpe *S'well* 00-03; rtd 03; Perm to Offic *S'well* from 03. *6 Ringwood Avenue, Mansfield, Nottingham NG18 4DA* Tel (01623) 422745

PARSONS, Canon Marlene Beatrice. b 43. Wilson Carlile Coll. **dss** 76 **d** 87 **p** 94. Coulsdon St Jo *S'wark* 76-79; Hill *Birm* 79-86; Dioc Lay Min Adv 80-90; Vice Prin WMMTC 86-90; Dioc Dir of Ords *Birm* 90-04; Dean of Women's Min 90-04; Hon Can Birm Cathl 89-04; rtd 04; Perm to Offic *Birm* from 04. *20 Copperbeech Close, Birmingham B32 2HT* Tel 0121-427 2632

PARSONS, Miss Mary Elizabeth. b 43. Wilson Carlile Coll 65. **dss** 78 **d** 87 **p** 94. Chapl Asst Chu Hosp Ox 78-89; Chapl 89-93; rtd 93; NSM Sandford-on-Thames *Ox* 94-00. *20 Copperbeech Close, Birmingham B32 2HT* Tel 0121-426 4527

PARSONS, Canon Michael William Semper. b 47. St Cath Coll Ox BA69 MA74 DPhil74 Selw Coll Cam BA77 MA81. Ridley Hall Cam 75. **d** 78 **p** 79. C Edmonton All SS *Lon* 78-81; SPCK Research Fell Dur Univ 81-84; Hon Lect Th 84-85; SPCK Fell N of England Inst for Chr Educn 84-85; P-in-c Derby St Aug *Derby* 85-95; TR Walbrook Epiphany 95-96; Dioc Voc Adv 86-96; P-in-c Hempsted *Glouc* 96-00; Dir of Ords 96-04; Dir Curates' Tr 00-04; Prin WEMTC from 04; Hon Can Glouc Cathl from 03. *6 Spa Villas, Montpellier, Gloucester GL1 1LB* Tel (01452) 524550 E-mail principal@wemtc.freeserve.co.uk *or* mwsparsons@btinternet.com

PARSONS, Canon Robert Martin. b 43. Qu Coll Cam BA65 MA69. ALCD68. **d** 68 **p** 69. C Chapeltown *Sheff* 68-71; C Sheff St Jo 71-75; V Swadlincote *Derby* 75-91; RD Repton 81-91; P-in-c Gresley 82-86; R Etwall w Egginton 91-93; Can Res Derby Cathl 93-98; P-in-c Belper 98-03; V from 03; Hon Can Derby Cathl from 98. *St Peter's Vicarage, Chesterfield Road, Belper DE56 1FD* Tel (01773) 822148 E-mail canonparsons@totalise.co.uk

PARSONS, Roger John. b 37. Sarum Th Coll 62. **d** 65 **p** 66. C Bitterne Park *Win* 65-69; C Clerkenwell H Redeemer w St Phil *Lon* 69-72; C Willesden St Andr 72-76; C St Laur in Thanet *Cant* 76-81; Chapl Luton and Dunstable Hosp 81-86; Chapl St Mary's Hosp Luton 81-86; C Luton All SS w St Pet *St Alb* 81-86; Trustee St Benedict's Trust from 85; TV E Dereham *Nor* 86-88; TV E Dereham and Scarning 89; Perm to Offic 89-93. *478 Station Road, Sheringham NR26 8RG*

PARSONS, Stephen Christopher. b 45. Keble Coll Ox BA67 MA72 BLitt78. Cuddesdon Coll 68. **d** 70 **p** 71. C Whitstable All SS *Cant* 70-71; C Croydon St Sav 71-74; Perm to Offic *Ox* 74-76; C St Laur in Thanet *Cant* 76-79; V Lugwardine w Bartestree and

Weston Beggard *Heref* 79-87; V Lechlade *Glouc* 87-03; R Edin St Cuth *Edin* from 03. *6 Westgarth Avenue, Colinton, Edinburgh EH13 0BD* Tel 0131-441 3557
E-mail stephen@parsons252262.freeserve.co.uk

PARSONS, Stephen Drury. b 54. Qu Mary Coll Lon BSc76 CCC Cam MSc79. Westcott Ho Cam 79. **d** 82 **p** 83. C Stretford All SS *Man* 82-85; C Newton Heath All SS 85-86; V Ashton St Jas 86-90; Perm to Offic from 01. *150 Henrietta Street, Ashton-under-Lyne OL6 8PH* Tel 0161-308 2852

PARTINGTON, The Ven Brian Harold. b 36. OBE02. St Aid Birkenhead 60. **d** 63 **p** 64. C Barlow Moor *Man* 63-66; C Deane 66-68; V Patrick *S & M* 68-96; Bp's Youth Chapl 68-77; RD Peel 76-96; P-in-c German St Jo 77-78; V 78-96; P-in-c Foxdale 77-78; V 78-96; Can St German's Cathl 85-96; Adn Man 96-05; V Douglas St Geo 96-04; rtd 04. *Brambles, Patrick Village, Peel, Isle of Man IM5 3AH* Tel (01624) 844173
E-mail archd-sodor@mcb.net

PARTINGTON, John. *See* PARTINGTON, Peter John

PARTINGTON, Kenneth. b 41. Lanc Univ MA86. Ripon Hall Ox. **d** 70 **p** 71. C Atherton *Man* 70-72; C Kippax *Ripon* 72-75; V Cartmel Fell *Carl* 75-95; V Crosthwaite Kendal 75-95; V Witherslack 75-95; V Winster 78-95; rtd 01; Perm to Offic *Carl* from 01. *9 Castle Park, Kendal LA9 7AX* Tel (01539) 723963

PARTINGTON, Kevin. b 51. Huddersfield Poly BA73. St Jo Coll Nottm DCM93. **d** 93 **p** 94. C Salterhebble All SS *Wakef* 93-96; V Pontefract All SS 96-03; TR Dewsbury from 03. *The Rectory, 16A Oxford Road, Dewsbury WF13 4JT* Tel (01924) 465491 *or* 457057 E-mail kevin.partington@btopenworld.com

PARTINGTON, Peter John. b 57. Peterho Cam MA. St Jo Coll Nottm 79. **d** 81 **p** 82. C Cov H Trin *Cov* 81-85; C Woking St Jo *Guildf* 85-87; C 94-99; R Busbridge 87-94; Dir of Ords 94-03; P-in-c Winchcombe, Gretton, Sudeley Manor etc *Glouc* 03-05; TR Winchcombe from 05. *The Vicarage, Langley Road, Winchcombe, Cheltenham GL54 5QP* Tel (01242) 602368
E-mail revpjp@aol.com

PARTON, John Michael. b 44. Bradf & Ilkley Community Coll MA93. **d** 04 **p** 05. NSM Horbury w Horbury Bridge *Wakef* from 04. *106 Lennox Drive, Wakefield WF2 8LF* Tel and fax (01924) 360395 E-mail johnmparton@btinternet.com

PARTRIDGE, Alan Christopher. b 55. Thames Poly BA77 Ex Univ PGCE78. St Jo Coll Nottm MA00. **d** 00 **p** 01. C Woking St Jo *Guildf* 00-03; C Ely from 03. *20 Barton Road, Ely CB7 4DE* Tel (01353) 615408 E-mail alanc.partridge@lineone.net

PARTRIDGE, Anthony John. b 38. Univ of Wales (Lamp) BA61 Linacre Ho Ox BA63 K Coll Lon PhD77. St Steph Ho Ox 61. **d** 64 **p** 65. C Sydenham All SS *S'wark* 64-67; Hon C 68-74; Lic to Offic from 74; Prin Lect Thames Poly 75-92; Greenwich Univ from 92; rtd 03. *40 Upwood Road, London SE12 8AN,* or *University of Greenwich, Wellington Street, London SE18 6PF* Tel (020) 8318 9901 *or* 8854 2030

PARTRIDGE, Canon David John Fabian. b 36. Ball Coll Ox BA60 MA. Westcott Ho Cam 60. **d** 62 **p** 63. C Halliwell St Thos *Man* 62-65; C St Martin-in-the-Fields *Lon* 65-69; R Warblington w Emsworth *Portsm* 69-01; Hon Can Portsm Cathl 84-01; rtd 01. *7 Wensley Gardens, Emsworth PO10 7RA* Tel (01865) 558630

PARTRIDGE, Ian Starr. b 36. Linc Th Coll 87. **d** 89 **p** 90. C Barton upon Humber *Linc* 89-92; P-in-c Barkwith Gp 92-97; R 97-02; rtd 02; Perm to Offic *Linc* from 02; RD Calcewaithe and Candleshoe 03-05. *Altair, 4 Thames Street, Louth LN11 7AD* Tel (01507) 600398 E-mail ian@altair.org.uk

PARTRIDGE, Miss Margaret Edith. b 35. Birm Univ DipTh68. Gilmore Ho 63. **dss** 85 **d** 87 **p** 94. Amblecote *Worc* 85-89; Par Dn 87-89; C Borehamwood *St Alb* 89-94; TV 94-00; rtd 00; Perm to Offic *Birm* from 01. *4 Cornerstone Drive, Maryland Drive, Birmingham B31 2AT* Tel 0121-476 0854

PARTRIDGE, Martin David Waud. b 38. Ox NSM Course 86. **d** 89 **p** 90. NSM Wargrave *Ox* 89-97; NSM Schorne from 97. *The Rectory, Church Street, Quainton, Aylesbury HP22 4AP* Tel (01296) 655237

PARTRIDGE, Michael John. b 61. St Edm Hall Ox BA83 MA89 St Jo Coll Dur BA86. Cranmer Hall Dur 84. **d** 87 **p** 88. C Amington *Birm* 87-90; C Sutton Coldfield H Trin 90-93; P-in-c W Exe *Ex* 93-01; RD Tiverton 96-00; V Tiverton St Geo and St Paul from 01. *St Paul's Vicarage, Bakers Hill, Tiverton EX16 5NE* Tel (01884) 255705
E-mail mike@stpaulstiv.freeserve.co.uk
or m.partridge@tesco.net

PARTRIDGE, Ronald Malcolm. b 49. Lon Univ DipTh73 DAC94. Bris Bapt Coll LTh74 Cuddesdon Coll 74. **d** 75 **p** 76. C Bris St Andr Hartcliffe *Bris* 75-78; C E Bris 78-82; V Easton All Hallows 82-85; TV Brighton St Pet w Chpl Royal and St Jo *Chich* 85-86; TV Brighton St Pet and St Nic w Chpl Royal 86-88; C-in-c Bermondsey St Hugh CD *S'wark* 88-90; Asst Chapl Gt Ormond Street Hosp for Sick Children Lon 91-94; Asst Chapl Gt Ormond Street Hosp for Children NHS Trust 94-97. *29 All Saints Street, Hastings TN34 3BJ* Tel (01424) 715219

PARTRIDGE, Ronald William. b 42. Shimer Coll Illinois BA64. Cant Sch of Min 93. **d** 96 **p** 97. NSM Upchurch w Lower Halstow *Cant* from 96. *4 The Green, Lower Halstow, Sittingbourne ME9 7DT* Tel (01795) 842007
E-mail revdron.partridge@virgin.net

PARTRIDGE, Canon Timothy Reeve. b 39. Lon Univ BSc60 AKC60. Wells Th Coll 60. **d** 62 **p** 63. C Glouc St Cath *Glouc* 62-65; C Sutton St Nicholas *Linc* 65-74; R Bugbrooke *Pet* 74-95; R Bugbrooke w Rothersthorpe 95-04; RD Daventry 81-88; Can Pet Cathl 83-04; Warden of Par Ev 96-02; rtd 04. *54 Thorney Leys, Witney OX28 5LS* Tel (01993) 864926
E-mail canontp@aol.com

PASCHAL, Brother. *See* WORTON, David Reginald

PASCOE, Michael Lewis. b 43. OLM course 96. **d** 99 **p** 00. OLM Crowan and Treslothan *Truro* 99-02; C from 02; OLM Penponds 01-02; C Penponds from 02. *Genesis, Bosparva Lane, Leedstown, Hayle TR27 6DN* Tel (01736) 850425
E-mail revdmike@supanet.com

PASK, Howard. b 54. St Jo Coll Nottm. **d** 99 **p** 00. C Todmorden *Wakef* 99-02; P-in-c Hebden Bridge 02-03; P-in-c Heptonstall 02-03; V Hebden Bridge and Heptonstall from 03. *The Vicarage, 12 Becketts Close, Heptonstall, Hebden Bridge HX7 7LJ* Tel (01422) 842138 Mobile 07779-243176
E-mail howard@thepasksare.screaming.net

PASKETT, Ms Margaret Anne. b 45. York Univ BSc81 Leeds Univ MEd83. NEOC 84. **d** 87 **p** 94. Par Dn Marske in Cleveland *York* 87-91; C 92-96; Dioc Adv for Diaconal Mins 92-96; P-in-c Hemingbrough from 96. *The Vicarage, Hemingbrough, Selby YO8 7QG* Tel (01757) 638528

PASKINS, David James. b 52. Univ of Wales (Lamp) BA73 Trin Hall Cam BA76 MA81. Westcott Ho Cam 74. **d** 77 **p** 78. C St Peter-in-Thanet *Cant* 77-80; C Swanage *Sarum* 80-82; R Waldron *Chich* 82-92; R Bere Ferrers *Ex* 92-96; V Lockerley and E Dean w E and W Tytherley *Win* 96-03; R Cranborne w Boveridge, Edmondsham etc *Sarum* from 03. *The Rectory, Grugs Lane, Cranborne, Wimborne BH21 5PX* Tel (01725) 517232

PASSANT, Keith. b 39. St Jo Coll Dur BA62 CertEd70. St Alb Minl Tr Scheme 77. **d** 87 **p** 88. C Hatfield Hyde *St Alb* 87-93; rtd 93; Perm to Offic *St Alb* from 93. *26 Monk's Rise, Welwyn Garden City AL8 7NF* Tel (01707) 332869

PASTERFIELD, Canon Dunstan Patrick. b 17. Clare Coll Cam BA49 MA53. Cuddesdon Coll 49. **d** 51 **p** 51. C Dennington *St E* 51-53; Canada from 53; Hon Can Calgary 78-82. *12 Houston Road, Regina SK, Canada, S4V 0G4* Tel (001) (306) 761 9185 Fax 761 2608 E-mail dppasterfield@net1fx.com

PATCH, Simon John. b 63. Aus Nat Univ BA87. Chich Th Coll BTh95. **d** 95 **p** 96. C Ifield *Chich* 95-99; TV 99-03; C Stepney St Dunstan and All SS *Lon* from 03. *St Faith's House, Shandy Street, London E1 4ST* Tel (020) 7790 4194
E-mail simon_patch@lineone.net

PATCHELL, Miss Gwendoline Rosa (Wendy). b 49. Goldsmiths' Coll Lon BA69 TCert70. Trin Coll Bris DipHE92. **d** 92 **p** 94. C Ashton-upon-Mersey St Mary *Ches* 92-98; TV Hemel Hempstead *St Alb* from 98. *St Paul's Vicarage, 23 Saturn Way, Hemel Hempstead HP2 5NY* Tel (01442) 255023
E-mail hemelpcc@surfaid.com

PATCHING, Colin John. b 47. Linc Th Coll 84. **d** 86 **p** 87. C Farnley *Ripon* 86-89; C Didcot St Pet *Ox* 89-92; P-in-c Steventon w Milton from 92. *The Vicarage, 73 Field Gardens, Steventon, Abingdon OX11 6TF* Tel (01235) 831243

PATE, Barry Emile Charles. b 50. NE Lon Poly BA80 CQSW80. S'wark Ord Course 85. **d** 88 **p** 89. NSM E Dulwich St Jo *S'wark* 88-92; C Farnborough *Roch* 92-94; C Broxbourne w Wormley *St Alb* 94-00; V Wilbury from 00. *Church House, 103 Bedford Road, Letchworth Garden City SG6 4DU* Tel and fax (01462) 623119 E-mail b.pate@ntlworld.com

PATEL, Miss Urmila Devi. b 59. Essex Univ BSc82. Chich Th Coll 90. **d** 92 **p** 94. Par Dn Leek and Meerbrook *Lich* 92-94; C 94-97; TV Hackney Marsh *Lon* 97-01. *Address withheld by request*

PATEMAN, Edward Brian. b 29. Leeds Univ BA51. Qu Coll Birm 51. **d** 53 **p** 54. C Stockton St Pet *Dur* 53-57; Lect Bolton St Pet 57-58; V Coxhoe 58-65; V Dalton le Dale 65-93; RD Houghton 72-75; R Hawthorn 88-93; rtd 93. *27 Atherton Drive, Houghton le Spring DH4 6TA* Tel 0191-385 3168

PATEN, Richard Alfred. b 32. Ch Coll Cam BA56 MA60 CEng60 MICE60. Ripon Hall Ox 61. **d** 63 **p** 64. C Oadby *Leic* 63-67; C Pet St Mark *Pet* 67-71; Chapl Community Relns 71-95; Bp's Dioc Chapl 73-85; rtd 97; Perm to Offic *Pet* from 93. *19 The Lindens, 86 Lincoln Road, Peterborough PE1 2SN* Tel (01733) 562089

PATERNOSTER, Canon Michael Cosgrove. b 35. Pemb Coll Cam BA59 MA63. Cuddesdon Coll 59. **d** 61 **p** 62. C Surbiton St Andr *S'wark* 61-63; Chapl Qu Coll Dundee 63-68; Dioc Supernumerary *Bre* 63-68; Chapl Dundee Univ 67-68; Sec Fellowship of SS Alb and Sergius 68-71; R Dollar *St And* 71-75; R Stonehaven *Bre* 75-90; Hon Can St Paul's Cathl Dundee from 81; R Aberdeen St Jas *Ab* 90-00; rtd 00; Perm to Offic *B & W* from 00. *12 Priest Row, Wells BA5 2PY*

PATERSON (née SOAR), Mrs Angela Margaret. b 59. Aston Univ MSc81 MCIPD82. St Alb and Ox Min Course 97. **d** 00

p 01. NSM Icknield *Ox* from 00. *86 Hill Road, Watlington OX49 5AF* Tel (01491) 614034
E-mail angela@patersonlink.co.uk

PATERSON, David. b 33. Ch Ch Ox BA55 MA58. Linc Th Coll 56. **d** 58 **p** 59. C Kidderminster St Mary *Worc* 58-60; C Wolverhampton St Geo *Lich* 60-64; V Loughborough St Pet *Leic* 64-04; rtd 04; Perm to Offic *Ox* from 05. *487 Marston Road, Marston, Oxford OX3 0JQ* Tel (01865) 726842
E-mail davidpaterson129@hotmail.com

PATERSON, Douglas Monro. b 30. Em Coll Cam BA54 MA57. Tyndale Hall Bris 55. **d** 57 **p** 58. C Walcot *B & W* 57-60; C Portman Square St Paul *Lon* 60-62; Lect Oak Hill Th Coll 60-62; Min Hampstead St Jo Downshire Hill Prop Chpl *Lon* 62-65; Lect All Nations Chr Coll Ware 62-65; Rwanda 67-73; C Edin St Thos *Edin* 73-75; Lect Northumbria Bible Coll 73-94; Perm to Offic *Edin* 75-94; Lic to Offic *Newc* 76-94; rtd 94; Perm to Offic *Ox* from 94. *3 Penn Mead, Church Road, Penn, High Wycombe HP10 8NY* Tel (01494) 812496

PATERSON, Geoffrey Gordon. b 45. Cant Univ (NZ) LTh69. **d** 69 **p** 70. New Zealand 69-74; P-in-c Astwood Bank w Crabbs Cross *Worc* 78-80; New Zealand from 80; V Halswell-Prebbleton from 80. *19 Ridder Place, Christchurch 8003, New Zealand* Tel (0064) (3) 322 7787 *or* 365 3211

PATERSON, Gordon Ronald (Ron). b 16. MBE57. Ripon Hall Ox 58. **d** 59 **p** 60. C Warblington w Emsworth *Portsm* 59-62; V Swanmore St Barn 62-85; RD Bishop's Waltham 79-82; rtd 85; Perm to Offic *Win* 85-95 and *Portsm* from 85. *28 Eastways, Bishops Waltham, Southampton SO32 1EX* Tel (01489) 895671

PATERSON, James Beresford. b 21. DSC42. St Andr Univ MPhil85 FRSA93. Westcott Ho Cam 59. **d** 61 **p** 62. C Woodbridge St Mary *St E* 61-64; R Broughty Ferry *Bre* 64-72; Dioc Supernumerary 72-75; Sec Scottish Ch Action for World Development 72-79; P-in-c Glencarse 76-84; Dioc Sec 79-84; Hon Can St Paul's Cathl Dundee 79-89; rtd 84; Perm to Offic *Bre* and *St E* from 84. *67 Ipswich Road, Woodbridge IP12 4BT* Tel (01394) 383512

PATERSON, Mrs Jennifer Ann. b 49. Brooklands Tech Coll 69. S Dios Minl Tr Scheme 85. **d** 88 **p** 95. C Hale *Guildf* 88-92; NSM Seale, Puttenham and Wanborough 95-01; rtd 01; Perm to Offic *Guildf* 94-95 and from 01. *4 St George's Close, Badshot Lea, Farnham GU9 9LZ* Tel (01252) 316775
E-mail buao91@exchange.uk.com

✠**PATERSON, The Rt Revd John Campbell.** b 45. Auckland Univ BA66. St Jo Coll Auckland. **d** 69 **p** 70 **c** 95. C Whangarei New Zealand 69-71; V Waimate Maori N Pastorate 71-76; Co-Missr Auckland Maori Miss 76; Chapl Qu Victoria Sch 76-82; CF 76-84; Sec Bishopric of Aotearoa 78-87; Prov Sec 86-92; Gen Sec Angl Ch in Aotearoa, NZ and Polynesia 92-95; Bp Auckland from 95; Presiding Bp and Primate New Zealand 98-04. *PO Box 37-242, Parnell, Auckland 1033, New Zealand* Tel (0064) (9) 302 7202 Fax 302 7217 E-mail bishop.auckland@xtra.co.nz

PATERSON, John Thomas Farquhar. b 38. TCD BA61 MA64 BD71. CITC 63. **d** 63 **p** 64. C Drumglass *Arm* 63-65; C Dublin St Bart *D & G* 66-68; Min Can St Patr Cathl Dublin 67-83; Asst Dean of Residence TCD 68-72; C-in-c Dublin St Mark *D & G* 68-71; I Dublin St Bart w Leeson Park 72-78; Dean Kildare *M & K* 78-89; I Kildare w Kilmeague and Curragh 78-89; Lect Past Liturgy CITC 85-91; Hon Sec Gen Syn 85-91; Dean Ch Ch Cathl Dublin *D & G* 89-04; I Dublin Ch Ch Cathl Gp 89-04; rtd 04. *22 Corr Castle, Howth, Dublin 15, Irish Republic* Tel and fax (00353) (1) 839 5773 E-mail paterson@iol.ie

PATERSON, Michael Séan. b 61. Heythrop Coll Lon BD89 MA95 Univ of Wales (Lamp) MMin04. **d** 04 **p** 05. C Stonehaven *Bre* from 04. *7 Allardice Street, Stonehaven AB39 2BN* Tel (01569) 760261 E-mail rev.pilgrim@btinternet.com

PATERSON, Nigel John Merrick. b 53. Lanc Univ BEd75 Open Univ MA89. Dioc OLM tr scheme 99. **d** 01 **p** 02. OLM N Walsham w Antingham *Nor* from 01. *Marshgate Cottage, Marshgate, North Walsham NR28 9LG* Tel (01692) 406259 Mobile 07786-381361
E-mail nigelpaterson@marshgatecottage.freeserve.co.uk

PATERSON, Rex Douglas Trevor. b 27. AKC54. **d** 55 **p** 56. C Maidenhead St Luke *Ox* 55-58; C Littlehampton St Mary *Chich* 58-62; V Woodingdean 62-73; V Ferring 73-94; rtd 94; Perm to Offic *Chich* from 94. *14 Hurst Avenue, Worthing BN11 5NY* Tel (01903) 504252

PATERSON, Mrs Rita. **d** 04 **p** 04. C Muchalls *Bre* from 04. *34 Cairngrassie Circle, Portlethen, Aberdeen AB12 4TZ* Tel (01224) 780574

PATERSON, Canon Robert Mar Erskine. b 49. St Jo Coll Dur BA71 MA82. Cranmer Hall Dur. **d** 72 **p** 73. C Harpurhey St Steph and Harpurhey Ch Ch *Man* 72-73; C Sketty *S & B* 73-78; R Llangattock and Llangynidr 78-83; V Gabalfa *Llan* 83-94; TR Cowbridge 94-00; Prin Officer Ch in Wales Coun for Miss and Min from 00; Metrop Can from 04. *Council for Mission and Ministry, 39 Cathedral Road, Cardiff CF11 9XF* Tel (029) 2034 8209 *or* (01446) 793150 Fax (029) 2038 7835
E-mail principal.cmm@churchinwales.org.uk

PATERSON, Robin Fergus (Robert). b 32. Moore Th Coll Sydney 83. **d** 87 **p** 89. Singapore 87-88; NSM Crieff *St And* 88-92; NSM Comrie 88-92; R Dunkeld 93-98; R Strathtay 93-98; rtd 98; Lic to Offic *St And* and *Eur* from 98. *Corsie Hill House, Corsiehill, Perth PH2 7BN* Tel (01738) 446621

PATERSON, Robin Lennox Andrew. b 43. N Ord Course 84. **d** 87 **p** 88. C Manston *Ripon* 87-91; P-in-c Leeds All So 91-95; V 95-98; V Middleton St Mary from 98. *Middleton Vicarage, 198 Town Street, Leeds LS10 3TJ* Tel 0113-270 5689 Mobile 07778-860178 E-mail rlap@ntlworld.com

PATERSON, Rodney John. b 62. Keele Univ BA84. St Jo Coll Nottm MA98. **d** 98 **p** 99. C Huddersfield H Trin *Wakef* 98-01; P-in-c Charlton Kings H Apostles *Glouc* from 01. *The Vicarage, Langton Grove Road, Charlton Kings, Cheltenham GL52 6JA* Tel (01242) 512254 E-mail rodpaterson@fish.co.uk

PATERSON, Ron. *See* PATERSON, Gordon Ronald

PATERSON, Stuart Maxwell. b 37. Kelham Th Coll 57 Lich Th Coll 58. **d** 60 **p** 61. C Ilkeston St Mary *Derby* 60-64; V Somercotes 64-70; R Wingerworth 70-73; P-in-c Hawick *Edin* 92-95; R 95-00; rtd 00; Perm to Offic *Ab* from 05. *40 North Street, Inverurie AB51 4RS* Tel (01467) 624727
E-mail mpate37706@aol.com

PATERSON, Mrs Susan Ann. b 57. St Hilda's Coll Ox MA84. EMMTC DTPS95. **d** 95 **p** 96. NSM Evington *Leic* 95-98; NSM Humberstone 98-99; C 99-03; TV Melton Mowbray from 03. *26 Firwood Road, Melton Mowbray LE13 1SA*
E-mail spaterson@leicester.anglican.org

PATEY, The Very Revd Edward Henry. b 15. Hertf Coll Ox BA37 MA45 Liv Univ Hon LLD80. Westcott Ho Cam 38. **d** 39 **p** 40. C Colchester St Mary V *Chelmsf* 39-42; C Bishopwearmouth St Mich *Dur* 42-50; Youth Chapl 46-50; V Oldland *Bris* 50-52; Youth Sec BCC 52-56; Asst Gen Sec 56-58; Can Res Cov Cathl *Cov* 58-64; Select Preacher Ox Univ 61; Dean Liv 64-82; rtd 82; Perm to Offic *Bris* 82-03. *The College of St Barnabas, Blackberry Lane, Lingfield RH7 6NG*

PATIENT, Terence Ian. b 35. Open Univ BA83. LNSM course 94. **d** 96 **p** 97. OLM Old Catton *Nor* from 96. *8 Players Way, Norwich NR6 7AU* Tel (01603) 427899

PATO, Luke Luscombe Lungile. b 49. Fort Hare Univ BA76 Manitoba Univ MA80. St Bede's Coll Umtata DipTh71. **d** 73 **p** 75. S Africa 73-81 and from 92; Canada 81-90; Tutor Coll of Ascension Selly Oak 90-92. *PO Box 62098, Marshalltown, 2107 South Africa* Tel (0027) (11) 763 2510 *or* 492 1380 Mobile 83-367 3961 E-mail luke@cpsa.org.za

PATON, David. *See* PATON, Preb John David Marshall

PATON, George Hemsell. b 23. Wadh Coll Ox MA49. Oak Hill Th Coll 50. **d** 52 **p** 53. C Earlham St Anne *Nor* 52-54; C Darfield *Sheff* 54-56; Area Sec CMS *Ely* 56-62; Area Sec CMS *St E* and *Nor* 56-66; P-in-c Kemp Town St Mark *Chich* 66-67; V Kemp Town St Mark and St Matt 67-71; R Ripe w Chalvington 71-76; R Laughton w Ripe and Chalvington 77-78; V Iford w Kingston and Rodmell 78-90; rtd 90; Perm to Offic *Chich* from 90. *77 Springett Avenue, Ringmer, Lewes BN8 5QT* Tel (01273) 812754

PATON, Canon Ian James. b 57. Jes Coll Cam MA78 PGCE79. Westcott Ho Cam MA81. **d** 82 **p** 83. C Whitley Ch Ch *Ox* 82-84; Bp's Dom Chapl 84-86; Chapl Wadh Coll Ox 86-90; C Ox St Mary V w St Cross and St Pet *Ox* 86-90; Can and Vice Provost St Mary's Cathl Edin 90-94; R Edin St Mary 90-94; R Haddington and Dunbar 94-97; R Edin Old St Paul from 97; Can St Mary's Cathl from 04. *Lauder House, 39 Jeffrey Street, Edinburgh EH1 1DH* Tel 0131-556 3332
E-mail rector@osp.org.uk

PATON, Preb John David Marshall. b 47. Barrister-at-Law (Middle Temple) 71. St Steph Ho Ox 81. **d** 83 **p** 84. C Bethnal Green St Matt w St Jas the Gt *Lon* 83-86; P-in-c St Geo-in-the-East St Mary 86-89; V 89-92; P-in-c Bethnal Green St Barn 92-96; AD Tower Hamlets 92-96; Dir Post-Ord Tr 92-99; P-in-c St Vedast w St Mich-le-Querne etc from 97; P-in-c St Botolph without Bishopgate from 97; AD The City from 00; Preb St Paul's Cathl from 04. *St Vedast's Rectory, 4 Foster Lane, London EC2V 6HH* Tel (020) 7606 3998, 7588 3388 *or* 7606 1863 Fax 7638 1256 E-mail botolph.bgate@care4free.net *or* rector@botolph.org.uk

PATON, John William Scholar. b 52. Mert Coll Ox BA74 MA95. St Steph Ho Ox 93. **d** 95 **p** 96. C Sherborne w Castleton and Lillington *Sarum* 95-98; Succ S'wark Cathl *S'wark* 98-01; Chapl Medical and Dental Students K Coll Lon 98-01; P-in-c Purley St Mark from 01; P-in-c Purley St Swithun from 05. *St Mark's Vicarage, 22 Peaks Hill, Purley CR8 3JE* Tel (020) 8660 7204
E-mail john_w_s_paton@email.msn.com

PATON, The Ven Michael John Macdonald. b 22. Magd Coll Ox BA49 MA54. Linc Th Coll 52. **d** 54 **p** 55. C Gosforth All SS *Newc* 54-57; V Norton Woodseats St Chad *Sheff* 57-67; Sen Chapl Sheff United Hosps 67-70; Chapl Weston Park Hosp Sheff 70-78; V Sheff St Mark Broomhall *Sheff* 70-78; Adn Sheff 78-87; Can Res Sheff Cathl 78-87; rtd 88; Perm to Offic *Sheff* from 88. *947 Abbeydale Road, Sheffield S7 2QD* Tel 0114-236 6148

PATON-WILLIAMS, David Graham. b 58. Warwick Univ BA81 Selw Coll Cam BA86 MA90 Newc Univ MA92. Ridley Hall Cam 84. **d** 87 **p** 88. C S Westoe *Dur* 87-90; C Newton Aycliffe 90-91; TV 91-93; Chapl Univ Coll of Ripon and York St Jo 93-98; Min Can Ripon Cathl *Ripon* 93-98; R Bedale 98-02; P-in-c Leeming 98-02; R Bedale and Leeming from 03; AD Wensley from 05. *The Rectory, North End, Bedale DL8 1AF* Tel (01677) 422103 E-mail david.paton-williams@virgin.net

PATRICIA, Sister. *See* PERKINS, Patricia Doris

PATRICIA ANN, Sister. *See* GORDON, Sister Patricia Ann

PATRICK, Charles. *See* PATRICK, Peter Charles

PATRICK, Hugh Joseph. b 37. TCD BA62 MA66. **d** 63 **p** 64. C Dromore Cathl *D & D* 63-66; C Lurgan Ch the Redeemer 66-70; C Rothwell *Ripon* 70-73; V Thurnscoe St Hilda *Sheff* 73-78; V Wales 78-02; P-in-c Thorpe Salvin 78-82; RD Laughton 93-98; rtd 02; Perm to Offic *Sheff* from 02. *5 Fairfax Avenue, Worksop S81 7RH* Tel (01909) 477622 E-mail hugh@patrick46.fsnet.co.uk

PATRICK, James Harry Johnson. b 67. Birm Poly LLB88 Barrister 89. STETS 96 St Steph Ho Ox 99. **d** 99 **p** 00. Hon C Clifton All SS w St Jo *Bris* from 99. *4 Clifton Park Road, Bristol BS8 3HL* Tel 0117-908 0460 Fax 930 3813 Mobile 07768-340344 E-mail jp@guildhallchambers.co.uk

PATRICK, John Andrew. b 62. St Jo Coll Dur BA84. Ripon Coll Cuddesdon 87. **d** 89 **p** 90. C Frankby w Greasby *Ches* 89-92; C Boston *Linc* 92-95; P-in-c Graffoe Gp 95-97; V 97-02; P-in-c New Sleaford from 02. *The Vicarage, Market Place, Sleaford NG34 7SH* Tel (01529) 302177 E-mail japatrick1@aol.com

PATRICK, John Peter. b 23. AKC. **d** 52 **p** 53. C S Westoe *Dur* 52-55; C Woodhouse *Wakef* 55-58; C Batley All SS 58-59; V Upperthong 59-75; V Slaithwaite w E Scammonden 75-80; V Donington *Linc* 80-92; rtd 92; Perm to Offic *Linc* 92-01. *Little Paddock, 140 Main Road, Hundleby, Spilsby PE23 5NQ* Tel (01790) 752304

PATRICK, Peter Charles. b 64. Leeds Univ BA86 Fitzw Coll Cam BA91 MA95. Ridley Hall Cam 89. **d** 92 **p** 93. C Barton upon Humber *Linc* 92-96; TV Gt Grimsby St Mary and St Jas 96-03; RD Grimsby and Cleethorpes 99-03; R Middle Rasen Gp from 03. *The Vicarage, North Street, Middle Rasen, Market Rasen LN8 3TS* Tel (01673) 842249 E-mail charles.patrick@talk21.com

PATSTON, Raymond Sidney Richard. b 26. Kelham Th Coll 47. **d** 51 **p** 52. C Hammersmith H Innocents *Lon* 51-53; C Acton Green St Pet 53-56; Area Sec E Counties UMCA 56-62; C Chesterton St Luke *Ely* 56-59; R Downham Market w Bexwell 61-71; V Clee *Linc* 71-97; rtd 97. *75 Littlefield Lane, Grimsby DN34 4NU* Tel (01472) 349788

PATTEN (née STARNS), Mrs Helen Edna. b 43. St Hilda's Coll Ox BA65 Maria Grey Coll Lon CertEd70. Trin Coll Bris 73 Oak Hill Th Coll 81. **dss** 82 **d** 87 **p** 94. Tunbridge Wells St Jo *Roch* 82-86; Patcham *Chich* 86-91; Par Dn 87-91; Par Dn Eckington w Handley and Ridgeway *Derby* 91-94; C 94-95; TV 95-98; Chapl St Mich Hospice 98-03; rtd 03; Hon C Fairlight, Guestling and Pett *Chich* from 04. *Bethel, Eight Acre Lane, Three Oaks, Hastings TN35 4NL* Tel (01424) 752052

PATTERSON, Alfred Percy. **d** 85 **p** 87. NSM Aghalee *D & D* 85-91; C Gilford 91-93; Bp's C 93-95; I 95-00; rtd 00. *Brookdale, 723 Upper Newtownards Road, Belfast BT4 3NU* Tel (028) 9029 4741 E-mail revap.patterson@ntlworld.com

PATTERSON, Andrew John. b 56. Master Mariner 85 Riversdale Coll OND76. Qu Coll Birm 85. **d** 88 **p** 89. C Newc St Phil and St Aug *Newc* 88-92; Chapl Hunter's Moor Hosp 91-92; Asst Chapl R Victoria Infirmary Newc 92-96; V Whitley *Newc* from 96; Chapl Hexham Gen Hosp from 96. *The Vicarage, Whitley, Hexham NE46 2LA* Tel (01434) 673379

PATTERSON, Anthony. b 43. Moore Th Coll Sydney BTh82. **d** 83 **p** 83. Australia 83-91; C Darfield *Sheff* 91-94; TR Marfleet *York* 94-99; TV Heeley and Gleadless Valley *Sheff* 99-04; TR from 04; AD Attercliffe from 04. *Heeley Vicarage, 151 Gleadless Road, Sheffield S2 3AE* Tel 0114-255 7718 E-mail tony@yahoo.co.uk

PATTERSON, Charles David Gilliat. b 40. Lon Univ DipTh74. Oak Hill Th Coll 71. **d** 74 **p** 75. C Brompton H Trin *Lon* 74-77; C Spring Grove St Mary 77-80; V Bures *St E* 80-92; R Bath Weston St Jo w Kelston *B & W* 92-01; rtd 01; Perm to Offic *Ox* from 02. *Grove Mill, Mill Lane, Grove, Wantage OX12 7HU* Tel (01235) 772013

PATTERSON, Colin Hugh. b 52. CertEd75 St Pet Coll Ox MA77 Univ of Wales (Cardiff) MPhil90. Trin Coll Bris DipHE86. **d** 87 **p** 88. C Blackb Sav *Blackb* 87-90; C Haughton le Skerne *Dur* 90-93; Adult Educn Adv from 93. *24 Monks' Crescent, Durham DH1 1HD* Tel 0191-386 1691 *or* 374 6013 Fax 384 7529 E-mail colin.patterson@durham.anglican.org

PATTERSON, Colin Peter Matthew. b 62. Newc Poly BA84. St Steph Ho Ox 92. **d** 94 **p** 95. C Cullercoats St Geo *Newc* 94-97; Shrine P Shrine of Our Lady of Walsingham 97-99; P-in-c Harlow St Mary Magd *Chelmsf* 99-00; V from 00. *St Mary Magdalene's Vicarage, 3 Oaklands Drive, Harlow CM17 9BE* Tel (01279) 453848 E-mail frcolin@mmharlow.fsnet.co.uk

PATTERSON, Mrs Diane Rosemary. b 46. WMMTC 88. **d** 91 **p** 94. C Hill *Birm* 91-95; Perm to Offic 95-96; C Shottery St Andr *Cov* 96-01; C Hunningham from 01; C Wappenbury w Weston under Wetherley from 01; C Long Itchington and Marton from 01; C Offchurch from 01; RD Southam from 02. *The Vicarage, School Lane, Hunningham, Leamington Spa CV33 9DS* Tel (01926) 633630

PATTERSON, Hugh John. b 38. Southn Univ MPhil76. AKC63. **d** 64 **p** 65. C Epsom St Martin *Guildf* 64-65; Chapl Ewell Coll 65-68; Asst Chapl and Lect Bp Otter Coll Chich 68-71; Lect Dudley Coll of Educn 71-77; Lect Wolv Poly 77-92; Wolv Univ 92-00; Chapl 89-00; Hon C Morville w Aston Eyre *Heref* from 82; Hon C Upton Cressett w Monk Hopton from 82; Hon C Acton Round from 82; rtd 01. *6 Victoria Road, Bridgnorth WV16 4LA* Tel (01746) 765298

PATTERSON, Ian Francis Riddell. b 31. TCD BA55. **d** 55 **p** 56. C Belfast St Mary *Conn* 55-59; C Finaghy 59-63; I Craigs w Dunaghy and Killagan 63-66; Belfast Trin Coll Miss 66-68; I Belfast H Redeemer 68-80; I Kilroot 80-90; I Kilroot and Templecorran 90-92; I Donagh w Tyholland and Errigal Truagh *Clogh* 92-97; rtd 97. *6 Orchard Park, Aughnacloy BT69 6HT* Tel (028) 8555 7854

PATTERSON, Jennifer Mary. *See* TAYLOR, Sister Jennifer Mary

PATTERSON, John. *See* PATTERSON, Norman John

PATTERSON, John. b 27. MBIM76. Bps' Coll Cheshunt 60. **d** 61 **p** 62. C Maidenhead St Luke *Ox* 61-65; Chapl RAF 65-72; V Ashton St Jas *Man* 72-78; USA 78-90; R Somercotes and Grainthorpe w Conisholme *Linc* 90-92; rtd 92; Perm to Offic *Linc* from 92. *9 Simpson Close, Barrow-upon-Humber DN19 7BL* Tel (01469) 30867

PATTERSON, John Norton. b 39. TCD BA64 MA68. **d** 65 **p** 66. C Belfast St Paul *Conn* 65-68; C Larne and Inver 68-72; I Ballintoy w Rathlin and Dunseverick 72-05; Miss to Seafarers 72-05; Can Belf Cathl 97-05; Adn Dalriada *Conn* 01-05; rtd 05. *31 Moycraig Road, Dunseverick, Bushmills BT57 8TB* Tel (028) 2073 0654

PATTERSON, Marjorie Jean. *See* BROWN, Mrs Marjorie Jean

PATTERSON, Neil Sydney. b 79. BNC Ox BA00 MA04. Ripon Coll Cuddesdon BA03. **d** 04. C Cleobury Mortimer w Hopton Wafers etc *Heref* from 04. *5 New Road Gardens, Cleobury Mortimer, Kidderminster DY14 8AW* Tel (01299) 272922 E-mail pattersonneil@hotmail.com

PATTERSON, Norman John. b 47. Peterho Cam BA69 ALCD. St Jo Coll Nottm 70. **d** 73 **p** 74. C Everton St Ambrose w St Tim *Liv* 73-74; C Everton St Pet 74-78; TV 79-84; C Aigburth 84-92; Dioc Adv for Past Care and Counselling 84-05; V Gt Crosby All SS 92-05; Crosslinks Uganda from 05. *PO Box 20, Hoimar, Uganda* E-mail patterson@crosslinks.org

PATTERSON, Patric Douglas MacRae. b 51. Wycliffe Hall Ox 73. **d** 76 **p** 77. C Bebington *Ches* 76-79; Canada from 79. *The Rectory, PO Box 10, Milford ON, Canada, K0K 2P0*

PATTERSON, Canon Philip Fredrick. b 50. Ulster Univ BSc QUB BD. **d** 82 **p** 83. C Lurgan Ch the Redeemer *D & D* 82-86; I Carrowdore w Millisle 86-89; I Knockbreda from 89; Dioc Registrar from 00; Preb Down Cathl from 00. *Knockbreda Rectory, 69 Church Road, Newtownbreda, Belfast BT8 4AN* Tel and fax (028) 9064 1493 E-mail pfpatterson@hotmail.com

PATTERSON, The Very Revd Susan Margaret. b 48. Otago Univ BA71 BD89 PhD92. Knox Coll Dunedin 84. **d** 88 **p** 89. New Zealand 88-91 and 92-97; C Dunedin St Martin 88-91; Tutor Otago Univ and Knox Coll 89-91; USA 91-92; Assoc P Hawke's Bay 92-96; Lect Trin Coll Bris 97-00; I Kildallan w Newtowngore and Corrawallen *K, E & A* 00-04; I Killala w Dunfeeny, Crossmolina, Kilmoremoy etc *T, K & A* from 04; Dean Killala from 05. *St Michael's Rectory, Ballina, Co Mayo, Irish Republic* Tel (00353) (96) 21654 Mobile 86-605 7829 E-mail kilmoremoy@killala.anglican.org

PATTERSON, Trevor Harold. b 60. QUB BA82 Stranmillis Coll PGCE83. Trin Coll Bris DipHE93. **d** 93 **p** 94. C Ashtead *Guildf* 93-98; V Richmond H Trin and Ch Ch *S'wark* from 98. *Holy Trinity Vicarage, Sheen Park, Richmond TW9 1UP* Tel (020) 8404 1114 E-mail trevor-patterson@holy-trinity-richmond.fsnet.co.uk

PATTERSON, William Alfred. b 54. Wycliffe Hall Ox 77. **d** 79 **p** 80. C Partington and Carrington *Ches* 79-81; Canada from 81. *Address temp unknown*

PATTIMORE, Daniel James. b 64. Nottm Univ MEng88 Lon Bible Coll BA94. Wycliffe Hall Ox 97. **d** 99 **p** 00. C Charlesworth and Dinting Vale *Derby* 99-03; NSM Norley, Crowton and Kingsley *Ches* 03-04; P-in-c Heanor *Derby* from 04. *The Vicarage, 1A Mundy Street, Heanor DE75 7EB* Tel (01773) 719800 Mobile 07973-406022 E-mail dan@pattimore.com

PATTIMORE (née GORDON), Mrs Kristy. b 72. Leeds Univ BA94 Newc Univ PGCE95. Wycliffe Hall Ox 98. **d** 01 **p** 02. C Hallwood *Ches* 01-04; NSM Heanor *Derby* from 04. *The Vicarage, 1A Mundy Street, Heanor DE75 7EB* Tel (01773) 719800 E-mail kristygordon@hotmail.com

PATTINSON, Richard Clive. b 46. Keble Coll Ox BA68 MA84. Carl and Blackb Dioc Tr Inst 98. **d** 00 **p** 01. C Hesket-in-the-Forest and Armathwaite *Carl* 00-04; C Inglewood Gp from 04. *The Rectory, Skelton, Penrith CA11 9SE* Tel (017684) 84295

PATTINSON, Robert James. St Mich Coll Llan. **d** 04 **p** 05. C Llanelli *St D* from 04. *The Clergy House, 44 Coldstream Street, Llanelli SA15 3BH*

PATTINSON, Sir William Derek. b 30. Kt90. Qu Coll Ox BA52 MA56. St Deiniol's Hawarden 90 Coll of Resurr Mirfield 92. **d** 91 **p** 92. NSM Pimlico St Gabr *Lon* from 91. *9 Strutton Court, Great Peter Street, London SW1P 2HH* Tel (020) 7222 6307

PATTISON, Anthony. b 50. MRPharmS73 Heriot-Watt Univ BSc72. Sarum & Wells Th Coll 85. **d** 87 **p** 88. C Cullercoats St Geo *Newc* 87-89; Ind Chapl 89-99; C Cramlington 89-91; TV 91-99; TR Benwell from 99. *Benwell Rectory, 5 Lynnwood Avenue, Newcastle upon Tyne NE4 6XB* Tel 0191-256 7020 Fax 256 7010 E-mail pattison@lineone.net

PATTISON, Prof George Linsley. b 50. Edin Univ MA72 BD77 Dur Univ PhD. Edin Th Coll 74. **d** 77 **p** 78. C Benwell St Jas *Newc* 77-80; P-in-c Kimblesworth *Dur* 80-83; R Badwell Ash w Gt Ashfield, Stowlangtoft etc *St E* 83-91; Dean of Chpl K Coll Cam 91-01; Lect Aarhus Univ Denmark 01-04; Lady Marg Prof Div Ox Univ from 04; Can Res Ch Ch *Ox* from 04. *Christ Church, Oxford OX1 1DP*

PATTISON, Stephen Bewley. b 53. Selw Coll Cam BA76. Edin Th Coll 76. **d** 78 **p** 80. C Gosforth All SS *Newc* 78-79; NSM St Nic Hosp Newc 78-82; Hon C Newc St Thos Prop Chpl *Newc* 80-82; Chapl Edin Th Coll 82-83; Lect Past Studies Birm Univ 83-88; Perm to Offic *Birm* 83-86 and 87-00; Hon C Moseley St Mary 86-87. *11A Salisbury Road, Moseley, Birmingham B13 8JS* Tel 0121-449 3023

PATTLE (née OLIVER), Mrs Suzanne Marie. b 66. LMH Ox BA88 SSEES Lon MA91. Trin Coll Bris BTS03. **d** 03 **p** 04. C Rainham *Roch* from 03. *60 Childscroft Road, Rainham, Gillingham ME8 7SN* Tel (01634) 238060 Mobile 07973-853959 E-mail suzanne@pattle.charitydays.co.uk

PATTMAN, Andrew. b 53. Didsbury Coll Man BEd75. Westcott Ho Cam. **d** 95 **p** 96. C Washington *Dur* 95-98; Children's Work Adv *St Alb* 98-02; Perm to Offic from 04. *110 Marshalswick Lane, St Albans AL1 4XE* Tel (01727) 841201

PAUL, Brother. *See* SINGLETON, Ernest George

PAUL, Ian Benjamin. b 62. St Jo Coll Ox BA84 MA88 Southn Univ MSc85 Nottm Univ BTh91 PhD98. St Jo Coll Nottm 89. **d** 96 **p** 97. C Longfleet *Sarum* 96-00; NSM 00-04; Th Adv Dioc Bd of Min 00-04; Lect St Jo Coll Nottm from 04. *St John's College, Chilwell Lane, Bramcote, Nottingham NG9 3DS* Tel 0115-925 1114 E-mail ibpaul@ntlworld.com

PAUL, Canon John Douglas. b 28. Edin Univ MA52. Ely Th Coll 52. **d** 54 **p** 55. C Portsea Ascension *Portsm* 54-56; Nyasaland 56-60; Portuguese E Africa 60-70; Adn Metangula 65-70; R Castle Douglas *Glas* 70-75; R Edin St Mark *Edin* 75-80; R Elgin w Lossiemouth *Mor* 80-92; Syn Clerk 89-91; Hon Can St Andr Cathl Inverness from 89; Dean Mor 91-92; rtd 92. *2 The Avenue, Gifford, Haddington EH41 4QX* Tel (01620) 810547

PAUL, John Matthew. b 61. K Coll Lon BA82 Fitzw Coll Cam BA88 MA92. Westcott Ho Cam 86. **d** 89 **p** 90. C Writtle w Highwood *Chelmsf* 89-94; Min Can and Chapl St Paul's Cathl *Lon* 94-96; Min Can and Sacr St Paul's Cathl 96-99; V Winchmore Hill St Paul from 99; AD Enfield from 04. *St Paul's Vicarage, Church Hill, London N21 1JA* Tel (020) 8886 3545 E-mail john.paul@london.anglican.org

PAUL, Naunihal Chand (Nihal). b 40. Allahabad Univ MA. Bangalore Th Coll BD. **d** 69 **p** 70. C Simla Ch Ch India 69-70; V Kangra w Dharamsala 70-74; C Urmston *Man* 75-77; P-in-c Farnworth St Pet 77-80; TV E Farnworth and Kearsley 80-83; TV Laindon St Martin and St Nic w Nevendon *Chelmsf* 83-90; R Laindon w Dunton from 90. *38 Claremont Road, Laindon, Basildon SS15 5PZ* Tel (01268) 411190 E-mail rupriwas@aol.com

PAUL, Roger Philip. b 53. Clare Coll Cam BA74 MA88 CertEd76. Westcott Ho Cam 78. **d** 81 **p** 82. C Coventry Caludon *Cov* 81-85; R Warmington w Shotteswell and Radway w Ratley 85-98; R Kirkby Stephen w Mallerstang etc *Carl* from 98. *The Vicarage, Vicarage Lane, Kirkby Stephen CA17 4QX* Tel (01768) 371204 *or* 372919 E-mail recto.kspc@btinternet.com

PAUL, Simon Nicholas. b 56. Hull Univ BA81 PGCE82. Trin Coll Bris BA95. **d** 95 **p** 96. C Cranleigh *Guildf* 95-99; P-in-c Broughton and Duddon *Carl* 99-04; Chapl Ranby Ho Sch Retford from 04. *Ranby House School, Retford DN22 5HX* Tel (01777) 703138

PAULRAJ, Jeyachandran. b 60. Annamalai Univ MA97. Hindustan Bible Inst BTh85 Tamilnadu Th Sem BD86 MTh92. **d** 92 **p** 94. India 92-04; C S Ockendon and Belhus Park *Chelmsf* from 04. *The Rectory, North Road, South Ockendon RM15 6QJ* Tel (01708) 853349 E-mail revpjchandran@hotmail.com

PAVEY, Canon Angela Mary. b 55. Hull Univ BA77 Nottm Univ BCombStuds84. Linc Th Coll 81. **dss** 84 **d** 87 **p** 94. Linc St Faith and St Martin w St Pet *Linc* 84-86; Chapl Boston Coll of FE 87-95; Asst Min Officer *Linc* 89-95; C Birchwood 95-97; Dioc Dir of Ords from 97; Can and Preb Linc Cathl from 00. *St Luke's Vicarage, Jasmine Road, Lincoln LN6 0YR* Tel (01522) 683507 Fax 804741 E-mail angela.pavey@ntlworld.com

PAVEY, Gordon Sidney Alfred. b 19. Lon Univ BD47 Leeds Univ MEd58. Chich Th Coll 40. **d** 42 **p** 43. C S Mymms K Chas *Lon* 42-44; C Bedford Park 44-48; C Taunton H Trin *B & W* 48-50; Area Sec (N Midl) UMCA 50-54; V Huddersfield St Thos *Wakef* 54-64; Youth Chapl 54-57; Lic to Offic *Blackb* 64-68 and *Bris* 68-95; Prin Lect Th Bris Poly 77-92; Prin Lect Th Univ of the W of England, Bris from 92; rtd 84. *12 Chartley, The Avenue, Sneyd Park, Bristol BS9 1PE* Tel 0117-968 4762

PAVEY, John Bertram. b 51. Keele Univ BA73 Hull Univ PGCE74 MEd95. Linc Th Coll 81. **d** 83 **p** 84. C Boultham *Linc* 83-86; R Fishtoft 86-95; P-in-c Birchwood 95-01; V from 01. *St Luke's Vicarage, Jasmin Road, Lincoln LN6 0YR* Tel (01522) 688665 E-mail j.pavey@ntlworld.com

PAVEY, Michael Trevor. b 32. Lon Univ BA80 Bris Univ MPhil92. ALCD59. **d** 59 **p** 60. C Nor St Pet Mancroft *Nor* 59-61; C N Walsham w Antingham 61-63; Chapl RAF 63-83; R Mark w Allerton *B & W* 83-02; rtd 02. *17 Millgreen Close, West Huntspill, Highbridge TA9 3QY* Tel (01278) 782814

PAVYER, Miss Jennifer Elizabeth. b 75. Ex Univ BSc96 Cam Univ BTh02. Westcott Ho Cam 99. **d** 02 **p** 03. C Stevenage St Andr and St Geo *St Alb* 02-05; C Harpenden St Nic from 05. *86 Tufnells Way, Harpenden AL5 3HG* Tel (01582) 762485 E-mail jenny.pavyer@ukgateway.net

PAWSEY, Jack Edward. b 35. Trin Coll Ox BA59 MA65. Westcott Ho Cam 64. **d** 66 **p** 67. Sec Coun Soc Aid *S'wark* 66-75; Race Relns Worker 75-78; Acting Sec Coun Soc Aid 78-82; Perm to Offic 84-86; Hon C Camberwell St Geo 86-98; Staff Cllr Westmr Past Foundn 87-97; Perm to Offic *S'wark* from 98. *20 Addington Square, London SE5 7JZ* Tel (020) 7701 8920

PAWSON (née ROYLE), Mrs Gillian Mary. b 57. Kingston Univ BA79 Roehampton Inst PGCE82. SEITE 99. **d** 02 **p** 03. C Wimbledon *S'wark* from 02. *50 Evelyn Road, London SW19 8NT* Tel (020) 8286 1030 E-mail gillypawson@blueyonder.co.uk

PAWSON, John. b 66. Moorlands Th Coll BA00 Wycliffe Hall Ox. **d** 02 **p** 03. C Bursledon *Win* from 02. *13 Redcroft Lane, Bursledon, Southampton SO31 8GS* Tel (023) 8040 4902 Mobile 07762-246947 E-mail john.pawson@virgin.net

PAWSON, Preb John Walker. b 38. Kelham Th Coll 58. **d** 63 **p** 64. C N Hull St Mich *York* 63-67; C Lower Gornal *Lich* 67-70; V Tipton St Jo 70-78; V Meir Heath 78-03; RD Stoke 88-98; Preb Lich Cathl 93-03; rtd 03; Perm to Offic *Nor* from 03. *39 Runton Road, Cromer NR27 9AT* Tel (01263) 511715 E-mail pawson.meirton@virgin.net

PAXON, Robin Michael Cuninghame. b 46. St Jo Coll Dur BA69. Westcott Ho Cam 69. **d** 71 **p** 72. C Croydon St Pet S End *Cant* 71-77; C Saffron Walden w Wendens Ambo and Littlebury *Chelmsf* 77-80; P-in-c Plaistow St Mary 80-83; TV Plaistow 83-89; TV Dovercourt and Parkeston 90-95; rtd 95. *20 Park Road, Harwich CO12 3BJ* Tel (01255) 551139

PAXTON, John Ernest. b 49. Ex Univ BA71. Westcott Ho Cam 74. **d** 74 **p** 75. C Redditch St Steph *Worc* 74-77; UAE 77-81; C Bolton St Pet *Man* 81-91; Ind Missr 81-91; TV Southampton (City Cen) *Win* 91-96; R S'wark Ch Ch *S'wark* 96-03; Sen Chapl S Lon Ind Miss 96-03; Adv to Bd of Soc Resp *Worc* from 03. *57 Drovers Way, Worcester WR3 8QD* Tel (01905) 456793 *or* 732819 E-mail jpaxton@cofe-worcester.org.uk

PAXTON, William Neil. b 60. Brunel Univ BSc88 MA90. Ripon Coll Cuddesdon 02. **d** 04 **p** 05. C Camberwell St Geo *S'wark* from 04. *131 Coleman Road, London SE5 7TF* Tel (020) 7703 2704

PAY, Norman John. b 50. St Jo Coll Dur BA72. Cranmer Hall Dur. **d** 74 **p** 75. C S Moor *Dur* 74-78; C Rawmarsh w Parkgate *Sheff* 78-80; C-in-c New Cantley CD 80-82; V New Cantley 82-89; V Doncaster St Leon and St Jude from 89; Asst Clergy In-Service Tr Officer 90-93. *St Leonard's Vicarage, Barnsley Road, Doncaster DN5 8QE* Tel (01302) 784858

PAYN, Peter Richard. b 33. Moore Th Coll Sydney LTh59. **d** 60 **p** 60. Australia 60-79; C Pittwater 60-61; C Kensington St Matt 61-63; C Melbourne St Jas w St Jo 63-65; V E Geelong St Matt 65-79; C Blackb Ch Ch w St Matt *Blackb* 79-81; V Lowestoft Ch Ch *Nor* 81-92; P-in-c Tunbridge Wells St Pet *Roch* 92-96; V 96-03; rtd 03. *3 rue Emile Bazillou, 24400 Mussidan, France* Tel (0033) (5) 53 81 24 97 E-mail richardpayn@aol.com

PAYNE, Alan. *See* PAYNE, Kenneth Alan

PAYNE, Arthur Edwin. b 37. K Alfred's Coll Win TCert59. St Mich Coll Llan 86. **d** 87 **p** 88. C Swansea St Gabr *S & B* 87-90; Chapl Univ of Wales (Swansea) 87-90; V Brynmawr 90-91; TV Wickford and Runwell *Chelmsf* 91-94; Chapl Runwell Hosp Wickford 91-94; P-in-c Wraxall *B & W* 94-95; Perm to Offic 95-97; V Rhymney *Mon* 97-98; rtd 98. *25 Weaver's House, New Wanstead, London E11 2SY* Tel (020) 8530 0302

PAYNE, Cyril Gordon. b 26. Bris Univ BA53. Linc Th Coll 53. **d** 55 **p** 56. C Southall H Trin *Lon* 55-58; C Christchurch *Win* 58-63; V Otterbourne 63-75; V Milford 75-90; rtd 90; Perm to

Offic *Win* from 90. *11 Oaklands, Lymington SO41 3TH* Tel (01590) 671274

PAYNE, David Charles. b 62. Univ of Wales (Abth) BLib84. St Jo Coll Nottm MA95. **d** 95 **p** 96. C Horncastle w Low Toynton *Linc* 95-99; V Metheringham w Blankney and Dunston 99-04; Chapl Sherwood Forest Hosps NHS Trust from 04. *Kings Mill Hospital, Mansfield Road, Sutton-in-Ashfield NG17 4JL* Tel (01623) 622515 ext 4137

PAYNE, David James. b 31. Clare Coll Cam BA54 MA61. Wycliffe Hall Ox 60. **d** 62 **p** 63. C Gt Faringdon w Lt Coxwell *Ox* 62-63; C Guildf Ch Ch *Guildf* 63-66; R Shackleford 66-73; R Peper Harow 66-73; R Odell *St Alb* 73-78; V Pavenham 73-78; Warden Home of Divine Healing Crowhurst 78-84; R Wraxall *B & W* 84-92; rtd 92; Perm to Offic *Glouc* from 92 and *Bris* from 00. *Langet End, Upper Up, South Cerney, Cirencester GL7 5US* Tel (01285) 860677

PAYNE, David Ronald. b 49. DMS77 Open Univ BA87. St Mich Coll Llan 88. **d** 90 **p** 91. C Oystermouth *S & B* 90-93; V Penllergaer 93-02; TV Llanelli *St D* from 02. *The Vicarage, Swiss Valley, Felinfoel, Llanelli SA14 8BS* Tel (01554) 773559

PAYNE, Canon Denis Alfred. b 22. Oriel Coll Ox BA50 MA53. Wells Th Coll 50. **d** 51 **p** 52. C Sheff St Geo and St Steph *Sheff* 51-55; Chapl Makerere Univ Uganda 55-67; Min Sec ACCM 67-69; Sen Selection Sec 69-73; Dir Post-Ord Tr and Further Tr for Clergy *St E* 73-84; Dioc Dir of Ords 73-87; Can Res St E Cathl 73-89; rtd 89; Perm to Offic *St E* from 90. *The Crooked House, Brussels Green, Darsham, Saxmundham IP17 3RN* Tel (01728) 668705

PAYNE, Elizabeth. b 50. Univ Coll Lon BSc92. St Mich Coll Llan 96. **d** 98 **p** 99. C Cyncoed *Mon* 98-03; TV 03-04. *7A Cader Idris Close, Risca, Newport NP11 6RP* Tel (01633) 619004

PAYNE, Mrs Elizabeth Barbara Trudy. b 48. K Coll Lon BA66 Lon Inst of Educn PGCE73. **d** 04. OLM Clapham Park St Steph *S'wark* from 04. *6 Clarence Road, Croydon CR0 2EN* Tel (020) 8689 5857 E-mail paynetrudy@hotmail.com

PAYNE, Frederick Gates (Eric). b 19. Jes Coll Cam BA40 MA43. Lon Coll of Div 40. **d** 42 **p** 43. C Walcot *B & W* 42-45; CF (EC) 45-48; Hd CMJ Miss Ethiopia 48-67; SW Org Sec CMJ 68-85; rtd 84; Perm to Offic *B & W* from 85 and *Truro* from 91. *83 Penn Lea Road, Bath BA1 3RQ* Tel (01225) 423092

PAYNE, James John Henry. b 26. MBE69. St Pet Hall Ox BA53 MA59. Tyndale Hall Bris 48 Linc Th Coll 53. **d** 53 **p** 54. Asst Chapl Mersey Miss to Seamen 53-55; C Stoneycroft All SS *Liv* 55-57; Chapl Igbobi Coll Yaba Nigeria 57-62; Chapl Lagos St Sav 62-88; Dir Lagos Ord Course 81-87; Hon Can Lagos 71-88; rtd 88; Perm to Offic *Ox* 88-93 and from 04; Hon C Uffington, Shellingford, Woolstone and Baulking 93-04. *1 Timberyard Cottages, Church Street, Shellingford, Faringdon SN7 7QA* Tel (01367) 710274
E-mail james@payne2277.freeserve.co.uk

PAYNE, John. *See* PAYNE, Victor John

PAYNE, John. b 58. Glas Univ BSc80 Edin Univ BD84. Edin Th Coll 81. **d** 90 **p** 90. C Dur St Nic *Dur* 90-94; Australia from 94; Chapl Toorak Coll Melbourne from 02. *11 Feathertop Chase, Burwood East, Melbourne, Vic, Australia 3151* Tel (0061) (3) 9887 8748 E-mail johnpayne@rabbit.com.au

PAYNE, John Percival. b 49. Nottm Univ BA70. Cuddesdon Coll 70. **d** 72 **p** 73. C Tilehurst St Mich *Ox* 72-76; C Cross Green St Sav and St Hilda *Ripon* 76-79; Chapl St Hilda's Priory Whitby 79-83; V Leeds Belle Is St Jo and St Barn *Ripon* 83-88; Chapl St Hilda's Sch Whitby 88-97; R Loftus and Carlin How w Skinningrove *York* 97-99; Chapl OHP 99-01; Teacher Qu Mary's Sch Thirsk from 02; Chapl from 03. *Queen Mary's School, Baldersby Park, Topcliffe, Thirsk YO7 3BZ* Tel (01765) 609786 *or* 575000 E-mail johnp-virgil@connectfree.co.uk

PAYNE, John Rogan. b 44. Episc Th Coll Sao Paulo. **d** 78 **p** 79. Brazil 78-86; C Ilkley All SS *Bradf* 86-88; R Elvington w Sutton on Derwent and E Cottingwith *York* 88-94. *Manor Farm House, East Flotmanby Road, Filey YO14 0HX* Tel (01723) 513969

PAYNE, Canon Joseph Marshall. b 17. TCD BA38 MA52. **d** 40 **p** 41. C Belfast St Aid *Conn* 40-43; C Ballynafeigh St Jude *D & D* 43-44; Chapl RAF 44-65; Asst Chapl-in-Chief RAF 65-72; QHC 70-72; V Malew *S & M* 72-82; RD Castletown 77-82; Can St German's Cathl 78-84; Treas 80-84; rtd 82; Perm to Offic *S & M* from 84. *4B Milner Towers, Port Erin, Isle of Man IM9 6AG* Tel (01624) 832039

PAYNE, Julia Kathleen. *See* PEATY, Julia Kathleen

PAYNE, Kenneth Alan. b 45. Pemb Coll Ox BA68 MA71. Qu Coll Birm 71. **d** 74 **p** 74. Hon C Perry Barr *Birm* 74-78; Hon C Ruislip Manor St Paul *Lon* 78-79; C Hawksworth Wood *Ripon* 79-84; R Stanningley St Thos 84-94; TR Kippax w Allerton Bywater 94-00; AD Whitkirk 95-00; P-in-c Lambley *S'well* from 00; Dioc Min Development Adv from 00; Dioc Dir of Min from 02. *The Rectory, 2 Cocker Beck, Lambley, Nottingham NG4 4QP* Tel 0115-931 3531 *or* (01636) 814331
E-mail alanp@southwell.anglican.org

PAYNE, Leonard John. b 49. St Jo Coll Nottm Dip Th & Min 95. **d** 95 **p** 96. C Trimley *St E* 95-98; TV Sole Bay from 98. *The Rectory, 59 Southwold Road, Wrentham, Beccles NR34 7JE* Tel (01502) 675208 Mobile 07879-457902
E-mail leonard.payne@stedmundsbury.anglican.org

PAYNE, Mark James Townsend. b 69. Van Mildert Coll Dur BA90. Ridley Hall Cam 92. **d** 94 **p** 95. C Angmering *Chich* 94-98; Dioc Ev and C Prestonville St Luke 98-04; P-in-c Scaynes Hill from 04. *The Vicarage, Vicarage Lane, Scaynes Hill, Haywards Heath RH17 7PB* Tel (01444) 831265

PAYNE, Matthew Charles. b 62. Ex Univ LLB85 All Nations Chr Coll BA95 Solicitor 89. Oak Hill Th Coll 99. **d** 01 **p** 02. C Angmering *Chich* 01-05; V Lowestoft Ch Ch *Nor* from 05. *The Vicarage, 16 Corton Road, Lowestoft NR32 4PL* Tel (01502) 572444 E-mail matthew@christ-church.info

PAYNE, Michael Frederick. b 49. St Jo Coll Nottm 81. **d** 83 **p** 84. C Hyson Green *S'well* 83-86; P-in-c Peckham St Mary Magd *S'wark* 86-90; V 90-05; Hon C Chenies and Lt Chalfont, Latimer and Flaunden *Ox* from 05. *The Rectory, Latimer, Chesham HP5 1UA* Tel (01494) 764196
E-mail mikefpayne@hotmail.com

PAYNE, Mrs Norma. b 48. Bris Univ BA70 Homerton Coll Cam PGCE71. STETS 98. **d** 01 **p** 02. NSM Cley Hill Warminster *Sarum* 01-04; TV from 04. *The Vicarage, 6 Homefields, Longbridge Deverill, Warminster BA12 7DQ* Tel (01985) 841321

PAYNE, Mrs Penelope Kenward. b 42. LGSM64. Bp Otter Coll 94. **d** 94 **p** 98. NSM Portsea N End St Mark *Portsm* 94-05; NSM S Hayling from 05. *35 Saltmarsh Lane, Hayling Island PO11 0JT* Tel and fax (023) 9246 5259 *or* tel 9266 5753
E-mail pennie@ppayne.f9.co.uk

PAYNE, Mrs Priscilla Mary. b 40. **d** 04 **p** 05. NSM Ditton *Roch* from 04. *47 Bradbourne Lane, Ditton, Aylesford ME20 6PD* Tel (01732) 841257 E-mail priscilla.payne@tiscali.co.uk

PAYNE, Ralfe Dudley. b 22. Lon Univ BA50. Qu Coll Birm 50. **d** 52 **p** 53. C Tettenhall Wood *Lich* 52-57; C Tamworth 57-60; V Gayton w Fradswell 60-63; V Brockmoor 63-75; C Kinver 76-79; R Himley 79-89; V Swindon 79-89; rtd 89; Perm to Offic *Lich* and *Worc* from 89. *Highfield, Dunsley, Kinver, Stourbridge DY7 6LY* Tel (01384) 873612

PAYNE, Robert Christian. b 42. St Mich Coll Llan DipTh65. **d** 65 **p** 66. C Charlton Kings St Mary *Glouc* 65-69; C Waltham Cross *St Alb* 69-71; V Falfield *Glouc* 71-72; P-in-c Rockhampton 71-72; V Falfield w Rockhampton 72-76; Chapl HM Det Cen Eastwood Park 71-76; Chapl HM Youth Cust Cen Everthorpe 76-79; Chapl HM Youth Cust Cen Glen Parva 79-85; Pris Service Chapl Tr Officer 85-88; Chapl HM Pris Swinfen Hall 85-88; Asst Chapl Gen of Pris (SW) 88-90; Asst Chapl Gen of Pris 90-02; rtd 02; Sub Chapl HM YOI Stoke Heath and HM Pris Stafford from 02. *The Chaplaincy Team, HM Young Offender Institution, Stoke Heath, Market Drayton TF9 2JL* Tel (01630) 636116 E-mail bob.payne@ukgateway.net *or* bob.payne@hmps.gsi.gov.uk

PAYNE, Robert Harold Vincent. b 44. St Jo Coll York CertEd69. St Jo Coll Nottm 77. **d** 79 **p** 80. C Didsbury St Jas *Man* 79-80; C Didsbury St Jas and Em 80-83; V Southchurch Ch Ch *Chelmsf* 83-90; P-in-c Charles w Plymouth St Matthias *Ex* 90-94; Warden Lee Abbey 94-02; R Thorley *St Alb* from 02. *The Rectory, Vicerons Place, Bishop's Stortford CM23 4EL* Tel (01279) 659152 Fax 755179
E-mail bobpayne@stjamesthorley.freeserve.co.uk

PAYNE, Robert Sandon. b 48. Reading Univ BSc69 MRICS72. Ripon Coll Cuddesdon 77. **d** 80 **p** 81. C Bridgnorth, Tasley, Astley Abbotts and Oldbury *Heref* 80-83; P-in-c Wistanstow 83-92; P-in-c Acton Scott 86-92; P-in-c Dorrington 92-94; P-in-c Leebotwood w Longnor 92-94; P-in-c Smethcott w Woolstaston 92-94; P-in-c Stapleton 92-94; R Dorrington w Leebotwood, Longnor, Stapleton etc from 94. *The Rectory, Church Road, Dorrington, Shrewsbury SY5 7JL* Tel (01743) 718578

PAYNE, Rosemary Ann. b 46. SSC71 LSE LLB68. St Alb and Ox Min Course 97. **d** 00 **p** 01. NSM Wooburn *Ox* from 00; Bp's NSM Officer (Bucks) from 05. *30 Goddington Road, Bourne End SL8 5TZ* Tel (01628) 521677

PAYNE, Stephen Michael. b 55. **d** 03 **p** 04. C Plymouth Em, St Paul Efford and St Aug *Ex* from 03. *1 Yeo Close, Efford, Plymouth PL3 6ER* Tel (01752) 785576

PAYNE, Victor John. b 45. Open Univ BA81 Dip Psychotherapy 96. St Mich Coll Llan. **d** 70 **p** 71. C Ystrad Mynach *Llan* 70-72; C Whitchurch 72-75; CF (TA) 74-75; CF 75-93; V Talgarth and Llanelieu *S & B* 85-87; Chapl Mid-Wales Hosp 85-87; C Bassaleg *Mon* 93-96; TV 96-01; V Tongwynlais *Llan* from 01. *The Vicarage, 1 Merthyr Road, Tongwynlais, Cardiff CF15 7LE* Tel (029) 2081 0437

PAYNE, Warwick Martin. b 26. AKC51. **d** 52 **p** 53. C Mansfield SS Pet and Paul *S'well* 52-56; The Gambia 56-58; C Winlaton *Dur* 59-62; S Africa from 63; rtd 97. *7 Harvey Street, Harfield Village, Claremont, Cape Town, 7708 South Africa* Tel and fax (0027) (21) 683 0224

PAYNE COOK, Canon John Andrew Somerset. b 43. St Pet Coll Ox BA65 MA65. Coll of Resurr Mirfield 65. **d** 68 **p** 69. C St Mary-at-Latton *Chelmsf* 68-71; C Gt Berkhamsted *St Alb* 71-76; C-in-c N Brickhill CD 76-82; V N Brickhill and Putnoe

83-85; TR Tring 85-99; RD Berkhamsted 92-97; Hon Can St Alb 98-99; USPG 99-03; P-in-c Sandy Pt St Anne St Kitts-Nevis 00-03; P-in-c Ickleford w Holwell *St Alb* 03-05; P-in-c Pirton 03-05; R Holwell, Ickleford and Pirton from 05; Hon Can St Alb from 03. *The Vicarage, Crabtree Lane, Pirton, Hitchin SG5 3QE* Tel (01462) 712230 Fax 713597 E-mail jaspc@h-i-p.freeserve.co.uk

PAYNTER, Stephen Denis. b 59. Bath Univ BSc82 CertEd82. Trin Coll Bris BA89. **d** 89 **p** 90. C Nailsea Ch Ch *B & W* 89-92; C Farnborough *Guildf* 92-97; TV N Farnborough 97-98; V Ealing St Mary *Lon* from 98. *St Mary's Vicarage, St Mary's Road, London W5 5RH* Tel (020) 8567 0414 *or* 8579 7134 Fax 8840 4534 E-mail stevejen@lineone.net

PAYNTON, Paul Alexander. b 42. Linc Th Coll 72. **d** 74 **p** 75. C Uppingham w Ayston *Pet* 74-77; R Teigh w Whissendine 77-79; P-in-c Market Overton w Thistleton 77-79; R Teigh w Whissendine and Market Overton 79-95; V Irchester 95-00; rtd 04. *11 Mount Street, Lincoln LN1 3JE* Tel (01522) 560428

PAYTON, Canon Arthur Edward. b 16. Lambeth MA81. **d** 39 **p** 41. Brotherhood of St Paul from 36; St Kitts-Nevis 39-42; C Bedminster Down *Bris* 42-44; OCF 43-45; Org Sec Br Empire Leprosy Relief Assoc 44-49; P-in-c Toxteth Park St Jo and St Thos *Liv* 49-50; V 50-56; R Gt and Lt Wigborough w Salcot Virley *Chelmsf* 56-64; V Highwood 64-66; Hon C Feering 66-69; Hon C Kelvedon 69-82; Managing Dir Inter Ch Travel 54-82; Hon Can Gib Cathl *Eur* 73-84; rtd 81; P-in-c Wickmere w Lt Barningham and Itteringham *Nor* 84-88; Perm to Offic 88-00 and from 01. *The Grange, Sandy Lane, West Runton, Cromer NR27 9LT* Tel (01263) 837400

PAYTON, Paul John. b 59. Middx Poly MA90 LRAM79 GRSM80. Ripon Coll Cuddesdon. **d** 05. C Lancaster St Mary w St John and St Anne *Blackb* from 05. *25 Bishopdale Road, Lancaster LA1 5NF* Tel (01524) 844672 E-mail paytonpj@hotmail.com

PEACE, Brian. b 38. St Jo Coll Nottm DCM92. **d** 92 **p** 93. C Huddersfield H Trin *Wakef* 92-95; R Cheswardine, Childs Ercall, Hales, Hinstock etc *Lich* 95-00; TR 00-03; RD Hodnet 00-03; rtd 03. *2 Mouldsworth Close, Northwich CW9 8FT* Tel (01606) 333013 E-mail brian@peaceb.freeserve.co.uk

PEACE, Stuart Vaughan. d 04 **p** 05. OLM Dorking w Ranmore *Guildf* from 04. *95 Ashcombe Road, Dorking RH4 1LW* Tel (01306) 883002 E-mail stuart@peaces.freeserve.co.uk

PEACH, Malcolm Thompson. b 31. St Chad's Coll Dur BA56. Sarum Th Coll 56. **d** 58 **p** 59. C Beamish *Dur* 58-61; Chapl Dur Univ 61-65; NE England Sec SCM 61-65; C-in-c Stockton St Mark CD *Dur* 65-72; P-in-c Bishopwearmouth St Nic 72-81; V 81-85; V S Shields St Hilda w St Thos 85-95; Hon Chapl Miss to Seamen 85-95; P-in-c S Shields St Aid w St Steph *Dur* 92-95; rtd 95; Perm to Offic *Dur* from 95. *116 Mount Road, Sunderland SR4 7QD* Tel 0191-522 6216

PEACHELL, David John. b 45. Oak Hill Th Coll 85. **d** 86 **p** 87. C Prescot *Liv* 86-89; CF 89-98; P-in-c Hockering, Honingham, E and N Tuddenham *Nor* 98-02; rtd 02. *21 Brentwood, Eaton, Norwich NR4 6PN* Tel (01603) 880121

PEACOCK, Canon David. b 39. Liv Univ BA61 Lanc Univ MA71 Univ of the South (USA) Hon DD00 FRSA95. Westcott Ho Cam 84. **d** 84 **p** 85. Prin Lect St Martin's Coll Lanc 81-85; Hon C Lancaster St Mary *Blackb* 84-85; Prin Whitelands Coll 85-00; Pro Rector Surrey Univ 93-00; Hon C Roehampton H Trin *S'wark* 85-92; Hon C Putney St Mary 92-00; Hon Can S'wark Cathl 97-00; Perm to Offic *Blackb* from 00. *The Old Dairy, Keerside, Arkholme, Carnforth LA6 1AP* Tel (01524) 221706 E-mail keersidecowshed@aol.com

PEACOCK, John. b 34. ALCD60. **d** 60 **p** 61. C Addiscombe St Mary *Cant* 60-62; C Felixstowe St Jo *St E* 62-65; Chapl RAF 65-70; Australia from 71; C Panania 71-74; R Strathfield 74-80; Chapl Gladesville Hosp Sydney 81-94; Chapl Angl Retirement Villages Sydney 94-99; rtd 99. *511/6 Tarragal Glen Avenue, Erina, NSW, Australia 2250* Tel (0061) (2) 4367 0936

PEACOCK, Mrs Kate Rebecca. b 78. Hatf Coll Dur BA00. Westcott Ho Cam 01. **d** 03 **p** 04. C Cambridge Ascension *Ely* from 03. *2 Stretten Avenue, Cambridge CB4 3EP* Tel (01223) 462414 E-mail kate.peacock@btopenworld.com

PEACOCKE, Canon Arthur Robert. b 24. MBE93. Ex Coll Ox BA45 BSc47 MA48 DPhil48 DSc62 DD82 Birm Univ BD71. **d** 71 **p** 71. Fell and Tutor St Pet Coll Ox 65-73; Dean Clare Coll Cam 73-84; Lic to Offic *Ely* 73-85 and *Ox* 85-04; Dir Ian Ramsey Cen Ox 85-88; Warden SOSc from 87; Hon Chapl Ch Ch Ox 88-04; Hon Can Ch Ch *Ox* 94-04. *55 St John's Street, Oxford OX1 2LQ* Tel (01865) 512041

PEAD, Charles Henry. b 31. **d** 87 **p** 88. NSM Llanfrechfa and Llanddewi Fach w Llandegveth *Mon* 87-92; NSM Mamhilad and Llanfihangel Pontymoile 92-95; Lic to Offic from 96. *Jasmine, Caerleon Road, Llanfrechfa, Cwmbran NP44 8DQ* Tel (01633) 482685

PEAKE, Robert Ernest. b 27. Univ Coll Lon BSc51 FSS. Coll of Resurr Mirfield 83. **d** 85 **p** 86. C Linslade *Ox* 85-88; TV Gt Chesham 88-89; rtd 89; Hon C Princes Risborough w Ilmer *Ox* 93-98; Hon C Risborough 98-00. *Butley Cottage, Chestnut Way, Longwick, Princes Risborough HP27 9SD* Tel (01844) 344952

PEAKE, Canon Simon Jeremy Brinsley. b 30. Worc Coll Ox BA53 MA56. St Steph Ho Ox 53. **d** 57 **p** 58. C Eastbourne St Andr *Chich* 57-60; S Africa 60-69; C Claremont Ch the K 60-61; R Roodebloem All SS 61-65; R Maitland Gd Shep 65-69; Zambia 69-77; Assoc R Kitwe St Mich 69-71; Chapl Mindolo Ecum Foundn 71-77; Chapl Athens w Kifissia *Eur* 77-87; Chapl Vienna w Budapest and Prague 87-98; Chapl Vienna w Prague 98-00; Hon Can Malta Cathl 87-00; Adn E Adnry 95-00; rtd 00; Perm to Offic *B & W* and *Eur* from 00. *Rosedale, Queen Street, Keinton Mandeville, Somerton TA11 6EG* Tel (01458) 224483

PEAKE, Ms Sue. b 42. K Coll Dur BA63. SEITE 99. **d** 02 **p** 03. NSM Clapham Ch Ch and St Jo *S'wark* from 02. *20 Gauden Road, London SW4 6LT* Tel (020) 7627 4060

PEAL, Jacqueline. b 46. MCSP70. Cant Sch of Min 88. **d** 91 **p** 94. NSM Bexley St Jo *Roch* 91-97; NSM Crayford 91-94; C 94-97 and 00-01; C Dartford H Trin 97-00; Asst Chapl Thames Gateway NHS Trust from 01. *The Rectory, The Street, Ash, Sevenoaks TN15 7HA* Tel (01474) 872209 Fax as telephone E-mail peal@btinternet.com

PEAL, John Arthur. b 46. K Coll Lon BD70 AKC. **d** 71 **p** 72. C Portsea All SS w St Jo Rudmore *Portsm* 71-74; C Westbury *Sarum* 71-77; V Borstal *Roch* 77-82; Chapl HM Pris Cookham Wood 78-82; Chapl Erith and Distr Hosp 82-93; Chapl Qu Mary's Sidcup NHS Trust from 93; V Erith Ch Ch *Roch* 82-91; P-in-c Erith St Jo 86-91; V Bexley St Jo 91-00; R Ash from 00; R Ridley from 00. *The Rectory, The Street, Ash, Sevenoaks TN15 7HA* Tel and fax (01474) 872209 Mobile 07798-851583 E-mail peal@btinternet.com

PEAL, William John. b 26. K Coll Lon BSc47 AKC PhD52. St Jo Coll Nottm 79. **d** 80 **p** 81. C Coalville and Bardon Hill *Leic* 80-83; TV Melton Mowbray w Thorpe Arnold 83-86; TV Melton Gt Framland 86-90; rtd 90; Perm to Offic *Lich* from 91 and *Ches* 91-99. *20 Conway Road, Knypersley, Stoke-on-Trent ST8 7AL* Tel (01782) 513580

PEALL, Mrs Linda Grace. b 66. Westmr Coll Ox BEd88. EAMTC 99. **d** 02 **p** 03. NSM Blackwell All SS and Salutation *Dur* 02-04; NSM Darlington H Trin from 04. *3 Westfield Drive, Darlington DL3 9BB* Tel (01325) 362650 E-mail linda.peall@btopenworld.com

PEARCE, Adrian Francis. b 55. Westmr Coll Ox BTh05 SSC. S Dios Minl Tr Scheme 92. **d** 95 **p** 96. NSM Jersey St Jas *Win* from 95; NSM Jersey St Luke from 95; NSM Jersey St Mary from 01. *2 La Carriethe, Les Vaux, St Saviour, Jersey JE2 7US* Tel (01534) 873115 E-mail afpear@jerseymail.co.uk

PEARCE, Andrew John. b 66. Ex Univ BA89 Homerton Coll Cam PGCE93. St Mich Coll Llan Dip Past Th 94. **d** 96 **p** 97. C Llansamlet *S & B* 96-99; C Clydach 99-00; P-in-c Knighton, Norton, Whitton, Pilleth and Cascob 00-02; V from 02. *The Vicarage, Church Street, Knighton LD7 1AG* Tel (01547) 528566

PEARCE, Mrs Angela Elizabeth. b 36. K Coll Lon BSc58 CertEd59 BD79 AKC79. **dss** 79 **d** 87. Chapl Raines Sch 79-97; Homerton St Barn w St Paul *Lon* 79-85; Upper Chelsea St Simon 85-89; Hon Par Dn 87-89; Hon Par Dn Limehouse 89-97; Perm to Offic *St E* from 97. *50 Crown Street, Bury St Edmunds IP33 1QX* Tel (01284) 760016

PEARCE, Canon Brian Edward. b 39. Kelham Th Coll 59. **d** 64 **p** 65. C Smethwick St Matt *Birm* 64-68; C Kings Norton 68-72; TV 73-80; TR Swindon Dorcan *Bris* 80-91; Min Withywood CD 91-94; V Withywood 94-98; V Fishponds All SS 98-05; RD Bedminster 92-98; Hon Can Bris Cathl 97-05; rtd 05. *32 Brook Estate, Monmouth NP25 5AW* Tel (01600) 716057 E-mail rev.pearce@tesco.net

PEARCE, Clive. b 40. Univ of Wales (Lamp) BA63 Heythrop Coll Lon MA01. St Steph Ho Ox 63. **d** 65 **p** 66. C Acton Green St Pet *Lon* 65-67; C Eastcote St Lawr 67-73; V Hatch End St Anselm from 73. *Hatch End Vicarage, 50 Cedar Drive, Pinner HA5 4DE* Tel and fax (020) 8428 4111 Mobile 07710-900545 E-mail ecclesiaenavis@aol.com

PEARCE, Colin James. b 51. Trin Coll Bris DipTh96. **d** 96 **p** 97. C Kingswood *Bris* 96-00; TV Bedminster from 00. *St Dunstan's Vicarage, 66 Bedminster Down Road, Bristol BS13 7AA* Tel 0117-963 5977 E-mail colinjpearce@blueyonder.co.uk

PEARCE, Daniel. *See* PEARCE, William Philip Daniel

PEARCE, Desmond. b 30. Univ of Wales (Abth) BA52. EMMTC 85. **d** 88 **p** 89. NSM Chellaston *Derby* 88-90; NSM Walsall St Gabr Fulbrook *Lich* 90; C Stoke Lacy, Moreton Jeffries w Much Cowarne etc *Heref* 91-97; Perm to Offic *Mon* 98-00; P-in-c New Tredegar 00-03. *56 Bedwellty Road, Cefn Forest, Blackwood NP12 3HB* Tel (01443) 833015

PEARCE, Preb Eustace Kenneth Victor. b 13. Univ Coll Lon BSc65 St Pet Coll Ox Dip Anthropology 64 FRAI64. ALCD37. **d** 37 **p** 38. C Toxteth Park St Clem *Liv* 37-40; R Sutton 40-42; C Fordington *Sarum* 42-44; V Camberwell All SS *S'wark* 44-50; R Bucknall and Bagnall *Lich* 50-71; CF (TA) 66-81; V Audley *Lich* 71-81; Preb Lich Cathl 67-81; rtd 81; Chief Exec Evidence for Truth Broadcasting Assn from 83; Perm to Offic *Ches* from 83;

Chich 83-97; *Lich* 83-95. *15 Kinnersley Avenue, Kidsgrove, Stoke-on-Trent ST7 1AP,* or *13 Lismore Road, Eastbourne BN21 3AY* Tel (01782) 773325, (01323) 725231 *or* (01782) 642000 Fax (01782) 641121 E-mail ucb@ucb.co.uk

PEARCE, Canon Gerald Nettleton. b 25. St Jo Coll Dur BA49 DipTh51. **d** 51 **p** 52. C Bury St Edmunds St Mary *St E* 51-54; C Attenborough w Bramcote and Chilwell *S'well* 54-56; V Selston 56-61; R Wilford 61-73; RD Bingham 73-84; P-in-c Holme Pierrepont w Adbolton 73-84; V Radcliffe-on-Trent 73-84; V Shelford 73-84; Hon Can S'well Minster 77-84; R Sigglesthorne and Rise w Nunkeeling and Bewholme *York* 84-91; RD N Holderness 86-90; Perm to Offic from 91; rtd 91; Rtd Clergy and Widows Officer (E Riding) *York* from 91. *Sutherland Bridge, Cropton, Pickering YO18 8EU* Tel (01751) 417420

PEARCE, Mrs Iris Rose. b 27. **d** 00 **p** 03. OLM Parkstone St Pet and St Osmund w Branksea *Sarum* 00-03; Chapl Asst Poole Hosp NHS Trust 00-03; Hon Asst Chapl from 03. *Flat 1 Pelham, 34 Lindsay Road, Poole BH13 6AY* Tel (01202) 769301 E-mail iris1pelham@aol.com

PEARCE, Mrs Janet Elizabeth. b 49. Somerville Coll Ox BA72 MA76 CertEd74. N Ord Course 85. **d** 88 **p** 94. Par Dn Helsby and Dunham-on-the-Hill *Ches* 88-94; C 94-96; C Norley, Crowton and Kingsley from 96; Dioc Adv in Spirituality from 02. *St John's House, Pike Lane, Kingsley, Frodsham WA6 8EH* Tel (01928) 788386

PEARCE, Preb John Frederick Dilke. b 32. Ex Coll Ox BA55 MA59. Westcott Ho Cam. **d** 57 **p** 58. C Dalston St Mark w St Bart *Lon* 57-60; C Chelsea Ch Ch 60-63; R Lower Homerton St Paul 63-81; Preb St Paul's Cathl 70-97; P-in-c Clapton Park All So 72-77; V 77-84; RD Hackney 74-79; R Homerton St Barn w St Paul 81-85; TR Hackney Marsh 85; P-in-c Upper Chelsea St Simon 85-89; AD Chelsea 88-89; R Limehouse 89-97; rtd 97; Perm to Offic *St E* from 97. *50 Crown Street, Bury St Edmunds IP33 1QX* Tel (01284) 760016 Fax 756306 E-mail john@jfdp.freeserve.co.uk

PEARCE, Jonathan. b 55. St Jo Coll Nottm BTh85. **d** 85 **p** 86. C Gt Chesham *Ox* 85-89; C Newport Pagnell w Lathbury and Moulsoe 89-93; TV Waltham H Cross *Chelmsf* from 93. *The Vicarage, Church Road, High Beach, Loughton IG10 4AJ* Tel (020) 8508 1791

PEARCE, Kenneth Jack. b 25. CIPFA. Linc Th Coll 62. **d** 63 **p** 64. C Wootton Bassett *Sarum* 63-66; C Broad Town 63-66; P-in-c Derby St Andr *Derby* 66-68; V Derby St Mark 68-87; rtd 87; Perm to Offic *St Alb* from 91. *117 Oaks Cross, Stevenage SG2 8LT* Tel (01438) 317385

PEARCE, Michael Hawkins. b 29. Sarum Th Coll 61. **d** 62 **p** 63. C Bedminster St Aldhelm *Bris* 62-65; C Bishopston 65-68; R Jacobstow w Warbstow *Truro* 68-74; V Treneglos 68-74; V St Teath 74-94; rtd 94; Perm to Offic *Truro* from 94. *32 Trenant Road, Tywardreath, Par PL24 1QJ* Tel (01726) 813658

PEARCE, Neville John Lewis. b 33. CBIM88 Leeds Univ LLB53 LLM54. Trin Coll Bris 90. **d** 91 **p** 92. NSM Bath Walcot *B & W* 91-93; P-in-c Swainswick w Langridge and Woolley 93-98; Perm to Offic from 98. *Penshurst, Weston Lane, Bath BA1 4AB* Tel (01225) 426925

PEARCE, Sacha Jane. b 64. Reading Univ BA92. RGN86 Ripon Coll Cuddesdon. **d** 00 **p** 01. C Tisbury *Sarum* 00-01; C Nadder Valley 01-04; V Seend, Bulkington and Poulshot from 04. *The Rectory, High Street, Seend, Melksham SN12 6NR* Tel (01380) 828615 E-mail sachapearce@piran.org.uk

PEARCE, Trevor John. b 27. FSR57. Roch Th Coll 65. **d** 67 **p** 68. C Cheriton Street *Cant* 67-69; C Willesborough w Hinxhill 69-73; V Devonport St Barn *Ex* 73-79; Chapl N Devon Healthcare NHS Trust 79-83; V Derby St Andr w St Osmund *Derby* 83-84; Chapl Derbyshire R Infirmary 83-92; Lic to Offic *Derby* 84-92; rtd 92; Perm to Offic *Derby* from 92. *4 Morrell Wood Drive, Belper DE56 0JD* Tel (01773) 828450

PEARCE, Valerie Olive. b 46. Whitelands Coll Lon CertEd67. SEITE 96. **d** 97 **p** 98. Sisters of the Ch 77-04; Lic to Offic *S'wark* 97-04. *Address temp unknown* Tel 07932-060075 (mobile)

PEARCE, Victor. *See* PEARCE, Preb Eustace Kenneth Victor

PEARCE, William Philip Daniel. b 26. Stanford Univ BA48 Leeds Univ CertEd64 MA75. Cuddesdon Coll 54. **d** 56 **p** 57. USA 56-60 and from 86; CR 60-84; C St Geo-in-the-East w St Paul *Lon* 84-86; rtd 02. *1037 Olympic Lane, Seaside, CA 93955, USA* Tel (001) (831) 393 2176 E-mail philipearce@juno.com

PEARKES, Nicholas Robin Clement. b 49. Ex Univ BA. Linc Th Coll. **d** 82 **p** 83. C Plymstock *Ex* 82-85; P-in-c Weston Mill 85-86; TV Devonport St Boniface and St Phil 86-99; R Broadhempston, Woodland, Staverton etc from 99. *The Rectory, Broadhempston, Totnes TQ9 6AU* Tel (01803) 813754 E-mail platypus@wordoflife.fsnet.co.uk

PEARMAIN, Andrew Neil. b 55. K Coll Lon BD79 AKC79. Ridley Hall Cam 79. **d** 81 **p** 82. C Cranleigh *Guildf* 81-84; P-in-c Frimley 85-86; C 86-87. *4 Laurel Close, Farnborough GU14 0PT*

PEARMAIN, Canon Brian Albert John. b 34. Lon Univ BD68. Roch Th Coll 63. **d** 66 **p** 67. C Shirley St Jo *Cant* 66-69; C Selsdon St Jo w St Fran 69-73; P-in-c Louth H Trin *Linc* 73-75; TV Louth 75-79; R Scartho 79-97; RD Grimsby and Cleethorpes 89-94; Can and Preb Linc Cathl 94-97; rtd 97; Perm to Offic *Linc* from 00. *45 Wensley Road, Leeds LS7 2LS* Tel 07944-675321 (mobile)

PEARS, Anthony John. b 58. Ripon Coll Cuddesdon 00. **d** 02 **p** 03. C Watton w Carbrooke and Ovington *Nor* 02-05; R Northanger *Win* from 05. *The Rectory, Gaston Lane, Upper Farringdon, Alton GU34 3EE* Tel (01420) 588398 E-mail tony.pears@virgin.net

PEARSE, Andrew George. b 46. Wycliffe Hall Ox 71. **d** 74 **p** 75. C Homerton St Luke *Lon* 74-77; C Chadderton Em *Man* 77-81; R Collyhurst 81-89; Area Sec (NE, E Midl and Scotland) SAMS 89-03; rtd 03; Chapl Co-ord St Leon Hospice York from 03. *9 Troutsdale Avenue, Rawcliffe, York YO30 5TR* Tel (01904) 332373 E-mail andrew.stleonards@virgin.net

PEARSE, Ronald Thomas Hennessy. b 26. AKC52. **d** 53 **p** 54. C Leic St Pet *Leic* 53-55; C Hanwell St Thos *Lon* 55-58; R Asfordby *Leic* 58-84; P-in-c Scalford w Wycombe and Chadwell 75-76; R Thurcaston 84-89; rtd 89; Perm to Offic *Leic* 89-90. *15 Burton Street, Loughborough LE11 2DT* Tel (01509) 215478

PEARSON, Canon Andrew George Campbell. b 41. Qu Coll Ox BA63 BA66. Wycliffe Hall Ox 63. **d** 71 **p** 72. C Gillingham St Mark *Roch* 71-72; C Billingshurst *Chich* 72-77; C Ches Square St Mich w St Phil *Lon* 77-82; Co-ord Busoga Trust 82-02; Dir from 02; Hon Can Busoga from 98; P-in-c St Marg Pattens *Lon* from 90; C Kensington St Mary Abbots w St Geo from 96. *15 Chadwin Road, London E13 8ND* Tel (020) 7476 6730 *or* 7623 6630 Fax 7283 2304 E-mail busogatrust@hotmail.com

PEARSON, Andrew John. b 59. Humberside Coll of Educn HND83. Westcott Ho Cam 86. **d** 89 **p** 90. C Knaresborough *Ripon* 89-92; C Wetherby 92-94; P-in-c Hunslet Moor St Pet and St Cuth 94-96; V 96-01; Dioc Environment Officer from 97; V Hawksworth Wood from 01. *St Mary's Vicarage, 50 Cragside Walk, Leeds LS5 3QE* Tel 0113-258 2923 E-mail lindrew@pearley.fsnet.co.uk

PEARSON, Ms Brenda Elizabeth Frances (Brandy). b 51. SEITE 00. **d** 03 **p** 04. NSM Finsbury Park St Thos *Lon* from 03. *42 Grenoble Gardens, London N13 6JG* Tel (020) 8365 8971 E-mail brandy@brandywine999.fsnet.co.uk

PEARSON, Canon Brian Robert. b 35. Leeds Univ BA59. Coll of Resurr Mirfield 59. **d** 61 **p** 62. C Chesterfield St Mary and All SS *Derby* 61-66; P-in-c Derby St Jo 66-72; P-in-c Derby St Anne 66-72; R Thorpe *Nor* 72-90; Hon Can Nor Cathl 85-90; RD Nor E 86-90; V Harrogate St Wilfrid *Ripon* 90-00; rtd 00; Perm to Offic *York* from 00. *Green Garth, 13 Cedar Glade, Dunnington, York YO19 5QZ* Tel (01904) 481232

PEARSON, Canon Brian William. b 49. FHSM Brighton Poly BSc71 City Univ MSc80 Westmr Coll Ox MTh94. S'wark Ord Course & Clapham Ord Scheme 76. **d** 79 **p** 80. Hon C Plumstead All SS *S'wark* 79-81; Perm to Offic *Chich* 81-83; Hon C Broadwater St Mary 83-88; Bp's Research and Dioc Communications Officer *B & W* 88-90; Dioc Missr 91; Abp's Officer for Miss and Evang and Tait Missr *Cant* 91-97; Abp's Dioc Chapl 91-97; Hon Can Cant Cathl 92-97; Gen Dir CPAS 97-00; P-in-c Leek Wootton *Cov* from 00; Dioc Officer for OLM from 00. *The Vicarage, 4 Hill Wootton Road, Leek Wootton, Warwick CV35 7QL* Tel (01926) 854832 Fax 859117 E-mail brian@bwpvic.fslife.co.uk

PEARSON, Mrs Béatrice Levasseur. b 53. Sorbonne Univ Paris LèsL74 MèsL75 Lon Inst of Educn PGCE76. Ripon Coll Cuddesdon 01. **d** 03 **p** 04. C Easthampstead *Ox* from 03. *St Michael's House, Crowthorne Road, Bracknell RG12 7ER* Tel (01344) 460041 Mobile 07786-653318 E-mail bea.acumen@zetnet.co.uk

PEARSON, Christian David John (Brother Christian). b 42. Open Univ BA76 CCC Cam BA79 MA83. AKC65. **d** 66 **p** 67. C Pallion *Dur* 66-68; C Peterlee 68-71; SSF from 71; Lic to Offic *Sarum* 71-73; Tanzania 74-75; Lic to Offic *Ely* 75-90; Asst Chapl Keble Coll Ox 82-83; Chapl St Cath Coll Cam 83-86; Chapl Down Coll Cam 86-90; Lic to Offic *Lon* from 90; Dep Warden and Chapl Lon Goodenough Trust 90-95. *66 Warwick Way, London SW1V 1RZ* Tel (020) 7828 0271

PEARSON, Christopher Ian. b 65. Thames Poly BA91 K Coll Lon MA96. Coll of Resurr Mirfield CPS93. **d** 93 **p** 94. C Newington St Mary *S'wark* 93-95; C Streatham St Pet 95-97; V Kennington Park St Agnes from 97. *The Vicarage, 37 St Agnes Place, London SE11 4BB* Tel (020) 7735 3860 E-mail vicar@saintagnes.org.uk

PEARSON, Christopher John. b 49. GRSM LRAM ARCM. Oak Hill NSM Course 81. **d** 84 **p** 85. NSM Barton Seagrave w Warkton *Pet* 84-86; C Kettering St Andr 86-88; V Nassington w Yarwell and Woodnewton 88-91; V Pet St Mark 91-03; P-in-c Gt Doddington and Wilby from 03. *The Vicarage, 72 High Street, Great Doddington, Wellingborough NN9 7TH* Tel and fax (01933) 226711

PEARSON, Colin Graham. b 58. St Jo Coll Nottm 01. **d** 04 **p** 05. C Mickleover All SS *Derby* from 04. *28 Earlswood Drive, Mickleover, Derby DE3 5LN* Tel (01332) 674604

PEARSON, David. *See* PEARSON, James David

PEARSON, David. b 57. Man Poly BA78. Trin Coll Bris 85. **d** 88 **p** 89. C Shawbury *Lich* 88-91; C Morton 88-91; C Stanton on Hine Heath 88-91; R Mattishall w Mattishall Burgh, Welborne etc *Nor* 91-00; RD Dereham in Mitford 98-00; Asst P Tawa Linden New Zealand from 00. *38 Westhaven Drive, Tawa, Wellington, New Zealand* Tel (0064) (4) 232 1929 *or* (4) 232 8448 E-mail dpearson.tawa@xtra.co.nz

PEARSON, Edgar. b 13. Tyndale Hall Bris 37. **d** 41 **p** 42. C Handforth *Ches* 41; Burma 42; India 42-47; Hon CF 47; Chile 50-55; Australia 55-65; R Dallinghoo and Pettistree *St E* 65-83; P-in-c Bredfield w Boulge 74-86; rtd 83; P-in-c Dallinghoo and Pettistree *St E* 83-86; Perm to Offic *Mon* from 86. *Maendy House, Penrhos, Raglan, Usk NP15 2LQ* Tel (01600) 780398

PEARSON, Fergus Tom. b 58. Middx Poly BA81 Moore Th Coll Sydney MA98. Oak Hill Th Coll BA95. **d** 92 **p** 93. C Mildmay Grove St Jude and St Paul *Lon* 92-95; Australia 96-98; C Heatherlands St Jo *Sarum* 98-03; V Hensingham *Carl* from 03. *St John's Vicarage, Egremont Road, Hensingham, Whitehaven CA28 8QW* Tel (01946) 692822 E-mail fpe@rson.justbrowsing.com

PEARSON, Geoffrey Charles. b 49. BSc ARCS. Oak Hill Th Coll. **d** 82 **p** 83. C Foord St Jo *Cant* 82-86; V Ramsgate St Luke 86-93; Chapl to People at Work in Cam *Ely* 93-01; Chapl HM Pris Chelmsf from 01. *HM Prison, 200 Springfield Road, Chelmsford CM2 6LQ* Tel (01245) 268651 E-mail geoffcp@aol.com

PEARSON, Canon Geoffrey Seagrave. b 51. St Jo Coll Dur BA72. Cranmer Hall Dur 72. **d** 74 **p** 75. C Kirkheaton *Wakef* 74-77; C-in-c Blackb Redeemer *Blackb* 77-82; V 82-85; Asst Home Sec Gen Syn Bd for Miss and Unity 85-89; Hon C Forty Hill Jes Ch *Lon* 85-89; Exec Sec BCC Evang Cttee 86-89; V Roby *Liv* from 89; AD Huyton from 02; Hon Can Liv Cathl from 03. *The Vicarage, 11 Church Road, Liverpool L36 9TL* Tel and fax 0151-489 1438 E-mail geoffpeo@hotmail.com

PEARSON, George Michael. b 31. FCA FBCS MIMC. Qu Coll Birm 86 Coll of Resurr Mirfield 89. **d** 88 **p** 90. NSM Solihull *Birm* 88-95; Perm to Offic from 95. *The Parsonage, 67A Hampton Lane, Solihull B91 2QD* Tel 0121-705 0288 Fax 704 0466 E-mail parsonpearson@pearwood.org.uk

PEARSON, Canon Harold (Brother Geoffrey). b 21. Ch Coll Cam BA43 MA46. Chich Th Coll 43. **d** 45 **p** 46. C Weymouth H Trin *Sarum* 45-48; SSF from 48; P-in-c Plaistow St Andr *Chelmsf* 53-57; Chapl Denstone Coll Uttoxeter 58; Papua New Guinea 59-70; Min Gen SSF 70-85; Hon Can Win Cathl *Win* from 81; Zimbabwe 86-98; rtd 91. *The Friary, Hilfield, Dorchester DT2 7BE* Tel (01300) 341345 Fax 341293

PEARSON, Canon Henry Gervis. b 47. Mansf Coll Ox BA72 MA76. St Jo Coll Nottm 72. **d** 74 **p** 75. C Southgate *Chich* 74-76; TV 76-82; V Debenham w Aspall and Kenton *St E* 82-91; Chapl to Suffolk Fire Service 88-91; RD Loes 89-91; TR Marlborough *Sarum* 91-02; RD Marlborough 94-02; Can and Preb Sarum Cathl from 99; Chapl Savernake Hosp Marlborough 91-94; Chapl E Wilts Health Care NHS Trust from 94; R Queen Thorne *Sarum* from 02; RD Sherborne from 04. *The Rectory, Trent, Sherborne DT9 4SL* Tel (01935) 851049 E-mail rectory@queen-thorne.freeserve.co.uk

PEARSON, Ian. b 49. Liv Univ BA71. S'wark Ord Course 79. **d** 82 **p** 83. Hon C Lavender Hill Ascension *S'wark* 82-84; Archivist USPG 82-85; Archivist Nat Soc 85-91; Lic to Offic *Lon* 84-86 and 88-90; Hon C Westmr St Matt 86-88; Perm to Offic *S'wark* 85-90 and *St Alb* 90-91; C Chesterfield St Mary and All SS *Derby* 91-95; R Bengeo *St Alb* 95-04; P-in-c Worc City St Paul and Old St Martin etc *Worc* from 04. *The Rectory, 7 Aldersey Close, Worcester WR5 3EH* Tel (01905) 764726 E-mail ianandlizpearson@waitrose.com

PEARSON, James David. b 51. Cape Town Univ BSocSc74. St Paul's Coll Grahamstown 76. **d** 78 **p** 79. S Africa 78-99; C St Geo Cathl Cape Town 78-80; R Caledon H Trin 80-84; R Tristan da Cunha St Mary 84-86; R Camps Bay St Pet 86-89; R Kuruman St Mary-le-Bourne w Wrenchville St Pet 89-91; R Amalinda Ch Ch 92-96; Asst P Cambridge St Mark 96-98; Asst P-in-c Kidds Beach St Mary and St Andr 99; C Prittlewell St Steph *Chelmsf* 00-04; TV Barking St Marg w St Patr from 04. *Christ Church Vicarage, Bastable Avenue, Barking IG11 0NG* Tel (020) 8594 1976 E-mail david_pearson@dsl.pipex.com

PEARSON, Canon James Stuart. b 28. St Jo Coll Dur BA57. Cranmer Hall Dur 57. **d** 58 **p** 59. C Halifax St Jo Bapt *Wakef* 58-63; V Alverthorpe 63-70; V Knottingley 70-78; Dioc Soc Resp Adv 78-87; V Woolley 78-94; Chapl Bretton Hall Coll of Educn 87-94; Hon Can Wakef Cathl 89-94; RD Chevet 93-94; rtd 94; Perm to Offic *York* from 96. *21 Orrin Close, York YO24 2RA* Tel (01904) 708521

PEARSON, James William. b 20. FCA59. Qu Coll Birm 75. **d** 78 **p** 79. NSM Beoley *Worc* 78-90; Perm to Offic from 90. *Ringwood, Rowney Green, Alvechurch, Birmingham B48 7QE* Tel (01527) 66952

PEARSON, The Very Revd Kevin. b 54. Leeds Univ BA75 Edin Univ BD79. Edin Th Coll 76. **d** 79 **p** 80. C Horden *Dur* 79-81; Chapl Leeds Univ *Ripon* 81-87; R Edin St Salvador *Edin* 87-93; Chapl Napier Poly 88-92; Chapl Napier Univ 92-94; Dioc Dir of Ords 90-95; Prov Dir of Ords from 91; Assoc R Edin Old St Paul 93-94; P-in-c Linlithgow 94-95; R Edin St Mich and All SS from 95; Can St Mary's Cathl from 03; Dean Edin from 04. *The Rectory, 203 Gilmore Place, Edinburgh EH3 9PN* Tel 0131-229 6368

PEARSON, Mrs Lindsey Carole. b 61. Cov Poly BA85 CQSW85. Westcott Ho Cam 86. **d** 89 **p** 94. Par Dn High Harrogate St Pet *Ripon* 89-93; Par Dn Moor Allerton 93-94; C 94-96; TV Seacroft 96-04; World Development Officer 99-04; Area Co-ord (N and W Yorks) Chr Aid from 04. *St Mary's Vicarage, 50 Cragside Walk, Leeds LS5 3QE* Tel 0113-258 2923 *or* 225 2900 E-mail lindrew@pearley.fsnet.co.uk

PEARSON, Michael Carden. b 38. Guy's Hosp Medical Sch MB63 BChir63 Down Coll Cam MA64 Lon Univ MSc94 FRCR75 FRCP94. St Steph Ho Ox 96. **d** 98 **p** 99. NSM Horsted Keynes *Chich* 98-99; NSM Worth 99-00; Chapl Gtr Athens *Eur* 00-01; P-in-c Staplefield Common *Chich* from 05. *Bleak House, Station Road, Horsted Keynes, Haywards Heath RH17 7ED* Tel (01825) 790617

PEARSON, Michael John. b 53. Southn Univ BTh78. Sarum Th Coll 74. **d** 78 **p** 79. C Paignton St Jo *Ex* 78-82; TV Ilfracombe, Lee, W Down, Woolacombe and Bittadon 82-85; TV Ilfracombe, Lee, Woolacombe, Bittadon etc 85-86; TV Barnstaple from 97; Chapl N Devon Healthcare NHS Trust 86-96; RD Barnstaple *Ex* 97-01. *The Rectory, Sowden Lane, Barnstaple EX32 8BU* Tel (01271) 373837

PEARSON, Nigel. *See* PEARSON, John Nigel

PEARSON, Pauline Hilary. b 54. BA77 PhD88 RN77 RHV79. NEOC 02. **d** 05. NSM Denton *Newc* from 05. *3 Belle Grove Place, Newcastle upon Tyne NE2 4LH* Tel 0191-232 5980 Mobile 07050-105918 E-mail p.h.pearson@ncl.ac.uk

PEARSON, Mrs Priscilla Dawn. b 45. Oak Hill Th Coll BA90. **d** 90 **p** 94. Par Dn Stanford-le-Hope w Mucking *Chelmsf* 90-94; C 94; C Colchester St Jo 94-96; Hon C Woking St Jo *Guildf* from 03. *13 Ashley Road, Woking GU21 8SR* Tel (01483) 723878

PEARSON, Raymond Joseph. b 44. AKC71. St Aug Coll Cant 71. **d** 72 **p** 73. C Wetherby *Ripon* 72-75; C Goring-by-Sea *Chich* 75-77; C Bramley *Ripon* 77-82; V Patrick Brompton and Hunton 82-94; V Crakehall 82-94; V Hornby 82-94; World Miss Officer 88-94; RD Wensley 92-94; V Bardsey from 94. *The Vicarage, Wood Acre Lane, Bardsey, Leeds LS17 9DG* Tel (01937) 572243

PEARSON, Robert James Stephen. b 52. Cov Poly BA74. St Steph Ho Ox 85. **d** 87 **p** 88. C Stoke Newington St Mary *Lon* 87-90; C Haggerston All SS 90-97; C Dalston H Trin w St Phil and Haggerston All SS 97-98; Chapl HM Pris Wandsworth 98-02; Chapl HM Pris Pentonville from 02. *HM Prison Pentonville, Caledonian Road, London N7 8TT* Tel (020) 7023 7000

PEARSON, Robert Lyon. b 57. St Jo Coll Nottm 90. **d** 92 **p** 93. C Netherton *Liv* 92-96; V Woolston 96-02; V Highfield from 02. *St Matthew's Vicarage, Billinge Road, Wigan WN3 6BL* Tel (01942) 222121 Fax 211332 E-mail vicar@stmatthewhighfield.org.uk

PEARSON, Roderick Percy. b 21. Linc Th Coll 74. **d** 75 **p** 76. C Darlington St Cuth w St Hilda *Dur* 75-80; V Bishop Middleham 80-91; rtd 91. *The Lever Flat, Christ's Hospital in Sherburn, Sherburn House, Durham DH1 2SE* Tel 0191-372 1753

PEARSON, Preb Roy Barthram. b 35. K Coll Lon 56. **d** 60 **p** 61. C Brookfield St Mary *Lon* 60-64; C St Marylebone St Cypr 64-70; V Tottenham All Hallows from 70; AD E Haringey 95-00; Preb St Paul's Cathl from 96. *The Priory, Church Lane, London N17 7AA* Tel (020) 8808 2470

PEARSON-MILES, David. b 37. St Jo Coll Nottm 74. **d** 76 **p** 77. C Hazlemere *Ox* 76-79; R Waddesdon w Over Winchendon and Fleet Marston 79-82; CF 82-92; P-in-c Barcombe *Chich* 92-94; R 94-00; rtd 00. *The Coach House, Holme Place, Oakford, Tiverton EX16 9DH* Tel (01398) 351495

PEART, John Graham. b 36. Bps' Coll Cheshunt 65. **d** 68 **p** 69. C Cheshunt *St Alb* 68-70; C St Alb St Pet 70-73; R Hunsdon and Widford 73-76; Ind Chapl 76-82; Chapl St Geo Hosp and Distr Gen Hosp Stafford 82-87; Chapl Qu Eliz Hosp and Bensham Hosp Gateshead 87-89; Chapl Garlands Hosp 89-94; P-in-c Cotehill and Cumwhinton *Carl* 89-94; V Irthington, Crosby-on-Eden and Scaleby 94-98; rtd 98; Chapl Douglas MacMillan Hospice Stoke-on-Trent 98-01; P-in-c Salt and Sandon w Burston *Lich* 01-02; TV Mid Trent 02-03; Perm to Offic from 04. *Foxgloves, Copper Glade, Stafford ST16 3RJ* Tel (01785) 259313 E-mail john@peart-family.fsnet.co.uk

PEART, Patricia Isidora. b 55. Westcott Ho Cam CTM99. **d** 99. C Holland-on-Sea *Chelmsf* 99-00; C Shrub End 00-01. *6 Whitsand Road, Manchester M22 4ZA*

PEAT, Mrs Ann Kathleen. b 40. TCert60. LNSM course 93. **d** 98 **p** 99. OLM Brumby *Linc* from 98. *36 Glover Road, Scunthorpe DN17 1AS* Tel (01724) 852609

PEAT, David James. b 62. Leeds Univ BA84. Cranmer Hall Dur 86. **d** 89 **p** 90. C Wetherby *Ripon* 89-92; C Beeston 92-95; Chapl

St Lawr Coll Ramsgate from 95. *St Lawrence College, College Road, Ramsgate CT11 7AE* Tel (01843) 582084 *or* 587666

PEAT, David William. b 37. Clare Coll Cam MA59 PhD62 FRAS63. Westcott Ho Cam 72. **d** 75 **p** 76. C Chesterton St Andr *Ely* 75-77; Chapl Univ Coll of Ripon and York St Jo 77-83; V E Ardsley *Wakef* 83-87; Prin Willesden Min Tr Scheme 87-94; NSM Headingley *Ripon* from 94; Research Lect Leeds Univ from 94; rtd 97. *12 North Grange Mews, Headingley, Leeds LS6 2EW* Tel 0113-275 3179
E-mail phy6dwp@phys-irc.leeds.ac.uk

PEAT, The Ven Lawrence Joseph. b 28. Linc Th Coll 55. **d** 58 **p** 59. C Bramley *Ripon* 58-61; V 65-73; R Heaton Norris All SS *Man* 61-65; P-in-c Southend St Erkenwald *Chelmsf* 73-74; TR Southend St Jo w St Mark, All SS w St Fran etc 74-79; V Skelsmergh w Selside and Longsleddale *Carl* 79-86; RD Kendal 84-89; TV Kirkby Lonsdale 86-89; Hon Can Carl Cathl 88-95; Adn Westmorland and Furness 89-95; rtd 95; Perm to Offic *Carl* from 95. *32 White Stiles, Kendal LA9 6DJ* Tel (01539) 733829

PEAT, Matthew. b 71. Bradf and Ilkley Coll BA97. Ripon Coll Cuddesdon BTh03. **d** 03 **p** 04. C Walney Is *Carl* from 03. *7 Irwell Road, Walney, Barrow-in-Furness LA14 3WA* Tel (01229) 474663 E-mail mpeat@fish.co.uk

PEATFIELD, Canon Alfred Charles Henry. b 22. New Coll Ox BA48 MA48. Ripon Hall Ox 48. **d** 51 **p** 52. C Hackney St Jo *Lon* 51-54; V Battersea St Paul *S'wark* 54-56; Malaya 56-63; Malaysia 63-70; Adn N Malaya 64-70; V Hornchurch St Andr *Chelmsf* 70-92; RD Havering 76-80; Hon Can Chelmsf Cathl 80-92; rtd 92; Perm to Offic *Chelmsf* from 92. *28 Moor Lane, Upminster RM14 1EB* Tel (01708) 220598

PEATMAN (née HUGHES), Mrs Debbie Ann. b 62. SS Hild & Bede Coll Dur BA83 St Jo Coll Dur BA89. Cranmer Hall Dur 87. **d** 90 **p** 94. C Edin Old St Paul *Edin* 90-91; NSM Greasley *S'well* 92-94; NSM Whitley *Cov* 94-02; C Lancaster St Thos *Blackb* from 02. *6 Beechwood Gardens, Lancaster LA1 4PH* Tel (01524) 66295 E-mail debbie@peatman.org.uk

PEATMAN, Michael Robert. b 61. Keble Coll Ox BA85 MA89 St Jo Coll Dur BA89. Cranmer Hall Dur 87. **d** 90 **p** 91. C Greasley *S'well* 90-94; P-in-c Whitley *Cov* 94-02; Dio Stewardship Adv 94-02; Sen Chapl St Martin's Coll *Blackb* from 02. *6 Beechwood Gardens, Lancaster LA1 4PH* Tel (01524) 66295 *or* 384260 E-mail m.peatman@ucsm.ac.uk

PEATTIE, The Ven Colin Hulme Reid. b 39. Natal Univ BSc59. Ripon Hall Ox 61. **d** 63 **p** 64. C Belmont *Lon* 63-65; S Africa 65-83 and from 85; R Durban St Columba 65-69; R Dundee St Jas 69-72; Chapl St Andr Sch Bloemfontein 72-76; R Pietermaritzburg St Alphege 76-83; V S Ossett *Wakef* 83-85; R York-cum-Ravensworth 85-93; R Stanger All SS 93-96; R Umhlali All So from 96; Adn N Coast from 01. *PO Box 222, Salt Rock, 4391 South Africa* Tel and fax (0027) (32) 947 2001 Mobile 82-413 8650 E-mail cpeattie@absamail.co.za

PEATY, Julia Kathleen. b 53. Salford Univ BSc75. STETS 96. **d** 99 **p** 00. NSM E Grinstead St Swithun *Chich* from 99. *15 Overton Shaw, East Grinstead RH19 2HN* Tel (01342) 322386 E-mail jkpeaty@aol.com

PEBERDY (née GARNETT), Mrs Alyson Susan. b 48. Trevelyan Coll Dur BA69 Reading Univ MA75. Ox Min Course 95. **d** 96 **p** 97. C New Windsor *Ox* 96-99; V Brockley Hill St Sav *S'wark* from 99; P-in-c Perry Hill St Geo 00-01; P-in-c Forest Hill St Aug 00-02. *St Saviour's Vicarage, 5 Lowther Hill, London SE23 1PZ* Tel (020) 8690 2499 E-mail alysonpeberdy@aol.com

PECK, David Warner. b 66. American Univ (Washington) BA88 Selw Coll Cam BA94 MA99. Westcott Ho Cam 92. **d** 95 **p** 96. C Weybridge *Guildf* 95-99; Bp's Chapl 99-05; Abp's Sec for Internat Development *Cant* from 05. *2 Lambeth Palace Cottages, Lambeth Road, London SE1 7JX* Tel (020) 7898 1243
E-mail david.peck@c-of-e.org.uk

PECK, Robert John. b 49. Bath Univ BSc72. STETS 00. **d** 03 **p** 04. NSM Stoke-next-Guildf from 03. *10 Eastgate Gardens, Guildford GU1 4AZ* Tel (01483) 854224 E-mail j_b@tesco.net

PECKETT, Desmonde Claude Brown. b 19. Ex & Truro NSM Scheme. **d** 77 **p** 78. NSM Charlestown *Truro* 77-89; Perm to Offic from 89. *Smugglers, Porthpean, St Austell PL26 6AY* Tel (01726) 72768

PECKHAM, Richard Graham. b 51. Sarum & Wells Th Coll 84. **d** 86 **p** 87. C Bishop's Cleeve *Glouc* 86-89; TV Ilfracombe, Lee, Woolacombe, Bittadon etc *Ex* 89-96; TV Sidmouth, Woolbrook, Salcombe Regis, Sidbury etc from 96; RD Ottery 98-02; Hon Chapl ATC from 98. *St Francis's Vicarage, Woolbrook Road, Sidmouth EX10 9XH* Tel (01395) 514522
E-mail rikpeckham@lineone.net *or* rikpeckham@hotmail.com

PEDDER, Brian. b 38. Carl Dioc Tr Inst 88. **d** 91 **p** 92. NSM Wigton *Carl* 91-93; C Cleator Moor w Cleator 93-96; P-in-c Grayrigg, Old Hutton and New Hutton 96-04; rtd 04. *5 Scholars Green, Wigton CA7 9QW* Tel (016973) 45346

PEDLAR, John Glanville. b 43. Ex Univ BA68. St Steph Ho Ox 68. **d** 70 **p** 71. C Tavistock and Gulworthy *Ex* 70-73; Prec Portsm Cathl *Portsm* 74-77; Prec St Alb Abbey *St Alb* 77-81; V Redbourn 81-98; PV Westmr Abbey 87-04; V Bedford St Paul *St Alb* from 98. *St Paul's Vicarage, 12 The Embankment, Bedford MK40 3PD* Tel (01234) 364638 *or* 340163
E-mail johnpedlar@btinternet.com

PEDLEY, Canon Betty. b 49. ALCM78 Leeds Univ BEd71 Ripon Coll of Educn CertEd70 Coll of Preceptors Dip Special Educn 81. N Ord Course 85. **d** 88. Par Dn Sowerby *Wakef* 88-92; Par Educn Adv and Youth Chapl 92-03; P-in-c Luddenden w Luddenden Foot from 03; Hon Can Wakef Cathl from 00. *The Vicarage, 50 Carr Field Drive, Luddenden, Halifax HX2 6RJ* Tel (01422) 882127 Fax 365479

✠**PEDLEY, The Rt Revd Geoffrey <u>Stephen</u>.** b 40. Qu Coll Cam BA64 MA67. Cuddesdon Coll 64. **d** 66 **p** 67 **c** 98. C Liv Our Lady and St Nic *Liv* 66-69; C Cov H Trin *Cov* 69-71; Zambia 71-77; P-in-c Stockton H Trin *Dur* 77-83; V Stockton St Pet 77-88; Chapl to The Queen 84-98; R Whickham *Dur* 88-93; Can Res Dur Cathl 93-98; Suff Bp Lancaster *Blackb* from 98; Hon Can Blackb Cathl from 98. *Shireshead Vicarage, Whinney Brow, Forton, Preston PR3 0AE* Tel (01524) 799900 Fax 799901
E-mail bishop.lancaster@ukonline.co.uk

PEDLEY, Nicholas Charles. b 48. CQSW75. Qu Coll Birm 88. **d** 90 **p** 91. C Stafford St Jo and Tixall w Ingestre *Lich* 90-93; C Kingswinford St Mary *Worc* 93-96; TV 96-97; C Cheswardine, Childs Ercall, Hales, Hinstock etc *Lich* 97-99; Chapl HM YOI Stoke Heath 97-99; rtd 99; Perm to Offic *Worc* from 00. *33 Comber Grove, Kinver, Stourbridge DY7 6EN* Tel (01384) 877219 E-mail nick@npedley48.freeserve.co.uk

PEDLOW, Henry Noel. b 37. QUB BA59. **d** 61 **p** 62. C Belfast St Phil *Conn* 61-66; C Belfast St Nic 66-70; I Eglantine 70-82; I Kilkeel *D & D* 82-89; I Belfast St Donard 89-03; rtd 03. *8 Old Mill Dale, Dundonalad, Belfast BT16 1WG* Tel (028) 9048 5416

PEEBLES, David Thomas. b 64. Bris Univ BA85 St Chad's Coll Dur PGCE86 Man Univ MA94. Coll of Resurr Mirfield 90. **d** 90 **p** 91. C Crewe St Andr *Ches* 90-93; Lect and Asst Dir Studies Mirfield 93-95; Chapl Qu Mary and Westf Coll *Lon* 95-00; P-in-c Bethnal Green St Matt w St Jas the Gt 97-99; Chapl LSE from 00; Bp's Adv on New Relig Movements from 01. *3 Bristol House, 80A Southampton Row, London WC1B 4BA* Tel (020) 7242 4794 *or* 7980 1204 E-mail d.peebles@lse.ac.uk

PEEK, Alan Nicholas. b 65. Ridley Hall Cam 02. **d** 04. C Much Woolton *Liv* from 04. *25 Linkside Road, Liverpool L25 9NX* Tel 0151-428 9458

PEEK, John Richard. b 51. Bris Univ BSc72 Nottm Univ BA75. St Jo Coll Nottm. **d** 76 **p** 77. C Hebburn St Jo *Dur* 76-78; C Dunston 78-81; R Armthorpe *Sheff* 81-86; RE Teacher K Edw VI Sch Southn 87-88; Chapl and Hd RE Casterton Sch Cumbria 89; Teacher Furze Platt Comp Sch Berks 89-90; Perm to Offic *Portsm* 90-96; Chapl Bearwood Coll Wokingham 96-98. *Address temp unknown*

PEEL, Mrs Christine Mary. b 44. Whitelands Coll Lon CertEd66. Portsm Dioc Tr Course. **d** 90. NSM Sheet *Portsm* 90-03; Perm to Offic *York* from 03. *11 Whiteoak Avenue, Easingwold, York YO61 3GB* Tel (01347) 823548

PEEL, David Charles. b 41. AKC75. St Aug Coll Cant 75. **d** 76 **p** 77. C Tynemouth Cullercoats St Paul *Newc* 76-79; C Tynemouth St Jo 79-84; Ldr Cedarwood Project 84-88 and from 91; Warden Communicare Ho 89-91; Min Killingworth 89-91. *116 Grey Street, North Shields NE30 2EG* Tel 0191-272 8743 *or* 259 0245

PEEL, Derrick. b 50. Open Univ BA82. Linc Th Coll 75. **d** 78 **p** 79. C Otley *Bradf* 78-82; V Shelf 82-94; P-in-c Buttershaw St Aid 89-94; TR Shelf w Buttershaw St Aid 94-95; V E Crompton *Man* 95-05; V Ware St Mary *St Alb* from 05. *St Mary's Vicarage, 31 Thunder Court, Ware SG12 0PT* Tel (01920) 464817

PEEL, John Bruce. b 30. TCD BA54 MA68. Wells Th Coll 69. **d** 70 **p** 71. C Wilmslow *Ches* 70-75; V Weston 75-83; V Henbury 83-95; Chapl Parkside Hosp Ches 83-95; rtd 95; Perm to Offic *Ches* from 95. *Winneba, 29 Hungerford Terrace, Crewe CW1 6HF* Tel (01270) 587464

PEEL, Capt Jonathan Sidney. b 37. CBE95 MC57 DL75. St Jo Coll Cam BA70 MA75. Dioc OLM tr scheme 97. **d** 00 **p** 01. NSM Ashmanhaugh, Barton Turf etc *Nor* from 00. *Barton Hall, Barton Turf, Norwich NR12 8AU* Tel (01692) 536250 Fax 536135

PEEL, Michael Jerome. b 31. Bris Univ BA55 MLitt73 St Cath Soc Ox DipTh59 Man Univ BD65 K Coll Lon PhD88. Wycliffe Hall Ox 57. **d** 59 **p** 60. C Stretford St Matt *Man* 59-61; C Chorlton upon Medlock 61-62; Chapl Man Univ 61-62; C Chorlton-cum-Hardy St Clem 62-65; V Chirbury *Heref* 65-68; P-in-c Marton 65-68; R Iver Heath *Ox* 68-87; V Linslade 87-95; rtd 95; Warden Coll of St Barn Lingfield 95-00; Lic to Offic *S'wark* 95-00; Perm to Offic *Chich* and *Roch* 95-00; *St E* from 00; *Chelmsf* from 01. *Poplar Meadow, Thedwastre Road, Thurston, Bury St Edmunds IP31 3QY* Tel (01359) 270296

PEELING, Mrs Pamela Mary Alberta. b 44. Oak Hill Th Coll 83. **dss** 86 **d** 87 **p** 94. NSM Moulsham St Luke *Chelmsf* 86-88; NSM N Springfield 88-95; C Basildon St Martin 95-97; TV Grays Thurrock 97-05; rtd 05. *4 Heron Road, Saxmundham IP17 1WR* Tel (01728) 604584 E-mail phil@ppeeling.freeserve.co.uk.

PEER, Charles Scott. b 69. Bris Univ BSc91 PGCE94. Trin Coll Bris BA02. **d** 02 **p** 03. C Dawlish *Ex* from 02. *1 Kingsdown Crescent, Dawlish EX7 0HP* Tel (01626) 863848 E-mail cspeer316@aol.com

PEERS, John Edward. b 39. Bps' Coll Cheshunt 60. **d** 63 **p** 64. C Crayford *Roch* 63-67; C Beckenham St Jas 67-69; C Winlaton *Dur* 69-72; P-in-c Silksworth 72-81; R Lt Bowden St Nic *Leic* 81-86; P-in-c Lt Bowden St Hugh 83-86; RD Gartree I 84-88; R Market Harborough Transfiguration 86-88; V Skipton Ch Ch *Bradf* 88-99; V Hambleton w Out Rawcliffe *Blackb* 99-03; rtd 03. *9 Holland Road, Leominster HR6 8PF* Tel (01568) 614794 E-mail sreep@hotmail.com

✠**PEERS, The Most Revd Michael Geoffrey.** b 34. Univ of BC BA56. Trin Coll Toronto LTh59 Hon DD78. **d** 59 **p** 60 **c** 77. C Ottawa St Thos 59-61; C Ottawa Trin 61-65; Chapl Carleton Univ 61-66; R Winnipeg St Bede 66-72; R Winnipeg St Martin w Middlechurch St Paul 72-74; Adn Winnipeg 69-74; R St Paul's Cathl Regina and Dean Qu'Appelle 74-77; Bp Qu'Appelle 77-82; Abp Qu'Appelle and Metrop Rupert's Land 82-86; Primate Angl Ch of Canada 86-04; rtd 04. *600 Jarvis Street, Toronto ON, Canada, M4Y 2J6* Tel (001) (416) 924 9199 Fax 924 0211 E-mail primate@national.anglican.ca

PEERS, Michael John. b 65. SS Paul & Mary Coll Cheltenham BA86. Ripon Coll Cuddesdon 88. **d** 91 **p** 92. C Birstall and Wanlip *Leic* 91-94; C Leic St Marg and All SS 94-96; TV The Abbey Leic 96-00; P-in-c Langley Park *Dur* 00-01; V from 01; P-in-c Esh 00-01; V from 01; P-in-c Hamsteels 00-01; V from 01; P-in-c Waterhouses 00-01; V from 01. *The Vicarage, Church Street, Langley Park, Durham DH7 9TZ* Tel 0191-373 9509 E-mail mjpeers@aol.com

PEERS, Richard Charles. b 65. K Alfred's Coll Win BEd88. Chich Th Coll BTh93. **d** 93 **p** 94. C Grangetown *York* 93-95; C Portsea St Mary *Portsm* 95-97; Perm to Offic 99-01; Chapl St Luke's Sch Southsea 01-03; Hon Chapl Portsm Cathl *Portsm* 01-03; Dep Hd Ch Sch Richmond from 03. *1 Glebe House, Waynflete Street, London SW18 3QG* Tel (020) 8879 7298 *or* 8940 6982 E-mail richard.peers1@btopenworld.com

PEET, Derek Edwin. b 26. Sheff Univ BA51 DipEd52 Lon Univ DipTh57. Qu Coll Birm 66. **d** 67 **p** 68. C Hebden Bridge *Wakef* 67-70; V Darton 70-79; TR Gleadless Valley *Sheff* 79-85; V Kirk Hallam *Derby* 85-96; rtd 96; Perm to Offic *Ripon* from 96. *44 Parkways Grove, Woodlesford, Leeds LS26 8TP* Tel 0113-282 3079 Mobile 07960-450038

PEET, John Christopher. b 56. Oriel Coll Ox BA80 MA83 Clare Coll Cam BA82 MA87. Ridley Hall Cam 80. **d** 83 **p** 84. C Menston w Woodhead *Bradf* 83-86; C Prenton *Ches* 86-89; V Harden and Wilsden *Bradf* 89-97; V Cononley w Bradley from 97. *The Vicarage, 3 Meadow Close, Cononley, Keighley BD20 8LZ* Tel (01535) 634369

PEET, John Michael. b 44. AKC67. **d** 68 **p** 72. C Battersea St Pet *S'wark* 68-69; C Sutton St Nic 69-74; C Perry Hill St Geo 74-78; TV Stepney St Dunstan and All SS *Lon* 78-81; P-in-c Stamford Hill St Bart 81-86; V 87-89; P-in-c Mile End Old Town H Trin 89-90; P-in-c Bromley All Hallows 89-90; TR Bow H Trin and All Hallows 90-03; V Mile End H Trin from 03. *Holy Trinity Vicarage, 28 Coborn Street, London E3 2AB* Tel (020) 8980 2074 Fax 8980 2247 E-mail michael@mpeet.fsnet.co.uk

PEGG, Brian Peter Richard (Bill). b 30. Ox NSM Course 77 Sarum & Wells Th Coll 82. **d** 83 **p** 84. C Furze Platt *Ox* 83-85; V Ashbury, Compton Beauchamp and Longcot w Fernham 85-94; Chapl Mlaga *Eur* 94-97; rtd 97; Hon C Shere, Albury and Chilworth *Guildf* 98-02; Perm to Offic *Linc* from 03. *31 King Street, Winterton, Scunthorpe DN15 9TP* Tel (01724) 734860

PEGG, Gerald Francis. b 37. FCII69 Birkbeck Coll Lon DipRS91. S'wark Ord Course 88. **d** 91 **p** 92. NSM Belmont *S'wark* 91-95; NSM Winchelsea and Icklesham *Chich* 95-02; rtd 02. *Lorien, 19 Manor Close, Icklesham, Winchelsea TN36 4BT* Tel (01424) 814735 Mobile 07711-582710 E-mail geraldpegg@cwcom.net

PEGLER, Frederic Arthur. b 19. Selw Coll Cam BA46 MA48. Qu Coll Birm 46. **d** 47 **p** 48. C Crawley *Chich* 47-49; C Rickmansworth *St Alb* 49-50; V Sark *Win* 50-52; PV S'well Minster *S'well* 52-55; Canada 55-84; rtd 84; Perm to Offic *St Alb* 84-85. *302 Goodwin Manor, 1148 Goodwin Street, Victoria BC, Canada, V8S 5H2* Tel (001) (250) 386 6514

PEILOW, Lynda Elizabeth Anne. b 74. CITC BTh97. **d** 97 **p** 98. C Castleknock and Mulhuddart, w Clonsilla *D & G* 97-00; C Dublin St Ann and St Steph 00-01; Min Can St Patr Cathl Dublin 00-01; I Clonsast w Rathangan, Thomastown etc *M & K* from 01. *The Rectory, Monasteroris, Edenderry, Co Offaly, Irish Republic* Tel (00353) (46) 973 1585 E-mail lpeilow@oceanfree.net *or* edenderry@kildare.anglican.org

PEIRCE, John. b 35. Worc Coll Ox BA59 MA64 Kent Univ MA96. Wycliffe Hall Ox 59. **d** 61 **p** 62. C Brompton H Trin *Lon* 61-64; C Wareham w Arne *Sarum* 64-68; V Sturminster Newton and Hinton St Mary 68-74; V Kingswood *Bris* 74-79; Dir Coun Chr Care *Ex* 79-89; Public Preacher 89-92; NSM Hackney *Lon* 90-94; NSM St Botolph Aldgate w H Trin Minories from 94; Co-ord Ch Action on Disability 90-98; Perm to Offic *Ex* 92-98. *3 Mile End Place, London E1 4BH* Tel (020) 7790 9418

PEIRCE, Canon John Martin. b 36. Jes Coll Cam BA59 MA65. Westcott Ho Cam 65. **d** 66 **p** 67. C Croydon St Jo *Cant* 66-70; C Fareham H Trin *Portsm* 70-71; TV 71-76; TR Langley Marish *Ox* 76-85; RD Burnham 78-82; Dir of Ords and Post-Ord Tr 85-01; Can Res Ch Ch 87-01; rtd 01. *8 Burwell Meadow, Witney, Oxford OX28 5JQ*

PEIRIS, Lionel James Harold (Brother Lionel). b 45. Serampore Coll BD71. Bp's Coll Calcutta 67. **d** 70 **p** 71. Sri Lanka 70-76 and 78-95; P Lect Colombo Coll 71-76 and 78-95; C Shirley *Birm* 76-78; P Brother SSF Auckland New Zealand 96-97; Australia from 97; Asst Chapl and Past Asst Annerley Hosp 97-98; Hon C Annerley St Phil 97-98; P-in-c from 99. *115 Cornwall Street, Annerley, Qld, Australia 4103* Tel (0061) (7) 3391 3915 Fax 3391 3916

PELHAM, John. b 36. New Coll Ox BA61 MA65. **d** 79 **p** 80. NSM Balerno *Edin* 79-91; Hon C W Linton 91-94; Hon C Penicuik 91-94; Dioc Supernumerary from 94. *2 Horsburgh Bank, Balerno EH14 7DA* Tel 0131-449 3934 E-mail john.pelham@argonet.co.uk

PELL, Charles Andrew. b 54. Leeds Univ CertEd77. Aston Tr Scheme 87 St Jo Coll Nottm 87. **d** 89 **p** 90. C Mottram in Longdendale w Woodhead *Ches* 89-90; C Handforth 90-93; P-in-c Walton Breck *Liv* 93-94; V 94-96; P-in-c Glyndyfrdwy and Llansantfraid Glyn Dyfrdwy *St As* 96-01; CF (ACF) from 93; V Rhodes *Man* from 01. *Rhodes Vicarage, Boardman Lane, Middleton, Manchester M24 4PU* Tel 0161-643 3224 Mobile 07831-279429 E-mail padre@milnet.uk.net

PELLEY, John Lawless. b 34. Oak Hill Th Coll 67. **d** 69 **p** 70. C Fareham St Jo *Portsm* 69-72; C Frogmore *St Alb* 72-76; V Standon 76-96; RD Bishop's Stortford 91-95; rtd 96; Perm to Offic *Ely* from 96. *7 Home Close, Histon, Cambridge CB4 9JL* Tel (01223) 234636

PELLY, Raymond Blake. b 38. Worc Coll Ox BA61 MA63 Geneva Univ DTh71. Linc Th Coll 61 Bossey Ecum Inst Geneva 62. **d** 63 **p** 64. C Gosforth All SS *Newc* 63-65; C N Lynn w St Marg and St Nic *Nor* 69-70; Vice-Prin Westcott Ho Cam 71-76; Warden St Jo Coll Auckland New Zealand 77-85; Visiting Lect Univ of Mass Boston USA 86-88 and 96; Chapl Victoria Univ of Wellington New Zealand 90-94; Asst P Wellington St Pet 92-94 and from 96; rtd 03. *12 Kio Crescent, Hataitai, Wellington 2, New Zealand* Tel (0064) (4) 386 3972 Mobile 21-486200 Fax (4) 386 3729 E-mail raymond.pelly@xtra.co.nz

PEMBERTON, Anthony Thomas Christie (Chris). b 57. BA. Cranmer Hall Dur 82. **d** 84 **p** 85. C Maidstone St Luke *Cant* 84-88; Chapl Ox Pastorate 88-98; V Cant St Mary Bredin *Cant* from 98. *St Mary Bredin Vicarage, 57 Nunnery Fields, Canterbury CT1 3JN* Tel (01227) 453777 E-mail vicar@smb.org.uk

PEMBERTON, Carrie Mary. b 55. St Hilda's Coll Ox BA78 Cam Univ PGCE82 Leeds Univ MA92 Newnham Coll Cam PhD98. Cranmer Hall Dur 83 NEOC 84. **dss** 86 **d** 87 **p** 94. NSM Leeds St Geo *Ripon* 86-87; Miss Partner CMS and Dir Women's Studies Angl Th Inst Zaïre 87-91; Perm to Offic *Pet* 92-94; NSM Bourn and Kingston w Caxton and Longstowe *Ely* 94-99; TV Elsworth w Knapwell 99; Min Cambourne LEP 00-01; Cen Chapl Yarlswood Immigration and Detention Cen 01-03; Perm to Offic *Ely* from 01; Chief Exec CHASTE from 04. *Elsworth Rectory, The Drift, Elsworth, Cambridge CB3 8JN* Tel and fax (01954) 267722 E-mail carrie.pemberton@ely.anglican.org

PEMBERTON, Crispin Mark Rugman. b 59. St Andr Univ MTh83. St Steph Ho Ox 84. **d** 86 **p** 87. C Acton St Alb w All SS *Lon* 86-88; C Acton Green 88-90; C Leckhampton SS Phil and Jas w Cheltenham St Jas *Glouc* 90-93; V Tuffley 93-97; RE Teacher Cheltenham Coll Jun Sch from 97; Perm to Offic *Glouc* 97-00. *Cheltenham College (Junior School), Bath Road, Cheltenham GL53 7LD* Tel (01242) 265617

PEMBERTON, David Charles. b 35. K Coll Lon 57. **d** 61 **p** 62. C Pokesdown St Jas *Win* 61-65; C W Derby St Mary *Liv* 65-67; C-in-c Cantril Farm St Jude CD 67-71; V Cantril Farm 71-74; V Devonport St Boniface *Ex* 75-83; V Stanwell *Lon* 83-00; AD Spelthorne 92-97; rtd 00. *23C Gordon Road, Ashford TW15 3ES* Tel (01784) 253420

PEMBERTON, Canon Jeremy Charles Baring. b 56. Mert Coll Ox MA77 Fitzw Ho Cam BA80 Leeds Univ MA92. Ridley Hall Cam 78. **d** 81 **p** 82. C Stranton *Dur* 81-84; C Leeds St Geo *Ripon* 84-87; CMS Miss Partner and Dir Angl Th Inst Zaïre 87-91; V Irchester *Pet* 92-94; R Bourn and Kingston w Caxton and Longstowe *Ely* 94-00; P-in-c Elsworth w Knapwell 99-00; P-in-c Boxworth 99-00; TR Papworth from 00; RD Bourn 98-03; Hon Can Ely Cathl from 05; Hon Can Boga from 05. *Elsworth Rectory, The Drift, Elsworth, Cambridge CB3 8JN* Tel and fax (01954) 267722 E-mail jeremy.pemberton@ely.anglican.org

PEMBERY, Gerald Marcus. b 29. Glouc Sch of Min 89. **d** 90 **p** 91. NSM Bream *Glouc* 90-97; rtd 97; Perm to Offic *Glouc* from 97. *Kings Wood, The Tufts, Bream, Lydney GL15 6HW* Tel (01594) 562750

PENBERTHY (formerly LEGG), Ms Joanna Susan. b 60. Newnham Coll Cam BA81 MA85. St Jo Coll Nottm DipTh82 MTh84 St Jo Coll Dur 83. **dss** 84 **d** 87 **p** 97. Haughton le Skerne *Dur* 84-85; Llanishen and Lisvane *Llan* 85-87; NSM 87-89; NSM Llanwddyn and Llanfihangel-yng-Nghwynfa etc *St As* 89-93; NSM Llansadwrn w Llanwrda and Manordeilo *St D* 93-95; Officer Div for Par Development Ch in Wales 95-99; P-in-c Cynwyl Gaeo w Llansawel and Talley *St D* 99-01; V from 01. *The Vicarage, Llanwrda SA19 8HD* Tel (01550) 777343 E-mail penber6487@aol.com

PENDLEBURY, Stephen Thomas. b 50. ACA78 Southn Univ BSc73. Ridley Hall Cam 86. **d** 88 **p** 89. C Birkenhead St Jas w St Bede *Ches* 88-91; V 91-00; V Ches St Paul from 00. *St Paul's Vicarage, 10 Sandy Lane, Chester CH3 5UL* Tel (01244) 351377 E-mail stpendleby@aol.com

PENDORF, Canon James Gordon. b 45. Drew Univ New Jersey BA67. Episc Th Sch Cam Mass STB71. **d** 71 **p** 71. USA 71-76; V Colne H Trin *Blackb* 76-80; Sen Dioc Stewardship Adv *Chelmsf* 80-83; Dioc Sec *Birm* 83-95; P-in-c Highgate 95-97; V 97-04; Dioc Stewardship Adv 95-04; AD Birm City Cen 96-02; Hon Can Birm Cathl 90-04; Par Resources Adv and Chapl St Nic Ch Cen *St E* from 04. *Little Park, Main Road, Woolverstone, Ipswich IP9 1AR* Tel (01473) 780295 *or* 298504 E-mail jim@stedmundsbury.anglican.org *or* pendorfs@compuserve.com

PENFOLD, Brian Robert. b 54. Lon Univ BSc75 Bris Univ PGCE77. Oak Hill Th Coll BA84. **d** 84 **p** 85. C Norwood St Luke *S'wark* 84-88; C Rayleigh *Chelmsf* 88-92; V New Barnet St Jas *St Alb* from 92. *The Vicarage, 11 Park Road, Barnet EN4 9QA* Tel and fax (020) 8449 4043 Mobile 07753-680839 E-mail brian@brpenfold.freeserve.co.uk

PENFOLD, Colin Richard. b 52. St Pet Coll Ox BA74 MA78. Ridley Hall Cam 81. **d** 84 **p** 85. C Buckhurst Hill *Chelmsf* 84-87; C Greenside *Dur* 87-90; V Cononley w Bradley *Bradf* 90-97; P-in-c Shipley St Paul and Frizinghall 97; V Shipley St Paul from 98. *The Vicarage, 47 Kirkgate, Shipley BD18 3EH* Tel (01274) 583652 Fax as telephone E-mail colin@thepenfolds.org.uk

PENFOLD, Marion Jean. b 49. NEOC 96. **d** 99 **p** 00. NSM Lesbury w Alnmouth *Newc* 99-02; C 02-03; NSM Longhoughton w Howick 99-02; C 02-03; TV N Tyne and Redesdale from 03. *The Vicarage, Otterburn, Newcastle upon Tyne NE19 1NP* Tel (01830) 520212 *or* (01665) 712698 E-mail marion.penfold@btinternet.com

PENFOLD, Canon Susan Irene. b 52. York Univ BA73 Bris Univ PhD77 Selw Coll Cam BA83 MA87. Ridley Hall Cam 81. **dss** 84 **d** 87 **p** 94. Buckhurst Hill *Chelmsf* 84-87; Hon C Greenside *Dur* 87-90; Hon C Cononley w Bradley *Bradf* 90-97; Assoc Dioc Dir of Ords 96-01; Hon C Shipley St Paul 97-00; Perm to Offic from 00; Dir of Ords and CME Officer *Wakef* 01-03; Dir of Ords and Dean of Min from 03; Hon Can Wakef Cathl from 04. *The Vicarage, 47 Kirkgate, Shipley BD18 3EH* Tel and fax (01274) 583652 *or* tel (01924) 371802 E-mail sue.penfold@wakefield.anglican.org

PENGELLEY, Peter John. b 22. Sarum & Wells Th Coll 72. **d** 74 **p** 75. C Midsomer Norton *B & W* 74-78; R Stogursey w Fiddington 78-88; Ind Chapl 80-88; rtd 88; Perm to Offic *B & W* from 89. *Rosslyn Cottage, Roadwater, Watchet TA23 0RB* Tel (01984) 640798

PENGELLY, Canon Geoffrey. b 50. Oak Hill Th Coll 86. **d** 88 **p** 89. C Redruth w Lanner and Treleigh *Truro* 88-91; TV Bolventor 91-92; V Egloskerry, N Petherwin, Tremaine and Tresmere from 92; C Lezant w Lawhitton and S Petherwin w Trewen from 03; Hon Can Truro Cathl from 03; RD Trigg Major from 04. *The Vicarage, Egloskerry, Launceston PL15 8RX* Tel (01566) 785365

PENISTAN, Richard Luke. b 74. Newc Univ BA97 St Jo Coll Cam BA02. Ridley Hall Cam 00. **d** 03 **p** 04. C E Twickenham St Steph *Lon* from 03. *30 Crown Road, Twickenham TW1 3EE* Tel 07971-663129 (mobile) E-mail richard@st-stephens.org.uk

PENMAN, John Bain. b 67. Aber Univ BD89 New Coll Edin MTh93 SSC96. Edin Th Coll CECM93. **d** 93 **p** 94. C Glas St Ninian *Glas* 93-96; C Ealing Ch the Sav *Lon* 96-98; P-in-c Kirkcaldy and Kinghorn *St And* 98-04; R Falkirk *Edin* from 04. *55 Kerse Lane, Falkirk FK1 1RX* Tel (01324) 623709 Mobile 07801-800633 E-mail jbainp@tiscali.co.uk

PENMAN, Miss Margaret Heather. b 50. St Martin's Coll Lanc CertEd71 Lanc Univ DipEd82 FRSA95. Carl Dioc Tr Inst 90. **d** 93 **p** 94. Headteacher Hesketh w Becconsall All SS C of E Sch 85-00; RE/Schools Adv *Liv* from 00; NSM Lostock Hall *Blackb* 93-95; NSM Leyland St Jas from 95. *9 Oakfield Drive, Leyland, Preston PR5 3XE* Tel (01772) 435927 *or* 812630 Fax 814721 E-mail heatherpenman@onetel.com

PENMAN, Robert George. b 42. St Jo Coll Auckland LTh66. **d** 65 **p** 66. C Mt Roskill New Zealand 65-68; C Henderson 69-70; V Glen Innes 71-72; C Alverstoke *Portsm* 73-74; CF 74-77; C Bridgwater St Mary w Chilton Trinity *B & W* 77-80; P-in-c Haselbury Plucknett w N Perrott 80-81; P-in-c Misterton 80-81; V Haselbury Plucknett, Misterton and N Perrott 81-89; P-in-c Appleton *Ox* from 89; P-in-c Besselsleigh w Dry Sandford 89-00; P-in-c Besselsleigh from 00. *The Rectory, Oaksmere, Appleton, Abingdon OX13 5JS* Tel (01865) 862458 E-mail bobpenman@aol.com

PENN, Canon Arthur William. b 22. Man Univ BA49. Wycliffe Hall Ox 49. **d** 51 **p** 52. C Bowdon *Ches* 51-53; C Alston w Garrigill *Newc* 53-56; V Kirkdale *York* 56-67; V Brampton *Carl* 67-83; RD Brampton 74-83; P-in-c Gilsland w Nether Denton 75-81; Hon Can Carl Cathl 78-88; P-in-c Gilsland 81-83; V Rockcliffe and Blackford 83-88; rtd 88; Perm to Offic *Carl* 88-99. *1 Well Lane, Warton, Carnforth LA5 9QZ* Tel (01524) 733079

PENN, Barry Edwin. b 46. Univ of Wales (Swansea) BA72. St Jo Coll Nottm 77. **d** 79 **p** 80. C New Barnet St Jas *St Alb* 79-83; TV Preston St Jo *Blackb* 83-92; V Patchway *Bris* 92-01; Perm to Offic from 01. *50 Eastfield Road, Westbury-on-Trym, Bristol BS9 4AG* Tel 0117-962 2862

PENN, Christopher Francis. b 34. ACII63. Wells Th Coll 68. **d** 70 **p** 71. C Andover w Foxcott *Win* 70-72; C Odiham w S Warnborough 72-75; C Keynsham w Queen Charlton *B & W* 75; C Keynsham 75-76; TV 76-82; R Chilcompton w Downside and Stratton on the Fosse 82-87; RD Midsomer Norton 84-86; V Bathford 87-90; V Avonmouth St Andr *Bris* 90-96; Ind Chapl 90-96; rtd 96; Perm to Offic *B & W* and *Bris* from 96. *53 Caernarvon Road, Keynsham, Bristol BS31 2PF* Tel 0117-986 2367

PENN, Christopher Wilson. b 60. Cranmer Hall Dur 98. **d** 00 **p** 01. C Wrockwardine Deanery *Lich* 00-03; P-in-c Llanymynech from 03; P-in-c Llanyblodwel and Trefonen from 03; P-in-c Morton from 03. *The Rectory, Rectory Lane, Pant, Oswestry SY10 9RA* Tel (01691) 831211 E-mail chrispy@fish.co.uk

PENN, Clive Llewellyn. b 12. Oak Hill Th Coll 47. **d** 48 **p** 49. C Deptford St Luke *S'wark* 48-50; C Guernsey St Sampson *Win* 50-54; Australia 55-65; V Jersey Gouray St Martin *Win* 66-71; rtd 77; Lic to Offic *Win* 71-86. *PO Box 679, Williamstown, S Australia 5351*

PENNAL, David Bernard. b 37. Ripon Hall Ox 64. **d** 67 **p** 68. C Moseley St Mary *Birm* 67-71; C Bridgwater St Mary w Chilton Trinity *B & W* 71-73; P-in-c Hilton w Cheselbourne and Melcombe Horsey *Sarum* 73-76; R Milton Abbas, Hilton w Cheselbourne etc 76-78; P-in-c Spetisbury w Charlton Marshall 78-88; R Spetisbury w Charlton Marshall etc 89-00; rtd 00. *2 St Leonard's Terrace, Blandford Forum DT11 7PF* Tel (01258) 454238

PENNANT, David Falconer. b 51. Trin Coll Cam MA73. Trin Coll Bris BD84 PhD88. **d** 86 **p** 87. C Bramcote *S'well* 86-88; C Woking St Jo *Guildf* 88-93. *30 Oriental Road, Woking GU22 7AW* Tel (01483) 768055 E-mail david.pennant@ntlworld.com

PENNELL (also COFFIN), Ms Pamela. b 45. EAMTC 94. **d** 97 **p** 98. NSM Moulsham St Luke *Chelmsf* 97-98; NSM Writtle w Highwood 98-00; Perm to Offic 01-04; NSM Gt Waltham w Ford End from 04. *33 Birch Lane, Stock, Ingatestone CM4 9NA* Tel (01277) 841270

PENNEY, David Richard John. b 39. St Jo Coll Dur BA63 DipTh65. Cranmer Hall Dur 63. **d** 67 **p** 68. C Chilvers Coton w Astley *Cov* 67-70; C Styvechale 70-72; P-in-c Shilton w Ansty 72-77; P-in-c Withybrook 74-77; R Easington w Liverton *York* 77-85; Dir Soc Resp *Sarum* 85-93; Perm to Offic *Blackb* 93-02; rtd 01. *8 William Street, Colne BB8 0HH* Tel (01282) 870076 Mobile 07966-157697

PENNEY, William Affleck. b 41. MBIM75 FRSA91. K Coll Lon BD63 AKC63 St Boniface Warminster 65. **d** 66 **p** 67. C Chatham St Steph *Roch* 66-70; Ind Chapl 70-77; P-in-c Bredhurst 70-72; Hon C S Gillingham 72-74; Hon C Eynsford w Farningham and Lullingstone 74-77; Bp's Dom Chapl 74-88; Hon Ind Chapl 77-88; Hon C Balham St Mary and St Jo *S'wark* 89-91; Perm to Offic *St Alb* 91-94; Hon C Bushey 94-05; rtd 05. *47 Devonshire Mews South, London W1G 6QT* Tel (020) 7935 0649 E-mail b.penney@ashtonpenney.com

PENNICEARD, Clifford Ashley. b 42. Monash Univ Aus BA65 DipEd71 Linacre Coll Ox BA67 Ox Univ MA70. St Steph Ho Ox 65. **d** 68 **p** 69. C S Leamington St Jo *Cov* 68-70; Australia from 70; P-in-c Wantirna 74; Assoc P N Brighton 76-80; P-in-c Euroa 84-91; P-in-c Nagumbie 93-95; R Manly St Paul from 98. *99 Ernest Street, Manly, Qld, Australia 4179* Tel (0061) (7) 3396 2746 Mobile 416-177732 Fax (7) 3396 3796 E-mail cliffpenn@powerup.com.au

PENNIECOOKE, Dorothy Victoria. b 45. Dioc OLM tr scheme 97. **d** 00 **p** 01. NSM Balham Hill Ascension *S'wark* from 00. *56 Lysias Road, London SW12 8BP* Tel (020) 8673 0037

PENNINGTON, Mrs Catherine Prudence. b 56. Man Poly BSc82 Sussex Univ MSc87 Flinders Univ Aus BTh00. Adelaide Coll of Div 96. **d** 00 **p** 01. C Glenelg Australia 00-01; NSM American Cathl Paris 01-02; C Is of Dogs Ch Ch and St Jo w St Luke *Lon* 02-03; C De Beauvoir Town St Pet 03-04; P-in-c Nazeing *Chelmsf* from 05; P-in-c Roydon from 05. *The Vicarage, Betts Lane, Nazeing, Waltham Abbey EN9 2DB* Tel (01992) 893167 Mobile 07800-822297 E-mail pennington@hotmail.com

PENNINGTON, Edward Francis Quentin. b 76. G&C Coll Cam BA97 MA01 Birm Univ MSc98. Oak Hill Th Coll BTh04. **d** 04 **p** 05. C Moulton *Pet* from 04. *8 Cubleigh Close, Moulton, Northampton NN3 7BG* Tel 07743-942931 (mobile) E-mail efqpennington@hotmail.com

PENNINGTON, Emma Louise. b 71. Ex Univ BA92 Kent Univ MA96. Ripon Coll Cuddesdon BA00. **d** 00 **p** 01. C Shepperton *Lon* 00-03; Chapl Worc Coll Ox from 03. *Worcester College, Oxford OX1 2HB,* or *4 School Yard, Stadhampton, Oxford OX44 7TT* Tel (01865) 278300 *or* 400194

PENNINGTON, Frederick William. b 11. K Coll Lon. **d** 55 **p** 56. C Tiverton St Pet *Ex* 55-58; R Bradford 58-66; R Thornbury 58-66; V N Molton w Twitchen 66-77; P-in-c Molland 68-77; rtd 77; Lic to Offic *Ex* 77-95; Perm to Offic from 95. *Sunset Cottage, 103 West Street, Hartland, Bideford EX39 6BQ* Tel (01237) 441206

PENNINGTON, John Kenneth. b 27. Man Univ LLB48. Linc Th Coll 51. **d** 52 **p** 53. C Wavertree H Trin *Liv* 52-56; C Rotherham *Sheff* 56-59; P-in-c Kanpur All So India 59-63; V Nelson St Phil *Blackb* 64-66; Area Sec USPG *Derby, Leic* and *S'well* 66-71; *Derby* and *Sheff* 71-75; C Nottingham St Mary *S'well* 75-78; C Nottingham St Mary and St Cath 78-92; rtd 93; Perm to Offic *S'well* from 93. *3 St Jude's Avenue, Nottingham NG3 5FG* Tel 0115-962 3420

PENNINGTON, John Michael. b 32. Em Coll Cam BA54 MA58 IEng AMIEE MIHEEM. Wells Th Coll 58. **d** 60 **p** 61. C Stockport St Geo *Ches* 60-64; V Congleton St Steph 64-68; Chapl Nor Sch 68-70; V Hattersley *Ches* 70-72; C-in-c Upton Priory CD 72-75; V Upton Priory 75-79; Perm to Offic *Newc* 83-87; V Tynemouth St Jo 87-94; P-in-c Cambois 94-97; Chapl Northd HA 94-97; Ashington and Wansbeck Hosps 94-97; rtd 97; Perm to Offic *Newc* from 97. *297 Wingrove Road North, Fenham, Newcastle upon Tyne NE4 9EE* Tel 0191-274 5281 Fax as telephone

PENNOCK, Mrs Christine. b 48. Bp Grosseteste Coll BEd71 Leeds Univ PGCE94 Teesside Univ PGDE95. NEOC 98. **d** 01 **p** 02. C Crowland *Linc* 01-05; P-in-c Ruskington from 05. *The Rectory, All Saints' Close, Ruskington, Sleaford NG34 9FP* Tel (01526) 832463 Mobile 07813-954043 E-mail chris@cpennock.fsnet.co.uk

PENNY, Alexander Stuart Egerton. b 52. Wolv Art Coll BA75. Ridley Hall Cam MA00. **d** 00 **p** 01. C Uttoxeter Area *Lich* 00-03; V Crosthwaite Keswick *Carl* from 03. *Crosthwaite Vicarage, Vicarage Hill, Keswick CA12 5QB* Tel (01768) 772509 E-mail stuartpenny@onetel.com

PENNY, David Roy. b 67. Wilson Carlile Coll 89 N Ord Course 00. **d** 03 **p** 04. C Hey *Man* from 03; C Waterhead from 03. *91 New Street, Lees, Oldham OL4 3LP* Tel 0161-621 0104 E-mail dpennyca@aol.com

PENNY, Diana Eleanor. b 51. Open Univ BA87 Birm Univ DipEd96. Nor Ord Course 87. **d** 89 **p** 94. NSM Gillingham w Geldeston, Stockton, Ellingham etc *Nor* 89-93; NSM Upton St Leonards *Glouc* 93-97; NSM Stiffkey and Cockthorpe w Morston, Langham etc *Nor* 97-03; NSM Stiffkey and Bale 03-04; C Lowestoft St Marg from 04. *5 Magdalen Close, Lowestoft NR32 4TP* Tel (01502) 564651 E-mail dep@dialstart.net

PENNY, Edwin John. b 43. Leeds Univ BA64. Coll of Resurr Mirfield 64. **d** 66 **p** 67. C Acocks Green *Birm* 66-69; C Wombourne *Lich* 69-71; C Wednesbury St Paul Wood Green 71-74; V Kingshurst *Birm* 74-79; Chapl All Hallows Convent Norfolk 79-82; Hon Chapl Overgate Hospice Yorkshire 82-84; Hon C Raveningham *Nor* 84-90; All Hallows Hosp Nor Past Team 90-93; P-in-c Upton St Leonards *Glouc* 93-97; Dioc Communications Officer 93-97; P-in-c Stiffkey and Cockthorpe w Morston, Langham etc *Nor* 97-03; P-in-c Gunthorpe w Bale w Field Dalling, Saxlingham etc 99-03; R Stiffkey and Bale 03-04; rtd 04; Perm to Offic *Nor* from 04. *5 Magdalen Close, Lowestoft NR32 4TP* Tel (01502) 564651

PENNY, Michael John. b 36. Linc Th Coll 78. **d** 80 **p** 81. C Knighton St Mary Magd *Leic* 80-83; TV Leic Resurr 83-85; V Blackfordby 85-95; V Blackfordby and Woodville 95-00; RD Akeley W 88-93; rtd 00; Perm to Offic *Nor* from 00. *15 Sarah's Road, Hunstanton PE36 5PA* Tel (01485) 534957

PENNY, Stuart. *See* PENNY, Alexander Stuart Egerton

PENRITH, Suffragan Bishop of. *See* NEWCOME, The Rt Revd James William Scobie

PENTELOW, Mrs Ysmena Rachael. b 73. St Andr Univ BD96 MLitt99. EAMTC 01. **d** 03 **p** 04. C Stevenage H Trin *St Alb* from 03. *413 Scarborough Avenue, Stevenage SG1 2QA* Tel (01707) 331053 Mobile 07798-654194 E-mail pentelow@waitrose.com

PENTLAND, Raymond Jackson. b 57. Wm Booth Memorial Coll CertEd79 Open Univ BA90 Westmr Coll Ox MTh02. St Jo Coll Nottm 86. **d** 88 **p** 89. C Nottingham St Jude *S'well* 88-90; Chapl RAF 90-05; Command Chapl RAF from 05. *Chaplaincy Services (RAF), HQ, Personnel and Training Command, RAF Innsworth, Gloucester GL3 1EZ* Tel (01452) 712612 ext 5164 Fax 510828 E-mail r.pentland@btopenworld.com

PENTREATH, Canon Harvey. b 29. Wells Th Coll 54. **d** 57 **p** 58. C Bris St Ambrose Whitehall *Bris* 57-60; C Leatherhead *Guildf* 60-63; C Haslemere 63-65; R Elstead 65-72; V Cuddington 73-80; Hon Can Guildf Cathl 80; V Helston *Truro* 80-85; RD Kerrier 84-86; TR Helston and Wendron 85-92; Hon Can Truro Cathl 88-92; rtd 93; Perm to Offic *Truro* from 93. *Penmarr, 15 Penarwyn Crescent, Heamoor, Penzance TR18 3JU* Tel (01736) 360133

PEOPLES, James Scott. b 59. TCD BA DipTh HDipEd90. **d** 85 **p** 86. C Carlow w Urglin and Staplestown *C & O* 85-90; Chapl Kilkenny Coll 90-91; I Portarlington w Cloneyhurke and Lea *M & K* 91-99; Dioc Youth Officer (Kildare) 92-99; I Lucan w Leixlip *D & G* from 99. *5 Uppercross, Ballyowen Lane, Ballydowd, Lucan, Co Dublin, Irish Republic* Tel (00353) (1) 624 9147

PEPPER, David Reginald. b 50. Lon Bible Coll. St Alb Minl Tr Scheme 89. **d** 92 **p** 93. NSM Cheshunt *St Alb* 92-95. *36 Salisbury Road, Hoddesdon EN11 0HX* Tel (01992) 410544

PEPPER, Leonard Edwin. b 44. Ex Univ BA71. Ripon Hall Ox 71. **d** 73 **p** 74. C Cottingham *York* 73-76; C Kingshurst *Birm* 76-79; Dir Past Studies St Steph Ho Ox 80-89; TV Aylesbury w Bierton and Hulcott *Ox* 89-91; TV High Wycombe 91-96; rtd 96. *19 Gardiner Street, Oxford OX3 7AW* Tel (01865) 66191

PEPPIATT, Martin Guy. b 33. Trin Coll Ox BA57 MA60. Wycliffe Hall Ox 57. **d** 59 **p** 60. C St Marylebone All So w SS Pet and Jo *Lon* 59-63; Kenya 65-69; V E Twickenham St Steph *Lon* 69-96; rtd 96. *Pipers Cottage, East End, North Leigh, Witney OX29 8ND* Tel (01993) 883001

PEPPIATT, Quintin Brian Duncombe. b 63. Ex Univ BSc85 St Luke's Coll Ex PGCE86. Ripon Coll Cuddesdon 89 Ch Div Sch of the Pacific (USA) 90. **d** 92 **p** 93. C Gt Ilford St Clem and St Marg *Chelmsf* 92-95; TV E Ham w Upton Park St Alb from 95. *1 Norman Road, London E6 6HN* Tel (020) 8471 8751 E-mail quintinpeppiatt@aol.com

PERCIVAL, Brian Sydney. b 37. Univ of Wales (Ban) BA61. N Ord Course 81. **d** 84 **p** 85. NSM Norbury *Ches* 84-88; P-in-c Werneth 88-04; RD Chadkirk 00-04; rtd 04. *21 Holly Road, High Lane, Stockport SK6 8HW* Tel (01663) 810217

PERCIVAL, Geoffrey. b 46. Ridley Hall Cam 73. **d** 76 **p** 77. C Eccleshill *Bradf* 76-79; C Otley 79-82; V Windhill 82-02; P-in-c Oakenshaw cum Woodlands from 03. *St Andrew's Vicarage, 589 Bradford Road, Bradford BD12 7EJ* Tel (01274) 608173

PERCIVAL, James Edward Charles. b 50. N Ord Course 92. **d** 95 **p** 96. C Broughton *Blackb* 95-99; P-in-c Blackb St Steph 99-03; P-in-c Freckleton from 03; Chapl E Lancs Hosps NHS Trust from 99. *Holy Trinity Vicarage, 3 Sunnyside Close, Freckleton, Preston PR4 1YJ* Tel (01772) 632209

PERCIVAL, James Frederick. b 74. New Coll Ox BA96 MA01 Barrister-at-Law (Middle Temple) 99. Ripon Coll Cuddesdon MA02. **d** 03 **p** 04. C Redhill St Matt *S'wark* from 03. *44 Ridgeway Road, Redhill RH1 6PH* Tel (01737) 213681 E-mail james.percival@fish.co.uk

PERCIVAL, Joanna Vera. b 52. Univ of San Francisco BA87. Ch Div Sch of Pacific MDiv94. **d** 94 **p** 94. Asst to R Almaden USA 94-95; NSM Ockham w Hatchford *Guildf* 95-96; C Cobham 96-00; Dioc Spirituality Adv 00-02; V Weston from 02. *All Saints' Vicarage, 1 Chestnut Avenue, Esher KT10 8JL* Tel (020) 8972 9118 E-mail joanna.percival@tesco.net

PERCIVAL, Martin Eric. b 45. Lon Univ BSc66 Linacre Coll Ox BA70 MA74. Wycliffe Hall Ox 67. **d** 70 **p** 71. C Anfield St Marg *Liv* 70-73; C Witney *Ox* 73-74; TV Bottesford w Ashby *Linc* 74-76; TV Grantham 76-80; R Coningsby w Tattershall 80-82; P-in-c Coleford w Holcombe *B & W* 82-83; V 83-84; Chapl Rossall Sch Fleetwood 84-88; Chapl Woodbridge Sch 88-02; R Downham w S Hanningfield *Chelmsf* 02-05; P-in-c Ramsden Bellhouse 02-05; P-in-c Leiston *St E* from 05. *St Margaret's Vicarage, 2 King Edward Road, Leiston IP16 4HQ* Tel (01728) 833408 E-mail revmepercival@lycos.co.uk

PERCIVAL, Richard Thomas. b 33. Edin Coll of Art Dip Town Planning 67 MRICS59 MRTPI67 FRICS71. Edin Dioc NSM Course 79. **d** 91 **p** 98. S Africa 91-94; RD Adnry of Kokstad 93-94; NSM Edin St Ninian *Edin* 94-01; rtd 01; Perm to Offic *Edin* from 01. *2/1 Fettes Rise, Edinburgh EH4 1QH* Tel 0131-552 5271 E-mail rtpercival@netscapeonline.co.uk

PERCIVAL, Robert Standring. b 27. Sheff Univ BA55 Aston Univ Dip Counselling 83. Qu Coll Birm 57. **d** 59 **p** 60. C Lightbowne *Man* 59-62; C Prestwich St Marg 62-63; V Pendlebury St Aug 63-68; Lect Glos Coll of Arts and Tech 68-93; NSM Glouc St Mary de Crypt w St Jo and Ch Ch *Glouc* 68-82; Perm to Offic 82-97 and from 01; rtd 92. *5 Firwood Drive, Gloucester GL4 0AB* Tel (01452) 522739

PERCY, Brian. b 34. **d** 93 **p** 94. OLM Walton *St E* 93-00; OLM Walton and Trimley 00-04; rtd 04; Perm to Offic *St E* from 04. *16 Lynwood Avenue, Felixstowe IP11 9HS* Tel (01394) 286782

PERCY, Christopher. *See* HEBER PERCY, Canon Christopher John

PERCY, Donald. b 45. Kelham Th Coll 66. **d** 71 **p** 72. C Hendon St Ignatius *Dur* 71-75; C Gorton St Mary and St Thos *Man* 75-77; C Middlesbrough St Thos *York* 77-82; Guyana 82-86;

P-in-c S Moor *Dur* 86-90; V 90-95; rtd 05. *8 Ritson Street, Stanley DH9 0NH* Tel (01207) 233918

PERCY, Mrs Emma Margaret. b 63. Jes Coll Cam BA85 MA89 St Jo Coll Dur BA89. Cranmer Hall Dur 87. **d** 90 **p** 94. C Bedford St Andr *St Alb* 90-94; Chapl Anglia Poly Univ *Ely* 94-97; P-in-c Millhouses H Trin *Sheff* 97-03; V 03-04; Chapl Trin Coll Ox from 05. *2 Orchard View, High Street, Cuddesdon, Oxford OX44 9HP* Tel (01865) 876211 E-mail mpercy@fish.co.uk *or* emma.percy@pmb.ox.ac.uk

PERCY, Gordon Reid. b 46. St Jo Coll Dur BA68 DipTh70. Cranmer Hall Dur 69. **d** 71 **p** 72. C Flixton St Jo *Man* 71-76; C Charlesworth *Derby* 76-77; P-in-c 77-87; P-in-c Dinting Vale 80-87; V Long Eaton St Jo 87-98; RD Ilkeston 92-98; R Torquay St Matthias, St Mark and H Trin *Ex* from 98. *The Rectory, Wellswood Avenue, Torquay TQ1 2QE* Tel (01803) 293280 *or* 214175 E-mail gordonpercy@minister.com *or* stmathiaschurch@minister.com

PERCY, Prof Martyn William. b 62. Bris Univ BA84 K Coll Lon PhD92 Sheff Univ MEd St Jo Coll Dur CCSk90. Cranmer Hall Dur 88. **d** 90 **p** 91. C Bedford St Andr *St Alb* 90-94; Chapl and Dir Th and RS Ch Coll Cam 94-97; Dir Th and RS SS Coll Cam 95-97; Dir Linc Th Inst 97-04; Hon C Millhouses H Trin *Sheff* 97-04; Hon Can Sheff Cathl 97-04; Can Th from 04; Sen Lect Relig and Soc Sheff Univ 97-00; Reader 00-02; Reader Man Univ 02-04; Prin Ripon Coll Cuddesdon from 04; Prof Th and Min Hartford Sem Connecticut from 02; Prof Th Educn K Coll Lon from 04. *Ripon College, Cuddesdon, Oxford OX44 9EX* Tel (01865) 874404 Fax 875431 Mobile 07941-072542 E-mail mpercy@ripon-cuddesdon.ac.uk *or* mpercy@hartsem.edu

PERDUE, Ernon Cope Todd. b 30. TCD BA52 MA BD56 MEd73 UCD Dip Psychology 76 MPsychSc80. TCD Div Sch 53. **d** 54 **p** 55. C Dublin Drumcondra w N Strand *D & G* 54-58; C Dublin Booterstown w Carysfort 58-60; Dean of Res TCD 60-68; C-in-c Dublin St Mark *D & G* 66-68; C-in-c Dublin St Steph 68-69; I Rathmichael 69-76; Careers Counsellor Wicklow Voc Sch 76-82; I Limerick *L & K* 82-87; Can Limerick Cathl 82-87; Dean Killaloe, Kilfenora and Clonfert 87-95; I Killaloe w Stradbally 87-95; rtd 95. *177 The Ash, Charleville Square Apt, Butterfield Avenue, Rathfarnham, Dublin, Irish Republic* Tel (00353) (1) 495 6061 Mobile 86-278 0354 E-mail eperdue@gofree.indigo.ie *or* ernonandheather@hotmail.com

PEREIRA, Melvyn Christopher. b 52. Oak Hill Th Coll BA04. **d** 04 **p** 05. C Kettering Ch the King *Pet* from 04. *9 Churchill Way, Kettering NN15 5DP* Tel (01536) 485772 Mobile 07810-816744 E-mail melvyn02@yahoo.co.uk

PERERA, Ms Chandrika Kumudhini. b 61. Qu Coll Birm. **d** 03 **p** 04. C Luton All SS w St Pet *St Alb* from 03. *St Peter's House, Harefield Road, Luton LU1 1TH* Tel (01582) 413706 E-mail chandy@fish.co.uk

PERERA, George Anthony. b 51. Edin Univ BD74. Linc Th Coll 74. **d** 76 **p** 77. Chapl Mabel Fletcher Tech Coll Liv 76-79; C Wavertree H Trin *Liv* 76-79; TV Maghull 79-94; V Hunts Cross 94-04; Chapl Park Lane Hosp Maghull 79-89; Asst Chapl Ashworth Hosp Maghull 89-04; Chapl R Liverpool and Broadgreen Univ Hosps NHS Trust from 05. *Broadgreen Hospital, Thomas Drive, Liverpool L14 3LB* Tel 0151-282 6000 Fax 254 2070

✠**PERHAM, The Rt Revd Michael Francis.** b 47. Keble Coll Ox BA74 MA78. Cuddesdon Coll 74. **d** 76 **p** 77 **c** 04. C Addington *Cant* 76-81; Bp's Dom Chapl *Win* 81-84; Sec C of E Doctrine Commn 79-84; TR Oakdale *Sarum* 84-92; Prec and Can Res Nor Cathl *Nor* 92-98; Provost Derby 98-00; Dean Derby 00-04; Bp Glouc from 04. *Bishopscourt, Pitt Street, Gloucester GL1 2BQ* Tel (01452) 410022 ext 271 Fax 308324 E-mail bshpglos@glosdioc.org.uk

PERKES, Brian Robert Keith. b 46. St Andr Univ BSc68. N Ord Course 91. **d** 94 **p** 95. NSM Witton *Ches* 94-98; Bp's Chapl 98-00; P-in-c Ashton Hayes from 98; P-in-c Delamere from 00. *The Vicarage, Church Road, Ashton, Chester CH3 8AB* Tel (01829) 751265 E-mail brkperkes@tinyworld.co.uk

PERKIN, David Arthur. b 30. Pemb Coll Ox BA54 MA58. Linc Th Coll 54. **d** 56 **p** 57. C St John's Wood *Lon* 56-61; Chapl Loughb Univ *Leic* 61-84; V Paddington St Jas *Lon* 84-92; rtd 92. *14 Englewood Road, London SW12 9NZ*

PERKIN, Jonathan Guy. b 52. Westmr Coll Ox BEd76. Trin Coll Bris 89. **d** 91 **p** 92. C Cullompton *Ex* 91-96; C Ashtead *Guildf* 96-01; V Egham 01-05; V Churchdown *Glouc* from 05. *The Vicarage, 5 Vicarage Close, Churchdown, Gloucester GL3 2NE* Tel (01452) 713203 E-mail jjperkin@btconnect.com

PERKIN, Paul John Stanley. b 50. Ch Ch Ox BA71 MA75 CertEd. Wycliffe Hall Ox 78. **d** 80 **p** 81. C Gillingham St Mark *Roch* 80-84; C Brompton H Trin w Onslow Square St Paul *Lon* 84-87; P-in-c Battersea Rise St Mark *S'wark* 87-92; V from 92; P-in-c Battersea St Pet and St Paul from 00. *St Mark's Vicarage, 7 Elsynge Road, London SW18 2HW* Tel (020) 8874 6023 *or* 7223 6188 E-mail mark.mail@ukonline.co.uk

PERKINS, Canon Alban Leslie Tate. b 08. Kelham Th Coll 28. **d** 34 **p** 35. SSM from 33; C Nottingham St Geo w St Jo *S'well* 34-37 and 68-72; S Africa 37-67 and 76-80; Can Bloemfontein Cathl from 52; Lesotho 72-76; Perm to Offic *Man* 81-86 and *Blackb* 86-90. *The Homestead, Prestwood, Stourbridge DY7 5AN* Tel (01384) 872555

PERKINS, Colin Blackmore. b 35. FCII65. Lon Coll of Div 68. **d** 70 **p** 71. C Hyson Green *S'well* 70-73; V Clarborough w Hayton 73-79; P-in-c Cropwell Bishop 79-84; P-in-c Colston Bassett 79-84; P-in-c Granby w Elton 79-84; P-in-c Langar 79-84; V Tithby w Cropwell Butler 79-84; R Cropwell Bishop w Colston Bassett, Granby etc 84-94; P-in-c Sutton Bonington w Normanton-on-Soar 94-01; rtd 01; Perm to Offic *Newc* from 01. *6 Ravensmede, Alnwick NE66 2PX* Tel (01665) 510445 E-mail cperk68836@aol.com

PERKINS, David. b 51. Sarum & Wells Th Coll. **d** 87 **p** 88. C New Mills *Derby* 87-90; V Marlpool 90-95; P-in-c Turnditch 95-02; Min in charge Belper Ch Ch and Milford 95-02; V Belper Ch Ch w Turnditch from 02; RD Duffield from 97; Chapl S Derbyshire Community and Mental Health Trust from 95. *Christ Church Vicarage, Bridge Street, Belper DE56 1BA* Tel (01773) 824974 E-mail revdaveperkins@aol.com

PERKINS, David John Elmslie. b 45. Dur Univ BA66 DipTh68 ATII75. Cranmer Hall Dur 66. **d** 69 **p** 70. C Wadsley *Sheff* 69-71; C Shortlands *Roch* 71-73; Perm to Offic *Lon* 76-78; *B & W* 78-80 and from 02; Lic to Offic 80-02; rtd 02. *Rainbow's End, Montacute Road, Stoke-sub-Hamdon TA14 6UQ* Tel (01935) 823314

PERKINS, Miss Julia Margaret. b 49. Linc Th Coll 85. **d** 87 **p** 94. Par Dn Owton Manor *Dur* 87-89; Par Dn Leam Lane 89-94; C 94; P-in-c Stockton St Chad 94-96; V 96-00; C Eppleton and Hetton le Hole from 00. *Lyons Rectory, High Street, Easington Lane, Houghton le Spring DH5 0JN* Tel 0191-526 8918

PERKINS, Julian John. b 67. Southn Univ BSc90 MSc92. Trin Coll Bris BA00 MPhil03. **d** 01 **p** 02. C Thornbury *Glouc* 01-04; C Tewkesbury w Walton Cardiff and Twyning from 04. *43 Cypress Road, Walton Cardiff, Tewkesbury GL20 7RB* Tel (01684) 292031 E-mail julian.perkins@zen.co.uk

PERKINS, Malcolm Bryan. b 20. SS Coll Cam BA41 MA45. Wycliffe Hall Ox 41. **d** 43 **p** 44. C Rainham *Roch* 43-47; C Bexley St Jo 47-50; P-in-c Chalk 50-51; V 51-56; V Borstal 56-61; Chapl St Bart Hosp Roch 59-74; P-in-c Strood St Mary *Roch* 61-65; R Wouldham 65-73; Chapl Medway Hosp Gillingham 65-67; Toc H Staff Padre (SE Region) 73-85; Hon C Roch 74-85; rtd 85; Perm to Offic *Roch* from 85 and *Cant* 85-04. *Roke Cottage, 3 Belgrave Terrace, Laddingford, Maidstone ME18 6BP* Tel (01622) 871774

PERKINS, Patricia Doris (Sister Patricia). b 29. Gilmore Ho 60. **dss** 73 **d** 87 **p** 01. CSA from 71; Sherston Magna w Easton Grey *Bris* 73-75; Cant St Martin and St Paul *Cant* 76-78; Kilburn St Aug w St Jo *Lon* 80-84; Abbey Ho Malmesbury 84-87; Hon Par Dn Bayswater 87-94; Chapl St Mary's Hosp Praed Street Lon 88-89; Chapl St Chas Hosp Ladbroke Grove 88-89; Dean of Women's Min *Lon* from 89; Dioc Dir of Ords 90-94; Hon Par Dn St Olave Hart Street w All Hallows Staining etc 94-01. *8/9 Verona Court, London W4 2JD* Tel (020) 8987 2799

PERKINSON, Neil Donald. b 46. Wycliffe Hall Ox 84. **d** 85 **p** 86. C Workington St Jo *Carl* 85-88; TV Cockermouth w Embleton and Wythop 88-93; TV St Laur in Thanet *Cant* 93-01; P-in-c Darlaston All SS *Lich* from 01; Ind Chapl Black Country Urban Ind Miss from 01. *All Saints' Vicarage, Walsall Road, Wednesbury WS10 9SQ* Tel 0121-526 6898 *or* (01902) 710407 E-mail n.perkinson@btinternet.com

PERKINTON, Keith Glyn. b 61. Humberside Poly BA83 Leeds Univ BA92. Coll of Resurr Mirfield 93. **d** 93 **p** 94. C Knowle H Nativity *Bris* 93-97; TV Brighton Resurr *Chich* 97-05; P-in-c Hangleton from 05. *The Vicarage, 127 Hangleton Way, Hove BN3 8ER* Tel (01273) 413044

PERKS, David Leonard Irving. b 38. Avery Hill Coll TCert61 Sussex Univ MA76. S Dios Minl Tr Scheme 84. **d** 87 **p** 88. NSM Lewes All SS, St Anne, St Mich and St Thos *Chich* 87-91; Chapl HM Pris Lewes 91-94; NSM Deanery of Lewes and Seaford *Chich* 94-96; C Peacehaven and Telscombe Cliffs 96-00; C Telscombe w Piddinghoe and Southease 96-00; rtd 00; Asst to RD Lewes and Seaford *Chich* from 00; Chapl S Downs Health NHS Trust from 01. *45 Fitzjohn Road, Lewes BN7 1PR* Tel (01273) 478719

PERKS, Edgar Harold Martin. b 31. Open Univ BA87. Glouc Sch of Min 85. **d** 88 **p** 89. NSM Bromfield *Heref* 88-89; NSM Culmington w Onibury 88-89; NSM Stanton Lacy 88-89; NSM Culmington w Onibury, Bromfield etc 90-98; Perm to Offic from 98. *The Oaklands, Bromfield Road, Ludlow SY8 1DW* Tel (01584) 875525

PERRENS, Everard George. b 15. St Cath Coll Cam BA37 MA42. Linc Th Coll 40. **d** 42 **p** 43. C Rugby St Andr *Cov* 42-44; CF 44-47; CMS 47-65; Uganda 47-65; Chapl St Marg Sch Bushey 65-74; Hon C Earlsdon *Cov* 75-79 and 80-83; C Allesley Park 79-80; rtd 80; Perm to Offic *Cov* from 83. *2 Beechwood Court, Rochester Road, Earlsdon, Coventry CV5 6AE* Tel (024) 7671 2821 E-mail perrenseg@ukf.net

PERRETT, David Thomas. b 48. Cranmer Hall Dur 80. **d** 82 **p** 83. C Stapleford *S'well* 82-86; V Ollerton 86-87; P-in-c Boughton 86-87; V Ollerton w Boughton 87-93; V Winklebury *Win* 93-05; P-in-c Gresley *Derby* from 05. *The Vicarage, 120 Church Street, Church Gresley, Swadlincote DE11 9NR* Tel (01283) 223983 E-mail dtp@dperrett.freeserve.co.uk

PERRETT, Mrs Jill. b 59. Trent Poly BA80 Leeds Poly CQSW82. STETS 99. **d** 02 **p** 03. C Mere w W Knoyle and Maiden Bradley *Sarum* from 02. *6 Ash Grove, Mere, Warminster BA12 6BX* Tel (01747) 861223 E-mail revjperrett@tiscali.co.uk

PERRICONE, Vincent James. b 50. Connecticut Univ BA74 Pontifical Univ Rome STB88 STL90 Glas Univ PhD98. **d** 89 **p** 90. In RC Ch 89-94; C Glas St Mary *Glas* 94-95; P-in-c Glas All SS and Glas H Cross 95-03. *Address temp unknown*

PERRIN, Michael Leonard. b 47. Shenstone Coll of Educn CertEd66 Lanc Univ BEd71. Dioc OLM tr scheme 97. **d** 01 **p** 02. OLM Aspull St Eliz *Liv* from 01. *21 Firs Park Crescent, Aspull, Wigan WN2 2SJ* Tel (01942) 257418 E-mail mikeperrin99@hotmail.com

PERRINS, Christopher Neville. b 68. St Steph Ho Ox 01. **d** 03 **p** 04. C Warrington St Elphin *Liv* from 03. *41 Parr Street, Warrington WA1 2JN* Tel (01925) 419211 E-mail revdcnperrins@aol.com

PERRINS, Harold. b 21. Kelham Th Coll 38. **d** 44 **p** 45. C Fenton *Lich* 44-49; C Talke 49-53; R Armitage 53-61; V Lapley w Wheaton Aston 61-65; V Priorslee 65-69; R Harlaston and V Edingale 69-77; V Shobnall 77-86; rtd 86; Perm to Offic *Lich* from 86. *20 Meadow Rise, Barton under Needwood, Burton-on-Trent DE13 8DT* Tel (01283) 713515

PERRINS, Mrs Lesley. b 53. St Hugh's Coll Ox BA74 S Bank Poly DCG75. S Dios Minl Tr Scheme CECM93. **d** 93 **p** 95. NSM Stoneleigh *Guildf* 93-94; NSM Haxby w Wigginton *York* 94-00; Asst Chapl York Health Services NHS Trust 99-00. *37 St John's Rise, Woking GU21 7PN* Tel (01483) 761427

PERRIS, Anthony. b 48. Univ of Wales (Abth) BSc69 Selw Coll Cam BA76 MA79. Ridley Hall Cam 74. **d** 77 **p** 78. C Sandal St Helen *Wakef* 77-80; C Plymouth St Andr w St Paul and St Geo *Ex* 80-87; TV Yeovil *B & W* 87-88; V Preston Plucknett from 88. *St James's Vicarage, 1 Old School Close, Yeovil BA21 3UB* Tel (01935) 429398 E-mail antonyperris@yahoo.com

PERRIS, John Martin. b 44. Liv Univ BSc66 Bris Univ DipTh70. Trin Coll Bris 69. **d** 72 **p** 73. C Sevenoaks St Nic *Roch* 72-76; C Bebington *Ches* 76-79; V Redland *Bris* 79-97; RD Horfield 91-97; R Barton Seagrave w Warkton *Pet* from 97. *The Rectory, St Botolph's Road, Kettering NN15 6SR* Tel (01536) 513629 *or* 414052 E-mail st.botolphs@ukgateway.net

PERROTT, John Alastair Croome. b 36. Univ of NZ LLB60. Clifton Th Coll 62. **d** 64 **p** 65. C Tunbridge Wells St Pet *Roch* 64-67; C Stanford-le-Hope *Chelmsf* 67-78; R Elmswell *St E* 78-02; rtd 02; Perm to Offic *St E* from 02. *7 Millfield Road, Barningham, Bury St Edmunds IP31 1DX* Tel (01359) 221909

PERRY, Alan David. b 64. Avery Hill Coll BA86 Lon Inst of Educn PGCE87 Greenwich Univ MA99. NTMTC 01. **d** 03 **p** 04. NSM Romford St Edw *Chelmsf* from 03. *1A Lyndhurst Drive, Hornchurch RM11 1JL* Tel (01708) 437852 Mobile 07946-730291 E-mail alan.perry80@ntlworld.com

PERRY, Andrew John. b 65. Wilson Carlile Coll St Steph Ho Ox BTh00. **d** 00 **p** 01. C Southwick St Mich *Chich* 00-03; P-in-c Upper St Leonards St Jo 03; R from 03. *St John's Rectory, 53 Brittany Road, St Leonards-on-Sea TN38 0RD* Tel (01424) 423367 Mobile 07900-981345 E-mail perry.rickard@virgin.net

PERRY, Andrew Nicholas. b 62. Westmr Coll Ox BA86. Trin Coll Bris MA91. **d** 91 **p** 92. C Bath Weston All SS w N Stoke *B & W* 91-93; C Bath Weston All SS w N Stoke and Langridge 93-95; P-in-c Longfleet *Sarum* 95-00; V from 00. *The Vicarage, 32 Alverton Avenue, Poole BH15 2QJ* Tel (01202) 723359 *or* tel and fax 253527 E-mail andrewperry@ukgateway.net

PERRY, Andrew William. b 44. R Agric Coll Cirencester NDA65 MRAC65 ADFM66. WMMTC 91. **d** 94 **p** 95. NSM Redmarley D'Abitot, Bromesberrow, Pauntley etc *Glouc* from 94. *Rye Cottage, Broomsgreen, Dymock GL18 2DP* Tel (01531) 890489 Fax 632552 E-mail aw@perry.net

PERRY, Anthony Henry. b 54. Leic Univ BA76. Aston Tr Scheme 89 Linc Th Coll 93. **d** 93 **p** 94. C Bartley Green *Birm* 93-97; V Bearwood from 97. *St Mary's Vicarage, 27 Poplar Avenue, Birmingham B17 8EG* Tel 0121-429 2165 E-mail trinity20@btopenworld.co.uk

PERRY, Anthony Robert. b 21. Birkbeck Coll Lon 39 Natal Univ 40. Kelham Th Coll 48. **d** 52 **p** 53. SSM 52-01; C Sheff St Cecilia Parson Cross *Sheff* 52-56; S Africa 56-59 and 70-88; Min Modderpoort St Aug 56-58 and 83-88; Lesotho 59-70; Min Ha Chooko St Jas 59; Min Teyateyaneng St Agnes 60; Min Morija 66-67 and 76; Chapl Natal Univ 70-74 and 76-77; Melbourne Australia 75; Asst P Durban St Paul 78; Chapl Addington Hosp Durban 79-82; Chapl Chich Th Coll 88-90; Willen Priory 90-92; St Ant Priory 92-97; Vassall Road Priory 98-99; Warminster Priory 99; Perm to Offic *S'wark* from 98 and *Sarum* from 01. *2 Saxon's Acre, Warminster BA12 8HT* Tel (01985) 212510 *or* tel and fax 308818

PERRY, Christopher Richard. b 78. St Jo Coll Dur BA00 Leeds Univ MA02. Coll of Resurr Mirfield 00. **d** 02 **p** 03. C Penzance St Mary w St Paul and St Jo *Truro* from 02. *11 Pendarves Road, Penzance TR18 2AJ* Tel (01736) 350979 E-mail father.perry@btopenworld.com

PERRY, Canon Colin Charles. b 16. K Coll Cam BA38 MA42. Westcott Ho Cam 39. **d** 40 **p** 41. C Champion Hill St Sav *S'wark* 40-42; C Redhill St Jo 42-44; Ghana 45-56; V Aldbourne *Sarum* 56-64; V Baydon 57-64; PC Salisbury St Fran 64-69; V 69-71; V Preston 71-81; RD Weymouth 75-79; Can and Preb Sarum Cathl 77-82; TR Preston w Sutton Poyntz and Osmington w Poxwell 81-82; rtd 82; Perm to Offic *Sarum* from 82. *6 The Ridgeway, Corfe Mullen, Wimborne BH21 3HS* Tel (01202) 697298

PERRY, David William. b 42. St Chad's Coll Dur BA64 DipTh66. **d** 66 **p** 67. C Middleton St Mary *Ripon* 66-69; C Bedale 69-71; C Marton-in-Cleveland *York* 71-75; V Skirlaugh w Long Riston, Rise and Swine from 75; N Humberside Ecum Officer from 75. *The Vicarage, Skirlaugh, Hull HU11 5HE* Tel (01964) 562259 E-mail david@perryskirlaugh.karoo.co.uk

PERRY, Edward John. b 35. AKC62. **d** 63 **p** 64. C Honicknowle *Ex* 63-65; C Ashburton w Buckland-in-the-Moor 65-70; V Cornwood 70-92; Asst Dir of Educn 71-92; Chapl Moorhaven Hosp 91-93; V Ermington and Ugborough *Ex* 92-00; rtd 00; Perm to Offic *Ex* from 01. *32 Finches Close, Elburton, Plymouth PL9 8DP* Tel (01752) 405364

PERRY, James Marcus. b 71. Ridley Hall Cam 02. **d** 04 **p** 05. C Cen Wolverhampton *Lich* from 04. *7 Merridale Avenue, Wolverhampton WV3 9RE* E-mail jimperry@operamail.com

PERRY, Mrs Joanna Teresa. b 60. K Coll Lon BD82. Trin Coll Bris ADMT96. **d** 96 **p** 00. C Thornbury *Glouc* 96-97; C Winchcombe, Gretton, Sudeley Manor etc 97-99; Sub Chapl HM Pris and YOI New Hall from 99. *HM Prison and YOI New Hall, Dial Wood, Flockton, Wakefield WF4 4AX* Tel (01924) 848307

✠**PERRY, The Rt Revd John Freeman.** b 35. Lon Coll of Div ALCD59 LTh74 MPhil86. **d** 59 **p** 60 **c** 89. C Woking Ch Ch *Guildf* 59-62; C Chorleywood Ch Ch *St Alb* 62; Min Chorleywood St Andr CD 63-66; V Chorleywood St Andr 66-77; RD Rickmansworth 72-77; Warden Lee Abbey 77-89; RD Shirwell *Ex* 80-84; Hon Can Win Cathl *Win* 89-96; Suff Bp Southampton 89-96; Bp Chelmsf 96-03; rtd 03. *Foxbury, Gutch Common, Shaftesbury SP7 9AZ* Tel (01747) 828416

PERRY, John Neville. b 20. Leeds Univ BA41. Coll of Resurr Mirfield 41. **d** 43 **p** 44. C Poplar All SS w St Frideswide *Lon* 43-50; V De Beauvoir Town St Pet 50-63; V Feltham 63-75; RD Hounslow 67-75; Adn Middx 75-82; R Orlestone w Snave and Ruckinge w Warehorne *Cant* 82-86; rtd 86; Perm to Offic *Chich* from 90. *73 Elizabeth Crescent, East Grinstead RH19 3JG* Tel (01342) 315446

PERRY, John Walton Beauchamp. b 43. Ex Coll Ox BA64 Sussex Univ MA67. EAMTC 82 Westcott Ho Cam 84. **d** 85 **p** 86. C Shrewsbury St Chad w St Mary *Lich* 85-89; V Batheaston w St Cath *B & W* 89-99; V Milborne Port w Goathill from 99. *The Vicarage, Bathwell Lane, Milborne Port, Sherborne DT9 5AN* Tel (01963) 250248 E-mail jwbperry@hotmail.com

PERRY, Jonathan Robert. b 55. St Jo Coll Nottm DipTh. **d** 82 **p** 83. C Filey *York* 82-84; C Rayleigh *Chelmsf* 84-88; Asst Chapl St Geo Hosp Linc 88-90; Chapl Gateshead Hosps NHS Trust 90-98; Chapl Gateshead Health NHS Trust from 98. *Queen Elizabeth Hospital, Sheriff Hill, Gateshead NE9 6SX* Tel 0191-403 2072 *or* 482 0000 ext 2072

PERRY, Lesley Anne. b 52. K Coll Lon BA73 MIPR99. SEITE DipTh99. **d** 99 **p** 00. NSM Fulham All SS *Lon* from 99. *Flat 3, 76 Philbeach Gardens, London SW5 9EY* Tel (020) 7373 3085 *or* 7419 5404 E-mail lesley.perry@universitiesuk.ac.uk

PERRY, Mrs Lynne Janice. b 48. **d** 90 **p** 97. NSM Llanfair Mathafarn Eithaf w Llanbedrgoch *Ban* 90-97; C Bangor 97-99; TV from 99; I Tregarth from 04; AD Ogwen from 02. *Tre-wen, 39 Tal-y-Cae, Tregarth, Bangor LL57 4AE* Tel (01248) 600997

PERRY, Martin Herbert. b 43. Cranmer Hall Dur 66. **d** 70 **p** 71. C Millfield St Mark *Dur* 70-74; C Haughton le Skerne 74-77; V Darlington St Matt 77-79; V Darlington St Matt and St Luke 79-84; TR Oldland *Bris* 84-91; V 91-01; rtd 01. *Address withheld by request*

PERRY, Martyn. b 57. S Wales Bapt Coll DipTh85 DPS86 Coll of Resurr Mirfield 89. **d** 90 **p** 91. In Bapt Ch 85-89; C Hornsey St Mary w St Geo *Lon* 90-93; V Pontlottyn w Fochriw *Llan* 93-97; R Cilybebyll from 97. *The Rectory, 7 Cwmnantllwyd Road, Gellinudd, Pontardawe, Swansea SA8 3DT* Tel (01792) 862118

PERRY, Canon Michael Charles. b 33. Trin Coll Cam BA55 MA59. Westcott Ho Cam 56. **d** 58 **p** 59. C Baswich *Lich* 58-60; Chapl Ripon Hall Ox 61-63; Chief Asst Home Publishing SPCK 63-70; Can Res Dur Cathl *Dur* 70-98; Adn Dur 70-93; Bp's Sen Chapl 93-98; rtd 98. *57 Ferens Park, Durham DH1 1NU* Tel 0191-386 1891

PERRY, Michael James Matthew. b 66. Bris Univ BSc87 MSc89 PhD93. Trin Coll Bris BA99. **d** 99 **p** 00. C Keynsham *B & W*

99-03; R Cam Vale from 03. *The Rectory, Englands Lane, Queen Camel, Yeovil BA22 7NN* Tel (01935) 850326 E-mail michaelperry@firenet.uk.com

PERRY, The Very Revd Robert Anthony. b 21. Leeds Univ BA47. Coll of Resurr Mirfield 47. **d** 49 **p** 50. C Middlesbrough St Jo the Ev *York* 49-54; Prin St Aug Sch Betong Malaysia 54-60; Provost Kuching 60-66; R Hasfield w Tirley *Glouc* 66-69; Asst Chapl HM Pris Man 69; Chapl HM Pris Gartree 70-73; P-in-c Mottingham St Edw *S'wark* 73-75; P-in-c Miri St Columba Malaysia 75-77; Warden Coll of Epiphany Kuching 77-79; P-in-c Presteigne w Discoed *Heref* 80-83; R Presteigne w Discoed, Kinsham and Lingen 83-86; rtd 86; Perm to Offic *Heref* 87-93 and *Linc* from 95; Chapl Laslett's *Worc* 91-92; P-in-c Ryhall w Essendine *Pet* 94-95; P-in-c Ryhall w Essendine and Carlby 95-96. *7 Balk Road, Ryhall, Stamford PE9 4HT* Tel (01780) 763938

PERRY, Russell Lee. b 38. Worc Coll Ox BA60 MA64. Carl and Blackb Dioc Tr Inst 98. **d** 98 **p** 99. NSM Grasmere *Carl* 98-01; rtd 01; Perm to Offic *S'well* from 01. *Dumble Howe, 3 Byron Gardens, Southwell NG25 0DW* Tel (01636) 815813

PERRY, Timothy Richard. b 64. Trin Coll Bris BA93. **d** 93 **p** 95. C Abingdon *Ox* 93-97; New Life Outreach/Fit Lives 97-01; Mountaintop Life Coaching Canada from 01. *363 Stellar Drive, Kelowna BC, Canada, V1W 4K4* Tel (001) (250) 764 2881 E-mail timperry@mountaintopcoach.com

PERRY, Valerie Evelyn. b 39. Southn Univ CertEd59 Lon Univ DipRS85. S'wark Ord Course 82. **dss** 85 **d** 87 **p** 94. NSM Romford St Edw *Chelmsf* 85-89; Par Dn 89-91; Asst Chapl Middx Hosp Lon 92-94; Chapl S Kent Hosps NHS Trust 94-98; Hon C Aylesham w Adisham *Cant* 98-00; Hon C Nonington w Wymynswold and Goodnestone etc 98-00; rtd 99; Perm to Offic *Truro* from 01. *115 Century Close, St Austell PL25 3UZ* Tel (01726) 813658

PERRY, William Francis Pitfield. b 61. Keble Coll Ox BA84 MA87. Ripon Coll Cuddesdon 94. **d** 96 **p** 97. C Brockworth *Glouc* 96-01; P-in-c Millbrook *Win* from 01. *58 Shirley Avenue, Shirley, Southampton SO15 5NJ* Tel (023) 8070 1896 E-mail fr.will@icxc.org

PERRY-GORE, Canon Walter Keith. b 34. Univ of Wales (Lamp) BA59. Westcott Ho Cam 60. **d** 61 **p** 62. C St Austell *Truro* 61-64; R H Innocents Barbados 64-71; Canada from 71; R New Carlisle 71-74; R N Hatley 74-96; rtd 96. *1115 Rue Massawippi, North Hatley PQ, Canada, J0B 2C0* Tel (001) (819) 842 4665 Fax 842 2176

PERRYMAN, Preb David Francis. b 42. Brunel Univ BSc64. Oak Hill Th Coll 74. **d** 76 **p** 77. C Margate H Trin *Cant* 76-80; R Ardingly *Chich* 80-90; V Bath St Luke *B & W* from 90; RD Bath 96-03; Preb Wells Cathl from 01. *St Luke's Vicarage, Hatfield Road, Bath BA2 2BD* Tel (01225) 311904 Fax 400975 E-mail david@stlukebath.org.uk

PERRYMAN, Graham Frederick. b 56. Southn Univ BA78 Reading Univ PGCE80. Aston Tr Scheme 90 Trin Coll Bris DipHE94. **d** 94 **p** 95. C Hamworthy *Sarum* 94-98; P-in-c Moreton and Woodsford w Tincleton 98-02; R 02-04; TV Melbury from 04. *The Vicarage, Tollerford Lane, Higher Frome Vauchurch, Dorchester DT2 0AT* Tel and fax (01300) 320284 E-mail revgfp@btopenworld.com

PERRYMAN, James Edward. b 56. Lon Bible Coll BA85 Oak Hill Th Coll 86. **d** 88 **p** 89. C Gidea Park *Chelmsf* 88-91; C Becontree St Mary 91-94; Chapl Lyon *Eur* 94-00; R Allington and Maidstone St Pet *Cant* from 00; Dioc Ecum Officer from 02. *The Rectory, 35 Poplar Grove, Allington, Maidstone ME16 0DE* Tel (01622) 758704 E-mail jim@me16.com

PERRYMAN, Canon John Frederick Charles. b 49. Mert Coll Ox BA71 MA74 MInstGA98. Ridley Hall Cam 72. **d** 74 **p** 75. C Shortlands *Roch* 74-78; Asst Chapl St Geo Hosp Lon 78-82; Chapl Withington Hosp Man 83-94; Chapl S Man Univ Hosps NHS Trust from 94; Hon Can Man Cathl *Man* from 00. *Withington Hospital, Nell Lane, Manchester M20 2LR,* or *24 Alan Road, Withington, Manchester M20 4WG* Tel 0161-291 4800 *or* 445 8111

PERSSON, Matthew Stephen. b 60. Dundee Univ BSc82 Bris Univ MA98. Wycliffe Hall Ox 88. **d** 91 **p** 92. C Bath Twerton-on-Avon *B & W* 91-94; Chapl HM Pris Shepton Mallet 94-97; Perm to Offic *B & W* 97-98; C Shepton Mallet w Doulting 98-00. *Ham Manor, Bowlish, Shepton Mallet BA4 5JR*

✠**PERSSON, The Rt Revd William Michael Dermot.** b 27. Oriel Coll Ox BA51 MA55. Wycliffe Hall Ox 51. **d** 53 **p** 54 **c** 82. C S Croydon Em *Cant* 53-55; C Tunbridge Wells St Jo *Roch* 55-58; V S Mimms Ch Ch *Lon* 58-67; R Bebington *Ches* 67-79; V Knutsford St Jo and Toft 79-82; Suff Bp Doncaster *Sheff* 82-92; rtd 93; Asst Bp B & W from 93. *Ryalls Cottage, Burton Street, Marnhull, Sturminster Newton DT10 1PS* Tel (01258) 820452

PERTH, Archbishop of. *See* CARNLEY, The Most Revd Peter Frederick

PERTH, Provost of. *See* FARQUHARSON, The Very Revd Hunter Buchanan

PERU, Bishop of. *See* GODFREY, The Rt Revd Harold William

PERUMBALATH, John. b 66. Calicut Univ BA86 Union Bibl Sem Pune BD90 Osmania Univ Hyderabad MA93. Serampore Th Coll MTh93. **d** 94 **p** 95. C Calcutta St Jo India 94-95; V Calcutta St Jas 95-00; V Calcutta St Thos 00-01; C Beckenham St Geo *Roch* 02-05; TV Northfleet and Rosherville from 05. *St Mark's Vicarage, 123 London Road, Northfleet, Gravesend DA11 9NH* Tel (01474) 535814 E-mail jperumbalath@btopenworld.com

PESCOD, John Gordon. b 44. Leeds Univ BSc70. Qu Coll Birm DipTh71. **d** 72 **p** 73. C Camberwell St Geo *S'wark* 72-75; Chapl R Philanthropic Soc Sch Redhill 75-80; P-in-c Nunney w Wanstrow and Cloford *B & W* 80-84; R Nunney and Witham Friary, Marston Bigot etc 84-87; R Milverton w Halse and Fitzhead 87-93; V Frome St Jo and St Mary 93-00; V Frome St Jo 01; V Woodlands 93-01; RD Frome 97-01; V Castle Cary w Ansford from 01. *The Vicarage, Church Street, Castle Cary BA7 7EJ* Tel (01963) 351615 E-mail jjpescod@fish.co.uk

PESHAWAR, Bishop of. *See* RUMALSHAH, The Rt Revd Munawar Kenneth

PESKETT, Richard Howard. b 42. Selw Coll Cam BA64 MA67. Ridley Hall Cam 64. **d** 68 **p** 69. C Jesmond H Trin *Newc* 68-71; Singapore 71-91; Lect Trin Coll Bris from 91; Vice-Prin Trin Coll Bris from 98. *Trinity College, Stoke Hill, Bristol BS9 1JP* Tel 0117-968 2803 *or* 968 3996 Fax 968 7470 E-mail howard.peskett@trinity-bris.ac.uk

PESKETT, Timothy Lewis. b 64. St Kath Coll Liv BA86. Chich Th Coll BTh90. **d** 90 **p** 91. C Verwood *Sarum* 90-91; C Southsea H Spirit *Portsm* 91-95; TV Burgess Hill St Jo w St Edw *Chich* 95-00; V Burgess Hill St Edw from 00. *7 Bramble Gardens, Burgess Hill RH15 8UQ* Tel (01444) 241300

PESTELL, Robert Carlyle. b 54. Aston Tr Scheme 89 Linc Th Coll 91. **d** 93 **p** 94. C Matson *Glouc* 93-97; P-in-c Charfield 97-01; R Charfield and Kingswood from 02. *The Rectory, 36 Wotton Road, Charfield, Wotton-under-Edge GL12 8TG* Tel (01454) 260489

PETCH, Douglas Rodger. b 57. Nottm Univ BSc79. All Nations Chr Coll Cam DipRS81 St Jo Coll Nottm MTS95. **d** 94 **p** 94. Nigeria 94-96; C Pendleton *Man* 96-98; P-in-c Werneth 98-03; C Oldham St Paul 98-03; CMS from 03. *CMS, 157 Waterloo Road, London SE1 8XA* Tel (020) 7928 8681 E-mail rodger@petchr.freeserve.co.uk

PETER, Christopher Javed. b 51. Peshawar Univ BA75. Qu Coll Birm 94. **d** 96 **p** 97. C Darwen St Pet w Hoddlesden *Blackb* 96-98; C Accrington 98-99; C Burnley St Andr w St Marg and St Jas 99-05; Chapl R Liverpool and Broadgreen Univ Hosps NHS Trust from 05. *Royal Liverpool University Hospital, Prescot Street, Liverpool L7 8XP* Tel 0151-706 2826 E-mail christopher.peter@rlbuht.nhs.uk

PETER DOUGLAS, Brother. *See* NEEDHAM, Brother Peter Douglas

PETERBOROUGH, Bishop of. *See* CUNDY, The Rt Revd Ian Patrick Martyn

PETERBOROUGH, Dean of. *See* BUNKER, The Very Revd Michael

PETERKEN, Canon Peter Donald. b 28. K Coll Lon BD51 AKC51. **d** 52 **p** 53. C Swanley St Mary *Roch* 52-55 and 62-65; C Is of Dogs Ch Ch and St Jo w St Luke *Lon* 55-57; R S Perrott w Mosterton and Chedington *Sarum* 57-59; Br Guiana 59-62; R Killamarsh *Derby* 65-70; V Derby St Luke 70-90; RD Derby N 79-90; Hon Can Derby Cathl 85-95; R Matlock 90-95; rtd 95; Perm to Offic *Derby* from 95. *64 Brayfield Road, Littleover, Derby DE23 6GT* Tel (01332) 766285

PETERS, Bill. *See* PETERS, Canon Cyril John

PETERS, Carl Richard. b 62. Ripon Coll Cuddesdon 95. **d** 97 **p** 98. C Coventry Caludon *Cov* 97-01; V Gt Grimsby St Andr w St Luke and All SS *Linc* 01-02; TV Leek and Meerbrook *Lich* from 02. *All Saints Vicarage, Compton, Leek ST13 5PT* Tel (01538) 382588 E-mail carljackie@petersc.freeserve.co.uk

PETERS, The Very Revd Christopher Lind. b 56. Oak Hill Th Coll. **d** 82 **p** 83. C Knockbreda *D & D* 82-84; C Lisburn Ch Ch Cathl *Conn* 84-87; I Kilmocomogue Union *C, C & R* 87-93; P-in-c Beara 92-93; I Killiney Ballybrack *D & G* 93-98; Dean Ross *C, C & R* from 98; Chan Cork Cathl from 98; I Ross Union from 98. *The Deanery, Rosscarbery, Co Cork, Irish Republic* Tel (00353) (23) 48166 E-mail peters@esatclear.ie

PETERS, Canon Cyril John (Bill). b 19. Fitzw Ho Cam BA42 MA45. Chich Th Coll 40. **d** 42 **p** 43. C Brighton St Mich *Chich* 42-45 and 47-50; CF (EC) 45-47; Hon CF from 47; Chapl Brighton Coll 50-69; R Uckfield *Chich* 69-96; R Isfield 69-96; R Lt Horsted 69-96; RD Uckfield 73-96; Can and Preb Chich Cathl 81-89; rtd 96; Perm to Offic *Chich* from 96. *Canon's Lodge, 9 Calvert Road, Uckfield TN22 2DB* Tel (01825) 766397

PETERS, David Alexander. b 72. K Coll Lon BA94. St Steph Ho Ox BA98. **d** 99 **p** 00. C Paddington St Jas *Lon* 99-03; PV Westmr Abbey from 01; V Reading H Trin *Ox* from 03; V Reading St Mark from 03. *Holy Trinity Presbytery, 32 Baker Street, Reading RG1 7XY* Tel 0118-957 2650 E-mail frpeters@hotmail.com

PETERS, David Lewis. b 38. Ch Ch Ox BA62 MA66. Westcott Ho Cam 63. **d** 65 **p** 66. C Oldham St Mary w St Pet *Man* 65-69;

C Stand 70-74; P-in-c Hillock 70-74; V 74-82; V Haslingden w Haslingden Grane *Blackb* 82-88; rtd 88; Perm to Offic *Blackb* and *Man* from 88. *4 Laurel Mount, Sowerby Bridge HX6 2ET* Tel (01422) 836194

PETERS, Geoffrey John. b 51. BCom BSc MDiv MInstC(Glas). Oak Hill Th Coll 85 Gujranwala Th Sem 90. **d** 87 **p** 88. C Forest Gate St Sav w W Ham St Matt *Chelmsf* 87-90; C Wembley St Jo *Lon* 90-92; Chapl Wembley Hosp 90-92; TV Manningham *Bradf* 92-97; Res Scheme Manager Anchor Trust from 02. *Address temp unknown* E-mail peters379@hotmail.com

PETERS, John Peter Thomas. b 63. Keble Coll Ox BL85. Wycliffe Hall Ox BA91. **d** 95 **p** 96. C Brompton H Trin w Onslow Square St Paul *Lon* 95-99; P-in-c Bryanston Square St Mary w St Marylebone St Mark 00-04; R from 04. *73 Gloucester Place, London W1U 8JW* Tel (020) 7487 3224 *or* 7258 5042

PETERS, John Thomas. b 58. Connecticut Univ BA80. St Jo Coll Nottm 84. **d** 87 **p** 88. C Virginia Water *Guildf* 87-93; R Grand Rapids Ch Ch USA 93-00; R Eden Prairie St Alb from 00. *14434 Fairway Drive, Eden Prairie, MN 557344, USA* E-mail johnpeters@isd.net

PETERS, Canon Kenneth. b 54. Univ of Wales (Cardiff) DipTh77 Newport Univ Tokyo MBA88 Greenwich Univ MA02 MIW96 CNI95. St Mich Coll Llan 74. **d** 77 **p** 78. C Mountain Ash *Llan* 77-80; Asst Chapl Mersey Miss to Seamen 80-82; Chapl RNR from 80; Chapl Miss to Seamen Japan 82-89; Hon Can Kobe from 85; Chapl Supt Mersey Miss to Seamen 89-93; Justice and Welfare Sec from 94; Hon C St Mich Paternoster Royal *Lon* from 94. *The Mission to Seafarers, St Michael Paternoster Royal, College Hill, London EC4R 2RL* Tel (020) 7248 5202 Fax 7248 4761 E-mail justice@missiontoseafarers.org

PETERS, Malcolm John. b 71. Leic Univ BA92. Oak Hill Th Coll BA03. **d** 03 **p** 04. C Braintree *Chelmsf* from 03. *183 Notley Road, Braintree CM7 1HG* Tel (01376) 326755 E-mail malcolm.peters@ukgateway.net

PETERS, Marilyn Ann. b 49. Open Univ BA90 Bris Poly DMS92. Qu Coll Birm 96. **d** 98 **p** 99. C Blakenall Heath *Lich* 98-01; TV Cen Telford from 01. *The Vicarage, Church Road, Dawley, Telford TF4 2AS* Tel (01952) 501655 Mobile 07754-435272 E-mail marilyn.peters1@virgin.net

PETERS, Canon Michael. b 41. Chich Th Coll 75. **d** 77 **p** 78. C Redruth *Truro* 77-79; TV 79-80; TV Redruth w Lanner 80-82; R St Mawgan w St Ervan and St Eval 82-86; Chapl HM Pris Liv 86-87; Chapl HM Pris Bris 87-01; Hon Can Bris Cathl *Bris* 96-01; P-in-c Middlezoy and Othery and Moorlinch *B & W* from 01. *The Vicarage, North Lane, Othery, Bridgwater TA7 0QG* Tel (01823) 698953 E-mail mikesandra@ukgateway.net

PETERS, Robert David. b 54. BA76. Oak Hill Th Coll 78. **d** 79 **p** 80. C Hyde St Geo *Ches* 79-83; C Hartford 83-86; V Lindow 86-96; V Throop *Win* from 96; AD Bournemouth from 03. *St Paul's Vicarage, 1 Chesildene Avenue, Bournemouth BH8 0AZ* Tel (01202) 531064 E-mail rob.peters@ukgateway.net

PETERS, Stephen Eric. b 45. Westcott Ho Cam 74. **d** 77 **p** 78. C Wanstead St Mary *Chelmsf* 77-79; C Leigh-on-Sea St Marg 79-81; P-in-c Purleigh 81-82; P-in-c Cold Norton w Stow Maries 81-82; R Purleigh, Cold Norton and Stow Maries 83-84; V Bedford Park *Lon* 84-87; Perm to Offic *Ex* 87-88 and from 93; TR Totnes and Berry Pomeroy 88-90; Chapl Ex Sch 91-93; Chapl St Marg Sch Ex 91-93. *20 South Street, Totnes TQ9 5DZ* Tel (01803) 867199

PETERSEN, Miss Jennifer Elizabeth. b 55. Aus Nat Univ BA78. Moore Th Coll Sydney BTh82 Wycliffe Hall Ox 92. **d** 94 **p** 95. In Presbyterian Ch 85-94; C Elloughton and Brough w Brantingham *York* 94-96; C Ealing St Mary *Lon* 96-00; Chapl Thames Valley Univ 96-00; Chapl Qu Mary and Westf Coll from 00. *24 Sidney Square, London E1 2EY* Tel (020) 7791 1973 *or* 7882 3179 E-mail j.e.petersen@qmul.ac.uk

PETERSON, David Gilbert. Sydney Univ BA65 MA74 Lon Univ BD68 Man Univ PhD78. Moore Th Coll Sydney ThL68. **d** 68 **p** 69. Australia 68-75 and 80-96; C Manly St Matt 68-70; Lect Moore Th Coll 71-75; C Cheadle *Ches* 75-78; Sen Can and R Wollongong Cathl 80-84; Lect Moore Th Coll 84-96; Prin Oak Hill Th Coll from 96; Perm to Offic *Lon* and *St Alb* from 96. *Oak Hill Theological College, Chase Side, London N14 4PS* Tel (020) 8449 0467 Fax 8441 5996 E-mail davidp@oakhill.ac.uk

PETERSON, Dennis. b 25. Oak Hill Th Coll 51. **d** 54 **p** 55. C Leyton All SS *Chelmsf* 54-56; C Leeds St Geo *Ripon* 56-58; V E Brixton St Jude *S'wark* 58-91; rtd 91; Perm to Offic *Chelmsf* from 91. *79 Cavendish Gardens, Westcliff-on-Sea SS0 9XP* Tel (01702) 334400

PETERSON, Canon John Louis. b 42. Concordia Coll (USA) BA65. Harvard Div Sch STB68 Virginia Th Sem Hon DD93. **d** 76 **p** 77. USA 76-82; Dean St Geo Coll Jerusalem 82-94; Can Res 82-94; Hon Can from 95; Hon Can Kalamazoo from 82; Hon Prov Can Cant Cathl *Cant* from 95; Sec Gen ACC 95-04; Hon Can Kaduna from 99; Hon Can St Paul's Cathl *Lon* from 00. *Address temp unknown*

PETERSON, Paul John. b 67. Trin Coll Bris 94. **d** 97 **p** 98. C Burney Lane *Birm* 97-01; C-in-c Bradley Stoke N CD *Bris* from 01. *106 Cooks Close, Bradley Stoke, Bristol BS32 0BB* Tel (01454) 856947 E-mail paul@petersonp.freeserve.co.uk

PETFIELD, Bruce le Gay. b 34. FHA. NEOC 76. **d** 79 **p** 80. NSM Morpeth *Newc* 79-86; C Knaresborough *Ripon* 86-87; V Flamborough *York* 87-94; V Bempton 87-94; rtd 94; Perm to Offic *York* from 94. *36 Maple Road, Bridlington YO16 6TE* Tel (01262) 676028 E-mail bruce.petfield@btinternet.com

PETIT, Andrew Michael. b 53. Em Coll Cam MA78. Trin Coll Bris. **d** 83 **p** 84. C Stoughton *Guildf* 83-87; C Shirley *Win* 87-92; V Cholsey *Ox* 92-04; C Streatley w Moulsford 03-04; V Cholsey and Moulsford from 04; Chapl W Berks Priority Care Services NHS Trust 92-03. *The Vicarage, Church Road, Cholsey, Wallingford OX10 9PP* Tel (01491) 651216 Mobile 07986-005618 E-mail apetit@lineone.net

PETITT, Michael David. b 53. BCombStuds. Linc Th Coll 79. **d** 82 **p** 83. C Arnold *S'well* 82-86; Asst Chapl HM Youth Cust Cen Glen Parva 86-87; V Blaby *Leic* 87-94; V Leagrave *St Alb* 94-98; R Badby w Newham and Charwelton w Fawsley etc *Pet* from 98; Dioc Voc Adv from 00; Dir Tr for Past Assts 01-03. *The Vicarage, Vicarage Hill, Badby, Daventry NN11 3AP* Tel (01327) 310239

PETRIE, Alistair Philip. b 50. Lon Univ DipTh76 Fuller Th Sem California DMin99. Oak Hill Th Coll 76. **d** 76 **p** 77. C Eston *York* 76-79; P-in-c Prestwick *Glas* 79-81; R 81-82; Canada from 82. *1224 Mission Ridge Road, Kelowna BC, Canada, V1W 3B2* Tel (001) (250) 764 8590 Fax 764 0683 E-mail alistair@partnershipministries.org

PETRIE, Ian Robert (Eric). b 53. Avery Hill Coll PGCE84. Oak Hill Th Coll BA83 Qu Coll Birm 93. **d** 95 **p** 96. C Sedgley All SS *Worc* 95-98; P-in-c Salwarpe and Hindlip w Martin Hussingtree from 98; Co-ord Chapl W Mercia Police from 98. *The Rectory, Salwarpe, Droitwich WR9 0AH* Tel (01905) 778757 E-mail eric@petrierev.freeserve.co.uk

PETRINE, Andrei. b 73. St Jo Coll Dur BA05. Cranmer Hall Dur 02. **d** 05. C Hounslow H Trin w St Paul *Lon* from 05. *185 Bath Road, Hounslow TW3 3BU* Tel (020) 8570 9741 Mobile 07723-026925 E-mail andreipetrine@hotmail.com

PETTENGELL, Ernest Terence. b 43. K Coll Lon. **d** 69 **p** 70. C Chesham St Mary *Ox* 69-72; C Farnborough *Guildf* 72-75; Asst Master K Alfred Sch Burnham-on-Sea 75-78; C Bishop's Cleeve *Glouc* 78-80; Chapl Westonbirt Sch 80-85; P-in-c Shipton Moyne w Westonbirt and Lasborough *Glouc* 80-85; V Berkeley w Wick, Breadstone and Newport 85-92; TV Weston-super-Mare Cen Par *B & W* 92-95; P-in-c Weston super Mare Em 96-99; Chapl Staffs Univ *Lich* 99-03; V Douglas All SS and St Thos *S & M* from 03. *St Thomas's Vicarage, Marathon Avenue, Douglas IM2 4JA* Tel (01624) 611503

PETTERSEN, Canon Alvyn Lorang. b 51. TCD BA73 Dur Univ BA75 PhD81. Sarum & Wells Th Coll 78. **d** 81 **p** 82. Chapl Clare Coll Cam 81-85; Fell and Chapl Ex Coll Ox 85-92; Research Fell Linc Coll Ox 92-93; V Frensham *Guildf* 93-02; Can Res Worc Cathl *Worc* from 02. *2 College Green, Worcester WR1 2LH* Tel (01905) 28854 E-mail alvynpettersen@worcestercathedral.org.uk

PETTERSSON, Helge. b 44. Oslo Univ. **p** 71. Brazil 71-75; USA 75-77; Belgium 77-83; Norway 83-88; R Norwegian Ch and Seamen's Miss Lon from 88; Perm to Offic *S'wark* 96-00; Chapl S'wark Cathl from 00; NSM Bermondsey Deanery *S'wark* from 02. *St Olav's Church, 1 St Olav's Square, Albion Street, London SE16 1JB* Tel (020) 7237 5587 *or* 8852 3264 Mobile 07802-301090 Fax 7237 7280 E-mail helge.pettersson@sifh.no

PETTET, Christopher Farley. b 54. Ox Univ BEd78. St Jo Coll Nottm 87. **d** 90 **p** 91. C Luton St Mary *St Alb* 90-93; C Fawley *Win* 93-97; P-in-c Amport, Grateley, Monxton and Quarley from 97. *The Vicarage, Amport, Andover SP11 8BE* Tel (01264) 772950 E-mail cpettet@fish.co.uk

PETTIFER, Bryan George Ernest. b 32. Qu Coll Cam BA55 MA59 Bris Univ MEd74. Wm Temple Coll Rugby 56 Ridley Hall Cam 57. **d** 59 **p** 60. C Attercliffe w Carbrook *Sheff* 59-61; C Ecclesall 61-65; Chapl City of Bath Tech Coll 65-74; Adult Educn Officer *Bris* 75-80; Dir Past Th Sarum & Wells Th Coll 80-85; Can Res St Alb 85-92; Prin St Alb Minl Tr Scheme 85-92; Prin Ox Area Chr Tr Scheme *Ox* 92-94; Perm to Offic 94-98; Min and Deployment Officer/Selection Sec ABM 94-97; rtd 97; Perm to Offic *Glouc* 98-00; *Sarum* and *Bris* from 98; *B & W* from 02; Rtd Clergy Officer Malmesbury Adnry *Bris* from 04. *23 Curlew Drive, Chippenham SN14 6YG* Tel (01249) 659823

PETTIFER, John Barrie. b 38. Linc Th Coll 63. **d** 65 **p** 66. C Stretford St Matt *Man* 65-67; C Stand 67-71; V Littleborough 71-00; rtd 00. *Littleborough Christian Centre, 43 Todmorden Road, Littleborough OL15 9EL* Tel (01706) 374074

PETTIFOR, Canon David Thomas. b 42. Ripon Coll Cuddesdon 78. **d** 81 **p** 82. C Binley *Cov* 81-84; P-in-c Wood End 84-88; V 88-92; V Finham 92-98; TV Coventry Caludon from 98; Hon Can Cov Cathl from 04. *Holy Cross Vicarage, 14 St Austell Road, Coventry CV2 5AE* Tel (024) 7663 5734 E-mail david@dtpettifor.fsnet.co.uk

PETTIGREW, Miss Claire Gabrielle. b 23. St Mich Ho Ox 55. **dss** 77 **d** 87 **p** 95. Nor Heartsease St Fran *Nor* 77-81; Heigham H

Trin 81-87; Dioc Lay Min Adv 83-87; Asst Dir of Ords 87-89; rtd 89; Lic to Offic *Nor* 89-97. *26 Capel Court, The Burgage, Prestbury, Cheltenham GL52 3EL* Tel (01242) 577541

PETTIGREW, Stanley. b 27. TCD BA49 MA62. Div Test. **d** 50 **p** 51. C Newcastle *D & D* 50-53; C Dublin Clontarf *D & G* 53-57; I Derralossary 57-62; Miss to Seamen 62-92; I Wicklow w Killiskey *D & G* 62-92; Can Ch Ch Cathl Dublin 87-92; rtd 92. *Corr Riasc, Bollarney South, Wicklow, Irish Republic* Tel (00353) (404) 69755

PETTINGELL, Hubert (Hugh). b 32. ACA54 FCA65 AKC58. **d** 59 **p** 60. C Mansfield SS Pet and Paul *S'well* 59-61; CMS Iran 61-66; C Wellington w W Buckland and Nynehead *B & W* 67-68; Warden Student Movement Ho Lon 68-69; R Holywell w Needingworth *Ely* 69-71; Dir Finance WCC 80-96; Perm to Offic *Eur* from 94; rtd 97. *Chemin du Pommier 22, CH-1218 Le Grand Saconnex, Geneva, Switzerland* Tel (0041) (22) 798 8586 E-mail hpettingell@hotmail.com

PETTIT, Anthony David. b 72. Univ of Cen England in Birm BA94 MA95 St Jo Coll Dur BA01. Cranmer Hall Dur 98. **d** 01 **p** 02. C Gt Malvern St Mary *Worc* 01-04; P-in-c Cradley 04-05; TV Halas from 05. *34 Beecher Road, Halesowen B63 2DJ* Tel (01384) 566928 E-mail revant@fish.co.uk

PETTITT, Maurice. b 13. Clare Coll Cam BA35 MA57 MusBac37. Lich Th Coll 56. **d** 57 **p** 58. Asst Chapl Wellingborough Sch 57-62; R Rounton w Welbury *York* 62-69; V Riccall 69-78; RD Escrick 73-78; rtd 78; Perm to Offic *York* from 78. *Holbeck House, Low Street, Lastingham, York YO62 6TJ* Tel (01751) 417517

PETTITT, Robin Adrian. b 50. MRTPI79 Newc Univ BA77. St Steph Ho Ox 81. **d** 83 **p** 84. C Warrington St Elphin *Liv* 83-87; C Torrisholme *Blackb* 87-93; P-in-c Charnock Richard 93-00; Dioc Par Development Officer 93-98; Sec Dioc Adv Cttee for the Care of Chs 98-99; C Broughton 00-01; rtd 01; Perm to Offic *Liv* from 03. *The Vicarage, 169 Church Road, Haydock, St Helens WA11 0NJ* Tel (01942) 727956

PETTITT, Canon Simon. b 50. Nottm Univ BTh74 CertEd. Kelham Th Coll 70. **d** 75 **p** 76. C Penistone *Wakef* 75-78; Dioc Youth Officer 78-80; Dioc Schs Officer *St E* 80-86; P-in-c Hintlesham w Chattisham 80-86; V Bury St Edmunds St Jo 86-93; RD Thingoe 88-92; Dioc Communications Officer 93-00; Hon Can St E Cathl from 93; P-in-c Exning St Martin w Landwade 00-01; V from 01; RD Mildenhall from 01. *The Vicarage, New River Green, Exning, Newmarket CB8 7HS* Tel (01638) 577413 Fax 578792 Mobile 07850-480533 E-mail simon.pettitt@stedmondsbury.anglican.org

PETTS, Mrs Anna Carolyn. b 44. St Mich Coll Sarum CertEd65. STETS 00. **d** 03 **p** 04. NSM Hordle *Win* from 03. *65 Ferndale Road, New Milton BH25 5EX* Tel (01425) 620856 E-mail carolyn.petts@ukgateway.net

PETTY, Alicia Christina Margaret. b 64. Wycliffe Hall Ox 01. **d** 03 **p** 04. C Ockbrook *Derby* from 03. *12 Appian Close, Borrowash, Derby DE72 3LY* Tel (01332) 666205

PETTY, Brian. b 34. Man Univ BA90 Melbourne Univ DipRE. St Aid Birkenhead 59. **d** 62 **p** 63. C Meole Brace *Lich* 62-65; Chapl RAF 65-69; Australia 70-75; P-in-c Kimbolton w Middleton-on-the-Hill *Heref* 76-79; P-in-c Pudleston-cum-Whyle w Hatfield, Docklow etc 76-79; P-in-c Haddenham *Ely* 79-80; V 80-84; V Fairfield *Derby* 84-90; Chapl St Geo Sch Ascot 90-93; TR Sampford Peverell, Uplowman, Holcombe Rogus etc *Ex* 93-99; RD Cullompton 95-99; rtd 99; Perm to Offic *Ex* 99-02; Hon C Diptford, N Huish, Harberton, Harbertonford etc from 02. *Woodrising, Fortescue Road, Sidmouth EX10 9QB* Tel (01395) 514203

PETTY, Duncan. *See* PETTY, William Duncan

PETTY, The Very Revd John Fitzmaurice. b 35. Trin Hall Cam BA59 MA65. Cuddesdon Coll 64. **d** 66 **p** 67. C Sheff St Cuth *Sheff* 66-69; C St Helier *S'wark* 69-75; V Hurst *Man* 75-88; AD Ashton-under-Lyne 83-87; Hon Can Man Cathl 86-88; Provost Cov 88-00; Dean Cov 00; rtd 00; Perm to Offic *Lich* from 01. *4 Granville Street, Copthorne, Shrewsbury SY3 8NE* Tel (01743) 231513

PETTY, Neil. b 40. Coll of Resurr Mirfield 04. **d** 04 **p** 05. NSM N Thornaby *York* from 04. *28 Bader Avenue, Thornaby, Stockton-on-Tees TS17 0HQ* Tel (01642) 761588 Mobile 07985-760490 E-mail neilpetty@hotmail.com

PETTY, Capt Stuart. b 56. Wilson Carlile Coll Dip Evang85 Chich Th Coll 91. **d** 93 **p** 94. CA from 88; C W Bromwich St Andr w Ch Ch *Lich* 93-96; Asst Chapl Walsall Hosps NHS Trust 96-00; Sen Chapl 00-03; Chapl Team Ldr R Wolv Hosps NHS Trust from 03. *The Chaplain's Office, New Cross Hospital, Wednesfield Road, Wolverhampton WV10 0QP* Tel (01902) 307999

PETTY, William Duncan. b 55. Ex Univ BSc76 Leic Univ PGCE77. Oak Hill Th Coll 97. **d** 99 **p** 00. C Burscough Bridge *Liv* 99-04; Min Tanhouse The Oaks CD from 04. *33 Elmers Green, Skelmersdale WN8 6RZ* Tel (01704) 892444 E-mail duncan@thepettys.freeserve.co.uk

PETZER, Garth Stephen. MBE99. Rhodes Univ BTh95. St Paul's Coll Grahamstown. **d** 88 **p** 91. S Africa 88-95; C Queenstown St Mich 88-89; C E London St Sav 90-93; R E London St Martin 93-95; Chapl RN 96-03 and from 04; CF 03-04; Perm to Offic *Nor* from 04. *Royal Naval Chaplaincy Service, Room 203, Victory Building, HM Naval Base, Portsmouth PO1 3LS* Tel (01705) 727903 Mobile 07801-637205 Fax (01705) 727112 E-mail polgear@btopenworld.com

PETZSCH, Diana Frances Louise. b 54. BA73 MA74 MLitt79 CertEd81. Edin Th Coll 93. **d** 96 **p** 97. C Perth St Jo *St And* 96-99; Asst Chapl Maidstone and Tunbridge Wells NHS Trust 99-01; Chapl from 01; Chapl HM Pris E Sutton Park 01. *1 Wheatfield Way, Cranbrook TN17 3LS* Tel (01580) 713113 E-mail dpetzsch@hotmail.com

PETZSCH, Hugo Max David. b 57. Edin Univ MA79 BD83 PhD95 FSAScot91. Edin Th Coll 80. **d** 83 **p** 84. C Dollar *St And* 83-86; New Zealand 86-90; P-in-c Alyth, Blairgowrie and Coupar Angus 90-91; Chapl Glenalmond Coll *St And* 91-98; Dep Headmaster Benenden Sch from 99; Perm to Offic *Cant* from 99. *Benenden School, Cranbrook TN17 4AA* Tel (01580) 240592

PEVERELL, Canon Paul Harrison. b 57. Hull Univ BA80. Ripon Coll Cuddesdon. **d** 82 **p** 83. C Cottingham *York* 82-85; V Middlesbrough St Martin 85-93; V Gt Ayton w Easby and Newton in Cleveland from 93; Hon Can Ho Ghana from 04. *The Vicarage, Low Green, Great Ayton, Middlesbrough TS9 6NN* Tel (01642) 722333 E-mail revpev@btopenworld.com

PEYTON, The Ven Nigel. b 51. JP87. Edin Univ MA73 BD76. Union Th Sem (NY) STM77 Edin Th Coll 73. **d** 76 **p** 77. Chapl St Paul's Cathl Dundee *Bre* 76-82; Dioc Youth Chapl 76-85; Chapl Invergowrie 79-82; P-in-c 82-85; Chapl Univ Hosp Dundee 82-85; V Nottingham All SS *S'well* 85-91; P-in-c Lambley 91-99; Chapl Bluecoat Sch Nottm 90-92; Dioc Min Development Adv *S'well* 91-99; Adn Newark from 99. *Dunham House, Westgate, Southwell NG25 0JL,* or *4 The Woodwards, Newark NG24 3GG* Tel (01636) 817206 *or* 612249 Fax 815882 *or* 611952 E-mail archdeacon-newark@southwell.anglican.org

PEYTON JONES, Mrs Dorothy Helen. b 58. LMH Ox BA79 MPhil80. Trin Coll Bris. **dss** 86 **d** 87 **p** 94. W Holloway St Luke *Lon* 86-89; Par Dn 87-89; C Glas St Oswald *Glas* 89-92; NSM Drumchapel 92-98; Perm to Offic *Ely* 98-03; NSM Chesterton St Andr from 03. *71 Humberstone Road, Cambridge CB4 1JD* Tel (01223) 523485 E-mail dorothypj@ntlworld.com

PHAIR, Neal David Stewart. b 70. Limerick Univ BA98 UCD HDipEd99 TCD MPhil02. CITC 99. **d** 02 **p** 03. C Ballymena w Ballyclug *Conn* from 02. *38 Ballee Road East, Ballymena BT42 3DH* Tel (028) 2564 7038 Mobile 07966-552016 E-mail nealphair@hotmail.com

PHARAOH, Carol Helen. b 63. Preston Poly BTech84. St Jo Coll Dur 96. **d** 98 **p** 99. C Heaton Ch Ch *Man* 98-02; TV Walkden and Lt Hulton from 02. *St John's Vicarage, Algernon Road, Walkden, Manchester M28 3RD* Tel 0161-790 2338 E-mail pharaohingham@freenetname.co.uk

PHARAOH, Douglas William. b 18. MSHAA56. Worc Ord Coll 68. **d** 69 **p** 70. C Gt Malvern Ch Ch *Worc* 69-71; Area Sec Leprosy Miss 71-72; P-in-c Gateshead St Cuth *Dur* 72-73; V New Seaham 73-76; P-in-c Wymeswold *Leic* 76-78; V Wymeswold and Prestwold w Hoton 78-80; P-in-c Grandborough w Willoughby and Flecknoe *Cov* 80-81; V 81-83; rtd 83; Perm to Offic *Cov* from 83. *11 Margetts Close, Kenilworth CV8 1EN* Tel (01926) 779026

PHEELY, William Rattray. b 35. EN(M)88. Edin Th Coll 57. **d** 60 **p** 61. C Glas St Mary *Glas* 60-63; C Salisbury St Martin *Sarum* 63-66; Guyana 66-82; V Bordesley St Oswald *Birm* 82-86; Perm to Offic *Birm* 86-00 and *Ex* 00-03; rtd 00. *Flat 2, 16 Westcliffe Road, Birkdale, Southport PR8 2BN* Tel (01704) 563346

PHEIFFER, John Leslie. b 18. Wells Th Coll. **d** 67 **p** 68. C Northwood Hills St Edm *Lon* 67-69; Chapl Twickenham Prep Sch 69-71; C Chobham w Valley End *Guildf* 71-76; C Highcliffe w Hinton Admiral *Win* 77-79; V Portswood St Denys 79-85; rtd 86. *4 Haywards Close, Felpham, Bognor Regis PO22 8HF* Tel (01243) 828985

PHELAN, Thomas Sylvester Patrick. b 36. Leic Univ DSS62 Southn Univ DASS79 CQSW79. Chich Th Coll 72. **d** 94 **p** 95. C Somers Town *Lon* 94-96; C Old St Pancras w Bedford New Town St Matt 96-97; Chapl Camden and Islington Community Health NHS Trust 96-97; OSB from 97; Lic Preacher *Ox* 97-02; Hon C Nor St Jo w St Julian *Nor* from 02. *14 Cyprus Street, Norwich NR1 3AX* Tel (01603) 610104

PHELPS, Canon Arthur Charles. b 26. St Cath Coll Cam BA50 MA55. Ridley Hall Cam 51. **d** 53 **p** 54. C Kirkdale St Lawr *Liv* 53-56; C Rainham *Chelmsf* 56-60; Min Collier Row St Jas CD 60-65; V Collier Row St Jas 65-75; R Thorpe Morieux w Preston and Brettenham *St E* 75-84; R Rattlesden w Thorpe Morieux and Brettenham 84-90; Hon Can St E Cathl 89-90; rtd 90; Perm to Offic *Truro* 90-00 and *St E* from 01. *8 Northfield Court, Aldeburgh IP15 5LU* Tel (01728) 454772

PHELPS, Ian James. b 29. Oak Hill Th Coll 53. **d** 56 **p** 57. C Peckham St Mary *S'wark* 56-59; R Gaddesby w S Croxton *Leic* 59-67; R Beeby 59-67; Asst Dioc Youth Chapl and Rural Youth Adv 65-67; CF (TA) 60-67; CF (R of O) 67-84; Youth Chapl *Leic* 67-85; Dioc Adult Educn Officer 85-91; Past Asst to Bp and Adn

Leic 91-94; rtd 94; Perm to Offic *Leic* 94-99; *S'wark* from 99. *6 Montague Graham Court, Kidbrooke Gardens, London SE3 0PD* Tel (020) 8305 2150

PHELPS, Ian Ronald. b 28. FLS58 Lon Univ BSc53 PhD57. Chich Th Coll 57. **d** 59 **p** 60. C Brighton Gd Shep Preston *Chich* 59-61; C Sullington 62-64; C Storrington 62-64; R Newtimber w Pyecombe 64-68; V Brighton St Luke 68-74; TV Brighton Resurr 74-76; V Peacehaven 76-94; rtd 94; Perm to Offic *Chich* from 94. *2 Kingston Green, Seaford BN25 4NB* Tel (01323) 899511

PHENNA, Timothy Peter. b 69. Ridley Hall Cam BTh01. **d** 01 **p** 02. C Woodseats St Chad *Sheff* 01-04; USA from 04. *2051 Braun Drive, Golden, CO 80401, USA* E-mail tpphenna@aol.com

PHILBRICK, Gary James. b 57. Southn Univ BA78 K Alfred's Coll Win CertEd79 ACertCM84 MA(Theol)00 Edin Univ BD86. Edin Th Coll 83. **d** 86 **p** 87. C Southampton Maybush St Pet *Win* 86-90; R Fawley 90-00; P-in-c Swaythling 00-04; V from 04. *Swaythling Vicarage, 357 Burgess Road, Southampton SO16 3BD* Tel (023) 8055 4231 Fax 8067 9787 E-mail gary.philbrick@dial.pipex.com

PHILIP, Mathew. b 54. **d** 05. NSM Patcham *Chich* from 05. *Hillside Lodge, 76 Redhill Drive, Brighton BN1 5FL* Tel (01273) 883726

PHILIP, Peter Wells. b 35. Ridley Hall Cam 64. **d** 67 **p** 68. C Tollington Park St Mark w St Anne *Lon* 67-70; C Battersea St Pet *S'wark* 70-72; Hon C Kennington St Mark 72-73; New Zealand 74-92 and from 94; Hon C Auckland St Paul 74; V Titirangi 74-80; Hon C Blockhouse Bay 80-92; Past Dir Chr Advance Min 80-84; Dir Evang Fellowship of NZ 87-90; C Finchley Ch Ch *Lon* 92-93; V Frankton 94-00; rtd 00. *608 Rolleston Street, Thames 2801, New Zealand* Tel (0064) (7) 868 5028 E-mail peterphilip@paradise.net.nz

PHILIP BARTHOLOMEW, Brother. *See* KENNEDY, Brother Philip Bartholomew

PHILIPPINES, Prime Bishop of the Episcopal Church in the. *See* SOLIBA, The Most Revd Ignacio Capuyan

PHILLIP, Isaiah Ezekiel. b 59. Univ of W Indies BA88. Codrington Coll Barbados 85. **d** 88 **p** 89. C St Jo Cathl Antigua 88-91; R St Geo Dominica 91-96; R All SS Antigua 96-01; P-in-c Handsworth St Mich *Birm* from 02. *St Michael's Vicarage, 20 Soho Avenue, Birmingham B18 5LB* Tel 0121-554 3521 Mobile 07985-680705 E-mail phillipisaiah@hotmail.com

PHILLIPS, Andrew Graham. b 58. Ex Univ BSc79. Chich Th Coll 84. **d** 87 **p** 88. C Frankby w Greasby *Ches* 87-89; C Liv St Chris Norris Green *Liv* 89-92; CF 92-97; Chapl RN from 00. *Royal Naval Chaplaincy Service, Room 203, Victory Building, HM Naval Base, Portsmouth PO1 3LS* Tel (023) 9272 7903 Fax 9272 7111

PHILLIPS, Canon Anthony Charles Julian. b 36. Lon Univ BD63 AKC63 G&C Coll Cam PhD67 St Jo Coll Ox MA75 DPhil80. Coll of Resurr Mirfield 66. **d** 66 **p** 67. C-in-c Chesterton Gd Shep CD *Ely* 66-69; Dean, Chapl and Fell Trin Hall Cam 69-74; Hon Bp's Chapl *Nor* 70-71; Chapl and Fell St Jo Coll Ox 75-86; Lect Th Jes Coll Ox 75-86; Lect Th Hertf Coll Ox 84-86; Hd Master K Sch Cant 86-96; Hon Can Cant Cathl *Cant* 87-96; Can Th Truro Cathl *Truro* 86-02; Perm to Offic from 02; rtd 01. *10 St Peter's Road, Flushing, Falmouth TR11 5TP* Tel (01326) 377217

PHILLIPS, Mrs Audrey Katherine. b 32. Lorain Coll Ohio BS73. Ox Min Course 88. **d** 91 **p** 94. NSM Princes Risborough w Ilmer *Ox* 91-94; P Assoc Marco Is St Mark USA 94-98; NSM Akeman *Ox* 98-00. *1 The Chestnuts, Kirtlington, Kidlington OX5 3UB* Tel (01869) 350194 E-mail 110145,601@compuserve.com

PHILLIPS, Benjamin Guy. b 75. Wycliffe Hall Ox. **d** 02 **p** 03. C Cockermouth w Embleton and Wythop *Carl* 02-05; V Stanwix from 05. *Stanwix Vicarage, Dykes Terrace, Carlisle CA3 9AS* Tel (01228) 514600 *or* 511430 E-mail benphillips@uk2k.com

PHILLIPS, Benjamin Lambert Meyrick. b 64. K Coll Cam BA86 MA90. Ridley Hall Cam 87. **d** 90 **p** 91. C Wareham *Sarum* 90-94; C Chipping Barnet w Arkley *St Alb* 94-96; V Bodicote *Ox* from 96; AD Deddington from 05. *The Vicarage, Wykham Lane, Bodicote, Banbury OX15 4BW* Tel (01295) 270174

PHILLIPS, Beryl. *See* PHILLIPS, Mrs Elizabeth Beryl

PHILLIPS, Bill. *See* PHILLIPS, Edward Leigh Bill

PHILLIPS, Mrs Brenda. b 41. St Hugh's Coll Ox BA63 MA68. **d** 04. OLM Sherborne w Castleton and Lillington *Sarum* from 04. *Court House Dairy, Thornford Road, Sherborne DT9 6PT* Tel (01935) 812738 E-mail phillips@courthousedairyfarm.freeserve.co.uk

PHILLIPS, Brian Edward Dorian William. b 36. Bris Univ BA58. Ripon Hall Ox 58. **d** 60 **p** 61. C Ross *Heref* 60-64; Chapl RAF 64-68; Hon C Fringford w Hethe and Newton Purcell *Ox* 68-73; Chapl Howell's Sch Denbigh 73-76; C Cleobury Mortimer w Hopton Wafers *Heref* 76-80; V Dixton 80-02; rtd 02; Perm to Offic *Heref* from 02. *37 Duxmere Drive, Ross-on-Wye HR9 5UW* Tel (01989) 562993 Mobile 07712-071558 E-mail brianphillips@u-genie.co.uk

PHILLIPS, Canon Brian Robert. b 31. Clare Coll Cam BA53 MA57. Linc Th Coll 54. **d** 56 **p** 57. C Tuffley *Glouc* 56-59; C Southgate Ch Ch *Lon* 59-62; R Luckington w Alderton *Bris* 62-69; V Highworth w Sevenhampton and Inglesham etc 69-84; Hon Can Bris Cathl 84-90; P-in-c Long Newnton 84-87; P-in-c Crudwell w Ashley 84-87; R Ashley, Crudwell, Hankerton, Long Newnton etc 87-90; rtd 90; Perm to Offic *Portsm* and *Win* from 90. *Hannington, Hospital Road, Shirrell Heath, Southampton SO32 2JR* Tel (01329) 834547

PHILLIPS, The Very Revd Christopher John. b 46. **d** 79 **p** 80. Hong Kong 79-04; Chapl Hong Kong Cathl 83-87; Dean Hong Kong 88-04; Perm to Offic *Ely* from 04. *12A Cambridge Road, Ely CB7 4HL* E-mail cjphil@netvigator.com

PHILLIPS, David Arthur. b 36. S Dios Minl Tr Scheme 90. **d** 94 **p** 95. NSM Canford Magna *Sarum* from 94. *32 Lynwood Drive, Wimborne BH21 1UG* Tel (01202) 848725

PHILLIPS, David Elwyn. b 17. St D Coll Lamp 62. **d** 64 **p** 65. C Ferndale *Llan* 64-68; C Port Talbot St Theodore 68-70; V Abercanaid 70-87; rtd 87; Perm to Offic *Llan* from 87. *Carmel, 13 Tyleri Gardens, Victor Road, Abertillery NP13 1EZ*

PHILLIPS, David Keith. b 61. New Coll Ox MA90. St Jo Coll Dur BA90. **d** 91 **p** 92. C Denton Holme *Carl* 91-94; C Chadderton Ch Ch *Man* 94-98; Sec Ch Soc from 98; Public Preacher *St Alb* from 98. *The Flat, 16 Rosslyn Road, Watford WD18 0JY* Tel (01923) 235111 Fax 800362 E-mail director@churchsociety.org.uk

PHILLIPS, David Thomas. b 47. NEOC 03. **d** 05. NSM Gt and Lt Driffield *York* from 05. *71B Eastgate North, Driffield YO25 6EB* Tel (01377) 253262 E-mail dphill9590@hotmail.com

PHILLIPS, Edward Leigh Bill. b 12. St Edm Hall Ox BA34 MA47. Wycliffe Hall Ox 33. **d** 35 **p** 36. Asst Chapl Dean Close Sch Cheltenham 35-37; C Highfield *Ox* 37-38; C-in-c Patcham Chr the K CD *Chich* 39-41; CF (EC) 41-46; R Ide Hill *Roch* 46-49; V Moulsecoomb *Chich* 49-52; V Kingston w Iford 52-75; V Iford w Kingston and Rodmell 75-78; RD Lewes 65-77; rtd 78; Perm to Offic *Glouc* from 78. *35 Woodland Green, Upton St Leonards, Gloucester GL4 8BD* Tel (01452) 619894

PHILLIPS, Edwin George. b 35. N Wales Baptist Coll 64. **d** 03 **p** 03. NSM Morriston *S & B* from 03. *146 Lingfield Avenue, Port Talbot SA12 6QA* Tel (01639) 886784 Mobile 07815-969913

PHILLIPS, Mrs Elizabeth Beryl. b 34. **d** 94 **p** 95. C N Farnborough *Guildf* 94-99; rtd 99; Perm to Offic *Sarum* from 00. *8 Byron Road, Wimborne BH21 1NX* Tel (01202) 883328

PHILLIPS, Elwyn. *See* PHILLIPS, David Elwyn

PHILLIPS, Mrs Emma Catharine. b 62. St Anne's Coll Ox BA84. Trin Coll Bris BA99. **d** 99 **p** 00. C Shawbury *Lich* 99-01; C Moreton Corbet 99-01; C Stanton on Hine Heath 99-01; C Cen Telford 01-02; TV from 03. *Church House, 15 Carwood, Stirchley, Telford TF3 1YA* Tel (01952) 595482

PHILLIPS, Geoffrey Clarke. b 50. SW Minl Tr Course 94. **d** 96 **p** 97. NSM Georgeham *Ex* 96-98; Chapl HM YOI Huntercombe and Finnamore 99-00; Chapl HM Pris Shepton Mallet 01-03. *Address temp unknown*

PHILLIPS, Canon Geoffrey John. b 23. BNC Ox BA47 MA56. Ridley Hall Cam 54. **d** 56 **p** 57. C Kettering St Andr *Pet* 56-59; C Tideswell *Derby* 59-62; Ceylon 62-65; R Gillingham w Geldeston and Stockton *Nor* 65-70; V Eaton 70-81; RD Nor S 71-81; Hon Can Nor Cathl 78-81; Chapl Vienna w Budapest and Prague *Eur* 81-87; rtd 87; Perm to Offic *Nor* from 87. *Mere Farmhouse, White Heath Road, Bergh Apton, Norwich NR15 1AY* Tel (01508) 480656

PHILLIPS, Ivor Lynn. b 44. Leeds Univ BA70. Cuddesdon Coll 69. **d** 71 **p** 72. C Bedlinog *Llan* 71-73; C Roath 73-77; TV Wolverhampton All SS *Lich* 77-78; TV Wolverhampton 78-81; Chapl Charing Cross Hosp Lon 81-91; Chapl Milan w Genoa and Lugano *Eur* 91-94; C Hampstead St Jo *Lon* 95-00; V Whitton St Aug from 00. *St Augustine's Vicarage, Hospital Bridge Road, Whitton, Twickenham TW2 6DE* Tel (020) 8894 3764 Fax 8894 4543 E-mail staug@respite.demon.co.uk

PHILLIPS, Mrs Janet Elizabeth. b 37. Bp Grosseteste Coll CertEd57. EMMTC 81. **dss** 84 **d** 87 **p** 94. Wisbech St Aug *Ely* 84-86; Cambridge St Jas 86-87; Par Dn 87-91; Par Dn Wisbech SS Pet and Paul 91-94; C 94-02; rtd 02; Hon C Elm and Friday Bridge w Coldham *Ely* from 03. *St Mark's Vicarage, 18 Main Road, Friday Bridge, Wisbech PE14 0HJ* Tel (01760) 339161

PHILLIPS, Jeffery Llewellyn. b 32. Sarum & Wells Th Coll. **d** 87 **p** 88. C Ringwood *Win* 87-90; V Somborne w Ashley 90-93; rtd 93; Perm to Offic *Win* from 93. *Queen's Acre, 3 Solent Avenue, Lymington SO41 3SD* Tel (01590) 673955

PHILLIPS, Mrs Jennifer Jean. b 36. Guildf Dioc Min Course 98. **d** 01 **p** 02. OLM New Haw *Guildf* from 01. *20 Lindsay Road, New Haw, Addlestone KT15 3BD* Tel (01932) 343853 E-mail jenny@20lindsayroad.fsnet.co.uk

PHILLIPS, John. b 50. ACIB74. N Ord Course 01. **d** 04. NSM Wavertree H Trin *Liv* from 04. *12 Montclair Drive, Liverpool L18 0HA* Tel 0151-722 2542 E-mail jpipps@hotmail.com

PHILLIPS, John David. b 29. G&C Coll Cam BA50 MA54 CertEd69. SW Minl Tr Course 85. **d** 87 **p** 88. NSM St Martin w

E and W Looe *Truro* 87-88; NSM St Merryn 88-94; rtd 94; Perm to Offic *Truro* from 94. *Restings, Plaidy, Looe PL13 1LF* Tel (01503) 262121

PHILLIPS, John Eldon. b 50. Univ of Wales (Cardiff) BEd85 MEd92. St Mich Coll Llan. **d** 90 **p** 91. NSM Merthyr Cynog and Dyffryn Honddu etc *S & B* 90-94; Lic to Offic *St D* 94-99; NSM Ystradgynlais *S & B* 95-99; Chapl Trin Coll Carmarthen 95-99; P-in-c Llanrhidian w Llanmadoc and Cheriton *S & B* 99-05; Dioc Press Officer from 02. *10 Pentre Nicklaus Village, Llanelli SA15 2DE* Tel (01554) 744770

PHILLIPS, John Reginald. b 64. St Steph Ho Ox BTh93. **d** 96 **p** 97. C Bognor *Chich* 96-99; TV Moulsecoomb 99-00; C Hove 00-05; P-in-c Mackworth St Fran *Derby* from 05. *St Francis's Vicarage, 78 Collingham Gardens, Derby DE22 4FQ* Tel (01332) 347690

PHILLIPS, John William Burbridge. b 39. Dur Univ BSc60 Lon Univ BD68. Tyndale Hall Bris 65. **d** 68 **p** 69. C Barton Seagrave *Pet* 68-71; C Northampton All SS w St Kath 71-75; R Irthlingborough 75-88; V Weedon Lois w Plumpton and Moreton Pinkney etc 88-95; rtd 95; Perm to Offic *Pet* 95-96. *Finca Morito 8, 12579 Alcoceber, Castellon, Spain*

PHILLIPS, Joseph Benedict. b 11. **d** 37 **p** 38. In RC Ch 37-43; C St Mary-at-Lambeth *S'wark* 47-50; C Woking St Jo *Guildf* 50-53; V Burton in Kendal *Carl* 53-59; V Bradf St Andr *Bradf* 59-66; rtd 76. *100 Ruskin Avenue, Lincoln LN2 4BT* Tel (01522) 534411

PHILLIPS, Judith Mary. b 46. Reading Univ BA67 Cardiff Coll of Educn PGCE86. St Mich Coll Llan 93. **d** 95 **p** 97. Lect Neath Coll 84-00; NSM Clydach *S & B* 95-00; Dep Chapl HM Pris Bris 00-01; Chapl HM Pris Eastwood Park from 01. *HM Prison, Eastwood Park, Falfield, Wotton-under-Edge GL12 8DB* Tel (01454) 262100 Fax 262101

PHILLIPS, Canon Kenneth John. b 37. Coll of Resurr Mirfield 67. **d** 67 **p** 68. C Blackb St Jas *Blackb* 67-69; C-in-c Lea CD 70-80; V Lea 80-84; P-in-c Priors Hardwick, Priors Marston and Wormleighton *Cov* 85-02; Sec Dioc Adv Cttee 85-99; RD Southam 89-95; Hon Can Cov Cathl 94-02; Dioc Rural Chs Officer 00-02; rtd 02; Hon C Gisburn *Bradf* from 02; Hon C Hellifield from 02. *10 Park Avenue, Hellifield, Skipton BD23 4EZ* Tel (01729) 850340 E-mail kcanonic@aol.com

PHILLIPS, Lamont Wellington Sanderson. b 33. S'wark Ord Course 73. **d** 76 **p** 78. NSM Tottenham St Paul *Lon* 76-83; P-in-c Upper Clapton St Matt 83-88; V 88-97; rtd 98. *24 Berkshire Gardens, London N18 2LF* Tel (020) 8807 7025

PHILLIPS, Lynn. *See* PHILLIPS, Ivor Lynn

PHILLIPS, Canon Martin Nicholas. b 32. Em Coll Cam BA57 MA61. Linc Th Coll 57. **d** 59 **p** 60. C Stocking Farm CD *Leic* 59-63; V Sheff Gillcar St Silas *Sheff* 63-71; V Birstall *Leic* 72-82; R Wanlip 72-82; V Birstall and Wanlip 82-88; TR Loughborough Em and St Mary in Charnwood 88-96; Hon Can Leic Cathl 90-96; rtd 96; Perm to Offic *Leic* from 96. *Foxhollow, 40A Lodge Close, Barrow upon Soar, Loughborough LE12 8ZL* Tel (01509) 416361

PHILLIPS, Mary Alice. b 53. Ripon Coll Cuddesdon 97. **d** 99 **p** 00. C Addiscombe St Mildred *S'wark* 99-02; TV Basingstoke *Win* from 02. *219 Paddock Road, Basingstoke RG22 6QP* Tel (01256) 464393 E-mail map13@tinyworld.co.uk

PHILLIPS, Michael John. b 54. JP. Trent Poly BA77. Sarum & Wells Th Coll 78. **d** 81 **p** 82. C Killay *S & B* 81-83; C Treboeth 83-85; Hong Kong 85-88; Japan 88-91; TR Is of Scilly *Truro* 91-95; TR Cwmbran *Mon* from 95. *The Rectory, Clomendy Road, Cwmbran NP44 3LS* Tel (01633) 489718

PHILLIPS, Michael Thomas. b 46. CQSW81. Linc Th Coll 89. **d** 90 **p** 91. C Hyson Green *S'well* 90-91; C Basford w Hyson Green 91-93; Chapl HM Pris Gartree 93-99; Chapl HM Pris Nottm from 99. *The Chaplaincy Office, HM Prison Nottingham, Perry Road, Sherwood, Nottingham NG5 3AG* Tel 0115-872 3040 Fax 872 3001

PHILLIPS, Mrs Patricia. b 45. Glouc Sch of Min 83. **dss** 86 **d** 87 **p** 94. Newent and Gorsley w Cliffords Mesne *Glouc* 86-95; C 87-95; P-in-c Childswyckham w Aston Somerville, Buckland etc 95-97; R 97-00, R Redmarley D'Abitot, Bromesberrow, Pauntley etc from 00. *The Rectory, Redmarley, Gloucester GL19 3HS* Tel and fax (01531) 620715 E-mail revpp@tesco.net

PHILLIPS, Patrick Noble Stowell. b 22. Edin Univ MA50 CertEd63. ALCD52. **d** 52 **p** 53. CMS 52-55; St Mark Nibo Nisi Niger 52-55; St Paul Awka 52-55; C Mossley Hill St Matt and St Jas *Liv* 55-57; V Milverton, Milbank and Elma Canada 57-60; Hd Ang Grammar Sch Benin 60-63; R Moresby *Carl* 63-66; V Mapleton and Clandeboye Canada 66-71; R Arthuret 71-88; rtd 88. *14 Gipsy Lane, Reading RG6 7HB* Tel 0118-926 4654

PHILLIPS, Miss Pauline. b 54. **d** 96 **p** 97. OLM Mossley *Man* from 96. *32 Mountain Street, Mossley, Ashton-under-Lyne OL5 0EZ* Tel (01457) 832363

PHILLIPS, Percy Graham. b 26. St Aid Birkenhead 46. **d** 51 **p** 52. C Wallasey St Hilary *Ches* 51-54; C Thrybergh *Sheff* 54-58; C Guernsey St Michel du Valle *Win* 58-60; V Heytesbury w Tytherington and Knook *Sarum* 60-65; V Stonebridge St Mich *Lon* 65-70; R Vernham Dean w Linkenholt *Win* 70-78; C Farnham *Guildf* 78-82; TV Cove St Jo 82-89; rtd 89. *22 Charts Close, Cranleigh GU6 8BH*

PHILLIPS, Peter. b 26. Oak Hill Th Coll 63. **d** 65 **p** 66. C Eastbourne All SS *Chich* 65-69; C St Alb St Paul *St Alb* 69-73; V Riseley w Bletsoe 73-84; R Arley *Cov* 84-91; rtd 91; Perm to Offic *B & W* from 91; Clergy Retirement and Widows' Officer 99-04. *1 Rutland Lodge, 19 Linden Road, Clevedon BS21 7SR* Tel (01275) 875801

PHILLIPS, Peter Miles Lucas. b 44. Reading Univ BA66 QUB DipEd69 Univ of Wales (Cardiff) MEd88. St Mich Coll Llan 90. **d** 92 **p** 93. Dep Hd Teacher Dynevor Sch 82-96; NSM Llangyfelach *S & B* 92-96; Dep Chapl HM Pris Liv 96-97; Chapl HM Pris Usk and Prescoed 97-01; Chapl HM Pris Bris 01-04; rtd 04; Perm to Offic *Bris* from 04. *7 St Lucia Close, Bristol BS7 0XS* Tel 0117-952 5859 E-mail revdpeterphillips@yahoo.co.uk

PHILLIPS, Robin Michael. b 33. AKC58. **d** 59 **p** 60. C Hanwell St Mellitus *Lon* 59-61; C St Margaret's-on-Thames 61-64; C Hangleton *Chich* 64-68; V Mellor *Derby* 68-95; RD Glossop 89-93; rtd 95; Hon C Bridekirk *Carl* 95-96. *87 George Lane, Bredbury, Stockport SK6 1DH*

PHILLIPS, Mrs Sandra Georgina. b 49. STETS 01. **d** 04 **p** 05. NSM Portsdown *Portsm* from 04. *3 Lyne Place, Waterlooville PO8 9TP* Tel (023) 9259 6801 Mobile 07778-921624 E-mail sandie@fish.co.uk

PHILLIPS, Canon Stephen. b 38. QUB BA60. Linc Th Coll 60. **d** 62 **p** 63. C Waddington *Linc* 62-65; C Gt Grimsby St Jas 65-72; V Kirmington 72-97; V Limber Magna w Brocklesby 73-97; V Brocklesby Park and R Croxton 97-04; RD Yarborough 92-00; Can and Preb Linc Cathl from 98; rtd 04. *The Stables, 14 Church Lane, Keelby, Grimsby DN41 8ED* Tel (01469) 561395 E-mail canstephil@glimreho.freeserve.co.uk

PHILLIPS, Thomas Wynford. b 15. Univ of Wales BA37 BD40. St Mich Coll Llan. **d** 43 **p** 44. C Shotton *St As* 43-46; C Rhyl 46-50; C Hall Green Ascension *Birm* 50-52; R Shustoke 52-55; P-in-c Maxstoke 52-55; V Clay Cross *Derby* 55-68; R Upton Magna *Lich* 68-73; V Withington 68-73; R Roche *Truro* 73-80; R Withiel 73-80; RD St Austell 76-80; rtd 80; Perm to Offic *Truro* from 80. *Brynawelon, Wheal Quoit Avenue, St Agnes TR5 0SJ* Tel (01872) 552862

PHILLIPS, Timothy Leo. b 72. Bris Univ BSc95 PhD99. Trin Coll Bris BA01 MA02. **d** 02 **p** 03. C Leic H Trin w St Jo *Leic* from 02; TV Ashby-de-la-Zouch and Breedon on the Hill from 05. *Holy Trinity Vicarage, 1 Trinity Close, Ashby-de-la-Zouch LE65 2GQ* Tel (01530) 412339 E-mail tim@bradingroad.fsnet.co.uk

PHILLIPS-SMITH, Edward Charles. b 50. AKC71. **d** 73 **p** 74. C Wolverhampton *Lich* 73-76; Chapl St Pet Colleg Sch Wolv 77-87; Hon C Wolverhampton *Lich* 78-87; V Stevenage St Pet Broadwater *St Alb* 87-89; Chapl Millfield Jun Sch Somerset 89-95; Lic to Offic *Ox* from 95. *Papplewick School, Windsor Road, Ascot SL5 7LH* Tel (01344) 621488

PHILLIPSON (née MACKAY), Alison. b 62. Teesside Univ BA00. NEOC 01. **d** 04 **p** 05. C Stokesley w Seamer *York* from 04. *23 Darnbrook Way, Nunthorpe, Middlesbrough TS7 0RA* Tel (01642) 324803 E-mail alisonphillipson@aol.com

PHILLIPSON-MASTERS, Miss Susan Patricia. b 52. Sussex Univ CertEd73 K Alfred's Coll Win BEd81 Leeds Univ MA04 FIST76 ACP80 ACertCM99. Trin Coll Bris 86. **d** 89 **p** 95. C Saltford w Corston and Newton St Loe *B & W* 89-94; C Uphill 94-97; C Nailsea Ch Ch w Tickenham 97-98; P-in-c Tredington and Darlingscott w Newbold on Stour *Cov* 98-00; P-in-c The Stanleys *Glouc* from 00. *The Rectory, Church Road, Leonard Stanley, Stonehouse GL10 3NP* Tel (01453) 826698 Fax 826712 E-mail sue.pm@btinternet.com

PHILLPOT, Donald John. b 27. St Jo Coll Dur BA53 DipTh55. **d** 55 **p** 56. C Southmead *Bris* 55-60; C Brislington St Luke 60-63; R Stapleton *Heref* 63-68; V Dorrington 63-68; P-in-c Astley Abbotts 68-78; R Bridgnorth w Tasley 68-78; V Lillington *Cov* 78-92; rtd 92; Perm to Offic *Glouc* from 92. *22 Williams Orchard, Highnam, Gloucester GL2 8EL* Tel (01452) 386844

PHILP (née NOBLE), Mrs Ann Carol. b 42. Sarum Dioc Tr Coll CertEd63 Southn Univ MA(Ed)89 MCIPD. S Dios Minl Tr Scheme 93. **d** 95 **p** 96. Dir Sarum Chr Cen *Sarum* 93-98; Chapl Sarum Cathl 95-02; Dioc NSM Officer 98-02; P-in-c Woodford Valley from 02; Dioc Dir of Ords from 02. *The Vicarage, Middle Woodford, Salisbury SP4 6NR* Tel (01722) 782310 *or* 411944 E-mail ann.philp@salisbury.anglican.org *or* annphilp@aol.com

PHILPOTT, Barbara May. *See* WILKINSON, Canon Barbara May

PHILPOTT, Canon John David. b 43. Leic Univ BA64. Trin Coll Bris 69. **d** 72 **p** 73. C Knutsford St Jo *Ches* 72-75; C Toft 72-75; C Bickenhill w Elmdon *Birm* 75-79; V Birm St Luke 79-91; RD Birm City 83-88; Hon Can Birm Cathl 89-91; V Chilvers Coton w Astley *Cov* 91-00; RD Nuneaton 95-00; Hon Can Cov Cathl 96-00; P-in-C Prague St Clem *Eur* from 00. *Vrsni 27, Praha 8, 18200 Kobylisy, Czech Republic* Tel (00420) (284) 688 8575 E-mail philpott@volny.cz

PHILPOTT, John Wilfred. b 44. K Coll Lon BD67 AKC67. **d** 68 **p** 69. C Norbury St Steph *Cant* 68-71; C Addiscombe St Mildred

71-75; V Whitfield w Guston 75-01; rtd 02; Perm to Offic *Cant* from 02. *9 Mannering Close, River, Dover CT17 0UD* Tel (01304) 825875

PHILPOTT, Ronald. b 38. IPFA69. Cranmer Hall Dur 88. **d** 89 **p** 90. NSM S Ossett *Wakef* 89-93; R Clitheroe St Jas *Blackb* 93-03; rtd 03; Perm to Offic *York* from 03. *8 Headland Close, Haxby, York YO32 3HW* Tel (01904) 758697

PHILPOTT, Preb Samuel. b 41. Kelham Th Coll 60. **d** 65 **p** 66. C Swindon New Town *Bris* 65-70; C Torquay St Martin Barton *Ex* 70-73; TV Withycombe Raleigh 73-76; V Shaldon 76-78; P-in-c Plymouth St Pet 78-80; V from 80; RD Plymouth Devonport 86-93 and 95-01; Preb Ex Cathl from 91. *St Peter's Vicarage, 23 Wyndham Square, Plymouth PL1 5EG* Tel (01752) 222007 Fax 257973 E-mail frphilpott@aol.com

PHILPOTT-HOWARD, John Nigel. b 54. Univ of Wales Coll of Medicine MB, BCh77 FRCPath83. SEITE 99. **d** 02 **p** 03. NSM Shooters Hill Ch Ch *S'wark* from 02. *80 Charlton Road, London SE7 7EY* Tel (020) 8858 4692 E-mail jphilpotth@cs.com

PHILPS, Mark Seymour. b 51. Worc Coll Ox BA73 MA78 Lon Univ MA75 Nottm Univ BA79. St Jo Coll Nottm 77. **d** 80 **p** 81. C Chadwell Heath *Chelmsf* 80-83; C Woodford Wells 83-87; V Tipton St Matt *Lich* 87-02; C Roxeth *Lon* 02-03; TR from 03. *Christ Church Vicarage, Roxeth Hill, Harrow HA2 0JN* Tel (020) 8423 3168 E-mail mphilps@aol.com

PHILSON, James Alexander Summers (Hamish). b 20. Edin Th Coll 48. **d** 51 **p** 52. C Falkirk *Edin* 51-53; R Dunblane *St And* 53-62; Australia from 62; R Beverley 62-64; R Victoria Park 64-75; R Cottesloe 75-85; rtd 85. *38 Allenswood Road, Greenwood, W Australia 6024* Tel (0061) (8) 9447 9523 Mobile 0416-001620 E-mail jasp@smartchat.net.au

PHIPPS, David John. b 46. Bris Univ BSc68 Ex Univ PhD94 Nottm Univ PGCE69. Trin Coll Bris 75. **d** 78 **p** 79. C Madron w Morvah *Truro* 78-80; C Kenilworth St Jo *Cov* 80-83; TV Barnstaple *Ex* 83-95; I Abercraf w Callwen w Capel Coelbren *S & B* 95-02; P-in-c Gulval and Madron *Truro* from 02. *The Rectory, Madron, Penzance TR20 8SW* Tel (01736) 360992 E-mail phippsdv@dialstart.net

PHIPPS, Canon Frederick George. b 30. Kelham Th Coll 50. **d** 54 **p** 55. C Staveley *Derby* 54-59; Korea 59-65; Australia from 65; Can Ballarat Ch Ch Cathl 84-95; rtd 95. *240 Lava Street, PO Box 297, Warrnambool, Vic, Australia 3280* Tel (0061) (3) 5562 6738

PHIPPS, John Maclean. b 14. Em Coll Cam BA38 MA50. Cuddesdon Coll 38. **d** 39 **p** 40. C Banbury *Ox* 39-41; P-in-c Cambois *Newc* 41-46; C Newport Pagnell *Ox* 47-53; V Speenhamland 53-71; V Buckland 72-79; V Littleworth 72-79; R Pusey 72-79; rtd 79; Perm to Offic *Chich* 84-93 and *St Alb* from 93. *Bushmead Court, Bushmead Avenue, Bedford MK40 3QW* Tel (01234) 365137

PHIZACKERLEY, The Ven Gerald Robert. b 29. Univ Coll Ox BA52 MA56. Wells Th Coll 52. **d** 54 **p** 55. C Carl St Barn *Carl* 54-57; Chapl Abingdon Sch 57-64; R Gaywood, Bawsey and Mintlyn *Nor* 64-78; RD Lynn 68-78; Hon Can Nor Cathl 75-78; Hon Can Derby Cathl *Derby* 78-96; P-in-c Ashford w Sheldon 78-90; Adn Chesterfield 78-96; rtd 96; Perm to Offic *Derby* and *Cov* from 96. *Archway Cottage, Hall Road, Leamington Spa CV32 5RA* Tel (01926) 332740

PHYPERS, David John. b 39. Leic Univ BA60 CertEd61 Lon Univ BD65. Linc Th Coll 76. **d** 78 **p** 79. NSM Normanton *Derby* 78-80; NSM Sinfin 80-87; Lic to Offic 87-88; P-in-c Denby and Horsley Woodhouse 88-00; P-in-c Wormhill, Peak Forest w Peak Dale and Dove Holes from 00; Adv for Chr Giving from 00. *Shalom, Hallsteads, Dove Holes, Buxton SK17 8BJ* Tel (01298) 813344 E-mail davidp@dial.webs.co.uk

PICK, David. b 44. Linc Th Coll 85. **d** 87 **p** 88. C Howden *York* 87-90; P-in-c Sledmere and Cowlam w Fridaythorpe, Fimer etc 90-91; V 91-96; rtd 96; Perm to Offic *York* from 96. *Westwood Close, 16 North Street, Nafferton, Driffield YO25 4JW* Tel (01377) 240360

PICK, William Harry. b 23. Open Univ BA77. St Aid Birkenhead 51. **d** 54 **p** 55. C Wigan St Geo *Liv* 54-57; V Newton-le-Willows 57-67; V Stoneycroft All SS 67-79; R N Meols 79-88; rtd 88; Perm to Offic *Liv* from 88. *8 Morley Road, Southport PR9 9JS* Tel (01704) 541428

PICKARD, Canon Frank Eustace. b 31. Lon Univ BScEcon52 St Cath Soc Ox BA56 MA63. St Steph Ho Ox. **d** 57 **p** 58. C Haydock St Jas *Liv* 57-59; C Davenham *Ches* 59-60; Asst Master St Dunstan's Sch Lon 60-63; Min Can Pet Cathl *Pet* 63-72; P-in-c Newborough 67-68; V 68-72; R Isham w Pytchley 72-76; R Abington 76-96; Can Pet Cathl 86-02; rtd 96; Hon C Weedon Lois w Plumpton and Moreton Pinkney etc *Pet* 96-02; Perm to Offic from 02. *19 Watersmeet, Northampton NN1 5SQ* Tel (01604) 239667

PICKARD, Mrs Patricia Anne. b 44. **d** 04 **p** 05. NSM Ovenden *Wakef* from 04. *46 Crag Lane, Halifax HX2 8NU* Tel (01422) 346948 E-mail ap.pickard@tiscali.co.uk

PICKARD, Stephen Kim. b 52. Newc Univ Aus BCom74 Van Mildert Coll Dur PhD90. Melbourne Coll of Div BD79 St Jo Coll Morpeth 77. **d** 80 **p** 80. Australia 80-82 and from 91; C Singleton 80-82; C Dur St Cuth *Dur* 82-84; Chapl Van Mildert Coll Dur 84-90; Chapl Trev Coll Dur 84-90; Lect United Th Coll Sydney 91-97; Dir St Mark's Nat Th Cen from 98; Assoc Prof and Hd Th Chas Sturt Univ from 99. *St Mark's National Theological Centre, 15 Blackall Street, Barton, ACT, Australia 2607* Tel (0061) (2) 6249 8647 *or* 6273 1572 Mobile 419-638020 Fax (2) 6273 4067 E-mail spickard@csu.edu.au

PICKARD, William Priestley. b 31. MCIPD72. Clifton Th Coll 56. **d** 59 **p** 60. C Upper Tulse Hill St Matthias *S'wark* 59-63; Asst Warden Shaftesbury Crusade Bris from 64; rtd 96. *45 Totterdown Road, Weston-super-Mare BS23 4LJ* Tel (01934) 628994

PICKEN, David Anthony. b 63. Lon Univ BA84 Kent Univ PGCE85 Nottm Univ MA96. Linc Th Coll 87. **d** 90 **p** 91. C Worth *Chich* 90-93; TV Wordsley *Worc* 93-97; TR 97-04; RD Kingswinford 01-04; TR High Wycombe *Ox* from 04. *The Rectory, 6 Priory Avenue, High Wycombe HP13 6SH* Tel (01494) 525602 E-mail dap@dircon.co.uk

PICKEN, James Hugh. b 51. Victoria Univ (BC) BMus75 ARCT73 Ox Univ MA94. Ripon Coll Cuddesdon BA79. **d** 80 **p** 81. C Jarrow *Dur* 80-83; SSF 83-93; Perm to Offic *Sarum* 86-92; Guardian Alnmouth Friary 92-94; Lic to Offic *Newc* 92-94; Canada from 94. *929-4th Street NW, Calgary AB, Canada, T2N 1P4* Tel (001) (403) 270 9661

PICKERING, Alastair David. b 72. Newc Univ BA94. Wycliffe Hall Ox 03. **d** 05. C Silverhill St Matt *Chich* from 05. *98 Sedlescombe Gardens, St Leonards-on-Sea TN38 0YW* Tel (01424) 720809 E-mail al@thepickerings.net

PICKERING, David Colville. b 41. Kelham Th Coll 61. **d** 66 **p** 67. C Chaddesden St Phil *Derby* 66-70; C New Mills 70-72; C Buxton 72-74; V Chesterfield St Aug 74-90; R Whittington 90-99; P-in-c Hathersage 99; P-in-c Bamford 99; R Hathersage w Bamford and Derwent from 00. *The Vicarage, Church Bank, Hathersage, Hope Valley S32 1AJ* Tel (01433) 650215 E-mail crispy@kupola.com

PICKERING, The Ven Fred. b 19. St Pet Hall Ox BA41 MA45. St Aid Birkenhead 41. **d** 43 **p** 44. C Leyland St Andr *Blackb* 43-46; C Islington St Mary *Lon* 46-48; NE Area Sec CPAS 48-51; V Burton All SS *Lich* 51-56; V Carl St Jo *Carl* 56-63; V Chitts Hill St Cuth *Lon* 63-74; RD E Haringey 68-73; Adn Hampstead 74-84; rtd 84; Perm to Offic *Pet* 84-93 and *Ex* 94-96. *8 Fosbrooke House, Clifton Drive, Lytham St Annes FY8 5RQ*

PICKERING, Geoffrey Craig. b 40. Newc Coll of Arts NDD61 Leic Coll of Art & Design ATD62 Leic Univ CertEd62. S Dios Minl Tr Scheme 90. **d** 93 **p** 94. C Horsham *Chich* 93-97; V Heathfield from 97. *The Vicarage, Old Heathfield, Heathfield TN21 9AB* Tel (01435) 862457

PICKERING, John Alexander. b 41. TCD BA63 MA66. CITC 65. **d** 65 **p** 66. C Magheralin *D & D* 65-67; C-in-c Outeragh *K, E & A* 67-68; I 68-71; Deputation Sec Hibernian Bible Soc 71-74; C-in-c Drumgoon and Ashfield 74-80; I Keady w Armaghbreague and Derrynoose *Arm* 80-83; I Drumcree from 83. *Drumcree Rectory, 78 Drumcree Road, Portadown, Craigavon BT62 1PE* Tel (028) 3833 3711

PICKERING, John David. b 38. **d** 86 **p** 86. NSM Ellon *Ab* 86-88; NSM Cruden Bay 86-88; Ind Chapl *Dur* 88-97; TV Jarrow 91-97; P-in-c Newton Hall 97-02; TV Dur N 02-03; rtd 03. *14 Denholm Avenue, Cramlington NE23 3FT* Tel (01670) 716619

PICKERING, John Michael Staunton. b 34. Sarum & Wells Th Coll 71. **d** 72 **p** 73. C Gaywood, Bawsey and Mintlyn *Nor* 72-77; P-in-c Foulsham 77-81; R Foulsham w Hindolveston and Guestwick 81-88; P-in-c Bacton w Edingthorpe w Witton and Ridlington 88-98; rtd 98; Perm to Offic *Nor* from 04. *East Lodge, Wardley Hill Road, Kirby Cane, Bungay NR35 2PQ*

PICKERING, John Roger. b 28. Fitzw Ho Cam BA52 MA56. Linc Th Coll 62. **d** 63 **p** 66. C Haxby w Wigginton *York* 63-64; CF 66-69; C Folkestone H Trin w Ch Ch *Cant* 71-73; P-in-c Buckland Newton *Sarum* 73-77; P-in-c Wootton Glanville and Holnest 73-77; P-in-c Osmington w Poxwell 77-80; C Eston w Normanby *York* 83-84; P-in-c Swine 84-90; rtd 90; Perm to Offic *Truro* from 90. *The Bull Pens, Treworder Farm, Ruan Minor, Helston TR12 7JL* Tel (01326) 290908 Fax 0870-0553945 E-mail pickering@ministry.demon.co.uk

PICKERING, Malcolm. b 37. Sarum Th Coll 65. **d** 68 **p** 69. C Milton *Portsm* 68-70; C Stanmer w Falmer and Moulsecoomb *Chich* 70-75; Chapl Brighton Coll of Educn 71-75; V Hooe and R Ninfield *Chich* 75-80; V Ventnor H Trin and Ventnor St Cath *Portsm* 80-88; Chapl St Cath Sch Ventnor 87-88; V Marton *Blackb* 88-97; P-in-c Badingham w Bruisyard, Cransford and Dennington *St E* 97-99; V Leiston 99-04; rtd 04. *38 Lethbridge Road, Wells BA5 2FW* Tel (01749) 676526 E-mail malcolm@totland-a.freeserve.co.uk

PICKERING, Mark Penrhyn. b 36. Liv Univ BA59 St Cath Coll Ox BA62 MA67. Wycliffe Hall Ox 60. **d** 63 **p** 64. C Claughton cum Grange *Ches* 63-67; C Newland St Jo *York* 67-72; TV Marfleet 72-76; V Kingston upon Hull St Nic 76-85; V Elloughton and Brough w Brantingham 85-88; Chapl R Hull Hosps NHS Trust 88-01; Perm to Offic *York* from 01.

St Nicholas, Beech Hill Road, Swanland, North Ferriby HU14 3QY Tel (01482) 634892 *or* 674427

PICKERING, Stephen Philip. b 52. St Jo Coll York CertEd75. Coll of Resurr Mirfield 77. **d** 79 **p** 80. C Wallsend St Luke *Newc* 79-82; Chapl RN 82-92; C-in-c Ryecroft St Nic CD *Sheff* 92-97; V Ryecroft St Nic 97-01; V Plymouth St Simon and St Mary *Ex* from 01. *St Simon's Vicarage, 86 Edith Avenue, Plymouth PL4 8TL* Tel (01752) 660654

PICKERING, William Stuart Frederick. b 22. K Coll Lon BD49 AKC49 PhD58 Manitoba Univ Hon DCL81. **d** 50 **p** 51. C Frodingham *Linc* 50-53; Lic to Offic Guildf & Linc 55-56; Tutor K Coll Lon 53-56; Canada 58-66; Lic to Offic *Newc* 66-87; rtd 87; Perm to Offic *Ely* 87-97 and from 03. *1 Brookfield Road, Coton, Cambridge CB3 7PT* Tel (01954) 210525

PICKETT, Brian Laurence. b 48. Reading Univ BA70 Qu Coll Birm BA73 MA77. Ripon Coll Cuddesdon. **d** 88 **p** 88. C Highcliffe w Hinton Admiral *Win* 88-91; P-in-c Colbury 91-01; P-in-c W End 01-04; V from 04. *St James's Vicarage, Elizabeth Close, Southampton SO30 3LT* Tel (023) 8047 2180 Fax 8047 7661

PICKETT, Ms Joanna Elizabeth. b 53. Leic Univ BA74 MA80 Lon Univ MTh95. Wycliffe Hall Ox 87. **d** 89 **p** 94. Chapl Southn Univ *Win* 89-94; C N Stoneham 94-95; NSM Colbury 97-01; NSM W End from 01. *St James's Vicarage, Elizabeth Close, Southampton SO30 3LT* Tel (023) 8047 2180 Fax 8047 7661

PICKETT, Mark William Leslie. b 60. Westhill Coll Birm BEd84. Trin Coll Bris DipHE95. **d** 95 **p** 96. C Hellesdon *Nor* 95-98; TV Thetford 98-03; R Clitheroe St Jas *Blackb* from 03. *The Rectory, Woone Lane, Clitheroe BB7 1BJ* Tel (01200) 423608 E-mail cloverfieldchurch@talk21.com

PICKETT, Peter Leslie. b 28. Guy's Hosp Medical Sch LDS RCS. S Dios Minl Tr Scheme 83. **d** 86 **p** 87. NSM Eastbourne H Trin *Chich* 86-88; P-in-c Danehill 88-93; rtd 93; Perm to Offic *Chich* from 93. *Springfield, 76 Meads Road, Eastbourne BN20 7QJ* Tel (01323) 731709 E-mail janpickett@lineone.net

PICKFORD (née PACKER), Mrs Catherine Ruth. b 76. Nottm Univ BA97 Anglia Poly Univ MA00. Westcott Ho Cam MA00. **d** 00 **p** 01. C Gosforth All SS *Newc* 00-04; TV Benwell from 04. *56 Dunholme Road, Newcastle upon Tyne NE4 6XE* Tel 0191-273 5356 E-mail catherine.p@blueyonder.co.uk

PICKLES, Mark Andrew. b 62. Edin Univ BA83. Cranmer Hall Dur 85. **d** 88 **p** 89. C Rock Ferry *Ches* 88-91; C Hartford 91-93; V Wharton 93-00; P-in-c Duffield *Derby* 00-05; V Duffield and Lt Eaton from 05. *St Alkmund's Vicarage, Vicarage Lane, Duffield, Belper DE56 4EB* Tel (01332) 841168 *or* 840536 Fax 842595 E-mail md@vicduff.freeserve.co.uk

PICKSTONE, Charles Faulkner. b 55. BNC Ox BA77 MA81 Leeds Univ BA80. Coll of Resurr Mirfield 78. **d** 81 **p** 82. C Birkenhead Priory *Ches* 81-84; Chapl Paris St Geo *Eur* 84; C Camberwell St Giles w St Matt *S'wark* 84-89; V Catford St Laur from 89; Asst RD E Lewisham 92-99. *St Laurence's Vicarage, 31 Bromley Road, London SE6 2TS* Tel (020) 8698 2871 *or* 8698 9706 E-mail charlston@mailbox.co.uk

PICKTHORN, Canon Charles Howard. b 25. Linc Coll Ox BA48 MA52. Sarum Th Coll 48. **d** 50 **p** 51. C High Harrogate Ch Ch *Ripon* 50-54; C Cheam *S'wark* 54-60; R Bourton-on-the-Water w Clapton *Glouc* 60-91; Chapl RAF 60-76; RD Stow *Glouc* 67-90; P-in-c Gt Rissington 68-81; Hon Can Glouc Cathl from 77; rtd 91; Perm to Offic *Glouc* from 91. *267 Prestbury Road, Prestbury, Cheltenham GL52 3EX* Tel (01242) 521447

PICKUP, Harold. b 17. St Pet Hall Ox BA39 MA46. Ridley Hall Cam 46 Melbourne Coll of Div DipRE67. **d** 47 **p** 48. C Middleton *Man* 47-50; V Gravesend St Mary *Roch* 51-57; Australia from 57; rtd 82. *7 Farview Avenue, Riverside, Tas, Australia 7250* Tel (0061) (3) 6327 4891

PICTON, Arthur David. b 39. Ch Ch Ox BA62 MA67. Chich Th Coll. **d** 65 **p** 66. C Hulme St Phil *Man* 65-67; C Swinton St Pet 67-71; R Stretford St Pet 71-79; P-in-c Knights Enham *Win* 79-86; R 86-89; V Basing 89-02; RD Basingstoke 93-99; Hon Can Win Cathl 96-02; rtd 02; Perm to Offic *Win* from 03. *11 Millers Road, Tadley RG26 4LW* Tel 0118-981 5782 E-mail david@picton51.freeserve.co.uk

PIDGEON, Warner Mark. b 68. Trin Coll Bris 00. **d** 02 **p** 03. C Fair Oak *Win* from 02. *Windfall, Chapel Drove, Horton Heath, Eastleigh SO50 7DL* Tel (023) 8069 4577 Mobile 07876-085054 E-mail warnermoira@supanet.com

PIDOUX, Ian George. b 32. Univ Coll Ox BA55 MA60. Coll of Resurr Mirfield 54. **d** 57 **p** 58. C Middlesbrough All SS *York* 57-60; C Haggerston St Aug w St Steph *Lon* 60-62; C Aylesford *Roch* 80-81; TV Rye *Chich* 81-84; P-in-c Bridgwater St Jo *B & W* 84-86; V 86-98; Chapl Bridgwater Hosp 91-98; rtd 98; Perm to Offic *B & W* from 98. *Pear Tree Cottage, 9 Greenway, North Curry, Taunton TA3 6NQ* Tel (01823) 490647 Fax as telephone E-mail igsepidoux@aol.com

PIDSLEY, Preb Christopher Thomas. b 36. ALCD61. **d** 61 **p** 62. C Enfield Ch Ch Trent Park *Lon* 61-66; C Rainham *Chelmsf* 66-70; V Chudleigh *Ex* 70-98; RD Moreton 86-91; Preb Ex Cathl 92-98; rtd 98. *Bellever, Shillingford Abbot, Exeter EX2 9QF* Tel (01392) 833588

PIERARD, Canon Beaumont Harold. b 21. MBE72 JP68. St Jo Coll Auckland. **d** 46 **p** 51. New Zealand 46-53; Chapl Hurstpierpoint Coll 53-54; Chapl Worksop Coll Notts 54-57; New Zealand from 57; Hon Can St Peter's Cathl Waikato 64-82. *287 Peachgrove Road, Hamilton, New Zealand* Tel (0064) (7) 855 7000

PIERCE, Alan. b 46. St Mark & St Jo Coll Lon TCert68 Southlands Coll Lon BEd75 K Coll Lon MA85. Lon Bible Coll DipTh72 N Ord Course 89. **d** 92 **p** 93. NSM Bolton St Thos *Man* 92-98; NSM Halliwell 98-00; NSM Bolton Breightmet St Jas from 00. *3 Astley Road, Bolton BL2 4BR* Tel (01204) 300071 Fax 401556

PIERCE, Anthony. *See* PIERCE, Canon Claude Anthony

✠**PIERCE, The Rt Revd Anthony Edward.** b 41. Univ of Wales (Swansea) BA63 Linacre Coll Ox BA65 MA71. Ripon Hall Ox 63. **d** 65 **p** 66 **c** 99. C Swansea St Pet *S & B* 65-67; C Swansea St Mary and H Trin 67-74; Chapl Univ of Wales (Swansea) 71-74; V Llwynderw 74-92; P-in-c Swansea St Barn 92-96; Dioc Dir of Educn 93-96; Can Brecon Cathl 93-99; Adn Gower 95-99; V Swansea St Mary w H Trin 96-99; Bp S & B from 99. *Ely Tower, The Avenue, Brecon LD3 9DE* Tel (01874) 622008 Fax as telephone

PIERCE, Brian William. b 42. St Steph Ho Ox 86. **d** 88 **p** 89. C Cudworth *Wakef* 88-93; TV Manningham *Bradf* 93-98; V Tipton St Jo *Lich* from 98. *St John's Vicarage, Upper Church Lane, Tipton DY4 9ND* Tel 0121-557 1793

PIERCE, Bruce Andrew. b 58. TCD BBS80 BTh89 Dub City Univ MA99 MA02. CITC 86. **d** 89 **p** 90. C Raheny w Coolock *D & G* 89-92; C Taney 92-93; I Lucan w Leixlip 93-98; Chapl Adelaide and Meath Hosp Dublin 98-02; C Haarlem *Eur* 02-03; Chapl Toronto Gen Hosp Canada 03-04; Chapl Princess Marg Hosp Toronto from 04. *11 Pinewood Avenue, Toronto ON, Canada, M6C 2V2* Tel (001) (416) 651 3330 *or* 946 4501 ext 4752 E-mail brupierce@hotmail.com

PIERCE, Canon Claude Anthony (Tony). b 19. OBE46. Magd Coll Cam BA47 MA49 BD53. Ely Th Coll 47. **d** 48 **p** 49. C Chesterfield St Mary and All SS *Derby* 48-51; Chapl Magd Coll Cam 51-56; Lect Th 54-56; Select Preacher Cam Univ 54; Australia from 56; Warden Wollaston Th Coll 56-70; Hon Can Perth 64-66; Can 66-85; Chapl Actors Ch Union 77-90; Chapl Univ of W Australia 81-84; Chapl and Sub-Warden St Geo Coll Crawley 81-84; rtd 85; Perm to Offic *Perth* from 85. *61 Hawkstone Street, Cottesloe, W Australia 6011* Tel (0061) (8) 9383 2719

PIERCE, David. *See* PIERCE, Thomas David Benjamin

PIERCE, Jeffrey Hyam. b 29. FBIM80 Chelsea Coll Lon BSc51. Ox NSM Course 86. **d** 88 **p** 89. NSM Gt Missenden w Ballinger and Lt Hampden *Ox* 88-93; NSM Penn 93-97; rtd 97; Perm to Offic *Ox* from 97. *Glebe Cottage, Manor Road, Penn, High Wycombe HP10 8HY* Tel (01494) 817179

PIERCE, Jonathan Douglas Marshall. b 70. UCD BA91. CITC BTh96. **d** 96 **p** 97. C Knockbreda *D & D* 96-99; L'Arche Community Dublin 99-00; C Taney *D & G* 00-03; I Kilmore and Inch *D & D* from 03. *The Rectory, 22 Church Road, Kilmore, Downpatrick BT30 9HR* Tel (028) 4483 0371 E-mail kilmore@down.anglican.org

PIERCE, Neil David. b 42. Cant Univ (NZ) BA63 MA64 Ch Ch Coll Cant Dip Teaching65. Coll of Resurr Mirfield. **d** 70 **p** 71. C Huddersfield SS Pet and Paul *Wakef* 70-74; Zimbabwe 75-04; Prec St Jo Cathl Bulawayo 75-81; Hd Master Cyrene Sch 82-99; P-in-c Figtree, Marula and Plumtree 82-99; Dioc Sec Matabeleland 00-04; R Barham Green St Fran 02-04; rtd 04; Perm to Offic *Lich* from 05. *20 Poplar Avenue, Walsall WS5 4EX* Tel (01922) 632888 Mobile 07833-530111 E-mail pierceneil@aol.com

PIERCE, Stephen Barry. b 60. Birm Univ BA81 MA82. Cranmer Hall Dur. **d** 85 **p** 86. C Huyton St Mich *Liv* 85-89; V Walton Breck Ch Ch 89-00; P-in-c Walton Breck 98-00; Resources Officer from 00. *39 Duke Street, Formby, Liverpool L37 4AP* Tel (01704) 833725

PIERCE, Thomas David Benjamin. b 67. Ulster Univ BA88. Oak Hill Th Coll DipHE92 BA94. **d** 94 **p** 95. C Cromer *Nor* 94-97; C Belfast St Donard *D & D* 97-99; C Holywood 99-00; I Kilwarlin Upper w Kilwarlin Lower from 00. *Kilwarlin Rectory, 9 St John's Road, Hillsborough BT26 6ED* Tel (028) 9268 3299

PIERCE, William Johnston. b 32. N Ord Course. **d** 89 **p** 90. NSM Gt Crosby St Luke *Liv* 89-96; Perm to Offic from 96. *1 Forton Lodge, Blundellsands Road East, Liverpool L23 8SA* Tel 0151-924 2400

PIERCE-JONES, Alan. b 74. Coll of Ripon & York St Jo BA98. St Mich Coll Llan 98. **d** 00 **p** 01. C Port Talbot St Theodore *Llan* 00-02; TV Neath 02-05; P-in-c Lt Marsden w Nelson St Mary *Blackb* from 05; P-in-c Nelson St Bede from 05. *St Paul's Vicarage, Bentley Street, Nelson BB9 0BS* Tel (01282) 615888 E-mail fr.alan@apj.org.uk

PIERCY, Elizabeth Claire. *See* FRANCE, Mrs Elizabeth Claire

PIERPOINT, The Ven David Alfred. b 56. **d** 86 **p** 88. NSM Athboy w Ballivor and Killallon *M & K* 86-88; NSM Killiney Ballybrack *D & G* 88-89; NSM Narraghmore and Timolin w

Castledermot etc 89-91; Chan V St Patr Cathl Dublin 90-96; C Dublin St Patr Cathl Gp *D & G* 92-95; V Dublin Ch Ch Cathl Gp from 95; Can Ch Ch Cathl Dublin from 95; Adn Dublin from 04. *The Vicarage, 30 Phibsborough Road, Dublin 7, Irish Republic* Tel (00353) (1) 830 4601 Mobile 87-263 0402 E-mail dpier@iol.ie

PIGGOT, Alan Robert Lennox. b 62. Peterho Cam BA84 MA88. Westcott Ho Cam 00. **d** 02 **p** 03. C Dalston H Trin w St Phil and Haggerston All SS *Lon* 02-04; C Stoke Newington St Mary 04-05; C Hackney Wick St Mary of Eton w St Aug from 05. *St Mary's House, Eastway, London E9 5JA* Tel 07743-294532 (mobile) E-mail anglicalan@onetel.net.uk

PIGGOTT, The Ven Andrew John. b 51. Qu Mary Coll Lon BSc(Econ)72. St Jo Coll Nottm 83. **d** 86 **p** 87. C Dorridge *Birm* 86-89; TV Kidderminster St Geo *Worc* 89-94; V Biddulph *Lich* 94-99; Min and Voc Adv CPAS 99-01; Patr Sec 01-05; Adn Bath and Preb Wells Cathl *B & W* from 05. *56 Grange Road, Saltford, Bristol BS31 3AG* Tel (01225) 873609 Fax 874110 E-mail adbath@bathwells.anglican.org

PIGGOTT, Clive. b 47. St Luke's Coll Ex CertEd69. LNSM course 93. **d** 96 **p** 97. OLM Malden St Jas *S'wark* from 96. *84 Manor Drive North, New Malden KT3 5PA* Tel (020) 8337 0801

PIGGOTT, Raymond George. b 16. Leeds Univ BA38. Coll of Resurr Mirfield 38. **d** 40 **p** 41. C Leic St Mark *Leic* 40-42; C Munster Square St Mary Magd *Lon* 42-47; Chapl RN 47-53; C Felixstowe St Jo *St E* 53-54; V Barney w Thursford *Nor* 54-56; V Ilkley St Marg *Bradf* 56-65; V Roughey *Chich* 65-80; P-in-c Lynch w Iping Marsh 80-83; rtd 83; Perm to Offic *Chich* from 85. *Flat 2, Bramwell Lodge, Brighton Road, Terry's Cross, Woodmancote, Henfield BN5 9SX* Tel (01273) 493749

PIGOTT, Canon Graham John. b 44. Lon Univ BD73 Nottm Univ MPhil84 MEd94. St Jo Coll Nottm. **d** 81 **p** 82. C Beeston *S'well* 81-84; P-in-c W Bridgford 84-88; V Wilford Hill from 88; AD W Bingham 97-04; Hon Can S'well Minster from 04. *The Parsonage, Boundary Road, West Bridgford, Nottingham NG2 7DB* Tel 0115-923 3492 E-mail graham@gjpigott.fsnet.co.uk

PIGOTT, Canon John Drummond. b 26. TCD Div Test50 BA50 MA56. **d** 51 **p** 52. C Belfast St Phil *Conn* 51-54; C Jordanstown 54-56; Chapl RAF 56-59; R Upper Clatford w Goodworth Clatford *Win* 59-65; V Warley Woods *Birm* 65-74; RD Warley 72-74; V Boldmere 74-97; Hon Can Birm Cathl 81-97; RD Sutton Coldfield 88-93; rtd 97; Perm to Offic *B & W* from 97. *Clatford House, 41 Farriers Green, Monkton Heathfield, Taunton TA2 8PP* Tel (01823) 413552

PIGOTT, Nicholas John Capel. b 48. Qu Coll Birm 75. **d** 78 **p** 79. C Belmont *Dur* 78-79; C Folkestone St Sav *Cant* 79-82; C Birm St Geo *Birm* 82-85; V Stevenage St Hugh and St Jo *St Alb* 85-91; TV Totnes w Bridgetown, Berry Pomeroy etc *Ex* 91-02; Asst P 02-04; rtd 04. *27 Croft Road, Ipplepen, Newton Abbot TQ12 5SS* Tel (01803) 813664 E-mail njsa@pigott.freeserve.co.uk

PIGREM, Terence John (Tim). b 39. Middx Univ BA97 MA01. Oak Hill Th Coll 66. **d** 69 **p** 70. C Islington St Andr w St Thos and St Matthias *Lon* 69-73; C Barking St Marg w St Patr *Chelmsf* 73-75; TV 75-76; C W Holloway St Luke *Lon* 76-79; V 79-95; P-in-c Abbess Roding, Beauchamp Roding and White Roding *Chelmsf* 95-96; R S Rodings from 96; RD Dunmow 97-02. *The Rectory, Stortford Road, Leaden Roding, Dunmow CM6 1GY* Tel (01279) 876387 E-mail pigrem@btinternet.com

PIIR, The Very Revd Gustav Peeter. b 61. St Olaf Coll Minnesota BA83 Saskatchewan Univ MDiv86. **p** 88. Asst Toronto St Pet Canada 88-92; Asst Chas Ch Tallinn Estonia 92-95; R Tallinn H Spirit from 95; Dean Tallinn from 99; P-in-c Tallinn SS Tim and Titus *Eur* from 00. *Pühavaimu 2, Tallinn 10123, Estonia* Tel (00372) 646 4430 Mobile 51-76159 Fax 644 1487 E-mail praost@hot.ee

PIKE, Mrs Amanda Shirley Gail. b 69. Cranmer Hall Dur 99. **d** 01 **p** 02. C Boston Spa *York* 01-03; C Elloughton and Brough w Brantingham 03-05; P-in-c Eggleston *Dur* from 05; P-in-c Middleton-in-Teesdale w Forest and Frith from 05. *The Rectory, 1 Hude, Middleton-in-Teesdale, Barnard Castle DL12 0QW* Tel (01833) 641013 Mobile 07968-543569 E-mail amanda@ichthos.me.uk

PIKE, David Frank. b 35. BA Lon Univ TCert CEng MIMechE. S Dios Minl Tr Scheme 82. **d** 85 **p** 86. NSM Lancing w Coombes *Chich* 85-88; R Albourne w Sayers Common and Twineham 88-94; V Wisborough Green 94-04; rtd 04. *42 Greenoaks, Lancing BN15 0HE* Tel (01903) 766209

PIKE, George Richard. b 38. Birm Univ BSc57. WMMTC 79. **d** 82 **p** 83. NSM Edgbaston St Bart *Birm* 82-89; NSM S Yardley St Mich from 89. *138 Charlbury Crescent, Birmingham B26 2LW* Tel and fax 0121-783 2818 E-mail kepi@geopi.fsnet.co.uk

PIKE, Horace Douglas. b 13. AKC48. **d** 48 **p** 49. C Todmorden *Wakef* 48-52; P-in-c Lundwood 52-55; V Gawber 55-59; V Baildon *Bradf* 59-71; R Burnsall 72-78; rtd 78; P-in-c Birdsall w Langton *York* 81-86; Perm to Offic from 86. *18 Southfield Close, Rufforth, York YO23 3RE* Tel (01904) 738418

PIKE, James. b 22. TCD 66. **d** 68 **p** 69. C Clooney *D & R* 68-72; I Ardstraw 72-76; I Ardstraw w Baronscourt 76-86; I Ardstraw w Baronscourt, Badoney Lower etc 76-92; Can Derry Cathl 90-92; rtd 92. *19 Knockgreenan Avenue, Omagh BT79 0EB* Tel (028) 8224 9007 Fax 8225 1382

PIKE, Paul Alfred. b 38. Bognor Regis Coll of Educn CertEd58 MIL88. Wycliffe Hall Ox 83. **d** 84 **p** 85. C Penn Fields *Lich* 84-89; OMF Internat Japan 89-03; rtd 03; Perm to Offic *Bris* from 03. *18 Silverlow Road, Nailsea, Bristol BS48 2AD* Tel (01275) 856270 E-mail papike@attglobal.net

PIKE, Peter John. b 53. Southn Univ BTh86 Lanc Univ PhD00. Sarum & Wells Th Coll 81. **d** 84 **p** 85. C Broughton *Blackb* 84-88; V Woodplumpton 88-93; Asst Dir of Ords and Voc Adv 89-93; P-in-c Barnacre w Calder Vale 93-98; V Briercliffe 98-04; AD Burnley 01-04; V Bempton w Flamborough, Reighton w Speeton *York* from 04. *The Vicarage, Church Street, Flamborough, Bridlington YO15 1PE* Tel (01262) 850336 E-mail revpeterpike@hotmail.com

PIKE, Robert James. b 47. Kelham Th Coll 66. **d** 70 **p** 71. C Cov St Pet *Cov* 70-74; C Bilton 74-76; P-in-c Southall St Geo *Lon* 76-81; V S Harrow St Paul 81-86; C Hillingdon St Jo 86-88; Chapl Hillingdon Hosp & Mt Vernon Hosp Uxbridge 88-90; Perm to Offic 91-96. *6 Salt Hill Close, Uxbridge UB8 1PZ* Tel (01895) 235212

PIKE, Timothy David. b 68. Collingwood Coll Dur BA90 Leeds Univ BA94. Coll of Resurr Mirfield 92. **d** 95 **p** 96. C Owton Manor *Dur* 95-98; C Old St Pancras w Bedford New Town St Matt *Lon* 98-03; CR 03-04; P-in-c Hornsey H Innocents *Lon* from 04; C Stroud Green H Trin from 04. *99 Hillfield Avenue, London N8 7DG* Tel (020) 8340 1300 E-mail fathertimpike@hotmail.com

PILCHER, Mrs Jennifer. b 42. **d** 04 **p** 05. OLM Eastry and Northbourne w Tilmanstone etc *Cant* from 04. *1 Long Drive, Church Street, Eastry, Sandwich CT13 0HN* Tel (01304) 611472 E-mail jennifer.p@torview1.freeserve.co.uk

PILDITCH, Miss Patricia Desiree. b 21. **dss** 82 **d** 87 **p** 94. Barnstaple *Ex* 82-87; NSM Barnstaple 87-01; Asst Chapl N Devon Healthcare NHS Trust 82-01; Perm to Offic *Ex* from 01. *4 The Mews, Bydown, Swimbridge, Barnstaple EX32 0QB* Tel (01271) 830770

PILGRIM, Colin Mark. b 56. BA77 Geneva Univ Cert Ecum Studies 84. Westcott Ho Cam 81. **d** 84 **p** 85. C Chorlton-cum-Hardy St Clem *Man* 84-87; C Whitchurch *Bris* 87-89; V Bedminster Down 89-95; Dioc Youth Officer 95-01; Hon C Stoke Bishop 96-01; V Henleaze from 01. *St Peter's Vicarage, 17 The Drive, Henleaze, Bristol BS9 4LD* Tel 0117-962 0636 *or* 962 3196 E-mail markpilgrimis@aol.com

PILGRIM, Donald Eric. b 55. Cant Univ (NZ) BA80 LTh87. St Jo Coll Auckland 81. **d** 81 **p** 82. New Zealand 81-85 and from 86; C Southampton Maybush St Pet *Win* 85-86. *212 Hoon Hay Road, Christchurch 2, New Zealand* Tel (0064) (3) 338 4277 Fax as telephone

PILGRIM, Ms Judith Mary. b 44. Westcott Ho Cam 88. **d** 90 **p** 94. C Probus, Ladock and Grampound w Creed and St Erme *Truro* 90-94; Par Dn Nottingham All SS *S'well* 94; C 94-97; Asst Chapl to the Deaf 94-97; Perm to Offic *S'well* 97-00; *Ox* 00-01; P-in-c Zennor *Truro* from 02; P-in-c Towednack from 02. *The Vicarage, Nancledra, Penzance TR20 8LQ* Tel (01736) 740548

PILGRIM, Kenneth George. b 49. **d** 01 **p** 02. OLM Alkham w Capel le Ferne and Hougham *Cant* 01-03; Perm to Offic *Nor* from 04. *Sunny Oak, 27 Fakenham Road, Beetley, Dereham NR20 4BT* Tel (01362) 861265 E-mail ken@prilgrim12.freeserve.co.uk

PILGRIM, Mark. *See* PILGRIM, Colin Mark

PILKINGTON, Miss Anne. b 57. Aston Tr Scheme 88 N Ord Course 90. **d** 93 **p** 94. C Wythenshawe Wm Temple Ch *Man* 93-96; P-in-c 96-99; TV Wythenshawe from 99. *William Temple Vicarage, Robinswood Road, Manchester M22 6BU* Tel 0161-437 3194 E-mail a.pilky@fish.co.uk.

PILKINGTON, Charles George Willink. b 21. Trin Coll Cam BA42 MA64. Westcott Ho Cam. **d** 63 **p** 64. C Pendleton St Thos *Man* 63-65; C Brindle Heath 63-65; C Chorlton-cum-Hardy St Clem 65-68; R Withington St Chris 68-88; rtd 88; Perm to Offic *Man* from 88. *32 Rathen Road, Withington, Manchester M20 9GH* Tel 0161-434 5365

PILKINGTON, Canon Christopher Frost. b 23. Trin Coll Cam BA50 MA60. Ridley Hall Cam 50. **d** 52 **p** 53. C St Jo in Bedwardine *Worc* 52-55; V Worc St Mark 55-60; V Bromsgrove St Jo 60-68; R Bris St Steph w St Nic and St Leon *Bris* 68-81; P-in-c 81-82; Hon Can Bris Cathl 79-82; Hon Chapl Cancer Help Cen Bris 82-89; rtd 89; Perm to Offic *Bris* from 90. *Apple Acre, Tunbridge Road, Chew Magna, Bristol BS40 8SP* Tel (01275) 333545

PILKINGTON, Edward Russell. b 39. ALCD65. **d** 65 **p** 66. C Eccleshill *Bradf* 65-68; C Billericay St Mary *Chelmsf* 68-72; V New Thundersley 72-78; R Theydon Garnon 78-82; V Gidea Park 82-04; rtd 04. *19 Tryon Close, Swindon SN3 6HG* Tel (01793) 433495

PILKINGTON, John Rowan. b 32. Magd Coll Cam BA55 MA59. Ridley Hall Cam 57. **d** 59 **p** 60. C Ashtead *Guildf* 59-61; C Wimbledon *S'wark* 62-65; R Newhaven *Chich* 65-75; R Farlington *Portsm* 75-89; V Darlington St Mark w St Paul *Dur* 89-97; rtd 97; Perm to Offic *Portsm* from 98. *38 Main Road, Emsworth PO10 8AU* Tel (01243) 375830

PILKINGTON, Timothy William. b 54. Nottm Univ BA85. Linc Th Coll 82. **d** 85 **p** 86. C Newquay *Truro* 85-88; C Cockington *Ex* 88-91; R St John w Millbrook *Truro* 91-97; V Northampton St Matt *Pet* 97-02; TR Solihull *Birm* from 02. *The Rectory, St Alphege Close, Church Hill Road, Solihull B91 3RQ* Tel 0121-705 0069 *or* 705 5350 Fax 704 0646

PILKINGTON OF OXENFORD, The Revd Canon Lord (Peter). b 33. Jes Coll Cam BA55 MA59. Westcott Ho Cam 58. **d** 59 **p** 60. C Bakewell *Derby* 59-62; Chapl Eton Coll 62-75; Hd Master K Sch Cant 75-85; Hon Can Cant Cathl *Cant* 75-90; High Master St Paul's Sch Barnes 86-92; Chmn Broadcasting Complaints Commn 92-96; Hon C Pimlico St Mary Bourne Street *Lon* 92-05. *Oxenford House, Dowlish Wake, Ilminster TA19 0PP* Tel (01460) 52813 Fax 55280

✠**PILLAR, The Rt Revd Kenneth Harold.** b 24. Qu Coll Cam BA48 MA53. Ridley Hall Cam 48. **d** 50 **p** 51 **c** 82. C Childwall All SS *Liv* 50-53; Chapl Lee Abbey 53-57; V New Beckenham St Paul *Roch* 57-62; V Cant St Mary Bredin *Cant* 62-65; Warden Lee Abbey 65-70; V Waltham Abbey *Chelmsf* 70-82; RD Chigwell 76-78; RD Epping Forest 78-82; Suff Bp Hertford *St Alb* 82-89; rtd 89; Asst Bp Sheff from 89. *75 Dobcroft Road, Sheffield S7 2LS* Tel 0114-236 7902

PIMENTEL, Peter Eric. b 55. BA. Ridley Hall Cam. **d** 82 **p** 83. C Gt Ilford St Andr *Chelmsf* 82-85; Chapl Basingstoke Distr Hosp 85-88; TV Grays Thurrock *Chelmsf* 88-96; P-in-c Barton *Portsm* 96-99; V from 99; Dioc Ecum Officer 96-02. *St Paul's Vicarage, Staplers Road, Newport PO30 2HZ* Tel (01983) 522075 Mobile 07949-366625 Fax 08701-303386 E-mail peter@pimentel.freeserve.co.uk

PIMM, Robert John. b 57. Bris Univ BA78 ACIB82. Trin Coll Bris 92. **d** 94 **p** 95. C Long Benton *Newc* 94-98; TV Bath Twerton-on-Avon *B & W* from 98. *Ascension Vicarage, 35A Claude Avenue, Bath BA2 1AG* Tel (01225) 405354 E-mail robertpimm@tiscali.co.uk

PINCHBECK, Miss Caroline Rosamund. b 70. Hatf Coll Dur BA93. Wesley Ho Cam MA00. **d** 02 **p** 03. C Mawnan *Truro* from 02. *The Rectory, Old Church Road, Mawnan Smith, Falmouth TR11 5HY* Tel (01326) 250280 E-mail crp@wesley71.freeserve.co.uk

PINCHES, Donald Antony. b 32. Pemb Coll Cam BA55 MA60 Linacre Coll Ox BA67. Wycliffe Hall Ox 64. **d** 67 **p** 68. C Aylesbury *Ox* 67-71; C Compton Gifford *Ex* 71-74; TV Lydford, Brent Tor, Bridestowe and Sourton 74-77; V Shiphay Collaton 77-97; rtd 97; Perm to Offic *Ex* from 98. *3 Malderek Avenue, Preston, Paignton TQ3 2RP* Tel (01803) 698003

PINDER, Canon John Ridout. b 43. Peterho Cam BA65 MA69. Cuddesdon Coll 65. **d** 73 **p** 74. C Leavesden All SS *St Alb* 73-76; Gen Sec Melanesian Miss 77-89; P-in-c Harpsden *Ox* 82-89; R Farlington *Portsm* 89-02; R Liss from 02; RD Portsm 96-01; Hon Can Portsm Cathl from 01. *The Rectory, 111 Station Road, Liss GU33 7AQ* Tel (01730) 890085 Fax 892654 E-mail john@jrpinder.freeserve.co.uk

PINDER-PACKARD, John. b 47. Lon Univ BSc. N Ord Course 81. **d** 84 **p** 85. NSM Mosbrough *Sheff* 84-85; C Norton 85-88; V New Whittington *Derby* 88-04; P-in-c Newbold and Gt Barlow 99-00; Chapl Whittington Hall Hosp 88-04; R Barlborough and Renishaw *Derby* from 04. *The New Rectory, Church Street, Barlborough, Chesterfield S43 4EP* Tel (01246) 570621

PINE, David Michael. b 41. Lich Th Coll 68. **d** 71 **p** 72. C Northam *Ex* 71-74; R Toft w Caldecote and Childerley *Ely* 74-80; R Hardwick 74-80; V Ipswich St Andr *St E* 80-84; P-in-c Hazelbury Bryan w Stoke Wake etc *Sarum* 84-91; R Hazelbury Bryan and the Hillside Par 91-93; V Steep and Froxfield w Privett *Portsm* 93-00; rtd 00. *Amberley, High Road, Nettlestone, Seaview PO34 5DZ* Tel (01983) 563734

PINES, Christopher Derek. b 65. Lon Univ MB, BS89. Oak Hill Th Coll DipHE93 BA93. **d** 93 **p** 94. C Heref St Pet w St Owen and St Jas *Heref* 93-97; Min Can and Chapl St Alb Abbey *St Alb* 97-03; Chapl St Alb Sch from 03. *1 Fishpool Street, St Albans AL3 4RS* Tel (01727) 846508

PINFIELD, Leslie Arthur. b 57. Birm Univ BMus79 Univ Coll Lon Dip Librarianship 90. St Steph Ho Ox DipMin94. **d** 94 **p** 95. C Bath Bathwick *B & W* 94-98; TV Swindon New Town *Bris* from 98. *St Luke's Vicarage, 3 Briar Fields, Swindon SN1 2QN* Tel (01793) 536679 Fax as telephone

PINK, Canon David. b 34. Qu Coll Cam BA58 MA62. Linc Th Coll 58. **d** 60 **p** 61. C Lt Ilford St Mich *Chelmsf* 60-63; Lect Boston 63-65; V Kirton in Holland *Linc* 65-71; V Spittlegate 71-77; Ecum Officer Lincs and S Humberside 77-85; Can and Preb Linc Cathl from 77; P-in-c Canwick 77-87; R Washingborough w Heighington 87-88; R Washingborough w Heighington and Canwick 88-90; rtd 90; Perm to Offic *Linc* from 90. *The Old School, Swarby, Sleaford NG34 8TG*

PINKERTON, Ms Patricia Edith. b 38. California Univ BA72 MA75 BTh80. Ch Div Sch of the Pacific (USA). **d** 81 **p** 82. USA 81-88; C Coleford w Staunton *Glouc* 88-92; Dn-in-c St Briavels w Hewelsfield 92-94; P-in-c 94-97; rtd 97; Perm to Offic *Glouc* from 97. *Lammas Cottage, 7 Stephens Place, Broadwell, Coleford GL16 7BJ* Tel (01594) 810321

PINNELL, George. b 39. NTMTC 96. **d** 99 **p** 00. NSM Hillingdon St Jo *Lon* from 99. *127 Cobden Close, Uxbridge UB8 2YH* Tel 07951-124976 (mobile) E-mail pinneg@tiscali.co.uk

PINNER, John Philip. b 37. K Coll Lon BA59 AKC59 Lon Inst of Educn PGCE60. Westcott Ho Cam 69. **d** 71 **p** 72. C Dover St Mary *Cant* 71-74; Chapl Felsted Sch 74-81; Chapl Rathkeale Coll New Zealand 81-02; rtd 02. *PO Box 133, Greytown, Wairarapa, New Zealand 5953* Tel (0064) (6) 304 8301 E-mail cheri.john.pinner@xtra.co.nz

PINNER, Canon Terence Malcolm William. b 35. Southn Univ MA89. AKC59. **d** 60 **p** 61. C Eltham St Barn *S'wark* 60-64; S Africa 64-67 and 69-74; USPG 67-69; Sec for Home Affairs Conf of Br Miss Socs 74-76; P-in-c Hinstock *Lich* 76-79; Adult Educn Officer 76-79; Adult RE Officer 79-83; Chapl Southn Univ *Win* 83-88; Tutor S Dios Minl Tr Scheme 88-92; Dioc Dir of Ords *Win* 88-98; Hon Can Win Cathl 92-00; P-in-c Old Alresford and Bighton 93-00; rtd 00; Perm to Offic *Win* from 01. *47 Buriton Road, Winchester SO22 6JF* Tel (01962) 884215 Mobile 07889-177203

PINNINGTON, Mrs Gillian. b 59. St Kath Coll Liv BEd81 Chester Coll of HE BTh02. N Ord Course 99. **d** 02 **p** 03. C Roby *Liv* from 02. *42 Buttermere Road, Bowring Park, Liverpool L16 2NN* Tel 0151-489 5910 E-mail pinny@supanet.com

PINNINGTON, Canon Suzanne Jane. b 66. Trevelyan Coll Dur BA89. St Steph Ho Ox 95. **d** 97 **p** 98. C Oakham, Hambleton, Egleton, Braunston and Brooke *Pet* 97-00; V Cottingley *Bradf* from 00; Hon Can Bradf Cathl from 04. *6 Woodvale Crescent, Bingley BD16 4AL* Tel (01274) 562278

PINNOCK, Geoffrey Gilbert. b 16. K Coll Lon 47. **d** 50 **p** 51. C Paddington St Mich w All SS *Lon* 50-52; S Africa 52-57; Perm to Offic *Lon* 57-66; Acting Chapl Nat Hosp Qu Square Lon 60; St Steph Hosp Chelsea 61-62; Asst Chapl Univ Coll Hosp Lon 62-66; USA 66-72; Perm to Offic *Lon* 72-73 and *S'wark* 73-74; C Battersea St Phil w St Bart 74-75; P-in-c Boconnoc w Bradoc *Truro* 75-81; rtd 81. *11 Drove Acre Road, Oxford OX4 3DF* Tel (01865) 247355

PINNOCK, Giles Antony. b 67. Leic Univ BA88 MA93 SSC. St Steph Ho Ox BTh04. **d** 02 **p** 03. C Stony Stratford *Ox* from 02; C Calverton from 02. *St Birinus' House, 9 Bunsty Court, Stony Stratford, Milton Keynes MK11 1NJ* Tel (01908) 561675 Mobile 07792-971375 Fax 08714-332362 E-mail gilespinnock@btinternet.com

PINNOCK, Martyn Elliott. b 47. Dartmouth RN Coll 65. Linc Th Coll 93. **d** 93 **p** 94. C Fordingbridge *Win* 93-97; V St Minver *Truro* 97-01; P-in-c Luray Ch Ch USA 01-02; V Steeton *Bradf* from 02. *The Vicarage, 2 Halsteads Way, Steeton, Keighley BD20 6SN* Tel (01535) 652877 Mobile 07817-036655 Fax (01535) 653950 E-mail nguage@railwayrev.force9.co.uk

PINSENT, Ewen Macpherson. b 30. Edin Th Coll 67. **d** 69 **p** 70. C Holt *Nor* 69-72; R Kelso *Edin* 72-82; R Blendworth w Chalton w Idsworth etc *Portsm* 82-90; R Blendworth w Chalton w Idsworth 90-92; rtd 92; Perm to Offic *Sarum* from 94. *The Cross House, Childe Okeford, Blandford Forum DT11 8ED* Tel (01258) 860803

PIPER, Canon Andrew. b 58. Magd Coll Ox BA79 MA83. Chich Th Coll 80. **d** 83 **p** 84. C Eastbourne St Mary *Chich* 83-88; TV Lewes All SS, St Anne, St Mich and St Thos 88-93; TR Worth 93-03; Can Res and Prec Heref Cathl *Heref* from 03. *1 The Close, Hereford HR1 2NG* Tel (01432) 266193 Fax 374220 E-mail precentor@herefordcathedral.org

PIPER, Canon Clifford John. b 53. Aber Univ CSS88. Moray Ord Course 91. **d** 93 **p** 94. C Invergordon St Ninian *Mor* 93-96; NSM Tain 96-98; P-in-c 98-03; P-in-c Invergordon St Ninian 00-03; P-in-c Forres from 03; Can St Andr Cathl Inverness from 00. *St John's Rectory, Victoria Road, Forres IV36 3BN* Tel (01309) 672856 Mobile 07779-404735 E-mail cliffpiper@onet.co.uk

PIPER, Gary Quentin David. b 42. Nottm Coll of Educn TCert65 Maria Grey Coll Lon DipEd71. Oak Hill Th Coll 75. **d** 78 **p** 79. NSM Fulham St Matt *Lon* 78-85; V from 85; AD Hammersmith 86-92. *St Matthew's Vicarage, 2 Clancarty Road, London SW6 3AB* Tel (020) 7731 3272 E-mail revgarypiper@hotmail.com

PIPER, Graham. b 58. Southn Univ BTh91. Chich Th Coll 88. **d** 91 **p** 92. C Horsham *Chich* 91-94; TV Haywards Heath St Wilfrid 94-99; Dioc Voc Adv 96-99; V Bamber Bridge St Aid *Blackb* 99-04; V Hawes Side and Marton Moss from 04. *The Vicarage, Hawes Side Lane, Blackpool FY4 5AH* Tel (01253) 697937 Mobile 07816-525843

PIPER, John Howard. b 09. St Chad's Coll Dur BA31. **d** 32 **p** 34. Asst Chapl Denstone Coll Uttoxeter 32-34; C Knowle H Nativity *Bris* 34-41; C Sidmouth St Nic *Ex* 41-44; Chapl RAFVR 44-46; C Cov St Mark *Cov* 46-49; C Paignton St Jo *Ex* 49-55; C Devonport St Budeaux 55-57; V Whitleigh 57-68; R

Rearsby w Ratcliffe on the Wreake *Leic* 68-78; P-in-c Thrussington 77-78; R Rearsby w Ratcliffe-on-the-Wreake etc 78-82; rtd 82; Perm to Offic *Leic* from 82. *52 Avenue Road, Queniborough, Leicester LE7 3FA* Tel 0116-260 6605

PIPER, Kenneth John. b 29. St Luke's Coll Ex TCert53 Leeds Univ DipEd67. S Dios Minl Tr Scheme 79. **d** 82 **p** 83. NSM Bradford w Oake, Hillfarrance and Heathfield *B & W* 82-87; Chapl to Norway and Scandinavia Lay Tr Officer *Eur* 87-89; R Durrington *Sarum* 90-94; P-in-c Antony w Sheviock *Truro* 94-00; rtd 00; Perm to Offic *Truro* 01-03. *5 Manor Ride, Brent Knoll, Highbridge TA9 4DY* Tel (01278) 760347

PIPPEN, Canon Brian Roy. b 50. St D Coll Lamp DipTh73. **d** 73 **p** 74. C Maindee *Mon* 73-77; TV Cwmbran 77-84; V Newport Ch Ch 84-90; R Pontypool from 90; RD Pontypool from 98; Can St Woolos Cathl from 01. *The Vicarage, Trevethin, Pontypool NP4 8JF* Tel (01495) 762228

PIRET, Michael John. b 57. State Univ NY BA79 Univ of Michigan MA80 PhD91 Mert Coll Ox MLitt89. Edin Th Coll 90. **d** 92 **p** 93. C St Andr Cathl Inverness *Mor* 92-94; Dean of Div and Chapl Magd Coll Ox from 94. *Magdalen College, Oxford OX1 4AU* Tel (01865) 276027

PIRRIE, Stephen Robin. b 56. Kent Univ BA79 Cam Univ MA83 Barrister 80. EAMTC 94. **d** 97 **p** 98. C King's Lynn St Marg w St Nic *Nor* 97-99; C Bideford, Northam, Westward Ho!, Appledore etc *Ex* 99-00; TV 00-03. *Address withheld by request*

PITCHER, Canon David John. b 33. Ely Th Coll 55. **d** 58 **p** 59. C Kingswinford St Mary *Lich* 58-61; C Kirkby *Liv* 61-66; R Ingham w Sutton *Nor* 66-72; V Lakenham St Jo 72-76; R Framlingham w Saxtead *St E* 76-91; RD Loes 82-89; Hon Can St E Cathl 85-99; R Woodbridge St Mary 91-99; rtd 99; Perm to Offic *St E* from 00. *25 Coucy Close, Framlingham, Woodbridge IP13 9AX* Tel (01728) 621580

PITCHER, George Martell. b 55. Birm Univ BA77 Middx Univ BA05. NTMTC 02. **d** 05. NSM St Bride Fleet Street w Bridewell etc *Lon* from 05. *88 Elfindale Road, London SE24 9NW* Tel (020) 7733 1587 Mobile 07778-917182
E-mail george@luther.co.uk

PITCHER, Robert Philip. b 47. Westhill Coll Birm DipEd70. Trin Coll Bris 90. **d** 92 **p** 93. C Llansamlet *S & B* 92-96; V Caereithin 96-02; V Llanidloes w Llangurig *Ban* from 02; AD Arwystli from 04. *The Vicarage, Trefeglwys Road, Llanidloes SY18 6HZ* Tel (01686) 412370 E-mail bob.pitcher@openworld.com

PITCHER, Ronald Charles Frederick. b 21. AKC50. **d** 51 **p** 52. C Burnage St Marg *Man* 51-53; C Heywood St Jas 53-55; C Newall Green CD 55-61; V Newall Green St Fran 61-73; Chapl Wythenshawe Hosp Man 64-73; C-in-c Danesholme CD *Pet* 73-81; V Estover *Ex* 81-91; rtd 91; Perm to Offic *Sarum* from 92. *18 East Wyld Road, Weymouth DT4 0RP* Tel (01305) 771916

PITCHER, Simon John. b 63. Reading Univ BA85. Ridley Hall Cam 00. **d** 02 **p** 03. C Lightcliffe *Wakef* 02-05; P-in-c Heckmondwike from 05; C Liversedge w Hightown from 05; C Roberttown w Hartshead from 05. *The Vicarage, Church Street, Heckmondwike WF16 0AX* Tel (01924) 405881
E-mail sjp@ukgateway.net

PITCHFORD, Herbert John. b 34. Dur Univ BA60. Ridley Hall Cam 60. **d** 62 **p** 63. C Heref St Martin *Heref* 62-68; R Much Birch w Lt Birch 68-78; P-in-c Much Dewchurch w Llanwarne and Llandinabo 73-78; R Much Birch w Lt Birch, Much Dewchurch etc 78-80; V Grange Park St Pet *Lon* 80-91; V Wylde Green *Birm* 91-01; rtd 01; Perm to Offic *Glouc* and *Worc* from 03. *Woodlands, Eaton Road, Malvern WR14 4PE* Tel (01684) 575893 Mobile 07870-841150
E-mail revjpitchford@woodlands45.freeserve.co.uk

PITE, Sheila Reinhardt. *See* STEVENSON, Mrs Sheila Reinhardt

PITHERS, Canon Brian Hoyle. b 34. Chich Th Coll 63. **d** 66 **p** 67. C Wisbech SS Pet and Paul *Ely* 66-70; V Fenstanton 70-75; V Hilton 70-75; V Habergham Eaves St Matt *Blackb* 75-85; P-in-c Habergham Eaves H Trin 78-85; V Burnley St Matt w H Trin 85-86; TR Ribbleton 86-92; V Torrisholme 92-00; Hon Can Blackb Cathl 97-00; rtd 01; Perm to Offic *Blackb* from 01. *37 Dallam Avenue, Morecambe LA4 5BB* Tel (01524) 424786
E-mail brianpithers@supanet.com

PITKIN, James Mark. b 62. Man Univ BSc83 MRAeS90 CEng90 Glos Univ BA(Theol)03. STETS DipTh99. **d** 99 **p** 00. C Chilworth w N Baddesley *Win* 99-03; V Lockerley and E Dean w E and W Tytherley from 03. *The Vicarage, The Street, Lockerley, Romsey SO51 0JF* Tel (01794) 340635 Mobile 07931-736166 Fax 08701-674691 E-mail jamespitkin@priest.com

PITKIN, Mrs Susan Margaret. b 60. Man Univ BA84 Surrey Univ BA03. STETS 00. **d** 03 **p** 04. C Southampton Maybush St Pet *Win* from 03. *St Peter's House, Lockerley Crescent, Southampton SO16 4BP* Tel (023) 8077 5014 Mobile 07752-891052 E-mail suepitkin@minister.com

PITMAN, Roger Thomas. b 64. St Mich Coll Llan BTh00. **d** 00 **p** 01. C Caerphilly *Llan* 00-02; C Coity w Nolton from 02. *Y Lletty, Heol yr Ysgol, Coity, Bridgend CF35 6BL* Tel (01656) 652540 E-mail way-follower@hotmail.com

PITT, Mrs Beatrice Anne. b 50. I M Marsh Coll of Physical Educn CertEd71 Open Univ BA01. Trin Coll Bris 80. **d** 82 **p** 97. C Rhyl w St Ann *St As* 82-86; CMS 86-92; Jt Co-ord Dioc Bible Schs Bukavu Zaïre 88-92; NSM Penycae *St As* 92-98; Hon Rep for CMS *St As* and *Ban* 93-98; NSM Killesher *K, E & A* 98-01; P-in-c Killinagh w Kiltyclogher and Innismagrath 98-01; P-in-c Firbank, Howgill and Killington *Bradf* 01-05; rtd 05. *20 Thornsbank, Sedbergh LA10 5LF* Tel (01539) 622095
E-mail anne@pitt.euro1net.com

PITT, George. b 52. QUB BD79 MTh88. CITC 81. **d** 81 **p** 82. C Belfast St Mary *Conn* 81-86; CMS 86-92; Zaïre 88-92; V Penycae *St As* 92-98; I Killesher *K, E & A* 98-01; Educn Adv Ch of Ireland Bps' Appeal 01-03. *20 Thornsbank, Sedbergh LA10 5LF* Tel (01539) 622095

PITT, Karen Lesley Finella. *See* TIMMIS, Mrs Karen Lesley Finella

PITT, Robert Edgar. b 37. Chich Th Coll 70. **d** 73 **p** 74. C Knowle *Bris* 73-77; C Wells St Cuth w Coxley and Wookey Hole *B & W* 77-81; TV Wellington and Distr 81-94; V Burnham 94-02; Chapl Taunton and Somerset NHS Trust 94-02; rtd 02; Perm to Offic *Sarum* from 03. *Redmaye, 119 High Street, Burbage, Marlborough SN8 3AA* Tel (01672) 810651

PITT, Canon Trevor. b 45. Hull Univ BA66 MA69 Open Univ DipEd91. Linc Th Coll 68 Union Th Sem (NY) STM70. **d** 70 **p** 71. C Sheff St Geo *Sheff* 70-74; TV Gleadless Valley 74-78; TR 78-79; P-in-c Elham *Cant* 79-82; V Elham w Denton and Wootton 82-91; Vice Prin Cant Sch of Min 81-91; Six Preacher Cant Cathl *Cant* 85-91; Prin NEOC *Newc* from 91; Hon Can Newc Cathl from 91; Perm to Offic *Ripon* and *York* from 91. *Greenview House, Hamsterley, Bishop Auckland DL13 3QF,* or *NEOC, Ushaw College, Durham DH7 9RH* Tel and fax (01388) 488898 *or* tel 0191-373 7600 fax 373 7601
E-mail trevorpitt@aol.com *or* tpitt@neoc.org.uk

PITT, Mrs Valerie. b 55. Liv Univ BA77. STETS 02. **d** 05. NSM Oxshott *Guildf* from 05. *166 Manor Green Road, Epsom KT19 8LL* Tel (01372) 721776
E-mail curate.oxshott@btinternet.com

PITTIS, Stephen Charles. b 52. Sheff Univ MA01. Oak Hill Th Coll DipTh75. **d** 76 **p** 77. C Win Ch Ch *Win* 76-79; Chapl Dorset Inst of HE and Bournemouth and Poole Coll of FE *Sarum* 79-84; V Woking St Paul *Guildf* 84-97; Dir of Faith Development *Win* from 97. *60 Upper Brook Street, Winchester SO23 8DG* Tel (01962) 854133

PITTS, Canon Evadne Ione (Eve). b 50. Qu Coll Birm. **d** 89 **p** 94. C Bartley Green *Birm* 89-93; TD Kings Norton 93-94; TV 94-98; P-in-c Highters Heath 98-00; V from 00; Hon Can Birm Cathl from 05. *Immanuel Vicarage, Pickenham Road, Birmingham B14 4TG* Tel 0121-430 7578

PITTS, The Very Revd Michael James. b 44. Worc Coll Ox BA67. Qu Coll Birm 67. **d** 69 **p** 70. C-in-c Pennywell St Thos and Grindon St Oswald CD *Dur* 69-72; C Darlington H Trin 72-74; Chapl Dunkerque w Lille Arras etc Miss to Seamen *Eur* 74-79; V Tudhoe *Dur* 79-81; Chapl Helsinki w Moscow *Eur* 81-85; Chapl Stockholm 85-88; Hon Can Brussels Cathl 87-88; Canada from 88; Hon Chapl Miss to Seafarers from 88; Dean and R Ch Ch Cathl Montreal from 91. *18 Weredale Park, Westmount PQ, Canada, H3A 2B8* Tel (001) (514) 843 6577 Fax 847 1316
E-mail mjpitts@ibm.net

PITYANA, Prof Nyameko Barney. b 45. K Coll Lon BD81 Cape Town Univ PhD95 Trin Coll Hartford (USA) Hon DD96. Ripon Coll Cuddesdon 82. **d** 82 **p** 83. C Woughton *Ox* 82-85; V Highters Heath *Birm* 85-88; Dir Progr to Combat Racism WCC 88-92; Hon C Geneva *Eur* 88-92; S Africa from 93; Sen Lect RS Cape Town Univ 93-95; Chair Human Rights Commission 95-01; Prin and Vice Chan UNISA from 01. *PO Box 69334, Bryanston, 2021 South Africa* Tel and fax (0027) (12) 341 5583 Mobile 83-379 1329 E-mail pityanb@mweb.co.za

PIX, Stephen James. b 42. Ex Coll Ox BA64 MA68 Univ of Wales (Cardiff) LLM97. Clifton Th Coll 66. **d** 68 **p** 69. C St Helens St Helen *Liv* 68-71; Lic to Offic *S'wark* 71-76; Hon C Wallington H Trin 76-84; V Osmotherley w E Harlsey and Ingleby Arncliffe *York* 84-89; V Ox St Mich w St Martin and All SS *Ox* 89-01; rtd 01; Perm to Offic *St E* from 01. *South Farm, Windmill Hill, Long Melford, Sudbury CO10 9AD* Tel (01787) 466198

PIZZEY, Canon Lawrence Roger. b 42. Dur Univ BA64. Westcott Ho Cam 65. **d** 67 **p** 68. C Bramford *St E* 67-71; Tutor Woodbridge Abbey 71-77; Asst Chapl Woodbridge Sch 71-77; P-in-c Flempton w Hengrave and Lackford *St E* 77-85; R Culford, W Stow and Wordwell 77-85; P-in-c Acton w Gt Waldingfield 85-89; V 89-95; P-in-c Sudbury and Chilton 95-98; R from 98; RD Sudbury from 96; Hon Can St E Cathl from 00. *The Rectory, Christopher Lane, Sudbury CO10 2AS* Tel (01787) 372611 E-mail lrp.sudbury@virgin.net

PLACE, Donald Lee Andrew. b 37. **d** 74 **p** 79. C Stainton-in-Cleveland *York* 79-81; TV Loughton St Jo *Chelmsf* 81-83; Chapl Worc R Infirmary and Hosps 83-85; rtd 95. *c/o Miss M J Place, 929 South Braddock Avenue, Pittsburgh, PA 15221, USA*

PLACE, Rodger Goodson. b 37. St Chad's Coll Dur BA60. **d** 62 **p** 63. C Pontesbury I and II *Heref* 62-65; C Heref St Martin 65-68; V Ditton Priors 68-75; R Neenton 68-75; P-in-c Aston Botterell w Wheathill and Loughton 69-75; P-in-c Burwarton w

N Cleobury 69-75; P-in-c Dacre w Hartwith *Ripon* 75-76; V 76-82; V Wyther Ven Bede 82-92; P-in-c Roundhay St Jo 92-97; V 97-00; rtd 00; Perm to Offic *York* from 00. *72 Field Lane, Thorpe Willoughby, Selby YO8 9FL* Tel (01757) 703174

PLACE, Thomas Richard. b 59. Ridley Hall Cam 93. **d** 93 **p** 94. C Huyton St Geo *Liv* 93-97; CF from 97. *c/o MOD Chaplains (Army)* Tel (01980) 615804 Fax 615800

PLAISTER, Keith Robin. b 43. K Coll Lon BD65 AKC65. **d** 66 **p** 67. C Laindon w Basildon *Chelmsf* 66-71; V Gt Wakering 71-78; P-in-c Foulness 78; V Gt Wakering w Foulness 78-90; C Witham 91-94; TV 94-99; P-in-c Sandon from 99; P-in-c E Hanningfield from 99. *The Rectory, Rectory Chase, Sandon, Chelmsford CM2 7SQ* Tel (01245) 472262
E-mail keithplaister@hotmail.com

PLANT, Caroline Mary. b 56. Ripon Coll Cuddesdon 01. **d** 03 **p** 04. C Gnosall *Lich* from 03. *17 Fountain Fold, Gnosall, Stafford ST20 0DR* Tel (01785) 822001
E-mail carolineplant@yahoo.co.uk

PLANT, Mrs Edith Winifred Irene (Ewith). b 31. Liv Univ BEd71. Cranmer Hall Dur 81. **dss** 83 **d** 87. Countesthorpe w Foston *Leic* 83-86; Loughborough All SS and H Trin 86-90; Par Dn 87-90; Par Dn Thurnby Lodge 90-91; rtd 91; Perm to Offic *Leic* 91-96 and *Ab* from 97. *Craighall Cottage, 26 South Road, Ellon AB41 9NP* Tel (01358) 723628

PLANT, Mrs Glenys. b 49. ALA71. EMMTC 95. **d** 98 **p** 99. C Allestree *Derby* 98-01; rtd 01; Perm to Offic *Derby* from 01. *3 Stoodley Pike Gardens, Allestree, Derby DE22 2TN* Tel (01332) 552697

PLANT, John Frederick. b 61. Man Univ BA82 MEd95. Qu Coll Birm 83. **d** 85 **p** 86. C Kersal Moor *Man* 85-88; Chapl Aston Univ *Birm* 88-94; TR Market Bosworth, Cadeby w Sutton Cheney etc *Leic* 94-00; P-in-c The Sheepy Gp 98-00; TR Bosworth and Sheepy Gp from 00; P-in-c Nailstone and Carlton w Shackerstone from 04. *The Rectory, Park Street, Market Bosworth, Nuneaton CV13 0LL* Tel (01455) 290239
E-mail jplant@leicester.anglican.org

PLANT, Michael Ian. b 47. Man Univ MEd85 GNSM68. St Jo Coll Nottm 97. **d** 99 **p** 00. NSM St D Cathl *St D* 99-01; NSM Dewisland from 01. *Lower Treginnis, St Davids, Haverfordwest SA62 6RS* Tel (01437) 720840 Fax 721350

PLANT, Nicholas. b 58. MAAT87. St Alb and Ox Min Course 95. **d** 98 **p** 99. OLM W Slough *Ox* 98-04; OLM Burnham w Dropmore, Hitcham and Taplow from 04. *The Pines, 6A Green Lane, Burnham, Slough SL1 8DR* Tel (01628) 604532 Mobile 07802-363835 Pager 07625-349908
E-mail nick@theplants.freeserve.co.uk

PLANT, Richard. b 41. Open Univ BSc93. Qu Coll Birm 88. **d** 90 **p** 91. C Skelmersdale St Paul *Liv* 90-93; R Golborne 93-00; R Hesketh w Becconsall *Blackb* from 00. *All Saints' Rectory, Silverdale, Hesketh Bank, Preston PR4 6RZ* Tel (01772) 814798
E-mail richard.plant1@btinternet.com

PLANT, Richard George Nicholas. b 45. Man Univ BA67. Coll of Resurr Mirfield 68. **d** 71 **p** 72. C Cleckheaton St Jo *Wakef* 71-74; P-in-c Adel *Ripon* 74-78; V Ireland Wood 78-82; V Armley w New Wortley 82-92; R Garforth from 92. *The Rectory, Church Lane, Garforth, Leeds LS25 1NR* Tel 0113-286 3737
E-mail nick@plant.go-legend.net

PLANT, Robert David. b 28. Birm Univ BSc49 Ch Ch Coll Cant MA98. St Deiniol's Hawarden 74. **d** 76 **p** 80. NSM Llandrillo-yn-Rhos *St As* 76-79; NSM St Nicholas at Wade w Sarre and Chislet w Hoath *Cant* from 79. *4 Sandalwood Drive, St Nicholas-at-Wade, Birchington CT7 0PE* Tel (01843) 847276

PLATT, Andrew Martin Robert. b 41. Oak Hill Th Coll 74. **d** 76 **p** 77. C St Alb St Paul *St Alb* 76-79; V Gazeley w Dalham and Moulton *St E* 79-85; V Gazeley w Dalham, Moulton and Kentford 85-86; RD Mildenhall 84-86; P-in-c Saxmundham 86-89; R 89-97; P-in-c Sudbury w Ballingdon and Brundon 97-98; V 98-04; rtd 04; Co Ecum Officer *Nor* from 04; Perm to Offic *Nor* and *St E* from 04. *21 Homefield Paddock, Beccles NR34 9NE* Tel (01502) 717744

PLATT, David. *See* PLATT, William David

PLATT, Harold Geoffrey. b 27. Down Coll Cam BA50 MA52. Ridley Hall Cam 51. **d** 53 **p** 54. C Cambridge St Paul *Ely* 53-56; C-in-c Cam St Martin CD 56-57; R Lower Broughton St Clem *Man* 57-66; P-in-c Salford St Matthias w St Simon 62-66; Lic to Offic *Man* 66-76 and *Worc* 76-82; Hon C Belbroughton *Worc* 83-86; Hon C Belbroughton w Fairfield and Clent 86-90; NSM Hagley 87-90; rtd 90; Co-ord for Decade of Evang 90-95; Perm to Offic *Nor* from 95. *Brecklands Cottage, Brecklands Green, North Pickenham, Swaffham PE37 8LG* Tel (01760) 441581

PLATT, John Dendy. b 24. Magd Coll Cam BA49 MA55. Wells Th Coll 50. **d** 52 **p** 53. C Headley All SS *Guildf* 52-56; C Haslemere 56-58; R Skelton w Hutton-in-the-Forest *Carl* 59-71; rtd 89. *17 Primula Drive, Norwich NR4 7LZ* Tel (01603) 504272

PLATT, John Emerson. b 36. Pemb Coll Ox BA59 MA65 DPhil77 Hull Univ MTh72. Cuddesdon Coll 59. **d** 61 **p** 62. C Adlington *Blackb* 61-64; C Sutton St Mich *York* 64-68; C Ox St Giles *Ox* 68-71; Asst Chapl Pemb Coll Ox 68-69; Chapl 69-02; rtd 02. *Apple Tree Cottage, Church Road, Wilmcote, Stratford-upon-Avon CV37 9XD*

PLATT, Mrs Katherine Mary. b 29. ARIBA51 Sheff Univ BA51. Westcott Ho Cam 76. **dss** 79 **d** 87. Chesterton Gd Shep *Ely* 78-84; Whitton St Aug *Lon* 84-86; Dean of Women's Min 86-94; Hampton St Mary 86-94; Par Dn 87-94; rtd 94; Perm to Offic *Ches* from 94. *56 Mereheath Park, Knutsford WA16 6AU* Tel (01656) 651192

PLATT, Michael Robert. b 39. SS Coll Cam BA61 MA85 Nottm Univ PGCE62. Cuddesdon Coll 62. **d** 64. C Far Headingley St Chad *Ripon* 64-65; Asst Master Belmont Coll Barnstaple 65-68; Asst Master Qu Coll Taunton 68-00; Ho Master 72-83; Hd Geography 89-00; rtd 00. *8 Court Hill, Taunton TA1 4SX* Tel (01823) 270687 Fax as telephone

PLATT, William David. b 31. St Chad's Coll Dur BA54. Coll of Resurr Mirfield 54. **d** 56 **p** 57. C Bethnal Green St Jo w St Simon *Lon* 56-60; C Pinner 60-65; V N Hammersmith St Kath 65-72; V Woodham *Guildf* 72-88; Chapl Community of St Mary V Wantage 88-96; rtd 96; NSM Blewbury, Hagbourne and Upton *Ox* 96-03. *14 Radley House, Marston Ferry Road, Oxford OX2 7EA* Tel (01865) 556019

PLATTEN, Aidan Stephen George. b 76. Ripon Coll Cuddesdon BTh03. **d** 03 **p** 04. C Woodbridge St Mary *St E* from 03. *40 Old Barrack Road, Woodbridge IP12 4ET* Tel (01394) 384842

PLATTEN, Gregory Austin David. b 78. Worc Coll Ox BA00 Ox Univ MTh05. Ripon Coll Cuddesdon 01. **d** 03 **p** 04. C St John's Wood *Lon* from 03. *3 Cochrane Street, London NW8 7PA* Tel (020) 7722 4766 E-mail gregoryplatten@ukonline.co.uk

✠**PLATTEN, The Rt Revd Stephen George.** b 47. Lon Univ BEd72 Trin Coll Ox BD03 UEA Hon DLitt03. Cuddesdon Coll 72. **d** 75 **p** 76 **c** 03. C Headington *Ox* 75-78; Chapl and Tutor Linc Th Coll 78-83; Can Res Portms Cathl and Dir of Ords *Portsm* 83-89; Abp's Sec for Ecum Affairs *Cant* 90-95; Hon Can Cant Cathl 90-95; Dean Nor 95-03; Bp Wakef from 03. *Bishop's Lodge, Woodthorpe Lane, Wakefield WF2 6JL* Tel (01924) 255349 Fax 250202 E-mail bishop@bishopofwakefield.org.uk

PLATTS, Mrs Hilary Anne Norrie. b 60. SRN81 K Coll Lon BD85 AKC85. Ripon Coll Cuddesdon 86. **d** 88 **p** 94. C Moulsham St Jo *Chelmsf* 88-90; Chapl Reading Univ *Ox* 90-99; C Calcot 90-92; NSM Reading Deanery 99-00; Perm to Offic *Birm* from 00; Chapl Birm Specialist Community Health NHS Trust from 01; Chapl N Warks NHS Trust from 03. *All Saints' Vicarage, 2 Walsall Road, Sutton Coldfield B74 4QJ* Tel 0121-308 5315

PLATTS, Timothy Caradoc. b 61. LMH Ox BA83 MA88 St Cross Coll Ox DPhil88. Ripon Coll Cuddesdon 87. **d** 89 **p** 90. C Whitley Ch Ch *Ox* 89-95; P-in-c Earley St Nic 95-98; V 98-00; V Four Oaks *Birm* from 00. *All Saints' Vicarage, 2 Walsall Road, Sutton Coldfield B74 4QJ* Tel 0121-308 5315

PLAXTON, Canon Edmund John Swithun. b 36. AKC60. **d** 61 **p** 62. C Crofton Park St Hilda w St Cypr *S'wark* 61-65; C Coulsdon St Jo 65-69; V Forest Hill St Paul 69-80; V Belmont 80-93; V Lingfield and Crowhurst 93-01; Hon Can S'wark Cathl 97-01; rtd 01. *Tynymaes, Y Fron, Upper Llandwrog, Caernarfon LL54 7BW* Tel (01286) 880188
E-mail edmundrachel@aol.com

PLAYER, Leslie Mark. b 65. Ridley Hall Cam CTM95. **d** 95 **p** 96. C Belper *Derby* 95-98; C Hamworthy *Sarum* 98-03; R W Downland from 03. *The Rectory, 97 Mill End, Damerham, Fordingbridge SP6 3HU* Tel (01725) 518642

PLAYLE, Ms Merrin Laura. b 58. Univ of Wales (Swansea) BSc79. Ridley Hall Cam 99. **d** 01 **p** 02. C Haslemere and Grayswood *Guildf* from 01. *16 Chatsworth Avenue, Haslemere GU27 1BA* Tel (01428) 643928
E-mail merrin.playle@btopenworld.com

PLEDGER, Miss Alison Frances. b 56. Univ of Wales (Cardiff) BA79 K Alfred's Coll Win PGCE80. Linc Th Coll 89. **d** 91 **p** 94. Par Dn Soham *Ely* 91-94; C Ely 94-96; C Rusthall *Roch* 97-00; V Alkborough *Linc* from 00. *The Vicarage, Back Street, Alkborough, Scunthorpe DN15 9JJ* Tel (01724) 721126

PLEDGER, Mrs Nicola. b 55. Lon Bible Coll BA94. St Alb and Ox Min Course 99. **d** 01 **p** 02. C Ware Ch Ch *St Alb* from 01. *10 Cromwell Road, Ware SG12 7JZ* Tel (01920) 467918
E-mail alanic@freenetname.co.uk

PLESSIS, John Kenneth. b 69. Univ of Wales (Cardiff) BSc91 BA05 Univ of Wales (Swansea) PhD03 PGCE92. St Mich Coll Llan 03. **d** 05. C Haverfordwest St Mary and St Thos w Haroldston *St D* from 05. *The Vicarage, Camrose, Haverfordwest SA62 6JE* Tel (01437) 710990 Mobile 07868-750228
E-mail john@plessis.fslife.co.uk

PLIMLEY, Canon William. b 17. St Aid Birkenhead 50. **d** 52 **p** 53. C Norbury *Ches* 52-55; V Laisterdyke *Bradf* 55-83; RD Calverley 65-78; Hon Can Bradf Cathl 67-83; rtd 83; Perm to Offic *Bradf* from 83. *465 Bradford Road, Pudsey LS28 8ED* Tel (01274) 664862

PLIMMER, Wayne Robert. b 64. St Chad's Coll Dur BA85. St Steph Ho Ox 86. **d** 88 **p** 89. C Cockerton *Dur* 88-91; C Poulton-le-Fylde *Blackb* 91-93; V Darton *Wakef* from 93; P-in-c Cawthorne from 04. *The Vicarage, 6 Jacob's Hall Court, Darton, Barnsley S75 5LY* Tel (01226) 384596
E-mail wayne@wplimmer.freeserve.co.uk

PLOWMAN, Richard Robert Bindon. b 38. Solicitor 61. Ridley Hall Cam 76. **d** 78 **p** 79. C Combe Down w Monkton Combe *B & W* 78-81; C Combe Down w Monkton Combe and S Stoke 81-83; V Coxley w Godney, Henton and Wookey 83-03; RD Shepton Mallet 95-01; rtd 03. *Hyland House, Lower Rudge, Frome BA11 2QE* Tel (01373) 831316

PLUCK, Richard. b 60. Southn Univ BTh90. Aston Tr Scheme 84 Sarum & Wells Th Coll 86. **d** 90 **p** 91. C Harpenden St Nic *St Alb* 90-94; CF from 94. *c/o MOD Chaplains (Army)* Tel (01980) 615804 Fax 615800

PLUMB, Gordon Alan. b 42. Leeds Univ BA. Sarum & Wells Th Coll. **d** 82 **p** 83. C Biggleswade *St Alb* 82-86; TV Grantham *Linc* 86-95; P-in-c Saxby All Saints 95-97; P-in-c Bonby 95-97; P-in-c Horkstow 95-97; P-in-c S Ferriby 95-97; P-in-c Worlaby 95-97; R S Ferriby from 97; V Bonby from 97; V Horkstow from 97; R Saxby All Saints from 97; V Worlaby from 97. *The Rectory, 1 Church Lane, Saxby-All-Saints, Brigg DN20 0QE* Tel (01652) 618747 E-mail gplumb2000@aol.com

PLUMLEY, Paul Jonathan. b 42. St Jo Coll Nottm 71. **d** 74 **p** 75. C Mile Cross *Nor* 74-77; P-in-c Wickham Skeith *St E* 77-79; P-in-c Stoke Ash, Thwaite and Wetheringsett 77-79; Assoc Min Woodbridge St Jo 80-81; Chapl RAF 81-86; Perm to Offic *Roch* 86-95; R Hever, Four Elms and Mark Beech 95-00; Sen Chapl Maidstone and Tunbridge Wells NHS Trust from 00. *Chaplains' Office, Woodlands House, Pembury Hospital, Tonbridge Road, Tunbridge Wells TN2 4QJ* Tel (01892) 673920 *or* 823535 ext 3920 Mobile 07887-851042 E-mail paul.plumley@nhs.net

PLUMMER, Mrs Deborah Ann. b 49. St Hugh's Coll Ox BA71 MA75. St Alb Minl Tr Scheme 82. **dss** 85 **d** 87 **p** 94. Ickenham *Lon* 85-88; Par Dn 87-88; C Northolt St Mary 88-92; Chapl Lee Abbey 92-95; P-in-c Kintbury w Avington *Ox* 95-01; Lect Bolton St Pet *Man* from 01. *3 Ivy Bank Road, Bolton BL1 7EQ* Tel (01204) 602697 E-mail revd.debby@virgin.net

PLUMMER, Frances. b 36. Lon Univ BA DipRS. S'wark Ord Course. **dss** 82 **d** 87 **p** 94. NSM Salfords *S'wark* from 87; Dean MSE (Croydon) from 99. *50 Park View Road, Salfords, Redhill RH1 5DN* Tel (01293) 785852

PLUMMER, Miss June Alice. b 29. Bris Univ BA50 CertEd51. Sarum & Wells Th Coll 89. **d** 89 **p** 94. NSM Hanham *Bris* 89-97; rtd 97; Perm to Offic *Bris* from 97. *11 Glenwood Drive, Oldland Common, Bristol BS30 9RZ* Tel 0117-949 8667

PLUMPTON, Paul. b 50. Keble Coll Ox BA72 MA76. St Steph Ho Ox 72. **d** 74 **p** 75. C Tonge Moor *Man* 74-76; C Atherton 76-79; V Oldham St Jas 79-99; V Oldham St Jas w St Ambrose from 99. *The Vicarage, Yates Street, Oldham OL1 4AR* Tel 0161-633 4441

PLUMPTRE, John Basil. b 25. Pemb Coll Cam BA49 MA54 CertEd52. Launde Abbey 75. **d** 75 **p** 76. C Leic St Pet *Leic* 75-80; C Stanford on Soar *S'well* 81-90; C Rempstone 81-90; C Costock 81-90; C E Leake 81-90; rtd 91; Perm to Offic *Leic* 92-03 and *S'well* from 98. *14 Outwoods Road, Loughborough LE11 3LY* Tel (01509) 215452

PLUNKETT, Michael Edward. b 38. MBE04. Leeds Univ BSc61. Ely Th Coll 61. **d** 63 **p** 64. C Kirkby *Liv* 63-68; Lect Stockton-on-Tees 68-72; Lic to Offic *Dur* 72-73; TV Stockton 73-75; V Cantril Farm *Liv* 75-81; Soc Resp Officer 81-89; V Melling 81-91; TR Speke St Aid 91-04; rtd 04. *1 The Ridge, Bishops Castle SY9 5AB* Tel (01588) 630018

PLUNKETT, Canon Peter William. b 30. Oak Hill Th Coll. **d** 61 **p** 62. C Fazakerley Em *Liv* 61-64; C St Helens St Mark 64-68; V Kirkdale St Paul N Shore 68-79; P-in-c Bootle St Mary w St Jo 77-79; V Bootle St Mary w St Paul 79-81; V Goose Green 81-89; V W Derby St Jas 89-98; Hon Can Liv Cathl 97-98; rtd 98. *50 Trinity Crescent, West Shore, Llandudno LL30 2PQ* Tel (01492) 872109

PLYMING, Philip James John. b 74. Rob Coll Cam BA96 St Jo Coll Dur BA00 DMS01. Cranmer Hall Dur 98. **d** 01 **p** 02. C Chineham *Win* from 01. *6 Copse View Close, Chineham, Basingstoke RG24 8EZ* Tel (01256) 357030 E-mail philip.plyming@lineone.net

PLYMOUTH, Archdeacon of. *See* WILDS, The Ven Anthony Ronald

PLYMOUTH, Suffragan Bishop of. *Vacant*

PNEMATICATOS, Nicholas Peter Anthony. b 59. N Lon Univ BA92 Lon Univ MA93. Ripon Coll Cuddesdon DipMin95. **d** 95 **p** 96. C Yeovil St Mich *B & W* 95-98; Chapl Yeovil Coll 95-96; Chapl RN 98-02; Chapl RAF from 02. *Chaplaincy Services (RAF), HQ, Personnel and Training Command, RAF Innsworth, Gloucester GL3 1EZ* Tel (01452) 712612 ext 5164 Fax 9272 7111

POARCH, Canon John Chilton. b 30. Bris Univ BA54. Ridley Hall Cam 54. **d** 56 **p** 57. C Swindon Ch Ch *Bris* 56-59; C Corsham 59-61; Seychelles 61-63; V Brislington St Cuth *Bris* 63-69; Adn Seychelles 69-72; V Warmley *Bris* 72-86; R Syston 72-86; RD Bitton 79-85; P-in-c Bitton 80-86; Hon Can Bris Cathl 82-95; P-in-c Langley Fitzurse 86-94; Dioc Dir of Ords 86-94; Dir Ord Tr 94-95; P-in-c Draycot Cerne 87-94; rtd 95; Perm to Offic *Bris* from 95 and *B & W* 98-01; Officer for the Welfare of Rtd Mins Bris Adnry *Bris* from 01; Dioc Convenor Rtd Clergy Assn from 01. *86 Stanshaws Close, Bradley Stoke, Bristol BS32 9AF* Tel (01454) 619053

POCOCK, Mrs Gillian Margaret. b 35. Nottm Univ BA57. Cranmer Hall Dur 82. **dss** 83 **d** 87 **p** 94. Bearpark *Dur* 83-88; Hon Par Dn 87-88; Par Dn S Hetton w Haswell 88; Asst RD Dur 89-90; Chapl St Aid Coll Dur 89-93; Par Dn Esh *Dur* 90-92; P-in-c 92-99; P-in-c Hamsteels 97-99; P-in-c Langley Park 98-99; rtd 99. *11 Cooke's Wood, Broom Park, Durham DH7 7RL* Tel 0191-386 1140 E-mail gillian.pocock@lineone.net

POCOCK, Lynn Elizabeth. b 48. Coll of Wooster Ohio BA69 CertEd71. Qu Coll Birm 73. **dss** 82 **d** 87 **p** 94. Gleadless *Sheff* 82-85; Thorpe Hesley 85-92; Par Dn 87-92; NSM Ribbesford w Bewdley and Dowles *Worc* 92-03; Perm to Offic from 03. *2 Waterworks Road, Worcester WR1 3EX* Tel (01905) 612634

POCOCK, Canon Nigel John. b 47. Lon Univ BSc68 Birm Univ MA83. Lambeth STh78 Oak Hill Th Coll 69. **d** 72 **p** 73. C Tunbridge Wells St Jas *Roch* 72-75; C Heatherlands St Jo *Sarum* 75-78; V Leic St Chris *Leic* 78-83; R Camborne *Truro* 83-97; RD Carnmarth N 91-96; Hon Can Truro Cathl 92-97; V Old Windsor *Ox* from 97. *The Vicarage, Church Road, Old Windsor, Windsor SL4 2PQ* Tel (01753) 865778 Fax as telephone E-mail njpocock@ruan.freeserve.co.uk

PODGER, Richard Philip Champeney. b 38. K Coll Cam BA61 MA66. Cuddesdon Coll 62. **d** 64 **p** 65. C Doncaster St Geo *Sheff* 64-68; C Orpington All SS *Roch* 68-74; W Germany 76-88; Chapl Kassel *Eur* 83-88; TV Whitstable *Cant* 88-94; Perm to Offic from 95; Chapl E Kent NHS and Soc Care Partnership Trust from 02. *3 Alcroft Grange, Tyler Hill, Canterbury CT2 9NN* Tel (01227) 462038 E-mail podger@centrespace.freeserve.co.uk

POGMORE, Canon Edward Clement. b 52. Sarum & Wells Th Coll 76. **d** 79 **p** 80. C Calne and Blackland *Sarum* 79-82; TV Oakdale 82-89; Min Creekmoor LEP 82-89; Chapl Geo Eliot Hosp Nuneaton 89-94; Chapl Nuneaton Hosps 89-94; Chapl Geo Eliot Hosp NHS Trust Nuneaton from 94; Chapl Co-ord for N Warks from 94; Perm to Offic *Leic* from 91; Hon Can Cov Cathl *Cov* from 00. *The Chaplaincy, George Eliot Hospital, College Street, Nuneaton CV10 7DJ* Tel (024) 7686 5046, 7686 5281 *or* 7635 1351 ext 3528 E-mail edpog@hotmail.com *or* edward.pogmore@geh-tr.wminds.nhs.uk

✠**POGO, The Most Revd Sir Ellison Leslie.** b 47. KBE01. St Jo Coll Auckland LTh. **d** 79 **p** 79 **c** 81. Asst P Anderson's Bay New Zealand 79-81; Solomon Is from 81; Bp Ysabel 81-94; Abp Melanesia and Bp Cen Melanesia from 94. *Archbishop's House, PO Box 19, Honiara, Solomon Islands* Tel (00677) 21137 *or* 26101 Fax 21098 *or* 22072 E-mail epogo@comphq.org.sb

POIL, Canon Ronald Wickens. b 30. AKC56. **d** 57 **p** 58. C Willesborough *Cant* 57-60; Chapl RAF 60-76; P-in-c Edith Weston w Normanton *Pet* 65-67; V Southbourne *Chich* 76-80; P-in-c W Thorney 76-80; RD Westbourne 78-91; V Southbourne w W Thorney 80-96; Can and Preb Chich Cathl 90-96; rtd 96; Perm to Offic *Portsm* from 97. *33 Mays Lane, Stubbington, Fareham PO14 2EW*

POINTS, John David. b 43. Qu Coll Birm 78. **d** 80 **p** 81. C Wednesbury St Paul Wood Green *Lich* 80-85; V 93-01; V Sedgley St Mary 85-93; TR Wednesfield from 01; AD Wolverhampton from 03. *The Rectory, 9 Vicarage Road, Wednesfield, Wolverhampton WV11 1SB* Tel (01902) 731462

POLASHEK, Miss Stella Christine. b 44. Leic Poly MA85. EMMTC 92. **d** 95 **p** 96. NSM Appleby Gp *Leic* from 95; Chapl Leic Gen Hosp NHS Trust 99-00; Chapl Univ Hosps Leic NHS Trust from 00. *38 Mawbys Lane, Appleby Magna, Swadlincote DE12 7AA* Tel (01530) 272707

POLE, David John. b 46. Bath Academy of Art BA72. Trin Coll Bris 84. **d** 86 **p** 87. C Bris St Mary Redcliffe w Temple etc *Bris* 86-90; V Alveston 90-98; V Alveston and Littleton-on-Severn w Elberton from 98. *The Vicarage, Gloucester Road, Alveston, Bristol BS35 3QT* Tel (01454) 414810 Fax as telephone E-mail david.pole@dial.pipex.com

POLE, Francis John Michael. b 42. FRSA64 AMInstTA65 MInstTA00 CQSW74 MCMI99. St Jo Sem Wonersh 62. **d** 67 **p** 68. In RC Ch 67-75; NSM Walthamstow St Pet *Chelmsf* 75; NSM Penge Lane H Trin *Roch* 76-77; NSM Shirley St Jo *Cant* 77-79; Assoc Chapl The Hague *Eur* 79-83; V Norbury St Steph and Thornton Heath *Cant* 83-84; *S'wark* 85-00; Sen Dioc Police Chapl 95-00; Sen Chapl Sussex Police from 00; Nat Co-ord Police Chapl from 00; TV Crawley *Chich* from 00; Ind Missr for Crawley from 00. *35 Turnpike Place, Crawley RH11 7UA* Tel (01293) 513264 Mobile 07740-941565 E-mail francis.pole@virgin.net

POLHILL, Mrs Christine. b 46. Nottm Coll of Educn CertEd67. St Alb Minl Tr Scheme 81 Qu Coll Birm BA00. **dss** 84 **d** 87 **p** 94. St Alb St Mary Marshalswick *St Alb* 84-94; Hon Par Dn 87-94; C Cottered w Broadfield and Throcking 94-96; P-in-c 96-99; C Ardeley 94-96; P-in-c 96-99; C Weston 94-96; Perm to Offic *Lich* 99-00; C Lich St Mich w St Mary and Wall from 00. *Little Hayes, Beaudesert Park, Cannock Wood, Rugeley WS15 4JJ* Tel (01543) 674474 E-mail polhill@surfaid.org.uk

POLITT, Robert William. b 47. ARCM LGSM68. Oak Hill Th Coll 73. **d** 76 **p** 77. C Bexleyheath St Pet *Roch* 76-82; TV

Southgate *Chich* 82-90; Chapl N Foreland Lodge Sch Basingstoke 90-98; R Sherfield-on-Loddon and Stratfield Saye etc *Win* from 98. *The Rectory, 33 Northfield Road, Sherfield-on-Loddon, Hook RG27 0DR* Tel (01256) 882209 E-mail 113225.103@compuserve.com

POLKINGHORNE, Canon John Charlton. b 30. KBE97. Trin Coll Cam BA52 PhD55 MA56 ScD74 FRS74. Westcott Ho Cam 79. **d** 81 **p** 82. NSM Chesterton St Andr *Ely* 81-82; C Bedminster St Mich *Bris* 82-84; V Blean *Cant* 84-86; Dean Trin Hall Cam 86-89; Pres Qu Coll Cam 89-96; Can Th Liv Cathl *Liv* from 94; rtd 95; Six Preacher Cant Cathl *Cant* from 96; Perm to Offic *Ely* from 96. *74 Hurst Park Avenue, Cambridge CB4 2AF* Tel (01223) 360743

POLL, Martin George. b 61. Kent Univ BA83. Ripon Coll Cuddesdon 84. **d** 87 **p** 88. C Mill Hill Jo Keble Ch *Lon* 87-90; Chapl RN from 90. *Royal Naval Chaplaincy Service, Room 203, Victory Building, HM Naval Base, Portsmouth PO1 3LS* Tel (023) 9272 7903 Fax 9272 7111

POLLAK, Canon Peter Henry. b 18. Worc Ord Coll 67. **d** 69 **p** 70. C Claines St Jo *Worc* 69-73; R Grimley w Holt 73-88; RD Martley and Worc W 84-88; Hon Can Worc Cathl 85-88; rtd 88; Perm to Offic *Worc* from 88. *2 Tweenways, Main Road, Kempsey, Worcester WR5 3JY* Tel (01905) 820351

POLLARD, Mrs Ann Beatrice. b 46. **d** 03 **p** 04. OLM Mirfield *Wakef* from 03. *9 Manor Drive, Mirfield WF14 0ER* Tel (01924) 495322 Mobile 07751-630609 E-mail annrich@pollard5910fsnet.co.uk

POLLARD, Mrs Christine Beryl. b 45. DCR DNM. N Ord Course 86. **d** 89 **p** 94. Par Dn Ingrow cum Hainworth *Bradf* 89-94; C Nuneaton St Nic *Cov* 94-98; P-in-c Bourton w Frankton and Stretton on Dunsmore etc from 98. *The Rectory, Main Street, Frankton, Rugby CV23 9PB* Tel (01926) 632805

POLLARD, Canon Clifford Francis. b 20. AKC49. **d** 50 **p** 51. C Leominster *Heref* 50-53; C Luton St Mary *St Alb* 53-56; V Stopsley 56-60; Chapl Toc H (Kent and Sussex) 60-64; R Mersham *Cant* 64-68; Asst Dir of Educn 68-69; Dir of Educn 69-87; Hon Can Cant Cathl 72-91; rtd 87; Perm to Offic *Cant* from 03. *6 Lady Wootton's Green, Canterbury CT1 1NG* Tel (01227) 761674

POLLARD, David. b 55. LSE BSc77. Trin Coll Bris DipHE80. **d** 80 **p** 81. Canada 81-84; C-in-c Hillsfield and Monkspath LEP *Birm* 85-89; BCMS 89-93; Crosslinks 93-95; Spain 89-94; V Doncaster St Jas *Sheff* 95-98; rtd 98. *6 Mulberry Way, Armthorpe, Doncaster DN3 3UE* Tel (01302) 833404

POLLARD, David John Athey. b 44. ACP74 Culham Coll Ox CertEd69. St Jo Coll Nottm LTh88. **d** 88 **p** 89. C Illogan *Truro* 88-91; R Roche and Withiel 91-95; TV Maidstone St Martin *Cant* 95-97; C Parkwood CD 95-97; R Lanreath *Truro* 97-99; V Pelynt 97-99; R Lanreath, Pelynt and Bradoc 99-03; rtd 03. *Melyn Brea, 11 Mill Hill, Lostwithiel PL22 0HB* Tel (01208) 871541 E-mail david.pollard@totalise.co.uk

POLLARD, Canon David Stanley. b 49. Lon Univ BD80 AKC80 Bradf Univ MA. **d** 80 **p** 81. CGA 78-89; C Manningham St Mary and Bradf St Mich *Bradf* 80-83; P-in-c 83-84; TV Manningham 84-85; C 86-87; Lic to Offic 85-89; P-in-c Sidlesham *Chich* 89-94; Chapl Chich Coll of Tech 90-94; R Petworth *Chich* from 94; R Egdean from 94; RD Petworth from 95; Can and Preb Chich Cathl from 03. *The Rectory, Rectory Lane, Petworth GU28 0DB* Tel (01798) 342505 E-mail dspollard49@btinternet.com

POLLARD, Eric John. b 43. Chich Th Coll 83. **d** 85 **p** 86. C Brighton St Matthias *Chich* 85-90; C E Grinstead St Swithun 90-96; C Hove 96-00; P-in-c Brighton St Matthias from 00. *St Matthias's Vicarage, 45 Hollingbury Park Avenue, Brighton BN1 7JQ* Tel (01273) 508178 E-mail eric.pollard@btinternet.com

POLLARD, James Adrian Hunter. b 48. St Jo Coll Nottm BTh78. **d** 78 **p** 79. C Much Woolton *Liv* 78-81; CMS 81-84; V Toxteth Park Ch Ch *Liv* 85-90; CF from 90; Perm to Offic *S'wark* 92-94. *c/o MOD Chaplains (Army)* Tel (01980) 615804 Fax 615800

POLLARD, John Edward Ralph. b 40. ALCD68. **d** 67 **p** 68. C Ollerton *S'well* 67-71; C Walton H Trin *Ox* 71-74; P-in-c Cuddington w Dinton 74-77; V Haddenham 74-77; V Kingsey 75-77; V Haddenham w Cuddington and Kingsey 77-85; RD Aylesbury 80-85; V Haddenham w Cuddington, Kingsey etc 85-87; V Furze Platt 87-96; rtd 97. *113 Thame Road, Haddenham, Aylesbury HP17 8EH* Tel (01844) 290582

POLLARD, Matthew Rupert. b 66. St Jo Coll Nottm. **d** 03 **p** 04. C Huddersfield St Pet *Wakef* from 03; Asst Chapl Huddersfield Univ from 03. *75 St John's Road, Birkby, Huddersfield HD1 5EA* Tel (01484) 303299 E-mail m.pollard@hud.ac.uk

POLLARD, Mrs Patricia Julie. b 46. Open Univ BA97. Cant Sch of Min 93. **d** 96 **p** 97. NSM Eastling w Ospringe and Stalisfield w Otterden *Cant* 96-04; rtd 04; Perm to Offic *Cant* from 04. *7 Arthur Salmon Close, Faversham ME13 7PS* Tel (01795) 535407 E-mail nunc.dim@tesco.net

POLLARD, Roger Frederick. b 32. Sheff Univ BSc52 K Coll Lon PGCE55 Lanc Univ MA78. Linc Th Coll 56. **d** 58 **p** 59. C Catford St Laur *S'wark* 58-63; Ghana 63-66; C Fulford *York* 66-67; C Camberwell St Geo *S'wark* 67; Asst Master Roch Valley Sch Milnrow 68-69; S Craven Sch Cross Hills 69-91; rtd 91; Perm to Offic *Bradf* 69-93 and *B & W* from 93. *Little Garth, Rectory Lane, Dowlish Wake, Ilminster TA19 0NX* Tel (01460) 52594

POLLARD, Stephen. b 59. Coll of Resurr Mirfield 96. **d** 98 **p** 99. C Lt Lever *Man* 98-02; P-in-c Westleigh St Pet from 02. *St Peter's Vicarage, 6 Malham Close, Leigh WN7 4SD* Tel (01942) 673626

POLLARD, Vaughan. b 59. Aston Tr Scheme 90 Trin Coll Bris DipHE92. **d** 92 **p** 93. C Nailsea H Trin *B & W* 92-95; C Acomb St Steph *York* 95-97; P-in-c Moldgreen *Wakef* 97-99; P-in-c Rawthorpe 97-99; V Moldgreen and Rawthorpe from 99. *The Vicarage, 35 Church Street, Huddersfield HD5 9DL* Tel and fax (01484) 424432

POLLINGER (née WHITFORD), Mrs Judith. b 41. Ex Univ TCert78 BEd79 Plymouth Univ 95. SW Minl Tr Course 92. **d** 95 **p** 96. NSM St Endellion w Port Isaac and St Kew *Truro* from 95; Convenor Bp's Gp for Min of Healing from 04. *4 Marshalls Way, Trelights, Port Isaac PL29 3TE* Tel (01208) 880181 E-mail rev.judith@endellion.fslife.co.uk

POLLINGTON, Miss Ann Elizabeth Jane. b 56. Univ Coll Chich BA00. Ripon Coll Cuddesdon 00. **d** 02 **p** 03. C Honiton, Gittisham, Combe Raleigh, Monkton etc *Ex* from 02. *5 Glen Farm Crescent, Honiton EX14 2GX* Tel (01404) 549734 E-mail annp@fish.co.uk

POLLIT, Preb Michael. b 30. Worc Coll Ox BA54 MA58. Wells Th Coll 54. **d** 56 **p** 57. C Cannock *Lich* 56-59; C Codsall 59-62; V W Bromwich St Pet 62-67; R Norton in the Moors 67-76; RD Leek 72-76; V Shrewsbury St Chad 76-87; V Shrewsbury St Chad w St Mary 87-95; Preb Lich Cathl 81-95; P-in-c Shrewsbury St Alkmund 91-95; rtd 95; Perm to Offic *Heref* 96-99. *Pentreheyling House, Churchstoke, Montgomery SY15 6HU* Tel (01588) 620273

POLLIT, Ruth Mary. *See* LILLINGTON, Mrs Ruth Mary

POLLITT, Graham Anthony. b 48. BA79. Oak Hill Th Coll 76. **d** 79 **p** 80. C Rusholme H Trin *Man* 79-82; TV Southgate *Chich* 82-83; C Burgess Hill St Andr 83-86; Chapl St Martin's Coll of Educn *Blackb* 86-90; Chapl Cheltenham and Glouc Coll of HE 90-98; Perm to Offic *Glouc* 98-99; C Bispham *Blackb* 99-04; P-in-c Caton w Littledale from 04. *The Vicarage, 153 Brookhouse Road, Brookhouse, Lancaster LA2 9NX* Tel (01524) 770300

POLLOCK, Christopher John. b 62. TCD BTh89 QUB BD. CITC 86. **d** 89 **p** 90. C Agherton *Conn* 89-91; C Ballymoney w Finvoy and Rasharkin 91-93; I Derryvolgie 93-03; I Saintfield *D & D* from 03. *The Vicarage, 11 Lisburn Road, Saintfield, Ballynahinch BT24 7AL* Tel (028) 9751 0286 E-mail chriswenda@talk21.com

POLLOCK, Duncan James Morrison. b 54. MBE95 QGM75. Nottm Univ BCombStuds83. Linc Th Coll 80. **d** 83 **p** 84. C Folkestone St Mary and St Eanswythe *Cant* 83-85; CF 85-98; R Broughton, Bossington, Houghton and Mottisfont *Win* 98-00; I Groomsport *D & D* from 00. *32 Bangor Road, Groomsport, Bangor BT19 6JF* Tel (028) 9146 4476

POLLOCK, Hugh Gillespie. b 36. Oak Hill Th Coll 61. **d** 64 **p** 65. C Maidstone St Luke *Cant* 64-68; C Washfield *Ex* 68-71; C Washfield, Stoodleigh, Withleigh etc 71-73; Chapl Lee Abbey 73-76; V Dersingham *Nor* 76-80; P-in-c Anmer 79-80; P-in-c Shernbourne 79-80; R Dersingham w Anmer and Shernborne 80-89; RD Heacham and Rising 87-89; C Barnstaple *Ex* 89-94; P-in-c Atherington and High Bickington 94-96; P-in-c Burrington 94-96; TV Newton Tracey, Horwood, Alverdiscott etc 96-98; rtd 99; Perm to Offic *Ex* 99-01; C Diptford, N Huish, Harberton, Harbertonford etc from 01. *The Vicarage, Harberton, Totnes TQ9 7SA* Tel (01803) 868445

POLLOCK, James Colin Graeme. b 53. St Chad's Coll Dur BA76. Ripon Coll Cuddesdon 77. **d** 78 **p** 79. C Hartlepool St Oswald *Dur* 78-81; C Hartlepool St Aid 81-84; V Dawdon from 84; V Seaham Harbour from 03. *The Vicarage, Melbury Street, Seaham SR7 7NF* Tel 0191-581 2317

POLLOCK, John Charles. b 23. Trin Coll Cam BA46 MA48 Samford Univ (USA) Hon DLitt02. Ridley Hall Cam 49. **d** 51 **p** 52. C Portman Square St Paul *Lon* 51-53; Ed *The Churchman* 53-58; R Horsington *B & W* 53-58; Perm to Offic *Ex* 61-98 and from 00; rtd 88. *Rose Ash House, Rose Ash, South Molton EX36 4RB* Tel (01769) 550403

POLOMSKI, Elias Robert Michael. b 42. **d** 85 **p** 86. In RC Ch 85-90; C Headington Quarry *Ox* 91-94; Chapl St Alb Abbey *St Alb* 94-97; Chapl St Alb Sch 94-97; P-in-c Streatley w Moulsford *Ox* 97-03; C 03-04; P-in-c Streatley from 04. *The Vicarage, Vicarage Lane, Streatley, Reading RG8 9HX* Tel (01491) 872191

POMERY, David John. b 45. SS Mark & Jo Coll Chelsea CertEd67. Chich Th Coll 75. **d** 77 **p** 78. C Coseley Ch Ch *Lich* 77-79; C Stocksbridge *Sheff* 79-81; V Bentley 81-87; Asst Master Radlett Prep Sch 87-03; P-in-c Barton Bendish w Beachamwell and Shingham *Ely* from 03; P-in-c Fincham from 03; P-in-c Shouldham from 03; P-in-c Marham from 03; P-in-c Shouldham

Thorpe from 03. *The Rectory, Church Road, Barton Bendish, King's Lynn PE33 9DP* Tel (01366) 348063 E-mail revdjpomery@supanet.com

POMFRET, Albert. b 23. Univ of Wales (Cardiff) BSc57 MTh95 Lon Univ MA69 FCP83 Potchefstroom Univ PhD02. Oak Hill NSM Course 72. **d** 75 **p** 76. NSM Dartford Ch Ch *Roch* 75-80; Perm to Offic 80-92; Perm to Offic *Ex* from 92. *9 St Margaret's Court, Exe Street, Topsham, Exeter EX3 0JL* Tel (01392) 873404

POND, Geraldine Phyllis. b 53. SRN74. St Jo Coll Nottm MA97. **d** 97 **p** 98. C Ancaster Wilsford Gp *Linc* 97-01; P-in-c Harlaxton Gp from 01; Chapl Linc Distr Healthcare NHS Trust from 01. *The Rectory, 6 Rectory Lane, Harlaxton, Grantham NG32 1HD* Tel (01476) 567059 E-mail revgpond@aol.com

POND, Nigel Peter Hamilton. b 40. AKC65. **d** 66 **p** 67. C E Dereham w Hoe *Nor* 66-69; C Chapl RN 69-85; TR Woughton *Ox* 85-93; Chapl Milton Keynes Gen Hosp 85-93; RD Milton Keynes *Ox* 90-93; R Olney w Emberton 93-97; R Olney 97-03; rtd 03. *11 Gippingstone Road, Bramford, Ipswich IP8 4DR* Tel (01473) 741887 E-mail nigel@npond.freeserve.co.uk

PONSONBY, Simon Charles Reuben. b 66. Bris Univ MLitt96. Trin Coll Bris BA94. **d** 95 **p** 96. C Thorpe Edge *Bradf* 95-98; Pastorate Chapl Ox St Aldate *Ox* from 98. *14 Walton Street, Oxford OX1 2HG* Tel (01865) 552849 *or* 244713 Fax 201543 E-mail simon.ponsonby@staldates.org.uk

PONT, Gordon John Harper. b 35. Glas Univ BSc56 BD65. Edin Th Coll 56. **d** 59 **p** 60. C Dunfermline *St And* 59-62; C Motherwell *Glas* 62-65; R Largs 65-68; Dioc Supernumerary *Bre* 68-71; Chapl Dundee Univ 68-73; R Dundee St Luke 71-74; NSM Dundee St Paul 74-99; Hon Chapl St Paul's Cathl Dundee 74-99; Dioc Sec 96-02; rtd 02. *Dalhouzie, 11 West Moulin Road, Pitlochry PH16 5EA* Tel (01796) 472745 E-mail gordon.pont@tesco.net

PONTEFRACT, Archdeacon of. *See* GREENER, The Ven Jonathan Desmond Francis

PONTEFRACT, Suffragan Bishop of. *See* ROBINSON, The Rt Revd Anthony William

PONTER, John Arthur. b 37. Univ of Wales (Abth) BA61 Linacre Coll Ox BA63 MA68 UEA PhD81. Wycliffe Hall Ox 61. **d** 63 **p** 64. C Gidea Park *Chelmsf* 63-67; C-in-c Colchester St Anne CD 67-69; V Colchester St Anne 69-72; Chapl UEA *Nor* 72-78; Chapl Chelmsf Cathl *Chelmsf* 78-79; Chapl Chelmsf Cathl Cen 78-84; V Moulsham St Jo 79-85; Dir Man Chr Inst and Chr Leadership Course 85-92; Educn Officer N Federation for Tr in Min 85-92; TR Stantonbury and Willen *Ox* 92-02; rtd 02. *1 Highveer Croft, Tattenhoe, Milton Keynes MK4 3BN* Tel (01908) 520329 E-mail ponter@msn.com

PONTIN, Colin Henry. b 37. Trin Coll Bris. **d** 83 **p** 84. C Downend *Bris* 83-86; C Riverside *Ox* 86-88; V Eton w Eton Wick and Boveney 88-90; TV Riverside 91-95; V Churt *Guildf* 95-02; rtd 02; Perm to Offic *Win* from 03. *22 Shearsbrook Close, Bransgore, Christchurch BH23 8HF* Tel (01425) 673918 Mobile 07989-173259 E-mail colinpontin@lineone.net

POOBALAN, Isaac Munuswamy. b 62. RGN84 Edin Univ BD94 MTh97 Aber Univ MPhil98. Edin Th Coll 91. **d** 94 **p** 95. C Edin St Pet *Edin* 94-97; P-in-c Aberdeen St Clem *Ab* 97-01; R Aberdeen St Jo from 01. *The Rectory, 15 Ashley Road, Aberdeen AB10 6RU* Tel (01224) 591527 E-mail i.poovan@abdn.ac.uk

POODHUN, Canon Lambert David. b 30. Natal Univ BA53. Edin Th Coll 54. **d** 56 **p** 57. S Africa 56-76; Adn Durban 75-76; C Upton cum Chalvey *Ox* 77-80; Chapl Kingston Hosp Surrey 80-81; Chapl Tooting Bec Hosp Lon 81-84; Chapl Hurstwood Park Hosp Haywards Heath 84-01; Chapl St Fran Hosp Haywards Heath 84-94; Chapl Mid Sussex NHS Trust 94-01; Can and Preb Chich Cathl *Chich* from 93; Hon C Haywards Heath St Rich from 01. *8 Nursery Close, Haywards Heath RH16 1HP* Tel (01444) 440938 E-mail lambertpoodhun@aol.com

POOLE, Andrew John. b 52. EMMTC 98. **d** 01 **p** 02. NSM Scraptoft *Leic* from 01. *64 Scalborough Close, Countesthorpe, Leicester LE8 5XH* Tel 0116-277 4949

POOLE, Clifford George. b 36. Keble Coll Ox BA61 MA65 Lon Univ PGCE75. S'wark Ord Course 83. **d** 86 **p** 87. C W Dulwich All SS and Em *S'wark* 86-90; Chapl Luxembourg *Eur* 90-02; rtd 02; P-in-c Alderton, Gt Washbourne, Dumbleton etc *Glouc* 02-05; TV Winchcombe from 05. *The Vicarage, Church Road, Alderton, Tewkesbury GL20 8NR* Tel (01242) 620238

POOLE, David. b 54. **d** 02 **p** 04. OLM Chase Terrace *Lich* from 02. *435 Littleworth Road, Hednesford, Cannock WS12 5HZ* Tel (01543) 422218 E-mail dave.poole@tesco.net

POOLE, Mrs Denise June. b 49. Leic Univ BSc70 Bradf and Ilkley Coll DipAdEd85. N Ord Course 90. **d** 93 **p** 94. C Horton and Bradf St Oswald Chapel Green *Bradf* 93-97; Chapl Co-ord Bradf Hosps NHS Trust 97-00; V Bradf St Aug Undercliffe *Bradf* from 00. *St Augustine's Vicarage, Undercliffe Lane, Bradford BD3 0DW* Tel (01274) 305604 E-mail denise@undercliffe.org.uk

POOLE, Edward John. b 53. Hull Univ BA81 Heythrop Coll Lon MA04. St Steph Ho Ox 81. **d** 83 **p** 84. C Stevenage St Andr and St Geo *St Alb* 83-86; Tutor St Paul's Th Coll Madagascar 86-88; V Weston and P-in-c Ardeley *St Alb* 88-96; P-in-c Cottered w Broadfield and Throcking 94-96; Chapl Bucharest w Sofia *Eur* 96-98; Chapl HM Pris Lewes 98-03; Chapl HM Pris Featherstone from 03. *HM Prison, New Road, Featherstone, Wolverhampton WV10 7PU* Tel (01902) 703125

POOLE, Frederick Harold. b 14. Clifton Th Coll 54. **d** 56 **p** 56. C Bucknall and Bagnall *Lich* 56-60; R Chorlton on Medlock St Steph *Man* 60-68; rtd 79. *Victoria House Residential Home, 166 Church Street, Wallasey CH44 8AL*

POOLE, Helen Margaret. b 39. SRN. SW Minl Tr Course. **d** 94 **p** 95. NSM Ludgvan *Truro* 94-97; NSM Paul 97-02; NSM St Buryan, St Levan and Sennen 02-04; rtd 04. *Underhill Farmhouse, St Levan, Penzance TR19 6JS* Tel (01736) 810842 Fax 810858 E-mail helenandbob@fish.co.uk

POOLE, Ian Richard Morley. b 62. Birm Univ MB, ChB85 MRCGP90 DRCOG90. St Jo Coll Nottm MTh02. **d** 02 **p** 03. C Willenhall H Trin *Lich* from 02. *13 Wesley Road, Willenhall WV12 5QT* Tel (01922) 429262 E-mail woodchipper@blueyonder.co.uk

POOLE, James Christopher. b 73. Peterho Cam BA94 MA98. Aston Tr Scheme 96 Wycliffe Hall Ox 97. **d** 00 **p** 01. C Wimbledon Park St Luke *S'wark* 00-04; Miss Partner Crosslinks from 04; Kenya from 05. *12 Copsewood Road, Ashurst, Southampton SO40 7DL* E-mail james@realfire.org

POOLE, Miss Joan Wendy. b 37. Sarum Dioc Teacher Tr Coll CertEd57 Dalton Ho Bris DipTh66 Trin Coll Bris 86. **d** 87 **p** 94. Par Dn Longfleet *Sarum* 87-89; Par Dn Hamworthy 89-94; C 94-97; rtd 97; Perm to Offic *Sarum* from 97. *35 Borley Road, Poole BH17 7DT* Tel (01202) 256377

POOLE, John. *See* POOLE, Edward John

POOLE, Martin Bryce. b 59. Reading Univ BSc80. St Jo Coll Nottm 81. **d** 87 **p** 88. NSM Tulse Hill H Trin and St Matthias *S'wark* 87-99; NSM Hove *Chich* 00-01; Perm to Offic from 01. *14 Pembroke Avenue, Hove BN3 5DA* Tel and fax (01273) 747919 E-mail mb.poole@ntlworld.com

POOLE, Martin Ronald. b 59. Aston Univ BSc81 Leeds Univ BA86. Coll of Resurr Mirfield 84. **d** 87 **p** 88. C Sheff St Cath Richmond Road *Sheff* 87-90; C W Hampstead St Jas *Lon* 90-94; V Colindale St Matthias from 94. *St Matthias' Vicarage, Rushgrove Avenue, London NW9 6QY* Tel (020) 8205 8783 Fax 08701-289048 E-mail martin@mpoole57.freeserve.co.uk

POOLE, Peter William. b 35. St Pet Hall Ox BA59 MA63. Wells Th Coll 59. **d** 61 **p** 62. C Cheriton Street *Cant* 61-64; C Birchington w Acol 64-67; V Newington 67-73; P-in-c Lower Halstow 72-73; V Bearsted 73-76; V Lane End w Cadmore End *Ox* 84-89; R Chalfont St Giles 89-99; rtd 99; Perm to Offic *Guildf* from 01. *Primrose Cottage, St Nicholas Avenue, Cranleigh GU6 7AQ* Tel (01483) 272703

POOLE, Richard Eric. b 65. Huddersfield Poly BEng87. Trin Coll Bris BA98. **d** 98 **p** 99. C Sandal St Helen *Wakef* 98-01; TV Southgate *Chich* from 01. *St Andrew's Vicarage, Weald Drive, Crawley RH10 6NU* Tel (01293) 531828

POOLE, Roy John. b 26. Lon Univ BD54. St Jo Coll Lon LTh54. **d** 54 **p** 55. C Benwell St Aid *Newc* 54-57; Australia 57-61 and from 74; R Bradford cum Beswick *Man* 61-66; Area Sec Chr Aid Dept BCC 66-68; Regional Supervisor (S and E England) Chr Aid 68-74; rtd 91. *14 Chungking Grove, Stratton, W Australia 6056* Tel (0061) (8) 9250 2652 E-mail roy@echidna.id.au

POOLE, Stuart. b 33. CEng65 FIEE85 Loughb Coll DLC55 Lon Univ BScEng55 Man Univ MSc76. **d** 91 **p** 92. NSM Cheadle *Ches* 91-03; Perm to Offic from 03. *1 Dene House, Green Pastures, Stockport SK4 3RB* Tel 0161-432 6426 Fax as telephone E-mail stuart.poole@ukgateway.net

POOLE, Wendy. *See* POOLE, Miss Joan Wendy

POOLEY, Peter Owen. b 32. Kelham Th Coll 54. **d** 58 **p** 59. C Paddington St Mary Magd *Lon* 58-62; R Rockland St Mary w Hellington *Nor* 62-67; Asst Master Thos Lethaby Sch 67-70; St Phil Gr Sch Edgbaston 70-74; Lordswood Gr Sch 74-80; Hon C Edgbaston St Geo *Birm* 77-80; R Elton *Ely* 80-01; P-in-c Stibbington and Water Newton 80-01; R Elton w Stibbington and Water Newton 01-02; rtd 02; Perm to Offic *Linc* from 03. *1 Warrenne Keep, Stamford PE9 2NX* Tel (01780) 751646

POOLMAN, Alfred John. b 46. K Coll Lon BD69 AKC69 Sheff Univ Dip Psychotherapy 83. St Aug Coll Cant 69. **d** 70 **p** 71. C Headingley *Ripon* 70-74; C Moor Allerton 75-78; C Monk Bretton *Wakef* 78-80; V Copley and Chapl Halifax Gen Hosp 80-90; R Llanfynydd *St As* from 90. *The Rectory, Llanfynydd, Wrexham LL11 5HH* Tel (01978) 762304 E-mail john.poolman@tesco.net

POOLMAN, Mrs Carole Margaret. b 53. St As & Ban Minl Tr Course 98. **d** 01 **p** 02. NSM Pontblyddyn *St As* from 01. *The Rectory, Llanfynydd, Wrexham LL11 5HH* Tel (01978) 762304 E-mail carole.poolman@tesco.net

POOLTON, Martin Ronald. b 60. Kingston Poly BSc81 Salford Univ MSc83 Bp Grosseteste Coll PGCE85 FRGS81 SSC. Cuddesdon Coll DipMin95. **d** 97 **p** 98. C Penzance St Mary w St Paul *Truro* 97-99; C Northampton St Matt *Pet* 99-01; R

Jersey St Pet *Win* from 01. *The Rectory, La Rue du Presbytère, St Peter, Jersey JE3 7ZH* Tel and fax (01534) 481805 E-mail poolton@onetel.com

POPE, Preb Charles Guy. b 48. AKC70. St Aug Coll Cant 70. **d** 71 **p** 72. C Southgate Ch Ch *Lon* 71-74; C N St Pancras All Hallows 74-77; C Hampstead St Steph 74-77; V New Southgate St Paul 77-86; V Brookfield St Mary from 86; P-in-c Brookfield St Anne, Highgate Rise 88-99; AD S Camden 95-00; Preb St Paul's Cathl from 04. *St Mary's Vicarage, 85 Dartmouth Park Road, London NW5 1SL* Tel (020) 7267 5941 Mobile 07770-693435 Fax (020) 7482 2136 E-mail guypope@blueyonder.co.uk

POPE, Canon Colin. b 51. Brasted Place Coll 74. Linc Th Coll 75. **d** 78 **p** 79. C W Derby Gd Shep *Liv* 78-81; C-in-c Westbrook St Phil CD 81-82; V Westbrook St Phil 82-87; V Orrell and Chapl Billinge Hosp Wigan 87-96; V Southport Em *Liv* from 96; P-in-c Birkdale St Pet from 04; AD N Meols from 00; Hon Can Liv Cathl from 03. *Emmanuel Vicarage, 12 Allerton Road, Southport PR9 9NJ* Tel and fax (01704) 532743 E-mail cpope@fish.co.uk

POPE, David Allan. b 20. Oriel Coll Ox BA45 MA72. Ely Th Coll 45. **d** 47 **p** 48. C Folkestone St Mary and St Eanswythe *Cant* 47-51; V Tovil 51-54; R E Horsley *Guildf* 54-63; R Ivychurch w Old Romney and Midley *Cant* 63-65; P-in-c Brenzett w Snargate and Snave 64-65; P-in-c Newchurch 64-65; P-in-c St Mary in the Marsh 64-65; P-in-c Burmarsh 64-65; R Broadstairs 65-73; P-in-c Berwick *Chich* 73-76; P-in-c Arlington 73-75; P-in-c Selmeston w Alciston 74-76; R Berwick w Selmeston and Alciston 76; P-in-c Rusper 76-79; R Colsterworth *Linc* 79-81; P-in-c Ingworth 81-85; P-in-c Alby w Thwaite *Nor* 81-85; P-in-c Erpingham w Calthorpe 81-85; P-in-c Aldborough w Thurgarton 83-85; rtd 85; Perm to Offic *Nor* from 85. *Burgate Lodge, Saddle Bow, King's Lynn PE34 3AR* Tel (01553) 617599

POPE, Donald Keith. b 35. Sarum & Wells Th Coll 81. **d** 76 **p** 77. Hon C Caerleon *Mon* 76-82; C 82-83; V Pontypool 83-86; R Grosmont and Skenfrith and Llangattock etc 86-98; RD Abergavenny 93-98; rtd 98. *24 Incline Way, Ridgewood Gardens, Saundersfoot SA69 9LX* Tel (01834) 812089

POPE, Miss Elizabeth Mercy. b 51. Man Univ BSc73 Ex Univ PGCE74. Trin Coll Bris 99. **d** 01 **p** 02. C Bardsley *Man* 01-05; P-in-c Oldham St Paul from 05. *St Paul's Vicarage, 55 Belgrave Road, Oldham OL8 1LU* Tel 0161-624 1068 E-mail elizabeth.pope@lineone.net

POPE, Guy. *See* POPE, Preb Charles Guy

POPE, Michael John. b 37. Sarum Th Coll 62. **d** 65 **p** 66. C Broseley w Benthall *Heref* 65-68; C Shrewsbury St Giles *Lich* 68-71; P-in-c Shrewsbury St Geo 71-75; V 75-79; V Gnosall 79-00; RD Eccleshall 92-00; rtd 00; Perm to Offic *Lich* from 01. *Rivendell, 2 Dark Lane, Broseley TF12 5LH* Tel (01952) 883960

POPE, Michael Ronald. b 41. Bps' Coll Cheshunt 65. **d** 68 **p** 69. C Lyonsdown H Trin *St Alb* 68-72; C Seaford w Sutton *Chich* 72-76; R Hurstpierpoint 76-80; rtd 99. *34 Wilton Road, Shanklin PO37 7BZ* Tel (01983) 863602

POPEJOY, Wilfred. b 28. St Jo Coll Nottm 88. **d** 88. Hon C Donisthorpe and Moira w Stretton-en-le-Field *Leic* 88-98; rtd 98; Perm to Offic *Leic* from 99. *79 Donisthorpe Lane, Moira, Swadlincote DE12 6BB* Tel (01283) 760476

POPELY, David Charles. K Coll Lon BA00. SEITE 00. **d** 03. NSM Catford St Laur *S'wark* 03-05. *143 Killearn Road, London SE6 1BS* Tel (020) 8473 4248 Fax 8464 7814 Mobile 07947-309197 E-mail dave.popely@btinternet.com

POPHAM, Neil Andrew. b 69. Trin Coll Ox BA91 DPhil96 MA05 St Jo Coll Dur BA05. Cranmer Hall Dur 03. **d** 05. C Quarry Bank *Worc* from 05. *71 New Street, Quarry Bank, Brierley Hill DY5 2AZ* Tel (01384) 561350

POPP, Miss Julia Alice Gisela. b 45. Univ of BC BA71. St Jo Coll Nottm 78. **dss** 81 **d** 87 **p** 94. Woking St Mary *Guildf* 81-83; Hornsey Rise St Mary w St Steph *Lon* 83-87; Par Dn Hornsey Rise Whitehall Park Team 87-91; Par Dn Sutton St Nic *S'wark* 91-94; C 94-98; Missr Sutton Town Cen 91-98; TV Hackney Marsh *Lon* from 98. *105 Mayola Road, London E5 0RG* Tel and fax (020) 8533 4034 E-mail j.popp@btinternet.com

POPPLE, The Ven Dennis. b 31. Master Mariner 58. Vancouver Sch of Th LTh72 San Francisco Th Sem DMin89 St Aid Birkenhead 59. **d** 62 **p** 63. C Walkden Moor *Man* 62-65; Canada from 65; Admin Adn 87-96; rtd 96. *8580 General Currie Road, Suite 113, Richmond BC, Canada, V6Y 3V5*

POPPLETON, Julian George. b 63. St Chad's Coll Dur BA85 PGCE86 Cam Univ DipRS94 Surrey Univ BA02. STETS 99. **d** 02 **p** 03. NSM Harnham *Sarum* from 02; Chapl K Edw VI Sch Southn from 02. *19 Thompson Close, Salisbury SP2 8QU* Tel (01722) 334272 *or* (023) 8070 4561 E-mail jgp@kes.hants.sch.uk

POPPLEWELL, Andrew Frederick. b 53. St Jo Coll Dur BA75. Wycliffe Hall Ox 76. **d** 78 **p** 79. C Clifton *York* 78-81; C Lich St Chad *Lich* 82-84; V Laisterdyke *Bradf* 84-99. *Clifton, 210A Leeds Road, Eccleshill, Bradford BD2 3JU* Tel (01274) 637651

PORT MORESBY, Bishop of. *See* FOX, The Rt Revd Peter John

PORTEOUS, Canon Eric John. b 34. AKC58. **d** 59 **p** 60. C Wandsworth St Paul *S'wark* 59-62; C Leeds St Pet *Ripon* 62-66; V Wortley de Leeds 66-72; RD Armley 70-72; R Woolwich St Mary w H Trin *S'wark* 72-77; Sub-Dean Woolwich 74-77; P-in-c Woolwich St Mich 75-77; R Woolwich St Mary w St Mich 77-79; Chapl Whipps Cross Hosp Lon 79-96; Lic to Offic *Chelmsf* 79-86; Hon Can Chelmsf Cathl 86-96; rtd 96; Perm to Offic *Chelmsf* from 96. *128 Grove Hill, London E18 2HZ* Tel (020) 8530 5660

PORTEOUS, Michael Stanley. b 35. S'wark Ord Course 70. **d** 73 **p** 74. C Barnes St Mich *S'wark* 73-76; Chapl Greycoat Hosp Sch 76-78; C Brighton Annunciation *Chich* 78-80; Chapl Ch Hosp Horsham 80-85; TV Moulsecoomb *Chich* 85-88; R W Blatchington 88-99; rtd 99; Perm to Offic *Chich* from 99. *15 Mariners Close, Shoreham-by-Sea BN43 5LU*

PORTER, Andrew William. b 69. Bris Univ BSc91 BA01 PGCE94. Trin Coll Bris 98. **d** 01 **p** 02. C Ipsley *Worc* 01-04; V Fairfield *Liv* from 04. *St John's Vicarage, 19 Lockerby Road, Liverpool L7 0HG* Tel 0151-263 4001 E-mail andrew.porter@bigfoot.com

PORTER, Anthony. *See* PORTER, Canon David Anthony

PORTER, Canon Anthony. b 52. Hertf Coll Ox BA74 MA78 Fitzw Ho Cam BA76 MA80. Ridley Hall Cam 74. **d** 77 **p** 78. C Edgware *Lon* 77-80; C Haughton St Mary *Man* 80-83; P-in-c Bacup Ch Ch 83-87; V 87-91; R Rusholme H Trin from 91; Hon Can Man Cathl from 04. *Holy Trinity Rectory, Platt Lane, Manchester M14 5NF* Tel 0161-224 1123 Fax 224 1144 E-mail tony@plattchurch.org

PORTER, Arthur William. b 29. St Deiniol's Hawarden 70. **d** 70 **p** 71. C Ruislip St Martin *Lon* 70-80; V Kingsbury H Innocents 80-94; rtd 94; Perm to Offic *Sarum* from 94. *24 Belle Vue Road, Salisbury SP1 3YG* Tel (01722) 331314

PORTER, Barbara Judith. *See* JEAPES, Mrs Barbara Judith

PORTER, Brian John Henry. b 33. SW Minl Tr Course 78. **d** 81 **p** 82. NSM Plymouth St Andr w St Paul and St Geo *Ex* 81-85; Perm to Offic 85-87; NSM Devonport St Barn 87-90; C Brampton St Thos *Derby* 90-95; Asst Chapl Amsterdam w Den Helder and Heiloo *Eur* 95-97; rtd 97; Perm to Offic *Glouc* 99-00. *2 Abbotsdene, 6 Cudnall Street, Charlton Kings, Cheltenham GL53 8HT*

PORTER, Brian Meredith. b 39. Monash Univ Aus BA66 Trin Hall Cam BA75 MA79 New England Univ NSW BLitt79 MLitt85 ACT ThD01. Cuddesdon Coll 68. **d** 68 **p** 71. Australia 68-73 and from 75; C Kew 68-69; K Sch Parramatta 70-73; Perm to Offic *Ely* 73; Chapl Canberra Gr Sch 75-82; Chapl Ivanhoe Gr Sch 83-97; Sen Chapl Melbourne Gr Sch from 98. *Melbourne Grammar School, Domain Road, South Yarra, Vic, Australia 3141* Tel (0061) (3) 9882 8740 *or* 9868 7157 Mobile 407-552425 Fax (3) 9882 4137 E-mail bporter@mgs.vic.edu.au

PORTER, Damian Michael. b 66. Linc Th Coll BTh92. **d** 92 **p** 93. C Pelsall *Lich* 92-96; V Greenlands *Blackb* 96-00; V St Annes St Anne from 00. *St Anne's Vicarage, 4 Oxford Road, Lytham St Annes FY8 2EA* Tel (01253) 722725 E-mail dmp@oxrd.fsnet.co.uk

PORTER, Canon David Anthony (Tony). b 34. Wycliffe Hall Ox 73. **d** 75 **p** 76. C Watford St Luke *St Alb* 75-78; C Worting *Win* 78-81; V Snettisham *Nor* 81-82; P-in-c Ingoldisthorpe 81-82; C Fring 81-82; R Snettisham w Ingoldisthorpe and Fring 82-84; Chapl Asst Colchester Gen Hosp 87-88; Chapl Maidstone Hosp 88-94; Chapl Mid Kent Healthcare NHS Trust 94-98; Hon Can Cant Cathl *Cant* 97-98; rtd 98; Perm to Offic *Nor* and *Ely* from 98. *The Greys, 12 Hawthorn Close, Watlington, King's Lynn PE33 0HD* Tel (01558) 811301

PORTER, David Michael. b 37. Coll of Ripon & York St Jo BA88. Ely Th Coll 61. **d** 64 **p** 65. C Clun w Chapel Lawn *Heref* 64-67; C Scarborough St Mary w Ch Ch, St Paul and St Thos *York* 67-69; C Fulford 69-71; V Strensall 71-78; Chapl Claypenny and St Monica's Hosps 78-91; V Easingwold w Raskelf *York* 78-91; TR York All SS Pavement w St Crux and St Martin etc 91-97; R York All SS Pavement w St Crux and St Mich 97-02; rtd 02; Perm to Offic *York* from 02. *10 Hall Rise, Haxby, York YO32 3LP* Tel (01904) 769823

PORTER, David Michael. b 46. Nottm Univ BMedSci80 BM82 BS82. EMMTC 94. **d** 97 **p** 98. NSM Edwinstowe *S'well* 97-99. *Gorsethorpe Cottage, Edwinstowe, Mansfield NG21 9HJ* Tel (01623) 844657

PORTER, David Rowland Shelley. b 46. City of Liv Coll of HE CertEd69. STETS 00. **d** 03 **p** 04. NSM Whitehawk *Chich* from 03. *33 Warleigh Road, Brighton BN1 4NT* Tel (01273) 703499 E-mail davejanera@aol.com

PORTER, Howard. b 56. S Glam Inst HE CertEd78. St Mich Coll Llan 99. **d** 01 **p** 02. C Maindee *Mon* from 01. *16 Kensington Place, Newport NP19 8GL* Tel (01633) 281053

PORTER, James Richard. b 73. Lon Univ BMedSci97 MB, BS98. Oak Hill Th Coll MTh05. **d** 05. C Cromer *Nor* from 05. *18 Vicarage Road, Cromer NR27 9DQ* Tel (01263) 514352

PORTER, John Dudley Dowell. b 33. St Edm Hall Ox BA60 MA61. Qu Coll Birm 57. **d** 59 **p** 60. C Londonderry *Birm* 59-62; C Tettenhall Regis *Lich* 62-65; Chapl RAF 65-69; V Wombourne

Lich 69-75; V Rickerscote 75-81; P-in-c Chapel Chorlton 81-85; P-in-c Maer 81-85; P-in-c Whitmore 81-85; R Chapel Chorlton, Maer and Whitmore 85-92; TR Wednesfield 92-00; rtd 00; P-in-c Haughton St Anne *Man* 00-03; P-in-c Nord Pas de Calais *Eur* from 04. *37 Rue Principale, 62130 Framecourt, France* Tel (0033) (3) 21 04 36 35

PORTER, Canon Prof Joshua Roy. b 21. Mert Coll Ox BA42 MA47. St Steph Ho Ox 42. **d** 45 **p** 46. C Portsea St Mary *Portsm* 45-47; Bp's Dom Chapl *Chich* 47-49; Chapl and Lect Oriel Coll Ox 49-62; Tutor Oriel Coll Ox 50-62; Lect Th Ox Univ 50-62; Prof Th Ex Univ 62-86; Can and Preb Chich Cathl *Chich* 65-88; Wiccamical Preb Chich Cathl from 88; rtd 86; Lic to Offic *Lon* from 87. *36 Theberton Street, London N1 0QX* Tel (020) 7354 5861

PORTER, Miss Joy Dove. b 50. Lon Univ PGCE83 Ex Univ CPS86. Lon Bible Coll BA81 Wycliffe Hall Ox 89. **d** 91 **p** 94. Par Dn Chalgrove w Berrick Salome *Ox* 91-92; Par Dn Chipping Norton 92-94; C 94-95; Hong Kong 96-97; Chapl Rouen Miss to Seamen *Eur* 97-00; P-in-c Rouen All SS 97-00. *Address temp unknown*

PORTER, Kenneth Wilfred. b 27. St Aid Birkenhead 58. **d** 61 **p** 62. C Queensbury *Bradf* 61-63; C Oldham St Paul *Man* 63-65; V Wardle 65-91; Chapl Birch Hill Hosp 84-91; rtd 91; Perm to Offic *Man* 91-97 and *Liv* 97-03. *19 Knowsley Drive, Leigh WN7 3LY*

PORTER, Malcolm Derek. b 53. BSc. NTMTC. **d** 05. C Woodford Wells *Chelmsf* from 05. *St Stephen's Vicarage, 41 Fraser Road, London E17 9DD* Tel (020) 8520 1785

PORTER, Mrs Marie-Jeanne. b 60. EMMTC 95. **d** 98 **p** 99. NSM Warsop *S'well* 98-04. *Gorsethorpe Cottage, Edwinstowe, Mansfield NG21 9HJ* Tel (01623) 844657

PORTER, Matthew James. b 69. Nottm Univ BA90. Wycliffe Hall Ox BTh93. **d** 96 **p** 97. C Dore *Sheff* 96-00; V Woodseats St Chad from 00. *St Chad's Vicarage, 9 Linden Avenue, Sheffield S8 0GA* Tel 0114-274 5086 Fax as telephone E-mail office@stchads.org

PORTER, Michael Edward. b 44. Trin Coll Bris 75. **d** 77 **p** 78. C Corby St Columba *Pet* 77-81; C Rainham *Chelmsf* 81-82; TV 82-92; P-in-c S Hornchurch St Jo and St Matt 92-95; V Anerley *Roch* from 95; AD Beckenham from 05. *The Vicarage, 234 Anerley Road, London SE20 8TJ* Tel (020) 8778 4800 E-mail mike@christchurchanerley.freeserve.co.uk

PORTER, Roy. *See* PORTER, Canon Prof Joshua Roy

PORTER, Mrs Susan Patricia June. b 53. STETS 00. **d** 03. NSM Wilton w Netherhampton and Fugglestone *Sarum* from 03. *24 Belle Vue Road, Salisbury SP1 3YG* Tel (01722) 331314 E-mail revporter@sarum1220.fsnet.co.uk

PORTER, William Albert. b 28. Univ of NZ BA51 MA52. Coll of Resurr Mirfield 53. **d** 55 **p** 56. C Perry Barr *Birm* 55-58; New Zealand 59-62; Fiji 62-67; Can and Prec H Trin Cathl Suva 65-67; C Wimbledon *S'wark* 68; Asst Chapl HM Pris Liv 69-70; Chapl 79-87; Chapl HM Pris Brixton 70-74; Chapl HM Pris Long Lartin 74-79; Chapl HM Pris Nottm 87-90; P-in-c Sneinton St Matthias *S'well* 90-93; rtd 94; Perm to Offic *Glouc* from 01. *40 Duke Street, Cheltenham GL52 6BP* Tel (01242) 262198

PORTER-PRYCE, Ms Julia Frances. b 57. Man Univ BA78 Leic Univ MPhil94. NTMTC 93. **d** 96 **p** 97. C Stoke Newington Common St Mich *Lon* 96-99; C Is of Dogs Ch Ch and St Jo w St Luke 99-02; V De Beauvoir Town St Pet from 02. *St Peter's Vicarage, 86 De Beauvoir Road, London N1 5AT* Tel (020) 7254 5670 E-mail juliap@freeuk.com

PORTEUS, James Michael. b 31. Worc Coll Ox BA55 MA58. Cuddesdon Coll. **d** 57 **p** 58. C Fleetwood St Pet *Blackb* 57-60; C Ox St Mary V *Ox* 60-62; Staff Sec SCM Ox 60-62; Chapl Univ of Chicago USA 62-69 and 86-91; Chapl Lon Univ *Lon* 69-74; V Hampstead Garden Suburb 74-86; Min Livingston LEP *Edin* 91-96; rtd 96; P-in-c Portree *Arg* 96-05. *3 Camustianavaig, Portree IV51 9LQ* Tel (01478) 650223

PORTEUS, Canon Robert John Norman. b 50. TCD BA72 MA76. CITC 75. **d** 75 **p** 76. C Portadown St Mark *Arm* 75-79; I Ardtrea w Desertcreat 79-83; I Annaghmore 83-98; I Derryloran from 98; Can Arm Cathl from 98; Preb from 01. *Derryloran Rectory, 13 Loy Street, Cookstown BT80 8PZ* Tel and fax (028) 8676 2261 E-mail derryloran@armagh.anglican.org

PORTHOUSE, Canon John Clive. b 32. Lon Univ BD58. Tyndale Hall Bris 55 Oak Hill Th Coll 58. **d** 60 **p** 61. C Leyton All SS *Chelmsf* 60-62; C Kendal St Thos *Carl* 62-64; V Flimby 64-68; V Sidcup St Andr *Roch* 68-74; V Beckenham St Jo 74-86; RD Beckenham 80-86; V Southborough St Pet w Ch Ch and St Matt 86-96; TR 96-97; Hon Can Roch Cathl 96-97; rtd 97; Perm to Offic *Carl* from 98. *148 Stainbank Road, Kendal LA9 5BE* Tel (01539) 736106

PORTHOUSE, Roger Gordon Hargreaves. b 39. Tyndale Hall Bris 66. **d** 69 **p** 70. C Wellington w Eyton *Lich* 69-71; C Cheadle *Ches* 71-75; R Frettenham w Stanninghall *Nor* 75-81; R Spixworth w Crostwick 75-81; V Hailsham *Chich* 81-04; RD Dallington 96-03; rtd 05. *19 Cornmill Gardens, Polegate BN26 5NJ* Tel (01323) 487372 E-mail rporthouse@btclick.com

PORTLOCK, John Anthony. b 37. WMMTC 96. **d** 99 **p** 00. NSM Lyddington w Stoke Dry and Seaton etc *Pet* 99-05; NSM Bulwick, Blatherwycke w Harringworth and Laxton from 05. *7 Chestnut Close, Uppingham LE15 9TQ* Tel (01572) 823225 E-mail portlocklydd@aol.com

PORTSDOWN, Archdeacon of. *See* LOWSON, The Ven Christopher

PORTSMOUTH, Bishop of. *See* STEVENSON, The Rt Revd Kenneth William

PORTSMOUTH, Dean of. *See* BRINDLEY, The Very Revd David Charles

PORTWOOD, Prof Derek. b 31. Keele Univ MA69 PhD79. Lon Coll of Div ALCD57. **d** 57 **p** 58. C Laisterdyke *Bradf* 57-60; C-in-c Westlands St Andr CD *Lich* 60-66; V Westlands St Andr 66-69; rtd 96; Perm to Offic *Ely* 96-00. *51 River Lane, Cambridge CB5 8HP* Tel (01223) 311044 Fax as telephone

POSKITT, Mark Sylvester. b 63. Loughb Univ BSc84. St Jo Coll Nottm MA95. **d** 97 **p** 98. C Brigg, Wrawby and Cadney cum Howsham *Linc* 97-00; TV Howden *York* from 00. *The Vicarage, Portington Road, Eastrington, Goole DN14 7QE* Tel (01430) 410282 E-mail msposkitt@tesco.net

POST, David Charles William. b 39. Jes Coll Cam BA61 MA65. Oak Hill Th Coll 61. **d** 63 **p** 64. C Orpington Ch Ch *Roch* 63-66; C Fulwood *Sheff* 66-68; V Lathom *Liv* 68-75; V Poughill *Truro* 75-78; V Braddan and Santan *S & M* 78-79; Dioc Missr 78-79; V Sherburn in Elmet *York* 79-91; P-in-c Kirk Fenton 84-85; V Thornthwaite cum Braithwaite and Newlands *Carl* 91-93; R Wheldrake w Thorganby *York* 93-04; P-in-c Elvington w Sutton on Derwent and E Cottingwith 03-04; rtd 04. *Cheviot, 5 Mayfield Crescent, Middle Rasen, Market Rasen LN8 3UA* Tel (01673) 843388

POST, Oswald Julian. b 48. Derby Lonsdale Coll BEd79. EMMTC. **d** 84 **p** 85. Travelling Sec Rwanda Miss 79-89; Hon C Hulland, Atlow, Bradley and Hognaston *Derby* 84-89; V Wormhill, Peak Forest w Peak Dale and Dove Holes 89-99; P-in-c Youlgreave, Middleton, Stanton-in-Peak etc from 99. *The Vicarage, Church Street, Youlgrave, Bakewell DE45 1WL* Tel (01629) 636285

POSTILL, John Edward. b 35. Oak Hill Th Coll 64. **d** 67 **p** 68. C Southgate *Chich* 67-70; C Bowling St Jo *Bradf* 70-74; TV Winfarthing w Shelfanger *Nor* 74-79; R Slaugham *Chich* 79-97; C Busbridge and Hambledon *Guildf* 97-03; rtd 03. *Dora Cottage, Beech Hill, Hambledon, Godalming GU8 4HL* Tel (01428) 687968 E-mail jandjpostill@talk21.com

POSTILL, Canon Richard Halliday. b 37. Hull Univ BSc59. Westcott Ho Cam 66. **d** 68 **p** 69. C Wylde Green *Birm* 68-72; C Kingswinford St Mary *Lich* 72-76; V Yardley Wood *Birm* 76-86; V Acocks Green 86-02; AD Yardley 93-00; Hon Can Birm Cathl 99-02; rtd 02; Perm to Offic *Birm* from 03. *32 Longmore Road, Shirley, Solihull B90 3DY* Tel 0121-744 6217 E-mail richardh@postill.fsbusiness.co.uk

POSTLES, Donald. b 29. MPS51 Birm Univ DipTh59 MA65. Qu Coll Birm 56. **d** 59 **p** 60. C Southport H Trin *Liv* 59-62; C Prescot 62-63; V Wigan St Steph 63-71; V Farnworth 71-84; V Mossley Hill St Barn 84-92; rtd 93. *43 The Broadway, Abergele LL22 7DD* Tel (01745) 826165

POSTON, Jonathan David. b 59. Ches Coll of HE MTh05. N Ord Course 01. **d** 04 **p** 05. C Prestwich St Mary *Man* from 04. *49 Cromwell Road, Prestwich, Manchester M25 1HR* Tel and fax 0161-798 6352 Mobile 07754-517797 E-mail revjp@poston.org.uk

POTHEN, Simon John. b 60. Westmr Coll Ox BA86. Ripon Coll Cuddesdon 86. **d** 88 **p** 89. C Southgate Ch Ch *Lon* 88-91; C Tottenham St Mary 91-93; TV Gt Grimsby St Mary and St Jas *Linc* 93-96; R Friern Barnet St Jas *Lon* 96-02; V Pinner from 02. *The Vicarage, 2 Church Lane, Pinner HA5 3AA* Tel (020) 8866 3869 *or* 8866 2676 Mobile 07939-523366 E-mail spothen@btconnect.com

POTIPHER, John Malcolm Barry. b 42. St Alb Minl Tr Scheme 79. **d** 82 **p** 83. Chapl Herts Fire Brigade 82-91; NSM Chambersbury *St Alb* 82-84; NSM Hemel Hempstead 84-86; NSM Digswell and Panshanger 86-92; P-in-c Pirton 92-95; rtd 95; Perm to Offic *St Alb* from 95. *66 Peartree Lane, Welwyn Garden City AL7 3UH* Tel and fax (01707) 886953 E-mail john.potipher@ntlworld.com

POTTER, Charles Elmer. b 42. Georgetown Univ (USA) BS65 Valparaiso Univ JD73. Wycliffe Coll Toronto MDiv81. **d** 81 **p** 82. C Southport Ch Ch *Liv* 81-84; Chapl Lee Abbey 84-87; Australia 87-93; P-in-c Aldingham and Dendron and Rampside *Carl* 93-96; P-in-c Aldingham, Dendron, Rampside and Urswick 96-99; V Bexley St Mary *Roch* from 99. *The Vicarage, 29 Hill Crescent, Bexley DA5 2DA* Tel (01322) 523457 Fax as telephone E-mail cpotter@lineone.net

POTTER, The Very Revd Christopher Nicholas Lynden. b 49. Leeds Univ BA71. St As Minl Tr Course 90. **d** 93 **p** 94. C Flint *St As* 93-96; V Llanfair DC, Derwen, Llanelidan and Efenechtyd 96-01; Dean and Lib St As Cathl from 01; V St As 01-03; TR from 03. *The Deanery, Upper Denbigh Road, St Asaph LL17 0RL* Tel (01745) 583597 E-mail chris_potter@talk21.com

POTTER, Clement. *See* POTTER, Keith Clement

POTTER, Clive Geoffrey. b 55. Aston Tr Scheme 88 Sarum & Wells Th Coll 90. **d** 92 **p** 93. C Epsom Common Ch Ch *Guildf* 92-97; TV Westborough 97-98; TR from 98. *St Francis's Vicarage, Beckingham Road, Guildford GU2 8BU* Tel (01483) 504228

POTTER, Desmond. b 54. St Paul's Coll Grahamstown DipTh85. **d** 88 **p** 88. S Africa 88-98; V Newton *Ches* from 98. *St Michael's House, 56 Queensbury Road, Wirral CH48 6EP* Tel 0151-625 8517 Fax as telephone E-mail church@thepotters.me.uk

POTTER, Harry Drummond. b 54. Em Coll Cam BA76 MA79 MPhil81 LLB92 Barrister 93. Westcott Ho Cam 79. **d** 81 **p** 82. C Deptford St Paul *S'wark* 81-84; Chapl Selw Coll Cam 84-87; Chapl Newnham Coll Cam 84-87; Chapl HM Pris Wormwood Scrubs 87-88; Chapl HM YOI Aylesbury 88-93; NSM Camberwell St Giles w St Matt *S'wark* 93-03; Perm to Offic from 03. *19 Dobell Road, London SE9 1HE* Tel (020) 7067 1500 E-mail tuahousis@hotmail.com

POTTER, Canon James David. b 35. AKC66. **d** 67 **p** 68. C Longbridge *Birm* 67-70; Lic to Offic 71-73; V N Harborne 73-78; V Smethwick H Trin w St Alb 78-83; V Blurton *Lich* 83-90; V Dordon *Birm* 90-98; RD Polesworth 91-96; Hon Can Birm Cathl 96-98; rtd 98; Perm to Offic *Birm* from 98. *49 Winstanley Road, Stechford, Birmingham B33 8UH* Tel 0121-783 2734

POTTER, John Daniel. b 29. Sydney Univ BA50. St Jo Coll Morpeth ThL51. **d** 51 **p** 53. Australia 52-65 and from 71; C High Harrogate Ch Ch *Ripon* 65-66; Chapl St Mary's Sch Wantage 66-68; Chapl St Jo Sch and NSM St Andr Cathl Singapore 68-71; OCF 68-71; rtd 95; Lic to Offic *Eur* 95-97. *200 Castella Road, Toolangi, Vic, Australia 3777* Tel (0061) (3) 5962 9449

POTTER, John Dennis. b 39. Ealing Tech Coll. S Dios Minl Tr Scheme 92. **d** 94 **p** 95. NSM Box w Hazlebury and Ditteridge *Bris* 94-98. *Address temp unknown*

POTTER, John Ellis. b 45. SSC. Sarum & Wells Th Coll 82. **d** 84 **p** 85. C Wootton Bassett *Sarum* 84-88; TV Swindon New Town *Bris* 88-96; V Milber *Ex* from 96. *St Luke's Vicarage, 10 Laburnum Road, Newton Abbot TQ12 4LQ* Tel (01626) 365837

POTTER, Canon John Henry. b 26. Lon Univ BA50. Oak Hill Th Coll 50. **d** 52 **p** 53. C Islington St Mary *Lon* 52-55; C Kinson *Sarum* 55-58; V Upper Holloway St Jo *Lon* 58-65; R Illogan *Truro* 65-69; P-in-c Ilfracombe SS Phil and Jas *Ex* 69-72; V 72-76; R Poole *Sarum* 76-87; RD Poole 80-85; Can and Preb Sarum Cathl 83-91; P-in-c Charmouth and Catherston Leweston 87-91; rtd 91; Perm to Offic *Sarum* 91-99; Perm to Offic *Win* 91-00. *11 Park Terrace, Tenby SA70 7LY* Tel (01834) 843647

POTTER, Judith Anne. CertEd. **d** 05. OLM Shere, Albury and Chilworth *Guildf* from 05. *3 Bank Terrace, Gomshall Lane, Shere, Guildford GU5 9HB* Tel (01483) 203352 E-mail judyp@btopenworld.com

POTTER, Keith Clement. b 39. Leeds Univ CertSS78 Bradf Univ MA81. Chich Th Coll 62. **d** 64 **p** 65. C Doncaster Ch Ch *Sheff* 64-68; C Tong *Bradf* 68-70; V Bradf St Columba w St Andr 70-79; V Yeadon St Andr 79-02; rtd 02. *6 Main Street, Balintore, Tain IV20 1UE*

POTTER, Kenneth Benjamin. Open Univ BA GLCM. NEOC 84. **d** 87 **p** 88. NSM Ryton w Hedgefield *Dur* 87-95; P-in-c Harby w Thorney and N and S Clifton *S'well* from 95. *The Rectory, Front Street, South Clifton, Newark NG23 7AA* Tel (01522) 778258 E-mail kenneth.b.potter@btinternet.com

POTTER, Mrs Linda. b 47. Cranmer Hall Dur 92. **d** 94 **p** 95. C Shildon w Eldon *Dur* 94-98; P-in-c Castleside 98-04; TR Gt Aycliffe and Chilton from 04. *St Clare's Rectory, St Cuthbert's Way, Newton Aycliffe DL5 5NT* Tel (01325) 313613 E-mail linda.potter@durham.anglican.org

POTTER, Preb Malcolm Emmerson. b 48. Bedf Coll Lon BSc70. St Jo Coll Nottm DPS75. **d** 75 **p** 76. C Upton (Overchurch) *Ches* 76-78; CPAS Staff 78-84; Development Officer St Jo Coll Nottm 84-86; P-in-c Wellington, All SS w Eyton *Lich* 86-95; V from 95; Preb Lich Cathl from 99. *All Saints' Vicarage, 35 Crescent Road, Wellington, Telford TF1 3DW* Tel (01952) 641251 Fax 401807 E-mail malcolmepotter@blueyonder.co.uk

POTTER, Peter Maxwell. b 46. Univ of Wales (Swansea) BA69 Univ of BC MA71. Sarum & Wells Th Coll 83. **d** 85 **p** 86. C Bradford-on-Avon *Sarum* 85-88; C Harnham 88-91; P-in-c N Bradley, Southwick and Heywood 91-96; V Sale St Anne *Ches* 96-00; R Largs *Glas* from 00. *St Columba's Rectory, Aubery Crescent, Largs KA30 8PR* Tel and fax (01475) 673143 E-mail peshar@lineone.net

POTTER, Canon Phillip. b 54. Stirling Univ BA75. Trin Coll Bris 82. **d** 84 **p** 85. C Yateley *Win* 84-88; V Haydock St Mark *Liv* from 88; Hon Can Liv Cathl from 03. *St Mark's Vicarage, 2 Stanley Bank Road, St Helens WA11 0UW* Tel (01744) 23957 Fax 602641 E-mail info@stmarkshaydock.org

POTTER, Richard Antony. b 36. K Coll Cam BA60 MA64. Ridley Hall Cam 60. **d** 62 **p** 63. C Luton w E Hyde *St Alb* 62-72; V Lyonsdown H Trin 72-85; R Broxbourne w Wormley 85-02; rtd 02; C Thorverton, Cadbury, Upton Pyne etc *Ex* from 02. *The Vicarage, Newton St Cyres, Exeter EX5 5BN* Tel (01392) 851386

POTTER, Miss Sharon Jane. b 63. Suffolk Coll BSc96 K Coll Lon MSc00 RGN91. **d** 04. OLM Ipswich All Hallows *St E* from 04. *9 Norman Crescent, Ipswich IP3 9JY* Tel (01473) 421087 Mobile 07795-168600 E-mail sharon.jane@potterdome.fsnet.co.uk

POTTER, Stephen Michael. b 55. Oak Hill Th Coll 93. **d** 95 **p** 96. C Chesterfield H Trin and Ch Ch *Derby* 95-99; P-in-c S Normanton from 99. *The Rectory, Church Street, South Normanton, Alfreton DE55 2BT* Tel (01773) 811273

POTTER, Canon Timothy John. b 49. Bris Univ BSc71. Oak Hill Th Coll 73. **d** 76 **p** 77. C Wallington H Trin *S'wark* 76-79; C Hampreston *Sarum* 79-81; TV Stratton St Margaret w S Marston etc *Bris* 81-87; P-in-c Hatfield Heath *Chelmsf* 87-89; P-in-c Sheering 87-89; R Hatfield Heath and Sheering from 90; Hon Can Chelmsf Cathl from 02. *The Vicarage, Broomfields, Hatfield Heath, Bishop's Stortford CM22 7EH* Tel (01279) 730288 E-mail tim.potter1@btinternet.com

POTTIER, Ronald William. b 36. S'wark Ord Course 73. **d** 76 **p** 77. NSM Lower Sydenham St Mich *S'wark* 76-98; NSM Sydenham All SS from 98. *12 Neiderwald Road, London SE26 4AD* Tel (020) 8699 4375

POTTS, Heather Dawn. b 52. **d** 98 **p** 99. C Attleborough w Besthorpe *Nor* 98-01; R Bunwell, Carleton Rode, Tibenham, Gt Moulton etc from 01; RD Depwade from 03. *The Rectory, Chapel Road, Carleton Rode, Norwich NR16 1RN* Tel (01953) 789218

POTTS, James. b 30. K Coll Lon BD56 AKC56. **d** 57 **p** 58. C Brighouse *Wakef* 57-59; Tanganyika 59-64; Tanzania 64-71; C-in-c Athersley and New Lodge CD *Wakef* 71-73; V Athersley 73-77; V Madeley *Lich* 77-85; V Baswich 85-93; RD Stafford 88-95; rtd 93. *16A Christchurch Lane, Lichfield WS13 8BA* Tel (01543) 418808

POTTS, Mrs Jill. b 46. Open Univ BA89. STETS 02. **d** 05. NSM Corfe Mullen *Sarum* from 05. *5 Orchard Lane, Corfe Mullen, Wimborne BH21 3SU* Tel (01202) 695988 E-mail jill@steveandjill.me.uk

POTTS, William Gilbert. b 17. Bps' Coll Cheshunt 46. **d** 49 **p** 50. C Fenton *Lich* 49-52; C W Bromwich St Andr 52-53; C Ashbourne w Mapleton and Clifton *Derby* 53-57; V Beighton *Sheff* 57-64; V Winshill *Derby* 64-82; rtd 82; Perm to Offic *Derby* from 82. *28 Roydon Close, Mickleover, Derby DE3 0PN* Tel (01332) 516328

POULARD, Christopher. b 39. FCA64. Ridley Hall Cam 82. **d** 84 **p** 85. C N Walsham w Antingham *Nor* 84-86; C Oulton Broad 86-90; TV Raveningham 90-94; R Raveningham Gp 94-99; RD Loddon 98-99; Perm to Offic *Chelmsf* from 99; rtd 04. *Cuddington, Colam Lane, Little Baddow, Chelmsford CM3 4SY* Tel (01245) 224221 Fax 221394 E-mail chris@poulard.org.uk

POULSON, Ms Anna Louise. b 73. Univ Coll Dur BA94 K Coll Lon MA97. Ridley Hall Cam 98. **d** 02 **p** 03. C Ealing St Mary *Lon* from 02. *St John's Vicarage, Church Avenue, Southall UB2 4DH* Tel (020) 8571 3027 Mobile 07929-348621 E-mail anna.poulson@kcl.ac.uk

POULSON, Mark Alban. b 63. Bath Coll of HE BEd86 Anglia Poly Univ MA03. Ridley Hall Cam. **d** 00 **p** 01. C Alperton *Lon* 00-03; P-in-c Southall Green St Jo from 03. *St John's Vicarage, Church Avenue, Southall UB2 4DH* Tel (020) 8574 2055 E-mail mpoulson@fish.co.uk

POULTER, Canon Alan John. b 39. St Aid Birkenhead 64. **d** 67 **p** 68. C Heswall *Ches* 67-72; V Bredbury St Mark 72-78; V Oxton 78-97; RD Birkenhead 93-97; TR Ches Team 97-02; Hon Can Ches Cathl 96-02; rtd 02; Perm to Offic *Ches* from 03. *21 Bevyl Road, Parkgate, Neston CH64 6RP* Tel 0151-336 6288 E-mail ajohn1@aol.com

POULTER, Joseph William. b 40. Dur Univ BA61 BA66 DipTh67. Cranmer Hall Dur 66. **d** 67 **p** 68. C Harlow New Town w Lt Parndon *Chelmsf* 67-71; C Washington *Dur* 71-77; Producer Metro Radio from 75; C-in-c Town End Farm CD 77-83; V Sunderland Town End Farm 83-03; TV N Wearside from 03. *Town End Farm House, Bootle Street, Sunderland SR5 4EY* Tel 0191-536 3823 Fax 537 3744 E-mail joepoulter@tinyworld.co.uk

POULTNEY, Wilfred Howard. b 25. SSC87. Qu Coll Birm 71. **d** 73 **p** 74. NSM S Leamington St Jo *Cov* 73-85; NSM Holbrooks 85-95; NSM Walsall St Gabr Fulbrook *Lich* from 95. *28 Walstead Road, Walsall WS5 4LX* Tel (01922) 868067

POULTON, Arthur Leslie. b 28. K Coll Lon BA53 AKC53 BD60 Leic Univ MA85. Tyndale Hall Bris 53. **d** 55 **p** 56. C New Catton St Luke *Nor* 55-56; C Earlham St Anne 56-58; C Chorleywood Ch Ch *St Alb* 58-61; R E Barnet 61-64; Ches Coll of HE 64-87; Chapl 64-84; Sen Lect 66-87; Dir of Studies Course in Chr Studies *Chelmsf* 87-94; P-in-c Gt Canfield 87-94; rtd 94; Perm to Offic *Ches* from 96. *Chaldon, Great Mollington, Chester CH1 6LG* Tel (01244) 851338

POULTON, Ian Peter. b 60. Lon Univ BSc(Econ)83 TCD DipTh86 Open Univ BA94. **d** 86 **p** 87. C Newtownards *D & D* 86-89; I Bright w Ballee and Killough 89-96; Relig Adv Downtown Radio 91-96; I Larne and Inver *Conn* 96-99; I Killiney Ballybrack *D & G* from 99. *Killiney Rectory, 21 Killiney*

Avenue, Killiney, Co Dublin, Irish Republic Tel and fax (00353) (1) 285 6180 E-mail poulton@oceanfree.net

POULTON, Katharine Margaret. b 61. Man Univ BA83 TCD DipTh87. **d** 87 **p** 91. C Bangor St Comgall *D & D* 87-91; C Seagoe 91-96; C Kilwaughter w Cairncastle and Craigy Hill *Conn* 96-99; C Greystones *D & G* 99-00; Bp's C Dublin St Geo and St Thos from 00. *Killiney Rectory, 21 Killiney Avenue, Killiney, Co Dublin, Irish Republic* Tel and fax (00353) (1) 285 6180 E-mail poulton@oceanfree.net

POULTON, Neville John. b 48. STETS. **d** 02. NSM Portsea St Cuth *Portsm* from 02. *18 Belgravia Road, Portsmouth PO2 0DX* Tel (023) 9236 1104 Mobile 07768-661796 E-mail momac@fish.co.uk

POUNCE, Alan Gerald. b 34. Lon Univ BSc55 Dip Counselling. Wycliffe Hall Ox 57. **d** 59 **p** 60. C Wednesfield Heath *Lich* 59-61; C Heref St Pet w St Owen *Heref* 61-63; R Gt w Lt Dunham *Nor* 63-69; Asst Master Windsor Boys' Sch 69-94; rtd 94; Perm to Offic *Ox* 69-99; Lic to Offic from 99. *38 Longdown Road, Sandhurst GU47 8QG* Tel (01344) 772870

POUNCEY, Christopher Michael Godwin. b 52. Reading Univ BSc74 Wycliffe Hall Ox BA77 MA. SW Minl Tr Course 03. **d** 04 **p** 05. NSM S Molton w Nymet St George, High Bray etc *Ex* from 04. *Brightley Barton, Umberleigh EX37 9AL* Tel (01769) 540405 Mobile 07977-930045 E-mail cmgpouncey@hotmail.com

POUNCEY, Canon Cosmo Gabriel Rivers. b 11. Qu Coll Cam BA32 MA36. Cuddesdon Coll 33. **d** 34 **p** 35. C Kennington St Jo *S'wark* 34-44; Sec Ch Educn League 43-46; V Woodham *Guildf* 46-63; Hon Can Guildf Cathl 62-63; V Tewkesbury w Walton Cardiff *Glouc* 63-81; P-in-c Tredington w Stoke Orchard and Hardwicke 63-81; RD Tewkesbury 68-81; Hon Can Glouc Cathl 72-81; P-in-c Deerhurst w Apperley 74-80; rtd 81; Perm to Offic *Glouc* 81-97; *Worc* 81-93; *Sarum* from 93. *Bridehead, Littlebredy, Dorchester DT2 9JA* Tel (01308) 482356

POUND, Canon Keith Salisbury. b 33. St Cath Coll Cam BA54 MA58. Cuddesdon Coll 55. **d** 57 **p** 58. C St Helier *S'wark* 57-61; Tr Officer Hollowford Tr & Conf Cen Sheff 61-64; Warden 64-67; R S'wark H Trin 68-74; P-in-c Newington St Matt 68-74; R S'wark H Trin w St Matt 74-78; RD S'wark and Newington 73-78; TR Thamesmead 78-86; Sub-Dean Woolwich 84-86; RD Greenwich 85-86; Hon Can S'wark Cathl 85-86; Chapl Gen of Pris 86-93; Chapl to The Queen 88-03; Chapl HM Pris Grendon and Spring Hill 93-98; rtd 98; Perm to Offic *Chich* from 99. *Adeleine, Pett Road, Pett, Hastings TN35 4HE* Tel (01424) 813873

POUNDE, Nigel. b 46. Edin Univ MA69 Union Th Sem (NY) STM01. Cranmer Hall Dur DipTh71. **d** 72 **p** 73. C Southsea St Simon *Portsm* 72-75; C Clayton w Keymer *Chich* 75-79; Malaysia 80-86; TV Wolverhampton *Lich* 87-97; Dioc Inter-Faith Officer 92-97; Care Services Manager Terrence Higgins Trust 97-00; USA 00-01; R Newport-on-Tay *St And* 01-02; Edin Warrant from 03. *11/11, Dudley Avenue South, Edinburgh EH6 4PH* Tel 0131-553 7401 Mobile 07941-151075 E-mail nigel.pounde@virgin.net

POVEY, John Michael. b 44. St Jo Coll Nottm BTh76. **d** 76 **p** 77. USA from 76. *67 East, Pittsfield, MA 01201, USA* E-mail jmp@berkshire.net

POVEY, Canon Kenneth Vincent. b 40. AKC62. **d** 63 **p** 64. C Crewe Ch Ch *Ches* 63-66; C Neston 66-69; C Kensington St Mary Abbots w St Geo *Lon* 69-72; R Ches H Trin *Ches* 72-81; Chapl Copenhagen w Aarhus *Eur* 81-86; R Gawsworth *Ches* 86-98; Hon Can Ches Cathl 92-98; rtd 98; Perm to Offic *Ches* from 98. *The White House, Bishopton Drive, Macclesfield SK11 8TR*

POVEY, William Peter. b 36. JP85. MRCS61 LRCP61 FFPHM79 FRIPHH DRCOG HonFChS Liv Univ DPH68 Man Univ MSc82. N Ord Course 90. **d** 93 **p** 94. Dioc Drug Liaison Officer *Ches* from 93; NSM Latchford Ch Ch 93-00; NSM Daresbury 00-03; rtd 03; Perm to Offic *Ches* from 03 and *Ex* from 04. *Owls' Nest, 9A The Square, Ugborough, Ivybridge PL21 0NT* Tel (01752) 691654 E-mail povey@excite.co.uk

POW, Miss Joyce. b 29. RGN55 SCM57 RSCN60 RNT73. St Jo Coll Nottm CertCS88. **d** 88 **p** 94. Hon Par Dn Largs *Glas* 88-94; Hon C 94-00. *15 Shuma Court, Skelmorlie PA17 5EJ* Tel (01475) 520289

POWE, David James Hector. b 50. Brighton Poly CertMS86. Wycliffe Hall Ox 88. **d** 90 **p** 91. C Ventnor St Cath *Portsm* 90-92; Chapl HM Pris Belmarsh 93-94 and 98-04; Chapl HM Pris Lewes 94-97; Chapl HM Pris Bris from 04. *The Chaplain's Office, HM Prison, Cambridge Road, Bristol BS7 8PS* Tel 0117-372 3246 *or* 372 3100

POWE, Eric James. b 23. Univ of Wales (Lamp) BA50 BD61. St Steph Ho Ox 50. **d** 52 **p** 53. C Ramsgate H Trin *Cant* 52-54; C Buckland in Dover 54-57; CF 57-73; Dep Asst Chapl Gen 72-73; R Broadstairs *Cant* 73-94; rtd 94; Perm to Offic *Cant* from 94. *34 Palm Bay Avenue, Cliftonville, Margate CT9 3DF* Tel (01843) 294673

POWELL, Canon Anthony James. b 51. Sarum & Wells Th Coll 78. **d** 79 **p** 80. C Larkfield *Roch* 79-83; C Leybourne 79-83; V Borough Green from 83; Hon Can Roch Cathl from 04. *The Vicarage, 24 Maidstone Road, Borough Green, Sevenoaks TN15 8BD* Tel and fax (01732) 882447

POWELL, Charles David. b 38. St Pet Coll Saltley CertEd61 ACP74. St Alb and Ox Min Course 96. **d** 99 **p** 00. NSM Ampthill w Millbrook and Steppingley *St Alb* 99-04; RD Ampthill from 03. *65 Blenheim Crescent, Luton LU3 1HD* Tel (01582) 457553 Mobile 07811-260675 E-mail rev.davidpowell@btinternet.com

POWELL, Christopher John. b 71. K Coll Lon BA94 AKC94. Coll of Resurr Mirfield 95. **d** 97 **p** 98. C Botley *Portsm* 97-01; C Portsea N End St Mark from 01. *St Francis House, 186 Northern Parade, Portsmouth PO2 9LU* Tel (023) 9266 2467 E-mail cjp@powellcj.freeserve.co.uk

POWELL, Colin Arthur. b 32. Hatf Coll Dur BA53. Oak Hill Th Coll 56. **d** 58 **p** 59. C Leyland St Andr *Blackb* 58-61; C Lancaster St Thos 61-64; C Tranmere St Cath *Ches* 64-65; R Cheetham Hill *Man* 65-81; TV Oldham 81-86; TV Rochdale 86-97; Chapl Rochdale Healthcare NHS Trust 94-97; rtd 97; Perm to Offic *Man* 00-03. *103 Parsonage Road, Withington, Manchester M20 4NU* Tel 0161-434 2409

POWELL, David. *See* POWELL, Charles David

POWELL, Mrs Diane. b 41. SW Minl Tr Course 85. **d** 88 **p** 94. Hon C St Merryn *Truro* 88-92; Dn-in-c Gerrans w St Anthony in Roseland 92-94; P-in-c 94-00; Asst Chapl R Cornwall Hosps Trust 00-04; rtd 04; Perm to Offic *Truro* from 04. *Windsway, Sandy Common, Constantine Bay, Padstow PL28 8JL* Tel (01841) 521610 E-mail diannick@msn.com

POWELL, Dudley John. b 44. Tyndale Hall Bris 65. **d** 69 **p** 70. C Blackb Sav *Blackb* 69-71; C Rodbourne Cheney *Bris* 71-74; P-in-c Kingsdown 74-79; V 79-80; V Stoke Gifford 80-90; TR 90-91; Ancient World Outreach Albania 91-03; Perm to Offic *Bris* from 91 and *Win* from 03. *30 Homechurch House, 31 Purewell, Christchurch BH23 1EH* Tel (01202) 481379 E-mail dudleyberat@tesco.net

POWELL, Eleanor Ann. b 55. Gwent Coll Newport CertEd76 Univ of Wales BA82. Qu Coll Birm 82. **d** 83 **p** 94. C Caereithin *S & B* 83-86; C Bishopston 86-88; Dioc Children's Officer *Glouc* 88-94; Hon Can Glouc Cathl 94-01; P-in-c The Edge, Pitchcombe, Harescombe and Brookthorpe 94-00; Dioc Adv for Women's Min 94-01; V Churchdown St Jo 00-01; Offg Chapl RAF from 00; Chapl United Bris Healthcare NHS Trust from 01. *The Chaplaincy Office, Bristol Royal Infirmary, Marlborough Street, Bristol BS2 8HW* Tel 0117-928 2136 E-mail eleanor.powell@btinternet.com

POWELL, Eric Michael. b 46. St As Minl Tr Course. **d** 04. NSM Gwersyllt *St As* from 04. *16 Foster Road, Wrexham LL11 2LT* Tel (01978) 365455 E-mail empowell@tiscali.co.uk

POWELL, Preb Frank. b 29. AKC52. **d** 53 **p** 54. C Stockingford *Cov* 53-56; C Netherton St Andr *Worc* 56-60; P-in-c W Bromwich St Jo *Lich* 60-66; C W Bromwich Gd Shep w St Jo 60-66; V 66-69; V Bilston St Leon 69-76; P-in-c Hanbury 76-82; V Hanbury w Newborough 83-86; V Basford 86-92; Preb Lich Cathl 87-92; rtd 92; Perm to Offic *Ches* from 92. *Pippins, 15 Jubilee Terrace, Nantwich CW5 7BT* Tel (01270) 610688 E-mail frank@fjpowell.fsnet.co.uk

POWELL, Gary Charles. b 62. UWIST BSc84. Coll of Resurr Mirfield 92. **d** 95 **p** 96. C Roath *Llan* 95-00; V Llansawel, Briton Ferry from 00. *The Vicarage, 251 Neath Road, Briton Ferry, Neath SA11 2SL* Tel (01639) 812200

POWELL, Geoffrey Peter. b 25. Chich Th Coll 54. **d** 56 **p** 57. C Bris St Agnes w St Simon *Bris* 56-58; C Sherston Magna w Easton Grey 58-62; V Wanborough 62-75; R Lyddington w Wanborough 75-80; V St Cleer *Truro* 80-90; rtd 91; Perm to Offic *Bris, Truro* and *Sarum* from 91. *The Old Bakery, Oare, Marlborough SN8 4JQ* Tel (01672) 562627

POWELL, John. b 44. St Luke's Coll Ex CertEd66 Univ of Wales (Lamp) MA02. Glouc Sch of Min 81. **d** 84 **p** 85. NSM Stroud and Uplands w Slad *Glouc* 84-89; Chapl Eliz Coll Guernsey 89-92; C Llandudno *Ban* 92-93; TV 94-96; V Dwygyfylchi 96-02; V Cardigan w Mwnt and Y Ferwig w Llangoedmor *St D* from 02. *The Vicarage, Napier Gardens, Cardigan SA43 1EG* Tel (01239) 612722 E-mail parchjohnpowell@lycos.co.uk

POWELL, John Keith Lytton. b 52. S Dios Minl Tr Scheme 91. **d** 94 **p** 95. NSM Bridgwater H Trin *B & W* 94-97; P-in-c Hatch Beauchamp w Beercrocombe, Curry Mallet etc 97-02; P-in-c Staple Fitzpaine, Orchard Portman, Thurlbear etc 97-02; R Beercrocombe w Curry Mallet, Hatch Beauchamp etc 02-05; P-in-c Exford, Exmoor, Hawkridge and Withypool from 05. *The Rectory, Exford, Minehead TA24 7LX* Tel (01643) 831586

POWELL, Miss Katherine. b 56. Sydney Univ BSS79 Lon Univ DipApTh84. Wycliffe Hall Ox 84. **dss** 86 **d** 87 **p** 94. Broadwater St Mary *Chich* 86-87; Par Dn 87-91; Asst Chapl Ch Hosp Horsham 91-96; Australia from 96; Chapl Glennie Sch from 97. *The Glennie School, Herries Street, Toowoomba, Qld, Australia 4350* Tel (0061) (7) 4637 9359 *or* 4688 8808 Fax 4688 8848 E-mail powellk@glennie.qld.edu.au

POWELL, Kelvin. b 49. Wycliffe Hall Ox 71. **d** 74 **p** 75. C Prescot *Liv* 74-77; C Ainsdale 77-79; V Bickershaw 79-85; R Hesketh w

Becconsall *Blackb* 85-99; Perm to Offic *Ox* from 03. *43 Sharman Beer Court, Southern Road, Thame OX9 2DD*

POWELL, Llewellyn. b 28. Glouc Th Course 67. **d** 70 **p** 71. C Quinton *Glouc* 70-73; P-in-c 74-76; V Church Honeybourne w Cow Honeybourne 76-83; R Pebworth w Dorsington and Honeybourne 83-87; rtd 87; Perm to Offic *St D* from 87. *Bodathro Bungalow, Llangynin, St Clears, Carmarthen SA33 4LD* Tel (01994) 448301

POWELL, Mark. b 57. Bath Univ BSc78 PhD81. Ripon Coll Cuddesdon BA84 MA88. **d** 85 **p** 86. C Evesham *Worc* 85-88; V Exhall *Cov* 88-96; V Leavesden All SS *St Alb* 96-00; V Ealing St Pet Mt Park *Lon* from 00. *St Peter's Vicarage, 56 Mount Park Road, London W5 2RU* Tel and fax (020) 8997 1620 E-mail mark.powell4@btinternet.com

POWELL, Martin. b 71. St Steph Ho Ox BTh00. **d** 00 **p** 01. C Caterham *S'wark* 00-03; V New Addington from 03. *St Edward's Vicarage, Cleves Crescent, Croydon CR0 0DL* Tel (01689) 845588

POWELL, Michael. *See* POWELL, Eric Michael

POWELL, Pamela. b 56. Univ of Wales BEd79 Goldsmiths' Coll Lon MA82. St As Minl Tr Course 00. **d** 03 **p** 04. C Wrexham *St As* from 03. *16 Foster Road, Wrexham LL11 2LT* Tel (01978) 365455 Mobile 07711-053565 E-mail pampowell@micro-plus-web.net

POWELL, Patricia. STETS. **d** 03 **p** 04. NSM Woodford Valley *Sarum* from 03. *Hawthorn Cottage, Great Durnford, Salisbury SP4 6AZ* Tel (01722) 782546 E-mail pmpowell@lineone.net

POWELL, Ralph Dover. b 49. ARMCM70. Chich Th Coll 71. **d** 74 **p** 75. C Coppenhall *Ches* 74-77; C Heref H Trin *Heref* 77-80; V Crewe St Barn *Ches* from 80. *St Barnabas' Vicarage, West Street, Crewe CW1 3AX* Tel (01270) 212418 E-mail westtstreet@netscapeonline.co.uk

POWELL, Raymond Leslie. b 35. AKC61. **d** 62 **p** 63. C Hendon St Mary *Lon* 62-67; C Huntingdon All SS w St Jo *Ely* 67-75; V Huntingdon St Barn 75-79; P-in-c Sawston 79-81; V 81-00; P-in-c Babraham 85-00; RD Shelford 89-94; rtd 00; Perm to Offic *Nor* from 01. *14 Appletree Lane, Roydon, Diss IP22 4FL* Tel (01379) 641412

POWELL, Richard Penry. b 15. Dur Univ LTh38. St Aid Birkenhead 34. **d** 38 **p** 39. C Brierley Hill *Lich* 38-42; C Derby St Chad *Derby* 42-45; C Uttoxeter w Bramshall *Lich* 45-47; V Alton 47-60; V Bradley-in-the-Moors 48-60; R Drayton Bassett 60-64; Min Canwell CD 60-64; V Wrockwardine 64-80; V Uppington 64-80; rtd 80; Perm to Offic *Lich* from 80. *34 Herbert Avenue, Wellington, Telford TF1 2BS* Tel (01952) 242528

POWELL, Robert John. b 65. Trin Coll Bris BA92. **d** 92 **p** 93. C Biggin Hill *Roch* 92-95; C Edgware *Lon* 95-01; Area Sec SAMS (NW England and N Wales) 01-04; TV Upper Holloway *Lon* from 04. *The Vicarage, 43 Dresden Road, London N19 3BG* Tel (020) 7686 2293

POWELL, Roger Roy. b 68. Thames Poly BSc91. Ripon Coll Cuddesdon BTh94. **d** 94 **p** 95. C Leic St Jas *Leic* 94-98; C The Abbey Leic 98-00; TV 00-05; P-in-c Leic St Paul 01-05; Youth Chapl 98-05; P-in-c Ridgeway *Sarum* from 05. *The Rectory, 3 Butts Road, Chiseldon, Swindon SN4 0NN* Tel (01793) 740369 E-mail revd.rpowell@btopenworld.com

POWELL, Stuart William. b 58. K Coll Lon BD80 AKC80. Ripon Coll Cuddesdon 86. **d** 88 **p** 89. C Horden *Dur* 88-90; C Northolt Park St Barn *Lon* 90-93; V Castle Vale St Cuth *Birm* 93-00; V Stockland Green from 00. *The Vicarage, Bleak Hill Road, Birmingham B23 7EL* Tel and fax 0121-373 0130 Mobile 07889-887358 Pager 07336-734456 E-mail spowell@talk21.com

POWELL, Valerie Isabelle Dawn Frances. b 69. Ripon Coll Cuddesdon BTh02. **d** 01 **p** 02. C Newport St Andr *Mon* 01-03; C Monmouth w Overmonnow etc from 03. *St Thomas's Vicarage, Overmonnow, Monmouth NP25 3ES* Tel (01600) 719039 E-mail val_powell@yahoo.co.uk

POWER, Alan Edward. b 26. Worc Coll Ox BA50 MA53. Lich Th Coll. **d** 57 **p** 58. C Summerfield *Birm* 57-60; C Oldbury 60-63; V Short Heath 63-97; rtd 97; Perm to Offic *Birm* from 97. *8 Southam Drive, Sutton Coldfield B73 5PD* Tel 0121-355 8923

POWER, David Michael. b 56. BA81 BEd. Oak Hill Th Coll. **d** 81 **p** 82. C Warblington w Emsworth *Portsm* 81-84; C-in-c Hartplain CD 84-88; V Hartplain 88-91; Adv in Evang 91-97; V Portsea St Cuth from 97. *St Cuthbert's Vicarage, 2 Lichfield Road, Portsmouth PO3 6DE* Tel (023) 9282 7071 Fax as telephone

POWER, Canon Ivor Jonathan. b 43. Lambeth STh87 CITC 66. **d** 69 **p** 70. C Dromore Cathl *D & D* 69-71; C Enniscorthy *C & O* 71-74; I Youghal *C, C & R* 74-78; I Youghal Union 78-81; I Athlone w Benown, Kiltoom and Forgney *M & K* 81-98; Can Meath 87-98; Dir of Ords (Meath) 91-97; I Dublin Crumlin w Chapelizod *D & G* from 98; Can Ch Ch Cathl Dublin from 05. *St Mary's Rectory, 118 Kimmage Road West, Dublin 12, Irish Republic* Tel (00353) (1) 455 5639 Fax 456 0006 E-mail crumlin@dublin.anglican.org

POWER, James Edward. b 58. Nottm Univ BSc81 Leeds Univ BA85. Coll of Resurr Mirfield 83. **d** 86 **p** 87. C Cadoxton-juxta-Barry *Llan* 86-89; Chapl Harrow Sch from 89. *35 West Street, Harrow HA1 3EG* Tel (020) 8872 8234 E-mail jep@harrowschool.org.uk

POWER, Mrs Jeanette. b 57. Oak Hill Th Coll BA81. **dss** 82 **d** 87 **p** 94. Warblington w Emsworth *Portsm* 82-84; Hartplain CD 84-87; Hon C Hartplain 87-91; Community Mental Health Chapl Havant and Petersfield from 91; NSM Wickham 93-97; NSM Portsea St Cuth from 97; Team Chapl Portsm Hosps NHS Trust from 01. *St Cuthbert's Vicarage, 2 Lichfield Road, Portsmouth PO3 6DE* Tel (023) 9282 7071 Fax as telephone

POWIS, Michael Ralph. b 63. St Jo Coll Nottm BTh95. **d** 95 **p** 96. C Dibden *Win* 95-00; V Hedge End St Luke from 00. *16 Elliot Rise, Hedge End, Southampton SO30 2RU* Tel (01489) 786717 E-mail mike.powis@ukgateway.net *or* mike.powis@fish.co.uk

POWLES, Charles Anthony. b 39. EAMTC. **d** 88 **p** 89. NSM Hemsby *Nor* 88-93; NSM Bradwell from 01. *94 Winifred Way, Caister-on-Sea, Great Yarmouth NR30 5PE* Tel (01493) 720096 E-mail charles.powles@rjt.co.uk

POWLES, Michael Charles. b 34. Reading Univ BSc56 Lon Univ PGCE83. Qu Coll Birm DipTh60. **d** 60 **p** 61. C Goodmayes All SS *Chelmsf* 60-65; C Surbiton St Matt *S'wark* 65-78; Lect Woolwich Coll 79-99; rtd 99. *Spring Cottage, 3 Rushett Close, Thames Ditton KT7 0UR* Tel (020) 8398 9654

POWLEY, Mark Thomas. b 75. Nottm Univ BA96 Birm Univ PGCE98. Wycliffe Hall Ox 01. **d** 03 **p** 04. C Addiscombe St Mary Magd w St Martin *S'wark* from 03. *68 Elgin Road, Croydon CR0 6XA* Tel (020) 8654 2126 E-mail mpowley@fish.co.uk

POWLEY, Robert Mallinson. b 39. Fitzw Coll Cam MA65. Ridley Hall Cam 61. **d** 63 **p** 64. C Bermondsey St Mary w St Olave, St Jo etc *S'wark* 63-67; C Moseley St Anne *Birm* 67-69; Lic to Offic *Man* 72-77; Hon C Walshaw Ch Ch 77-88; V Prestwich St Gabr 88-94; Bp's Dom Chapl 88-94; P-in-c Hargrave *Ches* 94-05; Exec Officer Bd for Soc Resp 94-05; Hon Can Ches Cathl 00-05; rtd 05. *4 Bron y Cae, Terrace Walk, Llanfairfechan LL33 0EW* Tel (01248) 689200

POWNALL, Lydia Margaret. *See* HURLE, Mrs Lydia Margaret

POWNALL, Stephen. b 56. St Jo Coll Nottm BA02. **d** 02 **p** 03. C Herne Hill *S'wark* from 02. *8 Ruskin Walk, London SE24 9LZ* Tel (020) 7274 3663 E-mail steve@sbpownall.fsworld.co.uk

POWNE, Peter Rebbeck Lamb. b 23. Sarum & Wells Th Coll 80. **d** 83 **p** 84. C Calne and Blackland *Sarum* 83-86; V Netheravon w Fittleton and Enford 86-93; rtd 93; Perm to Offic *Sarum* from 93. *2 Oak Lane, Figheldean, Salisbury SP4 8JS* Tel (01980) 670356

POYNTING, Charles Robert Macvicar. b 23. Hertf Coll Ox BA48 MA48. Wells Th Coll 48. **d** 50 **p** 51. C Gt Bookham *Guildf* 50-52; C Epsom Common Ch Ch 52-55; V Ashton H Trin *Man* 55-62; V Belfield 62-82; V Digby *Linc* 82-92; rtd 92; Perm to Offic *Ox* 93-00. *Digby Cottage, Noke, Oxford OX3 9TX* Tel (01865) 842794

✠**POYNTZ, The Rt Revd Samuel Greenfield.** b 26. TCD BA48 MA51 BD53 PhD60 Ulster Univ Hon DLitt95. TCD Div Sch Div Test50. **d** 50 **p** 51 **c** 78. C Dublin St Geo *D & G* 50-52; C Bray 52-55; C Dublin St Michan w St Paul 55-59; Sec and Sch Insp Ch Educn Soc for Ireland 56-75; I Dublin St Steph 59-67; I Dublin St Ann 67-70; I Dublin St Ann w St Steph 70-78; Adn Dublin 74-78; Bp C, C & R 78-87; Bp Conn 87-95; rtd 95. *10 Harmony Hill, Lisburn BT27 4EP* Tel (028) 9267 9013

PRADELLA, Henry. b 54. St Mary's Coll Twickenham BEd. NTMTC 97. **d** 00 **p** 01. NSM Hainault *Chelmsf* 00-04; C Romford Gd Shep Collier Row from 04. *121 Beattyville Gardens, Ilford IG6 1JZ* Tel (020) 8270 3922

PRAGNELL, John William. b 39. Lon Univ BD65. Lambeth STh87 LTh88. **d** 65 **p** 66. C Bitterne *Win* 65-68; C Hatfield Hyde *St Alb* 68-73; Kuwait 73-75; Chapl Leavesden Hosp and Abbots Langley Hosp 75-88; Chapl Watford Gen Hosp 86-88; V St Alb St Steph *St Alb* 88-95; RD St Alb 91-95; P-in-c Copythorne *Win* 95-02; Dioc Ecum Officer 95-02; Hosp Chapl Adv (Bournemouth Adnry) 00-02; rtd 02; Perm to Offic *Sarum* from 03. *10 South Mill Close, Amesbury, Salisbury SP4 7HR* Tel (01980) 622372

PRAGNELL, Michael John. b 40. Down Coll Cam BA62 PhD65 MA66 FIQA81 MRSC CChem MSOSc88. Ox NSM Course 81. **d** 84 **p** 85. NSM High Wycombe *Ox* 84-98; C Beercrocombe w Curry Mallet, Hatch Beauchamp etc *B & W* 98-05; rtd 05. *2 Listers Court, Listers Hill, Ilminster TA19 0DP* Tel (01460) 54212

PRAGNELL, Ms Sandra Ann. b 53. Hull Univ BA75 TCD BTh01 Dub City Univ MA04. CITC 98. **d** 01 **p** 02. C Castleknock and Mulhuddart, w Clonsilla *D & G* 01-05; PV Ch Ch Cathl Dublin 03-05; I Dundalk w Heynestown *Arm* from 05; I Ballymascanlan w Creggan and Rathcor from 05. *The Rectory, Old Golf Links Road, Blackrock, Co Louth, Irish Republic* Tel (00353) (42) 932 1402 Mobile 87-265 8592 E-mail dundalk@armagh.anglican.org

PRAILL, David William. b 57. York Univ BA79 FRGS90. Cranmer Hall Dur 81. **d** 82 **p** 83. C Digswell and Panshanger *St Alb* 82-84; CMS 84-89; Course Dir St Geo Coll Jerusalem 85-89; Dir McCabe Educn Trust 90-91; Dir St Luke's Hospice

Harrow and Wembley from 91; Perm to Offic *S'wark* from 91 and *Lon* 94-97. *1A St Ann's Crescent, London SW18 2ND* Tel (020) 8870 3694

PRANCE, Jeremy Roy. b 64. St Jo Coll Nottm BA99. **d** 99 **p** 00. C Bramcote *S'well* 99-04; C Bestwood Em w St Mark from 04. *45 Pine Hill Close, Nottingham NG5 9DA* Tel 0115-927 9547 E-mail jez.prance@ntlworld.com

PRANCE, Nicholas David. b 55. St Luke's Coll Ex CertEd77 RMN83. EMMTC 95. **d** 98 **p** 99. NSM Radford St Pet *S'well* 98-99. *27 Stiles Road, Arnold, Nottingham NG5 6RE* Tel 0115-953 4890 Mobile 07966-524581 E-mail nick@prance.freeserve.co.uk

PRANCE, Robert Penrose. b 47. Southn Univ DipTh. Sarum & Wells Th Coll 69. **d** 72 **p** 73. C Gillingham and Fifehead Magdalen *Sarum* 72-76; P-in-c Edmondsham 76-80; P-in-c Woodlands 76-80; P-in-c Wimborne St Giles 76-80; P-in-c Cranborne 77-80; R Cranborne w Boveridge, Edmondsham etc 80-83; Chapl Sherborne Sch 83-93; V Stoke Gabriel and Collaton *Ex* 93-99; Dep PV Ex Cathl 95-99; Chapl Shiplake Coll Henley from 99. *Shiplake College, Shiplake Court, Shiplake, Henley-on-Thames RG9 4BW* Tel 0118-940 2455 *or* 940 5258

PRASAD, Andrew. b 53. Ewing Coll, Allahabad BA75. Bp's Coll Calcutta BD81 Presbyterian Th Coll Seoul ThM88. **d** 79 **p** 81. *48 Ederline Avenue, London SW16 4SA* Tel (020) 8764 0633 E-mail a.prasad@pgen.net

PRASADAM, Goruganthula Samuel Narayanamurthy (Sam). b 34. Andhra Univ India BA57. Bangalore Th Coll BD65 Union Th Sem (NY) STM68. **d** 62 **p** 65. India 62-74; C Llanbeblig w Caernarfon and Betws Garmon etc *Ban* 75-76; C Norbury *Ches* 77-78; V Aberaman and Abercwmboi *Llan* 78-83; N Sec CMS 83-87; V Luton All SS w St Pet *St Alb* 87-96; rtd 99. *15 Rossons Road, Taverham, Norwich NR8 6RE*

PRASADAM, Canon Jemima. b 38. MBE05. BD61 BA87. Cranmer Hall Dur 86. **d** 87 **p** 94. Par Dn Luton All SS w St Pet *St Alb* 87-94; C 94-96; P-in-c Lozells St Paul and St Silas *Birm* from 96; Hon Can Birm Cathl from 05. *St Silas's Vicarage, 103 Heathfield Road, Birmingham B19 1HE* Tel 0121-523 5645 E-mail prasadam@fish.co.uk

PRASADAM, Madhu Smitha. b 64. Qu Coll Birm. **d** 03 **p** 04. C Blackheath *Birm* from 03. *25 Garland Crescent, Halesowen B62 9NJ* Tel 0121-421 4821 E-mail prasadam@fish.co.uk

PRASADAM, Samuel. *See* PRASADAM, Goruganthula Samuel Narayanamurthy

PRATT, Basil David. b 38. Ripon Hall Ox 64. **d** 67 **p** 68. C Lewisham St Jo Southend *S'wark* 67-68; C Caterham Valley 68-70; CF 70-93. *St Michael's, Bankend Road, Dumfries DG1 4AL* Tel (01387) 267933

PRATT, Christine Fiona. *See* BLACKMAN, Christine Fiona

PRATT, Edward Andrew. b 39. Clare Coll Cam BA61 MA65. Clifton Th Coll 63. **d** 66 **p** 67. C Southall Green St Jo *Lon* 66-69; C Drypool St Columba w St Andr and St Pet *York* 69-71; P-in-c Radbourne *Derby* 71-74; R Kirk Langley 71-78; V Mackworth All SS 71-78; V Southsea St Simon *Portsm* 78-97; rtd 97; Perm to Offic *Sarum* from 97. *7 Bay Close, Swanage BH19 1RE*

PRATT, Mrs Janet Margaret. b 40. Herts Coll BEd78. St Alb Minl Tr Scheme 78. **dss** 81 **d** 87 **p** 94. High Wych and Gilston w Eastwick *St Alb* 81-87; Hon Par Dn 87-89; Par Dn Histon *Ely* 89-94; C 94-97; Par Dn Impington 89-94; C 94-97; R Bardney *Linc* from 97. *The Rectory, 10 Church Lane, Bardney, Lincoln LN3 5TZ* Tel (01526) 398595 E-mail janet@jmpratt.freeserve.co.uk

PRATT, John. b 37. **d** 99 **p** 00. OLM St Enoder *Truro* from 99. *Chyteg, Newquay Road, St Columb Road, St Columb TR9 6PY* Tel and fax (01726) 860747

PRATT, John Anthony. b 38. Selw Coll Cam BA61 MA65. Qu Coll Birm DipTh66. **d** 66 **p** 67. C Harrow Weald All SS *Lon* 66-69; C St Pancras w St Jas and Ch Ch 69-74; C Saffron Walden *Chelmsf* 74-75; TV Saffron Walden w Wendens Ambo and Littlebury 75-79; V St Mary-at-Latton 79-88; Chapl Princess Alexandra Hosp Harlow 82-88; RD Harlow *Chelmsf* 83-88; R Tolleshunt Knights w Tiptree and Gt Braxted 88-03; rtd 03; Perm to Offic *Cov* from 03. *2 Erica Drive, Whitnash, Leamington Spa CV31 2RS* Tel (01926) 428609 E-mail japratt@fish.co.uk

PRATT, Kenneth George. b 21. EAMTC 81. **d** 84 **p** 85. NSM March St Jo *Ely* 84-87; Chapl Doddington Community Hosp 86-93; Chapl NW Anglia Healthcare NHS Trust from 93; P-in-c Doddington w Benwick *Ely* 87-94; rtd 94; Perm to Offic *Ely* from 94. *2 Windsor Drive, March PE15 8DF* Tel (01354) 658814 *or* 740481

PRATT, Michael. *See* HARRIS, Michael

PRATT, Canon Richard David. b 55. Linc Coll Ox BA77 MA81 Birm Univ PhD01 Nottm Univ BCombStuds84. Linc Th Coll 81. **d** 84 **p** 85. C Wellingborough All Hallows *Pet* 84-87; TV Kingsthorpe w Northampton St Dav 87-92; V Northampton St Benedict 92-97; P-in-c Carl St Cuth w St Mary *Carl* from 97; Dioc Communications Officer from 97; Hon Can Carl Cathl from 02. *St Cuthbert's Vicarage, West Walls, Carlisle CA3 8UF* Tel (01228) 521982 E-mail pratt@fish.co.uk *or* communications@carlislediocese.org.uk

PRATT, Samuel Charles. b 40. ALAM59. Oak Hill Th Coll 69. **d** 71 **p** 72. C Upper Holloway St Jo *Lon* 71-73; C Bucknall and Bagnall *Lich* 73-76; V Liv St Mich *Liv* 76-80; Chapl R Liv Hosp 80-94; Chapl R Liv Univ Hosp NHS Trust 94-01; V Billinge *Liv* from 01. *St Aidan's Vicarage, 91 Newton Road, Billinge, Wigan WN5 7LB* Tel (01744) 892210 Mobile 07957-367114 E-mail sp001f3678@blueyonder.co.uk

PRATT, Stephen Samuel. b 67. Univ Coll Ches BA88 Keele Univ PGCE89. Oak Hill Th Coll BA00. **d** 00 **p** 01. C Goodmayes All SS *Chelmsf* 00-03; TV Chell *Lich* from 03. *The Vicarage, 110 Sprinkbank Road, Stoke-on-Trent ST6 6HZ* Tel (01782) 823090 E-mail rev@steppratt.worldonline.co.uk

PRATT, Canon William Ralph. b 47. Keble Coll Ox BA69 MA73. Linc Th Coll 70. **d** 72 **p** 73. C Ifield *Chich* 72-78; TV 78; C Brighton St Pet w Chpl Royal and St Jo 79-83; P-in-c Hove St Jo 83-87; Dioc Communications Officer 87-00; Can and Preb Chich Cathl from 90; V Ringmer from 00. *The Vicarage, Vicarage Way, Ringmer, Lewes BN8 5LA* Tel (01273) 812243 E-mail wrpratt@btinternet.com

PREBBLE, The Ven Albert Ernest. b 08. Univ of NZ BA31 MA32 St Jo Coll Auckland 32. **d** 32 **p** 33. New Zealand 32-63; Adn Waimate 44-49; Adn Manukau 49-56; V Gen and Adn Auckland 56-63; Perm to Offic *Pet* from 59; V Greenhill St Jo *Lon* 63-72; rtd 73. *12 Saxon Court, Wessex Way, Bicester OX26 6AX* Tel (01869) 324861

PRECIOUS, Sally Joanne. *See* WRIGHT, Sally Joanne

PREECE, Barry Leslie. b 48. Lich Th Coll 68. **d** 71 **p** 72. C Ewell *Guildf* 71-74; C York Town St Mich 75-77; P-in-c Ripley 77-81; Chapl HM Det Cen Send 77-81; V Cuddington *Guildf* 81-88; V Cobham 88-03; R E and W Clandon from 03. *The Rectory, The Street, West Clandon, Guildford GU4 7RG* Tel and fax (01483) 222573 E-mail revpreece@aol.com *or* rev.preece@btinternet.com

PREECE, Colin George. b 51. Bernard Gilpin Soc Dur 71 Chich Th Coll 72. **d** 75 **p** 76. C Upper Gornal *Lich* 75-78; C Wednesbury St Paul Wood Green 78-81; V Oxley 81-89; V Kennington *Cant* 89-03; RD E Charing 92-98; P-in-c Ashford from 03. *The College, Church Yard, Ashford TN23 1QG* Tel (01233) 620672 E-mail cpreece@globalnet.co.uk

PREECE, Joseph. b 23. Univ of Wales (Ban) BA50 Univ of Wales (Swansea) DipSocSc51 LSE Cert Child Care 52 Lon Univ DBRS72. NW Ord Course 73. **d** 73 **p** 74. C Claughton cum Grange *Ches* 73-74; C Barnston 74-75; R Aldford and Bruera 75-80; V Wincle and Wildboarclough 80-82; P-in-c Cleeton w Silvington *Heref* 82-86; P-in-c Farlow 82-86; V Stottesdon 82-86; R Stottesdon w Farlow, Cleeton and Silvington 86-88; rtd 88; Perm to Offic *Heref* from 91. *Lingholm, Woodhall Drive, Hanwood, Shrewsbury SY5 8JU* Tel (01743) 860946

PREECE, Mark Richard. b 61. St Paul's Cheltenham BA85. Linc Th Coll 85. **d** 87 **p** 88. C Coity w Nolton *Llan* 87-89; C Penarth w Lavernock 89-92; V Ewenny w St Brides Major 92-99; V Canton St Luke 99-02; TR Canton Cardiff from 02. *Canton Rectory, 12 Thompson Avenue, Cardiff CF5 1EY* Tel (029) 2056 2022 Fax as telephone E-mail mrpree@globalnet.co.uk

PREECE, Ronald Alexander. b 29. Lon Univ BD56. ALCD55. **d** 56 **p** 57. C Rusholme H Trin *Man* 56-59; Teacher Kidbrooke Sch Lon 59-60; Brazil 60-63; Perm to Offic *Cant* 63-70; Teacher Abp's Sch Cant 64-70; OMF 70-94; SW Regional Dir 76-94; Perm to Offic *Bris* 76-94; rtd 94; Perm to Offic *Cant* from 98. *5 Tonford Lane, Canterbury CT1 3XU* Tel (01227) 471061

PREMRAJ, Deborah Devashanthy. b 66. Bangalore Univ BSc87 BEd92 Serampore Univ BD91. United Th Coll Bangalore 87. **d** 96 **p** 97. Deacon Vedal India 96-97; Presbyter Madurantakam 97-02; Perm to Offic *S'wark* 02-05; C Battersea Fields from 05. *All Saints' Vicarage, 100 Prince of Wales Drive, London SW11 4BD* Tel (020) 7498 6306 Mobile 07851-789156 E-mail debu_csi@yahoo.mail

PREMRAJ, Dhanaraj Charles. b 63. Madras Univ BA86 MA88 Heythrop Coll Lon MTh03. United Th Coll Bangalore BD92. **d** 93 **p** 94. India 93-02; Perm to Offic *S'wark* 02-05; C Battersea Fields from 05. *All Saints' Vicarage, 100 Prince of Wales Drive, London SW11 4BD* Tel and fax (020) 7622 3809 Mobile 07742-699371 E-mail allssbat@fish.co.uk

PRENTICE, Brian. b 40. St Jo Coll Nottm 81. **d** 83 **p** 84. C W Bromwich All SS *Lich* 83-86; C Tettenhall Wood 86-89; TV 89-90; V Essington 90-98; TR Willenhall H Trin from 98; P-in-c Bentley from 05; AD Wolverhampton from 03. *Short Heath Vicarage, 20 Church Road, Willenhall WV12 5PT* Tel (01922) 476416

PRENTICE, Mark Neil. b 73. Ex Univ BA94. Wycliffe Hall Ox MTh00. **d** 00 **p** 01. C Tulse Hill H Trin and St Matthias *S'wark* 00-04; C Langham Place All So *Lon* from 04. *25 Fitzroy Street, London W1T 6DR* Tel (020) 7287 1360

PRENTICE, Michael Charles. b 35. Bps' Coll Cheshunt 59. **d** 62 **p** 63. C Lon Docks St Pet w Wapping St Jo *Lon* 62-66; C Cranford 66-70; C Bethnal Green St Jas the Gt w St Jude 70-71; C Walsingham and Houghton *Nor* 71-73; C Southall Ch Redeemer *Lon* 73; V Acton Vale St Thos 73-78; P-in-c Stow Bardolph w Wimbotsham and Stow Bridge *Ely* 78-80; R

Woodford *Pet* 80-94; rtd 98. *Doric Cottage, 1 Low Road, Wretton, King's Lynn PE33 9QN* Tel (01366) 500210

PRENTIS, Calvert Clayton. b 62. Aston Tr Scheme 93 St Jo Coll Nottm 95. **d** 97 **p** 98. C Wood End *Cov* 97-00; TV Leeds St Geo *Ripon* 00-05; Asst Dioc Dir of Ords 02-05; P-in-c Huddersfield H Trin *Wakef* from 05. *Holy Trinity Vicarage, 132 Trinity Street, Huddersfield HD1 4DT* E-mail calvert.prentis@ntlworld.com

PRENTIS, Richard Hugh. b 36. Ch Coll Cam BA60 MA64. Sarum Th Coll 69. **d** 71 **p** 72. C Bath Bathwick St Mary *B & W* 71-76; Bp's Dom Chapl *Lich* 76-80; PV Lich Cathl 76-80; V Longton St Mary and St Chad 80-84; V Shifnal 84-94; P-in-c Badger 84-85; P-in-c Ryton 84-85; P-in-c Beckbury 84-85; rtd 94. *23A The Close, Lichfield WS13 7LD* Tel (01543) 411234

PRESCOTT, David John. b 51. St Kath Coll Liv BEd73. N Ord Course 00. **d** 03. C Southport Em *Liv* from 03. *28 Elswick Green, Southport PR9 9XT* Tel (01704) 227294 Mobile 07762-943138

PRESCOTT, Thomas Robert. b 41. St Mich Coll Llan DipTh95. **d** 95 **p** 96. C Abertillery w Cwmtillery w Six Bells *Mon* 95-99; V Llanhilleth 99-03; rtd 03. *70 Glandwr Street, Abertillery NP13 1TZ* Tel (01495) 216782

PRESCOTT, William Allan. b 57. **d** 93 **p** 94. C Horsell *Guildf* 93-98; R Guernsey St Sav *Win* from 98; Chapl Guernsey Airport from 03. *St Saviour's Rectory, Neuf Chemin Road, Guernsey GY7 9FQ* Tel (01481) 263045 Fax 267145 E-mail prescott@guernsey.net

PRESS, Richard James. b 45. Southn Univ CertEd67. Sarum & Wells Th Coll 92. **d** 92 **p** 93. C Bradford-on-Avon *Sarum* 92-95; P-in-c Rowde and Poulshot 95-98; R Rowde and Bromham 98-01; Chapl Wilts and Swindon Healthcare NHS Trust 98-00; P-in-c Chickerell w Fleet *Sarum* from 01. *The Rectory, East Street, Chickerell, Weymouth DT3 4DS* Tel (01305) 784915 E-mail revrichardpress@yahoo.co.uk

PRESS, William John. b 72. QUB MEng94 BTh. **d** 99 **p** 00. C Knockbreda *D & D* 99-03; C Dundonald 03-05; I Annalong from 05. *Kilhorne Rectory, 173 Kilkeel Road, Annalong, Newry BT34 4TN* Tel (028) 4376 8246

PRESTIDGE, Colin Robert. b 58. W Sussex Inst of HE BEd86 Open Univ BA01. STETS 01. **d** 04 **p** 05. NSM Crofton *Portsm* from 04; Asst Chapl E Hants Primary Care Trust from 04. *96 Titchfield Road, Stubbington, Fareham PO14 2JB* Tel (01329) 664375 E-mail colin@prestidge.org.uk

PRESTNEY, Mrs Patricia Christine Margaret. b 49. UEA BEd94. Oak Hill Th Coll 84. **d** 87 **p** 94. NSM Lawford *Chelmsf* 87-95; Chapl Benenden Sch 95-97; Chapl St Jo Coll Ipswich 97-00; R Lawford *Chelmsf* from 00. *The Rectory, Church Hill, Lawford, Manningtree CO11 2JX* Tel (01206) 392659 Fax 396039 E-mail patprestney@yahoo.com

PRESTON, David Francis. b 50. BNC Ox BA72 MA78. St Steph Ho Ox 72. **d** 74 **p** 75. C Beckenham St Jas *Roch* 74-79; C Hockley *Chelmsf* 81-83; C Lamorbey H Redeemer *Roch* 83-89; V Gillingham St Barn 89-00; Perm to Offic from 00. *109 Sunnymead Avenue, Gillingham ME7 2EA* Tel (01634) 856492

PRESTON, Mrs Deborah Anne. b 46. GTCL67. Carl and Blackb Dioc Tr Inst 01. **d** 04. OLM Kirkby Lonsdale *Carl* from 04. *The Old Schoolhouse, Kirkby Lonsdale, Carnforth LA6 2DX* Tel (015242) 72509 Mobile 07799-246380 E-mail deborah@jpreston83.freeserve.co.uk

PRESTON, Donald George. b 30. St Alb Minl Tr Scheme 77. **d** 80 **p** 81. NSM Elstow *St Alb* 80-87; NSM Goldington 87-94; Perm to Offic from 95. *106 Putnoe Street, Bedford MK41 8HJ* Tel (01234) 267313

PRESTON, Frederick John. b 32. MBE72. Oak Hill Th Coll 54. **d** 57 **p** 58. C Hove Bp Hannington Memorial Ch *Chich* 57-59; C-in-c Knaphill *Guildf* 60-62; CF 62-69; V Otterton *Ex* 69-71; CF 71-79; NSM 79-84; Chapl ICS 84-89; rtd 89; Perm to Offic *Nor* 96-98 and *Chich* from 98. *24 Patcham Mill Road, Stone Cross, Pevensey BN24 5PA* Tel (01323) 766644

PRESTON, James Martin. b 31. Trin Coll Cam MA55 Ch Ch Ox MA57. Virginia Th Sem 57 S'wark Ord Course 87. **d** 88 **p** 88. NSM Blackheath Ascension *S'wark* 88-95; NSM Lewisham St Mary 95-97; NSM Catford St Laur 97-99; Perm to Offic *Chich* from 99. *4 Aymer Road, Hove BN3 4GA* Tel (01273) 884177 Fax as telephone E-mail prestonm@clara.net

PRESTON, John. b 26. St Aid Birkenhead 58. **d** 52 **p** 52. In RC Ch 50-57; C Chadderton Ch Ch *Man* 58-59; C Didsbury Ch Ch 59-63; R Cheetham St Jo 63-96; rtd 96; Perm to Offic *Man* from 96. *119 Bury Old Road, Prestwich, Manchester M25 0EQ* Tel 0161-773 1131 Mobile 07949-200372 E-mail johnprestonuk@aol.com

PRESTON, John Baker. b 23. Lon Univ BA49. Oak Hill Th Coll 46. **d** 51 **p** 52. C Fazakerley Em *Liv* 51-55; C Eastbourne H Trin *Chich* 55-57; V Blackheath St Jo *S'wark* 57-65; Perm to Offic *Cant* 69-91; rtd 88. *43 Wedgwood Drive, Poole BH14 8ES*

PRESTON, John Michael. b 40. K Coll Lon BD63 AKC63 Lon Univ BA81 Southn Univ PhD91. St Boniface Warminster. **d** 65 **p** 66. C Heston *Lon* 65-67; C Northolt St Mary 67-72; Trinidad and Tobago 72-74; P-in-c Aveley *Chelmsf* 74-78; V 78-82; C Eastleigh *Win* 82-84; C-in-c Boyatt Wood CD 84-87; V W End 87-00; P-in-c Newton Valence, Selborne and E Tisted w Colemore 00-03; rtd 03; Perm to Offic *Portsm* from 03; Chapl SSB from 03. *29 Selsmore Road, Hayling Island PO11 9JZ* Tel (023) 9263 7673 E-mail john.preston@ukgateway.net

PRESTON, Mrs Junko Monica. b 38. Aoyama Gakuin Tokyo BA. **d** 92 **p** 93. C St Paul's Cathl Wellington from 92. *60A Messines Road, Karori, Wellington, New Zealand* Tel (0064) (4) 476 7902

PRESTON, Martin. *See* PRESTON, James Martin

PRESTON, Michael Christopher. b 47. Hatf Coll Dur BA68. Ripon Coll Cuddesdon 75. **d** 78 **p** 79. C Epsom St Martin *Guildf* 78-82; C Guildf H Trin w St Mary 82-86; V Epsom St Barn from 86. *St Barnabas' Vicarage, Hook Road, Epsom KT19 8TU* Tel (01372) 722874 E-mail rev@m-c-preston.demon.co.uk

PRESTON, Canon Percival Kenneth. b 16. Ch Ch Ox BA38 MA48. Cuddesdon Coll 38. **d** 40 **p** 45. C Jersey St Helier *Win* 40-46; C Ox SS Phil and Jas *Ox* 46-48; C Westbury-on-Trym H Trin *Bris* 48-50; Min Lawrence Weston CD 50-55; V Horfield St Greg 55-81; Hon Can Bris Cathl 74-82; RD Horfield 76-81; rtd 81; Perm to Offic *Bris* from 82 and *Glouc* from 83. *56 Gloucester Road, Rudgeway, Bristol BS35 3RT* Tel (01454) 612794

PRESTON, Reuben James. b 65. York Univ BSc86 MEng87 Derby Coll of Educn Cert Rural Studies89 Birm Univ PGCE97. Westcott Ho Cam 88. **d** 91 **p** 92. C Weoley Castle *Birm* 91-94; TV Malvern Link w Cowleigh *Worc* 94-96; Perm to Offic *Birm* 96-99; C Bordesley St Benedict from 99. *27 Haughton Road, Handsworth, Birmingham B20 3LE* Tel 0121-686 9304 Fax 686 9276 E-mail frreuben@england.com

PRESTON, William. b 25. St Cath Coll Cam BA46 MA50 Reading Univ MSc79. Oak Hill Th Coll 48. **d** 50 **p** 51. C Hyson Green *S'well* 50-52; C Lenton 52-55; Kenya 55-62; Bethany Sch Goudhurst 62-69; Cranbrook Sch Kent 69-90; Perm to Offic *Cant* from 64; *Roch* from 66; rtd 90. *29 Orchard Way, Horsmonden, Tonbridge TN12 8LA* Tel (01892) 722616

PRESTON-THOMAS, Canon Colin Barnabas Rashleigh. b 28. K Coll Lon 48 Edin Th Coll 51. **d** 53 **p** 54. C Edin St Dav *Edin* 53-54; Chapl St Ninian's Cathl Perth *St And* 54-55; Prec St Ninian's Cathl Perth 55-60; Chapl HM Pris Perth 55-60; P-in-c Inverkeithing *St And* 60; R 61-72; P-in-c Rosyth 60; R 61-72; Syn Clerk 68-93; Can St Ninian's Cathl Perth 68-93; R Forfar 72-82; Dioc Sec 80-90; R Kilmaveonaig 82-93; R Pitlochry 82-93; rtd 93; Hon Can St Ninian's Cathl Perth *St And* from 93. *14 Muirend Grove, Perth PH1 1JW* Tel (01738) 627807

PRESTWOOD, Ms Jayne Marie. b 64. Man Univ BA86 Nottm Univ MA93. Linc Th Coll MA94. **d** 94 **p** 95. C Reddish *Man* 94-98; Dioc Drugs Misuse Project Worker 98-00; P-in-c N Reddish 00-04; P-in-c Haughton St Anne from 04; Tr Officer for Reader Tr from 04. *St Anne's Rectory, St Anne's Drive, Denton, Manchester M34 3EB* Tel 0161-336 2374 E-mail jayne@jayneprestwood.fsnet.co.uk

PRETT, Alan. b 39. **d** 05. OLM Styvechale *Cov* from 05. *11 Pleydell Close, Coventry CV3 3EF* Tel (024) 7630 7584

PREVETT, Mark Norman. b 59. Univ of Wales (Cardiff) BD88. St Mich Coll Llan 85. **d** 88 **p** 89. C Brynmawr *S & B* 88-90; C Bassaleg *Mon* 90-92; R Blaina and Nantyglo 92-97; TV Halas *Worc* 97-04; RD Dudley 00-04; TR Totton *Win* from 04. *The Rectory, 92 Salisbury Road, Totton, Southampton SO40 3JA* Tel (023) 8086 5103 E-mail prevtherev@btopenworld.com

PREVITE, The Ven Anthony Michael Allen. b 41. TCD DipTh88. CITC 85. **d** 88 **p** 89. C Galway w Kilcummin *T, K & A* 88-91; I Omey w Ballynakill, Errislannan and Roundstone 91-93; Dean Tuam 93-96; I Tuam w Cong and Aasleagh 93-96; Adn Tuam from 96; Can Tuam Cathl from 96; I Omey w Ballynakill, Errislannan and Roundstone from 96. *The Rectory, Church Hill, Clifden, Co Galway, Irish Republic* Tel and fax (00353) (95) 21147 E-mail aprevite@eircom.net

PREWER, Dennis. b 30. Kelham Th Coll 50. **d** 54 **p** 55. C Stockport St Thos *Ches* 54-58; C Gt Grimsby St Mary and St Jas *Linc* 58-62; V Gt Harwood St Jo *Blackb* 62-64; V Scarcliffe *Derby* 64-70; Org Sec CECS 70-92; Dios Liv, Ban and St As 70-78; Dio Man 78-92; Lic to Offic *Ches* 70-92; Perm to Offic *Man* 78-96; rtd 92; Perm to Offic *Ches* from 92. *19 Alan Drive, Marple, Stockport SK6 6LN* Tel 0161-427 2827

PRICE, Miss Alison Jane. b 63. NNEB84. Aston Tr Scheme 91 Westcott Ho Cam CTM95. **d** 95 **p** 96. C Upper Norwood All SS *S'wark* 95-99; V Mitcham St Barn from 99. *St Barnabas' Vicarage, Thirsk Road, Mitcham CR4 2BD* Tel (020) 8648 2571 E-mail alison.price@lineone.net

PRICE, Mrs Alison Mary. b 48. K Alfred's Coll Win CertEd69. **d** 01. Par Dn Magor *Mon* from 01. *Greenwillow, Church Road, Undy, Caldicot NP26 3EN* Tel (01633) 880557

PRICE, Alun. b 60. Bradf Univ BSc82 Loughb Univ MSc88 Univ Coll Ches BTh04. N Ord Course 01. **d** 04 **p** 05. NSM Bramley *Sheff* from 04. *65 Far Golden Smithies, Swinton, Mexborough S64 8DD* Tel (01709) 579487 E-mail potty@witheringheights.plus.com

PRICE, Alun Huw. b 47. MBE91. St D Coll Lamp DipTh70. **d** 70 **p** 71. C Carmarthen St Dav *St D* 70-73; V Betws Ifan 73-77; CF 77-03. *Address temp unknown*

PRICE, Anthony Ronald. b 49. Linc Coll Ox BA71 MA83 St Jo Coll Dur BA78. **d** 79 **p** 80. C St Alb St Paul *St Alb* 79-81; C Wootton 81-85; C Lydiard Millicent w Lydiard Tregoz *Bris* 85-86; TV The Lydiards 86-91; V Marston *Ox* 91-95; V Marston w Elsfield from 95; RD Cowley 97-02. *The Vicarage, Elsfield Road, Marston, Oxford OX3 0PR* Tel (01865) 247034 E-mail tonyprice@stnicsmarston.freeserve.co.uk

PRICE, Carol Ann. b 46. St Jo Coll Nottm 02. **d** 03 **p** 04. NSM Derby St Alkmund and St Werburgh *Derby* 03-04; NSM Charlesworth and Dinting Vale from 04. *52 Statham Street, Derby DE22 1HQ* Tel (01332) 609111 Mobile 07787-522127 E-mail carol_price@ntlworld.com

PRICE, Christine. b 66. Leic Univ BA94. EAMTC 98. **d** 01 **p** 02. C Jersey St Helier *Win* from 01. *3 Myrtle Grove, 42 St Johns Road, St Helier, Jersey JE2 3LD* Tel (01534) 515401 Mobile 07971-026711 E-mail christineprice@jerseymail.co.uk

PRICE, Mrs Christine Janice. b 45. Sarum & Wells Th Coll 83. **dss** 86 **d** 87 **p** 94. Roxbourne St Andr *Lon* 86-90; NSM 87-90; NSM Roxeth Ch Ch and Harrow St Pet 90-93; NSM Roxeth 93-94; C 94-96; C Costessey *Nor* 96-98; rtd 98; Perm to Offic *Nor* from 98. *Kingfishers, 212A Taverham Road, Taverham, Norwich NR8 6SU* Tel and fax (01603) 868036 E-mail chrisjpri@aol.com

PRICE, Canon Clive Stanley. b 42. ALCD69. **d** 69 **p** 70. C Chenies and Lt Chalfont *Ox* 69-75; R Upper Stour *Sarum* 75-79; C-in-c Panshanger CD *St Alb* 79-82; TV Digswell and Panshanger 82-86; P-in-c St Oswald in Lee w Bingfield *Newc* from 86; Dioc Ecum Officer from 86; Hon Can Newc Cathl from 97; AD Bellingham from 00. *St Oswald's Vicarage, Wall, Hexham NE46 4DU* Tel (01434) 681354 E-mail cliveprice@wallvicarage.freeserve.co.uk

PRICE, Dai. *See* PRICE, William Haydn

PRICE, David. b 27. Wycliffe Hall Ox 61. **d** 63 **p** 64. C Bucknall and Bagnall *Lich* 63-67; C Abingdon w Shippon *Ox* 67-76; Israel 76-84; V S Kensington St Luke *Lon* 84-92; P-in-c S Kensington St Jude 88-92; rtd 92; Hon C Hordle *Win* 92-97; Perm to Offic 97-98; Perm to Offic *Worc* from 98. *9 Hanley Road, Malvern WR14 4PQ* Tel (01684) 568532

PRICE, David Gareth Michael. b 64. Ex Univ BA86 Kent Univ MA87 FSS. Wycliffe Hall Ox BTh94. **d** 97 **p** 98. C Godalming *Guildf* 97-00; C-in-c Elvetham Heath LEP 00-02; Min from 02. *Church House, 30 Chineham Close, Fleet GU51 1BF* Tel (01252) 695067 Fax 695068 E-mail pricesinfleet@ntlworld.com

PRICE, Canon David Rea. b 39. St Aid Birkenhead 61. **d** 63 **p** 64. C Green Street Green *Roch* 63-66; C Gillingham St Mary 66-69; C New Windsor St Jo *Ox* 69-72; V Winkfield 72-80; RD Bracknell 78-86; V Sunningdale 80-86; TR Wimborne Minster and Holt *Sarum* 86-96; R Wimborne Minster 96-01; Chapl Wimborne Hosp 86-01; RD Wimborne 88-98; Can and Preb Sarum Cathl 92-01; P-in-c Witchampton, Stanbridge and Long Crichel etc 00-01; rtd 01; Perm to Offic *Ex* from 01. *14 The Broadway, Exmouth EX8 2NW* Tel (01395) 269811 E-mail rea@14broadway.eclipse.co.uk

PRICE, Canon David Trevor William. b 43. Keble Coll Ox BA65 MA69 MEHS79 FRHistS79 FSA95. Sarum & Wells Th Coll 72. **d** 72 **p** 73. Lect Univ of Wales (Lamp) *St D* 70-87; Sen Lect 87-97; Chapl 79-80; Dean of Chpl 90-91; Public Preacher 72-86; Dioc Archivist 82-98; P-in-c Betws Bledrws 86-97; Hon Can St D Cathl 90-92; Can 92-00; V Cydweli and Llandyfaelog 97-00; P-in-c Myddle *Lich* from 00; P-in-c Broughton from 00; P-in-c Loppington w Newtown from 02; Perm to Offic *St As* from 01. *The Rectory, Myddle, Shrewsbury SY4 3RX* Tel (01939) 290811 Mobile 07811-712911 E-mail rector@myddle.net

PRICE, Dawson. b 31. OBE. Peterho Cam BA52. Oak Hill NSM Course 88. **d** 91 **p** 92. NSM Harpenden St Nic *St Alb* 91-99; rtd 99; Perm to Offic *Win* from 99. *8 Kimberley Close, Fair Oak, Eastleigh SO50 7EE* Tel (023) 8069 2273

PRICE, Derek Henry. b 51. Trin Coll Bris BA98. **d** 98 **p** 99. C Bayston Hill *Lich* 98-02; R Barrow St Paul *Carl* from 02. *St Paul's Rectory, 353 Abbey Road, Barrow-in-Furness LA13 9JY* Tel (01229) 821546 E-mail dh.price@virgin.net

PRICE, Canon Derek William. b 27. St Pet Hall Ox BA51 MA55. Qu Coll Birm 51. **d** 53 **p** 54. C St Marylebone St Mark Hamilton Terrace *Lon* 53-57; C Stevenage *St Alb* 57-63; Jamaica 63-67; R Bridgham and Roudham *Nor* 67-80; R E w W Harling 69-80; Hon Can Nor Cathl 75-92; RD Thetford and Rockland 76-86; P-in-c Kilverstone 80-87; P-in-c Croxton 80-87; TR Thetford 80-87; R Castleacre w Newton, Rougham and Southacre 87-92; Perm to Offic 92-99 and from 00; P-in-c Easton w Colton and Marlingford 99-00. *Fourways, King's Road, Dereham NR19 2AG* Tel (01362) 691660

PRICE, Chan Desmond. b 23. St D Coll Lamp BA50. **d** 51 **p** 52. C Llwynypia *Llan* 51-52; C Ystradyfodwg 52-54; C Watford Ch Ch *St Alb* 54-56; Chapl RAF 56-68; R Dinas and Llanllawer *St D* 68-72; V Llandeilo Fawr w Llandyfeisant 72-79; V Llandeilo Fawr and Taliaris 79-91; Can St D Cathl 83-91; Chan 89-91; RD Llangadog and Llandeilo 90-91; rtd 91; Hon Can St D Cathl *St D* from 91. *24 Diana Road, Llandeilo SA19 6RS* Tel (01558) 824039

PRICE, Canon Edward Glyn. b 35. Univ of Wales (Lamp) BA55. Ch Div Sch of the Pacific (USA) BD58. **d** 58 **p** 59. C Denbigh *St As* 58-65; V Llanasa 65-76; V Buckley 76-91; Dioc RE Adv 77-88; RD Mold 86-91; Can St As Cathl from 87; Preb and Sacr from 95; V Llandrillo-yn-Rhos 91-00; rtd 00. *7 Rhodfa Criccieth, Bodelwyddan, Rhyl LL18 5WL* Tel (01745) 571286

PRICE, Frank Lea. b 69. SS Coll Cam BA92 Solicitor 96. Oak Hill Th Coll BA99. **d** 99 **p** 00. C Hinckley H Trin *Leic* 99-04; C Cambridge H Sepulchre *Ely* from 04. *1 Pretoria Road, Cambridge CB4 1HD* Tel (01223) 518299 Fax 327331 E-mail frank.price@stag.org

PRICE, Frank Watkin. b 22. ALCM37 Univ of Wales (Lamp) BA45. St Mich Coll Llan 45. **d** 47 **p** 48. C Cwmaman *St D* 47-50; C Llanelli 50-52; Chapl RAF 52-68; Hd RE Amman Valley Comp Sch 68-85; Hd Master Lower Sch 75-85; R St Nicholas w Bonvilston and St George-super-Ely *Llan* 85-92; rtd 92; Perm to Offic *Llan* and *St D* from 92. *13 Pedair Erw Road, Cardiff CF14 4NU* Tel (029) 2061 8356

PRICE, Frederick Leslie. b 30. Oak Hill Th Coll 59. **d** 61 **p** 62. C Hougham in Dover Ch Ch *Cant* 61-64; R Plumbland and Gilcrux *Carl* 64-95; rtd 95; Perm to Offic *Carl* from 98. *1 Beech Hill, Oughterside, Aspatria, Carlisle CA7 2QA* Tel (01697) 320255

PRICE, Geoffrey David Gower. b 46. NDA NCA. Oak Hill Th Coll. **d** 83 **p** 84. C Gt Baddow *Chelmsf* 83-86; C Hampreston *Sarum* 86-88; TV 88-93; P-in-c Drayton in Hales *Lich* 93-97; V 97-99; P-in-c Adderley and Moreton Say 93-97; R Ipswich St Helen, H Trin, and St Luke *St E* 99-05; V E Bedfont *Lon* from 05. *St Mary's Vicarage, 9 Hatton Road, Bedfont, Feltham TW14 8JR* Tel (020) 8751 0088

PRICE, Gerald Andrew. b 31. NEOC. **d** 84 **p** 85. C Monkseaton St Mary *Newc* 84-87; V Cowgate 87-94; C Beltingham w Henshaw 94-96; C Haydon Bridge 94-96; rtd 96; Perm to Offic *Newc* from 96. *24 Hallstile Bank, Hexham NE46 3PQ* Tel (01434) 603374

PRICE, Glyn. *See* PRICE, Canon Edward Glyn

PRICE, Mrs Jean Amelia. b 44. St Alb and Ox Min Course 99. **d** 02 **p** 03. OLM N Buckingham *Ox* from 02. *15 Highlands Road, Buckingham MK18 1PN* Tel (01280) 815125 E-mail jeanprice@tinyworld.co.uk

PRICE, John Francis. b 32. Qu Coll Cam BA54 MA. Ridley Hall Cam 54. **d** 56 **p** 57. C Leic H Apostles *Leic* 56-60; V Forest Gate St Mark *Chelmsf* 60-71; V Harold Hill St Geo 72-79; R Loughton St Mary 79-83; TR Loughton St Mary and St Mich 83-88; R Kirby-le-Soken w Gt Holland 88-92; rtd 92; Perm to Offic *Chelmsf* from 00. *97 Kings Parade, Holland-on-Sea, Clacton-on-Sea CO15 5JH* Tel (01255) 813202

PRICE, John Joseph. b 44. Ridley Hall Cam 89. **d** 92 **p** 93. C Glenfield *Leic* 92-97; Relig Affairs Adv BBC Radio Leics 93-97; Midl Regional Co-ord Crosslinks 97-05; NSM Werrington *Pet* 04-05; P-in-c Pet St Mark and St Barn from 05. *59A Peterborough Road, Castor, Peterborough PE5 7AL* Tel (01733) 380025 E-mail jprice@onetel.net

PRICE, John Newman. b 32. St Alb Minl Tr Scheme 80. **d** 83 **p** 84. NSM Bedford St Pet w St Cuth *St Alb* 83-88; C Lt Berkhamsted and Bayford, Essendon etc 88-92; P-in-c Benington w Walkern 92-99; rtd 99; Perm to Offic *St Alb* from 00. *21 Wendover Drive, Bedford MK41 9QY* Tel (01234) 313373

PRICE, Canon John Richard. b 34. Mert Coll Ox BA58 MA62. Westcott Ho Cam 58. **d** 60 **p** 61. C Man St Aid *Man* 60-63; C Bramley *Ripon* 63-67; V Leeds All Hallows w St Simon 67-74; P-in-c Wrangthorn 73-74; V Claughton cum Grange *Ches* 74-78; V Mottram in Longdendale w Woodhead 78-88; RD Mottram 79-88; Hon Can Ches Cathl 86-99; R Nantwich 88-99; rtd 99; Perm to Offic *Bradf* 99-00; P-in-c Cowling from 00. *21 Mill Croft, Cowling, Keighley BD22 0AJ* Tel (01535) 637699

PRICE, Joseph Roderick (Rod). b 45. St Mich Coll Llan 71. **d** 75 **p** 76. C Fleur-de-Lis *Mon* 75-79; CF 79-99; rtd 99. *c/o MOD Chaplains (Army)* Tel (01980) 615804 Fax 615800

PRICE, Preb Lawrence Robert. b 43. LICeram71 N Staffs Poly CertCT66 Manager's Dip in Ceramic Tech 74. St Jo Coll Dur 76. **d** 78 **p** 79. C Harlescott *Lich* 78-80; C Cheddleton 80-83; P-in-c Calton 83-84; P-in-c Cauldon 83-84; P-in-c Grindon 83-84; P-in-c Waterfall 83-84; R Calton, Cauldon, Grindon and Waterfall 85-88; P-in-c Kingsley 95-01; R Kingsley and Foxt-w-Whiston from 01; RD Cheadle from 98; Preb Lich Cathl from 00. *The Rectory, Holt Lane, Kingsley, Stoke-on-Trent ST10 2BA* Tel (01538) 754754 Fax 754431 E-mail preblrprice@aol.com

PRICE, Leslie. *See* PRICE, Frederick Leslie

PRICE, Mari Josephine. b 43. St Hugh's Coll Ox BA65 Ox Univ MA69 DipEd66. Llan Dioc Tr Scheme 93. **d** 97 **p** 98. NSM Lisvane *Llan* 97-02; NSM Roath 02-03; Hon Chapl Llan Cathl from 03. *23 Ty Draw Road, Roath, Cardiff CF23 5HB* Tel (029) 2045 6757 Mobile 07850-019883

PRICE, Martin Randall Connop. b 45. Lon Univ BSc71 Fitzw Coll Cam BA75 MA79 Univ of Wales (Swansea) PhD02. Ridley

Hall Cam 73. **d** 76 **p** 77. C Keynsham *B & W* 76-79; Ind Chapl *Sheff* 79-83; V Wortley 79-83; R Hook Norton w Gt Rollright, Swerford etc *Ox* 83-91; V Shiplake w Dunsden 91-03; P-in-c Harpsden 02-03; R Shiplake w Dunsden and Harpsden from 03. *The Rectory, Shiplake, Henley-on-Thames RG9 4BS* Tel 0118-940 1306

PRICE (née ALDERTON), Mrs Mary Louise. b 54. Nottm Univ BSc75 IPFA87. EAMTC 02. **d** 05. NSM Melbourn *Ely* from 05; NSM Meldreth from 05. *4 Barrons Green, Shepreth, Royston SG8 6QN* Tel (01763) 261569 E-mail mary@price10051.fsnet.co.uk

PRICE, Michael Graham. b 62. Ex Coll Ox BA84. Linc Th Coll 84. **d** 86 **p** 87. C Salford St Phil w St Steph *Man* 86-90; R Man Gd Shep 90-95; V Netherton St Andr *Worc* 95-99; Chapl Bloxham Sch from 00. *Bloxham School, Bloxham, Banbury OX15 4PQ* Tel (01295) 720222

PRICE, Morris John. b 39. **d** 03 **p** 04. OLM Gt Wyrley *Lich* from 03. *42 Huthill Lane, Walsall WS6 6PB* Tel (01922) 412846 E-mail normoss@ukonline.co.uk

PRICE, Norman. *See* PRICE, William Norman

PRICE, Canon Norman Havelock. b 28. Univ of Wales (Lamp) BA52. St Mich Coll Llan 52. **d** 54 **p** 55. C Maindee *Mon* 54-58; V Llantilio Crossenny and Llanfihangel Ystern etc 58-64; V Mon St Thos-over-Monnow 64-65; V Mon St Thos-over-Monnow and Wonastow 65-71; V Overmonnow w Wonastow and Michel Troy 71-93; RD Monmouth 84-93; Can St Woolos Cathl 91-93; rtd 93; Hon Can St Woolos Cathl *Mon* 93-96; Lic to Offic from 93. *17 Cinderhill Street, Monmouth NP25 5EY* Tel (01600) 714587

✠**PRICE, The Rt Revd Peter Bryan.** b 44. Redland Coll of Educn CertEd66. Oak Hill Th Coll 72. **d** 74 **p** 75 **c** 97. C Portsdown *Portsm* 74-78; Chapl Scargill Ho 78-80; P-in-c Addiscombe St Mary *Cant* 80-81; V 81-84; V Addiscombe St Mary *S'wark* 85-88; Can Res and Chan S'wark Cathl 88-92; Gen Sec USPG 92-97; Area Bp Kingston *S'wark* 97-02; Bp B & W from 02. *The Palace, Wells BA5 2PD* Tel (01749) 672341 Fax 679355 E-mail bishop@bathwells.anglican.org

PRICE, Peter Charles. b 27. Angl Th Coll (BC) DipTh61. **d** 61 **p** 62. Canada 61-66; C St Mary-at-Latton *Chelmsf* 66-68; C Bearsted *Cant* 68-74; TV Ebbw Vale *Mon* 74-77; V Llanfihangel Crucorney w Oldcastle etc 77-87; V St Paul's Cathl St Helena 87-90; V Llanishen w Trellech Grange and Llanfihangel etc *Mon* 90-94; rtd 94; Perm to Offic *Heref* from 95. *1 Kynaston, Much Marcle, Ledbury HR8 2PD* Tel (01531) 670687

PRICE, Canon Philip. b 24. Tyndale Hall Bris 50. **d** 55 **p** 56. Kenya 55-75; R Gt Horkesley *Chelmsf* 75-89; rtd 89; Perm to Offic *Chelmsf* from 89; Hon Can Kitale from 02. *229 Meadgate Avenue, Great Baddow, Chelmsford CM2 7NJ* Tel (01245) 251499

PRICE, Raymond Francklin. b 30. Wycliffe Hall Ox 61. **d** 62 **p** 63. C Bilston St Leon *Lich* 62-67; C Keighley *Bradf* 67-70; V Mangotsfield *Bris* 70-79; Ind Chapl *Birm* 79-86; C Birm St Martin 84-85; C Birm St Martin w Bordesley St Andr 85-86; V Edgbaston St Aug 86-99; rtd 99; Perm to Offic *Birm* from 00. *35 Middle Park Road, Selly Oak, Birmingham B29 4BH* Tel 0121-475 4458

PRICE, Rod. *See* PRICE, Joseph Roderick

PRICE, Roland Kendrick. b 41. Cam Univ MA64 Essex Univ PhD69. St Alb and Ox Min Course CBTS95. **d** 95 **p** 96. NSM Cholsey *Ox* 95-97; Asst Chapl The Hague *Eur* from 99. *Bentinckstraat 129, 2582 ST Den Haag, The Netherlands* Tel (0031) (70) 358 9240 *or* 355 5359 Fax 354 1023 E-mail churchoffice@stjohnandstphilip.org

PRICE, Stanley George. b 32. FRICS69. Trin Coll Bris 84. **d** 85 **p** 86. C Newport w Longford and Chetwynd *Lich* 85-88; V Ipstones w Berkhamsytch and Onecote w Bradnop 88-97; rtd 98; Perm to Offic *B & W* 98-03; P-in-c Rodney Stoke w Draycott from 03. *St Aidan, Rectory Way, Lympsham, Weston-super-Mare BS24 0EN* Tel (01934) 750323 E-mail stanley-price@supanet.com

PRICE, Timothy Fry. b 51. NE Lon Poly CQSW. St Jo Coll Nottm 85. **d** 87 **p** 88. C Church Stretton *Heref* 87-91; V Sinfin *Derby* 91-00; Regional Adv (SW) CMJ 00-03; Nat Field Co-ord from 03; Perm to Offic *B & W, Bris* and *Glouc* from 01. *98 Furnham Road, Chard TA20 1BE* Tel (01460) 61308 E-mail nfc@cmj.org.uk

PRICE, Victor John. b 35. Oak Hill Th Coll 62. **d** 65 **p** 66. C Rainham *Chelmsf* 65-70; V Dover St Martin *Cant* 70-78; V Madeley *Heref* 78-90; P-in-c Derby St Pet and Ch Ch w H Trin *Derby* 90-91; V 91-96; P-in-c Morley w Morley 96-00; rtd 00; Perm to Offic *S'well* from 03. *4 Holmefield, Farndon, Newark NG24 3TZ* Tel (01636) 611788

PRICE, William. *See* PRICE, Canon David Trevor William

PRICE, William Haydn (Dai). b 20. Sarum & Wells Th Coll 77. **d** 80 **p** 81. NSM Alverstoke *Portsm* 80-85; rtd 85; Perm to Offic *Portsm* from 85. *15 Amersham Close, Alverstoke, Gosport PO12 2RU* Tel (023) 9258 0965

PRICE, William Norman. b 52. GRNCM73. N Ord Course 86. **d** 89 **p** 90. C Lower Broughton Ascension *Man* 89-91; Min Can and Succ St E Cathl *St E* 92-96; Prec 94-96; V Par *Truro* 96-00; V Musbury *Blackb* from 00. *St Thomas's Vicarage, 1 Flaxmoss Close, Haslingden, Rossendale BB4 4PX* Tel and fax (01706) 221923 E-mail golfsierra999@aol.com

PRICE-ROBERTS, Mervyn. b 29. Trin Coll Carmarthen TCert51 Univ of Wales DipRE52 BEd79. St Mich Coll Llan 89 Ban Ord Course 84. **d** 87 **p** 88. NSM Bangor *Ban* 87-89; V Llandygai w Tregarth 89-97; rtd 97; Perm to Offic *Ban* from 97. *17 Parc Hen Blas Estate, Llanfairfechan LL33 0RW* Tel (01248) 680305

PRICHARD, Canon Thomas John. b 16. Univ of Wales (Ban) BA38 MA72 Keele Univ PhD81 FRHistS82. Chich Th Coll 38. **d** 39 **p** 40. C Blaenau Ffestiniog *Ban* 39-41; C Machynlleth *Ban* 41-42; C Llanfabon *Llan* 42-44; C Ystradyfodwg 44-50; V Dinas w Penygraig 50-69; RD Rhondda 64-69; Can Llan Cathl 66-84; R Neath w Llantwit 69-84; Dioc Archivist 70-84; rtd 84; Perm to Offic *Ban* from 97. *Tros-yr-Afon, Llangwnnadl, Pwllheli LL53 8NS* Tel (01758) 612832

PRIDAY, Gerald Nelson. b 35. Glouc Th Course. **d** 85 **p** 88. NSM Eardisland *Heref* 85-91; NSM Aymestrey and Leinthall Earles w Wigmore etc 85-91; NSM Kingsland 85-91; NSM Eye, Croft w Yarpole and Lucton 91-94; NSM Heref All SS 94-96; NSM Letton w Staunton, Byford, Mansel Gamage etc 96-98; rtd 98; Perm to Offic *Heref* from 99. *4 Lime Close, Ludlow SY8 2PP* Tel (01584) 876910

PRIDDIN, Mrs Maureen Anne. b 46. Leeds Univ BA67 Nottm Univ DipEd68. EMMTC 82. **dss** 85 **d** 87 **p** 94. Mickleover St Jo *Derby* 85-87; Hon Par Dn 87-94; Assoc P from 94; Dioc World Development Officer 87-90. *7 Portland Close, Mickleover, Derby DE3 9BZ* Tel (01332) 513672 E-mail mpriddin@argonet.co.uk

✠**PRIDDIS, The Rt Revd Anthony Martin.** b 48. CCC Cam BA69 MA73 New Coll Ox DipTh71 MA75. Cuddesdon Coll 69. **d** 72 **p** 73 **c** 96. C New Addington *Cant* 72-75; Chapl Ch Ch Ox 75-80; Lic to Offic *Ox* 76-80; TV High Wycombe 80-86; P-in-c Amersham 86-90; R 90-96; RD Amersham 92-96; Hon Can Ch Ch 95-96; Suff Bp Warw *Cov* 96-04; Hon Can Cov Cathl 96-04; Bp Heref from 04. *The Bishop's House, The Palace, Hereford HR4 9BN* Tel (01432) 271355 Fax 343047 E-mail bishop@diooffice.freeserve.co.uk

PRIDEAUX, Humphrey Grevile. b 36. CCC Ox BA59 MA63 Birm Univ CertEd66 Lon Univ DipEd73 Open Univ BA87. Linc Th Coll 59. **d** 61 **p** 62. C Northampton St Matt *Pet* 61-62; C Milton *Portsm* 62-65; Perm to Offic *Birm* 65-66; Hd of RE Qu Mary's Gr Sch Walsall 66-69; Lect St Martin's Coll Lanc 69-80; Perm to Offic *Portsm* 80-86; Hon C Fareham H Trin 86-87; Hon C Bishop's Waltham 87-94; NSM P-in-c W Meon and Warnford 94-03. *6 Rectory Close, Alverstoke, Gosport PO12 2HT* Tel (023) 9250 1794

PRIDGEON, Paul Garth Walsingham. b 45. Sussex Univ BA69 CertEd. Glouc Sch of Min 87. **d** 87 **p** 88. NSM Cirencester *Glouc* 87-97; NSM Northleach w Hampnett and Farmington etc 97-03; Perm to Offic from 03. *4 Abbey Way, Cirencester GL7 2DT* Tel (01285) 656860

PRIDIE, William Raleigh. b 49. Bris Univ BEd72 Dip Mgt82 ACP82 FCollP83. SW Minl Tr Course 90. **d** 93 **p** 94. C Kingstone w Clehonger, Eaton Bishop etc *Heref* 93-96; P-in-c Kimbolton w Hamnish and Middleton-on-the-Hill 96-97; P-in-c Bockleton w Leysters 96-97; CME Officer 96-00; TV Leominster 97-00; R Fownhope w Mordiford, Brockhampton etc from 00. *The Rectory, Fownhope, Hereford HR1 4PS* Tel (01432) 860365

PRIDMORE, John Stuart. b 36. Nottm Univ BA62 MA67 Lon Inst of Educn PhD00. Ridley Hall Cam 62. **d** 65 **p** 66. C Camborne *Truro* 65-67; Tutor Ridley Hall Cam 67-68; Chapl 68-71; Asst Chapl K Edw Sch Witley 71-75; Chapl 75-86; Tanzania 86-88; Angl Chapl Hengrave Hall Cen 88-89; C St Martin-in-the-Fields *Lon* 89-95; TR Hackney 95-03; V St John-at-Hackney from 03. *The Rectory, 356 Mare Street, London E8 1HR* Tel (020) 8985 5374 E-mail john.pridmore@btinternet.com

PRIEST, Helen Elizabeth. *See* MACE, Mrs Helen Elizabeth

PRIEST, Richard Mark. b 63. Oak Hill Th Coll BA90. **d** 90 **p** 91. C Okehampton w Inwardleigh *Ex* 90-94; C Okehampton w Inwardleigh, Bratton Clovelly etc 94; CF from 94. *c/o MOD Chaplains (Army)* Tel (01980) 615804 Fax 615800

PRIESTLEY, Canon Alan Charles. b 41. Lon Univ BD69. Kelham Th Coll 64 Wm Temple Coll Rugby 65. **d** 65 **p** 66. C Edgbaston St Aug *Birm* 65-68; C Chelmsley Wood 68-72; TV 72-76; V Hazelwell from 76; Dioc Communications Officer 83-94; Bp's Press Officer from 85; Hon Can Birm Cathl from 87. *The Vicarage, 316 Vicarage Road, Birmingham B14 7NH* Tel 0121-444 4469 Mobile 07720-936729 Fax 0121-444 8184 E-mail apriestley@waitrose.com

PRIESTLEY, Canon John Christopher. b 39. Trin Coll Ox BA60. Wells Th Coll 61. **d** 68 **p** 69. C Habergham All SS *Blackb* 68-70; C Padiham 70-75; V Colne Ch Ch 75-98; Chapl to The Queen from 90; RD Pendle *Blackb* 91-96; P-in-c Foulridge 97-98; TV Colne and Villages 98-02; Hon Can Blackb Cathl 00-02; rtd 02; Perm to Offic *Blackb* from 02. *11 Chapman Court, Barnoldswick BB18 5EE* Tel (01282) 812308

PRIESTLEY, Rosemary Jane. *See* LAIN-PRIESTLEY, Ms Rosemary Jane

PRIESTLY, Thomas Herbert. b 67. Ulster Univ BA91. CITC BTh94. **d** 94 **p** 95. C Ballymena w Ballyclug *Conn* 94-99; I Dunmurry from 99. *The Rectory, 27 Church Avenue, Dunmurry, Belfast BT17 9RS* Tel (028) 9061 0984

PRIESTNALL, Reginald Hayward. b 22. Jes Coll Cam BA44 MA47. Ridley Hall Cam 44. **d** 45 **p** 46. C Streatham Immanuel *S'wark* 45-48; C Barking St Marg *Chelmsf* 48-51; R Bonsall *Derby* 51-53; P-in-c Mackworth St Fran 53-54; V 54-67; Chapl Kingsway Hosp Derby 61-67; V Rockingham w Caldecote *Pet* 67-71; V Northampton St Mich 71-77; V Ketton 77-89; RD Barnack 86-89; rtd 89. *Lavender Cottage, 486 Earlham Road, Norwich NR4 7HP* Tel (01603) 503435

PRIESTNER, Hugh. b 45. Nottm Univ BTh75. Linc Th Coll 71. **d** 75 **p** 76. C Seaton Hirst *Newc* 75-78; C Longbenton St Bart 78-81; P-in-c Glendale Gp 81-82; TV 83-88; Chapl Stafford Acute Hosps 88-89; Tr Co-ord W Cumberland Hosp 89-92; Chapl Fair Havens Hospice 94-98; Chapl Walsgrave Hosps NHS Trust 98-00; Chapl Univ Hosps Cov and Warks NHS Trust from 00. *Walsgrave General Hospital, Clifford Bridge Road, Coventry CV2 2DX* Tel (024) 7653 8950 *or* 7660 2020 ext 8950 E-mail hughpriestner@netscapeonline.co.uk

PRIGG, Patrick John. b 53. K Coll Lon BD82. Sarum & Wells Th Coll 89. **d** 92 **p** 93. C Wavertree St Mary *Liv* 92-96; Chapl Sandown Coll 92-96; P-in-c Glemsford, Hartest w Boxted, Somerton etc *St E* 96-99; R from 99. *The Rectory, 6 Lion Road, Glemsford, Sudbury CO10 7RF* Tel (01787) 282164 E-mail revpat@glemsfordrectory.freeserve.co.uk

PRIME, Geoffrey Daniel. b 12. Lich Th Coll 32. **d** 35 **p** 36. C Uttoxeter w Bramshall *Lich* 35-42; P-in-c Newborough w Ch Ch on Needwood 42-43; V Pattingham 43-55; V Longstone *Derby* 55-62; Org Sec CECS *Derby, Linc, Sheff* and *S'well* 62-65; Perm to Offic *Derby* 62-00; rtd 77. *Westside Mill Farm, Hulme End, Buxton SK17 0EY* Tel (01298) 84461

PRIMROSE, David Edward Snodgrass. b 55. St Jo Coll Cam MA80. Trin Coll Bris BA92. **d** 87 **p** 92. Pakistan 87-89; C Glouc St Paul *Glouc* 92-96; R Badgeworth, Shurdington and Witcombe w Bentham 96-03; V Thornbury and Oldbury-on-Severn w Shepperdine from 03; RD Hawkesbury from 04. *The Vicarage, 27 Castle Street, Thornbury, Bristol BS35 1HQ* Tel (01454) 413209 *or* 281900 E-mail primrose@blueyonder.co.uk

PRINCE (née RUMBLE), Mrs Alison Merle. b 49. Surrey Univ BSc71. Trin Coll Bris BA89. **d** 89 **p** 94. Par Dn Willesden Green St Gabr *Lon* 89-91; Par Dn Cricklewood St Gabr and St Mich 92; Par Dn Herne Hill *S'wark* 92-94; C 94-95; Chapl Greenwich Healthcare NHS Trust 95-96; TV Sanderstead All SS *S'wark* 97-03; TV Kegworth, Hathern, Long Whatton, Diseworth etc *Leic* from 04. *The Rectory, Presents Lane, Belton, Loughborough LE12 9UN* Tel (01530) 223447

PRINCE (née GRIFFITHS), Caroline Heidi Ann. b 66. Ex Univ BA88. Linc Th Coll 90. **d** 90 **p** 97. Chapl St Woolos Cathl *Mon* 90-94; C Newport St Woolos 90-94; C Abergavenny Deanery 94-96; TV Cwmbran 96-97; V Llantilio Crossenny w Penrhos, Llanvetherine etc from 97. *The Vicarage, Llantilio Crossenny, Abergavenny NP7 8SU* Tel (01600) 780240

PRINCE, Helena. b 23. Lightfoot Ho Dur 59. **dss** 66 **d** 87 **p** 94. W Derby St Mary *Liv* 65-85; rtd 85; Perm to Offic *Liv* 85-04. *5 Dominic Close, Liverpool L16 1JZ* Tel 0151-722 0263

PRINCE, Mrs Melanie Amanda. b 71. St D Coll Lamp BA92 Univ of Wales (Cardiff) MPhil93. St Mich Coll Llan 96. **d** 98 **p** 99. C Aberavon *Llan* 98-01; C Gabalfa from 01. *27 Pen-y-Bryn Road, Gabalfa, Cardiff CF14 3LG* Tel (029) 2025 4089

PRING, Althon Kerrigan (Kerry). b 34. AKC58. **d** 59 **p** 60. C Limehouse St Anne *Lon* 59-61; C Lt Stanmore St Lawr 61-64; C Langley Marish *Ox* 64-68; P-in-c Radnage 68-72; P-in-c Ravenstone w Weston Underwood 72-75; P-in-c Stoke Goldington w Gayhurst 72-75; R Gayhurst w Ravenstone, Stoke Goldington etc 75-85; P-in-c 85-86; RD Newport 78-80; TV Woughton 86-90; P-in-c Nash w Thornton, Beachampton and Thornborough 90-94; R 94-96; rtd 96; Perm to Offic *Ox* from 99. *Kingsmead, 9 Malting Close, Stoke Goldington, Newport Pagnell MK16 8NX* Tel (01908) 551345

PRINGLE, The Ven Cecil Thomas. b 43. TCD BA65. CITC 66. **d** 66 **p** 67. C Belfast St Donard *D & D* 66-69; I Cleenish *Clogh* 69-80; I Mullaghdun 78-80; I Rossory from 80; Preb Clogh Cathl 86-89; Adn Clogh from 89. *Rossory Rectory, Derryhonnelly Road, Enniskillen BT74 7JE* Tel (028) 6632 2874

PRINGLE, Graeme Lindsley. b 59. St Cath Coll Cam BA81 MA85. St Jo Coll Nottm Dip Th Studies 94. **d** 94 **p** 95. C Binley *Cov* 94-99; V Allesley Park and Whoberley from 99. *St Christopher's Vicarage, 99 Buckingham Rise, Coventry CV5 9HF* Tel (024) 7667 2879 E-mail graeme@stchristopher.org.uk

PRINGLE, Miss Janyce Mary. b 32. ARCM53 LRAM54 Ex Univ DipAdEd70 MPhil85. SW Minl Tr Course 83. **dss** 86 **d** 87 **p** 94. NSM Torquay St Matthias, St Mark and H Trin *Ex* 86-98; Chapl Asst Torbay Hosp Torquay 86-89; Perm to Offic *Ex* from 98. *Pendower, Wheatridge Lane, Torquay TQ2 6RA* Tel (01803) 607136

PRINGLE, John Richard. b 55. Lon Univ AKC76 CertEd77 Open Univ BA84. Chich Th Coll 78. **d** 78 **p** 79. C Northampton St Matt *Pet* 78-81; C Delaval *Newc* 81-84; V Newsham from 84; RD Bedlington 93-98. *St Bede's Vicarage, Newcastle Road, Newsham, Blyth NE24 4AS* Tel and fax (01670) 352391

PRINGLE, Victor. b 43. St Barn Coll Adelaide BA72 ACT ThDip72. **d** 73 **p** 75. Australia 73-80; C Murray Bridge 75; C O'Halloran Hill 76; Chapl R Adelaide Hosp and C Wakerville 77-78; R Clarence Town 78-80; C Lavender Hill Ascension *S'wark* 80-81; Australia from 81; Asst P Sydney St Laur from 82. *3/1A Avenue Road, Mosman, Sydney, NSW, Australia 2008* Tel (0061) (2) 9969 8294

PRINS, Canon Stanley Vernon. b 30. TD76. Dur Univ BSc54 MA69. Ripon Hall Ox 56. **d** 58 **p** 59. C Benwell St Jas *Newc* 58-61; Asst Chapl Newc Univ 61-65; CF (TA) from 64; C-in-c Whorlton H Nativity Chpl Ho Estate *Newc* 65-72; TV Whorlton 73-76; V Humshaugh 76-83; P-in-c Simonburn 82-83; P-in-c Wark 82-83; RD Bellingham 83-93; R Humshaugh w Simonburn and Wark 83-96; Hon Can Newc Cathl 88-96; rtd 96; Perm to Offic *Newc* from 96. *Woodside Cottage, Scrogwood, Bardon Mill, Hexham NE47 7AA* Tel (01434) 344876

PRIOR, David Clement Lyndon. b 40. Trin Coll Ox BA63 MA66. Ridley Hall Cam 65. **d** 67 **p** 68. C Reigate St Mary *S'wark* 67-72; S Africa 72-79; Can Cape Town 76-79; C Ox St Aldate w H Trin *Ox* 79-82; C Ox St Aldate w St Matt 82-84; USA 84-85; V Ches Square St Mich w St Phil *Lon* 85-95; P-in-c Mayfair Ch Ch 85-97; Public Preacher from 95; P-in-c St Botolph without Aldersgate 97-00. *2 North Lane, Wiston, Steyning BN44 3DQ* Tel (01903) 893566

PRIOR (née CHIUMBU), Esther Tamisa. b 73. Univ of Zimbabwe BSc95. Trin Coll Bris BA02. **d** 03 **p** 04. NSM Redland *Bris* 03-05; C Deptford St Jo w H Trin *S'wark* from 05. *3 Orchard Hill, London SE13 7QZ* Tel (020) 8694 1892 E-mail prior@esthermatt.freeserve.co.uk

PRIOR, Gregory Stephen. b 68. Geo Whitfield Coll S Africa BTh90. **d** 95 **p** 96. In C of E in S Africa 95-01; Min for Miss Muswell Hill St Jas w St Matt *Lon* 01-04; P-in-c Wandsworth All SS *S'wark* from 04. *Wandsworth Vicarage, 11 Rusholme Road, London SW15 3JX* Tel (020) 8788 7400 E-mail greg@wandsworthparish.co.uk

PRIOR, Canon Ian Graham. b 44. Lon Univ BSc(Econ)71. Oak Hill Th Coll DipHE80. **d** 80 **p** 81. C Luton Ch Ch *Roch* 80-83; TV Southgate *Chich* 83-93; V Burgess Hill St Andr from 93; RD Hurst 98-04; Can and Preb Chich Cathl from 03. *St Andrew's Vicarage, 2 Cants Lane, Burgess Hill RH15 0LG* Tel (01444) 232023

PRIOR, Ian Roger Lyndon. b 46. St Jo Coll Dur BA68. Lon Coll of Div 68. **d** 70 **p** 71. C S Croydon Em *Cant* 70-73; Perm to Offic *S'wark* 73-85; Dir Overseas Personnel TEAR Fund 73-79; Dep Dir 79-83; Fin and Admin Dir CARE Trust and CARE Campaigns 85-92; NSM New Malden and Coombe *S'wark* from 85; Dir Careforce from 92. *39 Cambridge Avenue, New Malden KT3 4LD* Tel (020) 8949 0912 *or* 8942 3331

PRIOR, James Murray. b 39. Edin Univ BCom64. St And Dioc Tr Course 85. **d** 90 **p** 91. NSM Kirriemuir *St And* 90-02; NSM Forfar 90-02; NSM Dundee St Jo *Bre* from 02; NSM Dundee St Ninian from 02. *Thornton Farm, Birkhill, Cupar KY15 4QN* Tel (01382) 330132

PRIOR, John Gilman Leathes. b 15. Qu Coll Cam BA37 MA41. Ridley Hall Cam 37. **d** 39 **p** 40. C Ipswich St Marg *St E* 39-41; CF 41-46; V Springfield H Trin *Chelmsf* 46-49; V Guildf Ch Ch *Guildf* 49-63; V Camberley St Paul 63-74; V Crondall 75-77; V Crondall and Ewshot 77-80; rtd 80; Perm to Offic *Win* from 80; *Guildf* 82-96; *Portsm* from 84. *Bungalow 116, Clare Park, Farnham GU10 5DT* Tel (01252) 855088

PRIOR, Preb John Miskin. b 27. Lon Univ BSc(Econ)48. Westcott Ho Cam 49. **d** 51 **p** 52. C Bedminster St Fran *Bris* 51-55; C Sherston Magna w Easton Grey 55-57; C Yatton Keynell 57-61; C Castle Combe 57-61; C Biddestone w Slaughterford 57-61; V Bishopstone w Hinton Parva 61-66; V Marshfield w Cold Ashton 66-82; P-in-c Tormarton w W Littleton 68-82; RD Bitton 73-79; R Trull w Angersleigh *B & W* 82-91; RD Taunton 84-90; Preb Wells Cathl 90-91; Chapl Huggens Coll Northfleet 91-97; rtd 92; Hon PV Roch Cathl *Roch* from 98; Perm to Offic from 99. *Buff Cottage, 7 St Margarets Street, Rochester ME1 1TU* Tel (01634) 846422

PRIOR, Canon Kenneth Francis William. b 26. St Jo Coll Dur BA49. Oak Hill Th Coll 46. **d** 49 **p** 50. C S Mimms Ch Ch *Lon* 49-52; C Eastbourne H Trin *Chich* 52-53; V Onslow Square St Paul *Lon* 53-65; V Hove Bp Hannington Memorial Ch *Chich* 65-70; R Sevenoaks St Nic *Roch* 70-87; Hon Can Roch Cathl 82-87; C-in-c Hampstead St Jo Downshire Hill Prop Chpl *Lon* 87-90; rtd 89; Perm to Offic *Chelmsf* from 89; *Lon* from 90; *St Alb* 90-99 and *Ex* from 00. *22 Barnfield Road, Torquay TQ2 6TN* Tel (01803) 606760

PRIOR, Canon Kenneth George William. b 17. Bris Univ BA39. Bible Churchmen's Coll Bris 35. **d** 40 **p** 41. C Toxteth Park

St Clem *Liv* 40-43; C Edge Hill St Cypr 43-45; C Garston 45-48; V Plymouth St Jude *Ex* 48-55; V Longfleet *Sarum* 55-82; Chapl Poole Gen Hosp 55-76; RD Poole *Sarum* 75-80; Can and Preb Sarum Cathl 77-82; rtd 82; Perm to Offic *Sarum* 82-00. *22 Ramsay Hall, 11-13 Byron Road, Worthing BN11 3HN* Tel (01903) 214880 E-mail kgwprior@aol.com

PRIOR, Matthew Thomas. b 74. Rob Coll Cam BA97 MA00. Trin Coll Bris BA04 MA05. **d** 05. C Deptford St Jo w H Trin *S'wark* from 05. *3 Orchard Hill, London SE13 7QZ* Tel (020) 8694 1892 E-mail prior@esthermatt.freeserve.co.uk

PRIOR, Nigel John. b 56. Bris Univ BA78. Westcott Ho Cam 79. **d** 81 **p** 82. C Langley All SS and Martyrs *Man* 81-82; C Langley and Parkfield 82-84; C Bury St Jo w St Mark 84-87; R Man Clayton St Cross w St Paul 87-99; P-in-c Mark Cross *Chich* 99-00; V Mayfield from 99. *The Vicarage, High Street, Mayfield TN20 6AB* Tel (01435) 873180

PRIOR, Stephen Kenneth. b 55. Rhode Is Coll (USA) BA78. Wycliffe Hall Ox 79. **d** 82 **p** 83. C Aberavon *Llan* 82-85; P-in-c New Radnor and Llanfihangel Nantmelan etc *S & B* 85-86; R 86-90; V Llansamlet 90-94; P-in-c Chester le Street *Dur* 94-96; R 96-01; R Caldbeck, Castle Sowerby and Sebergham *Carl* from 01; Dir of Ords from 04. *The Rectory, Caldbeck, Wigton CA7 8EW* Tel (016974) 78233
E-mail rectory@priors.freeserve.co.uk

PRIORY, Barry Edwin. b 44. FCIS Open Univ BA81. Qu Coll Birm 84. **d** 86 **p** 87. C Boldmere *Birm* 86-89; C Somerton w Compton Dundon, the Charltons etc *B & W* 89-93; R Porlock w Stoke Pero from 93; RD Exmoor 97-03. *The Rectory, Parsons Street, Porlock, Minehead TA24 8QL* Tel (01643) 863172
E-mail barry.priory@virgin.net

PRISTON, David Leslie. b 28. Lon Bible Coll 49 Oak Hill Th Coll 66. **d** 66 **p** 67. C Heref St Pet w St Owen *Heref* 66-71; R Beeby *Leic* 72-88; R Gaddesby w S Croxton 72-88; R S Croxton Gp 88-93; rtd 93; Perm to Offic *S'well* from 93. *20 Central Avenue, Chilwell, Nottingham NG9 4DU* Tel 0115-922 7643

PRITCHARD, Antony Robin. b 53. Van Mildert Coll Dur BSc74 SS Paul & Mary Coll Cheltenham CertEd75. St Jo Coll Nottm DipTh82 DPS84. **d** 84 **p** 85. C Desborough *Pet* 84-87; C Rushden w Newton Bromswold 87-91; R Oulton St Mich *Nor* from 91. *The Rectory, Christmas Lane, Oulton, Lowestoft NR32 3JX* Tel (01502) 565722

PRITCHARD, Brian James. ACIS85. St Alb and Ox Min Course 99. **d** 01 **p** 02. NSM Newbury *Ox* from 01; Perm to Offic *St D* from 05. *The Chase, Garden Close Lane, Wash Common, Newbury RG14 6PP* Tel (01635) 42613 Fax 35976
E-mail brianjp@waitrose.com

PRITCHARD, Brian James Pallister. b 27. CCC Cam BA51 MA66. Westcott Ho Cam 51. **d** 53 **p** 54. C Attercliffe w Carbrook *Sheff* 53-58; V New Bentley 58-60; Chapl Park Hill Flats Sheff 60-67; P-in-c Sheff St Swithun *Sheff* 67-72; V Welton *Linc* 72-92; RD Lawres 86-92; rtd 92; Perm to Offic *Derby* from 92. *Bridgeways, Milford Lane, Bakewell DE45 1DX* Tel (01629) 813553

PRITCHARD, Mrs Carol Sandra. b 52. St Aid Coll Dur BA74 Bris Univ PGCE75 UEA 95. EAMTC DipHE99. **d** 99 **p** 00. NSM Oulton St Mich *Nor* from 99. *The Rectory, Christmas Lane, Oulton, Lowestoft NR32 3JX* Tel (01502) 565722

PRITCHARD, Colin Ivor. b 44. Lon Inst of Educn TCert65. Chich Th Coll 66. **d** 69 **p** 70. C Kettering St Mary *Pet* 69-72; Chapl Clayesmore Sch Blandford 72-74; Asst Chapl Ellesmere Coll 74-77; C Duston *Pet* 77-80; V Wellingborough St Andr 80-89; R Sedlescombe w Whatlington *Chich* 89-01; V Bexhill St Barn from 01. *St Barnabas' Vicarage, Cantelupe Road, Bexhill-on-Sea TN40 1JG* Tel (01424) 212036

PRITCHARD, Colin Wentworth. b 38. K Coll Lon 59 St Boniface Warminster 59. **d** 63 **p** 64. C Putney St Marg *S'wark* 63-67; C Brixton St Matt 67-70; C Milton *Portsm* 70-74; V Mitcham St Mark *S'wark* 74-82; R Long Ditton 82-94; V Earlsfield St Andr 94-03; RD Wandsworth 98-03; rtd 03. *38 Hartfield Road, Seaford BN25 4PW* Tel (01323) 894899
E-mail colin@loavesandfishes.f2s.com

PRITCHARD, Mrs Coral. b 37. F L Calder Coll Liv TCert58 Lanc Univ BA97. Carl and Blackb Dioc Tr Inst 99. **d** 02 **p** 03. OLM Stalmine w Pilling *Blackb* from 02. *Heyswood House, Head Dyke Lane, Pilling, Preston PR3 6SJ* Tel (01253) 790335
E-mail pritchard@heyswood.freeserve.co.uk

PRITCHARD, Canon David Paul. b 47. BA FRCO LTCL. Wycliffe Hall Ox 80. **d** 82 **p** 83. C Kidlington *Ox* 82-84; P-in-c Marcham w Garford 84-85; V 86-96; RD Abingdon 91-96; R Henley w Remenham 96-04; Can Res Ely Cathl *Ely* from 04. *The Precentor's House, 32 High Street, Ely CB7 4JU* Tel (01353) 660335 E-mail david.pritchard@cathedral.ely.anglican.org

PRITCHARD, Donald Oliver. b 22. Qu Coll Birm 73. **d** 75 **p** 76. Hon C Dunchurch *Cov* 75-83; P-in-c Mells w Buckland Dinham, Elm, Whatley etc *B & W* 83-84; R 84-88; rtd 88; Perm to Offic *Truro* from 88. *Moonrakers, Pengelly, Callington PL17 7DZ* Tel (01579) 84329

✠**PRITCHARD, The Rt Revd John Lawrence.** b 48. St Pet Coll Ox BA70 MA73 DipTh70 Dur Univ MLitt93. Ridley Hall Cam 70. **d** 72 **p** 73 **c** 02. C Birm St Martin *Birm* 72-76; Asst Dir RE *B & W* 76-80; Youth Chapl 76-80; P-in-c Wilton 80-88; Dir Past Studies Cranmer Hall Dur 89-93; Warden 93-96; Adn Cant and Can Res Cant Cathl *Cant* 96-02; Suff Bp Jarrow *Dur* from 02. *Bishop's House, Ivy Lane, Gateshead NE9 6QD* Tel 0191-491 0917 Fax 491 5116
E-mail bishop.of.jarrow@durham.anglican.org

PRITCHARD, Jonathan Llewelyn. b 64. Edin Univ MA87 Leeds Univ MA89 PhD99. Ripon Coll Cuddesdon 98. **d** 00 **p** 01. C Skipton H Trin *Bradf* 00-04; P-in-c Keighley All SS from 04. *All Saints' Vicarage, 21 View Road, Keighley BD20 6JN* Tel (01535) 665312 E-mail jonathan@japritchard.me.uk

PRITCHARD, Miss Kathryn Anne. b 60. St Cath Coll Ox MA Bradf Univ DIT. St Jo Coll Dur. **d** 87. Par Dn Addiscombe St Mary *S'wark* 87-90; CPAS Staff 90-92; Perm to Offic *Cov* 92-95; Producer Worship Progr BBC Relig Broadcasting 94-99; Publicity Manager Hodder & Stoughton Relig Books 99-01; Commissioning and Product Development Manager Ch Ho Publishing from 01. *Church House, Great Smith Street, London SW1P 3NZ* Tel (020) 7898 1485
E-mail kathryn.pritchard@c-of-e.org.uk

PRITCHARD, Kenneth John. b 30. Liv Univ BEng51. NW Ord Course 72. **d** 74 **p** 75. C Ches Team *Ches* 74-78; Miss to Seamen 78-84; V Runcorn St Jo Weston *Ches* 78-84; V Gt Meols 84-98; rtd 98; Perm to Offic *Ches* and *Liv* from 99. *13 Fieldlands, Scarisbrick, Southport PR8 5HQ* Tel (01704) 514600

PRITCHARD, Malcolm John. b 55. Bradf Univ BA85 CQSW85. St Jo Coll Nottm 86. **d** 88 **p** 89. C Peckham St Mary Magd *S'wark* 88-93; V Luton St Matt High Town *St Alb* from 93. *St Matthew's Vicarage, 85 Wenlock Street, Luton LU2 0NN* Tel (01582) 732320 E-mail b4mjp2c@ntlworld.com

PRITCHARD, Michael Owen. b 49. Trin Coll Carmarthen CertEd71. St Mich Coll Llan 71. **d** 73 **p** 74. C Conwy w Gyffin *Ban* 73-76; TV Dolgellau w Llanfachreth and Brithdir etc 76-78; Dioc Children's Officer 77-86; V Betws y Coed and Capel Curig 78-83; CF (TAVR) from 79; V Betws-y-Coed and Capel Curig w Penmachno etc *Ban* 83-86; Chapl Claybury Hosp Woodford Bridge 86-96; Chapl Team Leader Forest Healthcare NHS Trust Lon from 96. *Dept of Spiritual and Religious Care, Whipps Cross Hospital, Whipps Cross Road, London E11 1NR* Tel (020) 8539 5522 *or* 8989 3813 E-mail mopritchard@aol.com

PRITCHARD, Mrs Norma Kathleen. b 32. Birm Univ BA53 CertEd54. EMMTC 81. **dss** 84 **d** 87 **p** 94. Derby St Alkmund and St Werburgh *Derby* 84-90; Par Dn 87-90; Par Dn Derby St Andr w St Osmund 90-94; C 94-96; Assoc Min Alvaston 96-02; rtd 02; Perm to Offic *Derby* and *S'wark* from 02. *44 Evans Avenue, Allestree, Derby DE22 2EN* Tel (01332) 557702

PRITCHARD, Peter Benson. b 30. FPhS60 LCP68 Univ of Wales (Lamp) BA51 St Cath Coll Ox DipTh57 Lon Univ PGCE68 DipEd70 Liv Univ MEd74 PhD81. Ripon Hall Ox 55. **d** 58 **p** 59. C Wavertree H Trin *Liv* 58-60; C Sefton 60-61; C-in-c Thornton CD 61-64; Chapl Liv Coll Boys' Sch 64-70; Hon C Wavertree St Bridget 70-89; Lect CF Mott Coll of Educn 70-76; Sen Lect Liv Coll of HE 76-83; Liv Poly 83-87; Perm to Offic *Liv* 90-96 and *Ches* from 90; Chapl St Jo Hospice Wirral from 93; Tutor Open Univ 90-95; rtd 95. *68 Gleggside, West Kirby, Wirral CH48 6EA* Tel 0151-625 8093

PRITCHARD, Peter Humphrey. b 47. Univ of Wales (Ban) BA70 MA98 Liv Univ PGCE73. Qu Coll Birm 85. **d** 87 **p** 88. C Llanbeblig w Caernarfon and Betws Garmon etc *Ban* 87-90; R Llanberis w Llanrug 90-94; R Llanfaethlu w Llanfwrog and Llanrhuddlad etc 94-99; R Llanfair Mathafarn Eithaf w Llanbedrgoch 99-05; rtd 05. *4 Penlon Gardens, Bangor LL57 1AQ*

PRITCHARD, Simon Geraint. b 61. Coll of Ripon & York St Jo BA85 Ex Univ PGCE88. Cranmer Hall Dur 98. **d** 00 **p** 01. C Heysham *Blackb* 00-01; C Morecambe St Barn 01-03; C Standish from 03. *St Wilfrid's House, 7 Rectory Lane, Standish, Wigan WN6 0XA* Tel (01257) 425806

PRITCHARD, Thomas. b 14. Ch Ch Ox BA37 MA40. Westcott Ho Cam 37. **d** 38 **p** 39. C Rugby St Andr *Cov* 38-45; Mauritius 45-49; V Ipswich All Hallows *St E* 49-61; Hon Can St E Cathl 58-61; V Ex St Dav *Ex* 62-81; rtd 81; Perm to Offic *Ex* from 81. *3 Mill Cottages, Exton, Exeter EX3 0PH* Tel (01392) 873018

PRITCHARD, Thomas James Benbow. b 47. St Paul's Cheltenham CertEd69 Univ of Wales (Cardiff) BEd79 MSc85. SW Minl Tr Course 96. **d** 99 **p** 00. NSM St Enoder *Truro* 99-01; P-in-c Roche and Withiel 01-05; V Llangollen w Trevor and Llantysilio *St As* from 05. *The Vicarage, Abbey Road, Llangollen LL20 8SN* Tel (01978) 860231
E-mail tjb_pritchard@btopenworld.com

PRITCHARD, The Ven Thomas William. b 33. Keele Univ BA55 DipEd55 Univ of Wales (Cardiff) LLM94. St Mich Coll Llan 55. **d** 57 **p** 58. C Holywell *St As* 57-61; C Ruabon 61-63; V 77-87; R Pontfadog 63-71; R Llanferres, Nercwys and Eryrys 71-77; Dioc Archivist 76-98; Can St As Cathl 84-98; RD Llangollen 86-87; Adn Montgomery 87-98; V Berriew and Manafon 87-98; rtd 98. *4 Glynne Way, Hawarden, Deeside CH5 3NL* Tel (01244) 538381

PRITCHETT, Antony. b 63. Kent Univ BA86. Westcott Ho Cam 96. **d** 98 **p** 99. C Broughton Astley and Croft w Stoney Stanton *Leic* 98-02; V Gawber *Wakef* from 02; Chapl Barnsley Hospice from 02. *The Vicarage, Church Street, Gawber, Barnsley S75 2RL* Tel (01226) 207140 E-mail antony.pritchett@tinyworld.co.uk

PRITCHETT, Mrs Beryl Ivy. b 48. Worc Coll of Educn TCert69. WMMTC 02. **d** 05. NSM Brockmoor *Worc* from 05. *7 Muirville Close, Wordsley, Stourbridge DY8 5NR* Tel (01384) 271470 Mobile 07790-563479 E-mail beryl.pritchett@btinternet.com

PRITT, Stephen. b 06. AKC31. **d** 31 **p** 32. C Witton *Blackb* 31-34; C St Annes St Thos 34-37; PC Ennerdale *Carl* 37-40; V Amblecote *Worc* 40-45; V Wolverley 46-48; V Warrington H Trin *Liv* 48-55; V Thornham w Titchwell *Nor* 55-58; Clerical Org Sec CECS *Cant, Chich, Roch* and *Win* 58-60; R Helhoughton w Raynham *Nor* 60-80; rtd 80; Perm to Offic *Glouc* 80-93. *23 Addiscombe Road, Weston-super-Mare BS23 4LT* Tel (01934) 622795

PRIVETT, Peter John. b 48. Qu Coll Birm 75. **d** 78 **p** 79. C Moseley St Agnes *Birm* 78-81; V Kingsbury 81-87; P-in-c Dilwyn and Stretford *Heref* 87-90; Dioc Children's Adv 87-01; TV Leominster 90-98; NSM from 98; Dioc Millennium Officer 98-01. *165 Bargates, Leominster HR6 8QT* Tel (01568) 613176

PROBART, Raymond. b 21. Sarum Th Coll 49. **d** 51 **p** 52. C Padiham *Blackb* 51-54; C Burnley St Pet 54-56; V Heyhouses 56-60; V Douglas 60-88; rtd 88; Perm to Offic *B & W* 88-98; *Glouc* from 03. *6 Capel Court, The Burgage, Prestbury, Cheltenham GL52 3EL* Tel (01242) 235771

PROBERT, Beverley Stuart. b 42. Dioc OLM tr scheme. **d** 01 **p** 02. OLM Canford Magna *Sarum* from 01. *Blaenafon, 102 Knights Road, Bournemouth BH11 9SY* Tel (01202) 571731

PROBERT, Christopher John Dixon. b 54. Univ of Wales (Cardiff) DipTh77 DPS78 Univ of Wales (Ban) BTh95 MTh97. St Mich Coll Llan 74. **d** 78 **p** 79. C Aberdare St Fagan *Llan* 78-79; C Cadoxton-juxta-Barry 79-81; R Llanfynydd *St As* 81-84; V Gosberton Clough and Quadring *Linc* 84-86; TV Coventry Caludon *Cov* 86-88; V Llanrhian w Llanhywel and Llanrheithan *St D* 88-91; V Tregaron w Ystrad Meurig and Strata Florida 91-93; Chapl Tregaron Hosp 91-93; Tutor St D NSM Course 89-93; V Betws-y-Coed and Capel Curig w Penmachno etc *Ban* 93-98; Warden of Readers 96-98; V Lt Drayton *Lich* 98-04; P-in-c North Hill and Lewannick *Truro* from 04; P-in-c Lezant w Lawhitton and S Petherwin w Trewen from 04; OCF from 01. *The Rectory, North Hill, Launceston PL15 7PQ* Tel (01566) 786976 Mobile 07718-667177 E-mail chris@probert1.co.uk

PROBERT, Canon Edward Cleasby. b 58. St Cath Coll Cam BA80 MA84. Ripon Coll Cuddesdon BA84. **d** 85 **p** 86. C Esher *Guildf* 85-89; V Earlsfield St Andr *S'wark* 89-94; V Belmont 94-04; Can Res and Chan Sarum Cathl *Sarum* from 04. *24 The Close, Salisbury SP1 2EH* Tel (01722) 555193 E-mail eprobert@ukgateway.packardbell.org

PROBETS, Canon Desmond. b 26. AKC50. **d** 51 **p** 52. C Finsbury St Clem *Lon* 51-52; C Kenton 52-62; Sub Warden St Pet Th Coll Siota Solomon Is 62-64; Hd Master All Hallows Sch Pawa Ugi 64-69; Hon Can Honiara from 67; Dean 69-72; V Timperley *Ches* 72-92; RD Bowdon 77-87; Hon Can Ches Cathl 82-92; rtd 92; Perm to Offic *Wakef* from 92. *24 Shelley Close, Penistone, Sheffield S36 6GT* Tel (01226) 766402

PROCTER, Andrew David. b 52. St Jo Coll Ox BA74 MA BA86. Trin Coll Bris 74. **d** 77 **p** 78. C Barnoldswick w Bracewell *Bradf* 77-80; P-in-c Kelbrook 80-82; V 82-87; V Heaton St Barn 87-93; V Swanley St Paul *Roch* from 93. *The Vicarage, Rowhill Road, Swanley BR8 7RL* Tel (01322) 662320

PROCTER, Robert Hendy. b 31. Trin Hall Cam BA54 MA58. Edin Dioc NSM Course 88. **d** 93 **p** 94. NSM Edin Ch Ch *Edin* 93-94; TV from 94. *2 Braid Avenue, Edinburgh EH10 6DR* Tel 0131-447 1140 E-mail revhend@aol.com *or* hendy@6a.org.uk

PROCTOR, Kenneth Noel. b 33. St Aid Birkenhead 61. **d** 63 **p** 64. C Oldham St Paul *Man* 63-66; C Davyhulme St Mary 66-69; V Norden w Ashworth 69-00; rtd 00. *4 Bankscroft, Hopwood, Heywood OL10 2NG* Tel (01706) 364197

PROCTOR, Michael John. b 59. Cranmer Hall Dur 93. **d** 93 **p** 94. C Leatherhead *Guildf* 93-98; V Henlow and Langford *St Alb* 98-01; V Marton-in-Cleveland *York* from 01; Min Coulby Newham LEP from 03. *The Vicarage, Stokesley Road, Marton-in-Cleveland, Middlesbrough TS7 8JU* Tel (01642) 326305 E-mail mlm.proctor@virgin.net

PROCTOR, Michael Thomas. b 41. Ch Ch Ox BA65 MA67. Westcott Ho Cam 63. **d** 65 **p** 66. C Monkseaton St Mary *Newc* 65-69; Pakistan 69-72; C Willington *Newc* 72-77; TV Willington 77-79; Ed Sec Nat Soc 79-84; P-in-c Roxwell *Chelmsf* 79-84; Bp's Ecum Officer 85-00; Dir of Miss and Unity 85-94; P-in-c Gt Waltham w Ford End 94-00; Hon Can Chelmsf Cathl 85-00; rtd 00; Dir Chelmsf Counselling Foundn from 00. *Claremont, South Street, Great Waltham, Chelmsford CM3 1DP* E-mail mtproctor@lineone.net

PROCTOR, Canon Noel. b 30. MBE93. St Aid Birkenhead 62. **d** 64 **p** 65. C Haughton le Skerne *Dur* 64-67; R Byers Green 67-70; Chapl HM Pris Eastchurch 70-74; Chapl HM Pris Dartmoor 74-79; Chapl HM Pris Man 79-95; Hon Can Man Cathl *Man* 91-95; rtd 95; Perm to Offic *Man* from 95. *222 Moor Lane, Salford M7 3QH* Tel 0161-792 1284

PROCTOR, Canon Susan Katherine. b 44. **d** 89 **p** 94. Par Dn Beighton *Sheff* 89-91; Par Dn Aston cum Aughton and Ulley 91-93; Par Dn Aston cum Aughton w Swallownest, Todwick etc 93-94; TV 94-96; P-in-c Aston cum Aughton w Swallownest and Ulley 01-02; TR 02-05; R Dinnington 96-01; AD Laughton 98-03; Hon Can Sheff Cathl 98-05; rtd 05. *69 Ings Mill Avenue, Clayton West, Huddersfield HD8 9QG* Tel (01484) 866189 Mobile 07768-293588 E-mail sueproctor@lineone.net

PROFIT, David Hollingworth. b 17. Man Univ BA38. Cuddesdon Coll 40. **d** 41 **p** 42. C Kings Heath *Birm* 41-43; S Africa from 43. *Braehead House, 1 Braehead Road, Kenilworth, 7708 South Africa* Tel (0027) (21) 762 6041

PROPHET, Canon John Roy Henderson. b 10. Dur Univ LTh48 BA49. ALCD34. **d** 34 **p** 35. C Low Leyton *Chelmsf* 34-37; C Canvey Is 37-38; P-in-c Walthamstow St Andr 38-39; V 39-44; V Jesmond H Trin *Newc* 44-48; V Fenham St Jas and St Basil 48-61; V Blaby *Leic* 61-73; Hon Can Leic Cathl 70-80; R Church Langton w Thorpe Langton and Tur Langton 73-80; rtd 80; Perm to Offic *Leic* and *Pet* from 80. *24 Stuart Court, High Street, Kibworth, Leicester LE8 0LR* Tel 0116-279 6880

PROSSER, Gillian Margaret. b 40. Lon Inst of Educn TCert61. **d** 99. OLM Cwmbran *Mon* from 99. *25 Forest Close, Coed Eva, Cwmbran NP44 4TE* Tel (01633) 866716

PROSSER, Hugh. *See* PROSSER, Richard Hugh Keble

PROSSER, Jean. b 40. Open Univ BA84 Surrey Univ PhD94. **d** 02. OLM Grosmont and Skenfrith and Llangattock etc *Mon* from 01. *Yew Tree Farm, Llangattock Lingoed, Abergavenny NP7 8NS* Tel (01873) 821405 E-mail jean.prosser@talk21.com

PROSSER, Malcolm George. b 22. Univ of Wales (Lamp) BA44. St Mich Coll Llan 44. **d** 45 **p** 46. C Llantwit Fardre *Llan* 45-49; C Roath 49-58; V Trealaw 58-66; V High Littleton *B & W* 66-87; rtd 87. *141 Westway, Broadstone BH18 9LQ* Tel (01202) 694280

PROSSER, Canon Rhys. b 51. BA74 Bris Univ CertEd75 Southn Univ BTh83 Hull Univ MA93. Sarum & Wells Th Coll 77. **d** 80 **p** 81. C Wimbledon *S'wark* 80-83; C St Helier 83-88; TV Gt and Lt Coates w Bradley *Linc* 88-95; P-in-c Saxilby Gp 95-97; R from 97; RD Corringham from 01; Can and Preb Linc Cathl from 03. *The Rectory, 1 Westcroft Drive, Saxilby, Lincoln LN1 2PT* Tel (01522) 702427

PROSSER, Richard Hugh Keble. b 31. Trin Coll Cam BA53 MA57 Leeds Univ PGCE63. Cuddesdon Coll 55. **d** 57 **p** 58. C Wigan All SS *Liv* 57-60; CR 62-87; St Aug Miss Penhalonga Zimbabwe 64-90; R Pocklington and Owsthorpe and Kilnwick Percy etc *York* 90-00; rtd 00; Perm to Offic *Sarum* from 02. *26 Fleur de Lis, Middlemarsh Street, Poundbury, Dorchester DT1 3GX* Tel (01305) 260329

PROSSER, Stephanie. b 42. Linc Th Coll 94. **d** 96 **p** 99. NSM Linc St Nic w St Jo Newport *Linc* 96-99; NSM Saxilby Gp from 99. *The Rectory, 1 Westcroft Drive, Saxilby, Lincoln LN1 2PT* Tel (01522) 702427

PROTHERO, Brian Douglas. b 52. St Andr Univ MTh75 Dundee Univ CertEd77. Linc Th Coll 84. **d** 86 **p** 87. C Thornbury *Glouc* 86-89; V Goodrington *Ex* 89-04; R Weybridge *Guildf* from 04. *The Rectory, 3 Churchfields Avenue, Weybridge KT13 9YA* Tel (01932) 842566 Mobile 07715-364389 E-mail brian.prothero@eidosnet.co.uk

PROTHERO, David John. b 43. St Pet Coll Ox BA66 MA70. St Steph Ho Ox 68. **d** 70 **p** 71. C Kirkby *Liv* 70-72; C St Marychurch *Ex* 72-74; V Marldon 74-83; Chapl HM Pris Channings Wood 78-83; V Torquay St Martin Barton *Ex* 83-91; P-in-c Bath Bathwick *B & W* 91-93; R from 93. *Bathwick Rectory, Sham Castle Lane, Bath BA2 6JL* Tel (01225) 460052 E-mail david@djprothero.fsnet.co.uk

PROTHERO, John Martin. b 32. Oak Hill Th Coll 64. **d** 66 **p** 67. C Tipton St Martin *Lich* 66-69; C Wednesfield Heath 69-72; Distr Sec BFBS 72-85; Lic to Offic *S'well* 73-86; Hon C Gedling 73; V Willoughby-on-the-Wolds w Wysall and Widmerpool 86-97; rtd 98. *The Elms, Vicarage Hill, Aberaeron SA46 0DY* Tel (01545) 570568

PROTHEROE, Rhys Illtyd. b 50. St D Coll Lamp DipTh74. **d** 74 **p** 75. C Pen-bre *St D* 74-76; C Carmarthen St Dav 76-78; V Llanegwad 78-79; V Llanegwad w Llanfynydd 79-82; V Gors-las 82-95; RD Dyffryn Aman 94-95; V Llan-llwch w Llangain and Llangynog from 95. *The Vicarage, Llan-llwch, Carmarthen SA31 3RN* Tel (01267) 236805

PROTHEROE, Canon Robin Philip. b 33. St Chad's Coll Dur BA54 DipTh56 MA60 Nottm Univ MPhil75 Ox Univ DipEd62. **d** 57 **p** 58. C Roath *Llan* 57-60; Asst Chapl Culham Coll Abingdon 60-64; Sen Lect RS Trent (Nottm) Poly *S'well* 64-84; Perm to Offic 64-66; Lic to Offic 66-84; P-in-c Barton in Fabis 70-73; P-in-c Thrumpton 70-73; Dir of Educn *Bris* 84-98; Hon Can Bris Cathl 85-98; Selector for ACCM 88-91; ABM from 91; Bp's Insp of Th Colls from 88; Perm to Offic from 98. *29 Barley Croft, Bristol BS9 3TG* Tel 0117-968 3245 Fax 968 4826 E-mail robinprotheroe@aol.com

PROUD, Andrew John. b 54. K Coll Lon BD79 AKC79. Linc Th Coll 79. **d** 80 **p** 81. C Stansted Mountfitchet *Chelmsf* 80-83; TV Borehamwood *St Alb* 83-90; C Bp's Hatfield 90-92; R E Barnet 92-01; Chapl Adis Ababa St Matt Ethiopia from 02. *PO Box 109, Adis Ababa, Ethiopia* Tel (00251) (1) 112623 Fax 551907 E-mail smac@telecom.net.et

PROUD, David John. b 56. Leeds Univ BA77 Dur Univ CertEd78. Ridley Hall Cam 85. **d** 88 **p** 89. C Lindfield *Chich* 88-91; TV Horsham 91-97; V Ware Ch Ch *St Alb* from 97; RD Hertford and Ware 04-05; Chapl E Herts NHS Trust 97-00; Chapl E and N Herts NHS Trust from 00. *The Vicarage, 15 Hanbury Close, Ware SG12 7BZ* Tel and fax (01920) 463165 E-mail davidproudccware@aol.com

PROUDLEY, Sister Anne. b 38. Edin Univ BSc60. St Alb and Ox Min Course 97. **d** 00 **p** 01. CSJB from 00; NSM Blackbird Leys *Ox* 00-04; Lic to Offic from 04; Chapl to the Homeless from 05. *The Priory, 2 Springhill Road, Begbroke, Kidlington OX5 1RX* Tel (01865) 855331 E-mail annecsjb@csjb.org.uk

PROUDLOVE, Lee Jason. b 70. Lon Bible Coll BA94 Bris Univ MA01. Trin Coll Bris 00. **d** 01 **p** 02. C Morden *S'wark* 01-04; Miss Partner CMS from 04. *CMS, Partnership House, 157 Waterloo Road, London SE1 8UU* Tel (020) 7928 8681 Mobile 07941-896235 E-mail lproudlove@hotmail.com

PROUDMAN, Canon Colin Leslie John. b 34. K Coll Lon BD60 MTh63. Wells Th Coll 60. **d** 61 **p** 62. C Radlett *St Alb* 61-64; Canada from 64; Hon Can Toronto from 86; Dean Div Toronto Div Coll 90-92; rtd 97. *#1802, 77 Maitland Place, Toronto ON, Canada, M4Y 2V6* Tel (001) (416) 923 4235

PROUSE, Ms Carole Maureen. b 45. N Ord Course. **dss** 86 **d** 87 **p** 95. NSM Coalville and Bardon Hill *Leic* 87-90; Perm to Offic 90-95; NSM Thorpe Acre w Dishley 95-96; P-in-c Packington w Normanton-le-Heath 96-01; Chapl HM Pris Low Newton 01-04; Asst Chapl from 04. *HM Prison Low Newton, Finchale Avenue, Brasside, Durham DH1 5YA* Tel 0191-386 1141

PROUT, Hubert Douglas. b 18. St D Coll Lamp BA38. **d** 41 **p** 42. C Low Leyton *Chelmsf* 41-44; CF 44-47; C Wanstead St Mary *Chelmsf* 47-50; Perm to Offic *Llan* 52-56; C Wirksworth w Carsington *Derby* 56-58; C Idridgehay 56-58; V Kirk Hallam 58-84; rtd 84; Perm to Offic *Llan* from 85. *9 Caldy Close, Porthcawl CF36 3QL* Tel (01656) 786479

PROUT, Mrs Joan. b 42. Gipsy Hill Coll of Educn TCert63. LNSM course 95. **d** 97 **p** 98. OLM Whitton *Sarum* from 97. *22 Ermin Close, Baydon, Marlborough SN8 2JQ* Tel (01672) 540465 E-mail joan.prout@genie.co.uk

PROVOST, Ian Keith. b 47. CA Tr Coll IDC73 Ridley Hall Cam CTM93. **d** 93 **p** 94. C Verwood *Sarum* 93-97; P-in-c Redlynch and Morgan's Vale 97-02; TV Plymstock and Hooe *Ex* from 02. *The Vicarage, 9 St John's Drive, Hooe, Plymouth PL9 9SD* Tel (01752) 403076 E-mail ian@provost.free-online.co.uk

PROWSE, Mrs Barbara Bridgette Christmas. b 41. R Holloway Coll Lon BA62. **d** 91 **p** 94. C Kingsthorpe w Northampton St Dav *Pet* 91-97; V Northampton St Jas 97-02; rtd 02; Perm to Offic *Truro* from 02. *36 Carn Basavern, St Just, Penzance TR19 7QX* Tel (01736) 787994 E-mail bbc@prowseb.freeserve.co.uk

PRUDOM, William Haigh. b 26. STh79 APhS81 Hull Univ MPhil88. St D Coll Lamp 60. **d** 62 **p** 63. C Aylesford *Roch* 62-63; C Margate St Jo *Cant* 63-66; V Long Preston *Bradf* 66-73; C Darlington St Cuth *Dur* 73-75; V Ticehurst *Chich* 75-79; P-in-c Flimwell 78-79; V Ticehurst and Flimwell 79-81; R Spennithorne w Finghall and Hauxwell *Ripon* 81-91; rtd 91; Perm to Offic *Ripon* from 91. *9 Sydall's Way, Catterick Village, Richmond DL10 7ND* Tel (01748) 818604

PRUEN, Canon Edward Binney. b 56. K Coll Lon BD77 AKC77. St Jo Coll Nottm DPS79. **d** 79 **p** 80. C Kidderminster St Mary *Worc* 79-82; C Woking St Jo *Guildf* 82-84; Chapl Asst R Marsden Hosp Lon and Surrey 84-86; C Stapleford *S'well* 86-88; Min Winklebury CD *Win* 88; V Winklebury 88-93; Chapl Ld Mayor Treloar Coll Alton from 93; Hon Can Win Cathl *Win* from 05. *2 St Joseph's Cottage, Upper Froyle, Alton GU34 4JY* Tel (01420) 23893 *or* 526400 Fax 526426 E-mail ed.pruen@treloar.org.uk

PRUEN, Hugh Barrington. b 18. AKC50. **d** 50 **p** 51. C Westmr St Steph w St Jo *Lon* 50-53; R Didmarton w Oldbury-on-the-Hill and Sopworth *Glouc* 53-56; V Ches St Jo *Ches* 56-64; R Skegness *Linc* 64-71; V Heckington w Howell 71-79; R Ashley w Weston by Welland and Sutton Bassett *Pet* 79-83; rtd 83; Perm to Offic *Linc* 83-00. *Ashleigh, Church Road, Old Bolingbroke, Spilsby PE23 4HF* Tel (01790) 763504

PRYCE, Donald Keith. b 36. Man Univ BSc. Linc Th Coll 69. **d** 71 **p** 72. C Heywood St Jas *Man* 71-74; P-in-c 74-75; V 75-86; R Ladybarn from 86; Chapl S Man Coll from 87; Chapl Christie Hosp NHS Trust Man from 93. *St Chad's Rectory, 1 St Chad's Road, Withington, Manchester M20 9WH* Tel 0161-445 1185

PRYCE, Robin Mark. b 60. Sussex Univ BA82 Cam Univ MA94. Westcott Ho Cam 84 United Th Coll Bangalore 85. **d** 87 **p** 88. C W Bromwich All SS *Lich* 87-90; Chapl Sandwell Distr Gen Hosp 90; Fell and Chapl CCC Cam 90-02; Tutor 92-02; Dean of Chpl 96-02; V Smethwick *Birm* from 02. *Old Church Vicarage, 93A Church Road, Smethwick, Warley B67 6EE* Tel 0121-558 1763 Fax as telephone E-mail markpryce@btopenworld.com

PRYCE, William Robert. b 28. MBE91. **d** 79 **p** 80. NSM Leverstock Green *St Alb* 79-80; Perm to Offic *Sheff* 80-84; NSM Sheff St Barn and St Mary 84-90; NSM Alveley and Quatt *Heref* 91-93; Perm to Offic from 93. *5 Wren Way, Bicester OX26 6UJ*

PRYKE, Jonathan Justin Speaight. b 59. Trin Coll Cam BA80 MA85. Trin Coll Bris BD85. **d** 85 **p** 86. C Corby St Columba *Pet* 85-88; C Jesmond Clayton Memorial *Newc* from 88. *15 Lily Avenue, Newcastle upon Tyne NE2 2SQ* Tel 0191-281 9854

PRYOR, Derek John. b 29. Lon Univ DipTh57 BD63 Birm Univ MEd74. Linc Th Coll 79 Chich Th Coll 79. **d** 80 **p** 81. Hon C Youlgreave *Derby* 80-82; Hon C Stanton-in-Peak 80-82; Hon C Ingham w Cammeringham w Fillingham *Linc* 82-87 and 92-99; Chapl Bp Grosseteste Coll Linc 83-84; Dioc Schs Officer *Linc* 87-92; rtd 92. *Walnut Cottage, Chapel Lane, Fillingham, Gainsborough DN21 5BP* Tel (01427) 668276 Fax 667956 E-mail john.pryor@btinternet.com

PRYOR, William Lister Archibald. b 39. Trin Coll Cam BA67 MA69 DipEd68. Ox NSM Course 72. **d** 75 **p** 90. NSM Summertown *Ox* 75-76; NSM Wolvercote w Summertown from 76; Perm to Offic *Nor* 93-04. *23 Harbord Road, Oxford OX2 8LH* Tel and fax (01865) 515102

PRYS, Deiniol. b 53. Univ of Wales (Ban) DipTh82 BTh91 Univ of Wales (Cardiff) DPS83. St Mich Coll Llan 82. **d** 83 **p** 84. C Llanbeblig w Caernarfon and Betws Garmon etc *Ban* 83-86; TV Amlwch 86-88; V Llanerch-y-medd 89-92; R Llansadwrn w Llanddona and Llaniestyn etc from 92. *The Rectory, Llansadwrn, Porthaethwy LL59 5SL* Tel (01248) 810534 Mobile 07740-541316

PRYSE, Hugh Henry David. b 58. St Chad's Coll Dur BA81 SS Coll Cam PGCE82 K Coll Lon MA96. St Steph Ho Ox 94. **d** 96 **p** 97. C Branksome St Aldhelm *Sarum* 96-00; TV Hove *Chich* 00-05; R Ex St Jas *Ex* from 05. *The Rectory, 45 Thornton Hill, Exeter EX4 4NR* Tel (01392) 431297 *or* 420407

PRYSOR-JONES, John Glynne. b 47. Heythrop Coll Lon MA94 Liv Univ CQSW73 Birm Univ DPS80. Westcott Ho Cam 88. **d** 90 **p** 91. C Mitcham St Mark *S'wark* 90-93; V Dudley St Fran *Worc* 93-99; R Woodchurch *Ches* 99-01; Hd Past Care Services Chorley and S Ribble NHS Trust and Preston Acute Hosps NHS Trust 01-02; Hd Past Care Services Lanc Teaching Hosps NHS Trust from 02. *Royal Preston Hospital, Sharoe Green Lane, Fulwood, Preston PR2 9HT* Tel (01772) 522350 *or* 700797 Fax 522447 E-mail john.prysor-jones@lthtr.nhs.uk

PRYTHERCH, David. b 30. Down Coll Cam BA54 MA58 Lon Univ CertEd68 DipAdEd71. Coll of Resurr Mirfield 54. **d** 56 **p** 57. C Blackpool St Steph *Blackb* 56-61; R Matson *Glouc* 61-65; Chapl St Elphin's Sch Matlock 65-85; V Thornton-le-Fylde *Blackb* 85-94; RD Poulton 91-94; rtd 94; Perm to Offic *Ches* from 96. *8A Dunraven Road, West Kirby, Wirral CH48 4DS*

PRZYWALA, Karl Andrzej. b 63. Univ Coll Dur BA85 Chas Sturt Univ NSW BTh04. St Mark's Nat Th Cen Canberra 01. **d** 04. C Houghton le Spring *Dur* 04-05; C Chester le Street from 05. *4 Hilda Terrace, Chester le Street DH2 2JE* Tel 0191-389 4388 E-mail karl_sydney@yahoo.co.uk

PUCKRIN, Christopher. b 47. Oak Hill Th Coll. **d** 82 **p** 83. C Heworth H Trin *York* 82-84; C Sherburn in Elmet 84-85; P-in-c Kirk Fenton 85-86; P-in-c Kirkby Wharfe 85-86; V Kirk Fenton w Kirkby Wharfe and Ulleskelfe 86-87; C York St Mich-le-Belfrey 87-94; P-in-c Barnstaple *Ex* 94-97; TV 97-00; V Woodside *Ripon* from 00. *St James's Vicarage, 1 Scotland Close, Horsforth, Leeds LS18 5SG* Tel 0113-258 2433

PUDDEFOOT, John Charles. b 52. St Pet Coll Ox BA74 Edin Univ BD78. Edin Th Coll 76. **d** 78 **p** 79. C Darlington H Trin *Dur* 78-81; Ind Chapl *Chich* 81-84; Asst Master Eton Coll 84-93; Hd Mathematics from 93; Lic to Offic *Ox* from 85. *Eton College, Windsor SL4 6DB* Tel (01753) 671320 E-mail j.puddefoot@etoncollege.org.uk

PUDGE, Mark Samuel. b 67. K Coll Lon BD90 AKC90 Heythrop Coll Lon MA99. Ripon Coll Cuddesdon 91. **d** 93 **p** 94. C Thorpe Bay *Chelmsf* 93-96; TV Wickford and Runwell 97-00; Management Consultant Citizens' Advice Bureau from 00; Hon C Paddington St Jo w St Mich *Lon* from 03. *Flat 2, 12 Connaught Street, London W2 2AF*

PUDNEY, Malcolm Lloyd. b 48. SEITE 99. **d** 01 **p** 02. NSM S Nutfield w Outwood *S'wark* from 01. *The Rookery, Broadbridge Lane, Smallfield, Horley RH6 9RF* Tel (01342) 842463 Mobile 07860-464836 E-mail yendup@xalt.co.uk

PUERTO RICO, Bishop of. *See* ALVAREZ-VELAZQUEZ, The Rt Revd David Andres

PUGH, Brian. *See* PUGH, William Bryan

PUGH, Harry. b 48. K Coll Lon BD70 AKC71 Lanc Univ MA89. **d** 72 **p** 73. C Milnrow *Man* 72-75; P-in-c Rochdale Gd Shep 75-78; TV Rochdale 78-79; Perm to Offic *Liv* 79-82; C Darwen St Cuth *Blackb* 82-85; C Darwen St Cuth w Tockholes St Steph 85-86; V Burnley St Steph 86-93; R Hoole 93-01; P-in-c Porthleven w Sithney *Truro* from 01. *The Vicarage, Pendeen Road, Porthleven, Helston TR13 9AL* Tel (01326) 562419

PUGH, Ronald Keith. b 32. Jes Coll Ox BA54 MA57 DPhil57. Ripon Hall Ox 56. **d** 59 **p** 60. C Bournemouth St Mich *Win* 59-61; Asst Chapl Bryanston Sch 61-66; Chapl Cranleigh Sch Surrey 66-68; Lic to Offic *Win* from 68; Lect K Alfred Coll Winchester 68-97; rtd 97; Sec and Treas Win and Portsm Dioc Clerical Registry from 97. *Church House, 9 The Close, Winchester SO23 9LS* Tel (01962) 844644 *or* 857249 Fax 877316 E-mail clerical.registry@ukgateway.net

PUGH, Stephen Gregory. Southn Univ BEd77. Linc Th Coll 85. **d** 87 **p** 88. C Harpenden St Nic *St Alb* 87-90; C Stevenage All SS Pin Green 90-93; V Stotfold and Radwell 93-00; V Gt Ilford St Marg and St Clem *Chelmsf* from 00. *The Vicarage, 70 Brisbane Road, Ilford IG1 4SL* Tel (020) 8554 7542 Mobile 07905-370410 E-mail stephenpugh@waitrose.com

PUGH, Miss Wendy Kathleen. b 48. Newnham Coll Cam BA69 MA75. Trin Coll Bris 93. **d** 95 **p** 96. C Hailsham *Chich* 95-99; C Frimley *Guildf* from 99. *4 Warren Rise, Frimley, Camberley GU16 8SH* Tel (01276) 66740 E-mail wkpugh@aol.com

PUGH, William Bryan (Brian). b 34. Ridley Hall Cam 59. **d** 61 **p** 62. C Oseney Crescent St Luke w Camden Square St Paul *Lon* 61-64; C N Wembley St Cuth 64-67; CF 67-88; QHC 85-88; Chapl Heathfield Sch Ascot 88-95; rtd 99; Perm to Offic *Ox* and *Guildf* from 99. *3 College Close, Camberley GU15 4JU* Tel (01276) 503702 E-mail w.pugh@ntlworld.com

PUGMIRE, Canon Alan. b 37. Lon Univ DipTh63. Tyndale Hall Bris 61. **d** 64 **p** 65. C Islington St Steph w St Bart and St Matt *Lon* 64-66; C St Helens St Mark *Liv* 66-71; R Stretford St Bride *Man* 71-82; R Burnage St Marg 82-02; AD Heaton 88-98; Hon Can Man Cathl 98-02; rtd 02; Perm to Offic *Man* from 02. *20 Shortland Crescent, Manchester M19 1SZ* Tel 0161-431 3476 Fax as telephone E-mail alan@apugmire.freeserve.co.uk

PUGSLEY, Anthony John. b 39. ACIB. Oak Hill Th Coll 89. **d** 90 **p** 91. C Chadwell *Chelmsf* 90-94; P-in-c Gt Warley Ch Ch 94-01; V Warley Ch Ch and Gt Warley St Mary 01-04; rtd 04. *3 Southcliffe Court, Southview Drive, Walton on the Naze CO14 8EP* Tel (01255) 850967 E-mail revtony@aol.com

PULESTON, Mervyn Pedley. b 35. K Coll Lon BD60 AKC60. **d** 61 **p** 62. C Gt Marlow *Ox* 61-65; P Missr Blackbird Leys CD 65-70; V Kidlington 70-85; R Hampton Poyle 70-85; TR Kidlington w Hampton Poyle 85-86; Chapl Geneva *Eur* 86-92; TV Dorchester *Ox* 92-00; rtd 00. *55 Benmead Road, Kidlington OX5 2DB* Tel (01865) 372360 E-mail mpuleston@aol.com

PULFORD, Christopher. b 59. Pemb Coll Ox BA81 MA87. Trin Coll Bris 82. **d** 84 **p** 85. C Parr *Liv* 84-87; Chapl Berkhamsted Colleg Sch Herts 87-92; Development Dir React from 92. *c/o React, St Luke's House, 270 Sandycombe Road, Kew, Richmond TW9 3NA* Tel (020) 8940 2575 Fax 8940 2050

PULFORD, John Shirley Walter. b 31. Jes Coll Cam BA55 MA59. Cuddesdon Coll 55. **d** 57 **p** 58. C Blackpool St Steph *Blackb* 57-60; N Rhodesia 60-63; V Newington St Paul *S'wark* 63-68; C Seacroft *Ripon* 68-70; Chapl HM Pris Liv 70-72; Chapl HM Pris Linc 72-73; Student Cllr Linc Colls of Art and Tech 73-79; Cam Univ Counselling Service 79-96; Dir 82-96; rtd 96. *59 Cromer Road, North Walsham NR28 0HB* Tel (01692) 404320

PULFORD, Canon Stephen Ian. b 25. Clifton Th Coll 53. **d** 56 **p** 57. C Heref St Jas *Heref* 56-58; R Coberley w Cowley *Glouc* 58-94; P-in-c Colesborne 75-94; Hon Can Glouc Cathl 84-94; RD Cirencester 88-89; rtd 94; Perm to Offic *Glouc* from 94. *16 Bafford Grove, Charlton Kings, Cheltenham GL53 9JE* Tel (01242) 524261

PULLAN, Ben John. b 43. Univ of Wales (Cardiff) MSc(Econ)83. Bris Minl Tr Scheme 74. **d** 77 **p** 78. NSM Westbury-on-Trym St Alb *Bris* 77-91; NSM Henleaze 91-03; NSM Bishopston and St Andrews from 05. *14 Linden Grange, Claremont Avenue, Bristol BS7 8JB* Tel 0117-944 4946 E-mail ben@bpullan.wanadoo.co.uk

PULLAN, Lionel Stephen. b 37. Keble Coll Ox BA58 MA62 ARCO58 FIST77 SSC. Cuddesdon Coll 58. **d** 60 **p** 61. C Tranmere St Paul *Ches* 60-63; C Higher Bebington 63-64; Perm to Offic 64-70; Hon C Luton St Chris Round Green *St Alb* 70-72; Hon C Hitchin H Sav 72-73; Hon C Welwyn 73-75; Hon C Welwyn w Ayot St Peter 75-78; Hon C Kimpton w Ayot St Lawrence 78-82; Hon C Stevenage St Andr and St Geo 82-85; Deputation Appeals Org CECS 85-90; V Sundon *St Alb* 90-03; rtd 03; Perm to Offic *St Alb* from 03. *139 Turnpike Drive, Luton LU3 3RB* Tel and fax (01582) 573236 E-mail wingchaplain@bedscambswgatc.org

PULLEN, James Stephen. b 43. Lon Univ BSc64 PGCE65 Linacre Coll Ox BA68. St Steph Ho Ox 66. **d** 68 **p** 69. C Chorlton-cum-Hardy St Clem *Man* 68-71; C Doncaster St Leon and St Jude *Sheff* 72-73; Chapl St Olave's and St Sav Schs Orpington 73-75; Chapl Haileybury Coll 75-01; Second Master 99-01; V St Ives *Ely* from 01. *The Vicarage, Westwood Road, St Ives PE27 6DH* Tel (01480) 463254 E-mail james.pullen@ely.anglican.org

PULLEN, Paul Anthony. b 58. Trin Coll Bris 96. **d** 98 **p** 99. C Helston and Wendron *Truro* 98-01; P-in-c Carbis Bay w Lelant from 01. *The Vicarage, Porthrepta Road, Carbis Bay, St Ives TR26 2LD* Tel (01736) 796206 E-mail paul.pullen@btopenworld.com

PULLEN, Roger Christopher. b 43. Lon Univ BSc65 PGCE90. Wells Th Coll 65. **d** 67 **p** 68. C S w N Hayling *Portsm* 67-69; C Farlington 69-73; V Farington *Blackb* 73-80; V Chorley All SS 80-83; V Kingsley *Ches* 83-92; R Cilcain and Nannerch and Rhydymwyn *St As* 92-99; Dioc MU Admin *Guildf* 99-02; Hon C Bramley and Grafham 99-00; Perm to Offic 00-02. *Ewhurst, 6 Chichester Way, Selsey, Chichester PO20 0PJ* Tel (01243) 601684 Mobile 07989-732729 E-mail roger_pullen@lineone.net

PULLEN, Timothy John. b 61. BNC Ox BA84. Cranmer Hall Dur 93. **d** 96 **p** 97. C Allesley *Cov* 96-00; V Wolston and Church Lawford from 00. *The Vicarage, Brook Street, Wolston, Coventry CV8 3HD* Tel (024) 7654 0778 *or* 7654 2722 E-mail tim.pullen@lineone.net

PULLIN, Andrew Eric. b 47. Kelham Th Coll 67 Linc Th Coll 71. **d** 73 **p** 74. C Pershore w Wick *Worc* 73-75; C Pershore w Pinvin, Wick and Birlingham 75-77; TV Droitwich 77-80; V Woburn Sands *St Alb* 80-85; Perm to Offic *B & W* 85-87. *85 Weymouth Road, Frome BA11 1HJ* Tel (01373) 472170

PULLIN, Christopher. b 56. St Chad's Coll Dur BA77 Heythrop Coll Lon MA04. Ripon Coll Cuddesdon 78 Ch Div Sch of Pacific 79. **d** 80 **p** 81. C Tooting All SS *S'wark* 80-85; V New Eltham All SS 85-92; V St Jo in Bedwardine *Worc* from 92; RD Martley and Worc W from 03. *St John's Vicarage, 143 Malvern Road, Worcester WR2 4LN* Tel (01905) 422327 *or* 420490 Fax 425569 E-mail vicar@stjohninbedwardine.co.uk

PULLIN, Peter Stanley. b 29. MA MSc CEng. Trin Coll Bris 87. **d** 88 **p** 89. NSM Rugby St Andr *Cov* 88-90; NSM Aylesbeare, Rockbeare, Farringdon etc *Ex* 90-98; Perm to Offic 99-04. *25 Ashley Road, Bathford, Bath BA1 7TT* Tel (01225) 852050

PULLIN, Stephen James. b 66. S Bank Univ BEng89 Open Univ MBA98. Trin Coll Bris BA04. **d** 04 **p** 05. C Soundwell *Bris* from 04. *33 Syston Way, Kingswood, Bristol BS15 1UE* Tel 0117-961 1890 Mobile 07866-700881 E-mail stephenjpullin@aol.com

PULLINGER, Mrs Catherine Ann. b 54. York Univ BA76. Oak Hill Th Coll DipHE93. **d** 93 **p** 97. NSM Luton St Paul *St Alb* 93-99; NSM Luton Lewsey St Hugh from 99. *52 Wheatfield Road, Luton LU4 0TR* Tel (01582) 606996 Fax 472726 E-mail cathy@pullinger.net

PULLINGER, Ian Austin. b 61. Oak Hill Th Coll. **d** 96 **p** 97. C Weston *Win* 96-00; TV The Ortons, Alwalton and Chesterton *Ely* from 00. *32 Fraserburgh Way, Orton Southgate, Peterborough PE2 6SS* Tel (01733) 394185 E-mail ianpullinger@bigfoot.com

PULLINGER, Peter Mark. b 53. Heythrop Coll Lon MA97. Ridley Hall Cam 01. **d** 03 **p** 04. C Clapham Park St Steph *S'wark* from 03. *6 Blenheim Gardens, London SW2 5ET* Tel 07796-956774 (mobile) E-mail mark@pullinger.net

PULMAN, Edgar James. b 17. Selw Coll Cam BA48 MA53. ALCD50. **d** 50 **p** 51. C Lee Gd Shep *S'wark* 50-52; C Stoke sub Hamdon *B & W* 52-53; V 53-58; C Norton sub Hamdon 52-53; R 53-58; Singapore 58-62; V Finchley H Trin *Lon* 63-76; C Norton sub Hamdon, W Chinnock, Chiselborough etc *B & W* 77-78; Perm to Offic 79-01; rtd 82. *The Orangery, The Manor House, Norton-sub-Hamdon, Stoke-sub-Hamdon TA14 6SJ* Tel (01935) 881521

PULMAN, John. b 34. Nottm Univ Cert Th & Past Studies 81. EMMTC 78. **d** 81 **p** 82. NSM Mansfield SS Pet and Paul *S'well* 81-83; C Mansfield Woodhouse 83-86; V Flintham 86-99; R Car Colston w Screveton 86-99; Chapl HM YOI Whatton 87-90; Chapl HM Pris Whatton 90-99; rtd 99; Perm to Offic *S'well* from 99 and *Derby* from 00. *101 Ling Forest Road, Mansfield NG18 3NQ* Tel (01623) 474707

PUMPHREY, Norman John Albert. b 21. Nor Ord Course 76. **d** 77 **p** 78. NSM Aylsham *Nor* 77-94; Chapl St Mich Hosp Aylsham 88-99; Perm to Offic *Nor* from 94. *12 Buxton Road, Aylsham, Norwich NR11 6JD* Tel (01263) 733207

PUNSHON, George Wilson. b 30. Bris Univ BSc Michigan State Univ MSc DipEd. Ripon Hall Ox 71 DipTh. **d** 73 **p** 74. C Knighton St Mary Magd *Leic* 73-76; V Donisthorpe and Moira w Stretton-en-le-Field 76-82; R Gt Bowden w Welham, Glooston and Cranoe 82-86; Zimbabwe 87-89 and 00-04; Perm to Offic *Pet* 96-00; V Ascension Is 97-98; Chapl Peterho Sch Marondera 00-04. *101 The Downs, Nottingham NG11 7EA*

PUNSHON, Canon Keith. b 48. JP. Jes Coll Cam BA69 MA73 Birm Univ DipTh73 MA77. Qu Coll Birm 71. **d** 73 **p** 74. C Yardley St Edburgha *Birm* 73-76; Chapl Eton Coll 76-79; V Hill *Birm* 79-86; CF (TA) from 79; V S Yardley St Mich *Birm* 86-96; Can Res Ripon Cathl *Ripon* from 96. *St Peter's House, Minster Close, Ripon HG4 1QP* Tel (01765) 604108 E-mail postmaster@riponcathedral.org.uk

PURCHAS, Canon Catherine Patience Ann. b 39. St Mary's Coll Dur BA61. St Alb Minl Tr Scheme 77. **dss** 80 **d** 87 **p** 94. RE Resource Cen 80-81; Relig Broadcasting Chiltern Radio 81-87; Wheathampstead *St Alb* 81-00; Hon Par Dn 87-94; Hon C 94-00; Relig Broadcasting Beds Radio from 88; Bp's Officer for Women from 93; Bp's Officer for NSMs and Asst Dir of Ords 93-00; Assoc Dioc Dir of Ords 00-03; Hon Can St Alb 96-00; rtd

03. *14 Horn Hill, Whitwell, Hitchin SG4 8AS* Tel and fax (01438) 871668 E-mail patience@purchas.fsworld.co.uk

PURCHAS, Canon Thomas. b 35. Qu Coll Birm 59. **d** 62 **p** 63. C Bp's Hatfield *St Alb* 62-71; R Blunham 71-78; P-in-c Tempsford w Lt Barford 71-78; R Blunham w Tempsford and Lt Barford 78-80; R Wheathampstead 80-00; RD Wheathampstead 92-99; Hon Can St Alb 99-00; rtd 00; RD Hitchin 00-02; Perm to Offic *St Alb* from 00. *14 Horn Hill, Whitwell, Hitchin SG4 8AS* Tel and fax (01438) 871668

PURDY, Canon John David. b 44. Leeds Univ BA65 DipTh74 MPhil76. Coll of Resurr Mirfield 72. **d** 75 **p** 76. C Marske in Cleveland *York* 75-78; C Marton-in-Cleveland 78-80; V Newby 80-87; V Kirkleatham 87-95; V Kirkbymoorside w Gillamoor, Farndale etc from 95; Can and Preb York Minster from 98; RD Helmsley from 99. *The Vicarage, Kirkbymoorside, York YO62 6AZ* Tel (01751) 431452

PURSER, Alan Gordon. b 51. Leic Univ BSc73. Wycliffe Hall Ox 74. **d** 77 **p** 78. C Beckenham Ch Ch *Roch* 77-81; TV Barking St Marg w St Patr *Chelmsf* 81-84; R Kensington S Africa 84-88; Min Hadley Wood St Paul Prop Chpl *Lon* 88-03; UK Team Ldr Crosslinks from 03. *18 Salmon Lane, London E14 7LZ* Tel (020) 7702 8741 Mobile 07802-888439 E-mail apurser@crosslinks.org

PURVEY-TYRER, Neil. b 66. Leeds Univ BA87 MA88. Westcott Ho Cam 88. **d** 90 **p** 91. C Denbigh and Nantglyn *St As* 90-92; Chapl Asst Basingstoke Distr Hosp 92-95; TV Cannock *Lich* 95-99; V Northampton H Sepulchre w St Andr and St Lawr *Pet* 99-02; Dioc Co-ord for Soc Resp from 99; TR Duston Team from 02. *The Rectory, 22 Berrywood Drive, Northampton NN5 6GB* Tel (01604) 752591 E-mail ntyrer@waitrose.com

PURVIS, Canon Colin. b 19. Kelham Th Coll 37. **d** 44 **p** 45. C Hebburn St Cuth *Dur* 44-47; C Sunderland 47-50; C Darlington St Cuth 50-53; C-in-C Humbledon St Mary V CD 53-58; C-in-c Bishopwearmouth St Mary V w St Pet CD 58-62; V Heworth St Mary 62-76; RD Gateshead 69-76; R Egglescliffe 76-84; Hon Can Dur Cathl 83-92; rtd 84. *4 Duke's Drive, Newcastle upon Tyne NE3 5NT* Tel 0191-236 6394

PURVIS, Lynn. b 58. St Jo Coll Dur BA97. Cranmer Hall Dur 94. **d** 98 **p** 99. C Gt Aycliffe *Dur* 98-02; Chapl N Tees and Hartlepool NHS Trust from 02. *University Hospital of North Tees, Hardwick Road, Stockton-on-Tees TS19 8PE* Tel (01642) 624714 E-mail lpurvis@nth.nhs.uk

PURVIS, Ms Sandra Anne. b 56. Univ Coll Ches BTh01. N Ord Course 98. **d** 01 **p** 02. C Blackpool St Jo *Blackb* from 01. *52 Leeds Road, Blackpool FY1 4HJ* Tel (01253) 624036 Mobile 07967-136992 E-mail sandraapurvis@aol.com

PURVIS, Canon Stephen. b 48. AKC70. **d** 71 **p** 72. C Peterlee *Dur* 71-75; Dioc Recruitment Officer 75-79; V Stevenage All SS Pin Green *St Alb* 79-88; TR Borehamwood 88-00; RD Aldenham 94-98; V Leagrave from 00; Hon Can St Alb from 02. *St Luke's Vicarage, High Street, Leagrave, Luton LU4 9JY* Tel and fax (01582) 572737 E-mail stephenpurvis@lycos.co.uk

PUSEY, Ian John. b 39. Sarum Th Coll 69. **d** 71 **p** 72. C Waltham Abbey *Chelmsf* 71-75; TV Stantonbury *Ox* 75-80; P-in-c Bletchley 80-84; R 84-00; RD Milton Keynes 96-00; P-in-c Lamp from 00; AD Newport from 04. *The Rectory, High Street, Haversham, Milton Keynes MK19 7DT* Tel and fax (01908) 312136 E-mail ian.pusey@virginnet.co.uk

PUTNAM, Mrs Gillian. b 43. WEMTC 00. **d** 02 **p** 03. NSM Milton *B & W* from 02. *6 Miller Close, Weston-super-Mare BS23 2SQ* Tel (01934) 416917 E-mail gillianputnam@yahoo.co.uk

✠**PWAISIHO, The Rt Revd William Alaha.** b 48. Bp Patteson Th Coll (Solomon Is) 71. **d** 74 **p** 75 **c** 81. Solomon Is 74-76; New Zealand 78-79; Solomon Is 79-95; Dean Honiara 80-81; Bp Malaita 81-89; Asst Bp Ches from 97; C Sale St Anne 97-99; R Gawsworth from 99. *The Rectory, Church Lane, Gawsworth, Macclesfield SK11 9RJ* Tel (01260) 223201 Mobile 07711-241625 E-mail bishop.gawsworth@virgin.net

PYATT, Noel Watson. b 34. AKC57. **d** 58 **p** 59. C Prenton *Ches* 58-61; C Cheadle Hulme All SS 61-63; P-in-c Hattersley 63-66; V 66-70; V Ches St Paul 70-99; rtd 99; Perm to Offic *Sheff* 99-02. *273 School Road, Sheffield S10 1GQ* Tel 0114-266 9944

PYBURN, Canon Alan. b 29. G&C Coll Cam BA51 MA55. Westcott Ho Cam 53. **d** 55 **p** 56. C Barnard Castle *Dur* 55-57; Chapl G&C Coll Cam 57-60; V Dallington *Pet* 60-72; V Ox St Giles *Ox* 72-79; P-in-c Remenham 79-94; R Henley 79-94; RD Henley 84-94; Hon Can Ch Ch 90-95; R Henley w Remenham 94-95; rtd 95. *Pippin Cottage, Well Hill, Finstock, Chipping Norton OX7 3BU* Tel (01993) 868651

PYBUS, Antony Frederick. b 54. Birm Univ BA77. St Jo Coll Dur 78. **d** 81 **p** 82. C Ches H Trin *Ches* 81-84; C W Hampstead St Jas *Lon* 84-89; V Alexandra Park St Andr 89-93; V Alexandra Park from 93. *The Vicarage, 34 Alexandra Park Road, London N10 2AB* Tel (020) 8883 3181 *or* 8444 6898 E-mail office@alexandrapark.org *or* vicar@alexandrapark.org

PYE, Alexander Frederick. b 61. St Mich Coll Llan Dip Practical Th 95. **d** 95 **p** 96. C Griffithstown *Mon* 95-97; P-in-c Bistre *St As* 97-99; P-in-c Penmaen and Crumlin *Mon* 99-00; V 00-02; R Govilon w Llanfoist w Llanelen from 02. *The Rectory, Merthyr Road, Govilon, Abergavenny NP7 9PT* Tel (01873) 832703

PYE, Canon Allan Stephen. b 56. Univ of Wales (Lamp) BA78 Lanc Univ MA85 MPhil87. Westcott Ho Cam 79. **d** 81 **p** 82. C Scotforth *Blackb* 81-85; C Oswaldtwistle All SS 85-87; V Wrightington 87-91; Chapl Wrightington Hosp 87-91; P-in-c Hayton St Mary *Carl* 91-93; V Hayton w Cumwhitton 93-98; RD Brampton 96-98; Hon Can Carl Cathl from 97; P-in-c Hawkshead and Low Wray w Sawrey 98-03; V Hawkshead and Low Wray w Sawrey and Rusland etc from 03. *The Vicarage, Vicarage Lane, Hawkshead, Ambleside LA22 0PD* Tel (01539) 436301 E-mail stephen.pye@virgin.net

PYE, Gay Elizabeth. b 46. RN67 RM68. BD73. **d** 96 **p** 96. NSM Castle Church *Lich* 96-00; Chapl HM Pris Shrewsbury 97-00; Perm to Offic *Lich* from 00; *Carl, Ches* and *Derby* from 01. *Castle Church Vicarage, 18 Castle Bank, Stafford ST16 1DJ* Tel and fax (01785) 600943 *or* tel 223673 E-mail gay.pye@bfbs.org.uk

PYE, James Timothy. b 58. Oak Hill Th Coll BA90. **d** 90 **p** 91. C Normanton *Derby* 90-94; R Talke *Lich* 94-04; R Knebworth *St Alb* from 04. *The Rectory, 15 St Martin's Road, Knebworth SG3 6ER* Tel (01438) 224102 E-mail jimpye@fish.co.uk

PYE, Joseph Terence Hardwidge. b 41. MRICS64. Trin Coll Bris 70. **d** 73 **p** 74. C Blackb Ch Ch *Blackb* 73-76; OMF 77-90; Korea 77-90; V Castle Church *Lich* from 90. *Castle Church Vicarage, 18 Castle Bank, Stafford ST16 1DJ* Tel (01785) 223673

PYE, Michael Francis. b 53. New Coll Ox BA75 MA78 DPhil78. STETS 97. **d** 00 **p** 01. C Fareham H Trin *Portsm* from 00. *12 Greenwood Close, Fareham PO16 7UF* Tel (01329) 280380 E-mail mike@pye229.freeserve.co.uk

PYE, Nicholas Richard. b 62. Univ Coll Lon BA84 Man Univ PGCE87 Anglia Poly Univ MA03. Ridley Hall Cam CTM98. **d** 98 **p** 99. C Epsom Common Ch Ch *Guildf* 98-01; C Harrow Trin St Mich *Lon* 01-03; V Finchley St Paul and St Luke from 03. *St Paul's Vicarage, 50 Long Lane, London N3 2PU* Tel (020) 8346 8729 E-mail revpye@xalt.co.uk

PYE, Sandra Anne. *See* ELLISON, Ms Sandra Anne

PYE, Stephen. *See* PYE, Canon Allan Stephen

PYKE, Alan. b 37. Trin Coll Bris BA87. **d** 87 **p** 88. CA 58-87; C Ipswich St Mary at Stoke w St Pet *St E* 87-90; R Creeting St Mary, Creeting St Peter etc 90-98; C S Trin Broads *Nor* 98-02; rtd 03; Perm to Offic *Nor* from 03. *20 Bell Meadow, Martham, Great Yarmouth NR29 4UA* Tel (01493) 740048 E-mail alanpyke@scs-datacom.co.uk

PYKE, Barry John. b 62. Qu Mary Coll Lon BSc84 Southn Univ BTh94 Open Univ BA96 FGS84. Sarum & Wells Th Coll 91. **d** 94 **p** 95. C Bengeworth *Worc* 94-96; C Worc City St Paul and Old St Martin etc 96-99; R Chipping Ongar w Shelley *Chelmsf* from 99; RD Ongar from 04. *The Rectory, Shackletons, Ongar CM5 9AT* Tel (01277) 362173 E-mail bpyke@care4free.net

PYKE, Richard Ernest. b 50. Sarum & Wells Th Coll. **d** 82 **p** 83. C Bushey *St Alb* 82-85; C Gt Berkhamsted 85-89; V St Alb St Mary Marshalswick 89-00; TR Bp's Hatfield from 00; RD Welwyn Hatfield from 03. *The Rectory, 1 Fore Street, Hatfield AL9 5AN* Tel and fax (01707) 262072 E-mail richard.pyke@btopenworld.com

PYKE, Mrs Ruth Cheryl. b 56. Bath Coll of HE BA78 W Lon Inst of HE PGCE80. St Alb and Ox Min Course 95. **d** 98 **p** 99. C Leavesden All SS *St Alb* 98-02; C St Alb St Steph from 02. *The Rectory, 1 Fore Street, Hatfield AL9 5AN* Tel and fax (01707) 262072 *or* (01727) 730746 E-mail ruth.pyke@tesco.net

PYKE, Thomas Fortune. b 62. St Chad's Coll Dur BA85 Fitzw Coll Cam BA88. Ridley Hall Cam 86. **d** 89 **p** 90. C Hitchin *St Alb* 89-94; Chapl Aston Univ *Birm* 94-99; V Birm St Paul from 99; Th Ecum Officer Birm Bd for Miss from 01. *71 Wellington Road, Birmingham B15 2ET* Tel and fax 0121-440 3407 Mobile 07753-616499 E-mail tom.pyke@virgin.net

PYLE, John Alan. b 31. Qu Coll Birm. **d** 69 **p** 70. C Fenham St Jas and St Basil *Newc* 69-72; C Monkseaton St Pet 72-74; C Morpeth 74-78; R Bothal 78-83; TV Willington 83-91; R Chollerton w Birtley and Thockrington 91-97; rtd 97; Perm to Offic *Newc* from 97. *37 Ullswater Drive, Killingworth, Newcastle upon Tyne NE12 6GX* Tel 0191-268 6044

PYM, David Pitfield. b 45. Nottm Univ BA65 Ex Coll Ox DPhil68. Ripon Hall Ox 66. **d** 68 **p** 69. C Nottingham St Mary *S'well* 68-72; Chapl RN 72-76 and 79-84; Chapl Worksop Coll Notts 76-79; R Avon Dassett w Farnborough and Fenny Compton *Cov* from 84. *The Rectory, Avon Dassett, Southam CV47 2AS* Tel (01295) 690305

PYM, Francis Victor. b 24. ARIBA52 DipArch52. St Jo Coll Dur 74. **d** 76 **p** 77. C Keighley *Bradf* 76-79; Chapl Bethany Fellowship 79-87; Lic to Offic *Chich* from 87; Dir Joshua Chr Trust from 88; Research Asst Ho of Lords from 89; Dir Gp Apologetics Initiative from 92. *Bolney House, Bolney, Haywards Heath RH17 5QR* Tel (01444) 881877

PYM, Gordon Sydney. b 19. Worc Ord Coll 59. **d** 61 **p** 62. C Highweek *Ex* 61-63; C Plymouth Em 63-66; V Kilnhurst *Sheff* 66-69; V Owston 69-72; V Hensall 72-75; rtd 75; Perm to Offic *Sheff* from 75. *6 Greno Road, Swinton, Mexborough S64 8RP* Tel (01709) 586884

PYNE, Robert Leslie. b 51. Lanchester Poly BA72 Solicitor 75 Leeds Univ DipTh78 Portsm Univ Dip Criminal Justice Studies 98. Coll of Resurr Mirfield 76. **d** 79 **p** 80. C Clifton All SS w St Jo *Bris* 79-81; Bp's Dom Chapl *Ox* 81-84; TV High Wycombe 84-90; Chapl RN from 90. *Royal Naval Chaplaincy Service, Room 203, Victory Building, HM Naval Base, Portsmouth PO1 3LS* Tel (023) 9272 7903 Fax 9272 7111

PYNN, Catherine. b 45. Reading Univ BSc67. St Alb and Ox Min Course 93. **d** 96 **p** 97. NSM Caversham St Pet and Mapledurham etc *Ox* 96-00; Chapl Bradfield Coll Berks from 00; NSM Aldermaston w Wasing and Brimpton *Ox* from 05; NSM Woolhampton w Midgham and Beenham Valance from 05. *Park Corner, 27 Silchester Road, Pamber Heath, Tadley RG26 3ED* Tel 0118-970 1646 Mobile 07717-726410

✠**PYTCHES, The Rt Revd George Edward David.** b 31. Bris Univ BA54 Nottm Univ MPhil84. Tyndale Hall Bris 51. **d** 55 **p** 56 **c** 70. C Ox St Ebbe *Ox* 55-58; C Wallington H Trin *S'wark* 58-59; Chile 59-77; Suff Bp Valparaiso 70-72; Bp Chile, Bolivia and Peru 72-77; V Chorleywood St Andr *St Alb* 77-96; rtd 96; Perm to Offic *St Alb* from 96. *Red Tiles, Homefield Road, Chorleywood, Rickmansworth WD3 5QJ* Tel (01923) 283763 Fax 283762

PYTCHES, Preb Peter Norman Lambert. b 32. Univ Coll Lon 52 Lon Univ BD57 Bris Univ MLitt67 Southn Univ PhD81 K Coll Lon MA00 Potchefstroom Univ MTh03 Lambeth STh74. Tyndale Hall Bris 53. **d** 57 **p** 58. C Heatherlands St Jo *Sarum* 57-61; C Cromer *Nor* 61-63; V Plymouth St Jude *Ex* 63-71; V Heatherlands St Jo *Sarum* 71-76; Dir Past Tr Oak Hill Th Coll 76-81; V Finchley Ch Ch *Lon* 81-91; AD Cen Barnet 86-91; V Forty Hill Jes Ch 91-97; Preb St Paul's Cathl 92-97; rtd 97; Perm to Offic *Lon* from 98. *25 Weardale Gardens, Enfield EN2 0BA* Tel and fax (020) 8366 5126

Q

QUANCE, John David. b 42. Kelham Th Coll 61. **d** 67 **p** 68. C Southgate Ch Ch *Lon* 67-70; C Norbury St Phil *Cant* 70-73; Asst Chapl Middx Hosp Lon 73-80; R Failsworth St Jo *Man* 80-95; Australia 84-85; P-in-c Healey *Man* 95-04; V Islamabad Pakistan 00-01. *4 Elm Grove, Rochdale OL11 3RZ* Tel (01706) 343473 Mobile 07876-742189

QUARMBY, David John. b 43. St Jo Coll Dur BA64 Lon Univ CertEd70 Man Univ MEd89 Sheff Univ MA99. Ridley Hall Cam 65. **d** 67 **p** 68. C Bournville *Birm* 67-71; V Erdington St Chad 71-73; Lic to Offic *Blackb* 73-83; Perm to Offic *Man* 83-90 and from 98; C Oldham St Paul 90-98; Hon C from 98; Cllr Huddersfield Poly 90-92; Huddersfield Univ 92-01. *30 College Avenue, Oldham OL8 4DS* Tel 0161-626 2771 E-mail davidquarmby@dqnet.freeserve.co.uk

QUARRELL, John Beck. b 39. Hull Coll of Educn CertEd59. Chich Th Coll 67. **d** 70 **p** 71. C Horbury *Wakef* 70-71; C Sowerby 71-73; V Brotherton 74-80; Chapl Pontefract Gen Hosp 78-80; V Staincliffe *Wakef* 80-88; Chapl Staincliffe Hosp 82-88; R Farndon w Thorpe, Hawton and Cotham *S'well* from 89. *The Rectory, 3 Marsh Lane, Farndon, Newark NG24 3SS* Tel (01636) 705048

QUARTON, Robert Edward. b 43. EMMTC 84. **d** 87 **p** 88. C Gresley *Derby* 87-88; C Clay Cross 88-90; C N Wingfield, Clay Cross and Pilsley 90-91; R Darley from 91; P-in-c S Darley, Elton and Winster from 03; RD Wirksworth from 03. *The Rectory, 15 Hall Rise, Darley Dale, Matlock DE4 2HD* Tel (01629) 734257 E-mail robertquarton@clara.co.uk

QUASH, Canon Jonathan Ben. b 68. Peterho Cam BA90 MA94 PhD99. Westcott Ho Cam 91. **d** 95 **p** 96. NSM Cambridge St Mary Less *Ely* 95-96; Asst Chapl Peterho Cam 95-96; Chapl Fitzw Coll Cam 96-99; Fell 98-99; Tutor Wesley Ho Cam 96-99; Fell and Dean Peterho Cam from 99; Can Th Cov Cathl *Cov* from 04. *Peterhouse, Cambridge CB2 1RD* Tel (01223) 338217 E-mail jbq1000@cam.ac.uk

✠**QUASHIE, The Rt Revd Kobina Adduah.** b 34. ACIS60 Univ of Ghana LLB71 LLM74 DipTh80. **d** 78 **p** 78 **c** 92. Ghana 78-80 and 92-02; Chapl Middx Hosp Lon 80; Funding Officer USPG 80-92; Hon Can Kumasi from 86; Hon Can Koforidua from 86; Hon Can Accra from 87; Bp Cape Coast 92-02; rtd 02. *32 Chandos Road, London NW2 4LU* Tel (020) 8452 5721

QUAYLE, Margaret Grace. b 28. Gipsy Hill Coll of Educn TCert48 Lon Univ BA53 Liv Univ MPhil78. LNSM course 95. **d** 98 **p** 99. OLM Gt Crosby St Luke *Liv* 98-03; Perm to Offic from 03. *Clwyd, 9 Myers Road West, Liverpool L23 0RS* Tel 0151-924 1659

QUENNELL, Brian Michael. b 19. **d** 74 **p** 75. C Oakham w Hambleton and Egleton *Pet* 74-78; V Denford w Ringstead 78-87; Perm to Offic 87-99; rtd 87. *9 The Hollies, St Christopher's Home, Abington Park Crescent, Northampton NN3 3AD* Tel (01604) 232729

QUIBELL, Edward Villiers. b 71. Anglia Poly BSc93 Hughes Hall Cam PGCE94. Trin Coll Bris BA03. **d** 03 **p** 04. C Swindon Ch Ch *Bris* from 03. *58 Upham Road, Swindon SN3 1DN* Tel (01793) 521296 Mobile 07771-854980 E-mail ed@equibell.fsnet.co.uk

QUIBELL, Mrs Susan Elizabeth. b 50. **d** 03 **p** 04. OLM Aldridge *Lich* from 03. *23 Highfield Way, Walsall WS9 8XF* Tel (01922) 456083 E-mail sue.quibell@virgin.net

QUICK, John Michael. b 46. N Counties Coll Newc TCert68 Birkbeck Coll Lon BSc73 FRGS70. St Alb and Ox Min Course 97. **d** 00 **p** 01. OLM New Windsor *Ox* from 00. *White Roses, 45 York Road, Windsor SL4 3PA* Tel (01753) 865557 Mobile 07977-754822 E-mail littlefrquick@aol.com

QUICK, Roger Aelfred Melvin Tricquet. b 55. Leeds Univ BA79 PGCE81. Coll of Resurr Mirfield BA94. **d** 96 **p** 97. C Chapel Allerton *Ripon* 96-00; C Ireland Wood 00-03; Hon C 03-04; Chapl Strathallan Sch from 04. *Jacaranda, Strathallan School, Forgandenny, Perth PH2 9EN* Tel (01738) 813509 E-mail father@priest.com

QUIGLEY, Adam. **d** 03 **p** 04. NSM Castlerock w Dunboe and Fermoyle *D & R* from 03. *41 Queens Park, Coleraine BT51 3JS* Tel (028) 7035 5191

QUIGLEY, Andrew. b 72. New Coll Ox BA96 Bris Univ PGCE98. St Jo Coll Nottm MTh03. **d** 04 **p** 05. C Burbage w Aston Flamville *Leic* from 04. *46 Salisbury Road, Hinckley LE10 2AR* Tel (01455) 617464 E-mail a.quigley@ntlworld.com

QUIGLEY, Donna Maree. Ulster Univ BEd BTh. **d** 01 **p** 02. C Portadown St Columba *Arm* 01-03; I Derryvolgie *Conn* from 04. *The Rectory, 35 Kirkwoods Park, Lisburn BT28 3RR* Tel (028) 9260 7370 E-mail donna_quigley@yahoo.co.uk

QUIGLEY, John Christopher. b 41. Pontifical Lateran Univ STL68. **d** 67 **p** 68. P-in-c N Bersted *Chich* from 03. *330 Chichester Road, Bognor Regis PO21 5AU* Tel (01243) 823800 Mobile 07792-718875 E-mail john.quigley4@btinternet.com

QUIGLEY, William. b 46. Ulster Univ BA86. CITC BTh98. **d** 98 **p** 99. C Ballymoney w Finvoy and Rasharkin *Conn* 98-01; I Eglish w Killylea *Arm* from 01. *154 Killylea Road, Armagh BT60 4LN* Tel and fax (028) 3756 8320

QUILL, John Stephen. b 51. Nottm Univ DipTh78. Linc Th Coll 76. **d** 79 **p** 80. C Sawbridgeworth *St Alb* 79-81; C Watford Ch Ch 81-85; Dioc Soc Services Adv *Worc* 85-90; Adv to Bd of Soc Resp 90-95. *Address temp unknown*

QUILL, Canon Walter Paterson. b 35. **d** 60 **p** 61. C Glendermott *D & R* 60-63; I Kilbarron 63-66; I Kilcronaghan w Ballynascreen 66-81; I Derg w Termonamongan from 81; Can Derry Cathl from 89; Preb Howth St Patr Cathl Dublin from 94. *13 Strabane Road, Castledreg BT81 7HZ* Tel (028) 8167 1362 E-mail walter.quill@talk21.com

QUILLIAM, Miss Anne Eleanor Scott. b 31. Bedf Coll Lon BA54 CertEd55. Dalton Ho Bris 59. **d** 87. Par Dn Toxteth St Philemon w St Gabr and St Cleopas *Liv* 87-92; rtd 92; Perm to Offic *S & M* from 92. *13 Raad ny Gabbil, Castletown, Isle of Man IM9 1HH* Tel (01624) 822375

QUIN, David Christopher. b 42. St Alb and Ox Min Course 97. **d** 00 **p** 01. NSM Blunham, Gt Barford, Roxton and Tempsford etc *St Alb* from 00. *The Rectory, Park Lane, Blunham, Bedford MK44 3NJ* Tel and fax (01767) 640690 Mobile 07867-664924 E-mail davidcquin@aol.com

QUIN, Eric Arthur. b 22. Magd Coll Cam BA46 MA48 Lon Univ BD56. Bps' Coll Cheshunt 46. **d** 48 **p** 49. C Luton St Andr *St Alb* 48-50; C Barnoldswick w Bracewell *Bradf* 50-52; PC Bradf St Sav 52-57; P-in-c Gt w Lt Wymondley *St Alb* 57-58; P-in-c St Ippolyts 57-58; V 58-70; RD Hitchin 68-70; V Haynes 70-87; rtd 87; Perm to Offic *Ches* from 87. *Annabel's Cottage, The Lydiate, Wirral CH60 8PR* Tel 0151-342 8650

QUIN, John James Neil. b 31. Ox Univ MA DipEd53. Qu Coll Birm 61. **d** 63 **p** 64. C Cannock *Lich* 63-68; V Sneyd Green 68-78; V Stafford St Paul Forebridge 78-90; TV Tettenhall Regis 90-98; rtd 98; Perm to Offic *Ex* from 00. *Watcombe House, 28 Barnpark Road, Teignmouth TQ14 8PN* Tel (01626) 772525

QUINE, Christopher Andrew. b 38. St Aid Birkenhead 61. **d** 64 **p** 65. C Hunts Cross *Liv* 64-67; C Farnworth and C-in-c Widnes St Jo 67-71; V Clubmoor 71-78; V Formby H Trin 78-99; V Arbory and Santan *S & M* 99-03; rtd 03. *17 Fieldlands, Southport PR8 5HQ* Tel (01704) 540569

QUINE, David Anthony. b 28. Qu Coll Cam BA52 MA59. Ridley Hall Cam 53. **d** 55 **p** 56. C Beckenham Ch Ch *Roch* 55-59; C Normanton *Derby* 59-60; V Low Elswick *Newc* 60-66; V Houghton *Carl* 66-68; Lic to Offic *York* 68-71; Chapl Monkton Combe Sch Bath 71-85; rtd 85; Perm to Offic *Carl* from 85. *Briar Cragg, Gale Rigg, Ambleside LA22 0AZ* Tel (01539) 433563

QUINE, Canon Ernest Kendrick Leigh. b 21. St Jo Coll Dur BA50 MA55 DipTh51 Nottm Univ DPhil68. **d** 51 **p** 52. C

Grassendale *Liv* 51-52; C Shrewsbury St Alkmund *Lich* 52-54; C-in-c Park Estate St Chris CD *Leic* 54-61; V Belgrave St Pet 61-93; Hon Can Leic Cathl 67-93; rtd 93; Perm to Offic *Leic* from 93. *63 Somerset Drive, Glenfield, Leicester LE3 8QW* Tel 0116-232 1994

✠**QUINLAN, The Rt Revd Alan Geoffrey.** b 33. Kelham Th Coll 54. **d** 58 **p** 59 **c** 88. C Bedford Leigh *Man* 58-61; S Africa from 61; Suff Bp Cape Town (Cen Region) 88-98; rtd 98. *132 Woodley Road, Plumstead, Cape Town, 7800 South Africa*

QUINN, Canon Arthur Hamilton Riddel. b 37. TCD BA60 MA64 BD67. **d** 61 **p** 62. C Belfast H Trin *Conn* 61-63; C Belfast St Mary Magd 63-64; Chapl Hull Univ *York* 64-69; Chapl Keele Univ *Lich* 69-74; P-in-c Keele 72-74; V Shirley St Jo *Cant* 74-84; V Shirley St Jo *S'wark* from 85; RD Croydon Addington from 95; Hon Can S'wark Cathl from 03. *The Vicarage, 49 Shirley Church Road, Croydon CR0 5EF* Tel (020) 8654 1013 Fax 8656 4568 E-mail stjohn@shirleychurchrd.freeserve.co.uk

QUINN, Cecil Hugh. b 24. Oak Hill Th Coll 74. **d** 76 **p** 77. C Bedford St Jo and St Leon *St Alb* 76-79; Deputation Sec Irish Ch Miss 79-89; I Rathmullan w Tyrella *D & D* 80-96; rtd 96. *Riverside Court, 9/1 Warriston Road, Edinburgh EH7 4HJ* Tel 0131-557 6438

QUINN, Derek John. b 55. TCD BTh88. **d** 88 **p** 89. C Mossley *Conn* 88-91; I Cappagh w Lislimnaghan *D & R* from 91; Bp's Dom Chapl from 00; Dioc Warden of Readers from 04. *Erganagh Rectory, 1 Erganagh Road, Omagh BT79 7SX* Tel (028) 8224 2572

QUINN, Eugene Frederick. b 35. Allegheny Coll (USA) AB57 Univ of California MA66 MA69 PhD70. Vancouver Sch of Th DipTh74. **d** 74 **p** 75. C Washington St Columba USA 74-75 and 78-81; Chapl Prague *Eur* 75-78; C Chevy Chase All SS USA 81-82 and 86-90; Chapl Nat Cathl Washington 81-82 and from 95; C Washington Epiphany 83 and 86-88; V Bowie St Jas 83-84; Chapl Warsaw 93-95. *5702 Kirkside Drive, Chevy Chase, MD 20815-7116, USA* E-mail efquinn@msn.com

QUINN, George Bruce. b 23. MBE05. **d** 82 **p** 83. NSM Douglas St Ninian *S & M* from 82. *85 Port-e-Chee Avenue, Douglas IM2 5EZ* Tel (01624) 674080

QUINN, John James. b 46. TCD BA70 PhD76. St Jo Coll Nottm. **d** 81 **p** 82. C Gorleston St Andr *Nor* 81-84; R Belton 84-90; R Burgh Castle 84-90; R Belton and Burgh Castle from 90. *The Rectory, Beccles Road, Belton, Great Yarmouth NR31 9JQ* Tel (01493) 780210

QUINN, Kenneth Norman. b 40. QUB BSc62 CEng MICE. CITC 80. **d** 85 **p** 86. NSM Seapatrick *D & D* 85-91; Lic to Offic from 91. *4 Knollwood, Seapatrick, Banbridge BT32 4PE* Tel (028) 4062 3515 E-mail ken.quinn@nireland.com

QUINN, Marjorie. d 94 **p** 97. NSM Hawarden *St As* 94-05; Lic to Offic from 05. *21 Hawarden Way, Mancot, Deeside CH5 2EL* Tel (01244) 531639

QUINNELL, Peter Francis. b 48. St Steph Ho Ox DipMin95. **d** 95 **p** 96. C Tewkesbury w Walton Cardiff *Glouc* 95-99; R Stratton, N Cerney, Baunton and Bagendon from 99. *The Rectory, 94 Gloucester Road, Cirencester GL7 2LJ* Tel (01285) 653359 E-mail quinnell.rectory@amserve.net

QUINT, Mrs Patricia Mary. b 51. Milton Keynes Coll of Ed CertEd76 Open Univ BA77 Lon Univ MA99. St Alb Minl Tr Scheme 90. **d** 93 **p** 94. C Hertford St Andr *St Alb* 93-96; C Bromham w Oakley and Stagsden 96-00; V Stotfold and Radwell from 00. *The Vicarage, 61 Church Road, Stotfold, Hitchin SG5 4NE* Tel and fax (01462) 730218 E-mail revquint@ntlworld.com

QUIREY, Mrs Edith. b 56. CITC 98. **d** 01 **p** 02. C Belfast St Mich *Conn* from 01. *696 Crumlin Road, Belfast BT14 8AD* Tel (028) 9029 9057

R

✠**RABENIRINA, The Most Revd Remi Joseph.** b 38. Antananarivo Univ LèsL83. St Paul's Coll Ambatoharanana 61 St Chad's Coll Dur 64 Bossey Ecum Inst Geneva. **d** 67 **p** 68 **c** 84. Dn Toamasina St Jas Madagascar 67; R St Matt Pro-Cathl Antsiranana 68-73; R Ambohimangakely St Jo 73-84; Angl Chapl Antananarivo Univ 73-84; Bp Antananarivo from 84; Abp Indian Ocean from 95. *Evêché Anglican, Lot VK 57 Ter Ambohimanoro, 101 Antananarivo, Madagascar* Tel (00261) (20) 222 0827 Mobile 3311-20827 Fax (00261) (20) 226 1331 E-mail eemdanta@dts.mg

RABIN, Peter David. b 62. Southlands Coll Lon BA86. Aston Tr Scheme 88 Ripon Coll Cuddesdon BTh93. **d** 93 **p** 94. C Hornsey St Mary w St Geo *Lon* 93-97; V Cricklewood St Pet from 97. *St Peter's Vicarage, 5 Farm Avenue, London NW2 2EG* Tel (020) 8450 9043 Fax 8208 4146 E-mail frrabin@dsl.pipex.com

RABJOHNS, Alan. b 40. Leeds Univ BA62. Coll of Resurr Mirfield 62. **d** 64 **p** 65. C Ashington *Newc* 64-67; C Upton cum Chalvey *Ox* 67-76; V Roath St Sav *Llan* from 76; AD Cardiff from 03. *St Saviour's Vicarage, 115 Splott Road, Cardiff CF24 2BY* Tel (029) 2046 1203

RABLEN, Antony Ford. b 52. St Jo Coll Nottm. **d** 82 **p** 83. C Clifton *York* 82-85; TV Marfleet 85-92; P-in-c Welton w Melton 92-00; TR Sutton St Jas and Wawne 00-05. *St Andrew's Vicarage, Malvern Avenue, Harrow HA2 9ER* Tel (020) 8422 3633

RABLEN, Mrs Christine Mary. b 52. Trevelyan Coll Dur BA74 Hull Univ BA92 Leeds Univ MA94. N Ord Course 00. **d** 02 **p** 03. C Sutton St Mich *York* 02-05; V Roxbourne St Andr *Lon* from 05. *St Andrew's Vicarage, Malvern Avenue, Harrow HA2 9ER* Tel (020) 8422 3633 E-mail christine@rablen4394.fsnet

RABY, Malcolm Ernest. b 47. St Jo Coll York BEd73. N Ord Course 81. **d** 84 **p** 85. NSM Chadkirk *Ches* 84-88; Consultant E England CPAS 88-94; C Ely 94-96; TV Ely 96-98; P-in-c Over from 98; Dioc Adv in Miss and Evang from 98; P-in-c Long Stanton w St Mich from 02. *The Vicarage, Horseware, Over, Cambridge CB4 5NX* Tel and fax (01954) 230329 E-mail mission@ely.anglican.org

RACE, Alan. b 51. Bradf Univ BTech73 Birm Univ MA82. Ripon Coll Cuddesdon 73. **d** 76 **p** 77. C Tupsley *Heref* 76-79; Asst Chapl Kent Univ *Cant* 79-84; Dir Studies S'wark Ord Course 84-94; R Aylestone St Andr w St Jas *Leic* from 94. *The Rectory, Old Church Street, Leicester LE2 8ND* Tel 0116-299 7624 Fax 299 7653 E-mail arace@leicester.anglican.org

RACE, Christopher Keith. b 43. St Paul's Coll Grahamstown 76. **d** 78 **p** 80. S Africa 78-83; Angl Chapl Stellenbosch Univ 79-81; R Kalk Bay 81-83; Dioc Admin Botswana and Personal Asst to Abp Cen Africa 83-86; P-in-c E Kalahari 83-86; V Tanworth St Patr Salter Street *Birm* 86-96; P-in-c Rothiemurchus *Mor* 96-01; Perm to Offic *Glouc* 02-03; P-in-c Kemble, Poole Keynes, Somerford Keynes etc 03-04; R from 04. *The Vicarage, Kemble, Cirencester GL7 6AG* Tel (01285) 770049 E-mail maeve.race@btinternet.com

RACE, John Arthur. b 37. St Alb and Ox Min Course 95. **d** 98 **p** 99. OLM Haddenham w Cuddington, Kingsey etc *Ox* from 98. *8 The Closes, Haddenham, Aylesbury HP17 8JN* Tel (01844) 290180

RACE, Stephen Peter. b 69. SS Hild & Bede Coll Dur BA93. St Steph Ho Ox 00. **d** 02 **p** 03. C Wigton *Carl* 02-05; V Dodworth *Wakef* from 05. *The Vicarage, Green Road, Dodworth, Barnsley S75 3RT* Tel (01226) 206276

RACTLIFFE, Dudley John. b 38. Man Univ BA62 Birm Univ DPS69. Ridley Hall Cam 63. **d** 66 **p** 67. C Radford *Cov* 66-68; C Haslemere *Guildf* 69-73; V Perry Beeches *Birm* 73-78; V Worle *B & W* 78-88; Dioc Ecum Officer 88-93; R Dowlishwake w Kingstone, Chillington etc 88-93; TR Swanage and Studland *Sarum* 93-01; rtd 01; Perm to Offic *B & W* from 02. *12 Sid Lane, Sidmouth EX10 9AN* Tel (01395) 579712

RADCLIFFE, Canon Albert Edward. b 34. Lon Univ BD63. St Aid Birkenhead Ch Div Sch of the Pacific (USA) 61. **d** 62 **p** 63. C Knotty Ash St Jo *Liv* 62-64; C Blundellsands St Nic 64-66; Chapl Haifa St Luke Israel 66-69; V Tonge w Alkrington *Man* 69-77; R Ashton St Mich 77-91; AD Ashton-under-Lyne 87-91; Can Res Man Cathl 91-00; rtd 00; Perm to Offic *Man* from 01. *26 St Chad's Road, Withington, Manchester M20 4WH* Tel 0161-445 1327

RADCLIFFE, David Jeffrey. b 52. Linc Th Coll 77. **d** 79 **p** 80. C Poulton-le-Fylde *Blackb* 79-84; V Ingol 84-88; R Lowther and Askham *Carl* 88-96; R Lowther and Askham and Clifton and Brougham from 96. *The Rectory, Lilac House, Lowther, Penrith CA10 2HH* Tel (01931) 712277

RADCLIFFE, Eileen Rose (Rosie). b 54. Carl Dioc Tr Inst 92. **d** 95 **p** 96. NSM Gt Salkeld w Lazonby *Carl* 95-96; NSM Dacre 99-02; Perm to Offic from 02. *The Rectory, Lilac House, Lowther, Penrith CA10 2HH* Tel (01931) 712277

RADCLIFFE, John Frederick. b 39. Dioc OLM tr scheme 99. **d** 01 **p** 02. OLM Meltham *Wakef* from 01. *13 Orchard Close, Meltham, Huddersfield HD9 4EG* Tel (01484) 348806

RADCLIFFE, Mrs Rosemary. b 45. SW Minl Tr Course 87. **d** 90 **p** 94. NSM Devoran *Truro* 90-93; Dn-in-c N Newton w St Michaelchurch, Thurloxton etc *B & W* 93-94; P-in-c 94-00; Chapl to the Deaf 93-96; P-in-c Whipton *Ex* 00-01; rtd 01; Perm to Offic *Truro* from 03. *76 Upland Crescent, Truro TR1 1NE* Tel (01872) 273906

RADCLIFFE, Rosie. *See* RADCLIFFE, Eileen Rose

✠**RADFORD, The Rt Revd Andrew John.** b 44. Trin Coll Bris 72. **d** 74 **p** 75 **c** 98. C Shirehampton *Bris* 74-78; C Henleaze 78-80; Producer Relig Progr BBC Radio Bris 74-80; V Bath St Barn w Englishcombe *B & W* 80-85; Dioc Communications Officer

Glouc 85-93; Producer Relig Progr Severn Sound Radio 85-93; Hon Can Glouc Cathl 91-98; Development and Tr Officer Ch Ho Westmr 93-98; Abps' Adv for Bps' Min 98; Suff Bp Taunton *B & W* from 98; Preb Wells Cathl from 98. *Bishop's Lodge, West Monkton, Taunton TA2 8LU* Tel (01823) 413526 Fax 412805 E-mail bishoptaunton@talk21.com

RADFORD, Vincent Arthur. b 45. Ches Coll of HE CertEd69. **d** 05. OLM Westhoughton and Wingates *Man* from 05. *64 Molyneux Road, Westhoughton, Bolton BL5 3EU* Tel (01942) 790091 E-mail vincent.radford@ntlworld.com

RADLEY, Mrs Jean Frances. b 40. Man Univ RGN62 Univ Coll Lon RSCN65 Preston Poly DN89 Cen Lancs Univ BSc95. Carl and Blackb Dioc Tr Inst 98. **d** 00 **p** 01. OLM Kendal St Geo *Carl* from 00. *3 Castle Street, Kendal LA9 7AD* Tel (01539) 740811 Mobile 07714-020189 E-mail jeanradley@onetel.com

RADLEY, Richard Brian. b 68. St Jo Coll Nottm 02. **d** 04 **p** 05. C Utley *Bradf* from 04. *1 Westview Way, Keighley BD20 6JD* Tel (01535) 664379 E-mail radley@radleyfamily.fsnet.co.uk

RADLEY, Stephen Gavin. b 62. K Coll Lon BSc83 AKC83 St Jo Coll Dur BA87. Cranmer Hall Dur 85. **d** 89 **p** 90. C Darlington St Matt and St Luke *Dur* 89-92; P-in-c Chilton 92-96; P-in-c Marley Hill 96-01. *Address temp unknown*

RADLEY, Stephen John. b 68. Lancs Coll of Agric NDA89. St Jo Coll Nottm BTh96. **d** 96 **p** 97. C Boulton *Derby* 96-00; Chapl RAF from 00. *Chaplaincy Services (RAF), HQ, Personnel and Training Command, RAF Ainsworth, Gloucester GL3 1EZ* Tel (01452) 712612 ext 5164 Fax 510828 E-mail steve.radley@cwcom.net

RAE SMITH, Tristram Geoffrey. b 57. Clare Coll Cam BA79 MA83 St Jo Coll Dur BA04. Cranmer Hall Dur 02. **d** 04 **p** 05. C Bradford-on-Avon Ch Ch *Sarum* from 04; C Westwood and Wingfield from 04. *22 Christchurch Road, Bradford-on-Avon BA15 1TB* Tel (01225) 862130 Mobile 07751-306272

RAFFAY, Julian Paul. b 60. Stirling Univ BSc84. Cranmer Hall Dur BA90. **d** 90 **p** 91. C Adel *Ripon* 90-93; C Leeds Halton St Wilfrid 93-95; Asst Chapl S Derbys Mental Health NHS Trust 95-97; TV Gleadless *Sheff* 97-01; V Deepcar from 01. *St John's Vicarage, 27 Carr Road, Deepcar, Sheffield S36 2PQ* Tel 0114-288 5138 E-mail julian@saintjohns.co.uk

RAGAN, Mrs Jennifer Mary. b 39. Linc Th Coll 71. **dss** 80 **d** 87 **p** 94. Hackney *Lon* 80-84; Hornchurch St Andr *Chelmsf* 84-88; Par Dn 87-88; Par Dn Ingrave St Steph CD 88-90; Par Dn Gt Parndon 90-94; C 94-99; TV from 99. *14 Deer Park, Harlow CM19 4LD* Tel (01279) 431133

RAGBOURNE, Miss Pamela Mary. b 27. CertEd47. Dalton Ho Bris 53. **dss** 76 **d** 87 **p** 94. CPAS Staff 68-79; Tottenham St Jo *Lon* 79-81; Gt Cambridge Road St Jo and St Jas 82-84; Camberley St Paul *Guildf* 84-86; rtd 87; Perm to Offic *Glouc* 87-93; and from 97; NSM Winchcombe, Gretton, Sudeley Manor etc 93-97. *14 Crispin Close, Winchcombe, Cheltenham GL54 5JY* Tel (01242) 603469

RAHI, Hakim Banta Singh. b 36. Union Bibl Sem Yavatmal BD71. **d** 74 **p** 74. India 74-83; In URC 83-88; Perm to Offic *Birm* 88-93; Ecum Evang Asian Community 88-93. *8 Temple Street, Bilston WV14 0NU* Tel (01902) 491392

RAHILLY, Philip James. b 54. Univ of Wales (Cardiff) BD86. Wycliffe Hall Ox 86. **d** 88 **p** 89. C Knightwick w Doddenham, Broadwas and Cotheridge *Worc* 88; C Martley and Wichenford, Knightwick etc 89-91; C Worc St Barn w Ch Ch 91-92; TV Kidderminster St Mary and All SS w Trimpley etc 92-95; P-in-c Childe Okeford, Okeford Fitzpaine, Manston etc *Sarum* 95-00; P-in-c Shilling Okeford 99-00; R Okeford from 00. *The Rectory, Rectory Lane, Child Okeford, Blandford Forum DT11 8DT* Tel (01258) 860547

RAI, Mrs Mary Anne. b 61. La Sainte Union Coll BTh83 PGCE84. Trin Coll Bris DipTh85. **dss** 86 **d** 87 **p** 99. Bury St Edmunds St Mary *St E* 86-89; Par Dn 87-89; Perm to Offic 90-93; Perm to Offic *Cov* 94-99 and from 02; NSM Styvechale 99-01. *61 Malthouse Lane, Kenilworth CV8 1AD* Tel (01926) 732223 E-mail kal.rai@virgin.net

RAIKES, Miss Gwynneth Marian Napier. b 51. Somerville Coll Ox MA72 Lon Univ BD81. Trin Coll Bris 79. **dss** 81 **d** 98 **p** 98. Asst Chapl Bris Poly *Bris* 81-86; Beckenham Ch Ch *Roch* 86-98; C 98-00; Dean of Women and Dir Past Tr Oak Hill Th Coll from 00; Perm to Offic *Lon* from 03. *5 Farm Lane, London N14 4PP* Tel (020) 8441 0490 *or* 8441 5996 Mobile 07866-651272 E-mail marianr@oakhill.ac.uk

RAIKES, Canon Myles Kenneth. b 23. New Coll Ox BA47 MA51. Wells Th Coll 47. **d** 49 **p** 50. C Chelmsf Cathl *Chelmsf* 49-51; C Stratford St Jo 51-53; P-in-c Hockerill *St Alb* 53-55; V 55-63; Chapl Herts and Essex Hosp Bp's Stortford 56-63; V Bushey Heath *St Alb* 63-70; R Digswell 70-77; Hon Can St Alb 76-77; P-in-c Meare *B & W* 77-81; P-in-c W Coker 82-83; Dioc Ecum Officer 84-88; C Ilminster w Whitelackington 84-85; C S Petherton w the Seavingtons 85-87; rtd 88; Perm to Offic *B & W* from 88. *7 West Street, South Petherton TA13 5DQ* Tel (01460) 241056

RAIKES, Canon Peter. b 37. St Mich Coll Llan 78. **d** 80 **p** 81. C Roath *Llan* 80-82; V Resolven 82-86; V Resolven w Tonna 86-92; RD Neath 89-01; V Skewen 92-02; Can Llan Cathl 97-02; rtd 02. *2 Kennedy Drive, Pencoed, Bridgend CF35 6TW* Tel (01656) 862317

RAIKES, Robert Laybourne. b 32. Wells Th Coll 59. **d** 61 **p** 62. C Poplar All SS w St Frideswide *Lon* 61-66; C Grendon Underwood w Edgcott *Ox* 66-68; C Swan 68-71; V Whitchurch Canonicorum w Wooton Fitzpaine etc *Sarum* 71-81; P-in-c Branksome St Aldhelm 81-82; V 82-91; V Pitminster w Corfe *B & W* 91-92; rtd 92; Chapl Madeira *Eur* 93-95; Perm to Offic *Glouc* 95-98; Hon C Broadwell, Evenlode, Oddington, Adlestrop etc 98-01; Lic to Offic *Eur* from 02. *28 Coopers Lane, Abingdon OX14 5GW* Tel (01235) 523426

RAILTON, John Robert Henry. b 45. Reading Univ BSc68 PhD82 FCIB79. S Dios Minl Tr Scheme 82. **d** 85 **p** 86. NSM Wickham *Portsm* 85-89; C Bridgemary 89-90; V 90-96; TR Ridgeway *Sarum* 96-02; TR Whitton from 02. *The Rectory, Back Lane, Ramsbury, Marlborough SN8 2QH* Tel (01672) 520235 E-mail rector@whittonteam.org.uk

RAILTON, Sandra. b 46. S Dios Minl Tr Scheme 82. **dss** 85 **d** 87 **p** 94. Catherington and Clanfield *Portsm* 85-86; Lee-on-the-Solent 86-89; C 87-89; Par Dn Burnham w Dropmore, Hitcham and Taplow *Ox* 89-94; TV Wallingford w Crowmarsh Gifford etc 94-98; Dioc Dir Ords (OLM) Berks 96-99; TV Ridgeway *Sarum* 98-02; Dioc Voc Adv 99-02; TV Whitton from 02; RD Marlborough from 04. *The Rectory, Back Lane, Ramsbury, Marlborough SN8 2QH* Tel (01672) 520235 E-mail vicar@whittonteam.org.uk

RAILTON-CROWDER, Mrs Mary. b 51. RN72 RM91 MIOSH93 Luton Univ BA96. St Alb and Ox Min Course 98. **d** 01 **p** 02. NSM Elstow *St Alb* 01-04; Ecum Chapl De Montford Univ 02-04; C Douglas All SS and St Thos *S & M* from 04. *All Saints' House, 62 Ballabrooie Way, Douglas, Isle of Man IM1 4HB* Tel (01624) 621547 E-mail revmrc@yahoo.com

RAINBIRD, Ms Ruth Patricia. b 40. SRN62. OLM course 98. **d** 01 **p** 02. OLM Limpsfield and Titsey *S'wark* from 01. *73 Stoneleigh Road, Oxted RH8 0TP* Tel (01883) 713683

RAINBOW, Preb Gerald Anton Hayward. b 15. St Edm Hall Ox BA38 MA41. Linc Th Coll 38. **d** 39 **p** 40. C Monkwearmouth St Andr *Dur* 39-43; Chapl RAFVR 43-47; V Claverley *Heref* 47-57; V Leominster 57-80; RD Leominster 60-80; Preb Heref Cathl 67-95; P-in-c Eyton 69-80; rtd 80; Perm to Offic *Heref* 89-01. *Whingate Cottage, Corby Hill, Carlisle CA4 8PN* Tel (01228) 562586

RAINE, Alan. b 49. MIPD93. NEOC DipHE95. **d** 95 **p** 96. NSM Jarrow *Dur* from 95; Chapl S Tyneside Coll from 97. *49 Brixham Crescent, Jarrow NE32 3SL* Tel 0191-489 3042 Fax as telephone

RAINE, David. b 58. Dur Univ MBA96 Open Univ BA96 MCIM99 MCIPD03. NEOC 01. **d** 04 **p** 05. NSM N Wearside *Dur* from 04. *5 Maydown Close, Sunderland SR5 3DZ* Tel 0191-549 7262 E-mail davidraine@dunelm.org.uk

RAINE, Patrick John Wallace. b 21. DFC. Sarum & Wells Th Coll 72. **d** 74 **p** 75. C Chandler's Ford *Win* 74-76; R Highclere and Ashmansworth w Crux Easton 76-84; R Copythorne and Minstead 84-87; rtd 87; P-in-c Breamore *Win* 91-95; Perm to Offic *Win* 95-03; *Sarum* 98-03; *Cov* from 03. *11 Wenbrook Close, Attleborough, Nuneaton CV11 4LJ* Tel (024) 7634 9871

RAINE, Stephen James. b 49. Lanchester Poly DipAD69 Sheff Poly BA80. N Ord Course 85. **d** 86 **p** 87. C Cottingham *York* 86-90; V Dunscroft Ch Ch *Sheff* 90-92; V Dunscroft St Edwin 92-96; V Kettering St Mary *Pet* from 96. *The Vicarage, 175 Avondale Road, Kettering NN16 8PN* Tel (01536) 512736 Fax as telephone E-mail evangelist24@aol.com

RAINER, John Charles. b 54. Ex Univ BA76 DipTh78 CertEd78 Hull Univ MBA02. St Jo Coll Nottm 86. **d** 88 **p** 89. C Fletchamstead *Cov* 88-94; V Leic H Apostles *Leic* 94-03; V Shipley St Pet *Bradf* from 03. *The Vicarage, 2 Glenhurst Road, Shipley BD18 4DZ* Tel (01274) 584488 E-mail johnrainer@btopenworld.com

RAINES, Mrs Gisela Rolanda. b 58. Groningen Univ Kandidaats 80. K Coll Lon BD83. **dss** 84 **d** 87 **p** 94. Charlton St Luke w H Trin *S'wark* 84-87; Par Dn 87; Chapl Imp Coll *Lon* 87-91; Hon C Birch w Fallowfield *Man* 94-95; P-in-c Withington St Chris 95-03; C Man St Ann from 03. *197 Old Hall Lane, Manchester M14 6HJ* Tel 0161-224 6643 E-mail gisela@fish.co.uk

RAINES, William Guy. b 46. Lon Univ BSc69 MSc70 Ox Univ BA80. Ripon Coll Cuddesdon 78. **d** 81 **p** 82. C W Drayton *Lon* 81-84; C Charlton St Luke w H Trin *S'wark* 84-87; Chapl K Coll Lon 87-94; Chapl Imp Coll 91-94; P-in-c Birch w Fallowfield *Man* 94-95; R from 95. *197 Old Hall Lane, Manchester M14 6HJ* Tel 0161-224 1310 E-mail wraines@emmental.demon.co.uk

RAINEY, Graeme Norman. b 66. Van Mildert Coll Dur BA88 Reading Univ MA01. Ridley Hall Cam 93. **d** 93 **p** 94. C Maltby *Sheff* 93-96; Chapl Reading Univ *Ox* 96-04; Chapl Downe Ho Sch Berks from 04. *Pickering, St Mary's Paddock, The Ridge, Cold Ash, Thatcham RG18 9JX* Tel (01635) 865112 *or* 204771 E-mail chaplain@downehouse.net

RAINFORD, Robert Graham. b 55. Lanc Univ CertEd76 BEd77. St Steph Ho Ox 81. **d** 83 **p** 84. C Burnley St Cath w St Alb and

St Paul *Blackb* 83-86; C-in-c Hawes Side St Chris CD 86-89; V Hawes Side 89-03; P-in-c Marton Moss 01-03; AD Blackpool 00-03; Hon Can Blackb Cathl 01-03; Sen Chapl to Bp Dover *Cant* 03-05. *Address temp unknown*

RAINSBERRY, Edward John. b 24. TCD BA48 MA58. TCD Div Sch Div Test49. **d** 49 **p** 50. C Abbeystrewry Union *C, C & R* 49-52; Chapl RAF 52-58; V Long Compton *Cov* 58-84; R Whichford 58-84; V Long Compton, Whichford and Barton-on-the-Heath 84-95; rtd 95; Perm to Offic *Cov* 95-01; *Ox* and *Pet* from 95. *12 Portway Gardens, Aynho, Banbury OX17 3AR* Tel (01869) 810417

RAINSBURY, Mark James. b 56. NE Lon Poly BA79. Oak Hill Th Coll BA87. **d** 88 **p** 89. C Tonbridge St Steph *Roch* 88-95; C Hampreston *Sarum* 95-97; TV 97-99; Perm to Offic *Win* from 03. *Old Orchard, Church Lane, West Parley, Ferndown BH22 8TS* Tel (01202) 590042

RAINSFORD, Peter John. b 31. FCP72. Qu Coll Birm 75. **d** 77 **p** 78. Hon C Lich St Chad *Lich* 77-81; C 82; C Coseley Ch Ch 82-84; V Wednesbury St Bart 84-91; Chapl Sandwell Distr Gen Hosp 89-91; rtd 91; Perm to Offic *Lich* from 91. *157 Broadway, Walsall WS1 3HD* Tel (01922) 624526
E-mail p.j.rainsford@tinyonline.co.uk

RAISTRICK, Brian. b 38. St Paul's Cheltenham TCert60 Ex Univ AdDipEd68 Newc Univ MEd76 UEA PhD86. Westcott Ho Cam 92. **d** 93 **p** 94. C Haverhill w Withersfield, the Wrattings etc *St E* 93-95; P-in-c Horringer cum Ickworth 95-02; P-in-c Risby w Gt and Lt Saxham and Westley 99-02; P-in-c Chevington w Hargrave and Whepstead w Brockley 00-02; R Horringer 02; RD Thingoe 99-01; rtd 03; Perm to Offic *St E* from 03. *Greenways, Westwood, Great Barton, Bury St Edmunds IP31 2SF* Tel (01284) 787372 *or* 747372
E-mail brian@raistrick.freeserve.co.uk

RAITH, Robert. b 31. Edin Univ MA61. Coll of Resurr Mirfield 57. **d** 59 **p** 60. C Edin St Jas *Edin* 59-61; P-in-c 76-77; Asst Prov Youth Org 61-65; C Dalmahoy 61-65; C Edin St Mark 66-76; Dioc Supernumerary 77-78; P-in-c Edin St Luke 78-79; Perm to Offic from 79; Pilsdon Community 87-90. *Address withheld by request*

RAITT, Derek. b 41. K Coll Lon BD63 AKC63. **d** 64 **p** 65. C Blackb St Jas *Blackb* 64-67; C Burnley St Pet 67-69; V Foulridge 69-74; V Euxton 74-91; V Penwortham St Mary 91-00; P-in-c Halton w Aughton from 00. *The Rectory, High Road, Halton, Lancaster LA2 6PU* Tel (01524) 811370

RAJ-SINGH, Reji. b 52. Sidney Webb Coll of Educn CertEd79 N Lon Poly BEd90 Heythrop Coll Lon MA02. St Alb and Ox Min Course 02. **d** 05. NSM Paddington St Jas *Lon* from 05. *3 Greek Court, 14A Old Compton Street, London W1D 4TH* Tel (020) 7278 0372 Mobile 07050-041232

RAJA, John Joshva. b 65. Serampore Coll MTh93 Leic Univ MA96 New Coll Edin 96. **d** 93 **p** 94. India 93-95; Hon C Leic H Spirit *Leic* 95-96; Hon C Edin H Cross *Edin* 96-99. *43 Scotland Street, Edinburgh EH3 6PY* Tel 0131-557 3797 Fax as telephone
E-mail j.raja@sms.ed.ac.uk

RAJKOVIC, Michael. b 52. Sheff Univ BMet74 MMet75 PhD79 St Jo Coll Nottm MA95 Lon Bible Coll MPhil03. Cranmer Hall Dur 93. **d** 95 **p** 96. C Harrow Weald All SS *Lon* 95-98; C Woodford Wells *Chelmsf* 98-02; V Bricket Wood *St Alb* from 02. *20 West Riding, Bricket Wood, St Albans AL2 3QP* Tel (01923) 681107 E-mail mrajk30852@aol.com

RAJKUMAR, Peniel Jesudason Rufus. b 77. Sri Venkateswara Univ India BA98 MA02 BD03. **d** 05. NSM Upper Holloway *Lon* from 05. *10 St Peter's Church, Anatola Road, London N19 5HN* Tel (020) 7561 9888 Mobile 07796-477586
E-mail rufus_peniel@rediffmail.com

RAKE, David John. b 47. Nottm Univ BA68 PhD73. Wycliffe Hall Ox DipTh73. **d** 74 **p** 75. C Radcliffe-on-Trent *S'well* 74-77; P-in-c Upwell St Pet *Ely* 77-79; P-in-c Outwell 77-79; Chapl Warw Univ *Cov* 79-86; V Kenilworth St Nic 86-98; P-in-c Tintagel *Truro* from 98; Bp's Adv on Spiritual Formation from 98. *The Vicarage, Vicarage Hill, Tintagel PL34 0DJ* Tel (01840) 770315

RALPH, Brian Charles. b 66. St Steph Ho Ox 89. **d** 92 **p** 93. C Yeovil St Mich *B & W* 92-95; TV St Jo on Bethnal Green *Lon* 95-01; P-in-c Bethnal Green St Barn 01-03; V from 03. *12 Chisenhale Road, London E3 5TG* Tel (020) 8983 3426, 8806 4130 *or* 7247 1448 E-mail brianralph@btinternet.com

RALPH, Nicholas Robert. b 63. Lanc Univ BSc85. Westcott Ho Cam BA91 CTM92. **d** 92 **p** 93. C Fareham H Trin *Portsm* 92-95; C Portsea St Cuth 95-96; V Hayling Is St Andr 96-03; V N Hayling St Pet 96-03; Soc Resp Adv from 03. *100 St Thomas's Street, Portsmouth PO1 2HE* E-mail nralph@bigfoot.com

RALPH, Richard Gale. b 51. Pemb Coll Ox BA73 MA78 DPhil78 FRSA90. S Dios Minl Tr Scheme 84. **d** 87 **p** 88. NSM St Leonards Ch Ch and St Mary *Chich* from 87; NSM St Pancras H Cross w St Jude and St Pet *Lon* 87-94; Prin Westmr Coll Ox 96-00. *St Alban, 11 The Mount, St Leonards-on-Sea TN38 0HR* Tel (01424) 422722

RALPHS, John Eric. b 26. St Cath Coll Ox BA52 MA56 MBAP66. Wycliffe Hall Ox 53. **d** 53 **p** 54. C Wolvercote *Ox* 53-55; Chapl Asst Radcliffe Infirmary Ox 54-62; Chapl Dragon Sch Ox 55-68; Asst Chapl HM Pris Ox 58-61; Jun Chapl Mert Coll Ox 59-62; Chapl St Hugh's Coll Ox 62-67; Priest-Psychotherapist from 68; Lic to Offic *Ox* from 83; rtd 91. *209 Woodstock Road, Oxford OX2 7AB* Tel (01865) 515550

RALPHS, Robert Brian. b 31. Qu Coll Birm 75. **d** 78 **p** 79. Hon C Wednesbury St Jo *Lich* 78-80; Hon C Wednesbury St Paul Wood Green 80-81; Perm to Offic 81-96; Hon C W Bromwich Gd Shep w St Jo 96. *204 Bromford Lane, West Bromwich B70 7HX* Tel 0121-553 0119

RALPHS, Sharon Ann. *See* SIMPSON, Mrs Sharon Ann

RAMELL, John Edwin. b 25. Bris Univ BA55. Tyndale Hall Bris. **d** 56 **p** 57. C New Milverton *Cov* 56-60; V Wombridge *Lich* 60-70; TR Chell 70-82; V Congleton St Pet *Ches* 82-90; rtd 90; Perm to Offic *Ox* from 92. *10 Newland Close, Eynsham, Witney OX29 4LE* Tel (01865) 880180

RAMPTON, Paul Michael. b 47. St Jo Coll Dur BA69 MA73 K Coll Lon PhD85 Westmr Coll Ox MTh99. Wycliffe Hall Ox 72. **d** 73 **p** 74. C Folkestone H Trin w Ch Ch *Cant* 73-77; P-in-c Kingsdown 77-79; P-in-c Ringwould w Oxney 77-79; R Ringwould w Kingsdown 79-83; V Maidstone St Paul 83-88; V Maidstone St Martin 88-95; V Steyning *Chich* from 95; R Ashurst from 95; RD Storrington 99-03. *St Andrew's Vicarage, Station Road, Steyning BN44 3YL* Tel and fax (01903) 813256

RAMPTON, Canon Valerie Edith. b 41. Nottm Univ BSc63 MSc66 BA79. Gilmore Course 78. **dss** 82 **d** 87 **p** 94. Sneinton St Chris w St Phil *S'well* 80-87; Par Dn 87-88; Par Dn Stapleford 88-93; Dioc Adv on Women in Min 90-01; Dn-in-c Kneesall w Laxton and Wellow 93-94; V 94-02; Hon Can S'well Minster 97-02; rtd 02; Perm to Offic *Linc* and *S'well* from 02. *Tansy Cottage, Hillside, Beckingham, Lincoln LN5 0RQ* Tel (01636) 626665 E-mail valerie.rampton@btinternet.com

RAMSARAN (or COOPER), Susan Mira. b 49. K Coll Lon BA70 Univ Coll Lon MA72 PhD78. Ripon Coll Cuddesdon BA92. **d** 93 **p** 94. C Selling w Throwley, Sheldwich w Badlesmere etc *Cant* 93-97; P-in-c Shipbourne *Roch* 97-99; P-in-c Plaxtol 97-99; R Shipbourne w Plaxtol from 99; RD Shoreham from 01. *The Rectory, The Street, Plaxtol, Sevenoaks TN15 0QG* Tel (01732) 810319

RAMSAY, Canon Alan Burnett. b 34. AKC62. **d** 63 **p** 64. C Clapham H Trin *S'wark* 63-67; C Warlingham w Chelsham and Farleigh 67-71; P-in-c Stockwell St Mich 71-78; V Lingfield 78-85; P-in-c Crowhurst 83-85; V Lingfield and Crowhurst 85-92; RD Godstone 88-92; V Mitcham St Mark 92-00; Hon Can S'wark Cathl 93-00; rtd 00; Perm to Offic *Cant* from 00. *Kent House, 9 Scotton Street, Wye, Ashford TN25 5BU* Tel (01233) 813730 E-mail aramsay@fish.co.uk

RAMSAY, Preb Carl Anthoney St Aubyn. b 55. WMMTC 88. **d** 90 **p** 91. C Wednesfield Heath *Lich* 90-94; V Willenhall St Anne 94-03; V Pelsall from 03; Preb Lich Cathl from 04. *The Vicarage, 39 Hall Lane, Pelsall, Walsall WS3 4JN* Tel (01922) 682098
E-mail spreeboy@talk21.com

RAMSAY, Christopher. b 68. St Jo Coll Dur BA90. Wycliffe Hall Ox BTh94. **d** 97 **p** 98. C Cricklewood St Gabr and St Mich *Lon* 97-01; P-in-c Southall St Geo from 01. *1 Lancaster Road, Southall UB1 1NP* Tel (020) 8574 1876
E-mail christopher.ramsay@btinternet.com

RAMSAY, Eric Nicolson. b 29. **d** 94 **p** 95. C Forfar *St And* 94-99 and from 00; C Kirriemuir 94-99 and from 00; Asst Chapl Gtr Athens *Eur* 99-00. *4 Beechwood Place, Kirriemuir DD8 5DZ* Tel (01575) 572029 E-mail ericaileenramsay@tinyworld.co.uk

RAMSAY, James Anthony. b 52. Wadh Coll Ox BA75 MA. **d** 86 **p** 87. C Olney w Emberton *Ox* 86-89; V Blackbird Leys 89-02; Chapl Bucharest w Sofia *Eur* 02-05; P-in-c Lt Ilford St Barn *Chelmsf* from 05; Chapl E Lon Univ from 05. *St Barnabas' Vicarage, Browning Road, London E12 6PB* Tel (020) 8472 2777

RAMSAY, Kenneth William. b 18. ALCD48. **d** 52 **p** 53. C Southall Green St Jo *Lon* 52-57; Asst Chapl Lee Abbey 57-60; Perm to Offic *Portsm* 69-80 and *Sarum* 77-87; rtd 87; Hon C Burstow *S'wark* 87-98; Perm to Offic from 98. *3 Park Close, Strood Green, Betchworth RH3 7JB* Tel (01737) 843470
E-mail ramsay@iname.com

RAMSAY, Kerry. b 59. Heythrop Coll Lon MA94. Westcott Ho Cam 92. **d** 94 **p** 96. C Westville St Eliz S Africa 95-96; C Charlton St Luke w H Trin *S'wark* 96-99; C Cambridge Gt St Mary w St Mich *Ely* 99-04; V Sunninghill *Ox* from 04. *Sunninghill Vicarage, Church Lane, Ascot SL5 7DD* Tel (01344) 620727 Mobile 07984-172334

RAMSAY, Max Roy MacGregor. b 34. Ball Coll Ox MA58. Qu Coll Birm 82. **d** 84 **p** 85. C Hale *Ches* 84-86; C Nantwich 87; V Haslington w Crewe Green 87-91; P-in-c Dunham Massey St Marg and St Mark 92-95; rtd 95; Perm to Offic *Ches* from 95. *6 Comber Way, Knutsford WA16 9BT* Tel (01565) 632362
E-mail max@rmramsay.fsnet.co.uk

RAMSBOTTOM, Mrs Julie Frances. b 54. Trevelyan Coll Dur BA76. S'wark Ord Course 88. **d** 91 **p** 94. Par Dn Bray and Braywood *Ox* 91-94; C 94-97; R W Woodhay w Enborne,

Hampstead Marshall etc from 97. *The Rectory, Enborne, Newbury RG20 0HD* Tel (01635) 34427
E-mail julie.ramsbottom@talk21.com

RAMSBURY, Area Bishop of. *Vacant*

RAMSDEN, Canon Arthur Stuart. b 34. Kelham Th Coll 56. **d** 61 **p** 62. C Featherstone *Wakef* 61-63; C Barnsley St Pet 63-67; V Charlestown 67-70; V Middlestown 70-77; V Purston cum S Featherstone 77-04; Hon Can Wakef Cathl 95-04; rtd 04. *31 Barnsley Road, Cawthorne, Barnsley S75 4HW* Tel (01226) 790696

RAMSDEN, Peter Stockton. b 51. Univ Coll Lon BSc74 Leeds Univ DipTh76 MA92. Coll of Resurr Mirfield 74. **d** 77 **p** 78. C Houghton le Spring *Dur* 77-80; C S Shields All SS 80-83; Papua New Guinea 83-90 and 93-96; P-in-c Micklefield *York* 90-93; V Long Benton *Newc* from 96. *The Vicarage, 3 Station Road, Benton, Newcastle upon Tyne NE12 8AN* Tel 0191-266 2015
E-mail vicar.stbarts@talk21.com

RAMSDEN, Raymond Leslie. b 49. Open Univ BA86. **d** 78 **p** 79. C Greenhill St Jo *Lon* 78-85; C Staines St Mary and St Pet 85-90; V Hounslow St Steph from 90. *St Stephen's Vicarage, Parkside Road, Hounslow TW3 2BP* Tel (020) 8570 3056
E-mail revrramsden@hotmail.com

RAMSDEN, Stuart. *See* RAMSDEN, Canon Arthur Stuart

RAMSEY-HARDY, Stuart John Andrew. b 46. St Jo Coll Dur BA69. Wycliffe Hall Ox 69. **d** 74 **p** 75. C Stoke Newington St Mary *Lon* 74-77; C Hersham *Guildf* 78-79; Hon C Thames Ditton 79-83. *23 New Row, London WC2N 4LA* Tel (020) 7836 2217

RAMSHAW, Marcus John. b 71. St Andr Univ MTheol93 York Univ MA94. Cranmer Hall Dur 94. **d** 96 **p** 97. C Hythe *Cant* 96-00; Chapl Down Coll Cam 01-03; NSM Cam St Edw *Ely* from 03. *10 Holyrood Close, Cambridge CB4 3NE* Tel (01223) 360298 Mobile 07793-064455 E-mail mjr62@cam.ac.uk

RANCE, Miss Eleanor Jane. b 72. K Coll Lon BA93 AKC93 Dur Univ MA96. Cranmer Hall Dur DMS96. **d** 96 **p** 97. C Barnes St Mary *S'wark* 96-97; C Barnes 97-99; Chapl RAF from 99. *Chaplaincy Services (RAF), HQ, Personnel and Training Command, RAF Innsworth, Gloucester GL3 1EZ* Tel (01452) 712612 ext 5164 Fax 510828

RANDALL, Anthony. *See* RANDALL, James Anthony

RANDALL, Colin Antony. b 57. SS Paul & Mary Coll Cheltenham BEd78. Trin Coll Bris BD84. **d** 84 **p** 85. C Denton Holme *Carl* 84-87; C Brampton RD 87-90; R Hanborough and Freeland *Ox* 90-99; P-in-c Croglin *Carl* from 99; P-in-c Holme Eden 99-05; P-in-c Wetheral w Warwick 99-05; R Holme Eden and Wetheral w Warwick from 05. *St Paul's Vicarage, Warwick Bridge, Carlisle CA4 8RF* Tel (01228) 560332
E-mail carandall@freeuk.com

RANDALL, Preb Colin Michael Sebastian. b 50. Aston Univ BSc72. Qu Coll Birm 72. **d** 75 **p** 76. C Tonge w Alkrington *Man* 75-78; C Elton All SS 78-82; P-in-c Bridgwater H Trin *B & W* 82-86; V 86-90; V Bishops Hull 90-00; TR Wellington and Distr from 00; Preb Wells Cathl from 05. *The Rectory, 72 High Street, Wellington TA21 8RF* Tel (01823) 662248
E-mail colinms.randall@virgin.net

RANDALL, Canon Edmund Laurence. b 20. AM80. CCC Cam BA40 MA47. Wells Th Coll 47. **d** 49 **p** 50. C Bournemouth St Luke *Win* 49-52; Fell and Lect Selw Coll Cam 52-57; Chapl 53-57; Prin Ely Th Coll 57-59; Can Res Ely Cathl *Ely* 57-59; Australia from 60; Chapl St Fran Coll Brisbane 60-64; Warden St Barn Coll Adelaide 64-85; Hon Can Wangaratta from 89; rtd 85. *44 Mackay Street, Wangaratta, Vic, Australia 3677* Tel (0061) (3) 5721 9007

RANDALL, Elizabeth. *See* BILLETT, Mrs Elizabeth Nicola

RANDALL, Gareth John. b 49. Southn Univ BA72 PGCE73 ACP80. Oak Hill Th Coll 90. **d** 93 **p** 94. Dir of Studies Dame Alice Owen's Sch Potters Bar 84-95; Dir of Personnel 95-00; Asst Hd from 00; NSM S Mymms K Chas *St Alb* 93-98; NSM Potters Bar from 98. *Peterslea, 196 Barnet Road, Potters Bar EN6 2SE* Tel (01707) 651958 *or* 622847
E-mail randallg42@thegrid.org.uk

RANDALL, Ian Neville. b 39. Oriel Coll Ox BA62 MA65. St Steph Ho Ox 62. **d** 65 **p** 66. C Perivale *Lon* 65-68; C Fulham St Jo Walham Green 68-73; C Cowley St Jas *Ox* 73-79; TV 79-82; V Didcot St Pet 82-93; P-in-c Clewer St Andr 93-04; rtd 04. *12 Westmead Road, Fakenham NR21 8BL* Tel (01328) 862443

RANDALL, James Anthony. b 36. ACIB69 Kent Univ DipTh80. Ridley Hall Cam 68. **d** 70 **p** 71. C Rusthall *Roch* 70-74; V Shorne 74-79; V Bexleyheath Ch Ch 79-89; R Stone 89-98; rtd 98; Perm to Offic *Roch* from 99. *6 Sandling Way, St Mary's Island, Chatham ME4 3AZ* Tel (01634) 890603

RANDALL, Canon John Terence. b 29. St Cath Coll Cam BA52 MA59. Ely Th Coll 52. **d** 54 **p** 55. C Luton Ch Ch *St Alb* 54; C Dunstable 54-57; C Ely 57-60; C March St Jo 60-62; Area Sec (S Midl) UMCA 62-64; Area Sec USPG *Birm* and *Cov* 65-76; P-in-c Avon Dassett w Farnborough *Cov* 76-78; P-in-c Fenny Compton 76-78; R Avon Dassett w Farnborough and Fenny Compton 78-84; V New Bilton 84-94; RD Rugby 89-94; Hon Can Cov Cathl 93-94; rtd 94; Perm to Offic *Cov* and *Pet* from 94; *Leic* from 96. *52 Cymbeline Way, Rugby CV22 6LA* Tel (01788) 816659

RANDALL, Julian Adrian. b 45. Open Univ BA78 Stirling Univ MSc94 MIPD St Andr Univ PhD01. St Jo Sem Wonersh 68. **d** 70 **p** 71. Asst P Mortlake w E Sheen *S'wark* 71-72; Asst P Welling 72-74; Asst P Tunbridge Wells H Trin w Ch Ch *Roch* 74-79; NSM Dunfermline *St And* 96-98; P-in-c Elie and Earlsferry 98-03; P-in-c Pittenweem 98-03; Asst P St Andrews St Andr from 03; Dir Progr Business Sch St Andr Univ from 03. *10 Forbes Place, St Andrews KY16 9UJ* Tel (01334) 477761
E-mail jrandall@randall.co.uk

RANDALL, Kelvin John. b 49. JP80. K Coll Lon BD71 AKC71 Birm Univ PGCE72 Trin Coll Carmarthen MPhil97 Univ of Wales (Ban) PhD00. St Jo Coll Nottm DPS73. **d** 74 **p** 75. C Peckham St Mary Magd *S'wark* 74-78; C Portsdown *Portsm* 78-81; C-in-c Crookhorn Ch Cen CD 81-82; R Bedhampton 82-90; Bp's Chapl for Post-Ord Tr 84-89; RD Havant 87-89; P-in-c Bournemouth St Jo w St Mich *Win* 90-94; V 94-97; Chapl Talbot Heath Sch Bournemouth 90-94; Research Fell Trin Coll Carmarthen 97-00; C Portswood St Denys *Win* from 00. *The Vicarage, 54 Whitworth Crescent, Southampton SO18 1GD* Tel (023) 8067 2108 Fax 8067 1757 E-mail kjrandall@argonet.co.uk

RANDALL, Mrs Lynda Lorraine. b 44. Sarum & Wells Th Coll 89. **d** 91 **p** 94. Par Dn Chesterton St Andr *Ely* 91-94; C 94-95; C Linton 95-96; TV Linton 96-99; R Byfield w Boddington and Aston le Walls *Pet* from 99. *The Rectory, 55 Church Street, Byfield, Daventry NN11 6XN* Tel (01327) 260204
E-mail lynda@chrislyn.demon.co.uk

RANDALL, Miss Marian Sally. b 49. Trin Coll Bris 75. **dss** 80 **d** 87 **p** 94. Peckham St Mary Magd *S'wark* 80-83; Sutton Ch Ch 83-97; Par Dn 87-94; C 94-97; P-in-c S Merstham from 97. *The Vicarage, Battlebridge Lane, Redhill RH1 3LH* Tel (01737) 642722

RANDALL, Martin Trevor. b 51. St Jo Coll Dur BA74. Trin Coll Bris 74. **d** 77 **p** 78. C Ashton-upon-Mersey St Mary *Ches* 77-80; C Everton St Sav w St Cuth *Liv* 80-82; V W Derby Gd Shep 82-91; P-in-c Toxteth Park Ch Ch 91-94; P-in-c Toxteth Park St Bede 91-94; V Toxteth Park Ch Ch w St Bede 95-97; Chapl HM Pris Altcourse from 97. *HM Prison Altcourse, Higher Lane, Liverpool L9 7LH* Tel 0151-522 2000 ext 2395 Fax 522 2121

RANDALL, Canon Samuel Paul. b 59. Leeds Univ MA90. Ridley Hall Cam 84. **d** 87 **p** 88. C Kingston upon Hull St Nic *York* 87-89; CF 89-93; TV Bramley *Ripon* 93-96; Dioc Ecum Officer *Dur* 97-01; P-in-c Holmside 97-01; Bp's Officer for Ch in the World *Bradf* from 02; Hon Can Bradf Cathl from 04. *The Vicarage, Morton Lane, East Morton, Keighley BD20 5RS* Tel (01274) 561640 Mobile 07967-120070

RANDELL, David Peter. b 48. Trin Coll Bris BA88. **d** 92 **p** 93. C Wells St Cuth w Wookey Hole *B & W* 92-95; TV Wellington and Distr 95-05; R Chenderit *Pet* from 05. *The Rectory, Marston St Lawrence, Banbury OX17 2DB* Tel (01295) 712279
E-mail revrandell@supanet.com

RANDELL, John Harrison. b 35. Lon Univ BD62. Chich Th Coll 77. **d** 78 **p** 78. C Ribbleton *Blackb* 78-82; V Barton 82-00; rtd 00; Perm to Offic *Blackb* from 00. *6 Royds Avenue, Morecambe LA3 1PA* Tel (01524) 850269

RANDELL, Phillip John. b 45. Lon Univ DipTh68 BD73 CertEd. Linc Th Coll 67. **d** 68 **p** 69. C Henbury *Bris* 68-71; C Summertown *Ox* 71-73; C Liskeard w St Keyne *Truro* 73-75; Chapl Coll of SS Mark and Jo Plymouth 75-79; Tanzania 80-82; R Alvescot w Black Bourton, Shilton, Holwell etc *Ox* 82-87; R St Gennys, Jacobstow w Warbstow and Treneglos *Truro* 87-97; rtd 97; Perm to Offic *Truro* from 01. *14 Merlin's Way, Tintagel PL34 0BP* Tel (01840) 770559

RANDOLPH-HORN, David Henry. b 47. Nottm Univ BA69 Keele Univ CQSW71. Qu Coll Birm 80. **d** 82 **p** 83. C Hamstead St Paul *Birm* 82-84; V Aston St Jas 84-94; Hon C Leytonstone H Trin Harrow Green *Chelmsf* 93-99; Sec Inner Cities Relig Coun 94-99; Assoc Dir Leeds Ch Inst from 99; P-in-c Heptonstall *Wakef* 99-02; P-in-c Farnley *Ripon* from 03. *23 Spencer Place, Leeds LS7 4DQ,* or *20 New Market Street, Leeds LS1 6DG* Tel 0113-229 7546 *or* 245 4700 Fax 391 7939
E-mail david.hrh@virgin.net

RANGER, Keith Brian. b 34. Down Coll Cam BA58 MA63. Glas NSM Course 58. **d** 81 **p** 82. OMF Internat 81-99; Ethnic Min Co-ord 90-99; Hong Kong 81-89; Perm to Offic *Ches* 89-93 and from 99; *Man* 93-99; rtd 99. *144 Newton Street, Macclesfield SK11 6RW* Tel (01625) 439184
E-mail 101613.3107@compuserve.com

RANKIN, John. *See* RANKIN, Canon William John Alexander

RANKIN, John Cooper. b 24. Glas Univ MA44 Lon Univ BD53. Edin Th Coll 48. **d** 50 **p** 51. C Dundee St Mary Magd *Bre* 50-52; Chapl R Merchant Navy Sch Bearwood 53-60; Min Can Bris Cathl *Bris* 60-66; Lic to Offic *Lich* 66-69; Prin Lect Bp Otter Coll Chich 69-84; rtd 84. *28 Worcester Road, Chichester PO19 5DW* Tel (01243) 789467 E-mail johnrankin@cs.com

RANKIN, Joyce. d 03 **p** 04. C Dublin St Ann and St Steph *D & G* from 03. *151 The Northumberlands, Lower Mount Street, Dublin 2, Irish Republic* Tel (00353) (1) 662 5935 E-mail fejoycer@eircom.net

RANKIN, Stephen Brian. b 65. Salford Univ BSc88. Trin Coll Bris 95. **d** 97 **p** 98. C Ashton-upon-Mersey St Mary *Ches* from 97. *109 Ascot Avenue, Sale M33 4GT* Tel 0161-976 1693 E-mail srankin@breathemail.net

RANKIN, Canon William John Alexander. b 45. Van Mildert Coll Dur BA68 Fitzw Coll Cam BA73 MA77. Westcott Ho Cam 71. **d** 74 **p** 75. C St John's Wood *Lon* 74-78; Chapl Clifton Coll Bris 78-86; P-in-c The Claydons *Ox* 86-91; R 91-93; R Clare w Poslingford, Cavendish etc *St E* 93-04; R Stour Valley from 04; Hon Can St E Cathl from 05. *The Vicarage, 14 High Street, Clare, Sudbury CO10 8NY* Tel (01787) 278501

RANKINE, Christopher Barry. b 66. Portsm Poly BA88. Linc Th Coll BTh93. **d** 93 **p** 95. C Farlington *Portsm* 93-96; C Alverstoke 96-98; C Romsey *Win* 98-00; P-in-c W Andover from 00. *The Vicarage, 17 Millway Road, Andover SP10 3EU* Tel (01264) 392541 E-mail chris.rankine@lineone.net

RANN, Preb Harry Harvey. b 18. Sarum Th Coll 47. **d** 50 **p** 51. C Victoria Docks Ascension *Chelmsf* 50-52; C Christchurch *Win* 52-56; C Mill Hill Jo Keble Ch *Lon* 56-57; V Woolfold *Man* 57-62; Dean's Chapl and PV Ex Cathl *Ex* 62-77; Sacr 65-77; Succ 73-77; V Colyton 77-84; R Colyton and Southleigh 84-86; RD Honiton 84-86; Preb Ex Cathl 84-87; TR Colyton, Southleigh, Offwell, Widworthy etc 86-87; rtd 87; Perm to Offic *Ex* from 87. *4 Scattor View, Bridford, Exeter EX6 7JF* Tel (01647) 252741

RANN, Ruth. b 32. **d** 03 **p** 04. NSM Exminster and Kenn *Ex* 03-04; C Kenton, Mamhead, Powderham, Cofton and Starcross from 04. *All Saints' House, Kenton, Exeter EX6 8NG* Tel (01626) 890451

RANSOME, Arthur. b 21. St Jo Coll Nottm 71. **d** 72 **p** 72. Israel 72-76; C Virginia Water *Guildf* 76-79; P-in-c Peper Harow 79-82; P-in-c Shackleford 79-82; P-in-c Seale 82-89; rtd 89; Perm to Offic *Truro* 89-99. *Tudor Lodge, 60 East Church Street, Xenia, OH 45385, USA*

RANSON, Canon Arthur Frankland. b 50. St Jo Coll Dur BA73. Wycliffe Hall Ox 73. **d** 75 **p** 76. C Bare *Blackb* 75-78; C Scotforth 78-81; V Leyland St Ambrose 81-02; AD Leyland 96-02; P-in-c Blackb St Silas from 02; Hon Can Blackb Cathl from 00. *St Silas's Vicarage, Preston New Road, Blackburn BB2 6PS* Tel (01254) 671293 E-mail arthur.ranson@ntlworld.com

RANSON, George Sidney. b 28. Open Univ BA78. NEOC 85. **d** 86 **p** 87. NSM Acomb H Redeemer *York* 86-88; C Warton St Oswald w Yealand Conyers *Blackb* 88-90; V Pilling 90-95; rtd 95; Perm to Offic *Blackb* from 95. *18 Cotswold Road, Lytham St Annes FY8 4NN*

RANSON, Terence William James. b 42. AKC64 MTh87 STM88 AFAIM91. St Boniface Warminster 64. **d** 65 **p** 66. C Walton St Mary *Liv* 65-69; C Ipswich St Mary le Tower *St E* 69-71; Chapl Mersey Miss to Seamen 71-74; V N Keyham *Ex* 74-79; Australia 79-91; Sen Chapl and State Sec Fremantle Miss to Seamen 79-91; V N Mymms *St Alb* 91-04; rtd 04. *23 Pennine Close, Hereford HR4 0TE* Tel (01432) 278363

RANTALA, Tapani Pellervo. b 61. Helsinki Univ 81. **p** 91. Finland 91-02; Project Sec Par Work Cen 01-94; Asst Sec to Abp Turku and Finland 94-00; Dir and Chapl Finnish Ch in Lon from 02. *The Finnish Church in London, 33 Albion Street, London SE16 7JG* Tel (020) 7237 1261 Fax 7237 1245 E-mail tapani.rantala@btclick.com

RANYARD, Michael Taylor. b 43. Nottm Univ BTh74. Linc Th Coll 71. **d** 74 **p** 75. C Sutton in Ashfield St Mary *S'well* 74-76; Hon C Lewisham St Mary *S'wark* 76-77; C Rushmere *St E* 77-79; R Hopton, Market Weston, Barningham etc 79-83; Chr Educn and Resources Adv *Dur* 83-93; Prin Adv to Dioc Bd of Educn *Blackb* 93-98; Asst P Blackb Cathl 98-99; rtd 99; Perm to Offic *Heref* from 99. *72 Wyedean Rise, Belmont, Hereford HR2 7XZ* Tel and fax (01432) 355452 E-mail smranyard@xalt.co.uk *or* michaelranyard@beeb.net

RAO, Norma Ruoman. b 63. Westmr Coll Ox BTh97. Westcott Ho Cam 99. **d** 01 **p** 02. C Endcliffe *Sheff* 01-04; C Rotherham from 04. *7 Oxley Court, Rotherham S60 2ER* Tel (01709) 365145 E-mail norma@rrao.junglelink.co.uk

RAPHAEL, Brother. *See* PARKER, Ramon Lewis

RAPHAEL, The Ven Timothy John. b 29. Leeds Univ BA53. Coll of Resurr Mirfield. **d** 55 **p** 56. C Westmr St Steph w St Jo *Lon* 55-60; V Welling *S'wark* 60-63; New Zealand 63-72; Dean Dunedin 65-72; V St John's Wood *Lon* 72-83; AD Westmr St Marylebone 82-83; Adn Middx 83-96; rtd 96; Perm to Offic *Glouc* from 96. *121 Hales Road, Cheltenham GL52 6ST* Tel (01242) 256075

RAPHOE, Archdeacon of. *See* HARTE, The Ven Matthew Scott

RAPHOE, Dean of. *See* HAY, The Very Revd John

RAPKIN, Kevern. b 39. St D Coll Lamp BA62 Univ of Wales BD72. Lich Th Coll 63. **d** 65 **p** 66. C Hanley w Hope *Lich* 65-68; C Woodchurch *Ches* 68-70; C Abbots Langley *St Alb* 70-73; Australia 73-00 and from 04; R Mt Pleasant 73-80; R Rockingham and Safety Bay 80-90; R Lesmurdie 90-00; C Sholing *Win* 00-04; rtd 04. *15 Gamage Way, Lockridge, W Australia 6054* Tel (0061) (8) 9377 0332

RAPLEY, Frederick Arthur. b 27. Roch Th Coll 67. **d** 69 **p** 70. C Tenterden St Mildred w Smallhythe *Cant* 69-75; P-in-c Sittingbourne H Trin w Bobbing 75-85; V 85-89; rtd 89; Hon C Luton St Andr *St Alb* 89-92; Perm to Offic *St Alb* 92-98; *Cant* 98-02; *St E* from 02. *The Rectory, Clopton, Woodbridge IP13 6SE* Tel (01473) 738943

RAPLEY, Mrs Joy Naomi. b 41. Portsm Poly CertEd63 Open Univ BA79. Sarum & Wells Th Coll 87. **d** 89 **p** 94. Par Dn Welwyn Garden City *St Alb* 89-92; Chapl S Beds Community Healthcare Trust 92-98; C Wilbury *St Alb* 94-95; NSM St Mary's Bay w St Mary-in-the-Marsh etc *Cant* 98-02; NSM New Romney w Old Romney and Midley 98-02; Asst Chapl E Kent NHS and Soc Care Partnership Trust 99-02; P-in-c Clopton w Otley, Swilland and Ashbocking *St E* from 02. *The Rectory, Clopton, Woodbridge IP13 6SE* Tel (01473) 738943 E-mail revraps@aol.com

RAPSEY, Preb Peter Nigel. b 46. K Coll Lon BD68 AKC68. St Boniface Warminster. **d** 69 **p** 70. C Walton-on-Thames *Guildf* 69-73; C Fleet 73-77; P-in-c The Collingbournes and Everleigh *Sarum* 77-79; TV Wexcombe 79-84; R Wokingham St Paul *Ox* 84-93; Chapl Warminster Sch 93-96; V Frome Ch Ch *B & W* 96-04; P-in-c Evercreech w Chesterblade and Milton Clevedon from 04; RD Frome 01-03; Dir of Ords from 03; Preb Wells Cathl from 04. *The Vicarage, Church Lane, Evercreech, Shepton Mallet BA4 6HU* Tel (01749) 830322 E-mail ccfrome@fish.co.uk

RASHBROOK, Alan Victor. b 42. S'wark Ord Course. **d** 75 **p** 76. Hon C Woking St Mary *Guildf* 75-83. *Hope Cottage, Robin Hood Lane, Sutton Green, Guildford GU4 7QG* Tel (01483) 762760

RASON, Frederick George. b 26. Qu Coll Birm 68. **d** 69 **p** 70. C Weymouth H Trin *Sarum* 69-72; P-in-c Yatesbury 72-73; P-in-c Cherhill 72-73; R Oldbury 73-76; R W Parley 76-91; rtd 91; Perm to Offic *Sarum* from 91 and *Win* from 92. *4 Knoll Gardens, St Ives, Ringwood BH24 2LW* Tel (01425) 475761

RASTALL, Preb Thomas Eric. b 19. St Aid Birkenhead 62. **d** 63 **p** 64. C Leek St Luke *Lich* 64-67; V Brown Edge 67-74; P-in-c Croxden 74-78; V Denstone 74-81; P-in-c Ellastone 78-81; V Denstone w Ellastone and Stanton 81-91; RD Uttoxeter 87-91; Preb Lich Cathl 89-91; rtd 91; Perm to Offic *Cov* 91-01. *10 Vicarage Close, Burton, Carnforth LA6 1NP* Tel (01524) 782386

RATCLIFF, The Ven David William. b 37. Edin Th Coll 59. **d** 62 **p** 63. C Croydon St Aug *Cant* 62-65; C Selsdon St Jo w St Fran 65-69; V Milton Regis St Mary 69-75; Hon Min Can Cant Cathl 75-91; Asst Dir of Educn 75-91; Dioc Adv in Adult Educn and Lay Tr 75-91; Hon Pres Protestant Assn for Adult Educn in Eur 82-88; Chapl Frankfurt-am-Main 91-98; Adn Scandinavia *Eur* 96-05; Chapl Stockholm w Gävle and Västerås 98-02; rtd 05; Perm to Offic *Cant* from 02. *9 The Orchards, Elham, Canterbury CT4 6TR* Tel (01303) 840624 Fax 840871 E-mail archdeacon.david@zen.co.uk

RATCLIFFE, Canon Michael David. b 43. Lon Univ BSc65 Southn Univ PGCE67 Lon Univ BA75 Lanc Univ MA84. Cranmer Hall Dur 75. **d** 77 **p** 78. C Blackpool St Thos *Blackb* 77-81; V Oswaldtwistle St Paul from 81; RD Accrington 97-03; Hon Can Blackb Cathl from 00. *29 Mayfield Avenue, Oswaldtwistle, Accrington BB5 3AA* Tel (01254) 231038 Fax 390273 E-mail mratossy@tiscali.co.uk

RATCLIFFE, Peter William Lewis. b 30. Birm Univ BSc55 Lon Univ BD58. Tyndale Hall Bris 55. **d** 58 **p** 59. C Cambridge St Andr Less *Ely* 58-61; R Wistow 61-74; R Bury 61-74; V Rainham *Chelmsf* 74-85; R Wennington 75-85; V Heacham *Nor* 85-87; P-in-c Sedgeford w Southmere 85-87; V Heacham and Sedgeford 87-95; rtd 95; Perm to Offic *Nor* from 95. *22 Birchfield Gardens, Mulbarton, Norwich NR14 8BT* Tel (01508) 570511 E-mail p&mratcliffe@mulb.fsnet.co.uk

RATCLIFFE, Mrs Roosevelta (Rosie). b 60. K Coll Lon BA97 MA99. SEITE 98. **d** 01 **p** 02. C Croydon St Matt *S'wark* 01-04; Chapl S Lon and Maudsley NHS Trust from 04; Hon C Sanderstead All SS *S'wark* from 05. *Bethlem Royal Hospital, Monks Orchard Road, Beckenham BR3 3BX* Tel (020) 8777 6611 Fax 8777 1668

RATHBAND, Kenneth William. b 60. Edin Univ BD86. Edin Th Coll 82. **d** 86 **p** 87. NSM Dundee St Paul *Bre* 86-88; TV Dundee St Martin 88-89; NSM Edin SS Phil and Jas *Edin* 90-91; R Alyth *St And* from 91; R Blairgowrie from 91; R Coupar Angus from 91. *10 Rosemount Park, Blairgowrie PH10 6TZ* Tel (01250) 872431 *or* 874583 E-mail krathband@zetnet.co.uk

RATHBONE, Mrs Elizabeth. b 51. Lon Univ MB, BS76 MRCGP80. WMMTC 03. **d** 03 **p** 04. C Tettenhall Regis *Lich* from 03. *11 Harwin Close, Wolverhampton WV6 9LF* E-mail liz.rathbone1@btinternet.com

RATHBONE, Mrs Isobel. b 48. Girton Coll Cam MA70 Leeds Univ MA02 Solicitor 81. NEOC 02. **d** 05. NSM Moor Allerton

Ripon from 05. *32 Claremont Road, Leeds LS6 4EB* Tel and fax 0113-274 7716 Mobile 07775-656257
E-mail isobel@rathbone32.fsnet.co.uk

RATHBONE, Paul. b 36. BNC Ox BA58 MA62. Wycliffe Hall Ox. 58. **d** 60 **p** 61. C Carl St Jo *Carl* 60-63; C Heworth w Peasholme St Cuth *York* 63-68; V Thorganby w Skipwith and N Duffield 68-83; V Bishopthorpe and Acaster Malbis 83-01; rtd 01; Perm to Offic *York* from 01. *12 Whitelass Close, Thirsk YO7 1FG* Tel (01845) 523347 E-mail prathbon@fish.co.uk

RATHBONE, Stephen Derek. b 61. Wycliffe Hall Ox. **d** 00 **p** 01. C W Kirby St Bridget *Ches* 00-03; P-in-c Rainow w Saltersford and Forest from 03. *The Vicarage, Rainow, Macclesfield SK10 5TZ* Tel (01625) 572013 E-mail steve.rathbone@virgin.net

RATINGS, Canon John William. b 37. St Pet Coll Ox BA62 MA71. Cuddesdon Coll 62. **d** 64 **p** 65. C Langley All SS and Martyrs *Man* 64-68; C Easthampstead *Ox* 68-71; V Wargrave 71-02; V Wargrave w Knowl Hill from 02; RD Sonning 88-98; Hon Can Ch Ch from 97; Provost Woodard Corp (S Division) from 00. *The Vicarage, Station Road, Wargrave, Reading RG10 8EU* Tel 0118-940 2202 Fax 940 1470
E-mail jratings@aol.com

RATTENBERRY, Christopher James. b 59. Solicitor York Univ BA80. St Jo Coll Nottm 91. **d** 93 **p** 94. C Porchester *S'well* 93-98; P-in-c Daybrook 98-04; V from 04; AD Nottingham N from 01. *St Paul's Vicarage, 241 Oxclose Lane, Nottingham NG5 6FB* Tel 0115-926 2686 E-mail revdcjr@aol.com

✠**RATTERAY, The Rt Revd Alexander Ewen.** b 42. Codrington Coll Barbados 61. **d** 65 **p** 66 **c** 96. C S Kirkby *Wakef* 66-68; C Sowerby St Geo 68-71; V Airedale w Fryston 71-80; Bermuda from 80; Adn Bermuda 94-96; Bp Bermuda from 96. *Bishop's Lodge, PO Box HM 769, Hamilton HM CX, Bermuda* Tel (001) (441) 292 2967 *or* 292 6987 Fax 296 0592 *or* 292 5421
E-mail bishopratteray@ibl.bm

RATTIGAN, Paul Damian. b 61. Reading Univ BSc87 Liv Hope MA00 Sussex Univ PGCE88. Qu Coll Birm 93. **d** 95 **p** 96. C Parr *Liv* 95-99; P-in-c St Helens St Matt Thatto Heath 99-01; V from 01; Dioc Voc Adv from 02. *St Matthew's Vicarage, St Matthew's Grove, St Helens WA10 3SE* Tel (01744) 24644
E-mail pdr@st.matthewschurch.com

RATTUE, James. b 69. Ball Coll Ox BA91 MA04 Leic Univ MA93. St Steph Ho Ox 03. **d** 05. C Weybridge *Guildf* from 05. *87 Greenlands Road, Weybridge KT13 8PS* Tel (01932) 821196 Mobile 07952-615499 E-mail jamesrattue@hotmail.com

RAVALDE, Canon Geoffrey Paul. b 54. St Cuth Soc Dur BA76 SS Coll Cam BA86 MA90 Lon Univ MTh91 Barrister 78. Westcott Ho Cam 84. **d** 87 **p** 88. C Spalding *Linc* 87-91; P-in-c Wigton *Carl* 91-92; V from 92; RD Carl 95-00; Hon Can Carl Cathl from 96. *The Vicarage, Longthwaite Road, Wigton CA7 9JR* Tel (01697) 342337

RAVEN, Barry. b 48. Sarum & Wells Th Coll 69. **d** 72 **p** 73. C Henbury *Bris* 72-76; P-in-c S Marston w Stanton Fitzwarren 76-78; TV Stratton St Margaret w S Marston etc 78-80; P-in-c Coalpit Heath 80-84; V 84-91; R Ashley, Crudwell, Hankerton, Long Newnton etc from 91; RD N Wilts from 99. *The Rectory, 1 Days Court, Crudwell, Malmesbury SN16 9HG* Tel (01666) 577118 E-mail barry.raven@talk21.com

RAVEN, Mrs Margaret Ann. b 54. Westmr Univ BSc76 City Univ MSc87. Ridley Hall Cam 03. **d** 05. C Woodhall Spa Gp *Linc* from 05. *26 St Leonards Avenue, Woodhall Spa LN10 6TA* Tel (01526) 351358 E-mail ann.raven@btopenworld.com

RAVEN, Margaret Hilary. b 45. Dur Univ BA67 Man Univ MEd73. Wesley Th Sem Washington MDiv95. **d** 96 **p** 97. USA 96-01; Asst R Martinsburg Trin Ch 96-99; Assoc R Toms River Ch Ch 99-00; Perm to Offic *Edin* from 02. *32 Montpelier Park, Edinburgh EH10 4NJ* Tel 0131-228 4790
E-mail mthrraven@hotmail.com

RAVEN, Roger Ian Thomas-Ambrose. b 65. Girton Coll Cam BA87 MA91 PGCE88 Cranfield Univ MSc92 Leeds Univ BA01. Coll of Resurr Mirfield 99. **d** 01 **p** 02. C Cantley *Sheff* 01-05; V Up Hatherley *Glouc* from 05. *The Vicarage, Hatherley Road, Cheltenham GL51 6HX* Tel (01242) 236979
E-mail r.raven@btinternet.com

RAVEN, Tony. b 39. Garnett Coll Lon CertEd65 MIEE72 CEng72. St Alb and Ox Min Course 94. **d** 97 **p** 98. NSM Lt Berkhamsted and Bayford, Essendon etc *St Alb* 97-01; P-in-c Lt Hadham w Albury 01-05; rtd 05. *Church View, Church Hill, Stalbridge, Sturminster Newton DT10 2LR*
E-mail t_raven@btopenworld.com

RAVENS, David Arthur Stanley. b 30. Jes Coll Ox BA53 MA61 Lon Univ BD63. Wells Th Coll 61. **d** 63 **p** 64. C Seacroft *Ripon* 63-70; TV 70-73; Teacher Sir Wm Borcase's Sch Marlow 73-87; rtd 95. *44 Arthursdale Grange, Scholes, Leeds LS15 4AW* Tel 0113-273 6648

RAVENSCROFT, The Ven Raymond Lockwood. b 31. Leeds Univ BA53. Coll of Resurr Mirfield 54. **d** 55 **p** 56. C Goodwood S Africa 55-57; C St Jo Cathl Bulawayo S Rhodesia 57-59; R Francistown Bechuanaland 59-62; C St Ives *Truro* 62-64; V Falmouth All SS 64-68; V St Stephens by Launceston 68-73; P-in-c Launceston St Thos 68-73; V Launceston St Steph w St Thos 73-74; TR Probus, Ladock and Grampound w Creed and St Erme 74-88; RD Powder 77-81; Hon Can Truro Cathl 82-88; P-in-c St Erme 84-85; Adn Cornwall and Can Lib Truro Cathl 88-96; rtd 96; Perm to Offic *Truro* from 96 and *Ex* from 00. *19 Montpelier Court, St David's Hill, Exeter EX4 4DP* Tel (01392) 430607

RAVENSDALE, Jonathan Christopher. b 56. Aston Tr Scheme 90 Chich Th Coll DipTh94. **d** 94 **p** 95. C Leytonstone St Marg w St Columba *Chelmsf* 94-97; P-in-c Leytonstone St Andr 97-01; Voc Adv Richborough *Cant* and Barking from 97; V Walthamstow St Mich from 01. *St Michael's Vicarage, 9 Palmerston Road, London E17 6PQ* Tel (020) 8520 6328

✠**RAWCLIFFE, The Rt Revd Derek Alec.** b 21. OBE71. Leeds Univ BA42. Coll of Resurr Mirfield 42. **d** 44 **p** 45 **c** 74. C Claines St Geo *Worc* 44-47; Solomon Is 47-58; New Hebrides 58-80; Adn S Melanesia 59-74; Asst Bp Melanesia 74-75; Bp New Hebrides 75-80; Bp Glas 81-91; rtd 91; Asst Bp Ripon 91-96; Lic to Offic from 96. *7 Dorset Avenue, Leeds LS8 3RA* Tel 0113-249 2670 E-mail derek.rawcliffe@lineone.net

RAWDING, Andrew. b 70. Cranmer Hall Dur 00. **d** 02 **p** 03. C Enfield St Andr *Lon* 02-05. *38 Victoria Street, Armagh BT61 9DT* Tel (028) 3751 8018 E-mail therawdings@fish.co.uk

RAWDON-MOGG, Timothy David. b 45. St Jo Coll Dur BA76. Cuddesdon Coll 75. **d** 77 **p** 78. C Wotton St Mary *Glouc* 77-80; C Ascot Heath *Ox* 80-82; V Woodford Halse w Eydon *Pet* 82-88; V Shrivenham w Watchfield and Bourton *Ox* 88-00; R Horsted Keynes *Chich* from 00. *The Rectory, Station Road, Horsted Keynes, Haywards Heath RH17 7ED* Tel (01825) 790317

RAWE, Alan Charles George. b 29. ALCD56. **d** 56 **p** 57. C W Kilburn St Luke w St Simon and St Jude *Lon* 56-59; Lect Watford St Mary *St Alb* 59-61; R Ore *Chich* 61-69; R Moreton *Ches* 69-80; V Coppull *Blackb* 80-83; Miss to Seamen 83-94; Felixstowe Seafarers' Cen 88-94; rtd 94; Perm to Offic *Blackb* from 94. *15 Starfield Close, Lytham St Annes FY8 4QA* Tel (01253) 733647

RAWLING, Miss Jane Elizabeth. b 51. Birm Univ BSc73 St Jo Coll York CertEd75. St Jo Coll Nottm LTh84. **dss** 84 **d** 87 **p** 94. Southsea St Jude *Portsm* 84-87; C 87-88; C St Paul's Cray St Barn *Roch* 88-91; Hon C from 91; SE Regional Co-ord BCMS Crosslinks 91-01; Perm to Offic *S'wark* 97-01; Sec for Bps' Selection Conf and CME Sec Min Division from 01. *50 Batchwood Green, Orpington BR5 2NF,* or *Church House, Great Smith Street, London SW1P 3NZ* Tel (01689) 871467 *or* (020) 7898 1424 Fax (020) 7898 1421
E-mail jane.rawling@c-of-e.org.uk

RAWLING, Stephen Charles. b 43. Man Univ BSc64 Bris Univ MSc71 DipTh73. Sarum & Wells Th Coll 71. **d** 73 **p** 74. C Bris St Andr Hartcliffe *Bris* 73-76; C Westlands St Andr *Lich* 76-78; R Darlaston St Lawr 78-90; TR Bloxwich from 90. *All Saints' Vicarage, 3 Elmore Row, Bloxwich, Walsall WS3 2HR* Tel (01922) 476598

RAWLINGS, Miss Brenda Susan. b 48. Sussex Univ CertEd69 DipHE81. Oak Hill Th Coll 85. **d** 87 **p** 94. Par Dn Green Street Green *Roch* 87-90; Par Dn Collier Row St Jas and Havering-atte-Bower *Chelmsf* 90-94; C 94; C Greenstead 94-98; R 98-00; TR Greenstead w Colchester St Anne from 00. *The Rectory, 74 Howe Close, Colchester CO4 3XD* Tel (01206) 865762
E-mail ammasue@greenstead.fslife.co.uk

RAWLINGS, Gayle Ann Mary. b 53. Toronto Univ MD76 BA88 K Coll Lon MA89 FRCP(C)81. Westcott Ho Cam 01. **d** 03 **p** 04. C Ex St Thos and Em *Ex* from 03. *13 Sydney Road, Exeter EX2 9AJ* Tel (01392) 213445 E-mail rawlings@fish.co.uk

RAWLINGS, Preb John Edmund Frank. b 47. AKC69. St Aug Coll Cant 69. **d** 70 **p** 71. C Rainham *Roch* 70-73; C Tattenham Corner and Burgh Heath *Guildf* 73-76; Chapl RN 76-92; V Tavistock and Gulworthy *Ex* from 92; Chapl Kelly Coll Tavistock 93-02; RD Tavistock *Ex* 97-02; Preb Ex Cathl from 99. *The Vicarage, 5A Plymouth Road, Tavistock PL19 8AU* Tel (01822) 612162 *or* 616673 E-mail tavychurch@eurobell.co.uk

RAWLINGS, Canon Philip John. b 53. St Jo Coll Nottm BTh83. **d** 83 **p** 84. C Blackley St Andr *Man* 83-87; C Halliwell St Pet 87-93; R Old Trafford St Bride from 93; AD Stretford 98-05; Hon Can Man Cathl from 04. *St Bride's Rectory, 29 Shrewsbury Street, Old Trafford, Manchester M16 9BB* Tel 0161-226 6064
E-mail philjr@zetnet.co.uk

RAWLINGS, Susan. *See* RAWLINGS, Miss Brenda Susan

RAWLINS, Clyde Thomas. b 28. **d** 02. NSM Leeds St Aid *Ripon* from 02. *26 Gledhow Wood Close, Leeds LS8 1PN* Tel 0113-266 7731

RAWLINSON, Curwen. b 32. MBE73. Leeds Univ CertEd55 Man Univ DipEd56 Open Univ BA80. Sarum Th Coll 59. **d** 61 **p** 62. C Wigan St Mich *Liv* 61-63; CF 63-78; Dep Asst Chapl Gen 78-80; Asst Chapl Gen 80-85; QHC 83-98; R Uley w Owlpen and Nympsfield *Glouc* 85-98; RD Dursley 89-96; rtd 98; Perm to Offic *Glouc* from 98. *Cark House, 6 Groves Place, Fairford GL7 4BJ* Tel (01285) 711009

RAWLINSON, James Nigel. b 56. Em Coll Cam BA77 MB, BCh80 FRCSE86 FFAEM98. WMMTC 95. **d** 98 **p** 99.

NSM Bath Weston All SS w N Stoke and Langridge *B & W* from 98; Perm to Offic *Bris* from 98; Consultant Bris R Infirmary from 99. *Glen Boyd House, 38 Court View, Wick, Bristol BS30 5QP*

RAWLINSON, John. b 47. Guy's Hosp Medical Sch BSc67 MB, BS71 MRCS. EAMTC 89. **d** 92 **p** 93. NSM Tilbrook *Ely* from 92; NSM Covington from 92; NSM Catworth Magna from 92; NSM Keyston and Bythorn from 92; Chapl Chu Coll Cam from 98. *The Malt House, 42 Stonely, Huntingdon PE28 0EH* Tel (01480) 860263 Fax 861590 E-mail dingleberry@lineone.net

RAWLINSON, Rowland. b 20. Leeds Univ CertEd41 Liv Univ DipAdEd68 Open Univ BA74. St Deiniol's Hawarden 79. **d** 80 **p** 81. Hon C Barnston *Ches* 80-82; C 82-85; Hon C Higher Bebington 85-92; rtd 92; Perm to Offic *Ches* from 94. *18 Winston Grove, Moreton, Wirral CH46 0PQ* Tel 0151-677 5641

RAWSON, Michael Graeme. b 62. York Univ BA84 Ox Univ BA88. St Steph Ho Ox 86. **d** 89 **p** 90. C Brighouse St Martin *Wakef* 89-92; C Brighouse and Clifton 92-93; V Gomersal 93-04; Bp's Dom Chapl and Publicity Officer from 04. *Bishop's Lodge, Woodthorpe Lane, Wakefield WF2 6JL* Tel (01924) 255349 E-mail michael.rawson@bishopofwakefield.org.uk

RAY, Mrs Joanna Zorina. b 55. AIMLS78 K Coll Lon BSc77 Garnett Coll Lon PGCE80 Lon Inst of Educn MA92. S'wark Ord Course 84. **d** 87 **p** 94. NSM Carshalton *S'wark* 87-91; NSM Sutton New Town St Barn 91-93; NSM Knighton St Mary Magd *Leic* 93-94; C Leic H Spirit 94-98; Chapl for Deaf People 94-98; Chapl St Andr Hosp Northn 99-03; Perm to Offic *S'well* from 04. *37 Torvill Drive, Nottingham NG8 2BU* Tel 07802-300799 (mobile) E-mail revdjoannaray@cs.com

RAY, John Mead. b 28. OBE79. St Andr Univ MA50 DipEd51. CMS Tr Coll Chislehurst 60. **d** 70 **p** 71. Miss Partner CMS 70-95; C Sparkhill St Jo *Birm* 87-90; C Sparkbrook Em 87-90; C Sparkhill w Greet and Sparkbrook 90; Deanery Missr 90-95; rtd 95; Perm to Offic *Birm* from 95. *190 Sarehole Road, Birmingham B28 8EF* Tel 0121-777 6143

RAY, Robin John. b 44. Sarum & Wells Th Coll 72. **d** 74 **p** 75. C Bourne Valley *Sarum* 74-78; P-in-c Dilton's-Marsh 78-82; V 82-87; V Taunton Lyngford *B & W* 87-93; R Exford, Exmoor, Hawkridge and Withypool 93-04; ACORA Link Officer and Rural Affairs Officer 93-04; rtd 04. *Leigholt Farm, Somerton Road, Street BA16 0SU* Tel (01458) 841281

RAYBOULD, James Clive Ransford. b 37. Wolv Univ BSc62 Anglia Poly Univ MBA94 PhD01. Cranmer Hall Dur 81. **d** 83 **p** 84. C Cannock *Lich* 83-86; P-in-c Leek Wootton *Cov* 86-89; Dioc Tr Adv 86-89; TV Cannock *Lich* 89; Assoc Lect Anglia Poly Univ *Chelmsf* from 90; rtd 00. *73 Eastwood Old Road, Leigh-on-Sea SS9 4RS* Tel (01702) 522277

✠**RAYFIELD, The Rt Revd Lee Stephen.** b 55. Southn Univ BSc78 Lon Univ PhD81 SOSc95. Ridley Hall Cam 93. **d** 93 **p** 94 **c** 05. C Woodford Wells *Chelmsf* 93-97; P-in-c Furze Platt *Ox* 97-05; AD Maidenhead and Windsor 00-05; Suff Bp Swindon *Bris* from 05. *Mark House, Field Rise, Swindon SN1 4HP* Tel and fax (01793) 538654 E-mail bishop.lee@bristol.anglican.org *or* rayfield@btinternet.com

RAYMENT, Andrew David. b 45. Univ of Wales (Lamp) BA68 Univ of Wales (Abth) MA70. Ridley Hall Cam 78. **d** 80 **p** 81. C Costessey *Nor* 80-83; C Earlham St Anne 83-90; V Old Catton 90-96; Perm to Offic *Pet* from 00; Min Partnership Development Officer from 04; Adult Educn Officer and Post Ord Tr Co-ord from 05. *Peterborough DBF, Bouverie Court, 6 The Lakes, Northampton NN4 7YD* Tel (01604) 887047 *or* (01327) 340359 E-mail andrew@hrayment.wanadoo.co.uk

RAYMENT, Mrs Helen Elizabeth. b 46. Keswick Hall Coll CertEd67. EAMTC 92. **d** 95 **p** 96. NSM Old Catton *Nor* 95-96; Perm to Offic *Pet* 01-02; P-in-c Weedon Bec w Everdon and Dodford 02-03; V from 03. *The Vicarage, Church Street, Weedon, Northampton NN7 4PL* Tel (01327) 340359 E-mail revdh@hrayment.wanadoo.co.uk

RAYMENT-PICKARD, Hugh Douglas John. b 61. Kent Univ BA84 Em Coll Cam BA87 Lon Univ PhD97. Westcott Ho Cam 85. **d** 88 **p** 89. C St Jo on Bethnal Green *Lon* 88-91; C Hackney 91-92; TV 92-95; V Notting Dale St Clem w St Mark and St Jas from 95; AD Kensington from 01. *12 St Ann's Villas, London W11 4RS* Tel (020) 7221 3548 Fax 7221 8810 E-mail hugh@clementjames.co.uk

RAYMER, Victoria Elizabeth. b 46. Wellesley Coll (USA) BA68 Harvard Univ MA69 JD78 PhD81. St Steph Ho Ox BA86 Qu Coll Birm 88. **d** 89 **p** 94. Par Dn Bushey *St Alb* 89-94; C Eaton Socon 94-98; V Milton Ernest, Pavenham and Thurleigh 98-01; Dir Studies Westcott Ho Cam from 01. *1 Short Street, Cambridge CB1 1LB* Tel (01223) 352922 *or* tel and fax 741011 E-mail ver21@cam.ac.uk

RAYMONT, Philip Richard. b 56. Univ of Qld BA79 BEdSt86 Melbourne Univ MEd00 MACE. **d** 04. *Selwyn College, Cambridge CB3 9DQ* Tel (01223) 572638 Fax 331720 E-mail prr22@cam.ac.uk

RAYNER, David. b 49. Trin Hall Cam BA72 MA75. Westcott Ho Cam 75. **d** 78 **p** 79. C Chorlton-cum-Hardy St Clem *Man* 78-81; C Cambridge Gt St Mary w St Mich *Ely* 81-84; V Camberwell St Geo *S'wark* 84-88; Warden Trin Coll Cen Camberwell 84-88; Warden Bp Mascall Cen *Heref* 89-90; V Smethwick H Trin w St Alb *Birm* 90-92; P-in-c W Smethwick 90-92; P-in-c Smethwick SS Steph and Mich 92-95; V Smethwick Resurr 92-99; RD Warley 93-97; Sec Inner Cities Relig Coun 99-03; Perm to Offic *Lon* from 99. *Address temp unknown*

RAYNER, Canon George Charles. b 26. Bps' Coll Cheshunt 50. **d** 52 **p** 53. C Rowbarton *B & W* 52-56; V Taunton H Trin 56-63; Chapl Taunton and Somerset Hosp 60-63; V Lower Sandown St Jo *Portsm* 63-69; R Wootton 69-89; Hon Can Portsm Cathl 84-89; rtd 89; Perm to Offic *B & W* 89-92 and *Portsm* from 98; P-in-c Six Pilgrims *B & W* 93-02. *The Bungalow, 1 Alresford Road, Shanklin PO37 6HX* Tel (01983) 867304

RAYNER, Paul Anthony George. b 39. Dur Univ BA60 Lon Univ BD68 Cape Town Univ MA79. Lon Coll of Div 65. **d** 68 **p** 69. C Crookes St Thos *Sheff* 68-72; S Africa 72-79; P-in-c S Shoebury *Chelmsf* 80-84; R 84-97; V Loughton St Mich 97-04; rtd 04. *36 Amberley Road, Buckhurst Hill IG9 5QW* Tel (020) 8504 7434 E-mail prayner@globalnet.co.uk

RAYNER, Richard Noel. b 24. Lon Univ BD51. Oak Hill Th Coll 50. **d** 52 **p** 53. C Plymouth St Jude *Ex* 52-55; V Walthamstow St Luke *Chelmsf* 55-61; V Romford Gd Shep Collier Row 61-65; V Slough *Ox* 65-72; V Heworth w Peasholme St Cuth *York* 72-75; V Heworth H Trin 75-81; V Okehampton w Inwardleigh *Ex* 81-89; RD Okehampton 87-89; rtd 89; Perm to Offic *Ex* 90-98 and *B & W* from 90. *Redlands, 5 Ladymeade, Ilminster TA19 0EA* Tel (01460) 52491

RAYNER, Mrs Shirley Christine. b 54. SEITE 02. **d** 05. NSM Croydon St Pet *S'wark* from 05; NSM Croydon St Aug from 05. *59 Ewhurst Avenue, South Croydon CR2 0DL* Tel (020) 8651 2266

RAYNER, Stewart Leslie. b 39. St Jo Coll Dur BA61 DipTh66 MA73. Cranmer Hall Dur. **d** 67 **p** 68. C Whiston *Sheff* 67-70; C Doncaster St Geo 70-74; Chapl Doncaster R Infirmary 70-74; R Adwick-le-Street *Sheff* 74-85; V Totley 85-91; Asst Chapl Pastures Hosp Derby 91-94; Asst Chapl Kingsway Hosp Derby 91-94; Asst Chapl S Derby Mental Health Services 91-94; P-in-c Etwall w Egginton *Derby* 94-99; R from 99; RD Longford 96-01. *St Helen's Rectory, Main Street, Etwall, Derby DE6 6LP* Tel (01283) 732349 E-mail slrayner@fish.co.uk

RAYNES, Andrew. b 60. R Holloway Coll Lon BA83. Wycliffe Hall Ox 93. **d** 95 **p** 96. C Crowborough *Chich* 95-99; V Blackb Ch Ch w St Matt *Blackb* from 99; AD Blackb and Darwen from 03. *The Vicarage, Brandy House Brow, Blackburn BB2 3EY* Tel (01254) 56292 E-mail andrewraynes@btopenworld.com

RAYNHAM, Mrs Penelope Anne. b 44. SW Minl Tr Course 97. **d** 00 **p** 01. OLM S Hill w Callington *Truro* from 00. *Bramblings, Honicombe Corner, Harrowbarrow, Callington PL17 8JN* Tel (01822) 833065 E-mail penny@bramvista.co.uk

RAYNOR, Duncan Hope. b 58. Ex Coll Ox MA80 MA82 Birm Univ PGCE88 MLitt93. Qu Coll Birm 82. **d** 84 **p** 85. C Kings Heath *Birm* 84-87; Perm to Offic from 87; Hd of RE Alderbrook Sch Solihull 88-94; Chapl K Edw Sch Birm from 94. *134 Addison Road, Birmingham B14 7EP* Tel 0121-684 3407 *or* 472 1672 E-mail dhr@kes.bham.sch.uk

RAYNOR, Michael. b 53. Lanc Univ BA74 MSc75. Ripon Coll Cuddesdon BA84 MA99. **d** 85 **p** 86. C Gt Crosby St Faith *Liv* 85-88; V Warrington St Barn 88-97; V Orford St Andr from 97; AD Warrington 99-05; Hon Can Liv Cathl 03-05. *St Andrew's Vicarage, Poplars Avenue, Orford, Warrington WA2 9UE* Tel (01925) 631903 E-mail mjraynor@care4free.net

RAYNOR-SMITH, Charles Alfred Walter. b 12. Sarum Th Coll. **d** 55 **p** 56. C Oakdale St Geo *Sarum* 55-58; C Swanage 58-62; V Colehill 62-81; rtd 81; Perm to Offic *Sarum* from 81. *19 Tatnam Road, Poole BH15 2OW* Tel (01202) 681996

RAZZALL, Charles Humphrey. b 55. Worc Coll Ox BA76 MA81 Qu Coll Cam BA78. Westcott Ho Cam 76. **d** 79 **p** 80. C Catford (Southend) and Downham *S'wark* 79-83; V Crofton Park St Hilda w St Cypr 83-87; UPA Officer 87-92; TV Oldham *Man* 87-01; AD Oldham 92-99; Hon Can Man Cathl 98-01; R Coppenhall *Ches* from 01. *The Rectory, 198 Ford Lane, Crewe CW1 3TN* Tel (01270) 215151

REA, Simon William John. b 60. G&C Coll Cam MA Univ of Wales (Ban) PGCE Victoria Univ Wellington MA. Ridley Hall Cam 02. **d** 04 **p** 05. C Moreton *Ches* from 04. *9 Kinnerton Close, Wirral CH46 6HT* Tel 0151-605 1241 *or* 604 0049 Mobile 07905-699185 E-mail simonrea@gmx.net

READ, Andrew Gordon. b 40. Nottm Univ BA69 MRICS63 FRICS86. Cuddesdon Coll 70. **d** 70 **p** 71. C E Retford *S'well* 70-72; C Woodthorpe 72-76; P-in-c Newark St Leon 76-78; Perm to Offic *Roch* 79-91. *The Gables, 148 Hastings Road, Battle TN33 0TW* Tel (01424) 773044

READ, Charles William. b 60. Man Univ BA81 Man Poly CertEd82. St Jo Coll Nottm 86. **d** 88 **p** 89. C Oldham *Man* 88-90; C Urmston 90-94; P-in-c Broughton St Jas w St Clem and St Matthias 94-96; TV Broughton 96-99; Tutor Cranmer Hall

Dur from 99. *St John's College, 3 South Bailey, Durham DH1 3RJ* Tel 0191-374 3579 Fax 374 3573 E-mail c.w.read@durham.ac.uk

READ, Geoffrey Philip. b 61. Bris Univ LLB82. Wycliffe Hall Ox 85. **d** 88 **p** 89. C Dorking St Paul *Guildf* 88-92; TV Westborough 92-97; TR 97-98; Chapl Basle *Eur* from 98; P-in-c Freiburg-im-Breisau 98-01. *St Johanns-Ring 92, CH-4056 Basle, Switzerland* Tel (0041) (61) 321 7477 Fax 321 7476 E-mail geoff.read@datacomm.ch

READ, James Arthur. b 51. Nottm Coll of Educn BEd74. EMMTC 84. **d** 87 **p** 88. C Weoley Castle *Birm* 87-91; C W Smethwick 91-92; C Smethwick Resurrection 92; TV Atherton *Man* 92-97; P-in-c Facit 97-00; V Whitworth w Facit from 00. *The Vicarage, Market Street, Whitworth, Rochdale OL12 8LU* Tel (01706) 853931 E-mail james.read@phonecoop.coop

READ, John. b 33. Worc Coll Ox BA56 MA60. Chich Th Coll 56. **d** 58 **p** 59. C Babbacombe *Ex* 58-60; C Heavitree 60-63; V Swimbridge 63-69; V Ex St Matt 69-80; P-in-c Ex St Sidwell 79-80; R Ex St Sidwell and St Matt 80-83; Chapl Warneford Hosp Leamington Spa 83-89; Chapl S Warks Hosps 83-89; Chapl Dur and Ches le Street Hosps 89-95; Chapl Dryburn Hosp 89-95; rtd 95; NSM Tamworth *Lich* 95-98; Perm to Offic *Cov* from 02. *30 Wattfield Close, Rugeley WS15 1ER* Tel (01889) 575427

READ, John du Sautoy. **d** 66 **p** 67. V Choral Derry Cathl *D & R* 66-67; Dean's V Derry Cathl 67; S Africa from 69. *33 Town Street, Potchefstroom, 2520 South Africa* Tel (0027) (148) 297 8580

READ, John Samuel. b 33. Fitzw Ho Cam BA56. Clifton Th Coll 62. **d** 64 **p** 65. C Sneinton St Chris w St Phil *S'well* 64-67; C Huyton St Geo *Liv* 67-70; Lic to Offic *Blackb* 70-72; V Moldgreen *Wakef* 72-84; V Rawtenstall St Mary *Man* 84-91; Chapl Rossendale Gen Hosp 84-91; R Earsham w Alburgh and Denton *Nor* 91-98; P-in-c Ditchingham, Hedenham and Broome 94-98; rtd 98; Perm to Offic *Nor* and *St E* from 98. *7 Pine Tree Close, Worlingham, Beccles NR34 7EE* Tel (01502) 712585

READ, Mrs Julie Margaret. b 61. Keble Coll Ox BA82 Univ of Wales (Ban) PGCE83. WEMTC 97. **d** 00 **p** 01. C Bishop's Castle w Mainstone, Lydbury N etc *Heref* 00-03; R Pembridge w Moor Court, Shobdon, Staunton etc from 03. *The Rectory, Manley Crescent, Pembridge, Leominster HR6 9EB* Tel (01544) 388998

READ, Maureen Elizabeth. b 52. Man Metrop Univ BEd93 Chester Coll of HE BTh99. N Ord Course 95. **d** 98 **p** 99. NSM Leesfield *Man* 98-99; C 99-02; TV Heywood from 02. *The Vicarage, 27 Heys Lane, Heywood OL10 3RD* Tel (01706) 368053

READ, Michael Antony. b 75. Lanc Univ BA99 St Jo Coll Dur BA01. Cranmer Hall Dur 99. **d** 02 **p** 03. C Stanley *Liv* from 02. *25 Eaton Road, West Derby, Liverpool L12 7JJ* Tel 0151-226 3134

READ, Nicholas George. b 51. Chelsea Coll Lon BSc72 PhD81 Spurgeon's Coll Dip Counselling 97. SEITE 97. **d** 00 **p** 01. NSM Beckenham St Jo *Roch* 00-03; P-in-c Penge Lane H Trin from 03. *Holy Trinity Vicarage, 64 Lennard Road, London SE20 7LX* Tel (020) 8778 8113 Mobile 07904-317488 E-mail hancompro@aol.com

READ, Nicholas John. b 59. OBE99. Keble Coll Ox BA81 MSc82 MA85. Ox Min Course 92. **d** 95 **p** 96. NSM Charlbury w Shorthampton *Ox* 95-98; Dir Rural Stress Information Network 96-00; Chapl for Agric *Heref* from 98. *The Rectory, Manley Crescent, Pembridge, Hereford HR6 9EB* Tel (01544) 388998

READ, Canon Robert Edgar. b 47. Kelham Th Coll 66. **d** 70 **p** 71. C Harton Colliery *Dur* 70-75; C Wilmslow *Ches* 76-80; V Gatley 80-92; V Offerton from 92; RD Stockport 00-05; Hon Can Ches Cathl from 03. *St Alban's Vicarage, 1A Salcombe Road, Offerton, Stockport SK2 5AG* Tel 0161-480 3773 E-mail reread@talk21.com

READ, Victor. b 29. Lon Univ BD58. ALCD57. **d** 58 **p** 59. C Wimbledon *S'wark* 58-61; C Lt Marlow *Ox* 61-64; V Wootton *Linc* 64-67; R Croxton 64-67; V Ulceby 64-67; V Linc St Pet in Eastgate w St Marg 67-73; V W Wimbledon Ch Ch *S'wark* 73-94; rtd 94; Perm to Offic *Pet* from 94. *27 Nightingale Drive, Towcester NN12 6RA* Tel (01327) 352027

✠**READE, The Rt Revd Nicholas Stewart.** b 46. Leeds Univ BA70. Coll of Resurr Mirfield 70. **d** 73 **p** 74 **c** 04. C Coseley St Chad *Lich* 73-75; C Codsall 75-78; V Upper Gornal 78-82; V Mayfield *Chich* 82-88; RD Dallington 82-88; V Eastbourne St Mary 88-97; RD Eastbourne 88-97; Can and Preb Chich Cathl 90-97; Can 97-04; Min The Hydneye CD 91-93; Adn Lewes and Hastings 97-04; Bp Blackb from 04. *Bishop's House, Ribchester Road, Blackburn BB1 9EF* Tel (01254) 248234 Fax 246668 E-mail bishop@bishopofblackburn.org.uk

READE, Richard Barton. b 66. Wolv Poly BA88. Ripon Coll Cuddesdon BA91 MA97. **d** 92 **p** 93. C Wilnecote *Lich* 92-96; C Penkridge Team 96-98; P-in-c Basford 98-04; P-in-c Matlock Bank *Derby* from 04. *All Saints' Vicarage, Smedley Street, Matlock DE4 3JG* Tel (01629) 584107 E-mail richardreade3@supanet.com

READER, Christine Sarah. STETS. **d** 00 **p** 01. NSM N Waltham and Steventon, Ashe and Deane *Win* from 00. *5 Church Farm Close, North Waltham, Basingstoke RG25 2BN* Tel (01256) 397503

READER, John. b 53. Trin Coll Ox BA75 MA79 Man Univ DSPT83 MPhil87 Univ of Wales (Ban) PhD02. Ripon Coll Cuddesdon 76. **d** 78 **p** 79. C Ely 78-80; C Baguley *Man* 80-83; TV Kirkby Lonsdale *Carl* 83-86; V Lydbury N *Heref* 86-89; P-in-c Hopesay w Edgton 86-89; R Lydbury N w Hopesay and Edgton 89-90; Tutor Glouc Sch for Min 86-88; Vice-Prin 88-90; Dir Past Th Sarum & Wells Th Coll 90-92; P-in-c Elmley Lovett w Hampton Lovett and Elmbridge etc *Worc* from 92; Assoc Tr and Educn Officer 92-02; Ind Chapl from 01. *The Rectory, Elmley Lovett, Droitwich WR9 0PU* Tel (01299) 251798 E-mail john-reader@4thenet.co.uk

READER, The Ven Trevor Alan John. b 46. Lon Univ BSc68 MSc70 Portsm Poly PhD72. S Dios Minl Tr Scheme 83. **d** 86 **p** 87. C Alverstoke *Portsm* 86-89; P-in-c Hook w Warsash 89-95; V 95-98; P-in-c Blendworth w Chalton w Idsworth 98-03; Dioc Dir NSM 98-04; Adn Is of Wight from 03; Bp's Liaison Officer for Pris from 03. *5 The Boltons, Kite Hill, Wootton Bridge, Ryde PO33 4PB* Tel (01983) 884432

READER-MOORE, Anthony. b 43. Kent Univ BA80 Hull Univ MA83 SSC02. Linc Th Coll. **d** 82 **p** 83. C Addiscombe St Mildred *Cant* 82-84; C Addiscombe St Mildred *S'wark* 85-86; R N Wheatley, W Burton, Bole, Saundby, Sturton etc *S'well* 86-93; Rural Officer 89-93; P-in-c Alford w Rigsby *Linc* 93-97; V 97-00; P-in-c Bilsby w Farlesthorpe 93-97; V 97-00; P-in-c Hannah cum Hagnaby w Markby 93-97; R 97-00; P-in-c Well 93-97; R 97-00; P-in-c Saleby w Beesby and Maltby 93-97; R 97-00; V Wellingborough All Hallows *Pet* from 00. *12 Bush Close, Wellingborough NN8 3GL* Tel (01933) 222002 E-mail tonyreadermoore@yahoo.co.uk

READING, Canon Laurence John. b 14. DSC44. Lon Univ BD39 AKC39. **d** 39 **p** 40. C Prittlewell *Chelmsf* 39-42; Chapl RNVR 42-46; C-in-c Prittlewell St Pet CD 46-60; V Shrub End *Chelmsf* 60-64; Tr Officer Bd of Educn Adult Cttee 64; Sec 65-72; Can Heref Cathl *Heref* 72-82; rtd 82; Perm to Offic *Chelmsf* from 82. *Albemarle House, Guithavon Road, Witham CM8 1HD*

READING, Mrs Lesley Jean. b 49. GNSM70 Trent Park Coll of Educn CertEd71. N Ord Course 98. **d** 01 **p** 02. NSM Eccles *Man* 01-05; P-in-c Heywood St Jas from 05. *St James's Vicarage, 46 Bury Old Road, Heywood OL10 3JD* Tel (01706) 369754 E-mail readinglesley@hotmail.com

READING, Miss Siân Jacqueline Mary. b 64. Westcott Ho Cam CTM95. **d** 95 **p** 96. C Northampton St Alb *Pet* 95-98; TV Duston Team from 98. *St Francis House, Eastfield Road, Duston, Northampton NN5 6TQ* Tel (01604) 753679 E-mail sianreading@tinyonline.co.uk

READING, Area Bishop of. *See* COTTRELL, The Rt Revd Stephen Geoffrey

REAGON, Darrol Franklin. b 46. Univ of Wales (Cardiff) DipTh76. St Mich Coll Llan 74. **d** 76 **p** 77. C Llandrillo-yn-Rhos *St As* 76-78; C Hawarden 78-81; V Northwich St Luke and H Trin *Ches* 81-85; V Moulton *Linc* 85-91; V Scunthorpe Resurr 91-92; P-in-c Branston 92-94; R Branston w Nocton and Potterhanworth from 94. *The Rectory, Abel Smith Gardens, Branston, Lincoln LN4 1NN* Tel (01522) 791296

REAKES, Richard Frank. b 68. STETS 02. **d** 05. NSM Shepton Mallet w Doulting *B & W* from 05. *Ashdene, Frome Road, Doulting, Shepton Mallet BA4 4QQ* Tel (01749) 880271 Fax 880105 E-mail reakes4@aol.com

REAKES-WILLIAMS, Gordon Martin. b 63. St Cath Coll Cam BA86 MA89. St Jo Coll Dur BA90. **d** 91 **p** 92. C Harold Wood *Chelmsf* 91-94; Chapl Leipzig *Eur* from 95. *Schreberstrasse 14B, 04109 Leipzig, Germany* Tel (0049) (341) 302 7951 Mobile 177-240 4207 Fax (341) 993 8844 E-mail earwig@t-online.de

REALE, Mrs Kathleen. b 38. Carl Dioc Tr Course 83. **dss** 86 **d** 87 **p** 94. Dalston *Carl* 86-87; Par Dn 87-90; Par Dn Westward, Rosley-w-Woodside and Welton 87-90; Par Dn Thursby 89-90; Dn-in-c Gt Salkeld w Lazonby 90-94; P-in-c 94-97; rtd 97; Perm to Offic *Carl* from 98. *4 Low Moorlands, Carlisle CA5 7NX* Tel (01228) 711749

REANEY, Mrs Beverly Jane. b 58. Nottm Univ BA81. S Wales Ord Course 00. **d** 03 **p** 04. NSM Llanharry *Llan* from 03. *The Rectory, High Street, Nelson, Treharris CF46 6HA* Tel and fax (01443) 450335 E-mail beverly.j.reaney@rhondda-cynon-taf.gov.uk

REANEY, Christopher Thomas. b 60. Univ of Wales (Lamp) BA82. St Mich Coll Llan DipTh85. **d** 85 **p** 86. C Maindee *Mon* 85-87; C Griffithstown 88-89; V Treherbert w Treorchy *Llan* 89-99; V Treorchy and Treherbert 99-02; R Llanfabon from 02. *The Rectory, High Street, Nelson, Treharris CF46 6HA* Tel and fax (01443) 450335

REARDON, Bernard Morris Garvin. b 13. Keble Coll Ox BA35 MA38. Ripon Hall Ox 35. **d** 37 **p** 38. C Saffron Walden *Chelmsf* 37-38; C Shenfield 38-40; P-in-c 40-41; CF (EC) 41-46; V Hornchurch H Cross *Chelmsf* 46-47; R Kelly w Bradstone *Ex*

47-59; R Parham and Wiggonholt w Greatham *Chich* 59-63; Sen Lect, Reader, and Hd Relig Studies Newc Univ 63-78; rtd 78; Perm to Offic *Newc* from 78. *2 The Grove, Benton, Newcastle upon Tyne NE12 9PE* Tel 0191-266 1574

REASON, Jack. b 28. St Alb Minl Tr Scheme 77. **d** 80 **p** 81. NSM Luton Lewsey St Hugh *St Alb* 80-85; C Bideford *Ex* 85-88; R Northlew w Ashbury 88-93; R Bratton Clovelly w Germansweek 88-93; rtd 93; Perm to Offic *Ex* from 94. *2 Bay View Court, Bay View Road, Northam, Bideford EX39 1TJ* Tel (01237) 472150

REAST, Eileen Joan. *See* BANGAY, Mrs Eileen Joan

RECORD, Canon John. b 47. St Chad's Coll Dur BA71. Westcott Ho Cam 71. **d** 73 **p** 74. C Paddington St Jo w St Mich *Lon* 73-75; C Witney *Ox* 75-78; P-in-c Lt Compton and Chastleton 78-80; R Lt Compton w Chastleton, Cornwell etc 80-83; V Hawkhurst *Cant* 83-97; RD W Charing 89-95; Hon Can Cant Cathl 96-97; P-in-c Devizes St Jo w St Mary *Sarum* from 97; P-in-c Devizes St Pet 00-04; RD Devizes from 98; Can and Preb Sarum Cathl from 02. *The Rectory, 39 Long Street, Devizes SN10 1NS* Tel and fax (01380) 723705
E-mail rector@stjohndevizes.fsnet.co.uk

RECORD, Sister Marion Eva. b 25. MRCS50 LRCP50 Leeds Univ FFARCS57 Lon Univ BD79. **dss** 78 **d** 87 **p** 94. OHP from 72; Chapl Hull Univ *York* 72-78; Chapl York Univ 78-80; Lic to Offic 80-95; Perm to Offic from 95; rtd 96. *St Hilda's Priory, Sneaton Castle, Whitby YO21 3QN* Tel (01947) 602079

REDDIN, Mrs Christine Emily. b 46. Essex Univ BA67. STETS 01. **d** 04 **p** 05. NSM Burpham *Guildf* from 04. *The Corner House, Sutton Green Road, Guildford GU4 7QD* Tel (01483) 714708 Mobile 07764-677898 E-mail c.reddin@btinternet.com

REDDING, Benjamin James. b 73. K Coll Lon BSc94 PGCE95. Oak Hill Th Coll BA05. **d** 05. C Angmering *Chich* from 05. *7 Beech View, Angmering, Littlehampton BN16 4DE* Tel (01903) 784459 E-mail benjamesredding@yahoo.co.uk

REDDING, Roger Charles. b 45. Chich Th Coll 87. **d** 89 **p** 90. C Yeovil St Mich *B & W* 89-93; P-in-c Salisbury St Mark *Sarum* 93-94; Lic to Offic 94-96; TV Chalke Valley from 96; Chapl to Travelling People from 02; Perm to Offic *B & W* from 03. *The Vicarage, May Lane, Ebbesbourne Wake, Salisbury SP5 5JL* Tel (01722) 780408

REDDINGTON, Gerald Alfred. b 34. Lon Univ DipRS79. S'wark Ord Course 76. **d** 79 **p** 79. NSM St Vedast w St Mich-le-Querne etc *Lon* 79-85; Dir Past Support Gp Scheme 83-86; Hon C St Marylebone All SS 85-90; V Ealing St Barn 90-99; rtd 99; Perm to Offic *Portsm* from 88 and *Lon* from 02. *The Orange Tree, Madeira Road, Seaview PO34 5BA* Tel (01983) 617026
E-mail rev.redd@btinternet.com

REDEYOFF, Neil Martyn. b 69. Nottm Univ BA01. St Jo Coll Nottm 98. **d** 01 **p** 02. C Grange St Andr and Runcorn H Trin *Ches* 01-04; R Darfield *Sheff* from 04. *The Rectory, Church Street, Darfield, Barnsley S73 9JX* Tel (01226) 752236
E-mail neil@redeyoff.wanadoo.co.uk

REDFEARN, James Jonathan. b 62. Newc Univ BA83 PGCE89. Cranmer Hall Dur 95. **d** 95 **p** 96. C Kidsgrove *Lich* 95-97. *56 Holly Avenue, Jesmond, Newcastle upon Tyne NE2 2QA* Tel 0191-281 9046 E-mail jaredfearn@compuserve.com

REDFEARN, John William Holmes. Sheff Univ BA30 MA31 DipEd31. **d** 33 **p** 34. C Bishopwearmouth St Mich *Dur* 33-35; Asst Master Bede Coll Sch Sunderland 31-45; Chapl Berkhamsted Colleg Sch Herts 45-55; Chapl Haberdashers' Aske's Sch Elstree 56-72; Perm to Offic *Lon* 61-76; rtd 72. *184 Cardiff Road, Llandaff, Cardiff CF5 2AD* Tel (029) 2056 7692

REDFEARN, Michael. b 42. Open Univ BA78 Hull Univ MA84 BA86. Bernard Gilpin Soc Dur 63 St Aid Birkenhead 64. **d** 68 **p** 69. C Bury St Pet *Man* 68-71; C Swinton St Pet 71-74; Ind Chapl *Bris* 74-79 and 80-81; Ind Chapl Australia 79-80; Ind Chapl *York* 81-86; V Southill and Course Dir St Alb Minl Tr Scheme 86-93; Dep Chapl HM Pris Wandsworth 94; Chapl HM YOI and Rem Cen Feltham 94-97; Chapl HM YOI Aylesbury 97-02; rtd 02; Asst Chapl Palma de Mallorca *Eur* from 04. *Calle Xarxes Los Ciclamens 7, El Pinaret, 07470 Puerto Pollensa, Mallorca, Spain* Tel (0034) 971 866 689 Mobile 696-391584

REDFEARN, Ms Tracy Anne. b 66. Heythrop Coll Lon BD88. Ripon Coll Cuddesdon 91. **d** 93 **p** 94. C Haslemere *Guildf* 93-97; TV Gt Grimsby St Mary and St Jas *Linc* 97-00; P-in-c Legbourne 00-01; P-in-c Raithby 00-01; P-in-c Wold-Marsh Gp 00-01; V Legbourne and Wold Marsh 01-05; C Brumby from 05. *All Saints' Vicarage, 159 Warwick Road, Scunthorpe DN16 1HH* Tel (01724) 860345 E-mail tracy.redfearn@btopenworld.com

✠**REDFERN, The Rt Revd Alastair Llewellyn John.** b 48. Ch Ch Ox BA70 MA74 Trin Coll Cam BA74 MA79 Bris Univ PhD01. Qu Coll Birm 75. **d** 76 **p** 77 **c** 97. C Tettenhall Regis *Lich* 76-79; Tutor Ripon Coll Cuddesdon 79-87; Hon C Cuddesdon *Ox* 83-87; Can Res Bris Cathl *Bris* 87-97; Dioc Dir Tr 91-97; Suff Bp Grantham *Linc* 97-05; Dean Stamford 98-05; Can and Preb Linc Cathl 00-05; Bp Derby from 05. *The Bishop's House, 6 King Street, Duffield, Belper DE56 4EU* Tel (01332) 840132 Fax 842743 E-mail bishop@bishopofderby.org

REDFERN, Paul. b 48. Ulster Univ BA88. CITC BTh94. **d** 94 **p** 95. C Belfast St Aid *Conn* 94-97; I Belfast St Mark 97-03; I Kilbride from 03. *Kilbride Rectory, 7 Rectory Road, Doagh, Ballyclare BT39 0PT* Tel (028) 9334 0225

REDGERS, Brian. b 42. St Jo Coll Dur BA65 Keswick Hall Coll PGCE75. Westcott Ho Cam 65. **d** 67 **p** 68. C Rushmere *St E* 67-73; Lic to Offic from 73. *44 Belvedere Road, Ipswich IP4 4AB* Tel (01473) 273829

REDGRAVE, Cecil Goulden. b 14. Oak Hill Th Coll 37. **d** 41 **p** 42. C Higher Openshaw *Man* 41-43; C Ashton St Jas 43-44; C Chadderton Ch Ch 44-46; V Thornton *Leic* 46-49; V Fairlight *Chich* 49-60; V New Milverton *Cov* 60-76; R Tredington and Darlingscott w Newbold on Stour 76-83; rtd 83; Perm to Offic *Cov* from 83. *30 Elmdene Road, Kenilworth CV8 2BX* Tel (01926) 857118

REDGRAVE, Canon Christine Howick. b 50. AIAT73. Trin Coll Bris 75. **dss** 78 **d** 87 **p** 94. Watford *St Alb* 78-83; Maidenhead St Andr and St Mary *Ox* 83-85; Bracknell 85-96; Par Dn 87-94; TV 94-96; P-in-c Woolhampton w Midgham and Beenham Valance 96-04; Asst Dir of Ords 95-04; Dir of Ords (Reading and Dorchester) from 04; Hon Can Ch Ch from 00. *41 North Street, Marcham, Abingdon OX13 6NQ* Tel (01865) 391756
E-mail ordberk@oxford.anglican.org

REDHEAD, Edward. b 30. St Deiniol's Hawarden 60. **d** 63 **p** 64. C Mottram in Longdendale w Woodhead *Ches* 63-67; V Rivington *Man* 67-72; V Bloxwich *Lich* 72-75; Hon C Lich St Chad 82-84; P-in-c Bromfield w Waverton *Carl* 84-85; V 85-90; P-in-c W Newton 84-85; V 85-90; R Harrington 90-93; rtd 93. *Tigh-na-Mara, 2-3 Caroy, Struan, Isle of Skye IV56 8FQ* Tel (01470) 572338

REDHOUSE, Mark David. b 67. BTEC NC86. Oak Hill Th Coll BA94. **d** 94 **p** 95. C Fulham St Mary N End *Lon* 94-96; C Hove Bp Hannington Memorial Ch *Chich* 96-01; V Horam from 01; RD Dallington from 04. *The Vicarage, Horebeech Lane, Horam, Heathfield TN21 0DT* Tel (01435) 812563

REDKNAP, Clive Douglas. b 53. Trin Coll Bris BA95. **d** 95 **p** 96. C Patcham *Chich* 95-00; C Wadhurst and Stonegate 00-03; P-in-c Hollington St Jo 03-05; V from 05. *The Vicarage, 94 Lower Glen Road, St Leonards-on-Sea TN37 7AR* Tel (01424) 751103

REDMAN, Anthony James. b 51. Reading Univ BSc72 FRICS95. EAMTC 01. **d** 03 **p** 04. NSM Bury St Edmunds All SS w St Jo and St Geo *St E* from 03. *The Cottage, Great Livermere, Bury St Edmunds IP31 1JG* Tel (01359) 269335 Fax (01284) 704734
E-mail tony@tandcredman.fsnet.co.uk *or* info@whitcp.co.uk

REDMAN, Canon Arthur Thomas. b 28. Dur Univ BA52 PGCE. Ridley Hall Cam 62. **d** 63 **p** 64. C Heaton St Barn *Bradf* 63-66; C Hitchin St Mary *St Alb* 66-70; P Missr 72-75; Hd RE Stopsley High Sch Luton 66-70; Hd Humanities and Modern Studies Hewett Sch Nor 70-72; Perm to Offic *Nor* 70-72; V Swanwick and Pentrich *Derby* 75-80; Warden of Readers 78-97; Dir Bp's Cert 78-88; V Allestree 80-96; P-in-c Morley 82-85; Hon Can Derby Cathl 86-96; RD Duffield 88-96; rtd 96; Hon C Bretby w Newton Solney *Derby* 96-97; Chapl and Development Officer Children in Distress 97-01; Dir St Barn Project Romania from 01. *9 Ludgate Walk, Mackworth, Derby DE22 4HQ* Tel (01332) 521733 Fax 551569

REDMAN, Canon Douglas Stuart Raymond. b 35. MCIOB64. Roch Th Coll 66. **d** 68 **p** 69. C Shortlands *Roch* 68-71; V 80-00; R Kingsdown 71-76; R Chatham St Mary w St Jo 76-80; RD Beckenham 90-00; Hon Can Roch Cathl 93-00; rtd 00; Perm to Offic *Cant* from 01. *25 Hovendens, Sissinghurst, Cranbrook TN17 2LA* Tel (01580) 714600 Fax as telephone

REDMAN, Julia Elizabeth Hithersay. *See* WHITE, Mrs Julia Elizabeth Hithersay

REDVERS HARRIS, Jonathan Francis. b 60. Solicitor 87 Southn Univ LLB81 Univ of Wales (Cardiff) LLM94. Ridley Hall Cam 87. **d** 90 **p** 91. C Enfield St Jas *Lon* 90-93; PV Llan Cathl *Llan* 93-96; Succ 94-96; V Houghton Regis *St Alb* 96-03; V Ryde All SS *Portsm* from 03. *14 Argyll Street, Ryde PO33 3BZ* Tel (01983) 565953 E-mail j.redvers_harris@virgin.net

REDWOOD, Canon David Leigh. b 32. Glas Univ DipSW78. Edin Th Coll 57. **d** 59 **p** 60. C Stirling *Edin* 59-61; C Glas Ch Ch *Glas* 61-64; P-in-c Glas Ascension 64-66; R 66-69; R Hamilton 69-74; R Callander *St And* 74-76; Hon C 76-78; R Lochearnhead 74-76; R Killin 74-76; Hon C Doune 76-78; Hon C Aberfoyle 78-85; R Dunfermline 85-97; TR W Fife Team Min 85-97; Can St Ninian's Cathl Perth 90-97; Syn Clerk 93-97; rtd 97. *8 Strathmore Avenue, Dunblane FK15 9HX* Tel and fax (01786) 825493 E-mail david.redwood@care4free.net

REDWOOD, Marion. b 47. **d** 00. NSM Abercarn and Cwmcarn *Mon* from 00. *30 John Street, Cwmcarn, Crosskeys, Newport NP11 7EH* Tel (01495) 271910

REECE, Donald Malcolm Hayden. b 36. CCC Cam BA58 MA62. Cuddesdon Coll 58. **d** 60 **p** 61. C Latchford St Jas *Ches* 60-63; C Matlock and Tansley *Derby* 63-67; C-in-c Hackenthorpe Ch Ch CD 67-70; C Salisbury Cathl Rhodesia 70-73; V Leic St Pet *Leic* 74-82; V Putney St Marg *S'wark* 82-91; Home Sec Coun for Chr Unity 92-97; Hon C Wandsworth St Anne 94-97; V Shepherd's

Bush St Steph w St Thos *Lon* 97-04; rtd 04. *7 Duke Street, Oxford OX2 0HX* Tel (01865) 792678

REECE, Paul Michael. b 60. Southn Univ BA81. Coll of Resurr Mirfield 83. **d** 85 **p** 86. C Borehamwood *St Alb* 85-89; C Potters Bar 89-92; R Lt Stanmore St Lawr *Lon* from 92; AD Harrow 97-02; Chapl R Nat Orthopaedic Hosp NHS Trust from 92. *Whitchurch Rectory, St Lawrence Close, Edgware HA8 6RB* Tel (020) 8952 0019 Mobile 07860-690503 Fax (020) 8537 0547 E-mail paul.reece@london.anglican.org

REECE, Roger Walton Arden. b 56. Dioc OLM tr scheme 97. **d** 00 **p** 01. OLM Chadderton St Luke *Man* 00-04; OLM Chadderton St Matt w St Luke from 04. *186 Broadway, Chadderton, Oldham OL9 9JH* Tel 0161-284 6824 Mobile 07855-234862 E-mail rogerandhilary@aol.com

REED, Adam Michael Frederick. b 73. Humberside Univ BA95. Cranmer Hall Dur 96. **d** 99 **p** 00. C Northallerton w Kirby Sigston *York* 99-03; R Middleton, Newton and Sinnington from 03. *St Andrew's House, 15 Carr Lane, Middleton, Pickering YO18 8PU* Tel (01751) 474858

REED, Alan Ronald. b 44. Sarum Th Coll 66. **d** 68 **p** 70. C Ifield *Chich* 68-71; C Perivale *Lon* 71-72; C Ruislip St Martin 72-75; C Burgess Hill St Jo *Chich* 76-78; V Shoreham Beach 78-80; V Roughey 80-97; P-in-c Rusper 84-86; V Hove St Barn and St Agnes from 97. *St Barnabas' Vicarage, 88 Sackville Road, Hove BN3 3HE* Tel (01273) 732427

REED, Ms Annette Susan. b 54. Birm Univ BA76 Univ of Wales (Cardiff) CQSW78. Qu Coll Birm 84. **d** 87 **p** 94. C Churchover w Willey *Cov* 89-92; C Clifton upon Dunsmore and Newton 89-92; C Walsgrave on Sowe 92-95; C Cov E 92-95; C Burbage w Aston Flamville *Leic* 95-98; C Hinckley St Mary 95-98; C The Sheepy Gp 98-00; TV Bosworth and Sheepy Gp from 00. *The Rectory, Church Lane, Sheepy Magna, Atherstone CV9 3QS* Tel (01827) 881082 E-mail annettereed@greatsheep.freeserve.co.uk

REED, Brian. b 43. Bris Univ BSc65 Nottm Univ DipTh76. Linc Th Coll 73. **d** 76 **p** 77. C S Ashford Ch Ch *Cant* 76-78; C Spring Park 78-83; V Barming Heath from 83. *St Andrew's Vicarage, 416 Tonbridge Road, Maidstone ME16 9LW* Tel (01622) 726245

REED, Christopher John. b 42. Selw Coll Cam BA64 MA68 Dur Univ DipTh66. Cranmer Hall Dur 64. **d** 67 **p** 68. C Gt Ilford St Andr *Chelmsf* 67-70; P-in-c Bordesley St Andr *Birm* 70-72; V 72-80; V Crofton St Paul *Roch* 80-98; V Yalding w Collier Street from 98; RD Paddock Wood from 01. *The Vicarage, Vicarage Road, Yalding, Maidstone ME18 6DR* Tel (01622) 814182 E-mail chris.lysbeth@yaldingvicarage.freeserve.co.uk

REED, Colin. *See* REED, Matthew Colin

REED, Colin Bryher. b 58. York Univ BA80 RGN86. Ridley Hall Cam 93. **d** 95 **p** 96. C Grays North *Chelmsf* 95-99; Chapl Plymouth Hosps NHS Trust 99-02; Hd Chapl Services Norfolk and Nor Univ Hosp NHS Trust from 02. *The Chaplaincy, Norfolk and Norwich University Hospital, Colney Lane, Norwich NR4 7UZ* Tel (01603) 286286 *or* 287470 E-mail colin.reed@norfolk-norwich.thenhs.com

REED, Colin Charles Gilmour. b 40. LCP75 FCP86 St Luke's Coll Ex TCert63 Lon Univ DipTh69 La Trobe Univ Vic MA94. Tyndale Hall Brisbane 67. **d** 69 **p** 70. C Weston-super-Mare Ch Ch *B & W* 69-71; Kenya 71-79; Australia 80-99; CMS from 84; Tanzania from 99. *PO Box 282, Iringa, Tanzania* Tel (00255) (26) 270 2894 Mobile 74-420 6453 E-mail colinreed@maf.org *or* cwreed@cms.org.au

REED, David. *See* REED, Richard David

REED, Canon Douglas Victor. b 19. AKC41 Middlebury Coll (USA) Hon DD51. St Steph Ho Ox 41. **d** 42 **p** 43. C Poplar St Sav w St Gabr and St Steph *Lon* 42-44; C Bedford St Paul *St Alb* 44-45; Asst Org Sec SPCK 46-47; V Belvedere St Aug *Roch* 47-52; V Chislehurst Annunciation 52-85; Hon Can Roch Cathl 81-85; rtd 85; Perm to Offic *Roch* 85-94. *6 Crown Lane, Chislehurst BR7 5PL* Tel (020) 8467 3360

REED, Mrs Elizabeth Christine. b 43. Lon Bible Coll Lon Univ BD65. WMMTC 95. **d** 97 **p** 98. NSM Ledbury *Heref* from 97; Chapl Bromsgrove Sch from 99. *The Old Barn, Perrystone Hill, Ross-on-Wye HR9 7QX* Tel (01989) 780439 *or* (01527) 579679 Fax (01527) 576177 E-mail ereed@bromsgrove-school.co.uk

REED, Ethel Patricia Ivy. *See* WESTBROOK, Mrs Ethel Patricia Ivy

REED, Geoffrey Martin. b 51. Univ of Wales (Cardiff) BA73 Open Univ PGCE98. Oak Hill Th Coll 73. **d** 76 **p** 77. C Swansea St Nic *S & B* 76-78; C Sketty 78-84; V Glasbury and Llowes 84-86; V Glasbury and Llowes w Clyro and Betws 86-01; R Teme Valley S *Worc* 01-04. *The Rectory, Broadheath, Tenbury Wells WR15 8QW* Tel (01886) 853286 Mobile 07977-229103 E-mail martin.reed@clara.co.uk

REED, Harvey. *See* REED, William Harvey

REED, Jack. b 23. Bris Univ BA49 Lon Univ BD51. Tyndale Hall Bris. **d** 51 **p** 52. C Crookes St Thos *Sheff* 51-54; C Cheltenham St Mark *Glouc* 54-56; R Bickenhill w Elmdon *Birm* 56-60; V Sparkbrook Ch Ch 60-66; V Drypool St Columba w St Andr and St Pet *York* 66-80; TR Drypool 80-83; P-in-c Thwing 83-85; P-in-c Rudston w Boynton and Kilham 83-85; V 85-87; Perm to Offic from 87; rtd 88. *32 Dower Rise, Swanland, North Ferriby HU14 3QT* Tel (01482) 632649

REED, The Ven John Peter Cyril. b 51. BD78 AKC78. Ripon Coll Cuddesdon 78. **d** 79 **p** 80. C Croydon St Jo *Cant* 79-82; Prec St Alb Abbey *St Alb* 82-86; R Timsbury and Priston *B & W* 86-93; Chapl Rural Affairs Bath Adnry 87-93; P-in-c Ilminster w Whitelackington 93-94; TR Ilminster and Distr 94-99; Adn Taunton from 99. *4 Westerkirk Gate, Staplegrove, Taunton TA2 6BQ* Tel (01823) 323838 Fax 325420 E-mail adtaunton@bathwells.anglican.org

REED, Capt John William. b 57. Sussex Univ BSc79. N Ord Course 95. **d** 97 **p** 98. C Padgate *Liv* 97-99; C Orford St Marg 99-01; V from 01. *St Margaret's Vicarage, St Margaret's Avenue, Warrington WA2 8DT* Tel and fax (01925) 631937 E-mail john@scobiem.freeserve.co.uk

REED, Martin. *See* REED, Geoffrey Martin

REED, Matthew Colin. b 50. Edin Univ BD82. Edin Th Coll 72. **d** 84 **p** 85. C Edin St Pet *Edin* 84-87; P-in-c Linlithgow 87-94; P-in-c Bathgate 87-91; Chapl HM Pris Polmont 91-94; R Motherwell *Glas* 94-97; R Wishaw 94-97; Hon Asst P Edin St Fillan *Edin* from 00; Chapl HM Pris Edin from 02. *HM Prison Edinburgh, 33 Stenhouse Road, Edinburgh EH11 3LN* Tel 0131-444 3115 E-mail colin.reed@sps.gov.uk

REED, Matthew Graham. b 68. Nottm Univ BEng89 Roehampton Inst MSc03. Ripon Coll Cuddesdon BA92 MA97. **d** 93 **p** 94. C Oxton *Ches* 93-97; TV Gt Marlow w Marlow Bottom, Lt Marlow and Bisham *Ox* 97-02; Hd Lon and SE Team Chr Aid from 02. *52A Oak Tree Road, Marlow SL7 3EG* Tel (01628) 483568 E-mail mreed@christian-aid.org

REED, Canon Pamela Kathleen. b 38. EMMTC. **dss** 84 **d** 87 **p** 94. Cambridge Ascension *Ely* 84-88; Par Dn 87-88; Par Dn Cherry Hinton St Andr 88-90; C 91-95; C Teversham 91-95; V Chesterton St Geo 95-04; Hon Can Ely Cathl from 00; rtd 04. *17 Woodland Road, Sawston, Cambridge CB2 4DT* Tel (01223) 832571 E-mail pamk.reed@hotmail.com

REED, Richard David. b 32. Trin Coll Carmarthen K Alfred's Coll Win CertEd54 Ex Univ MA02. **d** 91 **p** 92. NSM Dale and St Brides w Marloes *St D* 91-96; P-in-c Blisland w St Breward *Truro* 96-99; rtd 99; Perm to Offic *Truro* from 99 and *St D* from 02. *25 West Haven Estate, Cosheston, Pembroke Dock SA72 4UL* Tel (01646) 685806

REED, Robert Chase. b 47. Emerson Coll Boston (USA) BSc70 TCD HDipEd72. **d** 87 **p** 88. Aux Min Taney *D & G* 87-97; Res Hd Master Wesley Coll Dub from 87; Succ St Patr Cathl Dublin 93-97; Treas St Patr Cathl Dublin from 96. *Embury House, Wesley College, Dublin 16, Irish Republic* Tel and fax (00353) (1) 296 8010 *or* 298 7343 E-mail bobreed@indigo.ie

REED, Simon John. b 63. Trin Coll Ox BA86 MA90. Wycliffe Hall Ox BA90. **d** 91 **p** 92. C Walton H Trin *Ox* 91-96; P-in-c Hanger Hill Ascension and W Twyford St Mary *Lon* 96-01; V from 01. *The Ascension Vicarage, Beaufort Road, London W5 3EB* Tel and fax (020) 8566 9920 E-mail coa@surfaid.org

REED, William Harvey. b 47. K Coll Lon BD69 AKC69. St Aug Coll Cant 69. **d** 70 **p** 71. C Stockton St Mark CD *Dur* 70-72; C Billingham St Cuth 72-76; C S Westoe 76-79; V Chilton Moor 79-87; R Hutton *Chelmsf* 87-95; V Hullbridge from 95. *The Vicarage, 93 Ferry Road, Hullbridge, Hockley SS5 6EL* Tel (01702) 232017 E-mail revharveyreed@whsmithnet.co.uk

REEDE, Samuel William. b 24. TCD BA48 MA52 BD55. CITC 50. **d** 50 **p** 51. C Waterford Ch Ch *C & O* 50-54; C Cregagh *D & D* 54-59; Hd S Ch Miss Ballymacarrett 59-67; Chapl Stranmillis Coll Belf 64-68; Can Raphoe Cathl *D & R* 67-92; I Raphoe w Raymochy 67-68; I Raphoe w Raymochy and Clonleigh 68-92; Dean Raphoe 80-92; rtd 92. *Rooskey, Newtowncunningham, Co Donegal, Irish Republic* Tel (00353) (74) 915 6426

REEDER, Angela Lilian. **d** 99 **p** 00. OLM Eastington, Frocester, Haresfield etc *Glouc* 99-04; Perm to Offic from 04. *St Loy Cottage, West End, Stonehouse GL10 3SL* Tel (01453) 827446

REES, Anthony John. b 49. St Jo Coll Dur BA72 DipTh73 MA77 Man Univ MEd89. **d** 74 **p** 75. C Smethwick St Matt w St Chad *Birm* 74-77; C Bolton St Pet *Man* 77-80; R Cheetham St Mark 80-88; V Mottram in Longdendale w Woodhead *Ches* 88-93; V Mottram in Longdendale 93-02; V Chirk *St As* from 02. *The Vicarage, Trevor Road, Chirk, Wrexham LL14 5HD* Tel (01691) 778519

REES, Antony. *See* REES, Percival Antony Everard

REES, Brian. b 48. McGill Univ Montreal BA74 St Andr Univ BD76 PhD80. Montreal Dioc Th Coll 76. **d** 80 **p** 81. Canada 80-85; C Montreal St Jas and Chapl Concordia Univ 80-82; R Rawdon Ch Ch 82-85; Chapl Bedford Sch 85-92; Hd Master Bedford Prep Sch 92-97; Hd Master Pilgrims' Sch from 97. *The Pilgrims' School, 3 The Close, Winchester SO23 9LT* Tel (01962) 854189 E-mail hmsecretary@pilgrims-school.co.uk

REES, Brynley Mervyn. b 18. Univ of Wales BA38. Lon Coll of Div 40. **d** 41 **p** 42. C Walthamstow St Luke *Chelmsf* 41-43; C Birm Bp Ryder *Birm* 43-46; V W Bromwich St Paul *Lich* 46-52; V Handforth *Ches* 52-60; V St Alb Ch Ch *St Alb* 60-84; rtd 84; C Weobley w Sarnesfield and Norton Canon *Heref* 84-91; Perm to

Offic from 92. *2 Nelson Cottage, Bridge Sollars, Hereford HR4 7JN* Tel (01981) 590296

REES, Celia Pamela. b 48. St D Coll Lamp BA70. LNSM course 97. **d** 98 **p** 99. OLM Leominster *Heref* from 98. *Rivendell, 50 Oldfields Close, Leominster HR6 8TL* Tel (01568) 616581 *or* 612124

REES, Mrs Christine Deryn Irving. b 57. Nottm Univ BSc Sheff Univ MA. Qu Coll Birm. **d** 00 **p** 01. NSM Astwood Bank *Worc* 00-01; C 01-03; TV Dronfield w Holmesfield *Derby* from 03. *43 Firthwood Road, Dronfield S18 3BW* Tel (01246) 411251 *or* 413893

REES, Christopher John. b 40. Dur Univ BA62. Ridley Hall Cam 62. **d** 64 **p** 65. C Wilmslow *Ches* 64-70; C Birkenhead St Pet w St Matt 70-75; V Lostock Gralam 75-83; R Davenham 83-96; P-in-c Aldford and Bruera 96-05; rtd 05. *15 Chapel Close, Comberbach, Northwich CW9 6BA* Tel (01606) 891366 E-mail cjrees@surfaid.org

REES, Canon David Frederick. b 21. SS Coll Cam BA48 MA52. Sarum Th Coll 48. **d** 50 **p** 51. C Blackb St Luke *Blackb* 50-53; C St Annes St Thos 53-55; V Choral York Minster *York* 55-62; V Penwortham St Mary *Blackb* 62-90; RD Leyland 70-84; Hon Can Blackb Cathl 79-90; rtd 90; Perm to Offic *Blackb* from 91. *4 Queensdale Close, Walton-le-Dale, Preston PR5 4JU* Tel (01772) 259010

REES, David Grenfell. b 18. St D Coll Lamp BA40 Qu Coll Birm 42. **d** 43 **p** 44. C Llangeinor *Llan* 43-47; C Cadoxton-juxta-Barry 47-53; C St Andrews Major 53-60; V Dyffryn 60-84; rtd 84; Perm to Offic *Llan* from 84. *10 Tyn-yr-Heol Road, Bryncoch, Neath SA10 7EA* Tel (01639) 644488

REES, Chan David Philip Dunn Hugh. b 38. Jes Coll Ox BA60 MA64 Ox Univ DipEd67. Westcott Ho Cam 62. **d** 64 **p** 65. C Salford St Phil w St Steph *Man* 64-66; Perm to Offic *St A* 66-67 and *Derby* 67-74; Chapl St Marg C of E High Sch Aigburth Liv 74-83; V Meliden and Gwaenysgor *St As* from 84; Dioc Adv for Schs 85-91; Warden of Readers 89-91; Dioc Dir of Ords 91-00; Hon Can St As Cathl 93-95 and from 95; Chan from 96. *The Vicarage, Meliden, Prestatyn LL19 8HN* Tel (01745) 856220

REES, David Richard. b 60. St Mich Coll Llan DipTh84. **d** 84 **p** 85. C Llanstadwel *St D* 84-86; C Carmarthen St Dav 86-91; V Llanrhian w Llanhywel and Carnhedryn etc 91-99; V Spittal w Trefgarn and Ambleston w St Dogwells from 99. *The Vicarage, Spittal, Haverfordwest SA62 5QP* Tel (01437) 741505

REES, Ms Diane Eluned. b 61. Univ of Wales (Ban) BSc82 Em Coll Cam PGCE83 Univ of Wales (Swansea) MEd87 CPsychol AFBPsS. St Jo Coll Nottm CTM93 BTh95 MA96. **d** 96 **p** 97. C Hall Green St Pet *Birm* 96-00; P-in-c Bozeat w Easton Maudit *Pet* 00-03; C Putney St Mary *S'wark* 03-04; TV from 04. *17 Fanthorpe Street, London SW15 1DZ* Tel (020) 8887 7164 E-mail dereeswdt@aol.com

REES, Eric Vernon. b 19. St Jo Coll Dur BA41 MA44. St Andr Pampisford 43. **d** 43 **p** 44. C Tollington Park St Mark *Lon* 43-51; C Edmonton All SS 51-66; C N St Pancras All Hallows 66-68; C-in-c Enfield St Giles CD 68-80; C Edmonton All SS 80-82; C Edmonton All SS w St Mich 82-90; rtd 90; Perm to Offic *Lon* from 90. *45 Monmouth Road, London N9 0JB* Tel (020) 8807 4329

REES, Glyn. b 63. St Bede's Coll Umtata 85. **d** 87 **p** 87. C Turffontein S Africa 87-88; Chapl S African Defence Force 89-90; P-in-c Nigel 91-92; C Kempton Park and Edenvale 92-93; TR Secunda 94-98; R Brakpan 99-00; R Whitwell *Derby* 00-05; R Wodonga Australia from 05. *225 Beechworth Road, Wodonga, Vic, Australia 3690* Tel (0061) (2) 6056 5795 *or* tel and fax 6024 2053

REES, Grenfell. *See* REES, David Grenfell

REES, Gruffydd Nicholas. b 23. Univ of Wales (Lamp) BA46. Wycliffe Hall Ox 46. **d** 48 **p** 49. C Fishguard *St D* 48-51; C Betws w Ammanford 51-53; C Carmarthen St Dav 53-57; C Epsom St Martin *Guildf* 57-62; V Llanbister and Llanbadarn Fynydd w Llananno *S & B* 62-75; R New Radnor and Llanfihangel Nantmelan etc 75-84; R Llangenni and Llanbedr Ystrad Yw w Patricio 84-88; rtd 88. *Trefilan, 26 Lakeside Avenue, Llandrindod Wells LD1 5NT* Tel (01597) 825451

REES, Ian Kendall. b 66. St Mich Coll Llan 98. **d** 00 **p** 01. C Barry All SS *Llan* 00-03; Assoc P Grangetown 03-05; P-in-c Pyle w Kenfig from 05. *The Vicarage, Pyle Road, Pyle, Bridgend CF33 6PG* Tel (01656) 740500 E-mail ian@rees1966.fsnet.co.uk

REES, Ivor. *See* REES, The Rt Revd John Ivor

REES, Jennifer Mary. *See* MORRELL, Mrs Jennifer Mary

REES, Joanna Mary. *See* STOKER, Mrs Joanna Mary

REES, John. *See* REES, Canon Vivian John Howard

✠**REES, The Rt Revd John Ivor.** b 26. Univ of Wales (Abth) BA50. Westcott Ho Cam 50. **d** 52 **p** 53 **c** 88. C Fishguard w Llanychar *St D* 52-55; C Llangathen w Llanfihangel Cilfargen 55-57; P-in-c Uzmaston and Boulston 57-59; V Slebech and Uzmaston w Boulston 59-65; V Llangollen and Trevor *St As* 65-74; RD Llangollen 70-74; R Wrexham 74-76; Can St As Cathl 75-76; Dean Ban 76-88; V Ban Cathl Par 79-88; Asst Bp St D 88-91; Adn St D 88-91; Bp St D 91-95; rtd 95; Hon Fell Trin Coll Carmarthen from 96. *Llys Dewi, 45 Clover Park, Haverfordwest SA61 1UE* Tel (01437) 764846

REES, John Martin Rawlins Gore. b 30. St D Coll Lamp BA53. **d** 55 **p** 57. C Mold *St As* 55-56; C Broughton 56-59; C Newtown 59-61; V Penycae 61-73; V Northop 73-83; V Bickerton w Bickley *Ches* 83-91; Lic to Offic 91-95; rtd 95. *Hafod, 9 High Park, Gwernaffield, Mold CH7 5EE* Tel (01352) 740412

REES, Canon John Philip Walford. b 41. St D Coll Lamp BA62 Linacre Coll Ox BA64 MA69 Univ of Wales (Cardiff) BD73. Wycliffe Hall Ox 62. **d** 64 **p** 65. C Reading St Jo *Ox* 64-67; V Patrick *S & M* 67-68; C Pontypool *Mon* 68-70; Area Sec CMS *Glouc, Heref* and *Worc* 70-75; V Bream *Glouc* 75-91; Team Ldr Ichthus Chr Fellowship 91-96; TV Glyncorrwg w Afan Vale and Cymmer Afan *Llan* 96-99; R Llandogo and Tintern *Mon* 99-00; R Llandogo w Whitebrook Chpl and Tintern Parva from 00; AD Monmouth from 02; Hon Can St Woolos Cathl from 05. *The Rectory, Llandogo, Monmouth NP25 4TW* Tel (01594) 530887

REES, The Ven John Wynford Joshua. b 24. Univ of Wales (Lamp) BA52. **d** 53 **p** 54. C Aberystwyth *St D* 53-60; V Llanyre w Llanfihangel Helygen, Llanwrthwl etc *S & B* 60-71; R Llanyre w Llanfihangel Helygen and Diserth 71-87; V Llanllyr-yn-Rhos w Llanfihangel Helygen 87-94; RD Maelienydd 74-87; Hon Can Brecon Cathl 77-79; Can Res 79-94; Treas 83-87; Adn Brecon 87-94; rtd 94. *Denebrook, Ithan Road, Llandrindod Wells LD1 6AS* Tel (01597) 823573

REES, Canon Judith Margaret. b 39. Southn Univ BTh89. **dss** 86 **d** 87 **p** 94. Sanderstead All SS *S'wark* 86-87; Par Dn 87; Dir Cottesloe Chr Tr Progr *Ox* 89-99; Par Dn Gt Horwood 89-91; Par Dn Winslow w Gt Horwood and Addington 91-94; C 94-99; RD Claydon 96-99; Hon Can Ch Ch 97-99; rtd 99; Perm to Offic *Sarum* from 01. *Sidney Cottage, 111 Lower Road, Salisbury SP2 9NH* Tel (01722) 410050

✠**REES, The Rt Revd Leslie Lloyd.** b 19. Kelham Th Coll 36. **d** 42 **p** 43 **c** 80. C Roath St Sav *Llan* 42-45; Asst Chapl HM Pris Cardiff 42-45; Chapl HM Pris Dur 45-48; V Princetown *Ex* 48-55; Chapl HM Pris Dartmoor 48-55; Chapl HM Pris Win 55-62; Chapl Gen of Pris 62-80; Hon Can Cant Cathl *Cant* 66-80; Chapl to The Queen 71-80; Suff Bp Shrewsbury *Lich* 80-86; rtd 86; Hon Asst Bp Win from 87. *c/o G H Rees Esq, 31 Collin Road, Kendal LA9 5LH*

REES, Matthew Haydn Brinley. b 69. Wycliffe Hall Ox. **d** 03 **p** 04. C Ox St Aldate *Ox* from 03. *11 Duke Street, Oxford OX2 0HX* Tel (01865) 728866 *or* 254811 Mobile 07811-149305 E-mail matt.rees@staldates.org.uk

REES, Michael. *See* REES, Canon Richard Michael

REES, Michael Lloyd. b 51. St D Coll Lamp DipTh74. **d** 74 **p** 75. C Cardigan w Mwnt and Y Ferwig *St D* 74-77; Min Can St D Cathl 77-81; TV Aberystwyth 81-83; Dioc Children's Adv 83-92; V Pen-boyr 83-88; V Henfynyw w Aberaeron and Llanddewi Aberarth 88-99; RD Glyn Aeron 95-99; V Gors-las from 99. *The Vicarage, 56 Black Lion Road, Cross Hands, Llanelli SA14 6RU* Tel (01269) 842561

REES (née CURRY), Mrs Pauline Carol. b 46. WMMTC 94. **d** 98 **p** 99. OLM Leominster *Heref* from 98. *Crossways Cottage, Leysters, Leominster HR6 0HR* Tel (01568) 750300 *or* 612124 Mobile 07702-238395

REES, Percival Antony Everard. b 35. Pemb Coll Ox BA56 MA59. Clifton Th Coll 58. **d** 60 **p** 61. C Heatherlands St Jo *Sarum* 60-65 and 69-70; India 65-69; V W Hampstead St Luke *Lon* 70-82; Lect Oak Hill Th Coll 82-86; V Enfield Ch Ch Trent Park *Lon* 87-00; rtd 00; Perm to Offic *Chelmsf* from 00. *10 Winchester Road, Frinton-on-Sea CO13 9JB* Tel (01255) 852464

REES, Philip. *See* REES, Canon John Philip Walford

REES, Canon Richard John Edward Williams. b 36. Univ of Wales (Lamp) BA58. St Mich Coll Llan 58. **d** 60 **p** 61. C St Issells *St D* 60-64; C Llanedy 64-67; V Whitchurch w Solva and St Elvis 67-77; V Whitchurch w Solva and St Elvis w Brawdy etc 77-01; RD Dewisland and Fishguard 73-01; Can St D Cathl 87-01; Treas 97-01; rtd 01. *The Smithy, Cheriton, Stackpole, Pembroke SA71 5BZ*

REES, Canon Richard Michael. b 35. St Pet Hall Ox BA57 MA61. Tyndale Hall Bris 57. **d** 59 **p** 60. C Crowborough *Chich* 59-62; C Clifton Ch Ch w Em *Bris* 62-64; V Clevedon Ch Ch *B & W* 64-72; V Cambridge H Trin *Ely* 72-84; Chief Sec CA 84-90; Can Res Ches Cathl *Ches* 90-00; Vice-Dean 93-00; Dioc Missr 90-00; Cheshire Co Ecum Officer 91-99; rtd 00; Perm to Offic *Nor* from 01. *65 Tennyson Avenue, King's Lynn PE30 2QJ* Tel (01553) 691982

REES, Ronald Benjamin Dennis. b 44. Univ of Wales (Ban) BTh00. St Mich Coll Llan 00. **d** 00 **p** 01. C Llanbedrog w Llannor and Llangian *Ban* 00-02; P-in-c Llanllyfni 02-03; R 03-05; R Dolgellau w Llanfachreth and Brithdir etc from 05. *The Rectory, Pencefn Road, Dolgellau LL40 2YW* Tel (01341) 422225

REES, Stephen Philip. b 70. St Luke's Coll Ex BA. Oak Hill Th Coll BA03. **d** 03 **p** 04. C Moreton-in-Marsh w Batsford,

Todenham etc *Glouc* from 03. *32 Croft Holm, Moreton-in-Marsh, Gloucester GL56 0JH* Tel (01608) 652199 E-mail zipyzac@globalnet.com

REES, Miss Susan Mary. b 61. Univ of Wales (Cardiff) BSc82. Ripon Coll Cuddesdon 00. **d** 02 **p** 03. C Penarth All SS *Llan* 02-05; C Roath from 05. *St Anne's House, 3 Snipe Street, Cardiff CF24 3RB* Tel (029) 2049 3940

REES, Canon Vivian John Howard. b 51. Southn Univ LLB72 Ox Univ BA79 MA84 Leeds Univ MPhil84. Wycliffe Hall Ox 76. **d** 79 **p** 80. C Moor Allerton *Ripon* 79-82; Sierra Leone 82-86; Lic to Offic *Ox* from 86; Jt Dioc Reg from 98; Dep Prov Reg 98-00; Prov Reg from 00; Legal Adv ACC from 98; Hon Prov Can Cant Cathl *Cant* from 01. *Oxford Diocesan Registry, 16 Beaumont Street, Oxford OX1 2LZ* Tel (01865) 241974 Fax 726274 E-mail oxford@winckworths.co.uk

REES, William David Cledwyn. b 25. FRGS54 Qu Coll Cam BA49 DipEd50 MA52 Univ of Wales MA75 PhD81. St Deiniol's Hawarden 63. **d** 65 **p** 66. Hon C Rhyl w St Ann *St As* 65-72; Chapl and Lect St Mary's Coll Ban 72-77; Lic to Offic *Ban* 72-77; Lect Univ of Wales (Ban) from 77; Chapl 77-84; Sec Dioc Schs Cttee 84-86. *Anwylfa, Fron Park Avenue, Llanfairfechan LL33 0AS* Tel (01248) 680054

REESE, Preb John David. b 49. Cuddesdon Coll 73. **d** 76 **p** 77. C Kidderminster St Mary *Worc* 76-81; Malaysia 81-85; V Bishop's Castle w Mainstone *Heref* 85-91; RD Clun Forest 87-91; V Tupsley 91-93; P-in-c Hampton Bishop and Mordiford w Dormington 91-93; V Tupsley w Hampton Bishop from 93; RD Heref City 96-02; Preb Heref Cathl from 96. *The Vicarage, 107 Church Road, Hereford HR1 1RT* Tel (01432) 274490

REEVE, Canon Brian Charles. b 36. Lon Univ BSc57 BD60. Tyndale Hall Bris 58. **d** 61 **p** 62. C Eccleston St Luke *Liv* 61-63; C Upton (Overchurch) *Ches* 63-65; C Pemberton St Mark Newtown *Liv* 65-68; V Macclesfield Ch Ch *Ches* 68-74; V Stone Ch Ch *Lich* 74-84; RD Trentham 77-84; V Hoole *Ches* 84-94; Chapl Ches City Hosp 84-91; P-in-c Alderley *Ches* 94-01; Dioc Warden of Readers 94-00; Hon Can Ches Cathl 94-01; rtd 01; Perm to Offic *Ches* from 02. *73 Spring Gardens, Leek ST13 8DD* Tel (01538) 387321

REEVE, David Michael. b 44. St Cath Coll Cam BA67 MA71. Coll of Resurr Mirfield 68. **d** 70 **p** 71. C Willingdon *Chich* 70-73; C Hove All SS 73-76; C Moulsecoomb 76-80; R Singleton 80-90; V E Dean 80-90; V W Dean 80-90; R Hurstpierpoint 90-99; R Kingston Buci from 99. *The Rectory, Rectory Road, Shoreham-by-Sea BN43 6EB* Tel (01273) 592591

REEVE, John Richard. b 65. Southn Univ BA86 La Sainte Union Coll PGCE88. Ripon Coll Cuddesdon 95. **d** 97 **p** 98. C Hale w Badshot Lea *Guildf* 97-00; TV Totton *Win* from 00. *The Vicarage, Ringwood Road, Woodlands, Southampton SO40 7GX* Tel (023) 8066 3267 E-mail johnreeve6@aol.com

REEVE, Kenneth John. b 42. Sarum & Wells Th Coll 91. **d** 93 **p** 94. C Thorpe St Matt *Nor* 93-96; P-in-c S Lynn 96-99; Perm to Offic 03-04; P-in-c Gt and Lt Ellingham, Rockland and Shropham etc from 04. *The Rectory, Rectory Lane, Great Ellingham, Attleborough NR17 1LD* E-mail kenrevreeve@hotmail.com

REEVE, Kenneth Robert. b 23. St Cath Coll Ox BA49 MA53. Sarum Th Coll 64. **d** 68 **p** 69. Hon C Farleigh Hungerford w Tellisford *B & W* 68-71; Perm to Offic Virgin Is 71-72; Hon C Norton St Philip 72-74; Hon C Hinton Charterhouse 72-74; Seychelles 74-76; Perm to Offic *B & W* 77-89; *Chich* 78-82. *Address temp unknown*

REEVE, Michael. *See* REEVE, David Michael

REEVE, Richard Malcolm. b 64. Reading Univ BSc85. Trin Coll Bris BA92. **d** 92 **p** 93. C Northolt St Mary *Lon* 92-95; C Acton Green 95-98; V Hayes St Edm from 98. *St Edmund's Vicarage, 1 Edmund's Close, Hayes UB4 0HA* Tel (020) 8573 6913 E-mail richardmreeve@aol.com

REEVE, Richard Noel. b 29. MB, ChB. St Deiniol's Hawarden. **d** 84 **p** 85. Hon C Norton *Ches* 84-85; C Filey *York* 85-87; TV Brayton 87-90; rtd 90; Perm to Offic *Man* 90-93 and *Lich* from 99; Res Min Bicton, Montford w Shrawardine and Fitz *Lich* 97-99. *26 Windsor Road, Stafford ST17 4PA* Tel (01785) 252607

REEVE, Preb Roger Patrick. b 42. Fitzw Coll Cam BA65 MA68. Coll of Resurr Mirfield. **d** 67 **p** 68. C Barnstaple St Pet w H Trin *Ex* 67-74; V Ernesettle 74-78; V Braunton 78-05; RD Barnstaple 85-93 and 01-03; Preb Ex Cathl from 92; rtd 05. *27 Westacott Meadow, Barnstaple EX22 8QX* Tel (01271) 326927 E-mail rogerreeve@cwcom.net

REEVES, Christopher. b 30. Nottm Univ BA53. Wells Th Coll 53. **d** 55 **p** 56. C Rowbarton *B & W* 55-59; C Cant St Greg *Cant* 59-61; Chapl Schiedam Miss to Seamen *Eur* 61-67; V Barkingside H Trin *Chelmsf* 67-97; rtd 97; Perm to Offic *Truro* from 00. *3 Albany Close, Goonown, St Agnes TR5 0XE* Tel (01872) 552976

REEVES, David Eric. b 46. Sarum Th Coll 68. **d** 71 **p** 72. C Guildf H Trin w St Mary *Guildf* 71-74; C Warmsworth *Sheff* 74-78; V Herringthorpe 78-90; V Cleveleys *Blackb* from 90; RD Poulton 94-00. *The Vicarage, Rough Lea Road, Thornton-Cleveleys FY5 1DP* Tel (01253) 852153

REEVES, Donald St John. b 34. Qu Coll Cam BA57 MA61. Cuddesdon Coll 62. **d** 63 **p** 64. C Maidstone All SS w St Phil *Cant* 63-65; Bp's Dom Chapl *S'wark* 65-68; V St Helier 69-80; R Westmr St Jas *Lon* 80-98; Dir Soul of Eur Project from 98; rtd 98; Perm to Offic *Ex* from 00. *The Coach House, Church Street, Crediton EX17 2AQ* Tel (01363) 775100 Fax 773911 E-mail donalreeve@aol.com

REEVES, Elizabeth Anne. *See* THOMAS, Mrs Elizabeth Anne

REEVES, Gillian Patricia. b 46. S'wark Ord Course 87. **d** 90 **p** 94. Par Dn Shirley St Geo *S'wark* 90-94; C 94-96; C Caterham 96-98; TV from 98. *St Luke's Vicarage, 8 Whyteleafe Hill, Whyteleafe CR3 0AA* Tel (020) 8660 4015

REEVES, Graham. b 65. Southn Univ BTh94 Univ Coll Chich MA04. Chich Th Coll 91. **d** 94 **p** 95. C Cardiff St Mary and St Steph w St Dyfrig etc *Llan* 94-95; C Roath 95-98; Chapl Sussex Weald and Downs NHS Trust 98-02; Chapl W Sussex Health and Soc Care NHS Trust from 02. *45 Abbottsbury, Bognor Regis PO21 4RT*

REEVES, John Graham. b 44. Kelham Th Coll 64. **d** 69 **p** 71. C Aston cum Aughton *Sheff* 69-71; C Ribbleton *Blackb* 72-74; C Cleveleys 74-75; P-in-c Huncoat 75-77; V 77-82; V Knuzden 82-92; V Sandylands from 92. *St John's Vicarage, 2 St John's Avenue, Morecambe LA3 1EU* Tel (01524) 411299

REEVES, Ms Karen Susan. b 56. Bris Univ BA78. Ripon Coll Cuddesdon 02. **d** 05. C De Beauvoir Town St Pet *Lon* from 05. *16 De Beauvoir Road, London N1 5SU* Tel (020) 7254 1671 Mobile 07967-604439 E-mail karen.reeves6@btinternet.com

REEVES, Kenneth William. b 38. TCD 67. **d** 69 **p** 70. C Killowen *D & R* 69-70; I Ardara 70-76; TV Quidenham *Nor* 76-81; V Swaffham 81-86; Chapl Nor Coll of Educn 86-91; P-in-c Lakenham St Alb *Nor* 86-91; rtd 92; Perm to Offic *Nor* 92-98 and from 05; P-in-c Trowse 99-03; P-in-c Nerja and Almuécar *Eur* 03-04. *15 Morris Close, Stoke Holy Cross, Norwich NR14 8LL* Tel (01508) 494583 E-mail revkenn@aol.com

REEVES, Maria Elizabeth Ann. *See* COULTER, Mrs Maria Elizabeth Ann

REEVES, Michael Richard Ewert. b 74. Girton Coll Cam MA00. Oak Hill Th Coll 98. **d** 02 **p** 03. NSM Langham Place All So *Lon* from 02. *83 Boundary Road, London NW8 0RG* Tel (020) 7625 5840 *or* 7580 3522 E-mail mreeves@dsl.pipex.com

REEVES, Nicholas John Harding. b 44. Open Th Coll BA99 Nottm Univ MA02. ALCD69. **d** 69 **p** 70. C Upton (Overchurch) *Ches* 69-72; C Woodlands *Sheff* 72-74; C-in-c Cranham Park CD *Chelmsf* 74-79; V Cranham Park 79-88; R Aldridge *Lich* 88-02; Dioc Officer for Evang *Carl* from 03; C Eden, Gelt and Irthing from 03. *The New Vicarage, Irthington, Carlisle CA6 4NJ* Tel (01697) 741864 Mobile 07714-245506 E-mail the7reeves@aol.com

✠**REEVES, The Rt Revd Sir Paul Alfred.** b 32. GCMG85 GCVO86 QSO90. Univ of NZ BA55 MA56 St Pet Coll Ox BA61 MA65 Hon DCL85 Wellington Univ (NZ) Hon LLD89 Gen Th Sem NY Hon DD92. St Jo Coll Auckland LTh58. **d** 58 **p** 60 **c** 71. New Zealand 58-59 and from 64; C Ox St Mary V *Ox* 59-61; C Kirkley *Nor* 61-63; C Lewisham St Mary *S'wark* 63-64; Bp Waiapu 71-79; Bp Auckland 79-85; Abp New Zealand 80-85; Gov Gen NZ 85-90; ACC Rep at United Nations 91-93; Asst Bp New York 91-94; Dean Te Rau Kahikatea Th Coll Auckland 94-95. *16E Cathedral Place, Parnell, Auckland, New Zealand* Tel (0064) (9) 302 2913 *or* 373 7599 ext 4754 Fax 308 2312 E-mail sirpaulreeves@dra.co.nz

REGAN, Brian. b 46. MBIM80. WMMTC 88. **d** 91 **p** 92. C Cov St Jo *Cov* 91-94; FSJ from 93; V Tile Hill *Cov* from 94. *St Oswald's Vicarage, 228 Jardine Crescent, Coventry CV4 9PL* Tel (024) 7646 5072 E-mail brian@revregan.freeserve.co.uk

REGAN, Noel Henry Likely. b 49. **d** 99 **p** 00. C Taunagh w Kilmactranny, Ballysumaghan etc *K, E & A* from 99. *Gurteen Farm, Cliffoney, Co Sligo, Irish Republic* Tel (00353) (71) 916 6253

REGAN, Paul John. b 67. Southn Univ BA88 PhD96 St Jo Coll Dur BA98. Cranmer Hall Dur 96. **d** 99 **p** 00. C St Alb St Pet *St Alb* 99-03; TV Smestow Vale *Lich* from 03. *Swindon Vicarage, 12 St John's Close, Swindon, Dudley DY3 4PQ* Tel (01384) 273429 *or* (01902) 897700

REGAN, Philip. b 49. Qu Mary Coll Lon BSc MSc. Wycliffe Hall Ox 81. **d** 83 **p** 84. Hon C Scotforth *Blackb* 83-89; P-in-c Combe St Nicholas w Wambrook *B & W* 89-01; V from 01; P-in-c Whitestaunton 89-01; R from 01. *The Vicarage, Combe St Nicholas, Chard TA20 3NJ* Tel (01460) 62121

REGINALD, Brother. *See* BOX, Reginald Gilbert

REID, Alec. *See* REID, William Alexander

REID, Amanda Joy. *See* MARRIOTT, Mrs Amanda Joy

REID, Andrew John. b 47. Birm Univ BEd70 Man Univ MEd76. S'wark Ord Course 88. **d** 88 **p** 89. NSM Westerham *Roch* 88-90; Chapl Abp Tenison's Sch Kennington from 90. *Archbishop Tenison's School, 55 Kennington Oval, London SE11 5SR* Tel (020) 7435 3771 *or* 7435 6126

REID, Christopher Jason. b 69. Trin Coll Bris 01. **d** 03 **p** 04. C Woodley *Ox* from 03. *8 Caldbeck Drive, Woodley, Reading RG5 4LA* Tel 0118-944 0690 E-mail cjasonreid@hotmail.com

REID, Canon Colin Guthrie. b 30. **d** 56 **p** 57. C Kendal St Thos *Carl* 56-59; C Crosthwaite Keswick 59-60; R Caldbeck w Castle Sowerby 60-76; RD Wigton 69-70; P-in-c Sebergham 75-76; R Caldbeck, Castle Sowerby and Sebergham 76-93; Hon Can Carl Cathl 88-93; rtd 93; Perm to Offic *Carl* from 93. *Mellbreak, Longthwaite Road, Wigton CA7 9JR* Tel (01697) 345625

REID, Mrs Diane Mary. b 73. Lanc Univ BMus94 Huddersfield Univ PGCE98. Trin Coll Bris BA04. **d** 04 **p** 05. C Reading St Agnes w St Paul and St Barn *Ox* from 04. *8 Caldbeck Drive, Woodley, Reading RG5 4LA* Tel 0118-944 0690 E-mail dianem_clark@hotmail.com

REID, Donald. b 58. Glas Univ LLB79 Pemb Coll Ox MPhil81 Edin Univ BD85. Edin Th Coll 82. **d** 85 **p** 86. C Greenock *Glas* 85-88; C Baillieston 88-91; R 91-95; C Glas St Serf 88-91; R 91-95; Chapl Glas Univ 89-00; Chapl Glas Caledonian Univ 89-00; Chapl Strathclyde Univ 89-00; TP Glas St Mary 95-00; Assoc P 00-04; C Edin St Jo *Edin* from 04. *Flat 2, 3 Randolph Place, Edinburgh EH3 7TQ* Tel 0131-226 7757 E-mail dreid212@aol.com

✠**REID, The Rt Revd Gavin Hunter.** b 34. OBE00. K Coll Lon BA56. Oak Hill Th Coll 56. **d** 60 **p** 61 **c** 92. C E Ham St Paul *Chelmsf* 60-63; C Rainham 63-66; Publications Sec CPAS 66-71; Hon C St Paul's Cray St Barn *Roch* 68-71; Ed Sec USCL 71-74; Hon C Woking St Jo *Guildf* 72-92; Sec for Evang CPAS 74-92; Consultant Missr CPAS and BMU Adv 90-92; Suff Bp Maidstone *Cant* 92-00; Six Preacher Cant Cathl 92-97; rtd 00; Perm to Offic *Nor* and *St E* from 00. *Furzefield, 17 Richard Crampton Road, Beccles NR34 9HN* Tel (01502) 717042 Fax 710739 Mobile 07941-770549 E-mail gavin@reids.org

REID, Geraldine Felicity (Jo). b 47. RGN69. EMMTC 95. **d** 98 **p** 99. NSM Skellingthorpe w Doddington *Linc* 98-02; NSM Hykeham from 02. *Tol Peden, Monson Park, Skellingthorpe, Lincoln LN6 5UE* Tel (01522) 828402 *or* 828403 E-mail tolpedn@ntlworld.com

REID, Gordon. *See* REID, Canon William Gordon

REID, Herbert Alan. b 31. AKC55. **d** 56 **p** 57. C Penwortham St Mary *Blackb* 56-59; C-in-c Penwortham St Leon CD 59-63; V Brierfield 63-72; V Warton St Paul 72-79; V Read in Whalley 79-98; rtd 98; Perm to Offic *Blackb* from 98. *Paslew House, 6 The Sands, Whalley, Blackburn BB7 9TL* Tel (01254) 824620

REID, Hugh Gamble. b 33. Roch Th Coll 63. **d** 64 **p** 64. C Martin w Thornton *Linc* 64-66; Bp's Youth Chapl 66-69; C Alford w Rigsby 66-69; Chapl HM Borstal Everthorpe 69-71; Chapl HM Pris Dur 71-74; Chapl HM Pris Wakef 74-77; V Northowram *Wakef* 77-79; Chapl HM Pris Coldingley 79-81; Chapl HM Rem Cen Risley 81-85; Chapl HM Pris Holloway 85-88; C Guilden Morden *Ely* 88-89; C Shingay Gp 90; R Upwell Ch Ch 90-93; R Welney 90-93; rtd 93; Perm to Offic *Ely* from 93. *Banff, 23 Northwold, Ely CB6 1BG* Tel (01353) 663924

REID, James. b 46. Strathclyde Univ BSc69. WMMTC 88. **d** 91 **p** 92. C Attleborough *Cov* 91-95; V Walsall Pleck and Bescot *Lich* 95-99; TR Chell from 99. *The Rectory, 203 St Michael's Road, Stoke-on-Trent ST6 6JT* Tel (01782) 838708

REID, Jason. *See* REID, Christopher Jason

REID, Jo. *See* REID, Geraldine Felicity

REID, Lucinda Jane. b 57. Dur Univ BA78. Ripon Coll Cuddesdon 79. **dss** 81 **d** 85 **p** 85. Birtley *Dur* 81-84; Canada from 84. *127 Glasgow Street North, Guelph ON, Canada, N1H 4W5* Tel (001) (519) 821 7419 E-mail lreid@uoguelpha.ca

REID, Mrs Pauline Ann. b 57. EAMTC 00. **d** 03 **p** 04. C Silverstone and Abthorpe w Slapton etc *Pet* from 03. *The Rectory, 2 Tews End Lane, Paulerspury, Towcester NN12 7NQ* Tel (01327) 811670 Mobile 07812-831869 E-mail p.reid@tiscali.co.uk

REID, Peter Ivor. b 30. Qu Coll Cam BA53 MA72. St Mich Coll Llan 78. **d** 80 **p** 81. C Llantwit Major and St Donat's *Llan* 80-83; C Llantwit Major 83-84; V Laleston w Tythegston 84; V Laleston w Tythegston and Merthyr Mawr 84-88; V Roath 88-98; rtd 98. *18 Woolaston Avenue, Cardiff CF23 5AD* Tel (029) 2075 3306

REID, Robert. *See* McLEAN-REID, Robert

REID, Stewart Thomas. b 45. Liv Hope MA01. Oak Hill Th Coll 66. **d** 70 **p** 71. C Normanton *Derby* 70-73; C Leyland St Andr *Blackb* 73-78; V Halliwell St Luke *Man* 78-95; V Southport Ch Ch *Liv* from 95. *The Vicarage, 12 Gloucester Road, Southport PR8 2AU* Tel (01704) 565120

REID, William Alexander (Alec). b 23. Melbourne Univ BA48 ACT ThL50. Trin Coll Melbourne 46. **d** 51 **p** 52. Australia 51-52, 58-71 and from 81; C Kennington St Jo *S'wark* 53; C Westmr St Matt *Lon* 53-56; C Balkwell *Newc* 56-58; Malaysia 71-76; Papua New Guinea 76-81; rtd 89. *7/55A Coorigil Road, Carnegie, Vic, Australia 3163* Tel (0061) (3) 9569 9217

REID, Canon William Gordon. b 43. Edin Univ MA63 Keble Coll Ox BA66 MA72. Edin Th Coll 63 Cuddesdon Coll 66. **d** 67 **p** 68. C Edin St Salvador *Edin* 67-69; Chapl and Tutor Sarum Th Coll 69-72; R Edin St Mich and All SS *Edin* 72-84; Provost St Andr Cathl Inverness *Mor* 84-87; Chapl Ankara *Eur* 87-89; Chapl Stockholm w Gävle and Västerås 89-92; V Gen to Bp Eur 92-02; Can Gib Cathl 92-98; Adn in Eur 96-98; P-in-c St Mich Cornhill w St Pet le Poer etc *Lon* 97-98; Dean Gib *Eur* 98-00; Adn Italy and Malta 00-03; Chapl Milan w Genoa and Varese 00-03; R Philadelphia St Clem USA from 04. *St Clement's Church, 2013 Appletree Street, Philadelphia, PA 19103, USA* Tel (001) (215) 563 1876 Fax 563 7627

REIDE, Ms Susannah Louise Court. b 69. Clare Coll Cam BA91. Trin Coll Bris BA04. **d** 04 **p** 05. C Marlborough *Sarum* from 04. *10 Alexandra Terrace, Marlborough SN8 1DA* Tel (01672) 515983

REIGATE, Archdeacon of. *See* KAJUMBA, The Ven Daniel Steven Kimbugwe

REILLY, Frederick James. b 29. CITC 70. **d** 73 **p** 74. C Agherton *Conn* 73-75; C Ballymena 75-82; I Ballyscullion *D & R* 82-04; Can Derry Cathl 03-04; rtd 04. *11 Swilly Drive, Portstewart BT55 7FJ* Tel (028) 7083 5788

REILLY, Thomas Gerard. b 38. **d** 64 **p** 64. In RC Ch 64-73; Hon C Clapton Park All So *Lon* 73-76; Hon C Haggerston All SS 76-78; Hon C Walthamstow St Sav *Chelmsf* 79-85; P-in-c Forest Gate Em w Upton Cross 85-89; V 89-92; V Chaddesden St Phil *Derby* 92-01; RD Derby N 95-00; rtd 01; Perm to Offic *B & W* from 01. *4 Rose Lane, Crewkerne TA18 7ER* Tel (01460) 72613 E-mail ger_mon@totalise.co.uk

REILY, Paul Alan. b 59. UEA BA81. St Jo Coll Nottm DTS91 MA92. **d** 92 **p** 93. C Westcliff St Mich *Chelmsf* 92-96; P-in-c Barkingside St Cedd 96-98; V 98-01; V Leyton St Cath and St Paul from 01; AD Waltham Forest from 04. *St Catherine's Vicarage, Fairlop Road, London E11 1BL* Tel (020) 8539 6361 E-mail paul@reily.co.uk

REINDORP, Canon David Peter Edington. b 52. TD05. Trin Coll Cam BA82 MA86 CQSW77 DASS77. Westcott Ho Cam 79. **d** 83 **p** 84. C Chesterton Gd Shep *Ely* 83-85; C Hitchin *St Alb* 85-88; R Landbeach and V Waterbeach *Ely* 88-97; OCF 88-97; CF(V) from 92; RD Quy *Ely* 94-97; V Cherry Hinton St Jo from 97; RD Cambridge from 04; Hon Can Ely Cathl from 05. *St John's Vicarage, 9 Luard Road, Cambridge CB2 2PJ* Tel (01223) 247451 *or* tel and fax 241316 E-mail david.reindorp@talk21.com

REINDORP, Canon Michael Christopher Julian. b 44. Trin Coll Cam BA67 MA70 K Coll Lon MA99. Cuddesdon Coll 67 United Th Coll Bangalore 68. **d** 69 **p** 70. C Poplar *Lon* 69-74; V Chatham St Wm *Roch* 74-84; R Stantonbury *Ox* 84-87; TR Stantonbury and Willen 87-92; P-in-c Richmond St Mary w St Matthias and St Jo *S'wark* 92-95; TR from 96; Hon Can S'wark Cathl from 03. *The Vicarage, Ormond Road, Richmond TW10 6TH* Tel and fax (020) 8940 0362 E-mail rector@richmondteam.freeserve.co.uk

REISS, Prof Michael Jonathan. b 58. Trin Coll Cam BA78 MA82 PhD82 PGCE83 FIBiol90 Open Univ MBA02. EAMTC 87. **d** 90 **p** 91. Lect Cam Univ 88-94; Reader 94-00; NSM Comberton *Ely* 90-94; NSM Deanery of Bourn 94-96 and 99-00; P-in-c Boxworth and Elsworth w Knapwell 96-99; Perm to Offic 99-03; Prof Science Educn Inst of Educn Lon Univ from 01; P-in-c Toft w Caldecote and Childerley *Ely* from 03. *Institute of Education, University of London, 20 Bedford Way, London WC1H 0AL* Tel (020) 7612 6776 E-mail m.reiss@ioe.ac.uk

REISS, Peter Henry. b 62. Hertf Coll Ox BA85 MA91 Natal Univ MA95. St Jo Coll Nottm 95. **d** 95 **p** 96. C Sherwood *S'well* 95-00; TV Bestwood 00-03; V Bestwood Park w Rise Park 03-04; Tr Officer CME and Laity Development *Man* from 04. *Board for Ministry and Society, 5th Floor, Church House, 90 Deansgate, Manchester M3 2GJ* Tel 0161-828 1410 Fax 828 1485 E-mail preiss@manchester.anglican.org

REISS, Canon Robert Paul. b 43. Trin Coll Cam BA67 MA71. Westcott Ho Cam 67. **d** 69 **p** 70. C St John's Wood *Lon* 69-73; Bangladesh 73; Chapl Trin Coll Cam 73-78; Selection Sec ACCM 78-85; Sen Selection Sec 83; TR Grantham *Linc* 86-96; RD Grantham 92-96; Adn Surrey and Hon Can Guildf Cathl *Guildf* 96-05; Can Westmr Abbey from 05. *1 Little Cloister, London SW1P 3PL* Tel (020) 7654 4804 Fax 7654 4811 E-mail robert.reiss@westminster-abbey.org

REITH, Robert Michael. b 55. Oak Hill Th Coll BA83. **d** 83 **p** 84. C Kendal St Thos *Carl* 83-87; C Leyland St Andr *Blackb* 87-92; V Leyland St Jo 92-94; TR Dagenham *Chelmsf* 94-03; V from 03. *The Vicarage, Church Lane, Dagenham RM10 9UL* Tel (020) 8592 1339 E-mail mike.reith1@ntlworld.com

RENDALL, Canon John Albert. b 43. Hull Univ BTh84 MA89. Ripon Hall Ox 65. **d** 68 **p** 69. C Southsea St Simon *Portsm* 68-71; C Wallington H Trin *S'wark* 71-77; P-in-c Rufforth w Moor Monkton and Hessay *York* 77-79; R from 79; P-in-c Long Marston 77-79; R from 79; RD New Ainsty 85-97; P-in-c Healaugh w Wighill, Bilbrough and Askham Richard from 02; P-in-c Tockwith and Bilton w Bickerton from 03; Can and Preb York Minster from 94; Chapl Purey Cust Nuffield Hosp from 82. *The Vicarage, Wetherby Road, Rufforth, York YO23 3QF* Tel and fax (01904) 738262 E-mail nata@supanet.com

RENDALL, Richard John. b 54. Wadh Coll Ox BA76 LLB76 MA92 Solicitor 78. Wycliffe Hall Ox 90. **d** 92 **p** 93. C Heswall *Ches* 92-98; R High Ongar w Norton Mandeville *Chelmsf* 98-04; R Broadwell, Evenlode, Oddington, Adlestrop etc *Glouc* from

04. *The Rectory, Broadwell, Moreton-in-Marsh GL56 0TU* Tel (01451) 831866 E-mail rendalls@talk21.com

RENDELL, Jason. b 68. **d** 05. Chapl to Bp Stepney *Lon* from 05. *63 Coborn Road, London E3 2DB* Tel (020) 8981 2323 Fax 8981 8015

RENDLE, Graham Barton. b 40. **d** 99 **p** 00. OLM Rougham, Beyton w Hessett and Rushbrooke *St E* from 99. *Appletrees, Bury Road, Beyton, Bury St Edmunds IP30 9AB* Tel (01359) 270924

RENFREY, Edward Donald John-Baptist. b 53. ACT DipTh76. **d** 76 **p** 77. Australia 76-84 and from 99; C Naracoorte 76-77; P-in-c Kingston w Robe 78-81; R 81-84; Chapl RN 84-99; Chapl R Aus Navy from 99. *5/7 Bayview Street, Fannie Bay, NT, Australia 0820* Tel (0061) (8) 409-662823 (mobile) E-mail edwardrenfrey@hotmail.com.au

RENISON, Gary James. b 62. SS Hild & Bede Coll Dur BA83. Ridley Hall Cam 84. **d** 86 **p** 87. C Stapenhill w Cauldwell *Derby* 86-89; C Cheadle Hulme St Andr *Ches* 89-92; Min Cheadle Hulme Em CD 92-95; P-in-c Bar Hill *Ely* from 95. *108 Stonefield, Bar Hill, Cambridge CB3 8TE* Tel (01954) 781629 *or* tel and fax 206120 E-mail gjr@renison.ndo.co.uk

RENNARD, Edward Lionel. b 51. CertEd72 Nottm Univ BTh80. Linc Th Coll 76. **d** 80 **p** 81. C Old Brumby *Linc* 80-82; C-in-c Gt Grimsby St Matt Fairfield CD 82-86; V Fairfield St Matt 86-88; V Hykeham 88-91; TR 91-00; TR Blyth Valley *St E* from 00. *The Rectory, Highfield Road, Halesworth IP19 8SJ* Tel and fax (01986) 872331 *or* tel 872602 Mobile 07939-220416 E-mail e.l.rennard@ntlworld.com

RENNARD, Margaret Rose. b 49. CertEd75. Linc Th Coll 76. **d** 87 **p** 94. C Fairfield St Matt *Linc* 87-88; C Hykeham 88-00; Chapl HM Pris Morton Hall 91-00; Asst Chapl HM Pris Blundeston from 00; Chapl Allington NHS Trust from 00; Perm to Offic *St E* from 01. *The Rectory, Highfield Road, Halesworth IP19 8SU* Tel and fax (01986) 872331 *or* tel 872602 E-mail margaret.rennard@ntlworld.com

RENNIE, Iain Hugh. b 43. Ripon Coll Cuddesdon 88. **d** 90 **p** 91. C Poulton-le-Sands w Morecambe St Laur *Blackb* 90-94; V Hornby w Claughton 94-02; V Hornby w Claughton and Whittington etc from 02. *The Vicarage, Main Street, Arkholme, Carnforth LA6 1AX* Tel (015242) 21238

RENNIE, Paul Antony. b 58. Heriot-Watt Univ BSc82 Edin Univ LTh. **d** 87 **p** 88. C Nairn *Mor* 87-90; C Forres 87-90; C Edin St Pet *Edin* 90-92; Dep Chapl HM Pris Leeds 92; Chapl HM YOI Hindley 93-95; Chapl HM Pris Liv 95-97; Chapl RAF from 97. *Chaplaincy Services (RAF), HQ, Personnel and Training Command, RAF Ainsworth, Gloucester GL3 1EZ* Tel (01452) 712612 ext 5164 Fax 510828

RENNIX, Raymond Latham. b 37. QUB BTh02. CITC 00. **d** 03 **p** 04. Aux Min Killaney w Carryduff *D & D* from 03. *5 Brompton Court, Dromara, Dromore BT25 2DQ* Tel (028) 9753 3167 Mobile 07977-584053 E-mail ray.rennix@u.genie.co.uk

RENSHAW, Mrs Anne-Marie Louise. b 71. St Hilda's Coll Ox MA96 Fitzw Coll Cam BA97. Ridley Hall Cam 95. **d** 98 **p** 99. C Norton *St Alb* 98-02; TV Borehamwood 02-05; TV Elstree and Borehamwood from 05. *Holy Cross Vicarage, 1 Warren Grove, Borehamwood WD6 2QU* Tel (020) 8953 2183 E-mail alr@fish.co.uk

RENSHAW, Anthony. b 40. McGill Univ Montreal LTh87 DipMin87. Montreal Dioc Th Coll 83. **d** 87 **p** 88. Canada 87-90; P-in-c Ainsdale *Liv* 90-91; V 91-98; V Singleton w Weeton *Blackb* 98-03; rtd 03. *20 The Windrush, Rochdale OL12 6DY* Tel (01706) 341420 E-mail tonyrenshaw@tiscali.co.uk

RENSHAW, David William. b 59. Oak Hill Th Coll BA85. **d** 85 **p** 86. C Shawbury *Lich* 85-88; V Childs Ercall and R Stoke upon Tern 88-92; V Stoneleigh *Guildf* 92-97; RD Epsom 95-97; Chapl Scarborough and NE Yorks Healthcare NHS Trust 97-99; Chapl St Cath Hospice Scarborough 97-99; R Meppershall w Campton and Stondon *St Alb* 99-01; C Bedford St Andr 02; rtd 02. *11 Albany Road, Bexhill-on-Sea TN40 1BY* Tel (01424) 731526 E-mail dwrenshaw@onetel.com

RENSHAW, Peter Selwyn Kay. b 29. Keble Coll Ox BA52 MA64. St Steph Ho Ox 52. **d** 64 **p** 65. Lic to Offic *Ox* 64-66; Chapl RN 66-70; Chapl Br Emb and Athens St Paul *Eur* 71-74; Gothenburg 74-75; Chapl RN Sch Haslemere 75-81; Costa Blanca *Eur* 81-82; R Ewelme *Ox* 83-85; R Ewelme, Brightwell Baldwin, Cuxham w Easington 85-92; rtd 92. *Lovedays House, Painswick, Stroud GL6 6QB* Tel (01452) 812811

RENSHAW, Susan Kathryn. b 55. Shenstone Coll of Educn CertEd77. WMMTC 99. **d** 02 **p** 03. C Sedgley All SS *Worc* 02-05; C Gornal and Sedgley from 05. *23 Sunningdale Road, Dudley DY3 3PP* Tel (01902) 661184 Mobile 07932-750410 E-mail skrenshaw@btinternet.com

RENSHAW, Timothy John. b 65. Trin Coll Carmarthen BA86. St Jo Coll Nottm MA97. **d** 97 **p** 98. C Calverton *S'well* 97-01; C Epperstone 97-01; C Gonalston 97-01; C Oxton 97-01; P-in-c Shireoaks 01-05; Dioc Adv on Notts Coalfield 01-05; Project Manager Cathl Breakfast and Archer Projects *Sheff* from 05. *The Cathedral, 4-7 East Parade, Sheffield S1 2ET* Tel 0114-275 1650 *or* 279 7042

RENWICK, Canon Colin. b 30. St Aid Birkenhead. **d** 59 **p** 60. C Drypool St Columba w St Andr and St Pet *York* 59-62; C Wigan St Cath *Liv* 62-64; Min Thornton CD 64-77; V Thornton 77-97; RD Bootle 83-89; Hon Can Bauchi from 93; rtd 97; Perm to Offic *Ches* from 97. *27 Briar Drive, Heswall, Wirral CH60 5RN* Tel 0151-342 3308

RENYARD, Christopher. b 52. Open Univ BA87. Coll of Resurr Mirfield 81. **d** 84 **p** 85. C Heckmondwike *Wakef* 84-88; C Harpenden St Nic *St Alb* 88-95; Asst Chapl Salisbury Health Care NHS Trust 95-01; Chapl Team Ldr from 01. *The Chaplain's Office, Salisbury District Hospital, Salisbury SP2 8BJ* Tel (01722) 429271 E-mail chaplains.department@shc-tr.swest.nhs.uk

RENYARD, Paul Holmwood. b 42. K Coll Lon BD65 AKC65. **d** 66 **p** 67. C Croydon St Aug *Cant* 66-69; C Farnham *Guildf* 69-72; V Capel 72-78; Asst Dir RE 72-78; Asst Dir RE *Roch* 78-83; Hon C Roch 78-83; V Holdenhurst *Win* 83-95; V Pennington from 95. *The Vicarage, 29 Ramley Road, Pennington, Lymington SO41 8LH* Tel (01590) 672646 E-mail paul@renyard.fsnet.co.uk

REPATH, George David. b 43. Univ of Wales (Lamp) DipTh68 Kellogg Coll Ox MSt96. **d** 68 **p** 69. C Cardiff St Jo *Llan* 68-73; C Gt Stanmore *Lon* 73-77; V Stratfield Mortimer *Ox* 77-85; RD Bradfield 82-85; P-in-c Mortimer W End w Padworth 83-85; V Bray and Braywood from 85. *The Vicarage, Bray, Maidenhead SL6 2AB* Tel (01628) 621527

REPATH, John Richard. b 48. Univ of Wales (Cardiff) DipTh75. St Mich Coll Llan 72. **d** 75 **p** 76. C Canton St Jo *Llan* 75-79; C Burghclere w Newtown and Ecchinswell w Sydmonton *Win* 80-83; R Bewcastle and Stapleton *Carl* 83-88; P-in-c Kirklinton w Hethersgill and Scaleby 86-88; R Bewcastle, Stapleton and Kirklinton etc 88-97; rtd 97; P-in-c New Galloway *Glas* from 97. *The Rectory, Kenbridge Road, New Galloway, Castle Douglas DG7 3RP* Tel (01644) 420235

REPTON, Suffragan Bishop of. *See* HAWTIN, The Rt Revd David Christopher

RESCH, Michael Johann. b 63. NTMTC DTPS99. **d** 99 **p** 00. C Cullompton *Ex* 99-01; C Cullompton, Willand, Uffculme, Kentisbeare etc 01-03; P-in-c Sittingbourne H Trin w Bobbing *Cant* from 03. *Holy Trinity Vicarage, 47 London Road, Sittingbourne ME10 1NQ* Tel (01795) 472724 Mobile 07866-922918 E-mail mikeresch@aol.com

RESTALL, Miss Susan Roberta. b 45. MSc. Sarum & Wells Th Coll 79. **dss** 82 **d** 87 **p** 94. Dorchester *Sarum* 82-84; Portland All SS w St Pet 84-87; Par Dn 87; TD Yate New Town *Bris* 87-94; TV 94-95; Chapl Birm Heartlands and Solihull NHS Trust 95-01; rtd 01; Perm to Offic *Birm* from 03. *12 Croft Road, Yardley, Birmingham B26 1SG* Tel 0121-783 3325

REVELEY, James Stewart. b 69. Goldsmiths' Coll Lon BMus92. Ch Div Sch of the Pacific (USA) 95 Ripon Coll Cuddesdon BA97. **d** 96 **p** 97. C Goldington *St Alb* 96-00; C Harpenden St Nic 00-04; V Boxmoor St Jo from 04. *St John's Vicarage, 10 Charles Street, Hemel Hempstead HP1 1JH* Tel and fax (01442) 255382 E-mail revjumble@aol.com

REVELEY, Mrs Valerie Mary. b 39. Lon Inst of Educn BEd77. St Alb and Ox Min Course 96. **d** 99 **p** 00. OLM Olney *Ox* from 99. *36 Oxleys, Olney MK46 5PH* Tel (01234) 713989

REVELL, Patrick Walter Millard. b 32. Wells Th Coll 65. **d** 67 **p** 68. C Leic St Jas *Leic* 67-74; V Quorndon 74-82; TR Camelot Par *B & W* 82-90; RD Cary 90-96; RD Bruton 90-96; V Castle Cary w Ansford 90-97; rtd 97; Perm to Offic *B & W* and *Sarum* from 97. *80 Sheepland Lane, Sherborne DT9 4BP* Tel (01935) 813083

REVERA, Susan Mary. *See* LEATHLEY, Susan Mary

REW, Eric Malcolm. b 63. UEA BSc84 PGCE89. Qu Coll Birm 98. **d** 00 **p** 01. C Shepshed *Leic* 00-03; C Shepshed and Oaks in Charnwood 03-04; TV Kingsthorpe w Northampton St Dav *Pet* from 04. *The Vicarage, 42 Fallow Walk, Northampton NN2 8DE* Tel (01604) 471948 E-mail rev.rew@fish.co.uk

REX, Keith Leslie Herbert. b 30. K Coll Lon 53. **d** 55 **p** 56. C Shepton Mallet *B & W* 55-58; C Cheshunt *St Alb* 58-60; V Weston-super-Mare St Andr Bournville *B & W* 60-67; R Charlton Adam w Charlton Mackrell 67-69; rtd 90. *46 Petherton Gardens, Hengrove, Bristol BS14 9BS*

REYNISH, David Stuart. b 52. Nottm Univ BEd75. Linc Th Coll 72. **d** 77 **p** 78. C Boston *Linc* 77-80; C Chalfont St Peter *Ox* 80-84; V Thursby *Carl* 84-88; R Iver Heath *Ox* 88-03; V Kelvedon and Feering *Chelmsf* from 03. *The Vicarage, Church Street, Kelvedon, Colchester CO5 9AL* Tel (01376) 571172

REYNOLDS, Alan Martin. b 53. Sarum & Wells Th Coll 73. **d** 77 **p** 78. C Glan Ely *Llan* 77-84; V Pontyclun w Talygarn 84-97; Perm to Offic from 97. *The Orchards, Stow Hill, Newport NP20 4EA* Tel (01633) 215841 E-mail martin.reynolds1@virgin.net

REYNOLDS, Alan Thomas William. b 43. Lon Univ BSc64. Linc Th Coll 64. **d** 66 **p** 67. C Leic St Pet *Leic* 66-70; C Huntington *York* 70-72; Jamaica 72-76; V Stechford *Birm* 76-83; P-in-c

Hampton in Arden 83-86; V 87-93; Chapl E Birm Hosp 86-88; Chapl Parkway Hosp Solihull 88-93; V Moseley St Anne *Birm* 93-02; V Kerry and Llanmerewig and Dolfor *St As* from 02; AD Cedewain from 03. *The Vicarage, 47 Willans Drive, Kerry, Newtown SY16 4DB* Tel (01686) 670466

REYNOLDS, Alfred Stanley. b 18. Birm Univ BSc39 Open Univ BA88. St Deiniol's Hawarden 69. **d** 70 **p** 71. NSM Illogan *Truro* 70-85; Perm to Offic *Sarum* from 86. *42 Cloford Close, Trowbridge BA14 9DH* Tel (01225) 763542

REYNOLDS, Mrs Angela Heather. b 44. Wye Coll Lon BSc66 Birm Univ CertEd67. EAMTC 94. **d** 97 **p** 98. NSM Barnham Broom *Nor* 97-99; C Easton w Colton and Marlingford 99-00; P-in-c Easton, Colton, Marlingford and Bawburgh from 00. *Easton Vicarage, 107 Dereham Road, Easton, Norwich NR9 5ES* Tel (01603) 880197 E-mail revangel@fish.co.uk

REYNOLDS, David Hammerton. b 39. St Jo Coll Dur BA62. Qu Coll Birm DipTh63. **d** 65 **p** 66. C N Ormesby *York* 65-68; C Hessle 68-71; V Sherburn in Elmet 71-79; V Fulford 79-87; Resp for Clergy In-Service Tr York Area 82-87; C Egloskerry *Truro* 87; TV Bolventor 87-90; TR Brayton *York* from 90; RD Selby from 04. *The Rectory, Doncaster Road, Brayton, Selby YO8 9HE* Tel (01757) 704707 E-mail dhr@breathemail.net

REYNOLDS, David James. b 48. St Jo Coll Dur BA72 Lanc Univ MA85. Cranmer Hall Dur 69. **d** 73 **p** 74. C Formby H Trin *Liv* 73-77; P-in-c Widnes St Paul 77-80; V Southport St Paul 80-87; P-in-c Mawdesley *Blackb* 87-91; R from 91; Chapl Derian Ho Children's Hospice 93-97. *Mawdesley Rectory, Green Lane, Ormskirk L40 3TH* Tel (01704) 822203 E-mail davidreynolds@tinyworld.co.uk

REYNOLDS, Canon John Lionel. b 34. JP. Westmr Coll Ox MTh00. Chich Th Coll 58. **d** 61 **p** 62. C Whitkirk *Ripon* 61-64; C Tong *Bradf* 64-68; V Chisledon and Draycot Foliatt *Sarum* 68-74; TR Ridgeway 74-76; RD Marlborough 74-76; V Calne and Blackland 76-89; RD Calne 77-84; Can and Preb Sarum Cathl 80-02; V Woodford Valley 89-02; rtd 02; Perm to Offic *Sarum* from 02 and *Win* from 03. *Rose Court, Church Hill, Lover, Salisbury SP5 2PL* Tel (01725) 512311

REYNOLDS, John Stewart. b 19. St Edm Hall Ox BA42 MA45 BLitt50 FSA81. Ridley Hall Cam 42. **d** 44 **p** 45. C Ox St Clem *Ox* 44-46; C-in-c Ox All SS w St Martin 46-49; R Easton-on-the-Hill *Pet* 49-56; R Besselsleigh w Dry Sandford *Ox* 56-85; Lect Wycliffe Hall Ox 71-78; rtd 85; Perm to Offic *Ox* from 85. *Linden Lodge, 59 St Mary's Road, Oxford OX4 1PZ* Tel (01865) 727386

REYNOLDS, Mandy Elizabeth. b 59. NTMTC 99. **d** 02 **p** 03. NSM Wembley St Jo *Lon* 02-04; CF from 04. *c/o MOD Chaplains (Army)* Tel (01980) 615804 Fax 615800 E-mail mandyreynoldsuk@yahoo.co.uk

REYNOLDS, Martin. *See* REYNOLDS, Alan Martin

REYNOLDS, Michael. *See* REYNOLDS, Richard Michael

REYNOLDS, Mrs Michelle Angela. b 70. Ridley Hall Cam 02. **d** 04 **p** 05. C Hoddesdon *St Alb* from 04. *St Catherine's House, Pauls Lane, Hoddesdon EN11 8TR* Tel (01992) 443724 E-mail michellea_reynolds@hotmail.com

REYNOLDS, Paul Andrew. b 57. BA86. Trin Coll Bris 83. **d** 86 **p** 87. C Reading St Jo *Ox* 86-90; C Dorridge *Birm* 90-95; TV Riverside *Ox* from 95. *The Vicarage, 69A Eton Wick Road, Windsor SL4 6NE* Tel (01753) 852268

REYNOLDS, Paul Frederick. b 56. Lon Bible Coll DRBS78 St Jo Coll Nottm 90. **d** 92 **p** 93. C Hyde St Geo *Ches* 92-96; P-in-c Delamere 96-00; Asst Dir Par Support and Development 96-98; Acting Dir 98-00; V Handforth from 00. *The Vicarage, 36 Sagars Road, Handforth, Wilmslow SK9 3EE* Tel (01625) 250559 *or* 532145 E-mail paul.reynolds@saintchads.fsnet.co.uk

REYNOLDS, Philip Delamere. b 53. Leeds Univ CertEd74 Nottm Univ BCombStuds82. Linc Th Coll 79. **d** 82 **p** 83. C Huddersfield St Jo *Wakef* 82-85; C Barkisland w W Scammonden 85-87; P-in-c Skelmanthorpe from 87. *St Aidan's Vicarage, Radcliffe Street, Skelmanthorpe, Huddersfield HD8 9AF* Tel (01484) 863232 E-mail northmist@thales.demon.co.uk

REYNOLDS, Raymond Ernest. b 29. Nottm Univ MPhil89. Lambeth STh84 CA Tr Coll 50 Chich Th Coll 58. **d** 60 **p** 61. C Leeds St Marg *Ripon* 60-62; C Beeston *S'well* 62-64; R Farnley *Ripon* 64-76; R Higham-on-the-Hill w Fenny Drayton *Leic* 76-81; R Higham-on-the-Hill w Fenny Drayton and Witherley 81-90; V Sutton *Ely* 90-94; R Witcham w Mepal 90-94; rtd 94; C Nantwich *Ches* 94-96; Perm to Offic from 96. *4 St Alban's Drive, Nantwich CW5 7DW* Tel (01270) 623534

REYNOLDS, Richard Michael. b 42. St Steph Ho Ox 65. **d** 67 **p** 68. C Kidderminster St Mary *Worc* 67-70; Guyana 70-73; TV N Creedy *Ex* 73-80; R Holsworthy w Hollacombe 80-86; R Holsworthy w Hollacombe and Milton Damerel from 86; Chapl N Devon Healthcare NHS Trust from 94. *The Rectory, Bodmin Street, Holsworthy EX22 6BH* Tel (01409) 253435 E-mail michael@rnlds85.freeserve.co.uk

REYNOLDS, Roderick Bredon (Rory). b 58. Man Univ BA80. Ripon Coll Cuddesdon 93. **d** 95 **p** 96. C Hitchin *St Alb* 95-98; C Stevenage St Andr and St Geo 98-00; P-in-c High Wych and Gilston w Eastwick from 00. *The Rectory, High Wych, Sawbridgeworth CM21 0HX* Tel (01279) 600894 Mobile 07970-070827 E-mail roryreynolds@mac.com

REYNOLDS, Mrs Rosemary Joan. b 46. WMMTC 00. **d** 03 **p** 04. NSM Brandwood *Birm* from 03. *23 Chanston Avenue, Birmingham B14 5BD* Tel 0121-444 7015 E-mail hello@frankandrosemary.freeserve.co.uk

REYNOLDS, Simon Andrew. b 65. ARCM85 UEA MA00. Westcott Ho Cam 98. **d** 00 **p** 01. C Ex St Thos and Em *Ex* 00-03; Min Can and Succ St Paul's Cathl *Lon* from 03; Warden Coll Min Cans from 04. *8A Amen Court, London EC4M 7BU* Tel (020) 7248 6115 *or* 7246 8338 E-mail succentor@stpaulscathedral.org.uk

RHAM, Canon John Theodore. b 27. Magd Coll Cam BA50 MA65. Sarum Th Coll 50. **d** 52 **p** 53. C Harborne St Pet *Birm* 52-54; C Coleshill 54-56; C Falmouth K Chas *Truro* 56-59; R St Ewe 59-68; RD St Austell 65-68; V Budock 68-93; RD Carnmarth S 77-84; Hon Can Truro Cathl 80-93; rtd 93; France from 94. *Villa Budoc, 136 route de Bernis, Langlade, 30980 Gard, France*

RHODES, Adrian Michael. b 48. K Coll Lon BD71 AKC71 DPST76. Qu Coll Birm 71. **d** 72 **p** 73. C Bury St Jo *Man* 73-75; Chapl N Man Gen Hosp 75-77; C Crumpsall *Man* 75-77; Chapl Walsall Manor and Bloxwich Hosps 77-83; Chapl Walsall Gen Hosp 81-83; Chapl Man R Infirmary 83-94; Chapl St Mary's Hosp Man 83-94; Chapl Man R Eye Hosp 83-94; Chapl Cen Man Healthcare NHS Trust 94-00; Perm to Offic *Man* from 00. *58 Errwood Road, Burnage, Manchester M19 2QH* Tel 0161-224 1739 E-mail adrian@rhodes.net

RHODES, Anthony John. b 27. Mert Coll Ox BA50 MA53 DipTh53. St Steph Ho Ox 52. **d** 54 **p** 55. C Northampton St Alb *Pet* 54-57; C Oakham 57-60; P-in-c S Queensferry *Edin* 60-74; V Mitcham St Olave *S'wark* 74-81; V Owston *Linc* 81-92; V W Butterwick 81-92; rtd 92. *1 Trentside, Owston Ferry, Doncaster DN9 1RS* Tel (01427) 728237

RHODES, Arthur. b 31. Dur Univ BA58. Cranmer Hall Dur 57. **d** 59 **p** 60. C Kirkdale St Lawr *Liv* 59-61; C Litherland St Phil 61-64; V St Helens St Matt Thatto Heath 64-67; V Samlesbury *Blackb* 67-79; Lic to Offic 80-01; Perm to Offic from 01. *88 Deborah Avenue, Fulwood, Preston PR2 9HU* Tel (01772) 712212

RHODES, Benjamin. b 71. Portsm Univ BSc93. Westcott Ho Cam 94. **d** 97 **p** 98. C Upminster *Chelmsf* 97-01; Asst Chapl Lewisham Hosp NHS Trust 01-05; Sen Chapl Barts and The Lon NHS Trust from 05; NSM St Bart Less *Lon* from 05. *The Royal London Hospital, Whitechapel Road, London E1 1BB* Tel (020) 7377 7385 E-mail ben.rhodes@bartsandthelondon.nhs.uk

RHODES, Christine. *See* RHODES, Lois Christine

RHODES, David. b 34. St Chad's Coll Dur BA60. **d** 61 **p** 62. C Dudley St Jo *Worc* 61-64; C-in-c Stourbridge St Mich Norton CD 64-68; V Astwood Bank w Crabbs Cross 69-78; Dioc Ecum Officer 73-78; TR Hackney *Lon* 78-88; R St Giles Cripplegate w St Bart Moor Lane etc 88-00; rtd 00; Perm to Offic *Chelmsf* from 00. *4 Freshwell Gardens, Saffron Walden CB10 1BZ* Tel (01799) 522912

RHODES, David George. b 45. Univ of Wales (Abth) BA66. Trin Coll Bris 83. **d** 85 **p** 86. C Brinsworth w Catcliffe *Sheff* 85-89; V Mortomley St Sav 89-90; V Mortomley St Sav High Green 90-99; V Totley from 99. *All Saints' Vicarage, 37 Sunnyvale Road, Sheffield S17 4FA* Tel 0114-236 2322 E-mail drhodes@toucansurf.com

RHODES, David Grant. b 43. Ex Univ BA66 Leeds Univ DipAdEd75. Sarum & Wells Th Coll 69. **d** 72 **p** 73. C Mirfield *Wakef* 72-75; V Batley St Thos 75-80; Dioc Adult Educn Officer 76-80; Hon C Huddersfield St Jo 85-86; Dir BRF 86-87; V Robert Town *Wakef* 87-94; Project Worker 'Faith in Leeds' 94-99; Hon C Potternewton *Ripon* 95-99; Chapl Missr Children's Soc 99-03; Hon C Leeds City *Ripon* 99-03; rtd 03. *2 Moorland Road, York YO10 4HF* Tel (01904) 651749 Mobile 07712-006930 E-mail rhodes@freeuk.com

RHODES, Duncan. b 35. Leeds Univ BSc56. Local Minl Tr Course 90. **d** 93 **p** 94. OLM Saddleworth *Man* from 93. *Holden Cottage, 21 Spurn Lane, Diggle, Oldham OL3 5QP* Tel (01457) 872399 E-mail dunrhodes@aol.com

RHODES, Mrs Heather. b 32. **d** 88. Par Dn Purley St Mark *S'wark* 89-94; C 94-98; rtd 98; Hon C Purley St Mark *S'wark* 00-05; Perm to Offic from 05. *24 Highfield Road, Purley CR8 2JG* Tel (020) 8660 1486

RHODES, Canon John Lovell. b 33. MBE81. Lon Univ BD59. St Aid Birkenhead 55. **d** 59 **p** 60. C Bradf St Clem *Bradf* 59-61; C Heeley *Sheff* 61-66; Ind Chapl *Linc* 66-81; Sen Ind Chapl 81-98; RD Grimsby and Cleethorpes 76-83; Can and Preb Linc Cathl 77-98; Chapl Franklin Coll 92-98; rtd 98; Perm to Offic *Linc* 98-01. *19 Augusta Close, Grimsby DN34 4TQ* Tel (01472) 343167

RHODES, Jonathan Peter. b 69. Coll of Ripon & York St Jo BA96. N Ord Course 01. **d** 04 **p** 05. C High Harrogate Ch Ch *Ripon* from 04. *7 Kingsway Drive, Harrogate HG1 5NJ* Tel (01423) 526846

RHODES, Lois Christine. b 34. Lon Univ BSc61. Glouc Sch of Min 84. **d** 87 **p** 94. NSM Weobley w Sarnesfield and Norton Canon *Heref* 87-92; NSM Letton w Staunton, Byford, Mansel Gamage etc 87-92; Asst Chapl Heref Hosps NHS Trust from 93. *Bellbrook, Bell Square, Weobley, Hereford HR4 8SE* Tel (01544) 318410 *or* (01432) 355444

RHODES, Matthew Ivan. b 66. Bris Univ BA89 Birm Univ MPhil95. Qu Coll Birm BD93. **d** 94 **p** 95. C Willenhall H Trin *Lich* 94-97; Chapl Maadi St Jo Egypt 97-00; P-in-c Middleton *Birm* from 00; P-in-c Wishaw from 00; P-in-c Curdworth from 05. *The Rectory, Glebe Fields, Curdworth, Sutton Coldfield B76 9ES* Tel (01675) 470384 E-mail catmat30@hotmail.com

RHODES, Robert George. b 41. Man Univ BSc62. Ripon Hall Ox DipTh73. **d** 74 **p** 75. C Banbury *Ox* 74-77; TV Banbury 77-81; P-in-c Long Horsley *Newc* 81-86; Adult Educn Adv 81-86; TR Wolverton *Ox* 86-97; P-in-c Bledlow w Saunderton and Horsenden 97-98; TV Risborough 98-02; Warden of Readers 97-02; USPG Belize from 02. *6 Sixth Street, King's Park, Belize City, Belize* Tel (00501) (2) 237949, 233660 *or* 233664 E-mail bandjrhodes@hotmail.com

RHODES-WRIGLEY, James. b 35. AKC59. **d** 60 **p** 61. C S Harrow St Paul *Lon* 60-66; V Hendon Ch Ch 66-71; V Northolt Park St Barn 71-92; rtd 92; Hon C Whyke w Rumboldswhyke and Portfield *Chich* from 96. *4 Gordon Avenue, Donnington, Chichester PO19 8QY* Tel (01243) 781664

RHYDDERCH, David Huw. b 48. Univ of Wales (Cardiff) DipTh73. St Mich Coll Llan 70. **d** 73 **p** 74. C Gelligaer *Llan* 73-76; C Penarth All SS 76-78; V Resolven 78-81; V Ystrad Rhondda w Ynyscynon 81-93; RD Rhondda 89-93; R St Andrews Major w Michaelston-le-Pit from 93. *The Rectory, Lettons Way, Dinas Powys CF64 4BY* Tel (029) 2051 2555

RICE, Brian Keith. b 32. Peterho Cam BA55 MA59. Seabury-Western Th Sem BD57 STM67 MDiv79 Linc Th Coll. **d** 57 **p** 58. C Winchmore Hill St Paul *Lon* 57-60; C Derby St Werburgh *Derby* 60-63; C Mackworth St Fran 63-66; Chapl Kingsway Hosp Derby 63-66; Educn Sec USPG 66-72; Dir of Educn *Birm* 72-84; Chapl St Chad's Hosp Birm 77-84; Soc Resp Officer *Dur* 84-97; rtd 97; Perm to Offic *Dur* from 97; *York* from 98. *Jasmine Cottage, 16 Forest Lane, Kirklevington, Yarm TS15 9LY* Tel (01642) 780396

RICE, Brian Thomas. b 46. Univ of Wales (Cardiff) BD77. St Mich Coll Llan 75. **d** 77 **p** 78. C Llanelli *St D* 77-79; P-in-c Llandygwydd and Cenarth w Cilrhedyn 79-80; V 80-83; V Llandingat w Myddfai from 83; AD Llangadog and Llandeilo from 91. *The New Vicarage, 42 Broad Street, Llandovery SA20 0AY* Tel (01550) 720524

RICE, David. b 57. Nottm Univ BA79. Ripon Coll Cuddesdon 80. **d** 82 **p** 83. C Cirencester *Glouc* 82-86; R Theale and Englefield *Ox* 86-00; TR Wallingford from 00. *The Rectory, 22 Castle Street, Wallingford OX10 8DW* Tel (01491) 202188

RICE, Franklin Arthur. b 20. FRICS49. St Alb Minl Tr Scheme 77. **d** 80 **p** 81. NSM Hoddesdon *St Alb* 80-84; Perm to Offic *Guildf* from 85. *1 Oatlands Court, St Mary's Road, Weybridge KT13 9QE* Tel (01932) 846462

RICE, John Leslie Hale. b 38. Lon Univ BScEng60 BD68 FCMI. EMMTC 73. **d** 76 **p** 77. NSM Allestree St Nic *Derby* 76-90; Lic to Offic from 90. *14 Gisborne Crescent, Allestree, Derby DE22 2FL* Tel (01332) 557222

RICE, Lt Cdr Peter Langford. b 49. RN Coll Dartmouth 70 RN Coll Greenwich 78. STETS 97. **d** 00 **p** 01. NSM Salisbury St Fran and Stratford sub Castle *Sarum* 00-03; P-in-c W Highland Region *Arg* from 03. *St Moluag's Diocesan Centre, Croft Avenue, Oban PA34 5JJ* Tel (01631) 570870 Mobile 07966-793717 Fax (01631) 570441 E-mail pincwest@aol.com

RICE-OXLEY, John Richard. b 44. Keble Coll Ox BA66 MA69 Dur Univ MA85. Lon Coll of Div 68. **d** 70 **p** 71. C Eastwood *S'well* 70-73; Youth Adv CMS 73-78; V Mansfield St Jo *S'well* 78-82; P-in-c Thornley *Dur* 82-85; P-in-c Darlington St Matt and St Luke 85-87; V 87-98; V Hornsea w Atwick *York* from 98; P-in-c Aldbrough, Mappleton w Goxhill and Withernwick from 05. *The Vicarage, 9 Newbeggin, Hornsea HU18 1AB* Tel (01964) 532531

RICH, Brian John. b 49. Reading Univ BSc70. Guildf Dioc Min Course 94. **d** 97 **p** 98. OLM Stoke Hill *Guildf* from 97. *Roewen, 1 Trentham Crescent, Old Woking, Woking GU22 9EW* Tel (01483) 829541 E-mail btrich@ntlworld.com

RICH, Canon Christopher Robin. b 49. LSE MSc(Econ)95. Brasted Th Coll 70 Sarum & Wells Th Coll 72. **d** 74 **p** 75. C Sholing *Win* 74-76; C Southampton Maybush St Pet 76-79; R Fawley 79-90; Ind Chapl 83-90; Dir Soc Resp 90-99; Hon Can Win Cathl 96-99; Dir Soc Resp *Blackb* from 99. *24 Bosburn Drive, Mellor Brook, Blackburn BB2 7PA* Tel (01254) 676281 E-mail chris.rich@blackburn.anglican.org

RICH, Nicholas Philip. b 49. St Cuth Soc Dur BA74 PGCE75 Coll of Ripon & York St Jo CertEd83. Linc Th Coll 86. **d** 88 **p** 89. C W Acklam *York* 88-91; Chapl St Geo Sch Harpenden 91-95; Lic to Offic *St Alb* 91-95; rtd 95. *57 Knowlwood Road, Todmorden OL14 6PB* Tel (01706) 810551

RICH, Paul Michael. b 36. OBE87. Sarum Th Coll 62. **d** 65 **p** 66. C Woodbridge St Mary *St E* 65-68; C W Wycombe *Ox* 68-70; CF 70-88; Lic to Offic *S & B* 88-90; V Crondall and Ewshot *Guildf* from 91. *The Vicarage, Farm Lane, Crondall, Farnham GU10 5QE* Tel (01252) 850379

RICH, Peter Geoffrey. b 45. Oak Hill Th Coll 74. **d** 77 **p** 78. C Blackheath St Jo *S'wark* 77-80; C Surbiton St Matt 80-87; V St Alb St Luke *St Alb* 87-98; V Gravesend St Aid *Roch* from 98. *The Vicarage, St Gregory's Crescent, Gravesend DA12 4JL* Tel (01474) 352500 E-mail angela_richuk@yahoo.co.uk

RICH, Thomas. b 52. St Jo Coll Nottm 86. **d** 88 **p** 89. C Netherton *Liv* 88-91; P-in-c Bootle Ch Ch 91-93; V from 93. *Christ Church Vicarage, 1 Breeze Hill, Bootle L20 9EY* Tel 0151-525 2565 Mobile 07958-784313 E-mail tom@richchurch.freeserve.co.uk

RICHARDS, Alan Grenville. b 41. Kelham Th Coll 64. **d** 69 **p** 70. C Northolt St Mary *Lon* 69-75; V Fatfield *Dur* 75-84; V Beighton *Sheff* 84-91; V Endcliffe 91-94; Deputation Appeals Org Children's Soc 94-98; V Cheriton All So w Newington *Cant* from 98. *All Souls Vicarage, 1 Ashley Avenue, Cheriton, Folkestone CT19 4PX* Tel (01303) 275483

RICHARDS, Andrew David Thomas. b 55. St Jo Coll Dur BA76 Roehampton Inst PGCE84 FRSA96. St Steph Ho Ox 76. **d** 78 **p** 79. C Shirley *Birm* 78-80; C Cowley St Jo *Ox* 80-82; Perm to Offic *Win* 84-88 and *Sarum* 88-92; NSM Hazelbury Bryan and the Hillside Par *Sarum* 92-94; Chapl Rossall Sch Fleetwood 94-99; Min Can Ely Cathl and Chapl K Sch Ely 99-03; Sen Chapl and Hd RS Wellington Coll Berks from 03. *Chapel Hill, Wellington College, Crowthorne RG45 7PT* Tel (01344) 444104 Mobile 07952-341837 E-mail adtr@wellington-college.berks.sch.uk

RICHARDS, Anthony Francis. b 26. Edin Univ 45 Wadh Coll Ox BA51 MA54. Ridley Hall Cam 50. **d** 52 **p** 53. C Finchley Ch Ch *Lon* 52-55; C Maidenhead St Andr and St Mary *Ox* 55-59; Lect All Nations Chr Coll Ware 58-59; V High Wycombe Ch Ch *Ox* 59-63; P-in-c 63-66; V Terriers 63-73; USA 70-71; V Cinderford St Steph w Littledean *Glouc* 73-80; V Clacton St Paul *Chelmsf* 80-93; New Zealand 88-89; rtd 93. *Mont, 58230 Ouroux-en-Morvan, Montsauche, France* Tel (0033) (3) 86 78 24 44 E-mail anthony.richards@libertysurf.fr

RICHARDS, Mrs April Deborah. b 42. Man Univ BSc63. S Dios Minl Tr Scheme 82. **dss** 85 **d** 87 **p** 94. Catherington and Clanfield *Portsm* 85-89; C 87-89; C E Meon and Langrish 89-95; Chapl Portsm Hosps NHS Trust 92-95; P-in-c Blackmoor and Whitehill *Portsm* 95-98; V 98-05; RD Petersfield 99-04; rtd 05. *Ryber House, 4 Castle Hill, East Leake, Loughborough LE12 6LX*

RICHARDS, Basil Ernest. b 18. Lich Th Coll 51. **d** 53 **p** 54. C Kidderminster St Mary *Worc* 53-55; C Northfield *Birm* 55-56; Hon C Gt Malvern Ch Ch *Worc* 78-84; Perm to Offic from 84; Chapl Laslett's Almshouses 84-88; rtd 88. *42 Viscount Cobham Court, Pickersleigh Road, Malvern WR14 2RJ* Tel (01684) 565441

RICHARDS, Brian. b 39. Open Univ BA78. N Ord Course 65 St Deiniol's Hawarden 94. **d** 94 **p** 94. C St Mellons and Michaelston-y-Fedw *Mon* 94-96; P-in-c Michaelston-y-Fedw 96-02; P-in-c Haarlem *Eur* from 02. *Closenberg Bastion 8, 1991 SP Velserbroek, The Netherlands* Tel (0031) (23) 547 3760

RICHARDS, Brian William. b 45. Spurgeon's Coll Lon BA88 MTh99. Guildf Dioc Min Course 01. **d** 03 **p** 04. NSM Howell Hill w Burgh Heath *Guildf* from 03. *2 Canford Court, 88A Epsom Road, Sutton SM3 9ES* Tel (020) 8330 1196 E-mail brianmeg@globalnet.co.uk

RICHARDS, Charles Dennis Vincent. b 37. AKC61. **d** 62 **p** 63. Chapl St Ninian's Cathl Perth *St And* 62-64; C Pimlico St Mary Graham-street *Lon* 64-66; C St Marylebone Ch Ch w St Barn 66-68; C Wood Green St Mich 68-69; Min S Kenton Annunciation CD 69-77; P-in-c Wembley Park St Aug 70-73; Hon C Paddington St Jo w St Mich 77-94; Perm to Offic 77-79; Lic to Offic from 79; rtd 02. *Flat B, 10 Bathurst Street, London W2 2SD* Tel (020) 7262 5633

RICHARDS, Charles Edmund Nicholas. b 42. Trin Coll Cam BA64 MA68. Westcott Ho Cam 64. **d** 66 **p** 67. C Rugby St Andr *Cov* 66-72; TV Basingstoke *Win* 72-77; R Rotherhithe St Mary w All SS *S'wark* from 77; RD Bermondsey 81-91. *The Rectory, 72 St Marychurch Street, London SE16 4JE* Tel (020) 7231 2465

RICHARDS, Christopher Mordaunt. b 40. New Coll Ox BA63 MA72 Bris Univ MB, ChB72. Cuddesdon Coll 63. **d** 65 **p** 81. C Bris St Mary Redcliffe w Temple etc *Bris* 65-66; Perm to Offic 66-72; Hon C Keynsham *B & W* 81-90; Perm to Offic 90-93. *4 St Ronans Avenue, Bristol BS6 6EP* Tel 0117-974 4062

RICHARDS, Daniel James. b 40. St D Coll Lamp DipTh66. **d** 66 **p** 67. C Kingswinford H Trin *Lich* 66-69; C Banbury *Ox* 69-71; C Aylesbury 71-73; C-in-c Stoke Poges St Jo Manor Park CD 73-78; R W Slough 78-80; R Ilchester w Northover, Limington, Yeovilton etc *B & W* 80-90; RD Ilchester 81-91; RD Martock 89-91; TR Bruton and Distr 90-97; R Axbridge w Shipham and Rowberrow 97-04; rtd 04; Clergy Retirement and Widows' Officer *B & W* from 05. *1 Quaperlake Street, Bruton BA10 0HA* Tel (01749) 812386 E-mail revdanrich@aol.com

RICHARDS, Canon David. b 30. Bris Univ BA52. St Mich Coll Llan 52. **d** 54 **p** 55. C Llangynwyd w Maesteg *Llan* 54-56; Iran 57-61 and 62-66; C Skewen *Llan* 61-62; V Cwmbach 66-76; Warden of Ords 71-77; R Coity w Nolton 76-96; Can Llan Cathl 88-96; rtd 96; Perm to Offic *Llan* and *Mon* from 96. *Inglewood, 5 Hopewell Close, Bulwark, Chepstow NP16 5ST* Tel (01291) 628912

RICHARDS, David Arnold. b 56. Wycliffe Hall Ox 76. **d** 81 **p** 82. C Skewen *Llan* 81-84; C Barking St Marg w St Patr *Chelmsf* 84-85; TV 85-90; Chapl Barking Hosp 87-88; P-in-c Stratford St Jo and Ch Ch w Forest Gate St Jas *Chelmsf* 90-97; V Stratford St Jo w Ch Ch and St Jas from 97. *Stratford Vicarage, 20 Deanery Road, London E15 4LP* Tel (020) 8534 8388 *or* 8503 1913 E-mail office@stjohnse15.freeserve.co.uk

RICHARDS, David Gareth. b 60. Hull Univ BA83 Birm Univ DipTh91. Qu Coll Birm 89. **d** 92 **p** 93. C Knowle *Birm* 92-96; Assoc R Edin St Paul and St Geo *Edin* 96-00; R from 00. *11 East Fettes Avenue, Edinburgh EH4 1DN* Tel 0131-332 3904 *or* 556 1355 Fax 556 0492 E-mail dave@pandgchurch.org.uk

RICHARDS, Dennis. b 48. St Mich Coll Llan DipTh95. **d** 97 **p** 98. C Cwmbran *Mon* 97-00; TV from 00. *St Peter's Vicarage, 30 Longhouse Grove, Henllys, Cwmbran NP44 6HQ* Tel (01633) 867613 E-mail rockrchrds@aol.com

RICHARDS, James Johnston. b 59. Solicitor 84 Lon Bible Coll BA90 Dur Univ MA97. Cranmer Hall Dur 90. **d** 92 **p** 93. C Harrow Trin St Mich *Lon* 92-95; C Kendal H Trin *Carl* 95-99; R Windermere from 99. *The Rectory, Longlands Road, Bowness-on-Windermere, Windermere LA23 3AS* Tel (01539) 443063 E-mail rector@stmartin.org.uk

RICHARDS, Mrs Jane Valerie. b 43. Westf Coll Lon BA64 Birm Univ CertEd65. S Dios Minl Tr Scheme 84. **d** 87 **p** 94. NSM Locks Heath *Portsm* 87-90; Asst Chapl Qu Alexandra Hosp Portsm 90-92; Chapl Portsm Hosps NHS Trust 92-95; Asst to RD Fareham *Portsm* 95-96; C Locks Heath 95-96; Chapl Southn Univ Hosps NHS Trust 96-03; rtd 03; Perm to Offic *Portsm* from 97 and *Win* from 03. *16 Lodge Road, Locks Heath, Southampton SO31 6QY* Tel (01489) 573891 E-mail dick@richards9934.freeserve.co.uk

RICHARDS, John. b 20. Univ of Wales (Lamp) BA40 Keble Coll Ox BA42 MA46 BLitt48 FSA70. Westcott Ho Cam. **d** 43 **p** 44. C Chirk *St As* 43; CF 44-45; C Bollington St Jo *Ches* 46-50; V Macclesfield St Pet 50-56; Lect Macclesfield Coll of FE 53-56; V New Brighton All SS 56-67; Master Wellington Sch Wirral 61-65 and 67-82; CF (TA) 62-69; Sen CF (TA) 69-86; V Hoylake *Ches* 67-86; Chapl Hoylake Cottage Hosp 67-86; rtd 86; Perm to Offic *Ches* from 86. *Ithaca, 56 Cleveley Road, Wirral CH47 8XR* Tel 0151-632 5135

RICHARDS, Preb John Francis. b 37. Dur Univ BA61. Wells Th Coll 61. **d** 63 **p** 64. C Sherwood *S'well* 63-67; C Bishop-wearmouth St Mich *Dur* 67-69; C Egg Buckland *Ex* 69-75; CF (ACF) 72-02; V Plymouth St Jas Ham *Ex* 75-83; V Plympton St Mary 83-02; RD Plymouth Moorside 88-93 and 96-01; Preb Ex Cathl from 91; rtd 02; Clergy Widow(er)s Officer *Ex* from 02. *24 Trewithy Drive, Plymouth PL6 5TY* Tel (01752) 214442 E-mail jfr-sjr@fish.co.uk

RICHARDS, John George. b 48. Qu Coll Birm 87. **d** 89 **p** 90. C Acocks Green *Birm* 89-92; TV Shirley 92-96; P-in-c Yardley Wood 96-00; V from 00. *Christ Church Vicarage, School Road, Yardley Wood, Birmingham B14 4EP* Tel 0121-436 7726 E-mail rev.johnrichards@btinternet.com

RICHARDS, John Henry. b 34. CCC Cam BA57 MA75. St Mich Coll Llan BD77. **d** 77 **p** 78. C Llangynwyd w Maesteg *Llan* 77-79; C Cardiff St Jo 79-82; Asst Chapl Univ of Wales (Cardiff) 79-82; V Penmark w Porthkerry 82-83; R Stackpole Elidor w St Petrox *St D* 83-85; R St Petrox w Stackpole Elidor and Bosherston etc 85-99; rtd 99. *20 Williamson Street, Pembroke SA71 4ER* Tel (01646) 672472

RICHARDS, John Michael. b 53. Coll of Ripon & York St Jo TCert76 Open Univ BA81. Cranmer Hall Dur 93. **d** 93 **p** 94. C Wath-upon-Dearne *Sheff* 93-95; R Warmsworth 95-01; R Sprotbrough from 01. *The Rectory, 42A Spring Lane, Sprotborough, Doncaster DN5 7QG* Tel (01302) 853203 Fax as telephone

RICHARDS, John Stanley. b 39. St Jo Coll Dur BA60. Ridley Hall Cam 61. **d** 64 **p** 65. C Fordingbridge w Ibsley *Win* 64-67; CF (TA) 64-68; C Bitterne Park *Win* 67-68; C Pokesdown All SS 68-70; Fell Qu Coll Birm 70-71; C Chesterton St Andr *Ely* 71-73; Asst Chapl Canford Sch Wimborne 73-77; Assoc Dir Fountain Trust 77-80; NSM New Haw *Guildf* 81-84; Dir Renewal Servicing from 81. *Crossover Cottage, Riverside, Staines TW18 8NH,* or *PO Box 463, Staines TW18 3WL*

RICHARDS, John William. b 29. Southn Univ BSc55. Sarum & Wells Th Coll 78. **d** 81 **p** 82. NSM Woking St Mary *Guildf* 81-85; C Addlestone 85-87; C S Gillingham *Roch* 87-89; Hon C W Byfleet *Guildf* 91-95; rtd 94; Perm to Offic *Sarum* from 95. *16 Normandy Way, Poundbury Whitfield, Dorchester DT1 2PP* Tel (01305) 251529

RICHARDS, Julian. b 25. Wycliffe Hall Ox 71. **d** 73 **p** 74. C Hessle *York* 73-76; P-in-c Rowley 76-82; Chapl HM Pris Hull 79-82; P-in-c Boldre *Win* 82-83; P-in-c Boldre w S Baddesley 83; V 83-93; rtd 93; RD Alton *Win* 93-98; Perm to Offic *Portsm* and *Win* from 98; Clergy Widows Officer (Win Adnry) 00-04. *Manor End, Worldham Hill, East Worldham, Alton GU34 3AX* Tel (01420) 86894 E-mail julian.richards@manorend.fsnet.co.uk

RICHARDS, Keith David. b 50. Didsbury Coll of Educn CertEd72. S'wark Ord Course 79. **d** 82 **p** 83. NSM Walworth *S'wark* 82-85; Chapl Derbyshire Coll of HE 85-87; V Rottingdean *Chich* 87-93; TR Crawley 93-97; V Arundel w Tortington and S Stoke from 97; RD Arundel and Bognor from 04. *The Vicarage, 26 Maltravers Street, Arundel BN18 9BU* Tel (01903) 885209 *or* 882262 Fax 882201 E-mail keith@arundel2000.freeserve.co.uk

RICHARDS, Kelvin. b 58. Univ of Wales (Abth) BSc80 MA88. Ripon Coll Cuddesdon BA82. **d** 83 **p** 84. C Killay *S & B* 83-86; C Morriston 86-89; R Llangattock and Llangyndir from 89; RD Crickhowell from 02. *The Rectory, Llangattock, Crickhowell NP8 1PH* Tel (01873) 810270

RICHARDS, Llewelyn. b 15. St Deiniol's Hawarden 73. **d** 75 **p** 76. NSM Corwen and Llangar *St As* 75-85; Past Care Gwyddelwern 78-85; rtd 85. *120 Maesyfallen, Corwen LL21 9AD* Tel (01490) 412195

RICHARDS, Mrs Mary Edith. b 33. SW Minl Tr Course 85. **d** 87 **p** 94. NSM Kea *Truro* 87-88; Asst Chapl Bris Poly *Bris* 88-91; C E Clevedon and Walton w Weston w Clapton *B & W* 91-96; rtd 96; Hon C Probus, Ladock and Grampound w Creed and St Erme *Truro* from 97; Mental Health Chapl Cornwall Healthcare NHS Trust 97-01. *62 Midway Drive, Uplands Park, Truro TR1 1NQ* Tel (01872) 277556

RICHARDS, Nicholas. *See* RICHARDS, Charles Edmund Nicholas

RICHARDS, Norman John. b 47. BSc. Ridley Hall Cam. **d** 83 **p** 84. C Luton St Fran *St Alb* 83-86; R Aspenden and Layston w Buntingford 86-95; P-in-c Westmill 94-95; R Aspenden, Buntingford and Westmill from 95. *The Vicarage, Vicarage Road, Buntingford SG9 9BH* Tel and fax (01763) 271552 E-mail nrichardsvic@aol.com

RICHARDS, Robert Graham. b 42. St Jo Coll Nottm 77. **d** 80 **p** 81. C Radipole and Melcombe Regis *Sarum* 80-83; TV Billericay and Lt Burstead *Chelmsf* 84-91; UK Dir CMJ 91-95; Chief Exec Nat Bibl Heritage Cen Ltd Trust 95-97; C Chorleywood St Andr *St Alb* 97-00; Perm to Offic *Sarum* from 01; Chapl Lee Abbey 02-05. *33 Stowell Crescent, Wareham BH20 4PT* Tel and fax (01929) 557124 E-mail rev_rob_richards@yahoo.co.uk

RICHARDS, Shaun. b 62. SSC. St Steph Ho Ox DipMin95. **d** 97 **p** 98. C Willesden Green St Andr and St Fran *Lon* 97-01; P-in-c Pentonville St Silas w All SS and St Jas 01; V from 02. *St Silas House, 45 Cloudesley Road, London N1 0EL* Tel (020) 7278 1101 E-mail fathershaun@one-richards.freeserve.co.uk

RICHARDS, Simon Granston. b 47. Nottm Univ BTh72 ALCD72. St Jo Coll Nottm 68. **d** 72 **p** 73. C Waltham Abbey *Chelmsf* 72-77; TV Basildon St Martin w H Cross and Laindon etc 77-80; V Grayshott *Guildf* 80-88; V Eccleston Ch Ch *Liv* 88-92; V Berkeley w Wick, Breadstone and Newport *Glouc* 92-02; P-in-c Stone w Woodford and Hill 99-02; V Berkeley w Wick, Breadstone, Newport, Stone etc 02-05; RD Dursley 96-02; V Bisley, Chalford, France Lynch, and Oakridge from 05; Chapl Severn NHS Trust from 94. *The Vicarage, Cheltenham Road, Bisley, Stroud GL6 7BJ* Tel (01452) 770056 E-mail simongr@tiscali.co.uk

RICHARDS, Stuart Anthony. b 70. K Coll Lon BA92 AKC92 Keble Coll Ox BA97 MA02. St Steph Ho Ox MTh02. **d** 99 **p** 00. C Reading All SS *Ox* 99-02; C Solihull *Birm* from 02. *17 Church Hill Close, Solihull B91 3JB* Tel 0121-704 0897

RICHARDS, Canon Thomas John Wynzie. b 25. St D Coll Lamp BA49. **d** 51 **p** 52. C Llandybie *St D* 51-53; V 71-87; C Llandegai *Ban* 53-56; R Llanymawddwy 56-57; Chapl Nat Nautical Sch Portishead 57-71; RD Dyffryn Aman *St D* 78-85; Can St D Cathl 83-92; Treas St D Cathl 89-92; V Pencarreg and Llanycrwys 87-92; rtd 92. *Maes Teifi, Cwmann, Lampeter SA48 8DT* Tel (01570) 423354

RICHARDS, Canon William Hughes. b 37. St D Coll Lamp BA58. **d** 60 **p** 61. C Llandysul *St D* 60-63; C Llanelli 63-65; V Llanddewi Brefi w Llanbadarn Odwyn 65-73; V Pen-bre 73-83; V Llangunnor w Cwmffrwd 83-88; V Cardigan w Mwnt and Y Ferwig 88-99; V Cardigan w Mwnt and Y Ferwig w Llangoedmor 99-01; Can St D Cathl 89-01; Treas 01; rtd 01. *Hafan Gobaith, 6 Cwrt y Gloch, Peniel, Carmarthen SA32 7HW* Tel (01267) 235995

RICHARDS, Canon William Neal. b 38. ALCD63. **d** 63 **p** 64. C Otley *Bradf* 63-65; C Leamington Priors St Mary *Cov* 65-67; CMS 67-69; Kenya 69-74; Asst Provost and Can Res Nairobi 70-74; V Gt Malvern St Mary *Worc* 74-86; Chapl Kidderminster Health Distr 86-91; RD Kidderminster *Worc* 89-91; R Martley and Wichenford, Knightwick etc 91-01; rtd 01; Perm to Offic *Worc* from 01. *Bay Tree Cottage, 32 Pump Street, Malvern WR14 4LU* Tel (01684) 569658

RICHARDSON, Aidan. *See* RICHARDSON, James Aidan

RICHARDSON, Andrew John. b 44. Ex Univ CertEd69. Trin Coll Bris 83. **d** 82 **p** 83. Kenya 82-87; Dioc Educn Sec *Maseno N* 83-89; Chapl Brentwood Sch Essex 88; Chapl Scarborough Coll 88-01; TV Parkham, Alwington, Buckland Brewer etc *Ex* from 01; RD Hartland from 03. *The Rectory, Old Market Drive, Woolsery, Bideford EX39 5QF* Tel (01237) 431571 E-mail rev.andy-ros@care4free.net

RICHARDSON, Aubrey. *See* RICHARDSON, John Aubrey

RICHARDSON, Charles Leslie Joseph. b 54. St Jo Coll Dur BA76. Coll of Resurr Mirfield 76. **d** 79 **p** 80. C Folkestone St Mary and St Eanswythe *Cant* 79-83; C Maidstone St Martin 83-86; Selection Sec and Voc Adv ACCM 86-91; PV Westmr Abbey 87-91; R Hastings St Clem and All SS *Chich* 91-98; RD Hastings 92-97; V E Dulwich St Jo *S'wark* from 98; Dioc Voc Adv from 99. *St John's Vicarage, 62 East Dulwich Road, London SE22 9AU* Tel (020) 7639 3807

RICHARDSON, Clive John. b 57. Trin Coll Bris DipHE82 Oak Hill Th Coll BA83 Bris Univ MA00. **d** 83 **p** 84. C Woking St Pet *Guildf* 83-86; C Worplesdon 86-90; V Rowledge 90-03; V Rowledge and Frensham from 03. *The Vicarage, Church Lane, Rowledge, Farnham GU10 4EN* Tel (01252) 792402 E-mail clive@rowvic.freeserve.co.uk

RICHARDSON, David. b 71. Edin Univ MA93 Stranmillis Coll PGCE94 PhD98. CITC BTh02. **d** 02 **p** 03. C Coleraine *Conn* from 02. *49 Avonbrook Gardens, Coleraine BT52 1SS* Tel (028) 7034 3671 E-mail darube@btopenworld.com

RICHARDSON, David Anthony. b 41. Kelham Th Coll 57. **d** 66 **p** 67. C Tong *Bradf* 66-68; C Richmond St Mary *S'wark* 68-71; C Sanderstead All SS 71-74; TV 74-78; R Beddington 78-92; V Dormansland 92-98; RD Godstone 95-98; USA from 98; Assoc R Tucson St Phil in the Hills from 98. *St Philip's in the Hills, PO Box 65840, Tucson, AZ 85728-5840, USA* Tel (001) (520) 299 6421 Fax 299 0712 E-mail richardsond@juno.com

RICHARDSON, Canon David Gwynne. b 39. AMIMinE. K Coll Lon 60. **d** 64 **p** 65. C Birtley *Dur* 64-67; Bp's Soc and Ind Adv 67-77; TV Brayton *York* 78-92; Ind Chapl 78-92; Chapl IMinE from 85; R Monk Fryston and S Milford 92-04; RD Selby 93-04; Can and Preb York Minster 03-04; rtd 04; Perm to Offic *York* from 04. *14 Beechcroft, Brayton, Selby YO8 9EP* Tel (01757) 704121 E-mail d.grich@freeuk.com

RICHARDSON, David John. b 50. MA LLB FCIArb. S'wark Ord Course. **d** 85 **p** 86. NSM S Croydon Em *S'wark* from 85. *20 Hurst View Road, South Croydon CR2 7AG* Tel (020) 8688 4947 *or* 8688 6676 E-mail dr.personal@13kbw.law.co.uk

RICHARDSON, The Very Revd David John Leyburn. b 46. Univ of Qld BA69. St Barn Coll Adelaide ACT ThL70 Melbourne Coll of Div BD75. **d** 70 **p** 71. Australia 70-75 and from 79; Perm to Offic *Birm* 75-76; C Cambridge Gt St Mary w St Mich *Ely* 76-79; Dean Adelaide 89-99; Dean Melbourne from 99. *St Paul's Cathedral, 209 Flinders Lane, Melbourne, Vic, Australia 3000* Tel (0061) (3) 9650 3791 *or* 9419 3364 Fax 9419 4364 E-mail drichardson@stpaulscathedral.org.au

RICHARDSON, Preb Douglas Stanley. b 23. Bps' Coll Cheshunt 55. **d** 57 **p** 58. C Hampton St Mary *Lon* 57-61; V W Twyford 61-69; V Notting Hill St Pet 69-78; V Staines St Pet 78-83; P-in-c Staines St Mary 81-83; V Staines St Mary and St Pet 83-92; AD Spelthorne 83-92; Preb St Paul's Cathl 92; rtd 92; Perm to Offic *Win* from 92. *22 Rooks Down Road, Badgers Farm, Winchester SO22 4LT* Tel (01962) 863687

RICHARDSON, Edward John. b 39. Westmr Coll Ox MTh98. Lich Th Coll 62. **d** 65 **p** 66. C Chessington *Guildf* 65-70; TV Trunch *Nor* 70-75; V Stoneleigh *Guildf* 75-79; Perm to Offic *S'wark* 92-94; Hon C Kingston All SS w St Jo 94-99; C 99-04; rtd 04; Perm to Offic *S'wark* 04-05; P-in-c Burpham *Chich* from 05. *The Vicarage, Burpham, Arundel BN18 9RJ* Tel (01903) 882948

RICHARDSON (née WOOD), Elaine Mary. b 51. SRN74. SEITE 00. **d** 03 **p** 04. C Hythe *Cant* from 03. *2 Palmarsh Avenue, Hythe CT21 6NT* Tel (01303) 261699 E-mail elaine.longview@virgin.net

RICHARDSON, Canon Eric Hatherley Humphrey. b 12. Qu Coll Ox BA35 MA46. Westcott Ho Cam 35. **d** 36 **p** 37. C Stoke Newington St Mary *Lon* 36-39; S Africa from 39. *PO Box 2289, Cramerview, 2060 South Africa* Tel (0027) (11) 787 7813 E-mail ceric@kon.co.za

RICHARDSON, Geoffrey Stewart. b 47. St Jo Coll Ox BA69 MA73. St Steph Ho Ox 70. **d** 72 **p** 73. C Roxbourne St Andr *Lon* 72-75; C Woodford St Barn *Chelmsf* 75-80; V Goodmayes St Paul 80-87; R Stow in Lindsey *Linc* 87-92; P-in-c Coates 87-92; P-in-c Willingham 87-92; R Stow Gp 92-01; RD Corringham 93-01; R Shaldon, Stokeinteignhead, Combeinteignhead etc *Ex* from 01. *The Rectory, Torquay Road, Shaldon, Teignmouth TQ14 0AX* Tel (01626) 872396

RICHARDSON, Graeme James. b 75. Oriel Coll Ox BA97. Ripon Coll Cuddesdon MPhil02. **d** 03 **p** 04. C Hatfield Hyde *St Alb* from 03. *Church House, Hollybush Lane, Welwyn Garden City AL7 4JS* Tel (01707) 338835 E-mail graeme.richardson@theology.ox.ac.uk

RICHARDSON, Gwynne. *See* RICHARDSON, Canon David Gwynne

RICHARDSON, James Aidan. b 28. St Chad's Coll Dur BA51 DipTh54. **d** 54 **p** 55. C Ferryhill *Dur* 54-56; C Stirling *Edin* 56-58; P-in-c Bo'ness 58-64; P-in-c Linlithgow 58-64; V Linthwaite *Wakef* 64-79; RD Blackmoorfoot 77-79; V Clifton 79-92; P-in-c Hartshead 83-88; rtd 92; Perm to Offic *Wakef* from 92. *10B Brooke Street, Cleckheaton BD19 3RY* Tel (01274) 874587

RICHARDSON, James Arthur. b 19. MC44. MRICS53 Lon Univ BSc51. Ridley Hall Cam 60. **d** 62 **p** 62. C Wandsworth All SS *S'wark* 62-65; V Streatham Park St Alb 65-87; rtd 87; Perm to Offic *Chich* from 87. *18 Crunden Road, Eastbourne BN20 8LW* Tel (01323) 737711

RICHARDSON, James Horner. b 19. Ch Coll Cam BA42 MA45. Ridley Hall Cam 41. **d** 43 **p** 44. C Normanton *Derby* 43-47; C Far Headingley St Chad *Ripon* 47-48; C High Harrogate St Pet 48-50; CF 50-53; Hon CF from 53; V Chadderton Em *Man* 53-59; V Huyton St Mich *Liv* 59-70; V Ormskirk 70-80; Hon Chapl ATC 71-80; V Giggleswick *Bradf* 80-82; P-in-c Rathmell 80-82; V Giggleswick and Rathmell w Wigglesworth 82-84; rtd 84; Hon Chapl Spennithorne Hall *Ripon* from 84; Hon C Aysgarth and Bolton cum Redmire from 84; Perm to Offic *Bradf* from 97. *25 Longdale Avenue, Settle BD24 9BB* Tel (01729) 823793

RICHARDSON, Canon James John. b 41. Hull Univ BA63 Sheff Univ DipEd64 FRSA91. Cuddesdon Coll 66. **d** 69 **p** 70. C Wolverhampton St Pet *Lich* 69-72; P-in-c Hanley All SS 72-75; R Nantwich *Ches* 75-82; Hon Can Ripon Cathl *Ripon* 82-88; V Leeds St Pet 82-88; Exec Dir Coun of Chrs and Jews 88-92; P-in-c Brington w Whilton and Norton *Pet* 93-96; P-in-c Church Brampton, Chapel Brampton, Harleston etc 94-96; TR Bournemouth St Pet w St Swithun, H Trin etc *Win* from 96; P-in-c Bournemouth St Aug from 01. *St Peter's Rectory, 18 Wimborne Road, Bournemouth BH2 6NT* Tel and fax (01202) 554058 E-mail canonrichardson@ntlworld.com

RICHARDSON, John. *See* RICHARDSON, Edward John

RICHARDSON, John. b 41. Qu Coll Birm 69. **d** 72 **p** 73. C Ormskirk *Liv* 72-74; C Doncaster St Geo *Sheff* 74-77; R Hemsworth *Wakef* 77-79; V Penallt *Mon* 79-85; R Amotherby w Appleton and Barton-le-Street *York* 85-89; P-in-c Hovingham 86-89; P-in-c Slingsby 86-89; TR Street 89-90; R Skelton w Shipton and Newton on Ouse 90-93; V Alsager St Mary *Ches* 93-96; V Grangetown *York* 96-00; V E Coatham 00-02; V Coatham and Dormanstown 02-04; P-in-c York St Lawr w St Nic from 04. *St Lawrence's Vicarage, 11 Newland Park Close, York YO10 3HW* Tel (01904) 411916

RICHARDSON, John. b 47. Linc Th Coll 78. **d** 80 **p** 81. C Keighley St Andr *Bradf* 80-83; V Hugglescote w Donington *Leic* 83-84; V Hugglescote w Donington-le-Heath and Ellistown 84-86; TR Hugglescote w Donington, Ellistown and Snibston 86-97; RD Akeley S 87-96; Chapl ATC 84-97; R Hallaton w Horninghold, Allexton, Tugby etc *Leic* 97-00; Rural Officer (Leic Adnry) 97-00; rtd 00; Perm to Offic *Pet* from 04. *13 Normanton Drive, Oakham LE15 6FG* Tel (01572) 770755 E-mail jcrichardson@home.gb.com

RICHARDSON, John. b 55. Lon Univ BEd BD Kent Univ MA. St Steph Ho Ox. **d** 83 **p** 84. C Thornbury *Glouc* 83-86; C Sheff St Cecilia Parson Cross *Sheff* 86-87; C Clacton St Jas *Chelmsf* 87-90; R Gt and Lt Tey w Wakes Colne and Chappel from 90. *The Rectory, Brook Road, Great Tey, Colchester CO6 1JF* Tel (01206) 211481 E-mail revjohn.richardson@virgin.net

RICHARDSON, John Aubrey. b 33. NEOC 90. **d** 93 **p** 94. NSM Warkworth and Acklington *Newc* 93-03; Perm to Offic from 03. *Harvest Lodge, 27 Acklington Village, Morpeth NE65 9BL* Tel (01670) 760761

RICHARDSON, John Hedley. b 45. Leeds Univ BA72. Qu Coll Birm 72. **d** 74 **p** 75. C Chaddesden St Phil *Derby* 74-76; Perm to Offic 76-86; TV Old Brampton and Loundsley Green 86-91; R Caston w Griston, Merton, Thompson etc *Nor* 91-95; RD Breckland 94-99; P-in-c Hockham w Shropham Gp of Par 94-95; R Caston, Griston, Merton, Thompson etc 95-02; P-in-c Clifton St Jas *Sheff* 02-03; V from 03. *Clifton Vicarage, 10 Clifton Crescent North, Rotherham S65 2AS* Tel (01709) 363082 *or* 836308 Fax as telephone

✠**RICHARDSON, The Rt Revd John Henry.** b 37. Trin Hall Cam BA61 MA65. Cuddesdon Coll 61. **d** 63 **p** 64 **c** 94. C Stevenage *St Alb* 63-66; C Eastbourne St Mary *Chich* 66-68; V Chipperfield St Paul *St Alb* 68-75; V Rickmansworth 75-86; RD Rickmansworth 77-86; V Bishop's Stortford St Mich 86-94; Hon Can St Alb 87-94; Suff Bp Bedford 94-02; rtd 02; Hon Asst Bp Carl from 03; Hon Asst Bp Newc from 03. *The Old Rectory, Bewscastle, Carlisle CA6 6PS* Tel (01697) 748389

RICHARDSON, John Humphrey. b 33. Dur Univ BA57. Chich Th Coll 57. **d** 59 **p** 60. C Bexhill St Barn *Chich* 59-61; C Stanmer w Falmer and Moulsecoomb 61-64; C Ifield 64-70; R Earnley and E Wittering 70-79; V Stamford All SS w St Pet *Linc* 79-81; R Stamford St Jo w St Clem 79-81; RD Aveland and Ness w Stamford 80-87; V Stamford All SS w St Jo 81-92; P-in-c Metheringham w Blankney 92-94; V Metheringham w Blankney and Dunston 94-98; rtd 98; Perm to Offic *Chich* from 99. *68 Bishopsgate Walk, Chichester PO19 6FQ* Tel (01243) 536864

RICHARDSON, Canon John Malcolm. b 39. Glas Univ MA60 BD63. Andover Newton Th Coll STM65 Edin Th Coll 84. **d** 84 **p** 85. C Edin Old St Paul *Edin* 84-86; R Leven *St And* 86-90; R Newport-on-Tay 90-96; R Tayport 90-96; Can St Ninian's Cathl Perth from 93; R Forfar from 96. *The Rectory, 24 St James's Road, Forfar DD8 1LG* Tel and fax (01307) 463440

RICHARDSON, John Peter. b 50. Keele Univ BA72. St Jo Coll Nottm 73. **d** 76 **p** 77. C Blackheath *Birm* 76-81; P-in-c Sparkbrook Ch Ch 81-83; Chapl NE Lon Poly *Chelmsf* 83-92; Chapl E Lon Univ 92-99; Hon C Stratford St Jo w Ch Ch and St Jas 83-99; C 99-00; C Henham and Elsenham w Ugley from 00. *39 Oziers, Elsenham, Bishop's Stortford CM22 6LS* Tel (01279) 813703 Mobile 07931-506913
E-mail j.p.richardson@virgin.net

RICHARDSON, John Stephen. b 50. Southn Univ BA71. St Jo Coll Nottm 72. **d** 74 **p** 75. C Bramcote *S'well* 74-77; C Radipole and Melcombe Regis *Sarum* 77-80; P-in-c Stinsford, Winterborne Came w Whitcombe etc 80-83; Asst Dioc Missr 80-83; V Nailsea Ch Ch *B & W* 83-90; Adv on Evang 86-90; Provost Bradf 90-00; Dean Bradf 00-01; V Wye w Brook *Cant* from 01; C Westwell, Hothfield, Eastwell and Boughton Aluph from 04; AD W Bridge from 03; Chapl Wye Coll Kent *Lon* from 01. *The Vicarage, Cherry Garden Crescent, Wye, Ashford TN25 5AS* Tel (01233) 812450 E-mail wyechurch@ic.ac.uk

RICHARDSON, Canon John Stuart. b 46. Trin Coll Ox BA68 MA71 DPhil73 FRSE96. **d** 79 **p** 80. NSM St Andrews St Andr *St And* 79-87; Chapl St Andr Univ 80-87; Prof Classics Edin Univ from 87; TV Edin St Columba *Edin* from 87; Hon Can St Mary's Cathl from 00. *29 Merchiston Avenue, Edinburgh EH10 4PH* Tel 0131-228 3094 E-mail j.richardson@ed.ac.uk

RICHARDSON, John Thandule. b 49. Bradf and Ilkley Coll BSc80 Lanc Univ MA97. Carl and Blackb Dioc Tr Inst 94. **d** 97 **p** 98. NSM Lea *Blackb* 97-02; NSM Broughton 02-04; NSM Lanercost, Walton, Gilsland and Nether Denton *Carl* from 04. *6 Irthing Park, Gilsland, Carlisle CA8 7DL* Tel (01697) 747652
E-mail johntr123@aol.com

RICHARDSON, John William. b 56. Bp Otter Coll BA85 Chich Th Coll 85. **d** 87 **p** 88. C E Preston w Kingston *Chich* 87-89; C Goring-by-Sea 89-90; TV Aldrington 91-92; V Sompting 92-02; P-in-c Margate All SS *Cant* from 02; P-in-c Westgate St Sav from 02. *The Vicarage, Thanet Road, Westgate-on-Sea CT8 8PB* Tel (01843) 831869 E-mail revjohnrichardson@btopenworld.com

RICHARDSON, Joseph Edmund. b 27. St Chad's Coll Dur BA49. Sarum Th Coll 51. **d** 52 **p** 53. C Far Headingley St Chad *Ripon* 52-56; C Hoylake *Ches* 56-58; R Halton *Ox* 58-65; R Davenham *Ches* 65-76; V Sale St Anne 76-84; R Delamere 84-88; rtd 88; Perm to Offic *Ex* 94-99. *10 Glenthorne Road, Exeter EX4 4QU* Tel (01392) 438539

RICHARDSON, Mrs Kathleen Beatrice. b 50. Carl and Blackb Dioc Tr Inst 02. **d** 04 **p** 05. NSM Kirkby Thore w Temple Sowerby and Newbiggin *Carl* from 04. *The Rectory, Kirkby Thore, Penrith CA10 1UR* Tel (017683) 62075 Mobile 07950-950273 E-mail katmalric@aol.com

RICHARDSON, Laurence Leigh. b 71. Trin Coll Carmarthen BA92 PGCE93 Univ of Wales (Cardiff) BTh97 FGMS04. St Mich Coll Llan 94. **d** 97 **p** 98. C Carmarthen St Pet *St D* 97-01; Chapl Carmarthenshire Coll 99-01; P-in-c Abergwili w Llanfihangel-uwch-Gwili etc *St D* 01-03; V from 03; CF(V) from 01. *The Vicarage, Wellfield Road, Abergwili, Carmarthen SA31 2JQ* Tel (01267) 234189 E-mail landcat10a@aol.com

RICHARDSON, Mrs Linda Joan. b 58. Univ of Wales BSc80. St Alb and Ox Min Course 01. **d** 04 **p** 05. NSM W Wycombe w Bledlow Ridge, Bradenham and Radnage *Ox* from 04. *Long Acre, Greenend Road, Radnage, High Wycombe HP14 4BY* Tel (01494) 484607 Fax 484608
E-mail linda.richardson@long-acre.co.uk

RICHARDSON, Maurice. b 12. **d** 66 **p** 67. C Hawksworth w Scarrington *S'well* 66-69; V Lowdham 69-77; rtd 77; Perm to Offic *S'well* from 77 and *Leic* from 82. *Old Orchard, Granby, Nottingham NG13 9PR* Tel (01949) 50860

RICHARDSON, Preb Neil. b 46. Southn Univ BTh83. Sarum & Wells Th Coll 71. **d** 74 **p** 75. C Oldham St Mary w St Pet *Man* 74-77; C-in-c Holts CD 77-82; R Greenford H Cross *Lon* from 82; Preb St Paul's Cathl from 02. *The Rectory, Oldfield Lane, Greenford UB6 9JS* Tel (020) 8578 1543
E-mail neil@holycross.ndo.co.uk
or neilandmarion2001@hotmail.com

✠**RICHARDSON, The Rt Revd Paul.** b 47. Qu Coll Ox BA68 BA70 MA75. Harvard Div Sch 70 Cuddesdon Coll 71. **d** 72 **p** 73 **c** 87. C Earlsfield St Jo *S'wark* 72-75; Asst Chapl Oslo St Edm *Eur* 75-77; Papua New Guinea 77-95; Miss P Nambaiyufu 77-79; Lect Newton Th Coll 79-81; Prin 81-85; Dean Port Moresby 85-86; Bp Aipo Rongo 87-95; Bp Wangaratta 95-97; Asst Bp Newc from 98. *Close House, St George's Close, Jesmond, Newcastle upon Tyne NE2 2TF* Tel 0191-281 2556 *or* 285 2220 Fax 284 6933

RICHARDSON, Paul. b 58. Univ of Wales (Cardiff) BSc80. Ridley Hall Cam 81. **d** 84 **p** 85. C Stanwix *Carl* 84-87; Ind Chapl 87-89; Staff P Dalton-in-Furness 87-89; V Marton Moss *Blackb* 89-95; P-in-c Prestwich St Gabr *Man* 95-00; Bp's Dom Chapl 95-00; V Westbury *Sarum* 00-02; TR White Horse from 02; RD Heytesbury from 04. *The Vicarage, Bitham Lane, Westbury BA13 3BU* Tel (01373) 822209
E-mail paul.richardson8@btinternet.com

RICHARDSON, Pauline Kate. *See* JENKINS, Pauline Kate

RICHARDSON, Robin John. b 71. Bris Univ BA01 Loughb Univ BEng92 PGCE93. Trin Coll Bris 98. **d** 01 **p** 02. C Sidmouth, Woolbrook, Salcombe Regis, Sidbury etc *Ex* 01-04; CF from 04. *c/o MOD Chaplains (Army)* Tel (01980) 615804 Fax 615800
E-mail strangways@xalt.co.uk

RICHARDSON, Simon James. b 51. Loughb Univ BSc82 Nottm Univ MA99. EMMTC 96. **d** 99 **p** 00. C Market Harborough and The Transfiguration etc *Leic* 99-02; Chapl Loughb Univ from 02; C Loughborough All SS w H Trin 02-04. *13 Spinney Hill Drive, Loughborough LE11 3LB* Tel (01509) 237761

RICHARDSON, Simon John. b 56. Univ of Wales (Ban) BA77. Ridley Hall Cam 81. **d** 84 **p** 85. C Luton St Mary *St Alb* 84-88; C Middleton *Man* 88-91; Sweden from 91; *Enebacken, Racksätter, 732 97 Arboga, Sweden* Tel (0046) (589) 70103

RICHARDSON, Simon Kay Caoimhn. b 74. St Jo Coll Dur BA96. Wycliffe Hall Ox 01. **d** 03 **p** 04. C Folkestone H Trin w Ch Ch *Cant* from 03; C Sandgate St Paul w Folkestone St Geo from 03. *St George's House, 133 Shorncliffe Road, Folkstone CT20 3PB* Tel (01303) 248675 Mobile 07771-800846
E-mail simonkcrichardson@hotmail.com

RICHARDSON, Miss Susan. b 58. Cranmer Hall Dur. **d** 87 **p** 94. Par Dn Stokesley *York* 87-91; Par Dn Beverley St Nic 91-94; P-in-c Cloughton 94-97; Tr Officer E Riding Adnry from 94; V Cloughton and Burniston w Ravenscar etc 97-99; V Middlesbrough St Oswald from 99. *St Oswald's Vicarage, Lambton Road, Middlesbrough TS4 2RG* Tel (01642) 816156

RICHBOROUGH, Suffragan Bishop of (Provincial Episcopal Visitor). *See* NEWTON, The Rt Revd Keith

RICHENS, Canon Geoffrey Roger. b 23. ALCD52. **d** 52 **p** 53. C St Helens St Helen *Liv* 52-56; V Widnes St Mary 56-80; V Skelmersdale St Paul 80-93; Hon Can Liv Cathl 89-93; rtd 93; Perm to Offic *Liv* from 93 and *Blackb* from 98. *43 West View, Parbold, Wigan WN8 7NT* Tel (01257) 463143

RICHERBY, Canon Glynn. b 51. K Coll Lon BD73 AKC73. St Aug Coll Cant 73. **d** 74 **p** 75. C Weston Favell *Pet* 74-78; Prec Leic Cathl *Leic* 78-81; V Glen Parva and S Wigston 81-93; Dir Post-Ord Tr 86-95; V Leic St Jas from 93; Dir CME from 95; Hon Can Leic Cathl from 98. *St James the Greater Vicarage, 216 London Road, Leicester LE2 1NE* Tel 0116-254 4113
E-mail glynn@leicester.anglican.org

RICHES, Canon John Kenneth. b 39. CCC Cam BA61 MA65. Kirchliche Hochschule Bethel 61 Westcott Ho Cam 62. **d** 65 **p** 66. C Costessey *Nor* 65-68; Chapl and Fell SS Coll Cam 68-72; Lect Glas Univ 72-86; Sen Lect 86-91; Prof Div and Bibl Criticism Glas Univ from 91; Chmn Balmore Trust from 80; Lic to Offic *Glas* from 85; Can St Mary's Cathl from 01; rtd 04. *Viewfield House, Balmore, Torrance, Glasgow G64 4AE* Tel (01360) 620254 E-mail j.riches@divinity.gla.ac.uk

RICHES, Malcolm Leslie. b 46. St Jo Coll Nottm Dip Th & Min 94. **d** 94 **p** 95. C Swaythling *Win* 94-97; P-in-c Boldre w S Baddesley 97-01; V 01-03; V Ellingham and Harbridge and Hyde w Ibsley from 03. *The Vicarage, Frogham Hill, Stuckton, Fordingbridge SP6 2HH* Tel (01425) 650853
E-mail malcolm.riches@ukgateway.net

RICHEUX, Marc Stephen. b 66. Man Univ BA89. Trin Coll Bris BA00. **d** 00 **p** 01. C Plumstead St Jo w St Jas and St Paul *S'wark* 00-04; V Streatham Park St Alb from 04. *St Alban's Vicarage, 5 Fayland Avenue, London SW16 1SR* Tel (020) 8677 4521 *or* 8769 5415 E-mail mricheux@clara.co.uk

RICHEY, Robert Samuel Payne. b 23. TCD BA46. **d** 48 **p** 49. C Moy *Arm* 48-50; I Killinagh w Kiltyclogher *K, E & A* 50-60; I Killinagh w Kiltyclogher and Innismagrath 60-72; I Killinagh w Kiltyclogher, Killargue etc 72-91; I Killinagh w Kiltyclogher and Innismagrath 91-98; Sec Dioc Bd Educn 64-98; Dioc Sec (Kilmore) 72-98; Dioc Info Officer (Kilmore) 81-98; Can Kilmore Cathl 80-98; Preb Mulhuddart St Patr Cathl Dublin 94-98; rtd 98. *Rockview, Blacklion, Co Cavan, Irish Republic* Tel and fax (00353) (71) 985 3010
E-mail robkathrichey@eircom.net

✠**RICHMOND, The Rt Revd Francis Henry Arthur.** b 36. TCD BA59 MA66 Strasbourg Univ BTh60 Linacre Coll Ox MLitt64. Wycliffe Hall Ox 60. **d** 63 **p** 64 **c** 86. C Woodlands *Sheff* 63-66; Chapl Sheff Cathl 66-69; V Sheff St Geo 69-77; Chapl Sheff Univ 74-77; Warden Linc Th Coll 77-86; Can and Preb Linc Cathl *Linc* 77-86; Suff Bp Repton *Derby* 86-98; Hon Can Derby Cathl 86-98; rtd 98; Hon Asst Bp Ox from 99. *39 Hodges Court, Oxford OX1 4NZ* Tel (01865) 790466

RICHMOND, Gordon Hazlewood. b 33. Launde Abbey 77. **d** 79 **p** 80. C Leic St Paul *Leic* 79-81; C Shepshed 81-84; V Ryhall w Essendine *Pet* 84-91; RD Barnack 89-91; V Gretton w

Rockingham 91-98; rtd 98; Perm to Offic *Pet* from 98; *Leic* from 99. *Malvern, 2 Linwal Avenue, Houghton-on-the-Hill, Leicester LE7 9HD* Tel 0116-241 7638

RICHMOND, Patrick Henry. b 69. Ball Coll Ox BA90 Green Coll Ox MA94 DPhil94. Wycliffe Hall Ox BA96. **d** 97 **p** 98. C Leic Martyrs *Leic* 97-01; Chapl St Cath Coll Cam from 01. *8 South Green Road, Cambridge CB3 9JP* Tel (01223) 324035 *or* 338300 E-mail chaplain@caths.cam.ac.uk

RICHMOND, Peter James. b 54. Ex Univ PGCE95. St Jo Coll Nottm. **d** 80 **p** 81. C Ogley Hay *Lich* 80-83; C Trentham 83-85; P-in-c Wolverhampton St Jo 85-89; P-in-c Loppington w Newtown 89-93; P-in-c Edstaston 89-93; Perm to Offic *Ex* 94-95; P-in-c Weston Zoyland w Chedzoy *B & W* 95-03; Chapl Somerset Partnership NHS and Soc Care Trust 97-03; Lead Chapl E Kent NHS and Soc Care Partnership Trust from 03; Hon C St Nicholas at Wade w Sarre and Chislet w Hoath *Cant* from 04. *St Martin's Hospital, Littlebourne Road, Canterbury CT1 1TD* Tel (01227) 812047 E-mail peter.richmond@ekentmht.nhs.uk

RICHMOND, Mrs Yvonne Lorraine. b 63. WEMTC 96. **d** 99 **p** 00. NSM Magor *Mon* 99-00; NSM Kenilworth St Jo *Cov* 00-05; Chapl for Evang Cov Cathl from 05. *Birchwood, Red Lane, Kenilworth CV8 1PB* Tel (024) 7647 1039 E-mail yvonne.richmond@care4free.net

RICHMOND, Archdeacon of. *See* GOOD, The Ven Kenneth Roy

RICKARDS, Bruce Walter. b 69. NTMTC 98. **d** 01 **p** 02. NSM St Marg Lothbury and St Steph Coleman Street etc *Lon* from 01. *85A Toynbee Road, London SW20 8SJ* Tel (020) 8540 4150 Mobile 07850-655102 E-mail byrickards@btinternet.com *or* bruce_rickards@eigmail.com

RICKETTS, Allan Fenn. b 46. Open Univ BA76. Cranmer Hall Dur 68. **d** 71 **p** 72. C Rowley Regis *Birm* 71-72; C The Quinton 72-74; C Brierley Hill *Lich* 74-77; TV Chelmsley Wood *Birm* 77-82; TV Ross w Brampton Abbotts, Bridstow and Peterstow *Heref* 82-88; R Linton w Upton Bishop and Aston Ingham 88-96. *13 Falaise Close, Ross-on-Wye HR9 5UT* Tel (01989) 565077

RICKETTS, Mrs Diane. NTMTC. **d** 01 **p** 02. NSM Nazeing *Chelmsf* from 01; NSM Roydon from 01. *38 Paternoster Close, Waltham Abbey EN9 3JX* Tel (01992) 764415 E-mail diane_ricketts@yahoo.co.uk

RICKETTS, Canon Kathleen Mary. b 39. Southlands Coll Lon TCert59 Univ of W Aus BA79. Westcott Ho Cam 81. **dss** 83 **d** 87 **p** 94. All Hallows by the Tower etc *Lon* 83-88; C 87-88; C Hall Green Ascension *Birm* 88-91; Chapl Birm Children's Hosp 91-94; Chapl Birm Children's Hosp NHS Trust 94-99; Hon Can Birm Cathl *Birm* 96-99; rtd 99; Perm to Offic *Birm* from 00. *22 Holly Drive, Birmingham B27 7NF* Tel 0121-706 1087

RICKETTS, Mrs Linda Elizabeth. b 52. RNMH85. EAMTC 98. **d** 01 **p** 02. C Loddon, Sisland, Chedgrave, Hardley and Langley *Nor* from 01. *All Saints' House, 6 Farm Close, Chedgrave, Norwich NR14 6HQ* Tel (01508) 528310

RICKETTS, Peter William. b 28. DLC53. St Alb Minl Tr Scheme 76. **d** 79 **p** 80. NSM Hertford All SS *St Alb* 79-86; R Blunham w Tempsford and Lt Barford 86-93; rtd 93; Perm to Offic *St Alb* 93-02 and *Sarum* from 03. *7 Rashley Road, Chickerell, Weymouth DT3 4AT* Tel (01305) 781892

RICKMAN, Peter Alan. b 68. Ripon Coll Cuddesdon BTh97. **d** 97 **p** 98. C Bitterne Park *Win* 97-01; Chapl St Paul's Colleg Sch Hamilton NZ 01-04; Sub Chapl HM Pris Win 04-05; P-in-c Bransgore *Win* from 05. *St Mary's Vicarage, Ringwood Road, Bransgore, Christchurch BH23 8JH* Tel (01425) 672327 Mobile 07789-684481 E-mail pizzarev@aol.com

RIDDEL, Canon Robert John. b 37. CITC 65. **d** 68 **p** 69. C Derryloran *Arm* 68-74; I Keady w Armaghbreague and Derrynoose 74-80; I Mullaghdun *Clogh* 80-84; I Cleenish 80-84; I Fivemiletown from 84; Can Clogh Cathl from 91; Preb Donaghmore St Patr Cathl Dublin from 95. *The Rectory, 160 Ballagh Road, Fivemiletown BT75 0QP* Tel (028) 8952 1030 E-mail r.j.riddel@btinternet.com

RIDDELL, Morris Stroyan. b 34. Lon Univ DipTh59 BD69. Tyndale Hall Bris 57. **d** 60 **p** 60. S Africa 60-63; C Mowbray 60-62; V Addington Ch Ch 62-63; V N Grimston w Wharram Percy and Wharram-le-Street *York* 63-67; V Kirby Grindalythe 63-67; P-in-c Weaverthorpe w Helperthorpe and Luttons 65-67; P-in-c Settrington 65-67; P-in-c Wintringham 65-67; P-in-c Thorpe Bassett 65-67; R Bris St Jo w St Mary-le-Port *Bris* 67-70; Dir Bris Samaritans 67-70; Chapl HM Pris Long Lartin 71-74; Chapl HM Pris Brixton 74-78; Chapl Cane Hill Hosp Coulsdon 78-85; Chapl HM Rem Cen Latchmere Ho 85-89; rtd 95. *Flat 5, 30 Montpelier Crescent, Brighton BN1 3JJ* Tel (01273) 329229

RIDDELSDELL, Canon John Creffield. b 23. Selw Coll Cam BA47 MA52 Lon Univ BD70. Ridley Hall Cam 47. **d** 49 **p** 50. C Kilburn St Mary *Lon* 49-52; Kenya 52-77; V Gt Ilford St Andr *Chelmsf* 77-88; rtd 88; Perm to Offic *Chelmsf* from 88. *Waverley, Mill Lane, Walton on the Naze CO14 8PE* Tel (01255) 850213

RIDDING, George. b 24. Oriel Coll Ox BA50 MA57. Wells Th Coll 60. **d** 61 **p** 62. C Countess Wear *Ex* 61-62; Chapl Ex Sch 62-64; India 64-68; Hd Master W Buckland Sch Barnstaple 68-78; USPG 78-82; P-in-c Broadhembury w Payhembury *Ex* 82-83; P-in-c Plymtree 82-83; R Broadhembury, Payhembury and Plymtree 83-89; rtd 89; Perm to Offic *Sarum* from 89. *3 Cann Lodge Gardens, Shaftesbury SP7 8HU* Tel (01747) 851390

RIDDING, William Thomas. b 54. Southn Univ BTh. Sarum & Wells Th Coll 80. **d** 83 **p** 84. C Verwood *Sarum* 83-86; TV Gillingham 86-01; RD Blackmore Vale 95-01; P-in-c Stalbridge 01-02; R Stalbridge and Stock from 02. *The Rectory, Church Hill, Stalbridge, Sturminster Newton DT10 2LR* Tel (01963) 362859 E-mail williamridding@beeb.net

RIDDLE, Kenneth Wilkinson. b 20. St Cath Soc Ox BA42 MA46. Ripon Hall Ox 42. **d** 43 **p** 44. C Lowestoft St Marg *Nor* 43-47; C Luton St Mary *St Alb* 47-49; V Sundon w Streatley 49-52; R Pakefield *Nor* 52-59; V Nor St Pet Mancroft 59-60; R E w W Harling 60-65; P-in-c Bridgham and Roudham 60-61; R 61-65; R Lowestoft St Marg 65-68; rtd 85. *9 Clare Court, Clarence Road, Fleet GU51 3XX* Tel (01252) 617450

RIDEOUT, Canon Gordon Trevor. b 38. BA87 Westmr Coll Ox MTh96. Lon Coll of Div 58. **d** 62 **p** 63. C Southgate *Chich* 62-65; Chapl Dr Barnardo's Barkingside and Woodford Bridge 65-67; CF 67-73; V Nutley *Chich* 73-79; V Eastbourne All SS 79-03; Chapl Moira Ho Sch E Sussex 79-03; Chapl Brighton Poly *Chich* 80-92; Chapl Brighton Univ 92-03; rtd 03; Can and Preb Chich Cathl *Chich* from 90; RD Eastbourne from 97. *9 Filching Close, Polegate BN26 5NU* Tel (01323) 482660

RIDER, Andrew. b 62. RMN85 Nottm Univ BTh90 K Coll Lon MA96. Aston Tr Scheme 85 St Jo Coll Nottm 87. **d** 90 **p** 91. C Luton Ch Ch *Roch* 90-93; C w resp for Clubhouse Langham Place All So *Lon* 93-03; P-in-c Spitalfields Ch Ch w All SS 03-04; R from 04. *The Rectory, 2 Fournier Street, London E1 6QE* Tel (020) 7247 0790 *or* 7247 7202 Fax 7247 5921 E-mail arider@clara.co.uk

RIDER, Canon Dennis William Austin. b 34. St Aid Birkenhead 58. **d** 61 **p** 62. C Derby St Aug *Derby* 61-64; C Sutton *Liv* 64-67; R Stiffkey w Morston, Langham Episcopi etc *Nor* 67-71; V Buxton w Oxnead 71-79; R Lammas w Lt Hautbois 72-79; R Gaywood, Bawsey and Mintlyn 79-91; RD Lynn 89-91; Hon Can Nor Cathl 90-99; R E Dereham and Scarning 91-98; TR 98-99; RD Dereham in Mitford 95-98; rtd 99; Perm to Offic *Nor* from 01. *37A Holt Road, Fakenham NR21 8BW* Tel (01328) 856018

RIDER, Geoffrey Malcolm. b 29. Selw Coll Cam BA53 MA56 Lon Inst of Educn PGCE68. Coll of Resurr Mirfield 53. **d** 55 **p** 56. C S Elmsall *Wakef* 55-60; C Barnsley St Mary 60-63; V Cleckheaton St Jo 63-67; Public Preacher *S'wark* 67-92; rtd 92; Succ Kimberley Cathl S Africa 92-95; Perm to Offic *S'wark* 95-03; Chapl and Hon Min Can Ripon Cathl *Ripon* from 04. *35 Kirkby Road, Ripon HG4 2EY* Tel (01765) 690517

RIDER, Neil Wilding. b 35. St Jo Coll Dur BA59 DipTh61 Univ of Wales (Lamp) MA00. Cranmer Hall Dur 59. **d** 62 **p** 63. C Blackb St Barn *Blackb* 62-64; C Chadderton Em *Man* 64-69; C Deane 69-72; V Coldhurst 72-75; Perm to Offic *Ely* 76-78; C Didsbury Ch Ch *Man* 78-80; Perm to Offic *St D* from 80; rtd 00. *Caergrawnt, Llandovery Road, Cwmann, Lampeter SA48 8EL* Tel (01570) 422921

RIDGE, Aubrey. b 25. Oak Hill Th Coll 67. **d** 68 **p** 69. C Gorleston St Andr *Nor* 68-70; C Hamworthy *Sarum* 70-75; P-in-c Pitsea *Chelmsf* 75-78; R 78-81; P-in-c Stoke Ash, Thwaite and Wetheringsett *St E* 81-85; P-in-c Bedingfield and Thorndon w Rishangles 81-85; P-in-c Thorndon w Rishangles, Stoke Ash, Thwaite etc 85-86; P-in-c Risby w Gt and Lt Saxham and Westley 86-90; rtd 90; Perm to Offic *Sarum* 90-93; Hon C Milford *Win* 93-96; Perm to Offic 96-99. *5 Oak Tree Court, Whitby Road, Milford on Sea, Lymington SO41 0UJ* Tel (01590) 643504

RIDGE, Haydn Stanley. b 24. Univ of Wales (Lamp) BA51 Bris Univ CertEd52. Qu Coll Birm 56. **d** 56 **p** 57. C Blackheath *Birm* 56-60; Div Master Guernsey Gr Sch 60-75; Perm to Offic *Win* 60-62; Hon C Guernsey St Steph 62-96; Dep Hd Master St Peter Port Sch 75-80; Hd Master St Sampson Sch 75-87; rtd 91; Perm to Offic *Win* 96-00. *St David, Les Cherfs, Castel, Guernsey GY5 7HG* Tel (01481) 56209

RIDGE, James Scott. b 77. Ex Univ BSc99 Anglia Poly Univ BTh05. Westcott Ho Cam 02. **d** 05. C Halstead Area *Chelmsf* from 05. *47 Tidings Hill, Halstead CO9 1BL* Tel (01787) 475528 Mobile 07796-647343 E-mail james@ridge.clara.co.uk

RIDGEWAY, David. b 59. St Chad's Coll Dur BSc80 Cam Univ CertEd81. Ripon Coll Cuddesdon 84. **d** 87 **p** 88. C Kempston Transfiguration *St Alb* 87-90; C Radlett 90-95; P-in-c Heath and Reach 95-98; V 98-01; V St Alb St Steph from 01; AD St Alb from 05. *St Stephen's Vicarage, 14 Watling Street, St Albans AL1 2PX* Tel (01727) 862598 Fax 07092-109111 E-mail davidridgeway@eggconnect.net

RIDGEWELL, Miss Mary Jean. b 54. Dur Univ BA76 PGCE77. Ridley Hall Cam 89. **d** 91 **p** 94. Par Dn Trowbridge St Jas *Sarum* 91-94; C 94-95; Chapl Lee Abbey 95-96; NSM Bradford Peverell, Stratton, Frampton etc *Sarum* 96-97; Chapl HM Pris and Young Offender Inst Guys Marsh from 97. *HM Prison and YOI, Guy's*

Marsh, Shaftesbury SP7 0AH Tel (01747) 853344 ext 325 Fax 851584 E-mail mary@jridgewell.fsnet.co.uk

RIDGWAY, David. b 28. Trin Hall Cam BA54 MA58. Westcott Ho Cam 54. **d** 56 **p** 57. C Milton *Portsm* 56-59; CF 59-63; R Gosforth *Carl* 63-70; V Walney Is 70-76; P-in-c Irthington 76-78; P-in-c Crosby-on-Eden 77-78; V Irthington, Crosby-on-Eden and Scaleby 79-93; rtd 93. *11 Woodleigh, Walton, Brampton CA8 2DS* Tel (01697) 73252

RIDGWAY, Mrs Janet Elizabeth Knight. b 40. St Alb Minl Tr Scheme 83. **dss** 86 **d** 87 **p** 94. Tring *St Alb* 86-87; Hon Par Dn 87-94; Hon C from 94. *Barleycombe, Trooper Road, Aldbury, Tring HP23 5RW* Tel and fax (01442) 851303 E-mail rev.j.ridgway@breathemail.net

RIDGWELL, Graham Edgar Charles. b 46. LGSM71 Open Univ BA82 UEA DPSE88 Leeds Univ MA04. **d** 02 **p** 03. NSM Whitby w Aislaby and Ruswarp *York* 02-05; Hon TV Linton *Ely* from 05. *The Vicarage, Park Lane, Castle Camps, Cambridge CB1 6SR* Tel (01799) 584803 E-mail ridgwell@onetel.com

RIDING, Pauline Alison. *See* BICKNELL, Mrs Pauline Alison

RIDINGS, Neil Arthur. b 66. Man Poly BEd90. St Jo Coll Nottm 01. **d** 01 **p** 02. C Holyhead *Ban* 01-05; TV from 05. *St Seiriol's House, Gors Avenue, Holyhead LL65 1PB* Tel (01407) 764780

RIDLEY, Alfred Forbes. b 34. Bps' Coll Cheshunt 62. **d** 65 **p** 66. C Prittlewell St Mary *Chelmsf* 65-69; R Paulerspury *Pet* 69-73; P-in-c Wicken 71-73; V W Haddon w Winwick 73-83; RD Brixworth 80-83; R Guernsey St Philippe de Torteval *Win* 83-92; R Guernsey St Pierre du Bois 83-92; R Blakesley w Adstone and Maidford etc *Pet* 92-99; rtd 99; Perm to Offic *Pet* from 99. *4 Plessey Close, Towcester NN12 6HY* Tel (01327) 358664

RIDLEY, Andrew Roy. b 55. St Pet Coll Ox BA77. Ripon Coll Cuddesdon 78. **d** 79 **p** 80. C Bollington St Jo *Ches* 79-83; V Runcorn St Mich 83-94; Dioc Chapl to MU 92-98; RD Frodsham 94-98; V Helsby and Dunham-on-the-Hill 94-98; P-in-c Alvanley 94-98; R Whitchurch *Lich* from 98; RD Wem and Whitchurch from 01. *The Rectory, Church Street, Whitchurch SY13 1LB* Tel and fax (01948) 662342

RIDLEY, David Gerhard. b 60. Southn Univ BSc82 Bath Univ PGCE83. Qu Coll Birm 91. **d** 93 **p** 94. C Faversham *Cant* 93-97; Min Folkestone St Aug CD 97-01; V Dover St Mary from 01; P-in-c Guston from 02. *The Vicarage, Taswell Street, Dover CT16 1SE* Tel (01304) 206842 E-mail davidridley@bigfoot.com

RIDLEY, Derek. b 40. Newc Univ BSc74. Cranmer Hall Dur 75. **d** 78 **p** 79. C Upperby St Jo *Carl* 78-81; C Penrith w Newton Reigny 81; C Penrith w Newton Reigny and Plumpton Wall 81-82; TV 82-86; V Cadishead *Man* 86-99; R Asfordby and P-in-c Ab Kettleby Gp *Leic* 99-02; P-in-c Old Dalby and Nether Broughton 99-01; rtd 02. *32 Carleton Place, Penrith CA11 8LW* Tel (01768) 890676

RIDLEY, Jay. b 41. Birm Univ BA63. St Steph Ho Ox 63. **d** 65 **p** 66. C Woodford St Mary *Chelmsf* 65-67; C Prittlewell St Mary 67-70; C-in-c Dunscroft CD *Sheff* 70-74; Asst Chapl HM Pris Wormwood Scrubs 75-77; Chapl HM Rem Cen Ashford 77-84; Chapl HM YOI Feltham 84-91; Chapl HM Pris Ashwell 91-00; C Oakham, Hambleton, Egleton, Braunston and Brooke *Pet* from 00. *45 Trent Road, Oakham LE15 6HE* Tel (01572) 756086 E-mail j.ridley@zetnet.co.uk

RIDLEY, Mrs Lesley. b 46. Cranmer Hall Dur 75. **dss** 78 **d** 87 **p** 94. Upperby St Jo *Carl* 78-81; Penrith w Newton Reigny and Plumpton Wall 81-86; Cadishead *Man* 86-99; Par Dn 87-94; C 94-99; C Asfordby and Ab Kettleby Gp *Leic* 99-02; rtd 02. *32 Carleton Place, Penrith CA11 8LW* Tel (01768) 890676

RIDLEY, Louise. b 59. Lanc Univ BA81 LGSM83. Cranmer Hall Dur 01. **d** 03 **p** 04. C Sheff St Cuth *Sheff* from 03. *112 Whiteways Road, Sheffield S4 8EU* Tel 0114-261 1605

RIDLEY, Canon Michael Edward. b 37. Ex Univ MA90. St Boniface Warminster AKC62. **d** 63 **p** 64. C Chapel Allerton *Ripon* 63-67; C Epsom St Martin *Guildf* 67-70; C Claxby w Normanby-le-Wold etc *Linc* 70-72; V Leake 72-75; R Harlaxton w Wyville and Hungerton 75-80; R Stroxton 76-80; Dioc Stewardship Adv *Portsm* 80-86; P-in-c Rowlands Castle 80-82; C Blendworth w Chalton w Idsworth etc 83-86; TV N Creedy *Ex* 86-90; R W Downland *Sarum* 90-02; RD Chalke 92-97 and 98-00; Can and Preb Sarum Cathl 00-02; rtd 02; Perm to Offic *Truro* from 03. *6 Cole Moore Meadow, Tavistock PL19 0ES* Tel (01822) 610799

RIDLEY, Michael Laurence. b 59. BA81. Ripon Coll Cuddesdon 81. **d** 83 **p** 84. C Bollington St Jo *Ches* 83-88; V Thelwall 88-95; V Weaverham 95-05; RD Middlewich 99-05; V Stockton Heath from 05. *The Vicarage, 91 Walton Road, Stockton Heath, Warrington WA4 6NR* Tel (01925) 261396

RIDLEY, Peter John. b 39. Keble Coll Ox BA61. Tyndale Hall Bris 61. **d** 63 **p** 64. C Clifton Ch Ch w Em *Bris* 63-67; C Lambeth St Andr w St Thos *S'wark* 67-69; V W Hampstead St Cuth *Lon* 69-77; V Eynsham *Ox* 77-85; RD Woodstock 82-84; V Nicholforest and Kirkandrews on Esk *Carl* 85-96; P-in-c E Knoyle, Semley and Sedgehill *Sarum* 96-04; rtd 04. *The Castle, Castle Street, Hilton, Appleby-in-Westmorland CA16 6LX* Tel (017683) 51682

RIDLEY, Simon. b 33. Magd Coll Ox BA54 MA58 BD66. Linc Th Coll 54. **d** 57 **p** 58. C St John's Wood *Lon* 57-60; Abp's Dom Chapl *Cant* 60-61; V N Wootton *B & W* 61-66; Lect Wells Th Coll 61-65; Hong Kong 66-70; TR Basingstoke *Win* 70-73; rtd 96; Perm to Offic *Cant* from 96. *Oxney House, The Street, Wittersham, Tenterden TN30 7ED* Tel (01797) 270215

RIDLEY, Stephen James. b 57. St Pet Coll Ox MA83. Ripon Coll Cuddesdon 80. **d** 82 **p** 83. C Heald Green St Cath *Ches* 82-85; Chapl Ches Coll 85-90; Dioc Press Officer 85-90; Chapl Birkenhead Sch Merseyside 90-96; Lic to Offic *Ches* 90-96; Chapl Barnard Castle Sch from 96. *3 Old Courts, Barnard Castle School, Newgate, Barnard Castle DL12 8UN* Tel (01833) 690222

RIDLEY, Stewart Gordon. b 47. K Coll Lon AKC72. St Aug Coll Cant 72. **d** 73 **p** 74. C Armley w New Wortley *Ripon* 73-77; C Hawksworth Wood 77-79; C Rothwell w Lofthouse 79-81; R Whitwood *Wakef* 81-87; R Ingoldmells w Addlethorpe *Linc* 87-92; RD Calcewaithe and Candleshoe 89-92; V Settle *Bradf* 92-05; P-in-c Waddington from 05; P-in-c Hurst Green and Mitton from 05; Dioc Chapl MU from 93. *The Vicarage, Slaidburn Road, Waddington, Clitheroe BB7 3JQ* Tel (01200) 423589

RIDLEY, Vic. *See* RIDLEY, David Gerhard

RIDOUT, Canon Christopher John. b 33. K Coll Lon BD57 AKC57 MA92. **d** 58 **p** 59. C Roxeth Ch Ch *Lon* 58-62; CMS 62-63; Kenya 63-75; C Gt Malvern St Mary *Worc* 75-79; R Bredon w Bredon's Norton 79-98; RD Pershore 91-97; Hon Can Worc Cathl 92-98; rtd 98; Perm to Offic *Glouc* from 98. *5 Belworth Drive, Hatherley, Cheltenham GL51 6EL* Tel (01242) 231765

RIDYARD, Preb John Gordon. b 33. St Aid Birkenhead 59. **d** 62 **p** 63. C Lancaster St Mary *Blackb* 62-65; C Bushbury *Lich* 65-68; V Darlaston All SS 68-76; TV Wolverhampton St Mark 76-78; TV Wolverhampton 78-82; V Bishopswood 82-89; V Brewood 82-89; RD Penkridge 83-89; R Newcastle w Butterton 89-98; Preb Lich Cathl 82-03; rtd 98; V in The Close and Perm to Offic *Lich* from 98. *Upper Flat, Vicars' Hall, Beacon Street, Lichfield WS13 7AD* Tel (01543) 306297

RIDYARD, Malcolm Charles. b 32. St D Coll Lamp BA54 Wycliffe Hall Ox 54. **d** 56 **p** 57. C Widnes St Paul *Liv* 56-59; C Ashton-in-Makerfield St Thos 59-61; India 62-71; Area Sec CMS *B & W*, *Bris* and *Sarum* 71-80; P-in-c Church Coniston *Carl* 80-87; P-in-c Torver 80-87; R Bootle, Corney, Whicham and Whitbeck 87-97; rtd 98; Perm to Offic *Birm* from 98. *140 Quinton Road West, Quinton, Birmingham B32 2RH* Tel 0121-422 3895

RIEM, Canon Roland Gerardus Anthony. b 60. St Chad's Coll Dur BSc82 Kent Univ PhD86 Heythrop Coll Lon MA99. St Jo Coll Nottm 86. **d** 89 **p** 90. C Deal St Leon and St Rich and Sholden *Cant* 89-92; Sen Chapl Nottm Univ *S'well* 92-98; Minl Development Officer STETS 98-06; Can Res Win Cathl *Win* from 05. *5A The Close, Winchester SO23 9LS* Tel (01962) 857216 Fax 857201 E-mail roland.riem@winchester-cathedral.org.uk

RIESS, Trevor William. b 54. Down Coll Cam MA76 CertEd77. St Jo Coll Nottm 84. **d** 86 **p** 87. C Stainforth *Sheff* 86-88; Chapl St Jas Choir Sch Grimsby 89; C Lowestoft and Kirkley *Nor* 89-90; TV 90-94; TV Lowestoft St Marg 94-95; Chapl Lothingland Hosp 90-95; V Gorleston St Mary *Nor* 95-05; P-in-c Scole, Brockdish, Billingford, Thorpe Abbots etc from 05. *The Rectory, Norwich Road, Scole, Diss IP21 4DY* Tel (01379) 740250

RIGBY, Francis Michael. b 29. Glouc Sch of Min. **d** 90 **p** 91. NSM Alvescot w Black Bourton, Shilton, Holwell etc *Ox* 90-92; P-in-c Gt w Lt Tew 92-95; P-in-c Bishop's Frome w Castle Frome and Fromes Hill *Heref* 96-99; P-in-c Acton Beauchamp and Evesbatch 96-99; Perm to Offic from 00. *Barn Acre, Bishop's Frome, Worcester WR6 5AV* Tel (01885) 490204

RIGBY, Harold. b 34. Nottm Univ BA56 St Cath Soc Ox BA58 MA62 Man Poly PGCE77. Ripon Hall Ox 56. **d** 58 **p** 59. C Didsbury St Jas and Em *Man* 58-61; C Bury St Jo 61-64; P-in-c Lostock St Thos and St Jo 64-76; Hon C Davyhulme St Mary 76-79; Lic Preacher from 79; Perm to Offic *Ches* from 79; rtd 99. *17 Atwood Road, Didsbury, Manchester M20 0TA* Tel 0161-445 7454

RIGBY, Joseph. b 37. Open Univ BA72. Ox NSM Course. **d** 78 **p** 79. NSM Earley St Pet *Ox* 78-80; C Penzance St Mary w St Paul *Truro* 80-82; V Mevagissey 82-83; P-in-c St Ewe 83; R Mevagissey and St Ewe 83-90; rtd 90; Perm to Offic *Truro* from 90. *5 The Close, Upland Crescent, Truro TR1 1LY* Tel (01872) 240440

RIGBY, Michael. *See* RIGBY, Francis Michael

RIGBY, Michael John. b 52. MA MSc. Ridley Hall Cam. **d** 82 **p** 83. C Reading St Jo *Ox* 82-86; C Wallington H Trin *S'wark* 86-92; Pastor Foundns Chr Fellowship Trust Ch from 92. *14 Dinorben Court, Woodcote Road, Wallington SM6 0PZ* Tel (020) 8647 8649

RIGBY, William. b 51. Leic Univ BSc(Econ)72 Newc Poly BSc82. Cranmer Hall Dur 86. **d** 88 **p** 89. C Morpeth *Newc* 88-92; R St John Lee 92-00; Chapl to the Deaf from 92; P-in-c Chapel House from 00. *The Vicarage, 44 Queensbury Drive, North*

Walbottle, Newcastle upon Tyne NE15 9XF Tel 0191-267 4069 Fax 229 0232 E-mail bill.rigby1@btopenworld.com

RIGELSFORD, Mrs Anne Catharina (Ank). b 44. EAMTC 99. **d** 02 **p** 03. NSM Cambridge H Cross *Ely* from 02. *19 Clare Street, Cambridge CB4 3BY* Tel (01223) 368150 Mobile 07932-846395 E-mail ank@rigelsford.freeserve.co.uk

RIGGS, Sidney James. b 39. Bps' Coll Cheshunt 62. **d** 63 **p** 64. C S'wark St Geo *S'wark* 63-66; C Plymouth Crownhill Ascension *Ex* 66-69; Asst Youth Chapl *Glouc* 69-71; Hon Min Can Glouc Cathl 71-74; Min Can Glouc Cathl 74-76; V Glouc St Mary de Lode and St Nic 76-92; R Rodborough 92-04; RD Stonehouse 94-96; rtd 04; Perm to Offic *Glouc* from 05. *6 Severn Road, Stonehouse GL10 2DL* Tel (01453) 824682

RIGNEY, James Thomas Walpole. b 59. Sydney Univ BA82 MA88 Pemb Coll Ox DPhil95 CCC Cam BA00 MA04. Westcott Ho Cam 98. **d** 01 **p** 02. C Cambridge St Jas *Ely* 01-04; Chapl and Fell Magd Coll Cam from 05. *Magdalene College, Cambridge CB3 0AG* Tel (01223) 332129 E-mail jtr22@cam.ac.uk

RILEY, David Leo. b 51. S Bank Univ MSc95. Dioc OLM tr scheme 97. **d** 00 **p** 01. NSM Bellingham St Dunstan *S'wark* from 00. *117 Whitefoot Lane, Bromley BR1 5SB* Tel (020) 8516 4544 E-mail driley3020@aol.com

RILEY, John Graeme. b 55. St Jo Coll Dur BA78. Trin Coll Bris 79. **d** 81 **p** 82. C Hensingham *Carl* 81-84; C Preston St Cuth *Blackb* 84-87; V Blackb Ch Ch w St Matt 87-98; Chapl Qu Park Hosp Blackb 87-94; V Shevington *Blackb* 98-04; V Euxton from 04. *The Vicarage, Wigan Road, Euxton, Chorley PR7 6JH* Tel (01257) 262102

RILEY, Preb John Martin. b 37. St D Coll Lamp BA62 DipTh63. **d** 63 **p** 64. C Conwy w Gyffin *Ban* 63-68; P-in-c Llanfachraeth 68-70; TV Dolgellau, Llanfachreth, Brithdir etc 70-72; V Beddgelert 72-78; Dioc Youth Chapl 72-78; V Tywyn 78-82; V Tywyn w Aberdyfi 82-95; V Llanegryn w Aberdyfi w Tywyn 95-03; RD Ystumaner 87-01; AD 01-03; Can Ban Cathl 90-97; Preb from 97; rtd 03; Perm to Offic *Ban* from 03. *Llwyncelyn, Corris, Machynlleth SY20 9SP* Tel (01654) 761769 E-mail jrile001@fish.co.uk

RILEY, The Very Revd Kenneth Joseph. b 40. OBE03. Univ of Wales BA61 Linacre Ho Ox BA64 MA68. Wycliffe Hall Ox 61. **d** 64 **p** 65. C Fazakerley Em *Liv* 64-66; Chapl Brasted Place Coll Westerham 66-69; Chapl Oundle Sch 69-74; Chapl Liv Cathl *Liv* 74-75; Chapl Liv Univ 74-93; V Mossley Hill St Matt and St Jas 75-83; RD Childwall 82-83; Can Res Liv Cathl 83-93; Treas 83-87; Prec 87-93; Dean Man 93-05; rtd 05. *145 Turning Lane, Southport PR8 5HZ*

RILEY, Mrs Lesley Anne. b 54. Totley Thornbridge Coll TCert75. Trin Coll Bris DipHE81. **dss** 81 **d** 87 **p** 98. Hensingham *Carl* 81-84; Preston St Cuth *Blackb* 84-87; Hon Par Dn Blackb Ch Ch w St Matt 87-98; Asst Dir of Ords 96-00; Dir of Ords from 00; Hon C Shevington 98-04. *The Vicarage, Wigan Road, Euxton, Chorley PR7 6JH* Tel (01257) 262102

RILEY, Ms Linda. b 67. St Jo Coll Nottm BA00. **d** 00 **p** 01. C Ince Ch Ch *Liv* from 00. *70 Belle Green Lane, Ince, Wigan WN2 2EP* Tel (01942) 495831 Mobile 07944-377732

RILEY, Martin. *See* RILEY, Preb John Martin

RILEY, Martin Shaw. b 47. Selw Coll Cam BA71 Cam Univ CertEd72 MA75. Sarum & Wells Th Coll 85. **d** 87 **p** 88. C Tuffley *Glouc* 87-91; Hon Min Can Glouc Cathl from 88; P-in-c Barnwood 91-94; V 94-99; P-in-c Highnam, Lassington, Rudford, Tibberton etc 99-04; R from 04. *The Rectory, Maidenhall, Highnam, Gloucester GL2 8DL* Tel (01452) 525567 E-mail rileys25@tesco.net

RILEY, Michael Charles. b 57. Ball Coll Ox BA79 MA83 Ex Univ CertEd80. Edin Th Coll 84. **d** 86 **p** 87. C Newc St Geo *Newc* 86-89; C Chiswick St Nic w St Mary *Lon* 89-90; V Chiswick St Paul Grove Park from 90. *St Paul's Vicarage, 64 Grove Park Road, London W4 3SB* Tel (020) 8987 0312 E-mail michaelc.riley@virgin.com

RILEY, Preb Patrick John. b 39. Leeds Univ BA62. Coll of Resurr Mirfield 62. **d** 64 **p** 65. C Rowbarton *B & W* 64-72; P-in-c Farleigh Hungerford w Tellisford 72-73; P-in-c Rode, Rode Hill and Woolverton 72-73; R Rode Major 73-85; RD Frome 78-85; V Glastonbury w Meare and W Pennard 85-01; Preb Wells Cathl 90-01; rtd 01; Perm to Offic *Sarum* from 02. *24 Tanyard Lane, Shaftesbury SP7 8HW* Tel (01747) 850361

RILEY, Peter Arthur. b 23. Kelham Th Coll 40. **d** 51 **p** 52. C Aston cum Aughton *Sheff* 51-53; C Doncaster Ch Ch 53-55; Trinidad and Tobago 55-59; C-in-c Leic St Chad CD *Leic* 59-62; Jamaica 62-77; V Abertillery *Mon* 77-83; R Panteg 83-88; rtd 88; Hon C Dartmouth *Ex* 88-99; Lic to Offic *Mon* from 99. *The Bungalow, Clewer Court, Newport NP20 4LQ* Tel (01633) 766870

RILEY, Canon William. b 24. St Aid Birkenhead 48. **d** 51 **p** 52. C Edgehill St Dunstan *Liv* 51-53; C Halsall 53-57; V Prestolee *Man* 57-62; P-in-c Ringley 60-62; R Tarleton *Blackb* 62-92; RD Leyland 84-89; Hon Can Blackb Cathl 90-92; rtd 92; Perm to Offic *Blackb* from 92. *114 Liverpool Road, Hutton, Preston PR4 5SL* Tel (01772) 614267

RILEY-BRALEY, Robert James. b 57. Ch Ch Ox BA82 Ch Ch Ox MA82 Down Coll Cam BA83 MA87 K Coll Lon MA98 Surrey Univ PGCE92. Ridley Hall Cam 81. **d** 84 **p** 85. C Thames Ditton *Guildf* 84-87; C Gravesend St Geo *Roch* 87-91; Perm to Offic *Lon* 91-92; *Blackb* 92-95; *S'wark* 95-02; C Stevenage St Mary Shephall w Aston *St Alb* from 02. *31 Harefield, Stevenage SG2 9NG* Tel (01438) 749695 E-mail ril.bral@virgin.net

RIMELL, Gilbert William. b 22. Llan Dioc Tr Scheme 76. **d** 81 **p** 82. NSM Laleston w Tythegston and Merthyr Mawr *Llan* 81-94; rtd 94; Perm to Offic *Llan* from 94. *75 Bryntirion Hill, Bridgend CF31 4BY* Tel (01656) 658002

RIMMER, Andrew Malcolm. b 62. Magd Coll Cam BA84 MA88. Wycliffe Hall Ox 86. **d** 88 **p** 89. C Romford Gd Shep Collier Row *Chelmsf* 88-92; C Hazlemere *Ox* 92-97; V Crookhorn *Portsm* from 97. *The Vicarage, 87 Perseus Place, Waterlooville PO7 8AW* Tel (023) 9226 7647 *or* tel and fax 9225 5527 E-mail a.rimmer@tesco.net

RIMMER, Anthony Robert Walters. b 41. Hull Univ BA63. Coll of Resurr Mirfield 64. **d** 66 **p** 67. C Leeds All SS *Ripon* 66-69; C Kippax 69-72; C Preston St Jo *Blackb* 72-76; TV 76-83; P-in-c Glasson Ch Ch 83-86; Chapl Lanc R Infirmary 83-86; Chapl Dunkirk Miss to Seafarers *Eur* 86-01; rtd 01; Perm to Offic *Blackb* from 02. *The Haws, 1 Wartonwood View, Carnforth LA5 9DE* Tel (01524) 733974 Mobile 07967-004850

RIMMER, Clive. *See* RIMMER, John Clive

RIMMER, Canon David Henry. b 36. Ex Coll Ox BA60 MA65. Linc Th Coll 62. **d** 64 **p** 65. C Liv Our Lady and St Nic *Liv* 64-66; C Daybrook *S'well* 66-69; Chapl St Mary's Cathl *Edin* 69-71; R Kirkcaldy *St And* 71-78; R Haddington *Edin* 78-83; R Dunbar 79-83; R Edin Gd Shep 83-01; Hon Can St Mary's Cathl 98-01; rtd 01. *4/15 Orchard Brae Avenue, Edinburgh EH4 2HW* Tel 0131-539 0283

RIMMER, Janet. *See* SPICER, Dorothy Janet Rosalind

RIMMER, John Clive. b 25. Oak Hill Th Coll 63. **d** 65 **p** 66. C Earlestown *Liv* 65-69; C-in-c Dallam CD 69-74; V Southport SS Simon and Jude 74-83; V Westhead 83-90; Chapl Ormskirk Hosp Liv 84-90; rtd 90; Perm to Offic *Liv* from 90. *14 Hurlston Drive, Ormskirk L39 1LD* Tel (01695) 570838

RIMMER, Mrs Margaret. b 55. St Jo Coll Dur BA05 SRN77 SCM78. Cranmer Hall Dur 00. **d** 02 **p** 03. C Aysgarth and Bolton cum Redmire *Ripon* from 02. *Swan Bungalow, Redmire, Leyburn DL8 4HA* Tel (01969) 625031 Mobile 07815-297758 E-mail margaret.rimmer1@tesco.net

RIMMER, Paul Nathanael. b 25. Jes Coll Ox BA48 MA50. Wycliffe Hall Ox 48. **d** 50 **p** 51. C Douglas St Thos *S & M* 50-52; C Windermere St Martin *Carl* 52-55; India 55-59; V Marston *Ox* 59-90; RD Cowley 69-73; rtd 90. *32 Ulfgar Road, Wolvercote, Oxford OX2 8AZ* Tel (01865) 352567

RIMMER, Peter Anthony. b 39. St As Minl Tr Course 90. **d** 96 **p** 97. NSM Abergele *St As* 96-00; C Bodelwyddan from 00. *17 Lon-y-Mes, Abergele LL22 7JG* Tel (01745) 833222

RIMMER, Roy Malcolm. b 31. Fitzw Ho Cam BA58 MA62. Tyndale Hall Bris 54. **d** 59 **p** 60. C Ox St Clem *Ox* 59-62; The Navigators 62-70; Oslo St Edm *Eur* 62-64; Public Preacher *S'wark* 64-66; Perm to Offic *Ox* 66-70; C Portman Square St Paul *Lon* 70-75; R Rougham *St E* 75-87; P-in-c Rushbrooke 78-87; P-in-c Beyton and Hessett 86-87; V Newmarket All SS 87-93; rtd 93; Perm to Offic *Ely* from 93 and *St E* from 98. *Ramsey House, 3 Oakfield Place, Old Station Road, Newmarket CB8 8GA* Tel (01638) 660852

RIMMINGTON, Gerald Thorneycroft. b 30. Lon Univ BSc56 PhD64 Leic Univ MA59 Nottm Univ MEd72 PhD75 FCP66. **d** 76 **p** 78. Canada 76-79; Lic to Offic *Leic* 79-80; R Paston *Pet* 81-86; V Cosby *Leic* 86-90; Dir CME 87-90; R Barwell w Potters Marston and Stapleton 90-95; rtd 95; Perm to Offic *Leic* from 95; RD Guthlaxton I 03-04. *7 Beechings Close, Countesthorpe, Leicester LE8 5PA* Tel 0116-277 7155

RINDL, Antony William. b 64. Doncaster Coll of Educn HND88. St Jo Coll Nottm 97. **d** 99 **p** 00. C Syston *Leic* 99-03; TV Colne and Villages *Blackb* from 03; AD Pendle from 05. *The Vicarage, Skipton Road, Foulridge, Colne BB8 7NP* Tel (01282) 870959 E-mail rindl-@fish.co.uk

RINGER, Philip James. b 47. Ox Min Course 88. **d** 91 **p** 92. NSM Chalfont St Peter *Ox* 91-95; TV Combe Martin, Berrynarbor, Lynton, Brendon etc *Ex* 96-03; R Wriggle Valley *Sarum* from 03. *The Rectory, Church Street, Yetminster, Sherborne DT9 6LG* Tel (01935) 872237 E-mail revphil@supanet.com

RINGLAND, Tom Laurence. b 61. SS Hild & Bede Coll Dur BSc83. Trin Coll Bris BA89. **d** 89 **p** 90. C Southgate *Chich* 89-92; C Polegate 92-96; P-in-c Coalville and Bardon Hill *Leic* 96-98; V from 98. *Christ Church Vicarage, London Road, Coalville LE67 3JA* Tel (01530) 838287 E-mail tringland@aol.com

RINGROSE, Brian Sefton. b 31. Clare Coll Cam BA54 MA58 Lon Univ PGCE55. Tyndale Hall Bris 56. **d** 58 **p** 59. C Ox St Ebbe *Ox* 58-60; C Erith St Paul *Roch* 60-61; India 61-75; P-in-c Ox St Matt *Ox* 75-78; Interserve (Scotland) 78-96; Perm to Offic *Glas* 78-96; rtd 96. *1 Napier Road, Edinburgh EH10 5BE* Tel 0131-447 2012 E-mail brianringrose@aol.com

RINGROSE, The Ven Hedley Sidney. b 42. Open Univ BA79. Sarum Th Coll 65. **d** 68 **p** 69. C Bishopston *Bris* 68-71; C Easthampstead *Ox* 71-75; V Glouc St Geo w Whaddon *Glouc* 75-88; RD Glouc City 83-88; Hon Can Glouc Cathl 86-98; V Cirencester 88-98; RD Cirencester 89-97; Adn Cheltenham from 98; Hon Can Glouc Cathl from 98. *The Sanderlings, Thorncliffe Drive, Cheltenham GL51 6PY* Tel (01242) 522923 Fax 235925 E-mail archdchelt@star.co.uk

RINTAMÄKI, Juha Matti Sakari. b 69. **d** 02. Chapl Finnish Ch in Lon from 03; Lic to Offic *S'wark* from 04. *The Finnish Church in London, 33 Albion Street, London SE16 7HZ* Tel (020) 7237 1261 Fax 7237 1245 Mobile 07768-870614 E-mail juha.rintamaki@finnishchurch.org.uk

RIO GRANDE, Bishop of. *See* KELSHAW, The Rt Revd Terence

RIOCH, Mrs Wenda Jean. b 35. Sarum & Wells Th Coll 84. **d** 87 **p** 94. Par Dn Basingstoke *Win* 87-91; Par Dn Catshill and Dodford *Worc* 91-94; C 94-98; TV Ottery St Mary, Alfington, W Hill, Tipton etc *Ex* 98-05; rtd 05. *76 Gardeners Green, Shipton Bellinger, Tidworth SP9 7TA* Tel (01980) 842334 E-mail wrioch@aol.com

RIORDAN, Sean Charles. b 67. Loughb Univ BA89. St Jo Coll Nottm MA98. **d** 99 **p** 00. C Ockbrook *Derby* 99-03; Asst Chapl Tervuren *Eur* from 03. *Zikkelstraat 13, 1970 Wezembeek-Oppem, Belgium* Tel (0032) (2) 767 3025 *or* 688 0988 E-mail sean.riordan@stpaulstervuren.org

RIPLEY, Preb Geoffrey Alan. b 39. Dur Univ BA62. St Aid Birkenhead. **d** 64 **p** 65. C E Herrington *Dur* 64-67; Hon C Hodge Hill CD *Birm* 68-70; Youth Chapl *Liv* 70-75; Chapl Liv Cathl 70-78; Bp's Dom Chapl 75-78; V Wavertree St Bridget 78-87; Lay Tr Adv *B & W* 87-95; Dioc Chapl MU 92-01; R S Petherton w the Seavingtons 95-01; Chapl E Somerset NHS Trust 95-01; Preb Wells Cathl *B & W* 97-01; rtd 02; Perm to Offic *B & W* from 02. *20 Overleigh, Street BA16 0TL* Tel (01458) 446766

RIPON AND LEEDS, Bishop of. *See* PACKER, The Rt Revd John Richard

RIPON, Dean of. *See* METHUEN, The Very Revd John Alan Robert

RIPPINGALE, Denis Michael. b 29. Leeds Univ BA52. Coll of Resurr Mirfield 52. **d** 54 **p** 55. C S Kirkby *Wakef* 54-58; C King Cross 58-60; C Derby St Thos *Derby* 60-63; V Altofts *Wakef* 63-71; V S Elmsall 71-84; V Marsden 84-92; rtd 92. *61 Viking Road, Bridlington YO16 7PW* Tel (01262) 601838

RISBY, John. b 40. Lon Univ. Lambeth STh82 Oak Hill Th Coll 64. **d** 67 **p** 68. C Fulham Ch Ch *Lon* 67-68; C Ealing St Mary 68-70; C Chitts Hill St Cuth 70-73; C Hove Bp Hannington Memorial Ch *Chich* 73-76; V Islington St Jude Mildmay Park *Lon* 76-82; P-in-c Islington St Paul Ball's Pond 78-82; V Mildmay Grove St Jude and St Paul 82-84; R Hunsdon w Widford and Wareside *St Alb* from 84; RD Hertford 91-96. *The Rectory, Acorn Street, Hunsdon, Ware SG12 8PB* Tel (01920) 870171 E-mail jrisby@tiscali.co.uk

RISDON, John Alexander. b 42. Lon Univ DipTh66. Clifton Th Coll 66. **d** 68 **p** 69. C Ealing Dean St Jo *Lon* 68-72; C Heref St Pet w St Owen *Heref* 72-74; Ord Cand Sec CPAS 74-77; Hon C Bromley Ch Ch *Roch* 74-77; TV Cheltenham St Mary, St Matt, St Paul and H Trin *Glouc* 77-86; R Stapleton *Bris* 86-00; R Bedhampton *Portsm* from 00. *The Rectory, Bidbury Lane, Bedhampton, Havant PO9 3JG* Tel (023) 9248 3013 Fax as telephone E-mail pam@bedhamptonrectory.freeserve.co.uk

RISHTON, Mrs Tracy Jane. b 67. St Jo Coll Nottm 01. **d** 04 **p** 05. C Earby *Bradf* from 04; C Kelbrook from 04. *St Mary's Vicarage, Vicarage Road, Kelbrook, Barnoldswick BB18 6TQ* Tel (01282) 841607 E-mail tracy@rishton.info

RISING, Sidney Frederick. b 28. EMMTC 73. **d** 76 **p** 77. NSM W Bridgford *S'well* 76-79; C 79-82; V Whatton w Aslockton, Hawksworth, Scarrington etc 82-87; Chapl HM Det Cen Whatton 82-87; Chapl Notts Police 87-93; Rural Officer *S'well* 87-89; P-in-c Perlethorpe 88-90; P-in-c Norton Cuckney 89-90; P-in-c Staunton w Flawborough 90-93; P-in-c Kilvington 90-93; rtd 93. *5 St Leonard's Cottages, London Road, Newark NG24 1TQ* Tel (01636) 610318

RITCHIE, Angus William Mark. b 74. Magd Coll Ox BA94 BPhil96 MA98. Westcott Ho Cam 96. **d** 98 **p** 99. C Plaistow and N Canning Town *Chelmsf* 98-02; TV 02-04; Dir Contextual Th Cen R Foundn of St Kath in Ratcliffe from 05; Hon C Gt Ilford St Luke from 05; Fells' Chapl Magd Coll Ox from 05. *The Royal Foundation of St Katharine, 2 Butcher Row, London E14 8DS* Tel (020) 7790 3540 Fax 7702 7603 E-mail director@theology-centre.org

RITCHIE, Brian Albert. b 34. Open Univ BA80 Birm Univ MA84. Qu Coll Birm 60. **d** 63 **p** 64. C S Leamington St Jo *Cov* 63-67; C-in-c Canley CD 67-70; Perm to Offic 71-80; Hon C Cov H Trin 82-88; R Hatton w Haseley, Rowington w Lowsonford etc 88-97; rtd 97; Perm to Offic *Cov* from 98. *10 Margetts Close, Kenilworth CV8 1EN*

RITCHIE, David John Rose. b 48. St Jo Coll Dur BA72 DipTh74. **d** 74 **p** 75. C Harold Wood *Chelmsf* 74-79; TV Ipsley *Worc* 79-84; Chapl Vevey w Château d'Oex and Villars *Eur* 84-93; V Stoke Bishop *Bris* from 93. *The Vicarage, Mariner's Drive, Bristol BS9 1QJ* Tel 0117-968 1858 *or* 968 7449 E-mail churchmanager@stmarymagdalenestokebishop.org.uk

RITCHIE, David Philip. b 60. Hatf Coll Dur BA85. Wycliffe Hall Ox 85. **d** 87 **p** 88. C Chadwell *Chelmsf* 87-90; C Waltham H Cross 90-94; TV Becontree W 94-98; TR 98-01; Lay Tr Officer from 01; C Lt Waltham 02-05; C Gt and Lt Leighs and Lt Waltham from 05. *Glebelands, Boreham Road, Great Leighs, Chelmsford CM3 1PP* Tel (01245) 362644 E-mail pritchie@chelmsford.anglican.org

RITCHIE, Miss Jean. b 30. Lon Univ CertEd51 Dip Ch Development 71. Trin Coll Bris DipTh79. **dss** 79 **d** 87 **p** 94. Ox St Ebbe w H Trin and St Pet *Ox* 79-87; Par Dn 87-91; rtd 91; Perm to Offic *B & W* 91-94 and from 96; NSM Clevedon St Andr and Ch Ch 94-96. *63 Holland Road, Clevedon BS21 7YJ* Tel (01275) 871762

RITCHIE, Philip. *See* RITCHIE, David Philip

RITCHIE, Philip Simon James. b 68. Man Univ BA90 Sussex Univ MA98 Leeds Univ MA01 Man Metrop Univ PGCE92. Coll of Resurr Mirfield 99. **d** 01 **p** 02. C Brighton St Nic *Chich* 01-04; P-in-c Chich St Wilfrid from 04. *St Wilfrid's House, 7 Durnford Close, Chichester PO19 3AG* Tel (01243) 783853 E-mail phil@sonrit.fsnet.co.uk

RITCHIE, Robert Peter. b 57. St Pet Coll Ox BA81 St Jo Coll Cam MPhil83. SEITE 97. **d** 00 **p** 01. NSM Kingston All SS w St Jo *S'wark* from 00. *7 Gibbon Road, Kingston-upon-Thames KT2 6AD* E-mail robert@rsritchie.freeserve.co.uk

RITCHIE, Canon Samuel. b 31. Lon Coll of Div 65. **d** 67 **p** 68. C Westlands St Andr *Lich* 67-70; V Springfield H Trin *Chelmsf* 70-82; Chapl HM Pris Chelmsf 70-82; Chapl HM Pris Brixton 82-84; Chapl HM Pris Hull 84-86; Sen Chapl HM Prison Wymott 86-95; NW Area Chapl Co-ord 86-95; rtd 95; P-in-c Helmingham w Framsden and Pettaugh w Winston *St E* 96-97; Perm to Offic from 03. *Hillcrest, 3 Highfield Drive, Claydon, Ipswich IP6 0EY* Tel (01473) 833798

RITCHIE, William James. b 62. TCD MA84 DipTh86. **d** 86 **p** 87. C Enniscorthy *C & O* 86-89; Asst Chapl Alexandria Egypt 89-91; Bp's C Kells Gp *C & O* 91-92; I Kells Union *M & K* 92-99; Warden of Readers 93-97; Dioc Ecum Officer 97-99; Min Can St Patr Cathl Dublin 97-99; I Clondehorkey w Cashel *D & R* 99-00; I Dublin St Bart w Leeson Park *D & G* 00-04; I Tullow w Shillelagh, Aghold and Mullinacuff *C & O* from 04. *The Rectory, Barrack Street, Tullow, Co Carlow, Irish Republic* Tel and fax (00353) (59) 915 1481 E-mail tullow@leighlin.anglican.org

RITSON, Canon Gerald Richard Stanley (Bill). b 35. CCC Cam BA59 MA63. Linc Th Coll 59. **d** 61 **p** 62. C Harpenden St Jo *St Alb* 61-65; C Goldington 65-69; R Clifton 69-76; Sec to Dioc Past Cttee 76-87; P-in-c Aldenham 76-87; Hon Can St Alb 80-87; Can Res St Alb 87-00; rtd 00; Perm to Offic *S'wark* from 00. *97 Mitre Road, London SE1 8PT* Tel (020) 7633 0012

RIVERS, Arthur. b 20. Oak Hill Th Coll 52. **d** 53 **p** 54. C Wigan St Cath *Liv* 53-56; V Parr Mt 56-60; V Burscough Bridge 60-79; V Holmesfield *Derby* 79-86; rtd 86; Hon C Warton St Oswald w Yealand Conyers *Blackb* 86-88; Perm to Offic *Blackb* from 88 and *Carl* 88-04. *125A Thelwall New Road, Thelwall, Warrington WA4 2HR* Tel (01925) 600442

RIVERS, David John. b 51. St Jo Coll Nottm. **d** 84 **p** 85. C Woodthorpe *S'well* 84-88; C Hyson Green St Paul w St Steph 88; Asst Chapl Colchester Gen Hosp 89-91; Chapl Leeds Teaching Hosps NHS Trust 91-05; rtd 05; Perm to Offic *Ripon* from 05. *28 Palace Road, Ripon HG4 1ET* Tel (01765) 606227 Mobile 07810-430245 E-mail woollrivers@msn.com

RIVERS, John Arthur. b 21. EAMTC 79. **d** 81 **p** 82. NSM Blakeney w Cley, Wiveton, Glandford etc *Nor* 81-86; Hon C Cromer 86-87; Perm to Offic from 87. *28 Compit Hills, Cromer NR27 9LJ* Tel (01263) 513051

RIVETT, Andrew George. b 52. Lon Univ MB, BS76 LRCP76 MRCS76. Oak Hill Th Coll 85. **d** 87 **p** 88. C Stanford-le-Hope w Mucking *Chelmsf* 87-90; C Slough *Ox* 90-93; TV Totton *Win* 93-99. *NHS Library, South Academic Block, Southampton General Hospital, Tremonar Road, Southampton SO16 6YD* Tel (023) 8077 7222

RIVETT, Leonard Stanley. b 23. MSSCLE82 St Jo Coll Dur BA47 DipTh49 York Univ Cert Local Hist 88. **d** 49 **p** 50. C Chorlton-cum-Hardy St Clem *Man* 49-53; C-in-c Wythenshawe Wm Temple Ch CD 53-57; Area Chapl Toc H (E and W Yorkshire) 57-62; V Norton juxta Malton *York* 62-74; Warden Wydale Hall 74-83; R Elvington w Sutton on Derwent and E Cottingwith 83-88; rtd 88; Perm to Offic *York* from 88; Offg Chapl RAF from 90. *47 Ryecroft Avenue, York YO24 2SD* Tel (01904) 705364

RIVETT, Peter John. b 42. St Jo Coll Dur BA71 DipTh72. Cranmer Hall Dur. **d** 72 **p** 73. C Newland St Jo *York* 72-76; TV Marfleet 76-82; V Oxhey All SS *St Alb* 82-93; TR Swanborough *Sarum* 93-98; TV Pewsey and Swanborough 98-01; USPG from 01. *USPG, Partnership House, 157 Waterloo Road, London SE1 8XA* Tel (020) 7928 8681

RIVIERE, Jonathan Byam Valentine. b 54. Cuddesdon Coll. **d** 83 **p** 84. C Wymondham *Nor* 83-88; TV Quidenham 88-94; P-in-c Somerleyton w Ashby, Fritton and Herringfleet 94; R Somerleyton, Ashby, Fritton, Herringfleet etc 95-03; R Sandringham w W Newton and Appleton etc from 03; P-in-c Castle Rising from 03; P-in-c Hillington from 03; Dom Chapl to The Queen from 03. *The Rectory, Sandringham PE35 6EH* Tel (01485) 540587 E-mail jonathan-riviere@lineone.net

RIVIERE, Mrs Tanagra June (Tana). b 41. S Dios Minl Tr Scheme 88. **d** 91. NSM Medstead w Wield *Win* 91-94; NSM Bishop's Sutton and Ropley and W Tisted 94-96. *The Drey, Paice Lane, Medstead, Alton GU34 5PT* Tel (01420) 563330 Fax as telephone

RIX, Patrick George. b 30. Magd Coll Ox BA54 DipEd55 MA57. Ridley Hall Cam 58. **d** 60 **p** 61. C Dur St Nic *Dur* 60-62; Asst Chapl Wrekin Coll Telford 62-70; Asst Chapl Gresham's Sch Holt 70-80; Chapl Bloxham Sch 80-86; rtd 86; P-in-c Swanton Abbott w Skeyton *Nor* 89; Perm to Offic from 89. *5 Rye Close, North Walsham NR28 9EY* Tel (01692) 402649

ROACH, Kenneth Thomas. b 43. St Andr Univ BD69 Fitzw Coll Cam BA71 MA76. Westcott Ho Cam 69. **d** 71 **p** 72. C Glas St Marg *Glas* 71-73; CF 73-76; R Johnstone *Glas* 76-85; R Bearsden 85-96; TR from 96; CF (TA) from 86. *34 Roman Road, Bearsden, Glasgow G61 2SQ* Tel 0141-942 0386

ROACH, Lynne Elisabeth. *See* DAVIES, Mrs Lynne Elisabeth

ROACHE, Anthony. b 60. Nazarene Th Coll Man BA78. **d** 99 **p** 00. C Bury St Mary *Man* 99-02; P-in-c Ringley w Prestolee from 02; Voc Adv from 04; CF(V) from 03. *The Vicarage, 9 Stoneleigh Drive, Radcliffe, Manchester M26 1FZ* Tel (01204) 573742 E-mail roachefamily@ntlworld.com

ROAKE, Anthony Richard Garrard. b 52. Keble Coll Ox BA75 MA80. Wycliffe Hall Ox 75. **d** 77 **p** 78. C Clifton *S'well* 77-80; V Lapley w Wheaton Aston *Lich* 80-86; V Bournemouth St Andr *Win* 86-98; V Fernhurst *Chich* from 98. *The Vicarage, Church Road, Fernhurst, Haslemere GU27 3HZ* Tel (01428) 652229 E-mail tonyrgr@gmail.com

ROAN, Canon William Forster. b 21. St Chad's Coll Dur BA47 DipTh49. **d** 49 **p** 50. C Barrow St Jas *Carl* 49-52; C-in-c Westf St Mary CD 52-58; V Westfield St Mary 58-61; R Greystoke 61-69; V Workington St Jo 70-86; Hon Can Carl Cathl 72-86; RD Solway 77-84; rtd 86; Perm to Offic *Carl* from 86. *41 Chiswick Street, Carlisle CA1 1HJ* Tel (01228) 521756

ROBARTS, Mrs Freda Margaret. b 43. Open Univ BA86. St As Minl Tr Course 98. **d** 04. NSM Berriew *St As* from 04. *Bryn Awel, Llanrhaeadr ym Mochnant, Oswestry SY10 0DJ* Tel (01691) 780056

ROBB, Ian Archibald. b 48. K Coll Lon 68. **d** 72 **p** 73. C E Ham w Upton Park *Chelmsf* 72-74; C Leckhampton SS Phil and Jas w Cheltenham St Jas *Glouc* 74-79; P-in-c Cheltenham St Mich 79-90; V Lower Cam w Coaley from 90. *St Bartholomew's Vicarage, 99 Fairmead, Cam, Dursley GL11 5JR* Tel (01453) 542679 E-mail ia_jdr@lineone.net

ROBB, Robert Hammond Neill. b 46. Open Univ BA89 Man Univ 66. St Deiniol's Hawarden 87. **d** 87 **p** 88. C Lache cum Saltney *Ches* 87-89; V Norley and Crowton 89-97; P-in-c Kingsley 95-97; V Norley, Crowton and Kingsley 97-98; V Neston from 98. *The Vicarage, High Street, Neston CH64 9TZ* Tel 0151-353 1000 E-mail celtic.robb@btopenworld.com

ROBB, Timothy Simon. b 72. Cant Univ (NZ) BMus94 LTCL94 Lon Bible Coll BTh98. Trin Coll Bris MA03. **d** 03 **p** 04. C Bedford Ch Ch *St Alb* from 03. *161 Dudley Street, Bedford MK40 3SY* Tel (01234) 301708 Mobile 07808-521382 E-mail curate@christchurchbedford.org.uk

ROBBIE, James Neil. b 68. Strathclyde Univ BEng90. Oak Hill Th Coll BTh02. **d** 05. C Wolverhampton St Luke *Lich* from 05. *36 Pencombe Drive, Wolverhampton WV4 5EW*

ROBBINS, Angela Mary. *See* WEAVER, Canon Angela Mary

ROBBINS, David Leslie. b 43. Univ Coll Lon BSc65 Nottm Univ CertEd66. EMMTC 96. **d** 00 **p** 01. NSM Newark *S'well* 00-04; NSM S'well H Trin from 04. *21 Woodland View, Southwell NG25 0AG* Tel (01636) 812641 Mobile 07773-361042 E-mail dlrobbins1@hotmail.com

ROBBINS, David Ronald Walter. b 47. Sarum & Wells Th Coll 85. **d** 87 **p** 88. C Meir Heath *Lich* 87-89; C Collier Row St Jas and Havering-atte-Bower *Chelmsf* 89-93; C Tamworth *Lich* 93-97; P-in-c Hulland, Atlow, Bradley and Hognaston *Derby* 97-98; P-in-c Kniveton 97-98; R Hulland, Atlow, Kniveton, Bradley and Hognaston 98-02; R Widford *Chelmsf* from 02. *The Rectory, 3 Canuden Road, Widford, Chelmsford CM1 2SU* Tel (01245) 346329 Fax 346365 E-mail robbinsdrw@btinternet.com

ROBBINS, Mrs Janet Carey. b 41. Ox Univ BA63 MA95 PGCE81 Univ of Wales (Lamp) 92. St D Dioc Tr Course 96. **d** 98 **p** 99. NSM Llanfihangel Ystrad and Cilcennin w Trefilan etc *St D* 98-01; NSM Quantock Towers *B & W* 02-03; rtd 03. *Rhydyfran, Cribyn, Lampeter SA48 7NH* Tel (01570) 470349

ROBBINS, Martin Charles. b 68. Thames Valley Univ BA91. Ripon Coll Cuddesdon BTh00. **d** 00 **p** 01. C Thatcham *Ox* 00-03; CF from 03. *c/o MOD Chaplains (Army)* Tel (01980) 615804 Fax 615800

ROBBINS, Peter Tyndall. b 25. Magd Coll Ox BA46 DipTh47 MA51. Westcott Ho Cam 48. **d** 50 **p** 51. C Bury St Paul *Man* 50-53; C Swinton St Pet 53-55; V Prestwich St Hilda 55-59; V Lower Halstow *Cant* 59-63; V Charing w Lt Chart 63-73; V Basing *Win* 73-83; V Kingsclere 83-90; rtd 90; Perm to Offic *Birm* 91-00; Asst RD Tamworth *Lich* 91-95; Perm to Offic from 95. *1 Smyth Flat, St John's Hospital, St John Street, Lichfield WS13 6PB* Tel (01543) 415197 E-mail robbinspb@tesco.net

ROBBINS, Richard Harry. b 14. Lon Univ BD47 Keble Coll Ox DipTh50. ALCD41. **d** 41 **p** 42. C Enfield St Geo *Lon* 41-44; CF (EC) 44-48; Perm to Offic *Ox* 48-49; CF 49-55; Chile 55-86; rtd 86. *61 Richmond Wood Road, Bournemouth BH8 9DQ* Tel (01202) 512247

ROBBINS, The Ven Stephen. b 53. K Coll Lon BD74 AKC74. St Aug Coll Cant 75. **d** 76 **p** 77. C Tudhoe Grange *Dur* 76-80; C-in-c Harlow Green CD 80-84; V Gateshead Harlow Green 84-87; CF from 87; Chapl R Memorial Chpl Sandhurst from 01; Adn for the Army from 04. *c/o MOD Chaplains (Army)* Tel (01980) 615804 Fax 615800

ROBBINS, Walter. b 35. **d** 72 **p** 73. Argentina 73-82; Adn N Argentina 80-82; C Southborough St Pet w Ch Ch and St Matt *Roch* 82-86; V Sidcup St Andr 86-95; V Grain w Stoke 95-00; rtd 00; Perm to Offic *Roch* from 00; *Cant* from 01. *Mariners, Imperial Avenue, Minster on Sea, Sheerness ME12 2HG* Tel (01795) 876588

ROBBINS-COLE, Adrian Peter. b 62. LSE BSc(Econ)84 K Coll Lon MA96. Ch Div Sch of the Pacific (USA) 90 Ripon Coll Cuddesdon BA92. **d** 93 **p** 94. C S Dulwich St Steph *S'wark* 93-97; V Motspur Park 97-04; RD Merton 01-04; R Peterborough All SS USA from 04. *49 Concord Street, Peterborough, NH 03458, USA*

ROBBINS-COLE, Ms Sarah Jane. b 68. Vermont Univ BA90 K Coll Lon MA00. Ch Div Sch of the Pacific (USA) 92 Ripon Coll Cuddesdon BA95. **d** 95 **p** 96. C W Dulwich All SS *S'wark* 95-98; Chapl K Coll Sch Wimbledon 98-04; Hon C Motspur Park *S'wark* 98-04; USA from 04. *49 Concord Street, Peterborough, NH 03458, USA*

ROBERT, Brother. *See* ATWELL, Robert Ronald

ROBERT HUGH, Brother. *See* KING-SMITH, Philip Hugh

ROBERTS, Aelwyn. *See* ROBERTS, Joseph Aelwyn

ROBERTS, Alan Moss. b 39. CEng68 MIMechE68 MIMarE68. St Jo Coll Nottm 77. **d** 79 **p** 80. C Bromsgrove St Jo *Worc* 79-83; C Edgbaston St Germain *Birm* 83-89; R Broadhembury, Payhembury and Plymtree *Ex* from 89. *The Rectory, Broadhembury, Honiton EX14 3LT* Tel (01404) 841240 E-mail alanmossroberts@lineone.net

ROBERTS, Mrs Andrea Joan. b 46. Liv Poly ALA68 St Jo Coll Dur BA73 PGCE74. Cranmer Hall Dur 70 Carl and Blackb Dioc Tr Inst 03. **d** 04 **p** 05. NSM Garstang St Thos *Blackb* from 04. *The Vicarage, 5 Lancaster Road, Cockerham, Lancaster LA2 0EB* Tel and fax (01524) 791390 E-mail michael.andrea.r@ukonline.co.uk

ROBERTS, Preb Andrew Alexander. b 49. Open Univ BA75. Bp Otter Coll CertEd70 Sarum & Wells Th Coll 76. **d** 80 **p** 81. NSM Dorchester *Sarum* 80-85; C Swanage and Studland 85-87; TV 87-94; TR Bridgnorth, Tasley, Astley Abbotts, etc *Heref* from 94; Preb Heref Cathl from 03. *The Rectory, 16 East Castle Street, Bridgnorth WV16 4AL* Tel (01746) 763256 *or* 767174 E-mail andyaroberts@talk21.com

ROBERTS, Andrew John. b 55. Newc Univ BA77. EMMTC 00. **d** 03 **p** 04. NSM Church Langton cum Tur Langton etc *Leic* from 03. *Oaks Ridge House, 53A Oaks Road, Great Glen, Leicester LE8 9EG* Tel and fax 0116-259 3392 Mobile 07971-059048 E-mail roberts.andrew@btopenworld.com

ROBERTS, Anne Judith. b 44. CertEd65 DipEd78 Open Univ BA82 Dip Counselling 91. S Dios Minl Tr Scheme 86. **d** 89 **p** 94. Hon Par Dn S Kensington H Trin w All SS *Lon* 89-92; NSM Barnes *S'wark* 92-04; S'wark OLM Scheme 98-04. *5 Avenue Gardens, London SW14 8BP* Tel (020) 8878 5642 E-mail revjr@surfaid.org

ROBERTS, Mrs Anne Marie. b 55. York Univ BA77 Nottm Univ DipTh81. St Jo Coll Nottm 80 WMMTC 93. **d** 96 **p** 97. NSM Meole Brace *Lich* from 96; Chapl Robert Jones/Agnes Hunt Orthopaedic NHS Trust from 98; Chapl Prestfelde Sch Shrewsbury from 99. *The Vicarage, Vicarage Road, Shrewsbury SY3 9EZ* Tel (01743) 231744 *or* 362399 E-mail mbvicarage@aol.com

ROBERTS, Anthony. *See* ROBERTS, John Anthony Duckworth

ROBERTS, Arthur. *See* ROBERTS, John Arthur

ROBERTS, Barrie Moelwyn Antony. b 43. RN Coll Dartmouth 63 Trin Coll Carmarthen CertEd70 Birm Poly BA83. Qu Coll Birm 00. **d** 04 **p** 05. NSM Bartley Green *Birm* from 04. *34 Wheats Avenue, Harborne, Birmingham B17 0RJ* Tel 0121-426 2501 E-mail b.roberts@lineone.net

ROBERTS, Barry. *See* ROBERTS, Ronald Barry

ROBERTS, Bernard John. b 21. Ox NSM Course 79. **d** 82 **p** 83. NSM Wendover *Ox* 82-01; NSM Wendover and Halton from 01. *19 The Paddocks, Wendover, Aylesbury HP22 6HE* Tel (01296) 623445

ROBERTS, Brian David. b 44. Ball Coll Ox BA66 FRSA00. **d** 03. OLM Guildf H Trin w St Mary *Guildf* from 03. *Risby, Upper Guildown Road, Guildford GU2 4EZ* Tel (01483) 570556 Mobile 07979-766471 Fax (020) 7631 6224
E-mail roberts@risby83.freeserve.co.uk

ROBERTS, Bryan Richard. b 55. Univ of Wales (Cardiff) BD80. St Mich Coll Llan 78. **d** 80 **p** 81. C Finham *Cov* 80-83; Asst Youth Officer *Nor* 83-86; R N and S Creake w Waterden 86-91; P-in-c E w N and W Barsham 86-91; Chapl Epsom Coll 91-01; Chapl Gresham's Sch Holt from 01. *10 Kelling Road, Holt NR25 6RT* Tel (01263) 713234

ROBERTS, Charles Richard Meyrick. b 53. Huddersfield Poly ARCM75 BA75. St Paul's Coll Grahamstown DipTh91. **d** 92 **p** 92. S Africa 92-94; C Bath Abbey w St Jas *B & W* 94-98; P-in-c Chew Magna w Dundry 98-00; R Chew Magna w Dundry and Norton Malreward from 00; P-in-c Chew Stoke w Nempnett Thrubwell from 03. *The Rectory, 24 High Street, Chew Magna, Bristol BS40 8PW* Tel (01275) 332199
E-mail chewrector@hotmail.com

ROBERTS, Christopher Michael. b 39. CCSk93 Man Univ DipAE79. Qu Coll Birm 62. **d** 64 **p** 65. C Milton next Gravesend Ch Ch *Roch* 64-68; C Thirsk w S Kilvington *York* 68-69; V Castleton *Derby* 69-75; TV Buxton w Burbage and King Sterndale 75-79; Perm to Offic 84-87; NSM Marple All SS *Ches* 87-90; Chapl Asst St Helens Hosp *Liv* 90-91; Chapl Asst Whiston Co Hosp Prescot 90-91; Chapl Asst Rainhill Hosp Liv 90-91; Chapl R United Hosp Bath 91-94; Chapl R United Hosp Bath NHS Trust 94-99; Sen Chapl Birm Children's Hosp NHS Trust 99-04; rtd 04; Perm to Offic *Birm* from 04. *6 Myring Drive, Sutton Coldfield B75 7RZ* Tel 0121-329 2547
E-mail chrismirob@aol.com

ROBERTS, Colin Edward. b 50. Sarum & Wells Th Coll. **d** 83 **p** 84. C Harton *Dur* 83; C S Shields All SS 83-85; C Thamesmead *S'wark* 85-87; TV 87-89; C Streatham St Pet 89-90 and 92; Zimbabwe 90-92; V Earlsfield St Jo *S'wark* from 92. *St John's Vicarage, 40 Atheldene Road, London SW18 3BW* Tel (020) 8874 2837 Fax 08088-742816
E-mail vicar@stjohnthedivine.freeserve.co.uk

ROBERTS, Canon Cyril. b 41. St Deiniol's Hawarden. **d** 84 **p** 85. C Maltby *Sheff* 84-86; TR Gt Snaith from 86; AD Snaith and Hatfield from 03; Hon Can Sheff Cathl from 05. *The Orchard, Pontefract Road, Snaith, Goole DN14 9JS* Tel (01405) 860866 Mobile 07702-004870 E-mail cyril@holyburrows.fsnet.co.uk

ROBERTS, David. b 44. Ex Univ BA65. St Steph Ho Ox 65. **d** 67 **p** 68. C Southwick St Columba *Dur* 67-72; C-in-c Southwick St Cuth CD 72-79; R Alyth *St And* 79-84; R Blairgowrie 79-84; R Coupar Angus 79-84; P-in-c Taunton St Jo *B & W* from 84; Chapl Somerset Coll of Arts and Tech from 84. *17 Henley Road, Taunton TA1 5BW* Tel (01823) 284176
E-mail scat.chap@virgin.net

ROBERTS, David Alan. b 38. Open Univ BA82. Ripon Hall Ox 71. **d** 73 **p** 74. C W Bridgford *S'well* 73-77; V Awsworth w Cossall 77-82; V Oxclose *Dur* 82-94; P-in-c New Seaham 94-04; rtd 04. *8 Hazel Road, Gateshead NE8 2EP* Tel 0191-460 9919

ROBERTS, David Charles. b 53. Poly of Wales CertEd76 Open Univ BA82 BA93 Univ of Wales MEd87. St Mich Coll Llan 96. **d** 98 **p** 99. C Whitchurch *Llan* 98-00; Chapl Univ of Wales (Cardiff) from 00. *6 Gwaun Llwyfen, Nelson, Treharris CF46 6HY* Tel (01443) 450995 E-mail droberts@uwic.ac.uk

ROBERTS, Preb David Henry. b 38. St Chad's Coll Dur BA60. Qu Coll Birm DipTh62. **d** 62 **p** 63. C Stonehouse *Glouc* 62-65; C Hemsworth *Wakef* 65-69; V Newsome 69-76; R Pontesbury I and II *Heref* 76-03; RD Pontesbury 83-93; Preb Heref Cathl from 85; rtd 03; Perm to Offic *Heref* from 03. *14 Beaconsfield Park, Ludlow SY8 4LY* Tel (01584) 878568
E-mail dhroberts@lineone.net

ROBERTS, Canon David John. b 36. Man Univ BSc58. St D Coll Lamp 65. **d** 67 **p** 68. C Rhosllannerchrugog *St As* 67-70; R Cerrigydrudion w Llanfihangel Glyn Myfyr etc 70-75; R Llanrwst and Llanddoget 75-77; R Llanrwst and Llanddoget and Capel Garmon 77-84; RD Llanrwst 77-84; V Abergele 84-01; RD Rhos 94-00; Hon Can St As Cathl 95-96; Can Cursal St As Cathl 96-01; rtd 01. *Brithdir, Abergele Road, Bodelwyddan, Rhyl LL18 5SR* Tel (01745) 585807

ROBERTS, Dewi. b 57. LWCMD77 Cyncoed Coll CertEd78. St Mich Coll Llan. **d** 84 **p** 85. C Clydach *S & B* 84-88; V Glantawe 88-94; V Loughor from 94. *The Rectory, 109 Glebe Road, Loughor, Swansea SA4 6SR* Tel (01792) 891958

ROBERTS, Dewi James Llewelyn. b 63. United Th Coll Abth 83. **d** 96 **p** 97. C Llandudno *Ban* 96-02; C Bodedern w Llanfachraeth and Llechgynfarwy 99-02; C Llanfaethlu w Llanfwrog and Llanrhuddlad etc 99-02; V Newcastle Emlyn w Llandyfriog etc *St D* from 02. *The Vicarage, Newcastle Emlyn SA38 9LL* Tel (01239) 710385 E-mail dewi.roberts@which.net

ROBERTS, Diane. b 45. Bris Univ CertEd66 BEd82. STETS 02. **d** 05. NSM Kinson *Sarum* from 05. *6 Herbert Road, Woodfalls, Salisbury SP5 2LF* Tel (01725) 510894
E-mail robertsdiane1@aol.com

ROBERTS, Dilwyn Carey. b 38. St Deiniol's Hawarden 74. **d** 76 **p** 77. C Glanadda *Ban* 76-77; TV Amlwch, Rhosybol, Llandyfrydog etc 77-81; V Llanllechid 81-85; V Caerhun w Llangelynin 85-87; V Caerhun w Llangelynin w Llanbedr-y-Cennin 87-92; rtd 93. *67 St Georges Drive, Conwy LL31 9PR*

ROBERTS, Donald James. b 26. Sarum & Wells Th Coll 83. **d** 86 **p** 87. NSM Corfe Castle, Church Knowle, Kimmeridge etc *Sarum* 86-88 and 91-95; C Broadstone 88-91; rtd 91; Perm to Offic *Sarum* 95-98 and *St E from 01. 42 Priory Court, Nacton, Ipswich IP10 0JU* Tel (01473) 711242

ROBERTS, Edward. *See* ROBERTS, Canon Henry Edward

ROBERTS, Edward John Walford. b 31. Trin Coll Carmarthen CertEd. St D Dioc Tr Course. **d** 79 **p** 80. NSM Burry Port and Pwll *St D* 79-98; NSM Swansea St Jas *S & B* 98-02; Lic to Offic from 02. *1A Woodlands Terrace, Uplands, Swansea SA1 6BR*

ROBERTS, Canon Edward Owen. b 38. K Coll Lon BD63 AKC63. **d** 64 **p** 65. C Auckland St Andr and St Anne *Dur* 64-67; C Cheltenham St Paul *Glouc* 67-68; Asst Master Colne Valley High Sch Linthwaite 69-71; V Meltham Mills *Wakef* 71-75; R Emley 75-88; RD Kirkburton 80-88; V Huddersfield H Trin 88-04; RD Huddersfield 89-99; Hon Can Wakef Cathl 92-04; rtd 04; Perm to Offic *York* from 04. *2B Queen Street, Filey YO14 9HB* Tel (01723) 515535 E-mail edwardr@fish.co.uk

ROBERTS, The Ven Elwyn. b 31. Univ of Wales (Ban) BA52 Keble Coll Ox BA54 MA59. St Mich Coll Llan 54. **d** 55 **p** 56. C Glanadda *Ban* 55-57; V 66-71; Lib and Lect St Mich Coll Llan 57-66; Dir Post-Ord Tr *Ban* 70-90; R Llandudno 71-83; Can Ban Cathl 77-78; Chan Ban Cathl 78-83; Adn Meirionnydd 83-86; R Criccieth w Treflys 83-86; Adn Ban 86-99; rtd 99; Perm to Offic *Ban* from 99. *6 Min Menai, Eithinog, Bangor LL57 2LB* Tel (01248) 355515

ROBERTS, Eric. b 40. Ban Ord Course 90 St Mich Coll Llan 92. **d** 93 **p** 94. Min Can Ban Cathl *Ban* 93-97; R Llanllyfni 97-02; V Llandysul w Bangor Teifi w Henllan etc *St D* from 02; AD Emlyn from 04. *The Vicarage, Tanyfron, Well Street, Llandysul SA44 4DR* Tel (01559) 362277

ROBERTS, Graham Miles. b 59. Open Univ BA95. Trin Coll Bris 90. **d** 92 **p** 93. C Charles w Plymouth St Matthias *Ex* 92-96; Chapl Plymouth Univ 92-94; TV Liskeard, St Keyne, St Pinnock, Morval etc *Truro* 96-99; P-in-c Bournemouth St Andr *Win* 99-04; V from 04. *St Andrew's Vicarage, 53 Bennett Road, Bournemouth BH8 8QQ* Tel (01202) 396022
E-mail graham_roberts@ntlworld.com

ROBERTS, Canon Henry Edward (Ted). b 28. Oak Hill Th Coll 53. **d** 56 **p** 57. C Edgware *Lon* 56-58; C Bedworth *Cov* 58-61; V Bethnal Green St Jas Less *Lon* 61-73; V Old Ford St Mark Victoria Park 61-73; V Bethnal Green St Jas Less w Victoria Park 73-78; RD Tower Hamlets 76-78; Can Res Bradf Cathl *Bradf* 78-82; Dioc Dir Soc Resp 78-82; V Bermondsey St Jas w Ch Ch *S'wark* 82-90; P-in-c Bermondsey St Anne 82-90; Hon Can S'wark Cathl 90-93; Gen Adv for Inner City Min 90-93; rtd 93. *12 Bromeswell Road, Ipswich IP4 3AS* Tel (01473) 288956

ROBERTS, James. *See* ROBERTS, William James

ROBERTS, James Arthur. b 34. Lon Univ BSc56. Bps' Coll Cheshunt 58. **d** 60 **p** 61. C Upper Holloway St Steph *Lon* 60-62; C March St Jo *Ely* 62-65; V Coldham 65-70; V Friday Bridge 65-70; PC Ridgeway *Derby* 70-72; P-in-c Gleadless *Sheff* 72-74; TR 74-79; P-in-c Catfield *Nor* 79-82; P-in-c Ingham w Sutton 79-82; R Aldwincle w Thorpe Achurch, Pilton, Wadenhoe etc *Pet* 82-91; R Barby w Kilsby 91-96; RD Daventry 92-96; rtd 96; Perm to Offic *Ely* 96-00. *29 Whiteacres, Whittlesey, Peterborough PE7 1XR* Tel (01733) 351602

ROBERTS, Jane Elizabeth. b 53. SEITE 98. **d** 01 **p** 02. NSM Mitcham Ascension *S'wark* from 01. *39 Castleton Road, Mitcham CR4 1NZ* Tel (020) 8764 6423 Mobile 07790-703710
E-mail janeroberts@nasuwt.net

ROBERTS, Miss Janet Lynne. b 56. Trin Coll Bris 76. **dss** 82 **d** 87 **p** 94. Dagenham *Chelmsf* 82-86; Huyton St Mich *Liv* 86-91; Par Dn 87-91; C Aughton Ch Ch 91-98; TV Parr 98-05; TR from 05. *St Paul's Vicarage, 75 Chain Lane, St Helens WA11 9QF* Tel and fax (01744) 734335
E-mail church@stpaulschainlane.freeserve.co.uk

ROBERTS, Mrs Jasmine Cynthia. b 46. Cant Sch of Min 88. **d** 91. NSM Sandwich *Cant* from 91; Asst Dir of Ords from 02. *The Rectory, Knightrider Street, Sandwich CT13 9ER* Tel and fax (01304) 613138 E-mail jasmineroberts@supanet.com

ROBERTS, Jeffrey David. b 25. St Cath Coll Cam BA46 MA50 Lon Univ BSc58. **d** 65 **p** 66. Hd Master Adams' Gr Sch Newport Shropshire 59-73; Hd Master St Geo Sch Gravesend 74-82. *Corner House, Keyston, Huntingdon PE28 0RD* Tel (01832) 710254

ROBERTS, John Anthony Duckworth. b 43. K Coll Lon BD65 AKC65. St Boniface Warminster 65. **d** 66 **p** 67. C Wythenshawe Wm Temple Ch CD *Man* 66-69; C Bradford-on-Avon *Sarum* 69-72; Chapl Dauntsey's Sch Devizes 72-73; CF 73-77; P-in-c Verwood *Sarum* 77-81; V 81-86; V Clitheroe St Mary *Blackb* 86-97; R Paget St Paul Bermuda 97-03; rtd 03. *The Old Coach House, Forwood, Minchinhampton, Stroud GL6 9AB* Tel (01453) 835811

ROBERTS, John Arthur. b 37. Man Univ BScTech59 CEng68 MIEE68. Cranmer Hall Dur DipTh71. **d** 71 **p** 72. C Wellington w Eyton *Lich* 71-75; P-in-c Newton Flowery Field *Ches* 75-80; V Dunham Massey St Marg 80-91; Chapl Countess of Ches Hosp NHS Trust 91-02; Chapl W Cheshire NHS Trust 94-02; NSM Plas Newton *Ches* 99-02; rtd 02; Perm to Offic *Ches* from 02. *29 Well Lane, Chester CH2 2HL* Tel (01244) 409579 Mobile 07816-752516

ROBERTS, John Charles. b 50. Nottm Univ BA71 Cam Univ BA73. Westcott Ho Cam 71. **d** 73 **p** 74. C Newark St Mary *S'well* 73-77; Chapl RAF 77-93; Lic to Offic *Bris* 93-95. *Address temp unknown*

ROBERTS, John Charles Welch. b 39. UMIST BSc60. Oak Hill NSM Course 91 SW Minl Tr Course 92. **d** 94 **p** 95. NSM Washfield, Stoodleigh, Withleigh etc *Ex* from 94. *East Sidborough, Loxbeare, Tiverton EX16 8DA* Tel and fax (01884) 256302 E-mail john@sidborough.freeserve.co.uk

ROBERTS, Canon John Hugh. b 42. K Alfred's Coll Win CertEd72 Open Univ BA75. Wells Th Coll 65. **d** 67 **p** 68. C Wareham w Arne *Sarum* 67-70; C Twyford *Win* 70-72; Asst Teacher Rawlins Sch Leics 72-74; V Nassington w Yarwell *Pet* 74-77; Asst Teacher Sponne Sch Towcester 78-92; RD Brackley 94-03; P-in-c Helmdon w Stuchbury and Radstone etc 93-03; P-in-c Weedon Lois w Plumpton and Moreton Pinkney etc 02-03; R Astwell Gp 03-05; Can Pet Cathl 01-05; rtd 05. *Pimlico House, Pimlico, Brackley NN13 5TN* Tel (01280) 850378 E-mail rev.roberts@virgin.net

ROBERTS, Canon John Mark Arnott. b 54. K Coll Lon AKC75 CertEd76. Chich Th Coll 77. **d** 77 **p** 78. C Ashford *Cant* 77-82; V St Mary's Bay w St Mary-in-the-Marsh etc 82-91; R Sandwich from 91; AD Sandwich from 00; Hon Can Cant Cathl from 03; C Woodnesborough w Worth and Staple from 04. *The Rectory, Knightrider Street, Sandwich CT13 9ER* Tel and fax (01304) 613138 E-mail revdmarkroberts@supanet.com

ROBERTS, Canon John Victor. b 34. St Edm Hall Ox BA58 MA62. Tyndale Hall Bris 58. **d** 60 **p** 61. C Southport Ch Ch *Liv* 60-62; C Pemberton St Mark Newtown 62-65; V Blackb Sav *Blackb* 65-71; Chapl Blackb and Lancs R Infirmary and Park Lee Hosp 65-71; V Parr *Liv* 71-73; TR 73-80; R Much Woolton 80-02; RD Childwall 84-89; AD Liv S 89-00; Hon Can Liv Cathl 95-02; rtd 02; Perm to Offic *Liv* from 02; Hon Chapl Liv Cathl from 04. *8 Cherry Vale, Liverpool L25 5PX* Tel and fax 0151-428 8290 E-mail canonjvr@hotmail.com

ROBERTS, John Victor. b 40. GIPE61. Qu Coll Birm 83. **d** 85 **p** 86. C Ludlow *Heref* 85-89 and 92-93; P-in-c Coreley and Doddington 89-92; P-in-c Knowbury 89-92; TV Ludlow, Ludford, Ashford Carbonell etc 93-02; rtd 02; Perm to Offic *Heref* from 02. *The Fold, 10 Whitemeadow Close, Craven Arms SY7 9QP* Tel (01588) 672093

ROBERTS, Jonathan George Alfred. b 60. Lon Univ BD. Qu Coll Birm. **d** 84 **p** 85. C Shepshed *Leic* 84-86; C Braunstone 86-87; Dioc Youth Adv *Dur* 88-92; Nat Youth Officer Gen Syn Bd of Educn 92-94; P-in-c Washington *Dur* 94-95; R 95-99; Regional Co-ord for Community Work Assessment Consortium for the NE from 99; Perm to Offic *Dur* from 99 and *Newc* from 01. *10 Brierville, Durham DH1 4QE* Tel 0191-383 9148 *or* 514 6150 E-mail cwacnee@aol.com

ROBERTS, Joseph Aelwyn. b 18. Univ of Wales (Lamp) BA40. St Mich Coll Llan 41. **d** 42 **p** 43. C Llanllyfni *Ban* 42-44; Min Can Ban Cathl 44-52; V Llandegai 52-88; Dioc Dir for Soc Work 73-88; rtd 88; Perm to Offic *Ban* from 88. *The Vicarage, Llandygai, Bangor LL57 4LA* Tel (01248) 353711

ROBERTS, Judith. *See* ROBERTS, Anne Judith

ROBERTS, Ms Judith. b 55. Collingwood Coll Dur BA76 Goldsmiths' Coll Lon PGCE77. SW Minl Tr Course 00. **d** 03 **p** 04. C Burrington, Chawleigh, Cheldon, Chulmleigh etc *Ex* from 03. *The Rectory, Chawleigh, Chulmleigh EX18 7HJ* Tel (01769) 580660 E-mail judith75@yahoo.com

ROBERTS, Mrs Kathleen Marie. b 50. Th Ext Educn Coll 94. **d** 00 **p** 01. S Africa 00-02; C Crediton, Shobrooke and Sandford etc *Ex* from 03. *50 Beech Park, Pounds Hill, Crediton EX17 1HW* Tel (01363) 777924

ROBERTS, Keith Mervyn. b 55. St Pet Coll Birm CertEd76 LGSM78. Qu Coll Birm 89. **d** 91 **p** 92. C Hall Green St Pet *Birm* 91-95; TV Warwick *Cov* 95-00; P-in-c Bishop's Tachbrook from 00; Dioc Communications Officer 03-04; Dir Communications from 04; Relig Affairs Correspondent BBC Radio Cov & Warw 95-01; Presenter/Producer from 01. *The Vicarage, 24 Mallory Road, Bishops Tachbrook, Leamington Spa CV33 9QX* Tel and fax (01926) 426922 E-mail mervynrob@aol.com *or* mervyn.roberts@covcofe.org

ROBERTS, Canon Kenneth William Alfred. b 26. Roch Th Coll 63. **d** 65 **p** 66. C Waterlooville *Portsm* 65-67; C Honicknowle *Ex* 67-68; C Christchurch *Win* 68-69; C Shiphay Collaton *Ex* 70-71; CF 71-74; R Bassingham *Linc* 74-75; V Carlton-le-Moorland w Stapleford 74-75; R Thurlby w Norton Disney 74-75; V Aubourn w Haddington 74-75; Chapl R Hosp Sch Holbrook 75-78; P-in-c Copdock w Washbrook and Belstead *St E* 78-79; P-in-c Brandeston w Kettleburgh 79-82; Chapl Brandeston Hall Sch 79-84; Chapl Lisbon *Eur* 84-86; Can and Chan Malta Cathl 86-89; R Wimbotsham w Stow Bardolph and Stow Bridge etc *Ely* 89-91; rtd 91; Perm to Offic *St E* 91-98. *2 Valley Farm Bungalows, Combs Lane, Stowmarket IP14 2NL* Tel (01449) 674746

ROBERTS, Preb Kevin Thomas. b 55. Qu Coll Cam BA78 MA82 Nottm Univ BA82. St Jo Coll Nottm 80. **d** 83 **p** 84. C Beverley Minster *York* 83-86; C Woodley St Jo the Ev *Ox* 86-91; V Meole Brace *Lich* from 91; RD Shrewsbury from 98; Preb Lich Cathl from 02. *The Vicarage, Vicarage Road, Shrewsbury SY3 9EZ* Tel (01743) 231744 *or* tel and fax 362399 E-mail mbvicarage@aol.com

ROBERTS, Laurence James. b 51. Sussex Univ BEd73. Sarum & Wells Th Coll 75. **d** 78 **p** 79. C Rotherhithe St Mary w All SS *S'wark* 78-81; Public Preacher 81-84; Ind Chapl 81-84; Hon P Nunhead St Silas 82-84; TV Plaistow *Chelmsf* 84-89; Chapl Newham Gen Hosp and Plaistow Hosp 84-96; Tutor Community Nursing Services 89-96; Tutor Westmr Past Foundn from 90; Perm to Offic *Chelmsf* from 90; Lect E Lon Univ from 92. *40 Boleyn Road, London E7 9QE* Tel (020) 8472 2430 E-mail laurence.roberts@virgin.net

ROBERTS, Ms Leanne Kelly. b 74. St Hilda's Coll Ox BA95 MA02 Em Coll Cam BA01. Westcott Ho Cam 99. **d** 02 **p** 03. C Hampton All SS *Lon* 02-05; Chapl Hertf Coll Ox from 05. *Hertford College, Catte Street, Oxford OX1 3BW* Tel (01865) 279400 E-mail leanneroberts_uk@yahoo.co.uk

ROBERTS, Miss Marguerite Mary Grace. b 43. Keswick Hall Coll CertEd65 Sussex Univ BEd74 UEA MA86. EAMTC 97. **d** 00 **p** 01. Hon C Cambridge St Mark *Ely* from 00. *5 Eachard Road, Cambridge CB3 0HZ* Tel (01223) 359167

ROBERTS, Mark. *See* ROBERTS, Canon John Mark Arnott

ROBERTS, Martin Vincent. b 53. LRAM72 Birm Univ BA76 MA77 PhD82. Ripon Coll Cuddesdon 76. **d** 78 **p** 79. C Perry Barr *Birm* 78-81; Sen Chapl and Lect W Sussex Inst of HE 81-86; Leic Poly *Leic* 86-92; Sen Chapl De Montfort Univ 92-95; TV Leic H Spirit 86-89; TR 89-95; V Baswich *Lich* 95-01; V Selly Oak St Mary *Birm* from 01. *St Mary's Vicarage, 923 Bristol Road, Selly Oak, Birmingham B29 6ND* Tel 0121-472 0250 E-mail martin@mroberts48.fsnet.co.uk

ROBERTS, Matthew Garnant. b 13. St D Coll Lamp BA37. **d** 37 **p** 38. C St Brides Minor *Llan* 37-39; C Iford *Win* 39-43; C Bournemouth St Alb 43-46; Chapl RAF 47-68; P-in-c Hinton Ampner w Bramdean *Win* 68-70; R 70-74; R Hinton Ampner w Bramdean and Kilmeston 74-78; rtd 78; Lic to Offic *B & W* 79-96. *The Granary, Quaperlake Street, Bruton BA10 0NA* Tel (01749) 812545

ROBERTS, Mervyn. *See* ROBERTS, Keith Mervyn

ROBERTS, Michael Brian. b 46. Oriel Coll Ox BA68 MA72 St Jo Coll Dur BA73. Cranmer Hall Dur 71. **d** 74 **p** 75. C St Helens St Helen *Liv* 74-76; C Goose Green 76-78; C Blundellsands St Nic 78-80; V Fazakerley St Nath 80-87; V Chirk *St As* 87-01; V Cockerham w Winmarleigh and Glasson *Blackb* from 01. *The Vicarage, 5 Lancaster Road, Cockerham, Lancaster LA2 0EB* Tel and fax (01524) 791390 E-mail michael.andrea.r@ukonline.co.uk

ROBERTS, Michael Frederick. b 46. Sarum Th Coll 86. **d** 88 **p** 89. C Reading St Matt *Ox* 88-91; NSM Douglas St Geo and St Barn *S & M* 91-93; V Malew from 93. *Malew Vicarage, Crossag Road, Ballasalla, Isle of Man IM9 3EF* Tel (01624) 822469 E-mail malew@globalnet.co.uk

ROBERTS, Canon Michael Graham Vernon. b 43. Keble Coll Ox BA65. Cuddesdon Coll 65 Ch Div Sch of the Pacific (USA) MDiv67. **d** 67 **p** 68. C Littleham w Exmouth *Ex* 67-70; Chapl Clare Coll Cam 70-74; V Bromley St Mark *Roch* 74-79; Tutor Qu Coll Birm 79-85; TR High Wycombe *Ox* 85-90; Vice-Prin Westcott Ho Cam 90-93; Prin from 93; Hon Can Ely Cathl *Ely* from 04. *Westcott House, Jesus Lane, Cambridge CB5 8BP* Tel (01223) 741020 *or* 741010 Fax 741002 E-mail mgvr2@cam.ac.uk

ROBERTS, Nia Wyn. b 64. Univ of Wales (Ban) BA86 PGCE87 CQSW90 Anglia Poly Univ MA00. Westcott Ho Cam 98. **d** 00 **p** 01. C Rhyl w St Ann *St As* 00-03; R Bala from 03. *Y Rheithordy, 13 Heol-y-Castell, Bala LL23 7YA* Tel (01678) 521047 Mobile 07833-302312

ROBERTS, Nicholas John. b 47. Lon Univ BD70 AKC70 MTh78 Surrey Univ MSc93. St Aug Coll Cant 70. **d** 71 **p** 72. C Tividale *Lich* 71-74; C St Pancras H Cross w St Jude and St Pet *Lon* 74-76; C Camberwell St Giles *S'wark* 76-78; Chapl Ch Coll Cam 78-82; V Kingstanding St Luke *Birm* 82-85; Chapl St Chas Hosp Ladbroke Grove 85-96; Chapl Princess Louise Hosp Lon 85-96; Chapl Paddington Community Hosp 85-96; Chapl Cen Middx Hosp NHS Trust 96-99; Chapl St Mary's NHS Trust Paddington 99-04; Chapl Sisters of the Ch from 04. *32 Burnell Avenue, Richmond TW10 7YE* Tel (020) 8549 1060 Mobile 07984-892635 E-mail nick@norlon.freeserve.co.uk

ROBERTS, Mrs Patricia Frances. b 62. Roehampton Inst BEd85. Trin Coll Bris 93. **d** 96 **p** 97. NSM Buckhurst Hill *Chelmsf* 96-99;

NSM Gt Baddow from 99. *124 Beehive Lane, Chelmsford CM2 9SH* Tel (01245) 269026
E-mail tudorandtricia@ezekiel124.fsnet.co.uk

ROBERTS, Paul Carlton. b 57. Worc Coll Ox BA78 MA86 CertEd. St Jo Coll Nottm 84. **d** 87 **p** 88. C Hazlemere *Ox* 87-91; C Woodley St Jo the Ev 91-92; TV Woodley 92-03; R Coulsdon St Jo *S'wark* from 03. *The Rectory, 232 Coulsdon Road, Coulsdon CR5 1EA* Tel (01737) 552152 Fax as telephone
E-mail robertspc@fish.co.uk

ROBERTS, Paul John. b 60. Man Univ BA82 Man Poly PGCE83 Man Univ PhD91. St Jo Coll Nottm 83. **d** 85 **p** 86. C Burnage St Marg *Man* 85-88; Tutor Trin Coll Bris 88-00; R Cotham St Sav w St Mary and Clifton St Paul *Bris* from 00. *12 Belgrave Road, Bristol BS8 2AB* Tel 0117-377 1086
E-mail proberts1@blueyonder.co.uk

ROBERTS, Peter Francis. b 59. N Illinois Univ BSc81 Leeds Univ BA87. Coll of Resurr Mirfield 85. **d** 88 **p** 89. C Leeds All So *Ripon* 88-92; Asst Dioc Youth Chapl 91-92; USPG Belize 92-94; V Collingham w Harewood *Ripon* 95-01; World Miss Officer 95-01; Chapl Dubai and Sharjah w N Emirates 01-03; R Merritt Is USA from 03. *PO Box 541025, Merritt Island, FL 32953, USA* Tel (001) (321) 452 5260 E-mail stlukes1@bellsouth.net

ROBERTS, Peter Gwilym. b 42. N Ord Course 78. **d** 81 **p** 82. NSM Seaforth *Liv* 81-83; TV Kirkby 83-88; Dioc Adv on UPA 88-91; P-in-c Southport H Trin 91-94; S Africa from 94; rtd 00. *PO Box 44108, Linden, Gauteng, 2104 South Africa* Tel (0027) (11) 475 4439 *or* 475 1314 Fax 475 8284

ROBERTS, Peter Reece. b 43. Chich Th Coll 73. **d** 75 **p** 76. C Cadoxton-juxta-Barry *Llan* 75-79; C Brixham w Churston Ferrers *Ex* 79-81; C Bexhill St Pet *Chich* 81-84; R Heene from 84; RD Worthing 89-97. *Heene Rectory, 4 Lansdowne Road, Worthing BN11 4LY* Tel (01903) 202312 Fax as telephone

ROBERTS, Philip Alan. b 59. Chich Th Coll 85. **d** 88 **p** 89. C Friern Barnet St Jas *Lon* 88-93; C Farnham Royal w Hedgerley *Ox* 93-02; TV Southend *Chelmsf* from 02. *39 St John's Road, Westcliff-on-Sea SS0 7JY* Tel (01702) 433327

ROBERTS, Philip Anthony. b 50. St Jo Coll Dur BA73. Wycliffe Hall Ox 75. **d** 77 **p** 78. C Roby *Liv* 77-79; C Ainsdale 79-80; C Pershore w Pinvin, Wick and Birlingham *Worc* 80-83; Chapl Asst Radcliffe Infirmary Ox 83-88; John Radcliffe and Littlemore Hosps Ox 83-88; Chapl R Victoria and Bournemouth Gen Hosps 88-91; Chapl Heref Co Hosp 91-94; Chapl Heref Hosps NHS Trust from 94. *The County Hospital, Union Walk, Hereford HR1 2ER* Tel (01432) 364139 *or* 355444

ROBERTS, Canon Phillip. b 21. Sarum Th Coll 55. **d** 57 **p** 58. C Salisbury St Mich *Sarum* 57-60; Australia 60-63; V Westbury *Sarum* 63-73; TR Dorchester 73-80; Can and Preb Sarum Cathl 75-87; R Upper Chelsea H Trin w St Jude *Lon* 80-87; rtd 87; Perm to Offic *Sarum* from 87; V of Close Sarum Cathl 89-95. *112 Harnham Road, Salisbury SP2 8JW* Tel (01722) 323291

ROBERTS, The Ven Raymond Harcourt. b 31. CB84. St Edm Hall Ox BA54 MA58. St Mich Coll Llan 54. **d** 56 **p** 57. C Bassaleg *Mon* 56-59; Chapl RNR 57-59; Chapl RN 59-84; Chapl of the Fleet and Adn for the RN 80-84; QHC 80-84; Hon Can Gib Cathl *Eur* 80-84; Gen Sec JMECA 85-89; C Hale *Guildf* 85-89; Hon Chapl Llan Cathl *Llan* 90-95; Lic to Offic from 95. *8 Baynton Close, Llandaff, Cardiff CF5 2NZ* Tel (029) 2057 8044

ROBERTS, Miss Rebecca Mary. b 71. Glam Univ BA92 Chelt & Glouc Coll of HE PGCE93. Qu Coll Birm BA02. **d** 03. C Greenstead w Colchester St Anne *Chelmsf* from 03. *St Anne's Vicarage, Compton Road, Colchester CO4 4BQ* Tel (01206) 522378 E-mail bricklanebek@hotmail.com

ROBERTS, Richard. b 23. Univ of Wales BA48. St Mich Coll Llan 48. **d** 50 **p** 51. C Pwllheli *Ban* 50-53; C Llangelynnin 53-57; V Llanwnog w Penstrowed 57-68; R Llanrwst and Llanddoget *St As* 68-75; RD Llanrwst 73-75; V Llandrillo-yn-Rhos 75-90; rtd 91; Perm to Offic *Ban* from 91 and *St A from 97. 2 Bryn Ithel, Abergele LL22 8QB* Tel (01745) 826353

ROBERTS, Canon Richard Stephanus Jacob (Steph). b 28. TCD BA51 MA57. TCD Div Sch Div Test51. **d** 51 **p** 52. C Orangefield *D & D* 51-54; Miss to Seamen 51-94; Portuguese E Africa 51-65; Ceylon 65-68; Chapl Miss to Seamen Dublin 68-72; Chapl Miss to Seamen Southn 72-94; Sen Chapl Ch on the High Seas 72-94; Hon Can Win Cathl *Win* 82-94; rtd 94; Perm to Offic *Win* from 94. *25 Bassett Crescent West, Southampton SO16 7EB* Tel (023) 8079 0734

ROBERTS, Ronald Barry. b 40. S Dios Minl Tr Scheme 80. **d** 83 **p** 85. NSM Wedmore w Theale and Blackford *B & W* 83-85; C Odd Rode *Ches* 85-87; V Eaton and Hulme Walfield 87-04; rtd 04; Perm to Offic *Ches* from 04. *Iona, 8 Belmont Avenue, Sandbach CW11 1BX* Tel (01270) 766124
E-mail barryroberts@uwclub.net

ROBERTS, Mrs Rosamunde Mair. b 59. RN80. STETS 98. **d** 01 **p** 02. C Farnham *Guildf* 01-04; C Fleet from 04. *38 Oasthouse Drive, Fleet GU51 2UL* E-mail rosmairroberts@hotmail.com

ROBERTS, Mrs Rosanne Elizabeth. b 51. Glouc Sch of Min 85. **d** 88 **p** 94. NSM Charlton Kings St Mary *Glouc* 88-93; C Leckhampton SS Phil and Jas w Cheltenham St Jas 93-96; R Ashchurch from 96. *The Rectory, Ashchurch, Tewkesbury GL20 8JZ* Tel (01684) 293729

ROBERTS, Miss Sandra June. b 58. Univ Coll Ches BA96. Qu Coll Birm 98. **d** 98 **p** 99. C Mold *St As* 98-01; V Llandrillo and Llandderfel from 01; AD Penllyn and Edeirnion from 04. *The Vicarage, Llandrillo, Corwen LL21 0SW* Tel (01490) 440224

ROBERTS, Stephanus. *See* ROBERTS, Canon Richard Stephanus Jacob

ROBERTS, Stephen Bradley. b 66. K Coll Lon BD90 Wycliffe Hall Ox 89. **d** 91 **p** 92. C W Hampstead St Jas *Lon* 91-94; TV Uxbridge 94-98; Chapl Brunel Univ 98-04; Vice Prin St Mich Coll Llan from 04. *St Michael's College, 54 Cardiff Road, Llandaff, Cardiff CF5 2YJ* Tel (029) 2083 8004 *or* 2055 1780
E-mail sr@stmichaels.ac.uk

ROBERTS, The Ven Stephen John. b 58. K Coll Lon BD81 Heythrop Coll Lon MTh99. Westcott Ho Cam. **d** 83 **p** 84. C Riverhead w Dunton Green *Roch* 83-86; C St Martin-in-the-Fields *Lon* 86-89; Warden Trin Coll Cen Camberwell 89-99; V Camberwell St Geo *S'wark* 89-99; RD Camberwell 97-99; Treas and Can Res S'wark Cathl 00-05; Sen Dioc Dir of Ords 00-05; Adn Wandsworth from 05. *2 Alma Road, London SW18 1AB* Tel (020) 8874 8567
E-mail stephen.roberts@southwark.anglican.org

ROBERTS, Miss Susan Emma. b 60. La Sainte Union Coll BTh93. St Steph Ho Ox DipMin94. **d** 96 **p** 97. C Petersfield *Portsm* 96-00; P-in-c Ashprington, Cornworthy and Dittisham *Ex* 00-04; TV Totnes w Bridgetown, Berry Pomeroy etc from 04; RD Totnes from 03. *The Rectory, Priory View, Cornworthy, Totnes TQ9 7HN* Tel (01803) 732384
E-mail sue.cornworthy@zoom.co.uk

ROBERTS, Sydney Neville Hayes. b 19. K Coll Lon 38. Cuddesdon Coll 45. **d** 47 **p** 48. C Aylesbury *Ox* 47-52; CF 52-69; R Theale w N Street *Ox* 69-76; R Theale and Englefield 76-85; rtd 85; Perm to Offic *Ox* from 89. *34 Stonebridge Road, Steventon, Abingdon OX13 6AU* Tel (01235) 834777

ROBERTS, Mrs Sylvia Ann. b 40. Stockwell Coll Lon TCert60. S Dios Minl Tr Scheme 81. **dss** 84 **d** 87 **p** 94. Crookhorn *Portsm* 84-88; Hon Par Dn Bedhampton 88-89; Par Dn Southampton (City Cen) *Win* 89-91; TD 91-94; TV 94-96; V Merton St Jo *S'wark* from 96; P-in-c Colliers Wood Ch Ch from 01. *St John's Vicarage, High Path, London SW19 2JY* Tel (020) 8542 3283

ROBERTS, Tegid. b 47. **d** 87 **p** 88. Lic to Offic *Ban* 87-93; NSM Llandinorwig w Penisa'r-waen 93-99; Lic to Offic 99-00; Dioc Officer for Children and Schs from 00; Min Can Ban Cathl 00-05; V Llandwrog and Llanwnda from 05. *Arwel, Llanrug, Caernarfon LL55 3BA* Tel (01286) 870760
E-mail tr@roberts485.freeserve.co.uk

ROBERTS, Terry Harvie. b 45. Sarum & Wells Th Coll 87. **d** 89 **p** 90. C Weymouth H Trin *Sarum* 89-93; TV Basingstoke *Win* 93-98; P-in-c Win St Barn from 98. *St Barnabas' Vicarage, Trussell Crescent, Winchester SO22 6DY* Tel and fax (01962) 882728 E-mail stbarnabas.winchester@ukgateway.net

ROBERTS, Canon Thomas Ewart. b 17. VRD65. Liv Univ BA41. St Aid Birkenhead 39. **d** 41 **p** 42. C Bowdon *Ches* 41-44; V Dunham Massey St Marg 47-52; Chapl RNVR 44-47 and 53-58; Chapl RNR 58-67; Ind Chapl *S'wark* 52-55; C-in-c Woolwich H Trin CD 52-55; Chapl R Arsenal Woolwich 52-55; PC Selsdon *Cant* 55-59; V Dover St Mary 59-71; RD Dover 59-71; Hon Can Cant Cathl 67-71 and 81-84; V Chesterfield St Mary and All SS *Derby* 71-75; V Tenterden St Mildred w Smallhythe *Cant* 75-82; RD W Charing 81-82; rtd 82; Asst Chapl Kent and Cant Hosp 82-91; Perm to Offic *Cant* from 84. *56 The Gateway, Dover CT16 1LQ* Tel (01304) 216311

ROBERTS, Tudor Vaughan. b 58. Newc Univ BA81. All Nations Chr Coll 91 Trin Coll Bris BA94. **d** 96 **p** 97. C Buckhurst Hill *Chelmsf* 96-99; TV Gt Baddow from 99. *124 Beehive Lane, Chelmsford CM2 9SH* Tel (01245) 269026
E-mail tudorandtricia@ezekiel124.fsnet.co.uk

ROBERTS, Tunde. *See* ROBERTS, Vincent Akintunde Tunde

ROBERTS, Vaughan Edward. b 65. Selw Coll Cam BA88 MA91. Wycliffe Hall Ox 89. **d** 91 **p** 92. C Ox St Ebbe w H Trin and St Pet *Ox* 91-95; Student Pastor 95-98; R from 98. *St Ebbe's Rectory, 2 Roger Bacon Lane, Oxford OX1 1QE* Tel (01865) 248154
E-mail vroberts@stebbes.org.uk

ROBERTS, Vaughan Simon. b 59. Univ of Wales (Ban) BA80 Bath Univ PhD99. McCormick Th Sem Chicago MA82 Westcott Ho Cam 83. **d** 85 **p** 86. C Bourne *Guildf* 85-89; Chapl Phyllis Tuckwell Hospice Farnham 88-89; Chapl Bath Univ *B & W* 89-96; NSM Bath Ch Ch Prop Chpl 90-96; P-in-c 92-96; P-in-c Chewton Mendip w Ston Easton, Litton etc 96-03; Dioc Voc Adv 96-99; Dir of Ords 99-03; TR Warwick *Cov* from 03. *St Mary's Vicarage, The Butts, Warwick CV34 4SS* Tel (01926) 492909 Fax as telephone
E-mail vaughan.roberts@btinternet.com

ROBERTS, Vincent Akintunde Tunde. b 55. Kingston Poly BA(Econ)81. S'wark Ord Course. **d** 91 **p** 92. Hon C Brixton Road Ch Ch *S'wark* 91-96; C Mitcham St Barn 96-99; P-in-c Stoke Newington St Olave *Lon* 99-03; V from 03. *St Olave's*

Vicarage, Woodberry Down, London N4 2TW Tel and fax (020) 8800 1374 E-mail tunde.roberts@talk21.com

ROBERTS, Vivian Phillip. b 35. Univ of Wales BD78. St D Coll Lamp 57. **d** 60 **p** 61. C Cwmaman *St D* 60-64; R Puncheston, Lt Newcastle and Castle Bythe 64-72; V Brynamman 72-77; V Brynaman w Cwmllynfell 77-83; V Pen-bre 83-00; rtd 00. *40 New Road, Llanelli SA15 3DR* Tel (01554) 755506

ROBERTS, Wallace Lionel. b 31. Univ of Wales (Lamp) BA58. St D Coll Lamp 55. **d** 59 **p** 60. C Astley Bridge *Man* 59-61; Asst Master Stand Gr Sch 61-66; Hon C Stand 61-66; Hon CF Aden 66-67; Lect Stockport Tech Coll 67-70; Hon C Heaton Moor *Man* 67-70; Chapl Qu Sch Rheindahlen 70-76; Hon CF 70-76; Swaziland 76-85; Chapl Oporto *Eur* 86-89; Chapl Hordle Ho Sch Milford-on-Sea 89-90; C Portishead *B & W* 91-96; rtd 96; Perm to Offic *B & W* from 96. *44 Hallett's Way, Portishead, Bristol BS20 6BT* Tel (01275) 817484

ROBERTS, William James (Jim). b 55. Hughes Hall Cam PGCE78. Lon Bible Coll BA77 NEOC 92. **d** 94 **p** 95. NSM York St Mich-le-Belfrey *York* from 94. *12 Bishop's Way, York YO10 5JG* Tel (01904) 413479

ROBERTS, Wynne. b 61. Univ of Wales (Ban) BTh92. Ridley Hall Cam 85. **d** 87 **p** 88. Min Can Ban Cathl and C Ban Cathl Par *Ban* 87-90; V Ynyscynhaearn w Penmorfa and Porthmadog 90-94; TV Bangor 94-04; Chapl NW Wales NHS Trust from 99. *North West Wales NHS Trust, Ysbyty Gwynedd, Penrhosgarnedd, Bangor LL57 2PW* Tel (01248) 384384 Fax 370629 E-mail wynne.roberts@nww-tr.wales.nhs.uk

ROBERTSHAW, John Sean. b 66. Cranmer Hall Dur 90. **d** 93 **p** 94. C Morley St Pet w Churwell *Wakef* 93-96; TV Upper Holme Valley 96-01; TR from 01; CF (TA) from 98. *The Vicarage, Kirkroyds Lane, New Mill, Holmfirth HD9 1LS* Tel and fax (01484) 683375 Mobile 07980-289727 E-mail vcar@dialstart.net

ROBERTSHAW, Jonothan Kempster Pickard Sykes. b 41. AKC65. **d** 66 **p** 67. C Perranzabuloe *Truro* 66-69; Miss to Seamen 69-76; Hong Kong 69-72; Namibia 73-76; TV Probus, Ladock and Grampound w Creed and St Erme *Truro* 76-79; TV N Hill w Altarnon, Bolventor and Lewannick 79-80; P-in-c Lansallos 80-84; R 84-96; P-in-c Talland 80-84; V 84-96; V Madron 96-01; P-in-c Gulval 99-01; V Gulval and Madron 01; rtd 01. *9 Redwood Drive, Aston-on-Clun, Craven Arms SY7 8EZ* Tel (01588) 660760

ROBERTSON, Agnes Muriel Hodgson. b 20. Edin Univ MA41. St And NSM Tr Scheme. **d** 91 **p** 94. NSM Lochgelly *St And* 91-92; Par Dn Glenrothes 92-94; NSM 94-98; NSM Leven 94-01; NSM St Andrews St Andr 94-01; NSM Lochgelly 94-01; rtd 98; P Cupar *St And* 01-04. *5 Bathgate Court, Cupar KY15 4LP* Tel (01334) 653543

ROBERTSON, Ms Beverley Ann. b 57. Qu Coll Birm 98. **d** 01 **p** 02. C Sutton Coldfield H Trin *Birm* from 01. *1 Trinity Hill, Sutton Coldfield B72 1TA* Tel 0121-354 4689 E-mail bev_robertson@yahoo.com

ROBERTSON, Brian Ainsley. b 50. Warwick Univ BSc72. St Jo Coll Nottm 94. **d** 94 **p** 95. C Leic Martyrs *Leic* 94-97; C Oadby 97-98; TV 98-02; P-in-c Ashby-de-la-Zouch St Helen w Coleorton 02-05; P-in-c Breedon cum Isley Walton and Worthington 03-05; TR Ashby-de-la-Zouch and Breedon on the Hill from 05. *The Rectory, 4 Upper Packington Road, Ashby-de-la-Zouch LE65 1EF* Tel (01530) 414404 E-mail b-robertson@sthelens-ashby.fsnet.co.uk

ROBERTSON, Charles Kevin. b 64. Virginia Poly & State Univ BA85 Dur Univ PhD99. Virginia Th Sem MDiv93. **d** 93 **p** 94. P-in-c USA 93-96; NSM Neville's Cross St Jo CD *Dur* 96-97; NSM Esh 97-99; R Milledgeville St Steph USA from 99. *Box 309, Milledgeville, GA 31059-0309, USA* E-mail rector@ststephensga.org

ROBERTSON, Charles Peter. b 57. Aston Tr Scheme 92 Linc Th Coll 94. **d** 96 **p** 97. C Holbeach *Linc* 96-99; C S Lafford 01-03; P-in-c from 03. *The Rectory, 16 West Street, Folkingham, Sleaford NG34 0SW* Tel (01529) 497617

ROBERTSON, David. *See* ROBERTSON, Thomas John

ROBERTSON, David John. b 54. Sheff Univ BA76. Ridley Hall Cam 77. **d** 79 **p** 80. C Downend *Bris* 79-83; C Yate New Town 83-85; TV 85-87; TV High Wycombe *Ox* 87-97; RD Wycombe 91-97; P-in-c Haley Hill *Wakef* 97-99; V Ovenden from 97. *St George's Vicarage, 2 Bracewell Drive, Wheatley, Halifax HX3 5BT* Tel (01422) 354153

ROBERTSON, Edward Macallan. b 28. Aber Univ MA49 Qu Coll Ox BLitt51. Coll of Resurr Mirfield 53. **d** 55 **p** 56. C Swindon New Town *Bris* 55-60; R Hawick *Edin* 60-69; R Alloa *St And* 70-73; Lic to Offic *Edin* 74-78; P-in-c Bathgate 78-82; P-in-c Linlithgow 78-82; Hon C Strathtay *St And* 82-90; P-in-c Auchterarder 90-93; P-in-c Muthill 90-93; rtd 93. *Coruisk, 65 Smithfield Crescent, Blairgowrie PH10 6UE* Tel (01250) 874427

ROBERTSON, Ernest Ian. b 22. Bede Coll Dur BA49. Wycliffe Hall Ox 49. **d** 51 **p** 52. C Jarrow St Paul *Dur* 51-54; C Sedgefield 54-56; V Eighton Banks 56-60; Chapl Shotley Bridge Gen Hosp 60-81; V Benfieldside *Dur* 60-87; Chapl HM Det Cen Medomsley 61-87; rtd 87. *10 Beddell House Residential Home, Durham DH1 2SE* Tel 0191-372 1992

ROBERTSON, Iain Michael. b 67. Trin Coll Bris 03. **d** 05. C E Clevedon w Clapton in Gordano etc *B & W* from 05. *33 Ash Grove, Clevedon BS21 7JZ* Tel (01275) 340346

ROBERTSON, Ian Hugh. b 44. Lanc Univ MA91 ARCM65 LGSM64 FRSA. St Mark's Dar-es-Salaam 80. **d** 83 **p** 83. SSF 73-82; Zimbabwe 83-87; TV Barrow St Geo w St Luke *Carl* 87-90; V Reigate St Mark *S'wark* 90-98; P-in-c Accrington St Jo w Huncoat *Blackb* 98-99; V from 99. *St John's Vicarage, 11 Queen's Road, Accrington BB5 6AR* Tel and fax (01254) 234587 E-mail ianrobertson@uwclub.net

ROBERTSON, James Alexander. b 46. Ox Univ MTh99. Sarum & Wells Th Coll 72. **d** 75 **p** 76. C Monkseaton St Pet *Newc* 75-78; C Prudhoe 78-79; TV Brayton *York* 79-84; V Redcar 84-93; V Selby Abbey 93-96; V Monkseaton St Pet *Newc* from 96; AD Tynemouth from 98. *St Peter's Vicarage, 6 Elmwood Road, Whitley Bay NE25 8EX* Tel and fax 0191-252 1991 E-mail jim.a.robertson@blueyonder.co.uk

ROBERTSON, James Macaulay. b 51. St Jo Coll Dur BA73. Oak Hill Th Coll. **d** 00 **p** 01. C Holdenhurst and Iford *Win* 00-04; V Marden *Cant* from 04. *The Vicarage, Haffenden Close, Marden, Tonbridge TN12 9DR* Tel (01622) 831379 E-mail robo@fish.co.uk

ROBERTSON, John Charles. b 61. St Pet Coll Ox BA81 Trin Coll Cam BA89. Ridley Hall Cam 87. **d** 90 **p** 91. C Kenilworth St Jo *Cov* 90-94; Chapl York Univ *York* 94-00; V Grove *Ox* from 00. *The Vicarage, Main Street, Grove, Wantage OX12 7LQ* Tel (01235) 766484 E-mail jroberts@fish.co.uk

ROBERTSON, Mrs Josephine Anne. b 51. CertEd72 Ch Ch Coll Cant BSc91. Dioc OLM tr scheme 99. **d** 02 **p** 03. OLM Folkestone H Trin w Ch Ch *Cant* from 02; Chapl Dover Coll 02-05. *100 Surrenden Road, Folkestone CT19 4AQ* Tel (01303) 277330 Mobile 07905-954504 E-mail jo.robertson@ntlworld.com

ROBERTSON, Kathryn. b 58. Leeds Univ BA05. N Ord Course 02. **d** 05. C Dewsbury *Wakef* from 05. *73A Chickenley Lane, Dewsbury WF12 8QD* Tel (01924) 260510

ROBERTSON, Mrs Linda Margaret. b 51. Somerville Coll Ox BA71 MA76 Aber Univ MSc72. STETS 00. **d** 03 **p** 04. NSM Hursley and Ampfield *Win* from 03. *35 Winnington, Fareham PO15 6HP* Tel (01329) 239857 E-mail revlindarob@yahoo.co.uk

ROBERTSON, Muriel. *See* ROBERTSON, Agnes Muriel Hodgson

ROBERTSON, Canon Paul Struan. b 45. St Jo Coll Dur BA73 Newc Univ Aus BEdSt79 MA95. **d** 72 **p** 73. C Chester le Street *Dur* 72-73; Australia 73-88 and from 89; C Hamilton 73-77; C Cessnock 77-79; R Scone 79-88; V Collierley w Annfield Plain *Dur* 88-89; R New Lambton from 89; AD Newc W from 96; Lect St Jo Coll Morpeth from 97; Can Newc Cathl from 01. *122 St James Road, PO Box 292, New Lambton, NSW, Australia 2305* Tel (0061) (2) 4957 1173 *or* 4952 2218 Fax 4957 1788 E-mail saints@idl.net.au

ROBERTSON, Mrs Priscilla Biddulph. b 25. St And Dioc Tr Course 87. **d** 90 **p** 94. C St Andrews St Andr *St And* from 90. *8 Balrymonth Court, St Andrews KY16 8XT* Tel (01334) 474976

ROBERTSON, Scott. b 64. Edin Univ BD90. Edin Th Coll 86. **d** 90 **p** 91. C Glas Gd Shep and Ascension *Glas* 90-92; P-in-c 92-97; P-in-c Ardrossan from 97; P-in-c Irvine St Andr LEP from 97; P-in-c Dalry from 97. *31 Milgarholm Avenue, Irvine KA12 0EL* Tel and fax (01294) 278341 Mobile 07703-709176 E-mail revscottrobertson@talk21.com

ROBERTSON, Stephen Andrew. b 60. Strathclyde Univ BSc82. Trin Coll Bris 92. **d** 92 **p** 93. C Vange *Chelmsf* 92-96; V Creeksea w Althorne, Latchingdon and N Fambridge from 96. *The Vicarage, Fambridge Road, Althorne, Chelmsford CM3 6BZ* Tel (01621) 740250 E-mail stephen.r@quista.net

ROBERTSON, Stuart Lang. b 40. Glas Univ MA63 Edin Univ MTh97. St Jo Coll Nottm 72. **d** 75 **p** 76. C Litherland St Jo and St Jas *Liv* 75-78; C Edin St Thos *Edin* 78-81; Chapl Edn Univ and C Edin St Pet 81-83; R Edin St Jas 83-91; Miss to Seamen 83-91; Crosslinks 91-05; Hon Chapl St Petersburg *Eur* 93-98; Chapl Warsaw 98-04; Asst Chapl Barcelona 04-05; rtd 05. *3 Pentland Villas, Juniper Green EH14 5EQ* Tel 0131-453 4755 E-mail jensinerob@yahoo.co.uk

ROBERTSON, Thomas John (David). b 15. Univ of Wales BA38 Lon Univ DipTh64 DipEd66. St Steph Ho Ox 38. **d** 40 **p** 41. C Welshpool *St As* 40-42; C Shotton 42-45; C Colwyn Bay 45-48; V Choral St As Cathl 48-49; R Newmarket 49-53; V Woolfold *Man* 53-57; V Bury St Thos 57-61; Hd of RE Bramhall Gr Sch 61-74; V Taddington and Chelmorton *Derby* 74-80; rtd 80; Perm to Offic *Derby* 80-87; *Ches* and *Man* 80-95; *S'wark* 95-03; *Roch* 01-03. *The Coach House, Halstead Hall, Halstead, Sevenoaks TN14 7DH*

ROBIN, John Bryan Carteret. b 22. Trin Coll Ox BA48 MA55. Cuddesdon Coll 49. **d** 77 **p** 78. Chapl Rishworth Sch Ripponden 76-81; Australia from 82; Chapl Geelong Gr Sch 82-84; P-in-c

Queenscliff St Geo 86-94; rtd 94. *8 Heron Court, Point Lonsdale, Vic, Australia 3225* Tel (0061) (3) 5258 4432

ROBIN, Peter Philip King. b 23. Trin Coll Cam BA48 MA81. Cuddesdon Coll 49. **d** 51 **p** 52. C Bethnal Green St Matt *Lon* 51-54; Papua New Guinea 54-75; R Elsing w Bylaugh *Nor* 76-85; R Lyng w Sparham 76-85; P-in-c Holme Cultram St Mary *Carl* 85-88; rtd 88; Perm to Offic *Carl* 88-99 and from 02. *191 Brampton Road, Carlisle CA3 9AX* Tel (01228) 545293

ROBINS, Christopher Charles. b 41. St Mich Coll Llan 66. **d** 68 **p** 69. C Bideford *Ex* 68-71; C Dawlish 71-74; V Laira 74-81; P-in-c Dodbrooke 81-83; P-in-c Churchstow w Kingsbridge 81-83; R Kingsbridge and Dodbrooke from 83. *The Rectory, Church Street, Kingsbridge TQ7 1NW* Tel (01548) 856231

ROBINS, Douglas Geoffrey. b 45. Open Univ BA90. Ex & Truro NSM Scheme. **d** 81 **p** 83. NSM Kenwyn *Truro* 81-84; Public Preacher 84-00; NSM Truro St Paul and St Clem 00-04; P-in-c Gerrans w St Anthony-in-Roseland and Philleigh from 04. *The Rectory, The Square, Gerrans, Portscatho, Truro TR2 5GA* Tel (01872) 580277

ROBINS, Ian Donald Hall. b 28. K Coll Lon BD51 AKC51 Lanc Univ MA74. **d** 52 **p** 53. C St Annes St Thos *Blackb* 52-55; C Clitheroe St Mary 55-57; V Trawden 57-67; Hd of RE St Chris C of E Sch Accrington 67-76; P-in-c Hugill *Carl* 76-82; Asst Adv for Educn 76-82; Chapl St Martin's Coll of Educn *Blackb* 82-86; V St Annes St Marg 86-91; rtd 91; Perm to Offic *Blackb* from 91. *20 Painter Wood, Billington, Blackburn BB7 9JD* Tel (01254) 824930

ROBINS, Mrs Mary Katherine. b 34. FRGS Bris Univ BSc55 CertEd56. St Alb Minl Tr Scheme. **dss** 84 **d** 87 **p** 94. N Mymms *St Alb* 84-92; Hon Par Dn 87-92; NSM Northaw 92-95; Hon C Westmr St Jas *Lon* 95-00; Perm to Offic *St Alb* from 95. *15 Bluebridge Road, Brookmans Park, Hatfield AL9 7UW* Tel (01707) 656670 E-mail maryrob@eclipse.co.uk

ROBINS, Terrence Leslie. b 38. Kingston Poly 56 CEng67 FIMechE78. N Ord Course 99. **d** 00 **p** 01. Bp's Adv for Elderly People in Res Care *Wakef* from 98; Hon C Cumberworth, Denby and Denby Dale 00-03; P-in-c from 03. *Cruck Cottage, Cumberworth Lane, Denby Dale, Huddersfield HD8 8RU* Tel and fax (01484) 866000 E-mail robinslt@aol.com

ROBINS, Ms Wendy Sheridan. b 56. Lanc Univ BA77. EAMTC 93. **d** 93 **p** 94. Dir of Communications and Resources *S'wark* from 92; NSM Walthamstow St Pet *Chelmsf* from 93; Hon C S'wark Cathl *S'wark* from 02. *17 Hillcrest Road, London E17 4AP,* or *Trinity House, 4 Chapel Court, Borough High Street, London SE1 1HW* Tel (020) 8523 0016 *or* 7403 8686 Fax 7403 4770 E-mail wendy.s.robins@southwark.anglican.org

ROBINSON, Alan Booker. b 27. Keble Coll Ox BA51 MA56. Sarum Th Coll 51. **d** 53 **p** 54. C Leeds All So *Ripon* 53-56; C Ilkley St Marg *Bradf* 57-59; V Carlton *Wakef* 59-66; OCF 66-92; V Hooe *Ex* 66-95; RD Plympton 81-83; RD Plymouth Sutton 86-91; rtd 95; Perm to Offic *Ripon* from 95. *1 Charlton Court, Knaresborough HG5 0BZ* Tel (01423) 860884 E-mail robalb@beeb.net

ROBINSON, Albert. b 15. Roch Th Coll 60. **d** 61 **p** 62. C Limpsfield and Titsey *S'wark* 61-64; R Grimston w Congham *Nor* 64-73; P-in-c Roydon All SS 64-73; V Gt w Lt Plumstead 73-81; rtd 81; Perm to Offic *Glouc* 81-91. *63 Marleyfield Way, Churchdown, Gloucester GL3 1JW* Tel (01452) 855178

ROBINSON, Alison Jane. b 55. WEMTC 99. **d** 02 **p** 03. C Bishop's Cleeve *Glouc* from 02. *2A Orchard Road, Bishops Cleeve, Cheltenham GL52 8LX* Tel (01242) 675471 Mobile 07773-721238 E-mail alisonjane.robinson@btinternet.com

ROBINSON, Andrew David. b 61. St Cath Coll Ox BA84 MA01 RMN89. Trin Coll Bris 97. **d** 02. C Southmead *Bris* 02-03; C Kington St Michael and Chippenham St Paul w Hardenhuish etc 03-04; NSM Barlby w Riccall *York* from 05. *13 The Crescent, Riccall, York YO19 6PL* Tel (01757) 249248 E-mail room_2_live@yahoo.co.uk

ROBINSON, Canon Andrew Nesbitt. b 43. AKC67. **d** 68 **p** 69. C Balsall Heath St Paul *Birm* 68-71; C Westmr St Steph w St Jo *Lon* 71-75; Chapl Sussex Univ *Chich* from 75; Chapl Brighton Poly 75-92; Chapl Brighton Univ 92-93; P-in-c Stanmer w Falmer from 80; Can and Preb Chich Cathl from 98. *St Laurence House, Park Street, Brighton BN1 9PG* Tel (01273) 606928 *or* 606755

ROBINSON, Andrew Stephen. b 49. Lanc Univ BA71 Worc Coll of Educn PGCE72 Glam Univ Dip Educn Mgt 82. St Mich Coll Llan 90. **d** 95 **p** 96. NSM Llangattock and Llangyndir *S & B* 95-04; P-in-c Llanfeugan w Llanthetty etc from 04. *17 Pencommin, Llangynidr, Crickhowell NP8 1LT* Tel (01874) 730034

✠**ROBINSON, The Rt Revd Anthony William.** b 56. CertEd. Sarum & Wells Th Coll. **d** 82 **p** 83 **c** 02. C Tottenham St Paul *Lon* 82-85; TV Leic Resurr *Leic* 85-89; TR 89-97; RD Christianity N 92-97; P-in-c Belgrave St Pet 94-95; Hon Can Leic Cathl 94-97; Adn Pontefract *Wakef* 97-03; Suff Bp Pontefract from 02; Can Res Wakef Cathl from 05. *Pontefract House, 181A Manygates Lane, Sandal, Wakefield WF2 7DR* Tel (01924) 250781 Fax 240490 E-mail bishop.pontefract@wakefield.anglican.org

ROBINSON, Arthur Robert Basil. b 32. ACP67 St Jo Coll Dur BA56 Bradf Univ MA84. Wycliffe Hall Ox 56. **d** 58 **p** 59. C Pemberton St Mark Newtown *Liv* 58-62; CF 62-65; Asst Master Colne Valley High Sch Linthwaite 65-69; Asst Chapl HM Pris Man 69; Chapl HM Borstal Roch 69-74; Peru 74-77; V Golcar *Wakef* 77-83; Admin Sheff Fam Conciliation Service 84-91; Warden St Sampson's Cen York 91-00; rtd 00. *Morangie, 2A Brecksfield, Skelton, York YO30 1YD* Tel (01904) 470558

ROBINSON, Arthur William. b 35. Dur Univ BSc60. Clifton Th Coll 60. **d** 62 **p** 63. C Ox St Clem *Ox* 62-65; Chile 65-77; V Hoxton St Jo w Ch Ch *Lon* 78-88; TV Gateacre *Liv* 88-00; rtd 00; Perm to Offic *Liv* from 00. *86 Kingsthorne Park, Liverpool L25 0QS* Tel 0151-486 2588 E-mail arthelrob@aol.com

ROBINSON, Brian John Watson. b 33. St Cath Coll Cam BA56 MA60. Westcott Ho Cam 57. **d** 58 **p** 59. C Whitworth w Spennymoor *Dur* 58-62; India 62-66; P-in-c Preston St Steph *Blackb* 66-72; V Ashton-on-Ribble St Andr 72-79; Lic to Offic 79-82; V Preston St Jude w St Paul 82-97; Chapl N Tyneside Health Care NHS Trust 94-97; rtd 97; Perm to Offic *Blackb* from 97. *50 Green Acres, Fulwood, Preston PR2 7DB* Tel (01772) 861516

ROBINSON, Canon Bryan. b 32. Fitzw Ho Cam BA56. Ely Th Coll 56. **d** 58 **p** 59. C Fleetwood St Pet *Blackb* 58-65; V Burnley St Andr 65-74; V Burnley St Marg 65-74; V Burnley St Andr w St Marg 74-97; RD Burnley 85-91; P-in-c Burnley St Jas 92-97; Hon Can Blackb Cathl 94-97; rtd 97; Perm to Offic *Blackb* from 97. *50 Fountains Avenue, Simonstone, Burnley BB12 7PY* Tel (01282) 776518

ROBINSON, Mrs Christine. b 50. Nottm Univ BA71. EAMTC 01. **d** 04 **p** 05. NSM Prittlewell w Westcliff *Chelmsf* from 04. *Pasadena, St John's Road, Benfleet SS7 2PT* Tel (01702) 557000 E-mail chris.peterbryanco@btinternet.com

ROBINSON, Christopher Gordon. b 49. Ridley Hall Cam. **d** 82 **p** 83. C Stanton *St E* 82-85; C Lawshall 85-86; P-in-c Lawshall w Shimplingthorne and Alpheton 86-89; TV Oakdale *Sarum* 89-99; V Easton H Trin w St Gabr and St Lawr and St Jude *Bris* 99-05; C S Molton w Nymet St George, High Bray etc *Ex* from 05. *The Rectory, Parsonage Lane, South Molton EX36 3AX* Tel (01769) 572411

ROBINSON, Christopher James. b 52. St Pet Coll Birm CertEd74. OLM course 97. **d** 99 **p** 00. OLM Wilnecote *Lich* from 99. *55 Sycamore, Wilnecote, Tamworth B77 5HB* Tel (01827) 282331 E-mail chrisrobinson5@compuserve.com

ROBINSON, Daffyd Charles. b 48. Qu Coll Birm 77. **d** 80 **p** 85. C Abington *Pet* 80-82; C Immingham *Linc* 85-90; R Willoughby from 90. *The Rectory, Station Road, Willoughby, Alford LN13 9NA* Tel and fax (01507) 462045 E-mail rector@willoughby-lincs.org.uk

ROBINSON, Mrs Danielle Georgette Odette. b 47. SEITE 98. **d** 01 **p** 02. NSM Reigate St Mary *S'wark* from 01; Chapl Surrey and Sussex Healthcare NHS Trust from 01; Perm to Offic *Chich* from 01. *10 Doran Gardens, Doran Drive, Redhill RH1 6AY* Tel (01737) 772380

ROBINSON, David. b 42. Sarum & Wells Th Coll. **d** 82 **p** 83. C Billingham St Cuth *Dur* 82-86; V Longwood *Wakef* 86-94; C Athersley 94-97; P-in-c Brotherton 97-02; rtd 02; Perm to Offic *York* from 03. *The Vicarage, Market Weighton Road, Holme-on-Spalding-Moor, York YO43 4AG* Tel (01430) 860379

ROBINSON, Canon David Hugh. b 47. Linc Th Coll 76. **d** 79 **p** 80. C Bulkington *Cov* 79-82; P-in-c Whitley 82-87; Chapl Walsgrave Hosp Cov 87-94; Chapl Walsgrave Hosps NHS Trust 94-97; Hon Can Cov Cathl *Cov* 92-98; Perm to Offic 98-01; Succ Cov Cathl from 01. *95 Potters Green Road, Coventry CV2 2AN* Tel (024) 7662 2683 E-mail david.robinson@coventrycathedral.org.uk

ROBINSON, David Mark. b 55. Univ Coll Dur BSc76 Leic Univ MA80 CQSW80. Cranmer Hall Dur 86. **d** 88 **p** 89. C Shipley St Pet *Bradf* 88-92; P-in-c Ingrow cum Hainworth 92-97; V Bramhope *Ripon* from 97. *The Vicarage, 26 Leeds Road, Bramhope, Leeds LS16 9BQ* Tel 0113-284 2543 E-mail stgiles@onetel.com

ROBINSON, David Michael Wood. b 28. Glas Univ BSc50 Lon Univ BD54. **d** 57 **p** 57. C Erith St Jo *Roch* 57-58; Japan 58-71; R Holton and Waterperry *Ox* 71-88; RD Aston and Cuddesdon 88-92; R Holton and Waterperry w Albury and Waterstock 88-94; Chapl Ox Poly 90-92; Chapl Ox Brookes Univ 92-94; rtd 94. *72 Divinity Road, Oxford OX4 1LJ* Tel (01865) 245466

ROBINSON, Capt Denis Hugh. b 53. SS Mark & Jo Coll Plymouth CertEd75. Sarum & Wells Th Coll 88. **d** 91 **p** 92. NSM Bisley and W End *Guildf* from 91; Asst Chapl Gordon's Sch Woking 91-94; Chapl from 94. *40 Malthouse Lane, West End, Woking GU24 9JE* Tel (01276) 857624 E-mail steviedenrob@aol.com

ROBINSON, Dennis Winston. b 42. QUB BScEng68. CITC. **d** 88 **p** 89. NSM Mullavilly *Arm* 88-92; NSM Arm St Mark 92-95; C Portadown St Mark 95-98; I Aghavea *Clogh* from 98. *The Rectory, Brookeborough, Enniskillen BT94 4EE* Tel (028) 8953 1210 E-mail dw.robinson@btopenworld.com

ROBINSON, Derek Charles. b 43. S'wark Ord Course 91. **d** 94 **p** 95. NSM Abbey Wood *S'wark* from 94. *19 Silverdale Road, Bexleyheath DA7 5AB* Tel (01322) 523870

ROBINSON, Douglas. b 48. Nottm Univ BEd70 Lon Univ BD74 Union Th Sem Virginia MA75. **d** 75 **p** 76. C Southport Ch Ch *Liv* 75-78; V Clubmoor 78-85; Chapl Epsom Coll 85-88; Chapl Dauntsey's Sch Devizes 89-95; Perm to Offic *Eur* from 95. *Im Grünen Weg 1, Hangen Wiesheim 55234, Germany* Tel (0049) (6375) 941575 E-mail reverendrobinson@t-online.de

ROBINSON, Elizabeth Carole Lesley. b 67. CITC 99. **d** 02 **p** 03. NSM Clonfert Gp *L & K* from 02. *Camelot, Lusmagh, Banagher, Co Offaly, Irish Republic* Tel and fax (00353) (509) 51598 Mobile 87-909 1561 E-mail kandlrobinson@eircom.net

ROBINSON, Eric Charles. b 47. Lon Univ BD71 Lanc Univ MA97. Carl and Blackb Dioc Tr Inst 94. **d** 97 **p** 98. NSM Carl St Cuth w St Mary *Carl* 97-99; C Kendal H Trin 99-01; P-in-c Arthuret from 01; P-in-c Nicholforest and Kirkandrews on Esk from 01. *Arthuret Rectory, Arthuret Drive, Longtown, Carlisle CA6 5SG* Tel (01228) 791338

ROBINSON, Frank. *See* ROBINSON, John Francis Napier

ROBINSON, George. b 27. HNC59. Oak Hill Th Coll 59. **d** 61 **p** 62. C Branksome St Clem *Sarum* 61-64; Australia from 64; rtd 80. *24 Abingdon Road, Roseville, NSW, Australia 2069* Tel (0061) (2) 9416 4330 Fax 9416 9936
E-mail mandgrobinson@ozemail.com.au

ROBINSON, Mrs Gillian Dawn. b 69. Edin Univ BD91. Trin Coll Bris 94. **d** 96 **p** 97. C Totton *Win* 96-00; P-in-c Roughtown *Man* from 00. *St John's Vicarage, Carrhill Road, Mossley, Ashton under Lyne OL5 0BL* Tel (01457) 836139
E-mail gill@robinson.camnews.net

ROBINSON, Mrs Hazel. b 61. RGN83 RSCN83. St Jo Coll Nottm 02. **d** 04 **p** 05. C Toton *S'well* from 04. *29 Johnson Way, Chilwell, Nottingham NG9 6RJ* Tel 0115-973 1535 Mobile 07944-440941

ROBINSON, Ian. b 57. Nottm Univ BTh87 MA97. Linc Th Coll 84. **d** 87 **p** 88. C Bottesford w Ashby *Linc* 87-90; TV 90-95; P-in-c Caistor w Clixby 95-00; P-in-c Grasby 95-00; P-in-c Searby w Owmby 95-00; V Caistor Gp from 00; RD W Wold from 01. *The Vicarage, 1 Cromwell View, Caistor, Lincoln LN7 6UH* Tel (01472) 851339 E-mail ianrobinson5@compuserve.com

ROBINSON, Ian Cameron. b 19. OBE72. Em Coll Cam BA40 MA44. Linc Th Coll 71. **d** 72 **p** 73. C Ipswich St Aug *St E* 72-74; V Darsham 74-84; V Westleton w Dunwich 74-84; RD Saxmundham 79-83; rtd 84; Perm to Offic *St E* 84-03. *Corner House, Rectory Street, Halesworth IP19 8BS* Tel (01986) 873573

ROBINSON, Mrs Jane Hippisley. b 41. Somerville Coll Ox MA66 K Coll Lon PGCE. S Dios Minl Tr Scheme 88. **d** 91. NSM Ealing St Pet Mt Park *Lon* 91-96; NSM N Acton St Gabr 96-00; Perm to Offic from 00. *60 Madeley Road, London W5 2LU* Tel (020) 8991 0206
E-mail rogerrobinson@madeley.freeserve.co.uk

ROBINSON, Mrs Janet. b 34. Milton Keynes Coll of Ed CertEd77 Open Univ BA78. WMMTC 89. **d** 92 **p** 94. NSM Roade and Ashton w Hartwell *Pet* 92-94; NSM Potterspury, Furtho, Yardley Gobion and Cosgrove 94-99; rtd 99; Perm to Offic *Pet* from 99. *73 Eastfield Crescent, Yardley Gobion, Towcester NN12 7TT* Tel (01908) 542331

ROBINSON, Mrs Jean Anne. b 50. Lon Univ BPharm72 MRPharmS73 Southn Univ BTh98. STETS 95. **d** 98 **p** 99. NSM Frimley *Guildf* 98-03; NSM Worplesdon from 03; Chapl Ashford and St Pet Hosp NHS Trust from 04. *4 Chequer Tree Close, Knaphill, Woking GU21 2PB* Tel (01483) 481825
E-mail jean@knaphill21.fsnet.co.uk

ROBINSON, Jennifer Elizabeth. b 53. Sheff Hallam Univ BA96. N Ord Course 01. **d** 04. NSM Fishlake w Sykehouse and Kirk Bramwith etc *Sheff* from 04. *The Fold, 5 Old School Close, Armthorpe, Doncaster DN3 2SA* Tel (01302) 830087
E-mail jenny@ardyne.freeserve.co.uk

ROBINSON, John Francis Napier (Frank). b 42. St Edm Hall Ox BA64 MA68 Lon Univ DipTh68. Clifton Th Coll 65. **d** 68 **p** 69. C Southport Ch Ch *Liv* 68-71; C Coleraine *Conn* 71-74; Deputation Sec (Ireland) BCMS 74-76; TV Marfleet *York* 76-81; V Yeadon St Jo *Bradf* 81-95; P-in-c Rounds Green *Birm* 95-00; V 00-02; rtd 02; Perm to Offic *S'well* from 03. *61 Clumber Avenue, Beeston, Nottingham NG9 4BH* Tel 0115-922 1704

ROBINSON, The Very Revd John Kenneth. b 36. K Coll Lon BD61 AKC61. **d** 62 **p** 63. C Poulton-le-Fylde *Blackb* 62-65; C Lancaster St Mary 65-66; Chapl HM Pris Lanc 65-66; Chapl St Jo Sch Singapore 66-68; V Colne H Trin *Blackb* 68-71; Dir Educn Windward Is 71-74; V Skerton St Luke *Blackb* 74-81; Area Sec (E Anglia) USPG 81-91; Hon Min Can St E Cathl *St E* 82-91; Chapl Gtr Lisbon *Eur* 91-00; Adn Gib 94-02; Can Gib Cathl 94-00; Dean Gib 00-03; rtd 03. *9 Poplar Drive, Coppull, Chorley PR7 4LS* Tel (01257) 470042

ROBINSON, John Leonard William. b 23. Lon Univ BA50. Bps' Coll Cheshunt 50. **d** 52 **p** 53. C Victoria Docks Ascension *Chelmsf* 52-55; C Kilburn St Aug *Lon* 55-63; C Westmr St Jas 63-81; V Compton, the Mardens, Stoughton and Racton *Chich* 81-93; V Stansted 85-93; rtd 93; Perm to Offic *St Alb* from 93 and *Lon* from 96. *19 Greenhill Park, Barnet EN5 1HQ* Tel (020) 8449 3984

ROBINSON, Jonathan William Murrell. b 42. Univ of Wales (Lamp) MA01. Sarum Th Coll 65. **d** 68 **p** 69. C Tooting All SS *S'wark* 68-71; C Bourne *Guildf* 71-76; Dir Grail Trust from 76; Dir Grail Trust Chr Community Cen Burtle *B & W* 78-82; Hon C Willesden Green St Gabr *Lon* 78-82; V Stoke St Gregory w Burrowbridge and Lyng *B & W* 82-90; Dir Grail Retreat Cen from 90; NSM Aymestrey and Leinthall Earles w Wigmore etc *Heref* 92-96; rtd 01; Perm to Offic *Heref* from 01. *The Liberty, Arthurs Gate, Montgomery SY15 6QU* Tel and fax (01686) 668502

ROBINSON, Kathryn Elizabeth. b 55. Hull Univ BA76 K Coll Lon MSc86 St Hilda's Coll Ox PGCE77. NTMTC 03. **d** 05. NSM Leytonstone St Jo *Chelmsf* from 05. *54 Corbett Road, London E17 3JZ* Tel (020) 8503 6023
E-mail kthryrbnsn@aol.com

ROBINSON, Keith. b 48. Lon Univ BA75 BD77 AKC77. Westcott Ho Cam 77. **d** 78 **p** 79. C Bow w Bromley St Leon *Lon* 78-81; C Leighton Buzzard w Eggington, Hockliffe etc *St Alb* 81-88; PV Westmr Abbey 82-90; V Bulkington w Shilton and Ansty *Cov* 88-95; P-in-c Salisbury St Martin *Sarum* 95-00; P-in-c Laverstock 95-00; R Salisbury St Martin and Laverstock from 00; RD Salisbury 98-03. *The Rectory, Tollgate Road, Salisbury SP1 2JJ* Tel (01722) 504813 *or* tel and fax 503123
E-mail frkeithssm@yahoo.co.uk

ROBINSON, Kenneth. *See* ROBINSON, The Very Revd John Kenneth

ROBINSON, Kenneth Borwell. b 37. Lon Univ BA62. Ridley Hall Cam 68. **d** 70 **p** 71. C Walthamstow St Jo *Chelmsf* 70-74; P-in-c Becontree St Alb 74-78; P-in-c Heybridge w Langford 78-84; TV Horley *S'wark* 84-98; C Oxted and Tandridge 98-02; rtd 02; Perm to Offic *Portsm* from 03. *49 Osborne Road, East Cowes PO32 6RZ* Tel (01983) 295736

ROBINSON, Lesley. *See* ROBINSON, Elizabeth Carole Lesley

ROBINSON, Leslie. b 31. St Aid Birkenhead 56. **d** 59 **p** 60. C Hugglescote w Donington *Leic* 59-61; C Greenside *Dur* 61-63; C-in-c New Cantley CD *Sheff* 63-66; V Choral Heref Cathl *Heref* 66-67; R Easton-on-the-Hill *Pet* 67-69; Hon Min Can Pet Cathl 68-69; C Weston-super-Mare St Jo *B & W* 69-70; V Winkleigh *Ex* 70-72; V Thorpe Acre w Dishley *Leic* 72-78; V Cloughton *York* 78-79; V Hedon w Paull 79-81; V Bywell *Newc* 81-86; V Wymeswold and Prestwold w Hoton *Leic* 86-97; rtd 97; Perm to Offic *Leic* 97-98. *19 Ambleside Close, Loughborough LE11 3SH* Tel (01509) 263790

ROBINSON, Miss Margaret. b 32. S'wark Ord Course 83. **dss** 86 **d** 87 **p** 94. Finsbury St Clem w St Barn and St Matt *Lon* 86-87; Par Dn St Giles Cripplegate w St Bart Moor Lane etc 87-94; C 94-95; rtd 95; Perm to Offic *Win* 95-00; Hon Chapl Win Cathl 98-00. *10 Barnfield Road, Petersfield GU31 4DQ* Tel (01730) 268056

ROBINSON, Michael John. b 45. Nottm Univ BA66. Linc Th Coll 78. **d** 79 **p** 80. C Aston cum Aughton *Sheff* 79-80; C Rotherham 80-82; TV Howden *York* 82-86; V Heywood St Jas *Man* 86-92; V Astley 92; R Blackley St Paul 92-97; V Hale and Ashley *Ches* from 97. *St Peter's Vicarage, 1 Harrop Road, Hale, Altrincham WA15 9BU* Tel 0161-928 4182 Fax 928 9702

ROBINSON, Monica Dorothy. b 40. St Alb and Ox Min Course 99. **d** 01 **p** 02. NSM Bedford St Andr *St Alb* from 01. *Shoyswell, Radwell Road, Milton Ernest, Bedford MK44 1RY* Tel (01234) 824366 E-mail mdrobinson@btopenworld.com

ROBINSON, The Ven Neil. b 29. St Jo Coll Dur BA52 DipTh54. **d** 54 **p** 55. C Kingston upon Hull H Trin *York* 54-58; V Glen Parva and S Wigston *Leic* 58-68; Hon Can Leic Cathl 68-83; RD Sparkenhoe I 69-83; R Market Bosworth w Shenton 69-83; Can Res Worc Cathl *Worc* 83-87; Adn Suffolk *St E* 87-94; rtd 94; Perm to Offic *Ripon* from 94. *16 Mallorie Court, Ripon HG4 2QG* Tel (01765) 603075

ROBINSON, Norman Leslie. b 50. Liv Univ BSc71. Lon Bible Coll BA78 Wycliffe Hall Ox 78. **d** 80 **p** 81. C Bebington *Ches* 80-83; C St Helens St Helen *Liv* 83-90; P-in-c Westward, Rosley-w-Woodside and Welton *Carl* from 90; P-in-c Thursby from 98. *The Vicarage, Rosley, Wigton CA7 8AU* Tel (01697) 343723
E-mail normalrevs@aol.com

ROBINSON, Canon Paul Leslie. b 46. Dur Univ BA67 Nottm Univ DipTh73. Linc Th Coll 71. **d** 74 **p** 75. C Poynton *Ches* 74-76; C Prenton 76-78; V Seacombe 78-88; V Stalybridge St Paul 88-00; P-in-c Wallasey St Hilary 00-04; R from 04; Urban Min Officer from 96; Hon Can Ches Cathl from 98. *St Hilary's Rectory, Church Hill, Wallasey CH45 3NH* Tel 0151-638 4771 E-mail paul@revrobinson.fsnet.co.uk

ROBINSON, Paul Leslie. b 65. St Steph Ho Ox 95. **d** 97 **p** 98. C Upholland *Liv* 97-01; V Lydiate and Downholland from 01; P-in-c Halsall from 04. *The Vicarage, Church Lane, Lydiate, Liverpool L31 4HL* Tel 0151-526 0512
E-mail frpaul.robinson@btopenworld.com

ROBINSON, Peter Charles. b 53. Open Univ BA83. Oak Hill Th Coll 85. **d** 87 **p** 88. C Nottingham St Ann w Em *S'well* 87-89; C Worksop St Anne 89-92; V S Ramsey St Paul *S & M* 92-99; Can

St German's Cathl 98-99; P-in-c Goostrey and Dioc Dir of Ords *Ches* 99-03; P-in-c Aldeburgh w Hazlewood *St E* 03-04. *Flat 1, 45 The Thoroughfare, Woodbridge IP12 1AH* Tel (01394) 383804 Mobile 07941-202524 E-mail pcrwoodbridge@aol.com

ROBINSON, Peter Edward Barron. b 40. Open Univ BSc99. Sarum & Wells Th Coll 76. **d** 78 **p** 79. C Petersfield w Sheet *Portsm* 78-82; R Bentworth and Shalden and Lasham *Win* 82-88; R W Horsley *Guildf* 88-00; rtd 00; Perm to Offic *B & W* from 01. *Byways, Kingstone, Ilminster TA19 0NT* Tel (01460) 259016 E-mail peb.robinson@ntlworld.com

ROBINSON, Peter John Alan. b 61. St Jo Coll Cam BA83 MA87. St Jo Coll Dur BA92 PhD97. **d** 95 **p** 96. C N Shields *Newc* 95-99; P-in-c Byker St Martin from 99; P-in-c Byker St Mich w St Lawr from 01. *St Martin's Vicarage, 152 Roman Avenue, Newcastle upon Tyne NE6 2RJ* Tel 0191-265 5931 E-mail pjarobison@lineone.net

ROBINSON, Peter McCall. b 24. Worc Coll Ox BA48 MA50. Wells Th Coll 48. **d** 50 **p** 51. S Africa 50-54; C Stoke Poges *Ox* 55-57; S Africa 57-71; V Payhembury *Ex* 71-79; R Cheriton w Tichborne and Beauworth *Win* 79-81; S Africa 81-82; V Marystowe, Coryton, Stowford, Lewtrenchard etc *Ex* 82-85; V Blackawton and Stoke Fleming 85-88; rtd 88; Perm to Offic *Ex* from 89. *2 Langwells Court, Blackawton, Totnes TQ9 7BG* Tel (01803) 712827

ROBINSON, Philip. b 38. S Dios Minl Tr Scheme 88. **d** 91 **p** 92. NSM Ickenham *Lon* 91-95; P-in-c 95-04; P-in-c Hayes St Anselm 98-99; P-in-c Harlington 98-00; AD Hillingdon 97-03; rtd 04; Perm to Offic *Lon* and *Eur* from 04. *5 Preston Court, 4 Fairfield Road, Uxbridge UB8 1DQ* Tel 07956-570176 (mobile) *or* (0033) (4) 93 76 88 71 E-mail philip@stjean.fslife.co.uk

ROBINSON, Raymonde Robin. b 43. St Jo Coll Dur BA66. Chich Th Coll 67. **d** 70 **p** 71. C Ealing St Barn *Lon* 70-72; C Pinner 72-75; C Clerkenwell H Redeemer w St Phil 75-80; TV Kingsthorpe w Northampton St Dav *Pet* 80-89; R Letchworth *St Alb* 89-95; V Noel Park St Mark *Lon* from 95. *St Mark's Vicarage, Ashley Crescent, London N22 6LJ* Tel (020) 8888 3442

ROBINSON, Richard Hugh. b 35. St Jo Coll Cam BA58 MA62. Ridley Hall Cam 58. **d** 60 **p** 81. C Cheadle Hulme St Andr *Ches* 60-62; Hon C Alvanley 62-64; Perm to Offic *York* 64-80; Hon C Elloughton and Brough w Brantingham 80-86; C 86-87; Ext Dir CMJ 87-88; NSM Appleby *Carl* 91-93; Perm to Offic *Carl* and *York* 93-98; *Ely* from 01; rtd 00. *26 Paradise Street, Cambridge CB1 1DR* Tel (01223) 328833 Fax 328838

ROBINSON, Canon Roger George. b 24. Qu Coll Cam BA46 MA50. Ridley Hall Cam 46. **d** 48 **p** 49. C Gorleston St Andr *Nor* 48-51; C Drypool St Andr and St Pet *York* 51-54; P-in-c Kingston upon Hull St Aid Southcoates 54-55; V 55-60; V Clifton 60-70; Chapl Clifton Hosp York 61-70; V Far Headingley St Chad *Ripon* 70-81; RD Headingley 72-81; Hon Can Ripon Cathl 81; Perm to Offic from 81; R Drayton w Felthorpe *Nor* 81-91; rtd 91. *24 St Matthew's Walk, Leeds LS7 3PS* Tel 0113-269 6307

ROBINSON, Ronald Frederick. b 46. Brasted Place Coll 72. Oak Hill Th Coll 74. **d** 76 **p** 77. C Pennington *Man* 76-77; C Bedhampton *Portsm* 77-79; C Portsea N End St Mark 79-82; V 90-92; R Rowner 82-90; Perm to Offic *Portsm* 93-02; P-in-c Bury and Houghton *Chich* 96-97; P-in-c Coldwaltham and Hardham 96-97; P-in-c Bury w Houghton and Coldwaltham and Hardham 97-98; V 98; Past Sec Ch Union 98-02; P-in-c Portsea Ascension *Portsm* from 02. *The Vicarage, 98 Kirby Road, Portsmouth PO2 0PW* Tel (023) 9266 0123 Fax 9266 7499 E-mail fr.robinson@talk21.com

ROBINSON, Roy David. b 35. AKC59. **d** 60 **p** 61. C Acocks Green *Birm* 60-62; C Shirley 62-65; C Haslemere *Guildf* 65-70; R Headley w Box Hill 70-85; V Hinchley Wood 85-00; rtd 00; Perm to Offic *Guildf* from 02. *1 Park Road, Slinfold, Horsham RH13 0SD* Tel (01403) 791640

ROBINSON, Prof Simon John. b 51. Edin Univ MA72 PhD89 Ox Univ BA77. Wycliffe Hall Ox 75. **d** 78 **p** 79. C Haughton le Skerne *Dur* 78-81; Chapl Asst N Tees Hosp Stockton-on-Tees 81-83; C Norton St Mary *Dur* 81-83; Chapl Heriot-Watt Univ *Edin* 83-90; R Dalmahoy 83-90; Chapl Leeds Univ *Ripon* 90-04; P-in-c Leeds Em 90-04; Prof Ethics Leeds Metrop Univ from 04; NSM Leeds City from 05. *14 Parkside Green, Leeds LS6 4NY* Tel 0113-274 6297 *or* 233 5070 Mobile 07801-745401 E-mail s.j.robinson@leeds.ac.uk

ROBINSON, Stuart Peter. b 59. Moore Th Coll Sydney BTh85 ACT DipTh86. **d** 87 **p** 87. Australia 87-98 and from 01; C Miranda St Paul 87-88; C Doonside St Jo 88-89; R Quakers Hill St Steph 89-97; Perm to Offic *Ox* from 96; Chapl Tervuren *Eur* 98-01; P-in-c Liège 98-00; Dioc Ev and Ch Growth Consultant *Sydney* from 01. *Dept of Evangelism, St Andrew's House, Sydney Square, PO Box A295, Sydney South, NSW, Australia 1235* Tel (0061) (2) 9265 1582 Fax 9267 8601 E-mail robinson.stuart@bigpond.com *or* dofe@ozemail.com

ROBINSON, Mrs Teresa Jane. b 56. St Alb and Ox Min Course 98. **d** 01 **p** 02. OLM Cookham *Ox* 01-03; OLM The Cookhams from 03. *7 Golden Ball Lane, Maidenhead SL6 6NW* Tel (01628) 634107 E-mail terrie@7goldenball.freeserve.co.uk

ROBINSON, Canon Thomas Fisher. b 20. St Jo Coll Dur BA49. **d** 50 **p** 51. C Pendlebury St Jo *Man* 50-54; C Davyhulme St Mary 54-56; V Litherland St Andr *Liv* 56-62; V Wigan St Cath 62-67; V Garston 67-88; Hon Can Liv Cathl 85-88; rtd 88; Perm to Offic *Liv* from 88. *208 Mather Avenue, Liverpool L18 9TG* Tel 0151-475 7870

ROBINSON, Thomas Hugh. b 34. CBE89. TCD BA55 MA71. **d** 57 **p** 58. C Belfast St Clem *D & D* 57-60; Kenya 61-64; I Youghal *C, C & R* 64-66; CF 66-89; Dep Chapl Gen 86-89; TR Cleethorpes *Linc* 90-98; R 98-99; rtd 99; Perm to Offic *Glouc* from 99 and *Worc* from 03. *Brailes View House, Landgate, Blockley, Moreton-in-Marsh GL56 9BX* Tel (01386) 701189

ROBINSON, Timothy James. b 59. Middx Poly BA84 Coll of Ripon & York St Jo PGCE00. St Steph Ho Ox 88. **d** 91 **p** 92. C W Acklam *York* 91-95; P-in-c N Ormesby 95-96; V 96-99; Teacher Hall Garth Sch Middlesbrough from 99; Perm to Offic *Ripon* from 99. *The Yellow House, Copt Hewick, Ripon HG4 5BY* Tel (01765) 690744 E-mail timrobinson2000@aol.com

ROBINSON, Virgil Austin Anderson. b 38. Univ of SW Louisiana BS62 Loyola Univ Chicago MPS88. St Steph Ho Ox 77 St Geo Coll Jerusalem 81. **d** 79 **p** 80. NSM Bicester w Bucknell, Caversfield and Launton *Ox* 79-82; USA from 82; R Northbrook St Giles 83-90; R Woodstock St Anne 91; Chapl NW Univ and R Park Ridge St Anselm 92; Dean St Paul's Cathl Fond du Lac 93-95; R Chicago St Paul and the Redeemer 96-98; R Milwaukee St Paul from 98. *1527 Chapel Court, Northbrook, IL 60062, USA*

ROBINSON, William Pitchford. b 50. Nottm Univ BTh75. Kelham Th Coll 71. **d** 75 **p** 76. C Bow w Bromley St Leon *Lon* 75-79; Hon C Barkingside St Geo *Chelmsf* 79-82; Chapl Claybury Hosp Woodford Bridge 79-85; Hon C Barkingside St Fran *Chelmsf* 82-85; Australia from 86. *Address temp unknown*

ROBLIN, The Ven Graham Henry. b 37. OBE83. AKC61. St Boniface Warminster 60. **d** 62 **p** 63. C St Helier *S'wark* 62-66; CF 66-81; Dep Asst Chapl Gen 81-83; Warden RAChD Cen Bagshot 83-85; Asst Chapl Gen (BOAR) 86-89; Dep Chapl Gen 89-93; Adn for the Army 90-93; QHC 87-93; R Bere Regis and Affpuddle w Turnerspuddle *Sarum* 93-01; rtd 01; Perm to Offic *B & W* and *Sarum* from 02. *Croft Cottage, High Street, Yetminster, Sherborne DT9 6LF* Tel (01935) 873795

ROBOTTOM, David Leonard Douglas. b 40. Qu Coll Birm 80 Sarum & Wells Th Coll 81. **d** 83 **p** 84. C Uppingham w Ayston and Wardley w Belton *Pet* 83-87; TV Sidmouth, Woolbrook and Salcombe Regis *Ex* 87-91; TV Sidmouth, Woolbrook, Salcombe Regis, Sidbury etc 91-95; R Bradninch and Clyst Hydon from 95; RD Cullompton from 03. *The Rectory, 27 West End Road, Bradninch, Exeter EX5 4QS* Tel (01392) 881264 E-mail su2312@eclipse.co.uk

ROBSON, Alan. *See* ROBSON, Gilbert Alan

ROBSON, Angus William. b 13. Kelham Th Coll 32. **d** 38 **p** 39. C Regent Square St Pet *Lon* 38-40; C Mill End *St Alb* 40-45; CF 43-45; P-in-c Luton St Pet 45; Perm to Offic *St Alb* 45-46; V Sark *Win* 46-50; V Jersey St Jas 50-75; Chapl HM Pris Jersey 60-75; rtd 78; Perm to Offic *Win* 78-98. *Flat 1, La Petite Carrière, Wellington Road, St Helier, Jersey JE2 4RJ* Tel (01534) 31656

ROBSON, Claire English. b 62. Middx Poly BEd88. Westcott Ho Cam 96. **d** 99 **p** 00. C Dorchester *Sarum* 99-02; C Kilburn St Mary w All So and W Hampstead St Jas *Lon* 02-04; Min Can and Chapl St Paul's Cathl from 04. *7B Amen Court, London EC4M 7BU* Tel (020) 7246 8323 E-mail chaplain@stpaulscathedral.org.uk

ROBSON, Featherstone. b 30. Southn Univ CertEd52 Nottm Univ DipEd74. Oak Hill Th Coll 55. **d** 58 **p** 59. C Illogan *Truro* 58-60; Chapl Bedstone Sch Shropshire 60-61; Hd RE John Hampden Gr Sch High Wycombe 61-67; Teacher Larkmead Sch Abingdon 68-71; Teacher Dorking Gr Sch 71-76; Ho Master Scarisbrick Hall Sch Ormskirk 77-78; Chapl Dean Close Jr Sch Cheltenham 78-79; Asst Chapl K Edw Sch Witley 79-81; Deputation Sec for England, Irish Ch Miss 82-86; rtd 86; Perm to Offic *Ox* 86-00. *71 Springfield Drive, Abingdon OX14 1JF* Tel (01235) 533421

ROBSON, Gilbert Alan. b 30. St Pet Hall Ox BA53 MA57. Linc Th Coll 56. **d** 57 **p** 58. C Chatham St Mary w St Jo *Roch* 57-59; Sub Warden Roch Th Coll 59-62; Min Can Roch Cathl *Roch* 59-62; Bp's Dom Chapl 61-64; Chapl Roch Th Coll 62-64; R Wouldham *Roch* 62-64; Chapl Nor Coll of Educn 65-68; Sen Lect in Div 68-72; V Shotwick *Ches* 72-74; Dioc Dir of Ords 72-74; Bp's Dom Chapl 72-74; Hd of Div Eton Coll Windsor 74-89; R Wrotham *Roch* 89-95; rtd 95; Perm to Offic *Nor* from 95. *3 Staden Park, Trimingham, Norwich NR11 8HX* Tel (01263) 834887

ROBSON, Howard. *See* ROBSON, John Howard

ROBSON, Preb Ian Leonard. b 32. K Coll Lon MA00. Bps' Coll Cheshunt 61. **d** 63 **p** 64. C Croxley Green All SS *St Alb* 63-65; C Harpenden St Nic 65-68; V Redbourn 68-72; V Ashford St Matt *Lon* 72-77; V Kensington St Mary Abbots w St Geo 77-97; AD Kensington 94-97; Preb St Paul's Cathl 96-97; rtd 97; Perm to Offic *Chich* from 97. *Wepham Lodge, Wepham, Arundel BN18 9RA* Tel (01903) 884667 E-mail robsonoblate@aol.com

ROBSON, James Edward. b 65. Pemb Coll Ox BA88. Wycliffe Hall Ox 91. **d** 94 **p** 95. C Enfield Ch Ch Trent Park *Lon* 94-98; C Oakwood St Thos 98-00; Hon C from 00; Perm to Offic from 02; Tutor Oak Hill Th Coll from 00. *1 Ruston Gardens, London N14 4PF* Tel (020) 8440 3122 E-mail jamesr@oakhill.ac.uk

ROBSON, John Howard. b 60. Newc Univ BA81 ACIB87. Cranmer Hall Dur 98. **d** 00 **p** 01. C Hethersett w Canteloff w Lt and Gt Melton *Nor* 00-04; R Brooke, Kirstead, Mundham w Seething and Thwaite from 04. *The Vicarage, 105 The Street, Brooke, Norwich NR15 1JU* Tel (01508) 550378

ROBSON, John Phillips. b 32. LVO99. St Edm Hall Ox. AKC58. **d** 59 **p** 60. C Huddersfield SS Pet and Paul *Wakef* 59-62; Asst Chapl Ch Hosp Horsham 62-65; Chapl 65-80; Sen Chapl Wellington Coll Berks 80-89; Chapl to RVO and Qu Chpl of the Savoy 89-02; Chapl to The Queen 93-02; rtd 02; Extra Chapl to The Queen from 02. *A2 Odhams Walk, London WC2H 9SA* Tel (020) 7240 7662

ROBSON, Mrs Margery June. b 44. Darlington Tr Coll CertEd65. St Steph Ho Ox 92. **d** 94 **p** 95. C Tuffley *Glouc* 94-98; V Darlington St Mark w St Paul *Dur* 98-03; Chapl Metro Cen Gateshead from 03. *23 Carr House Mews, Consett DH8 6FD* Tel (01207) 581270

ROBSON, Martin Douglas. b 62. St Andr Univ MTh85 Cam Univ PGCE88 Edin Univ MTh94. Edin Th Coll CECM94. **d** 94 **p** 95. C Perth St Ninian *St And* 94-97; P-in-c Lockerbie *Glas* 97-01; P-in-c Moffat 97-01; R Edin St Fillan *Edin* from 01. *St Fillan's Rectory, 8 Buckstone Drive, Edinburgh EH10 6PD* Tel 0131-445 2942 E-mail martin@robson31.fsnet.co.uk

ROBSON, Pamela Jean. b 44. CTM97. **d** 97 **p** 98. NSM W Ewell *Guildf* 97-01; NSM Wotton and Holmbury St Mary from 02. *The Rectory, Holmbury St Mary, Dorking RH5 6NL* Tel (01306) 730285 E-mail pamandbrianrobson@hotmail.com

ROBSON, Canon Patricia Anne. b 40. MBE99. CertEd60. SW Minl Tr Course 85. **d** 87 **p** 94. Dioc Youth Officer *Truro* 87-92; Hon C Paul 87-92; Hon C Kenwyn St Geo 88-92; Dn-in-c St Enoder 92-94; P-in-c from 94; P-in-c Newlyn St Newlyn from 03; Hon Can Truro Cathl from 98; RD Pydar 02-03. *St Enoder Rectory, Summercourt, Newquay TR8 5DF* Tel (01726) 860724 Fax as telephone E-mail intercelt@aol.com

ROBSON, Paul Coutt. b 37. Leeds Univ BA60. Coll of Resurr Mirfield 63. **d** 64 **p** 65. C Stokesay *Heref* 64-66; C St Geo Cathl Cape Town 66-68; R Roodebloem All SS 68-70; Chapl HM Pris Man 70-71; Chapl HM Borstal Feltham 71-74; Chapl HM Borstal Hollesley Bay 74-78; Chapl HM Pris Grendon and Spring Hill 78-85; Chapl HM Pris Nor 85-92; Chapl HM YOI and Remand Cen Brinsford 92-99; rtd 99; Perm to Offic *Heref* 00-01; P-in-c Wistanstow 01-04. *Pilgrims, Henley Common, Church Stretton SY6 6RS* Tel (01694) 781221 E-mail smrpcr@lineone.net

ROBSON, Peter Cole. b 45. Clare Coll Cam BA66 MA70 Oriel Coll Ox BLitt69 MLitt70. Coll of Resurr Mirfield 70. **d** 71 **p** 72. C Gt Grimsby St Mary and St Jas *Linc* 71-73; Chapl BNC Ox 73-76; R Timsbury *B & W* 76-79; P-in-c Blanchland w Hunstanworth *Newc* 80-83; rtd 87. *c/o J W T Robson Esq, 54 Linkfield Road, Mountsorrel, Leicester LE12 7DL*

ROBSON, Stephen Thomas. b 54. Chich Th Coll 84. **d** 86 **p** 87. C Newc St Fran *Newc* 86-89; C Gateshead St Cuth w St Paul *Dur* 89-91; TV Stanley 91-96; V Sugley *Newc* from 96. *Sugley Vicarage, Lemington, Newcastle upon Tyne NE15 8RD* Tel 0191-267 4633

ROBSON, William. b 34. FCIS66 FCCA80. Sarum & Wells Th Coll 77. **d** 79 **p** 80. C Lymington *Win* 79-81; CF 81-93; V Barton Stacey and Bullington etc *Win* 93-98; rtd 98; Hon C Knaresborough *Ripon* 98-01; Perm to Offic *Newc* 03-04; Hon C Barrow upon Soar w Walton le Wolds *Leic* from 04; Hon C Wymeswold and Prestwold w Hoton from 04. *The Vicarage, 5 The Stockwell, Wymeswold, Loughborough LE12 6UF* Tel (01509) 889568 E-mail maibill@aol.com

ROBUS, Keith Adrian. b 59. Chich Th Coll 85. **d** 88 **p** 89. C Greenhill St Jo *Lon* 88-92; C Willesden St Matt 92-02; V N Acton St Gabr from 02. *St Gabriel's Vicarage, 15 Balfour Road, London W3 0DG* Tel (020) 8992 5938 E-mail keith@robus.demon.co.uk

ROBY, Richard James. b 33. Imp Coll Lon BSc54 Lon Inst of Educn PGCE55. St Alb Minl Tr Scheme 82. **d** 85 **p** 86. NSM Bushey *St Alb* 85-92; NSM Wootton 92-00; rtd 00; Perm to Offic *St Alb* from 00. *5 Powis Mews, Flitwick, Bedford MK45 1SU* Tel (01525) 718529 E-mail richard.roby@ntlworld.com

ROCHDALE, Archdeacon of. *See* BALLARD, The Ven Andrew Edgar

ROCHE, Miss Alison Mary. b 70. Man Univ BSc91 Nottm Univ PGCE94. St Jo Coll Nottm MA(TS)00. **d** 01 **p** 02. C Leic Martyrs *Leic* from 01. *4 Purbeck Close, Wigston LE18 2JY* Tel 0116-257 1887 E-mail aroche@fish.co.uk

ROCHE, Barry Robert Francis. b 40. Lon Univ BD66 Ox Univ MTh93. Clifton Th Coll 63. **d** 68 **p** 69. C Beckenham Ch Ch *Roch* 68-72; C Chester le Street *Dur* 72-74; C-in-c N Bletchley CD *Ox* 74-78; R Luton Ch Ch *Roch* 78-92; Chapl All SS Hosp Chatham 78-92; TR Glascote and Stonydelph *Lich* 92-99; RD Tamworth 95-99; V Oulton Broad *Nor* 99-05; rtd 05. *24 Lakeside Close, Nantyglo, Ebbw Vale NP23 4EG*

ROCHESTER, Thomas Robson. b 33. NEOC 85. **d** 90 **p** 91. NSM Glendale Gp *Newc* 90-03; rtd 03; Perm to Offic *Newc* from 03. *Cushat Law, Thropton, Morpeth NE65 7HX* Tel (01669) 62079 E-mail trochester2@aol.com

ROCHESTER, Archdeacon of. *See* LOCK, The Ven Peter Harcourt D'Arcy

ROCHESTER, Bishop of. *See* NAZIR-ALI, The Rt Revd Michael James

ROCHESTER, Dean of. *See* NEWMAN, The Very Revd Adrian

ROCK, Mrs Jean. b 37. Gilmore Course 76. **dss** 79 **d** 87 **p** 97. Douglas St Matt *S & M* 79-81; Marown 81-83; Chapl Asst Oswestry and Distr Hosp 83-87; Oswestry St Oswald *Lich* 83-90; Par Dn 87-90; C-in-c Pont Robert and Pont Dolanog *St As* 90-97; V 97; rtd 97; Perm to Offic *Lich* from 99. *10 Wharf Cottages, Rhoswiel, Weston Rhyn, Oswestry SY10 7TD* Tel (01691) 773766

ROCKALL, Miss Valerie Jane. b 42. City of Cov Coll CertEd63. St Alb Minl Tr Scheme 78. **dss** 81 **d** 87 **p** 94. Asst Hd Wigginton Sch Tring 73-90; Boxmoor St Jo *St Alb* 81-87; NSM Hemel Hempstead 87-90; Par Dn Ampthill w Millbrook and Steppingley 90-93; TD Southampton (City Cen) *Win* 93-94; TV 94-99; P-in-c Aveley and Purfleet *Chelmsf* from 99. *The Vicarage, Mill Road, Aveley, South Ockendon RM15 4SR* Tel (01708) 891242

ROCKEY, Antony Nicolas. b 65. Kingston Poly BEng89 CEng94 MICE94 MCIWEM95. Carl and Blackb Dioc Tr Inst 02. **d** 05. C Cockermouth w Embleton and Wythop *Carl* from 05. *High Garth, Lorton Road, Cockermouth CA13 9DF*

RODD, Philip Rankilor. b 60. Ex Univ BA79 K Coll Lon PGCE85. Ridley Hall Cam 03. **d** 05. C Heigham H Trin *Nor* from 05. *14 Trinity Street, Norwich NR2 2BQ* Tel (01603) 614231 E-mail info@trinitynorwich.org

RODEL, Mark Neil. b 71. Southn Univ BA96. STETS 02. **d** 05. C Southsea St Jude *Portsm* from 05. *92 Marmion Road, Southsea PO5 2BB* Tel (023) 9287 6156 Mobile 07748-272360 Pager 07654-325425 E-mail mark@rodel.net

RODEN, Jo. *See* LOVERIDGE, Ms Joan Margaretha Holland

RODEN, John Michael. b 37. St Jo Coll York CertEd64 Open Univ BA82 MA92 York Univ DPhil96. Ripon Hall Ox 71. **d** 73 **p** 74. C Saltburn-by-the-Sea *York* 73-77; Chapl St Pet Sch York 77-82; Warden Marrick Priory *Ripon* 83; Hon C Appleton Roebuck w Acaster Selby *York* 84-85; P-in-c 86-03; Youth Officer 86-03; Sen Chapl Selby Coalfield Ind Chapl 96-03; rtd 03; Perm to Offic *York* from 03. *Ebor Cottage, 8 Copmanthorpe Grange, Copmanthorpe, York YO23 3TN* Tel (01904) 744826 E-mail rodenjohn@lineone.net

RODEN, Michael Adrian Holland. b 60. Ripon Coll Cuddesdon 82. **d** 85 **p** 86. C S Lambeth St Anne and All SS *S'wark* 85-88; C Wandsworth St Paul 88-90; C Ox St Mary V w St Cross and St Pet *Ox* 90-94; Chapl Wadh Coll Ox 90-94; R Steeple Aston w N Aston and Tackley *Ox* 94-02; TR Hitchin *St Alb* from 02. *The Rectory, 21 West Hill, Hitchin SG5 2HZ* Tel (01462) 434017 *or* 452758

RODERICK, Philip David. b 49. Univ of Wales (Swansea) BA70 Univ of Wales (Abth) BD77 Lon Univ CertEd71. Linc Th Coll 80. **d** 80 **p** 81. C Llanfair-is-gaer and Llanddeiniolen *Ban* 80-82; TV Holyhead w Rhoscolyn w Llanfair-yn-Neubwll 82-84; Chapl and Lect Th Univ of Wales (Ban) 84-88; Warden Angl Chapl Cen 84-88; Prin Bucks Chr Tr Scheme *Ox* 88-94; Dir Chiltern Chr Tr Progr 88-94; Dir Quiet Garden Trust from 92; Dir The Wells Inst from 96; V Amersham on the Hill *Ox* 96-04; Ldr Contemplative Fire from 04; Perm to Offic from 04. *21 Elm Close, Weston Turville, Aylesbury HP22 5SS* Tel (01296) 614597 E-mail philiproderick@btinternet.com

RODFORD, Canon Brian George. b 50. Hatf Poly BEd84. **d** 79 **p** 80. Hon C St Alb St Steph *St Alb* 79-85; Chapl St Mary's Sch 81-90; Sen Teacher 83-90; Hon C Hendon St Mary and Golders Green *Lon* 85-90; Hon C Winchmore Hill H Trin 90-95; V Ponders End St Matt 95-02; Dir Chain Foundn Uganda from 02; Can All SS Cathl Kampala from 02; Perm to Offic *St Alb* from 04. *Simon's Acre, 17 Pagasvlei Road, Constantia, 7806 South Africa* Tel (0027) (21) 794 8940 *or* (01727) 850382 E-mail brodford_chain@hotmail.com

RODGER, Canon Raymond. b 39. Westmr Coll Ox MTh93. Bps' Coll Cheshunt 62. **d** 63 **p** 64. C Frodingham *Linc* 63-66; Asst Chapl St Geo Hosp Lon 66-69; C Waltham *Linc* 69-73; V Nocton 73-86; P-in-c Potter Hanworth 74-86; P-in-c Dunston 77-86; RD Graffoe 81-92; Can and Preb Linc Cathl from 85; V Nocton w Dunston and Potterhanworth 86-92; Bp's Dom Chapl 92-05; Gen Preacher 92-05; rtd 05. *13 Lupin Road, Lincoln LN2 4GB* Tel (01522) 536723 Mobile 07803-123975 E-mail canrod@hotmail.com

RODGERS, Canon Cyril George Hooper. b 20. Qu Coll Birm 50. **d** 52 **p** 53. C Bishop's Cleeve *Glouc* 52-56; V Nailsworth 56-61; Chapl Longford's Approved Sch Minchinhampton 56-57; CF (TA) 58-62; R Upwell Ch Ch *Ely* 61-66; CF (TA - R of O) 62-87; V Wiggenhall St Germans and Islington *Ely* 66-76; RD Lynn

Marshland 68-76; R Woolpit *St E* 76-84; RD Lavenham 78-87; Hon Can St E Cathl 84-87; R Woolpit w Drinkstone 84-87; rtd 87; Perm to Offic *St E* from 87. *Fox Farm, Wetherden, Stowmarket IP14 3NE* Tel (01359) 40364

RODGERS, David. b 26. Sarum Th Coll 63. **d** 65 **p** 66. C Combe Down *B & W* 65-68; V Leigh Woods 68-76; R Wellow w Foxcote and Shoscombe 76-79; C Wells St Cuth w Coxley and Wookey Hole 79-82; P-in-c Wookey w Henton 79-82; V Ercall Magna *Lich* 82-89; V Rowton 82-89; RD Wrockwardine 84-88; rtd 89; Perm to Offic *B & W* from 98. *27 Wood Close, Wells BA5 2GA*

RODGERS, Preb Frank Ernest. b 46. Tyndale Hall Bris 68. **d** 71 **p** 72. C Madeley *Heref* 71-74; C Littleover *Derby* 74-77; V Clodock and Longtown w Craswell and Llanveyno *Heref* 77-79; P-in-c St Margaret's w Michaelchurch Eskley and Newton 77-79; V Clodock and Longtown w Craswall, Llanveynoe etc from 79; RD Abbeydore 90-96; Preb Heref Cathl from 96. *The Vicarage, Longtown, Hereford HR2 0LD* Tel (01873) 860289

RODGERS, John Terence Roche. b 28. TCD BA53 MA57 ACII. Bps' Coll Cheshunt. **d** 57 **p** 58. C Templecorran *Conn* 57-60; C Derriaghy 60-61; C Antrim All SS 62-64; I Belfast St Steph 64-79; I Dunmurry 79-94; Can Belf Cathl 92-94; rtd 94. *8 Aberdelghy Park, Lambeg, Lisburn BT27 4QF* Tel (028) 9266 0430

RODGERS, Richard Thomas Boycott. b 47. Lon Univ MB, BS70 FRCS81. St Jo Coll Nottm DipTh77. **d** 77 **p** 78. C Littleover *Derby* 77-80; Lect Birm St Martin w Bordesley St Andr *Birm* 89-90; Perm to Offic from 90. *63 Meadow Brook Road, Birmingham B31 1ND* Tel 0121-476 0789
E-mail dick.rodgers@charis.co.uk

RODHAM, Morris. b 59. Hatf Coll Dur BA81 St Jo Coll Dur PGCE85 Bris Univ MA93. Trin Coll Bris DipHE92. **d** 93 **p** 94. C New Milverton *Cov* 93-97; V Leamington Priors St Mary from 97. *The Vicarage, 28 St Mary's Road, Leamington Spa CV31 1JP* Tel (01926) 778507 *or* tel and fax 778505
E-mail morris/helen@stmaryschurch.swinternet.co.uk

RODLEY, Ian Tony. b 48. Qu Coll Birm 77. **d** 80 **p** 81. C Baildon and Dioc Children's Adv *Bradf* 80-85; V Bradf St Wilfrid Lidget Green 85-90; Chapl to the Deaf 88-90; V Otley 90-98; C Wolverton *Ox* 98-03; TR Bramley *Ripon* from 03. *St Peter's Vicarage, 8 Hough Lane, Leeds LS13 3NE* Tel 0113-255 5180
E-mail ianrod@clara.co.uk

RODRIGUEZ, Luis Mario. b 64. Occidental Coll (USA) BA86 S California Univ MA93. St Steph Ho Ox MTh99. **d** 98 **p** 99. C Battersea Ch Ch and St Steph *S'wark* 98-02; C Pimlico St Pet w Westmr Ch Ch *Lon* from 02. *3 St Peter's House, 119 Eaton Square, London SW1W 9AL* Tel (020) 7235 4480
E-mail lum.rod@virgin.net

RODRIGUEZ-VEGLIO, Francis Bonny. b 33. SSC. Sarum Th Coll 62. **d** 64 **p** 65. C Alnwick St Paul *Newc* 64-68; V Horton w Piddington *Pet* 68-79; P-in-c Preston Deanery 68-79; CF (ACF) 75-82; TV Is of Scilly *Truro* 79-82; Hon Chapl Miss to Seamen 79-82; Perm to Offic *Pet* 86-88; C Leic Ch Sav *Leic* 88-91; V Kirkwhelpington, Kirkharle, Kirkheaton and Cambo *Newc* 91-95; Perm to Offic *Pet* from 95. *Gemacq Cottage, 14 Daventry Road, Norton, Daventry NN11 2ND* Tel (01327) 872030
E-mail francis.andree@tiscali.co.uk

RODWELL, Barry John. b 39. Birm Univ CertEd59 Cam Univ DipAdEd77. Ridley Hall Cam 67. **d** 70 **p** 71. C Sudbury St Greg and St Pet *St E* 70-73; Hd RE Hedingham Sch 73-80; R Sible Hedingham *Chelmsf* 80-85; RE Adv 85-93; V Gt Burstead 93-00; rtd 00; Perm to Offic *Nor* from 00. *The Nutshell, 11 Filbert Road, Loddon, Norwich NR14 6LW* Tel (01508) 522949
E-mail nutshell@tesco.net

RODWELL (née VINCENT), Mrs Jacqueline Margaret. b 59. Glos Univ BA04. WEMTC 01. **d** 04 **p** 05. NSM Cheltenham St Mark *Glouc* from 04. *27 Hatherley Court Road, Cheltenham GL51 3AG* Tel (01242) 697541
E-mail the.rodwells@blueyonder.co.uk

RODWELL, Canon John Stanley. b 46. Leeds Univ BSc68 Southn Univ PhD74. Cuddesdon Coll 71. **d** 74 **p** 75. Hon C Horfield H Trin *Bris* 74-75; Hon C Skerton St Luke *Blackb* 75-77; Lic to Offic from 77; Hon Can Blackb Cathl from 03. *7 Derwent Road, Lancaster LA1 3ES* Tel (01524) 62726

ROE, Mrs Caroline Ruth. b 57. Birm Univ BA80 PGCE93. Wycliffe Hall Ox 81. **dss** 84 **d** 87 **p** 96. Olveston *Bris* 84-87; Par Dn 87; NSM Alveley and Quatt *Heref* 87-94; Bp's Voc Officer 90-94; Hon C Loughborough Em and St Mary in Charnwood *Leic* 97-98; C Hathern, Long Whatton and Diseworth w Belton etc 98-00; Perm to Offic 01-04; Chapl Univ Hosps Leic NHS Trust from 04. *4 John's Lee Close, Loughborough LE11 3LH* Tel (01509) 260217 *or* 0116-256 3413

ROE, Frank Ronald. b 31. Brasted Th Coll Westcott Ho Cam 55. **d** 57 **p** 58. C S w N Hayling *Portsm* 57-61; Hong Kong 61-77; Sen Chapl St Jo Cathl 61-66; Asst Chapl 77; Sen Chapl Miss to Seamen 66-69; Australia from 77; Hon Chapl Miss to Seafarers from 77; rtd 96. *166 Dempster Street, PO Box 838, Esperance, W Australia 6450* Tel (0061) (8) 9071 4207 *or* 9071 6811/22 Mobile 417-172272 Fax 9072 1073
E-mail revfrank@bigpond.com

ROE, Canon Joseph Thorley. b 22. AKC49 DipAdEd Hull Univ PhD90. K Coll Lon 46. **d** 50 **p** 51. C Methley *Ripon* 50-53; C Richmond 53-55; V Leeds Gipton Epiphany 55-60; C of E Youth Coun Tr Officer 60-64; Sec Youth Dept BCC 64-67; Prin Lect Bretton Hall Coll Wakef 67-74; Sec for Miss and Unity *Ripon* 74-78; Dioc Missr and Bp's Dom Chapl 75-78; Can Res Carl Cathl *Carl* 78-82; Dioc Dir of Tr 78-82; Dioc Adult Educn Officer *Wakef* 82-88; Hon Can Wakef Cathl 83-88; Dir of Educn 85-88; rtd 88; Perm to Offic *Wakef* from 88. *29 Milnthorpe Drive, Wakefield WF2 7HU* Tel (01924) 256938

ROE, Peter Harold. b 37. K Coll Lon BD62 AKC62. **d** 63 **p** 64. C Knowle St Barn *Bris* 63-65; C Leckhampton St Pet *Glouc* 65-68; V Shaw Hill *Birm* 68-73; V Hobs Moat 73-90; V Packwood w Hockley Heath 90-99; rtd 99; Perm to Offic *Blackb* from 99. *14 Worcester Avenue, Garstang, Preston PR3 1EY* Tel (01995) 605775

ROE, Robert Henry. b 22. LCP57. Westcott Ho Cam 72. **d** 74 **p** 75. Hd Master St Mary's Primary Sch Saffron Walden 74-83; NSM Saffron Walden w Wendens Ambo and Littlebury *Chelmsf* 75-86; Perm to Offic *Nor* from 86. *Larchmount, High Street, Cley, Holt NR25 7RG* Tel (01263) 740369

ROE, Robin. b 28. CBE MC68. TCD BA52 MA55. **d** 53 **p** 54. C Dublin Sandford *D & G* 53-55; CF 55-81; QHC 77-81; R Merrow *Guildf* 81-89; rtd 89; Perm to Offic *Guildf* from 89. *Lansdowne, 6 Mitchells Close, Shalford, Guildford GU4 8HY* Tel (01483) 563852

ROE, Thorley. *See* ROE, Canon Joseph Thorley

ROEMMELE, Michael Patrick. b 49. TCD BA72 MA76. **d** 73 **p** 74. C Portadown St Columba *Arm* 73-77; C Drumachose *D & R* 77-80; Bahrain 79-83; Cyprus 79-83; Chapl RAF 83-00; CF from 00. *c/o MOD Chaplains (Army)* Tel (01980) 615804 Fax 615800

ROESCHLAUB, Robert Friedrich. b 39. Purdue Univ BSc63. Berkeley Div Sch MDiv66. **d** 66 **p** 66. USA 66-77; Hon C Tilehurst St Cath *Ox* 78-79; Hon C Tilehurst St Mich 79-82; P-in-c Millom H Trin w Thwaites *Carl* 82-85; P-in-c Millom 85-89; R Dunstall w Rangemore and Tatenhill *Lich* 89-93; rtd 94; Perm to Offic *Carl* from 98. *20 Pannatt Hill, Millom LA18 5DB* Tel (01229) 772185

ROEST, Wilma. b 62. Utrecht Univ MA88 Roehampton Inst PGCE92. SEITE 96. **d** 99 **p** 00. C Merton St Mary *S'wark* 99-02; TV N Lambeth from 02. *De Pastorie, 10 Wincott Street, London SE11 4NT* Tel (020) 7820 9445 E-mail wilma.roest@virgin.net

ROFF, Andrew Martin. b 42. Bede Coll Dur BSc65. Westcott Ho Cam 65. **d** 70 **p** 71. C Ches St Mary *Ches* 70-73; Min Can Blackb Cathl *Blackb* 73-76; P-in-c Blackb St Jo 74-75; V Longton 76-81; Chapl Trin Coll Glenalmond 82-83; R Allendale w Whitfield *Newc* 83-92; V Gosforth St Nic 92-97; Dioc Supernumerary *Mor* from 01. *Rowan Glen, Upper Braefindon, Culbokie, Dingwall IV7 8GY* Tel (01349) 877762
E-mail 106770.3175@compuserve.com

ROFF, Canon John Michael. b 47. St Chad's Coll Dur BSc69. Westcott Ho Cam 70. **d** 72 **p** 73. C Lancaster St Mary *Blackb* 72-75; C Dronfield *Derby* 75-76; TV 76-80; TR N Wingfield, Pilsley and Tupton 80-85; V Ilkeston St Mary 85-90; V Stockport St Geo *Ches* 90-94; TR Stockport SW 94-00; RD Stockport 95-00; Dioc Ecum Officer 92-99; Hon Can Ches Cathl 98-00; Can Res 00-04; rtd 04; Perm to Offic *Blackb* from 05. *14 Westbourne Road, Lancaster LA1 5DB* Tel (01524) 841621
E-mail roff@roff.org.uk

ROGAN, Canon John. b 28. St Jo Coll Dur BA49 MA51 DipTh54 Open Univ BPhil81. **d** 54 **p** 55. C Ashton St Mich *Man* 54-57; C Sharrow St Andr *Sheff* 57-61; Ind Chapl 57-61; Sec C of E Ind Cttee 61-66; V Leigh St Mary *Man* 66-78; RD Leigh 71-78; Hon Can Man Cathl 75-78; Provost St Paul's Cathl Dundee *Bre* 78-83; R Dundee St Paul 78-83; Soc Resp Adv *Bris* 83-93; Can Res Bris Cathl 83-93; rtd 93; Perm to Offic *Bris* from 93. *84 Concorde Drive, Bristol BS10 6PX* Tel 0117-950 5803

ROGER ALEXANDER, Brother. *See* BOHUN, Brother Roger Alexander

ROGERS, Canon Alan David. b 24. K Coll Cam BA47 MA50. Cuddesdon Coll 50. **d** 52 **p** 53. C Saffron Walden *Chelmsf* 52-54; C Walthamstow St Mich 54-57; Madagascar 57-66; Qu Coll Birm 66-67; Lect Div Weymouth Coll 67-73; Lic to Offic *Sarum* from 69; Hd of Relig and Th Depts Dorset Inst of Educn 73-82; Hon Can Antananarivo from 84; rtd 89. *4 Fossett Way, Wyke Regis, Weymouth DT4 9HD* Tel (01305) 779942

ROGERS, Mrs Angela. **d** 00 **p** 01. OLM Bridgnorth, Tasley, Astley Abbotts, etc *Heref* from 00. *18 St Nicholas Road, Bridgnorth WV15 5BW* Tel (01746) 762013

ROGERS, Brian Robert. b 36. Open Univ BA80. St Jo Coll Nottm 70. **d** 72 **p** 73. C Ealing St Mary *Lon* 72-74; C Greenside *Dur* 74-75; Lic to Offic 75-85; Perm to Offic *Lich* 85-95; rtd 97; Perm to Offic *Sarum* from 97. *71 Alderney Avenue, Poole BH12 4LF* Tel (01202) 772103

ROGERS, Brian Victor. b 50. Trin Coll Bris 75. **d** 78 **p** 79. C Plumstead St Jo w St Jas and St Paul *S'wark* 78-83; P-in-c Gayton *Nor* 83-85; P-in-c Gayton Thorpe w E Walton 83-85; P-in-c Westacre 83-85; P-in-c Ashwicken w Leziate 83-85; R

Gayton Gp of Par 85-91; R Rackheath and Salhouse 91-96; P-in-c Warmington, Tansor, Cotterstock and Fotheringhay *Pet* 96-97; V Warmington, Tansor and Cotterstock etc from 97. *The Vicarage, Warmington, Peterborough PE8 6TE* Tel (01832) 280263 E-mail brian.rogers@cwcom.net

ROGERS, Christopher Antony. b 47. N Ord Course 79. **d** 81 **p** 82. C Chesterfield St Aug *Derby* 81-84; C Chaddesden St Phil 84-86; R Whitwell 86-95; V W Burnley All SS *Blackb* 95-01; V Ashford St Hilda *Lon* from 01. *St Hilda's Vicarage, 8 Station Crescent, Ashford TW15 3HH* Tel (01784) 254237 *or* 245712 E-mail christopher.rogers@london.anglican.org

ROGERS, Clive Trevor Thorne. b 49. St Alb and Ox Min Course 02. **d** 05. NSM Beaconsfield *Ox* from 05. *23 Stratton Road, Beaconsfield HP9 1HR* Tel (01494) 675298 E-mail clive_rogers@btinternet.com

ROGERS, Clive William. b 62. Selw Coll Cam BA83 MA87 MEng93 Southn Univ BTh90. Chich Th Coll 87. **d** 90 **p** 91. C Leic St Aid *Leic* 90-93; P-in-c Ryhall w Essendine *Pet* 93-94; Lic to Offic *Ely* 94-03; Perm to Offic 00-04; Lic to Offic *Sarum* from 04. *4 The Sidings, Downton, Salisbury SP5 3QZ* Tel (01725) 512141

ROGERS, Cyril David. b 55. Birm Univ BA76 BTheol. Sarum & Wells Th Coll 80. **d** 83 **p** 84. C Leagrave *St Alb* 83-87; TV Langtree *Ox* 87-97; R Ballaugh *S & M* from 97. *The Rectory, Ballacrosha, Ballaugh, Isle of Man IM7 5AQ* Tel (01624) 897873

ROGERS, Damon. b 66. Cov Univ BEng92 Wolv Univ PGCE94 Warwick Univ BPhil02. Cranmer Hall Dur 01. **d** 03. C Heigham St Thos *Nor* from 03. *363 Earlham Road, Norwich NR2 3RQ* Tel (01603) 506121

ROGERS, David. b 48. Univ of Wales (Ban) BA69. Westcott Ho Cam 70. **d** 72 **p** 73. C Rainbow Hill and Tolladine *Worc* 72-75; C Astwood Bank w Crabbs Cross 75-79; V Cradley 79-90; V Beoley from 90; RD Bromsgrove from 00. *The Vicarage, Church Hill, Beoley, Redditch B98 9AR* Tel (01527) 63976 E-mail davidrogers@santiago.plus.com

ROGERS, David Alan. b 55. City of Lon Poly BA77 MCIT82. Linc Th Coll 88. **d** 90 **p** 91. C Kingston upon Hull St Nic *York* 90-93; P-in-c Kingston upon Hull St Mary 93-96; N Humberside Ind Chapl 93-02; Dir Leeds Ch Inst *Ripon* 02-04; Chief Officer Hull Coun for Voluntary Service from 04. *Hull Council for Voluntary Service, 29 Anlaby Road, Hull HU1 2PG* Tel (01482) 324474 Fax 580565

ROGERS, The Ven David Arthur. b 21. Ch Coll Cam BA47 MA52. Ridley Hall Cam 47. **d** 49 **p** 50. C Stockport St Geo *Ches* 49-53; R Levenshulme St Pet *Man* 53-59; V Sedbergh *Bradf* 59-74; P-in-c Cautley w Dowbiggin 59-60; V 60-74; P-in-c Garsdale 59-60; V 60-74; V Sedbergh, Cautley and Garsdale 74-79; P-in-c Firbank, Howgill and Killington 73-77; RD Sedbergh 59-73; RD Ewecross 73-77; Hon Can Bradf Cathl 67-77; Adn Craven 77-86; rtd 86; Lic to Offic *Bradf* from 86; Perm to Offic *Blackb* from 87 and *Carl* from 89. *Borrens Farm, Leck, Carnforth LA6 2JG* Tel (01524) 271616

ROGERS, David Barrie. b 46. S Dios Minl Tr Scheme 89. **d** 93. NSM Old Alresford and Bighton *Win* 93-96; Dep Warden Dioc Retreat Ho (Holland Ho) Cropthorne *Worc* 96-98; Warden Stacklands Retreat Ho W Kingsdown 98-03; Hon C Kingsdown *Roch* 98-03; Warden St Pet Bourne Cen from 03. *St Peter's Bourne Centre, 40 Oakleigh Park South, London N20 9JU*

ROGERS, David Martyn. b 56. Univ of Wales (Lamp) BA77 K Coll Lon BD79 AKC79 St Kath Coll Liv DipEd86 Liv Univ BPhil94. Chich Th Coll 79. **d** 80 **p** 81. C Hockerill *St Alb* 80-85; Perm to Offic *St As* 85-87; C Kilburn St Mary *Lon* 87-90; V New Longton *Blackb* from 90; Chapl to Lancs Constabulary from 90. *All Saints' Vicarage, Station Road, New Longton, Preston PR4 4LN* Tel (01772) 613347

ROGERS, George Hutchinson. b 51. Windsor Univ Ontario BSW75. Wycliffe Coll Toronto MDiv78. **d** 78 **p** 78. Canada 78-99; C Tonbridge SS Pet and Paul *Roch* 99-03; V Werrington *Pet* from 03. *The Vicarage, 51 The Green, Werrington, Peterborough PE4 6RT* Tel (01733) 571649 E-mail ghrogers@nildram.co.uk

ROGERS, Ian Colin. b 73. Wolv Univ BA95. Coll of Resurr Mirfield BA99. **d** 00 **p** 01. C Lon Docks St Pet w Wapping St Jo *Lon* 00-03; P-in-c Hammersmith St Luke from 03. *St Luke's Vicarage, 450 Uxbridge Road, London W12 0NS* Tel (020) 8749 7523 E-mail fr.ianrogers@ntlworld.com

ROGERS, The Very Revd John. b 34. Univ of Wales (Lamp) BA55 Oriel Coll Ox BA58 MA61. St Steph Ho Ox 57. **d** 59 **p** 60. C Roath St Martin *Llan* 59-63; Br Guiana 63-66; Guyana 66-71; V Caldicot *Mon* 71-77; V Monmouth 77-84; RD Monmouth 81-84; TR Ebbw Vale 84-93; RD Blaenau Gwent 86-93; Can St Woolos Cathl 88-93; Dean Llan 93-99; V Llandaff w Capel Llanilltern 93-99; rtd 99. *Fron Lodge, Llandovery SA20 0LJ* Tel (01550) 720089

ROGERS, John. b 61. St Jo Coll Nottm. **d** 05. C Otley *Bradf* from 05. *30 Newall Hall Park, Otley LS21 2RD*

ROGERS, John Arthur. b 47. MBIM. Edin Dioc NSM Course 90. **d** 92. C Middlesbrough St Martin *York* 92-93; NSM The Trimdons *Dur* 00-05; NSM Upper Skerne from 05. *9 Coronation Terrace, Trimdon Village, Trimdon Station TS29 6PQ* Tel (01429) 881119

ROGERS, John Robin. b 36. St Alb Minl Tr Scheme 78. **d** 81 **p** 82. NSM Digswell and Panshanger *St Alb* 81-84; C Welwyn w Ayot St Peter 85-92; R Wilden w Colmworth and Ravensden 92-99; rtd 99; Perm to Offic *St Alb* 99-02. *37 The Birches, Shobdon, Leominster HR6 9NG* Tel (01568) 708903

ROGERS, John William Trevor. b 28. Qu Coll Birm. **d** 85 **p** 86. NSM Dunchurch *Cov* 85-95; Perm to Offic from 95. *15 Hillyard Road, Southam, Leamington Spa CV47 0LD* Tel (01926) 813469

ROGERS, Canon Kenneth. b 33. Cuddesdon Coll 68. **d** 69 **p** 70. C Perranzabuloe *Truro* 69-71; C Truro St Paul 71-74; P-in-c Kenwyn St Geo 74-87; RD Powder 81-88; Hon Can Truro Cathl 87-98; TR Bodmin w Lanhydrock and Lanivet 87-98; RD Trigg Minor and Bodmin 89-93; rtd 98; Perm to Offic *Truro* from 98. *25 Paul Row, Truro TR1 1HH* Tel (01872) 261007

ROGERS, Canon Llewelyn. Univ of Wales (Lamp) BA59. St Mich Coll Llan. **d** 61 **p** 62. C Holywell *St As* 61-64; C Hawarden 64-70; R Bodfari 70-73; V Rhosymedre 73-78; V Llansantffraid-ym-Mechain 77-83; V Llansantffraid-ym-Mechain and Llanfechain 83-98; RD Llanfyllin 84-88; V Pont Robert, Pont Dolanog, Garthbeibio etc 98-01; Can St As Cathl 98-01; rtd 01. *17 Maes y Berllan, Llanymynech SY22 6PJ*

ROGERS, Mrs Lynne Rosemary. b 49. CITC 00. **d** 03 **p** 04. Aux Min Ferns w Kilbride, Toombe, Kilcormack etc *C & O* from 03. *The Corner House, Clone, Ferns, Co Wexford, Irish Republic* Tel (00353) (54) 66961 Mobile 87-677 4408 E-mail lynnerogers@eircom.net

ROGERS, Malcolm Dawson. b 63. SS Hild & Bede Coll Dur BA84 Selw Coll Cam BA88. Ridley Hall Cam 86. **d** 89 **p** 90. C Ipswich St Jo *St E* 89-93; CMS Russia 93-95; C Holloway St Mary Magd *Lon* 95-97; V 97-05; V Bury St Edmunds St Mary *St E* from 05. *St Mary with St Peter Vicarage, 78 Hardwick Lane, Bury St Edmunds IP33 2RA* Tel (01284) 763416 E-mail malcolmrogers@onetel.com

ROGERS, Malcolm Kenneth. b 72. Liv Inst of Educn BA93. St Jo Coll Nottm MA95 LTh96. **d** 96 **p** 97. C W Derby St Luke *Liv* 96-00; V Huyton Quarry from 00. *St Gabriel's Vicarage, 2 St Agnes Road, Huyton, Liverpool L36 5TA* Tel 0151-489 2688 E-mail malcolm.rogers@huytondeanery.org

ROGERS, Mark James. b 64. Univ of Wales (Lamp) BA. Qu Coll Birm. **d** 89 **p** 90. C Dudley St Aug Holly Hall *Worc* 89-93; C Worc St Barn w Ch Ch 93-94; TV 94-97; USPG Belize 97-00; Canada from 00. *St Columba's Rectory, 4020 Hingston Avenue, Montreal QC, Canada, H4A 2J7*

ROGERS, Martin Brian. b 53. LNSM course 89. **d** 92 **p** 93. OLM Collyhurst *Man* from 92. *8 Greenford Road, Crumpsall, Manchester M8 0NW* Tel 0161-740 4614

ROGERS, Martin Stephen. b 28. St Edm Hall Ox BA50 MA54. Cuddesdon Coll 50. **d** 52 **p** 53. C Reading St Mary V *Ox* 52-54; C Buxton *Derby* 54-57; Australia 58-64; Lect Cuddesdon Coll 65-73; Chapl Littlemore Hosp Ox 65-74; Dept of Educn Cam Univ 73-76; Chapl Univ Coll of Ripon and York St Jo 76-93; Postgraduate Medical Educn Adv Leeds Univ 90-93; rtd 93; Perm to Offic *Ex* from 98. *Freshwater, 4 Marles Close, Awliscombe, Honiton EX14 3GA* Tel (01404) 44296

ROGERS, Maurice George Walden. b 23. AKC51. **d** 52 **p** 53. C Bedford All SS *St Alb* 52-56; C Southfields St Barn *S'wark* 56-58; C Chingford SS Pet and Paul *Chelmsf* 58-61; V Gt Ilford St Luke 61-72; V Woodford St Barn 72-89; rtd 89; Perm to Offic *Chelmsf* from 89 and *Win* from 93. *The Coach House, 13 Bodorgan Road, Bournemouth BH2 6NQ* Tel (01202) 291034

ROGERS, Michael Andrew. b 47. OBE91. FRAeS96. Ripon Coll Cuddesdon. **d** 01 **p** 02. C Bromsgrove St Jo *Worc* 01-04; R Berrow w Pendock, Eldersfield, Hollybush etc from 04. *The Vicarage, Berrow, Malvern WR13 6JN* Tel (01684) 833230 E-mail mandmrogers@btinternet.com

ROGERS, Michael Ernest. b 34. Sarum & Wells Th Coll 83. **d** 85 **p** 86. C Roehampton H Trin *S'wark* 85-88; V Ryhill *Wakef* 88-94; V S Elmsall 94-00; rtd 00; Perm to Offic *Derby* from 00. *The Willows, 49 Main Street, Weston-on-Trent, Derby DE72 2BL* Tel (01332) 700273

ROGERS, Canon Michael Hugh Walton. b 52. K Coll Lon BD73 AKC73. St Aug Coll Cant 74. **d** 75 **p** 76. C Eastbourne St Andr *Chich* 75-78; C Uppingham w Ayston *Pet* 78-82; V Eye 82-90; R Cottesmore and Barrow w Ashwell and Burley 90-04; C from 04; C Greetham and Thistleton w Stretton and Clipsham 01-05; P-in-c from 05; RD Rutland 95-00; Can Pet Cathl from 01. *The Rectory, 38 Main Street, Cottesmore, Oakham LE15 7DJ* Tel (01572) 812202 E-mail mhwrogers@btinternet.com

ROGERS, Canon Noel Desmond. b 26. TD71. Univ of Wales (Lamp) BA51. **d** 53 **p** 54. C Rhyl w St Ann *St As* 53-58; V Everton St Geo *Liv* 58-64; R Newton in Makerfield Em 64-74; V Rostherne w Bollington *Ches* from 74; P-in-c Over Tabley and High Legh 93-98; RD Knutsford 85-96; Hon Can Ches Cathl from 87; CF (TA) 59-75; CF (R of O) 75-81. *The Vicarage, Rostherne Lane, Rostherne Village, Knutsford WA16 6RZ* Tel (01565) 830595

ROGERS, Mrs Pamela Rose. b 46. Keswick Hall Coll CertEd68. S Dios Minl Tr Scheme 92. **d** 95 **p** 96. NSM Axbridge w Shipham and Rowberrow *B & W* from 95; Bp's Officer for Ordained NSM (Wells Adnry) from 02. *28 Beech Road, Shipham, Winscombe BS25 1SB* Tel (01934) 842685

ROGERS, Mrs Patricia Anne. b 54. Lon Univ BD. Trin Coll Bris. **d** 87 **p** 94. Hon C Gayton Gp of Par *Nor* 87-91; Hon C Rackheath and Salhouse 91-96; Chapl to the Deaf 91-96; Chapl to the Deaf *Pet* 96-00; Visual Communications from 00. *1-2 Lees Cottages, Poole Lane, Thornton-le-Moors, Chester CH2 4JE*

ROGERS, Philip John. b 52. Univ of Wales CertEd74 Nottm Univ BTh79. St Jo Coll Nottm 76. **d** 79 **p** 80. C Stretford St Bride *Man* 79-84; P-in-c Plumstead St Jo w St Jas and St Paul *S'wark* 84-85; V from 85. *St John's Vicarage, 176 Griffin Road, London SE18 7QA* Tel (020) 8855 1827
E-mail philipjrogers@ukonline.co.uk

ROGERS (née GOLDER), Mrs Rebecca Marie (Beki). b 71. Brunel Univ BA94. Trin Coll Bris BA02. **d** 02 **p** 03. C Short Heath *Birm* from 02; NSM Roxeth *Lon* from 05. *58 Drury Road, Harrow HA1 4BW* Tel (020) 8423 1913
E-mail bekirogers@hotmail.com

ROGERS, Richard Anthony. b 46. Ex Coll Ox BA69 Birm Univ DipTh70. Qu Coll Birm 70. **d** 71 **p** 72. C Shirley *Birm* 71-74; Chapl Solihull Sch 74-78; Hon C Cotteridge *Birm* 78-84; Hon C Hill 84-93; Hd RE Kings Norton Sch from 93; Perm to Offic from 93. *48 Jordan Road, Sutton Coldfield B75 5AB* Tel 0121-308 0310

ROGERS, Richard Jonathan. b 64. Trin Coll Bris BTh96. **d** 96 **p** 97. C Carterton *Ox* 96-00; Crosslinks 00-03; Perm to Offic *B & W* from 00. *11 East End Avenue, Warminster BA12 9NF* Tel (01985) 214123

ROGERS, Canon Robert. b 42. Bernard Gilpin Soc Dur 66 St Aid Birkenhead 67 Ridley Hall Cam 69. **d** 70 **p** 71. C Childwall St Dav *Liv* 70-73; C Huntington *York* 73-76; TR Brayton 76-89; RD Selby 84-89; V New Malton 89-98; RD Bulmer and Malton 97-98; Asst Chapl York Health Services NHS Trust 98-99; Sen Chapl from 99; Can and Preb York Minster *York* from 03. *York District Hospital, Wiggington Road, York YO31 8HE* Tel (01904) 725579 E-mail bob.rogers@york.nhs.uk

ROGERS, Robert Charles. b 55. St Pet Coll Birm CertEd77 Warwick Univ MA99 Univ Coll Worc PGCertEBD00. St Jo Coll Nottm 87. **d** 89 **p** 90. C Wellesbourne *Cov* 89-93; R Bourton w Frankton and Stretton on Dunsmore etc 93-97; Behaviour Support Teacher Warks LEA from 98; Lic to Offic from 98. *18 Waring Way, Dunchurch, Rugby CV22 6PH* Tel (01788) 817361

ROGERS, Robin. *See* ROGERS, John Robin

ROGERS, Ronald James. b 31. Bris Univ BA56 St Cath Soc Ox BA58 MA65. Wycliffe Hall Ox 56. **d** 58 **p** 59. C Gt Yarmouth *Nor* 58-62; C Newington St Mary *S'wark* 67-69; C Liv Our Lady and St Nic w St Anne *Liv* 78-83; C Pimlico St Pet w Westmr Ch Ch *Lon* 83-85; Chapl Westmr City Sch 85-87; P-in-c Pimlico St Sav *Lon* 87-96; rtd 96; Chapl Izmir (Smyrna) w Bornova *Eur* 96-01; P-in-c Palermo w Taormina from 01. *Chaplaincy Residence, via Stabile Mariana 118B, 90139 Palermo, Sicily* Tel and fax (0039) (09) 158 5220

ROGERS, Ms Sally Jean. b 54. Univ of Wales (Lamp) BA77 Nottm Univ BTh87. Linc Th Coll 84. **d** 87 **p** 94. Par Dn Bris St Mary Redcliffe w Temple etc *Bris* 87-90; Par Dn Greenford H Cross *Lon* 90-94; C 94-96; TV Hemel Hempstead *St Alb* 96-02; Perm to Offic from 02. *62 Clarence Road, London E17 6AQ* Tel (020) 8531 4992

ROGERS, Trevor. *See* ROGERS, John William Trevor

ROGERS, William. *See* ROGERS, Clive William

ROGERS, William Arthur. b 41. Lon Univ BA64 CertEd. Chich Th Coll 79. **d** 81 **p** 82. C Chandler's Ford *Win* 81-84; R Bentley and Binsted 84-94; P-in-c The Lulworths, Winfrith Newburgh and Chaldon *Sarum* 94-99; rtd 99. *2 Hazel Close, Teignmouth TQ14 8RN* Tel (01626) 879183

ROGERSON, Anthony Carroll. b 37. Trin Coll Ox BA59 MA63 MIPD92. St Alb and Ox Min Course 96. **d** 98 **p** 99. NSM Radley and Sunningwell *Ox* 98-02; Perm to Offic from 02. *Noggins, 35 Lower Radley, Abingdon OX14 3AY* Tel (01235) 550214
E-mail tonyrogerson@cygnet.org.uk

✠**ROGERSON, The Rt Revd Barry.** b 36. Leeds Univ BA60 Bris Univ Hon LLD93. Wells Th Coll 60. **d** 62 **p** 63 **c** 79. C S Shields St Hilda w St Thos *Dur* 62-65; C Bishopwearmouth St Nic 65-67; Lect Lich Th Coll 67-71; Vice-Prin 71-72; Lect Sarum & Wells Th Coll 72-74; V Wednesfield St Thos *Lich* 75-79; TR Wednesfield 79; Suff Bp Wolverhampton 79-85; Bp Bris 85-02; rtd 02; Hon Asst Bp B & W from 03. *Flat 2, 30 Albert Road, Clevedon BS21 7RR* Tel (01275) 541964
E-mail barry.rogerson@blueyonder.co.uk

ROGERSON, Cecil Theodore. b 59. St Paul's Coll Grahamstown DipTh81. **d** 81 **p** 83. S Africa 81-97; TV Wordsley *Worc* from 97. *1 Denleigh Road, Kingswinford DY6 8QB* Tel and fax (01384) 278692 Mobile 07960-380729
E-mail ctroger@blueyonder.co.uk

ROGERSON, Colin Scott. b 30. St Andr Univ MA55. Edin Th Coll. **d** 57 **p** 58. C Byker St Ant *Newc* 57-59; C Newc St Geo 59-63; C Wooler 63-67; V Tynemouth St Aug 67-75; C Dur St Marg *Dur* 75-88; P-in-c Hebburn St Jo 88-95; rtd 95; Perm to Offic *Dur* from 95. *6 Edlingham Road, Durham DH1 5YS* Tel 0191-386 1956

ROGERSON, Canon David George. b 38. St Chad's Coll Dur BA60 Newc Univ DipEd67. **d** 63 **p** 64. C Wallsend St Luke *Newc* 63-67; C Delaval 67-70; V Long Benton St Mary 70-81; V N Sunderland 81-03; Warden Seahouses Dioc Hostel 81-03; Miss to Seafarers 81-03; Hon Can Newc Cathl *Newc* 02-03; rtd 03; Perm to Offic *Nor* from 03. *7 Marsh Lane, Wells-next-the-Sea NR23 1EG* Tel (01328) 710814

ROGERSON, Canon Ian Matthew. b 45. Bede Coll Dur CertEd67 Open Univ BA76. Oak Hill Th Coll DipHE81. **d** 83 **p** 84. C Haughton St Mary *Man* 83-86; V Ramsbottom St Andr from 86; P-in-c Edenfield and Stubbins from 04; AD Bury from 96; Hon Can Man Cathl from 04. *St Andrew's Vicarage, 2 Henwick Hall Avenue, Ramsbottom, Bury BL0 9YH* Tel and fax (01706) 826482

ROGERSON, Prof John William. b 35. Man Univ BD61 DD75 Linacre Ho Ox BA63 MA67 Aber Univ Hon DD98 Friedrich Schiller Univ DrTheol05. Ripon Hall Ox 61. **d** 64 **p** 66. C Dur St Oswald *Dur* 64-67; Lect Th Dur Univ 64-75; Sen Lect 75-79; Lic to Offic *Dur* 67-79; Lic to Offic *Sheff* from 79; Prof Bibl Studies Sheff Univ 79-96; Hd of Dept 79-94; Hon Can Sheff Cathl *Sheff* 82-95. *60 Marlborough Road, Sheffield S10 1DB* Tel 0114-268 1426

ROLAND, Andrew Osborne. b 45. Mert Coll Ox BA66 DPM69. Cranmer Hall Dur BA84. **d** 84 **p** 85. C Streatham St Leon *S'wark* 84-87; C Kingston All SS w St Jo 87-94; P-in-c Hackbridge and Beddington Corner from 94. *All Saints' Vicarage, New Road, Mitcham CR4 4JL* Tel (020) 8648 3650

ROLFE, Charles Edward. b 34. Wells Th Coll 68. **d** 70 **p** 71. C Bath Twerton-on-Avon *B & W* 70-79; TV Wellington and Distr 79-85; P-in-c Frome Ch Ch 85-89; V 89-94; Chapl Victoria Hosp Frome 85-94; Chapl St Adhelm's Hosp Frome 88-94; rtd 94; NSM Fordingbridge *Win* 95-01; NSM Hale w S Charford 95-01; NSM Fordingbridge and Breamore and Hale etc 01-05. *14 Ashford Close, Fordingbridge SP6 1DH* Tel (01425) 652684
E-mail charles@rolfe14.freeserve.co.uk

ROLFE, Joseph William. b 37. Qu Coll Birm 78. **d** 81 **p** 82. NSM Tredington and Darlingscott w Newbold on Stour *Cov* 81-91; NSM Brailes from 91; NSM Sutton under Brailes from 91; NSM Shipston Deanery from 98. *35 Manor Lane, Shipston-on-Stour CV36 4EF* Tel (01608) 661737

ROLFE, Paul Douglas. b 46. MIBC90. N Ord Course 90. **d** 93 **p** 94. C Urmston *Man* 93-96; V Lawton Moor 96-03; P-in-c Burnage St Nic from 03. *408 Kingsway, Burnage, Manchester M19 1PL* Tel 0161-432 7009
E-mail paul.d.rolfe@btinternet.com

ROLLETT, Robert Henry. b 39. Leeds Univ BA61 Leic Univ CertEd62. Linc Th Coll 77. **d** 79 **p** 80. C Littleport *Ely* 79-82; P-in-c Manea 82-83; V 83-85; P-in-c Wimblington 82-83; R 83-85; V Thorney Abbey 85-93; P-in-c The Ramseys and Upwood 93-94; TR 94-99; rtd 99; P-in-c Scalford w Goadby Marwood and Wycombe etc *Leic* 99-00. *2 Stockerston Crescent, Uppingham, Oakham LE15 9UB* Tel (01572) 823685

ROLLINS, David. b 65. Nene Coll Northampton DipSW93 De Montfort Univ BA98. St Steph Ho Ox 99. **d** 01 **p** 02. C Leic St Aid *Leic* 01-05; P-in-c Corringham *Chelmsf* from 05; P-in-c Fobbing from 05. *The Rectory, Church Road, Corringham, Stanford-le-Hope SS17 9AP* Tel (01375) 673074
E-mail drollins@drollins.freeserve.co.uk

ROLLINSON, Canon John Knighton. b 14. FRCO34 Sheff Univ BMus36 AKC48. **d** 49 **p** 50. C Ilkeston St Mary *Derby* 49-53; C Wirksworth w Carsington 53-55; PC Dethick, Lea and Holloway 55-64; R Whittington 64-81; Chapl Whittington Hall Hosp 64-82; P-in-c New Whittington 78-81; rtd 81; Perm to Offic *Derby* from 81. *75 Yew Tree Drive, Somersall, Chesterfield S40 3NB* Tel (01246) 568647

ROLLS, Peter. b 40. Leeds Inst of Educn CertEd. N Ord Course 80. **d** 83 **p** 84. NSM Meltham *Wakef* from 83. *14 Heather Road, Meltham, Huddersfield HD7 3EY* Tel (01484) 340342

ROLPH, Pauline Gladys. b 30. SRN51 SCM53 HVCert65. Oak Hill Th Coll 88. **d** 90 **p** 94. Hon C Chingford St Anne *Chelmsf* 90-96; rtd 96; Perm to Offic *Sarum* from 96. *1 Black Lawn, Gillingham SP8 4SD* Tel (01747) 822502 Fax 821474

ROLPH, Reginald Lewis George. b 29. Open Univ BA74. Bps' Coll Cheshunt 55. **d** 58 **p** 59. C Perivale *Lon* 58-61; C Wokingham St Paul *Ox* 61-63; C Letchworth *St Alb* 63-78; Perm to Offic from 78; rtd 93. *22 Souberie Avenue, Letchworth Garden City SG6 3JA* Tel (01462) 684596

ROLSTON, Cyril Willis Matthias. b 29. CITC 66. **d** 68 **p** 69. C Portadown St Mark *Arm* 68-71; I Loughgilly w Clare 71-81; Dir of Ords from 72; Asst Chapl Craigavon Area Hosp Gp Trust 80-96; I Moy w Charlemont *Arm* 81-96; Preb Arm Cathl 92-96; rtd 96; Chapl Armagh and Dungannon Health and Soc Services from 96. *19 Lower Parklands, Dungannon BT71 7JN* Tel (028) 8772 5910

ROLSTON, John Ormsby. b 28. TCD BA51 MA59 BD63. CITC 51. **d** 51 **p** 52. C Belfast St Mary Magd *Conn* 51-55; C Knock *D & D* 55-59; P-in-c Gilnahirk 59-63; I 63-66; I Belfast St Jas *Conn* 66-79; I Belfast St Jas w St Silas 79-96; Can Belf Cathl 82-96; Prec Belf Cathl 88-96; Adn Conn 88-96; rtd 96; Dioc C *Conn* 96-98. *5 Springburn Park, Lisburn BT27 5QZ* Tel (028) 9267 8932 E-mail j.o.rolston@lineone.net

ROLTON, Patrick Hugh. b 49. Sarum & Wells Th Coll 72. **d** 74 **p** 75. C Roch 74-79; C Edenbridge 79-81; R N Cray 81-97; rtd 97. *45 Chalk Pit Avenue, Orpington BR5 3JJ* Tel (01689) 872916

ROM, Norman Charles. b 24. S'wark Ord Course 63. **d** 66 **p** 67. C Leatherhead *Guildf* 66-71; Chapl HM Pris Cant 71-74; Chapl HM Pris Pentonville 74-85; Chapl HM Pris Stocken 85-87; P-in-c Empingham *Pet* 85-87; R Empingham and Exton w Horn w Whitwell 87-94; rtd 94; Perm to Offic *Pet* from 94 and *Linc* from 03. *11 Dundee Drive, Stamford PE9 2TR* Tel (01780) 482051

ROMANIS, Adam John Aidan. b 57. Pemb Coll Ox BA78 MA83. Westcott Ho Cam 81. **d** 84 **p** 85. C Northfield *Birm* 84-88; TV Seaton Hirst *Newc* 88-93; V Newc Ch Ch w St Ann 93-99; V Cowley St Jo *Ox* from 99. *The Vicarage, 271 Cowley Road, Oxford OX4 2AJ* Tel (01865) 242396 E-mail adamox4@aol.com

ROMER, William Miller. b 35. Brown Univ Rhode Is BA57. MDiv60. **d** 60 **p** 60. USA 60-03; P-in-c Lake Luzerne St Mary 60-64; Asst Min Hanover St Andr 64-65; V NY St Boniface 65-70; P-in-c Troy St Luke 70-71; R Rochester Redeemer 98-03; NSM Rathkeale w Askeaton, Kilcornan and Kilnaughtin *L & K* from 03. *The Rectory, Cragmore, Askeaton, Co Limerick, Irish Republic* Tel and fax (00353) (61) 398857 Mobile 87-236 8552 E-mail molroms@aol.com

RONAYNE, Peter Henry. b 34. FCA68. Oak Hill Th Coll 64. **d** 66 **p** 67. C Chesham St Mary *Ox* 66-69; C Worthing H Trin *Chich* 69-74; V Shoreditch St Leon w St Mich *Lon* 74-82; P-in-c Norwood St Luke *S'wark* 82-85; V 85-94; V W Norwood St Luke 94-99; RD Streatham 87-91; rtd 99; Perm to Offic *S'wark* 00-04. *54 Maywater Close, South Croydon CR2 0LS* Tel (020) 8651 9743

RONCHETTI, Quentin Marcus. b 56. Ripon Coll Cuddesdon 79. **d** 80 **p** 81. C Eastbourne St Mary *Chich* 80-83; C Moulsecoomb 83-85; TV 85-90; V Findon Valley 90-97; V Shoreham Beach from 97. *The Vicarage, West Beach, Shoreham-by-Sea BN43 5LF* Tel (01273) 453768

RONE, The Ven James. b 35. St Steph Ho Ox 79. **d** 80 **p** 81. C Stony Stratford *Ox* 80-82; P-in-c Fordham St Pet *Ely* 82-83; V 83-89; P-in-c Kennett 82-83; R 83-89; Can Res Ely Cathl 89-95; Treas 92-95; Adn Wisbech 95-02; Hon Can Ely Cathl 95-02; Bp's Adv for Hosp Chapl 96-02; rtd 03; Perm to Offic *Ely* from 03. *Little Housing, 32 Lumley Close, Ely CB7 4FG* Tel (01353) 667088

ROOKE, James Templeman. b 43. Saltley Tr Coll Birm CertEd65. EMMTC 82. **d** 84 **p** 85. NSM Bassingham *Linc* 84-89; NSM Hykeham 89-94; Sub Chapl HM Pris Morton Hall 94; P-in-c Borrowdale *Carl* 94-97; Chapl Keswick Sch 94-97; NSM Hykeham *Linc* 97-02; Sub Chapl HM Pris Morton Hall 97-00; NSM Swinderby *Linc* from 02; CF (ACF) from 00. *The Chestnuts, Main Street, Norton Disney, Lincoln LN6 9JU* Tel (01522) 788315

ROOKE, John George Michael. b 47. St Jo Coll Dur BA72. Cranmer Hall Dur 71. **d** 74 **p** 75. C Skelmersdale St Paul *Liv* 74-78; TV Speke St Aid 78-81; Ind Chapl 81-85; V Knotty Ash St Jo from 85. *St John's Vicarage, Thomas Lane, Liverpool L14 5NR* Tel 0151-228 2396

ROOKE, The Ven Patrick William. b 55. Open Univ BA85. Sarum & Wells Th Coll 75. **d** 78 **p** 79. C Mossley *Conn* 78-81; C Ballywillan 81-83; I Craigs w Dunaghy and Killagan 83-88; I Ballymore *Arm* 88-94; Asst Prov and Dioc Registrar 92-94; Hon V Choral Arm Cathl 93-94; I Agherton *Conn* from 94; Preb and Can Conn Cathl from 01; Adn Dalriada from 05. *The Rectory, 59 Strand Road, Portstewart BT55 7LU* Tel (028) 7083 2538 *or* 7083 3277 E-mail rooke59@hotmail.com *or* rector@aghertonparish.freeserve.co.uk

ROOKWOOD, Colin John. b 40. TCD BA64 MA68 Lon Univ PGCE67. Clifton Th Coll 67. **d** 70 **p** 71. C Eccleston Ch Ch *Liv* 70-75; V Penge St Jo *Roch* 75-82; V Childwall All SS *Liv* 82-91; Chapl Bethany Sch Goudhurst 91-03; Perm to Offic *Roch* from 01; rtd 03. *3 Spout Lane, Brenchley, Tonbridge TN12 7AP* Tel (01892) 725547 E-mail carolrookwood@aol.com

ROOM, Canon Frederick John. b 24. St Jo Coll Ox BA49 MA53. Wells Th Coll 49. **d** 51 **p** 52. C Bradford cum Beswick *Man* 51-54; C Halliwell St Marg 54-56; C Farnham Royal *Ox* 56-58; C-in-c Farnham Royal S CD 58-70; TV Thetford *Nor* 70-89; Sen Ind Missr 75-89; Hon Can Nor Cathl 77-89; rtd 89; Perm to Offic *Nor* from 89. *61 Beechwood Drive, Thorpe St Andrew, Norwich NR7 0LN* Tel (01603) 435930

ROOME, Mrs Alison Morag Venessa. b 48. Bp Lonsdale Coll TCert71. EMMTC 98. **d** 01 **p** 02. NSM Alfreton *Derby* from 01. *55 Dovedale Crescent, Belper DE56 1HJ* Tel (01773) 825635 E-mail aliroome@lineone.net

ROOMS, Canon Nigel James. b 60. Leeds Univ BSc81 Nottm Univ MA95 CEng86 MIChemE86. Cranmer Hall Dur 87. **d** 90 **p** 91. C Chell *Lich* 90-94; Min Moshi St Marg Tanzania 94-01; Dir Th Educn by Ext 94-01; Hon Can Arusha from 01; Dioc Dir of Tr *S'well* from 02. *12 Lingwood Lane, Woodborough, Nottingham NG14 6DX* Tel 0115-965 4380 *or* (01636) 817231 Fax (01636) 815084 E-mail nigel.rooms@southwell.anglican.org

ROOSE-EVANS, James Humphrey. b 27. St Benet's Hall Ox BA52 MA56. **d** 81 **p** 81. NSM Kington and Weobley *Heref* from 81; NSM Primrose Hill St Mary w Avenue Road St Paul *Lon* from 82. *71 Belsize Park Gardens, London NW3 4JP* Tel (020) 7722 5660

ROOT, Canon Howard Eugene. b 26. Univ of S California BA45 St Cath Soc Ox BA51 Magd Coll Cam MA53 Magd Coll Ox MA70. Ripon Hall Ox 49. **d** 53 **p** 54. C Trumpington *Ely* 53; Asst Lect Div Cam Univ 53-57; Lect 57-66; Fell and Chapl Em Coll Cam 54-56; Fell and Dean 56-66; Wilde Lect Ox Univ 57-60; Delegated Observer Second Vatican Coun 63-65; Prof Th Southn Univ 66-81; Hon Chapl Win Cathl *Win* 66-67; Can Th 67-80; Chmn Abp's Commn on Marriage 68-71; Consultant Lambeth Confs 68 and 88; Jt Ed *Journal of Th Studies* 69-74; Pope Adrian VI Prof Univ of Louvain 79; St Aug Can Cant Cathl *Cant* 80-91; Dir Angl Cen Rome 81-91; Abp Cant's Cllr on Vatican Affairs 81-91; Visiting Prof Pontifical Gregorian Univ Rome 84-91; Preceptor Malling Abbey from 93. *26 St Swithun Street, Winchester SO23 9HU*

ROOT, Preb John Brereton. b 41. Lon Univ BA64 Em Coll Cam BA66 MA. Ridley Hall Cam 64. **d** 68 **p** 69. C Harlesden St Mark *Lon* 68-73; C Lower Homerton St Paul 73-76; Chapl Ridley Hall Cam 76; Vice-Prin 76-79; V Alperton *Lon* from 79; AD Brent 95-00; Preb St Paul's Cathl from 01. *The Vicarage, 34 Stanley Avenue, Wembley HA0 4JB* Tel and fax (020) 8902 1729 *or* tel 8900 0222 Fax 8902 6231 E-mail stjames2000@breathemail.net

ROOTES, William Brian. b 44. St And NSM Tr Scheme 88. **d** 91. NSM Auchterarder *St And* 91-97; NSM Muthill 91-97; Dioc Sec 98-00; Treas Action of Chs Together in Scotland from 01. *Drummond Park Farm, Logiealmond, Perth PH1 3TJ* Tel (01738) 880477 Fax 880709

ROOTHAM, Gerald Raymond. b 47. **d** 02 **p** 03. OLM Mattishall w Mattishall Burgh, Welborne etc *Nor* from 02. *Norfolk Wing, Letton Hall, Shipdham, Thetford IP25 7SA* Tel (01362) 820886

ROPER, David John. b 53. St Steph Ho Ox 93. **d** 95 **p** 96. C Hunstanton St Mary w Ringstead Parva etc *Nor* 95-98; TV E Dereham and Scarning 98-00; R Barham w Bishopsbourne and Kingston *Cant* from 00; C Nonington w Wymynswold and Goodnestone etc from 00; AD E Bridge from 01; Hon Min Can Cant Cathl from 03. *The Rectory, The Street, Barham, Canterbury CT4 6PA* Tel (01227) 831340 E-mail david.roper@clara.co.uk

ROPER, Douglas. b 72. Teesside Univ BA93. Oak Hill Th Coll BA00. **d** 00 **p** 01. C Rugby St Matt *Cov* 00-03; C Mancetter 03-04. *Address temp unknown* Tel 07940-544024 (mobile) E-mail doug.roper@tesco.net

ROPER, Glenn. b 51. York Univ MA91 Caerleon Coll of Educn CertEd73. **d** 04 **p** 05. NSM Ovenden *Wakef* from 04. *113 Meadow Drive, Halifax HX3 5JZ* Tel (01422) 368086 E-mail glenn@roper.fsnet.co.uk

ROPER, Michael Darwin Alston. b 66. Leeds Univ BA03. Coll of Resurr Mirfield 01. **d** 03 **p** 04. C Mortlake w E Sheen *S'wark* from 03. *5 Vernon Road, London SW14 8NH* Tel (020) 8487 9565 E-mail gore_lodge@yahoo.co.uk

ROPER, Neil Vincent James. **d** 98 **p** 99. C Port Talbot St Theodore *Llan* 98-00; C Newton Nottage 00-03; C Treorchy and Treherbert 03; Chapl Quainton Hall Sch Harrow from 04. *Quainton Hall School, Hindes Road, Harrow HA1 1RX* Tel (020) 8427 1304

ROPER, Terence Chaus. b 35. K Coll Lon 56. St Boniface Warminster 59. **d** 60 **p** 61. C Forton *Portsm* 60-63; USA from 63; C Arlington St Alban 63-65; C Dallas St Thos 65-67; R Dallas Our Lady of Grace 67-73; R Irving Redeemer 73-76; R Dallas Transfiguration 76-99; R Philadelphia H Trin from 99. *1815 John F Kennedy Boulevard #2308, Philadelphia, PA 19103, USA* Tel (001) (215) 587 6873 *or* 567 1267

ROPER, Canon Timothy Hamilton. b 34. Qu Coll Cam BA57 MA61. Sarum Th Coll 57. **d** 59 **p** 60. C Kingsthorpe *Pet* 59-62; C Kirkby *Liv* 62-65; Chapl Rossall Sch Fleetwood 65-84; R Arthingworth, Harrington w Oxendon and E Farndon *Pet* 84-99; RD Brixworth 89-94; Can Pet Cathl 94-99; rtd 99. *47 Cromwell Crescent, Market Harborough LE16 8JN* Tel (01858) 468032

ROSAMOND, Derek William. b 49. Linc Th Coll 87. **d** 89 **p** 90. C Coventry Caludon *Cov* 89-93; Urban Regeneration Chapl S Tyneside *Dur* 93-96; TV Sunderland 96-04; Community P SW Stockton from 04; P-in-c Stockton St Paul from 04. *65 Bishopton Road, Stockton-on-Tees TS18 4PE* Tel (01642) 895868 E-mail derekrosamond@hotmail.com

ROSCOE, David John. b 64. UEA BA87 Selw Coll Cam BA93. Aston Tr Scheme 89 Westcott Ho Cam CTM94. **d** 94 **p** 95. C

Ditton St Mich *Liv* 94-98; TV Kirkby 98-99; V Wigan St Steph 99-03; Jt P-in-c Aspull and New Springs 02-03; V New Springs and Whelley from 03; Chapl Wrightington Wigan and Leigh NHS Trust from 03. *St Stephen's Vicarage, 141 Whelley, Wigan WN2 1BL* Tel (01942) 242579

ROSCOE, Simon Nicolas. b 51. SEITE 02. **d** 04. C Whitstable *Cant* from 04. *Middle Heronden, Heronden Road, Eastry, Sandwich CT13 0ET* E-mail snr@studio-ics.com

ROSE, Andrew David. b 45. BA81. Oak Hill Th Coll 78. **d** 81 **p** 82. C Northwood Em *Lon* 81-86; V Iver *Ox* 86-95; R Frinton *Chelmsf* from 95. *The Rectory, 22 Queens Road, Frinton-on-Sea CO13 9BL* Tel (01255) 674664 E-mail rose@rectory-frinton.freeserve.co.uk

ROSE, Anthony James. b 47. Trin Coll Bris BD72. **d** 73 **p** 74. C Halliwell St Pet *Man* 73-76; CF 76-94; R Colchester Ch Ch w St Mary V *Chelmsf* 94-01; RD Colchester 98-01; P-in-c Boreham from 01. *The Vicarage, Church Road, Boreham, Chelmsford CM3 3EG* Tel (01245) 450607 E-mail ajrose@dial.pipex.com

ROSE, Anthony John. b 53. Birm Univ BA79. Trin Coll Bris 84. **d** 86 **p** 87. C The Quinton *Birm* 86-90; R Abbas and Templecombe w Horsington *B & W* 90-98; V New Thundersley *Chelmsf* from 98. *St George's Vicarage, 89 Rushbottom Lane, Benfleet SS7 4DN* Tel (01268) 792088 E-mail anthony.rose@ukonline.co.uk

ROSE, Canon Barry Ernest. b 35. Chich Th Coll 58. **d** 61 **p** 62. C Forest Gate St Edm *Chelmsf* 61-64; Antigua 64-66; Dominica 66-69; V St Mary-at-Latton *Chelmsf* 69-79; V Stansted Mountfitchet 79-88; V Halstead St Andr w H Trin and Greenstead Green 88-00; RD Halstead and Coggeshall 91-95; RD Hinckford 95-98; Hon Can Chelmsf Cathl 96-00; rtd 00; Perm to Offic *Chelmsf* from 00. *26 Gurton Road, Coggeshall CO6 1QA* Tel (01376) 563988 Mobile 07984-546638 E-mail jbrose@talk21.com

ROSE, Canon Bernard Frederick. b 47. **d** 91 **p** 92. OLM Ipswich St Thos *St E* from 91; Hon Can St E Cathl from 05. *84 Chesterfield Drive, Ipswich IP1 6DN* Tel (01473) 462390

ROSE, Charles. *See* ROSE, Westmoreland Charles Edward

ROSE, Christopher John. b 66. Edin Univ BSc88. EAMTC 97. **d** 00 **p** 01. NSM Cambridge St Paul *Ely* from 00. *6 Montreal Road, Cambridge CB1 3NP* Tel (01223) 511241 *or* 213162 E-mail chris.rose@romseymill.org.uk

ROSE, David. *See* ROSE, John David

ROSE, Eve. b 63. Leeds Univ BA85. Qu Coll Birm 99. **d** 01 **p** 02. C Seacroft *Ripon* 01-04; Chapl Hull and E Riding Community Health NHS Trust from 04. *West House, Westwood Hospital, Woodlands, Beverley HU17 8BU* Tel (01482) 886500 Mobile 07771-851725 Fax (01482) 886633

ROSE, Miss Geraldine Susan. b 47. Trin Coll Bris BD78. **dss** 78 **d** 87 **p** 94. Tonbridge St Steph *Roch* 78-80; Littleover *Derby* 80-88; Par Dn 87-88; Par Dn Wombwell *Sheff* 88-94; C 94-96; rtd 96; Perm to Offic *Sheff* from 96. *5 Wheatcroft, Conisbrough, Doncaster DN12 2BL* Tel (01709) 867761 E-mail sroserhodon@onetel.net.uk

ROSE, Canon Gordon Henry. b 23. St Cath Soc Ox BA48 MA53. Wells Th Coll 49. **d** 50 **p** 51. C Bournemouth St Andr *Win* 50-55; R Bishopstoke 55-92; Hon Can Win Cathl 82-92; rtd 92; Perm to Offic *Win* from 92. *44 Westbury Court, Hedge End, Southampton SO30 0HN* Tel (01489) 781309

ROSE, Harry. *See* ROSE, Lionel Stafford Harry

ROSE, Ingrid Elizabeth. b 57. Univ of Wales (Abth) BA78 DipEd79. Trin Coll Carmarthen 84. **d** 87 **p** 01. NSM Ysbyty Cynfyn w Llantrisant and Eglwys Newydd *St D* 87-90 and 92-95. *Ystwyth Villa, Pontrhydygroes, Ystrad Meurig SY25 6DS* Tel (01974) 282398

ROSE, John Clement Wansey. b 46. New Coll Ox BA71 MA72. Ripon Hall Ox 70. **d** 72 **p** 73. C Harborne St Pet *Birm* 72-76; TV Kings Norton 76-81; V Maney 81-02; R Condover w Frodesley, Acton Burnell etc *Heref* from 02. *The Vicarage, Condover, Shrewsbury SY5 7AA* Tel (01743) 872251

ROSE, John David. b 40. Dioc OLM tr scheme 97. **d** 00 **p** 01. OLM Prescot *Liv* from 00. *18 Eccleston Gardens, St Helens WA10 3BL* Tel (01744) 736168 Mobile 07808-350859 Fax 0151-426 5121

ROSE, Canon Judith Anne. b 36. Newnham Coll Cam BA57 MA65 K Coll Lon PhD91. Ripon Coll Cuddesdon. **d** 87 **p** 94. Par Dn Kettering All SS *Pet* 87-92; P-in-c Aldwincle w Thorpe Achurch, Pilton, Wadenhoe etc 92-97; R 97-03; RD Oundle 98-03; Adv in Women's Min 01-03; Can Pet Cathl 01-03; rtd 03. *15 Standish Court, Campaign Avenue, Peterborough PE2 9RR* Tel (01733) 553272 E-mail canons.rose@virgin.net

ROSE, Judith Barbara. b 51. TCert72. St Alb and Ox Min Course 96. **d** 99 **p** 00. OLM Stantonbury and Willen *Ox* from 99. *16 Runnymede, Giffard Park, Milton Keynes MK14 5QL* Tel (01908) 618634 Fax as telephone

ROSE, The Ven Kathleen Judith. b 37. Lon Univ DipTh66. Lon Bible Coll BD73 St Mich Ho Ox 64. **dss** 76 **d** 87 **p** 94. Leeds St Geo *Ripon* 76-81; Bradf Cathl *Bradf* 81-85; S Gillingham *Roch* 85-87; Par Dn 87-90; RD Gillingham 88-90; Bp's Dom Chapl 90-95; Asst Dir of Ords 90-95; Hon Can Roch Cathl 93-02; Acting Adn Tonbridge 95-96; Adn Tonbridge 96-02; rtd 02; Perm to Offic *B & W* from 03. *4 Glebelands Close, Cheddar BS27 3XP* Tel (01934) 741708 Mobile 07736-616382

ROSE, Lionel Stafford Harry. b 38. MBE93. Wells Th Coll 69. **d** 71 **p** 72. C Minchinhampton *Glouc* 71-73; C Thornbury 73-75; R Ruardean 75-80; V Whiteshill 80-84; CF 84-93; Chapl HM Pris Kirkham 93-95; Chapl HM Pris Wymott 95-01; Chapl HM Pris Rye Hill 01; rtd 01; Perm to Offic *Ely* from 02. *4 Samian Close, Highfield, Caldecote, Cambridge CB3 7GP*

ROSE, Mrs Lynda Kathryn. b 51. Barrister-at-Law (Gray's Inn) 81 Ex Univ BA73 Ox Univ BA86. Wycliffe Hall Ox 87. **d** 87 **p** 94. C Highfield *Ox* 87-88; C Ox St Clem 89-93; Dir Anastasis Min 93-99; NSM Ambrosden w Merton and Piddington 94-99; Pres Assn Chr Writers from 99. *95 Staunton Road, Oxford OX3 7TR* Tel (01865) 768774

ROSE, Canon Paul Rosamond. b 32. Trin Hall Cam BA56 MA60. Westcott Ho Cam 57. **d** 59 **p** 60. C Wandsworth St Anne *S'wark* 59-61; C Tormohun *Ex* 61-64; S Rhodesia 64-65; Rhodesia 65-67; Min Can, Prec and Sacr Pet Cathl *Pet* 67-72; V Paddington St Jo w St Mich *Lon* 72-79; PV Westmr Abbey 74-79; Min Can and Prec Cant Cathl *Cant* 79-84; V Rothwell w Orton *Pet* 84-87; R Rothwell w Orton, Rushton w Glendon and Pipewell 87-97; Can Pet Cathl 94-97; rtd 97; Chapl Heidelberg *Eur* 98; Perm to Offic *Pet* from 97; *Lon* and *Eur* from 98; *Ely* from 03. *15 Standish Court, Campaign Avenue, Peterborough PE2 9RR* Tel (01733) 553272 E-mail canons.rose@virgin.net

ROSE, Robert Alec Lewis. b 41. Man Univ BSc64. Wycliffe Hall Ox 85. **d** 87 **p** 88. C Vange *Chelmsf* 87-91; C Langdon Hills 91-94; P-in-c Bentley Common 94-00; P-in-c Kelvedon Hatch 94-00; P-in-c Navestock 94-00; R Bentley Common, Kelvedon Hatch and Navestock from 00. *The Rectory, 2 Church Road, Kelvedon Hatch, Brentwood CM14 5TJ* Tel and fax (01277) 373486 E-mail robdaphnerose@talk21.com

ROSE, Susan. *See* ROSE, Miss Geraldine Susan

ROSE, Mrs Susan Margaret. b 59. Westmr Coll of Educn BEd81. St Alb and Ox Min Course 95. **d** 98 **p** 99. C N Petherton w Northmoor Green *B & W* 98-01; P-in-c 01-03; P-in-c N Newton w St Michaelchurch, Thurloxton etc 01-03; R Alfred Jewel from 03. *The Dower House, North Petherton, Bridgwater TA6 6SE* Tel (01278) 662429 E-mail rev.suerose@virgin.net

ROSE, Miss Susan Mary. b 36. TCert56. Dalton Ho Bris 68 Trin Coll Bris 74. **dss** 81 **d** 87 **p** 94. Brinsworth w Catcliffe *Sheff* 75-77; Scargill Ho 77-83; Netherthorpe *Sheff* 83-87; Tutor Trin Coll Bris 87-96; V Normanton *Wakef* 96-01; rtd 01; Perm to Offic *Sheff* from 01 and *Wakef* from 02. *23 Kendal Vale, Worsborough Bridge, Barnsley S70 5NL* Tel (01226) 771590

ROSE, Timothy Edward Francis. b 72. Univ of Wales (Cardiff) BD93 MA95 K Coll Lon PhD98. Wycliffe Hall Ox MTh03. **d** 01 **p** 02. C Jesmond H Trin and Newc St Barn and St Jude *Newc* 01-04; Chapl R Holloway and Bedf New Coll *Lon* from 04. *10 Willow Walk, Englefield Green, Egham TW20 0DQ* Tel (01784) 471497 *or* 443070 Mobile 07709-722325 E-mail tim.rose@rhul.ac.uk

ROSE, Westmoreland Charles Edward. b 32. St Jo Coll Nottm 85. **d** 87 **p** 88. C Fairfield *Derby* 87-90; V Linton and Castle Gresley 90-01; rtd 01; Perm to Offic *Derby* from 01. *17 Radcliffe Drive, Derby DE22 3LB* Tel (01332) 207271

ROSE-CASEMORE, Claire Pamela. b 63. St Paul's Cheltenham BA84 St Luke's Coll Ex PGCE85 Anglia Poly Univ MA02. Ridley Hall Cam 95. **d** 97 **p** 98. Par Dn Kingsthorpe w Northampton St Dav *Pet* 97-98; C 98-01; TV Daventry, Ashby St Ledgers, Braunston etc from 01. *The Rectory, 71 High Street, Braunston, Daventry NN11 7HS* Tel (01788) 890235 E-mail clairerc@btopenworld.com

ROSE-CASEMORE, John. b 27. Chich Th Coll. **d** 55 **p** 56. C Epsom Common Ch Ch *Guildf* 55-58; C Hednesford *Lich* 58-60; V Dawley 60-65; R Puttenham and Wanborough *Guildf* 65-72; R Frimley 72-83; RD Surrey Heath 76-81; R Ludgershall and Faberstown *Sarum* 83-86; R Tidworth, Ludgershall and Faberstown 86-92; rtd 92; Perm to Offic *Ex* from 93. *5 Culvery Close, Woodbury, Exeter EX5 1LZ* Tel (01395) 233426

ROSE-CASEMORE, Miss Penelope Jane. b 56. Bris Univ CertEd77 BEd78. Westcott Ho Cam 83. **dss** 85 **d** 87 **p** 94. Waterloo St Jo w St Andr *S'wark* 85-87; Par Dn 87-88; Asst Chapl Gt Ormond Street Hosp for Sick Children Lon 88-90; Par Dn Balham St Mary and St Jo *S'wark* 90-94; C 94-96; Par Dn Upper Tooting H Trin 90-94; C 94-96; TV Clapham Team 96-01; V Clapham Ch Ch and St Jo from 02; AD Clapham from 05. *Christchurch Vicarage, 39 Union Grove, London SW8 2QT* Tel and fax (020) 7622 3552

ROSEDALE, John Richard. b 54. N Ord Course 02. **d** 05. NSM Hadfield *Derby* from 05. *43 Spire Hollin, Glossop SK13 7BJ* Tel (01457) 857441 E-mail john@glossop.org

ROSEWEIR, Clifford John. b 43. Glas Univ MA64 Kingston Poly Dip Personnel Mgt 81 MIPD81. S'wark Ord Course 83. **d** 84 **p** 85. NSM Redhill H Trin *S'wark* 84-89; P-in-c Croydon St Martin 89-92; Perm to Offic 92-93; Hon C Wallington H Trin 93-94; V Croydon Ch Ch 94-97. *206 Bridle Road, Shirley,*

Croydon CR0 8HL Tel (020) 8765 7629 *or* 8777 2820 Mobile 07850-480058

ROSHEUVEL, Canon Siegfried Winslow Patrick. b 39. Goldsmiths' Coll Lon BA86 Westmr Coll Ox MTh01. Codrington Coll Barbados 64. **d** 68 **p** 68. Guyana 68-75; C Worksop Priory *S'well* 75-78; Area Sec USPG *Chelmsf* and *St Alb* 78-92; *Lon* 88-92; Dep Chapl HM Pris Wandsworth 92-93; Chapl HM Pris Wealstun 93-96; Sen Chapl HM Pris Brixton 96-04; rtd 04; Can Cape Coast from 94; Hon Chapl S'wark Cathl *S'wark* from 97. *9 Holmewood Gardens, London SW2 3RS* Tel (020) 8671 7604 E-mail patrick@bunta.fsworld.co.uk

ROSIER, The Rt Revd Stanley Bruce. b 28. Univ of W Aus BSc48 Ox Univ BA52 MA56. Westcott Ho Cam 53 Melbourne Coll of Div DipRE63. **d** 54 **p** 55 **c** 67. C Ecclesall *Sheff* 54-57; Australia from 57; Can Perth 66-67; Adn Northam 67; Bp Willochra 70-87; Asst Bp 90-92; R Parkside 87-94; rtd 94. *5A Fowler's Road, Glenunga, S Australia 5064* Tel (0061) (8) 8379 5213 E-mail bfrosier@senet.com.au

ROSKELLY, James Hereward Emmanuel. b 57. BSc ACSM80. Cranmer Hall Dur 83. **d** 86 **p** 87. C Dunster, Carhampton and Withycombe w Rodhuish *B & W* 86-90; C Ealing St Mary *Lon* 90-93; Chapl R Marsden Hosp Lon and Surrey 93-95; CF 95-03; TV Rayleigh *Chelmsf* from 03. *St Michael's House, 13 Sir Walter Raleigh Drive, Rayleigh SS6 9BJ* Tel 07989-442434 (mobile) E-mail jamesroskelly@aol.com

ROSKILLY, John Noel. b 33. DRCOG60 MRCGP68 Man Univ MB, ChB58. St Deiniol's Hawarden 74. **d** 75 **p** 76. NSM Bramhall *Ches* 75-86; V Capesthorne w Siddington and Marton 86-91; Dioc Dir of Counselling 84-93; Bp's Officer for NSM 87-93; NSM Macclesfield St Paul 92-93; rtd 93; Perm to Offic *Ches* from 93. *North View, Hawkins Lane, Rainow, Macclesfield SK10 5TL* Tel (01625) 501014

ROSKROW, Neil. b 27. FBCO80. St Alb Minl Tr Scheme 82. **d** 85 **p** 86. NSM Digswell and Panshanger *St Alb* 85-90; P-in-c Gt Gaddesden 90-95; P-in-c Lt Gaddesden 92-95; rtd 96; Perm to Offic *St Alb* from 96. *Trewinard, 64 New Road, Welwyn AL6 0AN* Tel (01438) 714132

ROSKROW, Mrs Pamela Mary. b 25. St Alb Minl Tr Scheme. **dss** 85 **d** 87 **p** 94. Digswell and Panshanger *St Alb* 85-90; Hon Par Dn 87-90; Hon Par Dn Gt Gaddesden 90-94; Hon C 94-95; Hon Par Dn Lt Gaddesden 92-94; Hon C 94-95; Perm to Offic from 96. *Trewinard, 64 New Road, Welwyn AL6 0AN* Tel (01438) 714132

ROSOMAN, Richard John. b 59. Ripon Coll Cuddesdon 90. **d** 92 **p** 93. C Cradley *Worc* 92-96; Ind Chapl and C Coseley Ch Ch 96-00; V Malvern H Trin and St Jas 00-04. *Address temp unknown* E-mail louise@mrosoman.freeserve.co.uk

ROSS, Alexander. *See* ROSS, David Alexander

ROSS, Canon Anthony McPherson. b 38. OBE. Univ of Wales (Lamp) BA60 Lon Univ BD63. St Mich Coll Llan 60. **d** 61 **p** 62. C Gabalfa *Llan* 61-65; Chapl RN 65-93; QHC 89-93; P-in-c Coln St Aldwyns, Hatherop, Quenington etc *Glouc* 93-95; V from 95; RD Fairford 96-04; Hon Can Glouc Cathl from 02. *The Vicarage, Coln St Aldwyns, Cirencester GL7 5AG* Tel (01285) 750013 E-mail tonyross-cheqs@care4free.net

ROSS, Mrs Audrey Ruth. b 42. Herts Coll BA86. St Alb and Ox Min Course 99. **d** 02 **p** 03. NSM Leavesden All SS *St Alb* from 02. *33 Pine Grove, Bushey WD23 2DY* Tel (01923) 233667

ROSS, David Alexander (Alex). b 46. Lon Univ DipTh73. Oak Hill Th Coll 73. **d** 75 **p** 76. C Northwood Em *Lon* 75-80; R Eastrop *Win* 80-86; V Hove Bp Hannington Memorial Ch *Chich* 86-93; V Muswell Hill St Jas w St Matt *Lon* from 93. *St James's Vicarage, 2 St James's Lane, London N10 3DB* Tel (020) 8444 2579 *or* 8883 6277 Fax 8883 4459 E-mail churchoffice@st-james.org.uk *or* alex.ross@st-james.org.uk

ROSS, Preb Duncan Gilbert. b 48. Lon Univ BSc70. Westcott Ho Cam 75. **d** 78 **p** 79. C Stepney St Dunstan and All SS *Lon* 78-84; V Hackney Wick St Mary of Eton w St Aug 84-95; P-in-c Bow Common 95-03; V from 03; Preb St Paul's Cathl from 95. *St Paul's Vicarage, Leopold Street, London E3 4LA* Tel and fax (020) 7987 4941 E-mail duncan.ross5@btinternet.com

ROSS, Frederic Ian. b 34. Man Univ BSc56. Westcott Ho Cam 58 Episc Th Sem Mass DipTh61. **d** 62 **p** 63. C Oldham *Man* 62-65; Sec Th Colls Dept SCM 65-69; Teacher Man Gr Sch 69-84; V Shrewsbury H Cross *Lich* 84-02; rtd 02; Perm to Offic *Heref* from 02. *The Paddock, Plealey Road, Annscroft, Shrewsbury SY5 8AN* Tel (01743) 860327

ROSS, Henry Ernest. b 40. NW Ord Course 70. **d** 73 **p** 74. NSM Litherland St Phil *Liv* 73-75; C Newton-le-Willows 75-77; P-in-c Walton St Luke 77-79; V from 79; RD Walton 84-89. *46 Somerset Drive, Southport PR8 3SN* Tel (01704) 571287 E-mail harry.ross@rossfamily.fsnet.co.uk

ROSS, John. b 41. Wells Th Coll 66. **d** 69 **p** 70. C Newc St Gabr *Newc* 69-71; C Prudhoe 71-75; Hon C Shotley 75-87; Hon C Whittonstall 75-87; P-in-c Wallsend St Pet 93-94. *11 Weston Avenue, Whickham, Newcastle upon Tyne NE16 5TS* Tel 0191-488 1546

ROSS, John Colin. b 50. Oak Hill Th Coll 84. **d** 86 **p** 87. C Stowmarket *St E* 86-89; C Wakef St Andr and St Mary *Wakef* 89-91; R Gt and Lt Whelnetham w Bradfield St George *St E* 91-94; V Newmarket All SS 94-02; V Erith St Paul *Roch* 02-04; P-in-c Combs and Lt Finborough *St E* from 04. *The Rectory, 135 Poplar Hill, Combs, Stowmarket IP14 2AY* Tel (01449) 612076 Mobile 07904-124227 E-mail rev.ross@virgin.net

ROSS, Malcolm Hargrave. b 37. Dur Univ BSc58. Westcott Ho Cam 63. **d** 64 **p** 65. C Armley St Bart *Ripon* 64-67; USPG 67-71; Trinidad and Tobago 67-71; V New Rossington *Sheff* 71-75; Bp's Missr in E Lon 75-82; P-in-c Haggerston All SS 75-82; V Bedford Leigh *Man* 82-85; Area Sec USPG *Bris* and *Glouc* 85-90; Bp's Officer for Miss and Evang *Bris* 90-94; P-in-c Lacock w Bowden Hill 90-94; V Sherston Magna, Easton Grey, Luckington etc from 94. *The Vicarage, Green Lane, Sherston, Malmesbury SN16 0NP* Tel (01666) 840209 E-mail mross@fish.co.uk

ROSS, Oliver Charles Milligan. b 58. Lon Univ BA80 St Edm Ho Cam BA85. Ridley Hall Cam 84. **d** 87 **p** 88. C Preston St Cuth *Blackb* 87-90; C Paddington St Jo w St Mich *Lon* 90-95; V Hounslow H Trin w St Paul from 95; P-in-c Isleworth St Mary 01-02. *The Vicarage, 66 Lampton Road, Hounslow TW3 4JD* Tel (020) 8570 3892 *or* 8570 3066 Fax 8570 8886 E-mail oliver.ross@london.anglican.org

ROSS, Ms Rachel Anne. b 64. York Univ BSc85 SS Coll Cam PGCE86 Sheff Univ MA97 Coll of Ripon & York St Jo MA00. N Ord Course 97. **d** 00 **p** 01. C Pendleton *Man* 00-04; P-in-c Salford Ordsall St Clem 03-04; P-in-c Salford St Ignatius and Stowell Memorial 03-04; R Ordsall and Salford Quays from 04. *The Rectory, Parsonage Close, Salford M5 3GS* Tel 0161-872 0800 Mobile 07884-371688

ROSS, Canon Raymond John. b 28. Trin Coll Cam BA52 MA57. St Steph Ho Ox 52. **d** 54 **p** 55. C Clifton All SS *Bris* 54-58; C Solihull *Birm* 58-66; C-in-c Hobs Moat CD 66-67; V Hobs Moat 67-72; R Newbold w Dunston *Derby* 72-95; RD Chesterfield 78-91; Hon Can Derby Cathl 86-95; rtd 96; Perm to Offic *Derby* from 96. *Threeways, Bridge Hill, Belper DE56 2BY* Tel (01773) 825876

ROSS, Vernon. b 57. Portsm Poly BSc79 RGN86. Trin Coll Bris DipHE91. **d** 91 **p** 92. C Fareham St Jo *Portsm* 91-94; P-in-c Witheridge, Thelbridge, Creacombe, Meshaw etc *Ex* 94-00; TR Barnstaple from 00. *The Rectory, 4 Northfield Lane, Barnstaple EX31 1QB* Tel (01271) 345958

ROSS-McCABE, Mrs Philippa Mary Seton. b 63. Natal Univ BA83 HDipEd86 Bris Univ BA01. Trin Coll Bris 99. **d** 01 **p** 02. C Burpham *Guildf* from 01. *8 Selbourne Road, Burpham, Guildford GU4 7JP* Tel and fax (01483) 456602 E-mail p.ross-mccabe@ntlworld.com

ROSS, Dean of. *See* PETERS, The Very Revd Christopher Lind

✠**ROSSDALE, The Rt Revd David Douglas James.** b 53. Westmr Coll Ox DipApTh90 MA91 Surrey Univ MSc01. K Coll Lon 72 Chich Th Coll 80. **d** 81 **p** 82 **c** 00. C Upminster *Chelmsf* 81-86; V Moulsham St Luke 86-90; V Cookham *Ox* 90-00; RD Maidenhead 94-00; Hon Can Ch Ch 99-00; Suff Bp Grimsby *Linc* from 00; Can and Preb Linc Cathl from 00. *Bishop's House, Church Lane, Irby, Grimsby DN37 7JR* Tel (01472) 371715 Fax 371716 E-mail rossdale@btinternet.com

ROSSETER, Miss Susan Mary. b 46. Man Univ BA67 Edin Univ DASS71. St Jo Coll Nottm LTh84. **d** 87 **p** 94. Par Dn Bromley Common St Aug *Roch* 87-88; C Pudsey St Lawr and St Paul *Bradf* 88-95; C Haughton le Skerne *Dur* 95-00; C Wilnecote *Lich* from 00. *5 Avill, Hockley, Tamworth B77 5QE* Tel (01827) 251816

ROSSITER, Donald William Frank. b 30. **d** 80 **p** 81. NSM Abergavenny St Mary w Llanwenarth Citra *Mon* 80-96; NSM Govilon w Llanfoist w Llanelen from 92. *10 Meadow Lane, Abergavenny NP7 7AY* Tel (01873) 855648

ROSSITER, Gillian Alice. b 56. SRN75 RSCN75 Chester Coll of HE Dip Counselling 96. N Ord Course 98. **d** 01 **p** 02. NSM Neston *Ches* 01-03; C from 03. *Ivy Cottage, 10 Burton Road, Little Neston, South Wirral CH64 9RE* Tel 0151-336 7369

ROSSITER, Raymond Stephen David. b 22. MBE99. St Deiniol's Hawarden 75. **d** 76 **p** 77. NSM Sale St Anne *Ches* 76-90; Perm to Offic from 90; rtd 91. *75 Temple Road, Sale M33 2FQ* Tel 0161-962 3240

ROSSLYN SMITH, Mrs Katherine Dorothy Nevill. b 40. STETS 97. **d** 00 **p** 01. NSM Tisbury *Sarum* 00-01; NSM Nadder Valley 01-03; NSM Chalke Valley from 03. *Swallowdale, The Quarry, Tisbury, Salisbury SP3 6HR* Tel (01747) 871605

ROSSLYN-SMITH, Mrs Kirsten Louise. b 73. Nottm Trent Univ BA96. St Jo Coll Nottm MTh05. **d** 05. C Tunbridge Wells St Jas *Roch* from 05. *3 Andrews Close, Tunbridge Wells TN2 3PA* Tel (01892) 531297

ROSTILL, Brian. b 50. K Alfred's Coll Win BTh00. Cranmer Hall Dur 01. **d** 03 **p** 04. C Knights Enham *Win* 03-05; C Knight's Enham and Smannell w Enham Alamein from 05. *2 Madrid Road, Andover SO10 1JR* Tel (01264) 324269 E-mail rostill@tiscali.co.uk

ROSTRON, Derek. b 34. St Mich Coll Llan 65. **d** 67 **p** 68. C Morecambe St Barn *Blackb* 67-70; C Ribbleton 70-72; V Chorley All SS 72-79; C Woodchurch *Ches* 79-80; V Audlem 80-03; RD Nantwich 87-97; rtd 04; Perm to Offic *Lich* from 04. *30 St Matthew's Drive, Derrington, Stafford ST18 9LU* Tel (01785) 246349

ROTHERHAM, Eric. b 36. Clifton Th Coll 63. **d** 67 **p** 68. C Gt Crosby St Luke *Liv* 67-69; C Sutton 69-71; V Warrington St Paul 72-79; Lic to Offic 79-80; Perm to Offic *Ches* and *Liv* from 80; rtd 01. *7 Paul Street, Warrington WA2 7LE* Tel (01925) 633048

ROTHERY, Cecil Ivor. b 24. St Jo Coll Winnipeg 50. **d** 53 **p** 54. Canada 53-72; C Gainsborough All SS *Linc* 72-74; R Fleet 74-79; P-in-c Wrawby 79-80; C Glanford Bridge 79-80; rtd 80; Perm to Offic *S'well* 80-83 and *Sheff* 83-93. *129 Queen Street, Retford DN22 7DA* Tel (01777) 701551

ROTHERY, Jean. b 44. **d** 98 **p** 99. NSM Purley *Ox* from 98. *Oak Lea, Tidmarsh Road, Tidmarsh, Reading RG8 8ER* Tel 0118-984 3625

ROTHERY, Robert Frederick (Fred). b 34. Lon Coll of Div 67. **d** 69 **p** 70. C Burscough Bridge *Liv* 69-72; C Chipping Campden *Glouc* 72-75; P-in-c Didmarton w Oldbury-on-the-Hill and Sopworth 75-77; R Boxwell, Leighterton, Didmarton, Oldbury etc 77-83; R Stow on the Wold 83-00; RD Stow 90-99; rtd 00. *12 Phillips Road, Marnhull, Sturminster Newton DT10 1LF* Tel (01258) 820668

ROTHWELL, Bryan. b 60. St Edm Hall Ox BA81 MA85. Trin Coll Bris. **d** 85 **p** 86. C Carl St Jo *Carl* 85-88; C Ulverston St Mary w H Trin 88-90; P-in-c Preston St Mary *Blackb* 90-96; P-in-c St John's in the Vale w Wythburn *Carl* 96-99; R St John's-in-the-Vale, Threlkeld and Wythburn from 99; Warden Dioc Youth Cen from 96; RD Derwent from 05. *The Rectory, Threlkeld, Keswick CA12 4RT* Tel (017687) 79714 E-mail bryan.rothwell@btinternet.com

ROTHWELL, Edwin John. b 53. Lanc Univ BA74 PhD79. Sarum & Wells Th Coll 88. **d** 90 **p** 91. C Malvern Link w Cowleigh *Worc* 90-94; R Bowbrook N 94-00; Asst Chapl Swindon and Marlborough NHS Trust 00-03; Chapl E Somerset NHS Trust from 03. *Chaplain's Office, Yeovil District Hospital, Higher Kingston, Yeovil BA21 4AT* Tel (01935) 475122 E-mail rothe@est.nhs.uk

ROTHWELL, Harold. b 34. AKC58. K Coll Lon St Boniface Warminster. **d** 59 **p** 60. C Old Brumby *Linc* 59-62; P-in-c Sheff St Steph w St Phil and St Ann *Sheff* 62-64; V Caistor w Holton le Moor and Clixby *Linc* 67-77; Chapl Caistor Hosp 67-77; Org Sec CECS *Ex* and *B & W* 77-81; P-in-c Deeping Fen *Linc* 78-81; C Boston 86-88; C Spilsby w Hundleby 88-91; C Bracebridge Heath 91-94; rtd 94; Perm to Offic *Linc* from 94. *47 Ridgeway, Nettleham, Lincoln LN2 2TL* Tel (01522) 751610

ROTHWELL, Michael John Hereward. *See* HEREWARD-ROTHWELL, Canon Michael John

ROTHWELL, Steven. b 68. Roehampton Inst BA99 Cam Univ MA02. Westcott Ho Cam 00. **d** 02 **p** 03. C Chesterton Gd Shep *Ely* from 02. *19 Hurrell Road, Cambridge CB4 3RQ* Tel (01223) 464348 E-mail srothwell44@hotmail.com

ROTHWELL-JACKSON, Christopher Patrick. b 32. St Cath Soc Ox BA58 MA61 Bris Univ PGCE66. St Steph Ho Ox 55. **d** 59 **p** 60. C E Clevedon All SS *B & W* 59-62; C Midsomer Norton 62-65; Asst Teacher St Pet Primary Sch Portishead 66-68; Clevedon Junior Sch 68-72; Dep Hd Clevedon All SS Primary Sch 72-75; Lic to Offic 69-75; Hd Master Bp Pursglove Sch Tideswell 75-90; Lic to Offic *Derby* 76-95; rtd 90; Perm to Offic *Ex* from 95. *Rosedale, Hookway, Crediton EX17 3PU* Tel (01363) 772039

ROUCH, David Vaughan. b 36. Oak Hill Th Coll 67. **d** 69 **p** 70. C Denton Holme *Carl* 69-74; V Litherland St Jo and St Jas *Liv* 74-95; V Pemberton St Mark Newtown from 95; P-in-c Wigan St Barn Marsh Green from 03. *The Vicarage, Victoria Street, Wigan WN5 9BN* Tel (01942) 206954 Fax 742869 E-mail drouchatjennyr@blueyonder.co.uk

ROUCH, Peter Bradford. b 66. BNC Ox MA87 Peterho Cam MA99. Westcott Ho Cam 96. **d** 99 **p** 00. C E Dulwich St Jo *S'wark* 99-02; Jun Research Fell St Steph Ho Ox 02-04; P-in-c Man Apostles w Miles Platting *Man* from 05. *St George's Rectory, 10 Redacre Road, Manchester M18 8RU* Tel 0161-220 7353 Mobile 07952-262616 E-mail revrouch@aol.com

ROULSTON, Joseph Ernest. b 52. MIBiol77 FRSC86 MRCPath93 FLS94 BNC Ox BA74 MA78 Lon Univ PhD81. Edin Dioc NSM Course 83. **d** 86 **p** 87. C Edin St Hilda *Edin* 86-88; C Edin St Fillan 86-88; NSM Edin St Mich and All SS 88-97; Dioc Chapl Gen from 96. *16 Summerside Street, Edinburgh EH6 4NU* Tel 0131-554 6382 *or* tel and fax 536 2703 Mobile 07703-200944 E-mail j.e.roulston@ed.ac.uk

ROUND, Keith Leonard. b 49. Sarum & Wells Th Coll 88. **d** 90 **p** 91. C Meir *Lich* 90-95; V Burslem St Werburgh from 95. *The Presbytery, Haywood Road, Stoke-on-Trent ST6 7AH* Tel (01782) 837582

ROUND, Malcolm John Harrison. b 56. Lon Univ BSc77 BA81. Oak Hill Th Coll. **d** 81 **p** 82. C Guildf St Sav w Stoke-next-Guildford *Guildf* 81-85; C Hawkwell *Chelmsf* 85-88; R Balerno *Edin* from 88. *53 Marchbank Drive, Balerno EH14 7ER* Tel 0131-449 4127

ROUNDHILL, Andrew (John). b 65. CCC Cam BA87. Ripon Coll Cuddesdon BTh93. **d** 93 **p** 94. C Lancaster Ch Ch w St Jo and St Anne *Blackb* 93-97; Chapl Loretto Sch Musselburgh 97-02; Chapl Hong Kong Cathl from 02. *D2 On Lee, 2 Mount Davis Road, Pok Fu Lam, Hong Kong* Tel (00852) 2817 8774 *or* 2523 4157 E-mail roundhill@netvigator.com

ROUNDTREE, James Clabern (Clay). b 75. Oklahoma Univ BFA98 York Univ MA00. St Steph Ho Ox BA02. **d** 03 **p** 04. C Yarm *York* from 03. *8 Merlay Close, Yarm TS15 9TE* Tel (01642) 787322 E-mail clayroundtree@hotmail.com

ROUNDTREE, Samuel William. b 19. TCD BA42 MA54. CITC 43. **d** 43 **p** 44. C Waterford Ch Ch *C & O* 44-47; I Tallow w Kilwatermoy 47-51; I Kiltegan w Stratford (and Rathvilly from 60) 51-62; Treas Leighlin Cathl 62-78; Preb Ossory Cathl 62-78; I Dunleckney 62-82; Chan Ossory and Leighlin Cathls 78-80; Prec 80-82; I New w Old Ross, Whitechurch, Fethard etc 82-88; Adn Ferns 86-88; rtd 88. *Killincarrig House, Killincarrig Road, Greystones, Co Wicklow, Irish Republic* Tel (00353) (1) 287 4428

ROUNTREE, Canon Richard Benjamin. b 52. NUI BA73. CITC 76. **d** 76 **p** 77. C Orangefield *D & D* 76-80; C Dublin Zion Ch *D & G* 80-83; I Dalkey St Patr 83-97; I Powerscourt w Kilbride from 97; Dioc Dir Decade of Evang 90-96; Can Ch Ch Cathl Dublin from 92; Treas from 04. *Powerscourt Rectory, Enniskerry, Bray, Co Wicklow, Irish Republic* Tel and fax (00353) (1) 286 3534 E-mail rountree@indigo.ie *or* powerscourt@glendalough.anglican.org

ROUSE, Graham. b 58. Sheff City Coll of Educn CertEd79 Leic Univ DipEd84. Cranmer Hall Dur 90. **d** 92 **p** 93. C Longridge *Blackb* 92-96; P-in-c Fairhaven 96-97; V from 97. *Fairhaven Vicarage, 83 Clifton Drive, Lytham St Annes FY8 1BZ* Tel (01253) 734562 E-mail fairhavenstpaul@btopenworld.com

ROUTH, Canon Eileen Rosemary. b 41. Cant Sch of Min 82. **dss** 85 **d** 87 **p** 94. Folkestone St Sav *Cant* 85-90; Par Dn 87-90; Par Dn Woodnesborough w Worth and Staple 90-91; Dn-in-c 91-94; V 94-96; V Maidstone St Martin 96-99; Hon Can Cant Cathl 99; rtd 99; Perm to Offic *Cant* from 00. *31 Tile Kiln Hill, Blean, Canterbury CT2 9EE* Tel (01227) 464052

ROUTH, William John. b 60. Magd Coll Ox BA81 MA92. Ripon Coll Cuddesdon 93. **d** 95 **p** 96. C Longton *Blackb* 95-99; V Sutton Coldfield St Chad *Birm* from 99. *St Chad's Vicarage, 41 Hollyfield Road, Sutton Coldfield B75 7SN* Tel 0121-329 2995 E-mail john.routh@btinternet.com

ROW, Mrs Pamela Anne. b 54. Open Univ BA86 MA92 Homerton Coll Cam BEd75. N Ord Course 94. **d** 96 **p** 97. NSM Neston *Ches* 96-01; Chapl Heref Cathl Sch from 02. *4 Harley Court, Hereford HR1 2NA* Tel (01432) 363508 *or* 363511

ROWBERRY, Christopher Michael. b 58. Univ of Wales (Lamp) MA04 Plymouth Univ CQSW85. Qu Coll Birm 94. **d** 96 **p** 97. C Lytchett Minster *Sarum* 96-00; TV Totton *Win* from 00. *The Vicarage, Eling Hill, Totton, Southampton SO40 9HF* Tel (023) 8086 6426 E-mail stmarythevirgin@btinternet.com

ROWBERRY, Michael James. b 46. Sussex Univ BA74. Edin Th Coll 85. **d** 87 **p** 92. C Wolvercote w Summertown *Ox* 87-88; NSM Cov St Fran N Radford *Cov* 91-95; Perm to Offic 95-98; C Doncaster Intake *Sheff* 98-00; C Doncaster H Trin 98-00; C-in-c St Edm Anchorage Lane CD from 00. *St Edmund's House, Anchorage Lane, Spotborough, Doncaster DN5 8DT* Tel (01302) 781986

ROWDON, John Michael Hooker. b 27. Witwatersrand Univ BA52. Ridley Hall Cam 52. **d** 54 **p** 55. C Broadwater St Mary *Chich* 54-56; C Streatham Immanuel w St Anselm *S'wark* 56-59; Nigeria 60-62; C All Hallows Lon Wall *Lon* 62-66; Warden Toc H Tower Hill 64-66; Australia from 66; rtd 92. *PO Box 120, Balingup, W Australia 6253*

ROWE, Andrew Gidleigh Bruce. b 37. AKC62. St Boniface Warminster. **d** 63 **p** 64. C Midsomer Norton *B & W* 63-68; Chapl RN 68-84; Chapl Heathfield Sch Ascot 84-86; Hon C Winkfield and Cranbourne *Ox* 84-86; TV Wellington and Distr *B & W* 86-95; R Chewton Mendip w Ston Easton, Litton etc 95-96; Perm to Offic *Ex* from 96; rtd 99. *Merrymeet, Posbury, Crediton EX17 3QF* Tel (01363) 772262

ROWE, Andrew Robert. b 64. Westmr Coll Ox BA85 PGCE86. Ridley Hall Cam CTM95. **d** 95 **p** 96. C Broadheath *Ches* 95-99; V E Ardsley *Wakef* from 99. *The Vicarage, Church Lane, East Ardsley, Wakefield WF3 2LJ* Tel (01924) 822184 E-mail andyr@rowe6423.freeserve.co.uk

ROWE, Canon Antony Silvester Buckingham. b 26. St Jo Coll Dur 53. **d** 55 **p** 56. C Holbrooks *Cov* 55-59; V Cov St Mary 59-83; RD Cov S 72-82; Hon Can Cov Cathl 76-92; R Harbury and Ladbroke 83-92; rtd 92; Perm to Offic *Cov* and *Glouc* from 92. *3 Cotswold Edge, Mickleton, Chipping Campden GL55 6TR* Tel (01386) 438622

ROWE, Arthur John. b 35. TCD 73. **d** 76 **p** 77. C Bangor Abbey *D & D* 76-78; I Kilbarron *D & R* 78-79; I Kilbarron w Rossnowlagh 79-82; P-in-c Hockering *Nor* 82-85; P-in-c

Honingham w E Tuddenham 82-85; P-in-c N Tuddenham 82-85; R Hockwold w Wilton *Ely* 85-95; R Weeting 85-95; rtd 95; Perm to Offic *Nor* from 05. *Orchard Villa, Back Lane, Castle Acre, King's Lynn PE32 2AR*

ROWE, Canon Bryan. b 50. Carl Dioc Tr Course 87. **d** 90 **p** 91. C Kells *Carl* 90-93; P-in-c Aspatria w Hayton 93-02; R Workington St Mich from 02; RD Solway from 99; Hon Can Carl Cathl from 99. *St Michael's Rectory, Dora Crescent, Workington CA14 2EZ* Tel (01900) 602311

ROWE, The Ven Christine Elizabeth. b 55. Southn Univ BEd77. Ripon Coll Cuddesdon 83. **dss** 86 **d** 87 **p** 94. Denham *Ox* 86-87; Par Dn 87-89; Par Dn Aylesbury 89; Par Dn Aylesbury w Bierton and Hulcott 89-93; NSM Caversham St Jo 93-99; Chapl HM Pris Reading 93-98; Chapl Mothers' Union 95-00; Chapl R Berks and Battle Hosps NHS Trust 96-00; P-in-c Vancouver St Thos Canada 00-01; R from 01; Adn Burrard from 04. *782 East King's Road, North Vancouver BC, Canada, V7K 1E3* Tel (001) (604) 987 6307 *or* 434 6111 Fax 434 9592 E-mail archburrard@aol.com

ROWE, David Brian. b 58. Trin Coll Bris DipHE82. **d** 83 **p** 84. C Radipole and Melcombe Regis *Sarum* 83-86; C Cranham Park *Chelmsf* 86-88; Assoc Min and Par Missr Eastrop *Win* 88-92; P-in-c Arborfield w Barkham *Ox* 92-97; Asst Dioc Adv in Evang *S'well* 97-02; P-in-c Wilford from 00. *The Rectory, Main Road, Nottingham NG11 7AJ* Tel 0115-981 5661 E-mail wilfordchurch@aol.com

ROWE, Geoffrey Lewis. b 44. Univ of Wales (Lamp) BA. Ripon Coll Cuddesdon 80. **d** 82 **p** 83. C Milber *Ex* 82-84; TV Withycombe Raleigh 84-90; R Clyst St Mary, Clyst St George etc from 90. *The Rectory, 40 Clyst Valley Road, Clyst St Mary, Exeter EX5 1DD* Tel (01392) 874363

ROWE, Miss Joan Patricia. b 54. Trin Coll Bris BA87. **d** 88 **p** 94. C Radstock w Writhlington *B & W* 88-92; C Nailsea H Trin 92-96; P-in-c Shapwick w Ashcott and Burtle from 96. *The Vicarage, Vicarage Lane, Shapwick, Bridgwater TA7 9LR* Tel (01458) 210260 E-mail joanrowe@ic24.net

ROWE, John Goring. b 23. McGill Univ Montreal BA48 BD51 Selw Coll Cam BA53. Montreal Dioc Th Coll LTh51. **d** 51 **p** 52. C N Clarendon Canada 51; C Trumpington *Ely* 51-53; Hon C Bow Common *Lon* 53-84; rtd 88. *10 Cordelia Street, London E14 6DZ* Tel (020) 7515 4681

ROWE, Peter Anthony. b 46. Univ Coll Dur BA68 Birkb Coll Lon MA91 Heythrop Coll Lon MTh02 Barrister 78 Solicitor 85. SEITE 95. **d** 98 **p** 99. NSM Ashford *Cant* 98-03; Perm to Offic from 04. *1 Woodside Villas, Ashford Road, Hamstreet, Ashford TN26 2DT* Tel (01233) 732172 Fax (01227) 450498 E-mail peterrowe@girlings.com

ROWE, Peter Farquharson. b 19. Selw Coll Cam BA41. Westcott Ho Cam 41. **d** 43 **p** 44. C Putney St Mary *S'wark* 43-47; C Lewisham St Jo Southend 47-54; V Mitcham Ascension 54-65; V Eltham Park St Luke 65-77; V Ravensthorpe w E Haddon and Holdenby *Pet* 77-84; rtd 84; Perm to Offic *Ex* 84-89; *Sarum* 89-92; *Win* from 92. *28 Gordon Avenue, Winchester SO23 0QQ* Tel (01962) 869806

ROWE, Philip William. b 57. Southn Univ BSc78. Lambeth STh86 Trin Coll Bris 82. **d** 85 **p** 86. C Tooting Graveney St Nic *S'wark* 85-89; V Abbots Leigh w Leigh Woods *Bris* 89-96; V Almondsbury 96-98; P-in-c Littleton on Severn w Elberton 96-98; V Almondsbury and Olveston from 98; AD Bris W from 00. *The Vicarage, Sundays Hill, Almondsbury, Bristol BS32 4DS* Tel (01454) 613223 E-mail philip.w.rowe@btopenworld.com

ROWE, Shiela. *See* JOHNSON, Mrs Shiela

ROWE, Canon Stanley Hamilton. b 18. St Pet Hall Ox BA48 MA52. ALCD50. **d** 50 **p** 51. C Leyton St Paul *Chelmsf* 50-52; CMS Nigeria 52-65; P-in-c Becontree St Cedd *Chelmsf* 65-67; Hd of RE Jo Hampden Sch High Wycombe 67-83; Perm to Offic *Ox* 67-84 and from 86; rtd 83; Hon P-in-c Aston Rowant w Crowell *Ox* 84-86; Hon Can Oke-Osun from 94. *37 Greenwood Avenue, Chinnor OX39 4HW* Tel (01844) 351278 E-mail shrowe@fish.co.uk

ROWE, Stephen Mark Buckingham. b 59. SS Mark & Jo Coll Plymouth BA81. Ripon Coll Cuddesdon 83. **d** 86 **p** 87. C Denham *Ox* 86-89; C Aylesbury w Bierton and Hulcott 89-90; TV 90-93; V Caversham St Jo 93-00; Canada from 00; Sen Chapl Miss to Seafarers 00-01; P-in-c Surrey Epiphany 01-02; R from 02. *782 East King's Road, North Vancouver BC, Canada, V7K 1E3* Tel (001) (604) 987 6307 *or* tel and fax 588 4511 E-mail rowesmb@aol.com

ROWE, Mrs Vanda Sheila. b 63. STETS 95. **d** 98 **p** 99. C Marlborough *Sarum* 98-01; TV Pewsey and Swanborough from 01. *The Vicarage, Church Road, Woodborough, Pewsey SN9 5PH* Tel (01672) 851746 E-mail vanda@vanda33.freeserve.co.uk

ROWELL, Canon Alan. b 50. Lon Univ BSc71 AKC71. Trin Coll Bris DipTh75. **d** 75 **p** 76. C W Hampstead St Cuth *Lon* 75-78; C Camborne *Truro* 78-81; V Pendeen w Morvah from 81; Hon Can Truro Cathl from 03. *The Vicarage, Pendeen, Penzance TR19 7SE* Tel (01736) 788777

✠**ROWELL, The Rt Revd Douglas Geoffrey.** b 43. CCC Cam BA64 MA68 PhD68 Keble Coll Ox DD97. Cuddesdon Coll. **d** 68 **p** 69 **c** 94. Asst Chapl New Coll Ox 68-72; Chapl Keble Coll Ox 72-94; Wiccamical Preb Chich Cathl *Chich* 81-01; Suff Bp Basingstoke *Win* 94-01; Bp Eur from 01. *Bishop's Lodge, Church Road, Worth, Crawley RH10 7RT,* or *14 Tufton Street, London SW1P 3QZ* Tel (01293) 883051 *or* (020) 7898 1155 Fax (01293) 884479 *or* (020) 7898 1166 E-mail bishop@dioceseineurope.org.uk

ROWELL, Frank. b 22. Chich Th Coll 50. **d** 52 **p** 53. C Ipswich All SS *St E* 52-56; R Earl Stonham 56-65; R Clopton 65-83; R Otley 65-83; R Clopton w Otley, Swilland and Ashbocking 83-88; rtd 88; Perm to Offic *St E* from 90. *37 Riverview, Melton, Woodbridge IP12 1QU* Tel (01394) 385449

ROWELL, Mrs Gillian Margaret. b 56. Lon Bible Coll BA96. St Alb and Ox Min Course DipMin99. **d** 99 **p** 00. NSM The Lee *Ox* 99-04; NSM Hawridge w Cholesbury and St Leonard 99-04. *81 Eskdale Avenue, Chesham HP5 3AY* Tel (01494) 772833

ROWELL, William Kevin. b 51. Reading Univ BSc71. Linc Th Coll 78. **d** 80 **p** 81. C Cannock *Lich* 80-83; Ind Chapl 83-86; C Ketley and Oakengates 83-86; R Norton in the Moors 86-93; RD Leek 92-93; P-in-c Minsterley and Habberley *Heref* 93-01; RD Pontesbury 99-01; Miss Adv USPG *Heref, Worc* and *Glouc* 01-03; NSM Wenlock *Heref* 02-03; R Llandysilio and Penrhos and Llandrinio etc *St As* from 04. *The Rectory, Rhos Common, Four Crosses, Llanymynech SY22 6RW* Tel (01691) 830533 E-mail bilkro@btinternet.com

ROWETT, David Peter. b 55. Univ Coll Dur BA76. Ripon Coll Cuddesdon 82. **d** 84 **p** 85. C Yeovil *B & W* 84-88; C Yeovil St Mich 88-89; V Fairfield St Matt *Linc* 89-05; P-in-c Barton upon Humber from 05. *The Vicarage, Beck Hill, Barton-upon-Humber DN18 5EY* Tel (01652) 632202 E-mail david.rowett@aol.com

ROWETT, Mrs Margaret Pettigrew Coupar. b 33. Sarum & Wells Th Coll 84. **dss** 86 **d** 87 **p** 95. Widley w Wymering *Portsm* 86-88; C 87-88; Par Dn Plympton St Mary *Ex* 88-91; rtd 91; NSM St Mewan *Truro* 94-96; Perm to Offic from 97. *Epiphany Cottage, 9 Socotra Drive, Trewoon, St Austell PL25 5SQ* Tel (01726) 71450

ROWLAND, Andrew John William. b 60. STETS 98. **d** 01 **p** 02. NSM Verwood *Sarum* 01-02; C from 02. *46 Crane Drive, Verwood BH31 6QB* Tel (01202) 825505 E-mail ar@fish.co.uk

ROWLAND, Barry William. b 59. St Jo Coll Nottm Dip Th & Min 95 BA95. **d** 95 **p** 96. C Welling *Roch* 95-98; C Green Street Green and Pratts Bottom 98-02; V New Beckenham St Paul from 02. *St Paul's Vicarage, Brackley Road, Beckenham BR3 1RB* Tel (020) 8650 3400 Mobile 07808-239668 E-mail bazzavic@hotmail.com

ROWLAND, Prof Christopher Charles. b 47. Ch Coll Cam BA69 MA73 PhD75. Ridley Hall Cam 72. **d** 75 **p** 76. Lect RS Newc Univ *Newc* 74-79; Hon C Benwell St Jas 75-78; Hon C Gosforth All SS 78-79; Dean Jes Coll Cam 79-91; Asst Lect Div Cam Univ 83-85; Lect Div 85-91; Lic to Offic *Ely* 79-91; Prof of Exegesis of H Scripture Ox Univ from 91; Fell Qu Coll Ox from 91; Can Th Liv Cathl *Liv* from 05. *Queen's College, Oxford OX1 4AW* Tel (01865) 279120

ROWLAND, Ms Dawn Jeannette. b 38. RSCN61 RGN63. S'wark Ord Course 81. **dss** 84 **d** 87 **p** 94. Par Dn Croydon H Sav *S'wark* 84-89; NSM Riddlesdown from 89. *9 Hartley Hill, Purley CR8 4EP* Tel (020) 8660 6270

ROWLAND, Derek John. b 47. St Jo Coll Nottm 84. **d** 86 **p** 87. C Porchester *S'well* 86-89; V Fairfield *Liv* 89-96; V Buckfastleigh w Dean Prior *Ex* from 96. *The Vicarage, Glebelands, Buckfastleigh TQ11 0BH* Tel (01364) 644228

ROWLAND, Eric Edward James. b 35. Leeds Univ BA62. Coll of Resurr Mirfield 61. **d** 63 **p** 64. C S Kirkby *Wakef* 63-65; C Headingley *Ripon* 65-70; V Osmondthorpe St Phil 70-79; R Sandy *St Alb* 79-00; RD Biggleswade 85-94; rtd 00; Perm to Offic *Ely* from 01. *3 Tower Road, Ely CB7 4HW* Tel (01353) 664359

ROWLAND, Geoffrey Watson. b 17. **d** 55 **p** 56. BCMS 55-65; Burma 55-65; C Blackheath Park St Mich *S'wark* 65-71; V W Bromwich St Paul *Lich* 71-76; Chapl Community Relns *Lon* 77-83; C Southall Green St Jo 83; rtd 83; Perm to Offic *Lon* from 83. *3 Amber Court, Longford Avenue, Southall UB1 3QR* Tel (020) 8574 3442

ROWLAND, Jennifer Norah. b 48. Worc Coll of Educn CertEd70 Open Univ BA83 ACIB. WMMTC 96. **d** 99 **p** 00. C Stratford-upon-Avon, Luddington etc *Cov* 99-03; P-in-c Ditton Priors w Neenton, Burwarton etc *Heref* from 03. *The Vicarage, Ditton Priors, Bridgnorth WV16 6SQ* Tel (01746) 712636 E-mail jenny@rowland4.demon.co.uk

ROWLAND, Mrs June Mary. b 46. SRN67. EMMTC 03. **d** 05. NSM Grantham *Linc* from 05. *The Vicarage, The Grove, Grantham NG31 7PU* Tel (01476) 572380 E-mail junerowlandhome@aol.com

ROWLAND, Robert William. b 51. Birm Univ BA72 Univ of Wales (Cardiff) DPS73. St Mich Coll Llan 72. **d** 74 **p** 75. C Connah's Quay *St As* 74; C Shotton 74-76; C Llanrhos 76-81; V Dyserth and Trelawnyd and Cwm from 81; RD St As from 94. *The Vicarage, Dyserth, Rhyl LL18 6DB* Tel (01745) 570750

ROWLAND, Stanley George. b 48. Middx Univ BA86. NTMTC 95. **d** 98 **p** 99. NSM Enfield St Geo *Lon* 98-02; C Grantham *Linc* 02-03; V Grantham, Earlesfield from 03. *The Vicarage, The Grove, Grantham NG31 7PU* Tel (01476) 572380 E-mail sgrathome@aol.com

ROWLAND JONES, Sarah Caroline. b 59. LVO93 OBE97. Newnham Coll Cam BA80 MA84 Nottm Univ BTh98. St Jo Coll Nottm 96. **d** 99 **p** 00. C Wrexham *St As* 99-02; S Africa from 02. *Bishopshaven, PO Box 420, Malmesbury, 7299 South Africa* E-mail sarahrj@surfaid.org

ROWLANDS, The Ven Emyr Wyn. b 42. St Mich Coll Llan 69. **d** 70 **p** 71. C Holyhead w Rhoscolyn *Ban* 70-74; V Bodedern w Llechgynfarwy and Llechylched etc 74-88; R Machynlleth and Llanwrin 88-97; R Machynlleth w Llanwrin and Penegoes from 97; AD Cyfeiliog and Mawddwy from 96; Can Ban Cathl 97-03; Can and Preb Ban Cathl from 03; Adn Meirionnydd from 04. *The Rectory, Newtown Road, Machynlleth SY20 8HE* Tel (01654) 702261

ROWLANDS, Forrest John. b 25. LSE BSc(Econ)51. Chich Th Coll 54. **d** 56 **p** 57. C Hove St Phil *Chich* 56-58; C Haywards Heath St Wilfrid 58-62; R Kingston by Sea 62-74; rtd 90. *130 Thorpe Road, Norwich NR1 1RH* Tel (01603) 473587

ROWLANDS, Gareth Richard. b 70. Univ of Wales BA93. St Steph Ho Ox BTh93. **d** 96 **p** 97. C Shotton *St As* 96-00; TV Wrexham and Chapl Maelor Hosp 00-03; Chapl Co-ord Ches and Ellesmere Port Hosps 03-05; Lead Chapl Princess Alexandra Hosp NHS Trust from 05. *Dept of Pastoral and Spiritual Care, Princess Alexandra Hospital, Hamstel Road, Harlow CM20 1QX* Tel (01279) 444455 ext 2717 E-mail gareth.rowlands@pah.nhs.uk

ROWLANDS, Graeme Charles. b 53. K Coll Lon BD74 AKC74. St Aug Coll Cant 75. **d** 76 **p** 77. C Higham Ferrers w Chelveston *Pet* 76-79; C Gorton St Mary and St Thos *Man* 79-81; C Reading H Trin *Ox* 81-89; P-in-c Kentish Town St Silas *Lon* 89-92; V 92-98; P-in-c Haverstock Hill H Trin w Kentish Town St Barn 93-98; V Kentish Town St Silas and H Trin w St Barn from 98. *St Silas's House, 11 St Silas's Place, London NW5 3QP* Tel (020) 7485 3727 E-mail ssilas@fish.co.uk

ROWLANDS, Mrs Jacqueline Adèle. b 43. Golds Coll Lon CertEd65 BEd72. St Alb Minl Tr Scheme 82. **dss** 85 **d** 87 **p** 05. Bromham w Oakley *St Alb* 85-88; Par Dn 87-88; Par Dn Bromham w Oakley and Stagsden 88-89; Perm to Offic 04-05; Hon C Bedford St Andr from 05. *2A Rosemary Drive, Bromham, Bedford MK43 8PL* Tel (01234) 403841

ROWLANDS, Canon John Henry Lewis. b 47. Univ of Wales (Lamp) BA68 Magd Coll Cam BA70 MA74 Dur Univ MLitt86. Westcott Ho Cam 70. **d** 72 **p** 73. C Aberystwyth *St D* 72-76; Chapl Univ of Wales (Lamp) 76-79; Youth Chapl 76-79; Dir Academic Studies St Mich Coll Llan 79-84; Sub-Warden 84-88; Warden 88-97; Lect Univ of Wales (Cardiff) *Llan* 79-97; Asst Dean 81-83; Dean 93-97; Dean of Div Univ of Wales 91-95; Dir of Ords 85-88; V Whitchurch 97-02; TR from 02; Hon Can Llan Cathl 90-97; Can from 97; Chan from 02; Chapl Cardiff Community Healthcare NHS Trust from 97. *The Vicarage, 6 Penlline Road, Cardiff CF14 2AD* Tel (029) 2062 6072 Fax as telephone E-mail office@parishofwhitchurch.freeserve.co.uk

ROWLANDS, Canon Joseph Haydn. b 36. Univ of Wales (Lamp) BA61 DipTh63. **d** 63 **p** 64. C Llanfairisgaer *Ban* 63-68; R Maentwrog w Trawsfynydd 68-75; V Henfynyw w Aberaeron and Llanddewi Aberarth *St D* 75-80; R Trefdraeth *Ban* 80-84; V Llandysul *St D* 84-98; V Llandysul w Bangor Teifi w Henllan etc 98-01; Hon Can St D Cathl 88-90; Can St D Cathl from 90; RD Emlyn 92-01; rtd 01. *1 Llys Ystrad, Johnstown, Carmarthen SA31 3PU*

ROWLANDS, Kenneth Albert. b 41. MA DipAE. NW Ord Course 70. **d** 73 **p** 74. NSM Hoylake *Ches* 73-80; NSM Oxton 80-82; Perm to Offic 82-00; C Stoneycroft All SS *Liv* 92-94; V Mossley Hill St Barn 94-03; rtd 03. *77 Queens Avenue, Meols, Wirral CH47 0LT* Tel 0151-632 3033

ROWLANDS, Marc Alun. b 62. Univ of Wales (Abth) BSc84 St D Coll Lamp MPhil89 PhD95. Wycliffe Hall Ox 97. **d** 99 **p** 00. C Betws w Ammanford *St D* 99-01; C Carmarthen St Pet 01-02; P-in-c Llanpumsaint w Llanllawddog 02-05. *Address temp unknown* E-mail marc_rowlands@hotmail.com

ROWLANDS, Michael Huw. b 62. Birm Univ BA85 Univ of Wales (Cardiff) BD88. St Mich Coll Llan 85. **d** 88 **p** 89. C Penarth All SS *Llan* 88-91; V Martletwy w Lawrenny and Minwear etc *St D* 91-99; CF 99-02; P-in-c Nolton w Roch *St D* 02-04; R Nolton w Roch and St Lawrence w Ford etc from 04. *Calbern, Simpson Cross, Haverfordwest SA62 6EP* Tel (01437) 710209

ROWLANDS, Richard. b 34. St Mich Coll Llan 59. **d** 62 **p** 63. C Tywyn *Ban* 62-65; C Dwygyfylchi 65-69; V Carno and Trefeglwys 69-71; CF 71-83. *Rhyd Casadog, Ty'n Lon Po, Holyhead LL65 3AQ* Tel (01407) 720843

ROWLANDS, Robert. b 31. Roch Th Coll. **d** 68 **p** 69. C Hooton *Ches* 68-71; V Stretton 71-88; P-in-c Appleton Thorn and Antrobus 87-88; V Stretton and Appleton Thorn 88-00; rtd 00; Perm to Offic *Carl* from 01. *Uplands, Redhills Road, Arnside, Carnforth LA5 0AT* Tel (01524) 761612

ROWLANDS, Simon David. b 66. **d** 99 **p** 00. C St Peter-in-Thanet *Cant* 99-03; Chapl Cant Ch Ch Univ Coll from 03. *Canterbury Christ Church University College, North Holmes Road, Canterbury CT1 1QU* Tel (01227) 767700 E-mail sdr5@cant.ac.uk

ROWLANDS, Mrs Valerie Christine. b 54. St As Minl Tr Course 99. **d** 02 **p** 03. NSM Llanbedr DC w Llangynhafal, Llanychan etc *St As* 02-04; Chapl St As Cathl from 04. *1 Llys Trewithan, St Asaph LL17 0DJ* Tel (01745) 583264

ROWLEY, Christopher Francis Elmes. b 48. St Jo Coll Dur BA70 St Luke's Coll Ex PGCE71. St Steph Ho Ox 76. **d** 78 **p** 79. C Parkstone St Pet w Branksea and St Osmund *Sarum* 78-81; TV 82-85; P-in-c Chard Gd Shep Furnham *B & W* 85-89; P-in-c Dowlishwake w Chaffcombe, Knowle St Giles etc 88-89; R Chard, Furnham w Chaffcombe, Knowle St Giles etc 89-91; V Stoke St Gregory w Burrowbridge and Lyng 91-04; RD Taunton 01-04; TV Wellington and Distr from 04. *All Saints' Vicarage, 62 Rockwell Green, Wellington TA21 9BX* Tel (01823) 662742 E-mail cft-arowley@supanet.com

ROWLEY, David Michael. b 39. N Ord Course 87. **d** 90 **p** 91. C Stainland *Wakef* 90-93; V Hayfield *Derby* 93-99; P-in-c Chinley w Buxworth 98-99; V Glossop 99-04; RD Glossop 96-04; rtd 04. *8 Weavers Close, Belper DE56 0HZ* Tel (01773) 882690

ROWLEY, Jennifer Jane Elisabeth. b 61. LMH Ox BA84 MA92. EAMTC 99. **d** 02 **p** 03. C Kingsthorpe w Northampton St Dav *Pet* 02-04; C Kettering SS Pet and Paul from 04. *2 Moorhouse Way, Kettering NN15 7LX* Tel (01536) 516150 E-mail jenny@peterandpaul.org.uk

ROWLEY, John. **d** 05. OLM Mitford *Newc* from 05. *Thistledene, Fulbeck, Morpeth NE61 3JU* Tel (01670) 515915

ROWLEY, Susan. **d** 01. OLM Fazeley *Lich* from 01. *76 Reindeer Road, Fazeley, Tamworth B78 3SW* Tel (01827) 250431 *or* 289414 E-mail rowley_sue@hotmail.com

ROWLEY-BROOKE, Mrs Marie Gordon. b 46. ARIAM69. Ripon Coll Cuddesdon 00. **d** 02 **p** 03. C Leckhampton SS Phil and Jas w Cheltenham St Jas *Glouc* 02-05; I Nenagh *L & K* from 05. *St Mary's Rectory, Church Road, Nenagh, Co Tipperary, Irish Republic* Tel (00353) (67) 32598 E-mail trumpetplayer@zoom.co.uk

ROWLING, Canon Catherine. b 55. Man Poly BEd77. Westcott Ho Cam 83 NEOC 85. **dss** 86 **d** 87 **p** 94. Gt Ayton w Easby and Newton in Cleveland *York* 86-89; Par Dn 87-89; Chapl Teesside Poly 89-92; Chapl Teesside Univ 92-96; Dioc Adv for Diaconal Mins 96-98; Dean of Women's Min from 98; Co Dir of Ords 98-05; Dioc Dir from 05; Dioc Moderator Reader Tr 99-04; Can and Preb York Minster from 01. *The Rectory, Cemetery Road, Thirsk YO7 1PR* Tel (01845) 523183 E-mail cathyrowling@aol.com

ROWLING, Richard Francis. b 56. BA. Westcott Ho Cam. **d** 84 **p** 85. C Stokesley *York* 84-87; C Stainton-in-Cleveland 87-90; V New Marske 90-96; V Wilton 92-96; P-in-c Ingleby Greenhow w Bilsdale Priory, Kildale etc 96-98; V 98-03; TR Thirsk from 03; Abp's Adv for Rural Affairs from 98; RD Mowbray from 04. *The Rectory, Cemetery Road, Thirsk YO7 1PR* Tel (01845) 523183 E-mail rfrowling@aol.com

ROWNTREE, Peter. b 47. St D Coll Lamp BA68 Univ of Wales (Cardiff) MA70. St Steph Ho Ox 70. **d** 72 **p** 73. C Stanwell *Lon* 72-75; C Northolt St Mary 75-79; Chapl Ealing Gen Hosp 79-83 and 87-94; Chapl Ealing Hosp NHS Trust 94-99; Chapl W Lon Healthcare NHS Trust 94-99; Chapl Cherry Knowle Hosp Sunderland 83-87; Chapl Ryhope Hosp Sunderland 83-87; Sen Co-ord Chapl Univ Coll Lon Hosps NHS Foundn Trust from 99. *The Chaplaincy, The Middlesex Hospital, Mortimer Street, London W1T 3AA* Tel (020) 7636 8333 E-mail peter.rowntree@uclh.org

ROWSELL, Canon John Bishop. b 25. Jes Coll Cam BA49 MA55. Ely Th Coll 49. **d** 51 **p** 52. C Hackney Wick St Mary of Eton w St Aug *Lon* 51-55; C Is of Dogs Ch Ch and St Jo w St Luke 55-56; C Reading St Mary V *Ox* 56-59; V Hightown *Wakef* 59-69; R Harlton *Ely* 69-81; V Haslingfield 69-81; V Methwold 81-95; RD Feltwell 81-95; R Northwold 82-95; Hon Can Ely Cathl 84-99; P-in-c Hockwold w Wilton 95-99; P-in-c Weeting 95-99; Perm to Offic from 00. *Reed House, High Street, Hilgay, Downham Market PE38 0LH* Tel (01366) 387662

ROWSON, Frank. b 40. CEng67 MIStructE67. Sarum & Wells Th Coll 87. **d** 90 **p** 91. NSM Ore Ch Ch *Chich* 90-98; NSM Fairlight, Guestling and Pett 98-00; rtd 00; Perm to Offic *Chich* from 01. *149 Priory Road, Hastings TN34 3JD* Tel (01424) 439802

ROWSTON, Geoffrey. b 34. Sarum Th Coll 59. **d** 62 **p** 63. C Ashburton w Buckland-in-the-Moor *Ex* 62-65; C Basingstoke *Win* 65-68; V Netley 68-78; V W End 78-87; R Alderbury and W Grimstead *Sarum* 87-91; P-in-c Whiteparish 89-91; TR Alderbury Team 91-99; rtd 99; Perm to Offic *Cov* from 99. *34 Oldbutt Road, Shipston-on-Stour CV36 4EG* Tel (01608) 663024

✠**ROWTHORN, The Rt Revd Jeffery William.** b 34. Societas Liturgica MNAAL MHSA Ch Coll Cam BA57 MA62 Oriel Coll Ox BLitt72. Berkeley Div Sch DD87 Cuddesdon Coll 61 Union Th Sem (NY) BD61. **d** 62 **p** 63 **c** 87. C Woolwich St Mary w H Trin *S'wark* 62-65; R Garsington *Ox* 65-68; USA from 68; Chapl and Dean Union Th Sem NY 68-73; Assoc Prof Past Th Yale and Berkeley Div Schs 73-87; Suff Bp Connecticut 87-93; Bp in Charge Convocation of American Chs in Eur 94-01; Asst Bp Eur from 95; Asst Bp Spain from 97; Asst Bp Portugal from 97; rtd 01. *17 Woodland Drive, Salem, CT 06420, USA* Tel (001) (860) 859 3377

✠**ROXBURGH, The Rt Revd James William.** b 21. St Cath Coll Cam BA42 MA46. Wycliffe Hall Ox 42. **d** 44 **p** 45 **c** 83. C Folkestone H Trin w Ch Ch *Cant* 44-47; C Handsworth St Mary *Birm* 47-50; V Bootle St Matt *Liv* 50-56; V Drypool St Columba w St Andr and St Pet *York* 56-65; V Barking St Marg *Chelmsf* 65-73; P-in-c Barking St Patr 65-73; Hon Can Chelmsf Cathl 72-77; V Barking St Marg w St Patr 73-75; TR 75-77; Adn Colchester 77-83; Suff Bp Barking 83-84; Area Bp Barking 84-90; rtd 90; Asst Bp Liv from 91. *Flat 3, Grantham, 8 Park Road West, Southport PR9 0JS* Tel (01704) 536834

ROXBY, Gordon George. b 39. Lon Univ BSc61. Coll of Resurr Mirfield 61. **d** 63 **p** 64. C Fleetwood St Pet *Blackb* 63-66; C Kirkham 66-68; V Runcorn St Jo Weston *Ches* 68-78; R Moston St Chad *Man* 78-86; V Bury St Pet 86-99; AD Bury 86-96; Hon Can Man Cathl 97-99; V Sandiway *Ches* 99-05; Initial Minl Tr Officer 99-04; rtd 05. *16 St Joseph's Way, Nantwich CW5 6TE* Tel (01270) 619898 E-mail wekan@surfaid.org

ROY, Jennifer Pearl. *See* DREW, Mrs Jennifer Pearl

ROYALL, Preb Arthur Robert. b 19. Lambeth MA. Qu Coll Birm 51. **d** 53 **p** 54. C Ashford St Matt *Lon* 53-56; V Heap Bridge *Man* 56-59; V Whitton St Aug *Lon* 59-64; R Poplar All SS w St Frideswide 64-71; P-in-c Bromley St Mich 64-71; P-in-c Poplar St Sav w St Gabr and St Steph 68-71; R Poplar 71-73; R Bow w Bromley St Leon 73-76; P-in-c Mile End Old Town H Trin 73-76; P-in-c Bethnal Green St Barn 73-75; RD Poplar 65-66; RD Tower Hamlets 68-76; Preb St Paul's Cathl 73-86; Clergy Appts Adv 76-85; Perm to Offic *Nor* 77-98 and *Ely* 78-98; rtd 86; Perm to Offic *Lon* 86-91. *5 Ramsay Hall, 11-13 Byron Road, Worthing BN11 3HN* Tel (01903) 230688

ROYDEN, Charles. b 60. Wycliffe Hall Ox BA86 MA91. **d** 87 **p** 88. C Bidston *Ches* 87-91; V N Brickhill and Putnoe *St Alb* 91-92; V Bedf St Mark from 93. *The Vicarage, Calder Rise, Bedford MK41 7UY* Tel and fax (01234) 342613 *or* tel 309175 Mobile 07973-113861 E-mail vicar@thisischurch.com

ROYDEN, Eric Ramsay. b 29. St Deiniol's Hawarden 75. **d** 77 **p** 78. Hon C Tranmere St Paul w St Luke *Ches* 77-81; C Eastham 81; V New Brighton All SS 81-95; P-in-c 95-97; rtd 95; Perm to Offic *Ches* from 97. *14 Kinglass Road, Bebington, Wirral CH63 9AJ*

ROYDEN, Ross Eric. b 55. Lon Bible Coll BA77 Nottm Univ MTh82. Wycliffe Hall Ox 79. **d** 81 **p** 82. C Moreton *Ches* 81-84; Chapl and Tutor Bedf Coll of HE *St Alb* 84-93; R Banchory *Ab* 93-00; R Kincardine O'Neil 93-00; V Kowloon Tong Ch Ch Hong Kong from 00. *Christ Church Vicarage, 2 Derby Road, Kowloon Tong, Kowloon, Hong Kong* Tel (00852) 2338 4433 Fax 2338 8422 E-mail rossroyden@aol.com

ROYDS, John Caress. b 20. Qu Coll Cam BA47 MA52. **d** 74 **p** 75. C Kettering St Andr *Pet* 74-76; Dioc Dir of Educn and R Loddington w Cransley 76-81; V Northampton St Jas 81-85; CMS Pakistan 85-86; rtd 87; Perm to Offic *Sarum* from 90. *16B Donaldson Road, Salisbury SP1 3AD* Tel (01722) 332293

ROYLANCE, Mrs Margaret. b 47. St Mary's Coll Chelt CertEd68. Cant Sch of Min 93. **d** 96 **p** 97. NSM Tenterden St Mildred w Smallhythe *Cant* from 96; Chapl Ashford Sch from 96. *5 Southgate Road, Tenterden TN30 7BS* Tel (01580) 762332

ROYLE, Antony Kevan. b 50. Lon Univ BSc71 FIA76. Trin Coll Bris 76. **d** 79 **p** 80. C Chell *Lich* 79-82; C Leyland St Andr *Blackb* 82-86; V Blackb Sav 86-95; Chapl Blackb R Infirmary and Park Lee Hosp 86-95; Chapl E Lancs Hospice 86-95; TR Walton H Trin *Ox* 95-01; NSM Wendover Deanery from 01. *4 Darley Close, Aylesbury HP21 7EA* Tel (01296) 582470 Mobile 07796-143905

ROYLE, Michael Arthur. b 38. Univ of Wales (Ban) BSc61 Lon Univ DipTh63. St Jo Coll Nottm 81. **d** 82 **p** 83. C Boulton *Derby* 82-85; C Belper 85-87; P-in-c Smalley and Morley 87-95; RD Heanor 89-94; V Charlesworth and Dinting Vale 95-02; rtd 02; Perm to Offic *Ches* from 02 and *Derby* from 03. *Kaiama, 55 Cross Lane, Marple, Stockport SK6 7PZ* Tel 0161-427 6453 E-mail royle@fish.co.uk

ROYLE, Canon Peter Sydney George. b 34. K Coll Lon BD57 AKC57. **d** 58 **p** 59. C St Helier *S'wark* 58-62; Australia 62-68; P-in-c Sydenham St Phil *S'wark* 69-72; V Leigh Park *Portsm* 72-85; RD Havant 77-82; V S w N Hayling 85-96; V S Hayling 96-97; Hon Can Portsm Cathl 95-97; rtd 97; Perm to Offic *Ex* from 97. *Fairbank, 74 Newton Road, Bishopsteignton TQ14 9PP* Tel (01626) 779252

ROYLE, Canon Roger Michael. b 39. AKC61 Lambeth MA90. **d** 62 **p** 63. C Portsea St Mary *Portsm* 62-65; C St Helier *S'wark* 65-68; Succ S'wark Cathl 68-71; Warden Eton Coll Dorney Par Project *Ox* 71-74; Conduct Eton Coll 74-79; Lic to Offic *S'wark* 79-90; Chapl Ld Mayor Treloar Coll Alton 90-92; Hon C Froyle and Holybourne *Win* 90-92; Hon Can and Chapl S'wark Cathl *S'wark* 93-99; Perm to Offic from 99; rtd 04. *Address withheld by request*

ROYLE, Canon Stanley Michael. b 43. K Coll Lon BD69 AKC69 Man Univ MA75. St Aug Coll Cant 71. **d** 72 **p** 73. C Timperley *Ches* 72-76; Perm to Offic 76-81; R Milton Abbas, Hilton w Cheselbourne etc *Sarum* 81-86; Dir of Ords 86-01; Adv on CME 86-98; Can and Preb Sarum Cathl from 89; Bp's Dom Chapl 98-01; Lic to Offic from 01. *Three Firs, Blandford Road, Sturminster Marshall, Wimborne BH21 4AF* Tel (01258) 857326

RUAHA, Bishop of. *See* MTETEMELA, The Most Revd Donald Leo

RUCK, John. b 47. Bris Univ BSc68 Birm Univ MPhil92. All Nations Chr Coll MA03. **d** 80 **p** 83. OMF Internat from 78; Indonesia 80-86 and 87-91; Perm to Offic *Birm* 86-87 and 91-98; Lic to Offic from 03; Lect Crowther Hall CMS Tr Coll Selly Oak 00-04; CMS from 04. *121 Bournbrook Road, Birmingham B29 7BY* Tel 0121-415 4036 E-mail johnanne@ruckja.freeserve.co.uk

RUDALL, Mark Edward. b 53. Regent's Park Coll Ox BA80 MA84. Ripon Coll Cuddesdon 00. **d** 01 **p** 02. In Bapt Min 80-00; C Wallingford *Ox* 01-03; Dioc Dir Communications *Guildf* from 04. *Diocesan House, Quarry Street, Guildford GU1 3XG* Tel (01483) 571826 Mobile 07779-654975 E-mail mark.rudall@cofeguildford.org.uk *or* mark.rudall@ntlworld.com

RUDD, Charles Robert Jordeson. b 34. TCD BA56 MA65 BD65. **d** 57 **p** 58. C Lurgan Redeemer *D & D* 57-61; C Lisburn Ch Ch Cathl *Conn* 61-62; C Willowfield *D & D* 62-66; I Drumgooland w Kilcoo 66-75; I Moira 75-95; I Magherally w Annaclone 95-02; Can Belf Cathl 90-02; rtd 02. *12 Thorn Heights, Banbridge BT32 4BF* Tel (028) 4062 8995

RUDD, Colin Richard. b 41. AKC64. **d** 65 **p** 66. C N Stoneham *Win* 65-70; V Rotherwick, Hook and Greywell 70-74; R Hook w Greywell 74-78; Toc H 78-89; V Buckland *Ox* 89-98; V Littleworth 89-98; R Pusey 89-98; R Gainfield 98-99; RD Vale of White Horse 96-99; rtd 99. *Alcudia, Bilbrook, Minehead TA24 6HE* Tel (01984) 640021

RUDD, Canon Julian Douglas Raymond. b 19. Leeds Univ BA40. Coll of Resurr Mirfield 40. **d** 42 **p** 43. C Bury St Edmunds St Jo *St E* 42-46; C Holborn St Alb w Saffron Hill St Pet *Lon* 46-49; V Bournemouth St Fran *Win* 49-60; RD Bournemouth 56-60; R Old Alresford 60-70; RD Alresford 60-70; Hon Can Win Cathl 62-70; V Warwick St Mary *Cov* 70-76; V Warwick St Mary w St Nic 76-83; Hon Can Cov Cathl 76-84; TR Warwick 83-84; RD Warwick 77-79; rtd 84; Perm to Offic *Sarum* 84-98. *The College of St Barnabas, Blackberry Lane, Lingfield RH7 6NJ* Tel (01342) 870441

RUDD, Robert. *See* RUDD, Charles Robert Jordeson

RUDD, Robert Arthur. b 33. ALCD60. **d** 60 **p** 61. C Blackb Sav *Blackb* 60-63; C Huyton St Geo *Liv* 63-65; V Bickershaw 65-72; Asst Chapl HM Pris Liv 72-73; Chapl HM Pris Birm 73-78; Chapl HM Pris Parkhurst 78-86; Chapl HM Pris Camp Hill 86-92; Chapl St Mary's Hosp Newport 92-95; rtd 95; Perm to Offic *Portsm* from 95. *The Elms, 13 Horsebridge Hill, Newport PO30 5TJ* Tel (01983) 524415

RUDDLE, Canon Donald Arthur. b 31. MBE04. Linc Th Coll 64. **d** 66 **p** 67. C Kettering SS Pet and Paul *Pet* 66-70; V Earlham St Anne *Nor* 70-79; V E Malling *Roch* 79-95; RD Malling 84-93; Hon Can Roch Cathl 88-95; Chapl Nord Pas de Calais *Eur* 95-98; rtd 98; Perm to Offic *Eur* from 98. *5 Windmill Lane, Faversham ME13 7GT* Tel (01795) 533461 E-mail don.ruddle@tiscali.co.uk

RUDDOCK, Brian John. b 45. Dur Univ BA66 Nottm Univ MEd91. Westcott Ho Cam 67. **d** 69 **p** 70. C Ross *Heref* 69-72; C Kettering SS Pet and Paul *Pet* 72-75; P-in-c Colchester St Steph *Chelmsf* 75-77; TR Colchester St Leon, St Mary Magd and St Steph 77-84; R March St Pet *Ely* 84-89; R March St Mary 84-89; RD March 87-89; Dioc Unemployment Officer *Sheff* 89-94; Resource and Development Officer CCWA 96-02. *46 Tanners Field, Amesbury, Salisbury SP4 7SF* Tel (01980) 623072

RUDDOCK, Bruce. *See* RUDDOCK, Canon Reginald Bruce

RUDDOCK, Canon Charles Cecil. b 28. TCD Dip Bibl Studies. TCD Div Sch. **d** 57 **p** 58. C Belfast St Mary *Conn* 57-59; C Carnmoney 59-61; C Belfast St Aid 61-63; I Kiltegan w Rathvilly *C & O* 63-69; C Newtownards *D & D* 69-72; Australia 72-83; I Mallow Union *C, C & R* 83-89; I Fenagh w Myshall, Aghade and Ardoyne *C & O* 89-95; Can Ossory and Leighlin Cathls 92-95; rtd 95; Perm to Offic *Glouc* from 95. *26 Arundel Drive, Rodborough, Stroud GL5 3SH* Tel (01453) 766484

RUDDOCK, Edgar Chapman. b 48. St Jo Coll Dur BA70 MA76. Cranmer Hall Dur 70. **d** 74 **p** 75. C Birm St Geo *Birm* 74-78; R

78-83; S Africa 83-91; Dir Tr Dio St Jo 83-86; P-in-c Mandini 86-87; Prov Dir Tr 88-91; TR Stoke-upon-Trent *Lich* 91-02; Internat Relns Sec USPG from 03. *USPG, Partnership House, 157 Waterloo Road, London SE1 8XA* Tel (020) 7928 8681 E-mail edrud@cix.co.uk

RUDDOCK, Kenneth Edward. b 30. TCD BA52 QUB MTh79. CITC 53 Div Test. **d** 53 **p** 54. C Ballymena *Conn* 53-56; C Belfast St Thos 56-60; I Tomregan w Drumlane *K, E & A* 60-68; I Belfast St Luke *Conn* 68-80; Miss to Seamen 80-96; I Whitehead and Islandmagee *Conn* 80-96; Can Lisburn Cathl 90-96; Dioc Info Officer from 90; Chan Conn Cathl 96; rtd 96; Dioc C *Conn* from 98. *24 Fourtowns Manor, Ahoghill, Ballymena BT42 1RS* Tel (028) 2587 8966 Mobile 07970-639067

RUDDOCK, Leonard William. b 58. CITC 91. **d** 94 **p** 95. NSM Roscrea w Kyle, Bourney and Corbally *L & K* from 94. *Short Corville, Roscrea, Co Tipperary, Irish Republic* Tel (00353) (505) 22034

RUDDOCK, Norman Trevor. b 35. TCD BA57 MA60 HDipEd62. TCD Div Sch 58. **d** 58 **p** 59. C Belfast St Steph *Conn* 58-60; C Dublin Ch Ch Leeson Park *D & G* 60-63; Perm to Offic 63-73; USA 70-72; I Killanne *C & O* 73-81; I Castlepollard and Oldcastle w Loughcrew etc *M & K* 84-93; Can Meath 92-93; I Wexford w Ardcolm and Killurin *C & O* 93-04; I Taghmon w Horetown and Bannow 95-04; P-in-c Kilscoran w Killinick and Mulrankin 02-04; Treas Ferns Cathl 96-98; Chan 98-03; Prec 03-04; rtd 04. *5 Richmond Terrace, Spawell Road, Wexford, Irish Republic* Tel and fax (00353) (53) 42905 Mobile 87-791 5901

RUDDOCK, Canon Reginald Bruce. b 55. AGSM77. Chich Th Coll. **d** 83 **p** 84. C Felpham w Middleton *Chich* 83-86; C Portsea St Mary *Portsm* 86-88; P-in-c Barnes St Mich *S'wark* 88-95; Dir Angl Cen Rome 95-99; Hon Can American Cathl Paris from 96; Can Res Worc Cathl *Worc* 99-04; Can Res Pet Cathl *Pet* from 04. *The Chapter Office, Minster Precincts, Peterborough PE1 1XS* Tel (01733) 343342 E-mail bruce.ruddock@peterborough-cathedral.org.uk

RUDEN, Lars Olav. b 43. **d** 00 **p** 01. OLM Bamford *Man* 00-05; P-in-c Healey from 05. *Healey Vicarage, 10 Healey Avenue, Rochdale OL12 6EG* Tel (01706) 657386 Mobile 07743-509193 E-mail larsruden.norge@virgin.net

RUDIGER, David John. b 42. MCMI91. Ox Min Course CBTS94. **d** 94 **p** 95. NSM Woughton *Ox* from 94. *32 Forest Rise, Eaglestone, Milton Keynes MK6 5EU* Tel (01908) 668474 E-mail david@rudiger2.freeserve.co.uk

RUDKIN, Simon David. b 51. Bradf Univ BA74 K Coll Lon BD77 AKC77. Coll of Resurr Mirfield 77. **d** 78 **p** 79. C Flixton St Mich *Man* 78-81; C Atherton 81-84; V Lever Bridge 84-91; P-in-c Pennington w Lindal and Marton *Carl* 91-96; P-in-c Pennington and Lindal w Marton and Bardsea 96-00; V Morland, Thrimby, Gt Strickland and Cliburn from 00; P-in-c Kirkby Thore w Temple Sowerby and Newbiggin from 04; P-in-c Bolton from 05; P-in-c Crosby Ravensworth from 05. *The Vicarage, Morland, Penrith CA10 3AX* Tel (01931) 714620

RUDMAN, David Walter Thomas. b 48. Lon Univ DipTh70 BD72. Oak Hill Th Coll 68. **d** 72 **p** 73. C Plymouth St Jude *Ex* 72-75; C Radipole *Sarum* 76-77; Warden St Geo Ho Braunton 77-03; R Georgeham *Ex* 88-03; Dioc Adv in Adult Tr 97-03; TV S Molton w Nymet St George, High Bray etc from 03; Dioc Adv in OLM from 03. *The Rectory, Kingsnymphton, Umberleigh EX37 9ST* Tel (01769) 580457 E-mail davidrudman@ntlworld.com

RUEHORN, Eric Arthur. b 33. St Aid Birkenhead 58. **d** 61 **p** 62. C Harpurhey Ch Ch *Man* 61-65; V Roughtown 65-74; V Hawkshaw Lane 74-99; rtd 99; Perm to Offic *Man* from 00. *29 Hunstanton Drive, Bury BL8 1EG* Tel 0161-761 3983

RUFF, Brian Chisholm. b 36. Lon Univ BD66 ACA60 FCA70. Oak Hill Th Coll 63. **d** 67 **p** 68. C Cheadle *Ches* 67-72; Educn and Youth Sec CPAS 72-76; V New Milverton *Cov* 76-90; V Westbourne Ch Ch Prop Chpl *Win* 90-01; rtd 02; Perm to Offic *Win* from 02 and *Sarum* from 03. *19 Hardy Road, West Moors, Wimborne BH22 0EX* Tel (01202) 868733 E-mail bcr@ruffys.fsnet.co.uk

RUFF, Michael Ronald. b 49. K Coll Lon BD72 AKC72. St Aug Coll Cant 72. **d** 73 **p** 74. C Old Shoreham *Chich* 73-76; Chapl Ellesmere Coll 77-81; Chapl Grenville Coll Bideford 81-87; Chapl Stamford Sch from 87; Perm to Offic *Linc* 87-99. *9 Vence Close, Stamford PE9 2LZ1* Tel (01780) 766567

RUFFLE, Preb John Leslie. b 43. ALCD66. **d** 66 **p** 67. C Eastwood *S'well* 66-70; C Keynsham w Queen Charlton *B & W* 70-75; P-in-c Weston-super-Mare Em 75; TV Weston-super-Mare Cen Par 75-84; V Yatton Moor 84-91; TR 91-98; P-in-c Chew Stoke w Nempnett Thrubwell 98-03; Dioc Adv in Past Care and Counselling from 03; Preb Wells Cathl from 97. *16 Mendip Road, Weston-super-Mare BS23 3HA* Tel (01934) 612254 Fax 612104 E-mail john@vicpress01.freeserve.co.uk

RUFFLE, Peter Cousins. b 19. Lon Univ BD42. ALCD42. **d** 42 **p** 43. C Highbury Ch Ch *Lon* 42-46; CMS Missr Bihar India 46-52; Youth Adv CMS 52-57; Hon C Bromley St Jo *Roch* 54-57; V Walton Breck *Liv* 57-60; V Aigburth 60-66; Prin Wilson Carlile Coll of Evang 66-74; Can Res Blackb Cathl *Blackb* 74-78; V Meole Brace *Lich* 78-85; rtd 85; Perm to Offic *Portsm* and *Win* 85-03; *York* from 03. *20 Dulverton Hall, Esplanade, Scarborough YO11 2AR* Tel (01723) 340120

RUFLI, Alan John. b 63. TCD BA89. **d** 91 **p** 92. C Donaghcloney w Waringstown *D & D* 91-94; C Knock 94-95; I Rathcoole *Conn* 95-01; I Holmpatrick w Balbriggan and Kenure *D & G* from 01. *Holmpatrick Rectory, Miller's Lane, Skerries, Co Dublin, Irish Republic* Tel (00353) (1) 849 2247 E-mail rufrev@aol.com

RUGEN, Peter. b 60. Crewe & Alsager Coll BEd86. Trin Coll Bris MA00. **d** 00 **p** 01. C Shipley St Pet *Bradf* 00-04; P-in-c Riddlesden from 04; P-in-c Morton St Luke from 04. *The Vicarage, St Mary's Road, Riddlesden, Keighley BD20 5PA* Tel (01535) 603419

RUGG, Andrew Philip. b 47. Kent Univ BA82. Sarum & Wells Th Coll 83. **d** 85 **p** 86. C Harlesden All So *Lon* 85-90; TV Benwell *Newc* 90-97; V Weetslade 97-00; rtd 00; Perm to Offic *York* from 00. *36 Whenby Grove, York YO31 9DS* Tel and fax (01904) 652567 Mobile 07980-390051

RUGMAN, Mrs Hazel. b 47. R Holloway Coll Lon BA68 ACIS89. N Ord Course 01. **d** 03. NSM Sandbach *Ches* from 03. *High Trees, 157 Sandbach Road North, Alsager, Stoke-on-Trent ST7 2AX* Tel (01270) 876386 Mobile 07762-706120 Fax (01270) 883737 E-mail pjrugman@btinternet.com

✠**RUHUMULIZA, The Rt Revd Jonathan.** b 56. Makumira Univ Coll Tanzania BD89. Butare Th Sch Rwanda 78. **d** 82 **p** 83 **c** 91. C Kigeme Rwanda 82-84; Manager and Chapl Kigeme High Sch 83-86 and 90-91; Manager and Chapl Kigeme Hosp 89-90; Asst Bp Butare 91-92; Prov Sec 92-93; Asst Bp Kigali 93; Coadjutor Bp 93-95; Bp 95-97; Miss Bp Cameroon 98-04; Hon Asst Bp Worc from 05; C Droitwich Spa from 05. *St Nicholas' Vicarage, Ombersley Close, Droitwich WR9 8JY* Tel (01905) 771516 E-mail bspjrmuliza@yahoo.co.uk

✠**RUMALSHAH, The Rt Revd Munawar Kenneth (Mano).** b 41. Punjab Univ BSc60 Serampore Coll BD65 Karachi Univ MA68 Cam Univ PGCE86. Bp's Coll Calcutta DipTh65. **d** 65 **p** 66 **c** 94. Pakistan 65-69 and 89-99; C H Trin Cathl Karachi 65-69; C Roundhay St Edm *Ripon* 70-73; Area Sec CMS *Ripon* and *York* 74-78; Asst Home Sec York Prov 73-78; Educn Sec BCC 78-81; P-in-c Southall St Geo *Lon* 81-88; USPG 89-03; Gen Sec 99-03; Bp Peshawar 94-99 and from 03; Hon Asst Bp S'wark 99-03. *St John's Cathedral, 1 Sir-Syed Road, Peshawar, NWFP, 25000, Pakistan* Tel (0092) (91) 276519 Fax 277499 E-mail manor@uspg.org.uk

RUMBALL, Preb Frank Thomas. b 43. Sarum & Wells Th Coll 72. **d** 74 **p** 75. C Bromyard *Heref* 74-78; TV Ewyas Harold w Dulas 78-79; TV Ewyas Harold w Dulas, Kenderchurch etc 79-81; C Minsterley 81-82; P-in-c Eye, Croft w Yarpole and Lucton 82-91; R Condover w Frodesley, Acton Burnell etc 91-01; Preb Heref Cathl 97-01; rtd 01; Perm to Offic *Heref* from 01. *The Old School, Pitchford, Shrewsbury SY5 7DW* Tel (01694) 731256

RUMBALL, William Michael. b 41. Surrey Univ BSc63 Birm Univ PhD66 Open Univ BA75 MIM66 MINucE73 FIMMM03. Wycliffe Hall Ox 78. **d** 80 **p** 81. C S Molton, Nymet St George, High Bray etc *Ex* 80-83; V S Hetton w Haswell *Dur* 83-90; V S Wingfield and Wessington *Derby* 90-99; rtd 99; Hon C Brailsford w Shirley and Osmaston w Edlaston *Derby* 01-03; Perm to Offic from 03. *4 Hawthorn Close, Ashbourne DE6 1HW* Tel (01335) 343203 E-mail wm.rumball@virgin.net

RUMBLE, Alison Merle. *See* PRINCE, Mrs Alison Merle

RUMBOLD, Bernard John. b 43. **d** 73 **p** 75. Hon C Alotau Papua New Guinea 73-76; C Gt Burstead *Chelmsf* 76-77; Chapl RAF 77-93; Chapl HM Pris Featherstone 93-95; C Wordsley *Worc* 95-96; TV 96-99; Chapl Dudley Gp of Hosps NHS Trust 96-99; R Teme Valley N *Worc* 99-02; rtd 02; P-in-c Brompton Regis w Upton and Skilgate *B & W* from 03; Perm to Offic *Sarum* from 03. *The Vicarage, Brompton Regis, Dulverton TA22 9NL* Tel (01398) 371438

RUMBOLD, Graham Charles. b 44. Open Univ BA79. S Dios Minl Tr Scheme 76. **d** 79 **p** 80. NSM Widley w Wymering *Portsm* 79-82; Chapl Cynthia Spencer Unit Manfield Hosp 82-94; Chapl Northampton Community Healthcare NHS Trust 94-01; Chapl Northants Healthcare NHS Trust from 01; NSM Weston Favell *Pet* 93-95; NSM Northampton St Matt from 98. *3 Calstock Close, Northampton NN3 3BA* Tel (01604) 627389

RUMENS, Canon John Henry. b 21. AKC49. **d** 50 **p** 51. C Wareham w Arne *Sarum* 50-54; V Alderholt 54-59; R Salisbury St Edm 59-72; RD Salisbury 69-72; R Trowbridge H Trin 72-79; P-in-c Sturminster Marshall 79-83; V 83-85; Can and Preb Sarum Cathl 72-85; rtd 85; Perm to Offic *Sarum* from 85. *20 Constable Way, Salisbury SP2 8LN* Tel (01722) 334716

RUMENS, Ms Katharine Mary. b 53. UEA BEd76. Westcott Ho Cam 90. **d** 92 **p** 94. Par Dn E Ham w Upton Park St Alb *Chelmsf* 92-94; C 94-95; C Waterloo St Jo w St Andr *S'wark* 95-00; Chapl S Bank Cen and Chapl Lon Weekend TV 95-00; R St Giles Cripplegate w St Bart Moor Lane etc *Lon* from 00. *The Rectory,*

4 The Postern, Wood Street, London EC2Y 8BJ Tel and fax (020) 7588 3013 *or* tel 7638 1997
E-mail rumens@stgileschurch.com

RUMING, Canon Gordon William. b 27. Kelham Th Coll 45. **d** 52 **p** 53. C Baildon *Bradf* 52-55; C Prestbury *Glouc* 55-60; C Penzance St Mary *Truro* 60-61; R Calstock 61-92; Hon Can Truro Cathl 79-92; RD E Wivelshire 85-91; rtd 92; Perm to Offic *Truro* from 92 and *Ex* from 99. *3 Derry Avenue, Plymouth PL4 6BH* Tel (01752) 661986

RUMSEY, Andrew Paul. b 68. Reading Univ BA89. Ridley Hall Cam MA98. **d** 97 **p** 98. C Harrow Trin St Mich *Lon* 97-01; V Gipsy Hill Ch Ch *S'wark* from 01. *Christ Church Vicarage, 1 Highland Road, London SE19 1DP* Tel (020) 8670 0385
E-mail vicar@gipsyhill.org.uk

RUMSEY, Ian Mark. b 58. Van Mildert Coll Dur BSc79 St Jo Coll Dur BA89. Cranmer Hall Dur 87. **d** 90 **p** 91. C Dalston *Carl* 90-94; C Wreay 92-94; TV Cockermouth w Embleton and Wythop 94-04; Adv for Post-Ord Tr 97-00; V Hurdsfield *Ches* from 04. *197A Hurdsfield Road, Macclesfield SK10 2PX* Tel (01625) 424587

RUNCORN, David Charles. b 54. BA77 Ox Poly Dip Psychology 88. St Jo Coll Nottm 77. **d** 79 **p** 80. C Wealdstone H Trin *Lon* 79-82; Chapl Lee Abbey 82-87; C Ealing St Steph Castle Hill *Lon* 89-90; V 90-96; Dir Past and Evang Studies Trin Coll Bris 96-03; Dir Min Development *Lich* from 03. *The Vicarage, 35 Church Street, Littleover, Derby DE23 6GF* Tel (01332) 767802 E-mail david.runcorn@lichfield.anglican.org

RUNCORN, Canon Dennis Brookes. b 22. Ch Coll Cam BA47 MA52. Ridley Hall Cam 47. **d** 49 **p** 50. C Ashtead *Guildf* 49-53; Hong Kong 54-62; Prin CMS Tr Coll Chislehurst 62-67; V Shortlands *Roch* 67-80; RD Beckenham 73-80; Hon Can Roch Cathl 78-87; V Shorne 80-87; rtd 87; Perm to Offic *Derby* from 87. *14 Hollowood Avenue, Littleover, Derby DE23 6JD* Tel (01332) 765859

RUNCORN, Jacqueline Ann. *See* SEARLE, Jacqueline Ann

RUNDELL, Simon Philip. b 67. Univ of N Lon BSc95 Leeds Univ BA01 RGN90. Coll of Resurr Mirfield 99. **d** 01 **p** 02. C Southsea H Spirit *Portsm* 01-04; P-in-c Elson from 04. *St Thomas's Vicarage, 21 Elson Road, Gosport PO12 4BL* Tel (023) 9258 2824 E-mail simon@rundell.org.uk

RUNDLE, Mrs Beryl Rosemary. b 28. Bris Univ BA49 CertEd50. S Dios Minl Tr Scheme 83. **dss** 86 **d** 87. Tangmere *Chich* 86-87; Hon Par Dn 87-92; Boxgrove 86-87; Hon Par Dn 87-92; Hon Par Dn Eastbourne St Sav and St Pet 92-98; Perm to Offic *Portsm* and *Chich* from 98. *22 Sovereign Drive, Southsea PO4 8XX* Tel (01705) 826859

RUNDLE, Hilary. b 65. St Hugh's Coll Ox BA88 Cheltenham & Glouc Coll of HE PGCE90. Trin Coll Bris 01. **d** 03 **p** 04. C Chipping Sodbury and Old Sodbury *Glouc* from 03. *23 Couzens Close, Chipping Sodbury, Bristol BS37 6BT* Tel (01454) 320951
E-mail hilaryrundle@hotmail.com

RUNDLE, Nicholas John. b 59. Southn Univ BA80. St Steph Ho Ox BTh84. **d** 84 **p** 85. C E Preston w Kingston *Chich* 84-87; Chapl RAF 87-91; Australia from 91; Assoc P Magill 91-93; R Grange 93-98; R Hawthorn 98-02; Chapl and Past Care Co-ord Mission Australia from 03. *Mission Australia, 49 Flinders Street, Adelaide, S Australia 5000* Tel (0061) (8) 8370 3583 *or* 8223 5428 Mobile 403-183005 Fax (8) 8223 6425
E-mail rundlen@mission.com.au

RUNDLE, Penelope Anne. b 36. St Hugh's Coll Ox MA59 Lon Univ DAA64. S Dios Minl Tr Scheme 85. **d** 88 **p** 94. Hon Par Dn Mere w W Knoyle and Maiden Bradley *Sarum* 88-91; Hon Par Dn Upper Stour 91-94; Hon C 94-02; rtd 02; Perm to Offic *Sarum* from 02. *7 Prospect Place, Ann Street, Salisbury SP1 2EA* Tel (01722) 411774

RUSCHMEYER, Henry Cassell. b 44. Union Coll NY BA66 Bank St Coll of Ed NY MEd73 NY Univ MA88. Gen Th Sem (NY) MD78. **d** 78 **p** 79. USA 78-89 and from 97; NSM Wilton Place St Paul *Lon* 89-97. *PO Box 25012, Sarasota, FL 34277, USA*

RUSCOE, Canon John Ernest. b 32. Dur Univ BA57. Qu Coll Birm 57. **d** 59 **p** 60. C Jarrow St Paul *Dur* 59-63; C Whitburn 63-65; V S Hylton from 65; Hon Can Dur Cathl from 85. *The Vicarage, Vicarage Lane, Sunderland SR4 0QB* Tel 0191-534 2325

RUSDELL-WILSON, Arthur Neville. b 43. Lon Univ BScEng65 Linacre Coll Ox BA70 MA74 ACGI. St Steph Ho Ox 68. **d** 71 **p** 72. C Whitton St Aug *Lon* 71-73; C Chiswick St Nic w St Mary 73-76; C Littlehampton St Jas *Chich* 76-81; C Littlehampton St Mary 76-81; C Wick 76-81; V Whitworth St Bart *Man* 81-88; V Shaw 88-98; rtd 03. *21 Fairview Avenue, Goring-by-Sea, Worthing BN12 4HT* Tel (01903) 242561
E-mail arthur@shawvic.demon.co.uk

RUSH, Paul Andrew. b 57. Lon Bible Coll BA79 Anglia Poly Univ MA03. Ridley Hall Cam 98. **d** 00 **p** 01. C Bar Hill *Ely* 00-03; Dioc Evang Officer *Leic* from 03. *38 Park Hill Drive, Leicester LE2 8HR* Tel 0116-224 1788
E-mail rev.paul.rush@ntlworld.com

RUSHER, James Victor Francis. b 28. RMA. Ridley Hall Cam 58. **d** 60 **p** 61. C Kensington St Helen w H Trin *Lon* 60-63; C Edgbaston St Bart *Birm* 63-66; V Summerfield 66-71; V Knowle 71-82; Perm to Offic 82-93; Chapl Parkway Hosp Solihull 85-93; rtd 93. *4 Froxmere Close, Solihull B91 3XG* Tel 0121-705 4514

RUSHFORTH, Richard Hamblin. b 40. Keble Coll Ox BA62 MA71. Chich Th Coll 62. **d** 64 **p** 65. C St Leonards Ch Ch *Chich* 64-79; Org Sec Fellowship of St Nic 79-81; V Portslade St Nic and St Andr from 81; Min Portslade Gd Shep CD 88-89. *The Vicarage, South Street, Portslade, Brighton BN41 2LE* Tel (01273) 418090

RUSHTON, David William. b 70. St Chad's Coll Dur BA96. St Steph Ho Ox DipTh98. **d** 98 **p** 99. C Hornsey St Mary w St Geo *Lon* 98-01; C Thamesmead *S'wark* 01-02; Asst Chapl King's Coll Hosp NHS Trust from 02. *The Chaplain's Office, King's College Hospital, Denmark Hill, London SE5 9RS* Tel (020) 7346 3522 Fax 7346 4059
E-mail rev.rushton@kingsch.nhs.uk

RUSHTON, Canon James David. b 39. Dur Univ BA61. Cranmer Hall Dur. **d** 64 **p** 65. C Upper Armley *Ripon* 64-67; C Blackpool Ch Ch *Blackb* 67-70; V Preston St Cuth 70-79; V Denton Holme *Carl* 79-96; P-in-c Preston All SS *Blackb* 96-00; V 00-04; AD Preston 98-03; Hon Can Blackb Cathl from 00; rtd 04. *3 Evergreen Avenue, Leyland PR25 3AW* Tel (01772) 451717
E-mail james@jamesrushton.wanadoo.co.uk

RUSHTON, Ms Janet Maureen. b 46. Keele Univ BA68 Leic Univ PGCE69. Wycliffe Hall Ox BTh94. **d** 94 **p** 95. C Harrow St Mary *Lon* 94-98; C Putney St Mary *S'wark* 98-02; P-in-c Wolvercote w Summertown *Ox* from 02. *The Vicarage, 37 Lonsdale Road, Oxford OX2 7ES* Tel (01865) 556079
E-mail janrushton@lineone.net

RUSHTON, Malcolm Leslie. b 47. Bris Univ BSc69 Birm Univ PhD72 Fitzw Coll Cam BA74. Ridley Hall Cam 72. **d** 75 **p** 76. C Cullompton *Ex* 75-79; Chapl Univ Coll *Lon* 79-87; Chapl R Veterinary Coll Lon 87-90; Chapl R Free Medical Sch 87-90. *Flat 3, 13 Belsize Grove, London NW3 4UX* Tel (020) 7722 1989 Fax as telephone

RUSHTON, Philip William. b 38. Open Univ BA87. Clifton Th Coll 62. **d** 65 **p** 66. C Brixton St Paul *S'wark* 65-67; C Aldridge *Lich* 67-69; C Bushbury 69-71; Chapl Nat Nautical Sch Portishead 71-72; Chapl RAF 72-79; P-in-c Bolton on Swale *Ripon* 79-87; P-in-c The Cowtons 80-82; V 82-89; CF (TA) from 88; R Litcham, Kempston, Lexham, Mileham, Beeston etc *Nor* 89-95; P-in-c Tittleshall w Godwick 93-95; R Litcham w Kempston, E and W Lexham, Mileham etc 95-96; P-in-c Scole, Brockdish, Billingford, Thorpe Abbots etc 96-98; R 98-01; rtd 01; Perm to Offic *St E* and *Carl* from 01. *Helm Lea, Kirkby Thore, Penrith CA10 1UA* Tel and fax (01768) 361597
E-mail philipwrushton@hotmail.com

RUSHTON, Mrs Samantha Jayne. b 65. St Hilda's Coll Ox MA87. Trin Coll Bris BA05. **d** 05. C Highworth w Sevenhampton and Inglesham etc *Bris* from 05. *14 Brookfield, Highworth, Swindon SN6 7HY* Tel (01793) 763197
E-mail sam.rushton@xalt.co.uk

RUSHTON, Mrs Susan Elizabeth. b 44. Univ of Wales (Cardiff) BA65. Bris Sch of Min 83. **dss** 86 **d** 87 **p** 94. Westbury-on-Trym H Trin *Bris* 86-91; Hon Par Dn 87-91; C Wotton St Mary *Glouc* 91-94; Chapl United Bris Healthcare NHS Trust 94-98; P-in-c Frampton Cotterell *Bris* from 94; P-in-c Iron Acton from 98. *The Rectory, Rectory Road, Frampton Cotterell, Bristol BS36 2BP* Tel and fax (01454) 772112 E-mail susan.rushton@onetel.com

RUSHTON, Mrs Valerie Elizabeth Wendy. b 40. Birm Univ BSocSc62 DPS87. WMMTC 86. **d** 89 **p** 94. C Nuneaton St Nic *Cov* 89-93; C Stockingford 93-96; TV Watling Valley *Ox* 96-01; rtd 02; Perm to Offic *Ox* from 02. *106 Moreton Road, Buckingham MK18 1IP* Tel (01280) 824942

RUSK, The Very Revd Frederick John. b 28. QUB BA50 TCD 52. **d** 53 **p** 54. C Ballymoney *Conn* 53-56; C Belfast St Nic 56-59; I Broomhedge 59-65; RE Insp 64-66; I Belfast St Simon 65-78; I Ballymena w Ballyclug 78-88; I Belfast St Nic 88-98; Preb Conn Cathl 84-86; Treas 86-90; Prec 90; Chan Conn Cathl 90-95; Dean Conn 95-98; rtd 98. *28 Banbridge Road, Lurgan, Craigavon BT66 7EQ* Tel (028) 3832 9763

RUSK, Michael Frederick. b 58. Cam Univ BA MA Dur Univ MA98. Westcott Ho Cam 81. **d** 84 **p** 85. C Altrincham St Geo *Ches* 84-87; Chapl Collingwood and Grey Coll *Dur* 87-90; Lect Dur Univ 89-99; C-in-c Neville's Cross St Jo CD 90-99; TR Oadby *Leic* from 99; RD Gartree II from 00. *St Peter's Rectory, 1 Leicester Road, Oadby, Leicester LE2 5BD* Tel 0116-271 2135
E-mail m.f.rusk@leicester.anglican.org

RUSS, Canon Timothy John. b 41. AKC64. Sarum Th Coll 66. **d** 66 **p** 67. C Walthamstow St Pet *Chelmsf* 66-70; C Epping St Jo 70-73; C Stepney St Dunstan and All SS *Lon* 73-75; Youth Officer 75-79; Tutor YMCA Nat Coll Walthamstow 79-84; Hon C St Botolph Aldgate w H Trin Minories *Lon* 82-89; Selection Sec ACCM 84-89; Dir St Marylebone Healing and Counselling Cen 89-92; Gen Sec Inst of Relig and Medicine 89-92; Hon C Hoxton St Anne w St Columba *Lon* 90-92; P-in-c St Dennis *Truro* from 92; Par Development Adv 92-99; Dir Minl

Tr from 99; Hon Can Truro Cathl from 01. *The Rectory, Carne Hill, St Dennis, St Austell PL26 8AZ* Tel (01726) 822317 Fax as telephone E-mail timruss@tesco.net

RUSSELL, Adrian Camper. b 45. Chich Th Coll 79. **d** 81 **p** 82. C Marton *Blackb* 81-84; C Haslemere *Guildf* 84-85; V Hartlepool H Trin *Dur* 85-89; P-in-c Cornforth 89-94; R Auchterarder *St And* 94-97; R Muthill 94-97; P-in-c Kenton Ascension *Newc* from 97. *Kenton Vicarage, Creighton Avenue, Newcastle upon Tyne NE3 4UN* Tel 0191-285 7803 Fax as telephone E-mail acr0210@btinternet.com

✠**RUSSELL, The Rt Revd Anthony John.** b 43. St Chad's Coll Dur BA65 Trin Coll Ox DPhil71. Cuddesdon Coll 65. **d** 70 **p** 71 **c** 88. C Hilborough w Bodney *Nor* 70-73; P-in-c Preston-on-Stour w Whitchurch *Cov* 73-76; P-in-c Atherstone on Stour 73-76; V Preston on Stour and Whitchurch w Atherstone 77-88; Can Th Cov Cathl 77-88; Chapl Arthur Rank Cen 73-82; Dir 83-88; Chapl to The Queen 83-88; Area Bp Dorchester *Ox* 88-00; Bp Ely from 00. *The Bishop's House, Ely CB7 4DW* Tel (01353) 662749 Fax 669477 E-mail bishop@ely.anglican.org

RUSSELL, Canon Brian Kenneth. b 50. Trin Hall Cam BA73 MA76 Birm Univ MA77 PhD83. Cuddesdon Coll 74. **d** 76 **p** 77. C Redhill St Matt *S'wark* 76-79; Dir Studies NEOC 79-83; P-in-c Merrington *Dur* 79-83; Dir of Studies and Lect Linc Th Coll 83-86; Selection Sec and Sec Cttee for Th Educn ABM 86-93; Bp's Dir for Min *Birm* from 93; Hon Can Birm Cathl from 99. *175 Harborne Park Road, Harborne, Birmingham B17 0BH* Tel 0121-426 0429 Fax 428 1114 E-mail b.russell@birmingham.anglican.org

RUSSELL, Brian Robert. b 61. QUB BA BD92 TCD DipTh85. **d** 85 **p** 86. C Dublin Drumcondra w N Strand *D & G* 85-87; C Carrickfergus *Conn* 87-90; I Kilmegan w Maghera *D & D* 90-96; I Bailieborough w Knockbride, Shercock and Mullagh *K, E & A* 96-00; I Kilbarron w Rossnowlagh and Drumholm *D & R* from 00. *The Rectory, Lisminton, Ballintra, Co Donegal, Irish Republic* Tel and fax (00353) (74) 973 4025 E-mail bestrussell@eircom.net

RUSSELL, Bruce Harley. b 57. Ch Ch Ox BA79 Roehampton Inst PGCE80. Ripon Coll Cuddesdon. **d** 99 **p** 00. C Bracknell *Ox* 99-03; TV Langley Marish from 03. *St Francis's Vicarage, 21 Lynward Avenue, Slough SL3 7BJ* Tel (01753) 557150 E-mail bhrussell@supanet.com

RUSSELL, Christopher Ian. b 68. St Jo Coll Dur BA91 St Edm Coll Cam MPhil96. Ridley Hall Cam 93. **d** 96 **p** 97. C Deptford St Jo w H Trin *S'wark* 96-99; Soul Survivor Watford *St Alb* 99-01; C Reading St Mary w St Laur *Ox* from 01. *9 Mansfield Road, Reading RG1 6AL* Tel 0118-956 0559 E-mail chris@belindarussell.freeserve.co.uk

RUSSELL, David Edward. **d** 52 **p** 53. C St Mich Cathl Barbados 53-56; Perm to Offic *Chich* and *Roch* from 98. *Address temp unknown*

RUSSELL, David John. b 57. Sarum & Wells Th Coll BTh94. **d** 94 **p** 95. C Glouc St Geo w Whaddon *Glouc* 94-98; P-in-c Wickwar w Rangeworthy 98-01; R Wickwar, Rangeworthy and Hillesley from 02. *The Rectory, High Street, Wickwar, Wotton-under-Edge GL12 8NP* Tel (01454) 294267 E-mail davidrussell@classicfm.net

RUSSELL, David Robert. b 43. Brasted Th Coll 66 Sarum Th Coll 68. **d** 70 **p** 71. C Leintwardine *Heref* 70-73; C Bridgnorth w Tasley 73-75; Australia from 75; R Lockridge 75-80; R Bellevue and Darlington 80-87; Snr Chapl DCS 93; R Carlisle and Rivervale from 95; AD Vic Park from 98. *239 Orrong Road, Rivervale, W Australia 6103* Tel (0061) (8) 9470 5861 Fax 9470 5862 E-mail drussl@smartchat.net.au

RUSSELL, Canon Derek John. b 30. St Pet Hall Ox BA54 MA58. Qu Coll Birm 54. **d** 56 **p** 57. C Boxley *Cant* 56-59; C Whitstable All SS 59-63; Chapl HM Pris Wormwood Scrubs 63-65 and 71-89; Chapl HM Pris Stafford 65-69; Pentonville 70; SE Regional Chapl 74-81; Chapl HM Rem Cen Latchmere Ho 74-77; Asst Chapl Gen of Pris 81-83; Dep 83-90; Hon Can Cant Cathl *Cant* 86-90; rtd 90; Perm to Offic *Cant* from 90. *25 Pier Avenue, Whitstable CT5 2HQ* Tel (01227) 276654

RUSSELL, Ms Elizabeth Marilyn Vivia. b 50. LRAM70 GRSM72. Westcott Ho Cam 95. **d** 97 **p** 98. C Alton St Lawr *Win* 97-01; C St Martin-in-the-Fields *Lon* from 01. *5 Aldwyn House, Davidson Gardens, London SW8 2HX* Tel (020) 7766 1108 E-mail clergy@smitf.org

RUSSELL, Eric Watson. b 39. FCA76. Clifton Th Coll 66. **d** 69 **p** 70. C Kinson *Sarum* 69-73; C Peckham St Mary Magd *S'wark* 73-77; TV Barking St Marg w St Patr *Chelmsf* 77-82; V Lozells St Paul and St Silas *Birm* 82-95; RD Aston 89-94; P-in-c Barston and C Knowle 95-04; I Kells Union *M & K* from 04. *The Rectory, Navan Road, Kells, Co Meath, Irish Republic* Tel (00353) (46) 929 3626 Mobile 86-066 3165 E-mail ericrussell@eircom.net

RUSSELL, The Ven Harold <u>Ian</u> Lyle. b 34. Lon Coll of Div ALCD59 BD60. **d** 60 **p** 61. C Iver *Ox* 60-63; C Fulwood *Sheff* 63-67; V Chapeltown 67-75; RD Tankersley 73-75; V Nottingham St Jude *S'well* 75-89; AD Nottingham Cen 86-89; Hon Can S'well Minster 88-89; Adn Cov 89-00; rtd 01; Chapl to The Queen 97-04; Perm to Offic *S'well* from 01. *5 Old Acres, Woodborough, Nottingham NG14 6ES* Tel 0115-965 3543

RUSSELL, Ms Isoline Lucilda (<u>Lyn</u>). b 41. **d** 03 **p** 04. OLM Camberwell St Giles w St Matt *S'wark* from 03. *124 Hindman's Road, London SE22 9NH* Tel (020) 8299 4431

RUSSELL, James Anthony Tomkins. b 67. Oak Hill Th Coll BA99. **d** 99 **p** 00. C Chadwell *Chelmsf* 99-03; C Patcham *Chich* from 03. *32 Fairview Rise, Brighton BN1 5GL* Tel (01273) 503926 E-mail jamesandannabel@aol.com

RUSSELL, Mrs Janet Mary. b 53. Univ of Wales BSc74 BArch76. Ox Min Course 91. **d** 94 **p** 95. C Watlington w Pyrton and Shirburn *Ox* 94-97; C Icknield 97-98; TV Wallingford 98-05; Par Development Adv (Berks) from 05. *The Rectory, Marsh Baldon, Oxford OX44 9LS* Tel (01865) 343215 E-mail revrussell@btopenworld.com

RUSSELL, Canon John Arthur. b 29. AKC62. **d** 63 **p** 64. C Fareham H Trin *Portsm* 63-67; R Greatham w Empshott 67-79; V Ham St Andr *S'wark* 79-87; P-in-c Battersea St Luke 87-92; V 92-96; Hon Can S'wark Cathl 95-96; rtd 97; Perm to Offic *S'wark* 97-03. *Toni Llido 4, 2, apt 5, 03730 Puerto de Javea, Alicante Province, Spain* Tel (0034) (96) 579 0587

RUSSELL, John Bruce. b 56. Ripon Coll Cuddesdon. **d** 95 **p** 96. C Newport Pagnell w Lathbury and Moulsoe *Ox* 95-98; P-in-c Wing w Grove 98-03; AD Mursley 02-03. *49 Tring Road, Aylesbury HP20 1LD* E-mail john@russvic.freeserve.co.uk

RUSSELL, John Graham. b 35. G&C Coll Cam BA58 MA62. Westcott Ho Cam 59. **d** 61 **p** 62. C Durleigh *B & W* 61-66; C Bridgwater St Mary w Chilton Trinity 61-66; C Far Headingley St Chad *Ripon* 66-72; P-in-c Leeds St Matt Lt London 72-79; V Rowley Regis *Birm* 79-84; V Hall Green Ascension 84-95; Deanery P Warley Deanery 95-00; rtd 01; Perm to Offic *Birm* from 01. *1 Stapylton Avenue, Harborne, Birmingham B17 0BA* Tel 0121-426 4529 E-mail pmr@russellp21.fsnet.co.uk

RUSSELL, John Richard. b 53. Westmr Coll Ox MTh01 FRSA02. Spurgeon's Coll 77 Ripon Coll Cuddesdon 01. **d** 01 **p** 02. Chapl RAF from 85; Perm to Offic *St Alb* from 04. *Chaplaincy Services (RAF) HQ, Personnel and Training Command, RAF Innsworth, Gloucester GL3 1EZ* Tel (01452) 712612 ext 5164 Fax 510828

RUSSELL, Canon Jonathan Vincent Harman. b 43. K Coll Lon 68. **d** 69 **p** 70. C Addington *Cant* 69-73; C Buckland in Dover w Buckland Valley 73-76; P-in-c Selling 76-85; P-in-c Throwley w Stalisfield and Otterden 79-85; R Selling w Throwley, Sheldwich w Badlesmere etc 85-95; Hon Min Can Cant Cathl 83-94; Hon Can Cant Cathl from 94; RD Ospringe 90-95; P-in-c Elham w Denton and Wootton 95-01; V from 01. *The Vicarage, Vicarage Lane, Elham, Canterbury CT4 6TT* Tel (01303) 840219

RUSSELL, Jonathan Wingate. b 55. BSc BA DMS Dip Ind Mgt. St Jo Coll Nottm 81. **d** 84 **p** 85. C Southsea St Jude *Portsm* 84-87; P-in-c Shorwell w Kingston 87-92; V from 92; P-in-c Gatcombe 87-92; R from 92; P-in-c Chale 89-92; R from 92; RD W Wight 96-01. *The Vicarage, 5 Northcourt Close, Shorwell, Newport PO30 3LD* Tel (01983) 741044 Fax as telephone E-mail russells@shorwellvicarage.freeserve.co.uk

RUSSELL, Lloyd George Winkler. b 19. Hatf Coll Dur BA49. **d** 45 **p** 46. Jamaica 45-48 and 50-52 and 82-85; Perm to Offic *Dur* 48-50; *Lon* 53-58; *S'wark* 53-59; *Roch* 58-81 and 85-03; rtd 85; Perm to Offic *S'wark* 85-03. *39 Pembroke Road, Bromley BR1 2RT* Tel (020) 8460 1498

RUSSELL, Lyn. *See* RUSSELL, Ms Isoline Lucilda

RUSSELL, Mrs Madeleine. b 41. **d** 04 **p** 05. NSM Halifax H Trin and St Jude *Wakef* from 04. *Holy Trinity Vicarage, 9 Love Lane, Halifax HX1 2BQ* Tel (01422) 352446

RUSSELL, Martin Christopher. b 48. St Jo Coll Dur BA70. Coll of Resurr Mirfield 72. **d** 74 **p** 75. C Huddersfield St Pet *Wakef* 74-77; Trinidad and Tobago 78-85; V S Crosland *Wakef* 86-00; P-in-c Helme 86-00; P-in-c Halifax H Trin 00-02; P-in-c Halifax St Jude 00-02; V Halifax H Trin and St Jude from 02. *Holy Trinity Vicarage, 9 Love Lane, Halifax HX1 2BQ* Tel (01422) 352446

RUSSELL, Michael John. b 38. Clifton Th Coll 68. **d** 68 **p** 69. C Cranham Park CD *Chelmsf* 68-70; C Bucknall and Bagnall *Lich* 70-77; P-in-c Tintwistle *Ches* 77-79; V 79-86; New Zealand from 86; rtd 03. *144 Winchester Street, Ashurst, New Zealand* Tel (0064) (6) 326 8547

RUSSELL, Morris Charles. b 14. AKC36. **d** 37 **p** 38. C Tottenham St Phil *Lon* 37-39; C Winchmore Hill H Trin 39-41; CF (EC) 41-46; V Thornham w Titchwell *Nor* 46-51; R Newmarket St Mary *St E* 51-59; R Ipswich St Matt 59-66; V Auckland St Matt New Zealand 67-79; rtd 79. *3A Princes Street, Cambridge, New Zealand* Tel (0064) (7) 823 1128

RUSSELL, Canon Neil. b 47. Nottm Univ CPS81 Ox Univ DipApTh95. EMMTC 78. **d** 81 **p** 82. NSM Wyberton *Linc* 81-84; C 84-85; V Frampton 85-93; Agric Chapl and Countryside Officer 88-93; P-in-c Stamford All SS w St Jo 93-97; V from 97; RD Aveland and Ness w Stamford from 00; Can and

Preb Linc Cathl from 02. *All Saints' Vicarage, Casterton Road, Stamford PE9 2YL* Tel and fax (01780) 756942 E-mail nrussell@onetel.com

RUSSELL, Mrs Noreen Margaret. b 39. Man Univ BA60 Lon Univ PGCE61 BD66. WMMTC 90. **d** 91 **p** 94. NSM Swynnerton and Tittensor *Lich* 91-97; C Draycott-le-Moors w Forsbrook from 97. *40 Old Road, Barlaston, Stoke-on-Trent ST12 9EQ* Tel (01785) 372992

RUSSELL, The Ven Norman Atkinson. b 43. Chu Coll Cam BA65 MA69 Lon Univ BD70. Lon Coll of Div 67. **d** 70 **p** 71. C Clifton Ch Ch w Em *Bris* 70-74; C Enfield Ch Ch Trent Park *Lon* 74-77; R Harwell w Chilton *Ox* 77-84; P-in-c Gerrards Cross 84-88; P-in-c Fulmer 85-88; R Gerrards Cross and Fulmer 88-98; Hon Can Ch Ch 95-98; RD Amersham 96-98; Adn Berks from 98. *Foxglove House, Love Lane, Donnington, Newbury RG14 2JG* Tel (01635) 552820 Fax 522165 E-mail archdber@oxford.anglican.org

RUSSELL, Peter Richard. b 60. Ch Ch Coll Cant BA99. SEITE 02. **d** 05. NSM Margate All SS *Cant* from 05; NSM Westgate St Sav from 05. *40 Dane Road, Birchington CT7 9PT* Tel (01843) 843237 E-mail minnisbay@hotmail.com

RUSSELL, Ralph Geoffrey Major. b 19. St Aug Coll Cant 47 Sarum Th Coll 48. **d** 50 **p** 51. C Redruth *Truro* 50-55; C Hayes St Mary *Lon* 55-56; C W Wycombe *Ox* 56-62; V New Bradwell w Stantonbury 62-73; P-in-c Gt Linford w Willen and Gt and Lt Woolstone 62-64; P-in-c Linslade 74-75; V 75-87; rtd 87; Perm to Offic *Ox* 87-04 and *Pet* 89-04. *22 Manormead, Tilford Road, Hindhead GU26 6RA* Tel (01428) 602573

RUSSELL, Richard Alexander. b 44. Univ of Wales (Abth) BA65 McMaster Univ Ontario MA67 Bris Univ MA73 PGCE74 MEd76. Trin Coll Bris DipHE81. **d** 82 **p** 83. C Hartlepool St Paul *Dur* 82-85; P-in-c Bath Widcombe *B & W* 85-88; V 88-00; rtd 00. *76 Waterside Way, Radstock, Bath BA3 3YQ* Tel (01761) 433217 E-mail 113135.2044@compuserve.com

RUSSELL, Roger Geoffrey. b 47. Worc Coll Ox BA69 MA73. Cuddesdon Coll 70. **d** 72 **p** 73. C Anlaby Common St Mark *York* 72-75; C Wilton Place St Paul *Lon* 75-86; R Lancing w Coombes *Chich* from 86; RD Worthing 97-05. *The Vicarage, 63 Manor Road, Lancing BN15 0EY* Tel (01903) 753212

RUSSELL, William Warren. b 52. QUB BSocSc74. CITC 74. **d** 77 **p** 78. C Agherton *Conn* 77-79; C Lisburn Ch Ch Cathl 79-83; I Magheradroll *D & D* from 83. *The Rectory, 18 Church Road, Ballynahinch BT24 8LP* Tel (028) 9756 2289 Mobile 07810-222906 E-mail rev_wwrussell@hotmail.com

RUSSELL-SMITH, Mark Raymond. b 46. New Coll Edin MTh91. St Jo Coll Dur BA71 Cranmer Hall Dur DipTh72. **d** 72 **p** 73. C Upton (Overchurch) *Ches* 72-75; C Deane *Man* 75-77; UCCF Travelling Sec 77-80; Lic to Offic *York* 78-81; BCMS 81-92; Kenya 81-92; P-in-c Slaidburn *Bradf* from 92; P-in-c Long Preston w Tosside from 97. *The Rectory, Slaidburn, Clitheroe BB7 3ER* Tel (01200) 446238

RUST, Jonathan Kenneth. b 62. Reading Univ BSc84. Ridley Hall Cam. **d** 00 **p** 01. C Holloway St Mary Magd *Lon* from 00. *59 Bride Street, London N7 8RN* Tel (020) 7607 1316 E-mail j.rust@tiscali.co.uk

RUSTED, Mrs Mary Elizabeth. b 44. **d** 00 **p** 01. OLM Mildenhall *St E* from 00. *Spring Hall Farm, Cooks Drove, West Row, Bury St Edmunds IP28 8QL* Tel (01638) 715054

RUSTELL, Anthony. b 77. Ch Ch Ox BA98 MSt01 MA02. St Steph Ho Ox 98. **d** 01 **p** 02. NSM Ox St Barn and St Paul *Ox* 01-04; P-in-c N Hinksey and Wytham from 04. *The Vicarage, 81 West Way, Oxford OX2 9JY* Tel (01865) 242345 E-mail anthony.rustell@keble.ox.ac.uk

✠**RUSTON, The Rt Revd John Harry Gerald.** b 29. SS Coll Cam BA52 MA56. Ely Th Coll 52. **d** 54 **p** 55 **c** 83. C Leic St Andr *Leic* 54-57; OGS from 55; C Cuddesdon and Tutor Cuddesdon Coll 57-61; C Sekhukhuniland S Africa 62-70; Prin St Fran Coll 67-70; Can Pretoria 68-76; Sub Dean 71-76; Adn Bloemfontein 76-83; Suff Bp Pretoria 83-91; Bp St Helena 91-99; rtd 99; Perm to Offic *Roch* from 99. *The College of St Barnabas, Blackberry Lane, Lingfield RH7 6NJ* Tel (01342) 870892

RUTHERFORD, Anthony Richard. b 37. Culham Coll Ox TCert62 Lon Univ DipAdEd68 Sussex Univ MA77. S'wark Ord Course 83. **d** 86 **p** 87. Hon C Tunbridge Wells St Luke *Roch* 86-88; C Bromley SS Pet and Paul 88-90; V Wragby *Linc* 90-94; Asst Min Officer 90-94; V Penge Lane H Trin *Roch* 94-02; rtd 02. *6 Ashley Gardens, Tunbridge Wells TN4 8TY* Tel (01892) 541009 E-mail rutherfordtony@hotmail.com

RUTHERFORD, Arthur Ernest. b 26. Saltley Tr Coll Birm CertEd53 Loughb Coll of Educn DipEd54. Sarum & Wells Th Coll 91. **d** 92 **p** 93. NSM Lilliput *Sarum* 92-96; Perm to Offic from 96. *Kirinyaga, 8 Jennings Road, Poole BH14 8RY* Tel (01202) 748777

RUTHERFORD, Daniel Fergus Peter. b 65. Hatf Coll Dur BA86 CertEd87. Ridley Hall Cam 88. **d** 90 **p** 91. C Harold Wood *Chelmsf* 90-94; C Hove Bp Hannington Memorial Ch *Chich* 94-97; Chapl City of Lon Freemen's Sch Ashtead Park from 97. *City Of London Freemen's School, Park Lane, Ashtead KT21 1ET* Tel (01372) 277933 Fax 276728

RUTHERFORD, David Lesslie Calderwood. b 29. Master Mariner 55 Open Univ BA76 Open Th Coll BA99 Univ of Wales (Lamp) MTh05. **d** 91 **p** 92. Dioc Moderator for Reader Tr *St E* 90-95; OLM Acton w Gt Waldingfield 91-00; rtd 00; Perm to Offic *St E* from 00. *18 Gotsfield Close, Acton, Sudbury CO10 0AS* Tel (01787) 374169 Mobile 07774-680862 E-mail david@rutherfordpriest.freeserve.co.uk

✠**RUTHERFORD, The Rt Revd Graeme Stanley.** b 43. Cranmer Hall Dur BA77 MA78 ACT 66. **d** 66 **p** 67 **c** 00. Australia 66-73 and from 77; C Bendigo St Paul 66-70; V Pyramid Hill 70-73; C Holborn St Geo w H Trin and St Bart *Lon* 73-74; C Dur St Nic *Dur* 74-77; R Kyabram 77-82; I Malvern 82-87; I Camberwell St Jo 87-00; Can Melbourne Cathl 91-00; Asst Bp Newcastle from 00. *10 Pangari Place, PO Box 9095, Wyoming, NSW, Australia 2250* Tel (0061) (2) 4329 2902 Fax 4329 5501 E-mail bishopgraeme@bigpond.com

RUTHERFORD, Ian William. b 46. Univ of Wales (Lamp) BA68. Cuddesdon Coll 68. **d** 70 **p** 71. C Gosforth All SS *Newc* 70-72; C Prestbury *Glouc* 73-76; Chapl RN 76-93; TV Redruth w Lanner and Treleigh *Truro* 93-94; V Paulsgrove *Portsm* 94-99; V Leeds Belle Is St Jo and St Barn *Ripon* from 99. *The Vicarage, 30 Low Grange View, Leeds LS10 3DT* Tel 0113-271 7821

RUTHERFORD, Janet Elizabeth. b 37. Leic Univ Dip Counselling 98. S'wark Ord Course 86. **d** 89. NSM Plaistow St Mary *Roch* 89-90; NSM Linc St Botolph *Linc* 91-93. *6 Ashley Gardens, Tunbridge Wells TN4 8TY* Tel (01892) 541009

RUTHERFORD, Canon John Bilton. b 23. Qu Coll Birm 49. **d** 52 **p** 53. C Newc H Cross *Newc* 52-57; C Longbenton St Bart 57-60; V High Elswick St Phil 60-66; V Walker 66-74; I Benwell St Jas 74-81; Hon Can Newc Cathl 80-90; V Lesbury w Alnmouth 81-90; RD Alnwick 86-89; Perm to Offic from 90; rtd 90. *68 Worcester Way, Woodlands Park, Wideopen, Newcastle upon Tyne NE4 5JE* Tel 0191-236 4785

RUTHERFORD, Peter George. b 34. Nor Ord Course 73. **d** 76 **p** 77. NSM New Catton Ch Ch *Nor* 76-79; NSM Eaton 79-80; NSM Nor St Steph 81-92; Perm to Offic 92-94 and from 99; P-in-c Earlham St Mary 94-99; RD Nor S 98-99; rtd 99. *126 Colman Road, Norwich NR4 7AA* Tel and fax (01603) 457629 E-mail pgr457629@aol.com

RUTHERFORD, Peter Marshall. b 57. St Andr Univ MTheol81 Ulster Univ MA96. CITC 83. **d** 83 **p** 84. C Stormont *D & D* 83-85; CF 85-01; Asst Chapl Gen 01-02; Asst Chapl Milan w Genoa and Varese *Eur* 03-04; I Castlepollard and Oldcastle w Loughcrew etc *M & K* from 04. *St Michael's Rectory, Castlepollard, Mullingar, Co Westmeath, Irish Republic* Tel (00353) (44) 61123

RUTHERFORD (née ERREY), Ms Rosalind Elisabeth. b 52. St Hugh's Coll Ox BA74 Goldsmiths' Coll Lon PGCE78 Surrey Univ BA02. STETS 99. **d** 02 **p** 03. C Earley St Pet *Ox* from 02. *33 Clevedon Drive, Earley, Reading RG6 5XF* Tel 0118-987 4118 E-mail rosalind@rutherfords.fsnet.co.uk

RUTLEDGE, Canon Christopher John Francis. b 44. Lon Univ BSc67 Clare Coll Cam PGCTh70 FE TCert80 Univ of Wales MPhil94 PhD99. Sarum Th Coll 67. **d** 70 **p** 71. C Birm St Pet *Birm* 70-73; C Calne and Blackland *Sarum* 73-76; P-in-c Derry Hill 76-78; V 78-81; P-in-c Talbot Village 81-82; V from 82; Can and Preb Sarum Cathl from 95. *The Vicarage, 20 Alton Road, Bournemouth BH10 4AE* Tel (01202) 513646 *or* 529349 E-mail christopher.rutledge@ntlworld.com

RUTLEDGE, Francis George. b 62. TCD BA83 DipTh86 BTh90. **d** 86 **p** 87. C Holywood *D & D* 86-89; C Willowfield 89-91; I Kilmakee *Conn* 91-97; I Carrigrohane Union *C, C & R* 97-04; I Donacavey w Barr *Clogh* from 04. *The Rectory, 247 Tattyreagh Road, Fintona, Omagh BT78 2DA* Tel and fax (028) 8284 1644 E-mail francisrutledge@utvinternet.com

RUTT, Mrs Celia Mary Avril. b 43. Cranmer Hall Dur. **d** 02 **p** 03. NSM Heworth H Trin *York* 02-05; NSM Acomb St Steph from 05. *226 Shipton Road, York YO30 5RZ* Tel (01904) 627384 E-mail crutt@fish.co.uk

RUTT, Canon Denis Frederic John. b 17. Kelham Th Coll 34. **d** 41 **p** 42. C Luton Ch Ch *St Alb* 41-46; R Yaxham and Welborne *Nor* 54-61; R Kirkley 61-71; RD Lothingland 65-71; R N Lynn w St Marg and St Nic 71-76; Can Res and Prec Lich Cathl *Lich* 76-83; rtd 83; Perm to Offic *Bradf* 83-99. *22 Stuart Court, High Street, Kibworth, Leicester LE8 0LR* Tel 0116-279 6321

RUTT-FIELD, Benjamin John. b 48. Chich Th Coll. **d** 90 **p** 91. C Wickford and Runwell *Chelmsf* 90-94; V Goodmayes St Paul from 94. *St Paul's Vicarage, 20 Eastwood Road, Ilford IG3 8XA* Tel (020) 8590 6596 E-mail frbenjaminruttfield@yahoo.co.uk

RUTTER, Canon Allen Edward Henry (Claude). b 28. Qu Coll Cam BA52 MA56 DipAgr53. Cranmer Hall Dur DipTh58. **d** 59 **p** 60. C Bath Abbey w St Jas *B & W* 59-60; C E Dereham w Hoe *Nor* 60-64; R Cawston 64-69; Chapl Cawston Coll 64-69; P-in-c Felthorpe w Haveringland 64-69; S Africa 69-73; P-in-c Over and Nether Compton, Trent etc *Sarum* 73-80; RD Sherborne 77-87; P-in-c Oborne w Poyntington 79-80; P-in-c Queen

Thorne 80-96; Can and Preb Sarum Cathl 86-96; rtd 96; Perm to Offic *B & W* 98-99 and from 00; P-in-c Thorncombe w Winsham and Cricket St Thomas 99; C Chard and Distr 99-00. *Home Farm, Chilson, South Chard, Chard TA20 2NX* Tel (01460) 221368

RUTTER, John Edmund Charles. b 53. Qu Coll Cam MA76. St Jo Coll Nottm MA93. **d** 93 **p** 94. C Penge St Jo *Roch* 93-97; Bp's C Bangor Primacy *D & D* 97-04; I Glenavy w Tunny and Crumlin *Conn* from 04. *The Vicarage, 30 Crumlin Road, Glenavy, Crumlin BT29 4LG* Tel and fax (028) 9442 2361 E-mail jecrutter@hotmail.com

RUTTER, Martin Charles. b 54. Wolv Poly BSc75 Southn Univ BTh81. Sarum & Wells Th Coll 76. **d** 79 **p** 80. C Cannock *Lich* 79-82; C Uttoxeter w Bramshall 82-86; V W Bromwich St Jas 86-97; P-in-c W Bromwich St Paul 89-97; V W Bromwich St Jas w St Paul 97-02; RD W Bromwich 94-02; V Gt Barr from 02. *22 Lodge Road, Walsall WS5 3JY* Tel 0121-357 5813

RUTTER, Ronald. b 47. SS Hild & Bede Coll Dur TCert71 Open Univ BA81 CMath MIMA. Carl and Blackb Dioc Tr Inst. **d** 00 **p** 01. NSM Heversham and Milnthorpe *Carl* from 00. *Ellerslie, Woodhouse Lane, Heversham, Milnthorpe LA7 7EW* Tel and fax (01539) 564260 E-mail ron_rutter@hotmail.com

RWANDA, Archbishop of. *See* KOLINI, The Most Revd Emmanuel Musaba

RYALL, John Francis Robert. b 30. New Coll Ox BA52 MA57. Westcott Ho Cam 52. **d** 54 **p** 55. C Petersfield w Sheet *Portsm* 54-56; C Portsea St Mary 56-62; C Warblington w Emsworth 62-65; C Freshwater 65-67; R Frating w Thorrington *Chelmsf* 67-73; R Gt Yeldham 74-76; P-in-c Lt Yeldham 75-76; R Gt w Lt Yeldham 76-80; P-in-c Thorley *Portsm* 80-82; P-in-c Shalfleet 80-82; V 82-95; V Calbourne w Newtown 82-95; rtd 95; Perm to Offic *Portsm* from 95. *Weald House, Main Road, Wellow, Yarmouth PO41 0SZ* Tel (01983) 760783

RYALL, Michael Richard. b 36. TCD BA58 MA65 HDipEd66. TCD Div Sch Div Test58. **d** 58 **p** 59. C Dublin St Geo *D & G* 58-62; CF 62-65 and 68-90; CF (TAVR) 67-68; C Dublin Rathmines *D & G* 65-66; Dungannon Sec Sch 66-68; R Yardley Hastings, Denton and Grendon etc *Pet* 90-01; rtd 01; Perm to Offic *Portsm* and *Guildf* from 02. *Hollow House, Hill Brow Road, Liss GU33 7PX* Tel (01730) 895161 Mobile 07968-111258

RYALLS, Craig James. b 74. Bris Univ BA96 Peterho Cam BA01. Ridley Hall Cam 99. **d** 02 **p** 03. C Bearsted w Thurnham *Cant* from 02. *19 Fulbert Drive, Bearsted, Maidstone ME14 4PU* Tel (01622) 631192 E-mail craig.ryalls@btopenworld.com

RYAN, David Peter. b 64. Aston Univ BSc86. Linc Th Coll BTh94. **d** 94 **p** 95. C Horsforth *Ripon* 94-97; C Bedale 97-98; P-in-c Startforth and Bowes and Rokeby w Brignall 98-00; V 00-04; P-in-c Warndon St Nic *Worc* from 04; Dioc Ecum Officer from 04. *The Vicarage, 4 Daty Croft, Home Meadow, Worcester WR4 0JB* Tel (01905) 616109 E-mail davidryannow@netscapeonline.co.uk

RYAN, Graham William Robert (Gregg). b 51. CITC 90 St Jo Coll Nottm CertCS93. **d** 93 **p** 94. NSM Clonsast w Rathangan, Thomastown etc *M & K* 93-97; Dioc Communications Officer 96-97; Press Officer from 97; Dioc C from 97. *Millicent Hall, Millicent South, Sallins, Naas, Co Kildare, Irish Republic* Tel (00353) (45) 879464 Fax 875173 E-mail gregg.ryan@irishrail.ie

RYAN, James Francis. b 47. Surrey Univ BSc. St Jo Coll Nottm. **d** 83 **p** 84. C Littleover *Derby* 83-86; C Chipping Sodbury and Old Sodbury *Glouc* 86-89; V Pype Hayes *Birm* 89-99; R W Winch w Setchey, N Runcton and Middleton *Nor* from 99. *The Rectory, Rectory Lane, West Winch, King's Lynn PE33 0NR* Tel (01553) 840835

RYAN, Canon Maureen. **d** 98 **p** 99. C Tuam w Cong and Aasleagh *T, K & A* from 98; Preb Kilmactalway St Patr Cathl Dublin from 01; Can Tuam Cathl *T, K & A* from 05. *Marshal's Park, Rinville, Oranmore, Galway, Irish Republic* Tel and fax (00353) (91) 794599 E-mail ryans@iol.ie

RYAN, Roger John. b 47. Surrey Univ MA00. Lon Bible Coll BA79 Oak Hill Th Coll 79. **d** 80 **p** 81. C Luton St Fran *St Alb* 80-83; R Laceby *Linc* 83-88; V Summerstown *S'wark* from 88. *St Mary's Vicarage, 46 Wimbledon Road, London SW17 0UQ* Tel (020) 8946 9853

RYAN, Canon Stephen John. b 49. Univ of Wales (Swansea) BA70 Bris Univ DipTh73. Sarum & Wells Th Coll 70. **d** 73 **p** 74. C Llantrisant *Llan* 73-77; V Treherbert w Treorchy 77-89; Youth Chapl 80-85; RD Rhondda 84-89; V Aberdare St Fagan 89-02; RD Cynon Valley 97-02; TR Neath from 02; Can Llan Cathl from 02; AD Neath from 04. *The Rectory, 23 London Road, Neath SA11 1LE* Tel (01639) 644612

RYCRAFT, Mrs Rosemary Ives Stewart. b 49. Westmr Coll Ox BTh00 SRN72 SCM74. St Alb and Ox Min Course 00. **d** 03 **p** 04. NSM New Marston *Ox* from 03. *15 Jack Straws Lane, Headington, Oxford OX3 0DL* Tel (01865) 791075 E-mail rosemary.rycraft@btopenworld.com

RYDER, Canon Derek Michael. b 36. St Cath Coll Cam BA60 MA64. Tyndale Hall Bris 61. **d** 63 **p** 64. C Hampreston *Sarum* 63-66; Asst Chapl Brentwood Sch Essex 66-72; Chapl Ipswich Sch 72-77; Home Sec CMJ 77-87; TR Wexcombe *Sarum* 87-99; RD Pewsey 89-99; Can and Preb Sarum Cathl 97-99; rtd 99; Perm to Offic *Ox* and *Sarum* from 00. *31 The Green, Calne SN11 8DJ* Tel (01249) 821797

RYDER, Jennifer Ann. *See* HAYNES, Mrs Jennifer Ann

RYDER, John Merrick. b 55. Natal Univ BA75 BA77. St Pet Coll Natal 81. **d** 82 **p** 83. S Africa 84-88; St Helena 88-91; C Havant *Portsm* 91-95; P-in-c Godshill 95-99; V from 99; P-in-c Wroxall 99-02. *The Vicarage, Church Hill, Godshill, Ventnor PO38 3HY* Tel (01983) 840895 E-mail rfrjohn@aol.com

RYDER, Lisle Robert Dudley. b 43. Selw Coll Cam BA68 MA72. Sarum Th Coll 69. **d** 71 **p** 72. C Lowestoft St Marg *Nor* 71-75; Chapl Asst Oxon Area HA 76-79; C Littlehampton St Jas *Chich* 79-85; C Littlehampton St Mary 79-85; C Wick 79-85; Chapl Worc R Infirmary 85-94; Chapl Worc R Infirmary NHS Trust 94-00; Chapl Worcs Acute Hosps NHS Trust 00-03; Hon Can Worc Cathl *Worc* 89-04; P-in-c Pyworthy, Pancrasweek and Bridgerule *Ex* from 04. *The Rectory, Pyworthy, Holsworthy EX22 6SU* Tel (01409) 253547

RYDER-WEST, Keith. b 63. Sunderland Poly BSc86. Chich Th Coll 92 Coll of Resurr Mirfield BTh95. **d** 95 **p** 96. C Rawmarsh w Parkgate *Sheff* 95-96; C Armley w New Wortley *Ripon* 96-99; V Altofts *Wakef* from 99. *The Vicarage, Altofts, Normanton WF6 2QG* Tel (01924) 892299

RYDINGS, Donald. b 33. Jes Coll Ox BA57 MA61. Linc Th Coll 57. **d** 59 **p** 60. C Poulton-le-Fylde *Blackb* 59-62; C Ox St Mary V *Ox* 62-66; Staff Sec SCM 62-66; C-in-c Bourne End St Mark CD *Ox* 66-74; R Hedsor and Bourne End 74-76; P-in-c Gt Missenden w Ballinger and Lt Hampden 76-93; RD Wendover 79-89; V Gt Missenden w Ballinger and Lt Hampden 93-02; rtd 02. *16 Marroway, Weston Turville, Aylesbury HP22 5TQ* Tel (01296) 612281

RYE, David Ralph. b 33. AKC59. **d** 60 **p** 61. C Rushmere *St E* 60-64; C Barnham Broom w Kimberley, Bixton etc *Nor* 64-76; TV Barnham Broom 76-82; TR 82-95; P-in-c Reymerston w Cranworth, Letton, Southburgh etc 85-95; rtd 95; Perm to Offic *Nor* from 95. *5A Yarmouth Road, Norwich NR7 0EA* Tel (01603) 439717

RYELAND, John. b 58. K Coll Lon BD80 AKC80. Linc Th Coll 80. **d** 81 **p** 82. C Enfield St Jas *Lon* 81-84; C Coulsdon St Andr *S'wark* 84-87; C-in-c Ingrave St Steph CD *Chelmsf* 87-97; Dir Chr Healing Miss from 97; NSM Paddington St Steph w St Luke *Lon* 97-99. *8 Cambridge Court, 210 Shepherd's Bush Road, London W6 7NJ* Tel (020) 7603 8118 Fax 7603 5224 E-mail chm@healingmission.org

RYLANDS, Mrs Amanda Craig. b 52. Homerton Coll Cam CertEd75 All Nations Chr Coll Dip Miss82. Trin Coll Bris 83. **dss** 85 **d** 87 **p** 94. Chippenham St Andr w Tytherton Lucas *Bris* 85-87; Par Dn Stockport St Geo *Ches* 87-91; Par Dn Acton and Worleston, Church Minshull etc 91-94; C 94-97; Dioc Adv for Min Among Children 95-97; NSM Langport Area Chs *B & W* 97-98 and 99-01; TV 98-99; Asst Dioc Voc Adv 00-01; Perm to Offic *Ex* 02-03; C Tedburn St Mary, Whitestone, Oldridge etc from 04; Dioc Dir of Ords from 05. *The Rectory, Church Lane, Cheriton Bishop, Exeter EX6 6HY* Tel (01647) 24702

RYLANDS, Canon Mark James. b 61. SS Hild & Bede Coll Dur BA83. Trin Coll Bris BA87. **d** 87 **p** 88. C Stockport St Geo *Ches* 87-91; V Acton and Worleston, Church Minshull etc 91-97; TR Langport Area Chs *B & W* 97-02; Dioc Missr *Ex* from 02; Can Res Ex Cathl from 02. *The Rectory, Church Lane, Cheriton Bishop, Exeter EX6 6HY* Tel (01647) 24702 *or* (01392) 459378 E-mail fishing@exeter.anglican.org

RYLE, Denis Maurice. b 16. OBE70. St Aid Birkenhead 35. **d** 39 **p** 40. C Parr *Liv* 39-42; C Widnes St Paul 42-44; C Much Woolton 44-45; CF 45-58; Sen CF 58-65; Dep Asst Chapl Gen 65-73; P-in-c Latimer w Flaunden *Ox* 73-85; rtd 85; Perm to Offic *York* from 90. *5 Church Close, Wheldrake, York YO19 6DP* Tel (01904) 898124

RYLEY, Canon Patrick Macpherson. b 30. Pemb Coll Ox BA54 Lon Univ BD56. Clifton Th Coll 54. **d** 56 **p** 57. C Ox St Clem *Ox* 56-59; Burma 60-66; Kenya 68-75; V Lynn St Jo *Nor* 76-92; V King's Lynn St Jo the Ev 92-95; RD Lynn 78-83; Hon Can Nor Cathl 90-95; rtd 95; Perm to Offic *Bradf* from 95. *106 Little Lane, Ilkley LS29 8JJ* Tel (01943) 817026

RYLEY, Timothy Patrick. b 64. Man Univ BA86. St Jo Coll Nottm Dip Th Studies 92 MA93. **d** 93 **p** 94. C Pendlebury St Jo *Man* 93-97; P-in-c Norris Bank 97-01; Age Concern from 01. *213 Green Lane, Heaton Moor, Stockport SK4 2NS* Tel 0161-975 0151

RYMER, David John Talbot. b 37. Chich Th Coll 63. **d** 66 **p** 67. C Tuffley *Glouc* 66-69; Rhodesia 69-79; P-in-c S Kensington St Jude *Lon* 79-82; V 82-88; P-in-c Ambergate *Derby* 88-91; P-in-c Heage 88-91; R Ambergate and Heage 91-96; P-in-c Findern 96-01; V 01-03; P-in-c Willington 96-01; V 01-03; rtd 03; Perm to Offic *Derby* from 03. *2 Glebe Close, Long Lane, Dalbury Lees, Ashbourne DE6 5BJ* Tel (01332) 824165 E-mail david.rymer@amserve.net

RYRIE, Alexander Crawford. b 30. Edin Univ MA52 BD55 Glas Univ MLitt75. New Coll Edin 52 Union Th Sem (NY) STM56. **d** 83 **p** 83. Hon C Edin St Mary *Edin* 83-85; R Jedburgh 85-95; rtd 95. *Boisils, Bowden, Melrose TD6 0ST* Tel (01835) 823226

RYRIE, Mrs Isabel. b 31. ABPsS73 CPsychol88 Edin Univ MA51 Glas Univ MEd70. Moray Ho Edin DipRE52. **d** 89 **p** 94. Bp's Dn *Edin* 89-91; NSM Edin St Mary 91-98; rtd 98. *Boisils, Bowden, Melrose TD6 0ST* Tel (01835) 823226 E-mail ryrie@onetel.com

S

SABAH, Bishop of. *See* YONG, The Most Revd Datuk Ping Chung

SABAN, Ronald Graham Street. b 28. Bps' Coll Cheshunt 60. **d** 62 **p** 63. C Maidstone St Martin *Cant* 62-66; C Croydon St Sav 66; rtd 94. *34 Kingsway, Caversham, Reading RG4 6RA* Tel 0118-947 9454

SABELL, Michael Harold. b 42. Open Univ BA78 Surrey Univ MSc. Sarum & Wells Th Coll 77. **d** 80 **p** 81. NSM Shirley *Win* 80-82; NSM Finham *Cov* 82-85; Chapl to the Deaf *Win* 81-82; *Cov* 82-85; *Sheff* 85-89; *Lich* 89-96; *St Alb* 96-01; P-in-c Gt and Lt Wymondley *St Alb* 96-01; R Ingoldsby *Linc* 01-04; R Old Somerby 01-04; R Ropsley 01-04; R Sapperton w Braceby 01-04; rtd 04; Perm to Offic *Lich* from 05. *35 Charlemont Avenue, West Bromwich B71 3BY* Tel 0121-588 2094

SABEY-CORKINDALE, Charmaine Clare. b 58. DipCOT87 SROT87. St Alb and Ox Min Course. **d** 02 **p** 03. NSM St Ippolyts *St Alb* 02-03; C Hitchin from 03. *5 Lavender Way, Hitchin SG5 2LU* Tel (01462) 435497

SACHS, Andrew James. b 73. Reading Univ BSc94 Kingston Univ PGCE96. Wycliffe Hall Ox BTh05. **d** 05. C Upper Sunbury St Sav *Lon* from 05. *41 Wolsey Road, Sunbury-on-Thames TW16 7TU* E-mail andysachs@freeuk.com

SACKLEY (née WITT), Mrs Caroline Elizabeth. b 51. Surrey Univ BSc04. STETS 02. **d** 05. C Graffoe Gp *Linc* from 05. *6 Heath Road, Navenby, Lincoln LN5 0TT* Tel (01522) 813759 E-mail sackleys@btopenworld.com

SADDINGTON, Peter David. b 42. Cranmer Hall Dur. **d** 84 **p** 85. C Tudhoe Grange *Dur* 84-86; C Monkwearmouth St Andr 86-88; V Burnopfield 88-94; P-in-c Greenside 94-96; V 96-04; rtd 04. *19 The Lawns, Ryton Village, Ryton NE40 3QN* Tel 0191-413 6881

SADGROVE, The Very Revd Michael. b 50. Ball Coll Ox BA71 MA75. Trin Coll Bris 72. **d** 75 **p** 76. Lic to Offic *Ox* 75-77; Tutor Sarum & Wells Th Coll 77-82; Vice-Prin 80-82; V Alnwick *Newc* 82-87; Vice-Provost, Can Res and Prec Cov Cathl *Cov* 87-95; Provost Sheff 95-00; Dean Sheff 00-03; Dean Dur from 03. *The Deanery, The College, Durham DH1 3EQ* Tel 0191-384 7500 Fax 386 4267 E-mail michael.sadgrove@durhamcathedral.co.uk

SADLER, Ann Penrith. b 50. STETS. **d** 01 **p** 02. C Len Valley *Cant* 01-04; P-in-c Aylesham w Adisham from 04; C Nonington w Wymynswold and Goodnestone etc from 04. *The Rectory, Dorman Avenue North, Aylesham, Canterbury CT3 3BL* Tel (01304) 840266 E-mail sadler@ferring39.fsnet.co.uk

SADLER, The Ven Anthony Graham. b 36. Qu Coll Ox BA60 MA64. Lich Th Coll 60. **d** 62 **p** 63. C Burton St Chad *Lich* 62-65; V Rangemore and Dunstall 65-72; V Abbots Bromley 72-79; V Pelsall 79-90; RD Walsall 82-90; P-in-c Uttoxeter w Bramshall 90-97; P-in-c Stramshall 90-97; P-in-c Kingstone w Gratwich 90-97; P-in-c Checkley 90-97; P-in-c Marchington w Marchington Woodlands 90-97; P-in-c Leigh 93-97; TR Uttoxeter Area 97; Adn Walsall 97-04; Preb Lich Cathl 87-04; rtd 04. *Llidiart Newydd, Llanrhaeadr-ym-Mochnant, Oswestry SY10 0ED* Tel (01691) 780276

SADLER, John Ernest. b 45. Nottm Univ BTh78. Linc Th Coll 74. **d** 78 **p** 79. C Brampton St Thos *Derby* 78-81; TV Coventry Caludon *Cov* 81-85; P-in-c High Elswick St Phil *Newc* 85; P-in-c Newc St Aug 85; V Newc St Phil and St Aug 86-94; P-in-c Newc Epiphany 94-99; Perm to Offic from 00; Ch Development Worker from 01. *1 Albermarle Avenue, Newcastle upon Tyne NE2 3NQ* Tel 0191-285 1724 *or* 262 1680 E-mail jjsadler@btinternet.com *or* john@umtp.org

SADLER, Michael Stuart. b 57. Wycliffe Hall Ox 78. **d** 81 **p** 82. C Henfynyw w Aberaeron and Llanddewi Aberarth *St D* 81-88; V Llanddewi Rhydderch w Llangattock-juxta-Usk etc *Mon* from 88. *The Vicarage, Llanddewi Rhydderch, Abergavenny NP7 9TS* Tel (01873) 840373

SAGAR, Brian. b 39. Sarum & Wells Th Coll 78. **d** 80 **p** 81. C Radcliffe St Thos and St Jo *Man* 80-82; P-in-c Charlestown 82-85; R Gt Lever 85-89; Chapl Cov Ch Housing Assn *Cov* 89-92; V Wing w Grove *Ox* 92-97; P-in-c Diddington *Ely* 97-00; P-in-c Lt Paxton 97-00; P-in-c Southoe 97-00; P-in-c Lever Bridge *Man* from 00. *St Stephen's Vicarage, Radcliffe Road, Bolton BL2 1NZ* Tel (01204) 528300

SAGE, Andrew George. b 58. Chich Th Coll 83. **d** 85 **p** 86. C Rawmarsh w Parkgate *Sheff* 85-87; C Fareham SS Pet and Paul *Portsm* 87-89; C Southsea H Spirit 89-91; P-in-c Nuthurst *Chich* 91-93; R 93-95; V Hangleton 95-04; Chapl Worthing and Southlands Hosps NHS Trust 01-04; V Blackpool St Steph *Blackb* from 04. *The Vicarage, St Stephen's Avenue, Blackpool FY2 9RB* Tel (01253) 351484 E-mail andrewsage@aol.com

SAGE, Canon Jesse. b 35. Trin Hall Cam BA61 MA65. Chich Th Coll 61. **d** 63 **p** 64. C Feltham *Lon* 63-67; S Africa 67-72 and from 96; R Abbas and Temple Combe *B & W* 72-75; R Abbas and Templecombe w Horsington 76-77; Chapl Agric and Rural Soc in Kent *Cant* 78-95; Hon Can Cant Cathl 90-95; R Gonubie St Martin by the Sea 96-00; P-in-c Komga St Paul 98-00; Hon Can Grahamstown from 02; rtd 00. *30 Hazy Ridge, Swallow Lane, Gonubie, 5257 South Africa* Tel (0027) (43) 732 1298 Mobile 82-651 6698 Fax (43) 732 1317 E-mail jessesage@qwest.co.za

SAGE, John Arthur. b 32. MInstP Lon Univ BSc54. St Alb Minl Tr Scheme 78. **d** 81 **p** 82. NSM Stevenage St Mary Shephall *St Alb* 81-86; NSM Stevenage St Mary Shephall w Aston 86-87; C St Peter-in-Thanet *Cant* 87-98; rtd 98; Perm to Offic *Cant* from 99. *3 West Cliff Road, Broadstairs CT10 1PU* Tel (01843) 603471

SAGOVSKY, Canon Nicholas. b 47. CCC Ox BA69 St Edm Ho Cam PhD81. St Jo Coll Nottm BA73. **d** 74 **p** 75. C Newc St Gabr *Newc* 74-77; C Cambridge Gt St Mary w St Mich *Ely* 81; Vice-Prin Edin Th Coll 82-86; Dean of Chpl Clare Coll Cam 86-97; Wm Leech Prof Fell Newc Univ *Newc* 97-02; Liv Hope Univ Coll 02-04; Can Westmr Abbey from 04. *3 Little Cloister, Westminster Abbey, London SW1P 3PL* Tel (020) 7654 4808 E-mail nicholas.sagovsky@westminster-abbey.org

SAINSBURY, Peter Donald. b 67. K Coll Lon MA04. Ridley Hall Cam 98. **d** 00 **p** 01. C Longfleet *Sarum* 00-04; Chapl Glos Univ from 04. *21 Sandford Mill Road, Cheltenham GL53 7QH* Tel (01242) 690440 *or* 543400 E-mail psainsbury@glos.ac.uk

✠**SAINSBURY, The Rt Revd Roger Frederick.** b 36. Jes Coll Cam BA58 MA62. Clifton Th Coll. **d** 60 **p** 61 **c** 91. C Spitalfields Ch Ch w All SS *Lon* 60-63; Missr Shrewsbury Ho Everton 63-74; P-in-c Everton St Ambrose w St Tim *Liv* 67-74; Warden Mayflower Family Cen Canning Town *Chelmsf* 74-81; P-in-c Victoria Docks St Luke 78-81; V Walsall *Lich* 81-87; TR 87-88; Adn W Ham *Chelmsf* 88-91; Area Bp Barking 91-02; Moderator Ch's Commn for Racial Justice 99-02; rtd 02; Hon Asst Bp B & W from 03. *Abbey Lodge, Battery Lane, Portishead, Bristol BS20 7JD* Tel (01275) 847082 E-mail bishoproger.abbey@btopenworld.com

SAINT, Arthur James Maxwell. b 10. St Jo Coll Ox BA31 MA35. Cuddesdon Coll 34. **d** 35 **p** 36. C Stoke upon Trent *Lich* 35-37; Hd Master St Thos Sch Kuching Sarawak 37-41; C Shrewsbury St Mary 42-43; V Shawbury 43-48; V Cheltenham St Steph *Glouc* 48-60; Chapl Guy's Hosp Lon 60-65; V Ox SS Phil and Jas *Ox* 65-76; rtd 76. *The College of St Barnabas, Blackberry Lane, Lingfield RH7 6NJ* Tel (01342) 870256

SAINT, David Gerald. b 45. Sarum & Wells Th Coll 72. **d** 75 **p** 76. C Wellingborough All Hallows *Pet* 75-79; R Kislingbury w Rothersthorpe 79-83; V Kings Heath 83-85; Relig Progr Producer BBC Radio Northn from 85; Perm to Offic *Pet* from 86. *71 Stanwell Way, Wellingborough NN8 3DD* Tel (01933) 675995

ST ALBANS, Archdeacon of. *See* CUNLIFFE, The Ven Helen Margaret

ST ALBANS, Bishop of. *See* HERBERT, The Rt Revd Christopher William

ST ALBANS, Dean of. *See* JOHN, The Very Revd Jeffrey Philip Hywel

ST ANDREWS, DUNKELD AND DUNBLANE, Bishop of. *See* CHILLINGWORTH, The Rt Revd David Robert

ST ANDREWS, DUNKELD AND DUNBLANE, Dean of. *See* MacALISTER, The Very Revd Randal George Leslie

ST ASAPH, Archdeacon of. *See* THOMAS, The Ven Elwyn Bernard

ST ASAPH, Bishop of. *See* DAVIES, The Rt Revd John Stewart

ST ASAPH, Dean of. *See* POTTER, The Very Revd Christopher Nicholas Lynden

ST DAVIDS, Archdeacon of. *See* HOLDSWORTH, The Ven John Ivor

ST DAVIDS, Bishop of. *See* COOPER, The Rt Revd Carl Norman

ST DAVIDS, Dean of. *See* EVANS, The Very Revd John Wyn

ST EDMUNDSBURY AND IPSWICH, Bishop of. *See* LEWIS, The Rt Revd John Hubert Richard

ST EDMUNDSBURY, Dean of. *See* ATWELL, The Very Revd James Edgar

ST GERMANS, Suffragan Bishop of. *See* SCREECH, The Rt Revd Royden

ST HELENA, Bishop of. *See* SALT, The Rt Revd John William

ST JOHN-CHANNELL, Michael Alister Morrell. b 53. Bris Univ BEd76 MA01. Ripon Coll Cuddesdon 76. **d** 78 **p** 79. C Portsea St Mary *Portsm* 78-81; PV Linc Cathl *Linc* 82-85; P-in-c Linc St Mary-le-Wigford w St Benedict etc 82-85; R Cranford *Lon* 85-92; V Staines St Mary and St Pet 92-99; V Cirencester *Glouc* from 99; RD Cirencester from 01. *Cirencester Vicarage, 1 Dollar Street, Cirencester GL7 2AJ* Tel (01285) 653142 Fax 652442 E-mail mstjc@hotmail.com

ST JOHN NICOLLE, Jason Paul. b 66. Mert Coll Ox BA88 Called to the Bar (Inner Temple) 95. Ripon Coll Cuddesdon 01. **d** 04 **p** 05. C Kidlington w Hampton Poyle *Ox* from 04. *29 Andersons Close, Kidlington OX5 1ST* Tel (01865) 378059

ST JOHN NICOLLE, Michael George. b 29. St Jo Coll Dur BA52 DipEd. **d** 70 **p** 71. C Lt Bowden St Nic *Leic* 70; C Knighton St Jo 71-74; R Desford 74-81; R Tarrant Valley *Sarum* 81-85; R Jersey St Jo *Win* 85-94; rtd 94; Perm to Offic *Win* from 94. *Les Noyers, Les Chenoles, St John, Jersey JE3 4FB* Tel (01534) 865276

SALENIUS, Richard Mark. b 57. K Coll Lon BD79 AKC79. Linc Th Coll 79. **d** 80 **p** 81. C St Marylebone w H Trin *Lon* 80-84; C Sale St Anne *Ches* 84-87; V Macclesfield St Jo 87-96; V Brightlingsea *Chelmsf* 96-05. *Address temp unknown* E-mail richard.salenius@btinternet.com

SALES, Canon Patrick David. b 43. K Coll Lon AKC68 BD74 Kent Univ MA00. **d** 69 **p** 70. C Maidstone All SS w St Phil *Cant* 69-72; C Chart next Sutton Valence 72-74; C Birchington w Acol 75-77; V Boughton under Blean w Dunkirk 77-83; V Herne 83-03; P-in-c Hoath 98-03; TV Whitstable from 03; Hon Min Can Cant Cathl 83-01; Hon Can from 01; RD Reculver 86-92; AD from 01; Dioc Adv in Liturgy from 00. *The Vicarage, Church Street, Whitstable CT5 1PG* Tel (01227) 272308 E-mail patrick@sales64.freeserve.co.uk

SALISBURY, Anne Ruth. b 37. Dalton Ho Bris 63. **d** 87 **p** 94. C Harrow Trin St Mich *Lon* 87-98; C Paddington Em and W Kilburn St Luke w St Simon and St Jude 99-03; rtd 03. *Address temp unknown* Tel 07986-868667 (mobile) E-mail annesals@fish.co.uk

SALISBURY, Harold Gareth. b 21. St Pet Hall Ox BA42 MA46. Wycliffe Hall Ox 42. **d** 44 **p** 45. C Pet St Mark *Pet* 44-46; India 47-63; V Duddo *Newc* 63-70; V Norham 63-70; V Norham and Duddo 70-78; V Snaith *Sheff* 78-86; P-in-c Cowick 78-86; TR Gt Snaith 86; rtd 86; Perm to Offic *Pet* from 87. *33 Nightingale Drive, Towcester NN12 6RA* Tel (01327) 353674

SALISBURY, John Forbes. b 16. St Jo Coll Dur 46. **d** 50 **p** 51. C Gt Malvern Ch Ch *Worc* 50-53; C Dudley St Jo 53-57; V Manningham St Luke *Bradf* 57-62; V Riddlesden 62-67; V Tosside 67-79; Lic to Offic 80-84; rtd 81; Perm to Offic *Bradf* 84-99. *14 Victoria Mill, Belmont Wharf, Skipton BD23 1RL* Tel (01756) 701411

SALISBURY, Peter Brian Christopher. b 58. UMIST BSc80 MBCS85. Sarum & Wells Th Coll BTh92. **d** 92 **p** 93. C Stanmore *Win* 92-95; V Chilworth w N Baddesley from 95. *The Vicarage, 33 Crescent Road, North Baddesley, Southampton SO52 9HU* Tel (023) 8073 2393 E-mail peter@chilworthchurch.org

SALISBURY, Canon Roger John. b 44. Lon Univ BD67. Lon Coll of Div 66. **d** 68 **p** 69. C Harold Wood *Chelmsf* 68-73; V Dorking St Paul *Guildf* 73-82; R Rusholme H Trin *Man* 82-90; TR Gt Chesham *Ox* from 90; RD Amersham 98-04; Hon Can Ch Ch from 02. *The Rectory, Church Street, Chesham HP5 1HY* Tel (01494) 783629 Fax 791745 E-mail rsalisbury@greatchesham.freeserve.co.uk

SALISBURY, Canon Tobias. b 33. Em Coll Cam BA60. Ripon Hall Ox 60. **d** 62 **p** 63. C Putney St Mary *S'wark* 62-65; C Churchdown St Jo *Glouc* 65-67; V Urchfont w Stert *Sarum* 67-73; R Burton Bradstock w Shipton Gorge and Chilcombe 73-79; P-in-c Long Bredy w Lt Bredy and Kingston Russell 75-79; TR Bride Valley 79-86; V Gt and Lt Bedwyn and Savernake Forest 86-97; Can and Preb Sarum Cathl 92-98; rtd 98; Perm to Offic *B & W* from 98. *Anfield, Hayes Lane, Compton Dundon, Somerton TA11 6PB* Tel (01458) 274459

SALISBURY, Bishop of. *See* STANCLIFFE, The Rt Revd David Staffurth

SALISBURY, Dean of. *See* OSBORNE, The Very Revd June

SALMON, Alan Clive. b 63. SSC99 Bris Univ BA84 Univ of Wales (Cardiff) DPS85. St Mich Coll Llan 84. **d** 86 **p** 87. C Llanelli *St D* 86-88; C Roath St German *Llan* 88-90; V Nevern and Y Beifil w Eglwyswrw and Meline etc *St D* 90-92; In RC Ch 92-99; Perm to Offic *S'wark* 99-00; Hon C Lavender Hill Ascension etc 00-01; TP Glas E End *Glas* from 01. *21 Swinton Road, Baillieston, Glasgow G69 6DS* Tel 0141-771 3000 *or* 778 4392 Mobile 07763-133775 E-mail alan.salmon@benedictiness.org.uk

SALMON, Andrew Ian. b 61. St Jo Coll Nottm BTh88. **d** 88 **p** 89. C Collyhurst *Man* 88-92; P-in-c Pendleton St Ambrose 92-95; TV Pendleton 95-99; TR 99-04; P-in-c Salford Sacred Trin and St Phil from 04. *St Philip's Rectory, 6 Encombe Place, Salford M3 6FJ* Tel 0161-834 2041 E-mail rev.andy@btinternet.com

SALMON, Andrew Meredith Bryant. b 30. Jes Coll Cam BA54 MA58. Ridley Hall Cam 54. **d** 56 **p** 57. C Enfield Ch Ch Trent Park *Lon* 56-58; Chapl Monkton Combe Sch Bath 58-71; Chapl Milton Abbey Sch Dorset 71-89; TV Bride Valley *Sarum* 89-96; rtd 97; Perm to Offic *Sarum* from 97. *1 Barnhill Road, Wareham BH20 5BD* Tel (01929) 554039

SALMON, Anthony James Heygate. b 30. CCC Ox BA53 MA57. Cuddesdon Coll 54. **d** 56 **p** 57. C S Norwood St Mark *Cant* 56-59; S Africa 59-69; Chapl USPG Coll of the Ascension Selly Oak 69-74; P-in-c Frinsted 74-78; R Harrietsham *Cant* 74-85; P-in-c Ulcombe 81-85; V Chobham w Valley End *Guildf* 85-95; rtd 95; Perm to Offic *St Alb* from 95. *24 Elmwood, Welwyn Garden City AL8 6LE* Tel (01707) 333694

SALMON, Bernard Bryant. b 24. Trin Hall Cam BA50 MA54. Wells Th Coll 50. **d** 52 **p** 53. C Stockton St Pet *Dur* 52-55; C Longbenton St Bart *Newc* 55-58; R Cramlington 58-71; V Winscombe *B & W* 71-91; RD Locking 78-86; rtd 91; Perm to Offic *B & W* from 91. *Scaddens House, Scaddens Lane, Rodney Stoke, Cheddar BS27 3UR* Tel (01749) 870194

SALMON, Mrs Constance Hazel. b 25. R Holloway Coll Lon BSc46. Lon Bible Coll 66 Gilmore Course 71. **dss** 80 **d** 87 **p** 96. Sidcup St Andr *Roch* 80-88; NSM 87-88; Perm to Offic 88-96; NSM Eynsford w Farningham and Lullingstone from 96. *43 Old Mill Close, Eynsford, Dartford DA4 0BN* Tel (01322) 866034

SALMON, Jonathan. b 66. Univ Coll of Swansea BSc(Econ)88 Sussex Univ MA95 MPhil95. Wycliffe Hall Ox 01. **d** 03 **p** 04. C Bowling St Jo *Bradf* from 03. *79 Bowling Hall Road, Bradford BD4 7LN* Tel (01274) 735332 Mobile 07814-674027 E-mail jonathan@jsalmon1.fsnet.co.uk

SALMON, Mrs Margaret Penny. b 37. Leeds Univ BA59 CertEd60. SW Minl Tr Course 85. **d** 88 **p** 94. NSM Yelverton, Meavy, Sheepstor and Walkhampton *Ex* from 88. *Hinnies, Leg-o-Mutton Corner, Yelverton PL20 6DJ* Tel (01822) 853310 E-mail peggysalmon@compuserve.com

SALMON, Mark Harold. b 62. Trin Coll Bris. **d** 00 **p** 01. C Bath Weston All SS w N Stoke and Langridge *B & W* 00-04; P-in-c Harlescott *Lich* from 04. *Harlescott Vicarage, Meadow Farm Drive, Shrewsbury SY1 4NG* Tel (01743) 362883 E-mail mark.salmon@xalt.co.uk

SALMON, Philip John. b 63. Oak Hill Th Coll 96. **d** 98 **p** 99. C Kington w Huntington, Old Radnor, Kinnerton etc *Heref* 98-02; TV Radipole and Melcombe Regis *Sarum* from 02. *The Vicarage, 74 Field Barn Drive, Weymouth DT4 0EF* Tel (01305) 778995 Mobile 07771-688226 E-mail pip@fish.co.uk

SALMON, Richard Harold. b 35. Fitzw Ho Cam BA57. Clifton Th Coll 57. **d** 59 **p** 60. C Blackheath Park St Mich *S'wark* 59-61; C St Alb St Paul *St Alb* 61-63; Malaysia 63-75; OMF 63-65; C Telok Anson St Luke 63-65; V Kuantan Pehang Epiphany 65-75; P-in-c March St Wendreda *Ely* 75-76; R 76-85; V Congresbury w Puxton and Hewish St Ann *B & W* 85-00; rtd 00; Perm to Offic *Truro* 00-01 and *B & W* from 02. *2 Wisteria Avenue, Hutton, Weston-super-Mare BS24 9QF* Tel (01934) 813750 E-mail richard.salmon@talk21.com

SALMON, The Very Revd Thomas Noel Desmond Cornwall. b 13. TCD BA35 MA49 BD42. TCD Div Sch 35. **d** 37 **p** 38. C Bangor St Comgall *D & D* 37-40; C Belfast St Jas *Conn* 40-41; C Larne and Inver 42-44; Clerical V Ch Ch Cathl Dublin *D & G* 44-45; Lect TCD 45-89; C Dublin Rathfarnham *D & G* 45-50; Hon Clerical V Ch Ch Cathl Dublin 45-63; I Tullow 50-62; I Dublin St Ann 62-67; Preb Dunlavin St Patr Cathl Dublin 63-67; Dean Ch Ch Cathl Dublin *D & G* 67-89; I Dublin Ch Ch Cathl Gp 76-89; rtd 89. *c/o Mrs I Sherwood, Hillcrest, Kilmolin, Enniskerry, Co Wicklow, Irish Republic*

SALMON, William John. b 50. Lon Univ BSc72 DipEd73. Cranmer Hall Dur 76. **d** 79 **p** 80. C Summerstown *S'wark* 79-81; C Hampreston *Sarum* 81-86; V Sundon *St Alb* 86-90; Dep Chapl HM Young Offender Inst Glen Parva 90-91; Chapl HM Pris Whitemoor 91-95; Chapl HM Pris Blundeston 95-04; Chapl HM Pris Belmarsh from 04. *HM Prison Belmarsh, Western Way, London SE28 0EB* Tel (020) 8331 4523 Fax 8331 4401 E-mail william.salmon@hmps.gsi.gov.uk *or* bill.salmon@fish.co.uk

SALMON, Mrs Yvonne Delysia. b 40. Cant Sch of Min 00. **d** 03 **p** 04. OLM Boughton Monchelsea *Cant* from 03. *Elderden Farm Cottage, Maidstone Road, Staplehurst, Tonbridge TN12 0RN* Tel (01622) 842598 E-mail y.salmon@tesco.net

SALONIA, Ivan. b 38. Open Univ BA81 N Lon Poly MA85 CQSW78. Milan Th Coll (RC) 60. **d** 63 **p** 64. In RC Ch Hong Kong 64-73; Hon C Woolwich St Thos *S'wark* 89-91; C Greenwich St Alfege w St Pet and St Paul 91-93; C Kidbrooke St Jas 93-95; TV 95-02; rtd 02; Perm to Offic *S'wark* from 03. *247 Hook Lane, Welling DA16 2NZ* Tel (020) 8306 2862 *or* 8298 1309 Fax 8306 6859 Mobile 07946-085065 E-mail ivanus_magnus@hotmail.com

SALOP, Archdeacon of. *See* HALL, The Ven John Barrie

SALT, Canon David Christopher. b 37. Univ of Wales (Lamp) BA59. Sarum Th Coll 59. **d** 61 **p** 62. C Kidderminster St Mary *Worc* 61-66; Ind Chapl 66-72; R Knightwick w Doddenham, Broadwas and Cotheridge 72-82; Chapl Worc Coll of HE 72-82; V Redditch St Steph *Worc* 82-02; P-in-c Tardebigge 84-88; RD Bromsgrove 91-00; Hon Can Worc Cathl 92-02; rtd 02; Perm to

Offic *Worc* from 03. *7 Longmoor Close, Redditch B97 6SX* Tel (01527) 68735

SALT, David Thomas Whitehorn. b 32. K Coll Lon AKC56 BD57. **d** 57 **p** 58. New Hebrides 57-63; Solomon Is 63-66; C Hawley H Trin *Guildf* 66-68; V Shelf *Bradf* 68-73; R Checkendon *Ox* 73-81; RD Henley 78-84; TR Langtree 81-84; Chapl Hungerford Hosp 84-89; V Hungerford and Denford *Ox* 84-89; P-in-c Harpsden 89-95; Gen Sec Melanesian Miss 89-95; rtd 95; Perm to Offic *Sarum* from 95. *7 Milton Road, Pewsey SN9 5JJ* Tel (01672) 569124

✠**SALT, The Rt Revd John William.** b 41. Kelham Th Coll 61. **d** 66 **p** 67 **c** 99. C Barrow St Matt *Carl* 66-70; Lesotho 70-77; S Africa 77-99; OGS from 81; Superior from 96; Dean Eshowe Cathl and Adn S Zululand 89-99; Bp St Helena from 99. *Bishopsholme, PO Box 62, St Helena, South Atlantic Ocean* Tel (00290) 4471 Fax 4728 E-mail bishop@helanta.sh *or* jsalt@ogs.net

SALT, Leslie. b 29. Linc Th Coll 68. **d** 69 **p** 69. C Alford w Rigsby *Linc* 69-75; V Torksey 75-94; R Kettlethorpe 77-94; V Marton 77-94; V Newton-on-Trent 77-94; rtd 94; Perm to Offic *Linc* 94-97. *2 Holdenby Close, Lincoln LN2 4TQ*

SALT, Neil. b 64. Univ of Wales (Ban) BA85 Edin Univ BD89 Man Metrop Univ BSc97. Edin Th Coll 86. **d** 89 **p** 90. C Stretford All SS *Man* 89-93; P-in-c Smallbridge 93; P-in-c Wardle 93; V Smallbridge and Wardle 93-94; Perm to Offic *Wakef* 94-01; Hon C Ripponden from 01; Chapl Rishworth Sch Ripponden from 02. *Christ Church Vicarage, 6 Long Meadow, Barkisland, Halifax HX4 0AR* Tel (01422) 825987 E-mail salt@fish.co.uk

SALTER, Arthur Thomas John. b 34. TD88. AKC60. **d** 61 **p** 62. C Ealing St Pet Mt Park *Lon* 61-65; C Shepherd's Bush St Steph w St Thos 65-66; C Holborn St Alb w Saffron Hill St Pet 66-70; P-in-c Barnsbury St Clem 70-77; P-in-c Islington St Mich 70-77; V Pentonville St Silas w All SS and St Jas 70-00; CF (TAVR) from 75; Gen Sec Angl and E Chs Assn from 76; Chmn from 90; P-in-c St Dunstan in the West *Lon* 79-99; rtd 00. *1 St James's Close, Bishop Street, London N1 8PH* Tel (020) 7359 0250

SALTER, Christopher. *See* SALTER, Nigel Christopher Murray

SALTER, George Alfred. b 25. TCD BA47 MA. CITC 49. **d** 49 **p** 50. C Rathdowney *C & O* 49-51; C Cork St Luke *C, C & R* 51-53; I Fermoy Union 53-55; I Cork St Luke w St Ann 55-73; Can Ross Cathl 69-88; Can Cork Cathl 69-88; Treas 88-94; I Cork St Luke Union 73-94; Preb Tymothan St Patr Cathl Dublin 88-94; rtd 94. *Mount Vernon House, 66 Wellington Road, Cork, Irish Republic* Tel (00353) (21) 450 6844

SALTER, Janet Elizabeth. b 48. Leeds Univ CertEd69. SW Minl Tr Course 92. **d** 95 **p** 98. C Coleshill *Birm* 95-97; Hon C St Dennis *Truro* 97-00; TV Gillingham *Sarum* 00-04; V Stour Vale from 04. *The Vicarage, Kington Magna, Gillingham SP8 5EW* Tel and fax (01747) 838494 E-mail kmvicarage@tiscali.co.uk

SALTER, John. *See* SALTER, Arthur Thomas John

SALTER, Canon John Frank. b 37. Dur Univ BA62 DipTh64. Cranmer Hall Dur 62. **d** 64 **p** 65. C Bridlington Priory *York* 64-67; Travelling Sec IVF 67-70; V Stoughton *Guildf* 70-02; RD Guildf 89-94; Hon Can Guildf Cathl 99-02; rtd 03. *7 Aldershot Road, Guildford GU2 8AE* Tel (01483) 511165 E-mail j.salter@btinternet.com

SALTER, John Leslie. b 51. AKC76. Coll of Resurr Mirfield 77. **d** 78 **p** 79. C Tottenham St Paul *Lon* 78-82; P-in-c Castle Vale *Birm* 82-83; TV Curdworth w Castle Vale 83-90; V Castle Vale St Cuth 90-92; V Wantage *Ox* from 93; AD Wantage from 01. *The Vicarage, The Cloisters, Wantage OX12 8AQ* Tel (01235) 762214 E-mail thevicar@wantage.parish.clara.net

SALTER, Nigel Christopher Murray. b 46. Loughb Univ BTech. Ripon Coll Cuddesdon 79. **d** 81 **p** 82. C Glouc St Aldate *Glouc* 81-84; C Solihull *Birm* 84-88; V Highters Heath 88-97; Asst Chapl Greenwich Healthcare NHS Trust 97-01; Asst Chapl Qu Eliz Hosp NHS Trust 01-03; P-in-c Leaton and Albrighton w Battlefield *Lich* from 03. *Leaton Vicarage, Baschurch Road, Bomere Heath, Shrewsbury SY4 3PN* Tel (01939) 290259

SALTER, Richard. b 24. Edin Th Coll 46. **d** 48 **p** 49. C Dundee St Salvador *Bre* 48-51; C Watford St Andr *St Alb* 51-54; C Oxhey St Matt 54-58; V Robert Town *Wakef* 58-62; V Watford St Jo *St Alb* 62-98; rtd 98; Perm to Offic *St Alb* from 98. *1 Beechfield Court, Grandfield Avenue, Watford WD17 4UE* Tel (01923) 231659

SALTER, Roger John. b 45. Trin Coll Bris 75. **d** 79 **p** 80. C Bedminster St Mich *Bris* 79-82; C Swindon Ch Ch 82-84; V Bedminster Down 84-89; P-in-c Northwood *Portsm* 89-93; P-in-c W Cowes H Trin 89-92; V Cowes H Trin and St Mary 92-94; USA from 94. *1300 Panorama Drive, Vestavia Hills, AL 35216, USA* Tel (001) (205) 823 7967

SALTWELL, Ms Kathleen. b 48. Edin Univ BD00 Cam Univ MA02. Westcott Ho Cam 00. **d** 02 **p** 03. C Worc SE *Worc* from 02. *24 Albert Road, Worcester SR5 1EB* Tel (01905) 356656 E-mail kathsaltwell@hotmail.com

SALWAY, Canon Donald Macleay. b 31. St Pet Hall Ox BA54 MA59. Oak Hill Th Coll 54. **d** 56 **p** 57. C Holloway St Mary w St Jas *Lon* 56-67; V Cambridge St Phil *Ely* 67-81; V Mile Cross *Nor* 81-96; RD Nor N 89-95; Hon Can Nor Cathl 91-96; rtd 96; Perm to Offic *B & W* from 96; C Langport Area Chs 98-00. *Lype House, Long Load, Langport TA10 9LD* Tel (01458) 241623

SAMBELL, David John. b 31. St Aid Birkenhead 60. **d** 63 **p** 64. C Sutton St Geo *Ches* 63-67; C Alsager St Mary 67-71; V Crewe St Pet 71-81; V Upton Priory 81-99; rtd 99; Perm to Offic *Ches* from 01. *19 Woodfield Close, Connah's Quay, Deeside CH5 4RF* Tel (01244) 814462

SAMBROOK, Kenneth Henry. b 42. N Ord Course 04. **d** 05. NSM Wistaston *Ches* from 05. *6 Westfield Drive, Wistaston, Crewe CW2 8ES* Tel (01270) 662455 E-mail kensambrook@beeb.net

SAMMAN, Peter Bryan. b 27. TCD BA53. Coll of Resurr Mirfield 53. **d** 55 **p** 56. C Adlington *Blackb* 55-57; C Church Kirk 57-60; V Briercliffe 60-67; V Lancaster Ch Ch 67-74; V Lostock Hall 74-85; V Morecambe St Barn 85-91; rtd 91; Perm to Offic *Blackb* from 91. *14 Wentworth Crescent, Morecambe LA3 3NX* Tel (01524) 425208

SAMMÉ, Raymond Charles. b 50. Trent Poly MIBiol80 Anglia Poly Univ MA03. Oak Hill Th Coll 85. **d** 87 **p** 88. C Holmer w Huntington *Heref* 87-90; C Derby St Alkmund and St Werburgh *Derby* 90-93; V Romford Gd Shep Collier Row *Chelmsf* from 93. *Good Shepherd Vicarage, 97 Collier Row Lane, Romford RM5 3BA* Tel (01708) 726423 E-mail ray.samme@btinternet.com

SAMMON, Helen Mary. b 57. Newnham Coll Cam MA79 Bris Univ MB, ChB82 MRCGP98. WEMTC 00. **d** 03 **p** 04. NSM Painswick, Sheepscombe, Cranham, The Edge etc *Glouc* from 03. *Windycot, Cranham, Gloucester GL4 8HS* Tel (01452) 813159 E-mail helen.sammon@doctors.org.uk

SAMMONS, Miss Elizabeth Mary. b 71. RN94 RHV98. Wycliffe Hall Ox 03. **d** 05. C Stoke Gifford *Bris* from 05. *56 Simmonds View, Stoke Gifford, Bristol BS34 8HL* Tel (01454) 776662 E-mail wizsammons@hotmail.com

SAMMONS, John Trevor. b 22. Birm Univ BA48. Ripon Hall Ox. **d** 50 **p** 51. C The Quinton *Birm* 50-55; V Birm St Luke 55-70; Chapl Birm Skin Hosp 56-70; P-in-c No Man's Heath *Lich* 70-82; R Newton Regis w Seckington and Shuttington *Birm* 70-86; rtd 87; Perm to Offic *Birm* from 87. *39 Kurtus, Dosthill, Tamworth B77 1NX* Tel (01827) 283875

SAMPFORD, John Alfred. b 36. Lich Th Coll 58. **d** 61 **p** 62. C Lambeth St Phil *S'wark* 61-65; C Beddington 65-69; V Hampstead Ch Ch *Lon* 69-79; V Enfield Chase St Mary 79-02; rtd 02; Perm to Offic *Ches* from 02. *Ellisland, Bryn Gwyn Lane, Northop Hall, Mold CH7 6JT* Tel (01244) 810635

SAMPSON, Brian Andrew. b 39. **d** 94 **p** 95. C Glemsford, Hartest w Boxted, Somerton etc *St E* 94-96; C Pentlow, Foxearth, Liston and Borley *Chelmsf* 96-97; P-in-c 97-04; C N Hinckford from 04. *The Rectory, The Street, Foxearth, Sudbury CO10 7JG* Tel (01787) 313132 E-mail captainbrianca@waitrose.co.uk

SAMPSON, Clive. b 38. St Jo Coll Cam BA61 MA64. Ridley Hall Cam 63. **d** 65 **p** 66. C Tunbridge Wells St Jo *Roch* 65-69; Travelling Sec Scripture Union 69-79; V Maidstone St Luke *Cant* 79-94; rtd 98. *64-70 rue Compans A3 274, 75019 Paris, France* Tel (0033) (1) 40 18 12 72

SAMPSON, Desmond William John. b 25. FRICS60. Roch Th Coll 63. **d** 65 **p** 66. C Hythe *Cant* 65-70; V Alkham w Capel le Ferne and Hougham 70-76; V Wingham w Elmstone and Preston w Stourmouth 76-86; RD E Bridge 81-86; C Hythe 86-91; rtd 91; Perm to Offic *Cant* from 91. *25 Albert Road, Hythe CT21 6BP* Tel (01303) 268457

SAMPSON, Jeremy John Egerton. b 23. Dur Univ BSc45. Wells Th Coll 46. **d** 48 **p** 49. C Longbenton St Bart *Newc* 48-51; Singapore 51-62; V Killingworth *Newc* 62-76; V Consett *Dur* 76-90; RD Lanchester 80-85; rtd 90; Perm to Offic *Dur* and *York* from 90. *6 Kilkenny Road, Guisborough TS14 7LE* Tel (01287) 632734

SAMPSON, Julian Robin Anthony. b 78. St D Coll Lamp BA00. St Steph Ho Ox 01. **d** 03. C Notting Hill All SS w St Columb *Lon* 03-04; C Staines St Mary and St Pet from 04. *12 Romana Court, Sidney Road, Staines TW18 4QJ* Tel (01784) 442487 E-mail jrasampson@yahoo.co.uk

SAMPSON, Terence Harold Morris. b 41. ACA64 FCA75. Bps' Coll Cheshunt 64. **d** 67 **p** 68. C Penrith St Andr *Carl* 67-72; V Carl St Barn 72-80; TR Carl H Trin and St Barn 80-84; Chapl Cumberland Infirmary 83-84; R Workington St Mich *Carl* 84-01; Hon Can Carl Cathl 89-01; RD Solway 90-95; Perm to Offic from 02. *16 Poplar Street, Keswick CA12 5BW*

SAMS, Michael Charles. b 34. FCA62. Ox NSM Course 81. **d** 84 **p** 85. NSM Abingdon *Ox* 84-92 and 99-04; P-in-c Shippon 92-99; Perm to Offic from 04. *13 Hound Close, Abingdon OX14 2LU* Tel (01235) 529084

SAMSON, Hilary Lynn. b 50. SW Minl Tr Course. **d** 03 **p** 04. NSM St Agnes and Mithian w Mount Hawke *Truro* from 03. *12 Newton Road, Troon, Camborne TR14 7SJ* Tel (01209) 713247 E-mail hilarysamson@lineone.net

SAMUEL, Alwin. **d** 81 **p** 83. Pakistan 81-03; Interfaith Worker and Dioc Adv *Ox* from 03. *Flat 1, 14 Magdalen Road, Oxford OX4 1RW*

SAMUEL, Brother. *See* DOUBLE, Richard Sydney

SAMUEL, Canon James Louis. b 30. Birm Poly CQSW72 Open Univ BA77. Sarum Th Coll 59. **d** 61 **p** 62. C Dursley *Glouc* 61-63; C Matson 63-65; C Leckhampton SS Phil and Jas 65-66; C Blakenall Heath *Lich* 67-69; P-in-c Dudley St Aug Holly Hall *Worc* 81-86; V 86-94; RD Dudley 87-93; Hon Can Worc Cathl 88-94; rtd 94; Perm to Offic *Worc* 94-96 and from 98; C Kidderminster St Mary and All SS w Trimpley etc 96-98. *44 Broadwaters Drive, Kidderminster DY10 2RY* Tel (01562) 68533 E-mail jimsam@sagainternet.co.uk

✠**SAMUEL, The Most Revd Kunnumpurathu Joseph.** b 42. Union Bibl Sem Yavatmal BRE68 Selly Oak Coll CPS85 Texas Chr Univ MDiv86. **d** 68 **c** 90. Ch of S India from 68; Bp E Kerala from 90; Moderator Ch of S India 99-04. *CSI Bishop's House, Melukavumattom PO, Kottayam 686 652, Kerala State, India* Tel (0091) (482) 291026 Fax 291044

SAMUEL, Luther Fiaz. b 47. Karachi Univ BA83. St Thos Th Coll Karachi BTh88. **d** 88 **p** 89. Pakistan 88-96; Oman 96-03; Perm to Offic *Lich* 03-04; NSM Walsall from 04; Minority Ethnic Angl Concerns Officer 04-05; Asian Missr from 05. *16 Bescot Drive, Walsall WS2 9DF* Tel (01543) 631814 Mobile 07901-718371 E-mail revlfs@hotmail.com

SAMUEL, Mrs Mary Rose. b 42. Newc Univ BA65 Bris Univ CQSW67. STETS 95. **d** 98 **p** 99. C Waltham on the Wolds, Stonesby, Saxby etc *Leic* 98-01; P-in-c Wymondham w Edmondthorpe, Buckminster etc 01-04; R S Framland from 04. *The Rectory, Sycamore Lane, Wymondham, Melton Mowbray LE14 2AZ* Tel (01572) 787238 Fax 787499 E-mail maryrose.samuel@virgin.net

SAMUEL, Oliver Harold. b 53. **d** 05. OLM Old Trafford St Bride *Man* from 05. *115 Northumberland Road, Old Trafford, Manchester M16 9PY* Tel 0161-876 5055

SAMUEL, Stuart. b 48. AKC70. St Aug Coll Cant 70. **d** 71 **p** 72. C Golcar *Wakef* 71-77; V Brampton St Mark *Derby* 77-79; P-in-c Hathern *Leic* 79-83; R Hathern, Long Whatton and Diseworth 83-90; R Hathern, Long Whatton and Diseworth w Belton etc 90-97; RD Akeley E 92-96; P-in-c Waltham on the Wolds, Stonesby, Saxby etc 97-02; P-in-c Wymondham w Edmondthorpe, Buckminster etc 97-01; P-in-c High Framland Par 97-01; P-in-c Helpringham w Hale *Linc* from 02. *The Vicarage, 2 Vicarage Lane, Helpringham, Sleaford NG34 0RP* Tel (01529) 421435 E-mail stuart@marymag.freeserve.co.uk

SAMUELS, Canon Ann Elizabeth. b 51. Birm Univ BA73 CertEd74. Trin Coll Bris 85. **d** 87 **p** 94. Par Dn Moreton *Ches* 87-91; Par Dn Halton 91-94; C 94-03; Bp's Adv for Women in Min 94-96; Asst Dir of Ords 96-03; RD Frodsham 99-03; Chapl Halton Gen Hosp NHS Trust 99-03; V Higher Bebington *Ches* from 03; Hon Can Ches Cathl from 01. *The Vicarage, King's Road, Bebington, Wirral CH63 8LX* Tel 0151-608 4429 E-mail vicar@higher.bebington.fsnet.co.uk

SAMUELS, Canon Christopher William John. b 42. AKC66. **d** 67 **p** 68. C Kirkholt *Man* 67-72; C-in-c Houghton Regis St Thos CD *St Alb* 72-76; R Tarporley *Ches* 76-83; R Ches St Mary from 83; RD Ches 95-02; Hon Can Ches Cathl from 97; Chapl to The Queen from 01. *The Rectory, Overleigh Road, St Mary-without-the-Walls, Chester CH4 7HL* Tel (01244) 671202 Fax 682034 E-mail cwjsamuels@tiscali.co.uk

SAMUELS, Raymond John. b 49. Qu Mary Coll Lon BSc73 Essex Univ CertEd74. Trin Coll Bris 85. **d** 87 **p** 88. C Moreton *Ches* 87-91; V Halton 91-02; Dioc Dir of Ords from 03. *The Vicarage, King's Road, Bebington, Wirral CH63 8LX* Tel 0151-608 4429 E-mail samuels@ddo-chester.fsnet.co.uk

SAMUELS, Miss Sheila Mary. b 57. St Andr Univ MA79 Wolfs Coll Ox MLitt82 PGCE83. Trin Coll Bris BA89. **d** 89 **p** 94. C Skirbeck H Trin *Linc* 89-96; Perm to Offic 00-03; rtd 04. *61 Oak Crescent, Boston PE21 9EZ* Tel (01205) 311851

SAMWAYS, Denis Robert. b 37. Leeds Univ BA62. Coll of Resurr Mirfield 62. **d** 64 **p** 65. C Clun w Chapel Lawn *Heref* 64-69; C Pocklington w Yapham-cum-Meltonby, Owsthorpe etc *York* 69-71; C Millington w Gt Givendale 69-71; R Hinderwell w Roxby 71-76; Hon C 80-91; Hon C Loftus 76-80; V Boosbeck w Moorsholm 91-95; R Kirby Misperton w Normanby, Edston and Salton 95-02; rtd 02. *7 High Street, Gatehouse of Fleet, Castle Douglas DG7 2HR* Tel (01557) 814095

SAMWAYS, John Feverel. b 44. BA DipTh. Trin Coll Bris 81. **d** 83 **p** 84. C Patcham *Chich* 83-86; C Ox St Aldate w St Matt *Ox* 86-94; R Ox St Matt 95-97; TR Keynsham *B & W* from 97. *St John's Rectory, 1 The Park, Keynsham, Bristol BS31 2BL* Tel 0117-986 3354 E-mail john.samways@blueyonder.co.uk

✠**SAN SI HTAY, The Most Revd Samuel.** BA. **d** 67 **c** 89. Asst Pastor Indaw Burma 67-69; P-in-c Mawbi 70-76; Prin H Cross Coll 76-91; Asst Bp Yangon 91-93; Gen Sec Myanmar 93-01; Abp Myanmar and Bp Yangon from 01. *Bishopscourt, 140 Pyidaungsu Yeiktha Road, Dagon, Yangon 11191, Myanmar* Tel (0095) (1) 246813 Fax 251405 E-mail cpm.140@mptmail.net.mm

✠**SANANA, The Rt Revd Rhynold Ewaruba.** b 39. Newton Th Coll 60 St Barn Coll Adelaide 71 St Aug Coll Cant 75. **d** 67 **p** 67 **c** 76. Papua New Guinea 67-72, 73-90 and from 92; Asst P Dogura Cathl 67-69; Asst P Popondetta Resurr 69-70; St Barn Coll Adelaide Australia 72-73; Dean Dogura and Adn E Region 74-76; Asst Bp New Guinea 76-77; Bp Dogura 77-89; Asst P Lakenham St Mark *Nor* 90-92; rtd 99. *Melanesian Brotherhood, Haruro, PO Box 29, Popondetta, Oro Province, Papua New Guinea*

SANDAY, Robert Ward. b 55. Sarum & Wells Th Coll 89. **d** 91 **p** 92. C Swindon Ch Ch *Bris* 91-94; V Lyddington and Wanborough and Bishopstone etc 94-00; Chapl to the Deaf *Win* from 00. *3 Wheat Close, Chandlers Ford, Eastleigh SO53 4HA* Tel (023) 8027 0551

SANDBERG, Canon Peter John. b 37. Lon Univ LLB59. Lon Coll of Div 67. **d** 69 **p** 70. C Hailsham *Chich* 69-72; C Billericay St Mary *Chelmsf* 72-77; TV Billericay and Lt Burstead 77-83; R Thundersley 83-02; RD Hadleigh 90-00; Hon Can Chelmsf Cathl 00-02; rtd 02; Perm to Offic *Chelmsf* from 02. *Hethersett, School Road, Pentlow, Sudbury CO10 7JR* Tel (01787) 281006 E-mail psandberg@compuserve.com

SANDELLS-REES, Kathy Louise. *See* JONES, Ms Kathy Louise

SANDERS, Colin Anthony Wakefield. b 26. Wadh Coll Ox MA55. Ox NSM Course 89. **d** 90 **p** 91. NSM Eynsham and Cassington *Ox* 90-95; NSM Bladon w Woodstock 95-05; NSM Blenheim from 05. *Little Firs, 41 Bladon Road, Woodstock OX20 1QD* Tel (01993) 813357

SANDERS, Diana Faye. b 46. Auckland Univ MA68 LSE PhD75. Westcott Ho Cam 02. **d** 04 **p** 05. NSM Cottenham *Ely* from 04. *48 Tenison Manor, Cottenham, Cambridge CB4 8XL* Tel (01954) 205420

SANDERS, Diana Louise. b 59. Southn Univ BSc80 ACA83. STETS 95. **d** 98 **p** 99. NSM Alderbury Team *Sarum* 98-01; NSM Clarendon from 01. *Park Cottage, West Dean, Salisbury SP5 1JQ* Tel (01794) 340355

SANDERS, Graham Laughton. b 32. Kelham Th Coll 52. **d** 56 **p** 57. C Glouc St Paul *Glouc* 56-60; India 61-68; V Heaton St Martin *Bradf* 68-76; V Gt Waltham *Chelmsf* 76-79; V Gt Waltham w Ford End 79-87; Sec Dioc Liturg Cttee 78-87; TR Guiseley w Esholt *Bradf* 87-94; rtd 97; Perm to Offic *Bradf* from 95; *York* from 98; *Ripon* from 03. *4 Marlborough Road, Shipley BD18 3NX* Tel (01274) 587896 Mobile 07808-123165 Fax (01274) 593529 E-mail glmcesanders@aol.com

SANDERS, Henry William. b 36. **d** 62 **p** 64. C Nottingham St Ann *S'well* 62-65; C Dagenham *Chelmsf* 65-67; C W Thurrock 67-73; C W Ham 73-78; rtd 01. *Lancaster House, Serene Place, Broadstairs CT10 1LN* Tel (01843) 862853

SANDERS, Herbert. b 21. Clifton Th Coll 51. **d** 53 **p** 54. C Laisterdyke *Bradf* 53-56; C Bingley All SS 56-59; V Oxenhope 59-66; Lic to Offic *Linc* 66-81 and from 95; rtd 81. *12 Low Toynton Road, Horncastle LN9 5LL*

SANDERS, Canon Hilary Clare. b 57. Hull Univ BA79 UEA CertEd81. EAMTC 83. **dss** 85 **d** 87 **p** 94. Haverhill w Withersfield, the Wrattings etc *St E* 85-87; Hon Par Dn Melton 87-94; Hon C 94-99; Dioc Dir Educn (Schools) 88-99; P-in-c Earl Soham w Cretingham and Ashfield from 99; P-in-c Boulge w Burgh, Grundisburgh and Hasketon from 05; Hon Can St E Cathl from 04. *The Rectory, Woodbridge Road, Grundisburgh, Woodbridge IP13 6UF* Tel (01473) 735749 E-mail claresanders@suffolkonline.net

SANDERS, James Alexander. b 29. **d** 65 **p** 66. Australia 65-78; C Enfield St Jas *Lon* 78-81; rtd 94. *Apt 8, 82 Sandy Bay Road, Battery Point, Tas, Australia 7004*

SANDERS, Canon Mark. b 57. Hull Univ BA79 Cam Univ BA82. Westcott Ho Cam 80. **d** 83 **p** 84. C Haverhill w Withersfield, the Wrattings etc *St E* 83-87; P-in-c Melton 87-91; R 91-98; Dioc Dir Post-Ord Tr from 97; Asst Dioc Dir of Ords 98-99; Dioc Dir of Ords from 99; Dioc Dir of CME 99-01; Hon Can St E Cathl from 01. *The Rectory, Woodbridge Road, Grundisburgh, Woodbridge IP13 6UF* Tel (01473) 735749 E-mail mark@stedmundsbury.anglican.org *or* msanders@fish.co.uk

SANDERS, Preb Michael Barry. b 45. Fitzw Coll Cam BA67 MA71 Lon Univ BD71. St Jo Coll Nottm 68 Lon Coll of Div. **d** 71 **p** 72. C Ashtead *Guildf* 71-74; Chapl St Jo Coll Cam 75-79; V Dorridge *Birm* 79-89; TR Walsall *Lich* 89-01; Preb Lich Cathl 97-01; Chapl The Hague *Eur* from 01. *Riouwstraat 2, 2585 HA The Hague, The Netherlands* Tel (0031) (70) 355 5359 Fax 306 0758 *or* 354 1023 E-mail churchoffice@stjohnandstphilip.org

SANDERS, Nigel Wilding. b 29. Mert Coll Ox MA55. Ox Min Course 91. **d** 92 **p** 93. NSM Maidenhead St Andr and St Mary *Ox* 92-97; NSM Furze Platt 97-04; rtd 04. *Fry's Barn, Home Farm, Barton, Winscombe BS25 1DX* Tel (01934) 843818 E-mail nigelisan@btinternet.com

SANDERS, Mrs Nora Irene. b 29. Lon Univ BA50 CertEd51. WMMTC 74. **dss** 78 **d** 87 **p** 94. Dorridge *Birm* 78-87; Par Dn 87-90; rtd 90; Hon C Tanworth *Birm* 94-96; Perm to Offic from 96. *8 Cransley Grove, Solihull B91 3ZA* Tel 0121-705 2391

SANDERS (née SHAW), Mrs Pamela Joyce. b 54. Liv Univ BA76. WEMTC 02. **d** 05. C Leominster *Heref* from 05. *8 Radnor View, Leominster HR6 8TF* Tel (01568) 620539

SANDERS, Roderick David Scott. b 58. Southn Univ BA80 CertEd81. Cranmer Hall Dur 85. **d** 88 **p** 89. C Luton St Mary *St Alb* 88-93; P-in-c Clovelly *Ex* 93-94; P-in-c Woolfardisworthy and Buck Mills 93-94; TV Parkham, Alwington, Buckland Brewer etc 94-98; NSM Cove St Jo *Guildf* 98-03; NSM Guildf All SS from 03; NSM Guildf Ch Ch w St Martha-on-the-Hill from 03. *Christ Church Vicarage, 25 Waterden Road, Guildford GU1 2AZ* Tel (01483) 568886 Mobile 07720-856460 E-mail rod.sanders@ntlworld.com

SANDERS (née COLLINGRIDGE), Mrs Susan Rachel. b 61. St Mary's Coll Dur BA83. Cranmer Hall Dur 85. **d** 88 **p** 94. Par Dn Luton St Mary *St Alb* 88-93; Perm to Offic *Ex* 93-94; NSM Parkham, Alwington, Buckland Brewer etc 94-98; TV Cove St Jo *Guildf* 98-03; V Guildf Ch Ch w St Martha-on-the-Hill from 03. *Christ Church Vicarage, 25 Waterden Road, Guildford GU1 2AZ* Tel (01483) 568886 Mobile 07711-549976 E-mail susie.sanders@ntlworld.com *or* susiesanders@dunelm.org.uk

SANDERS, Mrs Wendy Elizabeth. b 49. Carl Dioc Tr Course 87. **d** 90 **p** 94. NSM Bampton w Mardale *Carl* 90-92; C Walney Is 92-94; C Stanwix 94-98; TV Chippenham St Paul w Hardenhuish etc *Bris* 98-03; TV Kington St Michael 98-03; RD Chippenham 99-03; TR Cockermouth w Embleton and Wythop *Carl* from 03. *The Rectory, Lorton Road, Cockermouth CA13 9DU* Tel (01900) 823269 Mobile 07980-598892 E-mail wendy@parishofcockermouth.org.uk

SANDERS, William John. b 48. Liv Inst of Educn BA80. Wycliffe Hall Ox 81. **d** 83 **p** 84. C Netherton *Liv* 83-87; P-in-c Wavertree St Bridget 87-97; V Wavertree St Bridget and St Thos from 97. *The Vicarage, Ashfield, Wavertree, Liverpool L15 1EY* Tel 0151-733 1117

SANDERSON, Colin James. b 54. Univ of Wales MA95 SEN SRN. St Mich Coll Llan 85. **d** 87 **p** 88. C Merthyr Dyfan *Llan* 87-90; C Cadoxton-juxta-Barry 90-91; V Llangeinor 91-99; Lic to Offic from 04. *99 West Lee, Cowbridge Road East, Cardiff CF11 9DT* Tel (029) 2039 8771 Mobile 07713-742365

SANDERSON, Daniel. b 40. AKC66. **d** 67 **p** 68. C Upperby St Jo *Carl* 67-72; V Addingham 72-75; V Ireleth w Askam 75-02; C Dalton-in-Furness and Ireleth-with-Askam 02-05; Hon Can Carl Cathl 95-05; RD Furness 01-04; rtd 05. *52 Parklands Drive, Askam-in-Furness LA16 7JP*

SANDERSON, Canon Gillian. b 47. Cranmer Hall Dur 80. **dss** 82 **d** 87 **p** 94. Allesley *Cov* 82-86; Warwick 86-00; C 87-94; TV 94-00; Hon Can Cov Cathl 94-00; Perm to Offic from 00. *45 Buckley Road, Lillington, Leamington Spa CV32 7QG* Tel (01926) 459749 Mobile 07714-193776 E-mail gillian@canon-sanderson.freeserve.co.uk

SANDERSON, Paul. b 59. Univ of Wales (Abth) BSc80 Ches Coll of HE PGCE81 Man Univ MEd92. **d** 05. OLM Bury St Jo w St Mark *Man* from 05. *261 Walmersley Road, Bury BL9 6NX* Tel 0161-764 3452 E-mail paul261@fsmail.net

SANDERSON, Canon Peter Oliver. b 29. St Chad's Coll Dur BA52. **d** 54 **p** 55. C Houghton le Spring *Dur* 54-59; R Linstead Jamaica 59-63; Chapl RAF 63-67; P-in-c Winksley cum Grantley and Aldfield w Studley *Ripon* 67-68; V 68-74; V Leeds St Aid 74-84; Can and Provost St Paul's Cathl Dundee *Bre* 84-91; R Dundee St Paul 84-91; USA from 91; rtd 94; Interim Dean Trin Cathl Iowa from 05. *Trinity Cathedral Deanery, 1103 Main Street, Davenport, IA 52803, USA* Tel (001) (563) 323 8902 E-mail deanhtrincat@aol.com

SANDERSON, Peter Richard Fallowfield. b 18. St Cath Soc Ox BA41 MA46. Chich Th Coll 41. **d** 42 **p** 44. C Bishops Hull St Jo *B & W* 42-48; C Ox St Paul *Ox* 48-49; Perm to Offic *Ex* 49-55; V Poundstock *Truro* 56-74; P-in-c Hove St Patr *Chich* 74-79; P-in-c Buxted St Mary 79-82; P-in-c Hadlow Down 79-82; P-in-c Buxted and Hadlow Down 82-83; rtd 83; Perm to Offic *Chich* 83-00. *Nova Scotia, 48 Parklands Road, Hassocks BN6 8JZ* Tel (01273) 843117

SANDERSON, Scott. b 42. Oak Hill Th Coll. **d** 82 **p** 83. C Galleywood Common *Chelmsf* 82-88; P-in-c Newport w Widdington 88-92; V Newport 92-98; V Walton le Soken from 98. *The Vicarage, Martello Road, Walton on the Naze CO14 8BP* Tel (01255) 675452 E-mail scott.sanderson@lineone.net

SANDES, Canon Denis Lindsay. b 46. CITC BTh86. **d** 89 **p** 90. C Bandon Union *C, C & R* 89-92; I Kells Gp *C & O* from 92; Can Leighlin Cathl from 03. *The Priory, Kells, Co Kilkenny, Irish Republic* Tel (00353) (56) 772 8367 Mobile 86-647 5056 E-mail hello@ossory.anglican.org

SANDFORD, The Revd and Rt Hon Lord (John Cyril Edmondson). b 20. DSC43. Dartmouth RN Coll. Westcott Ho Cam 56. **d** 58 **p** 60. C Harpenden St Nic *St Alb* 58-63; Perm to Offic 63-66; Chapl for Miss and Ecum St Alb 63-66; Chmn Redundant Chs Cttee Ch Commrs 82-88; rtd 85. *27 Ashley Gardens, Ambrosden Avenue, London SW1P 1QD* Tel (020) 7834 5722

SANDFORD, Nicholas Robert. b 63. Kent Univ BA84 Univ of Wales (Cardiff) BD87. St Mich Coll Llan 84. **d** 87 **p** 88. C Neath w Llantwit *Llan* 87-90; C Cardiff St Jo 90-94; R Cilybebyll 94-97; Chapl HM Pris Swansea 95-97; Chapl HM Pris Parc (Bridgend) 97-04; Chapl HM Pris Usk and Prescoed from 04. *HM Prison Usk, 47 Maryport Street, Usk NP15 1XP* Tel (01291) 671600

SANDFORD, Paul Richard. b 47. Em Coll Cam BA69 MA73. Wycliffe Hall Ox 72. **d** 75 **p** 76. C Upper Holloway St Pet *Lon* 75-77; C Finchley St Paul Long Lane 77-81; Ind Chapl *Newc* 81-88; TV Cramlington 81-88; TV Dronfield *Derby* 88-90; TV Dronfield w Holmesfield 90-02; P-in-c Sinfin from 02; RD Derby S from 02. *St Stephen's Vicarage, 311 Sinfin Lane, Sinfin, Derby DE24 9GP* Tel (01332) 760135 E-mail paul.sandford@dwhteamparish.free-online.co.uk

SANDHAM, Shaun Graham. b 60. Cranmer Hall Dur 02. **d** 04 **p** 05. C Workington St Mich *Carl* from 04. *31 Clifton Court, Workington CA14 3HR* Tel (01900) 607434 Mobile 07778-334356

SANDHAM, Stephen McCourt. b 41. K Coll Lon BD65 AKC65. **d** 66 **p** 67. C Stockton St Pet *Dur* 66-69; C Bishopwearmouth Gd Shep 69-71; C Bishopwearmouth St Mich w St Hilda 71-75; V Darlington St Mark w St Paul 75-82; P-in-c Sunderland St Chad 82-87; R Shincliffe 87-98; P-in-c from 98; Chapl Sherburn Hosp Dur from 98. *Shincliffe House, Sherburn Hospital, Durham DH1 2SE* Tel 0191-372 2890

SANDOM, Miss Carolyn Elizabeth. b 63. Homerton Coll Cam BEd85. Wycliffe Hall Ox BTh93. **d** 94. C St Helen Bishopsgate w St Andr Undershaft etc *Lon* 94-96; C Cambridge H Sepulchre *Ely* 96-05. *12 Eden Street, Cambridge CB1 1EL* Tel (01223) 578016 E-mail carrie@sandom63.freeserve.co.uk

SANDS, Colin Robert. b 38. JP84. Chester Coll CertEd64. N Ord Course 82. **d** 85 **p** 86. Hd Master St Andr Magull Primary Sch 80-00; NSM Bootle Ch Ch *Liv* 85-94; NSM Maghull 94-01; rtd 01; Perm to Offic *Carl* and *Liv* from 01. *16 Strafford Drive, Bootle L20 9JW* Tel 0151-525 8709 *or* (01768) 863968

SANDS, Frederick William. b 25. St Deiniol's Hawarden 86. **d** 87 **p** 88. Chapl Asst Leic Gen Hosp 87-89; Chapl 89-95; rtd 95; Perm to Offic *Leic* from 95. *Cobblestones, Laughton, Lutterworth LE17 6QE* Tel 0116-240 3163

SANDS, Nigel Colin. b 39. Dur Univ BA64 MA68. Oak Hill Th Coll 65. **d** 67 **p** 68. C Skelmersdale St Paul *Liv* 67-71; C Childwall All SS 71-72; V Wavertree St Bridget 72-78; P-in-c Welford w Wickham and Gt Shefford *Ox* 78-86; P-in-c Boxford w Stockcross and Speen 84-86; R Welford w Wickham and Gt Shefford, Boxford etc from 86. *The Rectory, Wickham, Newbury RG20 8HD* Tel (01488) 608244

SANDS, William James. b 55. Nottm Univ LTh83 Birm Univ MA99. St Jo Coll Nottm 80. **d** 83 **p** 84. C St Mary-at-Latton *Chelmsf* 83-86; R Mvurwi Zimbabwe 86-87; C-in-c Barkingside St Cedd *Chelmsf* 87-89; C Woodford St Mary w St Phil and St Jas 87-89; P-in-c Elmsett w Aldham *St E* 89-92; P-in-c Kersey w Lindsey 89-92; R Esigodini Zimbabwe 92-96; Sub Dean Harare 97; Chapl Algarve *Eur* 98-00; V Castle Bromwich St Clem *Birm* 00; V from 00. *St Clement's Vicarage, Lanchester Way, Castle Bromwich, Birmingham B36 9JG* Tel and fax 0121-747 4460 E-mail billsands@onetel.com

SANER-HAIGH, Robert James. b 73. Birm Univ BA94 MPhil98. Wycliffe Hall Ox BA04. **d** 05. C Appleby *Carl* from 05. *92 Rivington Park, Appleby-in-Westmorland CA16 6HU* Tel (017683) 53636 E-mail robsaner@btinternet.com

SANGSTER, Andrew. b 45. K Coll Lon BD67 AKC67 BA71 MA84 Lon Inst of Educn MPhil93 LLB97 FCollP. St Boniface Warminster. **d** 69 **p** 70. C Aylesford *Roch* 69-72; C Shirley *Win* 73-76; V Woolston 76-79; Prov Youth Chapl Ch in Wales 79-82; Chapl Collegiate Sch New Zealand 82-89; Chapl Eton Coll 89-92; Hd Master St Edm Sch Hindhead 92-96; Hd Master Thos Prep Sch Lon 96-99; V Ormesby St Marg w Scratby, Ormesby St Mich etc *Nor* 99-04; Chapl Bromley Coll from 04. *The Chaplain's House, Bromley College, London Road, Bromley BR1 1PE* Tel (020) 8464 3558

SANKEY, Julian. b 52. Qu Coll Ox BA74 MA79. St Jo Coll Nottm 84. **d** 86 **p** 87. C New Barnet St Jas *St Alb* 86-89; C Mansfield SS Pet and Paul *S'well* 89-94; Chapl St Luke's Hospice Sheff from 94. *St Luke's Hospice, Little Common Lane, Sheffield S11 9NE, 20 Fulney Road, Sheffield S11 7EW* Tel 0114-236 9911 *or* 266 5689 Fax 262 1242

SANKEY, Terence Arthur Melville. b 51. CertTS. Trin Coll Bris 87. **d** 89 **p** 90. C Chalke Valley W *Sarum* 89-93; NSM Chalke from 93; Chapl HM Pris Dorchester from 99. *HM Prison Dorchester, 7 North Square, Dorchester DT1 1JD* Tel (01305) 266021 E-mail terry@rkhaye.globalnet.co.uk

SANSBURY, Canon Christopher John. b 34. Peterho Cam BA57 MA. Westcott Ho Cam 58. **d** 59 **p** 60. C Portsea N End St Mark *Portsm* 59-63; C Weeke *Win* 63-71; V N Eling St Mary 71-78; R Long Melford *St E* 78-00; P-in-c Shimpling and Alpheton 98-00; Hon Can St E Cathl 97-00; rtd 00; Perm to Offic *St E* from 00. *2 Deacon's Close, Lavenham, Sudbury CO10 9TT* Tel (01787) 248068

SANSOM, John Reginald. b 40. St Jo Coll Nottm 73. **d** 75 **p** 76. C Ipswich St Marg *St E* 75-79; P-in-c Emneth *Ely* 79-85; P-in-c Hartford 85-86; TV Huntingdon 86-91; R Sawtry 91-97; R

Sawtry and Glatton 97-99; TV Ely from 99. *44 Bentham Way, Ely CB6 1BS* Tel (01353) 664964 E-mail jsansom@bentham44.freeserve.co.uk

SANSOM, Canon Michael Charles. b 44. Bris Univ BA66 St Jo Coll Dur PhD74. Cranmer Hall Dur 68. **d** 72 **p** 73. C Ecclesall *Sheff* 72-76; Lic to Offic *Ely* 76-88; Dir of Studies Ridley Hall Cam 76-88; Vice-Prin 79-88; Dir of Ords *St Alb* from 88; Can Res St Alb from 88. *4D Harpenden Road, St Albans AL3 5AB* Tel (01727) 833777 E-mail ddo@stalbans.anglican.org

SANSOM, Robert Arthur. b 29. St Aid Birkenhead 60. **d** 62 **p** 63. C Sutton in Ashfield St Mary *S'well* 62-65; V Holbrooke *Derby* 65-70; Canada from 70; R North Saanich St Andr and H Trin 70-80; R Oak Bay St Mary 80-84; R Saanichton St Mary 84-89; rtd 89. *1-9871 Resthaven Drive, Sidney BC, Canada, V8L 3E9*

SANSOME, Geoffrey Hubert. b 29. Man Univ BA53. Qu Coll Birm DipTh62. **d** 62 **p** 63. C Prenton *Ches* 62-68; P-in-c Liscard St Thos 68-72; V Kingsley 72-83; V Wybunbury w Doddington 83-91; V Marbury 91-99; rtd 99; Perm to Offic *Blackb* from 00 and *Ches* from 01. *21 Ash Drive, Warton, Preston PR4 1DD* Tel (01772) 633799

SANSUM, Canon David Henry. b 31. Bris Univ BA52 MA63. St Aid Birkenhead 54. **d** 56 **p** 57. C Henleaze *Bris* 56-59; C Stratton St Margaret 59-60; C Stoke Bishop 60-64; V Stechford *Birm* 64-76; V Ashbourne w Mapleton *Derby* 76-98; P-in-c Thorpe 77-83; V Ashbourne St Jo 81-98; RD Ashbourne 91-98; Hon Can Derby Cathl 95-98; rtd 98; Perm to Offic *Bris* and *Glouc* from 98. *Greenleaze, Main Road, Easter Compton, Bristol BS35 5SQ* Tel (01454) 632563

✠**SANTER, The Rt Revd Mark.** b 36. Qu Coll Cam BA60 MA64 Lambeth DD99. Westcott Ho Cam. **d** 63 **p** 64 **c** 81. Tutor Cuddesdon Coll 63-67; C Cuddesdon *Ox* 63-67; Fell and Dean Clare Coll Cam 67-72; Tutor 68-72; Prin Westcott Ho Cam 73-81; Hon Can Win Cathl *Win* 78-81; Area Bp Kensington *Lon* 81-87; Bp Birm 87-02; rtd 02; Hon Asst Bp *Worc* from 02 and *Birm* from 03. *81 Clarence Road, Kings Heath, Birmingham B13 9UH* Tel 0121-441 2194

✠**SANTOS DE OLIVEIRA, The Most Revd Orlando. c** 97. Bp S Brazil from 97; Primate of Brazil from 03. *Caxia Postal 11.510, Teresópolis, Porto Alegre, RS, 90870-970, Brazil* Tel (0055) (51) 3318 6200 *or* 3318 6031 Fax as telephone E-mail osoliveira@ieab.org.br

SANTRA, Jagat Ranjan. b 54. Utkal Univ BA74 Serampore Univ BD81 MTh88. **p** 00. Perm to Offic *Edin* from 02. *41 Jeffrey Street, Edinburgh EH1 1DH* Tel 0131-556 9035 *or* 650 7993 E-mail jagat_s@hotmail.com

SANTRAM, Philip James. b 27. MA Delhi Univ BSc48 Serampore Univ BD53. Bp's Coll Calcutta 49. **d** 52 **p** 54. India 52-66; Lect Bp's Coll Calcutta 61-65; Ethiopia 66-68; C Horton *Bradf* 68-71; C Whitley Ch Ch *Ox* 71-72; P Missr Tilehurst St Mary CD 72-76; V Tilehurst St Mary 76-78; Canada from 78; rtd 92. *2306 Glazebrook Circle, Oakville ON, Canada, L6M 5B5* Tel (001) (905) 469 4652

SAPSFORD, John Garnet. b 38. **d** 76 **p** 76. C Whiteshill *Glouc* 76-81; Australia from 81. *11/24A Thomas Street, Ringwood, Vic, Australia 3134* Tel (0061) (3) 9876 0609 E-mail sapsford@melbpc.org.au

SAPWELL, Mrs Lynette. b 51. Sussex Univ BEd73 Middx Univ BA03. NTMTC 00. **d** 03 **p** 04. NSM Rochford *Chelmsf* from 03. *23 Briar Close, Hockley SS5 4HD* Tel (01702) 207167 E-mail lyn@sapwell.fsnet.co.uk

SARALIS, Preb Christopher Herbert. b 34. Univ of Wales BA54 St Cath Coll Ox BA56 MA60. Wycliffe Hall Ox. **d** 57 **p** 58. C Abergavenny St Mary w Llanwenarth Citra *Mon* 57-61; C Bridgwater St Mary w Chilton Trinity *B & W* 61-65; V Berrow 65-72; RD Burnham 72-76; R Berrow and Breane 72-76; V Minehead 76-92; RD Exmoor 80-86; Preb Wells Cathl 84-92; V Bovey Tracey SS Pet, Paul and Thos w Hennock *Ex* 92-99; rtd 99; Perm to Offic *B & W* from 99. *1 Broadway Road, Horton, Ilminster TA19 9RX* Tel (01460) 52416 E-mail saralis@fish

SARAPUK, Susan. b 59. Lon Univ BA80 Univ of Wales PGCE81. St Mich Coll Llan DPS90. **d** 90 **p** 97. C Morriston *S & B* 90-94; C Swansea St Pet 94-97; P-in-c Llangyfelach 97-98; V 98-02; C Sketty from 02. *13 Edison Crescent, Clydach, Swansea SA6 5JF* Tel (01792) 843521

SARGANT, John Raymond. b 38. CCC Cam BA61 MA70. Westcott Ho Cam 64 Harvard Div Sch 66. **d** 67 **p** 68. C Croydon St Jo *Cant* 67-72; Sec Zambia Angl Coun 72-75; P-in-c Bradford-on-Avon Ch Ch *Sarum* 76-81; V 81-90; TV Marlborough 90-03; Dioc Inter-Faith Adv 90-00; Can and Preb Sarum Cathl 92-01; rtd 03. *48 Summerhill Road, Lyme Regis DT7 3DT* Tel (01297) 445922

SARGEANT, Anthony. d 00 **p** 01. NSM Goostrey *Ches* from 00. *Greenbank House, Astbury Village Green, Congleton CW12 4RQ* Tel (01260) 272116

✠**SARGEANT, The Rt Revd Frank Pilkington.** b 32. St Jo Coll Dur BA55. Cranmer Hall Dur 57. **d** 58 **p** 59 **c** 84. C Gainsborough All SS *Linc* 58-62; C Gt Grimsby St Jas 62-66; V Hykeham 66-73; Dir In-Service Tr and Adult Educn *Bradf* 73-84; Can Res Bradf Cathl 73-77; Adn Bradf 77-84; Suff Bp Stockport *Ches* 84-94; Bp at Lambeth (Hd of Staff) *Cant* 94-99; rtd 99; Hon Asst Bp Eur from 99; Perm to Offic *Ches* from 99. *32 Brotherton Drive, Trinity Gardens, Salford M3 6BH* Tel 0161-839 7045 E-mail franksargeant68@hotmail.com

SARGEANT, George Henry. b 19. Bps' Coll Cheshunt 60. **d** 62 **p** 63. C Woodbridge St Jo *St E* 62-64; C Ipswich St Thos 64-68; C-in-c Gt w Lt Wratting 69-70; R 70-77; C-in-c Barnardiston 69-70; R 71-77; rtd 84; Lic to Offic *Nor* 90-99; Perm to Offic *Cant* from 02. *11 Langley Gardens, Cliftonville, Margate CT9 3EB* Tel (01843) 224788

SARGEANT, Kenneth Stanley. b 19. Lon Coll of Div 68. **d** 70 **p** 71. C E Ham St Paul *Chelmsf* 70-73; C Southborough St Pet w Ch Ch and St Matt *Roch* 73-77; Chapl Joyce Green Hosp Dartford 77-88; R Greenhithe St Mary *Roch* 77-88; rtd 88; Perm to Offic *Chich* from 88. *2 Westfield Close, Polegate BN26 6EF* Tel (01323) 488153

SARGEANTSON, Kenneth William. b 30. **d** 90 **p** 91. NSM The Marshland *Sheff* 90-93; NSM Goole 93-97; Perm to Offic from 97. *97 High Street, Swinefleet, Goole DN14 8AH* Tel (01405) 704256 E-mail kensergantson@aol.com

SARGENT, Miss Ann. b 65. **d** 98 **p** 99. C Bris St Andr Hartcliffe *Bris* 98-01; P-in-c Flax Bourton *B & W* from 01; P-in-c Barrow Gurney from 01. *The Rectory, Main Road, Flax Bourton, Bristol BS48 3QJ* Tel (01275) 461179

SARGENT, Charles Edward. b 68. K Coll Lon BD89 Leeds Univ MA96. Coll of Resurr Mirfield 94. **d** 96 **p** 97. C Notting Dale St Clem w St Mark and St Jas *Lon* 96-00; P-in-c S Kensington St Aug 00-04; Chapl Imp Coll 00-04; Chapl Brunel Univ from 04. *26 Church Road, Uxbridge UB8 3NA* Tel (01895) 203308 E-mail charles_sargent@priest.com

SARGENT, David Gareth. b 63. Sheff Univ BA85. Cranmer Hall Dur BA93. **d** 96 **p** 97. C Norbury *Ches* 96-01; V Hooton from 01. *Hooton Vicarage, Chester Road, Little Sutton, Ellesmere Port CH66 1QF* Tel 0151-339 2020 E-mail revdave.sargent@talk21.com

SARGENT, Derek Connor. b 66. TCD BTh99 St Jo Coll Nottm CertCS99 Cert Counselling 01. CITC 96. **d** 99 **p** 00. C Waterford w Killea, Drumcannon and Dunhill *C & O* 99-01; C 01-03; I Dublin Clontarf *D & G* from 03. *The Rectory, 15 Seafield Road West, Clontarf, Dublin 3, Irish Republic* Tel (00353) (1) 833 1181 E-mail clontarf@dublin.anglican.org

SARGENT, Preb Richard Henry. b 24. Man Univ BA50. Ridley Hall Cam 50. **d** 52 **p** 53. C Rusholme H Trin *Man* 52-54; C Cheadle *Ches* 54-59; V Cheadle Hulme St Andr 59-67; V Bushbury *Lich* 67-73; V Castle Church 73-89; RD Stafford 81-88; Preb Lich Cathl 87-89; rtd 89. *57 Deanshill Close, Stafford ST16 1BW* Tel (01785) 605335

SARGISSON, Conrad Ralph. b 24. Keble Coll Ox BA46 MA50. Wells Th Coll 48. **d** 50 **p** 51. C Charlton Kings St Mary *Glouc* 50-53; C Prestbury 53-55; V St Briavels 55-58; V Lanteglos by Fowey *Truro* 58-62; V Penzance St Mary 62-73; RD Penwith 72-73; V Westbury-on-Trym H Trin *Bris* 73-79; P-in-c Blisland w St Breward *Truro* 79-83; V Mylor w Flushing 83-91; rtd 91; Perm to Offic *Heref* 91-93; P-in-c St Hilary *Truro* 93-96; Perm to Offic from 96. *Cassacawn Farmhouse, Blisland, Bodmin PL30 4JU* Tel (01208) 850371

SARMEZEY, George Arpad. b 61. Qu Mary Coll Lon BA83 Goldsmiths' Coll Lon PGCE86. Westcott Ho Cam CTM92. **d** 92 **p** 93. C Eastville St Anne w St Mark and St Thos *Bris* 92-94; C Stratton St Margaret w S Marston etc 94-97; Asst Chapl Northn Gen Hosp NHS Trust 97-00; Sen Chapl from 00. *Northampton General Hospital, Billing Road, Northampton NN1 5BD* Tel (01604) 545773 Fax 544608 E-mail george.sarmezey@ngh-tr.anglox.nhs.uk

SARUM, Archdeacon of. *See* JEANS, The Ven Alan Paul

SASADA, Benjamin John. b 33. EAMTC. **d** 82 **p** 83. NSM Dickleburgh, Langmere, Shimpling, Thelveton etc *Nor* 82-88; NSM Diss 88-95; P-in-c Dickleburgh, Langmere, Shimpling, Thelveton etc 95-99; rtd 99; Perm to Offic *St E* from 84 and *Nor* from 99. *The Grange, Walcott Green, Diss IP22 3SS* Tel (01379) 642174

SASSER, Col the Ven Howell Crawford. b 37. Maryland Univ BA72 Geo Mason Univ Virginia MA74 Westmr Coll Ox MTh97. Washington Dioc Course 75. **d** 77 **p** 78. USA 77 and from 05; W Germany 77-80; Somalia 80-83; Cyprus 84-92; Chapl Montreux w Gstaad *Eur* 92-97; Chapl Oporto 97-05; Adn Gib 02-05; rtd 05. *11944 Artery Drive, Fairfax, VA 22030, USA*

SATTERFORD, Douglas Leigh. b 18. DSC42. Ripon Hall Ox 59. **d** 60 **p** 61. C Sanderstead All SS *S'wark* 60-65; V Lyminster *Chich* 65-85; V Poling 66-85; rtd 85; Perm to Offic *Chich* 85-88; *St E* 88-00; *Cant* 00-03. *5 Grovelands, Old Ashford Road, Lenham, Maidstone ME17 2QR* Tel (01622) 850675

SATTERLY, Gerald Albert. b 34. Lon Univ BA56 Ex Univ Hon BA. Wycliffe Hall Ox 58. **d** 60 **p** 61. C Southborough St Pet *Roch* 60-63; C S Lyncombe *B & W* 63-66; V Sheff St Barn *Sheff* 66-69; R Adwick-le-Street 69-73; V Awre and Blakeney *Glouc* 73-82; P-in-c Newnham 80-82; V Newnham w Awre and Blakeney 82-90; R Instow *Ex* 90-98; V Westleigh 90-98; rtd 98; Perm to Offic *Ex* and *Truro* from 99. *Tryst Lea, 2 Cameron Close, Maer Lane, Bude EX23 8SP*

✠SATTERTHWAITE, The Rt Revd John Richard. b 25. CMG91. Leeds Univ BA46. Coll of Resurr Mirfield 48. **d** 50 **p** 51 **c** 70. C Carl St Barn *Carl* 50-53; C Carl St Aid and Ch Ch 53-55; Asst Gen Sec C of E Coun on Foreign Relns 55-59; C St Mich Paternoster Royal *Lon* 55-59; P-in-c 59-65; Gen Sec C of E Coun on Foreign Relns 59-70; V St Dunstan in the West *Lon* 59-70; Hon Can Cant Cathl *Cant* 63-70; Gen Sec Abp's Commn on RC Relns 65-70; Suff Bp Fulham *Lon* 70-80; Bp Gib 70-80; Bp Eur 80-93; Dean Malta 70-93; rtd 93; Hon Asst Bp Carl 94-01 and from 04; Perm to Offic 01-04. *25 Spencer House, St Paul's Square, Carlisle CA1 1DG* Tel (01228) 594055

SAUL, Norman Stanley. b 30. St Aid Birkenhead 51. **d** 54 **p** 55. C S Shore H Trin *Blackb* 54-57; C Poulton-le-Fylde 57-59; PC Freckleton 59-66; V Blackb St Luke 66-68; V Barton 68-72; V Foxdale *S & M* 72-77; V Maughold 77-90; CF (ACF) 80-86; rtd 90; Perm to Offic *Blackb* from 90. *15 Croft Meadow, Bamber Bridge, Preston PR5 8HX* Tel (01772) 314475

SAUNDERS, Andrew Vivian. b 44. Leeds Univ BA65. Coll of Resurr Mirfield 66. **d** 68 **p** 69. C Goodmayes St Paul *Chelmsf* 68-71; C Horfield H Trin *Bris* 71-75; C Oldland 75-77; Ind Chapl *B & W* 77-80; P-in-c Buckland Dinham w Elm, Orchardleigh etc 77-78; P-in-c Buckland Dinham 78-80; V Westfield 80-90; R Clutton w Cameley 90-99; C Christchurch *Win* 99-05; rtd 05. *8 Mill House Court, Willow Vale, Frome BA11 1BG* Tel (01373) 467683

SAUNDERS, Barry. *See* SAUNDERS, John Barry

SAUNDERS, Brian Gerald. b 28. Pemb Coll Cam BA49 MA53. Cuddesdon Coll 63. **d** 66 **p** 67. NSM Gt Berkhamsted *St Alb* 66-87; P-in-c Lt Gaddesden 87-92; rtd 92; Perm to Offic *Ox* 92-94; *St Alb* from 92; *Pet* from 95; *Linc* from 01; Hon C Newton Longville w Stoke Hammond and Whaddon 94-01. *2 Bruce Close, Lincoln LN2 1SL* Tel (01522) 523193

SAUNDERS, Canon Bruce Alexander. b 47. St Cath Coll Cam BA68 MA72. Cuddesdon Coll 68. **d** 71 **p** 72. C Westbury-on-Trym H Trin *Bris* 71-74; Hon C Clifton St Paul 74-78; Asst Chapl Bris Univ 74-78; TV Fareham H Trin *Portsm* 78-84; TR Mortlake w E Sheen *S'wark* 84-97; RD Richmond and Barnes 89-94; Can Missr for Ch in Soc 97-03; Can Res S'wark Cathl from 03; C-in-c Bermondsey St Hugh CD from 03. *7 Temple West Mews, West Square, London SE11 4TJ* Tel (020) 7735 0143 *or* 7367 6706 Fax 7367 6725
E-mail bruce.saunders@southwark.anglican.org

SAUNDERS, David. b 28. Keble Coll Ox BA50 DipTh51 MA59. Cuddesdon Coll 51. **d** 53 **p** 54. C Mexborough *Sheff* 53-56; C Sheff St Cuth 56-60; V New Bentley 60-67; V Grimsby All SS *Linc* 67-78; V Caistor w Clixby 78-88; P-in-c Grasby 78-94; Chapl Caistor Hosp 78-94; P-in-c Searby w Owmby *Linc* 79-94; V Dunholme 88-92; P-in-c Welton and Dunholme w Scothern 92-94; rtd 94; Perm to Offic *Linc* from 94. *2 Oundle Close, Washingborough, Lincoln LN4 1DR* Tel (01522) 793164

SAUNDERS, Gareth John McKeith. b 71. St Andr Univ BD93 Edin Univ MTh99. TISEC 99. **d** 99 **p** 00. C St Andr Cathl *Ab* 99-03; C Edin St Salvador *Edin* from 03; C Edin Gd Shep from 03. *St Salvador's Rectory, 54 Drum Brae Park, Edinburgh EH12 8TF* Tel 0131-467 2418 Mobile 07732-356123
E-mail gareth@garethjmsaunders.co.uk

SAUNDERS, Geoffrey David. b 51. Bris Univ BSc73. Dioc OLM tr scheme. **d** 01 **p** 02. OLM Rockland St Mary w Hellington, Bramerton etc *Nor* from 01. *13 The Street, Rockland St Mary, Norwich NR14 7ER* Tel (01508) 538550
E-mail geoffsaunders@waitrose.com

SAUNDERS, Graham Howard. b 53. Hatf Poly BSc77. Trin Coll Bris BA86. **d** 86 **p** 87. C Birm St Martin w Bordesley St Andr *Birm* 86-89; C Olton 89-96; TV Bedminster *Bris* 96-02; P-in-c Farnham Royal w Hedgerley *Ox* from 02. *The Rectory, Victoria Road, Farnham Common, Slough SL2 3NJ* Tel (01753) 643233 Fax 644130

SAUNDERS, Ivor John. b 37. Wolv Poly CQSW81. **d** 04 **p** 05. OLM Wolverhampton St Jude *Lich* from 04. *34 Wrottesley Road, Wolverhampton WV6 8SF* Tel (01902) 751162
E-mail ivor.wendy@box3.fsnet.co.uk

SAUNDERS, James Benedict John. b 72. St Aid Coll Dur BA93 St Jo Coll Cam PhD97 St Jo Coll Dur BA00. Cranmer Hall Dur 98. **d** 01 **p** 02. C Sole Bay *St E* 01-04; P-in-c Teigh w Whissendine and Market Overton *Pet* from 04; Asst Chapl HM Pris Ashwell from 04. *The Vicarage, 3 Paddock Close, Whissendine, Oakham LE15 7HW* Tel (01664) 474864 Mobile 07952-498814
E-mail revjames@supanet.com

SAUNDERS, Mrs Joan Mary (Jo). b 44. Univ Coll Lon BA66 PGCE67. EAMTC 00. **d** 03 **p** 04. NSM Gt and Lt Casterton w Pickworth and Tickencote *Pet* from 03. *Mellstock, Bourne Road, Essendine, Stamford PE9 4LH* Tel (01780) 480479
E-mail josaunders@btinternet.com

SAUNDERS, John Barry. b 40. Chich Th Coll. **d** 83 **p** 84. C St Breoke *Truro* 83-84; C St Breoke and Egloshayle 84-87; V Treverbyn 87-96; RD St Austell 91-96; V Perranzabuloe 96-03; rtd 03; Perm to Offic *Truro* from 04. *48 Cormorant Drive, St Austell PL25 3BA* Tel (01726) 71994

SAUNDERS, Canon John Michael. b 40. Brasted Th Coll 66 Clifton Th Coll 68. **d** 70 **p** 71. C Homerton St Luke *Lon* 70-74; SAMS 74-97; Brazil 74-91; P-in-c Horsmonden *Roch* 91-97; Area Sec (SE England) SAMS 91-97; V Gillingham St Mark *Roch* from 97. *The Vicarage, Vicarage Road, Gillingham ME7 5UA* Tel (01634) 851818 Fax 570489
E-mail info@stmarkschurchgillingham.co.uk

SAUNDERS, Kenneth John. b 35. Linc Th Coll 73. **d** 75 **p** 76. C Boultham *Linc* 75-79; V Swinderby 79-87; V Cherry Willingham w Greetwell 87-95; P-in-c S Kelsey Gp 95-98; P-in-c N Kelsey 95-98; P-in-c Kelsey Gp 98-00; rtd 00; Perm to Offic *Linc* from 01. *Pew End, 17 Wentworth Drive, Dunholme, Lincoln LN2 3UH* Tel (01673) 862930

SAUNDERS, Malcolm Walter Mackenzie. b 34. Em Coll Cam BA58 MA62. Wycliffe Hall Ox 58. **d** 60 **p** 61. C Northampton St Giles *Pet* 60-63; C Northampton St Alb 63-66; V Corby St Columba 66-84; Nat Dir Evang Explosion 84-91; Lic to Offic *Pet* 84-91; V Ketton 91-92; R Ketton w Tinwell 92-01; rtd 01. *35 Main Street, Barrowden, Oakham LE15 8EQ* Tel (01572) 747036

SAUNDERS, Mrs Margaret Rose. b 49. Newnham Coll Cam BA71 St Jo Coll York PGCE72 Herts Univ Dip Counselling 96. St Alb Minl Tr Scheme 85. **d** 88 **p** 94. Hon Par Dn Gt Berkhamsted *St Alb* 88-90; Hon Chapl Asst Gt Ormond Street Hosp for Sick Children Lon 88-90; Asst Chapl Aylesbury Vale HA 90-92; Chapl Milton Keynes Gen NHS Trust 92-98; Chapl Milton Keynes Community NHS Trust 92-98; C Newport Pagnell w Lathbury and Moulsoe *Ox* 98-01; TV Grantham *Linc* 01-02; P-in-c Grantham, Manthorpe 02-04; Chapl United Lincs Hosps NHS Trust from 01. *2 Bruce Close, Lincoln LN2 1SL* Tel (01522) 523193 *or* 537403
E-mail margaret@saunderstd.fsnet.co.uk

SAUNDERS, Mark Richard. *See* VASEY-SAUNDERS, Mark Richard

SAUNDERS, Martin Paul. b 54. K Coll Lon BD76 AKC76 Univ of Northumbria at Newc DipSW96. Westcott Ho Cam 77. **d** 78 **p** 79. C Seaton Hirst *Newc* 78-81; Regional Chapl Hong Kong Miss to Seamen 81; C Egglescliffe *Dur* 81-82; Chapl to Arts and Recreation 81-84; C Jarrow 82-84; TV 84-88; V Southwick St Columba 88-94; Perm to Offic from 94. *55 The Meadows, Burnopfield, Newcastle upon Tyne NE16 6QW* Tel (01207) 271242 Mobile 07710-325197
E-mail martinsaunders@derwentheights.freeserve.co.uk

SAUNDERS, Martyn Leonard John. b 69. Magd Coll Cam MEng92. Wycliffe Hall Ox BA97. **d** 98 **p** 99. C Quinton Road W St Boniface *Birm* 98-02; TV Barnsbury *Lon* from 02. *5 Huntingdon Street, London N1 1BU* Tel (020) 7700 4097 *or* 7837 0720 E-mail martyn.saunders@london.anglican.org

SAUNDERS, Michael. b 38. Charing Cross Hosp Medical Sch MB, BS62 FRCPEd74 FRCP78 MSOSc84. NEOC 82. **d** 84 **p** 85. Lic to Offic *York* 84-92; Tutor NEOC 84-93; NSM Stokesley *York* 92-93; C Ripon Cathl *Ripon* 93-95; Perm to Offic *York* from 93; NSM Gt and Lt Ouseburn w Marton cum Grafton etc *Ripon* from 95. *College Grove, 2 College Lane, Masham HG4 4HE* Tel (01765) 866306
E-mail michael.saunders@btinternet.com

SAUNDERS, Michael Walter. b 58. CChem MRSC84 Grey Coll Dur BSc79. Wycliffe Hall Ox 86. **d** 89 **p** 90. C Deane *Man* 89-93; TV Eccles 93-02; Chapl Eccles Sixth Form Coll 96-02; Dioc Adv on Evang *Man* 98-02; C Yateley *Win* 02-03; C Yateley and Eversley from 03. *The Rectory, Glaston Hill Road, Eversley, Hook RG27 0LX* Tel 0118-973 6595
E-mail mikethevicar@thesaunders.plus.com

SAUNDERS, Moira Ruth Forbes. b 76. Birm Univ BA99. Ridley Hall Cam 02. **d** 04 **p** 05. C Welling *Roch* from 04. *52 Clifton Road, Welling DA16 1QD*

SAUNDERS, Canon Reginald Frederick. b 15. LNSM course 76. **d** 79 **p** 80. NSM Perth St Ninian *St And* from 79; NSM Stanley from 79; Hon Can St Ninian's Cathl Perth from 04. *31 Muirend Road, Perth PH1 1JU* Tel (01738) 626217

SAUNDERS, Canon Richard Charles Hebblethwaite. b 17. Qu Coll Ox BA40 DipTh41 MA42. Westcott Ho Cam 41. **d** 42 **p** 43. C Darnall *Sheff* 42-45; India 46-49; V Thornton-le-Street w Thornton-le-Moor etc *York* 49-52; V Eastwood *Sheff* 52-62; V Bris St Ambrose Whitehall *Bris* 62-75; P-in-c Easton All Hallows 65-68; TR E Bris 75-77; P-in-c Colerne 77-82; P-in-c N Wraxall 77-82; RD Chippenham 80-82; Hon Can Bris Cathl 82; rtd 82; Hon C Honiton, Gittisham, Combe Raleigh, Monkton etc *Ex* from 85. *St Michael's Cottage, Gittisham, Honiton EX14 3AH* Tel (01404) 850634

SAUNDERS, Richard George. b 54. BNC Ox BA76 MA81. St Jo Coll Nottm 82. **d** 85 **p** 86. C Barrow St Mark *Carl* 85-89; C Cranham Park *Chelmsf* 89-97; TV Kinson *Sarum* 97-00; TR from 00. *St Philip's Vicarage, 41 Moore Avenue, Kinson, Bournemouth BH11 8AT* Tel and fax (01202) 581135 *or* fax 581485 E-mail dick.saunders@ntlworld.com

SAUNDERS, Ronald. b 37. ACP67 St Pet Coll Birm CertEd62 CertRE62 Memorial Univ Newfoundland CertEd80 Columbia Univ MA82 PhD87 Cert Counselling 95. Sarum Th Coll 69. **d** 68 **p** 70. Malawi 68-72; Lic to Offic 68-70; C Blantyre 71-72; C Kensington St Mary Abbots w St Geo *Lon* 72-73; C

Bournemouth St Fran *Win* 73-75; Canada 75-81; I Twillingate 76; Lic to Offic 77-81; C Gt Marlow *Ox* 81-82; Area Org Leprosy Miss 82-85; V Penycae *St As* 85-87; TV Wrexham 87-89; Lic to Offic *Ox* 90-91; Chapl Morden Coll Blackheath 91-97; Master Wyggeston's Hosp Leic 97-03. *4 Visdelou Terrace, Shotley Gate, Ipswich IP9 1RP*

SAUNDERS, Sheila Lilian. b 42. **d** 03 **p** 04. OLM Walworth St Pet *S'wark* from 03. *9 Wooler Street, London SE17 2ED* Tel (020) 7252 5045 E-mail sheila.saunders3@btopenworld.com

SAUNDERS, Valerie. b 40. Bedf Coll Lon BSc62 Lon Inst of Educn PGCE63. **d** 03 **p** 04. NSM Dingwall *Mor* from 03; NSM Strathpeffer from 03. *Chessbury, 12 Firthview, Dingwall IV15 9PF* Tel (01349) 865445 E-mail chessbury@btopenworld.com

SAUNDERS, Ms Wendy Jennifer. b 49. S'wark Ord Course 86. **d** 95 **p** 96. Bp's Adv for Urban Min and Leadership *S'wark* 90-91; C Thamesmead 95-98; P-in-c Eltham St Sav from 98. *St Saviour's Vicarage, 98 Middle Park Avenue, London SE9 5JH* Tel (020) 8850 6829 Mobile 07802-603754 E-mail wendy.saunders@sunday.surfaid.org

SAUNT, James Peter Robert. b 36. Chich Th Coll 73. **d** 75 **p** 76. C Portland All SS w St Pet *Sarum* 75-78; P-in-c Bratton 78-81; V 81-94; Chapl HM Pris Erlestoke 80-94; P-in-c Oldbury *Sarum* 94-99; R 99-01; rtd 01; Perm to Offic *Sarum* from 02. *Elms, Waddon, Portesham, Weymouth DT3 4ER* Tel (01305) 871553

SAUSBY, John Michael. b 39. AKC. **d** 63 **p** 64. C Crosland Moor *Wakef* 63-65; C Halifax St Jo Bapt 65-67; V Birkby 67-77; V Holmfirth 77-89; TR Upper Holme Valley 89-01; rtd 01. *15 River Holme View, Brockholes, Huddersfield HD9 7BP* Tel (01484) 667228

SAVAGE, Andrew Michael. b 67. Wye Coll Lon BSc89 Cranfield Inst of Tech MSc91. Wycliffe Hall Ox 93. **d** 96 **p** 97. C Ecclesall *Sheff* 96-99; TV Kirk Ella and Willerby *York* from 99. *St Luke's Vicarage, 2A Chestnut Avenue, Willerby, Hull HU10 6PA* Tel (01482) 658974 E-mail savos@btinternet.com

SAVAGE, Canon Christopher Marius. b 46. Hull Univ MA94 FRSA99. Bps' Coll Cheshunt 66 Qu Coll Birm 68. **d** 70 **p** 71. C Battersea St Luke *S'wark* 70-75; TV Newbury *Ox* 75-80; R Lich St Mary w St Mich *Lich* 80-85; V Chessington *Guildf* 85-91; Ind Chapl *Win* 91-00; Chapl Basingstoke Coll of Tech 91-00; V Newc Ch Ch w St Ann *Newc* from 00. *The Vicarage, 11 Gibson Street, Newcastle upon Tyne NE1 6PY* Tel and fax 0191-232 0516 Mobile 07711-272567 E-mail cpsavage@btinternet.com

SAVAGE, Graham John. b 47. Univ of Wales (Ban) BSc69 PhD78. CITC 89. **d** 92 **p** 94. Lic to Offic *D & D* from 92; NSM Down Cathl 94-97; NSM Lecale Gp from 97. *7 Cedar Grove, Ardglass, Downpatrick BT30 7UE* Tel (028) 4484 1501

SAVAGE, Helen. b 55. Birm Univ BA76 Dur Univ BA82 MA90 Newc Univ MLitt83. Cranmer Hall Dur 80. **d** 83 **p** 84. C Newc St Gabr *Newc* 83-86; Adult Educn Adv 86-94; V Bedlington 94-04. *103 Holyfields, West Allotment, Newcastle upon Tyne NE27 0EU* Tel 0191-266 8782 E-mail hsavage@beeb.net

SAVAGE, Mrs Hilary Linda. b 48. RGN71 RM86. WMMTC 89. **d** 92 **p** 94. C Quinton Road W St Boniface *Birm* 92-96; P-in-c Edgbaston SS Mary and Ambrose 96-01; V 01-02; TV Cramlington *Newc* from 02. *1 Cateran Way, Cramlington NE23 6EX* Tel (01670) 714271

SAVAGE, Mrs Jennifer Anne. b 52. CertEd73. N Ord Course 96. **d** 99 **p** 00. C Haworth *Bradf* 99-02; R from 02. *The Rectory, 81 West Lane, Haworth, Keighley BD22 8EN* Tel (01535) 640293 *or* 642169

SAVAGE, John. b 48. Bris Univ BEd76. SW Minl Tr Course 94. **d** 97 **p** 98. C Falmouth K Chas *Truro* 97-00; P-in-c Mabe from 00; Chapl Miss to Seafarers from 00. *The Vicarage, Church Road, Mabe Burnthouse, Penryn TR10 9HN* Tel (01326) 373201

SAVAGE, Jonathan Mark. b 57. Kingston Poly BSc79 MSc89 Roehampton Inst PGCE80. Ridley Hall Cam 94. **d** 96 **p** 97. C Ely 96-99; TV Huntingdon from 99; C Gt w Lt Stukeley from 04. *The Vicarage, 3A Longstaff Way, Hartford, Huntingdon PE28 7XT* Tel (01480) 434463 E-mail marksavage@onetel.com

SAVAGE, Leslie Walter. b 15. Cranmer Hall Dur 63. **d** 65 **p** 66. C Stanwix *Carl* 65-69; V Bolton w Cliburn 69-74; V Holme *Blackb* 74-81; rtd 81; Perm to Offic *Chich* from 81. *42 Wilton Road, Bexhill-on-Sea TN40 1HX* Tel (01424) 223829

SAVAGE, Michael Atkinson. b 33. St Pet Hall Ox BA57 MA61. Tyndale Hall Bris 57. **d** 59 **p** 60. C Rugby St Matt *Cov* 59-62; C Welling *Roch* 62-66; V Bowling St Steph *Bradf* 66-73; V Ben Rhydding 73-92; RD Otley 87-92; TR Quidenham *Nor* 92-97; R Quidenham Gp 97-99; rtd 99; Perm to Offic *Bradf* from 00. *42 Hollins Lane, Utley, Keighley BD20 6LT* Tel (01535) 606790

SAVAGE, Paul James. b 58. Liv Univ BA81. Wycliffe Hall Ox 88. **d** 91 **p** 92. C Litherland St Phil *Liv* 91-94; CMS from 94. *Church Mission Society, Partnership House, 157 Waterloo Road, London SE1 8UU* Tel (020) 7928 8681 Fax 7401 3215

SAVEGE, Timothy. b 38. **d** 00 **p** 01. OLM Blyth Valley *St E* from 00. *2 Chequer Square, Bury St Edmunds IP33 1QZ* E-mail tim.savege@btinternet.com

SAVIGEAR, Miss Elfrida Beatrice. b 49. Wye Coll Lon BSc71 Edin Univ DipAE72 Bath Univ MSc85 Lambeth STh94. Trin Coll Bris Dip Th Studies 90 Ridley Hall Cam 91. **d** 93 **p** 94. C Ross w Brampton Abbotts, Bridstow, Peterstow etc *Heref* 93-97; P-in-c Butlers Marston and the Pillertons w Ettington *Cov* 97-99; P-in-c Alderminster and Halford 97-99; P-in-c Bicknoller w Crowcombe and Sampford Brett *B & W* 99-00; P-in-c Stogumber w Nettlecombe and Monksilver 99-00; R Quantock Towers from 00. *The Rectory, 11 Trendle Lane, Bicknoller, Taunton TA4 4EG* Tel (01984) 656262 E-mail elfrida@bicknollerrectory.freeserve.co.uk

SAVILE, Canon Ian Keith Wrey. b 26. Trin Hall Cam BA50 MA54. Ridley Hall Cam 51. **d** 53 **p** 54. C Bootle St Matt *Liv* 53-56; C Birkdale St Jo 56-57; V Barrow St Mark *Carl* 57-64; V Wandsworth All SS *S'wark* 64-74; RD Wandsworth 69-74; V S'well H Trin *S'well* 74-80; Bp's Adv on Evang 74-80; V Canford Magna *Sarum* 80-88; TR 88; RD Wimborne 85-88; Can and Preb Sarum Cathl 86-88; Patr Sec CPAS 88-93; rtd 93; Perm to Offic *Cov* 88-93 and *Sarum* from 93. *23A Avenue Road, Wimborne BH21 1BS* Tel (01202) 880210

SAVILL, David. b 27. TD69 and Bar 75. Em Coll Cam BA49 MA52. Ridley Hall Cam 50. **d** 52 **p** 53. Chapl St E Cathl *St E* 52-54; C St Martin-in-the-Fields *Lon* 54-57; V Sunbury 57-67; V Heston 67-73; Hon C Mettingham w Ilketshall St John *St E* 73-79; Hon C Mettingham 79-80; Chapl Felixstowe Coll 80-90; rtd 90; Perm to Offic *B & W* from 90. *30 Victoria Court, 2 Victoria Avenue, Chard TA20 1GA* Tel (01460) 239835

SAVILLE, Andrew. b 66. Worc Coll Ox BA92 MA92 Cov Univ PhD00. Wycliffe Hall Ox. **d** 95 **p** 96. C Tonbridge SS Pet and Paul *Roch* 95-99; NSM Bromley Ch Ch 99-03; Dir Bromley Chr Tr Cen 99-03; C Fordham *Chelmsf* from 03. *The Rectory, Wood Lane, Fordham Heath, Colchester CO3 9TR* Tel (01206) 242112 E-mail andy@savilles.org.uk

SAVILLE, Preb David James. b 39. Ch Ch Ox BA60 MA64. Clifton Th Coll 61. **d** 63 **p** 64. C Darfield *Sheff* 63-66; C St Leonards St Leon *Chich* 66-68; Cand Sec CPAS 69-74; Hon C Bromley Ch Ch *Roch* 69-74; V Taunton St Jas *B & W* 74-80; RD Taunton N 78-80; V Chorleywood Ch Ch *St Alb* 80-90; RD Rickmansworth 86-90; Adv for Evang Edmonton *Lon* 91-96; Dioc Adv for Evang 96-01; TR Hackney Marsh from 01; Preb St Paul's Cathl from 97. *St Barnabas' Rectory, 111 Homerton High Street, London E9 6DL* Tel (020) 8533 1156 E-mail david.j.saville@tesco.net

SAVILLE, Edward Andrew. b 47. Leeds Univ CertEd70 Open Univ BA75. Carl Dioc Tr Inst. **d** 90 **p** 91. C Accrington St Jo w Huncoat *Blackb* 90-93; C Standish 93-95; V Brierfield from 95; AD Pendle 98-05. *The Vicarage, 5 Reedley Farm Close, Reedley, Burnley BB10 2RB* Tel and fax (01282) 613235 E-mail e.saville@btinternet.com

SAVILLE (née McCULLAGH), Mrs Elspeth Jane Alexandra. b 68. Man Univ BSc90. Wycliffe Hall Ox BTh95. **d** 95 **p** 96. C Huddersfield H Trin *Wakef* 95-98; NSM Tonbridge SS Pet and Paul *Roch* 98-99; NSM Bromley Ch Ch 99-03; NSM Fordham *Chelmsf* from 03. *The Rectory, Wood Lane, Fordham Heath, Colchester CO3 9TR* Tel (01206) 242112

SAVILLE, Canon Jeremy David. b 35. Oriel Coll Ox BA59 MA62. Chich Th Coll 58. **d** 60 **p** 61. C Tynemouth Cullercoats St Paul *Newc* 60-63; C Hexham 63-65; Lic to Offic *Ox* 65-68; Chapl Cuddesdon Coll 65-68; R Holt *Nor* 68-73; P-in-c Kelling w Salthouse 68-71; R Edgefield 71-73; R Hoe 73-78; R E Dereham w Hoe 73-80; V E Dereham 80-81; R Scarning w Wendling 78-81; R Beckenham St Geo *Roch* 81-89; Hon Can Roch Cathl 86-89; R Ashdon w Hadstock *Chelmsf* 89-01; RD Saffron Walden 97-01; Hon Can Chelmsf Cathl 00-01; rtd 01; Perm to Offic *Nor* from 01. *8B Hillside, Sheringham NR26 8DB* Tel (01263) 820164

SAVILLE, Mrs Margaret. b 46. SW Minl Tr Course 93. **d** 94 **p** 95. C Over St Chad *Ches* 94-98; V Crewe All SS and St Paul from 98. *All Saints' Vicarage, 79 Stewart Street, Crewe CW2 8LX* Tel (01270) 560310

SAWARD, Canon Michael John. b 32. Bris Univ BA55. Tyndale Hall Bris. **d** 56 **p** 57. C Croydon Ch Ch Broad Green *Cant* 56-59; C Edgware *Lon* 59-64; Sec Liv Coun of Chs 64-67; Radio and TV Officer CIO 67-72; Hon C Beckenham St Jo *Roch* 70-72; V Fulham St Matt *Lon* 72-78; V Ealing St Mary 78-91; AD Ealing E 79-84; P-in-c Ealing St Paul 86-89; Preb St Paul's Cathl 85-91; Can Res and Treas St Paul's Cathl 91-00; rtd 01. *6 Discovery Walk, London E1W 2JG* Tel and fax (020) 7702 1130

SAWLE, Martin. b 49. Solicitor 74 Dundee Univ LLB70. N Ord Course 87. **d** 90 **p** 91. NSM Longton *Blackb* 90-92; P-in-c Hoghton 92-04; Perm to Offic from 04. *38 Chepstow Gardens, Garstang, Preston PR3 1TJ* E-mail martin@sawleandco.com

SAWLE, Ralph Burford. b 14. Lich Th Coll 34. **d** 37 **p** 38. C Sawley *Derby* 37-40; C Walthamstow St Barn *Chelmsf* 40-43; P-in-c Hanley All SS *Lich* 43-46; V Hanford 46-52; V Malins Lee 52-57; V Ocker Hill 57-61; V Werrington *Truro* 61-72; RD Trigg Major 66-72; V St Giles on the Heath w Virginstow 68-72; V St Neot 72-79; rtd 79; Perm to Offic *Win* from 79. *32 Cavendish Close, Romsey SO51 7HT* Tel (01794) 516132

SAWYER, Andrew William. b 49. AKC71 St Aug Coll Cant 71. **d** 72 **p** 73. C Farnham *Guildf* 72-75; C Dawlish *Ex* 75-78; R Colkirk w Oxwick, Whissonsett and Horningtoft *Nor* 78-82; R Colkirk w Oxwick w Pattesley, Whissonsett etc 82-90; V

Hungerford and Denford *Ox* from 90. *The Vicarage, Parsonage Lane, Hungerford RG17 0JB* Tel (01488) 682844

SAWYER, Derek Claude. b 33. ALCD58. **d** 58 **p** 59. C Kirby Muxloe *Leic* 58-60; C Braunstone 60-65; Mauritius 65-68; V Knighton St Mich *Leic* 68-82; Chapl Kifissia *Eur* 82; Lic to Offic *Glouc* 85-87; V Glouc St Aldate 87-01; rtd 01; R Capisterre w Dieppe Bay Town St Kitts from 01. *St Paul's Rectory, St Paul's Village, PO Box 539, Basseterre, St Kitts* Tel (001) (869) 466 6398 Fax as telephone E-mail raitasawyer@caribsurf.com

SAWYER, Graham Anthony Christian Paul. b 61. St Chad's Coll Dur BA82. **d** 98 **p** 02. C Roseneath New Zealand 98-99; Ind Chapl Sydney Australia 99-00; C Pontypool *Mon* 01-02; TV 02-03; C Newport St Andr 03-04. *Address temp unknown* E-mail graham.sawyer@excite.com

✠SAXBEE, The Rt Revd John Charles. b 46. Bris Univ BA68 St Jo Coll Dur PhD74. Cranmer Hall Dur 68. **d** 72 **p** 73 **c** 94. C Compton Gifford *Ex* 72-77; P-in-c Weston Mill 77-80; V 80-81; TV Cen Ex 81-87; Jt Dir SW Minl Tr Course 81-92; Preb Ex Cathl 88-92; Adn Ludlow *Heref* 92-01; Preb Heref Cathl 92-01; P-in-c Wistanstow 92-94; P-in-c Acton Scott 92-94; Suff Bp Ludlow 94-01; Bp Linc from 01. *The Bishop's House, 13 Eastgate, Lincoln LN2 1QQ* Tel (01522) 534701 Fax 511095 E-mail bishlincoln@claranet.co.uk

SAXBY, Martin Peter. b 52. St Jo Coll Dur BA77. Cranmer Hall Dur 74. **d** 78 **p** 79. C Peckham St Mary Magd *S'wark* 78-81; C Ramsey *Ely* 81-84; P-in-c Yaxham *Nor* 84-89; P-in-c Welborne 84-89; P-in-c Mattishall w Mattishall Burgh 84-89; R Mattishall w Mattishall Burgh, Welborne etc 89-90; V Rugby St Matt *Cov* from 90. *St Matthew's Vicarage, 7 Vicarage Road, Rugby CV22 7AJ* Tel (01788) 330442 *or* 330447 Fax 08701-391160 E-mail martinpa@stmatthews.org.uk

SAXBY, Steven Michael Paul. b 70. Fitzw Coll Cam BA98 MA02. Aston Tr Scheme 92 Linc Th Coll 94 Westcott Ho Cam 95. **d** 98 **p** 01. C E Ham w Upton Park St Alb *Chelmsf* 98-00; C Barking St Marg w St Patr 00-02; Waltham Forest Deanery Development Worker from 02; NSM Walthamstow 02-03; V Walthamstow St Pet from 03. *St Peter's Vicarage, 121 Forest Rise, London E17 3PW* Tel (020) 8520 3854 E-mail saxby@fish.co.uk

SAXTON, James. b 54. Lanc Univ BEd77 Hull Univ MEd85. Linc Th Coll 84. **d** 86 **p** 87. C Moor Allerton *Ripon* 86-90; C Knaresborough 90-92; TV Seacroft 92-95; V Ireland Wood 95-00; TV Becontree S *Chelmsf* from 02. *St Alban's Vicarage, Vincent Road, Dagenham RM9 6AL* Tel (020) 8595 1042

✠SAY, The Rt Revd Richard David. b 14. KCVO88. Ch Coll Cam BA38 MA41 Lambeth DD61 Kent Univ Hon DCL87. Ridley Hall Cam 38. **d** 39 **p** 40 **c** 61. C Croydon St Jo *Cant* 39-43; C St Martin-in-the-Fields *Lon* 43-50; Asst Sec C of E Youth Coun 42-44; Gen Sec 44-47; Gen Sec BCC 47-55; R Bp's Hatfield *St Alb* 55-61; Hon Can St Alb 57-61; Bp Roch 61-88; High Almoner 70-88; rtd 88; Hon Asst Bp Cant from 88. *23 Chequers Park, Wye, Ashford TN25 5BB* Tel (01233) 812720

SAYER, Derek John. b 32. St Steph Ho Ox 55. **d** 58 **p** 58. C Tottenham All Hallows *Lon* 58-61; C Letchworth *St Alb* 61-63; Chapl RADD 63-64 and 66-82; C Lancing St Mich *Chich* 64-66; C Dorking w Ranmore *Guildf* 89-92; V Holmwood 92-95; Perm to Offic 95-04; rtd 97. *Richeldis, 24 Chalkpit Lane, Dorking RH4 1ER* Tel (01306) 882610

SAYER, Canon William Anthony John. b 37. St Mich Coll Llan 60. **d** 64 **p** 65. C Gorleston St Andr *Nor* 64-67; P-in-c Witton w Ridlington 67-71; P-in-c Honing w Crostwight 67-71; V Bacton w Edingthorpe 67-71; CF 71-84; Miss to Seafarers from 84; R Holkham w Egmere w Warham, Wells and Wighton *Nor* 84-02; RD Burnham and Walsingham 87-92; Hon Can Nor Cathl 97-02; rtd 02; Perm to Offic *Nor* from 02. *Greenway Lodge, Mill Road, Wells-next-the-Sea NR23 1RF* Tel (01328) 711224

SAYERS, Karen Jane. b 69. Sheff Univ BMus90. Ripon Coll Cuddesdon 00. **d** 02 **p** 03. C Dunstable *St Alb* 02-05; TV Elstree and Borehamwood from 05. *The Rectory, St Nicholas Close, Elstree, Borehamwood WD6 3EW* Tel (020) 8953 1411 E-mail karen.sayers@talk21.com

SAYERS, Simon Philip. b 59. Cam Univ MA81. Oak Hill Th Coll 83. **d** 85 **p** 86. C Alperton *Lon* 85-89; C Hornsey Rise Whitehall Park Team 89-90; TV 90-96; P-in-c Digswell and Panshanger *St Alb* 96-98; Min Panshanger CD 98-02; R Warblington w Emsworth *Portsm* from 02. *The Rectory, 20 Church Path, Emsworth PO10 7DP* Tel (01243) 372428 E-mail simonsayers@hotmail.com

SAYERS, Susan. b 46. Bp Otter Coll Chich BEd69 Middx Univ BA02. NTMTC 99. **d** 02 **p** 03. NSM Southend *Chelmsf* from 02; Asst Chapl HM Pris Bullwood Hall from 02. *3 Fairview Gardens, Leigh-on-Sea SS9 3PD* Tel (01702) 478280 E-mail susansayers@yahoo.com

SAYLE, Philip David. b 61. Nottm Univ BA98. St Jo Coll Nottm Dip Th & Min 94. **d** 94 **p** 95. C Helston and Wendron *Truro* 94-97; R St Stephen in Brannel 97-00; R Kenwyn w St Allen from 00. *The Vicarage, Kenwyn Church Road, Kenwyn, Truro TR1 3DR* Tel (01872) 263015 Fax 240333 E-mail pdsayle@btinternet.com

SAYWELL, Philip. b 33. Linc Th Coll 57. **d** 60 **p** 61. C Stepney St Dunstan and All SS *Lon* 60-63; C Calstock *Truro* 63-66; V Lanteglos by Fowey 66-73; Iran 73-77; R Cockley Cley w Gooderstone *Nor* 78-81; V Didlington 78-81; R Gt and Lt Cressingham w Threxton 78-81; R Hilborough w Bodney 78-81; R Oxborough w Foulden and Caldecote 78-81; UAE 81-84; Perm to Offic *Chich* 84-88; Nat Co-ord (UK) SOMA UK 85-88; rtd 93. *Riverside, Exford, Minehead TA24 7PX* Tel (01643) 831619 Fax 831416 E-mail philip.saywell@virgin.net

SCAIFE, Andrew. b 50. Ex Coll Ox BA73 MA76. Wycliffe Hall Ox 74. **d** 77 **p** 78. C Everton St Geo *Liv* 77-81; P-in-c Liv St Mich 81; TV St Luke in the City 81-86; V Litherland St Phil 86-96; Snr Chapl Wirral Hosp NHS Trust from 96. *Arrowe Park Hospital, Upton, Wirral CH49 5PE* Tel 0151-678 5111 ext 2275 *or* 632 0646 E-mail andrew.scaife@whnt.nhs.uk

SCALES, Barbara Marion. b 24. S'wark Ord Course. **dss** 82 **d** 87 **p** 94. St Helier *S'wark* 82-87; Hon Par Dn 87-89; Chapl Asst St Helier Hosp Carshalton 82-88; NSM Cheam Common St Phil *S'wark* 89-95; rtd 95; Perm to Offic *S'wark* 95-04. *51 Tonfield Road, Sutton SM3 9JP* Tel (020) 8644 3712

SCAMMAN (née BEWES), Mrs Helen Catherine. b 71. Leeds Univ BA94 York Univ PGCE95 Cam Univ BA01. Ridley Hall Cam 99. **d** 02 **p** 03. C Win Ch Ch *Win* from 02. *8 Juniper Close, Winchester SO22 4LU* Tel (01962) 865051 E-mail scampersons@yahoo.com

SCAMMAN, Jonathan Leitch. b 73. St Andr Univ MA96 Ex Coll Ox MPhil98 Cam Univ BA01. Ridley Hall Cam 99. **d** 02 **p** 03. C Win Ch Ch *Win* from 02. *8 Juniper Close, Winchester SO22 4LU* Tel (01962) 865051 E-mail scampersons@yahoo.com

SCAMMELL, Frank. b 56. Cam Univ MA. St Jo Coll Nottm BA83. **d** 82 **p** 83. C Stapenhill w Cauldwell *Derby* 82-86; TV Swanage and Studland *Sarum* 86-92; Min Southgate LEP *St E* 92-03; V Stoughton *Guildf* from 03. *Stoughton Vicarage, 3 Shepherds Lane, Guildford GU2 9SJ* Tel (01483) 561603 E-mail frankpippa@hotmail.com

SCAMMELL, John Richard Lyn. b 18. TD50. Bris Univ LLB45. Wycliffe Hall Ox 46. **d** 48 **p** 49. C Bishopston *Bris* 48-50; C Stoke Bishop 50-52; RAChD 53-73; P-in-c Bicknoller *B & W* 73-78; P-in-c Crowcombe 75-78; R Bicknoller w Crowcombe and Sampford Brett 78-81; Perm to Offic *B & W* 81-93; *Guildf* 84-00; rtd 83. *49 Farmerie Road, Hundon, Sudbury CO10 8HA* Tel (01440) 786461

SCANDINAVIA AND GERMANY, Archdeacon of. *Vacant*

SCANLON, Geoffrey Edward Leyshon. b 44. Coll of Resurr Mirfield. **d** 76 **p** 77. C Beamish *Dur* 76-79; C-in-c Bishopwearmouth St Mary V w St Pet CD 79-81; USA from 81. *1226 North Vermilion, Danville, IL 61832, USA* Tel (001) (217) 442 1677

SCANTLEBURY, James Stanley. b 48. St Jo Coll Dur BA69 Heythrop Coll Lon MTh80. Westcott Ho Cam 70. **d** 72 **p** 73. C Upperby St Jo *Carl* 72-75; C Guildf H Trin w St Mary *Guildf* 75-77; Order of St Aug 77-86; Chapl Austin Friars Sch Carl 80-86; Chapl Mayfield Coll E Sussex 86-88; Chapl H Trin Sen Sch Halifax 88-90; NSM Ripponden *Wakef* 88-90; V Torpenhow *Carl* 91-94; V Allhallows 91-94; V Falmouth All SS *Truro* 94-98; V Harden and Wilsden *Bradf* 98-02; rtd 03. *5 Westhill Avenue, Cullingworth, Bradford BD13 5BB* Tel (01535) 272980

SCARBOROUGH, John Richard Derek. b 32. Lon Univ BA54. Cuddesdon Coll 68. **d** 69 **p** 70. C Fulbeck *Linc* 69-72; C Bassingham 73-74; Lic to Offic 74-76 and 78-93; R Boothby Graffoe 76-77; R Navenby 76-77; V Wellingore w Temple Bruer 76-77; V Graffoe 77-78; NSM Bassingham 93-97; NSM Aubourn w Haddington 93-97; NSM Carlton-le-Moorland w Stapleford 93-97; NSM Thurlby w Norton Disney 93-97; Perm to Offic from 97. *Hales Cottage, 47 High Street, Navenby, Lincoln LN5 0DZ* Tel (01522) 811031

SCARGILL, Christopher Morris. b 57. UEA BA79 York Univ MA81 Leeds Univ CertEd81 Nottm Univ BTh89. Linc Th Coll 86. **d** 89 **p** 90. C Desborough *Pet* 89-92; C Buxton w Burbage and King Sterndale *Derby* 92-93; TV 93-98; V Ipstones w Berkhamsytch and Onecote w Bradnop *Lich* from 98. *The Vicarage, Church Lane, Ipstones, Stoke-on-Trent ST10 2LF* Tel (01538) 266313 E-mail candsscargill@aol.com

SCARISBRICK, Mrs Helen. b 60. Sheff Univ BA81 Sheff Poly PGCE82 Chester Coll of HE BTh99. N Ord Course 97. **d** 99 **p** 00. C Norbury *Ches* 99-03; P-in-c Cheadle Heath from 03. *The Vicarage, 8 Tillard Avenue, Stockport SK3 0UB* Tel 0161-477 3541 E-mail helen.scarisbrick@btopenworld.com

SCARR, Hazel Anne. b 44. Guildhall Sch of Music & Drama. St Alb and Ox Min Course. **d** 00 **p** 01. NSM Adderbury w Milton *Ox* 00-04; NSM Chadlington and Spelsbury, Ascott under Wychwood 04-05; NSM Hardington Vale *B & W* from 05. *The Rectory, 38 Church Lane, Rode, Frome BA11 6PN* Tel (01373) 831234 E-mail hazel@jandhscarr.sagehost.co.uk

SCARTH, John Robert. b 34. Leeds Univ BSc55 CertEd St Jo Coll Dur DipTh65. Cranmer Hall Dur 63. **d** 65 **p** 66. C Dewsbury All SS *Wakef* 65-68; V Shepley 68-72; Asst Master Kingston-upon-Hull Gr Sch 72-78; St Mary's C of E Sch Hendon 78-81; V Ossett cum Gawthorpe 81-88; R Tarrington w

Stoke Edith, Aylton, Pixley etc *Heref* 88-96; rtd 96; Perm to Offic *Wakef* 96-97 and from 98. *44 Gagewell Drive, Horbury, Wakefield WF4 6BS* Tel (01924) 272055

SCARTH, Maurice John. b 31. MInstPS AMBIM. St Deiniol's Hawarden 81. **d** 83 **p** 84. C Llandrillo-yn-Rhos *St As* 83-87; V Rhosymedre 87-91; V Kerry and Llanmerewig and Dolfor 91-93; rtd 93. *Homelands, 11A Compton Way, Abergele LL22 7BL* Tel (01745) 833783

SCATTERGOOD, William Henry. b 26. **d** 56 **p** 57. C Gilgandra Australia 56-57; C Bourke 57-60; P-in-c Cobar 61-64; V Miriam Vale 64-67; R Balranald 67-74; R Hillston 74-76; 76-84; V Lonan and Laxey *S & M* 84-92; rtd 92; Perm to Offic *Chich* from 92. *18 Coldstream House, Bramber Lane, Seaford BN25 1AF* Tel (01323) 492203

SCEATS, Preb David Douglas. b 46. Ch Coll Cam BA68 MA72 Bris Univ MA71. Clifton Th Coll 68. **d** 71 **p** 72. C Cambridge St Paul *Ely* 71-74; Lect Trin Coll Bris 74-83; V Shenstone *Lich* 83-86; Dioc Tr Officer 86-91; P-in-c Colton 86-90; Dir Local Min Development 91-98; Warden of Readers 91-96; C Lich St Chad 94-98; Dioc Board of Min Team Ldr 96-98; Preb Lich Cathl 96-98; Prin NTMTC from 99; Preb St Paul's Cathl *Lon* from 02. *North Thames Ministerial Training Course, Oak Hill, Chase Side, London N14 4PS* Tel (020) 8364 9442 Fax 8364 8889 E-mail principal@ntmtc.org.uk *or* niblick@mashie-niblick.clara.co.uk

SCHAEFER, Carl Richard. b 67. Coll of Resurr Mirfield 91. **d** 94 **p** 95. C Ribbleton *Blackb* 94-98; V Blackb St Thos w St Jude from 98; P-in-c Blackb St Mich w St Jo and H Trin from 03. *The Vicarage, Didsbury Street, Blackburn BB1 3JL* Tel (01254) 263259 E-mail carl@schaeferc.freeserve.co.uk

SCHARF, Brian Howard. b 39. Alberta Univ BA60. Trin Coll Toronto 60 Coll of Resurr Mirfield 61. **d** 63 **p** 65. C Vancouver St Faith Canada 63-65; C Broadstairs *Cant* 65-68. *3236 Robinson Road, North Vancouver BC, Canada, V7J 3E9* Tel (001) (604) 987 0219 E-mail brianscharf@shaw.ca

SCHARF, Ulrich Eduard Erich Julian. b 35. Melbourne Univ BA59 MA67 Linacre Coll Ox BA67 MA72 Lon Univ PhD81. Ripon Hall Ox 65. **d** 67 **p** 68. C Hackney St Jo *Lon* 68-71; Lic to Offic 71-75; Bp Stepney's Chapl 71-75; P-in-c Shadwell St Paul w Ratcliffe St Jas 75-90; R St Geo-in-the-East w St Paul 79-86; P-in-c W Ham *Chelmsf* 90-95; V from 95. *The Vicarage, Devenay Road, London E15 4AZ* Tel (020) 8519 0955

SCHARIAH, Canon Zechariah. b 43. Zürich Univ BD87. Baptist Th Sem Rueschlikon 83. **d** 93 **p** 93. Chapl to Miss to Minorities from 93; Perm to Offic *Eur* from 95; Can Dar es Salaam from 00. *Waldstrasse 17, CH 6015 Reussbühl, Switzerland* Tel (0041) (41) 260 7502 *or* tel and fax 260 7509 E-mail karibumade@hotmail.com

SCHEMANOFF, Ms Natasha Anne. b 50. CertEd71 DipTh96. **d** 96 **p** 97. C Freshford, Limpley Stoke and Hinton Charterhouse *B & W* 96-99; TV Worle 99-00; V Kewstoke w Wick St Lawrence from 00; Bp's Adv for Racial Justice from 00. *The Vicarage, 35 Kewstoke Road, Kewstoke, Weston-super-Mare BS22 9YE* Tel (01934) 416162

SCHIBILD, Nigel Edmund David. b 47. Oak Hill Th Coll BA81. **d** 81 **p** 82. C Eccleston Ch Ch *Liv* 81-85; P-in-c Sydenham H Trin *S'wark* 85-87; V 87-91; Chapl Mildmay Miss Hosp 91-98; Assoc V Beirut All SS Lebanon 99-04; C Westminster St Jas the Less *Lon* from 05. *5 Goodyer House, Tachbrook Street, London SW1V 2QF* Tel (020) 7821 6166 Fax 7976 5408 Mobile 07947-047555 E-mail nigel.schibild@sjtl.org

SCHILD, John. b 38. ALCD64. **d** 64 **p** 65. C Cheltenham Ch Ch *Glouc* 64-67; Area Sec CMS *Sheff* and *S'well* 67-73; Area Sec CMS *Chelmsf* and *St Alb* 73-76; V Lt Heath *St Alb* 76-88; R Bedford St Pet w St Cuth 88-94; P-in-c King's Walden and Offley w Lilley 94-98; V 98-03; rtd 03. *Trenarren, St Cleer, Liskeard PL14 5DN* Tel (01579) 347047 E-mail john@schild.demon.co.uk

SCHLEGER, Ms Maria Francesca. b 57. LSE BA78 SS Coll Cam BA84 MA89. Westcott Ho Cam 82. **dss** 85 **d** 87 **p** 94. De Beauvoir Town St Pet *Lon* 85-90; Par Dn 87-90; TD Bow H Trin and All Hallows 90-94; Dean of Women's Min (Stepney Area) 90-94; Perm to Offic *Birm* 94-98; NSM Stepney St Dunstan and All SS *Lon* 99-03; Chapl Mildmay Miss Hosp from 03. *75 Lansdowne Drive, London E8 3EP* Tel (020) 7683 0051 *or* 7613 6300 ext 6170 E-mail schleger@waitrose.com *or* chaplain@mildmay.org

SCHLUTER, Nathaniel David. b 71. Pemb Coll Ox BA93 MA97 Green Coll Ox DPhil98. Wycliffe Hall Ox BA. **d** 00 **p** 01. C Gerrards Cross and Fulmer *Ox* 00-05; Prin Johannesburg Bible Coll S Africa from 05. *PO Box 374, Auckland Park, 2006 South Africa* E-mail info@johannesburgbiblecollege.org

SCHMIDT, Mrs Karen Rosemarie. b 48. Surrey Univ BSc70 Solicitor 76. STETS 96. **d** 99 **p** 00. NSM Lee-on-the-Solent *Portsm* 99-05; P-in-c Purbrook from 05. *The Vicarage, 9 Marrels Wood Gardens, Purbrook, Waterlooville PO7 5RS* Tel (023) 9226 6170 Mobile 07990-518541 E-mail karenrschmidt@yahoo.co.uk

SCHNURR, Jutta. *See* MUELLER-SCHNURR, Mrs Jutta

SCHNURR, Martin. b 67. **p** 02. Chapl (Asst) Bris Univ *Bris* from 02. *12 St Paul's Road, Clifton, Bristol BS8 1LR* Tel 0117-973 3963 Fax 954 6602 E-mail martin.schnurr@bris.ac.uk

SCHOFIELD, Andrew Thomas. b 47. K Coll Lon BD70 AKC71 PGCE72. St Aug Coll Cant 70. **d** 81 **p** 82. C Whittlesey *Ely* 81-84; C Ramsey 84-87; P-in-c Ellington 87-94; P-in-c Grafham 87-94; P-in-c Spaldwick w Barham and Woolley 87-94; P-in-c Easton 87-94; R March St Jo 94-05; P-in-c Duxford from 05; P-in-c Hinxton from 05; P-in-c Ickleton from 05. *The Rectory, 13 St John's Street, Duxford, Cambridge CB2 4RA* Tel (01223) 832137 E-mail andrew.schofield@ely.anglican.org *or* _atschofield@msn.com

SCHOFIELD, David. b 43. Linc Th Coll 74. **d** 75 **p** 76. C Gainsborough All SS *Linc* 75-78; R Bolingbroke w Hareby 78-79; P-in-c Hagnaby 78-79; P-in-c Hagworthingham w Asgarby and Lusby 78-79; P-in-c Mavis Enderby w Raithby 78-79; P-in-c E Kirkby w Miningsby 78-79; R Bolingbroke 79-81; C-in-c Stamford Ch Ch CD 81-90; V Crowle 90-97; V Crowle Gp from 97. *The Vicarage, Church Street, Crowle, Scunthorpe DN17 4LE* Tel (01724) 710268

SCHOFIELD, David Leslie. b 40. MISM89. EMMTC 98. **d** 01 **p** 02. NSM Derby St Mark *Derby* 01-04. *72 Bromley Cross Road, Bromley Cross, Bolton BL7 9LT* Tel (01204) 303137

SCHOFIELD, Edward Denis. b 20. **d** 61 **p** 62. C Addiscombe St Mildred *Cant* 61-63; P-in-c Croydon St Jas 63-64; V 64-66; V Boughton under Blean 66-75; P-in-c Dunkirk 73-75; V Boughton under Blean w Dunkirk 75-76; V Sandgate St Paul 76-85; rtd 85; Perm to Offic *Ex* from 95. *53 Haydons Park, Honiton EX14 8TA* Tel (01404) 42584

SCHOFIELD, Gary. b 64. Ripon Coll Cuddesdon 97. **d** 99 **p** 00. C Exhall *Cov* 99-02; V Wales *Sheff* from 02. *The Vicarage, Manor Road, Wales, Sheffield S26 5PD* Tel (01909) 771111

SCHOFIELD, John Martin. b 47. Selw Coll Cam BA69 MA73. St Steph Ho Ox 70. **d** 72 **p** 73. C Palmers Green St Jo *Lon* 72-75; C Friern Barnet St Jas 75-80; V Luton St Aug Limbury *St Alb* 80-89; V Biddenham 89-94; Dir CME 89-94; Dir Minl Tr *Guildf* 94-99; Can Res Guildf Cathl 95-99; Perm to Offic from 03. *1 Addley House, 72-78 Molesey Road, Hersham, Walton-on-Thames KT12 4RG* Tel (01932) 227642 E-mail johnscho@hotmail.com

SCHOFIELD, John Verity. b 29. Jes Coll Ox BA52 DipTh53 MA56. Cuddesdon Coll 53. **d** 55 **p** 56. C Cirencester *Glouc* 55-59; R Stella *Dur* 59-67; Kenya 67-69; Asst Chapl St Paul's Sch Barnes 69-70; Chapl 71-80; Australia 81-83; Gen Sec Friends of Elderly & Gentlefolk's Help 83-94; Perm to Offic *Sarum* from 83; rtd 94. *Bishops Barn, Foots Hill, Cann, Shaftesbury SP7 0BW* Tel (01747) 853852

SCHOFIELD, Nigel Timothy. b 54. Dur Univ BA76 Nottm Univ BCombStuds83 FRCO. Linc Th Coll 80. **d** 83 **p** 84. C Cheshunt *St Alb* 83-86; TV Colyton, Southleigh, Offwell, Widworthy etc *Ex* 86-94; V Seaton 94-03; P-in-c Beer and Branscombe 01-03; V Seaton and Beer from 03; RD Honiton 99-03. *The Vicarage, Colyford Road, Seaton EX12 2DF* Tel (01297) 20391

SCHOFIELD, Canon Rodney. b 44. St Jo Coll Cam BA64 MA67 St Pet Hall Ox BA70 MA73. St Steph Ho Ox 68. **d** 71 **p** 72. C Northampton St Mary *Pet* 71-76; V Irchester 76-84; Lesotho 84-86; R W Monkton *B & W* 86-00; Asst Dir of Ords 87-89; Dir of Ords 89-99; Preb Wells Cathl 90-00; Lect Zomba Th Coll Malawi 00-03; Can Upper Shire from 03; Perm to Offic *Sarum* from 04. *15 Johnson's Courtyard, South Street, Sherborne DT9 3TD* Tel (01935) 814932 E-mail rodney.schofield@gmail.com

SCHOFIELD, Ms Sarah. b 70. Man Univ BA95. Qu Coll Birm 95. **d** 97 **p** 98. C Longsight St Luke *Man* 97-02; Tutor (Man Ho) Westcott Ho Cam 00-04; P-in-c Gorton St Phil *Man* from 02; P-in-c Abbey Hey from 04. *St Philip's Rectory, Lavington Grove, Manchester M18 7EQ* Tel 0161-231 2201 E-mail sarahschof@aol.com

SCHOFIELD, Timothy. *See* SCHOFIELD, Nigel Timothy

SCHOFIELD, Mrs Victoria Louise. b 56. Liv Poly BSc88 Liv Univ PGCE91. Wycliffe Hall Ox 00. **d** 02 **p** 03. C Hattersley *Ches* 02-05; P-in-c Runcorn St Mich from 05. *145 Greenway Road, Runcorn WA7 4NR* Tel (01928) 500993

SCHOLEFIELD, John. b 27. Leeds Univ BSc50. Wells Th Coll 51. **d** 53 **p** 54. C Ossett cum Gawthorpe *Wakef* 53-56; C Hebden Bridge 56-58; V Sowerby St Geo 58-64; V Darton 64-70; V Stoke Gabriel *Ex* 70-84; P-in-c Collaton St Mary 82-84; V Stoke Gabriel and Collaton 84-92; rtd 92; Perm to Offic *Ex* from 92. *25 Droridge, Dartington, Totnes TQ9 6JQ* Tel (01803) 863192

SCHOLEFIELD, Mrs Judith Lenore. b 45. RN66 Open Univ BA97. WEMTC 99. **d** 04. OLM Ledbury *Heref* from 04. *Oakland Lodge, The Homend, Ledbury HR8 1AR* Tel (01531) 632279

SCHOLES, Ms Victoria Prichard. b 68. Man Univ BSc89. St Jo Coll Nottm 97. **d** 00 **p** 01. C Macclesfield St Jo *Ches* 00-02; NSM 02-03; Perm to Offic from 03. *37 Princes Way, Macclesfield SK11 8UB* Tel (01625) 425049

SCHOLEY, Donald. b 38. Leeds Univ CertEd60. Lich Th Coll 69. **d** 72 **p** 73. C Blaby *Leic* 72-75; TV Daventry w Norton *Pet* 75-78; R Wootton w Quinton and Preston Deanery from 78. *The Rectory, 67 Water Lane, Wootton, Northampton NN4 6HH* Tel (01604) 761891

SCHOLFIELD, Peter. b 35. Sarum Th Coll 64. **d** 66 **p** 67. C S Kirkby *Wakef* 66-69; P-in-c Carlton 69-90; rtd 90; Perm to Offic *Wakef* from 90. *31 Springhill Avenue, Crofton, Wakefield WF1 1HA* Tel (01924) 863430

SCHOLLAR, Canon Pamela Mary. b 39. Southn Univ DipEd80. S Dios Minl Tr Scheme 89. **d** 92 **p** 94. NSM Bournemouth St Andr *Win* 92-94; NSM Pokesdown St Jas from 94; Hon Can Win Cathl from 02. *22 Bethia Road, Bournemouth BH8 9BD* Tel (01202) 397925 E-mail schollar@ukgateway.net

SCHOLZ, Terence Brinsley. b 44. St Martin's Coll Lanc MA98. Carl and Blackb Dioc Tr Inst 94. **d** 97 **p** 98. NSM St Annes St Thos *Blackb* 97-01; NSM Broughton 01-02; Perm to Offic 02-04; NSM Freckleton from 04. *14 Further Ends Road, Freckleton, Preston PR4 1RL* Tel (01772) 632966 Fax 635779 Mobile 07768-441400

SCHOOLING, Bruce James. b 47. Rhodes Univ BA73. St Paul's Coll Grahamstown 76. **d** 76 **p** 77. S Africa 76-86; C Wanstead St Mary *Chelmsf* 87-90; V Leigh-on-Sea St Jas 90-04. *249 Woodgrange Drive, Southend-on-Sea SS1 2SQ* Tel (01702) 613429 Mobile 07710-208476 E-mail b.schooling@btinternet.com

SCHRIMSHAW, Angela Anna Violet. b 51. SRN73 SCM76 Hull Univ HVCert93 BSc98. NEOC 01. **d** 04 **p** 05. NSM Welton w Melton *York* from 04. *22 Bricknell Avenue, Hull HU5 4JS* Tel (01482) 446609 E-mail schrim@schrim.karoo.co.uk

SCHRODER, Edward Amos. b 41. Cant Univ (NZ) BA64. Cranmer Hall Dur DipTh66. **d** 67 **p** 68. C St Marylebone All So w SS Pet and Jo *Lon* 67-71; USA from 71; Dean Gordon Coll 71-76; Asst to Bp Florida 76-79; R Orange Park 79-86; R San Antonio from 86. *510 Belknap, San Antonio, TX 78212, USA* Tel (001) (210) 736 3132 Fax 733 1432 E-mail rector@cecweb.org

SCHRYVER, Mrs Linda Jean. b 56. Ch Ch Coll Cant BSc00. SEITE 00. **d** 03 **p** 04. NSM Willesborough *Cant* from 03. *2 Church Cottages, Canterbury Road, Godmersham, Canterbury CT4 7DS* Tel (01227) 730750 Mobile 07768-566372 E-mail schryverl@tiscali.co.uk

SCHULD DE VERNY, Dietrich Gustave. *See* DE VERNY, David Dietrich

SCHUMAN, Andrew William Edward. b 73. Birm Univ BA95 MSc96 Bris Univ PhD00 FRGS02. Trin Coll Bris BA03 MA04. **d** 04 **p** 05. C Shirehampton *Bris* from 04. *11 Severn Road, Shirehampton, Bristol BS11 9TE* Tel 0117-938 0779 E-mail aschuman@fish.co.uk

SCHUNEMANN, Bernhard George. b 61. LRAM83 K Coll Lon BD86 AKC86. Ripon Coll Cuddesdon 88. **d** 90 **p** 91. C Kirkby *Liv* 90-93; C St Martin-in-the-Fields *Lon* 93-97; Chapl Br Sch of Osteopathy 93-97; P-in-c Littlemore *Ox* from 97. *The Vicarage, St Nicholas Road, Oxford OX4 4PP* Tel (01865) 437720 Fax 437719 E-mail bschunemann@compuserve.com

✠**SCHUSTER, The Rt Revd James Leo.** b 12. Keble Coll Ox BA35 MA44. St Steph Ho Ox 36. **d** 37 **p** 38 **c** 56. Chapl St Steph Ho Ox 39-49; CF (EC) 40-46; S Africa from 49; Bp St John's 56-79; Asst Bp George from 80. *19 Aanhuizen Street, Swellendam, 6743 South Africa* Tel (0027) (291) 42115

SCHUTTE, Ms Margaret Ann. b 50. Natal Univ BA71. St Alb and Ox Min Course. **d** 04 **p** 05. C Overbury w Teddington, Alstone etc *Worc* from 04. *20 Cornfield Way, Ashton-under-Hill, Evesham WR11 7TA* Tel (01386) 882263 Mobile 07811-820190 E-mail schuttefamily@tesco.net

SCHWIER, Paul David. b 55. LNSM course 94. **d** 96 **p** 97. OLM Pulham Market, Pulham St Mary and Starston *Nor* 96-99; OLM Dickleburgh and The Pulhams from 99. *Street Farm, Pulham Market, Diss IP21 4SP* Tel (01379) 676240

SCHWIER, Peter Andrew. b 52. **d** 91 **p** 92. NSM Fressingfield, Mendham etc *St E* from 91. *Valley Farm, Metfield, Harleston IP20 0JZ* Tel (01379) 586517

SCLATER, Jennifer. **d** 02. Par Dn Elgin w Lossiemouth *Mor* 02-04; NSM from 04. *82 Pluscarden Road, Elgin IV30 1SU* Tel (01343) 556469

SCLATER, John Edward. b 46. Nottm Univ BA68 St Edm Hall Ox CertEd71. Cuddesdon Coll 69. **d** 71 **p** 72. C Bris St Mary Redcliffe w Temple etc *Bris* 71-75; Chapl Bede Ho Staplehurst 75-79; Chapl Warw Sch 79; P-in-c Offchurch *Cov* 79-80; Belgium 81-89; Willen Priory 89-91; C Linslade *Ox* 91-94; P-in-c Hedsor and Bourne End 94-02; rtd 02; Perm to Offic *B & W* from 03. *3 East Court, South Horrington Village, Wells BA5 3HL* Tel (01749) 671349 E-mail john@jes07.freeserve.co.uk

SCOBIE, Geoffrey Edward Winsor. b 39. Bris Univ BSc62 MSc68 Birm Univ MA70 Glas Univ PhD78 FRSA96 AFBPsS. Tyndale Hall Bris 62. **d** 65 **p** 66. C Summerfield *Birm* 65-66; C Moseley St Anne 66-67; Lect Psychology Glas Univ from 67; Hon C Glas St Silas *Glas* 70-83; P-in-c 83-84; Hon R 84-85; TR 85-86; Team Chapl 86-88; Hon Asst Team Chapl 88-99; Assoc P Bishopbriggs from 99. *3 Norfolk Crescent, Bishopbriggs, Glasgow G64 3BA* Tel 0141-722 2907 E-mail gscobie@educ.gla.ac.uk

SCOONES, Roger Philip. b 48. DipTh. Trin Coll Bris. **d** 82 **p** 83. C Childwall All SS *Liv* 82-85; Bradf Cathl *Bradf* 85-90; V Congleton St Pet *Ches* 90-96; P-in-c Congleton St Steph 94-96; R Stockport St Mary from 96. *St Mary's Rectory, Gorsey Mount Street, Stockport SK1 4DU* Tel 0161-429 6564 *or* 480 1815 Fax 429 6564 E-mail roger@scoones9.freeserve.co.uk

SCORER, Canon John Robson. b 47. Westcott Ho Cam 73. **d** 75 **p** 76. C Silksworth *Dur* 75-78; C Newton Aycliffe 78-82; V Sherburn 82-83; V Sherburn w Pittington 83-89; P-in-c Croxdale 89-93; Chapl Dur Constabulary from 89; Chapl Dur Police Tr Cen 93-05; Hon Can Dur Cathl from 04. *1 Vicarage Close, Howden le Wear, Crook DL15 8RB* Tel and fax (01388) 764938

SCOTFORD, Bethan Lynne. b 44. Univ of Wales (Cardiff) BA67 PGCE68 Man Metrop Univ Dip Educn Mgt 86. St As Minl Tr Course 95. **d** 99 **p** 00. Fieldworker (Wales) USPG from 98; C Guilsfield w Pool Quay *St As* 99-02; R Corwen and Llangar w Gwyddelwern and Llawrybetws from 02. *The Rectory, Ffordd ty Cerrig, Corwen LL21 9RP* Tel (01490) 412278 Mobile 07802-656607 E-mail 114153.2024@compuserve.com

SCOTLAND, Nigel Adrian Douglas. b 42. McGill Univ Montreal MA71 Aber Univ PhD75 CertEd75 Bris Univ MLitt85. Gordon-Conwell Th Sem MDiv70 Lon Coll of Div ALCD66 LTh74. **d** 66 **p** 67. C Harold Wood *Chelmsf* 66-69; USA 69-70; R Lakefield Canada 70-72; Lic to Offic *Ab* 72-75; Chapl and Lect St Mary's Coll Cheltenham 75-79; Sen Lect 77-79; Chapl and Sen Lect Coll of SS Paul and Mary Cheltenham 79-84; NSM Cheltenham St Mark *Glouc* 85-92; Field Chair RS Cheltenham and Glouc Coll of HE 89-01; Glos Univ from 01; Prin Lect from 96; Perm to Offic *Glouc* from 92. *23 School Road, Charlton Kings, Cheltenham GL53 8BG* Tel (01242) 529167 E-mail nscotland@chelt.ac.uk

SCOTLAND, Primus of the Episcopal Church in. *See* CAMERON, The Most Revd Andrew Bruce

SCOTT, Adam. b 47. TD78. Ch Ch Ox BA68 MA72 City Univ MSc79 Barrister 72 FRSA95 CEng81 MIEE81 FIEE94. S'wark Ord Course 73. **d** 75 **p** 76. MSE Blackheath Park St Mich *S'wark* from 75; Dean for MSE, Woolwich from 90; Prof Fell St Andr Univ *St And* 96-97 and from 98; Perm to Offic from 96. *19 Blackheath Park, London SE3 9RW,* or *The Gateway, North Haugh, St Andrews KY16 9SS* Tel (020) 8852 3286 *or* (01334) 462800 Fax (020) 8852 6247 *or* (01334) 426812 E-mail adam.scott@btinternet.com

SCOTT, Preb Allan George. b 39. Man Univ BA61. Coll of Resurr Mirfield 61. **d** 63 **p** 64. C Bradford cum Beswick *Man* 63-66; P-in-c 66-72; Hon C Bramhall *Ches* 72-74; Hon C Tottenham St Jo *Lon* 74-76; Hon C Bush Hill Park St Steph 76-79; R Stoke Newington St Mary 79-02; Preb St Paul's Cathl from 91; P-in-c Brownswood Park 95-97; rtd 04. *8 West Hackney House, 15 Northwold Road, London N16 7HJ* Tel (020) 7923 0153

SCOTT, Andrew Charles Graham. b 28. Mert Coll Ox BA57 MA. Wells Th Coll 57. **d** 59 **p** 60. C Rugby St Andr *Cov* 59-64; Chapl RN 64-68; C Prenton *Ches* 68-71; V Tow Law *Dur* 71-81; RD Stanhope 77-81; V Bampton w Clanfield *Ox* 81-95; rtd 95; Perm to Offic *Ex* from 95. *99 Speedwell Crescent, Plymouth PL6 5SZ* Tel (01752) 773570

SCOTT, Barrie. b 63. Birm Univ BA85 Goldsmiths' Coll Lon PGCE86. St Steph Ho Ox 93. **d** 95 **p** 96. C Tilehurst St Mich *Ox* 95-98; Perm to Offic *Birm* from 98. *29 Beechwood Road, Great Barr, Birmingham B43 6JN* Tel 0121-358 3877 *or* 373 4807

SCOTT, Basil John Morley. b 34. Qu Coll Cam BA59 Banaras Hindu Univ MA65. Ridley Hall Cam 58. **d** 60 **p** 61. C Woking St Pet *Guildf* 60-63; India 63-83; TR Kirby Muxloe *Leic* 83-89; Asian Outreach Worker (Leic Martyrs) 89-95; Derby Asian Chr Min Project *Derby* 95-00; rtd 00; Perm to Offic *Ely* from 00. *14 Scotsdowne Road, Trumpington, Cambridge CB2 2HU* Tel (01223) 476565 E-mail 100600.233@compuserve.com

SCOTT, Brian. b 35. CCC Ox BA58. Coll of Resurr Mirfield 59. **d** 61 **p** 65. C Carl St Aid and Ch Ch *Carl* 61-62; Asst Master Hutton Gr Sch 63-65; Perm to Offic *Leic* 65-67; Lic to Offic 67-70; P-in-c Theddingworth 71-78; V Lubenham 71-78; Asst Chapl Oundle Sch 78-83; R Barrowden and Wakerley w S Luffenham *Pet* 83-98; rtd 98; Perm to Offic *Leic* and *Pet* from 98. *The Cedars, 3 Glaston Road, Preston, Oakham LE15 9NH* Tel (01572) 737242

SCOTT, Charles Geoffrey. b 32. St Jo Coll Cam BA54 MA58. Cuddesdon Coll 56. **d** 58 **p** 59. C Brighouse *Wakef* 58-61; C Bathwick w Woolley *B & W* 61-64; V Frome Ch Ch 64-78; R Winchelsea *Chich* 78-93; R Winchelsea and Icklesham 93-95; rtd 95; Perm to Offic *Chich* from 95. *Hickstead, Main Street, Iden, Rye TN31 7PT* Tel (01797) 280096

SCOTT, Christopher. *See* DAVIES, Christopher

SCOTT, Christopher John Fairfax. b 45. Magd Coll Cam BA67 MA71. Westcott Ho Cam 68. **d** 70 **p** 71. C Nor St Pet Mancroft *Nor* 70-73; Chapl Magd Coll Cam 73-79; V Hampstead Ch Ch *Lon* 79-94; rtd 00. *49 St Barnabas Road, Cambridge CB1 2BX* Tel (01223) 359421

SCOTT, Canon Christopher Michael. b 44. SS Coll Cam BA66 MA70. Cuddesdon Coll 66. **d** 68 **p** 69. C New Addington *Cant* 68-73; C Westmr St Steph w St Jo *Lon* 73-78; V Enfield St Mich 78-81; V Effingham w Lt Bookham *Guildf* 81-87; R Esher 87-98; RD Emly 91-96; R Bude Haven and Marhamchurch *Truro* from 98; Hon Can Truro Cathl from 03. *The Rectory, 8 Falcon Terrace, Bude EX23 8LJ* Tel (01288) 352318

SCOTT, Christopher Stuart. b 48. Surrey Univ BA92 MBPsS92. Sarum & Wells Th Coll 79. **d** 81 **p** 82. C Enfield Chase St Mary *Lon* 81-82; C Coalbrookdale, Iron-Bridge and Lt Wenlock *Heref* 82-86; P-in-c Breinton 86-89; Chapl Hickey's Almshouses Richmond 89-01. *164 Sheen Road, Richmond TW9 1XD* Tel (020) 8940 6560

SCOTT, Claude John. b 37. Qu Mary Coll Lon BSc60 PhD64 Lon Inst of Educn PGCE61 FRSA94. EAMTC 88. **d** 91 **p** 92. NSM Heigham H Trin *Nor* 91-98; Perm to Offic from 98. *17 Lime Tree Road, Norwich NR2 2NQ* Tel (01603) 455686 E-mail cjscott@btinternet.com

SCOTT, Colin. b 32. Dur Univ BA54. Coll of Resurr Mirfield 58. **d** 60 **p** 61. C Wallsend St Pet *Newc* 60-64; C Seaton Hirst 64-68; C Longbenton St Bart 68-70; V Benwell St Aid 70-77; V Sleekburn 77-89; P-in-c Cambois 77-88; V Longhoughton w Howick 89-96; rtd 96; Perm to Offic *Newc* from 96. *Pele Cottage, Hepple, Morpeth NE65 7LH* Tel (01669) 640258

✠**SCOTT, The Rt Revd Colin John Fraser.** b 33. Qu Coll Cam BA56 MA60. Ridley Hall Cam 56. **d** 58 **p** 59 **c** 84. C Clapham Common St Barn *S'wark* 58-61; C Hatcham St Jas 61-64; V Kennington St Mark 64-71; RD Lambeth 68-71; Vice-Chmn Dioc Past Cttee 71-77; Hon Can S'wark Cathl 73-84; TR Sanderstead All SS 77-84; Suff Bp Hulme *Man* 84-98; Chmn CCC 94-98; rtd 99; Hon Asst Bp Leic from 99; Perm to Offic *Derby* from 00. *The Priest House, Prior Park Road, Ashby-de-la-Zouch LE65 1BH* Tel (01530) 564403

SCOTT, Cuthbert Le Messurier. b 13. Wells Th Coll 60. **d** 61 **p** 62. C Highgate St Mich *Lon* 61-64; V Paddington St Jo w St Mich 64-72; V Shamley Green *Guildf* 72-83; rtd 83; Perm to Offic *Chich* 84-88 and from 95; Chapl St Dunstan's Hosp Brighton 88-95. *30 Manormead, Tilford Road, Hindhead GU26 6RA* Tel (01428) 604780

SCOTT, David. b 40. Rhodes Univ BA63. St Paul's Coll Grahamstown LTh65. **d** 65 **p** 66. S Africa 65-91; TV Cheltenham St Mark *Glouc* 92-96; R Swanscombe *Roch* from 96. *The Rectory, Swanscombe Street, Swanscombe DA10 0JZ* Tel (01322) 843160 E-mail davidscott@stpeterandstpaul.org.uk

SCOTT, Canon David Victor. b 47. St Chad's Coll Dur BA69. Cuddesdon Coll 69. **d** 71 **p** 72. C St Mary-at-Latton *Chelmsf* 71-73; Chapl Haberdashers' Aske's Sch Elstree 73-80; V Torpenhow *Carl* 80-91; V Allhallows 80-91; R Win St Lawr and St Maurice w St Swithun *Win* from 91; Warden Sch of Spirituality Win from 91; Hon Can Win Cathl from 02. *The Rectory, Colebrook Street, Winchester SO23 9LH* Tel (01962) 868056

SCOTT, Mrs Erica Jane. b 58. Trin Coll Bris BA02. **d** 02 **p** 03. C Ilminster and Distr *B & W* from 02. *145 Blackdown View, Ilminster TA19 0BG* Tel (01460) 53427 E-mail scott@ericaj.fsnet.co.uk

SCOTT, Francis Richard. b 63. St Jo Coll Nottm. **d** 00 **p** 01. C Huntington *York* 00-03; TV from 03. *402 Huntington Road, Huntington, York YO31 9HU* Tel (01904) 631345 E-mail fandfscott@aol.com

SCOTT, Gary James. b 61. Edin Univ BD87. Edin Th Coll 85. **d** 87 **p** 88. C Edin St Cuth *Edin* 87-90; R Peebles 90-92; P-in-c Innerleithen 92-96; R Penicuik 96-98; R W Linton 96-98; Lic to Offic from 98. *3 Crossburn Farm Road, Peebles EH45 8EG* Tel (01721) 721886

SCOTT, Geoffrey. *See* SCOTT, Charles Geoffrey

SCOTT, Canon Gordon. b 30. Man Univ BA51. St Jo Coll Dur 51. **d** 53 **p** 54. C Monkwearmouth St Andr *Dur* 53-55; C Stranton 55-56; C Chester le Street 56-59; V Marley Hill 59-62; Chapl Forest Sch Snaresbrook 62-66; Chapl Dunrobin Sch Sutherland 66-72; Chapl Pocklington Sch York 72-74; V Barton w Pooley Bridge *Carl* 74-80; RD Penrith 79-82; P-in-c Lazonby 80; R Gt Salkeld w Lazonby 80-90; Hon Can Carl Cathl 83-94; P-in-c Patterdale 90-94; rtd 94; Perm to Offic *Carl* 94-97. *48 Lakeland Park, Keswick CA12 4AT* Tel (01768) 775862

SCOTT, Guy Charles. b 61. Coll of Resurr Mirfield. **d** 00 **p** 01. C Abington *Pet* 00-03; P-in-c Mullion *Truro* from 03; C Cury and Gunwalloe w Mawgan from 03. *The Vicarage, Nansmellyon Road, Mullion, Helston TR12 7DH* Tel (01326) 240325

SCOTT, Mrs Helen Ruth. b 59. Surrey Univ BA97 K Coll Lon MA99 St Thos Hosp Lon SRN81 R Shrewsbury Hosp RM85. S'wark Ord Course DipRS92. **d** 92 **p** 94. NSM Richmond St Mary w St Matthias and St Jo *S'wark* 92-01; Chapl Hickey's Almshouses Richmond from 01. *164 Sheen Road, Richmond TW9 1XD* Tel (020) 8940 6560

SCOTT, Ian. b 45. MBChA87 MSSCh87. Qu Coll Birm 92. **d** 94 **p** 95. C Cropthorne w Charlton *Worc* 94-97; Asst Chapl Univ Hosp Birm NHS Trust 98-99; Chapl S Warks Combined Care NHS Trust 99-02; Chapl Worcs Acute Hosps NHS Trust from 02. *Kidderminster Hospital, Bewdley Road, Kidderminster DY11 6RJ* Tel (01562) 823424 E-mail ian.scott@worcsacute.wmids.nhs.uk

SCOTT, Ian Michael. b 25. Bris Univ BA50 Leic Univ DipEd51 Open Univ MA99. Bps' Coll Cheshunt 52. **d** 53 **p** 54. C Rotherhithe St Mary w All SS *S'wark* 53-55; C Lavender Hill Ascension 55-59; C Camberwell St Mich w All So w Em 59-60; C Kettering St Mary *Pet* 60-63; V Haverstock Hill H Trin w Kentish Town St Barn *Lon* 63-93; rtd 93; Perm to Offic *Nor* 93-96. *Los Molinos 8, 03726 Benitachell, Alicante, Spain* Tel (0034) (96) 574 1342 E-mail ian_benitachell@yahoo.co.uk

SCOTT, Mrs Inez Margaret Gillette. b 26. St Alb Minl Tr Scheme 76. **dss** 79 **d** 87 **p** 94. Preston w Sutton Poyntz and Osmington w Poxwell *Sarum* 83-86; Dorchester 86-96; Par Dn 87-88; NSM 88-96; rtd 88; Perm to Offic *Sarum* from 96. *14 Came View Road, Dorchester DT1 2AE* Tel (01305) 267547

SCOTT, James Alexander Gilchrist. b 32. Linc Coll Ox BA56 MA60. Wycliffe Hall Ox 56. **d** 58 **p** 59. C Shipley St Paul *Bradf* 58-61; Abp's Dom Chapl *York* 61-65; Brazil 65-68; V Grassendale *Liv* 68-77; V Thorp Arch w Walton *York* 77-89; RD Tadcaster 78-86; Chapl HM Pris Rudgate 77-82; Askham Grange 82-87; V Kirk Ella 89-92; TR 92-97; rtd 97; Perm to Offic *York* from 98. *Mount Royd, Potter Hill, Pickering YO18 8AD* Tel (01751) 476226

SCOTT, James William. b 39. S Dios Minl Tr Scheme 84. **d** 88 **p** 89. NSM Bremhill w Foxham and Hilmarton *Sarum* 88-94; NSM Derry Hill w Bremhill and Foxham from 94. *14 Bremhill, Calne SN11 9LA* Tel (01249) 813114

SCOTT, Mrs Janice Beasant. b 44. MCSP66 Middx Hosp Physiotherapy Sch Dip Town Planning 70. EAMTC 89. **d** 92 **p** 94. NSM Fakenham w Alethorpe *Nor* 92-95; C Eaton 95-99; R Dickleburgh and The Pulhams from 99; RD Redenhall from 03. *The Rectory, Station Road, Pulham Market, Diss IP21 4TE* Tel (01379) 676256 Mobile 07905-039243 E-mail revjanice@scott347.freeserve.co.uk

SCOTT, John. *See* SCOTT, The Ven William John

SCOTT, John. b 54. QUB BD79. CITC 80. **d** 81 **p** 82. C Willowfield *D & D* 81-83; C Newtownards 83-85; I Kilskeery w Trillick *Clogh* 85-90; Lic to Offic *D & D* 90-96; I Bright w Ballee and Killough 96-01; Perm to Offic from 01. *Ash Tree House, Moor Road, Ballyward, Castlewellan BT31 9TY* E-mail rev.john@virgin.net

SCOTT, John. b 54. Heriot-Watt Univ BA76 Leeds Univ BA97. Coll of Resurr Mirfield 95. **d** 97 **p** 98. C Bethnal Green St Matt w St Jas the Gt *Lon* 97-00; Asst Chapl Qu Mary and Westf Coll 97-00; C Heston 00-04; Inter-Faith Adv from 00. *73 Chilton Street, London W1U 6NW* Tel (020) 7935 8404 Mobile 07889-977593 E-mail jscott@no25.demon.co.uk

SCOTT, John David. b 52. St Jo Coll Ox BA74 MA78 Leeds Univ BA78. Coll of Resurr Mirfield 76. **d** 78 **p** 79. C Oundle *Pet* 78-81; C Dalston H Trin w St Phil *Lon* 81-85; V Ponders End St Matt 85-91; Chapl Bede Ho Staplehurst 91-03; Perm to Offic *Can* from 03 and *Lon* from 04. *1 The Cloisters, Gordon Square, London WC1H 0AG* Tel (01303) 240187 Mobile 07906-653807 E-mail john.scott@forwardinfaith.com

SCOTT, John Eric. b 16. FSA St Cath Coll Ox BA38 MA42. Ripon Hall Ox 39. **d** 40 **p** 41. C Heworth St Alb *Dur* 40-43; C Gateshead St Mary 43-45; Chapl and Sacr Ch Ch *Ox* 45-47; Ho Master Forest Sch Snaresbrook 55-81; P-in-c St Mich Cornhill w St Pet le Poer etc *Lon* 81-85; rtd 85. *17 Harman Avenue, Woodford Green IG8 9DS* Tel (020) 8505 7093

SCOTT, Preb John Gilbert Mortimer. b 25. St Edm Hall Ox BA49 MA52. Bps' Coll Cheshunt. **d** 51 **p** 52. C Ex St Thos *Ex* 51-54; C Wolborough w Newton Abbot 54-58; V Clawton 58-66; R Tetcott w Luffincott 58-66; RD Holsworthy 65-66; V Newton St Cyres 66-84; RD Cadbury 81-84; Preb Ex Cathl 84-02; P-in-c Bampton 84; P-in-c Clayhanger 84; P-in-c Petton 84; V Bampton, Morebath, Clayhanger and Petton 84-91; rtd 91. *Trelake, Bridgetown Hill, Totnes TQ9 5BA* Tel (01803) 867754

SCOTT, John Harold. b 46. Univ of Wales (Cardiff) BSc69. St Steph Ho Ox 69. **d** 72 **p** 73. C Skewen *Llan* 72-74; C Port Talbot St Theodore 74-77; P-in-c Bedlinog 77-78; V 78-85; R Penderyn w Ystradfellte and Pontneathvaughan *S & B* 85-04; R Penderyn Mellte from 04. *The Vicarage, Ystradfellte, Aberdare CF44 9JE* Tel (01639) 720405 Mobile 07711-961667 E-mail jhs46@tesco.net

SCOTT, John Peter. b 47. Open Univ BA80. Lambeth STh81 K Coll Lon 69 St Aug Coll Cant 74. **d** 75 **p** 76. C Dartford St Alb *Roch* 75-78; C-in-c Goring-by-Sea *Chich* 78-81; Chapl Wells and Meare Manor Hosps 81-86; CF (TAVR) 82-90; Chapl Pangbourne Coll 86-90; Min Reigate St Phil CD *S'wark* 90-92; P-in-c Reigate St Phil from 92; Chapl St Bede's Ecum Sch Reigate from 90. *The Parsonage, 102A Nutley Lane, Reigate RH2 9HA* Tel (01737) 244542

SCOTT, John Vickers. b 48. Open Univ BA88 MCIOB81. Carl and Blackb Dioc Tr Inst 02. **d** 05. NSM Penwortham St Leon *Blackb* from 05. *10 Cuerden Rise, Lostock Hall, Preston PR5 5YD* Tel and fax (01772) 490225 Mobile 07977-049829 E-mail scottjv@blueyonder.co.uk

SCOTT (née GOLDIE), Katrina Ruth. b 76. Fitzw Coll Cam BA97 MPhil00 MA01. Westcott Ho Cam 98. **d** 00 **p** 01. C Cov E *Cov* 00-04; V Willenhall from 04. *Willenhall Vicarage, Robin Hood Road, Coventry CV3 3AY* Tel (024) 7630 3266 E-mail katrinagoldie@hotmail.com

SCOTT, Keith Brounton de Salve. b 55. QUB BD. DipTh. **d** 83 **p** 84. C Belfast St Matt *Conn* 83-87; I Ardclinis and Tickmacrevan w Layde and Cushendun 87-01. *20 Princess Gardens, Holywood, Belfast BT18 0PN* Tel (028) 9042 2266 E-mail keithbscott@msn.com

SCOTT, Kenneth James. b 46. Bris Univ BA68. Trin Coll Bris 71. **d** 73 **p** 74. C Illogan *Truro* 73-76; C Camberley St Paul *Guildf* 76-81; R Bradford Peverell, Stratton, Frampton etc *Sarum* from 81; RD Dorchester 95-99. *The Rectory, Church Lane, Frampton, Dorchester DT2 9NL* Tel and fax (01300) 320429 E-mail kenscott@surfaid.org

SCOTT, Kevin Francis. b 51. Peterho Cam MA Mert Coll Ox DPhil76 CChem MRSC. Wycliffe Hall Ox BA83. **d** 83 **p** 84. C Ox St Ebbe w H Trin and St Pet *Ox* 83-86; P-in-c Prestonpans *Edin* 86-93; R Musselburgh 86-93; R Edin SS Phil and Jas from 93. *The Rectory, 5 Wardie Road, Edinburgh EH5 3QE* Tel 0131-552 4300 E-mail drkfs@aol.com

SCOTT, Kevin Peter. b 43. Reigate Coll of Art DipAD73. Coll of Resurr Mirfield 93. **d** 93 **p** 94. C Rushall *Lich* 93-97; P-in-c Goldenhill from 97. *St John's Vicarage, Drummond Street, Stoke-on-Trent ST6 5RF* Tel (01782) 782736

SCOTT, Kevin Willard. b 53. Westhill Coll Birm CYCW77 Open Univ BA96 Glos Univ MA03. Linc Th Coll 92. **d** 92 **p** 93. C Walton-on-Thames *Guildf* 92-97; R Matson *Glouc* 97-03; RD Glouc City 01-03; V Malden St Jo *S'wark* from 03; AD Kingston from 05. *5 Vicarage Close, Worcester Park KT4 7LZ* Tel (020) 8337 8830 E-mail kevinscott@fish.co.uk

SCOTT, Laurence Stanley. b 33. Open Univ BSc99. **d** 05. NSM Calstock *Truro* from 05. *88 Priory Close, Tavistock PL19 9DG* Tel (01822) 613227

SCOTT, Lester Desmond Donald. NUI BA89. CITC BTh92. **d** 92 **p** 93. C Killeshandra w Killegar and Derrylane *K, E & A* 92-95; C Kilmore w Ballintemple 92-95; I Fenagh w Myshall, Aghade and Ardoyne *C & O* from 95. *The Glebe House, Ballon, Carlow, Irish Republic* Tel and fax (00353) (59) 915 9367 Mobile 87-250 4322 E-mail lesterscott@oceanfree.net

SCOTT (née CURRELL), Mrs Linda Anne. b 62. K Alfred's Coll Win BEd84. Trin Coll Bris BA92. **d** 92 **p** 94. Par Dn Tunbridge Wells St Mark *Roch* 92-94; C 94-97; TV Walthamstow *Chelmsf* 97-02; Perm to Offic *Chelmsf* 02-04 and *S'wark* from 05. *35 Oswin Street, London SE11 4TF* Tel (020) 7735 4077 E-mail scottlindatim@aol.com

SCOTT, Canon Malcolm Kenneth Merrett. b 30. ACA53 FCA64. Clifton Th Coll 56. **d** 58 **p** 59. C Highbury Ch Ch *Lon* 58-60; CMS 60-61; Uganda 61-74; V Sunnyside w Bourne End *St Alb* 74-90; V Clapham 90-95; rtd 95. *10 The Ring, Little Haywood, Stafford ST18 0TP* Tel (01889) 881464

SCOTT, Nicholas Charles Andrew. b 74. Univ of Wales (Ban) BD95. Westcott Ho Cam 97. **d** 99 **p** 00. C Ryde H Trin and Swanmore St Mich *Portsm* 99-01; C Burbage w Aston Flamville *Leic* 01-04. *Willenhall Vicarage, Robin Hood Road, Coventry CV3 3AY* Tel (024) 7630 3266 E-mail ncascott@hotmail.com

SCOTT, Paul Malcolm. b 57. Sheff City Poly BA79 CPFA85. Ripon Coll Cuddesdon 98. **d** 00 **p** 01. C N Shields *Newc* 00-03; V Shiremoor from 03. *St Mark's Vicarage, Brenkley Avenue, Shiremoor, Newcastle upon Tyne NE27 0PP* Tel 0191-253 3291 E-mail paulmscott@scott2.freeserve.co.uk

SCOTT, Pauline Claire Michalak. b 55. St Anne's Coll Ox BA77 MA82 Dur Univ PGCE78. TISEC 98. **d** 01 **p** 02. NSM Papworth *Ely* from 01. *16 Granary Way, Cambourne, Cambridge CB3 6BQ* Tel (01954) 200795 Mobile 07855-395840 E-mail pauline.cm.scott@ntlworld.com

SCOTT, Peter Crawford. b 35. Ch Ch Ox BA56 MA61. Cuddesdon Coll 60. **d** 62 **p** 63. C Broseley w Benthall *Heref* 62-66; P-in-c Hughenden *Ox* 66-71; C Hykeham *Linc* 71-73; P-in-c Stottesdon *Heref* 73-76; Australia from 76; rtd 97. *6 Caldwell Place, Blacktown, Sydney, NSW, Australia 2148*

SCOTT, Peter James Douglas Sefton. b 59. OBE03. Edin Univ BD83. Edin Th Coll 81. **d** 83 **p** 84. C Helensburgh *Glas* 83-86; C-in-c Glas St Oswald 86-89; R 89-91; Chapl RN from 91. *Royal Naval Chaplaincy Service, Room 203, Victory Building, HM Naval Base, Portsmouth PO1 3LS* Tel (023) 9272 7903 Fax 9272 7111

SCOTT, Peter Lindsay. b 29. Keble Coll Ox BA54 MA58. Linc Th Coll 54. **d** 56 **p** 57. C Weston-super-Mare St Sav *B & W* 56-59; C Knowle H Nativity *Bris* 59-61; P-in-c Glas St Pet *Glas* 61-63; V Heap Bridge *Man* 63-73; V Rochdale St Geo w St Alb 73-86; R Droylsden St Andr 86-94; rtd 94; Perm to Offic *Man* from 94. *2 Chancel Place, Rochdale OL16 1FB* Tel (01706) 523270

SCOTT, Ruth. *See* SCOTT, Mrs Helen Ruth

SCOTT, Sara Rosamund. b 49. Portsm Poly BSc70 Plymouth Poly MPhil74. SEITE 97. **d** 00 **p** 01. NSM Rotherhithe H Trin *S'wark* 00-04; NSM Sydenham H Trin from 04; NSM Forest Hill St Aug from 04. *147 Jerningham Road, London SE14 5NJ* Tel (020) 7639 6311 Fax 7639 1842 E-mail sarascott@btinternet.com

SCOTT, Simon James. b 65. Ch Ch Ox BA87 MA90. Wycliffe Hall Ox 87. **d** 91 **p** 92. C Cheadle All Hallows *Ches* 91-95; Scripture Union 95-98; C Cambridge H Sepulchre *Ely* 98-05; R Lt Shelford from 05. *The Rectory, 2 Manor Road, Little Shelford, Cambridge CB2 5HF* Tel (01223) 843710 E-mail simon.scott@stag.org

SCOTT, Terence. b 56. QUB BSc77. CITC 77. **d** 80 **p** 81. C Ballymena *Conn* 80-83; C Antrim All SS 83-85; P-in-c Connor w Antrim St Patr 85-88; I Magherafelt *Arm* from 88; Hon V Choral Arm Cathl from 95. *St Swithin's Rectory, 1 Churchwell Lane, Magherafelt BT45 6AL* Tel and fax (028) 7963 2365 E-mail terrscott1@aol.com

SCOTT, Canon Theresa Anne. b 53. Bris Univ BSc75 Lon Univ PGCE76. Ox Min Course 89. **d** 92 **p** 94. NSM Wickham Bishops w Lt Braxted *Chelmsf* 92-93; NSM Drayton St Pet (Berks) *Ox* 94-01; NSM Convenor (Berks) 97-01; Bp's Officer for NSM 98-01; Bp's Adv for Women in Ord Min from 01; P-in-c Hurley and Stubbings 01-02; V Burchetts Green from 02; AD Maidenhead and Windsor from 05; Hon Can Ch Ch from 05. *The Vicarage, Burchetts Green Road, Burchetts Green, Maidenhead SL6 6QS* Tel (01628) 824454 E-mail theresa.scott@driftway.co.uk

SCOTT, Timothy Charles Nairne. b 61. Ex Univ BA83. Westcott Ho Cam 84. **d** 87 **p** 88. C Romford St Edw *Chelmsf* 87-89; Community Priest 89-94; P-in-c Leytonstone H Trin Harrow Green 94-97; V 97-02; Educn and Tr Adv (Bradwell Area) 02-04; R S'wark Ch Ch *S'wark* from 04. *35 Oswin Street, London SE11 4TF* Tel (020) 7735 4077 E-mail tim.scott@southwark.anglican.org

SCOTT, Trevor Ian. b 57. Culham Coll Ox CertEd79. EAMTC 97. **d** 98 **p** 99. NSM Waltham H Cross *Chelmsf* from 98. *Hartland Villas, 208 High Road, Broxbourne EN10 6QF* Tel (01992) 420376 *or* 450321 E-mail trevor.scott2@ntlworld.com

SCOTT, Vernon Malcolm. b 30. TCD BA57 MA60. TCD Div Sch Div Test56 Ridley Hall Cam 58. **d** 58 **p** 59. C Limehouse St Anne *Lon* 58-62; C N St Pancras All Hallows 62-66; V Enfield St Mich 66-77; R Tansor w Cotterstock and Fotheringhay *Pet* 77-81; R Barby w Onley 81-83; V Kilsby 81-83; R Barby w Kilsby 83-90; R Coxford Gp *Nor* 90-94; P-in-c South Raynham, E w W Raynham, Helhoughton, etc 94-96; R E and W Rudham, Houghton-next-Harpley etc 95-96; rtd 96; Perm to Offic *Nor* from 96. *5 Wells Road, Walsingham NR22 6DL* Tel (01328) 820151

SCOTT, Walter David Craig. b 22. Selw Coll Cam BA49 MA53. Sarum Th Coll 49. **d** 51 **p** 52. C Shildon *Dur* 51-55; Min Cleadon Park St Cuth CD 55-67; V Cleadon Park 67-71; V Bulkington *Cov* 72-83; RD Bedworth 76-79; V Bulkington w Shilton and Ansty 83-87; rtd 87; Perm to Offic *Cov* from 87. *8 Osprey Close, Nuneaton CV11 6TF* Tel (024) 7634 5561

SCOTT, William. b 20. MBE97. St Chad's Coll Dur BA46 Leeds Univ DipEd53 Dip Special Educn 78. **d** 60 **p** 61. CR 60-99; C Wolborough w Newton Abbot *Ex* 60-63; Chapl St Cath Sch Bramley 63-67; Chapl St Mary and St Anne's Sch Abbots Bromley 67-76; Perm to Offic *Cant* 77-90; Chapl Boulogne-sur-Mer w Calais and Lille *Eur* 87-90; Chapl Lille 90-97; rtd 97; Perm to Offic *Eur* from 97. *42 Westgate Court Avenue, Canterbury CT2 8JR* Tel (01227) 456277

SCOTT, William. b 44. Langham Towers Teacher Tr Coll TCert67 Sunderland Poly BEd78. NEOC 00. **d** 03 **p** 04. NSM Chester le Street *Dur* 03-04; P-in-c Byers Green from 04; C Spennymoor, Whitworth and Merrington from 04. *St Peter's Rectory, Byers Green, Spennymoor DL16 7NL* Tel (01388) 664994 Mobile 07808-078532

SCOTT, The Ven William John. b 46. TCD BA70. CITC. **d** 71 **p** 72. C Bangor St Comgall *D & D* 71-74; C Holywood 74-80; Dioc Min of Healing Team from 75; I Carnalea 80-90; N Ireland Wing Chapl ATC from 80; I Seapatrick *D & D* from 90; Treas Dromore Cathl from 02; Adn Dromore from 05. *The Rectory, 63 Lurgan Road, Banbridge BT32 4LY* Tel (028) 4062 2612 *or* 4062 2744 Fax 4066 9940 E-mail john@seapatrick.fsnet.co.uk

SCOTT, Preb William Sievwright. b 46. Edin Th Coll 67. **d** 70 **p** 71. C Glas St Ninian *Glas* 70-73; C Bridgwater St Fran *B & W* 73-77; R Shepton Beauchamp w Barrington, Stocklinch etc 77-81; P-in-c Cossington 82-84; P-in-c Woolavington 82-84; Chapl Community of All Hallows Ditchingham 84-91; V Pimlico St Mary Bourne Street *Lon* 91-02; P-in-c Pimlico St Barn 97-01; V 01-02; AD Westmr St Marg 97-04; Preb St Paul's Cathl from 00; Chapl to RVO and Qu Chpl of the Savoy from 02; Chapl to The Queen from 03. *The Queen's Chapel of the Savoy, Savoy Hill, London WC2R 0DA* Tel and fax (020) 7379 8088 *or* tel 7839 2048 Fax 7839 6017 E-mail wsssavoy@aol.com *or* bournebill@aol.com

SCOTT-BROMLEY, Mrs Deborah Joan. b 58. Surrey Univ BA01 Open Univ BA96. STETS 98. **d** 01 **p** 02. C Hale w Badshot Lea *Guildf* 01-05; V Bordon from 05. *St Mark's Vicarage, 58 Forest Road, Bordon GU35 0BP* Tel (01420) 477550 Mobile 07855-704849 E-mail d.scott.bromley@ntlworld.com

SCOTT-DEMPSTER, Canon Colin Thomas. b 37. Em Coll Cam BA65 MA68. Cuddesdon Coll 64. **d** 66 **p** 67. C Caversham *Ox* 66-69; Chapl Coll of SS Mark and Jo Chelsea 69-73; V Chieveley w Winterbourne and Oare *Ox* 73-02; RD Newbury 77-98; Hon Can Ch Ch 90-02; rtd 02. *Old Faskally House, Killiecrankie, Pitlochry PH16 5LG* Tel (01796) 473575 E-mail colin@faskally25.freeserve.co.uk

SCOTT-HAMBLEN, Shane. b 66. Webster Univ (USA) BMus89 St Thos Aquinas Univ Rome STB94 MA96 STL96 St Louis Univ 90. **d** 94 **p** 95. In RC Ch 94-97; C Staines St Mary and St Pet *Lon* 97-99; USA from 99; R Highlands St Mary from 02. *The Episcopal Church of St Mary, 1 Chestnut Street, Cold Spring, NY 10516, USA* Tel (001) (845) 265 2539

✠**SCOTT-JOYNT, The Rt Revd Michael Charles.** b 43. K Coll Cam BA65 MA68. Cuddesdon Coll 65. **d** 67 **p** 68 **c** 87. C Cuddesdon *Ox* 67-70; Tutor Cuddesdon Coll 67-71; Chapl 71-72; TV Newbury St Nic *Ox* 72-75; P-in-c Bicester 75-79; P-in-c Caversfield 75-79; P-in-c Bucknell 76-79; TR Bicester w Bucknell, Caversfield and Launton 79-81; RD Bicester and Islip 76-81; Can Res St Alb 82-87; Dir of Ords and Post-Ord Tr 82-87; Suff Bp Stafford *Lich* 87-92; Area Bp Stafford 92-95; Bp Win from 95. *Wolvesey, Winchester SO23 9ND* Tel (01962) 854050 Fax 897088 E-mail michael.scott-joynt@dial.pipex.com

SCOTT-OLDFIELD, Ivor Erroll Lindsay. b 21. Univ Coll Dur BA49. Sarum Th Coll 49. **d** 51 **p** 52. C Trowbridge St Jas *Sarum* 51-54; C Haggerston St Paul *Lon* 54-58; V Enfield SS Pet and Paul 58-61; V Kentish Town St Benet and All SS 61-68; Dir Gen RADD 68-87; rtd 87; Perm to Offic *Lon* from 87. *11E Prior Bolton Street, London N1 2NX*

SCOTT-THOMPSON, Ian Mackenzie. b 57. Ch Ch Ox BA78. St Jo Coll Nottm BA82. **d** 83 **p** 84. C Hartley Wintney, Elvetham, Winchfield etc *Win* 83-85; C Bitterne 85-89; V Iford 89-99; P-in-c Holdenhurst 95-99; TR Cove St Jo *Guildf* from 99; RD Aldershot from 03. *The Rectory, 55 Cove Road, Farnborough GU14 0EX* Tel (01252) 544544 E-mail ian.scott-thompson@virgin.net

SCRACE, David Peter. b 46. Sarum & Wells Th Coll 79. **d** 81 **p** 82. C Abbots Langley *St Alb* 81-85; TV Chippenham St Paul w Hardenhuish etc *Bris* 85-91; P-in-c Harnham *Sarum* 91-99; V from 99; RD Salisbury 93-98. *The Vicarage, Old Blandford Road, Salisbury SP2 8DQ* Tel (01722) 333564 E-mail d.scrace@btopenworld.com

SCRAGG, Michael John. b 39. BA93 Jas Cook Univ Townsville BCom97 MA01. ACT ThDip73. **d** 74 **p** 75. C Camp Hill Australia 74-77; C Chesterton Gd Shep *Ely* 77-79; Australia from 79; C Maryborough 79-80; V Biggenden 80-85; Chapl Wolston Park Hosp 85-91; P-in-c Taroom 91-96; C Noarlunga, Happy Valley and Willunga 96-97; rtd 98. *Eleebana, 1-11 Old Coach Way, PO Box 424, Yandina, Qld, Australia 4561* Tel (0061) (7) 5446 8774 Fax as telephone E-mail hapy5859@squirrel.com.au

SCREECH, Prof Michael. b 26. Ordre national du Mérite 83 Chevalier Légion d'Honneur 92. Univ Coll Lon BA50 Birm Univ DLitt59 Univ Coll Lon DLitt82 All So Coll Ox MA84 DLitt90 Ex Univ Hon DLitt93 Geneva Univ Hon DD98 FBA81 FRSL87. Ox Min Course 92. **d** 93 **p** 94. NSM Ox St Giles and SS Phil and Jas w St Marg *Ox* from 93; Extraordinary Fell Wolfs Coll Ox from 93; Chapl and Fell All So Coll Ox 01-03. *5 Swanston Field, Whitchurch on Thames, Reading RG8 7HP* Tel 0118-984 2513 Fax as telephone

✠**SCREECH, The Rt Revd Royden.** b 53. K Coll Lon BD74 AKC74. St Aug Coll Cant 75. **d** 76 **p** 77 **c** 00. C Hatcham St Cath *S'wark* 76-80; V Nunhead St Antony 80-87; P-in-c Nunhead St Silas 82-87; RD Camberwell 83-87; V New Addington 87-94; Selection Sec ABM 94-97; Sen Selection Sec Min Division Abps' Coun 97-00; Suff Bp St Germans *Truro* from 00. *32 Falmouth Road, Truro TR1 2HX* Tel (01872) 273190 Fax 277883 E-mail bishop@stgermans.truro.anglican.org

SCRINE, Ralph. b 19. Bris Univ BA40 Fitzw Ho Cam BA46 MA60 Lon Univ MPhil81. Westcott Ho Cam 45. **d** 46 **p** 47. C Moorfields *Bris* 46-51; P-in-c Biddestone w Slaughterford 51-52; P-in-c Lockleaze CD 52-60; V St Jas Less 60-65; Chapl Eliz Coll Guernsey 60-65; Lect Div Ch Ch Coll Cant 65-68; Chapl Ch Ch Coll of HE Cant 68-75; Sen Lect Ch Ch Coll Cant 68-84; rtd 84; Perm to Offic *Cant* 84-03. *14 Riverdale, Harbertonford, Totnes TQ9 7TJ* Tel (01803) 731046

✠**SCRIVEN, The Rt Revd Henry William.** b 51. Sheff Univ BA72. St Jo Coll Nottm DPS75. **d** 75 **p** 76 **c** 95. C Wealdstone H Trin *Lon* 75-79; SAMS Argentina 79-82; USA 82-83; SAMS Spain 84-90; Chapl Madrid w Bilbao *Eur* 90-95; Suff Bp Eur 95-02; Dean Brussels 95-97; Dir of Ords 97-02; Asst Bp Pittsburgh USA from 02. *1437 Greystone Drive, Pittsburgh, PA 15206, USA* Tel (001) (412) 362 1620 *or* 281 6131 Fax 471 5591 E-mail scriven@pgh.anglican.org

SCRIVEN, Hugh Alexander. b 59. Trin Coll Cam BA80. Cranmer Hall Dur 81. **d** 84 **p** 85. C Pudsey St Lawr and St Paul *Bradf* 84-87; C Madeley *Heref* 87-91; TV 91-00; V Edgbaston St Germain *Birm* from 00. *St Germain's Vicarage, 180 Portland Road, Birmingham B16 9TD* Tel 0121-429 3431

SCRIVENER, Robert Allan. b 54. Nottm Univ BEd78 Hull Univ BTh98 De Montfort Univ Leic MA99 Huddersfield Univ BA03. Linc Th Coll 79. **d** 80 **p** 81. C Sherwood *S'well* 80-83; C Burghclere w Newtown and Ecchinswell w Sydmonton *Win* 83-86; TV Hemel Hempstead *St Alb* 86-93; V Kingston upon Hull St Nic *York* 93-03; V Mansfield Woodhouse *S'well* from 03. *The Vicarage, 7 Butt Lane, Mansfield Woodhouse, Mansfield NG19 9JS* Tel (01623) 621875 E-mail allanbedbt@aol.com

SCRIVENS, Mrs Elaine. b 53. TCert74 Man Univ BEd75. NEOC. **d** 00 **p** 01. NSM E Coatham *York* 00-02; NSM Coatham and Dormanstown 02-04; Chapl Ven Bede Sch Ryhope from 04. *Ven Bede C of E Secondary School, Tunstall Bank, Sunderland SR2 0SX* Tel 0191-523 9745 Fax 523 9775

SCRIVENS, Ernest. b 25. Lon Univ DipTh53. Wycliffe Hall Ox ThL. **d** 62 **p** 63. C Chesham St Mary *Ox* 62-64; CF (S Rhodesia) 64-67; Jamaica 67-68; R Ardington w E Lockinge *Ox* 68-69; Miss to Seamen W Australia 69-79; V Yeadon St Jo *Bradf* 79-80; Australia from 81; rtd 88. *Villa 1101, 269 Binkdale Road, Wellington Point, Qld, Australia 4160*

SCROGGIE, Mrs Felicity Marie-Louise. b 62. Pemb Coll Ox BA86 St Andr Univ MPhil87. STETS BTh99. **d** 99 **p** 00. C Brondesbury St Anne w Kilburn H Trin *Lon* 99-02; V Sudbury St Andr from 02. *St Andrew's Vicarage, 956 Harrow Road, Wembley HA0 2QA* Tel (020) 8904 4016 E-mail felicity.scroggie@london.anglican.org

SCRUBY, The Ven Ronald Victor. b 19. Trin Hall Cam BA48 MA52. Cuddesdon Coll 48. **d** 50 **p** 51. Chapl K Edw VII Hosp Midhurst 50-53; C Rogate *Chich* 50-53; Ind Chapl Saunders-Roe E Cowes 53-58; V Eastney *Portsm* 58-65; RD Portsm 60-65; Adn Is of Wight 65-77; Adn Portsm 77-85; rtd 85; Perm to Offic *Chich* 85-94 and *Portsm* from 85. *Church House, Rogate, Petersfield GU31 5EA* Tel (01730) 821784

SCUFFHAM, Canon Frank Leslie. b 30. AKC56 DSRS68. **d** 57 **p** 58. C Kettering SS Pet and Paul *Pet* 57-59; Ind Chapl *Sheff* 60-61; Ind Chapl *Pet* 61-95; Can Pet Cathl 72-95; RD Corby 76-79; P-in-c Stoke Albany w Wilbarston 79; R 79-95; rtd 95; Perm to Offic *St E* from 95. *The Orchard, Earlsford Road, Mellis, Eye IP23 8EA* Tel (01379) 783378 E-mail fscuff@yahoo.co.uk

SCULLY, Hazel Mary. RGN SCM. **d** 01 **p** 02. NSM Portarlington w Cloneyhurke and Lea *M & K* from 01. *Lowtown, Coralstown, Kinnegad, Co Westmeath, Irish Republic* Tel (00353) (44) 74352 Mobile 87-281 3956 Fax (44) 74083

SCULLY, Kevin John. b 55. NIDA BDA96. St Steph Ho Ox 91. **d** 93 **p** 94. C Stoke Newington St Mary *Lon* 93-97; C Stepney St Dunstan and All SS 97-00; Dir of Ords from 97; Voc Adv from 97; P-in-c Bethnal Green St Matt w St Jas the Gt 00-02; R from 02. *The Rectory, Hereford Street, London E2 6EX* Tel and fax (020) 7739 7586 E-mail revkev@onetel.com

SCURR, Capt David. b 54. St Alb and Ox Min Course. **d** 05. C Thatcham *Ox* from 05. *28 London Road, Thatcham RG18 4LQ*

SCUTTER, Canon James Edward. b 36. OBE91. AKC59 St Boniface Warminster 59. **d** 60 **p** 61. C Tilbury Docks *Chelmsf* 60-63; Bechuanaland 63-65; Rhodesia 65-70; New Zealand 70-79; Singapore 79-81; New Zealand from 81; Prin Chapl NZ Defence Force 84-91; QHC from 84; Hon Can Wellington from 87. *32 Waitaheke Road, RD1, Otaki, New Zealand* Tel (0064) (4) 364 3260 E-mail jandhscutter@asiaonline.net.nz

SEABRIGHT, Mrs Elizabeth Nicola (Nicky). b 52. SRN73 HVCert78. WEMTC 01. **d** 04. NSM Ledbury *Heref* from 04. *The Grove Cottage, Fromes Hill, Ledbury HR8 1HP* Tel (01531) 640252 E-mail nicky.seabright@tesco.net

SEABROOK, Alan Geoffrey. b 43. ALCD65. **d** 66 **p** 67. C Bethnal Green St Jas Less *Lon* 66-70; C Madeley *Heref* 70-73; V Girlington *Bradf* 74-80; P-in-c Abdon w Clee St Margaret *Heref* 80-83; R Bitterley 80-83; P-in-c Cold Weston 80-83; P-in-c Hopton Cangeford 80-83; P-in-c Stoke St Milburgh w Heath 80-83; R Bitterley w Middleton, Stoke St Milborough etc from 83; RD Ludlow from 01. *The Rectory, Bitterley, Ludlow SY8 3HJ* Tel (01584) 890239

SEABROOK, Preb Geoffrey Barry. b 45. Open Univ BA77 DipEd Lon Univ MA(Ed)84. Chich Th Coll 66. **d** 69 **p** 70. C Tottenham All Hallows *Lon* 69-72; C Winchmore Hill H Trin 72-74; V Hornsey St Geo 74-82; P-in-c Hornsey St Mary 80-82; R Hornsey St Mary w St Geo from 82; P-in-c Hornsey H Innocents 84-92; AD W Haringey from 95; Preb St Paul's Cathl from 01. *Hornsey Rectory, 140 Cranley Gardens, London N10 3AH* Tel (020) 8883 6846 Fax 8352 0879 E-mail gb.seabrook@virgin.net

SEABROOK, Paul. b 60. Univ of Wales (Cardiff) BA81 Nottm Univ PGCE82. Ridley Hall Cam 01. **d** 03 **p** 04. C Wimborne Minster *Sarum* from 03. *29 Venator Place, Wimborne BH21 1DQ* Tel (01202) 887557 E-mail seabrooktribe@telco4u.net

SEABROOK, Mrs Penelope Anne. b 56. Hertf Coll Ox BA77 K Coll Lon MA98. SEITE 00. **d** 03 **p** 04. NSM Southfields St Barn *S'wark* from 03. *121 Home Park Road, London SW19 7HT* Tel (020) 8947 3113 E-mail pennyseabrook@hotmail.com

SEABROOK, Richard Anthony. b 68. Southn Univ BTh92. Chich Th Coll 92. **d** 92 **p** 93. C Cottingham *York* 92-94; C Hawley H

Trin *Guildf* 94-98; V Hockley *Chelmsf* 98-05; R Benalla Australia from 05. *Holy Trinity Rectory, 77 Arundel Street, Benalla, Vic, Australia 3672* Tel (0061) (3) 5762 2061 Fax 5762 7009

SEAFORD, Canon John Nicholas. b 39. Dur Univ BA67. St Chad's Coll Dur 68. **d** 68 **p** 69. C Bush Hill Park St Mark *Lon* 68-71; C Stanmore *Win* 71-73; V N Baddesley 73-76; V Chilworth w N Baddesley 76-78; V Highcliffe w Hinton Admiral 78-93; RD Christchurch 90-93; Hon Can Win Cathl 93-05; Dean Jersey 93-05; R Jersey St Helier 93-05; Chapl Jersey Airport 93-05; rtd 05. *Claremont, Buffetts Road, Sturminster Newton DT10 1DZ* Tel (01258) 471479

SEAL, Edward Hugh. b 10. ARCM31 Lon Univ BMus36. Wells Th Coll 46. **d** 48 **p** 49. C Midsomer Norton *B & W* 48-50; V Churt *Guildf* 50-57; V Pemberton St Jo *Liv* 57-63; R Poulton-le-Sands *Blackb* 63-78; rtd 78; Perm to Offic *Blackb* from 79. *3 Fern Bank, Lancaster LA1 4TT* Tel (01524) 67078

SEAL, Nicholas Peter. b 57. Ex Univ BA. Linc Th Coll 81. **d** 83 **p** 84. C Wareham *Sarum* 83-87; Chapl K Alfred Coll *Win* 87-91; V Stanmore 91-01; RD Win from 99; P-in-c Win St Matt from 01; Chapl Peter Symonds Coll Win from 01. *The Rectory, 44 Cheriton Road, Winchester SO22 5AY* Tel and fax (01962) 854849 E-mail peter.seal@ntlworld.com

SEAL, Philip Trevor. b 32. AKC55. **d** 56 **p** 57. C Godalming *Guildf* 56-60; C Tamworth *Lich* 60-61; R Lich St Chad 61-73; Chapl HM Youth Cust Cen Swinfen Hall 66-73; R Shere *Guildf* 74-88; RD Cranleigh 76-81; V Abbotsbury, Portesham and Langton Herring *Sarum* 88-97; rtd 97; Perm to Offic *Ex* from 01. *2 Moorlane Cottages, Poltimore, Exeter EX4 0AQ*

SEAL, Ronald Frederick. b 28. CA Tr Coll 50 Lich Th Coll 59. **d** 61 **p** 62. C Bedhampton *Portsm* 61-65; R N and S Kilworth *Leic* 65-71; R Barwell w Potters Marston and Stapleton 71-80; P-in-c Upper Stour *Sarum* 80-83; R Upper Stour 84-90; RD Heytesbury 87-89; Bermuda 90-92; Miss to Seamen 90-92; rtd 92; Perm to Offic *Sarum* from 92. *8 Briar Close, Wyke, Gillingham SP8 4SS* Tel (01747) 825462

SEAL (formerly MILLER), Mrs Rosamund Joy. b 56. Lon Univ BSc77 Whitelands Coll Lon PGCE80. EMMTC 92. **d** 94 **p** 96. NSM Grantham *Linc* 94-96; C Stamford All SS w St Jo 96-00; C Spalding from 00. *The Chantry, 7 Church Street, Spalding PE11 2PB* Tel (01775) 711355 *or* tel and fax 722631 E-mail rosamund.seal@spaldingchurches.org

SEAL, William Christopher Houston. b 50. Occidental Coll (USA) BA72. Ch Div Sch of the Pacific (USA) MDiv81. **d** 81 **p** 82. USA 81-88 and from 94; R Etton w Helpston *Pet* 88-94. *The Rectory, 171 Grove Street, Nevada City, CA 95959, USA*

SEALE, William Arthur. b 62. NUI BA84. CITC. **d** 87 **p** 88. C Drumragh w Mountfield *D & R* 87-90; I from 01; I Drumgath w Drumgooland and Clonduff *D & D* 90-01. *The Rectory, 8 Mullaghmenagh Avenue, Omagh BT78 5QH* Tel and fax (028) 8224 2130 E-mail drumragh@derry.anglican.org

SEALY, Daniel O'Neill. b 21. Oak Hill Th Coll 62. **d** 64 **p** 65. C Walcot *B & W* 64-67; Chapl RN 67-73; Nigeria 73-79; Libya 79-82; Tunisia 82-86; rtd 86; I Kilgariffe Union *C, C & R* 87-92. *Swanhill, Culver Street, Newent GL18 1JA*

SEALY, Canon Gordon William Hugh. b 27. Leeds Univ BA53 MA64. Coll of Resurr Mirfield 53. **d** 55 **p** 56. C Greenford H Cross *Lon* 55-58; Br Honduras 58-68; R Tarrant Gunville, Tarrant Hinton etc *Sarum* 68-74; V Leic St Paul *Leic* 74-96; Hon Can Leic Cathl 86-96; rtd 96. *Church Cottage, Maker Lane, Hoar Cross, Burton-on-Trent DE13 8QR* Tel (01283) 575738

SEALY, Stephen. b 52. K Coll Lon BD86 AKC86. Linc Th Coll 86. **d** 88 **p** 89. C Botley *Portsm* 88-91; Min Can and Prec Cant Cathl *Cant* 91-96; V Pembury *Roch* 96-04; V Sidcup St Jo from 04. *St John's Vicarage, 13 Church Avenue, Sidcup DA14 6BU* Tel and fax (020) 8300 0383 E-mail stephen@sealylink.freeserve.co.uk

SEAMAN, Canon Arthur Roland Mostyn. b 32. TCD BA55 DipEd56 Div Test56 MA58. Westcott Ho Cam 58. **d** 58 **p** 59. C Blackley St Pet *Man* 58-61; C Sanderstead All SS *S'wark* 61-62; V Heywood St Luke *Man* 62-70; Dir of Educn 70-85; Hon Can Man Cathl 74-95; R Chorlton-cum-Hardy St Werburgh 85-95; rtd 95; Perm to Offic *Newc* from 95. *10 The Haven, Beadnell, Chathill NE67 5AW* Tel (01665) 720510

SEAMAN, Canon Brian Edward. b 35. Dur Univ BA59. Cranmer Hall Dur. **d** 61 **p** 62. C Burnage St Marg *Man* 61-65; Chapl Mayflower Family Cen Canning Town *Chelmsf* 65-75; V High Elswick St Paul *Newc* 75-96; TV Glendale Gp 96-03; Hon Can Newc Cathl 82-03; rtd 03. *13 Rosebery Street, Ringstead, Kettering NN14 4BY* Tel (01933) 622615 E-mail learners@seaman.fsworld.co.uk

SEAMAN, Christopher Robert. b 34. St Jo Coll Ox BA58 MA74 Solicitor 62. Ox Min Course 92 St Alb and Ox Min Course 94. **d** 95 **p** 96. NSM Watlington w Pyrton and Shirburn *Ox* 95-97; NSM Icknield 97-98; Perm to Offic 98-99 and from 05; Hon C Shippon 99-04. *5 Curtyn Close, Abingdon OX14 1SE* Tel (01235) 520380

SEAMAN, Miss Miranda Kate. b 66. Univ Coll Lon BSc88 Solicitor 90. EAMTC 02. **d** 05. NSM S Weald *Chelmsf* from 05. *Hollyhock Cottage, 25 Common Lane, Stock, Ingatestone CM4 9LP* Tel (01277) 841921 *or* 210021 Mobile 07909-522763

SEAMAN, Paul Robert. b 61. Bp Grosseteste Coll BEd82. Chich Th Coll 83. **d** 86 **p** 87. C Tilehurst St Mich *Ox* 86-91; TV Moulsecoomb *Chich* 91-95; R Whyke w Rumboldswhyke and Portfield from 95. *St George's Rectory, 199 Whyke Road, Chichester PO19 7HQ* Tel (01243) 782535

SEAMAN (née HEWLINS), Mrs Pauline Elizabeth. b 47. Lon Univ BD68 AKC. Ox Min Course 93. **d** 96 **p** 97. NSM Radley and Sunningwell *Ox* 96-99; Chapl SS Helen and Kath Sch Abingdon 96-04; NSM Shippon *Ox* from 99; P-in-c from 05; Chapl SW Oxon Primary Care Trust from 05. *5 Curtyn Close, Abingdon OX14 1SE* Tel (01235) 520380

SEAMAN, Robert John. b 44. ACP DipEd. EAMTC. **d** 84 **p** 85. NSM Downham Market w Bexwell *Ely* 84-90; V Southea w Murrow and Parson Drove 90-97; V Guyhirn w Ring's End 90-97; V Newnham w Awre and Blakeney *Glouc* from 97; RD Forest N from 04. *The Vicarage, 1 Whetstones, Unlawater Lane, Newnham GL14 1BT* Tel (01594) 516648 Fax 510131 E-mail rj.seaman@btopenworld.com

SEAMER, Stephen James George. b 50. AKC73. Ridley Hall Cam 74. **d** 75 **p** 76. C Rustington *Chich* 75-78; C Bulwell St Jo *S'well* 78-79; P-in-c Camber and E Guldeford *Chich* 79-80; TV Rye 80-83; V Knowle *Birm* 83-87; Assoc Chapl Brussels Cathl *Eur* 87-88; P-in-c Tervuren 88-94; Chapl 94-98; P-in-c Liège 90-98; V Tonbridge SS Pet and Paul *Roch* from 98. *The Vicarage, 12 Church Street, Tonbridge TN9 1HD* Tel (01732) 770962 *or* 770961 Fax 358052 E-mail admin@tonbridgeparish.freeserve.co.uk

SEAR, Peter Lionel. b 49. Ex Univ BA72. Linc Th Coll 72. **d** 74 **p** 75. C Sheldon *Birm* 74-77; C Caversham *Ox* 77-81; C Caversham St Pet and Mapledurham etc 81-85; TR Thatcham 85-98; V Castle Cary w Ansford *B & W* 98-00; rtd 00; Perm to Offic *B & W* from 03. *Knowle Cottage, Lamyatt, Shepton Mallet BA4 6NP* Tel (01749) 813226

SEAR, Terence Frank. b 39. LDSRCSEng62 Univ Coll Lon BDS63. Portsm Dioc Tr Course 88. **d** 89. NSM Ryde H Trin *Portsm* 89-98; NSM Swanmore St Mich w Havenstreet 89-92; NSM Swanmore St Mich 92-98; NSM Wroxall 99-00; NSM Godshill 99-01; Perm to Offic from 02. *34 Whitehead Crescent, Wootton Bridge, Ryde PO33 4JF* Tel (01983) 883560

SEARE, Mrs Janice Mae. b 48. SEN. STETS 99. **d** 02 **p** 03. NSM Holdenhurst and Iford *Win* from 02. *Wood Farm, Holdenhurst Village, Bournemouth BH8 0EE* Tel (01202) 302468 Fax 391281 E-mail pj.seare@zoom.co.uk

SEARL, John. b 37. Southn Univ BSc58 Edin Univ PhD69. **d** 00 **p** 01. NSM Edin St Cuth *Edin* 00-03. *Tulach Ard, Badachro, Gairloch IV21 2AA* Tel (01445) 741231 E-mail m-jsearl@supanet.com

SEARLE, Charles Peter. b 20. Selw Coll Cam BA48 MA53. Ridley Hall Cam. **d** 50 **p** 51. C Becontree St Mary *Chelmsf* 50-53; P-in-c Bedford St Jo *St Alb* 53-56; R 56-60; V Weston-super-Mare Ch Ch *B & W* 60-70; V Woking Ch Ch *Guildf* 70-85; rtd 85; Perm to Offic *Ex* from 85. *Spinners, 15 Spindlebury, Cullompton EX15 1SY* Tel (01884) 33386 E-mail asearle@dialstart.net

SEARLE, David William. b 37. MASI89 ACIOB98. Dioc OLM tr scheme 96. **d** 99 **p** 00. OLM E Bergholt and Brantham *St E* from 99. *46 Chaplin Road, East Bergholt, Colchester CO7 6SR* Tel (01206) 298932

SEARLE, Capt Francis Robert. b 52. IDC74. CA Tr Coll 72 St Steph Ho Ox 88. **d** 90 **p** 91. CA from 72; C Lancing w Coombes *Chich* 90-93; V Hampden Park 93-00; P-in-c Eastchurch w Leysdown and Harty *Cant* 00-03; R from 03. *The Rectory, Warden Road, Sheerness ME12 4EJ* Tel (01795) 880205 E-mail francis.searle@churcharmy.net

SEARLE, Canon Hugh Douglas. b 35. St Cath Coll Cam BA59 MA63 Cranfield Inst of Tech MSc85. Oak Hill Th Coll 59. **d** 61 **p** 62. C Islington H Trin Cloudesley Square *Lon* 61-64; Chapl HM Pris Lewes 64-65; Chapl HM Borstal Roch 65-69; Chapl HM Youth Cust Cen Hollesley Bay Colony 70-74; Chapl HM Pris Parkhurst 74-78; P-in-c Barton *Ely* 78-84; V 84-00; P-in-c Coton 78-84; R 84-00; RD Bourn 81-94; Hon Can Ely Cathl 97-00; rtd 00; Perm to Offic *Ely* from 00. *38 Field End, Witchford, Ely CB6 2XE* Tel (01353) 659749 E-mail cfsw@ely.anglican.org

SEARLE, Jacqueline Ann. b 60. Whitelands Coll Lon BEd82 Bris Univ MA01. Trin Coll Bris 90. **d** 92 **p** 94. Par Dn Roxeth *Lon* 92-94; C Ealing St Steph Castle Hill 94-96; Tutor and Dean of Women Trin Coll Bris 96-03; P-in-c Littleover *Derby* 03-04; V from 04. *The Vicarage, 35 Church Street, Littleover, Derby DE23 6GF* Tel (01332) 767802 E-mail j.searle@ntlworld.com

SEARLE, John Francis. b 42. OBE98. FRCA70 FRSM84 Lon Univ MB, BS66. SW Minl Tr Course 92. **d** 95 **p** 96. NSM Ex St Leon w H Trin *Ex* 95-03; Assoc Staff Member SWMTC from 03; Perm to Offic *Truro* from 03. *Belle Isle Lodge, Belle Isle Drive, Exeter EX2 4RY* Tel (01392) 432153 E-mail johnlizex@aol.com

SEARLE, Mark Robin. b 73. Cen Sch Speech & Drama BA94. Trin Coll Bris BA03. **d** 03 **p** 04. C Cant St Mary Bredin *Cant*

from 03. *38 Nunnery Road, Canterbury CT1 3LS* Tel (01227) 455723 E-mail marksearle@btinternet.com

SEARLE, Michael Stanley. b 38. HNC60. AMIQ63. N Ord Course 93. **d** 95 **p** 96. NSM Hoole *Ches* 95-99; P-in-c Marbury from 99; P-in-c Tushingham and Whitewell from 02. *The Vicarage, Marbury, Whitchurch SY13 4LN* Tel (01948) 663758 Mobile 07850-720120 Fax (01948) 667479 E-mail mike.s.searle@btinternet.com

SEARLE, Michael Westran. b 47. Leeds Univ LLB68 Nottm Univ DipTh69. Cuddesdon Coll 69. **d** 71 **p** 72. C Norton St Mary *Dur* 71-74; C Westbury-on-Trym H Trin *Bris* 74-77; V Bedminster Down 77-84; V Bris Ch the Servant Stockwood 84-88; Dir of Tr *York* 88-00; R Dunnington from 00. *The Rectory, 30 Church Street, Dunnington, York YO10 5PW* Tel (01904) 489349 E-mail msearle@yorktrain.demon.co.uk

SEARLE, Philip Robert. b 67. Westcott Ho Cam. **d** 95 **p** 96. C Plymstock *Ex* 95-97; C Plymstock and Hooe 97-98; TV Stoke-upon-Trent *Lich* from 98. *All Saints' Vicarage, 540 Leek Road, Stoke-on-Trent ST1 3HH* Tel (01782) 205713 E-mail hairetic@surfaid.org

SEARLE, Ralph Alan. b 57. G&C Coll Cam BA79 MA83. Coll of Resurr Mirfield 81. **d** 83 **p** 84. C Cockerton *Dur* 83-86; C S Shields All SS 86-88; TV 88-96; Assoc P Worksop Priory *S'well* 96-97; Assoc P Paignton St Jo *Ex* 97-01; V Horfield St Greg *Bris* 01-03; Hon Min Can Bris Cathl 02-03. *2 Temple Gate, Temple End, High Wycombe HP13 5DY* Tel (01494) 437012 E-mail fr.ralph@tinyonline.co.uk

SEARLE-BARNES, Albert Victor. b 28. Sheff Univ BA48 Lon Univ BD53. ALCD53. **d** 53 **p** 54. C Iver *Ox* 53-55; C Attenborough w Bramcote *S'well* 55-59; C Bramcote 55-59; R Cratfield w Heveningham and Ubbeston *St E* 59-64; R Wick w Doynton *Bris* 64-70; Perm to Offic 70-72; V Downend 73-78; V Market Rasen *Linc* 78-86; R Linwood 79-86; V Legsby 79-86; R Green's Norton w Bradden *Pet* 86-88; V Hambledon *Portsm* 88-92; rtd 92; Perm to Offic *Glouc* from 92. *32 Oakland Avenue, Cheltenham GL52 3EP* Tel (01242) 227425

SEARLE-BARNES, Belinda Rosemary. b 51. ARCM72 GRSM73 Lon Univ Dip Past Th 91 MA93 Southn Univ DipMin96. Sarum Th Coll 93. **d** 96 **p** 97. NSM Pimperne, Stourpaine, Durweston and Bryanston *Sarum* 96-00; Asst Par Development Adv 98-00; Asst Chapl Bryanston Sch 98-00; TV Southampton (City Cen) *Win* 00-04; Chapl Godolphin Sch from 04. *The Godolphin School, Milford Hill, Salisbury SP1 2RA* Tel (01722) 430614

SEARS, Helen. *See* THAKE, Ms Helen

SEARS, Jacqueline Isabella. SRN69 DN84. NTMTC 95. **d** 99 **p** 00. NSM Hanwell St Mellitus w St Mark *Lon* 99-03; Asst Chapl Essex Rivers Healthcare NHS Trust 03-04; Chapl from 04; C Ipswich St Matt *St E* from 04. *4 Woodward Close, Ipswich IP2 0EA* Tel (01473) 214125 Mobile 07984-077990 E-mail jackie@searsfamily.fsnet.co.uk

SEARS, Jeanette. b 59. Man Univ BA80 PhD84 Lon Univ PGCE85. Wycliffe Hall Ox. **d** 92 **p** 94. NSM Ox St Aldate w St Matt *Ox* 92-94; NSM Ox St Aldate 95-96; Tutor Trin Coll Bris from 04. *Trinity College, Stoke Hill, Bristol BS9 1JP* Tel 0117-968 2803

SEARS, Michael Antony. b 50. Birm Univ BSc71 PGCE72. Linc Th Coll 78. **d** 80 **p** 81. C Willenhall H Trin *Lich* 80-83; C Caldmore 83-84; P-in-c 84-86; V 86-89; Abp Ilsley RC Sch Birm 89-97; TV Solihull *Birm* 98-02; R Castle Bromwich SS Mary and Marg from 02. *67 Chester Road, Castle Bromwich, Birmingham B36 9DP* Tel 0121-684 3031 Mobile 07740-537559 E-mail rector.castleb@fish.co.uk

SEATON, Canon James Bradbury. b 29. Ch Coll Cam BA53 MA57. Westcott Ho Cam 53. **d** 55 **p** 56. C Derby St Werburgh *Derby* 55-58; C Darlington St Cuth *Dur* 58-64; V Preston on Tees 64-72; TV Stockton H Trin 72-73; TV Cen Stockton 73-75; R Anstey *Leic* 75-89; RD Sparkenhoe III 81-89; Hon Can Leic Cathl 87-94; R Market Harborough Transfiguration 89-94; rtd 94; Perm to Offic *Glouc* from 94. *Wayside, Sheep Street, Chipping Campden GL55 6DW* Tel (01386) 841753

SEATON, Stuart Paul. b 75. Dur Univ BA96 Leeds Univ MA99. Coll of Resurr Mirfield 97. **d** 99 **p** 00. C Hatfield Hyde *St Alb* 99-02; Asst Chapl Aldenham Sch Herts 03-04; V Bushey Heath *St Alb* from 04. *St Peter's Vicarage, 19 High Road, Bushey Heath, Bushey WD23 1EA* Tel (020) 8950 1424 E-mail stuart@seaton.freeserve.co.uk

SEBER, Derek Morgan. b 43. Man Poly MA87 Man Metrop Univ MPhil96. Oak Hill Th Coll 71. **d** 73 **p** 74. C Collyhurst *Man* 73-76; C Radcliffe St Thos and St Jo 76-77; Ind Missr 77-89; P-in-c Hulme St Geo 77-83; Hon C Moss Side St Jas w St Clem 83-96; Project Officer Linking Up 89-96; Lic Preacher 90-96; P-in-c Cheetham St Jo 97; P-in-c Thornton Hough *Ches* from 97; Ind Chapl from 97. *All Saints' Vicarage, Raby Road, Thornton Hough, Wirral CH63 1JP* Tel and fax 0151-336 3429 *or* tel 336 1654 E-mail derek@morganseber.freeserve.co.uk

SECCOMBE, Marcus John. b 34. Oak Hill Th Coll 60. **d** 63 **p** 64. C Woodthorpe *S'well* 63-67; C Doncaster St Mary *Sheff* 67-72; V Owston 72-90; R Rossington 90-99; rtd 99; Perm to Offic *Sheff* from 99. *39 Marlborough Road, Doncaster DN2 5DF* Tel (01302) 321505 E-mail mark@secco9.freeserve.co.uk

SECOMBE, Preb Frederick Thomas. b 18. St D Coll Lamp BA40 St Mich Coll Llan 40. **d** 42 **p** 43. C Swansea St Mark *S & B* 42-44; C Knighton 44-46; C Machen *Mon* 46-49; C Newport St Woolos 49-52; Chapl St Woolos Hosp Newport 49-52; V Llanarth w Clytha, Llansantffraed and Bryngwyn *Mon* 52-54; R Machen and Rudry 54-59; V Swansea St Pet *S & B* 59-69; R Hanwell St Mary *Lon* 69-83; AD Ealing W 78-82; Preb St Paul's Cathl 81-83; rtd 83. *30 Westville Road, Penylan, Cardiff CF23 5AG* Tel (029) 2048 3978

SECRETAN, Ms Jenny Ruth. b 54. St Aid Coll Dur BA76 Ex Univ PGCE77 Dur Univ MA97. Linc Th Coll 81 Cranmer Hall Dur 83. **dss** 84 **d** 87 **p** 94. Asst Chapl Newc Poly *Newc* 84-86; Sunderland St Chad *Dur* 84-86; Bordesley St Oswald *Birm* 86-91; Par Dn 87-91; Assoc Soc Resp Officer *Dur* 92-95; Perm to Offic *Dur* and *Newc* 95-99. *14 Southwood Gardens, Newcastle upon Tyne NE3 3BU*

SEDANO, Juan Antonio. b 55. Centro de Discipulado Lima 85. **d** 88 **p** 88. Peru 88-90; Crosslinks 91-94; SAMS from 95; NSM Ingrave St Steph CD *Chelmsf* from 95. *5 The Chase, Middle Road, Ingrave, Brentwood CM13 3QT* Tel (01277) 810907 E-mail dan@sedano.freeserve.co.uk

SEDDON, Mrs Carol Susan. b 44. ARCM63 GNSM66 Man Univ CertEd67. Ripon Coll Cuddesdon. **d** 05. NSM Alsager St Mary *Ches* from 05; Asst Chapl HM YOI Stoke Heath from 05. *94 Dunnockfold Road, Alsager, Stoke-on-Trent ST7 2TW* Tel (01270) 878328 Mobile 07973-737038

SEDDON, Ernest Geoffrey. b 26. ARIBA51 Man Univ DipArch50 DipTh83 MA85. St Deiniol's Hawarden 80. **d** 80 **p** 81. C Dunham Massey St Marg *Ches* 80-83; P-in-c Warburton 82-87; P-in-c Dunham Massey St Mark 85-86; V 86-92; rtd 92; Perm to Offic *Ches* from 92. *7 Colwyn Place, Llandudno LL30 3AW* Tel (01492) 547639 *or* 642107

SEDDON, Philip James. b 45. Jes Coll Cam BA68 MA71 Birm Univ MPhil01. Ridley Hall Cam 67. **d** 70 **p** 71. C Tonge w Alkrington *Man* 70-74; CMS Nigeria 74-78; Lect St Jo Coll Nottm 78-79; Lic to Offic *Ely* 79-85; Chapl Magd Coll Cam 79-85; Lect Bibl Studies Selly Oak Colls 86-00; Lic to Offic *Birm* from 87; Lect Th Birm Univ from 00. *Department of Theology, University of Birmingham, Edgbaston, Birmingham B15 2TT* Tel 0121-414 3613 Fax 414 6866 E-mail p.j.seddon@bham.ac.uk

SEDEN, Martin Roy. b 47. Man Univ MSc Salford Univ PhD. EMMTC 79. **d** 82 **p** 83. NSM Knighton St Mary Magd *Leic* from 82. *139 Shanklin Drive, Leicester LE2 3QG* Tel 0116-270 2128 *or* 257 7404 E-mail rseden@dmu.ac.uk

SEDGEWICK, Clive Malcolm. b 56. Loughb Univ BSc78 UEA MA92 PGCE79. St Alb and Ox Min Course 00. **d** 04 **p** 05. NSM High Harrogate Ch Ch *Ripon* from 04. *11 Bogs Lane, Harrogate HG1 4DY* Tel (01423) 548548 Mobile 07903-326053 E-mail clivesedgewick@yahoo.com

SEDGLEY, Mrs Jean. b 41. Whitelands Coll Lon CertEd63. S Dios Minl Tr Scheme 92. **d** 95 **p** 96. NSM Haywards Heath St Wilfrid *Chich* 95-01; NSM Cuckfield from 01. *25 Pasture Hill Road, Haywards Heath RH16 1LY* Tel (01444) 413974

SEDGLEY, Canon Timothy John. b 42. St Jo Coll Ox BA63 MA68. Westcott Ho Cam 64. **d** 66 **p** 67. C Nor St Pet Mancroft *Nor* 66-70; V Costessey 70-79; RD Nor N 75-79; V Walton-on-Thames *Guildf* 79-05; RD Emly 86-91; Hon Can Guildf Cathl 86-05; Dir OLMs and NSMs 93-05; rtd 05. *6 St Paul's Court, Moreton-in-Marsh, Gloucester GL56 0ET* E-mail timsedgley@hotmail.com

SEDGWICK, Jonathan Maurice William. b 63. BNC Ox BA85 MA89 Leeds Univ BA88. Coll of Resurr Mirfield 86. **d** 89 **p** 90. C Chich St Paul and St Pet *Chich* 89-91; Dean of Div and Chapl Magd Coll Ox 91-94; Perm to Offic *S'wark* 97-00; Hon C E Dulwich St Jo from 00. *46 Wood Vale, London SE23 3EE* Tel (020) 8693 8129 E-mail jonathan@woodvale46.freeserve.co.uk

SEDGWICK, Peter Humphrey. b 48. Trin Hall Cam BA70 Dur Univ PhD83. Westcott Ho Cam 71. **d** 74 **p** 75. C Stepney St Dunstan and All SS *Lon* 74-77; P-in-c Pittington *Dur* 77-79; Lect Th Birm Univ 79-82; Hon C The Lickey *Birm* 79-82; Th Consultant for NE Ecum Gp *Dur* 82-88; Lect Th Hull Univ 88-94; Abp's Adv on Ind Issues *York* 88-94; Vice-Prin Westcott Ho Cam 94-96; Asst Sec Abps' Coun Bd for Soc Resp 96-04; NSM Pet St Barn *Pet* 96-98; Prin St Mich Coll Llan from 04. *St Michael's College, 54 Cardiff Road, Llandaff, Cardiff CF5 2YJ* Tel (029) 2056 3379 E-mail revgould@virgin.net

SEDLMAYR, Peter. b 53. Univ Coll Chich BA01. **d** 04. NSM Littlehampton and Wick *Chich* from 04. *83 Joyce Close, Wick, Littlehampton BN17 7JG* Tel (01903) 714968 Mobile 07941-921263 E-mail peterpaul@sedlmayr83.freeserve.co.uk

SEED, Richard Edward. b 55. UNISA BTh86 Westmr Coll Ox MEd. Kalk Bay Bible Inst S Africa DipTh79. **d** 80 **p** 81. S Africa 80-85 and 87-89; Zimbabwe 85-87; Asst Chapl Kingham Hill Sch Oxon 89-90; C Beckenham Ch Ch *Roch* 90-95; Chapl Düsseldorf

Eur 96-00; CMS from 00. *CMS, Partnership House, 157 Waterloo Road, London SE1 8UU* Tel (020) 7928 8681

SEED, The Ven Richard Murray Crosland. b 49. Leeds Univ MA91. Edin Th Coll 69. **d** 72 **p** 73. C Skipton Ch Ch *Bradf* 72-75; C Baildon 75-77; Chapl HM Det Cen Kidlington 77-80; TV Kidlington *Ox* 77-80; V Boston Spa *York* 80-99; P-in-c Newton Kyme 84-85; P-in-c Clifford 89-99; P-in-c Thorp Arch w Walton 98-99; Chapl Martin House Hospice for Children Boston Spa 85-99; RD New Ainsty *York* 97-99; Adn York from 99; R York H Trin Micklegate from 00. *Holy Trinity Rectory, Micklegate, York YO1 6LE* Tel (01904) 623798 Fax 628155 E-mail archdeacon.of.york@yorkdiocese.org

SEEL, Richard Malcolm. b 45. **d** 04 **p** 05. OLM Bacton w Edingthorpe w Witton and Ridlington *Nor* from 04; OLM Happisburgh, Walcott, Hempstead w Eccles etc from 04. *Seabrink, Beach Road, Bacton, Norwich NR12 0EP* Tel (01692) 650706 Mobile 07711-069680 E-mail richard@emerging-church.org

SEELEY, Jutta. *See* BRUECK, Ms Jutta

SEELEY, Martin Alan. b 54. Jes Coll Cam BA76 MA79. Ripon Coll Cuddesdon 76 Union Th Sem (NY) STM78. **d** 78 **p** 79. C Bottesford w Ashby *Linc* 78-80; USA 80-90; Selection Sec ABM 90-96; Sec for Continuing Minl Educn 90-96; V Is of Dogs Ch Ch and St Jo w St Luke *Lon* from 96. *Christ Church Vicarage, Manchester Road, London E14 3BN* Tel (020) 7538 1766 *or* 7987 1915 E-mail martin.seeley@london.anglican.org

SEGAL, Michael Bertram. b 20. Lon Univ BA44. Cuddesdon Coll 46. **d** 48 **p** 49. C Lewisham St Jo Southend *S'wark* 48-53; C Coulsdon St Andr 53-61; V S Wimbledon St Pet 61-71; V Crofton Park St Hilda w St Cypr 72-82; P-in-c Grendon w Castle Ashby *Pet* 82-85; V Gt Doddington 82-85; rtd 85; Perm to Offic *Cant* 85-02. *8 Manormead, Tilford Road, Hindhead GU26 6RA* Tel (01428) 602559

SEGRAVE-PRIDE, Mrs Philippa Louise. b 73. Westhill Coll Birm BTh96. Ripon Coll Cuddesdon 97. **d** 99 **p** 00. C Harborne St Pet *Birm* 99-02; TV Tring *St Alb* 02-04; TV Bp's Hatfield from 04. *St Michael's Vicarage, 31 Homestead Road, Hatfield AL10 0QJ* Tel (01707) 882276

SELBY, Miss Carole Janis. b 50. Chelsea Coll of Physical Educn CertEd71 Sussex Univ BEd72 K Coll Lon MA03. Westcott Ho Cam 93. **d** 95 **p** 96. C Worc St Barn w Ch Ch *Worc* 95-99; Min Turnford St Clem CD *St Alb* from 99; RD Cheshunt from 04. *St Clements House, 44 Hillview Gardens, Cheshunt, Waltham Cross EN8 0PE* Tel and fax (01992) 625098 E-mail c_selby@talk21.com

✠**SELBY, The Rt Revd Peter Stephen Maurice.** b 41. St Jo Coll Ox BA64 MA67 Episc Th Sch Cam Mass BD66 K Coll Lon PhD75. Bps' Coll Cheshunt 66. **d** 66 **p** 67 **c** 84. C Queensbury All SS *Lon* 66-69; C Limpsfield and Titsey *S'wark* 69-77; Assoc Dir of Tr 69-73; Vice-Prin S'wark Ord Course 70-72; Asst Dioc Missr *S'wark* 73-77; Dioc Missr *Newc* 77-84; Can Res Newc Cathl 77-84; Suff Bp Kingston *S'wark* 84-91; Area Bp 91-92; Wm Leech Professorial Fell Dur Univ 92-97; Asst Bp Dur 92-97; Asst Bp Newc 92-97; Bp Worc from 97; Hon Prof Univ Coll Worc from 98; Bp HM Pris from 01. *The Bishop's House, Hartlebury Castle, Kidderminster DY11 7XX* Tel (01299) 250214 Fax 250027 E-mail bishop.peter@cofe-worcester.org.uk

SELBY, Suffragan Bishop of. *See* WALLACE, The Rt Revd Martin William

SELDON, Francis Peter. b 58. St Jo Coll Nottm 98. **d** 00 **p** 01. C Styvechale *Cov* 00-02; C Cheylesmore 02-04; V from 04. *Christ Church Vicarage, 11 Frankpledge Road, Coventry CV3 5GT* Tel (024) 7650 2770

SELF, Canon David Christopher. b 41. Toronto Univ BSc62 MA64 K Coll Lon BD68 AKC68. **d** 69 **p** 70. C Tupsley *Heref* 69-73; Chapl Dur Univ *Dur* 73-78; TV Southampton (City Cen) *Win* 78-84; TR Dunstable *St Alb* 84-95; RD Dunstable 90-91; TR Bris St Paul's *Bris* from 95; RD Bris City 98-99; AD City 99-03; Hon Can Bris Cathl from 99. *St Paul's Rectory, 131 Ashley Road, Bristol BS6 5NU* Tel 0117-955 0150 *or* 955 1755 E-mail self@supanet.com

SELF, John Andrew. b 47. Pershore Coll of Horticulture CANP68. Trin Coll Bris 74 CMS Tr Coll Crowther Hall 76. **d** 81 **p** 83. CMS 77-91; Pakistan 77-91; Assoc V Bath Weston All SS w N Stoke *B & W* 91-92; V Sparkhill w Greet and Sparkbrook *Birm* from 92. *St John's Vicarage, 15 Phipson Road, Birmingham B11 4JE* Tel and fax 0121-449 2760 *or* tel 753 1415 E-mail john.self@stjohnsparkhill.org.uk

SELF, Peter Allen. b 41. S Dios Minl Tr Scheme 84. **d** 87 **p** 98. NSM Wilton *B & W* 87-91; NSM Taunton Lyngford 91-96; Asst Chapl Taunton and Somerset NHS Trust from 96. *20 Dyers Close, West Buckland, Wellington TA21 9JU* Tel (01823) 663408 Fax 663448

SELFE, John Ronald. b 41. EMMTC 85. **d** 95 **p** 96. OLM Mid Marsh Gp *Linc* from 95. *Bookend, 236 Eastgate, Louth LN11 8DA* Tel (01507) 603809 E-mail john.dorothyselfe@tiscali.co.uk

SELIM, Claes Eric. b 48. Uppsala Univ MA73 BD76. **p** 77. C Rasbo Sweden 77-80; P-in-c Hablingbo 81-85; P-in-c Öja and Huddunge 85-89; Dep Lect Uppsala Univ 81-89; Lect 89-95; V Öja 89-92; V Vänge 95-00; C Holbeach *Linc* 00-02; R Guernsey Ste Marie du Castel *Win* from 02; V Guernsey St Matt from 02. *Castel Rectory, La Rue de la Lande, Castel, Guernsey GY5 7EJ* Tel (01481) 256793

SELLER, James Stoddart. b 16. TD64. St Jo Coll Dur LTh45. Tyndale Hall Bris 40. **d** 44 **p** 45. C Cambridge St Andr Less *Ely* 44-47; C Holborn St Geo w H Trin *Lon* 47-48; C Whitby *York* 48-50; V Ravenscar 51-53; V Sledmere 53-60; P-in-c Huttons Ambo 57-60; R Burnby 60-89; R Londesborough 60-89; R Nunburnholme 60-89; P-in-c Shiptonthorpe w Hayton 78-89; rtd 89; Perm to Offic *York* from 89. *7 Wilton Road, Hornsea HU18 1QU* Tel (01964) 533160

SELLER, Prof Mary Joan. b 40. Qu Mary Coll Lon BSc61 Lon Univ PhD64 DSc82. S'wark Ord Course 89. **d** 91 **p** 94. NSM Hurst Green *S'wark* from 91. *11 Home Park, Oxted RH8 0JS* Tel (01883) 715675

SELLERS, Anthony. b 48. Southn Univ BSc71 PhD76. Wycliffe Hall Ox 84. **d** 86 **p** 87. C Luton St Mary *St Alb* 86-90; V Luton St Paul from 90. *St Paul's Vicarage, 37A Arthur Street, Luton LU1 3SG* Tel (01582) 481796 E-mail tsellers@route56.co.uk

SELLERS, George William. b 35. N Ord Course. **d** 89 **p** 90. NSM Rothwell *Ripon* from 89. *16 Thornegrove, Rothwell, Leeds LS26 0HP* Tel 0113-282 3522

SELLERS, Robert. b 58. Coll of Resurr Mirfield 90. **d** 92 **p** 93. C Wotton St Mary *Glouc* 92-95; TV Redruth w Lanner and Treleigh *Truro* 95-98; P-in-c Devoran 98-03; Bp's Dom Chapl 98-03; R Fountains Gp *Ripon* from 03. *Fountains Rectory, Winksley, Ripon HG4 3NR* Tel (01765) 658260 E-mail robert.sellers@ukonline.co.uk

SELLERS, Warren John. b 43. Bp Otter Coll Chich TCert73 W Sussex Inst of HE DipAdEd88. K Coll Lon 63 Sarum Th Coll 65. **d** 68 **p** 69. C Guildf H Trin w St Mary *Guildf* 68-72; Hon C Chich St Paul and St Pet *Chich* 72-73; C Epping St Jo *Chelmsf* 73-76; Hon C Pulborough *Chich* 76-90; Hon C Fleet *Guildf* 90-92; Teacher 73-89; Waltham Abbey St Lawr and H Cross Schs Essex 73-76; Pulborough St Mary, Easeboure & Bp Tuffnell Schs 76-89; Hd Teacher St Pet Jun Sch Farnborough 90-92; TV Upper Kennet *Sarum* 92-95; TR 95-03; rtd 03. *71 Bay Crescent, Swanage BH19 1RD*

SELLEY, Paul Edward Henry. b 47. Bris Univ BEd70 ALCM67 LTCL87. Sarum Th Coll 93. **d** 96 **p** 97. C Swindon Dorcan *Bris* 96-00; V Ashton Keynes, Leigh and Minety from 00. *The Vicarage, 23 Richmond Court, Ashton Keynes, Swindon SN6 6PP* Tel (01285) 861566 Fax as telephone E-mail paul.selley@which.net

SELLGREN, Eric Alfred. b 33. AKC61. **d** 62 **p** 63. C Ditton St Mich *Liv* 62-66; V Hindley Green 66-72; V Southport St Paul 72-80; Warden Barn Fellowship Winterborne Whitchurch 80-86; V The Iwernes, Sutton Waldron and Fontmell Magna *Sarum* 86-98; rtd 98; Perm to Offic *Sarum* from 98. *16 The Limes, Motcombe, Shaftesbury SP7 9QL* Tel (01747) 850747

SELLICK, Peter James. b 67. Wadh Coll Ox BA89. Edin Th Coll BD94. **d** 94 **p** 95. C Kippax w Allerton Bywater *Ripon* 94-97; C Stanningley St Thos 97-02; C W Bromwich All SS *Lich* from 02; Ind Chapl Black Country Urban Ind Miss from 02. *7 Hopkins Drive, West Bromwich B71 3RR* Tel 0121-588 3744

SELLIX, Martin Gordon. b 45. Ridley Hall Cam 74. **d** 76 **p** 77. C Crofton St Paul *Roch* 76-80; Ind Chapl *Chelmsf* 80-94; R Rayne 80-86; V Blackmore and Stondon Massey 86-94; RD Ongar 89-94; TR Liskeard, St Keyne, St Pinnock, Morval etc *Truro* 94-99; V Liskeard and St Keyne 99-05; Chapl Cornwall and Is of Scilly Mental Health Unit 96-02; Chapl N and E Cornwall Primary Care Trust 02-05; rtd 05. *Farthings, Quarry Road, Pensilva, Liskeard PL14 5NT* Tel (01579) 363565

SELLIX, Mrs Pamela Madge. b 47. Lon Univ BA68 PGCE68. SW Minl Tr Course 00. **d** 04 **p** 05. NSM Saltash *Truro* from 04. *Farthings, Quarry Road, Pensilva, Liskeard PL14 5NT* Tel (01579) 363565

SELLORS, Michael Harry. b 36. K Coll Lon 60 St Boniface Warminster 61. **d** 61 **p** 62. C Willesden St Mary *Lon* 61-64; C Aldershot St Mich *Guildf* 64-67; V Hale 67-84; P-in-c E w W Beckham *Nor* 84-85; P-in-c Bodham 84-85; V Weybourne w Upper Sheringham 84-85; R Kelling w Salthouse 84-85; R Weybourne Gp 85-91; V Hunstanton St Edm w Ringstead 91-97; Dean Jerusalem 97-02; rtd 02. *Cranford House, 56 Cromer Road, West Runton, Cromer NR27 9AD* Tel (01263) 837293

SELMAN, Cyril Allen. b 25. Wycliffe Hall Ox 64. **d** 65 **p** 65. C Thame *Ox* 65-69; V Beedon 69-87; R Peasemore 69-87; rtd 88; Perm to Offic *Ban* from 88. *7 North Street, North Tawton EX20 2DE* Tel (01837) 82785

SELMAN, Michael Richard. b 47. Sussex Univ BA68 Bris Univ MA70. Coll of Resurr Mirfield 71. **d** 73 **p** 74. C Hove All SS *Chich* 73-74; C Horfield H Trin *Bris* 74-78; P-in-c Landkey *Ex* 78-79; C Barnstaple and Goodleigh 78-79; TV Barnstaple, Goodleigh and Landkey 79-82; TR 82-84; P-in-c Sticklepath

83-84; TR Barnstaple 85; RD Barnstaple 83-85; TR Cen Ex 85-00; Chapl Aquitaine *Eur* from 00. *Le Presbytère, 1 Lotissement la Caussade, 33270 Floirac, France* Tel and fax (0033) (5) 56 40 05 12 E-mail michael.selman@wanadoo.fr

SELMES, Brian. b 48. Nottm Univ BTh74 Dur Univ MA97. Linc Th Coll 70. **d** 74 **p** 75. C Padgate *Liv* 74-77; C Sydenham St Bart *S'wark* 77-80; Chapl Darlington Memorial Hosp from 80; Chapl Darlington Memorial Hosp NHS Trust 94-98; Chapl S Durham Healthcare NHS Trust from 98. *Darlington Memorial Hospital, Hollyhurst Road, Darlington DL3 6HX* Tel (01325) 743029 *or* 359688 E-mail brian.selmes@smtp.sdhc-tr.northy.nhs.uk

SELVEY, Canon John Brian. b 33. Dur Univ BA54. Cuddesdon Coll 56. **d** 58 **p** 59. C Lancaster St Mary *Blackb* 58-61; C Blackb Cathl 61-65; Cathl Chapl 64-65; V Foulridge 65-69; V Walton-le-Dale 69-82; V Cleveleys 82-89; Hon Can Bloemfontein Cathl from 88; V Slyne w Hest *Blackb* 89-97; Hon Can Blackb Cathl 93-97; rtd 97; Perm to Offic *Carl* from 98. *Low Quietways, Borrowdale Road, Keswick CA12 5UP* Tel (01768) 773538

SELWOOD, Michael. b 40. Oak Hill Th Coll DipHE90 BA91. **d** 91 **p** 92. Canada 91-95; P-in-c Sherborne, Windrush, the Barringtons etc *Glouc* from 95. *The New Vicarage, Windrush, Burford OX18 4TS* Tel (01451) 844276 E-mail 106631.11@compuserve.com

SELWOOD, Robin. b 37. ALCD61. **d** 61 **p** 62. C Lenton *S'well* 61-63; C Norbury *Ches* 63-66; V Newton Flowery Field 66-75; V Kelsall 75-89; V Sale St Paul 89-02; rtd 02; P-in-c Langtoft w Foxholes, Butterwick, Cottam etc *York* from 02. *The Rectory, Church Lane, Langtoft, Driffield YO25 3TN* Tel (01377) 267226

SELWOOD, Timothy John. b 45. Lon Univ LLB66. Sarum Th Coll. **d** 83 **p** 84. NSM Colbury *Win* 83-85; NSM Copythorne and Minstead 85-90; Perm to Offic from 98. *Long Cottage, Mews Lane, Winchester SO22 4PS* Tel (01926) 860874

SELWYN, David Gordon. b 38. MEHS Clare Coll Cam BA62 MA66 New Coll Ox MA66. Ripon Hall Ox 62. **d** 64 **p** 65. C Ecclesall *Sheff* 64-65; Asst Chapl New Coll Ox 65-68; Lect Univ of Wales (Lamp) *St D* 68-98; Reader from 98; Perm to Offic from 68. *Address temp unknown*

SEMEONOFF, Canon Jean Mary Agnes. b 36. BSc56 Leic Univ CertEd57. EMMTC 84. **d** 87 **p** 94. Par Dn Leic H Spirit *Leic* 87 and 89-94; Chapl for Deaf People *Derby* 87-89; Chapl for Deaf People *Leic* 89-94; Hon Can Leic Cathl 92-99; rtd 94; Bp's Adv for Women's Min *Leic* 93-97; Min for Special Past Duties 94-99; Perm to Offic from 99. *107 Letchworth Road, Leicester LE3 6FN* Tel 0116-285 8854 E-mail semeonof@leicester.anglican.org

SEMEONOFF, Robert. b 40. Edin Univ BSc62 PhD67. EMMTC 81. **d** 84 **p** 85. NSM Leic H Spirit *Leic* 84-88 and 89-94; NSM Loughb Gd Shep 88-89; Asst Chapl Leic Univ 89-94; Min for Special Past Duties 94-98; Chapl Leic R Infirmary NHS Trust 98-01; Hon Asst Chapl Univ Hosps Leic NHS Trust from 01. *107 Letchworth Road, Leicester LE3 6FN* Tel 0116-285 8854 *or* 254 1414 ext 5487 E-mail semeonof@leicester.anglican.org

SEMPER, The Very Revd Colin Douglas. b 38. Keble Coll Ox BA62. Westcott Ho Cam 61. **d** 63 **p** 64. C Guildf H Trin w St Mary *Guildf* 63-67; Sec ACCM 67-69; Producer Relig Broadcasting Dept BBC 69-75; Overseas Relig Broadcasting Org BBC 75-79; Hd Relig Progr BBC Radio 79-82; Hon Can Guildf Cathl *Guildf* 80-82; Provost Cov 82-87; Can and Treas Westmr Abbey 87-97; Steward 87-90; rtd 97; Perm to Offic *Sarum* 97-03; Hon C Rowledge and Frensham *Guildf* from 03. *The Vicarage, Frensham, Farnham GU10 3DT* Tel (01252) 792137 E-mail sempers@freezone.co.uk

SEMPLE, Henry Michael. b 40. K Coll Lon BSc62 Birkbeck Coll Lon PhD67 CMath FIMA FCMI FRSA. S Dios Minl Tr Scheme. **d** 87 **p** 88. NSM Steyning *Chich* 87-91; Perm to Offic *Guildf* 87-91 and *Linc* 92-93; NSM Linc Cathl *Linc* 93-99; TR Headley All SS *Guildf* 99-02; V from 02. *All Saints' Rectory, High Street, Headley, Bordon GU35 8PP* Tel (01428) 717321 E-mail mandpsemple@waitrose.com

SEMPLE, Studdert Patrick. b 39. TCD BA66. CITC 66. **d** 67 **p** 68. C Orangefield *D & D* 67-70; USA 70-71; I Stradbally *C & O* 71-82; Ch of Ireland Adult Educn Officer 82-88; I Donoughmore and Donard w Dunlavin *D & G* 88-96; Bp's C Dublin St Geo and St Thos 96-99; Chapl Mountjoy Pris and Mater Hosps 96-99; rtd 99. *49 Richmond Park, Monkstown, Co Dublin, Irish Republic* Tel (00353) (1) 230 1712

SEN, Arani. b 61. R Holloway Coll Lon BA84 St Martin's Coll Lanc PGCE86 Open Univ MA94 Fitzw Coll Cam BA98 MA02. Ridley Hall Cam 96. **d** 99 **p** 00. C Mildmay Grove St Jude and St Paul *Lon* 99-02; C-in-c Southall Em CD from 02. *37 Dormers Wells Lane, Southall UB1 3HX* Tel (020) 8843 9556 *or* 8574 1890 E-mail rev.sen@virgin.net

SENIOR, Brian Stephen. b 55. Brighton Coll of Educn CertEd76. Oak Hill Th Coll DipHE93. **d** 93 **p** 94. C Hildenborough *Roch* 93-98; TV Tunbridge Wells St Jas w St Phil 98-04; V Tunbridge Wells St Phil from 04. *St Philip's Vicarage, Birken Road, Tunbridge Wells TN2 3TE* Tel (01892) 512071 E-mail revbssenior@beeb.net

SENIOR, David John. b 47. Oak Hill Th Coll. **d** 82 **p** 83. C Market Harborough *Leic* 82-85; TV Marfleet *York* 85-91; R Desford and Peckleton w Tooley *Leic* 91-96; P-in-c Hall Green Ascension *Birm* 96-99; V from 99; P-in-c Gospel Lane St Mich 97-03. *The Vicarage, 592 Fox Hollies Road, Birmingham B28 9DX* Tel 0121-777 3689

SENIOR, John Peter. b 23. Lon Univ BSc48. Edin Th Coll 63. **d** 65 **p** 66. C Marton *Blackb* 65-68; C Heysham 68-71; V Blackpool St Mich 71-79; V Heddon-on-the-Wall *Newc* 79-88; rtd 88; Perm to Offic *Wakef* from 88. *56 Thorpe Lane, Huddersfield HD5 8TA* Tel (01484) 530466

SENIOR, Patrick Nicolas Adam. b 63. Univ of Wales (Ban) BA86. Trin Coll Bris BA94. **d** 94 **p** 95. C Derringham Bank *York* 94-98; V Brownhill *Wakef* from 98. *The Vicarage, 24 Intake Lane, Brownhill, Batley WF17 0BT* Tel and fax (01924) 471999 E-mail pals@thedogcollar.fsnet.co.uk

✠**SENTAMU, The Most Revd and Rt Hon John Mugabi Tucker.** b 47. Makerere Univ Kampala LLB71 Selw Coll Cam BA76 MA MPhil79 PhD84. Ridley Hall Cam. **d** 79 **p** 79 **c** 96. Chapl HM Rem Cen Latchmere Ho 79-82; C Ham St Andr *S'wark* 79-82; C Herne Hill St Paul 82-83; P-in-c Tulse Hill H Trin 83-84; V Upper Tulse Hill St Matthias 83-84; V Tulse Hill H Trin and St Matthias 85-96; P-in-c Brixton Hill St Sav 87-89; Hon Can S'wark Cathl 93-96; Area Bp Stepney *Lon* 96-02; Bp Birm 02-05; Abp York from 05. *The Palace, Bishopthorpe, York YO23 3QE* Tel (01904) 707021 *or* 707022 Fax 709204 E-mail office@bishopthorpepalace.co.uk

SEOUL, Bishop of. *See* CHUNG, The Most Revd Matthew Chul Bum

SEPHTON, John. b 43. **d** 01 **p** 02. OLM Newburgh w Westhead *Liv* from 01; Asst Chapl HM Pris Risley from 02. *2 Ruff Lane, Ormskirk L39 4QZ* Tel (01695) 576774 *or* (01925) 763871 E-mail johnsephton@postmaster.co.uk

SEPPALA, Christopher James. b 59. St Jo Coll Dur BA82 Ch Ch Coll Cant CertEd92. Chich Th Coll 83. **d** 85 **p** 86. C Whitstable *Cant* 85-88; C S Ashford Ch Ch 88-91; Perm to Offic from 01. *9 Newton Road, Whitstable CT5 2JD* Tel (01227) 266411 E-mail xpristopheros@netscapeonline.co.uk

SERBUTT, Rita Eileen. b 33. Man Univ BA54 Univ of Wales (Cardiff) DipEd56 FRSA94. Dioc OLM tr scheme 98. **d** 01 **p** 02. OLM Balham St Mary and St Jo *S'wark* from 01. *5 Veronica Road, London SW17 8QL* Tel (020) 8772 1031 E-mail eileen.serbutt@virgin.net

SERJEANT, Frederick James. b 28. Lon Inst of Educn BEd77. AKC53 St Boniface Warminster 53. **d** 54 **p** 55. C Leytonstone St Marg w St Columba *Chelmsf* 54-58; C Parkstone St Pet w Branksea *Sarum* 58-59; V Reigate St Luke S Park *S'wark* 59-65; V Battersea St Pet 65-71; C-in-c Battersea St Paul 67-71; V W Mersea *Chelmsf* 71-73; P-in-c E Mersea 71-73; R W w E Mersea 73-75; rtd 93. *3 Church Hill View, Sydling, Dorchester DT2 9SY* Tel (01300) 341670

SERJEANT, Mrs Heather Faith. b 60. Stirling Univ BSc80 Ox Univ BTh04. Ripon Coll Cuddesdon 00. **d** 02 **p** 03. C Caversham and Mapledurham *Ox* from 02. *4A The Mount, Caversham, Reading RG4 7RU* Tel 0118-947 2729 E-mail heatherserjeant@aol.com

SERJEANT, John Frederick. b 33. K Coll Lon 52. **d** 56 **p** 57. C Over St Chad *Ches* 56-59; C-in-c Brinnington St Luke CD 59-63; V Brinnington 63-69; V Gatley 69-79; TV Halesworth w Linstead and Chediston *St E* 79-80; TV Halesworth w Linstead, Chediston, Holton etc 80-82; C Chesterfield St Mary and All SS *Derby* 82-88; Chapl Chesterfield R Hosp 82-88; Chapl Chesterfield and N Derbyshire R Hosp 88-95; rtd 95. *188 Queen Victoria Road, New Tupton, Chesterfield S42 6DW* Tel (01246) 863395

SERJEANTSON, John Cecil Myllles. b 36. Bp's Univ Lennoxville BA63 McGill Univ Montreal BD66. Montreal Dioc Th Coll LTh66. **d** 66 **p** 67. Canada 66-72 and from 79; C Westmount St Matthias 66-68; R Huntingdon w Ormstown 68-72; C Gt and Lt Driffield *York* 72-76; V Bilton St Pet 76-79; R Brome Montreal 79-01; rtd 01. *19 Mountain, South Bolton PQ, Canada, J0E 2H0* Tel (001) (450) 292 0850

SERMON, Michael John. b 61. Univ of Cen England in Birm ACIB85. Qu Coll Birm BA98 MA99. **d** 99 **p** 00. C W Heath *Birm* 99-03; V Blackheath from 03. *St Paul's Vicarage, 83 Vicarage Road, Halesowen B62 8HX* Tel 0121-559 1000 E-mail revsermon@aol.com

SERTIN, John Francis. b 22. Fitzw Ho Cam BA50 MA54. Tyndale Hall Bris. **d** 45 **p** 46. C Sidcup Ch Ch *Roch* 45-47; Chapl Fitzw Ho Cam 47-50; C-in-c St Paul's Cray St Barn CD *Roch* 50-59; V Chitts Hill St Cuth *Lon* 59-62; Sec Ch Soc 62-67; P-in-c Woburn Square Ch Ch *Lon* 67-77; R Holborn St Geo w H Trin and St Bart 67-80; R Donyatt w Horton, Broadway and Ashill *B & W* 80-92; rtd 92; Perm to Offic *B & W* 92-02. *23 Birstan Gardens, Andover SP10 4NY* Tel (01264) 334544

SERVANT, Canon Alma Joan. b 51. Nottm Univ BA76. Westcott Ho Cam 83. **dss** 85 **d** 87 **p** 94. Ordsall *S'well* 85-88; Par Dn 87-88; Par Dn Man Whitworth *Man* 88-94; TV 94-96; Chapl Man Poly 88-92; Chapl Man Metrop Univ 92-96; P-in-c Heaton Norris St Thos 96-00; P-in-c Hulme Ascension 00-05; R from 05; Hon

Can Man Cathl from 02. *The Rectory, Royce Road, Hulme, Manchester M15 5FQ* Tel 0161-226 5568

SERVANTE, Kenneth Edward. b 29. AKC55. **d** 56 **p** 57. C Chaddesden St Phil *Derby* 56-58; C Brampton St Thos 58-61; C Whitfield 61-63; V Derby St Paul 63-70; V Elmton 70-81; P-in-c Winster 81-82; P-in-c Elton 81-82; R S Darley, Elton and Winster 82-94; rtd 94; Perm to Offic *Derby* from 94. *13 Chestnut Avenue, Belper DE56 1LY* Tel (01773) 820513

SESSFORD, Canon Alan. b 34. Bps' Coll Cheshunt 65. **d** 66 **p** 67. C Highcliffe w Hinton Admiral *Win* 66-69; C Minehead *B & W* 70; C Chandler's Ford *Win* 70-73; V Burton and Sopley 73-00; RD Christchurch 93-98; Hon Can Win Cathl 98-00; rtd 00; Perm to Offic *Win* from 00; Chapl R Bournemouth and Christchurch Hosps NHS Trust from 01. *4 Benson Close, Bransgore, Christchurch BH23 8HX* Tel (01425) 673412

SETTERFIELD, Nicholas Manley. b 63. Colchester Inst of Educn BA89. St Steph Ho Ox 89. **d** 92 **p** 93. C Prestbury *Glouc* 92-96; R Letchworth *St Alb* 96-03; V Northampton St Matt *Pet* from 03. *St Matthew's Vicarage, 30 East Park Parade, Northampton NN1 4LB* Tel (01604) 713615
E-mail vicar@stmatthews-northampton.org

SETTIMBA, John Henry. b 52. Nairobi Univ BSc78 Leeds Univ MA91. Pan Africa Chr Coll BA78. **d** 78 **p** 80. Kenya 78-81; Uganda 81-85; C Allerton *Bradf* 86-87; C W Ham *Chelmsf* 87-91; C-in-c Forest Gate All SS 91-94; P-in-c 94-96; TV Hackney *Lon* 96-02. *63 Belvedere Court, Upper Richmond Road, London SW15 6HZ* Tel (020) 8789 8376

SEVILLE, Thomas Christopher John. b 57. Trin Hall Cam MA80. Coll of Resurr Mirfield 87. **d** 89 **p** 90. C Knowle *Bris* 89-93; CR from 93. *House of the Resurrection, Stocks Bank Road, Mirfield WF14 0BN* Tel (01924) 483315
E-mail tseville@mirfield.org.uk

SEWARD, Jolyon Frantom. b 57. Univ of Wales (Cardiff) BA81. Chich Th Coll 83. **d** 86 **p** 87. C Llanblethian w Cowbridge and Llandough etc *Llan* 86-88; C Newton Nottage 88-93; Dioc Children's Officer 88-98; V Penyfai w Tondu 93-01; TV Heavitree and St Mary Steps *Ex* from 01. *St Lawrence's Vicarage, 36 Lower Hill Barton Road, Exeter EX1 3EH* Tel (01392) 466302 *or* 677152 E-mail frjolyon@eurobell.co.uk

SEWARD, Nicholas. b 70. Imp Coll Lon BEng91 ACGI91. Cranmer Hall Dur BA96 MA98. **d** 98 **p** 99. C Bearsted w Thurnham *Cant* 98-02; Chapl and Hd RS Magd Coll Sch Ox from 02. *16 Rose Court, Hillsborough Road, Oxford OX4 3TA* Tel (01865) 717947 E-mail nseward@mcsoxford.org

SEWELL, Andrew. *See* SEWELL, John Andrew Clarkson

SEWELL, Andrew William. b 61. Nottm Univ BSc83. St Jo Coll Nottm 93. **d** 93 **p** 94. C Adel *Ripon* 93-96; C Far Headingley St Chad 96-98; Asst Dioc Missr 96-98; P-in-c Otham w Langley *Cant* 98-01; R from 01. *The Rectory, Church Road, Otham, Maidstone ME15 8SB* Tel (01622) 861470
E-mail asewell@aol.com

SEWELL, Barry. *See* SEWELL, John Barratt

SEWELL, Miss Elizabeth Jill. b 56. Reading Univ BSc77. Trin Coll Bris BA97. **d** 97 **p** 98. C Rothley *Leic* 97-01; TV Market Harborough and The Transfiguration etc from 01. *The Vicarage, 49 Ashley Way, Market Harborough LE16 7XD* Tel (01858) 463441 E-mail ejsewell@leicester.anglican.org

SEWELL, John Andrew Clarkson. b 58. Aston Tr Scheme 93 Ripon Coll Cuddesdon 95. **d** 97 **p** 98. C Horsham *Chich* 97-99; C Cleobury Mortimer w Hopton Wafers etc *Heref* 99-01; R 01-03; TV Ludlow, Ludford, Ashford Carbonell etc 03-04; Chapl Shropshire's Community NHS Trust 03-04. *Cumbria, Longridge Way, Weston-super-Mare BS24 7EB* E-mail jacsewell@aol.com

SEWELL, John Barratt (Barry). b 39. St Bart Hosp Medical Coll MB, BS63 DRCOG66. Ridley Hall Cam. **d** 92 **p** 93. C Ulverston St Mary w H Trin *Carl* 92-94; Asst Chapl R Cornwall Hosps Trust 94-98; Chapl 98-99; P-in-c Gerrans w St Anthony-in-Roseland and Philleigh *Truro* 00-03; rtd 03; Perm to Offic *Truro* from 04. *Cleswyth, Creegbrawse, St Day, Redruth TR16 5QF* Tel (01209) 821696 E-mail barry@cleswyth.freeserve.co.uk

SEWELL, Jonathan William. b 60. Lanc Univ BA82 BTh86. Linc Th Coll 83. **d** 86 **p** 87. C Ilkeston St Mary *Derby* 86-89; C Enfield Chase St Mary *Lon* 89-92; Dioc Youth Officer *Win* 92-97; P-in-c Headington St Mary *Ox* from 98. *St Mary's Vicarage, Bayswater Road, Headington, Oxford OX3 9EY* Tel (01865) 761886 E-mail jonathan.sewell@ntlworld.com

SEWELL, Peter Alexis. b 35. Lon Univ BSc61 PhD67 FRSC86. Cyprus & Gulf Ord Course 92. **d** 94 **p** 95. Cyprus and the Gulf 94-97; NSM Ormskirk *Liv* 97-01; Perm to Offic from 01. *Shakelady Hey, Sandy Lane, Lathom, Ormskirk L40 5TU* Tel and fax (01695) 572095

SEWELL, Richard Michael. b 62. Birm Univ BA84. SEITE 99. **d** 02 **p** 03. C Putney St Mary *S'wark* from 02. *8 Deodar Road, London SW15 2NN* Tel (020) 8785 3821
E-mail fieldsofgold@deodar15.fsnet.co.uk

SEWELL, Robin Warwick. b 42. Trin Coll Bris 80. **d** 82 **p** 83. C Hinckley H Trin *Leic* 82-85; C Broadwater St Mary *Chich* 85-89; Chapl Barcelona *Eur* 89-02; V Braintree St Paul *Chelmsf* from 02. *St Paul's Vicarage, Hay Lane, Braintree CM7 3DY* Tel (01376) 325095 E-mail robin@sewellgospel.fsnet.co.uk

SEWELL, Miss Sarah Frances. b 61. Wycliffe Hall Ox 87. **d** 91 **p** 94. C Binley *Cov* 91-94; Asst Chapl Derriford Hosp Plymouth 94-96; Chapl Stoke Mandeville Hosp NHS Trust 96-00; Chapl R Marsden NHS Trust from 00. *The Chaplain's Office, Royal Marsden Hospital, Downs Road, Sutton SM2 5PT* Tel (020) 8661 3074 *or* 8611 3074
E-mail sarah.sewell@rmh.nthames.nhs.uk

SEXTON, Canon Michael Bowers. b 28. SS Coll Cam BA52 MA56. Wells Th Coll 52. **d** 54 **p** 55. C Miles Platting St Luke *Man* 54-57; C Bradford cum Beswick 57-58; C-in-c Oldham St Chad Limeside CD 58-62; R Filby w Thrigby w Mautby *Nor* 62-72; P-in-c Runham 67-72; P-in-c Stokesby w Herringby 68-72; R Hethersett w Canteloff 72-85; V Ketteringham 73-84; RD Humbleyard 81-86; Hon Can Nor Cathl 85-93; R Hethersett w Canteloff w Lt and Gt Melton 85-86; V Hunstanton St Mary w Ringstead Parva, Holme etc 86-93; rtd 94; Perm to Offic *Nor* from 94. *3 Forge Close, Poringland, Norwich NR14 7SZ* Tel (01508) 493885

SEYMOUR, Dom Anthony Nicholas. b 39. QUB BA61. **d** 96 **p** 97. Community of Our Lady and St John 86-01; Perm to Offic *Win* from 01. *Alton Abbey, Abbey Road, Beech, Alton GU34 4AP* Tel (01420) 562145 *or* 563575 Fax 561691

SEYMOUR, David. b 43. Kelham Th Coll 60. **d** 68 **p** 69. C Cowley St Jas *Ox* 68-73; TV Lynton, Brendon, Countisbury, Lynmouth etc *Ex* 73-77; C-in-c Luton (Princes Park) CD *Roch* 78-79; V Rosherville 79-90; rtd 90. *4 Swinburne Drive, Lowry Hill, Carlisle CA3 0PY* Tel (01228) 597320
E-mail markbeech@boltblue.com

SEYMOUR, David Raymond Russell. b 56. Keble Coll Ox BA79 MA88. St Steph Ho Ox 79. **d** 81 **p** 82. C Tilehurst St Mich *Ox* 81-85; TV Parkstone St Pet w Branksea and St Osmund *Sarum* 85-91; V Bradford-on-Avon Ch Ch 91-01; P-in-c Sturminster Newton and Hinton St Mary 01-02; V Sturminster Newton, Hinton St Mary and Lydlinch from 02. *The Vicarage, Church Street, Sturminster Newton DT10 1DB* Tel (01258) 472531
E-mail davidseymour@ukonline.co.uk

SEYMOUR, Canon John Charles. b 30. Oak Hill Th Coll 51 and 55 Wycliffe Coll Toronto 54. **d** 57 **p** 58. C Islington St Andr w St Thos and St Matthias *Lon* 57-60; C Worthing St Geo *Chich* 60-63; V Thornton *Leic* 63-70; R Kirby Muxloe 70-81; TR 81-83; Hon Can Leic Cathl 82-93; RD Sparkenhoe I 83-88; R Market Bosworth w Shenton 83-87; TR Market Bosworth, Cadeby w Sutton Cheney etc 87-93; RD Sparkenhoe W 89-92; rtd 93. *7 Merton Close, Broughton Astley, Leicester LE9 6QP* Tel (01455) 282525

SEYMOUR, Nicholas. *See* SEYMOUR, Dom Anthony Nicholas

SEYMOUR, Paul Edward. b 62. Humberside Univ BA92. St Jo Coll Nottm 01. **d** 03 **p** 04. C Ingleby Barwick *York* from 03. *27 Berrington Gardens, Ingleby Barwick, Stockton-on-Tees TS17 0UH* Tel (01642) 763647 Mobile 07815-729831
E-mail paulseymour@tiscali.co.uk

SEYMOUR-WHITELEY, Richard Dudley. b 59. Leic Poly BSc80. Linc Th Coll 82. **d** 85 **p** 86. C Bushey *St Alb* 85-89; C Stevenage St Mary Shephall w Aston 89-93; P-in-c Blunham w Tempsford and Lt Barford 93-99; P-in-c The Stodden Churches 99-01; I Grey Abbey w Kircubbin *D & D* from 01. *The Rectory, 90 Newtownards Road, Greyabbey, Newtownards BT22 2QJ* Tel (028) 4278 8216 Mobile 07789-550508
E-mail richard@seymour-whiteley.wanadoo.co.uk

SHACKELL, Daniel William. b 42. **d** 95 **p** 96. Dir Spires Cen from 93; OLM Streatham St Leon *S'wark* 95-99; Lic to Offic from 99; Perm to Offic *Guildf* from 01. *83 Hillside, Banstead SM7 1EZ* Tel (01737) 361569 *or* (020) 8696 0943
E-mail dan@shackell83.freeserve.co.uk

SHACKELL, Kenneth Norman. b 26. S'wark Ord Course 66. **d** 69 **p** 70. NSM Greenwich St Alfege w St Pet and St Paul *S'wark* 69-95; Perm to Offic *Sarum* from 95. *17 Portman Drive, Child Okeford, Blandford Forum DT11 8HU* Tel and fax (01258) 861583

SHACKERLEY, Canon Albert Paul. b 56. K Coll Lon MA97. Chich Th Coll 91. **d** 93 **p** 94. C Harlesden All So *Lon* 93-96; P-in-c Chelmsf All SS *Chelmsf* 96-98; V 98-02; Can Res Sheff Cathl *Sheff* from 02. *9 Stumperlowe Hall Road, Sheffield S10 3QR* Tel 0114-230 4181 *or* 263 6066 Mobile 07786-927715
E-mail paul.shackerley@sheffield-cathedral.org.uk

SHACKLADY, Mrs Thelma. b 38. Liv Univ BA60. St Alb Minl Tr Scheme 89. **d** 92 **p** 94. NSM Luton St Andr *St Alb* 92-96; NSM Luton All SS w St Pet 96-03; Perm to Offic from 03. *45 Lilly Hill, Olney MK46 5EZ* Tel (01234) 712997
E-mail bill.shacklady@virgin.net

SHACKLEFORD, Richard Neal. b 40. Univ of Denver BA64 Univ of N Colorado MA74. St Steph Ho Ox 84. **d** 86 **p** 87. C Poulton-le-Fylde *Blackb* 86-88; USA from 88; Can St Jo Cathl Colorado 88-92; C Denver St Mich 92-96; R Lindenhurst St Boniface from 96. *100 46th Street, Lindenhurst, NY 11747, USA*

SHACKLETON, Canon Alan. b 31. Sheff Univ BA53. Wells Th Coll 54. **d** 56 **p** 57. C Ladybarn *Man* 56-58; C Bolton St Pet 58-61; V Middleton Junction 61-70; V Heywood St Luke 70-84; AD Rochdale 82-92; Hon Can Man Cathl 84-97; V Heywood St Luke w All So 85-86; TV Rochdale 86-91; TR 91-97; rtd 97; Perm to Offic *Man* from 97. *28 Taunton Avenue, Rochdale OL11 5LD* Tel (01706) 645335
E-mail alan@ashackleton.demon.co.uk

SHACKLETON, Ian Roderick. b 40. St Fran Coll Brisbane 69. **d** 72 **p** 72. C Toowoomba Australia 72-74; P-in-c Milmerran 74-75; R 75-78; C Birch St Agnes *Man* 79-80; P-in-c Newton Heath St Wilfrid and St Anne 80-87; NSM W Derby St Jo *Liv* 87-90; C 90-94; P-in-c Southport St Luke from 94; Asst Chapl HM Pris Liv from 94. *St Luke's Vicarage, 71 Hawkshead Street, Southport PR9 9BT* Tel (01704) 538703

SHACKLEY, Prof Myra Lesley. b 49. Southn Univ BA70 PhD75 Nottm Univ MA99 FRGS. EMMTC 96. **d** 99 **p** 00. NSM Ordsall *S'well* 99-02; Dioc Tourism Adv from 02; PV S'well Minster from 02. *47 Eldon Street, Tuxford, Newark NG22 0LG* Tel and fax (01777) 870838 Mobile 07889-691504
E-mail myra.shackley@ntu.ac.uk

SHAFEE, Kenneth Harold. b 30. ALA64. Ex & Truro NSM Scheme 78. **d** 81 **p** 82. NSM Littleham w Exmouth *Ex* 81-85; Custos St Jo Hosp Heytesbury 85-89; NSM Lydford, Brent Tor, Bridestowe and Sourton *Ex* 89-90; rtd 90; Perm to Offic *Ex* from 90. *The Firs, Exeter Road, Dawlish EX7 0LX* Tel (01626) 888326

SHAFTO, Robert James. b 38. FCA61. OLM course 96. **d** 99 **p** 00. OLM W Dulwich All SS *S'wark* from 99. *46 Cedar Close, London SE21 8HX* Tel (020) 8761 7395

SHAHZAD, Sulaiman. b 60. BA. Oak Hill Th Coll BA93. **d** 96 **p** 97. C Winchmore Hill St Paul *Lon* 96-00; TV Digswell and Panshanger *St Alb* from 00. *71 Haldens, Welwyn Garden City AL7 1DH* Tel (01707) 335537
E-mail sulishahzad@tiscali.co.uk

SHAIL, Canon William Frederick. b 15. Kelham Th Coll. **d** 41 **p** 42. C Deptford St Paul *S'wark* 41-44; C Lewisham St Mary 44-47; C Christchurch *Win* 47-52; R N Stoneham 52-68; V Bournemouth St Alb 68-78; V Burley Ville 78-84; rtd 84; Perm to Offic *Win* 84-97. *19 Halton Close, Bransgore, Christchurch BH23 8HZ* Tel (01425) 673064

SHAKESPEARE, James Douglas Geoffrey. b 71. Fitzw Coll Cam BA93 MA97 Man Univ MA96. Westcott Ho Cam 97. **d** 99 **p** 00. C Cherry Hinton St Jo *Ely* 99-02; Bp's Chapl and Policy Adv *Leic* from 02; P-in-c Birstall and Wanlip from 05. *St James's Rectory, 151 Birstall Road, Birstall, Leicester LE4 4DJ* Tel 0116-267 4517 E-mail shakespeare@jdgs.freeserve.co.uk

SHAKESPEARE, Steven. b 68. CCC Cam BA89 PhD94. Westcott Ho Cam 93. **d** 96 **p** 97. C Cambridge St Jas *Ely* 96-99; V Endcliffe and Chapl Sheff Hallam Univ *Sheff* 99-03; Chapl Liv Hope Univ Coll from 03. *Anglican Chaplaincy, Hope Park, Taggart Avenue, Liverpool L16 9JD* Tel 0151-291 3545
E-mail shakess@hope.ac.uk

SHAMBROOK, Roger William. b 46. Sarum & Wells Th Coll 78. **d** 83 **p** 84. OSP 76-82; C Southbourne St Kath *Win* 83-86; TV Bridport *Sarum* 86-01; Chapl Bridport Community Hosp 86-94; Chapl Dorset Community NHS Trust 94-01; P-in-c Torre All SS *Ex* from 01. *All Saints' Vicarage, 45 Barton Road, Torquay TQ1 4DT* Tel (01803) 328865

SHAND, Brian Martin. b 53. Univ Coll Lon BA76 PhD82. St Steph Ho Ox 85. **d** 87 **p** 88. C Uxbridge St Marg *Lon* 87-88; C Uxbridge 88-90; C Worplesdon *Guildf* 90-94; Relig Affairs Producer BBC Radio Surrey 90-94; V Weston 94-01; V Witley from 01. *The Vicarage, Petworth Road, Witley, Godalming GU8 5LT* Tel and fax (01428) 681872
E-mail allsaints.witley@btinternet.com

SHANKS, Canon Robert Andrew Gulval. b 54. Ball Coll Ox BA75 G&C Coll Cam BA79 Leeds Univ PhD90. Westcott Ho Cam 77. **d** 80 **p** 81. C Potternewton *Ripon* 80-83; C Stanningley St Thos 84-87; Lect Leeds Univ 87-91; Teaching Fell Lanc Univ *Blackb* 91-95; Research Fell in Th Cheltenham and Glouc Coll of HE 95-96; NSM Leeds City *Ripon* 95-96; P-in-c Upper Ryedale and CME Officer Cleveland Adnry *York* 97-04; Can Res Man Cathl *Man* from 04. *3 Booth-Clibborn Court, Salford M7 4PJ* Tel 0161-792 8820

SHANNON, Brian James. b 35. St Chad's Coll Dur BA59 DipTh61. **d** 61 **p** 62. C Palmers Green St Jo *Lon* 61-65; C Kenton 65-70; V Roxbourne St Andr 70-81; V Thorpe-le-Soken *Chelmsf* 81-91; V Gt Wakering w Foulness 91-99; rtd 99; Perm to Offic *Chelmsf* from 99. *154 Bournemouth Park Road, Southend-on-Sea SS2 5LT* Tel (01702) 464737

SHANNON, The Ven Malcolm James Douglas. b 49. TCD BA72 MA75. CITC 75. **d** 75 **p** 76. C Clooney *D & R* 75-78; I Kilcolman w Kiltallagh, Killorglin, Knockane etc *L & K* from 78; Adn Ardfert and Aghadoe 88-04; Adn Limerick from 04; Treas Limerick Cathl from 88; Dir of Ords from 91. *Kilcolman Rectory, Miltown, Killarney, Co Kerry, Irish Republic* Tel (00353) (66) 976 7302 Mobile 88-539 906 Fax (66) 976 7197

SHANNON, Canon Trevor Haslam. b 33. Selw Coll Cam BA57 MA61 Lon Univ BD69. Westcott Ho Cam 57. **d** 59 **p** 60. C Moss Side Ch Ch *Man* 59-62; V Woolfold 62-66; Chapl Forest Sch Snaresbrook 66-80 and 87-88; V Gt Ilford St Marg *Chelmsf* 88-90; TR Gt Ilford St Clem and St Marg 90-96; V 96-99; RD Redbridge 90-95; Hon Can Chelmsf Cathl 93-99; rtd 99; Perm to Offic *Nor* from 00. *Honeysuckle Cottage, Clubbs Lane, Wells-next-the-Sea NR23 1DP* Tel (01328) 711409

SHAPLAND, David Edward. b 26. Cuddesdon Coll 51. **d** 53 **p** 54. C Cranbrook *Cant* 53-55; Chapl St Cath Coll Cam 55-61; R Fittleworth *Chich* 62-65; Warden Bede Ho Staplehurst 65-69; Warden Llanerchwen Trust 70-91; Lic to Offic *S & B* 70-79; Perm to Offic *Chich* 79-91; rtd 91. *17 College Close, Westward Ho!, Bideford EX39 1BL* Tel (01237) 479566

SHARE, David James. b 30. Sarum Th Coll 56. **d** 58 **p** 59. C Whipton *Ex* 58-63; Min Tiverton St Andr Statutory Distr 63-69; RD Tiverton 67-74; V Tiverton St Andr 69-79; P-in-c Ex St Thos 79-80; TR Ex St Thos and Em 80-83; V Woodbury 83-95; rtd 95; Corps Chapl ATC 94-02; Perm to Offic *Ex* from 95. *57 Coombeshead Road, Newton Abbot TQ12 1PZ* Tel (01626) 362516

SHARLAND, Canon Marilyn. b 40. City of Birm Coll CertEd61. Oak Hill Th Coll 84. **dss** 86 **d** 87 **p** 94. Barkingside St Laur *Chelmsf* 86-87; Hon Par Dn 87-88; Hon Par Dn Hucclecote *Glouc* 88-89; C Coney Hill 89-98; P-in-c Tuffley 98-99; V from 99; Hon Can Glouc Cathl from 02. *St Barnabas' Vicarage, 200 Reservoir Road, Tuffley, Gloucester GL4 9SB* Tel (01452) 306535 Fax 535998 E-mail reverend.marilyn@euphony.net

SHARMAN, Hilary John. b 32. Leeds Univ BA58. Coll of Resurr Mirfield 58. **d** 60 **p** 61. C Hertford St Andr *St Alb* 60-64; C Harpenden St Nic 64-72; V High Cross from 72; V Thundridge from 72. *7 Ducketts Wood, Thundridge, Ware SG12 0SR* Tel (01920) 465561

SHARP, Alfred James Frederick. b 30. Oak Hill Th Coll 62. **d** 64 **p** 65. C Hanley Road St Sav w St Paul *Lon* 64-68; P-in-c Leverton *Linc* 68-84; Chapl Pilgrim Hosp Boston 76-84; P-in-c Benington w Leverton *Linc* 84; V Ch Broughton w Boylestone amd Sutton on the Hill *Derby* 84-89; R Ch Broughton w Barton Blount, Boylestone etc 89-94; rtd 94. *14 Edgefield, Weston, Spalding PE12 6RQ* Tel (01406) 370376

SHARP, Andrew Timothy. b 58. K Alfred's Coll Win BA79. Wycliffe Hall Ox 82. **d** 85 **p** 86. C Scarborough St Mary w Ch Ch and H Apostles *York* 85-89; C Luton St Fran *St Alb* 89-90; V 90-98; P-in-c Guernsey St Jo *Win* 98-01; V from 01; Vice-Dean Guernsey from 01. *St John's Vicarage, Les Amballes, St Peter Port, Guernsey GY1 1WY* Tel and fax (01481) 720879

SHARP, Mrs Barbara Elaine. b 52. Open Univ BA84. Ripon Coll Cuddesdon 01. **d** 03. C Timperley *Ches* from 03. *57 Heyes Lane, Timperley, Altrincham WA15 6DZ* Tel 0161-905 1994

SHARP, Bernard Harold. b 40. Linc Th Coll 64. **d** 67 **p** 68. C Newton Aycliffe *Dur* 67-69; C Leam Lane CD 69-71; Malawi 72-75; P-in-c Blakenall Heath *Lich* 75-77; TV Gateshead *Dur* 77-79; C Warmsworth *Sheff* 84; C Caerau w Ely *Llan* 85-92; V Cwmbach from 92. *The Vicarage, Bridge Road, Cwmbach, Aberdare CF44 0LS* Tel (01685) 878674

SHARP, Brian Phillip. b 48. Cant Sch of Min 85. **d** 88 **p** 89. C S Ashford Ch Ch *Cant* 88-92; C St Laur in Thanet 92-96; V Margate St Jo from 96. *The Vicarage, 24 St Peter's Road, Margate CT9 1TH* Tel (01843) 230766
E-mail brian.stjohn@cwcom.net

SHARP, Canon David Malcolm. b 33. Hertf Coll Ox BA56 MA59. Cuddesdon Coll 56. **d** 58 **p** 59. C Bris St Mary Redcliffe w Temple *Bris* 58-65; V Henleaze 65-75; V Nor St Pet Mancroft *Nor* 75-82; R Nor St Pet Mancroft w St Jo Maddermarket 82-98; Hon Can Nor Cathl 86-98; Dioc Eur Contact from 91; rtd 98; Perm to Offic *Nor* from 98. *The Pines, Field Lane, Fakenham NR21 9QX* Tel (01328) 864121
E-mail dmsharp.revcanon@ukonline.co.uk

SHARP, Mrs Heather Karin. b 48. **d** 04 **p** 05. OLM Blackrod *Man* from 04. *27 Hill Lane, Blackrod, Bolton BL6 5JW* Tel (01204) 693609 E-mail heatherksharp@hotmail.com

SHARP (née BROWN), Mrs Jane Madeline. b 54. **d** 97 **p** 98. C Aylestone St Andr w St Jas *Leic* 97-00; Hon C Knighton St Mary Magd from 00. *10 St Mary's Road, Leicester LE2 1XA* Tel 0116-270 6002 E-mail jbrown@leicester.anglican.org

SHARP, Mrs Janice Anne. b 54. Aston Tr Scheme 91 N Ord Course 93. **d** 96 **p** 97. C Skipton H Trin *Bradf* 96-00; V Buttershaw St Paul 00-02; Chapl Hull and E Yorks Hosps NHS Trust from 02. *The Hull Royal Infirmary, Anlaby Road, Hull HU3 2JZ* Tel (01482) 328541

SHARP, Nicholas Leonard. b 64. Grey Coll Dur BA85. St Jo Coll Nottm MA95. **d** 95 **p** 96. C Oakwood St Thos *Lon* 95-99; TV N Farnborough *Guildf* from 99; Chapl Farnborough Sixth Form Coll from 01. *The Vicarage, 45 Sand Hill, Farnborough GU14 8ER* Tel (01252) 543789
E-mail nick@sharp64.freeserve.co.uk

SHARP, Canon Reuben Thomas George (Tom). b 27. ALCD57. **d** 57 **p** 58. C Pudsey St Lawr *Bradf* 57-60; V Cononley w Bradley 60-63; Dioc Youth Chapl 60-63; Dioc Youth Officer *Wakef* 63-68; V Dewsbury All SS 68-84; RD Dewsbury 68-90; Hon Can Wakef Cathl 76-97; TR Dewsbury 84-90; V Cawthorne 90-97;

rtd 97; Perm to Offic *Man* from 99. *1 St Barnabas Drive, Littleborough OL15 8EJ* Tel (01706) 379298

SHARP, Preb Robert. b 36. FLCM58. St Aid Birkenhead 64. **d** 67 **p** 68. C Shipley St Paul *Bradf* 67-70; C-in-c Thwaites Brow CD 70-74; V Thwaites Brow 74-77; P-in-c Alberbury w Cardeston *Heref* 77-78; V 78-87; V Ford 77-87; V Claverley w Tuckhill 87-97; RD Bridgnorth 89-96; Preb Heref Cathl 91-97; rtd 97; Perm to Offic *Heref* 97-99 and from 01; C Stoke Lacy, Moreton Jeffries w Much Cowarne etc 99-00. *62 Biddulph Way, Ledbury HR8 2HN* Tel (01531) 631972

SHARP, Miss Sarah Elizabeth. b 67. Bp Otter Coll Chich BA89 Anglia Poly Univ MA00 Coll of Ripon & York St Jo PGCE90. Westcott Ho Cam 98. **d** 00 **p** 01. C Ross *Heref* 00-03; R Lower Windrush *Ox* from 03. *The Rectory, Main Road, Stanton Harcourt, Witney OX29 5RP* Tel (01865) 880249 E-mail sesharp@care4free.net

SHARPE, Canon Alan Brian. b 39. Lich Th Coll 64. **d** 67 **p** 68. C Croydon Woodside *Cant* 67-70; C Portsea St Mary *Portsm* 70-75; V Sheerness H Trin w St Paul *Cant* 75-83; V Hove St Patr w Ch Ch and St Andr *Chich* 83-90; V Hove St Patr from 90; Can and Preb Chich Cathl from 93. *St Patrick's Vicarage, 30 Cambridge Road, Hove BN3 1DF* Tel (01273) 327242

SHARPE, Anthony Mark. b 67. Leeds Univ BA01. Coll of Resurr Mirfield 99. **d** 01 **p** 02. C Acomb Moor *York* 01-02; C Norton juxta Malton 02-03; C W Buckrose 03-04; Chapl RN 04-05; R Teme Valley S *Worc* from 05. *The Rectory, Broadheath, Tenbury Wells WR15 8QW* Tel (01886) 853286

SHARPE, Canon Bruce Warrington. b 41. JP88. DMS(Ed)85 MCMI85. Ely Th Coll 62 St Steph Ho Ox 64. **d** 65 **p** 66. C Streatham St Pet *S'wark* 65-67; St Lucia 67-68; Hon C Leic St Matt and St Geo *Leic* 68-69; Hon C Catford St Laur *S'wark* 69-70; Hon C Deptford St Paul 70-75; Hon C Lamorbey H Redeemer *Roch* 76-83; Hon C Sidcup St Andr 88-99; Perm to Offic *Roch* 83-88 and 99-01; *Lon* from 97; *S'wark* from 98; Hon C Bickley from 01; Hon Can Windward Is from 01. *72 Faraday Avenue, Sidcup DA14 4JF* Tel (020) 8300 0695 *or* 8346 3522 E-mail canonbruce1@aol.com

SHARPE, Cecil Frederick. b 23. Edin Th Coll 52. **d** 54 **p** 55. C Falkirk *Edin* 54-56; C Kings Norton *Birm* 56-58; V Withall 58-80; Perm to Offic from 80; rtd 88. *35 Shirley Park Road, Shirley, Solihull B90 2BZ* Tel 0121-745 6905

SHARPE, David Francis. b 32. Ex Coll Ox BA56 MA59. St Steph Ho Ox 57. **d** 60 **p** 61. C Hunslet St Mary and Stourton *Ripon* 60-63; C Notting Hill St Jo *Lon* 63-68; V Haggerston St Mary w St Chad 68-78; P-in-c Haggerston St Aug w St Steph 73-78; V Haggerston St Chad 78-83; V Mill Hill St Mich 83-98; rtd 98; Chapl St Raphaël *Eur* 98-02; Perm to Offic *Lon* from 02. *15 Grahame Park Way, London NW7 2LA* Tel (020) 8959 0429 E-mail davidsharpe@waitrose.com

SHARPE, Derek Martin Brereton (Pip). b 29. Birkbeck Coll Lon BA60. NEOC 90. **d** 90 **p** 91. NSM Scarborough St Luke *York* 90-92; Asst Chapl Scarborough Distr Hosp 90-92; P-in-c Sherburn and W and E Heslerton w Yedingham *York* 92-99; Hon C Buckrose Carrs 99; rtd 99; Perm to Offic *York* from 00. *Byland Lodge, 68A Low Moorgate, Rillington, Malton YO17 8JW* Tel (01944) 759063

SHARPE, Gerard John. b 23. Westcott Ho Cam. **d** 64 **p** 65. C Thetford St Cuth w H Trin *Nor* 64-70; V Holme *Ely* 70-76; R Conington 70-76; R Glatton 74-93; V Holme w Conington 76-93; RD Yaxley 82-88; rtd 93; Perm to Offic *Ely* 93-00. *24 St Margaret's Road, Girton, Cambridge CB3 0LT* Tel (01223) 574246

SHARPE, Miss Joan Valerie. b 33. EMMTC 73. **dss** 84 **d** 88 **p** 94. Hon Par Dn Warsop *S'well* 88-94; Hon C 94-98; rtd 98; Perm to Offic *S'well* from 04. *1 Forest Court, Eakring Road, Mansfield NG18 3DP* Tel (01623) 424051

SHARPE, John Edward. b 50. St Jo Coll Dur BSc72. Cranmer Hall Dur 73. **d** 76 **p** 77. C Woodford Wells *Chelmsf* 76-79; C Ealing St Mary *Lon* 79-83; Min Walsall St Martin *Lich* 83-87; TV Walsall 87-96; R Glenfield *Leic* from 96; RD Sparkenhoe E from 03. *The Rectory, Main Street, Glenfield, Leicester LE3 8DG* Tel 0116-287 1604 E-mail jesharpe@leicester.anglican.org

SHARPE, Canon John Leslie. b 33. Open Univ BA75 Birm Univ DPS72 MInstGA89. Kelham Th Coll 54. **d** 58 **p** 59. C Charlton St Luke w St Paul *S'wark* 58-61; Papua New Guinea 62-70; Adn N Distr 68-70; P-in-c Southampton SS Pet and Paul w All SS *Win* 71-73; TV Southampton (City Cen) 73-75; Chapl SW Hants Psychiatric Services 75-93; Chapl Knowle Hosp Fareham 75-93; Hon Can Portsm Cathl *Portsm* 86-93; rtd 93; Perm to Offic *Sarum* from 98 and *Win* from 01. *Clare Cottage, 23 West Dean, Salisbury SP5 1JB* Tel (01794) 340028 Fax 342256 E-mail john@jlsharpe.freeserve.co.uk

SHARPE, The Ven Kenneth William. b 40. Univ of Wales (Lamp) BA61. Sarum Th Coll 61. **d** 63 **p** 64. C Hubberston *St D* 63-71; TV Cwmbran *Mon* 71-74; Dioc Children's Adv 72-82; Dioc Youth Chapl 74-82; V Dingestow and Llangovan w Penyclawdd and Tregaer 74-82; V Newport St Mark 82-97; Chapl Alltyryn Hosp Gwent 83-97; RD Newport *Mon* 93-97; Can St Woolos Cathl from 94; Adn Newport from 97. *The Archdeaconry, 93 Stow Hill, Newport NP20 4EA* Tel (01633) 215012

SHARPE, Mrs Margaret Theresa. b 48. Man Univ BEd70. Cranmer Hall Dur 72 WMMTC 90. **d** 91 **p** 94. C W Bromwich H Trin *Lich* 91-96; Asst Chapl Glenfield Hosp NHS Trust Leic 96-99; Chapl 99-00; Chapl Univ Hosps Leic NHS Trust 00-04; Chapl Team Ldr from 04. *Chaplains' Department, Glenfield Hospital, Groby Road, Leicester LE3 9QP* Tel 0116-256 3413 *or* 287 1604 E-mail margaret.sharpe@uhl-tr.nhs.uk

SHARPE, Mark. *See* SHARPE, Anthony Mark

SHARPE, Miss Mary. b 31. CQSW71. Dalton Ho Bris 58. **dss** 78 **d** 87 **p** 94. Upton (Overchurch) *Ches* 78-83; Harlescott *Lich* 83-84; New Brighton All SS *Ches* 85-89; Par Dn 87-89; rtd 89; Perm to Offic *Ches* from 89. *13 Manor Close, Neston CH64 6TE* Tel 0151-353 0456

SHARPE, Mrs Mary Primrose. b 22. Coll of St Matthias Bris CertEd. Gilmore Ho CertRK51 CMS Tr Coll Chislehurst. **dss** 81 **d** 87. Coley *Wakef* 81-87; Hon Par Dn 87-89; rtd 89; Perm to Offic *Bradf* 89-99. *54 Bradford Road, Menston, Ilkley LS29 6BX* Tel (01943) 877710

SHARPE, Peter Richard. b 55. Salford Univ BSc76 ACIB81. STETS 98. **d** 01 **p** 02. C Ex St Jas *Ex* 01-04; R S Hill w Callington *Truro* from 04. *The Rectory, Liskeard Road, Callington PL17 7JD* Tel (01579) 383341 Mobile 07767-251136 E-mail prshome@clara.net

SHARPE, Pip. *See* SHARPE, Derek Martin Brereton

SHARPE, Richard Gordon. b 48. Birm Univ BA69. St Jo Coll Nottm BA74. **d** 75 **p** 76. C Hinckley H Trin *Leic* 75-78; C Kingston upon Hull H Trin *York* 78-85; Chapl Marston Green Hosp Birm 85-88; Chapl Chelmsley Hosp Birm 86-88; TV Chelmsley Wood *Birm* 85-88; P-in-c Dosthill 88-93; V 93-97; R Desford and Peckleton w Tooley *Leic* from 97. *The Rectory, 27 Church Lane, Desford, Leicester LE9 9GD* Tel (01455) 822276 E-mail sharpeblackhorse@aol.com

SHARPE, Canon Roger. b 35. TCD BA60 MA63. Qu Coll Birm 60. **d** 62 **p** 63. C Stockton H Trin *Dur* 62-64; C Oakdale St Geo *Sarum* 64-68; V Redlynch and Morgan's Vale 68-86; RD Alderbury 82-86; V Warminster St Denys 86-88; R Upton Scudamore 86-88; V Horningsham 86-88; R Warminster St Denys, Upton Scudamore etc 88-95; Can and Preb Sarum Cathl 89-00; RD Heytesbury 89-95; Chmn Dioc Assn for Deaf from 91; P-in-c Corsley 92-95; TR Cley Hill Warminster 95-00; rtd 00; Perm to Offic *Sarum* from 01. *Woodside, Bugmore Lane, East Grimstead SP5 3SA* Tel (01722) 712753

SHARPE, Tony Ernest Charles. b 34. Dur Univ BA55. EAMTC 90. **d** 93 **p** 94. NSM Leigh-on-Sea St Jas *Chelmsf* 93-96; NSM Thorpe Bay 96-00; NSM Golden Cap Team *Sarum* from 00. *The Vicarage, Hawkchurch, Axminster EX13 5XB* Tel (01297) 678225

SHARPLES, Canon Alfred Cyril. b 09. Man Univ BA33. Linc Th Coll 33. **d** 35 **p** 36. C Rochdale *Man* 35-39; C Ashton St Mich 39-42; R Cheetham St Mark 42-46; V Tonge w Alkrington 46-51; V Hope St Jas 51-76; Hon Can Man Cathl 74-76; rtd 76; Perm to Offic *Ches* and *Man* from 77. *30 Greenbank Drive, Bollington, Macclesfield SK10 5LW* Tel 0161-207 5073

SHARPLES, David. b 41. Linc Th Coll 71. **d** 73 **p** 74. C Reddish *Man* 73-75; C Prestwich St Mary 76-78; V Ashton St Jas 78-86; V Hope St Jas from 86. *Hope Vicarage, Vicarage Close, Pendleton, Salford M6 8EJ* Tel 0161-789 3303

SHARPLES, David John. b 58. Lon Univ BD81 AKC81. Coll of Resurr Mirfield. **d** 82 **p** 83. C Prestwich St Mary *Man* 82-87; V Royton St Anne 87-02; AD Tandle 94-02; Dir of Ords from 02. *St Thomas's New Vicarage, Church Street, Milnrow, Rochdale OL16 3QS* Tel (01706) 291539 *or* 0161-708 9366 Fax 0161-792 6826 E-mail ddo@bishopscourt.manchester.anglican.org

SHARPLES, Derek. b 35. SS Paul & Mary Coll Cheltenham CertEd57 Liv Univ DipEd63 Man Univ MEd66 Bath Univ PhD72 Open Univ BA79 FCollP86. WMMTC 83. **d** 86 **p** 87. NSM Malvern H Trin and St Jas *Worc* 86-90; C St Jo in Bedwardine 90-92; R Belbroughton w Fairfield and Clent 92-00; rtd 00; Perm to Offic *Worc* from 00. *Witton, 16 Moorlands Road, Malvern WR14 1VA* Tel (01684) 575742 E-mail witton@clara.co.uk

SHARPLES, Mrs Jean. b 37. Padgate Coll of Educn TCert58. **d** 04 **p** 05. NSM Gerrans w St Anthony-in-Roseland and Philleigh *Truro* from 04. *Potterer's End, 18 Highertown, Portscatho, Truro TR2 5HP* Tel (01872) 580503 Mobile 07840-567933 E-mail jshar38429@aol.com

SHARPLES, Canon John Charles. b 29. St Jo Coll York TCert48 Lon Univ BSc55. St Deiniol's Hawarden 87. **d** 87 **p** 88. Hon C Wigan St Mich *Liv* 87-89; P-in-c New Springs 89-96; Hon Can Liv Cathl 97; rtd 97; Perm to Offic *Liv* from 97. *New Springs Vicarage, 7 Lealholme Avenue, Wigan WN2 1EH* Tel (01942) 243071

SHARPLES, Jonathan David. b 65. Lon Bible Coll BA95. Wycliffe Hall Ox 03. **d** 05. C Ashton-upon-Mersey St Mary *Ches* from 05. *23 Rydal Avenue, Sale M33 6WN* E-mail jonsharples@hotmail.com

SHARPLES, Ms Susan Margaret. b 58. SRN82 Worc Coll of Educn BA89. WMMTC 91. **d** 94 **p** 95. C Worc SE *Worc* 94-97; P-in-c Elmley Castle w Bricklehampton and Combertons 97-01; USA from 01. *Address temp unknown*

SHARPLEY, The Ven Roger Ernest Dion. b 28. Ch Ch Ox BA52 MA56. St Steph Ho Ox 52. **d** 54 **p** 55. C Southwick St Columba *Dur* 54-60; V Middlesbrough All SS *York* 60-81; P-in-c Middlesbrough St Hilda w St Pet 64-72; P-in-c Middlesbrough St Aid 79; V 79-81; RD Middlesbrough 70-81; Can and Preb York Minster 74-81; V St Andr Holborn *Lon* 81-92; Adn Hackney 81-92; rtd 92; Perm to Offic *Dur* from 92; Chapl Grey Coll Dur 96-01. *2 Hill Meadows, High Shincliffe, Durham DH1 2PE* Tel 0191-386 1908

SHAVE, Norman Rossen. b 60. G&C Coll Cam BA82 MA95 Newc Univ MB, BS85 MRCGP90. Cranmer Hall Dur 98. **d** 00 **p** 01. C Preston on Tees *Dur* 00-03; C Preston-on-Tees and Longnewton 03-04; V Norton St Mary from 04; P-in-c Stockton St Chad from 04. *2 Brambling Close, Norton, Stockton-on-Tees TS20 1TX* Tel (01642) 558888

SHAW, Alan. b 24. Man Univ BSc44 MSc48 PhD51. Ely Th Coll 55. **d** 57 **p** 58. C Orford St Marg *Liv* 57-59; C Bury St Mary *Man* 59-61; Perm to Offic *Liv* 61-71; V Beckermet St Jo *Carl* 71-76; V Lt Leigh and Lower Whitley *Ches* 76-80; V Latchford Ch Ch 80-91; rtd 91; Perm to Offic *Ches* and *Liv* from 91. *22 Pangbourne Close, Appleton, Warrington WA4 5HJ* Tel (01925) 269402

SHAW, Alan Taylor. b 52. Sarum & Wells Th Coll 88. **d** 90 **p** 91. C Beeston *Ripon* 90-93; C Stanningley St Thos 93-96; TV Seacroft 96-98; V Ryhill *Wakef* 98-02; rtd 03. *65 Hollingthorpe Avenue, Hall Green, Wakefield WF4 3NP*

SHAW, Alan Walter. b 41. TCD BA63 BAI63 Chu Coll Cam MSc66. **d** 94 **p** 95. NSM Drumcliffe w Kilnasoolagh *L & K* 94-97; NSM Kenmare w Sneem, Waterville etc from 97. *St Patrick's Rectory, Kenmare, Co Kerry, Irish Republic* Tel and fax (00353) (64) 41121 Mobile 87-678 8700 E-mail shawa@eircom.net *or* kenmare@ardfert.anglican.org

✠**SHAW, The Rt Revd Alexander Martin.** b 44. AKC67. **d** 68 **p** 69 **c** 04. C Glas St Oswald *Glas* 68-70; C Edin Old St Paul *Edin* 70-75; Chapl K Coll Cam 75-77; C St Marylebone All SS *Lon* 77-78; R Dunoon *Arg* 78-81; Succ Ex Cathl *Ex* 81-83; Dioc Miss and Ecum Officer 83-89; TV Cen Ex 83-87; Can Res St E Cathl *St E* 89-04; Prec 96-04; Bp Arg from 04. *The Pines, Ardconnel Road, Oban, Argyll PA34 5DR* Tel (01631) 566912 Mobile 07801-549615 E-mail alexandermartin.shaw@virgin.net

SHAW, Mrs Alison Barbara. b 55. Open Univ BA92. SW Minl Tr Course 98. **d** 01 **p** 02. NSM St Breoke and Egloshayle *Truro* 01-03; C Bodmin w Lanhydrock and Lanivet from 03. *The Vicarage, Rectory Road, Lanivet, Bodmin PL30 5HG* Tel (01208) 831743 E-mail alishaw2001@yahoo.co.uk

SHAW, Andrew Jonathan. b 50. Wycliffe Hall Ox 85. **d** 87 **p** 88. C Witton w Brundall and Braydeston *Nor* 87-89; C Brundall w Braydeston and Postwick 89-90; C Grayswood *Guildf* 90-91; P-in-c 91-99; Chapl RN Sch Haslemere 90-96; V Hendon St Paul Mill Hill *Lon* from 99. *St Paul's Vicarage, Hammers Lane, London NW7 4EA* Tel (020) 8959 1856 *or* tel and fax 8906 3793 E-mail parishoffice@stpaulsmillhill.freeserve.co.uk

SHAW, Ms Anne Lesley. b 50. SRN SCM ONC. Linc Th Coll 77. **dss** 80 **d** 87 **p** 94. Camberwell St Luke *S'wark* 80-85; Chapl Asst Lon Hosp (Whitechapel) 85-90; Chapl Lewisham Hosp 90-94; Chapl Hither Green Hosp 90-94; Chapl Sydenham Childrens' Hosp 90-94; Chapl Lewisham Hosp NHS Trust from 94. *The Chaplain's Office, University Hospital Lewisham, High Street, London SE13 6LH* Tel (020) 8333 3299 *or* 8333 3000 E-mail annie.shaw@uhl.nhs.uk

SHAW, Anne Patricia Leslie. b 39. MB, BS63 DA68 MRCS63 LRCP63. Qu Coll Birm 79. **dss** 81 **d** 87 **p** 94. Pinner *Lon* 81-84; Rickmansworth *St Alb* 84-87; NSM from 87. *37 Sandy Lodge Road, Moor Park, Rickmansworth WD3 1LP* Tel (01923) 827663 E-mail anneshaw@doctors.net.uk

SHAW, Anthony Keeble. b 36. K Alfred's Coll Win CertEd60 Birkbeck Coll Lon CPsychol98. SW Minl Tr Course 78. **d** 81 **p** 82. Hd Teacher Wolborough C of E Primary Sch 73-87; NSM E Teignmouth *Ex* 81-83; NSM Highweek and Teigngrace 83-87; Sub Chapl HM Pris Channings Wood 85-87; C Southbourne St Kath *Win* 87-89; Teaching 89-96; NSM Regent's Park St Mark *Lon* 93-96; P-in-c Winthorpe and Langford w Holme *S'well* 96-01; Dioc Chief Insp of Schs 96-01; rtd 01; Perm to Offic *Win* from 01. *Manlea Cottage, Centre Lane, Everton, Lymington SO41 0JP* Tel (01590) 645451

SHAW, Clive Ronald. b 54. UEA BA75 Hatf Coll Dur PGCE76. Carl and Blackb Dioc Tr Inst 99. **d** 02 **p** 03. C Westfield St Mary *Carl* from 02. *49 Sarsfield Road, Workington CA14 5DA* Tel (01900) 64976 E-mail c.shaw@rowan1.fslife.co.uk

SHAW, Colin Clement Gordon. b 39. RMN60 Thoracic Nursing Cert 62 DPS72. Linc Th Coll 65. **d** 67 **p** 68. C Tettenhall Regis *Lich* 67-70; C Tile Cross *Birm* 70-72; V Edstaston *Lich* 72-75; V Whixall 72-75; Chapl Stoke Mandeville Hosp and St Jo Hosp 75-90; Manor Ho Hosp and Tindal Gen Hosp Aylesbury 75-90; R Bledlow w Saunderton and Horsenden *Ox* 90-96; rtd 96. *5 Wyre Close, Haddenham, Aylesbury HP17 8AU* Tel (01844) 292741 E-mail ccg.shaw@btinternet.com

SHAW, Colin Martin. b 21. Oak Hill Th Coll 68. **d** 69 **p** 70. C Halliwell St Pet *Man* 69-72; V Tonge Fold 72-78; V Gresley *Derby* 78-82; V Gt Marsden *Blackb* 82-87; rtd 87; Perm to Offic *Ely* from 87. *60 Popes Lane, Warboys, Huntingdon PE28 2RN* Tel (01487) 822246

SHAW, David George. b 40. Lon Univ BD64. Tyndale Hall Bris 58. **d** 65 **p** 66. C Kirkdale St Lawr *Liv* 65-68; C Bebington *Ches* 68-70; V Swadlincote *Derby* 70-75; R Eyam 75-04; rtd 04. *86 Higher Street, Okeford Fitzpaine, Blandford Forum DT11 0RQ* Tel (01258) 860571 E-mail rector@eyamchurch.org

SHAW, David Michael. b 61. Univ Coll Dur BA83 Bris Univ BA97. Trin Coll Bris DipHE93. **d** 93 **p** 94. C Wotton-under-Edge w Ozleworth and N Nibley *Glouc* 93-97; P-in-c Jersey St Clem *Win* 97-98; R from 98. *The Rectory, La rue du Presbytere, St Clement, Jersey JE2 6RB* Tel (01534) 851992 E-mail st.clement@jerseymail.co.uk

SHAW, David Parlane. b 32. CITC. **d** 69 **p** 70. Bp's C Lower w Upper Langfield *D & R* 69-75; R Chedburgh w Depden and Rede *St E* 75-78; R Chedburgh w Depden, Rede and Hawkedon 79-82; R Desford *Leic* 82-83; R Desford and Peckleton w Tooley 84-91; P-in-c Ramsden Crays w Ramsden Bellhouse *Chelmsf* 91-95; rtd 95; Perm to Offic *Leic* from 95. *9 Hambleton Close, Leicester Forest East, Leicester LE3 3NA* Tel 0116-224 6507 E-mail david.shaw15@ntlworld.com

SHAW, David Thomas. b 45. Open Univ BA78. WMMTC 87. **d** 90 **p** 91. C Sheldon *Birm* 90-93; R Chelmsley Wood 93-02; TR Broughton Astley and Croft w Stoney Stanton *Leic* from 02. *The Rectory, St Mary's Close, Broughton Astley, Leicester LE9 6ES* Tel (01455) 283150

SHAW, Dennis Alfred Arthur. b 24. Wells Th Coll 64. **d** 65 **p** 66. C Redditch St Steph *Worc* 65-70; R Addingham *Bradf* 70-92; rtd 92; Perm to Offic *Bradf* from 92. *67 Crowther Avenue, Calverley, Pudsey LS28 5SA* Tel (01274) 611746

SHAW, Ernest Ronald. b 16. K Coll Lon BA38. Chich Th Coll 72. **d** 72 **p** 73. Chapl Cov Cathl *Cov* 72-78; Perm to Offic *Sarum* 79-80 and from 85; C Semley and Sedgehill 80-85; rtd 85. *Fairmead, Church Hill, Stour Row, Shaftesbury SP7 0QW* Tel (01747) 838350

SHAW, Mrs Felicity Mary. b 46. UEA BSc67 MSc68 Liv Inst of Educn DipRE87. N Ord Course 88. **d** 91 **p** 94. Par Dn Benchill *Man* 91-94; C 94-95; TV E Farnworth and Kearsley 95-98; TR 98-03; V Woodhall *Bradf* from 03. *St James's Vicarage, Galloway Lane, Pudsey LS28 8JR* Tel (01274) 662735 E-mail rev.flissshaw@tesco.net

SHAW, Frederick Hugh. b 16. CChem MRSC Dur Univ BSc49 MSc66. EMMTC 73. **d** 76 **p** 77. Hon C Wingerworth *Derby* 76-96; Perm to Offic from 96. *1 Frances Drive, Wingerworth, Chesterfield S42 6SJ* Tel (01246) 278321

SHAW, Gary Robert. b 59. **d** 85 **p** 86. C Dundonald *D & D* 85-87; I Tullaniskin w Clonoe *Arm* 87-94; Bp's C Stoneyford *Conn* 94-99; I Belfast St Nic 99-00; Chapl R Group of Hosps Health and Soc Services Trust 94-00; Lic to Offic *Conn* 00-04; Bp's C Monkstown from 04. *22 Rosemount Crescent, Newtownabbey BT37 0NH* Tel (028) 9096 4782 *or* 9036 9565 Mobile 07734-415869 E-mail gary.shaw1@ntlworld.com

SHAW, Canon Geoffrey Norman. b 26. Jes Coll Ox MA50. Wycliffe Hall Ox 49. **d** 51 **p** 52. C Rushden *Pet* 51-54; C Woking Ch Ch *Guildf* 54-59; V Woking St Paul 59-62; R St Leonards St Leon *Chich* 62-68; Lic to Offic *Sheff* 68-72; Vice-Prin and Lect Oak Hill Th Coll 72-79; Prin Wycliffe Hall Ox 79-88; Hon Can Ch Ch *Ox* 86-88; rtd 88; Lic to Offic *Nor* 88-91. *15A West Street, Kingham, Chipping Norton OX7 6YF* Tel (01608) 658006

SHAW, Gerald Oliver. b 32. K Coll Lon 56. **d** 60 **p** 61. C Burnley St Cuth *Blackb* 60-62; C Heysham 62-65; C-in-c Oswaldtwistle All SS CD 65-66; V Oswaldtwistle All SS 66-69; Chapl Leavesden Hosp Abbots Langley 69-75; Chapl Broadmoor Hosp Crowthorne 75-88; C Easthampstead *Ox* 88-92; P-in-c Beech Hill, Grazeley and Spencers Wood 92-97; rtd 97; Lic to Offic *Ox* from 99; Perm to Offic *Win* from 02. *1 Mortimer House Cottage, Mortimer Lane, Mortimer, Reading RG7 3PR* Tel 0118-933 3660

SHAW, Graham. b 44. Worc Coll Ox BA65. Cuddesdon Coll. **d** 69 **p** 70. C Esher *Guildf* 69-73; R Winford *B & W* 73-78; Chapl Ex Coll Ox 78-85; R Farnborough *Roch* 88-95; rtd 04. *2 Herons Place, Isleworth TW7 7BE* Tel (020) 8569 7839

SHAW, Canon Grahame David. b 44. Lich Th Coll 65. **d** 68 **p** 69. C Grange St Andr *Ches* 68-73; TV E Runcorn w Halton 73-74; TV Thamesmead *S'wark* 74-79; V Newington St Paul from 79; S'wark Adnry Ecum Officer from 90; RD S'wark and Newington 96-02; Hon Can S'wark Cathl from 99. *The Vicarage, Lorrimore Square, London SE17 3QU* Tel (020) 7735 2947 *or* 7735 8815 E-mail grahame.shaw@talk21.com

SHAW, Mrs Irene. b 45. Gilmore Course 80 NEOC 82. **dss** 83 **d** 87 **p** 94. Elloughton and Brough w Brantingham *York* 83-86; Westborough *Guildf* 86-88; C 87-88; C Shottermill 88-91; C Lamorbey H Redeemer *Roch* 91-97; V Belvedere All SS 97-02; P-in-c S Crosland *Wakef* 02-03; P-in-c Rashcliffe and Lockwood

02-03; TV Em TM 03-05; rtd 05. *10 Rowan Avenue, Beverley HU17 9UN*

SHAW, Canon Jane Alison. b 63. Ox Univ BA85 MA91 Harvard Div Sch MDiv88 Univ of California Berkeley PhD94. St Alb and Ox Min Course 96. **d** 97 **p** 98. Fell Regent's Park Coll Ox 94-01; Dean 98-01; Hon Cathl Chapl Ch Ch Ox from 00; Fell, Chapl and Dean of Div New Coll Ox from 01; NSM Ox St Mary V w St Cross and St Pet *Ox* 97-01; Hon Can Ch Ch from 05. *New College, Oxford OX1 3BN* Tel (01865) 279541 E-mail jane.shaw@theology.oxford.ac.uk

SHAW, Miss Jane Elizabeth. b 47. New Hall Cam BA68 MA72 Brunel Univ MPhil79 DipHSM71. NEOC 98. **d** 01 **p** 02. NSM Moor Allerton *Ripon* from 01. *101 St Anne's Road, Leeds LS6 3NZ* Tel 0113-275 8978 Fax 233 6997 E-mail j.e.shaw@leeds.ac.uk

SHAW, Mrs Jane Louise Claridge. b 66. Birm Poly BA87. WMMTC 00. **d** 03 **p** 04. C Longbridge *Birm* from 03. *6 Butter Walk, Birmingham B38 8JQ* Tel 0121-458 2950 E-mail louiseshaw6@yahoo.co.uk

SHAW, Mrs Janet Elaine. b 53. EMMTC 94. **d** 97 **p** 98. C Cleveleys *Blackb* 97-01; P-in-c Blackpool St Paul 01-03; V from 03. *St Paul's Vicarage, 253 Warbreck Hill Road, Blackpool FY2 0SP* Tel (01253) 350007 E-mail mail@vicstp.fsnet.co.uk

SHAW, John Boyde. b 52. St Jo Coll Nottm BA00. **d** 00 **p** 01. C Gorleston St Andr *Nor* 00-04; P-in-c Rockland St Mary w Hellington, Bramerton etc from 04. *The Rectory, 2 Rectory Lane, Rockland St Mary, Norwich NR14 7EY* Tel (01508) 538619 E-mail jshaw1@madasafish.com

SHAW, Jonathan. *See* SHAW, Andrew Jonathan

SHAW, Kenneth James. b 36. St Jo Coll Nottm 85 Edin Th Coll 88. **d** 87 **p** 89. NSM Troon *Glas* 87-89; C Glas St Mary 89-90; R Lenzie 90-01; Warden of Readers 96-01; rtd 01; Hon C Glas St Mary *Glas* from 02. *19 Mailerbeg Gardens, Moodiesburn, Glasgow G69 0JP* Tel (01236) 873987 E-mail ken@kjshaw.fsnet.co.uk

SHAW, Louise. *See* SHAW, Mrs Jane Louise Claridge

SHAW, Malcolm. b 46. Trin Coll Bris. **d** 01 **p** 02. C Bolsover *Derby* 01-05; R Brimington from 05. *The Rectory, Church Street, Brimington, Chesterfield S43 1JG* Tel (01246) 273103 Mobile 07713-624005 E-mail malshw@aol.com

SHAW, Malcolm Roy. b 47. Lon Univ BA69 Liv Poly CQSW76. NEOC 03. **d** 05. NSM Hunmanby w Muston *York* from 05. *31 Muston Road, Hunmanby, Filey YO14 0JY* Tel (01723) 890926

SHAW, Mrs Margaret Ann. b 58. Bp Otter Coll Chich BA80 SS Paul & Mary Coll Cheltenham PGCE81. EAMTC 00. **d** 03 **p** 04. C Langdon Hills *Chelmsf* from 03. *17 Oakham Close, Langdon Hills, Basildon SS16 6NX*

SHAW, Martin. *See* SHAW, The Rt Revd Alexander Martin

SHAW, Michael. *See* SHAW, Ralph Michael

SHAW, Michael Howard. b 38. Leeds Univ BSc61 Kent Univ DipTh90. Linc Th Coll 64. **d** 66 **p** 67. C W Hartlepool St Paul *Dur* 66-68; Asst Master Stockbridge Co Sec Sch 68; Totton Coll 69; Gravesend Boys' Gr Sch 70-72; Maidstone Gr Sch 72-94; Perm to Offic *Cant* and *Roch* from 70; rtd 03. *2 Bredgar Close, Maidstone ME14 5NG* Tel (01622) 673415

SHAW, Neil Graham. b 61. St Jo Coll Nottm LTh89. **d** 91 **p** 92. C Leamington Priors St Paul *Cov* 91-95; TV Bestwood *S'well* 95-99; Chapl HM YOI Thorn Cross from 99. *HM Young Offender Institution, Arley Road, Appleton, Warrington WA4 4RL* Tel (01925) 605085 Fax 262153

SHAW, Norman. b 33. Cranmer Hall Dur. **d** 82 **p** 83. C Beamish *Dur* 82-84; P-in-c Craghead 84-88; V Cleadon 88-98; rtd 98. *3 St Mary's Drive, Sherburn, Durham DH6 1RL* Tel 0191-372 2540 E-mail normandcon@aol.com

SHAW, Peter Haslewood. b 17. Pemb Coll Cam BA39 MA65. Worc Ord Coll 65. **d** 67 **p** 68. C S Kensington St Jude *Lon* 67-69; V Alderney *Win* 69-78; V Disley *Ches* 78-82; rtd 82; Chapl Athens w Kifissia, Patras and Corfu *Eur* 82-85; Hon C Las Palmas 84-85; Hon C Breamore *Win* 85-89. *Manor Cottage, Church Road, Greatworth, Banbury OX17 2DU* Tel (01295) 712102

SHAW, Ralph. b 38. Man Univ MEd70. Sarum & Wells Th Coll 78. **d** 80 **p** 81. C Consett *Dur* 80-84; P-in-c Tanfield 84-88; V 88-97; R S Shields St Aid and St Steph from 97. *The Rectory, 45 Lawe Road, South Shields NE33 2EN* Tel 0191-456 1831

SHAW, Ralph Michael. b 45. DipAdEd. Lich Th Coll 68. **d** 70 **p** 71. C Dewsbury All SS *Wakef* 70-75; TV Redcar w Kirkleatham *York* 75-76; Dioc Youth Officer *St Alb* 76-91; Lic to Offic from 91; Chief Exec Jo Grooms from 91. *18 Wyton, Welwyn Garden City AL7 2PF* Tel (01707) 321813 *or* (020) 7452 2000 Fax (020) 7452 2101 E-mail revmshaw@aol.com *or* mshaw@johngrooms.org.uk

SHAW, Richard. b 46. **d** 89 **p** 90. NSM Porchester *S'well* 89-91; NSM Daybrook from 04. *15 Harberton Close, Redhill, Nottingham NG5 8LA* Tel 0115-967 6884

SHAW, Preb Richard Tom. b 42. AKC69. St Aug Coll Cant 69. **d** 70 **p** 71. C Dunston St Nic *Dur* 70-73; C Maidstone All SS w St Phil and H Trin *Cant* 73-75; Chapl RN 75-79; V Barrow-on-Humber *Linc* 79-83; V Linc St Faith and St Martin w St Pet 83-91; V Clun w Bettws-y-Crwyn and Newcastle *Heref* from 91; RD Clun Forest from 94; P-in-c Hopesay from 98; Preb Heref Cathl from 02. *The Vicarage, Vicarage Road, Clun, Craven Arms SY7 8JG* Tel (01588) 640809

SHAW, Robert Christopher. b 34. Man Univ BA BD. Union Th Sem (NY) STM. **d** 82 **p** 83. C Sharlston *Wakef* 82-83; C Scissett St Aug 83-85; R Cumberworth w Denby Dale 85-90; P-in-c Denby 85-90; R Bolton w Ireby and Uldale *Carl* 90-95; rtd 95; Perm to Offic *York* from 95. *Stonecroft, Sproxton, York YO62 5EF* Tel (01439) 770178

SHAW, Robert William. b 46. Lon Univ BD69. St Aug Coll Cant 69. **d** 70 **p** 71. C Hunslet St Mary and Stourton *Ripon* 70-71; C Hunslet St Mary 71-74; C Hawksworth Wood 74-76; R Stanningley St Thos 76-84; V Potternewton 84-94; V Manston 94-02; P-in-c Beeston Hill H Spirit 02-04; P-in-c Hunslet Moor St Pet and St Cuth 02-04; V Beeston Hill and Hunslet Moor from 04. *St Peter's Vicarage, 139 Dewsbury Road, Leeds LS11 5NW* Tel 0113-277 2464

SHAW, Roderick Kenneth. b 37. MBIM77. Moray Ord Course 88. **d** 92 **p** 95. Hon C Grantown-on-Spey *Mor* 92-96; Hon C Rothiemurchus 92-00; P Companion Missr from 00. *The Cottage, Balliefurth, Grantown-on-Spey PH26 3NH* Tel (01479) 821496

SHAW, Mrs Rosemary Alice. b 44. CertEd65 CQSW78 Heythrop Coll Lon MA96 MA04. S'wark Ord Course 87. **d** 89 **p** 94. Par Dn Walworth *S'wark* 89-92; Par Dn E Dulwich St Jo 92-95; NSM 95-96; Eileen Kerr Mental Health Fell Maudsley Hosp 95-96; Chapl King's Healthcare NHS Trust 96-01; Sen Chapl Guy's and St Thos' Hosps NHS Trust Lon from 02; Hon C E Dulwich St Jo *S'wark* from 96. *19 Scutari Road, London SE22 0NN* Tel (020) 8693 6325 E-mail rosemary.shaw@gstt.sthames.nhs.uk

SHAW, Roy. *See* SHAW, Malcolm Roy

SHAW, Wendy Jane. b 54. Shenstone Coll of Educn CertEd75 Man Univ MEd90. EAMTC 01. **d** 05. C Thurton *Nor* from 05. *The Rectory, 2 Rectory Lane, Rockland St Mary, Norwich NR14 7EY* Tel (01508) 537045 Mobile 07830-306384 E-mail wendyjane.shaw@virgin.net

SHAYLER-WEBB, Peter. b 57. Bath Univ BSc81 BArch83. Ripon Coll Cuddesdon 93. **d** 95 **p** 96. C Bedford St Paul *St Alb* 95-99; C Dorking w Ranmore *Guildf* 99-04; R Sherwood Australia from 04. *41 Kathleen Street, Corinda, Qld, Australia 4075* Tel (0061) (7) 3278 2498 E-mail psw5957@aol.com

SHEA, Martyn Paul Leathley. b 66. City Univ BSc89. Wycliffe Hall Ox. **d** 00 **p** 01. C Ches Square St Mich w St Phil *Lon* 00-03; C Stamford St Geo w St Paul *Linc* from 03. *14 Queens Street, Stamford PE9 1QS* Tel (01780) 766248 *or* 481800 Mobile 07976-869467 E-mail associaterector@stgeorgeschurch.net

SHEAD, John Frederick Henry. b 38. ACP74 FCP81. Westcott Ho Cam 72. **d** 74 **p** 75. Hd Master Thaxted Co Primary Sch 70-85; Hon C Thaxted *Chelmsf* 74-85; C Saffron Walden w Wendens Ambo and Littlebury 86-88; P-in-c Wethersfield w Shalford 88-96; P-in-c Finchingfield and Cornish Hall End 94-96; V Finchingfield and Cornish Hall End etc 96-04; RD Braintree 95-00; rtd 04. *57 Kenworthy Road, Braintree CM7 1JJ* Tel (01376) 321783 E-mail jshead@finch31.freeserve.co.uk

SHEARCROFT, Sister Elizabeth Marion. b 57. SRN76. **d** 94 **p** 95. CA from 84; NSM Margate H Trin *Cant* 94-98; Chapl Thanet Healthcare NHS Trust 94-98; Chapl E Kent Hosps NHS Trust 99-02; C Kendal H Trin *Carl* 02-05; V Streatham Immanuel and St Andr *S'wark* from 05. *Immanuel Vicarage, 51A Guildersfield Road, London SW16 5LS* Tel (020) 8764 5103 E-mail liz@thekingsfishery.co.uk

SHEARD, Andrew Frank. b 60. York Univ BA81. St Jo Coll Nottm 92. **d** 94 **p** 95. C Uxbridge *Lon* 94-96; TV 96-99; P-in-c 99-01; TR from 01. *St Margaret's Vicarage, 72 Harefield Road, Uxbridge UB8 1PL* Tel (01895) 237853 *or* 258766 Fax 812194 E-mail andrewf.sheard@btinternet.com

SHEARD, Ernest. b 29. Linc Th Coll 73. **d** 74 **p** 75. NSM Birstall *Leic* 74-82; NSM Birstall and Wanlip 82-84; Asst Chapl Loughb Univ and Colls 75-90; Lic to Offic *Leic* 90-94; Perm to Offic from 94. *21 Orchard Road, Birstall, Leicester LE4 4GD* Tel 0116-267 3901

SHEARD, Gillian Freda. *See* COOKE, Ms Gillian Freda

SHEARD, Preb Michael Rowland. b 42. K Coll Lon BA Man Univ PhD. **d** 95 **p** 95. World Miss Officer *Lich* from 89; TV Willenhall H Trin *Lich* from 95; Preb Lich Cathl from 99; TV Willenhall H Trin from 03. *68 Sneyd Lane, Essington, Wolverhampton WV11 2DX* Tel (01922) 445844 Fax 491948 E-mail michael.sheard@btinternet.com

SHEARER, John Frank. b 35. Ex Univ BSc60. Tyndale Hall Bris 62. **d** 63 **p** 64. C Blackheath St Jo *S'wark* 63-67; R Nuffield *Ox* from 67. *The Rectory, Nuffield, Henley-on-Thames RG9 5SN* Tel (01491) 641305

SHEARING, Michael James. b 39. Lanc Univ BA71. Linc Th Coll. **d** 66 **p** 67. NSM Hartlepool St Paul *Dur* 66-76; Asst Master Dyke Ho Comp Sch Hartlepool 76-87; C Houghton le Spring 87; P-in-c Wheatley Hill 87-95; V Bishopwearmouth St Nic

95-97; R Cockfield and V Lynesack 97-04; rtd 04. *4 The Orchard, Barnard Castle DL12 8FB* Tel (01833) 630617 E-mail michael.shearing@durham.anglican.org

SHEARLOCK, The Very Revd David John. b 32. FRSA91 Birm Univ BA55. Westcott Ho Cam 56. **d** 57 **p** 58. C Guisborough *York* 57-60; C Christchurch *Win* 60-64; V Kingsclere 64-71; V Romsey 71-82; Dioc Dir of Ords 77-82; Hon Can Win Cathl 78-82; Dean Truro 82-97; R Truro St Mary 82-97; Chapl Cornwall Fire Brigade 91-97; rtd 98; Perm to Offic *Sarum* from 98. *3 The Tanyard, Shadrack Street, Beaminster DT8 3BG* Tel (01308) 863170

SHEARMAN, Michael Alan. b 22. Down Coll Cam BA44 MA48. Coll of Resurr Mirfield 46. **d** 48 **p** 49. C Bounds Green *Lon* 48-53; C Wembley Park St Aug 53-58; V Enfield St Luke 58-87; rtd 87; Perm to Offic *Nor* 87-02. *18 Thompson Avenue, Holt NR25 6EN* Tel (01263) 713072

SHEARS, Canon Michael George Frederick. b 33. Pemb Coll Cam BA57 MA68. St Steph Ho Ox 57. **d** 59 **p** 60. C Grantham St Wulfram *Linc* 59-68; R Waltham 68-80; R Barnoldby le Beck 74-80; RD Haverstoe 78-80; V Soham *Ely* 80-99; RD Fordham 83-95; Hon Can Ely Cathl 94-99; rtd 99; Perm to Offic *Nor* from 00. *Woodcutter's Cottage, 19 High Street, Wicklewood, Wymondham NR18 9QE* Tel (01953) 605535

SHEASBY, Adrian. b 29. Open Univ BA89. St Aid Birkenhead 54. **d** 57 **p** 58. C Foleshill St Paul *Cov* 57-60; C Pet St Jo *Pet* 60-65; V Maxey w Northborough 65-94; rtd 94; Perm to Offic *Pet* and *Linc* from 94. *26 Beech Close, Market Deeping, Peterborough PE6 8LL* Tel (01778) 347581

SHEATH, Allan Philip. b 48. SW Minl Tr Course 95. **d** 98 **p** 99. NSM Tiverton St Pet and Chevithorne w Cove *Ex* 98-03; C Honiton, Gittisham, Combe Raleigh, Monkton etc 03-04; TV from 04. *The Vicarage, Awliscombe, Honiton EX14 3PJ* Tel (01404) 42983 E-mail allan.sheath@virgin.net

SHEDD, Mrs Christine Elizabeth. b 49. City of Birm Coll CertEd70 St Jo Coll York MA02. N Ord Course 02. **d** 04 **p** 05. C Thornton St Jas *Bradf* from 04. *12 Middlebrook Way, Bradford BD8 0EJ* Tel (01274) 484161

SHEDDEN, Mrs Valerie. b 56. Ripon Coll of Educn CertEd77. Cranmer Hall Dur 81. **dss** 84 **d** 87 **p** 94. Tudhoe Grange *Dur* 84-85; Whitworth w Spennymoor 85-91; Par Dn 87-91; Par Dn E Darlington 91-94; P-in-c Bishop Middleham 94-00; Dioc RE Adv 94-00; V Heworth St Mary from 00. *Heworth Vicarage, High Heworth Lane, Gateshead NE10 0PB* Tel 0191-469 2111 E-mail val.shedden@talk21.com

SHEEHAN, Patrick Edward Anthony. b 37. Campion Ho Middx 58 English Coll Lisbon 62. **d** 67 **p** 69. In RC Ch 67-73; C Clapham H Spirit *S'wark* 73-75; P-in-c Wimbledon 75-77; Australia from 77; R Balga Good Shep 77-80; R Melville H Cross 80-85; Chapl R Newcastle Hosp 85-91; Chapl Jo Hunter Hosp 91-97; R Terrigal 97-01; rtd 01. *22 Abby Crescent, Ashmore, Qld, Australia 4214* Tel (0061) (7) 5564 7064

SHEEHY, Jeremy Patrick. b 56. Magd Coll Ox BA78 MA81 New Coll Ox DPhil90. St Steph Ho Ox 78. **d** 81 **p** 82. C Erdington St Barn *Birm* 81-83; C Small Heath St Greg 83-84; Dean Div, Fell and Chapl New Coll Ox 84-90; V Leytonstone St Marg w St Columba *Chelmsf* 90-96; P-in-c Leytonstone St Andr 93-96; Prin St Steph Ho Ox from 96. *St Stephen's House, 16 Marston Street, Oxford OX4 1JX* Tel (01865) 247874 Fax 794338 E-mail jeremy.sheehy@ssho.ox.ac.uk

SHEEKEY, Raymond Arthur. b 23. Chich Th Coll 51. **d** 53 **p** 54. C Ramsgate St Geo *Cant* 53-56; C Birchington w Acol 56-61; V Brabourne w Smeeth 61-79; RD N Lympne 75-78; Chapl Lenham Hosp 79-88; R Lenham w Boughton Malherbe 79-88; rtd 88; Perm to Offic *Bris* 88-97; Perm to Offic *Glouc* 98-99. *41 Barleycorn, Leybourne, West Malling ME19 5PS* Tel (01732) 847722

SHEEN, David Kenneth. b 70. Cov Univ BSc95 Univ of Wales (Cardiff) BA04. St Mich Coll Llan 01. **d** 04 **p** 05. C Cowbridge *Llan* from 04. *3 Leoline Close, Cowbridge CF71 7BU* Tel (01446) 773515 E-mail dk.sheen@btinternet.com

SHEEN, Canon John Harold. b 32. Qu Coll Cam BA54 MA58. Cuddesdon Coll 56. **d** 58 **p** 59. C Stepney St Dunstan and All SS *Lon* 58-62; V Tottenham St Jo 62-68; V Wood Green St Mich 68-78; P-in-c Southgate St Mich 77-78; R Kirkbride *S & M* 78-97; Chapl Ramsey Cottage Hosp 80-98; V Lezayre St Olave Ramsey 80-98; RD Ramsey 88-97; Can St German's Cathl 91-98; Dir of Ords 93-01; rtd 98; Perm to Offic *S & M* from 99. *Kentraugh Mill, Colby, Isle of Man IM9 4AU* Tel (01624) 832406

SHEEN, Canon Victor Alfred. b 17. Tyndale Hall Bris 47. **d** 49 **p** 50. Uganda 49-56; C Cheltenham St Mark *Glouc* 56-58; V W Streatham St Jas *S'wark* 58-65; V Clapham St Jas 65-86; RD Clapham and Brixton 75-82 and 85-86; Hon Can S'wark Cathl 80-86; rtd 86; Perm to Offic *Chich* from 86. *10 Porters Way, Polegate BN26 6AP* Tel (01323) 487487

SHEERAN, Antony. b 58. Birm Poly BA80. SEITE 02. **d** 05. NSM Mildmay Grove St Jude and St Paul *Lon* from 05. *26 Harcombe Road, London N16 0SA* Tel (020) 7275 9190 Mobile 07881-811586 E-mail tony.sheeran@marsh.com

SHEFFIELD, Julia. b 55. MCSP78 SRP78. NTMTC BA05. **d** 05. NSM Yiewsley *Lon* from 05. *30A Copperfield Avenue, Uxbridge UB8 3NX* Tel (01895) 237590 E-mail julishef@fish.co.uk

SHEFFIELD, Michael Julian. b 53. Brentwood Coll of Educn CertEd. Sarum & Wells Th Coll 76. **d** 79 **p** 80. C Locks Heath *Portsm* 79-83; C Ryde All SS 83-86; P-in-c Ryde H Trin 86-92; V 92-96; P-in-c Swanmore St Mich w Havenstreet 86-92; V Swanmore St Mich 92-96; V W Leigh 96-04; V Waterlooville from 04. *The Vicarage, 5 Deanswood Drive, Waterlooville PO7 7RR* Tel (023) 9226 2145 Mobile 07818-031902 E-mail mikejs99@hotmail.com

SHEFFIELD, Archdeacon of. *See* BLACKBURN, The Ven Richard Finn

SHEFFIELD, Bishop of. *See* NICHOLLS, The Rt Revd John

SHEFFIELD, Dean of. *See* BRADLEY, The Very Revd Peter Edward

SHEGOG, Preb Eric Marshall. b 37. City Univ MA88 FRSA92. Lich Th Coll 64. **d** 65 **p** 66. C Benhilton *S'wark* 65-68; Asst Youth Adv 68-70; V Abbey Wood 70-76; Chapl Sunderland Town Cen 76-83; C Bishopwearmouth St Mich w St Hilda *Dur* 76-83; Hd Relig Broadcasting IBA 84-90; Perm to Offic *Lon* 85-90 and *St Alb* 85-89; Hon C Harpenden St Nic *St Alb* 89-97; Dir Communications for C of E 90-97; Dir Communications *Lon* 97-00; Preb St Paul's Cathl 97-00; Acting Dioc Gen Sec 99; rtd 00; Perm to Offic *St Alb* from 00. *9 Colbron Close, Ashwell, Baldock SG7 5TH* Tel (01462) 743251

SHEHADI, Nabil Faouzi. b 58. Wycliffe Hall Ox 00. **d** 02 **p** 03. C Cobbold Road St Sav w St Mary *Lon* 02-05; V Internat Congregation Beirut All SS Lebanon from 05. *All Saints' Church, PO Box 11-2211, Riad El Solh, Beirut 1107 2100, Lebanon* Tel (00961) (4) 530551

SHELDON, Jennifer Christine. b 43. K Coll Lon BA99. NTMTC 00. **d** 02 **p** 03. NSM Poplar *Lon* from 02. *23 Lancaster Drive, London E14 9PT* Tel (020) 7538 2375 *or* 7538 9198 Fax 7538 1551 E-mail jensheldon@aol.com

SHELDON, Jonathan Mark Robin. b 59. Cam Univ MA83. Ridley Hall Cam 81. **d** 83 **p** 84. C Dulwich St Barn *S'wark* 83-86; C Worle *B & W* 86-88; V Chesterton St Andr *Ely* 88-97. *21 Chancery Lane, Thrapston, Kettering NN14 4JL* Tel (01832) 731173 E-mail jsheldon@agnet.co.uk

SHELDON, Martin David. b 67. Sussex Univ BA89. St Jo Coll Nottm MTh01. **d** 01 **p** 02. C Milton *Win* 01-05; V Lightwater *Guildf* from 05. *The Vicarage, 28 Broadway Road, Lightwater GU18 5SJ* Tel (01276) 472270 E-mail vicar@allsaintslightwater.org.uk

SHELDRAKE, Mrs Varlie Ivy. b 39. SRN64 SCM65 HVCert70. Dioc OLM tr scheme 00. **d** 03 **p** 04. OLM E w W Harling, Bridgham w Roudham, Larling etc *Nor* from 03. *Springfield, Lopham Road, East Harling, Norwich NR16 2PX* Tel (01953) 717404 E-mail varlie@eastharling.com

SHELLEY, Derrick Sydney David. b 38. Lon Univ LLB60 AKC65. Linc Th Coll 66. **d** 68 **p** 69. C Weybridge *Guildf* 68-72; Chapl Red Bank Schs 71-76; Perm to Offic *Blackb* 76-96; rtd 96; Perm to Offic *Truro* 96-03 and *Lich* from 04. *29 Lewis Close, Lichfield WS14 9UE* Tel (01543) 300567 E-mail notatmyage@ntlworld.com

SHELLEY, Robin Arthur. b 34. CEng MIMechE. St Jo Coll Nottm 85. **d** 87 **p** 88. C Countesthorpe w Foston *Leic* 87-90; V Enderby w Lubbesthorpe and Thurlaston 90-00; rtd 00; Perm to Offic *Leic* 00-03; *York* from 02. *10 West Leys Park, Swanland, North Ferriby HU14 3LS* Tel (01482) 637063

SHELLOCK, Norman Stanley. b 15. ATCL53 Dur Univ LTh38. St Aug Coll Cant 34. **d** 38 **p** 39. C Biscot *St Alb* 38-41; Br Guiana 41-59; Area Sec USPG *Ely* and *St E* 59-80; rtd 80; Perm to Offic *Nor* 80-81; *St E* from 81; *Ely* 81-97. *24 Runnymede Green, Bury St Edmunds IP33 2LH* Tel (01284) 703506

SHELLS, Canon Charles Harry. b 15. St Chad's Coll Dur BA38 MA43. **d** 39 **p** 40. C Almondbury *Wakef* 39-42; C Camberwell St Geo *S'wark* 42-47; V Newington St Paul 47-54; V Wandsworth St Anne 54-65; RD Wandsworth 63-65; R Trunch w Swafield *Nor* 65-71; R Bradfield 65-71; P-in-c Gimingham 65-71; P-in-c Trimingham 65-71; P-in-c Antingham w Thorpe Market 65-71; P-in-c Felmingham 65-68; P-in-c Suffield 65-68; P-in-c Gunton St Pet 65-71; RD Tunstead 65-68; Can Res Bris Cathl *Bris* 71-81; rtd 81; Lic to Offic *B & W* 81-96 and *Sarum* from 81; Perm to Offic *Bris* 81-02 and *B & W* from 88. *6 The Cloisters, South Street, Wells BA5 1SA* Tel (01749) 673961

SHELTON, Ian Robert. b 52. BEd74 Lon Univ MA79. Ripon Coll Cuddesdon BA81 MA90. **d** 82 **p** 83. C Wath-upon-Dearne w Adwick-upon-Dearne *Sheff* 82-86; TV Grantham *Linc* 86-93; P-in-c Waltham 93-97; R from 97; P-in-c Barnoldby le Beck 93-97; R from 97; RD Haverstoe from 01. *The Rectory, 95 High Street, Waltham, Grimsby DN37 0PN* Tel (01472) 822172

SHELTON, Ms Pauline Mary. b 52. K Coll Lon BA73. N Ord Course 96. **d** 99 **p** 00. C Baswich *Lich* 99-02; TV Stoke-upon-Trent from 02. *The Vicarage, Upper Belgrave Road, Stoke-on-Trent ST3 4QJ* Tel (01782) 324903 E-mail rev.pauline@virgin.net

SHEMILT, Lisa. b 69. St Jo Coll Nottm 03. **d** 05. C Walton St Jo *Derby* from 05. *8 Birkdale Drive, Chesterfield S40 3JL* Tel (01246) 207939 E-mail lisa@shemilt.fslife.co.uk

SHENTON, Canon Brian. b 43. Chich Th Coll 73. **d** 75 **p** 76. C Mill Hill Jo Keble Ch *Lon* 75-78; C New Windsor *Ox* 78-81; TV 81-82; P-in-c Cherbury 82-83; V Calcot 83-89; R Reading St Mary w St Laur from 89; P-in-c Reading St Matt 96-00; RD Reading from 95; Hon Can Ch Ch from 98. *Hamelsham, Downshire Square, Reading RG1 6NJ* Tel 0118-956 8163 *or* 957 1057 Mobile 07710-490250 E-mail stmaryshouserdg@waitrose.com

SHENTON, David. b 57. Aston Tr Scheme 91 Ripon Coll Cuddesdon DipMin95. **d** 95 **p** 96. C Thurmaston *Leic* 95-98; C Melton Mowbray 98-99; TV 99-01. *Address temp unknown*

SHEPHARD, Brian Edward. b 34. Magd Coll Cam BA56 MA60 Ox Univ CertEd71. Wycliffe Hall Ox 58. **d** 60 **p** 61. C Wigan St Cath *Liv* 60-62; C Kidderminster St Geo *Worc* 62-65; Lect CA Tr Coll Blackheath 65-70; Lect Hamilton Coll of Educn 70-77; Chapl Buchan Sch Castletown 77-88; Tutor Wilson Carlile Coll of Evang 88-89; C Andreas St Jude *S & M* 89-91; C Jurby 89-91; V Lezayre 91-02; rtd 02; Perm to Offic *S & M* from 02. *Keayn Ard, Queens Road, Port St Mary, Isle of Man IM9 5EP* Tel (01624) 833315 E-mail kyriosvoskos@manx.net

SHEPHEARD-WALWYN, John. b 16. Oriel Coll Ox BA38 MA44. Wells Th Coll 38. **d** 40 **p** 42. C Roch St Pet w St Marg *Roch* 41-44; C Lamorbey H Redeemer 44-49; C Edenbridge 49-56; V Rosherville 56-61; R Horwood and V Westleigh *Ex* 61-78; P-in-c Harberton w Harbertonford 78-82; rtd 82; Perm to Offic *Bris* 82-05. *5 Holly Road, Bramhall, Stockport SK7 1HH*

SHEPHERD, Canon Anthony Michael. b 50. Em Coll Cam BA72 MA76. Westcott Ho Cam 72. **d** 74 **p** 75. C Folkestone St Mary and St Eanswythe *Cant* 74-79; Bp's Dom Chapl *Ripon* 79-87; Dioc Communications Officer 79-87; V High Harrogate St Pet from 87; Hon Can Ripon Cathl from 99. *St Peter's Vicarage, 13 Beech Grove, Harrogate HG2 0ET* Tel (01423) 500901 E-mail ashepherd@bigfoot.com

SHEPHERD, Christopher Francis Pleydell. b 44. St Steph Ho Ox 68. **d** 69 **p** 70. C Milber *Ex* 69-72; C Ex St Thos 72-74; TV Ilfracombe, Lee and W Down 74-78; TV Ilfracombe, Lee, W Down, Woolacombe and Bittadon 78-80; P-in-c Tregony w St Cuby and Cornelly *Truro* 80-83; R 83-96; rtd 04. *2 Cherry Meadow, Cheriton Fitzpaine, Crediton EX17 4JX* Tel (01363) 866896

SHEPHERD, David. b 42. St Jo Coll Dur BA65 MA68 MLitt76. Edin Th Coll 66. **d** 68 **p** 69. Chapl St Paul's Cathl Dundee *Bre* 68-79; Chapl Dundee Univ 73-79; R Dundee St Mary Magd from 79; Hon Chapl Abertay Univ from 01. *14 Albany Terrace, Dundee DD3 6HR* Tel (01382) 223510

SHEPHERD, David Mark. b 59. Reading Univ BA81 Nottm Univ BTh86. Linc Th Coll 83. **d** 86 **p** 87. C Wilmslow *Ches* 86-89; C Bromborough 89-92; V Leasowe 92-97; V Oxhey St Matt *St Alb* from 97. *The Vicarage, St Matthew's Close, Eastbury Road, Watford WD19 4ST* Tel (01923) 241420 E-mail davidshepherd@matts52.fsnet.co.uk

SHEPHERD, Donald. *See* SHEPHERD, John Donald

SHEPHERD, Ernest John Heatley. b 27. TCD BA48 BD53. **d** 50 **p** 51. C Belfast St Mary Magd *Conn* 50-54; I Whitehouse 54-96; Can Conn Cathl 86-90; Co-ord Aux Min 87-96; Treas Conn Cathl 90; Prec Conn Cathl 90-96; rtd 96. *15 Downshire Gardens, Carrickfergus BT38 7LW* Tel (028) 9336 2243

SHEPHERD, Miss Jayne Elizabeth. b 57. Reading Univ BA78. Cranmer Hall Dur 79. **dss** 82 **d** 87 **p** 94. Wombourne *Lich* 82-85; Harlescott 85-90; Par Dn 87-90; Chapl Asst Qu Medical Cen Nottm Univ Hosp NHS Trust 90-97; Asst Chapl Cen Notts Healthcare NHS Trust 90-97; Chapl Pet Hosps NHS Trust 97-02; Chapl St Helens and Knowsley Hosps NHS Trust from 02. *Whiston Hospital, Warrington Road, Prescot L35 5DR* Tel 0151-426 1600 Fax 430 8478

SHEPHERD, Mrs Joan Francis Fleming. b 45. RGN66. **dss** 84 **d** 86 **p** 94. NSM Ellon *Ab* from 84; NSM Cruden Bay from 84; Bp's Chapl for Tr and Educn from 95. *Address temp unknown*

SHEPHERD, John Donald. b 33. Cranmer Hall Dur BA59 DipTh61. **d** 61 **p** 62. C Dewsbury All SS *Wakef* 61-63; C Chapelthorpe 63-66; V Stainland 66-70; Dioc Youth Chapl *Truro* 70-74; V Newquay 74-84; RD Pydar 81-84; Chapl Borocourt Mental Handicap Hosp 84-95; TR Langtree *Ox* 84-95; rtd 98; Perm to Offic *Lich* from 99. *21 Sparkham Close, Shrewsbury SY3 6BX* Tel (01743) 244453

SHEPHERD, The Very Revd John Harley. b 42. Melbourne Univ BA64 Union Th Sem (NY) MSacMus73 St Cath Coll Cam PhD80. Trin Coll Melbourne ThL66. **d** 67 **p** 68. Australia 67-70 and from 88; C Footscray W 67-68; C Brunswick 69-70; C Stretford St Matt *Man* 71; Asst P Sayville Long Is USA 72-77; Jo Stewart of Rannoch Scholar St Cath Coll Cam 77-80; C Cherry Hinton St Andr *Ely* 78-80; Chapl Ch Ch Ox 80-88; Chapl Univ W Australia 88-90; Dean Perth from 90. *St George's Cathedral, 38 St George's Terrace, Perth, W Australia 6000* Tel (0061) (8) 9325 5766 *or* 9322 7265 Fax 9325 5242 E-mail thedean@perthcathedral.org

SHEPHERD, John Martin. b 68. St Jo Coll Cam BA90. Oak Hill Th Coll BA96. **d** 96 **p** 97. C Rusholme H Trin *Man* 96-00; SAMS Brazil 00-03; TV Gt Chesham *Ox* from 03. *14A Manor Way, Chesham HP5 3BG* Tel (01494) 771471 E-mail john@theshepherds.org.uk

SHEPHERD, Canon John Michael. b 42. BNC Ox BA63 MA72. Coll of Resurr Mirfield 64. **d** 66 **p** 67. C Clapham H Spirit *S'wark* 66-69; C Kingston All SS 69-72; V Upper Tooting H Trin 73-80; V Wandsworth St Paul 80-90; P-in-c Mitcham SS Pet and Paul 90-92; V 92-97; RD Merton 96-97; V Battersea St Luke from 97; RD Battersea 01-04; Hon Can S'wark Cathl from 01. *52 Thurleigh Road, London SW12 8UD* Tel (020) 8673 6506

SHEPHERD, Mrs Julie Margaret. b 37. **d** 03 **p** 04. OLM Halliwell *Man* from 03. *Apple Cottage, 16 Grove Street, Bolton BL1 3PG* Tel (01204) 844508 Mobile 07742-667903 E-mail julie.shepherd@care4free.net

SHEPHERD, Keith Frederick. b 42. EMMTC 86. **d** 89 **p** 90. NSM Stocking Farm *Leic* 89-93; NSM Church Langton w Tur Langton, Thorpe Langton etc 93-99; TV Syston from 99. *The Parsonage, 20 Hoby Road, Thrussington, Leicester LE7 4TH* Tel (01664) 424962 E-mail shepherd@leicester.anglican.org

SHEPHERD, Michael John. b 54. St Chad's Coll Dur BA75 St Paul Univ Ottawa LCL81 Ottawa Univ MCL81. Ushaw Coll Dur 73. **d** 77 **p** 78. In RC Ch 77-93; NSM Evesham *Worc* 95-97; NSM Evesham w Norton and Lenchwick 97-99; NSM Badsey w Aldington and Offenham and Bretforton 99-03; R Ab Kettleby and Holwell w Asfordby *Leic* from 03. *The Rectory, 2 Church Lane, Asfordby, Melton Mowbray LE14 3RU* Tel (01664) 813130 E-mail mrvshep@btinternet.com

SHEPHERD, Mrs Pauline. b 53. Stockwell Coll of Educn TCert73. WMMTC 00. **d** 03 **p** 04. C Walsall Pleck and Bescot *Lich* from 03. *134 Birmingham Road, Aldridge, Walsall WS9 0AQ* Tel (01922) 452493 Mobile 07814-680304 E-mail andrew.shepherd2@which.net

SHEPHERD, Peter James. b 38. Dur Univ BA64. Ridley Hall Cam 64. **d** 66 **p** 67. C Luton Ch Ch *Roch* 66-70; C Belvedere All SS 70-71; C Wisley w Pyrford *Guildf* 71-75; V Thorney Abbey *Ely* 75-85; V Yaxley 85-93; RD Yaxley 88-92; P-in-c Feltwell 93-95; rtd 96; Perm to Offic *Ely* from 96. *51 Middlefield Road, Sawtry, Huntingdon PE28 5SH* Tel (01487) 834084

SHEPHERD, Peter William. b 48. Reading Univ BA71 Lon Univ BD80 Brighton Poly MPhil87 Lanc Univ MA94 Open Univ PhD04. Chich Th Coll 77. **d** 80 **p** 81. NSM Eastbourne St Sav and St Pet *Chich* 80-82; NSM Clitheroe St Mary *Blackb* from 82; Hd Master Wm Temple Sch Preston 83-88; Hd Master Canon Slade Sch Bolton from 89; Perm to Offic *Man* from 89. *Homestead, Eastham Street, Clitheroe BB7 2HY* Tel and fax (01200) 425053 *or* tel (01204) 333343 Fax (01204) 333340 E-mail pws.canonslade@btconnect.com

✠**SHEPHERD, The Rt Revd Ronald Francis.** b 26. Univ of BC BA48. AKC52 St Jo Coll Winnipeg Hon DD89. **d** 52 **p** 53 **c** 85. C Westmr St Steph w St Jo *Lon* 52-57; Canada from 57; Dean Edmonton 65-70; Dean Montreal 70-82; Bp BC 85-92; rtd 92; Hon V St Barn Miss San Diego USA 95-00. *Easter Hill, 110 Ensilwood Road, Salt Spring Island BC, Canada, V8K 1N1* Tel (001) (250) 537 1399

SHEPHERD, Thomas. b 52. SRN74 Man Univ BA79 Didsbury Coll Man PGCE83. N Ord Course 92. **d** 95 **p** 96. C Baguley *Man* 95-99; C Timperley *Ches* 99-03; V Sale St Paul from 03. *St Paul's Vicarage, 15 Springfield Road, Sale M33 7YA* Tel 0161-973 1042 E-mail revts@mac.com

SHEPHERD, Timothy Roy. b 34. Selw Coll Cam BA58. Linc Th Coll 62. **d** 64 **p** 65. C Selly Oak St Mary *Birm* 64-67; C Stockland Green 67-72; V Perry Common 72-76; V Holton-le-Clay *Linc* 76-84; V Habrough Gp 84-93; P-in-c Uffington 93-95; R Uffington Gp 95-99; rtd 99; Perm to Offic *Pet* from 99; *Linc* from 00. *Chapelside, Chapel Hill, Wootton, Woodstock OX20 1DX* Tel (01993) 813319

SHEPPARD, Ian Arthur Lough. b 33. Sarum & Wells Th Coll 71. **d** 74 **p** 75. C Bishop's Cleeve *Glouc* 74-77; Chapl RAF 77-81; V Gosberton *Linc* 81-87; V Leven Valley *Carl* 87-90; Deputation and Gen Appeals Org Children's Soc 90-98; rtd 98. *57 Seymour Grove, Eaglescliffe, Stockton-on-Tees TS16 0LE* Tel (01642) 791612 E-mail ian.sheppard@bluecarrots.com

SHEPPARD, Canon Martin. b 37. Hertf Coll Ox BA61 MA65. Chich Th Coll 63. **d** 65 **p** 66. C N Hull St Mich *York* 65-68; C Hove St Jo *Chich* 68-71; V Heathfield St Rich 71-77; V New Shoreham 77-94; V Old Shoreham 77-94; TR Rye 94-03; RD Rye 95-02; Can and Preb Chich Cathl 02-03; rtd 03. *62 St Pancras Road, Lewes BN7 1JG* Tel (01273) 474999

SHEPPARD, Norman George. b 32. Wolv Teacher Tr Coll CertEd73. St D Coll Lamp 57. **d** 59 **p** 60. C Burry Port and Pwll *St D* 59-64; SAMS 64-68; Chile 64-68; C Madeley *Heref* 68-69; Asst Master Madeley Court Sch 73-75; Gilbert Inglefield Sch Leighton Buzzard 75-80; USPG 80-81; Argentina from 80; rtd 95. *Santa Rosa 1650, Vincente Lopez, Province of Buenos Aires, Argentina* Tel (0054) (1) 797 9748

SHEPPARD, Roger Malcolm. b 47. Aston Univ MBA86 Wolv Poly PGCE88 Solicitor 74. WMMTC. **d** 01 **p** 02. NSM Castle

Vale St Cuth *Birm* from 01. *193 Dower Road, Sutton Coldfield B75 6SY* Tel 0121-682 3976 *or* 308 8850
E-mail roger_m_sheppard@hotmail.com

SHEPPARD, Stanley Gorton. b 18. St Jo Coll Dur 46. **d** 62 **p** 63. C Leic St Mark *Leic* 62-65; R Cole Orton 65-75; V Ashby Folville and Twyford w Thorpe Satchville 75-88; rtd 88; Perm to Offic *Ex* from 89. *1 Peak Coach House, Cotmaton Road, Sidmouth EX10 8SY* Tel (01395) 516124

SHEPPARD, Mrs Susan. b 59. Ex Univ BA80 MA99 SS Hild & Bede Coll Dur PGCE81. SW Minl Tr Course 95. **d** 98 **p** 99. NSM Stoke Canon, Poltimore w Huxham and Rewe etc *Ex* 98-01; Chapl St Pet High Sch Ex from 99; Tutor SWMTC from 05. *Autumn Haze, Rewe, Exeter EX5 4HA* Tel and fax (01392) 841284

SHEPTON, Robert Leonard McIntyre. b 35. Jes Coll Cam BA58 MA61. Oak Hill Th Coll 59. **d** 61 **p** 62. C Weymouth St Jo *Sarum* 61-63; Boys' Ldr Cam Univ Miss Bermondsey 63-66; Warden Ox-Kilburn Club 66-69; Chapl St D Coll Llandudno 69-77; Chief Instructor Carnoch Outdoor Cen 77-80; Chapl Kingham Hill Sch Oxon 80-92; rtd 92. *Innisfree, Duror, Appin PA38 4DA* Tel (01631) 730437 Fax 730382 E-mail bob@innisfree.free-online.co.uk

SHERBORNE, Archdeacon of. *See* TAYLOR, The Ven Paul Stanley

SHERBORNE, Area Bishop of. *See* THORNTON, The Rt Revd Timothy Martin

SHERDLEY, Mrs Margaret Ann. b 46. Chester Coll of HE BTh03. N Ord Course 00. **d** 03 **p** 04. NSM Fellside Team *Blackb* from 03. *23 Sandy Lane, Preesall, Poulton-le-Fylde FY6 0EJ* Tel (01253) 810894 Mobile 07931-592787
E-mail m.sherdley@btinternet.com

SHERGOLD, William Frank. b 19. St Chad's Coll Dur BA40 MA47. Coll of Resurr Mirfield 40. **d** 42 **p** 43. C Poplar All SS w St Frideswide *Lon* 42-49; V Hanworth All SS 49-58; V Hackney Wick St Mary of Eton w St Aug 59-64; V Paddington St Mary 64-69; V Charlton-by-Dover St Bart *Cant* 69-72; P-in-c Charlton-by-Dover SS Pet and Paul 70-72; R Charlton-in-Dover 72-78; R Tunstall 78-83; rtd 84; TV Poplar *Lon* 84; Hon C 84-92; Perm to Offic *Chich* 92-99 and *B & W* from 00. *78 Southover, Wells BA5 1UH* Tel (01749) 678803

SHERIDAN, Andrew Robert (Drew). b 61. Edin Univ MA83 Jordanhill Coll Glas PGCE86. TISEC 95. **d** 98 **p** 99. C Glas St Mary *Glas* 98-01; R Greenock from 01. *The Rectory, 96 Finnart Street, Greenock PA16 8HL* Tel (01475) 732441
E-mail drew@frsheridan.fsnet.co.uk

SHERIDAN, Mrs Deborah Jane. b 47. Kent Univ BA69 ALA73. WMMTC 90. **d** 93 **p** 94. NSM Lich St Chad *Lich* 93-03; NSM The Ridwares and Kings Bromley from 03; Chapl St Giles Hospice Lich from 98. *45 High Grange, Lichfield WS13 7DU* Tel (01543) 264363 *or* 416595 E-mail d.sheridan@postman.org.uk

SHERIDAN, Peter. b 37. Saltley Tr Coll Birm CertEd59 Leic Poly BEd82. N Ord Course 89. **d** 92 **p** 93. NSM Braunstone *Leic* 92-95; NSM Ratby cum Groby 95-98; NSM Newtown Linford 95-98; TV Bradgate Team 98-00; Perm to Offic 00-01; NSM Woodhouse, Woodhouse Eaves and Swithland from 01. *16 Turnpike Way, Markfield LE67 9QT* Tel (01530) 245166

SHERIFF (née WORRALL), Canon Suzanne. b 63. Trin Coll Bris BA86. **d** 87 **p** 94. Par Dn Kingston upon Hull St Nic *York* 87-91; Par Dn Kingston upon Hull St Aid Southcoates 91-94; C 94-96; TV Marfleet 96-00; TR from 00; Can and Preb York Minster from 01. *St Hilda's Vicarage, 256 Annandale Road, Hull HU9 4JU* Tel (01482) 799100
E-mail sue@sheriff256.freeserve.co.uk

SHERLOCK, Mrs Barbara Lee Kerney. b 48. Westcott Ho Cam. **d** 05. C Norton St Mary *Dur* from 05; C Stockton St Chad from 05. *71 The Glebe, Stockton-on-Tees TS20 1RD*

SHERLOCK, Charles Patrick. b 51. New Coll Ox BA73 MA76 Open Univ MBA00. Ripon Coll Cuddesdon 75. **d** 77 **p** 78. C Ashtead *Guildf* 77-81; Ethiopia 81-82; Chapl Belgrade w Zagreb *Eur* 82-84; USPG Ethiopia 84-91; R Dollar *St And* 91-97; Bursar Fistula Hosp Ethiopia 97-00; P-in-c Crieff *St And* 01-04; R from 04; P-in-c Comrie 01-04; R from 04; P-in-c Lochearnhead 01-04; R from 04. *The Ibert, Monzie, Crieff PH7 3LL* Tel (01764) 652619 *or* 656222 Mobile 07740-981951
E-mail cpsherlock@msn.com

SHERLOCK, Canon Desmond. b 31. K Coll Lon BD60 AKC60. **d** 61 **p** 62. C Mitcham Ascension *S'wark* 61-64; C Reigate St Luke S Park 64-67; V Aldersbrook *Chelmsf* 67-77; RD Redbridge 74-77; TR Witham 77-97; Hon Can Chelmsf Cathl 93-97; rtd 97; Perm to Offic *Chelmsf* from 98. *20 Chalks Road, Witham CM8 2JG* Tel (01376) 513004

SHERLOCK, Thomas Alfred. b 40. Aux Course 87. **d** 90 **p** 91. NSM Kilmallock w Kilflynn, Kilfinane, Knockaney etc *L & K* 90-94; C Templemore w Thurles and Kilfithmone *C & O* 95-98; I 98-00; I Castlecomer w Colliery Ch, Mothel and Bilbo from 00. *The Rectory, Castlecomer, Co Tipperary, Irish Republic* Tel and fax (00353) (56) 444 1677

SHERRATT, David Arthur. b 60. Univ of Wales (Lamp) BA82 Leeds Univ BA91. Coll of Resurr Mirfield 92. **d** 92 **p** 93. C St Jo on Bethnal Green *Lon* 92-95; C W Hampstead St Jas 95-98; V Abbey Wood *S'wark* from 98. *St Michael's Vicarage, 1 Conference Road, London SE2 0YH* Tel (020) 8311 0377

SHERRED, Peter William. b 47. Kent Univ BA69. SEITE 96. **d** 99 **p** 00. NSM Dover St Mary *Cant* 99-02; Perm to Offic from 02. *Copthorne, Dover Road, Guston, Dover CT15 5EN* Tel (01304) 203548 Fax 206950 E-mail copthorne@talk21.com

SHERRING, Patrick. b 55. Trent Park Coll of Educn BEd78 CertEd77 Lon Inst of Educn DipPSE88. Ridley Hall Cam 95. **d** 97 **p** 98. C Leyton St Mary w St Edw and St Luke *Chelmsf* 97-01; P-in-c Ingatestone w Buttsbury 01-04; V Ingatestone w Fryerning from 04. *The Rectory, 1 Rectory Close, Fryerning Lane, Ingatestone CM4 0DB* Tel (01277) 352562
E-mail patrick.sherring@ingatestoneparishchurch.org.uk

SHERRING, Toby Bruce. b 76. Ex Univ BA97 St Luke's Coll Ex PGCE98. St Steph Ho Ox MTh04. **d** 02 **p** 03. C W Derby St Jo *Liv* from 02. *St John's Vicarage, 2 Green Lane, Stoneycroft, Liverpool L13 7EA* Tel 0151-259 8587 *or* 228 2023
E-mail toby.sherring@ssho.oxon.org

SHERSBY, Brian Alfred. b 41. Clifton Th Coll 68. **d** 71 **p** 72. C Stoughton *Guildf* 71-74; C Heref St Pet w St Owen *Heref* 75-79; V Earlham St Mary *Nor* 79-91; R Murston w Bapchild and Tonge *Cant* from 91. *Bapchild Rectory, School Lane, Sittingbourne ME9 9NL* Tel (01795) 472929

SHERWIN, David Royston. b 56. HNC. St Jo Coll Nottm 84. **d** 89 **p** 90. C Conisbrough *Sheff* 89-95; V Wheatley Park 95-01; Dioc Adv for Evang 95-01; P-in-c Martley and Wichenford, Knightwick etc *Worc* from 01. *The Rectory, Martley, Worcester WR6 6QA* Tel and fax (01886) 888664
E-mail davidwin56@aol.com

SHERWIN, Mrs Jane. b 41. Kingston Coll of Art DipAD61. Sarum Th Coll 93. **d** 96 **p** 97. NSM Brightling, Dallington, Mountfield etc *Chich* 96-02; P-in-c Waldron from 02. *The Rectory, Sheepsetting Lane, Waldron, Heathfield TN21 0UY* Tel (01435) 862816

SHERWIN, Mrs Margaret Joyce. b 65. N Ord Course BTh99. **d** 99 **p** 00. C Litherland St Phil *Liv* 99-03; V Hindley Green from 03. *The Vicarage, 848 Atherton Road, Hindley, Wigan WN2 4SA* Tel (01942) 255833 E-mail revmarg@btopenworld.com

SHERWIN, Miss Margaret Miriam. b 32. **dss** 83 **d** 87 **p** 94. Holborn St Alb w Saffron Hill St Pet *Lon* 83-87; Par Dn 87-88; Par Dn Highgate St Mich 88-93; rtd 93; NSM Purbrook *Portsm* from 93. *16 Lombard Court, Lombard Street, Portsmouth PO1 2HU* Tel (023) 9283 8429

SHERWIN, Mrs Philippa Margaret. b 46. Lon Univ BDS70 LDSRCSEng70. LNSM course 98. **d** 99 **p** 00. OLM Queen Thorne *Sarum* from 99. *Holway Mill, Sandford Orcas, Sherborne DT9 4RZ* Tel (01963) 220380

SHERWOOD, David Charles. b 56. LRPS94. WEMTC 98. **d** 01 **p** 02. C Taunton Lyngford *B & W* 01-05; P-in-c Hemyock w Culm Davy, Clayhidon and Culmstock *Ex* from 05. *The Rectory, Hemyock, Cullompton EX15 3RQ* Tel (01823) 681589
E-mail revdcs@yahoo.co.uk

SHERWOOD, David James. b 45. Solicitor 69 Univ of Wales (Cardiff) LLM94. St Steph Ho Ox 81. **d** 83 **p** 84. C Westbury-on-Trym H Trin *Bris* 83-85; C Corringham *Chelmsf* 85-87; V Hullbridge 87-94; V Kenton *Lon* from 94. *St Mary's Vicarage, 3 St Leonard's Avenue, Harrow HA3 8EJ* Tel (020) 8907 2914 Fax 8933 7305 E-mail david.sherwood@ukonline.co.uk

SHERWOOD, Gordon Frederick. b 29. Sarum & Wells Th Coll 77. **d** 80 **p** 81. Hon C Weeke *Win* 80-82; C Kirk Ella *York* 82-85; P-in-c Burstwick w Thorngumbald 85-87; V 87-90; R Kirby Misperton w Normanby, Edston and Salton 90-94; rtd 94; Perm to Offic *Cant* from 95. *Sandycroft, Lewson Street, Norton, Faversham ME9 9JN* Tel (01795) 522696
E-mail gsherwood@onetel.com

SHERWOOD, Canon Ian Walter Lawrence. b 57. TCD BA80 DipTh82. **d** 82 **p** 84. C Dublin St Patr Cathl Gp *D & G* 82-83; Chapl Billinge Hosp Wigan 83-86; C Orrell *Liv* 83-86; Chapl Bucharest w Sofia *Eur* 86-89; Chapl Istanbul w Moda from 89; Can Malta Cathl from 97. *c/o FCO (Istanbul), King Charles Street, London SW1A 2AH* Tel (0090) (212) 251 5616
E-mail parson@tnn.net

SHERWOOD, Kenneth Henry. b 37. CITC 90. **d** 93 **p** 94. NSM Malahide w Balgriffin *D & G* 93-96; NSM Castleknock and Mulhuddart, w Clonsilla 96-97; NSM Leighlin w Grange Sylvae, Shankill etc *C & O* 97-04; rtd 04. *6 Beverton Way, Donabate, Co Dublin, Irish Republic*

SHERWOOD, Nigel John Wesley. b 58. DipTh. CITC 86. **d** 86 **p** 87. C Kilmore w Ballintemple, Kildallan etc *K, E & A* 86-89; I Tullow w Shillelagh, Aghold and Mullinacuff *C & O* 89-95; I Arklow w Inch and Kilbride *D & G* from 95; Sec SPCK Glendalough from 98. *The Rectory, Emoclew Road, Arklow, Co Wicklow, Irish Republic* Tel (00353) (402) 32439

SHERWOOD, Paul Steven. b 76. Southn Univ BA(QTS)98. Ripon Coll Cuddesdon 00. **d** 03 **p** 04. C Chilworth w N Baddesley *Win* from 03. *188 Rownhams Lane, North Baddesley, Southampton SO52 9LQ* Tel (023) 8073 3131
E-mail paul@baddesleychurch.org

SHERWOOD, Suffragan Bishop of. *Vacant*

SHEWAN, Alistair Boyd. b 44. Open Univ BA83 BSc95. Edin Th Coll 63. **d** 67 **p** 68. Prec St Andr Cathl Inverness *Mor* 67-69; C Shepherd's Bush St Steph w St Thos *Lon* 70-72; Hon C Edin St Mich and All SS *Edin* 73-75; Perm to Offic 75-81; Hon C Edin Old St Paul 81-86; NSM Edin St Columba 87-91; Asst Dioc Supernumerary from 91; C Edin St Ninian from 95. *3 Castle Wynd North, Edinburgh EH1 2NQ* Tel 0131-225 6537

SHEWAN, James William. b 36. Sarum Th Coll 61. **d** 63 **p** 64. C Rainbow Hill St Barn *Worc* 63-64; C Newton Aycliffe *Dur* 64-66; C Harton 66-69; V S Moor 69-72; CF 72-77; CF(V) from 81; P-in-c Benwell St Aid *Newc* 77-79; V Longhoughton w Howick 79-88; V Spittal and Scremerston 88-00; RD Norham 96-00; rtd 00; Perm to Offic *Newc* 00-04; Hon C Norham and Duddo from 04; Hon C Cornhill w Carham from 04; Hon C Branxton from 04. *The Vicarage, The Old School House, Branxton, Cornhill-on-Tweed TD12 4SW* Tel (01890) 820308

SHEWRING (née SMITH), Mrs Susan Helen. b 51. Univ of Cen England in Birm BEd87 Warwick Univ PGDE90. WMMTC 01. **d** 04 **p** 05. NSM Billesley Common *Birm* from 04. *48 St Helens Road, Solihull B91 2DA* Tel 0121-705 1845
E-mail sue_shewring@yahoo.co.uk

SHIELD, Barry Graham. b 39. Univ of Qld BA79 Univ of New England DipEd83 MLitt86 Kent Univ MA95 Washington Univ PhD00. St Fran Coll Brisbane DipTh85 McAuley Coll Brisbane GradDipRE84. **d** 83 **p** 84. Australia 83-00 and from 01; P-in-c Haselbury Plucknett, Misterton and N Perrott *B & W* 00-01. *21 Miller Street, PO Box 96, Taroom, Qld, Australia 4420* Tel (0061) (7) 4627 3158 Fax as telephone
E-mail barryshield1@bigpond.com

SHIELD, Graham Friend. b 63. Ripon Coll Cuddesdon. **d** 00 **p** 01. C Camborne *Truro* 00-03; P-in-c St Mawgan w St Ervan and St Eval from 03. *The Rectory, St Mawgan, Newquay TR8 4EZ* Tel (01637) 860023
E-mail graham@shieldfam.freeserve.co.uk

SHIELD, Ian Thomas. b 32. Hertf Coll Ox BA56 MA60 BLitt60. Westcott Ho Cam 59. **d** 61 **p** 62. C Shipley St Paul *Bradf* 61-64; Tutor Lich Th Coll 64-71; Chapl 67-71; V Dunston w Coppenhall *Lich* 71-79; TV Wolverhampton 79-86; rtd 87; Perm to Offic *Lich* from 87. *13 Duke Street, Penn Fields, Wolverhampton WV3 7DT* Tel (01902) 337037
E-mail ianshield@aol.com

SHIELDS, Mrs Jennifer Jill. b 39. Heref Coll of Educn CertEd74. St Alb and Ox Min Course 99. **d** 02 **p** 03. OLM Lenborough *Ox* from 02. *8 West Furlong, Padbury, Buckingham MK18 2BP* Tel (01280) 814474

SHIELDS, Canon Michael Penton. b 30. Bps' Coll Cheshunt. **d** 64 **p** 65. C Kingsbury St Andr *Lon* 64-67; C Friern Barnet All SS 67-69; V Colindale St Matthias 69-76; V Sevenoaks St Jo *Roch* 76-95; RD Sevenoaks 84-95; Chapl Sevenoaks Hosp 78-94; Chapl St Mich Sch Otford 90-95; Hon Can Roch Cathl *Roch* 94-95; rtd 95; Hon PV Roch Cathl *Roch* from 96; Perm to Offic from 01. *Flat 14, Bromley College, London Road, Bromley BR1 1PE* Tel (020) 8464 7906

SHILL, Kenneth Leslie. b 49. Leic Univ BA70 Lon Univ BD73. Ridley Hall Cam 75. **d** 77 **p** 78. C Harborne Heath *Birm* 77-83; V Mansfield St Jo *S'well* 83-93; Bp's Adv on Healing 89-93; Chapl Amsterdam w Heiloo *Eur* 93-95; TR Bath Twerton-on-Avon *B & W* 95-04; V Arnold *S'well* from 04. *St Mary's Vicarage, Church Lane, Arnold, Nottingham NG5 8HJ* Tel 0115-926 2946
E-mail shill1@tinyworld.co.uk

SHILLAKER, Mrs Christine Frances. b 39. Lon Univ DipTh61. Gilmore Ho 74. **dss** 86 **d** 87 **p** 94. Colchester St Leon, St Mary Magd and St Steph *Chelmsf* 86-89; Par Dn 87-89; Par Dn Colchester, New Town and The Hythe 89-94; C 94-96; P-in-c Ramsey w Lt Oakley 96-02; rtd 02; Perm to Offic *Chelmsf* from 02. *21 Nelson Road, Colchester CO3 9AP* Tel (01206) 570234

SHILLAKER, John. b 34. K Coll Lon BD60 AKC60. **d** 61 **p** 62. C Bush Hill Park St Mark *Lon* 61-65; C Milton *Win* 65-69; C-in-c Moulsham St Luke CD *Chelmsf* 69-78; V Moulsham St Luke 78-85; P-in-c Colchester St Leon, St Mary Magd and St Steph 85-86; R 86-89; R Colchester, New Town and The Hythe 89-96; rtd 96; Perm to Offic *Chelmsf* from 00. *21 Nelson Road, Colchester CO3 9AP* Tel (01206) 570234 Mobile 07889-816264

SHILLING, Ms Audrey Violet. b 26. Dur Univ BA69. CA Tr Coll 51 Cranmer Hall Dur 66. **d** 87 **p** 94. CA from 53; NSM Gillingham H Trin *Roch* 87-93; NSM Rainham 94-96; Perm to Offic from 96. *13 Guardian Court, London Road, Rainham, Gillingham ME8 7HQ* Tel (01634) 233654
E-mail audrey.shilling@diocese-rochester.org

SHILLINGFORD, Brian. b 39. Lich Th Coll 65. **d** 68 **p** 69. C Lewisham St Swithun *S'wark* 68-71; C Godstone 71-75; TV Croydon St Jo *Cant* 75-81; TV N Creedy *Ex* 81-93; TR 93-05; rtd 05. *Lyndbank, Albert Road, Crediton EX17 2BZ* Tel (01363) 877221 E-mail brianandkajshil@aol.com

SHILSON-THOMAS, Mrs Annabel Margaret. b 60. Jes Coll Ox BA82. Westcott Ho Cam 87. **d** 89 **p** 98. Par Dn Sydenham St Bart *S'wark* 89-93; Journalist CAFOD 95-03; Hon C Kingston All SS w St Jo *S'wark* 97-98; Perm to Offic *Ely* 00-03; Chapl Anglia Poly Univ 03-04; C Kingston All SS w St Jo *S'wark* from 04. *Church House, 30 Bloomfield Road, Kingston upon Thames KT1 2SE* Tel (020) 8546 9882

SHILSON-THOMAS, Hugh David. b 64. Ex Coll Ox BA86 MA98 K Coll Lon MA99. Westcott Ho Cam 87. **d** 89 **p** 90. C Sydenham All SS *S'wark* 89-92; C Lower Sydenham St Mich 89-92; Ecum Chapl Kingston Univ 93-98; Chapl Rob Coll Cam 98-03; Nat Adv for HE/Chapl Abps' Coun from 03. *Church House, Great Smith Street, London SW1P 3NZ* Tel (020) 7898 1513 E-mail hugh.shilson-thomas@c-of-e-org.uk

SHILVOCK, Geoffrey. b 47. Univ of Wales (Lamp) BA69. Sarum Th Coll 70. **d** 72 **p** 73. C Kidderminster St Mary *Worc* 72-78; P-in-c Gt Malvern Ch Ch 78-85; V Wolverley and Cookley from 85; RD Kidderminster 95-01. *The Vicarage, Wolverley, Kidderminster DY11 5XD* Tel (01562) 851133
E-mail geoffshilvock@hotmail.com

SHIMWELL, Canon Robert John. b 46. ARCM65. Trin Coll Bris 75. **d** 78 **p** 79. C Richmond H Trin *S'wark* 78-79; C Cullompton and Kentisbeare w Blackborough *Ex* 79-81; V S Cave and Ellerker w Broomfleet *York* 81-87; Chapl Lee Abbey 87-88; R Glas St Silas *Glas* 88-94; V Upton (Overchurch) *Ches* from 94; RD Wirral N 97-98; Hon Can Ches Cathl from 02. *The Vicarage, 20 Church Road, Upton, Wirral CH49 6JZ* Tel 0151-677 4810 *or* 677 1186 E-mail rob@shimwell.org

SHIN, Allen Kunho. b 56. Seabury-Western Th Sem MDiv96 STM01. **d** 96 **p** 96. C Manhattan St Mary USA 96-05; Chapl Keble Coll Ox from 05. *Keble College, Parks Road, Oxford OX1 3PG* Tel (01865) 272727 *or* 272700 Fax 272705

SHINE, Aisling Ann. RGN SCM. **d** 03 **p** 04. Aux Min Dublin Drumcondra w N Strand *D & G* from 03. *1 Roselawn Grove, Castleknock, Dublin 15, Irish Republic* Tel (00353) (1) 820 1797
E-mail shine1@eircom.net

SHINER, Michael Joseph. b 21. Chich Th Coll 51. **d** 53 **p** 54. C Weymouth H Trin *Sarum* 53-56; V Stanbridge w Tilsworth *St Alb* 56-63; V Powerstock w W Milton, Witherstone and N Poorton *Sarum* 67-73; V Knutsford St Cross *Ches* 73-75; Area Sec Age Concern Cornwall 75-86; Co Org W Sussex 80-86; rtd 86. *55 Tennyson Drive, Malvern WR14 2UL* Tel (01684) 563269

SHINN, William Raymond. b 22. Sarum & Wells Th Coll 71. **d** 73 **p** 74. C Letchworth St Paul *St Alb* 73-75; C Dunstable 76-78; TV 78-80; V Luton St Chris Round Green 80-88; rtd 88; Perm to Offic *St Alb* from 88. *31 Coleridge Close, Hitchin SG4 0QX* Tel (01462) 641883

SHINTON, Bertram David. b 41. K Coll Lon 62 Liv Univ PGCTh97. WMMTC 95. **d** 98 **p** 99. NSM Broseley w Benthall, Jackfield, Linley etc *Heref* from 98. *Gestiana, Woodlands Road, Broseley TF12 5PU* Tel (01952) 882765 *or* 0121-311 2104

SHIPLEY, Stephen Edwin Burnham. b 52. Univ Coll Dur BA74. Westcott Ho Cam 85. **d** 87 **p** 88. C Ipswich St Marg *St E* 87-90; P-in-c Stuntney *Ely* 90-95; Min Can, Prec and Sacr Ely Cathl 90-95; Producer Worship Progr BBC Relig Broadcasting from 95; Lic to Offic *Derby* from 96. *21 Devonshire Road, Buxton SK17 6RZ* Tel (01298) 78383 *or* 0161-244 3292 Fax 0161-244 3290 E-mail stephen.shipley@bbc.co.uk

SHIPP, Linda Mary. b 49. Cranmer Hall Dur 00. **d** 02 **p** 03. Hon Chapl among Deaf People *York* from 02; C Kirkleatham from 02; V Whorlton w Carlton and Faceby from 05. *Whorlton Vicarage, 18 Church Lane, Swainby, Northallerton DL6 3EA* Tel 07970-908517 (mobile) E-mail linda.shipp@btinternet.com

SHIPP, Susan. *See* HOLLINS, Patricia Susan

SHIPSIDES, Brian Kenneth. b 56. Reading Univ BA. Westcott Ho Cam 79. **d** 82 **p** 83. C Bramley *Ripon* 82-85; C Notting Dale St Clem w St Mark and St Jas *Lon* 85-90; Chapl N Lon Poly 90-92; Chapl Univ of N Lon 92-97; P-in-c Forest Gate All SS and St Edm *Chelmsf* from 97. *The Vicarage, 79 Claremont Road, London E7 0QA* Tel (020) 8534 7463 *or* 8472 8584

SHIPTON, Andrew James. b 60. Leeds Univ BA82 Univ of Northumbria at Newc MEd99. Cranmer Hall Dur 83. **d** 85 **p** 86. C Fishponds St Jo *Bris* 85-88; C Gosforth All SS *Newc* 88-91; V Long Benton St Mary 91-96; Chapl Univ of Northumbria at Newc from 96. *282 Wingrove Road North, Newcastle upon Tyne NE4 9EE* Tel 0191-274 9761 *or* 222 1679
E-mail andrew.shipton@unn.ac.uk

SHIPTON, Linda Anne. *See* GREEN, Mrs Linda Anne

SHIPTON (née WILSON), Mrs Marjorie Jayne. b 59. Hull Univ BA80 Leeds Univ MA01 K Alfred's Coll Win PGCE81. St Jo Coll Dur 85. **dss** 86 **d** 87 **p** 94. Ormesby *York* 86-89; Par Dn 87-89; Chapl Asst Newc Gen Hosp 89-91; Chapl 91-95; Dep Hd Chapl Newcastle upon Tyne Hosps NHS Trust from 95; NSM Whorlton *Newc* 94-97. *Royal Victoria Infirmary, Queen Victoria Road, Newcastle upon Tyne NE1 4LP* Tel 0191-232 5131

SHIRE, William Stanley. b 17. TCD BA39 MA43. **d** 40 **p** 41. C Dundalk *Arm* 40-43; C Portadown St Mark 43-45; P-in-c Mullaglass 45-51; I 51-57; C Attenborough w Bramcote and Chilwell *S'well* 57-58; V Lowdham 58-66; R Pilton w Wardenhoe and Stoke Doyle *Pet* 67-70; R Aldwincle w Thorpe Achurch, Pilton, Wadenhoe etc 70-82; rtd 82; Lic to Offic *Pet* 82-85; Perm to Offic from 85. *96 Glapthorne Road, Oundle, Peterborough PE8 4PS* Tel (01832) 272125

SHIRES, Alan William. b 36. Lon Univ BA60. Oak Hill Th Coll 57. **d** 61 **p** 62. C York St Paul *York* 61-64; C Southgate *Chich* 64-67; V Doncaster St Mary *Sheff* 67-75; Perm to Offic *Portsm* 75-96; Student Counsellor Portsm Poly 75-88; Hd Student Services Portsm Poly 88-96; rtd 96. *15 Broomfield Road, Admaston, Wellington TF5 0AR*

SHIRESS, Canon David Henry Faithfull. b 27. St Cath Coll Cam BA49 MA53. Ridley Hall Cam 51. **d** 53 **p** 54. C Southport Ch Ch *Liv* 53-55; C St Helens St Mark 55-58; V Shrewsbury St Julian *Lich* 58-67; V Blackheath Park St Mich *S'wark* 67-93; Sub-Dean Greenwich 81-90; RD Greenwich 90-91; Hon Can S'wark Cathl 89-93; rtd 93; Perm to Offic *Sarum* from 93. *35 Rempstone Road, Wimborne BH21 1SS* Tel (01202) 887845

SHIRLEY, Timothy Francis. b 25. Univ Coll Ox BA49 MA49. Qu Coll Birm 49. **d** 51 **p** 52. C Pimlico St Gabr *Lon* 51-56; C-in-c Hayes St Edm CD 56-65; V Fulham St Etheldreda 65-68; V Fulham St Etheldreda w St Clem 68-90; rtd 90; Perm to Offic *Worc* from 90. *70 St Dunstan's Crescent, Worcester WR5 2AQ* Tel (01905) 353930

SHIRLEY, Valerie Joy. b 42. LNSM course 93. **d** 96 **p** 97. OLM Sydenham H Trin *S'wark* from 96. *Flat 9, Faircroft, 5 Westwood Hill, London SE26 6BG* Tel (020) 8778 2551

SHIRRAS, The Ven Edward Scott. b 37. St Andr Univ BSc61. Clifton Th Coll 61. **d** 63 **p** 64. C Surbiton Hill Ch Ch *S'wark* 63-66; C Jesmond Clayton Memorial *Newc* 66-68; Youth Sec CPAS 68-71; Publications Sec 71-74; Asst Gen Sec 74-75; Hon C Wallington H Trin *S'wark* 69-75; V Roxeth Ch Ch *Lon* 75-82; V Roxeth Ch Ch and Harrow St Pet 82-85; AD Harrow 82-85; Adn Northolt 85-92; V Win Ch Ch *Win* 92-01; rtd 01; Perm to Offic *Ox* 01-02; P-in-c Marcham w Garford from 02. *1 All Saints Close, Marcham, Abingdon OX13 6PE* Tel (01865) 391319 E-mail shirras@ukgateway.net

SHIRRAS, Mrs Pamela Susan. b 41. St Andr Univ BSc62 Brunel Univ PGCE80. Wycliffe Hall Ox 04. **d** 05. NSM Marcham w Garford *Ox* from 05. *1 All Saints Close, Marcham, Abingdon OX13 6PE* Tel (01865) 391319 Mobile 07946-586616 E-mail shirras@ukgateway.net

SHIRRAS, Rachel Joan. *See* COLLINS, Rachel Joan

SHOCK, Rachel Alexandra. b 63. Nottm Trent Univ LLB94. EMMTC 95. **d** 98 **p** 00. NSM Radford All So w Ch Ch and St Mich *S'well* 98-99; NSM Lenton Abbey 99-02; NSM Wollaton from 02. *1 May Avenue, Wollaton, Nottingham NG8 2NE* Tel 0115-928 3626 E-mail racheltim.shock@ntlworld.com

SHOESMITH (née HALL), Mrs Judith Frances. b 64. SS Coll Cam BA85 MEng86 MA89 BTh02 CEng97. Ridley Hall Cam 99. **d** 02 **p** 03. C Drayton in Hales *Lich* from 02. *30 Berrisford Close, Market Drayton TF9 1LG* Tel (01630) 658977 E-mail jfh@franceshall.fsnet.co.uk

SHONE, The Very Revd John Terence. b 35. Selw Coll Cam BA58 MA64 Newc Univ MA92. Linc Th Coll 58. **d** 60 **p** 61. C St Pancras w St Jas and Ch Ch *Lon* 60-62; Chapl Aber Univ *Ab* 62-68; Chapl St Andr Cathl 62-65; V Gt Grimsby St Andr and St Luke *Linc* 68-69; Chapl Stirling Univ *St And* 69-80; R Bridge of Allan 69-86; P-in-c Alloa 77-85; Can St Ninian's Cathl Perth 80-89; P-in-c Dollar 81-86; Dean St Andr 82-89; Research and Development Officer 86-89; Dioc Supernumerary 86-89; TV Cullercoats St Geo *Newc* 89-00; rtd 00. *29 Redwell Place, Alloa FK10 2BT* Tel (01259) 215113 E-mail husnwif@aol.com

SHONE, Raymond. b 21. St Jo Coll Dur BA47 MA54 Brighton Poly Dip Counselling 81. Linc Th Coll 48. **d** 48 **p** 49. C Penn *Lich* 48-50; C Warblington w Emsworth *Portsm* 50-58; R Monks Risborough *Ox* 58-61; Chapl and Lect Bp Otter Coll Chich 61-66; Perm to Offic *Chich* from 66; Sen Lect Eastbourne Coll of Educn 66-76; E Sussex Coll of HE 76-79; Brighton Poly 79-80; Counsellor W Sussex Inst of HE 83-87; rtd 87. *28 Hawthorn Close, Chichester PO19 3DZ* Tel (01243) 774543

SHONE, Robert Alan. b 16. Qu Coll Cam BA38 MA42. St Steph Ho Ox 39. **d** 39 **p** 40. C W Derby Gd Shep *Liv* 39-41; C Wigan All SS 41-42; C Birch St Jas *Man* 42-45; C Wardleworth St Mary 45-47; R Withington St Chris 47-56; V Morley St Paul *Wakef* 56-63; V Wardleworth St Mary *Man* 63-73; V Wardleworth St Jas 66-73; V Wardleworth St Mary w St Jas 73-81; rtd 81; Perm to Offic *Man* from 81. *c/o C A J Shone Esq, 7 New Way, Whitworth, Rochdale OL12 8AN* Tel (01706) 852893

SHONE, Miss Ursula Ruth. b 34. Lon Univ DBRS59 Stirling Univ BA75 Open Univ BPhil88 Chester Coll of HE DipApTh00. **dss** 81 **d** 86 **p** 94. Bridge of Allan *St And* 81-85; Lochgelly 85-87; Chapl Cov Cathl *Cov* 87-90; Ind Chapl 87-90; Par Dn Ainsdale *Liv* 90-94; Dioc Science Adv 90-99; C Ainsdale 94-96; C Childwall St Dav 96-99; rtd 99; NSM Brechin *Bre* from 00. *4 Park Road, Brechin DD9 7AF* Tel (01356) 626087

SHOOTER, Robert David. b 44. Lon Univ BSc70 Lanc Univ MA94 CQSW72 LRAM92. N Ord Course 99. **d** 02 **p** 03. NSM Brierfield *Blackb* 02-04; NSM Briercliffe from 04. *234 Briercliffe Road, Burnley BB10 2NZ* Tel (01282) 412404

SHOOTER, Ms Susan. b 58. Nottm Univ BA81 PGCE82. St Jo Coll Nottm MA94. **d** 96 **p** 98. C Dartford H Trin *Roch* 96-97; C Crayford 97-00; V Bostall Heath from 00. *St Andrew's Parsonage, 276 Brampton Road, Bexleyheath DA7 5SF* Tel (020) 8303 9332 E-mail mistshoot@aol.com

SHORROCK, John Musgrave. b 29. TCD BA54 MA58. Bps' Coll Cheshunt 54. **d** 56 **p** 57. C Fleetwood St Pet *Blackb* 56-59; C Lancaster St Mary 59-61; C-in-c Blackpool St Wilfrid CD 61-65; V Blackpool St Wilfrid 65-67; Min Can and Sacr Cant Cathl *Cant* 67-70; V Chorley St Geo *Blackb* 71-78; P-in-c Bredgar w Bicknor and Huckinge *Cant* 78-82; P-in-c Frinsted w Wormshill and Milstead 78-82; R Bredgar w Bicknor and Frinsted w Wormshill etc 82-92; rtd 92; Perm to Offic *Cant* from 92; Clergy Widows Officer Cant Adnry from 97. *Bradgate, School Lane, Bekesbourne, Canterbury CT4 5ER* Tel (01227) 832133 E-mail shorrock@eurobell.co.uk

SHORT, Brian Frederick. b 29. St Jo Coll Nottm 70. **d** 72 **p** 73. C Walton *St E* 72-75; P-in-c Barking w Darmsden and Gt Bricett 75-78; P-in-c Ringshall w Battisford and Lt Finborough 75-78; TV Nor St Pet Parmentergate w St Jo *Nor* 78-88; R Winfarthing w Shelfanger w Burston w Gissing etc 88-90; rtd 90; Perm to Offic *Nor* from 92. *31 Nursery Gardens, Blofield, Norwich NR13 4JE* Tel (01603) 712396

SHORT, Bryan Raymond. b 37. Bris Univ BSc59 CertEd60. Dioc OLM tr scheme 00. **d** 02 **p** 03. OLM Kirkheaton *Wakef* from 02. *12 Bankfield Lane, Kirkheaton, Huddersfield HD5 0JG* Tel (01484) 425832

SHORT, Ms Clare. b 50. Leic Univ BA72 St Mary's Coll Twickenham PGCE73. S Dios Minl Tr Scheme 89. **d** 92 **p** 94. NSM Horsham *Chich* 92-99; Perm to Offic *Newc* from 04. *The Open Gate, Marygate, Holy Island, Berwick-upon-Tweed TD15 2SD* Tel (01289) 389222

SHORT, Eileen. b 45. Ex Univ BA66. N Ord Course 93. **d** 96 **p** 97. NSM Castleton Moor *Man* 96-98; NSM Chorlton-cum-Hardy St Clem 98-00; NSM Baguley from 00. *2 Netherwood Road, Northenden, Manchester M22 4BQ*

SHORT, Mrs Heather Mary. b 50. LWCMD71 Cardiff Coll of Educn CertEd72. WEMTC 98. **d** 01 **p** 02. C Heref S Wye *Heref* 01-05; P-in-c Bodenham w Hope-under-Dinmore, Felton etc from 05; P-in-c Marden w Amberley and Wisteston from 05; P-in-c Sutton St Nicholas w Sutton St Michael from 05. *The Vicarage, Bodenham, Hereford HR1 3JX* Tel (01568) 797370

SHORT, Canon John Sinclair. b 33. Oak Hill Th Coll 64. **d** 66 **p** 67. C Islington St Mary *Lon* 66-70; V Becontree St Mary *Chelmsf* 70-76; V New Malden and Coombe *S'wark* 76-90; RD Kingston 79-84; Hon Can S'wark Cathl 83-90; P-in-c Peldon w Gt and Lt Wigborough *Chelmsf* 90-93; rtd 93; Perm to Offic *S'wark* from 93. *22 Chart Lane, Reigate RH2 7BP* Tel (01737) 245244

SHORT, Canon John Timothy. b 43. Lon Univ DipTh67. Kelham Th Coll 63. **d** 68 **p** 69. C St Marylebone Ch Ch w St Barn *Lon* 68-70; C Southgate Ch Ch 70-72; P-in-c Mosser *Carl* 72-78; Dioc Youth Officer 72-78; R Heyford w Stowe Nine Churches *Pet* 78-87; V Northampton St Jas 87-96; RD Wootton 88-96; TR Kingsthorpe w Northampton St Dav from 96; Can Pet Cathl from 97. *The Rectory, 16 Green End, Kingsthorpe, Northampton NN2 6RD* Tel (01604) 717133 Fax as telephone E-mail tim@kingsthorpechurches.co.uk

SHORT, Kenneth Arthur. b 33. Tyndale Hall Bris 64. **d** 67 **p** 68. C E Twickenham St Steph *Lon* 67-71; C Paddock Wood *Roch* 71-74; SE Area Sec BCMS 74-82; Hon C Sidcup Ch Ch *Roch* 74-82; V Tollington Park St Mark w St Anne *Lon* 82-86; V Holloway St Mark w Em 86-89; R Alfold and Loxwood *Guildf* 89-98; rtd 98; Perm to Offic *Roch* from 00 and *Lon* from 02. *228 Ralph Perring Court, Stone Park Avenue, Beckenham BR3 3LX* Tel 020-8650 4859

SHORT, Martin Peter. b 54. Peterho Cam BA77 MA81. Wycliffe Hall Ox 77. **d** 79 **p** 80. C Shipley St Pet *Bradf* 79-82; C Becontree St Mary *Chelmsf* 82-86; V Bolton St Jas w St Chrys *Bradf* 86-92; Dioc Communications Officer 92-98; C Otley 92-98; Hd Media Tr Communications Dept Abps' Coun from 98; Hon C and Hon Chapl Bradf Cathl *Bradf* from 98. *3 Cathedral Close, Bradford BD1 4EG* Tel (01274) 777731

SHORT, Martin Ronald. b 57. Crewe & Alsager Coll CertEd78 Leic Univ BEd85. St Jo Coll Nottm 93. **d** 93 **p** 94. C Frankby w Greasby *Ches* 93-97; TV Horwich and Rivington *Man* 97-02; TV Turton Moorland Min from 02. *St Anne's Vicarage, High Street, Turton, Bolton BL7 0EH* Tel (01204) 856807

SHORT, Canon Michael John. b 38. Univ of Wales (Lamp) BA59. Sarum Th Coll 59. **d** 61 **p** 62. C Swansea St Nic *S & B* 61-64; C Oystermouth 64-69; V Merthyr Vale w Aberfan *Llan* 69-82; RD Merthyr Tydfil 76-82; R Caerphilly from 82; RD Caerphilly 83-04; Can Llan Cathl from 89; Prec from 02. *The Rectory, 2 St Martin's Road, Caerphilly CF83 1EJ* Tel (029) 2088 2992 Mobile 07831-742515

SHORT, Neil Robert. b 58. Loughb Univ BSc81 St Jo Coll Dur BA86. Cranmer Hall Dur 83. **d** 86 **p** 87. C Whitfield *Derby* 86-90; C Bradf St Aug Undercliffe *Bradf* 90-96; V Burscough Bridge *Liv* from 96. *St John's Vicarage, 253 Liverpool Road South, Ormskirk L40 7RE* Tel (01704) 893205 *or* 897852 E-mail neil@theshorts.go-plus.net

SHORT, Mrs Patricia Ann (Pip). b 41. K Coll Lon BA62 AKC62. **d** 00 **p** 01. NSM Etwall w Egginton *Derby* from 00; Chapl Asst S Derbyshire Acute Hosps NHS Trust from 00. *Ivy Cottage, 19 Monk Street, Tutbury, Burton-on-Trent DE13 9NA* Tel (01283) 813640 *or* (01332) 347141 Mobile 07711-823082 Fax 814373 E-mail pipshort@mail.com *or* pip.short@sdah-tr.trent.nhs.uk

SHORT, Robert Leslie. b 48. Em Coll Cam BA70 MA76. Wycliffe Hall Ox 87. **d** 92 **p** 92. Mexico 92-93; Chapl Repton Sch Derby 93-04; P-in-c Ibiza *Eur* from 04. *Address temp unknown*

SHORT, Timothy. *See* SHORT, Canon John Timothy

SHORT, Vincent Charles. b 57. Oak Hill Th Coll DipHE95. **d** 97 **p** 98. C Chatham St Phil and St Jas *Roch* 97-01; V Istead Rise from 01. *The Vicarage, Upper Avenue, Gravesend DA13 9DA* Tel (01474) 832403 Fax as telephone E-mail vcshort@fish.co.uk

SHORTER, Robert Edward. b 48. Ripon Coll Cuddesdon 89. **d** 91 **p** 92. C Braunton *Ex* 91-94; C Bishopsnympton, Rose Ash, Mariansleigh etc 94-96; TV 96-98; P-in-c E w W Harptree and Hinton Blewett *B & W* 98-03; Dioc Ecum Officer 98-03; rtd 03. *Fleur de la Passion, 61330 Torchamp, France* Tel (0033) (2) 33 38 56 53 E-mail outofit.shorter@wanadoo.fr

SHORTHOUSE, Raymond Trevor. b 34. DipAdEd Warwick Univ DPhil00. Ridley Hall Cam 68. **d** 70 **p** 71. C Gt Ilford St Andr *Chelmsf* 70-73; C Ludlow *Heref* 73-75; P-in-c Cressage w Sheinton 76-80; P-in-c Harley w Kenley 76-80; P-in-c Denby *Derby* 80-84; Adult Educn Officer 80-85; RD Heanor 83-84; V Chellaston 84-88; P-in-c Breadsall 88-98; Dioc Dir of Studies 88-96; rtd 98; P-in-c Symondsbury *Sarum* 99-04. *31 Sycamore Close, Clun Road, Craven Arms SY7 9AF* E-mail justin@shorthouse.netlineuk.net

SHORTT, Canon Noel Christopher. b 36. Open Univ BA76 Ulster Univ MA Dip Continuing Educn DPhil91. Bps' Coll Cheshunt 63. **d** 63 **p** 64. C Belfast St Mary *Conn* 63-66; C Agherton 66-68; Chapl RAF 68-69; I Duneane w Ballyscullion *Conn* 69-79; I Belfast St Steph w St Luke 79-89; I Ballyrashane w Kildollagh 89-99; Can Belfast St Anne 96-99; rtd 99. *2 Woodview Park, Ballymoney BT53 6DJ*

SHOTLANDER, Lionel George. b 27. Cant Univ (NZ) BA49 MA51. **d** 51 **p** 52. New Zealand 51-58 and 60-74; C Southsea St Pet *Portsm* 58-60; V Curdridge 74-85; R Durley 79-85; V Twyford and Owslebury and Morestead *Win* 85-91; rtd 91; Perm to Offic *Win* and *Portsm* from 91. *Cambria, High Street, Shirrell Heath, Southampton SO32 2JN* Tel (01329) 832353

SHOTTER, The Very Revd Edward Frank. b 33. Univ of Wales (Lamp) BA58. St Steph Ho Ox 58. **d** 60 **p** 61. C Plymouth St Pet *Ex* 60-62; Inter-Colleg Sec SCM (Lon) 62-66; Perm to Offic *Lon* 62-69; Dir Lon Medical Gp 63-89; Chapl Lon Univ Medical Students *Lon* 69-89; Dir Inst of Medical Ethics 74-89; Preb St Paul's Cathl *Lon* 77-89; Dean Roch 89-03; rtd 03; Perm to Offic *St E* from 04. *Hill House, School Road, Westhall, Halesworth IP19 8QZ* Tel (01502) 575364

SHOULER, Mrs Margaret Fiona. b 55. St Jo Coll Nottm. **d** 01 **p** 02. C Sherwood *S'well* from 01. *139 Appledore Avenue, Wollaton, Nottingham NG8 2RW* Tel 0115-928 3400 E-mail fionashouler@hotmail.com

SHOULER, Simon Frederic. b 54. Pemb Coll Cam MA79 FRICS89. EMMTC 82. **d** 85 **p** 86. NSM Asfordby *Leic* 85-89; Lic to Offic from 89. *1 West End, Long Clawson, Melton Mowbray LE14 4PE* Tel (01664) 822698 E-mail sshouler@oldmanorhouse.u-net.com

SHOZAWA, John. **d** 64. Canada 64-78 and 95-01; USA 78-95; rtd 01; Perm to Offic *Guildf* from 00. *4 Cromwell Place, Cranleigh GU6 7LF* Tel (01483) 267295

SHREEVE, The Ven David Herbert. b 34. St Pet Hall Ox BA57 MA61. Ridley Hall Cam 57. **d** 59 **p** 60. C Plymouth St Andr *Ex* 59-64; V Bermondsey St Anne *S'wark* 64-71; V Eccleshill *Bradf* 71-84; RD Calverley 78-84; Hon Can Bradf Cathl 83-84; Adn Bradf 84-99; rtd 99; Lic to Offic *Bradf* from 99; Perm to Offic *Ripon* from 00. *26 Kingsley Drive, Harrogate HG1 4TJ* Tel (01423) 886479

SHREWSBURY, Preb Michael Buller. b 30. St Jo Coll Dur BA54. Linc Th Coll 54. **d** 56 **p** 57. C Salford St Phil w St Steph *Man* 56-60; Chapl RN 60-63; Chapl HM Pris Pentonville 64-67; Bermuda 67-70; V Dalston H Trin w St Phil *Lon* 70-86; AD Hackney 79-84; Preb St Paul's Cathl 86-92; R Stepney St Dunstan and All SS 86-92; rtd 92; Perm to Offic *Lon* from 92. *Flat 1, 150 Wapping High Street, London E1W 3PH* Tel (020) 7480 5479

SHREWSBURY, Area Bishop of. *See* SMITH, The Rt Revd Alan Gregory Clayton

SHRIMPTON, Canon Aner Clive. b 14. Lon Univ BD39. ALCD39. **d** 39 **p** 40. C Ore Ch Ch *Chich* 39-41; C Battle 42-46; P-in-c S Patcham 46-52; V Ruddington *S'well* 52-84; Hon Can S'well Minster 78-84; rtd 84; Perm to Offic *S'well* from 84. *36 Brookview Drive, Keyworth, Nottingham NG12 5JN* Tel 0115-937 2795

SHRIMPTON, Mrs Sheila Nan. b 32. Qu Mary Coll Lon BA54 LSE CertSS55. St Chris Coll Blackheath 57. **dss** 83 **d** 87 **p** 94. Lic to Offic *B & W* 83-90; NSM Barkston and Hough Gp *Linc* 90-97; Asst Local Min Officer 90-97; C Brant Broughton and Beckingham 97-98; P-in-c Churchstanton, Buckland St Mary and Otterford *B & W* 98-02; rtd 02. *2 King William Mews, Church Street, Curry Rivel, Langport TA10 0HD* Tel (01458) 259293

SHRINE, Robert Gerald. b 44. Birm Univ BA65 Univ of Zambia PGCE70 Lanc Univ MA74 Open Univ BA80. St Jo Coll Nottm MA97. **d** 97 **p** 98. C Blackpool St Thos *Blackb* 97-99; Dioc Chapl among Deaf People *Wakef* and *Bradf* from 99. *The Vicarage, 80 Carr House Road, Halifax HX3 7RJ* Tel (Typetalk) 18002 (01274) 671576 Fax 677693 E-mail bob.shrine@ukonline.co.uk

SHRINE, Mrs Susan Elaine Walmsley. b 56. N Ord Course. **d** 02 **p** 03. C Bradshaw and Holmfield *Wakef* 02-04; TV Shelf w Buttershaw St Aid *Bradf* from 04. *The Vicarage, 80 Carr House Road, Halifax HX3 7RJ* Tel (01274) 671576 Fax 677693 E-mail sue.shrine@ukonline.co.uk

SHRISUNDER, David Shripat. b 29. Osmania Univ Hyderabad BA52 Serampore Univ BD59 Shivaji Univ Kolhapur MA69. Bp's Coll Calcutta 54. **d** 57 **p** 58. India 57-71, 72-75, 77-79 and 88-90; C Poona St Paul w Kirkee All SS 57-58; P I Bombay Em 58-61; I Solapur Epiphany 61-71, 72-75 and 88-90; Lect Dayanand Coll Solapur 69-71, 72-75 and 78-79; C Batley All SS *Wakef* 71-72; C Skegness *Linc* 75-77; C Derringham Bank *York* 80-81; TV Grays Thurrock *Chelmsf* 81-85; R Uddingston *Glas* 85-88; R Cambuslang 85-88; P-in-c Sinfin Moor *Derby* 90-94; rtd 94; Perm to Offic *Wakef* 94-96 and from 98. *8 Jessamine Street, Dewsbury WF13 3HY* Tel (01924) 489378

SHRIVES, Austen Geoffrey. b 28. Lon Univ BD68 MTh77. S'wark Ord Course. **d** 64 **p** 65. C Lower Sydenham St Mich *S'wark* 64-68; Miss to Seamen 68-74; V Epsom St Martin *Guildf* 74-84; V York Town St Mich 84-87; R Churchstanton, Buckland St Mary and Otterford *B & W* 87-93; rtd 93; Perm to Offic *Ex* 94-96; Perm to Offic *Heref* from 97. *16 Watling Street, Ross-on-Wye HR9 5UF*

SHUFFLEBOTHAM, Alastair Vincent. b 32. Nottm Univ CSocSc57. Lich Th Coll 63. **d** 65 **p** 66. C W Kirby St Bridget *Ches* 65-69; V Tranmere St Paul 69-71; V Tranmere St Paul w St Luke 71-78; V Neston 78-97; rtd 97. *Y-Clystyrau, 5 Tan-y-Bryn, Llanbedr Dyffryn Clwyd, Ruthin LL15 1AQ* Tel (01824) 704619

SHUKMAN, Ann Margaret. b 31. Girton Coll Cam BA53 MA58 LMH Ox DPhil74. WMMTC 80. **dss** 84 **d** 92 **p** 94. Steeple Aston w N Aston and Tackley *Ox* 84-96; NSM 92-96; rtd 96; Perm to Offic *Ox* from 96. *40 Woodstock Close, Oxford OX2 8DB* Tel (01865) 515907 Fax 310341

SHULER, Patricia Ann. b 52. Ridley Hall Cam 02. **d** 05. C Ipswich St Aug *St E* from 05. *18 Fitzmaurice Road, Ipswich IP3 9AX* E-mail tricia.shuler@gmail.com

SHUTT, Anthony John. b 57. Brunel Univ BSc79 DipHE89. Trin Coll Bris 87. **d** 89 **p** 90. C Epsom St Martin *Guildf* 89-95; P-in-c Send from 95. *St Mary's Vicarage, Vicarage Lane, Send, Woking GU23 7JN* Tel (01483) 222193

SHUTT, Laurence John. b 42. MPS64 MRPharmS88. St Steph Ho Ox 87 Llan Dioc Tr Scheme 80. **d** 84 **p** 85. NSM Whitchurch *Llan* 84-87; C Llanishen and Lisvane 88-90; V Middlestown *Wakef* 90-97; P-in-c Arnside *Carl* 97-04; Chapl RNR 89-04; rtd 04. *PO Box 59448, Pissouri, 4607 Limassol, Cyprus* Tel (00357) 2522 2507 Mobile 9913 8292 *or* 9913 9416 E-mail shasting@cytanet.com.cy

SHUTT, Nicholas Stephen. b 58. Qu Mary Coll Lon LLB80 Solicitor 83. SW Minl Tr Course 91. **d** 94 **p** 95. NSM Yelverton, Meavy, Sheepstor and Walkhampton *Ex* from 94. *12 Blackbrook Close, Walkhampton, Yelverton PL20 6JF* Tel (01822) 854653 E-mail nsshutt@aol.com

SIBANDA, Melusi Francis. b 72. Univ of Zimbabwe BSc96 BA99. Bp Gaul Th Coll Harare 97. **d** 98 **p** 99. C Bulawayo Cathl Zimbabwe 98-00; R Bulawayo St Marg 01-03; C Colne and Villages *Blackb* from 03. *13 Lancaster Street, Colne BB8 9AZ* Tel (01282) 871750 E-mail mfsibanda@hotmail.com

SIBBALD, Olwyn. *See* MARLOW, Mrs Olwyn Eileen

SIBLEY, Jonathan Paul Eddolls. b 55. Newc Univ BA77. Westcott Ho Cam 78 Ripon Coll Cuddesdon 85. **d** 87 **p** 88. C Waltham Cross *St Alb* 87-90; C Chalfont St Peter *Ox* 90-96; P-in-c Sulhamstead Abbots and Bannister w Ufton Nervet 96-02; P-in-c Sutton St Mary *Linc* from 02. *The Vicarage, Market Place, Long Sutton, Spalding PE12 9JJ* Tel and fax (01406) 362033 E-mail sibley.jon_jeanne@btinternet.com

SIBLEY, Peter Linsey. b 40. Selw Coll Cam BA61 MA63. Oak Hill Th Coll 79. **d** 81 **p** 82. C Crofton *Portsm* 81-84; TV Cheltenham St Mark *Glouc* 84-93; P-in-c Tewkesbury H Trin 93-96; V 96-05; RD Tewkesbury and Winchcombe 97-02; rtd 05. *14 Griffiths Avenue, Cheltenham GL51 7BH* Tel (01242) 514640 E-mail sibglos@aol.com

SIBSON, Canon Edward John. b 39. Brasted Th Coll 61 St Aid Birkenhead 63. **d** 65 **p** 66. C Gt Parndon *Chelmsf* 65-69; C Saffron Walden 69-72; P-in-c Colchester St Leon 72-77; Ind Chapl 72-80; TV Colchester St Leon, St Mary Magd and St Steph 77-80; V Layer de la Haye 80-90; R Chipping Ongar w

Shelley 90-98; RD Ongar 94-98; P-in-c High and Gd Easter w Margaret Roding 98-04; P-in-c Gt Canfield w High Roding and Aythorpe Roding 02-04; Hon Can Chelmsf Cathl 01-04; rtd 04. *73 Thaxted Road, Saffron Walden CB11 3AG* Tel (01799) 520007

SIBSON, Canon Robert Francis. b 46. Leeds Univ CertEd68. Sarum & Wells Th Coll 78. **d** 80 **p** 81. C Watford St Mich *St Alb* 80-83; TV Digswell and Panshanger 83-90; V Biggleswade 90-02; Chapl Bedford and Shires Health and Care NHS Trust 94-02; RD Biggleswade *St Alb* 96-01; Hon Can St Alb from 98; V Sawbridgeworth from 02. *The Vicarage, 144 Sheering Mill Lane, Sawbridgeworth CM21 9ND* Tel (01279) 723305 Fax 721541 E-mail robert.sibson@btinternet.com

SICHEL, Stephen Mackenzie. b 59. UEA BA80 Birm Univ MA95. Ripon Coll Cuddesdon 87. **d** 90 **p** 91. C Tettenhall Regis *Lich* 90-95; C Camberwell St Giles w St Matt *S'wark* 95-01; P-in-c Brixton St Matt 01-02; V Brixton St Matt w St Jude from 02. *The Vicarage, 5 St Matthew's Road, London SW2 1ND* Tel (020) 7274 3553

SIDAWAY, The Ven Geoffrey Harold. b 42. Kelham Th Coll 61. **d** 66 **p** 67. C Beighton *Derby* 66-70; C Chesterfield St Mary and All SS 70-72; P-in-c Derby St Bart 72-74; V 74-77; V Maidstone St Martin *Cant* 77-86; V Bearsted w Thurnham 86-00; RD Sutton 92-99; Hon Can Cant Cathl 94-00; Adn Glouc from 00. *Glebe House, Church Road, Maisemore, Gloucester GL2 8EY* Tel (01452) 528500 Fax 381528 E-mail archdglos@star.co.uk

SIDDALL, The Ven Arthur. b 43. Lanc Univ MA81 Surrey Univ PGCE94 MCMI96. ALCD67. **d** 67 **p** 68. C Formby H Trin *Liv* 67-70; C Childwall All SS 70-72; CMS 72-77; Bangladesh 74-77; V Clitheroe St Paul Low Moor *Blackb* 77-82; V Blackb St Gabr 82-90; Dep Gen Sec Miss to Seamen 90-93; Hon C Leatherhead *Guildf* 93-96; V Chipping and Whitewell *Blackb* 96-04; Rural Chapl 03-04; Chapl Naples w Sorrento, Capri and Bari *Eur* from 04; Adn Italy and Malta from 05. *Christ Church, Afsouth (Naples), BFPO 8, London* Tel (0039) (081) 411842 E-mail vicar@christchurch.it

SIDDLE, Michael Edward. b 33. Dur Univ BA54. St Aid Birkenhead 55. **d** 57 **p** 58. C Fazakerley Em *Liv* 57-59; C Farnworth 59-62; V Swadlincote *Derby* 62-70; Distr Sec (Northd and Dur) BFBS 70-72; Yorkshire 72-82; V Bamber Bridge St Aid *Blackb* 82-87; V Horsforth *Ripon* 87-00; rtd 00; Perm to Offic *Ripon* from 00. *28 Carr Bridge Drive, Cookridge, Leeds LS16 7JY* Tel 0113-261 0498 Mobile 07941-209069 E-mail mirisiddle@aol.com

SIDEBOTHAM, Canon Stephen Francis. b 35. Qu Coll Cam BA58 MA80. Linc Th Coll 58. **d** 60 **p** 61. C Bitterne Park *Win* 60-64; Hong Kong 64-83; Dean 76-83; Archdeacon 78-83; Chapl Gravesend and N Kent Hosp 83-94; R Gravesend St Geo *Roch* 83-94; RD Gravesend 91-94; P-in-c Rosherville 91-94; Acorn Chr Foundn from 94; rtd 97; Perm to Offic *Ox* 97-98. *87 Aston Abbotts Road, Weedon, Aylesbury HP22 4NH* Tel (01296) 640098

SIDEBOTTOM, Andrew John. *See* DAVIES, Andrew John

SIDEBOTTOM, George. b 16. TCD 43. **d** 49 **p** 50. C Drumholm and Rossnowlagh *D & R* 49-52; C Maghera 52-53; C Ches St Mary *Ches* 53-56; I Achill w Dugort, Castlebar and Turlough *T, K & A* 56-60; V Felmersham *St Alb* 60-81; w Bletsoe 62-79; R Bletsoe 60-62; rtd 81; Perm to Offic *St Alb* from 81. *2 Homebrook House, Cardington Road, Bedford MK42 0RL* Tel (01234) 356189

SIDES, Canon James Robert. b 37. TCD BA66. CITC 68. **d** 67 **p** 68. C Belfast St Clem *D & D* 67-70; C Antrim All SS *Conn* 70-73; I Tomregan w Drumlane *K, E & A* 73-80; I Killesher 80-97; Can Kilmore Cathl from 89; I Kildrumferton w Ballymachugh and Ballyjamesduff from 97. *Kildrumferton Rectory, Crosserlough, Co Cavan, via Kells, Irish Republic* Tel (00353) (49) 433 6211 Mobile 87-979 0080 E-mail kildrumferton@kilmore.anglican.org

SIEJKOWSKI, Piotr Jan. *See* ASHWIN-SIEJKOWSKI, Piotr Jan

SIEMENS, James Ryan. b 72. Manitoba Univ BA93 McGill Univ Montreal BTh96 MDiv97. **d** 97 **p** 98. C Basseterre St Geo Canada 97-98; R Nipawin St Jo 98-03; TV Swinton and Pendlebury *Man* from 03. *All Saints' Vicarage, 4 Banbury Mews, Wardley, Swinton, Manchester M27 9QZ* Tel 0161-794 5934 Mobile 07880-863858 E-mail father.james@swintonandpendlebury.org.uk

SIGRIST, Richard Martin. b 46. Bernard Gilpin Soc Dur 67 Sarum Th Coll 68. **d** 71 **p** 72. C Yeovil St Mich *B & W* 71-74; Chapl RN 74-84; TV Sidmouth, Woolbrook and Salcombe Regis *Ex* 84-86; TR 86-91; TR Sidmouth, Woolbrook, Salcombe Regis, Sidbury etc 91-94; RD Ottery 90-94; USA 94-99; P-in-c Devonport St Bart *Ex* 99-02; V from 02; RD Plymouth Devonport from 01. *St Bartholomew's Vicarage, 13 Outland Road, Plymouth PL2 3BZ* Tel (01752) 562623 E-mail rmsigrist@onetel.com

SILCOCK, Donald John. b 30. AKC59. **d** 60 **p** 61. C Hackney St Jo *Lon* 60-63; C-in-c Plumstead Wm Temple Ch Abbey Wood CD *S'wark* 63-68; C Felpham w Middleton *Chich* 68-74; R Ightham *Roch* 74-84; R Cliffe at Hoo w Cooling 84-92; RD Strood 85-91; rtd 92; Perm to Offic *Chich* from 92. *Puck's House, 26 Ancton Way, Elmer Sands, Middleton-on-Sea, Bognor Regis PO22 6JN* Tel (01243) 582589

SILINS, Jacqueline. *See* JOHNSON, Ms Jacqueline

SILK, David. *See* SILK, The Rt Revd Robert David

SILK, Ian Geoffrey. b 60. Pemb Coll Cam BA81 MA85. Trin Coll Bris BA89. **d** 89 **p** 90. C Linc St Giles *Linc* 89-93; P-in-c Linc St Geo Swallowbeck 93-98; V from 98; PV Linc Cathl from 01. *St George's Vicarage, 87 Eastbrook Road, Lincoln LN6 7EW* Tel (01522) 870881 E-mail revisilk@fish.co.uk

SILK, John Arthur. b 52. Selw Coll Cam BA73 MA77 K Coll Lon MTh80. Westcott Ho Cam 75. **d** 77 **p** 78. C Banstead *Guildf* 77-80; C Dorking w Ranmore 80-84; R Ringwould w Kingsdown *Cant* 84-95; V Thames Ditton *Guildf* from 95. *The Vicarage, Summer Road, Thames Ditton KT7 0QQ* Tel (020) 8398 3446 E-mail john@tdvic.fsnet.co.uk

SILK, Richard Trevor. b 67. St Steph Ho Ox 01. **d** 03 **p** 04. C St Marychurch *Ex* from 03. *28 Barewell Road, Torquay TQ1 4PA* Tel (01803) 326203 E-mail fr.richard@saint-marychurch.co.uk

✠**SILK, The Rt Revd Robert David.** b 36. Ex Univ BA58. St Steph Ho Ox 58. **d** 59 **p** 60 **c** 94. C Gillingham St Barn *Roch* 59-62; C Lamorbey H Redeemer 63-69; R Swanscombe SS Pet and Paul 69-71; P-in-c Swanscombe All SS 69-71; R Swanscombe 71-75; R Beckenham St Geo 75-80; Adn Leic 80-94; TR Leic H Spirit 82-88; Bp Ballarat 94-03; rtd 03; P-in-c Amberley w N Stoke and Parham, Wiggonholt etc *Chich* 03-04; Hon Asst Bp Ex from 04. *1 Centenary Way, Torquay TQ2 7SB* Tel (01803) 614456

SILK, Timothy James. b 73. Ox Brookes Univ BSc96. Oak Hill Th Coll BA99. **d** 99 **p** 00. C Stamford St Geo w St Paul *Linc* 99-02; C Arborfield w Barkham *Ox* from 02. *1 Meadow Barns, Park Lane, Finchampstead, Wokingham RG40 4QL* Tel 0118-973 6519 Fax 976 0285 E-mail timsilk@bigfoot.com

SILKSTONE, Thomas William. b 27. St Edm Hall Ox BA51 MA55 BD67. Wycliffe Hall Ox 51. **d** 53 **p** 54. C Aston SS Pet and Paul *Birm* 53-56; Div Master Merchant Taylors' Sch Crosby 56-62; Lect K Alfred's Coll Win 62-65; Sen Lect 65-75; Prin Lect 75-85; Lic to Offic *Win* 62-85; Perm to Offic *Truro* from 82; rtd 92. *Trevalyon, Lansallos, Looe PL13 2PX* Tel (01503) 72110

SILLER, Canon James Robert William. b 44. Pemb Coll Ox BA65 MA70. Westcott Ho Cam 67. **d** 70 **p** 71. C Spring Grove St Mary *Lon* 70-73; C Leeds St Pet *Ripon* 73-77; P-in-c Quarry Hill 73-77; V Gilling and Kirkby Ravensworth 77-82; P-in-c Melsonby 77-82; R Farnley 82-94; V Potternewton from 94; Hon Can Ripon Cathl 99-05; rtd 05. *4 Eskside Cottages, Eskdaleside, Grosmont, Whitby YO22 5PR*

SILLETT, Angela Veronica Isabel. *See* BERNERS-WILSON, Mrs Angela Veronica Isabel

SILLEY, Michael John. b 48. Ripon Coll Cuddesdon 82. **d** 84 **p** 85. C Frodingham *Linc* 84-87; V Ingham w Cammeringham w Fillingham 87-96; R Aisthorpe w Scampton w Thorpe le Fallows etc 87-96; RD Lawres 92-96; P-in-c N w S Carlton 93-96; P-in-c Brigg 96-97; V Brigg, Wrawby and Cadney cum Howsham 97-04; RD Yarborough 01-02; Bp's Dom Chapl from 05; Gen Preacher from 05. *Bishop's House, Eastgate, Lincoln LN2 1QQ* Tel (01522) 534701 E-mail michael.silley@lincoln.anglican.org

SILLIS, Andrew Keith. b 66. Wolv Poly BSc87. Aston Tr Scheme 91 Westcott Ho Cam 93. **d** 96 **p** 97. C Boyne Hill *Ox* 96-99; C Hayes St Nic CD *Lon* 99-00; C-in-c 00-05; V N Hayes St Nic from 05. *St Nicholas' Vicarage, Raynton Drive, Hayes UB4 8BG* Tel (020) 8573 4122 E-mail asillis@aol.com

SILLIS, Eric Keith. b 41. NW Ord Course 75. **d** 78 **p** 79. C Blackpool St Steph *Blackb* 78-82; V Huncoat 82-86; V Blackpool St Wilfrid 86-95; V Fleetwood St Dav from 95; Chapl Mothers' Union from 99. *St David's Vicarage, 211 Broadway, Fleetwood FY7 8AZ* Tel (01253) 779725 E-mail ksillis@stdavid.freeserve.co.uk *or* ksillis@fsnet.co.uk

SILLIS, Graham William. b 46. S'wark Ord Course 73. **d** 76 **p** 77. C Palmers Green St Jo *Lon* 76-79; C Dawlish *Ex* 79-81; V Ipswich St Thos *St E* 81-87; V Babbacombe *Ex* 87-95; C Tividale *Lich* 98-00; R Winchelsea and Icklesham *Chich* 00-03; V Derby St Luke *Derby* from 03. *St Luke's Vicarage, 48 Peet Street, Derby DE22 3RF* Tel (01332) 345720

SILLITOE, William John. b 37. Lich Th Coll 67. **d** 69 **p** 70. C Ettingshall *Lich* 69-71; C March St Jo *Ely* 72-74; P-in-c Kennett 74-77; V Fordham St Pet 74-77; V Castle Bromwich St Clem *Birm* 77-00; rtd 00; Perm to Offic *Birm* from 00. *St Clement's Croft, 11 Wood Green Road, Wednesbury WS10 9AX* Tel 0121-505 5954 E-mail mwm@fort34.freeserve.co.uk

SILLS, Canon Peter Michael. b 41. Barrister 76 Nottm Univ BA63 LLM68. S'wark Ord Course 78. **d** 81 **p** 82. C W Wimbledon Ch Ch *S'wark* 81-85; P-in-c Barnes H Trin 85-93; Wandsworth Adnry Ecum Officer 90-93; V Purley St Mark 93-00; Can Res Ely Cathl *Ely* from 00. *The Black Hostelry, The College, Ely CB7 4DL* Tel (01353) 645105 *or* 667735 E-mail peter.sills@cathedral.ely.anglican.org

SILVA, Peter John. b 47. Rhodes Univ BA73 HDipEd77 BEd79. St Paul's Coll Grahamstown 68. **d** 74 **p** 74. S Africa 74-98; C

Bloemfontein Cathl 74-75; Chapl Dioc Sch for Girls Grahamstown 75-79 and 89-95; Lect Rhodes Univ 79-81; Dir Academic Support Services Natal Univ 81-85; Regional Manager Performance and Educn Services 86; Dir Tape Aids for the Blind 87; R Overport Ch Ch 88-89; Dir Educn Projects Grahamstown Foundn 95-98; TV Abingdon *Ox* 99-02; Chief Exec Officer Peers Early Educn Partnership from 02. *Woodford Bridge Cottage, Drystone Hill, Enstone, Chipping Norton OX7 4AA* Tel (01608) 678627 *or* (01865) 395145 Mobile 07980-264472 E-mail peter.silva@virgin.net

SILVERMAN, Prof Bernard Walter. b 52. Jes Coll Cam BA73 MA76 PhD78 ScD89 Southn Univ BTh00 FRS97. STETS 97. **d** 99 **p** 00. Prof Statistics Bris Univ 93-03; Master St Pet Coll Ox from 03; Hon C Cotham St Sav w St Mary and Clifton St Paul *Bris* 99-05; Lic to Offic *Ox* from 05. *St Peter's College, Oxford OX1 2DL* Tel (01865) 278900
E-mail bernard.silverman@spc.ox.ac.uk

SILVERSIDES, Mark. b 51. Lon Univ BD73. St Jo Coll Nottm 74. **d** 76 **p** 77. C Hornchurch St Andr *Chelmsf* 76-80; P-in-c Becontree St Thos 80-85; TR Becontree W 85-86; CPAS Staff 86-92; New Media Producer from 92; Perm to Offic *Dur* 93-97. *15 Glenhurst Drive, Whickham, Newcastle upon Tyne NE16 5SH* Tel 0191-488 1937 E-mail msilversides@ambitnewmedia.com

SILVERTHORN, Alan. b 37. St Mich Coll Llan 62. **d** 65 **p** 66. C Machen and Rudry *Mon* 65-71; V New Tredegar 71-83; V Llanfrechfa and Llanddewi Fach w Llandegveth 83-04; rtd 04. *14 Davies Street, Ystrad Mynach, Hengoed CF82 8AD* Tel (01443) 816649

SILVESTER, Christine. b 51. WMMTC 02. **d** 05. NSM Walsall Wood *Lich* from 05. *31 Field Lane, Pelsall, Walsall WS4 1DN*

SILVESTER, David. b 59. Qu Mary Coll Lon BSc80 Nottm Univ BCombStuds85. Linc Th Coll 82. **d** 85 **p** 86. C Walthamstow St Mary w St Steph *Chelmsf* 85-90; TV Barking St Marg w St Patr 90-96; V Mildmay Grove St Jude and St Paul *Lon* from 96; AD Islington from 03. *The Vicarage, 71 Marquess Road, London N1 2PT* Tel fax (020) 7226 5924
E-mail dsilve5737@aol.com *or* stjudeandstpaul@aol.com

SILVESTER, Stephen David. b 59. Chu Coll Cam BA80 MA83 Man Univ PGCE82. St Jo Coll Nottm 88. **d** 91 **p** 92. C Nottingham St Jude *S'well* 91-96; V Gamston and Bridgford from 96; AD W Bingham from 04. *10 Scafell Close, West Bridgford, Nottingham NG2 6RJ* Tel 0115-982 5993
E-mail steve@st-lukes-gamston.org

SIM, David Hayward. b 29. Qu Coll Birm 57. **d** 59 **p** 60. C Foleshill St Laur *Cov* 59-62; C Kenilworth St Nic 62-64; V Devonport St Aubyn *Ex* 64-69; V Frampton *Linc* 69-74; V Gainsborough St Geo 74-82; V Sturminster Newton and Hinton St Mary *Sarum* 82-89; R Stock and Lydlinch 82-89; Dorchester 89-94; Chapl HM Pris Dorchester 89-94; rtd 95; Perm to Offic *Sarum* from 95. *12 Eldridge Close, Dorchester DT1 2JS* Tel (01305) 269262

SIMCOCK, Canon Michael Pennington. b 27. Qu Coll Cam BA50 MA52. Bps' Coll Cheshunt 50. **d** 52 **p** 53. C Andover w Foxcott *Win* 52-55; C Eastleigh 55-57; Min Tadley St Mary CD 57-67; V Altarnon and Bolventor *Truro* 67-70; V Treleigh 70-87; RD Carnmarth N 75-91; Hon Can Truro Cathl 82-92; R Redruth w Lanner 87-88; TR Redruth w Lanner and Treleigh 88-92; rtd 92; Perm to Offic *Truro* from 92. *1C Stratton Place, Falmouth TR11 2ST*

SIMCOX, Stephen Roy. b 59. Ridley Hall Cam 02. **d** 04 **p** 05. C The Ramseys and Upwood *Ely* from 04. *The Vicarage, Thatchers Close, Upwood, Ramsey, Huntingdon PE26 2PN* Tel (01487) 815492 E-mail stevesimcox@bigfoot.com

SIMESTER, Paul Stephen. b 57. Oak Hill Th Coll 97. **d** 99 **p** 00. C Branksome Park All SS *Sarum* 99-03; TV Wareham from 03. *St Martin's Vicarage, 9 Keysworth Drive, Wareham BH20 7BD* Tel (01929) 552756
E-mail associate.rector@warehamchurches.org.uk

SIMISTER, Charles Arnold. b 19. MM44. Edin Th Coll 49. **d** 52 **p** 53. C Glas Ch Ch *Glas* 52-57; C Worsley *Man* 57-60; V Downton *Sarum* 60-63; CF 63-84; R Kirkcudbright *Glas* 63-84; R Gatehouse of Fleet 63-84; rtd 84; Perm to Offic *Glas* from 84. *98 High Street, Kirkcudbright DG6 4TX* Tel (01557) 330747

SIMISTER, Norman Harold. b 39. Bris Univ BSc60. LNSM course 91. **d** 93 **p** 94. OLM Wainford *St E* from 93. *Romaine, 1 School Road, Ringsfield, Beccles NR34 8NZ* Tel (01502) 715549

SIMM, Michael Keith. b 63. Trin Coll Bris BA. **d** 00 **p** 01. C Ipswich St Matt *St E* 00-03; C Gorleston St Andr *Nor* from 03. *283 Lowestoft Road, Gorleston, Great Yarmouth NR31 6JW* Tel (01493) 667914 E-mail mike_simm@talk21.com

SIMMONDS, David Brian. b 38. Selw Coll Cam BA62 MA66 Heidelberg Univ 62. Ridley Hall Cam 63. **d** 65 **p** 66. C Newcastle w Butterton *Lich* 65-69; V Branston 69-97; V Branston w Tatenhill 97; RD Tutbury 95-97; rtd 97; Perm to Offic *Pet* 97-00; P-in-c Easton on the Hill, Collyweston w Duddington etc 00-02; Hon C Ketton, Collyweston, Easton-on-the-Hill etc 03-04. *8 Plover Road, Essendine, Stamford PE9 4UR*
E-mail davidbsimmonds@btinternet.com

SIMMONDS, Edward Alan. b 32. St Edm Hall Ox MA60. Ripon Coll Cuddesdon 88. **d** 89 **p** 90. NSM Ox St Mich w St Martin and All SS *Ox* 89-92; NSM Ox St Mary V w St Cross and St Pet 92-94; Chapl Lugano *Eur* 94-98; rtd 98; Perm to Offic *Ex* from 98. *Rokesdown, Higher Duryard, Pennsylvania Road, Exeter EX4 5BQ* Tel (01392) 270311
E-mail asimmonds@eclipse.co.uk

SIMMONDS, John. b 24. Sheff Univ BA50. Ridley Hall Cam 50. **d** 52 **p** 53. C Portsdown *Portsm* 52-55; C-in-c Fareham St Jo Ev CD 55-65; V W Streatham St Jas *S'wark* 65-73; V Congresbury *B & W* 73-75; P-in-c Puxton w Hewish St Ann and Wick St Lawrence 73-75; V Congresbury w Puxton and Hewish St Ann 75-84; Warden Home of Divine Healing Crowhurst 84-89; rtd 89. *Beach Villa, 14 The Beach, Clevedon BS21 7QU* Tel (01275) 342295

SIMMONDS, Paul Andrew Howard. b 50. Nottm Univ BSc73 Lon Univ DipTh78. Trin Coll Bris 75. **d** 78 **p** 79. C Leic H Trin w St Jo *Leic* 78-82; SW Regional Co-ord CPAS 83-86; Hd Adult Tr and Resources CPAS 86-95; C Wolston and Church Lawford *Cov* 89-03; Dioc Miss Adv 95-03; Research Dir Forward Vision from 03. *31 John Simpson Close, Wolston, Coventry CV8 3HX* Tel (024) 7654 3188 Fax 7654 0042
E-mail simmonds@bigfoot.com

SIMMONDS, Canon Paul Richard. b 38. AKC63. **d** 64 **p** 65. C Newington St Mary *S'wark* 64-67; C Cheam 68-73; P-in-c Stockwell Green St Andr 73-87; V 87-03; Hon Can S'wark Cathl 97-03; rtd 03. *Timbers, 37 Ocean Drive, Ferring, Worthing BN12 5QP* Tel (01903) 242679
E-mail mail@timbers37.freeserve.co.uk

SIMMONDS, Robert John. b 58. Aston Tr Scheme 92 Ripon Coll Cuddesdon DipMin96. **d** 96 **p** 97. C Southampton Thornhill St Chris *Win* 96-00; TV Basingstoke 00-05; Chapl Co-ord HM Pris Peterborough from 05. *HM Prison, Saville Road, Peterborough PE3 7PD* Tel (01733) 217593 Fax 217501
E-mail bobsimmondsvic@aol.com

SIMMONDS, Robert William. b 52. Nottm Univ BTh77 Birm Poly DCG79. Linc Th Coll 72. **d** 80 **p** 81. C Roehampton H Trin *S'wark* 80-83; TV Hemel Hempstead *St Alb* 83-90; V S Woodham Ferrers *Chelmsf* 90-94; rtd 94; Perm to Offic *Cant* from 03. *21 Copperfield Court, Rectory Road, Broadstairs CT10 1HE* Tel (01843) 863564
E-mail bobsimmonds@surefish.co.uk

SIMMONDS, William Hugh Cyril. b 08. Lon Univ DipOAS47. St Jo Hall Highbury. **d** 37 **p** 38. China 30-51; P-in-c Sinfin *Derby* 52-54; V Wolverhampton St Jude *Lich* 54-67; V S Malling *Chich* 67-78; rtd 78; Perm to Offic *Roch* 96-99. *6 Cornford House, Cornford Lane, Pembury, Tunbridge Wells TN2 4QS* Tel (01892) 824196

SIMMONS, Barry Jeremy. b 32. Leeds Univ BA54 MA62. Ridley Hall Cam 61. **d** 63 **p** 64. C Buttershaw St Aid *Bradf* 63-65; Jamaica 65-68; V Earby *Bradf* 68-73; Hong Kong 73-74; Bahrain 75-79; Chapl Luxembourg *Eur* 80-91; V Shoreham *Roch* 91-00; rtd 00; Perm to Offic *Glouc* and *Worc* from 01. *Touchdown, 57 Griffin Close, Stow on the Wold, Cheltenham GL54 1AY* Tel (01451) 831637

SIMMONS, Bernard Peter. b 26. CA Tr Coll 48 S'wark Ord Course 86. **d** 88 **p** 88. C Chatham St Wm *Roch* 88-91; rtd 91; P-in-c Underriver *Roch* 91-95; P-in-c Seal St Lawr 91-95; Perm to Offic *Pet* from 95. *5 Sycamore Drive, Desborough, Kettering NN14 2YH* Tel (01536) 763302

SIMMONS, Canon Brian Dudley. b 35. Master Mariner. St Steph Ho Ox 62. **d** 64 **p** 65. C Bournemouth St Pet *Win* 64-67; Miss to Seamen 67-71; Hon C Milton next Gravesend w Denton *Roch* 67-70; Hon C Gravesend St Geo 70-71; V Lamorbey H Trin 71-90; R Hever w Mark Beech 90-93; P-in-c Four Elms 90-93; R Hever, Four Elms and Mark Beech 93-94; V Langton Green 94-01; Hon Can Roch Cathl 91-01; rtd 01. *17 Chancellor House, Mount Ephraim, Tunbridge Wells TN4 8BT* Tel (01892) 617262

SIMMONS, Christopher John. b 49. Mert Coll Ox MA77. NEOC 88. **d** 90 **p** 91. C Kirkleatham *York* 90-93; P-in-c Barlby 93-95; V Barlby w Riccall 95-02; RD Derwent 98-01; R Pocklington and Owsthorpe and Kilnwick Percy etc from 02. *The Rectory, 29 The Balk, Pocklington, York YO42 2QQ* Tel (01759) 302133

SIMMONS, Eric. b 30. Leeds Univ BA51. Coll of Resurr Mirfield 51. **d** 53 **p** 54. C Chesterton St Luke *Ely* 53-57; Chapl Keele Univ *Lich* 57-61; CR from 63; Warden Hostel of the Resurr Leeds 66-67; Superior CR 74-87; R Foundn of St Kath in Ratcliffe 89-92; Prior St Mich Priory 93-97; rtd 98. *House of the Resurrection, Stocks Bank Road, Mirfield WF14 0BN* Tel (01924) 494318 Fax 490489

SIMMONS, Gary David. b 59. Trin Coll Bris BA86. **d** 87 **p** 88. C Ecclesfield *Sheff* 87-90; Min Stapenhill Immanuel CD *Derby* 90-96; V Stapenhill Immanuel 97-98; R Slaugham *Chich* from 98. *The Rectory, Brighton Road, Handcross, Haywards Heath RH17 6BU* Tel (01444) 400221

SIMMONS, Godfrey John. b 39. Open Univ BA81. St And NSM Tr Scheme 71 Edin Th Coll 77. **d** 74 **p** 74. Dioc Supernumerary *St And* 74-75 and 80-81; C Strathtay and Dunkeld 75-77; C

Bridge of Allan and Alloa 77-80; Asst Chapl Stirling Univ 77-80; Chapl 80; Min Crieff, Muthill and Comrie 80-81; R 81-85; Chapl HM Pris Perth 80-85; R Kirkwall and Stromness *Ab* 85-91; R Strichen 91-94; R Longside, Old Deer and Peterhead 91-92; Chapl HM Pris Peterhead 91-94; Miss to Seafarers 85-02; Hon Chapl (Scotland) 85-90; Hon Area Chapl (Scotland) 90-94; Chapl Supt Mersey Miss to Seafarers 94-02; TV Ch the K *Dur* from 02. *St George's Vicarage, South Moor, Stanley DH9 7EN* Tel and fax (01207) 230128 Mobile 07985-4458890 E-mail johnandjosimmons@onetel.com

SIMMONS, Miss Joan Yvonne. b 14. Gilmore Ho 57. **dss** 61 **d** 87. Harringay St Paul *Lon* 61-63; Belsize Park 63-69; Adult Educn Officer 69-78; rtd 78; Perm to Offic *Chich* from 87. *12 Whittington College, London Road, East Grinstead RH19 2QU* Tel (01342) 312781

SIMMONS, John. b 53. Carl Dioc Tr Course 82. **d** 85 **p** 86. C Wotton St Mary *Glouc* 85-88; P-in-c Amberley 88-92; R Burton Latimer *Pet* 92-98; RD Kettering 94-98; R Paston 98-01; V Irchester from 01. *The Vicarage, 19 Station Road, Irchester, Wellingborough NN29 7EH* Tel (01933) 312674 E-mail john@simmons6.freeserve.co.uk

SIMMONS, John Graham. b 54. Westf Coll Lon BSc75 Man Univ PGCE76 CertRE81. N Ord Course 89. **d** 92 **p** 93. C Thame w Towersey *Ox* 92-97; R Heydon, Gt and Lt Chishill, Chrishall etc *Chelmsf* from 97. *1 Hall Lane, Great Chishill, Royston SG8 8SG* Tel (01763) 838703 E-mail revsimm@aol.com

SIMMONS, John Harold. b 46. FCCA. Sarum & Wells Th Coll 86. **d** 89 **p** 90. NSM The Iwernes, Sutton Waldron and Fontmell Magna *Sarum* 89-01; NSM Iwerne Valley from 01. *Fourways, Shroton, Blandford Forum DT11 8QL* Tel (01258) 860515 E-mail fourways@compuserve.com

SIMMONS, Ms Marion. b 45. N Ord Course 95. **d** 98 **p** 99. NSM Stoneycroft All SS *Liv* 98-99; C 00-01; TV Fazakerley Em from 01. *St Paul's Vicarage, Formosa Drive, Liverpool L10 7LB* Tel 0151-521 3344 E-mail marionstpauls@aol.com

SIMMONS, Canon Maurice Samuel. b 27. St Chad's Coll Dur BA50 DipTh52 Newc Univ MA99 MPhil02. **d** 52 **p** 53. C S Shields St Hilda *Dur* 52-58; Youth Chapl 56-60; R Croxdale 58-81; Soc and Ind Adv to Bp Dur 61-70; Gen Sec Soc Resp Gp 70-75; Hon Can Dur Cathl from 71; Sec Dioc Bd for Miss and Unity 75-82; V Norton St Mary 81-92; RD Stockton 85-92; rtd 92. *11 Roecliffe Grove, Stockton-on-Tees TS19 8JU* Tel (01642) 618880 E-mail m.simmons1@ntlworld.com

SIMMONS, Peter. *See* SIMMONS, Bernard Peter

SIMMONS, Richard Andrew Cartwright. b 46. Trin Coll Bris 73. **d** 75 **p** 76. C Worting *Win* 75-80; R Six Pilgrims *B & W* 80-92; R Bincombe w Broadwey, Upwey and Buckland Ripers *Sarum* from 92. *The Rectory, 526 Littlemoor Road, Weymouth DT3 5PA* Tel (01305) 812542 E-mail rac_simmons@lineone.net

SIMMS, William Michael. b 41. DMA66 ACIS70 MCIPD75 Open Univ BA87. NEOC 84. **d** 87 **p** 88. NSM Croft *Ripon* 87; C 88; NSM Middleton Tyas and Melsonby 87; C 88; C Headingley 88-90; C Richmond w Hudswell 90-93; C-in-c Downholme and Marske 90-93; V Hawes and Hardraw from 93. *The Vicarage, Burtersett Road, Hawes DL8 3NP* Tel (01969) 667553

SIMON, Brother. *See* BROOK, Peter Geoffrey

SIMON, David Sidney. b 49. Univ of Wales (Abth) BSc(Econ)70 CDipAF76 Hull Univ MA83. NEOC 84. **d** 87 **p** 88. NSM Beverley St Mary *York* 87-94; NSM Beverley Deanery 94-98; Lect Humberside Coll of HE 87-90; Humberside Poly 90-92; Humberside Univ *York* 92-96; Lincs and Humberside Univ 96-98; Admin Rydal Hall *Carl* 98-01; Perm to Offic 01-02; NSM Cartmel Peninsula from 02. *3 Kents Bank House, Kentsford Road, Grange-over-Sands LA11 7BB* Tel (01539) 536762 E-mail dssimon@fish.co.uk

SIMON, Frederick Fairbanks. b 42. Ripon Coll Cuddesdon 74. **d** 77 **p** 78. C Cheddleton *Lich* 77-79; C Woodley St Jo the Ev *Ox* 79-82; V Spencer's Wood 82-85; P-in-c Steventon w Milton 85-87; Chapl Grenville Coll Bideford 87-95; rtd 96; Perm to Offic *Ex* 96-04. *Fairview Cottage, Link Road, Pillowell, Lydney GL15 4QY* Tel (01594) 560308

SIMON, Haydn Henry England. *See* ENGLAND-SIMON, Haydn Henry

SIMON, Oliver. b 45. Dur Univ BA67 Sussex Univ MA68 Sheff Univ MMinTheol94. Cuddesdon Coll 69. **d** 71 **p** 72. C Kidlington *Ox* 71-74; C Bracknell 74-78; V Frodsham *Ches* 78-88; R Easthampstead *Ox* 88-00; Chapl Ripon Coll Cuddesdon 00-05; Chapl Community of St Mary V Wantage 00-05; Chapl Pemb Coll Ox 03-04; TV Rugby St Andr *Cov* from 05. *The Vicarage, St John's Avenue, Rugby CV22 5HR* Tel (01788) 577331 E-mail oliversimon@dunelm.org.uk

SIMONS, Miss Christine. b 40. RGN62 RM64 RHV69. St Jo Coll Nottm 82. **dss** 84 **d** 87 **p** 94. Claygate *Guildf* 84-87; C Camberley St Paul 87-93; NSM 93-99; C Woking Ch Ch from 99. *4 Orchard Drive, Woking GU21 4BN* Tel (01483) 771551 Fax 888459 E-mail chris@christchurchwoking.org

SIMONS, Preb John Trevor. b 34. Lon Univ BD67. ALCD66. **d** 67 **p** 68. C Becontree St Mary *Chelmsf* 67-71; V Cranham Park 71-78; P-in-c Nailsea H Trin *B & W* 78-83; R 83-97; Sen Asst P 97-99; Preb Wells Cathl 90-99; rtd 99; Nat Dir Crosswinds Prayer Trust from 97; Perm to Offic *B & W* from 99. *11 Spring Hill, Worle, Weston-super-Mare BS22 9AP* Tel (01934) 624302 Fax as telephone E-mail crosswinds@btinternet.com

SIMONS, Mark Anselm. b 38. ARCM60. Oak Hill Th Coll 62. **d** 65 **p** 66. C Nottingham St Ann *S'well* 65-68; C N Ferriby *York* 68-75; P-in-c Sherburn 75-78; V Gt and Lt Driffield 78-93; Perm to Offic from 95; rtd 03. *7 Royal Crescent, Scarborough YO11 2RN* Tel (01723) 378056 E-mail m&f@bibleschool.go-plus.net

SIMONS, William Angus. b 18. Keble Coll Ox BA39 MA47. Cuddesdon Coll 40. **d** 41 **p** 42. C Poplar All SS w St Frideswide *Lon* 41-44 and 47-48; RAChD 44-47; C Is of Dogs Ch Ch and St Jo w St Luke *Lon* 48-54; V Fulham St Jas Moore Park 54-62; Ind Chapl *Worc* 62-63; Ind Missr R Foundn of St Kath in Ratcliffe 63-65; Chapl Hammersmith Hosp Lon 65-68; Chapl St Edm Hosp Northn 68-88; Chapl Northn Gen Hosp 68-72; P-in-c Northampton St Lawr *Pet* 72-76; C Northampton H Sepulchre w St Andr and St Lawr 76-81; rtd 81; Northants Past Coun Service from 76; Founder Dir 76-84; Supervisor from 84; Perm to Offic *Pet* from 81. *54 Park Avenue North, Northampton NN3 2JE* Tel (01604) 713767

SIMONSON, Canon Juergen Werner Dietrich. b 24. Lon Univ BD52. ALCD52. **d** 52 **p** 53. C W Kilburn St Luke w St Simon and St Jude *Lon* 52-56; Nigeria 57-63; Chapl CMS Tr Coll Chislehurst 64-65; Vice-Prin 65-67; Prin CMS Tr Coll Chislehurst 67-69; V Putney St Marg *S'wark* 69-81; RD Wandsworth 74-81; Hon Can S'wark Cathl 75-90; R Barnes St Mary 81-90; rtd 90; Perm to Offic *Win* from 90. *Elm Cottage, Horseshoe Lane, Ibthorpe, Andover SP11 0BY* Tel (01264) 736381

SIMPER, Rachel Dawn. *See* WATTS, Mrs Rachel Dawn

SIMPKINS, Frank Charles. b 19. MCIT52 MILT99. Oak Hill Th Coll 72. **d** 75 **p** 76. C Harrow Weald St Mich *Lon* 75-78; Hon C 81-84; P-in-c Dollis Hill St Paul 78-80; Chapl Northwick Park Hosp Harrow 81-83; Hon C Harrow Trin St Mich *Lon* 84-94; Perm to Offic from 94. *7 Milne Feild, Pinner HA5 4DP* Tel (020) 8428 2477

SIMPKINS, Canon Lionel Frank. b 46. UEA BSc68. Lambeth STh77 St Jo Coll Nottm ALCD72. **d** 73 **p** 74. C Leic H Apostles *Leic* 73-77; C Bushbury *Lich* 77-80; V Sudbury w Ballingdon and Brundon *St E* 80-96; Chapl Sudbury Hosps 80-96; RD Sudbury 88-96; Hon Can St E Cathl from 94; V Ipswich St Aug from 96; Warden of Readers from 03. *St Augustine's Vicarage, 2 Bucklesham Road, Ipswich IP3 8TJ* Tel (01473) 728654 E-mail office@st-augustines.freeserve.co.uk

SIMPKINS, Susan Carol. **d** 05. NSM Ruislip St Martin *Lon* from 05. *70 Park Avenue, Ruislip HA4 7UJ* Tel (01895) 630170 E-mail sue.simpkins@btopenworld.com

SIMPSON, Alan Eric. b 52. Ch Ch Ox BA73 MA77 Birm Univ PhD77 Dur Univ MA01 CPhys77 MInstP77. Cranmer Hall Dur 96. **d** 98 **p** 99. C Long Benton *Newc* 98-02; P-in-c Cresswell and Lynemouth from 02. *The Vicarage, 33 Till Grove, Ellington, Morpeth NE61 5ER* Tel (01670) 860242 E-mail fr.alan@talk21.com

SIMPSON, Alexander. b 31. Oak Hill Th Coll 74. **d** 76 **p** 77. Hon C Lower Homerton St Paul *Lon* 76-81; Hon C Homerton St Barn w St Paul 81-85; TV Hackney Marsh 85-87; V Kensington St Helen w H Trin 87-97; rtd 97; Perm to Offic *Derby* from 01. *18 Holymoor Road, Holymoorside, Chesterfield S42 7DX* Tel (01246) 567490

SIMPSON, Alison Jane. b 60. St Andr Univ BSc83 BD86 Princeton Univ MTh87. **d** 99 **p** 99. C Ellon *Ab* 99-02; R Huntly *Mor* from 02; R Keith from 02; R Aberchirder from 02. *Holy Trinity Rectory, Seafield Avenue, Keith AB55 5BS* Tel (01542) 882782 Mobile 07811-230648

SIMPSON, Andrew. b 48. Liv Univ BEng69. Sarum Th Coll 83. **d** 86 **p** 87. NSM Canford Magna *Sarum* from 86. *17 Sopwith Crescent, Wimborne BH21 1SH* Tel (01202) 883996 E-mail andrew.simpson6@virgin.net

SIMPSON, Charles Michael. b 38. St Cath Coll Cam MA64 Campion Hall Ox MA65 Heythrop Coll Lon STL69 K Coll Lon PhD71. **d** 68 **p** 69. Lect Th Lon Univ 72-84; Chapl Prince of Peace Community Greenwich 85-87; Retreat Dir St Beuno's Clwyd 87-91; P-in-c Selkirk *Edin* 91-94; P-in-c Offchurch *Cov* 94-96; Warden Offa Retreat Ho and Dioc Spirituality Adv 94-00; P-in-c Stoke Canon, Poltimore w Huxham and Rewe etc *Ex* 00-04; Dioc Adv in Adult Tr 00-04; rtd 04. *15 Shepherds Way, Stow on the Wold, Cheltenham GL54 1EA* Tel (01451) 831028

SIMPSON, David Charles Edward. b 51. NEOC 02. **d** 05. NSM York St Chad *York* from 05. *98 Brunswick Street, York YO23 1ED* Tel (01904) 635085

SIMPSON, David John. b 61. Univ Coll Dur BA85. Sarum & Wells Th Coll 89. **d** 91 **p** 92. C Selby Abbey *York* 91-94; C Romsey *Win* 94-97; Chapl Southn Univ 97-05; Chapl RN from 05. *Royal Naval Chaplaincy Service, Room 203, Victory Building, HM Naval Base, Portsmouth PO1 3LS* Tel (023) 9272 7900 Fax 727112

SIMPSON, Derek John. b 59. Oak Hill Th Coll BA89. **d** 89 **p** 90. C Alperton *Lon* 89-95; TR Brentford from 95; AD Hounslow from 02. *The Rectory, 3 The Butts, Brentford TW8 8BJ* Tel (020) 8568 6502 *or* 8568 7442 E-mail derek.simpson@btinternet.com

SIMPSON, Derrick. b 27. NW Ord Course 72. **d** 75 **p** 76. C Disley *Ches* 75-79; C Stockport St Geo 79-81; R Wistaston 81-90; Chapl Barony Hosp Nantwich 81-89; V Newton in Mottram *Ches* 90-93; rtd 93; Perm to Offic *Ches* from 93. *60 Dane Bank Avenue, Crewe CW2 8AD*

SIMPSON, Mrs Elizabeth Ann. b 59. Lon Bible Coll BA80 Trin Coll Bris 84. **dss** 86 **d** 97 **p** 98. Thornbury *Glouc* 86-87; Beckenham Ch Ch *Roch* 87-90; Heydon, Gt and Lt Chishill, Chrishall etc *Chelmsf* 90-93; Shirwell, Loxhore, Kentisbury, Arlington, etc *Ex* 93-97; NSM S Molton w Nymet St George, High Bray etc 97-99; C 99-03; P-in-c W Buckingham *Ox* from 03. *The Vicarage, Orchard Place, Westbury, Brackley NN13 5JT* Tel (01280) 704964 E-mail liz@surefish.co.uk

SIMPSON, Geoffrey Sedgwick. b 32. Hamilton Coll (NY) BA54 Wisconsin Univ MA Pemb Coll Cam PhD70. Gen Th Sem (NY) STB57. **d** 57 **p** 57. USA 57-77; Chapl Birm Univ *Birm* 77-80; V Shoreham *Roch* 80-90; TR Street *York* 90-02; rtd 02; Perm to Offic *Sarum* from 03. *The Laurels, Queen Street, Yetminster, Sherborne DT9 6LL* Tel (01935) 872915

SIMPSON, Mrs Georgina. b 46. Westmr Coll Ox BTh93 Birm Univ MA95 DipEd98. St Alb and Ox Min Course 95. **d** 97 **p** 98. NSM Littlemore *Ox* 97-98; C Ox St Giles and SS Phil and Jas w St Marg from 98. *85 Church Road, Sandford-on-Thames, Oxford OX4 4YA* Tel (01865) 512319
E-mail gs@stgileschurch.fsnet.co.uk

SIMPSON, Godfrey Lionel. b 42. Sarum Th Coll 63. **d** 66 **p** 67. C Leintwardine *Heref* 66-70; C Leominster 70-73; P-in-c Whitbourne 73-79; V Barlaston *Lich* 79-02; RD Trentham 85-00; P-in-c The Guitings, Cutsdean and Farmcote *Glouc* 02-03; P-in-c Upper and Lower Slaughter w Eyford and Naunton 02-03; R The Guitings, Cutsdean, Farmcote etc from 03. *The Rectory, Copse Hill Road, Lower Slaughter, Cheltenham GL54 2HY* Tel (01451) 810812

SIMPSON, Herbert. b 20. Carl Dioc Tr Course. **d** 82 **p** 83. NSM Barrow St Aid *Carl* 82; NSM Barrow St Jo 82-90; rtd 90; Perm to Offic *Carl* from 90. *3 Glenridding Drive, Barrow-in-Furness LA14 4PE* Tel (01229) 823707

SIMPSON, Mrs Janet Mary. b 42. New Coll Edin LTh94. EAMTC 99. **d** 00 **p** 01. C Aldringham w Thorpe, Knodishall w Buxlow etc *St E* 00-03; R Elmsett w Aldham, Hintlesham, Chattisham etc from 03. *The Rectory, Hadleigh Road, Elmsett, Ipswich IP7 6ND* Tel (01473) 658803
E-mail simpsonjanet@lineone.net

SIMPSON, The Very Revd John Arthur. b 33. OBE01. Keble Coll Ox BA56 MA60. Clifton Th Coll 56. **d** 58 **p** 59. C Low Leyton *Chelmsf* 58-59; C Orpington Ch Ch *Roch* 59-62; Tutor Oak Hill Th Coll 62-72; V Ridge *St Alb* 72-79; P-in-c 79-81; Dir of Ords and Post-Ord Tr 75-81; Hon Can St Alb 77-79; Can Res St Alb 79-81; Adn Cant and Can Res Cant Cathl *Cant* 81-86; Dean Cant 86-00; rtd 00; Perm to Offic *Cant* from 01. *Flat D, 9 Earls Avenue, Folkestone CT20 2HW*

SIMPSON, Canon John Bernard. b 40. ACP66 St Paul's Cheltenham CertEd62 Ox Univ MTh95. **d** 93 **p** 93. In URC 63-93; Asst to RD Lothingland *Nor* 93-94; RD from 99; C Hopton w Corton 93-94; P-in-c 94-99; TR Lowestoft St Marg from 99; Hon Can Nor Cathl from 01. *St Margaret's Rectory, 147 Hollingsworth Road, Lowestoft NR32 4BW* Tel (01502) 573046 Fax 538253 E-mail john.simpson5@tesco.net

SIMPSON, Canon John Lawrence. b 33. DL04. SS Coll Cam BA55 MA59 ARCM60 UWE Hon MMus. Wells Th Coll 63. **d** 65 **p** 66. Chapl Win Cathl *Win* 65-66; C Win St Bart 65-69; Chapl Repton Sch Derby 69-71; Hd of RE Helston Sch 71-78; P-in-c Curry Rivel *B & W* 79-80; R Curry Rivel w Fivehead and Swell 80-86; V Tunbridge Wells K Chas *Roch* 86-89; Can Res Bris Cathl *Bris* 89-99; rtd 99; Perm to Offic *B & W* from 00. *Yardes Cottage, Windmill Hill, Ilminster TA19 9NT* Tel (01823) 480593

SIMPSON, John Peter. b 39. ALCD66. **d** 66 **p** 67. C Woodside *Ripon* 66-69; C Burnage St Marg *Man* 69-72; V Rochdale Deeplish St Luke 72-80; R Lamplugh w Ennerdale *Carl* 80-04; rtd 04. *8 Queens Avenue, Seaton, Workington CA14 1DN* Tel (01900) 604215 E-mail revpetersim@supanet.com

SIMPSON, John Raymond. b 41. NSW Sch of Hypnotic Sciences Dip Clinical Hypnotherapy 87 Univ of S Aus GradDipEd92 MASCH87. Chich Th Coll 65. **d** 67 **p** 68. C Scarborough St Martin *York* 67-71; C Grangetown 71-72; Youth Chapl Bermuda 72-75; C Lewisham St Mary *S'wark* 76; Australia 76-99 and from 00; C Albany 76-78; R Carey Park 78-84; Chapl RAN 84-90; Chapl RAAF 90-99; Grace Cathl San Francisco USA 99-00; Chapl RANSR from 00. *PO Box 1419, Albany, W Australia 6332* Tel (0061) (8) 9841 6295, 9571 7009 *or* tel and fax 9571 7007 Fax 9481 6205
E-mail johnsimpson_94108@yahoo.com

SIMPSON, John Verrent. b 68. Univ of Wales (Cardiff) BScEcon93. Ripon Coll Cuddesdon BTh98. **d** 98 **p** 99. C Cardiff St Jo *Llan* 98-00; C Cen Cardiff 00-01; C Upper Chelsea H Trin w St Jude *Lon* 01-04; P-in-c Lt Missenden *Ox* from 05. *The Vicarage, Little Missenden, Amersham HP7 0RA* Tel (01494) 862008 Mobile 07779-136757 E-mail jvs@fish.co.uk

SIMPSON, Mrs June Hall. b 31. LRAM59 Sheff Univ BEd74. EMMTC 83. **dss** 86 **d** 87 **p** 94. NSM Carlton in Lindrick *S'well* 87-01; rtd 01. *Address temp unkown*
E-mail revjune@91windsor.freeserve.co.uk

SIMPSON, Kevin Gordon. b 54. QPM02. Univ of Wales BEd96 MCIPD94. St Mich Coll Llan. **d** 02 **p** 03. NSM Llantwit Fardre *Llan* from 02. *95 St Anne's Drive, Pontypridd CF38 2PB* Tel (01443) 207033 Mobile 07870-397494
E-mail k.g.simpson@btinternet.com

SIMPSON, Miss Margery Patricia. b 36. SRN57 SCM59. Oak Hill Th Coll BA86. **dss** 86 **d** 87 **p** 94. Rodbourne Cheney *Bris* 86-87; Par Dn 87-90; Par Dn Warmley 90-94; C Warmley, Syston and Bitton 94-95; TV Yate New Town 95-96; rtd 97; Perm to Offic *Sarum* from 97. *19 Wentworth Park, Stainburn, Workington CA14 1XP* Tel (01900) 61523

SIMPSON, Mark Lawrence. b 73. Oak Hill Th Coll BA03. **d** 03 **p** 04. C Leyland St Andr *Blackb* from 03. *3 Beech Avenue, Leyland PR25 3AL* Tel (01772) 622446

SIMPSON, Michael. *See* SIMPSON, William Michael

SIMPSON, Michael. *See* SIMPSON, Charles Michael

SIMPSON, Peter. *See* SIMPSON, John Peter

SIMPSON, Canon Peter Wynn. b 32. Birm Univ BA53. Ripon Hall Ox 55. **d** 57 **p** 58. C Leamington Priors H Trin *Cov* 57-60; C Croydon St Jo *Cant* 60-63; V Foleshill St Laur *Cov* 63-70; V Radford 70-79; RD Cov N 76-79; V Finham 79-91; RD Cov S 82-88; Hon Can Cov Cathl 83-91; rtd 91; Perm to Offic *Cov* from 91. *Faith Cottage, 118 Main Street, Wolston, Coventry CV8 3HP* Tel (024) 7654 3965

SIMPSON, Philip Alexander. b 54. Keele Univ BA79 CQSW79. CMS Tr Coll Selly Oak 85. **d** 89. CMS from 85; Pakistan 85-98; Regional Dir for Middle East and Pakistan from 98. *CMS, Partnership House, 157 Waterloo Road, London SE1 8UU* Tel (020) 7928 8681 Fax 7401 3215
E-mail phil.simpson@cms-uk.org

SIMPSON, Raymond James. b 40. Lon Coll of Div ALCD63 LTh74. **d** 63 **p** 64. C Longton St Jas *Lich* 64-68; C Upper Tooting H Trin *S'wark* 68-71; BFBS Distr Sec E Anglia 71-77; C-in-c Bowthorpe CD *Nor* 78-84; V Bowthorpe 84-96; Perm to Offic *Newc* from 96; Guardian Community of Aid and Hilda from 96. *Lindisfarne Retreat, Marygate, Holy Island, Berwick-upon-Tweed TD15 2SD* Tel and fax (01289) 389249
E-mail raysimpson@ndirect.co.uk

SIMPSON, Richard Lee. b 66. Keble Coll Ox BA88 MPhil91 Westmr Coll Ox PGCE89. Wycliffe Hall Ox 91. **d** 93 **p** 94. C Newc St Gabr *Newc* 93-97; P-in-c Jesmond H Trin from 97; P-in-c Newc St Barn and St Jude from 97. *Holy Trinity Vicarage, 63 Roseberry Crescent, Jesmond, Newcastle upon Tyne NE2 1EX* Tel 0191-281 1663 E-mail ricksimpson@lineone.net

SIMPSON, Robert Charles. b 46. Ridley Hall Cam. **d** 85 **p** 86. C Eastwood *S'well* 85-88; V Yardley St Cypr Hay Mill *Birm* 88-93; P-in-c Newent and Gorsley w Cliffords Mesne *Glouc* 93-95; R 95-05; Dioc Ecum Officer 04-05; P-in-c Glouc St Jas and All SS from 05. *The Vicarage, 1 The Conifers, Gloucester GL1 4LP* Tel (01452) 422349 E-mail robertcsimpson@onetel.com

SIMPSON, Robert David. b 61. Fitzw Coll Cam BA83 MA87 Bris Univ MLitt94. Trin Coll Bris DipHE87. **d** 87 **p** 88. C Beckenham Ch Ch *Roch* 87-90; C Heydon w Gt and Lt Chishill *Chelmsf* 90; C Chrishall 90; C Elmdon w Wendon Lofts and Strethall 90; C Heydon, Gt and Lt Chishill, Chrishall etc 91-93; TV Shirwell, Loxhore, Kentisbury, Arlington, etc *Ex* 93-97; TR S Molton w Nymet St George, High Bray etc 97-03. *The Vicarage, Orchard Place, Westbury, Brackley NN13 5JT* Tel (01280) 782893 E-mail revsimpson@supanet.com

SIMPSON, Robert John. NUU BA PGCE. **d** 03 **p** 04. Aux Min Ballymoney w Finvoy and Rasharkin *Conn* from 03. *28 Willowfield Park, Coleraine BT52 2NF* Tel (028) 7035 8552
E-mail srobertheather@aol.com

SIMPSON, Robert Theodore (Theo). b 34. Linc Coll Ox BA58 MA61 K Coll Lon PhD71 UNISA Dip Tertiary Educn 83 MEd85. Chich Th Coll 58. **d** 60 **p** 61. C Ellesmere Port *Ches* 60-63; CR 63-66; S Africa 68-88; Prin St Pet Coll 72-75; Pres Federal Th Sem 73-75; Sen Lect Th Swaziland Univ 83-87; Assoc Prof Th 87-88; Chapl and Lect Coll of SS Mark and Jo Plymouth 88-90; Tutor Simon of Cyrene Th Inst 90-92; Perm to Offic *S'wark* 91-92; P-in-c Shadwell St Paul w Ratcliffe St Jas *Lon* 92-01; rtd 01. *36 Whitton Dene, Hounslow TW3 2JT*
E-mail theo@cologon.org

SIMPSON, Roger Westgarth. b 51. Lon Univ BSc72. St Jo Coll Nottm 77. **d** 79 **p** 80. C St Marylebone All So w SS Pet and Jo *Lon* 79-85; R Edin St Paul and St Geo *Edin* 85-95; R Vancouver H Trin Canada 95-99; V York St Mich-le-Belfrey *York* from 99. *The Parish Centre, 11/12 Minster Yard, York YO1 7HH* Tel (01904) 624190 *or* 412470 Fax 622290
E-mail admin@st-michael-le-belfrey.org

SIMPSON, The Ven Samuel. b 26. TCD BA55 MA69 Div Test56. TCD Div Sch. **d** 56 **p** 57. C Coleraine *Conn* 56-60; I Donagh w Cloncha and Clonmany *D & R* 60-64; I Ballyscullion

64-81; Can Derry Cathl 78-96; I Errigal w Garvagh 81-96; Adn Derry 89-96; rtd 96. *53 Magheramenagh Drive, Atlantic Road, Portrush BT56 8SP* Tel (028) 7082 4292

SIMPSON (née RALPHS), Mrs Sharon Ann. b 55. St Mary's Coll Dur BA77. Cranmer Hall Dur 81. **dss** 83 **d** 87 **p** 94. Caverswall *Lich* 83-87; Par Dn 87-89; Asst Dioc Officer for Minl Tr *St As* 90-91; NSM Selkirk *Edin* 91-94; C Offchurch *Cov* 94-96; Warden Offa Retreat Ho and Dioc Spirituality Adv 94-00; C Stoke Canon, Poltimore w Huxham and Rewe etc *Ex* 00-04; Dioc Adv in Adult Tr 00-04; rtd 04. *15 Shepherds Way, Stow on the Wold, Cheltenham GL54 1EA* Tel (01451) 831028

SIMPSON, Mrs Susie Alexandra. b 58. Hertf Coll Ox BA81. St Steph Ho Ox BA98. **d** 99 **p** 00. C High Wycombe *Ox* 99-03; TV from 03. *The Vicarage, 175 Dashwood Avenue, High Wycombe HP12 3DB* Tel (01494) 474996 E-mail sas@fish.co.uk

SIMPSON, Thomas Eric. b 31. St Chad's Coll Dur BA55. Ely Th Coll 55. **d** 57 **p** 58. C Jarrow St Paul *Dur* 57-61; C Bishopwearmouth St Mary V w St Pet CD 61-63; V Chopwell 63-92; Chapl Norman Riding Hosp Tyne & Wear 79-83; Chapl Shotley Bridge Gen Hosp 83-90; rtd 92. *58 Tanmeads, Nettlesworth, Chester le Street DH2 3PY* Tel 0191-371 9814

SIMPSON, Ursula Lucy. b 51. St Anne's Coll Ox MA73 Leeds Univ MA05. N Ord Course 02. **d** 05. NSM York St Paul *York* from 05. *The Vicarage, Jubilee Terrace, York YO26 4YZ* Tel and fax (01904) 654214 E-mail u.simpson@btopenworld.com

SIMPSON, William Michael. b 45. Leeds Univ BA66 PGDipESL67. St Jo Coll Nottm 75. **d** 77 **p** 78. C Desborough *Pet* 77-80; P-in-c Arthingworth w Kelmarsh and Harrington 79-80; Hong Kong 80-85 and 92-00; P-in-c Stanley St Steph and Chapl St Steph Coll 80-85; Chapl St Jo Cathl 80-85; P-in-c Beetham and Milnthorpe *Carl* 85-92; V Kowloon Tong Ch Ch 92-00; V Ticehurst and Flimwell *Chich* from 00. *The Vicarage, Ticehurst, Wadhurst TN5 7AB* Tel (01580) 200316 E-mail mars8@tinyworld.co.uk

SIMS, Bernard David. b 40. Bris Coll Dip Tech Chemistry 63 Bath Univ BSc66. Ox Min Course 91. **d** 94 **p** 95. NSM Beedon and Peasemore w W Ilsley and Farnborough *Ox* 94-98; TV Blakenall Heath *Lich* from 98. *St Chad's Vicarage, Edison Road, Walsall WS2 7HT* Tel (01922) 612081 E-mail sims@beechdale.fsnet.co.uk

SIMS, Christopher Sidney. b 49. Wycliffe Hall Ox 74. **d** 77 **p** 78. C Walmley *Birm* 77-80; V Yardley St Cypr Hay Mill 80-88; V Stanwix *Carl* 88-96; RD Carl 89-95; Hon Can Carl Cathl 91-95; P-in-c Bassenthwaite, Isel and Setmurthy 96-00; P-in-c Bolton w Ireby and Uldale 96-00; P-in-c Allhallows 96-00; P-in-c Torpenhow 96-00; TR Binsey 00-03; V Shrewsbury H Cross *Lich* from 03. *1 Underdale Court, Underdale Road, Shrewsbury SY2 5DD* Tel (01743) 248859

SIMS, Graeme. *See* SIMS, Michael Graeme

SIMS, Canon James Henry. b 35. St Jo Coll Nottm 87. **d** 89 **p** 91. NSM Bangor Abbey *D & D* 89-93; C Holywood 93; Bp's C Kilbroney 93-01; Min Can Belf Cathl from 99; P-in-c Clonallon w Warrenpoint *D & D* from 01; Can Dromore Cathl from 03. *The Rectory, 8 Donaghaguy Road, Warrenpoint, Newry BT34 3RZ* Tel (028) 4175 3497

SIMS, Keith George. b 29. LNSM course 92. **d** 95 **p** 96. OLM Forest Hill St Aug *S'wark* 95-04. *68 Forest Hill Road, London SE22 0RS* Tel (020) 8693 7225

SIMS, Michael Graeme. b 37. SW Minl Tr Course 96. **d** 98 **p** 99. NSM Parkham, Alwington, Buckland Brewer etc *Ex* 98-00; NSM Blymhill w Weston-under-Lizard *Lich* from 00. *The Rectory, Blymhill, Shifnal TF11 8LH* Tel (01952) 850273

SIMS, Peter George Russell. b 36. Univ of Wales (Swansea) BA57. St Mich Coll Llan 63. **d** 65 **p** 66. C Brecon w Battle *S & B* 65-72; Min Can Brecon Cathl 65-72; V Llanfrynach and Cantref w Llanhamlach from 72. *The Rectory, Llanfrynach, Brecon LD3 7AJ* Tel (01874) 86667

SIMS, Sidney. b 20. Wycliffe Hall Ox. **d** 64 **p** 65. C Attenborough w Bramcote *S'well* 64-67; V Ramsey St Mary's w Ponds Bridge *Ely* 67-70; V Cambridge St Matt 70-85; Algeria 85-86; rtd 86, Perm to Offic *Nor* from 86. *Cockley Cottage, 66 Morston Road, Blakeney, Holt NR25 7BE* Tel (01263) 740184

SIMS, Vickie Lela. b 56. Iowa State Univ BA79. Ripon Coll Cuddesdon 00. **d** 02 **p** 03. C Grantham *Linc* from 02; P-in-c Coulsdon St Andr *S'wark* from 05. *St Andrew's Vicarage, Julien Road, Coulsdon CR5 2DN* Tel (020) 8660 0398 E-mail simstabbat@hotmail.com

SINCLAIR, Andrew John McTaggart. b 58. Ex Univ BA80. Westcott Ho Cam 81. **d** 84 **p** 85. C Aston cum Aughton and Ulley *Sheff* 84-87; C Rotherham 87-88; TV Edin Old St Paul *Edin* 88-93; Hon Angl Chapl Edin Univ and Moray Ho Coll 89-93; TV Dunstable *St Alb* 93-00; V Verwood *Sarum* from 00. *The Vicarage, 34 Dewlands Way, Verwood BH31 6JN* Tel (01202) 822298 *or* 813256 E-mail ansinclair@aol.com

SINCLAIR, Arthur Alfred. b 46. **d** 87 **p** 89. Hon C St Andr Cathl Inverness *Mor* 87-92; C 93-97; Chapl Asst Inverness Hosp 87-89; Dioc Chapl 87-89; NSM Culloden St Mary-in-the-Fields 89-92; P-in-c from 93; P-in-c Inverness St Jo from 93; Edin Th Coll 92-93; Chapl Raigmore Hosp NHS Trust Inverness from 93. *St John's Rectory, Southside Road, Inverness IV2 3BG* Tel (01463) 716288 E-mail sinclairstjohns@aol.com

SINCLAIR, Charles Horace. b 19. Keble Coll Ox BA40 MA44. Linc Th Coll 41. **d** 42 **p** 43. C Upper Norwood St Jo *Cant* 42-45; Chapl K Coll Auckland 46-50; Asst Chapl Haileybury Coll 51; Hd Master Prebendal Sch Chich 51-53; PV Chich Cathl *Chich* 51-53; Chapl and Sen Tutor Brookland Hall Welshpool 53-57; Hd Master St Aid Sch Denby Dale 57-64; Perm to Offic *Wakef* 58-64; rtd 84; Perm to Offic *Cant* from 84. *Oakstead, 94 Harbour Way, Folkestone CT20 1NB* Tel (01303) 250882 Mobile 07974-294886

SINCLAIR, Colin. b 30. **d** 84 **p** 85. NSM Ramoan w Ballycastle and Culfeightrin *Conn* 84-92. *4 Bushfoot Cottages, Portballintrae, Bushmills BT57 8RN* Tel (028) 2073 1551

SINCLAIR, Gordon Keith. b 52. MA. Cranmer Hall Dur. **d** 84 **p** 85. C Summerfield *Birm* 84-88; V Aston SS Pet and Paul 88-01; AD Aston 00-01; Hon Can Birm Cathl 00-01; V Cov H Trin *Cov* from 01. *4 Bishop's Walk, Coventry CV5 6RE* Tel (024) 7671 2114

SINCLAIR, Horace. *See* SINCLAIR, Charles Horace

SINCLAIR, Canon Jane Elizabeth Margaret. b 56. St Hugh's Coll Ox BA78 MA80 Nottm Univ BA82. St Jo Coll Nottm 80. **dss** 83 **d** 87 **p** 94. Herne Hill St Paul *S'wark* 83-86; Chapl and Lect St Jo Coll Nottm 86-93; Can Res Sheff Cathl *Sheff* 93-03; V Rotherham from 03; Hon Can Sheff Cathl from 03. *The Vicarage, 2 Heather Close, Rotherham S60 2TQ* Tel (01709) 364341

SINCLAIR, John Robert. b 58. Oak Hill Th Coll DipHE92. **d** 92 **p** 93. C Ponteland *Newc* 92-96; V Long Benton St Mary 96-01; V Newburn from 01. *The Vicarage, High Street, Newburn, Newcastle upon Tyne NE15 8LQ* Tel 0191-229 0522 Fax 267 0582 E-mail john.r.sinclair@lineone.net

✠**SINCLAIR, The Rt Revd Maurice Walter.** b 37. Nottm Univ BSc59 Leic Univ PGCE60. Tyndale Hall Bris 62 Nashotah Ho Hon DD01. **d** 64 **p** 65 **c** 90. C Boscombe St Jo *Win* 64-67; SAMS 67-02; Argentina 67-78; Personnel Sec 79-83; Asst Gen Sec 83-84; Prin Crowther Hall CMS Tr Coll Selly Oak 84-90; Bp N Argentina 90-02; Primate of S Cone 95-02; rtd 02; Hon Asst Bp Birm from 02. *55 Selly Wick Drive, Birmingham B29 7JQ* Tel 0121-471 2617 E-mail mandg@sinclair401.fsnet.co.uk

SINCLAIR, Michael David Bradley. b 42. N Ord Course Coll of Resurr Mirfield. **d** 97 **p** 98. NSM Settrington w N Grimston, Birdsall w Langton *York* 97-99; P-in-c W Buckrose from 99. *Witham Cottage, Langton, Malton YO17 9QP* Tel (01653) 658360

SINCLAIR, Nigel Craig. b 65. Teesside Poly BA87 Coll of Ripon & York St Jo MA00. St Jo Coll Dur BA93. **d** 94 **p** 95. C Marton-in-Cleveland *York* 94-97; TV Thirsk 97-02; V Pannal w Beckwithshaw *Ripon* from 02. *St Robert's Vicarage, 21 Crimple Meadows, Pannal, Harrogate HG3 1EL* Tel (01423) 870202 E-mail nsinclair@supanet.com

SINCLAIR, Peter. b 44. Oak Hill Th Coll. **d** 88 **p** 89. C Darlington H Trin *Dur* 88-91; C-in-c Bishop Auckland Woodhouse Close CD 91-98; P-in-c Consett from 98. *The Vicarage, 10 Aynsley Terrace, Consett DH8 5NF* Tel (01207) 502235

SINCLAIR, Peter Monteith. b 52. St Andr Univ BSc73. NEOC. **d** 01 **p** 02. NSM Darlington St Cuth *Dur* from 01. *Sundial Cottage, 7 Haughton Green, Darlington DL1 2DD* Tel (01325) 358424 Fax 361572 Mobile 07710-017625 E-mail peter@psld.co.uk

SINCLAIR, Robert Charles. b 28. Liv Univ LLB49 QUB LLM69 PhD82. Ely Th Coll 58. **d** 60 **p** 61. C Glenavy *Conn* 60-63; Chapl RN 63-67; C Cregagh *D & D* 67-68; Perm to Offic *Conn* from 69. *Juniper Cottage, 11A Glen Road, Glenavy, Crumlin BT29 4LT* Tel (028) 9445 3126

SINCLAIR, Robert Michael. b 41. CQSW81. Edin Th Coll 63. **d** 66 **p** 67. C Dunfermline *St And* 66-68; C Edin Old St Paul *Edin* 68-72; P-in-c Edin St Dav 72-77; Hon Dioc Supernumerary 77-96. *121/19 Comiston Drive, Edinburgh EH10 5QU* Tel 0131-447 5068

SINDALL, Canon Christine Ann. b 42. ALA69. EAMTC 84. **d** 87 **p** 94. NSM Sutton *Ely* 87-89; C Cambridge Ascension 89-94; TV 94-96; R Cheveley from 96; R Ashley w Silverley from 96; V Kirtling from 96; V Wood Ditton w Saxon Street from 96; RD Linton from 01; Hon Can Ely Cathl from 01. *The Rectory, 132 High Street, Cheveley, Newmarket CB8 9DG* Tel (01638) 730770 *or* tel and fax 731946 E-mail csindall@surfaid.org

SINGH, Balwant. b 32. BA60. Saharanpur Th Coll 50. **d** 53 **p** 58. India 53-67 and 71-73; Hon C Handsworth St Jas *Birm* 67-71; Hon C N Hinksey *Ox* 73-80; Lic to Offic 80-81; Hon C S Hinksey from 82. *9 Jersey Road, Oxford OX4 4RT* Tel (01865) 717277

SINGH, Thomas Balwant. b 62. Westmr Coll Ox BTh98. Wycliffe Hall Ox 98. **d** 00 **p** 01. C Houghton Regis *St Alb* 00-04; V Biscot from 04. *The Vicarage, 161 Bishopscote Road, Luton LU3 1PD* Tel (01582) 579410 E-mail thomassingh@hotmail.com

SINGH, Vivian Soorat. b 30. Trin Coll Cam BA MA53. Westcott Ho Cam 54. **d** 55 **p** 56. C Yardley Wood *Birm* 55-57; C Birm St Paul 57-59; Asst Master Framlingham Coll 59-72; Chapl 60-72; Chapl Wymondham Coll 72-75; Dep Hd Litcham High Sch 75-88; rtd 88; Perm to Offic *Nor* from 88. *Manor Cottage, Wendling Road, Longham, Dereham NR19 2RD* Tel (01362) 687382

SINGLETON, David Brinley (Brin). b 59. St Steph Ho Ox. **d** 00 **p** 01. C Soham *Ely* 00-01; C Soham and Wicken 02-04; P-in-c Capel St Mary w Lt and Gt Wenham *St E* from 04. *The Rectory, Days Road, Capel St Mary, Ipswich IP9 2LE* Tel (01473) 310759 E-mail brin.singleton@ukgateway.net

SINGLETON, Mrs Editha Mary. b 27. WMMTC 85. **dss** 84 **d** 87 **p** 94. Lich St Chad *Lich* 84-90; Hon Par Dn 87-90; Hon Par Dn Beaulieu and Exbury and E Boldre *Win* 90-94; Hon C 94-97; Perm to Offic from 97. *The Peregrine, The Lane, Fawley, Southampton SO45 1EY* Tel (023) 8089 4364

SINGLETON, Ernest George (Paul). b 15. St Aug Coll Cant 38. **d** 41 **p** 42. C Portsea N End St Mark *Portsm* 41-46; C Hendon St Mary *Lon* 46-48; CR 48-68; Lic to Offic *Wakef* 49-51; Lic to Offic *Lon* 52-56; S Africa 56-60; Prior St Teilo's Priory Cardiff 61-68; Perm to Offic *Lon* 68-91 and 93-95; rtd 80; Hon C Twickenham St Mary *Lon* 91-93. *Suite 268, Postnet X31, Saxonwold, Johannesburg, 2132 South Africa* Tel (0027) (11) 880 2982 Fax 442 4732

SINGLETON, Kenneth Miller. b 58. Oak Hill Th Coll 89. **d** 91 **p** 92. C Grove *Ox* 91-95; P-in-c Ashbury, Compton Beauchamp and Longcot w Fernham 95-99; C Kirkheaton *Wakef* 99-04. *34 Arlington Way, Huddersfield HD5 9TF* Tel (01484) 319592 E-mail kensingleton@hotmail.com

SINGLETON, Mary. *See* SINGLETON, Mrs Editha Mary

SINNAMON, Canon William Desmond. b 43. TCD BA65 MA80 MPhil95. CITC 66. **d** 66 **p** 67. C Seapatrick *D & D* 66-70; C Arm St Mark *Arm* 70-74; V Choral Arm Cathl 73-74; I Ballinderry 75-80; I Dublin St Patr Cathl Gp *D & G* 80-83; Preb Tipperkevin St Patr Cathl Dublin 80-83; I Taney *D & G* from 83; Can St Patr Cathl Dublin from 91; Treas 91-96; Chan from 96. *Taney Rectory, 6 Stoney Road, Dundrum, Dublin 14, Irish Republic* Tel (00353) (1) 298 4497 *or* tel and fax 298 5491 E-mail taney@dublin.anglican.org *or* parishoftaney@eircom.net

SINNICKSON, Charles. b 21. Princeton Univ BA44. Cuddesdon Coll 60. **d** 63 **p** 64. C Soho St Anne w St Thos and St Pet *Lon* 63-67; C Chelsea St Luke 67-72; Hon C S Kensington St Jude 72-81; NSM Upper Chelsea St Simon 81-86; NSM S Kensington St Aug 86-90; rtd 90; Perm to Offic *Lon* 90-02. *4 Cranley Mansion, 160 Gloucester Road, London SW7 4QF* Tel (020) 7373 2767

SINTON, Bernard. b 43. Leic Univ BSc66. Sarum & Wells Th Coll 87. **d** 90 **p** 91. NSM Horsham *Chich* from 90. *The Vicarage, Shipley Village, Shipley, Horsham RH13 8PH* Tel (01403) 741238

SINTON, Mrs Patricia Ann. b 41. RGN62 SCM64. STETS 95. **d** 98 **p** 99. NSM Horsham *Chich* 98-01; P-in-c Shipley from 01. *The Vicarage, Shipley Village, Shipley, Horsham RH13 8PH* Tel (01403) 741238

SINTON, Vera May. b 43. Somerville Coll Ox BA65 MA69 Bris Univ CertEd66. Trin Coll Bris DipHE81. **dss** 81 **d** 87 **p** 94. Broxbourne w Wormley *St Alb* 81-87; Hon Par Dn 87; Tutor All Nations Chr Coll Ware 81-87; Chapl St Hilda's Coll Ox 87-90; Tutor Wycliffe Hall Ox 87-98; NSM Ox St Clem *Ox* from 99; Tutor Ox Cen for Youth Min from 01; rtd 03. *22 Norham Gardens, Oxford OX2 6QD* Tel (01865) 514232 E-mail vera.sinton@wycliffe.ox.ac.uk

SIRMAN, Allan George. b 34. Lon Univ BA58. Oak Hill Th Coll 55. **d** 59 **p** 60. C Uphill *B & W* 59-61; C Morden *S'wark* 61-65; R Chadwell *Chelmsf* 65-75; V Wandsworth All SS *S'wark* 75-95; rtd 95; Perm to Offic *Ripon* from 95. *Marydale, Kingsley Drive, Middleham, Leyburn DL8 4PZ* Tel (01969) 624582 E-mail sirmans@freeuk.com

SIRR, The Very Revd John Maurice Glover. b 42. TCD BA63. CITC 65. **d** 65 **p** 66. C Belfast St Mary *Conn* 65-68; C Finaghy 68-69; I Drumcliffe w Lissadell and Munninane *K, E & A* 69-87; Preb Elphin Cathl 81-87; Dean Limerick and Ardfert *L & K* from 87; I Limerick City from 87; Chapl Limerick Pris from 87. *The Deanery, 7 Kilbane, Castletroy, Limerick, Irish Republic* Tel and fax (00353) (61) 338697 *or* tel 310293 Fax 315721 Mobile 87-254 1121 E-mail dean@limerick.anglican.org

SITCH, Keith Frank. b 40. Ex Univ BA63 Lon Univ MA95. S'wark Ord Course 72. **d** 75 **p** 76. NSM Romford St Edw *Chelmsf* 75-78; NSM Kidbrooke St Jas *S'wark* from 78. *92 Kidbrooke Park Road, London SE3 0DX* Tel (020) 8856 3843

✠SITSHEBO, The Rt Revd Wilson Timothy. b 52. UNISA BTh82 MTh93. St Bede's Coll Umtata DipTh77. **d** 79 **p** 80 **c** 01. Zimbabwe 80-96; Tutor United Coll of Ascension Selly Oak 96-01; Bp Matabeleland from 01. *PO Box 2422, Bulawayo, Zimbabwe* Tel (00263) (9) 61370 Fax 68353

SITWELL, Mrs Mary Elizabeth. b 49. Brighton Coll of Educn DipEd71 Sussex Univ BEd72. **d** 03. NSM Bishopstone *Chich* from 03; Chapl Roedean Sch Brighton from 03. *49 Fitzgerald Avenue, Seaford BN25 1AZ* Tel (01323) 892424 E-mail mes@roedean.co.uk

SIXSMITH, David. b 39. Lon Univ BD66. **d** 97 **p** 98. OLM Narborough w Narford *Nor* 97-99; OLM Pentney St Mary Magd w W Bilney 97-99; OLM Westacre 97-99; OLM Castle Acre w Newton and Southacre 97-99; C Hunstanton St Mary w Ringstead Parva etc 99-01; P-in-c Foulsham w Hindolveston and Guestwick from 01; P-in-c N Elmham w Billingford and Worthing from 02. *The Rectory, Guist Road, Foulsham, Dereham NR20 5RZ* Tel (01362) 683275

SIXTUS, Bernard. b 68. German Armed Forces Univ BA(Ed)93 Hamburg Univ PhD02 Leeds Univ MA03. Coll of Resurr Mirfield 01. **d** 03 **p** 04. C Paris St Geo *Eur* from 03. *7 rue Auguste Vacquerie, 75116 Paris, France* Tel (0033) (1) 47 20 64 95 E-mail frbernard@gmx.com

SIZER, Stephen Robert. b 53. Sussex Univ BA Ox Univ MTh94. Trin Coll Bris 80. **d** 83 **p** 84. C St Leonards St Leon *Chich* 83-86; C Guildf St Sav w Stoke-next-Guildford *Guildf* 86-89; R Stoke-next-Guildf 89-97; V Virginia Water from 97. *Christ Church Vicarage, Callow Hill, Virginia Water GU25 4LD* Tel and fax (01344) 842374 Mobile 07970-789549 E-mail stephen.sizer@btinernet.com *or* stephen@sizers.org

SKELDING, Mrs Hazel Betty. b 25. LGSM66 CertEd45. Gilmore Course 80. **dss** 83 **d** 87 **p** 94. Hinstock and Sambrook *Lich* 83-84; Asst Children's Adv RE 86-91; Hon Par Dn Alderbury Team *Sarum* 91-94; C 94-96; rtd 96; Perm to Offic *Sarum* from 96 and *Truro* from 01. *Spindrift, 3 Quilver Close, Gorran Haven, St Austell PL26 6JT* Tel (01726) 843764

SKELTON, Beresford. b 52. St Chad's Coll Dur BA74 SSC. Chich Th Coll 74. **d** 76 **p** 77. C Byker St Ant *Newc* 76-80; C Newc St Jo 80-82; Chapl Asst Newc Gen Hosp 80-81; Chapl Asst Freeman Hosp Newc 81-82; V Cresswell and Lynemouth *Newc* 82-88; P-in-c Millfield St Mary *Dur* 88-93; V from 93; P-in-c Bishopwearmouth Gd Shep from 04. *St Mary Magdalene's Vicarage, Wilson Street, Sunderland SR4 6HJ* Tel and fax 0191-565 6318

SKELTON, Dennis Michael. b 33. K Coll Lon BSc55. NEOC 76. **d** 79 **p** 80. NSM Pennywell St Thos and Grindon St Oswald CD *Dur* 79-84; V Heatherycleugh 84-99; V St John in Weardale 84-99; V Westgate 84-99; rtd 99; Perm to Offic *Dur* from 99. *52 Vicarage Close, New Silksworth, Sunderland SR3 1JF* Tel 0191-523 7135

SKELTON, Canon Henry John Nugent. b 13. Linc Th Coll 37. **d** 40 **p** 41. C Grantham St Wulfram *Linc* 40-43; Chapl RAFVR 43-47; V Heckington w Howell *Linc* 47-56; V Holbeach 56-73; RD Elloe E 68-73; Can and Preb Linc Cathl 70-73; rtd 78; Perm to Offic *St D* from 78. *Upton Castle, Cosheston, Pembroke Dock SA72 4SE* Tel (01646) 682435

SKELTON, Melvyn Nicholas. b 38. St Pet Coll Ox BA61 MA65 Selw Coll Cam BA63 MA68. Ridley Hall Cam 62. **d** 64 **p** 65. C St Marychurch *Ex* 64-66; C Bury St Edmunds St Mary *St E* 66-69; Hon C 69-78; Lic to Offic from 78; rtd 03. *Milburn House, The Street, Moulton, Newmarket CB8 8RZ* Tel (01638) 750563 *or* 712243

SKELTON, Canon Pamela Dora. b 38. Hull Coll of Educn DipEd60. Edin Th Coll 80. **dss** 78 **d** 86 **p** 94. Edin St Barn *Edin* 78-86; Dn-in-c 86-90; Dioc Youth Chapl 83-90; Min Edin Ch Ch 91-97; Chapl Lothian Primary Healthcare NHS Trust from 91; Hon Can St Mary's Cathl *Edin* from 00. *112 St Alban's Road, Edinburgh EH9 2PG* Tel 0131-667 1280 E-mail pdskelton@yahoo.com

SKEOCH, Canon David Windsor. b 37. Ch Ch Ox BA58 MA62. Westcott Ho Cam 73. **d** 74 **p** 75. NSM Pimlico St Mary Graham-street *Lon* 74-79; Bp's Dom Chapl *Truro* 79-81; Bp's Chapl *Lon* 81-83; V Pimlico St Gabr from 83; Can The Murray from 92. *St Gabriel's Vicarage, 30 Warwick Square, London SW1V 2AD* Tel and fax (020) 7834 7520 *or* 7834 2136

SKETCHLEY, Edward Sydney. b 20. Qu Coll Birm. **d** 49 **p** 50. C Bakewell *Derby* 49-53; PC Ridgeway 53-57; PC Abbey Dale 57-65; V Walsgrave on Sowe *Cov* 65-73; V Hound *Win* 73-90; rtd 90; Perm to Offic *Win* from 90 and *Portsm* from 02. *Cloisters, 1 Monks Way, Fareham PO14 3LU*

SKEVINGTON, Michael James. b 56. Natal Univ BA79. St Paul's Coll Grahamstown. **d** 82 **p** 83. S Africa 82-88 and from 90; C Slough *Ox* 88-90. *PO Box 38088, Point, 4069 South Africa* Tel (0027) (31) 337 7521 *or* 337 5573

SKIDMORE, Michael Anthony. **d** 98 **p** 99. NSM Rainworth *S'well* 98-00; NSM Blidworth 98-00; P-in-c Basford St Leodegarius 00-05; P-in-c Willoughby-on-the-Wolds w Wysall and Widmerpool from 05. *The Rectory, Keyworth Road, Wysall, Nottingham NG12 5QQ* E-mail mike.skidmore@breathemail.net

SKIDMORE, Mrs Sheila Ivy. b 36. **d** 87 **p** 94. Hon Par Dn Leic Resurr *Leic* 87-91; Par Dn Clarendon Park St Jo w Knighton St Mich 91-94; TV 94-01; rtd 01; Perm to Offic *Leic* from 01. *15 School Lane, Birstall, Leicester LE4 4EA* Tel 0116-267 3318 E-mail revd.sheila@theskidmores.f9.co.uk

SKILLEN, John Clifford Tainish. b 50. NUU BA72 MA82 QUB DipEd73 TCD BTh89. CITC 86. **d** 89 **p** 90. C Bangor Abbey *D & D* 89-92; I Kilwarlin Upper w Kilwarlin Lower 92-96; I Finaghy *Conn* from 96; Dioc Rep for Bps' Appeal from 97; Asst Ed *Church of Ireland Gazette* from 99. *St Polycarp's Rectory, 104 Upper Lisburn Road, Belfast BT10 0BB* Tel (028) 9062 9764 E-mail st-polycarp@utvinternet.com

SKILLINGS, Martyn Paul. b 46. St Chad's Coll Dur BA68. Linc Th Coll 68. **d** 70 **p** 71. C Stanley *Liv* 70-72; C Warrington St Elphin 72-75; Ind Chapl 75-76; V Surfleet *Linc* 88-92; V Burton St Chad *Lich* from 92. *The Vicarage, 113 Hunter Street, Burton-on-Trent DE14 2SS* Tel and fax (01283) 564044 Mobile 07887-854525 E-mail pedaller@care4free.net

SKILTON, The Ven Christopher John. b 55. Magd Coll Cam BA76 MA80. Wycliffe Hall Ox 77. **d** 80 **p** 81. C Ealing St Mary *Lon* 80-84; C New Borough and Leigh *Sarum* 84-88; TV Gt Baddow *Chelmsf* 88-95; TR Sanderstead All SS *S'wark* 95-04; P-in-c Sanderstead St Mary 02-04; RD Croydon S 00-04; Adn Lambeth from 04. *7 Hoadly Road, London SW16 1AE* Tel (020) 8769 4384 *or* 8785 1980 E-mail chris.skilton@southwark.anglican.org

SKINGLEY, Christopher George. b 49. K Coll Lon MA98. Oak Hill Th Coll BA90 Qu Coll Birm. **d** 00 **p** 01. C Enfield St Jas *Lon* 00-03; V Ramsgate St Mark *Cant* from 03. *St Mark's Vicarage, 198 Margate Road, Ramsgate CT12 6AQ* Tel (01843) 581042 E-mail chrisann@fish.co.uk

SKINNER, Arthur. b 38. **d** 97 **p** 98. NSM Selling w Throwley, Sheldwich w Badlesmere etc *Cant* from 97. *Bruckley Bungalow, Ashford Road, Badlesmere, Faversham ME13 0NZ* Tel (01233) 740666

✠**SKINNER, The Rt Revd Brian Antony.** b 39. Reading Univ BSc60. Tyndale Hall Bris 66. **d** 67 **p** 68 **c** 77. C Woking St Pet *Guildf* 67-70; Chile 70-86; Adn Valparaiso 76-77; Suff Bp Valparaiso 77-86; C Chorleywood St Andr *St Alb* 87-96; V Iver *Ox* from 96. *The Vicarage, Widecroft Road, Iver SL0 9QD* Tel and fax (01753) 653131 E-mail brianofiver@dolphinaccess.net

SKINNER, David Malcolm. b 26. CCC Cam BA55 MA59. Wells Th Coll 55. **d** 57 **p** 58. C Bris Lockleaze St Mary Magd w St Fran *Bris* 57-60; Sec C of E Radio and TV Coun 60-64; Sec Abps' Radio and TV Coun 64-67; V Ston Easton w Farrington Gurney *B & W* 67-70; rtd 70. *Glasha, Cromane, Killorglin, Co Kerry, Irish Republic* Tel (00353) (66) 69149

SKINNER, Mrs Elaine Teresa (Terri). b 55. Bath Univ BSc78. EMMTC 99. **d** 02 **p** 03. NSM Whitwick St Jo the Bapt *Leic* 02-05; NSM Thorpe Acre w Dishley from 05. *31 Stewart Drive, Loughborough LE11 5RU* Tel (01509) 843790 Mobile 07810-241381 E-mail terri.skinner@btopenworld.com

SKINNER, Graeme John. b 57. Southn Univ BSc79. Trin Coll Bris BA. **d** 86 **p** 87. C Bebington *Ches* 86-90; V Ashton-upon-Mersey St Mary from 90. *St Mary's Vicarage, 20 Beeston Road, Sale M33 5AG* Tel 0161-973 5118 Fax 973 3227 E-mail graeme@gjskinner.freeserve.co.uk

SKINNER, Mrs Jane Mary. b 59. Leeds Univ BA81. Cranmer Hall Dur 82. **dss** 84 **d** 87 **p** 94. Chatham St Phil and St Jas *Roch* 84-87; Hon Par Dn Church Coniston *Carl* 87-91; Hon Par Dn Torver 87-91; NSM Dalton-in-Furness 91-97; Chapl HM Pris Haverigg 92-97; Chapl Carl Hosps NHS Trust 97-01; Chapl N Cumbria Acute Hosps NHS Trust 01-02; TV Carl H Trin and St Barn *Carl* 98-02; Hon C W Swindon and the Lydiards *Bris* from 02; Chapl Swindon and Marlborough NHS Trust from 03. *The Rectory, Old Shaw Lane, Shaw, Swindon SN5 5PH* Tel (01793) 770568 Fax as telephone E-mail skinners@shawrectory.fsnet.co.uk

SKINNER, Mrs Jean. b 47. Univ of Northumbria at Newc BA03 RN68 RM70. NEOC 93. **d** 96 **p** 97. NSM Ch the King *Newc* 96-03; NSM City Cen Chapl from 03. *32 Easedale Avenue, Melton Park, Newcastle upon Tyne NE3 5TB* Tel 0191-236 3474 E-mail revjeanskinner@yahoo.com

SKINNER, Preb John Cedric. b 30. Bris Univ BA55 Lon Univ DipTh57. Tyndale Hall Bris 55. **d** 57 **p** 58. C St Leonard *Ex* 57-62; Univ Sec IVF 62-68; V Guildf St Sav *Guildf* 68-76; R Stoke next Guildf St Jo 74-76; R Guildf St Sav w Stoke-next-Guildford 76-84; R Ex St Leon w H Trin *Ex* 84-98; Chapl R W of England Sch for the Deaf 84-98; Preb Ex Cathl *Ex* 92-98; rtd 98; Perm to Offic *Ex* from 00. *386 Topsham Road, Exeter EX2 6HE* Tel (01392) 876540

SKINNER, John Richard. b 45. N Ord Course 84. **d** 87 **p** 88. C Allerton *Liv* 87-90; C Huyton St Mich 90-97; P-in-c Fairfield 97-03; rtd 04. *30 Duke Street, Formby, Liverpool L37 4AT* Tel (01704) 874899

SKINNER, John Timothy. b 55. Linc Th Coll 79. **d** 81 **p** 82. C Newton Aycliffe *Dur* 81-82; Perm to Offic *Newc* 95-01; Bermuda from 01. *St John's Church, PO Box HM 1856, Hamilton HM HX, Bermuda* Tel (001441) 292 6802

SKINNER, Leonard Harold. b 36. K Coll Lon BD62 AKC62. **d** 63 **p** 64. C Hackney Wick St Mary of Eton w St Aug *Lon* 63-66; C Palmers Green St Jo 66-70; V Grange Park St Pet 70-80; TV Hanley H Ev *Lich* 80-86; Chapl Sunderland Poly *Dur* 86-92; Chapl Sunderland Univ 92-93; P-in-c Hebburn St Oswald 93-01; rtd 01; Perm to Offic *Newc* from 01. *28 Brighton Grove, Whitley Bay NE26 1QH* Tel 0191-251 4891

SKINNER, Maurice Wainwright. b 30. St Jo Coll Ox BA53 MA59 FRSC70. Ox NSM Course. **d** 86 **p** 87. NSM Furze Platt *Ox* 86-94; NSM Hurley and Stubbings 94-00; rtd 00; Perm to Offic *Ox* from 00. *133 Beverley Gardens, Maidenhead SL6 6ST* Tel (01628) 624875

SKINNER, Michael Thomas. b 39. Open Univ BA88 BA90. S'wark Ord Course 73. **d** 78 **p** 79. NSM Orpington St Andr *Roch* 78-82; P-in-c from 99; NSM Orpington All SS 82-99; Assoc Bp's Officer for NSMs 90-98; Bp's Officer for NSMs from 98; Perm to Offic *S'wark* from 02. *The Vicarage, Anglesea Road, Orpington BR5 4AN* Tel and fax (01689) 823775 E-mail michael.skinner@rochester.anglican.org

SKINNER, Mrs Nicola Jayne. b 70. Birm Univ BA92. Cuddesdon Coll MTh. **d** 98 **p** 99. C Bartley Green *Birm* 98-01; Assoc Min Aurora Trin Ch Canada from 01. *Trinity Anglican Church, 79 Victoria Street, Aurora ON, Canada, L4G 1R3*

SKINNER, Peter William. b 47. SSC. Sarum & Wells Th Coll 85. **d** 87 **p** 88. C Latchford St Jas *Ches* 87-89; C Weymouth St Paul *Sarum* 89; Perm to Offic *Lon* 97-99; C Leic St Aid *Leic* 99-01; TV Staveley and Barrow Hill *Derby* 01-04; V Middlesbrough St Thos *York* from 04. *The Vicarage, 259 Normanby Road, Middlesbrough TS6 6TB* Tel (01642) 453679

SKINNER, Philip Harold. b 30. **d** 97 **p** 98. OLM Tisbury *Sarum* 97-01; rtd 01; Perm to Offic *Sarum* from 02. *Ladydown House, Vicarage Road, Tisbury, Salisbury SP3 6HY* Tel (01747) 870394

SKINNER, Raymond Frederick. b 45. St Jo Coll Dur BA67 Dur Univ MA93. Cranmer Hall Dur. **d** 70 **p** 71. C High Elswick St Paul *Newc* 70-76; V Newbottle *Dur* 76-87; Ind Chapl 81-87; RD Houghton 84-87; Oman 87-90; TR Morden *S'wark* from 90; Asst RD Merton from 91. *The Rectory, London Road, Morden SM4 5QT* Tel (020) 8648 3920 *or* 8658 0012 E-mail skinhicks@aol.com

SKINNER, Stephen John. b 52. Bris Univ BSc St Jo Coll Dur BA Dur Univ MLitt AIA. Cranmer Hall Dur. **d** 83 **p** 84. C Chatham St Phil and St Jas *Roch* 83-87; P-in-c Torver *Carl* 87-90; R 90-91; P-in-c Church Coniston 87-90; V 90-91; V Dalton-in-Furness 91-97; TR Carl H Trin and St Barn 97-02; TR W Swindon and the Lydiards *Bris* from 02. *The Rectory, Old Shaw Lane, Shaw, Swindon SN5 5PH* Tel (01793) 770568 Fax as telephone E-mail skinners@shawrectory.fsnet.co.uk

SKINNER, Terri. *See* SKINNER, Mrs Elaine Teresa

SKIPPER, Kenneth Graham. b 34. St Aid Birkenhead 65. **d** 68 **p** 69. C Newland St Aug *York* 68-71; C Newby 71-74; V Dormanstown 74-78; C-in-c Mappleton w Goxhill 78; C-in-c Withernwick 78; V Aldbrough w Cowden Parva 78; V Aldbrough, Mappleton w Goxhill and Withernwick 79-89; R Londesborough 89-96; R Burnby 90-96; R Nunburnholme and Warter 90-96; V Shiptonthorpe w Hayton 90-96; rtd 96. *18 Elder Crescent, Bowmore, Isle Of Islay PA43 7HU* Tel (01496) 810321 E-mail kenskipislay@aol.com

SKIPPER, Canon Lawrence Rainald. b 17. St Pet Hall Ox BA39 MA43. Wycliffe Hall Ox 39. **d** 41 **p** 41. C Aldershot H Trin *Guildf* 41-44; C Paignton Ch Ch *Ex* 44-48; V Paignton St Paul Preston 48-50; Chapl Trent Coll Nottm 50-56; Lic to Offic *Derby* 51-56; V Claughton cum Grange *Ches* 56-65; R Christleton 65-72; RD Ches 69-78; R Eccleston and Pulford 72-82; Hon Can Ches Cathl 74-82; rtd 82; Perm to Offic *Ches* from 82. *10 Westminster Terrace, Chester CH4 7LF* Tel (01244) 683178

SKIPPON, Kevin John. b 54. St Steph Ho Ox 78. **d** 81 **p** 82. C Gt Yarmouth *Nor* 81-84; C Kingstanding St Luke *Birm* 84-86; V Smethwick SS Steph and Mich 86-92; Chapl Derbyshire R Infirmary 92-94; Chapl Derbyshire R Infirmary NHS Trust 94-98; Chapl S Derbyshire Acute Hosps NHS Trust from 98. *Derbyshire Royal Infirmary, London Road, Derby DE1 2QY* Tel (01332) 347141 ext 2572 E-mail kevin.skippon@sdah-tr.trent.nhs.uk

SKIRROW, Paul Richard. b 52. Hull Univ BA82 Chester Coll of HE MTh00. N Ord Course 97. **d** 00 **p** 01. C St Luke in the City *Liv* 00-03; V Ditton St Mich w St Thos from 03; Asst Dir CME from 03. *The Vicarage, 339 Ditchfield Road, Widnes WA8 8XR* Tel and fax 0151-424 2502 E-mail paul.skirrow@btinternet.com

SKLIROS, Michael Peter. b 33. Clare Coll Cam BA57 MA62. Ridley Hall Cam 57. **d** 59 **p** 60. C Hornchurch St Andr *Chelmsf* 59-61; Asst Chapl Denstone Coll Uttoxeter 61-65; Chapl RAF 65-77; P-in-c Stowmarket *St E* 77-78; Lic to Offic 78-85; C Gt Finborough w Onehouse and Harleston 85-91; P-in-c 91; R Gt and Lt Bealings w Playford and Culpho 91-96; rtd 96; Hon Asst to Bp Brandon Canada from 03. *49 Almond Crescent, Brandon MB, Canada, R7B 1A2* Tel (001) (204) 726 9144 E-mail pifont@mts.net

SKOYLES, John Alan. b 32. Breakspear Coll 50 Christleton Hall 53. **d** 58 **p** 59. In RC Ch 59-80; Soc worker 80-99; NSM The Hydneye *Chich* 99-00; C Kenton, Mamhead, Powderham, Cofton and Starcross *Ex* 00-01. *Flat 3, 31 Ceylon Place, Eastbourne BN21 3JE*

SKRINE, Charles Walter Douglas. b 75. Qu Coll Ox BA98. Oak Hill Th Coll BA03. **d** 03 **p** 04. C St Helen Bishopsgate w St Andr

Undershaft etc *Lon* from 03. *64 Arbery Road, London E3 5DD* Tel (020) 8980 8596 *or* 7283 2231
E-mail charles@cwdskrine.freeserve.co.uk

SKUBLICS, Ernest. b 36. Sant' Anselmo Univ Rome STB62 Ottawa Univ MTh64 STL64 Nijmegen Univ DrTheol67. **d** 73 **p** 73. R Whitewood Canada 73-76; Chapl Manitoba Univ 76-77; Soc Worker 77-86; Registrar and Asst Prof Manitoba Univ 86-90; Assoc Dir Inst for Th Studies Seattle Univ USA 90-93; Dean Graduate Sch Mt Angel Sem Oregon 93-00; C Hawley H Trin *Guildf* from 04. *295 Fernhill Road, Farnborough GU14 9EW* Tel (01276) 34241 E-mail ej@skublics.freeserve.co.uk

SKUCE, David. b 56. NUU BSc79 QUB PGCE80 TCD BTh89. CITC 87. **d** 89 **p** 90. C Templemore *D & R* 89-92; I Kilbarron w Rossnowlagh and Drumholm 92-99; I Urney w Sion Mills from 99; Bp's Dom Chapl from 94. *The Rectory, 112 Melmount Road, Sion Mills, Strabane BT82 9PY* Tel (028) 8165 8020

SLACK, Canon Ellis Edward. b 23. Birm Univ BA51 MA53. Qu Coll Birm 51. **d** 53 **p** 53. C Leeds Halton St Wilfrid *Ripon* 53-56; R Stanningley St Thos 57-64; V N Dulwich St Faith *S'wark* 64-72; V Bethnal Green St Jo w St Simon *Lon* 72-78; TR Bethnal Green St Jo w St Bart 78-79; Can Res Portsm Cathl *Portsm* 79-83; Bp's Chapl for CME 79-83; V Woodplumpton *Blackb* 83-88; Dir Post-Ord Tr 83-88; rtd 88; Perm to Offic *York* from 88. *68 Ouse Lea, Shipton Road, York YO30 6SA* Tel (01904) 658263
E-mail ellis.slack@tesco.net

SLACK, Michael. b 53. St Jo Coll Dur BA74 Lon Univ PGCE79 RGN83. St Steph Ho Ox 74. **d** 76 **p** 77. C Wolverhampton St Steph *Lich* 76-77; NSM Bywell *Newc* 89-93; TV Cullercoats St Geo 93-98; TR from 98. *St George's Vicarage, Beverley Gardens, North Shields NE30 4NS* Tel and fax 0191-252 1817

SLADDEN, David. *See* SLADDEN, John David

SLADDEN, Duncan Julius Edward. b 25. K Coll Cam BA50 MA51. Cuddesdon Coll 51. **d** 53 **p** 54. C Huddersfield St Pet *Wakef* 53-55; C Reading St Mary V *Ox* 55-61; R Largs *Glas* 61-65; P-in-c Stevenage *St Alb* 65-70; R Johnstone *Glas* 70-76; Prayer Gp Adv Scottish Chs Renewal 76-81; Sec Scottish Episc Renewal Fellowship 81-84; R E Kilbride 85-90; rtd 90. *17 Bruce Avenue, Dunblane FK15 9JB* Tel (01786) 825520

SLADDEN, Canon John Cyril. b 20. Mert Coll Ox BA42 MA46 BD66. Wycliffe Hall Ox 46. **d** 48 **p** 49. C Oswestry St Oswald *Lich* 48-51; Tutor St Aid Birkenhead 51-53; R Todwick *Sheff* 53-59; V Lower Peover *Ches* 59-86; RD Knutsford 80-85; Hon Can Ches Cathl 80-86; rtd 86. *Rossa, Penmon, Beaumaris LL58 8SN* Tel (01248) 490207

SLADDEN, John David. b 49. RN Eng Coll Plymouth BSc74 St Edm Coll Cam MA86. Ridley Hall Cam 80. **d** 83 **p** 84. C St Bees *Carl* 83-85; Perm to Offic *Lich* 85-87; Miss Co-ord Down to Earth Evangelistic Trust 85-87; V Doncaster St Jas *Sheff* 87-94. *9 Teal Close, Chatteris PE16 6PR* Tel (01354) 694097

SLADE, Canon Adrian Barrie. b 47. K Alfred's Coll Win DipEd68. St Jo Coll Nottm BTh73 ALCD72. **d** 73 **p** 74. C Streatham Immanuel w St Anselm *S'wark* 73-76; C Chipping Barnet *St Alb* 76-78; C Chipping Barnet w Arkley 78-80; V Sundon 80-85; Soc Resp Officer *Glouc* from 86; Hon Can Glouc Cathl from 91. *38 Sydenham Villas Road, Cheltenham GL52 6DZ* Tel (01242) 253162 Fax 242672
E-mail glossr@star.co.uk

SLADE, Alfred Laurence. b 12. ACII. Roch Th Coll 67. **d** 69 **p** 70. Hon C Cliftonville *Cant* 69-71; Hon C Westgate St Jas 71-75; Perm to Offic *Sarum* 75-81; Perm to Offic *Cant* 81-93. *21 McKinlay Court, The Parade, Minnis Bay, Birchington CT7 9QG* Tel (01843) 46882

SLADE, Michael John. b 55. Trin Coll Bris 94. **d** 96 **p** 97. C Blagdon w Compton Martin and Ubley *B & W* 96-99; V Winscombe from 99; RD Locking from 05. *The Vicarage, Winscombe Hill, Winscombe BS25 1DE* Tel (01934) 843164
E-mail michaeljohnslade@aol.com

SLADE, Canon William Clifford. b 24. St Jo Coll Dur BA47 MA53. **d** 49 **p** 50. C Northallerton w Deighton and Romanby *York* 49-52; C Eston 52-54; V Anlaby Common St Mark 54-60; V Brompton w Snainton 60-67; R Stokesley 67-71; V Felixkirk w Boltby and Kirby Knowle 71-82; Abp's Adv for Spiritual Direction 82-86; C Topcliffe w Dalton and Dishforth 82-86; Can and Preb York Minster 79-86; Perm to Offic from 86; rtd 86. *Bede House, Beck Lane, South Kilvington, Thirsk YO7 2NL* Tel (01845) 522915

SLATER, Mrs Ann. b 46. Somerville Coll Ox BA67 MA71. WMMTC 92. **d** 95 **p** 96. C Northampton St Benedict *Pet* 95-99; TV Daventry, Ashby St Ledgers, Braunston etc from 99; R Heyford w Stowe Nine Churches and Flore etc from 05. *The Rectory, Church Lane, Nether Heyford, Northampton NN7 3LQ* Tel (01327) 342201 E-mail ann.slater@btinternet.com

SLATER, David. *See* SLATER, Canon Philip David

SLATER, Ian. **d** 04 **p** 05. NSM Gt Horton *Bradf* from 04. *Stable Cottage, 5 The Drive, Denholme, Bradford BD13 4DY* Tel (01274) 831437

SLATER, James Richard David. b 61. New Univ of Ulster BA83 TCD BTh89 Univ of Ulster MA92. CITC 86. **d** 89 **p** 90. C Clooney w Strathfoyle *D & R* 89-93; I Aghadowey w Kilrea 93-05; I Cumber Upper w Learmount from 05. *248B Glenshane Road, Killaloo, Londonderry BT47 3SN* Tel (028) 7130 1724

SLATER, John Albert. b 25. Lon Univ BA52. Oak Hill Th Coll 47. **d** 52 **p** 53. C Everton Em *Liv* 52-55; V Kirkdale St Paul N Shore 55-61; V Bacup St Sav *Man* 61-70; V Blackpool St Thos *Blackb* 70-84; rtd 84; Perm to Offic *Blackb* from 84. *18 Church Road, Thornton-Cleveleys FY5 2TZ* Tel (01253) 853330

SLATER, John Ralph. b 38. Kent Univ BA90. Linc Th Coll 71. **d** 73 **p** 74. C S Hackney St Mich w Haggerston St Paul *Lon* 73-74; C Leytonstone St Marg w St Columba *Chelmsf* 74-77; C Whitstable All SS w St Pet *Cant* 77-80; V Gt Ilford St Alb *Chelmsf* 80-83; V Clipstone *S'well* 83-87; rtd 87. *117 Canterbury Road, Westgate-on-Sea CT8 8NW* Tel (01227) 831593

SLATER, Mark Andrew. b 56. ARCS79 Imp Coll Lon BSc79. Ridley Hall Cam 87. **d** 89 **p** 90. C Northampton St Giles *Pet* 89-92; C Stopsley *St Alb* 92-93; C-in-c Bushmead CD 93-99; V St Alb St Luke from 99. *St Luke's Vicarage, 46 Cell Barnes Lane, St Albans AL1 5QJ* Tel (01727) 865399 Fax 865399
E-mail mark.slater@saint-lukes.co.uk

SLATER, The Ven Paul John. b 58. CCC Ox MA83 St Jo Coll Dur BA83. Cranmer Hall Dur 81. **d** 84 **p** 85. C Keighley St Andr *Bradf* 84-88; P-in-c Cullingworth and Dir Dioc Foundn Course 88-93; Bp's Personal Exec Asst 93-95; Warden of Readers 92-96; R Haworth 95-01; Bp's Officer for Min and Miss 01-05; Adn Craven from 05. *Woodlands, Nethergyll Lane, Cononley, Keighley BD20 8PB* Tel (01535) 635113
E-mail paul.slater@dial.pipex.com

SLATER, Canon Philip David. b 27. K Coll Lon 58. **d** 60 **p** 61. C Havant *Portsm* 60-67; C Leigh Park 68-69; Hants Co RE Adv 69-74; Gosport and Fareham RE Adv 74-82; Hon C Bishop's Waltham 76-82; V Bulford, Figheldean and Milston *Sarum* 82-93; RD Avon 85-95; Can and Preb Sarum Cathl 91-95; V Avon Valley 93-95; rtd 95; V of Close Sarum Cathl *Sarum* from 95; Chapl Godolphin Sch 95-04. *102 Coombe Road, Salisbury SP2 8BD* Tel (01722) 332529 E-mail voc@salcath.co.uk

SLATER, Robert Adrian. b 48. St Jo Coll Nottm 76. **d** 79 **p** 80. C Bedworth *Cov* 79-82; TV Billericay and Lt Burstead *Chelmsf* 82-88; V Rounds Green *Birm* 88-94. *11 Lewis Road, Birmingham B30 2SU* Tel 0121-689 2721 E-mail robslater@freeuk.com

SLATER, Thomas Ernest. b 37. Chelsea Coll Lon TCert60 Lon Univ BD71 NE Lon Poly DipG&C88. ALCD66. **d** 67 **p** 68. C Bootle Ch Ch *Liv* 67-72; C Stapleford *S'well* 72-75; Supt Tower Hamlets Miss 75-77; Hon C Stepney St Pet w St Benet *Lon* 78-79; Asst Chapl The Lon Hosp (Whitechapel) 79-83; Chapl 83-89; NSM Poplar *Lon* 89-92 and 94-02; Perm to Offic 92-94; rtd 02. *11 Elgin House, Cordelia Street, London E14 6EG* Tel (020) 7987 4504

SLATER, Victoria Ruth. b 59. Hertf Coll Ox BA82 MA87 Selw Coll Cam BA89 MA94. Westcott Ho Cam 86. **d** 89 **p** 94. Chapl Asst Man R Infirmary 89-90; Chapl 90-94; Chapl St Mary's Hosp Man 90-94; Chapl Ox Radcliffe Hosp NHS Trust 94-97; Chapl Sir Michael Sobell Ho Palliative Care Unit 97-05; Asst Soc Resp Adv *Ox* from 05. *Diocesan Church House, North Hinksey Lane, Botley, Oxford OX2 0NB* Tel (01865) 208214

SLATER, William Edward. b 51. Bolton Inst of Tech HNC77. Aston Tr Scheme 85 Oak Hill Th Coll 87. **d** 89 **p** 90. C Balderstone *Man* 89-94; V Newchapel *Lich* from 94; RD Stoke N from 99. *The Vicarage, 32 Pennyfield Road, Newchapel, Stoke-on-Trent ST7 4PN* Tel (01782) 782837
E-mail willslater@tinyworld.co.uk

SLATOR, Edward Douglas Humphreys. b 18. TCD BA41 MA47 Hull Univ BPhil75. **d** 43 **p** 44. C Taney *D & G* 43-46; Chapl St Columba's Coll Dub 46-60; I Killea *C & O* 60-73; C Taney *D & G* 74-80; P-in-c Rathmolyon w Castlerickard, Rathcore and Agher *M & K* 80-87; rtd 87; PV Ch Ch Cathl Dublin *D & G* from 93. *31 St John's, Park Avenue, Dublin 4, Irish Republic* Tel (00353) (1) 283 9395

SLATTER, Barrie John. b 44. Nottm Univ BSc66 FRICS97. Dioc OLM tr scheme 97. **d** 00 **p** 01. OLM Hundred River *St E* 00-03; C Sternfield, Benhall, Snape etc from 03. *The Rectory, Low Road, Stratford St Andrew, Saxmundham IP17 1LJ* Tel (01728) 603180 Mobile 07802-924738
E-mail rectory@barrieslatter.fsnet.co.uk

SLATTERY, Maurice Michael. b 43. Southlands Coll Lon TCert73 Lon Inst of Educn BEd74. S'wark Ord Course 91. **d** 94 **p** 95. NSM Malden St Jas *S'wark* 94-97; NSM Niton, Whitwell and St Lawrence *Portsm* 97-99; NSM Selsdon St Jo w St Fran *S'wark* 99-03; Perm to Offic *Portsm* 03-04; P-in-c St Lawrence from 04. *Marlbrook, Hunts Road, St Lawrence, Ventnor PO38 1XT* Tel (01983) 855801
E-mail maurice@slattery6800.fsnet.com

SLAUGHTER, Clive Patrick. b 36. St Paul's Coll Grahamstown DipTh78. **d** 77 **p** 78. S Africa 77-87; R Thorley w Bishop's Stortford H Trin *St Alb* 87-90; R Thorley 90-01; RD Bishop's Stortford 96-01; rtd 01; Perm to Offic *St Alb* 01-03; P-in-c Much Hadham 03-04; P-in-c Braughing w Furneux Pelham and Stocking Pelham from 04. *53 High Street, Hunsdon, Ware SG12 8QB* Tel (01279) 844955
E-mail clive.slaughter@virgin.net

SLAUGHTER, Canon Maurice Basil. b 20. Leeds Univ BA42. Coll of Resurr Mirfield 42. **d** 44 **p** 45. C Kingswinford St Mary *Lich* 44-46; C Roch St Nic w St Clem *Roch* 46-47; C Luton Ch Ch *St Alb* 47-50; V Birm St Marg Ladywood *Birm* 50-52; V Newsome *Wakef* 52-60; V Queensbury *Bradf* 60-63; V Skipton Ch Ch 63-78; Hon Can Bradf Cathl 67-85; RD Skipton 73-82; P-in-c Bolton Abbey 78-85; P-in-c Rylstone 78-85; P-in-c Arncliffe w Halton Gill 79-82; rtd 85; Perm to Offic *Bradf* 85-99; Perm to Offic *Wakef* 85-96; Perm to Offic *Ely* 96-00. *107 Lisle Close, Ely CB7 4AD* Tel (01353) 664541

SLEDGE, The Ven Richard Kitson. b 30. Peterho Cam BA52 MA57. Ridley Hall Cam 52. **d** 54 **p** 55. C Compton Gifford *Ex* 54-57; C Ex St Martin, St Steph, St Laur etc 57-63; V Dronfield *Derby* 63-76; TR 76-78; RD Chesterfield 72-78; Adn Huntingdon *Ely* 78-96; R Hemingford Abbots 78-89; Hon Can Ely Cathl 78-99; rtd 96; Bp's Dom Chapl *Ely* 96-99; Dioc Retirement Officer from 98; Perm to Offic from 99. *7 Budge Close, Brampton, Huntingdon PE29 4PL* Tel (01480) 380284 *or* (01353) 662749 Fax (01480) 437789

SLEDGE, Timothy Charles Kitson. b 64. Coll of Ripon & York St Jo BA87 York Univ MA88. Trin Coll Bris DipHE95 ADUT95. **d** 95 **p** 96. C Huddersfield St Thos *Wakef* 95-98; V Luddenden w Luddenden Foot 98-03; P-in-c Sowerby 02-03; Dioc Miss Enabler *Pet* from 03. *The Vicarage, Campbell Square, Northampton NN1 3EB* Tel (01604) 230563
E-mail tim@sledgey.freeserve.co.uk

SLEE, The Very Revd Colin Bruce. b 45. OBE01. K Coll Lon BD69 AKC69 FKC01. St Aug Coll Cant 69. **d** 70 **p** 71. C Nor Heartsease St Fran *Nor* 70-73; C Cambridge Gt St Mary w St Mich *Ely* 73-76; Chapl Girton Coll Cam 73-76; Tutor and Chapl K Coll Lon 76-82; Can Res and Sub-Dean St Alb 82-94; Provost S'wark 94-00; Dean S'wark from 00; Hon Lect Harvard Div Sch from 01. *The Provost's Lodging, 51 Bankside, London SE1 9JE* Tel (020) 7928 6414 *or* 7367 6731 Fax 7367 6725
E-mail colin.slee@southwark.anglican.org

SLEE, John Graham. b 51. Brunel Univ BTech73. Oak Hill Th Coll 85. **d** 87 **p** 88. C St Columb Minor and St Colan *Truro* 87-91; R St Mawgan w St Ervan and St Eval 91-02; RD Pydar 93-95; P-in-c St Just-in-Roseland and St Mawes from 02. *16 Waterloo Close, St Mawes, Truro TR2 5BD* Tel (01326) 270248 Fax as telephone E-mail jslee@priest.com

SLEEMAN, Matthew Timothy. b 68. St Cath Coll Cam BA90 MA95 PhD96. Wycliffe Hall Ox BA97. **d** 98 **p** 99. C Eynsham and Cassington *Ox* 98-02; Perm to Offic *Lon* from 03. *128 The Fairway, London N14 4NN* Tel (020) 8449 9891 *or* 8449 0467

SLEGG, John Edward. b 36. St Pet Coll Ox BA62 MA66. Ridley Hall Cam 62. **d** 64 **p** 65. C Perranzabuloe *Truro* 64-66; CF 66-86; V Poling *Chich* from 86; V Lyminster from 86. *The Vicarage, 3 Middle Paddock, Lyminster, Littlehampton BN17 7QH* Tel (01903) 882152 E-mail slegglymvic@aol.com

SLEIGHT, Gordon Frederick. b 47. AKC69. St Aug Coll Cant 69. **d** 70 **p** 71. C Boston *Linc* 70-74; P-in-c Louth St Mich and Stewton 74; TV Louth 74-81; V Crosby 81-95; P-in-c Nettleham 95-97; V 97-05; RD Lawres 04-05; rtd 05. *Elderbank, Stoer, Lochinver, Lairg IV27 4JE* Tel (01571) 855207
E-mail gordon@gsleight.freeserve.co.uk

SLIM, David Albert. b 49. Westhill Coll Birm CertEd72. Linc Th Coll 90. **d** 90 **p** 91. C Walmley *Birm* 90-93; R Marchwiel and Isycoed *St As* 93-03; TV Wrexham from 03. *The Vicarage, 37 Acton Gate, Wrexham LL11 2PW* Tel (01978) 266685

SLIPPER, Charles Callan. b 55. Lanc Univ BA77 PhD84. S Dios Minl Tr Scheme 91. **d** 93 **p** 94. Focolare Movement from 77; NSM N Acton St Gabr *Lon* 93-96; Perm to Offic from 96. *38 Audley Road, London W5 3ET* Tel (020) 8991 2022 *or* 8354 0763 Fax 8453 1621 E-mail callan@onetel.com

SLIPPER, Robert James. b 64. St Jo Coll Cam BA87 MA91. Wycliffe Hall Ox BA92. **d** 92 **p** 93. C Southgate *Chich* 92-95; C Stoughton *Guildf* 95-00; V Terrington St Clement *Ely* from 00. *The Vicarage, 27 Sutton Road, Terrington St Clement, King's Lynn PE34 4PQ* Tel (01553) 828430
E-mail robert@slipper.fsnet.co.uk

SLOANE, Isaac Reuben. b 16. TCD BA41 MA60. **d** 42 **p** 43. C Kinawley w H Trin *K, E & A* 42-44; I Gleneely w Culdaff *D & R* 44-54; I Ardstraw w Baronscourt, Badoney Lower etc 54-76; I Drumclamph w Drumquin 76-78; rtd 78. *c/o P Sloane Esq, 17 Kingsfort Lodge, Moira, Craigavon BT67 0QG*

SLOANE, Niall James. b 81. TCD BA03. CITC 03. **d** 05. C Agherton *Conn* from 05. *The Curatage, 23 Cappaghmore Manor, Portstewart BT55 7RD* Tel and fax (028) 7083 4606
E-mail curate.agherton@connor.anglican.org

SLOGGETT, Donald George. b 49. Trin Coll Bris 81. **d** 83 **p** 84. C Horfield H Trin *Bris* 83-86; C Highworth w Sevenhampton and Inglesham etc 86-88; P-in-c Upavon w Rushall *Sarum* 88-90; R Upavon w Rushall and Charlton 90-01; R Stoulton w Drake's Broughton and Pirton etc *Worc* from 01. *The Rectory, Manor Farm, Stoulton, Worcester WR7 4RS* Tel (01905) 840528
E-mail donsloggett@zetnet.co.uk

SLOW, Leslie John. b 47. Liv Univ BSc68 MSc69. N Ord Course 77. **d** 80 **p** 81. NSM Gt Horton *Bradf* from 80. *25 Grasleigh Way, Bradford BD15 9BE* Tel (01274) 491808

SLUMAN, Richard Geoffrey Davies. b 34. St Jo Coll Ox BA68 MA68. Sarum Th Coll 68. **d** 70 **p** 71. C Gt Yarmouth *Nor* 70-73; V Churchdown *Glouc* 73-82; P-in-c Blockley w Aston Magna 82-83; V Blockley w Aston Magna and Bourton on the Hill 83-94; rtd 94; Perm to Offic *Cov* from 94. *21 Manor Farm Road, Tredington, Shipston-on-Stour CV36 4NZ* Tel (01608) 662317

SLY, Canon Christopher John. b 34. Selw Coll Cam BA58 MA62. Wycliffe Hall Ox. **d** 60 **p** 61. C Buckhurst Hill *Chelmsf* 60-64; V Berechurch 64-75; V Southend St Sav Westcliff 75-87; R Wickham Bishops w Lt Braxted 87-99; RD Witham 87-96; Hon Can Chelmsf Cathl 93-99; rtd 99. *Ludlow Cottage, Church Lane, Little Leighs, Chelmsford CM3 1PQ* Tel (01245) 361489

SLYFIELD, John David. b 32. TD67. Roch Th Coll 66. **d** 68 **p** 69. C St Mary in the Marsh *Cant* 68-71; P-in-c Steeple Claydon *Ox* 71-76; P-in-c Middle w E Claydon 71-76; RD Claydon 73-78; R The Claydons 76-78; V S Westoe *Dur* 78-82; V Tideswell *Derby* 82-92; RD Buxton 84-91; rtd 92; Perm to Offic *Derby* 92-02; P-in-c Beeley and Edensor from 02. *The Vicarage, Edensor, Bakewell DE45 1PH* Tel (01246) 582180

SMAIL, Richard Charles. b 57. CCC Ox BA80 MA83. Ox Min Course 90. **d** 93 **p** 95. NSM Keble Coll Ox 93-96; Chapl, Fell and Lect BNC Ox 97-02; Perm to Offic *Ox* from 02. *Brasenose College, Oxford OX1 4AJ* E-mail richardsmail@supanet.com

SMAIL, Canon Thomas Allan. b 28. Glas Univ MA49 Edin Univ BD52. **d** 79 **p** 79. Vice-Prin St Jo Coll Nottm 80-85; TR Sanderstead All SS *S'wark* 85-94; Hon Can S'wark Cathl 91-94; rtd 94; Perm to Offic *S'wark* from 94. *36B Alexandra Road, Croydon CR0 6EU* Tel (020) 8656 9683
E-mail tasmail@blueyonder.co.uk

SMALE, Frederick Ronald. b 37. K Coll Lon BD60 AKC60. **d** 61 **p** 62. C Bearsted *Cant* 61-64; C Fishponds St Mary *Bris* 64-69; V Hartlip *Cant* 69-71; P-in-c Stockbury w Bicknor and Huckinge 69-71; V Hartlip w Stockbury 71-75; R River 75-85; V Birchington w Acol and Minnis Bay 85-00; rtd 00; Perm to Offic *Cant* from 01. *28 Margate Road, Broomfield, Herne Bay CT6 7BL* Tel (01227) 283880

SMALE, Ian Keith. b 53. Wycliffe Hall Ox. **d** 00 **p** 01. C Overton w Laverstoke and Freefolk *Win* 00-04; P-in-c E Dean w Friston and Jevington *Chich* from 04. *The Rectory, Gilberts Drive, East Dean, Eastbourne BN20 0DL* Tel (01323) 423266
E-mail ian@smale.fslife.co.uk

SMALL, David Binney. b 39. Brasted Th Coll 61 Westcott Ho Cam 63. **d** 65 **p** 66. C Milton *Portsm* 65-69; CF 69-92; R Wickwar w Rangeworthy *Glouc* 92-97; RD Hawkesbury 94-97; rtd 97; Perm to Offic *Glouc* from 97; Sub Chapl HM Pris Glouc from 98. *16 Wotton Road, Charfield, Wotton-under-Edge GL12 8TP* Tel and fax (01454) 261746

SMALL, Gordon Frederick. b 41. St Jo Coll Nottm 77. **d** 79 **p** 80. C Belper *Derby* 79-84; NSM Matlock Bath 90-91; C Ripley 91-93; TV Bucknall and Bagnall *Lich* 93-98; Assoc P Deal St Leon w St Rich and Sholden etc *Cant* from 98. *St Richard's Lodge, 7 St Richard's Road, Deal CT14 9JR* Tel (01304) 374674
E-mail gordon.small1@btopenworld.com

SMALL, Marcus Jonathan. b 67. Univ of Wales (Ban) BD94. Ripon Coll Cuddesdon 94. **d** 96 **p** 97. C Moseley St Mary *Birm* 96-99; TV Wenlock *Heref* from 99; R Eardisley w Bollingham, Willersley, Brilley etc from 05. *Church House, Church Road, Eardisley, Hereford HR3 6NN* Tel (01544) 327440
E-mail marcus@flying-goose.freeserve.co.uk

SMALL, Simon William. b 57. Worc Coll of Tech HNC77 DMA81. Cuddesdon Coll. **d** 98 **p** 99. C Kidderminster St Mary and All SS w Trimpley etc *Worc* 98-01; Chapl to Bp Dudley from 01. *4 Hemplands Road, Stourbridge DY8 1TX* Tel (01384) 826939 Mobile 07702-693414
E-mail simon.small@blueyonder.co.uk

SMALLDON, Canon Keith. b 48. Open Univ BA76 Newc Univ MA94. St Mich Coll Llan. **d** 71 **p** 72. C Cwmbran *Mon* 71-73; C Chepstow 73-75; Dioc Youth Adv *Bradf* 75-79; P-in-c Woolfold *Man* 82-85; Dioc Youth and Community Officer 82-90; P-in-c Thursby *Carl* 90-94; Dir of Clergy Tr 90-94; TR Daventry, Ashby St Ledgers, Braunston etc *Pet* 94-98; Chapl Danetre Hosp 94-98; TR Llantwit Major *Llan* 98-03; Can Res Brecon Cathl *S & B* from 03; Dioc Dir of Min from 03. *The Clergy House, Cathedral Close, Brecon LD3 9DP* Tel (01874) 623886 Fax 623716 E-mail keithsmalldon@aol.com

SMALLEY, Mrs Kathleen. b 23. Linc Th Coll 81. **dss** 84 **d** 87 **p** 94. Leominster *Heref* 84-85; Bridgnorth, Tasley, Astley Abbotts, etc 85-96; Hon C 87-96; Perm to Offic from 96. *8A Cliff Road, Bridgnorth WV16 4EY* Tel (01746) 766202

SMALLEY, The Very Revd Stephen Stewart. b 31. Jes Coll Cam BA55 MA58 PhD79. Eden Th Sem (USA) BD57 Ridley Hall Cam. **d** 58 **p** 59. C Portman Square St Paul *Lon* 58-60; Chapl Peterho Cam 60-63; Dean 62-63; Nigeria 63-69; Lect Th Man Univ 70-77; Can Res and Prec Cov Cathl *Cov* 77-87; Vice-Provost 86-87; Dean Ches 87-01; rtd 01; Perm to Offic *Glouc* from 02. *The Old Hall, The Folly, Longborough, Moreton-in-Marsh GL56 0QS* Tel (01451) 830238 E-mail stephen@sssss.fsworld.co.uk

SMALLMAN, Miss Margaret Anne. b 43. Hull Univ BSc64 Bris Univ CertEd65. St Jo Coll Nottm. **dss** 83 **d** 87 **p** 94. Bromsgrove St Jo *Worc* 83-88; Par Dn 87-88; Par Dn Stoke Prior, Wychbold and Upton Warren 88-90; TD Tettenhall Wood *Lich* 91-94; TV 94-99; P-in-c W Bromwich H Trin from 99; C W Bromwich Gd Shep w St Jo from 99; RD W Bromwich from 04. *Holy Trinity Vicarage, 1 Burlington Road, West Bromwich B70 6LF* Tel 0121-525 3595 E-mail mas@msmallman.fsnet.co.uk

SMALLMAN, Mrs Sheila Maxine. b 30. Lon Univ BSc51. St Jo Coll Nottm 91 Cant Sch of Min 92. **d** 97 **p** 98. NSM Benenden *Cant* 97-01; Asst Chapl Benenden Hosp 97-01; P-in-c Sandhurst 01-04; rtd 04. *Beacon Shaw, Rolvenden Road, Benenden, Cranbrook TN17 4BU* Tel and fax (01580) 240625 Mobile 07773-056253 E-mail barrysmallman@aol.com

SMALLS, Peter Harry. b 34. FCCA. LNSM course 96. **d** 97 **p** 98. OLM Narborough w Narford *Nor* 97-99; OLM Pentney St Mary Magd w W Bilney 97-99; OLM Castle Acre w Newton and Southacre 97-99; OLM Westacre 97-99; OLM Narborough w Narford and Pentney 99-02; Perm to Offic from 03. *Windward, Drapers Lane, Ditchingham, Bungay NR35 2JW* Tel (01986) 894667

SMALLWOOD, Simon Laurence. b 58. St Jo Coll Dur BSc80. Cranmer Hall Dur 89. **d** 92 **p** 93. C Stapenhill w Cauldwell *Derby* 92-96; TV Dagenham *Chelmsf* 96-03; V Becontree St Geo from 03. *The Vicarage, 86 Rogers Road, Dagenham RM10 8JX* Tel (020) 8593 2760

SMART, Barry Anthony Ignatius. b 57. Lanc Univ BEd79. St Steph Ho Ox 85. **d** 88 **p** 89. C Wantage *Ox* 88-91; C Abingdon 91-93; TV 93-95; C Princes Risborough w Ilmer 95-97; C Kingstanding St Luke *Birm* 97-00; V Small Heath from 00. *All Saints' Clergy House, 85 Jenkins Street, Small Heath, Birmingham B10 0PQ* Tel 0121-772 0621 Fax as telephone

SMART, Beryl. b 33. Sheff Univ BSc55 FIMgt83. Dioc OLM tr scheme 98. **d** 01 **p** 02. OLM Newchurch w Croft *Liv* from 01. *41 Culcheth Hall Drive, Culcheth, Warrington WA3 4PT* Tel (01925) 762655

SMART, Mrs Carol. b 45. SSF SRN67. S Dios Minl Tr Scheme 89. **d** 92 **p** 94. Chapl St Mary's Hosp NHS Trust 92-99; NSM Shorwell w Kingston *Portsm* 99-02; NSM Gatcombe 92-02; NSM Chale 92-02; Perm to Offic from 02. *20 Sydney Close, Shide, Newport PO30 1YG* Tel (01983) 526242 E-mail carol_smart@tssf.freeserve.co.uk

SMART, Clifford Edward James. b 28. Kelham Th Coll 48. **d** 53 **p** 54. C Blackb St Pet *Blackb* 53-56; Korea 56-65 and 66-93; C Birm St Aid Small Heath *Birm* 65-66; rtd 93. *6045 Glennaire Drive, St Louis, MO 63129-4761, USA* Tel (001) (314) 846 5927

SMART, Harry Gavin. b 67. St D Coll Lamp BA90. Westcott Ho Cam 90. **d** 94 **p** 95. C Thirsk *York* 94-97; C Sheff St Leon Norwood *Sheff* 97-99; Mental Health Chapl Sheff Care Trust from 99. *Longley Centre, Northern General Hospital, Herries Road, Sheffield S5 7AU* Tel 0114-226 1675 *or* 271 6310

SMART, Canon Haydn Christopher. b 38. Wells Th Coll 66. **d** 69 **p** 70. C Hillmorton *Cov* 69-72; C Duston *Pet* 72-75; V Woodford Halse 75-79; V Woodford Halse w Eydon 79-82; V Wellingborough All SS 82-92; RD Wellingborough 87-92; V Longthorpe 92-03; Can Pet Cathl 92-03; RD Pet 96-01; rtd 03; P-in-c Madeira *Eur* from 03. *The Parsonage, 20 rua do Quebra Costas, 9000 Funchal, Madeira* Tel (00351) (291) 220674 Fax (291) 220161 E-mail holytrinity@netmadeira.com

SMART, Mrs Hilary Jean. b 42. SOAS Lon BA63 CSocSc64 DASS67. EMMTC 85. **d** 88 **p** 94. Par Dn Walsall Pleck and Bescot *Lich* 88-94; C 94; TV Sheff Manor *Sheff* 94-02; Bp's Ecum Officer 94-02; rtd 02; Chapl Compton Hospice from 02; Perm to Offic *Heref* from 03. *Abbey Cottage, 42 High Street, Much Wenlock TF13 6AD* Tel (01952) 727062

SMART, John Francis. b 36. Keble Coll Ox BA59 MA69. Cuddesdon Coll 59. **d** 61 **p** 66. C Cannock *Lich* 61-63; Hon C Gt Wyrley 63-66; C Wednesfield St Thos 66-70; V Brereton 70-85; R E Clevedon and Walton w Weston w Clapton *B & W* 85-02; Chapl Southmead Health Services NHS Trust 85-99; Chapl N Bris NHS Trust 99-02; rtd 02. *Sunnymead, Ford Cross, South Zeal, Okehampton EX20 2JL* Tel (01837) 840233 E-mail andrsmart@tiscali.co.uk

SMART, Neil Robert. b 61. Bris Univ BVSc84. Ridley Hall Cam 01. **d** 03 **p** 04. C Shirley *Win* from 03. *16 Radway Road, Southampton SO15 7PW* Tel (023) 8077 9605 E-mail somesmarts@btopenworld.com

SMART, Richard Henry. b 22. St Jo Coll Dur 46 Clifton Th Coll 48. **d** 52 **p** 53. C Leeds St Geo *Ripon* 52-54; Kenya 54-56; C New Addington *Cant* 56-59; V Awsworth w Cossall *S'well* 59-63; BFBS Distr Sec E Anglia 63-70; Bp's Ecum Adv *Ely* 70-81; Dioc Missr 70-74; P-in-c Dry Drayton 74-81; Min Bar Hill LEP 74-81; P-in-c Madingley 80-81; V Sandylands *Blackb* 81-92; rtd 92; Perm to Offic *Pet* from 97; *Ely* 97-00; *Nor* from 98. *156 Ryeland Road, Duston, Northampton NN5 6XJ* Tel (01604) 758502

SMART, Richard Henry. b 23. Lon Univ BA51. Oak Hill Th Coll. **d** 53 **p** 54. C Bedworth *Cov* 53-56; C New Malden and Coombe *S'wark* 56-59; V Hanley Road St Sav w St Paul *Lon* 59-71; V Plumstead All SS *S'wark* 71-88; rtd 88; Perm to Offic *Chich* from 88. *2 Annington Road, Eastbourne BN22 8NG* Tel (01323) 726850

SMART, Sydney. b 15. TCD BA37 MA43. **d** 39 **p** 40. C Belfast St Mich *Conn* 39-42; P-in-c Belfast St Barn 42-46; I 46-60; I Belfast All SS 60-83; Can Belf Cathl 76-83; rtd 83. *49 Ballylenaghan Park, Belfast BT8 6WP* Tel (028) 9079 9028

SMEATON, William Brian Alexander. b 37. CITC 69. **d** 71 **p** 72. C Belfast St Luke *Conn* 71-81; I Tullyaughnish w Kilmacrennan and Killygarvan *D & R* 81-02; Bp's Dom Chapl 87-02; Can Raphoe Cathl 88-02; Dioc Radio Officer 90-02; rtd 02. *Bearna Ghaoithe, Drumcavney, Trentagh, Letterkenny, Co Donegal, Irish Republic* Tel (0353) (91) 37917 E-mail smeaton@indigo.ie

SMEDLEY, Christopher John. b 62. Trent Poly BSc90. St Jo Coll Nottm MA98. **d** 98 **p** 99. C Cotmanhay *Derby* 98-02; R Wilne and Draycott w Breaston from 02. *The Rectory, 68 Risley Lane, Breaston, Derby DE72 3AU* Tel (01332) 872242 E-mail smedley7@fish.co.uk

SMEDLEY, Paul Mark. b 59. Bris Univ BA80 Lanc Univ MA81. S Dios Minl Tr Scheme 89. **d** 92 **p** 93. NSM Acton St Mary *Lon* from 92. *12 Baldwyn Gardens, London W3 6HH* Tel (020) 8993 5527 *or* 8932 8497 Fax 8932 8315 E-mail paul@planningforum.co.uk

SMEETON (née GRESHAM), Mrs Karen Louise. b 75. Hull Univ LLB96. Ripon Coll Cuddesdon BA01. **d** 02 **p** 03. C Leesfield *Man* from 02. *124 Spring Lane, Lees, Oldham OL4 5BD* Tel 0161-652 6398

SMEETON, Nicholas Guy. b 74. Trin Hall Cam MA99. Ripon Coll Cuddesdon BA03. **d** 04 **p** 05. C Ashton Ch Ch *Man* from 04. *124 Spring Lane, Lees, Oldham OL4 5BD* Tel 0161-652 6398 E-mail nick@smeeton100.freeserve.co.uk

SMEJKAL, Yenda Marcel. b 68. Van Mildert Coll Dur BA97. Coll of Resurr Mirfield 97. **d** 99 **p** 00. C S Shields All SS *Dur* 99-03; TV N Wearside 03-04; P-in-c Sundon *St Alb* from 04. *St Mary's Vicarage, 1 Selina Close, Luton LU3 3AW* Tel (01582) 583076 E-mail yenda.smejkal@virgin.net

SMETHURST, David Alan. b 36. Lon Univ BD60 Man Univ MPhil84. Tyndale Hall Bris 57. **d** 61 **p** 62. C Burnage St Marg *Man* 61-63; P-in-c Whalley Range St Marg 63-65; R Haughton St Mary 65-74; R Ulverston St Mary w H Trin *Carl* 74-87; Dean Hong Kong 87; Dir Acorn Chr Healing Trust Resource Cen 88-93; V Epsom St Martin *Guildf* 93-00; RD Epsom 97-00; rtd 01; Perm to Offic *Carl* from 01. *3 Friars Ground, Kirkby-in-Furness LA17 7YB* Tel (01229) 889725 Fax as telephone E-mail friarsground@yahoo.com

SMETHURST, Gordon James. b 33. CEng FIStructE. N Ord Course 79. **d** 82 **p** 83. NSM Halliwell St Marg *Man* 82-87; NSM Bradshaw 87-88; Asst Chapl Bolton R Infirmary 88-95; Asst Chapl Bolton Gen Hosp 88-95; NSM Westhoughton and Wingates *Man* from 95. *91 Albert Road West, Bolton BL1 5ED* Tel (01204) 842561

SMETHURST, Gordon McIntyre. b 40. Man Univ BA62 BD69. Wells Th Coll 70. **d** 70 **p** 71. C Sandal St Helen *Wakef* 70-73; P-in-c Smawthorpe St Mich 73-75; P-in-c Whitwood 73-75; Hd RE Goole Gr Sch 75-79; S Hunsley Sch Melton 80-00; V Anlaby Common St Mark *York* 00-03; P-in-c Roos and Garton w Tunstall, Grimston and Hilston from 03. *The Rectory, Rectory Road, Roos, Hull HU12 0LD* Tel (01964) 671744

SMETHURST, Leslie Beckett. b 22. CEng. NW Ord Course 72. **d** 75 **p** 76. C Baguley *Man* 75-78; TV Droylsden St Mary 78-81; V Droylsden St Martin 81-86; rtd 87; Perm to Offic *Blackb* from 87. *27 Calf Croft Place, Lytham St Annes FY8 4PU* Tel (01253) 733159

SMILLIE, Linda Barbara. b 46. Oak Hill Th Coll 85. **d** 87 **p** 94. Par Dn Holloway St Mary w St Jas *Lon* 87-88; Par Dn Holloway St Mary Magd 88-90; Chapl W End Stores 90-91; C Holloway St Mark w Em 90-91; Hon C Islington St Mary 92-94; C-in-c Southall Em CD 95-01; rtd 01; Perm to Offic *Ox* 01-04; Hon C Hanger Hill Ascension and W Twyford St Mary *Lon* from 04. *48 Brentmead Gardens, London NW10 7ED* Tel (020) 8838 2542 E-mail rsmillie@freenetname.co.uk

SMITH, Alan. b 38. Tyndale Hall Bris 63. **d** 65 **p** 66. C New Milverton *Cov* 65-68; C Cheadle *Ches* 68-71; V Handforth 71-78; Asst Chapl HM Pris Styal 75-78; Chapl HM Pris Wormwood Scrubs 78-79; Chapl HM Borstal Wellingborough 79-83; R Rushden w Newton Bromswold *Pet* 83-96; Chapl Rushden Sanatorium 83-03; V Wollaston and Strixton *Pet* 96-03; rtd 03. *The Rectory, Main Street, Aldwincle, Kettering NN14 3EP* Tel (01832) 720613 E-mail revalan@fish.co.uk

✠**SMITH, The Rt Revd Alan Gregory Clayton.** b 57. Birm Univ BA78 MA79. Wycliffe Hall Ox 79. **d** 81 **p** 82 **c** 01. C Pudsey St Lawr *Bradf* 81-82; C Pudsey St Lawr and St Paul 82-84; Chapl Lee Abbey 84-90; TV Walsall *Lich* 90-97; Dioc Missr 90-97; Adn Stoke 97-01; Area Bp Shrewsbury from 01. *Athlone House, 68 London Road, Shrewsbury SY2 6PG* Tel (01743) 235867 Fax 243296 E-mail bishop.shrewsbury@lichfield.anglican.org

SMITH, Alan Leonard. b 51. Madeley Coll of Educn CertEd72. Trin Coll Bris DipTh95. **d** 95 **p** 96. C Taunton St Mary *B & W* 95-98; V Taunton Lyngford from 98; RD Taunton from 04. *St Peter's Vicarage, Eastwick Road, Taunton TA2 7HD* Tel (01823) 275085 E-mail alan@rasmith.fsnet.co.uk

SMITH, Alan Pearce Carlton. b 20. Trin Hall Cam BA40 MA45 LLB46. Westcott Ho Cam 76. **d** 78 **p** 79. NSM Cherry Hinton St Jo *Ely* 78-82; P-in-c Madingley and Dry Drayton 82-83; P-in-c Swaffham Bulbeck 84-88; rtd 88. *38 Alpha Road, Cambridge CB4 3DG* Tel (01223) 358124

SMITH, Alan Thomas. b 35. Ridley Hall Cam 82. **d** 84 **p** 85. C Bedworth *Cov* 84-89; R Carlton Colville w Mutford and Rushmere *Nor* 89-97; rtd 97; Perm to Offic *Nor* from 01. *17 St Martins Gardens, New Buckenham, Norwich NR16 2AX* Tel (01953) 860550 Mobile 07811-229493

SMITH, Alec John. b 29. AKC53. **d** 54 **p** 55. C Charlton Kings St Mary *Glouc* 54-56; C-in-c Findon Valley CD *Chich* 56-57; V Viney Hill *Glouc* 57-65; V Churchdown St Jo 65-66; V Bishop's Cannings *Sarum* 66-69; CF 69-88; V Douglas St Thos *S & M* 88-92; rtd 92; Perm to Offic *S & M* from 92. *Church Barn, Lonan Church Road, Laxey, Isle of Man IM4 7JX* Tel (01624) 861325

SMITH, Alexander Montgomery. b 36. TCD BA59 MA64 BD65. TCD Div Sch Div Test60. **d** 61 **p** 62. C Knock *D & D* 61-64; C Belfast St Thos *Conn* 64-66; Lect St Kath Coll Liv 66-69; Sen Lect 69-98; Asst Chapl St Kath Coll *Liv* 66-69; Chapl 69-80; NSM Allerton 80-98; NSM Christchurch *Win* from 98. *11 Magdalen Lane, Christchurch BH23 1PH* Tel (01202) 476103

SMITH, Alfred Lawrence. b 23. FCP84 Open Univ BA72 Birm Univ DipEd73. EMMTC 82. **d** 85 **p** 86. NSM Ashover *Derby* 85-86; NSM Ashover and Brackenfield 86-95; Perm to Offic from 95. *Cotton House Farm, Amber Lane, Ashover, Chesterfield S45 0DZ* Tel (01246) 590265

SMITH, Andrew Clifford. b 67. Ridley Coll Melbourne BMin00. AdDipTh01. **d** 01 **p** 01. C Clayton All SS Australia 01-03; C Gainsborough and Morton *Linc* from 03. *St George's Vicarage, Heapham Road, Gainsborough DN21 1SH* Tel (01427) 612717 E-mail smithbanda@hotmail.com

SMITH, Andrew John. b 37. Leeds Univ BA61. Coll of Resurr Mirfield 61. **d** 63 **p** 64. C W Hackney St Barn *Lon* 63-65; Dir and Chapl Northorpe Hall Trust Yorkshire 65-72; Warden Ox Ho Bethnal Green 72-78; Dir and Chapl The Target Trust 78-86; P-in-c Gt Staughton *Ely* 86-88; Norfolk DTI Educn Adv 88-91; Perm to Offic *Ex* 92-96 and from 98; C Widecombe-in-the-Moor, Leusdon, Princetown etc 96-97; rtd 97. *Mountjoy, Rilla Mill, Callington PL17 7NT*

SMITH, Andrew John. b 46. ACGI Lon Univ BScEng67 DIC PhD71 Trin Coll Ox DipTh74 Bath Univ MEd88 CEng96 MIEE96. Coll of Resurr Mirfield 74. **d** 76 **p** 77. C Swindon New Town *Bris* 76-78; C Southmead 78-79; Perm to Offic 79-91. *15 Dyrham Close, Bristol BS9 4TF* Tel 0117-942 8594

SMITH, Andrew John. b 53. Loughb Univ BTech74. Lon Bible Coll 95 St Jo Coll Nottm MA98. **d** 99 **p** 00. C Hailsham *Chich* 99-02; P-in-c Worc St Mich *Worc* 02-03; TV Almondbury w Farnley Tyas *Wakef* from 03. *150 Fleminghouse Lane, Huddersfield HD5 8UD* Tel (01484) 545085 Fax 08701-322204 E-mail revdajsmith@talk21.com

SMITH, Andrew John. b 59. Birm Univ BSc80 PhD81. WMMTC 89. **d** 91 **p** 92. C Lower Mitton *Worc* 91-92; C Stourport and Wilden 92-95; TV Redditch, The Ridge 95-05; P-in-c Redditch St Steph 02-05; TR Redditch H Trin from 05; Ind Chapl 95-05; Chapl Redditch and Bromsgrove Primary Care Trust 01-05; V W Bromwich All SS *Lich* from 05. *All Saints' Vicarage, 90 Hall Green Road, West Bromwich B71 3LB* Tel 0121-588 3698

SMITH, Andrew Perry Langton. b 56. Sheff City Poly BSc79 Imp Coll Lon MSc80. Trin Coll Bris 89. **d** 91 **p** 92. C Littleover *Derby* 91-95; TV Walsall *Lich* from 95; Ind Chapl Black Country Urban Ind Miss from 95; Hon C Walsall St Paul from 05; Hon C Walsall Pleck and Bescot from 05. *21 Buchanan Road, Walsall WS4 2EW* Tel (01922) 634859 *or* 710407 E-mail aplsmith@fish.co.uk

SMITH, Mrs Anita Elisabeth. b 57. Westhill Coll Birm BEd79. Trin Coll Bris DipHE88 ADPS88. **d** 88 **p** 94. Par Dn Bermondsey St Anne *S'wark* 88-92; Par Dn Brockley Hill St Sav 92-94; C 94-99; Miss Partner CMS Kenya from 99. *CMS, PO Box 40360, Nairobi, Kenya*

SMITH, Ann Veronica. b 38. Doncaster Coll of Educn DipEd. Edin Dioc NSM Course 88. **d** 95 **p** 96. NSM S Queensferry *Edin* 95-99; NSM Falkirk from 99. *16 Mannerston, Linlithgow EH49 7ND* Tel (01506) 834361

SMITH (née JENNINGS), Mrs Anne. b 41. CertEd63 STh. Gilmore Ho 65. **dss** 71 **d** 87 **p** 94. Barton w Peel Green *Man* 71-76; Wythenshawe Wm Temple Ch 76-79; Rochdale 79-83; Chapl Rochdale Colls of FE 79-83; Hillock *Man* 83-88; Dn-in-c 87-88; Chapl Wakef Cathl *Wakef* 88-96; P-in-c Whitwell *Derby* 96-00; V Mansfield Woodhouse *S'well* 00-01; rtd 01; Perm to Offic *Carl* 02-05 and *Blackb* from 05. *The Reader's House, Slaidburn Road, Waddington, Clitheroe BB7 3JQ* Tel (01200) 425472

SMITH, Canon Anthony Charles. b 43. Sarum & Wells Th Coll 90. **d** 92 **p** 93. C Dartford H Trin *Roch* 92-95; V Northfleet 95-05; TR Northfleet and Rosherville from 05; Hon Can Roch Cathl from 05. *The Vicarage, The Hill, Northfleet, Gravesend DA11 9EU* Tel (01474) 566400 E-mail smithab@clara.net

SMITH, Anthony Cyril. b 40. K Coll Lon 65. **d** 69 **p** 70. C Crewkerne *B & W* 69-74; TV Hemel Hempstead *St Alb* 74-76; Asst Chapl K Coll Taunton 76-80; Chapl 80-02; rtd 02; Perm to Offic *B & W* from 03. *1 Castle Street, Stogursey, Bridgwater TA5 1TG* Tel (01278) 733577

SMITH, Anthony James. b 57. ACA Sheff Univ BA. Ridley Hall Cam 83. **d** 86 **p** 87. C Woking St Pet *Guildf* 86-90; C Reigate St Mary *S'wark* 90-94; CMS Kenya 94-00; Finance Team Ldr World Vision UK 00-05. *7 Shuttleworth Grove, Wavendon Gate, Milton Keynes MK7 7RX* Tel (01908) 586156 E-mail anthony.smith@summitskills.org.uk

SMITH, The Ven Anthony Michael Percival. b 24. G&C Coll Cam BA48 MA53. Westcott Ho Cam 48. **d** 50 **p** 51. C Leamington Priors H Trin *Cov* 50-53; Abp's Dom Chapl *Cant* 53-57; Chapl Norwood and Distr Hosp 57-66; V Norwood All SS 57-66; V Yeovil St Jo w Preston Plucknett *B & W* 66-72; RD Merston 68-72; Preb Wells Cathl 70-72; V Addiscombe St Mildred *Cant* 72-79; Adn Maidstone 79-89; Dir of Ords 80-89; Hon Can Cant Cathl 80-89; rtd 89; Perm to Offic *Cant* from 90; *Chich* 89-91 and from 93; RD Rye *Chich* 91-93. *The Garden House, Horseshoe Lane, Beckley, Rye TN31 6RZ* Tel (01797) 260514

SMITH, Antoinette. b 47. NTMTC AdDipTh98 ADPS98. **d** 98 **p** 99. NSM Chigwell and Chigwell Row *Chelmsf* 98-02; TV from 02. *St Winifred's Church House, 115 Manor Road, Chigwell IG7 5PS* Tel (020) 8500 4608 E-mail reverend@tonismith.freeserve.co.uk

SMITH, Miss Audrey. b 47. S'wark Ord Course 89. **d** 92 **p** 94. NSM Croydon St Aug *S'wark* 92-98; P-in-c Redmarley D'Abitot, Bromesberrow w Pauntley etc *Glouc* 98-00. *11 The Crofts, Newent GL18 1SQ* Tel (01531) 828316

SMITH, Mrs Audrey Isabel. b 20. Lon Univ. Qu Coll Birm IDC79. **dss** 84 **d** 87 **p** 94. NSM Kingston All SS w St Jo *S'wark* 87-95; Perm to Offic *Truro* from 95. *31 Copes Gardens, Truro TR1 3SN* Tel (01872) 261813

SMITH, Austin John Denyer. b 40. Worc Coll Ox BA62. Cuddesdon Coll 64. **d** 66 **p** 67. C Shepherd's Bush St Steph w St Thos *Lon* 66-69; C W Drayton 69-72; Chapl Sussex Univ *Chich* 72-79; V Caddington *St Alb* from 79. *The Vicarage, Collings Wells Close, Caddington, Luton LU1 4BG* Tel (01582) 731692 E-mail ajdsmith@lineone.net

SMITH, Mrs Barbara Jean. b 39. Bris Univ BA62 Surrey Univ PGCE93. S'wark Ord Course 83. **dss** 86 **d** 87 **p** 94. Hon Dss Chislehurst St Nic *Roch* 86; Hon Par Dn 87-90; Hon C Wrecclesham *Guildf* 90-94; Hon C Herriard w Winslade and Long Sutton etc *Win* 94-99; P-in-c 99-03; P-in-c Newnham w Nately Scures w Mapledurwell etc 99-03; rtd 03. *Hill Cottage, 282 Lovedean Lane, Waterlooville PO8 9RY* Tel (023) 9259 4426 E-mail barbarajsmith@btopenworld.com

SMITH, Mrs Barbara Mary. b 47. Doncaster Coll of Educn CertEd68. St Jo Coll Dur 82. **dss** 85 **d** 87 **p** 94. Beverley St Nic *York* 85-87; Par Dn 87; NSM S'wark H Trin w St Matt *S'wark* 89-90; Ind Chapl Teesside *York* 91-95; Hon C Middlesbrough St Chad 94-95; Perm to Offic *St Alb* from 96; Locum Chapl Anglia Poly Univ *Ely* 96-98; TV Linton 00-04; rtd 04. *26 Oak Close, Hexham NE46 2RE*

SMITH, Canon Barry. b 41. Univ of Wales (Lamp) BA62 Fitzw Ho Cam BA64 MA68 Man Univ MPhil91. Ridley Hall Cam. **d** 65 **p** 66. C Rhyl w St Ann *St As* 65-70; Chapl Scargill Ho 70-72; C Flint *St As* 72-74; V Broughton 74-86; Dioc Ecum Officer 82-86; RD Wrexham 82-86; R Wrexham 86-95; Can Cursal St As Cathl 86-95; Chan 95; Perm to Offic *S'wark* 97-02. *1 Acorn Keep, Rowhills, Farnham GU9 9BL* Tel (01252) 322111

SMITH, Barry Roy. b 46. STETS. **d** 00 **p** 04. NSM Blendworth w Chalton w Idsworth *Portsm* 00-05; Asst Chapl Portsm Hosps NHS Trust 03-05; Team Chapl from 05. *7A Durley Avenue, Waterlooville PO8 8XA* Tel (023) 9226 5620

SMITH, Beverley Anne. b 56. Univ of Wales Coll of Medicine MSc97 RN78 RM80 RHV87 Univ of Wales PGCE00. St Mich Coll Llan. **d** 05. NSM Whitchurch *Llan* from 05. *3 Solva Avenue, Cardiff CF14 0NP* Tel (029) 2076 1746 Mobile 07841-707525 E-mail beverley.anne@btinternet.com

SMITH, The Ven Brian. b 44. Westmr Coll Ox MTh95. Sarum & Wells Th Coll 71. **d** 74 **p** 75. C Pennywell St Thos and Grindon St Oswald CD *Dur* 74-77; Chapl RAF 77-95; P-in-c Keswick St Jo *Carl* 95-96; V 96-05; RD Derwent 98-05; Hon Can Carl Cathl 99-05; Adn Man *S & M* from 05; V Douglas St Geo from 05. *St George's Vicarage, 16 Devonshire Road, Douglas, Isle of Man IM2 3RB* Tel (01624) 675430 Fax 616136 E-mail archd-sodor@mcb.net

✠**SMITH, The Rt Revd Brian Arthur.** b 43. Edin Univ MA66 Fitzw Coll Cam BA68 MA72 Jes Coll Cam MLitt73. Westcott Ho Cam 66. **d** 72 **p** 73 **c** 93. Tutor and Lib Cuddesdon Coll 72-75; Dir of Studies 75-78; Sen Tutor Ripon Coll Cuddesdon

78-79; C Cuddesdon *Ox* 76-79; Dir Tr *Wakef* 79-87; P-in-c Halifax St Jo 79-85; Hon Can Wakef Cathl 81-87; Adn Craven *Bradf* 87-93; Suff Bp Tonbridge *Roch* 93-01; Hon Can Roch Cathl 93-01; Bp Edin from 01. *3 Eglinton Crescent, Edinburgh EH12 5DH* or *Bishop's Office, 21A Grosvenor Crescent, Edinburgh EH12 5EL* Tel 0131-226 5099 *or* 538 7044 Fax 538 7088 E-mail bishop@edinburgh.anglican.org

SMITH, Brian Godfrey. b 24. Chich Th Coll 63. **d** 65 **p** 66. C Newc H Cross *Newc* 65-68; C Redcar *York* 68-72; C Kirkleatham 68-72; V Wortley de Leeds *Ripon* 72-76; Chapl Costa del Sol E *Eur* 76-82; Chapl Estoril 82-84; V Worfield *Heref* 84-89; rtd 89; Perm to Offic *Heref* from 92. *2 Pineway, Lodge Farm, Bridgnorth WV15 5DT* Tel (01746) 764088

SMITH, Brian Michael. b 42. Kelham Th Coll 69. **d** 69 **p** 70. C Somers Town *Lon* 70-74; C Stamford Hill St Jo 74-75; C Stamford Hill St Bart 75-84; P-in-c Edmonton St Pet w St Martin 84-92; V from 92. *The Vicarage, St Peter's Road, London N9 8JP* Tel (020) 8807 2974 Fax 8887 0153 E-mail vicar@stpeteredmonton.freeserve.co.uk

SMITH, Canon Bridget Mary. b 46. Bp Otter Coll CertEd67 S Dios Minl Tr Scheme 88. **d** 91 **p** 94. C Pet H Spirit Bretton *Pet* 91-95; P-in-c Silverstone and Abthorpe w Slapton 95-03; R Silverstone and Abthorpe w Slapton etc from 03; Warden of Past Assts 00-06; Can Pet Cathl from 01. *The Vicarage, High Street, Silverstone, Towcester NN12 8US* Tel (01327) 857996 E-mail quickvic@lineone.net

SMITH, Mrs Carol. b 55. SEITE 01. **d** 04 **p** 05. C Epping Distr *Chelmsf* from 04. *76 The Plain, Epping CM16 6TW* Tel (01992) 560070 E-mail carolrev@gotadsl.co.uk

SMITH, Mrs Catherine Eleanor Louise. b 52. St Alb and Ox Min Course 99. **d** 02 **p** 03. NSM Denham *Ox* 02-05; NSM Penn Street from 05; Chapl Heatherwood and Wexham Park Hosp NHS Trust from 05. *55 Penn Road, Beaconsfield HP9 2LW* Tel and fax (01494) 670389

SMITH, Charles Henry Neville. b 31. Nottm Univ BA52 MA65. Sarum Th Coll 55. **d** 57 **p** 58. C Thirsk w S Kilvington *York* 57-60; C Linthorpe 60-61; V Danby 61-66; Chapl United Cam Hosps 66-76; Chapl Lanc Moor Hosp 76-84; Hon Can Blackb Cathl *Blackb* 81-84; Asst Sec Gen Syn Hosp Chapl Coun 84-88; Hon C Lee St Marg *S'wark* 84-88; Chapl Guy's Hosp Lon 88-96; rtd 96; Hon Chapl S'wark Cathl *S'wark* from 96. *57 Belmont Park, London SE13 5BW* Tel (020) 8318 9993

SMITH, Charles Rycroft (Ryc). b 46. Sarum & Wells Th Coll 76. **d** 78 **p** 79. C Heref St Martin *Heref* 78-81; C Southampton Maybush St Pet *Win* 81-83; R The Candover Valley 83-99; RD Alresford 90-99; P-in-c Guernsey St Andr 99-01; R from 01; Vice-Dean Guernsey from 02. *The Rectory, rue des Morts, St Andrews, Guernsey GY6 8XN* Tel and fax (01481) 238568 E-mail ryc@starectory.fsnet.co.uk

SMITH, Charles Septimus. b 23. Bris & Glouc Tr Course. **d** 79 **p** 80. NSM Bris St Agnes and St Simon w St Werburgh *Bris* 79-86; C 86-87; C Bris St Paul's 87-89; rtd 89. *2432 Jarvis Street West, Mississauga ON, Canada, L5C 2P6*

SMITH, Christine. b 46. **d** 97 **p** 98. C Salterhebble All SS *Wakef* 97-01; P-in-c Siddal from 01. *St Mark's Vicarage, 15 Whitegate Road, Siddal, Halifax HX3 9AD* Tel (01422) 844511

SMITH, Christine Lydia. *See* CARTER, Mrs Christine Lydia

SMITH, Christopher Blake Walters. b 63. Univ of Wales (Cardiff) BMus84 BD88 LLM95. St Mich Coll Llan 85. **d** 88 **p** 89. C Aberdare *Llan* 88-93; V Tongwynlais 93-00; Dioc Dir Post-Ord Tr from 95; Dom Chapl Bp Llan and Warden of Ords from 01. *Pendinas, The Cathedral Green, Llandaff, Cardiff CF5 2EB* Tel and fax (029) 2056 2649 E-mail cbw@csmith20.freeserve.co.uk

SMITH, Canon Christopher Francis. b 46. K Coll Lon BD68 AKC68. St Aug Coll Cant 69. **d** 70 **p** 71. C Norwood All SS *Cant* 70-72; Asst Chapl Marlborough Coll 72-76; C Deal St Leon w Sholden *Cant* 77-81; P-in-c Benenden 81-83; V from 83; P-in-c Sandhurst w Newenden from 04; Hon Can Cant Cathl from 03; AD Tenterden from 05; Chapl Benenden Sch 81-92; Chapl Benenden Hosp from 91. *The Vicarage, The Green, Benenden, Cranbrook TN17 4DL* Tel (01580) 240658 E-mail christopherfrancissmith@yahoo.co.uk

SMITH, Christopher James. b 72. Newc Univ BSc94. Wycliffe Hall Ox BTh01. **d** 02 **p** 03. C Cambridge H Trin *Ely* 02-04; Assoc R Zion Ch USA from 04. *Zion Church, 5167 Main Street, Manchester Center, VT 05255, USA* Tel (001) (802) 362 1987 E-mail revsmith@ntlworld.com

SMITH, Christopher Matthew. b 67. New Coll Ox BA89 MA93 Homerton Coll Cam PGCE90. St Steph Ho Ox BA94. **d** 95 **p** 96. C Wantage *Ox* 95-99; Dom Chapl to Bp Horsham *Chich* 99-01; V Beckenham St Mich w St Aug *Roch* from 01. *St Michael's Vicarage, 120 Birkbeck Road, Beckenham BR3 4SS* Tel (020) 8778 6569

SMITH, Canon Christopher Milne. b 44. Selw Coll Cam BA66. Cuddesdon Coll 67. **d** 69 **p** 70. C Liv Our Lady and St Nic *Liv* 69-74; TV Kirkby 74-81; R Walton St Mary 81-91; Can Res Sheff Cathl *Sheff* 91-02; V Doncaster St Geo from 02; Bp's Adv on the Paranormal from 97; Hon Can Sheff Cathl from 03; Chapl to The Queen from 04. *The Vicarage, 98 Thorne Road, Doncaster DN2 5BJ* Tel (01302) 368796 *or* 323748

SMITH, Clarice Mary. b 25. St Mich Coll Llan 76. **dss** 77 **d** 80. Llangiwg *S & B* 77-80; C Llwynderw 80-84; C Newton St Pet 84-88; rtd 88. *33 Sherringham Drive, Newton, Swansea SA3 4UG* Tel (01792) 367984

SMITH, Clifford. b 31. Lon Univ DipTh60. St Aid Birkenhead 59. **d** 61 **p** 62. C Limehouse St Anne *Lon* 61-63; C Ashtead *Guildf* 63-66; R Bromley All Hallows *Lon* 66-76; V Hillsborough and Wadsley Bridge *Sheff* 76-89; V Stainforth 89-96; rtd 96; Hon C Hurst *Ox* from 97. *33 King Street Lane, Winnersh, Wokingham RG41 5AX* Tel 0118-978 9453

SMITH, Clive Leslie. b 50. Leeds Univ BA72 MA03 Ch Coll Liv PGCE73. Coll of Resurr Mirfield 75. **d** 77 **p** 78. C Goldington *St Alb* 77-81; C Cheshunt 81-84; V Watford St Pet 84-89; Chapl Leavesden Hosp Abbots Langley 89-94; Chapl St Alb and Hemel Hempstead NHS Trust 94-00; Chapl W Herts Hosps NHS Trust 00-01; Sen Chapl Doncaster and Bassetlaw Hosps NHS Trust from 01; Perm to Offic *S'well* from 02. *Chaplaincy Department, Doncaster Royal Infirmary, Armthorpe Road, Doncaster DN2 5LT* Tel (01302) 381484 *or* 881351 E-mail chaplaincy.department@dbh.nhs.uk

SMITH, Colin. b 39. MBE. Open Univ BA80 LRSC65 CChem88 FRSC88. NEOC 94. **d** 97 **p** 98. NSM Jesmond H Trin *Newc* from 97; NSM Newc St Barn and St Jude from 97. *1 Cayton Grove, Newcastle upon Tyne NE5 1HL* Tel 0191-267 9519 E-mail colinandevelyn@btopenworld.com

SMITH, Colin Graham. b 59. Hatf Poly BA82 CQSW82. Trin Coll Bris BA88. **d** 88 **p** 89. C Bermondsey St Jas w Ch Ch *S'wark* 88-92; V Brockley Hill St Sav 92-99; Miss Partner CMS Kenya from 99. *CMS, PO Box 40360, Nairobi, Kenya*

SMITH, Colin Richard. b 53. Liv Poly BA80 Liv Univ MTD83. Oak Hill Th Coll 84. **d** 86 **p** 87. C Ormskirk *Liv* 86-89; V Wigan St Cath 89-94; C St Helens St Helen 94-99; TV from 99. *211A Dentons Green Lane, St Helens WA10 6RU* Tel (01744) 453681

SMITH, Mrs Corinne Anne. b 52. St Andr Univ MTh91. St Alb and Ox Min Course 95. **d** 97. C Abingdon *Ox* 97-02; Chapl Pemb Coll Ox 02-03; Chapl Ox Radcliffe Hosps NHS Trust from 03. *The John Radcliffe Hospital, Headley Way, Headington, Oxford OX3 9DU* Tel (01865) 741166 *or* 226090 E-mail corinne.smith@vizzavi.net

SMITH, Craig Philip. b 61. Huddersfield Poly HND82 Sheff City Poly BA86. St Jo Coll Nottm Dip Th Studies 92 DipMM93. **d** 93 **p** 94. C Bramley and Ravenfield *Sheff* 93-95; C Bramley and Ravenfield w Hooton Roberts etc 95-97; C Rainham w Wennington *Chelmsf* 97-00; TV Gainsborough and Morton *Linc* 00-03; V Catshill and Dodford *Worc* from 03. *The Vicarage, 403 Stourbridge Road, Catshill, Bromsgrove B61 9LG* Tel (01527) 579619 E-mail catshill.vicarage@btopenworld.com

SMITH, Darren John Anthony. b 62. Nottm Univ BCombStuds84. Linc Th Coll 84. **d** 86 **p** 87. C Leic Ascension *Leic* 86-90; C Curdworth w Castle Vale *Birm* 90; C Castle Vale St Cuth 90-91; C Kingstanding St Luke 91-92; P-in-c 92-93; V from 93; P-in-c Kingstanding St Mark 01-02. *St Luke's Clergy House, 49 Caversham Road, Kingstanding, Birmingham B44 0LW* Tel 0121-354 3281 Fax 680 4919

SMITH, David. *See* SMITH, Terence David

SMITH, David Charles Stuart. CertEd53 Wheaton Coll Illinois MA74. Oak Hill Th Coll 61. **d** 61 **p** 62. Australia 61-72, 75-89 and from 90; Wellington Coll Berks 72-75; C Luton Lewsey St Hugh *St Alb* 90; rtd 96. *Address temp unknown* E-mail sgejmsmith@bigpond.com.au

SMITH, David Earling. b 35. AKC60. **d** 61 **p** 62. C Knebworth *St Alb* 61-63; C Chipping Barnet 64-66; C S Ormsby w Ketsby, Calceby and Driby *Linc* 66-69; R Claxby w Normanby-le-Wold 69-74; R Nettleton 69-74; R S Kelsey 69-74; R N Owersby w Thornton le Moor 69-74; R Stainton-le-Vale w Kirmond le Mire 69-74; V Ancaster 74-79; Warden and Chapl St Anne Bedehouses Linc 79-89; C Linc Minster Gp 79-89; rtd 89; Perm to Offic *Linc* 90-02. *17 Egerton Road, Lincoln LN2 4PJ* Tel (01522) 510336 E-mail david@limani17.fsnet.co.uk

✠**SMITH, The Rt Revd David James.** b 35. AKC58 FKC99. **d** 59 **p** 60 **c** 87. C Gosforth All SS *Newc* 59-62; C Newc St Fran 62-64; C Longbenton St Bart 64-68; V Longhirst 68-75; V Monkseaton St Mary 75-82; RD Tynemouth 80-82; Hon Can Newc Cathl 81-87; Adn Lindisfarne 81-87; V Felton 82-83; Suff Bp Maidstone *Cant* 87-92; Bp HM Forces 90-92; Bp Bradf 92-02; rtd 02; Hon Asst Bp York from 02; Hon Asst Bp Eur from 02. *34 Cedar Glade, Dunnington, York YO19 5QZ* Tel (01904) 481225 E-mail david@djmhs.force9.co.uk

SMITH, Canon David John. b 32. Goldsmiths' Coll Lon BA76 LSE MSc79. Lon Coll of Div 68. **d** 70 **p** 71. C Clerkenwell St Jas and St Jo w St Pet *Lon* 70-73; P-in-c Penge St Paul *Roch* 74-78; V 78-89; RD Beckenham 86-89; Chapl Bromley and Sheppard's Colls 90-97; Perm to Offic *S'wark* 90-97; Dioc Clergy Widows and Retirement Officer *Roch* 90-97; Hon Can Roch Cathl 95-97; rtd 98; Perm to Offic *St Alb* from 98 and *Lon* from 99. *13 Park Way, Rickmansworth WD3 7AU* Tel (01923) 775963

SMITH, David John Parker. *See* EVANS, David Victor

SMITH, David Leonard. b 37. St Alb Minl Tr Scheme 84. **d** 91 **p** 92. NSM Potton w Sutton and Cockayne Hatley *St Alb* from 91. *11 Judith Gardens, Potton, Sandy SG19 2RJ* Tel (01767) 260583 E-mail davidlsmith@hotmail.com

SMITH, David Robert. b 54. Southn Univ BSc75 Loughb Univ MSc86 CEng84 MRAeS84. WEMTC 02. **d** 05. C Matson *Glouc* from 05. *58 Haycroft Drive, Matson, Gloucester GL4 6XX* Tel (01452) 311041 E-mail draesmith@btinternet.com

SMITH, David Roland Mark. b 46. Dur Univ BA68 ACP78 FRSA87 SSC88. Edin Th Coll 68. **d** 70 **p** 71. C Southwick St Columba *Dur* 70-74 and 81-82; Asst Chapl Univ of Wales (Cardiff) *Llan* 74-76; Hon C E Bris 76-78; Hon C Filton 78-79; Min Leam Lane CD *Dur* 80-81; Co-ord Chapl Service Sunderland Poly 81-86; Chapl Birm Univ *Birm* 86-95; Chapl Heathrow Airport *Lon* 95-00; rtd 00; Chapl Wolv Airport *Lich* from 00; Perm to Offic *Heref*, *Worc* from 00 and *Birm* from 02. *20 Carder Drive, Brierley Hill DY5 3SR* Tel (01384) 352045 Mobile 07778-876695 E-mail revdrmsmith@aol.com

SMITH, David Sidney Mark. b 54. Bris Univ BEd76. Ripon Coll Cuddesdon 77. **d** 79 **p** 80. C Wotton-under-Edge w Ozleworth and N Nibley *Glouc* 79-83; TV Malvern Link w Cowleigh *Worc* 83-93; Relig Affairs Producer BBC Heref and Worc 90-93; V Clevedon St Jo *B & W* from 93. *St John's Vicarage, 1 St John's Road, Clevedon BS21 7TG* Tel (01275) 872410 Fax 544005 E-mail dsms@blueyonder.co.uk

SMITH, David Stanley. b 41. Ox NSM Course. **d** 84 **p** 85. NSM Burghfield *Ox* 84-86; NSM Stratfield Mortimer 86-88; NSM Mortimer W End w Padworth 86-88; C St Breoke and Egloshayle *Truro* 88-93; V Penwerris from 93. *Penwerris Vicarage, 12 Stratton Terrace, Falmouth TR11 2SY* Tel (01326) 314263

SMITH, David Watson. b 31. Sarum Th Coll 63. **d** 65 **p** 66. C W Wimbledon Ch Ch *S'wark* 65-69; C Cheam 69-74; V Haslington *Ches* 74-83; V Haslington w Crewe Green 83-87; V Daresbury 87-98; rtd 98; Perm to Offic *Pet* from 98. *4 Wakefield Way, Nether Heyford, Northampton NN7 3LU* Tel (01327) 341561 E-mail rev.dw.smith@freeuk.com

SMITH, Canon David William. b 46. Sarum Th Coll 70. **d** 72 **p** 73. C Stokesley *York* 72-75; C Edin St Mich and All SS *Edin* 75-77; R Galashiels 77-85; R Yarm *York* 85-00; TR Whitby w Aislaby and Ruswarp from 00; P-in-c Fylingdales and Hawsker cum Stainsacre from 03; Can and Preb York Minster from 05. *The Rectory, Chubb Hill Road, Whitby YO21 1JP* Tel (01947) 602590

SMITH, Deborah Jane. b 62. Newc Poly BA83. STETS 00. **d** 03 **p** 04. C Dorchester *Sarum* from 03. *10 Treves Road, Dorchester DT1 2HD* Tel (01305) 260552 Mobile 07870-560354 E-mail smithsmania@btopenworld.com

SMITH, Mrs Deborah Louise. b 56. St Jo Coll Nottm Dip Counselling 97. WEMTC 02 N Ord Course 03. **d** 05. C Honley *Wakef* from 05; Chapl HM Pris and YOI New Hall from 05. *150 Fleminghouse Lane, Huddersfield HD5 8UD* Tel (01484) 545085 E-mail revdajsmith@talk21.com

SMITH, Mrs Decia Jane. b 47. ALAM66. WMMTC 92. **d** 95 **p** 96. C Edgbaston St Germain *Birm* 95-99; P-in-c Abbots Leigh w Leigh Woods *Bris* from 00. *The Vicarage, 51 Church Road, Abbots Leigh, Bristol BS8 3QU* Tel (01275) 373996 Fax 371799 E-mail revdecia@fish.co.uk

SMITH, Declan. *See* SMITH, Godfrey Declan Burfield

SMITH, Denis Richard. b 53. MA. St Jo Coll Nottm 83. **d** 85 **p** 86. C Hersham *Guildf* 85-88; C Thatcham *Ox* 88-91; V Shefford *St Alb* 91-02; P-in-c Tilehurst St Cath *Ox* from 02. *The Vicarage, Wittenham Avenue, Tilehurst, Reading RG31 5LN* Tel 0118-942 7786 E-mail revdenissmith@hotmail.com

SMITH, Dennis Austin. b 50. Lanc Univ BA71 Liv Univ PGCE72. NW Ord Course 74. **d** 77 **p** 78. NSM Seaforth *Liv* 77-83; NSM Gt Crosby St Faith 77-83; Hon C 83-98; Hon C Gt Crosby St Faith and Waterloo Park St Mary from 98; Asst Chapl Merchant Taylors' Sch Crosby 79-83; Chapl from 83. *16 Fir Road, Liverpool L22 4QL* Tel 0151-928 5065

SMITH, Derek Arthur. b 38. Chich Th Coll 63. **d** 66 **p** 67. C Cheadle *Lich* 66-70; C Blakenall Heath 70-72; P-in-c 76-77; TR 77-86; V Knutton 72-76; R Lich St Mary w St Mich 86-96; P-in-c Wall 90-96; R Lich St Mich w St Mary and Wall 96-98; V W Bromwich St Andr w Ch Ch 98-02; rtd 02. *20 Tiverton Drive, West Bromwich B71 1DA* Tel 0121-525 0260

SMITH, Derek Arthur Byott. b 26. Hull Univ MA89. S Dios Minl Tr Scheme 78. **d** 81 **p** 82. NSM Wimborne Minster and Holt *Sarum* 81-83; C Northampton St Alb *Pet* 83-85; Ind Chapl *York* 85-89; P-in-c Kingston upon Hull St Mary 88-89; P-in-c Newington w Dairycoates 89-93; rtd 93; Perm to Offic *York* from 93. *107 Cardigan Road, Bridlington YO15 3LP* Tel (01262) 678852

SMITH, Derek Arthur Douglas. b 26. Dur Univ BA51. Qu Coll Birm 58. **d** 60 **p** 61. C Evesham *Worc* 60-63; C Bollington St Jo *Ches* 63-68; V Thelwall 68-78; V Whitegate w Lt Budworth 78-92; rtd 92; Perm to Offic *Ches* from 92. *10 Newtons Crescent, Winterley, Sandbach CW11 9NS* Tel (01270) 589130

SMITH, Canon Derek Graham. b 52. St Cath Coll Cam BA74 MA77. Westcott Ho Cam 74. **d** 76 **p** 77. C Weymouth H Trin *Sarum* 76-79; P-in-c Bradpole 79; TV Bridport 79-84; R Monkton Farleigh, S Wraxall and Winsley 84-98; TR Melksham from 98; RD Bradford from 01; Chapl Wilts and Swindon Healthcare NHS Trust 00-02; Can and Preb Sarum Cathl *Sarum* from 03. *The Rectory, Canon Square, Melksham SN12 6LX* Tel (01225) 703262

SMITH, Diana Linnet. b 47. Sheff Univ BSc69 Goldsmiths' Coll Lon MA83 Trin Coll Carmarthen PhD99. EAMTC 02. **d** 03 **p** 04. C Oundle w Ashton and Benefield w Glapthorn *Pet* from 03. *The Rectory, Main Street, Aldwincle, Kettering NN14 3EP* Tel (01832) 720613 E-mail sdiana@fish.co.uk

SMITH, Donald Edgar. b 56. Oak Hill Th Coll 89. **d** 91 **p** 92. C Holloway St Mark w Em *Lon* 91-92; C Tollington 92-95; TV W Ealing St Jo w St Jas from 95. *23A Culmington Road, London W13 9NJ* Tel (020) 8566 3459 Fax 8566 3507 E-mail donthevic@btinternet.com

SMITH, The Ven Donald John. b 26. Univ of Wales LLM. Clifton Th Coll 50. **d** 53 **p** 54. C Edgware *Lon* 53-56; C Ipswich St Marg *St E* 56-58; V Hornsey Rise St Mary *Lon* 58-62; R Whitton and Thurleston w Akenham *St E* 62-75; Hon Can St E Cathl 73-91; Adn Suffolk 75-84; R The Rickinghalls 75-76; P-in-c Redgrave w Botesdale 75-76; R Redgrave cum Botesdale w Rickinghall 76-78; Adn Sudbury 84-91; rtd 91; Perm to Offic *Cov*, *Ox*, *St E* and *Worc* from 91; *Glouc* 91-96 and from 03. *St Peter's Cottage, Stretton-on-Fosse, Moreton-in-Marsh GL56 9SE* Tel (01608) 662790

✠**SMITH, The Rt Revd Donald Westwood.** b 28. Edin Th Coll 54 St D Coll Lamp 50. **d** 54 **p** 55 **c** 90. Asst Dioc Supernumerary *Ab* 54-55; Chapl St Andr Cathl 55-56; Canada 56-57; R Longside *Ab* 57-65; Mauritius 65-85; P-in-c St Geo-in-the-East St Mary *Lon* 85-86; Seychelles 86-87; Madagascar 87-99; Bp Toamasina 90-99. *Avenue Cote d'Emeraude, Morcellement Raffray, Albion, Mauritius* Tel (00230) 238 5966 E-mail tighdhonuil@hotmail.com

SMITH, Douglas David Frederick. b 28. Lon Univ BD53. ALCD53. **d** 53 **p** 54. C Fulham Ch Ch *Lon* 53-57; C Heatherlands St Jo *Sarum* 57-61; V Hyson Green *S'well* 61-66; Lic to Offic *York* 66-69; NE Area Sec CPAS 66-69; R Higher Openshaw *Man* 69-80; R Church w Chapel Brampton *Pet* 80-81; R Church and Chapel Brampton w Harlestone 81-86; Perm to Offic *Ox* from 86; rtd 89. *1 Maybush Walk, Olney MK46 5NA* Tel (01234) 712256

SMITH, Ms Elizabeth. b 46. Liv Inst of Educn CertEd67 Heythrop Coll Lon BD76 Lon Univ MPhil84. Westcott Ho Cam CTM92. **d** 92 **p** 94. Par Dn Moulsham St Jo *Chelmsf* 92-94; C 94-96; V Westcliff St Andr 96-00; V Sedgley St Mary *Worc* from 00. *St Mary's Vicarage, St Mary's Close, Dudley DY3 1LD* Tel (01902) 883310

SMITH (née HOWSE), Mrs Elizabeth Ann. b 39. Bath Academy of Art CertEd60 Warwick Univ BEd85. WMMTC 91. **d** 94 **p** 95. C Fletchamstead *Cov* 94-97; P-in-c Leamington Hastings and Birdingbury 97-03; P-in-c Grandborough w Willoughby and Flecknoe 97-03; V Leam Valley 03-05; rtd 05. *9 David Road, Rugby CV22 7PX* Tel (01788) 522584 E-mail beth_smith@leam5.freeserve.co.uk

SMITH, Miss Elizabeth Jane. b 50. Birm Univ BA72 DCG73. Trin Coll Bris 88. **d** 90 **p** 95. C Lowestoft and Kirkley *Nor* 90-94; TV Rugby St Andr *Cov* 94-01; C Shepton Mallet w Doulting *B & W* 01-03; R from 03; Chapl Mendip Primary Care Trust from 01. *23 Compton Road, Shepton Mallet BA4 5QR* Tel (01749) 346184 E-mail liz@revsmith.fsnet.co.uk

SMITH, Elizabeth Marion. b 52. ACA76 FCA82. Carl Dioc Tr Inst 91. **d** 94 **p** 95. C Appleby *Carl* 94-98; P-in-c Hesket-in-the-Forest and Armathwaite 98-04; P-in-c Skelton and Hutton-in-the-Forest w Ivegill 98-04; R Inglewood Gp from 04. *St Mary's Vicarage, High Hesket, Carlisle CA4 0HU* Tel (01697) 473320 Fax 473167 E-mail revdesmith@hotmail.com

SMITH, Eric Frederick. b 19. Lon Univ BA40 BD42. ALCD42. **d** 42 **p** 43. C Talbot Village *Sarum* 42-44; C S'wark St Jude *S'wark* 44-48; P-in-c Mottingham St Edward LD 48-56; V Lee Gd Shep w St Pet 56-67; Sub-Dean Lewisham 61-67; R Long Ditton 67-81; V Deal St Geo *Cant* 81-85; RD Sandwich 82-85; rtd 85; Perm to Offic *Cant* from 85; Chapl Cant Sch of Min 88-94. *Beach Cottage, 179 Beach Street, Deal CT14 6LE* Tel (01304) 367648

SMITH, Eustace. b 20. St Pet Hall Ox BA43 MA46. Wycliffe Hall Ox 43. **d** 46 **p** 46. C Tiverton St Pet *Ex* 46-47; C Lenton *S'well* 47-49; C Aston SS Pet and Paul *Birm* 49-53; V Bermondsey St Anne *S'wark* 53-59; V Buckminster w Sewstern *Leic* 59-74; V Buckminster w Sewstern, Sproxton and Coston 74-82; R Algarkirk *Linc* 82-88; V Fosdyke 82-88; rtd 89; Perm to Offic *Leic* 89-00. *32 Wordsworth Way, Measham, Swadlincote DE12 7ER* Tel (01530) 273765

SMITH (née DAVIS), Felicity Ann. b 40. Bris Univ MB, ChB63. Qu Coll Birm 83. **dss** 86 **d** 87 **p** 94. NSM Dioc Bd for Soc Resp *Cov* 86-96; NSM Leamington Spa H Trin and Old Milverton from 96. *14 Oakwood Grove, Warwick CV34 5TD* Tel (01926) 492452

SMITH, Francis Armand. b 10. Sarum Th Coll 59. **d** 61 **p** 62. C Marlborough *Sarum* 61-63; V Upavon w Rushall 63-76; rtd 76; Perm to Offic *S'wark* 76-93; *St Alb* 77-93; *Chich* 78-93. *15 High Street, Cowden, Edenbridge TN8 7JQ* Tel (01342) 850484

SMITH, Francis Christian Lynford. b 36. Padgate Coll of Educn TCert59 Lon Univ DipRE66. Cuddesdon Coll 72. **d** 74 **p** 75. C Catford St Laur *S'wark* 74-79; Mauritius 79-80; Chapl Dulwich Coll 81-91; Chapl St Mich Univ Sch Victoria Canada from 91; rtd 01. *Apartment 403, 2626 Blackwood Street, Victoria BC, Canada, V8T 3W3* Tel (001) (250) 598 3459 E-mail smudge4147@hotmail.com

SMITH, Francis James Prall. b 22. Nor Ord Course 73. **d** 76 **p** 77. NSM Gunthorpe w Bale *Nor* 76-82; NSM Friston *St E* 82-86; NSM Knodishall w Buxlow 82-86; NSM Aldringham w Thorpe, Knodishall w Buxlow etc 86-89; rtd 89; Perm to Offic *St E* from 90. *6 Bluebell Way, Worlingham, Beccles NR34 7BT* Tel (01502) 711528

SMITH, Francis Malcolm. b 44. Open Univ BA82 FCMI ACIB69. EAMTC 90. **d** 93 **p** 94. NSM Prittlewell *Chelmsf* from 93. *14 St James Avenue, Southend-on-Sea SS1 3LH* Tel (01702) 586680 Fax 291166

SMITH, Canon Frank. b 39. Nottm Univ CertEd65 Open Univ BA76. Paton Congr Coll Nottm 61 Cuddesdon Coll 69. **d** 69 **p** 70. C Davyhulme St Mary *Man* 69-72; PC Peak Forest and Wormhill *Derby* 72-78; R W Hallam and Mapperley 78-85; V Henleaze *Bris* 85-01; RD Clifton 93-99; Hon Can Bris Cathl 99-01; rtd 01; Perm to Offic *Derby* from 01. *4 Hall Court, The Village, West Hallam, Ilkeston DE7 6GS* Tel 0115-944 3474

SMITH, Mrs Gabrielle Lynette Claire. b 49. St Aid Coll Dur BA70 ARCM73. St Alb and Ox Min Course 95. **d** 98 **p** 99. NSM Gt Marlow w Marlow Bottom, Lt Marlow and Bisham *Ox* from 98. *29 Bovingdon Heights, Marlow SL7 2JR* Tel (01628) 482923

SMITH (née SAMPSON), Ms Gail Sampson. b 49. Towson State Univ (USA) BA85. Virginia Th Sem MDiv93. **d** 93 **p** 94. Assoc R Ellicott City St Jo USA 93-99; Perm to Offic *S'wark* 00-01; Hon C Kew St Phil and All SS w St Luke 01-02; The Netherlands from 02. *Zonnembloemlaan 30, 2111 ZH Aerdenhout, The Netherlands* E-mail ukrevgss@aol.com

SMITH, Gary Russell. b 56. Southn Univ BTh94. Cuddesdon Coll 94. **d** 96 **p** 97. C Southampton Maybush St Pet *Win* 96-00. *Address temp unknown*

SMITH, Gavin Craig. b 71. Ridley Hall Cam 02. **d** 04 **p** 05. C Heatons *Man* from 04. *St Paul's Rectory, 42 Lea Road, Stockport SK4 4JU* Tel 0161-283 3822 Mobile 07919-354796 E-mail gavinsmith1971@hotmail.com

SMITH, Geoffrey. *See* SMITH, Richard Geoffrey

SMITH, Geoffrey. b 45. Bernard Gilpin Soc Dur 65 Sarum Th Coll 66. **d** 69 **p** 70. C Hatfield *Sheff* 69-71; C Bolton St Pet *Man* 71-74; V Lt Hulton 74-78; P-in-c Newc St Andr *Newc* 78-87; Soc Resp Adv 78-87; Hon Can Newc Cathl 84-87; Dir Cen for Applied Chr Studies 87-91; Team Ldr Home Office Birm Drug Prevention Unit 91-93; Public Preacher *Birm* 87-93; C Brampton and Farlam and Castle Carrock w Cumrew *Carl* 93-96; ACUPA Link Officer 94-96; Can Res Bradf Cathl *Bradf* 96-00; Nat Dir Toc H from 00; Perm to Offic *Ox* 00-02; Hon C Biddenham *St Alb* from 02. *The Vicarage, 57 Church End, Biddenham, Bedford MK40 4AS* Tel (01234) 218914

SMITH, Canon Geoffrey Cobley. b 30. Bps' Coll Cheshunt 63. **d** 65 **p** 66. C Hockerill *St Alb* 65-68; C Evesham *Worc* 68-72; V Walberswick w Blythburgh *St E* 72-85; RD Halesworth 81-85; R Newmarket St Mary w Exning St Agnes 85-00; RD Mildenhall 86-00; Hon Can St E Cathl 87-00; rtd 00; Perm to Offic *St E* from 00. *78 Eastgate Street, Bury St Edmunds IP33 1YR* Tel (01284) 731061

SMITH, Geoffrey Keith. b 37. Lon Coll of Div 57. **d** 60 **p** 61. C Leek St Luke *Lich* 60-63; C Trentham 63-66; V Lilleshall 66-84; P-in-c Sheriffhales w Woodcote 83-84; V Lilleshall and Sheriffhales 84-87; P-in-c Haughton 87-91; R Derrington, Haughton and Ranton 91-03; RD Stafford 95-03; rtd 03. *19 Meadow Drive, Haughton, Stafford ST18 9HU* Tel (01785) 259076

SMITH, Geoffrey Raymond. b 49. AKC71. St Aug Coll Cant 71. **d** 72 **p** 73. C Hendon St Alphage *Lon* 72-75; C Notting Hill St Mich and Ch Ch 75-78; P-in-c Isleworth St Fran 78-83; P-in-c Chipping Ongar *Chelmsf* 83-84; R 84-86; R Shelley 84-86; R Chipping Ongar w Shelley 86-89; RD Ongar 88-89; P-in-c Harlow St Mary Magd 89-90; V 90-98; R Woodford St Mary w St Phil and St Jas from 98. *The Rectory, 8 Chelmsford Road, London E18 2PL* Tel (020) 8504 3472 E-mail geoffreysmith49@aol.com

SMITH, George Frederick. b 35. AKC59. **d** 60 **p** 61. C Radford *Cov* 60-64; C Kenilworth St Nic 64-67; V Burton Dassett 67-71; CF 71-74; V Lapley w Wheaton Aston *Lich* 74-80; V Gt Wyrley 80-90; V Shareshill 90-95; rtd 95. *Beili Tew Lodge, Llansawel, Llandeilo SA19 7LJ*

SMITH, Canon George Robert Henry. b 24. Chich Th Coll 49. **d** 52 **p** 53. C Glouc St Steph *Glouc* 52-56; V Parkend 56-65; P-in-c Clearwell 60-62; V Tuffley 65-82; Hon Can Glouc Cathl 81-95; R Leckhampton St Pet 82-94; rtd 94; NSM Westcote w Icomb and Bledington *Glouc* 95-98; Perm to Offic from 98. *1 The Paddocks, Church Lane, Bledington, Chipping Norton OX7 6XB* Tel (01608) 659194

SMITH, Gerald. b 36. Sarum Th Coll 61. **d** 63 **p** 64. C Menston w Woodhead *Bradf* 63-66; Chapl RAF 66-70; C Hoylake *Ches* 70-72; R Inverurie *Ab* 72-74; R Kemnay 72-74; TV Hucknall Torkard *S'well* 74-75; Falkland Is 75-78; V Luddenden w Luddenden Foot *Wakef* 79-86; V Scopwick Gp *Linc* 86-94; P-in-c Leasingham 94-96; rtd 96; Perm to Offic *Ex* from 96 and *Truro* from 00. *Ivy Cottage, Woolsery, Bideford EX39 5QS* Tel and fax (01237) 431298

SMITH, Mrs Gill. b 55. EAMTC 02. **d** 05. NSM Burwell w Reach *Ely* from 05. *22 Bloomsfield, Burwell, Cambridge CB5 0RA* Tel (01638) 743589 E-mail gillsmith.cam@virgin.net

SMITH, Mrs Gillian Angela. b 39. RGN60 RM62. All Nations Chr Coll IDC65. **d** 94 **p** 95. NSM Haydock St Mark *Liv* 94-96; Perm to Offic *Ely* 96-02; rtd 99; Hon C Milton *Win* 02-03; Perm to Offic *Ely* from 03. *15 The Sheltons, Frinton-on-Sea CO13 0LX* Tel (01255) 671041

SMITH, Godfrey Declan Burfield. b 42. TCD BA64 MA67 PGCE65. Irish Sch of Ecum Dip Ecum82 Sarum Th Coll. **d** 69 **p** 70. Zambia 70-75; Perm to Offic *D & G* 81-02; S Regional Sec (Ireland) CMS 81-99; Overseas Sec 87-93; Miss Personnel Sec 93-99; I Donoughmore and Donard w Dunlavin *D & G* from 02. *The Rectory, Donard, Co Wicklow, Irish Republic* Tel (00353) (45) 404631 Fax 404800 E-mail declansmith14@eircom.net

SMITH, Graeme Richard. b 65. Leeds Univ BA87 MA91 Birm Univ PhD97. Qu Coll Birm 87. **d** 89 **p** 90. C Daventry *Pet* 89-92; Perm to Offic *Birm* 92-97; Lect Th Westmr Coll Ox 97-00; Co Ecum Officer *Ox* 97-00; Sen Lect Ox Brookes Univ 00-02; Dean Non-Res Tr St Mich Coll Llan from 04. *St Michael's College, 54 Cardiff Road, Llandaff, Cardiff CF5 2YJ* Tel (029) 2083 8006 E-mail gs@stmichaels.ac.uk

SMITH, Graham. *See* SMITH, John Graham

SMITH, Graham. b 39. Univ of Wales (Ban) CertEd60 Lon Univ DipEd75. **d** 01 **p** 02. OLM Upper Holme Valley *Wakef* 01-05; NSM E Richmond *Ripon* from 05. *The Rectory, 13 Kneeton Park, Middleton Tyas, Richmond DL10 6SB* Tel (01825) 377562 Mobile 07887-952397 E-mail graham.smith50@btopenworld.com

SMITH, Graham Arthur James. b 43. MRICS68. STETS 98 Coll of Resurr Mirfield 01. **d** 01 **p** 02. NSM Broadstone *Sarum* from 01. *5 Durlston Road, Parkstone, Poole BH14 8PQ* Tel 07710-328685 (mobile) E-mail fr.graham.smith@talk21.com

SMITH, The Very Revd Graham Charles Morell. b 47. St Chad's Coll Dur BA74. Westcott Ho Cam 74. **d** 76 **p** 77. C Tooting All SS *S'wark* 76-80; TV Thamesmead 80-87; TR Kidlington w Hampton Poyle *Ox* 87-97; RD Ox 89-95; TR Leeds City *Ripon* 97-04; Hon Can Ripon Cathl 97-04; Dean Nor from 04. *The Deanery, Cathedral Close, Norwich NR1 4EG* Tel (01603) 218308 Mobile 07798-916321 E-mail graham@gcmsmith.org.uk *or* dean@cathedral.org.uk

SMITH, Graham David Noel. b 37. Oak Hill Th Coll 72. **d** 73 **p** 74. C Southborough St Pet w Ch Ch and St Matt *Roch* 73-76; C Bedworth *Cov* 76-79; R Treeton *Sheff* 79-84; V Riddlesden *Bradf* 84-96; RD S Craven 91-96; rtd 96; Hon C Ilkley All SS *Bradf* 97-03; Perm to Offic from 03. *26 Hawthorne Grove, Burley in Wharfdale, Ilkley LS29 7RF* Tel (01943) 864754 E-mail grahams@26hawthorne.freeserve.co.uk

SMITH, Canon Graham Francis. b 27. Leic Univ DSS51 Lon Univ BD57. Wells Th Coll 51. **d** 54 **p** 55. C Howe Bridge *Man* 54-57; C Hatfield Hyde *St Alb* 57-63; V Angell Town St Jo *S'wark* 63-73; V Wandsworth St Anne 73-85; P-in-c Wandsworth St Faith 75-78; RD Wandsworth 81-85; Hon Can S'wark Cathl 82-92; Mert Deanery Missr 85-92; rtd 92; Perm to Offic *Pet* from 97. *The Haven, 9 High Street, Syresham, Brackley NN13 5HL* Tel (01280) 850421

SMITH, Graham John. b 31. SSC. **d** 75 **p** 76. NSM Devonport St Mark Ford *Ex* 75-81; NSM Plympton St Maurice 81-90; V Ernesettle 90-03; P-in-c from 03; rtd 03. *St Aidan's Vicarage, 122 Rochford Crescent, Plymouth PL5 2QD* Tel (01752) 210241 E-mail graham.smith6@talk21.com

SMITH, Graham John. b 60. RN Eng Coll Plymouth BScEng84. Trin Coll Bris BA90 St Jo Coll Nottm MA00. **d** 90 **p** 91. C Herne *Cant* 90-93; Chapl RN 93-96; C Henfield w Shermanbury and Woodmancote *Chich* 96-98; Chapl Sussex Police 96-98; Chapl Portsm Hosps NHS Trust 98-00; P-in-c Cosham and Chapl Highbury Coll of FE Portsm 00-05; CME Officer *Portsm* 03-05; rtd 05. *The Vicarage, 269 Hawthorn Crescent, Cosham, Portsmouth PO6 2TL* Tel (023) 9238 7162 Mobile 07970-826160 E-mail gjsmith@first-web.co.uk

SMITH, Graham Russell. b 60. New Coll Ox BA81 MA89 Lon Univ BD89. Qu Coll Birm 02. **d** 04 **p** 05. C Yardley St Edburgha *Birm* from 04. *424 Church Road, Yardley, Birmingham B33 8PB* Tel 0121-783 7318 E-mail kiew.graham@virgin.net

SMITH, Grahame Clarence. b 32. Lich Th Coll 58. **d** 60 **p** 61. C New Sleaford *Linc* 60-63; R Tydd 63-76; V Barholm w Stowe 76-81; V Tallington 76-81; R Uffington 76-81; P-in-c W Deeping 76-77; R 77-81; R Uffington 81-92; rtd 92; Perm to Offic *Linc*

92-95. *Keeper's Cottage, Careby Road, Aunby, Stamford PE9 4EG* Tel (01780) 66386

SMITH, Greg Peter. b 60. Warwick Univ BA86 Qu Coll Birm BA99. WMMTC 97. **d** 99 **p** 00. C Binley *Cov* 99-04; P-in-c E Green from 04. *St Andrew's Vicarage, Church Lane, Eastern Green, Coventry CV5 7BX* Tel (024) 7642 2856 E-mail gregsmith31760@aol.com

SMITH, Gregory James. *See* CLIFTON-SMITH, Gregory James

SMITH, Canon Guy Howard. b 33. Man Univ BA54. Coll of Resurr Mirfield 60. **d** 62 **p** 63. C Oswestry H Trin *Lich* 62-66; Chapl RNR from 63; Prin St Aug Sch Betong Malaysia 66-69; V Willenhall St Anne *Lich* 69-79; P-in-c Willenhall St Steph 75-79; R Lilongwe St Pet Malawi 79-82; Adn Lilongwe 80-82; V Tettenhall Wood *Lich* 82-89; TR 89-91; TR Kidderminster St Jo and H Innocents *Worc* 91-99; rtd 99; Perm to Offic *Worc* from 99. *11 Church Walk, Stourport-on-Severn DY13 0AL* Tel and fax (01299) 822281 E-mail gandmsmith@talk21.com

SMITH, Mrs Gwendoline Anne. b 52. K Coll Lon BA97. SEITE 97. **d** 99 **p** 00. C Erith St Paul *Roch* 99-02; V Hadlow from 02. *The Vicarage, Maidstone Road, Hadlow, Tonbridge TN11 0DJ* Tel (01732) 850238 E-mail gwensmith@kent33.freeserve.co.uk

SMITH, Harold. *See* SMITH, Robert Harold

SMITH, Harold. b 20. Qu Coll Birm 77. **d** 80 **p** 81. NSM Gravelly Hill *Birm* 80-85; NSM Duddeston w Nechells 85-93; Perm to Offic from 93. *37 Dovey Tower, Duddeston Manor Road, Birmingham B7 4LE* Tel 0121-682 9417

SMITH, Harvey Jefferson. b 19. AMCT39 FIEE38 FIMechE52 FIPlantE67 ACIArb78. St Alb Minl Tr Scheme 81. **d** 88 **p** 97. NSM Hemel Hempstead *St Alb* 88-92 and 95-00; Perm to Offic 92-95 and from 00. *43 Garland Close, Hemel Hempstead HP2 5HU* Tel (01442) 266377

SMITH, Sister Hazel Ferguson Waide. b 33. Univ Coll Lon BA55. **dss** 64 **d** 87. CSA 58-77; St Etheldreda's Children's Home Bedf 64-85; Bedford St Paul *St Alb* 85-92; Par Dn 87-92; rtd 92; Perm to Offic *St Alb* from 92; *Ox* 93-00; Assoc Sister CSA from 03. *Paddock House, 6 Linford Lane, Willen, Milton Keynes MK15 9DL* Tel and fax (01908) 397267 Mobile 07789-654881 E-mail hazel@paddock-house.fsnet.co.uk

SMITH, Henry Neville. b 25. Chich Th Coll 53. **d** 54 **p** 55. C Oldham St Mary *Man* 54-56; C Mitcham St Olave *S'wark* 57-59; Succ Leic Cathl *Leic* 59-60; Chapl St Jas Hosp Balham 60-63; V Ivinghoe w Pitstone *Ox* 63-73; Chapl Qu Anne's Sch Caversham 73-90; rtd 90; Perm to Offic *Chich* from 90. *4 St Mary's Mews, Felpham, Bognor Regis PO22 7PE* Tel (01243) 822716

SMITH, Henry Robert. b 41. Lanchester Poly BSc66. Qu Coll Birm 75. **d** 78 **p** 79. Hon C Hillmorton *Cov* 78-81; Lic to Offic *S'well* 81-85; Hon C Radcliffe-on-Trent and Shelford etc 85-89; C Sutton in Ashfield St Mary 89-92; P-in-c Forest Town 92-98; P-in-c Babworth w Sutton-cum-Lound 98-02; P-in-c Scofton w Osberton 98-02; R Babworth w Sutton-cum-Lound and Scofton etc from 02. *St Bartholomew's Vicarage, Mattersey Road, Retford DN22 8PW* Tel (01777) 710007 *or* 703253 E-mail bobsmith@dircon.co.uk

SMITH, Howard Alan. b 46. Dip Counselling 81 St Jo Coll Dur BA73 DipTh74. **d** 74 **p** 75. C Brighton St Matthias *Chich* 74-77; C Henfield 77-78; C Henfield w Shermanbury and Woodmancote 78-80; R Northiam 80-87; Chapl St Ebba's Hosp Epsom 87-94; Chapl Qu Mary's Hosp Carshalton 87-94; Chapl Merton and Sutton Community NHS Trust 94-99; Chapl Epsom and St Helier NHS Trust from 99; Perm to Offic *Guildf* from 01. *St Helier Hospital, Wrythe Lane, Carshalton SM5 1AA* Tel (020) 8296 2306 *or* 8643 3300 E-mail hosmith@globalnet.co.uk

SMITH, Howard Gilbert. b 48. Leeds Univ BA69. St Steph Ho Ox BA71 MA75 Ridley Hall Cam 72. **d** 73 **p** 74. C Wallsend St Luke *Newc* 73-76; C Farnworth and Kearsley *Man* 76-77; P-in-c Farnworth All SS 77-78; TV E Farnworth and Kearsley 78-82; V Belfield 82-93; V Leesfield 93-04; V Northallerton w Kirby Sigston *York* from 04. *27 Mowbray Road, Northallerton DL6 1QT* Tel (01609) 770082

SMITH, Ian. b 62. Hull Univ BA83. Oak Hill Th Coll DipHE87 BA88. **d** 88 **p** 89. C W Hampstead St Luke *Lon* 88-90; C Woking St Pet *Guildf* 90-95; V Leyland St Jo *Blackb* 95-02; C Goole *Sheff* 02-03; P-in-c Sheff St Paul from 03. *St Paul's Vicarage, Wheata Road, Sheffield S5 9FP* Tel 0114-246 8494 E-mail stjohns@ukonline.co.uk

SMITH, Canon Ian Walker. b 29. Leeds Univ BA52. Coll of Resurr Mirfield 52. **d** 54 **p** 55. C Moulsecoomb *Chich* 54-61; Chapl K Sch Cant 61-62; C Crawley *Chich* 62-79; TV 79-81; R Clenchwarton *Ely* 81-94; RD Lynn Marshland 84-94; Hon Can Ely Cathl 88-94; Perm to Offic *Nor* 88-94; rtd 94; Perm to Offic *Ely* from 94. *27 Jubilee Drive, Dersingham, King's Lynn PE31 6YA* Tel (01485) 540203

SMITH, Irene Lillian. **d** 99 **p** 00. OLM Moston St Chad *Man* from 99. *1 Walmersley Road, Manchester M40 3RS* Tel 0161-682 5927 E-mail irenel.smith@ukgateway.net

SMITH, Mrs Irene Mary. b 43. Shenstone Coll of Educn CertEd64 Lon Univ BD77. OLM course 96. **d** 99 **p** 00. OLM Uttoxeter Area *Lich* from 99. *16 Teanhurst Close, Tean, Stoke-on-Trent ST10 4NN* Tel (01538) 722975 E-mail irene.smith2@tesco.net

SMITH, Miss Irene Victoria. b 45. SRN66 SCM69. **d** 03 **p** 04. OLM Lawton Moor *Man* from 03. *288 Wythenshawe Road, Manchester M23 9DA* Tel 0161-998 4100 Mobile 07889-116856

SMITH, James. *See* SMITH, Philip James

SMITH, James. b 26. NEOC 76. **d** 79 **p** 80. NSM Seaton Hirst *Newc* 79-82; NSM Cresswell and Lynemouth 82-88; NSM Cambois 88-93; rtd 93; Perm to Offic *Newc* from 93. *140 Pont Street, Ashington NE63 0PX* Tel (01670) 816557

SMITH, James Edward. b 30. Chich Th Coll 57. **d** 58 **p** 59. C Ellesmere Port *Ches* 58-61; C W Bromwich All SS *Lich* 61-63; Chapl RN 63-65; V Walton St Jo *Liv* 65-71; V Anfield St Columba 71-79; V Altcar 79-92; rtd 92; Perm to Offic *Linc* 93-02. *The Hollies, 43 Carlton Road, Bassingham, Lincoln LN5 9HB* Tel (01522) 788260

SMITH, James Harold. b 31. Ch Coll Tasmania ThL61. **d** 61 **p** 61. Australia 61-63, 66-85 and 92-94; Canada 64-65; Chapl St Chris Hospice Lon 86-87; Asst Chapl Brook Gen Hosp Lon 87-92; Asst Chapl Greenwich Distr Hosp Lon 87-92; Perm to Offic *S'wark* from 94. *Poplar Cottage, 80 Charlton Road, London SE7 7EY* Tel (020) 8858 4692

SMITH, James Henry. b 32. St Aid Birkenhead. **d** 65 **p** 66. C Wigan St Cath *Liv* 65-68; V Parkfield in Middleton *Man* 68-77; V Bolton Breightmet St Jas 77-97; rtd 97; Perm to Offic *Liv* from 97. *Flat 4, 14A Cropton Road, Formby, Liverpool L37 4AD* Tel (01704) 833682

SMITH, James William. b 47. SRN69 RMN70 MRIPHH69 MRSH92 Lambeth STh90 Sussex Coll of Tech MA95 SOAS Lon PhD95. Chich Th Coll 78. **d** 80 **p** 80. C Kenwyn *Truro* 80-82; C Haslemere *Guildf* 82-84; TV Honiton, Gittisham, Combe Raleigh, Monkton etc *Ex* 84-91; Chapl R Marsden Hosp Lon and Surrey 91-95; Perm to Offic *S'wark* 91-95; rtd 95; Perm to Offic *Sarum* from 96. *22 Thrift Close, Stalbridge, Sturminster Newton DT10 2LE* Tel (01963) 362445

SMITH, Janet. *See* SMITH, Ms Patricia Janet

SMITH, Mrs Janice Lilian. b 51. Open Univ BSc99. N Ord Course 98. **d** 01 **p** 02. NSM Yeadon St Jo *Bradf* from 01. *17 Silverdale Close, Guiseley, Leeds LS20 8BQ* Tel (01943) 877023 E-mail janice@mizzie.fsnet.co.uk

SMITH, Jeffery Donald Morris. b 23. **d** 53 **p** 54. S Rhodesia 53-61; R Old Deer *Ab* 61-63; R Fraserburgh 63-68; S Africa 68-73; P-in-c Bintree w Themelthorpe *Nor* 73-76; V Twyford w Guist 73-76; R Twyford w Guist and Bintry w Themelthorpe 76-80; RD Sparham 79-81; R Twyford w Guist w Bintry w Themelthorpe etc 81; TR Hempnall 81-84; R Catfield 84-89; R Ingham w Sutton 84-89; rtd 89; Perm to Offic *Nor* from 89. *27 Dale Road, Dereham NR19 2DD* Tel (01362) 697022

SMITH, Canon Jeffry Bradford. b 56. BA82. Ch Div Sch of the Pacific (USA) MDiv85 Ripon Coll Cuddesdon. **d** 86 **p** 87. C Frimley *Guildf* 87-91; R E and W Clandon 91-03; Chapl HM Pris Send 94-96; Chapl HM Pris Channings Wood 03-04; Can Res and Sub-Dean Bermuda from 04. *Cathedral of the Most Holy Trinity, Church Street, Hamilton HM CX, Bermuda* Tel (001) (441) 292 4033

SMITH, Mrs Jennifer Pamela. b 63. Girton Coll Cam BA85 MA88. Oak Hill Th Coll BA91. **d** 91 **p** 94. C Rawdon *Bradf* 91-93; Chapl Bradf Cathl 93-96; P-in-c Kelbrook 96-00; Asst Chapl Airedale NHS Trust from 01. *24 Greenacres, Skipton BD23 1BX* Tel (01756) 790852

SMITH, Jeremy John Hawthorn. b 52. Birm Univ BSc73 Lanc Univ MA97. Carl and Blackb Dioc Tr Inst 94. **d** 97 **p** 98. NSM Long Marton w Dufton and w Milburn *Carl* 97-00; NSM Hesket-in-the-Forest and Armathwaite 00-04; NSM Skelton and Hutton-in-the-Forest w Ivegill 00-04; NSM Ainstable 00-04; NSM Inglewood Gp from 04. *St Mary's Vicarage, High Hesket, Carlisle CA4 0HU* Tel (01697) 473320

SMITH, Jeremy Victor. b 60. Keble Coll Ox BA82. Chich Th Coll 83. **d** 85 **p** 86. C Alton St Lawr *Win* 85-88; C W Hampstead St Jas *Lon* 88-93; V St Geo-in-the-East St Mary 93-97. *18 The Grange, Grange Road, London W4 4DE* Tel (020) 8742 7104

SMITH, Jesse Lee. b 70. Man Univ BA93. Linc Th Coll DipMM94 Westcott Ho Cam MA95. **d** 96 **p** 97. C Gomersal *Wakef* 96-00; C Penarth All SS *Llan* 00-02; TV Cen Cardiff 02-03; V Hartlepool H Trin *Dur* from 03. *Holy Trinity Vicarage, Davison Drive, Hartlepool TS24 9BX* Tel (01429) 267618 E-mail jesse@frjesse.freeserve.co.uk

SMITH, John. *See* SMITH, Stephen John

SMITH, John Alec. b 37. Lon Coll of Div ALCD62 BD63. **d** 63 **p** 64. C Cromer *Nor* 63-66; C Barking St Marg *Chelmsf* 66-69; V Attercliffe *Sheff* 69-75; P-in-c Sheff St Barn 76-78; V Sheff St Barn and St Mary 78-89; Ind Chapl 78-89; RD Ecclesall 80-85; TR Chippenham St Paul w Hardenhuish etc *Bris* 89-00; V Kington St Michael 89-00; rtd 00. *82 Victoria Road, Bidford-on-Avon, Alcester B50 4AR* Tel (01793) 872932

SMITH, John Bartlett. b 50. ACIPD St Chad's Coll Dur BA73 Lanchester Poly Dip Ind Relns 80. Cuddesdon Coll 73. **d** 76 **p** 77. C Heref St Martin *Heref* 76-86; NSM Isleworth St Mary

Lon 86-89; NSM Millom *Carl* 89-92; NSM Balham St Mary and St Jo *S'wark* 92-04. *101 Gosberton Road, London SW12 8LG* Tel (020) 8675 1743

SMITH, John Denmead. b 44. Ox Univ BA65 MA69 DPhil71. Coll of Resurr Mirfield 72. **d** 75 **p** 76. Asst Chapl Win Coll from 75. *11 Kingsgate Street, Winchester SO23 9PD* Tel (01962) 861820

SMITH, John Eckersley. b 26. Univ of Wales (Lamp). St Aug Coll Cant Wycliffe Hall Ox 53. **d** 55 **p** 56. C Heywood St Jas *Man* 55-57; C Atherton 57-59; R Gorton All SS 59-65; C Northenden 73-75; V Charlestown 75-82; Perm to Offic from 85; rtd 91. *19 Arthur Street, Swinton, Manchester M27 0HP* Tel 0161-793 7707

SMITH, John Ernest. b 52. St Andr Univ MTh77. Wycliffe Hall Ox 78. **d** 79 **p** 80. C Bermondsey St Mary w St Olave, St Jo etc *S'wark* 79-87; P-in-c Whyteleafe 87-97; RD Caterham 96-98; P-in-c Merstham and Gatton from 98. *The Rectory, Gatton Bottom, Merstham, Redhill RH1 3BH* Tel (01737) 643755 Fax 642954 E-mail john_e_smith@talk21.com

SMITH, John Graham. b 32. **d** 78 **p** 79. NSM Hordle *Win* 78-00; rtd 00; Perm to Offic *Win* from 00. *3 Marryat Road, New Milton BH25 5LW* Tel (01425) 615701

SMITH, John Lawrence. b 43. Birm Univ BSc65. Linc Th Coll 67. **d** 70 **p** 71. C Frodingham *Linc* 70-75; TV Gt Grimsby St Mary and St Jas 75-83; V Wolverhampton St Andr *Lich* from 83. *St Andrew's Vicarage, 66 Albert Road, Wolverhampton WV6 0AF* Tel (01902) 712935

SMITH, Canon John Leslie. b 44. Trin Coll Cam BA65 MA71. Ripon Coll Cuddesdon 79. **d** 81 **p** 82. C Ollerton *S'well* 81-84; P-in-c Farndon and Thorpe 84-88; P-in-c Winthorpe and Langford w Holme 88-95; Dioc Chief Insp Ch Schs 88-95; Dir of Educn *Pet* 95-99; P-in-c Cottingham w E Carlton 97-99; Dir of Educn *Roch* from 99; Hon Can Roch Cathl from 04; P-in-c Bredgar w Bicknor and Frinsted w Wormshill etc *Cant* from 05. *The Vicarage, Parsonage Lane, Bredgar, Sittingbourne ME9 8HA* Tel (01622) 884387 *or* (01634) 843667 Fax (01634) 843674 E-mail john.smith@rochester.anglican.org

SMITH, John Macdonald. b 29. Ch Coll Cam BA52 MA56. Wells Th Coll 56. **d** 58 **p** 59. C Westbury-on-Trym H Trin *Bris* 58-60; C Reading St Giles *Ox* 60-63; V Kidmore End 63-82; rtd 82. *38 Main Road, Norton, Evesham WR11 4TL* Tel (01386) 870918

SMITH, John Malcolm. b 36. ACIB60. N Ord Course 81. **d** 84 **p** 85. NSM Bury St Pet *Man* from 84. *46 Ajax Drive, Bury BL9 8EF* Tel 0161-766 8378

SMITH, John Oswald Salkeld. b 32. Oak Hill Th Coll 57. **d** 60 **p** 61. C Peckham St Mary Magd *S'wark* 61-63; C Rodbourne Cheney *Bris* 63-67; V Bradf St Aug Undercliffe *Bradf* 67-74; P-in-c Hammersmith St Simon *Lon* 74-76; V Chelsea St Jo w St Andr 76-97; rtd 98. *2 Lawn Road, Guildford GU2 4DE*

SMITH, John Roger. b 36. Dur Univ BA59. Tyndale Hall Bris 59. **d** 61 **p** 62. C Chaddesden St Mary *Derby* 61-63; C Gresley 63-66; V Burton Ch Ch *Lich* 66-76; V Doncaster St Mary *Sheff* 76-92; R Barnburgh w Melton on the Hill etc 92-01; rtd 01; Perm to Offic *Bradf* from 03. *2 Fieldhead Drive, Cross Hills, Keighley BD20 7RJ* Tel (01535) 634062

SMITH, John Sydney. b 36. Loughb Coll ALA59 FLA68 FISM82 Lanc Univ MA97. Carl and Blackb Dioc Tr Inst 94. **d** 97 **p** 98. NSM Arthuret, Nicholforest and Kirkandrews on Esk *Carl* 97-02; rtd 02; Perm to Offic *Carl* from 01. *The Jays, 3 White House, Walton, Brampton CA8 2DJ* Tel (01697) 741114

SMITH, John Thomas. b 29. Shuttleworth Agric Coll NDA55 Keele Univ DASE72 Wolv Poly MPhil81 PhD87. WMMTC 87. **d** 91 **p** 92. NSM Drayton in Hales *Lich* 91-96; NSM Cheswardine, Childs Ercall, Hales, Hinstock etc 96-98; rtd 98; Perm to Offic *Lich* 98-00. *Red Bank House, Market Drayton TF9 1AY* Tel (01630) 652302

SMITH, John Thompson. b 30. Wycliffe Hall Ox 64. **d** 66 **p** 67. C Walsall *Lich* 66-69; V Stoke Prior *Worc* 69-75; Asst Gen Sec Red Triangle Club 75-85; R Tendring and Lt Bentley w Beaumont cum Moze *Chelmsf* 85-89; R Fairstead w Terling and White Notley etc 89-92; Chapl Heath Hosp Tendring 85-92; rtd 92; Perm to Offic *B & W* from 92. *1 Harvey Close, Weston-super-Mare BS22 7DW* Tel (01934) 514256

SMITH, John Trevor. b 47. GGSM. Coll of Resurr Mirfield 74. **d** 77 **p** 78. C Loughton St Jo *Chelmsf* 77-80; C Ruislip St Martin *Lon* 80-84; P-in-c Southall Ch Redeemer 84-91; V Kingsbury St Andr from 91. *St Andrew's Vicarage, 28 Old Church Lane, London NW9 8RZ* Tel (020) 8205 7447 Fax 8205 7652 E-mail johnt.smith@london.anglican.org

SMITH, John William. b 51. EAMTC 00. **d** 03 **p** 04. NSM Erpingham w Calthorpe, Ingworth, Aldborough etc *Nor* from 03. *18 Pound Lane, Aylsham, Norwich NR11 6DR* Tel (01263) 734761

SMITH, Jonathan Paul. b 60. Univ of Wales (Lamp) BA81. Wycliffe Hall Ox 82. **d** 84 **p** 85. C Baglan *Llan* 84-88; C Gabalfa 88-90; R Llangammarch w Llanganten and Llanlleonfel etc *S & B* 90-01; Dioc Missr 95-01; R Denbigh *St As* from 01. *The Rectory, 5 St David's Court, Denbigh LL16 3EJ* Tel (01745) 812284 E-mail mission@cadmarch.freeserve.co.uk

SMITH, Jonathan Peter. b 55. K Coll Lon BD77 AKC77 Cam Univ PGCE78. Westcott Ho Cam 79. **d** 80 **p** 81. C Gosforth All SS *Newc* 80-82; C Waltham Abbey *Chelmsf* 82-85; Chapl City Univ *Lon* 85-88; R Harrold and Carlton w Chellington *St Alb* 88-97; Chapl Beds Police 90-97; V Harpenden St Jo from 97; RD Wheathampstead 99-04. *St John's Vicarage, 5 St John's Road, Harpenden AL5 1DJ* Tel (01582) 467168 *or* 712776 E-mail oldtractorboy@tiscali.co.uk

SMITH, Joyce Mary. b 52. Lon Hosp BDS74 Nottm Univ MMedSc77 Lon Univ PhD84 MCCDRCS89. EAMTC. **d** 00 **p** 01. C Harlow St Mary and St Hugh w St Jo the Bapt *Chelmsf* 00-02; C Waltham H Cross 02-03; TV from 03. *St Lawrence House, 46 Mallion Court, Waltham Abbey EN9 3EQ* Tel (01992) 767916 E-mail joyce@smith2767fsnet.co.uk

SMITH, Julian. b 48. K Coll Lon 70. Linc Th Coll 71. **d** 73 **p** 74. C Taunton Lyngford *B & W* 73-76; TV Wellington and Distr 76-81; R Axbridge w Shipham and Rowberrow 81-96; Chapl St Jo Hosp Axbridge from 84; V Taunton St Andr *B & W* from 96. *St Andrew's Vicarage, 118 Kingston Road, Taunton TA2 7SR* Tel (01823) 332544 E-mail jandms@eurobell.co.uk

SMITH, Julian William. b 64. Liv Univ BSc85. Trin Coll Bris BA93. **d** 93 **p** 94. C Henfynyw w Aberaeron and Llanddewi Aberarth *St D* 93-97; V Llansantffraed and Llanbadarn Trefeglwys etc 97-05; V Llansantffraed w Llanrhystud and Llanddeiniol from 05. *The Vicarage, 11 Maes Wyre, Llanrhystud SY23 5AH* Tel (01974) 202336

SMITH, Keith. b 46. ACIB. S Dios Minl Tr Scheme 85. **d** 87 **p** 88. NSM W Worthing St Jo *Chich* 87-94; NSM Maybridge 94-96; C Durrington 96-01; V Pagham from 01. *The Vicarage, Church Lane, Pagham, Bognor Regis PO21 4NX* Tel (01243) 262713

SMITH, Kenneth Robert. b 48. K Coll Lon BD75 AKC75. St Aug Coll Cant 75. **d** 76 **p** 77. C Birtley *Dur* 76-80; V Lamesley 80-90; R Whitburn from 90. *The Rectory, 51 Front Street, Whitburn, Sunderland SR6 7JD* Tel 0191-529 2232

SMITH, Kenneth Victor George. b 37. ALCD61 Lon Univ BD62. **d** 62 **p** 63. Hon C Bromley Common St Aug *Roch* 62-66; Hon C Streatham Immanuel w St Anselm *S'wark* 66-68; Perm to Offic 68-78; Chapl Whitgift Sch and Ho Croydon 78-97; Hon C Sanderstead All SS 78-91; Hon C Croydon St Jo 91-97; rtd 02. *Bridle Ways, Haling Grove, South Croydon CR2 6DQ* Tel (020) 8680 4460

SMITH, Kevin. b 66. Westmr Coll Ox BA89. Chich Th Coll 90. **d** 92 **p** 93. C Worksop Priory *S'well* 92-96; V New Cantley *Sheff* 96-03; P-in-c Horden *Dur* from 03. *11 Shotton Road, Horden, Peterlee SR8 4RB*

SMITH, Laurence Sidney. b 37. Sarum & Wells Th Coll 70. **d** 73 **p** 74. C Surbiton St Matt *S'wark* 73-76; C Horley 76-81; V W Ewell *Guildf* 81-90; V W Byfleet 90-02; rtd 02; Perm to Offic *Glouc* from 03. *Candlemill Cottage, Millbank, George Street, Nailsworth, Stroud GL6 0AG* Tel (01453) 836432

SMITH, Lawrence Paul. b 51. Ch Ch Coll Cant CertEd72 Southn Univ BTh81. Chich Th Coll 76. **d** 79 **p** 80. C Margate St Jo *Cant* 79-84; R Eythorne w Waldershare 84-87; P-in-c Sibertswold w Coldred 85-87; P-in-c Barfreystone 85-87; R Eythorne and Elvington w Waldershare etc 87-97; Par Min Development Adv (Kensington Area) *Lon* from 97; NSM Isleworth St Fran from 00. *St Francis Vicarage, 865 Great West Road, Isleworth TW7 5PD* Tel (020) 8568 9098 *or* 8580 2142 Fax 8560 8113 E-mail lawrence.smith@london.anglican.org

SMITH, Lewis Shand. b 52. Aber Univ MA74 Edin Univ BD78. Edin Th Coll 74. **d** 77 **p** 78. C Wishaw *Glas* 77-79; P-in-c 79-80; C Motherwell 77-79; P-in-c 79-80; R Lerwick *Ab* 80-00; R Burravoe 80-00; Miss to Seafarers from 80; Can St Andr Cathl *Ab* 93-00; R Dumfries *Glas* 00-05. *Address temp unknown* E-mail shand.smith@talk21.com

SMITH, Mrs Linda Jean. b 61. Ripon Coll Cuddesdon DipMin99. **d** 99 **p** 00. C St Martin w Looe *Truro* 99-03; P-in-c Talland from 03; C Lanreath, Pelynt and Bradoc from 03. *Trelawne Glebe, Trelawne Cross, Pelynt, Looe PL13 2NA* Tel (01503) 272640 E-mail trelawnevicarage@ukonline.co.uk

SMITH, Linnet. *See* SMITH, Diana Linnet

SMITH, Miss Lorna Cassandra. b 43. Open Univ BA76. Cant Sch of Min 82. **dss** 86 **d** 87 **p** 94. Birchington w Acol and Minnis Bay *Cant* 86-87; Par Dn 87-92; C Addlestone *Guildf* 92-97; V Englefield Green from 97. *The Vicarage, 21 Willow Walk, Englefield Green, Egham TW20 0DQ* Tel and fax (01784) 432553 E-mail revlcs@aol.com

SMITH, Mrs Lorna Rosalind. b 53. Oak Hill NSM Course 89. **d** 92 **p** 94. NSM Squirrels Heath *Chelmsf* 92-94; NSM Stanford-le-Hope w Mucking 94-97; P-in-c Fobbing 97-04; P-in-c Tillingham from 04. *The Vicarage, 6 Bakery Close, Tillingham, Southminster CM0 7TT* Tel (01621) 778017 E-mail lornads24@aol.com

SMITH, Lynford. *See* SMITH, Francis Christian Lynford

SMITH (née THORNTON), Mrs Magdalen Mary. b 69. Warwick Univ BA90. Qu Coll Birm BD95. **d** 96 **p** 97. C Kirkby *Liv* 96-98; C Birm St Martin w Bordesley St Andr *Birm* 00-03; NSM Tilston and Shocklach *Ches* from 03. *The Rectory,*

41 Inveresk Road, Tilston, Malpas SY14 7ED Tel (01829) 250628 E-mail mags@smith.freeserve.co.uk

SMITH, Margaret Elizabeth. b 46. Bretton Hall Coll CertEd67. N Ord Course 85. **d** 88 **p** 94. Hon Par Dn Battyeford *Wakef* 88-89; Hon C Mirfield 89-91; Chapl HM Pris and YOI New Hall 90-95; Dn-in-c Flockton cum Denby Grange *Wakef* 91-94; P-in-c 94-96; V Scholes 96-01; P-in-c Buckden *Ely* 01-05; P-in-c Offord D'Arcy w Offord Cluny 01-05; R Buckden w the Offords from 05. *The Vicarage, Church Street, Buckden, St Neots PE19 5TL* Tel (01480) 810371 E-mail memagsmith@waitrose.com

SMITH, Mrs Marion Elizabeth. b 51. Bris Univ CertEd73 Middx Univ BA99. NTMTC AdDipTh98. **d** 98 **p** 99. NSM Cowley *Lon* 98-00; P-in-c Harlington from 00. *The Rectory, St Peter's Way, Hayes UB3 5AB* Tel (020) 8759 9569 Mobile 07803-617509 E-mail marion.smith@tiscali.co.uk

SMITH, Mark Andrew. b 59. **d** 85 **p** 86. S Africa 85-01; P St Mary Magdalene Port Elizabeth 88-89; R St Pet Cradock 89-92; R Alexandra Plurality 93; Chapl St Andr Coll Grahamstown 94-01; Chapl Denstone Coll Uttoxeter from 02. *Denstone College, Denstone, Uttoxeter ST14 5HN* Tel (01889) 590372 Mobile 07776-185474 Fax (01889) 590744

SMITH, Mark David. *See* LAYNESMITH, Mark David

SMITH, Mark Gordon Robert Davenport. b 56. St Jo Coll Dur BA77. Ridley Hall Cam 78. **d** 80 **p** 81. C Sheff St Jo *Sheff* 80-83; C Brightside w Wincobank 83-86; V Kimberworth Park 86-91; Consultant NE England CPAS 91-98; Nat Co-ord Cert in Evang Studies (CA) 98-04; Chapl for Deaf People *Derby* from 04. *6 Old Chester Road, Derby DE1 3SA* Tel 07702-269608 (mobile)

SMITH, Mark Graham. b 63. Ex Univ BA86 Lanc Univ PhD03. Westcott Ho Cam 87. **d** 90 **p** 91. C Cottingham *York* 90-92; C Guisborough 92-94; Sen Chapl St Martin's Coll *Blackb* 94-98; V Ashton-on-Ribble St Mich w Preston St Mark 98-03; V Scotforth from 03; Dioc World Development Adv from 00. *St Paul's Vicarage, 24 Scotforth Road, Lancaster LA1 4ST* Tel (01524) 32106 E-mail marklisasmith@aol.com

SMITH, Mark Peter. b 61. Reading Univ BA82 Open Univ BA93 MA97 Keele Univ PGCE84 Liv Univ MTh02. N Ord Course 99. **d** 02 **p** 03. C Wingerworth *Derby* from 02. *20 Longedge Rise, Wingerworth, Chesterfield S42 6NX* Tel (01246) 229532 E-mail mark@mpsosb1.demon.co.uk

SMITH, Mark Richard Samuel. b 63. UMIST BSc84. Cranmer Hall Dur 86. **d** 89 **p** 90. C Kersal Moor *Man* 89-93; C Halliwell St Pet 93-01; TV Stockport SW *Ches* 01-02. *Address temp unknown*

SMITH, Mark Winton. b 60. St Jo Coll Dur BA81 Barrister-at-Law (Middle Temple) 82. SEITE 01. **d** 04. NSM E Wickham *S'wark* from 04. *16 Watersmeet Way, London SE28 8PU* Tel and fax (020) 8310 5063 E-mail revdmarksmith@aol.com

SMITH, Martin David. b 52. LTCL Hull Univ BA75. Cuddesdon Coll 75. **d** 78 **p** 79. C Brentwood St Thos *Chelmsf* 78-80; C Reading St Giles *Ox* 80-91; R Colkirk w Oxwick w Pattesley, Whissonsett etc *Nor* 91-95; P-in-c Gt and Lt Ryburgh w Gateley and Testerton 94-95; P-in-c Hempton and Pudding Norton 94-95; P-in-c Nor St Pet Parmentergate w St Jo 95-03; R Nor St Jo w St Julian from 03. *The Rectory, 10 Stepping Lane, Norwich NR1 1PE* Tel (01603) 622509 Fax 628417 E-mail frmartinsmith@clara.net

SMITH, Martin Lee. b 47. Worc Coll Ox BA68 MA72. Cuddesdon Coll 68. **d** 70 **p** 71. C Digswell *St Alb* 70-71; C Cheshunt 71-73; Perm to Offic *Ox* 74-80; SSJE 76-02; USA from 81. *1245 4th Street SW E208, Washington, DC 20024, USA* E-mail martin.l.smith@worldnet.att.net

SMITH, Martin Stanley. b 53. Univ of Wales (Abth) BScEcon75. STETS DipTh99. **d** 99 **p** 00. NSM Woking Ch Ch *Guildf* from 99. *Brackenlea, Heather Close, Horsell, Woking GU21 4JR* Tel (01483) 714307 E-mail martin.wokingsmiffs@ntlworld.com

SMITH, Canon Martin William. b 40. K Coll Lon BD63 AKC63. **d** 64 **p** 65. C Ashford St Hilda CD *Lon* 64-67; Malaysia 67-71; V Lakenham St Mark *Nor* 72-85; V N Walsham w Antingham 85-01; P-in-c Neatishead, Barton Turf and Irstead 94-95; RD Tunstead 91-96; RD St Benet 96-99; Hon Can Nor Cathl from 93; V Wymondham from 01. *The Vicarage, 5 Vicar Street, Wymondham NR18 0PL* Tel (01953) 602269

SMITH, Martyn. b 52. CertEd73. Oak Hill Th Coll BA81. **d** 81 **p** 82. C Halliwell St Pet *Man* 81-86; V Cambridge St Martin *Ely* 86-89; Vineyard Chr Fellowship from 89. *Address temp unknown*

SMITH, Melvyn. *See* SMITH, Canon William Melvyn

SMITH, Merrick Thomas Jack. b 37. Glos Coll of Arts & Tech ONC57 CEng65 MCIBSE65. Oak Hill NSM Course 90. **d** 92 **p** 93. NSM Isleworth St Mary *Lon* 92-94; Perm to Offic *Birm* 94-96; NSM Warfield *Ox* 96-98; TV Wallingford 98-01; P-in-c Tredington and Darlingscott w Newbold on Stour *Cov* 01-03; rtd 03; Perm to Offic *Sarum* from 03. *7 Field End, Bideford EX39 3SH* E-mail smith.merrick@virgin.net

SMITH, Michael. *See* SMITH, The Ven Anthony Michael Percival

SMITH, Michael. b 54. Matlock Coll of Educn CertEd76 Nottm Univ BEd77. Ridley Hall Cam 87. **d** 89 **p** 90. C Ilkeston St Mary *Derby* 89-92; TV Wirksworth 92-98; RD Wirksworth 97-98; V Ashbourne w Mapleton 98-04. *Address temp unknown* E-mail revmikesmith@btinternet.com

SMITH, Michael David. b 57. BA80. St Steph Ho Ox 81. **d** 83 **p** 84. C Beaconsfield *Ox* 83-87; V Wing w Grove 87-92; R Farnham Royal w Hedgerley 92-01; P-in-c Cookham 01-03; V The Cookhams from 03. *The Vicarage, Church Gate, Cookham, Maidenhead SL6 9SP* Tel (01628) 523969 *or* 529661

SMITH, Michael Ian Antony. b 69. Warwick Univ BSc91. Oak Hill Th Coll BA95. **d** 95 **p** 96. C Cheadle *Ches* 95-98; C Hollington St Leon *Chich* 98-01; C Hartford *Ches* 01-04; V from 04. *The Vicarage, 7 The Green, Hartford, Northwich CW8 1QA* Tel (01606) 77557 *or* 783063 Fax 786758 E-mail miasmith@btopenworld.com

SMITH, Michael James. b 47. AKC69. St Aug Coll Cant 70. **d** 71 **p** 72. C Corby St Columba *Pet* 71-78; V Collierley *Dur* 78-80; CPAS Evang from 83. *56 Kingsmere, Chester le Street DH3 4DE* Tel 0191-209 2985

SMITH, Michael John. b 47. Lon Univ DipTh71. Kelham Th Coll 65. **d** 71 **p** 72. C Cov St Mary *Cov* 71-75; Chapl RN 75-90; CF 90-95; R Lynch w Iping Marsh and Milland *Chich* 95-03; RD Midhurst 98-03; Community Chapl Bielefeld Station Germany from 03. *Community Chaplain's Office, 7 Regt RLC, Catterick Barracks, Bielefeld, BFPO 39* Tel (0049) (521) 9254 3118 E-mail revmjsmith@hotmail.com

SMITH, Michael Keith John. b 66. Thames Poly BSc88. Linc Th Coll BTh95. **d** 95 **p** 96. C Birch St Agnes w Longsight St Jo w St Cypr *Man* 95-99; TV Pendleton from 99; P-in-c Lower Kersal from 03. *The Vicarage, 25 Brindle Heath Road, Salford M6 6GD* Tel 0161-737 2337 E-mail mkjsmith@supanet.com

SMITH, Michael Raymond. b 36. ARCM56 ARCO56 Qu Coll Cam BA59 MA63. Cuddesdon Coll 64. **d** 65 **p** 66. C Redcar *York* 65-70; V Dormanstown 70-73; Prec Worc Cathl *Worc* 73-77; TR Worc St Barn w Ch Ch 77-83; RD Worc E 79-83; V Eskdale, Irton, Muncaster and Waberthwaite *Carl* 83-87; Chapl Uppingham Sch 87-93; P-in-c Stoke Lacy, Moreton Jeffries w Much Cowarne etc *Heref* 93-01; Dioc Schs Officer 97-03; rtd 01. *Plough House, Wellington, Hereford HR4 8AT* Tel (01432) 839087 E-mail m.smith@hereford.anglican.org

SMITH, Michael Richard Guy. b 55. Man Univ BA77. Ripon Coll Cuddesdon 88. **d** 90 **p** 91. C Wallasey St Hilary *Ches* 90-93; C Howden *York* 93-94; TV 94-97; V Gt and Lt Driffield from 04. *The Vicarage, Downe Street, Driffield YO25 6DX* Tel (01377) 253394

SMITH, Neville. *See* SMITH, Charles Henry Neville

SMITH, Norman George. b 27. K Coll Lon BD52 AKC52. **d** 53 **p** 54. C Pennington *Man* 53-56; C Chorlton-cum-Hardy St Clem 56-57; V Heywood St Jas 57-63; R Bedhampton *Portsm* 63-81; V Win St Bart *Win* 81-92; RD Win 84-89; rtd 92; Perm to Offic *Win* from 92. *89 Priors Dean Road, Winchester SO22 6JY*

SMITH, Norman Jordan. b 30. Sarum Th Coll 57. **d** 60 **p** 61. C Parkend *Glouc* 60-61; C Clearwell 60-61; C W Tarring *Chich* 61-65; Australia 65-68; V Chidham *Chich* 68-94; rtd 95. *Potters Paradise, 82 Church Road, Hayling Island PO11 0NX*

SMITH, Preb Olwen. b 44. Birm Univ BA66 DPS68. Selly Oak Coll 67. **d** 87 **p** 94. Ind Chapl Black Country Urban Ind Miss *Lich* 84-98; TV Cen Wolverhampton from 94; Preb Lich Cathl from 99. *66 Albert Road, Wolverhampton WV6 0AF* Tel (01902) 712935 *or* 710407 Fax 685222 E-mail bcuim3@nascr.net

SMITH, Mrs Pamela Christina. b 46. St Alb and Ox Min Course 97. **d** 00 **p** 01. NSM Ironstone *Ox* from 00; Chapl Kath Ho Hospice from 00. *The Vicarage, Horley, Banbury OX15 6BJ* Tel (01295) 730951 E-mail pamela@banx.fsnet.co.uk

SMITH, Miss Pamela Frances. b 44. St Mary's Coll Chelt TCert65. WEMTC 91. **d** 94 **p** 95. NSM Badgeworth w Shurdington *Glouc* 94-95; NSM Badgeworth, Shurdington and Witcombe w Bentham 95-02; NSM The Lavingtons, Cheverells, and Easterton *Sarum* 02-05; C E Clevedon w Clapton in Gordano etc *B & W* from 05. *5 Chestnut Grove, Clevedon BS21 7LA* Tel (01275) 795080

SMITH, Ms Pamela Jane Holden. b 56. Warwick Univ BA78 Lon Inst of Educn PGCE82. Qu Coll Birm BA04. **d** 04 **p** 05. NSM Coventry Caludon *Cov* from 04. *34 Styvechale Avenue, Coventry CV5 6DX* Tel (024) 7667 2893 E-mail pam_holden_smith@hotmail.com *or* blue.sky@btopenworld.com

SMITH, Ms Patricia Janet. b 45. Oak Hill Th Coll 87. **d** 89 **p** 90. Canada 89-02; V Charminster and Stinsford *Sarum* from 02. *The Vicarage, Mill Lane, Charminster, Dorchester DT2 9QP* Tel (01305) 262477 E-mail plumsmith@tiscali.co.uk

SMITH, Paul. b 48. STETS 99. **d** 02 **p** 03. NSM Copthorne *Chich* from 02. *7 Heather Close, Copthorne, Crawley RH10 3PZ* Tel (01342) 714308 E-mail heatherclose@freenet.co.uk

SMITH, Paul. b 52. LNSM course 97. **d** 98 **p** 99. OLM Leominster *Heref* from 98. *32 The Meadows, Leominster HR6 8RF* Tel (01568) 615862 *or* 612124

SMITH, Paul Aidan. b 59. Birm Univ BA82. Wycliffe Hall Ox 82. **d** 85 **p** 86. C Selly Park St Steph and St Wulstan *Birm* 85-88; C Kensal Rise St Mark and St Martin *Lon* 88-91; V Water Eaton

Ox 91-00; TR Hale w Badshot Lea *Guildf* 00-02; TV Stantonbury and Willen *Ox* from 02. *2 Hooper Gate, Willen, Milton Keynes MK15 9JR* Tel (01908) 606689 Mobile 07930-308644 E-mail paul_a_smith@bigfoot.com

SMITH, Paul Allan. b 66. Ch Coll Cam BA88 MA00 PhD94. WMMTC 98 Ripon Coll Cuddesdon 99. **d** 00 **p** 01. C Moseley St Mary *Birm* 00-03; P-in-c Tilston and Shocklach *Ches* from 03; Officer for Initial Min Tr from 03. *The Rectory, 41 Inveresk Road, Tilston, Malpas SY14 7ED* Tel (01829) 250628 E-mail paul@smith291066.freeserve.co.uk

SMITH, Paul Andrew. b 55. St Chad's Coll Dur BA76. Chich Th Coll 78. **d** 80 **p** 81. C Habergham Eaves St Matt *Blackb* 80-83; C Ribbleton 83-86; V Rishton 86-05; RD Whalley 95-01; R Cottingham *York* from 05. *The Rectory, Hallgate, Cottingham HU16 4DD* Tel (01482) 847668 E-mail dreadnoughtfam@aol.com

SMITH, Paul Anthony. b 66. Ripon Coll Cuddesdon. **d** 00 **p** 01. C Prestwood and Gt Hampden *Ox* 00-05; P-in-c W Leigh *Portsm* from 05. *St Alban's Vicarage, Martin Road, Havant PO9 5TE* Tel (023) 9245 1751

SMITH, Preb Paul Gregory. b 39. Ex Univ BA61. St Steph Ho Ox 61. **d** 63 **p** 64. C Walthamstow St Mich *Chelmsf* 63-66; C Devonport St Mark Ford *Ex* 66-69; C Hemel Hempstead *St Alb* 69-71; TV 71-83; R Bideford *Ex* 83-96; TR Bideford, Northam, Westward Ho!, Appledore etc 96; Chapl Bideford and Torridge Hosps 83-96; P-in-c Ex St Jas *Ex* 96-98; R 98-03; Preb Ex Cathl from 95; rtd 03. *Valrose, Broad Lane, Appledore, Bideford EX39 1ND* Tel (01237) 423513 E-mail fatherpaulsmith@aol.com

SMITH, Mrs Pauline Frances. b 37. Bris Univ BA58 Lon Univ CertEd59. Sarum & Wells Th Coll 87. **d** 90 **p** 94. C Cobham *Guildf* 90-96; P-in-c Lower Wylye and Till Valley *Sarum* 96-97; TV Wylye and Till Valley 97-03; RD Stonehenge 01-03; rtd 03; Perm to Offic *Glouc* from 04. *267B London Road, Charlton Kings, Cheltenham GL52 6YG* Tel (01242) 222810

SMITH, Peter. b 36. Keele Univ BA60. Cuddesdon Coll 73. **d** 75 **p** 76. C Shrewsbury St Chad *Lich* 75-80; V Burton St Chad 80-90; P-in-c Berwick w Selmeston and Alciston *Chich* 90-91; R 91-02; rtd 02; Perm to Offic *Sarum* from 03. *40 Homefield, Child Okeford, Blandford Forum DT11 8EN* Tel (01258) 861833

SMITH, Peter. b 49. Ex Univ BSc69 PGCE73. Carl Dioc Tr Course. **d** 82 **p** 83. NSM Kendal H Trin *Carl* from 82. *55 Empson Road, Kendal LA9 5PR* Tel (01539) 721467 E-mail rev.p.smith@btinternet.com

SMITH, Peter Alexander. *See* GRAYSMITH, Peter Alexander

SMITH, Peter Denis Frank. b 52. Local Minl Tr Course. **d** 81 **p** 83. OLM Camberwell St Mich w All So w Em *S'wark* 81-95; OLM Croydon St Jo 95-04. *57 Alton Road, Croydon CR0 4LZ* Tel (020) 8760 9656

SMITH, Peter Francis Chasen. b 28. Leeds Univ BA54. Coll of Resurr Mirfield 54. **d** 56 **p** 57. C E Dulwich St Clem *S'wark* 56-59; C Sutton St Nic 59-62; C-in-c Wrangbrook w N Elmsall CD *Wakef* 62-68; Chapl St Aid Sch Harrogate 68-85; P-in-c Lower Nidderdale *Ripon* 85-93; rtd 93; Perm to Offic *Ripon* from 93 and *York* from 95. *Clematis Cottage, Main Street, Kilburn, York YO61 4AH* Tel (01347) 868394 E-mail peter.f.c.smith@btinternet.com

SMITH, Peter Henry. b 62. Bris Univ BA83. SEITE 96. **d** 99 **p** 00. C Romford St Edw *Chelmsf* 99-02; V Aldersbrook from 02. *St Gabriel's Vicarage, 12 Aldersbrook Road, London E12 5HH* Tel (020) 8989 0315 E-mail peterhxsmith@aol.com

SMITH, Peter Howard. b 55. St Andr Univ MTh78. Trin Coll Bris 78. **d** 79 **p** 80. C Handforth *Ches* 79-82; C Eccleston St Luke *Liv* 82-85; V Leyton St Paul *Chelmsf* 85-91; V Darwen St Barn *Blackb* 91-99; TR Bushbury *Lich* from 99. *The Rectory, 382 Bushbury Lane, Wolverhampton WV10 8JP* Tel (01902) 787688 *or* 782226 E-mail phsmith@dial.pipex.com

SMITH, Peter Howard. b 57. St Jo Coll Dur BSc78 Selw Coll Cam BA82 MA85. Ridley Hall Cam 80. **d** 83 **p** 84. C Welling *Roch* 83-87; C Hubberston w Herbrandston and Hasguard etc *St D* 87-89; C Hubberston 89-91; V Canley *Cov* 91-00; V Burney Lane *Birm* from 00; AD Yardley and Bordesley from 05. *Christ Church Vicarage, Burney Lane, Birmingham B8 2AS* Tel 0121-783 7455 E-mail peter@ccbl.org.uk

SMITH, Peter James. b 23. K Coll Lon 49. **d** 53 **p** 54. C Atherton *Man* 53-55; C Wokingham All SS *Ox* 55-56; C Doncaster St Geo *Sheff* 56-59; V Whitgift w Adlingfleet 59-62; Chapl Highcroft Hosp Birm 62-71; C Wolborough w Newton Abbot *Ex* 71-74; C Furze Platt *Ox* 74-78; Travelling Sec Ch Coun for Health and Healing 78-81; P-in-c Bisham *Ox* 82-90; rtd 90; NSM Hindhead *Guildf* 90-96; Perm to Offic *Guildf* 96-97 and *Portsm* from 97. *4 Copse Close, Liss GU33 7EW* Tel (01730) 894099

SMITH, Peter Michael. b 28. Open Univ BA75. K Coll Lon 52. **d** 56 **p** 57. C Pokesdown St Jas *Win* 56-59; C Weeke 59-63; V Hutton Roof *Carl* 63-69; V Barrow St Aid 69-72; V Preston Patrick 72-93; rtd 93; Chapl to the Deaf and Hard of Hearing *Carl* from 93; Perm to Offic from 93. *7 Green Road, Kendal LA9 4QR* Tel (01539) 726741 Mobile 07973-224289 E-mail peter@smith687.freeserve.co.uk

SMITH, Peter William. b 31. Glouc Th Course 74. **d** 77 **p** 77. C Coleford w Staunton *Glouc* 77; Hon C 77-87; P-in-c Alderton w Gt Washbourne 87-94; R Alderton, Gt Washbourne, Dumbleton etc 94-97; rtd 97; Perm to Offic *Ex* from 97. *5 Western Drive, Starcross, Exeter EX6 8EH* Tel (01626) 890115

SMITH, Philip David. b 55. Shoreditch Coll Lon BEd78. Oak Hill Th Coll BA98. **d** 98 **p** 99. C Cheltenham St Mary, St Matt, St Paul and H Trin *Glouc* 98-03; TV Cheltenham St Mark from 03. *3 Deacon Close, Cheltenham GL51 3NY* Tel (01242) 528567

SMITH, Philip Hathway. b 66. St Andr Univ MTh88. Coll of Resurr Mirfield 90. **d** 92 **p** 93. C Shrewsbury St Giles w Sutton and Atcham *Lich* 92-94; C Clayton 94-97; TV Hanley H Ev 97-02; C Croydon St Mich w St Jas *S'wark* 02-04; P-in-c Sydenham All SS from 04. *All Saints' Vicarage, 41 Trewsbury Road, London SE26 5DP* Tel (020) 8778 3065

SMITH, Philip James. b 32. St Alb Minl Tr Scheme. **d** 82 **p** 83. NSM Radlett *St Alb* 82-85; C 85-89; V Codicote 89-99; RD Hatfield 95-01; rtd 99; Perm to Offic *St Alb* from 00. *34 Cherry Tree Rise, Walkern, Stevenage SG2 7JL* Tel (01438) 861951

SMITH, Philip James. b 60. ACGI82 Imp Coll Lon BScEng82 Fitzw Coll Cam BA94. Ridley Hall Cam CTM95. **d** 95 **p** 96. C Aldborough w Boroughbridge and Roecliffe *Ripon* 95-99; V from 99. *The Vicarage, Church Lane, Boroughbridge, York YO51 9BA* Tel (01423) 322433 E-mail vicar@aldwithbb.freeserve.co.uk

SMITH, Philip Lloyd Cyril. b 22. Ch Coll Cam BA47 MA49. Wycliffe Hall Ox 47. **d** 49 **p** 50. C St Helens St Helen *Liv* 49-52; C Woking St Jo *Guildf* 52-56; R Burslem St Jo *Lich* 56-83; P-in-c Burslem St Paul 82-83; R Burslem 83-86; rtd 86; Perm to Offic *Sheff* 86-01. *Upper Treasurer's House, 42 Bromley College, London Road, Bromley BR1 1PE* Tel (020) 8290 1566

SMITH, Ralston Antonio. b 28. St Pet Coll Jamaica 53. **d** 56 **p** 57. Jamaica 56-60 and from 72; C Ex St Thos *Ex* 60-62; C Withycombe Raleigh 62-68; V Exwick 68-72; rtd 93. *PO Box 136, Anglican House, United Theological College, Kingston 7, Jamaica*

SMITH, Raymond Charles William. b 56. K Coll Lon BD78 AKC78. Coll of Resurr Mirfield 79. **d** 80 **p** 81. C Iffley *Ox* 80-83; C Wallingford w Crowmarsh Gifford etc 83-86; V Tilehurst St Mary 86-96; TR Haywards Heath St Wilfrid *Chich* from 96. *The Rectory, St Wilfrid's Way, Haywards Heath RH16 3QH* Tel (01444) 413300

SMITH, Canon Raymond Douglas. b 31. TCD BA53 MA56 BD56. **d** 54 **p** 55. C Belfast St Mich *Conn* 54-56; C Ballymacarrett St Patr *D & D* 56-58; CMS Tr Coll Chislehurst 58-60; Kenya (CMS) 60-71; Asst Gen Sec (Hibernian) CMS 71-74; Gen Sec CMS 74-86; CMS Ireland 76-86; Hon Can N Maseno from 78; I Powerscourt w Kilbride and Annacrevy *D & G* 86-96; Can Ch Ch Cathl Dublin 94-96; rtd 96. *Glencarrig Lodge, Kindlestown Upper, Delgany, Co Wicklow, Irish Republic* Tel (00353) (1) 287 3229

SMITH, Raymond Frederick. b 28. Lon Univ BSc51 Leeds Univ MA65. Oak Hill Th Coll 51. **d** 53 **p** 54. C Toxteth Park St Philemon *Liv* 53-56; C Halliwell St Pet *Man* 56-58; V Denton and Weston *Bradf* 58-66; V Normanton *Wakef* 66-81; RD Chevet 73-81; R Moreton *Ches* 81-90; rtd 90. *Cornerways, Station Road, Llanymynech SY22 6EG* Tel (01691) 839294

SMITH, Raymond George Richard. b 38. Univ of Wales (Ban) BSc61 MSc65. WMMTC 91. **d** 94 **p** 95. NSM Edgmond w Kynnersley and Preston Wealdmoors *Lich* 94-97; Chapl Princess R Hosp NHS Trust Telford 95-03; V Llandegfan w Llandysilio *Ban* from 03. *The Vicarage, Mona Road, Menai Bridge LL59 5EA* Tel (01248) 717265

SMITH, Raymond Horace David. b 30. Sir John Cass Coll Lon FIBMS61. Lon Coll of Div 64. **d** 67 **p** 68. C Shoreditch St Leon *Lon* 67-70; SAMS 71-73; Chile 71-80; P-in-c Castle Hedingham *Chelmsf* 80-83; P-in-c Cambridge St Phil *Ely* 83-86; V 86-91; Chapl Ibiza *Eur* 91-94; C Lowton St Mary *Liv* 94-96; rtd 96; Perm to Offic *Ely* 96-02 and from 03; *Win* 02-03. *15 The Sheltons, Frinton-on-Sea CO13 0LX* Tel (01255) 671041 E-mail camsmith@freeuk.com

SMITH, Canon Richard. b 47. Westmr Coll Ox MTh99. St D Coll Lamp DipTh75. **d** 75 **p** 76. C Aberavon *Llan* 75-78; Ind Chapl 78-81; TV Bournemouth St Pet w St Swithun, H Trin etc *Win* 81-85; Chapl Colchester Gen Hosp 85-94; Chapl Severalls Hosp Colchester 85-94; Sen Chapl Essex Rivers Healthcare NHS Trust from 94; Sen Chapl NE Essex Mental Health NHS Trust 94-01; Sen Chapl N Essex Mental Health Partnership NHS Trust from 01; Bp's Adv for Hosp Chapl *Chelmsf* from 99; Hon Can Chelmsf Cathl from 01. *The Chaplain's Office, Colchester General Hospital, Turner Road, Colchester CO4 5JL* Tel (01206) 742513 E-mail richard.smith@essexrivers.nhs.uk

SMITH, Richard Geoffrey. b 46. St Jo Coll Dur BA68 MA69. St Steph Ho Ox BA74 MA78. **d** 75 **p** 76. C Brentwood St Thos *Chelmsf* 75-78; C Corringham 78-81; R Shepton Beauchamp w Barrington, Stocklinch etc *B & W* 81-83; TV Redditch, The Ridge *Worc* 85-89; R Teme Valley N 89-98; Perm to Offic *Heref* from 02. *Churchbridge, Nash, Ludlow SY8 3AX* Tel (01584) 891329

SMITH, Richard Harwood. b 34. Sarum Th Coll 57. **d** 59 **p** 60. C Kington w Huntington *Heref* 59-62; Br Guiana 62-66; Guyana 66-69; C Broseley w Benthall *Heref* 69-70; Lic to Offic 70-76; USPG Area Sec (Dios Heref and Worc) 70-76; R Wigmore Abbey 76-84; V Eye w Braiseworth and Yaxley *St E* 84-96; P-in-c Bedingfield 84-96; P-in-c Occold 84-96; rtd 96. *33 Broad Street, Leominster HR6 8DD* Tel (01568) 610676

SMITH, Canon Richard Ian. b 46. Jes Coll Ox BA69 MA80. Ripon Hall Ox 69. **d** 70 **p** 71. C Eston *York* 70-76; TV E Ham w Upton Park St Alb *Chelmsf* 76-80; R Crook *Dur* 80-86; V Stanley 80-86; V Billingham St Cuth from 86; AD Stockton 92-01; Hon Can Dur Cathl from 98. *St Cuthbert's Vicarage, Church Road, Billingham TS23 1BW* Tel (01642) 659538 Fax 553236

SMITH, Richard Keith. b 44. Harper Adams Agric Coll NDA69. St Jo Coll Nottm. **d** 84 **p** 85. C Wirksworth w Alderwasley, Carsington etc *Derby* 84-87; R Hulland, Atlow, Bradley and Hognaston 87-96; P-in-c Long Compton, Whichford and Barton-on-the-Heath *Cov* from 96; P-in-c Wolford w Burmington from 97; P-in-c Cherington w Stourton from 97; P-in-c Barcheston from 97. *The Vicarage, Broad Street, Long Compton, Shipston-on-Stour CV36 5JH* Tel (01608) 684207

SMITH, Richard Michael. b 52. Lon Univ BA74. EAMTC 79. **d** 82 **p** 83. NSM Cambridge Ascension *Ely* 82-84; C Rainham *Roch* 84-88; V Southborough St Thos 88-96; P-in-c Shanklin St Sav *Portsm* 96-99; V from 99; P-in-c Lake 96-99; V from 99. *The Vicarage, Lake, Sandown PO36 9JT* Tel (01983) 405666

SMITH, Robert Harold. b 23. Lon Univ BA49. Oak Hill Th Coll 46. **d** 50 **p** 51. C Nottingham St Ann *S'well* 50-52; C-in-c Elburton CD *Ex* 52-57; V Lowestoft Ch Ch *Nor* 57-67; R Upton *Ex* 67-80; R Bressingham *Nor* 80-81; P-in-c N w S Lopham 80-81; P-in-c Fersfield 80-81; R Bressingham w N and S Lopham and Fersfield 81-87; rtd 87; Perm to Offic *Nor* from 87. *22 St Walstan's Road, Taverham, Norwich NR8 6NG* Tel (01603) 861285

SMITH, Robert Harrison. b 62. Lon Bible Coll BA90 Nottm Univ MA(TS)00 MA(MM)01 Cam Univ PGCE93. St Jo Coll Nottm 99. **d** 01 **p** 02. C Chatham St Phil and St Jas *Roch* 01-05; C Nailsea H Trin *B & W* from 05. *3 Wedmore Road, Nailsea, Bristol BS48 4PZ* Tel (01275) 790320
E-mail robandesther@rhsmith.freeserve.co.uk

✠**SMITH, The Rt Revd Robin Jonathan Norman.** b 36. Worc Coll Ox BA60 MA64. Ridley Hall Cam 60. **d** 62 **p** 63 **c** 90. C Barking St Marg *Chelmsf* 62-67; Chapl Lee Abbey 67-72; V Chesham St Mary *Ox* 72-80; RD Amersham 79-82; TR Gt Chesham 80-90; Hon Can Ch Ch 88-90; Suff Bp Hertford *St Alb* 90-01; rtd 01; Hon Asst Bp St Alb from 02. *7 Aysgarth Road, Redbourn, St Albans AL3 7PJ* Tel and fax (01582) 791964
E-mail bprobin@no7.me.uk

SMITH, Rodney Frederic Brittain. b 37. Jes Coll Cam BA61 MA64. St Steph Ho Ox 87. **d** 88 **p** 89. NSM Rainworth *S'well* 88-89; C Basford St Aid 89-91; C Sneinton St Cypr 91-94; P-in-c Sneinton St Matthias 94-96; V 96-02; P-in-c Sneinton St Steph w St Alb 01-02; rtd 02. *41A Cyprus Road, Nottingham NG3 5EB* Tel 0115-962 0378

SMITH, Rodney John Boughton. b 19. AKC41. Sarum Th Coll 41. **d** 42 **p** 43. C Frome St Jo *B & W* 42-44; C Eastbourne St Andr *Chich* 45-48; C Belvedere St Aug *Roch* 48-49; C Horsham *Chich* 49-55; V Kings Bromley *Lich* 55-60; V Porthill 60-68; V E Meon *Portsm* 68-84; V Langrish 76-84; rtd 84; Perm to Offic *Ex* 84-99. *3 Barton Orchard, Tipton St John, Sidmouth EX10 0AN* Tel (01404) 814673

SMITH, Roger. *See* SMITH, Thomas Roger

SMITH, Roger. *See* SMITH, John Roger

SMITH, Roger Owen. b 50. Univ of Wales (Abth) BA72 St Chad's Coll Dur CertEd73 FRGS. S'wark Ord Course 84. **d** 87 **p** 88. NSM Nunhead St Antony w St Silas *S'wark* 87-91; NSM Forest Hill St Aug 91-98; NSM Crofton Park St Hilda w St Cypr 91-98; NSM Brockley Hill St Sav 91-98; NSM Camberwell St Giles w St Matt 98-00; Perm to Offic *Cant* from 01. *22 Wear Bay Road, Folkestone CT19 6BN* Tel (01303) 259896

SMITH, Canon Roger Stuart. b 41. Chich Th Coll 65. **d** 66 **p** 67. C Garforth *Ripon* 66-70; C Hilborough Gp *Nor* 70-73; TV 73-78; V Mendham w Metfield and Withersdale *St E* 78-89; P-in-c Fressingfield w Weybread 86-89; R Fressingfield, Mendham etc 90-91; RD Hoxne 86-91; R Kelsale-cum-Carlton, Middleton, Theberton etc 91-01; C Yoxmere Conf 01-04; RD Saxmundham 96-03; Hon Can St E Cathl 97-04; rtd 04; Perm to Offic *St E* from 04. *Rookery Nook, The Green, St Margaret South Elmham, Harleston IP20 0PN* Tel (01986) 782465
E-mail canonroger@middleton3112.freeserve.co.uk

SMITH, Roger William. b 48. Imp Coll Lon BSc70. EAMTC. **d** 00 **p** 01. NSM Rothwell w Orton, Rushton w Glendon and Pipewell *Pet* from 00. *6A Kipton Close, Rothwell, Kettering NN14 6DR* Tel (01536) 710981
E-mail roger.smith@corusgroup.com

SMITH, Ronald. b 26. ALCD56. **d** 56 **p** 57. C Gravesend St Jas *Roch* 56-59; C-in-c Istead Rise CD 59-79; V Istead Rise 79-93; rtd 93; Perm to Offic *Roch* from 93. *114 Maidstone Road, Rochester ME1 3DT* Tel (01834) 829183

SMITH, Ronald Deric. b 21. Lon Univ BA46. Bps' Coll Cheshunt 59. **d** 61 **p** 62. C Crayford *Roch* 61-67; USA 67-68; C W Malling w Offham *Roch* 68-71; V Slade Green 71-78; V Bromley Common St Luke 78-91; rtd 91; Perm to Offic *S'wark* and *Roch* from 91. *5 Bromley College, London Road, Bromley BR1 1PE* Tel (020) 8464 0212

SMITH, Ronald Eric. b 43. EMMTC 93. **d** 93 **p** 94. NSM Wingerworth *Derby* 93-99; NSM Newbold w Dunston 99-01; NSM Loundsley Green from 01. *21 Windsor Drive, Wingerworth, Chesterfield S42 6TG* Tel (01246) 279004

SMITH, Canon Ronald James. b 36. Linc Th Coll 73. **d** 75 **p** 76. C Bilborough St Jo *S'well* 75-78; P-in-c Colwick 78-81; R 81-85; P-in-c Netherfield 78-81; V 81-85; C Worksop Priory 85-90; TV Langley and Parkfield *Man* 90-95; P-in-c Barton w Peel Green 95-01; Hon Can Tamale from 01; rtd 01; Perm to Offic *Man* from 01. *12 Bramhall Drive, Holmes Chapel, Crewe CW4 7EJ* Tel (01477) 544072
E-mail anne@vicarage01.freeserve.co.uk

SMITH, Ronald William. b 45. St Jo Coll York CertEd67. Chich Th Coll 70. **d** 73 **p** 74. C Scarborough St Martin *York* 73-76; C Stainton-in-Cleveland 76-80; V E Coatham 80-89; V Brookfield from 89. *Brookfield Vicarage, 89 Low Lane, Brookfield, Middlesbrough TS5 8EF* Tel (01642) 282241
E-mail revronsmith@ntlworld.com

SMITH, The Very Revd Rowan Quentin. b 43. AKC66. St Boniface Warminster 66. **d** 67 **p** 68. C Matroosfontein S Africa 67-69; C Bonteheuwel 70; C Plumstead All SS 71-72; P-in-c Grassy Park 72-77; CR 80-89; Chapl St Martin's Sch Rosettenville 80-88; Chapl Cape Town Univ 88-90; Prov Exec Officer 90-96; Can of Prov 93-96; Can Pastor St Geo Cathl 96; Dean Cape Town from 96. *The Deanery, 29 Upper Orange Street, Oranjezicht, 8001 South Africa* Tel (0027) (21) 465 2609 *or* 423 3371 Fax 423 8466 E-mail sgcdean@icon.co.za

SMITH, Preb Roy Leonard. b 36. Clifton Th Coll 63. **d** 66 **p** 67. C Clapham St Jas *S'wark* 66-70; C Kennington St Mark 70-74; C-in-c Southall Em CD *Lon* 74-83; V Stonebridge St Mich from 83; Preb St Paul's Cathl from 96. *St Michael's Vicarage, Hillside, London NW10 8LB* Tel (020) 8965 7443
E-mail prebroy@yahoo.co.uk

SMITH, Royston. b 55. EMMTC 87. **d** 90 **p** 91. NSM Shirland *Derby* 90-94; NSM Ashover and Brackenfield 95-01; NSM Ashover and Brackenfield w Wessington from 01. *Kirkdale Cottage, Oakstedge Lane, Milltown, Ashover, Chesterfield S45 0HA* Tel (01246) 590975
E-mail royston@kirkdalecottage.freeserve.co.uk

SMITH, Royston Burleigh. b 26. St Deiniol's Hawarden 76. **d** 79 **p** 80. C Prestatyn *St As* 79-83; V Kerry and Llanmerewig 83-90; C Rhyl w St Ann 90-91; rtd 91. *45 Clwyd Park, Kinmel Bay, Rhyl LL18 5EJ* Tel (01745) 337684

SMITH, Ruth. *See* SMITH, Ms Vivienne Ruth

SMITH, Ryc. *See* SMITH, Charles Rycroft

SMITH, Mrs Shirley Ann. b 46. RSCN68 RM82 RGN84 RHV86. Sarum & Wells Th Coll 89. **d** 93 **p** 94. C Totton *Win* 93-96; Chapl Portsm Hosps NHS Trust 96-98; V Lord's Hill *Win* 98-01; TV Beaminster Area *Sarum* 01-05; rtd 05. *7 The Moor, Puddletown, Dorchester DT2 8TE* Tel (01305) 849262

SMITH, Stephen. b 53. Leeds Poly CQSW78. Sarum & Wells Th Coll 87. **d** 89 **p** 90. C Redcar *York* 89-92; C Leeds St Aid *Ripon* 92-96; R Lanteglos by Camelford w Advent *Truro* 96-99; Chapl Hull and E Yorks Hosps NHS Trust 99-01. *Address temp unknown*

SMITH, Stephen. b 60. Coll of Resurr Mirfield 02. **d** 04 **p** 05. C Burnley St Cath w St Alb and St Paul *Blackb* from 04. *St Alban's House, 8 Mary Towneley Fold, Burnley BB10 4LZ* Tel (01282) 411348

SMITH, Stephen John. b 46. Kelham Th Coll 65. **d** 69 **p** 70. C Warsop *S'well* 69-73; C Heaton Ch Ch *Man* 73-75; V Bolton St Bede 75-78; R Bilborough w Strelley *S'well* 78-84; R E Leake 84-92; P-in-c Costock 84-92; P-in-c Rempstone 84-92; P-in-c Stanford on Soar 84-92; R E and W Leake, Stanford-on-Soar, Rempstone etc 92-97; RD W Bingham 92-97; V Swaffham *Nor* from 97; C Gt and Lt Dunham w Gt and Lt Fransham and Sporle from 03; RD Breckland from 02; Chapl NW Anglia Healthcare NHS Trust from 99. *The Vicarage, White Cross Road, Swaffham PE37 7QY* Tel and fax (01760) 721373
E-mail frjohnsmith@aol.com

SMITH, Stephen John. b 55. Lon Univ BD80. Trin Coll Bris 77. **d** 81 **p** 82. C Fulham St Matt *Lon* 81-86; C Stoke Gifford *Bris* 86-90; TV 90-01; rtd 01; Perm to Offic *Bris* from 01. *47 Saxon Way, Bradley Stoke, Bristol BS32 9AR* Tel (01454) 616429
E-mail steve@revsmith.freeserve.co.uk

SMITH, Canon Stephen John Stanyon. b 49. Sussex Univ BA81 Birm Univ MSocSc83. Westcott Ho Cam 83. **d** 85 **p** 86. C Four Oaks *Birm* 85-89; USA from 89; Asst P Cheyenne River Reservation 89-91; Miss P Rosebud Reservation 91-94; Assoc R Ivoryton and Essex 94-98; Can St Paul's Cathl Buffalo from 98.

100 Beard Avenue, Buffalo, NY 14214, USA Tel and fax (001) (716) 838 0240 *or* tel 855 0900 Fax 855 0910 E-mail stanyon@juno.com

SMITH, Stephen Thomas. b 55. Westcott Ho Cam 95. **d** 97 **p** 98. C Kempston Transfiguration *St Alb* 97-01; C Bromham w Oakley and Stagsden 01-05; TV Elstow from 05. *St Michael's Vicarage, Faldo Road, Bedford MK42 0EH* Tel (01234) 266920

SMITH, Steven Barnes. b 60. Cov Poly BA83 Leeds Univ BA86. Coll of Resurr Mirfield 84. **d** 87 **p** 88. C Darlington St Mark w St Paul *Dur* 87-89; C Prescot *Liv* 89-91; V Hindley Green 91-96; Asst Chapl Havering Hosps NHS Trust 96-98; Chapl Team Ldr Chelsea and Westmr Healthcare NHS Trust from 98. *Chelsea and Westminster Hospital, 369 Fulham Road, London SW10 9NH* Tel (020) 8746 8083 *or* 8746 8000 E-mail steven.smith@chelwest.nhs.uk

SMITH, Steven Gerald Crosland. b 48. Linc Th Coll 82. **d** 84 **p** 85. Chapl St Jo Sch Tiffield 84-87; C Towcester w Easton Neston *Pet* 84-87; P-in-c Kings Heath 87-89; V 89-93; TV N Creedy *Ex* from 93; RD Cadbury from 02. *The Vicarage, Cheriton Fitzpaine, Crediton EX17 4JB* Tel (01363) 866352 E-mail stevengcsmith@aol.com

SMITH, Susan. b 48. Swansea Coll of Educn 69 Open Univ Cert Business Studies89 FInstD87. Ox Min Course 93. **d** 96 **p** 97. C Burnham w Dropmore, Hitcham and Taplow *Ox* 96-00; TV Whitton *Sarum* 00-02; TV W Slough *Ox* from 02. *St Andrew's House, Washington Drive, Slough SL1 5RE* Tel (01628) 661994

SMITH, Miss Susan Ann. b 50. Bris Univ BA72 St Jo Coll York PGCE73. Ripon Coll Cuddesdon 97. **d** 99 **p** 00. C Swaffham *Nor* 99-02; R King's Beck from 02. *The Rectory, Aylsham Road, Felmingham, North Walsham NR28 0LD* Tel (01692) 402382

SMITH, Mrs Susan Jennifer. b 52. MCIPD90 DipTM90. St Alb and Ox Min Course 94. **d** 97 **p** 98. C Ascot Heath *Ox* 97-01; P-in-c Flixton St Mich *Man* from 01. *The Rectory, 348 Church Road, Urmston, Manchester M41 6HR* Tel 0161-748 2884 Fax as telephone E-mail saxoncross@talk21.com

SMITH, Terence. b 38. Lon Univ DipTh69 Brunel Univ BSc79 Cranfield Inst of Tech MSc80. Tyndale Hall Bris 67. **d** 69 **p** 70. C Cheylesmore *Cov* 69-71; C Leamington Priors St Paul 71-74; V Halliwell St Paul *Man* 74-75; Lect Uxbridge Coll 80-86; R Medstead w Wield *Win* 86-99; P-in-c Kennington *Ox* 99-03; V from 03. *The New Vicarage, The Avenue, Kennington, Oxford OX1 5AD* Tel (01865) 321504 E-mail ter.s@btinternet.com

SMITH, Terence David. b 59. **d** 02. NSM Myddle *Lich* from 02; NSM Broughton from 02; NSM Loppington w Newtown from 02. *Lamorna, Scholars' Lane, Loppington, Shrewsbury SY4 5RE* Tel 07703-183034 (mobile)

SMITH, Terrence Gordon. b 34. TD83. MCSP58 SRN60. St Mich Coll Llan 68. **d** 70 **p** 71. C Gelligaer *Llan* 70-73; CF (TA) 72-99; C Aberavon *Llan* 73-75; V Pontlottyn w Fochriw 75-77; V Kenfig Hill 77-84; V Dyffryn 84-99; rtd 99. *1 Gnoll Crescent, Neath SA11 3TF*

SMITH, Thomas Roger. b 48. Cant Sch of Min 77. **d** 80 **p** 81. NSM Folkestone St Sav *Cant* 80-82; NSM Lyminge w Paddlesworth, Stanford w Postling etc 82-85; Chapl Cant Sch of Min 82-91; R Biddenden and Smarden *Cant* 86-91; TR Totnes, Bridgetown and Berry Pomeroy etc *Ex* 91-96; P-in-c Haslingden w Grane and Stonefold *Blackb* 96-98; V from 98; RD Accrington from 03. *St James's Vicarage, Church Lane, Haslingden, Rossendale BB4 5QZ* Tel (01706) 215533 E-mail rsmith9456@aol.com

SMITH, Timothy. b 58. Trin Coll Bris 00. **d** 02 **p** 03. C Warminster Ch Ch *Sarum* from 02. *1 Brook Close, Warminster BA12 8SG* Tel (01985) 214569 E-mail timmy.smith@virgin.net

SMITH, Timothy Brian. b 62. Brisbane Coll BA(Theol)92. **d** 92 **p** 92. Australia 92-94 and from 96; C Grafton St Jo Ev 92-94; C Heald Green St Cath *Ches* 94-96; R Mid Richmond 96-01; I Belmont St Steph from 01. *42 Regent Street, Belmont, Vic, Australia 3216* Tel (0061) (3) 5243 2557 Mobile 412-673152 E-mail timsandy@turboweb.net.au

SMITH, Toni. *See* SMITH, Antoinette

SMITH, Tony. b 23. Roch Th Coll 62. **d** 64 **p** 65. Chapl TS Arethusa 64-67; C Frindsbury *Roch* 64-67; V Hadlow 67-78; R Wrotham 78-89; RD Shoreham 80-89; rtd 89; Perm to Offic *Roch* 89-05. *2 Craftman Cottages, Oxborough Road, Stoke Ferry, King's Lynn PE33 9SY* Tel (01366) 501497

SMITH, Trevor Andrew. b 60. St Jo Coll Dur BA86. Cranmer Hall Dur 83. **d** 87 **p** 88. C Guisborough *York* 87-90; C Northallerton w Kirby Sigston 90-95; R Middleton, Newton and Sinnington 95-01; Chapl St Luke's Hospice Plymouth from 01. *St Luke's Hospice, Stamford Road, Plymouth PL9 9XA* Tel (01752) 401172 *or* 316868 Fax 481878

SMITH, Trevor Bernard. b 33. Culham Coll of Educn CertEd70 Ox Poly BEd82. Oak Hill Th Coll 61. **d** 64 **p** 65. C Bispham *Blackb* 64-66; C Chesham St Mary *Ox* 66-68; Perm to Offic 90-94; rtd 96. *126 The Broadway, Herne Bay CT6 8HA* Tel (01227) 362665

SMITH, Vernon Hemingway. b 33. St Alb Minl Tr Scheme 83. **d** 86 **p** 87. NSM Leighton Buzzard w Eggington, Hockliffe etc *St Alb* 86-98; NSM Newbury *Ox* 98-03; rtd 03. *41 Orion Way, Leighton Buzzard LU7 8XJ* Tel (01525) 370304

SMITH, Ms Vivienne Ruth. b 57. St Jo Coll Dur BA79. N Ord Course 95. **d** 00 **p** 01. C Heckmondwike *Wakef* 00-03; TV Dewsbury from 03. *St John's Vicarage, 68 Staincliffe Road, Dewsbury WF13 4ED* Tel (01924) 458371 E-mail r2cstsmith@btinternet.com

SMITH, Walter. b 37. Westcott Ho Cam 67. **d** 69 **p** 70. C N Hull St Mich *York* 69-72; C Whitby 72-74; V Newington w Dairycoates 74-77; P-in-c Skipton Bridge 77-78; P-in-c Baldersby 77-78; TV Thirsk 77-88; P-in-c Topcliffe w Dalton and Dishforth 82-87; V Lythe w Ugthorpe 88-97; rtd 97; Perm to Offic *York* from 98. *102 Upgang Lane, Whitby YO21 3JW* Tel (01947) 605456

SMITH, Miss Wendy Hamlyn. b 41. ALA70 Open Univ BA85. Ridley Hall Cam 85. **d** 87 **p** 94. C Stroud H Trin *Glouc* 87-90 and 91-92; Australia 90-91; TD Stoke-upon-Trent *Lich* 92-94; TV 94-97; V Pheasey 97-02; P-in-c Barlaston from 02; Chapl Douglas Macmillan Hospice Blurton from 04. *The Vicarage, 2 Longton Road, Barlaston, Stoke-on-Trent ST12 9AA* Tel (01782) 372452 E-mail wendy@whsphea.fsnet.co.uk

SMITH, William Joseph Thomas. b 20. Chich Th Coll 54. **d** 55 **p** 56. C Laindon w Basildon *Chelmsf* 56-61; R Stifford 61-65; V Boreham 65-90; rtd 90; Perm to Offic *Chelmsf* from 90. *7 Trelawn, Church Road, Boreham, Chelmsford CM3 3EF* Tel (01245) 466930

SMITH, William Manton. b 64. Univ of Wales (Abth) LLB85 St Jo Coll Dur PGCE90. United Th Coll Abth BD89 St Jo Coll Nottm 91. **d** 93 **p** 94. C Coventry Caludon *Cov* 93-97; V Exhall from 97. *Exhall Vicarage, Ash Green, Coventry CV7 9AA* Tel (024) 7636 2997 E-mail william.smith@fish.co.uk

SMITH, Canon William Melvyn. b 47. K Coll Lon BD69 AKC69 PGCE70. St Aug Coll Cant 71. **d** 71 **p** 72. C Kingswinford H Trin *Lich* 71-73; Hon C Coseley Ch Ch 73-74; C Wednesbury St Paul Wood Green 75-78; V Coseley St Chad 78-91; TR Wordsley 91-93; RD Himley 83-93; TR Wordsley *Worc* 93-96; RD Himley 93-96; Stewardship and Resources Officer from 97; Hon Can Worc Cathl from 03. *14 Beech Tree Close, Kingswinford DY6 7DR* Tel (01384) 357062 *or* (01905) 20537 E-mail melvynsm@aol.com *or* msmith@cofe-worcester.org.uk

SMITH-CAMERON, Canon Ivor Gill. b 29. Madras Univ BA50 MA52. Coll of Resurr Mirfield. **d** 54 **p** 55. C Rumboldswyke *Chich* 54-58; Chapl Imp Coll *Lon* 58-72; Dioc Missr *S'wark* 72-92; Can Res S'wark Cathl 72-94; C Battersea Park All SS 92-94; Hon C 94-96; Hon C Battersea Fields 96-05; Co-ord All Asian Chr Consultation 92-93; rtd 94; Chapl to The Queen 95-99; Perm to Offic *S'wark* from 05. *24 Holmewood Gardens, London SW2 3RS* Tel (020) 8678 8977 E-mail holmewood24@surefish.co.uk

SMITHAM, Ann. *See* HOWELLS, Mrs Elizabeth Ann

✠**SMITHSON, The Rt Revd Alan.** b 36. Qu Coll Ox BA62 MA68. Qu Coll Birm DipTh64. **d** 64 **p** 65 **c** 90. C Skipton Ch Ch *Bradf* 64-68; C Ox St Mary V w St Cross and St Pet *Ox* 68-72; Chapl Qu Coll Ox 69-72; Chapl Reading Univ *Ox* 72-77; V Bracknell 77-83; TR 83-84; Can Res Carl Cathl *Carl* 84-90; Dir Dioc Tr Inst 84-90; Dioc Dir of Tr 85-90; Suff Bp Jarrow *Dur* 90-01; rtd 02. *St Crispin's, Crispin Street, Creetown, Newton Stewart DG8 7JT* Tel (01671) 820310

SMITHSON, Michael John. b 47. Newc Univ BA68 Lon Univ BD79 Dur Univ PGCE FRGS. Trin Coll Bris 76. **d** 79 **p** 80. C S Mimms Ch Ch *Lon* 79-81; Support and Public Relations Sec UCCF 82-84; R Frating w Thorrington *Chelmsf* 84-88; V Portsea St Luke *Portsm* 88-04. *52 Walmer Road, Portsmouth PO1 5AS* Tel 07802-482584 (mobile)

SMITHURST, Jonathan Peter. b 54. EMMTC DTPS94. **d** 94 **p** 95. NSM Bramcote *S'well* 94-03; NSM Attenborough from 03; Acting AD Beeston 98-99; AD from 99. *46 Sandy Lane, Beeston, Nottingham NG9 3GS* Tel 0115-922 6588 E-mail j.smithurst@ctlmail.co.uk

SMITS, Eric. b 29. **d** 61 **p** 62. C Thornaby on Tees St Paul *York* 61-66; R Brotton Parva 66-98; rtd 98. *7 Pikes Nurseries, Ludham, Great Yarmouth NR29 5NW* Tel (01692) 678156

SMOUT, Francis David James. b 36. TD. **d** 03 **p** 04. NSM Eyemouth *Edin* from 03. *Benedict House, Coldingham, Eyemouth TD14 5NE* Tel (01890) 771220 E-mail fdjsmout@fish.co.uk

SMOUT, Canon Michael John. b 37. St Pet Coll Ox BA61 MA75 Lon Univ BD64. Lon Coll of Div 62. **d** 64 **p** 65. C Toxteth Park St Philemon w St Silas *Liv* 64-69; C Everton St Sav 69-70; Missr E Everton Gp of Chs 70-74; V Everton St Sav w St Cuth 74-79; R Aughton St Mich 79-02; RD Ormskirk 82-89; AD 89-02; Hon Can Liv Cathl 92-02; rtd 02. *4 Victoria Road, Aughton, Ormskirk L39 5AU* Tel (01695) 423054

SMURTHWAITE, William. b 25. Brasted Th Coll 53 Edin Th Coll 54. **d** 57 **p** 58. C S Shields St Simon *Dur* 57-59; Miss to Seamen 59-72; Lagos Nigeria 59-63; Port of Spain Trinidad and Tobago 63-65; Port Chapl Immingham 65-72; Lic to Offic *Linc* 65-72; R Ladybank *St And* 73-90; R Cupar 73-90; rtd 90. *10 Park View, Balmullo, St Andrews KY16 0DN* Tel (01334) 870639

SMYTH, Anthony Irwin. b 40. TCD BA63 MA66. Clifton Th Coll 64. **d** 66 **p** 67. C Worthing St Geo *Chich* 66-69; SAMS Chile 70-75; Dir Th Educn Valparaiso 72-75; C Woodley St Jo the Ev *Ox* 76-80; V St Leonards St Ethelburga *Chich* 80-93; R Stopham and Fittleworth from 93; rtd 05; Perm to Offic *Portsm* and *Chich* from 05. *20 Grenehurst Way, Petersfield GU31 4AZ* Tel (01730) 260370 E-mail anthony.smyth@btinternet.com

SMYTH, Francis George. b 20. Ridley Hall Cam 64. **d** 65 **p** 66. C Ormskirk *Liv* 65-70; V Bicton *Lich* 70-90; Chapl HM Pris Shrewsbury 71-90; rtd 90; Perm to Offic *Lich* from 90. *41 Sutton Road, Shrewsbury SY8 6DL* Tel (01743) 360030

SMYTH, Gordon William. b 47. Open Univ BA. St Jo Coll Nottm 81. **d** 83 **p** 84. C St Keverne *Truro* 83-86; V Landrake w St Erney and Botus Fleming 86-95; RD E Wivelshire 94-95; V Highertown and Baldhu from 95. *All Saints' Vicarage, Highertown, Truro TR1 3LD* Tel (01872) 261944 E-mail asht194@hotmail.com

SMYTH, Canon Kenneth James. b 44. TCD BA67 MA72. **d** 68 **p** 69. C Bangor Abbey *D & D* 68-71; C Holywood 71-74; I Gilnahirk 74-82; I Newtownards w Movilla Abbey 82-89; I Newtownards from 89; Preb Wicklow St Patr Cathl Dublin from 93. *The Rectory, 36 Belfast Road, Newtownards BT23 4TT* Tel and fax (028) 9181 2527 *or* 9181 3193 E-mail kennethjsmyth@aol.com

SMYTH, Peter Charles Gordon. b 72. Univ of Wales (Ban) BA94 TCD BTh98. CITC. **d** 98 **p** 99. C Stillorgan w Blackrock *D & G* 98-02; Canada from 02. *2 Sydney Street, Thunder Bay ON, Canada, P7B 1P7*

SMYTH, Robert Andrew Laine (Brother Anselm). b 30. Trin Coll Cam BA53 MA59 Lon Univ PGCE60 DipEd65. **d** 79 **p** 80. SSF from 53; Min Prov Eur Prov SSF 79-91; Lic to Offic *Linc* 84-92; P-in-c Cambridge St Benedict *Ely* 92-93; V 93-00; rtd 00. *St Clare's House, 3 Pool Field Avenue, Birmingham B31 1ER* Tel 0121-476 1912

SMYTH, Trevor Cecil. b 45. Chich Th Coll 66. **d** 69 **p** 70. C Cookridge H Trin *Ripon* 69-73; C Middleton St Mary 73-75; C Felpham w Middleton *Chich* 75-78; P-in-c Wellington Ch Ch *Lich* 78-80; V 80-86; P-in-c W Wittering *Chich* 86; R W Wittering and Birdham w Itchenor 86-94; Perm to Offic 00; TV Withycombe Raleigh *Ex* from 01. *All Saints' Vicarage, Church Road, Exmouth EX8 1RZ* Tel (01395) 278534

SMYTHE, Mrs Angela Mary. b 53. St Jo Coll Nottm 85. **d** 87 **p** 94. Par Dn Forest Town *S'well* 87-90; Dn-in-c Pleasley Hill 90-94; V 94-03; AD Mansfield 98-03; P-in-c Sneinton St Chris w St Phil from 03. *St Christopher's Vicarage, 180 Sneinton Boulevard, Nottingham NG2 4GL* Tel 0115-950 5303 E-mail angiesmythe@aol.com

SMYTHE, Peter John Francis. b 32. Lon Univ LLB56 Barrister-at-Law (Middle Temple) 76. Wells Th Coll 56. **d** 58 **p** 59. C Maidstone All SS *Cant* 58-62; V Barrow St Jo *Carl* 62-65; V Billesdon w Goadby and Rolleston *Leic* 65-71; rtd 97. *Sherington House, 44 Priory Road, Malvern WR14 3DN* Tel and fax (01684) 573266

SMYTHE, Canon Ronald Ingoldsby Meade. b 25. Qu Coll Ox BA46 MA48. Ely Th Coll 51. **d** 54 **p** 55. C Wanstead St Mary *Chelmsf* 54-56; C-in-c Belhus Park CD 56-59; Min Belhus Park ED 59-62; V Hatfield Heath 62-78; Hon C Writtle 78-81; Hon C Writtle w Highwood 81-85; P-in-c Whatfield w Semer, Nedging and Naughton *St E* 85-89; Dir Ipswich Concern Counselling Cen from 85; Dioc Adv for Counselling 85-89; Dioc Adv for Counselling and Past Care 89-96; rtd 90; Hon Can St E Cathl *St E* 93-96; Perm to Offic from 96. *94 Wangford Road, Reydon, Southwold IP18 6NY* Tel (01502) 723413

SNAITH, Bryan Charles. b 33. Univ of Wales BSc55. St Mich Coll Llan 61. **d** 61 **p** 62. C Bargoed w Brithdir *Llan* 61-62; C Llanishen and Lisvane 62-71; Ind Chapl *Dur* 71-76; Ind Chapl *Worc* 76-81; P-in-c Stone 76-81; C Chaddesley Corbett 77-81; Ind Chapl *Chelmsf* 81-03; TV Colchester St Leon, St Mary Magd and St Steph 81-86; rtd 03. *4 Wren Close, Stanway, Colchester CO3 8ZB* Tel (01206) 767793 E-mail bryansnaith-colchester@msn.com

SNAPE, Sqn Ldr Bernard Reginald Roy. b 08. OBE56. Sarum Th Coll 69. **d** 69 **p** 70. C W Leigh *Portsm* 69-71; V Arreton 71-75; rtd 75; Perm to Offic *Sarum* from 75. *23 Shady Bower Close, Salisbury SP1 2RQ* Tel (01722) 328645

SNAPE, Gary John Stanley. b 50. STETS. **d** 05. NSM Fareham H Trin *Portsm* from 05. *51 Crescent Road, Locks Heath, Southampton SO31 6PE* Tel (01489) 589205

SNAPE, Harry. b 21. Qu Coll Birm 76. **d** 78 **p** 79. NSM Highters Heath *Birm* 78-82; NSM Stirchley 82-84; TV Corby SS Pet and Andr w Gt and Lt Oakley *Pet* 84-89; rtd 89; Perm to Offic *Chich* from 89. *Flat 19, Ramsey Hall, Byron Road, Worthing BN11 3HN* Tel (01903) 237663

SNAPE, Mrs Lorraine Elizabeth. b 52. STETS. **d** 02. NSM Titchfield *Portsm* from 02; Asst to RD Fareham from 05. *51 Crescent Road, Locks Heath, Southampton SO31 6PE* Tel (01489) 589205 E-mail lorrainesnape@tinyworld.co.uk

SNAPE, Paul Anthony Piper. b 44. **d** 98 **p** 99. OLM Tettenhall Wood and Perton *Lich* from 98. *24 Windsor Gardens, Castlecroft, Wolverhampton WV3 8LY* Tel (01902) 763577 E-mail p-snape@amserve.com

SNARE, Peter Brian. b 39. Cape Town Univ BSc63. SEITE 99. **d** 02 **p** 03. NSM Dymchurch w Burmarsh and Newchurch *Cant* from 02. *35 Shepherds Walk, Hythe CT21 6PW* Tel (01303) 269242 E-mail peter.snare@btinternet.com

SNASDELL, Canon Antony John. b 39. St Chad's Coll Dur BA63. **d** 65 **p** 66. C Boston *Linc* 65-70; Hon C Worksop Priory *S'well* 71-82; P-in-c Gt Massingham *Nor* 82-84; P-in-c Lt Massingham 82-84; P-in-c Harpley 82-84; R Gt and Lt Massingham and Harpley 84-91; R Thorpe 91-04; Hon Can Nor Cathl 03-04; rtd 04. *18 Lime Tree Avenue, Wymondham NR18 0EU* Tel (01953) 857509

SNEARY, Michael William. b 38. Brentwood Coll of Educn CertEd71 Open Univ BA79. Ely Th Coll 61. **d** 64 **p** 65. C Loughton St Jo *Chelmsf* 64-67; Youth Chapl 67-70; Hon C Ingrave 70-71; Teacher Harold Hill Gr Sch Essex 71-74; Ivybridge Sch 74-76; Coombe Dean Sch Plymouth 76-03; rtd 03. *The Lodge, 1 Lower Port View, Saltash PL12 4BY*

SNEATH, Canon Sidney Dennis. b 23. Leeds Univ BA50. Bps' Coll Cheshunt 50. **d** 52 **p** 53. C Nuneaton St Mary *Cov* 52-59; C-in-c Galley Common Stockingford CD 59-68; V Camp Hill w Galley Common from 68; Hon Can Cov Cathl from 80. *The Vicarage, Cedar Road, Nuneaton CV10 9DL* Tel (024) 7639 2523

SNELGAR, Canon Douglas John. b 17. DSC45. Trin Hall Cam BA48 MA53. Westcott Ho Cam 48. **d** 50 **p** 51. C Fareham SS Pet and Paul *Portsm* 50-53; C Ventnor St Cath 53-57; C Ventnor H Trin 53-57; V Steep 57-92; P-in-c Froxfield w Privett 88-92; Hon Can Portsm Cathl 85-92; rtd 92; Perm to Offic *Chich* and *Portsm* from 92. *37 South Acre, South Harting, Petersfield GU31 5LL* Tel (01730) 825142

✠**SNELGROVE, The Rt Revd Donald George.** b 25. TD72. Qu Coll Cam BA48 MA53 Hull Univ Hon DD97. Ridley Hall Cam. **d** 50 **p** 51 **c** 81. C Oakwood St Thos *Lon* 50-53; C Hatch End St Anselm 53-56; V Dronfield *Derby* 56-62; CF (TA) 60-73; V Hessle *York* 63-70; RD Hull 67-70 and 81-90; Can and Preb York Minster 69-81; Adn E Riding 70-81; R Cherry Burton 70-78; Suff Bp Hull 81-94; rtd 94; Hon Asst Bp Linc from 95. *Kingston House, 8 Park View, Barton-upon-Humber DN18 6AX* Tel (01652) 634484 E-mail donaldsnelgrove@aol.com

SNELL, Mrs Brigitte. b 43. BA85. EAMTC 86. **d** 89 **p** 94. NSM Cambridge Gt St Mary w St Mich *Ely* 89-91; Par Dn Cambridge St Jas 91-94; C 94-95; V Sutton 95-03; R Witcham w Mepal 95-03; rtd 03. *45 London Road, Harston, Cambridge CB2 5QQ* Tel (01223) 872839 E-mail brigittesnell@aol.com

SNELL, Colin. b 53. Trin Coll Bris 94. **d** 96 **p** 97. C Martock w Ash *B & W* 96-00; TV Wilton from 00. *St Michael's House, 1 Comeytrowe Lane, Taunton TA1 5PA* Tel (01823) 326525 E-mail stmikes@fish.co.uk *or* revsnell@fish.co.uk

SNELL, James Osborne. b 13. Selw Coll Cam BA35 MA39. Ely Th Coll 35. **d** 36 **p** 37. C Summertown *Ox* 36-38; C Fenny Stratford 38-43; C Rugeley *Lich* 43-47; V Dawley Parva 47-52; V New Bradwell w Stantonbury *Ox* 52-61; P-in-c Gt Linford 55-61; R Charlton-in-Dover *Cant* 61-69; R Ramsgate H Trin 69-78; rtd 79; Perm to Offic *Cant* from 79. *3 Glebe Close, St Margarets-at-Cliffe, Dover CT15 6AF* Tel (01304) 852210

SNELLGROVE, Martin Kenneth. b 54. City Univ BSc77 CEng80 MICE84. Aston Tr Scheme 85 Ridley Hall Cam 87. **d** 89 **p** 90. C Four Oaks *Birm* 89-92; TV Wrexham *St As* 92-01; R Hope from 01; AD Hawarden from 03. *The Rectory, Kiln Lane, Hope, Wrexham LL12 9PH* Tel (01978) 762127

SNELLING, Brian. b 40. **d** 69 **p** 70. C Slough *Ox* 69-72; C Hoole *Ches* 72-76; V Millbrook 76-80; V Homerton St Luke *Lon* 80-90; R Marks Tey w Aldham and Lt Tey *Chelmsf* 90-98; V Stebbing w Lindsell 98-04; V Stebbing and Lindsell w Gt and Lt Saling from 04. *The Vicarage, 7 Ruffels Place, Stebbing, Dunmow CM6 3TJ* Tel (01371) 856080 E-mail revbrians@aol.com

SNELSON, William Thomas. b 45. Ex Coll Ox BA67 Fitzw Coll Cam BA69 MA75. Westcott Ho Cam 67. **d** 69 **p** 70. C Godalming *Guildf* 69-72; C Leeds St Pet *Ripon* 72-75; V Chapel Allerton 75-81; V Bardsey 81-93; Dioc Ecum Officer 86-93; W Yorkshire Ecum Officer *Bradf* 93-97; Gen Sec Chs Together in England from 97; Perm to Offic *St Alb* from 97 and *Ely* from 03. *Churches Together in England, 27 Tavistock Square, London WC1H 9HH* Tel (020) 7529 8133 Fax 7529 8134 E-mail bill.snelson@cte.org.uk

SNOOK, Hywel Geraint. b 77. Aston Univ BSc99 Leeds Univ BA04. Coll of Resurr Mirfield 02. **d** 05. C Marton *Blackb* from 05. *14 Gorse Road, Blackpool FY3 9DZ*

SNOOK, Mrs Margaret Ann. b 41. S Dios Minl Tr Scheme. **d** 91 **p** 94. NSM Keynsham *B & W* from 91. *32 Hurn Lane, Keynsham, Bristol BS31 1RS* Tel 0117-986 3439

SNOOK, Walter Currie. *See* CURRIE, Walter

SNOW, Campbell Martin Spencer. b 35. JP75. Roch Th Coll 65. **d** 67 **p** 68. C Dover St Mary *Cant* 67-72; C Birchington w Acol 72-74; V Reculver 74-80; P-in-c New Addington 80-81; V 81-84; V New Addington *S'wark* 85-87; P-in-c Caterham Valley 87-99;

CF (ACF) 84-87; CF (TA) 87-92; OCF 92-95; rtd 99; Perm to Offic *S'wark* from 99; Widows' Officer 99-04. *28 The Crossways, Merstham, Redhill RH1 3NA* Tel (01737) 643388 E-mail csnow@waitrose.com

SNOW, Frank. b 31. Lon Univ BD57. **d** 83 **p** 84. Hon C Tweedmouth *Newc* 83-86; Hon C Berwick H Trin 86-89; Hon C Berwick St Mary 86-89; Hon C Berwick H Trin and St Mary 89-90; R Gt Smeaton w Appleton Wiske and Birkby etc *Ripon* 90-97; rtd 97; Perm to Offic *Ripon* from 97 and *Sheff* from 02. *11 The Green, Totley, Sheffield S17 4AT* Tel 0114-235 0024 E-mail frank@fcrsnow.freeserve.co.uk

SNOW, Martyn James. b 68. Sheff Univ BSc89. Wycliffe Hall Ox BTh95. **d** 95 **p** 96. C Brinsworth w Catcliffe and Treeton *Sheff* 95-97; CMS Guinea 98-01; V Pitsmoor Ch Ch *Sheff* from 01. *The Vicarage, 257 Pitsmoor Road, Sheffield S3 9AQ* Tel 0114-272 7756

SNOW, Miss Patricia Margaret. b 21. Dub Bible Coll 45 St Mich Ho Ox 51. **dss** 72 **d** 87 **p** 96. W Ham *Chelmsf* 72-78; Acomb St Steph *York* 78-83; rtd 83; NSM Northfleet *Roch* 96-01; Perm to Offic from 01. *29 Huggens' College, College Road, Northfleet, Gravesend DA11 9DL* Tel (01474) 369463

SNOW, Peter David. b 37. St Jo Coll Cam BA61 MA67. Ridley Hall Cam 62. **d** 64 **p** 65. C Kingshurst *Birm* 64-66; USA from 67; C Santa Barbara All SS 67-71; Can Missr for Youth Los Angeles 71-75; R Jackson St Jo 75-81; Asst R Bellevue Resurr 81-85; R Redmond H Cross 89-01; rtd 01; P-in-c Edmonds SS Hilda and Patr from 02. *927 36th Avenue, Seattle, WA 98122, USA* Tel (001) (206) 329 3784 E-mail peterorlisa@cs.com

SNOW, Peter Normington. b 23. St Jo Coll Ox BA48 MA52. Ely Th Coll 48. **d** 50 **p** 51. C Lower Gornal *Lich* 50-52; C Solihull *Birm* 52-56; V Emscote *Cov* 56-89; RD Warwick 67-77; rtd 89; Perm to Offic *Cov* from 89. *3 Park Lane, Harbury, Leamington Spa CV33 9HX* Tel (01926) 612410

SNOW, Richard John. b 57. Bris Univ BSc80. **d** 90 **p** 91. C Preston Plucknett *B & W* 90-95; TV Stratton St Margaret w S Marston etc *Bris* 95-02; R Box w Hazlebury and Ditteridge from 02. *The Vicarage, Church Lane, Box, Corsham SN13 8NR* Tel (01225) 744458 E-mail snows@fish.co.uk

SNOWBALL, Miss Deborah Jane. b 67. Middx Poly BEd90. Ripon Coll Cuddesdon 02. **d** 04 **p** 05. C Sawbridgeworth *St Alb* from 04. *St Mary's Lodge, Knight Street, Sawbridgeworth CM21 9AX* Tel (01279) 726696 E-mail deborahsnowball@surefish.co.uk

SNOWBALL, Dorothy Margaret. b 52. Sunderland Univ BA98. NEOC 98. **d** 01 **p** 02. NSM Heworth St Mary *Dur* from 01. *2 Oval Park View, Felling, Gateshead NE10 9DS* Tel 0191-469 5059 E-mail dsnowball@talk21.com

SNOWBALL, Michael Sydney. b 44. Dur Univ BA70 MA72 St Jo Coll Dur DipTh72. **d** 72 **p** 73. C Stockton St Pet *Dur* 72-75; C Dunston St Nic 75-77; C Dunston 77-78; C Darlington St Jo 78-81; V Chilton 81-91; V Brompton w Deighton *York* from 91. *The Vicarage, Brompton, Northallerton DL6 2QA* Tel (01609) 772436 E-mail mickthevic@aol.com

SNOWDEN, Miss Alice Isabel Glass. b 55. Lanc Univ BA77 Humberside Coll of Educn PGCE84. Ripon Coll Cuddesdon 91. **d** 94 **p** 95. C Mirfield *Wakef* 94-97; TV Guiseley w Esholt *Bradf* 97-02; V Bankfoot from 02. *St Matthew's Vicarage, Carbottom Road, Bradford BD5 9AA* Tel (01274) 726529 E-mail sobak@0800dial.com

SNOWDEN (née HALL), Mrs Elizabeth. b 58. Plymouth Poly BSc79 Birm Univ BA01 Lon Inst of Educn PGCE80. Qu Coll Birm 98. **d** 01. C Burntwood *Lich* 01-04; C and Youth Work Co-ord Ogley Hay from 04. *25 Snowdrop Close, Walsall WS8 7RN* Tel (01543) 454816

SNUGGS, David Sidney. b 49. Keble Coll Ox BA71 PGCE72 MA75. S Dios Minl Tr Scheme 89. **d** 92 **p** 93. C Bitterne *Win* 92-96; V Fair Oak from 96. *The Vicarage, Fair Oak Court, Fair Oak, Eastleigh SO50 7BG* Tel (023) 8069 2238

SNYDER, Miss Susanna Jane. b 78. Em Coll Cam BA00 MA04. Qu Coll Birm BA04. **d** 05. C Stoke Newington St Mary *Lon* from 05; C Brownswood Park from 05. *Downstairs Flat, St Mary's Rectory, Stoke Newington Church Street, London N16 9ES* Tel (020) 7254 6072 E-mail susannasnyder@btinternet.com

SNYDER GIBSON, Catherine. *See* GIBSON, Catherine Snyder

SOADY, Mark. b 60. RMN84 Univ of Wales BTh. St Mich Coll Llan 96. **d** 96 **p** 97. C Tenby *St D* 96-99; TV 99-03; Min Can St Woolos Cathl *Mon* from 03; CF(V) from 98. *Hebron, 9 Clifton Road, Newport NP20 4EW* Tel (01633) 267191 Mobile 07968-753978 E-mail marksoady@onetel.com

SOAR, Arthur Leslie. b 20. ACII. Linc Th Coll 82. **d** 83 **p** 84. NSM Chilham *Cant* 83-86; NSM Crundale w Godmersham 86-90; NSM Elmsted w Hastingleigh 86-90; rtd 90; Perm to Offic *Cant* from 90. *9 Redington, Lower Queens Road, Ashford TN24 8HW* Tel (01233) 625559

SOAR, Martin William. b 54. Wye Coll Lon BSc78. Wycliffe Hall Ox 86. **d** 88 **p** 89. C Henfynyw w Aberaeron and Llanddewi Aberarth *St D* 88-91; C Hubberston 91-93; P-in-c Low Harrogate St Mary *Ripon* 93-95; V from 95. *St Mary's Vicarage, 22 Harlow Oval, Harrogate HG2 0DS* Tel (01423) 502614 E-mail martinsoar@supanet.com

✠**SOARES, The Rt Revd Fernando da Luz.** b 43. Univ of Porto. **d** 71 **p** 72 **c** 80. Bp Lusitanian Ch from 80; Hon Asst Bp Eur from 95. *Rua Elias Garcia 107-1 Dto, 4430-091 Vila Nova de Gaia, Portugal* Tel (00351) (22) 375 4646 Fax 375 2016 E-mail fernandols@netc.pt *or* ilcae@mail.telepac.pt

SODADASI, David Anand Raj. b 63. Osmania Univ Hyderabad BCom85 MA99 Union Bibl Sem Pune BD95. United Th Coll Bangalore MTh00. **d** 01 **p** 02. C Jabalpur Cathl India 01-04; Lect Leonard Th Coll 00-04; Perm to Offic *Ox* 04-05; NSM Ray Valley from 05. *St Mary's House, High Street, Charlton-on-Otmoor, Kidlington OX5 2UQ* Tel (01865) 331124 Mobile 07906-924883 E-mail sdanandraj@hotmail.com

SODOR AND MAN, Bishop of. *See* KNOWLES, The Rt Revd Graeme Paul

SOER, Patricia Kathleen Mary. b 40. CertEd61. OLM course 96. **d** 99 **p** 00. OLM Deptford St Jo w H Trin *S'wark* from 99. *350 Wood Vale, London SE23 3DY* Tel (020) 8699 4616

SOFIELD, Martin. b 60. **d** 02 **p** 03. OLM Clifton *Man* from 02. *16 Ross Drive, Clifton, Swinton, Manchester M27 6PS* Tel 0161-959 6517 E-mail martin.sofield@ntlworld.com

SOGA, Hector Ian. b 47. Glas Univ MA70 BMus78 PhD90 Selw Coll Cam BA72 MA76. St And NSM Tr Scheme 87. **d** 88 **p** 89. NSM Dollar *St And* from 88. *2 Harviestoun Road, Dollar FK14 7HF* Tel (01259) 743169

SOKANOVIC (née HARRIS), Mrs Mary Noreen Cecily. b 58. Suffolk Coll BA97 RGN79 RN96. EAMTC 02. **d** 05. NSM Whitton and Thurleston w Akenham *St E* from 05. *Sideview, School Road, Coddenham, Ipswich IP6 9PS* Tel (01449) 760527 E-mail marysok@tiscali.co.uk

SOKOLOWSKI (née MAHON), Mrs Stephanie Mary. b 56. Liv Univ BSc80 SRN80. S'wark Ord Course 91. **d** 94 **p** 95. C Warlingham w Chelsham and Farleigh *S'wark* 94-97; C Godstone and Blindley Heath 97-04. *Address temp unkown* E-mail smsokol@aol.com

✠**SOLIBA, The Most Revd Ignacio Capuyan.** b 44. Univ of Philippines AB72. St Andr Th Sem Manila BTh73 MDiv88. **d** 73 **p** 74 **c** 91. Chapl St Paul's Memorial Sch 73-75; Officer-in-charge 75-76; P-in-c Balbalasang 74-76; V Balantoy 77-78 and 82-91; V Mt Data 79-81; Bp N Luzon 91-97; Prime Bp Philippines from 97. *PO Box 10321, Broadway Centrum, 1112 Quezon City, Philippines* Tel (0063) (2) 722 8478 *or* 721 5061 Fax 721 1923 E-mail soliba@edsamail.com.ph *or* soliba@hotmail.com

SOLOMON, Arthur Creagh. b 33. ACT LTh Ch Coll Hobart. **d** 62 **p** 63. Australia 62-67; C Addiscombe St Mildred *Cant* 67-68; Chapl Pierrepont Sch Frensham 69-72; R Clifton Campville w Chilcote *Lich* 72-95; P-in-c Thorpe Constantine 83-95; R Clifton Campville w Edingale 95; Perm to Offic *Derby* 96-98; rtd 98; Perm to Offic *S & M* from 98. *Poppy Cottage, Ballacannell, Laxey, Isle of Man IM4 7HD* Tel (01624) 861235

SOMERS-EDGAR, Carl John. b 46. Otago Univ BA69. St Steph Ho Ox 72. **d** 75 **p** 76. C Northwood H Trin *Lon* 75-79; C St Marylebone All SS 79-82; V Liscard St Mary w St Columba *Ches* 82-85; New Zealand from 85. *St Peter's Vicarage, 57 Baker Street, Caversham, Dunedin, New Zealand* Tel (0064) (3) 455 3961

SOMERS HESLAM, Peter. *See* HESLAM, Peter Somers

SOMERVELL, Mrs Katherine Mary. b 30. Edin Univ CQSW51. WMMTC 86. **d** 88 **p** 94. Par Dn Caldmore *Lich* 88-92; Par Dn Wilnecote 92-94; C 94-95; rtd 95; NSM Loppington w Newtown *Lich* 95-99. *3 Orchard Close, Cressage, Shrewsbury SY5 6BZ* Tel (01952) 510755

SOMERVILLE, David. b 58. QUB BEd. **d** 00 **p** 01. C Lisburn Ch Ch *Conn* 00-03; I Drumgath w Drumgooland and Clonduff *D & D* from 03. *The Rectory, 29 Cross Road, Hilltown, Newry BT34 5TF* Tel (028) 4063 1171 Mobile 07811-916825 E-mail revds@btinternet.com

SOMERVILLE, John William Kenneth. b 38. St D Coll Lamp 60. **d** 63 **p** 64. C Rhosllannerchrugog *St As* 63-67; C Llangystennin 67-70; V Gorsedd 70-77; V Gorsedd w Brynford and Ysgeifiog 77-02; RD Holywell 96-02; rtd 02. *15 Bryn Marl Road, Mochdre, Colwyn Bay LL28 5DT*

SOMMERVILLE, Prof Robert Gardner. b 27. Glas Univ MB50 ChB50 MD60 FRCPGlas67 Lon Univ FRCPath68. **d** 96 **p** 96. NSM Blairgowrie *St And* 96-97; NSM Coupar Angus 96-97; NSM Alyth 96-97; P-in-c Killin 97-99; Perm to Offic 99-01; P-in-c Tayport from 01. *Monkmyre, Myreriggs Road, Coupar Angus, Blairgowrie PH13 9HS* Tel and fax (01828) 627131 E-mail rgsommer@lineone.net

SONG, James. b 32. Lon Coll of Div 57. **d** 60 **p** 61. C Virginia Water *Guildf* 60-63; C Portman Square St Paul *Lon* 63-66; V Matlock Bath *Derby* 66-76; V Woking St Jo *Guildf* 76-94; RD Woking 87-92; rtd 94; Perm to Offic *Guildf* from 94. *Ash House, Churt, Farnham GU10 2NU* Tel and fax (01428) 714493

SOOSAINAYAGAM, Xavier. b 50. Sri Lanka Nat Sem BPh73 St Paul's Sem Trichy BTh77 S'wark Ord Course 89. **d** 76 **p** 77. In

RC Ch 76-89; C Streatham St Leon *S'wark* 89-94; C Merton St Jas 94-97; V Croydon H Sav from 97. *The Vicarage, 115 St Saviour's Road, Croydon CR0 2XF* Tel (020) 8684 1345 Mobile 07789-567842 E-mail xaviersoosai@hotmail.com

SOPER, Brian Malcolm. b 31. Lon Univ BSc53. Ripon Hall Ox 63. **d** 63 **p** 64. C Platt *Roch* 63-64; Chapl K Sch Roch 64-72; Chapl Repton Sch Derby 72-75; Chapl Bennett Memorial Dioc Sch Tunbridge Wells 75-84; Perm to Offic *Cant* 70-87 and *Chich* from 87. *Galliards, Landgate, Rye TN31 7LH* Tel (01797) 222897

SOPER, Jonathan Alexander James. b 64. Univ Coll Dur BA85. Wycliffe Hall Ox 94. **d** 96 **p** 97. C Bath Weston All SS w N Stoke and Langridge *B & W* 96-00; C Bryanston Square St Mary w St Marylebone St Mark *Lon* 00-04. *22 Mont le Grand, Exeter EX1 2PA* Tel (01392) 274728 E-mail enccontact@enc.eclipse.co.uk

SOPHIANOU, Neofitos Anthony (Tony). b 47. Sarum & Wells Th Coll 86. **d** 88 **p** 89. C St Peter-in-Thanet *Cant* 88-91; Perm to Offic *St Alb* 97-99; C Stevenage St Nic and Graveley 99-03; Perm to Offic 03-04; V Wheatley Park *Sheff* from 04. *The Vicarage, 278 Thorne Road, Doncaster DN2 5AJ* Tel (01302) 326041 E-mail tony.sophianou@ntlworld.com

SORENSEN, Ms Anna Katrine Elizabeth. b 58. Man Univ BA82 MPhil94 Open Univ PGCE95. Ripon Coll Cuddesdon 83. **d** 87 **p** 94. Par Dn Ashton H Trin *Man* 87-88; Asst Chapl St Felix Sch Southwold 89-90; Chapl 90-99; Hon Par Dn Reydon *St E* 89-92; Hon Par Dn Blythburgh w Reydon 92-94; Hon C 94-99; C Gislingham and Thorndon 99-03; P-in-c Billingborough Gp *Linc* from 03. *The Vicarage, 13 High Street, Billingborough, Sleaford NG34 0QG* Tel (01529) 240750 Mobile 07932-031479 E-mail anna_sor@yahoo.com

SOULSBY, Canon Michael. b 36. Dur Univ BSc57. Westcott Ho Cam 61. **d** 62 **p** 63. C Selly Oak St Mary *Birm* 62-66; C Kings Norton 66-72; TV 73-76; TR Sutton *Liv* 76-88; RD Prescot 84-88; P-in-c Orton Longueville *Ely* 88-96; RD Yaxley 92-02; TR The Ortons, Alwalton and Chesterton 96-04; Hon Can Ely Cathl from 94; rtd 04. *8 Leiston Court, Eye, Peterborough PE6 7WL* Tel (01733) 221124 E-mail m.soulsby@talk21.com

SOUPER, Patrick Charles. b 28. K Coll Lon BD55 AKC55. **d** 57 **p** 58. Chapl Derby City Hosp 57-62; Chapl Derby Cathl *Derby* 57-62; Asst Chapl Lon Univ *Lon* 62-64; C St Marylebone w H Trin 64-65; Chapl St Paul's Sch Barnes 65-70; Lect in Educn Southn Univ 70-87; rtd 87. *PO Box 11, 74100 Rethymnon, Crete, Greece* Tel (0030) (831) 31521 Fax 31903 E-mail pigiaki@phl.uoc.gr

SOUPPOURIS, Ms Gail Camilla. b 52. Essex Univ BA75. SEITE 02. **d** 05. C W Wickham St Fran and St Mary *S'wark* from 05. *St Mary's Vicarage, The Avenue, West Wickham BR4 0DX* Tel 07950-665051 (mobile)

SOURBUT, Philip John. b 57. Cam Univ BA MA. Cranmer Hall Dur BA. **d** 85 **p** 86. C Springfield All SS *Chelmsf* 85-88; C Roxeth Ch Ch and Harrow St Pet *Lon* 88-91; P-in-c Bath St Sav *B & W* 91-93; R Bath St Sav w Swainswick and Woolley 93-98; V Cullompton and R Kentisbeare w Blackborough *Ex* 98-01; TR Cullompton, Willand, Uffculme, Kentisbeare etc from 01. *Windyridge, 10 Willand Road, Cullompton EX15 1AP* Tel (01884) 34048 Fax 34747 E-mail psourbut@lineone.net

SOUTER, Ruth Rosemary. b 55. Dur Univ BEd77. EMMTC 00. **d** 03 **p** 04. C Braunstone Park CD *Leic* from 03. *16 Turville Road, Leicester LE3 1NY* Tel 0116-291 3040 E-mail ruthsouter@yahoo.com

SOUTER, William Ewen Logan. b 66. Em Coll Cam BA88 Univ Coll Lon PhD93. Trin Coll Bris BA94 MA97. **d** 97 **p** 98. C Harborne Heath *Birm* 97-01; TV Horsham *Chich* from 01. *St John's House, Church Road, Broadbridge Heath, Horsham RH12 3ND* Tel (01403) 265238 Mobile 07889-612861 E-mail ewen@souter.me.uk

SOUTH, Gillian. *See* HARWOOD, Mrs Gillian

SOUTH EAST ASIA, Archbishop of. *See* YONG, The Most Revd Datuk Ping Chung

SOUTHALL, Colin Edward. b 36. Lich Th Coll 63. **d** 65 **p** 82. C Wylde Green *Birm* 65-67; Perm to Offic 68-73; Perm to Offic *Pet* 73-81; Hon C Linc St Faith and St Martin w St Pet *Linc* 82-85; Hon C Gt Glen, Stretton Magna and Wistow etc *Leic* 85-93; Chapl Asst Leic R Infirmary 93-96; Hon C Fleckney and Kilby *Leic* 96-98; Perm to Offic from 99. *1 Spinney View, Great Glen, Leicester LE8 9EP* Tel 0116-259 2959

SOUTHAMPTON, Suffragan Bishop of. *See* BUTLER, The Rt Revd Paul Roger

SOUTHEE, Mrs Sandra Margaret. b 43. EAMTC 97. **d** 00 **p** 01. NSM Galleywood Common *Chelmsf* 00-02; NSM Moulsham St Jo from 02; Asst Chapl Mid-Essex Hosp Services NHS Trust from 02. *6 Hampton Road, Chelmsford CM2 8ES* Tel (01245) 475456

SOUTHEND, Archdeacon of. *See* LOWMAN, The Ven David Walter

SOUTHERN, Humphrey Ivo John. b 60. Ch Ch Ox BA82 MA86. Ripon Coll Cuddesdon 83. **d** 86 **p** 87. C Rainham *Roch* 86-90; C Walton St Mary *Liv* 90-92; C Walton-on-the-Hill 92; V Hale *Guildf* 92-96; TR 96-97; TR Hale w Badshot Lea 97-99; Dioc Ecum Officer 92-99; TR Tisbury *Sarum* 99-01; TR Nadder Valley from 01; RD Chalke from 00. *The Rectory, Park Road, Tisbury, Salisbury SP3 6LF* Tel and fax (01747) 870312 E-mail humphreysouthern@waitrose.com

SOUTHERN, John Abbott. b 27. Leeds Univ BA47. Coll of Resurr Mirfield. **d** 51 **p** 52. C Leigh St Mary *Man* 51-55; C Gt Grimsby St Jas *Linc* 55-58; V Oldham St Jas *Man* 58-60; V Haigh *Liv* 60-75; V Pemberton St Jo 75-98; rtd 98; Perm to Offic *Liv* from 00. *145 Moor Road, Orrell, Wigan WN5 8SJ* Tel (01942) 732132

SOUTHERN, Paul Ralph. b 48. Oak Hill Th Coll 85. **d** 87 **p** 88. C Chadwell Heath *Chelmsf* 87-91; P-in-c Tolleshunt D'Arcy w Tolleshunt Major 91-01; V Tolleshunt D'Arcy and Tolleshunt Major from 01. *8 Vicarage Close, Tolleshunt D'Arcy, Maldon CM9 8UG* Tel (01621) 860521

SOUTHERN CONE OF AMERICA, Primate of. *See* VENABLES, The Most Revd Gregory James

SOUTHERTON, Miss Kathryn Ruth. b 66. Univ of Wales (Lamp) BA88. Sarum & Wells Th Coll 90. **d** 92 **p** 97. C Connah's Quay *St As* 92-97; R Halkyn w Caerfallwch w Rhesycae 97-04; I Achonry w Tubbercurry and Killoran *T, K & A* from 04. *Back Acre, Carrowdubh, Strandhill, Sligo, Irish Republic* Tel (00353) (71) 68571

SOUTHERTON, Canon Peter Clive. b 38. MBE01. Univ of Wales (Lamp) BA59. Qu Coll Birm DipTh60. **d** 61 **p** 62. C Llandrillo-yn-Rhos *St As* 61-68; Bermuda 68-71; V Esclusham *St As* 72-82; V Prestatyn 82-04; Hon Can St As Cathl 96-04; rtd 04. *6 Llwyn Mesen, Prestatyn LL19 8NS* Tel (01745) 853176

SOUTHEY, George Rubidge. b 34. St Mich Coll Llan 84. **d** 86 **p** 87. C Hessle *York* 86-89; P-in-c Scarborough St Columba 89-92; V 92-99; rtd 99; Perm to Offic *Glouc* from 00. *19 Pochard Close, Quedgeley, Gloucester GL2 4LL* Tel (01452) 724004

SOUTHGATE, Graham. b 63. GIBiol85 Bris Poly Higher Dip Applied Biology 83 NE Surrey Coll of Tech PhD89. Ripon Coll Cuddesdon BTh93. **d** 93 **p** 94. C Tisbury *Sarum* 93-97; TV Chalke Valley 97-03; R Bratton, Edington and Imber, Erlestoke etc from 03. *The Vicarage, Upper Garston Lane, Bratton, Westbury BA13 4SN* Tel (01380) 830374 E-mail grahamsouthgate63@hotmail.com

SOUTHGATE, Patricia. **d** 03 **p** 04. OLM Parkstone St Pet and St Osmund w Branksea *Sarum* from 03. *60 Orchard Avenue, Poole BH14 8AJ* Tel (01202) 745081 E-mail pat.southgate@virgin.net

SOUTHGATE, Stephen Martin. b 61. Lanc Univ BA83 St Martin's Coll Lanc PGCE84. Cranmer Hall Dur DMS98. **d** 98 **p** 99. C Witton *Ches* 98-01; R Backford and Capenhurst from 01. *The Vicarage, Grove Road, Mollington, Chester CH1 6LG* Tel (01244) 851071 E-mail thesouthgates@beeb.net

SOUTHWARD, Douglas Ambrose. b 32. St Jo Coll Nottm LTh74 FBS02. ALCD57. **d** 57 **p** 58. C Otley *Bradf* 57-61; C Sedbergh 61-63; C Cautley w Dowbiggin 61-63; C Garsdale 61-63; PV Lich Cathl *Lich* 63-65; V Hope *Derby* 65-72; V Crosby Ravensworth *Carl* 72-82; V Bolton 74-82; Sec Dioc Past and Redundant Chs Uses Cttees 78-82; RD Appleby 78-82; Hon Can Carl Cathl 81-95; R Asby 81-82; V Hawkshead and Low Wray w Sawrey 82-98; P-in-c Windermere St Jo 84-89; RD Windermere 84-89; P-in-c Satterthwaite 94-95; rtd 98; Perm to Offic *Carl* from 98. *Hawthorn House, Town End, Witherslack, Grange-over-Sands LA11 6RL* Tel (01539) 552078

SOUTHWARD, James Fisher. b 57. St Martin's Coll Lanc BEd80. Chich Th Coll 83. **d** 86 **p** 87. C Woodford St Barn *Chelmsf* 86-89; TV Crawley *Chich* 89-95; V Higham and Merston *Roch* from 95; RD Strood from 02. *The Vicarage, Hermitage Road, Higham, Rochester ME3 7NE* Tel (01634) 717360 E-mail jfsouthward@yahoo.co.uk

SOUTHWARK, Archdeacon of. *See* IPGRAVE, The Ven Michael Geoffrey

SOUTHWARK, Bishop of. *See* BUTLER, The Rt Revd Thomas Frederick

SOUTHWARK, Dean of. *See* SLEE, The Very Revd Colin Bruce

SOUTHWELL, Peter John Mackenzie. b 43. New Coll Ox BA64 MA68. Wycliffe Hall Ox 66. **d** 67 **p** 68. C Crookes St Thos *Sheff* 67-70; Lect Sheff Univ 67-70; Sen Tutor Wycliffe Hall Ox from 70; Chapl Qu Coll Ox from 82. *The Queen's College, Oxford OX1 4AW* Tel (01865) 279143 *or* 553829 Fax 274215

SOUTHWELL, The Ven Roy. b 14. AKC42. **d** 42 **p** 43. C Wigan St Mich *Liv* 42-44; C Kennington St Jo *S'wark* 44-48; V Ixworth *St E* 48-51; P-in-c Ixworth Thorpe 48-51; V Bury St Edmunds St Jo 51-56; R Bucklesham w Brightwell and Foxhall 56-59; Dir RE 59-68; Hon Can St E Cathl 59-68; V Hendon St Mary *Lon* 68-71; Adn Northolt 70-80; rtd 80; Warden Community of All Hallows Ditchingham 83-89; Lic to Offic *Nor* 83-89; Perm to Offic from 89. *397 Sprowton Road, Norwich NR3 4HY* Tel (01603) 405977

SOUTHWELL, Bishop of. *See* CASSIDY, The Rt Revd George Henry

SOUTHWELL, Dean of. *See* LEANING, The Very Revd David

SOUTHWELL-SANDER, Canon Peter George. b 41. G&C Coll Cam BA64 MA67. Westcott Ho Cam 63. **d** 65 **p** 66. C

Maidstone All SS w St Phil *Cant* 65-68; C Cambridge Gt St Mary w St Mich *Ely* 68-71; Chapl Girton Coll Cam 69-73; V Clapham St Paul *S'wark* 73-77; V Merton St Mary 77-84; P-in-c Merton St Jo 77-79; Dir of Min *Chelmsf* 85-94; Can Res Chelmsf Cathl 85-94; Public Preacher 94-96; Perm to Offic 96-97; UK Adv Chicago Th Seminaries' DMin in Preaching from 95; USA from 96. *600 Salem End Road, Framingham, MA 01702, USA* Tel (001) (508) 875 5540

SOWDEN, Charles William Bartholomew. b 47. DipADO68. Local Minl Tr Course 90 LNSM course 96. **d** 97 **p** 98. OLM Saxonwell *Linc* from 97. *River View, 7 The Meadows, Long Bennington, Newark NG23 5EL* Tel (01400) 281596 E-mail charles.sowden1@btinternet.com

SOWDEN, Geoffrey David. b 57. Kingston Poly BA79. Wycliffe Hall Ox DipMin95. **d** 97 **p** 98. C Ware Ch Ch *St Alb* 97-02; V Highworth w Sevenhampton and Inglesham etc *Bris* from 02. *The Vicarage, 10 Stonefield Drive, Highworth, Swindon SN6 7DA* Tel (01793) 765554 E-mail the.sowdens@btinternet.com

SOWDON, Henry Lewis Malcolm. b 37. TCD BA. Bps' Coll Cheshunt. **d** 64 **p** 65. C Newport w Longford *Lich* 64-66; C Caverswall 66-69; Chapl Clayesmore Sch Blandford 69-72; Hon C Hornsey Ch Ch *Lon* 72-80; Chapl Gordon's Sch Woking 80-86; TV Hodge Hill *Birm* 86-91; Perm to Offic from 91; rtd 02. *157 Heathfield Road, Birmingham B19 1JD* Tel 0121-240 3557

SOWERBUTTS, Alan. b 49. Sheff Univ BSc70 PhD73 Qu Coll Cam BA75 MA79. Westcott Ho Cam 74. **d** 76 **p** 77. C Salesbury *Blackb* 76-80; V Lower Darwen St Jas 80-84; V Musbury 84-93; P-in-c Brindle 93-98; Sec Dioc Adv Cttee for the Care of Chs 93-98; V Read in Whalley from 98. *The Vicarage, George Lane, Read, Burnley BB12 7RQ* Tel (01282) 771361 E-mail anseres@ukonline.co.uk

SOWERBUTTS, Philip John. b 67. Chester Coll of HE BEd89 Edge Hill Coll of HE PGCE99. Oak Hill Th Coll BA03. **d** 03 **p** 04. C Kirk Ella and Willerby *York* from 03. *24 Redland Drive, Kirk Ella, Hull HU10 7UZ* Tel (01482) 653251 Mobile 07957-122836 E-mail philip-claire@hotmail.com

SOWERBY, Geoffrey Nigel Rake. b 35. St Aid Birkenhead 56. **d** 60 **p** 61. C Armley St Bart *Ripon* 60-63; Min Can Ripon Cathl 63-65; V Thornthwaite w Thruscross and Darley 65-69; V Leeds All SS 69-73; V Leyburn w Bellerby 73-81; R Edin Old St Paul *Edin* 81-86; V Hawes and Hardraw *Ripon* 86-92; Dioc Adv in Deliverance Min 91-92; rtd 92; Perm to Offic *Dur* and *Ripon* from 92. *6 Wycar Terrace, Bedale DL8 2AG* Tel (01677) 425860 Mobile 07944-383742 E-mail geoffreysowerby@onetel.com

SOWERBY, Mark Crispin Rake. b 63. K Coll Lon BD85 AKC85 Lanc Univ MA94. Coll of Resurr Mirfield 85. **d** 87 **p** 88. C Knaresborough *Ripon* 87-90; C Darwen St Cuth w Tockholes St Steph *Blackb* 90-92; V Accrington St Mary 92-97; Chapl St Chris High Sch Accrington 92-97; Chapl Victoria Hosp Accrington 92-97; Asst Dir of Ords *Blackb* 93-96; Voc Officer and Selection Sec Min Division 97-01; V Harrogate St Wilfrid *Ripon* 01-04; TR from 04. *St Wilfrid's Vicarage, 51B Kent Road, Harrogate HG1 2EU* Tel (01423) 503259 Mobile 07778-451145 E-mail mcrsowerby@aol.com *or* vicar@stwilfrids-harrogate.co.uk

SOWTER, Colin Victor. b 35. Ball Coll Ox BA56 MA59 DPhil60. Oak Hill NSM Course 88. **d** 91 **p** 92. NSM Cranleigh *Guildf* 91-93; NSM Wonersh 93-98; NSM Wonersh w Blackheath 98-05; rtd 05; Perm to Offic *Guildf* from 05. *Hollycroft, Grantley Avenue, Wonersh Park, Guildford GU5 0QN* Tel (01483) 892094 Fax 892894 E-mail sowter@lineone.net

SOX, Harold David. b 36. N Carolina Univ BA58. Union Th Sem (NY) MDiv61. **d** 61 **p** 61. USA 61-74; Hon C Richmond St Mary *S'wark* 74-79; Hon C Richmond St Mary w St Matthias and St Jo 79-82; Hon C Kensington St Mary Abbots w St Geo *Lon* 82-84 and 89-93; Perm to Offic 84-89; Hon C Beedon and Peasemore w W Ilsley and Farnborough *Ox* 93-94; Perm to Offic *Ox* 93-97 and *S'wark* 97-04. *20 The Vineyard, Richmond TW10 6AN* Tel (020) 8940 0094

SPACKMAN (née MORRISON), Mrs Ailsa. b 40. Qu Univ Kingston Ontario BA82. Montreal Dioc Th Coll. **d** 83 **p** 85. Canada 83-95; Dn Caspe 83-85; I Malbay Miss Par 85-92; Chapl Drummondville Penitentiary 92-93; rtd 93; Perm to Offic *Ex* from 99. *Cofton Lodge, Cofton Hill, Cockwood, Starcross, Exeter EX6 8RB* Tel (01626) 891584

SPACKMAN, Canon Peter John. b 37. Southn Univ BSc60. Westcott Ho Cam 65. **d** 66 **p** 67. C Boxmoor St Jo *St Alb* 66-69; C Alnwick St Paul *Newc* 69-72; C-in-c Stewart Town Jamaica 72-74; Canada 74-95; I Sept-Iles 74-77; R Baie Comeau 77-80; R Gaspe 80-92; Adn Gaspe 88-92; R Richmond 92-94; Hon Can Quebec 92-94; Perm to Offic *Ex* 95-97; Hon C Kenton, Mamhead, Powderham, Cofton and Starcross 97-02; Perm to Offic from 02. *Cofton Lodge, Cofton Hill, Cockwood, Starcross, Exeter EX6 8RB* Tel (01626) 891584 E-mail spackman1@btinternet.com

SPAFFORD, The Very Revd Christopher Garnett Howsin. b 24. St Jo Coll Ox BA48 MA54. Wells Th Coll 48. **d** 50 **p** 51. C Brighouse *Wakef* 50-53; C Huddersfield St Pet 53-55; V Hebden Bridge 55-61; R Thornhill 61-69; V Shrewsbury St Chad *Lich* 69-76; V Newc St Nic *Newc* 76-89; Provost Newc 76-89; rtd 89; Perm to Offic *Heref* from 93. *Low Moor, Elm Close, Leominster HR6 8JX* Tel (01568) 614395

SPAIGHT, Robert George. b 45. Ridley Hall Cam. **d** 84 **p** 85. C St Columb Minor and St Colan *Truro* 84-87; C Worksop St Jo *S'well* 87-89; V Barlings *Linc* from 89. *The Vicarage, Station Road, Langworth, Lincoln LN3 5BB* Tel (01522) 754233

SPANISH REFORMED CHURCH, Bishop of. *See* LÓPEZ LOZANO, The Rt Revd Carlos

SPANNER, Prof Douglas Clement. b 16. Lon Univ BSc46 PhD51 DSc72. LNSM course. **d** 73 **p** 75. Hon C Ealing St Mary *Lon* 73-78; Hon C Eynsham *Ox* 79-83; Hon C Grove 83-86; Lic to Offic from 86. *Shalom, Main Street, Grove, Wantage OX12 7JY* Tel (01235) 766845

SPANNER, Handley James. b 51. Lanchester Poly BSc73 BA. Oak Hill Th Coll 82. **d** 85 **p** 86. C Cov H Trin *Cov* 85-89; V Rye Park St Cuth *St Alb* 89-01; V Colney Heath St Mark from 01. *St Mark's Vicarage, St Mark's Close, Colney Heath, St Albans AL4 0NQ* Tel (01727) 822040 E-mail jamesspanner@aol.com

SPARHAM, Canon Anthony George. b 41. St Jo Coll Dur BA69 DipTh. Cranmer Hall Dur 66. **d** 71 **p** 72. C Bourne *Linc* 71-74; TV Tong *Bradf* 74-76; V Windhill 76-81; Dioc Dir of Educn *St E* 82-85; V Goostrey *Ches* 85-99; Dir Lay Tr 85-90; Jt Dir Lay Tr 90-97; Hon Can Ches Cathl from 94; R Wilmslow from 99. *The Rectory, 12 Broadway, Wilmslow SK9 1NB* Tel (01625) 523127 *or* 520309 E-mail tsparham@fish.co.uk

SPARKES, Colin Anthony. b 37. Surrey Univ MSc68 Bath Univ MEd83 MIEE. Ox NSM Course 78. **d** 81 **p** 82. NSM Shrivenham w Watchfield and Bourton *Ox* 81-84; NSM Shellingford 84-91; R Hawkinge w Acrise and Swingfield *Cant* 91-01; rtd 02; Perm to Offic *Cant* from 02. *Winkfield, Victoria Road, Kingsdown, Deal CT14 8DX* Tel (01304) 365662

SPARKES, Donald James Henry. b 33. Oak Hill Th Coll DipTh59. **d** 59 **p** 60. C Southall Green St Jo *Lon* 59-63; P-in-c Pitsmoor *Sheff* 63-70; V 70-73; P-in-c Wicker w Neepsend 70-73; V Pitsmoor w Wicker 73-79; V Pitsmoor w Ellesmere 79-86; V Pitsmoor Ch Ch 86-96; rtd 96; Perm to Offic *Derby* and *Sheff* from 96. *8 Grosvenor Mansions, Broad Walk, Buxton SK17 6JH* Tel (01298) 25134

SPARKS, Christopher Thomas. b 29. Lanc Univ PGCE69 Birm Univ 81. St D Coll Lamp BA53 Lich Th Coll 53. **d** 55 **p** 56. C Macclesfield St Mich *Ches* 55-59; C W Kirby St Bridget 59-61; V Altrincham St Jo 61-68; Lic to Offic *Blackb* 68-79; C Lancaster St Mary 79-83; Chapl HM Pris Lanc 83-84; Perm to Offic *Blackb* from 84; rtd 94. *1 Yealand Drive, Scotforth, Lancaster LA1 4EW* Tel (01524) 67507

SPARKS, Ian. b 59. Lanc Univ BSc(Econ)81. Cranmer Hall Dur 94. **d** 96 **p** 97. C Bowdon *Ches* 96-00; V Chelford w Lower Withington from 00. *The New Vicarage, Chelford, Macclesfield SK11 9AH* Tel (01625) 861231 E-mail ian@sparks5.freeserve.co.uk

SPARROW, Michael Kenneth. St Jo Coll Dur BA74. Coll of Resurr Mirfield 74. **d** 75 **p** 76. C N Hinksey *Ox* 75-78; C Portsea St Mary *Portsm* 78-85; V Midsomer Norton w Clandown *B & W* 85-93; Chapl Schiedam Miss to Seafarers *Eur* 93-03. *Address temp unknown*

SPEAKMAN, Anthony Ernest. b 43. **d** 71 **p** 72. C Newtown *St As* 71-72; C Holywell 72-75; C St Marylebone w H Trin *Lon* 75-77; V Camberwell St Phil and St Mark *S'wark* 77-80; Lic to Offic *Lon* 94-96; NSM Kensington St Jo from 96; rtd 99. *24 McAuley Close, Kennington Road, London SE1 7BX* Tel (020) 7928 8721 *or* 7602 3898

SPEAKMAN, Joseph Frederick. b 26. NW Ord Course 75. **d** 78 **p** 79. NSM Wallasey St Hilary *Ches* 78; C 79-82; V Marthall w Over Peover 82-91; rtd 91; Perm to Offic *Ches* from 91. *1 Kinnaird Court, Cliff Road, Wallasey CH44 3AX* Tel 0151-637 0109

SPEAR, Andrew James Michael. b 60. Dur Univ BA81. Ridley Hall Cam 83. **d** 86 **p** 87. C Haughton le Skerne *Dur* 86-90; C Eastbourne H Trin *Chich* 90-95; C Patcham 95-02; V Oldland *Bris* from 02. *Oldland Vicarage, Grangeville Close, Longwell Green, Bristol BS30 9YJ* Tel 0117-932 7178 *or* 932 3291 E-mail andrewjmspear@hotmail.com

SPEAR, Miss Jennifer Jane. b 53. Westhill Coll Birm BEd76. Trin Coll Bris DipHE84. **dss** 84 **d** 87 **p** 95. Reading St Jo *Ox* 84-90; Par Dn 87-90; Hon Par Dn Devonport St Barn *Ex* 90-91; Hon Par Dn Devonport St Mich 90-91; Par Dn Plymstock 91-94; C 94-97; TV Plymstock and Hooe from 97. *63 Plymstock Road, Plymstock, Plymouth PL9 7NX* Tel (01752) 405202

SPEAR, John Cory. b 33. Open Univ BA87. Ridley Hall Cam 68. **d** 70 **p** 71. C Gerrards Cross *Ox* 70-73; TV Washfield, Stoodleigh, Withleigh etc *Ex* 73-79; R Instow 79-90; V Westleigh 79-90; RD Hartland 82-89; V Pilton w Ashford 90-97; TR Barnstaple 97-99; rtd 99; Perm to Offic *Ex* from 00. *Abbots Lodge, Abbotsham Court, Abbotsham, Bideford EX39 5BH* Tel (01237) 476607

SPEAR, Sylvia Grace. b 36. St Chris Coll Blackheath 60. **dss** 76 **d** 87 **p** 94. S Wimbledon H Trin and St Pet *S'wark* 76-80; Lee Gd Shep w St Pet 80-95; Par Dn 87-94; C 94-95; rtd 95; Perm to Offic

Nor from 95. *19 Grovelands, Ingoldisthorpe, King's Lynn PE31 6PG* Tel (01485) 543469

SPEARS, Reginald Robert Derek. b 48. Trin Coll Ox BA72 MA75. Cuddesdon Coll 72. **d** 75 **p** 76. C Hampton All SS *Lon* 75-79; C Caversham *Ox* 79-81; C Caversham St Pet and Mapledurham etc 81-84; V Reading St Matt 84-94; V Earley St Pet from 94. *St Peter's Vicarage, 129 Whiteknights Road, Reading RG6 7BB* Tel 0118-926 2009 Fax as telephone E-mail derekspears@compuserve.com

SPECK, Ms Jane Elisabeth. b 72. Univ of Cen England in Birm BA94 St Jo Coll Dur BA01. Cranmer Hall Dur 98. **d** 02 **p** 03. C Stourport and Wilden *Worc* from 02. *143 Sutton Park Road, Kidderminster DY11 6JQ* Tel (01562) 820678 Mobile 07968-000362 E-mail janespeck@hotmail.com

SPECK, Preb Peter William. b 42. Univ of Wales BSc64 Birm Univ BA66 DPS67 MA71. Qu Coll Birm 64. **d** 67 **p** 68. C Rhosddu *St As* 67-71; C Wrexham 71-72; Asst Chapl United Sheff Hosps 72-73; Chapl N Gen Hosp Sheff 73-79; Chapl R Free Hosp Lon 79-95; Hon Sen Lect Sch of Med 87-95; Preb St Paul's Cathl *Lon* 92-95; Chapl Southn Univ Hosps NHS Trust 95-02; rtd 02; Public Preacher *Win* from 02; Visiting Fell Southn Univ from 02; Hon Sen Research Fell K Coll Lon from 02. *22 The Harrage, Romsey SO51 8AE* E-mail peter.speck@which.net

SPECK, Raymond George. b 39. Oak Hill Th Coll 64. **d** 67 **p** 68. C Stretford St Bride *Man* 67-70; C Roxeth Ch Ch *Lon* 70-74; V Woodbridge St Jo *St E* 74-85; R Jersey St Ouen w St Geo *Win* 85-98; rtd 98; Perm to Offic *Win* from 98. *Rosevale Lodge, rue du Craslin, St Peter, Jersey JE3 7BU* Tel (01534) 634987

SPEDDING, Geoffrey Osmond. b 46. Hull Univ BA67 Fitzw Coll Cam BA69 MA BD. **d** 70 **p** 71. C Bradf Cathl *Bradf* 70-73; C Sutton St Jas and Wawne *York* 73-76; TV Preston St Jo *Blackb* 76-82; TV Yate New Town *Bris* 82-87; TR Bestwood *S'well* 87-94; V Ravenshead 94-04; rtd 04. *Address withheld by request*

SPEDDING, William Granville. b 39. Tyndale Hall Bris BD60. **d** 62 **p** 63. C Man Albert Memorial Ch *Man* 62-65; Hd RE Whitecroft Sch Bolton 65-71; Co-ord Humanities Hayward Sch Bolton 71-93; Perm to Offic 65-67 and from 02; NSM New Bury 67-79; NSM Bolton St Paul w Em 79-86; NSM Pennington 86-02. *26 Milverton Close, Lostock, Bolton BL6 4RR* Tel (01204) 841248 E-mail info@hovercraft.org.uk

SPEEDY (née BRINDLEY), Mrs Angela Mary. b 44. Oak Hill Th Coll 93 N Ord Course 99. **d** 00 **p** 01. C Handforth *Ches* 00-03; R Whaley Bridge from 03. *St James's Rectory, Taxal Road, Whaley Bridge, High Peak SK23 7DY* Tel (01663) 719535 E-mail parish@rectorsretreat.fsnet.co.uk

SPEEDY, Canon Darrel Craven. b 35. St Chad's Coll Dur BA57. Wells Th Coll 57. **d** 59 **p** 60. C Frodingham *Linc* 59-63; V Heckington w Howell 63-71; V Barton upon Humber 71-79; R Tain *Mor* 79-85; Dioc Sec 82-85; Can St Andr Cathl Inverness 83-85; Syn Clerk 83-85; R Whaley Bridge *Ches* 85-01; RD Chadkirk 88-95; Hon Can Ches Cathl from 96; rtd 01; P-in-c Barthomley *Ches* from 01. *The Rectory, Rushy Lane, Barthomley, Crewe CW2 5PE* Tel (01270) 877112 E-mail darrel.speedy@btopenworld.com

SPEEKS, Mark William. b 62. Ex Univ BA82 Ex Coll Ox MSt83 Yale Univ MDiv02. **d** 02 **p** 02. C Los Angeles St Alban USA 02-03; NSM Kilburn St Mary w All So and W Hampstead St Jas *Lon* from 04. *Flat 1, 6 Upper John Street, London W1F 9HB* Tel (020) 7734 7699

SPEERS, Canon Samuel Hall. b 46. TCD BA70 MA75. Cuddesdon Coll 70. **d** 73 **p** 74. C Boreham Wood All SS *St Alb* 73-76; Madagascar 76-88; Hon Can Antananarivo from 85; R S Lafford *Linc* 88-02; RD Lafford 96-02; TR Chipping Barnet *St Alb* from 02. *The Rectory, 38 Manor Road, Barnet EN5 2JJ* Tel (020) 8449 3894 E-mail hall.speers@talk21.com

SPENCE, Brian Robin. b 39. St Chad's Coll Dur BA61. **d** 63 **p** 64. C Weston *Guildf* 63-67; Lesotho 67-68; C Chobham w Valley End *Guildf* 68-71; C Gt Yarmouth *Nor* 71-74; V Warnham *Chich* 74-81; V E Grinstead St Mary 81-86; V Crowthorne *Ox* 86-05; rtd 05; Hon C Theale and Englefield *Ox* from 05. *St Mark's House, Englefield, Reading RG7 5EP* Tel 0118-930 2227

SPENCE, Elizabeth. St Alb and Ox Min Course. **d** 05. NSM Cowley St Jas *Ox* from 05. *Address temp unknown*

SPENCE, James Knox. b 30. Worc Coll Ox BA55 MA58. Ridley Hall Cam. **d** 57 **p** 58. C W Hampstead Trin *Lon* 57-60; C Ox St Ebbe w St Pet *Ox* 61-64; Cand Sec CPAS 64-68; V Reading Greyfriars *Ox* 68-78; C St Helen Bishopsgate w St Andr Undershaft etc *Lon* 78-82; P-in-c Gt Baddow *Chelmsf* 82-86; V 86-88; TR 88-95; rtd 95; Hon C Wallingford *Ox* from 96. *15 High Street, Wallingford OX10 0BP* Tel (01491) 826814 E-mail jim@spence341.fsnet.co.uk

SPENCE, James Timothy. b 35. St Jo Coll Cam BA59 MA63. Wycliffe Hall Ox 59. **d** 61 **p** 62. C Stoke *Cov* 61-64; C Cambridge H Trin *Ely* 64-67; R Tarrington w Stoke Edith *Heref* 67-72; Dioc Youth Officer 67-72; Lic to Offic *Win* 72-75; R Falstone *Newc* 75-80; TV Bellingham/Otterburn Gp 80-82; Dioc Ecum Adv 82-87; V Dinnington 82-87; V Shap w Swindale *Carl* 87-93; P-in-c Bowness and Kirkbride w Newton Arlosh 93-00; rtd 00; Perm to Offic *Carl* from 02. *67 Clifford Road, Penrith CA11 8PT* Tel (01768) 866727

SPENCE, Canon John Edis. b 24. St Edm Hall Ox BA46 MA48. Westcott Ho Cam 47. **d** 48 **p** 49. C Newland St Jo *York* 48-50; Australia 50-54; C Uckfield *Chich* 54-55; Chapl RN 55-59 and 60-65; V Thornton-le-Street w Thornton-le-Moor etc *York* 59-60; Chapl RNR from 65; V St Germans *Truro* 65-73; V Tideford 65-73; P-in-c Sheviock 69-70; Perm to Offic 73-76; Dioc Chapl to Bp 76-78; C Newlyn St Newlyn 76-78; Chapl for Maintenance of the Min 78-87; Stewardship Adv 80-87; Hon Can Truro Cathl 84-89; Bp's Dom Chapl 87-89; P-in-c St Allen 87-89; rtd 89; Lic to Offic *Truro* 89-95; Perm to Offic *Ex* 91-98; Hon C Diptford, N Huish, Harberton, Harbertonford etc from 98. *26 Kerries Road, South Brent TQ10 9DA* Tel (01364) 72578

SPENCE, Mrs Moira Joan. b 44. St Alb and Ox Min Course 96. **d** 01 **p** 02. OLM Risborough *Ox* from 01. *37 Place Farm Way, Monks Risborough, Princes Risborough HP27 9JJ*

SPENCE, Canon Philip Arthur. b 39. Lon Univ BD71 Open Univ BA76. Westcott Ho Cam 78. **d** 78 **p** 79. In Methodist Ch 67-78; C Walthamstow St Pet *Chelmsf* 78-80; Dioc Adv on Evang 80-87; Dep Dir Dept of Miss (Evang Division) 80-85; P-in-c Greensted 80-86; Bp's Adv on Tourism 81-87; Asst Dir of Miss and Unity 85-87; R Greensted-juxta-Ongar w Stanford Rivers 86-87; V Cambridge St Mark *Ely* 87-95; Chapl Wolfs Coll Cam 87-95; Relig Adv Anglia TV 91-95; V Pet St Jo *Pet* 95-01; Can Res and Warden Pet Cathl 97-01; Can from 01; P-in-c Preston and Ridlington w Wing and Pilton from 01; Adult Educn Officer 01-05. *The Rectory, Ridlington Road, Preston, Oakham LE15 9NN* Tel (01572) 737287 E-mail philip.spence@talk21.com

SPENCE, The Very Revd Walter Cyril. b 19. TCD BA40 MA43 BD43. **d** 42 **p** 43. C Maghera *D & R* 43-48; C Roscommon *K, E & A* 48-50; I Ballysumaghan w Killery 50-55; I Tubbercurry w Kilmactigue *T, K & A* 55-60; I Achonry w Tubbercurry and Killoran 60-66; Can Achonry Cathl 62-66; Dean Tuam 66-81; I Tuam 66-81; Dioc Registrar 66-85; Preb Kilmactalway St Patr Cathl Dublin 67-85; I Kilmoremoy w Castleconnor, Easkey, Kilglass etc *T, K & A* 81-85; rtd 85. *Beth Shalom, 1 Gracefield Avenue, Dublin 5, Irish Republic*

SPENCELEY, Malcolm. b 40. Cranmer Hall Dur 78. **d** 80 **p** 81. C Redcar *York* 80-85; V Middlesbrough Ascension 85-93; V Newby from 93. *The Vicarage, 77 Green Lane, Scarborough YO12 6HT* Tel (01723) 363205

SPENCER, Andrew. b 47. St Matthias Coll Bris BEd70. **d** 04 **p** 05. Moderator for Reader Tr *Guildf* from 01; OLM Busbridge and Hambledon from 04. *24 Park Road, Godalming GU7 1SH* Tel (01483) 416333 E-mail andyspencer@godalming.ac.uk

SPENCER, Antony Wade. b 50. AIQS78 Birm Poly HNC74 Wolv Poly MCIOB76. Ridley Hall Cam CTM94. **d** 94 **p** 95. C Bury St Edmunds St Geo *St E* 94-96; Perm to Offic 96-97; C Rougham, Beyton w Hessett and Rushbrooke 97-99; TV Mildenhall from 99. *The Vicarage, 8 Church Lane, Mildenhall, Bury St Edmunds IP28 7ED* Tel (01638) 717331 Mobile 07710-298604 Fax 717557 E-mail antspencer@aol.com

SPENCER, Christopher Graham. b 61. Magd Coll Cam BA83 MA87 Bath Univ MSc84. St Jo Coll Nottm 93. **d** 93 **p** 94. C Ore *Chich* 93-97; V Deal St Geo *Cant* from 97. *The Vicarage, 8 St George's Road, Deal CT14 6BA* Tel (01304) 372587 E-mail vicar@stgeorgesdeal.org.uk

SPENCER, David William. b 43. EAMTC 80. **d** 81 **p** 82. NSM Wisbech St Aug *Ely* 81-84; C Whittlesey 84-86; R Upwell Ch Ch 86-90; R March St Pet and March St Mary 90-98; TV Stanground and Farcet 98-01; V Farcet 01-04; V Farcet Hampton from 04. *The Vicarage, Main Street, Farcet, Peterborough PE7 3AN* Tel (01733) 240286 E-mail davidspencer@freezone.co.uk

SPENCER, Derek Kenneth. b 67. St Jo Coll Nottm BA98. **d** 03 **p** 05. Storrington Deanery Youth Missr *Chich* from 01. *18 Ingram Road, Steyning BN44 3PF* Tel (01903) 813049 Mobile 07734-330678 E-mail noba@btinternet.com

SPENCER, Mrs Gail. STETS. **d** 03 **p** 04. NSM Wilton w Netherhampton and Fugglestone *Sarum* from 03. *68 Bouverie Avenue, Salisbury SP2 8DX* Tel (01722) 331128 E-mail gailespencer@yahoo.co.uk

SPENCER, Geoffrey. b 50. ALCM76 Nottm Univ CertEd78 ACertCM79 Open Univ BA84. Linc Th Coll 85. **d** 87 **p** 88. C Skegness and Winthorpe *Linc* 87-90; V Heckington 90-93; P-in-c Bottesford and Muston *Leic* 93-98; P-in-c Harby, Long Clawson and Hose 94-98; P-in-c Barkestone w Plungar, Redmile and Stathern 94-98; RD Framland 97-98; Perm to Offic *Linc* 03-05; Lic Preacher from 05. *The Vicarage, Yawling Gate Road, Friskney, Boston PE22 8QF* Tel (01754) 820418

SPENCER, Canon Gilbert Hugh. b 43. Lon Univ BD67. ALCD66. **d** 67 **p** 68. C Bexleyheath Ch Ch *Roch* 67-73; C Bexley St Jo 73-76; P-in-c Bromley St Jo 76-78; V 78-81; R Chatham St Mary w St Jo 81-91; V Minster-in-Sheppey *Cant* from 91; P-in-c Queenborough 99-05; AD Sittingbourne 94-00 and 03-04; Hon Can Cant Cathl from 99; Chapl Sheppey Community Hosp

91-98; Chapl Thames Gateway NHS Trust from 98. *The Vicarage, Vicarage Road, Minster-on-Sea, Sheerness ME12 2HE* Tel and fax (01795) 873185
E-mail gilbert_spencer@hotmail.com

SPENCER, Gordon Charles Craig. b 13. Oak Hill Th Coll 35. **d** 38 **p** 39. C Attenborough w Bramcote *S'well* 38-41; C Heanor *Derby* 41-45; P-in-c Eastwood *S'well* 45-46; R W Hallam *Derby* 46-66; PC Mapperley 51-66; RD Ilkeston 62-66; V Bathampton *B & W* 66-81; Chapl R Sch Bath 72-81; rtd 81; P-in-c Ditteridge *Bris* 81-86; Perm to Offic *B & W* from 86 and *Bris* 86-05. *26 Elm Grove, Bath BA1 7AZ* Tel (01225) 316570

SPENCER, Graham Lewis. b 48. St Jo Coll Nottm 80. **d** 82 **p** 83. C Leic St Anne *Leic* 82-85; P-in-c Frisby-on-the-Wreake w Kirby Bellars 85-86; TV Melton Gt Framland 86-93; V Upper Wreake 93-99; V Glen Magna cum Stretton Magna etc 99-05; rtd 05. *18 Chetwynd Drive, Melton Mowbray LE13 0HU* Tel (01664) 564266 E-mail graham.trish@lineone.net

SPENCER, Ian John. b 61. Qu Coll Birm 03. **d** 05. C Gt Malvern St Mary *Worc* from 05. *107 Court Road, Malvern WR14 3EF*

SPENCER, Joan. b 50. HND. LNSM course 96. **d** 98 **p** 99. OLM Norwich St Mary Magd w St Jas *Nor* from 98. *94 Mousehold Avenue, Norwich NR3 4RS* Tel (01603) 404471

SPENCER, John Edward. b 36. Bris Univ BA60. Tyndale Hall Bris 60. **d** 61 **p** 62. C St Helens St Mark *Liv* 61-64; Japan 65-70; Area Sec CMS *Leic* and *Pet* 70-71; Warden and Chapl Rikkyo Japanese Sch Rudgwick 71-73; Hd Master and Chapl Pennthorpe Sch Rudgwick 74-96; NSM Rudgwick *Chich* 95-96; rtd 96; Perm to Offic *Chich* from 96; *Guildf* 96-98; Hd Master Ardingly Coll Jun Sch Haywards Heath 97-98; Chapl Rowcroft Hospice Torquay 99-01; Hon C Bovey Tracey SS Pet, Paul and Thos w Hennock *Ex* from 99. *101 Churchfields Drive, Bovey Tracey, Newton Abbot TQ13 9QZ* Tel (01626) 836773

SPENCER, Mrs Margot Patricia Winifred. b 48. Coll of St Matthias Bris CertEd69 Farnborough Tech Coll 91. STETS 98. **d** 01 **p** 02. NSM Wonersh w Blackheath *Guildf* 01-05; NSM Busbridge and Hambledon from 05. *24 Park Road, Godalming GU7 1SH* Tel (01483) 416333
E-mail margotspencer@tinyworld.co.uk
or margot@wonershchurch.com

SPENCER, Neil Richard. b 49. Leeds Univ BA70 ALA72. WEMTC 96. **d** 99 **p** 00. NSM Ludlow, Ludford, Ashford Carbonell etc *Heref* 99-02; C Letton w Staunton, Byford, Mansel Gamage etc 02-05; P-in-c Ormesby St Marg w Scratby, Ormesby St Mich etc *Nor* from 05. *The Rectory, 11 Church View, Ormesby, Great Yarmouth NR29 3PZ* Tel (01493) 730234
E-mail nspencer@revd.freeserve.co.uk

SPENCER, Norman Ernest. b 07. **d** 74 **p** 75. NSM Olveston *Bris* 74-82; Perm to Offic from 82. *26 Park Crescent, Bristol BS16 1NZ* Tel 0117-956 8873

SPENCER, Peter Cecil. b 30. Lich Th Coll 58. **d** 61 **p** 62. C Alton St Lawr *Win* 61-63; C Bournemouth St Luke 63-66; C W End 67-70; C Reading St Mary V *Ox* 70-72; C-in-c Reading St Matt CD 72-76; V Reading St Matt 76-78; TV Sidmouth, Woolbrook and Salcombe Regis *Ex* 78-86; R Birch w Layer Breton and Layer Marney *Chelmsf* 86-96; rtd 96; Perm to Offic *Chelmsf* from 99. *11 Dray Court, Colchester Road, West Bergholt, Colchester CO6 3TD* Tel (01206) 243453

SPENCER, Peter Roy. b 40. CertEd. Sarum & Wells Th Coll 72. **d** 74 **p** 75. C Northampton St Alb *Pet* 74-77; TV Cov E *Cov* 77-90; V Erdington St Barn *Birm* 90-02; TR Erdington from 02. *The Vicarage, 26 Church Road, Birmingham B24 9AX* Tel 0121-373 0884 *or* 350 9945

SPENCER, Richard Dennis. b 50. Imp Coll Lon BSc71. NTMTC 93. **d** 96 **p** 97. C Leek and Meerbrook *Lich* 96-00; P-in-c Shrewsbury H Trin w St Julian from 00. *Holy Trinity Vicarage, Greyfriars Road, Shrewsbury SY3 7EP* Tel (01743) 244891
E-mail rds@htbv.org.uk

SPENCER, Richard Hugh. b 62. Univ of Wales (Cardiff) LLB84 BD88 Bris Univ MA92. St Mich Coll Llan 85. **d** 88 **p** 89. C Barry All SS *Llan* 88-90; Asst Chapl Univ of Wales (Cardiff) 90-92; Lect NT Studies 92-98; Tutor St Mich Coll Llan 92-98; R Llangenni and Llanbedr Ystrad Yw w Patricio *S & B* 98-00; Dir Post-Ord Tr 00; TV Cowbridge *Llan* 02-03; NSM from 03; Hd of Th Trin Coll Carmarthen from 03. *Trinity College, College Road, Carmarthen SA31 3EP* Tel (01267) 676767
E-mail r.spencer@trinity-cm.ac.uk

SPENCER, Richard William Edward. b 33. FSCA66. WMMTC 78. **d** 81 **p** 82. NSM The Lickey *Birm* 81-83; Area Sec (Warks and W Midl) Chr Aid 83-93; Perm to Offic *Worc* from 95 and *Heref* from 98. *Honey Hedge, 165 Godiva Road, Leominster HR6 8TB* Tel (01568) 620097

SPENCER, Robert. b 48. St Jo Coll Nottm CertCS93. **d** 93 **p** 94. NSM Ellon *Ab* 93-95 and from 99; NSM Cruden Bay 93-95; NSM Fraserburgh w New Pitsligo 95-99. *12 Riverview Place, Ellon AB41 9NW* Tel (01358) 723193 Fax (01224) 248505
E-mail spencer@netmatters.co.uk

SPENCER, Roy Primett. b 26. Oak Hill Th Coll 50. **d** 53 **p** 54. C Bedford St Pet *St Alb* 53-55; C Luton Ch Ch 55-58; C Nottingham St Mary *S'well* 58-60; V Middlestown *Wakef* 60-61; Chapl Crumpsall Hosp Man 61-66; R Fleet *Linc* 66-69; V Accrington St Paul *Blackb* 69-78; V Woodplumpton 78-83; P-in-c Preston St Luke 83-89; P-in-c Preston St Luke and St Oswald 89-90; Chapl Preston Hosp N Shields 83-91; rtd 91; Perm to Offic *Blackb* from 91. *5 Hollywood Avenue, Penwortham, Preston PR1 9AS* Tel (01772) 743783

SPENCER, Stephen Christopher. b 60. Ball Coll Ox BA82 DPhil90. Edin Th Coll 88. **d** 90 **p** 91. C Harlesden All So *Lon* 90-93; Zimbabwe 93-99; V Caton w Littledale *Blackb* 99-03; Dep Prin Carl and Blackb Dioc Tr Inst 99-03; Tutor N Ord Course from 03. *Northern Ordination Course, Luther King House, Brighton Grove, Manchester M14 5JP* Tel 0161-249 2511
E-mail s.spencer@ukgateway.net

SPENCER, Stephen Nigel Howard. b 53. Pemb Coll Ox BA75 MA03 Jes Coll Cam PGCE76. Trin Coll Bris 80. **d** 82 **p** 83. C Partington and Carrington *Ches* 82-85; C Brunswick *Man* 85-88; Chapl UEA *Nor* 88-92; rtd 92; Perm to Offic *Nor* 92-95. *43 College Lane, Norwich NR4 6TW* Tel (01603) 506815
E-mail howard.spencer@btinternet.com

SPENCER, Steven Christopher. b 47. RGN69 Westmr Coll Lon HND78. NTMTC 98. **d** 98 **p** 99. NSM Chatham St Phil and St Jas *Roch* from 98. *278 Churchill Avenue, Chatham ME5 0LH* Tel (01634) 302581 E-mail steve@scspencer.freeserve.co.uk

SPENCER, Mrs Susan. b 47. EMMTC 87. **d** 90 **p** 94. Par Dn Cotgrave *S'well* 90-94; C 94-98; P-in-c Rolleston w Fiskerton, Morton and Upton from 98; Asst Warden of Readers from 98. *The Vicarage, 29 Marlock Close, Fiskerton, Southwell NG25 0UB* Tel (01636) 830331 E-mail suespencer@fiskertonvcb.net

SPENCER, Mrs Susan Lesley. b 55. Dioc OLM tr scheme 97. **d** 00 **p** 01. OLM Middleton w Thornham *Man* from 00. *1 Westbrook Close, Rochdale OL11 2XY* Tel (01706) 350668
E-mail suespencer@bigfoot.com

SPENCER, Sylvia. **d** 98. Chapl Grampian Univ Hosp NHS Trust from 98. *Aberdeen Royal Infirmary, Foresterhill, Aberdeen AB9 2ZB* Tel (01224) 681818

SPENCER-THOMAS, Canon Owen Robert. b 40. Lon Univ BSc(Soc)70 LGSM96 MRTvS76. Westcott Ho Cam 70. **d** 72 **p** 73. C S Kensington St Luke *Lon* 72-76; Lect RS S Kensington Inst 74-76; Dir Lon Chs Radio Workshop & Relig Producer BBC 76-78; Relig Producer Anglia TV 78-95; Lic to Offic *Lon* 76-87; NSM Cambridge Ascension *Ely* from 87; Chapl St Jo Coll Sch Cam 93-98; Chapl St Bede's Sch Cam 96-97; Chapl Ch Coll Cam 97-01; Dioc Dir of Communications *Ely* from 02; Hon Can Ely Cathl from 04. *52 Windsor Road, Cambridge CB4 3JN* Tel and fax (01223) 358448 *or* tel (01353) 652701
E-mail owenst@btinternet.com

SPENDLOVE, Mrs Lindsay Kate. b 55. Man Univ LLB77 Essex Univ BA88. EAMTC 89. **d** 92 **p** 94. NSM Lexden *Chelmsf* 92-94; NSM Colchester Ch Ch w St Mary V 94-96; NSM Pleshey 97-02; Perm to Offic *St E* from 02. *Caer Colyn, Donkey Lane, Friston, Saxmundham IP17 1PL* Tel (01728) 688043
E-mail ikspendlove@supanet.com

SPERRING, Clive Michael. b 43. Oak Hill Th Coll 71. **d** 75 **p** 76. C Hawkwell *Chelmsf* 75-78; C-in-c Gt Baddow 78-82; New Zealand from 82. *49 Te Arawa Street, Orakei, Auckland 5, New Zealand* Tel (0064) (9) 528 4400 *or* 521 0296
E-mail revclive@xtra.co.nz

SPEYER, Nicholas Anthony. b 48. Lon Univ BD78 Sydney Univ BE70 Sheff Univ MPhil84. Moore Th Coll Sydney ThL77. **d** 79 **p** 79. Australia 79-82 and from 84; C Millhouses H Trin *Sheff* 82-84. *Address temp unknown* E-mail nspeyer@primus.com.au

SPICER, David John. b 52. Sussex Univ BA76 Lon Univ MTh78 Dip Psychotherapy 97. Westcott Ho Cam 77. **d** 79 **p** 80. C E Dulwich St Jo *S'wark* 79-82; C Richmond St Mary w St Matthias and St Jo 82-87; V Lewisham St Swithun 87-91; Chapl Community of All Hallows Ditchingham from 91. *St Edmund's House, All Hallows Convent, Ditchingham, Bungay NR35 2DZ* Tel (01986) 892139

SPICER (formerly RIMMER), Dorothy Janet Rosalind. b 49. Cen Sch of Art Lon BA72 Middx Poly ATD74 E Lon Univ MA98. Westcott Ho Cam. **d** 00 **p** 01. C Notting Hill St Jo and St Pet *Lon* 00-02; V Totternhoe, Stanbridge and Tilsworth *St Alb* from 02. *The Vicarage, Mill Road, Stanbridge, Leighton Buzzard LU7 9HX* Tel (01525) 210253 E-mail revjanetspicer@aol.com

SPICER, Leigh Edwin. b 56. Sarum & Wells Th Coll 78. **d** 81 **p** 82. C Harborne St Pet *Birm* 81-83; C Bloxwich *Lich* 83-87; Chapl RAF from 87. *Chaplaincy Services (RAF), HQ, Personnel and Training Command, RAF Innsworth, Gloucester GL3 1EZ* Tel (01452) 712612 ext 5164 Fax 510828

SPICER, Nicolas. b 61. Univ of Wales (Lamp) BA84. Coll of Resurr Mirfield 84. **d** 86 **p** 87. C Westbury-on-Trym H Trin *Bris* 86-89; C Willesden Green St Andr and St Fran *Lon* 89-93; Chapl Asst Charing Cross Hosp Lon 93-94; Asst Chapl Hammersmith Hosps NHS Trust 94-97; R Ardleigh and The Bromleys *Chelmsf* from 97. *The Rectory, Hall Road, Great Bromley, Colchester CO7 7TS* Tel (01206) 230344 E-mail nspicer@lineone.net

SPICER, Robert Patrick. b 39. FCA68. St Alb and Ox Min Course 94. **d** 97 **p** 98. NSM Riverside *Ox* 97-01; NSM Beaconsfield from 01; Perm to Offic *Lon* from 98. *The Parsonage,*

St Michael's Green, Beaconsfield HP9 2BN Tel (01494) 673464 E-mail robspic@msn.com

SPIERS, The Ven Graeme Hendry Gordon. b 25. ALCD52. **d** 52 **p** 53. C Addiscombe St Mary *Cant* 52-56; Succ Bradf Cathl *Bradf* 56-58; V Speke All SS *Liv* 58-66; V Aigburth 66-80; RD Childwall 75-79; Hon Can Liv Cathl 77-91; Adn Liv 80-91; rtd 91; Perm to Offic *Liv* 91-03. *19 Barkfield Lane, Liverpool L37 1LY* Tel (01704) 872902

SPIERS, Peter Hendry. b 61. St Jo Coll Dur BA82. Ridley Hall Cam 83. **d** 86 **p** 87. C W Derby St Luke *Liv* 86-90; TV Everton St Pet 90-95; V Everton St Geo 95-05; P-in-c Gt Crosby St Luke from 05. *St Luke's Vicarage, Liverpool Road, Crosby, Liverpool L23 5SE* Tel 0151-924 1737 E-mail pete@spiersfamily.eclipse.co.uk

SPIKIN, Simon John Overington. b 48. Nottm Univ BTh74. Linc Th Coll 70. **d** 75 **p** 76. C Sawbridgeworth *St Alb* 75-79; C Odiham w S Warnborough and Long Sutton *Win* 79-81; R Dickleburgh w Thelveton w Frenze and Shimpling *Nor* 81-82; P-in-c Rushall 81-82; R Dickleburgh, Langmere, Shimpling, Thelveton etc 82-96; rtd 96; Perm to Offic *Cant* from 01. *Marley Court, Kingston, Canterbury CT4 6JH* Tel (01227) 832405

SPILLER, Canon David Roger. b 44. St Jo Coll Dur BA70 Fitzw Coll Cam BA72 MA76 Nottm Univ DipAdEd80. Ridley Hall Cam 70. **d** 73 **p** 74. C Bradf Cathl *Bradf* 73-77; C Stratford-on-Avon w Bishopton *Cov* 77-80; Chapl Geo Eliot Hosp Nuneaton 80-90; V Chilvers Coton w Astley *Cov* 80-90; RD Nuneaton 84-90; Prin Aston Tr Scheme 90-97; C Kings Norton *Birm* 98-99; C Shirley 99-00; Dir of Min and Dioc Dir of Ords *Cov* from 00; Hon Can Cov Cathl from 04. *The Parsonage, Sambourne Lane, Sambourne, Redditch B96 6PA* Tel (01527) 892372 *or* (024) 7671 0504 Fax (024) 7671 0550 E-mail rogerspiller@btinternet.com

SPILLER, Edward William. b 32. Cranmer Hall Dur 80. **d** 82 **p** 83. C Kirkleatham *York* 82-85; R The Thorntons and The Otteringtons 85-00; rtd 01; Perm to Offic *York* from 01. *Carlton House, Topcliffe Road, Thirsk YO7 1RL* Tel (01845) 522811 E-mail rev.ted@skypilot.flyer.co.uk

SPILMAN, Derrick Geoffrey. b 27. Roch Th Coll 61. **d** 63 **p** 64. C Dover St Mary *Cant* 63-67; CF 67-71; Canada from 71; rtd 92. *5398 Walter Place, Burnaby BC, Canada, V5G 4K2* Tel (001) (604) 294 6816

SPILSBURY, Stephen Ronald Paul. b 39. Nottm Univ BSc69 MPhil72 Bris Univ PhD99. Linc Th Coll 71. **d** 64 **p** 65. In RC Ch 64-71; C Cricklade w Latton *Bris* 72-75; P-in-c Swindon All SS 76-81; V Lawrence Weston 81-95; RD Westbury and Severnside 89-91; rtd 99; Perm to Offic *Bris* from 03. *10 Woodside Grove, Bristol BS10 7RF* Tel 0117-959 1079 E-mail paul.spilsbury@btinternet.com

SPINDLER, Miss Jane Diana. b 54. Southn Univ BA75 CertEd76. Wycliffe Hall Ox 87. **d** 89 **p** 94. C Bishopsworth *Bris* 89-93; C Brislington St Luke 93-94; rtd 95; Perm to Offic *Bris* from 95. *143 Highridge Road, Bishopsworth, Bristol BS13 8HT* Tel 0117-935 8137

SPINK, Mrs Diana. b 40. Ex Univ BA63 PGCE64. St Alb and Ox Min Course 97. **d** 00 **p** 01. NSM Hemel Hempstead *St Alb* from 00. *39 Garland Close, Hemel Hempstead HP2 5HU* Tel (01442) 262133 Mobile 07808-184321 E-mail diana2spink@hotmail.com

SPINK, Canon George Arthur Peter. b 26. Oak Hill Th Coll 54. **d** 56 **p** 57. C Thurnby w Stoughton *Leic* 56-58; C-in-c Thurnby Lodge CD 58-59; Chapl Bonn w Cologne *Eur* 59-62; Chapl Vienna w Budapest and Prague 62-68; Chapl Cov Cathl *Cov* 68-70; Can Res Cov Cathl 70-77; Warden The Dorothy Kerin Trust Burrswood 77-81; Prior Omega Order from 80; Lic to Offic *Roch* 80-86; Lic to Offic *B & W* 86-95; rtd 89. *The Priory, Winford Manor, Winford, Bristol BS40 8DW* Tel (01275) 472262 Fax 472065

SPINKS, Prof Bryan Douglas. b 48. FRHistS85 St Chad's Coll Dur BA70 DipTh71 BD79 K Coll Lon MTh72 Dur Univ DD88 Yale Univ Hon MA98. **d** 75 **p** 76. C Witham *Chelmsf* 75-78; C Clacton St Jas 78-79; Chapl Chu Coll Cam 80-97; Lic to Offic *Ely* 80-97; Affiliated Lect Div Cam Univ 82-97; Perm to Offic *St Alb* 84-99; Prof Liturg Studies Yale Univ and Fell Morse Coll from 98; Perm to Offic *Ely* from 02. *Institute of Sacred Music, 409 Prospect Street, New Haven, CT 06511, USA* Tel (001) (203) 432 5186 E-mail bryan.spinks@yale.edu *or* bryspinkus@aol.com

SPINKS, Christopher George. b 53. Brighton Poly HND80. Oak Hill Th Coll BA88. **d** 88 **p** 89. C Hove Bp Hannington Memorial Ch *Chich* 88-92; Travelling Sec UCCF 92-95; Itinerant Min 95-98; Chapl Martlets Hospice Hove from 98; TV Hove *Chich* from 99. *35 St Heliers Avenue, Hove BN3 5RE* Tel (01273) 730027 E-mail chrisgspinks@hotmail.com

SPINKS, John Frederick. b 40. Westmr Coll Ox MTh97. Oak Hill Th Coll 79. **d** 82 **p** 83. NSM Roxbourne St Andr *Lon* 82-89; C Northwood H Trin 89-93; P-in-c Greenhill St Jo 93-96; V 96-04; rtd 04; Perm to Offic *Lon*, *Ox* and *St Alb* from 04. *Woodpecker Cottage, 232 Northwood Road, Harefield, Uxbridge UB9 6PT* Tel (01895) 822477 Mobile 07711-635199 E-mail john@spinks77.freeserve.co.uk

SPITTLE, Christopher Bamford. b 74. St Jo Coll Dur BA95. Ridley Hall Cam 97. **d** 99 **p** 00. C Netherton *Liv* 99-03; TR Sutton from 03. *St Michael's Vicarage, Gartons Lane, Clock Face, St Helens WA9 4RB* Tel (01744) 813738

SPITTLE, Robin. b 57. St Jo Coll Nottm 84. **d** 86 **p** 87. C Ipswich St Fran *St E* 86-91; Min Shotley St Mary CD 91-92; R Shotley 92-99; P-in-c Copdock w Washbrook and Belstead 93-99; V Kesgrave from 99. *The Vicarage, 18 Bell Lane, Kesgrave, Ipswich IP5 1JQ* Tel (01473) 622181 E-mail robin.spittle@lineone.net

SPIVEY, Colin. b 35. ACII61. Oak Hill Th Coll 74. **d** 76 **p** 77. C Egham *Guildf* 76-79; C Edgware *Lon* 79-83; R Haworth *Bradf* 83-95; Sub Chapl HM Pris Leeds 94-99; V Thorpe Edge *Bradf* 95-00; rtd 01; Perm to Offic *Ripon* from 01. *2 Woodhill View, Wetherby LS22 6PP* Tel (01937) 581508

SPIVEY, Canon Peter. b 19. Edin Th Coll 46. **d** 48 **p** 49. C Dewsbury Moor *Wakef* 48-50; C Mirfield 50-53; R Whitwood Mere 53-61; Chapl Castleford, Normanton and Distr Hosp 53-61; V Meltham *Wakef* 61-85; Chapl Moorview Hosp 61-68; RD Blackmoorfoot 79-85; Hon Can Wakef Cathl 81-85; rtd 85; Perm to Offic *Wakef* from 85. *3 Follett Avenue, Huddersfield HD4 5LW* Tel (01484) 654674

SPIVEY, Ronald. b 28. ACMA MInstAM. EMMTC 83. **d** 86 **p** 87. NSM Sutton St Mary *Linc* 86-98; Perm to Offic from 98. *5 Lancaster Drive, Long Sutton, Spalding PE12 9BD* Tel (01406) 362084 E-mail ron@spiveyr.freeserve.co.uk

SPOKES, David Lawrence. b 57. Nottm Univ BCombStuds85. Linc Th Coll 82. **d** 85 **p** 86. C Rushall *Lich* 85-89; TV Thornaby on Tees *York* 89-93; R Yardley Hastings, Denton and Grendon etc *Pet* from 02. *The Rectory, Castle Ashby Road, Yardley Hastings, Northampton NN7 1EL* Tel (01604) 696080

SPOKES, Keith John. b 29. EAMTC. **d** 84 **p** 85. NSM Bury St Edmunds St Mary *St E* 84-89; P-in-c Helmingham w Framsden and Pettaugh w Winston 89-92; rtd 93; Perm to Offic *St E* from 93. *16 Croft Rise, Bury St Edmunds IP33 2PY* Tel (01284) 706742

SPONG, Terence John. b 32. Roch Th Coll 63. **d** 66 **p** 67. C Forton *Portsm* 66-68; Rhodesia 68-80; Zimbabwe 80-84; R Christow, Ashton, Trusham and Bridford *Ex* 84-86; Chapl Puerto de la Cruz Tenerife *Eur* 86-93; Miss to Seamen 86-93; rtd 93; Perm to Offic *Win* from 93; Chapl R Bournemouth and Christchurch Hosps NHS Trust 97-98. *14B Stuart Road, Highcliffe, Christchurch BH23 5JS* Tel (01425) 277833

SPOONER, Anthony Patrick David. b 45. Univ Coll of Rhodesia Univ Coll of Nyasaland BA68 Nottm Univ DipTh72. Linc Th Coll 71. **d** 74 **p** 75. C Glynde, W Firle and Beddingham *Chich* 74-77; Rhodesia 77-80; Zimbabwe 80-86; P-in-c Clacton St Jas *Chelmsf* 86-90; V from 90. *St James's Vicarage, 44 Wash Lane, Clacton-on-Sea CO15 1DA* Tel (01255) 422007 E-mail revapdspooner@aol.com

SPOTTISWOODE, Anthony Derek. b 25. Solicitor 50 Pemb Coll Cam BA47 MA86. Sarum & Wells Th Coll 85. **d** 86 **p** 87. C Hampstead St Jo *Lon* 86-94; rtd 95; Perm to Offic *Lon* from 95. *Flat 6, 38-40 Eton Avenue, London NW3 3HL* Tel (020) 7435 6756

SPRATLEY, Deryck Edward. b 30. BSc. Oak Hill Th Coll 62. **d** 64 **p** 65. C Ramsgate St Luke *Cant* 64-67; C W Holloway St Dav *Lon* 67-73; V Upper Holloway St Pet 73-79; V Upper Holloway St Pet w St Jo 79-82; P-in-c Dagenham *Chelmsf* 82-88; P-in-c Becontree St Geo 84-88; TR Dagenham 88-93; rtd 93; Perm to Offic *Chelmsf* 93-01. *35 Upper Second Avenue, Frinton-on-Sea CO13 9LP* Tel (01255) 851216

SPRATT, Laurence Herbert. b 28. Linc Th Coll 76. **d** 78 **p** 79. C Mexborough *Sheff* 78-80; R Wrentham w Benacre, Covehithe, Frostenden etc *St E* 80-88; Perm to Offic *Arg* 89-90 and 91-98; P-in-c Inveraray 90-91; rtd 93. *19 Church Street, Ellesmere SY12 0HD*

SPRATT, Robert Percival. b 31. FCIOB MRSH ABEng. Carl Dioc Tr Inst 84. **d** 87 **p** 88. NSM Kendal St Thos *Carl* 87-89; Chapl HM Pris Preston 89-96; Dir Miss to Pris from 96; Perm to Offic *Blackb* from 96 and *Carl* from 97. *Missions to Prisons, PO Box 37, Kendal LA9 6GF* Tel and fax (01539) 720475

SPRAY, Canon Charles Alan Francis Thomas. b 27. ARSM51 Lon Univ BScEng51. Ridley Hall Cam 57. **d** 59 **p** 60. C Chich St Pancras and St Jo *Chich* 59-63; V Shipley 63-69; R Ore 70-85; V Burgess Hill St Andr 85-93; Can and Preb Chich Cathl 88-93; rtd 93; Perm to Offic *Chich* from 93. *6 Silverdale Road, Burgess Hill RH15 0EF* Tel (01444) 232149

SPRAY, John William. b 29. Sarum & Wells Th Coll 71. **d** 73 **p** 74. C Clayton *Lich* 73-77; V Hartshill 77-82; P-in-c Aston 82-83; P-in-c Stone St Mich 82-83; P-in-c Stone St Mich w Aston St Sav 83-84; R 84-90; rtd 90. *2 Belvoir Avenue, Trentham, Stoke-on-Trent ST4 8SY* Tel (01782) 644959

SPRAY, Mrs Josephine Ann. b 44. Nottm Coll of Educn TCert65. St Alb and Ox Min Course CBTS95. **d** 98 **p** 99. NSM Watford St Mich *St Alb* 98-02; P-in-c Turvey from 02. *The Rectory, Bamfords Lane, Turvey, Bedford MK43 8DS* Tel (01234) 881312 Fax 881817 E-mail jas@watfordgb.freeserve.co.uk

SPRAY, Richard Alan. b 43. EMMTC 85. **d** 88 **p** 89. NSM Cotgrave *S'well* 88-96; P-in-c Barton in Fabis 96-01; P-in-c

Thrumpton 96-01; P-in-c Kingston and Ratcliffe-on-Soar 96-01; P-in-c Blyth 01-02; P-in-c Scrooby 01-02; V Blyth and Scrooby w Ranskill from 02. *The Vicarage, St Martin's Close, Blyth, Worksop S81 8DW* Tel (01909) 591229
E-mail richard.spray@tesco.net

SPREADBRIDGE, Paul Andrew. b 49. Greenwich Univ CertEd02 Kent Univ BA05. SEITE 99. **d** 98 **p** 03. In RC Ch 98-01; NSM Chatham St Steph *Roch* 02-04; C Orpington All SS from 04. *99 Gillmans Road, Orpington BR5 4LD* Tel (01689) 838599 E-mail paul.spreadbridge@btopenworld.com

SPREADBURY, Joanna Mary Magdalen. b 65. Magd Coll Ox BA90 MA93 K Coll Lon PhD99. Westcott Ho Cam MA99. **d** 99 **p** 00. C Watford St Mich *St Alb* 99-03; C Leavesden All SS from 03. *49 Ross Crescent, Garston, Watford WD25 0DA* Tel (01923) 673129

SPREADBURY, John Graham. b 59. OLM course 96. **d** 99 **p** 00. OLM Billingborough Gp *Linc* from 99. *Osbourne House, 3-5 Low Street, Billingborough, Sleaford NG34 0QJ* Tel (01529) 240440

SPRENT, Michael Francis (Brother Giles). b 34. Ex Coll Ox BA58 MA62. Kelham Th Coll 58. **d** 61 **p** 62. C Plaistow St Andr *Chelmsf* 61-63; SSF from 61; Papua New Guinea 65-69; Hilfield Friary 69-74 and 77-78; Alnmouth Friary 74-76; Harbledown Friary 78-82; Sweden 76-77; TV High Stoy *Sarum* 77-78; Solomon Is 83-97; Perm to Offic *Sarum* from 97; rtd 99. *The Friary, Hilfield, Dorchester DT2 7BE* Tel (01300) 341345 Fax 341293

SPRIGGS, John David Robert. b 36. BNC Ox BA58 MA63. S'wark Ord Course 73. **d** 75 **p** 76. Lic to Offic *Ox* 75-97; Chapl Pangbourne Coll 95-97; Perm to Offic *Linc* from 97. *Glen House, Great Ponton Road, Boothby Pagnell, Grantham NG33 4DH* Tel (01476) 585756

SPRINGATE, Paul Albert Edward. b 48. Oak Hill Th Coll 81. **d** 83 **p** 84. C Pennycross *Ex* 83-87; TV Sileby, Cossington and Seagrave *Leic* 87-96; Chapl and Warden Harnhill Healing Cen from 96; Bp's Adv on Healing *Glouc* from 03. *Centre of Christian Healing, Harnhill Centre, Harnhill, Cirencester GL7 5PX* Tel (01285) 850283 Fax 850519
E-mail office@harnhillcentre.org.uk

SPRINGBETT, John Howard. b 47. Pemb Coll Cam BA70 MA74. Ridley Hall Cam 70. **d** 72 **p** 73. C Ulverston St Mary w H Trin *Carl* 72-76; V Dewsbury Moor *Wakef* 76-84; V Hoddesdon *St Alb* 84-00; RD Cheshunt 94-00; TR Shelf w Buttershaw St Aid *Bradf* 00-03; V Woodford Bridge *Chelmsf* from 03. *St Paul's Vicarage, 4 Cross Road, Woodford Green IG8 8BS* Tel (020) 8504 3815
E-mail springbett25@hotmail.com

SPRINGETT, Robert Wilfred. b 62. Nottm Univ BTh89. Linc Th Coll 86. **d** 89 **p** 90. C Colchester St Jas, All SS, St Nic and St Runwald *Chelmsf* 89-92; C Basildon St Martin w Nevendon 92-94; P-in-c Belhus Park 94-01; P-in-c S Ockendon 94-01; RD Thurrock 98-01; R Wanstead St Mary w Ch Ch from 01. *The Rectory, 37 Wanstead Place, London E11 2SW* Tel (020) 8989 9101 E-mail robert.springett@lineone.net

SPRINGETT, Simon Paul. b 56. Warwick Univ LLB78. Wycliffe Hall Ox 78. **d** 81 **p** 82. C Harlow St Mary and St Hugh w St Jo the Bapt *Chelmsf* 81-84; C Gt Clacton 84-86; R Rayne 86-91; Chapl RN from 91. *Royal Naval Chaplaincy Service, Room 203, Victory Building, HM Naval Base, Portsmouth PO1 3LS* Tel (023) 9272 7903 Fax 9272 7111

SPRINGFORD, Patrick Francis Alexander. b 45. Wycliffe Hall Ox 71. **d** 74 **p** 75. C Finchley Ch Ch *Lon* 74-79; CF from 79. *c/o MOD Chaplains (Army)* Tel (01980) 615804 Fax 615800

SPRINGHAM, Desmond John. b 32. Bris Univ BA56. Oak Hill Th Coll 56. **d** 58 **p** 59. C St Alb St Paul *St Alb* 58-61; C Reading St Jo *Ox* 61-66; R Worting *Win* 66-80; V Jersey St Andr 80-97; rtd 97; Perm to Offic *Sarum* from 97. *19 Balmoral Crescent, Dorchester DT1 2BN* Tel (01305) 268022

SPRINGTHORPE, Canon David Frederick. b 47. Open Univ BA. AKC72. **d** 73 **p** 74. C Dartford St Alb *Roch* 73-77; C Biggin Hill 77-80; R Ash 80-89; R Ridley 80-89; R Eynsford w Farningham and Lullingstone 89-94; V Barnehurst 94-04; RD Erith 98-04; R Keston from 04; Hon Can Roch Cathl from 02. *The Rectory, 24 Commonside, Keston BR2 6BP* Tel (01689) 853186 E-mail david.springthorpe@btopenworld.com

SPROSTON, Bernard Melvin. b 37. St Jo Coll Dur 77. **d** 79 **p** 80. C Westlands St Andr *Lich* 79-82; P-in-c Heage *Derby* 82-87; V Heath 87-02; rtd 02; Perm to Offic *Derby* from 02. *2 Upwood Close, Holmehall, Chesterfield S40 4UP* Tel (01246) 207401

SPROULE, Gerald Norman. b 26. TCD Dip Bibl Studies 60. **d** 60 **p** 61. C Monaghan *Clogh* 60-62; I Cleenish 62-68; I Magheracross 68-73; Admin Sec (Ireland) BCMS 73-79; I Belfast St Aid *Conn* 79-86; I Magherally w Annaclone *D & D* 86-94; rtd 94. *4 Hilden Park, Lisburn BT27 4UG* Tel (028) 9260 1528

SPURGEON, Michael Paul. b 53. MIEx. Linc Th Coll 83. **d** 85 **p** 86. C Lillington *Cov* 85-89; C Min Can Ripon Cathl *Ripon* 89-95; R Lower Nidderdale from 95. *Lower Nidderdale Rectory, 6 Old Church Green, Kirk Hammerton, York YO26 8DL* Tel (01423) 331142

SPURIN, Canon Richard Mark. b 28. Peterho Cam BA52 MA60. Wycliffe Hall Ox 54. **d** 55 **p** 56. C Foleshill St Laur *Cov* 55-58; C Atherstone 58-60; CMS 60-61; Kenya 61-73; C-in-c Ewell St Paul Howell Hill CD *Guildf* 73-82; V Netherton *Liv* 82-86; V Brandwood *Birm* 86-91; C Padiham *Blackb* 91-93; Hon Can Nambale Cathl Kenya from 92; rtd 93; Perm to Offic *Blackb* from 93. *11 Rosemount Avenue, Burnley BB11 2JU* Tel (01282) 421402

SPURLING, David John. b 35. Cam Univ MA62 Leeds Univ MPhil77. LNSM course 96. **d** 97 **p** 98. OLM Quidenham Gp *Nor* 97-02. *1A rue St Sebastien, 68230 Walbach, France*

SPURR, Andrew. b 58. St Jo Coll Dur BA80 LRPS02. Ripon Coll Cuddesdon 80 Roch Div Sch (USA) 84 Qu Coll Birm 92. **d** 93 **p** 94. C Rainham *Roch* 93-96; C Stansted Mountfitchet *Chelmsf* 96; C Stansted Mountfitchet w Birchanger and Farnham 97; R from 97. *The Rectory, 5 St John's Road, Stansted CM24 8JP* Tel (01279) 812203 Fax as telephone E-mail rector@stansted.net

SPURR, Roger Colin. b 29. Linc Th Coll. **d** 82 **p** 83. C Street w Walton *B & W* 82-85; R Stogumber w Nettlecombe and Monksilver 85-95; rtd 95; Perm to Offic *Newc* from 95. *15 Abbey Gate, Morpeth NE61 2XL* Tel (01670) 514561
E-mail rc-ke@spurr70.fsnet.co.uk

SPURRELL, John Mark. b 34. FSA87 CCC Ox BA57 DipTh58 MA61. Linc Th Coll 58. **d** 60 **p** 61. C Tilbury Docks *Chelmsf* 60-65; C Boston *Linc* 65-76; R Stow in Lindsey 76-85; P-in-c Willingham 76-85; P-in-c Coates 76-85; P-in-c Brightwell w Sotwell *Ox* 85-97; rtd 97; Perm to Offic *B & W* from 97. *10 The Liberty, Wells BA5 2SU* Tel (01749) 678966

SPURRIER, Richard Patrick Montague. b 25. Bris Univ BA59. Wycliffe Hall Ox 59. **d** 61 **p** 62. C S Lyncombe *B & W* 61-63; C Weston St Jo 63-64; rtd 90. *48 Longford Road, Melksham SN12 6AU* Tel (01225) 707419

SPURWAY, Christine Frances. b 54. Cuddesdon Coll DipMin98. **d** 98 **p** 99. C Coulsdon St Andr *S'wark* 98-02; P-in-c Riddlesdown from 02; RD Croydon S from 04. *St James's Vicarage, 1B St James's Road, Purley CR8 2DL* Tel (020) 8660 5436

SQUAREY, Canon Gerald Stephen Miles. b 36. Lich Th Coll 59. **d** 62 **p** 63. C Poplar All SS w St Frideswide *Lon* 62-64; C Heston 64-67; V Bradford Abbas w Clifton Maybank *Sarum* 67-74; P-in-c Corfe Castle 74-79; R 79-84; R Steeple w Tyneham, Church Knowle and Kimmeridge 79-84; R Corfe Castle, Church Knowle, Kimmeridge etc 84-90; P-in-c Pimperne 90-91; P-in-c Stourpaine, Durweston and Bryanston 90-91; R Pimperne, Stourpaine, Durweston and Bryanston 91-01; RD Milton and Blandford 91-01; Can and Preb Sarum Cathl 92-01; rtd 01; Bp's Dom Chapl *Sarum* from 02. *4 Water Lane, Salisbury SP2 7TE* Tel (01722) 326396

SQUIRE, Clenyg. b 31. TCert53. Cuddesdon Coll 89. **d** 90 **p** 91. NSM Hale and Ashley *Ches* 90-93; P-in-c Kingsley 93-95; Perm to Offic *Ches* and *Man* 95-03; *Newc* 00-03 and *Lon* from 04. *19 Priory Road, Hampton TW12 2NR* Tel (020) 8979 3579
E-mail clenyg@blueyonder.co.uk

SQUIRE, Geoffrey Frank. b 36. Ex & Truro NSM Scheme. **d** 83 **p** 84. NSM Barnstaple *Ex* 83-98; NSM Swimbridge w W Buckland and Landkey from 98. *Little Cross, Northleigh Hill, Goodleigh, Barnstaple EX32 7NR* Tel (01271) 344935

SQUIRE, Humphrey Edward. b 29. St Chad's Coll Dur BA55. Coll of Resurr Mirfield. **d** 57 **p** 58. C Newbold w Dunston *Derby* 57-59; C Thorpe *Nor* 59-61; Zanzibar 61-63; C Whittington *Derby* 63-64; R Drayton *Nor* 64-75; Chapl Dover Coll 75-83; TV Wareham *Sarum* 83-94; rtd 94; Perm to Offic *Sarum* from 94. *La Retraite, Burbidge Close, Lytchett Matravers, Poole BH16 6EG* Tel (01202) 623204

SQUIRE, Preb John Brinsmead. b 16. St Edm Hall Ox BA38 MA43. Linc Th Coll 38. **d** 40 **p** 40. C Knowle *Bris* 40-41; C Bath Bathwick *B & W* 41-45 and 48-51; C Walsall St Andr *Lich* 45-46; C Lower Gornal 47-48; V Bridgwater H Trin *B & W* 51-57; V Taunton St Andr 57-81; Preb Wells Cathl from 77; rtd 81. *Xanadu, 1 St Mary Street, Nether Stowey, Bridgwater TA5 1LJ* Tel (01278) 732957

SQUIRES, John Wallace Howden. b 45. Sydney Univ BA67 MTh97 Lon Univ BD75. Moore Th Coll Sydney ThL74 Melbourne Coll of Div DipRE75. **d** 76 **p** 76. Australia 76-78 and from 80; C Luton St Mary *St Alb* 78-79; Chapl Home of Divine Healing Crowhurst 79-80. *22 Moorehead Street, Redfern, NSW, Australia 2016* Tel (0061) (2) 9690 0206 *or* 9381 1730 Fax 9381 1909 E-mail j.squires@newcollege.unsw.edu.au

SQUIRES, The Ven Malcolm. b 46. St Chad's Coll Dur BA72. Cuddesdon Coll 72. **d** 74 **p** 75. C Headingley *Ripon* 74-77; C Stanningley St Thos 77-80; V Bradshaw *Wakef* 80-85; V Ripponden 85-89; V Barkisland w W Scammonden 85-89; V Mirfield 89-96; R Wrexham *St As* 96-02; Hon Can St As Cathl 00-01; Adn Wrexham from 01; R Llandegla from 02. *The Rectory, Llandegla, Wrexham LL11 3AW* Tel (01978) 790362
E-mail squiresmalcolm@aol.com

SSERUNKUMA, Michael Wilberforce. b 54. Trin Coll Bris DipHE88 BA90. Bp Tucker Coll Mukono 77. **d** 77 **p** 78. Uganda 77-87; C Gabalfa *Llan* 90-94; TV Cyncoed *Mon* 94-95; R Canton St Jo *Llan* 95-01; Asst Chapl R Berks and Battle Hosps NHS Trust 01-02; Chapl Team Ldr from 02. *The Chaplaincy, Royal Berkshire Hospital, London Road, Reading RG1 5AN* Tel 0118-987 7105

STABLES, Courtley Greenwood. b 13. Keble Coll Ox BA49 MA54. St Steph Ho Ox 48. **d** 50 **p** 51. C Watlington *Ox* 50-51; C Bracknell 51-55; Br Honduras 55-57; C Guildf H Trin w St Mary *Guildf* 57-61; Chapl Bedford Modern Sch 61-63; Sen Lect Coll of All SS Tottenham 63-72; Chmn Coun of Ch Schs Co 68-87; C St Andr Undershaft w St Mary Axe *Lon* 64-72; Hon C Uckfield *Chich* 72-94; rtd 78; Perm to Offic *Chich* from 94. *Abotslare, Pound Green, Buxted, Uckfield TN22 4JZ* Tel (01825) 732467

STABLES, Miss Katharine Ruth. b 45. R Holloway Coll Lon BA67. WMMTC 90. **d** 93 **p** 94. NSM Knutton *Lich* 93-05; NSM Silverdale and Alsagers Bank 93-96; Soc Resp Officer 96-99; Officer for NSMs 03-05; NSM Startforth and Bowes and Rokeby w Brignall *Ripon* from 05. *35 Low Startforth Road, Barnard Castle DL12 9AU* Tel (01833) 631697 E-mail kruth@btopenworld.com

STACE, Michael John. b 44. Open Univ BA80 MBEng MCMI. SEITE 94. **d** 97 **p** 98. NSM Cant St Dunstan w H Cross *Cant* 97-01; NSM Cant All SS from 01. *124 St Stephen's Road, Canterbury CT2 7JS* Tel (01227) 451169 Mobile 07831-174900 Fax 455627 E-mail michaelstace@btconnect.com

STACEY, Helen Norman. Edin Univ MB, ChB45 PhD49. S'wark Ord Course 82. **dss** 83 **d** 87 **p** 94. Notting Hill St Jo and St Pet *Lon* 83-85; Upper Kennet *Sarum* 85-87; Hon Par Dn 87-93; Perm to Offic from 93. *Greystones House, Green Street, Avebury, Marlborough SN8 1RE* Tel (01672) 539289

STACEY, Nicolas David. b 27. St Edm Hall Ox BA51 MA55. Cuddesdon Coll 51. **d** 53 **p** 54. C Portsea N End St Mark *Portsm* 53-58; Bp's Dom Chapl *Birm* 58-59; R Woolwich St Mary w H Trin *S'wark* 59-68; Borough Dean Greenwich 65-68; Dep Dir Oxfam 68-70; Perm to Offic *Ox* 68-71; P-in-c Selling *Cant* 76-78; Perm to Offic 79-84 and from 90; Six Preacher Cant Cathl 84-89; rtd 92. *The Old Vicarage, Selling, Faversham ME13 9RD* Tel (01227) 752833 E-mail nicholas@stacey.fsnet.co.uk

STACEY (née O'BRIEN), Mrs Shelagh Ann. b 55. RGN83 Bedf Coll Lon BSc77. N Ord Course 89. **d** 92 **p** 94. Par Dn S Elmsall *Wakef* 92-94; C 94-95; C Carleton 95-97; P-in-c 97-99; C E Hardwick 95-97; P-in-c 97-99; V Carleton and E Hardwick from 99. *The Vicarage, 10 East Close, Pontefract WF8 3NS* Tel (01977) 702478

STACEY, Timothy Andrew. b 58. Imp Coll Lon BSc79 York Univ PGCE83. St Jo Coll Nottm 94. **d** 94 **p** 95. C Chorleywood Ch Ch *St Alb* 94-99; P-in-c Chalfont St Giles *Ox* from 99; Chapl Bucks Chilterns Univ Coll from 99. *The Rectory, 2 Deanway, Chalfont St Giles HP8 4DX* Tel (01494) 872097 E-mail tands.stacey@virgin.net *or* tstace01@bcuc.ac.uk

STACEY, Canon Victor George. b 44. NUI BA69 QUB MTh. CITC 72. **d** 72 **p** 73. C Derriaghy *Conn* 72-76; C Knock *D & D* 76-79; I Ballymacarrett St Martin 79-86; I Dublin Santry w Glasnevin *D & G* 86-95; Bp's Dom Chapl from 90; I Dun Laoghaire from 95; Prov and Dioc Registrar from 95; Preb Maynooth St Patr Cathl Dublin from 97. *Christ Church Vicarage, 2 Park Road, Dun Laoghaire, Co Dublin, Irish Republic* Tel (00353) (1) 280 9537

STACKPOLE, Robert Aaron. b 59. Williams Coll Mass BA82 Oriel Coll Ox MLitt88. St Steph Ho Ox 88. **d** 90 **p** 91. C Kettering SS Pet and Paul *Pet* 90-93; Canada from 93. *Address temp unknown*

STAFF, Mrs Jean. b 44. CertEd64. EMMTC 81. **dss** 84 **d** 87 **p** 94. Old Brumby *Linc* 84-88; C 87-88; C Gainsborough St Geo 88-91; Dn-in-c 91-94; P-in-c 94-96; P-in-c Haxey 96-97; P-in-c Owston 96-97; V Haxey 97-04; V Owston 97-04; rtd 04. *5 South Furlong Croft, Epworth, Doncaster DN9 1GB*

STAFF, Susan. *See* JACKSON, Mrs Susan

STAFFORD, Christopher James. b 67. Birm Univ BSc88 PhD92. St Jo Coll Nottm MA98. **d** 99 **p** 00. C Westbrook St Phil *Liv* 99-03; R Newchurch w Croft from 03. *Newchurch Rectory, 17 Jackson Avenue, Culcheth, Warrington WA3 4ED* Tel (01925) 766300 E-mail cjstaff@surfaid.org

STAFFORD, David George. b 45. Qu Coll Birm 75. **d** 77 **p** 78. C Chesterfield St Aug *Derby* 77-80; C Ranmoor *Sheff* 80-83; V Bolton-upon-Dearne from 83. *The Vicarage, 41 Station Road, Bolton-upon-Dearne, Rotherham S63 8AA* Tel (01709) 893163

STAFFORD, Dhenis Dhelaney. b 58. Trin Coll Bris 02. **d** 04 **p** 05. C Norbury *Ches* from 04. *27 Davenport Road, Hazel Grove, Stockport SK7 4HA* Tel 0161-483 6922 Mobile 07976-665816 E-mail dhenis.stafford@norburypc.org.uk

STAFFORD, Canon John Ingham Henry. b 31. TCD BA52 MA58. **d** 53 **p** 55. C Clonallon *D & D* 53-56; C Belfast Malone St Jo *Conn* 56-59; Australia 59-64; Min Can Down Cathl *D & D* 64-68; Hd of S Ch Miss Ballymacarrett 68-73; I Bright w Killough 73-83; C Bangor Primacy 83-92; Can Down Cathl 90-92; I Urney w Sion Mills *D & R* 92-98; rtd 98. *14 Cleland Park North, Bangor BT20 3EN* Tel (028) 9145 6311 Mobile 07709-978874 E-mail jihstafford@yahoo.co.uk

STAFFORD, Mark Anthony. b 64. Huddersfield Univ BSc92. St Jo Coll Nottm MA98. **d** 98 **p** 99. C Stafford St Jo and Tixall w Ingestre *Lich* 98-01; C W Retford *S'well* 01; TV Retford from 02. *The Rectory, Rectory Road, Retford DN22 7AY* Tel (01777) 719816

STAFFORD, Matthew Charles. b 73. Wilson Carlile Coll 94 Ripon Coll Cuddesdon 99. **d** 99 **p** 00. C High Wycombe *Ox* 99-02; P-in-c Wrockwardine Wood *Lich* 02-04; R Oakengates and Wrockwardine Wood from 04. *The New Rectory, Church Road, Wrockwardine Wood, Telford TF2 7AH* Tel (01952) 613865 Mobile 07986-754478 E-mail jules.matthew@talk21.com

STAFFORD, Richard William (Billy). b 46. Ringsent Tech Inst TCert69. CITC 96. **d** 99 **p** 00. NSM Urney w Denn and Derryheen *K, E & A* from 99; NSM Annagh w Drumgoon, Ashfield etc from 00. *12 Cherrymount, Keadue Lane, Cavan, Co Cavan, Irish Republic* Tel (00353) (49) 437 1173 Mobile 87-240 4630 E-mail rwstafford@yahoo.com

STAFFORD, Area Bishop of. *See* MURSELL, The Rt Revd Alfred Gordon

STAFFORD-WHITTAKER, William Paul. b 69. Chich Th Coll 91. **d** 94 **p** 95. C Brighton Resurr *Chich* 94-97; C Holborn St Alb w Saffron Hill St Pet *Lon* 97-02; V Stanwell from 02. *Dunmore Cottage, 38 High Street, Stanwell, Staines TW19 7JS* Tel (01784) 252044 E-mail vicar.stanwell@btinternet.com

STAGG, Jeremy Michael. b 47. Leeds Univ BSc69 Fontainebleau MBA77. Sarum & Wells Th Coll 90. **d** 92 **p** 93. C Basing *Win* 92-96; P-in-c Barton, Pooley Bridge and Martindale *Carl* 96-99; Hon CMS Rep 96-99; C Burgh-by-Sands and Kirkbampton w Kirkandrews etc *Carl* 99-00; C Barony of Burgh 00-01; P-in-c Distington 01-05; Dioc Past Sec 00-05; TR Cheswardine, Childs Ercall, Hales, Hinstock etc *Lich* from 05. *The Vicarage, Childs Ercall, Market Drayton TF9 2DA* Tel (01952) 840229

STAGG, Canon Michael Hubert. b 39. St Chad's Coll Dur 58. **d** 63 **p** 64. C Weston-super-Mare St Sav *B & W* 63-66; P-in-c Fosdyke *Linc* 66-71; R Brompton Regis w Upton and Skilgate *B & W* 71-78; P-in-c Kidderminster St Jo *Worc* 78-80; P-in-c Cannington *B & W* 80-84; R Cannington, Otterhampton, Combwich and Stockland 84-87; Dioc Communications Officer *Nor* 88-93; Bp's Chapl 88-93; R Sprowston w Beeston 93-01; P-in-c Nor St Andr 01-04; P-in-c Nor St Geo Colegate 01-04; RD Nor N 95-04; Hon Can Nor Cathl 98-04; rtd 05; Perm to Offic *Nor* from 05. *31 Ash Grove, Norwich NR3 4BE* Tel (01603) 444549 *or* 479795 E-mail michaelstagg@waitrose.com

STAGG, Roy Ernest. b 48. **d** 01 **p** 02. OLM Birchington w Acol and Minnis Bay *Cant* 01-04; OLM St Laur in Thanet 04-05. *7 Minster Road, Acol, Birchington CT7 0JB* Tel (01843) 841551 E-mail roy@staggr.freeserve.co.uk

STAINER, Helene Lindsay. b 59. SW Minl Tr Course 01. **d** 04 **p** 05. NSM Ivybridge w Harford *Ex* from 04. *35 Savery Close, Ivybridge PL21 0JR* Tel (01752) 698361 E-mail helenestainer@aol.com

STAINER, Richard Bruce. b 62. Linc Th Coll 92. **d** 94 **p** 95. C N Walsham w Antingham *Nor* 94-97; R Cogenhoe and Gt and Lt Houghton w Brafield *Pet* from 97; RD Wootton from 01. *The Rectory, Church Street, Cogenhoe, Northampton NN7 1LS* Tel (01604) 891166 Fax as telephone E-mail r.stainer@tesco.net

STAINES, Edward Noel. b 26. Trin Coll Ox BA48 BSc49 MA52 MSc85. Chich Th Coll 51 57. **d** 57 **p** 58. C Eastbourne St Mary *Chich* 57-61; V Amberley w N Stoke 61-70; V Forest Row 70-75; V Bexhill St Aug 75-79; TR Ovingdean w Rottingdean and Woodingdean 79-85; V Rottingdean 85-86; Chapl Gtr Lisbon *Eur* 88; Chapl Marseille 90; rtd 90; Perm to Offic *Worc* from 86. *16 Conningsby Drive, Pershore WR10 1QX* Tel (01386) 554382

STAINES, Michael John. b 28. Trin Coll Ox BA52 MA56. Wells Th Coll 62. **d** 64 **p** 65. C Southwick St Mich *Chich* 64-67; TV Harling Gp *Nor* 67-73; P Missr S Chilterns Gp *Ox* 74-75; R W Wycombe w Bledlow Ridge, Bradenham and Radnage 76-93; RD Wycombe 83-87; rtd 93; Perm to Offic *Heref* and *Worc* from 93. *Upper Town Cottage, Berrington, Tenbury Wells WR15 8TH* Tel (01584) 811533 E-mail michael.staines@virgin.net

STAINSBY, Alan. b 48. NEOC 01. **d** 04 **p** 05. NSM Hart w Elwick Hall *Dur* from 04. *6 Church View, Shotton Colliery, Durham DH6 2YD* Tel 0191-526 5200 E-mail astainsbyshotton@aol.com

STALEY, Andrew. b 50. Rhode Is Univ BA83. Westcott Ho Cam 01. **d** 04 **p** 05. C Bridport *Sarum* from 04. *28 Watton Park, Bridport DT6 5NJ* Tel (01308) 420136 Mobile 07939-363731 E-mail seabury8@aol.com

STALKER, Harry. b 47. **d** 04. OLM Felixstowe SS Pet and Paul *St E* from 04. *2 Ascot Drive, Felixstowe IP11 9DW* Tel (01394) 210826 Fax 210663 Mobile 07710-221275 E-mail aitchess@clara.net

STALKER, William John. b 49. N Ord Course 89. **d** 91 **p** 92. C Formby H Trin *Liv* 91-94; V Stoneycroft All SS 94-03; Chapl R Liv Univ Hosp NHS Trust 94-03; P-in-c Lowton St Mary *Liv*

from 03. *The Vicarage, 1 Barford Drive, Lowton, Warrington WA3 1DD* Tel (01942) 607705

STALLARD, John Charles. b 34. Selw Coll Cam BA58 MA62. Ripon Hall Ox 62. **d** 64 **p** 65. C Hall Green Ascension *Birm* 64-66; C Sutton Coldfield H Trin 66-68; C-in-c Brandwood CD 68-71; Chapl Dame Allan's Schs Newc 71-74; V Warley Woods *Birm* 75-84; TR Droitwich *Worc* 84-87; P-in-c Dodderhill 84-87; TR Droitwich Spa 87-94; V Pensnett 94-00; rtd 00; Perm to Offic *St D* from 00. *Greengates, Cae Melyn, Aberystwyth SY23 2HA* Tel (01970) 624269 E-mail greengates@breathemail.net

STALLARD, Canon Mary Kathleen Rose. b 67. Selw Coll Cam BA88 Lon Inst of Educn PGCE90. Qu Coll Birm 91. **d** 93 **p** 97. C Newport St Matt *Mon* 93-96; P-in-c Ysbyty Cynfyn w Llantrisant and Eglwys Newydd *St D* 96-97; V 97-02; Min Can and Chapl St As Cathl *St As* 02-03; Can Res from 03. *Woodcroft, Upper Denbigh Road, St Asaph LL17 0BG* Tel (01745) 730064

STALLEY, Brian Anthony. b 38. Oak Hill Th Coll 60. **d** 63 **p** 64. C Summerstown *S'wark* 63-70; Surrey BFBS Sec 70-73; Manager Action Cen BFBS 73-76; R Branston *Linc* 76-91; rtd 91; Perm to Offic *Linc* from 91. *6 Sunningdale Grove, Washingborough, Lincoln LN4 1SP* Tel (01522) 794164 Mobile 07941-508445 Fax (01522) 794663 E-mail brian@bstalley.freeserve.co.uk

STAMFORD, Brian. b 37. **d** 91 **p** 92. CMS Uganda 88-95; P-in-c North Hill and Lewannick *Truro* 95-03; P-in-c Altarnon w Bolventor, Laneast and St Clether from 03. *The Vicarage, Altarnon, Launceston PL15 7SJ* Tel and fax (01566) 86108 E-mail brianstamford@btopenworld.com

STAMFORD, Dean of. *Vacant*

STAMP, Andrew Nicholas. b 44. Ex Univ BA67. Sarum Th Coll 67. **d** 69 **p** 70. C S Beddington St Mich *S'wark* 69-73; Tutor Sarum & Wells Th Coll 73-76; Chapl RN 76-81; C-in-c W Leigh CD *Portsm* 81-82; V W Leigh 82-87; R Botley 87-95; V Curdridge 94-95; R Durley 94-95; P-in-c Compton, the Mardens, Stoughton and Racton *Chich* from 95; P-in-c Stansted from 95; Tutor Bp Otter Coll Chich 95-98; Dioc Rural Officer *Chich* from 00. *The Vicarage, Compton, Chichester PO18 9HD* Tel (023) 9263 1252

STAMP, Ian Jack. b 47. Aston Tr Scheme 82 N Ord Course 83. **d** 86 **p** 87. C Tonge w Alkrington *Man* 86-89; V Heywood St Marg 89-98; P-in-c Heywood St Luke w All So 96-98; TR Heywood 98-01; V Bury St Jo w St Mark from 01. *St John's Vicarage, 270 Walmersley Road, Bury BL9 6NH* Tel 0161-764 3412 Fax as telephone E-mail revistamp@aol.com

STAMP, Philip Andrew. b 53. Linc Th Coll 86. **d** 88 **p** 89. C Barton w Peel Green *Man* 88-91; R Blackley H Trin from 91; P-in-c Lightbowne from 04. *Holy Trinity Rectory, Goodman Street, Manchester M9 4BW* Tel 0161-205 2879

STAMP, Richard Mark. b 36. St Chad's Coll Dur BA60 DipTh62. **d** 62 **p** 63. Australia 62-69 and from 72; C Greenhill St Jo *Lon* 69-72; rtd 01. *127 Hilda Drive, RMB Ravenswood, Harcourt, Vic, Australia 3453* Tel (0061) (3) 5435 3576 Fax as telephone E-mail stamp@netcon.net.au

STAMPS, Canon Dennis Lee. b 55. Biola Univ (USA) BA78 Trin Evang Div Sch (USA) MDiv83 MA87 Dur Univ PhD95. Westcott Ho Cam 90. **d** 92 **p** 93. C Moseley St Mary *Birm* 92-96; Dir WMMTC 96-01; Dean Qu Coll Birm 01-02; Minl Development Officer *St Alb* from 02; Can Res St Alb from 02. *7 Corder Close, St Albans AL3 4NH* Tel (01727) 841116 E-mail dstampsuk@aol.com

✠**STANAGE, The Rt Revd Thomas Shaun.** b 32. Pemb Coll Ox BA56 MA60 Nashotah Ho Wisconsin Hon DD86. Cuddesdon Coll 56. **d** 58 **p** 59 **c** 78. C Gt Crosby St Faith *Liv* 58-61; Min Orford St Andr CD 61-63; V Orford St Andr 63-70; S Africa from 70; Dean Kimberley 75-78; Suff Bp Johannesburg 78-82; Bp Bloemfontein 82-97; rtd 97; Acting Lect Th Univ of the Free State from 97. *PO Box 13598, Noordstad, Bloemfontein, 9301 South Africa* Tel (0027) (51) 436 7282

STANBRIDGE, The Ven Leslie Cyril. b 20. St Jo Coll Dur BA47 MA54. **d** 49 **p** 50. C Erith St Jo *Roch* 49-51; Tutor St Jo Coll Dur 51-55; Chapl 52-55; V Kingston upon Hull St Martin *York* 55-64; R Cottingham 64-72; Can and Preb York Minster 68-00; Succ Canonicorum from 88; RD Hull 70-72; Adn York 72-88; rtd 88; Perm to Offic *York* from 00. *39 Lucombe Way, New Earswick, York YO32 4DS* Tel (01904) 750812

✠**STANCLIFFE, The Rt Revd David Staffurth.** b 42. Trin Coll Ox BA65 MA68. Cuddesdon Coll 65. **d** 67 **p** 68 **c** 93. C Armley St Bart *Ripon* 67-70; Chapl Clifton Coll Bris 70-77; Dir of Ords *Portsm* 77-82; Can Res Portsm Cathl 77-82; Provost Portsm 82-93; Bp Sarum from 93. *South Canonry, 71 The Close, Salisbury SP1 2ER* Tel (01722) 334031 Fax 413112 E-mail dsarum@salisbury.anglican.org

STANDEN, David Charles. b 68. K Coll Lon BA91 AKC91 PGCE92 Lon Univ PhD00. Westcott Ho Cam 01. **d** 03 **p** 04. C Prittlewell *Chelmsf* from 03. *Oakleigh Cottage, 28 East Street, Southend-on-Sea SS2 6LH* Tel (01702) 603773 E-mail davidstanden@onetel.com

STANDEN, Mark Jonathan. b 63. LMH Ox BA85 Barrister 86. Ridley Hall Cam BA94 CTM95. **d** 95 **p** 96. C Sevenoaks St Nic *Roch* 95-99; R Angmering *Chich* from 99. *The Rectory, Rectory Lane, Angmering, Littlehampton BN16 4JU* Tel (01903) 784979

STANDEN McDOUGAL, Canon John Anthony Phelps. b 33. AKC58. **d** 59 **p** 60. C Ipswich St Marg *St E* 59-63; C Bury St Edmunds St Mary 63-65; C Wadhurst *Chich* 65-70; C Tidebrook 65-70; R Tollard Royal w Farnham *Sarum* 70-81; P-in-c Gussage St Michael and Gussage All Saints 71-76; R 76-81; RD Milton and Blandford 81-86; R Tollard Royal w Farnham, Gussage St Michael etc 82-86; Can and Preb Sarum Cathl 86-94; TR Bride Valley 86-94; rtd 94; Perm to Offic *Sarum* from 94. *Silverbridge Cottage, North Chideock, Bridport DT6 6LG* Tel (01297) 489408

STANDING, Victor. b 44. FRCO67 Lon Univ BMus66 Ox Univ DipTh77 Clare Coll Cam CertEd68. Ripon Coll Cuddesdon 75. **d** 78 **p** 79. C Wimborne Minster *Sarum* 78-80; TV Wimborne Minster and Holt 80-83; R Ex St Sidwell and St Matt *Ex* 83-94; Dep PV Ex Cathl 83-01; Chapl R Devon and Ex Hosp 83-94; Chapl W of England Eye Infirmary Ex 83-94; P-in-c Tedburn St Mary, Whitestone, Oldridge etc *Ex* 94-96; P-in-c Dunsford and Doddiscombsleigh 95-96; P-in-c Cheriton Bishop 95-96; R Tedburn St Mary, Whitestone, Oldridge etc 96-01; RD Kenn 97-01; V New Shoreham *Chich* from 01; V Old Shoreham from 01. *The Vicarage, Church Street, Shoreham-by-Sea BN43 5DQ* Tel (01273) 452109

STANDISH, Derrick Edgar. b 41. Univ of Wales (Lamp) BA67. Wycliffe Hall Ox 68. **d** 68 **p** 69. C Brynmawr *S & B* 68-69; C Morriston 69-74; V Merthyr Cynog and Dyffryn Honddu 74-76; R Llanwenarth Ultra *Mon* 76-83; V Abersychan and Garndiffaith 83-91. *7 Intermediate Road, Brynmawr, Ebbw Vale NP23 4SF*

STANDRING, Rupert Benjamin Charles. b 68. Pemb Coll Ox BA90 MA99. Ridley Hall Cam BA94. **d** 95 **p** 96. C Bromley Ch Ch *Roch* 95-99; Tutor Cornhill Tr Course 99-04; Hon C W Hampstead St Luke *Lon* 99-04; Perm to Offic from 99. *56 Langthorne Street, London SW6 6JY* Tel (020) 7385 4950 E-mail roo.bex@virgin.net

STANES, The Ven Ian Thomas. b 39. Sheff Univ BSc62 Linacre Coll Ox BA65 MA69. Wycliffe Hall Ox 63. **d** 65 **p** 66. C Leic H Apostles *Leic* 65-69; V Broom Leys 69-76; Warden Marrick Priory *Ripon* 76-82; Officer Miss, Min and Evang (Willesden Area) *Lon* 82-92; CME Officer 82-92; Preb St Paul's Cathl 89-92; Adn Loughborough *Leic* from 92. *The Archdeaconry, 21 Church Road, Glenfield, Leicester LE3 8DP* Tel 0116-231 1632 Fax 232 1593 E-mail stanes@leicester.anglican.org

STANESBY, Derek Malcolm. b 31. Leeds Univ BA56 Man Univ MEd75 PhD84 SOSc. Coll of Resurr Mirfield 56. **d** 58 **p** 59. C Lakenham St Jo *Nor* 58-61; C Welling *S'wark* 61-63; V Bury St Mark *Man* 63-67; R Ladybarn 67-85; Can and Steward Windsor 85-97; rtd 97; Perm to Office *Leic* and *Pet* from 00. *32 Elizabeth Way, Uppingham, Oakham LE15 9PQ* Tel (01572) 821298

STANFORD, Mark Roger. b 59. Cranmer Hall Dur 96. **d** 98 **p** 99. C Aughton Ch Ch *Liv* 98-02; TV Toxteth St Philemon w St Gabr and St Cleopas from 02; Chapl St Hilda's Priory and Sch Whitby from 03. *St Philemon's Vicarage, 40 Devonshire Road, Princes Park, Liverpool L8 3TZ* Tel 0151-727 1248 E-mail mark@stphilemons.org.uk

STANGHAN, Eileen. b 40. Whitelands Coll Lon CertEd75. LNSM course 95. **d** 98 **p** 99. OLM Reigate St Phil *S'wark* from 98. *20 Saxon Way, Reigate RH2 9DH* Tel (01737) 240920 *or* (01293) 430043

STANIFORD, Mrs Doris Gwendoline. b 43. Gilmore Course IDC79. **dss** 80 **d** 87 **p** 94. Hangleton *Chich* 80-82; Durrington 82-89; Par Dn 87-89; Chich Th Coll 83-89; C Crawley 89-97; Chapl Crawley Gen Hosp 89-97; Chapl St Cath Hospice 92-97; Dioc Voc Adv *Chich* 92-97; C Southwick St Mich 97-99; Asst Dir of Ords from 97; TV Ifield from 99. *St Alban's Vicarage, Gossops Drive, Crawley RH11 8LD* Tel (01293) 529848

STANLEY, Arthur Patrick. b 32. TCD BA54 Div Test55 MA64. **d** 55 **p** 56. C Waterford H Trin *C & O* 55-57; CF 58-74; Dep Asst Chapl Gen 74-83; USA 84-04; rtd 94. *10 Knights Court, Keyford, Frome BA11 1JD* Tel (01373) 301694 E-mail patnpaddy@hotmail.com

STANLEY, Baden Thomas. b 68. TCD BA91. CITC BTh94. **d** 94 **p** 95. C Seapatrick *D & D* 94-98; I Bray *D & G* from 98. *The Rectory, Church Road, Bray, Co Wicklow, Irish Republic* Tel and fax (00353) (1) 286 2968 Mobile 87-948 4408 E-mail bray@dublin.anglican.org

STANLEY, Canon John Alexander. b 31. OBE99. Tyndale Hall Bris. **d** 56 **p** 57. C Preston All SS *Blackb* 56-60; C St Helens St Mark *Liv* 60-63; V Everton St Cuth 63-70; P-in-c Everton St Sav 69-70; V Everton St Sav w St Cuth 70-74; V Huyton St Mich from 74; Hon Can Liv Cathl from 87; AD Huyton 89-02; Chapl to The Queen 93-01. *The Vicarage, Huyton Lane, Liverpool L36 7XE* Tel 0151-449 3900 Fax 480 6002 Mobile 07740-621833 E-mail huytonchurch@btconnect.com

STANLEY, Mrs Nicola Vere. b 56. STETS 99. **d** 02 **p** 03. C Bedford Park *Lon* from 02. *8 Birch Grove, London W3 9SN* Tel (020) 8992 0620 *or* 8994 1380 E-mail nvs@mosaicpublishing.co.uk

STANLEY, Patrick. *See* STANLEY, Arthur Patrick

STANLEY, Canon Simon Richard. b 44. Wells Th Coll 66. **d** 69 **p** 70. C Foleshill St Laur *Cov* 69-71; C Hessle *York* 71-75; P-in-c Flamborough 75-80; R Dunnington 80-92; P-in-c York St Barn 92-99; P-in-c York St Chad from 99; P-in-c York All SS Pavement w St Crux and St Mich from 03; P-in-c York St Denys from 04; Can and Preb York Minster from 05; Relig Progr Producer BBC Radio York from 94. *St Chad's Vicarage, 36 Campleshon Road, York YO23 1EY* Tel (01904) 674524 Fax 466516 E-mail simonstanley@clara.net

STANLEY-SMITH, James. b 29. Hatf Coll Dur BA54 DipEd55. S Dios Minl Tr Scheme 81. **d** 84 **p** 85. C Bournemouth St Jo w St Mich *Win* 84-87; R Hale w S Charford 87-94; rtd 94; Perm to Offic *Win* from 94. *10 Rownhams Way, Rownhams, Southampton SO16 8AE* Tel (023) 8073 2529 E-mail jstanley-smith@cwcom.net

STANNARD, Miss Beryl Elizabeth. b 36. SRN62 SCM64. Oak Hill Th Coll BA92. **d** 92 **p** 94. Par Dn Streatham Park St Alb *S'wark* 92-94; C 94-96; C Gerrards Cross and Fulmer *Ox* 96-01; rtd 01; Perm to Offic *Ox* from 02. *20 Wey Lane, Chesham HP5 1JH* Tel (01494) 774715

STANNARD, Brian. b 46. MICE71 MIStructE71. Cranmer Hall Dur 86. **d** 88 **p** 89. C Burnage St Marg *Man* 88-91; V Walmersley 91-03; TV Westhoughton and Wingates 03-04; rtd 04. *63 Portland Street, Southport PR8 5AF* Tel (01704) 534632 E-mail brian@stannardrev.fsnet.co.uk

STANNARD, The Ven Colin Percy. b 24. TD66. Selw Coll Cam BA47 MA49. Linc Th Coll 47. **d** 49 **p** 50. C St E Cathl *St E* 49-52; C-in-c Nunsthorpe CD *Linc* 52-55; CF (TA) 53-67; V Barrow St Jas *Carl* 55-64; V Upperby St Jo 64-70; R Gosforth 70-75; RD Calder 70-75; P-in-c Natland 75-76; V 76-84; RD Kendal 75-84; Hon Can Carl Cathl 75-84; Can Res Carl Cathl 84-93; Adn Carl 84-93; rtd 93; Perm to Offic *Carl* from 93. *51 Longlands Road, Carlisle CA3 9AE* Tel (01228) 538584

STANNARD, Canon Peter Graville. b 59. Univ of Wales (Abth) BSc(Econ)81. St Steph Ho Ox BA85 MA86. **d** 86 **p** 87. C Worksop Priory *S'well* 86-89; Prin St Nic Th Coll Ghana 89-96; Hon Can Koforidua from 93; TR Shelf w Buttershaw St Aid *Bradf* 96-99; P-in-c Heaton Norris St Thos *Man* 00-02; TV Heatons from 02. *St Thomas's Rectory, 6 Heaton Moor Road, Stockport SK4 4NS* Tel 0161-432 1912

STANTON, Ms Angela. b 59. Loughb Univ BSc80 Ch Coll Liv PGCE81. Westcott Ho Cam 03. **d** 05. C Atherton and Hindsford w Howe Bridge *Man* from 05. *St Anne's Vicarage, Powys Street, Atherton, Manchester M46 9AR* Tel (01942) 883902 E-mail angiestanton27@yahoo.co.uk

STANTON, Miss Barbara. b 51. Whitelands Coll Lon TCert72 DipNCTD77 Lon Univ BD86. WMMTC 89. **d** 92 **p** 94. NSM Hinckley St Mary *Leic* 92-97; P-in-c Husbands Bosworth w Mowsley and Knaptoft etc from 97; P-in-c Arnesby w Shearsby and Bruntingthorpe from 02; Bp's Ecum Adv 97-03; Dioc Rural Officer from 03. *The Rectory, Honeypot Lane, Husbands Bosworth, Lutterworth LE17 6LY* Tel (01858) 880351 E-mail barbarastanton@supanet.com

STANTON, Canon David John. b 60. St Andr Univ MTheol82 Ex Univ MA00 FSAScot89 FRSA98. Ripon Coll Cuddesdon 83. **d** 85 **p** 86. C Beckenham St Geo *Roch* 85-88; Asst Chapl Shrewsbury Sch 88-90; Hon C Shrewsbury All SS w St Mich *Lich* 88-90; P-in-c Abbotskerswell *Ex* 90-94; Chapl Plymouth Univ 92-97; P-in-c Bovey Tracey St Jo, Chudleigh Knighton etc 94-99; V Bovey Tracey St Jo w Heathfield 99-05; Dioc Voc Adv 95-05; Warden of Readers 96-03; Acting Dioc Dir of Ords 03-05; RD Moreton 98-05; Can Prec and Can Past Worc Cathl *Worc* from 05. *15A College Green, Worcester WR1 2LH* Tel (01905) 28854 Fax 611139 E-mail davidstanton@worcestercathedral.co.uk

STANTON, Gregory John. b 47. Sarum & Wells Th Coll 84. **d** 86 **p** 87. C Willenhall H Trin *Lich* 86-89; C Plympton St Mary *Ex* 89-91; V Milton Abbot, Dunterton, Lamerton etc from 91. *The Vicarage, The Parade, Milton Abbot, Tavistock PL19 0NZ* Tel (01822) 612732 E-mail gjstanton31@hotmail.com

STANTON, John Maurice. b 18. Univ Coll Ox BA45 MA45. Wycliffe Hall Ox 51. **d** 52 **p** 53. C Tonbridge SS Pet and Paul *Roch* 52-54; Hd Master Blundell's Sch Tiverton 59-71; Public Preacher *Ex* 71-72; C Ex St Matt 72-73; R Chesham Bois *Ox* 73-83; rtd 83; Perm to Offic *Ox* from 83. *16 Emden House, Barton Lane, Headington OX3 9JU* Tel (01865) 765206

STANTON, Miss Julie Elizabeth. b 59. Matlock Coll of Educn CertEd80. EMMTC 00. **d** 03 **p** 04. NSM Matlock Bath and Cromford *Derby* from 03. *35 Intake Lane, Cromford, Matlock DE4 3RH* Tel (01629) 822653 Mobile 07769-748276 Fax (01629) 760903 E-mail juliestanton@ukonline.com

STANTON, Ms Karen Janis. b 55. N Ord Course 00. **d** 03 **p** 04. C Withington St Paul *Man* 03-04; C Urmston from 04. *159 Irlam Road, Urmston, Manchester M41 6WF* Tel 0161-746 8573 Mobile 07814-254744 E-mail kaz@stanton.ndo.co.uk

STANTON, Thomas Hugh (Timothy). b 17. Trin Coll Cam BA38 MA45. Coll of Resurr Mirfield 46. **d** 47 **p** 48. C Camberwell St Geo *S'wark* 47-49; CR from 52; S Africa 54-87; rtd 87. *House of the Resurrection, Stocks Bank Road, Mirfield WF14 0BN* Tel (01924) 494318

STANTON-HYDE, Mrs Marjorie Elizabeth. b 37. TCert58. Cranmer Hall Dur 86. **d** 88 **p** 94. Par Dn Elmley Lovett w Hampton Lovett and Elmbridge etc *Worc* 88-91; Par Dn Wilden 88-91; Par Dn Hartlebury 88-91; Dn-in-c 91-94; P-in-c 94-97; R 97-98; rtd 98; Hon C Gt Malvern St Mary *Worc* 99-02; Warden Jes Hosp Cant 02-05; Chapl Worcs Community and Mental Health Trust from 05. *1 Link End House, 23 Pickersleigh Road, Malvern WR14 2RP* Tel (01684) 569589

STANTON-SARINGER, Maurice Charles. b 49. Bris Univ BSc71 PGCE72 Fitzw Coll Cam BA77 MA81. Ridley Hall Cam 75. **d** 78 **p** 79. C Gerrards Cross *Ox* 78-80; C Bletchley 80-83; Lic to Offic 83-91; Chapl Stowe Sch 83-91; R Sherington w Chicheley, N Crawley, Astwood etc *Ox* from 91; RD Newport 95-04. *The Rectory, 21 School Lane, Sherington, Newport Pagnell MK16 9NF* Tel (01908) 610521 E-mail saringer@telinco.co.uk

STANWAY, Peter David. b 48. K Coll Lon BD71. St Aug Coll Cant 72. **d** 73 **p** 74. C Maidstone All SS w St Phil and H Trin *Cant* 73-77; Canada 77-84; C Waterlooville *Portsm* 84-87; R Laughton w Ripe and Chalvington *Chich* 87-90; Chapl Witney Community Hosp 90-91; C Wheatley w Forest Hill and Stanton St John *Ox* 91-92; C Cowley St Jas 93-02; rtd 02. *22 Colleywood, Kennington, Oxford OX1 5NF* Tel (01865) 739342

STAPLE, Miss Patricia Ann. b 54. Birm Univ BA75. St Steph Ho Ox 00. **d** 02 **p** 05. C Dartmouth and Dittisham *Ex* 02-04; C Colyton, Musbury, Southleigh and Branscombe from 04. *29 Grove Hill, Colyton EX24 6ET* Tel (01297) 551369 Mobile 07719-129008 E-mail tricia_staple@hotmail.com

STAPLEFORD, Robin Duncan. b 62. St Jo Coll Nottm DipMin94 Aston Tr Scheme 92. **d** 96 **p** 97. C Evington *Leic* 96-99; TV Vale of Belvoir Par from 00. *The Vicarage, 1 Boyers Orchard, Harby, Melton Mowbray LE14 4BA* Tel (01949) 860269 E-mail stapleford.robin.d@ukonline.co.uk

STAPLES, David. b 35. Jes Coll Ox BA59 MA63 BD75. Linc Th Coll 59. **d** 61 **p** 62. C Kettering St Andr *Pet* 61-64; C Doncaster St Geo *Sheff* 64-66; Dioc Youth Chapl 66-71; V Mexborough 71-83; Chapl Montagu Hosp Mexborough 71-83; RD Wath *Sheff* 77-83; Hon Can Sheff Cathl 80-83; V W Haddon w Winwick *Pet* 83-88; RD Brixworth 83-89; V W Haddon w Winwick and Ravensthorpe 88-00; ACUPA Link Officer 90-00; rtd 00; Perm to Offic *Linc* from 00. *1 Sycamore Close, Bourne PE10 9RS* Tel (01778) 423121

STAPLES, Jeffrey Joseph. b 61. St Jo Coll Nottm 97. **d** 99 **p** 00. C Prenton *Ches* 99-03; P-in-c Wallasey St Nic 03-04; P-in-c New Brighton All SS 03-04; V Wallasey St Nic w All SS from 04. *St Nicholas' Vicarage, 22 Groveland Road, Wallasey CH45 8JY* Tel 0151-639 3589 E-mail jeffstaples4@hotmail.com

STAPLES, John Michael. b 45. STETS 94. **d** 97 **p** 98. C Tisbury *Sarum* 97-01; P-in-c Barford St Martin, Dinton, Baverstock etc 00-01; TV Nadder Valley from 01. *11A Tyndale's Meadow, Dinton, Salisbury SP3 5HU* Tel (01722) 717883 E-mail john_staples@talk21.com

STAPLES, John Wedgwood. b 42. Hertf Coll Ox BA64 MA. Wycliffe Hall Ox 64. **d** 66 **p** 67. C Yardley St Edburgha *Birm* 66-69; C Knowle 69-74; R Barcombe *Chich* 74-81; V Old Windsor *Ox* 81-96; P-in-c Pangbourne w Tidmarsh and Sulham 96-99; R from 99. *The Rectory, St James's Close, Pangbourne, Reading RG8 7AP* Tel 0118-984 2928 E-mail revd_john@staplesj.fsnet.co.uk

STAPLES, Peter. b 35. Jes Coll Ox BA59. Ripon Hall Ox 59. **d** 62 **p** 63. C Fairfield *Derby* 62-63; C Dore 63-66; C Wilne and Draycott w Breaston 66-71; The Netherlands from 72; Asst Chapl Utrecht w Amersfoort, Harderwijk and Zwolle *Eur* from 94. *Doldersweg 39C, 3712 BN Huis Ter Heide, Utrecht, The Netherlands* Tel (0031) (30) 693 1928

STAPLES, Canon Peter Brian. b 38. Bps' Coll Cheshunt 66. **d** 68 **p** 69. C Birkdale St Jas *Liv* 68-71; C Sevenoaks St Jo *Roch* 71-74; V Treslothan *Truro* 74-80; V Truro St Paul and St Clem 80-02; Hon Can Truro Cathl 98-02; rtd 02; Perm to Offic *St E* from 03. *25 Osmund Walk, Bury St Edmunds IP33 3UU* Tel (01284) 760620

STAPLES, Terence Malcolm. b 43. Trin Coll Bris MA01. BA95. **d** 95 **p** 96. C Bath St Sav w Swainswick and Woolley *B & W* 95-99; R Exton and Winsford and Cutcombe w Luxborough from 99. *The Rectory, Winsford, Minehead TA24 7JE* Tel (01643) 851301 E-mail staplest@freenet.co.uk

STAPLETON, The Very Revd Henry Edward Champneys. b 32. FSA74 Pemb Coll Cam BA54 MA58. Ely Th Coll 54. **d** 56 **p** 57. C York St Olave w St Giles *York* 56-59; C Pocklington w Yapham-cum-Meltonby, Owsthorpe etc 59-61; R Seaton Ross w Everingham and Bielby and Harswell 61-67; RD Weighton 66-67; R Skelton by York 67-75; V Wroxham w Hoveton *Nor* 75-81; P-in-c Belaugh 76-81; Can Res and Prec Roch Cathl *Roch* 81-88; Dean Carl 88-98; rtd 98; Perm to Offic *Wakef* from 98 and *York* from 03. *Rockland House, 20 Marsh Gardens, Honley, Huddersfield HD9 6AF* Tel (01484) 666629

STAPLETON, Leonard Charles. b 37. Chich Th Coll 75. **d** 77 **p** 78. C Crayford *Roch* 77-81; C Lamorbey H Redeemer 81-83; V

Belvedere St Aug 83-89; V Beckenham St Jas 89-02; rtd 02; Perm to Offic *Roch* 03-04 and *Win* from 04. *14 Howlett Close, Lymington SO41 9LA* Tel (01590) 679414

STAPLETON, Robert Michael Vorley. b 25. ALCD51. **d** 51 **p** 52. C Plymouth St Andr *Ex* 51-56; Chapl RN 56-60; C Surbiton St Matt *S'wark* 60-64; R Chenies and Lt Chalfont *Ox* 64-87; P-in-c Latimer w Flaunden 86-87; R Chenies and Lt Chalfont, Latimer and Flaunden 87-92; rtd 92. *Woodside, Swannaton Road, Dartmouth TQ6 9RL* Tel (01803) 832972

STAPLETON, Robert Vauvelle. b 47. Dur Univ BA70. Cranmer Hall Dur DipTh71. **d** 71 **p** 72. C Moreton *Ches* 71-73; C Monkwearmouth All SS *Dur* 73-76; C Stranton 76-79; P-in-c Kelloe 79-86; V New Shildon 86-96; R Stoke Albany w Wilbarston and Ashley etc *Pet* 96-04; P-in-c Somborne w Ashley *Win* from 04; Dioc Rural Officer from 04. *The New Vicarage, Romsey Road, Kings Somborne, Stockbridge SO20 6PR* Tel (01794) 388223 E-mail robertstapleton@hotmail.com

STARBUCK, Francis Tony. b 36. Kelham Th Coll 57. **d** 61 **p** 62. C Mansfield St Mark *S'well* 61-63; C Clifton H Trin CD 63-64; C Didcot *Ox* 67-71; P Missr California CD 71-75; R Barkham 74-75; V Hagbourne 75-82; V Maidenhead St Luke 82-87; New Zealand from 87; V Te Puke St Jo 87-96; Can Waiapu 90-94; V Clevedon All So 96-01; rtd 01. *12A Shepherds Road, Papakura, New Zealand* Tel (0064) (9) 299 8605

STARES, Brian Maurice William. b 44. St Deiniol's Hawarden 74. **d** 74 **p** 75. C Risca *Mon* 74-77; V Newport St Steph and H Trin 77-87; V Fleur-de-Lis 87-92; Chapl HM Pris Belmarsh 92-93; Chapl HM YOI Dover 93-98; Chapl HM YOI and Rem Cen Feltham 98-99; V Bishton *Mon* from 99. *The Vicarage, Station Road, Llanwern, Newport NP18 2DW* Tel (01633) 413457

STARES, Mrs Olive Beryl. b 33. Sarum Th Coll 83. **dss** 86 **d** 87 **p** 94. Crofton *Portsm* 86-87; Hon C 87-01; rtd 01. *62 Mancroft Avenue, Hill Head, Fareham PO14 2DD* Tel (01329) 668540

STARK, Mrs Beverley Ann. b 52. Bp Otter Coll CertEd73 EMMTC 92. **d** 92 **p** 94. Par Dn Bulwell St Jo *S'well* 92-94; C 94-97; TV Bestwood 97-03; V Bestwood Em w St Mark 03-04; R Scalford w Wycombe and Chadwell etc *Leic* from 04. *The Rectory, 23 Melton Road, Waltham on the Wolds, Melton Mowbray LE14 4AJ* Tel (01664) 464600 E-mail beverley.stark@ntlworld.com

STARK, John Jordan. b 40. Hull Univ BA62. St Chad's Coll Dur. **d** 64 **p** 65. C Buxton *Derby* 64-67; C Wolborough w Newton Abbot *Ex* 67-74; R Belstone 74-79; P-in-c Plymouth St Gabr 79-80; V from 80. *The Vicarage, 1 Peverell Terrace, Plymouth PL3 4JJ* Tel (01752) 663938

STARK, Margaret Alison. b 46. Univ of Wales BA70 BA71. St Mich Coll Llan DPS90. **d** 90 **p** 97. C Llanishen and Lisvane *Llan* 90-93; C Llanishen 93-94; C Aberavon 94-98; R Llanfabon 98-01; rtd 01. *4 Penarth House, 28 Stanwell Road, Penarth CF64 2EY* Tel (029) 2070 1303

STARK, Michael. b 35. Dur Univ BSc56 SEN58. Chich Th Coll 58. **d** 60 **p** 61. C Middlesbrough St Paul *York* 60-64; C S Bank 64-66; R Skelton in Cleveland 66-74; P-in-c Upleatham 66-67; R 67-74; Asst Chapl HM Pris Wormwood Scrubs 74-76; Asst Chapl HM Pris Liv 75-76; Chapl HM Pris Featherstone 76-83; Chapl HM Pris Ex 83-89; Chapl HM Pris Leic 89-97; rtd 97; Perm to Offic *Leic* and *S'well* from 99; P-in-c Rotterdam *Eur* from 04. *28 St Peters Road, Leicester LE2 1DA*

STARKEY, Gerald Dennis. b 34. Qu Coll Birm 79. **d** 82 **p** 83. C Wilnecote *Lich* 82-86; Min Stoke-upon-Trent 86-90; P-in-c W Bromwich St Pet 90-00; rtd 00; Perm to Offic *Lich* from 01. *6 Hazelwood Drive, Wednesfield, Wolverhampton WV11 1SH* Tel (01902) 726252

STARKEY, John Douglas. b 23. St Chad's Coll Dur BA47 DipTh48. **d** 48 **p** 49. C Horninglow *Lich* 48-52; C Lower Gornal 52-55; C-in-c W Bromwich Ascension CD 55-57; V Coseley Ch Ch 57-66; V Freehay 66-84; P-in-c Oakamoor w Cotton 78-84; R Dunstall w Rangemore and Tatenhill 84-88; rtd 88; Perm to Offic *Lich* and *Derby* from 88. *34 Park Crescent, Doveridge, Ashbourne DE6 5NE* Tel (01889) 566384

STARKEY, Michael Stuart. b 63. LMH Ox BA85 Nottm Univ BTh92 MA93. St Jo Coll Nottm 90. **d** 93 **p** 94. C Ealing St Mary *Lon* 93-95; C Brownswood Park 95-97; P-in-c 97-01; V Twickenham Common H Trin from 01. *Holy Trinity Vicarage, 1 Vicarage Road, Twickenham TW2 5TS* Tel (020) 8898 1168 E-mail revstarkey@yahoo.co.uk

STARKEY, Patrick Robin. b 37. **d** 64 **p** 65. C Tonbridge SS Pet and Paul *Roch* 64-68; Asst Chapl Sherborne Sch 68-72; Scripture Union 73-85; rtd 99. *14 Heol Twrch, Lower Cwmtwrch, Swansea SA9 2TD*

STARKEY, Simon Mark. b 36. Liv Univ BA78 MA96. Clifton Th Coll 63. **d** 66 **p** 67. C Ox St Ebbe w St Pet *Ox* 66-72; Community Chapl CPAS Kirkdale 72-75; TV Toxteth Park St Bede *Liv* 75-78; P-in-c 78-80; V 80-90; RD Toxteth 81-89; Chapl Univ Coll Ches 90-96; TV St Luke in the City *Liv* 96-03; rtd 03; Perm to Offic *Liv* from 03. *23 Merlin Street, Liverpool L8 8HY* Tel 0151-709 0208

STARKEY, Susan Anne. b 52. St Jo Coll Nottm. **d** 97 **p** 98. C Watford St Luke *St Alb* 97-02; C Oxhey All SS 02-04; V Findern *Derby* from 04; V Willington from 04. *The Vicarage, 66 Castle Way, Willington, Derby DE65 6BU* Tel (01283) 702203

STARKIE, Andrew Edward. b 70. Regent's Park Coll Ox BA91 MA95 Selw Coll Cam MPhil03 PhD03. Ridley Hall Cam 97. **d** 02 **p** 03. C Long Benton *Newc* from 02. *5 Balroy Court, Newcastle upon Tyne NE12 9AW* Tel 0191-270 2186 E-mail curate.stbarts@talk21.com

STARNES, Peter Henry. b 19. LTCL74 St Jo Coll Cam BA42 MA47 Ch Ch Coll Cant PGCE72. Linc Th Coll 42. **d** 44 **p** 45. C Gillingham *Sarum* 44-50; C St Peter-in-Thanet *Cant* 50-52; CF 52-55; Hon CF from 55; R Hothfield *Cant* 56-60; V Westwell 56-65; R Eastwell w Boughton Aluph 60-65; rtd 84. *Whitebeams, High Halden, Ashford TN26 3LY* Tel (01233) 850245

STARNS, Helen Edna. *See* PATTEN, Mrs Helen Edna

STARR, Michael Reginald. b 41. FICE71 Bris Univ BSc63 PhD66. Ox NSM Course 83. **d** 86 **p** 87. NSM Gt Faringdon w Lt Coxwell *Ox* 86-00; P-in-c Ashbury, Compton Beauchamp and Longcot w Fernham 00-03; NSM Shrivenham and Ashbury from 03. *The Vicarage, Ashbury, Swindon SN6 8LN* Tel (01793) 710231 E-mail michael_starr@compuserve.com

STARR, Michael Richard. b 43. Sarum Th Coll 65. **d** 68 **p** 69. C Plymouth St Pet *Ex* 68-72; C Blackpool St Paul *Blackb* 72-74; V Burnley St Cuth 74-79; C Eastbourne St Mary *Chich* 79-84; P-in-c Eastbourne Ch Ch 84-87; V 87-88; R Guernsey Ste Marie du Castel *Win* 88-01; V Guernsey St Matt 94-01; Vice-Dean Guernsey 99-01; P-in-c Win St Bart from 01. *Hyde Vicarage, 1 Abbey Hill Close, Winchester SO23 7AZ* Tel (01962) 852032

STARRS, Lindsey Carolyn. b 49. Alsager Coll of Educn CertEd70 Liv Inst of HE BEd85. Ripon Coll Cuddesdon 00. **d** 02 **p** 03. C Penkridge Team *Lich* from 02. *31 Saxon Road, Penkridge, Stafford ST19 5EP* Tel (01785) 716540 E-mail starrs@lstarrs.fsnet.com

STARTIN, Nicola Gail. b 57. K Coll Lon LLB79. St Steph Ho Ox 88. **d** 90 **p** 96. C Wellingborough All SS *Pet* 90-92; NSM Pyle w Kenfig *Llan* 94-95; Asst Chapl Mid Kent Healthcare NHS Trust 95-97; Chapl HM Pris E Sutton Park 97-00; Chapl HM Pris Haslar 00-02; Chapl Haslar Immigration Removal Cen from 02. *Haslar Immigration Removal Centre, 2 Dolphin Way, Gosport PO12 2AW* Tel (023) 9260 4047 E-mail nicola.startin@hmps.gsi.gov.uk

STATHAM, Brian Edward. b 55. K Coll Lon MA AKC76. St Steph Ho Ox 77. **d** 78 **p** 79. C Ches H Trin *Ches* 78-81; C Birkenhead Priory 81-82; TV 82-86; V Newton 86-91; SSF 91-94; TV Horsham *Chich* 95-99; Chapl Horsham Gen Hosp 95-99; TV Ches Team *Ches* 99-03; P-in-c Stockport St Matt from 03. *St Matthew's Vicarage, 99 Chatham Street, Stockport SK3 9EG* Tel 0161-480 5515 E-mail brianstatham@aol.com

STATHAM, John Francis. b 31. Kelham Th Coll 51. **d** 56 **p** 57. C Ilkeston St Mary *Derby* 56-58; C New Mills 58-59; V 69-81; C Newbold w Dunston 59-62; PC Ridgeway 62-69; RD Glossop 78-81; R Matlock 81-89; R Killamarsh 89-93; rtd 93; Perm to Offic *Derby* and *S'well* from 93. *33 Ackford Drive, The Meadows, Worksop S80 1YG* Tel (01909) 476031

STATHER, Thomas William John. b 79. Van Mildert Coll Dur BSc00. St Steph Ho Ox BTh04. **d** 04 **p** 05. C Colchester St Jas and St Paul w All SS etc *Chelmsf* from 04. *Benson House, 13 Roman Road, Colchester CO1 1UR* Tel (01206) 578401 E-mail jstather@dunelm.org.uk

STATON, Preb Geoffrey. b 40. Wells Th Coll 64. **d** 66 **p** 67. C Wednesfield St Thos *Lich* 66-69; C Cannock 69-72; V Cheddleton 72-82; RD Leek 77-82; V Harlescott 82-90; TR Penkridge Team 90-05; rtd 05; C Colton, Colwich and Gt Haywood *Lich* from 05; Preb Lich Cathl from 87. *The Vicarage, Main Road, Little Haywood, Stafford ST18 0TS* Tel (01889) 881262 E-mail geoffrey.staton@virgin.net

STATTER, Ms Deborah Hilary. b 55. **d** 00 **p** 01. OLM Everton St Pet *Liv* 00-02; OLM Everton St Pet w St Chrys 02-04; C from 04. *The Vicarage, 43 St Chrysostoms Way, Liverpool L6 2NQ* Tel and fax 0151-260 8289 Mobile 07952-105466

STAUNTON, Richard Steedman. b 25. Wadh Coll Ox BA49 MA50 BSc51. Cuddesdon Coll 63. **d** 64 **p** 65. C Wyken *Cov* 64-68; V Tile Hill 68-76; V Hillmorton 76-90; rtd 90; Perm to Offic *Ban* from 90. *2 Tan-y-fron, Corris Uchaf, Machynlleth SY20 9BN* Tel (01654) 761466

STAVELEY-WADHAM, Robert Andrew. b 43. ACII. Ridley Hall Cam 79. **d** 81 **p** 82. C Saffron Walden w Wendens Ambo and Littlebury *Chelmsf* 81-84; P-in-c Austrey and Warton *Birm* 84-87; Perm to Offic *Chich* 87-02; *Ely* 88-96; P-in-c Tillington from 02; P-in-c Duncton from 02; P-in-c Up Waltham from 02. *The Rectory, Tillington, Petworth GU28 9AH* Tel (01798) 345210

STEAD, Andrew Michael. b 63. BA84. Coll of Resurr Mirfield 84. **d** 87 **p** 88. C Wellingborough All Hallows *Pet* 87-90; Chapl St Alb Abbey *St Alb* 90-94; Chapl Aldenham Sch Herts 94-04; Ho Master from 01; Perm to Offic *St Alb* from 04. *Kennedy's House, Aldenham School, Elstree, Borehamwood WD6 3AJ* Tel (01923) 851621 Fax 854410 E-mail ams@aldenham.com

STEAD, Canon George Christopher. b 13. K Coll Cam BA35 MA38 LittD78 New Coll Ox BA35 Keble Coll Ox MA49 FBA80. Cuddesdon Coll 38. **d** 38 **p** 41. Perm to Offic *Newc* 38-39; C Newc St Jo 39; Lect Div K Coll Cam 38-49; Fell 38-49 and 71-85; Prof Fell 71-80; Asst Master Eton Coll 40-44; Fell and Chapl Keble Coll Ox 49-71; Select Preacher Ox Univ 58-59 and 61; Ely Prof Div Cam Univ 71-80; Can Res Ely Cathl *Ely* 71-80; rtd 80; Perm to Offic *Ely* from 81. *13 Station Road, Haddenham, Ely CB6 3XD* Tel (01353) 740575

STEAD, Philip John. b 60. Sheff Univ LLB82 City of Lon Poly ACII85. Linc Th Coll 95. **d** 95 **p** 96. C Warsop *S'well* 95-99; P-in-c Forest Town from 99. *The Vicarage, Old Mill Lane, Forest Town, Mansfield NG19 0EP* Tel (01623) 621120

STEAD, Timothy James. b 60. Ex Univ BSc82. St Steph Ho Ox DipMin95. **d** 95 **p** 97. C Broseley w Benthall, Jackfield, Linley etc *Heref* 95-99; TV Haywards Heath St Wilfrid *Chich* from 99. *Ascension Vicarage, 1 Sandy Vale, Haywards Heath RH16 4JH* Tel (01444) 450173

STEADMAN, Gloria Ann. b 44. **d** 04 **p** 05. NSM Farlington *Portsm* from 04. *Lane End House, 63 Glamorgan Road, Waterlooville PO8 0TS* Tel (023) 9259 5561

STEADMAN, Mark John. b 74. Southn Univ LLB95 Ch Coll Cam BA01 Barrister-at-Law (Inner Temple) 96. Westcott Ho Cam 99. **d** 02 **p** 03. C Portsea St Mary *Portsm* from 02. *1 St Mary Glebe, 32 Nutfield Place, Portsmouth PO1 4JF* Tel (023) 9283 0154 E-mail steadman@fish.co.uk

STEADMAN, Norman Neil. b 39. QUB BSc61 Leeds Univ MA03 TCD Div Test63. **d** 63 **p** 64. C Newtownards *D & D* 63-65; C Belfast Whiterock *Conn* 65-67; Asst Dean of Res QUB 67-71; Perm to Offic *St Alb* 71-73; Dioc Youth Officer 73-76; P-in-c Hitchin H Sav 76; TV Hitchin 77-84; V Brampton *Carl* 84-93; R Brampton and Farlam and Castle Carrock w Cumrew 93-98; C Carl H Trin and St Barn 98-04; Chapl Carl Hosps NHS Trust 98-01; Chapl N Cumbria Acute Hosps NHS Trust 01-04; Chapl North Lakeland Healthcare NHS Trust 98-01; Chapl N Cumbria Mental Health NHS Trust 01-04; rtd 04. *9 Newlands Road, Carlisle CA2 4JB* Tel (01228) 546229

STEADMAN-ALLEN, Miss Barbara. b 53. Trent Park Coll of Educn CertEd74 Birm Univ BMus77 ARCM83. Cranmer Hall Dur 88. **d** 90 **p** 94. C Chessington *Guildf* 90-94; C Chertsey 94-99; Chapl Box Hill Sch from 99; P-in-c Mickleham *Guildf* 99-01; C Leatherhead and Mickleham 01-04; TV Surrey Weald from 04. *The Vicarage, Horsham Road, Holmwood, Dorking RH5 4JX* Tel (01306) 889118 Mobile 07817-006254 E-mail bsa312@freenet.co.uk

STEADY, Miss Vilda May. b 51. Linc Th Coll 87. **d** 89 **p** 94. Par Dn Cannock *Lich* 89-91; Par Dn Hammerwich 91-94; C 94-95; Asst Chapl Eastbourne Hosps NHS Trust 95-97; Chapl Luton and Dunstable Hosp NHS Trust 97-01; Sen Chapl Jas Paget Healthcare NHS Trust from 01. *James Paget Hospital, Lowestoft Road, Gorleston, Great Yarmouth NR31 6LA* Tel (01493) 452452 *or* 452408 E-mail vilda.steady@jpaget.nhs.uk

STEAR, Michael Peter Hutchinson. b 47. Goldsmiths' Coll Lon TCert68. Wycliffe Hall Ox 71. **d** 74 **p** 75. C Streatham Vale H Redeemer *S'wark* 74-77; C-in-c Ramsgate St Mark *Cant* 77-82; V 82-83; Min Jersey St Paul Prop Chpl *Win* 83-94; TR Radipole and Melcombe Regis *Sarum* 94-00; Chapl Weymouth Coll 94-97; rtd 00; Perm to Offic *Sarum* from 01. *132 Preston Road, Preston, Weymouth DT3 6BH*

STEAR, Mrs Patricia Ann. b 38. Birm Univ BSc60. LNSM course 96. **d** 97 **p** 98. OLM Bradford Peverell, Stratton, Frampton etc *Sarum* from 97. *Westwood House, Bradford Peverell, Dorchester DT2 9SE* Tel (01305) 889227 Fax 889718 E-mail patstear@saqnet.co.uk

STEARN, Peter Reginald. b 38. ARCM. Linc Th Coll 75. **d** 77 **p** 78. C St Alb St Pet *St Alb* 77-79; C Bushey 79-82; V Kings Langley from 82. *The Vicarage, 1 The Glebe, Kings Langley WD4 9HY* Tel (01923) 262939

STEBBING, Christopher Henry. b 64. G&C Coll Cam MEng87 MA90. Cranmer Hall Dur 98. **d** 00 **p** 01. C Malin Bridge *Sheff* 00-04; V Sheff St Jo from 04. *St John's Vicarage, 91 Manor Oaks Road, Sheffield S2 5EA* Tel 0114-272 7423 *or* 272 8678 E-mail chris@stebbingfamily.go-plus.net

STEBBING, Michael Langdale (Nicolas). b 46. Univ of Zimbabwe BA68 Univ of S Africa MTh86. Coll of Resurr Mirfield. **d** 74 **p** 75. C Borrowdale *Carl* 74-75; P-in-c Chikwaka Rhodesia 76-77; S Africa 79-86; CR from 80. *House of the Resurrection, Stocks Bank Road, Mirfield WF14 0BN* Tel (01924) 494318

STEDDON, Peter James Raymond. b 46. St Edm Hall Ox BA67 MA71 FCIPD. STETS 96. **d** 99 **p** 00. NSM Goring w S Stoke *Ox* 99-03; Team Missr Langtree from 03. *Rectory Cottage, High Street, Whitchurch on Thames, Reading RG8 7DF* Tel 0118-984 1473 Mobile 07766-514874 E-mail petersteddon@hotmail.com

STEDMAN, Barrie John. b 49. Dioc OLM tr scheme 97. **d** 00 **p** 01. OLM Mildenhall *St E* from 00. *13 Bennett Road, Red Lodge, Bury St Edmunds IP28 8JT* Tel (01638) 750505 Mobile 07831-803622 Fax (01223) 455823 E-mail barriestedman@aol.com

STEDMAN, Preb Michael Sydney. b 34. MRICS58. Clifton Th Coll 62. **d** 65 **p** 66. C Lindfield *Chich* 65-68; C Gt Baddow *Chelmsf* 68-73; TV Ashby w Thurton, Claxton and Carleton *Nor* 73-75; P-in-c 75-85; TV Rockland St Mary w Hellington 73-75; P-in-c 75-85; TV Framingham Pigot 73-75; P-in-c 75-85; TV Bramerton w Surlingham 73-75; P-in-c 75-85; TV Bergh Apton w Yelverton 73-75; P-in-c 75-85; RD Loddon 78-85; R Church Stretton *Heref* 85-99; RD Condover 88-96; Preb Heref Cathl 94-99; rtd 99; Perm to Offic *St E* from 00. *44 The Mowbrays, Framlingham, Woodbridge IP13 9DL* Tel (01728) 724479 E-mail michael@stedmanm.freeserve.co.uk

STEDMAN, Robert Alfred. b 24. Qu Coll Birm 50. **d** 52 **p** 53. C Portchester *Portsm* 52-55; V Brighton St Anne *Chich* 55-61; V Salehurst 61-76; R Newhaven 76-90; rtd 90; Perm to Offic *Chich* 90-99. *12 Lady Wootton's Green, Canterbury CT1 1NG*

STEEL, Coralie Mary. b 47. Bedf Coll Lon BA69 Solicitor 73. St Mich Coll Llan 98. **d** 01 **p** 02. NSM Llangunnor w Cwmffrwd *St D* from 01. *Llwyn Celyn, 24 Picton Terrace, Carmarthen SA31 3BX* Tel (01267) 236369 E-mail coralie@fish.co.uk

STEEL, Graham Reginald. b 51. Cam Univ MA. Trin Coll Bris 80. **d** 83 **p** 84. C Gt Parndon *Chelmsf* 83-86; C Barking St Marg w St Patr 86-89; P-in-c Westcliff St Cedd 89-96; P-in-c Prittlewell St Pet 92-96; Chapl Southend Gen Hosp 89-92; V Prittlewell w Westcliff *Chelmsf* from 96. *The Vicarage, 122 Mendip Crescent, Westcliff-on-Sea SS0 0HN* Tel (01702) 525126 Fax 08701-643372 E-mail grahamsteel@blueyonder.co.uk

STEEL, Leslie Frederick. b 34. Webster Univ Geneva MA88. St Jo Coll Auckland 57 LTh65. **d** 59 **p** 60. New Zealand 59-71, 74-86 and from 04; Singapore 72-73; C Roslyn 59-62; V Waimea Plains 62-69; CF 70-73; V Dunstan 74-81; Adn Otago 77-82; V Anderson's Bay and Chapl Police Force 82-86; Can Dunedin Cathl 82-85; Adn Dunedin 85-86; Hon C Geneva *Eur* 87-90; Chapl Lausanne 90-97; Perm to Offic *Pet* 98-99; P-in-c Potterspury, Furtho, Yardley Gobion and Cosgrove 99-02; R Potterspury w Furtho and Yardley Gobion etc 02-04; rtd 04. *43 Fidelis Avenue, Snells Beach, Warkworth, Auckland, New Zealand* E-mail hestents@btinternet.com

STEEL, Norman William. b 53. Sarum & Wells Th Coll 85. **d** 87 **p** 88. C S Woodham Ferrers *Chelmsf* 87-91; V Woolavington w Cossington and Bawdrip *B & W* 91-99; P-in-c Pitminster w Corfe 99-02; Chapl Huish Coll Taunton from 99; rtd 02; Perm to Offic *B & W* from 02. *96 Burch's Close, Taunton TA1 4TS* Tel (01823) 423204 Fax 07986-370063 E-mail norman.steel@btinternet.com

STEEL, Richard John. b 57. Dur Univ BA79 Cam Univ MA86 Edin Univ MTh97. Ridley Hall Cam 81. **d** 84 **p** 85. C Hull St Jo Newland *York* 84-87; Relig Broadcasting Officer *Derby* 88-92; Dioc Communications Officer *Blackb* 92-97; Communication Dir CMS 97-05; Perm to Offic *Guildf* 97-00; NSM Stoke-next-Guildf 00-05; R Kirkheaton *Wakef* from 05. *The New Rectory, Church Lane, Kirkheaton, Huddersfield HD5 0BH* Tel (01484) 532410 E-mail richard.steel@ntlworld.com

STEEL, Thomas Molyneux. b 39. Man Univ BA61 Ox Univ DipPSA62. Ripon Hall Ox 61. **d** 63 **p** 64. C Newc H Cross *Newc* 63-66; P-in-c Man St Aid *Man* 66-71; R Failsworth St Jo 71-79; P-in-c Farnham Royal *Ox* 79-81; P-in-c Hedgerley 80-81; R Farnham Royal w Hedgerley 81-91; V Prescot *Liv* 91-03; rtd 03. *20 Barnet Way, London NW7 3BH* Tel (020) 8906 0271

STEELE, Alan Christopher. b 63. Cape Town Univ BA85 Univ of Zimbabwe BA91. Gaul Ho Harare 89. **d** 91 **p** 93. Zimbabwe 91-99; C Harare St Mary Magd 91-93; C Harare St Luke 93-95; Chapl Ruzawi Sch 96-99; CF from 99. *c/o MOD Chaplains (Army)* Tel (01980) 615804 Fax 615800

STEELE, Charles Edward Ernest. b 24. Cuddesdon Coll 72. **d** 74 **p** 75. C Rubery *Birm* 74-77; P-in-c Shaw Hill 77-79; V 79-82; C Curdworth 82-83; C Curdworth w Castle Vale 83-85; rtd 85; Perm to Offic *Birm* from 85. *3 Dominic Drive, Middleton Hall Road, Birmingham B30 1DW* Tel 0121-451 3372

STEELE, David Robert. b 29. Peterho Cam BA53 MA57. Oak Hill Th Coll 53. **d** 56 **p** 57. C Portman Square St Paul *Lon* 56-59; C Sevenoaks St Nic *Roch* 59-62; Kenya 63-65; Lic to Offic *Lon* 65-83; Chapl Steward's Trust Lon 65-72; Jt Gen Sec ICS 72-81; Dir 2 Tim 2 Trust from 82; Perm to Offic *Lon* 83-91 and *Win* from 83; rtd 94. *Worthy Park Grove, Abbots Worthy, Winchester SO21 1AN* Tel (01962) 882082

STEELE, Derek James. b 53. St Jo Coll Nottm CertRE. **d** 97 **p** 98. Aux Min Ballywillan *Conn* from 97. *106 Mountsandel Road, Coleraine BT52 1TA* Tel (028) 7035 1633

STEELE, Gerald Robert. b 25. St D Coll Lamp BA49. **d** 51 **p** 52. C Glyntaff *Llan* 51-63; V Llangeinor 63-73; R Cadoxton-juxta-Barry 73-91; Chapl Barry Community Hosp 73-91; Miss to Seamen 73-91; rtd 91; Perm to Offic *Llan* from 91. *74 Redbrink Crescent, Barry CF62 5TU* Tel (01446) 737554

STEELE, Canon Gordon John. b 55. Kent Univ BA76 Worc Coll Ox BA82 MA87. Coll of Resurr Mirfield 82. **d** 84 **p** 85. C Greenhill St Jo *Lon* 84-88; C Uxbridge St Andr w St Jo 88; TV Uxbridge 88-94; V Northampton St Alb *Pet* 94-01; V Pet St Jo from 01; RD Pet from 04; Can Pet Cathl from 04. *26 Minster Precincts, Peterborough PE1 1XZ* Tel (01733) 566265 E-mail gordonsteele@fish.co.uk

STEELE, Keith Atkinson. b 28. CEng MIMechE FInstMC. Qu Coll Birm Oak Hill Th Coll 80. **d** 81 **p** 82. NSM Westoning w Tingrith *St Alb* 81-87; NSM Chalgrave 87-88; P-in-c 88-96; RD Dunstable 91-96; Perm to Offic from 96. *Mariner's Lodge, Church Road, Westoning, Bedford MK45 5JW* Tel (01525) 714111

STEELE, Peter Gerald. b 44. Bournemouth Tech Coll BSc67 Essex Univ MSc69. Sarum & Wells Th Coll 91. **d** 93 **p** 94. C Beaminster Area *Sarum* 93-97; P-in-c Aldermaston w Wasing and Brimpton *Ox* from 97; P-in-c Woolhampton w Midgham and Beenham Valance from 05. *The Vicarage, Wasing Lane, Aldermaston, Reading RG7 4LX* Tel 0118-971 2281 E-mail petesteele@btopenworld.com

STEELE, Terence. b 54. Linc Th Coll 85. **d** 87 **p** 88. C New Sleaford *Linc* 87-90; V Cowbit 90-95; P-in-c Burgh le Marsh 95-97; P-in-c Orby 95-97; P-in-c Bratoft w Irby-in-the-Marsh 95-97; P-in-c Welton-le-Marsh w Gunby 95-97; V Burgh le Marsh from 97; R Bratoft w Irby-in-the-Marsh from 97; V Orby from 97; R Welton-le-Marsh w Gunby from 97; RD Calcewaithe and Candleshoe from 05. *The Vicarage, Glebe Rise, Burgh le Marsh, Skegness PE24 5BL* Tel (01754) 810216 E-mail father.terry@btclick.com

STEELE-PERKINS, Mrs Barbara Anita. b 46. Whitelands Coll Lon CertEd68 Spurgeon's Coll MTh98. STETS 99. **d** 01 **p** 02. Tutor Dioc Min Course *Guildf* from 95; NSM Wisley w Pyrford 01-04; NSM Haslemere and Grayswood from 04. *Church House, Church Close, Grayswood, Haslemere GU27 2DB* Tel (01428) 656504 E-mail barbara@steeleperkins.fsnet.co.uk

STEELE-PERKINS, Richard De Courcy. b 36. Clifton Th Coll 61. **d** 64 **p** 65. C Stoke Damerel *Ex* 64-65; C Washfield 65-68; P-in-c Wimbledon *S'wark* 68-70; Chapl Lambeth Hosp 70-74; Asst Chapl St Thos Hosp Lon 70-74; P-in-c Tawstock *Ex* 74-75; R 75-81; P-in-c Sticklepath 74-75; R 75-81; V Buckfastleigh w Dean Prior 81-91; TR Camelot Par *B & W* 91-94; Asst Chapl R Surrey Co and St Luke's Hosps NHS Trust 94-99; Asst Chapl Heathlands Mental Health Trust Surrey 94-99; P-in-c Ockham w Hatchford *Guildf* 99-01; rtd 02; Hon C E Horsley and Ockham w Hatchford and Downside *Guildf* 02-04; Perm to Offic from 04. *Church House, Church Close, Grayswood, Haslemere GU27 2DB* Tel (01428) 656504 E-mail richard@steele-perkins.fsnet.co.uk

STEEN, Canon Jane Elizabeth. b 64. Newnham Coll Cam BA88 MA90 PhD92. Westcott Ho Cam 93. **d** 96 **p** 97. C Chipping Barnet w Arkley *St Alb* 96-99; Chapl and Personal Asst to Bp S'wark 99-05; Hon Chapl S'wark Cathl 00-05; Chan and Can Th and Dir Min Tr from 05. *2 Harmsworth Mews, London SE11 4SQ* Tel (020) 7820 8079 E-mail jane.steen@southwark.anglican.org

STEER, Norman William. b 35. MBE00. SRN57. EAMTC 01. **d** 03 **p** 04. NSM Dickleburgh and The Pulhams *Nor* from 03. *Brook Cottage, Harleston Road, Starston, Harleston IP20 9NL* Tel (01379) 854245 Mobile 07941-473255 E-mail romans@steer.gointernet.co.uk

STEINBERG, Eric Reed (Joseph). b 65. Trin Coll Bris BA94. **d** 94 **p** 95. C Chigwell and Chigwell Row *Chelmsf* 94-99; Dir Y2000 99-00; Dir Jews for Jesus UK 00-05; Dir CMS from 05. *CMS, Partnership House, 157 Waterloo Road, London SE1 8UU* Tel (020) 7928 8681 E-mail kosherjoe@mac.com

STEINER, Eduard Samuel. b 52. Liv Univ MB, ChB74. EMMTC 93. **d** 96 **p** 97. NSM Ravenshead *S'well* 96-03; Lic to Offic from 03. *La Corbière, Cauldwell Drive, Mansfield NG18 4SL* Tel (01623) 653615 Mobile 07971-546470

STELL, Peter Donald. b 50. Leeds Univ 74 Southn Univ BA81 Man Univ 93 MInstM. Sarum & Wells Th Coll 78. **d** 81 **p** 82. C Rothwell w Lofthouse *Ripon* 81-85; TV Brayton *York* 85-87; Chapl Asst Leybourne Grange Hosp W Malling 87-88; Chapl Asst Kent, Sussex and Pembury Hosps Tunbridge Wells 87-88; C Spalding St Jo w Deeping St Nicholas *Linc* 87-93; Chapl S Lincs HA Mental Handicap Unit 88-93; Chapl HM Pris Liv 93-94; Chapl HM Pris Wayland 94-99; Chapl HM Pris Grendon and Spring Hill 99-02; Chapl HM Pris Rye Hill from 02. *HM Prison Rye Hill, Willoughby, Rugby CV23 8SZ* Tel (01788) 528800 ext 4410 Fax 523311

STENHOUSE, Joan Frances Fleming. b 45. RGN66. Ab Dioc Tr Course 82. **dss** 84 **d** 86 **p** 94. Ellon and Cruden Bay *Ab* 84-97; NSM 86-97; Bp's Chapl for Tr and Educn 95-00; Asst P Cuminestown 97-00; C Nova Scotia St Martin Canada from 00. *27 Birch Grove, Upper Tantallon NS, Canada, B3Z 1L1* E-mail jstenhouse@bwr.eastlink.ca

STENTIFORD, Mrs Pauline Cecilia Elizabeth. b 48. EAMTC 98. **d** 00 **p** 01. NSM Gt and Lt Bealings w Playford and Culpho *St E* 00-03; P-in-c from 03; RD Woodbridge from 05. *Sheepstor, Boyton, Woodbridge IP12 3LH* Tel (01394) 411469 E-mail pauline.stentiford@btopenworld.com

STEPHEN, Canon Kenneth George. b 47. Strathclyde Univ BA69 Edin Univ BD72. Edin Th Coll 69. **d** 72 **p** 73. C Ayr *Glas* 72-75; R Renfrew 75-80; R Motherwell 80-93; R Wishaw 80-93; Can St Mary's Cathl from 87; Syn Clerk from 87; R Kilmarnock from 93. *The Parsonage, 1 Dundonald Road, Kilmarnock KA1 1EQ* Tel (01563) 523577 E-mail ken.stephen@ukgateway.net

STEPHEN, Robert. b 63. Lon Bible Coll BA85 Westmr Coll Ox MTh96 FSAScot01. EMMTC. **d** 04 **p** 05. NSM Burbage w Aston Flamville *Leic* from 04. *Small Change, 4 Woodland Road, Hinckley LE10 1JG* Tel (01455) 615503 Mobile 07957-312892 E-mail revrstephen@hotmail.com

STEPHENI, Frederick William. b 28. TD73. FSAScot81 FRSA82 Cranfield Inst of Tech MSc82. Lambeth STh83 Qu Coll Birm 54. **d** 55 **p** 56. C Arnold *S'well* 55-57; P-in-c 57-58; P-in-c Hucknall Torkard 58-59; Chapl Stoke-on-Trent City Gen Hosp 59-62; Chapl N Staffs R Infirmary Stoke-on-Trent 59-62; CF (TA) 60-88; Chapl K Coll Hosp Lon 62-63; R Cotgrave *S'well* 63-76; V Owthorpe 63-76; Chapl Addenbrooke's Hosp Cam 76-88; Lic to Offic *Ely* 76-99; rtd 88; Perm to Offic *York* from 00. *64A Scarborough Road, Norton, Malton YO17 8AE* Tel (01653) 694995

STEPHENS, Anthony Wayne. b 54. Surrey Univ BSc80. St Jo Coll Nottm 02. **d** 04 **p** 05. C Preston w Sutton Poyntz and Osmington w Poxwell *Sarum* from 04. *8 Buddleia Close, Weymouth DT3 6SG* Tel (01305) 835096 E-mail tony.stephens@fish.co.uk

STEPHENS, Canon Archibald John. b 15. Selw Coll Cam BA37 MA44. Wells Th Coll 46. **d** 47 **p** 48. C Gt Malvern St Mary *Worc* 47-50; Nigeria 50-68 and 70-71; Hon Can Ondo 57-71; Hon Can Owerri from 71; C Swindon Ch Ch *Bris* 68-70; C-in-c Ash Vale CD *Guildf* 71-72; V Ash Vale 72-77; P-in-c Thursley 77-82; rtd 82; Perm to Offic *Guildf* from 85. *Fernhill, 12 Vicarage Lane, Farnham GU9 8HN* Tel (01252) 722514

STEPHENS, Grahame Frank Henry. b 33. **d** 02 **p** 03. OLM Woolwich St Mary w St Mich *S'wark* 02-05; Perm to Offic from 05. *121 The Drive, Bexley DA5 3BY* Tel (020) 8303 3546 Fax 8306 2155 Mobile 07775-796896

STEPHENS, Harold William Barrow. b 47. Lon Univ BEd71. S Dios Minl Tr Scheme 80. **d** 82 **p** 83. NSM Heytesbury and Sutton Veny *Sarum* 82-83; NSM Bishopstrow and Boreham 83-91; Dep Hd Master Westwood St Thos Sch Salisbury 91-99; P-in-c Market Lavington and Easterton 99-03; P-in-c W Lavington and the Cheverells 02-03; R The Lavingtons, Cheverells, and Easterton from 03. *The Vicarage, 14 Church Street, Market Lavington, Devizes SN10 4DT* Tel (01380) 813914 E-mail harold.stephens@ukonline.co.uk

STEPHENS, James Charles. b 62. Dip Analytical Chemistry. **d** 91 **p** 92. C Kilcolman w Kiltallagh, Killorglin, Knockane etc *L & K* from 91. *Kilderry, Miltown, Co Kerry, Irish Republic* Tel (00353) (66) 976 7735 E-mail jstephens@klinge.ie

STEPHENS, Mrs Jean. b 46. St As Minl Tr Course. **d** 89 **p** 97. NSM Gwernaffield and Llanferres *St As* 89-02; NSM Hawarden from 02. *Noddfa, Pen-y-Fron Road, Pantymwyn, Mold CH7 5EF* Tel (01352) 740037

STEPHENS, Mrs Joan. b 38. Dioc OLM tr scheme 97. **d** 00 **p** 01. OLM Irlam *Man* from 00. *77 Baines Avenue, Irlam, Manchester M44 6AS* Tel 0161-775 7538

STEPHENS, John. *See* STEPHENS, Canon Archibald John

STEPHENS, John Michael. b 29. MRICS52. Lich Th Coll 62. **d** 64 **p** 65. C Birchington w Acol *Cant* 64-70; V Tovil 70-79; V Brabourne w Smeeth 79-94; RD N Lympne 87-94; rtd 94; Perm to Offic *York* from 94. *Southacre, Kirby Mills, Kirkbymoorside, York YO62 6NR* Tel (01751) 432766

STEPHENS, Martin Nicholas. b 64. Brunel Univ BSc88 Nottm Univ MTh01. St Jo Coll Nottm 99. **d** 01 **p** 02. C Newchapel *Lich* 01-04; TV Bucknall from 04. *St John's Parsonage, 28 Greasley Road, Stoke-on-Trent ST2 8JE* Tel (01782) 542861

STEPHENS, Miss Mary. b 26. Reading Univ BA50 BEd51. Linc Th Coll. **d** 87 **p** 94. NSM Gt Grimsby St Mary and St Jas *Linc* 86-91; C 91-92; TD 92-94; TV 94-96; rtd 96; Perm to Offic *Linc* from 96. *33 Amesbury Avenue, Grimsby DN33 3HT* Tel (01472) 752340

STEPHENS, Michael. *See* STEPHENS, John Michael

STEPHENS, Paul. b 53. AGSM73 Newton Park Coll Bath PGCE74. Trin Coll Bris DipHE93. **d** 93 **p** 94. C S Molton w Nymet St George, High Bray etc *Ex* 93-97; R Norton Fitzwarren *B & W* 97-99; Chapl St Aug Sch Taunton 97-99; Chapl Monkton Combe Sch Bath from 99. *Monkton Combe School, Monkton Combe, Bath BA2 7HG* Tel (01225) 721116 *or* 721135

STEPHENS, Mrs Penny Clare. b 60. St Anne's Coll Ox BA83 Lon Inst of Educn PGCE85. Oak Hill Th Coll. **d** 99 **p** 00. C Turnham Green Ch Ch *Lon* 99-03; P-in-c Brasted *Roch* from 03. *The Rectory, Coles Lane, Brasted, Westerham TN16 1NR* Tel (01959) 565829

STEPHENS, Canon Peter John. b 42. Oriel Coll Ox BA64 MA67. Clifton Th Coll 63. **d** 68 **p** 68. C Lenton *S'well* 68-71; C Brixton Hill St Sav *S'wark* 71-73; P-in-c 73-82; TV Barnham Broom *Nor* 82-89; V Gorleston St Mary 89-94; RD Flegg (Gt Yarmouth) 92-94; P-in-c High Oak 94-97; RD Humbleyard 95-98; C Hingham w Wood Rising w Scoulton 96-97; TR High Oak, Hingham and Scoulton w Wood Rising 97-05; Hon Can Nor Cathl 99-05; rtd 05. *c/o Mrs J Roe, 31 Highbridge Walk,*

Aylesbury HP21 7SE Tel 07769-425349 *or* 07973-322513 (mobile) E-mail peterstephens@aol.com

STEPHENS, Preb Peter Stanley. b 33. ALCD59. **d** 59 **p** 60. C Paignton St Paul Preston *Ex* 59-64; V Buckland Monachorum 64-74; RD Tavistock 70-74; V Compton Gifford 74-85; RD Plymouth Sutton 83-86; Preb Ex Cathl 84-05; TR Plymouth Em w Efford 85-86; R Thurlestone w S Milton 86-98; rtd 98. *Headland View, 14 Court Park, Thurlestone, Kingsbridge TQ7 3LX* Tel and fax (01548) 560891

STEPHENS, Richard William. b 37. Dur Univ BSc62 DipTh64. Cranmer Hall Dur 62. **d** 64 **p** 65. C Hensingham *Carl* 64-67; C Norbury *Ches* 67-71; R Elworth and Warmingham 71-79; V Bootle St Matt *Liv* 79-89; P-in-c Litherland St Andr 79-83; P-in-c Failsworth H Trin *Man* 89-93; R 93-02; P-in-c Oldham St Barn 01-02; AD Oldham 99-02; rtd 02. *Cloverstone, 3 Craignair Street, Dalbeattie DG5 4AX* Tel (01556) 610627 E-mail revrstephens@btinternet.com

STEPHENS, Ronald John. b 13. Sarum Th Coll 56. **d** 57 **p** 58. C Calne *Sarum* 57-61; V Stanstead Abbots *St Alb* 61-82; rtd 82; Perm to Offic *Nor* from 82. *63 Beechlands Park, Southrepps, Norwich NR11 8NT* Tel (01263) 834893

STEPHENS, Canon Simon Edward. b 41. OBE97. Qu Coll Birm DPS68 PhD80. Bps' Coll Cheshunt 63. **d** 67 **p** 68. C Cov St Mark *Cov* 67-71; C Lillington 71-76; C-in-c Canley CD 76-79; V Canley 79-80; Chapl RN 80-97; Asst Chapl Menorca *Eur* 97-98; Chapl 98-99; Chapl Moscow from 99; Hon Can Malta Cathl from 01. *British Embassy - Moscow, FCO, King Charles Street, London SW1A 2AH* Tel (007) (095) 229 0990 Fax as telephone E-mail anglican@rol.ru

STEPHENS, Mrs Susanne Hilary. b 44. St Jo Coll Nottm. Guildf Dioc Min Course. **d** 00 **p** 01. OLM Camberley St Paul *Guildf* from 00. *Shire, Knightsbridge Road, Camberley GU15 3TS* Tel and fax (01276) 507693 Mobile 07714-217167 E-mail suestephens@onetel.com

STEPHENSON, David John. b 65. Bris Univ BSc(Soc)87 Dur Univ BA91. Cranmer Hall Dur 92. **d** 92 **p** 93. C Whickham *Dur* 92-94; C Sunderland Pennywell St Thos 94-97; V Stockton St Jo from 97; V Stockton St Jas from 99. *St John the Baptist Vicarage, 168 Durham Road, Stockton-on-Tees TS19 0DZ* Tel (01642) 674119 E-mail david.stephenson2@ntlworld.com

STEPHENSON, Canon Eric George. b 41. Bede Coll Dur CertEd63. Qu Coll Birm DipTh65. **d** 66 **p** 67. C Wakef St Jo *Wakef* 66-69; C Seaham w Seaham Harbour *Dur* 69-73; C Cockerton 73-75; Lic to Offic 75-85; V E Boldon from 85; AD Jarrow 92-01; Hon Can Dur Cathl from 93; Chapl to The Queen from 02. *39 Haversham Park, Sunderland SR5 1HW* Tel 0191-549 5278 E-mail eric.stephenson@btinternet.com

STEPHENSON, Ian Clarke. b 24. Lon Univ DipTh69. Tyndale Hall Bris 52. **d** 56 **p** 57. C Bedworth *Cov* 56-58; C Edgware *Lon* 58-65; R Biddulph Moor *Lich* 65-70; Hon C Biddulph 70-88; Hon C Burslem 85-88; New Zealand from 87; rtd 89. *5 Arthur Terrace, Balclutha, Otago, New Zealand* Tel (0064) (3) 418 2657

STEPHENSON, Jane. b 50. **d** 05. NSM Bunbury and Tilstone Fearnall *Ches* from 05. *The Mount, Hobb Hill, Tilston, Malpas SY14 7DU*

STEPHENSON, John Joseph. b 35. St Jo Coll Dur BA74. Qu Coll Birm 75. **d** 76 **p** 77. C Whitworth w Spennymoor *Dur* 76-79; V Eppleton 79-96; rtd 96; Perm to Offic *Dur* from 96. *29 Launceston Drive, Sunderland SR3 3QB* Tel 0191-528 2144

STEPHENSON (née BRYAN), Judith Claire. b 57. Aston Univ BSc79 PhD82 Trent Poly PGCE83. St Jo Coll Nottm BTh94 LTh95. **d** 95 **p** 96. C Wolverhampton St Matt *Lich* 95-99; Chapl Hull Univ *York* from 99. *21 Southwood Road, Cottingham HU16 5AE* Tel (01482) 847151

STEPHENSON, Juliet. b 69. St Jo Coll Dur BA05. Cranmer Hall Dur 03. **d** 05. C Retford *S'well* from 05. *1 Chapelgate, Retford DN22 6PJ* Tel (01777) 719908 E-mail juliet_stephenson@hotmail.com

STEPHENSON, Martin Woodard. b 55. St Cath Coll Cam BA77 MA82. Westcott Ho Cam 78. **d** 81 **p** 82. C Eastleigh *Win* 81-85; C Ferryhill *Dur* 85-87; Asst Dir of Ords 87-89; Chapl St Chad's Coll 87-89; TR Clarendon Park St Jo w Knighton St Mich *Leic* 89-98; P-in-c Hall Green St Pet *Birm* 98-99; V from 99. *St Peter's Vicarage, 33 Paradise Lane, Birmingham B28 0DY* Tel 0121-777 1935 E-mail martinw.stephenson@virgin.net

STEPHENSON, Nicolas William. b 22. Ely Th Coll 60. **d** 62 **p** 63. C S Westoe *Dur* 62-65; CR 68-74; Hon C Westgate Common *Wakef* 74-75; Lic to Offic 75-87; Asst Chapl HM Pris Wakef 84-87; rtd 87; Perm to Offic *Ripon* from 87. *24 Nicholson Court, 25 Fitzroy Drive, Leeds LS8 4AP* Tel 0113-248 5166

STEPHENSON, Canon Robert. b 36. St Chad's Coll Dur BA58 DipTh60. **d** 60 **p** 61. C Whickham *Dur* 60-63; C Gateshead St Mary 63-65; PC Low Team 65-67; R Stella 67-74; V Comberton *Ely* 74-04; RD Bourn 94-97; P-in-c Dry Drayton 97-01; Hon Can Ely Cathl 01-04; rtd 04. *1 Porthmore Close, Highfields, Caldecote, Cambridge CB3 7ZR* Tel (01954) 210638

STEPHENSON, Simon George. b 44. St Jo Coll Dur BA67. Trin Coll Bris 74. **d** 76 **p** 77. C Hildenborough *Roch* 76-82; C Bishopsworth *Bris* 82-85; C-in-c Withywood CD 85-90; TV Wreningham *Nor* 90-97; P-in-c Tasburgh w Tharston, Forncett and Flordon 94-97; TV High Oak, Hingham and Scoulton w Wood Rising 98-05; Asst Chapl HM Pris Wayland from 98. *The Chaplain's Office, HM Prison Wayland, Griston, Thetford IP25 6RL* Tel (01953) 804080 *or* 804100

STEPNEY, Area Bishop of. *See* OLIVER, The Rt Revd Stephen John

STERLING, Anne. *See* HASELHURST, Mrs Anne

STERLING, John Haddon. b 40. Pemb Coll Cam BA62 MA66. Cuddesdon Coll 63. **d** 65 **p** 66. S Africa 65-70; Chapl Bris Cathl *Bris* 71-74; Member Dioc Soc and Ind Team 71-74; Ind Chapl *Linc* 74-87; Ind Chapl *Ripon* 87-92; TV Hanley H Ev *Lich* 92-97; Min in Ind 92-97; P-in-c Hixon w Stowe-by-Chartley 97-02; P-in-c Fradswell, Gayton, Milwich and Weston 97-02; TR Mid Trent from 02. *The Vicarage, Stafford Road, Weston, Stafford ST18 0HX* Tel (01889) 270490

STERRY, Christopher. b 54. K Coll Lon BD77 AKC77. Episc Sem Austin Texas 78 St Jo Coll Nottm 79. **d** 80 **p** 81. C Huddersfield St Jo *Wakef* 80-84; V Middlestown 84-89; Chapl and Tutor N Ord Course 89-94; Lect Ches Coll of HE 93-94; NSM Padgate *Liv* 92-94; Bp's Dom Chapl *Blackb* 94-97; Chapl Whalley Abbey 94-97; Warden 97-04; V Whalley from 97. *The Vicarage, 40 The Sands, Clitheroe BB7 9TL* Tel (01254) 824679, 823249 *or* 828400 Mobile 07010-717992 Fax (01254) 828401 E-mail vicar@whalleypc.com

STERRY, Timothy John. b 34. Oriel Coll Ox BA58 MA62 DipTh60. Wycliffe Hall Ox 58. **d** 60 **p** 61. C Cromer *Nor* 60-64; Chapl Oundle Sch 64-72; Teacher Cheam Prep Sch 72-75; Hd Master Temple Grove Sch E Sussex 75-80; Team Ldr Scripture Union Independent Schs 81-99; rtd 00; Perm to Offic *Sarum* from 02. *60 Amberwood, Ferndown BH22 9JT* Tel (01202) 873053 E-mail tim@sterry.org

STEVEN, Canon David Bowring. b 38. AKC64. **d** 64 **p** 65. C Grantham St Wulfram *Linc* 64-68; S Africa 68-75; C Bramley *Ripon* 76-77; V Sutton Valence w E Sutton and Chart Sutton *Cant* 77-82; P-in-c Littlebourne 82-86; V Mansfield Woodhouse *S'well* 86-98; P-in-c Mullion *Truro* 98-03; RD Kerrier 01-03; Hon Can Truro Cathl 03 and from 04; rtd 03; Perm to Offic *Truro* from 03. *5 Guinea Port Parc, Wadebridge PL27 7BY* Tel (01208) 815393

STEVEN, James Henry Stevenson. b 62. CCC Cam MA84 St Jo Coll Dur BA87 K Coll Lon PhD99. Cranmer Hall Dur 84. **d** 87 **p** 88. C Welling *Roch* 87-91; C Bournemouth St Jo w St Mich *Win* 91-94; TV Bournemouth St Pet w St Swithun, H Trin etc 94-00; Chapl Bournemouth and Poole Coll of FE 94-00; Tutor Trin Coll Bris from 00. *Trinity College, Stoke Hill, Bristol BS9 1JP* Tel 0117-968 2803 E-mail james.steven@trinity-bris.ac.uk

STEVEN, Richard John. b 54. Oak Hill Th Coll BA99. **d** 99 **p** 01. Asst P Bluff Pt Australia 00-03; P-in-c Horsmonden *Roch* from 04. *The Rectory, Goudhurst Road, Horsmonden, Tonbridge TN12 8JU* Tel (01892) 722521 E-mail ra_steven@hotmail.com

STEVENETTE, John Maclachlan. b 30. St Pet Coll Ox MA60. Ripon Hall Ox 60. **d** 61 **p** 62. C Newhaven *Chich* 61-66; R Lynch w Iping Marsh 66-74; R Birdham w W Itchenor 74-78; R Byfleet *Guildf* 78-86; V Whittlesey *Ely* 86-90; TR Whittlesey and Pondersbridge 91; R Itchen Valley *Win* 91-99; rtd 99; Perm to Offic *Bris* from 00. *35 Ballard Chase, Abingdon OX14 1XQ* Tel (01235) 526706

STEVENETTE, Simon Melville. b 62. Hull Univ BA83. Wycliffe Hall Ox 84. **d** 87 **p** 88. C Carterton *Ox* 87-90; C Keynsham *B & W* 90-91; TV 91-98; Chapl Keynsham Hosp Bris 92-98; V Swindon Ch Ch *Bris* from 98. *Christ Church Vicarage, 26 Cricklade Street, Swindon SN1 3HG* Tel and fax (01793) 529166 *or* tel 522832 Mobile 07880-710172 E-mail simon@stevenette.freeserve.co.uk

STEVENS, Alan Robert. b 55. Warwick Univ BA77. St Jo Coll Nottm 87. **d** 89 **p** 90. C Ex St Leon w H Trin *Ex* 89-92; TV Rugby St Andr *Cov* 92-97; P-in-c N w S Kilworth and Misterton *Leic* 97-00. *Address temp unknown*

STEVENS, Andrew. *See* STEVENS, John David Andrew

STEVENS, Andrew Graham. b 54. BEd MA. Coll of Resurr Mirfield. **d** 83 **p** 84. C Leigh Park *Portsm* 83-87; TV Brighton Resurr *Chich* 87-94; V Plumstead St Nic *S'wark* from 94. *St Nicholas's Vicarage, 64 Purrett Road, London SE18 1JP* Tel (020) 8854 0461 Fax 8265 5065 E-mail frandrew@dircon.co.uk

STEVENS, Canon Anne Helen. b 61. Warwick Univ BA82 Fitzw Coll Cam BA90 MA94 Heythrop Coll Lon MTh99. Ridley Hall Cam 88. **d** 91 **p** 94. Par Dn E Greenwich Ch Ch w St Andr and St Mich *S'wark* 91-94; Chapl Trin Coll Cam 94-99; P-in-c Battersea St Mich *S'wark* from 99; Dir Readers' Tr from 99; Hon Can S'wark Cathl from 05. *93 Bolingbroke Grove, London SW11 6HA* Tel (020) 7228 1990

STEVENS, Anthony Harold. b 46. CEng71 MIStructE71 FIStructE87 MICE75 FICE92. St Mich Coll Llan 94. **d** 95 **p** 96. C Cardiff St Jo *Llan* 95-98; TV Cowbridge 98-01; R Eglwysilan from 01; AD Caerphilly from 04. *The Rectory, Brynhafod Road, Abertridwr, Caerphilly CF83 4BH* Tel (029) 2083 0220 E-mail tonstevens@aol.com

STEVENS, Brian Henry. b 28. Oak Hill Th Coll. **d** 69 **p** 70. C Chadwell *Chelmsf* 69-75; V Penge Ch Ch w H Trin *Roch* 75-85; V St Mary Cray and St Paul's Cray 85-93; rtd 93; Perm to Offic *Cant* from 93. *53 Middle Deal Road, Deal CT14 9RG*

STEVENS, Brian Henry. b 45. Open Univ BA80. S Dios Minl Tr Scheme 81. **d** 84 **p** 85. NSM S Malling *Chich* 84-86; C Langney 86-87; TV Wolverton *Ox* 87-88; V Welford w Sibbertoft and Marston Trussell *Pet* 88-91; V Hardingstone and Horton and Piddington from 91. *The Vicarage, 29 Back Lane, Hardingstone, Northampton NN4 6BY* Tel (01604) 760110 Fax 702547 Mobile 07710-207201 E-mail fr.brian@tesco.net

STEVENS, Cyril David Richard. b 25. NZ Bd of Th Studies. **d** 59 **p** 60. New Zealand 59-65 and 67-68; V Playford w Culpho and Tuddenham St Martin *St E* 65-67; R Rendham w Sweffling and Cransford 69-73; RD Saxmundham 72-74; R Rendham w Sweffling 73-95; rtd 95; Perm to Offic *St E* from 95. *Meadow Cottage, Low Road, Marlesford, Woodbridge IP13 0AW* Tel (01728) 746013

STEVENS, David Charles. b 31. Keble Coll Ox BA55 DipTh56 MA59. Wycliffe Hall Ox 55. **d** 57 **p** 58. C Plymouth St Andr *Ex* 57-60; S Rhodesia 61-65; Rhodesia 65-66; Asst Chapl Bryanston Sch 66-70; Chapl 70-73; P-in-c Shilling Okeford *Sarum* 73-76; Lic to Offic *Chelmsf* 76-86; Chapl Chigwell Sch Essex 76-86; R Tarrant Valley *Sarum* 86-94; rtd 94; Perm to Offic *Sarum* from 94. *Bumble Cottage, 3 Yondover, Loders, Bridport DT6 4NW* Tel (01308) 421025

STEVENS, David John. b 45. Bris Univ BA67 Lon Univ DipTh69. Clifton Th Coll. **d** 70 **p** 71. C Ex St Leon w H Trin *Ex* 70-75; P-in-c Lt Burstead *Chelmsf* 75-77; TV Billericay and Lt Burstead 77-81; P-in-c Illogan *Truro* 81-83; R St Illogan 83-96; RD Carnmarth N 96; V Highworth w Sevenhampton and Inglesham etc *Bris* 96-01; P-in-c Constantine *Truro* from 01; RD Kerrier from 03. *The Vicarage, Charlbury Heights, Constantine, Falmouth TR11 5UR* Tel (01326) 340259

STEVENS, David Lynne. b 59. Poly of Wales BA81. N Ord Course 99. **d** 02 **p** 03. C Horsforth *Ripon* from 02. *7 Featherbank Walk, Horsforth, Leeds LS18 4QN* Tel 0113-258 4653 Mobile 07748-477970 E-mail davidstev1@aol.com

STEVENS, David Norman. b 44. QPM91. EAMTC 01. **d** 03 **p** 04. NSM Necton, Holme Hale w N and S Pickenham *Nor* 03-05; Asst Chapl HM Pris Wayland from 04. *c/o Crockford, Church House, Great Smith Street, London SW1P 3NZ* E-mail david@stevens.go-plus.net

STEVENS, Douglas George. b 47. Lon Univ BA69. Westcott Ho Cam 69. **d** 72 **p** 73. C Portsea St Geo CD *Portsm* 72-75; C Portsea N End St Mark 75-79; Chapl NE Lon Poly *Chelmsf* 79-83; C-in-c Orton Goldhay CD *Ely* 83-87; V Elm 87-91; V Coldham 87-91; V Friday Bridge 87-91; R Woodston 91-98; P-in-c Fletton 94-98; rtd 98. *28 Francis Gardens, Peterborough PE1 3XX* Tel (01733) 755430

STEVENS, Frank Hayman. b 11. Univ Coll Ox BA32 MA38. Linc Th Coll 64. **d** 65 **p** 66. C Burnham *B & W* 65-68; V Kenn 68-69; P-in-c Kingston Seymour 68-69; R Kenn w Kingston Seymour 69-74; P-in-c Cossington 74-76; rtd 76; Perm to Offic *B & W* 76-98. *14 Eastgate Gardens, Taunton TA1 1RD* Tel (01823) 270436

STEVENS, Frederick Crichton. b 42. K Coll Lon BD78 AKC78. St Steph Ho Ox 78. **d** 79 **p** 80. C Newquay *Truro* 79-81; C St Martin-in-the-Fields *Lon* 81-85; P-in-c Soho St Anne w St Thos and St Pet 85-96; R 96-98; R Lostwithiel, St Winnow w St Nectan's Chpl etc *Truro* from 98; C Lanreath, Pelynt and Bradoc from 03. *The Rectory, 3 Springfield Close, Lostwithiel PL22 0ER* Tel (01208) 873448

STEVENS, Miss Gillian. b 51. K Alfred's Coll Win CertEd72. EAMTC 98. **d** 01 **p** 02. C March St Mary and March St Pet *Ely* 01-03; C Whittlesey, Pondersbridge and Coates 03-05; TV from 05. *8 The Grove, Whittlesey, Peterborough PE7 2RF* Tel and fax (01733) 202563 E-mail gill@stevens.net

STEVENS, James Anthony. b 47. Worc Coll Ox MA69. Trin Coll Bris 78. **d** 80 **p** 81. C Heref St Pet w St Owen and St Jas *Heref* 80-84; C Lowestoft and Kirkley *Nor* 84-85; TV 85-89; V Dorridge *Birm* 89-05; AD Shirley 02-05; R Sarratt and Chipperfield *St Alb* from 05. *The Vicarage, The Street, Chipperfield, Kings Langley WD4 9BJ* Tel (01923) 265848 E-mail jimandjudy@6manor.fsnet.co.uk

STEVENS, Jane. *See* KRAFT, Mrs Jane

STEVENS, Janice Hazel. b 42. **d** 00 **p** 01. Hon C Warlingham w Chelsham and Farleigh *S'wark* from 00; Chapl S Lon and Maudsley NHS Trust from 00. *7 Harrow Road, Warlingham CR6 9EY* Tel (01883) 626308 *or* (020) 8776 4361

STEVENS, John David Andrew. b 44. Wycliffe Hall Ox. **d** 68 **p** 69. C Standish *Blackb* 68-71; C Stonehouse *Glouc* 71-76; P-in-c Closworth *B & W* 76-77; P-in-c Barwick 76-77; TV Yeovil 77-80; R Chewton Mendip w Ston Easton, Litton etc 80-94; R Quantoxhead from 94; RD Quantock 95-01. *The New Rectory, Kilve, Bridgwater TA5 1DZ* Tel and fax (01278) 741501 E-mail andrewstevens@zetnet.co.uk

STEVENS, Martin Leonard. b 35. St Jo Coll Dur BA60 MA72. Oak Hill Th Coll 60. **d** 62 **p** 63. C Low Elswick *Newc* 62-65; C S Croydon Em *Cant* 65-69; Hon C 69-74; S England Dep Sec Irish Ch Miss 69-74; V Felling *Dur* 74-86; NSM Ches Square St Mich w St Phil *Lon* 92-96; rtd 95; Hon C Cullompton and Kentisbeare w Blackborough *Ex* 96-01; Perm to Offic *Cov* from 03. *11 Foxes Way, Warwick CV34 6AX* Tel (01926) 490864

STEVENS, Michael John. b 37. St Cath Coll Cam BA63. Coll of Resurr Mirfield 63. **d** 65 **p** 66. C Poplar All SS w St Frideswide *Lon* 65-71; Asst Chapl The Lon Hosp (Whitechapel) 71-74; Chapl St Thos Hosp Lon 75-96; Hospitaller St Bart Hosp Lon 96-05; P-in-c St Bart Less *Lon* 96-99; V 99-05; rtd 05; Perm to Offic *Chelmsf* from 03. *4 Stable Court, Charterhouse, Charterhouse Square, London EC1M 6AU* Tel (020) 7608 0072

STEVENS, Norman William. b 38. St Chad's Coll Dur BA61 DipTh63. **d** 63 **p** 99. C Wingate Grange *Dur* 63-64; NSM Bulkington w Shilton and Ansty *Cov* from 99. *60 Clinton Lane, Kenilworth CV8 1AT* Tel (01926) 858090 *or* (024) 7622 7597

STEVENS, Olive. b 48. Ex Univ BA04. SW Minl Tr Course 01. **d** 04 **p** 05. C Camborne *Truro* from 04. *6 St Meriadoc Road, Camborne TR14 7HL* Tel (01209) 613523 E-mail oste621439@aol.com

STEVENS, Penelope Ann. b 46. SW Minl Tr Course 96. **d** 99 **p** 00. NSM Halsetown *Truro* 99-02; P-in-c Breage w Germoe and Godolphin from 02. *The Vicarage, Breage, Helston TR13 9PN* Tel (01326) 573449 Mobile 07929-152234

STEVENS, Peter David. b 36. MRICS. Oak Hill Th Coll DipHE81. **d** 81 **p** 82. C Branksome St Clem *Sarum* 81-87; R Moreton and Woodsford w Tincleton 87-98; rtd 98; Hon C Hordle *Win* 98-02; Perm to Offic from 02. *34 Wisbech Way, Hordle, Lymington SO41 0YQ* Tel (01425) 628922

STEVENS, Philip Terence. b 55. Man Univ BSc76 Lon Univ BD81 St Jo Coll Dur MA86 MCMI MIED. Cranmer Hall Dur 81. **d** 83 **p** 84. C Withington St Paul *Man* 83-86; C Middleton 86-88; V Saddleworth 88-92; V Sheff St Paul *Sheff* 93-96; TR Sheff Manor 96-00; Perm to Offic 00-02; Soc Inclusion Manager Sheff City Coun from 00. *238 Carter Knowle Road, Sheffield S7 2EB* Tel 0114-250 8044

STEVENS, Richard William. b 36. AKC59. St Boniface Warminster 59. **d** 60 **p** 61. C Greenhill St Jo *Lon* 60-63; Chapl RAF 63-79; CF 79-01; rtd 01; Perm to Offic *Cant* from 02. *The Old Vicarage, Stockbury, Sittingbourne ME9 7UN* Tel (01795) 844891

STEVENS, Robin George. b 43. Leic Univ BA65. Cuddesdon Coll 74. **d** 74 **p** 75. C Hemel Hempstead *St Alb* 74-77; Chapl K Coll Sch Wimbledon 77-03; TV Wimbledon *S'wark* from 98. *9 Thornton Road, London SW19 4NE* Tel (020) 8946 4494

STEVENS, Simon Mark. b 72. Lon Univ BD Cam Univ MPhil. STETS 00. **d** 01 **p** 02. C Sholing *Win* from 01; Chapl Southn Univ from 05. *Chaplain's Lodge, St Mary's Church Close, Southampton SO18 2ST* Tel (023) 8055 8126 E-mail simon.m.stevens@btinternet.com

STEVENS, Mrs Susan Marjorie Earlam. b 52. RGN74 Ox Poly HVCert76. WMMTC 97. **d** 00 **p** 01. NSM Harborne St Faith and St Laur *Birm* 00-02; NSM Publow w Pensford, Compton Dando and Chelwood *B & W* from 03. *Woollard Place, Woollard, Pensford, Bristol BS39 4HU* Tel (01761) 490898

STEVENS, Miss Sylvia Joyce. b 41. Qu Mary Coll Lon BA63 Bris Univ CertEd64 St Jo Coll Dur BA77. Cranmer Hall Dur 75. **dss** 78 **d** 87 **p** 94. Chapl Trent (Nottm) Poly *S'well* 78-92; Chapl Nottm Trent Univ 92-93; CME Officer *Bris* 93-95; Tutor Trin Coll Bris 93-95; Hon C Chippenham St Pet *Bris* 93-95; C 95-97; R Everton and Mattersey w Clayworth *S'well* 97-03; rtd 03; Perm to Offic *S'well* from 04. *3 Claricoates Drive, Coddington, Newark NG24 2TF* Tel (01636) 611322

STEVENS, Thomas Walter. b 33. Bps' Coll Cheshunt. **d** 65 **p** 66. C Newc St Matt w St Mary *Newc* 65-69; C Wallsend St Luke 69-70; C Cranford *Lon* 70-87; C Fulwell St Mich and St Geo 87-90; C Teddington SS Pet and Paul and Fulwell 90-91; rtd 92; Perm to Offic *S'wark* from 92. *23A Samos Road, London SE20 7UQ* Tel (020) 8776 7960

✠**STEVENS, The Rt Revd Timothy John.** b 46. Selw Coll Cam BA68 MA72 DipTh. Ripon Coll Cuddesdon 75. **d** 76 **p** 77 **c** 95. C E Ham w Upton Park St Alb *Chelmsf* 76-80; TR Canvey Is 80-88; Dep Dir Cathl Cen for Research and Tr 82-84; Bp's Urban Officer 87-91; Hon Can Chelmsf Cathl 87-91; Adn W Ham 91-95; Suff Bp Dunwich *St E* 95-99; Bp Leic from 99. *Bishop's Lodge, 10 Springfield Road, Leicester LE2 3BD* Tel 0116-270 8985 Fax 270 3288 E-mail bptim@leicester.anglican.org

STEVENSON, Canon Alastair Rice. b 42. Open Univ BA78. Ripon Coll Cuddesdon 78. **d** 80 **p** 81. C Bexhill St Pet *Chich* 80-82; C Brighton St Matthias 82-84; C Swindon Ch Ch *Bris* 84-87; Bp's Soc and Ind Adv 87-97; P-in-c Swindon All SS w St Barn 97-01; V from 01; Hon Can Bris Cathl from 02. *The Vicarage, Southbrook Street, Swindon SN2 1HF* Tel (01793) 612385 Fax as telephone E-mail alastair@asteve.fsbusiness.co.uk

STEVENSON, Andrew James. b 63. IEng AMICE MIAT. SW Minl Tr Course 94. **d** 97 **p** 98. NSM Highertown and Baldhu

Truro from 97. *19 Hillcrest Avenue, Truro TR1 3NE* Tel (01872) 241880 E-mail andy@rebel.wanadoo.co.uk

STEVENSON, Beaumont. *See* STEVENSON, Canon Frank Beaumont

STEVENSON, Bernard Norman. b 57. Kent Univ BA78 Fitzw Coll Cam BA81 MA86. Ridley Hall Cam. **d** 82 **p** 83. C Mortlake w E Sheen *S'wark* 82-84; C Kensal Rise St Martin *Lon* 84-88; C Headstone St Geo 88-90; V Worfield *Heref* 90-95; R Hutton *B & W* from 95; RD Locking 04-05. *The Rectory, Church Lane, Hutton, Weston-super-Mare BS24 9SL* Tel (01934) 812366 E-mail bstevenson@clara.net

STEVENSON, Brian. *See* STEVENSON, Canon Robert Brian

STEVENSON, Brian. b 34. JP66. NW Ord Course 76. **d** 79 **p** 80. C Padiham *Blackb* 79-82; V Clitheroe St Paul Low Moor 82-89; V Blackb St Silas 89-01; rtd 01; Perm to Offic *Blackb* from 01. *1 Chatburn Close, Great Harwood, Blackburn BB6 7TL* Tel (01254) 885051

STEVENSON, Christopher James. b 43. TCD BA65 MA73 Em Coll Cam BA69 MA73. Westcott Ho Cam 68. **d** 70 **p** 71. C Newc H Cross *Newc* 70-72; C Arm St Mark *Arm* 72-73; C Dublin Crumlin *D & G* 73-76; Hon Clerical V Ch Ch Cathl Dublin 75-76; C-in-c Appley Bridge All SS CD *Blackb* 76-82; P-in-c Appley Bridge 82-91; Bp's C Clooncare w Killasnett, Lurganboy and Drumlease *K, E & A* from 91. *The Rectory, Manorhamilton, Co Leitrim, Irish Republic* Tel (00353) (71) 985 5041

STEVENSON, David Andrew. b 60. Trin Coll Bris BA92. **d** 92 **p** 93. C Nottingham St Sav *S'well* 92-96; P-in-c Darlaston All SS *Lich* 96-00; Ind Chapl Black Country Urban Ind Miss 96-00; C Darlaston St Lawr 99-00; TV Broadwater St Mary *Chich* from 00. *St Stephen's Vicarage, 37 Angola Road, Worthing BN14 8DU* Tel (01903) 523310

STEVENSON, Derick Neville. b 36. Open Univ BA76. Ridley Hall Cam 79. **d** 80 **p** 81. C Bonchurch *Portsm* 80-84; C-in-c Crookhorn Ch Cen CD 84-87; R Norton Fitzwarren *B & W* 87-96; P-in-c N Hartismere *St E* 96-01; rtd 01; Perm to Offic *Portsm* from 02. *Brambles, Main Road, Brighstone, Newport PO30 4AJ* Tel (01983) 740436

STEVENSON, Donald Macdonald. b 48. Lon Univ BSc(Econ)70 Leeds Univ MA72 Univ of Wales (Abth) PGCE73 Warwick Univ MEd78 UEA Dip Counselling 00. Oak Hill Th Coll BA88. **d** 88 **p** 89. C Gt Malvern St Mary *Worc* 88-92; Chapl Bedford Sch 92-98; Sen Chapl 96-98; Perm to Offic *St Alb* from 99 and *Ox* from 01. *94 Curlew Crescent, Bedford MK41 7HZ* Tel (01234) 217013 E-mail donstevenson100@hotmail.com

STEVENSON, Canon Frank Beaumont. b 39. Duke Univ (USA) BA61 MInstGA. Episc Th Sch Harvard MDiv64. **d** 64 **p** 64. USA 64-66; Zambia 66-68; Lect Th Ox Univ from 68; Bp's Tr Officer *Ox* 69-70; Chapl Keble Coll Ox 71-72; Chapl Oxon Mental Healthcare NHS Trust from 75; Officer for CME from 90; Dioc Adv Past Care from 90; Hon Can Ch Ch *Ox* from 98. *The School House, Wheatley Road, Stanton St John, Oxford OX33 1ET* Tel (01865) 351635 *or* 778911 E-mail 101531.3264@compuserve.com

STEVENSON, Gerald Ernest. b 35. S'wark Ord Course 80. **d** 83 **p** 84. NSM Eltham Park St Luke *S'wark* 83-88; Asst Chapl HM Pris Wormwood Scrubs 88-98; Perm to Offic *S'wark* 88-99; rtd 99; Hon C Eltham St Barn *S'wark* from 99. *7 Moira Road, London SE9 1SJ* Tel (020) 8850 2748

STEVENSON (née HALES), Ms Jan. b 65. TCD BEd85. CITC BTh94. **d** 94 **p** 95. C Lisburn Ch Ch Cathl *Conn* 94-99; C Coleraine 99-04. *Address temp unknown*

STEVENSON, John. b 39. Glas Univ MA64 Jordan Hill Coll Glas TCert65. St Jo Coll Nottm Edin Th Coll. **d** 87 **p** 88. NSM Moffat *Glas* 87-92; P-in-c Eastriggs 92-95; P-in-c Gretna 92-95; P-in-c Langholm 92-95; Israel 95-01; P-in-c Thurso *Mor* from 01; P-in-c Wick from 01. *5 Naver Place, Thurso KW14 8PZ* Tel (01847) 893393 E-mail john@kw147pz.co.uk

STEVENSON, John William. b 44. Salford Univ BSc66 E Warks Coll Dip Mgt73 Univ of S Africa BTh89. St Paul's Coll Grahamstown DipTh86. **d** 87 **p** 87. S Africa 87-93; V Broom Leys *Leic* from 93. *St David's Vicarage, 7 Greenhill Road, Coalville LE67 4RL* Tel (01530) 836262 E-mail stevensons@vicarage30.freeserve.co.uk

✠**STEVENSON, The Rt Revd Kenneth William.** b 49. Edin Univ MA70 Southn Univ PhD75 Man Univ DD87 FRHistS90. Sarum & Wells Th Coll 70. **d** 73 **p** 74 **c** 95. C Grantham w Manthorpe *Linc* 73-76; C Boston 76-80; Chapl and Lect Man Univ *Man* 80-86; TV Man Whitworth 80-82; TR 82-86; R Guildf H Trin w St Mary *Guildf* 86-95; Bp Portsm from 95. *Bishopsgrove, 26 Osborn Road, Fareham PO16 7DQ* Tel (01329) 280247 Fax 231538 E-mail bishports@portsmouth.anglican.org

STEVENSON, Leslie Thomas Clayton. b 59. TCD BA DipTh MPhil. **d** 83 **p** 84. C Dundela St Mark *D & D* 83-87; I Kilmore and Inch 87-92; R Donaghadee 92-99; I Portarlington w Cloneyhurke and Lea *M & K* from 99. *The Rectory, Portarlington, Co Laois, Irish Republic* Tel and fax (00353) (502) 40117

STEVENSON, Michael Richard Nevin. b 52. Univ Coll Lon MA77. CITC DipTh86. **d** 86 **p** 87. C Clooney w Strathfoyle *D & R* 86-89; CF from 89. *c/o MOD Chaplains (Army)* Tel (01980) 615804 Fax 615800

STEVENSON, Miss Pamela Mary. b 35. CQSW74. **d** 97 **p** 98. OLM Mitcham Ascension *S'wark* 97-05; Perm to Offic from 05. *7 Robin Hood Close, Mitcham CR4 1JN* Tel (020) 8764 8331 Mobile 07702-928204

STEVENSON, Peter John. b 70. Southn Univ BSc91 MSc93. Wycliffe Hall Ox 00. **d** 02 **p** 03. C Watford St Luke *St Alb* from 02. *19 Langley Road, Watford WD17 4PS* Tel (01923) 449165 Fax 246161 E-mail pete@stlukeswatford.org

STEVENSON, Richard Clayton. b 22. TCD BA48 MA56. CITC 48. **d** 48 **p** 49. C Belfast St Mary Magd *Conn* 48-51; C Bangor St Comgall *D & D* 51-54; I Comber 54-60; I Belfast St Barn *Conn* 60-70; I Belfast St Nic 70-88; Adn Conn 79-88; rtd 88. *42 Malone Heights, Belfast BT9 5PG* Tel (028) 9061 5006

STEVENSON, Robert. b 52. UWIST BSc73 MRTPI78 MCIM89. SEITE 03. **d** 05. NSM Woodnesborough w Worth and Staple *Cant* from 05. *The Old Rectory, 5 Cowper Road, Deal CT14 9TW* Tel (01304) 366003 E-mail robert@robstevenson.fsnet.co.uk

STEVENSON, Canon Robert Brian. b 40. QUB BA61 Qu Coll Cam BA67 MA71 Pemb Coll Ox BA69 BD76 MA76 Birm Univ PhD70. Cuddesdon Coll 69. **d** 70 **p** 71. C Lewisham St Jo Southend *S'wark* 70-73; C Catford (Southend) and Downham 73-74; Lect and Dir Past Studies Chich Th Coll 74-81; Acting Vice-Prin 80-81; V W Malling w Offham *Roch* from 81; RD Malling 93-02; Hon Can Roch Cathl from 98. *The Vicarage, 138 High Street, West Malling ME19 6NE* Tel (01732) 842245

STEVENSON, Canon Ronald. b 17. Leeds Univ BA38. Coll of Resurr Mirfield 38. **d** 40 **p** 41. C Pontefract All SS *Wakef* 40-44; C-in-c Lundwood CD 44-47; Area Sec Miss to Seamen 47-49; Chapl Lanc Moor Hosp 49-65; Chapl N Lancs and S Westmorland Hosps 65-75; Hon Can Blackb Cathl *Blackb* 71-75. *28 Slyne Road, Torrisholme, Morecambe LA4 6PA* Tel (01524) 410957

STEVENSON (née PITE), Mrs Sheila Reinhardt. b 60. St Jo Coll Dur BA82 Nottm Univ MA98. Oak Hill Th Coll BA88. **d** 88 **p** 94. Par Dn Derby St Aug *Derby* 88-92; C Brampton St Thos 92-95; Perm to Offic *St Alb* 95-96; P-in-c The Stodden Churches 96-98; P-in-c Croxton and Eltisley *Ely* 98-99; P-in-c Graveley w Papworth St Agnes w Yelling etc 98-99; Chapl Papworth Hosp NHS Trust 98-99; TV Braunstone *Leic* 99-02; P-in-c from 02. *36 Woodcote Road, Leicester LE3 2WD* Tel 0116-282 5272 E-mail sheila.pite@talk21.com

STEVENSON, Trevor Donald. b 59. TCD Div Sch BTh. **d** 91 **p** 92. C Magheralin w Dollingstown *D & D* 91-95; CMS Uganda 95-98; Dir Fields of Life from 98. *Tree Tops, Brides Glen Road, Shankill, Dublin 18, Irish Republic* Tel and fax (00353) (1) 282 0150 E-mail fieldsoflife@oceanfree.net

STEVENTON, Mrs June Lesley. b 61. Aston Tr Scheme 86 Sarum & Wells Th Coll BTh91. **d** 91 **p** 94. Par Dn Chatham St Steph *Roch* 91-94; C 94-96; Perm to Offic *York* 96-97 and *Liv* 97-00; V Abram *Liv* from 00; V Bickershaw from 00. *The Vicarage, 9 Lee Lane, Abram, Wigan WN2 5QU* Tel and fax (01942) 866396 E-mail abram.vicarage@btinternet.com

STEVENTON, Kenneth. b 59. Cuddesdon Coll 94. **d** 96 **p** 97. C Spalding *Linc* 96-99; R Sutterton, Fosdyke, Algarkirk and Wigtoft 99-05; P-in-c Staindrop *Dur* from 05; P-in-c Ingleton from 05; P-in-c Evenwood from 05. *St Mary's Vicarage, 7 Beechside, Staindrop, Darlington DL2 3PE* Tel (01833) 660237 E-mail revken@freeuk.co.uk

STEVINSON, Harold John Hardy. b 34. Selw Coll Cam BA57 MA61. Qu Coll Birm. **d** 59 **p** 60. C Bris St Mary Redcliffe w Temple *Bris* 59-63; C Caversham *Ox* 63-73; Soc Resp Officer *Dur* 74-82; Sec Dioc Bd for Miss and Unity 82-88; P-in-c Croxdale 82-88; P-in-c Leamington Hastings and Birdingbury *Cov* 88-96; rtd 96; Perm to Office *Cov* and *Glouc* from 96. *8 Greenways, Winchcombe, Cheltenham GL54 5LG* Tel (01242) 602195

STEVINSON, Mrs Josephine Mary. b 25. STh56. Cranmer Hall Dur 86. **dss** 86 **d** 87 **p** 94. Croxdale *Dur* 86-87; Lic to Offic 87-88; Lic to Offic *Cov* 88-96; NSM Leamington Hastings and Birdingbury 94-96; rtd 96; Perm to Offic *Glouc* from 96. *8 Greenways, Winchcombe, Cheltenham GL54 5LG* Tel (01242) 602195

STEWARD, Mrs Linda Christine. b 46. NE Lon Poly CQSW82. S'wark Ord Course 85. **d** 88 **p** 94. NSM E Ham w Upton Park St Alb *Chelmsf* 88-91; Chapl Newham Healthcare NHS Trust Lon 91-98; NSM Plaistow *Chelmsf* 91-96; NSM Plaistow and N Canning Town 96-98; P-in-c Rawreth w Rettendon from 98. *The Rectory, Church Road, Rawreth, Wickford SS11 8SH* Tel (01268) 766766 E-mail steward.linda@hotmail.com

STEWART, Alan. *See* STEWART, Hugh Alan

STEWART, Alan Valentine. b 47. CGLI Lic94 Univ Coll Galway BA98. **d** 97 **p** 98. C Mullingar, Portnashangan, Moyliscar, Kilbixy etc *M & K* 97-00; C Clane w Donadea and Coolcarrigan

from 00. *Baltrasna, Ashbourne, Co Meath, Irish Republic* Tel (00353) (1) 835 0997 *or* 814 0236
E-mail alanstewart@fasfinglas.ie

STEWART, Alexander Butler. b 25. TCD Dip Bibl Studies. **d** 58 **p** 59. C Holywood *D & D* 58-61; Miss to Seamen 61-64; Portuguese E Africa 61-64; I Donagh *D & R* 64-65; I Helen's Bay *D & D* 65-72; I Donegal w Killymard, Lough Eske and Laghey *D & R* 72-90; Can Raphoe Cathl 81-90; rtd 90; Lic to Offic *D & D* from 90. *12 Annes Court, Bangor BT20 3SX* Tel (028) 9145 7666

STEWART, Alice Elizabeth. b 42. **d** 00 **p** 01. C Cloughfern *Conn* from 00. *3 Fergus Court, Carrickfergus BT38 8HT* Tel (028) 9336 5721

STEWART (née BARBER), Mrs Anne Louise. b 71. QUB BA93 PGCE94. CITC 97. **d** 00 **p** 01. C Belfast Malone St Jo *Conn* from 00. *St George's Rectory, 28 Myrtlefield Park, Belfast BT9 6NF* Tel (028) 9066 7134 Mobile 07833-116512
E-mail stewartrevslb@yahoo.com

STEWART, Miss Betty. b 25. S'wark Ord Course 91. **d** 93 **p** 94. NSM Wandsworth Common St Mary *S'wark* 93-95; Asst P Hampton Hill *Lon* from 95. *71 Ormond Drive, Hampton TW12 2TL* Tel (020) 8979 2069

STEWART, Brian. b 59. BTh. **d** 91 **p** 92. C Ballywillan *Conn* 91-94; I Belfast St Geo from 94; Bp's Dom Chapl from 94; OCF from 00. *St George's Rectory, 28 Myrtlefield Park, Belfast BT9 6NF* Tel (028) 9066 7134 *or* 9023 1275

STEWART, Canon Charles. b 55. St Jo Coll Cam BA77 MA81 CertEd79. Wycliffe Hall Ox 85. **d** 87 **p** 88. C Bowdon *Ches* 87-90; C Bath Abbey w St Jas *B & W* 90-94; Can Res, Prec and Sacr Win Cathl *Win* from 94. *8 The Close, Winchester SO23 9LS* Tel and fax (01962) 856236 *or* 857211
E-mail charles.stewart@winchester-cathedral.org.uk

STEWART, Hugh Alan. b 67. Lon Inst BA91 Middx Univ BA03. Lon Bible Coll 96 NTMTC 00. **d** 03 **p** 04. C Gt Stanmore *Lon* from 03. *St John's House, 16 The Chase, Stanmore HA7 3RY* Tel (020) 8954 2627 E-mail h.alanstewart@tiscali.co.uk

STEWART, Canon Ian Guild. b 43. Edin Th Coll 89. **d** 84 **p** 85. NSM Dundee St Mary Magd *Bre* 84-87; NSM Dundee St Jo 87-90; C 90-92; NSM Dundee St Martin 87-90; C 90-92; R Montrose from 92; P-in-c Inverbervie from 92; Can St Paul's Cathl Dundee from 01. *The Rectory, 17 Panmure Place, Montrose DD10 8ER* Tel (01674) 672652

STEWART, James. *See* STEWART, Malcolm James

STEWART, James. b 32. Div Hostel Dub. **d** 69 **p** 70. C Belfast St Donard *D & D* 69-72; C Dundonald 72-74; I Rathmullan w Tyrella 74-80; I Belfast St Clem 80-97; I Moy w Charlemont *Arm* 97-04; rtd 04. *25 Barnish Road, Kells, Ballymena BT42 3PA* Tel (028) 2589 8787 Mobile 07833-791790
E-mail rev.jstewart@btopenworld.com

STEWART, Canon James Patrick. b 55. Keele Univ BA77 Birm Univ MA78. Ridley Hall Cam 86. **d** 88 **p** 89. C Boulton *Derby* 88-91; C Cove St Jo *Guildf* 91-92; TV 92-97; TR Tunbridge Wells St Jas w St Phil *Roch* 97-04; V Tunbridge Wells St Jas from 04; RD Tunbridge Wells from 99; Hon Can Roch Cathl from 05. *The Vicarage, 12 Shandon Close, Tunbridge Wells TN2 3RE* Tel and fax (01892) 530687 E-mail jimstewart@britlinks.co.uk

STEWART, James Richard. b 71. St Jo Coll Ox BA93 MA99. Cranmer Hall Dur BA98 DMS99. **d** 99 **p** 00. C Consett *Dur* 99-02; TV Kidderminster St Jo and H Innocents *Worc* from 02. *143 Sutton Park Road, Kidderminster DY11 6JQ* Tel (01562) 820678 E-mail jimthevic@hotmail.com

STEWART, Mrs Janet Margaret. b 41. Roehampton Inst CertEd62. Cranmer Hall Dur 67. **d** 87 **p** 94. Hon Par Dn Oulton Broad *Nor* 87-94; Hon C 94-97; Chapl Lowestoft Hosp 94-97; Perm to Offic *B & W* 97-98; C Quidenham Gp *Nor* 98-01; Asst Chapl Norfolk and Nor Univ Hosp NHS Trust from 00. *30 St Joseph's Road, Sheringham NR26 8JA* Tel (01263) 824497

STEWART, John. b 39. Oak Hill Th Coll 75. **d** 77 **p** 78. C Accrington Ch Ch *Blackb* 77-79; TV Darwen St Pet w Hoddlesden 79-86; R Coppull St Jo 86-04; rtd 04. *55 Bolton Road, Chorley PR7 3AU*

✠**STEWART, The Rt Revd John Craig.** b 40. Ridley Coll Melbourne LTh64. **d** 65 **p** 66 **c** 84. Australia 65-68 and from 70; C Prospect 65-67; C Mt Gambier 67-68; C Crawley *Chich* 68-70; I Frankston E 74-79; Gen Sec CMS Vic 79-84; Asst Bp Melbourne 84-01; W Region 84-91; N Region 91-94; E Region 94-01; V Gen 88-01; R Woodend 01-04; rtd 04. *PO Box 928, Bacchus Marsh, Vic, Australia 3440* Tel (0061) (3) 5367 0081
E-mail bishopjcstewart@bigpond.com

STEWART, Canon John Roberton. b 29. Sarum Th Coll 63. **d** 65 **p** 66. C Gillingham *Sarum* 65-70; R Langton Matravers 70-84; RD Purbeck 82-89; Can and Preb Sarum Cathl 83-90; R Kingston, Langton Matravers and Worth Matravers 84-90; Can Res Sarum Cathl 90-95; Treas 90-95; rtd 95; Perm to Offic *Sarum* from 95. *Hillrise, 26 Durlston Road, Swanage BH19 2HX* Tel (01929) 422802

STEWART, Canon John Wesley. b 52. QUB BD76 TCD 76. **d** 77 **p** 78. C Seagoe *D & D* 77-79; C Lisburn Ch Ch *Conn* 79-85; I Ballybay w Mucknoe and Clontibret *Clogh* 85-90; I Derryvullen S w Garvary from 90; Bp Dom Chapl 95-00; Glebes Sec from 95; Dioc Registrar from 98; Exam Can Clogh Cathl 98-00; Preb from 00. *The Rectory, Tullyharney, Enniskillen BT74 4PR* Tel and fax (028) 6638 7236
E-mail jva.stewart@care4free.net

STEWART, Louise. *See* STEWART, Mrs Anne Louise

STEWART, Malcolm James. b 44. TD78. York Univ BA66 K Coll Lon MA68 Lon Inst of Educn PGCE69 Solicitor 79. NEOC 89. **d** 93 **p** 94. NSM Upper Nidderdale *Ripon* 93-95; C Fountains Gp 95-98; V Catterick 98-03; P-in-c Culmington w Onibury, Bromfield etc *Heref* from 03. *The Vicarage, Bromfield, Ludlow SY8 2JP* Tel (01584) 856625

STEWART, Marcus Patrick Michael. b 66. Ox Univ BA89 MSc93 Cam Univ BA92. Ven English Coll Rome 89 Westcott Ho Cam 96. **d** 98 **p** 99. C Headington *Ox* 98-00; Hon C S Hinksey 00-01; CF 01-04; Chapl RN from 04. *Royal Naval Chaplaincy Service, Room 203, Victory Building, HM Naval Base, Portsmouth PO1 3LS* Tel (01705) 727903 Fax 727112

STEWART, Maxwell Neville Gabriel. b 33. Hertf Coll Ox BA58. Wycliffe Hall Ox DipTh59. **d** 60 **p** 61. C Perry Beeches *Birm* 60-62; Chapl Rosenberg Coll St Gallen 62-64; Perm to Offic *Chelmsf* 64-70; Warden Leics Poly 70-92; De Montfort Univ Leic 92-93; Hon C Leic St Mary *Leic* 74-79; Perm to Offic from 79; rtd 98. *25 Sidney Court, Norwich Road, Leicester LE4 0LR*

STEWART, Michael. b 65. St Jo Coll Nottm LTh89. **d** 89 **p** 90. C Ealing St Paul *Lon* 89-93; P-in-c N Wembley St Cuth 93-98; V 98-02; Assoc P Abbotsford Canada from 02. *St Matthew's Anglican Church, 2010 Guilford Drive, Abbotsford BC, Canada, V2S 5R2* E-mail mikes@stmatthewsanglicanchurch.com

STEWART, Canon Raymond John. b 55. TCD BA79 MA82. CITC Div Test77. **d** 79 **p** 80. C Clooney *D & R* 79-82; I Dunfanaghy 82-87; I Gweedore Union 85-87; Dioc Youth Adv 83-87; Bp's Dom Chapl 85-87; I Castledawson 87-03; I Tamlaght O'Crilly Upper w Lower from 03; Ed *D & R Dioc News* 89-93; Dioc Glebes Sec from 93; Stewardship Adv from 98; Can Derry Cathl from 99. *Hervey Hill Rectory, 16 Hervey Hill, Kilrea, Coleraine BT51 5TT* Tel and fax (028) 2954 0296 Mobile 07761-585412

STEWART, Stephen John. b 62. Oak Hill Th Coll. **d** 99 **p** 00. C Mile Cross *Nor* 99-04; TV Cove St Jo *Guildf* from 04. *Southwood Vicarage, 15 The Copse, Farnborough GU14 0QD* Tel (01252) 513422 E-mail stevestewartce@hotmail.com

STEWART, Susan Theresa. b 58. N Ord Course 01. **d** 04 **p** 05. C Lodge Moor St Luke *Sheff* from 04. *29 Worcester Road, Sheffield S10 4JH* Tel 0114-229 5813 Mobile 07966-695095

STEWART, William. **d** 01 **p** 02. NSM Kilroot and Templecorran *Conn* from 01. *63 Victoria Road, Carrickfergus BT38 7JJ* Tel (028) 9336 2145

STEWART, William James. b 58. BA. CITC DipTh. **d** 83 **p** 84. C Glenageary *D & G* 83-86; Rostrevor Renewal Cen 86-87; I Naas w Kill and Rathmore *M & K* 87-93; Min Dublin Ch Ch Cathl Gp *D & G* 93-04; CORE (St Cath Ch) 93-04; Chapl Rotunda Hosp 94-99; Chapl Dub Coll of Catering 94-04; Min Can St Patr Cathl Dublin 00-04. *Address temp unknown*

STEWART, William Jones. b 32. Trin Hall Cam BA55 MA59 Cam Univ CertEd56. Edin Th Coll 67. **d** 69 **p** 69. Chapl St Ninian's Cathl Perth *St And* 69-71; Bp's Dom Chapl *Ox* 71-75; V Lambourn 75-03; P-in-c Lambourne Woodlands 83-90; P-in-c Eastbury and E Garston 83-03; rtd 04. *9 Ascott Way, Newbury RG14 2FH* Tel (01635) 580244
E-mail stewart.clan4@btopenworld.com

STEWART-DARLING, Fiona Lesley. b 58. Kingston Poly GRSC79 Lon Univ PhD82 K Coll Lon MA99. Trin Coll Bris BA91. **d** 91 **p** 94. C Cirencester *Glouc* 91-94; Chapl Cheltenham and Glouc Coll of HE 94-97; Chapl Portsm Univ *Portsm* 97-04; Hon Chapl Portsm Cathl 97-04; Bp's Chapl in Docklands *Lon* from 04. *164 St Leonard's Road, London E14 6PW* Tel 07739-461090 (mobile)
E-mail fiona.stewart-darling@port.ac.uk

STEWART ELLENS, Gordon Frederick. *See* ELLENS, Gordon Frederick Stewart

STEWART-SYKES, Alistair Charles. b 60. St Andr Univ MA83 Birm Univ PhD92. Qu Coll Birm 86. **d** 89 **p** 90. C Stevenage St Andr and St Geo *St Alb* 89-92; C Castle Vale St Cuth *Birm* 92-93; Barbados 93-96; Assoc Min Hanley H Ev *Lich* 97-98; USA 98-01; V Sturminster Marshall, Kingston Lacy and Shapwick *Sarum* from 01. *The Vicarage, Newton Road, Sturminster Marshall, Wimborne BH21 4BT* Tel (01258) 857255 Fax 08701-358049 E-mail alistairstewartsykes@fish.co.uk

STEWART-SYKES, Teresa Melanie. b 64. Bris Univ BA85. Qu Coll Birm 87. **d** 89. Par Dn Stevenage St Andr and St Geo *St Alb* 89-92; Perm to Offic *Birm* 92-93; Barbados 93-97; C Meir Heath *Lich* 97-98; USA 98-01. *The Vicarage, Newton Road, Sturminster Marshall, Wimborne BH21 4BT* Tel (01258) 857255

STEYNOR, Victor Albert. b 15. Southn Univ DipEd62. S'wark Ord Course 68. **d** 71 **p** 72. C Bognor *Chich* 71-75; P-in-c Kenton and Ashfield w Thorpe *St E* 75-81; P-in-c Aspall 75-81; V

Debenham 75-81; V Debenham w Aspall and Kenton 81-82; rtd 82; Perm to Offic *St E* 82-03. *57 Denmark Road, Beccles NR34 9DL* Tel (01502) 711433

STIBBE, Mrs Hazel Mary. **d** 99 **p** 00. NSM Wolverhampton St Andr *Lich* 99-02; Lic to Offic *St As* from 03. *Braemar, Kerry Street, Montgomery SY15 6PG* Tel (01686) 668912

STIBBE, Mark William Godfrey. b 60. Trin Coll Cam BA83 MA86 Nottm Univ PhD88. St Jo Coll Nottm 83. **d** 86 **p** 87. C Stapleford *S'well* 86-90; C Crookes St Thos *Sheff* 90-93; Lect Sheff Univ 90-97; V Grenoside 93-97; V Chorleywood St Andr *St Alb* from 97. *St Andrew's Vicarage, 37 Quickley Lane, Chorleywood, Rickmansworth WD3 5AE* Tel (01923) 447111 Fax 447200 E-mail markstibbe@aol.com

STICKLAND, David Clifford. b 44. Surrey Univ BA01 CPFA68 MAAT77 FCCA80. STETS 98. **d** 01 **p** 02. NSM Greatham w Empshott and Hawkley w Prior's Dean *Portsm* from 01; Chapl Defence, Science and Tech Laboratory and QinetiQ from 02. *The Barn, Jolly Robins, Hawkley, Liss GU33 6NQ* Tel (01730) 827355 Mobile 07836-282561 Fax 827652 E-mail david_stickland@talk21.com

STICKLAND, Geoffrey John Brett. b 42. Open Univ BSc96. St D Coll Lamp. **d** 66 **p** 67. C Aberavon H Trin *Llan* 66-69; C-in-c Llanrumney CD *Mon* 69-72; C Tetbury w Beverston *Glouc* 72-75; V Hardwicke 75-82; R Hardwicke, Quedgeley and Elmore w Longney 82-98; V Quedgeley from 98. *The Rectory, School Lane, Quedgeley, Gloucester GL2 6PN* Tel (01452) 720411 E-mail geoffstickland@hotmail.com

STICKLEY, Mrs Annette Frances. b 44. Bp Otter Coll Chich 67. **d** 00. NSM Worth *Chich* from 00. *12 Woodlands, Pound Hill, Crawley RH10 3DL* Tel (01293) 873023

STIDOLPH, Canon Robert Anthony. b 54. GBSM76 ARCM75 FRSA92. St Steph Ho Ox 77. **d** 80 **p** 80. C Hove All SS *Chich* 80-84; TV Brighton Resurr 84-87; Chapl Cheltenham Coll 87-94; Sen Chapl and Hd RS Wellington Coll Berks 94-01; Hon Can Ch Ch *Ox* 00-04; Chapl and Asst Master Radley Coll 01-05; P-in-c Worth *Chich* from 05. *The Rectory, Church Road, Worth, Crawley RH10 7RT* Tel (01293) 882229

STIEVENARD, Alphonse Etienne Arthur. b 13. Selw Coll Cam BA36 MA40. Lon Coll of Div 36. **d** 37 **p** 38. C Northwood Em *Lon* 37-40; P-in-c Southborough St Pet *Roch* 40-44; V Leyton Ch Ch *Chelmsf* 44-51; V Jersey Millbrook St Matt *Win* 51-78; rtd 78; Perm to Offic *Win* from 78. *Le Ruisselet, Mont Rossignol, St Ouen, Jersey JE3 2LN* Tel (01534) 481215

STIFF, Canon Derrick Malcolm. b 40. Lich Th Coll 69. **d** 72 **p** 73. C Cov St Geo *Cov* 72-75; R Benhall w Sternfield *St E* 75-79; P-in-c Snape w Friston 75-79; V Cartmel *Carl* 79-87; R Sudbury and Chilton *St E* 87-94; P-in-c Lavenham 94-95; P-in-c Preston 94-95; R Lavenham w Preston 95-03; Min Can St E Cathl 90-00; Hon Can 00-03; RD Lavenham 95-03; rtd 03; Perm to Offic *St E* and *Sarum* from 03. *9 Fisherton Island, Salisbury SP2 7TG* Tel (01722) 320177 E-mail canonstiff@hotmail.com

STILEMAN, William Mark Charles. b 63. Selw Coll Cam BA85 MA89 PGCE86. Wycliffe Hall Ox. **d** 91 **p** 92. C Ox St Andr *Ox* 91-95; TV Gt Chesham 95-03; P-in-c Maidenhead St Andr and St Mary from 03. *St Mary's Vicarage, 14 Juniper Drive, Maidenhead SL6 8RE* Tel (01628) 624908

STILL, Colin Charles. b 35. Selw Coll Cam BA67 MA71. Cranmer Hall Dur DipTh68 United Th Sem Dayton STM69. **d** 69 **p** 70. C Drypool St Columba w St Andr and St Pet *York* 69-72; Abp's Dom Chapl 72-75; Recruitment Sec ACCM 76-80; P-in-c Ockham w Hatchford *Guildf* 76-80; R 80-90; Can Missr and Ecum Officer 80-90; Perm to Offic *Chich* from 92; rtd 96. *Flat 9, 16 Lewes Crescent, Brighton BN2 1GB* Tel (01273) 686014

STILL (née STACEY), Mrs Gillian. b 53. SW Minl Tr Course 94. **d** 97 **p** 98. NSM Peter Tavy, Mary Tavy, Lydford and Brent Tor *Ex* from 97. *The Rectory, Lydford, Okehampton EX20 4BH* Tel (01822) 820479 Mobile 07971-412511 E-mail gill_still@hotmail.com

STILL, Jonathan Trevor Lloyd. b 59. Ex Univ BA81 Qu Coll Cam BA84 MA88. Westcott Ho Cam 82. **d** 85 **p** 86. C Weymouth H Trin *Sarum* 85-88; Chapl for Agric *Heref* 88-93; V N Petherton w Northmoor Green *B & W* 93-00; V The Bourne and Tilford *Guildf* from 00; RD Farnham from 05. *The Vicarage, 2 Middle Avenue, Farnham GU9 8JL* Tel and fax (01252) 715505 E-mail jonstill@fish.co.uk

STILL, Kenneth Donald. b 37. St Aid Birkenhead 64. **d** 67 **p** 95. C Ainsdale *Liv* 67-68; C Kirkby 68-69; C Sutton 96-98; TV 98-03; rtd 03. *The Cottage, Wash Road, Kirton, Boston PE20 1QG* Tel (01205) 724043

STILLMAN, Roger John. b 47. St Steph Ho Ox 81. **d** 83 **p** 84. C St Helier *S'wark* 83-88; TV Rochdale *Man* 88-94; P-in-c Wokingham St Paul *Ox* 94-00; R 00-04; Chapl W Berks Priority Care Services NHS Trust 95-04. *13 Old School Place, Banbury OX16 4UB* Tel (01295) 257237 E-mail roger.stillman@btopenworld.com

STILLWELL, Wayne Anthony. b 68. Univ of Greenwich BA91. Oak Hill Th Coll 94. **d** 96 **p** 97. C Necton, Holme Hale w N and S Pickenham *Nor* 96-98; C Eastbourne H Trin *Chich* 98-03; V Chaddesden St Mary *Derby* from 03. *St Mary's Vicarage, 133 Chaddesden Lane, Chaddesden, Derby DE21 6LL* Tel (01332) 280924 E-mail w.stillwell@virgin.net

STILWELL, Malcolm Thomas. b 54. Coll of Resurr Mirfield 83. **d** 86 **p** 87. C Workington St Mich *Carl* 86-90; P-in-c Flimby 90-93; Perm to Offic 93-95; NSM Westfield St Mary from 95. *18 Moorfield Avenue, Workington CA14 4HJ* Tel (01900) 66757

STILWELL, Timothy James. b 65. Birm Univ BA87. Wycliffe Hall Ox 96. **d** 98 **p** 99. C Clifton Ch Ch w Em *Bris* 98-02; C Hammersmith St Paul *Lon* from 02. *30 Rannoch Road, London W6 9SR* Tel (020) 7385 5820 *or* 8746 5252 E-mail tim.stilwell@sph.org

STIMPSON, Nigel Leslie. b 60. St Martin's Coll Lanc BA92. Coll of Resurr Mirfield 94. **d** 94 **p** 95. C Heyhouses on Sea *Blackb* 94-96; C Torrisholme 96-99; V Ravensthorpe and Thornhill Lees w Savile Town *Wakef* from 99; TR Ribbleton *Blackb* from 05. *The Rectory, 238 Ribbleton Avenue, Ribbleton, Preston PR2 6QP* Tel (01772) 791747 E-mail nls@dircon.co.uk

STINSON, William Gordon. b 29. Lon Univ BSc50. Ely Th Coll 51. **d** 52 **p** 53. C Kingston upon Hull St Alb *York* 52-56; Br Guiana 56-61; V E and W Ravendale w Hatcliffe *Linc* 61-67; R Beelsby 61-67; P-in-c Ashby w Fenby and Brigsley 62-66; R 66-67; V New Cleethorpes 67-76; RD Grimsby and Cleethorpes 73-76; P-in-c Dovercourt *Chelmsf* 76-83; TR Dovercourt and Parkeston 83-91; RD Harwich 87-91; V Gosfield 91-95; rtd 95; Perm to Offic *Chelmsf* and *St E* from 95. *14 The Columbines, Melford Road, Cavendish, Sudbury CO10 8AB* Tel (01787) 281381

STIRK, Peter Francis. b 24. Linc Coll Ox BA49 MA53. Qu Coll Birm 49. **d** 50 **p** 51. C Beeston *Ripon* 50-68; P-in-c Kirby-on-the-Moor 68-71; V 71-81; P-in-c Cundall 73-81; V Kirby-on-the-Moor, Cundall w Norton-le-Clay etc 81-90; rtd 90. *Devonshire Cottage, Marton le Moor, Ripon HG4 5DJ* Tel (01423) 322330

STIRLING, Mrs Christina Dorita (Tina). b 48. Lon Univ BEd73. Wycliffe Hall Ox 87. **d** 89 **p** 94. Par Dn Thame w Towersey *Ox* 89-94; C 94-98; P-in-c Brill, Boarstall, Chilton and Dorton 98; R Bernwode from 98. *The Vicarage, 7 High Street, Brill, Aylesbury HP18 9ST* Tel (01844) 238325 Fax as telephone

STOCK, Lionel Crispian. b 58. ACMA85 ACIS94. Linc Th Coll BTh94. **d** 94 **p** 95. C Preston w Sutton Poyntz and Osmington w Poxwell *Sarum* 94-97; P-in-c Stalbridge 97-00; Hon C Hillingdon All SS *Lon* 01-05. *24 Ruskin Close, Kendal LA9 7LA* E-mail 106101.545@compuserve.com

STOCK, Nigel. *See* STOCK, The Rt Revd William Nigel

STOCK, Miss Ruth Vaughan. b 51. Birkbeck Coll Lon BA79 MA85. Wycliffe Hall Ox 91. **d** 93 **p** 94. Par Dn Toxteth St Philemon w St Gabr and St Cleopas *Liv* 93-94; C 94-97; TV from 97. *St Gabriel's Vicarage, 2 Steble Street, Liverpool L8 6QH* Tel 0151-708 7751

STOCK, The Very Revd Victor Andrew. b 44. AKC68 FRSA95. **d** 69 **p** 70. C Pinner *Lon* 69-73; Chapl Lon Univ 73-79; R Friern Barnet St Jas 79-86; R St Mary le Bow w St Pancras Soper Lane etc 86-02; P-in-c St Mary Aldermary 87-98; Dean Guildf from 02. *The Deanery, 1 Cathedral Close, Guildford GU2 7TL* Tel (01483) 560328 *or* 565287 Fax 303350 E-mail dean@guildford-cathedral.org

✠**STOCK, The Rt Revd William Nigel.** b 50. St Cuth Soc Dur BA72. Ripon Coll Cuddesdon DipTh75. **d** 76 **p** 77 **c** 00. C Stockton St Pet *Dur* 76-79; Papua New Guinea 79-84; V Shiremoor *Newc* 85-91; TR N Shields 91-98; RD Tynemouth 92-98; Hon Can Newc Cathl 97-98; Can Res Dur Cathl *Dur* 98-00; Chapl Grey Coll Dur 99-00; Suff Bp Stockport *Ches* from 00. *Bishop's Lodge, Back Lane, Dunham Town, Altrincham WA14 4SG* Tel 0161-928 5611 Fax 929 0692 E-mail bpstockport@chester.anglican.org

STOCK-HESKETH, Jonathan Philip. b 49. St Chad's Coll Dur BA Cam Univ CertEd Nottm Univ MTh PhD93 Dip Psychology 98. St Steph Ho Ox. **d** 83 **p** 84. C Leic St Phil *Leic* 83-86; C Loughborough Em 86-89; Lect Nottm Univ 95-04. *Address temp unknown* E-mail jshesketh@aol.com

STOCKBRIDGE, Alan Carmichael. b 33. MBE89. Keble Coll Ox BA55 MA62. Wycliffe Hall Ox 66. **d** 68 **p** 69. CF 68-78 and 82-92; Chapl Reading Sch 78-82; R Harrietsham w Ulcombe *Cant* 92-98; rtd 98; Perm to Offic *Eur* from 00. *R165, Avenida 5, S'algar, Menorca, Spain* Tel (0034) (971) 359833 Fax as telephone

STOCKBRIDGE, Nelson William. b 35. Trin Th Coll Auckland 61. **d** 84 **p** 85. New Zealand 85-86; C Shildon w Eldon *Dur* 87; C Norton St Mary 87-88; C Cottingham *York* 88-91; V Aldbrough, Mappleton w Goxhill and Withernwick 91-96; C Baildon *Bradf* 96-01; rtd 01; New Zealand from 02. *3 Alison Street, Rotorua, New Zealand 3201* Tel (0064) (7) 348 7327 E-mail nelsonandruth@xtra.co.nz

STOCKER, David William George. b 37. Bris Univ BA58 CertEd. Qu Coll Birm 59. **d** 60 **p** 61. C Sparkhill St Jo *Birm* 60-64; C Keighley *Bradf* 64-66; V Grenoside *Sheff* 66-83; V Sandbach *Ches* 83-01; rtd 01; Perm to Offic *Ches* from 01. *18 Mill Bridge Close, Crewe CW1 5DZ* Tel (01270) 212865

STOCKER, John Henry. b 48. Cov Univ BSc71 Sheff Univ BEd81 ACP88. St Mich Coll Llan 01. **d** 04 **p** 05. NSM Knighton, Norton, Whitton, Pilleth and Cascob *S & B* from 04. *Nantgaredig, Slough Lane, Presteigne LD8 2NH* Tel (01544) 267050 Mobile 07891-086631 E-mail johnstocker@supanet.com

STOCKER, Rachael Ann. *See* KNAPP, Mrs Rachael Ann

STOCKITT, Robin Philip. b 56. Liv Univ BA77 Crewe & Alsager Coll PGCE78 Open Univ Dip Special Needs 90. Ridley Hall Cam CTM95. **d** 97 **p** 98. C Billing *Pet* 97-01; P-in-c Freiburg-im-Breisau *Eur* from 01; Asst Chapl Basle from 01. *Am Kohlbach 16, 79199 Kirchzarten Burg-Hofen, Freiburg, Germany*

STOCKLEY, Mrs Alexandra Madeleine Reuss. b 43. Cranmer Hall Dur 80 Carl Dioc Tr Inst. **dss** 84 **d** 87 **p** 94. Upperby St Jo *Carl* 84-89; Par Dn 87-89; Dn-in-c Grayrigg, Old Hutton and New Hutton 90-94; P-in-c 94-95; P-in-c Levens 95-03; rtd 03; Perm to Offic *Carl* from 03. *Crowberry, Ulpha, Broughton-in-Furness LA20 6DZ* Tel (01229) 716875

STOCKLEY, Roland. b 23. St Jo Coll Dur BA47 DipTh49. **d** 49 **p** 50. C Rainbow Hill St Barn *Worc* 49-52; CF 52-57; V Broadwaters *Worc* 57-66; V Himbleton w Huddington 66-68; R Pedmore 68-88; rtd 88; Perm to Offic *Lich* and *Worc* from 90. *64 Hyperion Road, Stourbridge DY7 6SB* Tel (01384) 393463

STOCKPORT, Suffragan Bishop of. *See* STOCK, The Rt Revd William Nigel

STOCKS, Simon Paul. b 68. Rob Coll Cam BA89 MA93. Trin Coll Bris BA03. **d** 04 **p** 05. C Coulsdon St Jo *S'wark* from 04. *8 Waddington Avenue, Coulsdon CR5 1QE* Tel (01737) 553217 E-mail simon@spstocks.freeserve.co.uk

STOCKTON, Ian George. b 49. Selw Coll Cam BA72 MA76 Hull Univ PhD90. St Jo Coll Nottm PGCE74. **d** 75 **p** 76. C Chell *Lich* 75-78; C Trentham 78-80; R Dalbeattie *Glas* 80-84; P-in-c Scotton w Northorpe *Linc* 84-88; Asst Local Min Officer 84-88; Local Min Officer and LNSM Course Prin 88-97; TR Monkwearmouth *Dur* from 97. *The Rectory, 2A Park Avenue, Sunderland SR6 9PU* Tel 0191-548 6607 *or* 516 0135 E-mail ian.stockton@durham.anglican.org

STOCKWELL, John Nicholas. b 49. Trin Coll Bris 80. **d** 82 **p** 83. C Flixton St Jo *Man* 82-86; V Accrington Ch Ch *Blackb* 86-90; R Chulmleigh *Ex* 90-93; R Chawleigh w Cheldon 90-93; R Wembworthy w Eggesford 90-93; P-in-c Burwash Weald *Chich* 93-97; rtd 01. *23 John Street, Southampton SO14 3DR* Tel (023) 8033 3357 E-mail jnstockwell@aol.com

STODDART, David Easton. b 36. K Coll Dur BSc60 PhD66 CEng66 MIMechE66 FCMI72 FIQA76. WEMTC 92. **d** 95 **p** 96. OLM Stroud H Trin *Glouc* 95-99; OLM Woodchester and Brimscombe 99-00; NSM from 00; Jt Angl Chapl Severn NHS Trust from 99. *Dunelm, Pinfarthings, Amberley, Stroud GL5 5JJ* Tel (01453) 833028

STOKE-ON-TRENT, Archdeacon of. *See* STONE, The Ven Godfrey Owen

STOKER, Andrew. b 64. Coll of Ripon & York St Jo BA86. Coll of Resurr Mirfield 87. **d** 90 **p** 91. C Horton *Newc* 90-92; C Clifford *York* 92-96; P-in-c Cawood 96-98; P-in-c Ryther 96-98; P-in-c Wistow 96-98; R Cawood w Ryther and Wistow 98-04; P-in-c York St Clem w St Mary Bishophill Senior 04-05; R York St Clem w St Mary Bishophill from 05. *13 Nunthorpe Avenue, York YO23 1PF* Tel (01904) 624425

STOKER, Howard Charles. b 62. Linc Th Coll BTh93. **d** 93 **p** 94. C Hessle *York* 93-96; C Richmond w Hudswell *Ripon* 96-99; C Downholme and Marske 96-99; R Holt w High Kelling *Nor* from 99; RD Holt from 05. *The Rectory, 11 Church Street, Holt NR25 6BB* Tel (01263) 712048 Fax 711397 E-mail holtrectory@dialstart.com

STOKER, Mrs Joanna Mary. b 57. Leic Univ BA79 Nottm Univ BCombStuds83. Linc Th Coll 80. **dss** 83 **d** 87 **p** 94. Greenford H Cross *Lon* 83-87; Par Dn 87-89; Par Dn Farnham Royal w Hedgerley *Ox* 89-92; Dn-in-c Seer Green and Jordans 92-94; P-in-c 94-97; TV Stantonbury and Willen 97-03; TR Basingstoke *Win* from 03. *The Rectory, Church Street, Basingstoke RG21 7QT* Tel (01256) 326654 E-mail jostoker@jstoker29.freeserve.co.uk

STOKES, Albert Edward. b 21. TCD BA43 MA46 BD46. CITC 43. **d** 46 **p** 47. Lect Ch of Ireland Coll of Educn Dub 49-79; I Powerscourt w Kilbride and Annacrevy *D & G* 56-86; Ch Ch Cathl Dublin 70-86; rtd 86. *Cotehele, The Riverwalk, Ashford, Wicklow, Irish Republic* Tel (00353) (404) 40360

STOKES, Canon Andrew John. b 38. G&C Coll Cam BA60 MA64. Ripon Hall Ox 60. **d** 62 **p** 63. C Northampton All SS w St Kath *Pet* 62-65; C Endcliffe *Sheff* 65-68; Ind Missr 65-68; Sen Ind Chapl 69-74; P-in-c Bridport *Sarum* 75-79; TR 79-80; V Holbeach Marsh *Linc* 82-88; Bp's Dom Chapl 88-92; Can Res and Prec Linc Cathl 92-03; rtd 03; Perm to Offic *Linc* from 03. *2 Lupin Road, Lincoln LN2 4GD* Tel (01522) 537595 E-mail andrew.stokes@ntlworld.com

STOKES, Colin Arthur (Ted). b 59. Birm Univ BDS82. WEMTC 00. **d** 03 **p** 04. NSM Bromyard *Heref* from 03. *Solmor Paddocks, Linley Green Road, Whitbourne, Worcester WR6 5RE* Tel (01886) 821625

STOKES, David Francis Robert. b 53. Lon Inst of Educn PGCE76 Peterho Cam MA81 Trin Coll Bris BA87. Cranmer Hall Dur 01. **d** 03 **p** 04. C Salisbury St Mark *Sarum* from 03. *4 St Joseph's Close, Bishopdown, Salisbury SP1 3FX* Tel (01722) 327426 E-mail dsjs_stokes@lineone.net

STOKES, Miss Mary Patricia. b 39. St Hilda's Coll Ox BA62 MA66 Lanc Univ MA80 Bris Univ CertEd63. EMMTC 78. **d** 87 **p** 94. Par Dn Pheasey *Lich* 87-93; C Walton-on-Thames *Guildf* 93-05; rtd 05. *21 Brittain Road, Walton-on-Thames KT12 4LR* Tel (01932) 248945 E-mail marystokes1@excite.co.uk

STOKES, Michael John. b 34. Lich Th Coll 63. **d** 65 **p** 66. C Worplesdon *Guildf* 65-68; Chapl RAF 68-84; Asst Chapl-in-Chief RAF 84-89; QHC 87-95; V Chesterton w Middleton Stoney and Wendlebury *Ox* 89-95; RD Bicester and Islip 90-95; Chapl Kyrenia St Andr Cyprus 95-00; rtd 00; Perm to Offic *Ox* from 00. *Keeper's Cottage, Manor Farm Lane, Chesterton, Bicester OX25 1UD* Tel and fax (01869) 248744

STOKES, Roger Sidney. b 47. Clare Coll Cam BA68 MA72. Sarum & Wells Th Coll 69. **d** 72 **p** 73. C Keighley *Bradf* 72-74; C Bolton St Jas w St Chrys 74-78; V Hightown *Wakef* 78-85; Dep Chapl HM Pris Wakef 85-87; Chapl HM Pris Full Sutton 87-89; Perm to Offic *Wakef* 92-95; P-in-c Carlinghow 95-99; P-in-c Bedford St Martin *St Alb* from 99. *St Martin's Vicarage, 76 Clapham Road, Bedford MK41 7PN* Tel (01234) 357862 E-mail r.s.stokes.65@cantab.net

STOKES, Simon Colin. b 62. Nene Coll Northampton BSc83. Ridley Hall Cam CTM92. **d** 92 **p** 93. C New Catton Ch Ch *Nor* 92-96; P-in-c King's Lynn St Jo the Ev from 96; Chapl Coll of W Anglia from 01. *St John's Vicarage, Blackfriars Road, King's Lynn PE30 1NT* Tel (01553) 773034 E-mail simon@simonstokes.co.uk

STOKES, Ted. *See* STOKES, Colin Arthur

STOKES, Terence Harold. b 46. Open Univ BA89. Sarum & Wells Th Coll 71. **d** 73 **p** 74. C Blakenall Heath *Lich* 73-75; C Walsall Wood 75-78; C Northampton St Alb *Pet* 78-81; TV Swinton St Pet *Man* 81-85; V Daisy Hill 85-92. *8 Westbury Close, Westhoughton, Bolton BL5 3UL* Tel (01942) 819057

STOKES, Terence Ronald. b 35. Linc Th Coll. **d** 69 **p** 70. C Bramley *Ripon* 69-72; C Osbournby w Scott Willoughby *Linc* 72-74; C Hykeham 74-77; V Birchwood 77-94; P-in-c Scopwick Gp 94-00; rtd 01; Perm to Offic *Linc* from 01. *47 Paddock Lane, Metheringham, Lincoln LN4 3YG* Tel (01526) 321753

STOKES, Preb Terence Walter. b 34. Bps' Coll Cheshunt 62. **d** 64 **p** 65. C Wanstead St Mary *Chelmsf* 64-67; C St Alb Abbey *St Alb* 67-70; Asst Dir RE *B & W* 70-75; Youth Chapl 70-75; P-in-c Yeovil 75-77; TV 77-82; TR Wellington and Distr 82-99; RD Tone 89-96; Preb Wells Cathl 90-99; rtd 99; Perm to Offic *B & W* from 99. *57 Mountfields Avenue, Taunton TA1 3BW* Tel (01823) 351424

STOKES-HARRISON, David Neville Hurford. b 41. **d** 00 **p** 01. NSM Walsall *Lich* from 00. *6 Victoria Terrace, Walsall WS4 2DA* Tel (01922) 630657

STOKOE, Prof Rodney James Robert. b 20. Dur Univ BSc46 BA48 DipTh49. Crozer Th Sem Pennsylvania ThM67 Atlantic Sch of Th Halifax (NS) Hon DD87. **d** 49 **p** 50. C W Hartlepool St Paul *Dur* 49-53; R Edin Ch Ch *Edin* 53-57; P-in-c Bishopwearmouth St Gabr *Dur* 57-60; Canada from 60; Prof Div K Coll NS 60-71; Prof Past Th Atlantic Sch Th NS 71-85. *403 Prince Street, Ste 206, Truro NS, Canada, B2N 1E6* Tel (001) (902) 897 6129

STOKOE, Wayne Jeffrey (Jeff). b 56. Coll of Resurr Mirfield 94. **d** 96 **p** 97. C Sheff St Cath Richmond Road *Sheff* 96-99; V Edlington from 99; V Sheff St Cecilia Parson Cross from 05. *St Cecilia's Priory, 98 Chaucer Close, Sheffield S5 9QE* Tel 0114-232 1084 E-mail wjs@stokoej.freeserve.co.uk

STONE, Adrian Gordon. b 68. Trent Poly BSc89 Nottm Univ PGCE92. St Jo Coll Nottm 01. **d** 03 **p** 04. C Bayston Hill *Lich* from 03. *4 Newbrook Drive, Bayston Hill, Shrewsbury SY3 0QG* Tel (01743) 872956 Mobile 07739-043709 E-mail adrian@the-stone-family.net

STONE, Albert John. b 44. Loughb Univ BTech67 BSc. Sarum & Wells Th Coll 83. **d** 85 **p** 86. C Plymstock *Ex* 85-88; P-in-c Whitestone 88-92; P-in-c Oldridge 88-92; P-in-c Holcombe Burnell 88-92; R Tedburn St Mary, Whitestone, Oldridge etc 93-94; P-in-c Yarcombe w Membury and Upottery 94; P-in-c Cotleigh 94; V Yarcombe, Membury, Upottery and Cotleigh 95-99; P-in-c Bampton, Morebath, Clayhanger and Petton from 99. *The Vicarage, Station Road, Bampton, Tiverton EX16 9NG* Tel (01398) 331466 Fax as telephone E-mail ajstone@argonet.co.uk

STONE, Andrew Francis. b 43. AKC65. **d** 66 **p** 67. C Walthamstow St Mich *Chelmsf* 66-67; C Ealing St Barn *Lon* 67-70; C E Grinstead St Mary *Chich* 70-74; C-in-c The Hydneye CD 74-81; R Denton w S Heighton and Tarring Neville 81-93; V Eastbourne St Andr from 93. *St Andrew's Vicarage, 425 Seaside, Eastbourne BN22 7RT* Tel (01323) 723739

STONE, Miss Carol Ann. b 54. TD04. Leic Univ BA75 Qu Coll Cam BA77 MA81. Westcott Ho Cam 76. **d** 78 **p** 79. C Bradford-on-Avon *Sarum* 78-81; R Corsley 81-83; Chapl Dauntsey's Sch

Devizes 83-88; V Studley *Sarum* 89-94; Chapl Cheltenham Coll 94-95; Venezuela 95-96; V Upper Stratton *Bris* from 96; CF (ACF) 84-89; CF(V) 90-04. *The Vicarage, 67 Beechcroft Road, Swindon SN2 7RE* Tel (01793) 723095 Mobile 07702-342848 E-mail revcarolstone@btopenworld.com

STONE, Christopher. *See* STONE, Canon John Christopher

STONE, Christopher John. b 49. Lanc Univ MA89 Keele Univ MA92. Lambeth STh84 Linc Th Coll 78. **d** 81 **p** 82. C Bromley St Mark *Roch* 81-84; R Burgh-by-Sands and Kirkbampton w Kirkandrews etc *Carl* 84-89; Chapl N Staffs R Infirmary Stoke-on-Trent 89-93; Co-ord Staff Support Services N Staffs Hosp from 93. *5 Honeywood, Newcastle ST5 9PT* Tel (01782) 625134

STONE, Christopher Martyn Luke. b 78. Glam Univ BA99. St Steph Ho Ox 99. **d** 02 **p** 03. C Merthyr Tydfil Ch Ch *Llan* from 02. *7 Brynteg Terrace, Merthyr Tydfil CF47 0DP* Tel (01685) 386072 E-mail chrisstoneuk@yahoo.co.uk

STONE, David Adrian. b 56. Oriel Coll Ox BA78 MA83 BM, BCh83. Wycliffe Hall Ox 85. **d** 88 **p** 89. C Holborn St Geo w H Trin and St Bart *Lon* 88-91; C S Kensington St Jude 91-93; V 93-02; AD Chelsea 96-02; TR Newbury *Ox* from 02. *The Rectory, 64 Northcroft Lane, Newbury RG14 1BN* Tel (01635) 40326 *or* 47018 Mobile 07973-215927 Fax (01635) 30725 E-mail david@dandb.org.uk *or* rector@st-nicolas-newbury.org

STONE, Dominic Charles. b 63. HND85. Ridley Hall Cam CTM99. **d** 99 **p** 00. C Ashbourne w Mapleton *Derby* 99-02; TV Uttoxeter Area *Lich* from 02. *13 Moisty Lane, Marchington, Uttoxeter ST14 8JY* Tel (01283) 820030 E-mail dominicstone@fish.co.uk

STONE, Elizabeth Karen Forbes. *See* FORBES STONE, Elizabeth Karen

STONE, Geoffrey. *See* STONE, John Geoffrey Elliot

STONE, The Ven Godfrey Owen. b 49. Ex Coll Ox BA71 MA75 W Midl Coll of Educn PGCE72 Sheff Univ Dip Leadership, Renewal & Miss Studies 97. Wycliffe Hall Ox BA78. **d** 81 **p** 82. C Rushden w Newton Bromswold *Pet* 81-87; Dir Past Studies Wycliffe Hall Ox 87-92; TR Bucknall and Bagnall *Lich* 92-02; RD Stoke 98-02; Adn Stoke from 02; P-in-c Edensor from 04. *Archdeacon's House, 39 The Brackens, Newcastle ST5 4JL* Tel (01782) 663066 Fax 711165 E-mail archdeacon.stoke@lichfield.anglican.org

STONE, Ian Matthew. b 72. Ripon Coll Cuddesdon 03. **d** 05. C Hammersmith St Pet *Lon* from 05. *1st Floor Flat, 7 Ravenscourt Road, London W6 0UH* Tel (020) 8748 2695 E-mail matthew.stone1@virgin.net

STONE, Jeffrey Peter. b 34. Nottm Univ TCert72 BEd73. Lich Th Coll 58. **d** 61 **p** 62. C Newark St Mary *S'well* 61-65; C Sutton in Ashfield St Mich 65-69; Robert Smyth Sch Market Harborough 72-89; Perm to Offic *Leic* 88-90; R Waltham on the Wolds, Stonesby, Saxby etc 90-96; rtd 96; Perm to Offic *Leic* from 99. *71 Redland Road, Oakham LE15 6PH* Tel (01572) 756842

STONE, John. *See* STONE, Albert John

STONE, John Anthony. b 46. St Chad's Coll Dur BA68 Univ of Wales (Lamp) MA05. **d** 69 **p** 70. C New Addington *Cant* 69-72; C Tewkesbury w Walton Cardiff *Glouc* 72-76; C-in-c Dedworth CD *Ox* 76-82; V Dedworth 82-86; TV Chipping Barnet w Arkley *St Alb* 86-95; R Baldock w Bygrave 95-03; R Ches H Trin *Ches* from 03. *The Rectory, 50 Norris Road, Chester CH1 5DZ* Tel (01244) 372721 E-mail jastone@dunelm.org.uk

STONE, Canon John Christopher. b 53. Newc Univ BA74 Birkbeck Coll Lon MA77 MSTSD74 LGSM73 MIPR FRSA. Oak Hill NSM Course 89. **d** 92 **p** 93. NSM Southfleet *Roch* from 92; Dioc Communications Officer 96-03; Chapl Univ of Greenwich 98-99; Hon Can Roch Cathl from 02; Bp's Dom Chapl from 03; Bp's Media Adv from 03. *Bishopscourt Flat, St Margaret's Street, Rochester ME1 1TS* Tel (01634) 814439 *or* (01474) 707511 Fax (01634) 831136 E-mail chris.stone@rochester.anglican.org

STONE, John Geoffrey Elliot. b 20. Ch Coll Cam BA41 MA45. Ridley Hall Cam 47. **d** 49 **p** 50. C Wellingborough St Barn *Pet* 49-51; C Bexhill St Pet *Chich* 51-56; C Ifield 56-59; V Southwater 59-70; V Thornham w Titchwell *Nor* 70-74; R Copdock w Washbrook and Belstead *St E* 74-77; P-in-c Therfield *St Alb* 77-82; P-in-c Kelshall 77-82; C Littlehampton St Jas *Chich* 82-85; C Littlehampton St Mary 82-85; C Wick 82-85; TV Littlehampton and Wick 86; rtd 86; C Compton, the Mardens, Stoughton and Racton *Chich* 86-92; Perm to Offic *Nor* 92-96 and *Chich* from 96. *11 Ramsay Hall, Byron Road, Worthing BN11 3HN* Tel (01903) 212947

STONE, Martyn. *See* STONE, Christopher Martyn Luke

STONE, Matthew. *See* STONE, Ian Matthew

STONE, Michael Graham. b 33. FBCS. S Dios Minl Tr Scheme. **d** 83 **p** 84. NSM Chich St Paul and St Pet *Chich* 83-95; NSM Chich 95-98; rtd 98; Perm to Offic *Chich* 98-00; Hon C Chich St Paul and Westhampnett from 00. *125 Cedar Drive, Chichester PO19 3EL* Tel (01243) 784484

STONE, Michael John. b 33. Trin Hall Cam MA56 LLB58. EAMTC 78. **d** 80 **p** 81. NSM Whitton and Thurleston w Akenham *St E* 80-84; NSM Westerfield and Tuddenham w Witnesham 84-95; Dioc Chr Stewardship Adv 93-95; P-in-c Coddenham w Gosbeck and Hemingstone w Henley 95-98; Asst P 98-02; Asst P Crowfield w Stonham Aspal and Mickfield 98-02; Dioc Voc Adv 95-99; rtd 02; Perm to Offic *St E* from 02. *10 Coppice Close, Melton, Woodbridge IP12 1RX* Tel (01394) 385810 E-mail emjaystone@aol.com

STONE, Nigel John. b 57. Bedf Coll Lon BSc82 Lon Bible Coll MA95. St Jo Coll Nottm 82. **d** 85 **p** 86. C Battersea Park St Sav *S'wark* 85-87; C Battersea St Sav and St Geo w St Andr 87-89; P-in-c Brixton St Paul 89-92; V 92-97; Lay Tr Officer from 97; Hon Chapl S'wark Cathl from 97. *11 Wilkinson Street, London SW8 1DD* Tel (020) 7582 6424 *or* 8392 3742 E-mail nigel.stone@southwark.anglican.org

STONE, Philip William. b 58. Ridley Hall Cam 85. **d** 88 **p** 89. C Hackney Marsh *Lon* 88-97; V Kensal Rise St Mark and St Martin 97-04; TR from 04; AD Brent from 03. *Kensal Rise Vicarage, 93 College Road, London NW10 5EU* Tel (020) 8969 4598 E-mail philstone@freenet.co.uk *or* phil.stone@london.anglican.org

STONE, Richard Anthony. b 46. Hatf Coll Dur BA68 Nottm Univ DipTh71. Linc Th Coll 70. **d** 73 **p** 74. C Marske in Cleveland *York* 73-78; TV Haxby w Wigginton 78-87; V Osbaldwick w Murton 87-96; TV Willington *Newc* from 96; Chapl N Tyneside Coll of FE from 99. *The Vicarage, Berwick Drive, Wallsend NE28 9ED* Tel 0191-262 7518

STONEBANKS, David Arthur. b 34. Louvain Univ Belgium MA70. Coll of Resurr Mirfield 64. **d** 66 **p** 67. C Burgess Hill St Jo *Chich* 66-68; Chapl City Univ *Lon* 70-73; Chapl Strasbourg w Stuttgart and Heidelberg *Eur* 73-80; Chapl Geneva 80-86; Chapl Zürich w St Gallen and Winterthur 86-89; R Horsted Keynes *Chich* 89-99; rtd 99. *42 Home Park, Oxted RH8 0JU* Tel (01883) 732339

STONEHOLD, Wilfred Leslie. b 33. St Luke's Coll Ex TCert71. OLM course 98. **d** 99 **p** 00. OLM Harlescott *Lich* from 99. *19 Wendsley Road, Harlescott Grange, Shrewsbury SY1 3PE* Tel (01743) 369237

STONES, John Graham. b 49. Southn Univ BSc72. SW Minl Tr Course 91. **d** 94 **p** 95. C Okehampton w Inwardleigh, Bratton Clovelly etc *Ex* 94-97; TV Sidmouth, Woolbrook, Salcombe Regis, Sidbury etc 97-04; R Church Stretton *Heref* from 04. *The Rectory, Ashbrook Meadow, Carding Mill Valley, Church Stretton SY6 6JF* Tel (01694) 722585 E-mail stsid@lineone.net

STONESTREET, George Malcolm. b 38. MBE05. AKC61. **d** 62 **p** 63. C Leeds St Pet *Ripon* 62-64; C Far Headingley St Chad 64-67; V Askrigg w Stallingbusk 67-82; V Bramley 82-85; TR 85-94; V Eskdale, Irton, Muncaster and Waberthwaite *Carl* 94-03; rtd 03. *Northside, Grange, Keswick CA12 5UQ* Tel (01768) 777671 E-mail malcolm@dip.edi.co.uk

STONEY, The Ven Thomas Vesey. b 34. Oriel Coll Ox BA56 MA60. CITC 58. **d** 58 **p** 59. C Ballywillan *Conn* 58-61; C Carrickfergus 61-66; I Skerry w Rathcavan and Newtowncrommelin 66-92; Adn Dalriada 85-92; rtd 93. *Ardagh Lodge, Newport, Co Mayo, Irish Republic* Tel (00353) (98) 41150

STOODLEY, Peter Bindon. b 47. Linc Th Coll 89. **d** 91 **p** 92. C Holbeck *Ripon* 91-94; P-in-c Osmondthorpe St Phil 94-99; V Sowerby Bridge w Norland *Wakef* from 99. *The Vicarage, 62 Park Road, Sowerby Bridge HX6 2BJ* Tel (01422) 831253 E-mail buccaneer.stoodley@tinyonline.co.uk

STORDY, Richard Andrew. b 64. St Jo Coll Ox BA86 Barrister 86. Cranmer Hall Dur BA97. **d** 98 **p** 99. C Gt Horton *Bradf* 98-02; V Chapeltown *Sheff* from 02. *St John's Vicarage, 23 Housley Park, Chapeltown, Sheffield S35 2UE* Tel 0114-257 0966

STOREY, Gerard Charles Alfred. b 57. GRSC80 Thames Poly BSc80 Lon Univ PhD84. Wycliffe Hall Ox 84. **d** 87 **p** 88. C Broadwater St Mary *Chich* 87-92; TV 92-95; Chapl Northbrook Coll of Design and Tech 90-95; Oman 95-99; P-in-c Guernsey H Trin *Win* 99-01; V from 01. *Holy Trinity Vicarage, Brock Road, St Peter Port, Guernsey GY1 1RS* Tel and fax (01481) 724382 E-mail gerardsusi@gtonline.net

STOREY, Canon Michael. b 36. Chich Th Coll 73. **d** 75 **p** 76. C Illingworth *Wakef* 75-78; V Rastrick St Jo 78-87; V Crosland Moor from 87; Hon Can Wakef Cathl from 00. *The Vicarage, Church Avenue, Crosland Moor, Huddersfield HD4 5DF* Tel (01484) 422381

STOREY, Mrs Patricia Louise. b 60. TCD MA83. CITC BTh94. **d** 97 **p** 98. C Ballymena w Ballyclug *Conn* 97-00; C Glenavy w Tunny and Crumlin 00-04; I Londonderry St Aug *D & R* from 04. *St Augustine's Rectory, 4 Bridgewater, Londonderry BT47 6YA* Tel (028) 7134 7532 E-mail storeyp@rev.5.freeserve.co.uk

STOREY, Timothy. b 60. Trin Coll Bris DipHE94. **d** 94 **p** 95. C Bath Weston St Jo w Kelston *B & W* 94-98; C Shirley *Win* 98-03; R Blandford Forum and Langton Long *Sarum* from 03. *The Rectory, 2 Portman Place, Blandford Forum DT11 7DG* Tel (01258) 480092 E-mail t.storey@btopenworld.com

STOREY, William Earl Cosbey. b 58. Kent Univ BA MPhil. CITC DipTh86. **d** 82 **p** 83. C Drumglass w Moygashel *Arm* 82-86; I Crinken *D & G* 86-96; I Glenavy w Tunny and Crumlin

Conn 98-04. *St Augustine's Rectory, 4 Bridgewater, Londonderry BT47 6YA* Tel (028) 7134 7532
E-mail es@cofire.freeserve.co.uk

STOREY, William Leslie Maurice. b 31. Oak Hill Th Coll 67. **d** 69 **p** 70. C Wembley St Jo *Lon* 69-71; C Ealing Dean St Jo 71-75; V W Derby St Luke *Liv* 75-80; V Hunts Cross 80-83; Hon C Brixton St Paul *S'wark* 83-86; P-in-c 87-88; P-in-c Brixton Hill St Sav 83-86; rtd 88; Perm to Offic *S'wark* 88-02. *124 Surbiton Hill Park, Surbiton KT5 8EP* Tel (020) 8390 2821

STORR VENTER, Phillip. b 52. Barrister-at-Law (Gray's Inn) 74. S'wark Ord Course 90. **d** 93 **p** 94. NSM Bethnal Green St Barn *Lon* 93-97; Chapl Armenia and Georgia *Eur* 97-02; P-in-c Highgate All SS *Lon* from 02. *All Saint's Vicarage, Church Road, London N6 4QH* Tel (020) 8340 1123 Mobile 07762-109937 E-mail storrventer@btopenworld.com

STORY, Victor Leonard. b 45. St Mark & St Jo Coll Lon TCert66 Brighton Poly BSc74 LIMA74. Ripon Coll Cuddesdon 80. **d** 81 **p** 82. C Evesham *Worc* 81-85; P-in-c Ilmington w Stretton on Fosse and Ditchford *Cov* 85-90; P-in-c Ilmington w Stretton-on-Fosse etc 90-96; Chapl Vlissingen (Flushing) Miss to Seamen *Eur* 96-97; Chapl Rotterdam Miss to Seamen 97-99; R Gt w Lt Milton and Gt Haseley *Ox* from 99. *The Rectory, Great Milton, Oxford OX44 7PN* Tel (01844) 279498

STOTE, Mrs Pamela Anne. b 49. Dudley Coll of Educn TCert70 Open Univ BA83. WMMTC 97. **d** 00 **p** 01. NSM Cov St Geo *Cov* 00-03; NSM Whitley from 03. *St James's Church, 171 Abbey Road, Coventry CV3 4BG* Tel and fax (024) 7630 1617 Mobile 07905-230924 E-mail st.james@stote.force9.co.uk

STOTER, David John. b 43. MBE02. K Coll Lon AKC66. **d** 67 **p** 68. C Reading St Giles *Ox* 67-71; C Luton Lewsey St Hugh *St Alb* 71-73; Chapl Westmr Hosp Lon 73-79; Convenor of Chapls Notts Distr HA 79-94; Chapl Univ Hosp Nottm 79-94; Chapl Nottm Gen Hosp 79-02; Sen Chapl Qu Medical Cen Nottm Univ Hosp NHS Trust 94-02; Sen Chapl Notts Healthcare NHS Trust 94-02; Manager Chapl and Bereavement Services 94-02; R Gedling *S'well* from 02. *The Rectory, Rectory Drive, Gedling, Nottingham NG4 4BG* Tel 0115-961 3214

STOTT, Andrew David. b 61. N Ord Course 03. **d** 05. NSM Walton Breck *Liv* from 05. *401 Walton Lane, Liverpool L4 5RL* Tel 0151-521 7827 Mobile 07967-468014
E-mail andrew@stott401.fsnet.co.uk

STOTT, Antony. b 21. Bps' Coll Cheshunt 53. **d** 55 **p** 56. Australia 55-62; V Longbridge Deverill w Hill Deverill *Sarum* 62-66; V Bratton 66-74; R Marnhull 74-81; P-in-c Broad Chalke and Bower Chalke 81; P-in-c Ebbesbourne Wake w Fifield Bavant and Alvediston 81; P-in-c Berwick St John 81; V Chalke Valley W 81-87; rtd 87; Perm to Offic *Ex* from 87. *11 Luscombe Close, Ivybridge PL21 9TT* Tel (01752) 896142
E-mail revtony1@aol.com

STOTT, Christopher John. b 45. Lon Univ BD68. Tyndale Hall Bris. **d** 69 **p** 70. C Croydon Ch Ch Broad Green *Cant* 69-72; Ethiopia 73-76; Area Sec (SW) BCMS 76-78; Tanzania 78-85; R Harwell w Chilton *Ox* from 85; RD Wallingford 91-95. *The Rectory, Harwell, Didcot OX11 0EW* Tel (01235) 835365

STOTT, Eric. b 36. ALCD62. **d** 62 **p** 63. C Penn Fields *Lich* 62-65; C Normanton *Derby* 65-71; R Lower Broughton St Clem w St Matthias *Man* 71-79; V Chadderton Em 79-01; rtd 01; Perm to Offic *Glouc* from 01. *21 Laynes Road, Hucclecote, Gloucester GL3 3PU* Tel (01452) 534492 E-mail seric@fish.co.uk

STOTT, Frederick. b 23. Univ of Wales (Cardiff) CQSW71 Indiana Univ BD98. Sarum & Wells Th Coll 83. **d** 85 **p** 86. NSM Sholing *Win* 85-90; Perm to Offic *Portsm* from 89; *Win* from 90; *Sarum* from 93. *35 Broadwater Road, Southampton SO18 2DW* Tel (023) 8055 7193

STOTT, Gary. b 69. Leeds Univ BA92 St Jo Coll Dur MA99. Cranmer Hall Dur DMS99. **d** 99 **p** 00. C Farnley *Ripon* 99-03; V Manston from 03. *Manston Vicarage, Church Lane, Leeds LS15 8JB* Tel 0113-260 0348 *or* 264 5530
E-mail hgstott@fish.co.uk

STOTT, John Robert Walmsley. b 21. Trin Coll Cam BA45 MA50. Lambeth DD83 Ridley Hall Cam 44. **d** 45 **p** 46. C St Marylebone All So w SS Pet and Jo *Lon* 45-50; R 50-75; Hon C 75-88; Hon C Langham Place All So from 88; Chapl to The Queen 59-91; Extra Chapl to The Queen from 91; Dir Lon Inst of Contemporary Christianity 82-86; Pres from 86; rtd 91. *12 Weymouth Street, London W1W 5BY* Tel (020) 7580 1867

STOTT, Jonathan Robert. b 67. Ripon Coll Cuddesdon. **d** 01 **p** 02. C Anfield St Columba *Liv* 01-05; V Dovecot from 05. *Holy Spirit Vicarage, Dovecot Avenue, Liverpool L14 7QJ* Tel 0151-220 6611 Mobile 07971-876517
E-mail jonathan_r_stott@hotmail.com

STOTT, Miss Teresa. b 57. Linc Th Coll 94. **d** 94 **p** 95. C Lee-on-the-Solent *Portsm* 94-97; C Spalding St Jo w Deeping St Nicholas *Linc* 97-98; P-in-c Freiston w Butterwick 98-99; R Freiston w Butterwick and Benington 99-03; R Freiston, Butterwick w Bennington, and Leverton 03-04; C-in-c Cleethorpes St Fran CD from 04; Chapl Matthew Humberston Sch from 04. *St Francis House, 19B Sandringham Road, Cleethorpes DN35 9HA* Tel (01472) 691215

STOW, John Mark. b 51. Selw Coll Cam BA73 MA77. Linc Th Coll 76. **d** 78 **p** 79. C Harpenden St Jo *St Alb* 78-82; TV Beaminster Area *Sarum* 82-87; P-in-c Hawkchurch 87-90; P-in-c Marshwood Vale 87-88; TR Marshwood Vale 88-91; Past Co-ord Millfield Jun Sch from 93. *Chestnut House, Edgarley, Glastonbury BA6 8LL* Tel (01458) 832245

STOW, Peter John. b 50. Oak Hill Th Coll. **d** 89 **p** 90. C Forest Gate St Mark *Chelmsf* 89-94; V from 94. *St Mark's Vicarage, Tylney Road, London E7 0LS* Tel (020) 8555 2988
E-mail saintmarks@clara.net

STOW, Archdeacon of. *See* ELLIS, The Ven Timothy William

STOWE, Brian. b 32. Trin Coll Cam BA55 BA56 MA59. Ridley Hall Cam 55. **d** 57 **p** 58. C New Catton St Luke *Nor* 57-59; Chapl R Masonic Sch Bushey 59-70; Tutor Rickmansworth Sch Herts 70-71; Chapl Alleyn's Foundn Dulwich 71-75; Hon C Dulwich St Barn *S'wark* 71-75; Chapl Ellerslie Sch Malvern 75-92; Chapl Malvern Coll 92-93; TV Malvern Link w Cowleigh *Worc* 93-94; rtd 95; P-in-c Malvern St Andr *Worc* 95-96; Perm to Offic from 96. *31 Park View, Grange Road, Malvern WR14 3HG* Tel 07792-515307 (mobile) E-mail bandmstowe@onetel.com

STOWE, Nigel James. b 36. Bris Univ BSc57. Clifton Th Coll 59. **d** 61 **p** 62. C Ware Ch Ch *St Alb* 61-64; C Reigate St Mary *S'wark* 64-67; V Islington St Jude Mildmay Park *Lon* 67-75; V Penn Street *Ox* 75-01; rtd 01. *27 Snowdrop Way, Widmer End, High Wycombe HP15 6BL* Tel (01494) 717496

STOWE, Canon Rachel Lilian. b 33. Qu Coll Birm 79. **dss** 83 **d** 87 **p** 94. Dean w Yelden, Melchbourne and Shelton *St Alb* 82-87; Pertenhall w Swineshead 82-87; Bp's Officer for NSMs and Asst Dir of Ords 87-93; rtd 93; NSM The Stodden Churches *St Alb* 87-96; Hon Can St Alb 92-96; Convenor Dioc Adv Gp for Chr Healing *Ripon* 98-03; Perm to Offic *Ripon* from 97 and *York* from 98. *Preston Cottage, East Cowton, Northallerton DL7 0BD* Tel and fax (01325) 378173 Mobile 07860-618600
E-mail rachel@stowe2106.freeserve.co.uk

STRACHAN, Donald Philip Michael. b 37. St D Coll Lamp 60. **d** 62 **p** 63. C Aberdeen St Mary *Ab* 62-64; P-in-c Aberdeen St Paul 64-66; Chapl St Andr Cathl 65-68; Itinerant Priest *Mor* 68-73; R Coatbridge *Glas* 73-85; Chapl HM Pris Glas (Barlinnie) 84-87; Dioc Supernumerary *Glas* 85-94; rtd 94; Perm to Offic *Arg* from 87. *Reul na Mara, Claddach Kirkibost, Isle of North Uist HS6 5EP* Tel (01876) 580392

STRAFFORD, Nigel Thomas Bevan. b 53. Univ of Wales (Lamp) BA80. Sarum & Wells Th Coll 80. **d** 82 **p** 94. C Kidderminster St Mary *Worc* 82; C Kidderminster St Mary and All SS, Trimpley etc 82-83; Hon C Stockton St Mark *Dur* 84-86; Asst P Longwood *Wakef* 86-94; V Athersley 94-97; P-in-c Ferrybridge 97-03; P-in-c Holme and Seaton Ross Gp *York* 03-04; R from 04. *The Vicarage, Market Weighton Road, Holme-on-Spalding-Moor, York YO43 4AG* Tel (01430) 860248

STRAIN, Christopher Malcolm. b 56. Solicitor Southn Univ LLB77. Wycliffe Hall Ox 83. **d** 86 **p** 87. C Werrington *Pet* 86-89; C Broadwater St Mary *Chich* 89-94; TV Hampreston *Sarum* 94-00; P-in-c Parkstone St Luke 00-03; V from 03. *The Vicarage, 2 Birchwood Road, Parkstone, Poole BH14 9NP* Tel (01202) 741030

STRAIN, John Damian. b 49. Keele Univ BA72 Birkbeck Coll Lon MSc83 PhD89 AFBPsS89. STETS BTh00. **d** 00 **p** 01. NSM Hindhead *Guildf* 00-03; NSM Churt and Hindhead from 03. *Pinewoods, Church Lane, Grayshott, Hindhead GU26 6LY* Tel (01428) 607115 E-mail j.strain@surrey.ac.uk

STRANACK, The Very Revd David Arthur Claude. b 43. Chich Th Coll 65. **d** 68 **p** 69. C Forest Gate St Edm *Chelmsf* 68-69; C Colchester St Jas, All SS, St Nic and St Runwald 69-74; V Brentwood St Geo 74-82; V Nayland w Wiston *St E* 82-99; Hon Can St E Cathl from 94; R Hadleigh 99-02; V Hadleigh, Layham and Shelley from 02; RD Hadleigh from 99; Dean Bocking from 99. *The Deanery, Church Street, Hadleigh, Ipswich IP7 5DT* Tel (01473) 822218

STRANACK, Fay Rosemary. b 30. Lon Univ BSc55 PhD60. Westcott Ho Cam 88. **d** 89 **p** 94. NSM Denmead *Portsm* 89-98; rtd 98; Perm to Offic *Portsm* from 98. *35 Yew Tree Gardens, Denmead, Waterlooville PO7 6LH* Tel (023) 9225 6785

STRANACK, Canon Richard Nevill. b 40. Leeds Univ BA63. Coll of Resurr Mirfield 63. **d** 65 **p** 66. C Bush Hill Park St Mark *Lon* 65-68; C Brighton St Martin *Chich* 68-72; P-in-c Toftrees w Shereford *Nor* 72-74; V 74-81; P-in-c Pensthorpe 72-74; R 74-81; V Hempton and Pudding Norton 72-81; RD Burnham and Walsingham 78-81; V Par *Truro* 81-94; P-in-c St Blazey 87-91; Hon Chapl Miss to Seafarers from 81; V Stratton and Launcells *Truro* from 94; Hon Can Truro Cathl from 98; RD Stratton from 02; Chapl Cornwall Healthcare NHS Trust 97-02; Chapl N and E Cornwall Primary Care Trust from 02. *The Vicarage, Diddies Road, Stratton, Bude EX23 9DW* Tel (01288) 352254 Fax 356525

STRAND, The Very Revd Tyler Alan. b 51. Augustana Coll (USA) AB73. St Steph Ho Ox 74 Gen Th Sem (NY) MDiv78. **d** 77 **p** 78. USA 77-85 and 93-00; W Germany 85-90; Chapl Helsinki w Moscow *Eur* 91-93; Dean Makati Philippines from 00. *48 McKinley Road, Forbes Park, Makati, Metro Manila, Philippines* E-mail tastrand@cs.com

STRANGE, Alan Michael. b 57. Pemb Coll Ox BA79 MA89. Wycliffe Hall Ox BA84. **d** 84 **p** 85. C York St Paul *York* 84-87; Asst Chapl Brussels Cathl *Eur* 87-91; Assoc Chapl 91-95; P-in-c Heigham H Trin *Nor* 95-99; R from 99. *The Rectory, 17 Essex Street, Norwich NR2 2BL* Tel (01603) 622225
E-mail rector@trinitynorwich.org *or* big1al@ntlworld.com

STRANGE, Brian. b 47. QUB BA69. SW Minl Tr Course 98. **d** 01 **p** 02. NSM Georgeham *Ex* 01-03; P-in-c from 03. *2 Inglenook Cottages, St Mary's Road, Croyde, Braunton EX33 1PG* Tel (01271) 890961 E-mail brian@croyde.org

STRANGE, Bryan. b 26. Sarum & Wells Th Coll 73. **d** 75 **p** 76. C King's Worthy *Win* 75-78; C Wilton *B & W* 78-80; V Kewstoke w Wick St Lawrence 80-89; rtd 89; Perm to Offic *Ex* from 90. *29 Bluebell Avenue, Tiverton EX16 6SX*

STRANGE, Malcolm. b 58. Westmr Coll Ox MTh95. Sarum & Wells Th Coll 82. **d** 85 **p** 86. C Seaton Hirst *Newc* 85-88; C Ridgeway *Sarum* 88-89; TV 89-91; TV Newbury *Ox* 91-98; TR Bideford, Northam, Westward Ho!, Appledore etc *Ex* 98-01; RD Hartland 99-01. *Address withheld by request*

STRANGE, Canon Mark Jeremy. b 61. Aber Univ LTh82. Linc Th Coll 87. **d** 89 **p** 90. C Worc St Barn w Ch Ch *Worc* 89-92; V Worc St Wulstan 92-98; R Elgin w Lossiemouth *Mor* from 98; Can St Andr Cathl Inverness from 00; Syn Clerk from 03. *The Rectory, 8 Gordon Street, Elgin IV30 1JQ* Tel (01343) 547505
E-mail stranges@trinity-elgin.fsnet.co.uk

STRANGE, Michael Paul. b 46. Univ of Wales (Ban) BSc67 MSc71. SEITE 94. **d** 97 **p** 98. NSM Clapham Team *S'wark* 97-01; NSM Clapham H Trin and St Pet from 02; Asst Chapl HM Pris High Down 98-01; Asst Chapl HM Pris Wormwood Scrubs from 01; Perm to Offic *Lon* from 02. *HM Prison Wormwood Scrubs, Du Cane Road, London W12 0TU* Tel (020) 8588 3200 ext 3262 *or* 7228 9868
E-mail michael.strange@hmps.gsi.gov.uk

STRANGE, Canon Peter Robert. b 48. Univ Coll Lon BA69 Ex Coll Ox BA71 MA76. Cuddesdon Coll 71. **d** 72 **p** 73. C Denton *Newc* 72-74; C Newc St Jo 74-79; Chapl for Arts and Recreation 79-90; R Wallsend St Pet 79-86; Can Res Newc Cathl from 86; Angl Adv Tyne Tees TV from 90; Asst Dioc Dir of Ords *Newc* 94-98. *55 Queen's Terrace, Jesmond, Newcastle upon Tyne NE2 2PL* Tel 0191-281 0181 *or* 232 1939 Fax 230 0735
E-mail stnicholas@aol.com

STRANGE, Preb Robert Lewis. b 45. Sarum & Wells Th Coll 72. **d** 74 **p** 75. C Walthamstow St Barn and St Jas Gt *Chelmsf* 74-77; C Wickford 77-80; P-in-c Treverbyn *Truro* 80-83; V 83-86; Asst Stewardship Adv 82-96; V Newlyn St Pet from 86; Preb Trehaverock from 94; Hon Chapl Miss to Seafarers from 86. *St Peter's Vicarage, Newlyn, Penzance TR18 5HT* Tel (01736) 362678 Fax 351174 E-mail robert.sarov@tiscali.co.uk

STRANGE, William Anthony. b 53. Qu Coll Cam BA76 MA80 K Alfred's Coll Win CertEd77 Ox Univ DPhil89. Wycliffe Hall Ox 79. **d** 82 **p** 83. Tutor Wycliffe Hall Ox 82-87; C Aberystwyth *St D* 87; TV 87-91; V Llandeilo Fawr and Taliaris 91-96; Hd of Th and RS Trin Coll Carmarthen 96-01; V Carmarthen St Pet *St D* from 03. *St Peter's Vicarage, Church Street, Carmarthen SA31 1GW* Tel (01267) 237117

STRANRAER-MULL, The Very Revd Gerald Hugh. b 42. AKC69. St Aug Coll Cant 69. **d** 70 **p** 71. C Hexham *Newc* 70-72; C Corbridge w Halton 72; R Cruden Bay *Ab* from 72; R Ellon from 72; Can St Andr Cathl from 81; Dean Ab from 88; P-in-c Peterhead from 02. *The Rectory, Ellon AB41 9NP* Tel (01358) 720366 Fax 720256 E-mail saint.mary's@virgin.net

STRAPPS, Canon Robert David. b 28. St Edm Hall Ox BA52 MA56. Wycliffe Hall Ox 52. **d** 54 **p** 55. C Low Leyton *Chelmsf* 54-57; C Ox St Aldate w H Trin *Ox* 57-60; V Sandal St Helen *Wakef* 60-94; RD Chevet 81-93; Hon Can Wakef Cathl 92-94; rtd 94; Perm to Offic *Wakef* 94-98; *Glouc* and *Worc* from 94. *Brookside, Hill Road, Kemerton, Tewkesbury GL20 7JN* Tel (01386) 725515

STRASZAK, Edmund Norman. b 57. Coll of Resurr Mirfield 88. **d** 90 **p** 91. C Adlington *Blackb* 90-93; C Harrogate St Wilfrid and St Luke *Ripon* 93-95; V Chorley All SS *Blackb* from 95. *All Saints' Vicarage, Moor Road, Chorley PR7 2LR* Tel (01257) 265665 E-mail edmund@straszak.freeserve.co.uk

STRATFORD, Mrs Anne Barbara. Southn Univ CertEd58 Ox Univ MTh99. Qu Coll Birm 88. **d** 91 **p** 94. Officer Dioc Bd of Soc Resp (Family Care) *Lich* 85-97; NSM Kinnerley w Melverley and Knockin w Maesbrook 91-95; Chapl Robert Jones and Agnes Hunt Orthopaedic Hosp 95-97; NSM Maesbury *Lich* 95-96; P-in-c 96-97; Chapl Moreton Hall Sch from 96; P-in-c Ford *Heref* 97-02; V 02-05; P-in-c Alberbury w Cardeston 97-02; V 02-05; rtd 05; Perm to Offic *Lich* from 05. *Pentre Cleddar, Hengoed, Oswestry SY10 7AB* Tel (01691) 650469

STRATFORD, David. b 46. LNSM course 95. **d** 98 **p** 99. OLM Ditton St Mich w St Thos *Liv* from 98. *96 Clincton View, Widnes WA8 8RW* Tel 0151-423 4912

STRATFORD, The Ven Ralph Montgomery. b 30. TCD BA53 MA67. CITC 53. **d** 54 **p** 54. Dioc C *C & O* 54-55; C Waterford Ch Ch 55-56; I Ballisodare w Collooney 56-00; Adn Killala and Achonry *T, K & A* 69-00; Can Killala Cathl 69-00; Preb Kilmactalway St Patr Cathl Dublin 85-00; rtd 00. *Knoxpark House, Robinstown, Mullingar, Co Westmeath, Irish Republic* Tel (00353) (44) 35292

STRATFORD, Terence Stephen. b 45. Chich Th Coll 67. **d** 69 **p** 70. C Old Shoreham *Chich* 69-73; C New Shoreham 69-73; C Uckfield 73-75; C Lt Horsted 73-75; C Isfield 73-75; P-in-c Waldron 76-80; R 80-82; V Blacklands Hastings Ch Ch and St Andr 82-89; P-in-c Ovingdean 89-95; Dioc Ecum Officer 89-95; P-in-c Staplefield Common 95-00; Sussex Ecum Officer 95-01; V Ferring from 00. *The Vicarage, 19 Grange Park, Ferring, Worthing BN12 5LS* Tel (01903) 241645

STRATFORD, Timothy Richard. b 61. York Univ BSc82. Wycliffe Hall Ox 83. **d** 86 **p** 87. C Mossley Hill St Matt and St Jas *Liv* 86-89; C St Helens St Helen 89-91; Bp's Dom Chapl 91-94; V W Derby Gd Shep 94-03; TR Kirkby from 03. *The Rectory, Old Hall Lane, Liverpool L32 5TH* Tel and fax 0151-547 2155
E-mail tim.stratford@btinternet.com

STRATHIE, Duncan John. b 58. Heythrop Coll Lon MA02. Cranmer Hall Dur BA95. **d** 97 **p** 98. C Yateley *Win* 97-01; V Kempshott from 01; Dioc Convener of Voc Adv from 03. *The Vicarage, 171 Kempshott Lane, Kempshott, Basingstoke RG22 5LF* Tel (01256) 356400
E-mail duncan.strathie@ntlworld.com

STRATON, Christopher James. b 46. DipTh74. **d** 93 **p** 94. S Africa 93-00; Chapl Miss to Seamen 93-96; Asst P Gingindlovu All SS 97-99; R 99-00; P-in-c Tyldesley w Shakerley *Man* from 00. *11 Peel Hall Avenue, Tyldesley, Manchester M29 8TA* Tel (01942) 882914

STRATTA, Antony Charles (Tony). b 36. ACIS. S'wark Ord Course 82. **d** 85 **p** 86. C Southborough St Pet w Ch Ch and St Matt *Roch* 85-88; R Gt Mongeham w Ripple and Sutton by Dover *Cant* 88-96; rtd 96; Perm to Offic *St E* from 96. *Well House, The Great Yard, Rougham Green, Bury St Edmunds IP30 9JP* Tel (01284) 386140
E-mail antony.stratta@btinternet.com

STRATTON, Henry William. b 39. Bris Univ CertEd74 BEd75. Glouc Sch of Min 80. **d** 83 **p** 84. NSM Cainscross w Selsley *Glouc* 83-87; C Odd Rode *Ches* 87-92; V Runcorn H Trin 92-96; V Lostock Gralam 96-05; rtd 05. *10 The Beeches, Great Sutton, Ellesmere Port CH66 4UJ* E-mail harry@hstratton.fsnet.co.uk

STRATTON, John Jefferies. b 27. Bps' Coll Cheshunt 53. **d** 55 **p** 56. C Watford St Mich *St Alb* 55-60; C Stevenage 60-65; R Cottered w Broadfield and Throcking 65-82; RD Buntingford 75-82; V S Mimms St Mary and Potters Bar *Lon* 82-84; V Potters Bar *St Alb* 85-94; P-in-c Flamstead 94-96; rtd 94; Perm to Offic *B & W* from 97; Hon C Taunton H Trin from 97. *17 The Fairways, Sherford, Taunton TA1 3PA* Tel (01823) 330564

STRAUGHAN, Keith. b 60. Imp Coll Lon BSc81 Lon Univ PhD87 Imp Coll Lon ARCS81 CPhys87 MInstP87 Trin Coll Cam BA94. Westcott Ho Cam 94. **d** 97 **p** 98. C Abbots Langley *St Alb* 97-00; Chapl and Fell SS Coll Cam 00-03; Tutor from 00; Dean from 03. *The Chaplain, Sidney Sussex College, Cambridge CB2 3HU* Tel (01223) 338800 *or* 338870 Fax 338884
E-mail pastoral.dean@sid.cam.ac.uk

STRAW (née CAUDWELL), Mrs Juliet Lesley. b 49. Univ of Wales (Ban) BA70 Leeds Univ PGCE71. St Alb and Ox Min Course 00. **d** 03 **p** 04. NSM Stratfield Mortimer and Mortimer W End etc *Ox* from 03. *Clive Cottage, 68 Windmill Road, Mortimer Common, Reading RG7 3RL* Tel 0118-933 2648
E-mail juliet.straw@btinternet.com

STREATER, David Arthur. b 33. Oak Hill Th Coll 67. **d** 68 **p** 69. C Lindfield *Chich* 68-71; S Africa 71-86; R Kingham w Churchill, Daylesford and Sarsden *Ox* 86-91; Dir Ch Soc 91-98; Sec Ch Soc Trust 91-96; rtd 98; P-in-c Odell *St Alb* 98-03. *4 Cropredy Court, Buckingham MK18 1UX* Tel (01280) 817740
E-mail monty@ukgateway.net

STREATFEILD, Francis Richard Champion. b 22. Qu Coll Cam BA48 MA59. Cuddesdon Coll 48. **d** 50 **p** 51. C Houghton le Spring *Dur* 50-53; India 53-70; V Sacriston *Dur* 70-79; Area Sec USPG *Carl* 79-85; C Carl St Aid and Ch Ch *Carl* 85-88; rtd 88; Perm to Offic *Carl* 88-99. *Fenton Lane Head, How Mill, Carlisle CA4 9LD* Tel (01228) 70470

STREATFEILD, Peter Michael Fremlyn. b 53. Newc Univ BSc77 St Jo Coll Dur BA03. Cranmer Hall Dur 00. **d** 03 **p** 04. C Solway Plain *Carl* from 03. *Ivy Cottage, Langrigg, Wigton CA7 3LL* Tel (01697) 321310 E-mail peter@streatfeild-2001.freeserve.co.uk

STREET, Anthony James. b 57. Trin Coll Bris 79. **d** 85 **p** 87. SAMS 85-95; Chile 85-95; P-in-c Warley *Wakef* 96-99; V from 99. *The Vicarage, 466 Burnley Road, Warley, Halifax HX2 7LW* Tel (01422) 363623 E-mail familiastreet@btinternet.co.uk

STREET, Matthew Graham. b 61. Regent's Park Coll Ox BA83. Wycliffe Hall Ox 99. **d** 01 **p** 02. C Combe Down w Monkton Combe and S Stoke *B & W* 01-05; P-in-c Peasedown St John w Wellow from 05. *The Vicarage, 18 Church Road, Peasedown*

St John, Bath BA2 8AA Tel (01761) 432293 Mobile 07710-527070 Fax 08701-307814
E-mail mgstreet@hotmail.com

STREET, Peter Jarman. b 29. K Coll Lon BD59 AKC59. **d** 59 **p** 60. C Highters Heath *Birm* 59-60; C Shirley 60-62; Lect Cheshire Coll of Educn 62-66; St Pet Coll of Educn Birm 66-70; RE Adv Essex Co Coun 70-92; Hon C Gt Dunmow *Chelmsf* 71-85; Sen Insp RE and Humanities 74-92; R Gt w Lt Yeldham 85-92; RD Belchamp 90-92; rtd 92; Perm to Offic *Chelmsf* from 92. *18 Jubilee Court, Great Dunmow CM6 1DY* Tel (01371) 876871

STREET, Philip. b 47. Lon Univ BPharm68. NW Ord Course 75. **d** 78 **p** 79. C Heaton St Barn *Bradf* 78-81; C Evington *Leic* 82-84; R Wymondham w Edmondthorpe, Buckminster etc 84-88; V Gosberton Clough and Quadring *Linc* 88-95; Asst Local Min Officer 88-95; V Buttershaw St Paul *Bradf* 95-99; P-in-c Gt and Lt Casterton w Pickworth and Tickencote *Pet* 99-04; R from 04; P-in-c Exton w Horn from 02. *The Rectory, Main Street, Great Casterton, Stamford PE9 4AP* Tel (01780) 764036
E-mail philipenny@streetshome.freeserve.co.uk

STREETER, Christine Mary. *See* HADDON-REECE, Mrs Christine Mary

STREETER, David James. b 42. Pemb Coll Cam BA64 MA68. Qu Coll Birm 65. **d** 67 **p** 68. C Saffron Walden *Chelmsf* 67-71; C Shrub End 71-73; R Rayne 73-79; V Highams Park All SS 79-82; P-in-c Stradbroke w Horham and Athelington *St E* 82-87; R Stradbroke, Horham, Athelington and Redlingfield from 87; RD Hoxne 91-00. *The Rectory, Doctors Lane, Stradbroke, Eye IP21 5HU* Tel (01379) 384363 Mobile 07798-784179
E-mail david.streeter@stedmundsbury.anglican.org

STREETING, John William. b 52. ACertCM89 Cam Inst of Educn CertEd74 Birm Univ BEd77 FGMS98 FRSA98 Anglia Poly Univ MA99. St Steph Ho Ox 90. **d** 92 **p** 93. C Upminster *Chelmsf* 92-95; C Chingford SS Pet and Paul 95-97; Assoc V Chelsea St Luke and Ch Ch *Lon* 97-03; V Sheerness H Trin w St Paul *Cant* from 03; P-in-c Queenborough from 05; AD Sittingbourne from 04. *The Vicarage, 241 High Street, Sheerness ME12 1UR* Tel (01795) 662589
E-mail john@htsheerness.fsnet.co.uk

STREETING, Laurence Storey. b 14. VRD65. St Jo Coll Dur BA39 DipTh40 MA42. **d** 40 **p** 41. C Bishopwearmouth St Gabr *Dur* 40-46; Chapl RNVR 42-46; S Africa 46-49; Chapl Garden City Woodford Bridge 49-51; Chapl Village Home Barkingside 49-51; Chapl RAF 51-56; Chapl RNR 56-90; Asst Chapl Eliz Coll Guernsey 56-60; Chapl Eshton Hall Sch Gargrave 60-64; Perm to Offic *Cant* 64-65; R Guernsey St Sampson *Win* 65-71; St Vincent 72-76; Chapl Madeira *Eur* 76-80; rtd 80; Perm to Offic *Win* from 79. *Apartment 8, de Hubie Court, Les Cotils Christian Centre, St Peter Port, Guernsey GY1 1VV*

STRETCH, Richard Mark. b 53. LNSM course 91. **d** 93 **p** 94. OLM Stowmarket *St E* from 93. *91 Kipling Way, Stowmarket IP14 1TS* Tel (01449) 676219

STRETTON, George Peter. b 22. MBE. **d** 70 **p** 71. Malaysia 70-78; V Shireoaks *S'well* 79-85; Perm to Offic *B & W* from 86; rtd 87. *9 The Lerburne, Wedmore BS28 4ED* Tel (01934) 713244

STRETTON, Reginald John. b 37. MRPharmS63 CBiol70 MIBiol70 Man Univ BSc62 Nottm Univ PhD65. EMMTC 88. **d** 91 **p** 92. NSM Loughb Gd Shep *Leic* 91-94; P-in-c Burrough Hill Pars 94-02; rtd 02; Perm to Offic *Leic* and *S'well* from 02; *Derby* from 05. *19 Paddock Close, Quorn, Loughborough LE12 8BJ* Tel (01509) 412935
E-mail rstretton@leicester.anglican.org

STRETTON, Robert John. b 45. Lon Univ DipTh69. Kelham Th Coll. **d** 69 **p** 70. C Hendon St Ignatius *Dur* 69-73; C Middlesbrough St Thos *York* 73-77; OSB 77-78; V Brandon *Dur* 78-85; SSM from 85; Lic to Offic *Dur* 85-91; Tr in Evang Ch in Wales 91-94; Perm to Offic *S'wark* 94-01; Lesotho from 01. *Society of the Sacred Mission Priory, PO Box 1579, Maseru, Lesotho* Tel (00266) 315979

STREVENS, Brian Lloyd. b 49. St Jo Coll Dur BA70. Ripon Hall Ox 70. **d** 73 **p** 74. C Old Trafford St Jo *Man* 73-76; C Bolton St Pet 76-78; Org Sec Southn Coun of Community Service 78-92; Perm to Offic *Win* 82-86, 92-95 and from 01; Hon C Bitterne Park *Win* 86-92; Hon C N Stoneham 95-01. *186 Hill Lane, Southampton SO15 5DB* Tel (023) 8033 3301
E-mail hq@scaccs.org.uk

STREVENS, Richard Ernest Noel. b 34. Nottm Univ BA60. Linc Th Coll 60. **d** 62 **p** 63. C St Botolph Aldgate w H Trin Minories *Lon* 62-66; C Ealing St Steph Castle Hill 66-68; Hon C St Botolph without Bishopgate 68-76; V Clent *Worc* 76-86; V Pirbright *Guildf* 86-00; Perm to Offic *Ex* 69-98 and from 00; rtd 00. *83 Head Weir Road, Cullompton EX15 1NN* Tel (01884) 35823

STRIBLEY, William Charles Harold. b 29. SW Minl Tr Course 84. **d** 87 **p** 88. NSM Kenwyn St Geo *Truro* 87-92; NSM Truro St Paul and St Clem 92-98; Perm to Offic from 99. *54 Chirgwin Road, Truro TR1 1TT* Tel (01872) 272958

STRICKLAND (née CUTTS), Mrs Elizabeth Joan Gabrielle. b 61. St Jo Coll Dur BA83. Westcott Ho Cam 87. **d** 90 **p** 94. C Cayton w Eastfield *York* 90-92; NSM Biggin Hill *Roch* 93-96; Perm to Offic *Ox* 96-00; *Ely* 00-02; P-in-c Holywell w Needingworth *Ely* from 02. *Windswept, Holywell, St Ives PE27 4TQ* Tel (01480) 495275 *or* 460107
E-mail epstrickland@compuserve.com

STRICKLAND, Jonathan Edward Tully. b 56. Westf Coll Lon BSc78. Ridley Hall Cam 00. **d** 02 **p** 03. C Margate H Trin *Cant* from 02. *10 Richmond Avenue, Cliftonville, Margate CT9 2NG* Tel (01843) 295188 E-mail strickers@tesco.net

STRICKLAND, Canon Paul Lowndes. b 21. Linc Th Coll 46. **d** 49 **p** 50. C Oatlands *Guildf* 49-52; C Huddersfield St Jo *Wakef* 52-54; V Carlton 54-58; V Offton, Nettlestead and Willisham *St E* 58-61; CF (TA) 59-67; V Debenham *St E* 61-75; V Lakenheath 75-83; Hon Can St E Cathl 81-83; rtd 83; Perm to Offic *Chelmsf* from 01. *4 Albany Gardens East, Clacton-on-Sea CO15 6HW* Tel (01255) 426303

STRIDE, Clifford Stephen. b 21. Ex & Truro NSM Scheme. **d** 81 **p** 82. NSM Chulmleigh *Ex* 81-83; NSM Hardham *Chich* 87-93; NSM Coldwaltham and Hardham 93-97; NSM Bury w Houghton and Coldwaltham and Hardham from 97. *Ambleside, Sandy Lane, Watersfield, Pulborough RH20 1NF* Tel (01798) 831851

STRIDE, Edgar George. b 23. Tyndale Hall Bris 47. **d** 51 **p** 52. C Croydon Ch Ch Broad Green *Cant* 51-55; V W Thurrock *Chelmsf* 55-61; V Becontree St Mary 61-70; R Spitalfields Ch Ch w All SS *Lon* 70-89; rtd 89; Perm to Offic *Pet* from 89 and *Linc* 89-01. *23 Pembroke Road, Stamford PE9 1BS* Tel (01780) 756325

STRIDE, John David. b 46. Ex Univ BSc68. Oak Hill Th Coll DipHE88. **d** 88 **p** 89. C Ashtead *Guildf* 88-96; V Lodge Moor St Luke *Sheff* from 96. *St Luke's House, 18 Blackbrook Road, Sheffield S10 4LP* Tel 0114-230 5271 Fax 230 8109
E-mail vicar@stlukeslodgemoor.org.uk

STRIDE, John Michael. b 48. Oak Hill Th Coll BA77. **d** 80 **p** 81. C Edmonton All SS *Lon* 80-82; C Edmonton All SS w St Mich 82-83; C Wembley St Jo 83-85; P-in-c Hockering *Nor* 85-89; R Hockering, Honingham, E and N Tuddenham 89-91; V Tuckswood 91-93; Chapl HM Pris Leeds 93-94; Chapl HM Pris Littlehey 94-96; V Heeley *Sheff* 96-99; TR Heeley and Gleadless Valley 99-04; AD Attercliffe 02-04; V Goole from 04. *The Vicarage, 22 Clifton Gardens, Goole DN14 6AS* Tel (01405) 764259 E-mail mojnst@aol.com

STRIKE, Maurice Arthur. b 44. FRSA66. Sarum & Wells Th Coll 85. **d** 87 **p** 88. C Chippenham St Andr w Tytherton Lucas *Bris* 87-91; R Corfe Castle, Church Knowle, Kimmeridge etc *Sarum* 91-04; R Guernsey St Philippe de Torteval *Win* from 04; R Guernsey St Pierre du Bois from 04. *The Rectory, St Pierre du Bois, Guernsey GY7 9SB* Tel (01481) 263544
E-mail mauricestrike@stpeters.ndo.co.uk

STRINGER, Adrian Nigel. b 60. Univ of Wales (Cardiff) BD82 Lanc Univ PGCE83. Sarum & Wells Th Coll 86. **d** 88 **p** 89. C Barrow St Matt *Carl* 88-92; TV Westhoughton *Man* 92-94; I Inver w Mountcharles, Killaghtee and Killybegs *D & R* 94-96; V Tuckingmill *Truro* 96-01; Chapl R Alexandra and Albert Sch Reigate 01-03; I Desertlyn w Ballyeglish *Arm* from 03. *The Rectory, 24 Cookstown Road, Moneymore, Magherafelt BT45 7QF* Tel (028) 8674 8200
E-mail adrianstringer@gatton-park.org.uk

STRINGER, Harold John. b 36. Peterho Cam BA58. Ripon Hall Ox 62. **d** 64 **p** 65. C Hackney St Jo *Lon* 64-68; C Roehampton H Trin *S'wark* 68-71; P-in-c Southampton St Mich w H Rood, St Lawr etc *Win* 71-73; TV Southampton (City Cen) 73-82; Ind Chapl 77-82; V Notting Hill St Jo *Lon* 82-87; V Notting Hill St Pet 82-87; V Notting Hill St Jo and St Pet 87-01; AD Kensington 98-01; rtd 02; Perm to Offic *Lon* from 03. *56 Mountfield Road, London W5 2NQ* Tel (020) 8998 8049
E-mail mail@haroldandchristina.co.uk

STRINGER, Canon John Roden. b 33. AKC61. **d** 62 **p** 63. C Auckland St Helen *Dur* 62-63; C Hebburn St Cuth 63-67; V Cassop cum Quarrington 67-88; RD Sedgefield 84-88; V Lumley 88-98; Hon Can Dur Cathl 88-98; rtd 98; Perm to Offic *Dur* 98-03. *14 Pennine View Close, Carlisle CA1 3GW* Tel (01228) 550467

STROMMEN, Mrs Mary Natasha. b 52. Kent Univ BA73 Bp Otter Coll Chich PGCE74. EAMTC 00. **d** 03 **p** 04. NSM Oslo w Bergen, Trondheim and Stavanger *Eur* from 03. *Lykkestien 4, 7053 Ranheim, Norway* Tel (0047) 7391 3281
E-mail mary.strommen@c2i.net

STRONG, Christopher Patteson. b 43. Ridley Hall Cam. **d** 83 **p** 84. C Dalton-in-Furness *Carl* 83-87; V Wootton *St Alb* 87-02; RD Elstow 94-02; R Fowlmere, Foxton, Shepreth and Thriplow *Ely* from 02. *The Rectory, High Street, Fowlmere, Royston SG8 7SU* Tel and fax (01763) 208195
E-mail christopherpstrong@hotmail.com

STRONG, Jack. b 16. St Aid Birkenhead 52. **d** 54 **p** 55. C Radcliffe St Thos *Man* 54-58; V Chadderton St Mark 58-66; V Burgh-by-Sands w Kirkbampton *Carl* 66-83; R Burgh-by-Sands and Kirkbampton w Kirkandrews etc 83; rtd 83; Perm to Offic

Glouc 84-99. *Aballava, 18 Wincel Road, Winchcombe, Cheltenham GL54 5YE* Tel (01242) 603347

STRONG, John. *See* STRONG, Capt William John Leonard

STRONG, Canon John David. b 34. Cuddesdon Coll 59. **d** 61 **p** 62. C Gosforth All SS *Newc* 61-65; Chapl Malvern Coll 65-71; R Welford w Weston on Avon *Glouc* 72-79; V Nailsworth 79-01; RD Tetbury 83-00; Hon Can Glouc Cathl 91-01; rtd 01. *Glebe House, The Meads, Leighterton, Tetbury GL8 8UW* Tel (01666) 890236 E-mail canondavid@penshouse.freeserve.co.uk

STRONG (formerly BULMAN), Ms Madeline Judith. b 61. K Coll Lon BD AKC. **dss** 86 **d** 87 **p** 94. Shepperton *Lon* 86-88; Par Dn 87-88; Par Dn Brentford 88-94; C 94-96; V Cobbold Road St Sav w St Mary 96-04; Dean of Women's Min 99-02; Chapl Stamford Ho Secure Unit 02-04; Spiritual Cllr PROMIS from 04; Perm to Offic *Cant* from 04. *27 Winchelsea Street, Dover CT17 9ST* Tel 07973-954802 (mobile)

STRONG, Matthew John. b 60. Lon Univ BA81 Cam Univ BA84 MA89. Ridley Hall Cam 82. **d** 85 **p** 86. C Houghton *Carl* 85-89; C Hirwaun *Llan* 89-91; V Troedyrhiw w Merthyr Vale 91-95; Tutor Llan Ord Course 91-95. *22 Birch Lane, Oldbury B68 0NZ* Tel 0121-421 5978

STRONG, Rowan Gordon William. b 53. Victoria Univ Wellington BA76 Edin Univ PhD92 Melbourne Coll of Div ThM88. St Jo Coll (NZ) LTh80. **d** 77 **p** 78. C Kapiti New Zealand 77-79; C Palmerston N St Pet 79-81; V Shannon 81-83; Assoc P E Hill Australia 83-89; NSM Edin Old St Paul *Edin* 89-92; Tutor Edin Univ 91-92; Lect Murdoch Univ Australia from 92; Sen Lect from 02. *150 George Street, East Fremantle, W Australia 6158* Tel (0061) (8) 9339 0643 *or* 9360 6470 Mobile 439-988896 Fax (8) 9360 6480 E-mail r.strong@murdoch.edu.au

STRONG, Capt William John Leonard. b 44. CA Tr Coll 64 Chich Th Coll 87. **d** 89 **p** 90. CA from 66; C Mayfield *Chich* 89-92; C Seaford w Sutton 92-94; V Crawley Down All SS 94-97; rtd 01. *21 Carroll Close, Poole BH12 1PL* Tel (01202) 733940 Mobile 07944-670125

STROUD, David Alan. b 74. Kent Univ BA96 Ch Ch Coll Cant PGCE95. Westcott Ho Cam 02. **d** 04 **p** 05. C Liss *Portsm* from 04. *13 Kelsey Close, Liss GU33 7HR* Tel (01730) 893173

STROUD, The Ven Ernest Charles Frederick. b 31. St Chad's Coll Dur BA59 DipTh60. **d** 60 **p** 61. C S Kirkby *Wakef* 60-63; C Whitby *York* 63-66; C-in-c Chelmsf All SS CD *Chelmsf* 66-69; V Chelmsf All SS 69-75; V Leigh-on-Sea St Marg 75-83; Asst RD Southend 76-79; RD Hadleigh 79-83; Hon Can Chelmsf Cathl 82-83; Adn Colchester 83-97; rtd 97; Perm to Offic *Chelmsf* from 97. *St Therese, 67 London Road, Hadleigh, Benfleet SS7 2QL* Tel (01702) 554941 Fax 500789

STROUD, Canon Robert Owen. b 29. AKC56. **d** 57 **p** 58. C Aylesbury *Ox* 57-60; C Bexhill St Pet *Chich* 60-64; C Gosforth All SS *Newc* 64-66; V High Elswick St Phil 66-72; V Tynemouth Cullercoats St Paul 72-77; R Orlestone w Ruckinge w Warehorne *Cant* 77-81; RD N Lympne 79-81; V Folkestone H Trin w Ch Ch 81-83; TR Folkestone H Trin and St Geo w Ch Ch 83-90; V Folkestone H Trin w Ch Ch 90-93; RD Elham 90-93; Hon Can Cant Cathl 92-93; rtd 93; Perm to Offic *Ex* 94-02; *Cant* from 02. *27 Rochester Avenue, Canterbury CT1 3YE* Tel (01227) 767312

STROWGER, Mrs Patricia. **d** 04 **p** 05. NSM The Lavingtons, Cheverells, and Easterton *Sarum* from 04. *60 High Street, Littleton Panell, Devizes SN10 4ES* Tel (01380) 812840 E-mail pstrowger@waitrose.com

✠**STROYAN, The Rt Revd John Ronald Angus.** b 55. St Andr Univ MTheol76. Qu Coll Birm 81 Bossey Ecum Inst Geneva 82. **d** 83 **p** 84 **c** 05. C Cov E *Cov* 83-87; V Smethwick St Matt w St Chad *Birm* 87-94; V Bloxham w Milcombe and S Newington *Ox* 94-05; AD Deddington 02-05; Suff Bp Warw *Cov* from 05. *Warwick House, 139 Kenilworth Road, Coventry CV4 7AF* Tel (024) 7641 6200 Fax 7641 5254 E-mail bish.warwick@clara.net *or* jstroyan@fish.co.uk

STRUDWICK, Canon Vincent Noel Harold. b 32. Nottm Univ BA59 DipEd. Kelham Th Coll 52. **d** 59 **p** 60. Tutor Kelham Th Coll 59-63; Sub-Warden 63-70; C Crawley *Chich* 70-73; Adult Educn Adv 73-77; R Fittleworth 73-77; Planning Officer for Educn Milton Keynes 77-80; Dir of Educn *Ox* 80-89; Hon Can Ch Ch from 82; Continuing Minl Educn Adv 85-89; Dir Dioc Inst for Th Educn 89-97; Prin Ox Min Course 89-94; Prin St Alb and Ox Min Course 94-96; Fell and Tutor Kellogg Coll Ox 94-00; C Aylesbury w Bierton and Hulcott *Ox* 97-98. *31 The Square, Brill, Aylesbury HP18 9RP* Tel (01865) 280354 Fax 270309 E-mail vincent.strudwick@conted.ox.ac.uk

STRUGNELL, John Richard. b 30. Lon Univ BA52 Leeds Univ MA61 Univ of Qld PhD77. Wells Th Coll 54. **d** 56 **p** 57. C Leeds Halton St Wilfrid *Ripon* 56-59; C Moor Allerton 59-62; Australia from 65; rtd 95. *231 Grandview Road, Pullenvale, Qld, Australia 4069* Tel (0061) (7) 3374 1776

STRUTT, Peter Edward. b 40. St Alb and Ox Min Course 94. **d** 97 **p** 98. NSM Penn Street *Ox* 97-02; Perm to Offic from 02. *59 King's Ride, Penn, High Wycombe HP10 8BP* Tel (01494) 812418

STRUTT, Mrs Susan. b 45. Glouc Sch of Min 87. **d** 90 **p** 94. NSM Eye, Croft w Yarpole and Lucton *Heref* 90-94; C Leominster 94-96; P-in-c Bosbury w Wellington Heath etc 96-98; TV Ledbury from 98; Dioc Adv on Women in Min 99-03. *The Vicarage, Bosbury, Ledbury HR8 1QA* Tel (01531) 640225 E-mail suestrutt@strutts.fsnet.co.uk

STUART, Angus Fraser. b 61. Bedf Coll Lon BA83 K Coll Lon PhD91 St Jo Coll Dur BA92. Cranmer Hall Dur 90. **d** 93 **p** 94. C Twickenham St Mary *Lon* 93-96; Sen Chapl Bris Univ *Bris* 96-05; Hon C Bris St Mich and St Paul 96-98; P-in-c 98-00; Hon C Cotham St Sav w St Mary and Clifton St Paul 00-05; I W Vancouver St Fran in the Wood Canada from 05. *4773 South Piccadilly, West Vancouver BC, Canada, V7W 1J8* Tel (001) (604) 922 3531

STUART, Sister Ann-Marie Lindsay. b 41. Westmr Coll Lon CertEd69 Kent Univ BA80 Univ of Wales (Lamp) MA03. Franciscan Study Cen 76. **d** 99 **p** 00. NSM Sherborne w Castleton and Lillington *Sarum* 99-01; TV Golden Cap Team from 01. *The Rectory, 5 Georges Close, Charmouth, Bridport DT6 6RU* Tel (01297) 560409

STUART, Brother. *See* BURNS, The Rt Revd Stuart Maitland

STUART, Francis David. b 32. Barrister-at-Law Lon Univ BA54 AKC57. Ridley Hall Cam 62. **d** 64 **p** 65. C Addiscombe St Mildred *Cant* 64-67; Chapl RN 67-71; Lic to Offic *Liv* 76-80; TV Oldham *Man* 84-89; Chapl Oldham and Distr Gen Hosp 84-89; Chapl Oldham R Infirmary 86-89; Chapl R Oldham Hosp 89-94; Chapl Oldham NHS Trust 94-98; rtd 97; Perm to Offic *Man* 00-03. *17 rue de la Villeneuve, 56150 Baud, France* Tel (0033) (2) 97 51 11 38

STUART, Canon Herbert James. b 26. CB83. TCD BA48 MA55. **d** 49 **p** 50. C Sligo Cathl *K, E & A* 49-53; C Dublin Rathmines *D & G* 53-55; Chapl RAF 55-73; Asst Chapl-in-Chief RAF 73-80; Chapl-in-Chief and Archdeacon for the RAF 80-83; Can and Preb Linc Cathl *Linc* 81-83; R Cherbury *Ox* 83-87; Perm to Offic *Glouc* 87-97; Perm to Offic *Ox* 87-96; rtd 91. *1 Abbot's Walk, Lechlade GL7 3DB* Tel (01367) 253299

✠**STUART, The Rt Revd Ian Campbell.** b 42. New England Univ (NSW) BA70 CertEd70 Melbourne Univ DipEd77 MA92 MACE72 FAIM91. St Barn Coll Adelaide 84. **d** 85 **p** 85 **c** 92. Australia 85-99; Asst Bp N Queensland 96-99; Chapl Liv Hope Univ Coll from 99; Asst Bp Liv from 99. *The Chaplaincy, Liverpool Hope, Hope Park, Taggart Avenue, Liverpool L16 9JD* Tel 0151-291 3547 Fax 291 3873 E-mail stuarti@hope.ac.uk

STUART-LEE, Nicholas Richard. b 54. Wycliffe Hall Ox. **d** 83 **p** 84. C Costessey *Nor* 83-85; TV Dewsbury *Wakef* 85-90; R Rowlands Castle *Portsm* 90-00; V Nottingham St Jude *S'well* 00-03; TR Thame *Ox* from 03. *The Rectory, 3 Fish Ponds Lane, Thame OX9 2BA* Tel (01844) 212225 *or* 216097 E-mail nrsl@ciloros.fsnet.co.uk

STUART-SMITH, David. b 36. St Pet Coll Ox BA61 MA65. Tyndale Hall Bris. **d** 63 **p** 64. C Tooting Graveney St Nic *S'wark* 63-67; C Richmond H Trin 67-70; Lic to Offic 70-74; NSM Canonbury St Steph *Lon* 70-74; Travelling Sec IVF 70-74; Bangladesh 74-79; V Clapham Park St Steph *S'wark* 79-95; RD Streatham 83-87; Chapl Wye Coll Kent 95-01; P-in-c Wye w Brook *Cant* 95-01; P-in-c Hastingleigh 00-01; rtd 01; Perm to Offic *Cant* from 01. *40 Lancaster Close, Hamstreet, Ashford TN26 2JG* Tel (01233) 731049 E-mail dstuartsmi@aol.com

STUART-WHITE, William Robert. b 59. Ox Univ BA. Trin Coll Bris BA. **d** 86 **p** 87. C Upper Armley *Ripon* 86-91; P-in-c Austrey *Birm* 91-92; P-in-c Warton 91-92; V Austrey and Warton 92-98; R Camborne *Truro* from 98. *The Rectory, Rectory Gardens, Camborne TR14 7DN* Tel (01209) 613020 E-mail wstuartwhi@aol.com

STUBBINGS, Frank Edward. b 20. Fitzw Coll Cam BA48 MA53. Worc Ord Coll 60. **d** 61 **p** 62. C Rowbarton *B & W* 61-64; V Catcott 64-74; V Burtle 64-74; Chapl St Cath Sch Bramley 74-83; R Barkestone w Plungar, Redmile and Stathern *Leic* 83-87; rtd 87; Perm to Offic *B & W* 88-91; Hon C Lostwithiel, St Winnow w St Nectan's Chpl etc *Truro* from 91. *Gooseydown, Park Road, Lostwithiel PL22 0BU* Tel (01208) 872762

STUBBS, Ian Kirtley. b 47. Man Univ DipAE90. Kelham Th Coll 66. **d** 70 **p** 71. C Chandler's Ford *Win* 70-75; C Farnham Royal *Ox* 75-80; Ind Chapl 75-80; Ind Chapl *Man* 81-86; TV Oldham 81-86; TR Langley and Parkfield 86-88; Community Work Officer Dioc Bd of Soc Resp 88-90; Dir Laity Development 90-96; Nat Adv in Adult Learning C of E Bd of Educn 97-02; V Stalybridge *Man* from 02. *The Vicarage, 2 Tintagel Court, Astley Road, Stalybridge SK15 1RA* Tel and fax 0161-338 2368 Mobile 07712-451710 E-mail ianstubbs@surefish.co.uk

STUBBS, Stanley Peter Handley. b 23. Lon Univ BD52 Lille 3 Univ MèsL82. Ely Th Coll 55. **d** 55 **p** 56. C Fletton *Ely* 55-58; Hon Min Can Pet Cathl *Pet* 56-58; C Hounslow Heath St Paul *Lon* 58-63; CF (TA) 59-78; V Northampton St Alb *Pet* 63-76; R Brondesbury Ch Ch and St Laur *Lon* 76-93; rtd 93; Perm to Offic *Lon* from 93. *3 Westbury Lodge Close, Pinner HA5 3FG* Tel (020) 8868 8296

STUBBS, Canon Trevor Noel. b 48. Hull Univ DipMin AKC70. St Aug Coll Cant 73. **d** 74 **p** 75. C Heckmondwike *Wakef* 74-77; Australia 77-80; V Middleton St Cross *Ripon* 80-89; R Wool and E Stoke *Sarum* 89-95; TR Bridport from 95; Can and Preb Sarum Cathl from 03. *The Rectory, 84 South Street, Bridport DT6 3NW* Tel (01308) 422138 E-mail trevor.stubbs@uk.com *or* rrbridport@aol.com

STUBENBORD, Jess William. b 48. BA72. Trin Coll Bris 75. **d** 78 **p** 79. C Cromer *Nor* 78-82; C Gorleston St Mary 82-85; P-in-c Saxthorpe and Corpusty 85-89; P-in-c Blickling 86-89; R Saxthorpe w Corpusty, Blickling, Oulton etc 89-93; P-in-c Mulbarton w Kenningham 93-97; P-in-c Flordon 94-97; P-in-c Wreningham 95-97; R Mulbarton w Bracon Ash, Hethel and Flordon from 98. *The Rectory, The Common, Mulbarton, Norwich NR14 8JS* Tel (01508) 570296 E-mail jwstubenbord@aol.com

STUBLEY, Peter Derek. b 28. AKC57 Dur Univ MA79 PhD91. **d** 58 **p** 59. C Stockton St Chad *Dur* 58-61; V W Hartlepool St Oswald 61-66; Ind Chapl 66-76; Ind Chapl *York* 76-96; V Gt Totham *Chelmsf* 83; P-in-c Kingston upon Hull St Mary *York* 83-88; rtd 96; Perm to Offic *York* from 96. *8 Queens Way, Cottingham HU16 4EP* Tel (01482) 848718

STUCKES, Stephen. b 62. Trin Coll Bris. **d** 96 **p** 97. C Dunster, Carhampton and Withycombe w Rodhuish *B & W* 96-00; V Alcombe from 00. *The Vicarage, 34 Manor Road, Minehead TA24 6EJ* Tel (01643) 703285 E-mail sjstuckes@hotmail.com

STUDD, John Eric. b 34. Clare Coll Cam BA58 MA62. Coll of Resurr Mirfield 58. **d** 60 **p** 61. C Westmr St Steph w St Jo *Lon* 60-65; Australia 65-69; Hon C Kensington St Mary Abbots w St Geo *Lon* 70-71; P-in-c Monks Risborough *Ox* 72-77; P-in-c Gt and Lt Kimble 72-77; C Aylesbury 78; Chapl to the Deaf 78-82; Chapl Hants, Is of Wight and Channel Is Assn for Deaf 82-91; Chapl to the Deaf *Win* 91-99; rtd 99; Perm to Offic *Guildf* 82-96 and *Portsm* 82-99. *28 Elgin Way, Flagstaff Hill, S Australia 5159* Tel (0061) (8) 8370 4707 Fax 8370 6517 E-mail jonea@senet.com.au

STUDDERT, Michael John de Clare. b 39. Trin Coll Cam BA64 MA67 K Alfred's Coll Win PGCE74. Cuddesdon Coll 64. **d** 66 **p** 67. C Langley All SS and Martyrs *Man* 66-69; C Fleet *Guildf* 69-73; Teacher Guildf C of E Secondary Sch 73-77; Chapl Eagle Ho Sch Sandhurst 77-88; rtd 04. *Southlands, Churt Road, Hindhead GU26 6PF* Tel (01428) 604620

STUDDERT-KENNEDY, Andrew Geoffrey. b 59. Ch Ch Ox BA80 MA86. Ripon Coll Cuddesdon BA88. **d** 89 **p** 90. C Wimbledon *S'wark* 89-94; V Norbury St Oswald 94-02; RD Croydon N 99-02; TR Marlborough *Sarum* from 02. *The Rectory, 1 Rawlingswell Lane, Marlborough SN8 1AU* Tel (01672) 514357 *or* 512357 E-mail studdertk@supanet.com

STUDDERT-KENNEDY, Canon Christopher John. b 22. BNC Ox BA49 MA53. Wells Th Coll 49. **d** 51 **p** 52. C Bermondsey St Mary w St Olave and St Jo *S'wark* 51-54; C Clapham H Trin 54-56; V Putney St Marg 56-66; R Godstone 66-91; RD Godstone 76-88; Hon Can S'wark Cathl 80-91; rtd 91; Perm to Offic *Chich* from 91. *Orchard House, The Street, Washington, Pulborough RH20 4AS* Tel (01903) 892774

STUDHOLME, Muriel Isabel. b 25. **d** 96. NSM Bromfield w Waverton *Carl* 96-02; NSM Solway Plain from 02. *Yew Tree Cottage, Dundraw, Wigton CA7 0DP* Tel (01697) 342506

STURCH, Richard Lyman. b 36. Ch Ch Ox BA58 MA61 DPhil70. Ely Th Coll. **d** 62 **p** 63. C Hove All SS *Chich* 62-65; C Burgess Hill St Jo 65-66; C Ox St Mich w St Martin and All SS *Ox* 67-68; Tutor Ripon Hall Ox 67-71; Nigeria 71-74; Lect Lon Bible Coll 75-80; Lic to Offic *Lon* 75-80; TV Wolverton *Ox* 80-86; R Islip w Charlton on Otmoor, Oddington, Noke etc 86-01; rtd 01. *35 Broomfield, Stacey Bushes, Milton Keynes MK12 6HA* Tel (01908) 316779 E-mail rsturch@compuserve.com

STURMAN, Robert George. b 50. Nottm Univ BTh79. Linc Th Coll 75. **d** 79 **p** 80. C Cainscross w Selsley *Glouc* 79-83; TV Bottesford w Ashby *Linc* 83-88; V Prescot *Liv* 88-91; P-in-c Abenhall w Mitcheldean *Glouc* 93-97; R from 97; RD Forest N 99-04. *St Michael's Rectory, Hawker Hill, Mitcheldean GL17 0BS* Tel (01594) 542434

STURROCK, Marian Elizabeth. b 46. Westmr Coll Ox BTh97. St Mich Coll Llan 97. **d** 99 **p** 00. C Swansea St Pet *S & B* 99-03; Chapl Swansea NHS Trust 00-03; R Thundersley *Chelmsf* from 03. *St Peter's Rectory, Church Road, Thundersley, Benfleet SS7 3HG* Tel (01268) 566206 E-mail mesturrock@aol.com

STURT, Rock André Daniel. b 56. Liv Univ BSc79 Lon Univ CertEd80. Oak Hill Th Coll DipTh88 BA88. **d** 88 **p** 89. Chapl St Bede's Sch Cam 88-90; Par Dn Cambridge St Martin *Ely* 88-90; C 90-91; P-in-c Alwalton and Chesterton 91-96; TV The Ortons, Alwalton and Chesterton 96-03; R Gravesend St Geo *Roch* from 03. *St George's Rectory, 54 The Avenue, Gravesend DA11 0LX* Tel (01474) 534965 E-mail rcsturt@fish.co.uk

STUTZ, Clifford Peter. b 25. **d** 83 **p** 84. OLM Cusop w Blakemere, Bredwardine w Brobury etc *Heref* from 83. *Burnt House, Dorstone, Hereford HR3 5SX* Tel (01497) 831472

STUTZ, Ms Sally Ann. b 64. Univ of Wales BSc88 Leeds Metrop Univ MSc93 Birm Univ BD95 SRD90. Qu Coll Birm 93. **d** 96 **p** 97. C Middleton St Mary *Ripon* 96-00; C Wilmslow *Ches* 00-03; Dioc Adv in Chr Worship 00-03; Perm to Offic from 03. *1 Arundel Close, Knutsford WA16 9BZ* Tel (01565) 650919 E-mail sally.stutz@stutzsanyal.fsnet.co.uk

STYLER, Geoffrey Marsh. b 15. CCC Ox BA37 MA40 Cam Univ MA44. Union Th Sem (NY) STM39 Cuddesdon Coll 40. **d** 41 **p** 42. C Heckmondwike *Wakef* 41-44; Vice-Prin Westcott Ho Cam 44-48; Fell CCC Cam from 48; Lect Th Cam Univ 53-82; Select Preacher Ox Univ 55-57; Select Preacher Cam Univ 58 and 63; rtd 82; Perm to Offic *Ely* from 95. *Corpus Christi College, Cambridge CB2 1RH*

STYLER, Jamie Cuming. b 36. Sarum & Wells Th Coll 70. **d** 72 **p** 73. C Whipton *Ex* 72-75; C Paignton St Jo 76-78; V Topsham 78-88; V Plymouth St Simon 88-01; Chapl Plymouth Community Services NHS Trust 94-01; rtd 01; Perm to Offic *Ex* from 01. *Drey House, 27 Langham Way, Ivybridge PL21 9BX* Tel (01752) 691592

STYLES, Clive William John. b 48. WMMTC 87. **d** 90 **p** 91. C Burslem *Lich* 90-94; TV Wednesfield 94-99; V Ashwellthorpe, Forncett, Fundenhall, Hapton etc *Nor* from 99. *The Vicarage, 16 The Fields, Tacolneston, Norwich NR16 1DG* Tel (01953) 788227

STYLES, Canon Lawrence Edgar. b 19. AM88. Pemb Coll Cam BA48 MA52. Ridley Hall Cam. **d** 50 **p** 51. C Bishop's Stortford St Mich *St Alb* 50-53; V Tyldesley w Shakerley *Man* 53-60; Australia from 60; Can Melbourne 82-86; rtd 86. *25 Carson Street, Kew, Vic, Australia 3101* Tel (0061) (3) 9853 9749 Fax as telephone E-mail lstyles@co31.aone.net.au

STYLES, Nigel Charles. b 57. Keele Univ BA79 Rob Coll Cam BA92. Ridley Hall Cam CTM93. **d** 95 **p** 96. C Bedford Ch Ch *St Alb* 95-02; V Bramcote *S'well* from 02. *Bramcote Vicarage, Moss Drive, Bramcote, Beeston NG9 3NF* Tel 0115-925 5655 E-mail nigel@stylish.freeserve.co.uk

SUART, Geoffrey Hugh. b 49. Man Univ BSc70 Nottm Univ PGCE71. Oak Hill Th Coll. **d** 83 **p** 84. C Ogley Hay *Lich* 83-86; TV Wenlock *Heref* 86-90; TR Kirby Muxloe *Leic* 90-04; RD Sparkenhoe E 99-03; R Snettisham w Ingoldisthorpe and Fring *Nor* from 04. *The Vicarage, 18 Park Lane, Snettisham, King's Lynn PE31 7NW* Tel (01485) 541301 E-mail geoffsuart@talk21.com

SUCH, Colin Royston. b 62. UEA LLB83. Ripon Coll Cuddesdon 94. **d** 97 **p** 98. C Streetly *Lich* 97-00; P-in-c Wednesfield St Greg 00-04; V Rushall from 04. *Rushall Vicarage, 10 Tetley Avenue, Walsall WS4 2HE* Tel (01922) 624677

SUCH, Canon Howard Ingram James. b 52. Southn Univ BTh81 Lon Univ MA97. Sarum & Wells Th Coll 77. **d** 81 **p** 82. C Cheam *S'wark* 81-84; Prec Cant Cathl *Cant* 84-91; Hon Min Can Cant Cathl 84-03; V Borden 91-03; AD Sittingbourne 00-03; Can Res and Prec Sheff Cathl *Sheff* from 03. *The Cathedral, Church Street, Sheffield S1 1HA* Tel 0114-275 3434 Fax 278 0244 E-mail howard.such@sheffield-cathedral.org.uk

SUCH, Paul Nigel. b 52. FGA72 BTh84. Chich Th Coll 79. **d** 84 **p** 85. C Handsworth St Andr *Birm* 84-87; C Rugeley *Lich* 87-88; TV 88-91; R Longton 91-02; R Cov St Jo *Cov* from 02. *St John's Rectory, 9 Davenport Road, Coventry CV5 6QA* Tel (024) 7667 3203 Fax as telephone

SUCH, Royston Jeffery. b 46. Solicitor Univ Coll Lon LLB67. Sarum & Wells Th Coll 83. **d** 83 **p** 84. NSM Ringwood *Win* 83-90; R Bishop's Sutton and Ropley and W Tisted from 90. *The Vicarage, Lyeway Lane, Ropley, Alresford SO24 0DW* Tel (01962) 772205

SUCKLING, Keith Edward. b 47. CChem FRSC Darw Coll Cam PhD71 Liv Univ BSc87 DSc89. Oak Hill NSM Course 91. **d** 94 **p** 95. NSM Digswell and Panshanger *St Alb* from 94. *291 Knightsfield, Welwyn Garden City AL8 7NH* Tel (01707) 330022 E-mail keith@suckling291.freeserve.co.uk

SUDAN, Archbishop of the Episcopal Church of the. *See* MARONA, The Most Revd Joseph Biringi Hassan

SUDBURY, Archdeacon of. *See* COX, The Ven John Stuart

SUDDABY, Susan Eveline. b 43. Bedf Coll of Educn CertEd64 Bp Otter Coll Chich AdvCertEd86. S'wark Ord Course 93. **d** 96 **p** 97. NSM Rusthall *Roch* 96-00; C Northfleet 00-02. *51 Bowen Road, Tunbridge Wells TN4 8SU* Tel (01892) 534100

SUDDARDS, John Martin. b 52. Trin Hall Cam BA74 MA77 Barrister-at-Law 75. Qu Coll Birm 86. **d** 89 **p** 90. C Halstead St Andr w H Trin and Greenstead Green *Chelmsf* 89-93; P-in-c Gt w Lt Yeldham 93-97; P-in-c Toppesfield and Stambourne 93-97; R Upper Colne 97-01; RD Hinckford 98-01; TR Witham from 01. *The Vicarage, 7 Chipping Dell, Witham CM8 2JX* Tel (01376) 513509 E-mail john@protais.ndo.co.uk

SUDELL, Philip Henry. b 61. Thames Poly BScEng84 Lon Univ PGCE85. Wycliffe Hall Ox 89. **d** 92 **p** 93. C Worthing Ch the King *Chich* 92-96; C Muswell Hill St Jas w St Matt *Lon* from 96. *8 St James's Lane, London N10 3DB* Tel (020) 8883 7417 *or* 8883 6277 E-mail philip.sudell@st-james.org.uk

SUDRON, David Jeffrey. b 78. Univ Coll Dur BA99 MA00. St Steph Ho Ox 01. **d** 03 **p** 04. C Gt Grimsby St Mary and St Jas

Linc from 03. *3 Grosvenor Street, Grimsby DN32 0QH* Tel (01472) 356931 E-mail david.sudron@dunelm.org.uk

SUDWORTH, Frank. b 43. Open Univ BA92. Oak Hill Th Coll DipHE78. **d** 78 **p** 79. C Deane *Man* 78-81; C Worksop St Jo *S'well* 82-85; V Wollaton Park 85-90; P-in-c Lenton Abbey 85-86; V 86-90; V Upper Armley *Ripon* 90-97; RD Armley 92-95; Dep Chapl HM Pris Liv 97-98; P-in-c Low Moor H Trin *Bradf* 98-03; V Low Moor 03; P-in-c Wyke from 03. *Holy Trinity Vicarage, Park House Road, Low Moor, Bradford BD12 0HR* Tel (01274) 678859

SUFFERN, Richard William Sefton. b 57. Reading Univ BSc79. Trin Coll Bris DipHE90. **d** 90 **p** 91. C Radipole and Melcombe Regis *Sarum* 90-94; TV Cheltenham St Mark *Glouc* 94-99; R Whitnash *Cov* from 99. *St Margaret's Rectory, 2 Church Close, Whitnash, Leamington Spa CV31 2HJ* Tel (01926) 425070 E-mail rwss@btinternet.com

SUFFOLK, Archdeacon of. *See* ARRAND, The Ven Geoffrey William

SUFFRIN, Canon Arthur Charles Emmanuel. b 09. Selw Coll Cam BA30 MA34. Qu Coll Birm 34. **d** 35 **p** 36. C Winchmore Hill H Trin *Lon* 35-39; C Abbots Langley *St Alb* 39-42; CF (EC) 42-44; Public Preacher *St Alb* 44-47; C-in-c Luton St Chris Round Green CD 47-53; V Croxley Green All SS 53-63; V Hexton 63-68; V Pirton 68-74; Hon Can St Alb 65-75; RD Hitchin 71-74; rtd 74; Perm to Offic *Sarum* from 74. *Sampford House Nursing Home, 27 Shurnhold, Melksham SN12 8DD* Tel (01255) 707442

SUGDEN, Charles Edward. b 59. Magd Coll Cam MA81 PGCE82. Trin Coll Bris DipHE91. **d** 91 **p** 92. C Gidea Park *Chelmsf* 91-94; TV Melksham *Sarum* 94-01; NSM Poole from 02. *Hyghfoldes, Canford Magna, Wimborne BH21 3AD* Tel (01202) 887386 E-mail parsons.paddock@btinternet.com

SUGDEN, Canon Christopher Michael Neville. b 48. St Pet Coll Ox BA70 MA74 Nottm Univ MPhil74 Westmr Coll Ox PhD88. St Jo Coll Nottm 72. **d** 74 **p** 75. C Leeds St Geo *Ripon* 74-77; Assoc P Bangalore St Jo India 77-83; Lic to Offic *Ox* from 83; Can St Luke's Cathl Jos Nigeria from 00; Exec Dir Ox Cen for Miss Studies from 01. *Oxford Centre for Mission Studies, PO Box 70, Oxford OX2 6HB* Tel (01865) 556071 Fax 510823 E-mail csugden@ocms.ac.uk

SUGDEN, Kara Kerstin. b 58. Man Univ BSc81 W Midl Coll of Educn PGCE82. Trin Coll Bris BA91. **d** 91 **p** 96. NSM Gidea Park *Chelmsf* 91-94; NSM Melksham *Sarum* 95-01; Chapl Canford Sch Wimborne from 01. *Hyghfoldes, Canford Magna, Wimborne BH21 3AD* Tel (01202) 887386 *or* 841254 E-mail kks@canford.com *or* parsons.paddock@btinternet.com

SULLIVAN, Adrian Michael. b 55. Sarum & Wells Th Coll 85. **d** 87 **p** 88. C Louth *Linc* 87-90; P-in-c E and W Keal 90; P-in-c Marden Hill Gp 90-92; R from 92; RD Bolingbroke 97-00. *The Rectory, Hall Lane, West Keal, Spilsby PE23 4BJ* Tel (01790) 753534 E-mail rev.sully@ic24.net

SULLIVAN, Canon Julian Charles. b 49. Lon Univ BSc74 CertEd75. Wycliffe Hall Ox 80. **d** 83 **p** 84. C Southall Green St Jo *Lon* 83-87; C Wells St Cuth w Wookey Hole *B & W* 87-90; V Sheff St Barn and St Mary *Sheff* 90-91; V Sheff St Mary w Highfield Trin 91-95; V Sheff St Mary Bramall Lane from 95; P-in-c Endcliffe from 04; Hon Can Sheff Cathl from 01; AD Ecclesall from 01. *St Mary's Vicarage, 42 Charlotte Road, Sheffield S1 4TL* Tel 0114-272 4987 E-mail jandvsullivan@blueyonder.co.uk

SULLIVAN, Preb Nicola Ann. b 58. SRN81 RM84. Wycliffe Hall Ox BTh95. **d** 95 **p** 96. C Earlham St Anne *Nor* 95-99; Assoc V Bath Abbey w St Jas *B & W* 99-02; Chapl R Nat Hosp for Rheumatic Diseases NHS Trust 99-02; Bp's Chapl and Past Asst *B & W* from 02; Sub-Dean Wells from 03; Preb Wells Cathl from 03. *North Wing Flat, The Palace, Wells BA5 2PD* Tel (01749) 672341 Fax 679355 E-mail nicola.sullivan@bathwells.anglican.org

SULLIVAN, Canon Trevor Arnold. b 40. CITC 69. **d** 70 **p** 71. C Lurgan Ch the Redeemer *D & D* 71-72; C Tralee *L & K* 72-75; Irish Sch of Ecum 75-77; Ind Chapl *D & G* 77-80; I Ematris *Clogh* 80-84; I Aughrim w Ballinasloe etc *L & K* from 84; Can Limerick and Killaloe Cathls from 89. *The Rectory, Aughrim, Ballinasloe, Co Galway, Irish Republic* Tel and fax (00353) (90) 967 3735 Mobile 87-412194

SULLY, Andrew Charles. b 67. Southn Univ BA88 Birm Univ DPS91 MPhil95. Qu Coll Birm 90. **d** 93 **p** 94. C Maindee *Mon* 93-96; V Llanfihangel w Llanafan and Llanwnnws etc *St D* 96-02; PV St As Cathl *St As* from 02; TV St As from 03. *Woodcroft, Upper Denbigh Road, St Asaph LL17 0BG* Tel (01745) 730064

SULLY, Martin John. b 44. AIAS. St Jo Coll Nottm 80. **d** 82 **p** 83. C Lindfield *Chich* 82-86; V Walberton w Binsted 86-01; R Lewes St Jo sub Castro from 01. *St John's Rectory, 1 The Avenue, Lewes BN7 1BA* Tel (01273) 473080

SUMARES, Manuel. b 43. Stonehill Coll USA BA66 Dominican Coll of Philosophy and Th Ottawa BPh74 Catholic Univ of Portugal PhD84 Westmr Coll Ox BTh99. **d** 97 **p** 99. Hon Asst Chapl Oporto *Eur* 97-05; P-in-c from 05. *Casa do Brrio-Monsul, P-Pvoa de Lanhoso 4830, Portugal* Tel (00351) (253) 993067 E-mail op14089@mail.telepac.pt

SUMMERS, Jeanne. *See* SUMMERS, Preb Ursula Jeanne

SUMMERS, John Ewart. b 35. MIMechE66 Ex Univ MA95. ALCD69. **d** 69 **p** 70. C Fulham St Matt *Lon* 69-72; Chapl RN 72-81; V Devonport St Barn *Ex* 81-98; V Devonport St Mich and St Barn 98-00; rtd 00; Perm to Offic *Ex* from 00. *Box Cottage, Aish, South Brent TQ10 9JH* Tel (01364) 72976

SUMMERS (née PASCOE), Mrs Lorraine Eve. b 51. St Alb and Ox Min Course 98. **d** 01 **p** 02. NSM Sandon, Wallington and Rushden w Clothall *St Alb* from 01. *29 Stane Street, Clothall, Baldock SG7 6TS* Tel (01462) 892472 E-mail revles@surefish.co.uk

SUMMERS, Neil Thomas. b 58. Roehampton Inst BA93 K Coll Lon MA94 St Mary's Coll Strawberry Hill PGCE95. SEITE 97. **d** 00 **p** 01. NSM Richmond St Mary w St Matthias and St Jo *S'wark* from 00. *2 Ravensbourne Road, Twickenham TW1 2DH* Tel (020) 8892 8313 E-mail ntsummers@aol.com

SUMMERS, Paul Anthony. b 53. St Jo Coll York CertEd75. Coll of Resurr Mirfield 77. **d** 80 **p** 81. C Manston *Ripon* 80-83; Min Can and Prec Ripon Cathl 83-88; Chapl Univ Coll of Ripon and York St Jo 84-88; V Whitkirk *Ripon* 88-95; R Lower Wharfedale 95-00; AD Harrogate 98-00; rtd 04; Perm to Offic *Bradf* from 05. *16 Beacon Street, Addingham, Ilkley LS29 0QX* Tel (01943) 839552 E-mail paulsummers65@hotmail.com

SUMMERS, Canon Raymond John. b 41. Univ of Wales TCert63 Open Univ BA75. St Mich Coll Llan 77. **d** 77 **p** 78. NSM Mynyddislwyn *Mon* 77-81; NSM Abercarn 81-82; P-in-c 82-89; V 89-91; V Mynyddislwyn 91-95; TR from 95; RD Bedwellty 93-04; Can St Woolos Cathl from 01. *The Rectory, Vicarage Lane, Pontllanfraith, Blackwood NP12 2DP* Tel (01495) 224240

SUMMERS, Stephen Bruce. b 63. St Andr Univ MTheol95. STETS 98. **d** 00 **p** 01. C Bishop's Waltham *Portsm* 00-02; R Farlington from 02. *The Rectory, 27 Farlington Avenue, Cosham, Portsmouth PO6 1DF* Tel (023) 9237 5145 E-mail summertime@tiscali.co.uk

SUMMERS, Preb Ursula Jeanne. b 35. Birm Univ BA56 Liv Univ CertEd57. Glouc Sch of Min. **dss** 85 **d** 87 **p** 94. Fownhope *Heref* 85-87; Hon C 87; Brockhampton w Fawley 85-87; Hon C 87; C Marden w Amberley and Wisteston 88-94; P-in-c 94-02; RD Heref Rural 93-99; P-in-c Moreton-on-Lugg 96-02; Preb Heref Cathl 96-02; rtd 02; Perm to Offic *Heref* from 02. *99 Walkers Green, Marden, Hereford HR1 3EA* Tel (01432) 880497 E-mail rsatmarden@aol.com

SUMNER, Preb Gillian Mansell. b 39. St Anne's Coll Ox BA61 MA65 MLitt76. Wycliffe Hall Ox BA85. **dss** 86 **d** 87 **p** 94. Ox St Andr *Ox* 86-91; Hon C 87-91; Tutor Wycliffe Hall Ox 86-89; Prin Ox Area Chr Tr Scheme *Ox* 89-91; Vice-Prin Ox Min Course 89-91; Assoc Prin 91-94; Hon C Kirtlington w Bletchingdon, Weston etc 91-94; Hon Can Ch Ch 94; Local Min Officer *Heref* 95-02; P-in-c Wistanstow 95-98; Preb Heref Cathl from 97; Adv for NSM from 02. *Black Venn, Reeves Lane, Stanage, Knighton LD7 1NA* Tel (01547) 530281 E-mail gandmsumner@compuserve.com

SUMNER, John Gordon. b 46. CCC Cam BA68 MA72. Ridley Hall Cam 69. **d** 72 **p** 73. C Liskeard w St Keyne *Truro* 72-75; C Caversham *Ox* 75-81; V Swallowfield 81-93; Asst Chapl Reading Univ 81-93; C Glastonbury w Meare *B & W* 93-04; Ldr Quest Community from 93. *The White Cottage, 15 Bere Lane, Glastonbury BA6 8BD* Tel (01458) 832377 E-mail jsumner@fish.co.uk

SUMNERS, Ms Cristina Jordan. b 47. Vassar Coll (NY) BA73 BNC Ox MPhil85. Princeton Th Sem 73 Gen Th Sem (NY) MDiv76. **d** 78 **p** 82. USA 79-91 and from 02; Asst to R San Antonio St Dav 80-90; P-in-c Rockport Trin by Sea 90-91; Asst Chapl K Edw Sch Witley 93-95; Perm to Offic *Guildf* 93-96; NSM Guildf H Trin w St Mary 97-02; Educn Officer 98-00. *NDCBU 5798, Taos, NM 87571, USA*

SUMSION, Paul Henry. b 74. UMIST BSc97. Trin Coll Bris BA03. **d** 04 **p** 05. C Hawkshaw Lane *Man* from 04; C Holcombe from 04; Chapl Bury Coll of FE from 05. *19 Fernview Drive, Ramsbottom, Bury BL0 9XB* Tel (01204) 888060 E-mail paul.sumsion@fish.co.uk

SUNDERLAND, Christopher Allen. b 52. BA75 St Pet Coll Ox MA80 DPhil80 DipTh86. Trin Coll Bris 84. **d** 86 **p** 87. C Stratton St Margaret w S Marston etc *Bris* 86-90; V Barton Hill St Luke w Ch Ch 90-98; RD Bris City 94-98; Perm to Offic from 98; Research Assoc Churches' Coun for Ind & Soc Resp from 98. *50 Guest Avenue, Emersons Green, Bristol BS16 7GA* Tel 0117-957 4652 Fax as telephone E-mail csunderland@pavilion.co.uk

SUNDERLAND, Preb Geoffrey. b 21. St Edm Hall Ox BA43 MA47 DipTh47. St Steph Ho Ox 46. **d** 48 **p** 49. C Clifton All SS *Bris* 48-51; C Elland *Wakef* 52-54; C Devonport St Mark Ford *Ex* 55-56; C-in-c Plymouth St Jas Ham CD 56-59; V Plymouth St Jas Ham 59-63; Chapl K Coll Taunton 63-65; C Clifton All SS *Bris* 65-68; V Plymstock *Ex* 68-86; RD Plympton 76-81; Preb Ex Cathl 82-89; rtd 86; Perm to Offic *B & W* and *Ex* from 86.

22 Blackdown View, Sampford Peverell, Tiverton EX16 7BE Tel (01884) 821688 E-mail geoffrey.sunderland@tiscali.co.uk

SUNDERLAND, Wendy Jillian. b 47. **d** 99 **p** 00. OLM Bury St Edmunds St Mary *St E* from 99. *9 Crown Street, Bury St Edmunds IP33 1QU* Tel (01284) 766883 E-mail wendy.sunderland@btinternet.com

SUNDERLAND, Archdeacon of. *See* BAIN, The Ven John Stuart

SUNLEY, Denis John. b 50. **d** 02. OLM Cannock *Lich* from 02. *22 Huntsman's Rise, Huntington, Cannock WS12 4PH* Tel (01543) 570572

SURMAN, Malcolm Colin. b 48. Birm Univ CertEd72 Southn Univ BTh88. Sarum & Wells Th Coll 76. **d** 78 **p** 79. C Basingstoke *Win* 78-81; P-in-c Alton All SS 81-85; V 85-01; Chapl N Hants Loddon Community NHS Trust 84-01; P-in-c Burton and Sopley *Win* from 01. *The Vicarage, Preston Lane, Burton, Christchurch BH23 7JU* Tel (01202) 489807 Fax 475793 E-mail malcolm.surman@dsl.pipex.com

SURREY, Mrs Maureen. b 53. Man OLM Scheme 98. **d** 01 **p** 03. OLM Davyhulme Ch Ch *Man* 01-02; OLM Walkden and Lt Hulton from 03. *56 Abingdon Road, Urmston, Manchester M41 0GN* Tel 0161-748 3961 E-mail sidandmo@hotmail.com

SURREY, Archdeacon of. *Vacant*

SURRIDGE, Mrs Faith Thomas. b 45. Open Univ BA75 DipRD83 Lon Univ PGCE76 Ex Univ Dip Maths Educn 87 BPhil(Ed)96. SW Minl Tr Course 83. **dss** 85 **d** 87 **p** 94. St Breoke and Egloshayle *Truro* 85-87; NSM St Mawgan w St Ervan and St Eval 91-95; NSM St Columb Major w St Wenn 95-03; P-in-c from 03. *The Rectory, St Columb TR9 6AE* Tel (01637) 880252 E-mail ftsurridge@portablesl.ngfl.gov.uk

SURTEES, Brian Lawrence. NTMTC. **d** 01 **p** 02. NSM Hatfield Heath and Sheering *Chelmsf* from 01. *13 Bowes Drive, Ongar CM5 9AU* Tel (01277) 363607 E-mail bsurtees@aol.com

SURTEES, Timothy John de Leybourne. b 31. G&C Coll Cam BA54 MA58. Westcott Ho Cam 54. **d** 56 **p** 57. C Guisborough *York* 56-59; C Grantham St Wulfram *Linc* 59-61; V Cayton w Eastfield *York* 61-72; R Cheam *S'wark* 72-96; rtd 96; Perm to Offic *Heref* from 96. *Dove Cottage, Leysters, Leominster HR6 0HW* Tel (01568) 750203

SUSTINS, Nigel. b 46. Lon Univ BEd70. S'wark Ord Course 86. **d** 88 **p** 90. Hon C Mitcham St Mark *S'wark* 89-93; Perm to Offic 96-02. *Address temp unknown*

SUTCH, Christopher David. b 47. TD92. AKC69. St Aug Coll Cant 69. **d** 70 **p** 71. C Bris St Andr Hartcliffe *Bris* 70-75; C Swindon Dorcan 75-78; TV 78-79; P-in-c Alveston 79-83; V 83-89; RD Westbury and Severnside 86-89; CF (TA) 80-83; TR Yate New Town *Bris* 89-99; RD Stapleton 95-99; V Cainscross w Selsley *Glouc* from 99; AD Stonehouse from 04. *The Vicarage, 58 Cashes Green Road, Stroud GL5 4RA* Tel (01453) 755148 Fax as telephone E-mail davidandmegan@sutches25.freeserve.co.uk

SUTCH, Canon Christopher Lang. b 21. Oriel Coll Ox BA47 MA47. Cuddesdon Coll 47. **d** 49 **p** 50. C Westbury-on-Trym H Trin *Bris* 49-53; V Bedminster Down 53-58; V Hanham 58-74; R Brinkworth w Dauntsey 74-86; RD Malmesbury 79-85; Hon Can Bris Cathl 82-86; rtd 86; Hon C E Bris 86-91; Perm to Offic *Bris* from 91 and *Glouc* from 01. *36 Arrowsmith Drive, Stonehouse, Gloucester GL10 2QR* Tel (01453) 791896

SUTCLIFFE, Crispin Francis Henry. b 48. Keble Coll Ox BA69. Sarum & Wells Th Coll 73. **d** 74 **p** 75. C Truro St Paul *Truro* 74-77; S Africa 77-80; P-in-c Treslothan *Truro* 80-85; V 85-91; R Ilchester w Northover, Limington, Yeovilton etc *B & W* from 91. *The Rectory, Ilchester, Yeovil BA22 8LJ* Tel (01935) 840296

SUTCLIFFE, Canon David. b 29. Lon Univ BD57. Lon Coll of Div ALCD56. **d** 57 **p** 58. C Penn *Lich* 57-61; V Ashton St Pet *Man* 61-65; V Eccleshill *Bradf* 65-71; Lic to Offic 71-74; V Manningham St Luke 74-79; V Bolton St Jas w St Chrys 79-85; V Calverley 85-94; RD Calverley 88-93; Hon Can Bradf Cathl 89-94; rtd 94; Perm to Offic *Bradf* from 94. *49 Galloway Lane, Pudsey LS28 7UG* Tel 0113-257 4053 E-mail sutters@galloway89.freeserve.co.uk

SUTCLIFFE, Howard Guest. b 44. Fitzw Coll Cam BA66 MA70 Birm Univ MA75 Man Univ CertRS88. Westcott Ho Cam 73. **d** 74 **p** 75. C Chorlton-cum-Hardy St Clem *Man* 74-77; Chapl Chetham's Sch of Music 77-80; V Oldham St Paul *Man* 80-94; Lic to Offic 94-97; Co-ord Werneth and Freehold Community Development Project from 94; Perm to Offic from 01. *34 Lynn Street, Oldham OL9 7DW,* or *155 Windsor Road, Oldham OL8 1RG* Tel 0161-628 2235 E-mail sdickson@uk.packardbell.org

SUTCLIFFE, Ian. b 31. Surrey Univ BSc69. Qu Coll Birm 61. **d** 63 **p** 65. C W Wimbledon Ch Ch *S'wark* 63-65; C Battersea St Phil 65-66; C Kingston Hill St Paul 71-73; Lic to Offic *Carl* 75-96; rtd 96. *42 Hill Street, Arbroath DD11 1AB*

SUTCLIFFE, John Leslie. b 35. Liv Univ BA56. Sarum Th Coll 58. **d** 60 **p** 61. C Lytham St Cuth *Blackb* 60-62; C Altham w Clayton le Moors 62-65; C-in-c Penwortham St Leon CD 65-71; Ind Chapl *Liv* 71-74; V Orford St Andr 74-79; V Burnley St Cuth *Blackb* 79-88; Bp's Adv on UPA *Ripon* 88-94; Hon C Leeds Gipton Epiphany 88-94; I Carrickmacross w Magheracloone *Clogh* 94-01; rtd 01; Perm to Offic *Blackb* from 02. *1 Beckside, Barley, Burnley BB12 9JZ* Tel (01282) 449687

SUTCLIFFE, Peter John. b 58. BA. Linc Th Coll. **d** 82 **p** 83. C Skipton Ch Ch *Bradf* 82-85; C Tettenhall Regis *Lich* 85-86; TV 86-89; TV Warwick *Cov* 89-93; Relig Producer BBC Radio Cov & Warks 89-93; V Burley in Wharfedale *Bradf* 93-03; RD Otley 97-02; P-in-c Yeadon St Andr from 03. *St Andrew's Vicarage, Haw Lane, Yeadon, Leeds LS19 7XQ* Tel 0113-250 3989 E-mail peter.sutcliffe@btinternet.com

SUTER, Richard Alan. b 48. Rhodes Univ BA72 St Jo Coll Dur BA74 DipTh75. Cranmer Hall Dur 72. **d** 75 **p** 76. C Darlington H Trin *Dur* 75-77; C Wrexham *St As* 77-82; R Llansantffraid Glan Conwy and Eglwysbach 82-87; V Broughton 87-92; RD Wrexham 90-97; V Rossett 92-04; V Holt, Rossett and Isycoed from 04. *The Vicarage, Rossett, Wrexham LL12 0HE* Tel (01244) 570498 E-mail sutertribe@quista.net

SUTHERLAND, Alan. b 55. Sarum & Wells Th Coll. **d** 80 **p** 81. C Hessle *York* 80-83; USA from 83. *111 Fontaine Boulevard, Winchester, KY 40391, USA*

SUTHERLAND, Alistair Campbell. b 31. Lon Univ BSc50 Ex Univ BA77 CEng MIEE. Wycliffe Hall Ox 77. **d** 78 **p** 79. C Nottingham St Jude *S'well* 78-81; R Barton in Fabis 81-96; P-in-c Thrumpton 81; V 81-96; RD W Bingham 87-92; Dioc Adv on Ind Society 92-96; NSM Gotham 93-96; NSM Kingston and Ratcliffe-on-Soar 93-96; rtd 96; Perm to Offic *S'wark* 88-01 and *Ex* 99-05. *36 Pyrton Lane, Watlington OX49 5LX* Tel (01491) 612705

SUTHERLAND, Eric. b 54. AKC76. Sarum & Wells Th Coll 76. **d** 77 **p** 78. C Roehampton H Trin *S'wark* 77-80; C Tattenham Corner and Burgh Heath *Guildf* 80-84; V Guildf All SS 84-91; Dep Chapl HM Pris Wandsworth 91-92; Chapl HM YOI Huntercombe and Finnamore 92-97; Chapl HM Pris Liv from 97. *HM Prison, 68 Hornby Road, Liverpool L9 3DF* Tel 0151-525 9571

SUTHERLAND, Mark Robert. b 55. Univ of NZ LLB77 Lon Inst of Educn MA95 Birkbeck Coll Lon DAC89. Ripon Coll Cuddesdon 82. **d** 85 **p** 86. C Pinner *Lon* 85-88; C Sudbury St Andr 88-91; Perm to Offic *S'wark* 91-92; Chapl Maudsley Hosp Lon 91-94; Chapl Bethlem R Hosp Beckenham 91-94; Chapl Bethlem and Maudsley NHS Trust Lon 94-99; Presiding Chapl S Lon and Maudsley NHS Trust from 99. *The Maudsley Hospital, London SE5 8AZ* Tel (020) 7919 2815 E-mail mark.sutherland@slam.nhs.uk

SUTTLE, Neville Frank. b 38. Reading Univ BSc61 Aber Univ PhD64. **d** 76 **p** 77. NSM Penicuik *Edin* from 76. *44 St James's Gardens, Penicuik EH26 9DU* Tel and fax (01968) 673819

SUTTON, Brian Ralph. b 33. Trin Coll Bris DPS81 Sarum & Wells Th Coll. **d** 83 **p** 84. NSM Timsbury *B & W* 83-84; NSM Timsbury and Priston 85-88; V Thorncombe w Winsham and Cricket St Thomas 89-98; rtd 98; Perm to Offic *B & W* from 98. *The Old Coach House, Priston, Bath BA2 9ED* Tel (01761) 471494

SUTTON, Charles Edwin. b 53. Bris Univ BEd77 Ox Univ. Ripon Coll Cuddesdon 77. **d** 80 **p** 81. C Stanwix *Carl* 80-84; Warden Marrick Priory *Ripon* 84-88. *7 Beech Close, Baldersby, Thirsk YO7 4QB* Tel (01765) 640616

SUTTON, Colin Phillip. b 51. Birm Univ BA73. Chich Th Coll 73. **d** 75 **p** 76. C Penarth All SS *Llan* 75-77; C Roath 77-80; C Caerau w Ely 80-84; V Rhydyfelin 84-04; V Fairwater from 04. *St Peter's Parsonage, 211 St Fagans Road, Cardiff CF5 3DW* Tel (029) 2056 2551

SUTTON, David John. b 49. **d** 99 **p** 00. C Maesglas and Duffryn *Mon* 99-05; Cyprus from 05. *PO Box 61083, 8130 Kato Paphos, Cyprus*

SUTTON, David Robert. b 49. Birm Univ BA69 Ox Univ CertEd72. St Steph Ho Ox 70. **d** 72 **p** 73. C Clitheroe St Mary *Blackb* 72-75; C Fleetwood St Pet 75-78; V Calderbrook *Man* 78-88; V Winton from 88; Chapl Salford Mental Health Services NHS Trust from 92. *The Vicarage, Albany Road, Eccles, Manchester M30 8FE* Tel 0161-788 8991 E-mail frdavid@veronicon.freeserve.co.uk

SUTTON, Eves. *See* SUTTON, The Rt Revd Peter Eves

SUTTON, James William. b 41. Oak Hill Th Coll 81. **d** 84 **p** 85. NSM Chorleywood St Andr *St Alb* 84-00; Perm to Offic from 00. *Belmount, 7 Hillside Road, Chorleywood, Rickmansworth WD3 5AP* Tel (01923) 282806 Fax 447200 E-mail sutton@7hillside.freeserve.co.uk

SUTTON, Jeremy John Ernest. b 60. Ridley Hall Cam 83. **d** 86 **p** 87. C Seacombe *Ches* 86-88; C Northwich St Luke and H Trin 88-90; TV Birkenhead Priory 90-94; V Over St Chad 94-01; V Dunham Massey St Marg and St Mark from 01. *St Margaret's Vicarage, Dunham Road, Altrincham WA14 4AQ* Tel 0161-928 1609 Fax as telephone E-mail jerrysutton@dunhamvicarage.fsnet.co.uk

SUTTON, Canon John. b 47. St Jo Coll Dur BA70. Ridley Hall Cam 70. **d** 72 **p** 73. C Denton St Lawr *Man* 72-77; R 77-82; V High Lane *Ches* 82-88; V Sale St Anne 88-96; V Timperley from 96; Hon Can Ches Cathl from 01; RD Bowdon from 03. *The*

Vicarage, 12 Thorley Lane, Timperley, Altrincham WA15 7AZ Tel 0161-980 4330

SUTTON, John Stephen. b 33. Em Coll Cam BA57 MA61. Wycliffe Hall Ox 57. **d** 59 **p** 60. C Dagenham *Chelmsf* 59-62; C Bishopwearmouth St Gabr *Dur* 62-63; V Over Kellet *Blackb* 63-67; V Darwen St Barn 67-74; V Walthamstow St Jo *Chelmsf* 74-84; V Stebbing w Lindsell 84-98; RD Dunmow 94-98; rtd 98; Perm to Offic *Chich* from 98. *20 Firwood Close, Eastbourne BN22 9QL* Tel (01323) 504654

SUTTON, Canon John Wesley. b 48. Rolle Coll CertEd71. All Nations Chr Coll. **d** 76 **p** 77. Chile 76-77; Peru 79-84; Area Sec SAMS 84-88; Youth Sec SAMS 88-91; Personnel Sec SAMS from 91; Asst Gen Sec SAMS from 91; Perm to Offic *Chelmsf* from 84; *Ox* 85-96; *St Alb* from 85; *Lon* 88-97; Hon Can Peru from 93. *88 Horn Lane, Woodford Green IG8 9AH* Tel (020) 8505 7888 Fax (01892) 525797

✠**SUTTON, The Rt Revd Keith Norman.** b 34. Jes Coll Cam BA58 MA62. Ridley Hall Cam. **d** 59 **p** 60 **c** 78. C Plymouth St Andr *Ex* 59-61; Chapl St Jo Coll Cam 62-67; Chapl Bp Tucker Coll Uganda 68-72; Prin Ridley Hall Cam 73-78; Suff Bp Kingston *S'wark* 78-84; Bp Lich 84-03; rtd 03. *8 Summerleaze Crescent, Bude EX23 8HH* Tel (01288) 352614

SUTTON, Kingsley Edwin. b 70. TCD BTh94. **d** 97 **p** 98. C Belfast St Matt *Conn* 97-99; C Willowfield *D & D* 99-02; I Newry from 02. *Glebe House, Windsor Avenue, Newry BT34 1EQ* Tel (028) 3026 2621 E-mail kingsleydaphne@ukonline.co.uk

SUTTON, Canon Malcolm David. b 26. Selw Coll Cam BA47 MA52. Ridley Hall Cam 48. **d** 50 **p** 51. C Owlerton *Sheff* 50-52; C Kew *S'wark* 52-54; C Hornchurch St Andr *Chelmsf* 54-56; V Roxeth Ch Ch *Lon* 56-63; R Beccles St Mich *St E* 63-82; TR 82-94; RD Beccles 65-73; Hon Can St E Cathl 70-94; rtd 94; Perm to Offic *St E* from 94 and *Nor* from 95. *10 Merville, Carlton Colville, Lowestoft NR33 8UF*

SUTTON, Peter. b 20. Ely Th Coll 60. **d** 62 **p** 63. C Kippax *Ripon* 62-64; R Hamerton *Ely* 64-77; V Winwick 64-77; V Upton and Copmanford 70-77; V Bradworthy *Ex* 77-90; rtd 90; Perm to Offic *Truro* 90-98 and *Ex* from 98. *Mowhay Villa, Chilsworthy, Holsworthy EX22 7BQ* Tel (01409) 254900

SUTTON, Peter Allerton. b 59. Ex Univ BA85. Linc Th Coll 85. **d** 87 **p** 88. C Fareham H Trin *Portsm* 87-90; C Alverstoke 90-93; Chapl HM Pris Haslar 90-93; V Lee-on-the-Solent *Portsm* from 93; Warden of Readers 96-00. *St Faith's Vicarage, Victoria Square, Lee-on-the-Solent PO13 9NF* Tel (023) 9255 0269

✠**SUTTON, The Rt Revd Peter Eves.** b 23. CBE90. Wellington Univ (NZ) BA45 MA47. NZ Bd of Th Studies LTh48. **d** 47 **p** 48 **c** 65. C Wanganui New Zealand 47-50; C Bethnal Green St Jo *Lon* 50-51; C Bp's Hatfield *St Alb* 51-52; New Zealand from 52; V Berhampore 52-58; V Whangarei 58-64; Adn Waimate 62-64; Dean St Paul's Cathl Dunedin 64-65; Bp Nelson 65-90; Acting Primate of New Zealand 85-86; rtd 90. *3 Ngatiawa Street, Nelson 7001, New Zealand* Tel and fax (0064) (3) 546 6591

SUTTON, Philip Frank. b 55. Lon Univ HND76. St Alb and Ox Min Course CBTS95. **d** 95 **p** 96. NSM Akeman *Ox* 95-00; Chapl Ox Radcliffe Hosps NHS Trust 96-00; Sen Chapl R United Hosp Bath NHS Trust from 00; Dioc Adv Hosp Chapl from 04. *Royal United Hospital, Combe Park, Bath BA1 3NG* Tel (01225) 824039 Pager 07659-184873
E-mail suttonp@ruh-bath.swest.nhs.uk

SUTTON, Richard Alan. b 39. Reading Univ BSc61. Wycliffe Hall Ox 70. **d** 72 **p** 73. C Galleywood Common *Chelmsf* 72-76; Pakistan 76-79; C Walsall St Martin *Lich* 79-83; V Barton Hill St Luke w Ch Ch *Bris* 83-89; V Sidcup Ch Ch *Roch* 89-95; rtd 95; Perm to Offic *Roch* 95-98. *30 Mill Road Avenue, Angmering, Littlehampton BN16 4HS* Tel (01903) 856721

SUTTON, Richard John. b 45. Lon Inst of Educn CertEd68. St Alb Minl Tr Scheme 77 Linc Th Coll 81. **d** 82 **p** 83. C Royston *St Alb* 82-87; C Bp's Hatfield 87-95; P-in-c Kempston and Biddenham 95-05; P-in-c Rackheath and Salhouse *Nor* from 05. *The Rectory, 56 Green Lane West, Rackheath, Norwich NR13 6PG* Tel (01603) 720097
E-mail suttonsea@btinternet.com

SUTTON, Ronald. b 27. FSCA. NW Ord Course 76. **d** 79 **p** 80. C Helsby and Dunham-on-the-Hill *Ches* 79-81; R Church Lawton 81-92; RD Congleton 91-92; rtd 92; Perm to Offic *Ches* from 92. *79 Thornton Avenue, Macclesfield SK11 7XL* Tel (01625) 430212

SWABEY, Brian Frank. b 44. BA. Oak Hill Th Coll 79. **d** 82 **p** 83. C Clapham St Jas *S'wark* 82-84; C Wallington H Trin 84-88; Chapl Mt Gould Hosp Plymouth 88-89; V Plymouth St Jude *Ex* 88-92; Chapl RN 92-99; V Penn Fields *Lich* 99-01; rtd 01; Perm to Offic *Ex* from 01. *2 Drax Gardens, Crownhill, Plymouth PL6 5BJ* Tel (01752) 210643
E-mail brianswabey@eurobell.co.uk

SWABY, Anthony. *See* SWABY, Leward Anthony Woodrow

SWABY, Desrene. SEITE 00. **d** 03 **p** 04. NSM S'wark St Geo w St Alphege and St Jude *S'wark* from 03. *36 Gabriel House, 10 Odessa Street, London SE16 7HQ* Tel (020) 7231 9834

SWABY, Canon John Edwin. b 11. St Jo Coll Dur BA32 DipTh34 MA35 Leic Univ PhD83. **d** 34 **p** 35. C Louth w Welton-le-Wold *Linc* 34-40; V Scunthorpe St Jo 40-53; R Mablethorpe w Stain 53-60; P-in-c Theddlethorpe w Mablethorpe 53-54; R 54-60; RD E Louthesk 57-60; Acting RD Yarborough 64-70; V Barton upon Humber 60-71; Can and Preb Linc Cathl 69-77; V Barholm w Stowe 71-76; R Uffington and V Tallington 71-76; rtd 76; Perm to Offic *Linc* and *Pet* from 76. *6 Willoughby Drive, Empingham, Oakham LE15 8PZ* Tel (01780) 460719

SWABY, Keith Graham. b 48. Southn Univ BA75. St Steph Ho Ox 75. **d** 77 **p** 78. C Lt Stanmore St Lawr *Lon* 77-80; C Hove All SS *Chich* 80-83; C Haywards Heath St Wilfrid 83; TV 83-95; C Clayton w Keymer 95-02; rtd 02. *The Old String of Horses, 2 and 4 Stephenson's Lane, Brampton CA8 1RU* Tel (016977) 3803

SWABY, Leward Anthony Woodrow. b 60. Trin Coll Bris 86 Ripon Coll Cuddesdon 89. **d** 92 **p** 93. C Wembley St Jo *Lon* 92-95; C Northampton St Matt *Pet* 95-97; TV Kingsthorpe w Northampton St Dav 97-01; Asst Chapl Worcs Acute Hosps NHS Trust from 01. *Worcestershire Royal Hospital, Charles Hastings Way, Worcester WR5 1DD* Tel (01905) 763333 Fax 760186 E-mail anthony.swaby@worcsacute.wmids.nhs.uk

SWAIN, Allan. *See* SWAIN, Canon William Allan

SWAIN, David Noel. b 36. Wellington Univ (NZ) BA63 MA66. Coll of Resurr Mirfield 65. **d** 67 **p** 68. C Clapham H Trin *S'wark* 67-70; New Zealand 70-75; P-in-c Hermitage *Ox* 75-76; P-in-c Hampstead Norris 75-76; V Hermitage w Hampstead Norreys 76-80; TR Hermitage and Hampstead Norreys, Cold Ash etc 80-82; R Bingham *S'well* 82-94; rtd 94; Perm to Offic *S'well* from 94. *77 Trent Boulevard, West Bridgford, Nottingham NG2 5BE* Tel 0115-982 1222 E-mail dnswain77@aol.com

SWAIN, John Edgar. b 44. Lich Th Coll 67. **d** 69 **p** 70. C E Dereham w Hoe *Nor* 69-73; V Haugh *Linc* 73-74; R S Ormsby w Ketsby, Calceby and Driby 73-74; R Harrington w Brinkhill 73-74; R Oxcombe 73-74; R Ruckland w Farforth and Maidenwell 73-74; R Somersby w Bag Enderby 73-74; R Tetford and Salmonby 73-74; R Belchford 73-74; V W Ashby 73-74; C Attleborough *Nor* 74-78; Canada 78-90 and from 01; P-in-c Oxford Cen w Eastwood and Princeton 78-84; P-in-c Oldcastle w Colchester N 84-90; P-in-c Kirton w Falkenham *St E* 90-95; Chapl Suffolk Constabulary 90-01; P-in-c Gt and Lt Whelnetham w Bradfield St George 95-01; P-in-c Lawshall 98-01; R Wawa w White River and Hawk Junction from 01. *St Paul's Anglican Rectory, Second Avenue, Wawa ON, Canada, P0S 1K0* Tel (001) (705) 856 1336
E-mail j_eswain@hotmail.com

SWAIN, Canon John Roger. b 29. Fitzw Ho Cam BA55 MA59. Bps' Coll Cheshunt 55. **d** 57 **p** 58. C Headingley *Ripon* 57-60; C Moor Allerton 60-65; V Wyther Ven Bede 65-75; V Horsforth 75-86; P-in-c Roundhay St Edm 86-88; V 88-95; RD Allerton 89-94; Hon Can Ripon Cathl 89-95; rtd 95. *3 Harlow Court, Park Avenue, Leeds LS8 2JH* Tel 0113-218 8329

SWAIN, Preb Peter John. b 44. NCA63. Sarum & Wells Th Coll 86. **d** 88 **p** 89. C Beaminster Area *Sarum* 88-92; P-in-c Bromfield w Waverton *Carl* 92-98; P-in-c W Newton 92-98; Member Rural Life and Agric Team 93-96; Ldr 96-98; RD Solway 95-98; Hon Can Carl Cathl 96-98; TR Leominster *Heref* from 98; RD Leominster 98-05; Preb Heref Cathl from 03. *The Rectory, Church Street, Leominster HR6 8NH* Tel (01568) 612124

SWAIN, Raymond Thomas. b 60. Oak Hill Th Coll BA89. **d** 89 **p** 90. C New Clee *Linc* 89-93; TV Cheltenham St Mark *Glouc* 93-03; Ecum Chapl Glos Hosps NHS Trust from 03. *Cheltenham General Hospital, Sandford Road, Cheltenham GL53 7AN* Tel (01242) 222222 ext 4286 E-mail redder@blueyonder.co.uk

SWAIN, Ronald Charles Herbert. b 08. Dur Univ BA42 MA50. St Aug Coll Cant 29. **d** 32 **p** 33. C S Wimbledon H Trin *S'wark* 32-34; SPG China 34-40; Perm to Offic *Dur* and *Newc* 41-42; P-in-c Padgate Ch Ch *Liv* 42-46; Perm to Offic *S'wark* 46-47; Chapl RAF 47-54; CF 54-62; V Walsham le Willows *St E* 62-70; V Shipley *Chich* 70-74; rtd 74; Perm to Offic *St E* 74-02. *81 Westley Road, Bury St Edmunds IP33 3RU* Tel (01284) 761655

SWAIN, Mrs Sharon Juanita. b 46. Sussex Univ BA75 CertEd76 Heythrop Coll Lon MA04. Glouc Sch of Min 81. **dss** 84 **d** 87 **p** 94. Upton St Leonards *Glouc* 84-88; C 87-88; Children's Officer *Worc* 88-95; Min Can Worc Cathl 94-95; V Hanley Castle, Hanley Swan and Welland 95-01; R E Bergholt and Brantham *St E* from 01; RD Samford from 01. *The Rectory, Rectory Lane, Brantham, Manningtree CO11 1PZ* Tel (01206) 392646 Mobile 07880-705630 E-mail s.swain@freeuk.com

SWAIN, Canon William Allan. b 38. Kelham Th Coll 63. **d** 68 **p** 69. C Welwyn Garden City *St Alb* 68-72; C Romsey *Win* 72-74; C Weeke 74-78; V Bournemouth H Epiphany 78-91; P-in-c Moordown 91-94; V from 94; Hon Can Win Cathl from 04. *St John's Vicarage, 2 Vicarage Road, Bournemouth BH9 2SA* Tel (01202) 546400 E-mail allan.swain@themail.co.uk

SWAINSON, Norman. b 38. Salford Univ MSc75. St Jo Coll Nottm 77. **d** 79 **p** 80. C Levenshulme St Pet *Man* 79-84; R Jarrow Grange *Dur* 84-97; rtd 97; Perm to Offic *Ches* from 98.

176 George Street, Compstall, Stockport SK6 5JD Tel 0161-449 0551

SWALES, David James. b 58. Warwick Univ BA. Cranmer Hall Dur. **d** 84 **p** 85. C Eccleshill *Bradf* 84-88; C Prenton *Ches* 88-92; V Oakworth *Bradf* 92-00; V Bolton St Jas w St Chrys from 00. *St James's Vicarage, 1056 Bolton Road, Bradford BD2 4LH* Tel (01274) 637193

SWALES, Peter. b 52. ACIB78 Open Univ BA99. Ridley Hall Cam 85. **d** 87 **p** 88. C Allestree *Derby* 87-91; P-in-c Horsley 91-99; RD Heanor 97-99; V Heckmondwike *Wakef* 99-03; V Chellaston *Derby* from 03. *The Vicarage, St Peter's Road, Chellaston, Derby DE73 6UT* Tel (01332) 704835 E-mail swales.peter@talk21.com

SWALLOW, Mrs Alice Gillian. b 51. Birm Univ BA72 CertEd73. NEOC 82. **dss** 84 **d** 87 **p** 94. Morpeth *Newc* 84-86; Uttoxeter w Bramshall *Lich* 86-88; Par Dn 87-88; Par Dn Rocester 88; Chapl to the Deaf *Man* 88-90; Par Dn Goodshaw and Crawshawbooth 88-93; C Barkisland w W Scammonden *Wakef* 93-95; V Ripponden 95-97; rtd 97; Hon C Scholes *Wakef* from 02. *22 Scholes Lane, Scholes, Cleckheaton BD19 6NR* Tel (01274) 875529 E-mail jill_swallow@yahoo.co.uk

SWALLOW, John Allen George. b 28. St Jo Coll Dur BA53 DipTh54. **d** 54 **p** 55. C Billericay St Mary *Chelmsf* 54-57; C Bishop's Stortford St Mich *St Alb* 57-59; V Roxwell *Chelmsf* 59-64; V S Weald 64-81; R W w E Mersea 81-93; rtd 93; Perm to Offic *Chelmsf* from 93 and *St E* from 95. *72 Rembrandt Way, Bury St Edmunds IP33 2LT* Tel (01284) 725136

SWALLOW, John Brian. b 36. Trent Poly 78. **d** 84 **p** 85. C Cleveleys *Blackb* 84-87; V Blackpool St Mich 87-93; P-in-c Burnley St Steph 93-98; V 98-01; RD Burnley 97-00; rtd 01; Perm to Offic *Dur* from 02. *6 Chichester Walk, Haughton-le-Skerne, Darlington DL1 2SG*

SWAN, Duncan James. b 65. Imp Coll Lon BSc88 SS Coll Cam BA91 Cam Univ MA95. Ridley Hall Cam 89. **d** 92 **p** 93. C Stevenage St Andr and St Geo *St Alb* 92-95; C Harpenden St Nic 95-99; V Redbourn from 99. *The Vicarage, Church End, Redbourn, St Albans AL3 7DU* Tel (01582) 793122 E-mail duncpen@hotmail.com

SWAN, Owen. b 28. ACP71. Edin Th Coll 56. **d** 59 **p** 60. C Lewisham St Jo Southend *S'wark* 59-64; CF (TA) from 60; V Richmond St Luke *S'wark* 64-82; C-in-c Darlington St Hilda and St Columba CD *Dur* 82-84; R Feltwell *Ely* 84-87; R Holywell w Needingworth 87-97; rtd 97; P-in-c Gt Staughton *Ely* 97-02; P-in-c Hail Weston and Southoe 00-02; Perm to Offic *Ely* and *St E* from 02. *Primrose Cottage, Hawes Lane, Norton, Bury St Edmunds IP31 3LS* Tel (01359) 231108

SWAN, Philip Douglas. b 56. Wye Coll Lon BSc78 Qu Coll Cam MA81 CertEd81 Nottm Univ DipTh87. St Jo Coll Nottm 86. **d** 88 **p** 89. C Birm St Martin w Bordesley St Andr *Birm* 88-92; C Selly Park St Steph and St Wulstan 92-96; P-in-c The Lickey 96-98; V from 98. *The Vicarage, 30 Lickey Square, Rednal, Birmingham B45 8HB* Tel 0121-445 1262 E-mail swan@lickey30.freeserve.co.uk

SWAN, Preb Ronald Frederick. b 35. St Cath Coll Cam BA59 MA. Coll of Resurr Mirfield. **d** 61 **p** 62. C Staveley *Derby* 61-66; Chapl Lon Univ *Lon* 66-72; C St Martin-in-the-Fields 72-77; V Ealing St Barn 77-88; V Ealing St Steph Castle Hill 81-88; AD Ealing E 84-88; V Harrow St Mary 88-97; AD Harrow 89-94; Preb St Paul's Cathl from 91; Master R Foundn of St Kath in Ratcliffe from 97. *The Royal Foundation of St Katharine, Ratcliffe, 2 Butcher Row, London E14 8DS* Tel (020) 7790 3540 *or* 7790 8124 Fax 7702 7603 E-mail ron@stkatharine.demon.co.uk

SWANBOROUGH, Alan William. b 38. Southn Univ BEd75. Sarum & Wells Th Coll 77. **d** 80 **p** 81. NSM Ventnor H Trin *Portsm* 80-85; NSM Ventnor St Cath 80-85; Chapl Upper Chine Sch Shanklin from 85; NSM Shanklin St Blasius *Portsm* 91-93; P-in-c from 93. *The Rectory, Rectory Road, Shanklin PO37 6NS* Tel (01983) 862407

SWANEPOEL, David John. b 41. Rhodes Univ BA62 UNISA BA64 DipHE80 BTh84. **d** 75 **p** 76. S Africa 75-94; Dean George 85-89; NSM Hellingly and Upper Dicker *Chich* 94-99. *Providence House, Coldharbour Road, Upper Dicker, Hailsham BN27 3QE* Tel (01323) 843887

SWANN, Antony Keith. b 34. Lon Univ DipTh60. St Aid Birkenhead 58. **d** 61 **p** 62. C Bilston St Leon *Lich* 61-66; Sierra Leone 66-70; V W Bromwich St Phil *Lich* 70-75; Nigeria 76-78; R Church Lench w Rous Lench and Abbots Morton *Worc* 78-88; Chapl HM Pris Coldingley 88-90; Chapl HM Pris Leyhill 91-97; rtd 97; P-in-c Kemble, Poole Keynes, Somerford Keynes etc *Glouc* 97-02; Perm to Offic from 03. *30 Perry Orchard, Upton St Leonards, Gloucester GL4 8DQ*

SWANN, The Ven Edgar John. b 42. TCD BA66 MA70 BD77 HDipEd80. CITC 68. **d** 68 **p** 69. C Crumlin *Conn* 68-70; C Howth *D & G* 70-73; I Greystones from 73; Can Ch Ch Cathl Dublin from 90; Adn Glendalough from 93. *The Rectory, Greystones, Co Wicklow, Irish Republic* Tel (00353) (1) 287 4077 Mobile 87-255 7032 Fax (1) 287 3766 E-mail edgarjswann@eircom.net

SWANN, Canon Frederick David. b 38. **d** 69 **p** 70. C Lurgan Ch the Redeemer *D & D* 69-77; I Ardmore w Craigavon 77-79; I Comber 79-85; I Drumglass w Moygashel *Arm* from 85; Can Arm Cathl from 96; Preb 98-01; Treas from 01. *The Rectory, 26 Circular Road, Dungannon BT71 6BE* Tel (028) 8772 2614 E-mail derickswann@lineone.net

SWANN, Paul David James. b 59. Ch Ch Ox BA81 MA88. St Jo Coll Nottm Dip Th Studies 89 DPS90. **d** 90 **p** 91. C Old Hill H Trin *Worc* 90-94; V 94-02; C Worc City St Paul and Old St Martin etc from 02; Chapl Worc Tech Coll from 02. *21 Tower Road, Worcester WR3 7AF* Tel (01905) 731135 E-mail paul@swannfamily.co.uk

SWANSEA AND BRECON, Bishop of. *See* PIERCE, The Rt Revd Anthony Edward

SWANTON, John Joseph. b 61. Bradf and Ilkley Coll BA84 MCIH89 MRSH95. S Dios Minl Tr Scheme 92. **d** 95 **p** 96. NSM Shalford *Guildf* 95-99; NSM Compton w Shackleford and Peper Harow from 99. *90 Busbridge Lane, Godalming GU7 1QH* Tel (01483) 427160

SWARBRIGG, David Cecil. b 42. TCD BA64 MA67. **d** 65 **p** 66. C Lisburn Ch Ch *Conn* 65-67; C Thames Ditton *Guildf* 72-76; Chapl Hampton Sch Middx 76-97; rtd 97; Perm to Offic *Lon* from 97. *39 Harefield, Hinchley Wood, Esher KT10 9TY* Tel and fax (020) 8398 3950

SWART-RUSSELL, Phoebe. b 58. Cape Town Univ BA79 MA82 DPhil88. Ox NSM Course 89. **d** 90 **p** 94. C Riverside *Ox* 90-95; Hon C Chenies and Lt Chalfont, Latimer and Flaunden 96-00. *The Rectory, Latimer, Chesham HP5 1UA* Tel (01494) 762281

SWARTZ, Clifford Robert. b 71. Trin Coll Connecticut BA92 Trin Coll Cam BA99. Ridley Hall Cam 97. **d** 00 **p** 01. C Kirk Ella *York* 00-03; Regional Dir FOCUS USA from 03; Hon C Tariffville Trin Ch from 03. *242 Steele Road, West Hartford, CT 06117, USA* E-mail clifford@swartz.karoo.co.uk

SWAYNE, Jeremy Michael Deneys. b 41. Worc Coll Ox BA63 BM, BCh67 MRCGP71 FFHom91. **d** 00 **p** 01. NSM Fosse Trinity *B & W* 00-04; P-in-c from 04. *16 Folly Drive, Ditcheat, Shepton Mallet BA4 6QH* Tel (01749) 860371 Fax 860530 E-mail jem.swayne@btinternet.com

SWEATMAN, John. b 44. Open Univ BA89. Bernard Gilpin Soc Dur 67 Oak Hill Th Coll 68. **d** 71 **p** 72. C Rayleigh *Chelmsf* 71-73; C Seaford w Sutton *Chich* 73-77; Chapl RN 77-82; CF 82-85; V Hellingly and Upper Dicker *Chich* 85-90; Hon C Mayfield 95-96; P-in-c Malborough w S Huish, W Alvington and Churchstow *Ex* 96-02; V Ash w Westmarsh *Cant* from 02. *The Vicarage, Queen's Road, Ash, Canterbury CT3 2BG* Tel (01304) 812296 E-mail ash.church@tiscali.co.uk

SWEED, John William. b 35. Bernard Gilpin Soc Dur 58 Clifton Th Coll 59. **d** 62 **p** 63. C Shrewsbury St Julian *Lich* 62-64; C Sheff St Jo *Sheff* 64-70; V Doncaster St Jas 70-79; V Hatfield 79-00; RD Snaith and Hatfield 84-93; rtd 00; Perm to Offic *Sheff* from 00. *21 The Oval, Tickhill, Doncaster DN11 9HF* Tel (01302) 743293

SWEENEY, Andrew James. b 61. Wycliffe Hall Ox 96. **d** 96 **p** 97. C Bladon w Woodstock *Ox* 96-99; C Coleraine *Conn* 99-02; V Cogges and S Leigh *Ox* from 02. *Cogges Priory, Church Lane, Witney OX28 3LA* Tel (01993) 702155 Mobile 07720-472556 E-mail sweeney@coggespriory.freeserve.co.uk

SWEENEY, Robert Maxwell. b 38. Ch Ch Ox BA63 MA66 Birm Univ MA78. Cuddesdon Coll 63. **d** 65 **p** 66. C Prestbury *Glouc* 65-68; C Handsworth St Andr *Birm* 68-70; Asst Chapl Lancing Coll 70-73; V Wotton St Mary *Glouc* 74-79; V Ox St Thos w St Frideswide and Binsey *Ox* 79-03; Chapl Magd Coll Ox 82-88; rtd 03. *9 Bathville Mews, Cedar Court Road, Cheltenham GL53 7RE* Tel (01242) 254028

SWEET, Canon John Philip McMurdo. b 27. New Coll Ox BA49 MA52 Lambeth DD94 SNTS61. Westcott Ho Cam 53 Yale Div Sch 54. **d** 55 **p** 56. C Mansfield St Mark *S'well* 55-58; Chapl Selw Coll Cam 58-83; Dean of Chpl 83-94; Asst Lect Div Cam Univ 60-63; Lect 64-94; Wiccamical Preb Chich Cathl *Chich* from 62; rtd 94; Perm to Offic *Ely* from 99. *97 Barton Road, Cambridge CB3 9LL* Tel (01223) 353186

SWEET, Miss Lynette Jessica. b 59. Kent Univ BA80. Westcott Ho Cam 03. **d** 05. C Wilton w Netherhampton and Fugglestone *Sarum* from 05. *25 Riverside, Wilton, Salisbury SP2 0HW* Tel (01722) 744974 Mobile 07941-477727 E-mail lynette@sweet96.fsnet.co.uk

SWEET, Reginald Charles. b 36. Open Univ BA74. Ripon Hall Ox 61. **d** 62 **p** 63. C Styvechale *Cov* 62-65; Chapl RN 65-69 and 74-93; R Riddlesworth w Gasthorpe and Knettishall *Nor* 69-74; R Brettenham w Rushford 69-74; Perm to Offic 93-96; Chapl Miss to Seamen 96-99; rtd 99; Chapl Win St Cross w St Faith *Win* from 99. *The Chaplain's Lodge, The Hospital of St Cross, St Cross Road, Winchester SO23 9SD* Tel (01962) 853525 Mobile 07889-375085

SWEET, Vaughan Carroll. b 46. Aston Univ BSc69 MSc70. Linc Th Coll 89. **d** 91 **p** 92. C Uttoxeter w Bramshall *Lich* 91-95; P-in-c Hadley 95-98; V from 98; P-in-c Wellington Ch Ch from 03; RD Telford from 00; RD Telford Severn Gorge *Heref* 00-03.

The Vicarage, 19 Manor Road, Hadley, Telford TF1 5PN Tel (01952) 254251 Fax as telephone E-mail vaughan.sweet@virgin.net

SWEET-ESCOTT, Richard Mark. b 28. Hertf Coll Ox BA51 MA53. Westcott Ho Cam 56. **d** 58 **p** 59. C Leeds St Pet *Ripon* 58-62; C Littlehampton St Mary *Chich* 62-65; C Seaford w Sutton 65-72; P-in-c Burpham 72-75; V Easebourne 75-79; V Crawley Down All SS 79-93; rtd 93; Perm to Offic *Chich* from 93. *8 Buttsfield Lane, East Hoathly, Lewes BN8 6EF* Tel (01825) 841052

SWEETING, Paul Lee. b 68. Lanc Univ BSc90 St Martin's Coll Lanc PGCE92. Cranmer Hall Dur BA99. **d** 99 **p** 00. C Blackb St Gabr *Blackb* 99-03; R Falkland Is from 03. *The Deanery, 17 Ross Road, Stanley, Falkland Islands* Tel (00500) 21100 Fax 21842 E-mail sweeting@horizon.co.fk

SWENSSON, Sister Gerd Inger. b 51. Lon Univ MPhil85 Uppsala Univ 70. **dss** 74 **d** 87. In Ch of Sweden 74-75; Notting Hill *Lon* 75-77; CSA from 75; Abbey Ho Malmesbury 77-79; R Foundn of St Kath 79-81; Notting Hill All SS w St Columb *Lon* 81-84; Kensington St Mary Abbots w St Geo 85-89; C Bedford Park 91-95; Sweden from 95. *Christens Gård, Pl 8, St Slågarp, S-231 95 Trelleborg, Sweden* Tel and fax (0046) (40) 487059 Mobile 708-743994 E-mail tedeum@mail.bip.net

SWIFT, Ainsley Laird. b 56. Liv Univ BEd80. Ripon Coll Cuddesdon. **d** 94 **p** 95. C Prescot *Liv* 94-98; TV New Windsor *Ox* 98-01; P-in-c from 01. *The Vicarage, Hermitage Lane, Windsor SL4 4AZ* Tel (01753) 858720 *or* 855447 Fax 860839 E-mail ainsley@swift9485.fsnet.co.uk

SWIFT, Christopher James. b 65. Hull Univ BA86 Man Univ MA95. Westcott Ho Cam 89. **d** 91 **p** 92. C Longton *Blackb* 91-94; TV Chipping Barnet w Arkley *St Alb* 94-97; Chapl Wellhouse NHS Trust 97-98; Chapl Dewsbury Health Care NHS Trust 98-01; Hd Chapl Services Leeds Teaching Hosps NHS Trust from 01. *The Chaplaincy, St James's University Hospital, Beckett Street, Leeds LS9 7TF* Tel 0113-206 4658 Mobile 07786-510292 E-mail chris.swift@leedsth.nhs.uk

SWIFT, Christopher John. b 54. Linc Coll Ox BA76 MA Selw Coll Cam BA80. Westcott Ho Cam 79. **d** 81 **p** 82. C Portsea N End St Mark *Portsm* 81-84; C Alverstoke 84-87; V Whitton SS Phil and Jas *Lon* 87-94; R Shepperton from 94; AD Spelthorne 98-04. *The Rectory, Church Square, Shepperton TW17 9JY* Tel and fax (01932) 220511 E-mail christopher.swift@london.anglican.org

SWIFT (formerly LAKER), Mrs Grace. b 39. RN63. Sarum & Wells Th Coll BTh91. **d** 91 **p** 94. C Helston and Wendron *Truro* 91-95; Chapl Havering Hosps NHS Trust 95-02; NSM Rush Green *Chelmsf* 98-02; Bp's Adv for Hosp Chapl from 99. *The Vicarage, 111 Church Street, Billericay CM11 2TR* Tel (01277) 625947 E-mail graceswift@hotmail.com

SWIFT, Ian John Edward. b 46. NTMTC 99. **d** 02 **p** 03. NSM Basildon St Martin *Chelmsf* from 02. *79 Bull Lane, Rayleigh SS6 8LD* Tel (01268) 775593 Mobile 07799-888607 E-mail ian@swiftfamily.fsnet.co.uk

SWIFT, Jessica Suzanne. b 75. Univ of New Brunswick BSc99. Wycliffe Hall Ox 99. **d** 02 **p** 03. C Islington St Mary *Lon* 02-05; C Mildmay Grove St Jude and St Paul from 05. *306B Amhurst Road, London N16 7UE* Tel (020) 7923 0114 Mobile 07812-676240 E-mail swift_jessica@hotmail.com

SWIFT, Ms Pamela Joan. b 47. Liv Univ BSc68. NEOC 85. **d** 88 **p** 94. Par Dn Bermondsey St Jas w Ch Ch *S'wark* 88-91; Par Dn Middleton St Cross *Ripon* 91-92; C Leeds All So and Dioc Stewardship Adv 92-95; TR Bramley 95-99; Miss Adv USPG *Blackb, Bradf, Carl* and *Wakef* 99-01; Hon C Kildwick *Bradf* 99-01; R and Community P Glas St Matt *Glas* 01-05; rtd 05. *17 Trotternish Avenue, Staffin, Portree IV51 9JU* Tel (01470) 562710 Mobile 07833-938843 E-mail pamswift@lineone.net

SWIFT, Richard Barrie. b 33. Selw Coll Cam BA58 MA64. Ripon Hall Ox. **d** 60 **p** 61. C Stepney St Dunstan and All SS *Lon* 60-64; C Sidmouth St Nic *Ex* 64-72; P-in-c W Hyde St Thos *St Alb* 72-77; V Mill End 72-77; V Mill End and Heronsgate w W Hyde 77-82; V Axminster *Ex* 82-83; P-in-c Chardstock 82-83; P-in-c Combe Pyne w Rousdon 82-83; TR Axminster, Chardstock, Combe Pyne and Rousdon 83-94; rtd 94; Perm to Offic *Ex* from 94. *15 Paternoster Row, Ottery St Mary EX11 1DP* Tel (01404) 813102

SWIFT, Selwyn. b 41. Trin Coll Bris 73. **d** 76 **p** 77. C Melksham *Sarum* 76-79; TV 79-81; TV Whitton 81-84; V Derry Hill 84-89; R Bunwell, Carleton Rode, Tibenham, Gt Moulton etc *Nor* 89-01; RD Depwade 97-01; rtd 01. *2 Kembold Close, Bury St Edmunds IP32 7EF* Tel (01284) 701258

SWIFT, Stanley. b 47. ACIS71 Nottm Univ DipTh73 Open Univ BA86. Linc Th Coll 71. **d** 74 **p** 75. C Heaton St Barn *Bradf* 74-77; C Bexhill St Pet *Chich* 77-81; R Crowland *Linc* 81-86; RD Elloe W 82-86; R Upminster *Chelmsf* 86-95; P-in-c N Ockendon 94-95; V Rush Green 95-02; V Gt Burstead from 02. *The Vicarage, 111 Church Street, Billericay CM11 2TR* Tel (01277) 625947 E-mail stanswift@hotmail.com

SWINBURNE, Harold Noel. b 27. Univ Coll Lon BA49 St Chad's Coll Dur DipTh. **d** 53 **p** 54. C Cockerton *Dur* 53-57; C Wisbech St Aug *Ely* 57-59; V Chilton Moor *Dur* 59-71; Lect RS New Coll Dur 71-93; Lic to Offic *Dur* 71-85; V Bishopwearmouth St Nic 85-93; rtd 93. *39 Durham Moor Crescent, Durham DH1 5AS* Tel 0191-386 2603

SWINDELL, Anthony Charles. b 50. Selw Coll Cam BA73 MA77 Leeds Univ MPhil77. Ripon Hall Ox 73. **d** 75 **p** 76. C Hessle *York* 75-78; P-in-c Litlington w W Dean *Chich* 78-80; Adult Educn Adv E Sussex 78-80; TV Heslington *York* 80-81; Chapl York Univ 80-81; R Harlaxton *Linc* 81-91; RD Grantham 85-90; R Jersey St Sav *Win* from 91; Perm to Offic *Nor* 93-96. *The Rectory, Rectory Lane, St Saviour's Hill, St Saviour, Jersey JE2 7NP* Tel (01534) 736679

SWINDELL, Brian. b 35. St Jo Coll Nottm 86. **d** 88 **p** 89. C Wombwell *Sheff* 88-91; V Brinsworth w Catcliffe 91-93; TR Brinsworth w Catcliffe and Treeton 93-99; rtd 99; Perm to Offic *S'well* from 04. *36 Wasdale Close, West Bridgford, Nottingham NG2 6RG* Tel 0115-914 1125

SWINDELL, Richard Carl. b 45. Didsbury Coll Man CertEd67 Open Univ BA73 Leeds Univ MEd86. N Ord Course 79 Qu Coll Birm 77. **d** 82 **p** 83. Hd Teacher Moorside Jun Sch 78-96; NSM Halifax St Aug *Wakef* 82-92; NSM Huddersfield H Trin from 92; Family Life and Marriage Officer 96-02; Bp's Adv for Child Protection from 02. *13 Moor Hill Court, Laund Road, Salendine Nook, Huddersfield HD3 3GQ* Tel (01484) 640473 Mobile 07946-761364 E-mail rswin25004@aol.com

SWINDELLS, Jonathan Reid. b 66. Bp Otter Coll Chich BA90 Cam Univ PGCE93 Leeds Univ BA02. Coll of Resurr Mirfield 00. **d** 02 **p** 03. C Sherborne w Castleton and Lillington *Sarum* from 02. *69 Granville Way, Sherborne DT9 4AT* Tel (01935) 389333 Mobile 07790-430070 E-mail jonathan@swindellsj.fsworld.co.uk

SWINDELLS, Philip John. b 34. St Edm Hall Ox BA56 MA60. Ely Th Coll 56. **d** 58 **p** 59. C Upton cum Chalvey *Ox* 58-62; C Bishops Hull St Jo *B & W* 62-66; C Stevenage St Geo *St Alb* 66-71; V Stevenage All SS Pin Green 71-78; R Clophill 78-00; P-in-c Upper w Lower Gravenhurst 83-93; P-in-c Shillington 96-99; rtd 00; Perm to Offic *Ely* from 00. *10 Birchmead, Gamlingay, Sandy SG19 3ND* Tel (01767) 654136

SWINDLEHURST, Canon Michael Robert Carol. b 29. Worc Coll Ox BA52 MA56. Cuddesdon Coll 61. **d** 63 **p** 64. C Havant *Portsm* 63-66; C Hellesdon *Nor* 66-69; V Brightlingsea *Chelmsf* 69-95; Miss to Seamen 69-95; RD St Osyth *Chelmsf* 84-94; Hon Can Chelmsf Cathl 89-95; rtd 95; Perm to Offic *Chelmsf* from 95 and *St Alb* 95-98. *9 Radwinter Road, Saffron Walden CB11 3HU* Tel (01799) 513788

SWINDON, Suffragan Bishop of. *See* RAYFIELD, The Rt Revd Lee Stephen

SWINGLER, Preb Jack Howell. b 19. St Jo Coll Cam BA41 MA47. Ridley Hall Cam 46. **d** 48 **p** 49. C Yeovil St Jo w Preston Plucknett *B & W* 48-53; V Henstridge 53-79; P-in-c Charlton Horethorne w Stowell 78-79; R Henstridge and Charlton Horethorne w Stowell 79-85; RD Merston 74-84; Preb Wells Cathl 79-05; rtd 85; Perm to Offic *B & W* from 85. *St Andrew's, March Lane, Galhampton, Yeovil BA22 7AN* Tel (01963) 440842

SWINHOE, Terence Leslie. b 49. Man Univ BA71 PGCE72 Lon Univ BD95. N Ord Course. **d** 84 **p** 85. C Harborne St Pet *Birm* 84-87; V Warley *Wakef* 87-96; V Rastrick St Matt from 96. *St Matthew's Vicarage, 1 Vicarage Gardens, Brighouse HD6 3HD* Tel (01484) 713386 E-mail swinfam@aol.com

SWINN, Gerald Robert. b 40. Leeds Univ BSc60 Lon Univ BD70. Oak Hill Th Coll 63. **d** 66 **p** 67. C Weston-super-Mare Ch Ch *B & W* 66-69; C Harefield *Lon* 70-72; Lic to Offic *Sarum* from 72. *7 Witchampton Road, Broadstone BH18 8HY*

SWINN, Philip Daniel. b 65. Oak Hill Th Coll BA01. **d** 01 **p** 02. C Harpenden St Nic *St Alb* 01-04; TV Bp's Hatfield from 04. *St John's Vicarage, Hill View, Bishops Rise, Hatfield AL10 9BZ* Tel (01707) 262689 E-mail pd_swinn@swinns.co.uk

SWINNERTON, Ernest George Francis. b 33. Clare Coll Cam BA54 MA57. Linc Th Coll 56. **d** 58 **p** 59. C Kirkholt *Man* 58-61; C Swindon Ch Ch *Bris* 61-67; C-in-c Walcot St Andr CD 67-75; P-in-c Chilton Foliat *Sarum* 76; TV Whitton 76-85; V Bolton St Matt w St Barn *Man* 85-95; rtd 95; Perm to Offic *Man* from 95. *15 Orchard Close, Chelmsford CM2 9SL* Tel (01245) 491366

SWINTON, Garry Dunlop. b 59. SS Mark & Jo Coll Plymouth BA81 CertEd82. Ripon Coll Cuddesdon 85. **d** 88 **p** 89. C Surbiton St Andr and St Mark *S'wark* 88-92; Succ S'wark Cathl 92-97; P-in-c Wandsworth St Faith 97-01; Chapl YMCA Wimbledon 97-01; Chapl Greycoat Hosp Sch from 01; Chapl Westmr City Sch from 01. *4 Greenham Close, London SE1 7RP* Tel (020) 7261 9321 Mobile 07961-422303 E-mail garryswinton@hotmail.com

SWITHINBANK, Kim Stafford. b 53. SS Coll Cam BA77 MA80. Cranmer Hall Dur 78. **d** 80 **p** 81. C Heigham H Trin *Nor* 80-83; Chapl Monkton Combe Sch Bath 83-85; C Langham Place All So *Lon* 85-89; R Stamford St Geo w St Paul *Linc* 90-02; Chapl NW Anglia Healthcare NHS Trust 90-02; V Falls Ch Virginia

USA from 02. *2344 Brittany Parc Drive, Falls Church, VA 22043, USA* Tel (001) (703) 569 2377 E-mail kswithinbank@thefallschurch.org

SWITHINBANK, Mrs Penelope Jane. b 53. St Andr Univ MTheol74 Hughes Hall Cam PGCE75. Ridley Hall Cam 00. **d** 02. Falls Ch Virginia USA from 02. *2344 Brittany Parc Drive, Falls Church, VA 22043, USA* Tel (001) (703) 569 2377 E-mail womanbydesign@hotmail.com

SWITZERLAND, Archdeacon of. *See* WILLIAMS, The Ven John Richard

SWORD, Bernard James. b 46. **d** 04 **p** 05. NSM Millbrook *Ches* from 04. *114 Tennyson Avenue, Dukinfield SK16 5DR* Tel 0161-338 6180 Mobile 07866-446681 E-mail besword@aol.com

SWYER, David Martin. b 64. Univ of Wales (Abth) BA87 PGCE89. St Mich Coll Llan DipTh91. **d** 91 **p** 92. C Killay *S & B* 91-93; C Newton St Pet 93-95; R Albourne w Sayers Common and Twineham *Chich* from 95. *The Rectory, 5 The Twitten, Albourne, Hassocks BN6 9DF* Tel (01273) 832129

SWYER (née HARRIS), Mrs Rebecca Jane. b 67. **d** 91. C Sketty *S & B* 91-95. *The Rectory, 5 The Twitten, Albourne, Hassocks BN6 9DF* Tel (01273) 832129

SWYNNERTON, Brian Thomas. b 31. JP77. Ox Univ Inst of Educn 56 NY Univ BA74 PhD75 FRGS62 LCP62. Lich Th Coll 67. **d** 69 **p** 70. C Swynnerton *Lich* 69-71; CF (TAVR) 70-80; C Eccleshall *Lich* 71-74; C Croxton w Broughton 74-80; Chapl and Lect Stafford Coll 80-84; Chapl Naples w Sorrento, Capri and Bari *Eur* 84-85; Perm to Offic *Lich* from 85; Chapl Rishworth Sch Ripponden 85-88; Chapl Acton Reynald Sch Shrewsbury 88-96; Chapl Telford City Tech Coll from 96. *Hales Farm, Market Drayton TF9 2PP* Tel (01630) 657156

SYDNEY, Archbishop of. *See* JENSEN, The Most Revd Peter Frederick

SYER, Angela. b 48. ARCM69 Philippa Fawcett Coll CertEd71. Qu Coll Birm. **d** 00 **p** 01. C Oakdale *Sarum* 00-04; P-in-c Coxley w Godney, Henton and Wookey *B & W* from 04. *The Vicarage, Vicarage Lane, Wookey, Wells BA5 1JT* Tel (01749) 677244

SYKES, Mrs Clare Mary. b 61. WMMTC 93. **d** 96 **p** 97. C Tupsley w Hampton Bishop *Heref* 96-01; NSM Bromyard from 01; NSM Stanford Bishop, Stoke Lacy, Moreton Jeffries w Much Cowarne etc from 01. *The Vicarage, 28 Church Lane, Bromyard HR7 4DZ* Tel (01885) 482438 E-mail sykes@quista.net

SYKES, Gerald Alfred. b 58. Univ of Wales (Abth) BSc79 PhD84 Univ of Wales (Cardiff) BD98. St Mich Coll Llan 95. **d** 98 **p** 99. C Cardigan w Mwnt and Y Ferwig w Llangoedmor *St D* 98-01; P-in-c Brechfa w Abergorlech etc from 01. *The Rectory, Brechfa, Carmarthen SA32 7RA* Tel (01267) 202389 Fax as telephone E-mail sykesga@bigfoot.com *or* sykesga@freenet.co.uk

SYKES, Graham Timothy Gordon. b 59. ACIB89. St Jo Coll Nottm BTh92. **d** 92 **p** 93. C Kington w Huntington, Old Radnor, Kinnerton etc *Heref* 92-95; C Breinton 95-97; TV W Heref 97-98; Dioc Co-ord for Evang 95-01; V Bromyard from 01; P-in-c Stanford Bishop, Stoke Lacy, Moreton Jeffries w Much Cowarne etc from 01. *The Vicarage, 28 Church Lane, Bromyard HR7 4DZ* Tel (01885) 482438 E-mail sykes@quista.net

SYKES, Ian. b 44. Lon Univ DipTh Leic Univ DipEd. Bris Bapt Coll 64 Ripon Coll Cuddesdon 84. **d** 85 **p** 86. In Bapt Min 64-84; C Headington *Ox* 85-88; TV Bourne Valley *Sarum* 88-97; R Peter Tavy, Mary Tavy, Lydford and Brent Tor *Ex* from 97. *The Rectory, Mary Tavy, Tavistock PL19 9PP* Tel (01822) 810516

SYKES, James Clement. b 42. Keble Coll Ox BA64 MA71. Westcott Ho Cam 65. **d** 67 **p** 68. C Bishop's Stortford St Mich *St Alb* 67-71; Chapl St Jo Sch Leatherhead 71-73; Bermuda 74-79; V Northaw *St Alb* 79-87; Chapl St Marg Sch Bushey 87-98; R Guernsey St Sampson *Win* from 99. *The Rectory, Grandes Maisons Road, St Sampsons, Guernsey GY2 4JS* Tel (01481) 244710 Mobile 07781-111459

SYKES, Miss Jean. b 45. Leeds Univ BA66 Bris Univ CertEd67. Ripon Coll Cuddesdon 86. **d** 88 **p** 94. C N Huddersfield *Wakef* 88-91; TD 91-93; TV Kippax w Allerton Bywater *Ripon* from 93; AD Whitkirk from 05. *The Vicarage, 134 Leeds Road, Allerton Bywater, Castleford WF10 2HB* Tel 0113-286 9415 E-mail vicar@stmarykippax.org.uk

SYKES, Jeremy Gordon. b 63. Hull Univ BA85. St Alb Minl Tr Scheme 92 Ripon Coll Cuddesdon 97. **d** 99 **p** 00. C Ipswich St Mary-le-Tower *St E* 99-02; P-in-c Briston w Burgh Parva and Melton Constable *Nor* from 02. *The Vicarage, 1 Grange Close, Briston, Melton Constable NR24 2LY* Tel (01263) 860280 E-mail jeremy@sykes-uk.com

SYKES, Jeremy Jonathan Nicholas. b 61. Girton Coll Cam BA83 MA86. Wycliffe Hall Ox BA88. **d** 89 **p** 90. C Knowle *Birm* 89-92; Asst Chapl Oakham Sch 92-98; Chapl Giggleswick Sch from 98; Lic to Offic *Bradf* from 98. *Giggleswick School, Giggleswick, Settle BD24 0DE* Tel (01729) 825856 Fax as telephone E-mail jemsykes@globalnet.co.uk

SYKES, Canon John. b 39. Man Univ BA62. Ripon Hall Ox 61. **d** 63 **p** 64. C Heywood St Luke *Man* 63-67; C Bolton H Trin 67-71; Chapl Bolton Colls of H&FE 67-71; R Reddish *Man* 71-78; V Saddleworth 78-87; TR Oldham 87-04; Hon Can Man Cathl 91-04; rtd 04; Chapl to The Queen from 95. *53 Ivy Green Drive, Springhead, Oldham OL4 4PR* Tel 0161-678 6767 E-mail j.sykes@rdplus.net

✠**SYKES, The Rt Revd Prof Stephen Whitefield.** b 39. St Jo Coll Cam BA61 MA65. Ripon Hall Ox 63. **d** 64 **p** 65 **c** 90. Fell and Dean St Jo Coll Cam 64-74; Asst Lect Div Cam Univ 64-68; Lect 68-74; Van Mildert Prof Div Dur Univ 74-85; Can Res Dur Cathl *Dur* 74-85; Regius Prof Div Cam Univ 85-90; Hon Can Ely Cathl *Ely* 85-90; Bp Ely 90-99; Perm to Offic *Ban* from 90; Prin St Jo Coll Dur from 99; Hon Asst Bp Dur from 99. *Ingleside, Whinney Hill, Durham DH1 3BE* Tel 0191-384 6465 E-mail s.w.sykes@durham.ac.uk

SYKES, William George David. b 39. Ball Coll Ox BA63 MA68. Wycliffe Hall Ox 63. **d** 65 **p** 66. Chapl Bradf Cathl *Bradf* 65-69; Chapl Univ Coll Hosp Lon 69-78; Chapl Univ Coll Ox from 78. *Senior Common Room, University College, High Street, Oxford OX1 4BH* Tel (01865) 276663

SYLVESTER, Jeremy Carl Edmund. b 56. Cape Town Univ BA78 HDipEd79. Coll of Resurr Mirfield 84. **d** 87 **p** 88. S Africa 87-96; P-in-c Stoke Newington St Olave *Lon* 96-98; TV Plymouth Em, St Paul Efford and St Aug *Ex* 98-01; CMS from 01. *CMS, Partnership House, 157 Waterloo Road, London SE1 8UU* Tel (020) 7928 8681

SYLVIA, Keith Lawrence Wilfred. b 63. Chich Th Coll 85. **d** 88 **p** 89. C Newbold w Dunston *Derby* 88-91; C Heston *Lon* 91-95; V Brighton St Matthias *Chich* 95-00; C Hove St Patr 00-04; P-in-c Croydon St Andr *S'wark* from 04. *St Andrew's Vicarage, 6 St Peter's Road, Croydon CR0 1HD* Tel (020) 8688 6011 E-mail frkeithsylvia@hotmail.com

SYMES, Collin. b 20. Birm Univ BA47 MA48. Bps' Coll Cheshunt 56. **d** 58 **p** 59. C Enfield St Mich *Lon* 58-60; C Brondesbury St Anne w Kilburn H Trin 60-62; R Maidwell w Draughton *Pet* 62-66; R Yardley Hastings 66-68; V Denton 66-68; Hon C Rusthall *Roch* 68-85; Chapl W Kent Coll of FE 68-73; Chapl Chapl RN Sch Haslemere 81-84; rtd 84; Chapl St Elphin's Sch Matlock 85-86; Perm to Offic *Chich* from 86 and *Roch* from 99. *5 Castle Mount, 40 Carlisle Road, Eastbourne BN20 7TD* Tel (01323) 721099

SYMES, Percy Peter. b 24. Leeds Univ BA50. Coll of Resurr Mirfield 50. **d** 52 **p** 53. C Ox St Barn *Ox* 52-54; C Headington 54-56; C Abingdon w Shippon 56-61; V Reading St Luke 61-81; V Drayton St Pet (Berks) 81-89; rtd 89; Perm to Offic *Ox* 94-02. *Merrileas, 23 Hollesley Road, Alderton, Woodbridge IP12 3BX* Tel (01394) 410452

SYMES-THOMPSON, Hugh Kynard. b 54. Peterho Cam BA76 MA81. Cranmer Hall Dur. **d** 79 **p** 80. C Summerfield *Birm* 79-82; C Harlow New Town w Lt Parndon *Chelmsf* 82-83; Australia 84-89; TV Dagenham *Chelmsf* 89-95; R Cranfield and Hulcote w Salford *St Alb* from 95; Chapl Cranfield Univ from 02. *The Rectory, Court Road, Cranfield, Bedford MK43 0DR* Tel (01234) 750214 E-mail revhugh@symes-thom.freeserve.co.uk

SYMMONS, Roderic Paul. b 56. Chu Coll Cam BA77 MA81 Oak Hill Th Coll BA83 Fuller Th Sem California DMin90. **d** 83 **p** 84. C Ox St Aldate w St Matt *Ox* 83-88; Lic to Offic *LA* USA 89-90; R Ardingly *Chich* 90-99; RD Cuckfield 95-99; P-in-c Redland *Bris* from 99; Tutor Trin Coll Bris from 99. *Redland Vicarage, 151 Redland Road, Bristol BS6 6YE* Tel 0117-946 4691 Fax 946 6862 E-mail rod@redland.org.uk

SYMON, Canon John Francis Walker. b 26. Edin Univ MA50. Edin Th Coll 50. **d** 52 **p** 53. C Edin St Cuth *Edin* 52-56; CF 56-59; R Forfar *St And* 59-68; R Dunblane 68-85; Can St Ninian's Cathl Perth 74-91; Can Emer St Andr from 00; Chapl Trin Coll Glenalmond 85-91; rtd 91; P-in-c Killin *St And* from 95. *20 Cromlix Crescent, Dunblane FK15 9JQ* Tel (01786) 822449 E-mail walkersymon@freeola.com

SYMON, Canon Roger Hugh Crispin. b 34. St Jo Coll Cam BA59. Coll of Resurr Mirfield 59. **d** 61 **p** 62. C Westmr St Steph w St Jo *Lon* 61-66; P-in-c Hascombe *Guildf* 66-68; Chapl Surrey Univ 66-74; V Paddington Ch Ch *Lon* 74-78; V Paddington St Jas 78-79; USPG 80-87; Abp Cant's Acting Sec for Angl Communion Affairs 87-94; Can Res Cant Cathl *Cant* 94-02; rtd 02; Perm to Offic *Glouc* from 02. *5 Bath Parade, Cheltenham GL53 7HL* Tel (01242) 700645 E-mail rogersymon@blueyonder.co.uk

SYMONDS, Alan Jeffrey. b 56. Ridley Hall Cam CTM95. **d** 95 **p** 96. C Bath St Luke *B & W* 95-99; R Abbas and Templecombe w Horsington from 99. *The Rectory, 8 Church Hill, Templecombe BA8 0HG* Tel (01963) 370302 E-mail as@fish.co.uk

SYMONDS, James Henry. b 31. Ripon Hall Ox 67. **d** 69 **p** 70. C Southampton (City Cen) *Win* 69-71; CF 71-78; CF 79-90; P-in-c Arrington *Ely* 78-79; P-in-c Orwell 78-79; P-in-c Wimpole 78-79; P-in-c Croydon w Clopton 78-79; CF (R of O) 90-96; rtd 96; P-in-c Coughton, Spernall, Morton Bagot and Oldberrow *Cov* 99-02; Perm to Offic *Lich* from 00 and *Cov* from 02. *Thimble Cottage, Kings Coughton, Alcester B49 5QD* Tel (01789) 400814

SYMONS, Fernley Rundle. b 39. Peterho Cam BA61 MA71 Open Univ BSc99. St Steph Ho Ox 61. **d** 64 **p** 65. C Chesterton St Geo *Ely* 64-67; C Henleaze *Bris* 67-72; V Shirehampton 72-00; rtd 00; Perm to Offic *Bris* from 01. *Inglewood, 6 Westfield Close, Uphill,*

Weston-super-Mare BS23 4XQ Tel and fax (01934) 626855 Mobile 07950-051816 E-mail fernley@fanddsymons.net

SYMONS, Stewart Burlace. b 31. Keble Coll Ox BA55 MA59. Clifton Th Coll 55. **d** 57 **p** 58. C Hornsey Rise St Mary *Lon* 57-60; C Gateshead St Geo *Dur* 60-61; C Patcham *Chich* 61-64; R Stretford St Bride *Man* 64-71; V Waterloo St Jo *Liv* 71-83; R Ardrossan *Glas* 83-96; C-in-c Irvine St Andr LEP 83-96; Miss to Seamen 83-96; rtd 96; Perm to Offic *Carl* from 96. *8 Carlingdale, Burneside, Kendal LA9 6PW* Tel (01539) 728750

SYMS, Richard Arthur. b 43. Ch Coll Cam BA66 MA71. Wycliffe Hall Ox 66. **d** 68 **p** 69. C New Eltham All SS *S'wark* 68-72; Chapl to Arts and Recreation *York* and *Dur* 72-73; C Hitchin St Mary *St Alb* 73-76; TV Hitchin 77-78; Perm to Offic 78-97 and from 03; P-in-c Datchworth 97-03; rtd 03. *94 Pondcroft Road, Knebworth SG3 6DE* Tel and fax (01438) 811933 E-mail syms94@faxvia.net

SYNNOTT, Alan Patrick Sutherland. b 59. **d** 85 **p** 86. C Lisburn Ch Ch *Conn* 85-88; CF 88-95; I Galloon w Drummully *Clogh* 95-01; I Monkstown *Conn* 01-04. *Address temp unknown*

T

TABERN, James. b 23. St Aid Birkenhead 57. **d** 59 **p** 60. C Garston *Liv* 59-61; V Litherland St Paul Hatton Hill 61-72; V Gillingham St Mark *Roch* 72-79; V Lindow *Ches* 79-85; rtd 85; Perm to Offic *Liv* 86-91 and from 98; *Ches* from 97. *12 Dickinson Road, Formby, Liverpool L37 4BX* Tel (01704) 831131

TABERNACLE, Peter Aufrere. b 22. SSC. S'wark Ord Course 72. **d** 74 **p** 75. NSM Enfield St Geo *Lon* 74-80; C Corby Epiphany w St Jo *Pet* 80-83; V Wellingborough St Mark 83-88; P-in-c Wilby 83-88; rtd 88; Perm to Offic *Pet* from 88. *16 St Mary's Paddock, Wellingborough NN8 1HJ* Tel and fax (01933) 228570 E-mail p.tabernacle@btinternet.com

TABOR, James Hugh. b 63. Univ of W Aus BA85. Ripon Coll Cuddesdon 02. **d** 04 **p** 05. C Alverstoke *Portsm* from 04. *1 Newlands Avenue, Gosport PO12 3QX* Tel 07808-302481 (mobile)

TABOR, John Tranham. b 30. Ball Coll Ox BA56 MA58. Ridley Hall Cam 55. **d** 58 **p** 59. C Lindfield *Chich* 58-62; Tutor Ridley Hall Cam 62-63; Chapl 63-68; Warden Scargill Ho 68-75; R Berkhamsted St Mary *St Alb* 75-96; rtd 96; Perm to Offic *St Alb* from 96 and *Ox* 99-00. *2 Warwick Close, Aston Clinton, Aylesbury HP22 5JF* Tel and fax (01296) 631562 E-mail johntabor@customnet.co.uk

TABRAHAM, Canon Albert John. b 14. Birm Univ DipTh71. Coll of Resurr Mirfield 55. **d** 56 **p** 57. C Oldbury *Birm* 56-59; V Stockland Green 59-70; RD Aston 68-70; V Acocks Green 70-80; RD Yardley 74-77; Hon Can Birm Cathl 78-80; rtd 80; Hon C Duns *Edin* 80-01. *Muirfield Nursing Home, Main Street, Gullane EH31 2AA* Tel (01620) 842768

TADMAN, John Christopher. b 33. Lon Coll of Div 54. **d** 58 **p** 59. C Blackheath St Jo *S'wark* 58-61; C Surbiton Hill Ch Ch 61-64; R Cratfield w Heveningham and Ubbeston *St E* 65-70; R Kelsale w Carlton 70-74; R Ashurst *Roch* 74-76; V Fordcombe 74-77; P-in-c Penshurst 76-77; R Penshurst and Fordcombe 77-85; V Felsted *Chelmsf* 85-93; Resource Min Brentwood 93-98; Chapl Warley Hosp Brentwood 93-98; rtd 98; Perm to Offic *Glouc* 99-01; Jt P-in-c Staverton w Boddington and Tredington etc 01-04. *Fairways, Shaw Green Lane, Prestbury, Cheltenham GL52 3BP* Tel (01242) 582826

TAGGART, William Joseph. b 54. DipFD. DipTh. **d** 85 **p** 86. C Belfast St Mich *Conn* 85-90; Chmn Dioc Youth Coun 90-94; I Belfast St Kath from 90. *St Katharine's Rectory, 24 Lansdowne Road, Belfast BT15 4DB* Tel (028) 9077 7647 E-mail stkatharine@talk21.com

TAGUE, Russell. b 59. Aston Tr Scheme 90 Linc Th Coll 92. **d** 94 **p** 95. C Astley *Man* 94-97; Chapl HM YOI Swinfen Hall 97-00; Chapl HM Pris Risley 00-05; TV Kirkby *Liv* from 05. *The Vicarage, 6 Brampton Close, Liverpool L32 1BD*

TAILBY, Ms Jane Dorothy. b 56. Culham Coll of Educn BEd79. WEMTC 01. **d** 04 **p** 05. NSM Frampton Cotterell *Bris* from 04; NSM Iron Acton from 04. *47 Chedworth, Yate, Bristol BS37 8RY* Tel (01454) 313096 E-mail jdtailby@aol.com

TAILBY, Mark Kevan. b 36. K Coll Lon 60. **d** 64 **p** 65. C Newbold on Avon *Cov* 64-67; C Stratford-on-Avon w Bishopton 67-70; CF 70-76; P-in-c S Shoebury *Chelmsf* 76-79; P-in-c Stambridge 79-89; Chapl Rochford Gen Hosp 79-89; TV Dovercourt and Parkeston *Chelmsf* 89-93; P-in-c Colchester St Botolph w H Trin and St Giles 93-97; V 97-01; rtd 01; Perm to Offic *Worc* from 01; OCF from 93. *53 Jamaica Road, Malvern WR14 1TX* Tel (01684) 573869

TAILBY, Peter Alan. b 49. Chich Th Coll 83. **d** 85 **p** 86. C Stocking Farm *Leic* 85-88; C Knighton St Mary Magd 88-90; P-in-c Thurnby Lodge 90-98; P-in-c W Molesey *Guildf* from 98. *The Vicarage, 518 Walton Road, West Molesey KT8 2QF* Tel (020) 8979 3846 E-mail ptailby@netlineuk.net

TAINTON, Mrs Carol Anne. b 50. EMMTC 96. **d** 99 **p** 00. NSM Gamston and Bridgford *S'well* 99-03; P-in-c Lowdham w Caythorpe, and Gunthorpe 03-04; V from 04. *4 Hazelas Drive, Gunthorpe, Nottingham NG14 7FZ* Tel 0115-966 5922 E-mail revcaroltainton@ukonline.co.uk

TAIT, James Laurence Jamieson. b 47. St Jo Coll Dur 78. **d** 80 **p** 81. C Heyside *Man* 80-81; C Westhoughton 81-84; R Aldingham and Dendron and Rampside *Carl* 84-88; V Flookburgh 88-92; New Zealand from 92. *PO Box 5134, Palmerston North, New Zealand* Tel (0064) (6) 358 9134 *or* 358 5403 Fax 358 5403 E-mail stpeters@icon.nz

TAIT, Philip Leslie. b 52. Ex Univ BA73 Hull Univ PGCE74. NEOC 87. **d** 90 **p** 91. NSM Osbaldwick w Murton *York* 90-92; Chapl and Hd RS Berkhamsted Sch Herts 93-97; P-in-c Woodhorn w Newbiggin *Newc* 98; Chapl HM Pris Wolds 98-00; Chapl R Russell Sch Croydon 00-05; Chapl Hurstpierpoint Coll from 05. *Hurstpierpoint College, Malthouse Lane, Hurstpierpoint, Hassocks BN6 9JS* Tel (01273) 833636

TAIT (née DAVIS), Canon Ruth Elizabeth. b 39. St Andr Univ MA62 Moray Ho Coll of Educn DipEd63. Moray Ord Course 89. **dss** 90 **d** 94 **p** 95. Elgin w Lossiemouth *Mor* 90-96; C 94-96; NSM Dufftown *Ab* from 96; C Forres *Mor* 96-98; NSM Aberlour 98-03; Hon Can St Andr Cathl Inverness from 03. *Benmore, Burnbank, Birnie, Elgin IV30 8RW* Tel (01343) 862808 E-mail ruth.e.tait@btinternet.com

TAIT, Ms Valerie Joan. b 60. Open Univ BA96 SRN82 RSCN82 DN88. Trin Coll Bris 99. **d** 01 **p** 02. C W Heref from 01. *79 Bridle Road, Hereford HR4 0PW* Tel (01432) 273708 E-mail valtait@fish.co.uk

TALBOT, Alan John. b 23. BNC Ox BA49 MA55. Coll of Resurr Mirfield 49. **d** 51 **p** 52. C Hackney Wick St Mary of Eton w St Aug *Lon* 51-54; C Portsea St Sav *Portsm* 54-63; Chapl St Jo Coll Chidya Tanzania 63-65; P-in-c Namakambale 65-68; V Stepney St Aug w St Phil *Lon* 69-78; V Twickenham All Hallows 78-86; rtd 88; Perm to Offic *S'wark* from 88. *46 Brandon Street, London SE17 1NL* Tel (020) 7703 0719

TALBOT, Derek Michael (Mike). b 55. St Jo Coll Dur BSc77 Nottm Univ DipTh85. St Jo Coll Nottm 84. **d** 87 **p** 88. C Rushden w Newton Bromswold *Pet* 87-90; C Barton Seagrave w Warkton 90-95; V Kettering Ch the King 95-02; V Northwood Em *Lon* from 02; AD Harrow from 02. *Emmanuel Vicarage, 3 Gatehill Road, Northwood HA6 3QB* Tel (01923) 828914 *or* 845203 Mobile 07767-763715 Fax (01923) 845209 E-mail mike.talbot@lineone.net *or* mike.talbot@ecn.org.uk

TALBOT (née THOMSON), Mrs Elizabeth Lucy. b 74. Lanc Univ BA96 Bris Univ BA00 MA01. Trin Coll Bris 98. **d** 01 **p** 02. C Bitterne *Win* from 01; Chapl Dean Close Sch Cheltenham from 05. *Dean Close School, Shelburne Road, Cheltenham GL51 6HE* Tel (01242) 258000 Mobile 07977-115923 E-mail libby@thomson74.fslife.co.uk

TALBOT, George Brian. b 37. Qu Coll Birm 78. **d** 80 **p** 81. C Heref St Martin *Heref* 80-83; R Bishop's Frome w Castle Frome and Fromes Hill 83-90; P-in-c Acton Beauchamp and Evesbatch w Stanford Bishop 83-90; R Burstow *S'wark* 90-02; rtd 02. *Box No 237, Bellaluz 10.03, La Manga Club, 30385 Los Belones, Cartagena, Murcia, Spain* Tel (0034) (9) 6813 8103

TALBOT, John Herbert Boyle. b 30. TCD BA51 MA57. CITC 52. **d** 53 **p** 54. C Dublin St Pet *D & G* 53-57; Chan Vicar St Patrick's Cathl Dub 56-61; C Dublin Zion Ch 57-61; Chapl Asst St Thos Hosp Lon 61-64; Min Can and Sacr Cant Cathl *Cant* 64-67; R Brasted *Roch* 67-84; R Ightham 84-95; P-in-c Shipbourne 87-91; RD Shoreham 89-95; rtd 95; Perm to Offic *Roch* from 01. *12 Waterlakes, Edenbridge TN8 5BX* Tel (01732) 865729

TALBOT, John Michael. b 23. FRSM FRCPath68 Lon Univ MD52. S'wark Ord Course 75. **d** 78 **p** 79. NSM S Croydon Em *Cant* 78-81; Perm to Offic *Nor* 82-85 and from 96; NSM Hethersett w Canteloff w Lt and Gt Melton 85-96. *3 White Gates Close, Hethersett, Norwich NR9 3JG* Tel (01603) 811709

TALBOT, Mrs June Phyllis. b 46. Ripon Coll of Educn CertEd67. NEOC 88. **d** 91 **p** 94. NSM Cleadon *Dur* 91-97; Dioc Voc Adv from 94; NSM Bishopwearmouth St Gabr from 97. *66 Wheatall Drive, Whitburn, Sunderland SR6 7HQ* Tel 0191-529 2265

TALBOT (née KINGHAM), Canon Mair Josephine. b 59. Univ Coll Lon BA84. Ridley Hall Cam 85. **d** 88 **p** 94. C Gt Yarmouth *Nor* 88-94; Sen Asst P Raveningham Gp 94-99; Chapl Norfolk Mental Health Care NHS Trust 94-02; P-in-c Watton w Carbrooke and Ovington *Nor* from 02; Bp's Adv for Women's Min 01-04; Hon Can Nor Cathl from 02. *St Mary's Vicarage,*

Norwich Road, Watton, Thetford IP25 6DB Tel (01953) 881439 E-mail mair@mairtalbot.fsnet.co.uk

TALBOT, Mrs Margaret Eileen Coxon. b 52. STETS 01. **d** 04 **p** 05. NSM Herstmonceux and Wartling *Chich* from 04. *The Granary, Kitchenham Road, Ashburnham, Battle TN33 9NA* Tel (01424) 893605

TALBOT, Mrs Marian. b 25. Qu Coll Birm 76. **dss** 78 **d** 87 **p** 94. Droitwich *Worc* 78-87; Par Dn Droitwich Spa 87-88; Chapl Droitwich Hosps 83-88; Asst Chapl Alexandra Hosp Redditch 88-98; Perm to Offic 88-98; rtd 98; Perm to Offic *Truro* from 00. *Noten, 10 The Fairway, Mawnan Smith, Falmouth TR11 5LR* Tel (01326) 250035

TALBOT, Mike. *See* TALBOT, Derek Michael

TALBOT, Stephen Richard. b 52. BSc. Trin Coll Bris DipHE. **d** 84 **p** 85. C Tonbridge SS Pet and Paul *Roch* 84-89; P-in-c Hemingford Abbots *Ely* 89-96; P-in-c Hemingford Grey 89-01; P-in-c Ashburnham w Penhurst *Chich* from 01. *Agmerhurst Granary, Kitchenham Road, Ashburnham, Battle TN33 9NA* Tel (01424) 893605

TALBOT, Sister Susan Gabriel. b 46. Leeds Univ BA69 Man Poly CertEd70 Man Univ PhD00. N Ord Course 91. **d** 94 **p** 95. C Wythenshawe St Martin *Man* 94-98; P-in-c Cheetham St Jo 98-02; Lic Preacher 02-04; C Wilmslow *Ches* from 04. *34 Eaton Road, Bowdon, Altrincham WA14 3EH* Tel 0161-233 0630 E-mail susan@gabriel87.freeserve.co.uk

TALBOT-PONSONBY, Preb Andrew. b 44. Leeds Univ DipTh66. Coll of Resurr Mirfield 66. **d** 68 **p** 70. C Radlett *St Alb* 68-70; C Salisbury St Martin *Sarum* 70-73; P-in-c Acton Burnell w Pitchford *Heref* 73-80; P-in-c Frodesley 73-80; P-in-c Cound 73-80; Asst Dioc Youth Officer 73-80; P-in-c Bockleton w Leysters 80-81; V 81-92; P-in-c Kimbolton w Middleton-on-the-Hill 80-81; V Kimbolton w Hamnish and Middleton-on-the-Hill 81-92; P-in-c Wigmore Abbey 92-96; R 97-98; Preb Heref Cathl from 87; RD Leominster 97-98; Public Preacher from 98; Warden of Readers from 02. *Llan Retreat House, Twitchen, Clunbury, Craven Arms SY7 0HN* Tel (01588) 660417 E-mail llant-p@beeb.net

TALBOT-PONSONBY, Mrs Gillian. b 50. Sarum & Wells Th Coll 89. **d** 91 **p** 94. C Leominster *Heref* 91-92; NSM Wigmore Abbey 92-98; Public Preacher from 98; Asst Dioc Adv on Women in Min 99-03; Dioc Adv from 03. *Llan Retreat House, Twitchen, Clunbury, Craven Arms SY7 0HN* Tel (01588) 660417 E-mail llant-p@beeb.net

TALBOTT, Brian Hugh. b 34. RD78. St Pet Hall Ox BA57 MA64. Westcott Ho Cam. **d** 59 **p** 60. C Newc H Cross *Newc* 59-61; C Newc St Jo 61-64; Chapl RNR 63-91; Chapl Barnard Castle Sch 64-71; Chapl Bishop's Stortford Coll 71-96; Hon C Bishop's Stortford St Mich *St Alb* 71-96; rtd 96; Perm to Offic *B & W* from 96; Acting Chapl Wells Cathl Sch 97-98. *Four Seasons, Milton Lane, Wookey Hole, Wells BA5 1DG* Tel (01749) 679678

TALBOTT, Scott Malcolm. b 55. St Alb and Ox Min Course 00. **d** 03 **p** 04. NSM Watford St Andr *St Alb* from 03. *Elmhurst, 40 Berks Hill, Chorleywood, Rickmansworth WD3 5AH* Tel (01923) 282370 Mobile 07802-244877 E-mail scott.talbott@talk21.com

TALBOTT, Simon John. b 57. Pontifical Univ Maynooth BD81. **d** 81 **p** 82. In RC Ch 81-87; C Headingley *Ripon* 88-91; V Gt and Lt Ouseburn w Marton cum Grafton 91-97; Chapl Qu Ethelburga's Coll York 91-97; P-in-c Markington w S Stainley and Bishop Thornton *Ripon* 97-01; AD Ripon 97-01; P-in-c Epsom St Martin *Guildf* 01-02; V from 02. *35 Burgh Heath Road, Epsom KT17 4LP* Tel (01372) 743336 Fax 749193 E-mail s.talbott@virgin.net

TALING, Johannes Albert (Hans). b 59. St Jo Coll Nottm 93. EAMTC 00. **d** 02 **p** 03. C Littleborough *Man* 02-05; P-in-c N Buckingham *Ox* from 05. *The Rectory, South Hall, Maids Moreton, Buckingham MK18 1QD* Tel (01280) 813246 E-mail family@taling.fsnet.co.uk

TALLANT, John. b 45. Edin Th Coll 86. **d** 88 **p** 89. C Cayton w Eastfield *York* 88-90; C N Hull St Mich 90-91; V Scarborough St Sav w All SS 91-93; V Fleetwood St Nic *Blackb* 93-99; P-in-c Sculcoates St Paul w Ch Ch and St Silas *York* 99-03; P-in-c Hull St Mary Sculcoates 99-03; P-in-c Hull St Steph Sculcoates 99-03; R Woldsburn from 03. *The New Rectory, West End, Bainton, Driffield YO25 9NR* Tel (01377) 217622

TALLINN, Dean of. *See* PIIR, The Very Revd Gustav Peeter

TALLON, Jonathan Robert Roe. b 66. Rob Coll Cam BA88 MA92. St Jo Coll Nottm BTh94. **d** 97 **p** 98. C Bury St Jo w St Mark *Man* 97-01; P-in-c Cadishead from 01. *St Mary's Vicarage, Penry Avenue, Cadishead, Manchester M44 5ZE* Tel 0161-775 2171

TAMBLING, Peter Francis. b 20. St Pet Hall Ox BA47. Westcott Ho Cam. **d** 49 **p** 50. C Stockport St Mary *Ches* 49-51; C Westbury *Sarum* 52-56; R Bishopstrow and Boreham 56-64; R Zeals and Stourton 64-73; P-in-c Bourton w Silton 71-73; R Upper Stour 73-74; R Glenfield *Leic* 74-85; RD Sparkenhoe III 76-81; rtd 85; Perm to Offic *B & W* 86-94. *20 Balsam Fields, Wincanton BA9 9HF* Tel (01963) 34237

TAMPLIN, Peter Harry. b 44. Sarum & Wells Th Coll 71. **d** 73 **p** 74. C Digswell *St Alb* 73-76; C Chesterton St Luke *Ely* 76-82; V Chesterton St Geo 82-95; R Durrington *Sarum* from 95. *The Rectory, Church Street, Durrington, Salisbury SP4 8AL* Tel (01980) 594374 *or* 594471 E-mail petertamplin@hotmail.com

TAMPLIN, Roger Ian. b 41. K Coll Lon BD63 AKC63. St Boniface Warminster 60. **d** 64 **p** 65. C St Helier *S'wark* 64-68; C Camberwell St Giles 68-72; C Tanga St Aug Tanzania 72-73; P-in-c Brent Pelham w Meesden *St Alb* 74-78; P-in-c Anstey 75-78; rtd 01. *31 Shackleton Spring, Stevenage SG2 9DF* Tel (01438) 316031 E-mail roger.tamplin@ic24.net

TAMS, Gordon Thomas Carl. b 37. Leeds Univ BA60 Newc Univ MLitt84 Reading Univ CertEd61 LLCM76. Edin Dioc NSM Course 83. **d** 90 **p** 91. NSM Kelso *Edin* 90-92; P-in-c Coldstream 92-02; rtd 02. *47 Lennel Mount, Coldstream TD12 4NS* Tel (01890) 882479 E-mail tamsga@fish.co.uk

TAMS, Paul William. b 56. Huddersfield Poly CertEd77. EAMTC 87. **d** 90 **p** 91. NSM Mildenhall *St E* 90-93; NSM Brandon and Santon Downham w Elveden etc from 93. *38 Raven Close, Mildenhall, Bury St Edmunds IP28 7LF* Tel (01638) 715475 E-mail paultams@lineone.net

TANCOCK, Steven John. b 73. Westmr Coll Ox BTh01. St Steph Ho Ox 02. **d** 04 **p** 05. C Wincanton *B & W* from 04; C Pen Selwood from 04. *125 Cale Way, Wincanton BA9 9DB* Tel (01963) 824873

TANKARD, Reginald Douglas Alan. b 37. Sarum Th Coll 60. **d** 62 **p** 63. C Howden *York* 62-65; C Heckmondwike *Wakef* 65-67; CF 67-70; C Thornbury *Bradf* 82-88; P-in-c Rockcliffe and Blackford *Carl* 88-90; V 90-03; rtd 03. *21 Northgate, Almondbury, Huddersfield HD5 8RX* Tel (01484) 514426

TANN, Canon David John. b 31. K Coll Lon BD57 AKC57. **d** 58 **p** 59. C Wandsworth St Anne *S'wark* 58-60; C Sholing *Win* 60-64; Asst Chapl Lon Univ *Lon* 64-65; C Fulham All SS 65-68; Hon C 72-82; Lic to Offic 68-72; Teacher Godolphin and Latymer Sch Hammersmith 68-73; Ealing Boys Gr Sch 69-73; Hd of RE Green Sch Isleworth 73-82; V Dudley St Jas *Worc* 82-95; Chapl Burton Road Hosp Dudley 83-95; Hon Can Worc Cathl *Worc* 90-95; RD Dudley 93-95; rtd 95; Perm to Offic *Lon* from 97. *75 Parkview Court, Fulham High Street, London SW6 3LL* Tel (020) 7736 6018

TANNER, Preb Alan John. b 25. OBE97. SS Coll Cam 43 Linc Coll Ox BA52 MA65. Coll of Resurr Mirfield 52. **d** 54 **p** 55. C Hendon St Mary *Lon* 54-58; V S Harrow St Paul 58-60; Dir Coun for Chr Stewardship 60-65; Dir Lay Tr 65-71; Sec Coun for Miss and Unity 65-80; V St Nic Cole Abbey 66-78; Sec Gtr Lon Chs' Coun 76-83; P-in-c St Ethelburga Bishopgate 78-85; R St Botolph without Bishopgate 78-97; P-in-c All Hallows Lon Wall 80-97; Bp's Ecum Officer 81-97; AD The City 90-97; Preb St Paul's Cathl 91-97; P-in-c St Clem Eastcheap w St Martin Orgar 93-97; P-in-c St Sepulchre w Ch Ch Greyfriars etc 93-97; P-in-c St Kath Cree 93-97; P-in-c Smithfield St Bart Gt 94-95; rtd 97; Preacher of the Charterhouse 73-00; Perm to Offic *Lon* from 00; *B & W* from 01; *Cant* from 03. *Cricklewood Cottage, 34 Convent Road, Broadstairs CT10 3BE*

TANNER, Canon Frank Hubert. b 38. St Aid Birkenhead 63. **d** 66 **p** 67. C Ipswich St Marg *St E* 66-69; C Mansfield SS Pet and Paul *S'well* 69-72; V Huthwaite 72-79; Chapl to the Deaf 79-92; Hon Can S'well Minster 90-92; Chapl Northn and Rutland Miss to the Deaf 92-01; rtd 01; Perm to Offic *Truro* from 03. *The Tamarisks, Trenow Lane, Perranuthnoe, Penzance TR20 9NY* Tel (01736) 719426 E-mail franktanner@lineone.net

TANNER, Leonard John. **d** 03 **p** 04. C Taney *D & G* from 03. *Lisheen, Taney Park, Dundrum, Dublin 14, Irish Republic* Tel (00353) (1) 296 7106 *or* 298 5491 E-mail tanner1@eircom.net

TANNER, Mark Simon Austin. b 70. Ch Ch Ox BA92 MA96 St Jo Coll Dur BA98 Liv Univ MTh05. Cranmer Hall Dur 95. **d** 98 **p** 99. C Upton (Overchurch) *Ches* 98-01; V Doncaster St Mary *Sheff* from 01. *St Mary's Vicarage, 59 St Mary's Road, Doncaster DN1 2NR* Tel (01302) 342565 E-mail st.marys@fish.co.uk

TANNER, Mark Stuart. b 59. Nottm Univ BA81. Sarum & Wells Th Coll. **d** 85 **p** 86. C Radcliffe-on-Trent *S'well* 85; C Radcliffe-on-Trent and Shelford etc 85-88; C Bestwood 88-89; TV 89-93; Bp's Research Officer 93-97; P-in-c S'well H Trin 93-98; V from 98; AD S'well from 01. *Holy Trinity Vicarage, Westhorpe, Southwell NG25 0NB* Tel (01636) 813243 E-mail mark.tanner@tesco.net

TANNER, Martin Philip. b 54. Univ Coll Lon BSc(Econ)75. Ridley Hall Cam 79. **d** 82 **p** 83. C Bitterne *Win* 82-85; C Weeke 85-88; V Long Buckby w Watford *Pet* 88-96; P-in-c Desborough 96-97; R Desborough, Brampton Ash, Dingley and Braybrooke from 97. *The Vicarage, Lower Street, Desborough, Kettering NN14 2NP* Tel (01536) 760324 Fax 760854 E-mail revmtanner@aol.com

TANSILL, Canon Derek Ernest Edward. b 36. Univ of Wales (Lamp) BA61. Ripon Hall Ox 61. **d** 63 **p** 64. C Chelsea St Luke *Lon* 63-67; C-in-c Saltdean CD *Chich* 67-69; V Saltdean 69-73; V Billingshurst 73-82; RD Horsham 77-82 and 85-93; Can and Preb Chich Cathl from 81; R Bexhill St Pet 82-85; RD Battle and

Bexhill 84-86; V Horsham 85-86; TR from 86. *The Vicarage, The Causeway, Horsham RH12 1HE* Tel (01403) 272919 *or* 253762

TANZANIA, Archbishop of. *See* MTETEMELA, The Most Revd Donald Leo

TAPHOUSE, Bryan George. b 50. STETS DipTh98. **d** 98 **p** 99. NSM Romsey *Win* from 98. *2 Campion Drive, Romsey SO51 7RD* Tel (01794) 516022

TAPLIN, John. b 35. St Alb Minl Tr Scheme 78. **d** 81 **p** 82. NSM Knebworth *St Alb* 81-88; R Lt Hadham w Albury 88-00; rtd 00; Perm to Offic *St E* from 00. *77 Hepworth Road, Stanton, Bury St Edmunds IP31 2UA* Tel (01359) 250212 E-mail johntaplin@supanet.com

TAPLIN, Kim. b 58. Lon Bible Coll BA79 Homerton Coll Cam PGCE84. S Dios Minl Tr Scheme 94. **d** 94 **p** 95. C Sholing *Win* 94-97; P-in-c Rendcomb *Glouc* 97-00; Chapl Rendcomb Coll Cirencester 97-00; Chapl Clifton Coll Bris from 01. *The Chaplaincy, Clifton College, 83B Pembroke Road, Clifton BS8 3EA* Tel 0117-315 7257 *or* 315 7258

TAPLIN, Stewart Tennent Eaton. b 46. Lanc Univ Dip Teaching91 Melbourne Univ BEd92 GradDipEd94 MEd97. ACT ThL69 DipYL71. **d** 72 **p** 73. V Altham w Clayton le Moors *Blackb* 74-76; Can Res Blackb Cathl 76-78; Lic to Offic *Carl* 76-78; Australia from 78. *2 Boston Street, Ashwood, Vic, Australia 3147* Tel (0061) (3) 9888 3328 *or* 9845 7777 Fax 9845 7710

TAPPER, John A'Court. b 42. FCA64. Sarum & Wells Th Coll 89. **d** 91 **p** 92. C Ashford *Cant* 91-94; P-in-c Folkestone H Trin w Ch Ch 94-96; V from 96; P-in-c Sandgate St Paul w Folkestone St Geo from 01; AD Elham 00-05. *Holy Trinity Vicarage, 21 Manor Road, Folkestone CT20 2SA* Tel (01303) 253831 E-mail trinitybenefice@ic24.net

TARGETT, Kenneth. b 28. Qu Coll Birm 54. **d** 57 **p** 58. C Mansfield Woodhouse *S'well* 57-59; C Skipton Ch Ch *Bradf* 59-62; V Bradf St Jo 62-65; Perm to Offic 65-82; Australia 82-87; V Old Leake w Wrangle *Linc* 87-94; rtd 94; Perm to Offic *Linc* from 00. *The Sloop, Sea Lane, Old Leake, Boston PE22 9JA* Tel (01205) 871991 E-mail ken@thesloop.fsnet.co.uk

TARLETON, Canon Peter. b 46. TCD BA72 MA80 HDipEd77. TCD Div Sch Div Test 73. **d** 73 **p** 74. C Cork St Luke w St Ann *C, C & R* 73-75; C Dublin Drumcondra *D & G* 75-78; I Limerick City *L & K* 78-82; I Drumgoon w Dernakesh, Ashfield etc *K, E & A* 82-85; Chapl HM YOI Hindley 85-89; Chapl HM Pris Lindholme 89-99; Hon Can Sheff Cathl *Sheff* 98-99; Chapl HM Pris Leeds from 99; Perm to Offic *Sheff* 99-03. *HM Prison, 2 Gloucester Terrace, Armley, Leeds LS12 2TJ* Tel 0113-203 2704 E-mail peter.tarleton@hmps.gsi.gov.uk

TARLING, Paul. b 53. Oak Hill Th Coll BA. **d** 85 **p** 86. C Old Hill H Trin *Worc* 85-89; V Walford w Bishopswood *Heref* 89-90; P-in-c Goodrich w Welsh Bicknor and Marstow 89-90; R Walford and St John w Bishopswood, Goodrich etc 90-96; RD Ross and Archenfield 95-96; P-in-c Kington w Huntington, Old Radnor, Kinnerton etc 96-00; R from 00; RD Kington and Weobley from 02. *The Vicarage, Church Road, Kington HR5 3AG* Tel (01544) 230525

TARPER, Miss Ann Jennifer. b 47. SRN71 Nottm Univ BCombStuds82. Linc Th Coll 79. **dss** 83 **d** 87 **p** 96. Stamford All SS w St Jo *Linc* 82-85; Witham *Chelmsf* 85-90; Par Dn 87-90; Min and Educn Adv to Newmarch Gp Min *Heref* 90-93; Perm to Offic 93-95; Dep Chapl HM Pris Dur 95-97; Chapl HM Pris Foston Hall 97-00; Perm to Offic *Lich* 97-02; C W End *Win* from 02. *Galilee, 1 Gatcombe Gardens, West End, Southampton SO18 3NA* Tel (023) 8047 4535

TARR, James Robert. b 39. Bps' Coll Cheshunt 64. **d** 67 **p** 68. C Wortley de Leeds *Ripon* 67-69; C Hunslet St Mary and Stourton St Andr 70-73; V Moorends *Sheff* 73-77; V Cross Stone *Wakef* 77-83; V Chilworth w N Baddesley *Win* 83-90; V Andover St Mich 90-93; V W Andover 93-00; Chapl Mojacar *Eur* 00-02; rtd 02. *Les Courades, Vieux Cerier, 16350 Charente, France* Tel (0033) (5) 45 30 00 39

TARRANT, Canon Ian Denis. b 57. G&C Coll Cam BA MA Nottm Univ DipTh. St Jo Coll Nottm 81. **d** 84 **p** 85. C Ealing St Mary *Lon* 84-87; CMS from 87; Republic of Congo 88-98; Can Boga from 97; Sen Angl Chapl Nottm Univ *S'well* from 98. *The Chaplaincy, University Park, Nottingham NG7 2RD* Tel 0115-951 3927 *or* 951 3378 E-mail ian.tarrant@nottingham.ac.uk

TARRANT, John Michael. b 38. St Jo Coll Cam BA59 MA63 Ball Coll Ox BA62 MA76. Ripon Hall Ox 60. **d** 62 **p** 63. C Chelsea All SS *Lon* 62-65; Chapl and Lect St Pet Coll Saltley 66-70; Belize 70-74; V Forest Row *Chich* 75-87; Perm to Offic *Heref* 93-99; NSM Ross 99-00; P-in-c Guilsborough w Hollowell and Cold Ashby *Pet* from 00; Jt P-in-c Cottesbrooke w Gt Creaton and Thornby from 00. *The Vicarage, 15 Church Mount, Guilsborough, Northampton NN6 8QA* Tel (01604) 743508

TARRANT, Paul John. b 57. Chich Th Coll. **d** 82 **p** 83. C Southgate Ch Ch *Lon* 82-85; C Hornsey St Mary w St Geo 85-90; USA 90-96; R Edin Old St Paul *Edin* 96-97. *Address temp unknown*

TARREN, Eileen. b 46. Cranmer Hall Dur. **d** 02 **p** 03. NSM Pittington, Shadforth and Sherburn *Dur* from 02. *14 Berwick Chase, Peterlee SR8 1NQ*

TARRIS, Canon Geoffrey John. b 27. Em Coll Cam BA50 MA55. Westcott Ho Cam 51. **d** 53 **p** 54. C Abbots Langley *St Alb* 53-55; Prec St E Cathl *St E* 55-59; V Bungay H Trin w St Mary 59-72; RD S Elmham 65-72; V Ipswich St Mary le Tower 72-78; Hon Can St E Cathl 74-82; V Ipswich St Mary le Tower w St Lawr and St Steph 78-82; Can Res St E Cathl 82-93; Dioc Dir of Lay Min and Warden of Readers 82-87; Dioc Dir of Ords 87-93; rtd 93; Perm to Offic *Nor* and *St E* from 93; Hon PV Nor Cathl *Nor* from 94. *53 The Close, Norwich NR1 4EG* Tel (01603) 622136

TARRY, Gordon Malcolm. b 54. Leeds Univ BSc75. Lon Bible Coll BA83 Ridley Hall Cam. **d** 85 **p** 86. C Gt Ilford St Andr *Chelmsf* 85-89; C Rainham 89-92; C Rainham w Wennington 92-93; V Gt Ilford St Jo from 93; AD Redbridge from 01. *St John's Vicarage, 2 Regent Gardens, Ilford IG3 8UL* Tel (020) 8590 5884 E-mail gordontarry@yahoo.co.uk

TASH, Stephen Ronald. b 56. Warw Univ BEd79. WMMTC 88. **d** 91 **p** 92. C Studley *Cov* 91-95; P-in-c Salford Priors from 95; Dioc Youth Officer 95-00; P-in-c Temple Grafton w Binton from 00; P-in-c Exhall w Wixford from 03. *The Vicarage, Station Road, Salford Priors, Evesham WR11 8UX* Tel (01789) 772445 E-mail stevetash@aol.com

TASKER, Harry Beverley. b 41. BA76. Wycliffe Hall Ox 64. **d** 67 **p** 68. C Withington St Paul *Man* 67-71; C Bingley All SS *Bradf* 71-72; Chapl RAF 72-76; R Publow w Pensford, Compton Dando and Chelwood *B & W* 76-84; V Long Ashton 84-04; RD Portishead 86-91; rtd 04. *The Malthouse, Manor Court, Manor Lane, Ettington, Stratford-upon-Avon CV37 7TW* Tel (01789) 748290

TASSELL, Canon Dudley Arnold. b 16. K Coll Lon BD49 AKC49. **d** 49 **p** 50. C New Eltham All SS *S'wark* 49-55; V Catford St Andr 55-63; R Rotherhithe St Mary w All SS 63-77; RD Bermondsey 69-76; Hon Can S'wark Cathl 72-76; V Spring Park *Cant* 76-84; RD Croydon Addington 81-84; V Spring Park All SS *S'wark* 85-86; rtd 86; Perm to Offic *Guildf* from 86. *72 Sandy Lane, Woking GU22 8BH* Tel (01483) 762944

TASSELL, Mrs Stella Venetia. b 39. RGN60 RNT63 RMN66 RHV72. Guildf Dioc Min Course 97. **d** 01 **p** 02. OLM Woodham *Guildf* from 01. *72 Sandy Lane, Woking GU22 8BH* Tel (01483) 762944 Mobile 07790-521567 E-mail stella@stassell69.fsnet.co.uk

TATE, David. b 44. Open Univ BA78 CIPFA70. **d** 02 **p** 03. OLM N w S Wootton *Nor* from 02. *36 The Birches, South Wootton, King's Lynn PE30 3JG* Tel (01553) 672474 E-mail davidtate@allsts.freeserve.co.uk

TATE, Mrs Harriet Jane. b 62. Hull Univ BA84. Man OLM Scheme 99. **d** 02 **p** 03. OLM Heatons *Man* from 02. *70 Winchester Drive, Stockport SK4 2NU* Tel 0161-431 7051 E-mail harriettate@supanet.com

TATE, Henry Charles Osmond. b 13. K Coll Lon 64. **d** 65 **p** 66. C Boscombe St Andr *Win* 65-68; R Winfrith Newburgh w Chaldon Herring *Sarum* 68-78; V Chardstock *Ex* 78-82; rtd 82. *10 Stuart Court, High Street, Kibworth, Leicester LE8 0LR* Tel 0116-279 6380

TATE, James. b 56. DipAD80. Oak Hill Th Coll DipHE95. **d** 95 **p** 96. C Hammersmith St Simon *Lon* 95-98; C N Hammersmith St Kath 98-99; P-in-c from 99. *St Katherine's Vicarage, Primula Street, London W12 0RF* Tel (020) 8746 2213 *or* 8743 3951 E-mail jim@stkats.wanadoo.co.uk

TATE, John Robert. b 38. Dur Univ BA61 MA71. Cranmer Hall Dur. **d** 70 **p** 71. C Bare *Blackb* 70-73; V Over Darwen St Jas 73-81; V Caton w Littledale 81-98; rtd 98; Perm to Offic *Blackb* from 98. *19 Clifton Drive, Morecambe LA4 6SR* Tel (01524) 832840

TATE, Robert John Ward. b 24. St Jo Coll Morpeth ThL48. **d** 49 **p** 50. Australia from 49; Chapl RN 53-79; QHC 76-79; rtd 79. *58 Skye Point Road, Carey Bay, NSW, Australia 2283* Tel (0061) (2) 4959 2921

TATHAM, Andrew Francis. b 49. Grey Coll Dur BA71 Southlands Coll Lon DAM80 K Coll Lon PhD84 AKC88 FBCartS96. S'wark Ord Course 89. **d** 92 **p** 93. NSM Headley w Box Hill *Guildf* 92-02; TV Ilminster and Distr *B & W* from 02. *The Rectory, Broadway, Ilminster TA19 9RE* Tel (01460) 52559

TATTON-BROWN, Simon Charles. b 48. Qu Coll Cam BA70 MA78 Man Univ CQSW72. Coll of Resurr Mirfield 78. **d** 79 **p** 80. C Ashton St Mich *Man* 79-82; P-in-c Prestwich St Gabr 82-87; V 87-88; Bp's Dom Chapl 82-88; TR Westhoughton 88-96; TR Westhoughton and Wingates 97-00; V Chippenham St Andr w Tytherton Lucas *Bris* from 00; RD Chippenham from 03. *The Vicarage, 54A St Mary Street, Chippenham SN15 3JW* Tel (01249) 656834 E-mail stbrown@ukip.co.uk

TATTUM, Ian Stuart. b 58. N Lon Poly BA79 Lanc Univ Fitzw Coll Cam BA89. Westcott Ho Cam 87. **d** 90 **p** 91. C Beaconsfield *Ox* 90-94; C Bushey *St Alb* 94-96; P-in-c Pirton 96-01; P-in-c St Ippolyts from 00; P-in-c Gt and Lt Wymondley from 01. *The Vicarage, Stevenage Road, St Ippolyts, Hitchin SG4 7PE* Tel (01462) 457552

TATTUM, Ruth Margaret. *See* LAMPARD, Ms Ruth Margaret

TAULTY, Mrs Eileen. b 45. **d** 03. OLM Pemberton St Mark Newtown *Liv* from 03. *36 Alexandra Crescent, Wigan WN5 9JP* Tel (01942) 208021

TAUNTON, Archdeacon of. *See* REED, The Ven John Peter Cyril

TAUNTON, Suffragan Bishop of. *See* RADFORD, The Rt Revd Andrew John

TAVERNOR (née LLOYD), Mrs Eileen. b 50. FIBMS74 Liv Poly HNC72. N Ord Course 88. **d** 91 **p** 94. C Heref St Martin w St Fran *Heref* 91-95; P-in-c Bucknell w Chapel Lawn, Llanfair Waterdine etc 95-01; V from 01. *The Vicarage, Bucknell SY7 0AD* Tel (01547) 530340

TAVERNOR, James Edward. b 23. Lich Th Coll 41 St D Coll Lamp BA49. **d** 50 **p** 51. C Monmouth *Mon* 50-52; C Prestbury *Glouc* 52-53; C Newbold w Dunston *Derby* 53-55; C Buxton 67-69; Perm to Offic *Derby* 70-75, *Heref* 75-83 and *St D* 83-91; rtd 88. *12 Beech Close, Ludlow SY8 2PD* Tel (01584) 876502

TAVERNOR, William Noel. b 16. Lich Th Coll 37. **d** 40 **p** 41. C Ledbury *Heref* 40-43; C Kidderminster St Mary *Worc* 43-46; V Bettws-y-Crwyn w Newcastle *Heref* 46-50; V Upton Bishop 50-57; V Aymestrey and Leinthall Earles 57-65; P-in-c Shobdon 58-65; V Canon Pyon w Kings Pyon and Birley 65-88; rtd 88; Perm to Offic *Heref* from 97. *Vine Cottage, Kingsland, Leominster HR6 9QS* Tel (01568) 708817

TAVINOR, The Very Revd Michael Edward. b 53. Univ Coll Dur BA75 Em Coll Cam CertEd76 K Coll Lon MMus77 AKC77 ARCO77. Ripon Coll Cuddesdon BA81 MA86. **d** 82 **p** 83. C Ealing St Pet Mt Park *Lon* 82-85; Min Can, Prec and Sacr Ely Cathl *Ely* 85-90; P-in-c Stuntney 87-90; V Tewkesbury w Walton Cardiff *Glouc* 90-99; P-in-c Twyning 98-99; V Tewkesbury w Walton Cardiff and Twyning 99-02; Hon Can Glouc Cathl 97-02; Dean Heref from 02. *The Deanery, Cathedral Close, Hereford HR1 2NG* Tel (01432) 374203 Fax 374220 E-mail dean@herefordcathedral.co.uk

TAWN, Andrew Richard. b 61. Trin Coll Cam BA83 Ox Univ BA88. Ripon Coll Cuddesdon 86. **d** 89 **p** 90. C Dovecot *Liv* 89-93; TV Dorchester *Ox* 93-98; Student Supervisor Cuddesdon Coll 93-98; R Addingham *Bradf* from 98. *The Rectory, Low Mill Lane, Addingham, Ilkley LS29 0QP* Tel (01943) 830276 E-mail saintpeter@addinghamrectory.fsnet.co.uk

TAYLER, Raymond James. b 38. K Alfred's Coll Win TCert74. SW Minl Tr Course 98. **d** 01 **p** 02. NSM Mlaga *Eur* from 01. *Casa Palomero, Oficina de Correos, 29714 Salares, Málaga, Spain* Tel (0034) (95) 203 0461 E-mail rjtayler@yahoo.co.uk

TAYLOR, Alan Clive. b 48. Southn Univ BTh79. Sarum Th Coll 69. **d** 74 **p** 75. C Watford St Pet *St Alb* 74-78; C Broxbourne w Wormley 78-83; Chapl to the Deaf 83-91; V Shefford 83-91; R Portishead *B & W* 91-02; TR from 02. *66 Drakes Way, Portishead, Bristol BS20 6LD* Tel (01275) 842284 E-mail possetrector@aol.com

TAYLOR, Alan Gerald. b 33. Roch Th Coll 61 St Aid Birkenhead 61. **d** 63 **p** 64. C W Bridgford *S'well* 63-66; C E w W Barkwith *Linc* 66-69; V E Stockwith 69-76; V Morton 69-76; Countryside Officer 69-88; R Ulceby w Fordington 76-88; R Willoughby w Sloothby w Claxby 76-88; R Woolpit w Drinkstone *St E* 88-98; Rural Min Adv from 88; rtd 98; Perm to Offic *St E* from 01. *5 Finch Close, Stowmarket IP14 5BQ* Tel (01449) 614078

TAYLOR, Canon Alan Leonard. b 43. Chich Th Coll 67. **d** 69 **p** 70. C Walton St Mary *Liv* 69-73; C Toxteth St Marg 73-75; V Stanley 75-83; V Leeds St Aid *Ripon* from 84; Hon Can Ripon Cathl from 97. *The Vicarage, Elford Place West, Leeds LS8 5QD* Tel 0113-248 6992 E-mail cllr.ala.taylor@leeds.gov.uk

TAYLOR, Andrew David. b 58. Regent's Park Coll Ox BA81 MA86 Toronto Univ MDiv92 K Coll Lon MTh95. Westcott Ho Cam 85. **d** 87 **p** 89. C Leckhampton SS Phil and Jas w Cheltenham St Jas *Glouc* 87-91; P-in-c Swindon w Uckington and Elmstone Hardwicke 92-93; C Highgate St Mich *Lon* 94-97; Chapl R Holloway and Bedf New Coll *Guildf* 97-03. *Woodcote, Spring Woods, Virginia Water GU25 4PW* Tel (01344) 842955

TAYLOR, Ann. *See* TAYLOR, Margaret Ann

TAYLOR, Ms Anne Elizabeth. b 68. Ulster Univ BSc91 MA99. CITC BTh94. **d** 94 **p** 95. C Dublin Rathfarnham *D & G* from 94; Chapl Adelaide and Meath Hosp Dublin 01-03; Abp's Dom Chapl *D & G* from 03; Children's Min Officer Sunday Sch Soc of Ireland from 05. *Rathfarnham Rectory, Rathfarnham Road, Terenure, Dublin 6W, Irish Republic* Tel and fax (00353) (1) 490 5543 E-mail sundayschoolsociety@ireland.anglican.org

TAYLOR, Arthur Alfred. b 32. Univ Coll Ox MA56. Ox NSM Course 80. **d** 83 **p** 84. NSM Monks Risborough *Ox* 83-96; NSM Aylesbury Deanery from 96. *9 Place Farm Way, Monks Risborough, Princes Risborough HP27 9JJ* Tel (01844) 347197

TAYLOR, Arthur John. b 17. Lon Univ BD39 BA52. ALCD39. **d** 40 **p** 41. C Walthamstow St Andr *Chelmsf* 40-42; C Hitchin H Sav *St Alb* 44-45; Asst Chapl Felsted Sch 45-46; Asst Master K Sch Ely 56-80; Perm to Offic *Ely* 56-85; rtd 80; Perm to Offic *Mon* from 86. *44 Homeforge House, Goldwire Lane, Monmouth NP25 5HA* Tel (01600) 716269

TAYLOR, Arthur Robert. b 26. ACIS59. Oak Hill Th Coll 67. **d** 68 **p** 69. C Wilmington *Roch* 68-71; C Polegate *Chich* 71-73; R Chesterton w Haddon *Ely* 73-80; P-in-c Alwalton 73-75; R 75-80; R Sawtry 80-91; rtd 91; Perm to Offic *Roch* from 92. *10 Faraday Ride, Tonbridge TN10 4RL* Tel (01732) 358694 E-mail bp.haddon@virgin.net

TAYLOR, Miss Averil Mary. b 36. Sarum Dioc Tr Coll TCert56 Westmr Coll Ox TCert (Mus) 66. WEMTC 99. **d** 00 **p** 01. OLM Longden and Annscroft w Pulverbatch *Heref* from 00. *Sheaves, Lyth Bank, Lyth Hill, Shrewsbury SY3 0BE* Tel and fax (01743) 872071

TAYLOR, Avril Fiona. b 58. NEOC 02. **d** 05. NSM Byker St Silas *Newc* from 05. *125 Rawling Road, Gateshead NE8 4QS* E-mail avriltaylor@blueyonder.co.uk

TAYLOR, Bernard Richmond Hartley. b 30. Reading Univ MEd. S Dios Minl Tr Scheme 82. **d** 85 **p** 86. NSM Englefield Green *Guildf* 85-90; NSM Lyddington w Stoke Dry and Seaton *Pet* 90-95; rtd 95; Perm to Offic *Guildf* from 96. *Middleton House, 40 Bond Street, Egham TW20 0PY* Tel (01784) 435886

TAYLOR, Brian. b 38. MBIM Bris Univ BA60 Liv Univ BA70 Southn Univ MA90. Ridley Hall Cam 60. **d** 66 **p** 66. Nigeria 66-72; Perm to Offic *Derby* 74-78; Chapl Newbury Coll 76-94; P-in-c Shaw cum Donnington *Ox* 89-90; R from 90. *The Rectory, Well Meadow, Shaw, Newbury RG14 2DS* Tel (01635) 40450 *or* 41155 E-mail bt@shawchurch.freeserve.co.uk

TAYLOR, Brian. b 42. St Deiniol's Hawarden 78. **d** 80 **p** 81. C Mold *St As* 80-84; V Bagillt from 84. *The Vicarage, Bryntirion Road, Bagillt CH6 6BZ* Tel (01352) 732732 Mobile 07803-305956 E-mail brian@prayers.freeserve.co.uk

TAYLOR, Brian. b 61. St Mich Coll Llan DipTh91. **d** 94 **p** 95. C Aberdare *Llan* 94-97; V Cwmparc from 97. *The Vicarage, Vicarage Terrace, Cwmparc, Treorchy CF42 6NA* Tel (01443) 773303

TAYLOR, Brian John Chatterton. b 30. Trin Hall Cam BA53 Kent Univ MA57 Melbourne Univ BEd66 Lon Univ MA78. Westcott Ho Cam 53. **d** 55 **p** 56. C Leigh St Jo *Man* 55-57; C Ashton Ch Ch 57-58; Australia from 58; Miss to Seamen 58-60; Vic State High Schs 60-71; Sen Lect Toorak Teachers' Coll 72-80; Prin Lect Inst of Cath Educn 80-88; Co-ord RE Tintern Angl Girls' Gr Sch 89-93; Supernumerary Asst Redhill St Geo from 90. *RMB 6047, Merricks North, Vic, Australia 3926* Tel and fax (0061) (3) 5989 7564 Mobile 408-250630 E-mail sumptonv@surf.net

TAYLOR, Brian Valentine. b 34. St Deiniol's Hawarden 69. **d** 71 **p** 72. C Workington St Mich *Carl* 71-72; C Carl St Aid and Ch Ch 73-74; Chapl Rotterdam Miss to Seamen *Eur* 74-75; Asst Chapl Madrid 75-76; Chapl Marseille w St Raphaël, Aix-en-Provence etc 77-78; Chapl Alassio w Genoa and Rapallo 78-81; C Higher Broughton *Man* 82-83; P-in-c Cheetwood St Alb 83-84; Lic to Offic 84-85; rtd 85; Perm to Offic *Man* 85-97. *36A Station Road, Thornton-Cleveleys FY5 5HZ* Tel (01253) 827704

TAYLOR, Charles Derek. b 36. Trin Hall Cam BA59 MA62. Ripon Hall Ox 59. **d** 61 **p** 62. C Nottingham All SS *S'well* 61-64; C Binley *Cov* 64-67; C Stoke 67-70; R Purley *Ox* 70-74; V Milton *B & W* 74-93; RD Locking 86-87 and 90-93; V Wells St Cuth w Wookey Hole 93-98; rtd 98; Perm to Offic *Roch* from 00. *5 Banner Farm Road, Tunbridge Wells TN2 5EA* Tel (01892) 526825

TAYLOR, Canon Charles William. b 53. Selw Coll Cam BA74 MA78. Cuddesdon Coll 74. **d** 76 **p** 77. C Wolverhampton *Lich* 76-79; Chapl Westmr Abbey 79-84; V Stanmore *Win* 84-90; R N Stoneham 90-95; Can Res and Prec Lich Cathl *Lich* from 95. *23 The Close, Lichfield WS13 7LD* Tel (01543) 306140 *or* 306100 Fax 306109 E-mail charles.taylor@lichfield-cathedral.org

TAYLOR, Christopher Vincent. b 47. Cen Sch Speech & Drama DipDA71. Cranmer Hall Dur 94. **d** 96 **p** 97. C Kendal St Geo *Carl* 96-99; TV Wheatley *Ox* 99-03; TV Leeds City *Ripon* from 03. *Holy Trinity Vicarage, 28 Hawkswood Avenue, Leeds LS5 3PN* Tel 0113-259 0031

TAYLOR, Preb Clive Cavanagh. b 28. MBE91. Cranmer Hall Dur 61. **d** 63 **p** 64. C Wembley St Jo *Lon* 63-66; C Edmonton All SS 66-69; V Tottenham St Jo 69-76; RD E Haringey 73-76; Dir of Ords 76-85; Chapl Metrop Police Coll Hendon 76-93; Sen Chapl Metrop Police 78-93; V Temple Fortune St Barn 76-93; Preb St Paul's Cathl 78-93; AD W Barnet 79-85; rtd 93; Perm to Offic *Chich* from 93. *26 Wenthill Close, East Dean, Eastbourne BN20 0HT* Tel (01323) 422346

TAYLOR, Colin John. b 66. Witwatersrand Univ BCom87 BTh94. Wycliffe Hall Ox MTh97. **d** 97 **p** 98. C Denton Holme *Carl* 97-01; Bp's Dom Chapl from 01; Asst P Dalston w Cumdivock, Raughton Head and Wreay from 01; Dir CME 1-4 from 00. *The Vicarage, Wreay, Carlisle CA4 0RL* Tel (01697) 473883 *or* 476274 E-mail bishop.chaplain@carlislediocese.org.uk

TAYLOR, David. b 53. St Jo Coll Dur BA74 PGCE75. Sarum & Wells Th Coll 91. **d** 93 **p** 94. C Cheadle Hulme All SS *Ches* 93-97; V Macclesfield St Jo from 97; RD Macclesfield 03-05. *St John's Vicarage, 25 Wilwick Lane, Macclesfield SK11 8RS* Tel (01625) 424185 Fax 612511 E-mail david.taylor937@ntlworld.com

TAYLOR, David Christopher Morgan. b 56. Leeds Univ BSc77 Univ Coll Lon PhD80 Univ Coll Ches MEd96 SOSc MIBiol. N

Ord Course 91. **d** 94 **p** 95. Tutor Liv Univ *Liv* from 86; NSM Waterloo Ch Ch and St Mary 94-99; P-in-c Altcar 98-00; NSM Altcar and Hightown from 03. *20 Liverpool Road, Formby, Liverpool L37 4BW* Tel (01704) 873304 Fax 0151-794 5337 E-mail dcmt@liverpool.ac.uk *or* taylordcm@aol.com

TAYLOR, Dennis James. b 31. ACIS62. Ripon Hall Ox 63. **d** 68 **p** 69. C Baswich *Lich* 68-77; P-in-c Hastings H Trin *Chich* 77-81; V 81-86; R Catsfield and Crowhurst 86-01; rtd 01; Perm to Offic *B & W* from 01. *17 Clifford Avenue, Taunton TA2 6DJ* Tel (01823) 275716

TAYLOR, Derek. *See* TAYLOR, Charles Derek

TAYLOR, The Very Revd Derek John. b 31. Univ of Wales (Lamp) BA52 Fitzw Ho Cam BA54 MA58 Ex Univ CertEd70 Birm Univ AdCertEd92. St Mich Coll Llan 54. **d** 55 **p** 56. C Newport St Paul *Mon* 55-59; CF (TA) 57-59 and 62-64; CF 59-62; V Bettws *Mon* 62-64; V Exminster *Ex* 64-70; Hd of RE Heathcote Sch Tiverton 70-71; W Germany 71-75; Chapl R Russell Sch Croydon 75-79; Chapl St Andr Sch Croydon 79-84; P-in-c Croydon St Andr *Cant* 79-81; V 81-84; Chapl Bromsgrove Sch 84-89; Provost St Chris Cathl Bahrain 90-97; Hon Chapl Miss to Seamen 90-97; NSM Droitwich Spa *Worc* 97-99; Asst P Finstall 99-00; P-in-c Milngavie *Glas* 00-03; Perm to Offic *Worc* from 04. *19 Warwick Hall Gardens, Bromsgrove B60 2AU* Tel and fax (01527) 872144 Mobile 07946-644989 E-mail derek@derekandvaltaylor.wanadoo.co.uk

TAYLOR, Donald Alastair. b 26. Lon Univ BD Linc Coll Ox DPhil77. St Paul's Coll Mauritius. **d** 65 **p** 65. C Ware St Mary *St Alb* 65-66; Seychelles 66-78; SSJE from 68; Lect RS Middx Poly *Lon* 78-92. *74 Woodcote Road, Caversham, Reading RG4 7EX* Tel 0118-946 3965 Fax as telephone E-mail da.taylor3@ntlworld.com

TAYLOR, Edward Frank. b 23. Lon Univ BSc44. Chich Th Coll 50. **d** 52 **p** 53. C Manston *Ripon* 52-55; Chapl Chich Th Coll 55-59; PV Chich Cathl *Chich* 57-59; C Ifield 59-63; V Hangleton 63-73; V Wivelsfield 73-88; rtd 88; Perm to Offic *Bradf* 88-00. *8 Linkway, Westham, Pevensey BN24 5JB*

TAYLOR, Elizabeth. *See* TAYLOR, Mrs Mary Elizabeth

TAYLOR, Eric Hargreaves. b 21. Oak Hill Th Coll 47. **d** 51 **p** 52. C Tranmere St Cath *Ches* 51-54; V Constable Lee *Man* 54-62; V Camerton H Trin W Seaton *Carl* 62-71; V Ramsgate Ch Ch *Cant* 71-85; Chapl Ramsgate Gen Hosp 71-85; rtd 85; Perm to Offic *Cant* 85-90; *Blackb* 89-96; *Ches* from 96. *130 Ellesmere Road, Walton, Warrington WA4 6EF* Tel (01925) 268100

TAYLOR, Garry Kenneth. b 53. Edin Univ BMus75 Southn Univ BTh81 Ch Ch Coll Cant PGCE95. Sarum & Wells Th Coll 76. **d** 79 **p** 80. C Southsea H Spirit *Portsm* 79-82; C Croydon St Jo *Cant* 82-84; C Croydon St Jo *S'wark* 85-86; V Choral S'well Minster *S'well* 86-90; V Portsea St Alb *Portsm* 90-94; NSM Hamble le Rice *Win* 96-97; P-in-c Southampton St Jude 97-04; V Highcliffe w Hinton Admiral from 04. *The Vicarage, 33 Nea Road, Christchurch BH23 4NB* Tel (01425) 272761 E-mail garrykt@aol.com

TAYLOR, George Davidson. b 27. St Aid Birkenhead 60. **d** 62 **p** 63. C Urmston *Man* 62-65; V Shuttleworth 65-71; V Litherland St Phil *Liv* 71-85; rtd 85. *34 Beckwith Crescent, Harrogate HG2 0BQ* Tel (01423) 560023

TAYLOR, George James Trueman. b 36. Ripon Hall Ox 66. **d** 69 **p** 70. C Wavertree H Trin *Liv* 69-73; V Newton-le-Willows 73-79; V Stoneycroft All SS 79-83; V Haigh 83-04; Jt P-in-c Aspull and New Springs 02-03; rtd 04. *228 Wigan Road, Aspull, Wigan WN2 1DU* Tel (01942) 830430

TAYLOR, Canon Godfrey Alan. b 36. Oak Hill Th Coll DipTh60. **d** 61 **p** 62. C Herne Bay Ch Ch *Cant* 61-64; C Tunbridge Wells St Jas *Roch* 64-68; V Guernsey H Trin *Win* 68-81; V Boscombe St Jo 81-03; Hon Can Win Cathl 96-03; AD Bournemouth 99-03; rtd 03. *Bosnoweth Vean, 21 Cullen View, Probus, Truro TR2 4NY* E-mail godfreyrev@aol.com

TAYLOR, Canon Gordon. b 46. AKC68. St Aug Coll Cant 69. **d** 70 **p** 71. C Rotherham *Sheff* 70-74; P-in-c Brightside St Thos 74-79; P-in-c Brightside St Marg 77-79; V Brightside St Thos and St Marg 79-82; R Kirk Sandall and Edenthorpe 82-91; V Beighton 91-96; V Goole 96-03; AD Snaith and Hatfield 98-03; V Tickhill w Stainton from 03; Hon Can Sheff Cathl from 93. *The Vicarage, 2 Sunderland Street, Tickhill, Doncaster DN11 9QJ* Tel (01302) 742224

TAYLOR, Gordon Clifford. b 15. VRD56 and Bars 66. FSA Ch Coll Cam BA37 MA41. Ripon Hall Ox 37. **d** 38 **p** 39. C Ealing St Steph Castle Hill *Lon* 38-40; Chapl RNVR 40-58; Asst Master Eton Coll 46-49; R St Giles-in-the-Fields *Lon* 49-99; RD Finsbury and Holborn 54-67; Chapl RNR 58-70; rtd 99. *4 King Street, Emsworth PO10 7AZ* Tel (01243) 379400

TAYLOR, Graham Peter. b 58. NEOC 92. **d** 95 **p** 96. NSM Pickering w Lockton and Levisham *York* 95-96; C Whitby 96-98; C Whitby w Aislaby and Ruswarp 98-99; V Cloughton and Burniston w Ravenscar etc 99-04; rtd 04; Perm to Offic *York* from 04. *14 Duchy Avenue, Scalby, Scarborough YO13 0SE* Tel (01723) 377151

✠**TAYLOR, The Rt Revd Humphrey Vincent.** b 38. Pemb Coll Cam BA61 MA66 Lon Univ MA70. Coll of Resurr Mirfield 61. **d** 63 **p** 64 **c** 91. C N Hammersmith St Kath *Lon* 63-64; C Notting Hill St Mark 64-66; USPG 67-71; Malawi 67-71; Chapl Bp Grosseteste Coll Linc 72-74; Sec Chapls in HE Gen Syn Bd of Educn 75-80; Gen Sec USPG 80-91; Sec Miss Progr 80-84; Hon Can Bris Cathl *Bris* 86-91; Lic to Offic *S'wark* 89-91; Suff Bp Selby *York* 91-03; rtd 03; Hon Asst Bp *Glouc* and *Worc* from 03. *10 High Street, Honeybourne, Evesham WR11 7PQ* Tel (01386) 834846 E-mail humannetaylor@ukonline.co.uk

TAYLOR, Iain William James. b 41. Dioc OLM tr scheme 00. **d** 03 **p** 04. OLM Cant St Pet w St Alphege and St Marg etc *Cant* from 03. *11 Keyworth Mews, Canterbury CT1 1XQ* Tel (01227) 766585

TAYLOR, Ian. b 53. Saltley Tr Coll Birm CertEd75. LNSM course 92. **d** 95 **p** 96. OLM Heywood *Man* from 95. *818A Edenfield Road, Rochdale OL12 7RB* Tel (01706) 355738

TAYLOR, Mrs Jacqueline Margaret. b 56. Trin Coll Bris 02. **d** 04 **p** 05. C Bath St Luke *B & W* from 04. *59 Longfellow Avenue, Bath BA2 4SH* Tel (01225) 465099 E-mail wookeyjackie@hotmail.com

TAYLOR, Jamie Alexander Franklyn (James). b 73. Kent Univ BA95. Westcott Ho Cam. **d** 98 **p** 99. C Walton-on-Thames *Guildf* 98-02; C St Peter-in-Thanet *Cant* from 02; Chapl E Kent NHS and Soc Care Partnership Trust 03-05. *St Andrew's House, 29 Reading Street, Broadstairs CT10 3AZ* Tel and fax (01843) 868923

TAYLOR, Jan William Karel. b 59. QUB BD82 MSocSc89 TCD DipTh84. **d** 84 **p** 85. C Belfast St Simon w St Phil *Conn* 84-87; I Belfast St Paul 87-92; Chapl RAF from 92; Perm to Offic *Ban* from 97. *Chaplaincy Services (RAF), HQ, Personnel and Training Command, RAF Innsworth, Gloucester GL3 1EZ* Tel (01452) 712612 ext 5164 Fax 510828

TAYLOR, Jane Suzanne. b 54. Ex Univ BA73. SEITE 96. **d** 99 **p** 00. NSM Knaphill w Brookwood *Guildf* 99-00; C Frimley Green and Mytchett 00-04. *Rocknell Manor Farm, Westleigh, Tiverton EX16 7ES* Tel (01884) 829000

TAYLOR, Mrs Janette Elizabeth. b 44. Glouc Sch of Min 89. **d** 92 **p** 94. C Glouc St Geo w Whaddon *Glouc* 92-96; R Woolaston w Alvington and Aylburton from 96. *The Rectory, Main Road, Alvington, Lydney GL15 6AT* Tel (01594) 529387

TAYLOR, Jason Victor. b 71. Lon Bible Coll BTh01 St Jo Coll Dur MA03. Cranmer Hall Dur 01. **d** 03 **p** 04. C Ripley *Derby* from 03. *31 Porterhouse Road, Ripley DE5 3FL* Tel (01773) 743511 Mobile 07773-352963 E-mail jason_@talk21.com

TAYLOR, Miss Jean. b 37. Nottm Univ TCert58 Man Univ CertRS85. St Andr Coll Pampisford 62. **dss** 68 **d** 00 **p** 01. CSA 62-79; E Crompton *Man* 79-97; Chadderton St Luke 97-00; OLM 00-04; OLM Chadderton St Matt w St Luke from 04. *1A Crossley Street, Shaw, Oldham OL2 8EN* Tel (01706) 844061

TAYLOR, Mrs Jennifer Anne. b 53. Sussex Univ BEd75 Surrey Univ BA01. STETS 98. **d** 01 **p** 02. Chapl Salisbury Cathl Sch from 01; NSM Salisbury St Thos and St Edm *Sarum* from 01. *27 Viking Way, Salisbury SP2 8TA* Tel and fax (01722) 503081 E-mail geoffrey.taylor5@ntlworld.com

TAYLOR (née PATTERSON), Sister Jennifer Mary. b 41. CA Tr Coll IDC65. **dss** 77 **d** 87. CA from 65; Chapl Asst HM Pris Holloway 75-79; Ho Mistress Ch Hosp Sch Hertf 78-79; Chapl Asst RAChD 80-90; Germany 90-96; rtd 96; Perm to Offic *Eur* from 96. *Calle Odisea s/n, Edf Balcon del Mar, Apto 464, 38631 Las Galletas, Tenerife, Canary Islands* Tel (0034) (22) 732469

TAYLOR, John. b 58. Aston Tr Scheme 94 Ripon Coll Cuddesdon 96. **d** 98 **p** 99. C Southport Em *Liv* 98-03; V Hindley All SS from 03. *The Vicarage, 192 Atherton Road, Hindley, Wigan WN2 3XA* Tel and fax (01942) 255175 E-mail johntaylor@supanet.com

TAYLOR, John Alexander. b 54. S Dios Minl Tr Scheme 89. **d** 92 **p** 93. NSM Abbotts Ann and Upper and Goodworth Clatford *Win* 92-99; Perm to Offic 99-00; NSM Hatherden w Tangley, Weyhill and Penton Mewsey 00-02; NSM W Andover from 02. *256 Weyhill Road, Andover SP10 3LR* Tel (01264) 359160 E-mail john@w256.fsnet.co.uk

TAYLOR, Canon John Ambrose. b 19. K Coll Lon 45. Coll of Resurr Mirfield 49. **d** 50 **p** 51. C Helmsley *York* 50-55; V Nether w Upper Poppleton 55-63; V Ches St Oswald w Lt St Jo *Ches* 63-72; P-in-c Ches Lt St Jo 63-67; TV Ches 72-74; Hon Can Gib Cathl *Eur* 74-91; V Withyham St Jo *Chich* 74-88; RD Rotherfield 77-87; P-in-c Withyham St Mich 87; rtd 88; Perm to Offic *Chich* 88-00. *The College of St Barnabas, Blackberry Lane, Lingfield RH7 6NJ* Tel (01342) 870697

TAYLOR, John Andrew. b 53. Linc Th Coll 86. **d** 88 **p** 89. C Stanley *Liv* 88-91; V Wigan St Jas w St Thos 91-04; AD Wigan W 99-04; Hon Can Liv Cathl 03-04; V Prescot from 04. *The Vicarage, Vicarage Place, Prescot L34 1LA* Tel 0151-426 0716 *or* 426 6719

✠**TAYLOR, The Rt Revd John Bernard.** b 29. KCVO97. Ch Coll Cam BA50 MA54 Jes Coll Cam 52 Hebrew Univ Jerusalem 54. Ridley Hall Cam 55. **d** 56 **p** 57 **c** 80. C Morden *S'wark* 56-59; V Henham *Chelmsf* 59-64; V Elsenham 59-64; Sen Tutor Oak Hill Th Coll 64-65; Vice-Prin 65-72; V Woodford Wells *Chelmsf* 72-75; Dioc Dir of Ords 72-80; Adn W Ham 75-80; Bp St Alb

80-95; High Almoner 88-97; rtd 95; Hon Asst Bp Ely from 95; Hon Asst Bp Eur from 98. *22 Conduit Head Road, Cambridge CB3 0EY* Tel (01223) 313783
E-mail john.taylor6529@ntlworld.com

TAYLOR, John Denys. b 20. Leeds Univ BA49. Coll of Resurr Mirfield 49. **d** 51 **p** 52. C Leeds St Marg *Ripon* 51-54; India 54-59; C Gt Grimsby St Jas *Linc* 59-66; New Zealand from 66. *4A Brunton Place, Glenfield, Auckland 1310, New Zealand* Tel (0064) (9) 443 1671 Fax as telephone

TAYLOR, Canon John Michael. b 30. St Aid Birkenhead 56. **d** 59 **p** 60. C Chorley St Jas *Blackb* 59-62; C Broughton 62-64; Chapl St Boniface Coll Warminster 64-68; V Altham w Clayton le Moors *Blackb* 68-76; RD Accrington 71-76; Can Res Blackb Cathl 76-96; Tutor Carl and Blackb Dioc Tr Inst 88-96; rtd 96; Perm to Offic *Blackb* from 96. *Edenholme, 25 Gorse Road, Blackburn BB2 6LZ* Tel (01254) 693772

✠**TAYLOR, The Rt Revd John Mitchell.** b 32. Aber Univ MA54. Edin Th Coll 54. **d** 56 **p** 57 **c** 91. C Aberdeen St Marg *Ab* 56-58; R Glas H Cross *Glas* 58-64; R Glas St Ninian 64-73; R Dumfries 73-91; Chapl Dumfries and Galloway R Infirmary 73-91; Can St Mary's Cathl *Glas* 79-91; Bp Glas 91-98; Asst Bp from 99; rtd 98. *10 George Street, Castle Douglas DG7 1LN* Tel and fax (01556) 502593

TAYLOR, John Porter. b 48. Ex Univ BA71 MA76. Cranmer Hall Dur 93. **d** 93 **p** 94. C Ossett cum Gawthorpe *Wakef* 93-96; R Crofton 96-02; Chapl Mid Yorks Hosps NHS Trust from 03. *Pinderfields General Hospital, Aberford Road, Wakefield WF1 4EE* Tel (01924) 201688
E-mail john.taylor@panp-tr.northy.nhs.uk

TAYLOR, John Ralph. b 48. St Jo Coll Nottm BTh74. **d** 74 **p** 75. C Clitheroe St Jas *Blackb* 74-77; C Kidsgrove *Lich* 77-79; C Hawkwell *Chelmsf* 79-82; V Linc St Geo Swallowbeck *Linc* 82-92; rtd 92. *The Gables, Beck Lane, South Hykeham, Lincoln LN6 9PQ* Tel (01522) 692043

TAYLOR, Canon John Rowland. b 29. OBE74. St Mich Coll Llan 57. **d** 58 **p** 59. C Caerau St Cynfelin *Llan* 58-59; C Aberdare 59-61; Miss to Seamen 61-88; Tanganyika 61-64; Tanzania 64-73; Adn Dar-es-Salaam 65-73; V-Gen 67-73; Thailand 73-84; Chapl Rotterdam w Schiedam *Eur* 84-88; V Warnham *Chich* 88-98; rtd 98; Perm to Offic *Chich* 98-00; P-in-c Streat w Westmeston from 00. *The Rectory, Streat Lane, Streat, Hassocks BN6 8RX* Tel (01273) 890607

TAYLOR, Joseph Robin Christopher. b 34. St Aid Birkenhead 58. **d** 61 **p** 62. C Aldershot St Mich *Guildf* 61-64; C Fleet 64-68; R Manaton *Ex* 69-74; R N Bovey 69-74; V Dawlish 74-87; P-in-c Christow, Ashton, Trusham and Bridford 87-88; R 88-95; Perm to Offic *Ex* 95-98; *St E* from 98; rtd 99. *24 Edwin Panks Road, Hadleigh, Ipswich IP7 5JL* Tel (01473) 824262

TAYLOR, Kelvin John. b 53. Portsm Univ CertEd94 BA96. Trin Coll Bris 02. **d** 04 **p** 05. C Overton w Laverstoke and Freefolk *Win* from 04. *21 Lordsfield Gardens, Overton, Basingstoke RG25 3EW* Tel (01256) 771305

TAYLOR, Kingsley Graham. b 55. Univ of Wales (Cardiff) BD93. St Mich Coll Llan 90. **d** 93 **p** 94. C Llanelli *St D* 93-97; V Whitland w Cyffig and Henllan Amgoed etc from 97. *The Vicarage, North Road, Whitland SA34 0BH* Tel (01994) 240494
E-mail ktaylor559@aol.com

TAYLOR, Luke Alastare John. b 68. Brunel Univ BA97. Oak Hill Th Coll BA00. **d** 00 **p** 01. C Hanworth St Rich *Lon* 00-04; C E Twickenham St Steph from 04. *11 Brantwood Avenue, Isleworth TW7 7EX* Tel (020) 8847 3979
E-mail lukeandgissy@talk21.com

TAYLOR, Lyndon John. b 49. St Mich Coll Llan 92 DipMin93. **d** 95 **p** 96. NSM Swansea St Nic *S & B* 95-01; V Waunarllwydd from 01. *27 Gelli Gwyn Road, Morriston, Swansea SA6 7PP* Tel (01792) 775898

TAYLOR, Lynne. b 51. Sheff Univ BMet73 Salford Univ PhD80. Man OLM Scheme 98. **d** 01 **p** 02. OLM Turton Moorland Min *Man* from 01. *56 Station Road, Turton, Bolton BL7 0HA* Tel (01204) 852551

TAYLOR, Margaret Ann. b 46. LNSM course 96. **d** 98 **p** 99. OLM Newcastle w Butterton *Lich* from 98. *12 Silverton Close, Bradwell, Newcastle ST5 8LU* Tel (01782) 660174

TAYLOR, Marian Alexandra. b 62. Newc Univ BA85. Qu Coll Birm 89. **d** 91 **p** 96. C Earls Barton *Pet* 91-93; NSM Wellingborough St Barn 95-96; NSM Beaumont Leys *Leic* 96-97; Perm to Offic *Pet* 99-00; NSM Kingsthorpe w Northampton St Dav 00-04; TV from 04. *75 Kentstone Close, Northampton NN2 8UH* Tel (01604) 843471 Mobile 07749-047933 E-mail marian@kingsthorpechurches.co.uk

TAYLOR, Mark Edward. b 54. St Jo Coll Auckland LTh. **d** 78 **p** 79. New Zealand 78-86 and from 90; Chapl RN 86-88; Chapl RNZN 90-94; Can Wellington 94-96; P-in-c Albany Greenhithe from 96. *2/2 Whitcombe Road, Bucklands Beach, Manukau City 1704, Auckland, New Zealand* Tel (0064) (27) 495 1767
E-mail chalice@xtra.co.nz

TAYLOR, Mark Frederick. b 62. N Ireland Poly BA84 TCD DipTh87. **d** 87 **p** 88. C Ballymacarrett St Patr *D & D* 87-90; C Dundela St Mark 90-93; I Kilmore and Inch 93-02; I Whitehead and Islandmagee *Conn* from 02. *St Patrick's Rectory, 74 Cable Road, Whitehead, Carrickfergus BT38 9SJ* Tel and fax (028) 9337 3300

TAYLOR, Mark John. b 73. St Andr Univ MTheol99. Coll of Resurr Mirfield 01. **d** 03. C N Meols *Liv* from 03. *28 Hoole Lane, Banks, Southport PR9 8BD* Tel (01704) 506037
E-mail mtaylor@mirfield.org.uk

TAYLOR, Martyn Andrew Nicholas. b 66. **d** 96 **p** 97. C Stamford St Geo w St Paul *Linc* 96-03; R from 03. *St George's Rectory, 16 St George's Square, Stamford PE9 2BN* Tel (01780) 757343 *or* 481800 E-mail rector@stgeorgeschurch.net

TAYLOR, Mrs Mary Elizabeth. b 39. Dioc OLM tr scheme 98. **d** 01 **p** 02. OLM Parr *Liv* from 01. *16 Hignett Avenue, St Helens WA9 2PJ* Tel (01744) 21086

TAYLOR, Mrs Maureen. b 36. Lon Bible Coll BTh90 MA94. **d** 97 **p** 98. NSM Borehamwood *St Alb* 97-00; NSM Radlett 00-05; NSM Aldenham, Radlett and Shenley from 05. *57A Loom Lane, Radlett WD7 8NX* Tel (01923) 855197

TAYLOR, Michael. *See* TAYLOR, Canon John Michael

TAYLOR, Michael Alan. b 47. Bris Univ CertEd70 Lon Univ BD85. Trin Coll Bris 72. **d** 76 **p** 77. C Chilwell *S'well* 76-79; Chapl RAF 79-87; New Zealand from 87. *1 Merton Place, Bryndwr, Christchurch 8005, New Zealand* Tel (0064) (3) 352 4788 *or* 355 6901 Fax 355 6908
E-mail strategic@chch.planet.org.nz

TAYLOR, Michael Allan. b 50. Nottm Univ BTh80. St Jo Coll Nottm 76. **d** 80 **p** 81. C Bowling St Jo *Bradf* 80-82; C Otley 82-85; P-in-c Low Moor St Mark 85-92; P-in-c Bris St Andr w St Bart *Bris* 92-96. *25 Cornfield Close, Bradley Stoke, Bristol BS32 9DN* Tel (01454) 618677

TAYLOR, Michael Andrew James. b 40. Univ Coll Ches BTh96. **d** 99 **p** 00. NSM Halliwell *Man* from 99; TV from 03. *123 Smithills Dean Road, Bolton BL1 6JZ* Tel (01204) 491503

TAYLOR, Michael Barry. b 38. Bps' Coll Cheshunt 63. **d** 65 **p** 66. C Leeds St Cypr Harehills *Ripon* 65-68; C Stanningley St Thos 68-70; V Hunslet Moor St Pet and St Cuth 70-78; V Starbeck 78-00; rtd 00; Perm to Offic *Leic* from 00. *11 Aulton Crescent, Hinckley LE10 0XA* Tel (01455) 442218

TAYLOR, Michael Frank Chatterton. b 30. St Aid Birkenhead 59. **d** 61 **p** 62. C Knighton St Jo *Leic* 61-65; V Briningham *Nor* 65-86; R Melton Constable w Swanton Novers 65-86; P-in-c Thornage w Brinton w Hunworth and Stody 85-86; R Lyng w Sparham 86-90; R Elsing w Bylaugh 86-90; R Lyng, Sparham, Elsing and Bylaugh 90-95; RD Sparham 92-95; rtd 95; Perm to Offic *Portsm* from 95. *The Rhond, 33 Station Road, St Helens, Ryde PO33 1YF* Tel and fax (01983) 873531 Mobile 07989-274848 E-mail mfct@tesco.net

TAYLOR, Canon Michael Joseph. b 49. Gregorian Univ Rome STB72 PhL74 Birm Univ MA81. English Coll Rome 67. **d** 72 **p** 73. In RC Ch 72-83; Hon C Newport Pagnell w Lathbury *Ox* 83-86; TV Langley Marish 86-90; Vice Prin EMMTC *S'well* 90-97; Prin from 97; Hon Can S'well Minster from 00. *52 Parkside Gardens, Wollaton, Nottingham NG8 2PQ* Tel 0115-928 3111 *or* 951 4854 Fax 951 4817
E-mail emmtc@nottingham.ac.uk

TAYLOR, Michael Laurence. b 43. ARCM68 Ch Coll Cam BA66 MA70 CertEd72 MPhil90. Cuddesdon Coll 66. **d** 68 **p** 69. C Westbury-on-Trym H Trin *Bris* 68-72; Asst Chapl Wellington Coll Berks 72-76; C St Helier *S'wark* 76-78; TV Bedminster *Bris* 78-82; P-in-c Chippenham St Andr w Tytherton Lucas 82-88; V 88-89; Dioc Ecum Officer *B & W* 89-90; P-in-c Rodney Stoke w Draycott 89-90. *21 Bath Road, Wells BA5 3HP* Tel (01749) 670348

TAYLOR, Michael Noel. b 40. Leeds Univ BSc62 PGCE63. EMMTC 95. **d** 98 **p** 99. NSM Woodthorpe *S'well* 98-02; NSM Gedling Deanery 02-03; NSM Epperstone from 03; NSM Gonalston from 03; NSM Oxton from 03; NSM Calverton from 03; NSM Woodborough from 03. *16 Church Meadow, Calverton, Nottingham NG14 6HG* Tel 0115-847 3718 Mobile 07713-125771 Fax 0115-912 7671
E-mail michael.taylor21@ntlworld.com

TAYLOR, Michael Stewart. b 58. Univ of Wales (Cardiff) DipTh90. St Mich Coll Llan BTh91. **d** 91 **p** 92. C Llangunnor w Cwmffrwd *St D* 91-94; V Llansantffraed and Llanbadarn Trefeglwys etc 94-97; P-in-c Jersey St Andr *Win* 97-99; V from 99. *The Vicarage, St Andrew's Road, First Tower, St Helier, Jersey JE2 3JG* Tel and fax (01534) 734975
E-mail vicarmike@aol.com

TAYLOR, Nancy. b 49. SRN70 SCM72. Ox Min Course 88. **d** 91 **p** 94. Chapl Asst Stoke Mandeville Hosp Aylesbury 91-94; Asst Chapl Aylesbury Vale Community Healthcare NHS Trust 94-97; NSM Weston Turville *Ox* 91-99; Chapl Kneesworth Ho Hosp from 98. *Kneesworth House Hospital, Old North Road, Bassingbourn, Royston SG8 5JP* Tel (01763) 255700

TAYLOR, Neil Hamish. b 48. Open Univ BA00. Linc Th Coll 72. **d** 75 **p** 76. C Rotherham *Sheff* 75-78; C Doncaster St Geo 78-82; V Alston cum Garrigill w Nenthead and Kirkhaugh *Newc* 82-87; P-in-c Lambley w Knaresdale 82-87; TR Alston Team 87-88; V Maidstone St Paul *Cant* 88-98; OCF 89-94; Sen Chapl Mid Kent

Healthcare NHS Trust 98-00; Sen Chapl Maidstone and Tunbridge Wells NHS Trust 00-01; Perm to Offic *Roch* 98-02; R Eynsford w Farningham and Lullingstone from 02. *The Rectory, Pollyhaugh, Eynsford, Dartford DA4 0HE* Tel (01322) 863050 E-mail neil_h_taylor@hotmail.com

TAYLOR, Canon Nicholas Hugh. b 63. Cape Town Univ BA83 MA87 Dur Univ PhD91. **d** 96 **p** 97. Lect and Chapl Univ of Swaziland 95-98; Chapl St Mich Sch Manzini 96-98; Sen Lect Africa Univ Zimbabwe 98-01; Can Th Mutare Cathl from 99; Dioc Dir Th Educn 99-01; R Penhalonga St Aug 00-01; Assoc Prof Pretoria Univ S Africa 02-04; R Pretoria St Hilda 02-03; R Pretoria N St Mary 03; Hon C Smithfield St Bart Gt *Lon* 04; Prof and Research Fell Univ of Zululand from 04; Hon Tutor Ripon Coll Cuddesdon from 04; Perm to Offic *Nor* from 04 and *Ox* from 05. *Ripon College, Cuddesdon, Oxford OX44 9EX* Tel (01865) 874836 E-mail nhtaylor@dunelm.org.uk

TAYLOR, Nicholas James. b 46. St Chad's Coll Dur BA67 DipTh68. **d** 69 **p** 70. C Beamish *Dur* 69-74; C Styvechale *Cov* 74-77; P-in-c Wilmcote w Billesley 77-79; P-in-c Aston Cantlow 77-79; V Aston Cantlow and Wilmcote w Billesley 79-87; V Cov St Fran N Radford 87-97; RD Cov N 93-97; TR Wilton *B & W* from 97. *The Vicarage, Fons George, Wilton, Taunton TA1 3JT* Tel (01823) 284253 E-mail church@ta13jt.freeserve.co.uk

TAYLOR, Nigel Thomas Wentworth. b 60. Bris Univ BA82 Ox Univ BA86. Wycliffe Hall Ox 84. **d** 87 **p** 88. C Ches Square St Mich w St Phil *Lon* 87-91; C Roxeth Ch Ch and Harrow St Pet 91-93; TV Roxeth 93-97; V S Mimms Ch Ch from 97; AD Cen Barnet from 04. *Christ Church Vicarage, St Albans Road, Barnet EN5 4LA* Tel (020) 8449 0942 *or* 8449 0832 E-mail nigel.taylor@london.anglican.org

TAYLOR, Mrs Noelle Rosemary. b 58. NTMTC 02. **d** 05. C St Mary-at-Latton *Chelmsf* from 05. *146 Churchfield, Harlow CM20 3DD* Tel (01279) 315199

TAYLOR, Norman. b 26. CCC Cam BA49 MA52. Cuddesdon Coll 49. **d** 51 **p** 52. C Clitheroe St Mary *Blackb* 51-54; C Pontesbury I and II *Heref* 54-55; R Lt Wilbraham *Ely* 55-71; Chapl St Faith's Sch Cam 71-86; Hon C Chesterton St Andr *Ely* 87-91; rtd 91; Perm to Offic *Sarum* from 91 and *Ex* from 98. *Shire End West, Cobb Road, Lyme Regis DT7 3JP* Tel (01297) 442922

TAYLOR, Norman Adrian. b 48. St D Coll Lamp DipTh73. **d** 73 **p** 74. C Fleur-de-Lis *Mon* 73-75; C W Drayton *Lon* 75-79; C-in-c Hayes St Edm CD 79-85; V Hayes St Edm 85-87; V Pilton w Ashford *Ex* 87-89; V Sidley *Chich* 89-02; Chapl Hastings and Rother NHS Trust 00-02; V Durrington *Chich* from 02. *The Vicarage, Bramble Lane, Worthing BN13 3JE* Tel (01903) 693499 E-mail frnorman@bigfoot.com

TAYLOR, Norman Wyatt. b 23. Wells Th Coll 58. **d** 60 **p** 61. C Lawrence Weston *Bris* 60-63; V 63-69; V Bishop's Cannings *Sarum* 69-77; V Bishop's Cannings, All Cannings etc 77-80; V W Moors 80-87; rtd 88; Perm to Offic *Ex* 89-98. *3 Kits Close, Chudleigh, Newton Abbot TQ13 0LG* Tel (01626) 852733

TAYLOR, Mrs Patricia. d 05. C Wicklow w Killiskey *D & G* from 05. *14 The Courtyard, Friars Hill, Wicklow, Irish Republic* E-mail patcraig@eircom.net

TAYLOR, Patrick James. b 72. Magd Coll Cam BA96 MA99 MEng96. Ripon Coll Cuddesdon BA00. **d** 01 **p** 02. C Kenilworth St Nic *Cov* 01-05; TV Solihull *Birm* from 05. *45 Park Avenue, Solihull B91 3EJ* Tel 0121-705 4927 *or* 705 5350 E-mail patrick@solihullparish.org.uk

TAYLOR, Paul. b 63. RGN85. Sarum & Wells Th Coll 92 Linc Th Coll BTh95. **d** 95 **p** 96. C Boultham *Linc* 95-98; C Ditton St Mich w St Thos *Liv* 98-00; V Bickerstaffe and Melling from 00. *The Vicarage, Intake Lane, Bickerstaffe, Ormskirk L39 0EB* Tel (01695) 722304 E-mail revpaultaylor@onetel.com

TAYLOR, Paul Frank David. b 60. Leic Poly BSc84 MRICS87. Trin Coll Bris BA91. **d** 91 **p** 92. C Edin St Thos *Edin* 91-94; C Kempshott *Win* 94-98; C-in-c Hatch Warren CD 98-01; V Salisbury St Fran and Stratford sub Castle *Sarum* from 01. *The Vicarage, 52 Park Lane, Salisbury SP1 3NP* Tel (01722) 333762 E-mail paul@pfdt.freeserve.co.uk

TAYLOR, Paul Jeremy. b 72. Brunel Univ BSc96. Ridley Hall Cam 02. **d** 04 **p** 05. C Longfleet *Sarum* from 04. *43 Kingston Road, Poole BH15 2LR* Tel (01202) 253527 Mobile 07776-425621 E-mail pjtaylorsurfing@hotmail.com

TAYLOR, Paul Michael. b 66. EMMTC 03. **d** 05 **p** 05. C Derby St Pet and Ch Ch w H Trin *Derby* from 05. *The Vicarage, 16 Farley Road, Derby DE23 6BX* Tel (01332) 360790 E-mail office@stpetersderby.org.uk

TAYLOR, The Ven Paul Stanley. b 53. Ox Univ BEd75 MTh98. Westcott Ho Cam. **d** 84 **p** 85. C Bush Hill Park St Steph *Lon* 84-88; Asst Dir Post Ord Tr Edmonton Episc Area 87-94; Dir Post Ord Tr 94-00 and 02-04; V Southgate St Andr 88-97; V Hendon St Mary 97-01; V Hendon St Mary and Ch Ch 01-04; AD W Barnet 00-04; Adn Sherborne *Sarum* from 04; Can and Preb Sarum Cathl from 04. *Aldhelm House, West Stafford, Dorchester DT2 8AB* Tel and fax (01305) 269074 *or* tel (01258) 859110 E-mail adsherborne@salisbury.anglican.org *or* ptatstmarys@aol.com

TAYLOR, Peter. b 35. Sussex Univ MA72. Wells Th Coll 58. **d** 60 **p** 61. C Godalming *Guildf* 60-62; C Epsom St Martin 62-65; R E Clandon 65-75; R W Clandon 65-75; rtd 96; P-in-c Burpham *Chich* 96-04. *Jordan's Bank, 20 Penfold Place, Arundel BN18 9SA* Tel (01903) 885706 E-mail pburpham@globalnet.co.uk

TAYLOR, Peter. b 51. St Jo Coll Cam BA72 MA76. Ridley Hall Cam 73. **d** 76 **p** 77. C Roch 76-79; Perm to Offic *Ely* 79-99; Downham from 99. *Gravel Head Farm, Downham Common, Little Downham, Ely CB6 2TY* Tel and fax (01353) 698714 E-mail peter.taylor5@talk21.com

TAYLOR, Peter David. b 38. FCA. N Ord Course 77. **d** 80 **p** 81. C Penwortham St Mary *Blackb* 80-84; V Farington 84-92; V Euxton 92-04; rtd 04. *33 Aspendale Close, Longton, Preston PR4 5LJ* Tel (01772) 614795

TAYLOR, Canon Peter David. b 47. Liv Univ BEd74 Man Univ MEd78 Lanc Univ MA88. N Ord Course 78. **d** 81 **p** 82. C Formby H Trin *Liv* 81-84; V Stoneycroft All SS 84-91; Chapl St Kath Coll 91-96; Dioc RE Field Officer 91-96; Dioc Dir of Educn *Leic* from 96; Hon Can Leic Cathl from 98. *87 Main Street, Humberstone, Leicester LE5 1AE* Tel 0116-248 7450 Fax 251 1638 E-mail ptaylor@chouse.leicester.anglican.org

TAYLOR, The Ven Peter Flint. b 44. Qu Coll Cam BA65 MA69. Lon Coll of Div BD70. **d** 70 **p** 71. C Highbury New Park St Aug *Lon* 70-73; C Plymouth St Andr w St Paul and St Geo *Ex* 73-77; V Ironville *Derby* 77-83; P-in-c Riddings 82-83; R Rayleigh *Chelmsf* 83-96; Chapl HM YOI Bullwood Hall 85-90; RD Rochford *Chelmsf* 89-96; Adn Harlow from 96. *Glebe House, Church Lane, Sheering, Bishop's Stortford CM22 7NR* Tel (01279) 734524 Fax 734426 E-mail a.harlow@chelmsford.anglican.org

TAYLOR, Peter Graham. b 45. Liv Univ 86 TCert69 CQSW69. Local Minl Tr Course 91. **d** 94 **p** 95. NSM Holywell *St As* 94-97; C Llanrhos 97-02; rtd 02. *23 Merllyn Road, Rhyl LL18 4HG* Tel (01745) 336953 E-mail perunow@global.co.uk

TAYLOR, Peter John. b 40. Oak Hill Th Coll 62. **d** 65 **p** 66. C St Paul's Cray St Barn *Roch* 65-69; C Woking St Jo *Guildf* 69-77; R Necton w Holme Hale *Nor* 77-94; P-in-c N Pickenham w S Pickenham etc 94; R Necton, Holme Hale w N and S Pickenham from 95; RD Breckland 86-94; Hon Can Nor Cathl 98-03. *The Rectory, School Road, Necton, Swaffham PE37 8HT* Tel (01760) 722021

TAYLOR, Peter John. b 46. Tyndale Hall Bris 70. **d** 73 **p** 74. C Walshaw Ch Ch *Man* 73-75; C Rodbourne Cheney *Bris* 75-78; Asst Chapl HM Pris Pentonville 78-79; Chapl HM Borstal Roch 79-84; Chapl HM Pris Highpoint 84-90; Asst Chapl Gen of Pris from 90. *HM Prison Service Chaplaincy, PO Box 349, Stafford ST16 3DL* Tel (01785) 213456 Fax 227734

TAYLOR, Peter John. b 60. New Coll Edin LTh87. Edin Th Coll 83. **d** 87 **p** 88. C Edin SS Phil and Jas *Edin* 87-90; USA 90-92; R Glas St Oswald *Glas* 92-97; R Kirkcudbright from 97; R Gatehouse of Fleet from 97. *9 St Mary's Street, Kirkcudbright DG6 4AA* Tel and fax (01557) 330146 E-mail ptkbt@aol.com

TAYLOR, Peter John. b 71. St Andr Univ MA94 Sussex Univ PGCE99. Oak Hill Th Coll BA05. **d** 05. C Boscombe St Jo *Win* from 05. *167 Southcote Road, Bournemouth BH1 3SP* Tel (01202) 397802

TAYLOR, Peter Joseph. b 41. Bps' Coll Cheshunt 66. **d** 68 **p** 69. C Wollaton *S'well* 68-71; C Cockington *Ex* 71-74; V Broadhembury 74-79; V Broadhembury w Payhembury 79-81; V Gt Staughton *Ely* 81-86; Chapl HM YOI Gaynes Hall 81-91; R Offord D'Arcy w Offord Cluny *Ely* 86-01; V Gt Paxton 86-01; rtd 01; Perm to Offic *Ely* from 01. *9 Park Way, Offord Cluny, St Neots PE19 5RW* Tel (01480) 811662

TAYLOR, Mrs Rachel Sara. b 60. Univ Coll Lon BA81. SEITE 98. **d** 01 **p** 02. C Wimbledon *S'wark* 01-05; V Motspur Park from 05. *The Vicarage, 2 Douglas Avenue, New Malden KT3 6HT* Tel (020) 8942 3117 E-mail rachel@taylortalk.fsnet.co.uk

TAYLOR (or URMSON-TAYLOR), Ralph Urmson. Tulsa Univ MA72 Man Coll of Educn DipEd74 TCert82. Kelham Th Coll DipTh56. **d** 56 **p** 57. C Redcar *York* 57-59; C Bridlington Quay H Trin 59-62; C Sewerby w Marton 60-62; USA 62-02; Asst P Tulsa H Trin 62-65; Sacr 93-02; Chapl Holland Hall Sch 65-93; rtd 93. *Via Montecavallo 18, PG 06081 Assisi, Italy*

TAYLOR, Raymond. b 34. Lon Coll of Div 62. **d** 65 **p** 66. C Pennington *Man* 65-70; P-in-c Wombridge *Lich* 70-80; R S Normanton *Derby* 80-88; RD Alfreton 86-88; V Youlgreave, Middleton, Stanton-in-Peak etc 88-98; rtd 99; Perm to Offic *Derby* from 98. *4 Jeffries Avenue, Crich, Matlock DE4 5DU* Tel (01773) 856845

TAYLOR, Raymond George. b 39. Bucknell Univ BS59 Univ of Penn MS65 EdD66 Penn State Univ MPA77 Maine Univ MBA85. Episc Th Sch Cam Mass BD62. **d** 62 **p** 63. USA 62-04; C Chestnut Hill St Martin 62-66; V Warwick St Mary 70-77; Assoc P Smithfield St Paul 87-90; Assoc P Oriental St Thos 90-00; Superintendent of Schs Maine 77-86; Prof N Carolina State Univ 86-01; P-in-c Malaga w Almunecar *Eur* from 04. *Cortijo Moya, 29710 Periana, Malaga, Spain* Tel and fax (0034) 609-885479 Mobile 650-780087 E-mail cortijomoya@terra.es

TAYLOR, Raymond Montgomery. b 43. Oak Hill Th Coll 77. **d** 80 **p** 81. Hon C Cricklewood St Pet *Lon* 80-85; Hon C Golders Green 85-87; V New Southgate St Paul 87-00; AD Cen Barnet 96-00; V Thaxted *Chelmsf* from 00. *The Vicarage, Watling Lane, Thaxted, Dunmow CM6 2QY* Tel and fax (01371) 830221 E-mail furor@scribendi.freeserve.co.uk

TAYLOR, Richard David. b 44. Worc Coll Ox BA67 MA70. Coll of Resurr Mirfield 67. **d** 69 **p** 70. C Barrow St Geo w St Luke *Carl* 69-73; C Gosforth All SS *Newc* 73-80; TR Newc Epiphany 80-83; V Tynemouth Priory 83-91; TR Benwell 91-98; P-in-c Blyth St Cuth 98-01; V from 01. *The Vicarage, 29 Ridley Avenue, Blyth NE24 3BA* Tel (01670) 352410 E-mail rdtaylor@fish.co.uk

TAYLOR, Richard Godfrey. b 73. Pemb Coll Cam MA99. Oak Hill Th Coll BA00. **d** 00 **p** 01. C Brunswick *Man* 00-04; C Aldridge *Lich* from 04. *14 St Thomas Close, Aldridge, Walsall WS9 8SL* Tel (01922) 453942 E-mail fatboytaylor@hotmail.com

TAYLOR, Preb Richard John. b 21. Kelham Th Coll 38. **d** 45 **p** 46. C Tunstall Ch Ch *Lich* 45-48; C Uttoxeter w Bramshall 48-52; V Croxden 52-57; V Willenhall H Trin 57-68; R Edgmond 68-77; V Streetly 77-87; Preb Lich Cathl 78-87; rtd 87; Perm to Offic *Lich* from 87. *15 Covey Close, Lichfield WS13 6BS* Tel (01543) 268558

TAYLOR, Richard John. b 46. Ripon Coll Cuddesdon 85. **d** 85 **p** 86. C Moseley St Mary *Birm* 85-87; V Kingsbury 87-91; TR Hodge Hill 91-03; P-in-c 03-05; R Weston super Mare St Jo *B & W* from 05. *The Rectory, Cecil Road, Weston-super-Mare BS23 2NF* Tel (01934) 623399

TAYLOR, Robert. *See* TAYLOR, Arthur Robert

TAYLOR, Robert Stirling. b 62. Ball Coll Ox BA83 Leeds Univ PhD88 Nottm Trent Univ PGCE93. Cranmer Hall Dur 00. **d** 02 **p** 03. C Mansfield St Jo *S'well* 02-04; C Eastwood from 04. *8 Mercia Close, Giltbrook, Nottingham NG16 2XF*

TAYLOR, Robin. *See* TAYLOR, Joseph Robin Christopher

TAYLOR, Roger. b 21. Birkbeck Coll Lon BA50 Leeds Univ MA59 Essex Univ MPhil96. Oak Hill Th Coll 47. **d** 51 **p** 52. C Chadderton Ch Ch *Man* 51-55; V Bowling St Steph *Bradf* 55-63; SW Area Sec CPAS 63-68; V Felixstowe SS Pet and Paul *St E* 68-81; P-in-c Gt and Lt Thurlow w Lt Bradley 81-82; TV Haverhill w Withersfield, the Wrattings etc 82-84; R Hopton, Market Weston, Barningham etc 84-86; rtd 86; Perm to Offic *St E* from 87. *Chapel House, Lindsey, Ipswich IP7 6QA* Tel (01787) 211120

TAYLOR, Roger James Benedict. b 42. Glouc Sch of Min 89 WMMTC 95. **d** 96 **p** 97. OLM Cromhall w Tortworth and Tytherington *Glouc* 96-99; P-in-c Wistanstow *Heref* 99-01; Min Can Brecon Cathl *S & B* from 01. *The Almonry, Cathedral Close, Brecon LD3 9DP* Tel (01874) 622972

TAYLOR, Canon Roland Haydn. b 29. St Chad's Coll Dur BA53 DipTh55. **d** 55 **p** 56. C N Gosforth *Newc* 55-58; C Barnsley St Mary *Wakef* 58-61; V Brotherton 61-68; V Purston cum S Featherstone 68-76; RD Pontefract 74-94; R Badsworth 76-97; Hon Can Wakef Cathl 81-97; rtd 97. *57 Fairview, Carleton, Pontefract WF8 3NU* Tel (01977) 796564

TAYLOR, Mrs Rosemary Edith. b 47. Nottm Univ MA04 RGN68 RHV71. EMMTC 01. **d** 04 **p** 05. NSM Bassingham Gp *Linc* from 04. *5 Beck Lane, South Hykeham, Lincoln LN6 9PQ* E-mail natuna@btopenworld.com

TAYLOR, Roy. b 63. Ex Coll Ox BA86 Ox Univ MA89 York Univ PGCE87 Univ of Wales (Cardiff) BD97. St Mich Coll Llan 95. **d** 97 **p** 98. C Guisborough *York* 97-99; Chapl Rossall Sch Fleetwood 99-02; V Dolphinholme w Quernmore and Over Wyresdale *Blackb* from 02. *The Vicarage, Dolphinholme, Lancaster LA2 9AH* Tel (01524) 791300

TAYLOR, Roy Partington. b 33. Birm Univ BA54 PGCE55 Bulmershe Coll of HE MPhil87. St Alb and Ox Min Course 96. **d** 98 **p** 99. NSM Hurley and Stubbings *Ox* 98-02; NSM Burchetts Green 02-03; rtd 03; Perm to Offic *Ox* 03-04; Hon C Maidenhead St Andr and St Mary from 04; Lect Bp Hannington Inst Kenya 01-02; Prin from 04. *16 Highfield Road, Maidenhead SL6 5DF* Tel (01628) 625454 E-mail roy.taylor@telco4u.net

TAYLOR, Roy William. b 37. Ch Coll Cam BA61 MA64. Clifton Th Coll 61. **d** 63 **p** 64. C Blackb Sav *Blackb* 63-66; C Hensingham *Carl* 66-68; CMS Taiwan 69-79; TV Bushbury *Lich* 79-85; OMF 85-93; Hon C Wolverhampton St Jude *Lich* 93-94; P-in-c Torquay St Jo and Ellacombe *Ex* 94-99; R Instow and V Westleigh 99-03; RD Hartland 01-03; rtd 03. *31 Shore Road, Millisle, Newtownards BT22 2BT* Tel (028) 9186 2769

TAYLOR, Simon Dominic Kent. b 69. Surrey Univ BSc90 PGCE91 Sussex Univ MA(Ed)99 Bris Univ BA01. **d** 01 **p** 02. C Southgate *Chich* 01-04; TV from 04. *21 Anglesey Close, Crawley RH11 9HG* Tel (01293) 552287

TAYLOR, Simon John. b 72. Worc Coll Ox BA94 MPhil96 MA99 DPhil00. St Mich Coll Llan 00 Ven English Coll Rome 01. **d** 02 **p** 03. C Cotham St Sav w St Mary and Clifton St Paul *Bris* from 02. *182 St Michael's Hill, Bristol BS2 8DE* Tel 0117-377 9591 E-mail taylor@fish.co.uk

TAYLOR, Mrs Stella Isabelle. b 31. S Dios Minl Tr Scheme 86. **d** 89 **p** 94. NSM Haworth *Bradf* 89-91; Par Dn Keighley St Andr 92-94; C 94-96; rtd 97; Perm to Offic *Bradf* 97-00. *8 The Linkway, Westham, Pevensey BN24 5JB*

TAYLOR, Stephen. b 65. City Univ BSc87 Lon Univ PGCE90. NTMTC 95. **d** 98 **p** 99. NSM Enfield Chase St Mary *Lon* 98-02; Perm to Offic *Eur* 02-03; Chapl Bp Stopford's Sch Enfield 98-02 and from 03; C Hornsey St Mary w St Geo *Lon* from 03. *145A North View Road, London N8 7ND,* or *Bishop Stopford's School, Brick Lane, Enfield EN1 3PU* Tel and fax (020) 8340 1489 Mobile 07711-559107 E-mail father.taylor@virgin.net

TAYLOR, Stephen Gordon. b 35. Bris Univ BA60. Ridley Hall Cam 60. **d** 62 **p** 63. C Gt Baddow *Chelmsf* 62-65; C Portsdown *Portsm* 65-69; P-in-c Elvedon *St E* 69-70; R 70-75; P-in-c Eriswell 69-70; R 70-75; P-in-c Icklingham 69-70; R 70-75; Chapl St Felix Sch Southwold 75-77; R Lt Shelford w Newton *Ely* 77-96; rtd 96; Perm to Offic *Ely* from 96. *15 Church Close, Whittlesford, Cambridge CB2 4NY* Tel (01223) 830461

TAYLOR, Stephen James. b 48. Chich Th Coll 70. **d** 73 **p** 74. C Tottenham St Paul *Lon* 73-76; St Vincent 78-85; Grenada 85-88; C-in-c Hammersmith SS Mich and Geo White City Estate CD *Lon* 88-96; AD Hammersmith 92-96; P-in-c Hammersmith St Luke 94-96; USPG Brazil from 96. *Avenue Rio Branco 277/907, Cinelandia, Rio de Janeiro, RJ 20047-900, Brazil*

TAYLOR, Canon Stephen Ronald. b 55. Dur Univ MA99. Cranmer Hall Dur 80. **d** 83 **p** 84. C Chester le Street *Dur* 83-87; V Newbottle 87-92; V Stranton 92-00; TR Sunderland from 00; Hon Can Rift Valley Tanzania from 00. *6 Thornhill Terrace, Sunderland SR2 7JL* Tel 0191-514 0447 *or* 565 4066 E-mail stephen.taylor@durham.anglican.org

TAYLOR, Stewart. b 51. St Jo Coll Dur 74. **d** 77 **p** 78. C Norwood St Luke *S'wark* 77-81; C Surbiton Hill Ch Ch 81-91; V Cambridge St Phil *Ely* from 91. *St Philip's Vicarage, 252 Mill Road, Cambridge CB1 3NF* Tel (01223) 247652 *or* 414775 E-mail vicar@stphilipschurch.org.uk

TAYLOR, Canon Stuart Bryan. b 40. St Chad's Coll Dur BA64. **d** 66 **p** 67. C Portsea N End St Mark *Portsm* 66-70; C Epsom St Martin *Guildf* 70-76; Chapl Clifton Coll Bris 76-88; Dir Bloxham Project 88-93; Chapl Giggleswick Sch 93-95; Bp's Officer for Miss and Evang *Bris* 96-01; Bp's Adv for Past Care for Clergy and Families from 01; Hon Min Can Bris Cathl from 02; Chapl Bris Cathl Sch from 01; Hon Can Bris Cathl *Bris* from 04. *62 Providence Lane, Long Ashton, Bristol BS41 9DN* Tel (01275) 393625 *or* 0117-906 0100 E-mail stuart.taylor@bristoldiocese.org

TAYLOR, Mrs Teresa Mary. b 53. SRN76 SCM78 HVCert80. WEMTC 98. **d** 02 **p** 03. NSM Kingswood *Bris* from 02. *15 Hampton Street, Bristol BS15 1TP* Tel 0117-373 2410 E-mail testaylor@blueyonder.co.uk

TAYLOR, Thomas. b 33. Sarum & Wells Th Coll 77. **d** 80 **p** 81. NSM Heatherlands St Jo *Sarum* 80-82; TV Kinson 82-88; TV Shaston 88-98; Chapl Westmr Memorial Hosp Shaftesbury 88-98; rtd 98; Perm to Offic *Sarum* from 98. *10 Hanover Lane, Gillingham SP3 4TA* Tel (01747) 826569

TAYLOR, Thomas. b 42. St Jo Coll Dur BA64. Linc Th Coll 64. **d** 66 **p** 67. C Clitheroe St Mary *Blackb* 66-69; C Skerton St Luke 69-71; C-in-c Penwortham St Leon CD 71-72; V Penwortham St Leon 72-78; R Poulton-le-Sands 78-81; P-in-c Morecambe St Lawr 78-81; R Poulton-le-Sands w Morecambe St Laur 81-85; Chapl Ld Wandsworth Coll Hants 85-92; V Walton-le-Dale *Blackb* 92-94; P-in-c Samlesbury 92-94; V Walton-le-Dale St Leon w Samlesbury St Leon 95-96; RD Leyland 94-96; Hon C Tarleton from 03. *52 Hesketh Lane, Tarleton, Preston PR4 6AQ* Tel (01772) 813871

TAYLOR, Thomas Ronald Bennett. b 23. TCD BA46 MA54. Div Test. **d** 47 **p** 48. C Larne and Inver *Conn* 47-49; Chapl RAF 49-65; I Narraghmore w Fontstown and Timolin *D & G* 65-68; I Tynan w Middletown *Arm* 68-85; rtd 85. *34 Kernan Park, Portadown, Craigavon BT63 5QY* Tel (028) 3833 7230

TAYLOR, Willam Goodacre Campbell. *See* CAMPBELL-TAYLOR, William Goodacre

TAYLOR, William Austin. b 36. Linc Th Coll 65. **d** 67 **p** 68. C Tyldesley w Shakerley *Man* 67-71; R Cheetham St Mark 71-79; TR Peel 79-90; AD Farnworth 83-90; V Pelton *Dur* 90-96; rtd 96; Perm to Offic *Man* from 96. *36 Tynesbank, Worsley, Manchester M28 8SL* Tel 0161-790 5327

TAYLOR, William Henry. b 56. Kent Univ BA79 Lon Univ MTh81 Lanc Univ MPhil87 FRAS80. Westcott Ho Cam. **d** 83 **p** 84. C Maidstone All SS and St Phil w Tovil *Cant* 83-86; Abp's Adv on Orthodox Affairs 86-88; C St Marylebone All SS *Lon* 86-88; Chapl Guy's Hosp Lon 88; CMS Jordan 88-91; V Ealing St Pet Mt Park *Lon* 91-00; AD Ealing 93-98; Dean Portsm 00-02; P-in-c Notting Hill St Jo and St Pet *Lon* 02; V Notting Hill St Jo from 03. *St John's Vicarage, 25 Ladbroke Road, London W11 3PD* Tel (020) 7727 3439 *or* 7727 4262 E-mail vicar@stjohnsnottinghill.com

TAYLOR, William Richard de Carteret Martin. b 33. CCC Cam MA57. Westcott Ho Cam 58. **d** 59 **p** 60. C Eastney *Portsm* 59-63; Chapl RN 63-67 and 70-87; V Childe Okeford *Sarum* 67-70; V

Manston w Hamoon 67-70; QHC from 83; TR Tisbury *Sarum* 87-89; Chapl Hatf Poly *St Alb* 89-92; Chapl Herts Univ 92-98; rtd 98; Perm to Offic *Ely* from 00. *Lark Rise, 47A New Street, St Neots, Huntingdon PE19 1AJ* Tel (01480) 473598

TAYLOR, Capt William Thomas. b 61. Rob Coll Cam BA83 BA90. Ridley Hall Cam 88. **d** 91 **p** 92. C Bromley Ch Ch *Roch* 91-95; C St Helen Bishopsgate w St Andr Undershaft etc *Lon* 95-98; R from 98; R St Pet Cornhill from 01. *The Old Rectory, Merrick Square, London SE1 4JB* Tel (020) 7378 8186

TEAGUE, Gaythorne Derrick. b 24. MBE05. Bris Univ MB, ChB49 MRCGP53. **d** 74 **p** 75. NSM Bris St Andr Hartcliffe *Bris* 74-86; Perm to Offic *B & W* from 86. *Innisfree, Bell Square, Blagdon, Bristol BS40 7UB* Tel (01761) 462671

TEAGUE, Robert Hayden. b 15. Univ of Wales (Ban). Dorchester Miss Coll 36 St Deiniol's Hawarden. **d** 63 **p** 64. C Rhosddu *St As* 63-65; C Llanrhos 65-66; V Llangernyw, Gwytherin and Llanddewi 66-77; V Meliden and Gwaenysgor 77-83; rtd 83. *Priory House Residential Home, 63 Gronant Road, Prestatyn LL19 9LU* Tel (01745) 852650

TEAL, Andrew Robert. b 64. Birm Univ BA85 Ox Brookes Univ PGCE05. Ripon Coll Cuddesdon 86. **d** 88 **p** 89. C Wednesbury St Paul Wood Green *Lich* 88-92; TV Sheff Manor *Sheff* 92-97; Asst Dioc Post Ord Tr Officer 93-98; Tutor Ripon Coll Cuddesdon 92-97; V Tickhill w Stainton *Sheff* 97-02; Warden of Readers 98-02; Hd of Th Plater Coll 02-03; Hd of Th and Past Studies from 03; Perm to Offic *Ox* from 05. *Plater College, Pullens Lane, Oxford OX3 0DT* Tel (01865) 740500 Fax 740510 E-mail theologyteal@aol.com *or* andrew.teal@plater.ac.uk

TEALE, Adrian. b 53. Univ of Wales (Abth) BA74 CertEd77 MA80 Univ of Wales (Cardiff) MTh89. Wycliffe Hall Ox 78. **d** 80 **p** 81. C Betws w Ammanford *St D* 80-84; V Brynaman w Cwmllynfell 84-01; RD Dyffryn Aman 95-01; V Betws w Ammanford from 01. *The Vicarage, College Street, Ammanford SA18 3AB* Tel (01269) 592084

TEAR, Jeremy Charles. b 67. Westmr Coll Ox BA89 Birm Univ MA99 N Lon Poly 90 GradIPM90 MIPD94. Aston Tr Scheme 95 Qu Coll Birm 97. **d** 99 **p** 00. C Timperley *Ches* 99-03; V Macclesfield St Paul from 03. *St Paul's Vicarage, Swallow Close, Macclesfield SK10 1QN* Tel (01625) 422910 *or* 501773 E-mail revjtear@fish.co.uk

TEARE, Mrs Marie. b 46. Open Univ BA81 RSCN67. N Ord Course 95. **d** 98 **p** 99. C Brighouse and Clifton *Wakef* 98-01; V Waggoners *York* from 01; RD Harthill from 02. *The Vicarage, Pulham Lane, Wetwang, Driffield YO25 9XT* Tel (01377) 236410 E-mail marie.teare@lineone.net

TEARE, Canon Robert John Hugh. b 39. Bris Univ BSc62 Leeds Univ DipTh69. Coll of Resurr Mirfield 67. **d** 70 **p** 71. C Fareham SS Pet and Paul *Portsm* 70-73; Chapl K Alfred Coll *Win* 73-78; V Pokesdown St Jas 78-82; R Winnall from 82; RD Win 89-99; Hon Can Win Cathl from 92. *The Rectory, 22 St John's Street, Winchester SO23 0HF* Tel (01962) 863891 Fax 867298 E-mail rjh.teare@btinternet.com

TEARNAN, John Herman Janson. b 37. Bris Univ BSc59. Kelham Th Coll 62. **d** 66 **p** 67. C Kettering SS Pet and Paul *Pet* 66-71; Lic to Offic 71-85; Perm to Offic *St Alb* 82-85 and *Pet* 85-94; Chapl HM YOI Wellingborough 89-90; Chapl HM YOI Glen Parva 90-94; Guyana 94-03; rtd 03. *14 Rectory Walk, Barton Seagrave, Kettering NN15 6SP* Tel (01536) 510629

TEASDALE, Keith. b 56. Cranmer Hall Dur 86. **d** 88 **p** 89. C Crook *Dur* 88-92; V Dunston from 92; AD Gateshead W from 00. *St Nicholas' Vicarage, Willow Avenue, Dunston, Gateshead NE11 9UN* Tel 0191-460 0509 *or* fax and tel 460 9327 Mobile 07718-907660 E-mail stn@ukonline.co.uk

TEBBS, Richard Henry. b 52. Southn Univ BTh. Sarum & Wells Th Coll 75. **d** 78 **p** 79. C Cinderhill *S'well* 78-82; C Nor St Pet Mancroft *Nor* 82; C Nor St Pet Mancroft w St Jo Maddermarket 82-85; TV Bridport *Sarum* 85-94; TR Yelverton, Meavy, Sheepstor and Walkhampton *Ex* from 94. *The Rectory, St Paul's Church, Yelverton PL20 6AB* Tel (01822) 852362 E-mail tebbsfamily@rtebbs.fsnet.co.uk

TEBBUTT, Christopher Michael. b 55. St Jo Coll Nottm BA94. **d** 96 **p** 97. C Catherington and Clanfield *Portsm* 96-00; P-in-c Southbroom *Sarum* from 00. *Southbroom Vicarage, 31 Fruitfields Close, Devizes SN10 5JY* Tel (01380) 721441 *or* 723891 E-mail thetebbutts@southbroom.fslife.co.uk

TEBBUTT, Sandra Eileen. b 56. FBDO78. STETS 96. **d** 99 **p** 00. NSM Blendworth w Chalton w Idsworth *Portsm* 99-00; Chapl Wilts and Swindon Healthcare NHS Trust 00-05; Regional Manager Bible Soc from 05. *Southbroom Vicarage, 31 Fruitfields Close, Devizes SN10 5JY* Tel (01380) 723633 E-mail sandra.tebbutt@biblesociety.org.uk

TEBBUTT, Simon Albert. b 27. Westmr Coll Ox BTh04. Qu Coll Birm 88. **d** 89 **p** 90. NSM Northampton St Matt *Pet* 89-92; TV Duston Team 92-94; rtd 94; NSM Gt and Lt Houghton w Brafield on the Green *Pet* 94-96; NSM Cogenhoe and Gt and Lt Houghton w Brafield 96-97; Dioc Sec St Luke's Hosp for the Clergy from 00; Perm to Offic from 01. *Tanners, Moulton Lane, Boughton, Northampton NN2 8RF* Tel (01604) 843240

TEDD, Christopher Jonathan Richard. *See* HOWITZ, Christopher Jonathan Richard

TEDMAN, Alfred. b 33. AKC59. **d** 60 **p** 61. C Newington St Mary *S'wark* 60-64; C Milton *Portsm* 64-68; R Bonchurch 68-98; RD E Wight 78-83; P-in-c Whitwell 79-82; P-in-c St Lawrence 82-84; V Wroxall 84-98; rtd 99. *Winfrith House, Blackgang Road, Niton, Ventnor PO38 2BW*

TEE, John. b 59. **d** 82 **p** 83. C Walworth *S'wark* 82-85; Chapl RAF 85-89; CF 89-03. *Address temp unknown*

TEED, John Michael. b 44. Middx Univ BA04. NTMTC 01. **d** 04 **p** 05. NSM Hanworth All SS *Lon* from 04. *5 Island Close, Staines TW18 4YZ* Tel (01784) 458583 Mobile 07702-244078 E-mail johnteed@fish.co.uk

TEGALLY, Narinder Jit Kaur. b 57. RGN93. St Alb and Ox Min Course 99. **d** 02 **p** 03. NSM Welwyn Garden City *St Alb* 02-05; Asst Chapl R Free Hampstead NHS Trust from 05. *The Chaplain's Office, Royal Free Hospital, Pond Street, London NW3 2QG* Tel (020) 7830 2742 *or* 7794 0500 Fax 7830 2468 E-mail narinder@grove-house.org.uk

TEGGARTY, Samuel James Karl. b 53. Dundee Univ BSc77. CITC 98. **d** 01 **p** 02. NSM Newry *D & D* 01-03; NSM Kilkeel from 03. *79 Knockchree Avenue, Kilkeel, Newry BT34 4BP* Tel (028) 4176 9076 E-mail karl@teggarty.fsnet.co.uk

TEGGIN, John. b 26. **d** 83 **p** 84. NSM Dublin Sandford w Milltown *D & G* 84-93; Dir Leprosy Miss 86-96. *Apartment 4, 69 Strand Road, Sandymount, Dublin 4, Irish Republic* Tel (00353) (1) 261 1792

TELFER, Andrew Julian. b 68. Essex Univ BA94. Wycliffe Hall Ox BTh97. **d** 97 **p** 98. C Skelmersdale St Paul *Liv* 97-01; C Ashton-in-Makerfield St Thos 01-03; V Whiston from 03. *The Vicarage, 90 Windy Arbor Road, Prescot L35 3SG* Tel 0151-426 6329

TELFER, Canon Frank Somerville. b 30. Trin Hall Cam BA53 MA58. Ely Th Coll 53. **d** 55 **p** 56. C Liv Our Lady and St Nic *Liv* 55-58; Chapl Down Coll Cam 58-62; Bp's Chapl *Nor* 62-65; Chapl Kent Univ *Cant* 65-73; Can Res Guildf Cathl *Guildf* 73-95; rtd 96; Perm to Offic *Nor* from 96. *Holbrook, Glandford, Holt NR25 7JP* Tel (01263) 740586

TELFORD, Alan. b 46. St Jo Coll Nottm. **d** 83 **p** 84. C Normanton *Derby* 83-86; TV N Wingfield, Pilsley and Tupton 86-90; TV N Wingfield, Clay Cross and Pilsley 90-92; P-in-c Oakwood 92-94; V Leic St Chris *Leic* from 94. *The Vicarage, 84A Marriott Road, Leicester LE2 6NT* Tel 0116-283 2679 E-mail alan@saffron84a.freeserve.co.uk

TELFORD, Richard Francis. b 46. K Coll Lon 65. **d** 69 **p** 70. C Barkingside H Trin *Chelmsf* 69-72; C Wickford 72-77; P-in-c Romford St Jo 77-80; V 80-82; Perm to Offic 93-96. *Juglans, The Street, Wattisfield, Diss IP22 1NS*

TELLINI, Canon Gianfranco. b 36. Gregorian Univ Rome DTh65. Franciscan Sem Trent 57. **d** 61 **p** 61. In RC Ch 61-66; C Mill Hill Jo Keble Ch *Lon* 66; C Roxbourne St Andr 66-67; Lect Sarum Th Coll 67-69; Sen Tutor 69-74; Vice-Prin Edin Th Coll 74-82; Lect Th Edin Univ 74-95; R Pittenweem *St And* 82-85; R Elie and Earlsferry 82-85; R Dunblane 85-98; Can St Ninian's Cathl Perth from 90; rtd 99. *53 Buchan Drive, Dunblane FK15 9HW* Tel (01786) 823281 E-mail giant11@aol.com

TEMBEY, David. b 51. **d** 96 **p** 97. NSM Whitehaven *Carl* 96-00; NSM Holme Cultram St Cuth 00-02; NSM Holme Cultram St Mary 00-02; NSM Bromfield w Waverton 00-02; TV Solway Plain from 02. *The Vicarage, Abbeytown, Wigton CA7 4SP* Tel (01697) 361246 Fax 361506 E-mail tembey6@aol.com

TEMPERLEY, Robert Noble. b 29. JP. St Jo Coll York CertEd50 ACP52 Dur Univ DAES62. NEOC 85. **d** 88 **p** 88. NSM Ryhope *Dur* 88-97; rtd 98; Perm to Offic *Dur* from 98. *18 Withernsea Grove, Ryhope, Sunderland SR2 0BU* Tel 0191-521 1813

TEMPLE, Mrs Sylvia Mary. b 48. Ex Univ BA70 Univ of Wales (Abth) PGCE71. St D Dioc Tr Course 93. **d** 94 **p** 97. NSM Tenby *St D* 94-99; C 99-00; V Martletwy w Lawrenny and Minwear etc from 00. *St John's Rectory, Church Street, Templeton, Narberth SA67 8XX* Tel (01834) 861412

TEMPLE-WILLIAMS, Alexander. **d** 04 **p** 05. C Pontypool *Mon* from 04. *St Matthew's House, Victoria Road, Pontymoile, Pontypool NP44 5JU* Tel (01495) 752233

TEMPLEMAN (née WILLIAMS), Mrs Ann Joyce. b 50. St Hugh's Coll Ox BA72 MA75 PGCE73. Cranmer Hall Dur 03. **d** 05. NSM Peterlee *Dur* from 05. *The Vicarage, Manor Way, Peterlee SR8 5QW* Tel 0191-586 2630 Mobile 07919-620259 E-mail ann@templeman99.freeserve.co.uk

TEMPLEMAN, Peter Morton. b 49. Ch Ch Ox BA71 MA75 BTh75. Wycliffe Hall Ox 73. **d** 76 **p** 77. C Cheltenham St Mary, St Matt, St Paul and H Trin *Glouc* 76-79; Chapl St Jo Coll Cam 79-84; P-in-c Finchley St Paul Long Lane *Lon* 84-85; P-in-c Finchley St Luke 84-85; V Finchley St Paul and St Luke 85-99; V Peterlee *Dur* from 99. *The Vicarage, Manor Way, Peterlee SR8 5QW* Tel 0191-586 2630

TEMPLETON, Iain McAllister. b 57. HNC86. St Andr Coll Drygrange 80. **d** 85 **p** 86. In RC Ch 85-92; NSM Dornoch *Mor* 95; P-in-c Kirriemuir *St And* 95-99; R Eccleston *Blackb* from 99. *The Rectory, New Lane, Eccleston, Chorley PR7 6NA* Tel and fax (01257) 451206 E-mail fatheriain@aol.com *or* fatheriain@priest.com

TEN WOLDE, Christine Caroline. b 57. **d** 99 **p** 00. NSM Llanegryn w Aberdyfi w Tywyn *Ban* from 99. *Aber-groes, Abertafol, Aberdovey LL35 0RE* Tel (01654) 767047 Mobile 07977-108438 Fax 767572
E-mail curate@stpeterschurch.org.uk

TENNANT, Cyril Edwin George. b 37. Keble Coll Ox BA59 MA63 Lon Univ BD61 Ex Univ MA03. Clifton Th Coll 59. **d** 62 **p** 63. C Stapleford *S'well* 62-65; C Felixstowe SS Pet and Paul *St E* 65-69; V Gipsy Hill Ch Ch *S'wark* 69-84; V Lee St Mildred 84-90; V Ilfracombe SS Phil and Jas w W Down *Ex* 90-01; P-in-c Lundy Is 90-92; rtd 01; Perm to Offic *Ex* from 01. *23 Broadgate Close, Pilton, Barnstaple EX31 4AL* Tel (01271) 323517
E-mail candc.tennant@virgin.net

TER BLANCHE, Harold Daniel. b 35. St Paul's Coll Grahamstown LTh85. **d** 63 **p** 64. S Africa 63-82; Chapl Miss to Seamen 82-84; Chapl Grimsby Distr Gen Hosp 84-94; Chapl NE Lincs NHS Trust 94-00; rtd 00; Perm to Offic *Linc* from 00. *25 Collingwood Crescent, Grimsby DN34 5RG* Tel (01472) 276624 Fax 313995

TERESA, Sister. *See* WHITE, Sister Teresa Joan

✠**TEROM, The Rt Revd Zechariah James.** b 41. St Columba's Coll Hazaribagh BA64 Ranchi Univ MA66. Bp's Coll Calcutta BD71. **d** 71 **c** 86. C Hazaribagh India 71-73; Par P Manoharpur 73-76; Bp Chotanagpur from 86; Moderator Ch of N India from 01. *Bishop's Lodge, PO Box 1, Church Road, Ranchi 834 001, Bihar, India* Tel (0091) (651) 311181 Fax 311184 *or* 314184

TERRANOVA, Jonathan Rossano (Ross). b 62. Sheff Poly BA85. Oak Hill Th Coll BA88. **d** 88 **p** 89. C Carl St Jo *Carl* 88-91; C Stoughton *Guildf* 91-94; R Ditton *Roch* from 94; RD Malling from 02. *The Rectory, 2 The Stream, Ditton, Maidstone ME20 6AG* Tel (01732) 842027

TERRELL, Richard Charles Patridge. b 43. Wells Th Coll 69. **d** 71 **p** 72. C Shepton Mallet *B & W* 71-76; P-in-c Drayton 76-78; P-in-c Muchelney 76-78; TV Langport Area Chs 78-82; P-in-c Tatworth 82-89; V 89-96; R W Coker w Hardington Mandeville, E Chinnock etc from 96. *The Rectory, 7 Cedar Fields, West Coker, Yeovil BA22 9DB* Tel (01935) 862328

TERRETT, Mervyn Douglas. b 43. AKC65. **d** 66 **p** 67. C Pet St Mary Boongate *Pet* 66-69; C Sawbridgeworth *St Alb* 69-74; V Stevenage H Trin 74-85; Perm to Offic from 86. *Red Roofs, 20 Woodfield Road, Stevenage SG1 4BP* Tel (01438) 720152

TERRY, Christopher Laurence. b 51. FCA80. St Alb Minl Tr Scheme. **d** 83 **p** 84. Hon C Dunstable *St Alb* 83-89; C Abbots Langley 89-92; TV Chambersbury 92-99; Chapl Abbot's Hill Sch Herts 96-99; R Southwick St Mich *Chich* 99-03; RD Hove 00-03; Finance and Admin Sec Min Division Abps' Coun from 04; Perm to Offic *St Alb* from 04. *Ministry Division, Church House, Great Smith Street, London SW1P 3NZ* Tel (020) 7898 1393
E-mail christopher.terry@c-of-e.org.uk *or* tecrry@aol.com

TERRY, Colin Alfred. b 49. Trin Coll Bris. **d** 00 **p** 01. C Bexleyheath Ch Ch *Roch* 00-03; V Belvedere All SS from 03. *All Saints' Vicarage, Nuxley Road, Belvedere DA17 5JE* Tel (01322) 432169 E-mail colin.terry3@btopenworld.com

TERRY, Ms Helen Barbara. b 58. Keele Univ BA80 ATCL98. Ripon Coll Cuddesdon 01. **d** 03 **p** 04. C Cainscross w Selsley *Glouc* from 03. *48 Cashes Green Road, Cainscross, Stroud GL5 4LN* Tel (01453) 752792

TERRY, Ian Andrew. b 53. St Jo Coll Dur BA74 St Jo Coll York PGCE75 St Mary's Coll Twickenham MA99. Coll of Resurr Mirfield 78. **d** 80 **p** 81. C Beaconsfield *Ox* 80-83; C N Lynn w St Marg and St Nic *Nor* 83-84; Chapl and Hd RE Eliz Coll Guernsey 84-89; Chapl St Jo Sch Leatherhead 89-92; R Bisley and W End *Guildf* 92-02; Asst Chapl HM Pris Coldingley 99-02; Dioc Dir of Educn *Heref* from 02; Hon TV W Heref from 03. *The Vicarage, Breinton, Hereford HR4 7PG* Tel (01432) 265967 *or* 357864 E-mail iaterry@attglobal.net *or* i.terry@hereford.anglican.org

TERRY, James Richard. b 74. Linc Coll Ox BA95 ACA98. Oak Hill Th Coll BA03. **d** 03 **p** 04. C Harold Wood *Chelmsf* from 03. *48 Harold Court Road, Romford RM3 0YX* Tel (01708) 344127
E-mail james_terry1@hotmail.com

TERRY, John Arthur. b 32. S'wark Ord Course. **d** 66 **p** 67. C Plumstead All SS *S'wark* 66-69; C Peckham St Mary Magd 69-72; V Streatham Vale H Redeemer 72-80; R Sternfield w Benhall and Snape *St E* 80-84; V Stevenage St Mary Shephall *St Alb* 84-86; V Stevenage St Mary Shephall w Aston 86-90; V Cople w Willington 90-97; Chapl Shuttleworth Agric Coll 90-97; rtd 97; Perm to Offic *St E* from 98; *Nor* 98-04; *Ely* from 03. *2 Kestrel Drive, Brandon IP27 0UA* Tel (01842) 812055

TERRY, Justyn Charles. b 65. Keble Coll Ox BA86 St Jo Coll Dur BA95. Cranmer Hall Dur 92. **d** 95 **p** 96. C Paddington St Jo w St Mich *Lon* 95-99; V Kensington St Helen w H Trin from 99. *St Helen's Vicarage, St Helen's Gardens, London W10 6LP* Tel (020) 8968 7807 Fax 8969 5782
E-mail justyn.terry@london.anglican.org

TERRY, Stephen John. b 49. K Coll Lon BD72 AKC74. **d** 75 **p** 76. C Tokyngton St Mich *Lon* 75-78; C Hampstead St Steph w All Hallows 78-81; V Whetstone St Jo 81-89; TR Aldrington *Chich* from 89. *The Rectory, 77 New Church Road, Hove BN3 4BB* Tel (01273) 737915

TESTA, Luigi Richard Frederick. b 30. Nottm Univ Cert Th & Past Studies 85. **d** 85 **p** 86. NSM Castle Donington and Lockington cum Hemington *Leic* 85-95; Perm to Offic from 95. *40 Hillside, Castle Donington, Derby DE74 2NH* Tel (01332) 810823

TESTER, Clarence Albert. b 20. Qu Coll Birm 47. **d** 50 **p** 51. C Southmead *Bris* 50-53; C Knowle St Barn 53-55; Chapl Ham Green Hosp Bris 55-70; V Halberton *Ex* 70-85; rtd 85; Perm to Offic *B & W* 86-98. *Brays Batch, Chewton Mendip, Bath BA3 4LH* Tel (01761) 241218

TETLEY, Brian. b 38. St Jo Coll Dur BA82 ACA62 FCA72. Cranmer Hall Dur 80. **d** 83 **p** 84. C Chipping Sodbury and Old Sodbury *Glouc* 83-86; Chapl and Succ Roch Cath *Roch* 86-89; R Gravesend H Family w Ifield 89-93; Tutor Westcott Ho Cam 93-94 and 95-96; Tutor Ridley Hall and Prec Ely Cathl *Ely* 95; C Duxford, Hinxton and Ickleton 97; Perm to Offic 98-99; NSM Worc Cathl *Worc* 00-03; rtd 03; Perm to Offic *Worc* from 03. *15B College Green, Worcester WR1 2LH* Tel and fax (01905) 724157 E-mail btetley@cofe-worcester.org.uk

TETLEY, The Ven Joy Dawn. b 46. St Mary's Coll Dur BA68 Leeds Univ CertEd69 St Hugh's Coll Ox BA75 MA80 Dur Univ PhD88. NW Ord Course 77. **dss** 77 **d** 87 **p** 94. Bentley *Sheff* 77-79; Buttershaw St Aid *Bradf* 79-80; Dur Cathl *Dur* 80-83; Lect Trin Coll Bris 83-86; Chipping Sodbury and Old Sodbury *Glouc* 83-86; Dn Roch Cathl *Roch* 87-89; Hon Can Roch Cathl 90-93; Assoc Dir of Post Ord Tr 87-88; Dir Post Ord Tr 88-93; Hon Par Dn Gravesend H Family w Ifield 89-93; Prin EAMTC *Ely* 93-99; Adn Worc and Can Res Worc Cathl *Worc* from 99. *15B College Green, Worcester WR1 2LH* Tel and fax (01905) 724157 E-mail jtetley@cofe-worcester.org.uk

TETLEY, Matthew David. b 61. Bucks Coll of Educn BSc83. Sarum & Wells Th Coll BTh89. **d** 87 **p** 88. C Kirkby *Liv* 87-90; C Hindley St Pet 90-93; TV Whorlton *Newc* 93-96; V Newbiggin Hall 96-01; P-in-c Longhorsley and Hebron from 01; Chapl HM Pris Acklington from 01. *Address withheld by request*

TETLOW, John. b 46. St Steph Ho Ox 73. **d** 76 **p** 77. C Stanwell *Lon* 76-77; C Hanworth All SS 77-80; C Somers Town 80-83; TV Wickford and Runwell *Chelmsf* 83-90; P-in-c Walthamstow St Mich 90-96. *6A Bushwood, London E11 3AY* Tel (020) 8520 6328

TETLOW, Richard Jeremy. b 42. Trin Coll Cam MA66 Goldsmiths' Coll Lon CQSW74. Qu Coll Birm 81. **d** 83 **p** 84. C Birm St Martin *Birm* 83-85; C Birm St Martin w Bordesley St Andr 85-88; V Birm St Jo Ladywood 89-01; V Ladywood St Jo and St Pet from 01. *St John's Vicarage, Darnley Road, Birmingham B16 8TF* Tel 0121-454 0973
E-mail richardtetlow@fish.co.uk

TETZLAFF, Silke. b 67. Friedrich Schiller Univ 87 K Coll Lon BA97 AKC97 Anglia Poly Univ MA01. Westcott Ho Cam 99. **d** 01 **p** 02. C Leagrave *St Alb* 01-05; TV Baldock w Bygrave and Weston from 05. *The Vicarage, 14 Munts Meadow, Weston, Hitchin SG4 7AE* Tel (01462) 790330
E-mail silke.tetzlaff@ntlworld.com

TEVERSON, Ms Nicola Jane. b 65. SEITE. **d** 05. C Bromley St Mark *Roch* from 05. *8 Broadoaks Way, Bromley BR2 0UB*
E-mail nicky.teverson@btinternet.com

TEWKESBURY, Suffragan Bishop of. *See* WENT, The Rt Revd John Stewart

THACKER, Christine Mary. b 44. Simon Fraser Univ BC BA90. Vancouver Sch of Th MDiv93. **d** 92 **p** 93. R Kitimat Ch Ch Canada 93-00; C Boultham *Linc* from 00. *13 Earls Drive, Lincoln LN6 7TY* Tel (01522) 805183 E-mail c.thacker1@ntlworld.com

THACKER, Ian David. b 59. DCR81 DRI84. Oak Hill Th Coll BA91. **d** 91 **p** 92. C Illogan *Truro* 91-94; C Eglwysilan *Llan* 94-96; TV Hornsey Rise Whitehall Park Team *Lon* 96-97; TV Upper Holloway 97-01; Chapl HM YOI Huntercombe and Finnamore from 01. *HM Young Offender Institution, Huntercombe Place, Nuffield, Henley-on-Thames RG9 5SB* Tel (01491) 641711 *or* 641715 Fax 641902
E-mail ithacker@talk21.com

THACKER, James Robert. b 40. W Virginia State Coll BA63 Nashotah Ho Wisconsin BD66 Catholic Univ of America MSW76. **d** 66 **p** 66. USA 66-90; V War w Avondale and Keystone 66-68; R Wheeling w Bellaire and Martins Ferry 68-71; V Harpers Ferry 71-77; Assoc R Westhampton Beach 78-80; R Lynchburg 80-85; R Roanoke 85-90; R St Mark Bermuda 90-99; R Tokyo St Alb Japan 99-04. *Address temp unknown*
E-mail thacker_global@hotmail.com

THACKER, Jonathan William. b 53. Lon Univ BA74 Nottm Univ DipTh78. Linc Th Coll 76. **d** 79 **p** 80. C Bromyard *Heref* 79-82; C Penkridge w Stretton *Lich* 82-87; V Brothertoft Gp *Linc* 87-96; RD Holland W 92-95; P-in-c Crosby 96-01; V from 01; Chapl Scunthorpe and Goole Hosps NHS Trust 99-01; Chapl N Lincs and Goole Hosps NHS Trust 01. *St George's Vicarage, 87 Ferry Road, Scunthorpe DN15 8LY* Tel and fax (01724) 843328 *or* tel 843336 E-mail jon@han195.freeserve.co.uk

THACKER, Kenneth Ray. b 31. Open Univ BA73. Tyndale Hall Bris 56. **d** 59 **p** 60. C Penn Fields *Lich* 59-61; C Tipton St Martin 62-64; V Moxley 64-71; R Leigh 71-91; rtd 92; Perm to Offic *Lich* 92-03. *24 Rugby Close, Newcastle ST5 3JN* Tel (01782) 617812

THACKER, Roger Ailwyn Mackintosh. b 46. CCC Cam BA68 MA73. Westcott Ho Cam 68. **d** 70 **p** 71. C St John's Wood *Lon* 70-74; P-in-c Hammersmith St Paul 74-79; V 79-99; rtd 00; Perm to Offic *St Alb* from 01. *The New Vicarage, 21 Lower Mall, London W6 9DJ* Tel (020) 7741 1860 *or* 7748 3855

THACKRAY, John Adrian. b 55. Southn Univ BSc76 ACIB84. Coll of Resurr Mirfield 81. **d** 84 **p** 85. C Loughton St Jo *Chelmsf* 84-87; Chapl Bancroft's Sch Woodford Green 87-92; Sen Chapl K Sch Cant 92-01; Chapl Abp's Sch Cant 01-02; Hon Min Can Cant Cathl *Cant* from 93; Sen Chapl K Sch Roch from 02; Hon PV Roch Cathl *Roch* from 02. *King's School, Rochester ME1 1TE* Tel (01634) 812306
E-mail thereverendfather@hotmail.com

THACKRAY, William Harry. b 44. Leeds Univ CertEd66. Chich Th Coll 70. **d** 73 **p** 74. C Sheff St Cuth *Sheff* 73-76; C Stocksbridge 76-78; P-in-c Newark St Leon *S'well* 79-80; TV Newark w Hawton, Cotham and Shelton 80-82; V Choral S'well Minster 82-85; V Bawtry w Austerfield 85; P-in-c Misson 85; V Bawtry w Austerfield and Misson 86-93; RD Bawtry 90-93; P-in-c Balderton 93-03; P-in-c Coddington w Barnby in the Willows 98-03; V Biggleswade *St Alb* from 03. *The Vicarage, Shortmead Street, Biggleswade SG18 0AT* Tel (01767) 312243
E-mail vicar@biggleswadeparishchurch.co.uk

THAKE (née SEARS), Ms Helen. b 50. Birm Coll of Educn CertEd71. Qu Coll Birm 96. **d** 98 **p** 99. C Hadley *Lich* 98-01; C Cannock from 01. *9 Condor Grove, Heath Hayes, Cannock WS12 3YB* Tel (01543) 270107

THAKE, Preb Terence. b 41. ALCD65. **d** 66 **p** 67. C Gt Faringdon w Lt Coxwell *Ox* 66-70; C Aldridge *Lich* 70-73; V Werrington 73-82; Chapl HM Det Cen Werrington Ho 73-82; TR Chell *Lich* 82-94; Chapl Westcliffe Hosp 82-94; RD Stoke N 91-94; V Colwich w Gt Haywood 94-00; P-in-c Colton 95-00; R Colton, Colwich and Gt Haywood 00-04; RD Rugeley from 98; Preb Lich Cathl from 94; rtd 04. *9 Condor Grove, Heath Hayes, Cannock WS12 3YB* Tel (01543) 270919
E-mail terry.thake@btinternet.com

THAME, Miss Margaret Eve. b 31. SRN54 SCM55. Glouc Sch of Min 85. **d** 88 **p** 94. NSM Pittville All SS *Glouc* 88-94; NSM Cheltenham St Mich 94-02; Perm to Offic from 02. *13 Brighton Road, Cheltenham GL52 6BA* Tel (01242) 241228

THATCHER, Barbara Mary. b 25. Lon Univ BCom. **d** 90 **p** 94. NSM Helensburgh *Glas* 90-01. *228 West Princes Street, Helensburgh G84 8HA* Tel (01436) 672003

THATCHER, Stephen Bert. b 58. Greenwich Univ PGCE03. St Jo Coll Nottm LTh87 ALCD87. **d** 87 **p** 88. C Bargoed and Deri w Brithdir *Llan* 87-89; C Llanishen and Lisvane 89-91; V Llanwnda, Goodwick w Manorowen and Llanstinan *St D* 91-95; P-in-c Coberley, Cowley, Colesbourne and Elkstone *Glouc* 95-96; Dioc Rural Adv 95-96; R New Radnor and Llanfihangel Nantmelan etc *S & B* 96-00; Dioc Tourism Officer 96-99; Dioc Chs and Tourism Rep 97-00; CF from 00. *c/o MOD Chaplains (Army)* Tel (01980) 615804 Fax 615800
E-mail stephen.thatcher2@btopenworld.com

THAWLEY, The Very Revd David Laurie. b 24. St Edm Hall Ox BA47 MA49. Cuddesdon Coll 49. **d** 51 **p** 52. C Bitterne Park *Win* 51-56; C-in-c Andover St Mich CD 56-60; Australia from 60; Can Res Brisbane 64-72; Dean Wangaratta 72-89; rtd 89. *Lavender Cottage, 2 Bond Street, North Caulfield, Vic, Australia 3161* Tel (0061) (3) 9571 0513 Mobile 407-811870
E-mail dthawley@bigpond.com

THAYER, Michael David. b 52. Sarum & Wells Th Coll 77. **d** 80 **p** 81. C Minehead *B & W* 80-85; Chapl RN 85-89; TV Lowestoft and Kirkley *Nor* 89-92; Chapl St Helena Hospice Colchester 92-97; Chapl HM Pris Acklington 99-01; Chapl HM Pris Erlestoke 01-03; R S Tawton and Belstone *Ex* from 03. *The Rectory, South Tawton, Okehampton EX20 2LQ* Tel (01837) 849048 E-mail michael.thayer@btopenworld.com

THEAKER, David Michael. b 41. **d** 68 **p** 69. C Folkingham w Laughton *Linc* 68-71; C New Cleethorpes 71-74; P-in-c Gt Grimsby St Andr and St Luke 74-77; P-in-c Thurlby 77-79; Perm to Offic *Ely* from 00. *11 Willow Way, Hauxton, Cambridge CB2 5JB* Tel (01223) 873132

THEAKSTON, Ms Sally Margaret. b 62. UEA BSc84 Ox Univ BA89 K Coll Lon MA94. Ripon Coll Cuddesdon 86. **d** 89 **p** 94. Par Dn Hackney *Lon* 89-93; Par Dn Putney St Mary *S'wark* 93-94; C 94-96; Chapl RN 96-02; TR Gaywood *Nor* from 02. *St Faith's Rectory, Gayton Road, King's Lynn PE30 4DZ* Tel and fax (01553) 774662 Mobile 07904-070654
E-mail stheakston@aol.com

THELWELL, The Ven John Berry. b 49. Univ of Wales (Ban) BD72. Qu Coll Birm 73. **d** 73 **p** 74. C Minera *St As* 73-80; Dioc Youth Chapl 78-86; V Gwernaffield and Llanferres 80-93; Chapl Clwyd Fire Service 88-94; RD Mold 91-95; TR Hawarden 93-02; Can Cursal St As Cathl 95-02; Prec 98-02; Adn Montgomery from 02; V Berriew from 03. *The Vicarage, Berriew, Welshpool SY21 8PL* Tel (01686) 640223 Fax as telephone

THEOBALD, Graham Fitzroy. b 43. ALCD67. **d** 67 **p** 68. C Crookham *Guildf* 67-71; C York Town St Mich 71-74; V Wrecclesham 74-83; Chapl Green Lane Hosp 74-81; R Frimley 83-85; Chapl Frimley Park Hosp 83-85; Perm to Offic *Ox* 90-92; C Easthampstead 92-97; Chapl E Berks NHS Trust from 92. *Chaplain's Office, E Berks NHS Trust, Church Hill House, Crowthorne Road, Bracknell RG12 7EP* Tel (01344) 823279 Mobile 07721-408740
E-mail graham.theobald@eberks-tr.anglox.nhs.uk

THEOBALD, Henry Charles. b 32. Lon Univ DRBS63. S'wark Ord Course 60. **d** 63 **p** 64. C Battersea St Phil *S'wark* 63-65; C Caterham 65-68; C Reigate St Luke S Park 68-73; Chapl S Lon Hosp for Women & St Jas Hosp Balham 73-83; Chapl St Mary's Hosp Portsm 83-95; rtd 93; Perm to Offic *Portsm* from 93; Chapl SSB 93-02. *141 Warren Avenue, Southsea PO4 8PP* Tel (023) 9281 7443

THEOBALD, John Walter. b 33. St Aid Birkenhead 62. **d** 65 **p** 66. C Hindley All SS *Liv* 65-68; C Beverley Minster *York* 68-71; R Loftus 71-86; P-in-c Carlin How w Skinningrove 73-86; Dep Chapl HM Pris Leeds 86-89; Chapl HM Pris Rudgate 89-93; Chapl HM Pris Thorp Arch 89-93; Chapl HM Pris Leeds 93-97; V Leeds St Cypr Harehills *Ripon* 97-01; rtd 01; P-in-c Swillington *Ripon* 01-05. *8 Inverness Road, Garforth, Leeds LS25 2LS*

THEODOSIUS, Hugh John. b 32. Trin Coll Cam BA56 MA60. Cuddesdon Coll 56. **d** 58 **p** 59. C Milton *Win* 58-62; C Romsey 62-64; C Southampton Maybush St Pet 64-70; V Malden St Jo *S'wark* 70-81; V Billingborough *Linc* 81-94; V Horbling 81-94; V Sempringham w Pointon and Birthorpe 81-94; RD Aveland and Ness w Stamford 87-93; rtd 97; Perm to Offic *Linc* from 00 and *Ely* from 01. *Sempringham House, East Bank, Sutton Bridge, Spalding PE12 9YN* Tel (01406) 351977

THEODOSIUS, James William Fletcher. b 73. Univ of Wales (Cardiff) BA94 Selw Coll Cam BA04 Cant Ch Ch Univ Coll PGCE96. Westcott Ho Cam 02. **d** 05. C Chich St Paul and Westhampnett *Chich* from 05. *37 Somerstown, Chichester PO19 6AL* Tel (01243) 775199
E-mail booth.theodosius@virgin.net

THEODOSIUS, Richard Francis. b 35. Fitzw Coll Cam BA59. Lich Th Coll 69. **d** 71 **p** 72. C Bloxwich *Lich* 71-73; Chapl Blue Coat Comp Sch Walsall 71-73; Chapl Ranby Ho Sch Retford 73-96; P-in-c Norton Cuckney *S'well* 96-02; rtd 02. *Downlea, 51 Town Street, Lound, Retford DN22 8RT* Tel (01777) 818744

THETFORD, Suffragan Bishop of. *See* ATKINSON, The Rt Revd David John

THEWLIS, Andrew James. b 64. Man Univ BSc86. Cranmer Hall Dur 87. **d** 90 **p** 91. C Walshaw Ch Ch *Man* 90-95; P-in-c Jersey St Jo *Win* 95-98; R from 98. *The Rectory, La rue des Landes, St John, Jersey JE3 4AF* Tel (01534) 861677 Mobile 07797-723828 E-mail athewlis@itl.net

THEWLIS, Brian Jacob. b 24. Melbourne Univ BA49. Coll of Resurr Mirfield 52. **d** 53 **p** 54. C Wednesbury St Jas *Lich* 53-57; Chapl K Coll Auckland New Zealand 57-61; C Sidley *Chich* 59-60; Australia from 61; I Reservoir St Geo 61-68; I Malvern St Paul 68-82; I Beaumaris St Mich 82-87; I Frankston St Paul 87-94; rtd 94. *41 Sixth Street, Parkdale, Vic, Australia 3194* Tel (0061) (3) 9587 3095

THEWLIS, John Charles. b 49. Van Mildert Coll Dur BA70 PhD75. N Ord Course 78. **d** 81 **p** 82. NSM Hull St Mary Sculcoates *York* 81-83; C Spring Park *Cant* 83-84; C Spring Park All SS *S'wark* 85-86; V Eltham Park St Luke 86-01; R Carshalton from 01. *The Rectory, 2 Talbot Road, Carshalton SM5 3BS* Tel (020) 8647 2366
E-mail rector@jctclerk.demon.co.uk

THEWSEY, Robert Sydney. b 65. Ripon Coll Cuddesdon DipMin01. **d** 01 **p** 02. C Chorlton-cum-Hardy St Clem *Man* 01-04; P-in-c Stretford All SS from 04. *The Rectory, 233 Barton Road, Stretford, Manchester M32 9RB* Tel 0161-865 1350
E-mail robert.thewsey@btinternet.com

THICKE, James Balliston. b 43. Sarum & Wells Th Coll 74. **d** 77 **p** 78. C Wareham *Sarum* 77-80; TV 80-83; Dioc Youth Adv *Dur* 83-87; C Portishead *B & W* 87-90; V Westfield from 90; RD Midsomer Norton 98-04; Chapl Norton Radstock Coll of FE from 00. *Westfield Vicarage, Midsomer Norton, Bath BA3 4BJ* Tel (01761) 412105 Fax 419865

THIEME, Paul Henri. b 22. Old Cath Sem Amersfoort 46. **d** 50 **p** 50. The Netherlands 50-57 and from 79; Perm to Offic *York* 58-59; C Newland St Aug 59-63; V Kingston upon Hull St Sav and St Mark 63-73; V Middlesbrough St Aid 73-79; rtd 87. *Haagweg 174, 2282 AY Rijswijk ZH, The Netherlands* Tel (0031) (70) 390 9296

✠**THIRD, The Rt Revd Richard Henry McPhail.** b 27. Em Coll Cam BA50 MA55 Kent Univ Hon DCL90. Linc Th Coll 50. **d** 52 **p** 53 **c** 76. C Mottingham St Andr *S'wark* 52-55; C Sanderstead All SS 55-59; V Sheerness H Trin w St Paul *Cant* 59-67; V Orpington All SS *Roch* 67-76; RD Orpington 73-76; Hon Can Roch Cathl 74-76; Suff Bp Maidstone *Cant* 76-80; Suff

Bp Dover 80-92; rtd 92; Asst Bp B & W from 92. *25 Church Close, Martock TA12 6DS* Tel (01935) 825519

THIRLWELL, Miss Margaret. b 36. Bris Univ BA59 St Aid Coll Dur DipEd61. **d** 03 **p** 04. OLM Binfield *Ox* from 03. *70 Red Rose, Binfield, Bracknell RG42 5LD* Tel (01344) 423920 E-mail margaret@mthirlwell.fsnet.co.uk

THIRTLE, Ms Lucy Rachel. b 62. Ex Univ BA85. Cranmer Hall Dur 97. **d** 99 **p** 00. C Basingstoke *Win* 99-04; P-in-c Kingsclere from 04. *The Vicarage, Fox's Lane, Kingsclere, Newbury RG20 5SL* Tel (01635) 297344

THISELTON, Canon Prof Anthony Charles. b 37. Novi Testamenti Societas 75 Lon Univ BD59 K Coll Lon MTh64 Sheff Univ PhD77 Dur Univ DD93 Lambeth DD02. Oak Hill Th Coll 58. **d** 60 **p** 61. C Sydenham H Trin *S'wark* 60-63; Tutor Tyndale Hall Bris 63-67; Sen Tutor 67-70; Lect Bibl Studies Sheff Univ 70-79; Sen Lect 79-85; Prof Calvin Coll Grand Rapids 82-83; Special Lect Th Nottm Univ 86-88; Prin St Jo Coll Nottm 86-88; Prin St Jo Coll w Cranmer Hall Dur 88-92; Prof Chr Th Nottm Univ from 92; Can Th Leic Cathl *Leic* from 94. *Department of Theology, Nottingham University, University Park, Nottingham NG7 2RD* Tel 0115-951 5852 Fax 951 5887 E-mail thiselton@ntlworld.com

THISTLETHWAITE, Canon Nicholas John. b 51. Selw Coll Cam BA73 MA77 PhD80. Ripon Coll Cuddesdon BA78 MA83. **d** 79 **p** 80. C Newc St Gabr *Newc* 79-82; Chapl G&C Coll Cam 82-90; Lic to Offic *Ely* 82-90; V Trumpington 90-99; Can Res and Prec Guildf Cathl *Guildf* from 99. *3 Cathedral Close, Guildford GU2 7TL* Tel and fax (01483) 569682 *or* tel 565287 E-mail precentor@guildford-cathedral.org

THISTLEWOOD, Michael John. b 31. Ch Coll Cam BA53 MA57. Linc Th Coll 54. **d** 56 **p** 57. C N Hull St Mich *York* 56-59; C Scarborough St Mary 59-61; V Kingston upon Hull St Jude w St Steph 61-67; V Newland St Aug 67-72; Asst Master Bemrose Sch Derby 72-80; V Derby St Andr w St Osmund *Derby* 80-82; Lic to Offic *Ox* 84-95; rtd 88; Perm to Offic *Carl* 88-98 and *Derby* from 98. *1 Lincoln Green, Chellaston, Derby DE73 5QP* Tel (01332) 701995 E-mail michael@thistlewood4164.freeserve.co.uk

THODAY, Margaret Frances. b 38. **d** 03 **p** 04. OLM Roughton and Felbrigg, Metton, Sustead etc *Nor* from 03. *Flat 3, 4 Norwich Road, Cromer NR27 0AX* Tel (01263) 510945

THODY, Charles Michael Jackson. b 62. Linc Th Coll BTh94. **d** 94 **p** 95. C Immingham *Linc* 94-97; P-in-c Leasingham and Cranwell 97-01; P-in-c Bishop Norton, Wadingham and Snitterby 01-03; Chapl Doncaster and S Humber Healthcare NHS Trust 01-03; Chapl Notts Healthcare NHS Trust from 03. *Rampton Hospital, Retford DN22 0PD* Tel (01777) 247524 E-mail charles.thody@nottshc.nhs.uk

THOM, Alastair George. b 60. ACA86 G&C Coll Cam BA81 MA84. Ridley Hall Cam 88. **d** 91 **p** 92. C Lindfield *Chich* 91-94; C Finchley St Paul and St Luke *Lon* 94-98; P-in-c Paddington Em Harrow Road from 98; P-in-c W Kilburn St Luke w St Simon and St Jude from 98. *The Vicarage, 19 Macroom Road, London W9 3HY* Tel (020) 8962 0294 E-mail alastairthom@yahoo.co.uk

THOM, Christopher Henry. **d** 03 **p** 04. NSM Loose *Cant* from 03. *Old Hill House, Old Loose Hill, Loose, Maidstone ME15 0BN* Tel (01622) 744833 E-mail chthom@ukonline.co.uk

THOM, James. b 31. St Chad's Coll Dur BA53 DipTh57. **d** 57 **p** 58. C Middlesbrough St Thos *York* 57-60; C Hornsea and Goxhill 60-62; C S Bank 62-63; V Copmanthorpe 63-75; V Coxwold 75-77; RD Easingwold 77-82; V Coxwold and Husthwaite 77-87; Abp's Adv for Spiritual Direction 86-93; P-in-c Topcliffe 87-93; rtd 93; Perm to Offic *Ripon* and *York* from 93. *34 Hellwath Grove, Ripon HG4 2JT* Tel (01765) 605083

THOM, Thomas Kennedy Dalziel. b 29. Pemb Coll Cam BA53 MA57. St Steph Ho Ox 60. **d** 61 **p** 62. C Colchester St Jas, All SS, St Nic and St Runwald *Chelmsf* 61-64; USPG 65-70; Ghana 65-70; SSJE 71-72; Chapl Essex Univ *Chelmsf* 73-80; Sec Chapls in HE Gen Syn Bd of Educn 81-87; Partnership Sec and Dep Gen Sec USPG 87-92; Chapl Burrswood Chr Cen *Roch* 93-94; rtd 95; Hon C Kennington St Jo w St Jas *S'wark* 95-00; Perm to Offic from 00. *24 South Island Place, London SW9 0DX* Tel (020) 7582 2798

THOMAS, Adrian Leighton. b 37. St D Coll Lamp BA62 DipTh. **d** 63 **p** 64. C Port Talbot St Theodore *Llan* 63-70; V Troedrhiwgarth 70-73; C Sandhurst *Ox* 73-77; V Streatley 77-84; P-in-c Moulsford 81-84; V Streatley w Moulsford 84-90; P-in-c Sutton Courtenay w Appleford 90-00; V 00-02; AD Abingdon 96-02; rtd 02; P-in-c Lugano *Eur* from 02. *Via Pola 8, 6932 Breganzona, Switzerland* Tel (0041) (91) 968 1149 E-mail leighton@leightonthomas.demon.co.uk

THOMAS, Alan. *See* THOMAS, Thomas Alan

THOMAS, Aled Huw. b 59. Univ of Wales (Abth) BD81 DPS83. St Mich Coll Llan 84. **d** 85 **p** 86. C Llandeilo Fawr and Taliaris *St D* 85-86; P-in-c Llangrannog and Llandysiliogogo 86-88; Chapl RAF 88-92; R Ystradgynlais *S & B* 92-94; CF from 94. *c/o MOD Chaplains (Army)* Tel (01980) 615804 Fax 615800

THOMAS, The Ven Alfred James Randolph. b 48. St D Coll Lamp DipTh71. **d** 71 **p** 72. C Cydweli and Llandyfaelog *St D* 71-74; C Carmarthen St Dav 74-76; TV Aberystwyth 76-81; V Betws w Ammanford 81-93; RD Dyffryn Aman 90-93; V Carmarthen St Pet 93-02; Can St D Cathl 96-02; V Bronllys w Llanfilo *S & B* from 02; Adn Brecon from 03. *The Vicarage, Bronllys, Brecon LD3 0HS* Tel (01874) 711200

THOMAS, Andrew Herbert Redding. b 41. Lon Coll of Div 66. **d** 69 **p** 70. C Cromer *Nor* 69-72; Holiday Chapl 72-76; R Grimston w Congham 76-83; R Roydon All SS 76-83; C-in-c Ewell St Paul Howell Hill CD *Guildf* 83-89; V Howell Hill 89-95; RD Epsom 93-95; TR Beccles St Mich *St E* 95-04; P-in-c Worlingham w Barnby and N Cove 98-01; rtd 04; Perm to Offic *Nor* and *St E* from 04. *9A Corner Street, Cromer NR27 9HW* Tel (01263) 515091

THOMAS, Anne. *See* THOMAS, Miss Eileen Anne Harwood

THOMAS, Arthur Norman. b 17. St Aid Birkenhead 54. **d** 56 **p** 57. C Chapel Allerton *Ripon* 56-59; V Wyther Ven Bede 59-65; R Seacroft 65-70; TR 70-76; R Thornton Watlass w Thornton Steward and E Witton 76-86; rtd 86; Perm to Offic *Ripon* from 86. *10 St Andrew's Meadow, Kirkby Malzeard, Ripon HG4 3SW* Tel (01765) 658884

THOMAS, Arun. *See* THOMAS, John Arun

THOMAS, Austin George. b 23. Open Univ BA75. Wells Th Coll 65. **d** 67 **p** 68. C Brislington St Luke *Bris* 67-73; P-in-c Bris St Geo 73-74; P-in-c Bris St Leon Redfield 74-75; TV E Bris 75-80; R Lyddington w Wanborough 80-88; rtd 88; Perm to Offic *Bris* from 88. *11 College Road, Bristol BS16 2HN* Tel 0117-958 3511

THOMAS, Barry Wilfred. b 41. Univ of Wales (Cardiff) BD75. St Mich Coll Llan 72. **d** 75 **p** 76. C Porthmadog *Ban* 75-78; V Llanegryn and Llanfihangel-y-Pennant etc 78-82; Sec Dioc Coun for Miss and Unity 81-94; R Llanbeblig w Caernarfon and Betws Garmon etc 82-94; Can Ban Cathl 89-94; Chapl Monte Carlo *Eur* 95-00; V Llanfihangel Ystrad and Cilcennin w Trefilan etc *St D* from 00. *The Vicarage, Felinfach, Lampeter SA48 8AE* Tel (01570) 471073

THOMAS, Bernard. *See* THOMAS, The Ven Elwyn Bernard

THOMAS, Bryan. b 36. Univ of Wales (Abth) BA59. St Deiniol's Hawarden 68. **d** 70 **p** 71. C Llangynwyd w Maesteg *Llan* 70-72; V Cwmllynfell *St D* 72-76; V Gors-las 76-82; R Yarnbury *Sarum* 82-97; TR Wylye and Till Valley 97-02; RD Wylye and Wilton 94-98; rtd 02; Perm to Offic *Sarum* from 03. *11 Ebble Crescent, Warminster BA12 9PF* Tel (01985) 300519

THOMAS, The Ven Charles Edward (Ted). b 27. Univ of Wales (Lamp) BA51. Coll of Resurr Mirfield 51. **d** 53 **p** 54. C Ilminster w Whitelackington *B & W* 53-56; Chapl St Mich Coll Tenbury 56-57; C St Alb St Steph *St Alb* 57-58; V Boreham Wood St Mich 58-66; R Monksilver w Brompton Ralph and Nettlecombe *B & W* 66-74; P-in-c Nettlecombe 68-69; R S Petherton w the Seavingtons 74-83; RD Crewkerne 77-83; Adn Wells, Can Res and Preb Wells Cathl 83-93; rtd 93; Perm to Offic *St D* from 93. *Geryfelin, Pentre, Tregaron SY25 6JG* Tel (01974) 298102

THOMAS, Charles Moray Stewart Reid. b 53. BNC Ox BA74 MA79. Wycliffe Hall Ox 75. **d** 78 **p** 79. C Bradf Cathl *Bradf* 78-81; C Barnsbury St Andr and H Trin w All SS *Lon* 81-90; TV Barnsbury 90-99; Chapl Lon Goodenough Trust from 99. *The London Goodenough Trust, London House, Mecklenburgh Square, London WC1N 2AB* Tel (020) 7837 8888 E-mail morayt@goodenough.ac.uk

THOMAS, Cheeramattathu John. b 25. Travanscore Univ BA46 BT49 Serampore Coll BD55 United Th Coll Bangalore MA66. Andover Newton Th Coll. **d** 55 **p** 57. Singapore 55-60; Sarawak 60-65; C Eastham *Ches* 66-74; V Gt Sutton 75-83; USA from 83; rtd 91. *301 Eagle Lakes Drive, Friendswood, TX 77546, USA* Tel (001) (281) 996 7797

THOMAS, Clive Alexander. b 49. St Luke's Coll Ex CertEd71 Open Univ BA77. STETS 94. **d** 97 **p** 99. NSM Southwick St Mich *Chich* 97-01; C Bridport *Sarum* 01-04; TV Shaston from 04. *The Rectory, Bleke Street, Shaftesbury SP7 8AH* Tel (01747) 852547 E-mail rev.cathomas@lineone.net

THOMAS, Preb Colin Norman. b 41. Open Univ BA78. Trin Coll Bris 72. **d** 74 **p** 75. C Handforth *Ches* 74-77; C Bucknall and Bagnall *Lich* 77-80; TV 80-86; V Ogley Hay from 86; RD Lich 99-04; Preb Lich Cathl from 04. *St James's Vicarage, 37 New Road, Brownhills, Walsall WS8 6AT* Tel (01543) 372187 *or* 373251 E-mail thomas@colnor.freeserve.co.uk

✠**THOMAS, The Rt Revd David.** b 42. Keble Coll Ox BA64 BA66 MA67. St Steph Ho Ox 64. **d** 67 **p** 68 **c** 96. C Hawarden *St As* 67-69; Tutor St Mich Coll Llan 69-70; Chapl 70-75; Sec Ch in Wales Liturg Commn 70-75; Vice-Prin St Steph Ho Ox 75-79; Prin 82-87; V Chepstow *Mon* 79-82; Lic to Offic *Ox* 82-87; V Newton St Pet *S & B* 87-96; Can Brecon Cathl 94-96; RD Clyne 96; Prov Asst Bp from 96. *Bodfair, 3 White's Close, Belmont Road, Abergavenny NP7 5HZ* Tel (01873) 858780 Fax 858269 E-mail pab@churchinwales.org.uk

THOMAS, David Brian. b 45. MIEEE. St D Dioc Tr Course 82. **d** 85 **p** 86. NSM Llandysul *St D* 85-87; NSM Lampeter Pont

Steffan w Silian 88-92; NSM Lampeter and Ultra-Aeron 92-96; P-in-c Llanfihangel Genau'r-glyn and Llangorwen 96-97; V from 97; RD Llanbadarn Fawr from 00. *The Vicarage, Maes y Garn, Bow Street SY24 5DS* Tel (01970) 828638

THOMAS, David Edward. b 60. Univ of Wales (Lamp) BA83 LTh85. St Mich Coll Llan DPS86. **d** 86 **p** 87. C Killay *S & B* 86-89; P-in-c Newbridge-on-Wye and Llanfihangel Brynpabuan 89-90; V 90-91; V Brecon St David w Llanspyddid and Llanilltyd from 91. *The Vicarage, 26 St David's Crescent, Ffrwdgrech Road, Brecon LD3 8DP* Tel (01874) 622707

THOMAS, Canon David Geoffrey. b 24. AKC48. **d** 49 **p** 50. C Milford Haven *St D* 49-52; Miss to Seamen 52-53 and 68-81; C Pembroke St Mary w St Mich 53-54; R Rhoscrowther and Pwllcrochan 54-68; V Milford Haven 68-89; Can St D Cathl 77-89; Treas 85-89; rtd 89. *49 Pill Lane, Milford Haven SA73 2LD* Tel (01646) 695792

THOMAS, David Geoffrey. b 37. Univ of Wales (Cardiff) BA58. Launde Abbey 70 Qu Coll Birm 71. **d** 71 **p** 72. Hon C Fenny Drayton *Leic* 71-75; Chapl Community of the H Family Baldslow Chich 75-77; Perm to Offic *Chich* 77-79; P-in-c Mill End and Heronsgate w W Hyde *St Alb* 79-81; Sen Lect Watford Coll 82-91; R Walgrave w Hannington and Wold and Scaldwell *Pet* 91-01; rtd 01. *1 Cypress Close, Desborough, Kettering NN14 2XU* Tel (01536) 763749 Fax as telephone

THOMAS, The Very Revd David Glynne. b 41. Dur Univ BSc63. Westcott Ho Cam 64. **d** 67 **p** 68. C St John's Wood *Lon* 67-70; Min Can St Alb 70-72; Chapl Wadh Coll Ox 72-75; C Ox St Mary V w St Cross and St Pet *Ox* 72-75; Bp's Dom Chapl 75-78; P-in-c Burnham 78-82; TR Burnham w Dropmore, Hitcham and Taplow 82-83; Australia 83-87 and from 99; Can Res Worc Cathl *Worc* 87-99; Dean Brisbane from 99. *The Deanery, PO Box 421, Brisbane, Qld, Australia 4001* Tel (0061) (7) 3835 2236 *or* 3835 2231 Fax 3832 3173 E-mail brisdean@anglicanbrisbane.org.au

THOMAS, David Godfrey. b 50. St Chad's Coll Dur BA71 Fitzw Coll Cam BA74 MA78. Westcott Ho Cam 72. **d** 75 **p** 76. C Kirkby *Liv* 75-78; TV Cov E *Cov* 78-88; TR Canvey Is *Chelmsf* 88-92; R Wivenhoe from 92. *The Rectory, 44 Belle Vue Road, Wivenhoe, Colchester CO7 9LD* Tel (01206) 825174

THOMAS, David John. b 34. Univ of Wales (Swansea) St D Coll Lamp. St D Dioc Tr Course 85. **d** 88 **p** 89. NSM Cwmaman *St D* 88-96; Public Preacher from 96. *9 New School Road, Garnant, Ammanford SA18 1LL* Tel (01269) 823936

THOMAS, David Richard. b 48. BNC Ox BA71 MA74 Fitzw Coll Cam BA75 MA80 Lanc Univ PhD83. Ridley Hall Cam 73 Qu Coll Birm 79. **d** 80 **p** 81. C Anfield St Columba *Liv* 80-83; C Liv Our Lady and St Nic w St Anne 83-85; Chapl CCC Cam 85-90; V Witton *Blackb* 90-93; Bp's Adv on Inter-Faith Relns 90-93; Dir Cen for Study of Islam and Chr-Muslim Relns Selly Oak 93-04; Sen Lect Birm Univ *Birm* 99-04. *The Vicarage, Church Square, Melbourne, Derby DE73 8JH* Tel (01332) 864121

THOMAS, David Ronald Holt. b 28. Lich Th Coll 55. **d** 58 **p** 59. C Uttoxeter w Bramshall *Lich* 58-61; C Hednesford 61-66; R Armitage from 66; RD Rugeley 88-94. *The Rectory, Hood Lane, Armitage, Rugeley WS15 4AG* Tel (01543) 490278

THOMAS, David Thomas. b 44. St Cath Coll Cam BA66 MA70 St Jo Coll Dur DipTh68. **d** 71 **p** 72. C Chorlton-cum-Hardy St Clem *Man* 71-74; Chapl Salford Tech Coll 74-79; P-in-c Pendleton St Thos *Man* 75-77; V 77-80; TR Gleadless *Sheff* 80-90; RD Attercliffe 86-90; V Benchill *Man* 90-99; TV Wythenshawe 99-00; AD Withington 99-00; P-in-c Stretford St Matt from 00. *St Matthew's Rectory, 39 Sandy Lane, Stretford, Manchester M32 9DB* Tel 0161-865 2535 E-mail tom-hil@talk21.com

THOMAS, Canon David William. b 17. Univ of Wales BA63 MA67. St D Coll Lamp BA38 St Mich Coll Llan 39. **d** 41 **p** 43. C Cynwyl Gaeo w Llansawel *St D* 41-46; C Llandysul 46-48; V Clydau and Penrhydd w Castellan 48-55; V Llanfihangel Genau'r Glyn 55-67; V Llangynfelyn 58-62; V Pontyberem 67-76; V Llanilar w Rhostie and Llangwyryfon etc 76-83; Hon Can St D Cathl 78-83; rtd 83. *Nantydderwen, 138 Marged Street, Ammanford SA18 2NN* Tel (01269) 594986

THOMAS, David William Wallace. b 51. St Chad's Coll Dur BA72. St Mich Coll Llan 72. **d** 75 **p** 76. C Bargoed and Deri w Brithdir *Llan* 75-79; Hon C 79-81; V Nantymoel w Wyndham 81-84; Chapl RN from 84. *Royal Naval Chaplaincy Service, Room 203, Victory Building, HM Naval Base, Portsmouth PO1 3LS* Tel (023) 9272 7903 Fax 9272 7111

THOMAS, David Wynford. b 48. Univ of Wales (Abth) LLB70. Qu Coll Birm 76. **d** 79 **p** 80. C Swansea St Mary w H Trin and St Mark *S & B* 79-83; P-in-c Swansea St Mark 83-89; Lic to Offic 90. *74 Terrace Road, Swansea SA1 6HU*

THOMAS, Canon Dillwyn Morgan. b 26. Univ of Wales (Lamp) BA50. Qu Coll Birm 50. **d** 52 **p** 53. C Dowlais *Llan* 52-59; C Pontypridd St Cath 59-63; V Llanwynno 63-68; V Bargoed w Brithdir 68-74; V Bargoed and Deri w Brithdir 74-75; V Penarth All SS 75-88; Can Llan Cathl 86-88; rtd 88; Perm to Offic *Llan* from 88. *11 Baroness Place, Penarth CF64 3UL* Tel (029) 2025 1698

THOMAS, Dorothy Judith. b 47. Univ of Wales (Cardiff) BA68. Princeton Th Sem MDiv94 MTh96 San Francisco Th Sem DMin01. **d** 03 **p** 04. NSM Wargrave w Knowl Hill *Ox* from 03. *The Vicarage, Knowl Hill, Reading RG10 9YD* Tel (01628) 822732 E-mail djudthomas@hotmail.com

THOMAS (née THOMSON), Mrs Dorothy Lucille. b 39. Univ of Wales (Lamp). **d** 00. OLM Pontnewydd *Mon* from 00. *Raldoro, Mount Pleasant Road, Pontnewydd, Cwmbran NP44 1BD* Tel (01633) 771353

THOMAS, Edward. *See* THOMAS, The Ven Charles Edward

THOMAS, Edward Bernard Meredith. b 21. Leeds Univ BA44 Univ of Qld BEd68 BD72. Coll of Resurr Mirfield 47. **d** 49 **p** 50. C St Mary-at-Lambeth *S'wark* 49-54; C Portsea N End St Mark *Portsm* 54-56; V Portsea All SS 56-64; Australia from 64; rtd 92. *33 Highfield Street, Durack, Qld, Australia 4077* Tel (0061) (7) 3372 3517

THOMAS, Edward Walter Dennis. b 32. St Mich Coll Llan 61. **d** 63 **p** 64. C Loughor *S & B* 63-69; V Ystradfellte 69-74; V Dukinfield St Mark and St Luke *Ches* 74-04; Chapl Gtr Man Police 77-04; OCF from 88; rtd 04. *16 Boyd's Walk, Dukinfield SK16 4TW* Tel 0161-330 1324 E-mail revewdt@aol.com

THOMAS, Miss Eileen Anne Harwood. b 35. Univ of Wales (Swansea) BA59 Kent Univ MA80. Cant Sch of Min 80. **dss** 83 **d** 87 **p** 94. Mill Hill Jo Keble Ch *Lon* 83-86; The Lydiards *Bris* 86-92; Par Dn 87-92; C-in-c Woodgate Valley CD *Birm* 92-96; rtd 96; Perm to Offic *Truro* from 96. *2 Trelinnoe Gardens, South Petherwin, Launceston PL15 7TH* Tel (01566) 773380

THOMAS, Canon Eirwyn Wheldon. b 35. St Mich Coll Llan 58. **d** 61 **p** 62. C Glanadda *Ban* 61-67; R Llantrisant and Llandeusant 67-75; V Nefyn w Tudweiliog w Llandudwen w Edern 75-01; Can Ban Cathl 97-01; rtd 01. *11 Wenfro Road, Abergele LL22 7LE* Tel (01745) 823587

THOMAS (née REEVES), Mrs Elizabeth Anne. b 45. Sheff Univ BA67 PGCE75. SW Minl Tr Course 87. **d** 90 **p** 94. Par Dn Stoke Damerel *Ex* 90-93; Dioc Children's Adv *Bradf* 93-01; Par Dn Baildon 93-94; C 94-96; P-in-c Denholme Gate 96-01; P-in-c Tuxford w Weston and Markham Clinton *S'well* from 01. *The Vicarage, Lincoln Road, Tuxford, Newark NG22 0HP* Tel and fax (01777) 870713 E-mail liz@tuxford-vic.demon.co.uk

THOMAS, The Ven Elwyn Bernard. b 45. Univ of Wales (Swansea) BSc68. St Mich Coll Llan BD71. **d** 71 **p** 72. C Aberdare St Fagan *Llan* 71-74; C Merthyr Dyfan 74-76; R Dowlais 76-86; V Llangynwyd w Maesteg 86-00; Can Llan Cathl 98-00; Adn St As from 00; R Llandyrnog and Llangwyfan from 00. *The Rectory, Ffordd Las, Llandyrnog, Denbigh LL16 4LT* Tel (01824) 790777 Fax 790877 E-mail bernardthomas@bun.com

THOMAS, Canon Ernest Keith. b 49. Univ of Wales (Cardiff) DipTh76. St Mich Coll Llan 73. **d** 76 **p** 77. C Swansea St Gabr *S & B* 76-79; C Killay 79-81; S Africa 81-92 and from 96; Prec Kimberley Cathl 81-84; R Kimberley St Aug 84-92; R Kimberley St Alb 89-92; Can Kimberley Cathl 86-92; V Aberdare *Llan* 93-96; Sub-Dean Bloemfontein Cathl from 96. *PO Box 1523, Bloemfontein, 9300 South Africa* Tel (0027) (51) 447 5951

THOMAS, Canon Euros Lloyd. b 53. Bris Poly LLB75. St Mich Coll Llan DipTh79. **d** 79 **p** 80. C Llanelli *St D* 79-84; R Cilgerran w Bridell and Llantwyd from 84; P-in-c Clydau 00-04; RD Cemais and Sub-Aeron from 93; Can St D Cathl from 03. *The Rectory, Cilgerran, Cardigan SA43 2RZ* Tel (01239) 614500

THOMAS, Frank Lowth. b 22. Lon Coll of Div 64. **d** 66 **p** 67. C Walthamstow St Mary *Chelmsf* 66-68; C Bickenhill w Elmdon *Birm* 68-71; R Carlton Colville *Nor* 71-81; R Smallburgh w Dilham w Honing and Crostwight 81-85; rtd 85; Perm to Offic *Nor* from 86. *7 Mill Close, Salhouse, Norwich NR13 6QB* Tel (01603) 720376

THOMAS, Geler Harries. b 28. St D Coll Lamp BA55. St Mich Coll Llan. **d** 57 **p** 58. C Llanelli Ch Ch *St D* 57-62; V Llandyssilio and Egremont 62-69; V Llanedy 69-79; V Llangennech and Hendy 79-88; V Llanegwad w Llanfynydd 88-92; RD Llangadog and Llandeilo 89-90; rtd 92. *14 Llys-y-Ferin, Pont-ar-Gothi, Nantgaredig, Carmarthen SA32 7NF* Tel (01267) 290516

THOMAS, Geoffrey Brynmor. b 34. K Coll Lon BA56 AKC56. Ridley Hall Cam 58. **d** 60 **p** 61. C Harlow New Town w Lt Parndon *Chelmsf* 60-65; V Leyton All SS 65-74; V Haley Hill *Wakef* 74-82; R The Winterbournes and Compton Valence *Sarum* 82-89; TV Cheltenham St Mark *Glouc* 89-92; P-in-c Dowdeswell and Andoversford w the Shiptons etc 92-95; RD Northleach 92-95; rtd 95; Perm to Offic *B & W* from 96. *48 Riverside Walk, Midsomer Norton, Bath BA3 2PD* Tel (01761) 414146

THOMAS, Geoffrey Charles. b 30. St Jo Coll Nottm LTh ALCD64. **d** 64 **p** 65. C York St Paul *York* 64-67; C Cheltenham Ch Ch *Glouc* 67-70; V Whitgift w Adlingfleet *Sheff* 70-74; P-in-c Eastoft 72-74; V Mortomley St Sav 74-88; R Middleton Cheney w Chacombe *Pet* 88-93; rtd 94; Perm to Offic *York* from 94. *55 Oakland Avenue, York YO31 1DF* Tel (01904) 414082

THOMAS, Canon Geoffrey Heale. b 29. St Mich Coll Llan 58. **d** 60 **p** 61. C Llansamlet *S & B* 60-63; Nigeria 63-67; V Swansea St Nic *S & B* 67-80; CF (TA) 72; V Oystermouth *S & B* 80-98; Hon Can Brecon Cathl 92-96; Can 97-98; rtd 98. *19 Ffordd Dryden, Killay, Swansea SA2 7PA* Tel (01792) 206308

THOMAS, George. b 46. Leeds Univ BEd69. Cranmer Hall Dur 75. **d** 78 **p** 79. C Highfield *Liv* 78-83; V Chorley St Jas *Blackb* 83-02; P-in-c Blackb St Gabr from 02. *St Gabriel's Vicarage, 6 Charnwood Close, Blackburn BB2 7BT* Tel (01254) 581412 E-mail gt@fish.co.uk

THOMAS, Glyn. b 36. Lon Univ BPharm61. St Deiniol's Hawarden 80. **d** 82 **p** 83. C Rhyl w St Ann *St As* 83-85; R Llanycil w Bala and Frongoch and Llangower etc 85-03; RD Penllyn 96-03; rtd 03. *Blaen-y-Coed, 7 Lon Helyg, Abergele LL22 7JQ*

THOMAS, Gordon Herbert. b 43. Guildf Dioc Min Course 00. **d** 00 **p** 01. OLM Cove St Jo *Guildf* from 00. *13 Tay Close, Farnborough GU14 9NB* Tel (01252) 512347 E-mail ghthomas@talk21.com

THOMAS, Greville Stephen. b 64. Qu Coll Birm 94. **d** 96 **p** 97. C Hillingdon All SS *Lon* 96-99; C Acton Green 99-04; P-in-c Northolt St Mary from 04. *St Mary's Rectory, Ealing Road, Northolt UB5 6AA* Tel (020) 8841 5691 E-mail greville.thomas@london.anglican.org

THOMAS, Gwilym Ivor. b 20. St D Coll Lamp BA41 Univ of Wales MPhil95. **d** 43 **p** 44. C Llansadwrn w Llanwrda *St D* 43-47; C Llanedy 47-53; V Ambleston w St Dogwells 53-62; V Llansantffraed 62-70; V Llansantffraed and Llanbadarn Trefeglwys 70-80; V Llansantffraed and Llanbadarn Trefeglwys etc 80-85; RD Glyn Aeron 78-85; rtd 85. *Stanley House, 9 Hill Street, New Quay SA45 9QD* Tel (01545) 560167

THOMAS, Harald Daniel. b 34. FInstTT. **d** 97. Par Dn Pontnewydd *Mon* from 97. *Raldoro, Mount Pleasant Road, Pontnewydd, Cwmbran NP44 1BD* Tel (01633) 771353

THOMAS, Miss Hilary Faith. b 43. Ex Univ BA65 Southn Univ PGCE66. Trin Coll Bris DipHE92 DPS94. **d** 94 **p** 95. C Yeovil w Kingston Pitney *B & W* 94-98; V Brislington St Luke *Bris* from 98. *The Vicarage, St Luke's Gardens, Bristol BS4 4NW* Tel 0117-977 7633

THOMAS, Hugh. b 25. St D Coll Lamp BA50. **d** 51 **p** 52. C Penbre *St D* 51-55; P-in-c Moelgrove and Monington 55-63; V Llanfynydd 63-74; V Pontyates 74-80; V Pontyates and Llangyndeyrn 80-90; rtd 91. *90 Priory Street, Kidwelly SA17 4TY* Tel (01554) 890114

THOMAS, Hugh Vivian. b 57. Kingston Poly LLB80 Barrister-at-Law (Lincoln's Inn) 86. SEITE 02. **d** 05. NSM Knockholt w Halstead *Roch* from 05. *5 The Meadows, Halstead, Sevenoaks TN14 7HD* Tel (01959) 532664 E-mail hughvthomas@btopenworld.com

THOMAS, Canon Huw Glyn. b 42. Univ of Wales (Lamp) BA62 Linacre Coll Ox BA65 MA69. Wycliffe Hall Ox 62. **d** 65 **p** 66. C Oystermouth *S & B* 65-68; Asst Chapl Solihull Sch 68-69; Chapl 69-73; Selection Sec ACCM 73-78; C Loughton St Jo *Chelmsf* 74-77; V Bury St Jo *Man* 78-83; Dir of Ords 82-87; V Bury St Jo w St Mark 83-86; Can Res and Treas Liv Cathl *Liv* 87-95; Ethiopia from 95. *St Matthew's Church, PO Box 109, Addis Ababa, Ethiopia*

THOMAS, Ian Melville. b 50. Jes Coll Ox BA71 MA75. St Steph Ho Ox 71. **d** 73 **p** 74. PV St D Cathl *St D* 73-77; Chapl RAF 77-95; Command Chapl RAF 95-00; V Llanelli *St D* 01-02; TR from 02. *The Vicarage, 1 Cysgod y Llan, Llanelli SA15 3HD* Tel (01554) 772072

THOMAS, Ian William. b 53. Bedf Coll of Educn CertEd74. Ox Min Course 89. **d** 92 **p** 93. NSM Fenny Stratford *Ox* from 92. *5 Laburnum Grove, Bletchley, Milton Keynes MK2 2JW* Tel (01908) 644457

THOMAS, Canon Idris. b 48. St D Coll Lamp DipTh71. **d** 71 **p** 72. C Llanbeblig w Caernarfon and Betws Garmon etc *Ban* 71-75; P-in-c Llanaelhaiarn 75-77; R Llanaelhaearn w Clynnog Fawr from 77; RD Arfon 93-00; AD 02-04; Hon Can Ban Cathl from 99. *Y Rheithordy, Trefor, Caernarfon LL54 5HN* Tel (01286) 660547

THOMAS, Irene. b 42. **d** 04. OLM E Wickham *S'wark* from 04. *Address temp unknown*

THOMAS, Mrs Iris. b 18. Univ of Wales (Abth) BA39 DipEd40. Llan Ord Course. **d** 80 **p** 97. Hon C Tylorstown *Llan* 80-84; Hon C Ferndale w Maerdy 84-85; rtd 85; Perm to Offic *Llan* from 86. *1 Maerdy Court, Maerdy Road, Ferndale CF3 4BT* Tel (01443) 755235

THOMAS, Jennifer Monica. b 58. Wilson Carlile Coll Dip Evang82 Sarum & Wells Th Coll DipMin93. **d** 93 **p** 94. Par Dn Wandsworth St Paul *S'wark* 93-94; C 94-97; V Forest Hill 97-02; V Mitcham Ascension from 02. *The Vicarage, Sherwood Park Road, Mitcham CR4 1NE* Tel (020) 8764 1258

THOMAS, John. *See* THOMAS, Cheeramattathu John

THOMAS, John <u>Arun</u>. b 47. Bombay Univ BA69 MA72 Nottm Univ CertEd80. Oak Hill Th Coll 84. **d** 88 **p** 89. C Liv Ch Ch Norris Green *Liv* 88-89; C Wavertree St Mary 89-93; V St Mary Cray and St Paul's Cray *Roch* 93-96; India 96-99 and from 04; V Malabar Hill All SS 96-97; Hon Min Scotskirk 97-99; Prin Bombay Scottish Sch 97-99; Australia 99-04. *PO Box 4201, Malabar Hill, Mumbai, 400006, India* E-mail arunn51@hotmail.com

THOMAS, Canon John Herbert Samuel. b 34. Pemb Coll Cam BA57 MA64. St Mich Coll Llan 57. **d** 58 **p** 59. C Port Talbot St Theodore *Llan* 58-60; C Llantwit Major and St Donat's 60-67; P-in-c Barry All SS 67-74; V Dinas w Penygraig 74-85; V Pontypridd St Cath 85-90; V Pontypridd St Cath w St Matt 90-99; RD Pontypridd 90-99; Can Llan Cathl from 95; rtd 99. *Ty Canon, Salisbury Road, Abercynon, Mountain Ash CF45 4NU* Tel (01443) 742577

THOMAS, John <u>Roger</u>. Trin Coll Carmarthen BA. St Mich Coll Llan. **d** 03 **p** 04. C Cardigan w Mwnt and Y Ferwig w Llangoedmor *St D* from 03. *8 Heol y Wern, North Park Estate, Cardigan SA43 1NE* Tel (01239) 613685

THOMAS, John Thurston. b 28. Univ of Wales (Swansea) BSc48 DipEd49 Leeds Univ PhD58 CChem FRSC65. Glouc Sch of Min 88. **d** 90 **p** 91. NSM S Cerney w Cerney Wick and Down Ampney *Glouc* 90-96; Perm to Offic *Glouc* 96-01; *S & B* from 01. *4 Nicholl Court, Mumbles, Swansea SA3 4LZ* Tel (01792) 360098

THOMAS, Judith. *See* THOMAS, Dorothy Judith

THOMAS, Julian <u>Mark</u>. b 48. SW Minl Tr Course 00. **d** 03. C Okehampton w Inwardleigh, Bratton Clovelly etc *Ex* from 03. *19 Fern Meadow, Okehampton EX20 1PB* Tel (01837) 54263 E-mail jmthomas@fish.co.uk

THOMAS, Mrs June Marion. b 31. Univ of Wales BA53 DipEd54. NEOC 83. **dss** 86 **d** 87 **p** 94. Stockton St Pet *Dur* 86-87; Hon Par Dn 87-89; NSM Stockton St Mark 89-94; P-in-c 94-01; rtd 01. *50 Brisbane Grove, Stockton-on-Tees TS18 5BP* Tel (01642) 582408

THOMAS, Keith. b 55. Southlands Coll Lon TCert80. N Ord Course 92. **d** 95 **p** 96. NSM Knuzden *Blackb* 95-98; NSM Darwen St Pet w Hoddlesden 98-04; Tullyallan Sch Darwen 99-04; NSM Turton Moorland Min *Man* from 04. *20 Duxbury Street, Darwen BB3 2LA* Tel (01254) 776484

THOMAS, Kenneth. *See* THOMAS, Canon William Kenneth

THOMAS, Kimberley Ann. b 59. Cranmer Hall Dur 02. **d** 04 **p** 05. C Chesterton *Lich* from 04. *17 Checkley Road, Chesterton, Newcastle ST5 7TN* Tel (01782) 560246

THOMAS, Leighton. *See* THOMAS, Adrian Leighton

THOMAS, Leslie Richard. b 45. Lon Coll of Div 65. **d** 69 **p** 70. C Knotty Ash St Jo *Liv* 69-72; C Sutton 72-74; TV 74-77; V Banks 77-82; V Gt Crosby All SS 82-92; P-in-c Marthall and Chapl David Lewis Cen for Epilepsy *Ches* 92-02; V Bickerton, Bickley, Harthill and Burwardsley from 02; RD Malpas from 04. *The Vicarage, Harthill Road, Burwardsley, Chester CH3 9NU* Tel (01829) 771225

THOMAS, Mark. *See* THOMAS, Julian Mark

THOMAS, Mark Wilson. b 51. Dur Univ BA72 Hull Univ MA89. Ripon Coll Cuddesdon 76. **d** 78 **p** 79. C Chapelthorpe *Wakef* 78-81; C Seaford w Sutton *Chich* 81-84; V Gomersal *Wakef* 84-92; TR Almondbury w Farnley Tyas 92-01; RD Almondbury 93-01; Hon Can Wakef Cathl 99-01; P-in-c Shrewsbury St Chad w St Mary *Lich* from 01. *25 The Crescent, Town Walls, Shrewsbury SY1 1TH* Tel and fax (01743) 343761 E-mail saint.chads@ukonline.co.uk

THOMAS, Sister Mary Josephine. b 30. Ripon Dioc Tr Coll TCert50 Carl Dioc Tr Course 88. **d** 90 **p** 94. NSM Hawes Side *Blackb* 90-93; NSM St Annes St Marg 93-00; Perm to Offic from 00. *112 St Andrew's Road North, Lytham St Annes FY8 2JQ* Tel (01253) 728016

THOMAS, Michael Longdon Sanby. b 34. Trin Hall Cam BA55 MA60. Wells Th Coll 56. **d** 58 **p** 59. C Sandal St Helen *Wakef* 58-60; Chapl Portsm Cathl *Portsm* 60-64; V Shedfield 64-69; V Portchester 69-98; rtd 98. *188 Castle Street, Portchester, Fareham PO16 9QH* Tel (023) 9242 0416 Fax as telephone E-mail thomasfamily73@cwtv.net

THOMAS, Michael Rosser David. b 74. Kent Univ BA96. St Steph Ho Ox BTh02. **d** 02 **p** 03. C Aberavon *Llan* from 02. *The Parsonage, 9 James Street, Port Talbot SA13 1AR* Tel (01639) 680585 E-mail fr.michael@ntlworld.co.uk

THOMAS, Moray. *See* THOMAS, Charles Moray Stewart Reid

THOMAS, Nigel Bruce. b 63. St Jo Coll Nottm MA98. BD. **d** 97 **p** 98. C Millom *Carl* 97-02; R Bentham *Bradf* from 02. *The Vicarage, 27 Station Road, Bentham, Lancaster LA2 7LH* Tel (01524) 261321

THOMAS, Owen James. b 17. Univ of Wales BA38. Tyndale Hall Bris 38. **d** 40 **p** 41. C Wandsworth St Steph *S'wark* 40-43; C Dagenham *Chelmsf* 43-46; R Glas St Silas *Glas* 46-51; Tutor Lon Bible Coll 51-62; Chapl and Lect 62-76; P-in-c Woburn Square Ch Ch *Lon* 51-52; Aux Chapl US Airforce 66-68; Hon C Northwood Em *Lon* 70-76; V Canonbury St Steph 76-85; rtd 85; Perm to Offic *Chich* from 85. *22 Woodland Way, Fairlight, Hastings TN35 4AU* Tel (01424) 813613 E-mail oth83ogt@aol.com

THOMAS, Ms Pamela Sybil. b 38. Ripon Coll Cuddesdon 88. **d** 90 **p** 94. Par Dn Preston w Sutton Poyntz and Osmington w Poxwell *Sarum* 90-94; C 94-96; P-in-c Weymouth St Edm from 96; P-in-c Abbotsbury, Portesham and Langton Herring from 97; Chapl Westhaven Hosp Weymouth from 96. *The Rectory, Portesham, Weymouth DT3 4HB* Tel (01305) 871217

THOMAS, Canon Patrick Hungerford Bryan. b 52. St Cath Coll Cam BA73 MA77 Leeds Univ BA78 Univ of Wales PhD82. Coll of Resurr Mirfield 76. **d** 79 **p** 80. C Aberystwyth *St D* 79-81; C Carmarthen St Pet 81-82; R Llangeitho and Blaenpennal w Betws Leucu etc 82-84; Warden of Ords 83-86; R Brechfa w Abergorlech etc 84-01; V Carmarthen St Dav from 01; Can St D Cathl from 00. *St David's Vicarage, 4 Penllwyn Park, Carmarthen SA31 3BU* Tel (01276) 234183

THOMAS, Paul Richard. b 75. Univ of Wales (Cardiff) BA96 MA99. Ripon Coll Cuddesdon BA01. **d** 02 **p** 03. C Wanstead St Mary w Ch Ch *Chelmsf* from 02. *13 Wanstead Place, London E11 2SW* Tel (020) 8530 4970
E-mail alban.sergius@ntlworld.com

THOMAS, Canon Paul Robert. b 42. OBE02. N Ord Course. **d** 82 **p** 83. C Hull St Jo Newland *York* 82-84; P-in-c Rowley 84-87; Soc Resp Officer Hull 84-87; R Rowley w Skidby 87-88; TR Barking St Marg w St Patr *Chelmsf* 88-93; Gen Sec and Admin St Luke's Hosp for Clergy 93-03; Can and Preb Chich Cathl *Chich* from 98; P in O from 99; rtd 03; Perm to Offic *Nor* from 03. *St Anne's Cottage, 37 Scarborough Road, Walsingham NR22 6AB* Tel (01328) 820571

THOMAS, Paul Wyndham. b 55. Oriel Coll Ox BA76 BTh78 MA80. Wycliffe Hall Ox 77. **d** 79 **p** 80. C Llangynwyd w Maesteg *Llan* 79-85; TV Langport Area Chs *B & W* 85-90; P-in-c Thorp Arch w Walton *York* 90-93; Clergy Tr Officer 90-04; V Nether w Upper Poppleton 93-04; P-in-c Castle Town *Lich* from 04. *St Thomas's Vicarage, Doxey, Stafford ST16 1EQ* Tel (01904) 605964

THOMAS, Canon Peter George Hartley. b 38. AKC63. **d** 64 **p** 65. C Leigh Park St Fran CD *Portsm* 64-69; V Cosham 69-77; R Hayes *Roch* 77-01; Hon Can Roch Cathl 00-01; rtd 01; Perm to Offic *Heref* from 01. *Somershey, 71 High Street, Church Stretton SY6 6BY* Tel (01694) 723125

THOMAS, Peter James. b 53. Lon Univ BSc75. Trin Coll Bris 77. **d** 80 **p** 81. C Hucclecote *Glouc* 80-84; C Loughborough Em *Leic* 84-85; TV Parr *Liv* 85-92; V Eckington and Defford w Besford *Worc* 92-05; RD Pershore 00-05; P-in-c Norton sub Hamdon, W Chinnock, Chiselborough etc *B & W* from 05. *The Rectory, Cat Street, Chiselborough, Stoke-sub-Hamdon TA14 6TT* Tel (01935) 881202 E-mail pthomas5@aol.com

THOMAS, Peter Rhys. b 37. TCD BA59 MA72 MInstPkg MCIPD. **d** 72 **p** 73. C Cong *T, K & A* 73-75; I 75-77; C Bingley All SS *Bradf* 77-79; V Shelf 79-81; Producer Relig Broadcasting Viking Radio 81-84; P-in-c Croxton *Linc* 81-82; P-in-c Ulceby 81-82; P-in-c Wootton 81-82; P-in-c Ulceby Gp 82; V 82-84; R E and W Tilbury and Linford *Chelmsf* 84-89; I Celbridge w Straffan and Newcastle-Lyons *D & G* 89-93; I Youghal Union *C, C & R* 93-99; Dioc Communications Officer (Cork) 95-99; Can Cork Cathl 97-99; Preb Cloyne Cathl 97-99; rtd 99; Rep Leprosy Miss Munster from 00. *Abina Cottage, Ballykenneally, Ballymacoda, Co Cork, Irish Republic* Tel and fax (00353) (24) 98082 E-mail prthomas@iol.ie

THOMAS, Peter Wilson. b 58. BD AKC. Ripon Coll Cuddesdon. **d** 82 **p** 83. C Stockton St Pet *Dur* 82-85; TV Solihull *Birm* 85-90; V Rednal from 90. *St Stephen's Vicarage, Edgewood Road, Rednal, Birmingham B45 8SG* Tel 0121-453 3347

THOMAS, Philip Harold Emlyn. b 41. Cant Univ (NZ) BA64 MA77 Dur Univ PhD82. Melbourne Coll of Div BD68. **d** 68 **p** 69. Australia 68-71; New Zealand 71-77; Fell and Chapl Univ Coll Dur 77-83; V Heighington *Dur* from 84; AD Darlington 94-00. *The Vicarage, 15 East Green, Heighington, Newton Aycliffe DL5 6PP* Tel and fax (01325) 312134
E-mail philip.thomas@durham.anglican.org

THOMAS, Philip John. b 52. Liv Poly BSc74 Leeds Poly 77. Trin Coll Bris 94. **d** 96 **p** 97. C Skelton w Upleatham *York* 96-97; C Acomb St Steph 97-01; V Woodthorpe *S'well* from 01; Chapl Mothers' Union from 03. *St Mark's Vicarage, 37A Melbury Road, Nottingham NG5 4PG* Tel 0115-926 7859
E-mail stmarks.woodthorpe@ntlworld.com

THOMAS, Ramon Lorenzo. b 44. Victoria Univ Wellington BCA73 Mass Inst of Tech MSc80 CA73. Oak Hill Th Coll 89. **d** 97 **p** 98. NSM Yateley *Win* 97-99; Chairman Judah Trust from 99. *1 Dickens Way, Yateley GU46 6XX* Tel (01252) 682224
E-mail judahtrust@aol.com

THOMAS, Rhys. *See* THOMAS, Peter Rhys

THOMAS, Richard Frederick. b 24. Qu Coll Cam BA45 MA49. Ridley Hall Cam 47. **d** 49 **p** 50. C S Croydon Em *Cant* 49-51; Chapl and Ho Master Haileybury Coll 51-67; Jerusalem 67-73; Ho Master Bp Luffa Sch Chich 74-80; Lic to Offic *Chich* 75-77; Hon C Chich St Pancras and St Jo 78-80; R N Mundham w Hunston and Merston 80-89; Perm to Offic *Portsm* from 89; C Compton, the Mardens, Stoughton and Racton *Chich* 96-00; C Stansted 96-00; rtd 00; Perm to Offic *Chich* from 00. *16 Brent Court, Emsworth PO10 7JA* Tel (01243) 430613 Mobile 07947-518314 E-mail thomasrb@ntlworld.com

THOMAS, Richard Paul. b 50. MIPR. Wycliffe Hall Ox 74. **d** 76 **p** 77. C Abingdon w Shippon *Ox* 76-80; R Win All SS w Chilcomb and Chesil *Win* 80-88; Dioc Communications Officer 83-89; Dioc Communications Officer *Ox* from 89. *18 Eason Drive, Abingdon OX14 3YD* Tel (01235) 553360 *or* (01865) 208224 Pager 07623-946222 Fax (01865) 790470
E-mail richard.thomas@oxford.anglican.org

THOMAS, Robert Stanley. b 31. Lon Univ BD65 Man Univ MEd78. Sarum Th Coll 66. **d** 67 **p** 68. C Maltby *Sheff* 67-70; Lic to Offic *St Alb* 70-72; *Man* 72-79; *St As* 80-82; Dioc RE Adv *St As* 82-96; V Glyndyfrdwy and Llansantfraid Glyn Dyfrdwy 82-96; RD Edeirnion 88-96; rtd 96. *Lynward, 74 Middleton Road, Oswestry SY11 2LF* Tel (01691) 654326

THOMAS, Robin. b 27. Cen Sch of Art Lon NDD50. St Steph Ho Ox 89. **d** 89 **p** 90. NSM Clifton All SS w St Jo *Bris* 89-94; P-in-c Tintagel *Truro* 94-97; rtd 97; Perm to Offic *Truro* from 97. *22 Hendra Vean, Truro TR1 3TU* Tel (01872) 271276

THOMAS, Roderick Charles Howell. b 54. LSE BSc75. Wycliffe Hall Ox 91. **d** 93 **p** 94. C Plymouth St Andr w St Paul and St Geo *Ex* 93-95; C Plymouth St Andr and St Paul Stonehouse 95-99; P-in-c Elburton 99-05; V from 05. *St Matthew's Vicarage, 3 Sherford Road, Plymouth PL9 8DQ* Tel (01752) 402771
E-mail roderick.t@virgin.net

THOMAS, Roger. *See* THOMAS, John Roger

THOMAS, Ronald Buford. b 62. Memphis State Univ (USA) BA84 Emory Univ Atlanta MDiv88 Peterho Cam PhD02. Candler Sch of Th 84. **d** 93 **p** 94. USA 93-99; Asst P Salt Lake City St Paul 93-95; Assoc R 95-99; Perm to Offic *Ely* from 99. *Flat 2, 28 Parkside, Cambridge CB1 1JE* Tel (01223) 741432
E-mail rbt21@cam.ac.uk

THOMAS, Roy. *See* LUTHER THOMAS, The Ven Ilar Roy

THOMAS, Russen William. b 30. Univ of Wales (Lamp) BA55. St Mich Coll Llan 55. **d** 57 **p** 58. C Newport St Jo Bapt *Mon* 57-59; C Pembroke Dock *St D* 59-62; R St Florence and Redberth 62-69; V Newport St Julian *Mon* 69-79; V Stratton *Truro* 79-88; RD Stratton 83-88; V Lanteglos by Fowey 88-91; Hon Chapl Miss to Seafarers from 88; rtd 92; Chapl Playa de Las Americas Tenerife *Eur* 93-97; Perm to Offic *Cov* from 97. *St Peter's Cottage, Langford Budville, Wellington TA21 0QZ* Tel (01823) 400525 Mobile 07801-473862
E-mail wen.rus@virgin.net

THOMAS, Simon Jonathan Francklin. b 51. Sheff Univ BA72 Nottm Univ BA78 Open Univ MA02. St Jo Coll Nottm 76. **d** 80 **p** 80. SAMS Peru 80-82; C Camberwell All SS *S'wark* 82; SAMS Bolivia 83-95; C Ashtead *Guildf* from 96. *1 Oakfield Road, Ashtead KT21 2RE* Tel (01372) 813334 Fax 813352
E-mail simon@simonjfthomas.freeserve.co.uk

THOMAS, Preb Stephen Blayney. b 35. St D Coll Lamp BA62. Bp Burgess Hall Lamp DipTh63. **d** 63 **p** 64. C Ledbury *Heref* 63-67; C Bridgnorth w Tasley 67-68; C Clun w Chapel Lawn, Bettws-y-Crwyn and Newcastle 68-73; C Clungunford w Clunbury and Clunton, Bedstone etc 68-73; V Worfield 73-84; RD Bridgnorth 81-83; R Kingsland 84-96; P-in-c Eardisland 84-96; P-in-c Aymestrey and Leinthall Earles w Wigmore etc 84-96; R Kingsland w Eardisland, Aymestrey etc 97-99; Preb Heref Cathl 85-01; rtd 99; Perm to Offic *Heref* and *Worc* from 00. *28 Castle Close, Burford, Tenbury Wells WR15 8AY* Tel (01584) 819642

THOMAS, Stuart Grahame. b 54. Pemb Coll Cam BA77 MA81 ATCL97. Ridley Hall Cam 85. **d** 87 **p** 88. C Guildf H Trin w St Mary *Guildf* 87-91; V Churt 91-94; V Ewell St Fran from 94; Dioc Ecum Officer from 99. *St Francis's Vicarage, 61 Ruxley Lane, Epsom KT19 0JG* Tel (020) 8393 5616
E-mail revstuart.thomas@virgin.net

THOMAS, Canon Sydney Robert. b 44. Univ of Wales (Swansea) BA65 MA83. St D Coll Lamp LTh67. **d** 67 **p** 68. C Llanelli *St D* 67-77; V Pontyberem 77-01; TR Cwm Gwendraeth from 01; RD Cydweli 94-05; Can St D Cathl from 94; Chan 01-03; Treas from 03. *The Vicarage, 56 Llannon Road, Pontyberem, Llanelli SA15 5LY* Tel (01269) 870345

THOMAS, Theodore Eilir. b 36. Univ of Wales (Lamp) BA58. Sarum Th Coll 58. **d** 60 **p** 61. C Fenton *Lich* 60-63; C Stourport All SS and St Mich CD *Worc* 63-67; V Worc H Trin 67-74; P-in-c Dudley St Fran 74-79; V 79-83; R Plympton St Maurice *Ex* 83-03; rtd 03; P-in-c St John w Millbrook *Truro* from 04. *The Vicarage, Millbrook, Torpoint PL10 1BW* Tel (01752) 822264

THOMAS, Thomas. b 68. Selw Coll Cam BA90. Wycliffe Hall Ox 91. **d** 93 **p** 94. C Much Woolton *Liv* 93-97; V Carr Mill from 97. *St David's Vicarage, 27 Eskdale Avenue, St Helens WA11 7EN* Tel (01744) 732330 E-mail tomtom@fish.co.uk

THOMAS, Thomas Alan. b 37. K Coll Lon BD60 AKC60. St Boniface Warminster 60. **d** 61 **p** 62. C Washington *Dur* 61-65; C Bishopwearmouth St Mary V w St Pet CD 65-70; V Ruishton w Thornfalcon *B & W* 70-82; R Hutton 82-94; V Frome Ch Ch 94-96; Chapl Victoria Hosp Frome 94-96; R Camerton w Dunkerton, Foxcote and Shoscombe *B & W* 96-00; rtd 00; Perm to Offic *B & W* from 00. *12 Farrington Way, Farrington Gurney, Bristol BS39 6US* Tel (01761) 453434

THOMAS, Thomas John Samuel. b 21. St D Coll Lamp BA48. **d** 49 **p** 50. C Dafen and Llwynhendy *St D* 49-50; Chapl RAF 52-77; QHC 73-85; V Horsham *Chich* 77-85; rtd 85; Perm to Offic *St D* from 85. *1 Glynhir Road, Llandybie, Ammanford SA18 2TA* Tel (01269) 850726

THOMAS, Canon Thomas Vernon. b 21. St D Coll Lamp BA42 Selw Coll Cam BA44 MA48. St Mich Coll Llan 44. **d** 45 **p** 46. C St Brides Minor *Llan* 45-47; Ripon Cathl *Ripon* 47-50; Min Can and Succ Ripon Cathl 47-50; C Leeds St Pet 50-55; V Beeston 55-77; Hon Can Ripon Cathl 75-89; R Spofforth w Kirk Deighton 77-89; rtd 89; Perm to Offic *Ripon* from 89. *The Lodge, Main Street, East Keswick, Leeds LS17 9DB* Tel (01937) 573033

THOMAS, Virginia Jacqueline. b 48. UEA BA70. Yale Div Sch MDiv97. **d** 00 **p** 01. NSM Chelsea St Luke and Ch Ch *Lon* 00-04; NSM W Brompton St Mary w St Pet from 04; P-in-c from 05. *The Vicarage, 24 Fawcett Street, London SW10 9EZ* Tel (020) 7352 5880 *or* 7835 1440 Fax 7370 6562 E-mail ginny@stmarytheboltons.demon.co.uk

THOMAS, William George. b 29. JP. FRSA Birm Univ BA50 CertEd51. EAMTC 82. **d** 85 **p** 86. NSM Brampton *Ely* 85-87; NSM Bluntisham w Earith 87-89; P-in-c Foxton 89-95; rtd 95; Perm to Offic *Ely* from 95. *3 The Paddock, Bluntisham, Huntingdon PE28 3NR* Tel (01487) 842057

THOMAS, The Ven William Jordison. b 27. K Coll Cam BA50 MA55. Cuddesdon Coll 51. **d** 53 **p** 54. C Byker St Ant *Newc* 53-56; C Berwick H Trin 56-59; V Alwinton w Holystone and Alnham 59-70; V Alston cum Garrigill w Nenthead and Kirkhaugh 70-80; P-in-c Lambley w Knaresdale 72-80; RD Bamburgh and Glendale 81-83; TR Glendale Gp 80-83; Adn Northd and Can Res Newc Cathl 83-92; rtd 92; Perm to Offic *Newc* from 92. *Wark Cottage, Whittingham, Alnwick NE66 4RB* Tel (01665) 574300

THOMAS, Canon William Kenneth. b 19. Mert Coll Ox BA40 MA44. Westcott Ho Cam 40. **d** 42 **p** 43. C Brislington St Luke *Bris* 42-47; C Westbury-on-Trym St Alb 47-52; CF 49-51; V Oldland and Longwell Green *Bris* 52-71; V Minety w Oaksey 71-82; P-in-c 82-84; RD Malmesbury 73-79; Hon Can Bris Cathl 77-84; P-in-c Crudwell w Ashley 82-84; rtd 84; Perm to Offic *Bris* 84-03. *1 Oaktree Court, Portland Drive, Willen, Milton Keynes MK15 9LP* Tel (01908) 660618

THOMAS, The Ven William Phillip. b 43. Lich Th Coll 68. **d** 70 **p** 71. C Llanilid w Pencoed *Llan* 70-74; C Pontypridd St Cath 74-76; V Tonyrefail 76-84; Youth Chapl 78-80; RD Rhondda 81-84; R Neath w Llantwit 84-98; Adn Llan from 97; V Caerau w Ely 98-00. *6 Rachel Close, Cardiff CF5 2SH* Tel and fax (029) 2056 2991 E-mail jeanclev@talk21.com

THOMAS, William Rhys Ithel Phillips. b 16. St Jo Coll Dur BA38 DipTh41 MA42. **d** 41 **p** 42. C Newport H Trin *Mon* 41-43; CF (EC) 43-48; C Usk *Mon* 48-49; V Llanishen w Trellech Grange 49-56; CF (TA) 49-56; CF 56-60; Area Sec (E Distr) Miss to Seamen 60-62; R Gt and Lt Saxham w Westley *St E* 62-68; Lic to Offic 68-78; Chapl Asst Addenbrooke's Hosp Cam 78-81; rtd 81; Perm to Offic *Ely* 85-00. *c/o P D Thomas Esq, Flat 2, Garden House, Napier Place, London W14 8LG*

THOMAS ANTHONY, Brother. *See* DEHOOP, Brother Thomas Anthony

THOMASSON, Keith Duncan. b 69. St Pet Coll Ox BA91 MA97 Lon Inst of Educn PGCE92. Ripon Coll Cuddesdon BA01 Bossey Ecum Inst Geneva. **d** 02 **p** 03. C Lancaster St Mary w St John and St Anne *Blackb* 02-04; C Longridge from 04. *94 Higher Road, Longridge, Preston PR3 3SY* Tel (01772) 785997 E-mail keiththomasson@hotmail.com

THOMPSON, Adrian David. b 68. Univ of Wales (Abth) BSc93 PhD97 Bris Univ PGCE98. Wycliffe Hall Ox 93. **d** 05. C Blackb St Gabr *Blackb* from 05. *St Gabriel's House, 1 Chatsworth Close, Blackburn BB1 8QH* Tel (01254) 697632 *or* 246066 E-mail adrian.curate@btinternet.com

THOMPSON, Andrew David. b 68. Poly of Wales BSc90 Nottm Univ MA03. Wycliffe Hall Ox 98. **d** 00 **p** 01. C Oakwood *Derby* 00-04; Asst Chapl UAE from 05. *47 Dalelands, Telford TF3 2BG* E-mail andythompson1968@swissmail.org

THOMPSON, Mrs Angela Lorena Jennifer. b 44. St Alb and Ox Min Course CBTS99. **d** 99 **p** 00. NSM Chalfont St Giles *Ox* from 99. *3 The Leys, Chesham Bois, Amersham HP6 5NP* Tel (01494) 726654 E-mail angelalj70@hotmail.com

THOMPSON, Canon Anthony Edward. b 38. Bris Univ BA61. Ridley Hall Cam 61. **d** 63 **p** 64. C Peckham St Mary Magd *S'wark* 63-66; SAMS Paraguay 67-72; C Otley *Bradf* 72-75; TV Woughton *Ox* 75-82; P-in-c Lower Nutfield *S'wark* 82-02; V S Nutfield w Outwood 02-03; RD Reigate 91-93; Local Min Adv Croydon Episc Area 93-03; Hon Can S'wark Cathl 03; rtd 03. *3 The Curlews, Shoreham-by-Sea BN43 5UQ* Tel (01273) 440183 E-mail cc@nutfield99.freeserve.co.uk

THOMPSON, Athol James Patrick. b 34. St Paul's Coll Grahamstown 72. **d** 74 **p** 75. S Africa 74-83; P-in-c Dewsbury St Matt and St Jo *Wakef* 84; TV Dewsbury 84-93; Chapl Staincliffe and Dewsbury Gen Hosps Wakef 84-90; Chapl Dewsbury and Distr Hosp 90-93; V Shiregreen St Jas and St Chris *Sheff* 93-99; rtd 99; Perm to Offic *Sheff* from 99. *109 Park Avenue, Chapeltown, Sheffield S35 1WH* Tel 0114-245 1028

THOMPSON, Barry Pearce. b 40. St Andr Univ BSc63 Ball Coll Ox PhD66 Hull Univ MA82. NW Ord Course 76. **d** 79 **p** 80. C Cottingham *York* 79-82; V Swine 82-83; Lect Th Hull Univ 83-88; Ind Chapl *York* 83-85; Abp's Adv on Ind Issues 85-88; Can Res Chelmsf Cathl *Chelmsf* 88-98; Treas and Can Windsor 98-02; rtd 02; Perm to Offic *York* from 03. *44 Topcliffe Road, Sowerby, Thirsk YO7 1RB* Tel (01845) 525170 Mobile 07768-515790

THOMPSON, Brian. b 34. MRICS65 FRICS75. St Jo Coll Nottm 81. **d** 84 **p** 85. C Bletchley *Ox* 84-87; V Sneyd Green *Lich* 87-99; rtd 99; Perm to Offic *Lich* from 99. *85 Harrington Croft, West Bromwich B71 3RJ* Tel 0121-588 6120 E-mail brian.thompson40@btinternet.com

THOMPSON, Carrie Julia. b 77. Keble Coll Ox BA99 MA04. St Steph Ho Ox 02. **d** 04 **p** 05. C Camberwell St Giles w St Matt *S'wark* from 04. *Flat C, St Giles Centre, 81 Camberwell Church Street, London SE5 8RB* Tel (020) 7277 0685 E-mail mother.carrie@btinternet.com

THOMPSON, David. *See* THOMPSON, John David

THOMPSON, David Arthur. b 37. Clifton Th Coll. **d** 69 **p** 70. C Finchley Ch Ch *Lon* 69-72; C Barking St Marg w St Patr *Chelmsf* 72-75; TV 75-81; V Toxteth Park St Clem *Liv* 81-91; TR Parr 91-03; rtd 03; Perm to Offic *Sarum* from 03. *Charis, 72 Harkwood Drive, Hamworthy, Poole BH15 4PE* Tel (01202) 668904

THOMPSON, David John. b 17. Selw Coll Cam BA48 MA52. Ridley Hall Cam 48. **d** 50 **p** 51. C Denton Holme *Carl* 50-53; V Fulham St Mary N End *Lon* 53-62; V Wallington H Trin *S'wark* 62-74; R Hambledon *Guildf* 74-84; rtd 84; Perm to Offic *Chich* from 85. *1 Pond Willow, North Trade Road, Battle TN33 0HU* Tel (01424) 773000

THOMPSON, David John. b 64. Cranmer Hall Dur 92. **d** 95 **p** 96. C Poulton-le-Sands w Morecambe St Laur *Blackb* 95-99; V Farington Moss 99-02; V Lea from 02. *45 Abingdon Drive, Ashton-on-Ribble, Preston PR2 1EY* Tel (01772) 729197

THOMPSON, David Simon. b 57. Aston Univ BSc82 MRPharmS83. STETS 01. **d** 04 **p** 05. NSM Bournemouth H Epiphany *Win* from 04. *15 Cheriton Avenue, Bournemouth BH7 6SD* Tel (01202) 426764 Mobile 07763-052009 E-mail david_iford@hotmail.com

THOMPSON, Canon Donald Frazer. b 20. St Cath Coll Cam BA46 MA49. Coll of Resurr Mirfield 46. **d** 48 **p** 49. C Cheshunt *St Alb* 48-52; C Norton 52-56; V Wigan St Anne *Liv* 56-62; V Leeds St Aid *Ripon* 62-73; RD Allerton 70-73; R Adel 73-87; Hon Can Ripon Cathl 75-87; RD Headingley 85-87; rtd 87; Perm to Offic *Cov* from 87. *75 Cubbington Road, Leamington Spa CV32 7AQ* Tel (01926) 773298

THOMPSON, Edward Ronald Charles. b 25. AKC51. **d** 52 **p** 53. C Hinckley St Mary *Leic* 52-54; Asst Master St Geo Upper Sch Jerusalem 54-55; Chapl St Boniface Coll Warminster 56-59; R Hawkchurch w Fishpond *Sarum* 59-63; V Camberwell St Mich w All So w Em *S'wark* 63-67; P-in-c St Mary le Strand w St Clem Danes *Lon* 67-74; R 74-93; rtd 93; Perm to Offic *S'wark* from 95. *3 Woodsyre, Sydenham Hill, London SE26 6SS* Tel (020) 8670 8289

THOMPSON, Ms Eileen Carol. b 46. Lon Univ BA69. New Coll Edin MTh92. **d** 96 **p** 97. Par Dn Dhaka St Thos Bangladesh 96-97; Presbyter Madras H Cross w St Mich India 97-99; Presbyter in charge Madras St Mary 99-02; V Pallikunu St Geo and Palla Ch Ch 02-04; Min Livingston LEP *Edin* from 04. *53 Garry Walk, Livingston EH54 5AS* Tel (01506) 433451 E-mail eileenct@fish.co.uk

THOMPSON, Frederick Robert. b 15. Dur Univ LTh40. St Aug Coll Cant 37. **d** 40 **p** 41. C Northampton Ch Ch *Pet* 40-44; C Maidstone All SS *Cant* 44-46; India 46-57; Area Sec (Dios Birm and Lich) SPG 57-64; V Tutbury *Lich* 64-80; rtd 80; Perm to Offic *Sarum* from 80. *1 Panorama Road, Poole BH13 7RA* Tel (01202) 700735

THOMPSON, Garry John. b 49. Qu Coll Birm. **d** 96 **p** 97. C Wilnecote *Lich* 96-99; V Lapley w Wheaton Aston from 99; P-in-c Blymhill w Weston-under-Lizard from 99. *The Vicarage, Pinfold Lane, Wheaton Aston, Stafford ST19 9PD* Tel (01785) 840395 E-mail garrythompson@clergy.net

✠**THOMPSON, The Rt Revd Geoffrey Hewlett.** b 29. Trin Hall Cam BA52 MA56. Cuddesdon Coll 52. **d** 54 **p** 55 **c** 74. C Northampton St Matt *Pet* 54-59; V Wisbech St Aug *Ely* 59-66; V Folkestone St Sav *Cant* 66-74; Suff Bp Willesden *Lon* 74-79; Area Bp Willesden 79-85; Bp Ex 85-99; rtd 99; Hon Asst Bp Carl from 99. *Low Broomrigg, Warcop, Appleby-in-Westmorland CA16 6PT* Tel (01768) 341281

THOMPSON, Geoffrey Peter. b 58. St Pet Coll Ox BA80 MA82. SEITE 99. **d** 02 **p** 03. C Cheam *S'wark* from 02. *49 Brocks Drive, Sutton SM3 9UW* Tel (020) 8641 6535 E-mail gtchurch@dircon.co.uk

THOMPSON, George Harry Packwood. b 22. Qu Coll Ox BA48 MA48 BTh49. Qu Coll Birm 50. **d** 51 **p** 52. Lect Qu Coll Birm 51-53; C Coleshill *Birm* 51-53; Chapl and Lect Sarum Th Coll 53-55; Vice-Prin 55-64; V Combe *Ox* 64-85; Perm to Offic from 85; rtd 87. *12 Briar Thicket, Woodstock OX20 1NT* Tel (01993) 811915

THOMPSON, Preb Gordon Henry Moorhouse. b 41. Univ of Wales LLM95. K Coll Lon 63 St Boniface Warminster 66. **d** 67 **p** 68. C Leominster *Heref* 67-70; C Burford II w Greete and Hope Bagot 70-74; TV 74-89; C Burford III w Lt Heref 70-74; TV 74-89; C Tenbury 70-74; TV 74-89; TV Burford I 74-89; RD Ludlow 83-89; Preb Heref Cathl 85-97; rtd 89; Perm to Offic *Heref* from 89. *The Poplars, Bitterley Village, Ludlow SY8 3HQ* Tel (01584) 891093

THOMPSON, Harold Anthony. b 41. N Ord Course 84. **d** 87 **p** 88. C Leeds Belle Is St Jo and St Barn *Ripon* 87-90; V Leeds St Cypr Harehills 90-96; V Shadwell from 96. *The Vicarage, 2 Church Farm Garth, Leeds LS17 8HD* Tel 0113-273 7035

THOMPSON, Hewlett. *See* THOMPSON, The Rt Revd Geoffrey Hewlett

THOMPSON, Ian Charles. b 58. Wycliffe Hall Ox 80. **d** 83 **p** 84. C Knutsford St Jo and Toft *Ches* 83-86; C Birkenhead Ch Ch 86-88; V Balderstone *Man* 88-99; TR S Rochdale 00-01; AD Rochdale from 97; P-in-c Littleborough from 01. *The Vicarage, 19 Deardon Street, Littleborough OL15 9DZ* Tel (01706) 378334 Mobile 07796-174449
E-mail ian.thompson51@btopenworld.com

THOMPSON, Ian David. b 51. Hull Univ BSc72. N Ord Course 94. **d** 97 **p** 98. C Blackley St Andr *Man* 97-00; P-in-c from 00. *The Vicarage, Churchdale Road, Higher Blackley, Manchester M9 8NE* Tel 0161-740 2961

THOMPSON, Ian George. b 60. SEITE 99. **d** 02 **p** 03. NSM Walworth St Pet *S'wark* from 02. *223 Hollydale Road, London SE15 2AR* Tel (020) 7639 5015 Mobile 07985-582257

THOMPSON, Ian Malcolm. b 59. Wm Booth Memorial Coll CertEd79 Aber Univ BTh98 Selw Coll Cam MA02. Edin Th Coll CECM93. **d** 94 **p** 95. C Longside, Old Deer and Strichen *Ab* 94-96; R Aberdeen St Mary 96-99; Chapl and Dean of Chpl Selw Coll Cam 99-05; Chapl Newnham Coll Cam 99-05; Dean K Coll Cam from 05; Hon C Cambridge St Mary Less *Ely* from 03. *King's College, Cambridge CB2 1ST* Tel (01223) 331446
E-mail imt22@cam.ac.uk

THOMPSON, James. b 30. Dip Hypnotherapy 84 Nottm Univ DipEd65 DipTh65. Paton Congr Coll Nottm 61 Wycliffe Hall Ox 66. **d** 66 **p** 67. C Woodlands *Sheff* 66-69; R Firbeck w Letwell 69-71; V Milnsbridge *Wakef* 71-80; Chapl St Luke's Hosp Huddersfield 71-80; NSM Dewsbury 80-84; Lect Huddersfield Coll FE 80-84; Dioc Chapl Aber Hosps 84-89; Dioc Supernumerary *Ab* 84-89; R Buckie and Portsoy 89-94; rtd 95. *Peace Haven, Fron Park Road, Holywell, Flintwell CH8 7UY* Tel (01352) 712368

THOMPSON, James. b 37. Coll of Resurr Mirfield 64. **d** 67 **p** 68. C Shieldfield Ch Ch *Newc* 67-69; C Hendon *Dur* 69-74; V Gateshead St Chad Bensham 74-85; R Easington 85-90; Chapl Thorpe Hosp Easington 85-90; V Cassop cum Quarrington *Dur* from 90. *The Vicarage, Prince Charles Avenue, Bowburn, Durham DH6 5DL* Tel 0191-377 0347

THOMPSON, Jeremy James Thomas. b 58. Sunderland Univ BEd92. Cranmer Hall Dur 94. **d** 96 **p** 97. C Bedlington *Newc* 96-00; P-in-c Choppington 00-02; V from 02. *The Vicarage, Scotland Gate, Choppington NE62 5SX* Tel (01670) 822216
E-mail jeremyjtthompson@operamail.com

THOMPSON, John David. b 40. Lon Univ BD65 Ch Ch Ox DPhil69. St Steph Ho Ox 65. **d** 67 **p** 68. C Solihull *Birm* 67-71; C Biddestone w Slaughterford *Bris* 71-73; Lect Wells Th Coll 71-72; C Yatton Keynell *Bris* 71-73; C Castle Combe 71-73; V Braughing *St Alb* 74-77; R Digswell 77-82; TR Digswell and Panshanger 82-98; rtd 00. *7 Russell Street, Boddam, Peterhead AB42 3NG* Tel (01779) 473506

THOMPSON, John Michael. b 47. Nottm Univ BTh77 Hull Univ Cert Local & Regional Hist 90. Linc Th Coll 73. **d** 77 **p** 78. C Old Brumby *Linc* 77-80; C Grantham 80-81; TV 81-84; V Holton-le-Clay 84-94; V Holton-le-Clay and Tetney 94-97; R Humshaugh w Simonburn and Wark *Newc* from 97. *The Vicarage, Humshaugh, Hexham NE46 4AA* Tel (01434) 681304

THOMPSON, John Turrell. b 57. Sheff Univ BA(Econ)79 Southn Univ BTh88. Sarum & Wells Th Coll 83. **d** 86 **p** 87. C Tavistock and Gulworthy *Ex* 86-90; TV Pinhoe and Broadclyst 90-95; P-in-c Northam w Westward Ho! and Appledore 95-96; TV Bideford, Northam, Westward Ho!, Appledore etc 96-00; rtd 00; Perm to Offic *Ex* from 00. *Brambles Patch, 39 Westermore Drive, Roundswell, Barnstaple EX31 3XU*

THOMPSON, John Wilfred. b 44. CA Tr Coll 66 St Deiniol's Hawarden 84. **d** 85 **p** 86. C Rhyl w St Ann *St As* 85-87; R Fritwell w Souldern and Ardley w Fewcott *Ox* 87-97. *61 Blake Road, Bicester OX6 7HH*

THOMPSON (née LILLIE), Mrs Judith Virginia. b 44. LMH Ox BA66 Univ of E Africa DipEd67 Essex Univ MA73 Bris Univ Dip Counselling 92. Gilmore Course IDC82. **dss** 82 **d** 87 **p** 94. Lawrence Weston *Bris* 82-85; E Bris 85-95; Hon Par Dn 87-95; Chapl HM Rem Cen Pucklechurch 87-91; Chapl Asst Southmead Hosp Bris 91-95; C Knowle St Barn *Bris* 95-02; Bp's Adv for Past Care for Clergy and Families 97-00; Community Th St Mich Coll Llan 00-05; Dir In-House Tr 02-05; Chapl Worcs Acute Hosps NHS Trust from 05. *Worcestershire Royal Hospital, Charles Hastings Way, Worcester WR5 1DD* Tel (01905) 763333

THOMPSON, Kenneth. b 31. St Deiniol's Hawarden 84. **d** 87 **p** 88. Hon Par Dn Upton (Overchurch) *Ches* 87-90; NSM Tranmere St Cath 90-95; rtd 96; Perm to Offic *Ches* from 96. *33 Meadway, Upton, Wirral CH49 6JQ* Tel 0151-677 6433

THOMPSON, Kenneth (Brother Nathanael). b 29. St Deiniol's Hawarden 76. **d** 78 **p** 79. SSF from 62; C Llanbeblig w Caernarfon *Ban* 78-80; C Swansea St Gabr *S & B* 84-87; C Swansea St Mary w H Trin 87; C Dolgellau w Llanfachreth and Brithdir etc *Ban* 95-99; rtd 98. *Church House, Llanerchymedd LL71 8EG*

THOMPSON, Kevin. b 55. Sheff Univ BEd77. Oak Hill Th Coll. **d** 89 **p** 90. C Brinsworth w Catcliffe *Sheff* 89-92; V Kimberworth Park 92-97; V Grenoside 97-98; Perm to Offic from 98. *30 Arnold Avenue, Charnock, Sheffield S12 3JB* Tel 0114-239 6986
E-mail kevin.thompson10@virgin.net

THOMPSON, Mark William. b 52. St Jo Coll Nottm 77. **d** 81 **p** 82. C Barnsbury St Andr and H Trin w All SS *Lon* 81-84; C Addiscombe St Mary *Cant* 84; C Addiscombe St Mary *S'wark* 85-87; V Thorpe Edge *Bradf* 87-94; Chapl Essex Rivers Healthcare NHS Trust from 94. *Colchester General Hospital, Turner Road, Colchester CO4 5JL* Tel (01206) 747474 *or* 742513
E-mail mark.thompson@essexrivers.nhs.uk

THOMPSON, Martin Eric. b 52. FCCA. Trin Coll Bris 95. **d** 97 **p** 98. C Heref St Pet w St Owen and St Jas *Heref* 97-01; P-in-c Huntley and Longhope *Glouc* 01-02; R Huntley and Longhope, Churcham and Bulley from 03; P-in-c Worfield *Heref* from 05. *The Vicarage, Hallon, Worfield, Bridgnorth WV15 5JZ* Tel (01746) 716698 E-mail revmartin@lineone.net

THOMPSON, Matthew. b 68. CCC Cam BA90 MA94 MPhil94. Ridley Hall Cam 91. **d** 94 **p** 95. C Hulme Ascension *Man* 94-97; C Langley and Parkfield 97-98; TV 98-00; P-in-c Man Clayton St Cross w St Paul from 00; AD Ardwick from 03. *The Rectory, 54 Clayton Hall Road, Manchester M11 4WH* Tel 0161-223 0766

THOMPSON, Mervyn Patrick. b 59. Wilson Carlile Coll 84 Coll of Resurr Mirfield 90. **d** 92 **p** 93. C Sheff St Cath Richmond Road *Sheff* 92-95; V Thurnscoe St Hilda from 95; P-in-c Thurnscoe St Helen from 99. *The Vicarage, Hanover Street, Thurnscoe, Rotherham S63 0HJ* Tel (01709) 893259

THOMPSON, Michael. b 49. NEOC 83. **d** 86 **p** 87. C Ashington *Newc* 86-88; C Ponteland 88-91; TV Newc Epiphany 91-98; P-in-c Choppington 98-99; P-in-c Woldingham *S'wark* 99-02; TV Caterham 02-03; TV Saffron Walden w Wendens Ambo, Littlebury etc *Chelmsf* from 03. *Ashdon Vicarage, Radwinter Road, Ashdon, Saffron Walden CB10 2ET* Tel (01799) 584171
E-mail rev-thompson@lineone.net

THOMPSON, Michael Bruce. b 53. N Carolina Univ BA75 Dallas Th Sem ThM79 Virginia Th Sem 79 Ch Coll Cam PhD88. **d** 80 **p** 81. Asst Min New Bern N Carolina 80-83; Chair Youth and Evang and Renewal in E Carolina 81-83; Lect Greek Cam Univ 87-88; Lect St Jo Coll Nottm 88-95; Lect NT and Dir of Studies Ridley Hall Cam from 95; Vice-Prin from 00. *Dashwood House, Sidgwick Avenue, Cambridge CB3 9DA* Tel (01223) 741077 *or* 741066 Fax 741081 E-mail mbt2@cam.ac.uk

THOMPSON, Michael James. b 55. St Andr Univ MTh78 Dur Univ MA93. St Mich Coll Llan 78. **d** 79 **p** 80. C Aberavon *Llan* 79-81; C Kensington St Mary Abbots w St Geo *Lon* 81-85; Chapl Westmr Abbey 85-87; Sacrist 86-87; P-in-c Westmr St Marg 86-87; R Lowick w Sudborough and Slipton *Pet* 87-94; P-in-c Islip 87-94; Hon C Hampstead Ch Ch *Lon* 95-96; Hon C Smithfield St Bart Gt 95-96; V Sneinton St Steph w St Alb *S'well* 96-98; Perm to Offic *Lon* 98; R Stamford St Mary and St Martin *Linc* 98-04; I Dublin St Bart w Leeson Park *D & G* from 04. *The Parsonage, 12 Merlyn Road, Dublin 4, Irish Republic* Tel (00353) (1) 269 4813 E-mail stbartholomew@dublin.anglican.org

THOMPSON, Michael John. Cam Univ MA. **d** 00 **p** 01. OLM Badgeworth, Shurdington and Witcombe w Bentham *Glouc* from 00. *Cornerways, 1 Church Lane, Shurdington, Gloucester GL51 4TJ* Tel (01242) 862467
E-mail mthompson123@aol.com

THOMPSON (née LOCKHART), Ms Michelle. b 68. Man Univ BA89. Ripon Coll Cuddesdon 90. **d** 92 **p** 94. Par Dn Leigh St Mary *Man* 92-94; Asst Chapl HM Pris Full Sutton 95-97; V York St Hilda *York* 97-00; Dir Reader Tr and Local Min Development *Man* 00-03; Chapl HM Pris Styal from 04. *HM Prison, Styal Road, Styal, Wilmslow SK9 4HR* Tel (01625) 553000

THOMPSON, Neil Hamilton. b 48. SS Hild & Bede Coll Dur BEd72 Leic Univ MA75. S'wark Ord Course 77 Ven English Coll Rome. **d** 80 **p** 81. C Merton St Mary *S'wark* 80-82; C

Dulwich St Barn 82-84; V Shooters Hill Ch Ch 84-87; V S Dulwich St Steph 87-96; R Limpsfield and Titsey from 96. *The Rectory, Limpsfield, Oxted RH8 0DG* Tel (01883) 722812 *or* tel and fax 712512 E-mail neilthompson@houndofheaven.co.uk

THOMPSON, Patricia. b 60. SRN. NEOC 94. **d** 97 **p** 98. NSM Sunderland St Chad *Dur* from 97; Voc Adv from 99. *11 Friarsfield Close, Chapelgarth, Sunderland SR3 2RZ* Tel 0191-522 7911

THOMPSON, Patrick Arthur. b 36. Dur Univ BA59. Qu Coll Birm DipTh61. **d** 61 **p** 62. C W Wickham St Fran *Cant* 61-65; C Portchester *Portsm* 65-68; C Birchington w Acol *Cant* 68-71; V S Norwood St Mark 71-77; P-in-c Norbury St Oswald 77-81; V Norbury St Oswald *S'wark* 81-93; V Sutton New Town St Barn 93-00; rtd 00; Resident P Grantown-on-Spey *Mor* from 04. *Rose Cottage, Market Street, Forres IV36 1EF* Tel (01309) 675917

THOMPSON, Paul. b 58. Ox Univ BA. Ripon Coll Cuddesdon 80. **d** 83 **p** 84. Chapl Fazakerley Hosp 83-86; C Kirkby *Liv* 83-86; TV 86-89; Ind Chapl 86-89; Chapl Kirkby Coll of FE 86-89; CF 89-01; Chapl Epsom Coll from 01. *Epsom College, Epsom KT17 4JQ* Tel (01372) 821288 E-mail schaplain@epsomcollege.org.uk

THOMPSON, Paul. b 65. TCD BA87. CITC 87. **d** 89 **p** 90. C Orangefield w Moneyreagh *D & D* 89-92; I Dromara w Garvaghy 92-97; I Ramoan w Ballycastle and Culfeightrin *Conn* 97-00; Dep Chapl HM Pris Liv 00-01; Chapl HM YOI Portland from 01. *HM Young Offender Institution, The Grove, Portland DT5 1DL* Tel (01305) 820301 Fax 823718

THOMPSON, Paul Noble. b 54. Univ of Wales (Cardiff) BMus77. Coll of Resurr Mirfield DipTh79. **d** 80 **p** 81. C Bargoed and Deri w Brithdir *Llan* 80-83; C Whitchurch 83-84; V Porth w Trealaw 84-89; V Llanharan w Peterston-super-Montem 89-97; C Barry All SS 97-01; Youth Chapl 97-01; V Lisvane from 01. *The Vicarage, 2 Llwyn-y-Pia Road, Lisvane, Cardiff CF14 0SY* Tel (029) 2075 3338

THOMPSON, Mrs Pauline. b 44. EMMTC 81. **dss** 84 **d** 87 **p** 94. Derby St Aug *Derby* 84-87; Par Dn 87-88; Par Dn Boulton 88-90; Par Dn Allestree 91-94; C 94-97; Sub-Chapl HM Pris Sudbury 92-94; P-in-c Hartington, Biggin and Earl Sterndale *Derby* 97-01; rtd 01; Perm to Offic *Derby* from 01. *46 Hawthorn Court, Kedleston Road, Derby DE22 1FY* Tel (01332) 210127

THOMPSON, Peter Alrick. b 79. QUB BA01 TCD MPhil04 ARIAM99 ACertCM. CITC 01. **d** 03 **p** 04. C Clooney w Strathfoyle *D & R* from 03. *11 Mosley Park, Londonderry BT47 5HR* Tel (028) 7134 1966 E-mail curate.clooney@derry.anglican.org

THOMPSON, Peter Kerr. b 32. Kelham Th Coll. **d** 56 **p** 57. Solomon Is 56-76; Adn Malaita and Outer E Solomon 62-76; Adn N Melanesia 68-70; Australia from 76; R S Gulf 76-78; R Port Hedland 78-82; R Melville 85-88; R Childers 89-91; R Bundaberg W 91-92. *28 Saunders Street, Point Vernon, Qld, Australia 4655* Tel (0061) (7) 4124 3645

THOMPSON, Canon Peter Ross. b 26. St Jo Coll Cam BA47 MB, BChir50. Tyndale Hall Bris. **d** 60 **p** 61. C New Malden and Coombe *S'wark* 60-61; BCMS Burma 61-66; R Slaugham *Chich* 66-72; V Polegate 72-92; Can and Preb Chich Cathl 91-92; rtd 92; Perm to Offic *Guildf* from 92. *Tregenna, Barley Mow Lane, Knaphill, Woking GU21 2HX* Tel (01483) 480595

THOMPSON, Randolph. b 25. Lich Th Coll 63. **d** 65 **p** 66. C Boultham *Linc* 65-68; V Paddock *Wakef* 68-69; P-in-c Cornholme 69-71; V 71-72; Chapl Barnsley Hall & Lea Hosps Bromsgrove 72-84; V Hanley Castle, Hanley Swan and Welland *Worc* 84-89; rtd 89; Perm to Offic *Lich* from 90. *37 Hampton Fields, Oswestry SY11 1TL* Tel (01691) 658484

THOMPSON, The Very Revd Raymond Craigmile. b 42. Man Univ BTh. **d** 84 **p** 85. C Clooney *D & R* 84-86; I Urney w Sion Mills 86-92; I Derryvullen N w Castlearchdale *Clogh* 92-05; Chapl to Bp Clogh 02-05; Can Clogh Cathl 03-05; Dean Clogh from 05; I Clogh w Errigal Portclare from 05. *The Deanery, 10 Augher Road, Clogher BT76 0AD* Tel (028) 8554 9797 E-mail dean@clogher.anglican.org

THOMPSON, Richard Brian. b 60. Sheff Poly BSc83. Ripon Coll Cuddesdon 86. **d** 89 **p** 90. C Thorpe Bay *Chelmsf* 89-92; V Rushmere *St E* 92-97; Dep Chapl HM Pris Nor 97-98; Chapl HM Pris Wayland 98-01; Chapl HM Pris and YOI Hollesley Bay from 01. *The Chaplain's Office, Hollesley Bay Colony, Hollesley, Woodbridge IP12 3JW* Tel (01394) 411741 ext 325 Fax 411071

THOMPSON, Robert Craig. b 72. Univ Coll Dur BA92. Westcott Ho Cam 94. **d** 96 **p** 97. C Wigan All SS *Liv* 96-00; P-in-c Ladybrook *S'well* from 00. *St Mary's Vicarage, Bancroft Lane, Mansfield NG18 5LZ* Tel (01623) 621709 E-mail revrobert@tiscali.co.uk

THOMPSON, Robert George. b 71. K Coll Cam BA93 MA97. Ripon Coll Cuddesdon MTh95. **d** 97 **p** 98. C Ruislip St Martin *Lon* 97-01; Chapl Parkside Community NHS Trust Lon from 01. *Chaplain's Office, St Charles Community Hospital, Exmoor Street, London W10 6DZ* Tel (020) 8962 4146 E-mail robert.thompson@kc-pct.nhs.uk

THOMPSON, Roger Quintin. b 63. K Coll Lon BA85 AKC85 Nottm Univ PGCE86 MA96. Aston Tr Scheme 92 St Jo Coll Nottm 94. **d** 96. C Easton H Trin w St Gabr and St Lawr and St Jude *Bris* 96-00; C Lisburn Ch Ch Cathl *Conn* 00-04; I Kilwaughter w Cairncastle and Craigy Hill from 04. *Cairncastle Rectory, 15 Cairncastle Road, Ballygally, Larne BT40 2RB* Tel (028) 2858 3220 E-mail rogfi@fish.co.uk

THOMPSON, Ross Keith Arnold. b 53. Sussex Univ BA75 Bris Univ PhD82. Coll of Resurr Mirfield 80. **d** 82 **p** 83. C Knowle *Bris* 82-85; TV E Bris 85-94; V Bristol St Aid w St Geo 94-95; V Knowle St Barn and H Cross Inns Court 95-02; Tutor St Mich Coll Llan from 02. *St Michael's College, 54 Cardiff Road, Llandaff, Cardiff CF5 2YJ* Tel (02920) 563379

THOMPSON, Ruth Jean. *See* GOSTELOW, Mrs Ruth Jean

THOMPSON, Stephen Peter. b 45. Lon Univ BSc67 Lon Inst of Educn PGCE71 K Coll Lon BD77 AKC77 SOAS Lon BA82 Poona Univ MPhil85 PhD87 FRAS91. Ripon Coll Cuddesdon. **d** 00. NSM Bedford Park *Lon* 00-01; NSM Isleworth St Fran from 01. *11 The Elms, Vine Road, London SW13 0NE* Tel (020) 8876 5820 E-mail rev-mrs@spthompson.freeserve.co.uk

THOMPSON, Thomas Oliver. b 27. TCD 61. **d** 63 **p** 64. C Lisburn Ch Ch *Conn* 63-68; Chapl to Ch of Ireland Miss to Deaf and Dumb 68-76; I Glenavy w Tunny and Crumlin 77-92; rtd 92. *34 Strandview Avenue, Portstewart BT55 7LL* Tel (028) 7083 3267

THOMPSON, Canon Timothy. b 34. Fitzw Ho Cam BA59 MA64. Cuddesdon Coll 59. **d** 61 **p** 62. C Noel Park St Mark *Lon* 61-64; C Shrub End *Chelmsf* 64-67; New Zealand 67-70; R Tolleshunt Knights w Tiptree *Chelmsf* 70-81; R Colchester St Jas, All SS, St Nic and St Runwald 81-88; RD Colchester 84-88; Hon Can Chelmsf Cathl 85-88; Can Res Chelmsf Cathl 88-01; Vice-Provost 88-00; Vice-Dean 00-01; rtd 01. *44 Sixth Avenue, Chelmsford CM1 4ED* Tel (01245) 260382

THOMPSON, Timothy Charles. b 51. Lon Univ BSc73 AKC. Westcott Ho Cam 75. **d** 78 **p** 79. C Ipswich St Mary at Stoke w St Pet etc *St E* 78-81; Ind Chapl *Nor* 81-88; C Lowestoft and Kirkley 81-83; TV 83-88; V Coney Hill *Glouc* 88-94; P-in-c Caister *Nor* 94-00; R from 00. *The Rectory, Rectory Close, Caister-on-Sea, Great Yarmouth NR30 5EG* Tel (01493) 720287 E-mail tim.thompson@ukonline.co.uk

THOMPSON, Canon Timothy William. b 47. Bris Univ CertEd70 Open Univ BA78. EMMTC. **d** 88 **p** 89. C Scartho *Linc* 88-91; V Haxey 91-95; P-in-c Surfleet 95-00; Asst Local Min Officer 95-00; RD Elloe W 98-00; P-in-c Linc St Pet-at-Gowts and St Andr from 00; P-in-c Linc St Botolph from 00; RD Christianity from 02; Can and Preb Linc Cathl from 02. *St Peter-at-Gowts Vicarage, 1 Sibthorp Street, Lincoln LN5 7SP* Tel (01522) 530256 Mobile 07885-238813 Fax (01522) 531040 E-mail tim.thompson@virgin.net

THOMPSON, Canon Tom Malcolm. b 38. Dur Univ BA60 Man Univ MPhil93. Bps' Coll Cheshunt 60. **d** 62 **p** 63. C Standish *Blackb* 62-65; C Lancaster St Mary 65-67; V Chorley All SS 67-72; V Barrowford 72-78; RD Pendle 75-78; R Northfield *Birm* 78-82; RD Kings Norton 79-82; V Longton *Blackb* 82-94; RD Leyland 89-94; V Nunthorpe *York* 94-03; Can and Preb York Minster 98-03; RD Stokesley 00-03; rtd 03; Perm to Offic *Carl* from 03. *Wainstones, 6 Greengate Crescent, Levens, Kendal LA8 8QB* Tel (01539) 561409

THOMPSON-McCAUSLAND, Marcus Perronet. b 31. Trin Coll Cam BA54 MA60. Coll of Resurr Mirfield 57. **d** 59 **p** 60. C Perry Barr *Birm* 59-65; V Rubery 65-72; R Cradley *Heref* 72-82; P-in-c Storridge 72-82; P-in-c Mathon 72-82; P-in-c Castle Frome 72-82; Hon C Camberwell St Giles *S'wark* 82-87; Hon C Lydbury N *Heref* 88-89; Hon C Lydbury N w Hopesay and Edgton 89-94; Hon C Wigmore Abbey 95-01; Perm to Offic from 01. *18 Watling Street, Leintwardine, Craven Arms SY7 0LW* Tel (01547) 540228

THOMPSON-VEAR, John Arthur. b 76. Sunderland Univ BA98. St Steph Ho Ox BA02. **d** 03 **p** 04. C Plymouth Crownhill Ascension *Ex* from 03. *45 Southwell Road, Plymouth PL6 5BG* Tel (01752) 706466 E-mail frjohn_ruth@yahoo.co.uk

THOMPSTONE, Canon John Deaville. b 39. BNC Ox BA63 MA67. Ridley Hall Cam 63. **d** 65 **p** 66. C Hoole *Ches* 65-68; C Fulwood *Sheff* 68-71; V Skirbeck H Trin *Linc* 71-77; V Shipley St Pet *Bradf* 77-91; RD Airedale 82-88; V Poynton *Ches* 91-04; Hon Can Ches Cathl 02-04; rtd 04. *Greyfriars, Broadway Road, Childswickham, Broadway WR12 7HP* Tel (01386) 852930 E-mail john@thompstone.fsnet.co.uk

THOMSETT, Murray Richard. b 32. MBKSTS Kingston Tech Coll HND54. Oak Hill Th Coll 91. **d** 92 **p** 93. NSM Whitton SS Phil and Jas *Lon* 92-96; NSM Hampton All SS 96-02; Chapl Terminal 4 Heathrow Airport from 96. *27 Coombe Road, Hampton TW12 3PB* Tel (020) 8979 7549 *or* 8745 2700 E-mail murrayt@nildram.co.uk

THOMSON, Alexander Keith. b 38. Cranmer Hall Dur BA63. **d** 64 **p** 65. C Middleton *Man* 64-68; Chapl Rannoch Sch Perthshire 68-72; P-in-c Kinloch Rannoch *St And* 68-72; Asst Chapl Oundle Sch 72-94; Chapl Laxton Sch 88-94; Lic to Offic *Pet* 73-94; Perm to Offic 94-98; rtd 98. *Holly Lodge, Achurch Road, Thorpe Waterville, Kettering NN14 3ED*

THOMSON, Andrew Maitland. b 43. CA(Z)67 Univ Coll of Rhodesia & Nyasaland Dip Applied Economics 65. Westcott Ho Cam 78. **d** 80 **p** 81. Zimbabwe 80-92; P-in-c E w N and W Barsham *Nor* 92-95; P-in-c N and S Creake w Waterden 92-94; P-in-c Sculthorpe w Dunton and Doughton 92-94; R N and S Creake w Waterden, Syderstone etc from 95. *The Rectory, 18 Front Street, South Creake, Fakenham NR21 9PE* Tel (01328) 823433 E-mail rector@creake.surfaid.org

THOMSON, Canon Celia Stephana Margaret. b 55. LMH Ox MA83 Birkbeck Coll Lon MA87 K Coll Lon MA94. Sarum & Wells Th Coll 89. **d** 91 **p** 94. Par Dn Southfields St Barn *S'wark* 91-94; C 94-95; V W Wimbledon Ch Ch 95-03; Tutor SEITE 95-00; Voc Adv Lambeth Adnry 96-00; Can Res Glouc Cathl *Glouc* from 03. *3 Miller's Green, Gloucester GL1 2BN* Tel (01452) 415824 E-mail cthomson@gloucestercathedral.org.uk

THOMSON, Preb Clarke Edward Leighton. b 19. TD65. Pemb Coll Ox BA41 MA45. Wycliffe Hall Ox 44. **d** 45 **p** 46. C Penge Lane H Trin *Roch* 45-47; Egypt 47-50; C Chelsea All SS *Lon* 50-51; V 51-92; CF (TA) 52-69; Preb St Paul's Cathl *Lon* 86-92; rtd 92; Perm to Offic *Lon* from 93. *15 Redburn Street, London SW3 4DA* Tel (020) 7351 5371

THOMSON, The Ven David. b 52. Keble Coll Ox MA78 DPhil78 Selw Coll Cam BA80 MA84. Westcott Ho Cam 78. **d** 81 **p** 82. C Maltby *Sheff* 81-84; Sec Par and People 84-94; TV Banbury *Ox* 84-94; TR Cockermouth w Embleton and Wythop *Carl* 94-02; Adn Carl and Can Res Carl Cathl from 02. *2 The Abbey, Carlisle CA3 8TZ* Tel (01228) 523026 Mobile 07771-864550 Fax (01228) 594899
E-mail archdeacon.north@carlislediocese.org.uk

THOMSON, Elizabeth Jane. b 64. Univ Coll Ox MA85 DPhil89 Trin Coll Cam BA02 Moray Ho Coll of Educn PGCE90. Westcott Ho Cam 00. **d** 03 **p** 04. C Pilton w Croscombe, N Wootton and Dinder *B & W* from 03. *Hill House, Fayreway, Croscombe, Wells BA5 3RA* Tel (01749) 343427
E-mail ejt@ecosse.net

THOMSON, Elizabeth Lucy. *See* TALBOT, Mrs Elizabeth Lucy

THOMSON, James Maclaren. b 69. Grey Coll Dur BA91 Univ Coll Lon MA93. Wycliffe Hall Ox BA99. **d** 00 **p** 01. C Oulton Broad *Nor* 00-04; V Chatteris *Ely* from 04. *The Vicarage, Church Lane, Chatteris PE16 6JA* Tel (01354) 692173
E-mail oxthomson@aol.com

THOMSON, Canon John Bromilow. b 59. York Univ BA81 Wycliffe Hall Ox BA84 MA91 Nottm Univ PhD01. **d** 85 **p** 86. C Ecclesall *Sheff* 85-89; S Africa 89-92; Tutor St Paul's Coll Grahamstown 89-92; Asst P Grahamstown St Bart 90-92; Asst Lect Rhodes Univ 91-92; V Doncaster St Mary *Sheff* 93-01; Dir Min from 01; Hon Can Sheff Cathl from 01. *15 Grange View, Balby, Doncaster DN4 0XL* Tel (01302) 570205 *or* (01709) 309143 Fax (01709) 309108
E-mail john.thomson@sheffield.anglican.org

THOMSON, Julian Harley. b 43. AKC70. St Aug Coll Cant 70. **d** 71 **p** 72. C Wellingborough All Hallows *Pet* 71-74; Min Can, Prec and Sacr Ely Cathl *Ely* 74-80; P-in-c Stuntney 76-80; V Arrington 80-91; R Croydon w Clopton 80-91; R Orwell 80-91; R Wimpole 80-91; V Linton 91-96; R Bartlow 91-96; P-in-c Castle Camps 91-96; TR Linton 96-01; RD Linton 99-01; rtd 01; Perm to Offic *Nor* from 01. *Lavender Cottage, 7 Abbey Road, Great Massingham, King's Lynn PE32 2HN* Tel (01485) 520721

THOMSON, Keith. *See* THOMSON, Alexander Keith

THOMSON, Matthew James. b 63. Nottm Univ BA92 Univ of Wales (Ban). St Jo Coll Nottm 92. **d** 95 **p** 96. C Cosham *Portsm* 95-98; C Nailsea Ch Ch w Tickenham *B & W* 98-01; V Congresbury w Puxton and Hewish St Ann from 01; Bp's Healing Adv from 01. *The Vicarage, Station Road, Congresbury, Bristol BS49 5DX* Tel (01934) 833126
E-mail mndjthomson@netscapeonline.co.uk

THOMSON, Peter Ashley. b 36. Ox Univ BA74 MA78 MACE77. Ridley Coll Melbourne ThL57. **d** 59 **p** 60. Australia 59-62, 64-96 and from 01; C Fen Ditton *Ely* 62-63; V Upwood w Gt and Lt Raveley 63-64; C W Holloway St Luke *Lon* 96-97; 2000 by 2000 (Millennium Projects) Officer 97-01; rtd 02. *PO Box 498, Mansfield, Vic, Australia 3722* Tel (0061) (3) 5777 5635

THOMSON, Peter Malcolm. b 44. Trin Coll Bris 75. **d** 78 **p** 79. C Tonbridge St Steph *Roch* 78-82; R Cobham w Luddesdowne and Dode 82-90; V Wythall *Birm* 90-02; rtd 02; Perm to Offic *Birm* from 02. *37 Northbrook Road, Shirley, Solihull B90 3NR* Tel 0121-745 9042

THOMSON, Canon Richard Irving. b 32. Oak Hill Th Coll 57. **d** 60 **p** 61. C Kingston upon Hull H Trin *York* 60-63; C S Croydon Em *Cant* 63-66; V Shoreditch St Leon *Lon* 66-73; Chapl Vevey w Château d'Oex and Villars *Eur* 73-78; V Reigate St Mary *S'wark* 78-97; Hon Can S'wark Cathl 90-97; rtd 97; Perm to Offic *Win* from 97. *Little Heathfield, Forest Front, Dibden Purlieu, Southampton SO45 3RG* Tel (023) 8084 9613
E-mail richardithomson@compuserve.com

THOMSON, Richard William Byars. b 60. Birm Univ BA86. Ripon Coll Cuddesdon 86. **d** 88 **p** 89. C Moulsecoomb *Chich* 88-90; P-in-c Kirriemuir *St And* 90-94; P-in-c Piddletrenthide w Plush, Alton Pancras etc *Sarum* 94-02; P-in-c Milborne St Andrew w Dewlish 94-02; Chapl Milton Abbey Sch Dorset from 02. *Nether Fen, Milton Abbey, Blandford Forum DT11 0DA* Tel (01258) 881513 E-mail byars22@aol.com

THOMSON, Robert Douglass. b 37. Lon Univ TCert61 Newc Univ DAES70 Dur Univ BEd75. NEOC 76. **d** 79 **p** 80. NSM Shincliffe *Dur* 79-98; Chapl St Aid Coll Dur 93-99. *11 Hill Meadows, High Shincliffe, Durham DH1 2PE* Tel 0191-386 3358

THOMSON, Robin Alexander Stewart. b 43. Ch Coll Cam MA69 K Coll Lon MTh72. SEITE 94. **d** 96 **p** 97. NSM Wimbledon Em Ridgway Prop Chpl *S'wark* 96-02; NSM Tooting Graveney St Nic from 02. *2 Coppice Close, London SW20 9AS* Tel (020) 8540 7748 *or* 8770 9717 Fax 8770 9747
E-mail 100126.3641@compuserve.com

THOMSON, Canon Ronald. b 24. Leeds Univ BA49. Coll of Resurr Mirfield 49. **d** 51 **p** 52. C Sunderland *Dur* 51-54; C Attercliffe w Carbrook *Sheff* 54-57; V Shiregreen St Hilda 57-73; RD Ecclesfield 72-73; V Worsbrough 73-88; RD Tankersley 75-85; Hon Can Sheff Cathl 77-88; rtd 88; Perm to Offic *Sheff* from 88. *4 St Mary's Garden, Worsbrough, Barnsley S70 5LU* Tel (01226) 203553

THOMSON, Ronald Arthur. b 29. G&C Coll Cam BA53 MA57. Ripon Hall Ox. **d** 57 **p** 58. C Sanderstead All SS *S'wark* 57-60; C Kidbrooke St Jas 60-62; Chapl RAF 62-68; C Amersham *Ox* 68; R Watton at Stone *St Alb* 68-94; rtd 94. *Ashby, 65 Edmonds Drive, Aston Brook, Stevenage SG2 9TJ* Tel (01438) 362192

THOMSON, Russell. b 39. AKC62. **d** 63 **p** 64. C Hackney *Lon* 63-66; C Plumstead Wm Temple Ch Abbey Wood CD *S'wark* 66-69; TV Strood *Roch* 69-75; V Gillingham St Mary 75-89; V Roch 89-04; Chapl St Bart Hosp Roch 89-94; Chapl Medway NHS Trust 94-04; Chapl Wisdom Hospice 89-04; rtd 04. *Little Heath, Shepherds Way, Fairlight, Hastings TN35 4BD* Tel and fax (01424) 812526

THOMSON, Wendy Leigh. b 64. Trin W Univ Vancouver BA87. Wycliffe Hall Ox BTh99. **d** 00 **p** 01. C Oulton Broad *Nor* 00-04; C Chatteris *Ely* from 04. *The Vicarage, Church Lane, Chatteris PE16 6JA* Tel (01354) 692173 E-mail oxthomson@aol.com

THOMSON, Mrs Winifred Mary. b 35. St Mary's Coll Dur BA57 MA58 Lon Univ 86. Qu Coll Birm 79. **dss** 82 **d** 87 **p** 94. Leic H Spirit *Leic* 82-86; Oadby 86-87; Par Dn 87-92; rtd 93; Perm to Offic *Leic* 93-03. *140 Knighton Church Road, Leicester LE2 3JJ* Tel 0116-270 5863

THOMSON GIBSON, Thomas. *See* GIBSON, Thomas Thomson

THOMSON-GLOVER, Canon William Hugh. b 28. Trin Hall Cam BA52 MA56. Cuddesdon Coll 52. **d** 54 **p** 55. C Stepney St Dunstan and All SS *Lon* 54-58; C Tiverton St Andr *Ex* 58-60; P-in-c 60-63; Chapl Clifton Coll Bris 63-69; V Bris Lockleaze St Mary Magd w St Fran *Bris* 70-76; P-in-c Sherston Magna w Easton Grey 76-81; P-in-c Luckington w Alderton 76-81; V Sherston Magna, Easton Grey, Luckington etc 81-93; P-in-c Foxley w Bremilham 84-86; RD Malmesbury 88-93; Hon Can Bris Cathl 91-93; rtd 93; Perm to Offic *Ex* from 93. *Woodgate Farm House, Woodgate, Culmstock, Cullompton EX15 3HW* Tel (01884) 841465

THORBURN, Guy Douglas Anderson. b 50. Ridley Hall Cam. **d** 83 **p** 84. C Putney St Marg *S'wark* 83-87; R Moresby *Carl* 87-97; V Gt Clacton *Chelmsf* from 97. *St John's Vicarage, Valley Road, Clacton-on-Sea CO15 4AR* Tel (01255) 423435
E-mail revguy.thorburn@virgin.net

THORBURN, Peter Hugh. b 17. Worc Coll Ox BA41 MA43. Wells Th Coll 46. **d** 47 **p** 48. C Mill Hill Jo Keble Ch *Lon* 47-51; Lon Dioc Home Missr Colindale St Matthias 51; V 51-54; V Wigan St Mich *Liv* 54-65; USA 65-68; V Chipping Sodbury and Old Sodbury *Glouc* 68-72; Chapl Withington Hosp Man 72-82; rtd 82; Perm to Offic *B & W* from 83; *Bris* from 85; *Lon* 85-97; Warden Servants of Ch the K from 89. *8 Stoberry Crescent, Wells BA5 2TG* Tel (01749) 672919

THORBURN, Simon Godfrey. b 51. Newc Univ BSc73 Fitzw Coll Cam BA77 MA81. Westcott Ho Cam 75. **d** 78 **p** 79. C Stafford St Mary and St Chad *Lich* 78-79; C Stafford 79-82; C Tettenhall Regis 82-83; TV 83-90; Soc Resp Officer *S'wark* 90-97; V Edgbaston St Geo *Birm* from 97; AD Edgbaston from 03; Chapl St Geo Sch Edgbaston from 99. *St George's Vicarage, 3 Westbourne Road, Birmingham B15 3TH* Tel 0121-454 2303
E-mail thorbesp@aol.com

THORESEN, Ms Alveen Fern. b 46. Avondale Coll NSW BA(Ed)69 Newc Univ Aus BA76 New England Univ NSW MA82. St Alb and Ox Min Course 96. **d** 01 **p** 02. NSM Caversham and Mapledurham *Ox* from 01. *1 Crescent Court, Crescent Road, Reading RG1 5SJ* Tel 0118-926 7119
E-mail alveen.thoresen@mon.bbc.co.uk

THORLEY, Canon Barry. b 44. Westcott Ho Cam 70. **d** 73 **p** 74. C Camberwell St Giles *S'wark* 73-76; C Moseley St Mary *Birm* 76-78; V Birchfield 78-83; V Brixton St Matt *S'wark* 84-89; C Greenwich St Alfege 96-00; C Thamesmead 00-01; TR from 01; Hon Can Zanzibar from 04. *Thamesmead Rectory, 22 Manor Close, London SE28 8EY* Tel (020) 8312 9770 *or* 8310 6814

THORLEY, Mrs Mary Kathleen. b 53. OBE00. Univ of Wales (Swansea) BA74 Glos Coll of Educn PGCE75. St Mich Coll Llan 99. **d** 02 **p** 03. NSM Carmarthen St Pet *St D* from 02. *Bryn Heulog, Heol Penllanffos, Carmarthen SA31 2HL* Tel (01267) 235927

THORLEY-PAICE, Alan. *See* PAICE, Alan

THORN (formerly KINGS), Mrs Jean Alison. b 63. RGN85 Heythrop Coll Lon MTh. Cranmer Hall Dur BA90. **d** 91 **p** 93. Chapl Bris Poly *Bris* 91-92; Chapl UWE 92-95; Hon C Bris Lockleaze St Mary Magd w St Fran 91-95; C Fishponds All SS 95-96; Hon C 96-97; V Bris Ch the Servant Stockwood 97-01; Hon C Whitchurch 01-04. *The Rectory, Church Street, Burton Bradstock, Bridport DT6 4QS* Tel (01308) 898799

THORN, Mrs Pamela Mary. b 46. Brentwood Coll of Educn BEd78. EAMTC 01. **d** 04 **p** 05. NSM Waterbeach *Ely* from 04. *31 Lode Avenue, Waterbeach, Cambridge CB5 9PX* Tel (01223) 864262 Mobile 07989-491557
E-mail trevor-pam@tthorn.freeserve.co.uk

THORN, Peter. b 50. Man Poly BEd79. Ridley Hall Cam 82. **d** 84 **p** 85. C Aughton Ch Ch *Liv* 84-87; C Skelmersdale St Paul 87-90; Dioc Children's Officer 87-92; P-in-c Croft w Southworth 90-92; C Streatley *St Alb* 92-95; R Blofield w Hemblington *Nor* 95-96; P-in-c 96-99; Assoc Dioc Dir of Tr 97-99; V Sheff St Bart *Sheff* 99-01; P-in-c Shotley *St E* from 01. *The Vicarage, 2 Gate Farm Road, Shotley, Ipswich IP9 1QH* Tel (01473) 788166 Mobile 07810-363291 E-mail peterthorn15@hotmail.com

THORN, Robert Anthony D'Venning. b 54. AKC76. Chich Th Coll 75. **d** 77 **p** 78. C Bodmin *Truro* 77-80; TV N Hill w Altarnon, Bolventor and Lewannick 80-83; V Feock and Dioc Ecum Officer 83-90; Broadcasting Officer *Linc* 90-93; V Whitchurch *Bris* 93-04; TR Bride Valley *Sarum* from 04. *The Rectory, Church Street, Burton Bradstock, Bridport DT6 4QS* Tel (01308) 898799

THORNBOROUGH (née O'MEARA), Ms Colette Margaret Mary. b 63. Univ of Wales (Abth) BA85. Moorlands Bible Coll. **d** 98 **p** 99. C Much Woolton *Liv* 98-02; V Blundellsands St Nic from 02. *St Nicholas' Vicarage, Nicholas Road, Blundellsands, Liverpool L23 6TS* Tel 0151-924 3551
E-mail revcolette@aol.com

THORNBURGH, Richard Hugh Perceval. b 52. Sarum & Wells Th Coll. **d** 84 **p** 85. C Broadstone *Sarum* 84-87; TV Beaminster Area 87-95; TV Hanley H Ev *Lich* 96-01; R S Elmham and Ilketshall *St E* from 01. *Parsonage House, Low Street, Ilketshall St Margaret, Bungay NR35 1QZ* Tel and fax (01986) 781345
E-mail richard.thornburgh@btinternet.com

THORNBURY, Peter Dawson. b 43. Open Univ BA84 TCD BTh93. CITC 90. **d** 93 **p** 94. C Annagh w Drumgoon, Ashfield etc *K, E & A* 93-96; I Clondehorkey w Cashel *D & R* 96-98; I Mevagh w Glenalla 96-98; Bp's C Kilsaran w Drumcar, Dunleer and Dunany *Arm* from 98. *Kilsaran Rectory, Dromisken Road, Castlebellingham, Dundalk, Co Louth, Irish Republic* Tel (00353) (42) 937 2523 Mobile 86-805 1926

THORNE, Mrs Anita Dawn. b 46. Trin Coll Bris 84. **dss** 86 **d** 87 **p** 94. Asst Chapl Bris Poly *Bris* 86-88; Par Dn Olveston 88-94; P-in-c 94-96; P-in-c Portland All SS w St Pet *Sarum* 96-05; P-in-c Clutton w Cameley *B & W* from 05. *The Rectory, Main Road, Temple Cloud, Bristol BS39 5DA* Tel (01761) 451248 *or* 451315

THORNE, Mrs Anne. b 55. SW Minl Tr Course 95. **d** 98 **p** 99. C Crediton and Shobrooke *Ex* 98-01; C Crediton, Shobrooke and Sandford etc 01; C Beer and Branscombe 01-03; C Seaton and Beer from 03. *The Vicarage, Mare Lane, Beer, Seaton EX12 3NB* Tel (01297) 20996 E-mail vicarthorne@aol.com

THORNE, Mrs Marie Elizabeth. b 47. EMMTC 83. **dss** 86 **d** 87 **p** 94. Cleethorpes *Linc* 86-90; C 87-90; C Brigg 90-96; P-in-c New Waltham 96-00; V from 00. *The Vicarage, 41 Dunbar Avenue, New Waltham, Grimsby DN36 4PY* Tel (01472) 589998
E-mail thorne@fish.co.uk

THORNETT, Frederick Charles. b 34. Harris Coll CQSW68. LNSM course. **d** 85 **p** 86. OLM Skegness and Winthorpe *Linc* 85-90; C New Sleaford 90-92; P-in-c Harlaxton 92-95; R Harlaxton Gp 95-99; rtd 99; Perm to Offic *Linc* 99-02. *93 Boston Road, Spilsby PE23 5HH* Tel (01790) 754151

THORNEWILL, Canon Mark Lyon. b 25. ALCD56. **d** 56 **p** 58. C-in-c Bradf Cathl *Bradf* 56-59; C-in-c Otley 59-62; R Lifton *Ex* 62-66; R Kelly w Bradstone 62-66; USA from 66; Dir Past Care Norton Hosps Louisville KY 69-84; Hon Can Louisville Cathl from 70; rtd 90. *Soma House, 116 East Campbell Street, Frankfort, KY 40601, USA* Tel (001) (502) 696 9274
E-mail mthornewil@aol.com

THORNEYCROFT, Preb Pippa Hazel Jeanetta. b 44. Ex Univ BA65. Qu Coll Birm 85 WMMTC. **d** 88 **p** 94. NSM Albrighton *Lich* 88-90; NSM Beckbury, Badger, Kemberton, Ryton, Stockton etc 90-96; P-in-c Shareshill from 96; Dioc Adv for Women in Min 93-00; Preb Lich Cathl from 99; RD Penkridge from 01; Chapl to The Queen from 01. *The Vicarage, 11 Brookhouse Lane, Featherstone, Wolverhampton WV10 7AW* Tel and fax (01902) 727579 Mobile 07970-869011
E-mail pippa@thorneycroft.plus.com

THORNILEY, Richard James Gordon. b 56. Portsm Poly BA78. St Jo Coll Nottm MTh95. **d** 97 **p** 98. C Bowbrook S *Worc* 97-01; R Church Lench w Rous Lench and Abbots Morton etc from 01. *The Rectory, Station Road, Harvington, Evesham WR11 8NJ* Tel (01386) 870527 E-mail richardgill@rthorniley.fsnet.co.uk

THORNLEY, David Howe. b 43. Wycliffe Hall Ox 77. **d** 79 **p** 80. C Burgess Hill St Andr *Chich* 79-83; P-in-c Amberley w N Stoke 83-84; P-in-c Parham and Wiggonholt w Greatham 83-84; V Amberley w N Stoke and Parham, Wiggonholt etc 84-92; P-in-c S w N Bersted from 92. *121 Victoria Drive, Bognor Regis PO21 2EH* Tel (01243) 862018

THORNLEY, Geoffrey Pearson. b 23. Pemb Coll Cam BA47 MA52. Cuddesdon Coll. **d** 50 **p** 51. C Stepney St Dunstan and All SS *Lon* 50-53; Chapl RN 53-73; Bp's Dom Chapl *Linc* 73-75; P-in-c Riseholme 73-78; P-in-c Scothern w Sudbrooke 77-78; V Dunholme 75-85; Hon PV Linc Cathl 75-85; rtd 85; Chapl Allnutt's Hosp Goring Heath 85-96. *c/o E Hylton, Messrs Humphrey & Co, 8-9 The Avenue, Eastbourne BN21 3YA* Tel (01323) 730631 Fax 738355

THORNLEY, Canon Nicholas Andrew. b 56. St Jo Coll Nottm BTh81. **d** 81 **p** 84. C Frodingham *Linc* 81-84; P-in-c Belton 84-85; V 85-90; V Horncastle w Low Toynton 90-98; V High Toynton 98; R Greetham w Ashby Puerorum 98; RD Horncastle 94-98; TR Gainsborough and Morton from 98; Can and Preb Linc Cathl from 98. *Gainsborough Rectory, 32 Morton Terrace, Gainsborough DN21 1RQ* Tel (01427) 612965
E-mail nick@gains98.fsnet.co.uk

THORNS, Mrs Joanne. b 64. Sunderland Univ BSc86 MRPharmS. Cranmer Hall Dur DTM99. **d** 99 **p** 00. C Norton St Mary *Dur* 99-04; C Stockton St Chad 02-04; TV Dur N from 04. *31 York Crescent, Durham DH1 5PT* Tel 0191-386 8049
E-mail joanne.thorns@durham.anglican.org

THORNTON, Cecil. b 26. Lon Univ BD PhD ThD. Tyndale Hall Bris 47. **d** 50 **p** 51. C Kilmegan *D & D* 50-51; C Dromore Cathl 51-54; I Magherahamlet 54-60; I Inniskeel *D & R* 60-65; I Fahan Lower and Upper 65-88; Can Raphoe Cathl 79-88; rtd 88; Perm to Offic *Conn* from 91. *Cluain-Fois, 38 Ballywillan Road, Portrush BT56 8JN* Tel (028) 7082 4669

THORNTON, Darren Thomas. b 68. Wilson Carlile Coll 90 EAMTC 00. **d** 02 **p** 03. C E Dereham and Scarning *Nor* 02-05; Chapl UEA from 05; P-in-c Nor St Giles from 05. *St Giles's Vicarage, 44 Heigham Road, Norwich NR2 3AU* Tel (01603) 623724 E-mail darrenthornton@hotmail.com

THORNTON, David John Dennis. b 32. Kelham Th Coll 52. **d** 56 **p** 57. C New Eltham All SS *S'wark* 56-58; C Stockwell Green St Andr 58-62; V Tollesbury *Chelmsf* 62-74; P-in-c Salcot Virley 72-74; V Kelvedon 74-00; rtd 00; Perm to Offic *Nor* from 01. *The Old Stable, 24 Pauls Lane, Overstrand, Cromer NR27 0PE* Tel (01263) 579279

THORNTON, Howard Deyes. b 52. Canadian Th Sem MA99. **d** 01 **p** 03. NSM Hanborough and Freeland *Ox* 01-02; C Luton St Mary *St Alb* 02-04; Chapl Luton Univ from 02. *33 Felix Avenue, Luton LU2 7LE* Tel (01582) 724754 *or* 734111
E-mail oxfordpilgrims@hotmail.com

THORNTON, John. b 26. St Edm Hall Ox BA53 MA57. Westcott Ho Cam 53. **d** 55 **p** 56. C Woodhall Spa *Linc* 55-58; C Glouc St Steph *Glouc* 58-60; C Wotton St Mary 60-62; P-in-c Gt Witcombe 62-63; R 63-91; Chapl HM Pris Glouc 82-91; rtd 91; Perm to Offic *Glouc* from 91. *24 Spencer Close, Hucclecote, Gloucester GL3 3EA* Tel (01452) 619775

THORNTON, Magdalen Mary. *See* SMITH, Mrs Magdalen Mary

THORNTON, Peter Stuart. b 36. St Pet Hall Ox BA59 MA67. Cuddesdon Coll 59. **d** 61 **p** 62. C E Coatham *York* 61-64; C Scarborough St Martin 64-67; R Seaton Ross w Everingham and Bielby and Harswell 67-81; RD Weighton 75-85; P-in-c Thornton w Allerthorpe 80-81; R Seaton Ross Gp of Par 81-85; V York St Lawr w St Nic 85-01; Asst Chapl York Health Services NHS Trust 93-02; rtd 01; Perm to Offic *York* from 01. *138 Lawrence Street, York YO10 3EB* Tel (01904) 423648

THORNTON, Timothy Charles Gordon. b 35. Ch Ch Ox BA58 MA61. Linc Th Coll 60. **d** 62 **p** 63. C Kirkholt CD *Man* 62-64; Tutor Linc Th Coll 64-68; Chapl 66-68; Fiji 69-73; Chapl Brasted Place Coll Westerham 73-74; Can Missr *Guildf* 74-79; P-in-c Hascombe 74-79; V Chobham w Valley End 79-84; V Spelsbury and Chadlington *Ox* 84-87; V Chadlington and Spelsbury, Ascott under Wychwood 87-00; rtd 00; Perm to Offic *Carl* from 01. *The Old Cottage, Warcop, Appleby-in-Westmorland CA16 6NX* Tel (01768) 341239

✠**THORNTON, The Rt Revd Timothy Martin.** b 57. Southn Univ BA78 K Coll Lon MA97. St Steph Ho Ox 78. **d** 80 **p** 81 **c** 01. C Todmorden *Wakef* 80-82; P-in-c Walsden 82-85; Lect Univ of Wales (Cardiff) *Llan* 85-87; Chapl 85-86; Sen Chapl 86-87; Bp's Chapl *Wakef* 87-91; Dir of Ords 88-91; Bp's Chapl *Lon* 91-94; Dep P in O 92-01; Prin NTMTC 94-98; V Kensington St Mary Abbots w St Geo *Lon* 98-01; AD Kensington 00-01; Area Bp Sherborne *Sarum* from 01. *Sherborne House, Tower Hill, Iwerne Minster, Blandford Forum DT11 8NH* Tel (01747) 812766 E-mail tim.thornton@talk21.com

THOROGOOD, John Martin. b 45. Birm Univ BA68 PGCE69. Ox NSM Course 82. **d** 85 **p** 86. NSM Sunningdale *Ox* 85-90; Chapl St Geo Sch Ascot 88-90; TV Camelot Par *B & W* 90-97; V Evercreech w Chesterblade and Milton Clevedon 97-03; RD Cary and Bruton 96-03; R Dulverton and Brushford from 03; RD Exmoor from 05. *The Vicarage, High Street, Dulverton TA22 9DW* Tel (01398) 323425
E-mail rev@johnthevicar.freeserve.co.uk

THOROLD, Jeremy Stephen. b 59. **d** 04 **p** 05. OLM Gainsborough and Morton *Linc* from 04. *The Wheelhouse, Laughton Lane, Morton, Gainsborough DN21 3ET* Tel (01427) 610837 Mobile 07718-911714
E-mail jerry.thorold@lincs.pnn.police.uk

THOROLD, John Robert Hayford. b 16. K Coll Cam BA43 MA45. Cuddesdon Coll 42. **d** 42 **p** 43. C Cheltenham St Mary *Glouc* 42-44; C Limehouse St Anne *Lon* 44-45; Tutor Ripon Hall Ox 47-52; V Mitcham SS Pet and Paul *S'wark* 52-86; OGS from 53; rtd 87; Perm to Offic *Blackb* 87-96; Hon Fell St Deiniol's Lib Hawarden from 00. *St Deiniol's Library, Hawarden, Deeside CH5 3DF* Tel (01244) 532350

THOROLD, Canon John Stephen. b 35. Bps' Coll Cheshunt 61. **d** 63 **p** 64. C Cleethorpes *Linc* 63-70; V Cherry Willingham w Greetwell 70-77; P-in-c Firsby w Gt Steeping 77-79; R 79-86; R Aswardby w Sausthorpe 77-86; R Halton Holgate 77-86; R Langton w Sutterby 77-86; V Spilsby w Hundleby 77-86; R Lt Steeping 79-86; R Raithby 79-86; V New Sleaford 86-01; RD Lafford 87-96; Can and Preb Linc Cathl 98-01; rtd 01; Perm to Offic *Linc* from 01. *8 Ashwood Close, Horncastle LN9 5HA* Tel (01507) 526562

THOROLD, Trevor Neil. b 63. Hull Univ BA87. Ripon Coll Cuddesdon 87. **d** 89 **p** 90. C W Bromwich St Andr w Ch Ch *Lich* 89-93; Res Min Oswestry 93-97; P-in-c Petton w Cockshutt, Welshampton and Lyneal etc 97-05; Local Min Adv (Shrewsbury) 97-05; RD Ellesmere 98-02. *32 The Knolls, Bicton Heath, Shrewsbury SY3 5DR* Tel (01743) 352934

THORP, Adrian. b 55. Clare Coll Cam BA77 MA80 Lon Univ BD80. Trin Coll Bris 77. **d** 80 **p** 81. C Kendal St Thos *Carl* 80-83; C Handforth *Ches* 83-86; V Siddal *Wakef* 86-91; V Bishopwearmouth St Gabr *Dur* from 91. *The Vicarage, 1 St Gabriel's Avenue, Sunderland SR4 7TF* Tel 0191-567 5200

THORP, Catherine. b 57. St Luke's Coll Ex BEd79. Oak Hill Th Coll 93. **d** 96 **p** 02. NSM Watford Ch Ch *St Alb* 96-99; NSM Kings Langley from 99. *111 Barton Way, Croxley Green, Rickmansworth WD3 3PB* Tel and fax (01923) 442713
E-mail cthorp57@hotmail.com

THORP, Miss Eileen Margaret. b 31. **d** 95 **p** 96. NSM Daventry, Ashby St Ledgers, Braunston etc *Pet* 95-02; rtd 02; Perm to Offic *Pet* from 02. *Waterside, Dark Lane, Braunston, Daventry NN11 7HJ* Tel (01788) 890321

THORP, Mrs Helen Mary. b 54. Bris Univ BA75 MA(Theol)77 DipHE Dur Univ MA98. Trin Coll Bris 78. **d** 87 **p** 94. NSM Siddal *Wakef* 87-91; NSM Bishopwearmouth St Gabr *Dur* from 91; Voc Adv from 93. *The Vicarage, 1 St Gabriel's Avenue, Sunderland SR4 7TF* Tel 0191-567 5200

THORP, Mrs Maureen Sandra. b 47. Man OLM Scheme 92. **d** 95 **p** 96. OLM Heywood *Man* 95-01; P-in-c Shore from 01; P-in-c Calderbrook from 01. *The Vicarage, 4 Stansfield Hall, Littleborough OL15 9RH* Tel (01706) 378414
E-mail tel.mo@virgin.uk

THORP, Norman Arthur. b 29. DMA63. Tyndale Hall Bris 63. **d** 65 **p** 66. C Southsea St Jude *Portsm* 65-68; C Braintree *Chelmsf* 68-73; P-in-c Tolleshunt D'Arcy w Tolleshunt Major 73-75; V 75-83; R N Buckingham *Ox* 83-95; RD Buckingham 90-95; rtd 95; Perm to Offic *Ox* 97-00. *20 Swimbridge Lane, Furzton, Milton Keynes MK4 1JT* Tel (01908) 506342

THORP, Roderick Cheyne. b 44. Ch Ch Ox BA65 MA69. Ridley Hall Cam 66. **d** 69 **p** 70. C Reading Greyfriars *Ox* 69-73; C Kingston upon Hull St Martin *York* 73-76; C Heworth H Trin 76-79; C-in-c N Bletchley CD *Ox* 79-86; TV Washfield, Stoodleigh, Withleigh etc *Ex* 86-96; RD Tiverton 91-96; P-in-c Dolton 96-00; P-in-c Iddesleigh w Dowland 96-00; P-in-c Monkokehampton 96-00; rtd 00; P-in-c Etton w Dalton Holme *York* from 00. *The Rectory, Main Street, Etton, Beverley HU17 7PQ* Tel (01430) 810735 E-mail aranjay@freeuk.com

THORP, Stephen Linton. b 62. Trin Coll Bris BA92. **d** 92 **p** 93. C Knutsford St Jo and Toft *Ches* 92-96; TV Newton Tracey, Horwood, Alverdiscott etc *Ex* from 96. *The Rectory, Beaford, Winkleigh EX19 8NN* Tel (01805) 603213
E-mail slthorp@tiscali.co.uk

THORP, Timothy. b 65. St Steph Ho Ox BTh93. **d** 96 **p** 97. C Jarrow *Dur* 96-99; P-in-c N Hylton St Marg Castletown 99-02; C Felpham *Chich* from 02; Missr Arundel and Bognor from 02. *3 Byron Close, Bognor Regis PO22 6QU* Tel (01243) 582511
E-mail fathertimt@bigfoot.com

THORPE, Christopher David Charles. b 60. Cov Poly BA83. Ripon Coll Cuddesdon 85. **d** 88 **p** 89. C Norton *St Alb* 88-92; TV Blakenall Heath *Lich* 92-99; TR Bilston from 99. *St Leonard's Vicarage, Dover Street, Bilston WV14 6AW* Tel (01902) 491560
E-mail chris@christhorpe.org

THORPE, Donald Henry. b 34. St Aid Birkenhead 57. **d** 60 **p** 61. C Mexborough *Sheff* 60-64; C Doncaster St Leon and St Jude 64-67; V Doncaster Intake 67-74; V Millhouses H Trin 74-85; Prec Leic Cathl *Leic* 85-89; TR Melton Gt Framland 89-93; rtd 93; Perm to Offic *Sheff* and *S'well* from 93. *18 All Hallows Drive, Tickhill, Doncaster DN11 9PP* Tel (01302) 743129
E-mail dsthorpe@waitrose.com

THORPE, Kerry Michael. b 51. Lon Univ BD78. Oak Hill Th Coll DipTh76. **d** 78 **p** 79. C Upton (Overchurch) *Ches* 78-81; C Chester le Street *Dur* 81-84; V Fatfield 84-93; V Margate H Trin *Cant* 93-98; C from 98. *1 Wealdhurst Park, St Peter's, Broadstairs CT10 2LD* Tel (01843) 871183
E-mail kerrythorpe@harvestnac.freeserve.co.uk

THORPE, Lynne Gail. b 62. Dioc OLM tr scheme 99. **d** 02 **p** 03. OLM Ipswich St Jo *St E* from 02. *31 King Edward Road, Ipswich IP3 9AN* Tel (01473) 717833

THORPE, Martin Xavier. b 66. Collingwood Coll Dur BSc87 Bris Univ MPhil00 GRSC87. Trin Coll Bris BA94. **d** 94 **p** 95. C Ravenhead *Liv* 94-98; TV Sutton 98-02; Asst Dir CME from 01; V Westbrook St Phil from 02. *St Philip's Vicarage, 89 Westbrook Crescent, Warrington WA5 8TN* Tel and fax (01925) 654400
E-mail martinpol.thorpe@talk21.com
or martin.cme1-4@talk21.com

THORPE, Michael William. b 42. Lich Th Coll 67. **d** 70 **p** 71. C Walthamstow St Mich *Chelmsf* 70-71; C Plaistow St Andr 71; P-in-c Plaistow St Mary 72-74; TV Gt Grimsby St Mary and St Jas *Linc* 74-78; Chapl Grimsby Distr Hosps 78-83; Chapl Roxbourne, Northwick Park and Harrow Hosps 83-87; Chapl St Geo Linc and Linc Co Hosps 87-92; Chapl Ipswich Hosp NHS Trust 92-00; rtd 00. *Moselle Cottage, 68 Lacey Street, Ipswich IP4 2PH* Tel (01473) 421850

THORPE, Richard Charles. b 65. Birm Univ BSc87. Wycliffe Hall Ox 93. **d** 96 **p** 97. C Brompton H Trin w Onslow Square St Paul *Lon* 96-05; P-in-c Shadwell St Paul w Ratcliffe St Jas from 05. *St Paul's Rectory, 298 The Highway, London E1W 3DH* Tel (020) 7481 2883 E-mail ric.thorpe@stpaulsshadwell.org

THORPE, Trevor Cecil. b 21. Em Coll Cam BA47 MA52. Ridley Hall Cam 48. **d** 50 **p** 51. C Farnborough *Guildf* 50-53; C W Ham All SS *Chelmsf* 53-57; V N Weald Bassett from 57. *The Vicarage, Vicarage Lane, North Weald, Epping CM16 6AL* Tel (01992) 522246

THRALL, Canon Margaret Eleanor. b 28. Girton Coll Cam BA50 MA54 PhD60 Cam Univ BA52. Ban Ord Course 81. **d** 82 **p** 97. Asst Chapl Univ of Wales (Ban) *Ban* 82-88; Lect Th Univ of Wales (Ban) 83-96; Hon Can Ban Cathl *Ban* 94-98; rtd 98; Perm to Offic *Ban* from 98. *Address temp unknown*

THRELFALL-HOLMES, Miranda. b 73. Ch Coll Cam BA95 MA99 Univ Coll Dur MA97 PhD00 St Jo Coll Dur BA02. Cranmer Hall Dur 00. **d** 03 **p** 04. C Newc St Gabr *Newc* from 03. *26 Crompton Road, Heaton, Newcastle upon Tyne NE6 5QL* Tel 0191-276 0215 E-mail rev.miranda@dsl.pipex.com

THROSSELL, John Julian. b 30. Nottm Univ BSc53 Syracuse Univ PhD56. Oak Hill Th Coll 72. **d** 75 **p** 76. NSM Wheathampstead *St Alb* 75-82; V Codicote 82-88; NSM Halesworth w Linstead, Chediston, Holton etc *St E* 89-95; rtd 91. *2 Little Horringer Hall Cottages, Horringer, Bury St Edmunds IP29 5PN* Tel (01284) 735088

THROWER, Clive Alan. b 41. Sheff Univ BSc62 CEng90. EMMTC 76. **d** 79 **p** 80. C Derby Cathl *Derby* 79-86; C Spondon 86-91; Soc Resp Officer 86-91; Faith in the City Link Officer 88-91; Dioc Rural Officer 91; P-in-c Ashford w Sheldon 91; V Ashford w Sheldon and Longstone from 92; Dioc Rural and Tourism Officer from 96; RD Bakewell and Eyam from 04. *The Vicarage, Church Lane, Great Longstone, Bakewell DE45 1TB* Tel (01629) 640257 Fax 640657 E-mail clive@thrower.org.uk

THROWER, Martin Charles. b 61. EAMTC 95. **d** 98 **p** 99. NSM Ipswich St Bart *St E* 98-01; NSM Bury St Edmunds All SS w St Jo and St Geo 01-03; P-in-c Gt and Lt Whelnetham w Bradfield St George 03-04; P-in-c Lawshall 03-04; P-in-c Hawstead and Nowton w Stanningfield etc 03-04; R St Edm Way from 04; RD Lavenham from 05. *The Rectory, Harrow Green, Lawshall, Bury St Edmunds IP29 4PB* Tel (01284) 830855 E-mail martin.thrower@btinternet.com

THROWER, Philip Edward. b 41. Kelham Th Coll 61. **d** 66 **p** 67. C Hayes St Mary *Lon* 66-69; C Yeovil *B & W* 69-71; C Shirley St Jo *Cant* 71-77; P-in-c S Norwood St Mark 77-81; V 81-84; V S Norwood St Mark *S'wark* 85-97; V Malden St Jas from 97. *St James's Vicarage, 7 Bodley Road, New Malden KT3 5QD* Tel (020) 8942 1860 *or* 8942 5070

THRUSH, Margaret. b 37. St Mary's Coll Dur BA60. Cranmer Hall Dur BA96 DMS97. **d** 97 **p** 98. NSM Houghton le Spring *Dur* 97-03; NSM Pittington, Shadforth and Sherburn from 03. *45 Highgate, Durham DH1 4GA* Tel 0191-386 1958

THUBRON, Thomas William. b 33. Edin Th Coll 62. **d** 65 **p** 66. C Gateshead St Mary *Dur* 65-66; C Shildon 66-67; E Pakistan 68-71; Bangladesh 71-80; V Wheatley Hill *Dur* 80-87; V Dur St Giles 87-98; rtd 98. *The Old Vicarage, Gable Terrace, Wheatley Hill, Durham DH6 3RA* Tel (01429) 823940

THURBURN-HUELIN, David Richard. b 47. St Chad's Coll Dur BA69 Ex Univ MA98. Westcott Ho Cam 69. **d** 71 **p** 72. C Poplar *Lon* 71-76; Chapl Liddon Ho Lon 76-80; R Harrold and Carlton w Chellington *St Alb* 81-88; V Goldington 88-95; Dir OLM *Truro* 95-00; P-in-c Shipston-on-Stour w Honington and Idlicote *Cov* from 01. *Shipston Rectory, 8 Glen Close, Shipston-on-Stour CV36 4ED* Tel (01608) 661724 E-mail thurburn@fish.co.uk

THURGILL, Sally Elizabeth. b 60. **d** 02 **p** 03. OLM Mattishall w Mattishall Burgh, Welborne etc *Nor* from 02. *3 Dereham Road, Yaxham, Dereham NR19 1RF* Tel (01362) 692745 E-mail csmsthurgill@ukonline.co.uk

THURLOW, Ms Judith Mary Buller. b 44. Ch Ch Coll Cant CertEd63 Natal Univ DipEd78 BTh94 MTh00. **d** 95 **p** 96. S Africa 95-00; C Port Shepstone St Kath 95-98; C Durban St Paul 99-00; C Orpington All SS *Roch* 00-02; R Kingsdown from 02. *The Rectory, School Lane, West Kingsdown, Sevenoaks TN15 6JL* Tel and fax (01474) 852265 Mobile 07949-272106 E-mail judiththurlow@ukgateway.net

THURMER, Canon John Alfred. b 25. Oriel Coll Ox BA50 MA55 Ex Univ Hon DD91. Linc Th Coll 50. **d** 52 **p** 53. C Lt Ilford St Mich *Chelmsf* 52-55; Chapl and Lect Sarum Th Coll 55-64; Chapl Ex Univ *Ex* 64-73; Lect 64-85; Can Res and Chan Ex Cathl 73-91; rtd 91; Perm to Offic *Ex* from 91. *38 Velwell Road, Exeter EX4 4LD* Tel (01392) 272277

THURSFIELD, John Anthony. b 21. Magd Coll Ox BA47 MA51. Cuddesdon Coll 47. **d** 49 **p** 50. V Basing *Win* 60-72; Chapl Bonn w Cologne *Eur* 72-75; R E Clandon *Guildf* 75-79; R W Clandon 75-79; V Reydon *St E* 79-83; Perm to Offic *Heref* 84-93 and from 96; rtd 86. *Little Homend, The Homend, Ledbury HR8 1AR* Tel (01531) 632935

THURSTON, Ian Charles. b 54. SS Hild & Bede Coll Dur CertEd78. S Dios Minl Tr Scheme 87. **d** 89 **p** 90. C St Chris Cathl Bahrain 89-91; C All Hallows by the Tower etc *Lon* 91-97; V Tottenham H Trin 97-00; R Cheadle w Freehay *Lich* from 00. *The Rectory, Church Street, Cheadle, Stoke-on-Trent ST10 1HU* Tel (01538) 753337

THURTELL, Victoria Ann. b 59. St Jo Coll Dur BSc82 PGCE96. STETS 02. **d** 05. C Chickerell w Fleet *Sarum* from 05. *6 Marina Gardens, Weymouth DT4 9QZ* Tel (01305) 771216 E-mail vickythurtell@hotmail.com

TIBBO, George Kenneth. b 29. Reading Univ BA50 MA54. Coll of Resurr Mirfield 55. **d** 57 **p** 58. C W Hartlepool St Aid *Dur* 57-61; V Darlington St Mark 61-74; V Darlington St Mark w St Paul 74-75; R Crook 75-80; V Stanley 76-80; V Oldham St Chad Limeside *Man* 80-87; V Hipswell *Ripon* 87-95; OCF 90-95; rtd 95; P-in-c Nidd *Ripon* 95-01; Perm to Offic 02-04; Hon C Saddleworth *Man* from 04. *The Vicarage, Woods Lane, Dobcross, Oldham OL3 5AN* Tel (01457) 829702

TIBBS, Canon John Andrew. b 29. AKC53. **d** 54 **p** 55. C Eastbourne St Mary *Chich* 54-57; S Africa 57-62; C Bourne *Guildf* 62-64; Swaziland 64-68; V Sompting *Chich* 69-73; R Ifield 73-78; TR 78-83; V Elstow *St Alb* 83-89; rtd 90; Chapl Bedf Gen Hosp 90-95; Hon Can St Alb 91-95; Perm to Offic from 00. *19 Adelaide Square, Bedford MK40 2RN* Tel (01234) 308737

TICE, Richard Ian (Rico). b 66. Bris Univ BA88. Wycliffe Hall Ox BTh94. **d** 94 **p** 95. C Langham Place All So *Lon* from 94. *Basement Flat, 141 Cleveland Street, London W1T 6QG* Tel (020) 7388 3280 *or* 7580 3522 E-mail ricospa-grace@allsouls.org

TICKLE, Robert Peter. St Chad's Coll Dur BA74. St Steph Ho Ox 74. **d** 76 **p** 77. *5 Bramley Court, Orchard Lane, Harrold, Bedford MK43 7BG* Tel (01234) 721417

TICKNER, Canon Colin de Fraine. b 37. Chich Th Coll. **d** 66 **p** 67. C Huddersfield SS Pet and Paul *Wakef* 66-68; C Dorking w Ranmore *Guildf* 68-74; V Shottermill 74-91; RD Godalming 89-91; R Ockley, Okewood and Forest Green 91-97; Hon Can Guildf Cathl 96-97; rtd 97; Adv for Past Care *Guildf* from 97; Chapl St Cath Sch Bramley from 97. *11 Linersh Drive, Bramley, Guildford GU5 0EJ* Tel (01483) 898161

TICKNER, David Arthur. b 44. MBE89. AKC67. **d** 69 **p** 70. C Thornhill Lees *Wakef* 69-71; C Billingham St Aid *Dur* 71-74; TV 74-78; CF 78-98; Perm to Offic *Guildf* 96-98; R Heysham *Blackb* from 98. *The Rectory, Main Street, Heysham, Morecambe LA3 2RN* Tel and fax (01524) 851422 E-mail david.tickner@tesco.net

TICKNER, Geoffrey John. b 55. BD. St Mich Coll Llan. **d** 82 **p** 83. C Bourne *Guildf* 82-85; C Grayswood 85-90; V New Haw 90-02; RD Runnymede 98-02; P-in-c Stevenage H Trin *St Alb* from 02. *Holy Trinity Vicarage, 18 Letchmore Road, Stevenage SG1 3JD* Tel (01438) 353229 E-mail vicar@holytrinity-stevenage.info.

TIDESWELL, Mrs Lynne Maureen Ann. b 49. N Ord Course 02. **d** 05. NSM Stoke-upon-Trent *Lich* from 05. *14 High Lane, Cheddleton Heath Road, Leek ST13 7DY* Tel (01538) 361134 E-mail maureen@highlane.plus.com

TIDMARSH, Canon Peter Edwin. b 29. Keble Coll Ox BA52 MA56 DipEd. St Steph Ho Ox 52. **d** 54 **p** 55. C Stepney St Dunstan and All SS *Lon* 54-58; C Streatham St Pet *S'wark* 58-62; Chapl Shiplake Coll Henley 62-64; Hd Master All SS Choir Sch 64-68; C St Marylebone All SS *Lon* 64-68; V Cubert *Truro* from 68; Dir of Educn 69-85; Hon Can Truro Cathl from 73. *The Vicarage, St Cubert, Newquay TR8 5HA* Tel (01637) 830301 E-mail petwww@btinternet.com

TIDSWELL, David Alan. b 42. CEng73 FIEE84. St Steph Ho Ox 99. **d** 00 **p** 01. NSM Forest Row *Chich* from 00. *Manapouri, Hammerwood Road, Ashurst Wood, East Grinstead RH19 3SA* Tel (01342) 822808 Mobile 07932-537410

TIDY, John Hylton. b 48. AKC72 St Aug Coll Cant 72. **d** 73 **p** 74. C Newton Aycliffe *Dur* 73-78; V Auckland St Pet 78-84; V Burley in Wharfedale *Bradf* 84-92; Dean Jerusalem 92-97; V Surbiton St Andr and St Mark *S'wark* from 97; RD Kingston 00-05. *St Mark's Vicarage, 1 Church Hill Road, Surbiton KT6 4UG* Tel (020) 8399 6053 Fax 8390 4928 E-mail jhtidy@blueyonder.co.uk

TIERNAN, Paul Wilson. b 54. Man Univ BA76. Coll of Resurr Mirfield 77. **d** 79 **p** 80. C Lewisham St Mary *S'wark* 79-83; V Sydenham St Phil from 83. *St Philip's Vicarage, 122 Wells Park Road, London SE26 6AS* Tel (020) 8699 4930

TIGWELL, Brian Arthur. b 36. S'wark Ord Course 74. **d** 77 **p** 78. C Purley St Mark *S'wark* 77-80; TV Upper Kennet *Sarum* 80-85; V Devizes St Pet 85-99; Wilts Adnry Ecum Officer 88-99; RD Devizes 92-98; rtd 99; Perm to Offic *Sarum* from 01. *2 Lansdowne Court, Long Street, Devizes SN10 1NJ* Tel (01380) 726177

TILBY, Ms Angela Clare Wyatt. b 50. Girton Coll Cam BA72 MA76. Cranmer Hall Dur 77. **d** 97 **p** 98. Tutor Westcott Ho Cam 97-01; NSM Cherry Hinton St Jo *Ely* from 97; Vice-Prin Westcott Ho Cam from 01. *Westcott House, Jesus Lane, Cambridge CB5 8BP* Tel (01223) 741000 E-mail angelus@easynet.co.uk

TILDESLEY, Edward William David. b 56. SS Hild & Bede Coll Dur BEd79. St Alb and Ox Min Course 93. **d** 96 **p** 97. Chapl Shiplake Coll Henley 96-99; NSM Emmer Green *Ox* 96-99; Chapl Oakham Sch 99-00; TV Dorchester *Ox* from 00. *The Vicarage, Clifton Hampden, Abingdon OX14 3EF* Tel and fax (01865) 407784 Mobile 07803-131332 E-mail etildesley@home.gb.com

TILL, Barry Dorn. b 23. Jes Coll Cam BA49 MA49. Westcott Ho Cam 48. **d** 50 **p** 51. C Bury St Mary *Man* 50-53; Fell Jes Coll Cam 53-60; Chapl 53-56; Dean 56-60; Dean Hong Kong 60-64; Attached Ch Assembly 64-65; Prin Morley Coll Lon 66-87; Dir Baring Foundn 87-92; rtd 92. *44 Canonbury Square, London N1 2AW* Tel (020) 7359 0708

TILL, The Very Revd Michael Stanley. b 35. Linc Coll Ox BA60 MA67. Westcott Ho Cam. **d** 64 **p** 65. C St John's Wood *Lon* 64-67; Chapl K Coll Cam 67-70; Dean 70-80; V Fulham All SS and AD Hammersmith *Lon* 81-86; Adn Cant and Can Res Cant Cathl *Cant* 86-96; Dean Win from 96. *The Deanery, The Close, Winchester SO23 9LS* Tel and fax (01962) 853738 *or* 857203 E-mail the.dean@winchester-cathedral.org.uk

TILLBROOK, Richard Ernest. b 50. St Mark & St Jo Coll Lon CertEd71 ACP76. NTMTC DipTh99. **d** 99 **p** 00. Hd RE Davenant Foundn Sch Loughton 71-03; NSM High Laver w Magdalen Laver and Lt Laver etc *Chelmsf* 99-03; V Colchester St Barn from 03. *St Barnabas' Vicarage, 13 Abbot's Road, Colchester CO2 8BE* Tel (01206) 797481 Mobile 07818-440530

TILLER, Edgar Henry. b 22. ACP71 Open Univ BA78. Wells Th Coll 57. **d** 59 **p** 60. C Weston-super-Mare St Jo *B & W* 59-62; V Stoke Lane 62-67; V Leigh upon Mendip 62-67; Perm to Offic *Ex* from 67; rtd 91. *3 Byron Close, Pilton, Barnstaple EX31 1QH* Tel (01271) 372483

TILLER, The Ven John. b 38. Ch Ch Ox BA60 MA64 Bris Univ MLitt72. Tyndale Hall Bris 60. **d** 62 **p** 63. C Bedford St Cuth *St Alb* 62-65; C Widcombe *B & W* 65-67; Tutor Tyndale Hall Bris 67-71; Chapl 67-71; Lect Trin Coll Bris 71-73; P-in-c Bedford Ch Ch *St Alb* 73-78; Chief Sec ACCM 78-84; Hon Can St Alb 79-84; Can Res Heref Cathl *Heref* 84-04; Chan 84-02; Dioc Dir of Tr 91-00; Adn Heref 02-04; rtd 05. *2 Pulley Lane, Bayston Hill, Shrewsbury SY3 0JH* Tel (01743) 873595

TILLETT, Leslie Selwyn. b 54. Peterho Cam BA75 MA79 Leeds Univ BA80. Coll of Resurr Mirfield 78. **d** 81 **p** 82. C W Dulwich All SS and Em *S'wark* 81-85; R Purleigh, Cold Norton and Stow Maries *Chelmsf* 85-93; R Beddington *S'wark* 93-05; R Wensum Benefice *Nor* from 05. *The Rectory, Weston Longville, Norwich NR9 5JU* Tel (01603) 880563 E-mail selwyn@tillett.org.uk

TILLETT, Michael John Arthur. b 57. Ridley Hall Cam 96. **d** 98 **p** 99. C Framlingham w Saxtead *St E* 98-01; P-in-c Stoke by Nayland w Leavenheath and Polstead 01-03; R from 03. *The Vicarage, Church Street, Stoke by Nayland, Colchester CO6 4QH* Tel (01206) 262248 Mobile 07703-794548 E-mail revtillett@aol.com

TILLETT, Miss Sarah Louise. b 59. Regent Coll Vancouver MCS00. Wycliffe Hall Ox 01. **d** 03. C Knowle *Birm* from 03. *St Anne's Cottage, 1713 High Street, Knowle, Solihull B93 0LN* Tel (01564) 775672 Fax 779123 Mobile 07764-608796 E-mail sarah.tillett@knowleparishchurch.org.uk

TILLETT, Selwyn. *See* TILLETT, Leslie Selwyn

TILLEY, Canon David Robert. b 38. Kelham Th Coll 58. **d** 63 **p** 64. C Bournemouth St Fran *Win* 63-67; C Moulsecoomb *Chich* 67-70; C Ifield 70-75; TV Warwick *Cov* 76-85; P-in-c Alderminster 85-89; P-in-c Halford 85-89; Dioc Min Tr Adv 85-04; CME Adv 90-04; P-in-c Alderminster and Halford 90-96; Assoc Min Willenhall 96-04; Hon Can Cov Cathl 03-04; rtd 04. *17 Coventry Road, Baginton, Coventry CV8 3AD* Tel and fax (024) 7630 2508 E-mail david.tilley@sagainternet.co.uk

TILLEY, James Stephen (Steve). b 55. St Jo Coll Nottm BTh84. **d** 84 **p** 85. C Nottingham St Jude *S'well* 84-88; C Chester le Street *Dur* 88-92; Tr and Ed CYFA (CPAS) 92-94; Hd 94-02; Perm to Offic *Cov* 93-02; Hon C Leamington Priors St Paul from 02. *82 Leicester Street, Leamington Spa CV32 4TB* Tel (01926) 420320 *or* 427149 E-mail steve@godstuff.org.uk

TILLEY, Peter Robert. b 41. Bris Univ BA62. Sarum & Wells Th Coll 77. **d** 79 **p** 80. C Wandsworth St Paul *S'wark* 79-82; V Mitcham St Mark 82-91; RD Merton 89-91; R Walton St Mary *Liv* 91-92; TR Walton-on-the-Hill 92-98; rtd 98; P-in-c Ghent *Eur* from 98. *Begijnhoflaan 29, 9000 Gent, Belgium* Tel (0032) (9) 223 7691 Fax 320 7692 E-mail peter.tilley@pandora.be

TILLIER, Jane Yvonne. b 59. New Hall Cam BA81 PhD85. Ripon Coll Cuddesdon BA90. **d** 91 **p** 94. Par Dn Sheff St Mark Broomhill *Sheff* 91-94; C 94-95; Chapl Glouc Cathl *Glouc* 95-97; P-in-c Madeley *Lich* 97-03; P-in-c Betley 02-03; Chapl and Team Ldr Perm to Offic 03-04; Chapl Douglas Macmillan Hospice Blurton from 04. *Douglas Macmillan Hospice, Barlaston Road, Blurton, Stoke-on-Trent ST3 3NZ* Tel (01782) 344300 *or* 639720 E-mail jane.tillier@boltblue.com

TILLMAN, Miss Mary Elizabeth. b 43. S Dios Minl Tr Scheme 86. **d** 89 **p** 95. NSM Bridgemary *Portsm* 89-93; NSM Portsea All SS from 93; Adv in Min to People w Disabilities from 93. *391 Fareham Road, Gosport PO13 0AD* Tel (01329) 232589

TILLOTSON, Simon Christopher. b 67. Lon Univ BA90 Trin Coll Cam BA93 MA96 Sarum Dioc Tr Coll CertHE00. Ridley Hall Cam 91. **d** 94 **p** 95. C Paddock Wood *Roch* 94-98; C Ormskirk *Liv* 98-00; V Aylesford *Roch* from 00. *The Vicarage, Vicarage Close, Aylesford ME20 7BB* Tel (01622) 717434 Mobile 07946-527471 E-mail sct@tillotsons.freeserve.co.uk

TILLYER, Preb Desmond Benjamin. b 40. Ch Coll Cam BA63 MA67. Coll of Resurr Mirfield 64. **d** 66 **p** 67. C Hanworth All SS *Lon* 66-70; Chapl Liddon Ho Lon 70-74; V Pimlico St Pet w Westmr Ch Ch *Lon* from 74; AD Westmr St Marg 85-92; Preb St Paul's Cathl from 01. *1 St Peter's House, 119 Eaton Square, London SW1W 9AL* Tel and fax (020) 7235 4242 E-mail vicar@stpetereatonsquare.co.uk

TILSON, Canon Alan Ernest. b 46. TCD. **d** 70 **p** 71. C Londonderry Ch Ch *D & R* 70-73; I Inver, Mountcharles and Killaghtee 73-79; I Leckpatrick w Dunnalong 79-89; Bermuda from 89; Hon Can Bermuda Cathl from 96. *Holy Trinity Rectory, PO Box CR 186, Hamilton Parish CR BX, Bermuda* Tel (001) (441) 293 1710 Fax 293 4363

TILSTON, Derek Reginald. b 27. NW Ord Course. **d** 73 **p** 74. NSM Bury St Mark *Man* 73-77; NSM Holcombe 77-82; NSM Bury St Jo 82-83; NSM Bury St Jo w St Mark 83-84; C Bramley *Ripon* 85-87; TV 87-90; R Tendring and Lt Bentley w Beaumont cum Moze *Chelmsf* 90-92; rtd 93; Perm to Offic *St E* from 93. *Cobbler's Cottage, 19 The Street, Wissett, Halesworth IP19 0JE* Tel (01986) 874693

TILT, Dawn Caroline. b 59. Llan Ord Course. **d** 99 **p** 00. NSM Pyle w Kenfig *Llan* 99-00; NSM Ewenny w St Brides Major 00-04; Chapl HM Pris Parc (Bridgend) from 04. *The Chaplaincy Centre, HM Prison Parc, Heol Hopcyn John, Coity, Bridgend CF35 6AR* Tel (01656) 300200 Fax 300201 E-mail thetilts@hotmail.com

TILTMAN, Alan Michael. b 48. Selw Coll Cam BA70 MA74. Cuddesdon Coll 71. **d** 73 **p** 74. C Chesterton Gd Shep *Ely* 73-77; C Preston St Jo *Blackb* 77-79; Chapl Lancs (Preston) Poly 77-79; TV Man Whitworth *Man* 79-86; Chapl Man Univ (UMIST) 79-86; V Urmston 86-99; Dir CME 99-03; C Salford Sacred Trin and St Phil 99-02; V Buckley *St As* from 04. *St Matthew's Vicarage, 114 Church Road, Buckley CH7 3JN* Tel (01244) 550645 E-mail a.tiltman@zoo.co.uk

TIMBERLAKE, Neil Christopher. b 26. Kelham Th Coll 47. **d** 51 **p** 52. C Ardwick St Benedict *Man* 51-54; C Moss Side Ch Ch 54-55; C Stockport St Alb Hall Street *Ches* 55-57; C Cov St Jo *Cov* 57-60; V Heath *Derby* 60-68; R Bridgetown Australia 68-70; C Leyland St Ambrose *Blackb* 70-72; C Bilborough w Strelley *S'well* 72-74; V Langold 74-86; rtd 86. *7 Thirlmere Avenue, Colne BB8 7DD* Tel (01282) 863879

TIMBRELL, Keith Stewart. b 48. Edin Th Coll 72. **d** 74 **p** 75. C Chorley St Pet *Blackb* 74-77; C Altham w Clayton le Moors 77-79; Chapl Whittingham Hosp Preston 79-95; Trust Chapl Dorset Health Care NHS Trust from 95. *Chaplain's Office, St Ann's Hospital, 69 Haven Road, Poole BH13 7LN* Tel (01202) 708881 E-mail clerigo@btinternet.com

TIMBRELL, Maxwell Keith. b 28. St Jo Coll Morpeth ThL51. **d** 51 **p** 52. Australia 51-58 and 64-82; C Hanworth All SS *Lon* 59-63; V Ingleby Greenhow w Bilsdale Priory *York* 83-85; P-in-c Kildale 83-85; V Ingleby Greenhow w Bilsdale Priory, Kildale etc 85-96; rtd 96; Perm to Offic *York* from 96. *Jasmine House, Nunnington, York YO62 5US* Tel (01439) 748319

TIMMINS, Susan Katherine. b 64. Leic Univ BScEng85 MICE91. St Jo Coll Nottm MTh94. **d** 96 **p** 97. C Iver *Ox* 96-00; P-in-c Pendlebury St Jo *Man* from 00. *St John's Vicarage, 91 Broomhall Road, Pendlebury, Manchester M27 8XR* Tel 0161-925 0171 E-mail susanktimmins@aol.com

TIMMIS (née PITT), Mrs Karen Lesley Finella. b 62. Lon Univ BA84. Chich Th Coll BTh94. **d** 94 **p** 95. C Walton-on-the-Hill *Liv* 94-98; P-in-c Warrington St Barn 98-00; V from 00. *The Vicarage, 73 Lovely Lane, Warrington WA5 1TY* Tel (01925) 633556

TIMOTHY, Miss Bronwen Doris (Bonnie). b 57. Sheff City Poly BSc81 Univ of Wales (Cardiff) PGCE82. St Mich Coll Llan 99. **d** 02 **p** 03. C Tenby *St D* 02-04; C Lampeter and Llanddewibrefi Gp from 04. *Garthowen, Kingsmead, Lampeter SA48 7AP* Tel (01570) 421333 Mobile 07773-645694

TIMS, Brian Anthony. b 43. Solicitor 64. STETS 95. **d** 98 **p** 99. NSM Whitchurch w Tufton and Litchfield *Win* 98-02; NSM Appleshaw, Kimpton, Thruxton, Fyfield etc from 02. *St Peter's Vicarage, High Street, Shipton Bellinger, Tidworth SP9 7UF* Tel (01980) 842244 E-mail brian@btims.freeserve.co.uk

TINDALE, Guy Gordon Beaumont. b 67. St Andr Univ BSc90 Peterho Cam BA03. Westcott Ho Cam 01. **d** 04 **p** 05. C Gosforth All SS *Newc* from 04. *1 Northfield Road, Newcastle upon Tyne NE3 3UL* Tel 0191-284 8568 E-mail g.tindale@allsaints-gosforth.org.uk

TINGAY, Kevin Gilbert Xavier. b 43. Sussex Univ BA79. Chich Th Coll 79. **d** 80 **p** 81. C W Tarring *Chich* 80-83; TV Worth 83-90; R Bradford w Oake, Hillfarrance and Heathfield *B & W* 90-01; RD Tone 96-01; P-in-c Camerton w Dunkerton, Foxcote and Shoscombe from 01; Bp's Inter Faith Officer from 01; Bp's Adv for Regional Affairs from 01. *The Rectory, Skinners Hill, Camerton, Bath BA2 0PU* Tel and fax (01761) 470249 E-mail kgxt@compuserve.com

TINGLE, Michael Barton. b 31. Bps' Coll Cheshunt 65. **d** 67 **p** 68. C Totteridge *St Alb* 67-70; C Hitchin St Mary 70-73; V Gt Gaddesden 73-78; V Belmont *Lon* 78-86; V Burford w Fulbrook and Taynton *Ox* 86-94; V Burford w Fulbrook, Taynton, Asthall etc 94-97; rtd 97; Perm to Offic *St Alb* from 97. *10 Edenhall Close, Hemel Hempstead HP2 4ND* Tel (01442) 217674

TINKER, Christopher Graham. b 78. Collingwood Coll Dur BA00. Wycliffe Hall Ox 02. **d** 04 **p** 05. C Houghton *Carl* from 04. *167 Kingstown Road, Carlisle CA3 0AX* Tel (01228) 591600 E-mail christinker04@aol.com

TINKER, Preb Eric Franklin. b 20. OBE89. Ex Coll Ox BA42 MA46 City Univ Hon DD87 Lon Univ Hon DD89 Middx Univ Hon DD93. Linc Th Coll 42. **d** 44 **p** 45. C Gt Berkhamsted *St Alb* 44-46; C Rugby St Andr *Cov* 46-48; CF 48-49; Lon Sec SCM 49-51; Chapl Lon Univ *Lon* 51-55; V Handsworth St Jas *Birm* 55-65; V Enfield St Andr *Lon* 65-69; Preb St Paul's Cathl 69-90; Sen Chapl Lon Univs and Polys 69-90; Dir of Educn (Dios Lon and S'wark) 72-80; Gen Sec Lon Dioc Bd of Educn 80-82; rtd 90; Perm to Offic *Lon* from 90. *35 Theberton Street, London N1 0QY* Tel (020) 7359 4750

TINKER, Melvin. b 55. Hull Univ BSc Ox Univ MA. Wycliffe Hall Ox 80. **d** 83 **p** 84. C Wetherby *Ripon* 83-85; Chapl Keele Univ *Lich* 85-90; V Cheadle All Hallows *Ches* 90-94; V Hull St Jo Newland *York* from 94. *St John's Vicarage, Clough Road, Hull HU6 7PA* Tel (01482) 343658 E-mail melvin@tink.karoo.co.uk

TINNISWOOD, Robin Jeffries. b 41. K Coll Lon BScEng64. Wells Th Coll 67. **d** 70 **p** 71. C Yeovil St Mich *B & W* 70-72; C Gt Marlow *Ox* 72-74; C Christow, Ashton, Trusham and Bridford *Ex* 74-77; P-in-c Ex St Paul 77; TV Heavitree w Ex St Paul 78-79; TV Ifield *Chich* 79-85; Perm to Offic *S'wark* 98-01; P-in-c Cury and Gunwalloe w Mawgan *Truro* 01-03. *Address temp unknown*

TINSLEY, Bernard Murray. b 26. Nottm Univ BA51 Birm Univ DPS. Westcott Ho Cam 51. **d** 53 **p** 54. C Rotherham *Sheff* 53-56; C Goole 56-58; V Thorpe Hesley 58-61; R Alverdiscott w Huntshaw *Ex* 61-78; R Newton Tracey 61-78; R Beaford and Roborough 67-78; V St Giles in the Wood 67-78; V Yarnscombe 67-78; R Newton Tracey, Alverdiscott, Huntshaw etc 78-88; RD Torrington 81-86; rtd 88; Perm to Offic *Ex* from 88. *The Grange, Grange Road, Bideford EX39 4AS* Tel (01237) 471414

TINSLEY, Derek. b 31. ALCM65 BTh93 PhD97. NW Ord Course 73. **d** 76 **p** 77. C Gt Crosby St Faith *Liv* 76-80; V Wigan St Anne 80-85; V Colton w Satterthwaite and Rusland *Carl* 85-93; rtd 93; Perm to Offic *Liv* from 93. *Lyndale, 43 Renacres Lane, Ormskirk L39 8SG*

TINSLEY, Preb Derek Michael. b 35. Lon Coll of Div ALCD66 LTh. **d** 66 **p** 67. C Rainhill *Liv* 66-68; C Chalfont St Peter *Ox* 68-73; P-in-c Maids Moreton w Foxcote 73-74; P-in-c Akeley w Leckhampstead 73-74; P-in-c Lillingstone Dayrell w Lillingstone Lovell 73-74; R N Buckingham 74-82; RD Buckingham 78-82; P-in-c Alstonfield *Lich* 82-84; P-in-c Butterton 82-84; P-in-c Warslow and Elkstones 82-84; P-in-c Wetton 82-84; V Alstonfield, Butterton, Warslow w Elkstone etc 85-95; RD Alstonfield 82-95; Preb Lich Cathl 91-98; V Cheddleton 95-98;

Chapl St Edw Hosp Cheddleton 96-98; rtd 98; Perm to Offic *Lich* and *Derby* from 98. *3 Windsor Close, Manor Green, Ashbourne DE6 1RJ* Tel (01335) 346226

TIPLADY, Peter. b 42. MRCGP72 FFPHM86 Dur Univ MB, BS65. Carl Dioc Tr Course 86. **d** 89 **p** 90. NSM Wetheral w Warwick *Carl* 89-05; NSM Holme Eden and Wetheral w Warwick from 05. *Meadow Croft, Wetheral, Carlisle CA4 8JG* Tel (01228) 561611 *or* 603608 E-mail petertiplady@ncha.demon.co.uk

TIPP, Canon James Edward. b 45. Heythrop Coll Lon MA93. Oak Hill Th Coll 73. **d** 75 **p** 76. C St Mary Cray and St Paul's Cray *Roch* 75-78; C Southborough St Pet w Ch Ch and St Matt 78-82; R Snodland All SS w Ch Ch from 82; RD Cobham from 96; Hon Can Roch Cathl from 01. *The Vicarage, 11 St Katherine's Lane, Snodland ME6 5EH* Tel (01634) 240232 Fax as telephone E-mail jim@jtipp.freeserve.co.uk

TIPPER, Michael William. b 38. Hull Univ BSc59 MSc61. Em Coll Saskatoon 72. **d** 73 **p** 74. Canada 73-77, 79-80, 83-88 and from 91; R Amcotts *Linc* 77-79; V Aycliffe *Dur* 80-83; V Kneesall w Laxton and Wellow *S'well* 88-91; rtd 98. *106 Purdue Court West, Lethbridge AB, Canada, T1K 4R8*

TIPPING, Mrs Brenda Margaret. b 44. N Lon Univ CQSW85 Dur Univ MA96. St Alb and Ox Min Course 96. **d** 99 **p** 00. NSM Stevenage St Andr and St Geo *St Alb* 99-05; P-in-c S Mymms and Ridge from 05; Chapl among Deaf People from 05. *The Vicarage, 6 Hamilton Close, South Mimms, Potters Bar EN6 3PG* Tel (01707) 643142 E-mail ken@tipping1941.freeserve.co.uk

TIPPING, Canon John Woodman. b 42. AKC65. **d** 66 **p** 67. C Croydon St Sav *Cant* 66-70; C Plaistow St Mary *Roch* 70-72; V Brockley Hill St Sav *S'wark* 72-83; P-in-c Sittingbourne St Mary *Cant* 83-86; V 86-94; P-in-c Mersham w Hinxhill 94-03; P-in-c Mersham w Hinxhill and Sellindge from 03; P-in-c Sevington from 94; P-in-c Brabourne w Smeeth 95-00; AD N Lympne 95-02; Hon Can Cant Cathl from 03. *The Rectory, Bower Road, Mersham, Ashford TN25 6NN* Tel (01233) 502138 Fax as telephone E-mail jwtipping@talk21.com

TIPPLE, Neil. b 58. Loughb Univ BTech81 Aston Univ MSc86. WMMTC 01. **d** 04 **p** 05. C Cov E *Cov* from 04. *5 Waterloo Street, Coventry CV1 5JS* Tel (024) 7622 2045 Mobile 07792-198451 E-mail ginandwhisky@aol.com

TIRWOMWE, Stephen Warren. b 46. TCert73 Makerere Univ Kampala 81 Open Univ MA94 Leeds Univ MA01. Bp Tucker Coll Mukono DipTh82 BD88 All Nations Chr Coll 93. **d** 81 **p** 82. Uganda 87-97 and from 02; C Osmondthorpe St Phil *Ripon* 97-02; Dioc Miss Co-ord Kigezi from 02. *Abaho Ahurira, PO Box 1091, Kabale, Uganda* Tel (00256) (77) 870467 E-mail swtirwomwe@hotmail.com

TITCOMB, Mrs Claire. b 35. St Alb and Ox Min Course 95. **d** 98 **p** 99. OLM Witney *Ox* from 98; Assoc P for Min Development from 01. *30 Beech Road, Witney OX28 6LW* Tel (01993) 771234 E-mail claireroyt@clara.net

TITCOMBE, Peter Charles. *See* JONES, Peter Charles

TITFORD, Richard Kimber. b 45. UEA BA67. Ripon Coll Cuddesdon 78. **d** 80 **p** 80. C Middleton *Man* 80-83; P-in-c Edwardstone w Groton and Lt Waldingfield *St E* 83-90; R 90-02; P-in-c Boxford 00-02; C Assington w Newton Green and Lt Cornard 00-02; R Boxford, Edwardstone, Groton etc 02-03; rtd 03; Perm to Offic *St E* from 03. *2 Chestnut Mews, Friars Street, Sudbury CO10 2AH* Tel and fax (01787) 880303 E-mail titford@keme.co.uk

TITLEY, David Joseph. b 47. Ex Univ BSc Surrey Univ PhD. Wycliffe Hall Ox. **d** 82 **p** 83. C Stowmarket *St E* 82-85; C Bloxwich *Lich* 85-90; TV 90-95; V Prees and Fauls 95-00; V Clacton St Paul *Chelmsf* from 00. *The Vicarage, 7 St Alban's Road, Clacton-on-Sea CO15 6BA* Tel (01255) 424760 E-mail titleys@supanet.com

TITLEY, Robert John. b 56. Ch Coll Cam BA78 MA82. Westcott Ho Cam. **d** 85 **p** 86. C Lower Sydenham St Mich *S'wark* 85-88; C Sydenham All SS 85-88; Chapl Whitelands Coll of HE 88-94; V W Dulwich All SS from 94; RD Streatham from 04. *The Vicarage, 165 Rosendale Road, London SE21 8LN* Tel (020) 8670 0826

TIVEY, Nicholas. b 65. Liv Poly BSc89. Ridley Hall Cam CTM94. **d** 94 **p** 95. C Bromborough *Ches* 94-97; TV Walton H Trin *Ox* 97-01; Chapl HM Pris Wayland from 01. *The Chaplain's Office, HM Prison Wayland, Griston, Thetford IP25 6RL* Tel (01953) 858080

TIZZARD, Dudley Frank. b 19. Roch Th Coll 63. **d** 65 **p** 66. C Bearsted *Cant* 65-68; C Cant St Martin w St Paul 68-71; Chapl HM Pris Cant 68-71; V Petham w Waltham *Cant* 71-75; C Sevenoaks St Jo *Roch* 75-78; Perm to Offic *Cant* 78-84 and 87-01; rtd 84; Lic to Offic *Cant* 84-87. *96 Langlands Road, Cullompton EX15 1JB* Tel (01884) 38279

TIZZARD, Peter Francis. b 53. Oak Hill Th Coll DipHE88. **d** 90 **p** 91. C Letchworth St Paul w Willian *St Alb* 90-95; I Drumkeeran w Templecarne and Muckross *Clogh* 95-00; P-in-c Ramsgate Ch Ch *Cant* 00-02; V from 02. *24 St Mildred's Avenue, Ramsgate CT11 0HT* Tel (01843) 853732

TOAN, Robert Charles. b 50. Oak Hill Th Coll. **d** 84 **p** 85. C Upton (Overchurch) *Ches* 84-87; V Rock Ferry 87-99; RD Birkenhead 97-99; V Plas Newton from 99; P-in-c Ches Ch Ch from 03; RD Ches from 02. *St Michael's Vicarage, 22 Plas Newton Lane, Chester CH2 1PA* Tel (01244) 319677 *or* 315129 Fax 315129 E-mail bob.toan@xaltmail.com

TOBIN, Richard Francis. b 44. CertEd. Chich Th Coll 76. **d** 78 **p** 79. C W Leigh CD *Portsm* 78-79; C Halstead St Andr w H Trin and Greenstead Green *Chelmsf* 79-87; Youth Chapl 82-87; V S Shields St Simon *Dur* 87-04; V Ipswich All Hallows *St E* from 04. *All Hallows' Vicarage, Reynolds Road, Ipswich IP3 0JH* Tel (01473) 727467 E-mail ricktobin@btinternet.com

TODD, Alastair. b 20. CMG71. CCC Ox BA45 Lon Univ DipTh65. Sarum & Wells Th Coll 71. **d** 73 **p** 74. C Willingdon *Chich* 73-77; P-in-c Brighton St Aug 77-78; V Brighton St Aug and St Sav 78-86; rtd 86; Perm to Offic *Chich* from 86. *59 Park Avenue, Eastbourne BN21 2XH* Tel (01323) 505843

TODD, Canon Andrew John. b 61. Keble Coll Ox 80 Univ Coll Dur BA84 K Coll Lon MPhil98. Coll of Resurr Mirfield 85. **d** 87 **p** 88. C Thorpe *Nor* 87-91; Chapl K Alfred Coll *Win* 91-94; Sen Asst P E Dereham and Scarning *Nor* 94-97; Dir Studies EAMTC *Ely* 94-01; Vice-Prin 97-01; CME Officer *St E* from 01; Can Res St E Cathl from 01; Sub Dean from 04. *3 Crown Street, Bury St Edmunds IP33 1QX* Tel and fax (01284) 706813 Mobile 07785-560558 E-mail andrew.todd@stedmundsbury.anglican.org

TODD, Catherine Frances. b 61. Surrey Univ BSc84 Westmr Coll Ox BTh99 RGN84 RM86. EAMTC 96. **d** 99 **p** 00. NSM Sutton and Witcham w Mepal *Ely* 99-01; C Horringer *St E* 01-03; R from 03. *3 Crown Street, Bury St Edmunds IP29 5PY* Tel (01284) 706813

TODD, Clive. b 57. Linc Th Coll 89. **d** 91 **p** 92. C Consett *Dur* 91-93; C Bensham 93-95; P-in-c S Hetton w Haswell 95-98; R Ebchester and V Medomsley 98-04; P-in-c S Lawres Gp *Linc* from 04. *The Vicarage, 14 Church Lane, Cherry Willingham, Lincoln LN3 4AB* Tel (01522) 750356

TODD, Edward Peter. b 44. Cranmer Hall Dur 86. **d** 88 **p** 89. C Hindley All SS *Liv* 88-91; P-in-c Wigan St Steph 91-96; V 96-98; P-in-c N Meols 98-03; TR 03-05; rtd 05. *1B Nixons Lane, Southport PR8 3ES* Tel (01704) 572422 E-mail revtodd@btopenworld.com

TODD, George Robert. b 21. Sarum & Wells Th Coll 74. **d** 76 **p** 77. Hon C Wellington and Distr *B & W* 76-86; Perm to Offic from 86. *15 John Grinter Way, Wellington TA21 9AR* Tel (01823) 662828

TODD, Ian Campbell. b 68. Westcott Ho Cam. **d** 04 **p** 05. C Scotforth *Blackb* from 04. *St Paul's Vicarage, 24 Scotforth Road, Lancaster LA1 4ST* Tel (01524) 63000

TODD, Jeremy Stephen Bevan (Jez). b 69. Kent Univ Dip Mgt96. Trin Coll Bris BA92. **d** 97 **p** 98. C Tufnell Park St Geo and All SS *Lon* 97-99; Perm to Offic from 03. *Top Flat, 70 Perryn Road, London W3 7LT* Tel (020) 8743 2880

TODD, Joy Gertrude. b 28. Ox Univ MTh99 Lon Univ DipRS94. LNSM course. **d** 90 **p** 94. OLM Guildf H Trin w St Mary *Guildf* 90-99; Perm to Offic from 99. *165 Stoke Road, Guildford GU1 1EY* Tel (01483) 567500

TODD, Michael Edward. b 62. Brighton Poly BA84 Surrey Univ PGCE85. Ven English Coll Rome 98 SEITE 96. **d** 99. C Farnham *Guildf* 99-00; Chapl Surrey Inst Art and Design 99-00; Development Officer Surrey Univ *Guildf* 00-02; Progr Manager and Lect Croydon Coll from 02; Hon C Camberwell St Giles w St Matt *S'wark* from 04. *De Pastorie, 10 Wincott Street, London SE11 4NT* Tel (020) 7735 8191 Mobile 07946-701279 E-mail mikeytodd@hotmail.com

TODD, Nicholas Stewart. b 61. Open Univ BA03. Wycliffe Hall Ox 94. **d** 96 **p** 97. C Gt Wyrley *Lich* 96-99; V Leaton and Albrighton w Battlefield 99-02; R Holbrook, Stutton, Freston, Woolverstone etc *St E* from 02. *The Rectory, Fishponds Lane, Holbrook, Ipswich IP9 2QZ* Tel (01473) 327705 Mobile 07762-645174 E-mail nick@toddsrus.org

TODD, Canon Norman Henry. b 19. PhC Lon Univ BPharm42 Fitzw Ho Cam BA50 MA55 Nottm Univ PhD78. Westcott Ho Cam 50. **d** 52 **p** 53. C Aspley *S'well* 52-54; Chapl Westcott Ho Cam 55-58; V Arnold *S'well* 58-65; V Rolleston w Morton 65-69; Can Res S'well Minster 65-69; R Elston w Elston Chapelry 71-76; R E Stoke w Syerston 72-76; V Sibthorpe 72-76; Bp's Adv on Tr 76-83; C Averham w Kelham 76-80; V Rolleston w Morton 80-83; P-in-c Upton 80-83; V Rolleston w Fiskerton, Morton and Upton 83-88; Hon Can S'well Minster 82-88; rtd 88; Perm to Offic *S'well* from 88; Abps' Adv for Bps' Min 88-94. *39 Beacon Hill Road, Newark NG24 2JH* Tel (01636) 671857 E-mail n.todd1@ntlworld.com

TODD, William Colquhoun Duncan. b 26. AKC53 St Boniface Warminster 53. **d** 54 **p** 55. C Westmr St Steph w St Jo *Lon* 54-59; Win Coll Missr 60-72; C-in-c Leigh Park CD *Portsm* 59-69; V Leigh Park 69-72; R Bp's Hatfield *St Alb* 72-00; Angl Adv Southern TV 62-72; Thames TV 72-92; Carlton TV 93-00; rtd 00; Perm to Offic *St Alb* from 00. *15 Archway House, Park Street, Hatfield AL9 5BB* Tel (01707) 256268

TODD, Canon William Moorhouse. b 26. Lich Th Coll 54. **d** 57 **p** 58. C W Derby St Mary *Liv* 57-61; V Liv St Chris Norris Green 61-97; Hon Can Liv Cathl 92-97; rtd 97; Perm to Offic *Liv* from 97. *3 Haymans Grove, West Derby, Liverpool L12 7LD* Tel 0151-256 1712

TOFTS, Jack. b 31. Roch Th Coll 66. **d** 68 **p** 69. C Richmond *Ripon* 68-71; C Croydon St Jo *Cant* 71-74; P-in-c Welney *Ely* 74-78; P-in-c Upwell Ch Ch 74-79; V Gorefield 78-94; R Newton 78-94; R Tydd St Giles 78-94; rtd 96; Perm to Offic *Ely* from 96. *The Birches, Church Road, Walpole St Peter, Wisbech PE14 7NU* Tel (01945) 780455

TOLL, Brian Arthur. b 35. Ely Th Coll 62 Linc Th Coll 64. **d** 65 **p** 66. C Cleethorpes *Linc* 65-68; C Hadleigh w Layham and Shelley *St E* 69-72; R Claydon and Barham 72-86; P-in-c Capel w Lt Wenham 86-94; P-in-c Holton St Mary w Gt Wenham 87-91; R Capel St Mary w Lt and Gt Wenham 94-96; P-in-c Ipswich St Mary at the Elms 96-01; Bp's Adv on Deliverance and Exorcism 89-97; rtd 01; Perm to Offic *St E* from 01. *39 Derwent Road, Ipswich IP3 0QR* Tel (01473) 424305 E-mail batoll@ntlworld.com

TOLLEFSEN, Alida Thadden Maria (Alja). b 50. Utrecht Univ 89. St Steph Ho Ox 96. **d** 98 **p** 99. C Bramhall *Ches* 98-02; V Knutsford St Cross from 02. *The Vicarage, Mobberley Road, Knutsford WA16 8EL* Tel (01565) 632389 E-mail tollef@pncl.co.uk

TOLLER, Elizabeth Margery. b 53. Leeds Univ BA75. Ripon Coll Cuddesdon 84. **d** 87 **p** 00. Asst Chapl Leeds Gen Infirmary 87-90; Perm to Offic *Nor* 90-91; Chapl Lt Plumstead Hosp 92-93; Chapl Co-ord HM Pris Nor 93-95; Chapl Gt Yarmouth Coll 96-99; Perm to Offic *S'wark* 99-00; Hon C Wandsworth St Paul from 00; Hon Asst Chapl St Chris Hospice Lon from 03. *116 Augustus Road, London SW19 6EW* Tel (020) 8788 2024 E-mail mtoller@gmx.de

TOLLER, Heinz Dieter. b 52. NEOC 86. **d** 87 **p** 88. C Leeds Gipton Epiphany *Ripon* 87-90; R Coltishall w Gt Hautbois and Horstead *Nor* 90-99; V Wandsworth St Paul *S'wark* from 99; AD Wandsworth from 05. *116 Augustus Road, London SW19 6EW* Tel (020) 8788 2024 Fax 08702-843237 Mobile 07941-291120 E-mail htoller@gmx.de

TOLLERSON, Peter Joseph Moncrieff. b 65. Oak Hill Th Coll 99. **d** 01 **p** 02. C Ulverston St Mary w H Trin *Carl* 01-04; Chapl RAF from 04. *Chaplaincy Services (RAF), HQ, Personnel and Training Command, RAF Innsworth, Gloucester GL3 1EZ* Tel (01452) 712612 ext 5164 Fax 510828 E-mail pedroandcarmen@yahoo.com

TOLLEY, Canon George. b 25. Lon Univ BSc45 MSc48 PhD52 Sheff Univ Hon DSc83 Open Univ Hon DUniv84 Hon DSc86 FRSC CBIM. Linc Th Coll 65. **d** 67 **p** 68. C Sharrow St Andr *Sheff* 67-90; Hon Can Sheff Cathl 76-98. *74 Furniss Avenue, Sheffield S17 3QP* Tel 0114-236 0538

TOLWORTHY, Canon Colin. b 37. Chich Th Coll 64. **d** 67 **p** 68. C Hulme St Phil *Man* 67-70; C Lawton Moor 70-71; C Hangleton *Chich* 72-76; V Eastbourne St Phil 76-87; V Hastings H Trin from 87; Can and Preb Chich Cathl from 03. *Holy Trinity Vicarage, 72 Priory Avenue, Hastings TN34 1UG* Tel (01424) 441766 E-mail colintolworthy@hotmail.com

TOMALIN, Stanley Joseph Edward. b 66. Oak Hill Th Coll BA93. **d** 96 **p** 97. C Bitterne *Win* 96-00; C Hailsham *Chich* 00; P-in-c Hawkswood CD from 01. *15 Howlett Drive, Hailsham BN27 1QW* Tel (01323) 846680 E-mail tomalinstan@aol.com

TOMBLING, Canon Arthur John. b 32. St Jo Coll Cam BA54 MA58. Ridley Hall Cam 55. **d** 57 **p** 58. C Rushden *Pet* 57-59; Asst Chapl Repton Sch Derby 59-61; C Reigate St Mary *S'wark* 61-64; V Battersea Park St Sav 64-87; P-in-c Battersea St Geo w St Andr 74-87; V Battersea St Sav and St Geo w St Andr 87-95; P-in-c Battersea Park All SS 89-95; RD Battersea 85-90; Hon Can S'wark Cathl 89-95; rtd 95; Perm to Offic *Pet* from 95. *5 William Steele Way, Higham Ferrers, Rushden NN10 8LS* Tel (01933) 418072

TOMBS, Kenneth Roberts. b 42. Open Univ BA84. S Dios Minl Tr Scheme 92. **d** 95 **p** 96. Dep Hd Twyford C of E High Sch Acton 86-97; Chapl from 98; NSM Ickenham *Lon* from 95. *91 Burns Avenue, Southall UB1 2LT* Tel (020) 8574 3738 E-mail ken.tombs@tesco.net

TOMKINS, Clive Anthony. b 47. Cant Sch of Min 85. **d** 88 **p** 89. C Eastry and Northbourne w Tilmanstone etc *Cant* 88-91; R 91-96; P-in-c 96-97; Chapl Eastry Hosp 91-93; Chapl Cant and Thanet Community Healthcare Trust 93-97; P-in-c Woodchurch *Cant* 97-01; P-in-c Maidstone St Martin from 01. *St Martin's Vicarage, Northumberland Road, Maidstone ME15 7LP* Tel (01622) 676282 E-mail clivetomkins@hotmail.com

TOMKINS, Ian James. b 60. Univ of Wales (Cardiff) LLB81 Aston Business Sch MBA90. Ridley Hall Cam. **d** 00 **p** 01. C Bourton-on-the-Water w Clapton *Glouc* 00-04; P-in-c Broxbourne w Wormley *St Alb* from 04. *The Vicarage, Churchfields, Broxbourne EN10 7AU* Tel (01992) 462382 E-mail ian-tomkins@lineone.net

TOMKINS, James Andrew. b 66. R Holloway & Bedf New Coll Lon BA88. St Alb and Ox Min Course 01. **d** 04 **p** 05. C Lavendon w Cold Brayfield, Clifton Reynes etc *Ox* from 04. *33 The Glebe, Lavendon, Olney MK46 4HF* Tel (01234) 241623 E-mail jamestomkins@s-michaels.org.uk

TOMKINS, Jocelyn Rachel. *See* WALKER, Ms Jocelyn Rachel

TOMKINSON, Raymond David. b 47. RGN MSSCh. EAMTC 86. **d** 89 **p** 90. NSM Chesterton St Geo *Ely* 89-91; C Sawston 91-93; C Babraham 91-93; P-in-c Wimbotsham w Stow Bardolph and Stow Bridge etc 93-94; R 94-00; RD Fincham 94-97; Dir Old Alresford Place *Win* from 00; P-in-c Old Alresford and Bighton from 00. *The Rectory, Old Alresford Place, Old Alresford SO24 9DH* Tel (01962) 732780 E-mail raymond@tomkinson45.fsnet.co.uk

TOMLIN, Graham Stuart. b 58. Linc Coll Ox MA80 Ex Univ PhD96. Wycliffe Hall Ox BA85. **d** 86 **p** 87. C Ex St Leon w H Trin *Ex* 86-89; Tutor Wycliffe Hall Ox from 89; Vice-Prin from 98; Chapl Jes Coll Ox 89-94. *Wycliffe Hall, Oxford OX2 6PW* Tel (01865) 274210 Fax 274205 E-mail graham.tomlin@wycliffe.ox.ac.uk

TOMLIN, Keith Michael. b 53. Imp Coll Lon BSc75. Ridley Hall Cam 77. **d** 80 **p** 81. C Heywood St Jas *Man* 80-83; C Rochdale 83-84; TV 84-85; Chapl Rochdale Tech Coll 83-85; R Benington w Leverton *Linc* 85-99; R Leverton 99-01; Chapl HM Pris N Sea Camp 97-01; P-in-c Fotherby *Linc* from 01. *The Rectory, Peppin Lane, Fotherby, Louth LN11 0UG* Tel (01507) 602312 E-mail fotherby@kmtomlin.freeserve.co.uk

TOMLINE, Stephen Harrald. b 35. Dur Univ BA57. Cranmer Hall Dur DipTh61. **d** 61 **p** 62. C Blackley St Pet *Man* 61-66; V Audenshaw St Steph 66-90; V Newhey 90-01; rtd 01; Perm to Offic *Carl* from 01. *3 Humphrey Cottages, Stainton, Kendal LA8 0AD* Tel (01539) 560988

TOMLINSON, Anne Lovat. b 56. Edin Univ MA78 PhD85 MTh98. St Jo Coll Nottm CertCS87. **d** 93. Tutor TISEC from 93; Dir Past Studies from 98; Perm to Offic *Edin* from 93. *3 Bright's Crescent, Edinburgh EH9 2DB* Tel and fax 0131-668 1322 E-mail anniet@talk21.com

TOMLINSON, Arthur John Faulkner (Jack). b 20. Clare Coll Cam BA41 MA45. Ridley Hall Cam 46. **d** 48 **p** 49. C Hampstead Em W End *Lon* 48-50; C Kensington St Helen w H Trin 50-54; V Furneux Pelham w Stocking Pelham *St Alb* 54-62; R Sarratt 62-85; rtd 85; Perm to Offic *Nor* from 85. *5 Mead Close, Buxton, Norwich NR10 5EL* Tel (01603) 279470

TOMLINSON, Barry William. b 47. Clifton Th Coll 72. **d** 72 **p** 73. C Pennington *Man* 72-76; SAMS 76-80; Chile 77-80; C-in-c Gorleston St Mary CD *Nor* 80; Chapl Jas Paget Hosp Gorleston 81-87; V Gorleston St Mary *Nor* 80-88; P-in-c Gt w Lt Plumstead 88-89; R Gt w Lt Plumstead and Witton 89-93; R Gt and Lt Plumstead w Thorpe End and Witton 93-98; Chapl Lt Plumstead Hosp 88-94; Chapl Norwich Community Health Partnership NHS Trust 94-95; RD Blofield *Nor* 96-98; R Roughton and Felbrigg, Metton, Sustead etc 99-02; V Margate H Trin *Cant* 98-99; rtd 02; Perm to Offic *Nor* from 02. *12 Heath Road, Sheringham NR26 8JH* Tel (01263) 820266 E-mail bwtomlinson@lineone.net

TOMLINSON, David Robert. b 60. Kent Univ BSc82 Chelsea Coll Lon PGCE83 Jes Coll Cam BA92 MA96. Ridley Hall Cam CTM93. **d** 93 **p** 94. C Godalming *Guildf* 93-98; V Grays North *Chelmsf* from 98; RD Thurrock from 03. *St John's Vicarage, 8A Victoria Avenue, Grays RM16 2RP* Tel (01375) 372101 E-mail dtjtgrays@btinternet.com

TOMLINSON, David William. b 48. Lon Bible Coll MA95 Westcott Ho Cam 97. **d** 97 **p** 98. NSM W Holloway St Luke *Lon* 97-00; P-in-c 00-01; V from 01. *St Luke's Vicarage, Penn Road, London N7 9RE* Tel and fax (020) 7607 1504 E-mail revdavetomlinson@hotmail.com

TOMLINSON, Edward James. b 74. Homerton Coll Cam BEd96. Westcott Ho Cam 99. **d** 02 **p** 03. C Brentwood St Thos *Chelmsf* from 02. *Stokes House, St Thomas Road, Brentwood CM14 4DS* Tel (01277) 210323 Mobile 07788-855646 E-mail frtomlinson@yahoo.co.uk

TOMLINSON, Eric Joseph. b 45. Qu Coll Birm 70. **d** 73 **p** 74. C Cheadle *Lich* 73-76; C Sedgley All SS 77-79; V Ettingshall 79-94; P-in-c Longsdon 94; P-in-c Rushton 94; P-in-c Horton 94; V Horton, Lonsdon and Rushton Spencer from 94. *The Vicarage, Longsdon, Stoke-on-Trent ST9 9QF* Tel (01538) 385318

TOMLINSON, Frederick William. b 58. Glas Univ MA80 Edin Univ BD83. Edin Th Coll 80. **d** 83 **p** 84. C Cumbernauld *Glas* 83-86; C Glas St Mary 86-88; R Edin St Hilda *Edin* 88-01; R Edin St Fillan 88-01; R Edin St Pet from 01. *3 Bright's Crescent, Edinburgh EH9 2DB* Tel and fax 0131-668 1322 E-mail fred.tomlinson@talk21.com

TOMLINSON, Canon Ian James. b 50. K Coll Lon AKC72 Hull Univ MA90 Ox Univ MTh01. St Aug Coll Cant 72. **d** 73 **p** 74. C Thirsk w S Kilvington and Carlton Miniott etc *York* 73-76; C Harrogate St Wilfrid *Ripon* 76-79; R Appleshaw, Kimpton, Thruxton, Fyfield etc *Win* from 79; Dioc Adv in Past care and Counselling from 01; Hon Can Win Cathl from 04. *The Rectory, Ragged Appleshaw, Andover SP11 9HX* Tel (01264) 772414 Fax 771302 E-mail ian@raggedappleshaw.freeserve.co.uk

TOMLINSON, Jack. *See* TOMLINSON, Arthur John Faulkner

TOMLINSON, Mrs Jean Mary. b 32. K Coll Lon CertRK53 BEd75. S Dios Minl Tr Scheme 84. **d** 87 **p** 94. Hon Par Dn Spring Park All SS *S'wark* 87-92; Chapl HM YOI Hatfield 92-98; Perm to Offic *S'well* from 92. *6 Cheyne Walk, Bawtry, Doncaster DN10 6RS* Tel (01302) 711281

TOMLINSON (née MILLS), Mrs Jennifer Clare. b 61. Trin Hall Cam BA82 MA86. Ridley Hall Cam 88. **d** 91 **p** 94. C Busbridge *Guildf* 91-95; C Godalming 95-97; NSM 97-98; NSM Grays North *Chelmsf* from 98. *St John's Vicarage, 8A Victoria Avenue, Grays RM16 2RP* Tel (01375) 372101 E-mail dtjtgrays@btinternet.com

TOMLINSON, John Howard. b 54. MICE83 Newc Univ BSc76. Chich Th Coll 91. **d** 93 **p** 94. C Blewbury, Hagbourne and Upton *Ox* 93-96; C Cowley St Jas 96-97; TV 97-04; TR Upper Wylye Valley *Sarum* from 04. *The Rectory, 1 Bests Lane, Sutton Veny, Warminster BA12 7AU* Tel (01985) 840014 E-mail fj@care4free.net

TOMLINSON, John William Bruce. b 60. Univ of Wales (Abth) BA82 Man Univ MA90. Hartley Victoria Coll 87 Mar Thoma Th Sem Kottayam 90 Linc Th Coll 91. **d** 92 **p** 93. In Methodist Ch 90-91; C Sawley *Derby* 92-95; P-in-c Man Victoria Park *Man* 95-98; Dioc CUF Officer 95-98; Chapl St Anselm Hall Man Univ 96-98; V Shelton and Oxon *Lich* 98-04; Ecum Co-ord for Miss *Linc* from 04. *145 Yarborough Road, Lincoln LN1 1HP* Tel (01522) 532230 E-mail pelican@supanet.com

TOMLINSON, Matthew Robert Edward. b 61. St Chad's Coll Dur BA83 Univ of Wales (Cardiff) BD94. St Mich Coll Llan 92. **d** 94 **p** 95. C Abergavenny St Mary w Llanwenarth Citra *Mon* 94-96; PV Llan Cathl and Chapl Llan Cathl Sch 96-00; V Edgbaston St Aug *Birm* from 00. *St Augustine's Vicarage, 44 Vernon Road, Birmingham B16 9SH* Tel and fax 0121-454 0127 Mobile 07989-915499 E-mail jm.tomlinson@virgin.net

TOMPKINS, David John. b 32. Oak Hill Th Coll 55. **d** 58 **p** 59. C Northampton St Giles *Pet* 58-61; C Heatherlands St Jo *Sarum* 61-63; V Selby St Jas *York* 63-73; V Wistow 63-73; V Retford St Sav *S'well* 73-87; P-in-c Clarborough w Hayton 84-87; V Kidsgrove *Lich* 87-90; V Tockwith and Bilton w Bickerton *York* 90-97; rtd 97; Perm to Offic *Pet* from 00. *49 Wentworth Drive, Oundle, Peterborough PE8 4QF* Tel (01832) 275176

TOMPKINS, Francis Alfred Howard. b 26. St Jo Coll Dur BA50 DipTh52. **d** 52 **p** 53. C Islington St Mary *Lon* 52-55; Argentina 55-61; Field Supt SAMS 61-65; V Donington *Linc* 65-79; RD Holland W 69-78; V Silloth *Carl* 79-91; rtd 91; Perm to Offic *Linc* 91-00; *York* from 01. *17 Southfield Drive, North Ferriby HU14 3DU* Tel (01482) 632483

TOMPKINS, Michael John Gordon. b 35. JP76. Man Univ BSc58 MPS59. N Ord Course 82. **d** 85 **p** 86. C Abington *Pet* 85-87; TV Daventry 87-92; P-in-c Braunston 87-92; TV Daventry, Ashby St Ledgers, Braunston etc 92-93; R Paston 93-98; Perm to Offic *Ches* from 98; rtd 00. *19 Clarendon Close, Chester CH4 9BL* Tel (01244) 659147

TOMPKINS, Peter Michael. b 58. Open Univ BA92 SS Hild & Bede Coll Dur CertEd79. St Jo Coll Nottm MA96. **d** 96 **p** 97. C Bromfield w Waverton *Carl* 96-99; R Woldsburn *York* 99-01; TV E Farnworth and Kearsley *Man* 01-05; P-in-c Laceby and Ravendale Gp *Linc* from 05. *The Rectory, 4 Cooper Lane, Laceby, Grimsby DN37 7AX* Tel (01472) 870884

TOMS, Sheila Patricia. b 33. Cam Univ TCert54 Univ of Wales (Cardiff) BEd77 Univ of Wales (Swansea) ADC74. Llan Ord Course 90. **dss** 91 **d** 94 **p** 97. Canton St Luke *Llan* 91-94; NSM Peterston-super-Ely w St Brides-super-Ely 94-00; P-in-c Newport St Paul *Mon* from 00. *East Wing, Dingestow Court, Dingestow, Monmouth NP25 4DY* Tel (01600) 740262

TONBRIDGE, Archdeacon of. *See* MANSELL, The Ven Clive Neville Ross

TONBRIDGE, Suffragan Bishop of. *See* CASTLE, The Rt Revd Brian Colin

TONES, Kevin Edward. b 64. Hertf Coll Ox BA85. Ridley Hall Cam 88. **d** 91 **p** 92. C Warmsworth *Sheff* 91-92; C Thorne 92-96; V Greasbrough from 96. *The Vicarage, 16 Church Street, Greasbrough, Rotherham S61 4DX* Tel (01709) 551288 E-mail kevt@tesco.net

TONG, Canon Peter Laurence. b 29. Lon Univ BA50. Oak Hill Th Coll 52. **d** 54 **p** 55. C Everton St Chrys *Liv* 54-56; P-in-c Liv St Sav 56-59; V Blackb Sav *Blackb* 59-65; Chapl Blackb R Infirmary 63-65; V Islington St Andr w St Thos and St Matthias *Lon* 65-75; V Welling *Roch* 75-82; TR Bedworth *Cov* 82-94; Hon Can Cov Cathl 88-94; Hon Can Chile from 89; rtd 94; Perm to Offic *Roch* from 94. *46 Bladindon Drive, Bexley DA5 3BP* Tel (020) 8303 0085

TONGE, Brian. b 36. St Chad's Coll Dur BA58. Ely Th Coll 59. **d** 61 **p** 62. C Fleetwood St Pet *Blackb* 61-65; Chapl Ranby Ho Sch Retford 65-69; Hon C Burnley St Andr w St Marg *Blackb* 69-97; rtd 97; Perm to Offic *Blackb* from 97. *50 Fountains Avenue, Simonstone, Burnley BB12 7PY* Tel (01282) 776518

TONGE, Lister. b 51. K Coll Lon AKC74 Man Univ Cert Counselling 92 Loyola Univ Chicago MPS95. St Aug Coll Cant 74. **d** 75 **p** 76. C Liv Our Lady and St Nic w St Anne *Liv* 75-78; C Johannesburg Cathl S Africa 78-79; CR 79-91; Lic to Offic *Wakef* 83-91; Perm to Offic *Man* 89-94; USA 93-95; Perm to Offic *Liv* 95-96; Chapl Community of St Jo Bapt from 96; Chapl Ripon Coll Cuddesdon from 05. *38 Empress Court, Woodin's Way, Oxford OX1 1HF* E-mail listertonge@ntlworld.com

TONGE, Malcolm. b 53. Lancs Poly BA74 FCA77. NEOC 00. **d** 03 **p** 04. NSM Brookfield *York* from 03. *65 Belmont Avenue, Middlesbrough TS5 8EW* Tel (01642) 599209 E-mail malcolm.tonge@huntsman.com

TONGUE, Canon Paul. b 41. St Chad's Coll Dur BA63 DipTh64. **d** 64 **p** 65. C Dudley St Edm *Worc* 64-69; C Sedgley All SS *Lich* 69-70; V Amblecote *Worc* from 70; Hon Can Worc Cathl from 93; Chapl Dudley Gp of Hosps NHS Trust from 93; RD Stourbridge *Worc* 96-01. *The Vicarage, 4 The Holloway, Amblecote, Stourbridge DY8 4DL* Tel (01384) 394057 E-mail fatherpaul@freeuk.com

TONKIN, The Ven David Graeme. b 31. Univ of NZ LLB56 LLM57 Barrister-at-Law. Coll of Resurr Mirfield 57. **d** 59 **p** 60. C Hackney Wick St Mary of Eton w St Aug *Lon* 59-62; Chapl Worksop Coll Notts 62-68; Lic to Offic *S'well* 63-68; Jordan 68-74; New Zealand from 74; Can St Pet Cathl Waikato 88-89; Adn Waitomo 89-98; rtd 93. *Box 91, Owhango, New Zealand* Tel (0064) (7) 895 4738 Fax as telephone

TONKIN, Canon Richard John. b 28. Lon Coll of Div ALCD59 BD60. **d** 60 **p** 61. C Leic Martyrs *Leic* 60-63; C Keynsham *B & W* 63-66; V Hinckley H Trin *Leic* 66-74; RD Sparkenhoe II 71-74; R Oadby 74-84; Hon Can Leic Cathl 83-93; V Leic H Apostles 84-93; rtd 93; Perm to Offic *Leic* from 93. *39 Shackerdale Road, Wigston, Leicester LE8 1BQ* Tel 0116-281 2517

TONKINSON, Canon David Boyes. b 47. K Coll Lon BD71 AKC71. St Aug Coll Cant 71. **d** 72 **p** 73. C Surbiton St Andr *S'wark* 72-74; C Selsdon St Jo w St Fran *Cant* 75-81; V Croydon St Aug 81-84; V Croydon St Aug *S'wark* 85-89; C Easthampstead *Ox* 89-96; Ind Chapl 89-96; Chapl Bracknell Coll 93-96; Soc Resp Adv *Portsm* 96-02; Hon Can Portsm Cathl from 96; Ind Chapl *Win* from 02. *9 Grebe Close, Kempshott, Basingstoke RG22 5JU* Tel (01256) 810161 E-mail davidbanhim@aol.com

TOOBY, Anthony Albert. b 58. Sarum & Wells Th Coll 89. **d** 91 **p** 92. C Warsop *S'well* 91-95; C Ollerton w Boughton 95-98; V Girlington *Bradf* from 98. *The Vicarage, 27 Baslow Grove, Bradford BD9 5JA* Tel (01274) 544987

TOOGOOD, John Peter. b 73. Leeds Univ BA95. Ripon Coll Cuddesdon 98. **d** 00 **p** 01. C Sherborne w Castleton and Lillington *Sarum* 00-03; P-in-c Chieveley w Winterbourne and Oare *Ox* from 03. *The Vicarage, Church Lane, Chieveley, Newbury RG20 8UT* Tel (01635) 247566 Mobile 07748-822336 Fax (01635) 812206 E-mail john@thetoogoods.fsnet.co.uk

TOOGOOD, Ms Melanie Lorraine. b 57. K Coll Lon BD78 AKC78. Cuddesdon Coll 94. **d** 96 **p** 97. C Shepperton *Lon* 96-99; C Greenford H Cross 99-04; P-in-c Tufnell Park St Geo and All SS from 04. *St George's Vicarage, 72 Crayford Road, London N7 0ND* Tel (020) 7700 0383 E-mail melanietoogood@tesco.net *or* melanie@toogood.info

TOOGOOD, Noel Hare. b 32. Birm Univ BSc54. Wells Th Coll 59. **d** 61 **p** 62. C Rotherham *Sheff* 61-65; C Darlington St Jo *Dur* 65-70; V Burnopfield 70-81; P-in-c Roche *Truro* 81-84; P-in-c Withiel 81-84; R Roche and Withiel 84-91; RD St Austell 88-91; V Madron 91-96; rtd 96; Perm to Offic *Portsm* from 97. *Acorn Cottage, Oakhill Road, Seaview PO34 5AP*

TOOGOOD, Robert Charles. b 45. AKC70. St Aug Coll Cant 70. **d** 71 **p** 72. C Shepperton *Lon* 71-74; C Kirk Ella *York* 74-76; P-in-c Levisham w Lockton 76-81; P-in-c Ebberston w Allerston 76-81; R Kempsey and Severn Stoke w Croome d'Abitot *Worc* 81-92; V Bramley *Win* from 92. *The Vicarage, Silchester Road, Bramley, Basingstoke RG26 5DQ* Tel (01256) 881373

TOOGOOD, Robert Frederick. b 43. St Paul's Cheltenham CertEd65 DipPE65 Open Univ BA74. Trin Coll Bris DipHE95. **d** 95 **p** 96. C Southbroom *Sarum* 95-99; TV Langport Area Chs *B & W* 99-04; rtd 04. *49 Barrow Close, Marlborough SN8 2BE* Tel (01672) 511468 E-mail bob.toogood@ukonline.co.uk

TOOKE, Mrs Sheila. b 44. EAMTC 89. **d** 91 **p** 94. NSM March St Wendreda *Ely* 91-95; P-in-c Upwell Ch Ch 95-97; P-in-c Welney 95-97; P-in-c Manea 95-97; R Christchurch and Manea and Welney 97-03; rtd 03; Perm to Offic *Ely* from 03. *The Haven, 21 Wisbech Road, March PE15 8ED* Tel (01354) 652844 E-mail stooke@c-m-w.fsnet.co.uk

TOOKEY, Preb Christopher Tom. b 41. AKC67. **d** 68 **p** 69. C Stockton St Pet *Dur* 68-71; C Burnham *B & W* 71-77; R Clutton w Cameley 77-81; V Wells St Thos w Horrington from 81; RD Shepton Mallet 86-95; Preb Wells Cathl from 90; Chapl Bath and West Community NHS Trust from 95. *The Vicarage, 94 St Thomas's Street, Wells BA5 2UZ* Tel (01749) 672193 E-mail christophertookey@hotmail.com

TOOLEY, Geoffrey Arnold. b 27. Lon Coll of Div 55. **d** 58 **p** 59. C Chalk *Roch* 58-60; C Meopham 60-62; P-in-c Snodland and Paddlesworth 62-68; P-in-c Burham 68-76; C Riverhead w Dunton Green 76-79; C S w N Bersted *Chich* 79-83; C-in-c N

Bersted CD 83-96; rtd 97. *Hawksworth, Charnwood Road, Bognor Regis PO22 9DN*

TOOLEY, Norman Oliver. b 27. Roch Th Coll. **d** 65 **p** 66. C Gravesend St Mary *Roch* 65-68; C Ormskirk *Liv* 68-73; Chapl Merseyside Cen for the Deaf 73-78; C Bootle Ch Ch 78-80; C W Ham *Chelmsf* 80-86; Chapl RAD 86-92; rtd 92; Perm to Offic *Roch* 92-98. *6 Newton Terrace, Crown Lane, Bromley BR2 9PH* Tel (020) 8303 0085

TOON, John Samuel. b 30. Man Univ BA. Bps' Coll Cheshunt 64. **d** 65 **p** 66. C Newark St Mary *S'well* 65-67; C Clewer St Andr *Ox* 67-69; Canada 70, 73-76 and from 78; R Osgathorpe *Leic* 70-72; C Maidstone All SS w St Phil and H Trin *Cant* 76-78; rtd 95; Hon C Portage la Prairie St Mary 95-02; P-in-c N Peace Par 02-05; R Oshawa Gd Shep from 05. *St George's Residence, 104-505 Simcoe Street South, Oshawa ON, Canada, L1H 4J9* Tel (001) (905) 571 5976 E-mail fathertoon@sympatico.com

TOON, Peter. b 39. Lambeth STh65 K Coll Lon BD65 MTh67 Liv Univ MA72 Ch Ch Ox DPhil77. NW Ord Course 72. **d** 73 **p** 74. C Skelmersdale St Paul *Liv* 73-74; Lib Latimer Ho Ox 74-76; C Ox St Ebbe w St Pet *Ox* 74-76; Tutor Oak Hill Th Coll 76-82; Hon Lect St Giles-in-the-Fields *Lon* 76-82; Dir Post-Ord Tr *St E* 82-87; P-in-c Boxford 82-88; V Staindrop *Dur* 88-91; USA 91-01; P-in-c Biddulph Moor *Lich* 01-05; P-in-c Brown Edge 03-05; rtd 05. *23120 SE Black Nugget Road, Q2 Issaquah, WA 98029, USA* Tel (001) (425) 391 8281 E-mail tronascranner2000@yahoo.com

TOOP, Alan Neil. b 49. St Alb Minl Tr Scheme 79 Linc Th Coll 82. **d** 83 **p** 84. C Kempston Transfiguration *St Alb* 83-87; C Ludlow *Heref* 87-92; P-in-c Stokesay and Sibdon Carwood w Halford 92-01; P-in-c Acton Scott 96-01; RD Condover 96-00; V Minsterley from 01; R Habberley from 01. *The Vicarage, Minsterley, Shrewsbury SY5 0AA* Tel (01743) 791213

TOOP, Mrs Mary-Louise. b 55. Glouc Sch of Min 90. **d** 04 **p** 05. Dir of Ords *Heref* from 00; NSM Minsterley from 04; NSM Habberley from 04; NSM Hope w Shelve from 04. *The Vicarage, Minsterley, Shrewsbury SY5 0AA* Tel (01743) 790399 Mobile 07811-468480 E-mail maryloutoop@lineone.net

TOOP, William John. b 07. Lon Univ BSc27 K Coll Cam BA38 MA42. **d** 41 **p** 42. E Pakistan 41-44 and 46-47; Chapl Lahore Cathl 44; Ind Chapl *Man* 44-47; V Cofton *Ex* 48-52; R Torwood St Mark 52-79; P-in-c Torquay H Trin 74-79; R Torwood St Mark w H Trin 79; rtd 79; Lic to Offic *Ex* 79-95; Perm to Offic from 95. *Georgian House, Park Hill Road, Torquay TQ1 2DZ* Tel (01803) 201387

TOOTH, Nigel David. b 47. RMN69 Dip Counselling 96. Sarum & Wells Th Coll 71. **d** 74 **p** 75. C S Beddington St Mich *S'wark* 74-77; C Whitchurch *Bris* 77-83; TV Bedminster 83-87; Chapl Dorchester Hosps 87-94; Chapl Herrison Hosp Dorchester 87-94; Chapl W Dorset Gen Hosps NHS Trust from 94. *Dorset County Hospital, Williams's Avenue, Dorchester DT1 2JY* Tel (01305) 255198 *or* 889576

TOOVEY, Preb Kenneth Frank. b 26. K Coll Lon BD51 AKC51. **d** 52 **p** 53. C Munster Square St Mary Magd *Lon* 52-60; V Upper Teddington SS Pet and Paul 60-70; V Ruislip St Martin 70-81; RD Hillingdon 75-81; V Greenhill St Jo 81-91; Preb St Paul's Cathl 83-91; rtd 91; Perm to Offic *Lon* from 91. *10 Fort Road, Northolt UB5 5HH* Tel (020) 8842 2812

TOOZE, Margaret Elizabeth. b 27. St Mich Ho Ox 54. **dss** 83 **d** 89 **p** 94. Kenya 61-88; C Bath Walcot *B & W* 89-95; Perm to Offic from 95. *33 Walcot Court, Walcot Gate, Bath BA1 5UB* Tel (01225) 465642

TOPALIAN, Berj. b 51. Sheff Univ BA72 PhD77. Sarum Th Coll 95. **d** 97 **p** 98. NSM Clifton Ch Ch w Em *Bris* 97-98; C Bris St Mich and St Paul 98-99; C Cotham St Sav w St Mary and Clifton St Paul 99-01; V Pilning w Compton Greenfield from 01; Hon Min Can Bris Cathl from 04. *The Vicarage, The Glebe, Pilning, Bristol BS35 4LE* Tel (01454) 633409 E-mail berj.topalian@btopenworld.com

TOPHAM, Paul Raby. b 31. DipEd58 MIL66 Columbia Pacific Univ LTh80 MA81. SSC. **d** 85 **p** 86. Chapl St Paul's Prep Sch Barnes 85-91; Chapl Toulouse w Biarritz, Cahors and Pau *Eur* 91-94; Perm to Offic *Eur* from 94 and *Lon* 94-97; P-in-c St Margaret's-on-Thames *Lon* 97-00; Hon C Hounslow W Gd Shep from 00; Hon C Teddington SS Pet and Paul and Fulwell from 00. *5 Marlingdene Close, Hampton TW12 3BJ* Tel (020) 8979 4277 Mobile 07714-650980 E-mail rev@topham28.freeserve.co.uk

TOPPING, Kenneth Bryan Baldwin. b 27. Bps' Coll Cheshunt 58. **d** 59 **p** 60. C Fleetwood St Pet *Blackb* 59-63; V Ringley *Man* 63-70; V Cleator Moor w Cleator *Carl* 70-91; rtd 92; Perm to Offic *Blackb* from 92. *23 Harrow Avenue, Fleetwood FY7 7HD* Tel (01253) 681441

TOPPING, Norman. b 32. NW Ord Course 73. **d** 76 **p** 77. NSM Prenton *Ches* 76-79; C E Runcorn w Halton 79-80; C Halton 80; P-in-c Newton Flowery Field 80-81; V 81-86; V Bredbury St Mark 86-96; rtd 96; Perm to Offic *Ches* from 96. *18 Well Bank, Sandbach CW11 1FQ* Tel (01270) 764771

TOPPING, Roy William. b 37. MBE92. S Dios Minl Tr Scheme 91. **d** 92 **p** 93. Bahrain 89-94; Chapl Miss to Seamen Milford Haven 94-99; rtd 99; Perm to Offic *Sarum* from 00. *7 Lady Down View, Tisbury, Salisbury SP3 6LL* Tel (01747) 871909

TORDOFF, Donald William. b 45. Nottm Univ BA69. Qu Coll Birm 69. **d** 71 **p** 72. C High Harrogate Ch Ch *Ripon* 71-75; C Moor Allerton 75-80; V Bilton 80-92; R Spennithorne w Finghall and Hauxwell 92-01; rtd 01; Perm to Offic *Ripon* from 02. *4 Weavers Green, Northallerton DL7 8FJ* Tel (01609) 760155 E-mail dont@onetel.com

TORDOFF (née PARKER), Mrs Margaret Grace. b 40. SRN65 SCM67 HVCert73. Cranmer Hall Dur 81. **dss** 83 **d** 87 **p** 94. Bilton *Ripon* 83-87; C 87-92; Chapl Spennithorne Hall 92; NSM Spennithorne w Finghall and Hauxwell 92-00; rtd 00; Perm to Offic *M & K* and *Ripon* from 00. *4 Weavers Green, Northallerton DL7 8FJ* Tel (01609) 760155 E-mail margarett@onetel.com

TORODE, Brian Edward. b 41. FCollP93 St Paul's Cheltenham TCert63 Poitiers Univ Dip French Studies 62. WEMTC 90. **d** 93 **p** 94. Hd Master Elmfield Sch Cheltenham from 82; NSM Up Hatherley *Glouc* 93-94; NSM Cheltenham St Steph 93-95; NSM Cheltenham Em 94-95; NSM Cheltenham Em w St Steph from 95. *23 Arden Road, Leckhampton, Cheltenham GL53 0HG* Tel (01242) 231212

TORRENS, Marianne Rose. *See* ATKINSON, Marianne Rose

TORRENS, Robert Harrington. b 33. Trin Coll Cam BA56 MA61. Ridley Hall Cam 56. **d** 58 **p** 59. C Bromley SS Pet and Paul *Roch* 58-60; C Aylesbury *Ox* 60-63; V Eaton Socon *St Alb* 63-73; Lic to Offic 73-75; V Pittville All SS *Glouc* 75-84; Chapl Frenchay Hosp Bris 84-94; Chapl Manor Park Hosp Bris 84-94; Chapl St Pet Hospice Bris 94-98; P-in-c Chippenham *Ely* 98-01; P-in-c Snailwell 98-01; Perm to Offic *Ely* and *St E* from 01. *68 Barons Road, Bury St Edmunds IP33 2LW* Tel (01284) 752075 E-mail torrensatkinson@aol.com

TORRY, Alan Kendall. b 33. Ex & Truro NSM Scheme. **d** 77 **p** 79. NSM Truro St Paul *Truro* 77-80; TV Probus, Ladock and Grampound w Creed and St Erme 80-84; P-in-c Gulval 84-88; V 88-99; P-in-c Marazion 85-88; V 88-99; rtd 99. *5 Chyandaunce Close, Gulval, Penzance TR18 3BP* Tel (01736) 362944

TORRY, Malcolm Norman Alfred. b 55. St Jo Coll Cam BA76 MA80 K Coll Lon MTh79 LSE MSc96 Lon Univ BD78 PhD90 BA01. Cranmer Hall Dur 79. **d** 80 **p** 81. C S'wark H Trin w St Matt *S'wark* 80-83; C S'wark Ch Ch 83-88; Ind Chapl 83-88; V Hatcham St Cath 88-96; V E Greenwich Ch Ch w St Andr and St Mich 96-97; TR E Greenwich from 97; RD Greenwich Thameside 98-01. *St George's Vicarage, 89 Westcombe Park Road, London SE3 7RZ* Tel (020) 8858 3006 *or* 8305 2339 Fax 8305 1802 E-mail malcolm@mtorry.freeserve.co.uk

TOSTEVIN, Alan Edwin John. b 41. BA. Trin Coll Bris 83. **d** 86 **p** 87. C Hildenborough *Roch* 86-89; TV Ipsley *Worc* from 89. *29 Sheldon Road, Redditch B98 7QS* Tel (01527) 501092 Mobile 07952-191321 E-mail alan@tostevin41.freeserve.co.uk

TOTNES, Archdeacon of. *See* GILPIN, The Ven Richard Thomas

TOTTEN, Andrew James. b 64. QUB BA87 TCD BTh90. CITC. **d** 90 **p** 91. C Newtownards *D & D* 90-94; CF from 94. *c/o MOD Chaplains (Army)* Tel (01980) 615804 Fax 615800

TOTTERDELL, Mrs Rebecca Helen. b 57. Lon Bible Coll BA80. Oak Hill Th Coll 88. **d** 91 **p** 94. Par Dn Broxbourne w Wormley *St Alb* 91-94; C 94-95; C Stevenage St Nic and Graveley 95-99; P-in-c Benington w Walkern from 99; Asst Dir of Ords from 03. *The Rectory, Church End, Walkern, Stevenage SG2 7PB* Tel (01438) 861322 E-mail addo@stalbans.anglican.org

TOTTLE, Mrs Nicola Rachael. b 72. Trin Coll Bris 98. **d** 01 **p** 02. C Bassaleg *Mon* 01-05; TV High Wycombe *Ox* from 05. *St James's Vicarage, Plomer Hill, High Wycombe HP13 5NB* Tel (01494) 526896 E-mail nicky.tottle@fish.co.uk

TOUCHSTONE, Grady Russell. b 32. Univ of S California 51. Wells Th Coll 63. **d** 65 **p** 66. C Maidstone St Mich *Cant* 65-70; USA from 70; rtd 95. *1069 South Gramercy Place, Los Angeles, CA 90019-3634, USA* Tel (001) (323) 731 5822 Fax 731 5880

TOURNAY, Ms Corinne Marie Eliane Ghislaine. b 57. Louvain Univ Belgium Lic82 STB90 MA90. Cuddesdon Coll DipMin94. **d** 94 **p** 95. C Redhill St Jo *S'wark* 94-98; V Deptford St Pet from 98. *St Peter's Vicarage, Wickham Way, London SE4 1LT* Tel (020) 8469 0013

TOVAR, Miss Gillian Elaine. b 48. Sussex Univ CertEd69. Trin Coll Bris BA86. **dss** 86 **d** 87 **p** 94. Tonbridge SS Pet and Paul *Roch* 86-00; Par Dn 87-94; C 94-00; V Gillingham H Trin from 00. *Holy Trinity Vicarage, 2 Waltham Road, Gillingham ME8 6XQ* Tel (01634) 231690 E-mail gilltovar@supanet.com

TOVEY, John Hamilton. b 50. Cant Univ (NZ) BA72. St Jo Coll Nottm DipTh78 DPS80. **d** 80 **p** 81. C Hyson Green *S'well* 80-83; New Zealand from 83; C Cashmere 83-85; Chapl Christchurch Cathl 85-89; P-in-c Amuri 89-90; V 90-94; C Johnsonville and Churton Park 94-96; P-in-c Churton Park from 96. *13 Halswater Drive, Churton Park, Wellington, New Zealand* Tel (0064) (4) 478 4099 Fax 478 4087 E-mail john.tovey@xtra.co.nz

TOVEY, Phillip Noel. b 56. Lon Univ BA77 Lon Bible Coll BA83 Nottm Univ MPhil88 Lambeth STh95. St Jo Coll Nottm 85. **d** 87 **p** 88. C Beaconsfield *Ox* 87-90; C Banbury 90-91; TV 91-95;

Chapl Ox Brookes Univ 95-98; P-in-c Holton and Waterperry w Albury and Waterstock 95-97; TV Wheatley 97-98; Dioc Tr Officer from 98; C Wootton and Dry Sandford from 05. *2 Ashcroft Close, Oxford OX2 9SE* Tel (01865) 863224 *or* 863680 E-mail phillip.tovey@virgin.net

TOVEY, Canon Ronald. b 27. AKC51. **d** 52 **p** 53. C Glossop *Derby* 52-55; C Chorlton upon Medlock *Man* 55-57; C Hulme St Phil 55-57; C Hulme St Jo 55-57; C Hulme H Trin 55-57; Malawi 57-69; Lesotho 69-85; Adn S Lesotho 77-85; Hon Can Lesotho 85-92; R Reddish *Man* 85-92; rtd 92; Perm to Offic *Pet* from 92; *Linc* 99-02. *86 Kings Road, Oakham LE15 6PD* Tel (01572) 770628 E-mail ronshir@tovey2.fsnet.co.uk

TOWELL, Alan. b 37. Sarum & Wells Th Coll 86 WMMTC 87. **d** 89 **p** 90. C Boultham *Linc* 89-93; P-in-c Scunthorpe Resurr 93-97; rtd 97. *154 Upper Eastern Green Lane, Coventry CV5 7DN* Tel (024) 7646 1881

TOWELL, Geoffrey Leonard. b 37. K Coll Lon BA59. Linc Th Coll 59. **d** 61 **p** 62. C Ashbourne w Mapleton *Derby* 61-65; C Claxby w Normanby-le-Wold *Linc* 65-67; V Alkborough w Whitton 67-80; R W Halton 68-80; P-in-c Winteringham 75-80; V Alkborough 81-85; Dioc Ecum Officer 85-91; rtd 91. *40 Lady Frances Drive, Market Rasen, Lincoln LN8 3JJ* Tel (01673) 843983

TOWERS, Canon David Francis. b 32. G&C Coll Cam BA56 MA60. Clifton Th Coll 56. **d** 58 **p** 59. C Gresley *Derby* 58-63; V Brixton St Paul *S'wark* 63-75; V Chatteris *Ely* 75-87; RD March 82-87; Hon Can Ely Cathl 85-87; R Burnley St Pet *Blackb* 87-97; rtd 97; Perm to Offic *Bradf* from 99. *9 West View, Langcliffe, Settle BD24 9LZ* Tel (01729) 825803

TOWERS, John Keble. b 19. Keble Coll Ox BA41 MA57. Edin Th Coll 41. **d** 43 **p** 44. Chapl Dundee St Paul *Bre* 43-47; India 47-62; R Edin Ch Ch-St Jas *Edin* 62-71; V Bradf St Oswald Chapel Green *Bradf* 71-78; P-in-c Holme Cultram St Mary *Carl* 78-80; V 80-85; rtd 85; Perm to Offic *Glas* 85-92; Hon C Moffat 92-00. *Flat 22/20, Croft-an-Righ, Edinburgh EH8 8ED* Tel 0131-557 1385

TOWERS, The Very Revd Patrick Leo. b 43. AKC68 Hull Univ CertEd69. **d** 74 **p** 75. Japan 74-81; TV Bourne Valley *Sarum* 81-83; Dioc Youth Officer 81-83; Chapl Oundle Sch 83-86; I Rathkeale w Askeaton and Kilcornan *L & K* 86-89; I Nenagh 89-00; Can Limerick, Killaloe and Clonfert Cathls 97-00; Provost Tuam *T, K & A* from 00; Can from 00; I Galway w Kilcummin from 00. *The Rectory, Taylor's Hill, Galway, Irish Republic* Tel and fax (00353) (91) 521914 Mobile 86-814 0649 E-mail towers@iol.ie

TOWERS, Terence John. b 33. AKC60. **d** 61 **p** 62. C Bishopwearmouth Gd Shep *Dur* 61-65; V Runham *Nor* 65-67; R Stokesby w Herringby 65-67; V Ushaw Moor *Dur* 67-93; rtd 93. *8 Beech Court, Langley Park, Durham DH7 9XL* Tel 0191-373 0210

TOWLER, Canon David George. b 42. Cranmer Hall Dur 73. **d** 76 **p** 77. C Newbarns w Hawcoat *Carl* 76-80; V Huyton St Geo *Liv* 80-98; V Newburgh w Westhead from 98; AD Ormskirk from 01; Hon Can Liv Cathl from 03. *The Vicarage, Back Lane, Newburgh, Wigan WN8 7XB* Tel and fax (01257) 463267 E-mail davidtowler@postmaster.co.uk

TOWLER, John Frederick. b 42. Bps' Coll Cheshunt 62. **d** 66 **p** 67. C Lowestoft St Marg *Nor* 66-71; R Horstead 71-77; Warden Dioc Conf Ho Horstead 71-77; Prec Worc Cathl *Worc* 77-81; Min Can Worc Cathl 77-81; rtd 02. *42 Monks Road, Hyde, Winchester SO23 7EQ* Tel and fax (01962) 863451 Mobile 07787-504662 E-mail cjt@ptners.freeserve.co.uk

TOWLSON, George Eric. b 40. N Ord Course 80. **d** 83 **p** 84. NSM Wakef St Andr and St Mary *Wakef* 83-84; NSM Ox St Mich w St Martin and All SS *Ox* 84-86; Perm to Offic 86-87; NSM Hoar Cross w Newchurch *Lich* 87-93; C Wednesbury St Paul Wood Green 93-01; rtd 01; Perm to Offic *Lich* from 01. *58 Church Lane, Barton under Needwood, Burton-on-Trent DE13 8HX* Tel (01283) 713673

TOWNDROW, The Ven Frank Noel. b 11. K Coll Cam BA34 MA38. Coll of Resurr Mirfield 35. **d** 37 **p** 38. C Chingford SS Pet and Paul *Chelmsf* 37-40; Chapl RAFVR 40-47; P-in-c Grangemouth *Edin* 47-48; R 48-51; V Kirton in Lindsey *Linc* 51-53; R Manton 51-53; R Greenford H Cross *Lon* 53-62; V E Haddon *Pet* 62-66; R Holdenby 62-66; V Ravensthorpe 63-66; Can Res Pet Cathl 66-77; Adn Oakham 67-77; Chapl to The Queen 75-81; rtd 77; Perm to Offic *Pet* 77-96. *Rio, 14 Dundee Road, Perth PH2 7EY* Tel (01738) 441543

TOWNEND, John Philip. b 52. Southn Univ BTh95. Sarum & Wells Th Coll 89. **d** 91 **p** 92. C Sherborne w Castleton and Lillington *Sarum* 91-95; P-in-c Wool and E Stoke 95-98; Sacr and Chapl Westmr Abbey 98-01; P-in-c Brightwalton w Catmore, Leckhampstead etc *Ox* from 01; P-in-c Beedon and Peasemore w W Ilsley and Farnborough from 05. *The Rectory, Main Street, Chaddleworth, Newbury RG20 7EW* Tel (01488) 638566 E-mail john@jptownend.freeserve.co.uk

TOWNEND, Lee Stuart. b 65. Cranmer Hall Dur DipTM98. **d** 98 **p** 99. C Buxton w Burbage and King Sterndale *Derby* 98-01; V Loose *Cant* from 01. *The Vicarage, 17 Linton Road, Loose, Maidstone ME15 0AG* Tel (01622) 743513 E-mail leenliz@ukonline.co.uk

TOWNER, Colin David. b 39. St Pet Coll Ox BA61 MA65 Lon Univ BD63 ARCM72 LRAM73. Tyndale Hall Bris 61. **d** 64 **p** 65. C Southsea St Simon *Portsm* 64-67; C Penge St Jo *Roch* 67-70; V Leic St Chris *Leic* 70-74; Hon C Southsea St Jude *Portsm* 75-82; Perm to Offic 86-90 and 00-01; C Southsea St Pet 01-03; P-in-c from 03; P-in-c Portsea St Luke from 05. *St Peter's House, Playfair Road, Southsea PO5 1EQ* Tel (023) 9229 7296 E-mail sctowner@yahoo.com

TOWNER, Preb Paul. b 51. Bris Univ BSc72 BTh81. Oak Hill Th Coll 78. **d** 81 **p** 82. C Aspley *S'well* 81-84; R Gt Hanwood *Heref* 84-99; RD Pontesbury 93-99; Preb Heref Cathl from 96; P-in-c Heref St Pet w St Owen and St Jas from 99. *The Vicarage, 102 Green Street, Hereford HR1 2QW* Tel (01432) 273676 E-mail preb.paul@ukgateway.net

TOWNLEY, Canon Peter Kenneth. b 55. Sheff Univ BA78. Ridley Hall Cam 78. **d** 80 **p** 81. C Ashton Ch Ch *Man* 80-83; C-in-c Holts CD 83-88; R Stretford All SS 88-96; V Ipswich St Mary-le-Tower *St E* from 96; RD Ipswich from 01; Hon Can St E Cathl from 03. *St Mary le Tower Vicarage, 8 Fonnereau Road, Ipswich IP1 3JP* Tel and fax (01473) 252770 E-mail peter.k.townley@btinternet.com

TOWNLEY, The Very Revd Robert Keith. b 44. St Jo Coll Auckland LTh67. **d** 67 **p** 68. New Zealand 67-70; C Lisburn Ch Ch *Conn* 71-74; C Portman Square St Paul *Lon* 75-80; Chan Cork Cathl *C, C & R* 82-94; Dean Ross 82-94; I Ross Union 82-94; Dean Kildare *M & K* from 95; Hon CF from 95; I Kildare w Kilmeague and Curragh *M & K* from 95; P-in-c Newbridge w Carnalway and Kilcullen 95-97; P-in-c Geashill w Killeigh and Ballycommon 00-01. *Dean's House, Curragh Camp, Co Kildare, Irish Republic* Tel and fax (00353) (45) 441654

TOWNLEY, Roger. b 46. Man Univ BSc York Univ MSc. St Deiniol's Hawarden 82. **d** 84 **p** 85. C Longton *Blackb* 84-88; V Penwortham St Leon 88-92; V Wrightington from 92; Chapl Wrightington Hosp NHS Trust 92-01; Chapl Wrightington Wigan and Leigh NHS Trust from 01. *The Vicarage, Church Lane, Wrightington, Wigan WN6 9SL* Tel (01257) 451332 E-mail r.townley@talk21.com

TOWNROE, Canon Edward John. b 20. St Jo Coll Ox BA42 MA48 FKC59. Linc Th Coll 42. **d** 43 **p** 44. C Sunderland *Dur* 43-48; Chapl St Boniface Coll Warminster 48-56; Warden 56-69; Lic to Offic *Sarum* 48-93; Perm to Offic from 93; Can and Preb Sarum Cathl 69-93; rtd 85. *St Boniface Lodge, Church Street, Warminster BA12 8PG* Tel (01985) 212355

TOWNROE, Canon Michael Dakeyne. b 15. Linc Th Coll 35. **d** 38 **p** 39. C Grantham *Linc* 38-41; C W Grinstead *Chich* 41-44; C Pulborough 44-47; R Graffham w Woolavington 47-59; Chapl St Mich Sch Burton Park 47-59; RD Petworth *Chich* 56-59; R Bexhill St Pet 59-82; RD Battle and Bexhill 64-77; Can and Preb Chich Cathl 69-82; rtd 82; Perm to Offic *Chich* from 82. *Lauriston Nursing Home, 40 The Green, St Leonards-on-Sea TN38 0SY* Tel (01424) 447522

TOWNSEND, Allan Harvey. b 43. WMMTC 89. **d** 92 **p** 93. NSM Fenton *Lich* 92-96; C Tividale 96-98; P-in-c Saltley and Shaw Hill *Birm* from 98; P-in-c Washwood Heath from 01. *The Clergy House, St Saviour's Road, Birmingham B8 1HW* Tel 0121-689 8897 Fax 246 4335 E-mail frallan@stsaviours98.freeserve.co.uk

TOWNSEND, Anne Jennifer. b 38. Lon Univ MB, BS60 MRCS60 LRCP60. S'wark Ord Course 88. **d** 91 **p** 94. NSM Wandsworth St Paul *S'wark* from 91; Chapl Asst St Geo Hosp Tooting 91-92; Dean MSE 93-99. *89E Victoria Drive, London SW19 6PT* Tel (020) 8785 7675 E-mail anne.townsend@gmx.net

TOWNSEND, Christopher Robin. b 47. St Jo Coll Nottm LTh74. **d** 74 **p** 75. C Gt Horton *Bradf* 74-77; C Heaton St Barn 77-78; C Wollaton *S'well* 78-80; V Slaithwaite w E Scammonden *Wakef* from 80. *The Vicarage, Station Road, Slaithwaite, Huddersfield HD7 5AW* Tel (01484) 842748 E-mail robin@townsend69.fsnet.co.uk

TOWNSEND, Derek William (Bill). b 52. Fitzw Coll Cam BA74 Man Univ PhD89. St Jo Coll Nottm 91. **d** 91 **p** 92. C Hazlemere *Ox* 91-95; TV Banbury 95-98; V Banbury St Paul 98-01. *Address temp unknown*

TOWNSEND, Mrs Diane Rosalind. b 45. Stockwell Coll of Educn CertEd66 K Alfred's Coll Win BEd88. Sarum Th Coll 93. **d** 96 **p** 97. NSM Botley *Portsm* 96-00; NSM Curdridge 96-00; NSM Durley 96-00; NSM Buriton from 00. *41 North Lane, Buriton, Petersfield GU31 5RS* Tel (01730) 269390

TOWNSEND, Gary. b 65. Trin Coll Bris. **d** 00 **p** 01. C Minster-in-Sheppey *Cant* 00-04; C Tonbridge SS Pet and Paul *Roch* from 04. *12 Salisbury Road, Tonbridge TN10 4PB* Tel (01732) 357205

TOWNSEND, Canon John Clifford. b 24. St Edm Hall Ox BA48 MA49. Wells Th Coll. **d** 50 **p** 51. C Machen *Mon* 50-51; C Usk and Monkswood w Glascoed Chpl and Gwehelog 51-55; R Melbury Osmond w Melbury Sampford *Sarum* 55-60; Chapl RNVR 57-58; Chapl RNR 58-75; V Branksome St Aldhelm *Sarum* 60-70; R Melksham 70-73; TR 73-80; Can and Preb

Sarum Cathl 72-90; RD Bradford 73-80; P-in-c Harnham 80-81; V 81-90; RD Salisbury 80-85; rtd 90; Perm to Offic *Sarum* from 90. *19 Wyke Oliver Close, Preston, Weymouth DT3 6DR* Tel (01305) 833641

TOWNSEND, John Elliott. b 39. ALCD63. **d** 64 **p** 65. C Harold Wood *Chelmsf* 64-68; C Walton *St E* 68-72; V Kensal Rise St Martin *Lon* 72-83; V Hornsey Ch Ch 83-98; V Forty Hill Jes Ch from 98. *The Vicarage, Forty Hill, Enfield EN2 9EU* Tel (020) 8363 1935 Fax as telephone
E-mail john@jesuschurch.freeserve.co.uk

TOWNSEND, John Errington. b 20. St Aug Coll Cant 64. **d** 65 **p** 66. C Alverstoke *Portsm* 65-69; R Droxford 69-74; Soc Work Org Sec 74-78; Perm to Offic 82-01; rtd 85. *2 Vigo Mews, Parkwood Road, Tavistock PL19 0RG* Tel (01822) 615912

TOWNSEND, Mark Timothy. b 67. Aston Tr Scheme 93 Cuddesdon Coll 93. **d** 96 **p** 97. C Ludlow, Ludford, Ashford Carbonell etc *Heref* 96-99; TV Leominster from 99. *1A School Road, Leominster HR6 8NJ* Tel (01568) 612124

TOWNSEND, Peter. b 35. AKC63. **d** 64 **p** 65. C Norbury St Oswald *Cant* 64-67; C New Romney w Hope 67-69; C Westborough *Guildf* 69-74; P-in-c Wicken *Pet* 74-87; R Paulerspury 74-84; P-in-c Whittlebury w Silverstone 82-84; V Whittlebury w Paulerspury 84-87; V Greetham and Thistleton w Stretton and Clipsham 87-01; rtd 01; Perm to Offic *Pet* from 01. *26 King's Road, Oakham LE15 6PD* Tel (01572) 759286

TOWNSEND, Peter. b 37. Open Univ BA87. Wells Th Coll 67. **d** 69 **p** 70. C Desborough *Pet* 69-72; C Bramley *Ripon* 72-75; C-in-c Newton Hall LEP *Dur* 75-80; P-in-c Newton Hall 80-81; V Hartlepool St Luke 81-03; rtd 03. *348 Stockton Road, Hartlepool TS25 2PW* Tel (01429) 291651
E-mail townsendfamgo@ntlworld.com

TOWNSEND, Philip Roger. b 51. Sheff Univ BA78. Trin Coll Bris 78. **d** 80 **p** 81. C W Streatham St Jas *S'wark* 80-85; C Ardsley *Sheff* 85-88; V Crookes St Tim from 88. *St Timothy's Vicarage, 152 Slinn Street, Sheffield S10 1NZ* Tel 0114-266 1745
E-mail vicar@sttims.org.uk

TOWNSEND, Robert William. b 68. Univ of Wales (Ban) BA90. St Mich Coll Llan BTh93. **d** 93 **p** 95. C Dolgellau w Llanfachreth and Brithdir etc *Ban* 93-94; Min Can Ban Cathl 94-96; P-in-c Amlwch 96-97; R 97-99; R Llanfair-pwll and Llanddaniel-fab etc 99-03; P-in-c Llanilar w Rhostie and Llangwyryfon etc *St D* from 03; Dioc Schools Officer from 03. *The Vicarage, Llanilar, Aberystwyth SY23 4PD* Tel (01974) 241659 Mobile 07855-492006 E-mail robert@rectory.net

TOWNSEND, Robin. *See* TOWNSEND, Christopher Robin

TOWNSEND, William. *See* TOWNSEND, Derek William

TOWNSHEND, Charles Hume. b 41. St Pet Coll Ox BA64 MA69. Westcott Ho Cam 64. **d** 66 **p** 67. C Warlingham w Chelsham and Farleigh *S'wark* 66-75; R Old Cleeve, Leighland and Treborough *B & W* 75-85; R Bishops Lydeard w Bagborough and Cothelstone 85-95; V N Curry from 95. *The Vicarage, Moor Lane, North Curry, Taunton TA3 6JZ* Tel (01823) 490255 E-mail curryvic@fish.co.uk

TOWNSHEND, David William. b 57. Lon Univ PGCE80 Ox Univ MA85. Cranmer Hall Dur 81. **d** 84 **p** 85. C Barking St Marg w St Patr *Chelmsf* 84-87; Canada from 87. *Box 587, Westport ON, Canada, K0G 1X0* Tel (001) (613) 272 2664

TOWNSHEND, Edward George Hume. b 43. Pemb Coll Cam BA66 MA70. Westcott Ho Cam 68. **d** 70 **p** 71. C Hellesdon *Nor* 70-74; Ind Chapl 74-81; TV Lowestoft St Marg 74-79; TV Lowestoft and Kirkley 79-81; V Stafford St Jo *Lich* 81-85; P-in-c Tixall w Ingestre 81-85; V Stafford St Jo and Tixall w Ingestre 85-87; R Lich St Chad 87-99; RD Lich 94-99; P-in-c Hammerwich 94-96; C Hamstead St Paul *Birm* 99-02; Chapl Birm Airport 00-05; Sen Ind Chapl 02-05; rtd 05; Perm to Offic *Birm* from 05. *Hamstead Vicarage, 840 Walsall Road, Birmingham B42 1ES* Tel 0121-357 0950 Mobile 07931-928114
E-mail dryfly57@hotmail.com

TOY, Elizabeth Margaret. b 37. NDAD59 CQSW77. Oak Hill NSM Course 85. **d** 88 **p** 94. NSM Hildenborough *Roch* from 88. *2 Francis Cottages, London Road, Hildenborough, Tonbridge TN11 8NQ* Tel (01732) 833886

TOY, Canon John. b 30. Hatf Coll Dur BA53 MA62 Leeds Univ PhD82. Wells Th Coll 53. **d** 55 **p** 56. C Newington St Paul *S'wark* 55-58; S Sec SCM 58-60; Chapl Ely Th Coll 60-64; Chapl Gothenburg w Halmstad and Jönköping *Eur* 65-69; Asst Chapl St Jo Coll York 69-72; Sen Lect 72-79; Prin Lect 79-83; Can Res and Chan York Minster *York* 83-99; rtd 99; Perm to Offic *S'well* from 03. *11 Westhorpe, Southwell NG25 0ND* Tel and fax (01636) 812609

TOZE, Lissa Melanie. *See* GIBBONS, Ms Lissa Melanie

TOZE, Stephen James. b 51. Birm Univ BA79. Qu Coll Birm 76 Westcott Ho Cam 93. **d** 93 **p** 94. C Leominster *Heref* 93-94; R Gt Brickhill w Bow Brickhill and Lt Brickhill *Ox* 94-02; Rural Officer Buckm Adnry 95-02; V Wilshamstead and Houghton Conquest *St Alb* from 02. *The Vicarage, 15 Vicarage Lane, Wilstead, Bedford MK45 3EU* Tel (01234) 740423

TOZER, Frank William. b 21. Open Univ BSc94. Wells Th Coll 61. **d** 63 **p** 64. C Kemp Town St Mark *Chich* 63-65; C Crawley 65-73; V Heathfield 73-87; rtd 87; Perm to Offic *Chich* from 87. *30 Orchid Close, Eastbourne BN23 8DE* Tel (01323) 768270

TOZER, Reginald Ernest. b 25. St Aid Birkenhead 57. **d** 59 **p** 60. C Plaistow St Andr *Chelmsf* 59-62; P-in-c Clayton *Lich* 62-69; V E Ham w Upton Park *Chelmsf* 69-75; V Hatfield Peverel w Ulting 75-91; rtd 91; Perm to Offic *St E* from 91. *Basil's Place, 4 Church Road, Snape, Saxmundham IP17 1SZ* Tel (01728) 688895

TRAFFORD, Mrs Joyce. b 35. N Ord Course 84. **d** 87 **p** 94. Par Dn Chapelthorpe *Wakef* 87-94; C 94-98; rtd 98; Perm to Offic *Wakef* from 98. *1 Gillion Crescent, Durkar, Wakefield WF4 6PP* Tel (01924) 252033

TRAFFORD, Peter. b 39. Chich Th Coll. **d** 83 **p** 84. C Bath Bathwick *B & W* 83-86; Chapl RN 86-90; P-in-c Donnington *Chich* 90-99; V Jarvis Brook 99-04; rtd 04. *26 Bourne Way, Midhurst GU29 9HZ* Tel (01730) 815710

TRAFFORD-ROBERTS, Rosamond Jane. b 40. Qu Coll Birm BA. **d** 95 **p** 96. C Ledbury *Heref* 95-00; Lect St Botolph Aldgate w H Trin Minories *Lon* 00-05; Chapl Ho of St Barn-in-Soho 03-05; rtd 05. *47C St George's Square, London SW1V 3QN* Tel (020) 7828 1122 Mobile 07736-335959
E-mail revdros@hotmail.com

TRAILL, Geoffrey Conway. b 58. Ridley Coll Melbourne BA82 BTh87. **d** 85 **p** 85. Australia 85-87 and from 88; C Shrub End *Chelmsf* 87-88. *1 Albert Street, Point Lonsdale, Vic, Australia 3225* Tel (0061) (3) 5258 4624 Mobile 412-381225 Fax 5258 4623 E-mail gtraill@optusnet.com.au

TRAINOR, Mrs Lynn Joanna. b 65. Bris Univ BSc87 Ex Univ PGCE89. St Alb and Ox Min Course 99. **d** 02 **p** 03. C Ascot Heath *Ox* from 02. *The Parsonage, King Edward's Road, Ascot SL5 8PD* Tel (01344) 883772 E-mail lynn@lynnie.co.uk

TRANTER, John. b 51. St Jo Coll Nottm. **d** 00 **p** 01. C Gt Wyrley *Lich* 00-04; V Altham w Clayton le Moors *Blackb* from 04. *The Vicarage, Church Street, Clayton le Moors, Accrington BB5 5HT* Tel (01254) 384321

TRANTER, Stephen. b 61. Lanc Univ BA81 RGN87 RM89. Trin Coll Bris BA99. **d** 99 **p** 00. C Blackpool St Thos *Blackb* 99-03; P-in-c Blackb St Jas from 03; P-in-c Blackb St Steph from 04. *St James's Vicarage, Cromer Place, Blackburn BB1 8EL* Tel (01254) 56465 E-mail stranter@fish.co.uk

TRAPNELL, Canon Stephen Hallam. b 30. G&C Coll Cam BA53 MA57 Virginia Th Sem BD56 MDiv70 Hon DD02. Ridley Hall Cam 53. **d** 56 **p** 57. C Upper Tulse Hill St Matthias *S'wark* 56-59; C Reigate St Mary 59-61; V Richmond Ch Ch 61-72; P-in-c Sydenham H Trin 72-80; R Worting *Win* 80-92; Field Officer Decade of Evang 92-96; Can Shyogwe (Rwanda) from 93; rtd 96; Perm to Offic *Sarum* from 93 and *Win* from 96. *Downs Cottage, Rivar Road, Shalbourne, Marlborough SN8 3QE* Tel (01672) 870514 Fax 871439
E-mail stephen.trapnell@ukgateway.net

TRASK, Mrs Marion Elizabeth. b 54. Leic Univ BSc75 Brunel Univ PGCE76. Moorlands Bible Coll 82 Oak Hill Th Coll 93. **d** 96 **p** 97. C Bermondsey St Mary w St Olave, St Jo etc *S'wark* 96-00; C Peckham St Mary Magd 00-04. *14 The Peacheries, Chichester PO19 7TP* Tel (01243) 778843

TRASLER, Canon Graham Charles George. b 44. Ch Ch Ox BA65 MA69. Cuddesdon Coll 66. **d** 68 **p** 69. C Gateshead St Mary *Dur* 68-71; P-in-c Monkwearmouth St Pet 71-79; R Bentley and Binsted *Win* 79-84; R New Alresford w Ovington and Itchen Stoke 84-01; RD Alresford 99-01; P-in-c Stockbridge and Longstock and Leckford 01-03; R from 03; Hon Can Win Cathl from 05. *The Rectory, 11 Trafalgar Way, Stockbridge SO20 6ET* Tel and fax (01264) 810810
E-mail gtrasler@aol.com

TRATHEN, Paul Kevin. b 69. York Univ BA91 MA93 Jordanhill Coll Glas PGCE94 Middx Univ BA03. NTMTC 00. **d** 03 **p** 04. C Wickford and Runwell *Chelmsf* from 03. *8 Honington Close, Wickford SS11 8XB* Tel (01268) 560286 Mobile 07742-422175
E-mail paultrathen@aol.com

TRAVERS, Canon Colin James. b 49. St Pet Coll Ox BA70 MA74. Ridley Hall Cam 70. **d** 72 **p** 73. C Hornchurch St Andr *Chelmsf* 72-75; Youth Chapl 75-77; C Aldersbrook 75-77; V Barkingside St Laur 77-82; V Waltham Abbey 82-88; V S Weald 88-95; Co-ord NTMTC and Hon C Gt Warley and Ingrave St Nic 95-98; P-in-c Gt Canfield w High Roding and Aythorpe Roding 98-02; V Theydon Bois from 02; Hon Can Chelmsf Cathl from 01. *The Vicarage, 2 Piercing Hill, Theydon Bois, Epping CM16 7JN* Tel (01992) 814725
E-mail colin@revtravs.f9.co.uk

TRAVERS, John William. b 48. Open Univ BA84 Hull Univ MA86. Linc Th Coll 75. **d** 78 **p** 79. C Headingley *Ripon* 78-81; TV Louth *Linc* 81-89; P-in-c Shingay Gp *Ely* 89; R 90-95; V Hamble le Rice *Win* from 95. *The Vicarage, Hamble, Southampton SO31 4JF* Tel and fax (023) 8045 2148
E-mail jtravers@totalise.co.uk

TRAVES, Stephen Charles. b 44. Sheff City Coll of Educn CertEd66 Open Univ BA79. N Ord Course 96. **d** 99 **p** 00. NSM Barnsley St Pet and St Jo *Wakef* 99-02; NSM Cudworth from 02; NSM Lundwood from 02. *32 Osprey Avenue, Birdwell, Barnsley*

S70 5SH Tel and fax (01226) 286692 Mobile 07732-252353 *or* 07753-390942 E-mail stephen@traves2.freeserve.co.uk

TRAVIS, Mrs Jean Kathleen. b 42. **d** 03 **p** 04. OLM Benson *Ox* from 03. *25 Old London Road, Benson, Wallingford OX10 6RR* Tel (01491) 838713 E-mail jeantravis@tesco.net

TRAYNOR, Nigel Martin Arthur. b 58. St Jo Coll Nottm 94. **d** 96 **p** 97. C Wellington, All SS w Eyton *Lich* 96-00; P-in-c Pype Hayes *Birm* 00-02; TV Erdington from 02. *St Mary's Vicarage, 1162 Tyburn Road, Birmingham B24 0TB* Tel 0121-373 3534 E-mail nigelt6@msn.com *or* revnigel@yahoo.co.uk

TREACY, Richard James. b 74. Aber Univ BD Univ of Wales (Cardiff) MTh99. **d** 98 **p** 99. C Hillsborough *D & D* 98-02. *17 Kinedale Cottages, Ballynahinch BT24 8YW* Tel (028) 9756 4960 E-mail rjt1@tesco.net

TREADGOLD, The Very Revd John David. b 31. LVO90. Nottm Univ BA58. Wells Th Coll 58. **d** 59 **p** 60. V Choral S'well Minster *S'well* 59-64; CF (TA) 62-67 and 74-78; R Wollaton *S'well* 64-74; V Darlington St Cuth w St Hilda *Dur* 74-81; Chapl to The Queen 81-89; Can Windsor 81-89; Chapl in Windsor Gt Park 81-89; Dean Chich 89-01; rtd 01. *43 Priors Acre, Boxgrove, Chichester PO18 0ER* Tel (01243) 782385

TREANOR, Canon Desmond Victor. b 28. St Jo Coll Dur BA53 DipTh54 MA59. **d** 54 **p** 55. C Oakwood St Thos *Lon* 54-57; C Sudbury St Andr 57-59; V Lansdown *B & W* 59-66; V Derby St Werburgh *Derby* 66-68; V Leic St Anne *Leic* 68-75; V Humberstone 75-86; Hon Can Leic Cathl 78-93; P-in-c Leic St Eliz Nether Hall 81-86; RD Christianity N 82-86; R Gt Bowden w Welham, Glooston and Cranoe 86-93; RD Gartree I 88-93; rtd 93; Perm to Offic *Leic* and *Pet* from 93. *5 Brookfield Way, Kibworth, Leicester LE8 0SA* Tel 0116-279 2750

TREANOR, Terence Gerald. b 29. St Jo Coll Ox BA52 MA56. Wycliffe Hall Ox 52. **d** 54 **p** 55. C Hornsey Ch Ch *Lon* 54-57; C Cambridge H Trin *Ely* 57-60; V Doncaster St Mary *Sheff* 60-66; Chapl Oakham Sch 66-94; rtd 94; Perm to Offic *Leic* 94-99; *Linc* and *Pet* from 94. *35 Glebe Way, Oakham LE15 6LX* Tel (01572) 757495

TREASURE, Canon Andrew Stephen. b 51. Oriel Coll Ox BA73 MA77. St Jo Coll Nottm BA76. **d** 77 **p** 78. C Beverley Minster *York* 77-81; C Cambridge H Trin *Ely* 81-84; C Cambridge H Trin w St Andr Gt 84-85; V Eccleshill *Bradf* 85-98; P-in-c Bradf St Oswald Chapel Green 98-04; P-in-c Horton 98-04; V Lt Horton from 04; Hon Can Bradf Cathl from 04. *St Oswald's Vicarage, Christopher Street, Bradford BD5 9DH* Tel (01274) 522717

TREASURE, Geoffrey. b 39. Hatf Coll Dur BA61 Univ of Wales (Cardiff) DipEd62. Oak Hill NSM Course 90. **d** 93 **p** 94. NSM Forty Hill Jes Ch *Lon* 93-95; Consultant SW England CPAS 95-02; Perm to Offic *B & W* 95-04; P-in-c Stoke St Gregory w Burrowbridge and Lyng from 04. *Gable Cottage, West Lyng, Taunton TA3 5AP* Tel (01823) 490458 E-mail gtreasure@onetel.com

TREASURE, Mrs Joy Elvira. b 23. St Anne's Coll Ox MA50 CertEd. S Dios Minl Tr Scheme 80. **dss** 82 **d** 87 **p** 94. Tisbury *Sarum* 82-87; Hon Par Dn 87-91; rtd 92; Perm to Offic *Sarum* from 92. *Friars Lodge, 1 The Friary, Salisbury SP1 2HU* Tel (01722) 333741

TREASURE, Ronald Charles. b 24. Oriel Coll Ox BA48 MA52. Cuddesdon Coll. **d** 50 **p** 51. C Whitby *York* 50-54; C-in-c N Hull St Mich 54-58; V 58-62; V New Malton 62-89; RD Malton 63-75; rtd 89; Perm to Offic *York* from 89. *Castle Walls, Castlegate, Kirkbymoorside, York YO62 6BW* Tel (01751) 432916

TREASURE, Stephen. *See* TREASURE, Canon Andrew Stephen

TREBY, David Alan. b 47. FIBMS72 Bris Poly MSc90. St Jo Coll Nottm Dip Th Studies 94 MA95. **d** 95 **p** 96. C Camborne *Truro* 95-00; V Stoke Gabriel and Collaton *Ex* from 00. *The Vicarage, Stoke Gabriel, Totnes TQ9 6QX* Tel (01803) 782358 E-mail dave@treby.freeserve.co.uk

TREDENNICK, Canon Angela Nicolette (Nicky). b 38. SRN62 SCM63 Lon Inst of Educn HVCert66. S'wark Ord Course 87. **d** 90 **p** 94. NSM Charlwood *S'wark* 90-92; Par Dn Roehampton H Trin 92-94; C 94-97; RD Wandsworth 95-97; V Redhill St Matt from 97; RD Reigate 00-03; Hon Can S'wark Cathl from 05. *St Matthew's Vicarage, 27 Ridgeway Road, Redhill RH1 6PQ* Tel (01737) 761568

TREDWELL, Samantha Jane. b 69. Nottm Trent Univ BEd92. EMMTC 00. **d** 03 **p** 04. C Skegby w Teversal *S'well* from 03. *Teversal Parsonage, Fackley Road, Sutton-in-Ashfield NG17 3JA* Tel (01623) 550566 E-mail revtred@fish.co.uk

TREE, Robin Leslie. b 46. S Dios Minl Tr Scheme 89. **d** 92 **p** 93. NSM St Leonards Ch Ch and St Mary *Chich* 92-95; NSM Hastings H Trin 95-98; TV Bexhill St Pet 98-01; V Hampden Park from 01. *St Mary's Vicarage, 60 Brassey Avenue, Eastbourne BN22 9QH* Tel (01323) 503166 E-mail frrobin@1tree.freeserve.co.uk

TREEBY, Stephen Frank. b 46. Man Univ LLB67 Nottm Univ DipTh69 Lambeth STh01. Cuddesdon Coll 69. **d** 71 **p** 72. C Ashbourne w Mapleton *Derby* 71-74; C Boulton 74-76; Chapl Trowbridge Coll *Sarum* 76-79; TV Melksham 79-87; V Dilton's-Marsh 87-01; Chapl Westbury Hosp 87-01; R Spetisbury w Charlton Marshall etc *Sarum* from 01. *The Rectory, Spetisbury, Blandford Forum DT11 9DF* Tel (01258) 453153

TREEN, Preb Robert Hayes Mortlock. b 19. New Coll Ox BA46 MA46. Westcott Ho Cam 45. **d** 47 **p** 48. C Bath Abbey w St Jas *B & W* 47-52; PC Pill 52-61; R Bath St Sav 61-76; Preb Wells Cathl from 74; V Bishops Hull 76-84; RD Taunton S 77-81; RD Taunton 81-84; rtd 84; Perm to Offic *B & W* from 84. *13 The Leat, Bishops Lydeard, Taunton TA4 3NY* Tel (01823) 433437

TREETOPS, Ms Jacqueline. b 47. NEOC 83. **dss** 86 **d** 87 **p** 94. Low Harrogate St Mary *Ripon* 86-87; C Roundhay St Edm 87-95; C Potternewton 95-97; rtd 97; Perm to Offic *Ripon* from 01. *43 Lincombe Bank, Leeds LS8 1QG* Tel 0113-237 0474

TREFUSIS, Charles Rodolph. b 61. Hull Univ BA83. Wycliffe Hall Ox 85. **d** 90 **p** 91. C Blackheath St Jo *S'wark* 90-94; V Purley Ch Ch from 94. *The Vicarage, 38 Woodcote Valley Road, Purley CR8 3AJ* Tel (020) 8660 1790 E-mail ctrefusis@aol.com

TREGENZA, Matthew John. b 69. Univ of Wales (Lamp) BA92 SS Coll Cam PGCE93 Lon Univ MA01 FRGS96. Westcott Ho Cam 01. **d** 03 **p** 04. C Marnhull *Sarum* from 03. *2 Markstone Cottages, Duck Street, Child Okeford, Blandford Forum DT11 8ET* Tel (01258) 860100 *or* 863629 E-mail matthew@tregenza.clara.co.uk

TREHARNE, David Owen. b 73. Univ of Wales (Cardiff) BMus94 Bris Coll PGCE00 Bris Univ MEd04. Trin Coll Bris 94 St Mich Coll Llan 03. **d** 99 **p** 04. NSM Bassaleg *Mon* 99-00; C Caerphilly *Llan* from 04. *Church House, 71 Bartlett Street, Caerphilly CF83 1JT* Tel (029) 2088 2695 E-mail dtrevd@aol.com

TREHERNE, Canon Alan Thomas Evans. b 30. Univ of Wales (Lamp) BA53. Wycliffe Hall Ox. **d** 55 **p** 56. C Heref St Pet w St Owen *Heref* 55-57; India 57-72; C-in-c Netherley Ch Ch CD *Liv* 72-74; R Gateacre 74-75; TR 75-96; RD Farnworth 81-89; Hon Can Liv Cathl 94-96; rtd 96; Perm to Offic *Lich* 96-00; RD Oswestry 01-02. *19 Smale Rise, Oswestry SY11 2YL* Tel (01691) 671569 E-mail alan@treherne.co.uk

TRELLIS, The Very Revd Oswald Fitz-Burnell. b 35. Chich Th Coll 73. **d** 74 **p** 75. C Chelmsf All SS *Chelmsf* 74-78; C-in-c N Springfield CD 79-85; V Heybridge w Langford 85-94; Dean Georgetown Guyana 94-01; P-in-c Doddinghurst and Mountnessing *Chelmsf* 01-04; P-in-c Doddinghurst from 04. *The Rectory, Church Lane, Doddinghurst, Brentwood CM15 0NJ* Tel (01277) 821366

TREMBATH, Martyn Anthony. b 65. Leeds Univ BA86. Ripon Coll Cuddesdon. **d** 90 **p** 91. C Bodmin w Lanhydrock and Lanivet *Truro* 90-91; C St Erth 92-96; C Phillack w Gwithian and Gwinear 94-96; C Hayle 94-96; Asst Chapl R Free Hampstead NHS Trust 96-98; Sen Chapl R Cornwall Hosps Trust from 98. *Royal Cornwall Hospital, Truro TR1 3LJ* Tel (01872) 252883 *or* 250000

TREMELLING, Peter Ian. b 53. Ex & Truro NSM Scheme 94. **d** 96 **p** 98. NSM St Illogan *Truro* from 96. *38 Wheal Agar, Pool, Redruth TR15 3QL* Tel (01209) 210625

TREMLETT, Andrew. b 64. Pemb Coll Cam BA86 MA90 Qu Coll Ox BA88 MA95 Ex Univ MPhil96 Liv Univ PGCE03. Wycliffe Hall Ox 86. **d** 89 **p** 90. C Torquay St Matthias, St Mark and H Trin *Ex* 89-92; Miss to Seamen 92-94; Asst Chapl Rotterdam *Eur* 92-94; Chapl 94-95; TV Fareham H Trin *Portsm* 95-98; Bp's Dom Chapl 98-03; V Goring-by-Sea *Chich* from 03. *The Vicarage, 12 Compton Avenue, Goring-by-Sea, Worthing BN12 4UJ* Tel (01903) 242525 E-mail a.tremlett@btopenworld.com

TREMLETT, The Ven Anthony Frank. b 37. Ex & Truro NSM Scheme 78. **d** 81 **p** 82. C Southway *Ex* 81-82; P-in-c 82-84; V 84-88; RD Plymouth Moorside 86-88; Adn Totnes 88-94; Adn Ex 94-02; rtd 02. *57 Great Berry Road, Crownhill, Plymouth PL6 5AY* Tel (01752) 240052 E-mail tremlettaf@aol.com

TRENCHARD, Hubert John. b 26. S Dios Minl Tr Scheme. **d** 83 **p** 84. NSM Sturminster Marshall *Sarum* 83-87; NSM Blandford Forum and Langton Long 87-96. *20 Chapel Gardens, Blandford Forum DT11 7UY* Tel (01258) 459576

TRENCHARD, Hugh. b 50. Dur Univ BD72. St Mich Coll Llan 72. **d** 75 **p** 76. C Caerleon *Mon* 75-80; Dioc Chapl GFS 78-86; Asst Chapl Mon Sch 80-84; V Llanarth w Clytha, Llansantffraed and Bryngwyn *Mon* 80-84; TV Cyncoed 84-93; Prov Officer for Soc Resp 94-96; V Caerwent w Dinham and Llanfair Discoed etc from 96. *The Vicarage, Vicarage Gardens, Caerwent, Newport NP26 5BF* Tel (01291) 424984

TRENCHARD, Paul Charles Herbert Anstiss. b 53. Liv Univ LLB76. St Steph Ho Ox 77. **d** 80 **p** 81. C Torquay St Martin Barton *Ex* 80-84; R Ashprington, Cornworthy and Dittisham 84-92; R Barnwell w Tichmarsh, Thurning and Clapton *Pet* 92-04. *Place de la Courtille, 71460 St Gengoux le National, France* Tel (0033) (3) 85 92 64 47 E-mail trenchard@tiscali.fr

TRENDALL, Peter John. b 43. Oak Hill Th Coll 66. **d** 69 **p** 70. C Beckenham Ch Ch *Roch* 69-73; C Bedworth *Cov* 73-76; V Hornsey Rise St Mary *Lon* 76-82; P-in-c Upper Holloway St Steph 80-82; V Hornsey Rise St Mary w St Steph 82-84; V

Walthamstow St Mary w St Steph *Chelmsf* 84-85; TR 85-93; P-in-c Chigwell 93-94; TR Chigwell and Chigwell Row from 94. *The Rectory, 66 High Road, Chigwell IG7 6QB* Tel (020) 8500 3510 E-mail trendall@fish.co.uk

TRENDER, Lawrence. b 37. Bps' Coll Cheshunt 64. **d** 66 **p** 67. C Petersham *S'wark* 66-71; C Malden St Jo 71-73; R Thornham Magna w Thornham Parva *St E* 73-81; R Thornhams Magna and Parva, Gislingham and Mellis 81-87; P-in-c Mellis 73-81; P-in-c Gislingham 73-81; RD Hartismere 85-87; R Skipsea w Ulrome and Barmston w Fraisthorpe *York* 92-01; rtd 01; Perm to Offic *York* from 01. *Stone Cottage, 5 Far Lane, Bewholme, Driffield YO25 8EA* Tel (01964) 533020

TRESIDDER, Alistair Charles. b 65. Qu Coll Ox BA88. Cranmer Hall Dur 93. **d** 93 **p** 94. C Limehouse *Lon* 93-98; V W Hampstead St Luke from 98. *St Luke's Vicarage, 12 Kidderpore Avenue, London NW3 7SU* Tel (020) 7794 2634 *or* 7431 6317 E-mail alistairtresidder@yahoo.co.uk

TRETHEWEY, The Ven Frederick Martyn. b 49. Lon Univ BA70 DipTh77 Lambeth STh79. Oak Hill Th Coll 75. **d** 78 **p** 79. C Tollington Park St Mark w St Anne *Lon* 78-82; C Whitehall Park St Andr Hornsey Lane 82-87; TV Hornsey Rise Whitehall Park Team 87-88; V Brockmoor *Lich* 88-93; V Brockmoor *Worc* 93-01; Chapl Russells Hall Hosp Dudley 88-94; Chapl Dudley Gp of Hosps NHS Trust 94-01; RD Himley *Worc* 96-01; Hon Can Worc Cathl 99-01; Adn Dudley from 01. *15 Worcester Road, Droitwich WR9 8AA* Tel and fax (01905) 773301 E-mail fred.trethewey@ntlworld.com

TRETHEWEY, Richard John. b 74. Jes Coll Ox MA02. Wycliffe Hall Ox BA02. **d** 02 **p** 03. C Biddulph *Lich* from 02. *48 Thames Drive, Biddulph, Stoke-on-Trent ST8 7HL* Tel 07759-650572 (mobile) E-mail richard@trethewey.org.uk

TRETT, Peter John. b 44. LNSM course 96. **d** 97 **p** 98. OLM High Oak, Hingham and Scoulton w Wood Rising *Nor* from 97. *Holly House, High Common, Hardingham, Norwich NR9 4AE* Tel (01953) 850369

TREVELYAN, Preb James William Irvine. b 37. Selw Coll Cam BA64 MA67. Cuddesdon Coll 62. **d** 65 **p** 66. C Heston *Lon* 65-68; C Folkestone St Sav *Cant* 68-72; R Lenham w Boughton Malherbe 72-78; P-in-c Honiton, Gittisham, Combe Raleigh, Monkton etc *Ex* 78-79; R 79-83; TR 83-00; Chapl Ex and Distr Community Health Service NHS Trust 78-00; P-in-c Farway w Northleigh and Southleigh *Ex* 84-86; Preb Ex Cathl 95-00; rtd 00; Perm to Offic *Carl* from 02. *Bridge End, Barbon, Carnforth LA6 2LT* Tel (01524) 276530 E-mail jwitrevelyan@onetel.com

TREVOR, Canon Charles Frederic. b 27. Sarum Th Coll 54. **d** 56 **p** 57. C Sutton in Ashfield St Mich *S'well* 56-58; C Birstall *Leic* 58-61; V Prestwold w Hoton 61-66; V Thornton in Lonsdale w Burton in Lonsdale *Bradf* 66-74; V Kirkby Malham 74-85; P-in-c Coniston Cold 81-85; Hon Can Bradf Cathl 85-92; V Sutton 85-92; RD S Craven 86-91; rtd 92; Perm to Offic *Bradf* from 92. *5 Brooklyn, Threshfield, Skipton BD23 5ER* Tel (01756) 752640

TREVOR-MORGAN, Canon Basil Henry. b 27. Univ of Wales (Lamp) BA51. Wells Th Coll 51. **d** 53 **p** 54. C Chepstow *Mon* 53-56; C Halesowen *Worc* 56-59; CF (TA) 59-92; V Stourbridge St Thos *Worc* 59-76; Chapl Christchurch Hosp 76-92; V Christchurch *Win* 76-92; Hon Can Win Cathl 84-92; rtd 93; Perm to Offic *Sarum* 96-04. *2 Avon House, 112 Graham Road, Malvern WR14 2HX* Tel (01684) 561672

TREW, Mrs Ann Patricia. b 58. Ripon Coll Cuddesdon. **d** 00 **p** 01. C Hambleden Valley *Ox* 00-03; P-in-c Hedsor and Bourne End from 03. *The Rectory, 1 Wharf Lane, Bourne End SL8 5RS* Tel (01628) 523046 E-mail aptrew@btinternet.com

TREW, Jeremy Charles. b 66. Univ of Wales (Abth) BSc89 Leeds Univ MSc92. St Jo Coll Nottm MA94. **d** 97 **p** 98. C Roundhay St Edm *Ripon* 97-01; P-in-c Spofforth w Kirk Deighton from 01. *The Rectory, Church Lane, Spofforth, Harrogate HG3 1AF* Tel (01937) 590251

TREW, Robin Nicholas. b 52. UWIST BSc74. St Jo Coll Nottm 87. **d** 89 **p** 90. C Cov H Trin *Cov* 89-93; V Snitterfield w Bearley 93-02; R Allesley from 02. *The Rectory, Rectory Lane, Allesley, Coventry CV5 9EQ* Tel (024) 7640 2006 E-mail robtrew@lineone.net

TREWEEKS, Mrs Angela Elizabeth. b 35. Gilmore Ho IDC59. **dss** 59 **d** 87 **p** 94. Chapl Asst St Nic Hosp Newc 85-87; Chapl 87; Hon C Newc St Geo *Newc* 87-89; Chapl St Mary's Hosp Stannington 92-95; Hon C Rothbury *Newc* 94-96; rtd 95; Perm to Offic *Newc* from 96. *The Nook, Pondicherry, Rothbury, Morpeth NE65 7YS* Tel (01669) 620393

TRICKETT, Judith. b 50. Open Univ BA00. St Jo Coll Nottm 89. **d** 91 **p** 94. Par Dn Kimberworth *Sheff* 91-93; Dn-in-c Worsbrough Common 93-94; V 94-01; V Herringthorpe from 01. *The Vicarage, 493 Herringthorpe Valley Road, Rotherham S60 4LB* Tel (01709) 836052 Mobile 07974-404831

TRICKETT, Stanley Mervyn Wood. b 27. Lich Th Coll 64. **d** 66 **p** 67. C Kington w Huntington *Heref* 66-70; P-in-c Old Radnor 70-81; P-in-c Knill 70-81; V Shrewton *Sarum* 81-97; P-in-c Winterbourne Stoke 81-92; RD Wylye and Wilton 85-89; rtd 97; Perm to Offic *Sarum* from 97. *3 Oakwood Grove, Alderbury, Salisbury SP5 3BN* Tel (01722) 710275

TRICKETT, Preb Susan. b 42. JP89. S Dios Minl Tr Scheme 91. **d** 94 **p** 95. NSM Combe Down w Monkton Combe and S Stoke *B & W* 94-99; Dean Women Clergy 99-05; V High Littleton from 99; Preb Wells Cathl from 00. *Holy Trinity Vicarage, Church Hill, High Littleton, Bristol BS39 6HG* Tel (01761) 472097 E-mail susi.trickett@btinternet.com

TRICKEY, Christopher Jolyon. b 57. Barrister-at-Law 80 Jes Coll Cam BA79 MA83. Trin Coll Bris BA90. **d** 90 **p** 91. C Chesham Bois *Ox* 90-94; R Busbridge *Guildf* 94-98; P-in-c Hambledon 97-98; R Busbridge and Hambledon from 98; Chapl Godalming Coll from 01. *Busbridge Rectory, Brighton Road, Godalming GU7 1XA* Tel (01483) 418820 Fax 421267 E-mail rev_j_trickey@yahoo.co.uk

TRICKEY, Canon Frederick Marc. b 35. Dur Univ BA62. Cranmer Hall Dur. **d** 64 **p** 65. C Alton St Lawr *Win* 64-68; V Win St Jo cum Winnall 68-77; Angl Adv Channel TV from 77; R Guernsey St Martin *Win* 77-02; P-in-c Sark 02-03; Dean Guernsey 95-03; Hon Can Win Cathl 95-03; rtd 03. *L'Esperance, La Route des Camps, St Martin, Guernsey GY4 6AD* Tel (01481) 238441

TRICKLEBANK, Steven. b 56. Nottm Univ BTh88. Linc Th Coll 85. **d** 88 **p** 89. C Ditton St Mich *Liv* 88-91; C Wigan All SS 91-93; Chapl Aintree Hosps NHS Trust Liv 93-97; C-in-c St Edm Anchorage Lane CD *Sheff* 97-00; Chapl Doncaster R Infirmary and Montagu Hosp NHS Trust 97-00; V Stocksbridge *Sheff* 00-04; V Streatham Ch Ch *S'wark* from 04; V Streatham Hill St Marg from 04. *Christ Church Vicarage, 3 Christchurch Road, London SW2 3ET* Tel (020) 8674 5723 E-mail steventricklebank@hotmail.com

TRIFFITT, Jonathan Paul. b 74. St Jo Coll Nottm BA03. **d** 03 **p** 04. C W Kilburn St Luke w St Simon and St Jude *Lon* from 03; C Paddington Em Harrow Road from 03. *Flat 2, 228 Fernhead Road, London W9 3EH* Tel (020) 8968 8985 E-mail j.triffitt@btinternet.com

TRIGG, Jeremy Michael. b 51. Open Univ BA88. Ripon Coll Cuddesdon 80. **d** 81 **p** 82. C Roundhay St Edm *Ripon* 81-84; C Harrogate St Wilfrid and St Luke 84-87; TV Pocklington Team *York* 87-90; R Rowley w Skidby 90-97; TV Wolverton *Ox* 97-98; R from 98. *28 Harvester Close, Greenleys, Milton Keynes MK12 6LE* Tel (01908) 222802

TRIGG, Jonathan David. b 49. Ex Coll Ox BA71 MA75 Dur Univ PhD92. Cranmer Hall Dur BA82. **d** 83 **p** 84. C Enfield St Andr *Lon* 83-87; V Oakwood St Thos 87-96; AD Enfield 92-96; V Highgate St Mich from 96; AD W Haringey from 00. *The Vicarage, 10 The Grove, London N6 6LB* Tel and fax (020) 8347 5124 *or* 8340 7279 E-mail jaydeen6@supanet.com

TRILL, Barry. b 42. Chich Th Coll 65. **d** 68 **p** 69. C W Hackney St Barn *Lon* 68-73; TV Is of Dogs Ch Ch and St Jo w St Luke 73-78; P-in-c Hastings All So *Chich* 78-79; V 79-99; rtd 99; Perm to Offic *Chich* from 01. *12 Heathlands, Westfield, Hastings TN35 4QZ* Tel (01424) 753595

TRILL, Victor Alfred Mansfield. b 21. St Deiniol's Hawarden. **d** 81 **p** 82. Hon C Prestbury *Ches* 81-83; Hon C Church Hulme 83-85; V Marbury 85-90; rtd 90; Perm to Offic *Ches* from 90. *5 Maisterson Court, Nantwich CW5 5TZ* Tel (01270) 628948

TRIMBLE, Mrs Anne Inman. b 40. Kenton Lodge Tr Coll CertEd60 Cam Univ DipRS84. NEOC 89. **d** 92 **p** 94. NSM Longnewton w Elton *Dur* 92-94; rtd 94; Perm to Offic *Dur* 94-98. *Address temp unknown*

TRIMBLE, Canon John Alexander. b 33. Lon Univ BD65. Edin Th Coll 55. **d** 58 **p** 59. C Glas St Mary *Glas* 58-60; C Edin St Jo *Edin* 60-65; R Baillieston *Glas* 65-69; R Falkirk *Edin* 69-86; R Troon *Glas* 86-98; Can St Mary's Cathl 91-98; rtd 98; Perm to Offic *Newc* from 98. *4 Hencotes Mews, Hexham NE46 2DZ* Tel (01434) 603032

TRIMBLE, Thomas Henry. b 36. TCD DipTh82 BTh90. CITC 79. **d** 82 **p** 83. C Seapatrick *D & D* 82-85; I Magheracross *Clogh* 85-90; Bp's Appeal Sec 89-90; I Donegal w Killymard, Lough Eskc and Laghey *D & R* 90-01; Can Raphoe Cathl 93-01; rtd 01. *Tyrone House, Tullycullion, Donegal, Irish Republic* Tel (00353) (74) 974 0706

TRIMBY, George Henry. b 44. DipTh. Trin Coll Bris 84. **d** 86 **p** 87. C Newtown w Llanllwchaiarn w Aberhafesp *St As* 86-88; P-in-c Llanfair DC, Derwen, Llanelidan and Efenechtyd 88-90; V 90-95; V Llanasa from 95; P-in-c Whitford 98-02; AD Holywell from 03. *The Vicarage, Llanasa Road, Gronant, Prestatyn LL19 9TL* Tel (01745) 888797

TRIMMER, Miss Penelope Marynice. b 65. STETS 01. **d** 04 **p** 05. C Talbot Village *Sarum* from 04. *18 Hillside Road, Poole BH12 5DY* Tel (01202) 381088 Mobile 07733-172460

TRINDER, John Derek. b 28. Glouc Th Course 74. **d** 77 **p** 78. C Forest of Dean Ch Ch w English Bicknor *Glouc* 77; Hon C 77-79; Hon C Chepstow *Mon* 79-81; C Newport St Paul 81-82; V Dingestow and Llangovan w Penyclawdd and Tregaer 82-87; V Kirton in Holland *Linc* 87-93; rtd 93; Perm to Offic *Linc* 93-02. *3 Arkendale, Whittington College, London Road, Felbridge, East Grinstead RH19 2QU* Tel (01342) 326413

TRIPLOW, Keith John. b 44. Selw Coll Cam BA66 MA70. Chich Th Coll 70. **d** 72 **p** 73. C Ipswich All Hallows *St E* 72-76; C Dartford H Trin *Roch* 76-78; V Fyfield w Tubney and Kingston Bagpuize *Ox* from 78. *The Vicarage, Fyfield, Abingdon OX13 5LR* Tel (01865) 390803

TRIST, Richard McLeod. b 55. Univ of NSW BSEd76. Ridley Coll Melbourne BTh86 DipMin86. **d** 87 **p** 87. Australia 87-96 and from 01; C Langham Place All So *Lon* 97-01; V Camberwell St Mark from 01. *1 Canterbury Road, Camberwell, Vic, Australia 3124* Tel (0061) (3) 9897 1532 *or* 9882 3776 Fax 9882 6514 E-mail richard.trist@bigpond.com *or* stmarksc@bigpond.com

TRISTRAM, Canon Catherine Elizabeth. b 31. Somerville Coll Ox BA53 MA57. **dss** 83 **d** 87 **p** 94. Holy Is *Newc* 84-87; Hon C 87-01; Hon Can Newc Cathl 94-01; Perm to Offic from 01. *4 Lewins Lane, Holy Island, Berwick-upon-Tweed TD15 2SB* Tel (01289) 389306

TRISTRAM, Geoffrey Robert. b 53. K Coll Lon BA76 Pemb Coll Cam BA78 MA80. Westcott Ho Cam 77. **d** 79 **p** 80. C Weymouth H Trin *Sarum* 79-82; C Gt Berkhamsted *St Alb* 83-85; OSB 85-99; Asst Chapl Oundle Sch 86-88; Sen Chapl 88-91; R Welwyn w Ayot St Peter *St Alb* 91-99; Chapl Qu Victoria Hosp and Danesbury Home 91-99; SSJE USA from 99. *Society of St John the Evangelist, 980 Memorial Drive, Cambridge, MA 02138, USA* Tel (001) (617) 876 3037

TRISTRAM, Canon Michael Anthony. b 50. Solicitor 76 Ch Coll Cam BA72 MA76. Ripon Coll Cuddesdon 79. **d** 82 **p** 83. C Stanmore *Win* 82-85; R Abbotts Ann and Upper and Goodworth Clatford 85-92; V Pershore w Pinvin, Wick and Birlingham *Worc* 92-03; Hon Can Worc Cathl 00-03; Can Res Portsm Cathl *Portsm* from 03. *51 High Street, Portsmouth PO1 2LU* Tel (023) 9273 1282 *or* 9234 7605 Fax 9229 5480 E-mail michael.tristram@ntlworld.com

TRIVASSE, Keith Malcolm. b 59. Man Univ BA81 CertEd82 MPhil90 Birm Univ DipTh86 Dur Univ MA98. Qu Coll Birm 84. **d** 86 **p** 87. C Prestwich St Marg *Man* 86-88; C Orford St Marg *Liv* 88-90; TV Sunderland *Dur* 90-91; P-in-c N Hylton St Marg Castletown 91-95; R Bothal and Pegswood w Longhirst *Newc* 95-97; P-in-c Bury Ch King *Man* from 01; P-in-c Bury St Paul 01-03. *St Paul's Vicarage, Fir Street, Bury BL9 7QG* Tel 0161-761 6991 E-mail keith.trivasse@care4free.net

TRIVASSE, Ms Margaret. b 59. Dur Univ BA80 MA97 New Coll Dur PGCE01 Liv Univ MTh05. N Ord Course 01. **d** 04 **p** 05. NSM Radcliffe *Man* from 04. *St Paul's Vicarage, Fir Street, Bury BL9 7QG* Tel 0161-761 6991 E-mail margtriv@yahoo.co.uk

TRODDEN, Michael John. b 54. K Coll Lon BD77 AKC77 CertEd. Wycliffe Hall Ox 79. **d** 80 **p** 81. C Woodford St Mary w St Phil and St Jas *Chelmsf* 80-87; V Aldborough Hatch 87-96; R Ampthill w Millbrook and Steppingley *St Alb* from 96. *The Rectory, Rectory Lane, Ampthill, Bedford MK45 2EL* Tel (01525) 402320

TROLLOPE, David Harvey. b 41. BSc63. Lon Coll of Div 66. **d** 68 **p** 69. C Bermondsey St Jas w Ch Ch *S'wark* 68-71; CMS Namibia 71-72; Uganda 72-77; Kenya 77-82; V Gt Crosby St Luke *Liv* 82-04; rtd 04. *26 White House Lane, Heswall, Wirral CH60 1UQ* Tel 0151-342 2648

TROMANS, Kevin Stanley. b 57. St Martin's Coll Lanc BEd79. Aston Tr Scheme 90 Coll of Resurr Mirfield 92. **d** 94 **p** 95. C Rawdon *Bradf* 94-96; C Woodhall 96-98; V Liversedge w Hightown *Wakef* 98-02; V Bierley *Bradf* from 02. *St John's Vicarage, Bierley Lane, Bradford BD4 6AA* Tel and fax (01274) 681397 E-mail kevandkate@ktromans.freeserve.co.uk

TROMBETTI, Lynda Joan. b 52. **d** 03 **p** 04. OLM Dorking w Ranmore *Guildf* from 03. *Mead Cottage, Pilgrims Way, Westhumble, Dorking RH5 6AP* Tel and fax (01306) 884360 Mobile 07968-629364 E-mail theflyingtrombettis@compuserve.com

TROOD, James William. b 68. Cov Poly BSc90 St Jo Coll Dur PGCE91. St Jo Coll Nottm MTh02. **d** 02 **p** 03. C Anchorsholme *Blackb* from 02. *2 Norman Close, Thornton-Cleveleys FY5 3UA* Tel (01253) 854376 Mobile 07713-139571 E-mail jimtrood@breathemail.net

TROTMAN, Anthony Edward Fiennes. b 11. Ex Coll Ox BA33 MA56. Wycliffe Hall Ox 46. **d** 48 **p** 49. C Ballymacarrett St Patr *D & D* 48-51; C Dundela St Mark 51-52; R Corsley *Sarum* 52-59; R Chilmark 59-76; P-in-c Teffont Evias and Teffont Magna 73-75; rtd 76; Perm to Offic *Sarum* from 76. *17 Estcourt Road, Salisbury SP1 3AP* Tel (01722) 324857

TROTT, Stephen. b 57. Hull Univ BA79 Fitzw Coll Cam BA83 MA87 Univ of Wales (Cardiff) LLM03 FRSA86. Westcott Ho Cam 81. **d** 84 **p** 85. C Hessle *York* 84-87; C Kingston upon Hull St Alb 87-88; R Pitsford w Boughton *Pet* from 88; Sec CME 88-93; Chapl Northants Gr Sch from 91. *The Rectory, Humfrey Lane, Boughton, Northampton NN2 8RQ* Tel (01604) 845655 Fax 08701-305526 E-mail strott@btinternet.com

TROTTER, Harold Barrington (Barry). b 33. Sarum Th Coll 64. **d** 66 **p** 67. C Salisbury St Fran *Sarum* 66-69; Dioc Youth Officer 69-72; V Horton and Chalbury 69-73; R Frenchay *Bris* 73-81; V Henbury 81-99; rtd 99; Perm to Offic *Ex* 00-02; *Glouc* from 02. *14 Butlers Mead, Blakeney GL15 4EH* Tel (01594) 510176

TROUNSON, Ronald Charles. b 26. Em Coll Cam BA48 MA52. Ripon Hall Ox 54. **d** 56 **p** 57. C Plymouth St Gabr *Ex* 56-58; Chapl Denstone Coll Uttoxeter 58-76; Bursar 76-78; Prin St Chad's Coll Dur 78-88; R Easton on the Hill, Collyweston w Duddington etc *Pet* 89-94; NSM 94-99; RD Barnack 91-94; rtd 94; Perm to Offic *Pet* from 99. *c/o R Trounson Esq, 13 Orchard Drive, Durham DH1 1LA*

TROUT, Keith. b 49. Trin Coll Bris DipHE92. **d** 92 **p** 93. C Pudsey St Lawr and St Paul *Bradf* 92-97; V Burley *Ripon* from 97. *St Matthias Vicarage, 271 Burley Road, Leeds LS4 2EL* Tel 0113-278 5872 *or* 230 4408 E-mail keithtrout@stmatthias.co.uk

TRUBY, Canon David Charles. b 57. BA79. Linc Th Coll 79. **d** 82 **p** 83. C Stanley *Liv* 82-85; C Hindley St Pet 85-90; R Brimington *Derby* 90-98; Can Res Derby Cathl 98-03; TR Wirksworth from 03; Hon Can Derby Cathl from 04. *The Rectory, Coldwell Street, Wirksworth, Matlock DE4 4FB* Tel (01629) 824707 E-mail david.truby@btinternet.com

TRUDGILL, Harry Keith. b 25. LCP54 Leeds Univ DipEd49 Lon Univ BD61. St Deiniol's Hawarden 76. **d** 76 **p** 76. In Methodist Ch 58-75; C Glas St Marg *Glas* 76-78; R Lenzie 78-86; rtd 86; Perm to Offic *Bradf* from 86. *10 Wharfe View, Grassington, Skipton BD23 5NL* Tel (01756) 752114

TRUEMAN, Reginald. b 24. K Coll Cam BA47 MA49 Man Univ BD53. St Jo Coll Winnipeg Hon DD58 Ely Th Coll 48 Union Th Sem (NY) STM50. **d** 50 **p** 51. C Bolton St Pet *Man* 50-53; Hong Kong 53-61; Prin Union Th Coll 57-61; Lect K Coll Lon 61-74; Sen Lect N Co Coll of Educn 75-78; Teacher Manor Park Sch Newc 78-82; Lesotho 84-86; rtd 92. *22 The Square, Petersfield GU32 3HS* Tel (01730) 261341

TRUMAN, Miss Catherine Jane. b 64. Coll of Ripon & York St Jo BEd88. St Jo Coll Nottm 01. **d** 03 **p** 04. C Owlerton *Sheff* from 03. *195 Walkley Lane, Sheffield S6 2PA* Tel 0114-281 3541 E-mail jane.truman@btopenworld.com

TRUMAN, Miss Charlotte Jane. b 71. Birm Univ BPhil96. Westcott Ho Cam CTM99. **d** 99 **p** 00. C High Harrogate Ch Ch *Ripon* 99-03; P-in-c Oulton w Woodlesford from 03. *The Vicarage, 46 Holmsley Lane, Woodlesford, Leeds LS26 8RY* Tel 0113-282 0411 E-mail cjtruman@christchurch80.freeserve.co.uk

TRUMPER, Roger David. b 52. Ex Univ BSc74 K Coll Lon MSc75 Ox Univ BA80 MA85. Wycliffe Hall Ox 78. **d** 81 **p** 82. C Tunbridge Wells St Jo *Roch* 81-84; C Slough *Ox* 84-87; TV Shenley and Loughton 87-88; TV Watling Valley 88-93; R Byfleet *Guildf* 93-05; TV Sidmouth, Woolbrook, Salcombe Regis, Sidbury etc *Ex* from 05. *All Saints' Vicarage, All Saints' Road, Sidmouth EX10 8ES* Tel (01395) 515963 E-mail roger.thetrumpers@virgin.net

TRURO, Bishop of. *See* IND, The Rt Revd William

TRURO, Dean of. *Vacant*

TRUSS, Canon Charles Richard. b 42. Reading Univ BA63 Linacre Coll Ox BA66 MA69 K Coll Lon MPhil79. Wycliffe Hall Ox 64. **d** 66 **p** 67. C Leic H Apostles *Leic* 66-69; C Hampstead St Jo *Lon* 69-72; V Belsize Park 72-79; V Wood Green St Mich 79-82; TR Wood Green St Mich w Bounds Green St Gabr etc 82-85; R Shepperton 85-94; V Waterloo St Jo w St Andr *S'wark* from 94; RD Lambeth from 95; Hon Can S'wark Cathl from 01; Sen Chapl Actors' Ch Union from 04. *St John's Vicarage, 1 Secker Street, London SE1 8UF* Tel and fax (020) 7928 4470 *or* tel 7633 9819 E-mail rtruss@stjohnswaterloo.co.uk

TRUSTRAM, Canon David Geoffrey. b 49. Pemb Coll Ox BA71 MA76 Qu Coll Cam BA73 MA77. Westcott Ho Cam 74. **d** 75 **p** 76. C Surbiton St Mark *S'wark* 75-77; C Surbiton St Andr and St Mark 77-78; C Richmond St Mary 78-79; C Richmond St Mary w St Matthias and St Jo 79-82; P-in-c Eastry *Cant* 82-88; R Eastry and Northbourne w Tilmanstone etc 88-90; Chapl Eastry Hosp 82-90; V Tenterden St Mildred w Smallhythe *Cant* from 90; Hon Can Cant Cathl from 96; AD Tenterden 99-05. *The Vicarage, Church Road, Tenterden TN30 6AT* Tel (01580) 763118 Fax 761173 E-mail trustram@btinternet.com

TSANG, Wing Man. b 52. Lon Univ BSc74 MPhil84 MCB88 MRCPath88 FRCPath96. STETS 99. **d** 02 **p** 03. C Merthyr Tydfil Ch Ch *Llan* 02-05; TV Broadwater St Mary *Chich* from 05. *67 Normandy Road, Worthing BN14 7EA* Tel (07961) 839018 E-mail wing2699@hotmail.com

TSIPOURAS, John George. b 38. Trin Coll Bris 76. **d** 78 **p** 79. C Cheadle Hulme St Andr *Ches* 78-82; V Hurdsfield 82-03; rtd 03; P-in-c W Heath *Birm* from 04. *5 Ashfurlong Close, Balsall Common, Coventry CV7 7QA* Tel (01676) 534048 E-mail john@tsipouras.org.uk

TUAM, Archdeacon of. *See* PREVITE, The Ven Anthony Michael Allen

TUAM, Dean of. *See* GRIMASON, The Very Revd Alistair John

TUAM, KILLALA AND ACHONRY, Bishop of. *See* HENDERSON, The Rt Revd Richard Crosbie Aitken

TUAM, Provost of. *See* TOWERS, The Very Revd Patrick Leo

TUBBS, Preb Brian Ralph. b 44. AKC66. **d** 67 **p** 68. C Ex St Thos *Ex* 67-72; TV Sidmouth, Woolbrook and Salcombe Regis 72-77; R Ex St Jas 77-96; RD Christianity 89-95; Preb Ex Cathl from 95; V Paignton St Jo from 96; Chapl S Devon Healthcare NHS Trust from 96. *The Vicarage, Palace Place, Paignton TQ3 3AQ* Tel (01803) 559059 E-mail father_tubbs@compuserve.com

TUBBS, Canon Christopher Norman. b 25. G&C Coll Cam BA51 MA54. Wycliffe Hall Ox. **d** 52 **p** 53. C Neston *Ches* 52-55; C Nor St Pet Mancroft *Nor* 55-59; V Scalby *York* 59-68; V Scalby w Ravenscar and Staintondale 68-95; RD Scarborough 76-82; Can and Preb York Minster 85-96; rtd 95; Perm to Offic *York* from 96. *9 Mill Lane, West Ayton, Scarborough YO13 9JT* Tel (01723) 863211

TUBBS, Gary Andrew. b 59. Univ of Wales (Swansea) BA82 Bris Univ MSc84 Bris Poly PGCE84. Oak Hill Th Coll. **d** 00 **p** 01. C Stanwix *Carl* 00-02; C Carl H Trin and St Barn from 02. *St Barnabas' Rectory, Brookside, Carlisle CA2 7SU* Tel (01228) 515274 E-mail garytubbs@bigfoot.com

TUBBS, Mrs Margaret Amy. SW Minl Tr Course. **d** 01. OLM St Martin w Looe *Truro* from 01; Admin Epiphany Ho from 04. *The Stables, Port Looe, Looe PL13 2HZ* Tel (01503) 265628 E-mail stablesretreat@onetel.com

TUBBS, Peter Alfred. b 22. G&C Coll Cam BA48 MA53. Linc Th Coll 55. **d** 57 **p** 58. C Tettenhall Regis *Lich* 57-60; C Wellington Ch Ch 60-64; Asst Chapl Keele Univ 65-69; V Cardington *St Alb* 69-85; RD Elstow 77-82; C Sandy 85-89; rtd 89; Perm to Offic *St Alb* from 89. *1 Foster Grove, Sandy SG19 1HP* Tel (01767) 682803

TUCK, Andrew Kenneth. b 42. Kelham Th Coll 63. **d** 68 **p** 69. C Poplar *Lon* 68-74; TV 74-76; V Walsgrave on Sowe *Cov* 76-90; R Farnham *Guildf* from 90; Chapl Surrey Hants Borders NHS Trust from 90; RD Farnham *Guildf* 00-05. *The Rectory, Upper Church Lane, Farnham GU9 7PW* Tel (01252) 715412 E-mail andrew.tuck@ic24.net *or* farnhamrectory@tiscali.co.uk

TUCK, David John. b 36. St Cath Coll Cam BA61 MA65. Cuddesdon Coll 61. **d** 63 **p** 64. C Holt and Kelling w Salthouse *Nor* 63-68; Zambia 68-73; V Sprowston *Nor* 73-84; R Beeston St Andr 73-84; RD Nor N 81-84; V Pinner *Lon* 84-01; rtd 01; Perm to Offic *Lon* 02-04 and *St Alb* from 04; Hon C N Harrow St Alb *Lon* from 04. *119 High Street, Northwood HA6 1ED* Tel (01923) 825806 E-mail dandtuck@btinternet.com

TUCK, Gillian. b 40. SRN64 SCM66. Llan Dioc Tr Scheme 93. **d** 97 **p** 98. NSM Pontypridd St Cath w St Matt *Llan* 97-01; P-in-c Pontypridd St Matt and Cilfynydd 01-05; NSM Pontypridd St Matt and Cilfynydd w Llanwynno from 05. *4 Maes Glas, Coed y Cwm, Pontypridd CF37 3EJ* Tel (01443) 791049

TUCK, Nigel Graham. b 57. Chich Th Coll 82. **d** 85 **p** 86. C Port Talbot St Theodore *Llan* 85-87; C Llantrisant 87-90; TV Duston Team *Pet* 90-95; C Aldwick *Chich* 95-98; C-in-c N Bersted CD 98-00; V N Bersted 01-02; rtd 02. *102 Wallace Avenue, Worthing BN11 5QA*

TUCK, Ralph Thomas. b 42. Worc Coll Ox BA64 Bris Univ CertEd66 Leeds Univ DipFE81. N Ord Course 87. **d** 90 **p** 91. NSM S Crosland *Wakef* 90-93; NSM Helme 90-93; Perm to Offic from 93. *48 Kirkwood Drive, Huddersfield HD3 3WJ*

TUCK, Ronald James. b 47. S'wark Ord Course 75. **d** 78 **p** 79. C Upper Holloway St Pet w St Jo *Lon* 78-81; P-in-c Scottow and Swanton Abbott w Skeyton *Nor* 81-88; R Bradwell from 88. *The Rectory, Church Walk, Bradwell, Great Yarmouth NR31 8QQ* Tel (01493) 663219 E-mail revtuck@evemail.net

TUCKER, Andrew Michael. b 64. K Coll Lon BD87. Wycliffe Hall Ox DipMin95. **d** 95 **p** 96. C Moreton *Ches* 95-96; C Poynton 96-99; C Polegate *Chich* 99-02; C-in-c Lower Willingdon St Wilfrid CD from 03. *St Wilfrid's House, 90 Broad Road, Lower Willingdon, Eastbourne BN20 9RA* Tel (01323) 482088

TUCKER, Anthony Ian. b 50. CYCW78. CA Tr Coll 73 S'wark Ord Course 81. **d** 85 **p** 86. NSM E Ham w Upton Park St Alb *Chelmsf* 85-86; NSM S'well Minster *S'well* 86-90; C Rolleston w Fiskerton, Morton and Upton 90-93; P-in-c Teversal 93-96; Chapl Sutton Cen 93-96; P-in-c Norwell w Ossington, Cromwell and Caunton 96-04; Dioc Tourism Adv 96-04; V Balderton and Barnby-in-the-Willows from 04; AD Newark from 00. *The Vicarage, Main Street, Balderton, Newark NG24 3NN* Tel (01636) 704811 E-mail tony@cloud9-online.com

TUCKER, Desmond Robert. b 29. Bris Sch of Min 83. **d** 86 **p** 87. C Bris St Mich *Bris* 86-88; P-in-c 88-94; rtd 94; Perm to Offic *Bris* from 94. *94 Fremantle House, Dove Street, Bristol BS2 8LH* Tel 0117-924 6803

TUCKER, Douglas Greening. b 17. St Aid Birkenhead 49. **d** 52 **p** 53. C Jesmond Clayton Memorial *Newc* 52-56; C Fenham St Jas and St Basil 56-58; V Cowgate 58-62; V Elsham *Linc* 62-85; V Worlaby 62-85; V Bonby 73-85; rtd 85; Perm to Offic *Newc* 85-02. *Balintore, 4 Kilrymont Place, St Andrews KY16 8DH* Tel (01334) 476738

TUCKER, Harold George. b 21. St Aug Coll Cant 48 Sarum Th Coll 50. **d** 51 **p** 52. C S Molton w Nymet St George *Ex* 51-56; V Mariansleigh and Romansleigh w Meshaw 56-64; R Bratton Fleming 64-73; P-in-c Goodleigh 67-73; P-in-c Stoke Rivers 67-73; P-in-c Parracombe 69-73; P-in-c Martinhoe 69-73; R Whimple 73-86; rtd 86; Perm to Offic *Ex* and *Truro* from 86. *Lansdowne, The Crescent, Widemouth Bay, Bude EX23 0AE* Tel (01288) 361396

TUCKER, Ian Malcolm. b 46. S Dios Minl Tr Scheme 86. **d** 89 **p** 90. NSM Pill w Easton in Gordano and Portbury *B & W* 89-95; C Frome St Jo and St Mary 95-99; TV Redruth w Lanner and Treleigh *Truro* 99-04; P-in-c Par from 04; Hon Chapl Miss to Seafarers from 04. *The Vicarage, 42 Vicarage Road, Tywardreath, Par PL24 2PH* Tel (01726) 812775 E-mail iandm@btopenworld.com

TUCKER, John Yorke Raffles. b 24. Magd Coll Cam BA49 MA56. Westcott Ho Cam 49. **d** 51 **p** 52. C Shadwell St Paul w Ratcliffe St Jas *Lon* 51-54; C Preston Ascension 54-58; V S Hackney St Mich 58-67; V Belmont 67-78; V Sunbury 78-89; rtd 89; Perm to Offic *Ex* 89-93 and *B & W* from 93. *Tudor Cottage, Fivehead, Taunton TA3 6PJ* Tel (01460) 281330

TUCKER, Michael. b 33. **d** 84 **p** 85. NSM Sawston *Ely* 84-87; C Ely 87-90; P-in-c Barton Bendish w Beachamwell and Shingham 90-98; P-in-c Wereham 90-98; rtd 98; Perm to Offic *Nor* 99-04 and *Ely* from 00. *20 Priory Lane, King's Lynn PE30 5DU* Tel (01553) 774707

TUCKER, Canon Michael Owen. b 42. Lon Univ BSc66 Surrey Univ PhD69. Glouc Sch of Min 81. **d** 84 **p** 85. NSM Uley w Owlpen and Nympsfield *Glouc* 84-92; P-in-c Amberley from 92; Dioc NSM Officer from 94; Hon Can Glouc Cathl from 98; RD Stonehouse 99-04. *The Rectory, Amberley, Stroud GL5 5JG* Tel (01453) 878515 Fax 08704-320747 E-mail mike@tuckers.org.uk

TUCKER, Nicholas Harold. b 41. Reading Univ BSc66. N Ord Course 90. **d** 93 **p** 94. NSM Ilkley All SS *Bradf* 93-98; P-in-c Uley w Owlpen and Nympsfield *Glouc* from 98. *The Rectory, The Green, Uley, Dursley GL11 5SN* Tel (01453) 860249 Fax 861184 E-mail nick@tucker141.fsnet.co.uk

TUCKER, Nicholas John Cuthbert. b 74. Birm Univ BSc. Oak Hill Th Coll MTh04. **d** 04 **p** 05. C Bebington *Ches* from 04. *8 Rolleston Drive, Bebington, Wirral CH63 3DB* Tel 0151-645 1244 Mobile 07957-566714 E-mail njctucker@hotmail.com

TUCKER, Richard Parish. b 51. Cam Univ BA72 MA76 Lon Univ BD83. Wycliffe Hall Ox 80. **d** 83 **p** 84. C Wellington w Eyton *Lich* 83-84; C Walsall 84-88; TV Dronfield *Derby* 88-90; TV Dronfield w Holmesfield 90-98; V Sutton Coldfield St Columba *Birm* from 98. *St Columba's Vicarage, 280 Chester Road North, Sutton Coldfield B73 6RR* Tel 0121-354 5873 E-mail richardtucker@tiscali.co.uk

TUCKER, Stephen Reid. b 51. New Coll Ox BA72 MA76 Lon Univ DipC&G96. Ripon Coll Cuddesdon DipTh76. **d** 77 **p** 78. C Hove All SS *Chich* 77-80; Lect Chich Th Coll 80-86; V Portsea St Alb *Portsm* 86-90; Chapl and Dean of Div New Coll Ox 90-95; P-in-c Ovingdean *Chich* 96-01; Bp's Adv on CME 96-01; V Hampstead St Jo *Lon* from 01. *The Vicarage, 14 Church Row, London NW3 6UU* Tel (020) 7435 0553 *or* 7794 5808 E-mail stephentucker@surefish.co.uk

TUCKER, Mrs Susan. b 53. Stockwell Coll of Educn CertEd74. **d** 97 **p** 98. C Taunton St Andr *B & W* 97-01; V Bishops Hull from 01; Chapl St Marg Hospice from 01. *The Vicarage, Bishops Hull Hill, Bishops Hull, Taunton TA1 5EB* Tel (01823) 333032 E-mail suetucker@tuckers99.freeserve.co.uk

TUCKER, Vivian Clive Temple. b 39. Univ of Wales (Swansea) BSc60 Univ of Wales DipEd61. St As Minl Tr Course 93. **d** 96 **p** 97. NSM Gresford *St As* 96-04; NSM Holt, Rossett and Isycoed from 04. *8 Snowdon Drive, Ty Gwyn, Wrexham LL11 2UY* Tel (01978) 359226

TUCKETT, Christopher Mark. b 48. Qu Coll Cam MA71 Lanc Univ PhD79. Westcott Ho Cam 71. **d** 75 **p** 76. C Lancaster St Mary *Blackb* 75-77; Chapl and Fell Qu Coll Cam 77-79; Lect NT Man Univ 79-89; Sen Lect 89-91; Prof Bibl Studies 91-96; Lect NT Ox Univ from 96; Perm to Offic *Ches* from 93 and *Derby* from 98. *Pembroke College, Oxford OX1 1DW* Tel (01865) 276426 E-mail christopher.tuckett@theology.ox.ac.uk

TUDBALL, Arthur James. b 28. AKC54. **d** 54 **p** 55. C Munster Square St Mary Magd *Lon* 54-56; Malaysia 63-73 and 75-79; Brunei 73-75; Singapore from 79; rtd 89. *Marine Parade Post Office, PO Box 529, Singapore 914401* Tel (0065) 3422258 Fax 3422259

TUDGE, Paul Quartus. b 55. Leeds Univ BEd78. Cranmer Hall Dur 84. **d** 87 **p** 88. C Roundhay St Edm *Ripon* 87-90; C Leeds City 91; V Woodside 91-99; Warden of Readers 96-99; V Ilkley All SS *Bradf* from 99; RD Otley from 02. *The Vicarage, 58 Curly Hill, Ilkley LS29 0BA* Tel (01943) 607537 *or* 816035 Fax 607058 E-mail paultudge@btinternet.com

TUDGEY, Stephen John. b 51. Nottm Univ BTh81 Westmr Coll Ox MTh00. St Jo Coll Nottm LTh81. **d** 81 **p** 82. C Grays Thurrock *Chelmsf* 81-84; C Madeley *Heref* 84-87; R Chilcompton w Downside and Stratton on the Fosse *B & W* 87-03; P-in-c Falmouth K Chas *Truro* from 03; Hon Chapl Miss to Seafarers from 04. *The Rectory, 19 Trescobeas Road, Falmouth TR11 2JB* Tel (01326) 319141 E-mail steve.tudgey@tiscali.co.uk

TUDOR, David Charles Frederick. b 42. Sarum Th Coll 70. **d** 73 **p** 74. C Plymouth St Pet *Ex* 73-75; C Reddish *Man* 75-78; P-in-c Hamer 78-80; V Goldenhill *Lich* 80-87; V Meir 87-91; Chapl Asst Nottm City Hosp 91-94; Chapl Cen Sheff Univ Hosps NHS Trust 94-96; V Nottingham St Geo w St Jo *S'well* 96-04; rtd 05. *102 St Albans Road, Nottingham NG6 9HG* Tel 0115-975 0184 Mobile 07811-866348

TUDOR, David St Clair. b 55. K Coll Lon BD77 AKC77 K Coll Lon MTh89. Ripon Coll Cuddesdon 77. **d** 78 **p** 79. C Plumstead St Nic *S'wark* 78-80; C Redhill St Matt 80-83; C-in-c Reigate St Phil CD 83-87; Asst Sec Gen Syn Bd for Miss and Unity 87-88; Perm to Offic *S'wark* 94-97; TV Canvey Is *Chelmsf* 97-00; TR from 00. *St Nicholas House, 210 Long Road, Canvey Island SS8 0JR* Tel (01268) 682586 E-mail dstudor@tinyworld.co.uk

TUDOR, Malcolm George Henry Booth. b 36. Nottm Univ BA71. Linc Th Coll 72. **d** 60 **p** 61. In RC Ch 60-71; C Cinderhill *S'well* 72-74; P-in-c Broxtowe 74-78; Public Preacher from 75; P-in-c E Drayton w Stokeham 78-86; R E Markham and Askham 78-86; P-in-c Headon w Upton 78-86; V Llandinam w Trefeglwys w Penstrowed *Ban* 86-01; rtd 01; Perm to Offic *Ban* from 01. *14 Rhos-y-Maen Isaf, Llanidloes SY18 6LB* Tel (01686) 411192

TUFFEL, Kennedy Joseph. b 20. Worc Ord Coll 64. **d** 66 **p** 67. C Belmont *Lon* 66-68; C Goring-by-Sea *Chich* 68-72 and 81-89; NSM 89-96; V Barnham 72-78; Hon C W Worthing St Jo 78-81; rtd 89; Perm to Offic *Chich* from 96. *15 Mill House Gardens, Mill Road, Worthing BN11 4NE* Tel (01903) 700671

TUFFIELD, Canon Basil Thomas. b 23. Fitzw Ho Cam BA49 MA54. Wells Th Coll 50. **d** 52 **p** 53. C Charlton St Luke w St Paul *S'wark* 52-58; C Carshalton 58-65; V Carshalton Beeches 65-79; P-in-c Cross Canonby *Carl* 79-82; V 82-90; P-in-c Allonby w W Newton 81-82; V Allonby 82-90; RD Solway 84-90; Hon Can Carl Cathl 87-90; rtd 90; Perm to Offic *Carl* from 90. *Hafod y Cwm, Llandernog Road, Nannerch, Mold CH7 5RP* Tel (01352) 741234

TUFFIN, Mrs Gillian Patricia. b 43. S Dios Minl Tr Scheme 91. **d** 94 **p** 95. C Gidea Park *Chelmsf* 94-98; TV Stoke-upon-Trent *Lich* 98-01; NSM Northolt Park St Barn *Lon* from 02. *76 Stowe Crescent, Ruislip HA4 7SS* Tel (01895) 631858 E-mail tuffins@bun.com

TUFFNELL, Nigel Owen. b 65. Teesside Poly BSc90. St Jo Coll Nottm 91. **d** 94 **p** 95. C Guisborough *York* 94-97; P-in-c Northwold *Ely* 97-98; P-in-c Stoke Ferry w Wretton 97-98; P-in-c Whittington 97-98; R Northwold and Wretton w Stoke Ferry etc 98-03; Bp's Adv on Environmental issues 02-03; P-in-c Kegworth *Leic* 03; P-in-c Hathern, Long Whatton and Diseworth w Belton etc 03; TR Kegworth, Hathern, Long Whatton, Diseworth etc from 04. *The Rectory, 24 Nottingham Road, Kegworth, Derby DE74 2FH* Tel (01509) 673146 E-mail envadvisor@yahoo.co.uk

TUFNELL, Edward Nicholas Pember. b 45. Chu Coll Cam MA68. St Jo Coll Nottm BA73. **d** 73 **p** 74. C Ealing St Mary *Lon* 73-76; BCMS Tanzania 76-88; P-in-c Lt Thurrock St Jo *Chelmsf* 89-91; V Grays North 91-98; Chapl Thurrock Community Hosp Grays 89-98; P-in-c Bourton-on-the-Water w Clapton *Glouc* 98-05; R Bourton-on-the-Water w Clapton etc from 05. *The Rectory, School Hill, Bourton-on-the-Water, Cheltenham GL54 2AW* Tel (01451) 820386 E-mail edward@stlawbourton.freeserve.co.uk

TUFT, Preb Patrick Anthony. b 31. Selw Coll Cam BA56 MA60. Edin Th Coll 56. **d** 58 **p** 59. C Keighley *Bradf* 58-63; PV Chich Cathl *Chich* 63-68; Min Can St Paul's Cathl *Lon* 68-74; Hon Min Can St Paul's Cathl 74-94; V Chiswick St Nic w St Mary from 74; PV Westmr Abbey 74-79; AD Hounslow *Lon* 87-93; P-in-c Chiswick St Paul Grove Park 88-90; Preb St Paul's Cathl from 95. *Chiswick Vicarage, The Mall, London W4 2PJ* Tel (020) 8995 4717 Mobile 07768-892099 E-mail patrick@ptuft.freeserve.co.uk

TUGWELL, Elizabeth Ann. b 36. SW Minl Tr Course. **d** 94 **p** 95. NSM Ludgvan *Truro* 94-97; NSM St Hilary w Perranuthnoe 94-97; Perm to Offic 99-05; P-in-c Stranraer *Glas* from 05; P-in-c Portpatrick from 05. *Dally Farmhouse, Kirkcolm, Stanraer DG9 0QD* Tel (01776) 853582

TULL, Preb Christopher Stuart. b 36. Hertf Coll Ox BA60 MA64. Oak Hill Th Coll 60. **d** 62 **p** 63. C Stoodleigh *Ex* 62-71; C Washfield 62-71; TV Washfield, Stoodleigh, Withleigh etc 71-74; RD Tiverton 74-75; R Bishops Nympton w Rose Ash 75-77; V Mariansleigh 75-77; TR Bishopsnympton, Rose Ash, Mariansleigh etc 77-99; RD S Molton 80-87 and 95-99; Preb Ex Cathl 84-99; rtd 99. *The Old Smithy, Challacombe, Barnstaple EX31 4TU* Tel (01598) 763201

TULLETT, Peter Watts. b 46. Qu Coll Birm 92. **d** 94 **p** 95. C Worle *B & W* 94-96; Chapl HM YOI Portland 96-01; Perm to Offic *B & W* 02-04; NSM Uphill from 04. *2 Ferry Lane, Lympsham, Weston-super-Mare BS24 0BT* Tel (01934) 814284

TULLOCH, Richard James Anthony. b 52. Wadh Coll Ox BA74 Selw Coll Cam BA79. Ridley Hall Cam 76. **d** 79 **p** 80. C Morden *S'wark* 79-83; C Jesmond Clayton Memorial *Newc* 83-94; V New Borough and Leigh *Sarum* from 94. *The Vicarage, 15 St John's Hill, Wimborne BH21 1BX* Tel (01202) 883490

TULLOCH, Walter Harold. b 16. AIMLS53 MRSH62. St Deiniol's Hawarden 79. **d** 79 **p** 80. NSM Maghull *Liv* 79-86; rtd 86; Perm to Offic *Liv* from 86. *8 Tailor's Lane, Maghull, Liverpool L31 3HD* Tel 0151-526 1936

TULLY, David John. b 56. St Jo Coll Dur BA77 Nottm Univ PGCE78. Ridley Hall Cam 81. **d** 84 **p** 85. C Gosforth St Nic *Newc* 84-86; C Newburn 86-90; TV Whorlton 90-96; V 96-00; R Gateshead Fell *Dur* from 00. *The Rectory, 45 Shotley Gardens, Low Fell, Gateshead NE9 5DP* Tel 0191-440 2190 E-mail david.tully@tesco.net

TULLY, Janet Florence. b 43. **d** 03 **p** 04. OLM Margate St Jo *Cant* from 03. *29 Grotto Gardens, Margate CT9 2BX* Tel (01843) 224979

TUNBRIDGE, Canon Genny Louise. b 64. Clare Coll Cam BA85 St Cross Coll Ox DPhil93 Birm Univ BD95. Qu Coll Birm 93. **d** 96 **p** 97. C Boston *Linc* 96-00; Lect 00-01; Prec Chelmsf Cathl *Chelmsf* from 01; Can Res from 03. *The Precentor's House, 1B Rainsford Avenue, Chelmsford CM1 2PJ* Tel (01245) 257306 *or* 294482 Fax 294499 E-mail precentor@chelmsfordcathedral.org.uk

TUNBRIDGE, John Stephen. b 31. Keble Coll Ox BA54 MA59. Ely Th Coll 54. **d** 56 **p** 57. C Upper Norwood All SS w St Marg *Cant* 56-57; C Ramsgate St Geo 57-60; P-in-c 76-84; C Folkestone St Mary and St Eanswythe 60-62; R Gt Chart 62-67; V Womenswold 67-76; C-in-c Aylesham CD 67-76; R Harbledown 84-94; Perm to Offic *St D* from 94; rtd 96. *Ashdown, 11 Castle Road, St Ishmaels, Haverfordwest SA62 3SF* Tel (01646) 636584

TUNLEY, Timothy Mark. b 61. Ridley Hall Cam 89. **d** 92 **p** 93. C Aldborough w Boroughbridge and Roecliffe *Ripon* 92-95; C Knaresborough 95-98; V Swaledale 98-05; TV Seacroft from 05; Dioc Adv for NSM from 03. *51 St James Approach, Leeds LS14 6JJ* Tel 0113-273 1396 E-mail timtunley@hotmail.com

TUNNICLIFFE, Mrs Jean Sarah. b 36. RGN69. Glouc Sch of Min 89. **d** 92 **p** 94. NSM Dixton *Heref* from 92. *Bryn Awelon, 21 Ridgeway, Wyesham, Monmouth NP25 3JX* Tel (01600) 714115

TUNNICLIFFE, Canon Martin Wyndham. b 31. Keele Univ BA56. Qu Coll Birm 59. **d** 60 **p** 61. C Castle Bromwich SS Mary and Marg *Birm* 60-65; V Shard End 65-73; R Over Whitacre w Shustoke 73-78; V Tanworth 78-98; RD Solihull 89-94; Hon Can Birm Cathl 91-98; rtd 98; Perm to Offic *Birm* from 98. *202 Ralph Road, Shirley, Solihull B90 3LE* Tel 0121-745 6522 Fax as telephone E-mail martin@202rr.freeserve.co.uk

TUNNICLIFFE, Mrs Siv. b 33. Stockholm Univ MPhil58. St Alb and Ox Min Course 94. **d** 97 **p** 98. OLM Wingrave w Rowsham, Aston Abbotts and Cublington *Ox* from 97; OLM Wing w Grove from 04. *Baldway House, Wingrave, Aylesbury HP22 4PA* Tel and fax (01296) 681374

TUNSTALL, Barry Anthony. b 29. Sarum Th Coll 53. **d** 55 **p** 56. C Croxley Green All SS *St Alb* 55-58; C Apsley End 58-63; V N Mymms 63-81; R Kirkby Overblow *Ripon* 81-94; rtd 94; Perm to Offic *B & W* from 01. *8 Lower Silk Mill, Darshill, Shepton Mallet BA4 5HF* Tel (01749) 344761

TUPLING, Mrs Catherine Louise. b 74. Westhill Coll Birm BTh96. Wycliffe Hall Ox 01. **d** 03 **p** 04. C Belper *Derby* from 03. *48 Arkwright Avenue, Belper DE56 0HY* Tel (01773) 599119 E-mail cltupling@tup-house.freeserve.co.uk

TUPPER, Michael Heathfield. b 20. St Edm Hall Ox BA41 MA46. Ridley Hall Cam 41. **d** 43 **p** 44. C Win Ch Ch *Win* 43-45; Chapl Monkton Combe Sch Bath 45-48; Asst Chapl Shrewsbury Sch 48-59 and 60-79; Kenya 59-60; Hon C Bayston Hill *Lich* 80-98; rtd 98; Perm to Offic *Lich* from 99. *9 Eric Lock Road, Bayston Hill, Shrewsbury SY3 0HQ* Tel (01743) 722674

TURAY, Prince Eddie Solomon. b 60. Sierra Leone Th Hall 82. **d** 85 **p** 87. Sierra Leone 85-91; Hon C Gt Cambridge Road St Jo and St Jas *Lon* 94-97; C Edmonton St Aldhelm 97-00; Perm to Offic 01-02. *Address temp unknown*

✠**TURNBULL, The Rt Revd Anthony Michael Arnold.** b 35. CBE03 DL05. Keble Coll Ox BA58 MA62 Dur Univ Hon DD03. Cranmer Hall Dur. **d** 60 **p** 61 **c** 88. C Middleton *Man* 60-61; C Luton w E Hyde *St Alb* 61-65; Dir of Ords *York* 65-69; Abp's Dom Chapl 65-69; Chapl York Univ 69-76; V Heslington 69-76; Chief Sec CA 76-84; Can Res Roch Cathl *Roch* 84-88; Adn Roch 84-88; Bp Roch 88-94; Bp Dur 94-03; rtd 03; Hon Asst Bp Cant from 03. *67 Strand Street, Sandwich CT13 9HN* Tel (01304) 611389 E-mail bstmt@btopenworld.com

TURNBULL, Brian Robert. b 43. Chich Th Coll 71. **d** 74 **p** 75. C Norbury St Phil *Cant* 74-76; C Folkestone St Sav 76-77; Hon C Tong *Lich* 83-88; C Jarrow *Dur* 88-89; TV 89-94; P-in-c Hartlepool St Oswald 94-96; V 96-04; rtd 04. *23 The Open, Newcastle upon Tyne NE1 4DB* Tel 0191-221 2312 E-mail frbrian@turnbull23.freeserve.co.uk

TURNBULL, James Awty. b 28. Solicitor Bradf Univ HonDLaws97. Cranmer Hall Dur 89. **d** 89 **p** 90. NSM Bolton Abbey *Bradf* 89-98; Perm to Offic from 98. *Deerstones Cottage, Deerstones, Skipton BD23 6JB*

TURNBULL, Michael. *See* TURNBULL, The Rt Revd Anthony Michael Arnold

TURNBULL, Michael Francis. b 62. Liv Univ BTh99. N Ord Course 95. **d** 98 **p** 99. C Birkenhead Ch Ch *Ches* 98-02; P-in-c Leasowe from 02. *St Chad's Vicarage, 70 Castleway North, Wirral CH46 1RW* Tel 0151-677 6889 Mobile 07904-067153 Fax 0151-677 3210 E-mail mike@theturnbulls.info

TURNBULL, Peter Frederick. b 64. SS Mark & Jo Coll Plymouth BA85. Sarum & Wells Th Coll BTh91. **d** 91 **p** 92. C Upper Norwood All SS *S'wark* 91-95; Chapl HM Pris Dorchester 95-98; C Dorchester *Sarum* 95-98; NSM Melbury 98-99; C Maltby *Sheff* 99-02; TV from 02. *The Rectory, 69 Blyth Road, Maltby, Rotherham S66 7LF* Tel (01709) 812684 Mobile 07747-132717 E-mail p.turnbull@dogcollar.org.uk

TURNBULL, Richard Duncan. b 60. Reading Univ BA82 St Jo Coll Dur BA92 Dur Univ PhD97 Ox Univ MA05 MICAS85. Cranmer Hall Dur 90. **d** 94 **p** 95. C Portswood Ch Ch *Win* 94-98; V Chineham 98-05; Prin Wycliffe Hall Ox from 05. *Wycliffe Hall, 54 Banbury Road, Oxford OX2 6PW* Tel (01865) 274200 Fax 274215 E-mail richard.turnbull@wycliffe.ox.ac.uk

TURNBULL, William George. b 25. Lich Th Coll 63. **d** 65 **p** 66. C Nunhead St Silas *S'wark* 65-69; C Portishead *B & W* 69-73; C Holsworthy w Cookbury *Ex* 73-76; P-in-c Bridgerule 76-79; P-in-c Pyworthy w Pancraswyke 77-79; P-in-c Pyworthy, Pancrasweek and Bridgerule 79-80; R 80-81; V Otterton and Colaton Raleigh 81-90; rtd 90; Chapl Convent Companions Jes Gd Shep W Ogwell 90-94; Perm to Offic *Chich* from 94 and *S'wark* from 00. *College of St Barnabas, Blackberry Lane, Lingfield RH7 6NJ* Tel (01342) 870585

TURNER, Alan James. b 40. Oak Hill Th Coll BA81. **d** 81 **p** 82. C Bradley *Wakef* 81-84; C Sandal St Helen 84-86; P-in-c Sileby *Leic* 86-87; TR Sileby, Cossington and Seagrave 87-94; R Hollington St Leon *Chich* 94-01; R Frant w Eridge from 01. *The Rectory, Frant, Tunbridge Wells TN3 9DX* Tel (01892) 750638

TURNER, Alan Roy. b 51. Sheff Univ BA96 MA99. EMMTC. **d** 00 **p** 01. C Bladon w Woodstock *Ox* 00-03; Chapl Cokethorpe Sch Witney 01-03; TV Brize Norton and Carterton *Ox* from 03. *8 Trefoil Way, Carterton OX18 1JQ* Tel (01993) 844175 E-mail beverley@agathos.fs.net.uk

TURNER, Albert Edward. b 41. Glouc Sch of Min 83. **d** 89 **p** 90. C Woodford St Mary w St Phil and St Jas *Chelmsf* 89-91; R Greatworth and Marston St Lawrence etc *Pet* 91-99; R Somersham w Pidley and Oldhurst *Ely* 99-02; rtd 02. *83 Horslow Street, Potton, Sandy SG19 2NX* Tel (01767) 260566 Mobile 07950-097525 E-mail aet546@hotmail.com

TURNER, Alison Joan. b 66. EAMTC. **d** 97 **p** 98. Perm to Offic *Chelmsf* 97-01; PV Ex Cathl *Ex* from 04. *6 Cathedral Close, Exeter EX1 1EZ* Tel (01392) 272498 Mobile 07958-276651

TURNER, Andrew John. b 52. St Jo Coll Nottm LTh. **d** 83 **p** 84. C Framlingham w Saxtead *St E* 83-86; P-in-c Badingham w Bruisyard and Cransford 86-88; P-in-c Dennington 86-88; R Badingham w Bruisyard, Cransford and Dennington 88-91; Chapl RAF from 91. *Chaplaincy Services (RAF), HQ, Personnel and Training Command, RAF Innsworth, Gloucester GL3 1EZ* Tel (01452) 712612 ext 5164 Fax 510828 E-mail andrewandliz@turner211274.fsnet.co.uk

TURNER, Ann. *See* TURNER, Mrs Patricia Ann

TURNER, Mrs Ann Elizabeth Hamer. b 38. Ex Univ BA59 PGCE60. Trin Coll Bris 84. **dss** 86 **d** 87 **p** 94. Bath St Luke *B & W* 86-87; Hon C 87-91; Chapl Dorothy Ho Foundn 89-91; C Bath Twerton-on-Avon 91-94; TV 94-96; rtd 98; Perm to Offic *Ex* from 00. *4 Beech Park, West Hill, Ottery St Mary EX11 1UH* Tel (01404) 813476

TURNER, Anthony John. b 49. DipMin. St Mich Coll Llan 89. **d** 91 **p** 92. C Coity w Nolton *Llan* 91-95; R Castlemartin w Warren and Angle etc *St D* 95-04; TV Monkton from 04; OCF 95-01. *The Rectory, Angle, Pembroke SA71 5AN* Tel (01646) 641368

TURNER, The Ven Antony Hubert Michael. b 30. FCA63 Lon Univ DipTh56. Tyndale Hall Bris 54. **d** 56 **p** 57. C Nottingham St Ann *S'well* 56-58; C Cheadle *Ches* 58-62; PC Macclesfield Ch Ch 62-68; Lic to Offic *S'wark* 68-74; Home Sec BCMS 68-74; V Southsea St Jude *Portsm* 74-86; P-in-c Portsea St Luke 75-80; RD Portsm 79-84; Hon Can Portsm Cathl 85-86; Adn Is of Wight 86-96; rtd 96; Perm to Offic *Portsm* from 96. *15 Avenue Road, Hayling Island PO11 0LX* Tel (023) 9246 5881

TURNER, Benjamin John. b 45. Bolton Inst of Tech CEng MICE. N Ord Course 82. **d** 85 **p** 86. C Worsley *Man* 85-88; V Elton St Steph 88-95; Asst P Greystoke, Matterdale, Mungrisdale etc *Carl* 95-98; TV Gd Shep TM 98-01; Asst Chapl Leeds Teaching Hosps NHS Trust from 01. *St James's University Hospital, Beckett Street, Leeds LS9 7TF* Tel 0113-243 3144

TURNER, Mrs Beryl Rose. b 31. Nottm Univ CertEd75 BEd76. **dss** 84 **d** 87 **p** 94. Mortomley St Sav *Sheff* 84-86; Whitgift w Adlingfleet and Eastoft 86; The Marshland 86-87; Par Dn Goole 87-94; C 94; rtd 95; Perm to Offic *Sheff* from 95. *49 Colonel's Walk, Goole DN14 6HJ* Tel (01405) 769193

TURNER, Canon Carl Francis. b 60. St Chad's Coll Dur BA81. St Steph Ho Ox 83. **d** 85 **p** 86. C Leigh-on-Sea St Marg *Chelmsf* 85-88; C Brentwood St Thos 88-90; TV Plaistow 90-95; P-in-c 95-96; TR Plaistow and N Canning Town 96-01; Prec and Can Res Ex Cathl *Ex* from 01. *6 Cathedral Close, Exeter EX1 1EZ* Tel (01392) 272498 E-mail precentor@exeter-cathedral.org.uk

TURNER, Charles Maurice Joseph. b 13. **d** 79 **p** 80. NSM Brislington St Luke *Bris* 79-83; NSM Bris Ch Ch w St Ewen and All SS 83-84; NSM Bris St Steph w St Nic and St Leon 83-84; NSM City of Bris 84-89; Perm to Offic 89-98. *31 Eagle Road, Bristol BS4 3LQ* Tel 0117-977 6329

TURNER, Mrs Christina Caroline. b 64. **d** 99 **p** 00. C Castle Church *Lich* 99-02; C Rugby St Andr *Cov* 02-03; TV from 03. *63A Lower Hillmorton Road, Rugby CV21 3TQ* Tel (01788) 544381 E-mail tina.turner@tinyworld.co.uk

TURNER, Mrs Christine. b 42. EMMTC. **d** 94 **p** 95. Asst Chapl Qu Medical Cen Nottm Univ Hosp NHS Trust 94-97; NSM Hickling w Kinoulton and Broughton Sulney *S'well* 94-97; NSM Cotgrave 97-99; P-in-c Willoughby-on-the-Wolds w Wysall and Widmerpool 99-04; rtd 04. *The Rosarie, Milcombe, Banbury OX15 4RS* Tel (01295) 722330 E-mail revd.christine@care4free.net

TURNER, Christopher Gilbert. b 29. New Coll Ox BA52 MA55. Ox Min Course 91. **d** 92 **p** 93. Hon C Hook Norton w Gt Rollright, Swerford etc *Ox* from 92. *Rosemullion, High Street, Great Rollright, Chipping Norton OX7 5RQ* Tel (01608) 737359

TURNER, Christopher James Shepherd. b 48. Ch Ch Ox BA70 MA74. Wycliffe Hall Ox 71. **d** 74 **p** 75. C Rusholme H Trin *Man* 74-78; C Chadderton Ch Ch 78-80; V 80-89; V Selly Park St Steph and St Wulstan *Birm* 89-99; P-in-c Locking *B & W* from 99; Chapl Weston Hospice from 99. *The Vicarage, The Green, Locking, Weston-super-Mare BS24 8DA* Tel (01934) 823556 Fax as telephone E-mail chris@turner2075.fslife.co.uk

TURNER, Christopher Matthew. b 68. Brunel Univ BSc90. Cranmer Hall Dur 01. **d** 03 **p** 04. C Hykeham *Linc* from 03. *28 Sycamore Crescent, Lincoln LN6 0RR* Tel (01522) 688274 E-mail c.turner@which.net

TURNER, Colin Peter John. b 42. Clifton Th Coll 63. **d** 66 **p** 67. C Kinson *Sarum* 66-68; C York St Paul *York* 68-72; Org Sec (SE Area) CPAS 73-78; TV Radipole and Melcombe Regis *Sarum* 78-87; R Radstock w Writhlington *B & W* from 90; R Kilmersdon w Babington from 90; RD Midsomer Norton from 04. *The Rectory, 1 Bristol Road, Radstock, Bath BA3 3EF* Tel (01761) 433182 E-mail stnicholasradstock@lineone.net

TURNER, Canon David Stanley. b 35. Westmr Coll Ox BA84 MISM69 MISE69. WMMTC 86. **d** 87 **p** 88. NSM Worc St Mich *Worc* 87-90; Min Shelfield St Mark CD *Lich* 90-95; C Walsall Wood 90-95; Min Can and Chapl St Woolos Cathl *Mon* 95-97; V Tredegar St Jas 97-05; Hon Can St Bart's Cathl Barrackpore from 96; rtd 05. *St James's Vicarage, Poplar Road, Tredegar NP22 4LH* Tel (01495) 722510

TURNER, Derek John. b 54. Univ of Wales (Ban) BSc81 PhD86. St Jo Coll Nottm. **d** 87 **p** 88. C Pelsall *Lich* 87-91; C Stratford-on-Avon w Bishopton *Cov* 91-99; R Leire w Ashby Parva and Dunton Bassett *Leic* from 00. *The Rectory, Dunton Road, Leire, Lutterworth LE17 5HD* Tel (01455) 209421 Mobile 07713-832676 Fax 08707-060402 E-mail frderek@cesmail.net

TURNER, Donald. b 29. S'wark Ord Course. **d** 71 **p** 72. C Hounslow St Steph *Lon* 71-76; Hon C Isleworth St Jo 76-78; C Brighton St Pet w Chpl Royal *Chich* 78-80; C Brighton St Pet w Chpl Royal and St Jo 80-85; P-in-c St Leonards SS Pet and Paul 85-87; V 87-91; rtd 91; Hon C Malborough w S Huish, W Alvington and Churchstow *Ex* 93-98; Chapl Las Palmas *Eur* 98-01; Perm to Offic *Ex* from 02. *15 Coombe Meadows, Chillington, Kingsbridge TQ7 2JL* Tel (01548) 531440

TURNER, Edgar. *See* TURNER, Canon Robert Edgar

TURNER, Edward. *See* TURNER, Albert Edward

TURNER, Canon Edward Robert. b 37. Em Coll Cam BA62 BTh66 MA67. Westcott Ho Cam 64. **d** 66 **p** 67. C Salford St Phil w St Steph *Man* 66-69; Chapl Tonbridge Sch 69-81; Adv for In-Service Tr *Roch* 81-89; Dir of Educn 81-96; Can Res Roch Cathl 81-00, Vice-Dean Roch Cathl 88-00; Dioc Adv on Community Affairs 96-00; Consultant Rochester 2000 Trust and Bp's Consultant on Public Affairs 00-02; Perm to Offic *Nor* from 01; rtd 02. *Glebe House, Church Road, Neatishead, Norwich NR12 8BT* Tel (01692) 631295

TURNER, Mrs Eileen Margaret. b 45. Goldsmiths' Coll Lon TCert66 Chester Coll of HE MTh02. N Ord Course 90. **d** 93 **p** 94. Par Dn Sandal St Cath *Wakef* 93-94; C 94-96; P-in-c Hammerwich *Lich* 96-02; Dir OLM Course 96-02; Dir Ext Studies St Jo Coll Nottm from 02. *St John's College, Chilwell Lane, Bramcote, Beeston, Nottingham NG9 3DS* Tel 0115-925 1114 Mobile 07774-623769 E-mail e.turner@stjohns-nottm.ac.uk

TURNER, Mrs Elaine. b 58. Birm Univ BSc79 CEng84 MICE84 MIStructE85. **d** 04 **p** 05. OLM Walesby *Linc* from 04. *Rose Cottage, Normanby-le-Wold, Market Rasen LN7 6SS* Tel (01673) 828142 E-mail elaine-turner58@supanex.com

TURNER, Miss Elizabeth Jane. b 67. Leeds Univ BEng88. Trin Coll Bris 93. **d** 96 **p** 97. C Eccles *Man* 96-00; P-in-c Barrow *Ches*

from 00; Dioc Ecum Officer from 00. *The Rectory, Mill Lane, Great Barrow, Chester CH3 7JF* Tel (01829) 740263 E-mail jane.turner@chester.anglican.org

TURNER, Canon Francis Edwin. b 29. Sarum Th Coll 54. **d** 57 **p** 58. C Cheriton Street *Cant* 57-61; C Willesborough w Hinxhill 61-64; P-in-c Betteshanger w Ham 64-65; R Northbourne w Betteshanger and Ham 64-70; R Northbourne, Tilmanstone w Betteshanger and Ham 70-74; V Sittingbourne St Mich 74-94; RD Sittingbourne 78-84; Hon Can Cant Cathl 84-94; rtd 94. *6 Cherry Grove, Hungerford RG17 0HP* Tel (01488) 682683

TURNER, Canon Frederick Glynne. b 30. Univ of Wales (Lamp) BA52. St Mich Coll Llan 52. **d** 54 **p** 55. C Aberaman *Llan* 54-60; C Oystermouth *S & B* 60-64; V Abercynon *Llan* 64-71; V Ton Pentre 71-73; TR Ystradyfodwg 73-77; R Caerphilly 77-82; V Whitchurch 82-96; Can Llan Cathl 84-96; Prec 95-96; rtd 96; Perm to Offic *Llan* from 96. *83 Newborough Avenue, Llanishen, Cardiff CF14 5DA* Tel (029) 2075 4443

TURNER, Miss Gaynor. b 44. LNSM course 93. **d** 96 **p** 97. NSM Salford Sacred Trin *Man* 96-99; Asst Chapl among Deaf People from 96; Lic Preacher from 99. *19 Ellesmere Avenue, Worsley, Manchester M28 0AL*

TURNER, Geoffrey. b 46. St Deiniol's Hawarden 85. **d** 87 **p** 88. C Loughor *S & B* 87-89; C Swansea St Pet 89-90; R New Radnor and Llanfihangel Nantmelan etc 90-96; V Ystalyfera from 96; RD Cwmtawe from 00. *The Vicarage, Ystalyfera, Swansea SA9 2EP* Tel (01639) 842257

TURNER, Geoffrey. b 51. Selw Coll Cam BA75 PGCE75 MA78. N Ord Course 90. **d** 93 **p** 94. C E Crompton *Man* 93-96; C Heywood St Luke w All So 96-98; TV Heywood 98-01; TR from 01. *St Luke's Vicarage, 26 Heywood Hall Road, Heywood OL10 4UU* Tel (01706) 360182

TURNER, Geoffrey Edwin. b 45. Aston Univ BSc68 Newc Univ MSc69 PhD72. Cranmer Hall Dur BA74 DipTh75. **d** 75 **p** 76. C Wood End *Cov* 75-79; V Huyton Quarry *Liv* 79-86; Press and Communications Officer *Ely* 86-94; P-in-c Gt w Lt Abington 86-94; P-in-c Hildersham 86-94; V Letchworth St Paul w Willian *St Alb* 94-01; P-in-c Willingham *Ely* 01-02; P-in-c Rampton 01-02; R Willingham from 02; R Rampton from 02. *The Rectory, 23 Rampton End, Willingham, Cambridge CB4 5ES* Tel (01954) 261225 E-mail geoffreyt@btinternet.com

✠**TURNER, The Rt Revd Geoffrey Martin.** b 34. Oak Hill Th Coll 60. **d** 63 **p** 64 **c** 94. C Tonbridge St Steph *Roch* 63-66; C Heatherlands St Jo *Sarum* 66-69; V Derby St Pet *Derby* 69-73; V Chadderton Ch Ch *Man* 73-79; R Bebington *Ches* 79-93; Hon Can Ches Cathl 89-93; RD Wirral N 89-93; Adn Ches 93-94; Suff Bp Stockport 94-00; rtd 00; Perm to Offic *Ches* from 00. *23 Lang Lane, West Kirby, Wirral CH48 5HG* Tel 0151-625 8504

TURNER, Gerald Garth. b 38. Univ of Wales (Lamp) BA61 St Edm Hall Ox BA63 MA67. St Steph Ho Ox 63. **d** 65 **p** 66. C Drayton in Hales *Lich* 65-68; Chapl Prebendal Sch Chich 68-70; PV Chich Cathl *Chich* 68-70; C Forest Row 70-72; V Hope *Derby* 72-78; Prec Man Cathl *Man* 78-86; Can Res 78-86; R Tattenhall and Handley *Ches* 86-04; rtd 04; Perm to Offic *S'well* from 04. *3 Westgate, Southwell NG25 0JN* Tel (01636) 815233 E-mail ggarthturner@hotmail.com

TURNER, Graham Colin. b 55. Bradf Univ BTech. Oak Hill Th Coll BA81. **d** 81 **p** 82. C Upper Armley *Ripon* 81-86; V Bordesley Green *Birm* 86-05; AD Yardley and Bordesley 00-05; TR Macclesfield Team Par *Ches* from 05. *The Rectory, 85 Beech Lane, Macclesfield SK10 2DY* Tel (01625) 426110 *or* 421984 E-mail grahamcturner@hotmail.com

TURNER, Mrs Heather Winifred. b 43. SRN65. Cant Sch of Min 89. **d** 90 **p** 94. Par Dn Orpington All SS *Roch* 90-93; Chapl to the Deaf 93-00; P-in-c Wrotham 95-01; TV E Dereham and Scarning *Nor* 01-02; rtd 02; Perm to Offic *Nor* 02-04; C Darsham *St E* from 04; C Middleton cum Fordley and Theberton w Eastbridge from 04; C Westleton w Dunwich from 04; C Yoxford, Peasenhall and Sibton from 04. *Nightingale House, 3 Heathlands, St George's Lane, Reydon, Southwold IP18 6RW* Tel (01502) 723386 E-mail heather-@fish.co.uk

TURNER, Henry John Mansfield. b 24. Magd Coll Cam BA45 MA48 Man Univ PhD85. Westcott Ho Cam 48. **d** 50 **p** 51. C Crosby *Linc* 50-52; C Chorlton upon Medlock *Man* 52-55; Inter-Colleg Sec SCM (Man) 52-55; C Leigh St Mary *Man* 55-57; V Rochdale Gd Shep 57-62; India 63-67; V Becontree St Geo *Chelmsf* 67-71; R Weeley 71-79; Chapl St Deiniol's Lib Hawarden 79-80; Sub-Warden 80-86; Perm to Offic *Chelmsf* from 86; Hon C St Botolph without Bishopgate *Lon* from 87. *Merrywood, 25 Fourth Avenue, Frinton-on-Sea CO13 9DU* Tel (01255) 677554

TURNER, James Alfred. b 34. Ox Coll FE MCIPS76. Ox Min Course 91. **d** 94 **p** 95. NSM Kidlington w Hampton Poyle *Ox* from 94. *11 St Mary's Close, Kidlington, Oxford OX5 2AY* Tel (01865) 375562

TURNER, James Henry. b 51. N Ord Course 99. **d** 02 **p** 03. NSM Middleton St Cross *Ripon* from 02. *38 Acre Crescent, Middleton, Leeds LS10 4DJ* Tel 0113-277 2681 E-mail jamesjpturner@aol.com

TURNER, Jane. *See* TURNER, Miss Elizabeth Jane

TURNER, Canon Jessica Mary. b 60. SS Coll Cam BA81 PGCE82. Trin Coll Bris 88. **d** 91 **p** 94. Par Dn Preston Em *Blackb* 91-94; C Bamber Bridge St Aid 94-95; Chapl Preston Acute Hosps NHS Trust 95-98; Chapl Blackpool Victoria Hosp NHS Trust 98-03; Chapl Blackpool, Fylde and Wyre Hosps NHS Trust from 03; Hon Can Blackb Cathl *Blackb* from 02. *Chaplaincy Office, Victoria Hospital, Whinney Heys Road, Blackpool FY3 8NR* Tel (01253) 303876 *or* 899791 E-mail jessica.turner@bfwhospitals.nhs.uk

TURNER, John. *See* TURNER, Henry John Mansfield

TURNER, John David Maurice. b 22. Keble Coll Ox BA45 MA48. Ripon Hall Ox 69. **d** 70 **p** 71. C Crowthorne *Ox* 70-73; V Cropredy w Gt Bourton 73-79; V Cropredy w Gt Bourton and Wardington 80-83; Perm to Offic *Ox* and *Pet* 83-03; rtd 87. *14 Stuart Court, High Street, Kibworth, Leicester LE8 0LR* Tel (01858) 881378

TURNER, John William. b 43. Sheff Univ BSc73. Wycliffe Hall Ox 86. **d** 88 **p** 89. C Clayton *Bradf* 88-91; C Horton 91-92; V Bankfoot 92-01; V Holland-on-Sea *Chelmsf* from 01. *The Vicarage, 297 Frinton Road, Holland-on-Sea, Clacton-on-Sea CO15 5SP* Tel (01255) 812420 E-mail john.turner15@virgin.net

TURNER, Canon Keith Howard. b 50. Southn Univ BA71. Wycliffe Hall Ox 72. **d** 75 **p** 76. C Enfield Ch Ch Trent Park *Lon* 75-79; C Chilwell *S'well* 79-83; P-in-c Linby w Papplewick 83-90; R from 90; Hon Can S'well Minster from 02. *The Rectory, Main Street, Linby, Nottingham NG15 8AE* Tel 0115-963 2346 E-mail k.h.turner@btopenworld.com

TURNER, Keith Stanley. b 51. ACIB80. NTMTC DTPS99. **d** 99 **p** 00. C S Hornchurch St Jo and St Matt *Chelmsf* from 99. *16 Wells Gardens, Rainham RM13 7LU* Tel (01708) 554274

TURNER, Kevin Louis Sinclair. b 60. St Jo Coll Nottm BA00. **d** 00 **p** 01. C Mount Pellon *Wakef* 00-03; P-in-c Sowerby from 03. *37 Hops Lane, Halifax HX3 5FB* Tel and fax (01422) 362416 E-mail kevin@kevinturner.freeserve.co.uk

TURNER, Lawrence John. b 43. Kelham Th Coll 65. **d** 70 **p** 71. C Lower Gornal *Lich* 70-73; C Wednesbury St Paul Wood Green 73-74; C Porthill 75-77; C Wilton *York* 77-80; P-in-c 80-82; R Jersey St Martin *Win* from 82; Chmn Jersey Miss to Seamen from 82. *The Rectory, La rue de la Croix au Maitre, St Martin, Jersey JE3 6HW* Tel (01534) 854294 E-mail ljturner@jerseymail.co.uk

TURNER, Leslie. b 29. NE Lon Poly BSc87. St Jo Coll Dur 50 St Aid Birkenhead 51. **d** 54 **p** 55. C Darwen St Cuth *Blackb* 54-56; C Haslingden w Grane and Stonefold 56-59; V Oswaldtwistle St Paul 59-65; Chapl Belmont and Henderson Hosps Sutton 65-71; St Ebba's Hosp Epsom 65-71; Qu Mary's Carshalton 67-71; Lic to Offic *Pet* 71-94; Chapl Princess Marina & St Crispin's Hosps 71-87; Chapl Northn Gen Hosp 87-94; Chapl Manfield Hosp Northn 87-94; Chapl St Edm Hosp Northn 87-94; rtd 94; Perm to Offic *Pet* from 94. *20 Banbury Close, Northampton NN4 9UA* Tel (01604) 769233

TURNER, Mrs Lorraine Elizabeth. b 67. Brunel Univ BSc90 Open Univ MA96. Cranmer Hall Dur 01. **d** 03 **p** 04. C Birchwood *Linc* from 03. *28 Sycamore Crescent, Lincoln LN6 0RR* Tel (01522) 688274 E-mail lorraine.t@which.net

TURNER, Mark. b 60. Aston Tr Scheme 87 Sarum & Wells Th Coll BTh92. **d** 92 **p** 93. C New Sleaford *Linc* 92-94; C Bottesford and Muston *Leic* 94-98; C Harby, Long Clawson and Hose 94-98; C Barkestone w Plungar, Redmile and Stathern 94-98; P-in-c Thurnby Lodge 98-00; C Aylestone Park CD 00-03; P-in-c Areley Kings *Worc* 03-05; R from 05. *14 Dunley Road, Stourport-on-Severn DY13 0AX* Tel (01299) 829557 E-mail revturner@tinyworld.co.uk

TURNER, Mark Richard Haythornthwaite. b 41. TCD MA67 Linc Coll Ox BA68. Wycliffe Hall Ox 65. **d** 68 **p** 69. C Birtley *Newc* 68-71; C Cambridge Gt St Mary w St Mich *Ely* 71-74; Chapl Loughb Univ *Leic* 74-79; P-in-c Keele *Lich* 80-85; Chapl Keele Univ 80-85; P-in-c Ashley 85-95; P-in-c Mucklestone 86-95; R Farnborough *Roch* 95-00; P-in-c Upper Tean *Lich* from 00; Local Min Adv (Stafford) from 00. *The Vicarage, Vicarage Road, Tean, Stoke-on-Trent ST10 4LE* Tel (01538) 722227

TURNER, Martin John. b 34. Trin Hall Cam BA55 MA59. Cuddesdon Coll 58. **d** 60 **p** 61. C Rugby St Andr *Cov* 60-65; C Cov Cathl 65-68; USA 68-70; V Rushmere *St E* 70-82; V Monkwearmouth St Pet *Dur* 82-90; V Bathford *B & W* 90-99; rtd 99; Perm to Offic *B & W* from 00. *The Vicarage, 35 Kewstoke Road, Kewstoke, Weston-super-Mare BS22 9YE* Tel (01934) 645654 Mobile 07929-231167 E-mail turnerschemanoff@aol.com

TURNER, Mrs Maureen. b 55. Leeds Univ BA78 MA01. St Jo Coll Nottm 84. **d** 87 **p** 94. Par Dn Darlaston St Lawr *Lich* 87-91; C Stratford-on-Avon w Bishopton *Cov* 91-98; Chapl Myton Hamlet Hospice 98-01; NSM Leire w Ashby Parva and Dunton Bassett *Leic* 00-01; Chapl Team Ldr Univ Hosps Leic NHS Trust from 01. *Leicester Royal Infirmary, Infirmary Square, Leicester LE1 5WW* Tel 0116-258 5487 E-mail maureen.turner@uhl-tr.nhs.uk

TURNER, Maurice. *See* TURNER, Charles Maurice Joseph

TURNER, Maurice William. b 27. Sarum Th Coll 53. **d** 56 **p** 57. C Thornhill *Wakef* 56-60; V Gawber 60-71; V Alverthorpe 71-74; V Shelton and Oxon *Lich* 74-81; P-in-c Battlefield w Albrighton 81-82; V Leaton 81-82; V Leaton and Albrighton w Battlefield 82-92; rtd 92; Perm to Offic *Lich* 93-96 and *Heref* from 96. *10 Melbourne Rise, Bicton Heath, Shrewsbury SY3 5DA* Tel (01743) 352667

TURNER, Michael Andrew. b 34. K Coll Cam BA59 MA62. Cuddesdon Coll 59. **d** 61 **p** 62. C Luton St Andr *St Alb* 61-64; V 70-77; C-in-c Northolt St Mary *Lon* 64-70; Perm to Offic *St Alb* 77-93; Dep Hd and Chapl Greycoat Hosp Sch 86-93; P-in-c Shilling Okeford *Sarum* 93-99; Chapl Croft Ho Sch Shillingstone 93-99; rtd 99; V of Close Sarum Cathl *Sarum* from 02. *12 Berkshire Road, Harnham, Salisbury SP2 8NY* Tel (01722) 504000 E-mail voc@salcath.co.uk

TURNER, Michael John Royce. b 43. St Jo Coll Dur BA65. Chich Th Coll 65. **d** 67 **p** 68. C Hodge Hill *Birm* 67-71; C Eling, Testwood and Marchwood *Win* 71-72; TV 72-77; R Kirkwall *Ab* 77-85; R Drumlithie *Bre* from 85; R Drumtochty from 85; R Fasque from 85; R Laurencekirk from 85. *Beattie Lodge, Laurencekirk AB30 1HJ* Tel and fax (01561) 377380 E-mail mjrturner@zoo.co.uk

TURNER, Canon Nicholas Anthony. b 51. Clare Coll Cam BA73 MA77 Keble Coll Ox BA77 MA81. Ripon Coll Cuddesdon 76. **d** 78 **p** 79. C Stretford St Matt *Man* 78-80; Tutor St Steph Ho Ox 80-84; V Leeds Richmond Hill *Ripon* 84-91; Offg Chapl RAF and V Ascension Is 91-96; Can Th St Helena Cathl from 94; V Raynes Park St Sav *S'wark* 96-01; P-in-c Broughton, Marton and Thornton *Bradf* from 01. *The Rectory, Broughton, Skipton BD23 3AN* Tel (01282) 842332 E-mail nicholas.turner@bradford.anglican.org

TURNER (née SYMINGTON), Mrs Patricia Ann. b 46. SRN68 RMN71 SCM72. St Steph Ho Ox 82. **dss** 84 **d** 87. Buttershaw St Aid *Bradf* 84-87; TD Manningham 87-91; Ascension Is 91-96; Par Dn Raynes Park St Sav *S'wark* 96-01; Par Dn Broughton, Marton and Thornton *Bradf* from 01; Assoc Dioc Dir of Ords from 04; RD Skipton from 05. *The Rectory, Broughton, Skipton BD23 3AN* Tel (01282) 842332 E-mail ann.turner@bradford.anglican.org

TURNER, Peter Carpenter. b 39. Oak Hill Th Coll 63. **d** 66 **p** 67. C Chadwell *Chelmsf* 66-69; C Braintree 69-73; R Fyfield 73-87; P-in-c Moreton 77-87; C-in-c Bobbingworth 82-87; P-in-c Willingale w Shellow and Berners Roding 84-87; V E Ham St Geo 87-04; rtd 04. *9 Llandovery House, Chipka Street, London E14 3LE* Tel (020) 7987 5902 E-mail detox.uk@btinternet.com *or* petercturner@btinternet.com

TURNER, The Ven Peter Robin. b 42. CB98. AKC65 St Luke's Coll Ex PGCE70 Open Univ BA79 Westmr Coll Ox MTh96. St Boniface Warminster 65. **d** 66 **p** 67. C Crediton *Ex* 66-69; Perm to Offic 69-70; Chapl RAF 70-88; Asst Chapl-in-Chief RAF 88-95; Chapl-in-Chief RAF 95-98; QHC 92-98; Can and Preb Linc Cathl *Linc* 95-98; Chapl Dulwich Coll 98-02; Bp's Dom Chapl *S'well* from 02; Hon Can S'well Minster from 02. *8 Raysmith Close, Southwell NG25 0BG* Tel and fax (01636) 816764 Mobile 07860-583475 E-mail pr.turner@lineone.net *or* chaplain@southwell.anglican.org

TURNER, Philip William. b 25. CM65. Worc Coll Ox BA50 MA62. Chich Th Coll 49. **d** 51 **p** 52. C Armley St Bart *Ripon* 51-56; P-in-c Crawley *Chich* 56-62; V Northampton St Matt *Pet* 62-66; Relig Broadcasting Org BBC Midl Region 66-71; Asst Master Brian Mill Sch Droitwich 71-73; Chapl Eton Coll 73-75; Chapl Malvern Coll 75-84; Chapl St Jas and Abbey Schs Malvern 84-86; rtd 90; Perm to Offic *Worc* from 90. *181 West Malvern Road, Malvern WR14 4AY* Tel (01684) 563852

TURNER, Canon Robert Edgar. b 20. TCD BA42 MA51. Linc Th Coll 44. **d** 45 **p** 46. C Kings Heath *Birm* 45-51; Min Can Belf Cathl 51-63; Dean of Res QUB 51-58; Bp's Dom Chapl *D & D* 56-67; I Belfast St Geo *Conn* 58-90; Can Belf Cathl 71-76; Preb Clonmethan St Patr Cathl Dublin 76-90; Dioc Registrar *Conn* from 82; rtd 90. *19 Cricklewood Park, Belfast BT9 5GU* Tel (028) 9066 3214 Fax 9058 6843 E-mail returner@ntlworld.com *or* registrar@connor.anglican.org

TURNER, Robin Edward. b 35. Selw Coll Cam BA57 MA63. Qu Coll Birm 57. **d** 63 **p** 64. C Aveley *Chelmsf* 63-67; C Upminster 67-71; R Goldhanger w Lt Totham 71-80; R Lt Baddow 80-00; Hon Chapl New Hall Sch Essex 80-00; rtd 00; Perm to Offic *Nor* from 00. *29 Swann Grove, Holt NR25 6DP* Tel (01263) 711330

TURNER, Canon Roger Dyke. b 39. Trin Coll Bris 79. **d** 81 **p** 82. C Clevedon St Andr *B & W* 81-82; C Clevedon St Andr and Ch Ch 83-85; R Freshford, Limpley Stoke and Hinton Charterhouse 85-88; V Kenilworth St Jo *Cov* 88-04; RD Kenilworth 90-98; Hon Can Cov Cathl 00-04; rtd 04; Perm to Offic *Birm* from 04. *8 Priors Close, Balsall Common, Coventry CV7 7FJ* Tel (01676) 533370

TURNER, Roy. *See* TURNER, Alan Roy

TURNER, St John Alwin. b 31. Dur Univ BA57 MA61. Cranmer Hall Dur DipTh58. **d** 59 **p** 60. C W Hartlepool St Paul *Dur* 59-62; C S Shore H Trin *Blackb* 62-65; V Huncoat 65-67; Org Sec (Dios Ripon and York) CMS 67-72; V Harrogate St Mark *Ripon* 72-94; rtd 96; Perm to Offic *Linc* from 01. *2 The Tilney, Whaplode, Spalding PE12 6UW* Tel (01406) 371390

TURNER, Susan. b 58. Man Univ BA89. N Ord Course 89. **d** 92 **p** 94. NSM Balderstone *Man* 92-93; NSM E Crompton 93-94; Hon C 94-96; Chapl Man Coll of Arts and Tech 92-96; Asst Chapl S Man Univ Hosps NHS Trust 96-97; Chapl Burnley Health Care NHS Trust 97-03; Chapl Cen Man/Man Children's Univ Hosp NHS Trust from 02. *Chaplaincy Office, Manchester Royal Infirmary, Oxford Road, Manchester M13 9WL* Tel 0161-276 45824

TURNER, Sylvia Jean. b 46. Lon Univ 72 Open Univ BA77. Westcott Ho Cam CTM95. **d** 95 **p** 96. C Whitstable *Cant* 95-99; R Wigmore Abbey *Heref* from 99. *The Rectory, Watling Street, Leintwardine, Craven Arms SY7 0LL* Tel (01547) 540235 E-mail sylvia.turner@virgin.net

TURNER, Tina. b 60. St Jo Coll Nottm BA02. **d** 02 **p** 03. C Halifax All So and St Aug *Wakef* from 02. *37 Hops Lane, Halifax HX3 5FB* Tel (01422) 360758 E-mail tina@tturner.junglelink.co.uk

TURNER, Valerie Kay. b 50. SS Paul & Mary Coll Cheltenham BEd72. WMMTC 97 Wycliffe Hall Ox 99. **d** 00 **p** 01. C Cheltenham St Luke and St Jo *Glouc* 00-04; P-in-c Forest of Dean Ch Ch w English Bicknor from 04; P-in-c Lydbrook 04-05. *Lydbrook Vicarage, Church Hill, Lydbrook GL17 9SW* Tel (01594) 861510 E-mail valmark@freenetname.co.uk

TURNER, Canon Walter John. b 29. Bris Univ BA53. Clifton Th Coll 49. **d** 54 **p** 55. C W Bromwich All SS *Lich* 54-58; C-in-c Oxley 58-60; V 60-65; V Wednesfield St Thos 65-74; RD Shifnal 75-83; V Boningale 75-83; V Shifnal 75-83; Preb Lich Cathl 80-83; Can Res and Prec Lich Cathl 83-94; rtd 94; Perm to Offic *Lich* from 94. *9 Kestrel Close, Newport TF10 8QE* Tel (01952) 820758

TURNER, William Edward. b 41. Keble Coll Ox BA63 MA73. Linc Th Coll 76. **d** 78 **p** 79. C Lich St Chad *Lich* 78-80; Chapl Trent (Nottm) Poly *S'well* 80-89; Chapl Lancs (Preston) Poly *Blackb* 89-92; Chapl Cen Lancs Univ 92-04; rtd 04. *Lunesdale, Rowgate, Kirkby Stephen CA17 4SP* Tel (017683) 72554

TURNER-CALLIS, Mrs Gillian Ruth. b 79. Aber Univ BD03. Wycliffe Hall Ox MTh05. **d** 05. C Shepshed and Oaks in Charnwood *Leic* from 05. *12 Smithy Way, Shepshed, Loughborough LE12 9TQ* Tel (01509) 505510 Mobile 07974-139881 E-mail gill.turner-callis@gmail.com

TURNER-LOISEL, Mrs Elizabeth Anne. b 57. Lanc Univ BA79 MA80 York Univ PGCE81. EMMTC 96. **d** 99 **p** 00. C Eastwood *S'well* and Chapl Nat Sch Hucknall 99-04; P-in-c Annesley w Newstead *S'well* from 04. *The Vicarage, Annesley Cutting, Annesley, Nottingham NG15 0AJ* Tel (01773) 780778 E-mail rev.liz@virgin.net

TURNOCK, Geoffrey. b 38. Leeds Univ BSc61 PhD64 MSOSc. EMMTC 84. **d** 87 **p** 88. NSM Oadby *Leic* 87-00; NSM Okeford *Sarum* 00-04; NSM Dorchester from 05. *10 Billingsmoor Lane, Poundbury, Dorchester DT1 3WT* Tel (01305) 757177

TURP, Paul Robert. b 48. Oak Hill Th Coll BA79. **d** 79 **p** 80. C Southall Green St Jo *Lon* 79-83; V Shoreditch St Leon w St Mich 83-88 and from 00; TR Shoreditch St Leon and Hoxton St Jo 88-00. *The Vicarage, 36 Hoxton Square, London N1 6NN* Tel (020) 7739 2063 E-mail paul@shoreditch0.demon.co.uk

TURPIN, Canon John Richard. b 41. St D Coll Lamp BA63 Magd Coll Cam BA65 MA70. Cuddesdon Coll 65. **d** 66 **p** 67. C Tadley St Pet *Win* 66-71; V Southampton Thornhill St Chris 71-85; V Ringwood from 85; Hon Can Win Cathl from 99. *The Vicarage, 65 Southampton Road, Ringwood BH24 1HE* Tel (01425) 473219 E-mail johnturpin@ringwoodparish.org.uk

TURPIN, Raymond Gerald. b 35. LNSM course 94. **d** 97 **p** 98. OLM Brockley Hill St Sav *S'wark* from 97. *60 Bankhurst Road, London SE6 4XN* Tel (020) 8690 6877 *or* 8311 2000

TURRALL, Albert Thomas George. b 19. Linc Th Coll 64. **d** 66 **p** 67. C Rowley Regis *Birm* 66-69; R Astley *Worc* 69-74; V Montford w Shrawardine *Lich* 74-77; R Montford w Shrawardine and Fitz 77-84; rtd 84; Perm to Offic *Heref* 86-98 and *Lich* from 86. *15 Highbury Close, Shrewsbury SY2 6SN* Tel (01743) 249831

TURRELL, Peter Charles Morphett. b 47. Dioc OLM tr scheme 98. **d** 01 **p** 02. OLM Carshalton Beeches *S'wark* from 01. *62 Stanley Park Road, Carshalton SM5 3HW* Tel (020) 8669 0318

TURRELL, Stephen John. b 35. Lon Univ DipRS85. S'wark Ord Course. **d** 83 **p** 84. NSM W Wickham St Jo *Cant* 83-84; Chapl Guild of St Bride from 83; NSM Addington *S'wark* 85-92; NSM Blendworth w Chalton w Idsworth *Portsm* 92-97; Perm to Offic 97-01; Hon C Storrington *Chich* from 01. *9 Longland Avenue, Storrington, Pulborough RH20 4HY* Tel (01903) 741272

TURTON, Arthur Bickerstaffe. b 19. Oak Hill Th Coll 46. **d** 48 **p** 49. C Rawtenstall St Mary *Man* 48-51; C Islington St Mary *Lon* 51-52; V Lozells St Silas *Birm* 52-56; V Streatham Park St Alb *S'wark* 56-60; Org Sec CPAS Metrop Area 60-64; V Southborough St Pet *Roch* 64-68; P-in-c Southborough St Matt 67-68; V Southborough St Pet w Ch Ch and St Matt 68-76; V

Histon *Ely* 76-82; rtd 84; Perm to Offic *Chich* 82-88; *Ely* 88-99. *1172 Greenwood Avenue, Victoria BC, Canada, V9A 5M1* Tel (001) (250) 385 0062

TURTON, Douglas Walter. b 38. Kent Univ BA77 Surrey Univ MSc90 Univ of Wales (Ban) DPhil04. Oak Hill Th Coll 77. **d** 78 **p** 79. C Cant St Mary Bredin *Cant* 78-80; P-in-c Thornton Heath St Paul 80-81; V 81-84; V Thornton Heath St Paul *S'wark* 85-91; R Eastling w Ospringe and Stalisfield w Otterden *Cant* 91-00; rtd 00. *16 Weatherall Close, Dunkirk, Faversham ME13 9UL* Tel (01227) 752244

TURTON, Neil Christopher. b 45. Wycliffe Hall Ox 77. **d** 79 **p** 80. C Guildf Ch Ch *Guildf* 79-83; C Godalming 83-86; V Wyke 86-92; R Frimley 92-02; RD Surrey Heath 97-02; V All SS Bay Head NJ USA from 02. *All Saints Rectory, 509 Lake Avenue, Bay Head, NJ 08742, USA* E-mail neil.turton@virgin.net

TURTON, Paul Edward. b 26. St Pet Hall Ox BA50 MA55. Qu Coll Birm 50. **d** 52 **p** 53. C Selly Oak St Mary *Birm* 52-55; C Ward End 55-57; I Netherton CD *Liv* 57-64; V Brockley Hill St Sav *S'wark* 64-68; Perm to Offic 68-70; Dir of Educn *Nor* 70-75; Dep Dir Nat Soc Cen Camberwell 75-77; Dir Nat Soc RE Cen Kensington 78-84; C Eastbourne St Mary *Chich* 84-86; rtd 86; Perm to Offic *Chich* from 87. *32 Churchill Close, Eastbourne BN20 8AJ* Tel (01323) 638089

TUSCHLING, Ruth Mary Magdalen. b 65. Freiburg Univ MA94 CCC Cam PhD04. Westcott Ho Cam BA97. **d** 98 **p** 99. C Hampstead St Jo *Lon* 98-01; Perm to Offic *Ely* 02-04; OSB from 04. *Burford Priory, 30 Priory Lane, Burford OX18 4SQ* Tel (01993) 823605 E-mail ruth@burfordosb.org.uk

✠TUSTIN, The Rt Revd David. b 35. Magd Coll Cam BA57 MA61 Lambeth DD98. Cuddesdon Coll 58. **d** 60 **p** 61 **c** 79. C Stafford St Mary *Lich* 60-63; C St Dunstan in the West *Lon* 63-67; Asst Gen Sec C of E Coun on Foreign Relns 63-67; V Wednesbury St Paul Wood Green *Lich* 67-71; V Tettenhall Regis 71-79; RD Trysull 76-79; Suff Bp Grimsby *Linc* 79-00; Can and Preb Linc Cathl 79-00; rtd 00; Hon Asst Bp Linc from 01. *The Ashes, Tunnel Road, Wrawby, Brigg DN20 8SF* Tel (01652) 655584 Fax as telephone E-mail tustindavid@hotmail.com

TUTTON, Canon John Knight. b 30. Man Univ BSc51. Ripon Hall Ox 53. **d** 55 **p** 56. C Tonge w Alkrington *Man* 55-57; C Bushbury *Lich* 57-59; R Blackley St Andr *Man* 59-67; R Denton Ch Ch 67-95; Hon Can Man Cathl 90-95; rtd 95; Hon C Exminster and Kenn *Ex* 96-01; Perm to Offic from 01. *2 Hescane Park, Cheriton Bishop, Exeter EX6 6JP* Tel (01647) 24651 E-mail johnktutton@onetel.com

✠TUTU, The Most Revd Desmond Mpilo. b 31. UNISA BA K Coll Lon BD MTh FKC78. St Pet Rosettenville LTh. **d** 60 **p** 61 **c** 76. S Africa 60-62; C Golders Green St Alb *Lon* 62-65; C Bletchingley *S'wark* 65-66; S Africa 67-70; Lesotho 70-72; Assoc Dir Th Educn Fund WCC 72-75; C Lee St Aug *S'wark* 72-75; Dean Johannesburg 75-76; Bp Lesotho 76-78; Asst Bp Johannesburg 78-85; Bp Johannesburg 85-86; Abp Cape Town 86-96; rtd 96. *PO Box 1092, Milnerton, 7435 South Africa* Tel (0027) (21) 552 7524 Fax 552 7529 E-mail mpilo@iafrica.com

TWADDELL, Canon William Reginald. b 33. TCD Dip Bibl Studies 61. **d** 62 **p** 63. C Belfast Whiterock *Conn* 62-65; I Loughgilly w Clare *Arm* 65-71; I Milltown 71-84; I Portadown St Mark 84-01; Preb Arm Cathl 88-96; Treas 96-98; Prec 98-01; rtd 01. *Tea Cottage, 19 Birches Road, Portadown BT62 1LS* Tel (028) 3885 2520

TWEDDELL, Christopher Noel. b 66. Auckland Univ BA93. St Jo Coll Auckland. **d** 92 **p** 93. New Zealand 92-97; C Maindee *Mon* 97-98; Hong Kong from 98. *55A Seabird Lane, Discovery Bay, Lantau Island, Hong Kong*

TWEDDLE, David William Joseph. b 28. ATCL56 Dur Univ BSc50 Open Univ BA97. Wycliffe Hall Ox 54. **d** 56 **p** 57. C Darlington H Trin *Dur* 56-60; P-in-c Prestonpans *Edin* 60-63; PV Linc Cathl *Linc* 63-65; C Pet St Jo *Pet* 65-71; Hon Min Can Pet Cathl 68-93; V Southwick w Glapthorn 71-83; P-in-c Benefield 80-83; R Benefield and Southwick w Glapthorn 83-93; RD Oundle 84-89; rtd 94; Perm to Offic *Ely* and *Pet* from 94. *6 Barton Square, Ely CB7 4DF* Tel (01353) 614393

TWEED, Andrew. b 48. Univ of Wales (Cardiff) BA69 Trin Coll Carmarthen MA97. St Deiniol's Hawarden. **d** 81 **p** 84. NSM Llandrindod w Cefnllys *S & B* 81-87; NSM Llandrindod w Cefnllys and Disserth from 87. *Gwenallt, Wellington Road, Llandrindod Wells LD1 5NB* Tel (01597) 823671 E-mail andrewtweed1@aol.com

TWEEDIE-SMITH, Ian David. b 60. Newc Univ BA83. Wycliffe Hall Ox 83. **d** 85 **p** 86. C Hatcham St Jas *S'wark* 85-89; C Bury St Edmunds St Mary *St E* 89-02; TV Woking St Pet *Guildf* from 02. *The Vicarage, 66 Westfield Road, Woking GU22 9NG* Tel (01483) 770779 Fax 770786 E-mail iantweediesmith@waitrose.com

TWEEDY, Andrew Cyril Mark. b 61. Man Univ BA(Econ)81. St Alb and Ox Min Course 98. **d** 01 **p** 02. C Carterton *Ox* 01-03; C Brize Norton and Carterton 03-04; V Bromham w Oakley and Stagsden *St Alb* from 04. *The Vicarage, 47 Stagsden Road, Bromham, Bedford MK43 8PY* Tel (01234) 823268 Mobile 07870-549393 E-mail andrew@tweedy.psa-online.com

TWIDELL, Canon William James. b 30. St Mich Coll Llan 58. **d** 60 **p** 61. C Tonge w Alkrington *Man* 60-63; C High Wycombe All SS *Ox* 63-65; P-in-c Elkesley w Bothamsall *S'well* 65-66; V Bury St Thos *Man* 66-72; V Daisy Hill 72-84; R Flixton St Mich 84-00; AD Stretford 88-98; Hon Can Man Cathl 97-00; rtd 00; Perm to Offic *Man* and *Ches* from 00. *11 Mercer Way, Nantwich CW5 5YD* Tel (01270) 620328

TWINLEY, David Alan. b 66. Ox Univ BTh00. St Steph Ho Ox 97. **d** 00 **p** 01. C Saffron Walden w Wendens Ambo, Littlebury etc *Chelmsf* 00-03; V Bury w Houghton and Coldwaltham and Hardham *Chich* from 03. *The New Vicarage, Church Lane, Bury, Pulborough RH20 1PB* Tel (01798) 839057 E-mail frdavid@twinley.me.uk

TWISLETON, John Fiennes. b 48. St Jo Coll Ox BA69 MA73 DPhil73. Coll of Resurr Mirfield DipTh75. **d** 76 **p** 77. C New Bentley *Sheff* 76-79; P-in-c Moorends 79-80; V 80-86; USPG 86-90; Coll of the Ascension Selly Oak 86-87; Prin Alan Knight Tr Cen Guyana 87-90; V Holbrooks *Cov* 90-96; Edmonton Area Missr *Lon* 96-01; Dioc Adv for Miss and Renewal *Chich* from 01; C Haywards Heath St Rich from 01. *27 Gatesmead, Haywards Heath RH16 1SN* Tel (01444) 414658 Fax as telephone E-mail john@twisleton.co.uk

TWISLETON, Peter. b 50. Linc Th Coll. **d** 84 **p** 85. C Bodmin w Lanhydrock and Lanivet *Truro* 84-87; C Par 87-90; R St Breoke and Egloshayle 90-93; R Bude Haven and Marhamchurch 93-97; V Horbury w Horbury Bridge *Wakef* from 98. *St Peter's Vicarage, Horbury, Wakefield WF4 6AS* Tel (01924) 273477

TWISLETON-WYKEHAM-FIENNES, Oliver William. *See* FIENNES, The Very Revd the Hon Oliver William

TWISS, Dorothy Elizabeth. Gilmore Ho 68 Linc Th Coll 70. **d** 87 **p** 94. Chapl Asst RAF 78-91; TV Pewsey *Sarum* 91-95; Chapl HM Pris Drake Hall 95-01; Chapl HM Pris Ford 01-03; rtd 03; Perm to Offic *Portsm* from 05. *24 Linda Grove, Cowplain, Waterlooville PO8 8UX* Tel 07929-650284 (mobile) E-mail dorothy@dtwiss.freeserve.co.uk

TWITTY, Miss Rosamond Jane. b 54. Univ of Wales (Ban) BSc75 CertEd76. Trin Coll Bris BA89. **d** 90 **p** 94. Par Dn Lt Thurrock St Jo *Chelmsf* 90-94; C 94-95; C Upper Armley *Ripon* from 95. *115A Heights Drive, Leeds LS12 3TG* Tel 0113-263 7240 E-mail janetwitty@supanet.com

TWOHIG, Brian Robert. b 48. La Trobe Univ Vic BA77 PhD86. St Mich Th Coll Crafers 70. **d** 72 **p** 73. Australia 72-78 and 80-82; C Leatherhead *Guildf* 78-80; TV New Windsor *Ox* 82-92; V Sheff St Cuth *Sheff* 92-97; rtd 97; Perm to Offic *Chich* from 98. *26A Bloomsbury Street, Brighton BN2 1HQ*

TWOMEY, Jeremiah Francis (Derry). b 50. Man Poly BA83 Univ of Wales (Ban) PGCE85 Real Colegio de Escoceses Valladolid Spain. NEOC 92. **d** 94 **p** 95. C Beverley St Nic *York* 94-96; V Anlaby Common St Mark 96-99; Ind Chapl *Newc* from 99. *20 Tynedale Close, Wylam NE41 8EX* Tel and fax (01661) 853884 E-mail chaplain@derry-nim-ntyneside.org.uk

TWOMEY, Jeremiah Thomas Paul. b 46. CITC 87. **d** 87 **p** 88. C Derryloran *Arm* 87-90; I Brackaville w Donaghendry and Ballyclog 90-97; I Mohill w Farnaught, Aughavas, Oughteragh etc *K, E & A* 97-00; Bp's C Belfast Whiterock *Conn* from 00. *8 Lyndhurstview Road, Lyndhurst Meadows, Belfast BT13 3XR* Tel (028) 9072 1134 E-mail ptwomey@esatclear.ie

TWYFORD, Canon Arthur Russell. b 36. ALCD60. **d** 60 **p** 61. C Speke All SS *Liv* 60-64; Asst Dioc Youth Officer *Ox* 64-70; R Maids Moreton w Foxcote 64-72; P-in-c Lillingstone Dayrell w Lillingstone Lovell 70-72; V Desborough *Pet* 72-88; P-in-c Brampton Ash w Dingley 73-77; P-in-c Braybrook 73-77; R Brampton Ash w Dingley and Braybrooke 77-88; RD Kettering 79-87; Can Pet Cathl 81-95; R Stanwick w Hargrave 88-95; rtd 95; Perm to Offic *Pet* 95-05. *rue Jean Brouel Cazals, 46250 Lot, France* E-mail artwyford@aol.com

TYDEMAN, Canon Richard. b 16. St Jo Coll Ox BA39 MA43. Ripon Hall Ox 38. **d** 39 **p** 40. C Langley St Mich *Birm* 39-41; C Ipswich All SS *St E* 41-45; P-in-c Ipswich St Helen 45-46; V Woodbridge St Jo 46-53; V Newmarket All SS 53-63; RD Newmarket 54-63; Hon Can St E Cathl 59-63; R St Sepulchre w Ch Ch Greyfriars etc *Lon* 63-81; Dep Min Can St Paul's Cathl 63-81; Preacher Lincoln's Inn 72-81; rtd 81; Perm to Offic *St E* from 82. *10 Colneis Road, Felixstowe IP11 9HF* Tel (01394) 283214

TYDEMAN, Rosemary. *See* WILLIAMS, Mrs Rosemary

TYE, Eric John. b 37. St Alb Minl Tr Scheme 78. **d** 81 **p** 82. NSM Rushden St Mary w Newton Bromswold *Pet* from 81. *31 Morris Avenue, Rushden NN10 9PB* Tel (01933) 353274

TYE, John Raymond. b 31. Lambeth STh64 Linc Th Coll 66. **d** 68 **p** 69. C Crewe St Mich *Ches* 68-71; C Wednesfield St Thos *Lich* 71-76; P-in-c Petton w Cockshutt 76-79; P-in-c Hordley 79; P-in-c Weston Lullingfield 79; R Petton w Cockshutt and Weston Lullingfield etc 79-81; V Hadley 81-84; R Ightfield w Calverhall 84-89; V Ash 84-89; R Calton, Cauldon, Grindon and Waterfall 89-96; RD Alstonfield 95-96; rtd 96. *38 Aston Street, Wem, Shrewsbury SY4 5AU*

TYERS, Canon John Haydn. b 31. Lon Univ BSc51 Open Univ BA00. Ridley Hall Cam 53. **d** 55 **p** 56. C Nuneaton St Nic *Cov*

55-58; C Rugby St Andr 58-62; V Cov St Anne 62-71; V Keresley and Coundon 71-78; V Atherstone 78-85; P-in-c Pleshey *Chelmsf* 85-91; Warden Pleshey Retreat Ho 85-91; Hon Can Chelmsf Cathl *Chelmsf* 86-91; P-in-c Ash *Lich* 91-96; P-in-c Ightfield w Calverhall 91-96; rtd 96; Perm to Offic *Heref* from 97. *7 Brook Road, Pontesbury, Shrewsbury SY5 0QZ* Tel (01743) 790354

TYERS, Philip Nicolas. b 56. Nottm Univ BTh84. St Jo Coll Nottm 80. **d** 84 **p** 85. C Rugby St Matt *Cov* 84-88; TV Cov E 88-95; P-in-c Preston St Matt *Blackb* 95-96; TR Preston Risen Lord from 96. *St Matthew's Vicarage, 20 Fishwick View, Preston PR1 4YA* Tel (01772) 794312 E-mail tyers-5@fish.co.uk

TYLDESLEY, Mrs Vera. b 47. Man Coll of Educn BEd80. LNSM course 95. **d** 98 **p** 99. OLM Pendlebury St Jo *Man* from 98. *7 Kingsway, Swinton, Manchester M27 4JU* Tel 0161-736 3845

TYLER, Alan William. b 60. Univ of Wales (Ban) DipTh84. Ridley Hall Cam 84. **d** 86 **p** 87. C Bedwellty *Mon* 86-89; C St Mellons and Michaelston-y-Fedw 89-92; V Abersychan and Garndiffaith 92-97; Chapl Glan Hafren NHS Trust 97-99; Sen Chapl Gwent Healthcare NHS Trust from 99; Lic to Offic *Mon* from 97. *The Royal Gwent Hospital, Cardiff Road, Newport NP20 2UB* Tel (01633) 234234 *or* 871457

TYLER, Alison Ruth. b 51. Keele Univ BA74 Birm Univ CQSW78. S'wark Ord Course 93. **d** 95 **p** 96. NSM Hatcham St Cath *S'wark* 95-99; Dep Chapl HM Pris Brixton 99-02; Chapl HM Pris Wormwood Scrubs from 02. *HM Prison Wormwood Scrubs, Du Cane Road, London W12 0TU* Tel (020) 8588 3200 *or* 7207 0756 Fax 8749 5655 E-mail ar.tyler@ntlworld.com *or* alison.tyler01@hmps.gsi.gov.uk

TYLER, Andrew. b 57. Univ of Wales (Lamp) BA79 Warw Univ MA80 Man Univ BD86. Coll of Resurr Mirfield 83. **d** 87 **p** 88. C Glen Parva and S Wigston *Leic* 87-90; C Didcot All SS *Ox* 90-92; Asst Chapl Chu Hosp Ox 92-93; NSM Caversham St Andr *Ox* 93-97; Co-ord Tr Portfolio (Berks) 96-97; P-in-c Nor St Giles *Nor* 97-99; P-in-c Norwich St Mary Magd w St Jas 99-00; V from 00. *St Mary's Vicarage, 10 Crome Road, Norwich NR3 4RQ* Tel and fax (01603) 661381 E-mail xatyler@aol.com

TYLER, Brian Sidney. b 32. MIPI79. Chich Th Coll 62. **d** 64 **p** 65. C Brighton St Mich *Chich* 64-69; C-in-c Southwick St Pet 69-75; Perm to Offic 80; NSM Brighton Resurr 93-94; Chapl St Dunstan's Hosp Brighton 93-95; C Brighton St Matthias *Chich* 95-02; Hon C from 02; rtd 02. *318 Ditchling Road, Brighton BN1 6JG* Tel (01273) 559292

TYLER, David Stuart. b 69. Hull Univ BSc91 ACA94. Wycliffe Hall Ox 01. **d** 03 **p** 04. C Ashby-de-la-Zouch St Helen w Coleorton *Leic* 03-05; C Ashby-de-la-Zouch and Breedon on the Hill from 05. *5 Ulleswater Crescent, Ashby-de-la-Zouch LE65 1FH* Tel (01530) 413166
E-mail catherine@somervilletyler.freeserve.co.uk

TYLER (née FOSTER), Mrs Frances Elizabeth. b 55. Linc Th Coll 81. **dss** 84 **d** 87 **p** 94. Hampton All SS *Lon* 84-87; Par Dn Brentford 87-91; NSM Walsgrave on Sowe *Cov* from 91; Dioc Adv for Women's Min from 97. *The Vicarage, 4 Farber Road, Coventry CV2 2BG* Tel (024) 7661 5152
E-mail revftyler@aol.com

TYLER, Mrs Gaynor. b 46. Univ of Wales (Abth) BA68. S'wark Ord Course 87. **d** 90 **p** 94. NSM Reigate St Luke S Park *S'wark* 90-97; Deanery NSM Maelienydd *S & B* 97-04; NSM Cwmddauddwr w St Harmon's and Llanwrthwl from 04. *Dyffryn Farm, Llanwrthwl, Llandrindod Wells LD1 6NU* Tel (01597) 811017

TYLER, Graham Reginald. b 25. CEng65 Aber Univ CertCS95. Moray Ord Course 90. **d** 95. Hon C Thurso *Mor* from 95; Hon C Wick from 95. *11 Houston Terrace, Thurso KW14 8PX* Tel (01847) 893876 E-mail grahamtyler@easicom.com

TYLER, John Arthur Preston. b 19. Em Coll Cam BA42 MA46. Wycliffe Hall Ox 42. **d** 44 **p** 45. C Rodbourne Cheney *Bris* 44-47; C Worthing Ch Ch *Chich* 48-50; C Streatham Park St Alb *S'wark* 50-59; R Wickhambreaux and Stodmarsh *Cant* 59-65; R Ickham w Wickhambreaux and Stodmarsh 65-85; rtd 85; Perm to Offic *Ox* 86-89 and *Cant* from 89. *Church Orchard, Church Lane, Kingston, Canterbury CT4 6HY* Tel (01227) 830193

TYLER, John Thorne. b 46. Selw Coll Cam BA68 MA71 Ex Univ DipEd70. Sarum & Wells Th Coll 70. **d** 72 **p** 73. C Frome St Jo *B & W* 72-74; Chapl Huish Coll Taunton 74-93; Hon C Stoke St Gregory w Burrowbridge and Lyng *B & W* 77-93; P-in-c Shepton Beauchamp w Barrington, Stocklinch etc 93-94; TV Ilminster and Distr 94-98; rtd 99; Hon C Quantock Towers *B & W* 99-01; P-in-c Stogursey w Fiddington from 01. *The Rectory, High Street, Stogursey, Bridgwater TA5 1PL* Tel (01278) 732884 E-mail tyleruk@hotmail.com

TYLER, The Ven Leonard George. b 20. Liv Univ BA41 Ch Coll Cam BA46 MA50. Westcott Ho Cam. **d** 43 **p** 44. C Toxteth Park Ch Ch *Liv* 43-44; Ceylon 46-50; R Bradford cum Beswick *Man* 50-55; V Leigh St Mary 55-66; RD Leigh 57-62; Adn Rochdale 62-66; Prin Wm Temple Coll 66-73; R Easthampstead *Ox* 73-85; rtd 85; Perm to Offic *Ox* from 85. *11 Ashton Place, Kintbury, Hungerford RG17 9XS* Tel (01488) 658510

TYLER, Malcolm. b 56. Kent Univ BSc77 Cam Univ BA84. Ridley Hall Cam 82. **d** 85 **p** 86. C Twickenham St Mary *Lon* 85-88; C Acton St Mary 88-91; V Walsgrave on Sowe *Cov* from 91. *The Vicarage, 4 Farber Road, Coventry CV2 2BG* Tel (024) 7661 5152 *or* 7661 8845 E-mail stmaryssowe@aol.com

TYLER, Samuel John. b 32. Lon Univ BD57. Oak Hill Th Coll 57. **d** 58 **p** 59. C W Ham All SS *Chelmsf* 58-61; V Berechurch 61-64; R Aythorpe w High and Leaden Roding 64-72; Perm to Offic 73-74; P-in-c Gt Ilford St Jo 74-76; V 76-92; rtd 92. *21 Ash Green, Canewdon, Rochford SS4 3QN* Tel (01702) 258526

TYLER (née WAITE), Mrs Sheila Margaret. b 25. SRN47 Lon Univ DipTh73. Trin Coll Bris 71. **dss** 79 **d** 87 **p** 94. Easton H Trin w St Gabr and St Lawr *Bris* 79-80; Westbury-on-Trym St Alb 81-85; rtd 85; Hon Par Dn Henleaze *Bris* 87-94; Hon C 94-95; Chapl Stoke Park and Purdown Hosps Stapleton 88-90; Perm to Offic *Bris* from 95; *B & W* 95-00; *Chich* 01-02. *6 Gracey Court, Woodland Road, Broadclyst, Exeter EX5 3GA* Tel (01392) 462872

TYLER, William Stanley. b 12. Ripon Hall Ox 54. **d** 55 **p** 56. C Upton *Ex* 55-58; V E Stonehouse 58-68; R Woodleigh and Loddiswell 68-76; rtd 76. *c/o Miss D A Tyler, 26 Fairmile House, 30 Twickenham Rd, Teddington TW11 8BA*

TYNDALL, Daniel Frank. b 61. Aston Tr Scheme 90 Sarum & Wells Th Coll BTh93. **d** 93 **p** 94. C Wolverhampton *Lich* 93-96; Assoc V Bris St Mary Redcliffe w Temple etc *Bris* 96-01; V Earley St Nic *Ox* from 01. *St Nicolas' Vicarage, 53 Sutcliffe Avenue, Reading RG6 7JN* Tel 0118-966 3563 Fax as telephone E-mail danieltyndall@bigfoot.com

TYNDALL, Mrs Elizabeth Mary. b 30. St Andr Univ MA51 Hughes Hall Cam CertEd52 Birm Univ DPS81. Qu Coll Birm 81. **dss** 83 **d** 87 **p** 94. Rugby St Andr *Cov* 83-87; Par Dn Feltham *Lon* 87-91; rtd 92; NSM Vale of White Horse Deanery *Ox* from 93. *4 Folly View Road, Faringdon SN7 7DH* Tel (01367) 240977

TYNDALL, Jeremy Hamilton. b 55. St Jo Coll Nottm BTh81 LTh81. **d** 81 **p** 82. C Oakwood St Thos *Lon* 81-84; C Upper Holloway St Pet w St Jo 84-87; TV Halewood *Liv* 87-96; P-in-c Yardley St Edburgha *Birm* 96-99; V 99-01; R Eugene St Thos USA from 01. *St Thomas's Episcopal Church, 1465 Coburg Road, Eugene, OR 97401, USA* Tel (001) (541) 343 5241

TYNDALL, Simon James. b 54. LSE BSc(Econ)77 Lon Univ PGCE82 Open Univ MA98. St Jo Coll Nottm 88. **d** 90 **p** 91. C Yeovil w Kingston Pitney *B & W* 90-94; V Rastrick St Jo *Wakef* 94-01; TR Chippenham St Paul w Hardenhuish etc *Bris* from 01. *The Rectory, 9 Greenway Park, Chippenham SN15 1QG* Tel (01249) 657216 E-mail sjt@fish.co.uk

TYNDALL, Canon Timothy Gardner. b 25. Jes Coll Cam BA50. Wells Th Coll 50. **d** 51 **p** 52. C Warsop *S'well* 51-55; R Newark St Leon 55-60; V Sherwood 60-75; P-in-c Bishopwearmouth St Mich w St Hilda *Dur* 75-85; RD Wearmouth 75-85; Hon Can Dur Cathl 83-90; Chief Sec ACCM 85-90; rtd 90; Perm to Offic *Lon* and *S'wark* from 90. *29 Kingswood Road, London W4 5EU* Tel (020) 8994 4516

TYNEY, Canon James Derrick. b 33. TCD. **d** 62 **p** 63. C Ballynafeigh St Jude *D & D* 62-64; C Bangor St Comgall 64-69; I Clonallon w Warrenpoint 69-75; I Groomsport 75-00; Can Belf Cathl 93-00; Dioc Registrar *D & D* 95-00; rtd 00. *27 Sandringham Drive, Bangor BT20 5NA* Tel (028) 9145 5670

TYRER, Ms Jayne Linda. b 59. Goldsmiths' Coll Lon BA81 CertEd82. Sarum & Wells Th Coll 85. **d** 87 **p** 95. C Rochdale *Man* 87-88; Par Dn Heywood St Luke w All So 88-91; Hon Par Dn Burneside *Carl* from 91; Chapl Kendal Hosps 91-94; Chapl Westmorland Hosps NHS Trust 94-98; Chapl Morecambe Bay Hosps NHS Trust from 98. *St Oswald's Vicarage, Burneside, Kendal LA9 6QX* Tel (01539) 722015
E-mail jayne.tyrer@wgh.mbht.nhs.uk

TYREUS, Per Jonas Waldemar (Peter). b 45. Uppsala Univ 66. **p** 71. Sweden 71-00; C Pelton *Dur* 00-03; C Chester le Street from 03. *16 Park Road North, Chester le Street DH3 3SD* Tel 0191-388 6801 E-mail peter@petertyreus.plus.com

TYRREL, John Cockett. b 16. Qu Coll Cam BA38 MA42. Ridley Hall Cam 38. **d** 40 **p** 41. C Southall H Trin *Lon* 40-43; Chapl RNVR 43-46; S Africa 46-50; Australia from 50; rtd 81; Perm to Offic *Canberra and Goulburn* from 81. *20/58 Shackleton Circuit, Mawson, ACT, Australia 2607* Tel (0061) (2) 6286 1317

TYRRELL, The Very Revd Charles Robert. b 51. SRN73 Open Univ BA80. Oak Hill Th Coll 74. **d** 77 **p** 78. C Halewood *Liv* 77-80; C St Helens St Helen 80-83; V Banks 83-88; New Zealand from 88; Can Wellington 88-94; Dean Nelson from 94. *The Deanery, 365 Trafalgar Street, Nelson, New Zealand* Tel (0064) (3) 548 8574 *or* 548 1008 Fax 548 3264
E-mail charles.tyrell@clear.net.nz

TYRRELL, John Patrick Hammond. b 42. Cranmer Hall Dur 62. **d** 65 **p** 66. C Edin St Jo *Edin* 65-68; Chapl RN 68-72; Hong Kong 72-74 and 78-82; Area Sec SE Asia SOMA UK 78-82; V Westborough *Guildf* 74-78; C Yateley *Win* 82-83; C-in-c Darby Green CD 83-88; V Darby Green 88-96; V Chineham 96-97; rtd 02. *5 Blacksmith's Court, Metheringham, Lincoln LN4 3YQ* Tel (01526) 322147 E-mail john_tyrrell42@hotmail.com

TYRRELL, Stephen Jonathan. b 39. Sheff Univ BA62. Clifton Th Coll. **d** 65 **p** 66. C Rodbourne Cheney *Bris* 65-68; C Lillington *Cov* 68-72; P-in-c Bishop's Itchington 73-78; V 78-86; V Kingston upon Hull St Nic *York* 86-92; TV Cheltenham St Mary, St Matt, St Paul and H Trin *Glouc* 92-04; rtd 04; Perm to Offic *Glouc* from 05. *96A Fosseway Avenue, Moreton-in-Marsh GL56 0AE* Tel (01608) 812350

TYSOE, James Raymond. b 19. Qu Coll Birm 70. **d** 75 **p** 76. NSM Cov E *Cov* 75-85; NSM Cov Cathl 85-87; Perm to Offic *Glouc* from 87. *Wisma Mulia, Bridge Road, Frampton on Severn, Gloucester GL2 7HE* Tel (01452) 740890

TYSON, Mrs Frances Mary. b 44. Reading Univ BScAgr68 Wolv Univ PGCE91. St Jo Coll Nottm 01. **d** 02 **p** 03. NSM Walsall *Lich* from 02; NSM Walsall St Paul from 05; NSM Walsall Pleck and Bescot from 05. *191 Birmingham Road, Walsall WS1 2NX* Tel (01922) 725285

TYSON, Mrs Nigella Jane. b 44. RGN66 Kent Univ BA95. SEITE 96. **d** 97 **p** 98. NSM Aylesham w Adisham, Nonington w Wymynswold and Goodnestone etc *Cant* 97-00; P-in-c Kingsland w Eardisland, Aymestrey etc *Heref* 00-04; R from 04. *The Rectory, Kingsland, Leominster HR6 9QW* Tel (01568) 708255 Fax 708062 *or* 08701-324310 E-mail nigella@kingslandgroup.org.uk

TYSON, Canon William Edward Porter. b 25. St Cath Coll Cam BA49 MA52. Ridley Hall Cam 49. **d** 51 **p** 52. C Wilmslow *Ches* 51-54; C Astbury 54-57; V Macclesfield St Pet 57-62; V Over Tabley 62-70; V High Legh 62-70; CF (TA) 64-91; V Church Hulme *Ches* 70-91; Chapl Cranage Hall Hosp 70-91; Hon Can Ches Cathl *Ches* 82-91; RD Congleton 85-90; rtd 91; Perm to Offic *Ches* and *Carl* from 91. *59 Kirkhead Road, Allithwaite, Grange-over-Sands LA11 7DD* Tel (01539) 535291

U

UCHIDA, Job Minoru. b 28. St Paul's Univ Tokyo BA51. Cen Th Coll Tokyo. **d** 54 **p** 55. Japan 54-56 and 59-89; SSM 56-58; Chapl to Japanese in UK 89-99; Hon C W Acton St Martin *Lon* 95-99; rtd 99. *9 Park View Way, Mansfield NG18 2RN* Tel (01623) 656947

UDAL, Miss Joanna Elizabeth Margaret. b 64. SS Hild & Bede Coll Dur BSc86. Ripon Coll Cuddesdon BTh94. **d** 97 **p** 98. C Whitton St Aug *Lon* 97-00; Asst to Abp Sudan from 00. *Provincial Office, Episcopal Church of the Sudan, PO Box 604, Khartoum, Sudan* Tel (00249) (11) 485718 Fax 485717 E-mail ecsprovince@hotmail.com

UDDIN, Mohan. b 52. Sussex Univ BA74 PGCE75 Lon Bible Coll MA87 Brunel Univ PhD98 Anglia Poly Univ MA02. Ridley Hall Cam 99. **d** 03 **p** 04. C Hornchurch St Andr *Chelmsf* from 03. *55A Chelmsford Drive, Upminster RM14 2PH* Tel (01708) 452705 E-mail mohan.uddin@btopenworld.com

UDY, John Francis. b 24. ACA51 FCA61 ATII65. EMMTC 78. **d** 81 **p** 82. NSM Kirton in Holland *Linc* 81-89; NSM Sutterton w Fosdyke and Algarkirk 89-94; rtd 94; Perm to Offic *Linc* 99-02. *26 Grosvenor Road, Frampton, Boston PE20 1DB* Tel (01205) 722043

UFFINDELL, David Wilfred George. b 37. Qu Coll Birm 72. **d** 75 **p** 76. NSM Harlescott *Lich* from 75. *13 Kenley Avenue, Heath Farm, Shrewsbury SY1 3HA* Tel (01743) 352029 Fax as telephone E-mail revuffindell@aol.com

UFFINDELL, Harold David. b 61. Down Coll Cam MA87. Wycliffe Hall Ox BA86 MA91 Oak Hill Th Coll 86. **d** 87 **p** 88. C Kingston Hill St Paul *S'wark* 87-91; C Surbiton St Matt 91-98; V Sunningdale *Ox* from 98. *The Vicarage, Sidbury Close, Sunningdale, Ascot SL5 0PD* Tel (01344) 620061 E-mail david@htpcsunn.freeserve.co.uk

UGANDA, Archbishop of. *See* OROMBI, The Most Revd Henry Luke

UGWUNNA, Sydney Chukwunma. b 45. Nebraska Wesleyan Univ BSc67 Univ of Nebraska, Linc MSc70 Wayne State Univ PhD79. Virginia Th Sem MDiv96. **d** 96 **p** 97. USA 96-98; C Knaresborough *Ripon* 98-02; Nigeria from 02. *St Stephen's Cathedral, Umuahia, Nigeria*

ULLMANN, Clair. *See* FILBERT-ULLMANN, Mrs Clair

UMPLEBY, Mark Raymond. b 70. Trin Coll Bris BA99. **d** 99 **p** 00. C Birstall *Wakef* 99-02; TV N Huddersfield from 02. *The Vicarage, 8 Oakdean, Fixby, Huddersfield HD2 2FA* Tel (01484) 358194 E-mail markumpleby@hotmail.com

UMZIMVUBU, Bishop of. *See* DAVIES, The Rt Revd Geoffrey Francis

UNDERDOWN, Steven. Hull Univ BSc75 CertEd76 K Coll Lon PhD02. **d** 88 **p** 04. CSWG 82-02; Lic to Offic *Chich* from 88; NSM Hove from 03; Chapl Brighton and Sussex Univ Hosps NHS Trust from 03. *29 Brunswick Place, Hove BN3 1ND* Tel (01273) 747889 E-mail stevenunderdown@onetel.com

UNDERHILL, Edward Mark Thomas. b 24. Univ Coll Dur BA50. St Aid Birkenhead 50. **d** 52 **p** 53. C Meopham *Roch* 52-54; Prin Kigari Coll Kenya 55-57; PC Gateshead St Geo *Dur* 57-68; V from 68. *St George's Vicarage, 327 Durham Road, Gateshead NE9 5AJ* Tel 0191-487 5587

UNDERHILL, Robin. b 31. Marymount Coll California BA89 Woodbury Univ California BSc90. Claremont Sch of Th MA92. **d** 93 **p** 94. USA 93-01; Asst P Beverly Hills All SS 93-00; Pastor San Fernando St Simon 00-01; rtd 01; P-in-c Stranraer *Glas* 01-04; P-in-c Portpatrick 01-04. *The New Parsonage, 2 Meadowbank, Stranraer DG9 0HF* Tel (01776) 705053 Mobile 07890-598245 E-mail stranraerpiskies@onetel.com

UNDERHILL, Stanley Robert. b 27. Cant Sch of Min. **d** 82 **p** 83. C New Addington *Cant* 82-84; C Cannock *Lich* 84-86; TV 86-88; R Dymchurch w Burmarsh and Newchurch *Cant* 88-92; rtd 92; Chapl Menorca *Eur* 92-94; Perm to Offic *Cant* 94-04. *Charterhouse, Charterhouse Square, London EC1M 6AN* Tel (020) 7490 5059 Mobile 07970-954958 E-mail stanunder@aol.com

UNDERWOOD, Adrian Anthony. b 67. **d** 02 **p** 03. C Sparkhill w Greet and Sparkbrook *Birm* from 02. *132 Oakwood Road, Sparkhill, Birmingham B11 4HD* Tel 0121-777 6093 Mobile 07752-001698 E-mail stjohns-sparkhill@charis.co.uk

UNDERWOOD, Brian. b 35. Dur Univ BA57 Keble Coll Ox PGCE76 Dur Univ MA72. Clifton Th Coll 57. **d** 59 **p** 60. C Blackpool Ch Ch *Blackb* 59-61; C New Malden and Coombe *S'wark* 61-64; Travel Sec Pathfinders 64-68; Chapl Chantilly *Eur* 68-69; Home Sec CCCS 69-71; P-in-c Gatten St Paul *Portsm* 71-72; Chapl Lyon w Grenoble and Aix-les-Bains *Eur* 72-75; Asst Chapl Trent Coll Nottm 76-80; Chapl Qu Eliz Gr Sch Blackb 80-85; R Bentham St Jo *Bradf* 85-92; V St Alb Ch Ch *St Alb* 92-00; rtd 00; Perm to Offic *St Alb* from 00. *16 Mitford Close, Bedford MK41 8RF* Tel (01234) 407856

UNDERWOOD, Charles Brian. b 23. Leeds Univ BA48 CertEd. Coll of Resurr Mirfield 48. **d** 50 **p** 51. C Tilehurst St Mich *Ox* 50-53; C Leic St Paul *Leic* 53-54; Youth Chapl 54-61; V Leic St Geo 57-59; R Harby 59-61; New Zealand 61-62; Dioc Youth Chapl *Bradf* 63-72; R Carleton-in-Craven 63-76; V Twyning *Glouc* 76-88; RD Tewkesbury 81-88; rtd 88; Perm to Offic *Glouc* from 00. *Chavender, 9 Ellendene Drive, Pamington, Tewkesbury GL20 8LU* Tel (01684) 772504 E-mail brian@chavender.fsnet.co.uk

UNDERWOOD, David Richard. b 47. AKC69 St Osyth Coll of Educn PGCE72. St Aug Coll Cant 69. **d** 70 **p** 92. C Witham *Chelmsf* 70-71; Teacher 71-82; Hd Teacher Gt Heath Sch Mildenhall 82-91; NSM Chevington w Hargrave and Whepstead w Brockley *St E* 82-91; Par Dn Haverhill w Withersfield, the Wrattings etc 91-92; TV 92-94; P-in-c Bury St Edmunds St Jo 94-99; RD Thingoe 95-99; P-in-c Bury St Edmunds St Geo 98-99; Dioc Dir of Educn 99-04; Hon Can St E Cathl 03-04. *51 Beverley Road, Ipswich IP4 4BU* Tel (01473) 273343 Mobile 07710-522074

UNDERWOOD, Jack Maurice. b 13. Leeds Univ BA36 Lon Univ BD41. Coll of Resurr Mirfield 36. **d** 38 **p** 39. C Kidderminster St Mary and All SS, Trimpley etc *Worc* 38-40; C Hornsey St Mary *Lon* 40-42; Chapl RAFVR 42-46; V Middleton *Birm* 50-53; Prin Stroud Court Ox 60-71; Perm to Offic *Eur* 73-78; rtd 78. *Willow Lea, Hatford, Faringdon SN7 8JF* Tel (01367) 710364

UNDERWOOD, John Alan. b 40. Glos Coll of Arts & Tech BSc88 Ox Poly CertEd84 MBCS74. St Alb and Ox Min Course 96. **d** 99 **p** 00. OLM Eynsham and Cassington *Ox* from 99. *17 Witney Road, Eynsham, Oxford OX29 4PH* Tel (01865) 881254 *or* 301305 Fax 301301 E-mail junderw549@aol.com

UNGOED-THOMAS, Peter. b 27. Pemb Coll Ox BA51 MA67. St Mich Coll Llan. **d** 60 **p** 61. C Llangeinor *Llan* 60-64; I Dublin Donnybrook *D & G* 64-67; RAChD 67-70; Chapl Leigh C of E Schs 70-74; C Leigh St Mary *Man* 70-74; Lect Warley Coll 74-86; Perm to Offic *Birm* and *St D* from 75; Lect Sandwell Coll of F&HE from 86; rtd 94. *93 Heol Felin-Foel, Llanelli SA15 3JQ*

UNITED STATES OF AMERICA, Presiding Bishop of. *See* GRISWOLD, The Most Revd Frank Tracy

✠**UNO, The Most Revd James Toru. c** 98. Bp Kita Kanto from 98; Primate of Nippon Seikokai from 02. *NSKK Provincial Office, 65 Yarai-cho, Shinjuku-ku, Tokyo, 162-0805, Japan* Tel (0081) (48) 642 2680 Fax 648 0358 *or* 476 7484

UNSWORTH, Philip James. b 41. UEA BEd82 Nottm Coll of Educn CertEd63 Nottm Univ DipEd72. EAMTC 94. **d** 97 **p** 98. NSM Hethersett w Canteloff w Lt and Gt Melton *Nor* 97-00; P-in-c Blofield w Hemblington from 00. *The Rectory, 10 Oakwood, Blofield, Norwich NR13 4JQ* Tel (01603) 713160

UNSWORTH, Thomas Foster. b 28. Lon Univ BA56. Lich Th Coll 60. **d** 62 **p** 63. C Northfield *Birm* 62-64; C The Lickey 64-66;

V Forcett *Ripon* 66-68; V Leyburn 68-73; V Bellerby 68-73; Chapl Whittingham Hosp Preston 73-79; V Freckleton *Blackb* 79-83; V S Yardley St Mich *Birm* 83-86; V Sutton w Carlton and Normanton upon Trent etc *S'well* 86-90; rtd 90; Chapl St Raphaël *Eur* 90-97; Perm to Offic *Cant* from 99. *4 Elm House, Bartholomew Street, Hythe CT21 5BY* Tel (01303) 237686

UNWIN, Barry. b 70. Sheff Univ BA91. Oak Hill Th Coll BA05. **d** 05. C Hebburn St Jo *Dur* from 05; C Jarrow Grange from 05. *St Oswald's Vicarage, St Oswald's Road, Hebburn NE31 1HR* Tel 0191-420 8245 E-mail barry_unwin@bigfoot.com

UNWIN, Christopher Michael Fairclough. b 31. Dur Univ BA57. Linc Th Coll 65. **d** 67 **p** 68. C S Shields St Hilda w St Thos *Dur* 67-73; R Tatsfield *S'wark* 73-81; RE Adv to Ch Secondary Schs 73-81; V Newc St Gabr *Newc* 81-96; RD Newc E 96; rtd 96; Perm to Offic *Dur* and *Newc* from 96. *2 The Cottage, West Row, Greatham, Hartlepool TS25 2HW* Tel (01429) 872781

UNWIN, The Ven Kenneth. b 26. St Edm Hall Ox BA48 MA52. Ely Th Coll 49. **d** 51 **p** 52. C Leeds All SS *Ripon* 51-55; C Dur St Marg *Dur* 55-59; V Dodworth *Wakef* 59-69; V Royston 69-73; V Wakef St Jo 73-82; Hon Can Wakef Cathl 80-82; RD Wakef 80-81; Adn Pontefract 82-92; rtd 92; Perm to Offic *Bradf* and *Wakef* from 92. *2 Rockwood Close, Skipton BD23 1UG* Tel (01756) 791323

UNWIN, Michael. *See* UNWIN, Christopher Michael Fairclough

UPCOTT, Derek Jarvis. b 26. CEng FIMechE FBIM. S'wark Ord Course 81. **d** 84 **p** 85. NSM Gt Chesham *Ox* 84-99; Perm to Offic *St Alb* 90-99 and *Ox* from 99. *Bluff Cottage, Blackthorne Lane, Ballinger, Great Missenden HP16 9LN* Tel (01494) 837505 E-mail derek.upcott@activelives.co.uk

UPHILL, Ms Ann Carol. b 54. Westcott Ho Cam 95. **d** 97 **p** 98. C Strood St Nic w St Mary *Roch* 97-01; R Footscray w N Cray from 01. *The Rectory, Rectory Lane, Sidcup DA14 5BP* Tel and fax (020) 8300 7096 Mobile 07802-883121 E-mail annuphill@lineone.net

UPHILL, Keith Ivan. b 35. Keble Coll Ox BA70 MA74. Wycliffe Hall Ox 67. **d** 70 **p** 71. C Maghull *Liv* 70-73; V Wroxall *Portsm* 73-77; TV Fareham H Trin 77-82; C Havant 82-84; P-in-c Merton St Jo *S'wark* 84-85; V 85-95; rtd 95; Perm to Offic *Portsm* from 95. *20 Wilby Lane, Anchorage Park, Portsmouth PO3 5UF* Tel (023) 9266 6998

UPPER SHIRE, Bishop of. *See* MALANGO, The Most Revd Bernard Amos

UPRICHARD, Jervis. b 17. **d** 42 **p** 43. C Kilmegan w Maghera *D & D* 42-45; C Ballymacarrett St Patr 45-46; C Kilmegan 46-47; C Belfast St Aid *Conn* 48-50; I Naas w Killashee *M & K* 50-53; I Outeragh w Fenagh *K, E & A* 53-60; V Edgeside *Man* 60-66; rtd 82; Perm to Offic *Man* 82-91. *c/o Miss A Uprichard, 6 Murray Terrace, Ladywell, Motherwell ML1 3PZ*

UPTON, Anthony Arthur. b 30. Leic Univ MA97 PhD03. Wells Th Coll 61. **d** 63 **p** 64. C Milton *Portsm* 63-67; Chapl RN 67-83; V Foleshill St Laur *Cov* 83-91; rtd 91; Perm to Offic *Cov* from 91. *Redlands Bungalow, Banbury Road, Lighthorne CV35 0AH*

UPTON, Ms Caroline Tracey. b 67. Lon Univ BMus90 Edin Univ BD94. Edin Th Coll 91. **d** 94 **p** 95. C Edin St Martin *Edin* 94-96; Hon C Edin St Pet 97-99; C 99-01; Chapl Lothian Univ Hosps NHS Trust from 01. *10 (3F1) Montagu Terrace, Edinburgh EH3 5QX* Tel 0131-552 0731 E-mail cu.olut@care4free.net

UPTON, Christopher Martin. b 53. Bp Grosseteste Coll CertEd74. EAMTC 94. **d** 97 **p** 98. NSM Gorleston St Andr *Nor* 97-05; NSM Bradwell from 05. *27 Curlew Way, Bradwell, Great Yarmouth NR31 8QX* Tel (01493) 668184

UPTON, Clement Maurice. b 49. Linc Th Coll 88. **d** 90 **p** 91. C Northampton St Alb *Pet* 90-93; V Laxey *S & M* 93-96; V Lonan 93-96; V Hipswell *Ripon* 96-01; V Wellingborough St Andr *Pet* from 01; Chapl Northants Police from 05. *St Andrew's Vicarage, Berrymoor Road, Wellingborough NN8 2HU* Tel (01933) 222692

UPTON, Donald George Stanley. b 16. Peterho Cam BA38 MA44. Westcott Ho Cam 39. **d** 40 **p** 41. C Ashbourne w Mapleton *Derby* 40-43; V Mackworth All SS 43-51; Chapl Bps' Coll Cheshunt 51-54; Chapl Haileybury Coll 54-58; Qu Eliz Gr Sch Barnet 59-60; Alleyne's Gr Sch Stevenage 60-69; Lic to Offic *St Alb* 69-97; Perm to Offic from 97; Chapl St Alb High Sch for Girls 69-73; Ch Hosp Sch Hertf 73-80; rtd 80. *2 The Square, Braughing, Ware SG11 2QS*

UPTON, Ms Julie. b 61. Ripon Coll Cuddesdon 87. **d** 88 **p** 94. C Kirkstall *Ripon* 88-91; Par Dn E Greenwich Ch Ch w St Andr and St Mich *S'wark* 91-94; C 94; Perm to Offic *S'wark* 01-03 and *St E* 02-03; NSM Manningham *Bradf* 03-04; TV Bramley *Ripon* from 04. *St Margaret's Vicarage, Newlay Lane, Leeds LS13 2AJ* Tel 0113-257 4811 E-mail julieupton@beeb.net

UPTON, Martin. *See* UPTON, Christopher Martin

UPTON, Michael Gawthorne. b 29. AKC53. **d** 54 **p** 55. C Middleton *Man* 54-57; C Plymouth St Andr *Ex* 57-59; Dep Dir of Educn *Cant* 59-63; Hon C Riverhead *Roch* 63-70; Youth Chapl 63-70; Lic to Offic *Ex* 70-94; Chr Aid Area Sec (Devon and Cornwall) 70-94; Chr Aid SW Region Co-ord 73-89; rtd 94; Perm to Offic *Ex* from 94. *Otter Dell, Harpford, Sidmouth EX10 0NH* Tel (01395) 568448

UPTON, Mrs Susan Dorothy. b 53. Bp Grosseteste Coll CertEd74 Nottm Univ BEd75. EAMTC 99. **d** 02 **p** 03. NSM Bradwell *Nor* from 02. *27 Curlew Way, Bradwell, Great Yarmouth NR31 8QX* Tel (01493) 668184 E-mail sue-upton@talk21.com

UPTON-JONES, Peter John. b 38. Selw Coll Cam BA63 MA67 Liv Univ CertEd64. N Ord Course 90. **d** 92 **p** 93. NSM Formby H Trin *Liv* 92-00; P-in-c Lezayre St Olave Ramsey *S & M* 00-03; V from 03; P-in-c Kirkbride 00-03; R from 03. *The Rectory, Bride, Isle of Man IM7 4AT* Tel (01624) 880351

URMSON-TAYLOR, Ralph. *See* TAYLOR, Ralph Urmson

✠**URQUHART, The Rt Revd David Andrew.** b 52. Ealing Business Sch BA77. Wycliffe Hall Ox 82. **d** 84 **p** 85 **c** 00. C Kingston upon Hull St Nic *York* 84-87; TV Drypool 87-92; V Cov H Trin *Cov* 92-00; Hon Can Cov Cathl 99-00; Suff Bp Birkenhead *Ches* from 00. *Bishop's Lodge, 67 Bidston Road, Prenton CH43 6TR* Tel 0151-652 2741 Fax 651 2330 E-mail bpbirkenhead@chester.anglican.org

URQUHART, Canon Edmund Ross. b 39. Univ Coll Ox BA62 MA68. St Steph Ho Ox 62. **d** 64 **p** 65. C Milton *Win* 64-69; C Norton *Derby* 69-73; V Bakewell from 73; RD Bakewell and Eyam 95-04; Hon Can Derby Cathl 02-05; rtd 05; Perm to Offic *Derby* from 05. *1 Hambleton Close, Ashbourne DE6 1NG* Tel (01335) 346454

URQUHART, Ian Garnham. b 46. Univ Coll Lon LLB71 Univ Coll Ches 97. Wycliffe Hall Ox 98. **d** 99 **p** 00. NSM Barnston *Ches* from 99. *5 St Peter's Close, Heswall, Wirral CH60 0DU* Tel and fax 0151-342 3588 Mobile 07770-823373 E-mail ian@papintalo.demon.co.uk

URSELL, David John. b 45. R Agric Coll Cirencester NDA70 MRAC70. SW Minl Tr Course 92. **d** 95 **p** 96. NSM Dolton *Ex* from 95; Rural Convenor from 95. *Aller Farm, Dolton, Winkleigh EX19 8PP* Tel (01805) 804414 *or* 804737 E-mail ursell@farmersweekly.net

URSELL, Canon Philip Elliott. b 42. Univ of Wales BA66 Ox Univ MA82. St Steph Ho Ox 66. **d** 68 **p** 69. C Newton Nottage *Llan* 68-71; Asst Chapl Univ of Wales (Cardiff) 71-77; Chapl Wales Poly 74-77; Lic to Offic *Llan* from 77; Chapl Em Coll Cam 77-82; Prin Pusey Ho Ox 82-02; Warden Ascot Priory from 85; Lic to Offic *Ox* from 82; Can Rio Grande from 05. *St Edward's, Ascot Priory, Priory Road, Ascot SL5 8RT* Tel (01344) 885157 E-mail ascot.priory@ic24.net

✠**URWIN, The Rt Revd Lindsay Goodall.** b 56. Heythrop Coll Lon MA03. Ripon Coll Cuddesdon 77. **d** 80 **p** 81 **c** 93. C Walworth *S'wark* 80-83; V N Dulwich St Faith 83-88; Dioc Missr *Chich* 88-93; OGS from 91; Area Bp Horsham *Chich* from 93; Can Chich Cathl from 93. *Bishop's House, 21 Guildford Road, Horsham RH12 1LU* Tel (01403) 211139 Fax 217349 E-mail bishhorsham@clara.net

URWIN, Preb Roger Talbot. b 22. Ex Coll Ox BA43 MA47. Sarum Th Coll 48. **d** 50 **p** 50. C Weymouth H Trin *Sarum* 50-53; V Netheravon w Fittleton 53-57; CF (R of O) 56-77; V Townstall w Dartmouth *Ex* 57-66; V Dartmouth St Petrox 58-66; RD Ipplepen 61-66; V Littleham w Exmouth 66-72; TR 72-87; RD Aylesbeare 69-73; P-in-c Withycombe Raleigh 72-74; Preb Ex Cathl 82-87; rtd 87; Perm to Offic *Truro* from 87. *Bishop's Lodge, Kelly Park, St Mabyn, Bodmin PL30 3RL* Tel (01208) 841606

USHER, George. b 30. Univ of Wales (Swansea) BSc51. St Deiniol's Hawarden 73. **d** 75 **p** 76. NSM Clun w Chapel Lawn *Heref* 75-78; NSM Clun w Chapel Lawn, Bettws-y-Crwyn and Newcastle 79-80; C Shrewsbury St Giles *Lich* 80-83; C Shrewsbury St Giles w Sutton and Atcham 83-84; R Credenhill w Brinsop and Wormsley etc *Heref* 84-98; rtd 98; Perm to Offic *Ex* from 02. *1 Trinity Court, The Esplanade, Sidmouth EX10 8BE* Tel (01395) 513889 E-mail georgeusher@clara.net

USHER, Graham Barham. b 70. Edin Univ BSc93 CCC Cam BA95 MA00. Westcott Ho Cam 93 St Nic Th Coll Ghana 96. **d** 96 **p** 97. C Nunthorpe *York* 96-99; V N Ormesby 99-04; R Hexham *Newc* from 04. *The Rectory, Eilansgate, Hexham NE46 3EW* Tel (01434) 603121 E-mail rector@hexhamabbey.org.uk

USHER, Robin Reginald. b 50. AKC74. St Aug Coll Cant 75. **d** 76 **p** 77. C Hulme Ascension *Man* 76-80; P-in-c Newall Green St Fran 80-85; C Atherton 85-87; TV 87-90; V Leigh St Jo 90-99; Chapl Wigan and Leigh Health Services NHS Trust 93-99; V Milnrow *Man* from 99. *The Vicarage, 40 Eafield Avenue, Milnrow, Rochdale OL16 3UN* Tel (01706) 642988

USHER-WILSON, Lucian Neville. b 36. Linc Coll Ox MA63 St Andr Univ DipEd64 Open Univ BA75. St Steph Ho Ox 91. **d** 94 **p** 96. NSM Compton and Otterbourne *Win* 94-96; NSM Shill Valley and Broadshire *Ox* from 96. *The Tallat, Westwell, Burford OX18 4JT* Tel (01993) 822464 E-mail neville.vw@virgin.net

UTLEY, Canon Edward Jacob. b 24. AKC52. **d** 53 **p** 54. C Pontefract St Giles *Wakef* 53-56; C Bexhill St Pet *Chich* 56-60; Chapl Asst Bexhill Hosp 56-60; Chapl Dudley Road Hosp Birm 60-89; RD Birm City *Birm* 75-82; Hon Can Birm Cathl 80-89; rtd 89; Perm to Offic *Birm* from 89. *St Raphael, 50 Wheatsheaf Road, Edgbaston, Birmingham B16 0RY* Tel 0121-454 2666

UTTLEY, Mrs Valerie Gail. b 43. Man Univ BA64. N Ord Course 80. **dss** 83 **d** 87 **p** 94. Otley *Bradf* 83-87; Hon Par Dn 87-89; Par Dn Calverley 89-92; Ind Chapl *Ripon* 92-97; C

Kirkstall 95-97; V Lofthouse from 97. *The Vicarage, 8 Church Farm Close, Lofthouse, Wakefield WF3 3SA* Tel (01924) 823286 E-mail gailuttley@yahoo.co.uk

UWADIAE, Amos Diebogheneruo. b 69. Ibadan Univ Nigeria BA99 MA02. Immanuel Coll Ibadan 92. **d** 95 **p** 96. Nigeria 95-03; C Ibadan All So 95-96; Asst V Ibadan St Jas 96-99; V Kokori St Luke 99-00; Can St Andr Cathl Warri 01-03; C Addlestone *Guildf* from 04. *Church House, Albert Road, Addlestone KT15 2PX* Tel (01932) 821176 Mobile 07780-843540 E-mail amosuwadiaeus@yahoo.com

V

VAIL, David William. b 30. Dur Univ BA56 Sheff Univ DipEd71. Oak Hill Th Coll 56. **d** 58 **p** 59. C Toxteth Park St Bede *Liv* 58-61; Kenya 61-77; Chapl Versailles *Eur* 77-82; Gen Sec Rwanda Miss 82-88; V Virginia Water *Guildf* 88-96; rtd 96; Perm to Offic *Ox* from 98. *36 Silverthorne Drive, Caversham, Reading RG4 7NS* Tel 0118-954 6667

VAIZEY, Martin John. b 37. AKC64. **d** 65 **p** 66. C Bishopwearmouth Gd Shep *Dur* 65-69; C Darlington H Trin 69-72; V Easington Colliery 72-80; C-in-c Bishopwearmouth St Mary V w St Pet CD 80-85; V Sunderland Springwell w Thorney Close 85-88; R Witton Gilbert 88-96; P-in-c Wingate Grange 96-99; V Wheatley Hill and Wingate w Hutton Henry from 99. *The Vicarage, North Road East, Wingate TS28 5BW* Tel (01429) 837968

VALE, Thomas Stanley George. b 52. Chich Th Coll 85. **d** 87 **p** 88. C Leic St Phil *Leic* 87-90; C Knighton St Mary Magd 90-93; P-in-c Leic St Chad 93-97; V 97-01; V Blackfordby and Woodville from 01. *11 Vicarage Close, Blackfordby, Swadlincote DE11 8AZ* Tel (01524) 219445 E-mail tvale@webleicester.co.uk

VALENTINE, Derek William. b 24. S'wark Ord Course 65. **d** 68 **p** 69. NSM Battersea St Luke *S'wark* 68-77; NSM Fenstanton *Ely* 77-88; Perm to Offic *Bradf* 88-96. *Address withheld by request*

VALENTINE, Hugh William James. b 56. Bradf Univ BA83 CQSW. S'wark Ord Course 86. **d** 89 **p** 90. NSM Stoke Newington Common St Mich *Lon* 89-92; NSM Westmr St Jas from 92; Bp's Adv in Child Protection (Stepney Area) from 96; Bp's Adv in Child Protection *Ox* from 96. *The Clerk's House, 127 Kennington Road, London SE11 6SF* Tel (020) 7735 3138 E-mail hugh.valentine@london.anglican.org

VALENTINE, Jeremy Wilfred. b 38. NW Ord Course 76. **d** 79 **p** 80. C Cundall *Ripon* 79-82; TV Huntington *York* 82-87; V Sand Hutton from 87; RD Buckrose and Bulmer and Malton 98-02. *The Vicarage, Sand Hutton, York YO41 1LB* Tel (01904) 468443 Fax 468670 E-mail jeremyvalentine@tinyworld.co.uk

VALENTINE, John Harvey. b 63. Ch Ch Ox BA85 MA85. Ridley Hall Cam BA92. **d** 93 **p** 94. C Heigham H Trin *Nor* 93-97; C Ches Square St Mich w St Phil *Lon* 97-00; C Brompton H Trin w Onslow Square St Paul 00-02; P-in-c Holborn St Geo w H Trin and St Bart from 02. *13 Doughty Street, London WC1N 2PL* Tel (020) 7404 9606 *or* 7404 4407 Mobile 07736-066091 Fax (020) 7831 0588 E-mail john.valentine@sgtm.org

VALIANT, Mrs Lesley Jean. b 51. Whitelands Coll Lon CertEd74 Univ Coll Chich BA99. STETS 99. **d** 01 **p** 02. NSM Bedhampton *Portsm* 01-04; C Southsea St Jude 04-05; Asst to RD Portsm from 04. *59 Kent Road, Southsea PO5 3EL* Tel (023) 9236 8141 Mobile 07751-168228 E-mail valiants@globalnet.co.uk

VALLINS, Canon Christopher. b 43. Lich Th Coll 63. **d** 66 **p** 67. C Cuddington *Guildf* 66-70; C Aldershot St Mich 70-73; V W Ewell 73-81; R Worplesdon 81-89; Chapl Merrist Wood Coll of Agric 81-89; RD Guildf 86-89; Chapl Epsom Health Care NHS Trust 89-99; Sen Chapl Epsom and St Helier NHS Trust from 99; Chapl Horton Hosp Epsom 95-98; Bp's Adv on Healing *Guildf* from 97; Hon Can Guildf Cathl from 01. *Little Watermead, Reigate Road, Hookwood, Horley RH6 0HD* Tel (01293) 824188 *or* (01372) 735322 Fax (01372) 735187 E-mail chrisvallins@yahoo.co.uk

VALLIS, Brett Paul Stanley. b 72. G&C Coll Cam BA93 St Jo Coll Dur BA01. Cranmer Hall Dur 99. **d** 02 **p** 03. C Monkseaton St Mary *Newc* 02-05; P-in-c Fatfield *Dur* from 05. *14 Ewesley, Washington NE38 9JG* E-mail vallisbrett@yahoo.co.uk

VAN BEVEREN, Mrs Susan Margaret. b 64. St Hugh's Coll Ox BA85 MA89. Trin Th Sch Melbourne 95. **d** 96 **p** 96. Ind Chapl Inter-Ch Trade and Ind Miss Australia 96-99; NSM Amsterdam w Den Helder and Heiloo *Eur* 00-03; Officer for Miss in Work and Economic Life *Ox* from 03. *14 Elm Road, Reading RG6 5TS* Tel 0118-986 4718 E-mail svan.beveren@well-centre.org

VAN CARRAPIETT, Timothy Michael James. b 39. Chich Th Coll 60. **d** 63 **p** 64. C Sugley *Newc* 63-65; C Newc St Fran 65-69; P-in-c Wrangbrook w N Elmsall CD *Wakef* 69-74; P-in-c Flushing *Truro* 74-75; P-in-c Mylor w Flushing 75-76; P-in-c St Day 76-82; R Aldrington *Chich* 82-87; V Bexhill St Barn 87-01; rtd 01; Perm to Offic *St E* from 01. *Bear-Wuff Cottage, 9 Tacon Road, Felixstowe IP11 2DT* Tel (01394) 271338

VAN CULIN, Canon Samuel. b 30. OBE. Princeton Univ AB52. Virginia Th Sem DB55 Hon DD77 Gen Th Sem NY Hon DD83. **d** 55 **p** 56. USA 55-83; Sec Gen ACC 83-94; Hon C All Hallows by the Tower etc *Lon* 89-04; Hon Can Cant Cathl *Cant* 83-94; Hon Can Ibadan from 83; Hon Can Jerusalem from 84; Hon Can S Africa from 89; Hon Can Honolulu from 91; rtd 94; Hon Can Nat Cathl USA from 04. *3900 Watson Place, NW B-5D, Washington DC 20016, USA*

VAN D'ARQUE, Christopher Simon Wayne. b 62. St Jo Coll Dur BA99. **d** 99 **p** 00. C Letchworth St Paul w Willian *St Alb* 99-02; C Westminster St Jas the Less *Lon* 02-03; V W Bessacarr *Sheff* from 03. *The Vicarage, 39 Sturton Close, Doncaster DN4 7JG* Tel (01302) 538487 E-mail clan.vandarque@virgin.net

VAN DE KASTEELE, Peter John. b 39. Magd Coll Cam BA61 MA65. Clifton Th Coll 61. **d** 63 **p** 64. C Eastbourne H Trin *Chich* 63-66; C N Pickenham w S Pickenham etc *Nor* 66-70; R Mursley w Swanbourne and Lt Horwood *Ox* 70-80; Admin Sec Clinical Th Assn from 83; Gen Dir 88-99; Perm to Offic *Glouc* from 83; Hon C Westcote w Icomb and Bledington 88-89; rtd 99. *St Mary's House, Church Westcote, Chipping Norton OX7 6SF* Tel (01993) 830193

van de WEYER, Robert William Bates. b 50. Lanc Univ BA76. S'wark Ord Course 78. **d** 81 **p** 82. Warden Lt Gidding Community from 77; Hon C Gt w Lt Gidding and Steeple Gidding *Ely* 81-83; P-in-c 83-93; P-in-c Winwick 83-93; P-in-c Hamerton 83-93; P-in-c Upton and Copmanford 83-93; Perm to Offic from 93. *Woodend, Upton, Huntingdon PE28 5YF* Tel (01480) 890333

VAN DEN BERG, Jan Jacob. b 56. Sarum & Wells Th Coll 86. **d** 88 **p** 89. C Glouc St Aldate *Glouc* 88-91; C Ollerton w Boughton *S'well* 91-95; P-in-c Scrooby 95-00; P-in-c Blyth 97-00; C Brampton and Farlam and Castle Carrock w Cumrew *Carl* 00-02; TV Eden, Gelt and Irthing 02-05; P-in-c Rockcliffe and Blackford from 05. *The Vicarage, Rockcliffe, Carlisle CA6 4AA* Tel (01228) 674209 E-mail jan@vandenberg.fsnet.co.uk

VAN DEN BERGH, Victor Michael Cornelius. b 53. ALBC92. Ridley Hall Cam 02. **d** 03 **p** 04. C Tamworth *Lich* from 03. *19 Perrycrofts Crescent, Tamworth B79 8UA* Tel (01827) 65926 Mobile 07770-900712 E-mail vic_vdb@btinternet.com

van den HOF, Ariadne Rolanda Magdalena. b 71. Univ of Wales (Cardiff) MTh96. Old Cath Sem Amersfoort 90 St Mich Coll Llan 98. **d** 99 **p** 00. C Dolgellau w Llanfachreth and Brithdir etc *Ban* 99-01; Min Can Ban Cathl 01-02; P-in-c Trefdraeth w Aberffraw, Llangadwaladr etc 02-03; R from 03. *The Rectory, 1 Maes Glas, Bethel, Bodorgan LL62 5NW* Tel (01407) 840190 E-mail ariadne@telco4u.net

VAN DER HART, William Richard. b 76. Homerton Coll Cam BEd99. Wycliffe Hall Ox BTh04. **d** 04 **p** 05. C Bryanston Square St Mary w St Marylebone St Mark *Lon* from 04. *17 Homer Row, London W1 4AP* Tel (020) 7402 4993 Mobile 07968-132129 E-mail vanders@tinyworld.co.uk

van der LINDE, Herbert John. b 43. Rhodes Univ BA66. Coll of Resurr Mirfield. **d** 68 **p** 69. C Kingston St Luke *S'wark* 68-75; C Chipping Campden w Ebrington *Glouc* 75-78; V Cheltenham St Pet 78-84; V Bussage from 84. *St Michael's Vicarage, Bussage, Stroud GL6 8BB* Tel (01453) 883556

VAN DER PUMP, Charles Lyndon. b 25. FRCM. S'wark Ord Course 86. **d** 88 **p** 89. NSM Primrose Hill St Mary w Avenue Road St Paul *Lon* 88-02; Perm to Offic from 02. *48 Canfield Gardens, London NW6 3EB* Tel and fax (020) 7624 4517 E-mail office@smvph.freeserve.co.uk

VAN DER TOORN, Mrs Stephne. b 53. Natal Univ BA73. **d** 93 **p** 95. NSM Pretoria St Mary S Africa 93-01; C Fawley *Win* from 01. *15 Long Lane Close, Holbury, Southampton SO45 2LE* Tel (023) 8089 1809 Mobile 07984-026897 E-mail vandertoorn@btinternet.com

van der VALK, Jesse. b 59. Nottm Univ BTh84 Birm Univ MPhil88 Avery Hill Coll PGCE85. St Jo Coll Nottm 81. **d** 88 **p** 89. C Droitwich Spa *Worc* 88-92; V Hartshead and Hightown *Wakef* 92-96; R Woolwich St Mary w St Mich *S'wark* from 96; USPG (Lon Volunteers and Co-workers Team) from 97. *The Rectory, 43 Rectory Place, London SE18 5DA* Tel (020) 8854 2302 E-mail jessevdvalk@aol.com

VAN KOEVERING, Mrs Helen Elizabeth Parsons. b 60. SS Hild & Bede Coll Dur BA82 Trin Coll Bris MPhil99. S Wales Ord Course 01. **d** 02 **p** 03. C Bettws *Mon* 02-03; Bp's Sec Niassa Mozambique from 03. *CP 264, Lichinga, Niassa, Mozambique* Tel (00258) 712 0735 Fax as telephone E-mail mark@koev.freeserve.co.uk *or* diocese.niassa@teledata.mz

✠**VAN KOEVERING, The Rt Revd Mark Allan.** b 57. Michigan State Univ BSc79 MSc85. Trin Coll Bris BA99. **d** 99 **p** 00 **c** 03. C Bettws *Mon* 99-01; P-in-c 01-03; Bp Niassa Mozambique from 03. *Diocese do Niassa, CP 264, Lichinga, Niassa, Mozambique* Tel (00258) 712 0735 Fax as telephone E-mail mark@koev.freeserve.co.uk *or* diocese.niassa@teledata.mz

VAN KRIEKEN VANNERLEY, David. *See* VANNERLEY, David van Krieken

VAN LEER, Samuel Wall. b 67. Virginia Univ BA90 California Univ MA91 St Jo Coll Dur BA01. Cranmer Hall Dur 99. **d** 02 **p** 03. C Berne w Neuchâtel *Eur* 02-05; Chapl E Netherlands from 05. *Ijsselsingel 86, 6991 ZT Rheden, The Netherlands* Tel (0031) (26) 495 0620

VAN LEEUWEN, The Ven Dirk Willem. b 45. Utrecht Univ LLD71. Th Faculty Brussels 71 S'wark Ord Course 80. **d** 82 **p** 83. Asst Chapl Brussels Cathl *Eur* 82-84; Chapl Haarlem 84-93; Chapl Antwerp St Boniface from 94; Chapl Charleroi 94-00; P-in-c Ypres 97-99; P-in-c Leuven 98-99; Can Brussels Cathl from 96; Chapl Knokke from 01; P-in-c Ostend 01-03; P-in-c Bruges 01-03; V Gen to Bp Eur from 02; Adn NW Eur from 05. *Grétrystraat 39, B-2018 Antwerp, Belgium* Tel (0032) (3) 239 3339 Fax 230 4797 E-mail dirk.vanleeuwen@scarlet.be

VAN STRAATEN, Christopher Jan. b 55. Bris Univ BA77 Natal Univ HDipEd78. Oak Hill Th Coll DipHE92. **d** 92 **p** 93. C Woodley *Ox* 92-96; V Gillingham St Aug *Roch* from 96. *St Augustine's Vicarage, Rock Avenue, Gillingham ME7 5PW* Tel (01634) 850288 E-mail chris.vanstraaten@sagk.org.uk

van WENGEN, Rosemary Margaret. b 38. Westf Coll Lon BA60 Univ of Leiden MA77 PhD81. SEITE 98. **d** 01 **p** 02. NSM Benenden *Cant* from 01; NSM Sandhurst w Newenden from 04. *Beach House, Grange Road, St Michaels, Tenterden TN30 6EF* Tel (01580) 764857 Fax 761405 E-mail rvanwengen@aol.com

VAN ZANDBERGEN, Karen. *See* BURNETT-HALL, Mrs Karen

VANDERSTOCK, Alan. b 31. St Jo Coll Dur BA57. Cranmer Hall Dur DipTh59. **d** 59 **p** 60. C Kersal Moor *Man* 59-62; C-in-c Lower Kersal CD 63-67; Lic Preacher *Cant* from 67; Sen Tutor Heath Clark High Sch Croydon 73-83; Dep Hd Teacher Norbury Manor High Sch Croydon 83-86; Sen Master Shirley High Sch Croydon 86-92; rtd 92. *17 Snowbell Road, Kingsnorth, Ashford TN23 3NF* Tel (01233) 503889

VANDYCK, Mrs Salli Diane Seymour. b 39. Grenoble Univ Dip French Studies 57 DipTT77 AIL75 CertFE93. S'wark Ord Course 93 SEITE 93. **d** 96 **p** 97. NSM Chertsey *Guildf* 96-98; NSM Ross *Heref* 98-03; rtd 03; Perm to Offic *Heref* from 03. *The Rectory, Linton, Ross-on-Wye HR9 7RX* Tel (01989) 720472

VANN, Ms Cherry Elizabeth. b 58. ARCM78 GRSM80. Westcott Ho Cam 86. **d** 89 **p** 94. Par Dn Flixton St Mich *Man* 89-92; Chapl Bolton Inst of F&HE 92-98; Par Dn Bolton St Pet 92-94; C 94-98; TV E Farnworth and Kearsley 98-04; TR from 04; Chapl among Deaf People 98-04. *195 Harrowby Street, Farnworth, Bolton BL4 9QU* Tel (01204) 572455 E-mail cvannskye@aol.com

VANN, Canon Paul. b 41. St D Coll Lamp DipTh65. **d** 65 **p** 66. C Griffithstown *Mon* 65-67; C Llanfrechfa All SS 67-71; Dioc Youth Chapl 69-74; Chapl St Woolos Cathl 71-72; P-in-c Llanrumney 72-76; V 76-97; Asst Chapl HM Pris Cardiff 75-78; RD Bassaleg *Mon* 90-99; R Machen from 97; Can St Woolos Cathl from 01. *The Rectory, Rectory Gardens, Chatham, Machen, Caerphilly CF83 8SU* Tel (01633) 440321

VANNERLEY, David van Krieken. b 50. Ch Ch Coll Cant CertEd71 Kent Univ BA78. SEITE 00. **d** 05. NSM St Laur in Thanet *Cant* from 05. *34 Cherry Gardens, Herne Bay CT6 5QE* Tel (01227) 369096 E-mail vannerley@aol.com

VANNOZZI, Canon Peter. b 62. Lon Univ BA83. Ripon Coll Cuddesdon BA86 MA91. **d** 87 **p** 88. C Kenton *Lon* 87-90; C Fleet *Guildf* 90-93; V Northwood Hills St Edm *Lon* 93-97; AD Harrow 95-97; V S Dulwich St Steph *S'wark* 97-05; RD Dulwich 02-05; Can Res Wakef Cathl *Wakef* from 05. *3 Cathedral Close, Wakefield WF1 2DP* Tel and fax (01924) 210007 E-mail petervannozzi@yahoo.co.uk

VANSTON, The Ven William Francis Harley. b 24. TCD BA48 MA52. **d** 48 **p** 49. C Belfast St Mary *Conn* 48-51; C Dublin Rathfarnham *D & G* 51-58; I Narraghmore w Fontstown and Timolin 58-65; I Arklow 65-67; I Arklow w Inch 67-73; I Arklow w Inch and Kilbride 73-89; RD Rathdrum 77-89; Adn Glendalough 83-89; rtd 89. *11 Seabank Court, Sandycove, Dun Laoghaire, Co Dublin, Irish Republic* Tel (00353) (1) 280 4575

VANSTONE, Preb Walford David Frederick. b 38. Open Univ BA81. AKC69. **d** 70 **p** 71. C Feltham *Lon* 70-75; TV E Runcorn w Halton *Ches* 75-80; V Grange St Andr 80-82; V Hampton All SS *Lon* from 82; P-in-c Teddington SS Pet and Paul and Fulwell 99-00; AD Hampton 95-03; Preb St Paul's Cathl from 99; Chapl Richmond Coll from 02. *All Saints' Vicarage, 40 The Avenue, Hampton TW12 3RS* Tel (020) 8979 2102 Fax 8255 6118 E-mail wvanstone@aol.com

VARAH, Paul Hugh. b 46. St Deiniol's Hawarden 83. **d** 85 **p** 86. C Prestatyn *St As* 85-87; P-in-c Hawarden 87-88; TV 88-89; V Esclusham 89-96; V Connah's Quay from 96. *The Vicarage, Church Hill, Connah's Quay, Deeside CH5 4AD* Tel (01244) 830224 Fax as telephone

VARGAS, Eric Arthur Dudley. b 27. BD. S Dios Minl Tr Scheme 81. **d** 83 **p** 84. C Farncombe *Guildf* 83-86; R Ockley, Okewood and Forest Green 86-90; V Kirdford *Chich* 90-93; rtd 93; Perm to Offic *Chich* and *Portsm* from 93. *33 Park Crescent, Emsworth PO10 7NT* Tel (01243) 430611

VARGESON, Peter Andrew. b 53. Wycliffe Hall Ox 85. **d** 87 **p** 88. C Yateley *Win* 87-92; V Bursledon from 92; AD Eastleigh from 99. *The Vicarage, School Road, Bursledon, Southampton SO31 8BW* Tel (023) 8040 2821 *or* 8040 6021 E-mail peter.vargeson@ukgateway.net

VARLEY (née TRIM), Elizabeth Ann. b 52. Homerton Coll Cam BEd75 Van Mildert Coll Dur PhD85 St Jo Coll Dur BA96. NEOC 94. **d** 96 **p** 97. C Sedgefield *Dur* 96-99; Dir Post-Ord Tr (Stepney Area) *Lon* 99-02; V Hipswell *Ripon* from 02. *The Vicarage, 7 Forest Drive, Colburn, Catterick Garrison DL9 4PN* Tel (01748) 833320 E-mail elizabeth_varley@hotmail.com

VARLEY, Robert. b 36. St Jo Coll Cam BA57 MA64 Man Poly PGCE92. NW Ord Course 71. **d** 74 **p** 75. C Wallasey St Hilary *Ches* 74-77; V Rock Ferry 77-81; Perm to Offic *Man* 82-83; Hon C E Farnworth and Kearsley 83-86; Hon C Walkden Moor 86-87; C 87-89; V Lt Hulton 89-90; Perm to Offic from 97. *66 Normanby Road, Worsley, Manchester M28 7TS* Tel 0161-790 8420

VARNEY, Donald James. b 35. Chich Th Coll 84. **d** 86. NSM Liss *Portsm* 86-05; rtd 05; Perm to Offic *Portsm* from 05. *12 Birch Close, Liss, Petersfield GU33 7HS* Tel (01730) 893945

VARNEY, Peter David. b 38. Univ Coll Dur BA61 MA64. Qu Coll Birm 61. **d** 64 **p** 65. C Newington St Paul *S'wark* 64-66; C Camberwell St Mich w All So w Em 66-67; Malaysia 67-68; Hon C Croxley Green All SS *St Alb* 69; Perm to Offic *Roch* 69-72 and 74-84; Asst Chapl CSJB 72-73; Asst Sec Chrs Abroad 74-79; Dir Bloxham Project 84-86; Perm to Offic *Cant* 84-85 and *S'wark* 85-86; P-in-c Thornage w Brinton w Hunworth and Stody *Nor* 87-88; P-in-c Briningham 87-88; P-in-c Melton Constable w Swanton Novers 87-88; Perm to Offic from 88; Chapl Yare and Norvic Clinics and St Andr Hosp Nor 90-95; rtd 03. *9 Coslany Street, Norwich NR3 3DT* Tel (01603) 462237 E-mail pv@onetel.com

VARNEY, Stephen Clive. b 59. Qu Mary Coll Lon BSc80 Sussex Univ MSc82 Southn Univ BTh88. Sarum & Wells Th Coll 83. **d** 86 **p** 87. C Riverhead w Dunton Green *Roch* 86-91; V Bostall Heath 91-99; V Bromley St Mark from 99. *St Mark's Vicarage, 51 Hayes Road, Bromley BR2 9AE* Tel (020) 8460 6220 Mobile 07961-117578

VARNEY, Wilfred Davies. b 10. Sarum & Wells Th Coll 71. **d** 71 **p** 72. C Glouc St Paul *Glouc* 71-74; V Lydbrook 74-77; rtd 77; Hon C Felpham w Middleton *Chich* 77-80; Hon C Overbury w Alstone, Teddington and Lt Washbourne *Worc* 80-82; Perm to Offic *Nor* 82-87 and 91-93; P-in-c Nor St Andr 87-91; Perm to Offic *Guildf* 93-00. *11 Manormead, Tilford Road, Hindhead GU26 6RA* Tel (01428) 606652

VARNEY, William James Granville. b 22. St D Coll Lamp 62. **d** 65 **p** 66. C Burry Port and Pwll *St D* 65-68; V Strata Florida 68-71; V Llandyfriog, Llanfair Trelygen, Troedyraur etc 71-78; OCF 78; R Aberporth w Tremain and Blaenporth *St D* 78-87; P-in-c Penbryn and Betws Ifan w Bryngwyn 88-92; rtd 92. *Alma, Tan y Groes, Cardigan SA43 2JT* Tel (01239) 810217

VARNHAM, Gerald Stanley. b 29. Sarum & Wells Th Coll 74. **d** 77 **p** 78. Hon C Portchester *Portsm* 77-86; Perm to Offic from 88. *15 Southampton Road, Fareham PO16 7DZ* Tel (01329) 234182

VARNON, Nicholas Charles Harbord. b 45. St Luke's Coll Ex CertEd71 Open Univ BA83 BPhil91 MA94 Univ of Wales MPhil00. St Mich Coll Llan 91. **d** 93 **p** 94. C Pontypridd St Cath w St Matt *Llan* 93-97; P-in-c Sutton St Nicholas w Sutton St Michael *Heref* 97-04; P-in-c Withington w Westhide 97-04; P-in-c Weybourne Gp *Nor* from 04; CF (ACF) from 00. *The Rectory, The Street, Weybourne, Holt NR25 7SY* Tel (01263) 588268

VARQUEZ, Leo Bacleon. b 61. St Andr Th Sem Manila LTh86. **d** 86 **p** 86. Philippines 86-97; P St Andr 86-91; P St Isidore 92-94; SSF 95-99; NSM Edin St Jo *Edin* 98-99; NSM Mill End and Heronsgate w W Hyde *St Alb* 99-00; Asst Chapl HM Pris Featherstone 00-02; C Hednesford *Lich* 00-04; C Kingstanding St Luke *Birm* from 04. *83 Landswood Close, Birmingham B44 0LF* Tel 0121-254 8304 E-mail leovarquez@yahoo.co.uk

VARTY, John Eric. b 44. Tyndale Hall Bris 68. **d** 71 **p** 72. C Barrow St Mark *Carl* 71-74; C Cheadle *Ches* 74-82; V Cheadle All Hallows 82-89; V Alsager Ch Ch from 89. *Christ Church Vicarage, 43 Church Road, Alsager, Stoke-on-Trent ST7 2HS* Tel (01270) 873727 *or* 0161-247 2000 E-mail vartyj1j2@clara.co.uk

VARTY, Robert. b 46. LRAM. Sarum & Wells Th Coll 84. **d** 86 **p** 87. C Plympton St Mary *Ex* 86-89; TV Northam w Westward Ho! and Appledore 89-95; P-in-c Wigginton *St Alb* 95-00; TV Tring 95-00; rtd 00; Clergy Widow(er)s Officer *Ex* 02-04; Perm to

Offic *Ex* 01-04 and *Eur* from 05. *La Butte, 61110 Bellou-sur-Huisne, France* Tel (0033) (2) 33 25 55 64 E-mail varty.robert@wanadoo.fr

VASEY, Arthur Stuart. b 37. Qu Coll Birm 68. **d** 71 **p** 72. C Shelf *Bradf* 71-73; Australia 74-76; Chapl St Jo Hosp Linc 76-79; P-in-c Tanfield *Dur* 79-84; C Birtley 84-85; C Middlesbrough St Thos *York* 85-86; rtd 02. *Glen Esk, 3 Quarry Bank, Malton YO17 7HA*

VASEY-SAUNDERS, Mrs Leah Beverley. b 77. Huddersfield Univ BMus98 St Jo Coll Dur BTh03. Cranmer Hall Dur 00. **d** 03 **p** 04. C Whorlton *Newc* 03-04; NSM Newc St Geo from 05. *52 Fern Avenue, Jesmond, Newcastle upon Tyne NE2 2QX* Tel 0191-239 9775 E-mail leahb.vasey-saunders@virgin.net

VASEY-SAUNDERS, Mark Richard. b 74. Coll of Ripon & York St Jo BA95 St Jo Coll Dur BA00. Cranmer Hall Dur 98. **d** 01 **p** 02. C Ponteland *Newc* 01-04; Chapl Newc Univ from 04. *52 Fern Avenue, Jesmond, Newcastle upon Tyne NE2 2QX* Tel 0191-281 5166 E-mail revmarksaunders@fish.co.uk

VAUGHAN, Andrew Christopher James. b 61. Univ of Wales (Lamp) BA82. Linc Th Coll 84. **d** 84 **p** 85. C Caerleon *Mon* 84-86; C Magor w Redwick and Undy 86-88; Ind Chapl 84-94; Linc Ind Miss *Linc* from 94. *4 Grange Close, Canwick, Lincoln LN4 2RH* Tel and fax (01522) 528266 Mobile 07702-468549 E-mail vaughanlim@tesco.net

VAUGHAN, Brian John. b 38. Lich Th Coll 65. **d** 68 **p** 69. C Fisherton Anger *Sarum* 68-70; C Wareham w Arne 70-73; Australia from 73; Asst P Mt Lawley 73; R Dalwallinu 73-76; R Morawa 75-78; Field Officer Bible Soc of W Australia 78-81; Assoc P Mt Lawley 82-86; R Pinjarra 86-96; R Manjimup 96-00; rtd 00. *Milborne, 6 Steeple Retreat, Busselton, W Australia 6280* Tel (0061) (8) 9751 1225 E-mail sherton@optusnet.com.au

VAUGHAN, Carole Ann. b 47. Leeds Univ CertEd68. STETS 95. **d** 98 **p** 99. NSM Oakley w Wootton St Lawrence *Win* from 98. *The Rectory, Glebe Lane, Worting, Basingstoke RG23 8QA* Tel (01256) 331531 E-mail carole@cjvaughan.co.uk

VAUGHAN, Charles Jeremy Marshall. b 52. Man Univ BSc75 LTh. St Jo Coll Nottm 83. **d** 85 **p** 86. C Epsom Common Ch Ch *Guildf* 85-88; C Woking Ch Ch 88-93; R Worting *Win* from 93. *The Rectory, Glebe Lane, Worting, Basingstoke RG23 8QA* Tel (01256) 331531 E-mail jeremy@cjvaughan.co.uk

VAUGHAN, Edward Michael. b 59. Univ of NSW BA80 Sydney Univ DipEd81. Moore Th Coll Sydney BTh87. **d** 89 **p** 89. C Jannali Australia 89-91; C Rozelle 92-94; R Darling Street 95-05; I Crinken *D & G* from 05. *15 Shrewsbury Hall, Shankill, Co Dublin, Irish Republic* Tel (00353) (1) 282 4391 Mobile 87-904 2092 E-mail ed@crinken.com

VAUGHAN, Idris Samuel. b 46. Sarum Th Coll 70. **d** 72 **p** 73. C Workington St Jo *Carl* 72-76; C Foley Park *Worc* 76-79; P-in-c Hayton St Mary *Carl* 79; V 79-85; Chapl Asst Univ Hosp Nottm 85-90; Chapl Asst Nottm Gen Hosp 85-90; Chapl Stafford Distr Gen Hosp 90-94; Chapl Chase Hosp Cannock 90-94; Chapl Mid Staffs Gen Hosps NHS Trust from 94. *The Chaplain's Office, Stafford District General Hospital, Weston Road, Stafford ST16 3RS* Tel (01785) 230930 *or* 257731 ext 4930

VAUGHAN, Jeffrey Charles. b 45. S'wark Ord Course 85. **d** 88 **p** 89. NSM Tottenham St Paul *Lon* 88-91; C Hendon St Alphage 91-95; V Enfield SS Pet and Paul from 95. *The Vicarage, 177 Ordnance Road, Enfield EN3 6AB* Tel (01992) 719770 Fax (020) 8292 8456

VAUGHAN, Jeremy. *See* VAUGHAN, Charles Jeremy Marshall

VAUGHAN, John. b 30. Sarum Th Coll 53. **d** 56 **p** 57. C Wigan St Andr *Liv* 56-59; Australia 59-64; P-in-c Riddings *Derby* 64-71; R Hasland 71-80; V Temple Normanton 71-80; TV Dronfield 80-86; V Bradwell 86-95; rtd 95; Perm to Offic *Derby* from 95. *11 Millstone Close, Dronfield Woodhouse, Dronfield S18 8ZL* Tel (01246) 415647

VAUGHAN, Patrick Handley. b 38. TCD BA60 BD65 Selw Coll Cam BA62 MA66 Nottm Univ PhD88. Ridley Hall Cam 61. **d** 63 **p** 64. Min Can Bradf Cathl *Bradf* 63-66; Uganda 67-73; P-in-c Slingsby *York* 74-77; Tutor NW Ord Course 74-77; P-in-c Hovingham *York* 74-77; Prin EMMTC *S'well* 77-90; Hon Can Leic Cathl *Leic* 87-90; Assoc Lect Open Univ from 94. *113 Upperthorpe Road, Sheffield S6 3EA* Tel 0114-272 2675

✠**VAUGHAN, The Rt Revd Peter St George.** b 30. Selw Coll Cam BA55 MA59 BNC Ox MA63. Ridley Hall Cam. **d** 57 **p** 58 **c** 89. C Birm St Martin *Birm* 57-63; Chapl Ox Pastorate 63-67; Asst Chapl BNC Ox 63-67; Ceylon 67-72; New Zealand 72-75; Prin Crowther Hall CMS Tr Coll Selly Oak 75-83; Adn Westmorland and Furness *Carl* 83-89; Hon Can Carl Cathl 83-89; Area Bp Ramsbury *Sarum* 89-98; Can and Preb Sarum Cathl 89-98; rtd 98; Hon Asst Bp Bradf 98-01; Hon Can Bradf Cathl from 98; Perm to Offic *Glouc* from 01; Hon Asst Bp Bris from 02. *Willowbrook, Downington, Lechlade GL7 3DL* Tel (01367) 252216

VAUGHAN, Preb Roger Maxwell. b 39. AKC62. **d** 63 **p** 64. C W Bromwich All SS *Lich* 63-65; C Wolverhampton 65-70; V Tunstall Ch Ch 70-79; V Tunstall 79; V Abbots Bromley 79-86; P-in-c Blithfield 85-86; V Abbots Bromley w Blithfield 86-93; V Stafford St Jo and Tixall w Ingestre 93-04; Preb Lich Cathl from 99; rtd 04; Perm to Offic *Lich* from 04. *51 Crestwood Drive, Stone ST15 0LW* Tel (01785) 812192 E-mail salrog.vaughan@btinternet.com

VAUGHAN, Trevor. b 41. TD91. Cen Lancs Univ BA91. Linc Th Coll 66. **d** 69 **p** 70. C Wyken *Cov* 69-72; C Stratford-on-Avon w Bishopton 72-73; P-in-c Monks Kirby w Withybrook and Copston Magna 73-75; P-in-c Wolvey, Burton Hastings and Stretton Baskerville 73-77; P-in-c Withybrook w Copston Magna 73-77; V Heyhouses *Blackb* 77-80; CF (TA) from 79; V Chorley St Geo *Blackb* 80-83; R Bolton by Bowland w Grindleton *Bradf* 83-89; V Settle 89-91; R Broughton, Marton and Thornton 91-00; V Morecambe St Barn *Blackb* 00-03; P-in-c Sabden and Pendleton from 03. *St Nicholas' Vicarage, Westley Street, Sabden, Clitheroe BB7 9EH* Tel (01282) 771384

VAUGHAN-JONES, Canon John Paschal. b 18. Keble Coll Ox BA39 MA43. St Steph Ho Ox 39. **d** 41 **p** 42. C Laindon w Basildon *Chelmsf* 41-43 and 47-49; CF 43-47; R Chipping Ongar *Chelmsf* 49-83; R Shelley 49-83; RD Ongar 72-82; Hon Can Chelmsf Cathl 78-83; rtd 83; Perm to Offic *Chelmsf* from 03. *Armadale, 3 Great Lane, Malborough, Kingsbridge TQ7 3SA* Tel (01548) 562138

VAUGHAN-WILSON, Jane Elizabeth. b 61. Magd Coll Ox MA87. Cranmer Hall Dur. **d** 89 **p** 94. Par Dn Ormesby *York* 89-93; Dn-in-c Middlesbrough St Agnes 93-94; P-in-c 94-95; TV Basingstoke *Win* 95-03; Perm to Offic *Truro* from 03. *4 Tolver Road, Penzance TR18 2AG* Tel (01736) 351825

VAYRO, Mark Shaun. b 66. Aston Tr Scheme 88 Linc Th Coll BTh93. **d** 93 **p** 94. C Northampton St Mich w St Edm *Pet* 93-96; TV Duston Team 96-98; V Elm and Friday Bridge w Coldham *Ely* 98-01. *125 Spalding Road, Pinchbeck, Spalding LN11 3UE*

VEEN, Keith Henry. b 46. **d** 01 **p** 02. OLM Croydon St Pet *S'wark* 01-02; OLM Croydon Ch Ch from 02. *91 The Ridgeway, Croydon CR0 4AH* Tel (020) 8688 3565 E-mail keithveen@veenco.fsnet.co.uk

VELLACOTT, John Patrick Millner. b 29. Ox NSM Course 86. **d** 89 **p** 90. NSM Cholsey *Ox* 89-93; Chapl Nerja *Eur* 93-97; rtd 97; Perm to Offic *Truro* 97-00; *Glouc* 00-02 and *Carl* from 03. *5 Stonycroft Drive, Arnside, Carnforth LA5 0EE* Tel (01524) 762800

VELLACOTT, Peter Graham. b 38. Seale-Hayne Agric Coll NDA59. EAMTC 90. **d** 93 **p** 94. NSM Framlingham w Saxtead *St E* 93-95; NSM Brandeston w Kettleburgh 95-99; NSM Easton 95-99; P-in-c Brandeston w Kettleburgh and Easton from 99. *Soham House, Brandeston, Woodbridge IP13 7AX* Tel (01728) 685423

✠**VENABLES, The Most Revd Gregory James.** b 49. Lon Univ CertEd74. **d** 84 **p** 84 **c** 93. SAMS from 77; Paraguay 78-90; C Rainham *Chelmsf* 90-92; C Rainham w Wennington 92-93; Aux Bp Peru and Bolivia 93-95; Bp Bolivia 95-00; Asst Primate of S Cone 95-02; Bp Coadjutor Argentina 00-02; Dioc Bp from 02; Presiding Bp of S Cone from 01. *Conesa 1925 1B, (1428) Belgrano, Capital Federal, Buenos Aires, Argentina* Tel (0054) (11) 4342 4618 *or* 4783 0272 Fax 4784 1277 E-mail bpgreg@ciudad.com.ar

VENABLES, Canon Margaret Joy. b 37. Bp Otter Coll CertEd57 S Dios Minl Tr Scheme 86. **d** 89 **p** 94. NSM Wilton *B & W* 89-91; C Taunton St Andr 91-97; P-in-c Haynes *St Alb* 97-03; P-in-c Clophill 00-03; R Campton, Clophill and Haynes from 03; RD Shefford from 01; Hon Can St Alb from 05. *The Vicarage, 4A North Lane, Haynes, Bedford MK45 3PW* Tel (01234) 381235 *or* (01727) 854532 E-mail margsv@waitrose.com

VENABLES, Philip Richard Meredith. b 58. Magd Coll Ox BA79 CertEd80. Wycliffe Hall Ox 85. **d** 88 **p** 89. C Gillingham St Mark *Roch* 88-93; V Penge St Jo from 93. *The Vicarage, St John's Road, London SE20 7EQ* Tel (020) 8778 6176 E-mail philip@venables01.freeserve.co.uk

VENESS, Allan Barry. b 39. Lon Inst of Educn TCert60 Sussex Univ BEd81 Univ Coll Chich Dip Th & Min 99. Bp Otter Coll 94. **d** 97. NSM Felpham *Chich* 97-01; NSM Aldwick from 01. *95 Limmer Lane, Felpham, Bognor Regis PO22 7LP* Tel (01243) 583230 Fax 582471

VENEZUELA, Bishop of. *See* GUERRERO, The Rt Revd Orlando

VENN, Prof Richard Frank. b 49. Leeds Univ BSc72 Strathclyde Univ PhD77 CChem FRSC97. Ridley Hall Cam 04. **d** 05. C Margate H Trin *Cant* from 05. *10 Richmond Avenue, Margate CT9 2NG* Tel (01843) 295188 Mobile 07967-146842 E-mail dickvenn@talktalk.net

✠**VENNER, The Rt Revd Stephen Squires.** b 44. Birm Univ BA65 Linacre Coll Ox BA67 MA71 Lon Univ PGCE72. St Steph Ho Ox 65. **d** 68 **p** 69 **c** 94. C Streatham St Pet *S'wark* 68-71; C Streatham Hill St Marg 71-72; C Balham Hill Ascension 72-74; V Clapham St Pet 74-76; Bp's Chapl to Overseas Students 74-76; P-in-c Studley *Sarum* 76; V 76-82; V Weymouth H Trin 82-94; RD Weymouth 88-93; Can and Preb Sarum Cathl 89-94; Suff Bp Middleton *Man* 94-99; Suff Bp Dover *Cant* from 99. *The Bishop's Office, Old Palace, Canterbury CT1 2EE* Tel (01227) 459382 Fax 784985 E-mail bishop@bishcant.org

VENNING, Nigel Christopher. b 50. K Coll Lon BD75 AKC75. St Aug Coll Cant 75. **d** 76 **p** 77. C Minehead *B & W* 76-80; C Fawley *Win* 80-83; P-in-c Whitestaunton and Combe St Nicholas w Wambrook *B & W* 83-89; R Staplegrove 89-01; P-in-c Norton Fitzwarren 00-01; R Staplegrove w Norton Fitzwarren 01-03; R Blackdown 03-05; RD Taunton 96-01; rtd 05. *Crispin House, 5 Mendip Edge, Weston-super-Mare BS24 9JF* E-mail nigelvenning@lycos.co.uk

✠**VERCOE, The Most Revd Whakahuihui.** b 28. MBE70. **d** 51 **p** 52 **c** 81. C Feilding NZ 51-53; P-in-c Wellington Maori Pastorate 53-54; P-in-c Wairarapa 55-57; Pastor Rangitikei-Manawatu 58-61; CF 61-71; Chapl Waipounamu Coll 71-75; P Ohinemutu 76-78; Pastor Ruatoki-Whakatane and Adn Maori work 78-81; Bp Aotearoa from 81; Abp New Zealand from 04. *PO Box 146, Rotorua, New Zealand* Tel (0064) (7) 348 6093 *or* 347 9241 Fax 348 6091 E-mail wvercoe@aot.ang.org.nz

VERE HODGE, Preb Francis. b 19. MC43. Worc Coll Ox BA46 MA46. Cuddesdon Coll 46. **d** 48 **p** 49. C Battle *Chich* 48-54; R Iping 54-58; R Linch 54-58; V Kingswood *S'wark* 58-65; V Moorlinch w Stawell and Sutton Mallet *B & W* 65-79; R Greinton 68-79; RD Glastonbury 75-79; P-in-c Lydeard St Lawrence w Combe Florey and Tolland 79-84; Preb Wells Cathl 79-98; rtd 84; Perm to Offic *B & W* 84-99 and *Ex* from 99. *1 Gracey Court, Woodland Road, Broadclyst, Exeter EX5 3GA* Tel (01392) 469005

VERE NICOLL, Charles Fiennes. b 55. Solicitor 79. St Alb and Ox Min Course 96. **d** 99 **p** 00. NSM Basildon w Aldworth and Ashampstead *Ox* from 99. *Ashvine, Westridge, Highclere, Newbury RG20 9RY* Tel 07768-238128 (mobile) E-mail cfvnicoll@aol.com

VEREKER, Jennifer Lesley. b 45. Totley Hall Coll CertEd66. WMMTC 96. **d** 99 **p** 00. NSM Rugby St Andr *Cov* 99-03; TV Gt and Lt Coates w Bradley *Linc* from 03. *St Nicolas' Vicarage, Great Coates Road, Great Coates, Grimsby DN37 9NS* Tel (01472) 882495 E-mail jenny@cjpvereker.freeserve.co.uk

VEREY, Christopher Douglas. b 46. St Chad's Coll Dur BA68 MA70. Ripon Coll Cuddesdon 02. **d** 04 **p** 05. NSM Yate New Town *Bris* from 04. *2 The Green, Heathend, Wotton-under-Edge GL12 8AR* E-mail chrisverey@tiscali.com.uk

✠**VERNEY, The Rt Revd Stephen Edmund.** b 19. MBE45. Ball Coll Ox BA48 MA48. **d** 50 **p** 51 **c** 77. C Gedling *S'well* 50-52; C-in-c Clifton CD 52-57; V Clifton St Fran 57-58; Dioc Missr *Cov* 58-64; V Leamington Hastings 58-64; Can Res Cov Cathl 64-70; Can Windsor 70-77; Suff Bp Repton *Derby* 77-85; Hon Can Derby Cathl 77-85; Dioc Dir of Post-Ord Tr 83-85; rtd 86; Perm to Offic *Ox* 86-91; Asst Bp Ox from 91. *Charity School House, Church Road, Blewbury, Didcot OX11 9PY* Tel (01235) 850004

VERNON, Bryan Graham. b 50. Qu Coll Cam BA72 MA76. Qu Coll Birm 73. **d** 75 **p** 76. C Newc St Gabr *Newc* 75-79; Chapl Newc Univ 79-91; Lect Health Care Ethics from 91; Chmn Newc Mental Health Trust 91-94; Perm to Offic from 94. *34 Queens Road, Jesmond, Newcastle upon Tyne NE2 2PQ* Tel 0191-281 3861 E-mail b.g.vernon@ncl.ac.uk

VERNON, John Christie. b 40. Imp Coll Lon BScEng62 ACGI62. Linc Th Coll 63. **d** 65 **p** 66. C Barnard Castle *Dur* 65-69; CF 69-90; Asst Chapl Gen 90-92; Chapl Ellesmere Coll 92-99; Perm to Offic *Lich* 99-01; NSM Ellesmere Deanery 01-05; P-in-c Petton w Cockshutt, Welshampton and Lyneal etc from 05; RD Ellesmere from 02. *The Drift House, Lake House Mews, Grange Road, Ellesmere SY12 9DE* Tel (01691) 623765 Mobile 07778-312226 E-mail john.vernon@which.net

VERNON, Matthew James. b 71. Collingwood Coll Dur BSc93. Westcott Ho Cam BA96 CTM97. **d** 97 **p** 98. C Guildf H Trin w St Mary *Guildf* 97-01; Chapl St Jo Cathl Hong Kong from 01. *St John's Cathedral, Garden Road, Hong Kong* Tel (00852) 2523 4157 Fax 2521 7830 E-mail vernon@stjohnscathedral.org.uk

VERNON, Robert Leslie. b 47. Sarum & Wells Th Coll 73. **d** 76 **p** 77. C Hartlepool St Luke *Dur* 76-79; C Birm St Geo *Birm* 79-82; V Bordesley Green 82-86; Dioc Youth Officer *Carl* 86-89; P-in-c Holme 86-89; Dioc Youth Adv *Newc* 89-95; V Ulgham and Widdrington 95-01; P-in-c Pokesdown St Jas *Win* from 01. *St James's Vicarage, 12 Harewood Avenue, Bournemouth BH7 6NQ* Tel (01202) 425918

VERWEY, Mrs Eileen Susan Vivien. b 41. Open Univ BA78 BA93 Goldsmiths' Coll Lon PGCE82. WEMTC 03. **d** 05. NSM Burghill *Heref* from 05; NSM Stretton Sugwas from 05; NSM Pipe-cum-Lyde and Moreton-on-Lugg from 05. *Mill Croft House, Staunton-on-Wye, Hereford HR4 7LW* Tel (01981) 500626

VESEY, Nicholas Ivo. b 54. Bris Univ BSc73. Cranmer Hall Dur 95. **d** 97 **p** 98. C Tunbridge Wells St Mark *Roch* 97-01; V New Catton St Luke w St Aug *Nor* from 01. *St Luke's Vicarage, 61 Aylsham Road, Norwich NR3 2HF* Tel (01603) 416973 E-mail nicholas.vesey@btopenworld.com

VESSEY, Andrew John. b 45. Bp Otter Coll CertEd67. Sarum & Wells Th Coll 84. **d** 86 **p** 87. C Framlingham w Saxtead *St E* 86-89; V Catshill and Dodford *Worc* 89-94; P-in-c Areley Kings 94-95; R 95-02; RD Stourport 00-02; TV Kidderminster St Jo and H Innocents 02-05; TR Cen Swansea *S & B* from 05. *The Rectory, 7 Eden Avenue, Uplands, Swansea SA2 0PS* Tel (01792) 298616 E-mail andrew@vessey.plus.com

VESSEY, Peter Allan Beaumont. b 36. R Agric Coll Cirencester Dip Estate Mgt 56. Lon Coll of Div ALCD65 LTh74. **d** 64 **p** 65. C Rayleigh *Chelmsf* 64-67; C Cambridge H Trin *Ely* 67-71; V Kingston upon Hull St Aid Southcoates *York* 71-80; V Swanwick and Pentrich *Derby* 80-94; Perm to Offic from 94; rtd 96. *2 Bakehouse Cottage, Scarthin, Cromford, Matlock DE4 3QF* Tel (01629) 825572 Fax 823988

VESTERGAARD, David Andrew. b 64. Reading Univ BSc86. Wycliffe Hall Ox 97. **d** 99 **p** 00. C Chadderton Ch Ch *Man* 99-02; V Wednesfield Heath *Lich* from 02. *Holy Trinity Vicarage, Bushbury Road, Wolverhampton WV10 0LY* Tel (01902) 738313 E-mail david@vestergaard.co.uk

VETTERS, Miss Shirley Jacqueline Margaret. b 34. S'wark Ord Course 85. **d** 88 **p** 94. NSM E Ham w Upton Park St Alb *Chelmsf* 88-91; C Birm St Martin w Bordesley St Andr *Birm* 91-04; Chapl to the Markets 91-04; rtd 04; Perm to Offic *Chelmsf* from 05. *62 South Street, Manningtree CO11 1BQ* Tel (01206) 393691

VEVERS, Geoffrey Martin. b 51. Oak Hill Th Coll. **d** 82 **p** 83. C Wealdstone H Trin *Lon* 82-84; C Harrow Trin St Mich 84-88; V Wandsworth St Steph *S'wark* 88-96; V Battersea Fields from 96; RD Battersea from 04. *St Saviour's Vicarage, 351A Battersea Park Road, London SW11 4LH* Tel (020) 7498 1642

VIBERT (née GREEN), Imogen Elizabeth. b 73. Birm Univ BA96 Cam Univ BTh02. Westcott Ho Cam 99. **d** 02 **p** 03. C Poplar *Lon* from 02. *6 Mountague Place, London E14 0EX* Tel (020) 7093 1452 *or* 7538 9198 E-mail ivibert@freeuk.com

VIBERT, Simon David Newman. b 63. Oak Hill Th Coll BA89. **d** 89 **p** 90. C Houghton *Carl* 89-92; C-in-c Buxton Trin Prop Chpl *Derby* 92-99; V Wimbledon Park St Luke *S'wark* from 99. *St Luke's Vicarage, 28 Farquhar Road, London SW19 8DA* Tel (020) 8946 3396 E-mail simon@wimbledonchurch.co.uk

VICARS, David. b 22. Leeds Univ BA48. Coll of Resurr Mirfield 48. **d** 50 **p** 51. C Newington St Paul *S'wark* 50-54; C Kingston St Luke 54-56; C Cirencester *Glouc* 56-59; Malaysia 59-66; Area Sec USPG *Llan, Mon, St D* and *S & B* 67-77; R Coychurch w Llangan and St Mary Hill *Llan* 77-90; rtd 90; Perm to Offic *Llan* from 90. *43 Bryn Rhedyn, Pencoed, Bridgend CF35 6TL* Tel (01656) 860920

VICARY, Canon Douglas Reginald. b 16. Trin Coll Ox BA38 BSc39 DipTh40 MA42. Wycliffe Hall Ox 39. **d** 40 **p** 41. Asst Chapl St Lawr Coll Ramsgate 40-45; C Collingtree w Courteenhall *Pet* 40-45; Tutor Wycliffe Hall Ox 45-47; Chapl 47-48; Chapl Hertf Coll Ox 45-48; Dir of Educn *Roch* 48-57; Min Can Roch Cathl 49-52; Can Res 52-57; Hon Can 57-75; Dir Post Ord Tr 52-57; Hd Master K Sch Roch 57-75; Can Res and Prec Wells Cathl *B & W* 75-88; Chapl to The Queen 77-87; rtd 88; Perm to Offic *B & W* from 88. *8 Tor Street, Wells BA5 2US* Tel (01749) 679137

VICK, Samuel Kenneth Lloyd. b 31. Univ of Wales (Lamp) BA53. Linc Th Coll. **d** 55 **p** 56. C Shotton *St As* 55-56; C Wrexham 56-61; C Knowle H Nativity *Bris* 61-67; V Mirfield Eastthorpe St Paul *Wakef* 67-78; V Altofts 78-98; rtd 98. *The Master's Lodge, Archbishop Holgate Hospital, Hemsworth, Pontefract WF96 4PP* Tel (01977) 610434

VICKERMAN, Canon John. b 42. Chich Th Coll 69. **d** 72 **p** 73. C Horbury *Wakef* 72-76; C Elland 76-78; V Glass Houghton 78-89; V Bruntcliffe 89-96; V King Cross from 96; RD Halifax from 00; Hon Can Wakef Cathl from 02. *The Vicarage, West Royd Avenue, Halifax HX1 3NU* Tel (01422) 352933

VICKERS, Dennis William George. b 30. RIBA72 York Univ MA91 IHBC99. Glouc Th Course 83. **d** 86 **p** 87. NSM Stokesay *Heref* 86-88; NSM Bucknell w Chapel Lawn, Llanfair Waterdine etc 88-92; NSM Wigmore Abbey 93-01; Perm to Offic from 01. *Reeves Holding, Reeves Lane, Stanage, Knighton LD7 1NA* Tel (01547) 530577 Fax 530773

VICKERS, Donald. Edge Hill Coll of HE DASE80 Univ of Wales (Ban) MEd87. N Ord Course 97. **d** 00 **p** 01. NSM Leigh St Mary *Man* 00-05; NSM Westleigh St Pet from 05. *21 Broom Way, Westhoughton, Bolton BL5 3TZ* Tel (01942) 815193 Mobile 07768-492581 E-mail don@dvickers20.freeserve.co.uk

VICKERS, Mrs Janice Audrey Maureen. b 56. Guildf Dioc Min Course 93. **d** 96 **p** 97. OLM Woking Ch Ch *Guildf* from 96. *7 Langdale Close, Woking GU21 4RS* Tel (01483) 720873 Fax 888459 E-mail rjvickers@aol.com *or* ccwoking@surfaid.org

VICKERS, Mrs Mary Janet. b 57. Westmr Coll Ox MTh97. St Jo Coll Nottm BTh85. **dss** 85 **d** 87 **p** 99. Worc City St Paul and Old St Martin etc *Worc* 85-89; Par Dn 87-89; World Miss Officer *Worc* 89-92; USPG 92-00; Lic to Offic *Eur* 95-99; Perm to Offic from 99; Perm to Offic Adnry of the Army from 97; NSM Cheswardine, Childs Ercall, Hales, Hinstock etc *Lich* 99-01; NSM Wrecclesham *Guildf* 01-02; NSM Pimperne, Stourpaine, Durweston and Bryanston *Sarum* 03-05; NSM Hipswell *Ripon* from 05. *5 Haig Road, Catterick Garrison DL9 3AH* Tel (01738) 833836 E-mail revsvickers@tiscali.co.uk

VICKERS, Michael. b 60. Cranmer Hall Dur BA98. **d** 98 **p** 99. C Monkwearmouth *Dur* 98-00; Kowloon St Andr Hong Kong from 00. *5 Waldo Villas, 202 Wong Chuk Wan, Sai Kung, New Territories, Hong Kong* Tel (00852) 2792 1873

✠**VICKERS, The Rt Revd Michael Edwin.** b 29. Worc Coll Ox BA56 MA56 Dur Univ DipTh59. **d** 59 **p** 60 **c** 88. C Bexleyheath Ch Ch *Roch* 59-62; Chapl Lee Abbey 62-67; V Hull St Jo Newland *York* 67-81; AD Cen and N Hull 72-81; Can and Preb York Minster 81-88; Adn E Riding 81-88; Area Bp Colchester *Chelmsf* 88-94; rtd 94; Asst Bp Blackb from 94. *2 Collingham Park, Lancaster LA1 4PD* Tel (01524) 848492 E-mail michael.e.vickers@lineone.net

VICKERS, Peter. b 56. St Jo Coll Nottm LTh85. **d** 85 **p** 86. C Worc St Barn w Ch Ch *Worc* 85-88; TV Kidderminster St Mary and All SS w Trimpley etc 88-92; Ind Chapl 88-92; CF from 92. *c/o MOD Chaplains (Army)* Tel (01980) 615804 Fax 615800 E-mail revsvickers@msn.com

VICKERS, Peter George. b 41. Local Minl Tr Course 90. **d** 93 **p** 94. OLM Cobham *Guildf* 93-04; OLM Cobham and Stoke D'Abernon from 04. *24 Station Road, Stoke D'Abernon, Cobham KT11 3BN* Tel (01932) 862497 E-mail revpetervickers@cobham82.fsnet.co.uk

VICKERS, Randolph. b 36. Newc Univ MA93 FCIM FInstD. St Alb Minl Tr Scheme 77. **d** 80 **p** 82. NSM Hitchin *St Alb* 80-87; NSM Luton Lewsey St Hugh 87-89; NSM Shotley *Newc* 89-01; rtd 01; Perm to Offic *Newc* from 01. *Beggar's Roost, 26 Painshawfield Road, Stocksfield NE43 7PF* Tel (01661) 842364 Fax as telephone E-mail rvickers@christian-healing.com

VICKERSTAFF, John Joseph. b 60. Dur Univ BEd82 Teesside Univ BA84 MA86 MPhil88 ARCO92. Westcott Ho Cam 97. **d** 97 **p** 98. C Halesworth w Linstead, Chediston, Holton etc *St E* 97-99; C Blyth Valley 99-00; TV Ch the King *Newc* 00-05; P-in-c Doveridge, Scropton, Sudbury etc *Derby* from 05. *The Rectory, Main Road, Sudbury, Ashbourne DE6 5HS* E-mail jvfb27@aol.com

VICKERY, Charles William Bryan. b 38. Lich Th Coll 63. **d** 65 **p** 66. C Hove St Barn *Chich* 65-73; Chapl Hostel of God Clapham 73-76; P-in-c Kingston St Luke *S'wark* 76-82; V 82-94; rtd 98. *63 Connaught Road, Teddington TW11 0QF* Tel (020) 8977 8628

VICKERY, Jonathan Laurie. b 58. Bretton Hall Coll BEd80. Wycliffe Hall Ox 81. **d** 84 **p** 85. C Gorseinon *S & B* 84-86; P-in-c Whitton and Pilleth and Cascob etc 86-87; R 87-91; V Crickhowell w Cwmdu and Tretower 91-02; P-in-c Downend *Bris* from 02. *Christ Church Vicarage, Shrubbery Road, Bristol BS16 5TB* Tel 0117-908 9868 E-mail vicar@christchurchdownend.com

VICKERY, Robin Francis. b 48. K Coll Lon BD73 AKC73. **d** 74 **p** 75. C Clapham St Jo *S'wark* 74-77; C Clapham Ch Ch and St Jo 75-77; C Reigate St Luke S Park 77-79; Hon C Clapham H Spirit 80-87 and from 02; Hon C Clapham Team 87-01; Perm to Offic *Lon* from 99. *13 Chelsham Road, London SW4 6NR* Tel (020) 7622 4792

VIDAL-HALL, Roderic Mark. b 37. Sheff Univ BSc60 Birm Univ DPS70. Lich Th Coll 62. **d** 64 **p** 65. C Ilkeston St Mary *Derby* 64-67; C Nether and Over Seale 67-70; V Chellaston 70-84; C Marchington w Marchington Woodlands *Lich* 84-97; C Kingstone w Gratwich 85-97; TV Uttoxeter Area 97-01; rtd 01. *Le Perhou, 22630 St Juvat, France* Tel (0033) (2) 96 88 16 34 E-mail mark@vidalhall.co.uk

VIGARS, Anthony Roy. b 54. St Jo Coll Dur BA75. Trin Coll Bris 77. **d** 78 **p** 79. C Barking St Marg w St Patr *Chelmsf* 78-81; C Littleover *Derby* 81-84; C-in-c Stapenhill Immanuel CD 84-90; V Meltham *Wakef* 90-97; V Reading St Jo *Ox* from 97. *St John's Vicarage, 50 London Road, Reading RG1 5AS* Tel 0118-931 1012 E-mail vigars@lineone.net

VIGEON, Canon Owen George. b 28. Peterho Cam BA52 MA57. Ely Th Coll 52. **d** 54 **p** 55. C Barrow St Luke *Carl* 54-58; Chapl St Jo Coll York 58-61; V Burnley St Steph *Blackb* 61-69; V Bilsborrow and Asst Dir RE 69-73; V St Annes St Thos 74-85; RD Fylde 80-85; R Halton w Aughton 85-93; Hon Can Blackb Cathl 92-93; rtd 93; Perm to Offic *Worc* 93-04 and *Cov* from 04. *10 Hall Lane, Coventry CV2 2AW* Tel (024) 7661 1712 E-mail owen@vigeon.freeserve.co.uk

VIGERS, Neil Simon. b 62. K Coll Lon BD84 MTh87. Linc Th Coll 88. **d** 90 **p** 91. C Chelsea St Luke and Ch Ch *Lon* 90-93; C Staines St Mary and St Pet 93-96; P-in-c Hook *Win* 96-02; R from 02. *The Rectory, London Road, Hook RG27 9EG* Tel (01256) 762268 E-mail neil@stjohnhook.fsnet.co.uk

VIGERS, Patricia Anne. b 31. Lon Inst of Educn TCert53. OLM course 96. **d** 99 **p** 00. OLM Betchworth *S'wark* from 99; OLM Buckland from 99. *5 Normanton, Buckland Road, Reigate RH2 9RQ* Tel (01737) 243698

VIGOR, Ms Margaret Ann. b 45. Ripon Coll Cuddesdon 85. **d** 87 **p** 96. Chapl Asst All SS Convent Ox 87-89; Par Dn Basildon St Martin w Nevendon *Chelmsf* 89-91; NSM Billingham St Cuth *Dur* from 96. *15 Mitchell Street, Hartlepool TS26 9EZ* Tel (01429) 867458

VILLAGE, Andrew. b 54. Collingwood Coll Dur BSc75 Edin Univ PhD80. Trin Coll Bris BA92. **d** 92 **p** 93. C Northampton St Giles *Pet* 92-95; R Middleton Cheney w Chacombe 95-04; Dir Cen for Min Studies Univ of Wales (Ban) *Ban* from 04. *Address temp unknown* E-mail andy@villages.fsnet.co.uk

VILLER, Canon Allan George Frederick. b 38. EAMTC 78. **d** 81 **p** 82. NSM Ely 81-85; V Emneth 85-92; V Littleport 92-03; RD Ely 98-03; Hon Can Ely Cathl from 01; rtd 03; Hon C Barton Bendish w Beachamwell and Shingham *Ely* from 03; Hon C Fincham from 03; Hon C Marham from 03; Hon C Shouldham from 03; Hon C Shouldham Thorpe from 03. *The Rectory, High Street, Fincham, King's Lynn PE33 9EL* Tel and fax (01366) 347491 E-mail allan@viller.net

VINCE, Mrs Barbara Mary Tudor. b 29. St Alb Minl Tr Scheme 79. **dss** 82 **d** 87 **p** 94. Northwood H Trin *Lon* 82-86; Belmont 86-89; Par Dn 87-89; rtd 90; Perm to Offic *Lon* from 90. *22 St Mary's Avenue, Northwood HA6 3AZ* Tel (01923) 825730

VINCE, David Eric. b 59. Birm Univ BA81 Nottm Univ BCombStuds85 Goldsmiths' Coll Lon PGCE90. Linc Th Coll 82. **d** 85 **p** 86. C Gt Malvern St Mary *Worc* 85-88; C All Hallows by the Tower etc *Lon* 88-90; Min St Giles Cripplegate w St Bart Moor Lane etc 90-92; R Salwarpe and Hindlip w Martin Hussingtree *Worc* 92-97; R Willersey, Saintbury, Weston-sub-Edge etc *Glouc* 97-03; P-in-c Quinton 02-03; R Mickleton, Willersey, Saintbury etc from 03; RD Campden from 01. *The Rectory, Weston-sub-Edge, Chipping Campden GL55 6QH* Tel (01386) 840292 Fax as telephone E-mail dev@amserve.com

VINCE, Raymond Michael. b 45. Lon Univ BD69 Bris Univ MA72 K Coll Lon MTh80 LSE MSc83. Tyndale Hall Bris 66. **d** 71 **p** 72. C Southsea St Jude *Portsm* 71-75; Hon C Islington St Mary *Lon* 75-83; Chapl N Lon Poly 75-83; USA from 83. *159 W Davis Boulevard, Tampa, FL 33606, USA* E-mail vince@tampabay.rr.com

VINCENT, Preb Alfred James. b 30. Bris Univ BA54 Lon Univ BD56. Tyndale Hall Bris 50. **d** 54 **p** 55. C Shrewsbury St Julian *Lich* 54-56; C Camborne *Truro* 56-59; V Kenwyn 59-68; Lic to Offic *St Alb* 68; Lect Qu Coll Birm 68-70; Lic to Offic *Birm* 68-70; V Bordesley St Oswald 70-76; V S Shields St Hilda w St Thos *Dur* 76-84; Hon Chapl Miss to Seafarers from 79; V Bude Haven *Truro* 84-89; R Bude Haven and Marhamchurch 89-92; RD Stratton 88-92; Preb St Endellion 90-95; rtd 92; P-in-c Chacewater *Truro* 92-95; Perm to Offic from 95. *5 Raymond Road, Redruth TR15 2HD* Tel (01209) 219263

VINCENT, Bruce Matthews. b 24. Univ of Wales (Swansea) Dip Youth Work 50 Open Univ BA76 Surrey Univ MPhil83. **d** 88 **p** 88. NSM Sidcup St Jo *Roch* 88-94; Perm to Offic from 94. *497 Footscray Road, London SE9 3UH* Tel (020) 8850 5450

VINCENT, Christopher Robin. b 30. Sarum Th Coll 57. **d** 60 **p** 61. C Frome St Jo *B & W* 60-64; V Puxton w Hewish St Ann and Wick St Lawrence 64-70; V Buckland Dinham w Elm 70-71; V Buckland Dinham w Elm, Orchardleigh etc 71-77; P-in-c Frome H Trin 77-90; Chapl St Adhelm's Hosp Frome 77-88; RD Frome *B & W* 85-89; V Kewstoke w Wick St Lawrence 90-94; rtd 94; Perm to Offic *B & W* from 94. *Willows Edge, 2 Westwood Close, Weston-super-Mare BS22 6JU* Tel (01934) 517425

VINCENT, David Cyril. b 37. Selw Coll Cam BA60 MA64. Coll of Resurr Mirfield 60. **d** 62 **p** 63. C Cheetwood St Alb *Man* 62-65; C Lawton Moor 65-67; V Wandsworth Common St Mary *S'wark* 67-84; RD Tooting 75-80; R Stoke D'Abernon *Guildf* 84-02; rtd 02. *29 North Street, Stoke-sub-Hamdon TA14 6QS* Tel (01935) 825438

VINCENT, George William Walter. b 13. ALCD40. **d** 40 **p** 41. C Hammersmith St Simon *Lon* 40-44; C Stowmarket *St E* 44-47; R Earl Stonham 47-55; R Alderton w Ramsholt and Bawdsey 55-86; rtd 86; Perm to Offic *St E* from 86. *c/o B Vincent Esq, Rectory House, Alderton, Woodbridge IP12 3BL* Tel (01394) 411306

VINCENT, Henry William Gordon. b 16. Leeds Univ BA42. Coll of Resurr Mirfield 42. **d** 44 **p** 45. C Bridgwater St Jo *B & W* 44-46; C Greenford H Cross *Lon* 46-52; C Teddington St Alb 52-55; V N Hammersmith St Kath 55-64; V Whitton St Aug 64-81; rtd 81; Perm to Offic *Sarum* from 81. *20 West Mills Road, Dorchester DT1 1SR* Tel (01305) 263933

VINCENT, James. *See* VINCENT, Preb Alfred James

VINCENT, John Leonard. b 61. Univ of Wales (Lamp) BA83 Southn Univ BTh87. Chich Th Coll 84. **d** 87 **p** 88. C Hampton All SS *Lon* 87-90; C Shepperton 90-95; V Whitton SS Phil and Jas 95-03; CF from 03. *c/o MOD Chaplains (Army)* Tel (01980) 615804 Fax 615800 E-mail pipnjim@aol.com

VINCENT, Michael Francis. b 48. CertEd70 Open Univ BA83. Sarum & Wells Th Coll 85. **d** 87 **p** 88. C Nuneaton St Mary *Cov* 87-90; C Stockingford 90-91; P-in-c 91-99; V from 99. *Stockingford Vicarage, 90 Church Road, Nuneaton CV10 8LG* Tel and fax (024) 7637 2089 E-mail mick@vincent4850.freeserve.co.uk

VINCENT, Canon Noel Thomas. b 36. Fitzw Ho Cam BA63 MA67. Ridley Hall Cam 60. **d** 63 **p** 64. C Fenham St Jas and St Basil *Newc* 63-67; C Prudhoe 67-70; V Holbrooke *Derby*

70-74; P-in-c Lt Eaton 72-74; P-in-c Osmaston w Edlaston 74-78; Hon C 78-85; Dioc Info Officer 74-78; Sen Producer Relig Progr BBC Man 82-91; Hon C Brailsford w Shirley and Osmaston w Edlaston *Derby* 85-86; Hon Can Derby Cathl 85-86; Perm to Offic *Ches* 86-92; Chief Producer BBC Relig Progr Lon 91-93; Chief Asst to Hd BBC Relig Broadcasting 93-95; Hon C Twickenham St Mary *Lon* 92-95; Can Res and Treas Liv Cathl *Liv* 95-02; rtd 02; Perm to Offic *Liv* from 03. *45 Duke Street, Formby, Liverpool L37 4AP* Tel (01704) 875938

VINCENT, Robin. *See* VINCENT, Christopher Robin

VINCENT, Roy David. b 37. Univ of Wales (Swansea) Dip Youth Work. Chich Th Coll 81. **d** 83 **p** 84. C Atherton *Man* 83-86; V E Crompton 86-95; P-in-c Burwash *Chich* 95-00; R 00-04; rtd 04. *1 Kelton Croft, Kirkland, Frizington CA26 3YE* Tel (01946) 861300

VINCER, Ms Louise Claire. b 69. Roehampton Inst BA90 Edin Univ MTh93. Westcott Ho Cam MA00. **d** 00 **p** 01. C Waltham H Cross *Chelmsf* 00-04; C Perry Hill St Geo w Ch Ch and St Paul *S'wark* from 04. *57 Kennington Park Road, London SE11 7JG* Tel (020) 7735 2807 E-mail lcvincer@ukonline.co.uk

VINCER, Canon Michael. b 41. Sarum & Wells Th Coll 77. **d** 80 **p** 81. Hon C Littleham w Exmouth *Ex* 80-92; Miss to Seamen 80-92; Area Sec USPG *Ex* and *Truro* 86-92; Ind Chapl Gtr Man Ind Miss *Man* from 92; Chapl Man Airport from 92; Lic Preacher from 92; Perm to Offic *Ches* from 92; Hon Can Man Cathl *Man* from 02. *10 Highfield Crescent, Wilmslow SK9 2JL* Tel (01625) 525982 *or* 0161-489 2838 Fax 0161-489 3909 E-mail mike.vincer@ntlworld.com *or* mike.vincer@manairport.co.uk

VINE, James David. b 67. Brighton Univ BSc95. St Steph Ho Ox. **d** 00 **p** 01. C Eastbourne St Mary *Chich* 00-03; V Stone Cross St Luke w N Langney from 03. *The Vicarage, 8 Culver Close, Eastbourne BN23 8EA* Tel (01323) 764473

VINE, John. b 24. Keble Coll Ox BA45 MA50. St Steph Ho Ox 45. **d** 48 **p** 49. C Hackney Wick St Mary of Eton w St Aug *Lon* 48-50; C Holborn St Alb w Saffron Hill St Pet 50-53; Chapl Ely Th Coll 53-56; Vice-Prin Ely Th Coll 56-60; Hon C St Leonards Ch Ch *Chich* 60-62; Chapl Lich Th Coll 62-67; R Wrington *B & W* 67-69; V Earl's Court St Cuth w St Matthias *Lon* from 69. *St Cuthbert's Clergy House, 50 Philbeach Gardens, London SW5 9EB* Tel (020) 7370 3263

VINE, Michael Charles. b 51. Worc Coll Ox BA73 MA80. Cuddesdon Coll 73. **d** 76 **p** 77. C Wallsend St Luke *Newc* 76-79; C Denton 79-81; V Sugley 81-91; V Shiremoor 91-02; R Wallsend St Pet and St Luke from 02. *148 Park Road, Wallsend NE28 7QS* Tel 0191-262 3723 E-mail vinemichael@freeuk.co.uk

VINE, Michael Derek. b 35. Ch Ch Ox BA58 MA63 Reading Univ PGCE. Ely Th Coll 58. **d** 60 **p** 61. C Syston *Leic* 60-63; C S Ascot *Ox* 63-66; Chapl RN 66-70; Perm to Offic *Portsm* 71-74; *Lon* 74-91; C Chepstow *Mon* 91-94; V Llantilio Pertholey w Bettws Chpl etc 94-00; rtd 00. *5 Chestnut Court, Abergavenny NP7 5JD*

VINE, Canon Neville Peter. b 54. K Coll Lon BD80 AKC80. Linc Th Coll 80. **d** 81 **p** 82. C Peterlee *Dur* 81-86; Chapl Peterlee Coll 84-86; V Auckland St Pet *Dur* 86-89; Perm to Offic 89-91; R Easington 91-99; R Easington, Easington Colliery and S Hetton 99-03; AD Easington 98-03; V Auckland St Andr and St Anne from 03; AD Auckland from 03; Hon Can Dur Cathl from 03. *4 Conway Grove, Bishop Auckland DL14 6AF* Tel (01388) 604397 E-mail neville.p.vine@lineone.net

VINER, Canon Leonard Edwin. b 20. Univ Coll Dur LTh41 BA43. St Aug Coll Cant 38. **d** 43 **p** 44. C W Molesey *Guildf* 43-45; Nyasaland 46-56 and 58-64; Malawi 64-71; C Roxbourne St Andr *Lon* 56-58; R Honing w Crostwight *Nor* 71-75; P-in-c E Ruston 71-73; V 73-75; P-in-c Witton w Ridlington 71-73; V 73-75; C Corby Epiphany w St Jo *Pet* 75-79; V Brigstock w Stanion 79-86; rtd 86; Asst Chapl Lisbon *Eur* 86-87; Chapl Tangier 87-89; Perm to Offic *Pet* from 90. *8 Clive Close, Kettering NN15 5BQ* Tel (01536) 519734

VINEY, Arthur William. b 32. BEd. S Dios Minl Tr Scheme. **d** 82 **p** 83. NSM Clayton w Keymer *Chich* 82-86; NSM Streat w Westmeston 86-94; rtd 94; Perm to Offic *Chich* from 94. *3 The Almshouses of the Holy Name, Brighton Road, Hurstpierpoint, Hassocks BN6 9EF* Tel (01273) 832570

VINEY, Peter. b 43. Ox NSM Course. **d** 76 **p** 77. NSM High Wycombe *Ox* from 76. *76 Westmead, Princes Risborough HP27 9HS* Tel (01844) 275461

VIPOND, Canon John. b 17. Lon Univ BD48. ALCD48. **d** 48 **p** 49. C Roxeth Ch Ch *Lon* 48-51; V 51-56; V Pudsey St Lawr *Bradf* 56-73; Hon Can Bradf Cathl 67-73; V St Austell *Truro* 73-83; rtd 83; Perm to Offic *Truro* from 83. *Wisteria, 15 Coffeelake Meadow, Lostwithiel PL22 0LT* Tel (01208) 873141

VIRDEN, Richard. b 40. K Coll Lon BSc61 Univ Coll Lon MSc62 PhD66. **d** 04. OLM N Tyne and Redesdale *Newc* from 04. *Ingram Cottage, West Woodburn, Hexham NE48 2SB* Tel (01434) 270334 E-mail richard.virden@ncl.ac.uk

VIRGO, Canon Leslie Gordon. b 25. Linc Th Coll 56. **d** 58 **p** 59. C Hatcham Park All SS *S'wark* 58-61; C Selsdon *Cant* 61-65; Chapl Warlingham Park Hosp Croydon 65-73; Dioc Adv on Past Care and Counselling from 74; R Chelsfield *Roch* from 74; Hon Can Roch Cathl from 83. *Chelsfield Rectory, Skibbs Lane, Orpington BR6 7RH* Tel (01689) 825749 E-mail leslie.virgo@tinyworld.co.uk

VIRTUE, Thomas James. b 32. QUB BA56 TCD 58 Liv Univ DipRS80. **d** 58 **p** 59. C Belfast St Mich *Conn* 58-61; C Belfast St Bart 61-63; I Tempo *Clogh* 63-66; P-in-c Glynn w Raloo and Templecorran *Conn* 66-70; TV Ellesmere Port *Ches* 70-74; TV Ches Team 74-83; V Gt Sutton 83-97; rtd 97; Perm to Offic *Ches* from 97. *48 Saughall Road, Blacon, Chester CH1 5EY* Tel (01244) 399531

VIVASH, Peter Henry. b 57. Hockerill Coll of Educn CertEd78 Chelmer Inst of HE CQSW85. Cranmer Hall Dur 90. **d** 92 **p** 93. C Malpas *Mon* 92-95; R Bettws 95-01; P-in-c Thornthwaite cum Braithwaite, Newlands etc *Carl* from 01; Dioc Rep CMS from 01; Warden of Readers *Carl* from 05. *Thornthwaite Vicarage, Braithwaite, Keswick CA12 5RY* Tel (01768) 778243 E-mail vivash@pvivash.fsnet.co.uk

VIVIAN, Adrian John. b 42. K Coll Lon BD65 AKC66. St Denys Warminster 62. **d** 66 **p** 67. C Bromley St Andr *Roch* 66-69; C Egg Buckland *Ex* 69-73; Perm to Offic 73-84; P-in-c Newton Ferrers w Revelstoke 84-87. *4 Fell Close, Yealmpton, Plymouth PL8 2EG* Tel (01752) 873116

VIVIAN, Thomas Keith. b 27. St Jo Coll Cam BA48 MA52. St Deiniol's Hawarden 76. **d** 80 **p** 81. Hd Master Lucton Sch Leominster 62-85; Lic to Offic *Heref* 80-85; P-in-c Chew Stoke w Nempnett Thrubwell *B & W* 85-88; R 88-97; P-in-c Norton Malreward 85-88; R 88-97; RD Chew Magna 92-97; rtd 97; Perm to Offic *B & W* and *Sarum* from 97. *Timberley, Sidmouth Road, Lyme Regis DT7 3ES* Tel (01297) 443547

VIVIAN, Victor Ivan. b 38. Nottm Poly LLB87. EMMTC DTPS94. **d** 94 **p** 95. NSM Bestwood *S'well* 94-99; Korea 99-03; rtd 03; Perm to Offic *S'well* from 03. *12 Deepdale Road, Wollaton, Nottingham NG8 2FU* Tel 0115-928 3954 E-mail viv.vivian@btinternet.com

VOAKE, Andrew James Frederick. b 28. Dur Univ BA55. Oak Hill Th Coll 51. **d** 55 **p** 56. C Uxbridge St Marg *Lon* 55; C Fulham St Matt 55-58; C Hove Bp Hannington Memorial Ch *Chich* 58-61; V Kirkdale St Lawr *Liv* 61-63; Chapl Millfield Sch Somerset 63-71; R Bp Latimer Memorial Ch *Birm* 71-73; R Birm Bishop Latimer w All SS 73-80; V Crondall and Ewshot *Guildf* 80-90; rtd 90; Perm to Offic *B & W* from 90. *1 St Aubyns Avenue, Weston-super-Mare BS23 4UJ* Tel (01934) 620587

✠**VOBBE, The Rt Revd Joachim Gerhard.** b 47. Bonn Univ DipTh72. **p** 72 **c** 95. Chapl Cologne *Eur* 72-74; Chapl Düsseldorf 74-77; R Blumberg 77-82; R Offenbach 82-95; Bp Bonn from 95; Asst Bp Eur from 99. *Gregor-Mendel-Strasse 28, D-53115 Bonn, Germany* Tel (0049) (228) 232285 Fax 238314 E-mail ordinariat@alt-katholisch.de

VOCKINS, Michael David. b 44. OBE96. Univ of Wales (Abth) BSc69. Glouc Sch of Min 85. **d** 88 **p** 89. NSM Cradley w Mathon and Storridge *Heref* from 88; RD Ledbury from 02; Perm to Offic *Worc* from 88. *Birchwood Lodge, Birchwood, Storridge, Malvern WR13 5EZ* Tel (01886) 884366 *or* (01905) 748474 E-mail michaelvockins@birchwoodlodge.fsnet.co.uk

VODEN, Capt Raymond William Lang. b 35. CQSW74. SW Minl Tr Course 85. **d** 88 **p** 89. CA from 60; NSM Bideford *Ex* 88-94; C Northlew w Ashbury 94; C Bratton Clovelly w Germansweek 94; TV Okehampton w Inwardleigh, Bratton Clovelly etc 94-01; Chapl Ex and Distr Community Health Service NHS Trust 94-01; Bp's Adv for Child Protection *Ex* 96-01; rtd 01; Hon C Calstock *Truro* 01; Perm to Offic *Ex* from 99 and *Truro* from 01. *1 School Lane, Harrowbarrow, Callington PL17 8BS* Tel (01579) 350135 E-mail ray.voden@btinternet.com

VOGT, Charles William Derek. b 36. Cert Analytical Psychology 85 SSC88. EMMTC 83. **d** 86 **p** 87. NSM Ilkeston H Trin *Derby* 86-87; C Derby St Anne and St Jo 87-90, TV Staveley and Barrow Hill 90-95; P-in-c Hasland 95-96; R 97-01; P-in-c Temple Normanton 95-96; V 97-01; rtd 01; Perm to Offic *Ex* from 01. *54 Old Bakery Close, Exeter EX4 2UZ* Tel (01392) 271943

VOGT, Robert Anthony. b 25. Jes Coll Cam BA50 MA54. S'wark Ord Course 60. **d** 63 **p** 64. C Sutton New Town St Barn *S'wark* 63-67; C Kidbrooke St Jas 67-72; V Wood End *Cov* 72-80; RD Cov E 77-80; R Kidbrooke St Jas *S'wark* 80-85; TR 85-90; rtd 90; Perm to Offic *S'wark* from 90. *16 Tristan Square, London SE3 9UB* Tel (020) 8297 2361

VOLTZENLOGEL, Timothy John. b 60. St Jo Coll Dur BA81. Wycliffe Hall Ox BTh00. **d** 00 **p** 01. C Eastbourne All SS *Chich* 00-04; V Church Langley *Chelmsf* from 04. *7 Ashworth Place, Harlow CM17 9PU* Tel (01279) 629950 E-mail tim@timv.freeserve.co.uk

VON BENZON, Charles Nicholas. b 54. Kent Univ BA78 Solicitor 79. S'wark Ord Course 82. **d** 85 **p** 86. NSM Bromley SS Pet and Paul *Roch* 85-87; Perm to Offic *Chich* 87-93; Ed *Newsletter among Ministers at Work* 89-93; Asst to RD

Dallington 93-95; C The Deverills *Sarum* 95; TV Cley Hill Warminster 95-01; R Fladbury w Wyre Piddle and Moor etc *Worc* from 01. *The Rectory, Station Road, Fladbury, Pershore WR10 2QW* Tel (01386) 860356
E-mail nicholasvonbenzon@btinternet.com

VON MALAISE, Nicolas Christoph Axel. b 62. Univ Coll Ox BA84. Ripon Coll Cuddesdon BA86. **d** 87 **p** 88. C Oxhey St Matt *St Alb* 87-90; C Northfield *Birm* 90-92; Asst Chapl Win Coll 92-05. *Address temp unknown*

VONBERG, Canon Michael. b 27. Lon Univ BA51. Wells Th Coll 58. **d** 59 **p** 60. C Bournemouth St Andr *Win* 59-61; C Milton 61-64; V Camberwell St Geo *S'wark* 64-74; V Kenley 75-94; RD Croydon S 85-93; Hon Can S'wark Cathl 89-94; rtd 94; Perm to Offic *Guildf* from 94. *81 Christchurch Mount, Epsom KT19 8LP*

VOOGHT, Canon Michael George Peter. b 38. St Pet Hall Ox BA61 MA65. Chich Th Coll 61. **d** 63 **p** 64. C E Dulwich St Jo *S'wark* 63-66; C Prestbury *Glouc* 66-72; R Minchinhampton 72-85; RD Stonehouse 79-85; V Thornbury 85-02; Hon Can Glouc Cathl 86-02; rtd 02; Perm to Offic *Glouc* from 03. *62 High Street, Thornbury, Bristol BS35 2AN* Tel (01454) 414915

VORLEY, Kenneth Arthur. b 27. Sarum Th Coll 65. **d** 67 **p** 68. C Ashbourne w Mapleton and Clifton *Derby* 67-71; R W Hallam and Mapperley 71-77; V Hemingford Grey *Ely* 78-88; rtd 88; Perm to Offic *Carl* 88-01 and from 03. *Glen Cottage, Braithwaite, Keswick CA12 5SX* Tel (01768) 778535

VOSS, Mrs Philomena Ann. b 35. Edge Hill Coll of HE CertEd55. St Alb Minl Tr Scheme 87 EAMTC 95. **d** 96 **p** 97. NSM Tye Green w Netteswell *Chelmsf* 96-03; NSM Ware St Mary *St Alb* from 03. *21 Queen's Road, Hertford SG13 8AZ* Tel (01992) 554676 E-mail annvoss@tesco.net

VOUSDEN, Canon Alan Thomas. b 48. K Coll Lon BSc69. Qu Coll Birm DipTh71. **d** 72 **p** 73. C Orpington All SS *Roch* 72-76; C Belvedere All SS 76-80; R Cuxton and Halling 80-86; V Bromley St Mark 86-98; Chapl Bromley Hosp 86-94; Chapl Bromley Hosps NHS Trust 94-98; V Rainham *Roch* from 98; Hon Can Roch Cathl from 99; RD Gillingham from 00. *The Vicarage, 80 Broadview Avenue, Gillingham ME8 9DE* Tel (01634) 231538 Fax 362023
E-mail alan-vousden@rainhamvic-kent.freeserve.co.uk

VOWLES, Miss Patricia. b 50. S'wark Ord Course 84. **d** 87 **p** 94. USPG 70-91; NSM Nunhead St Antony w St Silas *S'wark* 87-91; Par Dn Newington St Mary 91; Dn-in-c Camberwell St Mich w All So w Em 91; Par Dn 91-94; V from 94. *St Michael's Vicarage, 128 Bethwin Road, London SE5 0YY* Tel and fax (020) 7703 8686 *or* 7703 1491
E-mail p.vowles@btinternet.com

VOWLES, Canon Peter John Henry. b 25. Magd Coll Ox BA50 MA55. Westcott Ho Cam 50. **d** 52 **p** 53. C Kings Heath *Birm* 52-56; C Huddersfield St Pet *Wakef* 56-57; PC Perry Beeches *Birm* 57-64; V 64-72; R Cottingham *York* 72-83; R Man St Ann *Man* 83-91; Hon Can Man Cathl 83-91; rtd 91; Perm to Offic *Man* from 91. *10 Redshaw Close, Manchester M14 6JB* Tel 0161-257 2065

VROLIJK, Paul Dick. b 64. Delft Univ of Tech MSc88. Trin Coll Bris BA03. **d** 04 **p** 05. NSM Stoke Gifford *Bris* from 04. *95 Diana Gardens, Bradley Stoke, Bristol BS32 8DL* Tel (01454) 610544
E-mail paul@vrolijk.fsnet.co.uk

VYVYAN, John Philip. b 28. New Coll Ox BA51 MA59. Cuddesdon Coll 57. **d** 59 **p** 60. C Notting Hill St Mark *Lon* 59-61; USPG (Sarawak & Borneo) 61-64; V Adderbury w Milton *Ox* 64-93; rtd 93; Perm to Offic *Truro* from 93. *Forth Coth, Carnon Downs, Truro TR3 6LE* Tel (01872) 865740

W

WADDELL, Peter Matthew. b 75. Keble Coll Ox BA96 Fitzw Coll Cam MPhil98 PhD02. Westcott Ho Cam 98. **d** 02 **p** 03. C Oxton *Ches* 02-04; Chapl SS Coll Cam from 05. *Sidney Sussex College, Cambridge CB2 3HU* Tel (01223) 338872
E-mail peterwad@hotmail.com

WADDELL, Simon. b 60. Wellington Univ (NZ) BA81. St Jo Coll Auckland 86. **d** 88 **p** 89. New Zealand 88-97; Perm to Offic *Roch* 97-00; Hon C Roch St Marg from 00. *55 Fennel Close, Rochester ME1 1LW* Tel (020) 7898 1610 Fax 7898 1769

WADDINGTON, Gary Richard. b 69. St Chad's Coll Dur BSc91. St Steph Ho Ox BTh93. **d** 96 **p** 97. C Southsea H Spirit *Portsm* 96-00; V Paulsgrove from 00. *St Michael's Vicarage, Hempsted Road, Portsmouth PO6 4AS* Tel (023) 9237 8808 Mobile 07778-402490 E-mail frgaryw@btinternet.com

WADDINGTON, The Very Revd Robert Murray. b 27. Selw Coll Cam BA51 MA55. Ely Th Coll 51. **d** 53 **p** 54. C Bethnal Green St Jo w St Simon *Lon* 53-56; Australia 56-59 and 61-71; C Chesterton St Luke *Ely* 59-61; OGS from 60; Can Res Carl Cathl *Carl* 72-77; Bp's Adv for Educn 72-77; Hon Can Carl Cathl 77-84; Gen Sec Gen Syn Bd of Educn 77-84; Gen Sec Nat Soc 77-84; Dean Man 84-93; rtd 93; Perm to Offic *York* from 93. *6 Waverley Street, York YO31 7QZ* Tel (01904) 670200

WADDINGTON-FEATHER, John Joseph. b 33. FRSA87 Leeds Univ BA54 Keele Univ PGCE74. St Deiniol's Hawarden 75. **d** 77 **p** 78. NSM Longden and Annscroft w Pulverbatch *Heref* 77-84 and from 85; Chapl Asst HM Pris Shrewsbury 77-84 and from 85; Sudan 84-85; Chapl Prestfelde Sch Shrewsbury 86-96; rtd 96; Perm to Offic *Lich* from 99. *Fair View, Old Coppice, Lyth Bank, Bayston Hill, Shrewsbury SY3 0BW* Tel (01743) 872177 Fax as telephone E-mail john@feather-books.com

WADDLE, William. b 31. Linc Th Coll 64. **d** 66 **p** 67. C Tynemouth Priory *Newc* 66-69; C Longbenton St Bart 69-75; V Denton 75-81; V Beadnell 81; V Beadnell w Ellingham 81-93; RD Bamburgh and Glendale 83-92; Perm to Offic 93-99; rtd 93. *7 Hillside Road, Belford NE70 7NB* Tel (01668) 219 070

WADDY, Canon Lawrence Heber. b 14. Ball Coll Ox BA37 MA45. Westcott Ho Cam 39. **d** 40 **p** 41. Asst Master Win Coll 38-42 and 46-49; Chapl RNVR 42-46; Hd Master Tonbridge Sch 49-62; Lic Preacher *Roch* 50-63; Hon Can Roch Cathl 61-63; Hon Bp's Chapl 63; USA from 63; Chapl Bps' Sch 63-67; Hd Master and Chapl Santa Maria Internat Academy Chula Vista 67-69; Assoc Min Coronado Ch Ch 68-70; Lect California Univ San Diego 69-80; V San Diego Gd Samaritan 70-74; rtd 75; Hon Asst Min La Jolla St Jas-by-the-Sea from 75; Hon Can San Diego from 98. *5910 Camino de la Costa, La Jolla, CA 92037, USA* Tel (001) (858) 459 5221

WADE, Andrew John. b 50. R Agric Coll Cirencester NDA72. Trin Coll Bris DipHE86. **d** 86 **p** 87. C St Keverne *Truro* 86-89; TV Probus, Ladock and Grampound w Creed and St Erme 89-92; V Constantine 92-00; P-in-c Ludgvan 00-01; P-in-c Marazion 00-01; P-in-c St Hilary w Perranuthnoe 00-01; R Ludgvan, Marazion, St Hilary and Perranuthnoe from 01; RD Penwith from 03. *The Rectory, Ludgvan, Penzance TR20 8EZ* Tel (01736) 740784 E-mail andrewatludgvan@aol.com

WADE, Christopher John. b 54. Trent Poly BSc81 MRICS82 ACIArb88. Aston Tr Scheme 88 Trin Coll Bris. **d** 92 **p** 93. C Barnsley St Geo *Wakef* 92-95; C Whittle-le-Woods *Blackb* 95-99; P-in-c Bulwell St Jo *S'well* 99-03. *20 Westley Close, Whitley Bay NE26 4NR* Tel 08451-665277 Fax as telephone
E-mail chris@heavenfire.org

WADE, David Peter. b 65. St Jo Coll Nottm LTh92 DCM92. **d** 92 **p** 93. C Victoria Docks Ascension *Chelmsf* 92-95; P-in-c Victoria Docks St Luke 95-97; V from 97. *The Vicarage, 16A Ruscoe Road, London E16 1JB* Tel (020) 7476 2076
E-mail davenicky@hotmail.com

WADE, Geoffrey Adrian. b 61. Ripon Coll Cuddesdon. **d** 01 **p** 02. C Worc City St Paul and Old St Martin etc *Worc* 01-02; C Wordsley 02-04; TV Ilminster and Distr *B & W* from 04. *The Rectory, Church Street, Shepton Beauchamp, Ilminster TA19 0LQ* Tel (01460) 240228 E-mail wadesinsomerset@waitrose.com

WADE, Walter. b 29. Oak Hill Th Coll 64. **d** 66 **p** 67. C Denton Holme *Carl* 66-69; V Jesmond H Trin *Newc* 69-78; R Moresby *Carl* 78-87; P-in-c Langdale 87-94; Member Rural Life and Agric Team 93-94; rtd 94; Perm to Offic *Carl* from 94. *Manor Cottage, Fellside, Caldbeck, Wigton CA7 8HA* Tel (01697) 478214

WADE-STUBBS, Edward Pomery Flood. b 17. St Jo Coll Dur LTh39 BA40. Tyndale Hall Bris 36. **d** 40 **p** 41. C Burslem St Jo *Lich* 40-42; C Handsworth St Jas *Birm* 42-44; C Hawkhurst *Cant* 44-46; C Cheltenham St Mark *Glouc* 51-53; R Gt Witcombe 53-62; Canada 62-63; R Sutton Veny *Sarum* 63-66; V Norton Bavant 63-66; rtd 69; Perm to Offic *Sarum* 90-95. *c/o Thomson Snell and Passmore, 3 Lonsdale Gardens, Tunbridge Wells TN1 1NX*

WADEY, Ms Rachel Susan. b 71. Lanc Univ BA94 Ox Univ BA98. St Steph Ho Ox 95. **d** 98 **p** 99. C Poulton-le-Fylde *Blackb* 98-01; C Blackpool H Cross 01-03; V Skerton St Chad from 03. *St Chad's Vicarage, 1 St Chad's Drive, Lancaster LA1 2SE* Tel (01524) 63816 E-mail rachel_28_uk@yahoo.co.uk

WADGE, Alan. b 46. Grey Coll Dur BA68 MA72 St Chad's Coll Dur DipTh69. **d** 70 **p** 71. C Cockerton *Dur* 70-74; C Whitworth w Spennymoor 74-75; P-in-c Shipton Moyne w Westonbirt and Lasborough *Glouc* 75-80; Chapl Westonbirt Sch 75-80; V Dean Forest H Trin *Glouc* 80-83; Chapl Gresham's Sch Holt 83-91; R Ridgeway *Ox* from 91; RD Wantage 95-01. *The Rectory, Letcombe Regis, Wantage OX12 9LD* Tel (01235) 763805

WADHAM, Philip Andrew. b 41. Bradf Univ MA92. Vancouver Sch of Th BTh80. **d** 79 **p** 80. Canada 80-82 and 85-88; Ecuador 82-85; Area Sec USPG *Wakef* and *Bradf* 88-92; Perm to Offic *Bradf* 88-93; Canada from 93. *600 Jarvis Street, Toronto ON, Canada, K0G 1X0*

WADLAND, Douglas Bryan. b 33. K Coll Dur BA61 CQSW62. Oak Hill Th Coll 90. **d** 91 **p** 92. NSM Cowley *Lon* 91-93; Asst Chapl Hillingdon Hosp NHS Trust 91-93; P-in-c Wembley St Jo *Lon* 93-00; Chapl Cen Middx Hosp NHS Trust 93-00; rtd 00; Kenya 01-03; Hon C Alperton *Lon* from 03. *4 Selby Road, London W5 1LX* Tel (020) 8998 1839 E-mail wadland@lizbryan.freeserve.co.uk

WADMAN, Vera Margaret. b 51. EAMTC 97. **d** 00 **p** 01. NSM Burnham *Chelmsf* 00-02; NSM Creeksea w Althorne, Latchingdon and N Fambridge from 02. *Fernlea Cottage, 8 Fernlea Road, Burnham-on-Crouch CM0 8EJ* Tel (01621) 783963 E-mail verawadman@onetel.com

WADSWORTH (née REID), Mrs Alison Margaret. b 36. Bris Univ CertEd57. LNSM course 95. **d** 97 **p** 98. OLM Cley Hill Warminster *Sarum* from 97. *2 Saxon's Acre, Warminster BA12 8HT* Tel (01985) 212510

WADSWORTH, Andrew James. b 56. St Jo Coll Dur BA79 Cam Univ CertEd80 Lambeth STh95 FRSA99. Sarum & Wells Th Coll 84 Chich Th Coll 86. **d** 87 **p** 88. NSM Forest Row *Chich* 87-89; NSM E Grinstead St Swithun 87-89; C Shrewsbury St Chad w St Mary *Lich* 89-91; TV Honiton, Gittisham, Combe Raleigh, Monkton etc *Ex* 91-97; V Bulkington w Shilton and Ansty *Cov* from 97. *The Vicarage, School Road, Bulkington, Nuneaton CV12 9JB* Tel (024) 7631 2396 E-mail rev.andrew@wadswortha.fsnet.co.uk

WADSWORTH, Andrew John. b 67. Reading Univ BSc88 MRICS90. Wycliffe Hall Ox 99. **d** 01 **p** 02. C Plymouth St Andr and St Paul Stonehouse *Ex* 01-05; C Enfield Ch Ch Trent Park *Lon* from 05. *20 Heddon Road, Cockfosters, Barnet EN4 9LD* Tel (020) 8441 6444 E-mail awadsworth@waddy20.freeserve.co.uk

WADSWORTH, Jean. b 44. St Jo Coll Dur BA71. Cranmer Hall Dur 85. **d** 87 **p** 94. Par Dn Thamesmead *S'wark* 87-92; Par Dn Rotherhithe H Trin 92-94; C 94-98; V New Eltham All SS from 98; RD Eltham and Mottingham 01-05. *All Saints' Vicarage, 22 Bercta Road, London SE9 3TZ* Tel (020) 8850 9894

WADSWORTH, Canon Michael Philip. b 43. Qu Coll Ox BA65 MA68 DPhil75 Cam Univ PhD78. Ripon Hall Ox 67. **d** 70 **p** 71. C Sutton St Mich *York* 70-73; Lect Sussex Univ *Chich* 73-78; Hon C Hove St Jo 75-78; Fell and Chapl SS Coll Cam 78-81; Dir Th Studies 79-81; CF (TA) from 80; C Ditton St Mich *Liv* 81; TV 82-84; Dioc Lay Tr Officer 83-89; V Orford St Marg 84-89; V Haddenham *Ely* 89-98; V Wilburton 89-98; RD Ely 94-98; P-in-c Gt Shelford 98-01; Hon Can Ely Cathl 96-01; rtd 01; Perm to Offic *Ely* and *Linc* from 01. *9 Eastgate, Sleaford NG34 7DL* Tel (01529) 304251

WADSWORTH, Peter Richard. b 52. Qu Coll Ox BA73 MA77. Cuddesdon Coll 74 English Coll Rome 76. **d** 77 **p** 78. C High Wycombe *Ox* 77-81; C Farnham Royal w Hedgerley 81-84; Dioc Ecum Officer *Portsm* 84-90; V E Meon 84-96; V Langrish 84-96; V Elson 96-04; RD Gosport 96-02; V St Alb St Sav *St Alb* from 04. *St Saviour's Vicarage, 25 Sandpit Lane, St Albans AL1 4DF* Tel (01727) 851526 E-mail peter@hisstudy.freeserve.co.uk

WADSWORTH, Roy. b 37. NEOC 89. **d** 89 **p** 90. NSM Alne *York* from 89; Ind Chapl 94-03; rtd 02. *The Rosery, Tollerton, York YO61 1PX* Tel (01347) 838212

WAGGETT, Geoffrey James. b 49. Sarum & Wells Th Coll 83. **d** 85 **p** 86. C Newton Nottage *Llan* 85-88; TV Glyncorrwg w Afan Vale and Cymmer Afan 88-89; R 89-99; V Glyncorrwg and Upper Afan Valley 99-00; TR Ebbw Vale *Mon* from 00. *The Rectory, Eureka Place, Ebbw Vale NP23 6PN* Tel (01495) 301723

WAGSTAFF (née JONES), Ms Alison. b 40. K Coll Dur BA63 Man Univ CertEd64 New Coll Edin DPS92. TISEC 95. **d** 98 **p** 99. C Edin St Cuth *Edin* 98-00; Assoc P Edin St Columba from 00. *27 Cambridge Gardens, Edinburgh EH6 5DH* Tel and fax 0131-554 6702 *or* tel 551 1381 Fax 551 2771 E-mail hraw@onetel.com

WAGSTAFF, Andrew Robert. b 56. K Coll Lon BD79 AKC79. Coll of Resurr Mirfield 81. **d** 83 **p** 84. C Newark w Hawton, Cotham and Shelton *S'well* 83-86; C Dublin St Bart w Leeson Park *D & G* 86-89; V Nottingham St Geo w St Jo *S'well* 89-95; V Worksop Priory from 95. *The Vicarage, Cheapside, Worksop S80 2HX* Tel (01909) 472180

WAGSTAFF, The Ven Christopher John Harold. b 36. St D Coll Lamp BA62 DipTh63. **d** 63 **p** 64. C Queensbury All SS *Lon* 63-68; V Tokyngton St Mich 68-73; V Coleford w Staunton *Glouc* 73-83; RD Forest S 76-82; Adn Glouc 83-00; Hon Can Glouc Cathl 83-00; Hon Can St Andr Cathl Njombe (Tanzania) from 93; rtd 00; Perm to Offic *Glouc* from 00. *Karibuni, Collafield, Littledean, Cinderford GL14 3LG* Tel (01594) 825282

WAGSTAFF, Miss Joan. b 33. Gilmore Ho. **dss** 75 **d** 87 **p** 94. Ellesmere Port *Ches* 86-87; Par Dn 87-93; rtd 93; Perm to Offic *Ches* from 93. *41 Heywood Road, Great Sutton, South Wirral CH66 3PS* Tel 0151-348 0884

WAGSTAFF, Michael. b 59. R Holloway Coll Lon BA81. Coll of Resurr Mirfield 86. **d** 89 **p** 90. C Worksop Priory *S'well* 89-92; C Ab Kettleby Gp *Leic* 92-94; TV Leic Resurr 94-00; Dioc Soc Resp Officer *Sheff* from 00. *27 The Copse, Bramley, Rotherham S66 3TB* Tel (01709) 703672 E-mail michael.wagstaff@sheffield.anglican.org

WAGSTAFF, Robert William. b 36. Edin Th Coll 61. **d** 63 **p** 64. C Harringay St Paul *Lon* 63-64; C Mill Hill Jo Keble Ch 64-69; NSM N Lambeth *S'wark* 70-80; NSM Wilden, Hartlebury and Ombersley w Doverdale 80-97; C Shrawley, Witley, Astley and Abberley *Worc* 98-02; rtd 02; Perm to Offic *Worc* from 02. *The Red House, Quarry Bank, Hartlebury, Kidderminster DY11 7TE* Tel (01299) 250883

WAGSTAFFE, Eric Herbert. b 25. St Aid Birkenhead 55. **d** 57 **p** 58. C Harpurhey Ch Ch *Man* 57-60; R 60-69; V Pendlebury St Jo 69-84; V Hoghton *Blackb* 84-91; rtd 91; Perm to Offic *Blackb* 91-02 and *Man* from 95. *3 Chelwood Close, Bolton BL1 7LN* Tel (01204) 596048

WAIN, Phillip. b 54. Aston Tr Scheme 89 Linc Th Coll 93. **d** 93 **p** 94. C Witton *Ches* 93-97; R Lea Gp *Linc* from 97. *The Rectory, 18 Gainsborough Road, Lea, Gainsborough DN21 5HZ* Tel (01427) 613188

WAINAINA, Francis Samson Kamoko. b 51. St Jo Coll Dur MA89. Oak Hill Th Coll BA84. **d** 84 **p** 85. Kenya 84-88; C Upton (Overchurch) *Ches* 89-92; V Ellesmere St Pet *Sheff* 92-95; C York St Mich-le-Belfrey *York* 95-01; V Starbeck *Ripon* from 01. *The Vicarage, 78 High Street, Harrogate HG2 7LW* Tel (01423) 546477 *or* 889162 E-mail francis.wainaina@ntlworld.com

✠**WAINE, The Rt Revd John.** b 30. KCVO96. Man Univ BA51. Ridley Hall Cam 53. **d** 55 **p** 56 **c** 75. C W Derby St Mary *Liv* 55-58; C Sutton 58-60; V Ditton St Mich 60-64; V Southport H Trin 64-69; V Kirkby 69-71; TR 71-75; Suff Bp Stafford *Lich* 75-78; Preb Lich Cathl 75-78; Bp St E 78-86; Bp Chelmsf 86-96; Clerk of the Closet 89-96; rtd 96; Perm to Offic *St E* from 96. *Broadmere, Ipswich Road, Grundisburgh, Woodbridge IP13 6TJ* Tel (01473) 738296 E-mail bpjn@wainej.eclipse.co.uk

WAINE, Stephen John. b 59. Westcott Ho Cam 81. **d** 84 **p** 85. C Wolverhampton *Lich* 84-88; Min Can and Succ St Paul's Cathl *Lon* 88-93; V Romford St Edw *Chelmsf* from 93; P-in-c Romford St Jo from 02. *St Edward's Vicarage, 15 Oaklands Avenue, Romford RM1 4DB* Tel (01708) 740385 E-mail stephen@stephenwaine.freeserve.co.uk

WAINWRIGHT, John Pounsberry. b 42. St Steph Ho Ox 64. **d** 66 **p** 67. C Palmers Green St Jo *Lon* 66-70; C Primrose Hill St Mary w Avenue Road St Paul 70-71; P-in-c St John's Wood All SS 71-73; V Hendon All SS Childs Hill from 73. *All Saints' Vicarage, Church Walk, London NW2 2TJ* Tel (020) 7435 3182

WAINWRIGHT, Joseph Allan. b 21. K Coll Lon BD50 AKC50 Columbia Pacific Univ PhD82 Sussex Univ DPhil85. **d** 50 **p** 51. C Boston *Linc* 50-53; Chapl St Paul's Coll Cheltenham 53-62; Educn Sec BCC 62-66; Lect Moray Ho Coll of Educn Edin 66-78; Perm to Offic *Chich* 79-88; rtd 86. *Beggar's Roost, Lewes BN7 1LX* Tel (01273) 477453

WAINWRIGHT, Kevin Frank. b 46. Linc Th Coll 73. **d** 75 **p** 76. C Stand *Man* 75-78; C Radcliffe St Thos and St Jo 78-80; V Kearsley Moor from 80. *St Stephen's Vicarage, Blair Street, Kearsley, Bolton BL4 8QP* Tel (01204) 572535

WAINWRIGHT, Malcolm Hugh. b 47. Man Univ BA68 Nottm Univ MA89. St Jo Coll Nottm CTM97 MA98. **d** 98 **p** 99. NSM Cotgrave *S'well* 98-01; NSM Owthorpe 98-01; P-in-c Plumtree from 01; P-in-c Tollerton from 01. *St Peter's Rectory, Tollerton Lane, Tollerton, Nottingham NG12 4FW* Tel 0115-937 2349 E-mail mwainw7761@aol.com

WAINWRIGHT, Mrs Margaret Gillian. b 45. Qu Mary Coll Lon BA68. EAMTC 00. **d** 03 **p** 04. NSM Combs and Lt Finborough *St E* 03-05; NSM Creeting St Mary, Creeting St Peter etc from 05. *The Cottage, Elmswell Road, Wetherden, Stowmarket IP14 3LN* Tel (01359) 242653 E-mail margwain@btopenworld.com

WAINWRIGHT, Martin John. b 69. Loughb Univ BEng92. Trin Coll Bris BA98. **d** 98 **p** 99. C Chislehurst Ch Ch *Roch* 98-02; V Camberley St Mary *Guildf* from 02. *St Mary's House, 37 Park Road, Camberley GU15 2SP* Tel and fax (01276) 22085 *or* 685167 E-mail martin.wainwright@ntlworld.com

WAINWRIGHT, Maurice Sidney. b 30. Lon Univ BSc54. Bps' Coll Cheshunt 54. **d** 56 **p** 57. C Twickenham St Mary *Lon* 56-59; C Caversham *Ox* 59-61; Public Preacher *Chelmsf* 61-95; rtd 95. *60 Eastwood Road, London E18 1BU* Tel (020) 8989 1529

WAINWRIGHT, Pauline Barbara. *See* FLORANCE, Mrs Pauline Barbara

WAINWRIGHT, Peter Anthony. b 45. K Coll Lon BD73 MRICS67. Ridley Hall Cam 73. **d** 75 **p** 76. C Ashtead *Guildf* 76-79; V Woking St Paul 79-84; Perm to Offic *Ox* 87-92 and 03-05; P-in-c Harston w Hauxton and Newton *Ely* from 05. *The Vicarage, Church Street, Harston, Cambridge CB2 5NP* Tel (01223) 871832 Mobile 07814-835528 E-mail revpeterwainwright@tiscali.co.uk

WAINWRIGHT, Raymond Laycock. b 25. Lon Univ BD60. Ho of Resurr Mirfield 55. **d** 56 **p** 57. C Bingley All SS *Bradf* 56-58; C Almondbury *Wakef* 58-60; V Gawthorpe and Chickenley Heath

60-74; V New Mill 74-89; V Thurstonland 74-89; TV Upper Holme Valley 89-91; rtd 91; Perm to Offic *Wakef* from 91. *7 Greenlaws Close, Upperthong, Holmfirth HD9 3HN* Tel (01484) 683779

WAINWRIGHT, Robert Neil. b 52. NEOC 99. **d** 02 **p** 03. NSM Barlby w Riccall *York* 02-05; NSM Selby Abbey from 05. *33 Hillfield, Selby YO8 3ND* Tel (01757) 706216 Mobile 07768-390060 E-mail robbwain@yahoo.com

WAIT, Canon Alan Clifford. b 33. St Cath Soc Ox BA58 MA70. Coll of Resurr Mirfield. **d** 60 **p** 61. C Charlton St Luke w St Paul *S'wark* 60-67; C Caterham 67-72; V N Dulwich St Faith 72-83; RD Dulwich 78-83; V Purley St Barn 83-01; RD Croydon S 93-01; Hon Can S'wark Cathl 01; rtd 01; Perm to Offic *Cant* from 01. *Forgefield Oast, Church Hill, Bethersden, Ashford TN26 3AQ* Tel (01233) 820529

WAITE, Daniel Alfred Norman. b 42. **d** 04 **p** 05. OLM Gorleston St Andr *Nor* from 04. *15 Laburnum Close, Bradwell, Great Yarmouth NR31 8JB* Tel (01493) 664591 E-mail danwaite@bradwell15.fsnet.co.uk

WAITE, John Langton (Tony). b 10. Solicitor 34 ACP37 Man Univ 30. Wycliffe Hall Ox 37. **d** 39 **p** 40. C Hove Bp Hannington Memorial Ch *Chich* 39-41; C Walcot *B & W* 41-42; V Blackheath St Jo *S'wark* 42-48; V Leeds St Geo *Ripon* 48-58; V Woking St Jo *Guildf* 58-76; rtd 76; Perm to Offic *Portsm* from 82. *11 The Crescent, Alverstoke, Gosport PO12 2DH* Tel and fax (023) 9252 1458 E-mail tonywaite@cwcom.net

WAITE, Julian Henry. b 47. Open Univ BA98. Brasted Th Coll 68 Ridley Hall Cam 70. **d** 72 **p** 73. C Wollaton *S'well* 72-76; C Herne Bay Ch Ch *Cant* 76-79; P-in-c Mersham 79-87; Chapl Wm Harvey Hosp Ashford 79-87; Chapl R Cornwall Hosps Trust 79-87; R Mersham w Hinxhill *Cant* 87; V Marden 87-93; Chapl HM Pris Blantyre Ho 90-93; Chapl HM Pris Swaleside from 01. *HM Prison Swaleside, Eastchurch, Sheerness ME12 4AX* Tel (01795) 884042 Fax 884200

WAITE, Robin Derek. **d** 05. NSM Derringham Bank *York* from 05. *The Cottage, Melton Road, North Ferriby HU14 3ET* Tel (01482) 631162 E-mail rojaw@freezone.co.uk

WAITE, Sheila Margaret. *See* TYLER, Mrs Sheila Margaret

WAIYAKI, Canon Jennie. b 34. MBE88. ALA64. NEOC 89. **d** 92 **p** 94. NSM Ulgham and Widdrington *Newc* 92-97; Chapl Mothers' Union 96-02; Chapl Northumbria Healthcare NHS Trust from 97; NSM Longhorsley and Hebron *Newc* 97-04; Hon Can Newc Cathl from 02. *6 Woodburn Street, Stobswood, Morpeth NE61 5QD* Tel (01670) 791066

WAKE, Colin Walter. b 50. Oriel Coll Ox BA72 MA. Cuddesdon Coll 74. **d** 75 **p** 76. C Sandhurst *Ox* 75-78; C Faversham *Cant* 79-80; TV High Wycombe *Ox* 80-89; R Weston Favell *Pet* from 89; Chapl St Jo Hosp Weston Favell from 89. *The Rectory, Churchway, Weston Favell, Northampton NN3 3BX* Tel (01604) 784679 *or* 787117

WAKEFIELD, Allan. b 31. Qu Coll Birm 72. **d** 74 **p** 75. C Kingsthorpe w Northampton St Dav *Pet* 74-77; TV Clifton *S'well* 77-81; V Bilborough St Jo 81-85; R Bere Ferrers *Ex* 85-91; R Mevagissey and St Ewe *Truro* 91-96; rtd 96; Perm to Offic *Truro* 96-98; Hon C Malborough w S Huish, W Alvington and Churchstow *Ex* 98-02; Perm to Offic from 01. *4 Eden Cottages, Exeter Road, Ivybridge PL21 0BL* Tel (01752) 698724

WAKEFIELD, Andrew Desmond. b 55. K Coll Lon BD77 AKC77. Coll of Resurr Mirfield 77. **d** 78 **p** 79. C Mitcham Ascension *S'wark* 78-81; C Putney St Mary 81-86; TV Wimbledon 86-91; Ind Chapl from 90; Dioc Urban Missr 91-97; P-in-c S Wimbledon St Andr 91-97; V from 97. *105 Hartfield Road, London SW19 3TJ* Tel (020) 8542 1794 Fax 8542 6566 E-mail wakefieldandrew@hotmail.com

WAKEFIELD, Anne Frances. b 58. St Aid Coll Dur BSc79 Sheff Univ PGCE80. NTMTC 97. **d** 97 **p** 98. NSM Danbury *Chelmsf* 97-98; NSM Sherburn w Pittington *Dur* 98-01; Asst Chapl HM Pris Dur 01-03; Chapl HM YOI Northallerton 03-05; Chapl HM Pris Low Newton from 05. *HM Prison Low Newton, Finchale Avenue, Brasside, Durham DH1 5YA* Tel 0191-386 1141

WAKEFIELD, David Geoffrey. b 43. AMIC90. S'wark Ord Course 84. **d** 87 **p** 88. C Addiscombe St Mildred *S'wark* 87-89; C Reigate St Luke S Park 89-93; Chapl HM Pris Bullingdon 93-96; Chapl HM Pris Ranby 96-99; P-in-c Flintham *S'well* from 99; P-in-c Car Colston w Screveton from 99; Chapl HM Pris Whatton 99-03. *The Vicarage, Woods Lane, Flintham, Newark NG23 5LR* Tel and fax (01636) 525750 Mobile 07949-017823 E-mail david@thewakefields.freeserve.co.uk

WAKEFIELD, David Kenneth. b 64. Ridley Hall Cam 02. **d** 04 **p** 05. C Bures w Assington and Lt Cornard *St E* from 04. *19 Normandie Way, Bures CO8 5BE* Tel (01787) 228179 E-mail david@wakefield95.fsnet.co.uk

WAKEFIELD, Gavin Tracy. b 57. Van Mildert Coll Dur BSc78 Sheff Univ CertEd80 Kent Univ PhD98. St Jo Coll Nottm 83. **d** 86 **p** 87. C Anston *Sheff* 86-89; C Aston cum Aughton and Ulley 89-91; TV Billericay and Lt Burstead *Chelmsf* 91-98; Dir Miss & Past Studies Cranmer Hall Dur from 98. *7 Ferens Close, Durham DH1 1JX* Tel 0191-384 1229 E-mail gavin.wakefield@durham.ac.uk

WAKEFIELD, Kenneth. b 54. St Jo Coll Dur BA95. **d** 95 **p** 96. C E and W Leake, Stanford-on-Soar, Rempstone etc *S'well* 95-98; TV Launceston *Truro* 98-03; P-in-c Boyton, N Tamerton, Werrington etc from 03. *The Rectory, Werrington, Launceston PL15 8TP* Tel (01566) 773932

WAKEFIELD, Peter. b 48. Nottm Univ BTh72 DipAdEd85. St Jo Coll Nottm 68 ALCD72. **d** 72 **p** 73. C Hinckley H Trin *Leic* 72-75; C Kirby Muxloe 75-78; V Barlestone 78-85; TV Padgate *Liv* 85-88; V Quinton w Marston Sicca *Glouc* 91-97; rtd 97. *70 Holte Road, Aston, Birmingham B6 6RP* Tel 0121-328 0489

WAKEFIELD, Bishop of. *See* PLATTEN, The Rt Revd Stephen George

WAKEFIELD, Dean of. *See* NAIRN-BRIGGS, The Very Revd George Peter

WAKEHAM, Geoffrey. **d** 96 **p** 97. P-in-c Torrevieja *Eur* 96-00; Asst Chapl 00-01; rtd 01. *6 Juniper Court, Roundswell, Barnstaple EX31 3RL*

WAKEHAM-DAWSON, Andrew Whistler. b 65. Wye Coll Lon BSc87 Open Univ PhD94. STETS 98. **d** 01 **p** 02. NSM Paddington St Sav *Lon* 01-04. Chapl RAF from 04. *Chaplaincy Services (RAF), HQ, Personnel and Training Command, RAF Innsworth, Gloucester GL3 1EZ* Tel (01452) 712612 ext 5164 Fax 510828

WAKELIN, Brian Roy. b 53. Westf Coll Lon BSc74. STETS DipHE99. **d** 99 **p** 00. NSM Win Ch Ch *Win* from 99. *11 Elm Court, Elm Road, Winchester SO22 5BA* Tel (01962) 868679

WAKELIN, Paul Edward. b 60. St Steph Ho Ox 90. **d** 92 **p** 93. C Sevenoaks St Jo *Roch* 92-96; V Perry Street from 96. *All Saints' Vicarage, Perry Street, Gravesend DA11 8RD* Tel (01474) 534398

WAKELING, Bruce. b 50. Lon Univ BA74. Westcott Ho Cam 74. **d** 77 **p** 78. C Weymouth H Trin *Sarum* 77-82; TV Oakdale 82-89; R Clopton w Otley, Swilland and Ashbocking *St E* 89-98; V Rushmere from 98. *The Vicarage, 253 Colchester Road, Rushmere, Ipswich IP4 4SH* Tel (01473) 270976

WAKELING, Hugh Michael. b 42. Cape Town Univ BSc63 CEng82 FIChemE94. Wycliffe Hall Ox 71. **d** 74 **p** 75. C Kennington St Mark *S'wark* 74-78; C Surbiton Hill Ch Ch 78-80; NSM Richmond H Trin and Ch Ch 80-84; NSM California *Ox* 85-89 and from 00; NSM Arborfield w Barkham 89-00. *Pine Lodge, 52 Pine Drive, Finchampstead, Wokingham RG40 3LE* Tel 0118-973 4078

WAKELING, Mrs Joan. b 44. Hockerill Coll Cam CertEd65. S'wark Ord Course 76. **dss** 79 **d** 90 **p** 94. Surbiton Hill Ch Ch *S'wark* 79-80; Richmond H Trin and Ch Ch 80-84; California *Ox* 84-89; Arborfield w Barkham 89-00; NSM 90-00; Chapl Luckley-Oakfield Sch Wokingham 90-05; NSM Finchampstead *Ox* 00-05; P-in-c Raglan w Llandenny and Bryngwyn *Mon* from 05. *The Rectory, Primrose Green, Raglan, Usk NP15 2DU* Tel (01291) 690330 E-mail jwakelin@fish.co.uk

WAKELING, Rayner Alan. b 58. Portsm Poly BSc79 Bris Univ PGCE80. St Steph Ho Ox. **d** 01 **p** 02. C Willesden Green St Andr and St Fran *Lon* 01-05; V Greenhill St Jo from 05. *St John's Vicarage, 11 Flambard Road, Harrow HA1 2NB* Tel (020) 8907 7956 E-mail raynerwakeling@hotmail.com

WAKELY, Anthony Peter Robin. b 48. TCD BA71 Edin Univ PhD79 Milltown Inst Dub MA03. CITC 01. **d** 03 **p** 04. C Clones w Killeevan *Clogh* 03-05; P-in-c from 05; C Currin w Drum and Newbliss 03-05; P-in-c from 05. *The Rectory, Scotshouse, Clones, Co Monaghan, Irish Republic* Tel (00353) (47) 56962 E-mail robinwakely@hotmail.com

WAKELY, Marcus. b 40. Solicitor 62 FRSA88. EMMTC 84. **d** 87 **p** 88. NSM Carrington *S'well* 87-91; C Worksop Priory 91-95; V Sheff St Matt *Sheff* 95-01; rtd 01. *16 Park House Gates, Nottingham NG3 5LX* Tel 0115-960 9038

WAKELY, Roger. b 42. St Paul's Cheltenham CertEd. S'wark Ord Course 67. **d** 70 **p** 71. C Ealing St Mary *Lon* 70-76; Chapl Bp Wand Sch Sunbury-on-Thames 76-82; R Gaulby *Leic* 82-87; V Galleywood Common *Chelmsf* 87-95; Warden of Ords 89-95; rtd 95; Perm to Offic *Chelmsf* 95-99 and *Ex* from 99. *Linford, Broadway, Sidmouth EX10 8XH*

WAKELY, Simon Nicolas. b 66. K Alfred's Coll Win BA88. St Jo Coll Nottm 89. **d** 92 **p** 93. C Wymondham *Nor* 92-95; P-in-c Babbacombe *Ex* from 95. *Babbacombe Vicarage, 4 Cary Park, Torquay TQ1 3NH* Tel (01803) 323002 Mobile 07801-536181 E-mail finbar@tesco.net

WAKEMAN, Canon Hilary Margaret. b 38. EAMTC. **dss** 85 **d** 87 **p** 94. Heigham St Thos *Nor* 85-90; C 87-90; C Nor St Mary Magd w St Jas 90-91; Dn-in-c Norwich-over-the-Water Colegate St Geo 90-91; TD Norwich Over-the-Water 91-94; TV 94-96; Hon Can Nor Cathl 94-96; I Kilmoe Union *C, C & R* 96-01; Dir of Ords 99-01; rtd 01. *Skeagh, Schull, Co Cork, Irish Republic* Tel (00353) (28) 28263 E-mail wakeman@iol.ie

WAKERELL, Richard Hinton. b 55. Qu Coll Birm 81. **d** 84 **p** 85. C Gillingham St Mary *Roch* 84-87; C Kingswinford St Mary *Lich* 87-93; V Rickerscote 93. *70 Truro Drive, Plymouth PL5 4PB*

✠**WALDEN, The Rt Revd Graham Howard.** b 31. Univ of Qld BA52 MA54 Ch Ch Ox BLitt60 MLitt80. St Fran Coll Brisbane

ThL54. **d** 54 **p** 55 **c** 81. C W Hackney St Barn *Lon* 54-56; C Poplar St Sav w St Gabr and St Steph 57-58; Perm to Offic *Ox* 55-59; Australia from 59; Adn Ballarat 70-89; Bp in Hamilton 81-84; Asst Bp Ballarat 84-89; Bp The Murray 89-01; rtd 01. *13 O'Connor Place, Dubbo, NSW, Australia 2830* Tel (0061) (2) 6884 0883

WALDEN, Mrs Jane. b 55. Cartrefle Coll of Educn CertEd76 Chelt & Glouc Coll of HE BA01. WEMTC 02. **d** 05. NSM Minchinhampton *Glouc* from 05. *Rose Acre, London Road, Brimscombe, Stroud GL5 2TL* Tel (01453) 882314 E-mail jane_walden@hotmail.com

WALDEN, John Edward Frank. b 38. FInstSMM. Oak Hill Th Coll 67. **d** 69 **p** 70. C Rainham *Chelmsf* 69-73; P-in-c Bris H Cross Inns Court *Bris* 73-78; Conf and Publicity Sec SAMS 78-81; Hon C Southborough St Pet w Ch Ch and St Matt *Roch* 78-81; Exec Sec Spanish and Portuguese Ch Aid Soc 80-81; Hon C Tonbridge St Steph 81-84; R Earsham w Alburgh and Denton *Nor* 84-89; Perm to Offic from 01; rtd 03. *11 Hemmings Close, Norwich NR5 9EH*

WALES, David Neville. b 55. Rhodes Univ BA78 Open Univ BSc01 Dip Psych. Coll of Resurr Mirfield 80. **d** 82 **p** 83. Zimbabwe 82-88; C Linslade *Ox* 89-91; P-in-c Weston Turville from 91; Voc Adv from 99. *The Rectory, Church Walk, Weston Turville, Aylesbury HP22 5SH* Tel (01296) 613212 E-mail davidnwales@tiscali.co.uk

WALES, Archbishop of. *See* MORGAN, The Most Revd Barry Cennydd

WALFORD, Mrs Angela. b 44. Whitelands Coll Lon CertEd76. S Dios Minl Tr Scheme 85. **d** 92 **p** 94. NSM Boyatt Wood *Win* 92-99; Asst Chapl Epsom and St Helier NHS Trust from 99. *St Helier Hospital, Wrythe Lane, Carshalton SM5 1AA* Tel (020) 8296 2306 *or* 8644 4343 ext 2306

WALFORD, David. b 45. S'wark Ord Course 75. **d** 78 **p** 79. NSM Hackbridge and N Beddington *S'wark* 78-83; C Fawley *Win* 83-87; C-in-c Boyatt Wood CD 87-90; V Boyatt Wood 90-97; rtd 97; Perm to Offic *S'wark* 98-02; Assoc P S Beddington St Mich from 00; Hon Chapl Epsom and St Helier NHS Trust 00-03; Asst Chapl from 03. *58 Wolseley Road, Mitcham Junction, Mitcham CR4 4JQ* Tel (020) 8646 2841 E-mail wols@tinyworld.co.uk

WALFORD, David John. b 47. St Luke's Coll Ex CertEd68 K Coll Lon AKC71. St Aug Coll Cant 71. **d** 72 **p** 73. C Oxton *Ches* 72-77; C Neston 77-80; Youth Chapl 80-81; V Backford 80-81; C Woodchurch 81; Chapl Fulbourn Hosp and Ida Darw Hosp Cam 82-83; Chapl N Man Gen Hosp 83-86; Distr Chapl in Mental Health Ex HA from 86; Chapl R Devon and Ex Hosp (Wonford) 86-94; Chapl R Devon and Ex Healthcare NHS Trust from 94; Chapl Ex and Distr Community Health Service NHS Trust 94-01; Chapl Mid Devon Primary Care Trust from 01. *Royal Devon and Exeter Hospital, Barrack Road, Exeter EX2 5DW* Tel (01392) 402024 *or* 411611

WALFORD, David Sanderson. b 23. BEM49. Chich Th Coll 78. **d** 79 **p** 80. Hon C Chich St Pet *Chich* 79-81; C Chich St Paul and St Pet 81-83; P-in-c Wisbech St Aug *Ely* 83-86; rtd 88. *Sibford, Church Hill, Marnhull, Sturminster Newton DT10 1PU* Tel (01258) 820201

WALFORD, Frank Roy. b 35. Birm Univ MB, ChB58. Qu Coll Birm 78. **d** 80 **p** 81. Hon C Walsall Pleck and Bescot *Lich* 80-85; Chr Healing Cen Bordon 85-88; Dep Medical Dir St Wilfrid's Hospice Chich from 88; Perm to Offic *Chich* from 88. *15 Grove Road, Chichester PO19 8AR* Tel (01243) 533947

WALFORD, Robin Peter. b 46. Qu Coll Birm 75. **d** 78 **p** 79. C Radcliffe-on-Trent *S'well* 78-81; TV Newark w Hawton, Cotham and Shelton 81-84; P-in-c Forest Town 84-92; Co-ord Chapl Leeds Community and Mental Health Services 92-97; Perm to Offic *Ripon* from 97. *2A Weetwood Lane, Leeds LS16 5LS* Tel 0113-278 9953 E-mail walford@leedstherapy.fsnet.co.uk

WALKER, Alan Robert Glaister. b 52. K Coll Cam BA76 MA79 New Coll Ox MA84 Poly Cen Lon LLB91 Heythrop Coll Lon MTh93 Univ of Wales LLM96. St Steph Ho Ox 82. **d** 84 **p** 85. C St John's Wood *Lon* 84-86; Chapl Poly Cen Lon 87-92; Chapl Univ of Westmr 92-94; Chapl Univ Ch Ch the K 87-94; V Hampstead Garden Suburb from 94. *The Vicarage, 1 Central Square, London NW11 7AH* Tel and fax (020) 8455 7206 Mobile 07956-491037 E-mail fatherwalker@aol.com

WALKER, Albert William John. b 14. Linc Th Coll 43. **d** 45 **p** 46. C Ches St Mary *Ches* 45-48; C Hoylake 48-51; V Lower Tranmere 51-56; V Plumstead St Nic *S'wark* 56-66; V Merton St Jas 66-67; V Kingston St Luke 67-74; V Mickleton *Glouc* 74-79; rtd 79; Chapl Convent of St Mary at the Cross Edgware 79-87; Lic to Offic *Lon* 79-87; Perm to Offic *Carl* 87-95 and *Truro* from 95. *Shepherd's Fold, 4 Treza Road, Porthleven, Helston TR13 9NB* Tel (01326) 562104

WALKER, Allen Ross. b 46. Portsm Univ BA94 MA98. Chich Th Coll 86. **d** 88. C Cosham *Portsm* 88-91; Chapl Portsm Mental Health Community 91-97; Dn Portsm Deanery 91-97; Community Chapl Burnham Deanery *Ox* from 97. *21 Palmerstone Avenue, Langley, Slough SL3 7PU* Tel (01753) 522807 E-mail mrarwalker@aol.com

WALKER, Andrew Stephen. b 58. St Chad's Coll Dur BA80 Heythrop Coll Lon MA99. St Steph Ho Ox 83. **d** 85 **p** 86. C Fareham SS Pet and Paul *Portsm* 85-87; C St John's Wood *Lon* 87-93; V Streatham St Pet *S'wark* 93-98; Perm to Offic *Bris* and *S'wark* 98-00; R St Edm the King and St Mary Woolnoth etc *Lon* from 00. *St Mary Woolnoth Vestry, Lombard Street, London EC3V 9AN* Tel and fax (020) 7626 9701 Mobile 07931-745853 E-mail rector@marywoolnoth.org

WALKER, Mrs Angela Jean. b 55. St Jo Coll Nottm 03. **d** 05. C Kempshott *Win* from 05. *1 Lark Close, Basingstoke RG22 5PX* Tel (01256) 361747 E-mail ahiangel@aol.com

WALKER, Canon Anthony Charles St John. b 55. Trin Coll Ox MA80. Wycliffe Hall Ox 78. **d** 81 **p** 82. C Bradf Cathl *Bradf* 81-84; C Nottingham St Ann w Em *S'well* 84-88; V Retford St Sav 88-01; TR Retford from 02; AD Retford from 00; Hon Can S'well Minster from 04. *St Saviour's Vicarage, 31 Richmond Road, Retford DN22 6SJ* Tel and fax (01777) 703800 E-mail tony@tonywalker.f9.co.uk

WALKER, Canon Arthur Keith. b 33. Dur Univ BSc57 Fitzw Ho Cam BA60 MA64 Leeds Univ PhD68 FRSA94. Lich Th Coll 62. **d** 63 **p** 64. C Slaithwaite w E Scammonden *Wakef* 63-66; V N Wootton *B & W* 66-71; Lect Wells Th Coll 66-71; Can Res and Prec Chich Cathl *Chich* 71-80; TV Basingstoke *Win* 81-87; Can Res Win Cathl 87-03; rtd 03. *29 Sussex Street, Winchester SO23 8TG* Tel (01962) 864751 E-mail keith.walker@winchester-cathedral.org.uk

WALKER, Miss Bethany Helen. b 58. RGN80 DON80 Lon Univ DN83. Cranmer Hall Dur 86. **d** 89 **p** 94. C Newark *S'well* 89-93; rtd 93; Perm to Offic *S'well* from 93. *Julian House, 76 Peveril Road, Beeston, Nottingham NG9 2HU* Tel 0115-922 0672 E-mail bhelenw@fish.co.uk

WALKER, Brian Cecil. b 28. FCA62. Cranmer Hall Dur 68. **d** 70 **p** 71. C Heworth w Peasholme St Cuth *York* 70-73; C Attenborough w Chilwell *S'well* 73-75; C Chilwell 75-78; R Trowell 78-89; rtd 89; Perm to Offic *Worc* from 89 and *Birm* from 98. *1 Chaucer Road, Bromsgrove B60 2EE* Tel (01527) 579382

WALKER, Cameron. *See* WALKER, Canon John Cameron

WALKER, Christopher James Anthony. b 43. Sarum & Wells Th Coll 85. **d** 87 **p** 88. Hon C Durrington *Sarum* 87-89; CF 87-98; rtd 98. *Address temp unknown*

WALKER, Christopher John. b 52. ALA74. Chich Th Coll 75. **d** 78 **p** 79. C Reading All SS *Ox* 78-82; C Stony Stratford 82-84; C Wokingham All SS 84-90; V Headington St Mary 90-98; R S w N Moreton, Aston Tirrold and Aston Upthorpe from 98. *The Rectory, Church Lane, South Moreton, Didcot OX11 9AF* Tel and fax (01235) 812042 E-mail rwalker@brookes.ac.uk

WALKER, Christopher John Deville. b 42. St Jo Coll Dur BA69. Westcott Ho Cam 69. **d** 71 **p** 72. C Portsea St Mary *Portsm* 71-75; C Saffron Walden w Wendens Ambo and Littlebury *Chelmsf* 75-77; C St Martin-in-the-Fields *Lon* 77-80; V Riverhead w Dunton Green *Roch* 80-89; V Chatham St Steph 89-97; R Chislehurst St Nic 97-05; rtd 05. *2 Springbank, Shrewsbury Road, Church Stretton SY6 6HA* Tel (01694) 723444 E-mail chris.walker@diocese.rochester.org

WALKER, Canon David. b 48. Linc Th Coll 71. **d** 74 **p** 75. C Arnold *S'well* 74-77; C Crosby *Linc* 77-79; V Scrooby *S'well* 79-86; V Sutton in Ashfield St Mary 86-94; P-in-c Sutton in Ashfield St Mich 89-94; TR Birkenhead Priory *Ches* from 94; RD Birkenhead from 99; Hon Can Ches Cathl from 03. *St Anne's Vicarage, 29 Park Road West, Prenton CH43 1UR* Tel and fax 0151-652 1309 *or* tel 651 0050 E-mail dave.walker48@ntlworld.com

WALKER, Canon David Andrew. b 52. St Andr Univ MTh75 MA Hull Univ MPhil00. Linc Th Coll 79. **d** 81 **p** 82. C Hessle *York* 81-84; C N Hull St Mich 84-86; V from 86; AD Cen and N Hull from 99; RD Hull from 00; Can and Preb York Minster from 01. *St Michael's Vicarage, 214 Orchard Park Road, Hull HU6 9BX* Tel (01482) 803375 E-mail david@stmichaelsnorthhull.org.uk

WALKER, Canon David Grant. b 23. Bris Univ BA49 Ball Coll Ox DPhil54 FSA60 FRHistS62. **d** 62 **p** 62. NSM Swansea St Mary w H Trin *S & B* 62-86; Chapl and Lect Univ of Wales (Swansea) 62; Sen Lect 63-82; Dir Post-Ord Tr 65-93; Can Brecon Cathl from 72; Prec 79-90; Chan 90-93; Chapl Univ of Wales (Swansea) 75-76; Dir of In-Service Tr from 77; P-in-c Caereithin 86-87. *52 Eaton Crescent, Swansea SA1 4QN* Tel (01792) 472624

WALKER, David Ian. b 41. Dip Ch Music. Bernard Gilpin Soc Dur 64 Bps' Coll Cheshunt 65. **d** 68 **p** 69. C Todmorden *Wakef* 68-72; V Rastrick St Jo 72-77; V Crosland Moor 77-86; R Kirton in Lindsey w Manton *Linc* 86-99; R Grayingham 86-99; V Clee from 99; OCF from 88. *Old Clee Vicarage, 202 Clee Road, Grimsby DN32 8NG* Tel (01472) 691800 E-mail davidian@oldclee44.freeserve.co.uk

WALKER, David John. b 47. St Jo Coll Nottm 88. **d** 90 **p** 91. C Strood St Fran *Roch* 90-94; V Larkfield from 94. *The Vicarage, 206 New Hythe Lane, Larkfield, Maidstone ME20 6PT* Tel and fax (01732) 843349 E-mail davidjwalker@challenge1.freeserve.co.uk

✠**WALKER, The Rt Revd David Stuart.** b 57. Cam Univ MA. Qu Coll Birm DipTh. **d** 83 **p** 84 **c** 00. C Handsworth *Sheff* 83-86; TV Maltby 86-91; Ind Chapl 86-91; V Bramley and Ravenfield 91-95; R Bramley and Ravenfield w Hooton Roberts etc 95-00; Hon Can Sheff Cathl 00; Suff Bp Dudley *Worc* from 00. *Bishop's House, Bishop's Walk, Cradley Heath B64 7RH* Tel 0121-550 3407 Fax 550 7340 E-mail bishop.david@cofe-worcester.org.uk

WALKER, Dennis Richard. b 25. Bp Gray Coll Cape Town LTh57. **d** 57 **p** 58. S Africa 57-73; V Catterick *Ripon* 73-78; V Manston 78-86; rtd 86; Perm to Offic *York* from 90. *23 Promenade, Bridlington YO15 2QA* Tel (01262) 672131

WALKER, Derek Fred. b 46. Trin Coll Bris 71. **d** 74 **p** 75. C St Paul's Cray St Barn *Roch* 74-78; C Rushden w Newton Bromswold *Pet* 78-80; R Kirkby Thore w Temple Sowerby and Newbiggin *Carl* 80-83; V Coppull *Blackb* 83-87; V New Ferry *Ches* 87-96; R Akeman *Ox* from 96. *The Rectory, Alchester Road, Chesterton, Bicester OX26 1UW* Tel and fax (01869) 369815 E-mail akemanbenefice@yahoo.com

WALKER, Douglas. b 36. Lich Th Coll 61. **d** 63 **p** 64. C Bris St Ambrose Whitehall *Bris* 63-68; P-in-c Easton All Hallows 68-71; V Penhill 71-79; P-in-c Crundale w Godmersham *Cant* 79-83; P-in-c Elmsted w Hastingleigh 79-83; V Sheerness H Trin w St Paul 83-01; rtd 01; Perm to Offic *Worc* from 01. *21 Lower Ferry Lane, Callow End, Worcester WR2 4UN* Tel (01905) 831508

WALKER, Duncan Andrew. b 59. **d** 90 **p** 91. C Gorseinon *S & B* 90-91; C Morriston 92-94; V Llanelli Ch Ch *St D* 94-98; V Swansea St Jas *S & B* from 98. *St James's Vicarage, 1 Ffynone Drive, Swansea SA1 6DB* Tel (01792) 470532

✠**WALKER, The Rt Revd Edward William Murray (Dominic).** b 48. AKC73 Heythrop Coll Lon MA97 Brighton Univ Hon DLitt98 Univ of Wales LLM05. **d** 72 **p** 72 **c** 97. CGA 67-83; C Wandsworth St Faith *S'wark* 72-73; Bp's Dom Chapl 73-76; R Newington St Mary 76-85; RD S'wark and Newington 80-85; OGS from 83; Superior 90-96; V Brighton St Pet w Chpl Royal and St Jo *Chich* 85-86; P-in-c Brighton St Nic 85-86; TR Brighton St Pet and St Nic w Chpl Royal 86-97; RD Brighton 85-97; Can and Preb Chich Cathl 85-97; Area Bp Reading *Ox* 97-03; Bp Mon from 03. *Bishopstow, Stow Hill, Newport NP20 4EA* Tel (01633) 263510 Fax 259946 E-mail bishop.monmouth@churchinwales.org.uk

WALKER, Mrs Elizabeth. b 42. Sunderland Poly CQSW85. NEOC 91. **d** 94 **p** 00. NSM Stockton St Chad *Dur* from 94. *29 Bramble Road, Stockton-on-Tees TS19 0NQ* Tel (01642) 615332

WALKER, Mrs Elizabeth Margaret Rea. b 49. Ch Ch Coll Cant CertEd70. S'wark Ord Course 89. **d** 92 **p** 94. NSM Ash *Roch* 92-97; NSM Ridley 92-97; Chapl St Geo Sch Gravesend 92-97; P-in-c Burham and Wouldham *Roch* from 97; Assoc Dir of Ords from 97. *The Rectory, 266 Rochester Road, Burham, Rochester ME1 3RJ* Tel and fax (01634) 666862 Mobile 07931-356502 E-mail revdliz.walker@care4free.net

WALKER, Gavin Russell. b 43. FCA78. Coll of Resurr Mirfield 76. **d** 78 **p** 79. C Wakef St Jo *Wakef* 78-81; C Northallerton w Kirby Sigston *York* 81-83; V Whorlton w Carlton and Faceby 83-85; P-in-c Brotherton *Wakef* 85-89; Chapl Pontefract Gen Infirmary 85-89; V Earl's Heaton *Wakef* 89-97; TV Dewsbury 97-99; TV Egremont and Haile *Carl* 99-04; rtd 04. *Church How Cottage, Wasdale, Seascale CA20 1ET* Tel (01946) 726188 Mobile 07986-505886 E-mail staffa@lineone.net

WALKER, Geoffrey. *See* WALKER, Canon Philip Geoffrey

WALKER, Gerald Roger. b 41. K Coll Lon BD67 AKC67. **d** 68 **p** 69. C High Elswick St Phil *Newc* 68-70; C Goring-by-Sea *Chich* 70-75; R Selsey 75-81; V Hove St Andr Old Ch 81-91; V Copthorne 91-95; rtd 95; NSM Streat w Westmeston *Chich* 95-99; Perm to Offic *S'wark* from 00. *1 Glebe Cottages, Newdigate, Dorking RH5 5AA* Tel (01306) 631587

WALKER, Canon Graham. b 35. Ex Coll Ox BA58 BTh60 MA62 Leeds Univ MPhil80. Sarum Th Coll 60. **d** 61 **p** 62. C Guiseley *Bradf* 61-64; C Ingrow cum Hainworth 64-68; Lic to Offic 68-80; V Hellifield 80-01; RD Bowland 86-95; Hon Can Bradf Cathl 89-01; P-in-c Gisburn 94-01; rtd 01. *Shaw House, 3 Branstone Beck, High Bentham, Lancaster LA2 7LX* Tel (01524) 261125

WALKER, Canon Harvey William. b 26. Edin Univ MA52. St Steph Ho Ox 58. **d** 60 **p** 61. C Newc St Matt w St Mary *Newc* 60-64; V 64-94; Hon Can Newc Cathl 80-94; rtd 95; Perm to Offic *Newc* from 95. *21 Grosvenor Drive, Whitley Bay NE26 2JP* Tel 0191-252 1858

WALKER, Mrs Hazel. b 47. N Ord Course MA01. **d** 00 **p** 01. NSM Crofton *Wakef* from 00. *30 Heron Drive, Sandal, Wakefield WF2 6SW* Tel (01924) 259687 E-mail hazelw@heron55.freeserve.co.uk

WALKER, Helen Margaret. *See* WALKER, Miss Bethany Helen

WALKER, Hugh. *See* WALKER, John Hugh

WALKER, Ian Richard Stevenson. b 51. Univ of Wales (Lamp) BA73. Qu Coll Birm DipTh75. **d** 76 **p** 77. C Stainton-in-Cleveland *York* 76-79; C Fulford 79-81; C Kidderminster St Mary *Worc* 81-82; TV Kidderminster St Mary and All SS, Trimpley etc 82-86; R Keyingham w Ottringham, Halsham and Sunk Is *York* 86-98; RD S Holderness 94-98; R Scartho *Linc* from 98. *St Giles's Rectory, 44 Waltham Road, Grimsby DN33 2LX* Tel (01472) 872728 E-mail irsw@stgilesrec.fsnet.co.uk

WALKER, Jill Dorothy Ann. b 36. RGN58 Westmr Coll Ox DipApTh93. St Alb Minl Tr Scheme 89. **d** 96 **p** 97. NSM E Barnet *St Alb* 96-99; Asst Chapl Barnet and Chase Farm Hosps NHS Trust from 99. *2 Dean's Gardens, St Albans AL4 9LS* Tel (01727) 834436

WALKER, Mrs Jillian Francesca. b 41. **d** 99 **p** 00. OLM Blackbourne *St E* from 99. *The Woolpack, Bury Road, Ixworth, Bury St Edmunds IP31 2HX* Tel (01359) 230776 E-mail digger.walker@tiscali.co.uk

WALKER (née TOMKINS), Ms Jocelyn Rachel. b 64. Univ of Wales (Ban) BA85 Man Univ PGCE86. N Ord Course 98. **d** 01 **p** 02. C Chadderton St Matt *Man* 01-04; Chapl Asst Salford R Hosps NHS Trust from 04. *Chaplaincy Department, Hope Hospital, Stott Lane, Salford M6 8HD* Tel 0161-789 7373 E-mail joss.walker@tiscali.com

WALKER, John. *See* WALKER, Albert William John

WALKER, Canon John. b 51. Aber Univ MA74 Edin Univ BD78. Edin Th Coll 75. **d** 78 **p** 79. C Broughty Ferry *Bre* 78-81; P-in-c Dundee St Jo 81-85; Ind Chapl 83-88; R Dundee St Luke 85-95; R Inverurie *Ab* from 95; P-in-c Kemnay from 95; I Alford from 95; R Auchindoir from 95; Can St Andr Cathl from 01. *The Rectory, St Mary's Place, Inverurie AB51 3NW* Tel and fax (01467) 620470 E-mail jbwalker@cwcom.net

WALKER, John Anthony Patrick. b 58. Man Metrop Univ PGCE97. Trin Coll Bris BA86. **d** 86 **p** 87. C Canford Magna *Sarum* 86-90; TV Glyncorrwg w Afan Vale and Cymmer Afan *Llan* 90-96; Hd of RE Wentworth High Sch Eccles 97-99; Community Chapl and C Gorton St Phil *Man* 00-03; P-in-c Oldham St Paul 03-04. *Address temp unknown* E-mail johnwalker-uk@btinternet.com

WALKER, Canon John Cameron. b 31. St Andr Univ MA52. Edin Th Coll 63. **d** 65 **p** 66. C Edin H Cross *Edin* 65-67; C Perth St Jo *St And* 67-70; Chapl Angl Students Glas 70-74; Youth Chapl Warks Educn Cttee 75-77; Officer Gen Syn Bd of Educn 78-82; C W Hendon St Jo *Lon* 79-82; PV Westmr Abbey 82-84; Chapl Ghent w Ypres *Eur* 84-92; Chapl Ghent 92-98; Miss to Seamen 84-98; Can Brussels Cathl *Eur* 93-98; rtd 98. *Le Petit Clos, rue des Lilas, 11300 Bouriège, France* Tel and fax (0033) (4) 68 31 17 04

WALKER, John David. b 44. St Jo Coll Dur BA76. Cranmer Hall Dur 77. **d** 77 **p** 78. C Heworth H Trin *York* 77-81; P-in-c Allerthorpe and Barmby on the Moor w Fangfoss 81-83; TV Pocklington Team 84-89; P-in-c Hovingham 89; TV Street 89-92; R Dunnington 92-99; V Thorne *Sheff* 99-03; rtd 03; Perm to Offic *York* from 03. *9 Bishop Blunt Close, Hessle HU13 9NJ* E-mail john.d.walker@bt.internet.com

WALKER, John Frank. b 53. Leeds Univ BEd76 Ripon Coll of Educn CertEd75. NW Ord Course 78. **d** 81 **p** 82. NSM Whitkirk *Ripon* 81-82; C 82-85; V Sutton Courtenay w Appleford *Ox* 85-90; Dioc Children's Adv *S'wark* 90-94; V Walworth St Jo from 94; Youth and Children's Officer Woolwich Episc Area 95-99. *St John's Vicarage, 18 Larcom Street, London SE17 1NQ* Tel (020) 7703 4375

WALKER, John Frederick. b 21. St Jo Coll Dur BA47 DipTh49 MA51. **d** 49 **p** 50. C Normanton *Wakef* 49-51; C Northowram 51-53; V Gawthorpe and Chickenley Heath 53-59; V Haley Hill 59-74; V Hampsthwaite *Ripon* 74-86; P-in-c Killinghall 76-86; rtd 86; Perm to Offic *Bradf* from 86. *36 Rockwood Drive, Skipton BD23 1UW* Tel (01756) 799835

WALKER, John Howard. b 47. Brasted Th Coll 67 Clifton Th Coll 69. **d** 72 **p** 73. C Upton (Overchurch) *Ches* 72-76; Asst Chapl Liv Univ *Liv* 76-79; V Everton St Chrys 79-82; C Parr Mt 83-86; SAMS 86-94; Area Sec (NE and E Midl) SAMS 86-89; Paraguay 89-94; V Calverley *Bradf* from 95. *The Vicarage, Town Gate, Calverley, Pudsey LS28 5NF* Tel 0113-257 7968

WALKER, John Hugh. b 34. K Coll Lon BD57 AKC57 K Coll Lon MTh75 MA85 Lon Inst of Educn PGCE68. St Boniface Warminster 57. **d** 58 **p** 59. C Southend St Alb *Chelmsf* 58-61; V Gt Ilford St Alb 61-67; Perm to Offic 67-68; Hon C Forest Gate St Edm 68-74; Perm to Offic *Cant* 75-82 and from 87; R Dymchurch w Burmarsh and Newchurch 82-87; rtd 94. *14 Danes Court, Dover CT16 2QE* Tel (01304) 202233

WALKER, John Michael. b 32. Qu Coll Birm. **d** 57 **p** 58. C Ruddington *S'well* 57-60; C Horsham *Chich* 60-64; C Sullington 64-70; C Storrington 64-70; V Peasmarsh 70-73; V Washington 73-77; R Ashington, Washington and Wiston w Buncton 77-98; rtd 98; Perm to Offic *Chich* from 98. *The Granary, Staplefield Farm, Horsham Road, Steyning BN44 3AA*

WALKER, Canon John Percival. b 45. CITC 68. **d** 71 **p** 72. C Belfast St Clem *D & D* 71-74; C Magheraculmoney *Clogh* 74-78; C Lisburn St Paul *Conn* 78-81; I Belfast St Ninian 81-88; I Belfast St Mary 88-89; I Belfast St Mary w H Redeemer from 89; Preb Conn Cathl from 98; Treas Conn Cathl from 04. *St Mary's*

Rectory, 558 Crumlin Road, Belfast BT14 7GL Tel and fax (028) 9058 4540 *or* tel 9074 8423
E-mail john.walker18@ntlworld.com

WALKER, John Robert. b 50. NE Lon Poly BSc74 K Coll Lon PhD77. Trin Coll Bris BA93 MA95. **d** 96 **p** 97. C Bushbury *Lich* 96-00; TV Dewsbury *Wakef* 00-01. *183 Queens Drive, Ossett WF5 0NP* Tel (01924) 273837 E-mail revdjrw@aol.com

WALKER, Keith. *See* WALKER, Canon Arthur Keith

WALKER, Keith. b 48. Linc Th Coll 82. **d** 84 **p** 85. C Whickham *Dur* 84-87; C Trimdon Station 87; P-in-c 87-89; V 89-90; R Penshaw 90-98; P-in-c Shiney Row 92-95; P-in-c Herrington 93-95; rtd 98; Hon C Jersey St Brelade *Win* 01-03. *Hallgarth Heights, Kirk Merrington, Spennymoor DL16 7NY* Tel (01388) 827319

WALKER, Mrs Lesley Ann. b 53. Westmr Coll Ox MTh00. S Dios Minl Tr Scheme 85. **d** 88 **p** 94. Par Dn Oakdale *Sarum* 88-92; TD Bridgnorth, Tasley, Astley Abbotts, etc *Heref* 92-94; TV 94-03; Vice-Prin OLM Tr Scheme *Cant* 03-04. *28A West Cliff, Whitstable CT5 1DN*

WALKER, Mrs Linda Joan. b 47. **d** 04 **p** 05. OLM Blurton *Lich* from 04. *6 Thackeray Drive, Blurton, Stoke-on-Trent ST3 2HE* Tel (01782) 324895

WALKER, Mrs Margaret Joy. b 44. Westhill Coll Birm TCert66 Newc Univ MA93. CA Tr Coll 80. **dss** 86 **d** 87 **p** 94. Scargill Ho 86-87; Hon Par Dn Monkwearmouth St Andr *Dur* 87; Hon Par Dn Chester le Street 87-93; Hon Chapl Wells Cathl *B & W* 93-01; Perm to Offic *Cant* from 02. *1 Ensigne Cottages, Shalmsford Street, Chartham, Canterbury CT4 7RF* Tel (01227) 738690
E-mail margi@margiwalker.wanadoo.co.uk

WALKER, Margaret (Sister Lucy Clare). b 37. Guildf Dioc Min Course 99. **d** 01 **p** 02. CSP from 88; NSM Aldershot St Mich *Guildf* 01-04; NSM Chertsey, Lyne and Longcross from 04. *The Vicarage, Lyne Lane, Lyne, Chertsey KT16 0AJ* Tel (01932) 874405 Mobile 07960-247522

WALKER, Mark Robert Joseph George. b 66. Nottm Univ BA88 TCD PhD98. CITC 90. **d** 92 **p** 93. C Larne and Inver *Conn* 92-95; C Glynn w Raloo 92-95; Asst Chapl Royle Hosp Larne 92-94; Lect Th and Ch Hist Univ Coll Ches 95-00 and 00-01; Chapl NE Wales Inst of HE from 01; Dir Dioc Minl Tr Course *St As* from 01; C Wrexham from 01. *The Chaplaincy, Post Point 22, North East Wales Institute, Plas Coch College, Mold Road, Wrexham LL11 2AW* Tel (01978) 293336 Mobile 07798-483963 Fax (01978) 293254 E-mail m.walker@newi.ac.uk

WALKER, Preb Martin Frank. b 39. St Jo Coll Nottm 71. **d** 73 **p** 74. C Penn *Lich* 73-78; V Bentley 78-82; V Kinver 82-88; R Kinver and Enville 88-91; V Harlescott 91-02; R Broughton w Croxton and Cotes Heath w Standon 02-04; P-in-c from 04; Preb Lich Cathl from 00; rtd 04. *The Rectory, Station Road, Cotes Heath, Stafford ST21 6RS* Tel and fax (01782) 791549
E-mail martin.walker7@btinternet.com

WALKER, Martin John. b 52. Linc Coll Ox BA73 PGCE74 Château de Bossey Geneva Dip Ecum78. Cranmer Hall Dur BA78. **d** 79 **p** 80. C Harlow New Town w Lt Parndon *Chelmsf* 79-81; C Dorchester *Ox* 81-83; Chapl Bath Coll of HE 83-89; TV Southampton (City Cen) *Win* 89-91; Adv in RE and Resources *Sarum* 91-92; Hon C Northolt St Mary *Lon* 92-00; Chapl Bancroft's Sch Woodford Green 92-99; Chapl St Helen's Sch Northwood 99-00; Chapl Wellingborough Sch from 00; Perm to Offic *Lon* from 00. *Marsh House, Wellingborough School, Irthlingborough Road, Wellingborough NN8 2BX* Tel (01933) 222427 E-mail revmjwalker@yahoo.com

WALKER, Meuryn David. b 44. Bris Univ BSc66 Nottm Univ PGCE67. N Ord Course 97. **d** 00 **p** 01. NSM Wakef St Jo *Wakef* 00-02; NSM Horbury Junction from 02. *188 Stanley Road, Wakefield WF1 4AE* Tel (01924) 210797 Mobile 07775-583764
E-mail meuryn@blueyonder.co.uk

WALKER, Michael John. b 39. St D Coll Lamp BA61. St Aid Birkenhead 61. **d** 63 **p** 64. C Clifton *York* 63-66; C Marfleet 66-69; V Salterhebble St Jude *Wakef* 69-83; V Llangollen w Trevor and Llantysilio *St As* 83-93; RD Llangollen 87-93; V Kerry and Llanmerewig and Dolfor 93-01; RD Cedewain 97-01; rtd 01; Perm to Offic *Ban* from 01. *Sylfaen-y-Graig, 21 Garth Terrace, Porthmadog LL49 9BE* Tel (01766) 515192

WALKER, Nigel Maynard. b 39. ALCD66. **d** 67 **p** 68. C Southsea St Jude *Portsm* 67-70; C Addington S Africa 70-73; R 73-76; C Abingdon w Shippon *Ox* 76-80; V Upton (Overchurch) *Ches* 80-94; Chapl Brussels and Chan Brussels Cathl *Eur* 94-04; P-in-c Leuven 02-04; rtd 05; Perm to Offic *Cant* from 05. *25 Viking Court, Dumpton Park Drive, Broadstairs CT10 1RF* Tel (01843) 867535 E-mail nmw_sabbatical@hotmail.com

WALKER, Mrs Pamela Sarah. b 52. Somerville Coll Ox BA73 MA77 St Jo Coll Dur BA78. Cranmer Hall Dur 76. **dss** 79 **d** 87 **p** 94. Harlow New Town w Lt Parndon *Chelmsf* 79-81; Dorchester *Sarum* 82-83; Bath St Bart *B & W* 85-88; Hon Par Dn 87-88; Par Dn Warmley *Bris* 88-89; Par Dn Bitton 88-89; Par Dn Southampton (City Cen) *Win* 89-92; Par Dn Northolt St Mary *Lon* 92-94; R 94-04; R Corfe Mullen *Sarum* from 04. *The Rectory, 32 Wareham Road, Corfe Mullen, Wimborne BH21 3LE* Tel (01202) 692129 E-mail pswlkr@btinternet.com

WALKER, Paul Gary. b 59. Lon Univ BD. St Jo Coll Nottm 82. **d** 84 **p** 85. C Bowling St Steph *Bradf* 84-87; C Tong 87-90; P-in-c Oakenshaw cum Woodlands 90-97; V Wrose from 97; RD Calverley from 01. *St Cuthbert's Vicarage, 71 Wrose Road, Bradford BD2 1LN* Tel (01274) 611631
E-mail sqwalker@netcom.ca

WALKER, Paul Laurence. b 63. St Chad's Coll Dur BA84. Chich Th Coll BTh90. **d** 88 **p** 89. C Shildon w Eldon *Dur* 88-91; C Barnard Castle w Whorlton 91-93; C Silksworth 93-96; C-in-c Moorside St Wilfrid CD 96-99; V Norton St Mary 99-04; Chapl Manager Tees and NE Yorks NHS Trust from 04. *St Luke's Hospital, Marton Road, Middlesbrough TS4 3AF* Tel (01642) 516068 E-mail paul.walker@tney.northy.nhs.uk

WALKER, Pauline Ann. b 51. Open Univ BA87. St As Minl Tr Course 88. **d** 93 **p** 97. NSM Bistre *St As* 93-99; C Bistre 99-04; V Llay from 04. *The Vicarage, First Avenue, Llay, Wrexham LL12 0TN* Tel (01978) 852262

WALKER, Pauline Jean. b 49. St Hild Coll Dur BSc72 Homerton Coll Cam PGCE73 Nottm Univ MA96. All Nations Chr Coll 89 St Jo Coll Nottm 94. **d** 96 **p** 97. C Bitterne *Win* 96-01; CMS from 01. *CMS, Partnership House, 157 Waterloo Road, London SE1 8UU* Tel (020) 7928 8681

WALKER, Percival. *See* WALKER, Canon John Percival

WALKER, Peter Anthony. b 57. Pemb Coll Cam BA79 MA83 St Jo Coll Dur BA86. Cranmer Hall Dur 84. **d** 87 **p** 88. C Chesham Bois *Ox* 87-90; Chapl Bradf Cathl *Bradf* 90-93; TV W Swindon and the Lydiards *Bris* 93-99; V Keresley and Coundon *Cov* from 99. *Keresley Vicarage, 34 Tamworth Road, Coventry CV6 2EL* Tel and fax (024) 7633 2717
E-mail peter@st-thomas-keresley.org.uk

WALKER, Canon Peter Anthony Ashley. b 46. Chich Th Coll 67. **d** 70 **p** 71. C Stamford Hill St Thos *Lon* 70-74; C Bethnal Green St Matt 74-77; V Hackney Wick St Mary of Eton w St Aug 77-84; Warden Rydal Hall *Carl* 84-95; P-in-c Rydal 84-95; P-in-c Porthleven w Sithney *Truro* 95-01; RD Kerrier 96-01; Can Res Truro Cathl from 01; P-in-c Feock from 01. *The Vicarage, Feock, Truro TR3 6SD* Tel (01872) 862534
E-mail feockvic@btinternet.com

WALKER, Peter Jeffrey. b 46. Kelham Th Coll 65. **d** 70 **p** 71. C Middlesbrough All SS *York* 70-75 and 77-78; SSF 75-77; C-in-c Wrangbrook w N Elmsall CD *Wakef* 78-82; V Athersley 82-86; SSM 86-88; Perm to Offic *Dur* 88-89; V Hartlepool H Trin 89-95; Dep Chapl HM Pris Birm 95-96; Chapl HM Pris Moorland 96-01; Chapl HM Pris Full Sutton 01-04; Co-ord Chapl HM Pris Ford 04-05; P-in-c Ferrybridge *Wakef* from 05; P-in-c Brotherton from 05; OGS from 01. *St Andrew's Vicarage, 5 Pontefract Road, Ferrybridge, Knottingley WF11 8PN* Tel (01977) 672772

✠**WALKER, The Rt Revd Peter Knight.** b 19. Qu Coll Ox BA47 MA47 Cam Univ Hon DD78. Westcott Ho Cam 53. **d** 54 **p** 55 **c** 72. Asst Master Merchant Taylors' Sch Lon 50-56; C Hemel Hempstead St Mary *St Alb* 56-58; Fell Dean and Lect Th CCC Cam 58-62; Asst Tutor 59-62; Prin Westcott Ho Cam 62-72; Hon Can Ely Cathl *Ely* 66-72; Suff Bp Dorchester *Ox* 72-77; Can Res Ch Ch 72-77; Bp Ely 77-89; rtd 89; Hon Asst Bp Ox 89-95; Perm to Offic *Ely* from 95. *19 St Mark's Court, Barton Road, Cambridge CB3 9LE* Tel (01223) 363041

WALKER, Peter Ronald. Southn Univ BA72 K Alfred's Coll Win PGCE73. WMMTC 02. **d** 05. NSM Wellington Ch Ch *Lich* from 05. *4 Harvington Close, Wellington TF1 3EX* Tel (01952) 256927

WALKER, Peter Sidney Caleb. b 50. St Mich Th Coll Crafers 76. **d** 80 **p** 81. Australia 80-88; C Devonport 80-81; P-in-c Fingal Valley 81-84; R E Devonport and Spreyton 84-88; R Swallow *Linc* 88-94; R Selworthy, Timberscombe, Wootton Courtenay etc *B & W* 94-01; Chapl Costa del Sol W *Eur* 01-04. *Chafran, Johns Corner, Rosudgeon, Penzance TR20 9PJ* Tel (01736) 71004

WALKER, Peter Stanley. b 56. SRN RMN Nottm Univ BCombStuds. Linc Th Coll 80. **d** 83 **p** 84. C Woodford St Barn *Chelmsf* 83-86; C Brentwood St Thos 86-88; V Colchester St Barn 88-94; P-in-c Colchester St Jas, All SS, St Nic and St Runwald 94-96; R Colchester St Jas and St Paul w All SS etc from 96. *The Rectory, 76 East Hill, Colchester CO1 2QW* Tel (01206) 866802 Fax 799444
E-mail fatherpeter@walkerssc.freeserve.co.uk

WALKER, Peter William Leyland. b 61. CCC Cam BA82 MA86 PhD87 Ox Univ DPhil96. Wycliffe Hall Ox 87. **d** 89 **p** 90. C Tonbridge SS Pet and Paul *Roch* 89-93; Fell Tyndale Ho Cam 93-96; Tutor Wycliffe Hall Ox from 96; Hon C Abingdon *Ox* from 97. *Wycliffe Hall, 54 Banbury Road, Oxford OX2 6PW* Tel (01865) 274214 E-mail peter.walker@wycliffe.ox.ac.uk

WALKER, Canon Philip Geoffrey. b 47. St Jo Coll Dur BA70 Oriel Coll Ox BA72 MA76 Newc Univ MA93 Bris Univ PhD01. Ripon Hall Ox 70. **d** 74 **p** 75. C Sheff St Geo *Sheff* 74-77; C Cambridge Gt St Mary w St Mich *Ely* 77-81; V Monkwearmouth St Andr *Dur* 81-87; R Chester le Street 87-93; RD Chester-le-Street 89-93; Dioc Missr *B & W* 93-01; Can Res

Wells Cathl 94-01; Prin OLM Tr Scheme *Cant* 02-05; Prin Whitelands Coll Roehampton Inst from 05. *The Principal's Office, Whitelands College, Holybourne Avenue, London SW15 4JD* Tel (020) 8392 3500 Fax 8392 3531 E-mail drgeoffrey.walker@virgin.net

WALKER, Philip Kingsley. b 47. Ox Univ BA70 Univ of Wales DPS90. St Mich Coll Llan. **d** 90 **p** 91. C Maindee *Mon* 90-92; C Llanmartin 92-94; V Bishton 94-98; R Panteg 98-03; R Panteg w Llanfihangel Pontymoile from 03. *Panteg Rectory, The Highway, New Inn, Pontypool NP4 0PH* Tel (01495) 763724

WALKER, Raymond. b 28. Carl Dioc Tr Inst 83. **d** 86 **p** 87. NSM Gt Salkeld w Lazonby *Carl* 86-91; C Greystoke, Matterdale, Mungrisdale etc 91-92; TV 92-95; rtd 95. *Brackenrigg, Town Head, Lazonby, Penrith CA10 1AT* Tel (01768) 898314

WALKER, Richard David. b 45. Hull Univ BSc68. S Dios Minl Tr Scheme 92. **d** 95 **p** 96. NSM Horfield St Greg *Bris* 95-98; NSM Lawrence Weston and Avonmouth 98-00; Chapl HM Pris Leic 00-01; Chapl HM Pris Usk and Prescoed 01-03; Hon C Cromhall, Tortworth, Tytherington, Falfield etc *Glouc* from 04. *The Vicarage, Sundays Hill Lane, Falfield, Wotton-under-Edge GL12 8DQ* Tel (01454) 260033

WALKER, Richard John. b 67. Humberside Coll of Educn BSc88 Leeds Univ MSc(Eng)97 St Jo Coll Dur BA04. Cranmer Hall Dur 02. **d** 04 **p** 05. C Scarborough St Mary w Ch Ch and H Apostles *York* from 04. *13 Woodall Avenue, Scarborough YO12 7TH* E-mail lizzynrichard@tiscali.co.uk

WALKER, Richard Mainprize. b 43. Keele Univ BA DipEd. Wycliffe Hall Ox 84. **d** 86 **p** 87. C Guildf Ch Ch *Guildf* 86-90; V Bradley St Martin *Lich* from 90. *St Martin's Vicarage, King Street, Bradley, Bilston WV14 8PQ* Tel (01902) 493109

WALKER, Richard Mark. b 63. York Univ BSc84. St Jo Coll Nottm MA00. **d** 00 **p** 01. C Ben Rhydding *Bradf* 00-04; P-in-c Yeadon St Jo from 04. *St John's Vicarage, Barcroft Grove, Yeadon, Leeds LS19 7XZ* Tel 0113-250 2272 E-mail rwalker123@madasafish.com

WALKER, Roger. *See* WALKER, Gerald Roger

WALKER, Mrs Ruth. b 51. MAAT95. **d** 03 **p** 04. OLM Camberley St Mary *Guildf* from 03. *73 Verran Road, Camberley GU15 2ND* Tel (01276) 503551 E-mail trevorwalker@csma-netlink.co.uk

WALKER (née APPLETON), Mrs Ruth Elizabeth. b 58. St Jo Coll Dur BA79 Hughes Hall Cam PGCE80. St Jo Coll Nottm 86. **d** 88 **p** 94. Par Dn Princes Risborough w Ilmer *Ox* 88-90; C and Congr Chapl Bradf Cathl *Bradf* 90-93; C The Lydiards *Bris* 93-94; NSM W Swindon and the Lydiards 94-96; C Swindon St Jo and St Andr 96-98; Perm to Offic 98-99; C Keresley and Coundon *Cov* from 99; AD Cov N from 04. *Keresley Vicarage, 34 Tamworth Road, Coventry CV6 2EL* Tel and fax (024) 7633 2717 E-mail ruth@st-thomas-keresley.org.uk

WALKER, Sharon Anne. b 60. Derby Univ BA99. St Jo Coll Nottm. **d** 02 **p** 03. C Greetham and Thistleton w Stretton and Clipsham *Pet* 02-05; C Cottesmore and Barrow w Ashwell and Burley 02-05; P-in-c Pet St Mary Boongate from 05. *St Mary's Vicarage, 214 Eastfield Road, Peterborough PE1 4BD* Tel (01733) 343418

WALKER, Simon Patrick. b 71. Ch Ch Ox BA93. Wycliffe Hall Ox BTh94. **d** 97 **p** 98. C Abingdon *Ox* 97-01; Perm to Offic *Ches* from 01. *3 Gladstone Road, Headington, Oxford OX3 8LL* Tel (01865) 766356 *or* 08701-417077 E-mail simon@humanecogroup.com

WALKER, Stanley Frederick. b 48. St Jo Coll Nottm. **d** 84 **p** 85. C Ellesmere Port *Ches* 84-89; V Seacombe 89-97; C Lache cum Saltney 97-03; TV Wrexham *St As* from 03. *St Mark's Vicarage, Menai Road, Wrexham LL13 9LB* Tel (01978) 356647 Mobile 07802-960430 E-mail stanwalker@02.co.uk

WALKER, Stephen Michael Maynard. b 62. St Jo Coll Dur BA84. Trin Coll Bris 86. **d** 88 **p** 89. C Eastwood *S'well* 88-92; CF 92-02; C Marple All SS *Ches* from 02. *125 Church Lane, Marple, Stockport SK6 7LD* Tel 0161-427 3841

WALKER, Stephen Patrick. b 62. York Univ BSc83 PGCE84. St Jo Coll Nottm 87. **d** 90 **p** 91. C Hull St Jo Newland *York* 90-94; Min Grove Green LEP *Cant* 94-98; Children's Min Adv 96-98; TV Drypool *York* 98-99; TR 99-04; TR Binsey *Carl* from 04. *The Vicarage, Torpenhow, Wigton CA7 1HT* Tel (016973) 71541 E-mail stephen_p_walker@hotmail.com *or* binsey@fish.co.uk

WALKER, Mrs Susan Joy. b 52. Univ of Wales (Lamp) BA73 Hull Univ MA91. Qu Coll Birm 75. **dss** 83 **d** 87 **p** 94. Kidderminster St Mary and All SS, Trimpley etc *Worc* 83-86; Keyingham w Ottringham, Halsham and Sunk Is *York* 86-87; Hon Par Dn 87-94; Hon C 94-98; Chapl Hull Coll of FE 89-98; Chapl N Lindsey Coll *Linc* from 98. *St Giles's Rectory, 44 Waltham Road, Grimsby DN33 2LX* Tel (01472) 872728 *or* 294034 E-mail susanwalker@leggott.ac.uk *or* irsw@stgilesrec.fsnet.co.uk

WALKER, The Ven Thomas Overington. b 33. Keble Coll Ox BA58 MA61. Oak Hill Th Coll 58. **d** 60 **p** 61. C Woking St Paul *Guildf* 60-62; C St Leonards St Leon *Chich* 62-64; Travelling Sec IVF 64-67; Succ Birm Cathl *Birm* 67-70; V Harborne Heath 70-91; P-in-c Edgbaston St Germain 83-91; Hon Can Birm Cathl 80-91; RD Edgbaston 89-91; Adn Nottingham *S'well* 91-96; rtd 96; Perm to Offic *Heref* from 97. *6 Cornbrook, Clee Hill, Ludlow SY8 3QQ* Tel (01584) 890176

WALKER, Trevor John. b 51. Southn Univ BTh80. Sarum & Wells Th Coll 75. **d** 78 **p** 79. C Standish *Blackb* 78-81; P-in-c N Somercotes *Linc* 81-82; P-in-c S Somercotes 81-82; V Somercotes 82-85; R Binbrook Gp from 85. *The Rectory, Louth Road, Binbrook, Lincoln LN8 6BJ* Tel (01472) 398227 Fax 399547 E-mail priest1@compuserve.com

WALKER, Canon Walter Stanley. b 21. AKC42. Cuddesdon Coll 42. **d** 44 **p** 45. C Southport All SS *Liv* 44-47; Miss to Seamen 47-48; C-in-c Kelsall CD *Ches* 48-53; V Birkenhead St Mary w St Paul 53-61; Chapl Barony Hosp Nantwich 61-66; R Wistaston 61-66; R Bromborough 66-77; R Wallasey St Hilary 77-86; RD Wallasey 77-86; Hon Can Ches Cathl 80-86; rtd 86; Perm to Offic *Ches* from 86. *41 Seabank Road, Wirral CH60 4SN* Tel 0151-342 6543

WALKEY, Malcolm Gregory Taylor. b 44. Lon Univ. Kelham Th Coll 63. **d** 68 **p** 69. C Oadby *Leic* 68-72; TV Corby SS Pet and Andr w Gt and Lt Oakley *Pet* 72-79; R Ashton w Hartwell 79-86; TR Halesworth w Linstead, Chediston, Holton etc *St E* 86-91; P-in-c Laxfield 93-01; rtd 01; Perm to Offic *St E* from 02. *4 Church View, Holton, Halesworth IP19 8PB* Tel (01986) 872594

WALKLATE, Keith. b 46. FCIB MIEx FRSA. Ox Min Course 92. **d** 95 **p** 96. NSM Wykeham *Ox* from 95; CME Adv 96-97. *Holly Tree House, 17 Old Glebe, Upper Tadmarton, Banbury OX15 5TH* Tel (01295) 780273 Fax 780834 E-mail keithwalklate@btinternet.com

WALL, Colin. b 52. Hull Univ BEd74 Humberside Coll of Educn BA83. NEOC 02. **d** 05. NSM Hedon w Paull *York* from 05. *430 James Reckitt Avenue, Hull HU8 0JA* Tel (01482) 377041 E-mail colin@wal.karoo.co.uk

WALL, Canon David Oliver. b 39. TD JP. Bps' Coll Cheshunt 62. **d** 65 **p** 66. C Lt Ilford St Mich *Chelmsf* 65-68; CF 68-73; R Sudbourne w Orford *St E* 73-76; R Orford w Sudbourne and Chillesford w Butley 76-79; P-in-c Iken 76-79; R Drinkstone 79-82; R Rattlesden 79-82; R Chedburgh w Depden, Rede and Hawkedon 82-99; Sen Chapl ACF from 88; Chapl to Suffolk Fire Service *St E* 91-03; Hon Can St E Cathl 96-00; rtd 00; Perm to Offic *Ely* from 01. *Orford House, 43 Corsbie Close, Bury St Edmunds IP33 3ST* Tel (01284) 723232

WALL, Miss Elizabeth Anne. b 51. Birm Univ BDS73. WMMTC 97. **d** 00 **p** 01. NSM Lich St Chad *Lich* from 00. *Gaia Cottage, 15 Gaia Lane, Lichfield WS13 7LW* Tel (01543) 254891 Mobile 07711-557770 E-mail elizabeth.wall@9damstreet.co.uk

✠**WALL, The Rt Revd Eric St Quintin.** b 15. BNC Ox BA37 MA46. Wells Th Coll 37. **d** 38 **p** 39 **c** 72. C Boston *Linc* 38-41; Chapl RAFVR 41-45; V Sherston Magna w Easton Grey *Bris* 44-53; RD Malmesbury 51-53; V Cricklade w Latton 53-60; Bp's Chapl and Dioc Adv in Chr Stewardship 60-66; Hon Can Bris Cathl 60-72; V Westbury-on-Trym St Alb 66-72; RD Clifton 67-72; Suff Bp Huntingdon *Ely* 72-80; Can Res Ely Cathl 72-80; rtd 80; Perm to Offic *Nor* from 80; *St E* from 81; *Ely* 86-00; Hon Asst Bp Glouc from 00. *Forest House, Cinderhill, Coleford GL16 8HQ* Tel (01594) 832424

WALL, John Caswallen. b 60. York Univ BA83 MA85 Ox Univ BA89. St Steph Ho Ox 86. **d** 89 **p** 90. C Ifield *Chich* 89-94; C Brighton St Pet and St Nic w Chpl Royal 94-97; C Brighton St Pet w Chpl Royal 97-98; TV Newbury *Ox* from 98. *St George's Vicarage, 206 Andover Road, Newbury RG14 6NU* Tel (01635) 41249 Fax 524994 E-mail stgeorge@easynet.co.uk

WALL, Martyn Philip Lucas. b 17. Hertf Coll Ox BA38 MA43 Open Univ BA95. Wells Th Coll 69. **d** 71 **p** 72. C Highworth w Sevenhampton and Inglesham etc *Bris* 71-74; R Wick w Doynton 74-85; rtd 85; Perm to Offic *Sarum* from 85. *9 Woburn Close, Trowbridge BA14 9TJ* Tel (01225) 754323

WALL, Nicholas John. b 46. MBE02 TD01. Brasted Th Coll 69 Trin Coll Bris 71. **d** 73 **p** 74. C Morden *S'wark* 73-78; R Dunkeswell and Dunkeswell Abbey *Ex* 78-83; V Sheldon 78-83; P-in-c Luppitt 81-83; V Dunkeswell, Sheldon and Luppitt 83-03; V Dunkeswell, Luppitt, Sheldon and Upottery from 03; CF(V) from 87. *The Rectory, Dunkeswell, Honiton EX14 4RE* Tel (01404) 891243 E-mail nickandgrete@hotmail.com

WALL, Mrs Pauline Ann. b 39. Bris Sch of Min 87. **dss** 85 **d** 87 **p** 94. Bris Ch the Servant Stockwood *Bris* 85-99; Hon Par Dn 87-94; Hon C 94-99; Chapl St Brendan's Sixth Form Coll 90-99; rtd 99; Perm to Offic *Bris* from 99. *41 Ladman Road, Bristol BS14 8QD* Tel (01275) 833083

WALL, Philip. *See* WALL, Martyn Philip Lucas

WALL, Richard David. b 78. Ch Ch Ox BA99. St Steph Ho Ox 00. **d** 02 **p** 03. C Bocking St Mary *Chelmsf* 02-05; USA from 05. *St Clement's Church, 2013 Appletree Street, Philadelphia, PA 19103, USA* Tel (001) (215) 563 1876 Fax 563 7627 E-mail frrichardwall@aol.com

WALL, Robert William. b 52. Ex Coll Ox MA Ex Univ BPhil77. Trin Coll Bris 80. **d** 83 **p** 84. C Blackb Sav *Blackb* 83-86; C

Edgware *Lon* 86-89; C Barnsbury 89-90; TV 90-99; V Dalston St Mark w St Bart from 99. *St Mark's Vicarage, Sandringham Road, London E8 2LL* Tel (020) 7254 4741 E-mail rob.wall@care4free.net

WALLACE, Preb Alastair Robert. b 50. St Cath Coll Cam BA71 MA75 Lon Univ BD75. Trin Coll Bris 72. **d** 75 **p** 76. C Ex St Leon w H Trin *Ex* 75-79; Chapl Ridley Hall Cam 79-80; R Bath St Mich w St Paul *B & W* 83-96; RD Bath 90-96; Sub-Dean Wells 96-99; Hon Asst Dioc Missr from 96; Preb Wells Cathl from 96; TR Ilminster and Distr from 99. *The Rectory, Court Barton, Ilminster TA19 0DU* Tel (01460) 52610 E-mail alastair.wallace@btinternet.com

WALLACE, Mrs Ann. b 29. CITC 92. **d** 95 **p** 96. Aux Min Abbeyleix w Ballyroan etc *C & O* from 95. *Knapton, Abbeyleix, Portlaoise, Co Laois, Irish Republic* Tel (00353) (502) 31010

WALLACE, Mrs Brenda Claire. b 52. Linc Th Coll 73 S'wark Ord Course 78. **dss** 80 **d** 87 **p** 94. Sutton at Hone *Roch* 80-83; Borstal 83-87; Hon Par Dn 87-89; HM Pris Cookham Wood 83-89; Asst Chapl 87-89; NSM Stansted Mountfitchet *Chelmsf* 89-96; NSM Stansted Mountfitchet w Birchanger and Farnham 97; C Hutton from 97. *The Rectory, 175 Rayleigh Road, Hutton, Brentwood CM13 1LX* Tel (01277) 215115 Fax 263407 E-mail huttonchurch@zetnet.co.uk

WALLACE, David Alexander Rippon. b 39. CEng MIEE. Ox Min Course 94. **d** 96 **p** 97. NSM Haddenham w Cuddington, Kingsey etc *Ox* 96-97; NSM Worminghall w Ickford, Oakley and Shabbington from 97. *11 Station Road, Haddenham, Aylesbury HP17 8AN* Tel (01844) 290670 E-mail revd@wallaces.org

WALLACE, Mrs Edwina Margaret. b 49. EMMTC 00. **d** 03 **p** 04. C Broughton Astley and Croft w Stoney Stanton *Leic* from 03. *The Rectory, Nock Verges, Stoney Stanton, Leicester LE9 4LR* Tel (01455) 271234 Mobile 07766-714261 E-mail em.wallace@btopenworld.com

WALLACE, Godfrey Everingham. *See* EVERINGHAM, Georgina Wendy

WALLACE, James Stephen. b 60. Plymouth Poly BSc81 St Martin's Coll Lanc 90. Westcott Ho Cam 96. **d** 98 **p** 99. C Newport Pagnell w Lathbury and Moulsoe *Ox* 98-02; USPG Sri Lanka from 02. *Devasarana Development Centre, Ibbagamuwa, Sri Lanka*

WALLACE, Julie Michele. b 58. Lon Univ Dip Counselling 88 Cert Counselling 92 Ox Univ MTh93 Univ Coll Lon MSc02. CA Tr Coll 77. **d** 88 **p** 94. Chapl Middx Poly *Lon* 86-90; Voc Adv CA 90-92; Member CA Counselling Service 92-96; Hon C Bellingham St Dunstan *S'wark* 91-96; TV Kidbrooke St Jas 96-99; Perm to Offic 99-01; Hon C Croydon Woodside 01-03. *6 Pantanas, Treharris CF46 5BN*

✠**WALLACE, The Rt Revd Martin William.** b 48. K Coll Lon BD70 AKC70. St Aug Coll Cant 70. **d** 71 **p** 72 **c** 03. C Attercliffe *Sheff* 71-74; C New Malden and Coombe *S'wark* 74-77; V Forest Gate St Mark *Chelmsf* 77-93; RD Newham 82-91; P-in-c Forest Gate Em w Upton Cross 85-89; Hon Can Chelmsf Cathl 89-03; P-in-c Forest Gate All SS 91-93; Dioc ACUPA Link Officer 91-97; P-in-c Bradwell on Sea 93-97; P-in-c St Lawrence 93-97; Ind Chapl Maldon and Dengie Deanery 93-97; Adn Colchester 97-03; Bp's Adv for Hosp Chapl 97-03; Suff Bp Selby *York* from 03. *Bishop's House, Barton-le-Street, Malton YO17 6PL* Tel (01653) 627191 Fax 627193 E-mail bishselby@clara.net

WALLACE (née ALEXANDER), Mrs Nancy Joan. b 42. Roehampton Inst TCert64 N Lon Univ CertCC70 PQCSW97 Ox Brookes Univ BA97. St Alb and Ox Min Course CBTS95. **d** 98 **p** 99. NSM Worminghall w Ickford, Oakley and Shabbington *Ox* 98-03. *11 Station Road, Haddenham, Aylesbury HP17 8AN* Tel (01844) 290670 Fax as telephone E-mail nancy@wallace.nildram.co.uk

WALLACE, Nicholas Robert. b 56. Trin Coll Bris DipHE95. **d** 95 **p** 96. C Fishponds St Jo *Bris* 95-98; P-in-c Barton Hill St Luke w Ch Ch 98-99; P-in-c Barton Hill St Luke w Ch Ch and Moorfields 99-00; R Binstead *Portsm* from 00; V Havenstreet St Pet from 00. *The Rectory, Pitts Lane, Ryde PO33 3SU* Tel (01983) 562890

WALLACE, Raymond Sherwood. b 28. Selw Coll Dunedin (NZ). **d** 52 **p** 54. C Roslyn New Zealand 52-54; C Invercargill 54-55; P-in-c Waitaki 55-58; C St Pancras H Cross w St Jude and St Pet *Lon* 58-64; C N Harrow St Alb 64-67; V Stroud Green H Trin 67-79; V Penwerris *Truro* 79-84; R Wymington w Podington *St Alb* 84-87; rtd 87; Perm to Offic *St Alb* from 87. *141 Dunsmore Road, Luton LU1 5JX* Tel (01582) 455882

WALLACE, Richard Colin. b 39. Mert Coll Ox BA61 MA64. St Chad's Coll Dur 69. **d** 71 **p** 72. Tutor St Chad's Coll Dur 71-72; P-in-c Kimblesworth *Dur* 72-74; Chapl Bradf Univ *Bradf* 74-79; C Bingley All SS 79-80; TV 80-89; V Earby from 89; P-in-c Kelbrook from 01; RD Skipton 00-05. *The Vicarage, Skipton Road, Earby, Barnoldswick BB18 6JL* Tel (01282) 842291

WALLACE, Richard Ernest. b 35. Ridley Coll Melbourne ThL61 ACT 61. **d** 61 **p** 62. Australia 61-67 and from 69; C Balwyn St Barn 61-62; C S Yarra 62-64; C Bentleigh St Jo 64-65; I Northcote 65-66; C Ipswich St Fran *St E* 67-69; I Belgrave 69-79; Dir Angl Renewal Min 79-82; I Blackburn St Jo 83-92; I Syndal St Jas 92-95; Sen Assoc P Glen Waverley 95-97. *49 Patterson Street, Ringwood East, Vic, Australia 3155* Tel (0061) (3) 9870 1000 Mobile 419-314060 Fax (3) 9870 1821 E-mail rwallace@melbpc.org.au

WALLACE, Richard John. b 56. Coll of Resurr Mirfield. **d** 82 **p** 83. C Catford St Laur *S'wark* 82-85; C Bellingham St Dunstan 85-87; V 87-95; TR Stanley *Dur* 95-99; V Cockerton from 99. *St Mary's Vicarage, Newton Lane, Cockerton, Darlington DL3 9EX* Tel (01325) 367092

WALLACE, Richard Samuel. b 17. TCD BA39 MA53. **d** 41 **p** 42. C Belfast St Steph *Conn* 41-43; C Hammersmith St Pet *Lon* 43-44; India 44-51; Perivale *Lon* 51-54; V Notting Hill St Mark 54-60; V Teddington St Mark 60-83; rtd 83; Perm to Offic *Ex* from 83. *St Christopher, 17 Hartley Road, Exmouth EX8 2SG* Tel (01395) 279595

WALLACE, Robert. b 52. Sussex Univ BSc73 Nottm Univ DipTh75. Linc Th Coll 73. **d** 76 **p** 77. C Plaistow St Mary *Roch* 76-79; C Dartford H Trin 79-83; V Borstal 83-89; Chapl The Foord Almshouses 83-89; Chapl HM Pris Cookham Wood 83-89; P-in-c Farnham *Chelmsf* 89-96; V Stansted Mountfitchet 89-96; R Stansted Mountfitchet w Birchanger and Farnham 97; R Hutton from 97. *The Rectory, 175 Rayleigh Road, Hutton, Brentwood CM13 1LX* Tel (01277) 215115 Fax 263407 E-mail huttonchurch@zetnet.co.uk

WALLER, Annalu. b 63. Cape Town Univ BSc83 MSc88 Dundee Univ PhD92. TISEC 01. **d** 04 **p** 05. NSM Dundee St Marg *Bre* 04-05; C from 05. *9 Invergowrie Drive, Dundee DD2 1RD* Tel (01382) 644570

WALLER, David Arthur. b 61. Leeds Univ BA83. Chich Th Coll 89. **d** 91 **p** 92. C Aldwick *Chich* 91-95; TV Crawley 95-00; V Walthamstow St Sav *Chelmsf* from 00. *St Saviour's Vicarage, 210 Markhouse Road, London E17 8EP* Tel (020) 8520 2036 E-mail d.a.waller@btinternet.com

WALLER, David James. b 58. Whitelands Coll Lon BA85 K Coll Lon MA95. Ripon Coll Cuddesdon 85. **d** 88 **p** 89. C Tettenhall Regis *Lich* 88-91; Chapl Univ of Greenwich *S'wark* 92-97; P-in-c Yiewsley *Lon* 97-01; TR Plymstock and Hooe *Ex* from 01. *The Rectory, 5 Cobb Lane, Plymstock, Plymouth PL9 9BQ* Tel (01752) 403126 E-mail david@waller2000.freeserve.co.uk

WALLER, Derek James Keith. b 54. Em Coll Cam BA75 PGCE76. Trin Coll Bris 88. **d** 91 **p** 92. C Church Stretton *Heref* 91-95; R Appleby Gp *Leic* 95-04; P-in-c Rushden St Pet from 04. *St Peter's Vicarage, 12 Kensington Close, Rushden NN10 6RR* Tel (01933) 356398 E-mail waller@leicester.anglican.org

WALLER, Mrs Elizabeth Alison. b 49. Open Univ BA89 Univ of Cen England in Birm MA99 Wolfs Coll Cam PGCE91. EAMTC 02. **d** 05. NSM Oundle w Ashton and Benefield w Glapthorn *Pet* from 05. *Priory Cottage, 40 Church Street, Stilton, Peterborough PE7 3RF* Tel (01733) 242412 E-mail lizwaller@waitrose.com

WALLER, Ms Elizabeth Jean. b 58. Keswick Hall Coll BEd BTh. Linc Th Coll 84. **d** 87 **p** 94. Par Dn Mile End Old Town H Trin *Lon* 87-90; Manna Chr Cen 90-91; Chapl LSE *Lon* 91-96; Hon C Soho St Anne w St Thos and St Pet 91-96; CARA from 96; NSM Notting Dale St Clem w St Mark and St Jas *Lon* 96-99; Perm to Offic 99-00. *55 Browning Avenue, Hanwell W7 1AX* Tel (020) 8578 3827

WALLER, Gordon Robert. b 50. Jes Coll Cam BA72 MA75. Dioc OLM tr scheme 00. **d** 03. OLM Tooting All SS *S'wark* from 03. *131 Ribblesdale Road, London SW16 6SP* Tel (020) 8769 6733 E-mail baldypevsner@yahoo.co.uk

WALLER, John. b 60. Man Univ BA84. St Jo Coll Nottm 85. **d** 87 **p** 88. C Chorlton-cum-Hardy St Clem *Man* 87-90; R Openshaw 90-95; Chapl Ancoats Hosp Man 93-95; TV Watling Valley *Ox* 95-96; TR 96-03; R Brickhills and Stoke Hammond from 03. *Kingswood, Pound Hill, Great Brickhill, Milton Keynes MK17 9AS* Tel (01525) 261062 E-mail john.waller1@virgin.net

WALLER, John Pretyman. b 41. Sarum Th Coll 68. **d** 71 **p** 72. C Ipswich St Jo *St E* 71-74; R Waldringfield w Hemley 74-78; P-in-c Newbourn 74-78; R Waldringfield w Hemley and Newbourn from 78. *The Rectory, Mill Road, Waldringfield, Woodbridge IP12 4PY* Tel (01473) 736247

✠**WALLER, The Rt Revd John Stevens.** b 24. Peterho Cam BA48 MA53. Wells Th Coll 48. **d** 50 **p** 51 **c** 79. C Hillingdon St Jo *Lon* 50-52; C Twerton *B & W* 52-55; C-in-c Weston-super-Mare St Andr Bournville CD 55-59; V Weston-super-Mare St Andr Bournville 59-60; R Yarlington 60-63; Youth Chapl 60-63; Tr Officer C of E Youth Coun 63-67; V Frindsbury w Upnor *Roch* 67-72; P-in-c Strood St Fran 67-72; P-in-c Strood St Mary 67-72; P-in-c Strood St Nic 67-72; TR Strood 72-73; RD Strood 67-73; R Harpenden St Nic *St Alb* 73-79; Suff Bp Stafford *Lich* 79-87; Asst Bp B & W 87-04; P-in-c Long Sutton w Long Load 87-88; TV Langport Area Chs 88-89; rtd 89. *102 Harnham Road, Salisbury SP2 8JW* Tel (01722) 329739 Fax 411492 E-mail jwaller@talk21.com

WALLER, Canon John Watson. b 35. Qu Mary Coll Lon BSc57. Wycliffe Hall Ox 58. **d** 61 **p** 62. C Pudsey St Lawr *Bradf* 61-65; V

74-82; V Mortomley St Sav *Sheff* 65-74; V Pudsey St Lawr and St Paul *Bradf* 82-88; Hon Can Bradf Cathl 84-88; RD Calverley 84-88; V Kingston upon Hull H Trin *York* 88-01; AD Cen and N Hull 94-99; Can and Preb York Minster 95-04; RD Hull 96-00; rtd 01; Perm to Offic *York* from 04. *7 Seven Wells, Amotherby, Malton YO17 6TT* Tel (01653) 691388
E-mail johnandmarywaller@hotmail.com

WALLER, Orlando Alfred. b 12. St Aid Birkenhead 39. **d** 41 **p** 42. C Birkenhead St Pet *Ches* 41-42; C Crewe St Barn 42-45; C Gatley 45-49; Min Heald Green St Cath CD 49-51; V Haslington w Crewe Green 51-54; Australia 54-59; V Runcorn St Jo Weston *Ches* 59-63; V Merrington *Dur* 63-70; P-in-c Bearpark 70-71; V 71-76; rtd 77. *22 Thornley Close, Broom Park, Durham DH7 7NN*

WALLER, Philip Thomas. b 56. Ex Coll Ox BA78 MA88. St Jo Coll Dur BA87. **d** 88 **p** 89. C Enfield St Andr *Lon* 88-91; C Belper *Derby* 91-95; P-in-c Oakwood from 95. *The Vicarage, 239 Morley Road, Oakwood, Derby DE21 4TB* Tel (01332) 667803 E-mail waller.family@clara.co.uk

WALLES, Bruce Andrew. b 54. Coll of Resurr Mirfield 90. **d** 92 **p** 93. C Maidstone St Martin *Cant* 92-96; TV Banbury *Ox* 96-98; V Banbury St Leon 98-04; V Aintree St Giles w St Pet *Liv* from 04. *St Giles's Vicarage, 132 Aintree Lane, Liverpool L10 8LE* Tel 0151-476 5554 E-mail wallba@ntlworld.com

WALLEY, Peter Francis. b 60. Bris Univ BSc82 CEng89 MICE89. Trin Coll Bris 96. **d** 98 **p** 99. C Ex St Jas *Ex* 98-01; Asst Chapl Brussels *Eur* 01-05; Bp's Dom Chapl *Lich* from 05. *Bishop's House, 22 The Close, Lichfield WS13 7LG* Tel (01543) 306000 Fax 306009 E-mail peter.walley@lichfield.anglican.org

WALLING, Mrs Carolyn. b 47. Rolle Coll CertEd69. Episc Div Sch Cam Mass MDiv87. **d** 86 **p** 87. Saudi Arabia 89; USA 94-96; Par Dn Mottingham St Andr *S'wark* 90; Par Dn Battersea St Mary 91-94; C Lee Gd Shep w St Pet 96. *50 Queen of Denmark Court, Finland Street, London SE16 1TB* Tel (020) 7231 3873 Fax as telephone

WALLINGTON, Martin John. b 59. St Alb and Ox Min Course 95. **d** 98 **p** 99. NSM Chorleywood St Andr *St Alb* 98-03; P-in-c Wooburn *Ox* from 03. *Wooburn Vicarage, Windsor Hill, Wooburn Green, High Wycombe HP10 0EH* Tel (01628) 521209

WALLINGTON, Paul. b 62. Birm Univ BCom83 ACA86. Trin Coll Bris BA94. **d** 94 **p** 95. C Chorley St Laur *Blackb* 94-97; C Darwen St Pet w Hoddlesden 97-98; TV 98-00; rtd 00. *551 Darwen Road, Dunscar, Bolton BL7 9RT* Tel (01204) 308637 E-mail thewallingtons@hotmail.com

WALLIS, Benjamin John. b 55. Wimbledon Sch of Art BA79. Chich Th Coll 92. **d** 94 **p** 95. C Battersea Ch Ch and St Steph *S'wark* 94-98; C Wood Green St Mich w Bounds Green St Gabr etc *Lon* 98-03; V Barkingside St Geo *Chelmsf* from 03. *St George's Vicarage, Woodford Avenue, Ilford IG2 6XQ* Tel (020) 8550 4149

WALLIS, David Peter. b 72. Ripon Coll Cuddesdon BTh03. **d** 03 **p** 04. C Eastbourne St Mary *Chich* from 03. *6 Bay Pond Road, Eastbourne BN21 1HX* Tel (01323) 733159

WALLIS, Ian George. b 57. Sheff Univ BA79 PhD92 St Edm Ho Cam MLitt87. Ridley Hall Cam 88. **d** 90 **p** 91. C Armthorpe *Sheff* 90-92; Chapl SS Coll Cam 92-95; Lic to Offic *Ely* 93-95; Hon C Chesterton Gd Shep 95; R Houghton le Spring *Dur* from 95; AD Houghton from 04. *The Rectory, Dairy Lane, Houghton le Spring DH4 5BH* Tel 0191-584 2198 Fax 512 1685

WALLIS, John Anthony. b 36. St Pet Coll Ox BA60 MA65. Clifton Th Coll 60. **d** 62 **p** 63. C Blackpool St Mark *Blackb* 62-65; C Leeds St Geo *Ripon* 65-69; Korea 69-74; Nat Sec (Scotland) OMF 75-78; Home Dir OMF 78-89; Hon C Sevenoaks St Nic *Roch* 78-89; Chapl The Hague *Eur* 89-95; V Northwood Em *Lon* 95-01; rtd 01; Perm to Offic *Nor* from 03. *Church Cottage, 61 Gayton Road, Grimston, King's Lynn PE32 1BG* Tel (01485) 600336 E-mail johna.wallis@virgin.net

WALLIS, Paul Anthony. b 65. Nottm Univ BTh90. St Jo Coll Nottm 87. **d** 90 **p** 91. C Somers Town *Lon* 90-93; P-in-c Southsea St Pet *Portsm* 93-94; Chapl Generation Min 95-00; Chapl-Gen from 02; R Kambah St Steph and Chapl Aus Nat Univ 00-02. *Jesus House, 26 Belmont Street, Southsea PO5 1ND* Tel (023) 9229 8019 E-mail ministry@paulwallis.com

WALLIS, Peter. b 42. K Coll Lon MB, BS68 MRCS AKC68. STETS 98. **d** 01. NSM Clymping and Yapton w Ford *Chich* from 01. *Chanters, 3 Second Avenue, Felpham, Bognor Regis PO22 7LJ* Tel (01243) 584080 Mobile 07885-542651
E-mail revdocpeterw@aol.com

WALLIS, Raymond Christopher. b 38. Lon Univ DipTh61 Moor Park Coll Farnham 62. Sarum Th Coll 63. **d** 66 **p** 67. C Allerton *Bradf* 66-68; C Langley Marish *Ox* 68-69; C Caister *Nor* 69-73; P-in-c E w W Bradenham 73-80; R Outwell *Ely* 80-84; R Upwell St Pet 80-84; V Bishopstone *Chich* 84-97; rtd 97; Perm to Offic *Chich* from 97. *The Moorings, Rattle Road, Westham, Pevensey BN24 5DS* Tel (01323) 766247

WALLIS, Roland Seabon. b 17. MBE44. Lon Univ BSc38 Ex Univ BSc57. St Aug Coll Cant 75. **d** 77 **p** 78. NSM Whitstable *Cant* 77-87; rtd 87; Perm to Offic *Cant* 87-01. *Appletree House Nursing Home, 352 Burton Road, Derby DE23 6AF*

WALLMAN-GIRDLESTONE, Jane Elizabeth. b 61. Homerton Coll Cam BEd83 Bell Educational Trust CertTESOL85 Open Univ AdDipEd88 Drama Studio Lon Dip Theatre88. St Steph Ho Ox 89 Sarum & Wells Th Coll BTh92. **d** 93 **p** 94. C Woodbridge St Mary *St E* 93-96; V Ipswich St Thos 96-00; Dir of Past Studies and Adv for Women's Min St Mich Coll Llandaff 00-02. *Isle View, The Clattach, Allanfeam, Inverness IV2 7HZ* Tel (01463) 230708 E-mail jane@sharing-space.co.uk

WALLS, Michael Peter. b 38. Cape Town Univ BA57 Lon Univ DipTh61. Wells Th Coll 59. **d** 61 **p** 62. C Morecambe St Barn *Blackb* 61-64; C Birm St Paul *Birm* 64-66; Ind Chapl 64-74; V Temple Balsall 66-74; Chapl Wroxall Abbey Sch 72-74; V Kings Heath *Birm* 74-76; Hon C Bordesley St Benedict 76-78; Sen Chapl Oakham Sch 78-83; P-in-c Leic St Sav *Leic* 83-85; P-in-c Knossington and Cold Overton 85-87; P-in-c Owston and Withcote 85-87; V Tilton w Lowesby 85-87; P-in-c 87; V Whatborough Gp 87-90; Bp's Adv Relns w People of Other Faiths 89-93; Hon Can Leic Cathl 89-93; V Leic St Mary 90-93; rtd 93; Perm to Offic *Ban* from 02. *Gwynt y Mor, 1A Bro Cymerau, Pwllheli LL53 5PY* Tel (01758) 613495
E-mail michael.w@tinyworld.co.uk.

WALLS, Roland Charles. b 17. CCC Cam BA48 MA52. Kelham Th Coll 34. **d** 40 **p** 41. C Manston *Ripon* 40-43; C Sheff St Cecilia Parson Cross *Sheff* 43-45; Perm to Offic *Ely* 45-48; Fell CCC Cam 48-62; Chapl 52-55; Dean of Chpl 55-58; Lect Kelham Th Coll 48-51; Bp's Dom Chapl *Ely* 51-52; Select Preacher Cam Univ 56; Select Preacher Ox Univ 77; Can Res Sheff Cathl *Sheff* 58-62; Hon C-in-c Roslin (Rosslyn Chpl) *Edin* 62-69; Lect Div Edin Univ 63-77; Community of the Transfiguration from 65. *23 Manse Road, Roslin EH25 9LF*

WALMISLEY, Andrew John. b 55. Ex Univ BA75. Ridley Hall Cam 76. **d** 78 **p** 79. C W Brompton St Mary w St Pet *Lon* 78-81; USA from 81. *2601 Derby Street, Berkeley, CA 94705, USA*
E-mail walmisley@aol.com

WALMSLEY, Derek. b 57. Oak Hill Th Coll DipHE91. **d** 91 **p** 92. C Bletchley *Ox* 91-95; C Utley *Bradf* 95-00; V from 00. *St Mark's Vicarage, Greenhead Road, Keighley BD20 6ED* Tel (01535) 607003

WALMSLEY, Jane. *See* LLOYD, Patricia Jane

WALMSLEY, John William. b 37. Hull Univ BA71 MA73 PhD81. Wycliffe Hall Ox 71. **d** 72 **p** 73. C Clifton *York* 72-74; C Acomb St Steph 74-76; P-in-c Newton upon Ouse 76-81; P-in-c Shipton w Overton 76-81; V York St Thos w St Maurice 81-89; V Barkingside St Laur *Chelmsf* 89-92; Dir Children in Distress 92-01; rtd 01. *2930 East Higgins Lake Drive, Roscommon, MI 48653, USA*

WALMSLEY-McLEOD, Paul Albert. b 56. St Cuth Soc Dur BA82 Cam Univ CertEd83. Westcott Ho Cam 85. **d** 87 **p** 88. C Gt Bookham *Guildf* 87-90; Asst Chapl St Chris Hospice Lon 90-93; Soc Care Team Member Phoenix Ho Fountain Project 93-95; C Catford (Southend) and Downham *S'wark* 95-96; TV 96-99; P-in-c Downham St Barn 00-02; R Friern Barnet St Jas *Lon* from 02. *The Rectory, 147 Friern Barnet Lane, London N20 0NP* Tel (020) 8445 7844
E-mail pawm_friernbarnet@hotmail.com

WALNE, John Clifford. b 29. Wycliffe Hall Ox. **d** 87 **p** 88. NSM Hedsor and Bourne End *Ox* 87-88; Hon C Lezayre St Olave Ramsey *S & M* 88-92; Hon C Kirkbride 88-92; P-in-c Berrington w Betton Strange *Heref* 92-97; rtd 97. *2 Bell Close, Beaconsfield HP9 1AT* Tel (01494) 670120

WALROND-SKINNER, Susan Mary. *See* PARFITT, Susan Mary

WALSALL, Archdeacon of. *See* JACKSON, The Ven Robert William

WALSER, Emil Jonathan. b 16. St Jo Coll Dur LTh38 BA39 MA43. Oak Hill Th Coll 35. **d** 39 **p** 40. C Holloway St Mary Magd *Lon* 39-42; C Pudsey St Lawr *Bradf* 42-46; R Whalley Range St Edm *Man* 46-52; V Mackworth All SS *Derby* 52-65; P-in-c Kirk Langley 57-59; R 59-65; V Baslow 65-82; RD Bakewell and Eyam 78-81; rtd 82; Perm to Offic *York* from 82. *2 Almond Grove, Filey YO14 9EH* Tel (01723) 515582

WALSER (née SHIELS), Mrs Rosalinde Cameron. b 47. Edin Univ MA68 Moray Ho Coll of Educn PGCE69. N Ord Course 92. **d** 95 **p** 97. NSM Scarborough St Mary w Ch Ch and H Apostles *York* 95-97; Chapl St Cath Hospice Scarborough 95-97; Chapl Scarborough Coll 95-97; P-in-c E Ayton *York* from 97. *29 Sea Cliff Road, Scarborough YO11 2XU* Tel (01723) 372382

WALSH, Bertram William Nicholas. b 21. TCD BA44. CITC 46. **d** 46 **p** 47. C Dublin St Pet w St Matthias *D & G* 46-47; Min Can St Patr Cathl Dublin 47-49; C Dublin St Jas *D & G* 47-49; Res Preacher Cork Cathl *C, C & R* 49-52; C Dublin St Bart *D & G* 52-54; Clerical V Ch Ch Cathl Dublin 54-58; Chapl St Columba's Coll Dub 60-87; rtd 87. *14 Linden Lea Park, Stillorgan, Co Dublin, Irish Republic* Tel (00353) (1) 288 7641

WALSH, David Christopher. b 59. Warwick Univ BA81 St Jo Coll Nottm BA83. Ripon Coll Cuddesdon 00. **d** 02 **p** 03. C Greenwich St Alfege *S'wark* from 02. *88 Ashburnham Grove, London SE10 8UJ* Tel (020) 8691 6856 Mobile 07957-656643
E-mail david@walsh.name

✠**WALSH, The Rt Revd Geoffrey David Jeremy.** b 29. Pemb Coll Cam BA53 MA58. Linc Th Coll 53. **d** 55 **p** 56 **c** 86. C Southgate Ch Ch *Lon* 55-58; SCM Sec Cam 58-61; C Cambridge Gt St Mary w St Mich *Ely* 58-61; V Moorfields *Bris* 61-66; R Marlborough *Sarum* 66-76; Can and Preb Sarum Cathl 73-76; Adn Ipswich *St E* 76-86; R Elmsett w Aldham 76-80; Suff Bp Tewkesbury *Glouc* 86-95; rtd 95; Perm to Offic *St E* from 95. *6 Warren Lane, Martlesham Heath, Ipswich IP5 3SH* Tel (01473) 620797

WALSH, Geoffrey Malcolm. b 46. Sarum & Wells Th Coll 82. **d** 84 **p** 85. C Wellington and Distr *B & W* 84-87; TV Axminster, Chardstock, Combe Pyne and Rousdon *Ex* 87-90; Chapl RN 90-94; R Huntspill *B & W* from 94. *The Rectory, Church Road, West Huntspill, Highbridge TA9 3RN* Tel (01278) 793950 Fax as telephone E-mail g.walsh1@ntlworld.co.uk

WALSH, John Alan. b 37. Chich Th Coll 63. **d** 66 **p** 67. C Wigan St Anne *Liv* 66-69; C Newport w Longford *Lich* 69-73; V Dunstall 73-83; V Rangemore 73-83; P-in-c Tatenhill 77-83; R Dunstall w Rangemore and Tatenhill 83; V Hartshill 83-03; rtd 03. *A9 Plumley Close, Vicars Cross, Chester CH3 5PD* Tel (01244) 310936

WALSH, Peter. b 64. Liv Univ BA86 Nottm Univ BTh90. Linc Th Coll 87. **d** 90 **p** 91. C Cantley *Sheff* 90-93; C Poulton-le-Fylde *Blackb* 93-95; V Blackpool St Steph 95-03; TR Ches Team *Ches* 03-05; V Ches St Oswald and St Thos from 05; Min Can Ches Cathl 04-05. *The Vicarage, 33 Abbots Grange, Chester CH2 1AJ* Tel (01244) 399990

WALSHE, Canon Brian. b 28. AKC49. St Boniface Warminster. **d** 54 **p** 55. C Southsea St Pet *Portsm* 54-57; C Portsea St Jo Rudmore 57-58; Warden Wellington Coll Miss Walworth 58-62; V Chesterfield St Aug *Derby* 62-68; R Langley Marish *Ox* 68-76; Chapl Manfield Hosp Northn 76-88; V Northampton St Alb *Pet* 76-88; Dir Mountbatten Community Trust from 76; Chief Exec Lon Youth Trust from 87; rtd 88; Perm to Offic *Pet* 88-93 and *Chich* from 93. *9/10 Warrior Court, 16 Warrior Way, St Leonards-on-Sea TN37 6BS*

WALSHE, Marie Sylvia. b 54. RGN RCNT. **d** 99 **p** 00. Aux Min Kilkeel *D & D* 99-00; Aux Min Down H Trin w Hollymount from 00; Aux Min Rathmullan w Tyrella from 00. *The Rectory, 10 Ballydonnell Road, Downpatrick BT30 8EN* E-mail kwalshe@talk21.com

WALT, Canon Trevor William. b 52. MBE03. RMN74 RNT79. Ox NSM Course 83. **d** 86 **p** 87. NSM Crowthorne *Ox* 86-89; Chapl Asst Broadmoor Hosp Crowthorne 86-89; Chapl from 89; Hon Can Ch Ch *Ox* from 00. *Broadmoor Hospital, Crowthorne RG45 7EG* Tel (01344) 773111 ext 4450

WALTER, Christopher Stuart Radclyffe. b 47. Sarum & Wells Th Coll 91. **d** 93 **p** 94. C Fakenham w Alethorpe *Nor* 93-96; P-in-c Buxton w Oxnead, Lammas and Brampton from 96; P-in-c Coltishall w Gt Hautbois and Horstead 99-05; P-in-c Marsham w Burgh-next-Aylsham from 05. *The Vicarage, Back Lane, Buxton, Norwich NR10 5HD* Tel (01603) 279394

WALTER, Donald Alex. b 34. Ripon Hall Ox 57. **d** 60 **p** 61. C Ealing St Steph Castle Hill *Lon* 60-63; Jamaica 63-80; V Twickenham Common H Trin *Lon* 81-00; rtd 00; Perm to Offic *Lon* from 03. *Ebenezer, 23 Hawley Close, Hampton TW12 3XX* Tel (020) 8941 5193 E-mail daw@maperche.co.uk

WALTER, Giles Robert. b 54. Cam Univ MA76. Cranmer Hall Dur 78. **d** 82 **p** 83. C Finchley Ch Ch *Lon* 82-86; C Cambridge H Sepulchre w All SS *Ely* 86-92; C Cambridge H Sepulchre 92-93; P-in-c Tunbridge Wells St Jo *Roch* 93-95; V from 95. *St John's Vicarage, 1 Amherst Road, Tunbridge Wells TN4 9LG* Tel (01892) 521183

WALTER, Ian Edward. b 47. Edin Univ MA69 Keble Coll Ox BA71 MA78. Cuddesdon Coll 71. **d** 73 **p** 74. C Greenock *Glas* 73-76; C Glas St Mary 76-79; Chapl Angl Students Glas 76-79; R Paisley St Barn 79-84; P-in-c Bolton St Phil *Man* 84-86; V 86-91; Dioc Ecum Officer 88-94; V Elton All SS 91-98; V Stalybridge 98-01; R Hawick *Edin* from 01. *St Cuthbert's Rectory, Rectory Close, Liddlesdale Road, Hawick TD9 0ET* Tel (01450) 372043 E-mail ian.walter@amserve.net

WALTER, Michael. b 36. AKC62. **d** 63 **p** 64. C Middlesbrough St Jo the Ev *York* 63-65; C Sherborne *Win* 65-68; C Bournemouth St Fran 68-69; Prec Newc Cathl *Newc* 69-71; C Dur St Marg *Dur* 72-74; P-in-c Deaf Hill cum Langdale 74-77; V Newington w Dairycoates *York* 77-88; Perm to Offic 88-92; C Feltham *Lon* 92-96; Perm to Offic 96-03; rtd 01. *15 Glanville Road, Bromley BR2 6LN* Tel (020) 8313 3390

WALTER, Noel. b 41. St D Coll Lamp DipTh66. **d** 66 **p** 67. C Mitcham Ascension *S'wark* 66-71; C Caterham 71-74; V Welling 74-82; C Warlingham w Chelsham and Farleigh 82-88; Chapl Warlingham Park Hosp Croydon 82-88; Chapl R Earlswood Hosp Redhill 88-90; Chapl Redhill Gen Hosp 88-91; Chapl E Surrey Hosp Redhill 88-96; Sen Chapl Gt Ormond Street Hosp for Children NHS Trust from 96; Perm to Offic *Ex* from 98. *Great Ormond Street Hospital, Great Ormond Street, London WC1N 3JH,* or *3 Carleton Villas, London NW5 2QU* Tel (020) 7405 9200, 7813 8232 *or* 7482 2133 E-mail walten@gosh.nhs.uk

WALTER, Peter John. b 44. CEng MIGasE. Chich Th Coll 80. **d** 82 **p** 83. C Leominster *Heref* 82-85; P-in-c Brimfield 85-90; P-in-c Orleton 85-90; R Orleton w Brimfield 91-95; rtd 04. *Mews Cottage, 39 West Street, Leominster HR6 8EP*

WALTER, Robin. b 37. Univ Coll Dur BA63 MA90 Linacre Coll Ox BA65 MA69. St Steph Ho Ox 63. **d** 66 **p** 68. C Peckham St Jo *S'wark* 66-69; Chapl Lon Univ *Lon* 69-70; C Dur St Marg *Dur* 70-74; R Burnmoor 74-79; Asst Master Barnard Castle Sch 79-97; NSM Barnard Castle Deanery 88-97; Hon C Whorlton *Dur* 82-88; P-in-c Redmarshall 97-01; R 01-03; P-in-c Bishopton w Gt Stainton 97-01; V 01-03; rtd 03; Perm to Offic *York* from 03 and *Worc* from 04. *The Laurels, Worcester Road, Great Witley, Worcester WR6 6HR* Tel (01299) 890190

WALTERS, Andrew Farrar. b 42. ACP67 St Luke's Coll Ex CertEd71. **d** 81 **p** 82. Hd Master and Warden St Mich Coll Tenbury 77-85; Chapl Ex Cathl Sch 85-87; Hd Master Homefield Sch Sutton 87-92; Hd Master Lich Cathl Sch 92-02; Hon C Sutton St Nic *S'wark* 87-92; Chan's V Lich Cathl *Lich* 93-02; rtd 02. *The Drey, Trallong, Brecon LD3 8HP* Tel and fax (01874) 636374 E-mail andrew.walter2@talk21.com

WALTERS, Christopher John Linley. b 24. St Pet Hall Ox BA47 MA49. Linc Th Coll 48. **d** 50 **p** 51. C Dartford Ch Ch *Roch* 50-53; C Oswestry St Oswald *Lich* 53-56; V Weston Rhyn 56-61; V Newcastle St Paul 61-70; V Pattingham 70-85; P-in-c Patshull 77-85; V Pattingham w Patshull 85-89; rtd 89; Perm to Offic *Heref* from 93. *Old School House, 19 Cardington, Church Stretton SY6 7JZ* Tel (01694) 771528

WALTERS, Christopher Rowland. b 47. Open Univ BA78 Univ of Wales PGCE94. **d** 02. Hd Master Mayflower Chr Sch Pontypool from 90; OLM Abergavenny H Trin *Mon* from 02. *Court Farm, Llanfihangel Pontymoel, Pontypool NP4 0JB* Tel (01495) 0740440 *or* 762323 Mobile 07967-945320 E-mail church@chriswalters.co.uk

WALTERS, David Michael Trenham. b 46. Open Univ BA86. St D Coll Lamp DipTh69. **d** 69 **p** 70. C Killay *S & B* 69-72; CF 72-89 and 91-01; Chapl Eagle Ho Prep Sch Crowthorne 89-91; Chapl R Memorial Chpl Sandhurst 97-01; P-in-c Llanyrnewydd *S & B* from 01. *Westwood Cottage, 65 Pennard Road, Pennard, Swansea SA3 2AD*

WALTERS, David Trevor. b 37. Ex Coll Ox BA58 MA62. St Steph Ho Ox 62. **d** 64 **p** 65. C Cardiff St Mary *Llan* 64-69; C Brecon w Battle *S & B* 69-73; Min Can Brecon Cathl 69-73; V Llanddew and Talachddu 73-78; V Cefncoed and Capel Nantddu 78-80; V Cefn Coed and Capel Nantddu w Vaynor etc 80-87; V Talgarth and Llanelieu 87-04; rtd 04. *16 Dan-y-Bryn, Glasbury, Hereford HR3 5NH* Tel (01497) 842966

WALTERS, Mrs Felicity Ann. b 56. WEMTC. **d** 01 **p** 02. C Glouc St Geo w Whaddon *Glouc* from 01. *82 Bodiam Avenue, Tuffley, Gloucester GL4 0TL* Tel (01452) 383578 E-mail felicitywalters@posthaste88.freeserve.co.uk

WALTERS, Canon Francis Raymond. b 24. Ball Coll Ox BA49 MA54. Wycliffe Hall Ox 51. **d** 53 **p** 54. C Boulton *Derby* 53-56; Lect Qu Coll Birm 56-64; Succ Birm Cathl *Birm* 56-58; C Harborne St Pet 58-64; V Leic St Nic *Leic* 64-74; Chapl Leic Univ 64-74; R Appleby 74-77; Dioc Dir of Educn 77-89; Hon Can Leic Cathl 77-91; P-in-c Swithland 77-91; rtd 91; Perm to Offic *Nor* from 91. *2 Beeston Common, Sheringham NR26 8ES* Tel (01263) 824414

WALTERS, Ian Robert. b 51. ACA75 FCA81. LNSM course 80. **d** 85 **p** 86. OLM Ingoldsby *Linc* from 85. *Dairy Farmhouse, Westby, Grantham NG33 4EA* Tel (01476) 585542 Fax 585066 E-mail ianwalters@cirebase.freeserve.co.uk

WALTERS, Ms Jennifer Betty. b 56. Birm Univ BA77. STETS. **d** 00 **p** 01. NSM Freemantle *Win* from 00. *115B Millbrook Road East, Southampton SO15 1HP* Tel (023) 8033 2613

WALTERS, John Philip Hewitt. b 50. Coll of Resurr Mirfield 72. **d** 73 **p** 74. C Llangiwg *S & B* 73-76; Min Can Brecon Cathl 76-79; C Brecon w Battle 76-79; V Merthyr Cynog and Dyffryn Honddu etc 79-83; V Llandeilo Tal-y-bont from 83. *The Vicarage, 28 Bolgoed Road, Pontardulais, Swansea SA4 8JE* Tel (01792) 882468

WALTERS, Leslie Ernest Ward. b 27. Wadh Coll Ox BA51 MA55. Ridley Hall Cam 55. **d** 57 **p** 58. C Heref St Pet w St Owen *Heref* 57-59; C Morden *S'wark* 59-61; V Felbridge 61-68; V Streatham Immanuel w St Anselm 68-81; V Cotmanhay *Derby* 81-92; Chapl Ilkeston Gen Hosp 81-88; Chapl Ilkeston Community Hosp 88-92; rtd 92; Perm to Offic *Nor* from 93. *Rokeby, 18 Taverham Road, Felthorpe, Norwich NR10 4DR* Tel (01603) 755134

WALTERS, Canon Michael William. b 39. Dur Univ BSc61. Clifton Th Coll 61. **d** 63 **p** 64. C Aldershot H Trin *Guildf* 63-66; C Upper Armley *Ripon* 66-69; NE Area Sec CPAS 69-75; V Hyde St Geo *Ches* 75-82; V Knutsford St Jo and Toft 82-97; P-in-c Congleton St Pet 97-98; TR Congleton 98-05; Hon Can Ches Cathl from 94; rtd 05; Hon C Davenham *Ches* from 05. *27 Alvanley Rise, Northwich CW9 8AY* Tel (01606) 333126

WALTERS, Nicholas Humphrey. b 45. K Coll Lon BD67 AKC67. **d** 68 **p** 69. C Weston *Guildf* 68-71; Chapl and Lect NE Surrey

Coll of Tech Ewell 71-77; Hon C Ewell 71-77; Warden Moor Park Coll Farnham 77-80; Tutor Surrey Univ *Guildf* from 80; Dir of Studies Guildf Inst from 82; Lic to Offic from 84. *9 Valley View, Godalming GU7 1RD* Tel (01483) 415106 *or* 562142

WALTERS, Peter. b 27. Leeds Univ BSc48 Univ of Wales (Abth) MSc52. Ripon Coll Cuddesdon 78. **d** 79 **p** 80. C Kingswood *Bris* 79-82; R Stanton St Quintin, Hullavington, Grittleton etc 82-88; rtd 88; Perm to Offic *Glouc* 88-97. *Holly Tree House, 12 Bethany Lane, West Cross, Swansea SA3 5TL* Tel (01792) 405197

WALTERS, Mrs Sheila Ann Beatrice. b 37. Bris Univ DipEd58. EMMTC 85. **d** 89 **p** 94. NSM Ashby-de-la-Zouch St Helen w Coleorton *Leic* 89-98; Perm to Offic 99-02; NSM Packington w Normanton-le-Heath 02-05. *Address temp unknown* E-mail churchmatters@sabwalters.co.uk

WALTHEW, Mrs Nancy Jennifer. b 39. Leeds Inst of Educn CertEd59. N Ord Course 92. **d** 95 **p** 96. NSM Wilmslow *Ches* 95-02; Perm to Offic from 04. *Ashburn, 13 Priory Road, Wilmslow SK9 5PS* Tel (01625) 525462

WALTON, Mrs Alison Claire. b 59. Homerton Coll Cam BEd82. Lon Bible Coll Oak Hill Th Coll BA90 MPhil92. **d** 92 **p** 98. C Bedford Ch Ch *St Alb* 92-94; Perm to Offic *St Alb* 94-95 and *S'well* 95-98; NSM Lenton Abbey *S'well* 98-99; Assoc Lect St Jo Coll Nottm 97-99; C Thorley *St Alb* 00-03; V Croxley Green St Oswald from 03. *St Oswald's Vicarage, 159 Baldwins Lane, Croxley Green, Rickmansworth WD3 3LL* Tel (01923) 232387 E-mail ali.walton@macunlimited.net

WALTON, Mrs Ann Beverley. b 56. Huddersfield Poly BSc78 Sheff Poly MPhil84 Coll of Ripon & York St Jo MA97. N Ord Course 00. **d** 03. C Ecclesfield *Sheff* from 03. *15 Nursery Drive, Ecclesfield, Sheffield S35 9XU* Tel 0114-234 9421 E-mail annbwalton@hotmail.com

WALTON, Brian. b 53. Sarum & Wells Th Coll 83. **d** 85 **p** 86. C Silksworth *Dur* 85-86; C Bishopwearmouth St Mich w St Hilda 86-88; Chapl RN 88-92; V Sugley *Newc* 92-95; Chapl Lemington Hosp 92-95; CF from 95. *c/o MOD Chaplains (Army)* Tel (01980) 615804 Fax 615800

WALTON, Mrs Camilla Iris. b 56. STETS 97. **d** 00 **p** 01. C Lyndhurst and Emery Down and Minstead *Win* 00-04; V Boldre w S Baddesley from 04. *The Vicarage, Pilley Hill, Pilley, Lymington SO41 5QF* Tel (01590) 677528 E-mail camillawalton@aol.com

WALTON, Frank. b 39. **d** 04. OLM Woodhorn w Newbiggin *Newc* from 04. *6 New Queen Street, Newbiggin-by-the-Sea NE64 6AZ* Tel (01670) 817568 E-mail notlaw@btopenworld.com

WALTON, The Ven Geoffrey Elmer. b 34. Dur Univ BA59. Qu Coll Birm DipTh61. **d** 61 **p** 62. C Warsop *S'well* 61-65; Dioc Youth Chapl 65-69; V Norwell 65-69; Recruitment Sec ACCM 69-75; V Weymouth H Trin *Sarum* 75-82; RD Weymouth 79-82; Can and Preb Sarum Cathl 81-00; Adn Dorset 82-00; P-in-c Witchampton and Hinton Parva, Long Crichel etc 82-96; V Witchampton, Stanbridge and Long Crichel etc 96-00; rtd 00; Perm to Offic *Sarum* from 01. *Priory Cottage, 6 Hibberds Field, Cranborne, Wimborne BH21 5QL* Tel (01725) 517167

WALTON, John Victor. b 45. Lon Univ BSc67. Linc Th Coll 79. **d** 81 **p** 82. C Stevenage St Mary Shephall *St Alb* 81-85; TV Bourne Valley *Sarum* 85-95; P-in-c Puddletown and Tolpuddle 95-02; R Puddletown, Tolpuddle and Milborne w Dewlish 02-04; rtd 04. *Serenity, Wootton Grove, Sherborne DT9 4DL* Tel (01935) 814435 E-mail life@clara.co.uk

WALTON, Kevin Anthony. b 64. St Chad's Coll Dur BA87 Dur Univ PhD99. Trin Coll Bris BA91. **d** 92 **p** 93. C Stranton *Dur* 92-95; C Hartlepool H Trin 95-96; V Sunderland St Mary and St Pet from 96; AD Wearmouth from 05. *The Clergy House, Springwell Road, Sunderland SR3 4DY* Tel 0191-528 3754 E-mail kevin.walton@durham.anglican.org

WALTON, Luke. b 64. Leeds Univ LLB87. Cranmer Hall Dur BA94. **d** 97 **p** 98. C Didsbury St Jas and Em *Man* 97-02; C Clifton Ch Ch w Em *Bris* from 02. *62 Clifton Park Road, Bristol BS8 3HN* Tel 0117-973 2128 Mobile 07799-414199 E-mail luke.w@fish.co.uk

WALTON, Mrs Marjorie Sandra. b 46. WMMTC 97. **d** 00 **p** 01. NSM The Whitacres and Shustoke *Birm* 00-04; NSM Water Orton from 04. *51 Station Road, Coleshill, Birmingham B46 2JB* Tel (01675) 464641

WALTON, Maurice James. b 31. Liv Univ BArch53 MCD54 RIBA54 MRTPI55. Wycliffe Hall Ox 93. **d** 94 **p** 95. NSM Billing *Pet* 94-97; NSM Brington w Whilton and Norton etc 97-02; rtd 02. *10A Sutton Street, Flore, Northampton NN7 4LE* E-mail wal.gill@virgin.net

WALTON, Reginald Arthur. b 40. St Jo Coll Nottm 80. **d** 81 **p** 82. C Woodthorpe *S'well* 81-84; P-in-c Nottingham St Andr 84-85; V 85-91; R Moreton *Ches* 91-01; P-in-c Whatton w Aslockton, Hawksworth, Scarrington etc *S'well* 01-05; V from 05. *The Vicarage, Main Street, Aslockton, Nottingham NG13 9AL* Tel (01949) 51040 E-mail reg@rwalton.fsworld.co.uk

WALTON, Stephen James. b 71. Mert Coll Ox BA92 MA97. Oak Hill Th Coll BA01. **d** 02 **p** 03. C Thurnby w Stoughton *Leic* from 02. *8 Sturrock Close, Thurnby, Leicester LE7 9QP* Tel 0116-241 9198 E-mail walton_stephen@hotmail.com

WALTON, Stephen John. b 55. Birm Univ BSc76 Fitzw Coll Cam BA79 MA82 Sheff Univ PhD97. Ridley Hall Cam 77. **d** 83 **p** 84. C Bebington *Ches* 83-86; Voc and Min Adv CPAS 86-92; Lic to Offic *St Alb* 86-94; Public Preacher 00-04; Bp's Dom Chapl 94-95; Lect St Jo Coll Nottm 95-99; Lect Lon Bible Coll 99-03; Sen Lect from 03. *St Oswald's Vicarage, 159 Baldwins Lane, Croxley Green, Rickmansworth WD3 3LL* Tel (01923) 232387 *or* 456326 Fax 456327 E-mail s.walton@londonbiblecollege.ac.uk

WAMBUNYA, Timothy Livingstone (Amboko). b 66. Simon of Cyrene Th Inst 93 Oak Hill Th Coll DipHE94 BA94. **d** 97 **p** 98. C Southall Green St Jo *Lon* 97-00; TV Tollington from 00. *Emmanuel Vicarage, 145 Hornsey Road, London N7 6DU* Tel (020) 7700 7110 Mobile 07770-887232 Fax (020) 7607 1737 E-mail t.wamb@virgin.net

WANDSWORTH, Archdeacon of. *See* ROBERTS, The Ven Stephen John

WANJIE, Lukas Macharia. b 50. Fitzw Coll Cam BA79 MA83 Birkbeck Coll Lon MSc98. St Paul's Coll Limuru 72 Ridley Hall Cam 76. **d** 75 **p** 76. C Uthiru St Pet Kenya 75-76; C Mill End and Heronsgate w W Hyde *St Alb* 79; V Westlands St Mark Nairobi 80-84; Prin Trin Bible Coll Nairobi 85-91; C St Alb St Steph 91-94; Perm to Offic 94-95; Race Relations Adv Croydon *S'wark* 95-01; V Bermondsey St Kath w St Bart from 01. *St Katharine's Vicarage, 90 Eugenia Road, London SE16 2RA* Tel (020) 7237 3679 E-mail lukas.wanjie@southwark.anglican.org

WANLISS, Hector. b 62. St Paul's Coll Grahamstown DipTh85. **d** 88 **p** 90. S Africa 88-97; P-in-c Aylesham w Adisham *Cant* 97-99; CF from 99. *c/o MOD Chaplains (Army)* Tel (01980) 615804 Fax 615800

WANN, Canon Denis Francis. b 27. TCD BA55 MA77 Div Test 56. **d** 56 **p** 57. C Belfast St Donard *D & D* 56-58; BCMS Tanzania 58-72; Hon Can Moro from 72; C Lurgan Ch the Redeemer *D & D* 72-73; Australia 73-91 and from 95; R Port Kembla 73-78; R Albion Park 78-84; RD Shoalhaven 79-82; Adn Wollongong and Camden 82-84; R Turramurra 84-91; I Bailieborough w Knockbride, Shercock and Mullagh *K, E & A* 91-95; rtd 95; Assoc Min Wollongong from 96. *4/28 Robertson Street, Coniston, NSW, Australia 2500* Tel (0061) (2) 4227 6906 Fax 4229 2144 E-mail dwann@telstra.easymail.com.au

WANSTALL, Noelle Margaret. *See* HALL, Canon Noelle Margaret

WANT, Mrs Angela Patricia. BA. EAMTC. **d** 05. NSM Newport and Widdington *Chelmsf* from 05. *3 Orchard Close, Newport, Saffron Walden CB11 3QT* Tel (01799) 540051

WANYOIKE, Julius Njuguna. b 70. Catholic Univ of E Africa BA99. Bp Kariuki Bible Coll 91. **d** 93 **p** 93. Kenya 93-03; Provost Thika 02-03; Perm to Offic *Birm* from 04. *2 Ripple Road, Birmingham B30 2RB* Tel 07742-975952 (mobile) E-mail wanyoikejrev@yahoo.com

WARBRICK, Quentin David. b 66. Jes Coll Ox BA88. Cranmer Hall Dur 89. **d** 92 **p** 93. C Birm St Martin w Bordesley St Andr *Birm* 92-96; C Handsworth St Jas 96-00; V Packwood w Hockley Heath from 00; AD Shirley from 05. *The Vicarage, Nuthurst Lane, Hockley Heath, Solihull B94 5RP* Tel (01564) 783121 E-mail qd@dwarbrick.fsnet.co.uk

WARBURTON, Andrew James. b 44. Oak Hill Th Coll 64. **d** 69 **p** 70. C New Milverton *Cov* 69-72; C Fulham St Matt *Lon* 72-76; C Chesham St Mary *Ox* 76-80; TV Gt Chesham 80-94; Chapl Paris St Mich *Eur* 94-97; Asst Chapl Amsterdam w Heiloo 97-00. *Burnbrae Cottage, Riccarton, Newcastleton TD9 0SN*

WARBURTON, John Bryce. b 33. St Aid Birkenhead 64. **d** 66 **p** 67. C Padiham *Blackb* 66-69; C Burnley St Pet 69-70; V Tideswell *Derby* 70-81; V Bollington St Jo *Ches* 81-91; V Capesthorne w Siddington and Marton 91-98; rtd 98; Perm to Offic *St E* from 98. *64 Friars Street, Sudbury CO10 2AG* Tel (01787) 371132

WARBURTON, Piers Eliot de Dutton. b 30. Cranmer Hall Dur BA65. **d** 65 **p** 66. C Grassendale *Liv* 65-68; Bermuda 68-71; R Sherborne *Win* 71-76; V Yateley 76-82; R Guernsey St Andr 82-89; V Hartley Wintney, Elvetham, Winchfield etc 89-98; rtd 98; Perm to Offic *Win* from 98; Clergy Widows Officer (Win Adnry) from 04. *Rowan Cottage, Station Road, Chilbolton, Stockbridge SO20 6AL* Tel (01264) 860275 E-mail b.warburton@rowan51.fsnet.co.uk

WARBURTON, Walter George. b 16. Bede Coll Dur BA40 DipTh42 MA43. **d** 41 **p** 42. C Witton *Blackb* 41-45; C Accrington Ch Ch 45-46; V Bolton St Barn *Man* 46-52; V Haslingden St Jo Stonefold *Blackb* 52-60; V Gt Marsden 60-81; rtd 81; Perm to Offic *Blackb* 81-02. *145 Halifax Road, Nelson BB9 0EL* Tel (01282) 697589

WARCHUS, Michael Edward George. b 37. Lon Univ DipTh67. Roch Th Coll 65. **d** 68 **p** 69. C Buckhurst Hill *Chelmsf* 68-71; C Stainton-in-Cleveland *York* 71-76; V Carlton and Drax 76-86; V Acomb St Steph 86-98; rtd 98; Perm to Offic *York* from 98 and *Ripon* from 00. *12 Tentergate Gardens, Knaresborough HG5 9BL* Tel (01423) 862887

WARD, Alan William. b 56. Trin Coll Bris 80. **d** 81 **p** 82. C New Ferry *Ches* 81-86; Dioc Youth Officer 86-91; C Charlesworth and Dinting Vale *Derby* 91-96; V Mickleover All SS from 96. *All Saints' Vicarage, Etwall Road, Mickleover, Derby DE3 0DL* Tel (01332) 513793 E-mail alanward3@tesco.net

WARD, Alfred John. b 37. Coll of Resurr Mirfield 93. **d** 93 **p** 94. C Hendon St Mary *Lon* 93-00; Chapl Convent of St Mary at the Cross Edgware 00-04; rtd 04; Perm to Offic *Cant* from 05. *60 Valley Road, Dover CT17 0QW* Tel (01304) 824767

WARD, Mrs Alisoun Mary. b 52. Univ of Wales BA74. Ridley Hall Cam 94. **d** 96 **p** 97. C S Woodham Ferrers *Chelmsf* 96-00; TV Southend 00-02. *160 Upper Fant Road, Maidstone ME16 8DJ* Tel (01622) 728202 E-mail rev_soun@hotmail.com

WARD, Andrew John. b 65. Cliff Th Coll 85 Trin Coll Bris BA99. **d** 99 **p** 00. C Belper *Derby* 99-03; TV Walbrook Epiphany from 03. *St James's Vicarage, 224 Osmaston Road, Derby DE23 8JX* Tel (01332) 265531 E-mail andyward@cwcom.net

WARD, Anthony Colin. b 55. Univ of Rhodesia BA76 Lambeth MA03. Wycliffe Hall Ox 78. **d** 80 **p** 81. Zimbabwe 80-85; S Africa 85-90; Asst P Leic H Trin w St Jo *Leic* 90-96; R Rainham w Wennington *Chelmsf* 96-05; C Cranham Park from 05. *226 Moor Lane, Upminster RM14 1HN* Tel (01708) 221711 Fax 08700-940113 E-mail wards@nildram.co.uk

WARD, Canon Anthony Peter. b 46. Bris Univ BSc67 Ox Univ DipEd68. St Jo Coll Nottm. **d** 82 **p** 83. C Hellesdon *Nor* 82-85; P-in-c Nor St Aug w St Mary 85-91; P-in-c Norwich-over-the-Water Colegate St Geo 85-90; Norfolk Churches' Radio Officer 85-95; TV Norwich Over-the-Water 91-95; V Gorleston St Andr from 95; RD Gt Yarmouth 98-02; Hon Can Nor Cathl from 03. *St Andrew's Vicarage, 16 Duke Road, Gorleston, Great Yarmouth NR31 6LL* Tel (01493) 663477 E-mail tonyward@fish.co.uk

WARD, Arthur John. b 32. Lon Univ BD57. St Aid Birkenhead 57. **d** 57 **p** 58. C Ecclesfield *Sheff* 57-60; C Fulwood 60-63; Tutor St Aid Birkenhead 63-66; R Denton St Lawr *Man* 66-74; CMS 74-82; TV Wolverhampton *Lich* 82-90; V Edgbaston SS Mary and Ambrose *Birm* 90-96; rtd 96; Perm to Offic *Heref* from 97. *Bramble Cottage, 6 Lower Forge, Eardington, Bridgnorth WV16 5LQ* Tel (01746) 764758

WARD, Miss Beverley Jayne. b 61. Bolton Inst of Educn CertEd97. St Steph Ho Ox 00. **d** 02. C Standish *Blackb* from 02. *69 Churchlands Lane, Standish, Wigan WN6 0XU* Tel 07811-907274 (mobile)

WARD, Brett Ernest. b 62. ACT ThL86. **d** 89 **p** 89. Australia 89-97; C Forton *Portsm* 97-99; P-in-c from 99. *The Vicarage, 10 Spring Garden Lane, Gosport PO12 1HY* Tel (023) 9250 3140 E-mail fr.brett@hisdesk1.demon.co.uk

WARD, Canon Calvin. b 34. Univ of Wales BA57 DipEd60 Fitzw Ho Cam BA63 MA67. Westcott Ho Cam 61. **d** 64 **p** 65. C Handsworth St Mich *Birm* 64-66; C Shaw Hill 66-69; V Windhill *Bradf* 69-76; V Esholt 76-81; V Oakworth 81-91; V Allerton 91-99; Hon Can Bradf Cathl 94-99; rtd 99; Perm to Offic *Bradf* from 99. *47 Wheatlands Drive, Heaton, Bradford BD9 5JN*

WARD, Christopher John William. b 36. Bps' Coll Cheshunt 66 Qu Coll Birm 68. **d** 69 **p** 70. C Wednesbury St Bart *Lich* 69-73; CF 73-93; rtd 93; Perm to Offic *Sarum* from 93. *6 Meadow View, Blandford Forum DT11 7JB* Tel (01258) 455140

WARD, David. b 40. St Jo Coll Nottm 83. **d** 85 **p** 86. C Aspley *S'well* 85-89; V 89-04; rtd 04. *150 Robins Wood Road, Nottingham NG8 3LD* Tel 0115-929 3231 Mobile 07971-092089 E-mail revd.d.ward@ic24.net

WARD, David Conisbee. b 33. St Jo Coll Cam BA54 MA59. S'wark Ord Course 77. **d** 80 **p** 81. NSM Surbiton St Matt *S'wark* 80-83; C Streatham Immanuel w St Anselm 83-84; P-in-c 84-87; V Hook 87-93; rtd 93; Perm to Offic *Chich* and *S'wark* from 94. *50 Elgar Avenue, Surbiton KT9 9JN* Tel (020) 8399 9679

WARD, Canon David Robert. b 51. Oak Hill Th Coll 74. **d** 77 **p** 78. C Kirkheaton *Wakef* 77-81; V Earl's Heaton 81-88; V Bradley from 88; Hon Can Wakef Cathl from 02. *The Vicarage, 3 St Thomas Gardens, Huddersfield HD2 1SL* Tel (01484) 427838

WARD, Edward. *See* WARD, William Edward

WARD, The Ven Edwin James Greenfield (Ted). b 19. LVO63. Ch Coll Cam BA46 MA48. Ridley Hall Cam 46. **d** 48 **p** 49. C E Dereham w Hoe *Nor* 48-50; V N Elmham w Billingford 50-55; Chapl to The Queen 55-90; Extra Chapl to The Queen from 90; R W Stafford w Frome Billet *Sarum* 67-84; Can and Preb Sarum Cathl 67-84; Adn Sherborne 67-84; rtd 85; Perm to Offic *Win* from 99. *14 Arle Close, Alresford SO24 9BG* Tel (01962) 735501

WARD, Canon Frances Elizabeth Fearn. b 59. St Andr Univ MTh83 Jes Coll Cam DipTh89 Man Univ PhD00 Lon Hosp RGN87. Westcott Ho Cam 87. **d** 89 **p** 94. Par Dn Westhoughton *Man* 89-93; Tutor Practical Th N Coll Man 93-98; Hon C Bury St Pet 93-98; C Unsworth 98-99; V Bury St Pet from 99; Bp's Adv on Women in Min from 02; Hon Can Man Cathl from 04; Perm to Offic *Carl* from 04. *St Peter's Vicarage, St Peter's Road, Bury BL9 9QZ* Tel 0161-764 1187 E-mail frankie@poward.fsnet.co.uk

WARD, Frank Neal. b 16. EAMTC 78. **d** 80 **p** 81. NSM Weybourne w Upper Sheringham *Nor* 80-84; NSM Kelling w Salthouse 80-84; NSM Briningham 84-92; NSM Brinton, Briningham, Hunworth, Stody etc 92-97; Perm to Offic from 97. *Newlands, The Street, Sharrington, Melton Constable NR24 2AB* Tel (01263) 860337

WARD, Frank Wyatt. b 30. Oak Hill NSM Course 84. **d** 92 **p** 94. NSM Paddington St Pet *Lon* from 92. *82 Hill Rise, Greenford UB6 8PE* Tel (020) 8575 5515

WARD, Garry William. b 67. RGN90 RM92. Qu Coll Birm 01. **d** 03 **p** 04. C Wednesfield *Lich* from 03. *18 Duke Street, Wednesfield, Wolverhampton WV11 1TH* Tel 07734-567860 (mobile) E-mail garry@pundle.co.uk

WARD, Geoffrey Edward. b 30. Linc Th Coll 62. **d** 64 **p** 65. C Oundle *Pet* 64-68; C Weston Favell 68-70; TV 70-72; R Cottingham w E Carlton 72-95; rtd 95; Perm to Offic *Pet* from 95. *4 Sovereigns Court, Saxonfields, Kettering NN16 9SS* Tel (01536) 520498

WARD, Prof Graham John. b 55. Fitzw Coll Cam BA80 Selw Coll Cam MA83. Westcott Ho Cam 87. **d** 90 **p** 91. C Bris St Mary Redcliffe w Temple etc *Bris* 90-92; Chapl Ex Coll Ox 92-94; Dean Peterho Cam 95-99; Prof Contextual Th Man Univ *Man* from 99. *Address temp unknown* E-mail graham.ward@man.ac.uk

WARD, Helen Frances. b 48. EAMTC 02. **d** 04 **p** 05. NSM Gorleston St Andr *Nor* from 04. *St Andrew's Vicarage, 16 Duke Road, Gorleston, Great Yarmouth NR31 6LL* Tel (01493) 664700 E-mail hward001@fish.co.uk

WARD, Ian Stanley. b 62. K Coll Lon BD83. Cranmer Hall Dur 84. **d** 86 **p** 87. C Moreton *Ches* 86-89; Chapl RAF from 89. *Chaplaincy Services (RAF), HQ, Personnel and Training Command, RAF Innsworth, Gloucester GL3 1EZ* Tel (01452) 712612 ext 5164 Fax 510828

WARD, Jayne. *See* WARD, Miss Beverley Jayne

WARD, John. *See* WARD, Arthur John

WARD, John Frederick. b 55. St Mich Coll Llan 81. **d** 84 **p** 85. C Pembroke Dock *St D* 84-86; PV Llan Cathl *Llan* 86-89; R St Brides Minor w Bettws 89-97; V Shard End *Birm* 97-04; V Twigworth, Down Hatherley, Norton, The Leigh etc *Glouc* from 04. *The Rectory, Tewkesbury Road, Twigworth, Gloucester GL2 9PQ* Tel (01452) 731483 E-mail wardjohn23@aol.com

WARD, John Raymond. b 31. St Jo Coll Dur BA54 DipTh56. **d** 56 **p** 57. C Leeds St Pet *Ripon* 56-60; C Seacroft 60-63; V Kirkstall 63-75; V Bramhope 75-95; rtd 96; Perm to Offic *Ripon* from 01. *94 Leeds Road, Bramhope, Leeds LS16 9AN* Tel 0113-230 0356

WARD, Prof John Stephen Keith. b 38. Univ of Wales (Cardiff) BA62 Linacre Coll Ox BLitt68 DD97 Trin Hall Cam MA72 DD97. Westcott Ho Cam 72. **d** 72 **p** 73. Lect Philosophy of Relig Lon Univ *Lon* 71-75; Hon C Hampstead St Jo 72-75; Dean Trin Hall Cam 75-82; Prof Moral and Soc Th K Coll Lon 82-85; Prof Hist and Philosophy of Relig 85-91; Regius Prof Div Ox Univ from 91; Can Res Ch Ch *Ox* from 91. *Christ Church, Oxford OX1 1DP* Tel (01865) 276246 E-mail keith.ward@chch.ox.ac.uk

WARD, John Stewart. b 43. St Jo Coll Dur BA66. Ripon Coll Cuddesdon 77. **d** 79 **p** 80. C High Harrogate Ch Ch *Ripon* 79-82; V Ireland Wood 82-86; Chapl Wells Cathl Sch 86-88; V Menston w Woodhead *Bradf* 88-95; R Bolton Abbey from 95; RD Skipton 98-00. *The Rectory, Bolton Abbey, Skipton BD23 6AL* Tel (01756) 710326 *or* 710238

WARD, Keith Raymond. b 37. Dur Univ BSc60. Chich Th Coll 63. **d** 65 **p** 66. C Wallsend St Luke *Newc* 65-68; C Wooler 68-74; V Dinnington 74-81; V Bedlington 81-93; V Stannington 93-99; rtd 99; Perm to Offic *Newc* from 00. *2 Ethel's Close, Gloster Meadows, Amble, Morpeth NE65 0GD* Tel (01665) 714357

WARD, Kenneth Arthur. b 22. St D Coll Lamp BA50 Chich Th Coll 50. **d** 52 **p** 53. C Wellingborough St Barn *Pet* 52-55; C Stevenage *St Alb* 55-58; R Daventry *Pet* 58-72; RD Daventry 68-76; R Daventry w Norton 73-79; R Daventry 79-82; V Pattishall w Cold Higham 82-88; rtd 88; Perm to Offic *Pet* from 89. *43 Inlands Rise, Daventry NN11 4DQ*

WARD, Kevin. b 47. Edin Univ MA69 Trin Coll Cam PhD76. **d** 78 **p** 79. CMS 75-92; Uganda 76-90; Qu Coll Birm 91; Perm to Offic *Birm* 91; C Halifax *Wakef* 91-92; P-in-c Charlestown 92-95; Lect Leeds Univ from 95. *8 North Grange Mews, Leeds LS26 2EW* Tel 0113-278 7801 E-mail trskw@leeds.ac.uk

WARD, Canon Leslie Alan James. b 38. K Coll Lon 58 St Boniface Warminster AKC61. **d** 62 **p** 63. C Earlham St Anne *Nor* 62-65; C Gt Yarmouth 65-70; R Belton 70-83; R Burgh Castle 71-83; Chapl Norfolk and Nor Univ Hosp NHS Trust 83-02; Chapl W Norwich and Colman Hosp 83-94; Hon Can Nor Cathl *Nor* 86-02; rtd 02; Perm to Offic *Nor* from 02. *32 Riverway Court, Recorder Road, Norwich NR1 1BP* Tel (01603) 631537

WARD, Lionel Owen. b 37. Univ of Wales (Cardiff) BA58 Univ of Wales (Swansea) DipEd59 MA65 Lon Univ PhD70. St Mich Coll Llan 83. **d** 85 **p** 86. NSM Swansea St Mary w H Trin *S & B* 85-89; P-in-c Swansea St Matt w Greenhill 89-00; TV Cen Swansea 00-01; Dioc Dir of Educn 97-01; RD Swansea 98-01; rtd 02. *96 Glanbrydan Avenue, Uplands, Swansea SA2 0JH* Tel (01792) 521144

WARD, Mrs Marjorie. b 38. Univ of Wales (Abth) BA59 DipEd60. N Ord Course 83. **dss** 86 **d** 87 **p** 94. Keighley St Andr *Bradf* 86-88; Hon Par Dn 87-88; Hon Par Dn Oakworth 88-90; C Allerton 91-99; rtd 99; Perm to Offic *Bradf* from 00. *47 Wheatlands Drive, Heaton, Bradford BD9 5JN*

WARD, Mark. b 62. Imp Coll Lon BScEng84 ACGI84. Wycliffe Hall Ox BTh93. **d** 93 **p** 94. C Parkham, Alwington, Buckland Brewer etc *Ex* 93-96; C S Molton w Nymet St George, High Bray etc 96-97; TV 97-05; TV Ottery St Mary, Alfington, W Hill, Tipton etc from 05. *The Vicarage, Newton Poppleford, Sidmouth EX10 0HB* Tel (01395) 568390
E-mail mark@thewards.fslife.co.uk

WARD, Matthew Alan James. b 69. Nottm Poly BSc91. Ridley Hall Cam 94. **d** 97 **p** 98. C Birchwood *Linc* 97-00; Chapl Cov Univ *Cov* from 00. *40 Spencer Avenue, Coventry CV5 6NP* Tel (024) 7667 5549 *or* 7688 8315 Fax 7688 8337
E-mail m.ward@coventry.ac.uk

WARD, Canon Michael Anthony. b 42. Sarum Th Coll 67. **d** 70 **p** 71. C Bridport *Sarum* 70-74; TV Swanborough 74-77; P-in-c Chute w Chute Forest 77-79; P-in-c Shalbourne w Ham 77-79; TR Wexcombe 79-86; V Southbroom 86-99; Can and Preb Sarum Cathl from 95; TR Alderbury Team 99-01; TR Clarendon from 01. *The Rectory, 5 The Copse, Alderbury, Salisbury SP5 3BL* Tel (01722) 710229
E-mail mwardclarendon@aol.com

WARD, Michael Henry. b 42. St Martin's Coll Lanc BA02. **d** 03 **p** 04. NSM S Shore H Trin *Blackb* from 03. *509A Lytham Road, Blackpool FY4 1TE* Tel (01253) 404204

WARD, Michael Paul. b 68. Regent's Park Coll Ox BA90 MA95 Peterho Cam BA01. Ridley Hall Cam 99. **d** 04 **p** 05. Chapl Peterho Cam from 04; NSM Gt Shelford *Ely* from 04. *Peterhouse, Cambridge CB2 1RD* Tel (01223) 338254
E-mail mpw27@cam.ac.uk

WARD, Michael Reginald. b 31. BNC Ox BA54 MA58. Tyndale Hall Bris 54. **d** 56 **p** 57. C Ealing St Mary *Lon* 56-59; C Morden *S'wark* 59-61; Area Sec (Midl and E Anglia) CCCS 61-66; V Chelsea St Jo *Lon* 66-73; P-in-c Chelsea St Andr 72-73; V Chelsea St Jo w St Andr 73-76; P-in-c Hawkesbury *Glouc* 76-80; P-in-c Alderley w Hillesley 79-80; P-in-c Bibury w Winson and Barnsley 80-85; V Barkby and Queniborough *Leic* 85-90; R Gunthorpe w Bale w Field Dalling, Saxlingham etc *Nor* 90-98; rtd 98; Perm to Offic *Heref* from 98 and *Glouc* from 00. *2 Rose Cottages, Victoria Road, Ledbury HR8 2DB* Tel (01531) 635515

WARD, Nigel Andrew. b 50. Peterho Cam BA72 MA76. Oak Hill NSM Course 89. **d** 92 **p** 93. NSM Frogmore *St Alb* from 92. *15 Park Street, St Albans AL2 2PE* Tel (01727) 872667

WARD, Patricia. b 43. QUB BA65. St Mich Coll Llan 89. **d** 91 **p** 97. NSM Swansea St Mary w H Trin *S & B* 91-98; C Glantawe 98-99; NSM 99-02; rtd 02. *96 Glanbrydan Avenue, Uplands, Swansea SA2 0JH* Tel (01792) 521144

WARD, Peter Garnet. b 28. GRSM51 LRAM. Ridley Hall Cam 59. **d** 61 **p** 62. C Maghull *Liv* 61-64; Kenya 64-73; Master St Leon Mayfield Sch Sussex 73-83; Perm to Offic *Chich* 74-75; P-in-c Coleman's Hatch 75-77; Lic to Offic 77-83; P-in-c Herstmonceux 83-84; P-in-c Wartling 83-84; R Herstmonceux and Wartling 84-94; rtd 94; Perm to Offic *Chich* from 94. *Old Jesolo, Cross Lane, Ticehurst, Wadhurst TN5 7HQ* Tel (01580) 201340

WARD, Canon Philip Paul Ben. b 35. Toronto Univ BA60. ALCD66. **d** 66 **p** 67. C Chenies and Lt Chalfont *Ox* 66-68; C Ardsley *Sheff* 68-70; C Finham *Cov* 70-73; V Terrington St Clement *Ely* 73-81; Hon Can Ch Ch Cathl Fredericton Canada from 93; rtd 98; P-in-c Fredericton Junction from 04. *4261 Heritage Drive, Tracy NB, Canada, E5L 1B2* Tel (001) (506) 368 9182 E-mail bethany@nbnet.nb.ca

WARD, Robert. b 60. Em Coll Cam BA81 MA85. Chich Th Coll. **d** 86 **p** 87. C Horfield H Trin *Bris* 86-90; C Stantonbury and Willen *Ox* 90; TV 90-96; V Knowle St Martin *Bris* from 96. *St Martin's Vicarage, 46 St Martin's Road, Bristol BS4 2NG* Tel 0117-977 6275 Fax as telephone
E-mail frrob@wardmail.fslife.co.uk

WARD, Robert Arthur Philip. b 53. Lon Univ BD82 Open Univ BA88. Qu Coll Birm 77. **d** 79 **p** 80. C Balsall Heath St Paul *Birm* 79-82; Chapl RAF 82-98; TR Blakenall Heath *Lich* 98-01. *St Winifred's Cottage, Maesbury Marsh, Oswestry SY10 8JA* Tel (01691) 679906

WARD, Robert Charles Irwin. b 48. Leic Univ LLB70 Called to the Bar (Inner Temple) 72. St Jo Coll Dur 78. **d** 80 **p** 81. C Byker St Mich w St Lawr *Newc* 80-85; Perm to Offic from 86; Dir Clarence Trust and NE Area Revival Min from 86; Asst Chapl HM Pris Frankland 91-95. *1 Hawthorn Villas, The Green, Wallsend NE28 7NT* Tel and fax 0191-234 3969 Mobile 07768-528181

WARD, Canon Robin. b 66. Magd Coll Ox BA87 MA91 K Coll Lon PhD03. St Steph Ho Ox 88. **d** 91 **p** 92. C Romford St Andr *Chelmsf* 91-94; C Willesden Green St Andr and St Fran *Lon* 94-96; V Sevenoaks St Jo *Roch* from 96; Chapl Invicta Community Care NHS Trust from 97; Hon Can Roch Cathl *Roch* from 04. *St John's Vicarage, 62 Quakers Hall Lane, Sevenoaks TN13 3TX* Tel (01732) 451710
E-mail stjohns7oaks@tinyworld.co.uk

WARD, Ronald Albert. b 29. Shoreditch Coll Lon TCert54. Spurgeon's Coll 85. **d** 03 **p** 04. NSM E Blatchington *Chich* from 03. *4 Albany Road, Seaford BN25 2QB* Tel (01323) 890977 Mobile 07962-120975
E-mail revronward.curate@btinternet.com

WARD (née NIXSON), Mrs Rosemary Clare. b 57. Westf Coll Lon BA79 Liv Univ MA80 MPhil82. Aston Tr Scheme 89 Trin Coll Bris BA94. **d** 94 **p** 95. C E Bris 94; C Bris St Andr Hartcliffe 94-98; C Downend 98-02; C Broad Blunsdon 02; P-in-c from 02; C Highworth w Sevenhampton and Inglesham etc from 02; Dioc Lay Tr Adv 02-05; Leadership Development Adv CPAS from 05. *25 Leam Road, Leamington Spa CV31 3PA* Tel (01926) 420193
E-mail rc@nixsonr.freeserve.co.uk

WARD, Mrs Sheena Mary. b 55. Newc Univ BA76 PGCE77. Dioc OLM tr scheme 98. **d** 00 **p** 01. OLM Cramlington *Newc* from 00. *17 Yarmouth Drive, Cramlington NE23 1TL* Tel (01670) 732211 E-mail sheena.ward@dsl.pipex.com

WARD, Simon William James. b 71. Dur Univ BA94 Westmr Coll Ox PGCE96. Ripon Coll Cuddesdon 98. **d** 00 **p** 01. C Aldershot St Mich *Guildf* 00-03; TV Sole Bay *St E* from 03. *The Rectory, 45 Wangford Road, Reydon, Southwold IP18 6PZ* Tel (01502) 722192 E-mail revdsimon@msn.com

WARD, Stanley. b 34. NEOC. **d** 84 **p** 85. NSM Jarrow *Dur* 84-90; P-in-c Thornley 90-99; rtd 99; Perm to Offic *Ex* from 00. *4 Church Walk, Thornley, Durham DH6 3EN* Tel and fax (01429) 821766

WARD, Stanley Gordon. b 21. Qu Coll Cam BA43 MA47. EMMTC 76. **d** 79 **p** 80. NSM Wollaton *S'well* 79-83; NSM Plympton St Mary *Ex* 84-88; Perm to Offic from 88. *60 Wain Park, Plympton, Plymouth PL7 2HX* Tel (01752) 344042

WARD, Stephen Philip. b 49. Sheff Univ BA72. St Steph Ho Ox 77. **d** 79 **p** 80. C Narborough *Leic* 79-80; C Brentwood St Thos *Chelmsf* 81-82; Perm to Offic *Leic* 03-05; NSM Leic St Mary from 05. *56 Moor Lane, Loughborough LE11 1BA* Tel (01509) 216945

WARD, Mrs Susan Elizabeth. b 50. N Ord Course 92. **d** 95 **p** 96. NSM Heyside *Man* from 95. *45 Fold Green, Chadderton, Oldham OL9 9DX* Tel 0161-620 2839

WARD, Timothy James. b 67. CCC Ox BA90 MA95 Edin Univ PhD99. Oak Hill Th Coll BA95. **d** 99 **p** 00. C Crowborough *Chich* 99-04; TV Hinckley H Trin *Leic* from 04. *Holy Trinity Vicarage, 1 Cleveland Road, Hinckley LE10 0AJ* Tel (01455) 442750 E-mail wardtmthy@aol.com

WARD, Timothy John Conisbee. b 62. New Coll Ox BA85 MA02 PGCE86. Wycliffe Hall Ox BA91. **d** 92 **p** 93. C Dorking St Paul *Guildf* 92-96; C Herne Hill *S'wark* 96-02; V Walberton w Binsted *Chich* from 02. *St Mary's Vicarage, The Street, Walberton, Arundel BN18 0PQ* Tel (01243) 551488

WARD, Timothy William. b 49. Open Univ BA74 Birm Univ BPhil(Ed)93. St Deiniol's Hawarden 78. **d** 79 **p** 80. Hon C Handsworth St Mary *Birm* 79-95; Perm to Offic from 95; Hon C Gt Barr *Lich* from 95. *3 Dale Close, Birmingham B43 6AS* Tel 0121-358 1880 *or* 248 7832
E-mail curate.greatbarr@btinternet.com

WARD, William Edward. b 48. FSAScot71. AKC71. **d** 72 **p** 73. C Heref St Martin *Heref* 72-77; C Blakenall Heath *Lich* 77-78; TV 78-82; V Astley, Clive, Grinshill and Hadnall 82-91; R Edgmond w Kynnersley and Preston Wealdmoors from 91; P-in-c Tibberton w Bolas Magna and Waters Upton from 02; Chapl Harper Adams Agric Coll from 96. *The Rectory, 37 High Street, Edgmond, Newport TF10 8JW* Tel (01952) 820217

WARD, William Francis. b 35. Ely Th Coll 61 Coll of Resurr Mirfield 64. **d** 64 **p** 65. C Byker St Ant *Newc* 64-67; C Glas St Marg *Glas* 67-69; R Glas Ascension 69-74; Chapl RNR 72-74; Chapl RN 74-78; R Arbroath *Bre* 78-99; Hon Chapl Miss to Seafarers from 78; P-in-c Auchmithie *Bre* 79-90; rtd 99. *1 Denholm Gardens, Letham, Angus DD8 2XT* Tel (01307) 818032 Fax 818924 E-mail billward@letham.fsworld.co.uk

WARD-BODDINGTON, Canon Douglas. b 20. MBE97. S'wark Ord Course 69. **d** 72 **p** 73. C S'wark Ch Ch *S'wark* 72-77; Admin S Lon Ind Miss 72-77; Chapl Algarve *Eur* 77-80 and 83-89; V Gen to Bp Eur 80-83; Can Gib Cathl 80-97; rtd 89; Chapl Oporto *Eur* 89-97; Chapl CSP 98-02; Perm to Offic *S'wark* 97-98; *Chich* 98-05; *Eur* from 97 and *Guildf* from 98. *The Warden's House, Hawley Green, Blackwater, Camberley GU17 9DN* Tel (01276) 34872 Mobile 07730-147153
E-mail wardboddington@freeuk.com

WARDALE, Harold William. b 40. BSc PhD. Wycliffe Hall Ox 83. **d** 85 **p** 86. C Bedminster St Mich *Bris* 85-89; TV Bishopston 89-96; V Lawrence Weston 96-98; V Lawrence Weston and Avonmouth 99-05; rtd 05. *3 Cleeve Rise, Newent GL18 1BZ* Tel (01531) 822390

WARDALE, Robert Christopher. b 46. Newc Univ BA69. Coll of Resurr Mirfield 77. **d** 79 **p** 80. C Cockerton *Dur* 79-84; P-in-c Hedworth 84-87; V 87-92; V Darlington H Trin from 92. *Holy*

Trinity Vicarage, 45 Milbank Road, Darlington DL3 9NL Tel (01325) 480444 E-mail chris.wardale@durham.anglican.org

WARDELL, Gareth Kevin. b 59. York Univ BA81 MA01. Ridley Hall Cam 03. **d** 05. C Selby Abbey *York* from 05. *49 Woodville Terrace, Selby YO8 8AJ* Tel (01757) 290289 *or* 703123 E-mail wardellgareth@hotmail.com

WARDELL, Stewart Francis. b 68. Chu Coll Cam BA89 Bris Univ MA95. Cuddesdon Coll BA98. **d** 98 **p** 99. C Brentwood St Thos *Chelmsf* 98-02; R Hawkinge w Acrise and Swingfield *Cant* from 02. *The Rectory, 78 Canterbury Road, Hawkinge, Folkestone CT18 7BP* Tel (01303) 892369

WARDEN, John Michael. b 41. Univ Coll Lon BA63 Trin Coll Ox BA65 MA. NEOC 80. **d** 82 **p** 83. NSM Osmotherley w E Harlsey and Ingleby Arncliffe *York* 82-86; V Kirkdale 86-97; V Kirkdale w Harome, Nunnington and Pockley from 98. *Kirkdale Vicarage, Main Road, Beadlam, Nawton, York YO62 7ST* Tel (01439) 771206

WARDEN, Richard James. b 57. Kent Univ BA79 K Coll Lon MTh86. Wycliffe Hall Ox 81. **d** 83 **p** 84. C Fulham St Mary N End *Lon* 83-85; CF 85-89; Chapl Wycombe Abbey Sch 89-01; Sen Chapl and Hd RS Wellington Coll Berks 01-04; P-in-c Finchampstead *Ox* from 04. *The Rectory, The Village, Finchampstead, Wokingham RG40 4JX* Tel 0118-973 2102 E-mail revrjw@hotmail.com

WARDLE, Canon John Alexander. b 30. TD73. Lon Univ BA59 Man Univ MA81. Oak Hill Th Coll 53. **d** 57 **p** 58. C Blackpool St Mark *Blackb* 57-60; C Tunbridge Wells St Jo *Roch* 60-62; V Maidstone St Luke *Cant* 62-69; CF (TA) 62-73; V Hartford *Ches* 69-79; R Barton Seagrave w Warkton *Pet* 79-96; Can Pet Cathl 94-96; rtd 96; Perm to Offic *Eur* from 96; SAMS Spain 96-99; Perm to Offic *Leic* and *Pet* from 99. *17 Westmorland Drive, Desborough, Kettering NN14 2XB* Tel (01536) 762558 E-mail abywardle@yahoo.com

WARDLE, John Argyle. b 47. St Jo Coll Dur BA71 ARCM67 CertEd73. **d** 73 **p** 74. C Mansfield SS Pet and Paul *S'well* 73-77; Chapl St Felix Sch Southwold 77-87; TV Haverhill w Withersfield, the Wrattings etc *St E* 87-90; V Choral S'well Minster *S'well* 90-99; Bp's Adv on Healing 94-99; R Bridlington Priory *York* from 99; RD Bridlington from 03. *The Rectory, Church Green, Bridlington YO16 7JX* Tel (01262) 672221 *or* 601938 E-mail jawardle@fish.co.uk

WARDLE-HARPUR, Canon James. b 31. St Jo Coll Dur BA55. Wells Th Coll 55. **d** 56 **p** 57. C Sheff St Cecilia Parson Cross *Sheff* 56-59; C Maltby 59-61; V Doncaster St Jude 61-64; Pakistan 64-68; R Man Victoria Park *Man* 68-75; V Foxton w Gumley and Laughton *Leic* 75-79; V Foxton w Gumley and Laughton and Lubenham 79-82; TR Leic Resurr 82-88; V Burrough Hill Pars 88-94; Hon Can Leic Cathl 88-94; rtd 96. *Laburnum Cottage, 1 Coates Lane, Starbotton, Skipton BD23 5HZ* Tel (01756) 760401

WARDMAN, Carol Joy. b 56. Lon Univ BA79. N Ord Course 91. **d** 94 **p** 95. NSM Hebden Bridge *Wakef* 94-97; NSM Sowerby from 97. *25 Scarr Head Road, Sowerby Bridge HX6 3PU* Tel (01422) 316723 *or* 0161-832 5253

WARDROBE, Bevan. b 26. Hatf Coll Dur BA53. Cuddesdon Coll 53. **d** 54 **p** 55. C Southgate Ch Ch *Lon* 54-59; PV Lich Cathl *Lich* 59-67; Asst Master Cathl Sch 59-67; Hd Master York Minster Song Sch 67-85; V Choral York Minster *York* 67-85; Chapl Rome *Eur* 85-91; rtd 91; Chapl San Remo *Eur* 91-96; Perm to Offic *Glouc* from 96. *3 Regency Gardens, Sandford Road, Cheltenham GL53 7AJ* Tel (01242) 242355

WARE, Canon John Lawrence. b 37. Nottm Univ BA59. Ridley Hall Cam 62. **d** 62 **p** 63. C Attercliffe *Sheff* 62-66; C Ranmoor 66-68; R Liddington *Bris* 68-74; Soc and Ind Adv 74-79; P-in-c Eastville St Thos 74-79; Hon Can Bris Cathl 76-01; V Kingswood 79-88; RD Bitton 85-87; P-in-c Broad Blunsdon 88-94; RD Cricklade 88-94; R The Blunsdons 94-01; rtd 01; Perm to Offic *Bris* from 01. *26 Dongola Road, Bishopston, Bristol BS7 9HP* Tel 0117-924 1304

WARE, Ms Judith Marian. b 52. St Hugh's Coll Ox BA74 MA PGCE75. Carl and Blackb Dioc Tr Inst 00. **d** 02 **p** 03. NSM Windermere St Mary and Troutbeck *Carl* 02-05; C Thornes St Jas w Ch Ch *Wakef* from 05; C Lupset from 05; Chapl Wakef Cathl Sch from 05. *The Vicarage, St James Court, Wakefield WF2 8DW* Tel (01924) 299889 E-mail jmware@ecosse.net

WARE, Stephen John. b 55. Univ of Wales (Lamp) BA76. Ripon Coll Cuddesdon 77. **d** 79 **p** 80. C Lighthorne *Cov* 79-82; Chapl RAF 82-05; Selection Sec Min Division 05; V Bloxham w Milcombe and S Newington *Ox* from 05. *The Vicarage, Church Street, Bloxham, Banbury OX15 4ET* Tel (01295) 720252

WAREHAM, Mrs Caroline. b 32. Lightfoot Ho Dur 55. **dss** 80 **d** 87 **p** 94. Stanwell *Lon* 80-88; Par Dn 87-88; C Epsom St Barn *Guildf* 88-95; C Aldershot St Mich 95-98; rtd 98; Perm to Offic *Sarum* from 00. *17 Homefield, Mere, Warminster BA12 6LT* Tel (01747) 861716

WAREHAM, Mrs Sheila. b 36. CertEd56. N Ord Course 85. **d** 88 **p** 94. NSM Lostock Hall *Blackb* 88-90; NSM Allithwaite *Carl* 90-91; NSM Windermere RD 91-94; P-in-c Colton 94-96; Perm to Offic from 97. *Lyng Nook, Church Road, Allithwaite, Grange-over-Sands LA11 7RD* Tel (01539) 535237

WARHAM, Mrs Jean. b 55. **d** 00 **p** 01. OLM Newcastle w Butterton *Lich* from 00. *166 High Street, Alsagers Bank, Stoke-on-Trent ST7 8BA* Tel (01782) 721505

WARHURST (née HART), Mrs Jane Elizabeth. b 56. Sheff Univ BA77 Man Poly DCG78. N Ord Course 98. **d** 01 **p** 02. C Edge Hill St Cypr w St Mary *Liv* from 01. *St Mary's Vicarage, Towerlands Street, Liverpool L7 8TT*

WARHURST, Richard. b 76. Univ Coll Chich BA99. St Steph Ho Ox 00. **d** 02 **p** 03. C New Shoreham *Chich* from 02; C Old Shoreham from 02. *17 Colvill Avenue, Shoreham-by-Sea BN43 5WN* Tel (01273) 464528

WARING, Graham George Albert. b 37. ACII62. Portsm Dioc Tr Course 86. **d** 87 **p** 02. Chapl Asst Qu Alexandra Hosp Portsm 87-92; NSM Portsea All SS *Portsm* 92-94; NSM Widley w Wymering 94-95; NSM Wisbech St Aug *Ely* 95-98; Chapl King's Lynn and Wisbech Hosps NHS Trust 96-00; NSM Leverington *Ely* 98-00; NSM Southea w Murrow and Parson Drove 98-00; Perm to Offic *York* 00-02; NSM Scarborough St Sav w All SS from 02. *28 Newby Farm Road, Newby, Scarborough YO12 6UN* E-mail graham.waring@virgin.net

WARING, Jeffery Edwin. b 53. Trin Coll Bris 80. **d** 83 **p** 84. C Harpurhey Ch Ch *Man* 83-86; TV Eccles 86-92; P-in-c Hamworthy *Sarum* 92-04; P-in-c Red Post from 04. *The Vicarage, East Morden, Wareham BH20 7DW* Tel (01929) 459244

WARING, John Valentine. b 29. St Deiniol's Hawarden 65. **d** 67 **p** 68. C Bistre *St As* 67-71; C Blackpool St Thos *Blackb* 71-72; R Levenshulme St Pet *Man* 72-87; R Caerwys and Bodfari *St As* 87-94; rtd 94. *13 St Mellors Road, Southdown Park, Buckley CH7 2ND* Tel (01244) 547290

WARING, Mrs Margaret Ruth. b 44. Keele Univ CertEd65. SW Minl Tr Course 86. **d** 90 **p** 94. Par Dn Tavistock and Gulworthy *Ex* 90-94; C 94-96; TV Axminster, Chardstock, All Saints etc 96-04; rtd 04; Perm to Offic *Ex* from 04. *5 The Battens, Stockland, Honiton EX14 9DS* Tel (01404) 881516

WARING, Roger. b 32. ACP66 CertEd56 Open Univ BA74. SW Minl Tr Course 83. **d** 86 **p** 87. NSM Ex St Sidwell and St Matt *Ex* 86-90; NSM Tavistock and Gulworthy 90-96; NSM Axminster, Chardstock, All Saints etc 96-99; Perm to Offic from 99. *5 The Battens, Stockland, Honiton EX14 9DS* Tel (01404) 881516

WARING, Mrs Sheila May. b 29. SS Paul & Mary Coll Cheltenham CertEd49. Oak Hill Th Coll 85. **dss** 86 **d** 87 **p** 94. Eastwood *Chelmsf* 86-92; NSM 87-92; Chapl Rochford Hosp 87-92; Chapl Southend Community Care Services NHS Trust 92-99; NSM Prittlewell St Pet *Chelmsf* 92-96; NSM Prittlewell w Westcliff 96-99; Perm to Offic from 99. *42 Manchester Drive, Leigh-on-Sea SS9 3HR* Tel (01702) 711046

WARKE, Alistair Samuel John. b 66. Ulster Univ BA89. CITC BTh92. **d** 92 **p** 93. C Arm St Mark *Arm* 92-95; I Killyman 95-04; Hon V Choral Arm Cathl 95-04. *Address temp unknown*

✠**WARKE, The Rt Revd Robert Alexander.** b 30. TCD BA52 BD60. Union Th Sem (NY) Dip Ecum60. **d** 53 **p** 54 **c** 88. C Newtownards *D & D* 53-56; C Dublin St Cath w St Victor *D & G* 56-58; C Dublin Rathfarnham 58-64; Min Can St Patr Cathl Dublin 59-64; I Dunlavin w Ballymore Eustace and Hollywood *D & G* 64-67; I Dublin Drumcondra w N Strand 67-71; I Dublin St Barn 67-71; I Dublin Zion Ch 71-88; Adn Dublin 80-88; Bp C, C & R 88-98; rtd 98. *6 Kerdiff Park, Monread Road, Naas, Co Kildare, Irish Republic* Tel (00353) (45) 898144 E-mail rawarke@eircom.net

WARLAND, Peter William. b 35. K Coll Lon 56. **d** 60 **p** 61. C Pemberton St Jo *Liv* 60-64; C Warrington St Elphin 64-66; V Farnworth All SS *Man* 66-71; Chapl RN 71-92; QHC 88-92; Chapl Greenbank and Freedom Fields Hosps Ex 92-00; Chapl St Luke's Hospice Plymouth 94-00; rtd 00; Perm to Offic *Ex* from 00. *122 Wingfield Road, Stoke, Plymouth PL3 4ER* Tel (01752) 561381

WARMAN, Canon John Richard. b 37. Pemb Coll Ox BA61 MA. Ridley Hall Cam 61. **d** 63 **p** 64. C Huyton St Mich *Liv* 63-67; Asst Chapl Liv Univ 67-68; Chapl 68-74; P-in-c Holbrooke *Derby* 74-80; P-in-c Lt Eaton 74-80; R Sawley 80-96; RD Ilkeston 82-92; Hon Can Derby Cathl 91-02; V Allestree 96-02; rtd 02; Perm to Offic *Derby* from 02. *27 Swanmore Road, Littleover, Derby DE23 3SD* Tel (01332) 510089 E-mail jnp.warman@cwcom.net

WARMAN, Miss Marion Alice. b 20. Newnham Coll Cam BA43 MA50. S'wark Ord Course 76. **dss** 79 **d** 87 **p** 94. Spring Grove St Mary *Lon* 79-87; Hon Par Dn 87-94; Hon C from 94; Chapl Asst W Middx Hosp Isleworth 80-93; Chapl Volunteer Hounslow and Spelthorne NHS Trust 93-04; Perm to Offic *Lon* from 93. *43 Thornbury Road, Isleworth TW7 4LE* Tel (020) 8560 5905

WARMAN, Philip Noel. b 64. Roehampton Inst BSc85 PGCE86. Ridley Hall Cam 99. **d** 01 **p** 02. C Burney Lane *Birm* from 01.

136 Burney Lane, Ward End, Birmingham B8 2AR Tel 0121-783 7935 Mobile 07718-294555 E-mail phil@warman23.fsnet.co.uk

WARNE, Miss Susan Annette. b 39. Man Univ BSc61 Nottm Univ DipEd62. **d** 00 **p** 01. OLM Kelsale-cum-Carlton, Middleton, Theberton etc *St E* 00-04; OLM Middleton cum Fordley and Theberton w Eastbridge from 04; OLM Yoxford, Peasenhall and Sibton from 01; OLM Darsham and Westleton w Dunwich from 04. *Wynkyns, 22 Oakwood Park, Yoxford, Saxmundham IP17 3JU* Tel (01728) 668410

WARNER, Alan Winston. b 51. Lon Univ BSc73. Coll of Resurr Mirfield 73. **d** 76 **p** 77. C Willenhall St Anne *Lich* 76-78; C Baswich 78-81; V Wednesfield St Greg 81-87; Chapl Frimley Park Hosp 87-94; Chapl Frimley Park Hosp NHS Trust 94-04; Team Ldr Shrewsbury and Telford NHS Trust from 04; OCF from 95. *The Princess Royal Hospital, Apley Castle, Telford TF1 6TF* Tel (01952) 641222 E-mail alanwarner@igclick.net

WARNER, Alison Mary. b 44. Pace Univ USA BA. St Alb and Ox Min Course 01. **d** 04 **p** 05. NSM Waterloo St Jo w St Andr *S'wark* from 04. *5 Mace Close, London E1W 2JX* Tel (020) 7481 9197 Mobile 07900-552665 E-mail ali@aliwarner.freeserve.co.uk

WARNER, Canon Andrew Compton. b 35. Fitzw Ho Cam BA58 MA62. Westcott Ho Cam 59. **d** 60 **p** 61. C Addlestone *Guildf* 60-64; C-in-c Ash Vale CD 64-71; V Hinchley Wood 71-80; R Gt Bookham 80-00; RD Leatherhead 88-93; Hon Can Guildf Cathl 99-00; rtd 00; Perm to Offic *Win* from 00. *5 Pearman Drive, Andover SP10 2SB* Tel (01264) 391325 E-mail dandawarner@yahoo.co.uk

WARNER, Clifford Chorley. b 38. Hull Univ MA88. EMMTC 76. **d** 79 **p** 80. NSM Swanwick and Pentrich *Derby* 79-88; NSM Allestree 88-98; Perm to Offic from 98. *17 Amber Heights, Ripley DE5 3SP* Tel (01773) 745089

WARNER, David. b 40. AKC63. **d** 64 **p** 65. C Castleford All SS *Wakef* 64-68; Warden Hollowford Tr and Conf Cen Sheff 68-72; R Wombwell *Sheff* 72-83; V Wortley w Thurgoland 83-95; RD Tankersley 88-93; V Worsbrough 95-00; P-in-c Bildeston w Wattisham *St E* 00-02; P-in-c Whatfield w Semer, Nedging and Naughton 00-02; R Bildeston w Wattisham and Lindsey, Whatfield etc 02-05; rtd 05; Perm to Offic *St E* from 05. *10 Magdalen Street, Eye IP23 7AJ* Tel (01379) 870459 Mobile 07050-111478

WARNER, David Leonard John. b 24. Kelham Th Coll 47. **d** 51 **p** 52. C Mill Hill St Mich *Lon* 51-54; C Pimlico St Sav 54-56; S Africa 56-68; V Bournemouth H Epiphany *Win* 68-78; V Whitchurch w Tufton and Litchfield 78-89; RD Whitchurch 79-89; rtd 89; Perm to Offic *Win* from 89; Hon Chapl Win Cathl from 97. *9 Sparkford Close, Winchester SO22 4NH* Tel (01962) 867343 E-mail david.warner@btinternet.com

WARNER, Dennis Vernon. b 46. Lon Univ BA68 K Coll Lon BD71. **d** 72 **p** 73. C W Bromwich All SS *Lich* 72-75; C Uttoxeter w Bramshall 75-79; NSM Stretton w Claymills from 79. *17 Shrewsbury Road, Stretton, Swadlincote DE13 0JF* Tel (01283) 548058 *or* (01543) 306030 E-mail dennis.warner@lichfield.anglican.org

WARNER, Canon George Francis. b 36. Trin Coll Ox BA60 MA64 Qu Coll Cam BA63. Westcott Ho Cam 61. **d** 63 **p** 64. C Birm St Geo *Birm* 63-66; C Maidstone All SS w St Phil and H Trin *Cant* 66-69; Chapl Wellington Coll Berks 69-78; TR Coventry Caludon *Cov* 78-95; Hon Can Cov Cathl 85-02; RD Cov E 89-95; P-in-c Leamington Priors All SS 95-02; P-in-c Leamington Spa H Trin and Old Milverton 95-02; rtd 02; Perm to Offic *Cov* from 02. *Coll Leys Edge, Fant Hill, Upper Brailes, Banbury OX15 5AY* Tel (01608) 685550

WARNER, James Morley. b 32. S'wark Ord Course 66. **d** 69 **p** 70. C S Mymms K Chas *Lon* 69-72; C Bush Hill Park St Steph 72-75; V W Hendon St Jo 75-98; rtd 98; Perm to Offic *Lon* 98-00; Hon C Wembley Park from 00. *46 Churchill Road, Kenton, Harrow HA3 0AY* Tel (020) 8907 8505

WARNER, John Philip. b 59. Keble Coll Ox BA80 MA84. St Steph Ho Ox 81. **d** 83 **p** 84. C Brighton Resurr *Chich* 83-87; C Paddington St Mary *Lon* 87-90; V Teddington St Mark and Hampton Wick St Jo 90-00; P-in-c Belgrade *Eur* 00-03; P-in-c St Magnus the Martyr w St Marg New Fish Street *Lon* from 03; P-in-c St Mary Abchurch from 04. *St Magnus the Martyr, Lower Thames Street, London EC3R 6DN* Tel (020) 7626 4481 E-mail rector@stmagnus.fsnet.co.uk

WARNER, Canon Martin Clive. b 58. St Chad's Coll Dur BA80 MA85. St Steph Ho Ox 82. **d** 84 **p** 85. C Plymouth St Pet *Ex* 84-88; TV Leic Resurr *Leic* 88-93; Admin Shrine of Our Lady of Walsingham 93-02; P-in-c Hempton and Pudding Norton *Nor* 98-00; Hon Can Nor Cathl 00-02; Can Res St Paul's Cathl *Lon* from 03. *3 Amen Court, London EC4M 7BU* Tel and fax (020) 7248 2559 E-mail pastor@stpaulscathedral.org.uk

WARNER, Mary. b 52. Univ of Wales (Swansea) BSc73 Aber Univ PhD77. NEOC 90. **d** 93 **p** 94. C Bensham *Dur* 93-96; Asst Chapl Newcastle upon Tyne Hosps NHS Trust 96-98; Chapl Hartlepool and E Durham NHS Trust 98-99; Chapl N Tees and Hartlepool NHS Trust 99-04; Chapl City Hosps Sunderland NHS Trust from 04. *The Chaplain's Office, Sunderland Royal Hospital, Kayll Road, Sunderland SR4 7TP* Tel 0191-569 9180 *or* 522 6444

WARNER, Canon Michael John William. b 41. Sarum Th Coll 68. **d** 71 **p** 72. C Plympton St Mary *Ex* 71-75; V St Goran w Caerhays *Truro* 75-78; V Bishops Tawton *Ex* 78-79; V Newport 78-79; Perm to Offic *Truro* 79-83; V St Stythians w Perranarworthal and Gwennap 83-93; Sec Dioc Adv Cttee 93-01; P-in-c Budock 93-97; P-in-c Tregony w St Cuby and Cornelly 97-03; C Probus, Ladock and Grampound w Creed and St Erme 02-03; Hon Can Truro Cathl 98-03; rtd 03; Perm to Offic *Truro* from 03. *98 Porthpean Road, St Austell PL25 4PN* Tel (01726) 64130 E-mail m.j.w.w@btinternet.com

WARNER, Nigel Bruce. b 51. St Jo Coll Cam BA72 MA76 ALCM67. Wycliffe Hall Ox 75. **d** 77 **p** 78. C Luton St Mary *St Alb* 77-80; Prec Dur Cathl *Dur* 80-84; R St John Lee *Newc* 84-91; V Lamesley *Dur* 91-98; V Bishopwearmouth St Nic from 98; AD Wearmouth 99-05. *St Nicholas' Vicarage, 200 Queen Alexandra Road, Sunderland SR3 1XQ* Tel 0191-522 6444 *or* 520 2127 E-mail nigel.warner@durham.anglican.org

WARNER, Philip. *See* WARNER, John Philip

WARNER, Canon Robert William. b 32. TCD BA54 MA65 BD65. TCD Div Sch Div Test56. **d** 56 **p** 57. C Wythenshawe St Martin CD *Man* 56-60; R Hulme St Steph w St Mark 60-66; R Droylsden St Mary 66-76; R Stand 76-97; AD Radcliffe and Prestwich 85-96; Hon Can Man Cathl 87-97; rtd 97; Perm to Offic *Man* from 99. *28 Cow Lees, Westhoughton, Bolton BL5 3EG* Tel (01942) 818823

WARNER, Terence. b 36. **d** 92 **p** 93. NSM Leek and Meerbrook *Lich* 92-98; NSM Odd Rode *Ches* 98-03; Perm to Offic *Lich* from 03. *36 Haig Road, Leek ST13 6BZ* Tel (01538) 371988

WARNES, Brian Leslie Stephen. b 40. Natal Univ BSocSc76. Kelham Th Coll 59. **d** 67 **p** 68. C Tonge Moor *Man* 67-71; S Africa 71-87; V Blean *Cant* 87-94; New Zealand from 94; V Te Awamutu St Jo 94-98; Chapl to Bp Christchurch 98-04; rtd 05. *13 Velma Crescent, Dinsdale, Hamilton, New Zealand* E-mail khotso@paradise.net.nz

WARNES, David John. b 50. Jes Coll Cam BA72 MA76 PGCE73. EAMTC 01. **d** 04 **p** 05. NSM Ipswich St Mary-le-Tower *St E* from 04; Chapl Ipswich Sch from 04. *6 Warrington Road, Ipswich IP1 3SG* Tel (01473) 281109 *or* 408300 Fax 400058 Mobile 07732-654603 E-mail david@warnes68.freeserve.co.uk

WARNES, Miss Marjorie. b 32. Leeds Inst of Educn CertEd53. St Jo Coll Nottm 85. **d** 87 **p** 94. C Leamington Priors St Mary *Cov* 87-97; rtd 97; Perm to Offic *Cov* from 97. *78 Lewis Road, Radford Semele, Leamington Spa CV31 1UQ* Tel (01926) 420811

WARNES, Warren Hugh. b 23. St Barn Coll Adelaide ThL49. **d** 50 **p** 50. Australia 50-58 and 60-62; C Northolt St Mary *Lon* 58-60 and 62-64; V Kings Heath *Pet* 64-71; V Rockingham w Caldecote 71-73; V Gretton w Rockingham and Caldecote 73-83; V Marston St Lawrence w Warkworth and Thenford 83-89; rtd 89; Perm to Offic *Pet* from 89; Officer for Clergy Widows (Northampton) from 90. *17 Thorpe Road, Earls Barton, Northampton NN6 0PJ* Tel (01604) 812935

WARR, Timothy Gerald. b 59. Trin Coll Bris BA86. **d** 88 **p** 89. C Yateley *Win* 88-91; C Chapel Allerton *Ripon* 91-93; V Wortley de Leeds 93-01; TR Borehamwood *St Alb* 01-05; TR Elstree and Borehamwood from 05. *The Rectory, 94 Shenley Road, Borehamwood WD6 1EB* Tel and fax (020) 8207 6603 *or* tel 8905 1365 E-mail tim.warr@btinternet.com

WARREN, The Very Revd Alan Christopher. b 32. CCC Cam BA56 MA60. Ridley Hall Cam 56. **d** 57 **p** 58. C Cliftonville *Cant* 57-59; C Plymouth St Andr *Ex* 59-62; Chapl Kelly Coll Tavistock 62-64; V Leic H Apostles *Leic* 64-72; Hon Can Cov Cathl *Cov* 72-78; Dioc Missr 72-78; Provost Leic 78-92; rtd 92; Perm to Offic *Nor* from 92. *9 Queen's Drive, Hunstanton PE36 6EY* Tel (01485) 534533

WARREN, Bunny. *See* WARREN, Gordon Lenham

✠**WARREN, The Rt Revd Cecil Allan.** b 24. Sydney Univ BA51 Qu Coll Ox BA56 MA59. ACT ThL52. **d** 50 **p** 51 **c** 65. Australia 50-83; Can Canberra and Goulburn 63-65; Asst Bp 65-72; Bp 72-83; Asst Bp Derby 83-89; TR Old Brampton and Loundsley Green 83-89; Hon Can Derby Cathl 83-89; rtd 89. *2/19 Sidney Street, Toowoomba, Australia 4350* Tel (0061) (7) 4638 4487

WARREN, Christopher Pelham. b 55. Middx Univ BA05. NTMTC 02. **d** 05. NSM Saffron Walden w Wendens Ambo, Littlebury etc *Chelmsf* from 05. *108 Debden Road, Saffron Walden CB11 4AL* Tel (01799) 500542 E-mail chris.warren@bbc.co.uk

WARREN, Clifford Frederick. b 32. Univ of Wales (Lamp) BA53. St Mich Coll Llan 54. **d** 56 **p** 57. C Whitchurch *Llan* 56-68; Lic to Offic 68-70; C Llanedeyrn *Mon* 70-76; R Machen 76-97; rtd 97; Lic to Offic *Mon* from 97. *1 Drury Close, Thornhill, Cardiff CF14 9BJ* Tel (029) 2076 5127

WARREN, David. b 39. S'wark Ord Course. **d** 87 **p** 88. NSM Mottingham St Andr *S'wark* from 87. *26 Longcroft, London SE9 3BQ* Tel (020) 8851 4824

WARREN, Desmond Benjamin Moore. b 22. TCD BA44 MA49. Bps' Coll Cheshunt 46. **d** 48 **p** 49. C Moulsham St Jo *Chelmsf*

48-52; C Colchester St Mary V 52-55; V Elmstead 55-63; R Sandy *St Alb* 63-78; P-in-c Westmill 78-79; P-in-c Gt Munden 78-79; R Westmill w Gt Munden 79-84; rtd 84; Lic to Offic (Lismore) *C & O* 84-90; Perm to Offic *C, C & R* 91-04. *Dee House, 11-13 Highworth Avenue, Cambridge CB4 2BQ* Tel (01223) 353161

WARREN, Eric Anthony. b 28. MBE. Ex & Truro NSM Scheme. **d** 83 **p** 84. NSM Chudleigh *Ex* 83-88; Perm to Offic from 88. *Lower Radway House, Bishopsteignton, Teignmouth TQ14 9SS* Tel (01626) 772135 *or* 779277

WARREN, Frederick Noel. b 30. TCD BA52 MA58 BD66 QUB PhD72. **d** 53 **p** 54. C Belfast St Matt *Conn* 53-56; C Belfast St Geo 56-59; I Castlewellan *D & D* 59-65; I Clonallon w Warrenpoint 65-69; I Newcastle 69-87; Can Belf Cathl 73-76; Preb Wicklow St Patr Cathl Dublin 76-88; I Dunfanaghy, Raymunterdoney and Tullaghbegley *D & R* 87-97; Preb Swords St Patr Cathl Dublin 89-97; rtd 97. *Runclevin, Dufanaghy, Letterkenny, Co Donegal, Irish Republic* Tel (00353) (74) 913 6635

WARREN, Geoffrey. *See* WARREN, Robert Geoffrey

WARREN, Geoffrey Richard. b 44. Middx Poly MA91 Middx Univ PhD01. Bps' Coll Cheshunt 66 Qu Coll Birm 68. **d** 69 **p** 70. C Waltham Cross *St Alb* 69-73; C Radlett 73-78; C Tring 78-80; TV Tring 80-95; V Watford St Andr from 95; RD Watford from 04. *St Andrew's Vicarage, 18 Park Road, Watford WD17 4QN* Tel (01923) 239265 E-mail geoffwarren@btinternet.com

WARREN, Mrs Gillian. b 53. Sheff Univ BA74 PGCE75. WMMTC 89. **d** 92 **p** 94. Par Dn Tettenhall Regis *Lich* 92-94; C 94-95; TV Bilston 95-00; R Lich St Chad 00-02; V Wednesbury St Paul Wood Green from 02. *St Paul's Vicarage, 68 Wood Green Road, Wednesbury WS10 9QT* Tel 0121-556 0687

WARREN, Gordon Lenham (Bunny). b 45. Wycliffe Hall Ox DipMin93. **d** 93 **p** 94. C Sunbury *Lon* 93-96; C Laleham 96-98; R Limehouse from 98. *Limehouse Rectory, 5 Newell Street, London E14 7HP* Tel (020) 7987 1502 E-mail cpsalm19@aol.com

WARREN, Preb Henry Fiennes. b 21. Keble Coll Ox BA42 MA47. Cuddesdon Coll 42. **d** 48 **p** 49. C Weston-super-Mare St Jo *B & W* 48-53; R Exford 53-75; RD Wiveliscombe 65-73; Preb Wells Cathl from 73; R W Monkton 75-86; rtd 86; Perm to Offic *B & W* from 86. *6 Brookside, Broadway, Ilminster TA19 9RT* Tel (01460) 57922

WARREN, James Randolph. b 54. St Paul's Cheltenham CertEd75 Bris Univ BEd76 Birm Univ MEd84. Ridley Hall Cam CTM92. **d** 92 **p** 93. C Boldmere *Birm* 92-95; V Torpoint *Truro* 95-01; Hon Chapl RN 98-01; V Shottery St Andr *Cov* from 01. *The Vicarage, Church Lane, Shottery, Stratford-upon-Avon CV37 9HQ* Tel (01789) 293381 Fax 296648

WARREN, Malcolm Clive. b 46. St D Coll Lamp. **d** 74 **p** 75. C Newport St Andr *Mon* 74-78; C Risca 78-79; V St Hilary Greenway 79-84; TV Grantham *Linc* 84-90; Ind Chapl *Linc* 87-90 and *Worc* 90-05; P-in-c Dudley St Aug Holly Hall *Worc* 95-96; Perm to Offic 96-97; TV Kidderminster St Mary and All SS w Trimpley etc 97-05; Ind Chapl *Bris* from 05. *The Glebe House, 1 McLaren Road, Avonmouth, Bristol BS11 9FE* Tel 0117-373 2546 Mobile 07971-222739
E-mail malcolm_warren@hotmail.com
or malcolmwarren9@aol.com

WARREN, Martin John. b 59. Ch Coll Cam BA81 MA85. St Jo Coll Nottm LTh85. **d** 86 **p** 87. C Littleover *Derby* 86-90; C Hermitage and Hampstead Norreys, Cold Ash etc *Ox* 90-91; TV 91-97; TV Hermitage 97-02; P-in-c Shebbear, Buckland Filleigh, Sheepwash etc *Ex* from 02. *The Rectory, Shebbear, Beaworthy EX21 5RU* Tel (01409) 281424 E-mail w.chara@fish.co.uk

WARREN, Michael John. b 40. Kelham Th Coll 59. **d** 64 **p** 65. C Withington St Chris *Man* 64-67; C Worsley 67-69; C Witney *Ox* 69-72; V S Hinksey 72-80; Canada 80-99 and from 02; C Verwood *Sarum* 99-00; rtd 00. *Apartment 3, 32 Lafayette Crescent, Lethbridge AB, Canada, T1K 4B6* Tel (001) (403) 317 0317

WARREN, Michael Philip. b 62. Nottm Univ GradDipPhys87. Oak Hill Th Coll BA91 MA04. **d** 94 **p** 95. C Tunbridge Wells St Jo *Roch* 94-98; Assoc Min Heydon, Gt and Lt Chishill, Chrishall etc *Chelmsf* 98-04; V Tunbridge Wells St Pet *Roch* from 04. *St Peter's Vicarage, Bayhall Road, Tunbridge Wells TN2 4TP* Tel (01892) 530384 E-mail elmdonvic@aol.com

WARREN, The Ven Norman Leonard. b 34. CCC Cam BA58 MA62. Ridley Hall Cam 58. **d** 60 **p** 61. C Bedworth *Cov* 60-63; V Leamington Priors St Paul 63-77; R Morden *S'wark* 77-88; TR 88-89; RD Merton 86-89; Adn Roch and Can Res Roch Cathl *Roch* 89-00; rtd 00; Perm to Offic *Roch* from 00. *1 Sandling Way, St Mary's Island, Chatham ME4 3AZ* Tel (01634) 891363

WARREN, Canon Paul Kenneth. b 41. Selw Coll Cam BA63 MA67. Cuddesdon Coll 64. **d** 67 **p** 68. C Lancaster St Mary *Blackb* 67-70; Chapl Lanc Univ 70-78; V Langho Billington 78-83; Bp's Dom Chapl and Chapl Whalley Abbey 83-88; R Standish 88-01; P-in-c Silverdale from 01; Hon Can Blackb Cathl from 91; RD Chorley 92-98. *The Vicarage, St John's Grove, Silverdale, Carnforth LA5 0RH* Tel (01524) 701268

WARREN, Peter. b 40. FCA64. Oak Hill Th Coll 77. **d** 79 **p** 80. C Newcastle w Butterton *Lich* 79-82; TV Sutton St Jas and Wawne *York* 82-87; V Ledsham w Fairburn 87-95; R Ainderby Steeple w Yafforth and Kirby Wiske etc *Ripon* 95-03; rtd 03. *Appletree House, 2 Harvest Close, York YO32 5SA* Tel (01904) 492181
E-mail rabbit@ainderbysteeple.fsnet.co.uk

WARREN, Peter John. b 55. Worc Coll of Educn CertEd76. Trin Coll Bris BA86. **d** 86 **p** 87. C W Streatham St Jas *S'wark* 86-91; P-in-c Edin Clermiston Em *Edin* 91-98; P-in-c Blackpool Ch Ch w All SS *Blackb* 98-03; V from 03. *The Vicarage, 23A North Park Drive, Blackpool FY3 8LR* Tel and fax (01253) 391235
E-mail revpwarren@blueyonder.co.uk

WARREN, Philip James. b 65. SS Paul & Mary Coll Cheltenham BA87 Hughes Hall Cam PGCE88 Kingston Univ MA93. St Jo Coll Nottm MA99. **d** 00 **p** 01. C Reigate St Mary *S'wark* 00-03; P-in-c Jersey Millbrook St Matt *Win* from 03; P-in-c Jersey St Lawr from 03. *The Rectory, La Rue de l'Eglise, St Lawrence, Jersey JE3 1FF* Tel (01534) 869013
E-mail philwarren@jerseymail.co.uk

WARREN, Canon Robert. b 54. TCD BA78 MA81. CITC 76. **d** 78 **p** 79. C Limerick City *L & K* 78-81; Dioc Youth Adv (Limerick) 79-86; I Adare w Kilpeacon and Croom 81-88; Bp's Dom Chapl 81-95; Dioc Registrar (Limerick etc) from 81; Dioc Registrar (Killaloe etc) from 86; I Tralee w Kilmoyley, Ballymacelligott etc from 88; Can Limerick, Killaloe and Clonfert Cathls 95-96; Chan from 97; Asst Dioc Sec *L & K* from 90; Preb Taney St Patr Cathl Dublin from 04. *St John's Rectory, Ashe Street, Tralee, Co Kerry, Irish Republic* Tel (00353) (66) 712 2245 *or* 712 4152 Mobile 87-252 1133 Fax (66) 712 9004
E-mail rwarren@indigo.ie

WARREN, Robert Geoffrey. b 51. DipHE. Trin Coll Bris 79. **d** 82 **p** 83. C Felixstowe SS Pet and Paul *St E* 82-86; V Gazeley w Dalham, Moulton and Kentford 86-90; P-in-c Ipswich St Clem w St Luke and H Trin 90-98; C Gt Finborough w Onehouse and Harleston 98-00; rtd 01; Perm to Offic *B & W* from 02. *11 Homefield, Locking, Weston-super-Mare BS24 8ED* Tel (01934) 824408

WARREN, Robert Irving. b 38. Univ of BC BA58 Ox Univ MA73. Angl Th Coll (BC) LTh61. **d** 61 **p** 63. Canada 61-89; R Northfield *Birm* from 89. *The Rectory, Rectory Road, Birmingham B31 2NA* Tel 0121-477 3111 *or* 475 1518

WARREN, Canon Robert Peter Resker. b 39. Jes Coll Cam BA63 MA. ALCD65. **d** 65 **p** 66. C Rusholme H Trin *Man* 65-68; C Bushbury *Lich* 68-71; V Crookes St Thos *Sheff* 71-90; TR 90-93; RD Hallam 78-83; Hon Can Sheff Cathl 82-93; Can Th Sheff Cathl 93-04; Nat Officer for Evang 93-04; Springboard Missr 98-04; rtd 04; Perm to Offic *Ripon* from 03. *Willow Bank House, Borrage Lane, Ripon HG4 2PZ* Tel (01765) 602996
E-mail robert.warren@ukgateway.net

WARREN, William Frederick. b 55. Sarum & Wells Th Coll 83. **d** 86 **p** 87. C E Greenwich Ch Ch w St Andr and St Mich *S'wark* 86-91; C Richmond St Mary w St Matthias and St Jo 91-95; TV 96-97; V Putney St Marg from 97. *St Margaret's Vicarage, 46 Luttrell Avenue, London SW15 6PE* Tel and fax (020) 8788 5522 *or* 8789 5932 E-mail wwarren@dircon.co.uk

WARRICK, Mark. b 54. Aston Univ BSc76 Nottm Univ BCombStuds83. Linc Th Coll 80. **d** 83 **p** 84. C Grantham *Linc* 83-87; C Cirencester *Glouc* 87-91; V Over *Ely* 91-97; V Deeping St James *Linc* from 97. *The Vicarage, 16 Church Street, Deeping St James, Peterborough PE6 8HD* Tel (01778) 345890 Fax 345877 E-mail vicar@dsj.org.uk

WARRILLOW, Brian Ellis. b 39. Linc Th Coll 81. **d** 83 **p** 84. C Tunstall *Lich* 83-85; C Shrewsbury H Cross 86-87; P-in-c Tilstock 88; P-in-c Whixall 88; V Tilstock and Whixall 89-92; TV Hanley H Ev 92-94; rtd 94; Perm to Offic *Lich* 01-02; P-in-c Menton *Eur* 02-05. *Soleil de Menton, 2 Avenue du Pigautier, 06500 Menton, France*
E-mail thewarrillows@netscapeonline.co.uk

WARRILOW, Mrs Christine. b 42. Lanc Univ BA86. N Ord Course 86. **d** 89 **p** 94. C Netherton *Liv* 89-92; C Cantril Farm 92-94; V 94-96; V Hindley Green 96-02; rtd 02; Perm to Offic *Liv* from 03. *10 Beacon View Drive, Upholland, Skelmersdale WN8 0HL*

WARRINGTON, Katherine Irene (Kay). b 44. Univ of Wales (Swansea) BSc67 DipEd68. St Mich Coll Llan 93. **d** 95. NSM Knighton and Norton *S & B* 95-98; NSM Llywel and Traeanglas w Llanulid 98-00; NSM Trallwng w Bettws Penpont w Aberyskir etc 00-04; Dioc Children's Officer from 96. *17 Ffordd Emlyn, Ystalyfera, Swansea SA9 2EW* Tel (01639) 842874

WARRINGTON, Archdeacon of. *See* BRADLEY, The Ven Peter David Douglas

WARRINGTON, Suffragan Bishop of. *See* JENNINGS, The Rt Revd David Willfred Michael

WARWICK, Gordon Melvin. b 31. N Ord Course 79. **d** 80 **p** 81. NSM Darrington *Wakef* 80-87; TV Almondbury w Farnley Tyas 87-95; rtd 95; Perm to Offic *Newc* from 95. *Andante, Christon Bank, Alnwick NE66 3ES* Tel (01665) 576742

WARWICK, Hugh Johnston. b 39. ARCM63. St Alb and Ox Min Course 97. **d** 00 **p** 01. NSM Rotherfield Peppard *Ox* 00-02; NSM

Rotherfield Peppard and Kidmore End etc from 02. *Middle Dale Cottage, 112 Shiplake Bottom, Peppard Common, Henley-on-Thames RG9 5HR* Tel 0118-972 3070 Fax as telephone E-mail hwarwick@cix.compulink.co.uk

WARWICK, Canon John Michael. b 37. Fitzw Ho Cam BA58 MA62. Ely Th Coll 58. **d** 60 **p** 61. C Towcester w Easton Neston *Pet* 60-63; C Leighton Buzzard *St Alb* 63-64; C Boston *Linc* 64-66; P-in-c Sutterton 66-72; V 72-74; V Sutton St Mary 74-84; V Bourne 84-02; Can and Preb Linc Cathl 89-02; RD Aveland and Ness w Stamford 93-00; Chapl Bourne Hosps Lincs 84-93; Chapl NW Anglia Healthcare NHS Trust 93-98; rtd 02. *24 Hurst Park Road, Twyford, Reading RG10 0EY* Tel 0118-932 0649

WARWICK, Neil Michael. b 64. Nottm Univ BA86. Ridley Hall Cam 03. **d** 05. C Towcester w Easton Neston *Pet* from 05. *35 Hazel Crescent, Towcester NN12 6UQ* Tel (01327) 323018 E-mail revwarwick@btinternet.com

WARWICK, Archdeacon of. *See* PAGET-WILKES, The Ven Michael Jocelyn James

WARWICK, Suffragan Bishop of. *See* STROYAN, The Rt Revd John Ronald Angus

WASEY, Kim Alexandra Clare. b 77. Man Univ BA99 Birm Univ MPhil03. Qu Coll Birm 00. **d** 02 **p** 03. C Rochdale *Man* 02-04; Chapl Man Univ from 04; Chapl Man Metrop Univ from 04. *38 Park Range, Manchester M14 5HQ* Tel 0161-275 2894 Mobile 07944-155772 E-mail kim.wasey@gmail.com

WASH, John. b 46. CEng MIStructE70. **d** 81 **p** 83. OLM Newington St Mary *S'wark* 81-04. *15 Canterbury Place, London SE17 3AD* Tel (020) 7582 9280

WASHINGTON, Nigel Leslie. b 50. St Paul's Cheltenham BEd73 Lon Univ MA83. St Alb and Ox Min Course 97. **d** 00 **p** 01. NSM Westoning w Tingrith *St Alb* from 00. *3 Avenue Mews, Flitwick, Bedford MK45 1BF* Tel (01525) 714442 *or* 636298 E-mail nigelwash@hotmail.com

WASHINGTON, Canon Patrick Leonard. b 44. Nottm Univ BSc66. St Steph Ho Ox 65. **d** 68 **p** 69. C Fleet *Guildf* 68-71; C Farnham 71-74; TV Staveley and Barrow Hill *Derby* 74-83; V Norbury St Phil *Cant* 83-84; V Norbury St Phil *S'wark* from 85; RD Croydon N 90-99; Hon Can S'wark Cathl from 01. *St Philip's Vicarage, 66 Pollards Hill North, London SW16 4NY* Tel (020) 8764 1812

WASSALL, Canon Keith Leonard. b 45. Bede Coll Dur TCert67. Chich Th Coll 68. **d** 71 **p** 72. C Upper Gornal *Lich* 71-74; C Codsall 74-75; TV Hanley All SS 75-79; Asst P Pembroke Bermuda 79-81; V Rickerscote *Lich* 81-92; P-in-c Coven 92-99; Asst Chapl HM Pris Featherstone 92-99; Can Res Bermuda 99-04; C Houghton le Spring *Dur* from 04; C Eppleton and Hetton le Hole from 04; C Lyons from 04. *28 Monteigne Drive, Bowburn, Durham DH6 5QB* Tel 0191-377 8709 E-mail klwassall@tiscali.co.uk

WASTELL, Canon Eric Morse. b 33. St Mich Coll Llan DipTh62. **d** 62 **p** 63. C Oystermouth *S & B* 62-65; Antigua 65-74; Hon Can Antigua 71-74; V Swansea St Gabr *S & B* 74-98; RD Clyne 88-96; Can Brecon Cathl from 90; rtd 98. *18 Belgrave Court, Walter Road, Uplands, Swansea SA1 4PY* Tel (01792) 466709

WASTIE, Canon David Vernon. b 37. Open Univ BA84. Chich Th Coll 79. **d** 81 **p** 82. C Bitterne Park *Win* 81-83; TV Chambersbury *St Alb* 83-87; V Jersey St Luke *Win* 87-95; P-in-c Jersey St Jas 87-93; V 93-95; V Southbourne St Kath 95-99; Hon Can Bukavu from 94; rtd 02. *8 Hazelby Road, Creswell, Worksop S80 4BB* Tel (01909) 720126 E-mail canonwastie@hotmail.com

WATCHORN, Canon Brian. b 39. Em Coll Cam BA61 MA65 Ex Coll Ox BA62. Ripon Hall Ox 61. **d** 63 **p** 64. C Bolton St Pet *Man* 63-66; Chapl G&C Coll Cam 66-74; V Chesterton St Geo *Ely* 75-82; Fell Dean and Chapl Pemb Coll Cam from 82; Lic to Offic *Ely* from 82; Hon Can Ely Cathl from 94; Chapter Can from 00. *7 Botolph Lane, Cambridge CB2 3RD* Tel (01223) 322378 *or* 338147 E-mail dean@pem.cam.ac.uk

WATERFIELD, Janet Lyn. b 60. WMMTC 99. **d** 02 **p** 03. C Bilston *Lich* from 02. *6 Hodnet Close, Bilston WV14 0UF* Tel 07905-539111 (mobile) E-mail janwaterfield@blueyonder.co.uk

WATERFORD, Dean of. *See* LESTER, The Very Revd Trevor Rashleigh

WATERHOUSE, Eric Thomas Benjamin. b 24. Lon Univ 60. Kelham Th Coll 47 Qu Coll Birm 50. **d** 51 **p** 52. C Wolverhampton St Pet *Lich* 51-56; C Lower Gornal 56-57; V Walsall St Mark 57-60; R Kington w Dormston *Worc* 60-64; R Worc St Clem 64-77; P-in-c Abberton, Naunton Beauchamp and Bishampton etc 77-80; R 80-92; rtd 92; Perm to Offic *Worc* from 92. *7 Hazel Avenue, Evesham WR11 1XT* Tel (01386) 421312

WATERHOUSE, Canon Peter. b 46. Leeds Univ DipTh68. Linc Th Coll 68. **d** 70 **p** 71. C Consett *Dur* 70-73; C Heworth St Mary 73-76; V Stockton St Chad 76-83; V Lanchester from 83; P-in-c Holmside from 03; AD Lanchester 90-99; Hon Can Dur Cathl from 03. *The Vicarage, 1 Lee Hill Court, Lanchester, Durham DH7 0QE* Tel (01207) 521170

WATERMAN, Canon Albert Thomas. b 33. Roch Th Coll 61. **d** 64 **p** 65. C Dartford St Alb *Roch* 64-67; V Ilkeston St Jo *Derby* 67-75; V Mackworth St Fran 75-79; V Dartford St Alb *Roch* 79-98; RD Dartford 84-97; Hon Can Roch Cathl 96-98; rtd 98. *19 Beachfield Road, Bembridge PO35 5TN* Tel (01983) 874286

WATERMAN, Mrs Jacqueline Mahalah. b 45. ALCM71. Cant Sch of Min 82. **dss** 85 **d** 87 **p** 94. Wavertree H Trin *Liv* 85-90; Par Dn 87-90; Par Dn Anfield St Columba 90-94; C 94; TV Speke St Aid 94-97; P-in-c Walton St Jo 97-99; V 99-01; C Baildon *Bradf* from 01. *93 Hoyle Court Road, Baildon, Shipley BD17 6EL* Tel (01274) 594456

WATERS, Arthur Brian. b 34. St Deiniol's Hawarden 71. **d** 73 **p** 74. C Bedwellty *Mon* 73-76; P-in-c Newport All SS 76-81; V Mynyddislwyn 81-91; C-in-c Maesglas Newport CD 91-95; V Maesglas and Duffryn 95-99; rtd 99. *3B Blaen-y-Pant Crescent, Blaen-y-Pant, Newport NP20 5QB*

WATERS, Brenda Mary. b 51. Bp Otter Coll. **d** 99. NSM Whyke w Rumboldswhyke and Portfield *Chich* from 99. *69 Chatsworth Road, Chichester PO19 7YA*

WATERS, Mrs Carolyn Anne. b 52. St Jo Coll Nottm BA02. **d** 00 **p** 01. NSM Frodsham *Ches* 00-02; C Penhill *Bris* from 02. *The Vicarage, Bremhill Close, Swindon SN2 5DS* Tel (01793) 721921 Mobile 07789-430317 E-mail caswaters@dsl.pipex.com

WATERS, David Keith. b 46. S Wales Bapt Coll DipTh73 DPS73 St Mich Coll Llan 93. **d** 93 **p** 94. In Bapt Ch 73-90; C Caerphilly *Llan* 93-97; TV Cwmbran *Mon* 97-99; R Gelligaer *Llan* from 99. *The Rectory, Church Road, Gelligaer, Hengoed CF82 8FW* Tel (01443) 830300

WATERS, Miss Jill Christine. b 43. CertEd64. Cranmer Hall Dur 82. **dss** 82 **d** 87 **p** 94. New Milverton *Cov* 82-86; Draycott-le-Moors w Forsbrook *Lich* 86-96; Par Dn 87-94; C 94-96; P-in-c Mow Cop from 96. *The Vicarage, 5 Congleton Road, Mow Cop, Stoke-on-Trent ST7 3PJ* Tel (01782) 515077

WATERS, John Michael. b 30. Qu Coll Cam BA53 MA58. Ridley Hall Cam 53. **d** 55 **p** 56. C Southport Ch Ch *Liv* 55-57; C Farnworth 57-62; V Blackb H Trin *Blackb* 63-70; Sec Birm Coun Chr Chs 70-77; Chapl Birm Cathl *Birm* 70-74; Dioc Ecum Officer 74-77; V Hednesford *Lich* 77-93; RD Rugeley 78-88; rtd 93; P-in-c Etton w Dalton Holme *York* 93-99; Perm to Offic from 00. *Blacksmith's Cottage, Middlewood Lane, Fylingthorpe, Whitby YO22 4UB* Tel (01947) 880422

WATERS, Mark. b 51. Southn Univ BTh85. Sarum & Wells Th Coll 79. **d** 82 **p** 83. C Clifton All SS w St Jo *Bris* 82-85; P-in-c Brislington St Anne 85-91; Dioc Soc Resp Officer *Sheff* 91-94; Community Org Citizen Organisation Foundn 94-00; NSM Rotherham 94-97; Hon C Gt Crosby St Faith and Waterloo Park St Mary *Liv* 97-00; NSM from 05; TV Kirkby 00-04; Project Development Manager Ch Action on Poverty 04-05. *30 Victoria Road West, Crosby, Liverpool L23 8UQ* Tel 0151-931 1031 E-mail mark_waters@beeb.net

WATERS, Nicholas Marshall Stephenson. b 35. Selw Coll Cam BA59 MA63. Wells Th Coll 59. **d** 61 **p** 62. C Eastbourne St Mary *Chich* 61-64; Asst Chapl Ardingly Coll 64-93; P-in-c Slindon, Eartham and Madehurst *Chich* 93-99; R 99-03; rtd 03. *Lyle House, School Lane, Fittleworth, Pulborough RH20 1JB* Tel (01798) 865778

WATERS, Stephen. b 49. Chich Th Coll 83. **d** 85 **p** 86. C Baildon *Bradf* 85-87; C Altrincham St Geo *Ches* 87-89; TV Ellesmere Port 89-91; P-in-c Crewe St Jo 91-93; V Mossley 93-98; TV Congleton 98-99; P-in-c Alvanley 99-02; V Penhill *Bris* from 02. *The Vicarage, Bremhill Close, Swindon SN2 5DS* Tel (01793) 721921 Mobile 07796-694139 E-mail frstephen.waters@dsl.pipex.com

WATERS, William Paul. b 52. Aston Tr Scheme 84 Chich Th Coll 86. **d** 88 **p** 89. C Tottenham St Paul *Lon* 88-91; C Stroud Green H Trin 91-95; TV Wickford and Runwell *Chelmsf* 95-98; Chapl Runwell Hosp Wickford 95-98; Chapl Qu Medical Cen Nottm Univ Hosp NHS Trust from 98. *Queen's Medical Centre University Hospital, Derby Road, Nottingham NG7 2UH* Tel 0115-924 9924 ext 43799 *or* 917 4412 Mobile 07711-721483 E-mail paul.waters@nottshc.nhs.uk

WATERSTONE, Albert Thomas. b 23. TCD BA45 BD67. CITC 46. **d** 46 **p** 47. C Kilkenny St Canice Cathl *C & O* 46-50; P-in-c Borris-in-Ossory w Aghavoe 50-51; I 52-54; I Fiddown w Kilmacow 54-64; I Tullamore w Lynally and Rahan *M & K* 64-73; I Tullamore w Durrow, Newtownfertullagh, Rahan etc 73-90; Can Meath 81-90; rtd 90. *Lynally House, Mocklagh, Blue Ball, Tullamore, Co Offaly, Irish Republic* Tel and fax (00353) (506) 21367

WATERSTREET, Canon John Donald. b 34. Trin Hall Cam BA58 MA62. Lich Th Coll 58. **d** 60 **p** 61. C Blackheath *Birm* 60-64; C Aston SS Pet and Paul 64-67; R Sheldon 67-77; RD Coleshill 75-77; V Selly Oak St Mary 77-89; RD Edgbaston 84-89; Hon Can Birm Cathl 86-00; R The Whitacres and Shustoke 89-97; C Acocks Green 97-00; rtd 00; Perm to Offic *Birm* from 00. *547 Fox Hollies Road, Hall Green, Birmingham B28 8RL* Tel 0121-702 2080

WATERTON, Dawn. b 46. WMMTC 95. **d** 98 **p** 99. NSM Nuneaton St Nic *Cov* from 98. *65 Main Street, Higham on the Hill, Nuneaton CV13 6AH* Tel (01455) 212861

WATES, John Norman. b 43. JP82. BNC Ox MA65 Solicitor 72 FRSA00. Dioc OLM tr scheme 99. **d** 02 **p** 03. OLM Chipstead *S'wark* from 02. *Elmore, High Road, Chipstead, Coulsdon CR5 3SB* Tel (01737) 557550 Fax 552918 E-mail john@jwates.com

WATHEN, Mark William Gerard. b 12. TD45. ACIB. K Coll Lon 31. **d** 82 **p** 82. Hon C Broadford *Arg* 82-91; Hon C Fort William 82-91; Hon C Portree 82-96; rtd 96. *Tollgate Cottage, Norwich Road, Marsham, Norwich NR10 5PX* Tel (01263) 732673

WATHERSTON, Peter David. b 42. Lon Univ BSc69 FCA76. Ridley Hall Cam 75. **d** 77 **p** 78. C Barnsbury St Andr *Lon* 77-78; C Barnsbury St Andr w H Trin 79-80; C Barnsbury St Andr and H Trin w All SS 81; Chapl Mayflower Family Cen Canning Town *Chelmsf* 81-96; Perm to Offic from 96; Co-ord First Fruit Charity from 97. *264 Plashet Grove, London E6 1DQ,* or *Latimer Hall, Cleves Road, London E6 1QF* Tel (020) 8470 6868 *or* 8548 4676 Fax 8548 4110 E-mail first.fruit@virgin.net

WATKIN, David Glynne. b 52. Univ of Wales (Lamp) BA74 PhD78 Wolv Univ PGCE87 MTS FRGS. **d** 02 **p** 03. OLM Wolverhampton St Matt *Lich* from 02. *3 Alder Dale, Wolverhampton WV3 9JF* Tel (01902) 710842 E-mail d.g.watkin@wlv.ac.uk

WATKIN, David William. b 42. FCA70. Qu Coll Birm 84. **d** 86 **p** 87. C Tunstall *Lich* 86-89; Camberwell Deanery Missr *S'wark* 89-95; V Trent Vale *Lich* 95-01; V Milton from 01. *The Vicarage, Baddeley Green Lane, Stoke-on-Trent ST2 7EY* Tel (01782) 534062

WATKIN, Prof Thomas Glyn. b 52. Pemb Coll Ox BA74 MA77 BCL75 Barrister-at-Law (Middle Temple) 76. Llan Dioc Tr Scheme 89. **d** 92 **p** 94. NSM Roath St Martin *Llan* from 92. *49 Cyncoed Road, Penylan, Cardiff CF23 5SB* Tel (029) 2049 5662

WATKINS, Alfred Felix Maceroni. b 20. Glouc Th Course 70. **d** 72 **p** 73. C Yate *Glouc* 72-75; V Parkend 75-90; rtd 90; Perm to Offic *Heref* from 93. *Leylines, 26 Southbank Road, Hereford HR1 2TJ* Tel (01432) 341014

WATKINS, Anthony John. b 42. St D Coll Lamp BA64 St Steph Ho Ox 64. **d** 66 **p** 67. C E Dulwich St Jo *S'wark* 66-71; C Tewkesbury w Walton Cardiff *Glouc* 71-75; Prec 75-81; Chapl Choral Ches Cathl *Ches* 75-81; V Brixworth w Holcot *Pet* from 81. *The Vicarage, Station Road, Brixworth, Northampton NN6 9DF* Tel (01604) 880286

WATKINS, Mrs Christine Dorothy (Sue). b 29. **d** 89 **p** 00. Deacon Port Macquarie Australia 89-95; Chapl Port Macquarie Gen Hosp 89-95; Perm to Offic *Chich* 97-00; NSM Crawley from 00. *2 Homethorne House, Oak Road, Crawley RH11 8AE* Tel (01293) 526055

WATKINS, Christopher. b 43. Sarum & Wells Th Coll 88. **d** 90 **p** 91. C Abergavenny St Mary w Llanwenarth Citra *Mon* 90-94; TV Cwmbran 94-96; TV Wordsley *Worc* from 00. *25 Middleway Avenue, Stourbridge DY8 5NB* Tel (01384) 861943 E-mail chriswat@blueyonder.co.uk

WATKINS, David James Hier. b 39. Trin Coll Carmarthen CertEd60 Univ of Wales DipEd67 BEd76. St Mich Coll Llan. **d** 90 **p** 91. NSM Oystermouth *S & B* from 90; Dioc Youth Chapl from 91; Lect Gorseinon Coll from 92. *10 Lambswell Close, Langland, Swansea SA3 4HJ* Tel (01792) 369742

WATKINS, Felix. *See* WATKINS, Alfred Felix Maceroni

WATKINS (née ROBERTS), Mrs Gwyneth. b 35. Univ of Wales (Swansea) BA MEd. St Mich Coll Llan 90. **d** 91 **p** 97. C Llanbadarn Fawr w Capel Bangor and Goginan *St D* 91-94; P-in-c Maenordeifi and Capel Colman w Llanfihangel etc 94-97; R 97-98; rtd 98. *Wenllys, Waunfarlais Road, Llandybie, Ammanford SA18 3NG*

WATKINS, Mrs Hilary Odette. b 47. New Hall Cam MA73. St Alb and Ox Min Course 98. **d** 01 **p** 02. NSM Appleton and Besselsleigh *Ox* 01-04; C Aisholt, Enmore, Goathurst, Nether Stowey etc *B & W* from 04. *The Rectory, Church Road, Spaxton, Bridgwater TA5 1DA* Tel (01278) 671265 E-mail hilary.watkins1@tesco.net

WATKINS, Jonathan. b 58. Padgate Coll of Educn BEd79. Trin Coll Bris 90. **d** 92 **p** 93. C Wallington H Trin *S'wark* 92-97; C Hartley Wintney, Elvetham, Winchfield etc *Win* 97-99; Chapl K Alfred's Coll Win from 99. *King Alfred's College, Sparkford Road, Winchester SO22 4NR* Tel (01962) 827246 *or* 827410 E-mail jonathan.watkins@wkac.ac.uk

WATKINS, Miss Lorna Ann Francis Charles. b 59. Trin Coll Carmarthen BEd82. St Steph Ho Ox 82. **d** 84 **p** 97. C Tenby and Gumfreston *St D* 84-89; C Pembroke Dock 89-91; Dn-in-c Cosheston w Nash and Upton 91-92; C Bassaleg *Mon* 92-94; C Mynyddislwyn 94-95; TV 95-99; R Herbrandston and Hasguard w St Ishmael's *St D* 99-05. *Address temp unknown*

WATKINS, Michael John. b 61. RGN90. Trin Coll Bris 03. **d** 05. C Bath Weston All SS w N Stoke and Langridge *B & W* from 05. *23 Lucklands Road, Bath BA1 4AX* Tel (01225) 310492 Mobile 07814-430782 E-mail mikeandsarah@xalt.co.uk

WATKINS, Michael Morris. b 32. MRCS60 LRCP60. St Jo Coll Nottm DPS78. **d** 81 **p** 81. C Hornchurch St Andr *Chelmsf* 81-84; P-in-c Snitterfield w Bearley *Cov* 84-90; V 90-92; rtd 93; Perm to Offic *Cov* from 93. *Glaslyn, Riverside, Tiddington Road, Stratford-upon-Avon CV37 7BD* Tel (01789) 298085 E-mail revdocmw@waitrose.com

WATKINS, Ms Betty Anne. *See* MOCKFORD, Mrs Betty Anne

WATKINS, Canon Peter. b 51. Oak Hill Th Coll BA. **d** 82 **p** 83. C Whitnash *Cov* 82-86; V Wolston and Church Lawford 86-99; RD Rugby 94-99; V Finham from 99; Hon Can Cov Cathl from 04. *St Martin's Vicarage, 136 Green Lane South, Coventry CV3 6EA* Tel and fax (024) 7641 8330 E-mail st-martins@freeuk.com

WATKINS, Peter Gordon. b 34. St Pet Coll Ox BA57 MA61. Wycliffe Hall Ox 58. **d** 59 **p** 60. C Wolverhampton St Geo *Lich* 59-60; C Burton St Chad 60-61; C Westmr St Jas *Lon* 61-63; USA 63-65; V Ealing Common St Matt *Lon* from 67. *St Matthew's Vicarage, 7 North Common Road, London W5 2QA* Tel (020) 8567 3820 E-mail peterwatkins@amserve.com

WATKINS, Robert Henry. b 30. New Coll Ox BA54 MA60. Westcott Ho Cam 59. **d** 60 **p** 61. C Newc H Cross *Newc* 60-63; C Morpeth 63-67; V Delaval 67-80; V Lanercost w Kirkcambeck and Walton *Carl* 80-90; rtd 90; Perm to Offic *Carl* from 90. *Lowpark, Loweswater, Cockermouth CA13 0RU* Tel (01900) 85242

WATKINS, Sue. *See* WATKINS, Mrs Christine Dorothy

WATKINS, Susan Jane. b 58. Qu Coll Birm. **d** 01 **p** 02. C Edgbaston St Germain *Birm* from 01. *410 Gillott Road, Birmingham B16 9LP* Tel 0121-242 3059 E-mail sue-watkins@blueyonder.co.uk

WATKINS, Canon William Hywel. b 36. St D Coll Lamp BA58. Wycliffe Hall Ox 58. **d** 61 **p** 62. C Llanelli *St D* 61-68; V Llwynhendy 68-78; V Slebech and Uzmaston w Boulston 78-01; RD Daugleddau 87-01; Hon Can St D Cathl 91-93; Can St D Cathl 93-01; rtd 01. *Nant-yr-Arian, Llanbadarn Fawr, Aberystwyth SY23 3SZ* Tel (01970) 623359 Fax as telephone

WATKINS-JONES, Arthur Basil. b 24. Sarum Th Coll 67. **d** 69 **p** 70. C Broadstone *Sarum* 69-73; P-in-c Winterbourne Stickland and Turnworth etc 73-76; R 76-78; P-in-c Lilliput 78-82; V 82-89; rtd 89; Perm to Offic *Sarum* from 89. *Oak Cottage, 31 Danecourt Road, Poole BH14 0PG* Tel (01202) 746074

WATKINS-WRIGHT, Richard Kenneth David. b 39. Westcott Ho Cam 66. **d** 70 **p** 71. C Bilton *Cov* 70-74; Asst Chapl St Geo Hosp Lon 74-75; Chapl Oakwood Hosp Maidstone 76-78; R Gt w Lt Gransden *Ely* 78-97; rtd 99; Perm to Offic *Ely* from 01. *Halsou, 5 De Lisle Close, Papworth Everard, Cambridge CB3 8UT* Tel (01480) 830746 E-mail richard@watkinswright.plus.com

WATKINSON, Adam John McNicol. b 68. Keble Coll Ox BA89 MA93 St Martin's Coll Lanc PGCE90. N Ord Course 01. **d** 03 **p** 04. NSM Croston and Bretherton *Blackb* from 03; Chapl Ormskirk Sch from 03. *2 Brookdale, Sheep Hill Lane, New Longton, Preston PR4 4XL* Tel (01772) 619844 E-mail adamjwatkinson@aol.com

WATKINSON, Neil. b 64. Univ Coll Lon BSc86 DipArch91. Oak Hill Th Coll BA04. **d** 04 **p** 05. C Maidenhead St Andr and St Mary *Ox* from 04. *1 Hemsdale, Maidenhead SL6 6SL* Tel (01628) 770951 *or* 638866 E-mail neil.watkinson@stmarysmaidenhead.org

WATKINSON, Ronald Frank. EAMTC. **d** 04 **p** 05. NSM Paston *Pet* from 04. *20 Welbourne, Peterborough PE4 6NH* Tel (01733) 571733 E-mail ronwatkinson@kingdomyouth.freeserve.co.uk

WATLING, His Honour Brian. b 35. QC79. K Coll Lon LLB56 Barrister 57. **d** 87 **p** 88. NSM Lavenham *St E* 87-90; NSM Nayland w Wiston 90-03; NSM Boxford, Edwardstone, Groton etc from 03. *The Red House, Boxford, Sudbury CO10 5HH*

WATLING, Sister Rosemary Dawn. b 32. Newnham Coll Cam BA70 MA73. Gilmore Course 70. **dss** 85 **d** 87 **p** 94. CSA 79-90; Paddington St Mary *Lon* 85-86; E Bris 86-87; Hon Par Dn 87; Par Dn Clifton H Trin, St Andr and St Pet 87-94; C 94-95; rtd 95; NSM Wraxall *B & W* 96-02; Perm to Offic from 02. *32 St Andrew's Mews, Wells BA5 2LB* Tel (01749) 673675

WATSON, Canon Alan. b 34. Lon Univ LLB58. Linc Th Coll 58. **d** 60 **p** 61. C Spring Park *Cant* 60-63; C Sheerness H Trin w St Paul 63-68; R Allington 68-73; P-in-c Maidstone St Pet 73; R Allington and Maidstone St Pet 73-99; Hon Can Cant Cathl 85-99; RD Sutton 86-92; rtd 99; Perm to Offic *B & W* and *Sarum* from 00. *68 Southgate Drive, Wincanton BA9 9ET* Tel (01963) 34368 E-mail alan@watson.orbitalnet.co.uk

WATSON, Alan. b 41. AKC64. St Boniface Warminster. **d** 65 **p** 66. C Hendon *Dur* 65-68; C Sheff St Cecilia Parson Cross *Sheff* 68-70; C Harton Colliery *Dur* 70-72; TV 72-74; R Gorton St Mary and St Thos *Man* 74-82; R Swinton St Pet 82-87; TR Swinton and Pendlebury 87-89; R Rawmarsh w Parkgate *Sheff* 89-94; P-in-c Dunscroft St Edwin 96-99; V from 99. *The Vicarage, 162 Station Road, Dunscroft, Doncaster DN7 4JR* Tel (01302) 841328 E-mail a.watsondunscroft@whsmithnet.co.uk

WATSON, Albert Victor. b 44. Ridley Hall Cam 85. **d** 87 **p** 88. C Hornchurch St Andr *Chelmsf* 87-94; P-in-c Tye Green w Netteswell 94-95; R from 95; RD Harlow 99-04. *The Rectory, Tawneys Road, Harlow CM18 6QR* Tel (01279) 425138 E-mail albert@watson2119.fsnet.co.uk

WATSON, Alfred Keith. b 39. Birm Univ BSc61. Ox Min Course 93. **d** 96 **p** 97. NSM Aylesbury w Bierton and Hulcott *Ox* 96-01; NSM Ludgvan, Marazion, St Hilary and Perranuthnoe *Truro* from 01. *The Rectory, St Hilary, Churchtown, Penzance TR20 9DQ* Tel (01736) 710229

WATSON, Andrew John. b 61. CCC Cam BA82 MA90. Ridley Hall Cam 84. **d** 87 **p** 88. C Ipsley *Worc* 87-91; C Notting Hill St Jo and St Pet *Lon* 91-96; V E Twickenham St Steph from 96; AD Hampton from 03. *St Stephen's Vicarage, 21 Cambridge Park, Twickenham TW1 2JE* Tel (020) 8607 9676 *or* 8892 5258 E-mail andrew@st-stephens.org.uk

WATSON, Anne-Marie Louise. *See* RENSHAW, Mrs Anne-Marie Louise

WATSON, Craig. b 60. Bath Univ BSc82 CertEd82 York St Jo Coll MA04. N Ord Course 00. **d** 03 **p** 04. NSM Thorpe Edge *Bradf* 03-04; NSM Halliwell St Pet *Man* from 04. *2 Holly Mill Crescent, Bolton BL1 8TX* Tel (01204) 458191 E-mail crw@canon-slade.bolton.sch.uk

WATSON, David. *See* WATSON, Canon Leonard Alexander David

WATSON, The Very Revd Derek Richard. b 38. Selw Coll Cam BA61 MA65. Cuddesdon Coll 62. **d** 64 **p** 65. C New Eltham All SS *S'wark* 64-66; Chapl Ch Coll Cam 66-70; Bp's Dom Chapl *S'wark* 70-73; V Surbiton St Mark 73-77; V Surbiton St Andr and St Mark 77-78; Can Res and Treas S'wark Cathl 78-82; Dioc Dir of Ords 78-82; P-in-c Chelsea St Luke *Lon* 82-85; R 85-87; P-in-c Chelsea Ch Ch 86-87; R Chelsea St Luke and Ch Ch 87-96; AD Chelsea 94-96; Dean Sarum 96-02; rtd 02. *Bede House, Paul's Mill, Penn, High Wycombe HP10 8NZ* Tel (01494) 816502

WATSON, Derek Stanley. b 54. NEOC DipHE95. **d** 95 **p** 96. C W Acklam *York* 95-98; C-in-c Ingleby Barwick CD 98-00; V Ingleby Barwick from 00. *St Francis's House, Barwick Way, Ingleby Barwick, Stockton-on-Tees TS17 0WD* Tel and fax (01642) 760171 E-mail derek@watson1954.freeserve.co.uk

WATSON, Mrs Diane Elsie. b 44. N Ord Course 92. **d** 95 **p** 96. C Grange St Andr *Ches* 95-00; C Runcorn H Trin 96-00; R Thurstaston from 00. *Thurstaston Rectory, Telegraph Road, Thurstaston, Wirral CH61 0HJ* Tel 0151-648 1816 E-mail diane.watson@virgin.net

WATSON, Preb Donald Wace. b 17. Qu Coll Cam BA39 MA43. Lich Th Coll 39. **d** 41 **p** 42. C W Bromwich St Andr *Lich* 41-43; C Fenton 43-47; C-in-c Birches Head CD 47-48; V Smethwick St Steph *Birm* 48-51; R Kingstone w Gratwich *Lich* 51-55; V Kinver 55-82; Preb Lich Cathl 78-82; rtd 82; Perm to Offic *Heref* from 89. *The Stables, King Street, Much Wenlock TF13 6BL* Tel (01952) 728364

WATSON, Mrs Elsada Beatrice (Elsie). b 30. Westhill Coll Birm CPS86. WMMTC. **d** 89 **p** 94. NSM Birm St Pet *Birm* 89-90; NSM Lozells St Paul and St Silas 90-93; Par Dn 93-94; C 94-96; Perm to Offic from 96; rtd 96. *4 Maidstone Road, Birmingham B20 3EH* Tel 0121-356 0626

WATSON, Geoffrey. b 48. Liv Univ BEd71. Linc Th Coll 81. **d** 83 **p** 84. C Hartlepool St Luke *Dur* 83-87; P-in-c Shadforth 87-94; Soc Resp Officer 87-94; Dioc Rural Development Adv 90-94; V Staveley, Ings and Kentmere *Carl* from 94. *The Vicarage, Kentmere Road, Staveley, Kendal LA8 9PA* Tel (01539) 821267 E-mail geof_watson@lineone.net

WATSON, Gordon Mark Stewart. b 67. Wolv Poly BA90 DipEd. CITC BTh95. **d** 95 **p** 96. C Ballymoney w Finvoy and Rasharkin *Conn* 95-98; I Brackaville w Donaghendry and Ballyclog *Arm* 98-01; I Killesher *K, E & A* from 01. *The New Rectory, Tully Two, Enniskillen BT92 1FN* Tel (028) 6634 8235 Mobile 07710-924660 E-mail killesher@kilmore.anglican.org

WATSON, Graeme Campbell Hubert. b 35. Ch Ch Ox BA58 BA59 MA61. Coll of Resurr Mirfield 59. **d** 61 **p** 62. C Edin St Mary *Edin* 61-63; C Carrington *S'well* 63-67; Tanzania 67-77; Tutor St Cyprian's Coll Ngala 67-69; Vice-Prin St Mark's Th Coll Dar es Salaam 69-73; P-in-c Dar es Salaam St Alb 74-77; P-in-c Kingston St Mary w Broomfield *B & W* 77-80; V 80-81; R Kingston St Mary w Broomfield etc 81-95; P-in-c Feock *Truro* 95-00; Tutor SWMTC 95-00; rtd 00; Perm to Offic *Truro* 00-02 and *Lon* from 02. *75 Winston Road, London N16 9LN* Tel (020) 7249 8701 E-mail gralizwatson@btinternet.com

WATSON, Hartley Roger. b 40. K Coll Lon. **d** 64 **p** 65. C Noel Park St Mark *Lon* 64-67; C Munster Square St Mary Magd 67-68; C Stamford Hill St Jo 68-70; Chapl RAF 70-76; R St Breoke *Truro* 76-84; P-in-c Egloshayle 82-84; R Wittering w Thornhaugh and Wansford *Pet* 84-00; RD Barnack 98-00; R Brigstock w Stanion and Lowick and Sudborough from 00. *The Rectory, Church Street, Brigstock, Kettering NN14 3EX* Tel (01536) 373371

WATSON, Henry Stanley. b 36. **d** 72 **p** 74. NSM Bethnal Green St Jas Less *Lon* 72-83; NSM Old Ford St Paul w St Steph and St Mark 83-88; NSM Bethnal Green St Jas Less 89-93; NSM Scarborough St Mary w Ch Ch and H Apostles *York* 93-97; P-in-c Seamer 97-03; rtd 03; Hon C Prees *Lich* from 03; Hon C Fauls from 03. *The Vicarage, Church Street, Prees, Whitchurch SY13 2EE* Tel (01948) 840243

WATSON, Canon Ian Leslie Stewart. b 50. Wycliffe Hall Ox 79. **d** 81 **p** 82. C Plymouth St Andr w St Paul and St Geo *Ex* 81-85; TV Ipsley *Worc* 85-90; V Woodley St Jo the Ev *Ox* 90-92; TR Woodley 92-95; Chapl Amsterdam w Den Helder and Heiloo *Eur* 95-01; Chief Exec ICS from 01; Can Gib Cathl *Eur* from 02; Perm to Offic *Cov* from 01 and *Worc* from 03. *Intercontinental Church Society, 1 Athena Drive, Tachbrook Park, Warwick CV34 6NL* Tel (01926) 430347 Fax 888092 E-mail ilwatson@ics-uk.org

WATSON, James Valentine John Giles. b 65. Newc Univ BA87 Ox Univ BA91 MA97. Ripon Coll Cuddesdon 89. **d** 92 **p** 93. C Newc St Geo *Newc* 92-95; TV Daventry, Ashby St Ledgers, Braunston etc *Pet* 95-00; V Woodplumpton *Blackb* 00-03; TR Wheatley *Ox* from 03. *The Vicarage, 18 London Road, Wheatley, Oxford OX33 1YA* Tel (01865) 872224 E-mail james@jvrswatson.freeserve.co.uk

WATSON, The Ven Jeffrey John Seagrief. b 39. Em Coll Cam BA61 MA65. Clifton Th Coll 62. **d** 65 **p** 66. C Beckenham Ch Ch *Roch* 65-69; C Southsea St Jude *Portsm* 69-71; V Win Ch Ch *Win* 71-81; V Bitterne 81-93; RD Southampton 83-93; Hon Can Win Cathl 91-93; Adn Ely 93-04; Hon Can Ely Cathl 93-04; rtd 04; Perm to Offic *Win* from 04. *7 Ferry Road, Hythe, Southampton SO45 5GB* Tel (023) 8084 1189

WATSON, John. b 34. AKC59. **d** 60 **p** 61. C Stockton St Pet *Dur* 60-64; C Darlington H Trin 64-66; V Swalwell 66-68; Perm to Offic *Dur* 68-69; *Leic* 69-74; *Man* 74-76; rtd 96. *The Flat, 194 Abington Avenue, Northampton NN1 4QA* Tel (01604) 624300 E-mail john.moirawatson@btopenworld.com

WATSON, John Calum. b 69. Spurgeon's Coll BD96. Trin Coll Bris MA03. **d** 03 **p** 04. C Richmond H Trin and Ch Ch *S'wark* from 03. *23 Grena Road, Richmond TW9 1XU* Tel (020) 8948 4476 E-mail john@allyu.org.uk

WATSON, Canon John Derrick. b 35. K Coll Lon 56. Edin Th Coll 60. **d** 61 **p** 62. C Fulham St Etheldreda *Lon* 61-64; P-in-c Stevenage H Trin *St Alb* 64-71; V 71-74; V Leagrave 74-84; RD Luton 80-82; V Eaton Socon 84-98; Hon Can St Alb 93-98; RD Biggleswade 94-96; rtd 98; Perm to Offic *Ely* and *St Alb* from 99. *14 Balmoral Way, Eynesbury, St Neots PE19 2RJ* Tel (01480) 404520

WATSON, Preb John Francis Wentworth. b 28. St Jo Coll Nottm LTh59. **d** 59 **p** 60. C Egham *Guildf* 59-62; C-in-c Ewell St Paul Howell Hill CD 62-66; R Ashtead 66-72; V Plymouth St Andr w St Paul and St Geo *Ex* 72-94; Angl Adv TV SW 83-93; Westcountry TV 93-94; Preb Ex Cathl 84-94; rtd 94; Perm to Offic *Ex* from 97. *Woodland House, Western Road, Ivybridge PL21 9AL* Tel (01752) 893735

WATSON, John Lionel. b 39. G&C Coll Cam BA61 MA65. Ridley Hall Cam 62. **d** 64 **p** 65. C Toxteth Park St Philemon w St Silas *Liv* 64-69; C Morden *S'wark* 69-73; C Cambridge St Phil *Ely* 73-74; Chapl Elstree Sch Woolhampton 74-77; R Woolhampton w Midgham *Ox* 77-81; R Woolhampton w Midgham and Beenham Valance 81-95; Perm to Offic *Win* from 97; rtd 00. *Westfield House, Littleton Road, Crawley, Winchester SO21 2QD* Tel (01962) 776892

WATSON, John Robertson Thomas. b 27. CITC 68. **d** 70 **p** 71. C Belfast St Steph *Conn* 71-73; Bp's C Swanlinbar w Templeport *K, E & A* 73-82; I Arvagh w Carrigallen, Gowna and Columbkille 82-97; Preb Kilmore Cathl 88-97; rtd 97. *75 Church Road, Dundonald, Belfast BT16 2LW* Tel (028) 9048 2520

WATSON, Jonathan Ramsay George. b 38. Oriel Coll Ox BA61 MA65 DipEd62. Ridley Hall Cam 88. **d** 90 **p** 91. C Locks Heath *Portsm* 90-94; V Erith St Paul *Roch* 94-01; rtd 01. *14 Park Crescent, Midhurst GU29 9ED* Tel (01730) 816145 E-mail jrgwatson@netscapeonline.co.uk

WATSON, Julie Sandra. b 59. Liv Poly BSc81 Teesside Poly PhD86. NEOC 99. **d** 02 **p** 03. NSM Redcar *York* from 02. *20 Talisker Gardens, Redcar TS10 2TG* Tel (01642) 478147 E-mail j.s.watson@tees.ac.uk

WATSON, Keith. *See* WATSON, Alfred Keith

WATSON, Kenneth Roy. b 27. CEng68 MIMechE68. EMMTC 83. **d** 86 **p** 87. NSM Ashby-de-la-Zouch St Helen w Coleorton *Leic* 86-90; R Breedon cum Isley Walton and Worthington 90-93; rtd 93; Perm to Offic *Leic* and *Derby* from 93. *9 Thornley Place, Ashbourne DE6 1PQ*

WATSON, Laurence Leslie. b 31. Keble Coll Ox BA55 MA59. Ely Th Coll. **d** 57 **p** 58. C Solihull *Birm* 57-60; C Digswell *St Alb* 60-62; V Smethwick St Steph *Birm* 62-67; V Billesley Common 67-95; rtd 95; Perm to Offic *Cov* and *Birm* from 95. *10 Redwing Close, Bishopton, Stratford-upon-Avon CV37 9EX* Tel (01789) 294569

WATSON, Canon Leonard Alexander David. b 37. Man Univ BSc59. Coll of Resurr Mirfield 62. **d** 64 **p** 65. C Rawmarsh w Parkgate *Sheff* 64-68; C Empangeni S Africa 69-74; TV E Runcorn w Halton *Ches* 74-79; TV Sanderstead All SS *S'wark* 79-86; TR Selsdon St Jo w St Fran 86-98; RD Croydon Addington 90-95; P-in-c Horne and Outwood 98-02; Hon Can S'wark Cathl 02-03; rtd 02; Perm to Offic *Win* from 03. *White Gables, Station Road, East Tisted, Alton GU34 3QX* Tel (01420) 588317 E-mail dadiwatson@hotmail.com

WATSON, Mark. *See* WATSON, Gordon Mark Stewart

WATSON, Michael Henry. b 44. Victoria Univ Wellington BA65 MA66. Wycliffe Hall Ox 75. **d** 77 **p** 78. C Farnborough *Roch* 77-81; New Zealand from 81. *PO Box 7023, Wellington South, New Zealand* Tel (0064) (4) 389 2760 *or* 389 9603 Fax 389 2109

WATSON, Michael Paul. b 58. Trin Coll Bris DipHE93. **d** 93 **p** 94. C Derby St Alkmund and St Werburgh *Derby* 93-99; USA from 00; Lt Rock St Andr 00-01; R Bridge Community Austin from 01. *10636 Floral Park Drive, Austin, TX 78759, USA* E-mail mike.bridgepoint@worldnet.att.net

WATSON, Nicholas Edgar. b 67. St Cath Coll Cam BA88 MA92. Wycliffe Hall Ox BA91. **d** 92 **p** 93. C Benfieldside *Dur* 92-95; C-in-c Stockton Green Vale H Trin CD 95-96; P-in-c Stockton H Trin 96-00; Chapl Ian Ramsey Sch Stockton 95-00; P-in-c Breadsall *Derby* from 00; Warden of Readers from 00. *The Rectory, 57 Rectory Lane, Breadsall, Derby DE21 5LL* Tel (01332) 831352 E-mail revnickw@derbyreaders.fsnet.co.uk

WATSON, Prof Paul Frederick. b 44. MRCVS69 RVC(Lon) BSc66 BVetMed69 Sydney Univ PhD73 Lon Univ DSc95. Oak Hill NSM Course 86. **d** 88 **p** 89. NSM Muswell Hill St Jas w St Matt *Lon* 88-96; NSM Edmonton St Aldhelm 96-01; Perm to Offic *Lon* and *St Alb* from 01. *50 New Road, Ware SG12 7BY* Tel (01920) 466941 E-mail pwatson@rvc.ac.uk

WATSON, Paul R. b 66. St Andr Univ MA89 Glas Univ BD95 MTh00. **d** 00 **p** 01. C Glas St Ninian *Glas* from 00. *416 Paisley Road, Glasgow G51 1BE* Tel 0141-427 4205 E-mail paulandlna@care4free.net

WATSON, Paul William. b 55. Huddersfield Poly BA. St Jo Coll Nottm. **d** 86 **p** 87. C Meltham Mills *Wakef* 86-89; C Meltham 89-90; TV Borehamwood *St Alb* 90-96; V Oswaldtwistle Immanuel and All SS *Blackb* from 96. *Immanuel Vicarage, New Lane, Oswaldtwistle, Accrington BB5 3QN* Tel (01254) 233962 *or* 382147 E-mail janet_paul@lineone.net

WATSON, Philip. b 60. RGN83. Qu Coll Birm 86. **d** 89 **p** 90. C Ordsall *S'well* 89-93; TV Benwell *Newc* 93-99; V Stocking Farm *Leic* from 99. *St Luke's Vicarage, 97 Halifax Drive, Leicester LE4 2DP* Tel 0116-235 3206

WATSON, Richard Frederick. b 66. Avery Hill Coll BA87. Trin Coll Bris 91. **d** 93 **p** 94. C Kempston Transfiguration *St Alb* 93-97; TV Dunstable 97-03; R E Barnet from 03; RD Barnet from 05. *The Rectory, 136 Church Hill Road, Barnet EN4 8XD* Tel (020) 8368 3840 *or* 8361 7524 E-mail rector.smeb@surefish.co.uk *or* rf.watson@btopenworld.com

WATSON, Richard Rydill. b 47. SSC. Sarum & Wells Th Coll 74. **d** 77 **p** 78. C Cayton w Eastfield *York* 77-80; C Howden 80-82; P-in-c Burton Pidsea and Humbleton w Elsternwick 82-83; V Dormanstown 83-87; V Cotehill and Cumwhinton *Carl* 87-89; Chapl Harrogate Distr and Gen Hosp 89-94; Chapl Harrogate Health Care NHS Trust 94-99; Asst Chapl Oldham NHS Trust 99-02; Asst Chapl Pennine Acute Hosps NHS Trust from 02; P-in-c Shaw *Man* from 99. *The Vicarage, 13 Church Road, Shaw, Oldham OL2 7AT* Tel (01706) 847369

WATSON, Robert Bewley. b 34. Bris Univ BA59. Clifton Th Coll 56. **d** 61 **p** 62. C Bebington *Ches* 61-65; C Woking St Jo *Guildf* 65-68; V Knaphill 68-98; rtd 98; Perm to Offic *Guildf* from 98. *Endrise, 1 Wychelm Road, Lightwater GU18 5RT* Tel (01276) 453822

WATSON, Roger. *See* WATSON, Hartley Roger

WATSON, The Ven Sheila Anne. b 53. St Andr Univ MA75 MPhil80. Edin Th Coll 79. **dss** 79 **d** 87 **p** 94. Bridge of Allan *St And* 79-80; Alloa 79-80; Monkseaton St Mary *Newc* 80-84; Adult Educn Officer *Lon* 84-87; Hon C Chelsea St Luke and Ch Ch 87-96; Selection Sec ABM 92-93; Sen Selection Sec 93-96; Adv on CME *Sarum* 97-02; Dir of Min 98-02; Can and Preb Sarum Cathl 00-02; Adn Buckingham *Ox* from 02. *Bede House, Paul's Hill, Penn, High Wycombe HP10 8NZ* Tel (01494) 814571 Fax 817946 E-mail archdbuc@oxford.anglican.org

WATSON, Stephanie Abigail. *See* MOYES, Mrs Stephanie Abigail

WATSON, Thomas Anthony. b 23. Chich Th Coll 50. **d** 52 **p** 53. C Ashburton w Buckland-in-the-Moor *Ex* 52-54; C Bideford 54-57; V Bishops Nympton 57-59; R Rose Ash 57-59; N Rhodesia 59-64; Zambia 64-65; V Honicknowle *Ex* 65-72; R Butterleigh 72-90; R Silverton 72-90; rtd 90; Chapl Palermo w Taormina *Eur* 90-93; Perm to Offic *Ex* from 93. *13A Lower North Street, Exeter EX4 3ET* Tel (01392) 424423

WATSON, Canon Timothy Patrick. b 38. ALCD66. **d** 66 **p** 67. C Northwood Em *Lon* 66-70; TV High Wycombe *Ox* 70-76; Gen Sec ICS 76-82; R Bath Weston All SS w N Stoke *B & W* 82-93; R Bath Weston All SS w N Stoke and Langridge 93-94; TR Cheltenham St Mary, St Matt, St Paul and H Trin *Glouc* 94-03; rtd 03; Perm to Offic *Glouc* from 04; Can Kitgum from 05. *The Gateways, Farm Lane, Leckhampton, Cheltenham GL53 0NN* Tel (01242) 514298 E-mail suejwatson@chelters.fsnet.co.uk

WATSON, Miss Violet Hazel. b 29. SRN52 SCM54 RSCN59. Linc Th Coll 83. **dss** 85 **d** 87. Hammersmith SS Mich and Geo White City Estate CD *Lon* 85-86; Sunbury 86; Fulham St Dionis Parson's Green 86-87; Par Dn 87; Perm to Offic *St Alb* 88-90. *Address temp unknown*

WATSON, William. b 36. Ripon Hall Ox 64. **d** 66 **p** 67. C Leamington Priors H Trin *Cov* 66-69; V Salford Priors 69-74; V Malin Bridge *Sheff* 74-79; Chapl Shrewsbury R Hosps 79-89; Chapl R Hallamshire Hosp Sheff 89-92; Chapl Cen Sheff Univ Hosps NHS Trust 92-93; P-in-c Alveley and Quatt *Heref* 93-96; Chapl N Gen Hosp NHS Trust Sheff 96-01; Chapl Weston Park Hosp Sheff 96-99; Chapl Cen Sheff Univ Hosps NHS Trust 99-01; rtd 96; Perm to Offic *Sheff* from 01. *396 Stannington Road, Stannington, Sheffield S6 5QQ* Tel 0114-232 4005

WATSON, William Henry Dunbar. b 31. Univ of W Ontario BA60. **d** 58 **p** 60. C Westmr St Jas *Lon* 58-60; Canada 60-04; Asst Chapl and Prec Gibraltar Cathl *Eur* from 04. *The Port Chaplain's Flat, Mission to Seafarers, North Mole, Gibraltar* Tel (00350) 41799 E-mail william.watson@sympatico.ca

WATSON, William Lysander Rowan. b 26. TCD BA47 MA50 Clare Coll Cam MA52 St Pet Hall Ox MA57. **d** 49 **p** 50. C Chapelizod and Kilmainham *D & G* 49-51; Tutor Ridley Hall Cam 51-55; Chapl 55-57; Chapl St Pet Coll Ox 57-93; Fell and Tutor 59-93; Sen Tutor 77-81; Vice Master 83-85; Lect Th Ox Univ 60-93; rtd 93. *Llandaff Barn, 11 Thames Street, Eynsham, Witney OX29 4HF* Tel (01865) 464198 E-mail lysander.watson@spc.ox.ac.uk

WATSON WILLIAMS, Richard Hamilton Patrick. b 31. SS Coll Cam BA57 MA62. St Aug Coll Cant. **d** 59 **p** 60. C Dorking St Paul *Guildf* 59-63; C Portsea St Mary *Portsm* 63-66; V Culgaith *Carl* 66-71; V Kirkland 66-71; V Wigton 72-79; Warden Dioc Conf Ho Crawshawbooth *Man* 79-82; P-in-c Crawshawbooth 79-82; Master Lady Kath Leveson Hosp 82-98; P-in-c Temple Balsall *Birm* 82-84; V 84-98; rtd 98; Perm to Offic *Glouc* from 98. *16 Barton Mews, Barton Road, Tewkesbury GL20 5RP* Tel (01684) 290509 E-mail squaredws@beeb.net

WATT, The Very Revd Alfred Ian. b 34. FRSA95. Edin Th Coll 57. **d** 60 **p** 61. Chapl St Paul's Cathl Dundee *Bre* 60-63; Prec 63-66; P-in-c Dundee H Cross 64-66; R Arbroath 66-69; R Perth St Ninian *St And* 69-82; Provost St Ninian's Cathl Perth 69-82; Can St Ninian's Cathl Perth 82-98; R Kinross 82-95; Dean St Andr 89-98; rtd 98. *33 Stirling Road, Milnathort, Kinross KY13 9XS* Tel and fax (01577) 865711

WATT, Prof William Montgomery. b 09. Edin Univ MA30 PhD44 Ball Coll Ox BA32 BLitt36 MA36 Aber Univ Hon DD66 Hamdard Univ Karachi Hon DLitt98. Cuddesdon Coll 38. **d** 39 **p** 40. C W Brompton St Mary *Lon* 39-41; C Edin Old St Paul *Edin* 41-43; Hon C 46-60; Jerusalem 43-46; Lect Edin Univ 46-53; Reader 53-64; Prof Arabic and Islamic Studies 64-79; Hon C Edin St Columba *Edin* 60-67; Hon C Dalkeith 80-93; Hon C Lasswade 80-93; rtd 93. *The Neuk, 2 Bridgend, Dalkeith EH22 1JT* Tel 0131-663 3197

WATT-WYNESS, Gordon. b 25. Cranmer Hall Dur 70 St Jo Coll Dur 70. **d** 72 **p** 73. C Scarborough St Mary w Ch Ch, St Paul and St Thos *York* 72-76; R Rossington *Sheff* 76-90; rtd 90; Perm to Offic *York* from 90. *15 Newton Court, Crescent Road, Filey YO14 4LL* Tel (01723) 516608

WATTERS, Mrs Kay. b 44. St Alb and Ox Min Course 98. **d** 01 **p** 02. OLM Prestwood and Gt Hampden *Ox* from 01; Chapl to Bp Buckingham from 04. *7 Widmere Field, Prestwood, Great Missenden HP16 0SP* Tel (01494) 865468 Mobile 07714-220241 Fax (01494) 862552

WATTERSON, Mrs Susan Mary. b 50. S & M Dioc Inst 84. **d** 87 **p** 94. NSM Rushen *S & M* 87-89; Hon Par Dn Castletown 89-94; C 94-96; Dioc Youth Officer 87-91; Bp's Adv for Healing Min 91-94; Asst Chapl Bris Univ *Bris* 96-99; Hon C Bris St Mich and St Paul 96-99; Project Leader Galway Chr Tr Inst 99-00; I Youghal Union *C, C & R* 00-03; Dir Ch's Min of Healing from 03. *26 Griffeen Glen Dene, Lucan, Co Dublin, Irish Republic*

WATTLEY, Jeffery Richard. b 57. Univ of Wales (Abth) BSc(Econ)79. Trin Coll Bris BA92. **d** 92 **p** 93. C Reading Greyfriars *Ox* 92-96; V Wonersh *Guildf* 96-98; V Wonersh w Blackheath from 98. *The Vicarage, The Street, Wonersh, Guildford GU5 0PF* Tel (01483) 893131 E-mail jrwattley@aol.com *or* jeff@wonershchurch.com

WATTS, Mrs Aline Patricia. b 57. St Jo Coll Nottm 02. **d** 04 **p** 05. C Lache cum Saltney *Ches* from 04. *69 Sandy Lane, Saltney, Chester CH4 8UB* Tel (01244) 683225 E-mail alinewatts@tiscali.co.uk

WATTS, Canon Anthony George. b 46. K Coll Lon BD69 AKC69 Lon Univ CertEd70. Sarum & Wells Th Coll 82. **d** 84 **p** 85. C Wimborne Minster and Holt *Sarum* 84-87; P-in-c Shilling Okeford 87-92; Chapl Croft Ho Sch Shillingstone 87-92; R W Parley *Sarum* 92-00; RD Wimborne 98-00; TR Cley Hill Warminster from 00; Can and Preb Sarum Cathl from 00. *The Rectory, 5 Church Street, Warminster BA12 8PG* Tel and fax (01985) 213456 E-mail tandgwatts@aol.com

WATTS, Anthony John. b 30. AKC59. **d** 60 **p** 61. C Whitburn *Dur* 60-63; C Croxdale 63-65; V Warrington St Pet *Liv* 65-70; V Peel *Man* 70-78; P-in-c Bury St Mark 78-81; V Davyhulme Ch Ch 81-99; Chapl Trafford Gen Hosp 89-94; Chapl Trafford Healthcare NHS Trust 94-98; rtd 99; Perm to Offic *Ches* from 00. *11 Brackenfield Way, Winsford CW7 2UX* Tel (01606) 590803

WATTS, David Henry. b 27. Ex Coll Ox BA50 MA55. Wells Th Coll 51. **d** 53 **p** 54. C Haslemere *Guildf* 53-55; C Chelmsf Cathl *Chelmsf* 55-58; Succ Chelmsf Cathl 55-58; V Chessington *Guildf* 58-62; Educn Officer Essex Educn Cttee 62-70; HMI of Schs 70-87; Hon C Wetherby *Ripon* 79-87; P-in-c Healaugh w Wighill, Bilbrough and Askham Richard *York* 87-89; Chapl HM Pris Askham Grange 87-96; rtd 89; Perm to Offic *York* from 98. *3 Westwood Way, Boston Spa, Wetherby LS23 6DX* Tel (01937) 845005

WATTS, Canon Frank Walter. b 30. St Boniface Warminster 53 K Coll Lon AKC54. **d** 54 **p** 55. C Llandough w Leckwith *Llan* 54-56; C Llanishen and Lisvane 56-59; C Gt Marlow *Ox* 59-60; R Black Bourton 60-63; V Carterton 60-63; C-in-c Brize Norton 61-63; V Brize Norton and Carterton 63-69; Australia from 69; Hon Can Perth from 78; rtd 95. *Villa 5, 178-180 Fern Road, Wilson, W Australia 6107* Tel and fax (0061) (8) 9258 4532 Mobile 408-094991 E-mail frawawa@southwest.com.au

WATTS, Fraser Norman. b 46. Magd Coll Ox BA68 MA74 K Coll Lon MSc70 PhD75 Magd Coll Cam DipTh90 CPsychol89 FBPsS80. Westcott Ho Cam 88. **d** 90 **p** 91. NSM Harston w Hauxton *Ely* 90-95; P-in-c 91-95; Fell Qu Coll Cam from 94; Lect Cam Univ from 94; Chapl Cam St Edw *Ely* from 95. *19 Grantchester Road, Cambridge CB3 9ED* Tel (01223) 359223 Fax 763003 E-mail fnw1001@hermes.cam.ac.uk

WATTS, Gordon Sidney Stewart. b 40. CITC 63. **d** 66 **p** 67. C Belfast St Steph *Conn* 66-69; CF 69-94; V Boldre w S Baddesley *Win* 94-96; P-in-c Warmfield *Wakef* 96-02; Sub Chapl HM Pris Wakef 97-02; Chapl Huggens Coll Northfleet from 02. *Chaplain's House, Huggens College, College Road, Northfleet DA11 9DL* Tel (01474) 352428 Fax 533091 E-mail gss.watts@virgin.net

WATTS, Graham Hadley Lundie. b 74. Man Metrop Univ BA95. Ridley Hall Cam 98. **d** 02 **p** 03. C Camberley St Paul *Guildf* from 02. *3 Upper Gordon Road, Camberley GU15 2HJ* Tel (01276) 700301 E-mail graham.watts7@ntlworld.com

WATTS, Ian Charles. b 63. Hull Univ BA85. Linc Th Coll 86. **d** 88 **p** 89. C W Kirby St Bridget *Ches* 88-93; V High Lane 93-00; P-in-c Newton in Mottram 00-04; P-in-c Burnley St Cuth *Blackb* from 04. *St James's Vicarage, Church Street, Briercliffe, Burnley BB10 2HU* Tel (01282) 423700 *or* 424978

WATTS, John Michael. d 04. OLM Ashtead *Guildf* from 04; Asst Chapl Guy's and St Thos' Hosps NHS Trust Lon from 04. *31 Broadhurst, Ashtead KT21 1QB* Tel (01372) 275134 E-mail jmwatts@waitrose.com

WATTS, John Robert. b 39. Leeds Univ BSc60 MSc63 DipEd63. Oak Hill Th Coll 88. **d** 90 **p** 91. C Partington and Carrington *Ches* 90-93; P-in-c Tintwistle 93-98; V Hollingworth w Tintwistle 98-04; RD Mottram 99-03; rtd 04. *16 Norley Drive, Vicars Cross, Chester CH3 5PG* Tel (01244) 350439 E-mail revrob@jrwatts.fsnet.co.uk

WATTS, John Stanley. b 28. LCP62 Birm Univ DipEd65 MEd72 Nottm Univ MPhil83. Qu Coll Birm 83. **d** 86 **p** 87. Lect Wolverhampton Poly 77-90; Hon C Dudley St Fran *Worc* 86-91; Lect Wolverhampton Univ 90-93; Hon C Sedgley St Mary 91-98; Perm to Offic from 98. *5 Warren Drive, Sedgley, Dudley DY3 3RQ* Tel (01902) 661265

WATTS, Mrs Mary Kathleen. b 31. Lon Univ DipRS73 BA86. Gilmore Ho 73. **dss** 77 **d** 87 **p** 94. Lower Streatham St Andr *S'wark* 77-88; C 87-88; C Streatham Immanuel w St Anselm 87-88; C Streatham Immanuel and St Andr 90-91; rtd 91; Perm to Offic *S'wark* 91-94; Hon C Norbury St Oswald from 94. *2 Beaufort Gardens, London SW16 3BP* Tel (020) 8764 6165

WATTS, Paul George. b 43. Nottm Univ BA67. Wells Th Coll 67. **d** 69 **p** 70. C Sherwood *S'well* 69-74; Chapl Trent (Nottm) Poly 74-80; V Nottingham All SS 80-84; Public Preacher from 84. *16 Grosvenor Avenue, Nottingham NG5 3DX* Tel 0115-960 9964 *or* 915 0640 E-mail paul.watts@nottinghamcity.gov.uk

WATTS (née SIMPER), Mrs Rachel Dawn. b 67. K Coll Lon BD89. Westcott Ho Cam 90. **d** 92 **p** 94. Par Dn Clitheroe St Mary *Blackb* 92-94; C 94-95; C Nor St Pet Mancroft w St Jo Maddermarket *Nor* 95-97; V Slyne w Hest *Blackb* 97-04; V Briercliffe from 04; Women's Min Adv from 00. *St James's Vicarage, Church Street, Briercliffe, Burnley BB10 2HU* Tel (01282) 423700

WATTS, Ms Rebecca Harriet. b 61. St Cath Coll Cam BA83 MA Welsh Coll of Music & Drama 84. Wycliffe Hall Ox 87. **d** 90 **p** 94. C Goldsworth Park *Guildf* 90-94; Chapl Wadh Coll Ox 94-97; C Ox St Mary V w St Cross and St Pet *Ox* 94-97; Chapl Somerville Coll Ox 97-98; Perm to Offic *Newc* 98-99 and from 02. *15 Woodbine Avenue, Gosforth, Newcastle upon Tyne NE3 4EU* Tel 0191-285 9840

WATTS, Robert. *See* WATTS, John Robert

WATTS, Roger Edward. b 39. S'wark Ord Course 85. **d** 88 **p** 89. C Belmont *S'wark* 88-92; R Godstone 92-97; R Godstone and Blindley Heath from 97. *The Rectory, 17 Ivy Mill Lane, Godstone RH9 8NK* Tel (01883) 742354

WATTS, Roger Mansfield. b 41. Univ of Wales (Cardiff) BSc63 CEng76 MIEE76. Chich Th Coll 89. **d** 91 **p** 92. C Chippenham St Andr w Tytherton Lucas *Bris* 91-93; C Henfield w Shermanbury and Woodmancote *Chich* 93-96; R Jedburgh *Edin* 96-99; R Wingerworth *Derby* from 99. *The Rectory, Longedge Lane, Wingerworth, Chesterfield S42 6PU* Tel (01246) 234242

WATTS, Ms Samantha Alison Lundie. b 70. Birm Univ BA92 Cam Univ BA01. Ridley Hall Cam 99. **d** 02 **p** 03. C Camberley St Paul *Guildf* from 02. *3 Upper Gordon Road, Camberley GU15 2HJ* Tel (01276) 700301 E-mail sami.watts@ntlworld.com

WATTS, Scott Antony. b 67. FRMetS99 MCMI00. EAMTC 00. **d** 03 **p** 04. NSM Brampton *Ely* from 03. *10 Link Drive, Brampton, Huntingdon PE28 4FE* Tel (01480) 411141 Mobile 07795-631139 E-mail rev.scott.watts@ntlworld.com

WATTS, Mrs Valerie Anne. b 44. UEA BEd79. EAMTC 90. **d** 93 **p** 94. NSM N Walsham w Antingham *Nor* from 93. *15 Millfield Road, North Walsham NR28 0EB* Tel (01692) 405119

WATTS, Wilfred Richard James. b 11. St Mich Coll Llan 64. **d** 66 **p** 66. C Coleford w Staunton *Glouc* 66-69; V Viney Hill 69-82; rtd 82; Perm to Offic *Glouc* 82-97. *c/o Mrs E M Sowerby, 22 Petvin Close, Street BA16 0SX*

WATTS, William Henry Norbury. b 51. CertEd. St Jo Coll Nottm 87. **d** 89 **p** 90. C S Molton w Nymet St George, High Bray etc *Ex* 89-93; TV Swanage and Studland *Sarum* from 93. *The Vicarage, School Lane, Studland, Swanage BH19 3AJ* Tel (01929) 450441 E-mail will.watts@tesco.net

WAUD, John David. b 31. N Ord Course 82. **d** 85 **p** 86. C Cayton w Eastfield *York* 85-88; R Brandesburton 88-93; R Beeford w Frodingham and Foston 93-99; rtd 99; Perm to Offic *York* from 00. *21 Lowfield Road, Beverley HU17 9RF* Tel (01482) 864726 E-mail jdw2@jdw2.karoo.co.uk

WAUDBY, Miss Christine. b 45. TCert66. Trin Coll Bris DipHE. **d** 90 **p** 94. C Weston-super-Mare Ch Ch *B & W* 90-94; C Blackheath *Birm* 94-99; Perm to Offic 99-03; NSM Ipsley *Worc* from 03. *The Rectory, Icknield Street, Redditch B98 0AN* Tel (01527) 521082

WAUDE, Andrew Leslie. b 74. Leeds Univ BA02. Coll of Resurr Mirfield 99. **d** 02 **p** 03. C Swinton and Pendlebury *Man* from 02. *46 Townsend Road, Swinton, Manchester M27 6SH* Tel 0161-794 1808 Mobile 07708-004478 E-mail fr_andrew@lycos.co.uk

WAUGH, Ian William. b 52. Bede Coll Dur DipEd74 BEd75. NEOC 99. **d** 02 **p** 03. NSM Benfieldside *Dur* from 02. *36 Muirfield Close, Shotley Bridge, Consett DH8 5XE* Tel (01207) 591923 Mobile 07808-412953 E-mail ian-barbara-waugh@lineone.net

WAUGH, Mrs Jane Leitch. b 38. DMusEd60 CertEd61 Toronto Univ MDiv83. Trin Coll Toronto 80. **d** 84 **p** 94. Canada 84-87; Par Dn Dunnington *York* 88-90; Perm to Offic 90-93 and from 96; NSM York St Olave w St Giles 93-96; rtd 98. *Moonrakers, Rectory Corner, Brandsby, York YO61 4RJ* Tel (01347) 888637

WAUGH, Nigel John William. b 56. TCD BA78 MA81. CITC 76. **d** 79 **p** 80. C Ballymena *Conn* 79-82; C Ballyholme *D & D* 82-84; I Bunclody w Kildavin *C & O* 84-86; I Bunclody w Kildavin and Clonegal 86-91; I Bunclody w Kildavin, Clonegal and Kilrush 91-98; Preb Ferns Cathl 88-91; Treas 91-96; Radio Officer (Cashel) 90-91; (Ferns) 92-98; Dioc Info Officer (Ferns) 91-98; Prec Ferns Cathl 96-98; I Delgany *D & G* from 98. *The Rectory, 8 Elsinore, Delgany, Greystones, Co Wicklow, Irish Republic* Tel (00353) (1) 287 4515 Fax 287 7578 E-mail delgany@glendalough.anglican.org

WAXHAM, Derek Frank. b 33. Oak Hill Th Coll 76. **d** 79 **p** 80. NSM Old Ford St Paul w St Steph and St Mark *Lon* 79-89; NSM Bow w Bromley St Leon from 89. *39 Hewlett Road, London E3 5NA* Tel (020) 8980 1748

WAY, Albert James. b 27. St D Coll Lamp BA61 DipTh63. **d** 63 **p** 64. C Neath w Llantwit *Llan* 63-68; C Watford St Jo *St Alb* 68; R Clayhidon *Ex* 68-76; V Llanbadog and Llanllowell *Mon* 76-83; V Llanhilleth 83-98; rtd 98. *9 Berthon Road, Little Mill, Pontypool NP4 0HE* Tel (01495) 785724

WAY, Miss Alison Janet. b 61. York Univ BSc83 FIBMS86. St Mich Coll Llan 02. **d** 04 **p** 05. C Basingstoke *Win* from 04. *1 The Glebe, Church Square, Basingstoke RG21 1QW* Tel (01256) 466694 Mobile 07817-586942 E-mail alison.way@tesco.net

WAY, Andrew Lindsay. b 43. Linc Th Coll 76. **d** 78 **p** 79. C Shenfield *Chelmsf* 78-82; C Waltham *Linc* 82-84; V New Waltham 84-89; R Duxford *Ely* 89-94; V Hinxton 89-94; V Ickleton 89-94; P-in-c Doddington w Benwick 94-97; P-in-c Wimblington 94-97; R Doddington w Benwick and Wimblington 97-98; R Eythorne and Elvington w Waldershare etc *Cant* from 98; AD Dover 00-03. *The Rectory, Barfrestone Road, Eythorne, Dover CT15 4AH* Tel (01304) 830241 Fax (08701) 255866 E-mail albeway@clara.co.uk

WAY, Anthony Hilton. b 21. Chich Th Coll 57. **d** 59 **p** 60. C Chich St Paul and St Bart *Chich* 59-61; C Hangleton 61-63; V Horam 63-70; V Ditchling 70-77; Asst Dioc Sec 77-83; Chapl Dioc Ch Ho 79-83; V Linchmere 83-91; rtd 91; Perm to Offic *Chich* from 91. *41 Heath Court, Heath Road, Haywards Heath RH16 3AF* Tel (01444) 415158

WAY, Mrs Barbara Elizabeth. b 47. Open Univ BA82 Hull Univ PGCE86. Linc Th Coll IDC78. **dss** 78 **d** 87 **p** 94. Shenfield

Chelmsf 78-82; Adult Educn Adv *Linc* 82-85; Dioc Lay Min Adv 85; New Waltham 82-89; Min 87-89; Tetney 86-89; Min 87-89; NSM Duxford *Ely* 89-94; NSM Ickleton 89-94; NSM Hinxton 89-94; Dir Past Studies EAMTC 91-94; Min Pampisford 92-94; P-in-c Coates 94-95; TV Whittlesey, Pondersbridge and Coates 95-98; Local Min Adv *Cant* 98-02; Dioc Dir of Reader Selection and Tr 00-02; Dioc Adv in Women's Min 02-04; P-in-c Whitfield w Guston from 02. *The Rectory, Barfrestone Road, Eythorne, Dover CT15 4AH* Tel (01304) 830241 Fax (08701) 255866 E-mail belway@clara.co.uk

WAY, Colin George. b 31. St Cath Coll Cam BA55 MA59 Lon Inst of Educn PGCE58. EAMTC. **d** 84 **p** 85. NSM Hempnall *Nor* 84-87; C Gaywood, Bawsey and Mintlyn 87-90; R Acle w Fishley and N Burlingham 90-96; RD Blofield 95-96; rtd 96; Perm to Offic *Nor* 96-97 and from 02; P-in-c Pulham Market, Pulham St Mary and Starston 97-99; Hon C Eaton 99-02. *347 Unthank Road, Norwich NR4 7QG* Tel (01603) 458363 E-mail cw@eatonparish.com

WAY, David. b 54. Pemb Coll Ox MA DPhil. Cranmer Hall Dur BA Cuddesdon Coll 83. **d** 85 **p** 86. C Chenies and Lt Chalfont *Ox* 85-87; C Chenies and Lt Chalfont, Latimer and Flaunden 87-88; Tutor and Dir Studies Sarum & Wells Th Coll 88-93; Selection Sec Min Division from 94; Sec Minl Educn Cttee from 94; Th Educn Sec Min Division from 99. *Ministry Division, Church House, Great Smith Street, London SW1P 3NZ* Tel (020) 7898 1405 Fax 7898 1421 E-mail david.way@mindiv.c-of-e.org.uk

WAY, David Charles. b 61. St Mich Coll Llan BTh94. **d** 97 **p** 98. C Cardiff St Mary and St Steph w St Dyfrig etc *Llan* 97-02; V Aberaman and Abercwmboi w Cwmaman from 02. *St Margaret's Vicarage, Gladstone Street, Aberaman, Aberdare CF44 6SA* Tel (01685) 872871 E-mail david.way@dtn.ntl.com

WAY, Lawrence William. b 32. St Mich Coll Llan 77. **d** 79 **p** 80. C Merthyr Dyfan *Llan* 79-82; V Abercynon 82-84; TV Cwmbran *Mon* 84-86; V Caerwent w Dinham and Llanfair Discoed etc 86-90; V Pontnewydd 90-93; rtd 93. *8 Ceredig Court, Llanyravon, Cwmbran NP44 8SA* Tel (01633) 865309 Fax 876830 E-mail frway.angelus@virgin.net

WAY, Michael David. b 57. K Coll Lon BD78 AKC78. St Steph Ho Ox 79. **d** 80 **p** 83. C Bideford *Ex* 80-81; Hon C Wembley Park St Aug *Lon* 81-84; C Kilburn St Aug w St Jo 84-89; V Earlsfield St Jo *S'wark* 89-92; Project Co-ord CARA 92-99; Consultant Cen Sch for Counselling and Therapy 99-00; Dir RADICLE *Lon* from 00. *14 St Peter's Gardens, London SE27 0PN* Tel (020) 8670 3439 *or* 7932 1129

WAYNE, Kenneth Hammond. b 31. Bps' Coll Cheshunt 58. **d** 61 **p** 62. C Eyres Monsell CD *Leic* 61-62; C Loughborough Em 62-65; C-in-c Staunton Harold 65-73; V Breedon w Isley Walton 65-73; V Leic St Phil 73-85; V Ault Hucknall *Derby* 85-95; rtd 95; Perm to Offic *S'well* from 96. *The Haven, 3 Burton Walk, East Leake, Loughborough LE12 6LB* Tel (01509) 852848

WAYTE, Christopher John. b 28. Lon Univ BSc54. Wells Th Coll 54. **d** 56 **p** 57. C Maidstone St Martin *Cant* 56-60; C W Wickham St Jo 60-61; C Birchington w Acol 61-64; C-in-c Buckland Valley CD 64-68; R Biddenden 68-80; Chapl ATC 71-86; P-in-c Boughton Monchelsea *Cant* 80-85; V St Margarets-at-Cliffe w Westcliffe etc 85-91; rtd 92; Perm to Offic *Cant* from 92. *9 St John's Road, Hythe CT21 4BE* Tel (01303) 263060 E-mail audrey@wayte93.freeserve.co.uk

WEALE, Colin Alexander. b 26. Univ of Wales (Lamp) BA49 Open Univ MPhil87 Middx Univ PhD96. Lambeth STh81 Sarum Th Coll 49. **d** 51 **p** 52. C Swansea St Mary and H Trin *S & B* 51-55; Min Can Brecon Cathl 55-59; C Brecon w Battle 55-59; V Llanbister and Llanbadarn Fynydd w Llananno 59-61; R Bengeo H Trin *St Alb* 61-69; R Bengeo 69-93; rtd 93; Perm to Offic *Nor* from 93. *1 Diana Way, Caister-on-Sea, Great Yarmouth NR30 5TP* Tel (01493) 377946

WEARMOUTH, Alan Wilfred. b 54. St Paul's Cheltenham CertEd75 Bris Univ BEd76. Glouc Sch of Min 85. **d** 88 **p** 89. NSM Coleford w Staunton *Glouc* from 88. *Windhover, Broadwell Bridge, Coleford GL16 7GA* Tel (01594) 832660

WEATHERHEAD, The Very Revd Thomas Leslie. b 13. Hatf Coll Dur BA37 LTh37. St Aug Coll Cant 32. **d** 37 **p** 38. C Beeston Hill H Spirit *Ripon* 37-40; C Wensley 40-42; Chapl RAFVR 42-47; C Leeds Halton St Wilfrid *Ripon* 47-48; V New Mills *Derby* 48-59; R Staveley 59-65; Dean and V-Gen Nassau 65-72; R Felmingham *Nor* 72-79; P-in-c Suffield 72-74; R 74-79; P-in-c Colby w Banningham and Tuttington 72-74; R 74-79; RD Tunstead 76-79; rtd 79; Perm to Offic *Ripon* from 79. *St Nicholas' Lodge, 25 Bishopton Lane, Ripon HG4 2QN* Tel (01765) 600413

WEATHERILL, Stephen Robert. b 70. Roehampton Inst BA98 Nottm Univ MA00. St Jo Coll Nottm 98. **d** 00 **p** 02. C Bridlington Priory *York* 00-01; NSM Kendal St Thos *Carl* from 02. *35 Church Street, Milnthorpe LA7 7DX* Tel (01539) 565871 E-mail stephen@pv-media.co.uk

WEATHERLEY, Miss Mary Kathleen. b 36. SRN57 SCM59 Midwife Teacher's Dip 72. SW Minl Tr Course 78. **dss** 82 **d** 87 **p** 94. Littleham w Exmouth *Ex* 82-84; Heavitree w Ex St Paul 85-87; Hon Par Dn 87-88; Chapl Asst R Devon and Ex Hosp 85-93; Lic to Offic *Ex* 88-94; NSM Littleham w Exmouth 94-98; Perm to Offic from 98. *38 Egremont Road, Exmouth EX8 1SA* Tel (01395) 265528

WEATHRALL, Ian Charles. b 22. OBE75. AKC47. **d** 47 **p** 48. C Southampton St Mary w H Trin *Win* 47-51; India from 51; Brotherhood of Ascension from 51; Hd 70-88; rtd 92. *7 Court Lane, Delhi 110 054, India* Tel (0091) (11) 396 8515

WEAVER, Alan William. b 63. Brighton Poly HNC88. Linc Th Coll 95. **d** 95 **p** 96. C Seaford w Sutton *Chich* 95-98; C Langney 98-01; P-in-c Haven CD from 02. *1 Columbus Drive, Eastbourne BN23 6RR* Tel (01323) 642897 Fax as telephone E-mail angyalanweaver@mistral.co.uk

WEAVER, Canon Angela Mary. b 48. WMMTC 92. **d** 95 **p** 96. C Hill *Birm* 95-99; V Hamstead St Paul from 99; AD Handsworth from 05; Hon Can Birm Cathl from 05. *Hamstead Vicarage, 840 Walsall Road, Birmingham B42 1ES* Tel 0121-357 8941 Mobile 07813-807853 E-mail angela.weaver@btconnect.com

WEAVER, Prof Arthur Kenneth (Ken). b 17. Trin Coll Cam BA30 MA44 MRAeS50. Ox NSM Course 81 Wycliffe Hall Ox 81. **d** 81 **p** 82. NSM Ashbury, Compton Beauchamp and Longcot w Fernham *Ox* 81-87; Perm to Offic from 87. *White Lodge, King's Lane, Longcot, Faringdon SN7 7SS* Tel (01793) 782364

WEAVER, Brian John. b 34. Oak Hill Th Coll 82. **d** 84 **p** 85. C Nailsea H Trin *B & W* 84-88; R Nettlebed w Bix and Highmore *Ox* 88-98; rtd 98; Hon C Warfield *Ox* from 99. *47 Walsh Avenue, Warfield, Bracknell RG42 3XZ* Tel (01344) 485379 E-mail bri_jac@onetel.com

WEAVER, David Anthony. b 43. Hatf Coll Dur BSc65. Lich Th Coll 68. **d** 71 **p** 72. C Walsall Wood *Lich* 71-75; C Much Wenlock w Bourton *Heref* 75-76; Canada 76-79 and 82; V Mow Cop *Lich* 79-82; P-in-c Burntwood 82-00; V from 00; Chapl St Matt Hosp Burntwood 83-95. *The Vicarage, Church Road, Burntwood, Walsall WS7 9EA* Tel (01543) 675014

WEAVER, Duncan Charles. b 60. St Jo Coll Nottm BA99. St Jo Coll Nottm DipTh94. **d** 94 **p** 95. C Watford *St Alb* 94-98; TV Bourne Valley *Sarum* 98-01; CF from 01. *c/o MOD Chaplains (Army)* Tel (01980) 615804 Fax 615800 E-mail dweaver385@aol.com

WEAVER, Fiona Margaret. b 61. Westcott Ho Cam 99. **d** 00 **p** 01. C Islington St Jas w St Pet *Lon* 00-03; Asst Chapl Univ of N Lon 00-02; Asst Chapl Lon Metrop Univ 01-03; Chapl from 03. *123 Calabria Road, London N5 1HS* Tel (020) 7359 5808 *or* 7133 2030 Fax 7133 2813 E-mail f.weaver@londonmet.ac.uk

WEAVER, Ian Douglas. b 65. Ridley Coll Melbourne BMin96. **d** 96 **p** 96. Australia 96-98 and from 03; TV Rushden St Mary w Newton Bromswold *Pet* 98-02; Dioc Youth Min Facilitator Melbourne from 03. *The Anglican Centre, 209 Flinders Lane, Melbourne, Vic, Australia 3000* Tel (0061) (3) 9653 4220 Mobile 409-604006 Fax (3) 9653 4268 E-mail iweaver@melbourne.anglican.com.au

WEAVER, Canon John. b 28. Ex Coll Ox BA51 MA55. St Steph Ho Ox 52. **d** 55 **p** 56. C Ex St Dav *Ex* 55-58; S Africa from 58; Hon Can St John's from 81; Adn Midl 84-95; Hon Can Pietermaritzburg from 95. *PO Box 56, Underberg, 3257 South Africa* Tel (0027) (33) 701 1124

WEAVER, Mrs Joyce Margaret. b 43. **d** 00 **p** 01. OLM Warrington St Ann *Liv* from 00. *71 Orford Avenue, Warrington WA2 8PQ* Tel (01925) 634993

WEAVER, Ken. *See* WEAVER, Prof Arthur Kenneth

WEAVER, Canon Michael Howard. b 39. Leeds Univ DipArch63 DLA69 Southn Univ MPhil95. Chich Th Coll 63. **d** 66 **p** 67. C Kidderminster St Jo *Worc* 66-69; Br Honduras 69-71; TV Droitwich *Worc* 71-76; V Arundel w Tortington and S Stoke *Chich* 76-96; P-in-c Clymping 84-87; RD Arundel and Bognor 88-93; Sub-Chapl HM Pris Ford 77-96; Hon Can Enugu from 94; V Lymington *Win* 96-04; Chapl Southn Community Services NHS Trust 96-04; rtd 04; Perm to Offic *Win* from 04 and *Portsm* from 05. *Dolphin Cottage, High Street, Freshwater PO40 9JU* Tel and fax (01983) 753786 E-mail junovicarage@hotmail.com

WEAVER, Canon William. b 40. Man Univ BA63 BD65. **d** 74 **p** 75. Lect Th Leeds Univ 67-91; Hon C Clifford *York* 82-86; Chapl K Edw Sch Birm 91-94; Provost Woodard Schs (Midl Division) 94-03; Hon Can Derby Cathl *Derby* from 96; Perm to Offic from 96. *20 St Peter's Garth, Thorner, Leeds LS14 3EE* Tel 0113-289 3689

WEBB, Canon Albert. b 22. AKC49. **d** 50 **p** 51. C Warsop *S'well* 50-52; V Cleeve Prior *Worc* 52-59; V Foley Park 59-66; V Evesham 66-87; RD Evesham 73-79; Hon Can Worc Cathl 75-87; rtd 87; Perm to Offic *Worc* from 87. *2 Dolphin Close, Worcester WR2 6BG* Tel (01905) 422230

WEBB, Anthony John. b 24. Sarum & Wells Th Coll 79. **d** 81 **p** 82. C Yeovil *B & W* 81-84; P-in-c Cossington 84-87; P-in-c Woolavington 84-87; P-in-c Bawdrip 87; V Woolavington w Cossington and Bawdrip 87-91; rtd 91; Perm to Offic *B & W* from 91. *4 Brue Crescent, Burnham-on-Sea TA8 1LR* Tel (01278) 787483

WEBB, Arthur Robert. b 33. FRSA LCP67 Lanc Univ MA82. Wells Th Coll 69. **d** 70 **p** 70. C W Drayton *Lon* 70-72; Hd Master

St Jas Cathl Sch Bury St Edmunds 72-86; Min Can St E Cathl *St E* 72-87; Succ St E Cathl 81-87; P-in-c Seend and Bulkington *Sarum* 87-88; V 88-91; R Heytesbury and Sutton Veny 91-96; rtd 96; Perm to Offic *B & W* from 96; *Sarum* from 98; and *Bris* from 00; P-in-c Las Palmas *Eur* from 04. *Calle Montevideo 2-7, 35007 Las Palmas de Gran Canaria, Canary Islands, Spain* Tel (0034) (928) 26702

WEBB, Mrs Barbara Mary. b 39. Bedf Coll Lon BA60 Cam Univ PGCE61. Wycliffe Hall Ox 00. **d** 02 **p** 03. NSM Cumnor *Ox* from 02. *50 West St Helen Street, Abingdon OX14 5BP* Tel (01235) 202873 E-mail derry_barbara@msn.com

WEBB, Mrs Brenda Lynn. b 45. Stockwell Coll of Educn CertEd66. EAMTC 97. **d** 00 **p** 01. NSM Saxmundham w Kelsale cum Carlton *St E* from 00; Teacher Beacon Hill Sch from 00. *The Rectory, Manor Gardens, Saxmundham IP17 1ET* Tel (01728) 604234 E-mail richard@saxrectory.freeserve.co.uk

WEBB, Christopher Scott. b 70. Univ of Wales (Abth) BSc. Trin Coll Bris BA96. **d** 96 **p** 97. C Dafen *St D* 96-98; C Cowbridge *Llan* 98-01; Officer for Renewal, Par Development and Local Ecum 01-04; V Llanfair Caereinion, Llanllugan and Manafon *St As* from 04. *The Vicarage, Parsons Bank, Llanfair Caereinion, Welshpool SY21 0RR* Tel (01938) 811335 E-mail chris@webbsworld.freeserve.co.uk

WEBB, Cyril George. b 19. Roch Th Coll 64. **d** 66 **p** 67. C Bournemouth St Andr *Win* 66-71; V Micheldever 71-72; V Micheldever and E Stratton, Woodmancote etc 72-79; V Bubwith w Ellerton and Aughton *York* 79-83; I Tomregan w Drumlane *K, E & A* 83-86; rtd 86; Perm to Offic *Cant* 90-98. *62 Columbia Avenue, Whitstable CT5 4EH* Tel (01227) 264687

WEBB, David Basil. b 30. Ch Coll Cam BA54 MA58. Ripon Hall Ox 54. **d** 55 **p** 56. C Wimbledon *S'wark* 55-57; Chapl Em Coll Cam 57-60; V Langley Mill *Derby* 60-64; R Farnborough *Roch* 64-73; R Dunstable *St Alb* 73-78; TR 78-84; RD Dunstable 81-84; TR Bemerton *Sarum* 84-90; V Haslingden w Grane and Stonefold *Blackb* 90-96; RD Accrington 92-95; rtd 96; Perm to Offic *Bradf* from 96. *22 Thwaites Avenue, Ilkley LS29 8EH* Tel (01943) 609762

WEBB, David William. b 30. MRINA Kent Univ DipTh84. Cant Sch of Min 86. **d** 89 **p** 90. NSM Sittingbourne St Mary *Cant* 89-95; Hon C Iwade 95-02; Perm to Offic from 02. *16 School Lane, Iwade, Sittingbourne ME9 8SE* Tel (01795) 424502

WEBB, Mrs Diane. b 45. LNSM course 91. **d** 93 **p** 94. OLM Stowmarket *St E* 93-05; OLM Haughley w Wetherden and Stowupland from 05. *36 Wordsworth Road, Stowmarket IP14 1TT* Tel (01449) 677880

WEBB, Diane Silvia. Birm Univ BA66 Dur Univ MA93. N Ord Course 82. **dss** 85 **d** 03 **p** 04. Wyther Ven Bede *Ripon* 85-86; Perm to Offic *York* 95-99; rtd 03; NSM Bow Common *Lon* from 03. *St Bartholomew's Vicarage, Buckhurst Street, London E1 5QT* Tel (020) 7247 8013 E-mail diane@webb.lcbroadband.co.uk

WEBB, Dominic Mark. b 68. Oriel Coll Ox BA91. Wycliffe Hall Ox BA93. **d** 96 **p** 97. C Cradley *Worc* 96-99; C Leyton Ch Ch *Chelmsf* 99-02; P-in-c St Helier *S'wark* from 02. *St Peter's Vicarage, Bishopsford Road, Morden SM4 6BH* Tel (020) 8648 6050 Mobile 07736-927115 E-mail domwebb@talk21.com

WEBB, Frances Mary. *See* BATTIN, Mrs Frances Mary

WEBB, Mrs Gillian Anne. b 49. Whitelands Coll Lon CertEd71 Heythrop Coll Lon MA04. St Alb Minl Tr Scheme 83. **dss** 86 **d** 87 **p** 94. Kempston Transfiguration *St Alb* 86-96; NSM 87-96; NSM Kempston All SS from 96. *2 Hillson Close, Marston Moreteyne, Bedford MK43 0QN* Tel (01234) 767256 E-mail webbg@marston2.freeserve.co.uk

WEBB, Gregory John. b 55. Man Univ LLB77. Oak Hill Th Coll 89. **d** 91 **p** 92. C Bury St Edmunds St Geo *St E* 91-94; P-in-c Bury St Edmunds All SS 94-02; TR Bury St Edmunds All SS w St Jo and St Geo from 02; RD Thingoe from 01. *All Saints' Vicarage, 59 Bennett Avenue, Bury St Edmunds IP33 3JJ* Tel (01284) 701063 E-mail gjwebb@fish.co.uk

WEBB, Harold William. b 37. St Chad's Coll Dur BA59. St Steph Ho Ox 59. **d** 61 **p** 62. C Plumstead St Nic *S'wark* 61-65; S Africa 65-70; Sacr Wakef Cathl *Wakef* 71-72; P-in-c Lane End *Ox* 72-76; V Lane End w Cadmore End 76-84; Chapl to the Deaf *Guildf* 84-96; V Roade and Ashton w Hartwell *Pet* 96-02; rtd 02; Perm to Offic *Guildf* from 03. *16 Harrow Drive, West Wittering, Chichester PO20 8EJ* Tel (01243) 673460

WEBB (née EDWARDS), Mrs Helen Glynne. b 57. SRN79 RMN81 Birkbeck Coll Lon MSc94. Wycliffe Hall Ox 88. **d** 90 **p** 94. Par Dn Clapham St Jas *S'wark* 90-94; Chapl Asst Southmead Health Services NHS Trust 94-97; Perm to Offic *Bris* from 97. *13 The Green, Olveston, Bristol BS35 4DN* Tel (01454) 615827 Fax as telephone

WEBB, Jennifer Rose. b 48. Leeds Univ BA70 Bedf Coll Lon CQSW72. LNSM course 93. **d** 96 **p** 97. OLM Ham St Rich *S'wark* from 96. *3 Locksmeade Road, Ham, Richmond TW10 7YT* Tel (020) 8948 0031 *or* 8547 6052

WEBB, John Christopher Richard. b 38. ACA63 FCA74. Wycliffe Hall Ox 64. **d** 67 **p** 68. C Hendon St Paul Mill Hill *Lon* 67-71; CF 71-93; R Bentworth and Shalden and Lasham *Win* 93-03; RD Alton 98-02; rtd 03. *Lower Farm Cottage, Church Street, Podimore, Yeovil BA22 8JE* E-mail john.c.r.webb@ukgateway.net

WEBB, Kenneth Gordon. b 47. Lon Univ MB, BS71 DRCOG73. Trin Coll Bris BA92. **d** 93 **p** 94. C Cheltenham St Mark *Glouc* 93-97; Banchang Ch Ch Thailand 97-02; P-in-c Duns *Edin* from 02. *The Rectory, Wellfield, Duns TD11 3EH* Tel (01361) 882209 E-mail kgwebb@xalt.co.uk

WEBB, Marjorie Valentine (Sister Elizabeth). b 31. Bedf Coll Lon Westmr Coll Ox MTh98. **d** 88 **p** 94. CSF from 55; Revd Mother 71-86; Lic to Bp Heref 86-90; Perm to Offic *Lon* 88-90; Lic to Offic *Lich* 90-91; *B & W* from 95; *Cant* 95-00; *Birm* 97-00; *Lich* from 00. *The Community of St Francis, 10 Halcrow Street, London E1 2EP* Tel (020) 7247 6233

WEBB, Martin George. b 46. SS Mark & Jo Coll Chelsea CertEd68 Leeds Univ MEd95. N Ord Course 82. **d** 85 **p** 86. NSM Brotherton *Wakef* 85-87; Perm to Offic *York* 95-98; NSM Bethnal Green St Barn *Lon* from 98. *St Bartholomew's Vicarage, Buckhurst Street, London E1 5QT* Tel (020) 7247 8013 *or* 7510 8945 E-mail martin@webb.lcbroadband.co.uk

WEBB, Michael David. b 59. K Coll Lon BD82 PGCE83. Ripon Coll Cuddesdon 88. **d** 90 **p** 91. C Broughton Astley *Leic* 90-93; C Hugglescote w Donington, Ellistown and Snibston 93-94; TV 94-98; R Castleford All SS and Whitwood *Wakef* 98-01; P-in-c Glass Houghton 98-01; TR Castleford 02; rtd 02. *7 St Peter's Close, Farndon, Newark NG24 3SN* Tel (01636) 702548 E-mail michael@webbs-web.co.uk

WEBB, Canon Michael John. b 49. Linc Coll Ox BA70 MA74. Linc Th Coll 70. **d** 72 **p** 73. C Tring *St Alb* 72-75; C Chipping Barnet 75-78; C Chipping Barnet w Arkley 78-82; TV Cullercoats St Geo *Newc* 82-89; V Newc H Cross 89-97; Chapl Mothers' Union 96-02; V Newc St Gabr *Newc* from 97; AD Newc E from 97; Hon Can Newc Cathl from 02. *St Gabriel's Vicarage, 9 Holderness Road, Heaton, Newcastle upon Tyne NE6 5RH* Tel 0191-276 3957 *or* fax and tel 265 5843 E-mail ruraldeaneast@ukgateway.net

WEBB, Nikola. *See* MARSHALL, Pauline Nikola

WEBB, Norma Fay. b 39. K Coll Dur BDS62. **d** 04 **p** 05. OLM Thornhill and Whitley Lower *Wakef* from 04. *24 High Street, Thornhill, Dewsbury WF12 0PS* Tel (01924) 463574 E-mail normafwebb@aol.com

WEBB, Peter Henry. b 55. Nottm Univ BA77 Sunderland Univ Dip Psychology 95. St Steph Ho Ox 77. **d** 79 **p** 80. C Lancing w Coombes *Chich* 79-82; C The Hydneye CD 82-84; C-in-c 84-86; Chapl Sunderland Distr Gen Hosp 86-94; Chapl City Hosps Sunderland NHS Trust from 94. *The Chaplain's Office, Sunderland Royal General Hospital, Kayll Road, Sunderland SR4 7TP* Tel 0191-565 6256 *or* 569 9180

WEBB, Rex Alexander Francis. b 32. Ely Th Coll 56. **d** 58 **p** 59. C Millbrook *Win* 58-60; Australia from 60; rtd 97. *54 Annaburoo Crescent, Tiwi, Darwin, NT, Australia 0810*

WEBB, Richard. b 38. Oak Hill NSM Course 91. **d** 94 **p** 95. NSM Hanwell St Mary w St Chris *Lon* 94-04; rtd 04; Perm to Offic *Cant* from 05. *1 Haffenden Meadow, Charing, Ashford TN27 0JR* Tel (01233) 714663

WEBB, Richard Frederick. b 42. Cant Sch of Min. **d** 84 **p** 85. C Ipswich St Clem w H Trin *St E* 84-87; R Rougham and Beyton w Hessett 87-91; R Rougham, Beyton w Hessett and Rushbrooke 91-92; P-in-c Woodbridge St Jo 92-98; P-in-c Saxmundham 98-04; P-in-c Kelsale-cum-Carlton, Middleton, Theberton etc 02-04; R Saxmundham w Kelsale cum Carlton from 04; RD Saxmundham from 03. *The Rectory, Manor Gardens, Saxmundham IP17 1ET* Tel (01728) 604234 E-mail richard@saxrectory.freeserve.co.uk

WEBB, Robert. *See* WEBB, Arthur Robert

WEBB, Rowland James. b 33. Roch Th Coll 64. **d** 67 **p** 68. C Tavistock and Gulworthy *Ex* 67-70; Chapl RN 70-86; R Mundford w Lynford *Nor* 86-90; V Burnham *Chelmsf* 90-98; rtd 98; Perm to Offic *Chelmsf* from 98. *4 Pine Drive, Ingatestone CM4 9EF*

WEBB, Timothy Robert. b 57. Univ of Wales (Abth) BA79 CQSW89 Univ of Wales (Ban) BTh03. **d** 03 **p** 04. C Machynlleth w Llanwrin and Penegoes *Ban* from 03. *Y Rheithordy, Penegoes, Machynlleth SY20 8NH* Tel (01654) 703214 Mobile 07765-298575

WEBB, William John. b 43. Cuddesdon Coll 68. **d** 71 **p** 72. C Weston Favell *Pet* 71-73; C Newport w Longford *Lich* 74-77; C Baswich 77-79; P-in-c Stonnall and Wall 79-83; V Prees and Fauls 83-95; V St Martin's from 95. *The Vicarage, St Martins, Oswestry SY11 3AP* Tel (01691) 772295

WEBBER, David Price. b 39. Chich Th Coll 90. **d** 91 **p** 92. NSM Shoreham Beach *Chich* 91-93; NSM Hove St Patr 93-96; Turks and Caicos Is from 96. *PO Box 24, Grand Turk, Turks and Caicos Islands, BWI*

WEBBER, The Very Revd Eric Michael. b 16. Lon Univ BD54 ATh(SA)55 Univ of Tasmania MEd77 MHums85. AKC43. **d** 43 **p** 44. C Clapham H Spirit *S'wark* 43-47; C Wimbledon 47-50; S Africa 50-58; Australia from 58; Dean Hobart 59-71; Sen Lect Relig Studies Tasmanian Coll Adv Educn 71-81; rtd 94.

5B Kendrick Court, Dynnyrne, Tas, Australia 7005 Tel (0061) (3) 6223 6413

WEBBER, John Arthur. b 45. Keble Coll Ox BA67 MA71 Gen Th Sem NY STM85. Cuddesdon Coll 70. **d** 71 **p** 72. C Penarth All SS *Llan* 71-74; USPG Bangladesh 75-84 and 85-91; USA 84-85; Asst P Stepney St Dunstan and All SS *Lon* 91-97; Bp's Adv on Inter-Faith Relns 91-04; P-in-c Bethnal Green St Barn 97-00; Dir of Ords 00-04; TR Llantwit Major *Llan* from 04. *The Rectory, High Street, Llantwit Major CF61 1SS* Tel (01446) 792324

WEBBER, Lionel Frank. b 35. Kelham Th Coll St Mich Coll Llan. **d** 60 **p** 61. C Bolton Sav *Man* 60-63; C Aberavon *Llan* 63-65; R Salford Stowell Memorial *Man* 65-69; V Aberavon H Trin *Llan* 69-74; TV Stantonbury *Ox* 74-76; TR Basildon St Martin w H Cross and Laindon *Chelmsf* 76-79; P-in-c Nevendon 77-79; RD Basildon 79-89; R Basildon St Martin w Nevendon 79-95; R Basildon St Martin 95-01; Hon Can Chelmsf Cathl 84-01; Chapl to The Queen 94-01; rtd 01. *12 Ramblers Way, Burnham-on-Crouch CM0 8LR* Tel (01621) 785152

WEBBER, Canon Michael Champneys Wilfred. b 48. Man Univ BA71 MA(Theol)78. Cuddesdon Coll 73. **d** 75 **p** 76. C Caterham *S'wark* 75-79; P-in-c Kidbrooke St Jas 79-84; TV 84-85; V Earls Barton *Pet* from 87; RD Wellingborough from 00; Can Pet Cathl from 04. *The Vicarage, 7 High Street, Earls Barton, Northampton NN6 0JG* Tel and fax (01604) 810447
E-mail michaelc.webber@btinternet.com

WEBBER, Raymond John. b 40. Lon Univ DipTh65. Linc Th Coll 84. **d** 85 **p** 86. C Helston *Truro* 85; C Helston and Wendron 85-90; TV 90-93; R Kenton, Mamhead, Powderham, Cofton and Starcross *Ex* 93-03; rtd 03; Perm to Offic *Truro* from 03. *1 Seton Gardens, Camborne TR14 7JS* Tel (01209) 711360

WEBBER, Thomas George Edward. b 63. LSE BSc84. Trin Coll Bris DipTh98. **d** 98 **p** 99. C Churchdown *Glouc* 98-02; TV Stoke Gifford *Bris* from 02. *The Vicarage, Mautravers Close, Bradley Stoke, Bristol BS32 8ED* Tel 0117-931 2222
E-mail tcwebber@lineone.net

WEBBER, Toby Roderic. b 75. St Jo Coll Dur BA96. Wycliffe Hall Ox BA01. **d** 02 **p** 03. C Chorley St Laur *Blackb* from 02. *57 Park Road, Chorley PR7 1QZ* Tel (01257) 274170 Fax 231374

WEBBLEY, Ms Rachel Catharine. b 75. Hatf Coll Dur BA98. Qu Coll Birm BA03. **d** 04 **p** 05. C Bicester w Bucknell, Caversfield and Launton *Ox* from 04. *34 Kennedy Road, Bicester OX26 2BQ* Tel (01869) 253691 E-mail rcwebbley@hotmail.com

WEBER, Douglas John Craig. b 20. Ex Coll Ox BA46 MA46. Sarum Th Coll. **d** 49 **p** 50. C Portsea N End St Mark *Portsm* 49-52; C Alverstoke 52-55; V Hook w Warsash 55-88; rtd 88; Perm to Offic *Portsm* from 88. *1 Trevose Way, Titchfield, Fareham PO14 4NG* Tel (01489) 583065

WEBLEY, Robin Bowen. b 32. Univ of Wales (Cardiff) DPS. St Mich Coll Llan 87. **d** 89 **p** 90. C St D Cathl *St D* 89-91; Min Can St D Cathl 89-91; R Castlemartin w Warren and Angle etc 91-94; Succ St D Cathl 94-00; rtd 00. *Whiteleys, Stepaside, Narberth SA67 8NS* Tel (01834) 813603

WEBSTER, The Very Revd Alan Brunskill. b 18. KCVO88. Qu Coll Ox BA39 MA43 BD54 City Univ Hon DD. Westcott Ho Cam 41. **d** 42 **p** 43. C Attercliffe w Carbrook *Sheff* 42-44; C Sheff Arbourthorne 44-46; Chapl and Lib Westcott Ho Cam 46-48; Vice-Prin 48-53; V Barnard Castle *Dur* 53-59; RD Barnard Castle 54-59; Warden Linc Th Coll 59-70; Can and Preb Linc Cathl *Linc* 64-70; Dean Nor 70-78; Dean St Paul's *Lon* 78-87; rtd 88; Perm to Offic *Nor* 88-01. *Rocket Lodge, High Street, Cley, Holt NR25 7RB* Tel (01263) 741022

WEBSTER, David Edward. b 39. K Coll Lon 60 Edin Th Coll 62. **d** 64 **p** 65. C Maghull *Liv* 64-69; R Wavertree St Mary 69-76; TV Greystoke, Matterdale and Mungrisdale *Carl* 76-81; R Lowton St Luke *Liv* 81-88; R Stoneleigh w Ashow and Baginton *Cov* 88-01; Chapl Nat Agric Cen 88-01; P-in-c Pennington and Lindal w Marton and Bardsea *Carl* 01-02; V from 02. *The Vicarage, Main Road, Swarthmoor, Ulverston LA12 0RZ* Tel and fax (01229) 583174 E-mail d.webster@ruralnet.org.uk

WEBSTER, David Leslie Holbarow. b 37. St Alb and Ox Min Course 00. **d** 02 **p** 03. NSM Hurst *Ox* 02-04; NSM Earley St Nic from 04. *515 Reading Road, Winnersh, Wokingham RG41 5HL* Tel 0118-979 4568 Fax 961 9575
E-mail dlhwebster@supanet.com

WEBSTER, David Robert. b 32. Selw Coll Cam BA56 MA60. Linc Th Coll 56. **d** 58 **p** 59. C Billingham St Cuth *Dur* 58-61; C Doncaster St Geo *Sheff* 61-64; Chapl Doncaster R Infirmary 61-64; V Lumley *Dur* 64-76; V Belmont 76-93; rtd 93. *25 Eldon Grove, Hartlepool TS26 9LY* Tel (01429) 425915
E-mail david.webster50@ntlworld.com

WEBSTER, Dennis Eric. b 39. Fitzw Ho Cam BA60 MA64 Linacre Coll Ox MA70 Lon Univ CertEd61. Wycliffe Hall Ox 62. **d** 65 **p** 66. C Herne Bay Ch Ch *Cant* 65-68; C Tulse Hill H Trin *S'wark* 68-69; Missr Kenya 70-75; Chapl Pierrepont Sch Frensham 75-91; R Chiddingfold *Guildf* 91-02; rtd 02; Perm to Offic *Guildf* from 02. *Sylvan Cottage, 24 Longdown Road, Lower Bourne, Farnham GU10 3JL* Tel (01252) 713919

WEBSTER, Derek Herbert. b 34. FRSA82 Hull Univ BA55 Lon Univ BD55 Leic Univ MEd68 PhD73. Lambeth STh67 Linc Th Coll 76. **d** 76 **p** 77. Lect Hull Univ from 72; Reader from 97; NSM Cleethorpes *Linc* from 76. *60 Queen's Parade, Cleethorpes DN35 0DG* Tel (01472) 693786
E-mail dwebster@edrev.demon.co.uk

WEBSTER, Mrs Diane Margaret. b 43. Oak Hill NSM Course 91. **d** 94 **p** 95. NSM Welwyn Garden City *St Alb* 94-99; P-in-c Burley Ville *Win* from 99; RD Christchurch from 03. *The Vicarage, Church Corner, Burley, Ringwood BH24 4AP* Tel (01425) 402303 E-mail dwebster@fish.co.uk

WEBSTER, Geoffrey William. b 36. St Alb Minl Tr Scheme 77. **d** 80 **p** 81. NSM Harlington *St Alb* 80-82; C Belmont *Dur* 82-86; R Gateshead Fell 86-94; P-in-c Hamsterley 94-95; V Hamsterley and Witton-le-Wear 95-02; rtd 02. *38A Owton Manor Lane, Hartlepool TS25 3AE* Tel (01429) 265798

WEBSTER, Canon Glyn Hamilton. b 51. SRN73. Cranmer Hall Dur 74. **d** 77 **p** 78. C Huntington *York* 77-81; V York St Luke 81-92; Chapl York Distr Hosp 81-92; Sen Chapl York Health Services NHS Trust 92-99; Can and Preb York Minster *York* 94-99; Can Res York Minster from 99; RD City of York 97-04; Assoc Dioc Dir of Ords from 05. *4 Minster Yard, York YO1 7JD* Tel (01904) 620877 Fax 557201 E-mail pastor@yorkminster.org

WEBSTER, John Bainbridge. b 55. Clare Coll Cam MA81 PhD82. **d** 83 **p** 84. Chapl and Dep Sen Tutor St Jo Coll Dur 83-86; Hon C Bearpark *Dur* 83-86; Assoc Prof Systematic Th Wycliffe Coll Toronto 86-93; Prof Systematic Th 93-95; Ramsay Armitage Prof Systematic Th 95-96; Lady Marg Prof Div Ox Univ 96-04; Can Res Ch Ch *Ox* 96-04. *Address temp unknown*
E-mail john.webster@christ-church.ox.ac.uk

WEBSTER, John Kelsey. b 62. St Alb and Ox Min Course 00. **d** 03 **p** 04. NSM Woolhampton w Midgham and Beenham Valance *Ox* from 03; NSM Aldermaston w Wasing and Brimpton from 05. *51 Stoneyfield, Beenham, Reading RG7 5ND* Tel 0118-971 4924 Mobile 07800-121246

WEBSTER, Canon Martin Duncan. b 52. Nottm Univ BSc74 DipTh76. Linc Th Coll 75. **d** 78 **p** 79. C Thundersley *Chelmsf* 78-81; C Canvey Is 81-82; TV 82-86; V Nazeing 86-99; RD Harlow 88-99; TR Waltham H Cross from 99; Hon Can Chelmsf Cathl from 00. *The Rectory, Highbridge Street, Waltham Abbey EN9 1DG* Tel and fax (01992) 762115
E-mail martin-webster@lineone.net

WEBSTER, Mrs Monica. b 39. DipCOT60. WMMTC 94. **d** 97 **p** 98. NSM Wolverton w Norton Lindsey and Langley *Cov* 97-01; Asst Chapl to the Deaf 97-01; NSM Stoneleigh w Ashow and Baginton 98-01; Chapl to the Deaf and Hard of Hearing *Carl* from 01; NSM Aldingham, Dendron, Rampside and Urswick from 02; NSM Pennington and Lindal w Marton and Bardsea from 02. *Trinkeld Vicarage, Main Road, Swarthmoor, Ulverston LA12 0RZ* Tel and fax (01229) 583174
E-mail revmonic@fish.co.uk

WEBSTER, Mrs Patricia Eileen. b 34. St Gabr Coll Lon TCert54. Gilmore Ho 56. **d** 87 **p** 94. Par Dn Belmont *Dur* 87-93; rtd 93. *25 Eldon Grove, Hartlepool TS26 9LY* Tel (01429) 425915
E-mail david.webster50@ntlworld.com

WEBSTER, Peter. b 26. MRICS FCIOB FASI. Cranmer Hall Dur 68. **d** 70 **p** 71. C Tickhill w Stainton *Sheff* 70-72; C Conisbrough 72-73; V Walkley 73-77; V Rawcliffe 77-84; V Barrow-on-Humber *Linc* 84; P-in-c Goxhill 84; V Barrow and Goxhill 84-91; rtd 91; Perm to Offic *Sheff* and *York* from 91. *1 Parsons Lane, Howden, Goole DN14 7BT* Tel (01430) 431637
E-mail cleric@fish.co.uk

WEBSTER, Rosamond Mary. *See* LATHAM, Ms Rosamond Mary

WEBSTER, Sarah Vernoy. b 38. Univ of Georgia BSc61. S'wark Ord Course 87. **d** 90 **p** 94. NSM Primrose Hill St Mary w Avenue Road St Paul *Lon* 90-01; Lic to Offic *Chelmsf* from 01; *Lon* from 01. *Birdhouse, 19 Beach Road, Lee-Over-Sands, Clacton-on-Sea CO16 8EX* Tel (01255) 820652
E-mail revsallywebster@aol.com

WEBSTER, Mrs Sheila Mary. b 22. Bedf Coll Lon CertSS43. Gilmore Ho 69. **dss** 81 **d** 87. Patcham *Chich* 77-83; Hove All SS 84-90; Hon Par Dn 87-90; rtd 90; Perm to Offic *Chich* from 90. *108 Surrenden Road, Brighton BN1 6WB* Tel (01273) 561222

WEBSTER-SMITH, Preb Alfred William. b 10. St Chad's Coll Dur BA32 MA35. **d** 33 **p** 34. C Riddlesdown *S'wark* 33-36; Tanganyika 36-51; Gen Sec UMCA 51-59; Lic to Offic *S'wark* 51-59; Hon Can Masasi from 57; Zambia 59-66; Can N Rhodesia 60-62; R Pontesbury I and II *Heref* 66-76; RD Pontesbury 66-76; Preb Heref Cathl 73-81; rtd 76; Perm to Offic *S'wark* 80-02. *The College of St Barnabas, Blackberry Lane, Lingfield RH7 6NJ* Tel (01342) 870609

WEDDERSPOON, The Very Revd Alexander Gillan. b 31. Jes Coll Ox BA54 MA61 Lon Univ BD62. Cuddesdon Coll. **d** 61 **p** 62. C Kingston All SS *S'wark* 61-63; Lect RE Lon Univ 63-66; Educn Adv C of E Sch Coun 66-70; Can Res Win Cathl *Win* 70-87; Treas 80-85; Vice-Dean 80-87; Dean Guildf 87-01; rtd 01; Perm to Offic *Guildf* from 01. *1 Ellery Close, Cranleigh GU6 8DF* Tel (01483) 548586 E-mail alex@wedderspoon.fsnet.co.uk

WEDGBURY, John William. b 53. RMCS BSc78. St Jo Coll Nottm 84. **d** 87 **p** 88. C Foord St Jo *Cant* 87-91; V Mangotsfield *Bris* 91-92; NSM Manselton *S & B* 00-02; P-in-c Caereithin 02-05; NSM Swansea St Thos and Kilvey from 05. *4 Ffynone Drive, Swansea SA1 6DD* Tel (01792) 464194

WEDGEWORTH, Canon Michael John. b 40. Nottm Univ BSc62. Wesley Ho Cam MA66. **d** 93 **p** 94. In Methodist Ch 66-93; NSM Feniscowles *Blackb* 93-96; Sec DBF 95-05; Hon P Blackb Cathl from 95; Lic to Offic from 96; Hon Can Blackb Cathl from 03. *46 Preston New Road, Blackburn BB2 6AH* Tel (01254) 260078 *or* 54421 Fax 699963
E-mail mike.wedgeworth@blackburn.anglican.org.uk

WEDGWOOD, George Peter. b 26. St Jo Coll Dur BA51 MA56. **d** 52 **p** 53. C Barrow St Mark *Carl* 52-54; Chapl Sedbergh Sch 54-57; P-in-c Dur St Cuth *Dur* 57-63; Chapl Dur High Sch 58-63; Chapl, Hd of Div and Sen Lect St Kath Coll *Liv* 63-69; Prin Lect 69-83; Hd of Div Liv Coll of HE 84-86; P-in-c Kirkoswald, Renwick and Ainstable *Carl* 86-88; rtd 88; Perm to Offic *Carl* 88-92 and *Liv* 92-97; Hon C Hawick *Edin* 02-05. *Lakeside View, Auchry, Turriff AB53 5TP* Tel (01888) 544619

WEDGWOOD, Keith. b 20. Hertf Coll Ox BA42 MA46. Wycliffe Hall Ox 42. **d** 43 **p** 44. C Hartlebury *Worc* 43-46; C Worc St Martin 46-49; Succ Derby Cathl *Derby* 49-52; V Choral Sarum Cathl *Sarum* 52-68; Succ 55-68; R Coverdale w Hillsboro Canada 68-72; P-in-c Osmington w Poxwell *Sarum* 72-77; TV The Iwernes and Sutton Waldron 77-78; P-in-c 78-81; V The Iwernes, Sutton Waldron and Fontmell Magna 81-85; rtd 85; Perm to Offic *Sarum* 85-05. *c/o A Wedgwood Esq, 9A Rosebery Road, Bournemouth BH5 2JH*

WEDGWOOD GREENHOW, Stephen John Francis. b 57. Man Univ BA82. Edin Th Coll MTh84. **d** 84 **p** 85. C Wythenshawe Wm Temple Ch *Man* 84-87; USA from 87. *556 North George Washington Blvd, Yuba City, CA 95993, USA* Tel (001) (530) 822 0691

WEEDEN, Simon Andrew. b 55. York Univ BA79. Wycliffe Hall Ox 88. **d** 90 **p** 91. C Gt Chesham *Ox* 90-94; P-in-c Haversham w Lt Linford, Tyringham w Filgrave 94-97; R Lamp 97-99; P-in-c Bramshott and Liphook *Portsm* 99-00; R from 00; RD Petersfield from 04. *The Rectory, 22 Portsmouth Road, Liphook GU30 7DJ* Tel (01428) 723119 Fax 725390
E-mail simon@weedens.freeserve.co.uk

WEEDING, Paul Stephen. b 62. Leic Poly BSc. Ripon Coll Cuddesdon 88. **d** 90 **p** 91. C Llanishen and Lisvane *Llan* 90-93; C Merthyr Tydfil Ch Ch 93-97; V Abercynon 97-03; Asst Chapl Qu Medical Cen Nottm Univ Hosp NHS Trust from 03. *Trust Headquarters, Derby Road, Nottingham NG7 2UH* Tel 0115-924 9924

✠**WEEKES, The Rt Revd Ambrose Walter Marcus.** b 19. CB70. AKC41 Linc Th Coll 41. **d** 42 **p** 43 **c** 77. C New Brompton St Luke *Roch* 42-44; Chapl RNVR 44-46; Chapl RN 46-69; Chapl of the Fleet and Adn for the RN 69-72; QHC from 69; Can Gib Cathl *Eur* 71-73; Chapl Tangier 72-73; Dean Gib 73-77; Aux Bp Eur 77-80; Suff Bp Eur 80-86; Dean Brussels 81-86; rtd 86; Asst Bp Roch 86-88; Asst Bp Eur from 89; Chapl Montreux w Gstaad 89-92; Perm to Offic *Lon* from 03. *Charterhouse, Charterhouse Square, London EC1M 6AN* Tel (020) 7251 4201

WEEKES, Cecil William. b 31. CITC. **d** 78 **p** 79. NSM Glenageary *D & G* 78-80; Bp's V Kilkenny Cathl *C & O* 80-83; I Carlow w Urglin and Staplestown 83-90; Can Leighlin Cathl 88-96; Can Ossory Cathl 88-96; I Lismore w Cappoquin, Kilwatermoy, Dungarvan etc 90-96; Dean Lismore 90-96; Chan Cashel Cathl 90-96; Prec Waterford Cathl 90-96; rtd 96. *The Cottage, Danesfort Road, Bennettsbridge, Co Kilkenny, Irish Republic* Tel and fax (00353) (56) 772 7711
E-mail cwweekes@eircom.net

WEEKES, David John. b 34. Magd Coll Cam BA59 MA68 Lon Univ PGCE68 Aber Univ MTh79. Clifton Th Coll 62. **d** 64 **p** 65. C Cheadle *Ches* 64-68; Uganda 69-73; Perm to Offic *St And* 73-74; Chapl and Hd of RE Fettes Coll Edin 74-94; Warden and Chapl Lee Abbey Internat Students' Club Kensington 94-01; rtd 01; Perm to Offic *Lon* 94-03. *Loaning Hill, Kilmany, Cupar KY15 4PT* Tel (01382) 330137 Mobile 07855-761970
E-mail davidweekes@hotmail.com

WEEKES, Robin Alasdair Rutley. b 73. Peterho Cam MA94. Wycliffe Hall Ox BA98 MA98. **d** 99 **p** 00. C Wimbledon Em Ridgway Prop Chpl *S'wark* from 99. *25 Richmond Road, London SW20 0PG* Tel (020) 8947 2029

WEEKS, Ms Jane Anne. b 61. UEA BA00. Aston Tr Scheme 95 EAMTC 97. **d** 00 **p** 01. C Hadleigh *St E* 00-02; C Hadleigh, Layham and Shelley 02-03; Chapl HM Pris Bullwood Hall from 03. *HM Prison and YOI Bullwood Hall, High Road, Hockley SS5 4TE* Tel (01702) 562838
E-mail weeks.clan@virgin.net.com

WEETMAN, Mrs Dorothy. b 41. **d** 03 **p** 04. OLM Prudhoe *Newc* from 03. *Station Gate East, Eltringham Road, Prudhoe NE42 6LA* Tel (01661) 834538

WEETMAN, Canon John Charles. b 66. Qu Coll Ox BA87 MA92. Trin Coll Bris BA91. **d** 91 **p** 92. C Hull St Jo Newland *York* 91-95; V Boosbeck w Moorsholm 95-02; V Redcar from 02; RD Guisborough from 99; Can and Preb York Minster from 05. *St Peter's Vicarage, 66 Aske Road, Redcar TS10 2BP* Tel (01642) 490700

WEIGHTMAN, Miss Andrea Frances. b 66. Sheff Univ BA87. Ridley Hall Cam 00. **d** 03. C Handforth *Ches* from 03. *61 Pickmere Road, Handforth, Wilmslow SK9 3TB* Tel (01625) 526207 Mobile 07974-946668

WEIGHTMAN, David Courtenay. b 47. FRICS88. **d** 04. OLM Oxted and Tandridge *S'wark* from 04. *13 Silkham Road, Oxted RH8 0NP* Tel (01883) 715420 Mobile 07739-456947 Fax (01883) 717336 E-mail david@survez.co.uk

WEIL, Thomas James. b 53. K Coll Lon BSc74 PhD79 AKC74. S Tr Scheme 95. **d** 97 **p** 99. NSM Stoughton *Guildf* 97-03; Perm to Offic *Lon* 03-05. *17 Lyons Drive, Guildford GU2 9YP* Tel (01483) 234535

WEIR, Graham Francis. b 52. GSM LASI. N Ord Course 88. **d** 91 **p** 92. NSM High Crompton *Man* 91-92; NSM Heyside 92-94; Asst Chapl Bolton Hosps NHS Trust 94-96; Chapl from 96; Dep Hd of Chapl from 04. *The Chaplain's Office, Royal Bolton Hospital, Minerva Road, Farnworth, Bolton BL4 0JR* Tel (01204) 390770 *or* 390390
E-mail graham.weir@boltonh-tr.nwest.nhs.uk

WEIR, John Michael Vavasour. b 48. K Coll Lon BD72 AKC72 MA00. **d** 73 **p** 74. C Hatfield Hyde *St Alb* 73-76; C Watford St Mich 76-79; Asst Chapl Oslo St Edm *Eur* 80-81; V Bethnal Green St Pet w St Thos *Lon* 81-04; Chapl Qu Eliz Hosp for Children Lon 81-98; Chapl Team Ldr Toc H from 01; Sen Chapl Dubai and Sharjah w N Emirates from 04. *Holy Trinity Dubai, PO Box 7415, Dubai, United Arab Emirates* Tel (00971) (4) 337 0247 E-mail chap7415@emirates.net.ae

WEIR, John William Moon. b 36. St Luke's Coll Ex CertEd69 Ex Univ BEd76. SW Minl Tr Course 82. **d** 85 **p** 86. NSM Meavy, Sheepstor and Walkhampton *Ex* 85-87; NSM Yelverton, Meavy, Sheepstor and Walkhampton from 87; Hd Master Princetown Primary Sch 86-94; Sub-Chapl HM Pris Dartmoor 86-94. *Goblin's Green, Dousland, Yelverton PL20 6ND* Tel (01822) 852671

WEIR, William Daniel Niall. b 57. UEA BA79. Ripon Coll Cuddesdon 80. **d** 83 **p** 84. C Chelsea St Luke *Lon* 83-87; PV Westmr Abbey 85-89; C Poplar *Lon* 87-88; TV 88-93; P-in-c Forest Gate Em w Upton Cross *Chelmsf* 93-97; V 97-99; Asst Chapl Southn Univ Hosps NHS Trust 99-00; Trust Chapl 00-03; R W Hackney St Barn *Lon* from 03. *The Rectory, 306 Amhurst Road, London N16 7UE* Tel (020) 7254 3235
E-mail niall.weir@bigfoot.com

WEISSERHORN, Julian Timothy David Moritz. b 74. K Coll Lon BA96 AKC96. Oak Hill Th Coll 02. **d** 04 **p** 05. C Chadwell *Chelmsf* from 04. *7 Cedar Road, Grays RM16 4ST* Tel (01375) 850940 E-mail julianweisserhorn@hotmail.com

WELANDER, Canon David Charles St Vincent. b 25. FSA. Lon Coll of Div BD47 ALCD47. **d** 48 **p** 49. C Heigham H Trin *Nor* 48-51; Tutor Oak Hill Th Coll 51-52; Chapl and Tutor Lon Coll of Div 52-56; V Iver *Ox* 56-63; V Cheltenham Ch Ch *Glouc* 63-75; RD Cheltenham 73-75; Can Res Glouc Cathl 75-91; rtd 91; Perm to Offic *Glouc* 91-98 and *Bris* from 91. *Willow Cottage, 1 Sandpits Lane, Sherston Magna, Malmesbury SN16 0NN* Tel (01666) 840180

WELBOURN, David Anthony. b 41. K Coll Lon BD63 AKC63 Sunderland Poly DMS77. St Boniface Warminster 63. **d** 64 **p** 65. C Stockton St Chad *Dur* 64-67; C S Westoe 69-74; Ind Chapl 69-80; Ind Chapl *Nor* 80-90; Ind and Commerce Officer *Guildf* from 90. *81 Collingwood Crescent, Guildford GU1 2NU* Tel and fax (01483) 825541 E-mail david@dwelbourn.freeserve.co.uk

WELBY, Alexander. *See* WELBY, Richard Alexander Lyon

WELBY, Canon Justin Portal. b 56. Trin Coll Cam BA78 MA90 St Jo Coll Dur BA91 Dip Minl Studies 92 MACT84. Cranmer Hall Dur 89. **d** 92 **p** 93. C Chilvers Coton w Astley *Cov* 92-95; R Southam 95-02; V Ufton 98-02; RD Southam 97-99; Can Res Cov Cathl from 02; Co-Dir Internat Min from 02. *35 Asthill Grove, Coventry CV3 6HN* Tel (024) 7650 5426 *or* 7652 1204 Fax 7652 1260 E-mail justin.welby@coventrycathedral.org.uk

WELBY, Peter Edlin Brown. b 34. Open Univ BA75. St Jo Coll Dur 75. **d** 77 **p** 78. C Auckland St Andr and St Anne *Dur* 77-79; C S Westoe 79-81; V Tudhoe 81-93; R Croxdale and Tudhoe 93-99; rtd 99. *Blyth House, 9 Rhodes Terrace, Nevilles Cross, Durham DH1 4JW* Tel 0191-384 8295

WELBY, Richard Alexander Lyon (Alex). b 58. St Jo Coll Nottm BTh81 LTh Leeds Univ MA93. Ridley Hall Cam 83. **d** 84 **p** 85. C Stoke Bishop *Bris* 84-88; V Bowling St Steph *Bradf* 88-95; P-in-c Hatherleigh, Meeth, Exbourne and Jacobstowe *Ex* from 95. *The Rectory, Hatherleigh, Okehampton EX20 3JY* Tel and fax (01837) 810314 Mobile 07966-409788
E-mail alex.welby@virgin.net

WELCH, Amanda Jane. b 58. **d** 04 **p** 05. OLM Worplesdon *Guildf* from 04. *Glenlea, Liddington New Road, Guildford GU3 3AH* Tel (01483) 233091 E-mail cofeworp@fish.co.uk

WELCH, David John. b 52. NTMTC 98. **d** 01 **p** 02. C Walthamstow *Chelmsf* from 01. *9 Church End, London E17 9RJ* Tel (020) 8509 3746 E-mail dwelch@fish.co.uk

WELCH, Derek. b 27. Keble Coll Ox BA51 MA57. Coll of Resurr Mirfield 51. **d** 53 **p** 54. C Middlesbrough St Jo the Ev *York* 53-58; C Oswaldtwistle Immanuel *Blackb* 58-59; V Accrington St Andr 59-65; V Salesbury 66-72; V Heyhouses on Sea 73-92; rtd 92; Perm to Offic *Blackb* from 92. *76 St Thomas's Road, Lytham St Annes FY8 1JR* Tel (01253) 781469

WELCH, Francis Hughan. b 16. Lon Univ BD67. S'wark Ord Course 67. **d** 70 **p** 71. Lic to Offic *St Alb* 70-71; C St Alb St Steph 71-75; P-in-c 75-80; Chapl St Alb City Hosp 80-90; Perm to Offic *Lon* 80-90; rtd 81; Perm to Offic *St Alb* 80-81 and 90-93; Hon C St Alb St Pet 81-89; Hon C St Alb St Mich 89-90; Perm to Offic *St D* from 93. *Bryntelor, Sarnau, Llandysul SA44 6QN* Tel (01239) 654573

WELCH, Gordon Joseph. b 47. Man Univ BSc68 PhD72. N Ord Course 84. **d** 87 **p** 88. NSM Upton Ascension *Ches* 87-98; Lic to Offic 99-00; NSM Backford and Capenhurst 00-02; NSM Ellesmere Port from 02; Hon Chapl ATC from 02. *6 St James's Avenue, Chester CH2 1NA* Tel (01244) 382196

WELCH, Canon Grant Keith. b 40. AKC63. **d** 64 **p** 65. C Nottingham St Mary *S'well* 64-68; V Cinderhill 68-73; R Weston Favell *Pet* 73-88; Master St Jo Hosp Weston Favell 73-88; Can Pet Cathl 83-88; P-in-c Gt Houghton 84-85; C Loughton St Jo *Chelmsf* 89-92; TR 92-05; AD Epping Forest 00-04; rtd 05. *7 Hayes Lane, Compton Dundon, Somerton TA11 6PB* Tel (01458) 272526 E-mail juliawelch@waitrose.com

WELCH, Harold Gerald. b 16. St Cath Soc Ox BA48 MA53. Wycliffe Hall Ox 48. **d** 50 **p** 51. C Ipswich St Jo *St E* 50-53; V Offton, Nettlestead and Willisham 53-58; V Lozells St Paul *Birm* 58-66; V Austrey 66-83; V Warton 66-83; rtd 83; Perm to Offic *Lich* from 88 and *Birm* 88-00. *2 Clifford Close, Tamworth B77 2DD* Tel (01827) 53678

WELCH, Ian Michael. b 59. Warwick Univ BA81 Connecticut Univ MA84. Ripon Coll Cuddesdon 00. **d** 02 **p** 03. C Lee St Aug *S'wark* from 02. *38 Marvels Lane, London SE12 9PE* Tel (020) 8857 4810

WELCH, John Harry. b 52. Oak Hill Th Coll 85. **d** 87 **p** 88. C Parr *Liv* 87-90; V W Derby St Luke 90-00; V Eccleston Park from 00. *St James's Vicarage, 159A St Helen's Road, Prescot L34 2QB* Tel 0151-426 6421

WELCH, Canon Michael Robin. b 33. MBE81. St Chad's Coll Dur BSc55. Wells Th Coll 57. **d** 59 **p** 60. C S Shields St Hilda *Dur* 59-63; CF (R of O) 61-88; Warden and Tr Officer Dioc Youth Cen *Newc* 63-68; Soc and Ind Adv *Portsm* 68-96; V Portsea All SS 72-85; V Swanmore St Barn 85-96; RD Bishop's Waltham 88-93; Hon Can Portsm Cathl 92-96; rtd 96; Perm to Offic *Sarum* from 96. *Southwell, Church Street, Mere, Warminster BA12 6LS* Tel (01747) 860047

WELCH, Mrs Pamela Jean. b 47. Girton Coll Cam MA76 K Coll Lon BD79 AKC79. Qu Coll Birm 79. **dss** 80 **d** 87. Tottenham H Trin *Lon* 80-84; Asst Chapl Bryanston Sch 84-87; Perm to Offic *Chich* 87-94; C Mornington St Mary New Zealand from 02. *23 Byron Street, Mornington, Dunedin, New Zealand* Tel and fax (0064) (3) 453 0052 E-mail nplwelch@xtra.co.nz

WELCH, Paul Baxter. b 47. Lanc Univ BEd74 MA75. St Alb Minl Tr Scheme 80. **d** 83 **p** 84. NSM Heath and Reach *St Alb* 83-84; Bp's Sch Adv *Win* 84-89; P-in-c Clungunford w Clunbury and Clunton, Bedstone etc *Heref* 89-93; V Wellingborough All SS *Pet* 93-01; R Pulborough *Chich* from 01; RD Storrington from 04. *The Rectory, 2 London Road, Pulborough RH20 1AP* Tel (01798) 875773 E-mail paul.welch@virgin.net

WELCH, Mrs Sally Ann. b 62. Pemb Coll Ox MA88. St Alb and Ox Min Course 96. **d** 99 **p** 00. NSM Abingdon *Ox* 99-01; P-in-c Kintbury w Avington 01-05; R Cherbury w Gainfield from 05. *The Rectory, Church Lane, Longworth, Abingdon OX13 5DX* Tel (01865) 820213 Mobile 07974-439630 E-mail sally.welch@virgin.net

WELCH, Stephan John. b 50. Hull Univ BA74 Lon Univ MTh98. Qu Coll Birm DipTh76. **d** 77 **p** 78. C Waltham Cross *St Alb* 77-80; P-in-c Reculver *Cant* 80-86; P-in-c Herne Bay St Bart 82-86; V Reculver and Herne Bay St Bart 86-92; V Hurley and Stubbings *Ox* 92-00; P-in-c Hammersmith St Pet *Lon* from 00; AD Hammersmith and Fulham from 01. *17 Ravenscourt Road, London W6 0UH* Tel (020) 8748 1781 *or* 8741 4848 Fax 8748 5453 E-mail stephanjwelch@dsl.pipex.com

WELCHMAN, Richard Neville de Beaufort. b 11. St Pet Hall Ox BA33 DipTh34 MA37. Wycliffe Hall Ox 33. **d** 34 **p** 35. C Plymouth St Andr *Ex* 34-40; CF 40-45; P-in-c Yelverton *Ex* 45-54; R Lifton 54-62; R Kelly w Bradstone 59-62; V Pinhoe 62-76; rtd 77; Lic to Offic *Ex* 77-95; Perm to Offic from 95. *8 Culvert Road, Stoke Canon, Exeter EX5 4BD* Tel (01392) 841503

WELDON, William Ernest. b 41. TCD BA62 MA66. **d** 64 **p** 65. C Belfast Trin Coll Miss *Conn* 64-67; C Carnmoney 67-71; Chapl RN 71-96; QHC 93-96; Hon C Holbeton *Ex* 96-01; Perm to Offic from 01. *3 Garden Close, Holbeton, Plymouth PL8 1NQ* E-mail billanddinahweldon@btopenworld.com

WELFORD, Gillian Margaret. BA. **d** 04 **p** 05. OLM Chiddingfold *Guildf* from 04. *15 Woodberry Close, Chiddingfold, Godalming GU8 4SF* Tel (01428) 683620 E-mail gwelford@fish.co.uk

WELHAM, Clive Richard. b 54. **d** 80 **p** 81. C Bellingham St Dunstan *S'wark* 80-84; Chapl Goldsmiths' Coll Lon 84-95; V Plumstead Ascension from 95. *The Ascension Vicarage, Thornhill Avenue, London SE18 2HS* Tel (020) 8854 3395

WELLER, David Christopher. b 60. UWIST BSc83. St Jo Coll Nottm MA94. **d** 96 **p** 97. C Wednesfield Heath *Lich* 96-99; TV Glascote and Stonydelph 99-05; Chapl Rio de Janeiro Ch Ch Brazil from 05. *Rua Real Grandeza 99, Botafogo, Rio de Janeiro, RJ 22281-030, Brazil* Tel (0055) (21) 2539 9488

WELLER, John Christopher. b 25. St Pet Hall Ox BA49 MA52 Nottm Univ BD57. Qu Coll Birm 50. **d** 51 **p** 52. C Nottingham All SS *S'well* 51-54; C-in-c Porchester St Jas CD 54-58; S Rhodesia 58-64; Zambia 64-71; V W Heath *Birm* 71-81; Warden and Chapl Resthaven Home Stroud 81-84; P-in-c Duddeston 84-85; Zimbabwe 85-90; Can Harare 87-90; rtd 90; P-in-c Ward End *Birm* 96-97; Perm to Offic from 97. *141 Yardley Fields Road, Birmingham B33 8RP* Tel 0121-784 0540

WELLER, Richard Morton. b 33. Selw Coll Cam BA57 MA61. Wells Th Coll 61. **d** 63 **p** 64. C Stockingford *Cov* 63-66; C Pontefract St Giles *Wakef* 66-68; C-in-c Stockton St Jas CD *Dur* 68-74; V E Ardsley *Wakef* 74-83; V Heckmondwike 83-91; V Birstall 91-96; RD Birstall 92-96; V Gawber 96-01; rtd 01; Perm to Offic *Wakef* from 02. *14 Callis Way, Penistone, Sheffield S36 6UH* Tel (01226) 379760

WELLER (née SPENCE), Susan Karen. b 65. Leeds Univ BSc86 Liv Univ PhD89. Wycliffe Hall Ox BA95. **d** 96 **p** 97. C Caverswall and Weston Coyney w Dilhorne *Lich* 96-00; C Wilnecote 00-05; Dioc Adv for Women in Min 00-04; Brazil from 05. *Rua Real Grandeza 99, Botafogo, Rio de Janeiro, RJ 22281-030, Brazil* Tel (0055) (21) 2539 9488

WELLING, Anthony Wyndham. b 29. Ely Th Coll 55. **d** 58 **p** 83. C Coppenhall St Paul *Ches* 58-60; Lic to Offic *Ox* 82; Hon C Cookham 83-03; Hon C The Cookhams from 03. *Broadway Barn, High Street, Ripley, Woking GU23 6AQ* Tel (01483) 225384

WELLINGTON, Bishop of. *See* BROWN, The Rt Revd Thomas John

WELLINGTON, Canon James Frederick. b 51. Leic Univ LLB72 Fitzw Coll Cam BA76. Ridley Hall Cam 74. **d** 77 **p** 78. C Mill Hill Jo Keble Ch *Lon* 77-80; C Wood Green St Mich 80-82; C Wood Green St Mich w Bounds Green St Gabr etc 82-83; V Stocking Farm *Leic* 83-90; V Gt Glen, Stretton Magna and Wistow etc 90-98; Warden of Readers 91-97; Hon Can Leic Cathl from 94; RD Gartree II 96-98; TR Syston from 98; RD Goscote from 00. *The Rectory, Upper Church Street, Syston, Leicester LE7 1HR* Tel 0116-260 8276 E-mail jhcwelli@leicester.anglican.org

WELLS, Adrian Mosedale. b 61. SW Minl Tr Course 96. **d** 99 **p** 00. NSM Kingskerswell w Coffinswell *Ex* 99-02; NSM Wolborough and Ogwell from 02. *St Bartholomew's House, 1 St Bartholomew Way, Ogwell, Newton Abbot TQ12 6YW* Tel (01626) 331147 E-mail awells@fish.co.uk

WELLS, Andrew Stuart. b 48. St Jo Coll Dur BA71 Man Metrop Univ PGCE04. Cranmer Hall Dur. **d** 74 **p** 75. C Walmsley *Man* 74-77; C Failsworth H Family 77-79; R Openshaw 79-90; V Hindsford 90-98. *1 Henry Street, Haslington, Crewe CW1 5PS* Tel (01270) 585303

WELLS, The Ven Anthony Martin Giffard. b 42. St Jo Coll Nottm 72. **d** 74 **p** 75. C Orpington Ch Ch *Roch* 74-78; P-in-c Odell *St Alb* 78-82; R 82-86; P-in-c Pavenham 78-82; V 82-86; RD Sharnbrook 81-86; R Angmering *Chich* 86-98; RD Arundel and Bognor 93-98; Chapl Paris St Mich *Eur* from 98; Adn France from 02. *11 bis rue de Surene, 75008 Paris, France* Tel (0033) (1) 42 66 10 08 *or* 47 42 70 88 Fax 47 42 74 75 E-mail archdeacon@saintmichaelsparis.org

WELLS, Antony Ernest. b 36. Oak Hill Th Coll 58. **d** 61 **p** 62. C Bethnal Green St Jas Less *Lon* 61-64; SAMS Paraguay 64-69; V Kirkdale St Athanasius *Liv* 69-73; SAMS Argentina 73-75; V Warfield *Ox* 75-81; V Fairfield *Liv* 81-83; C Rainhill 83-85; TV Cheltenham St Mark *Glouc* 85-89; P-in-c Forest of Dean Ch Ch w English Bicknor 89-95; rtd 97; C Pinhoe and Broadclyst *Ex* 02-04. *9 The Cricketers, Axminster EX13 5RG*

WELLS, Miss Cecilia Isabel. b 24. Bedf Coll Lon BA45. St Mich Ho Ox 56. **dss** 62 **d** 87. Chester le Street *Dur* 74-84; rtd 84; Perm to Offic *Ches* from 84. *12 Rectory Close, Nantwich CW5 5SW* Tel (01270) 627258

WELLS, Charles Francis. b 39. Oak Hill Th Coll. **d** 85 **p** 86. C Southend St Sav Westcliff *Chelmsf* 85-89; P-in-c E and W Horndon w Lt Warley 89-96; V E and W Horndon w Lt Warley and Childerditch 96-97; P-in-c Tillingham 97-04; rtd 04. *14 Irvington Close, Leigh-on-Sea SS9 4NJ* Tel (01702) 512041

WELLS, David. *See* WELLS, Canon William David Sandford

WELLS, David. b 63. Imp Coll Lon BSc85 ARCS85. EAMTC 97. **d** 00 **p** 01. C Sprowston w Beeston *Nor* 00-03; P-in-c Drayton w

Felthorpe from 03. *The Rectory, 46 School Road, Drayton, Norwich NR8 6EF* Tel (01603) 864749 E-mail david.wells@btinternet.com

WELLS, David Henry Nugent. b 20. St Chad's Coll Dur BA42 MA46. **d** 47 **p** 48. C Wednesbury St Paul Wood Green *Lich* 47-48; C Rugeley 48-50; C Hanley All SS 50-53; R Leigh 53-57; R Ashley and V Hales 57-64; V Alrewas and Wychnor 64-73; R Upton Magna and V Withington 73-81; R Uffington, Upton Magna and Withington 81-85; rtd 85; Perm to Offic *Lich* 85-00. *13 Belvidere Avenue, Shrewsbury SY2 5PF* Tel (01743) 365822

WELLS, Canon Edward Arthur. b 23. MBE97. SRN. Oak Hill Th Coll. **d** 57 **p** 58. C Wednesfield Heath *Lich* 57-60; R Mettingham w Ilketshall St John *St E* 60-62; R Sproughton w Burstall 62-74; V Ipswich St Nic 74-80; Hon Can St E Cathl 80-90; Chapl Ipswich Hosp 66-90; rtd 90; Perm to Offic *St E* from 90. *74 Christchurch Street, Ipswich IP4 2DH* Tel (01473) 254046

WELLS, George Reginald. b 11. K Coll Cam BA33. Cuddesdon Coll 33. **d** 34 **p** 35. C Penistone w Midhope *Wakef* 34-37; India 38-61; V Hagbourne *Ox* 61-74; P-in-c Gt Coxwell 74-80; P-in-c Buscot 74-80; P-in-c Coleshill 74-80; P-in-c Eaton Hastings 74-80; rtd 80; Perm to Offic *Glas* from 80. *c/o G I Wells Esq, 19 Mitchell Drive, Rutherglen, Glasgow G73 3QP* Tel 0141-647 2467

WELLS, Isabel. *See* WELLS, Miss Cecilia Isabel

WELLS, Jo Bailey. b 65. CCC Cam BA87 MA90 Minnesota Univ MA90 St Jo Coll Dur BA92 PhD97. Cranmer Hall Dur. **d** 95 **p** 96. Chapl Clare Coll Cam 95-98; Dean 98-01; Perm to Offic *Nor* 99-04; Tutor Ridley Hall Cam 01-05; Dir Angl Studies Duke Div Sch N Carolina USA from 05. *Duke University, Durham, NC 27708, USA* Tel (001) (919) 660 3400 Fax 660 3473

WELLS, John Michael. b 35. Mert Coll Ox BA58 MA61. Westcott Ho Cam 60. **d** 62 **p** 63. C Hornchurch St Andr *Chelmsf* 62-64; C Barking St Marg 64-66; C Wanstead H Trin Hermon Hill 66-69; V Elm Park St Nic Hornchurch 69-76; Offg Chapl RAF 69-76; R Wakes Colne w Chappel *Chelmsf* 76-79; Project Officer Cathl Cen for Research and Tr 79-81; Hon Chapl Chelmsf Cathl 79-81; Area Sec CMS *Chelmsf* and *Ely* 81-88; E Cen Co-ord 85-91; Area Sec *Chelmsf* and *St E* 88-91; Public Preacher *Chelmsf* 82-91; V Hanging Heaton *Wakef* 92-96; rtd 00; Perm to Offic *Chelmsf* from 00. *2 Clarkesmead, Tiptree, Colchester CO5 0BX* Tel (01621) 819899

WELLS, John Rowse David. b 27. Kelham Th Coll 53. **d** 57 **p** 58. SSM from 57; Lic to Offic *S'well* 57-59; Australia 59-65 and from 97; Tutor St Mich Th Coll 61-65; Lesotho 65-96; R Mantsonyane St Jas 67-77; Can SS Mary and Jas Cathl Maseru 77-96; Adn Cen Lesotho 85-95. *St Michael's Priory, 75 Watsons Road, Diggers Rest, Vic, Australia 3427* Tel (0061) (3) 9740 1618 Fax 9740 0007 E-mail ssm.melbourne@bigpond.com

WELLS, Leslie. b 61. **d** 04. OLM St Helier *S'wark* from 04. *59 Wigmore Road, Carshalton SM5 1RG* Tel (020) 8644 9203 E-mail leswells80@hotmail.com

WELLS, Lydia Margaret. b 50. St Aid Coll Dur BA72 Sheff Univ MPhil92 Leeds Univ MA00. N Ord Course 97. **d** 00 **p** 01. C Adwick-le-Street w Skelbrooke *Sheff* 00-03; V Doncaster Intake from 03. *The Vicarage, Kingston Road, Intake, Doncaster DN2 6LS* Tel (01302) 343119 Mobile 07977-740813 E-mail lydwells@tesco.net

WELLS, Mark Wynne-Eyton. b 20. Peterho Cam BA48 MA54. Westcott Ho Cam 48. **d** 50 **p** 51. C Heene *Chich* 50-53; C Sullington 53-57; R Slinfold 57-59; S Rhodesia 59-62; V Stoke by Nayland w Leavenheath *St E* 62-88; RD Hadleigh 71-76 and 85-86; rtd 88; Perm to Offic *Nor* from 88. *Red House, The Street, Great Snoring, Fakenham NR21 0AH* Tel (01328) 820641

WELLS, Michael John. b 46. Univ Coll Ox BA68 MA73 Solicitor 74. S Dios Minl Tr Scheme 92. **d** 95 **p** 96. NSM Brighton St Pet w Chpl Royal *Chich* 95-98; Sen C 99-04; NSM Brighton St Bart 98-99; rtd 04; Perm to Offic *Chich* from 04. *35 Park Crescent, Brighton BN2 3HB* Tel (01273) 600735

WELLS, Nicholas Anthony. b 60. Cranmer Hall Dur 88. **d** 91 **p** 92. C Accrington St Jo w Huncoat *Blackb* 91-94; C Douglas St Geo and St Barn *S & M* 94-95; C Douglas All SS and St Thos 95-97; V Onchan 97-03; V Netherton *Liv* from 03. *The Vicarage, 183 St Oswald's Lane, Bootle L30 5SR* Tel 0151-525 1882 E-mail nick.the-vic@virgin.net

WELLS, Peter Robert. b 59. Wilson Carlile Coll 78 Sarum & Wells Th Coll 87. **d** 89 **p** 90. CA from 81; C Mortlake w E Sheen *S'wark* 89-93; Dir St Marylebone Healing and Counselling Cen 93-97; TV N Lambeth *S'wark* 97-00; Chapl Trin Hospice Lon 97-03. *3 The Chase, London SW4 0NP* Tel (020) 7787 1000

WELLS, Philip Anthony. b 57. BA MPhil. Coll of Resurr Mirfield. **d** 84 **p** 85. C Wylde Green *Birm* 84-87; Chapl and Succ Birm Cathl 87-91; Bp's Dom Chapl 91-97; V Polesworth from 97. *The Vicarage, High Street, Polesworth, Tamworth B78 1DU* Tel (01827) 892340 E-mail polesworthabbey@aol.com

WELLS, Richard John. b 46. St Mich Coll Llan DipTh70 Cuddesdon Coll 70. **d** 71 **p** 72. C Kingston upon Hull St Alb *York* 71-75; C Addlestone *Guildf* 75-80; V Weston 80-88; V Milford 88-96; Chapl Milford Hosp Godalming 88-96; R Westbourne *Chich* from 96. *The New Rectory, Westbourne Road, Emsworth PO10 8UL* Tel (01243) 372867

WELLS, Robert Crosby. b 28. St Jo Coll Dur BA52. **d** 54 **p** 55. C S Shore H Trin *Blackb* 54-59; C-in-c Lea CD 59-69; V Ribby w Wrea 69-93; rtd 93; Perm to Offic *Blackb* from 93. *4 Myra Road, Fairhaven, Lytham St Annes FY8 1EB* Tel (01253) 739851

WELLS, The Ven Roderick John. b 36. Dur Univ BA63 Hull Univ MA85. Cuddesdon Coll 63. **d** 65 **p** 66. C Lambeth St Mary the Less *S'wark* 65-68; P-in-c 68-71; R Skegness *Linc* 71-77; P-in-c Winthorpe 77; R Skegness and Winthorpe 77-78; TR Gt and Lt Coates w Bradley 78-89; RD Grimsby and Cleethorpes 83-89; Can and Preb Linc Cathl 86-01; Adn Stow 89-01; V Hackthorn w Cold Hanworth 89-93; P-in-c N w S Carlton 89-93; rtd 01; Perm to Offic *Linc* and *Pet* from 01. *9 Hardwick Close, Oakham LE15 6FF* Tel (01572) 756532 E-mail wells1@wells1.netlineuk.net

WELLS, Mrs Sally Ursula. b 40. St Mark's Coll Canberra BTh93 Ripon Coll Cuddesdon 96. **d** 97 **p** 98. Asst Chapl Vienna *Eur* 97-02; Perm to Offic from 02. *Fugbachgasse 12/19, A-1020 Vienna, Austria* Tel and fax (0043) (1) 406 6354 E-mail wellsvienna@nusurf.at

WELLS, Canon Samuel Martin Bailey. b 65. Mert Coll Ox BA87 MA95 Edin Univ BD91 Dur Univ PhD96. Edin Th Coll 88. **d** 91 **p** 92. C Wallsend St Luke *Newc* 91-95; C Cherry Hinton St Andr *Ely* 95-97; C Teversham 95-97; P-in-c Earlham St Eliz *Nor* 97-03; RD Nor S 99-03; P-in-c Cambridge St Mark *Ely* 03-05; Wiccamical Preb Chich Cathl *Chich* 04-05; Dean Duke Chpl Duke Univ N Carolina USA from 05. *Duke University, Durham, NC 27708, USA* Tel (001) (919) 684 2177 Fax 681 8660 E-mail samwells@bigfoot.com

WELLS, Terry Roy John. b 45. EAMTC 89. **d** 92 **p** 93. C Martlesham w Brightwell *St E* 92-95; R Higham, Holton St Mary, Raydon and Stratford 95-00; TV Walton and Trimley from 00. *The Vicarage, Church Lane, Trimley St Martin, Felixstowe IP11 0SW* Tel (01394) 286388 E-mail terry.wells@tesco.net

WELLS, Canon William David Sandford. b 41. JP. Oriel Coll Ox BA64 MA66. Ridley Hall Cam 63. **d** 65 **p** 66. C Gt Malvern St Mary *Worc* 65-70; V Crowle 70-84; P-in-c Himbleton w Huddington 78-84; V E Bowbrook 84-89; Hon Can Worc Cathl from 84; RD Droitwich 84-96; R Bowbrook S from 89. *The Vicarage, Church Road, Crowle, Worcester WR7 4AT* Tel (01905) 381617 Fax 08701-623981 E-mail david@sandfordwells.freeserve.co.uk

WELLS, Archdeacon of. *See* MAURICE, The Ven Peter David

WELLS, Dean of. *See* CLARKE, The Very Revd John Martin

WELSBY, George Andrew. b 61. St Martin's Coll Lanc BA82 Leeds Univ BA98. Coll of Resurr Mirfield 96. **d** 98 **p** 99. C W Derby St Jo *Liv* 98-02; V Nuneaton St Mary *Cov* from 02. *St Mary's Abbey Vicarage, 99 Bottrill Street, Nuneaton CV11 5JB* Tel (024) 7638 2936

WELSH, Angus Alexander. b 30. Trin Coll Cam BA54 MA59 St Jo Coll Dur DipTh56. **d** 56 **p** 57. C Jesmond Clayton Memorial *Newc* 56-60; C Fenham St Jas and St Basil 60-62; V Bacup St Jo *Man* 62-68; Tristan da Cunha 68-71; St Vincent 72-78; R Heysham *Blackb* 78-88; V Blackb St Steph 88-96; rtd 96; Perm to Offic *Newc* from 96. *23 Low Stobhill, Morpeth NE61 2SF* Tel (01670) 513261

WELSH, Jennifer Ann. b 48. Univ Coll Lon BA. **d** 81 **p** 98. NSM Newport St Matt *Mon* 81-85; NSM Risca 85-04; NSM Maindee from 04. *470 Caerleon Road, Newport NP19 7LW* Tel (01633) 258287

WELSH, Jennifer Lee. b 59. Calgary Univ BSc81. Cam Episc Div Sch (USA) MDiv87. **d** 87 **p** 88. Canada 87-89; Asst Chapl HM Pris Linc 89-94; Perm to Offic *Win* 94-02 and *Lon* from 03. *Address temp unkown*

WELSH, Miss Mary Elizabeth. b 22. St Hilda's Coll Ox BA44 MA48 Lon Univ DipEd45 BD50. Lambeth STh64. **dss** 68 **d** 87 **p** 94. Ex St Mark *Ex* 70-82; Lic to Offic 82-85; Yatton Moor *B & W* 85-87; Perm to Offic from 87. *26 Rectory Way, Yatton, Bristol BS49 4JF* Tel (01934) 833329

WELSH, Maxwell Wilfred. b 29. Bp's Coll Calcutta 55. **d** 58 **p** 59. India 58-72; C Cannock *Lich* 73-76; C Wednesfield 76-79; V Milton 79-86; V Croxton w Broughton and Adbaston 86-00; rtd 00; Perm to Offic *Lich* from 01. *24 Churchfield Road, Eccleshall, Stafford ST21 6AG* Tel (01785) 850330

WELSH, Philip Peter. b 48. Keble Coll Ox BA69 MA73 Selw Coll Cam BA72 MA76. Westcott Ho Cam 71. **d** 73 **p** 74. C W Dulwich All SS and Em *S'wark* 73-76; C Surbiton St Andr and St Mark 76-79; Lect St Steph Coll Delhi India 79-81; V Malden St Jo *S'wark* 81-87; Min Officer *Linc* 87-94; TR Basingstoke *Win* 94-02; V Westmr St Steph w St Jo *Lon* from 02. *26 Vincent Square, London SW1P 2NJ* Tel (020) 7834 8981 *or* 7834 3865 E-mail norburyststephen@aol.com

WELSH, Robert Leslie. b 32. Sheff Univ BA54 St Jo Coll Dur DipTh58. **d** 58 **p** 59. C S Westoe *Dur* 58-62; C Darlington St Cuth 62-66; CF (TA) 64-67; V E Rainton *Dur* 66-85; R W Rainton 66-85; R Wolsingham and Thornley 85-97; rtd 97. *12 Lea Green, Wolsingham, Bishop Auckland DL13 3DU* Tel (01388) 528529

WELSMAN, Derek Brian. b 65. Trin Coll Bris DipTS99. **d** 99 **p** 00. C Ash *Guildf* 99-02; V Easebourne *Chich* from 02; Chapl K Edw VII Hosp Midhurst from 02. *The Priory, Easebourne, Midhurst GU29 0AJ* Tel (01730) 812655 *or* 813341

WELTERS, Mrs Elizabeth Ann. b 49. Bris Univ BSc70 Reading Univ PGCE71. St Alb and Ox Min Course 94. **d** 97 **p** 98. NSM Aylesbury w Bierton and Hulcott *Ox* 97-03; NSM Schorne from 03. *The Rectory, Rectory Drive, Waddesdon, Aylesbury HP18 0JQ* Tel (01296) 655069 *or* 651312 Mobile 07986-733645 E-mail lizwelters@waitrose.com

WEMYSS, Gary. b 52. Cranmer Hall Dur 79. **d** 80 **p** 81. C Blackb St Jas *Blackb* 80-83; C Padiham 83-86; V Stalmine 86-90; P-in-c Egton-cum-Newland and Lowick *Carl* 90-03; V Egton-cum-Newland and Lowick and Colton from 03; RD Furness from 04. *The Vicarage, Penny Bridge, Ulverston LA12 7RQ* Tel (01229) 861285 E-mail gwemyss@clara.co.uk

WENHAM, David. b 45. Pemb Coll Cam BA67 MA Man Univ PhD70. Ridley Hall Cam 81. **d** 84 **p** 85. Tutor Wycliffe Hall Ox 84-02; Dean from 02; NSM Shelswell *Ox* 96-02; NSM Cumnor from 03. *66 Pinnocks Way, Oxford OX2 9DQ* Tel (01865) 863712 E-mail david.wenham@wycliffe.ox.ac.uk

WENHAM, Michael Timothy. b 49. Pemb Coll Cam MA75. Wycliffe Hall Ox DipTh85. **d** 86 **p** 87. C Norbury *Ches* 86-89; V Stanford in the Vale w Goosey and Hatford *Ox* from 89. *The Vicarage, Church Green, Stanford in the Vale, Faringdon SN7 8HU* Tel (01367) 710267

WENHAM, Peter William. b 47. Pemb Coll Cam MA73 FRCS76 Cam Univ MD85. St Jo Coll Nottm 98. **d** 01 **p** 02. NSM Wollaton Park *S'well* from 01. *31 Sutton Passeys Crescent, Wollaton, Nottingham NG8 1BX* Tel 0115-970 2481

WENSLEY, Beryl Kathleen. *See* YATES, Mrs Beryl Kathleen

✠**WENT, The Rt Revd John Stewart.** b 44. CCC Cam BA66 MA70. Oak Hill Th Coll 67. **d** 69 **p** 70 **c** 96. C Northwood Em *Lon* 69-75; V Margate H Trin *Cant* 75-83; Vice-Prin Wycliffe Hall Ox 83-89; Adn Surrey *Guildf* 89-96; Chmn Dioc Coun for Unity and Miss 90-96; Suff Bp Tewkesbury *Glouc* from 96; Hon Can Glouc Cathl from 96. *Bishop's House, Church Road, Staverton, Cheltenham GL51 0TW* Tel (01242) 680188 Fax 680233 E-mail bshptewk@star.co.uk

WENZEL, Peggy Sylvia. STh. Gilmore Ho. **d** 88 **p** 94. Perm to Offic *Sarum* from 88; rtd 92. *Church Cottage, Church Street, Pewsey SN9 5DL* Tel (01672) 563834

WERNER, David Robert Edmund. b 33. Clifton Th Coll 61. **d** 63 **p** 64. C Holywell *St As* 63-68; C Llanrhos 68-70; R Tedburn St Mary *Ex* 71-91; RD Kenn 80-83; Perm to Offic from 92; rtd 98. *The Old Rectory, Church Lane, Tedburn St Mary, Exeter EX6 6EN* Tel (01647) 61253

WERNER, Canon Donald Kilgour. b 39. Univ of Wales BA61 Linacre Coll Ox BA64 MA67. Wycliffe Hall Ox 61. **d** 64 **p** 65. C Wrexham *St As* 64-69; Chapl Brasted Place Coll Westerham 69-73; Chapl Bris Univ *Bris* 73-76; Hon C Clifton St Paul 73-76; Chapl Keele Univ *Lich* 77-79; P-in-c Keele 77-79; C York St Mich-le-Belfrey *York* 79-83; Dir of Evang 79-83; R Holborn St Geo w H Trin and St Bart *Lon* 83-02; Hon Can Bujumbura from 99; Prof and Dean Th Light Univ Burundi from 03; Lic Preacher *Lon* 02-04; rtd 05. *7 Minstrel Close, Hucknall NG15 7NZ* Tel 0115-963 1504 Mobile 07837-181565 E-mail donaldinburundi@hotmail.com

WERRELL, Ralph Sidney. b 29. Hull Univ PhD02. Tyndale Hall Bris 54. **d** 56 **p** 57. C Penn Fields *Lich* 56-60; C Champion Hill St Sav *S'wark* 60-61; R Danby Wiske w Yafforth *Ripon* 61-65; P-in-c Hutton Bonville *York* 61-65; R Combs *St E* 65-75; V Bootle Ch Ch *Liv* 75-80; R Scole, Brockdish, Billingford, Thorpe Abbots etc *Nor* 80-83; R Southam w Stockton *Cov* 83-89; R Southam 89-94; rtd 95; Perm to Offic *Birm* and *Cov* from 95; *Lich* from 01. *Sameach, 2A Queens Road, Kenilworth CV8 1JQ* Tel and fax (01926) 858677

WERRETT, Olivia Margaret. b 50. Bp Otter Coll 00. **d** 03. NSM Bexhill St Pet *Chich* from 03. *127 Pebsham Lane, Bexhill-on-Sea TN40 2RP* Tel (01424) 214144 E-mail olivia@1950werrett.freeserve.co.uk

WERWATH, Wolfgang Albert Richard Kurt. b 22. Ripon Hall Ox 54. **d** 56 **p** 57. C Hamer *Man* 56-58; C N Reddish 58-59; V Chadderton St Luke 59-67; V Whitfield *Derby* 67-75; V Bretby w Newton Solney 75-88; rtd 88; Perm to Offic *Derby* from 88 and *S'well* from 90. *28 D'Ayncourt Walk, Farnsfield, Newark NG22 8DP* Tel (01623) 882635

WESSON, Preb John Graham. b 38. St Pet Coll Ox BA62 DipTh63 MA68. Clifton Th Coll 63. **d** 65 **p** 66. C Southport Ch Ch w St Andr *Liv* 65-68; C Ox St Ebbe w St Pet *Ox* 68-71; Chapl Poly Cen Lon 71-76; C-in-c Edin St Thos *Edin* 76-82; Dir Past Studies Trin Coll Bris 82-86; R Birm St Martin w Bordesley St Andr *Birm* 86-96; RD Birm City 88-95; Hon Can Birm Cathl 91-96; Dir Local Min Development *Lich* 96-98; Team Ldr Min Division 99-03; Team Ldr Bd of Min 99-03; C Lich St Mich w St Mary and Wall 96-03; Preb Lich Cathl 99-03; rtd 03. *11 Gordon Drive, Abingdon OX14 3SW* Tel (01235) 526088 E-mail john.wesson@lichfield.anglican.org

WEST, Alan David. b 61. Southn Univ BTh92 Thames Valley Univ MA97. Aston Tr Scheme 87 Sarum & Wells Th Coll 89. **d** 92 **p** 93. C S'wark St Geo the Martyr w St Jude *S'wark* 92-94; C S'wark St Geo w St Alphege and St Jude 95-96; V Boscoppa *Truro* 96-02; Chapl Mt Edgcumbe Hospice from 02. *Mount Edgcumbe Hospice, Porthpean Road, St Austell PL26 6AB* Tel (01726) 65711 Fax 66421 E-mail alan.west@hospice.cornwall.nhs.uk

WEST, Andrew Victor. b 59. Wycliffe Hall Ox 87. **d** 90 **p** 91. C Leyland St Andr *Blackb* 90-94; C Blackpool St Jo 94-96; TV Bedworth *Cov* 96-98; Chapl Cheltenham and Glouc Coll of HE 98-01; Chapl Glos Univ 01-03; Chapl St Martin's Coll *Carl* from 03; C Carl St Jo from 03. *68 Greystone Road, Carlisle CA1 2DG* Tel (01228) 520893

WEST, Arthur. b 20. Linc Th Coll 59. **d** 60 **p** 61. C Cottingham *York* 60-64; V Ruswarp w Sneaton 64-68; V Nether w Upper Poppleton 68-85; RD Ainsty 77-85; rtd 85; Perm to Offic *York* from 85. *8 River View, Linton on Ouse, York YO30 2BJ* Tel (01347) 848463

WEST, Bernard Kenneth. b 31. Linc Th Coll. **d** 67 **p** 68. C E Ham St Geo *Chelmsf* 67-71; C Gt Bookham *Guildf* 71-73; R Esperance Australia 73-76; C Dalkeith 76-79; P-in-c Carine 80-82; R Carine w Duncraig 82-84; C Ravensthorpe 85-87; rtd 87. *9 Beaufort Street, Katanning, W Australia 6317*

WEST, Bryan Edward. b 39. Avery Hill Coll CertEd69 BEd80 Kent Univ MA86. Cant Sch of Min 85. **d** 88 **p** 89. NSM Gravesend H Family w Ifield *Roch* 88-92; C Gravesend St Geo 92-95; NSM Hatcham Park All SS *S'wark* 95-98; Perm to Offic *Chelmsf* 95-98; NSM Ashingdon w S Fambridge 98-01; NSM Stambridge 98-01; NSM Canvey Is from 01; Chapl Southend Health Care NHS Trust from 99; rtd 04. *St Anne's House, 51 St Anne's Road, Canvey Island SS8 7LS* Tel (01268) 514412 E-mail roadbuilder@fish.co.uk

WEST, Miss Caroline Elisabeth. b 61. RGN84. Wycliffe Hall Ox DipMin95. **d** 95. NSM Eastrop *Win* from 95. *19 Beaulieu Court, Riverdene, Basingstoke RG21 4DQ* Tel (01256) 350389 *or* 464249 E-mail caroline.west@stmarys-basingstoke.org.uk

WEST, Mrs Christine Cecily. TCD BA60 MA63 HDipEd61. CITC 91. **d** 94 **p** 95. NSM Bray *D & G* 94-96; NSM Kilternan 96-99; Lic to Offic from 99. *55 Beech Park Road, Foxrock, Dublin 18, Irish Republic* Tel (00353) (1) 289 6374

WEST, Clive. b 35. QUB BD75 Stranmillis Coll TCert57 TCD DBS63 Lon Univ DipTh68. CITC 62. **d** 64 **p** 65. C Lisburn Ch Ch Cathl *Conn* 64-68; Asst Master Lisnagarvey Sec Sch Lisburn 68-70; C Belfast All SS 70-75; I 84-00; Can Belf Cathl 95-00; I Mullabrack w Kilcluney *Arm* 76-84; rtd 00. *16 Stormont Park, Belfast BT4 3GX* Tel (028) 9041 9317 E-mail clivewest@tiscali.co.uk

WEST, David Marshall. b 48. St Jo Coll Dur BA70. **d** 73 **p** 74. C Wylde Green *Birm* 73-76; C Wokingham St Paul *Ox* 76-79; V Hurst 79-88; V Maidenhead St Luke 88-95; C Whitley Ch Ch 95-99; P-in-c Reading Ch Ch 99-05; V from 05. *Christ Church Vicarage, 4 Vicarage Road, Reading RG2 7AJ* Tel 0118-987 1250 E-mail revdmwest@hotmail.com

WEST, Derek Elvin. b 47. Hull Univ BA69. Westcott Ho Cam 71. **d** 73 **p** 74. C Walthamstow St Pet *Chelmsf* 73-77; C Chingford SS Pet and Paul 77-80; TV W Slough *Ox* 80-88; Slough Community Chapl 88-95; TV Upton cum Chalvey from 95. *St Peter's Vicarage, 52 Montem Lane, Slough SL1 2QJ* Tel (01753) 520725

WEST, Mrs Elizabeth Maxine. b 47. Liv Univ BA69 Lon Inst of Educn PGCE70 K Coll Lon BA95 AKC. NTMTC. **d** 99 **p** 00. NSM Hornsey H Innocents *Lon* 99-00; NSM Highgate St Mich 00-03; C from 03. *West Villa, Inderwick Road, London N8 9JU* Tel (020) 8348 3042

WEST, Eric Edward. b 32. Leeds Univ BA60. Bps' Coll Cheshunt 63. **d** 64 **p** 65. C Biscot *St Alb* 64-71; V 71-02; rtd 03; Perm to Offic *St Alb* from 03. *134 Brompton Close, Luton LU3 3QU* Tel (01582) 581417

WEST, Eric Robert Glenn. b 55. QUB BA79 Man Univ DipEd80. CITC BTh92. **d** 92 **p** 93. C Enniskillen *Clogh* 92-95; I Lisbellaw 95-00; CF 00-03; I Annagh w Drumgoon, Ashfield etc *K, E & A* from 03. *8 Dannys Mill Road, Coles Hill, Enniskillen BT74 7FB* Tel (028) 6634 6870 Mobile 07980-269014

WEST, Harold Reginald. b 15. Dur Univ BA43 MA46. Coll of Resurr Mirfield 43. **d** 45 **p** 46. C Tynemouth H Trin W Town *Newc* 45-48; C Sugley 48-55; V Cresswell 55-61; V Newc St Luke 61-82; rtd 82; Perm to Offic *Newc* from 82. *42 Linden Road, Gosforth, Newcastle upon Tyne NE3 4HB* Tel 0191-284 4291

WEST, Henry Cyrano. b 28. K Coll Lon. **d** 51 **p** 52. C Braunstone *Leic* 51-53; C Wandsworth St Anne *S'wark* 53-55; C Raynes Park St Sav 55-58; CF 58-63; V Sculcoates *York* 63-71; P-in-c Kingston upon Hull St Jude w St Steph 67-71; Lic to Offic *Cov* 71-75 and *Man* 75-87; Hon C Hulme Ascension *Man* 87-94; rtd 91; Perm to Offic *Man* from 91. *6 King's Drive, Middleton, Manchester M24 4PB* Tel 0161-643 4410

WEST, Keith. *See* RYDER-WEST, Keith

WEST (formerly WINDIATE), Mrs Mary Elizabeth. b 49. Linc Th Coll 94. **d** 94 **p** 95. C Loughton St Jo *Chelmsf* 94-98; P-in-c Ashingdon w S Fambridge 98-01; P-in-c Stambridge 98-01; TV

Canvey Is from 01. *St Anne's House, 51 St Anne's Road, Canvey Island SS8 7LS* Tel (01268) 514412 E-mail mothermary2@tiscali.co.uk

WEST, Maxine. *See* WEST, Mrs Elizabeth Maxine

WEST, Canon Michael Brian. b 39. Bris Univ BSc60. Linc Th Coll 64. **d** 66 **p** 67. C Bp's Hatfield *St Alb* 66-69; Ind Chapl 69-81; Sen Ind Chapl 71-81; Hon Can St Alb 78-81; Sen Ind Chapl and Hon Can Sheff Cathl *Sheff* 81-01; Perm to Offic from 02; Dir Open Forum for Economic Regeneration 02-04; rtd 04. *23 Walton Road, Sheffield S11 8RE* Tel 0114-266 2188 E-mail mikepamwest@tinyworld.co.uk

WEST, Canon Michael Frederick. b 50. Trin Coll Ox BA72 MA76 UEA PhD96. Westcott Ho Cam 72. **d** 74 **p** 75. C Wolverhampton *Lich* 74-78; C Hanley H Ev 78-79; TV 79-82; Dioc Youth Officer *St E* 83-88; V Ipswich St Thos 88-95; Prin OLM Scheme 96-03; Hon Can St E Cathl 96-03; Can Res and Chan Linc Cathl *Linc* from 03; Dioc Dir Formation in Discipleship and Min from 03. *The Chancery, 11 Minster Yard, Lincoln LN2 1PJ* Tel (01522) 525610 *or* 544544 E-mail chancellor@lincolncathedral.com

WEST, Michael John. b 33. Imp Coll Lon BScEng54 ARSM54 CEng60 FIMM68 FEng89 Hon FIMM96. S'wark Ord Course 85. **d** 88 **p** 89. NSM Caterham *S'wark* 88-98; Perm to Offic *Lon* from 96; *Chich* from 97; *S'wark* from 98. *Minstrels, The Causeway, Horsham RH12 1HE* Tel (01403) 263437 Fax 249604 E-mail goodshepherd@btinternet.com

WEST, Michael Oakley. b 31. Open Univ BA97 DipEurHum97. Bris Bapt Coll 53 Wells Th Coll 62. **d** 63 **p** 64. C Swindon Ch Ch *Bris* 63-66; Libya 66-68; R Lydiard Millicent w Lydiard Tregoz *Bris* 68-75; V Breage w Germoe *Truro* 75-82; CMS 82-91; Chapl Tel Aviv 82-89; Chapl Shiplake Coll Henley 91-94; Asst Chapl Bryanston Sch 94-95; Perm to Offic *Eur* 95-97; rtd 96; Perm to Offic *Lon* 96-97; Lic to Offic Spokane USA from 97. *1932 East 25th Avenue, Spokane, WA 99203, USA*

WEST, Paul Leslie. b 57. OLM course 96. **d** 99 **p** 00. OLM Kinnerley w Melverley and Knockin w Maesbrook *Lich* from 99. *Braddan, Farm Hall, Kinnerley, Oswestry SY10 8EG* Tel (01691) 682600

WEST, Peter Harcourt. b 29. **d** 59 **p** 60. C Histon *Ely* 59-60; C Hampreston *Sarum* 60-61; C Braintree *Chelmsf* 61-63; Perm to Offic from 72; rtd 94. *Westgates, 139 Witham Road, Black Notley, Braintree CM77 8LR* Tel (01376) 323048

WEST, Canon Philip William. b 48. Magd Coll Ox BA70 MA78. St Jo Coll Nottm BA74. **d** 75 **p** 76. C Rushden w Newton Bromswold *Pet* 75-79; C Pitsmoor w Ellesmere *Sheff* 79-83; V Attercliffe 83-89; Ind Chapl 85-90; P-in-c Darnall 86-89; V Stannington from 89; P-in-c Sheff St Bart from 02; AD Hallam 96-02; Hon Can Sheff Cathl from 01. *The Vicarage, 214 Oldfield Road, Stannington, Sheffield S6 6DY* Tel 0114-234 5586 *or* 232 4490 E-mail philipwest@fish.co.uk

WEST, Reginald Roy. b 28. St Deiniol's Hawarden 74. **d** 74 **p** 75. C Abergavenny St Mary w Llanwenarth Citra *Mon* 74-77; V Tredegar St Jas 77-96; rtd 96; Lic to Offic *Mon* from 96. *2 Croesonen Park, Abergavenny NP7 6PD* Tel (01873) 857043

WEST, Stephen Peter. b 52. Liv Univ CertEd74. Oak Hill Th Coll 87. **d** 89 **p** 90. C Gateacre *Liv* 89-92; V Liv All So Springwood 92-02; TV Teignmouth, Ideford w Luton, Ashcombe etc *Ex* from 02. *The Vicarage, 3 Moors Park, Bishopsteignton, Teignmouth TQ14 9RH* Tel and fax (01626) 775247 E-mail spmwest@aol.com

WEST, Canon Thomas Roderic. b 55. BTh90. TCD Div Sch. **d** 86 **p** 87. C Dromore Cathl *D & D* 86-89; I Carrowdore w Millisle 89-95; I Moira from 95; Can Belf Cathl from 05. *The Rectory, 1 Main Street, Moira, Craigavon BT67 0LE* Tel (028) 9261 1268

WEST, Timothy Ralph. b 53. Bath Univ BSc75. Ridley Hall Cam 82. **d** 85 **p** 86. C Mildenhall *St E* 85-88; TV Melbury *Sarum* 88-92; TR 92-98; TR Preston w Sutton Poyntz and Osmington w Poxwell from 98. *The Rectory, Sutton Road, Preston, Weymouth DT3 6BX* Tel (01305) 833142 Mobile 07000-785720 E-mail t.r.west@psion.net

WEST AFRICA, Archbishop of. *See* AKROFI, The Most Revd Justice Ofei

WEST CUMBERLAND, Archdeacon of. *See* HILL, The Ven Colin

WEST HAM, Archdeacon of. *See* FOX, The Ven Michael John

WEST INDIES, Archbishop of. *See* GOMEZ, The Most Revd Drexel Wellington

WEST-LINDELL, Stein Erik. b 54. BA. Linc Th Coll 82. **d** 84 **p** 85. C Allington and Maidstone St Pet *Cant* 84-87; R Orlestone w Snave and Ruckinge w Warehorne 87-93; R Byfield w Boddington and Aston le Walls *Pet* 93-99; V Nor Lakenham St Alb and St Mark *Nor* from 99. *St Alban's Vicarage, Eleanor Road, Norwich NR1 2RE* Tel (01603) 621843

WESTALL, Jonathan Mark. b 67. Nottm Univ BSc88 K Coll Lon PGCE93 Dur Univ BA98. **d** 99 **p** 00. C St Helier *S'wark* 99-02; C Reading Greyfriars *Ox* from 02. *93 York Road, Reading RG1 8DU* Tel 0118-957 6436 E-mail jon@westall.clava.co.uk

✠**WESTALL, The Rt Revd Michael Robert.** b 39. Qu Coll Cam BA62 MA66. Cuddesdon Coll 63 Harvard Div Sch 65. **d** 66 **p** 67 **c** 01. C Heref St Martin *Heref* 66-70; India 70-83; Vice Prin Bp's Coll Calcutta 76-79; Prin 79-83; Tanzania 84-92 and from 01; Prin St Mark's Th Coll Dar-es-Salaam 84-92; R Alfrick, Lulsley, Suckley, Leigh and Bransford *Worc* 93-00; Bp SW Tanganyika 01-04; rtd 04. *Bishop's House, PO Box 32, Njombe, Tanzania* Tel (00255) (26) 278 2012 Fax 278 2403 E-mail punitha@africaonline.co.tz

WESTBROOK, Canon Colin David. b 36. Oriel Coll Ox BA59. St Steph Ho Ox DipTh60 MA63. **d** 61 **p** 62. C Roath St Martin *Llan* 61-66; C Roath 66-74; V Llantarnam *Mon* 74-79; V Newport St Jo Bapt from 79; Hon Can St Woolos Cathl 88-91; Can St Woolos Cathl from 91; Warden of Ords 91-99. *St John's Vicarage, Oakfield Road, Newport NP20 4LP* Tel (01633) 265581

WESTBROOK (née REED), Mrs Ethel Patricia Ivy. b 42. Bris Univ CertEd63. Cant Sch of Min 82. **dss** 84 **d** 87 **p** 94. Fawkham and Hartley *Roch* 84-85; Asst Dir of Educn 84-86; Cliffe at Hoo w Cooling 85-86; Corby SS Pet and Andr w Gt and Lt Oakley *Pet* 86-90; Par Dn 87-90; Par Dn Roch 90-94; C Rainham 94-99; V Joydens Wood St Barn 99-05; Dioc Chapl Mothers' Union 01-05; rtd 05; Hon C Banstead *Guildf* from 05; Perm to Offic *Roch* from 05. *14 Glenfield Road, Banstead SM7 2DG* Tel (01737) 353938 E-mail patwestbrook@wipe.fsnet.co.uk

WESTBY, Martyn John. b 61. Leeds Univ BA83. Trin Coll Bris 96. **d** 98 **p** 99. C Drypool *York* 98-01; P-in-c Cherry Burton from 01; Chapl Bp Burton Coll York from 01; Assoc Dioc Dir of Ords *York* from 05. *The Rectory, Main Street, Cherry Burton, Beverley HU17 7RF* Tel (01964) 503036

WESTCOTT, James John. b 55. St Jo RC Sem Surrey 76. **d** 81 **p** 82. In RC Ch 81-93; C Westmr St Steph w St Jo *Lon* 93-96; P-in-c Haggerston St Chad 96-01; V from 01. *St Chad's Vicarage, Dunloe Street, London E2 8JR* Tel (020) 7613 2229 E-mail chad@jameswestcott.co.uk

WESTERMANN-CHILDS, Miss Emma Jane. b 71. Univ of Wales (Ban) BA93 Ox Univ MTh99. Ripon Coll Cuddesdon 96. **d** 98 **p** 99. C Launceston *Truro* 98-01; P-in-c St Stephen in Brannel from 01. *The Rectory, 70 Rectory Road, St Stephen, St Austell PL26 7RL* Tel (01726) 822236 E-mail emma.childs@btinternet.com

WESTERN, Canon Robert Geoffrey. b 37. Man Univ BSc60. Qu Coll Birm DipTh62. **d** 62 **p** 63. C Sedbergh *Bradf* 62-65; PV Linc Cathl *Linc* 65-73; Hd Master Linc Cathl Sch 74-96; Can and Preb Linc Cathl *Linc* 74-96; rtd 97. *2 Guldrey House, Guldrey Lane, Sedbergh LA10 5DS* Tel (01539) 621426

WESTHAVER, George Derrick. b 68. St Mary's Univ Halifax NS BA92. Wycliffe Coll Toronto MDiv98. **d** 97 **p** 98. C Teversham and Cherry Hinton St Andr *Ely* 97-00; TV The Ramseys and Upwood 00-03; Chapl Linc Coll Ox from 03; Hon C Ox St Mich w St Martin and All SS *Ox* from 03. *Lincoln College, Oxford OX1 3DR,* or *14 Newton Road, Oxford OX1 4PT* Tel (01865) 279800 *or* 726775 E-mail george.westhaver@virgin.net

WESTLAKE, Michael Paul. b 34. Ex Coll Ox BA56 MA64. Wells Th Coll 59. **d** 61 **p** 62. C Southmead *Bris* 61-67; V Eastville St Thos 67-74; V Eastville St Thos w St Anne 74-83; P-in-c Easton St Mark 79-83; V Marshfield w Cold Ashton and Tormarton etc 83-01; rtd 01; Perm to Offic *Birm* from 03. *65 Duxford Road, Great Barr, Birmingham B42 2JD* Tel 0121-380 7030

WESTLAND, Richard Theodore. b 27. LNSM course. **d** 87 **p** 88. OLM Freiston w Butterwick *Linc* 87-97; rtd 97; Perm to Offic *Linc* from 97. *76 Brand End Road, Butterwick, Boston PE22 0JD* Tel (01205) 760572

WESTLEY, Stuart. b 24. Em Coll Cam BA48 MA52 Man Univ DASE84. Wells Th Coll 49. **d** 50 **p** 51. C Prestwich St Marg *Man* 50-53; C Tonge w Alkrington 53-55; C-in-c Oldham St Ambrose 55-58; Lic to Offic *Blackb* 58-70; Chapl Arnold Sch Blackpool 58-66; Asst Chapl Denstone Coll Uttoxeter 70-73; Chapl Ermysted's Gr Sch Skipton 73-85; Hon C Blackpool St Mich *Blackb* 75-77; Perm to Offic *Bradf* 77-78; Lic to Offic 78-85; C Padiham *Blackb* 85-89; rtd 89; Perm to Offic *Blackb* from 89. *20 Crichton Place, Blackpool FY4 1NS* Tel (01253) 347962 E-mail s.westley@amserve.net

WESTMINSTER, Archdeacon of. *Vacant*

WESTMINSTER, Dean of. *See* CARR, The Very Revd Arthur Wesley

WESTMORELAND, Mrs Diane Ruth. b 57. Man Univ BA78. NEOC 95. **d** 98 **p** 99. NSM Tadcaster w Newton Kyme *York* 98-99; C 99-02; P-in-c Stamford Bridge Gp from 02. *The Rectory, 8 Viking Road, Stamford Bridge, York YO41 1BR* Tel (01759) 371353 Mobile 07870-745506 E-mail diane@dianewestmoreland.com

WESTMORLAND AND FURNESS, Archdeacon of. *See* HOWE, The Ven George Alexander

WESTNEY, Michael Edward William. b 29. Lich Th Coll 64. **d** 65 **p** 66. C Hughenden *Ox* 65-68; C Banbury 68-71; TV Trunch *Nor* 71-78; V Reading St Matt *Ox* 78-83; TV W Slough 83-88; TR 88-94; rtd 94; Perm to Offic *Ox* 97-00. *59 Portland Close, Burnham, Slough SL2 2LT* Tel (01628) 660052

WESTON, Christopher James. b 20. G&C Coll Cam BA46 MA49. Ridley Hall Cam 47. **d** 49 **p** 50. C Neasden cum Kingsbury St Cath *Lon* 49-53; Singapore 53-55; Chapl Cheltenham Coll 56-63; V Clifton St Jas *Sheff* 63-70; P-in-c Stevenage St Nic *St Alb* 70-71; V 71-87; rtd 87; Perm to Offic *Ely* 87-99. *6 Allen Court, Hauxton Road, Trumpington, Cambridge CB2 2LU* Tel (01223) 510926

WESTON, Canon David Wilfrid Valentine. b 37. Lanc Univ PhD93. **d** 67 **p** 68. OSB 60-84; Lic to Offic *Ox* 67-84; Prior Nashdom Abbey 71-74; Abbot 74-84; C Chorley St Pet *Blackb* 84-85; V Pilling 85-89; Bp's Dom Chapl *Carl* 89-94; Can Res Carl Cathl from 94; Lib from 95; Vice-Dean 00. *3 The Abbey, Carlisle CA3 8TZ* Tel (01228) 521834

WESTON, Frederick Victor Henry. b 41. Qu Coll Cam BA63 MA67. St D Coll Lamp 63. **d** 65 **p** 66. C Grangetown *Llan* 65-67; C Cwmmer w Abercregan CD 67-69; C Haverhill *St E* 69-74; R Gt and Lt Whelnetham 74-79; Perm to Offic from 84; Chapl HM Pris Highpoint 92-98. *154 Southgate Street, Bury St Edmunds IP33 2AF* Tel (01284) 760800
E-mail victorweston@yahoo.com

WESTON, Gary James. b 72. Westmr Coll Ox BTh95. Wycliffe Hall Ox 02. **d** 04 **p** 05. C Barrow St Paul *Carl* from 04. *50 Furness Park Road, Barrow-in-Furness LA14 5PS* Tel (01229) 835558
E-mail gary.weston@ukonline.co.uk

WESTON, Ivan John. b 45. MBE88. Chich Th Coll 71. **d** 74 **p** 75. C Harlow St Mary Magd *Chelmsf* 74-77; Chapl RAF 77-00; Perm to Offic *Nor* 93-95 and *Ely* from 00. *2 The Furlongs, Needingworth, St Ives PE27 4TX* Tel (01480) 462107

WESTON, John Oglivy. b 30. St Pet Coll Ox BA66 MA70. Linc Th Coll 71. **d** 71 **p** 72. Lect Trent (Nottm) Poly 66-82; Hon C Long Clawson and Hose *Leic* 71-82; Hon C Bingham *S'well* 82-85; Lic to Offic 85-91; rtd 91; Perm to Offic *Heref* 91-97. *Mowbray Lodge, Marshbrook, Church Stretton SY6 6QE* Tel (01694) 781288

WESTON, Mrs Judith. b 36. MSR56 Open Univ BA75. St Jo Coll Nottm 84. **dss** 85 **d** 87 **p** 94. Huddersfield H Trin *Wakef* 85-87; Par Dn 87-91; Par Dn Wakef St Andr and St Mary 91-94; C 94-95; Chapl Huddersfield NHS Trust 95-98; rtd 96; Perm to Offic *Wakef* from 98. *Overcroft, 8A Newland Road, Huddersfield HD5 0QT* Tel (01484) 453591

WESTON, Canon Keith Aitken Astley. b 26. Trin Hall Cam BA51 MA55. Ridley Hall Cam 51. **d** 53 **p** 54. C Weston-super-Mare Ch Ch *B & W* 53-56; C Cheltenham St Mark *Glouc* 56-59; PC Clevedon Ch Ch *B & W* 59-64; R Ox St Ebbe w H Trin and St Pet *Ox* 64-85; RD Ox 71-76; Hon Can Ch Ch 81-85; Dir Post-Ord Tr *Nor* 85-90; Dioc Dir of Ords 85-91; P-in-c Nor St Steph 85-91; Hon Brigade Chapl Norfolk Co Fire Service 90-91; rtd 91; Hon C Thame *Ox* from 91. *18 Moor End Lane, Thame OX9 3BQ* Tel (01844) 215441

WESTON, Neil. b 51. Jes Coll Ox BA73 MA78. Ridley Hall Cam 74. **d** 76 **p** 77. C Ealing St Mary *Lon* 76-80; P-in-c Pertenhall w Swineshead *St Alb* 80-89; P-in-c Dean w Yelden, Melchbourne and Shelton 80-89; R The Stodden Churches 89-91; R Newhaven *Chich* 91-98; Miss to Seamen 91-98; P-in-c Radcliffe-on-Trent and Shelford etc *S'well* 98-04; R from 04. *The Rectory, 2 Vicarage Lane, Radcliffe-on-Trent, Nottingham NG12 2FB* Tel 0115-933 2203 E-mail neilweston@ntlworld.com

WESTON, Paul David Astley. b 57. Trin Hall Cam BA80 MA83 Westmr Coll Ox MPhil92 K Coll Lon PhD02. Wycliffe Hall Ox 83. **d** 85 **p** 86. C New Malden and Coombe *S'wark* 85-89; Lect Oak Hill Th Coll 89-97; Vice-Prin 97-00; Gen Sec UCCF 00-01; Assoc Lect Ridley Hall Cam 02-03; Tutor from 03; Perm to Offic *Ely* from 01. *31 Thornton Close, Girton, Cambridge CB3 0NF* Tel (01223) 276657 *or* 710115 E-mail pdaw2@cam.ac.uk

WESTON, Ralph Edward Norman. b 30. Worc Ord Coll 67. **d** 69 **p** 70. C Harborne St Pet *Birm* 69-71; CF 71-75; Chapl Oswestry Sch 75-85; Chapl Rotherham Distr Gen Hosp 85-95; CF (ACF) 87-95; TV Thorverton, Cadbury, Upton Pyne etc *Ex* 95-99; rtd 95; Perm to Offic *Ex* from 99. *10 Rogers Close, Tiverton EX16 6UW* Tel (01884) 259622 Fax as telephone

WESTON, Stephen John Astley. b 55. Aston Univ BSc77. Ridley Hall Cam 78. **d** 81 **p** 82. C Gt Chesham *Ox* 81-85; C Southport Ch Ch *Liv* 85-87; P-in-c Gayhurst w Ravenstone, Stoke Goldington etc *Ox* 87-91; R 91-96; RD Newport 92-95; V Chipping Norton 96-01; TR from 01; AD Chipping Norton from 02. *The Vicarage, Church Street, Chipping Norton OX7 5NT* Tel (01608) 642688 E-mail revsweston@lineone.net

WESTON, Timothy Bernard Charles. b 48. Dioc OLM tr scheme 00. **d** 03 **p** 04. OLM Watton w Carbrooke and Ovington *Nor* from 03. *The Oaks, Shipdham Road, Carbrooke, Thetford IP25 6SX* Tel (01362) 820292 E-mail timangie@dial.pipex.com

WESTON, Mrs Virginia Anne. b 58. UEA BSc79. Wycliffe Hall Ox 84. **d** 87 **p** 02. Par Dn New Malden and Coombe *S'wark* 87-89; Lic to Offic *Lon* 89-01; Lic to Offic *Ely* from 01; Chapl to People at Work in Cam from 02. *31 Thornton Close, Girton, Cambridge CB3 0NF* Tel (01223) 276657 *or* 710115
E-mail chaplain@htcambridge.org.uk
or virginiaweston@yahoo.co.uk

WESTWOOD, Canon John Richard. b 55. Clare Coll Cam BA77 MA81 Lambeth MA98. Ripon Coll Cuddesdon 77. **d** 79 **p** 80. C Oakham w Hambleton and Egleton *Pet* 79-81; C Oakham, Hambleton, Egleton, Braunston and Brooke 81-83; V Gt w Lt Harrowden and Orlingbury 83-90; V Wellingborough St Andr 90-99; RD Wellingborough 92-97; R Irthlingborough from 99; Warden of Readers 95-05; Can Pet Cathl from 97. *The Rectory, 79 Finedon Road, Irthlingborough, Wellingborough NN9 5TY* Tel (01933) 650278 E-mail john@johnwestwood.fsnet.co.uk

WESTWOOD, Peter. b 38. Open Univ BA76. AKC65. **d** 65 **p** 66. C Acomb St Steph *York* 65-68; Chapl HM Youth Cust Cen Onley 69-73; Chapl HM Pris Leic 73-77; Chapl HM Pris Maidstone 77-81; Chapl HM Pris Dur 81-87; Chapl HM Pris Brixton 87-93; Chapl HM Pris Wormwood Scrubs 93-98; Perm to Offic *S'wark* from 98; rtd 99. *St Stephen's Church, College Road, London SE21 7HN* Tel (020) 8693 0082

WESTWOOD, Richard Andrew. b 64. Nottm Univ BSc85 PGCE86. St Jo Coll Nottm 02. **d** 04 **p** 05. C Gt Wyrley *Lich* from 04. *6 Clover Ridge, Cheslyn Hay, Walsall WS6 7DP* Tel (01922) 419161 E-mail rrejas@ic24.net

WESTWOOD, Timothy. b 61. Wolv Poly DMS86 MBA91. WMMTC 95. **d** 98 **p** 99. NSM Sedgley St Mary *Worc* from 98. *5 Deborah Close, Wolverhampton WV2 3HS* Tel (01902) 831078
E-mail twestwood@cableinet.co.uk

WETHERALL, Canon Cecil Edward (Ted). b 29. St Jo Coll Dur 49. **d** 56 **p** 57. C Ipswich St Aug *St E* 56-59; R Hitcham 59-79; P-in-c Brettenham 61-63; P-in-c Kettlebaston 71-91; R Hitcham w Lt Finborough 79-91; P-in-c Preston 85-91; Hon Can St E Cathl 83-91; rtd 92; Perm to Offic *St E* 92-97; Asst Chapl Athens w Kifissia, Patras, Thessaloniki etc *Eur* 92-96. *Kastraki, Tolo, Nafplio, 21056 Argolis, Greece*

WETHERALL, Mrs Joanne Elizabeth Julia. b 62. NNEB81. STETS 02. **d** 05. NSM Godalming *Guildf* from 05. *58 Wolseley Road, Godalming GU7 3EA* Tel (01483) 415034
E-mail simon.wetherall@which.net

WETHERALL, Nicholas Guy. b 52. Lon Univ BMus73 Ox Univ CertEd75. Chich Th Coll 82. **d** 84 **p** 85. C Cleobury Mortimer w Hopton Wafers *Heref* 84-87; TV Leominster 87-92; V Cuckfield *Chich* from 92; RD Cuckfield 99-03. *The Vicarage, Broad Street, Cuckfield, Haywards Heath RH17 5LL* Tel (01444) 454007

WETHERELL, Ms Eileen Joyce. b 44. Westf Coll Lon BSc66. S Dios Minl Tr Scheme 89. **d** 92 **p** 94. Par Dn Southampton Maybush St Pet *Win* 92-94; C 94-96; TV Totton 96-04; V Hythe from 04; Dioc Adv for Women's Min from 02. *The Vicarage, 14 Atheling Road, Hythe, Southampton SO45 6BR* Tel (023) 8084 2461 E-mail eileenwetherell@btinternet.com

WETHERELL, Philip Anthony. b 45. Leic Univ MPhil87. AKC72. **d** 73 **p** 74. C Walthamstow St Sav *Chelmsf* 73-75; Chapl and Tutor Namibia Internat Peace Cen 75-76; C Knighton St Mary Magd *Leic* 76-80; TV Southampton (City Cen) *Win* 80-84; Miss Personnel Sec USPG 84-96; Admin Coun for Educn in World Citizenship 97-98; Development Officer Kaloko Trust UK from 98. *Flat D, 14 Asylum Road, London SE15 2RL* Tel (020) 7732 1601

WEYMAN, Canon Richard Darrell George. b 46. Lon Univ BA Bris Univ PhD. Sarum & Wells Th Coll. **d** 84 **p** 85. C Sherborne w Castleton and Lillington *Sarum* 84-88; V Malden St Jo *S'wark* 88-92; P-in-c Marnhull *Sarum* from 92; Dir Post Ord Tr from 92; Can and Preb Sarum Cathl from 99. *The Rectory, New Street, Marnhull, Sturminster Newton DT10 1PY* Tel (01258) 821130
E-mail dweyman@weyman.fsnet.co.uk

WEYMAN PACK-BERESFORD, John Derek Henry. b 31. Wells Th Coll 69. **d** 70 **p** 71. C Headley All SS *Guildf* 70-76; V Westcott 76-97; RD Dorking 84-89; rtd 97; Perm to Offic *Truro* from 99. *Kittiwake, Polurrian Cliff, Mullion, Helston TR12 7EW* Tel (01326) 240457

WEYMONT, Martin Eric. b 48. St Jo Coll Dur BA69 MA74 Fitzw Coll Cam PGCE73 Lon Inst of Educn PhD89 Open Univ BSc96. Westcott Ho Cam 71. **d** 73 **p** 74. C Blackheath *Birm* 73-76; Hon C Willesden St Matt *Lon* 76-77; Hon C Belmont 77-79; P-in-c W Twyford 79-85; NSM Cricklewood St Mich 85-88; Chapl St Pet Colleg Sch Wolv 88-91; Hon C Wolverhampton *Lich* 88-91; NSM Bickershaw *Liv* 91-97; P-in-c Mells w Buckland Dinham, Elm, Whatley etc *B & W* from 97. *The Rectory, Gay Street, Mells, Frome BA11 3PT* Tel (01373) 812320 Fax 813778

WHALE, Desmond Victor. b 35. Bris Sch of Min 81. **d** 84 **p** 85. Lic to Offic *Bris* 84-88; C Parr *Liv* 88-91; R Winfarthing w Shelfanger w Burston w Gissing etc *Nor* 91-00; RD Redenhall 97-99; rtd 00; Perm to Offic *Nor* from 00 and *Sarum* from 01. *47 Cornbrash Rise, Hilperton, Trowbridge BA14 7TS* Tel (01225) 768537 Mobile 07887-717052

WHALE, Canon Jeffery Walter George. b 33. Lon Univ BSc60. Cuddesdon Coll 60. **d** 62 **p** 63. C Rugby St Andr *Cov* 62-68; C-in-c Britwell St Geo CD *Ox* 68-77; P-in-c Datchet 77-78; TR Riverside 78-88; RD Burnham 83-87; Hon Can Ch Ch 85-01; TR New Windsor 88-01; rtd 01; Hon C Chenies and Lt Chalfont, Latimer and Flaunden *Ox* 01-03. *62 Eton Wick Road, Eton Wick, Windsor SL4 6JL* Tel and fax (01753) 865616 Mobile 07711-566167 E-mail jeffery.whale@ukgateway.net

WHALE, Noel Raymond. b 41. Ox Univ 67. **d** 70 **p** 71. C Amersham *Ox* 70-73; Australia from 73; C Geelong 73-76; P-in-c Altona 76-79; I 79-85; I Ivanhoe 86-97; Prec/Min Can St Paul's Cathl 97-01; I Bundoora St Pet from 01. *12 Alma Road, PO Box 1225, Bundoora, Vic, Australia 3083* Tel (0061) (3) 9467 4442 *or* 9467 3769 Mobile 412-196127 Fax (3) 9467 6642 E-mail jonahnoel@hotmail.com

WHALE, Peter Richard. b 49. Auckland Univ MA72 BSc73 Down Coll Cam BA74 MA79 Otago Univ BD78 Ex Univ PhD90. St Jo Coll Auckland 75. **d** 77 **p** 78. C Takapuna New Zealand 77-80; Chapl K Coll Auckland 81-85; TV Saltash *Truro* 85-90; Jt Dir SW Minl Tr Course 86-90; Preb St Endellion 89-90; Prin WMMTC 90-92; rtd 04. *6 Bluebell Walk, Coventry CV4 9XR* Tel (024) 7646 4894 E-mail petegray@btinternet.com

WHALES, Jeremy Michael. b 31. Bris Univ MA82. Lambeth STh72 Wycliffe Hall Ox 59. **d** 61 **p** 62. C W Wimbledon Ch Ch *S'wark* 61-64; Lect St Paul's Coll Cheltenham 64-67; Asst Chapl and Sen Lect 67-74; Chapl 74-78; Assoc Chapl and Sen Lect Coll of SS Paul and Mary Cheltenham 78-84; V Cheltenham St Luke and St Jo *Glouc* 85-92; rtd 92; Perm to Offic *Glouc* from 92; Clergy Widows Officer (Cheltenham Adnry) 96-99. *5 Robert Burns Avenue, Cheltenham GL51 6NU* Tel (01242) 527583

WHALEY, Stephen John. b 57. York Univ BA79. Cranmer Hall Dur BA85. **d** 86 **p** 87. C Selby Abbey *York* 86-90; V Derringham Bank from 90; AD W Hull 98-00. *110 Calvert Road, Hull HU5 5DH* Tel (01482) 352175

WHALLEY, Anthony Allen. b 41. Linc Th Coll 77. **d** 79 **p** 80. C Upton cum Chalvey *Ox* 79-83; R Newton Longville w Stoke Hammond and Whaddon 83-96; R Winslow w Gt Horwood and Addington from 99. *The Vicarage, Vicarage Road, Winslow, Buckingham MK18 3BJ* Tel (01296) 712564 E-mail laurence@winslow11.fsnet.co.uk

WHALLEY, Mrs Constance Mary. b 55. Carl and Blackb Dioc Tr Inst 99. **d** 02 **p** 03. NSM Garstang St Helen and St Michaels-on-Wyre *Blackb* from 02. *Brierfield, Stoney Lane, Goosnargh, Preston PR3 2WH* Tel (01995) 640652

WHALLEY, Edward Ryder Watson. b 31. G&C Coll Cam BA54 MA59. Westcott Ho Cam 55. **d** 57 **p** 58. C Ashton-on-Ribble St Andr *Blackb* 57-60; Chapl Magd Coll Cam 60-63; C Arnold *S'well* 63-67; rtd 96; Perm to Offic *Lon* from 03. *6 Cranleigh, 137-139 Ladbroke Road, London W11 3PX* Tel (020) 7727 1985

WHALLEY, George Peter. b 40. LNSM course 82. **d** 86 **p** 86. NSM Ellon *Ab* from 86; NSM Cruden Bay from 86. *128 Braehead Drive, Cruden Bay, Peterhead AB42 0NW* Tel (01779) 812511 Fax 812771 E-mail pwhalley@compuserve.com

WHALLEY, Jonathan Peter Lambert. b 60. Wm Booth Memorial Coll 87. St Jo Coll Nottm BA97. **d** 97 **p** 98. C Hattersley *Ches* 97-01; V The Marshland *Sheff* from 01; CF(V) from 02. *The Vicarage, Kings Causeway, Swinefleet, Goole DN14 8DH* Tel (01405) 704643

WHALLEY, Michael Thomas. b 30. AKC55. **d** 56 **p** 57. C Nottingham All SS *S'well* 56-58; C Clifton St Fran 58-60; C Mansfield SS Pet and Paul 60; V N Wilford St Faith 60-66; Asst Chapl HM Pris Man 66-67; Chapl HM Youth Cust Cen Dover 67-69; Lic to Offic *Linc* 70-75; Chapl HM Pris Aylesbury 75-79; C Aylesbury *Ox* 79-83; P-in-c Bierton w Hulcott 83-89; TV Aylesbury w Bierton and Hulcott 89-95; rtd 95; Perm to Offic *Linc* from 97. *17 Willowfield Avenue, Nettleham, Lincoln LN2 2TH* Tel (01522) 595372

WHALLEY, Peter. *See* WHALLEY, George Peter

✠**WHALON, The Rt Revd Pierre Welté.** b 52. Boston Univ BMus74 Duquesne Univ MMus81. Virginia Th Sem MDiv85. **d** 85 **p** 85 **c** 01. USA 85-01; R N Versailles All So 85-91; R Philadelphia St Paul 91-93; R Fort Pierce St Andr 93-01; Bp in Charge Convocation of American Chs in Eur from 01; Hon Asst Bp Eur from 02. *23 Avenue George V, 75008 Paris, France* Tel (0033) (1) 53 23 84 04 *or* tel and fax 47 20 02 23 E-mail bppwhalon@aol.com *or* cathedral@american.cathedral.com

WHARTON, Christopher Joseph. b 33. Keble Coll Ox BA57 MA61. **d** 79 **p** 80. NSM Harpenden St Nic *St Alb* 79-93; R Kimpton w Ayot St Lawrence 93-00; Perm to Offic from 00. *97 Overstone Road, Harpenden AL5 5PL* Tel (01582) 761164

WHARTON, Ms Gillian Vera. b 66. TCD BTh93 MPhil99 HDipEd02. CITC 90. **d** 93 **p** 94. C Glenageary *D & G* 93-96; PV Ch Ch Cathl Dublin from 96; Dioc Youth Officer 96-00; C Lucan w Leixlip 96-00; Chapl Rathdown Sch 00-04; I Dublin Booterstown *D & G* from 04; I Dublin Mt Merrion from 04. *The Rectory, Cross Avenue, Blackrock, Dublin 18, Irish Republic* Tel (00353) (1) 288 7118 Mobile 87-230 0767 E-mail gillwharton@hotmail.com *or* booterstown@dublin.anglican.org

✠**WHARTON, The Rt Revd John Martin.** b 44. Van Mildert Coll Dur BA69 Linacre Coll Ox BTh71 MA76. Ripon Hall Ox 69. **d** 72 **p** 73 **c** 92. C Birm St Pet *Birm* 72-75; C Croydon St Jo *Cant* 76-77; Dir Past Studies Ripon Coll Cuddesdon 77-83; C Cuddesdon *Ox* 79-83; Sec to Bd of Min and Tr *Bradf* 83-92; Dir Post-Ord Tr 84-92; Hon Can Bradf Cathl 84-92; Can Res Bradf Cathl 92; Bp's Officer for Min and Tr 92; Area Bp Kingston *S'wark* 92-97; Bp Newc from 97. *The Bishop's House, 29 Moor Road South, Newcastle upon Tyne NE3 1PA* Tel 0191-285 2220 Fax 284 6933 E-mail bishop@newcastle.anglican.org

WHARTON, Miss Kate Elizabeth. b 78. Leeds Metrop Univ BSc00. Wycliffe Hall Ox BTh05. **d** 05. C W Derby St Luke *Liv* from 05. *269 Princess Drive, Liverpool L12 6QG* E-mail kwharton@fish.co.uk

WHARTON, Richard Malcolm. b 69. Univ of Cen England in Birm BA91 PGCE92. Ripon Coll Cuddesdon BTh98. **d** 98 **p** 99. C Weoley Castle *Birm* 98-01; C Hall Green Ascension 01-04; P-in-c Gospel Lane St Mich from 03. *15 Raglan Road, Birmingham B5 7RA* Tel 0121-440 2196 E-mail rwharton@fish.co.uk

WHARTON, Susan Jane. b 58. Leeds Univ BSc79 Coll of Ripon & York St Jo MA00. N Ord Course 96. **d** 99 **p** 00. C Bingley All SS *Bradf* 99-03; P-in-c Weston w Denton from 03; P-in-c Leathley w Farnley, Fewston and Blubberhouses from 03. *The Vicarage, Askwith, Otley LS21 2HX* Tel (01943) 461139 E-mail wharton@nildram.co.uk

WHARTON, Thomas Anthony. b 21. Bps' Coll Cheshunt 49. **d** 52 **p** 53. C Beeston *S'well* 52-55; C Ambleside w Rydal *Carl* 55-58; V Northowram *Wakef* 58-65; V Chipping Norton *Ox* 65-86; Chapl Berne *Eur* 86-89; rtd 89; Perm to Offic *Glouc* from 89. *4 Bowling Green Crescent, Cirencester GL7 2HA* Tel (01285) 659043

WHARTON, Thomas Geoffrey. b 72. Glas Univ BA93. Westcott Ho Cam 03. **d** 05. C Linton in Craven *Bradf* from 05. *15 Brooklyn, Threshfield, Skipton BD23 5ER* E-mail tvwharton@onetel.com

WHATELEY, Stuart David. b 44. Ripon Hall Ox 71. **d** 73 **p** 74. C Chilvers Coton w Astley *Cov* 73-76; Chapl Miss to Seafarers from 76. *10 Merryman Garth, Hedon, Hull HU12 8NJ* Tel (01405) 764730 E-mail padre@marinersclub.org

WHATELEY, Thomas Roderick (Rod). b 52. St Jo Coll Nottm 94. **d** 96 **p** 97. C Willesborough *Cant* 96-99; P-in-c Cliftonville 99-03; R Orlestone w Snave and Ruckinge w Warehorne etc from 03. *The Rectory, Cock Lane, Ham Street, Ashford TN26 2HU* Tel (01233) 732274 E-mail rod.whateley@tiscali.co.uk

WHATLEY, Lionel Frederick. b 50. St Paul's Coll Grahamstown 77. **d** 79 **p** 80. C Uitenhage S Africa 79-80; R Newton Park 80-83; R Alexandria Plurality 83-84; R Waterberg 84-90; R Letaba 90-99; Adn NE 95-99; V Gen 97-99; R Ashington, Washington and Wiston w Buncton *Chich* 99-05; TV Langport Area Chs *B & W* from 05. *The Vicarage, 1 New Street, Long Sutton, Langport TA10 9JW* Tel (01458) 241260 E-mail whatley@onetel.com

WHATLEY, Roger James. b 49. Chich Th Coll 94. **d** 96 **p** 04. NSM Newport St Jo *Portsm* from 96. *Beechcroft, 46 Trafalgar Road, Newport PO30 1QG* Tel (01983) 825938

WHATMORE, Michael John. b 30. Bris Univ BA51 St Cath Soc Ox BA53 MA54. Wycliffe Hall Ox 56. **d** 56 **p** 58. C Bexley St Mary *Roch* 56-57; C Keston 57-59; C Bromley St Mark 59-61; Distr Sec (GB) Bible Soc 61-64; R Stanningley St Thos *Ripon* 64-67; V Speke All SS *Liv* 67-70; Teacher & Sen Tutor Barton Peveril Coll 70-92; rtd 92; Perm to Offic *Win* from 92. *26 Grebe Close, Milford on Sea, Lymington SO41 0XA* Tel (01590) 644892

WHATMOUGH, Michael Anthony (Tony). b 50. ARCO71 Ex Univ BA72. Edin Th Coll BD81. **d** 81 **p** 82. C Edin St Hilda and Edin St Fillan *Edin* 81-84; C Salisbury St Thos and St Edm *Sarum* 84-86; R 86-93; RD Salisbury 90-93; V Bris St Mary Redcliffe w Temple etc *Bris* 93-04. *Address temp unknown* E-mail tony@whatmough.org.uk

WHATSON, Mark Edwin Chadwick. b 57. CEng83 MIMechE83 Southn Univ BSc79. N Ord Course 86. **d** 88 **p** 91. NSM Church Hulme *Ches* 88-91; NSM Goostrey 91-95; NSM Hardwicke, Quedgeley and Elmore w Longney *Glouc* 95-98; C Thornbury 98-01; Ind Chapl 99-01; R Freshwater *Portsm* from 01; R Yarmouth from 01. *The Rectory, Afton Road, Freshwater PO40 9TS* Tel (01983) 752010 Fax as telephone E-mail mark.whatson@bigfoot.com

WHATTON, Miss Joanna Nicola. b 72. Liv Univ BA93 Bris Univ BA00 Homerton Coll Cam PGCE95. Trin Coll Bris 98. **d** 01 **p** 02. C Chislehurst St Nic *Roch* from 01. *Southbeech, Old Perry Street, Chislehurst BR7 6PP* Tel (020) 8467 1170

WHAWELL, Arthur Michael. b 38. SRN59. Sarum & Wells Th Coll 74. **d** 76 **p** 77. C Cottingham *York* 76-79; P-in-c Bessingby 79-84; P-in-c Carnaby 79-84; V Birchencliffe *Wakef* 84-87; Chapl Huddersfield R Infirmary 84-87; V St Bart Less *Lon* 87-95; Chapl St Bart Hosp Lon 87-95; P-in-c Wormingford, Mt Bures and Lt Horkesley *Chelmsf* 95-00; V 00-03; rtd 03. *Cherry Trees, Benefield Road, Upper Glapthorn, Peterborough PE8 5BQ* Tel (01832) 272500 E-mail michael@whawell.freeserve.co.uk

WHEALE, Alan Leon. b 43. HNC65 AKC69 Hull Univ MA92. St Aug Coll Cant 69 DipMin89. **d** 70 **p** 71. C Tamworth *Lich* 70-73; C Cheddleton 73-75; V Garretts Green *Birm* 75-78; V Perry Beeches 78-83; V Winshill *Derby* 83-84; Deputation Appeals Org (E Midl) CECS 84-86; C Arnold *S'well* 86-88; V Daybrook 88-96; R Clifton Campville w Edingale and Harlaston *Lich* 96-01; R Clifton Campville w Edingale and Harlaston from 96; P-in-c No Man's Heath 96-01; P-in-c Thorpe

Constantine from 96; P-in-c Elford from 97. *The Rectory, Main Street, Clifton Campville, Tamworth B79 0AP* Tel (01827) 373257 E-mail alan-wheale@supanet.com

WHEALE, Sarah Ruth. *See* BULLOCK, Mrs Sarah Ruth

WHEAT, Charles Donald Edmund. b 37. Nottm Univ BA70 Sheff Univ MA76. Kelham Th Coll 57. **d** 62 **p** 63. C Sheff Arbourthorne *Sheff* 62-67; Lic to Offic *S'well* 67-70; SSM from 69; Chapl St Martin's Coll Lanc 70-73; Prior SSM Priory Sheff 73-75; Lic to Offic *Sheff* 73-97; C Ranmoor 75-77; Asst Chapl Sheff Univ 75-77; Chapl 77-80; Prov SSM in England 81-91; Dir 82-89; Lic to Offic *Blackb* 81-88; V Middlesbrough All SS *York* 88-95; Roehampton Inst *S'wark* 96-97; Chapl OHP 97-98; Prior St Antony's Priory Dur 98-01; V Middlesbrough St Thos *York* 01-03; rtd 03; Hon C S Bank *York* from 03. *154 Carisbrooke Avenue, Thorntree, Middlesbrough TS3 9LS* Tel (01642) 210824 E-mail ssmmbro@aol.com

WHEATLEY, David. b 44. Dioc OLM tr scheme 00. **d** 02 **p** 03. OLM Castleford *Wakef* from 02. *124 Queens Park Drive, Castleford WF10 3AP* Tel (01977) 553885

WHEATLEY, David Maurice. b 69. Man Poly BA91. Wycliffe Hall Ox 02. **d** 05. C Cheltenham St Mary, St Matt, St Paul and H Trin *Glouc* from 05. *Trinity House, 100-102 Winchcombe Street, Cheltenham GL52 2NW* Tel (01242) 262306 Fax 515523 E-mail david.wheatley@trinityuk.org

WHEATLEY, Gordon Howard. b 29. Trin Coll Cam MA52. Lon Bible Coll. **d** 90 **p** 91. C Cockley Cley w Gooderstone *Nor* 90-94; C Didlington 90-94; C Gt and Lt Cressingham w Threxton 90-94; C Hilborough w Bodney 90-94; C Oxborough w Foulden and Caldecote 90-94; P-in-c Mundford w Lynford 94-98; P-in-c Ickburgh w Langford 94-98; P-in-c Cranwich 94-98; rtd 98; Perm to Offic *Nor* from 98. *6 Mount Close, Swaffham PE37 7NQ* Tel (01760) 722450

WHEATLEY, Ian James. b 62. Chich Th Coll BTh94. **d** 94 **p** 95. C Braunton *Ex* 94-97; Chapl RN from 97. *Royal Naval Chaplaincy Service, Room 203, Victory Building, HM Naval Base, Portsmouth PO1 3LS* Tel (023) 9272 7903 Fax 9272 7111

WHEATLEY, Jane. *See* WHEATLEY, Miss Sarah Jane

WHEATLEY, John. b 14. **d** 77 **p** 78. NSM Cambois *Newc* 77-87; rtd 87; Perm to Offic *Newc* from 87. *20 Cypress Gardens, Blyth NE24 2LP* Tel (01670) 353353

WHEATLEY, The Ven Paul Charles. b 38. Dur Univ BA61. Linc Th Coll 61. **d** 63 **p** 64. C Bishopston *Bris* 63-68; Youth Chapl 68-73; V Swindon St Paul 73-77; TR Swindon Dorcan 77-79; R Ross *Heref* 79-81; P-in-c Brampton Abbotts 79-81; RD Ross and Archenfield 79-91; TR Ross w Brampton Abbotts, Bridstow and Peterstow 81-91; Preb Heref Cathl 87-91; Adn Sherborne *Sarum* 91-03; P-in-c W Stafford w Frome Billet 91-03; rtd 03. *The Farthings, Bridstow, Ross-on-Wye HR9 6QF* Tel (01305) 264637 E-mail 101543.3471@compuserve.com

✠**WHEATLEY, The Rt Revd Peter William.** b 47. Qu Coll Ox BA69 MA73 Pemb Coll Cam BA71 MA75. Ripon Hall Ox 72. **d** 73 **p** 74 **c** 99. C Fulham All SS *Lon* 73-78; V St Pancras H Cross w St Jude and St Pet 78-82; P-in-c Hampstead All So 82-90; P-in-c Kilburn St Mary 82-90; P-in-c Kilburn St Mary w All So 90-95; V W Hampstead St Jas 82-95; Dir Post-Ord Tr 85-95; AD N Camden 88-93; Adn Hampstead 95-99; Area Bp Edmonton from 99. *27 Thurlow Road, London NW3 5PP* Tel (020) 7435 5890 Fax 7435 6049 E-mail bishop.edmonton@london.anglican.org

WHEATLEY, Miss Sarah Jane. b 45. St Gabr Coll Lon Dip Teaching67. St Alb Minl Tr Scheme 77. **d** 96 **p** 97. NSM Meppershall w Campton and Stondon *St Alb* 96-99; P-in-c Shillington 99-03; V Gravenhurst, Shillington and Stondon from 03. *All Saints' Vicarage, Vicarage Close, Shillington, Hitchin SG5 3LS* Tel (01462) 713797 *or* 731170 E-mail jane.wheatley5@btinternet.com

WHEATLEY PRICE, Canon John. b 31. Em Coll Cam BA54 MA58. Ridley Hall Cam 54. **d** 56 **p** 57. C Drypool St Andr and St Pet *York* 56-59; CMS 59-76; Uganda 60-74; Adn Soroti 72-74; Hon Can Soroti 78-97; Adn N Maseno Kenya 74-76; V Clevedon St Andr *B & W* 76-82; V Clevedon St Andr and Ch Ch 82-87; Chapl Amsterdam *Eur* 87-92; P-in-c Cromford *Derby* 92-95; P-in-c Matlock Bath 92-95; V Matlock Bath and Cromford 95-96; rtd 96; Perm to Offic *Sarum* 96-01 *or Birm* from 01. *2 Beausale Drive, Knowle, Solihull B93 0NS* Tel (01564) 730067 E-mail johnwheatleyprice@lineone.net

WHEATON, Christopher. b 49. St Jo Coll Nottm BTh80 LTh80. **d** 80 **p** 81. C Hatcham St Jas *S'wark* 80-83; C Warlingham w Chelsham and Farleigh 83-87; V Carshalton Beeches from 87; RD Sutton from 03. *The Vicarage, 38 Beeches Avenue, Carshalton SM5 3LW* Tel (020) 8647 6056 E-mail good.shepherd@btinternet.com

WHEATON, Canon David Harry. b 30. St Jo Coll Ox BA53 MA56 Lon Univ BD55. Oak Hill Th Coll 58. **d** 59 **p** 60. Tutor Oak Hill Th Coll 59-62; Prin 71-86; C Enfield Ch Ch Trent Park *Lon* 59-62; R Ludgershall *Ox* 62-66; V Onslow Square St Paul *Lon* 66-71; Chapl Brompton Hosp 69-71; Hon Can St Alb 76-96; V Ware Ch Ch 86-96; RD Hertford 88-91; Chapl to The Queen 90-00; rtd 96. *43 Rose Drive, Chesham HP5 1RR* Tel (01494) 783862

WHEATON, Canon Ralph Ernest. b 32. St Jo Coll Dur BA54. Cranmer Hall Dur DipTh58. **d** 58 **p** 59. C Evington *Leic* 58-63; V Bardon Hill 63-71; V Whitwick St Jo the Bapt 71-81; RD Akeley S 79-81; V Blyth *S'well* 81-96; P-in-c Scofton w Osberton 83-86; V 86-96; RD Worksop 83-93; Hon Can S'well Minster 86-96; P-in-c Langold 86-91; rtd 96; Perm to Offic *Linc* 99-02 and *S'well* from 02. *Petriburg, Main Street, Hayton, Retford DN22 9LL* Tel (01777) 705910

WHEBLE, Eric Clement. b 23. S'wark Ord Course 68. **d** 71 **p** 72. C Croydon H Trin *Cant* 71-78; Hon C Croydon St Sav 78-80; Hon C Norbury St Oswald 80-81; TV Selsdon St Jo w St Fran 81-84; TV Selsdon St Jo w St Fran *S'wark* 85-88; rtd 88; Perm to Offic *Portsm* and *Win* from 88. *23 Holmesland Drive, Botley, Southampton SO30 2SH* Tel (01489) 798050

WHEELDON, William Dennis. b 25. Leeds Univ BA51. Coll of Resurr Mirfield 52. **d** 54 **p** 56. CR 55-76; Barbados 59-66; Prin Coll of Resurr Mirfield 66-75; P-in-c New Whittington *Derby* 83-87; P-in-c Belper Ch Ch and Milford 87-90; rtd 90; Perm to Offic *Bradf* from 90. *10 Brooklyn, Threshfield, Skipton BD23 5ER* Tel (01756) 753187

WHEELER, Preb Alexander Quintin Henry (Alastair). b 51. Lon Univ BA73 Nottm Univ DipTh75. St Jo Coll Nottm 74. **d** 77 **p** 78. C Kenilworth St Jo *Cov* 77-80; C Madeley *Heref* 80-83; P-in-c Draycott-le-Moors *Lich* 83-84; P-in-c Forsbrook 83-84; R Draycott-le-Moors w Forsbrook 84-91; V Nailsea Ch Ch *B & W* 91-96; R Nailsea Ch Ch w Tickenham from 96; RD Portishead 95-01; Preb Wells Cathl from 03. *The Rectory, 1 Christ Church Close, Nailsea, Bristol BS48 1RT* Tel (01275) 853187 E-mail aqhw@aol.com

WHEELER, Andrew Charles. b 48. CCC Cam BA69 MA72 Makerere Univ Kampala MA72 Leeds Univ PGCE72. Trin Coll Bris BA88. **d** 88 **p** 88. CMS from 76; C Whitton *Sarum* 88-89; Egypt 89-92; Sudan 92-00; Abp's Sec for Angl Communion Affairs *Cant* 00-01; NSM Guildf St Sav *Guildf* from 02. *9 Hurley Gardens, Guildford GU4 7YH* Tel (01483) 532310 E-mail andrew.wheeler3@ntlworld.com

WHEELER, Anthony. *See* WHEELER, Richard Anthony

WHEELER, Anthony William. b 28. **d** 76 **p** 77. NSM Shirehampton *Bris* 76-98; Chmn Avonmouth Miss to Seamen from 76; rtd 98; Perm to Offic *Bris* from 98. *3 The Priory, Priory Gardens, Bristol BS11 0BZ* Tel 0117-982 2261

WHEELER (née MILLAR), Mrs Christine. b 55. City of Lon Poly BSc76 DipCOT81. S Dios Minl Tr Scheme 84. **d** 87 **p** 94. NSM Kingston Buci *Chich* 87-89; Par Dn Merstham and Gatton *S'wark* 89-94; C 94-96; R Rockland St Mary w Hellington, Bramerton etc *Nor* 96-04; Perm to Offic from 04. *Mayland, Low Road, Strumpshaw, Norwich NR13 4HU* Tel (01603) 713583 E-mail emailcw@btinternet.com

WHEELER, David Ian. b 49. Southn Univ BSc70 PhD78. N Ord Course 87. **d** 90 **p** 91. C Blackpool St Jo *Blackb* 90-94; R Old Trafford St Jo *Man* from 94. *St John's Rectory, Lindum Avenue, Old Trafford, Manchester M16 9NQ* Tel 0161-872 0500

WHEELER, David James. b 49. Leeds Univ MA95 CQSW74. S Dios Minl Tr Scheme 87. **d** 90 **p** 91. C Hythe *Cant* 90-92; C Knaresborough *Ripon* 92-97; Asst Soc Resp Officer 94-97; P-in-c Gt and Lt Ouseburn w Marton cum Grafton etc 97-01; V 01-05; Jt AD Ripon 01-05; V Cobbold Road St Sav w St Mary *Lon* from 05. *St Saviour's Vicarage, Cobbold Road, London W12 9LN* Tel (020) 8743 4769 E-mail sacerdote@btopenworld.com

WHEELER, Sister Eileen Violet. b 28. TCert48 Newnham Coll Cam MA52. Chich Th Coll 85. **dss** 86 **d** 87 **p** 95. Bexhill St Pet *Chich* 86-95; Hon Par Dn 87-90; Par Dn 90-94; NSM 94-95; rtd 94; Hon C Bexhill St Mark *Chich* 95-00; Perm to Offic 00-02; Hon C Horsham from 02. *St Mary's Lodge, Normandy, Horsham RH12 1JL* Tel (01403) 261407

WHEELER, Graham John. b 39. St Mich Coll Llan BD78. **d** 66 **p** 67. C Roath St Martin *Llan* 66-71; C Cadoxton-juxta-Barry 71-75; Perm to Offic 75-79; C Highcliffe w Hinton Admiral *Win* 79-83; C Milton 83-90; P-in-c Bournemouth St Ambrose from 90. *St Ambrose Vicarage, 72 West Cliff Road, Bournemouth BH4 8BE* Tel (01202) 764957

WHEELER, James Albert. b 49. Sarum & Wells Th Coll 74. **d** 76 **p** 77. C Orpington All SS *Roch* 76-79; C Roch 79-81; C Bexley St Jo 81-84; V Penge Lane H Trin 84-93; P-in-c Tunbridge Wells St Luke 93-99; V from 99. *St Luke's Vicarage, 158 Upper Grosvenor Road, Tunbridge Wells TN1 2EQ* Tel (01892) 521374

WHEELER, John David. b 31. Selw Coll Cam BA54 MA58. Ely Th Coll 54. **d** 56 **p** 57. C Charlton St Luke w St Paul *S'wark* 56-60; C Northolt St Mary *Lon* 61-63; V Bush Hill Park St Mark 64-71; V Ealing St Pet Mt Park 71-74; V Truro St Paul *Truro* 74-79; V Truro St Paul and St Clem 79-80; P-in-c Hammersmith St Sav *Lon* 80-83; V Cobbold Road St Sav w St Mary 83-96; rtd 96; Perm to Offic *Heref* 96-01; *Chich* from 01. *49 Magdalen Road, St Leonards-on-Sea TN37 6EU* Tel (01424) 714371

WHEELER, Julian Aldous. b 48. Nottm Univ BTh74. Kelham Th Coll 70. **d** 75 **p** 76. C Bideford *Ex* 75-79; Lic to Offic 79-86; Hon C Parkham, Alwington, Buckland Brewer etc 86-03. *Forge*

Cottage, Pump Lane, Abbotsham, Bideford EX39 5AZ Tel (01237) 473948 E-mail jwheeler@connectfree.co.uk

WHEELER, Preb Madeleine. b 42. Gilmore Course 76. **dss** 78 **d** 87 **p** 94. Ruislip Manor St Paul *Lon* 78-92; Par Dn 87-91; TD 91-92; Chapl for Women's Min (Willesden Episc Area) 86-95; P-in-c N Greenford All Hallows 94-00; Preb St Paul's Cathl 95-00; rtd 00; Perm to Offic *St Alb* from 00 and *Lon* from 02. *178A Harefield Road, Uxbridge UB8 1PP* Tel (01895) 257274

WHEELER, Nicholas Charles. b 50. Leic Univ BA72. SEITE 00. **d** 03 **p** 04. NSM Blackheath St Jo *S'wark* from 03. *52 Oakways, London SE9 2PD* Tel (020) 8859 7819

WHEELER, Nicholas Gordon Timothy. b 59. BCombStuds84. Linc Th Coll. **d** 84 **p** 85. C Hendon St Alphage *Lon* 84-87; C Wood Green St Mich w Bounds Green St Gabr etc 87-89; TV 89-93; R Cranford 93-02; V Ruislip St Mary from 02. *St Mary's Vicarage, 9 The Fairway, Ruislip HA4 0SP* Tel (020) 8845 3485 Mobile 07946-111968 E-mail nicholasgwheeler@aol.com

WHEELER, Nicholas Paul. b 60. Ox Univ BA86 MA91. Wycliffe Hall Ox 83. **d** 87 **p** 88. C Wood Green St Mich w Bounds Green St Gabr etc *Lon* 87-91; Chapl to Bp Edmonton 91-96; P-in-c Somers Town 96-03; P-in-c Old St Pancras w Bedford New Town St Matt 96-03; P-in-c Camden Town St Mich w All SS and St Thos 96-03; P-in-c Camden Square St Paul 96-03; TR Old St Pancras from 03. *The Vicarage, 191 St Pancras Way, London NW1 9NH* Tel (020) 7485 6837 *or* tel and fax 7424 0724

WHEELER, Richard Anthony (Tony). b 23. St Chad's Coll Dur BA46 MA48 DipTh48. **d** 48 **p** 49. C Kingswinford St Mary *Lich* 48-52; C Toxteth Park St Agnes *Liv* 52-54; V Upholland 54-64; R Dorchester H Trin w Frome Whitfield *Sarum* 64-73; TV Dorchester 73-87; rtd 87; Perm to Offic *Sarum* from 87. *30 Mountain Ash Road, Dorchester DT1 2PB* Tel (01305) 264811 E-mail peewheet@cix.compulink.co.uk

WHEELER, Canon Richard Roy. b 44. K Coll Lon BD72. St Aug Coll Cant. **d** 74 **p** 74. C Brixton St Matt *S'wark* 74-78; Dir St Matt Meeting Place Brixton 78-79; Sec BCC Community Work Resource Unit 79-82; TV Southampton (City Cen) *Win* 83-88; TR 88-98; Hon Can Win Cathl 94-98; Soc Resp Adv *St Alb* from 98; Can Res St Alb from 01. *Holywell Close, 43 Holywell Hill, St Albans AL1 1HE* Tel (01727) 856753 *o* 851748 Fax 830368 E-mail sro@stalbans.anglican.org

WHEELER, Mrs Sally Ann Violet. b 59. Westmr Coll Ox BEd81. St Alb and Ox Min Course 94. **d** 97 **p** 98. NSM Chippenham St Paul w Hardenhuish etc *Bris* 97-01; C Gtr Corsham and Lacock 01-04; TV from 04. *The Vicarage, Folly Lane, Lacock, Chippenham SN15 2LL* Tel (01249) 730272 E-mail wheelers.7@btinternet.com

WHEELHOUSE, Brian Clifford Dunstan. b 69. St Steph Ho Ox BTh93. **d** 96 **p** 97. C Brighton Resurr *Chich* 96-99; C Hangleton 99-00; Perm to Offic 00-01; C Kingstanding St Luke *Birm* 01-03; V Houghton Regis *St Alb* from 03. *The Vicarage, Bedford Road, Houghton Regis, Dunstable LU5 5DJ* Tel and fax (01582) 867593

WHEELWRIGHT, Michael Harvey. b 39. Bps' Coll Cheshunt 64. **d** 67 **p** 68. C Glen Parva and S Wigston *Leic* 67-70; C Evington 70-74; V Leic St Eliz Nether Hall 74-79; Chapl Prudhoe Hosp Northd 79-99; Perm to Offic *Dur* from 95 and *Newc* from 99; rtd 04. *6 Nunnykirk Close, Ovingham, Prudhoe NE42 6BP* Tel (01661) 835749

WHELAN, Canon John Bernard. b 17. Oak Hill Th Coll 38. **d** 47 **p** 48. C Ambleside w Rydal *Carl* 47-49; C Barrow St Luke 49-54; Korea 54-66; Japan 66-67; C Bury St Mary *Man* 68-71; Asst Chapl Crumpsall Hosp Man 71-73; Chapl N Man Gen Hosp 73-82; rtd 82; Chapl Las Palmas *Eur* 82-84; Asst Chapl Valletta w Sliema 84-93; Can Malta Cathl 87-93. *22 Westminster Rhiwlas, Northop Road, Flint CH6 5LH*

WHELAN, Miss Patricia Jean. b 33. ACA55 FCA82. Dalton Ho Bris 58. **dss** 64 **d** 87 **p** 94. Stapleford *S'well* 62-69; Aylesbury *Ox* 69-75; Bushbury *Lich* 75-77; Patchway *Bris* 77-81; Trin Coll Bris 81-82; W Swindon LEP 82-86; High Wycombe *Ox* 86-87; Par Dn 87-91; Par Dn Ox St Ebbe w H Trin and St Pet 91-93; rtd 93. *81 Cogges Hill Road, Witney OX28 3XU* Tel (01993) 779099

WHELAN, Peter Warwick Armstrong. b 34. Southn Univ BTh80 Open Univ BA80 DipHSW94 S Bank Univ 97. Sarum Th Coll 69. **d** 71 **p** 72. C Salisbury St Mark *Sarum* 71-73; C Solihull *Birm* 73-77; TR Shirley 77-86; Chapl Whittington Hosp NHS Trust 86-99; Chapl Camden and Islington Community Health NHS Trust 86-98; Perm to Offic *Ex* from 98; rtd 99. *Olde Court Coach House, Higher Lincombe Road, Torquay TQ1 2EX* Tel (01803) 212483

WHELAN, Raymond Keith. b 40. Cant Sch of Min 85. **d** 88 **p** 91. C Eastbourne St Andr *Chich* 88-93; C-in-c Parklands St Wilfrid CD 93-95; TV Chich 95-00; V Chich St Wilfrid 00-01; rtd 04. *9 Ruislip Gardens, Aldwick, Bognor Regis PO21 4LB* Tel (01243) 264865

WHERLOCK, Mrs Evalene Prudence. b 50. WEMTC 98. **d** 01 **p** 02. NSM Bishopsworth and Bedminster Down *Bris* from 01. *63 Bridgwater Road, Bedminster Down, Bristol BS13 7AX* Tel 0117-964 1035 Mobile 07899-932763 E-mail evawherlock@ukonline.co.uk

WHERRY, Anthony Michael. b 44. Nottm Univ BA65 Univ Coll Lon DAA66. WMMTC 88. **d** 91 **p** 92. NSM Worc City St Paul and Old St Martin etc *Worc* 91-95; NSM Worc E Deanery 95-02; NSM Worc SE from 02. *2 Redfern Avenue, Worcester WR5 1PZ* Tel (01905) 358532 Mobile 07780-677942 E-mail tony@wherry222.fsnet.co.uk

WHETTEM, Canon John Curtiss. b 27. Peterho Cam BA50 MA55. Wycliffe Hall Ox 50. **d** 52 **p** 53. C Clifton Ch Ch *Bris* 52-55; C Wandsworth All SS *S'wark* 55-58; V Soundwell *Bris* 58-63; Youth Chapl 63-68; Chapl Bris Cathl 64-68; R N Mundham w Hunston *Chich* 68-80; P-in-c Oving w Merston 75-80; TR Swanborough *Sarum* 80-92; RD Pewsey 84-89; rtd 92; Perm to Offic *Sarum* from 92. *32 Hogshill Street, Beaminster DT8 3AA* Tel (01308) 863050

WHETTER, Michael Arnold. b 30. Bris Univ BA51. Wells Th Coll 53. **d** 55 **p** 56. C Dursley *Glouc* 55-58; C Coppenhall *Ches* 58-61; R Ches H Trin 61-71; V Stockport St Alb Hall Street 72-90; V Offerton 90-91; Chapl Cherry Tree Hosp Stockport 72-91; Chapl Offerton Hosp Stockport 72-91; V Bollington St Jo *Ches* 91-00; rtd 00; Perm to Offic *Glouc* from 00. *Knapp Cottage, Selsley West, Stroud GL5 5LJ* Tel (01453) 822920

WHETTINGSTEEL, Raymond Edward. b 44. S Dios Minl Tr Scheme 79. **d** 82 **p** 83. NSM Sholing *Win* 82-84; C Southampton Maybush St Pet 84-89; V Hatherden w Tangley, Weyhill and Penton Mewsey from 89. *The Rectory, Penton Mewsey, Andover SP11 0RD* Tel (01264) 773554 E-mail ray_whettingsteel@btinternet.com

WHETTLETON, Timothy John. b 53. Univ of Wales (Swansea) BA74. St Mich Coll Llan DMS98 Dip Practical Th 99. **d** 99 **p** 00. C Llansamlet *S & B* 99-01; P-in-c Gowerton from 01. *The Vicarage, 14 Church Street, Gowerton, Swansea SA4 3EA* Tel (01792) 872266

WHETTON, Nicholas John. b 56. Open Univ BA94. St Jo Coll Nottm 83. **d** 86 **p** 87. C Hatfield *Sheff* 86-90; V Cornholme *Wakef* 90-96; P-in-c Livesey *Blackb* 96-99; V 99-03; P-in-c Ewood 96-97; Chapl HM Pris Hull from 03. *The Chaplain's Office, HM Prison Hull, Hedon Road, Hull HU9 5LS* Tel (01482) 282200

WHIFFEN, Canon William Timothy. b 25. SS Coll Cam BA50 MA54 FRSA94. Linc Th Coll. **d** 52 **p** 53. C Wigan St Mich *Liv* 52-56; India 57-69; V Clay Cross *Derby* 69-74; Sec (Overseas Division) USPG 74-79; TR Woughton *Ox* 79-85; P-in-c Seer Green and Jordans 85-91; Hon Can Ch Ch 91-92; rtd 91. *90 Booker Avenue, Bradwell Common, Milton Keynes MK13 8EF* Tel (01908) 677466

✠**WHINNEY, The Rt Revd Michael Humphrey Dickens.** b 30. Pemb Coll Cam BA55 MA59. Gen Th Sem (NY) STM90 Ridley Hall Cam 55. **d** 57 **p** 58 **c** 82. C Rainham *Chelmsf* 57-60; Hd Cam Univ Miss Bermondsey 60-67; Chapl 67-73; V Bermondsey St Jas w Ch Ch *S'wark* 67-73; Adn S'wark 73-82; Suff Bp Aston *Birm* 82-85; Bp S'well 85-88; Asst Bp Birm 88-95; Can Res Birm Cathl 92-95; rtd 96; Hon Asst Bp Birm from 96. *3 Moor Green Lane, Moseley, Birmingham B13 8NE* Tel 0121-249 2856 Fax as telephone E-mail michael.whinney@btinternet.com

WHINNEY, Nigel Patrick Maurice. b 43. Open Univ BA91. SW Minl Tr Course 95. **d** 97 **p** 98. NSM Ilminster and Distr *B & W* from 97; NSM Officer (Taunton Adnry) from 99; RD Crewkerne and Ilminster from 01. *The Monks Dairy, Isle Brewers, Taunton TA3 6QL* Tel (01460) 281975 E-mail pearls@harriet-whinney.co.uk

WHINTON, William Francis Ivan. b 35. N Ord Course 77. **d** 80 **p** 81. NSM Stockport St Mary *Ches* 80-82; NSM Disley 82-87; V Birtles 87-00; Dioc Officer for Disabled 89-00; rtd 00; Chapl for Deaf People *Ches* 00-04. *Allmeadows Cottage, Wincle, Macclesfield SK11 0QJ* Tel (01260) 227278

WHIPP, Antony Douglas. b 46. Leeds Univ BSc68 Lanc Univ PhD04. Ripon Coll Cuddesdon 84. **d** 86 **p** 87. C Dalston *Carl* 86-89; V Holme Cultram St Mary 89-96; V Holme Cultram St Cuth 89-96; V Kells 96-00; V Hartlepool St Aid *Dur* from 00. *St Aidan's Vicarage, St Aidan's Street, Hartlepool TS25 1SN* Tel (01429) 273539 Fax 232604 E-mail tony.whipp@durham.anglican.org

WHIPP, Margaret Jane. b 55. LMH Ox BA76 Sheff Univ MB, ChB79 MRCP82 FRCR86 Hull Univ MA99. N Ord Course 87. **d** 90 **p** 94. NSM Wickersley *Sheff* 90-98; Tutor Cranmer Hall Dur 98-99; Dir Practical Th NEOC 00-04; Ecum Chapl Ox Brookes Univ *Ox* from 04. *The Mullings, 71 Sandfield Road, Headington, Oxford OX3 6RW* Tel (01865) 765409 E-mail margaretwhipp@doctors.org.uk

WHITAKER, Anthony. b 50. SS Mark & Jo Coll Chelsea CertEd72 Middx Univ BA02. NTMTC 99. **d** 02 **p** 03. NSM Blackmore and Stondon Massey *Chelmsf* 02-05; C from 02. *3 Marks Avenue, Ongar CM5 9AY* Tel (01277) 363725 Mobile 07905-013017 E-mail whitaker_tony@hotmail.com

WHITAKER, Benjamin. *See* WHITAKER, Michael Benjamin

WHITAKER, David Arthur Edward. b 27. New Coll Ox BA50 MA55. Wells Th Coll 51. **d** 53 **p** 54. C W Bridgford *S'well* 53-56; CF 56-58; V Clifton St Fran *S'well* 58-63; Basutoland 63-66; Lesotho 66-69; R Buckerell *Ex* 69-76; R Feniton 69-76; P-in-c

Tiverton St Pet 76-79; R 79-92; rtd 92; Perm to Offic *Heref* from 92. *Wits End, Hereford Road, Weobley, Hereford HR4 8SW* Tel (01544) 318669

WHITAKER, Irene Anne. b 57. Dioc OLM tr scheme 99. **d** 01 **p** 02. OLM Parr *Liv* from 01. *369 Elephant Lane, St Helens WA9 5HF* Tel (01744) 637207 Mobile 07748-435224

WHITAKER, Margaret Scott. b 45. **d** 03 **p** 04. OLM Eaton *Nor* 03-05; NSM Sprowston w Beeston from 05. *6 Wroxham Road, Sprowston, Norwich NR7 8TZ* E-mail whitaker@supanet.com

WHITAKER, Michael Benjamin. b 60. Nottm Univ BA83. Sarum & Wells Th Coll 85. **d** 87 **p** 88. C Gt Grimsby St Mary and St Jas *Linc* 87-91; C Abingdon *Ox* 91-95; Chapl to the Deaf *Sarum* 95-00; Perm to Offic *Win* 97-00; Asst Chapl Chapl to the Deaf *Ox* from 00. *87 Bagley Wood Road, Kennington, Oxford OX1 5LY* Tel (01865) 736100 E-mail whitaker@tribeandclan.freeserve.co.uk

WHITBY, Suffragan Bishop of. *See* LADDS, The Rt Revd Robert Sidney

WHITCOMBE, William Ashley. b 78. UEA BA01. St Steph Ho Ox BTh04. **d** 04 **p** 05. C W Hendon St Jo *Lon* from 04. *2A Montagu Road, London NW4 3ES* Tel (020) 8202 2659 E-mail wawhitcombe@aol.com

WHITCROFT, Graham Frederick. b 42. Oak Hill Th Coll 64. **d** 66 **p** 67. C Cromer *Nor* 66-69; C Attercliffe *Sheff* 69-72; V Kimberworth Park 72-85; V Lepton *Wakef* from 85; RD Kirkburton from 98. *The Vicarage, 138 Wakefield Road, Lepton, Huddersfield HD8 0LU* Tel (01484) 602172 E-mail whitcroft@btopenworld.com

WHITE, Alan. b 18. Man Univ BSc39 MSc40 St Cath Soc Ox BA42 MA46 Leeds Univ MEd52. Ripon Hall Ox 40. **d** 42 **p** 43. C Leic St Marg *Leic* 42-45; Chapl and Asst Master Leeds Gr Sch 45-56; Lic to Offic *Worc* 56-89; Asst Master Bromsgrove Sch 56-72; Chapl 72-83; rtd 83; P-in-c Tardebigge *Worc* 89-00; Perm to Offic from 00. *25 Leadbetter Drive, Bromsgrove B61 7JG* Tel (01527) 877955

WHITE, Preb Alan. b 43. Ex Univ BA65. Chich Th Coll 65. **d** 68 **p** 69. C Upper Clapton St Matt *Lon* 68-72; C Southgate Ch Ch 72-76; P-in-c Friern Barnet St Pet le Poer 76-79; V 79-85; TR Ex St Thos and Em *Ex* from 85; RD Christianity from 99; Preb Ex Cathl from 03. *St Thomas's Vicarage, 57 Cowick Street, Exeter EX4 1HR* Tel (01392) 255219 E-mail revalan.white@btopenworld.com

WHITE, Alan Albert. b 29. Campion Ho Middx 74. **d** 77. In RC Ch 77-90; C Llanegryn w Aberdyfi w Tywyn *Ban* from 99. *7 Cantref, Twywn LL36 0BW* Tel (01654) 710745

WHITE, Mrs Alison Mary. b 56. St Aid Coll Dur BA78 Leeds Univ MA94. Cranmer Hall Dur 83. **dss** 86 **d** 87 **p** 94. NSM Chester le Street *Dur* 86-89; Dioc Adv in Local Miss 89-93; Hon Par Dn Birtley 89-93; Dir Past Studies Cranmer Hall Dur 93-98; Dir of Ords *Dur* 98-00; Springboard Missr *Dur* 00-02; Springboard Missr *Pet* 02-04; Adult Educn Officer from 05. *4 The Avenue, Dallington, Northampton NN5 7AN* Tel (01604) 581400 Fax 750925 E-mail alison.m.white@ukgateway.net

WHITE, Canon Andrew Paul Bartholomew. b 64. MIOT85 ABIST85. Ridley Hall Cam 86. **d** 90 **p** 91. C Battersea Rise St Mark *S'wark* 90-93; P-in-c Balham Hill Ascension 93-97; V 97-98; Dir Internat Min and Can Res Cov Cathl *Cov* 98-05; Iraq from 05; President Foundn for Reconciliation from 05. *The Croft, 66 Shepherds Way, Liphook GU30 7HH* Tel (01428) 723939 *or* (00964) (7901) 265723 E-mail andrew.white@frme.org.uk

WHITE, Andrew Peter. b 65. Lon Univ BA87. Sarum & Wells Th Coll BTh94. **d** 94 **p** 95. C Croydon St Matt *S'wark* 94-96; C S Wimbledon H Trin and St Pet 96-98; TV Droitwich Spa *Worc* 98-05; RD Droitwich 02-04; P-in-c Hartlebury from 05; Bp's Dom Chapl from 05. *Hartlebury Vicarage, Quarry Bank, Hartlebury, Kidderminster DY11 7TE* Tel (01299) 251738 E-mail andrew.white12@virgin.net

WHITE, Antony. *See* FELTHAM-WHITE, Antony James

WHITE, Canon Christopher Norman Hessler. b 32. TD76. St Cath Coll Cam BA56 MA60. Cuddesdon Coll 57. **d** 59 **p** 60. C Solihull *Birm* 59-62; C Leeds St Aid *Ripon* 62-65; CF (TA) 64-85; V Aysgarth *Ripon* 65-74; R Richmond 74-76; P-in-c Hudswell w Downholme and Marske 75-76; R Richmond w Hudswell 76-97; RD Richmond 75-80 and 93-97; Hon Can Ripon Cathl 89-97; Chapl St Fran Xavier Sch Richmond 89-97; rtd 97; Perm to Offic *Ripon* from 97. *Orchard House, Aske, Richmond DL10 5HN* Tel (01748) 850968

WHITE, Colin Davidson. b 44. St And Dioc Tr Course 86 Coates Hall Edin 90. **d** 88 **p** 89. NSM Glenrothes *St And* 88-89; P-in-c 89-90; P-in-c Leven 90-92; R 92-95; V Grimethorpe *Wakef* 95-01; P-in-c Kellington w Whitley 01-02; TV Knottingley and Kellington w Whitley from 02. *The Vicarage, 1 Manor Farm Close, Kellington, Goole DN14 0PF* Tel (01977) 663728 Mobile 07973-795560 Fax (01977) 663671 E-mail cicol@whitefam67.fsnet.co.uk

WHITE, Crispin Michael. b 42. Southn Univ MA98 FRSA94. Bps' Coll Cheshunt 62. **d** 65 **p** 66. C S Harrow St Paul *Lon* 65-67; C Mill Hill St Mich 67-68; I Labrador St Clem Canada 68-71; Toc H Padre (W Region) 71-75; (E Midl Region) 75-82; Ind Chapl *Portsm* 82-98; P-in-c Hatfield Broad Oak and Bush End *Chelmsf* 98-04; Ind Chapl from 04. *11 St Mary's Road, London E13 9AE* Tel (020) 8548 4659 E-mail crispin.white@eccr.org.uk

WHITE, David Christopher. b 51. Lon Univ LLB73. St Jo Coll Nottm 86. **d** 88 **p** 89. C Bulwell St Mary *S'well* 88-92; V Nottingham All SS 92-98; TR Clarendon Park St Jo w Knighton St Mich *Leic* 98-05; R Emmaus Par Team from 05; Bp's NSM Officer from 02. *The Rectory, 9 Springfield Road, Leicester LE2 3BB* Tel 0116-270 6097 E-mail dwhite@ntlworld.com

WHITE, David John. b 26. Leeds Univ BA53. Coll of Resurr Mirfield 53. **d** 55 **p** 56. C Brighton St Pet *Chich* 55-58; C Wednesbury St Jas *Lich* 58-60; C Bishops Hull St Jo *B & W* 60-61; R Morton *Derby* 61-62; In RC Ch 62-73; Lect Whitelands Coll Lon 72-75; R Tregony w St Cuby and Cornelly *Truro* 75-79; R Castle Bromwich SS Mary and Marg *Birm* 79-83; V Plymouth St Simon *Ex* 83-88; R Lapford, Nymet Rowland and Coldridge 88-93; RD Chulmleigh 93; rtd 93; Perm to Offic *Ex* 94-99. *The Belvedere, Peak Hill Road, Sidmouth EX10 8RZ* Tel (01395) 513365

WHITE, David Paul. b 58. Oak Hill Th Coll. **d** 84 **p** 85. C Toxteth Park St Clem *Liv* 84-87; C Woodford Wells *Chelmsf* 87-89; C Woodside Park St Barn *Lon* 89-90; TV Canford Magna *Sarum* 90-93; V York St Mich-le-Belfrey *York* 93-99; V St Austell *Truro* from 99. *The Vicarage, 1 Carnsmerry Crescent, St Austell PL25 4NA* Tel (01726) 73839 E-mail david@st-michael-le-belfry.org

WHITE, Derek. b 35. MBE97. **d** 84 **p** 85. C St Marylebone St Cypr *Lon* 84-96; Bp's Chapl for the Homeless 87-01; P-in-c St Mary le Strand w St Clem Danes 96-01; rtd 01; Perm to Offic *S'wark* from 04. *80 Coleraine Road, London SE3 7PE* Tel (020) 8858 3622

WHITE, Douglas Richard Leon (Rick). b 49. Linc Th Coll 81. **d** 83 **p** 84. C Warsop *S'well* 83-88; V Kirkby in Ashfield St Thos 88-93; Asst Chapl Qu Medical Cen Nottm Univ Hosp NHS Trust 93-98; Chapl Cen Notts Healthcare NHS Trust 98-01; Chapl Notts Healthcare NHS Trust 01-02; Chapl Geo Eliot Hosp NHS Trust Nuneaton from 02; Chapl Mary Ann Evans Hospice from 02. *George Eliot Hospital, College Street, Nuneaton CV10 7DJ* Tel (024) 7635 1351 E-mail rick.white@tesco.net

WHITE, Dudley William. b 33. Univ of Wales (Ban) BSc53. St Mich Coll Llan BD69. **d** 59 **p** 60. C Sketty *S & B* 59-66; R New Radnor and Llanfihangel Nantmelan 66-70; V Penyfai w Tondu *Llan* 70-77; V Swansea St Jude *S & B* 77-98; rtd 98. *37 Dunraven Road, Sketty, Swansea SA2 9LQ* Tel (01792) 201937

WHITE, Eric James. b 46. Man OLM Scheme. **d** 01 **p** 02. OLM Pennington *Man* from 01. *18 Clifton Road, Leigh WN7 3LS* Tel (01942) 678758

✠**WHITE, The Rt Revd Francis.** b 49. Univ of Wales (Cardiff) BSc(Econ)70 DSS71. St Jo Coll Nottm DipTh78. **d** 80 **p** 81 **c** 02. C Dur St Nic *Dur* 80-84; C Chester le Street 84-87; Chapl Dur and Ches le Street Hosps 87-89; V Birtley *Dur* 89-97; RD Chester-le-Street 93-97; Adn Sunderland and Hon Can Dur Cathl 97-02; Can Pet Cathl *Pet* from 02; Suff Bp Brixworth from 02. *4 The Avenue, Dallington, Northampton NN5 7AN* Tel (01604) 759423 Fax 750925 E-mail fw@bpofbrixworth.free-online.co.uk

WHITE, Frederick William Hartland. b 22. MBE62. Kelham Th Coll 39. **d** 45 **p** 46. C Newc St Jo *Newc* 45-50; CF 50-70; Asst Chapl Gen 70-74; Chapl Guards Chpl Lon 70-74; QHC from 73; V Harrow St Mary *Lon* 74-87; rtd 87; Perm to Offic *Sarum* from 87. *Whitesfield House, 5 Seend Cleeve, Melksham SN12 6PS* Tel (01380) 828525

WHITE, Canon Gavin Donald. b 27. Toronto Univ BA49 Lon Univ PhD70. Trin Coll Toronto BD61 Gen Th Sem (NY) STM68 St Steph Ho Ox 51. **d** 53 **p** 54. Canada 53-58; Zanzibar 59-62; Kenya 62-66; C Hampstead St Steph *Lon* 68-70; Lect Glas Univ 71-92; Lic to Offic *Glas* 71-90; rtd 92; Hon Can St Mary's Cathl *Glas* from 92; Hon C St Andrews All SS *St And* from 94. *85D Market Street, St Andrews KY16 9NX* Tel (01334) 477338 E-mail gavin.d.white@ukgateway.net

WHITE, Geoffrey Brian. b 54. Jes Coll Ox BA76 MA80. St Steph Ho Ox 76. **d** 79 **p** 80. C Huddersfield St Pet *Wakef* 79-82; C Flixton St Mich *Man* 82-84; TV Westhoughton 84-91; V Stevenage St Mary Shephall w Aston *St Alb* from 91; RD Stevenage from 01. *St Mary's Vicarage, 148 Hydean Way, Shephall, Stevenage SG2 9YA* Tel (01438) 351963

WHITE, Canon Geoffrey Gordon. b 28. Selw Coll Cam BA50 MA54. Cuddesdon Coll 51. **d** 53 **p** 54. C Bradford-on-Avon *Sarum* 53-56; C Kennington St Jo *S'wark* 56-61; V Leeds St Wilfrid *Ripon* 61-63; Chapl K Coll Hosp Lon 63-66; V Aldwick *Chich* 66-76; V Brighton Gd Shep Preston 76-93; Can and Preb Chich Cathl 90-93; rtd 93; Hon C Stepney St Dunstan and All SS *Lon* from 94. *Flat 65, Telfords Yard, London E1W 2BQ* Tel (020) 7480 6585 E-mail jwhite.telford@virgin.net

WHITE, Howard Christopher Graham. b 43. Leeds Univ BA65. Coll of Resurr Mirfield 67. **d** 67 **p** 68. C Friern Barnet St Jas *Lon*

67-71; P-in-c Uxbridge Moor 71-73; Asst Chapl RADD 73-77; Hon C Corringham *Chelmsf* 73-77; Team Ldr St Sav Cen for the Deaf Acton 77-84; Perm to Offic *Guildf* 86-94 and *Chich* from 94. *Chez Nous, St Saviour's Hill, St Saviour, Jersey JE2 7LF*

WHITE, Hugh Richard Bevis. b 55. New Coll Ox BA78 Ox Univ DPhil85. S'wark Ord Course 93. **d** 96 **p** 97. NSM Westcote Barton w Steeple Barton, Duns Tew etc *Ox* 96-99; NSM Ox St Mary V w St Cross and St Pet 99-01; V Deddington w Barford, Clifton and Hempton from 01. *28 Duns Tew, Bicester OX25 6JR* Tel (01869) 347889

WHITE, Ian Jeffrey. b 57. Leeds Univ BSc80 PhD86 BA05 CChem83 MRSC83. Coll of Resurr Mirfield 03. **d** 05. C Stanningley St Thos *Ripon* from 05. *The Rectory, Stanningley Road, Stanningley, Pudsey LS28 6NB* Tel 0113-257 8966 E-mail ian@stanningleyparish.org.uk

WHITE, Ian Terence. b 56. CertEd. Ripon Coll Cuddesdon 83. **d** 86 **p** 87. C Maidstone St Martin *Cant* 86-89; C Earley St Pet *Ox* 89-91; TV Schorne 91-96; V St Osyth *Chelmsf* 96-00; V The Suttons w Tydd *Linc* 00-04; rtd 04. *The Vicarage, 41 Chapelgate, Sutton St James, Spalding PE12 0EE* Tel (01945) 440457 E-mail revianwhite@aol.com

WHITE, Jack Chapman. b 27. St Louis Univ BSc49 Univ of Cincinnati PhD82. **d** 54 **p** 55. USA 54-62 and 65-94; C St Louis H Trin 54-55; C St Louis Ascension 54-56; P-in-c 56-57; P-in-c St Louis St Andr 57; Chapl Utica Coll Syracuse Univ NY 57-58; Adv and Asst Chapl Barnard Coll Columbia Univ 58-62; Can Res American Cathl Paris 62-65; Chapl American Coll France 62-65; Chapl Howard Univ Washington DC 65-66; Dir Youth Services Piedmont 66-67; Chapl Whittle Par on the Plains VA 66-67; Assoc Min Washington DC St Thos 68-74; Tutor Gestalt Inst Gt Duck Is 75; Dir Speakers Bureau Nat Cathls Assn (NYC) from 78; Izmir (Smyrna) w Bornova *Eur* 95-96; rtd 96. *PK 148 Pasapor, Alfancak, Izmir, Turkey 35220*

WHITE, Miss Janice. b 49. Trin Coll Bris IDC76. **d** 91 **p** 94. C Claygate *Guildf* 91-98; Assoc Min Stanford-le-Hope w Mucking *Chelmsf* from 98. *Glebe House, Wharf Road, Stanford-le-Hope SS17 0BY* Tel (01375) 645542

WHITE, Jeremy Spencer. b 54. St Luke's Coll Ex BEd78. Wycliffe Hall Ox 81. **d** 84 **p** 85. C S Molton w Nymet St George, High Bray etc *Ex* 84-87; TV 87-95; V Sway *Win* 95-00; P-in-c Uplyme w Axmouth *Ex* 00-03; R from 03. *The Rectory, Rhode Lane, Uplyme, Lyme Regis DT7 3TX* Tel (01297) 443256

WHITE, Jo. *See* WHITE, Julia Mary

WHITE, Canon John Austin. b 42. LVO04. Hull Univ BA64. Coll of Resurr Mirfield 64. **d** 66 **p** 67. C Leeds St Aid *Ripon* 66-69; Asst Chapl Leeds Univ 69-73; Chapl N Ord Course 73-82; Can and Prec Windsor from 82. *4 The Cloisters, Windsor Castle, Windsor SL4 1NJ* Tel (01753) 848787 E-mail john.white@stgeorges-windsor.org

WHITE, John Christopher. b 62. Keble Coll Ox BA84. Wycliffe Hall Ox 86. **d** 89 **p** 90. C Southway *Ex* 89-93; TV Plymouth Em, St Paul Efford and St Aug 93-99; Hon C Abbotskerswell from 99. *The Vicarage, Church Path, Abbotskerswell, Newton Abbot TQ12 5NY* Tel (01626) 334445 E-mail johnwhite@fish.co.uk

WHITE, John Cooper. b 58. LTCL79 K Alfred's Coll Win BEd82 Lon Univ MA92 FRSA94. St Steph Ho Ox 86. **d** 89 **p** 90. C Christchurch *Win* 89-93; P-in-c Bournemouth St Alb 93-94; V 94-00; P-in-c Southbourne St Kath 00-04; V from 04. *St Katharine's Vicarage, 7 Wollaston Road, Bournemouth BH6 4AR* Tel (01202) 423986 E-mail stkathnic@btinternet.com

WHITE, Canon John Francis. b 47. Qu Coll Cam BA69 MA73. Cuddesdon Coll 72. **d** 72 **p** 73. Sacr Wakef Cathl *Wakef* 72-73; Prec 73-76; V Thurlstone 76-82; P-in-c Hoyland Swaine 81-82; V Chapelthorpe from 82; RD Chevet from 96; Hon Can Wakef Cathl from 00. *The Vicarage, 3 Church Lane, Chapelthorpe, Wakefield WF4 3JF* Tel (01924) 255360 E-mail john@white3.demon.co.uk

WHITE, John Malcolm. b 54. Aston Univ BSc77. Trin Coll Bris BA87. **d** 87 **p** 88. C Harborne Heath *Birm* 87-91; C S Harrow St Paul *Lon* 91-93; TV Roxeth 93-96; V Derby St Alkmund and St Werburgh *Derby* from 96. *The Vicarage, 200 Duffield Road, Derby DE22 1BL* Tel and fax (01332) 348339

WHITE, John McKelvey. b 57. QUB BA TCD DipTh82. **d** 82 **p** 83. C Clooney *D & R* 82-84; C Belfast H Trin *Conn* 84-86; I Kilcronaghan w Draperstown and Sixtowns *D & R* 86-94; I Ballybeen *D & D* 94-04; I Lurgan St Jo from 04. *St John's Rectory, Sloan Street, Lurgan, Craigavon BT66 8NT* Tel (028) 3832 2770

WHITE, Canon John Neville. b 41. Edin Univ MA63. Cranmer Hall Dur DipTh65. **d** 65 **p** 66. C Sedgefield *Dur* 65-68; C Stoke *Cov* 68-72; V Wrose *Bradf* 72-90; V Farsley from 90; RD Calverley 93-98; Hon Can Bradf Cathl from 96. *The Vicarage, 9 St John's Avenue, Farsley, Pudsey LS28 5DN* Tel 0113-257 4009

WHITE, John William. b 37. CEng71 MIMechE71. St Alb and Ox Min Course 98. **d** 01 **p** 02. NSM Sandhurst *Ox* from 01. *21 Broom Acres, Sandhurst GU47 8PN* Tel (01344) 774349

WHITE (née REDMAN), Mrs Julia Elizabeth Hithersay. b 43. St Alb Minl Tr Scheme 87 St Alb and Ox Min Course 99. **d** 99 **p** 00. NSM Harpenden St Jo *St Alb* from 99. *The Folly, 71 Station Road, Harpenden AL5 4RL* Tel (01582) 763869

WHITE, Julia Mary (Jo). b 52. Harris Coll CertEd73 Man Univ BEd85 MEd87 PhD92. N Ord Course 00. **d** 03 **p** 04. C Ashbourne w Mapleton *Derby* from 03. *12 Meynell Rise, Ashbourne DE6 1RU* Tel (01335) 346446 E-mail jo@whiteshouse.plus.net

WHITE, Julian Edward Llewellyn. b 53. St D Coll Lamp BA79 Bp Burgess Hall Lamp 73 Chich Th Coll 79. **d** 79 **p** 80. C Newport St Mark *Mon* 79-83; TV Llanmartin 83-86; R Llandogo and Tintern 86-90 and 91-98; P-in-c St Paul and St Thos St Kitts-Nevis 90-91; V Mathern and Mounton w St Pierre from 98; AD Netherwent from 05. *St Tewdric's Vicarage, Mathern, Chepstow NP16 6JA* Tel (01291) 622317

WHITE, Justin Michael. b 70. Keble Coll Ox MEng93 Warwick Univ MA94 Trin Coll Cam BA00. Westcott Ho Cam 98. **d** 01 **p** 02. C Chippenham St Andr w Tytherton Lucas *Bris* 01-04; Chapl SS Helen and Kath Sch Abingdon from 04. *62 Sadlers Court, Abingdon OX14 2PA* Tel (01235) 521876 Mobile 07866-073023 E-mail jwhite9243@aol.com

WHITE, Keith. b 54. Liv Poly BA78 Lon Univ BD82. Wycliffe Hall Ox 78. **d** 81 **p** 82. C Edin St Thos *Edin* 81-84; C Fulwood *Sheff* 84-87; R Heigham H Trin *Nor* 87-95; Zimbabwe 95-97; V Ipswich St Jo *St E* from 97. *St John's Vicarage, Cauldwell Hall Road, Ipswich IP4 4QE* Tel (01473) 728034 E-mail keith@whites10.freeserve.co.uk

WHITE, Kenneth Charles. b 26. Tyndale Hall Bris 48. **d** 54 **p** 56. Uganda 54-55; Kenya 55-57; C Morden *S'wark* 57-60; V Ramsey St Mary's w Ponds Bridge *Ely* 60-66; V Leyton Ch Ch *Chelmsf* 66-81; V Totland Bay *Portsm* 81-91; rtd 91; Perm to Offic *Llan* from 91. *30 Pendwyallt Road, Whitchurch, Cardiff CF14 7EG* Tel (029) 2061 1529

WHITE, Malcolm Robert. b 46. Man Univ BSc68. St Jo Coll Dur 74. **d** 77 **p** 78. C Linthorpe *York* 77-81; C Sutton St Jas and Wawne 81-83; V Upper Holloway St Pet w St Jo *Lon* 83-95; TV Burnham w Dropmore, Hitcham and Taplow *Ox* 95-00; CMS Jordan from 00. *CMS, Partnership House, 157 Waterloo Road, London SE1 8UU* Tel (020) 7803 3318 Fax 7401 3215 E-mail malcolm@sleepy-hollow.freeserve.co.uk

WHITE, Marilyn Jeanne. b 32. Avery Hill Coll CertEd69. WMMTC 85. **d** 88 **p** 94. NSM Westbury-on-Severn w Flaxley and Blaisdon *Glouc* 88-98; Perm to Offic *B & W* from 98. *4 Minster Way, Bath BA2 6RQ* Tel (01225) 464450

WHITE (née DUNCOMBE), Mrs Maureen Barbara. b 42. Bris Univ BA63 Ox Univ DipEd64. Oak Hill Th Coll 87. **d** 89 **p** 00. NSM Wallington H Trin *S'wark* 89-91; Perm to Offic *Win* 99-00; NSM Totton from 00. *Meadowsweet, 132 Woodlands Road, Ashurst, Southampton SO40 7AP* Tel (023) 8029 2309 Mobile 07712-418224 E-mail meadowsweet@tiscali.co.uk

WHITE, Michael Godfrey. b 46. St Alb and Ox Min Course 98. **d** 02 **p** 03. OLM Shelswell *Ox* from 02. *11 Hardwick, Bicester OX27 8SS* Tel (01869) 278157 E-mail mike.doreenwhite@ntlworld.com

WHITE, Nicolas John. b 54. BEd. Wycliffe Hall Ox. **d** 83 **p** 84. C Islington St Mary *Lon* 83-87; Chapl Univ Coll 87-89. *36 Castelnau, London SW13 9RU*

WHITE, Patrick George Hilliard. Toronto Univ BA67 DMin93. Wycliffe Coll Toronto MDiv77. **d** 77 **p** 78. Canada 77-97; Bermuda from 97. *St John's Rectory, 15 Langton Hill, Pembroke HM 13, Bermuda*

✠**WHITE, The Rt Revd Paul Raymond.** b 49. Canberra Coll BTh86 DipMin87 Heythrop Coll Lon MTh89. St Mark's Coll Canberra 85. **d** 85 **p** 86 **c** 01. Australia 85-87, 89-92 and from 97; C N Goulburn 85-87; P-in-c Reigate St Phil *S'wark* 87-89; R Queanbeyan 89-92; V Redhill St Matt 92-97; V E Ivanhoe St Geo 97-00; Dir Th Educn from 00; Asst Bp Melbourne (W Region) from 01. *28, 43-51 Jeffcott Street, West Melbourne, Vic, Australia 3003* Tel (0061) (3) 9640 0163 *or* 9653 4220 Fax 9650 2184 E-mail pwhite@melbourne.anglican.com.au

WHITE, Peter Francis. b 27. St Edm Hall Ox BA51 MA55. Ridley Hall Cam 51. **d** 53 **p** 54. C Drypool St Columba *York* 53-56; V Dartford St Edm *Roch* 56-62; CF 62-78; R Barming *Roch* 78-89; rtd 89; Perm to Offic *Wakef* 89-98. *Middleton House Cottage, Middleton on the Hill, Ludlow SY8 4BE* Tel (01568) 750454

WHITE, Peter John. b 26. St Aid Birkenhead 57. **d** 60 **p** 61. C Toxteth Park St Gabr *Liv* 60-62; C Huyton St Mich 62-63; V Thornham w Gravel Hole *Man* 63-68; C Keighley *Bradf* 68-71; C Newington w Dairycoates *York* 71-75; C Frodingham *Linc* 75-80; R Mareham-le-Fen and Revesby 80-86; V Wrawby 86-91; V Melton Ross w New Barnetby 86-91; rtd 91; Perm to Offic *Linc* 91-95 and *Wakef* from 96. *3 Park Avenue, Wakefield WF2 8DS* Tel (01924) 201438

WHITE, Philip Craston. b 59. York Univ BA81 Nottm Univ PGCE84. Trin Coll Bris DipTS99. **d** 99 **p** 00. C Countesthorpe w Foston *Leic* 99-03; C-in-c Hamilton CD from 03. *2 Cransley Close, Hamilton, Leicester LE5 1QQ*

WHITE, Philip William. b 53. Bede Coll Dur CertEd75 Coll of Ripon & York St Jo MA01. St Jo Coll Nottm DCM91. **d** 91

p 92. C Clifton *York* 91-95; TV Heworth H Trin 95-01; P-in-c Scarborough St Jas w H Trin from 01; Tr Officer E Riding from 01. *St James's Vicarage, 24 Seamer Road, Scarborough YO12 4DT* Tel (01723) 361469 Mobile 07720-010066 E-mail phil@vicarage.netkonect.co.uk

WHITE, Canon Phillip George. b 33. Univ of Wales (Lamp) BA54. St Mich Coll Llan 54. **d** 56 **p** 57. C Tongwynlais *Llan* 56-58; C Mountain Ash 58-60; C Aberavon 60-62; Area Sec (Middx) CMS 62-64; V Treherbert *Llan* 64-76; P-in-c Treorchy 75-76; V Treherbert w Treorchy 76-77; V Pyle w Kenfig 77-99; RD Margam 86-99; Can Llan Cathl from 91; rtd 99. *8 Heol Fair, Porthcawl CF36 5LA* Tel (01656) 786297

WHITE, Mrs Priscilla Audrey. b 62. St Hugh's Coll Ox BA84 MA88. Wycliffe Hall Ox 87. **d** 89 **p** 94. Par Dn Southway *Ex* 89-93; NSM Plymouth Em, St Paul Efford and St Aug 93-99; P-in-c Abbotskerswell from 99. *The Vicarage, Church Path, Abbotskerswell, Newton Abbot TQ12 5NY* Tel (01626) 334445 E-mail priscillawhite@fish.co.uk

WHITE, Richard Alfred. b 49. DipSW CQSW. St Jo Coll Nottm. **d** 90 **p** 91. C Leic St Phil *Leic* 90-95; C Old Dalby and Nether Broughton 95-98; R Ibstock w Heather from 98. *The Rectory, 2 Hinckley Road, Ibstock LE67 6PB* Tel (01530) 260246 E-mail rwhite@leicester.anglican.org

WHITE, Richard Allen. b 25. Open Univ BA78 Southn Univ MPhil88 MTh95. Sarum & Wells Th Coll 78. **d** 81 **p** 82. NSM Bursledon *Win* 81-85; C W End 85-90; C Fareham SS Pet and Paul *Portsm* 90-95; Chapl St Chris Hosp Fareham 92-98; rtd 96; Perm to Offic *Portsm* and *Win* from 96. *11 Quay Haven, Swanwick, Southampton SO31 7DE* Tel (01489) 576529

WHITE, Richard Stanley. b 70. Trin Coll Bris BA02. **d** 03. C Haydock St Mark *Liv* from 03. *303 Park Street, Haydock, St Helens WA11 0BG* Tel (01744) 634026 E-mail richardwhite@stmarkshaydock.org

WHITE, Rick. *See* WHITE, Douglas Richard Leon

WHITE, Canon Robert Bruce. b 42. Sarum & Wells Th Coll 71. **d** 73 **p** 74. C Woodford St Barn *Chelmsf* 73-75; Youth Chapl 75-79; C-in-c Sutton 75-78; P-in-c 78-79; C-in-c Shopland 75-78; P-in-c 78-79; TR Southend St Jo w St Mark, All SS w St Fran etc 79-82; P-in-c Southend St Alb 80-82; TR Southend 82-89; P-in-c Brentwood St Thos from 89; RD Brentwood from 93; Hon Can Chelmsf Cathl from 97; Chapl NE Lon Mental Health Tr from 97. *The Vicarage, 91 Queen's Road, Brentwood CM14 4EY* Tel (01277) 225700 E-mail pilgrimclub@aol.com

WHITE, Canon Robert Charles. b 61. Mansf Coll Ox BA83. St Steph Ho Ox 83. **d** 85 **p** 86. C Forton *Portsm* 85-88; C Portsea N End St Mark 88-92; V Warren Park 92-00; P-in-c Leigh Park 94-96; V 96-00; Hon Can Portsm Cathl from 97; RD Havant 98-00; V Portsea St Mary from 00. *St Mary's Vicarage, Fratton Road, Portsmouth PO1 5PA* Tel (023) 9282 2687 *or* 9282 2990 Fax 9235 9320 E-mail revrcwhite@aol.com

WHITE, The Ven Robin Edward Bantry. b 47. TCD BA70 BD79. CITC 72. **d** 72 **p** 73. C Dublin Zion Ch *D & G* 72-76; Min Can St Patr Cathl Dublin 76-79; C Taney Ch Ch *D & G* 76-79; I Abbeystrewry Union *C, C & R* 79-89; I Douglas Union w Frankfield 89-02; I Moviddy Union from 02; Can Cork Cathl from 89; Can Ross Cathl 89-93; Adn Cork, Cloyne and Ross from 93. *Moviddy Rectory, Aherla, Co Cork, Irish Republic* Tel (00353) (21) 733 1511 Mobile 87-286 2178 E-mail archdeacon@cork.anglican.org

WHITE, Roderick Harry. b 55. Trin Coll Bris BA86. **d** 86 **p** 87. C Northampton St Giles *Pet* 86-89; C Godley cum Newton Green *Ches* 89-93; P-in-c 93-99; R Northiam *Chich* from 99. *The Rectory, 24 High Meadow, Northiam, Rye TN31 6GA* Tel (01797) 253118

WHITE, Roger David. b 37. Univ of Wales (Cardiff) BTh91. St Mich Coll Llan DipTh66. **d** 66 **p** 67. C Mountain Ash *Llan* 66-71; C Port Talbot St Theodore 71-74; V Caerhun w Llangelynin *Ban* 74-85; R Llanbedrog w Llannor w Llanfihangel etc 85-88; V Llangeinor *Llan* 88-90; V Spittal w Trefgarn and Ambleston w St Dogwells *St D* 90-98; V Abergwili w Llanfihangel-uwch-Gwili etc 98-00; rtd 00. *Tir Na Nog, 18 Bryn Cir, Llanerchymedd LL71 8EG* Tel (01248) 470159

WHITE, Roger Ian Scott. b 41. Leeds Univ BA62 Culham Coll Ox PGCE70. Coll of Resurr Mirfield 62. **d** 64 **p** 65. C Wotton-under-Edge *Glouc* 64-69; NSM Rugby St Andr *Cov* 71-80; W Germany 80-82; P-in-c Brinklow *Cov* 82-86; R 86-90; P-in-c Harborough Magna 82-86; R 86-90; P-in-c Monks Kirby w Pailton and Stretton-under-Fosse 82-86; V 86-90; Germany 90-92; V Lydgate w Friezland *Man* 92-01; Chapl Hamburg *Eur* from 01. *Englische Planke 1A, 20459 Hamburg, Germany* Tel (0049) (40) 439 2334 E-mail st.thomas.becket@t-online.de

✠**WHITE, The Rt Revd Roger John.** b 41. Eden Th Sem (USA) BA65 Seabury-Western Th Sem Hon DCL86 Kelham Th Coll. **d** 66 **p** 67 **c** 84. C Manston *Ripon* 66-69; USA from 69; R Alton St Paul 72-80; R Indianapolis Trin Ch 80-84; Bp Milwaukee 84-03; rtd 03. *700 Waters Edge Road, #25, Racine, WI 53402, USA* Tel (001) (262) 752 1415 Mobile 414-630 2883 Fax (262) 752 1514 E-mail rjwhite787@aol.com

WHITE, Ronald Henry. b 36. Bris Univ BSc58. SW Minl Tr Course 82. **d** 85 **p** 86. C Ivybridge *Ex* 85-87; C Ivybridge w Harford 87-88; V Blackawton and Stoke Fleming 88-95; V Stoke Fleming, Blackawton and Strete 95-00; RD Woodleigh 95-99; rtd 00; Perm to Offic *Ex* from 02. *10 Hollingarth Way, Hemyock, Cullompton EX15 3XB* Tel (01823) 681020

WHITE, Canon Roy Sidney. b 34. Sarum Th Coll 62. **d** 65 **p** 66. C Selsdon *Cant* 65-68; C Ranmoor *Sheff* 68-72; V Croydon St Andr *Cant* 72-78; Dir Abp Coggan Tr Cen 78-85; Dir of Chr Stewardship *S'wark* 85-91; Hon Can S'wark Cathl 85-91; Can Res S'wark Cathl 91-99; Vice Provost S'wark 91-99; rtd 99; Perm to Offic *Cant* from 00. *11 Beach Avenue, Birchington CT7 9JS* Tel (01843) 843414

WHITE, Mrs Ruth Anna. b 45. Aoyama Gakuin Tokyo BA68 Grenoble Univ. Westmr Coll Cam 83 EAMTC 98. **d** 99 **p** 00. NSM Leyton St Mary w St Edw and St Luke *Chelmsf* 99-03; NSM Leytonstone St Jo from 03; Asst Chapl among deaf and deaf-blind people from 99. *18A Barclay Road, London E11 3DG* Tel and fax (020) 8558 5692 Mobile 07960-580837 E-mail ruthwhite@surefish.co.uk

WHITE, Mrs Sally Margaret. b 59. Univ of Wales (Cardiff) BTh01. St Mich Coll Llan 99. **d** 01 **p** 02. C Berkeley w Wick, Breadstone, Newport, Stone etc *Glouc* 01-05; Co-ord Chapl HM Pris Bedf from 05. *HM Prison, St Loyes Street, Bedford MK40 1HG* Tel (01234) 358671 *or* 373000 ext 3053

WHITE, Sandy Dulcie. b 44. LNSM course 95. **d** 98 **p** 99. OLM W Streatham St Jas *S'wark* from 98. *242 Mitcham Lane, London SW16 6NU* Tel (020) 8677 9487

WHITE, Mrs Sheelagh Mary. NEOC 02. **d** 05. C Heworth St Alb *Dur* from 05. *28 Avenue Road, Gateshead NE8 4JD*

WHITE, Simon Inigo Dexter. b 58. York Univ BA80 Nottm Univ PGCE81. St Jo Coll Nottm 87. **d** 90 **p** 91. C Chadkirk *Ches* 90-94; C Stockport St Geo 94; TV Stockport SW 94-99; Chapl Stockport Gr Sch 94-99; P-in-c W Hallam and Mapperley *Derby* 99-02; P-in-c Stanley 99-02; R W Hallam and Mapperley w Stanley from 02. *The Rectory, The Village, West Hallam, Ilkeston DE7 6GR* Tel 0115-932 4695

WHITE, Simon James Hithersay. b 65. St Jo Coll Nottm 01. **d** 03 **p** 04. C Alnwick *Newc* from 03. *65 Allerburn Lea, Alnwick NE66 2NQ* Tel (01665) 510677 E-mail simonjhwhite@breathemail.net

WHITE, The Very Revd Stephen Ross. b 58. Hull Univ BA79 QUB DPhil93. Ripon Coll Cuddesdon BA84. **d** 85 **p** 86. C Redcar *York* 85-88; P-in-c Gweedore, Carrickfin and Templecrone *D & R* 88-92; Bp's Dom Chapl 91-92; Dean Raphoe 92-02; I Raphoe w Raymochy and Clonleigh 93-01; Dean Killaloe and Clonfert *L & K* from 02. *The Deanery, Killaloe, Co Clare, Irish Republic* Tel (00353) (61) 376687 E-mail dean@killaloe.anglican.org

WHITE, Mrs Susan Margaret. b 48. Univ of E Lon BA84 Brunel Univ MBA94 Anglia Poly Univ MA04. EAMTC 01. **d** 04 **p** 05. C Harwich Peninsula *Chelmsf* from 04. *19 Beacon Hill Avenue, Harwich CO12 3NR* Tel (01255) 240886 E-mail suewhite712@hotmail.com

WHITE, Sister Teresa Joan. b 36. Wellesley Coll (USA) BA58 Harvard Univ STB61 Lon Univ CertEd74 Hon DD86. **dss** 75 **d** 87 **p** 94. CSA from 72; Teacher Burlington-Danes Sch 74-76; Lect Inst of Chr Studies *Lon* 76-78; Gen Sec World Congress of Faiths 77-81; Lect Dioc Readers' Course *S'wark* 81-89; Asst Abp's Sec for Ecum Affairs 81-82; Ed *Distinctive Diaconate* from 81; Ed *DIAKONIA News* 87-03; Ed *Distinctive News of Women in Ministry* from 94; Lic to Offic *Lon* from 94; Chapl Angl Communion Office from 04. *St Andrew's House, 16 Tavistock Crescent, London W11 1AP* Tel and fax (020) 7221 4604 E-mail sister.teresa@london.anglican.org

WHITE, Trevor John. b 37. St Pet Coll Ox BA61 MA65 Lon Univ BD92. Wycliffe Hall Ox 61. **d** 63 **p** 64. C Walsall *Lich* 63-67; V Greasbrough *Sheff* 67-73; Chapl Nat Nautical Sch Portishead 73-82; Chapl Bris Cathl Sch 82-00; rtd 00; Perm to Offic *B & W* from 82 and *Bris* from 00. *4 Gardner Road, Portishead, Bristol BS20 7ER* Tel (01275) 847855

WHITE, Canon Vernon Philip. b 53. Clare Coll Cam BA75 MA79 Oriel Coll Ox MLitt80. Wycliffe Hall Ox. **d** 77 **p** 78. Tutor Wycliffe Hall Ox 77-83; Chapl and Lect Ex Univ 83-87; R Wotton and Holmbury St Mary *Guildf* 87-93; Dir of Ords 87-93; Can Res and Chan Linc Cathl *Linc* 93-01; Prin STETS from 01. *19 The Close, Salisbury SP1 2EE* Tel (01722) 424804 *or* 424820 E-mail vpwhite@stets.ac.uk

WHITE, William Frederick. b 30. St Jo Coll Nottm. **d** 02. NSM Hillingdon St Jo *Lon* from 02; Asst Chapl Hillingdon Hosp NHS Trust from 02. *31A Copperfield Avenue, Hillingdon, Uxbridge UB8 3NU* Tel (01895) 236746 *or* 279433 E-mail billwhite2001@btinternet.com

WHITE, William John. b 54. BSc. Wycliffe Hall Ox. **d** 84 **p** 85. C Bowdon *Ches* 84-87; C Chadkirk 87-90; R Wistaston from 90; RD Nantwich 98-01. *The Rectory, 44 Church Lane, Wistaston, Crewe CW2 8HA* Tel (01270) 665742 *or* 567119 E-mail billwhite@beeb.net

WHITE SPUNNER, Mrs Jessie Janet. b 37. SRN59 SCM61. CITC 91. **d** 94 **p** 95. NSM Shinrone w Aghancon etc *L & K* from 94. *Milltown Park, Shinrone, Birr, Co Offaly, Irish Republic* Tel and fax (00353) (505) 47035
E-mail shinrone@killaloe.anglican.org *or* janwspun@iol.ie

WHITEFIELD, Keith Russell. b 60. Aber Univ MA83 PhD91 Edin Univ BD91. Edin Th Coll 88. **d** 91 **p** 93. C Haddington *Edin* 91-94; C Dunbar 91-94; Miss P Wester Hailes St Luke from 94. *35/5 Wester Hailes Park, Edinburgh EH14 3AG*
E-mail keith.whitefield@cableinet.co.uk

WHITEHEAD, Alexander. *See* WHITEHEAD, Canon Matthew Alexander

WHITEHEAD, Barry. b 30. Oriel Coll Ox BA53 MA62. St Steph Ho Ox 53. **d** 55 **p** 56. C Edgehill St Dunstan *Liv* 55-58; C Upholland 58-61; Ind Chapl 61-90; CF (TA) 64-78; V Aspull *Liv* 77-96; rtd 96; Perm to Offic *Blackb* and *Liv* from 96; *Nor* from 01. *5 Sedgely, Standish, Wigan WN6 0BZ* Tel (01257) 427160

WHITEHEAD, Brian. b 36. SRN58. S'wark Ord Course 72. **d** 75 **p** 77. C Croydon St Aug *Cant* 75-78; C St Marychurch *Ex* 78-80; V Devonport St Mark Ford 80-87; V Castle Donington and Lockington cum Hemington *Leic* 87-98; Chapl Asmara St Geo Eritrea 98-99; Vice Provost All SS Cathl Cairo 99-00; Assoc P Abu Dhabi 00-01; rtd 01; Perm to Offic *Nor* from 01. *10 Bluebell Gardens, Wells-next-the-Sea NR23 1JJ* Tel (01328) 711139
E-mail britone@uk.packardbell.org

WHITEHEAD, Christopher Martin Field. b 36. ALCD62. **d** 62 **p** 63. C Higher Openshaw *Man* 62-63; C Halliwell St Pet 64-66; V Owlerton *Sheff* 66-75; V Hunmanby w Muston *York* 75-95; RD Scarborough 91-94; R Lockington and Lund and Scorborough w Leconfield 95-01; rtd 01; Perm to Offic *York* from 01. *59 Cornelian Drive, Scarborough YO11 3AL* Tel (01723) 377837

WHITEHEAD, Canon Derek. b 27. St Jo Coll Cam BA50 MA55 Lon Univ BD60 Lanc Univ PhD73. Wells Th Coll 55. **d** 56 **p** 57. C Lower Broughton Ascension *Man* 56-59; Chapl Highgate Sch Lon 63-65; Lect Div Preston Poly 65-79; Dir of Educn *Chich* 79-94; rtd 94; P-in-c Fletching *Chich* 93-03; Can and Preb Chich Cathl 82-98. *2 Sheffield Park House, Uckfield TN22 3QY* Tel (01825) 790734

WHITEHEAD, Frederick Keith. b 35. K Coll Lon BD58 AKC58. St Boniface Warminster 58. **d** 59 **p** 60. C S Shore H Trin *Blackb* 59-63; C Whitfield *Derby* 63-66; Lic to Offic 66-93; V Glossop 93-98; Chapl Shire Hill Hosp Glossop 93-99; rtd 99; Perm to Offic *Derby* from 98. *7 Badgers Way, Glossop SK13 6PP* Tel (01457) 852717

WHITEHEAD, Gordon James. b 42. Clifton Th Coll 66. **d** 73 **p** 74. Chile 73-87; C Coleraine *Conn* 87-94; I Errigle Keerogue w Ballygawley and Killeshil *Arm* 94-02; I Bright w Ballee and Killough *D & D* from 02. *Bright Rectory, 126 Killough Road, Downpatrick BT30 8LL* Tel (028) 4484 2229 Fax 4484 2766
E-mail whiteheads@bigfoot.com *or* bright@down.anglican.org

WHITEHEAD, Canon Hazel. b 54. K Coll Lon BD76 AKC76 Lon Univ CertTESOL89 Lambeth MA97. Oak Hill Th Coll 93. **d** 94 **p** 95. Tutor Dioc Min Course *Guildf* 94-96; Prin 96-05; C Oatlands 95-04; Dioc Dir Minl Tr from 05; Hon Can Guildf Cathl from 03. *The Vicarage, 5 Burwood Road, Walton-on-Thames KT12 4AA* Tel (01932) 269343 Fax 230274
E-mail hazel@guildforddmc.co.uk

WHITEHEAD, Ian Richard. b 63. St Jo Coll Nottm BA95. **d** 95 **p** 96. C Hillmorton *Cov* 95-97; C Whitnash 97-99; R Rolleston *Lich* from 99; V Anslow from 99. *The Rectory, Church Road, Rolleston-on-Dove, Burton-on-Trent DE13 9BE* Tel (01283) 810132 *or* 810151 E-mail revirwhite@aol.com

WHITEHEAD, Mrs Jennifer Jane. b 45. St Jo Coll York CertEd67. LNSM course 95. **d** 98 **p** 99. OLM Winterton Gp *Linc* from 98. *11 Queen Street, Winterton, Scunthorpe DN15 9TR* Tel (01724) 734027

WHITEHEAD, John Stanley. b 38. Jes Coll Cam BA63 MA67 MPhil. Westcott Ho Cam 63. **d** 64 **p** 65. C Batley All SS *Wakef* 64-67; C Mitcham St Mark *S'wark* 67-70; C Frindsbury w Upnor *Roch* 70-72; TV Strood 72-75; R Halstead 75-82; V Betley *Lich* 82-85; V Betley and Keele 85-01; Asst Chapl Keele Univ 82-01; rtd 01; Perm to Offic *Ches* from 02. *Paddock House, Longhill Lane, Hankelow, Crewe CW3 0JG* Tel (01270) 812607
E-mail john@whitehead400.freeserve.co.uk

WHITEHEAD, Canon Matthew Alexander. b 44. Leeds Univ BA65 St Chad's Coll Dur DipEd66 Birm Univ MA75. Qu Coll Birm DipTh68. **d** 69 **p** 70. C Bingley All SS *Bradf* 69-72; C Keele *Lich* 72-74; Asst Chapl Keele Univ 72-74; Bp's Dom Chapl *Dur* 74-80; V Escomb 74-80; V Witton Park 74-80; V Birtley 80-89; RD Chester-le-Street 84-89; V Stockton St Pet 89-00; V The Trimdons 00-03; Hon Can Dur Cathl 96-03; P-in-c Stow Gp *Linc* from 03; Dioc Warden of Readers from 03; Can and Preb Linc Cathl from 04. *The Rectory, Normanby Road, Stow, Lincoln LN1 2DF* Tel (01427) 788251
E-mail alexwhitehead@btopenworld.com

WHITEHEAD, Canon Michael Hutton. b 33. St Chad's Coll Dur 54. **d** 58 **p** 59. C Southwick St Columba *Dur* 58-64; V Hendon St Ignatius 64-70; P-in-c Sunderland 67-80; V Hendon 70-80; V Hendon and Sunderland 80-87; Hon Can Dur Cathl from 84; V Hartlepool St Aid 87-98; RD Hartlepool 91-95; rtd 98. *4 West Row, Greatham, Hartlepool TS25 2HW* Tel (01429) 872922

WHITEHEAD, Nicholas James. b 53. ACIB. Ridley Hall Cam 86. **d** 88 **p** 89. C Bourne *Guildf* 88-92; V Hersham from 92. *The Vicarage, 5 Burwood Road, Walton-on-Thames KT12 4AA* Tel (01932) 227445 Fax 230274
E-mail nick@nickhaze.demon.co.uk

WHITEHEAD, Paul Conrad. b 60. St Jo Coll Nottm LTh92. **d** 92 **p** 93. C Mansfield Woodhouse *S'well* 92-96; C Carlton-in-the-Willows 96-02; C Colwick 96-02; CF (TA) from 96; NSM Trowell, Awsworth and Cossall *S'well* from 04. *84 Hillside Road, Beeston, Nottingham NG9 3AT* Tel 0115-919 7030 Mobile 07973-727221 E-mail paulkirsten@ntlworld.com

WHITEHEAD, Philip. b 34. Kelham Th Coll 55. **d** 59 **p** 60. C Sugley *Newc* 59-62; C Alnwick St Paul 62-63; C Newc St Gabr 63-66; C Gosforth All SS 66-67; V Kenton Ascension 67-75; V Spittal 75-88; P-in-c Scremerston 81-88; V Cresswell and Lynemouth 88-96; Perm to Offic from 96; rtd 96. *13 Abbey Gate, Morpeth NE61 2XL* Tel (01670) 514953

WHITEHEAD, Robin Lawson. b 53. Bris Univ BA76 Lon Univ MA96. St Steph Ho Ox 77. **d** 80 **p** 81. C Cheshunt *St Alb* 80-83; C E Grinstead St Swithun *Chich* 83-85; V Friern Barnet St Pet le Poer *Lon* 85-92; R Friern Barnet St Jas 92-95; C Wood Green St Mich w Bounds Green St Gabr etc 96-97; TR Leic Resurr *Leic* 97-04; V Boston *Linc* from 04. *The Vicarage, Wormgate, Boston PE21 6NP* Tel (01205) 362992
E-mail robin@whitehead8606.fsnet.co.uk

WHITEHORN, Arthur Basil. b 24. Ox Univ MA50. WMMTC 81. **d** 84 **p** 85. NSM Bromsgrove St Jo *Worc* 84-94; Asst Chapl Bromsgrove and Redditch HA 84-89; Perm to Offic from 94. *15 Perry Lane, Bromsgrove B61 7JL* Tel (01527) 874857

WHITEHOUSE, Alan Edward. b 35. CEng66. Glouc Sch of Min 89. **d** 92 **p** 93. NSM Evesham *Worc* 92-96; NSM Evesham w Norton and Lenchwick 96-03; Perm to Offic from 03. *The Coppice, 56 Elm Road, Evesham WR11 3DW* Tel (01386) 442427 Fax 424334 E-mail alan.coppice@btopenworld.com

WHITEHOUSE, David Garner. b 70. Sheff Univ BEng91. EAMTC 03. **d** 05. NSM Cheadle *Ches* from 05. *1 Warren Avenue, Cheadle SK8 1NB* Tel 0161-428 3001

WHITEHOUSE, Nigel Andrew. b 57. St Mary's RC Sem Birm 75. **d** 80 **p** 81. In RC Ch 81-87; C Whittlesey and Pondersbridge *Ely* 92-94; P-in-c Newton 94-98; R 98-03; P-in-c Gorefield 94-98; V 98-03; P-in-c Tydd St Giles 94-98; R 98-03; TR Whittlesey, Pondersbridge and Coates from 03. *The Vicarage, St Mary's Street, Whittlesey, Peterborough PE7 1BG* Tel (01733) 203676
E-mail nigel.whitehouse@ntlworld.com

WHITEHOUSE, Canon Susan Clara. b 48. R Holloway Coll Lon BA70. Westcott Ho Cam 87. **d** 89 **p** 94. Par Dn Farnley *Ripon* 89-93; Dioc Development Rep from 92; C Bedale 93-96; C Thornton Watlass w Thornton Steward 93-96; V Aysgarth and Bolton cum Redmire from 96; Hon Can Ripon Cathl from 02; AD Wensley 03-05. *The Vicarage, Carperby, Leyburn DL8 4DQ* Tel (01969) 663235 E-mail suewhitehouse@carperby.fsnet.co.uk

WHITELEY, Donal Royston. b 27. Qu Coll Birm 54. **d** 57 **p** 58. C Handsworth St Mary *Birm* 57-60; C Kingswinford St Mary *Lich* 60-63; R Norton Canes 63-71; V Wetley Rocks 71-96; rtd 96; Perm to Offic *Derby* from 97. *7 Balmoral Road, Burton-on-Trent DE15 0JN* Tel (01283) 548312

WHITELEY, Canon Robert Louis. b 28. Leeds Univ BA48. Coll of Resurr Mirfield 50. **d** 52 **p** 53. C Hollinwood *Man* 52-55; Br Honduras 56-61; V Illingworth *Wakef* 61-68; V Westgate Common 68-75; Can Res Wakef Cathl 75-80; Hon Can Wakef Cathl 80-93; V Almondbury 80-82; TR Almondbury w Farnley Tyas 82-92; RD Almondbury 81-93; rtd 93; Perm to Offic *Wakef* from 93 and *Ox* from 98. *2 Woodclyffe Almshouses, Wargrave Hill, Wargrave, Reading RG10 8JH* Tel 0118-940 3877

WHITELOCK, Alfred Theodore. b 33. Bris Univ BTh58. Chich Th Coll 58. **d** 60 **p** 61. C Bris St Andr w St Bart *Bris* 60-62; USA from 69. *3025 Ivyland Road, Roanoke, VA 24014, USA* Tel (001) (540) 427 5073 E-mail pateral@yahoo.com

WHITELOCK, Mrs Susan Karen. b 62. STETS 98. **d** 01. NSM Portsea N End St Mark *Portsm* from 01. *404 Copnor Road, Portsmouth PO3 5EW* Tel 07903-414029 (mobile)

WHITEMAN, Canon Cedric Henry. b 28. Lich Th Coll 59. **d** 61 **p** 62. C Abington *Pet* 61-64; V Kettering St Andr 64-79; RD Kettering 73-79; Can Pet Cathl 77-79; V Rotherham *Sheff* 79-87; RD Rotherham 79-86; Hon Can Sheff Cathl 85-98; Bp's Dom Chapl 86-99; V Wentworth 87-91; rtd 91; Perm to Offic *Sheff* from 99. *11 Thornbrook Close, Chapeltown, Sheffield S35 2BB* Tel 0114-245 7479 E-mail cedric.whiteman@btinternet.com

WHITEMAN, Christopher Henry Raymond. b 51. Portsm Poly BA73 Worc Coll of Educn PGCE74 Open Univ BSc97. St Jo Coll Nottm DipTh90 MA99. **d** 90 **p** 91. C Rockland St Mary w Hellington, Bramerton etc *Nor* 90-93; P-in-c Gillingham w Geldeston, Stockton, Ellingham etc 93-94; R 94-04; R Culworth w Sulgrave and Thorpe Mandeville etc *Pet* from 04. *The Rectory, Queens Street, Culworth, Banbury OX17 2AT* Tel (01295) 760383

WHITEMAN, The Ven Rodney David Carter. b 40. Ely Th Coll 61. **d** 64 **p** 65. C Kings Heath *Birm* 64-70; V Rednal 70-79; V Erdington St Barn 79-89; RD Aston 81-86 and 88-89; Hon Can Birm Cathl 85-89; Adn Bodmin *Truro* 89-00; P-in-c Cardynham 89-94; P-in-c Helland 89-94; Hon Can Truro Cathl from 89; Adn Cornwall from 00. *Archdeacon's House, 3 Knights Hill, Kenwyn, Truro TR1 3UY* Tel (01872) 272866 Fax 242108 E-mail rodney@truro.anglican.org

WHITESIDE, Canon Peter George. b 30. St Cath Coll Cam BA55 MA61. Cuddesdon Coll 55. **d** 57 **p** 58. C Westmr St Steph w St Jo *Lon* 57-61; Chapl Clifton Coll Bris 61-70; Hd Master Linc Cathl Sch 71-73; Can and Preb Linc Cathl *Linc* 72-73; Australia 74-92; Prin and Chapl Wadhurst C of E Gr Sch 74-89; TV Brentford *Lon* 92-97; rtd 97. *c/o Mrs M Pretlove, 101 Camborne Road, Morden SM4 4JN*

WHITESIDE, Robert Henry. b 44. TCD BA67 MA71 HDipEd68. CITC 95. **d** 98 **p** 99. C Clonsast w Rathangan, Thomastown etc *M & K* 98-00; Chapl K Hosp Sch Dub from 00. *The King's Hospital, Palmerstown, Dublin 20, Irish Republic* Tel (00353) (1) 626 5933 Fax 623 0349

WHITFIELD, Charles. b 25. St Pet Hall Ox BA49 MA53. Ridley Hall Cam 49. **d** 51 **p** 52. C Ecclesfield *Sheff* 51-54; C Grassendale *Liv* 54-56; C Neasden cum Kingsbury St Cath *Lon* 56-58; C St Martin-in-the-Fields 58-59; V Bromley H Trin *Roch* 59-68; V Egg Buckland *Ex* 68-90; rtd 90; Perm to Offic *Ex* from 99. *23 Chapel Meadow, Buckland Monachorum, Yelverton PL20 7LR*

WHITFIELD, Joy Verity. *See* CHAPMAN, Mrs Joy Verity

WHITFIELD, Leslie Turnbull. b 43. Nottm Univ MA00 DipEE67 CEng72 MIEE72 DMS74 MCMI74. St Jo Coll Nottm 97. **d** 00 **p** 01. C Bottesford w Ashby *Linc* 00-03; P-in-c Mablethorpe w Trusthorpe from 03. *The Rectory, 88 Wellington Road, Mablethorpe LN12 1HT* Tel (01507) 473159 E-mail les.whitfield@ntlworld.com

WHITFIELD, Trevor. b 48. Bedf Coll Lon BSc71 Bris Univ PGCE73 Fitzw Coll Cam BA78 MA88. Ridley Hall Cam 76. **d** 79 **p** 80. C Battersea St Pet and St Paul *S'wark* 79-82; Chapl Stockholm w Uppsala *Eur* 82-83; C-in-c Roundshaw St Paul CD *S'wark* 83-89; Asst Chapl R Victoria Infirmary Newc 89-92; Asst Chapl Berne w Neuchâtel *Eur* 92-95; Chapl Utrecht w Amersfoort, Harderwijk and Zwolle 95-02; Chapl Maisons-Laffitte from 02. *15 avenue Carnot, 78600 Maisons-Laffitte, France* Tel (0033) (1) 39 63 34 97

WHITFIELD, William. b 47. Open Univ BA80 Univ of Wales (Cardiff) LLM95 FRSH81. STETS 01. **d** 04 **p** 05. NSM Marchwood *Win* from 04. *35 The Rowans, Marchwood, Southampton SO40 4YW* Tel (023) 8086 0399 E-mail wwhitfield60@hotmail.com

WHITFORD, Judith. *See* POLLINGER, Mrs Judith

WHITFORD (née FAULKNER), Mrs Margaret Evelyn. b 54. Goldsmiths' Coll Lon BEd77. EAMTC 98. **d** 01 **p** 02. C Grays Thurrock *Chelmsf* from 01. *The Rectory, Princess Margaret Road, East Tilbury, Tilbury RM18 8PB* Tel (01375) 840276 E-mail mrgrtfaulkner@aol.com

WHITFORD, William Laurence. b 56. Open Univ BA92 Liv Univ DipApTh96. N Ord Course 92. **d** 95 **p** 96. C Hindley All SS *Liv* 95-99; P-in-c E and W Tilbury and Linford *Chelmsf* 99-04; R from 04. *The Rectory, Princess Margaret Road, East Tilbury, Tilbury RM18 8PB* Tel (01375) 842220 E-mail laurence@whitfordw.freeserve.co.uk

WHITHAM, Ian Scott. b 66. Oak Hill Th Coll. **d** 01 **p** 02. C Yateley *Win* 01-03; C Yateley and Eversley from 03. *18 Hall Farm Crescent, Yateley GU46 7HT* Tel (01252) 647200 Mobile 07946-394467 E-mail ianwitham@yahoo.co.uk

WHITING, Antony Gerald Stroud. b 26. CITC 81. **d** 86 **p** 87. NSM Clonmel Union *C, C & R* 86-87; Cork St Fin Barre's Union 87-88; Lic to Offic 88-92; Bp's C Mallow Union 92-97; I 97-98; rtd 98. *Address temp unknown*

WHITING, Graham James. b 58. Bris Univ BSc81. Chich Th Coll 83. **d** 86 **p** 88. C Portslade St Nic and St Andr *Chich* 86-87; C W Tarring 87-91; C Seaford w Sutton 91-94; P-in-c Bournemouth St Clem *Win* 94-02; V Findon Valley *Chich* from 02. *The Vicarage, 29 Central Avenue, Worthing BN14 0DS* Tel (01903) 872900 E-mail graham.whiting@lineone.net

WHITING, Joseph Alfred. b 41. Oak Hill Th Coll 82. **d** 85 **p** 86. Hon C Sidcup St Andr *Roch* 85-88; C Southborough St Pet w Ch Ch and St Matt 88-92; C Aldridge *Lich* 92-97; TV Rye *Chich* 97-02; rtd 02. *71 Ash Tree Drive, West Kingsdown, Sevenoaks TN15 6LW* Tel (01474) 853202 E-mail joebarb@westking1.fsnet.co.uk

WHITING, Mark Justin Robert. b 70. St Steph Ho Ox 99. **d** 01 **p** 02. C Sevenoaks St Jo *Roch* 01-04; P-in-c Derby St Bart *Derby* from 04. *St Bartholomew's Vicarage, 49 Addison Road, Derby DE24 8FH* Tel and fax (01332) 347709 Mobile 07951-589024

WHITLEY, Eric Keir. b 47. Salford Univ BSc68. Trin Coll Bris 77. **d** 79 **p** 80. C Nottingham St Ann w Em *S'well* 79-83; V Donisthorpe and Moira w Stretton-en-le-Field *Leic* 83-91; V Thorpe Acre w Dishley 91-00; V Loughb Gd Shep from 00. *21 Parklands Drive, Loughborough LE11 2SZ* Tel (01509) 211005

WHITLEY, John Duncan Rooke. b 29. Trin Coll Cam BA51 MA55 Jordan Hill Coll Glas CertEd82. Coll of Resurr Mirfield 52. **d** 54 **p** 55. C Ashington *Newc* 54-59; C Chiswick St Nic w St Mary *Lon* 59-61; V Ware St Mary *St Alb* 61-71; Can Missr Edin 71-74; Chapl R Edin Hosp 71-74; Dioc Educn Officer *Edin* 71-74; Hon Asst Dioc Supernumerary from 74; Asst Chapl Lothian Primary Healthcare NHS Trust 95-04; Warrant from 99; TP Edin St Columba *Edin* from 99. *114 Viewforth, Edinburgh EH10 4LN* Tel and fax 0131-229 0130 Mobile 07774-402551 E-mail john.whitley@blueyonder.co.uk

WHITLEY, John William. b 46. TCD BA68. Cranmer Hall Dur BA71. **d** 71 **p** 72. C Belfast St Mary Magd *Conn* 71-73; C Toxteth St Philemon w St Gabr *Liv* 73-78; P-in-c Toxteth Park St Cleopas 78-88; TV Toxteth St Philemon w St Gabr and St Cleopas 89-95; P-in-c Litherland St Paul Hatton Hill 95-02; V from 02. *St Paul's Vicarage, Watling Avenue, Liverpool L21 9NU* Tel 0151-928 2705 E-mail anthea.whitley@virgin.net

WHITLEY (née ALLISON), Rosemary Jean. b 45. LTCL67. Trin Coll Bris 75 St Jo Coll Nottm 94. **d** 95 **p** 99. NSM Loughb Gd Shep *Leic* 95-98 and from 00; NSM Thorpe Acre w Dishley 98-00. *21 Parklands Drive, Loughborough LE11 2SZ* Tel (01501) 211005

WHITLOCK, Canon James Frederick. b 44. Ch Coll Cam BA75 MA78. Westcott Ho Cam 73. **d** 76 **p** 77. C Newquay *Truro* 76-79; P-in-c St Mawgan w St Ervan and St Eval 79-81; R 81; Bp's Dom Chapl 82-85; Dioc Dir of Ords 82-85; V Leagrave *St Alb* 85-89; TR Probus, Ladock and Grampound w Creed and St Erme *Truro* 89-95; V Penzance St Mary w St Paul 95-00; P-in-c Penzance St Jo 97-00; Hon Can Truro Cathl 98-00; rtd 00; Perm to Offic *Truro* from 00. *10 Barlandhu, Newlyn, Penzance TR18 5QT* Tel (01736) 330474

WHITMARSH, Mrs Pauline. **d** 04. OLM Bramshaw and Landford w Plaitford *Sarum* from 04. *Dovera, North Lane, Nomansland, Salisbury SP5 2BU* Tel (01794) 390534 E-mail plwhitmarsh@tiscali.co.uk

WHITMORE, Benjamin Nicholas. b 66. Imp Coll Lon BEng88. Cranmer Hall Dur 89. **d** 92 **p** 93. C Gt Wyrley *Lich* 92-95; C Hednesford 95-00; V Walsall Pleck and Bescot from 00; Hon C Walsall St Paul from 05; Hon C Walsall from 05. *St John's Vicarage, Vicarage Terrace, Walsall WS2 9HB* Tel (01922) 631989 E-mail bennyjo@vicres.fsnet.co.uk

WHITMORE, Edward James. b 36. Lon Univ BD66. Tyndale Hall Bris. **d** 68 **p** 69. Tanzania 68-76; Lic to Offic *Blackb* from 77. *74 Greencroft, Penwortham, Preston PR1 9LB* Tel (01772) 746522

WHITMORE, Miss Jane Frances. b 30. **dss** 79 **d** 87 **p** 94. Elloughton and Brough w Brantingham *York* 79-83; Foley Park *Worc* 83-87; C Frimley *Guildf* 87-96; rtd 96; Perm to Offic *Worc* from 96. *The Grange, 26 Middleton Road, Marlpool, Kidderminster DY11 5EY*

WHITMORE, Stephen Andrew. b 53. Sheff Univ BSc74. St Jo Coll Nottm 89. **d** 91 **p** 92. C Newbury *Ox* 91-95; TV High Wycombe from 95. *70 Marlow Road, High Wycombe HP11 1TH* Tel (01494) 438722 E-mail steve@stjohnschurch.freeserve.co.uk

WHITNALL, Robert Edward (Dominic). b 14. Magd Coll Ox BA37. Cuddesdon Coll 37. **d** 38 **p** 39. C Staveley *Derby* 38-44; CR from 47; S Africa 47-66; Hon C Battyeford *Wakef* from 68; rtd 84. *House of the Resurrection, Stocks Bank Road, Mirfield WF14 0BN* Tel (01924) 483335

WHITNEY, Charles Edward. b 46. Goldsmiths' Coll Lon BA71 TCert72 ACP75. WEMTC 01. **d** 04 **p** 05. NSM Tewkesbury w Walton Cardiff and Twyning *Glouc* from 04. *Sarn Hill Lodge, Bushley Green, Bushley, Tewkesbury GL20 6AD* Tel (01684) 296764

WHITTA, Rex Alfred Rought. b 28. Leeds Inst of Educn CertEd52 Open Univ BA88 Lon Univ CertTESOL89. Qu Coll Birm DipTh63. **d** 63 **p** 64. C Newland St Aug *York* 63-66; V Elloughton 66-68; P-in-c Brantingham 66-68; V Elloughton and Brough w Brantingham 68-74; TR Redcar w Kirkleatham 74-78; V Redcar 78-84; V Bassenthwaite, Isel and Setmurthy *Carl* 84-86; P-in-c Cloughton *York* 86-88; P-in-c Hackness w Harwood Dale 86-88; rtd 89; Perm to Offic *York* 89-03. *89 Uplands Avenue, Connah's Quay, Deeside CH5 4LF* Tel (01244) 831424 Mobile 07941-461823 E-mail whitta.rasl@virgin.net

WHITTAKER, Mrs Angela. b 68. Birm Univ BA89 St Martin's Coll Lanc PGCE91. NEOC 98. **d** 00 **p** 01. C Houghton le Spring *Dur* 00-04; TV Kirkby Lonsdale *Carl* from 04. *The Vicarage, Vicarage Lane, Kirkby Lonsdale, Carnforth LA6 2BA* Tel (01524) 272078

WHITTAKER, Brian Lawrence. b 39. Clifton Th Coll 63. **d** 66 **p** 67. C Whitton and Thurleston w Akenham *St E* 66-69; C Normanton *Wakef* 69-74; P-in-c Castle Hall and Dukinfield Ch Ch *Ches* 74-77; P-in-c Stalybridge H Trin and Ch Ch 74-77; V 77-83; TR Bucknall and Bagnall *Lich* 83-91; R Draycott-le-Moors w Forsbrook 91-05; rtd 05; Perm to Offic *Lich* from 05. *6 Rubens Way, Stoke-on-Trent ST3 7GQ* Tel (01782) 397765

WHITTAKER, Bryan. b 58. Southn Univ BTh82. Chich Th Coll 82. **d** 84 **p** 85. C Whitleigh *Ex* 84-88; C Corringham *Chelmsf* 88-92; V Rush Green 92-94. *361 Dagenham Road, Romford RM7 0XX*

WHITTAKER, Derek. b 30. OBE85. Liv Univ BEng51 PhD58 CEng65. **d** 93 **p** 95. Zambia 93-96; NSM Broom Leys *Leic* 97-00; rtd 00; Perm to Offic *Leic* from 00. *44 St David's Crescent, Coalville LE67 4SJ* Tel (01530) 831071

WHITTAKER, Edward Geoffrey. b 59. Birm Univ BSc82 Avery Hill Coll PGCE85 Dur Univ MA95. Westcott Ho Cam 97. **d** 99 **p** 00. C Neston *Ches* 99-02; V Rocester and Croxden w Hollington *Lich* from 02; RD Uttoxeter from 04. *The Vicarage, Church Lane, Rocester, Uttoxeter ST14 5JZ* Tel (01889) 590424

WHITTAKER, Garry. b 59. St Jo Coll Nottm 89. **d** 91 **p** 92. C Denton Ch Ch *Man* 91-95; P-in-c Waterhead 95-05; V Bacup and Stacksteads from 05. *10 Park Crescent, Bacup OL13 9RL* Tel (01706) 873362

WHITTAKER, James Rawstron. b 14. Worc Coll Ox BA38 MA46. Wells Th Coll 38. **d** 40 **p** 41. C York St Mary Bishophill Senior *York* 40-43; Hornsea w Bewholme 43-47; R Neen Sollars w Milson *Heref* 47-55; V Annscroft 55-70; R Pontesbury III 55-70; V Longden 55-70; V Almeley 70-80; P-in-c Kinnersley w Norton Canon 74-80; rtd 81; Perm to Offic *Heref* from 82. *Eign Gate House, 142 Eign Street, Hereford HR4 0AP* Tel (01432) 268961

WHITTAKER, Mrs Jennifer Margaret. b 43. Glas Univ MA64. St Alb and Ox Min Course 00. **d** 03 **p** 04. NSM Martley and Wichenford, Knightwick etc *Worc* from 03. *The Key Barn, Half Key, Malvern WR14 1UP* Tel (01886) 833897 E-mail jenniferwhittaker@virgin.net

WHITTAKER, Jeremy Paul. b 59. Ox Univ MA. Ripon Coll Cuddesdon 82. **d** 84 **p** 85. C Crowthorne *Ox* 84-87; C Westborough *Guildf* 87-88; TV 88-91; Chapl Pierrepont Sch Frensham 91-95; Perm to Offic *Guildf* from 95. *6 Springhaven Close, Guildford GU1 2JP*

WHITTAKER, Canon John. b 20. Ch Coll Cam BA47 MA49. Ridley Hall Cam 46. **d** 48 **p** 49. C Astley Bridge *Man* 48-51; C Kersal Moor 51-53; R Birch St Agnes 53-66; V New Bury 66-75; Hon Can Man Cathl 71-87; R Middleton 75-87; rtd 87; Perm to Offic *Man* from 87. *5 Farnborough Road, Bolton BL1 7HJ* Tel (01204) 595499

WHITTAKER, John. b 27. Oak Hill Th Coll 53. **d** 55 **p** 56. C Blackpool St Thos *Blackb* 55-57; C St Helens St Helen *Liv* 58-60; V Hensingham *Carl* 60-67; V Skelmersdale St Paul *Liv* 67-77; V Gt Faringdon w Lt Coxwell *Ox* 77-83; RD Vale of White Horse 80-83; rtd 83; Perm to Offic *Ox* 83-88; C Broughton Poggs w Filkins, Broadwell etc 88-95; C Shill Valley and Broadshire 95-96; Perm to Offic from 98. *26 The Pines, Faringdon SN7 8AU* Tel (01367) 241009

WHITTAKER, John. b 69. Leic Univ BA90 ACA93. Ripon Coll Cuddesdon BTh00. **d** 00 **p** 01. C Melton Mowbray *Leic* 00-03; P-in-c Barrow upon Soar w Walton le Wolds from 03. *The Rectory, 27 Cotes Road, Barrow upon Soar, Loughborough LE12 8JP* Tel (01509) 621834 E-mail johnhelena@tiscali.co.uk

WHITTAKER, Karl Paul. b 55. ATL. CITC BTh95. **d** 95 **p** 96. C Killowen *D & R* 95-99; I Annaghmore *Arm* 99-04; P-in-c Sunbury St Mary Australia from 04. *9 O'Shanassy Street, Sunbury, Vic, Australia 3429* Tel (0061) (3) 9744 1347 Fax 9740 8393 E-mail vicar.stmarys@bigpond.com

WHITTAKER, Canon Peter Harold. b 39. AKC62. **d** 63 **p** 64. C Walton St Mary *Liv* 63-67; C Ross *Heref* 67-70; R Bridgnorth St Mary 70-78; P-in-c Oldbury 70-78; TR Bridgnorth, Tasley, Astley Abbotts and Oldbury 78-81; RD Bridgnorth 78-81; Preb Heref Cathl 80-81; V Leighton Buzzard w Eggington, Hockliffe etc *St Alb* 81-92; RD Dunstable 84-85; R Barton-le-Cley w Higham Gobion and Hexton 92-04; Hon Can St Alb from 92; rtd 04. *12 Aldersley Way, Ruyton XI Towns, Shrewsbury SY4 1NE* Tel (01939) 260059

WHITTAKER, Robert Andrew. b 49. Open Univ BA75 Nottm Univ MA83 DipEd. Linc Th Coll 85. **d** 87 **p** 88. C Mansfield Woodhouse *S'well* 87-90; V Norwell w Ossington, Cromwell and Caunton 90-95; Chapl Ranby Ho Sch Retford 95-03. *Bishopsgate School, Englefield Green, Egham TW20 0YJ* Tel (01784) 432109

WHITTAKER, William Paul. *See* STAFFORD-WHITTAKER, William Paul

WHITTAM, Canon Kenneth Michael. b 26. Ball Coll Ox BA50 MA54. Cuddesdon Coll 50. **d** 52 **p** 53. C Adlington *Blackb* 52-55; C St Annes St Thos 55-58; R Halton w Aughton 58-62; R Colne St Bart 62-66; Chapl Highgate Sch Lon 66-75; V Shotwick *Ches* 75-89; Can Res Ches Cathl and Dioc Missr 75-85; Hon Can Ches Cathl 85-90; Clergy Study Officer 85-91; rtd 91; Perm to Offic *Ches* from 91. *22 Warwick Close, Little Neston, Neston CH64 0SR* Tel 0151-336 8541

WHITTINGHAM, Mrs Janet Irene. b 49. **d** 03 **p** 04. OLM Pendleton *Man* from 03. *24 Aylesbury Close, Salford M5 4FQ* Tel 0161-736 5878

WHITTINGHAM, Peter. b 58. Sheff Univ BA79 PGCE. St Jo Coll Nottm 88. **d** 90 **p** 91. C Northowram *Wakef* 90-93; C Airedale w Fryston 93-96; V Wrenthorpe from 96; P-in-c Alverthorpe from 02. *The Vicarage, 121 Wrenthorpe Road, Wrenthorpe, Wakefield WF2 0JS* Tel (01924) 373758

WHITTINGHAM, Ronald Norman. b 43. Linc Coll Ox BA65 MA68. Coll of Resurr Mirfield 65. **d** 67 **p** 68. C Horninglow *Lich* 67-69; C Drayton in Hales 69-70; C Uttoxeter w Bramshall 71-75; P-in-c Burton St Paul 75-80; V Shareshill 80-83; V Silverdale and Knutton Heath 83-89; P-in-c Alsagers Bank 83-89; V Silverdale and Alsagers Bank 89-92; V Honley *Wakef* 92-99; TV Hugglescote w Donington, Ellistown and Snibston *Leic* 99-02; TV Leic Presentation from 02. *St Chad's Clergy House, 145 Coleman Road, Leicester LE5 4LH* Tel 0116-276 6062 E-mail whittingham@leicester.anglican.org

WHITTINGTON, David John. b 45. OBE01. Qu Coll Ox BA67 MA71. Coll of Resurr Mirfield 69. **d** 71 **p** 72. Chapl St Woolos Cathl *Mon* 71-72; C Ox St Mary V w St Cross and St Pet *Ox* 72-76; Chapl Qu Coll Ox 72-76; V Stockton *Dur* 77-98; Hon Can Dur Cathl 93-98; Can Res and Dioc Dir Educn 98-03; Nat Sch Development Officer Abps' Coun from 03. *Church House, Great Smith Street, London SW1P 3NZ* Tel (020) 7898 1789 E-mail david.whittington@c-of-e.org.uk

WHITTINGTON, Peter Graham. b 68. Ox Poly BA90. Trin Coll Bris BA95. **d** 95 **p** 96. C Gateacre *Liv* 95-99; V Huyton St Geo 99-05; V Orrell from 05. *St Luke's Vicarage, 10 Lodge Road, Orrell, Wigan WN5 7AT* Tel (01695) 623410 E-mail whitts01@surfaid.org

WHITTINGTON, Richard Hugh. b 47. MBE74. Sarum & Wells Th Coll DipTh93. **d** 93 **p** 94. C Enfield St Jas *Lon* 93-96; P-in-c Ightham *Roch* 96-97; R 97-01; Chapl R Hosp Chelsea from 01. *The Chaplaincy, The Royal Hospital Chelsea, Royal Hospital Road, London SW3 4SL* Tel (020) 7881 5234 *or* 7881 5260 Mobile 07979-360025 Fax (020) 7881 5463 E-mail chaplain@chelsea-pensioners.org.uk

WHITTINGTON, Mrs Sharon Ann. b 56. Leeds Univ BA79 PGCE80. NEOC. **d** 00 **p** 01. NSM The Street Par *York* 00-03; P-in-c York St Thos w St Maurice from 03; NSM York St Olave w St Giles from 03; NSM York St Helen w St Martin from 04. *30 Marygate, York YO30 7BH* Tel (01904) 627401

WHITTLE, Alan. b 29. K Coll Lon BD52 AKC52. **d** 53 **p** 54. C Combe Down *B & W* 53-55; C Bath Twerton-on-Avon 55-57; Australia 57-66; R Aston Rowant w Crowell *Ox* 66-68; Lic to Offic *S'wark* 69-72; V Mitcham Ch Ch 72-92; rtd 92; Perm to Offic *S'wark* from 92. *117 May Cross Avenue, Morden SM4 4DF* Tel (020) 8540 0201

WHITTLE, Fred. b 17. Keble Coll Ox BA40 MA44. Cuddesdon Coll 40. **d** 41 **p** 42. C Northampton St Matt *Pet* 41-47; C W Molesey *Guildf* 47-49; C Isham *Pet* 49-51; V Warmington 51-58; R Orlingbury w Pytchley 58-71; R Gt w Lt Addington 71-82; rtd 82; Lic to Offic *Pet* 82-85; Perm to Offic from 85. *6 Coleman Street, Raunds, Wellingborough NN9 6NJ* Tel (01933) 624989

WHITTLE, Ian Christopher. b 60. Univ Coll Dur BA81 Fitzw Coll Cam BA88 MA91. Ridley Hall Cam 85. **d** 88 **p** 89. C S Petherton w the Seavingtons *B & W* 88-91; Asst Chapl The Hague *Eur* 91-97; P-in-c Gayton Gp of Par *Nor* 97-99; R Gayton, Gayton Thorpe, E Walton, E Winch etc from 99; RD Lynn from 02. *The Rectory, Grimston Road, Gayton, King's Lynn PE32 1QA* Tel (01553) 636227

WHITTLE, John William. b 46. Qu Mary Coll Lon BA68. Sarum & Wells Th Coll 84. **d** 86 **p** 87. C Blandford Forum and Langton Long etc *Sarum* 86-88; NSM Pimperne, Stourpaine, Durweston and Bryanston from 02. *The Cottage, Queens Road, Blandford Forum DT11 7JZ* Tel (01258) 454789 E-mail johnwwhittle@hotmail.com

WHITTLE, Naomi Clare. b 54. Colchester Inst of Educn BA75 Lon Univ PGCE76 Middx Univ MA(Theol)99 LGSM77. SEITE 95. **d** 98 **p** 99. C Catford (Southend) and Downham *S'wark* 98-02; P-in-c Shooters Hill Ch Ch 02; V from 02. *Christ Church Vicarage, 1 Craigholm, Shooters Hill, London SE18 3RR* Tel (020) 8856 5858 E-mail naomiwhittle@tiscali.co.uk

WHITTLE, Robin Jeffrey. b 51. Bris Univ BA72 Leic Univ CQSW75. Sarum & Wells Th Coll 85. **d** 87 **p** 88. C Henbury *Bris* 87-91; V Capel *Guildf* 91-96; Chapl among Deaf People from 96; Perm to Offic *Roch* and *S'wark* 97-99; P-in-c Walton-on-the-Hill 99-04; V Tattenham Corner from 04. *St Mark's Vicarage, St Mark's Road, Epsom KT18 5RD* Tel (01737) 353011 E-mail bob@whittle1.fsnet.co.uk

WHITTLE, Mrs Sheila Margaret. b 36. Glouc Th Course 83 NY Th Sem MA88 Vancouver Sch of Th. **d** 90 **p** 90. R Bulkley Valley Canada 90-93; C Dunbar St Phil 93; P-in-c Maple Ridge St Jo the Divine 93-95; Lethbridge St Mary the Virgin 95-97; NSM Portsea N End St Mark *Portsm* 97-98; P-in-c Lezant w Lawhitton and S Petherwin w Trewen *Truro* 98-02; rtd 02; Perm to Offic *Glouc* from 03. *5 Pennine Close, Walton Cardiff, Tewkesbury GL20 7PL* Tel (01684) 299981 E-mail whittle@beeb.net

WHITTLESEA, Grahame Stanley Jack Hammond. b 37. Kent Univ LLM95. **d** 05. OLM Blean *Cant* from 05. *24 Tyler Hill Road, Blean, Canterbury CT2 9HT* Tel (01227) 763373 Mobile 07866-037774 E-mail g.whittlesea@ukonline.co.uk

WHITTOCK (née MARBUS), Alida Janny. b 52. RGN78. STETS 00. **d** 03. NSM Weymouth H Trin *Sarum* from 03. *79 Clearmount Road, Weymouth DT4 9LE* Tel (01305) 786792 E-mail adamarbus@aol.com

WHITTOCK, Michael Graham. b 47. Hull Univ BA69 Fitzw Coll Cam BA71 MA76. Westcott Ho Cam 69 Union Th Sem Virginia 71. **d** 72 **p** 73. C Kirkby *Liv* 72-76; C Prescot 76-79; R Methley w Mickletown *Ripon* 79-92; RD Whitkirk 88-92; V Morley St Pet w Churwell *Wakef* 92-01; R Gt Hanwood *Heref* from 01; R Longden and Annscroft w Pulverbatch from 01. *The Rectory, Plealey Lane, Longden, Shrewsbury SY5 8ET* Tel (01743) 861003 Fax 861237

WHITTOME, Donald Marshall. b 26. Cam Univ BA50 MA53. S Dios Minl Tr Scheme. **d** 84 **p** 85. NSM Henfield w Shermanbury and Woodmancote *Chich* 84-93; P-in-c Poynings w Edburton, Newtimber and Pyecombe 93-97; rtd 97; Perm to Offic *Chich* from 97. *Quaker's Rest, 7 Dean Court Road, Rottingdean, Brighton BN2 7DE* Tel (01273) 705508 Fax 271475

WHITTON, Eric. b 33. N Lon Poly 78. Lon Coll of Div ALCD59 Western Th Sem Michigan 60. **d** 60 **p** 61. C Mortlake w E Sheen *S'wark* 60-64; C Surbiton St Matt 64-66; Youth Officer *Lon* 66-72; Tr Officer Gen Syn Bd of Educn 73-78; Visiting Lect Roehampton Inst of HE from 80; rtd 94. *31 Ovington Street, London SW3 2JA* Tel (020) 7584 8819

WHITTY, Gordon William. b 35. WMMTC. **d** 82 **p** 83. NSM Willenhall St Giles *Lich* 82-84; NSM Coseley Ch Ch 84-85; C 85-87; TV Hanley H Ev 87-91; P-in-c Meir 91-98; P-in-c Hanbury w Newborough and Rangemore 98-99; V 99-03; rtd 03. *14 Cardrona Close, Oakwood, Derby DE21 2JN* Tel (01332) 726320 E-mail gordonwhitty@vinweb.co.uk

WHITTY, Harold George. b 41. TCD BA64 MA67. CITC Div Test65. **d** 65 **p** 66. C Willowfield *D & D* 65-68; C Lisburn Ch Ch *Conn* 68-71; Bp's Dom Chapl 70-71; Asst Dir Exhibitions CMJ 71-72; C Enfield Ch Ch Trent Park *Lon* 72-75; TV Washfield, Stoodleigh, Withleigh etc *Ex* 75-83; R 83-84; TR 84-93; P-in-c Aylesbeare, Rockbeare, Farringdon etc 02-04; RD Tiverton 82-84; P-in-c Allithwaite *Carl* 93-97; TV Cartmel Peninsula 97-02; Local Min Officer 99-02; rtd 04. *Wagon Works, Jericho Street, Thorverton, Exeter EX5 5PA* Tel (01392) 860397 E-mail harold.whitty@btinternet.com

WHITWAM, Miss Diana Morgan. b 28. MCSP54 Brighton Poly Dip Counselling 82. **d** 93 **p** 94. OLM Stoke-next-Guildf 93-01; Perm to Offic from 02. *13 Abbots Hospital, High Street, Guildford GU1 3AJ* Tel (01483) 565977 E-mail dwhitwam@onetel.com

WHITWELL, Canon John Peter. b 36. Qu Coll Birm 62. **d** 65 **p** 66. C Stepney St Dunstan and All SS *Lon* 65-68; C Chingford SS Pet and Paul *Chelmsf* 68-71; V Walthamstow St Sav 71-78; P-in-c Lt Ilford St Mich 78-88; R 88-98; RD Newham 91-97; Hon Can Chelmsf Cathl 96-98; rtd 98; Perm to Offic *Ox* from 99. *152 Bath Road, Banbury OX16 0TT* Tel (01295) 266243 E-mail jandawhitwell@aol.com

WHITWELL, Martin Corbett. b 32. Pemb Coll Ox BA55 MA59. Clifton Th Coll 55. **d** 57 **p** 58. C Wolverhampton St Jude *Lich* 57-60; C Aldridge 60-66; Chapl Sandbach Co Secondary Sch 68-74; C Chipping Campden *Glouc* 70-71; Perm to Offic *Chich* 74-75; *Bris* 75-76; C Tranmere St Cath *Ches* 76-80; V Lt Leigh and Lower Whitley 80-90; rtd 90; Perm to Offic *Ches* from 90; *Heref* and *Lich* from 93. *11 Hollies Drive, Bayston Hill, Shrewsbury SY3 0NN* Tel (01743) 874241

WHITWELL, Timothy John. b 72. Westmr Coll Ox BTh97 Leeds Univ MA00 SSC. Coll of Resurr Mirfield 97. **d** 99 **p** 00. C Middlesbrough Ascension *York* 99-02; R Loftus and Carlin How w Skinningrove from 02. *The Rectory, 11 Micklow Lane, Loftus, Saltburn-by-the-Sea TS13 4JE* Tel (01287) 643702 Mobile 07715-137470 E-mail timothy.whitwell@talk21.com

WHITWORTH, Benjamin Charles Battams. b 49. CCC Ox BA71 MA85. Linc Th Coll 83. **d** 85 **p** 86. C Swanborough *Sarum* 85-88; C Sherborne w Castleton and Lillington 88-91; V Milborne Port w Goathill *B & W* 91-98; rtd 98; Perm to Offic *B & W* from 00. *13 The Avenue, Taunton TA1 1EA* Tel (01823) 272442

WHITWORTH, Canon Duncan. b 47. K Coll Lon BD69 AKC69. St Aug Coll Cant 69. **d** 70 **p** 71. C Tonge Moor *Man* 70-73; C Upper Norwood St Jo *Cant* 73-78; Asst Chapl Madrid *Eur* 78-82; Chapl Br Embassy Ankara 82-83; V Douglas St Matt *S & M* from 84; RD Douglas from 91; Can St German's Cathl from 96. *St Matthew's Vicarage, Alexander Drive, Douglas, Isle of Man IM2 3QN* Tel (01624) 676310

WHITWORTH, Canon Patrick John. b 51. Ch Ch Ox BA72 MA76 St Jo Coll Dur DipTh75 MA78. **d** 76 **p** 77. C York St Mich-le-Belfrey *York* 76-79; C Brompton H Trin w Onslow Square St Paul *Lon* 79-84; V Gipsy Hill Ch Ch *S'wark* 84-95; Hon Can Bauchi from 95; R Bath Weston All SS w N Stoke and Langridge *B & W* from 95; RD Bath from 03. *The Vicarage, Weston, Bath BA1 4BU* Tel (01225) 421159 E-mail pwhitworth1@compuserve.com

WHYBORN, Robert. b 42. Loughb Coll of Educn CSD69. N Ord Course 87. **d** 90 **p** 91. NSM Milnrow *Man* 90-97; NSM Greenfield 97-03; NSM Saddleworth from 03. *St Mary's Vicarage, 1 Park Lane, Greenfield, Oldham OL3 7DX* Tel (01457) 872346 Fax as telephone E-mail revrob8@aol.com

WHYBROW, Paul Andrew. b 59. St Paul's Cheltenham BEd80. Oak Hill Th Coll DipMin89 DipTh90 BA90 Wycliffe Hall Ox 95. **d** 97 **p** 98. C Magor *Mon* 97-00; V Poughill *Truro* from 00. *The Vicarage, Poughill, Bude EX23 9ER* Tel (01288) 355183 E-mail pa.whybrow@btinternet.com

WHYMAN, Oliver. b 27. ALCM52 LCP57. S'wark Ord Course 60. **d** 63 **p** 64. C Streatham Ch Ch *S'wark* 63-68; Lic to Offic 68-87; NSM Sutton New Town St Barn 87-92; rtd 92; Perm to Offic *S'wark* 92-00. *37 Jubilee Court, London Road, Thornton Heath CR7 6JL* Tel (020) 8684 5320

WHYSALL, Mrs Joan. b 42. Lady Mabel Coll DipEd64 Nottm Univ MA01. EMMTC 98. **d** 01 **p** 02. NSM Trowell, Awsworth and Cossall *S'well* from 01. *55 Trowell Park Drive, Trowell, Nottingham NG9 3RA* Tel 0115-875 2677 Mobile 07802-415036 Fax 08701-371114 E-mail joan.whysall@ntlworld.com

WHYTE, Alastair John. b 61. Coll of Ripon & York St Jo BA83 Lanc Univ MA95. Sarum & Wells Th Coll 83. **d** 85 **p** 86. C Chorley St Geo *Blackb* 85-88; C Poulton-le-Fylde 88-91; V Wesham 91-00; Chapl Wesham Park Hosp Preston 91-94; Chapl Blackpool, Wyre and Fylde Community NHS Trust 94-02; P-in-c Treales *Blackb* 98-00; V Garstang St Thos 00-02; AD Garstang 02. *Address withheld by request*

WHYTE, David. b 30. **d** 97 **p** 97. NSM Calne and Blackland *Sarum* 97-00; rtd 00; Perm to Offic *Sarum* from 01. *20 Castle Street, Calne SN11 0DX* Tel (01249) 817033

WHYTE, Duncan Macmillan. b 25. St Jo Coll Dur BA49 St Cath Soc Ox BA51 MA57. Wycliffe Hall Ox 49. **d** 51 **p** 53. C Garston *Liv* 51-56; C St Leonards St Leon *Chich* 56-59; V Southsea St Simon *Portsm* 59-66; Gen Sec Lon City Miss 66-92; Hon C Blackheath St Jo *S'wark* 66-92; rtd 92; Perm to Offic *Sarum* from 92. *1 The Meadows, Salisbury SP1 2SS* Tel (01722) 330528

WHYTE, Henry Lewis. b 38. Lon Coll of Div ALCD70 LTh74. **d** 70 **p** 71. C Crawley *Chich* 70-74; V Bermondsey St Jas w Ch Ch *S'wark* 74-82; V Kingston Hill St Paul 82-94; V Blackheath Park St Mich 94-02; rtd 02. *6 Horn Park Lane, London SE12 8UU* Tel (020) 8318 9837

WHYTE, Herbert Blayney. b 21. TCD BA43 MA53. **d** 44 **p** 45. C Dublin Crumlin *D & G* 44-47; Succ St Patr Cathl Dublin 47-50; Dioc Registrar (Ossory, Ferns and Leighlin) *C & O* 50-58; Bp's V and Lib Kilkenny Cathl 50-58; Bp's Dom Chapl 50-58; Preb Ossory Cathl 56-58; I Maryborough 58-68; Clerical V Ch Ch Cathl Dublin *D & G* 68-91; I Dublin Crumlin 68-91; Can Ch Ch Cathl Dublin 80-86; Chan 86-91; rtd 91. *238 Redford Park, Greystones, Co Wicklow, Irish Republic* Tel (00353) (1) 287 7264

WHYTE, Canon Robert Euan. b 44. St Pet Coll Ox BA67. Cuddesdon Coll 67. **d** 69 **p** 70. C Blackheath Ascension *S'wark* 69-73; BCC 73-87; NSM Lewisham St Swithun *S'wark* 73-76; NSM Heston *Lon* 76-77; NSM Rusthall *Roch* 77-87; C 87-88; V from 88; RD Tunbridge Wells 91-96; Hon Can Roch Cathl from 00. *The Vicarage, Bretland Road, Rusthall, Tunbridge Wells TN4 8PB* Tel (01892) 521357 Fax 537014 E-mail rewhyte@btinternet.com

WIBBERLEY, Anthony Norman. b 36. K Coll Lon BSc58 AKC58. Sarum & Wells Th Coll 76. **d** 79 **p** 80. Hon C Tavistock and Gulworthy *Ex* 79-86; R Hoby cum Rotherby w Brooksby, Ragdale & Thru'ton *Leic* 86-90; V Ingol *Blackb* 90-96; Perm to Offic *Ely* from 97; rtd 00. *13 Missleton Court, Cherry Hinton Road, Cambridge CB1 8BL*

WIBREW, Mrs Janet Anne. b 48. Win Sch of Art NDAD89. S Dios Minl Tr Scheme 89. **d** 92 **p** 94. NSM Basingstoke *Win* 92-95; Chapl N Hants Hosp 95-96; Asst Chapl Basingstoke Distr Hosp 97-99; NSM Cliddesden and Ellisfield w Farleigh Wallop etc *Win* 97-99. *High Meadows, Green Lane, Ellisfield, Basingstoke RG25 2QW* Tel (01256) 381387

WIBROE, Andrew Peter. b 56. K Coll Lon BD83 AKC83 Thames Poly PGCE91. Ripon Coll Cuddesdon 83. **d** 86 **p** 87. C Purley St Mark *S'wark* 86-88; C Boyne Hill *Ox* 89-90; Hon C Milton next Gravesend Ch Ch *Roch* from 90. *32 Ayelands, New Ash Green, Longfield DA3 8JN* Tel (01474) 879014 E-mail peterwibroe@aol.com

WICK, Patricia Anne. b 54. Lon Bible Coll BA80 Oak Hill Th Coll DipHE86. **dss** 86 **d** 87 **p** 94. Halliwell St Luke *Man* 86-87; Par Dn 87-91; Par Dn Drypool *York* 91-94; C 94-95; TV 95-97; Perm to Offic 98-99; CMS Uganda from 98. *PO Box 845, Arua, Uganda* E-mail t.wick@bushnet.net

WICKENS, Andrew Peter. b 63. St Jo Coll Dur BA85 Magd Coll Cam MEd97 PGCE95 ARCM84. Westcott Ho Cam 98. **d** 00 **p** 01. C Louth *Linc* 00-03; TV from 03; PV Linc Cathl from 01. *The Vicarage, Little Lane, Louth LN11 9DU* Tel and fax (01507) 601250 E-mail apw@tonality.freeserve.co.uk

WICKENS, Andrew St Lawrence John. b 63. Mert Coll Ox BA85 Birm Univ MPhil94. Qu Coll Birm 89. **d** 92 **p** 93. C Birchfield *Birm* 92-96; Perm to Offic 96-97; Zambia 97-00; CMS Kenya 01-05; P-in-c Dudley St Jas *Worc* from 05; Educn Chapl from 05. *St James's Vicarage, The Parade, Dudley DY1 3JA*

WICKENS, John Philip. b 33. Open Univ BA76. K Coll Lon 57. **d** 61 **p** 62. C Hatcham Park All SS *S'wark* 61-64; USA 64-66; Tutor Richmond Fellowship Coll 66-95; Hon C Sutton Ch Ch

S'wark 68-83; Hon C Benhilton 83-95; rtd 95; Perm to Offic *Worc* from 95. *West Villa, 196 West Malvern Road, Malvern WR14 4AZ* Tel (01684) 574043

WICKENS, Mrs Moira. b 56. S Dios Minl Tr Scheme 91. **d** 94. NSM Ifield *Chich* 94-96; C Saltdean 96-03; Schs Liaison Officer from 03; C Ovingdean from 03. *21 Ainsworth Avenue, Ovingdean, Brighton BN2 7BG* Tel (01273) 309546

WICKHAM, Mrs Jennifer Ruth. b 68. Univ of W Ontario BA91. Cranmer Hall Dur BA98. **d** 98 **p** 99. C Ponteland *Newc* 98-00; Assoc P Ottawa St Geo Canada from 01. *57A Tauvette Street, Ottawa ON, Canada, K1B 3A2* Tel (001) (613) 590 7921 *or* 235 1636 E-mail ajwickham@yahoo.com *or* revjw.stgeorge@cyberus.ca

WICKHAM, Lionel Ralph. b 32. St Cath Coll Cam BA57 MA61 PhD LRAM. Westcott Ho Cam 57. **d** 59 **p** 60. C Boston *Linc* 59-61; Tutor Cuddesdon Coll 61-63; V Cross Stone *Wakef* 63-67; Lect Th Southn Univ 67-78; Sen Lect 78-81; V Honley 81-87; Lect Cam Univ 87-00; NSM W Wratting *Ely* 89-00; NSM Weston Colville 89-00; rtd 00; Perm to Offic *Wakef* from 99. *19 Barrowstead, Skelmanthorpe, Huddersfield HD8 9UW* Tel (01484) 864185 E-mail lpatristic@aol.com

WICKHAM, Nicholas John. b 27. Trin Coll Cam BA51 MA56. Coll of Resurr Mirfield 54 Ox NSM Course 85. **d** 87 **p** 88. NSM Banbury *Ox* 87-92; rtd 92. *Address temp unknown*

WICKHAM, Canon Norman George. b 25. Kelham Th Coll 42. **d** 51 **p** 52. C Syston *Leic* 51-54; V Leic St Gabr 54-57; R Wingerworth *Derby* 57-69; TP Edin St Jo *Edin* 69-79; Can and Vice Provost St Mary's Cathl Edin 74-79; R Edin Ch Ch 79-88; Can St Mary's Cathl 86-91; rtd 88; Hon Can St Mary's Cathl *Edin* from 91. *The Coach House, 15 Spylaw Road, Edinburgh EH10 5BN* Tel 0131-447 1050 E-mail norman.wickham@btinternet.com

WICKHAM, Robert James. b 72. Grey Coll Dur BA94. Ridley Hall Cam 95. **d** 98 **p** 99. C Willesden St Mary *Lon* 98-01; C Somers Town 01-03; TV Old St Pancras from 03. *St Mary's House, Eversholt Street, London NW1 1BN* Tel (020) 7387 7301 E-mail somerstown@aol.com

WICKINGS, Luke Iden. b 59. Sheff Poly BA81. Oak Hill Th Coll BA90. **d** 90 **p** 91. C Fulham St Mary N End *Lon* 90-94; C Bletchley *Ox* 94-00; V W Norwood St Luke *S'wark* from 00. *The Vicarage, 6 Chatsworth Way, London SE27 9HR* Tel (020) 8670 2706 *or* 8761 0068

WICKREMASINGHE, Rosemary Ethel. b 32. Reading Univ ATD52 K Coll Lon BD85 AKC85. St Alb and Ox Min Course 93. **d** 96 **p** 97. NSM Godrevy *Truro* from 96. *10 Glebe Row, Phillack, Hayle TR27 5AJ* Tel (01736) 757850

WICKS, Christopher Blair. b 59. Oak Hill Th Coll BA88. **d** 88 **p** 89. C Edmonton All SS w St Mich *Lon* 88-92; C Southborough St Pet w Ch Ch and St Matt etc *Roch* 92-96; TV from 96. *72 Powder Mill Lane, Southborough, Tunbridge Wells TN4 9EJ* Tel (01892) 529098 E-mail chriswicks@tiscali.co.uk

WICKS, Mrs Susan Joyce. b 51. SEN80 CSS89. EMMTC 97. **d** 00 **p** 01. C Birstall and Wanlip *Leic* 00-04; R Fenn Lanes Gp from 04. *The Vicarage, High Street, Stoke Golding, Nuneaton CV13 6HE* Tel (01455) 212317 Mobile 07808-917164 E-mail sueterry.wicks@virgin.net

WICKS, Susan Lynn. b 66. Trin Coll Bris DipHE98. **d** 98 **p** 99. C Whitburn *Dur* 98-03; TV S Carl TM *Carl* from 03. *St Elisabeth's Vicarage, Arnside Road, Carlisle CA1 3QA* Tel (01228) 596427 E-mail suewicks@fish.co.uk

WICKSTEAD, Gavin John. b 46. St Chad's Coll Dur BA67. Linc Th Coll 82. **d** 84 **p** 85. C Louth *Linc* 84-87; P-in-c E Markham and Askham *S'well* 87-89; P-in-c Headon w Upton 87-89; P-in-c Grove 87-89; R E Markham w Askham, Headon w Upton and Grove 90-92; P-in-c Skegness and Winthorpe *Linc* 92-97; R 97-01; V Holbeach from 01; RD Elloe E from 05. *The Vicarage, 2 Church Walk, Holbeach, Spalding PE12 7DT* Tel (01406) 422185 E-mail wickstead@btopenworld.com

WIDDAS, Preb John Anderson. b 38. Kelham Th Coll 58. **d** 63 **p** 64. C Willenhall H Trin *Lich* 63-66; C Tamworth 66-69; V 86-96; V Chesterton 69-74; R Lich St Chad 74-86; RD Lich 77-86; Preb Lich Cathl 80-00; P-in-c Gentleshaw 80-82; P-in-c Farewell 80-82; RD Tamworth 91-95; V Walsall Wood 96-00; rtd 00; Chapl Burton Hosps NHS Trust 01-03; Perm to Offic *Lich* from 04. *90 Main Street, Alrewas, Burton-on-Trent DE13 7AE* Tel (01283) 792031

WIDDECOMBE, Canon Malcolm Murray. b 37. Tyndale Hall Bris 57. **d** 62 **p** 63. C Bris H Trin *Bris* 62-65; C Barton Hill St Luke w Ch Ch 65-67; P-in-c Bris St Phil and St Jacob w Em 67-74; V from 74; RD Bris City 79-85; Hon Can Bris Cathl from 86. *The Vicarage, 7 King's Drive, Bristol BS7 8JW* Tel and fax 0117-924 3169 *or* 929 3386 *or* tel 924 6299 E-mail wid@pipnjay.org.uk

WIDDECOMBE, Roger James. b 70. Wycliffe Hall Ox 01. **d** 03 **p** 04. C Downend *Bris* from 03. *8 Farm Court, Bristol BS16 6DF* Tel 0117-330 7885

WIDDESS, Mrs Margaret Jennifer. b 48. Bedf Coll Lon BA70 Clare Hall Cam PGCE75 Lambeth MA03. EAMTC 94. **d** 97 **p** 98. NSM Cambridge St Botolph *Ely* from 97. *69 Gwydir Street, Cambridge CB1 2LG* Tel (01223) 313908 E-mail margaret.widdess@ukonline.co.uk

WIDDICOMBE, Peter John. b 52. Univ of Manitoba BA74 St Cath Coll Ox MPhil77 St Cross Coll Ox DPhil90. Wycliffe Coll Toronto MDiv81. **d** 81 **p** 82. Canada 81-84 and from 93; C Ox St Andr *Ox* 84-86; Acting Chapl Trin Coll Ox 88; Linc Coll Ox 89; P-in-c Penn 90-93. *457 Northlake Drive, Waterloo ON, Canada, 2NV 2A4*

WIDDOWS, Christopher. *See* WIDDOWS, John Christopher

WIDDOWS, David Charles Roland. b 52. Hertf Coll Ox BA75 MA79. St Jo Coll Nottm BA77. **d** 79 **p** 80. C Blackley St Andr *Man* 79-83; P-in-c Rochdale Deeplish St Luke 83-84; V 84-92; TR Stoke Gifford *Bris* from 92. *The Vicarage, 24 North Road, Stoke Gifford, Bristol BS34 8PB* Tel 0117-923 6395 *or* 969 2486 E-mail admin@st-michaels-church.freeserve.co.uk

WIDDOWS, Edward John. b 45. ACertCM00. Lon Coll of Div 66. **d** 70 **p** 71. C Formby St Pet *Liv* 70-72; C Uckfield, Isfield and Lt Horsted *Chich* 72-73; C Babbacombe *Ex* 73-76; V Sithney *Truro* 76-78; RD Kerrier 77-78; V Bude Haven 78-84; P-in-c Laneast w St Clether and Tresmere 84-85; P-in-c N Hill w Altarnon, Bolventor and Lewannick 84-85; P-in-c Boyton w N Tamerton 84-85; P-in-c N Petherwin 84-85; R Collingham w S Scarle and Besthorpe and Girton *S'well* 85-92; R Guernsey St Michel du Valle *Win* 92-99; R Compton and Otterbourne 99-02; rtd 02; Perm to Offic *Pet* from 02. *Glebe Cottage, 4 Spring Back Way, Uppingham, Oakham LE15 9TT* Tel (01572) 821980 E-mail ewiddows01@aol.com

WIDDOWS, Heather Susan. b 45. Open Univ BA76. Moray Ord Course 91. **d** 96 **p** 97. NSM Kishorn *Mor* from 96. *2 Fasaich, Gairloch IV21 2DB* Tel and fax (01445) 712176 E-mail heatherwiddows@hotmail.com

WIDDOWS, John Christopher (Kit). b 46. Trin Coll Cam BA69 MA72. Cuddesdon Coll 69. **d** 71 **p** 72. C Herrington *Dur* 71-76; Chapl Nat Exhibition Cen 76-80; TV Chelmsley Wood *Birm* 76-80; V Halifax St Hilda *Wakef* 80-95; RD Halifax 92-95; AD Newc Cen *Newc* from 95; Master Newc St Thos Prop Chpl from 95; P-in-c Fawdon 99-00. *9 Chester Crescent, Newcastle upon Tyne NE2 1DH* Tel and fax 0191-232 9789 *or* tel 232 0842 E-mail kit@widdows-rev.fsnet.co.uk

WIDDOWSON, Charles Leonard. b 28. ALCD62. **d** 62 **p** 63. C Radcliffe-on-Trent *S'well* 62-66; R Newark Ch Ch 66-69; Australia from 69; rtd 93. *5 Sharrock Avenue, Cheltenham, Vic, Australia 3192* Tel (0061) (03) 9584 9004

WIDDOWSON, Robert William. b 47. Linc Th Coll 83. **d** 85 **p** 86. C Syston *Leic* 85-88; R Husbands Bosworth w Mowsley and Knaptoft etc 88-93; R Asfordby 93-98; P-in-c Ab Kettleby Gp 93-98; P-in-c Old Dalby and Nether Broughton 95-98; P-in-c Charlton Musgrove, Cucklington and Stoke Trister *B & W* 98-03; P-in-c Ashwick w Oakhill and Binegar from 03; Adv in Rural Affairs from 98. *The Rectory, Fosse Road, Oakhill, Bath BA3 5HU* Tel and fax (01749) 841688

WIDERMARK, Sussie Maria Elisabeth. b 58. Lund Univ Sweden BA87. Lund Inst Past Th 88. **p** 89. Sweden 89-00 and 01-03; C Barton upon Humber *Linc* 00-01; C Glenageary *D & G* from 03. *403 Rosses Court, Dun Laoghaire, Co Dublin, Irish Republic* Tel (00353) (1) 231 1192 E-mail mariawidermark@hotmail.com

WIFFEN, Richard Austin. b 58. St Pet Coll Ox BA80. Trin Coll Bris BA90. **d** 90 **p** 91. C Bowdon *Ches* 90-93; C Ellesmere Port 93-94; TV 94-02; Hon C from 02. *Lime Tree Farm, Stanney Lane, Little Stanney, Chester CH2 4HT* Tel 0151-355 1654

WIFFEN, Ronald. b 38. Open Th Coll BA99. SEITE 99. **d** 01 **p** 02. NSM Canvey Is *Chelmsf* 01-04; NSM Bowers Gifford w N Benfleet from 04. *40 Gladwyns, Basildon SS15 5JA* Tel (01268) 410492

WIFFIN, Susan Elizabeth. b 51. Edin Th Coll 93. **d** 96 **p** 97. NSM Jedburgh *Edin* 96-98; C Galashiels 98-01; P-in-c Fochabers and Dioc Miss Co-ord *Mor* 01-05; Can St Andr Cathl Inverness 03-05; Miss and Min Officer *Ab* from 05. *15 Corse Wynd, Kingswells, Aberdeen AB15 8TP* Tel (01224) 743955 Mobile 07753-684923 E-mail susan.wiffin@btopenworld.com

WIGFIELD, Thomas Henry Paul. b 26. Edin Th Coll 46. **d** 49 **p** 50. C Seaham w Seaham Harbour *Dur* 49-52; C Dur St Marg 52-54; V Fatfield 54-63; Asst Dir Chs' TV Cen 63-79; Perm to Offic *Lon* 63-91; Perm to Offic *St Alb* 66-91; Hd of Services Foundn for Chr Communication 79-84; Chs' Liaison Officer 84-91; rtd 91; Perm to Offic *Ox* from 91. *16 Fishers Field, Buckingham MK18 1SF* Tel (01280) 817893

WIGGEN, Richard Martin. b 42. Open Univ BA78 Hull Univ MA86. Qu Coll Birm 64. **d** 67 **p** 68. C Penistone w Midhope *Wakef* 67-70; C Leeds St Pet *Ripon* 70-73; Asst Youth Chapl *Glouc* 73-76; Youth Officer *Liv* 76-80; V Kirkstall *Ripon* 80-90; V Meanwood from 90. *Meanwood Vicarage, 9 Parkside Green, Leeds LS6 4NY* Tel 0113-275 7885 E-mail wiggen@btopenworld.com

WIGGINS, Gillian Holt. b 33. Birm Univ MB, ChB56. **d** 03. NSM Ascot Heath *Ox* from 03. *Keren, 2 Kiln Lane, Winkfield, Windsor SL4 2DU* Tel (01344) 884008 E-mail gilliwig@aol.com

WIGGINS, Karl Patrick. b 38. MRICS64 FRICS87. Trin Coll Bris BD72. **d** 72 **p** 73. C Hildenborough *Roch* 72-76; Hon C Reading St Barn *Ox* 76-78; Hon C Chieveley w Winterbourne and Oare 78-80; Hon C Earley St Nic 80-83; Hon C Reading St Jo 83-88; Hon C Beech Hill, Grazeley and Spencers Wood 88-98; rtd 98; Perm to Offic *Ox* 99. *Willow Cottage, 37 New Road, Bradford-on-Avon BA15 1AP* Tel (01225) 867007 E-mail kk-wiggins@msn.com

WIGGINTON, Canon Peter Walpole. b 20. Edin Th Coll 40. **d** 43 **p** 44. C Derby St Jas *Derby* 43-46; C Brimington 46; C Gedling *S'well* 46-49; PV S'well Minster 49-52; V Rolleston w Morton 52-56; R W Keal *Linc* 56-83; R E Keal 57-83; R E and W Keal 83-88; RD Bolingbroke 66-88; Can and Preb Linc Cathl 77-88; R Bolingbroke 83-88; R Toynton All Saints w Toynton St Peter 83-88; rtd 88; Chapl Trin Hosp Retford 88-05; Perm to Offic *S'well* from 91. *Trinity Cottage, River Lane, Retford DN22 7DZ* Tel (01777) 860352

WIGGLESWORTH, Mark. b 60. Clare Coll Cam BA82. St Jo Coll Nottm 89. **d** 92 **p** 93. C Brinsworth w Catcliffe *Sheff* 92-93; C Brinsworth w Catcliffe and Treeton 93-95; C Goole 95-96; V Askern from 96; AD Adwick from 05. *The Vicarage, Church Street, Askern, Doncaster DN6 0PH* Tel (01302) 700404 E-mail markandbethwig@yahoo.co.uk

WIGGS, Robert James. b 50. Pemb Coll Cam BA72 MA CertEd. Qu Coll Birm 78. **d** 80 **p** 81. C Stratford St Jo and Ch Ch w Forest Gate St Jas *Chelmsf* 80-83; C E Ham w Upton Park St Alb 83-86; TV 86-91; TR Grays Thurrock 91-99; Perm to Offic from 99. *113 Moulsham Street, Chelmsford CM2 0JN* Tel (01245) 359138

WIGHT, Dennis Marley. b 53. Southn Univ BTh87. Sarum & Wells Th Coll 82. **d** 85 **p** 86. C Gillingham *Sarum* 85-87; Appeals Org CECS from 87; Perm to Offic *Birm* 89-90; V Coseley Ch Ch *Lich* 90-93; V Coseley Ch Ch *Worc* 93-94; R Stoke Prior, Wychbold and Upton Warren 94-02; RD Droitwich 96-99; V Dale and St Brides w Marloes *St D* from 02; AD Roose from 05. *The Vicarage, Dale, Haverfordwest SA62 3RN* Tel (01646) 636255 E-mail dennis.wight@tesco.net

WIGHT (née JONES), Mrs Sian Hilary. b 54. CertEd75 Birm Univ BEd76 Southn Univ BTh87. Sarum & Wells Th Coll 82. **dss** 85 **d** 87 **p** 94. Ex St Sidwell and St Matt *Ex* 85-87; Par Dn 87-88; Perm to Offic *Lich* 89-90 and 93-96; Hon Par Dn Coseley Ch Ch 90-93; Hon Par Dn Coseley Ch Ch *Worc* 93-94; NSM Stoke Prior, Wychbold and Upton Warren 94-02; NSM Dale and St Brides w Marloes *St D* from 02. *The Vicarage, Dale, Haverfordwest SA62 3RN* Tel (01646) 636255

WIGHTMAN, William David. b 39. Birm Univ BA61. Wells Th Coll 61. **d** 63 **p** 64. C Rotherham *Sheff* 63-67; C Castle Church *Lich* 67-70; V Buttershaw St Aid *Bradf* 70-76; V Cullingworth 76-83; R Peterhead *Ab* 83-91; R Strichen, Old Deer and Longside 90-91; Provost St Andr Cathl 91-02; R Aberdeen St Andr 91-02; P-in-c Aberdeen St Ninian 91-02; Hon Can Ch Ch Cathl Connecticut from 91; rtd 02; Perm to Offic *York* from 04. *66 Wold Road, Pocklington, York YO42 2QG* Tel (01759) 301369 E-mail davidwightman@ntlworld.com

WIGLEY, Brian Arthur. b 31. Qu Coll Birm. **d** 82 **p** 83. C Houghton le Spring *Dur* 82-85; C Louth *Linc* 85-86; TV 86-89; Chapl City Hosp NHS Trust Birm 89-95; rtd 95; Perm to Offic *Ex* from 95. *3 Willows Close, Frogmore, Kingsbridge TQ7 2NY* Tel (01548) 531374

WIGLEY, Canon Harry Maxwell (Max). b 38. Oak Hill Th Coll 61. **d** 64 **p** 65. C Upton (Overchurch) *Ches* 64-67; C Gateacre *Liv* 67-69; C Chadderton Ch Ch *Man* 67; V Gt Horton *Bradf* 69-88; Hon Can Bradf Cathl 85-03; V Pudsey St Lawr and St Paul 88-96; V Yeadon St Jo 96-03; rtd 03; Hon Dioc Ev *Bradf* from 04. *20 Collier Lane, Baildon, Shipley BD17 5LN* Tel (01274) 581988 E-mail hjwigley@nascr.net

WIGLEY, Ms Jennifer. b 53. Bris Univ BA74 Birm Univ MA75 Ox Univ CertEd76. Qu Coll Birm 86. **d** 87 **p** 97. C Llangollen w Trevor and Llantysilio *St As* 87-89; C Swansea St Jas *S & B* 89-94; NSM Aberystwyth *St D* 95-98; Tutor St Mich Coll Llan 98-00; C Sketty *S & B* 98-00; Chapl Univ of Wales (Swansea) 00-02; Chapl Univ of Wales (Cardiff) *Llan* 02; Dep Dir S Wales Ord Course from 02; TV Cen Cardiff *Llan* from 03. *17 Chargot Road, Llandaff, Cardiff CF5 1EW* E-mail jennifer.wigley@ntlworld.com

WIGNALL, Daniel Robert Phillip. b 65. Ox Poly BEd88. St Jo Coll Nottm MA98. **d** 98 **p** 99. C Fletchamstead *Cov* 98-01; C Abingdon *Ox* from 01. *102 Gibson Close, Abingdon OX14 1XT* Tel (01235) 539172 Fax 08701-377372 E-mail danny.wignall@ntlworld.com

WIGNALL, Paul Graham. b 49. Lanc Univ BA72 Qu Coll Cam BA74 MA78. Westcott Ho Cam 72. **d** 74 **p** 75. C Chesterton Gd Shep *Ely* 74-76; Min Can Dur Cathl *Dur* 76-79; Tutor Ripon Coll Cuddesdon 80-84; P-in-c Aston Rowant w Crowell *Ox* 81-83; C Shepherd's Bush St Steph w St Thos *Lon* 84-85; P-in-c St Just-in-Roseland and St Mawes *Truro* 99-01; Dir Tr and Development from 01; C St Agnes and Mithian w Mount Hawke from 01. *The Vicarage, Mount Hawke, Truro TR4 8DE* Tel (01209) 891516 *or* (01872) 270162 E-mail paulwignall@supanet.com *or* dtd@truro.anglican.org

WIGRAM, Andrew Oswald. b 39. Lon Univ BD64. Bps' Coll Cheshunt 61. **d** 64 **p** 65. C Marton-in-Cleveland *York* 64-69; Kenya 69-82; Warden Trin Coll Nairobi 77-82; V Westcliff St Mich *Chelmsf* 82-95; RD Southend-on-Sea 89-94; R Cropwell Bishop w Colston Bassett, Granby etc *S'well* 95-05; rtd 05. *38 Pierremont Crescent, Darlington DL3 9PB* Tel (01325) 371473 E-mail andrew.wigram@ntlworld.com

WIGRAM, John Michael. b 67. Ex Univ BSc88. St Jo Coll Nottm MTh04. **d** 05. C Hazlemere *Ox* from 05. *Church House, 70 Georges Hill, Widmer End, High Wycombe HP15 6BH* Tel (01494) 713848 E-mail wigram@ntlworld.com

WIGRAM (née CHAPMAN), Mrs Rachel Grace. b 67. Ex Univ BA88. St Jo Coll Nottm 03. **d** 05. C Hazlemere *Ox* from 05. *Church House, 70 Georges Hill, Widmer End, High Wycombe HP15 6BH* Tel (01494) 713848 E-mail wigram@ntlword.com

WIGRAM, Miss Ruth Margaret. b 41. CertEd63. Cranmer Hall Dur 83. **dss** 84 **d** 87 **p** 94. Shipley St Paul and Frizinghall *Bradf* 84-87; Par Dn 87-90; Asst Dioc Dir of Ords 90-96; C Skipton H Trin 90-96; V Easby w Skeeby and Brompton on Swale etc *Ripon* from 96. *The Vicarage, St Paul's Drive, Brompton on Swale, Richmond DL10 7HQ* Tel (01748) 811840 E-mail ruth.wigram@lineone.net

WIGSTON, Kenneth Edmund. b 28. Lich Th Coll 55. **d** 58 **p** 59. C Sharrow St Andr *Sheff* 58-61; C Kidlington *Ox* 61-68; R Airdrie *Glas* 68-78; R Gartcosh 68-78; R Glas St Oswald 78-85; R Onich *Arg* 85-94; R Glencoe 85-94; R Ballachulish 85-94; rtd 94; Perm to Offic *Arg* from 94. *Old Croft Cottage, 18 Tigh a' phuirt, Glencoe, Ballachulish PH49 4HN* Tel (01855) 811503

WIKELEY, Canon John Roger Ian. b 41. AKC64. **d** 65 **p** 66. C Southport H Trin *Liv* 65-69; C Padgate Ch Ch 69-71; TV Padgate 71-73; R 73-74; TR 74-85; TR W Derby St Mary 85-98; V from 98; P-in-c W Derby St Jas from 04; AD W Derby from 89; Hon Can Liv Cathl from 94. *The Rectory, Meadow Lane, West Derby, Liverpool L12 5EA* Tel 0151-256 6600 Fax 226 4343 E-mail wikeley@wikeley.f9.co.uk

WIKNER, Richard Hugh. b 46. MSI. St Alb Minl Tr Scheme 79. **d** 94 **p** 95. NSM Lt Heath *St Alb* from 94. *Koinonia, 5 The Avenue, Potters Bar EN6 1EG* Tel (01707) 650437 E-mail hughwikner@lineone.net

WILBOURNE, David Jeffrey. b 55. Jes Coll Cam BA78 MA82. Westcott Ho Cam 79. **d** 81 **p** 82. C Stainton-in-Cleveland *York* 81-85; Chapl Asst Hemlington Hosp 81-85; R Monk Fryston and S Milford *York* 85-91; Abp's Dom Chapl 91-97; Dir of Ords 91-97; V Helmsley from 97. *Canons Garth, Helmsley, York YO62 5AQ* Tel (01439) 770236

WILBOURNE, Geoffrey Owen. b 29. Lich Th Coll 60. **d** 62 **p** 63. C Marfleet *York* 62-65; V Ellerton Priory w Aughton and E Cottingwith 65-70; TV Scalby w Ravenscar and Staintondale 70-73; V Kingston upon Hull St Nic 73-76; V Keyingham 76-85; V Hemingbrough 85-91; rtd 91; Perm to Offic *Derby* 91-00 and *York* from 02. *40 Knipe Point Drive, Scarborough YO11 3JT* Tel (01723) 355255

WILBRAHAM, David. b 59. Oak Hill Th Coll BA88. **d** 88 **p** 89. C Ince Ch Ch *Liv* 88-91; Min St Helens St Helen 91-93; Perm to Offic *Guildf* 96-99; NSM Hindhead 99-00; V 00-03; V Churt and Hindhead from 03. *The Vicarage, Wood Road, Hindhead GU26 6PX* Tel (01428) 605305 Mobile 07779-262302 E-mail davidwilbraham@lineone.net

WILBY, Mrs Jean (Sister Davina). b 38. Open Univ BA82. Wycliffe Hall Ox 83. **dss** 85 **d** 87 **p** 94. Maidenhead St Andr and St Mary *Ox* 85-87; C 87; TD Hermitage and Hampstead Norreys, Cold Ash etc 87-91; Lic to Offic 92-95; All SS Convent Ox 91-95; NSM Iffley *Ox* 94-95; C Denham 95-98; rtd 98; P-in-c Woolstone w Gotherington and Oxenton etc *Glouc* from 98. *The Rectory, 67 Malleson Road, Gotherington, Cheltenham GL52 4EX* Tel (01242) 675559

WILBY, Timothy David. b 59. Univ Coll Dur BA80 MA87. Ripon Coll Cuddesdon 81. **d** 83 **p** 84. C Standish *Blackb* 83-86; CF 86-89; V Chorley All SS *Blackb* 89-95; V Penwortham St Leon 95-00; TR Fellside Team from 00. *The Vicarage, Goosnargh Lane, Goosnargh, Preston PR3 2BN* Tel (01772) 865274 E-mail timwilby@aol.com *or* fellsiderector@aol.com

WILBY, Mrs Wendy Ann. b 49. St Hugh's Coll Ox BA71 MA93 Leeds Univ MA01 ARCM69 LRAM72. NEOC. **d** 90 **p** 94. Par Dn Barwick in Elmet *Ripon* 90-93; C High Harrogate St Pet 93-94; P-in-c Birstwith 94-01; AD Harrogate 00-01; Chapl St Aid Sch Harrogate 94-01; V Halifax *Wakef* from 01. *The Vicarage, Kensington Road, Halifax HX3 0HN* Tel and fax (01422) 365477 E-mail octave@wwilby.freeserve.co.uk

WILCOCK, Michael Jarvis. b 32. Dur Univ BA54. Tyndale Hall Bris 60. **d** 62 **p** 63. C Southport Ch Ch *Liv* 62-65; C St Marylebone All So w SS Pet and Jo *Lon* 65-69; V Maidstone St Faith *Cant* 69-77; Dir Past Studies Trin Coll Bris 77-82; V Dur St Nic *Dur* 82-98; rtd 98; Perm to Offic *Chich* from 98. *1 Tudor*

Court, 51 Carlisle Road, Eastbourne BN21 4JR Tel (01323) 417170

WILCOCK, Paul Trevor. b 59. Bris Univ BA Leeds Univ MA93. Trin Coll Bris 83. **d** 87 **p** 88. C Kirkheaton *Wakef* 87-90; Chapl Huddersfield Poly 90-92; Chapl Huddersfield Univ 92-93; Dir Student Services from 93; NSM Huddersfield H Trin from 92; Chapl W Yorkshire Police from 02. *25 Mendip Avenue, Huddersfield HD3 3QG* Tel (01484) 472675 Fax 473120 E-mail p.t.wilcock@hud.ac.uk

WILCOCK, Terence Granville. b 50. Open Univ BA82. EAMTC. **d** 02 **p** 03. NSM Oundle w Ashton and Benefield w Glapthorn *Pet* 02-04; NSM Crosscrake *Carl* from 04. *The Vicarage, Shyreakes Lane, Crosscrake, Kendal LA8 0AB* Tel (01539) 560333 E-mail terryatash@aol.com

WILCOCKSON, Stephen Anthony. b 51. Nottm Univ BA73 Ox Univ BA75 MA81. Wycliffe Hall Ox 73. **d** 76 **p** 77. C Pudsey St Lawr *Bradf* 76-78; C Wandsworth All SS *S'wark* 78-81; V Rock Ferry *Ches* 81-86; V Lache cum Saltney 86-95; V Howell Hill w Burgh Heath *Guildf* from 95; RD Epsom from 00. *St Paul's Vicarage, 17 Northey Avenue, Cheam, Sutton SM2 7HS* Tel (020) 8224 9927 E-mail stevewilcockson@yahoo.com

WILCOX, Anthony Gordon. b 41. Lon Coll of Div LTh67 ALCD67. **d** 67 **p** 68. C Cheltenham Ch Ch *Glouc* 67-72; C Beccles St Mich *St E* 72-74; TV 74-81; V Ipswich All SS from 81. *All Saints' Vicarage, 264 Norwich Road, Ipswich IP1 4BT* Tel (01473) 252975

WILCOX, Brian Howard. b 46. Westcott Ho Cam 71. **d** 73 **p** 74. C Kettering SS Pet and Paul *Pet* 73-78; V Eye 78-82; R Clipston w Naseby and Haselbech w Kelmarsh 82-90; V Hornsea w Atwick *York* 90-97; RD N Holderness 95-97; R Uckfield *Chich* from 97; R Isfield from 97; R Lt Horsted from 97. *The Rectory, Belmont Road, Uckfield TN22 1BP* Tel (01825) 762251

WILCOX, Colin John. b 43. St Mich Coll Llan DipTh84. **d** 86 **p** 87. C Newport St Andr *Mon* 86-88; C Llanmartin 88-90; TV 90-92; V Griffithstown from 92. *St Hilda's Vicarage, 2 Sunnybank Road, Griffithstown, Pontypool NP4 5LT* Tel (01495) 763641

✠**WILCOX, The Rt Revd David Peter.** b 30. St Jo Coll Ox BA52 MA56. Linc Th Coll 52. **d** 54 **p** 55 **c** 86. C St Helier *S'wark* 54-56; C Ox St Mary V *Ox* 56-59; Tutor Linc Th Coll 59-60; Chapl 60-61; Sub-Warden 61-63; India 64-70; R Gt w Lt Gransden *Ely* 70-72; Can Res Derby Cathl *Derby* 72-77; Warden EMMTC 73-77; Prin Ripon Coll Cuddesdon 77-85; V Cuddesdon *Ox* 77-85; Suff Bp Dorking *Guildf* 86-95; rtd 95; Hon Asst Bp Chich from 95. *4 The Court, Hoo Gardens, Willingdon, Eastbourne BN20 9AX* Tel (01323) 506108

WILCOX, David Thomas Richard. b 42. Down Coll Cam BA63 Regent's Park Coll Ox BA66 Tübingen Univ. **d** 95 **p** 96. C Bris St Mary Redcliffe w Temple etc *Bris* 95-97; TV Yate New Town 97-02; Hon C from 02; rtd 02. *The Vicarage, Shorthill Road, Westerleigh, Bristol BS37 8QN* Tel (01454) 312152

WILCOX, Graham James. b 43. Qu Coll Ox BA64 MA75 Lon Univ BD97 MTh02. Ridley Hall Cam 64. **d** 66 **p** 67. C Edgbaston St Aug *Birm* 66-69; C Sheldon 69-72; Asst Chapl Wrekin Coll Telford 72-74; C Asterby w Goulceby *Linc* 74-77; R 77-81; R Benniworth w Market Stainton and Ranby 77-81; R Donington on Bain 77-81; R Stenigot 77-81; R Gayton le Wold w Biscathorpe 77-81; V Scamblesby w Cawkwell 77-81; R Asterby Gp 81-88; V Sutton le Marsh 88-90; R Sutton, Huttoft and Anderby 90-98; R Fyfield, Moreton w Bobbingworth etc *Chelmsf* from 98. *The Rectory, Willingale Road, Fyfield, Ongar CM5 0SD* Tel (01277) 899255 E-mail wilcoxg4@aol.com

WILCOX, Haydon Howard. b 56. Sarum & Wells Th Coll. **d** 82 **p** 83. C Fishponds St Jo *Bris* 82-85; TV Hucknall Torkard *S'well* 85-91; R Bilsthorpe 91-99; R Eakring 91-99; P-in-c Maplebeck 91-99; P-in-c Winkburn 91-99; P-in-c Aldershot St Mich *Guildf* 99-03; V 03; Perm to Offic from 03. *46 Barn Meadow Close, Church Crookham, Aldershot GU52 0YB* Tel and fax (01252) 621639 E-mail haydonwilcox@mac.com

WILCOX, Canon Hugh Edwin. b 37. St Edm Hall Ox BA62 MA66. St Steph Ho Ox 62. **d** 64 **p** 65. C Colchester St Jas, All SS, St Nic and St Runwald *Chelmsf* 64-66; Hon C Clifton St Paul *Bris* 66-68; SCM 66-68; Sec Internat Dept BCC 68-76; Asst Gen Sec 74-76; V Ware St Mary *St Alb* 76-03; Hon Can St Alb 96-03; rtd 03; Perm to Offic *St Alb* from 03. *The Briars, 1 Briary Lane, Royston SG8 9BX* Tel (01763) 244212 E-mail h.wilcox@britishlibrary.net

WILCOX, Canon Jeffry Reed. b 40. MBE05. K Coll Lon AKC65 BA78. **d** 66 **p** 67. C Ryhope *Dur* 66-69; C Cockerton 69-71; P-in-c Pallion 71-82; R Streatham St Leon *S'wark* from 82; RD Streatham 92-00; Hon Can S'wark Cathl from 05. *The Rectory, 1 Becmead Avenue, London SW16 1UH* Tel (020) 8769 4366 *or* 8769 1216

WILCOX, John Bower. b 28. AKC55. **d** 58 **p** 59. C Orford St Marg *Liv* 58-60; C W Derby St Mary 60-63; Ind Chapl *Linc* 63-74; R Aisthorpe w W Thorpe and Scampton 63-74; R Brattleby 64-74; Ind Chapl *York* 74-89; P-in-c Middlesbrough St Cuth 89-93; Urban Development Officer 89-93; rtd 93; Perm to Offic *York* from 93. *5 Duncan Avenue, Redcar TS10 5BX* Tel (01642) 489683

WILCOX, Peter Jonathan. b 61. St Jo Coll Dur BA84 MA91 St Jo Coll Ox DPhil93. Ridley Hall Cam BA86. **d** 87 **p** 88. C Preston on Tees *Dur* 87-90; NSM Ox St Giles and SS Phil and Jas w St Marg *Ox* 90-93; TV Gateshead *Dur* 93-98; Dir Urban Miss Cen Cranmer Hall 93-98; P-in-c Walsall St Paul *Lich* from 98; Hon C Walsall Pleck and Bescot from 05; Hon C Walsall from 05. *St Paul's Vicarage, 57 Mellish Road, Walsall WS4 2DG* Tel (01922) 624963 *or* 626817

WILD, Alan James. b 46. LNSM course 94. **d** 97 **p** 98. OLM Walworth St Pet *S'wark* from 97. *67 Liverpool Grove, London SE17 2HP* Tel (020) 7708 1216

WILD, Hilda Jean. b 48. Linc Th Coll 95. **d** 95 **p** 96. C Newark *S'well* 95-99; V Earlsdon *Cov* from 99. *St Barbara's Vicarage, 24 Rochester Road, Coventry CV5 6AG* Tel (024) 7667 4057

WILD, Roger Bedingham Barratt. b 40. Hull Univ MA94. ALCD64. **d** 65 **p** 66. C Shipley St Pet *Bradf* 65-68; C Pudsey St Lawr 68-71; P-in-c Rawthorpe *Wakef* 71-73; V 73-78; V Ripon H Trin *Ripon* 78-93; RD Ripon 86-93; R Barwick in Elmet 93-01; OCF 79-93; CMS from 01. *Trinity Theological College, 490 Upper Bukit Timar Road, Singapore 678093* Tel (0065) 6762 3714 E-mail rbbwild@hotmail.com.uk *or* roger@ttc.edu.sg

WILDE, David Wilson. b 37. Lon Coll of Div ALCD61 BD62. **d** 62 **p** 63. C Kirkheaton *Wakef* 62-66; C Attenborough w Chilwell *S'well* 66-72; P-in-c Bestwood Park 72-83; R Kimberley from 83. *The Rectory, 1 Eastwood Road, Kimberley, Nottingham NG16 2HX* Tel 0115-938 3565 E-mail christwl@aol.co.uk

WILDEY, Canon Ian Edward. b 51. St Chad's Coll Dur BA72. Coll of Resurr Mirfield 72. **d** 74 **p** 75. C Westgate Common *Wakef* 74-77; C Barnsley St Mary 77-81; V Ravensthorpe 81-95; R Barnsley St Mary from 95; Dir of Educn from 96; Hon Can Wakef Cathl from 00. *The Rectory, 30 Victoria Road, Barnsley S70 2BU* Tel and fax (01226) 282270 E-mail ian@ewildey.freeserve.co.uk

WILDING, Canon Anita Pamela. b 38. MBE01. Blackpool and Fylde Coll of Further Tech TCert61. CMS Tr Coll Chislehurst 65. **dss** 89 **d** 92 **p** 93. CMS Kenya 87-04; Perm to Offic *York* from 04. *5 The Fairways, 35 The Esplanade, Knott End-on-Sea, Poulton-le-Fylde FY6 0AD* Tel (01253) 810642 E-mail wildingp@tiscali.co.uk

WILDING, David. b 43. K Coll Lon BD67 AKC67. **d** 68 **p** 69. C Thornhill *Wakef* 68-70; C Halifax St Jo Bapt 70-72; V Scholes 72-79; V Lightcliffe 79-97; rtd 97; Perm to Offic *Wakef* from 97. *10 Stratton Park, Rastrick, Brighouse HD6 3SN* Tel (01484) 387651

WILDING, Michael Paul. b 57. Chich Th Coll 82. **d** 85 **p** 86. C Treboeth *S & B* 85-87; C Llangiwg 87-88; V Defynnog w Rhydybriw and Llandeilo'r-fan 88-00; V Defynnog, Llandilo'r Fan, Llanulid, Llywel etc from 00. *The Vicarage, Sennybank, Sennybridge, Brecon LD3 8PP* Tel (01874) 638927

WILDING, Pamela. *See* WILDING, Canon Anita Pamela

WILDS, The Ven Anthony Ronald. b 43. Dur Univ BA64. Bps' Coll Cheshunt 64. **d** 66 **p** 67. C Newport Pagnell *Ox* 66-72; Zambia 72-75; V Chandler's Ford *Win* 75-85; V Andover w Foxcott 85-97; RD Andover 89-94; Hon Can Win Cathl 91-97; TR Solihull *Birm* 97-01; Hon Can Birm Cathl 00-01; Adn Plymouth *Ex* from 01. *33 Leat Walk, Roborough, Plymouth PL6 7AT* Tel (01752) 793397 Fax 774618 E-mail archdeacon.of.plymouth@exeter.anglican.org

WILES, Mrs Cathryn. b 51. BEd. **d** 04. NSM Wandsworth Common St Mary *S'wark* from 04. *10 Waldeck Grove, London SE27 0BE* Tel (020) 8761 4017 *or* 8682 6627 E-mail cathy.mail@virgin.net

WILES, Roger Kenneth. b 58. Witwatersrand Univ BA. St Paul's Coll Grahamstown. **d** 83 **p** 84. S Africa 83-99; C Johannesburg St Gab 83-84; C Belgravia St Jo 84-85; Chapl Jeppe Boys' High Sch 85-86; Chapl Witwatersrand Univ 86-93; R Edenvale Em 94-99; P-in-c Edin Clermiston Em *Edin* 99-05; V Poulton Lancelyn H Trin *Ches* from 05. *Address temp unknown* Tel 07909-574169 (mobile) E-mail roger@gam.co.za

WILESMITH, Miss Mary Adelaide. b 50. NNEB69. WEMTC 03. **d** 05. NSM Badgeworth, Shurdington and Witcombe w Bentham *Glouc* from 05. *32 Leyson Road, The Reddings, Cheltenham GL51 6RX* Tel (01452) 712635 Mobile 07947-254509

WILFORD (formerly GIBSON), Laura Mary. b 50. N Ord Course 85. **d** 88 **p** 94. Par Dn Foley Park *Worc* 88-90; Par Dn Kidderminster St Jo and H Innocents 90-94; TV 94-96; P-in-c Mamble w Bayton, Rock w Heightington etc 96-99; TV Cartmel Peninsula *Carl* 99-01; Jt Dir of Ords 00-01; P-in-c Worminghall w Ickford, Oakley and Shabbington *Ox* from 01. *The Rectory, 32A The Avenue, Worminghall, Aylesbury HP18 9LE* Tel (01844) 338839 E-mail laura.wilford@virgin.net

WILKERSON, Ms Valerie Anne. b 40. Leeds Univ BA62 RGN77 RM78. St Jo Coll Nottm 03. **d** 04 **p** 05. NSM Alrewas *Lich* from 04; NSM Wychnor from 04. *22 Chaseview Road, Alrewas, Burton-on-Trent DE13 7EL* Tel (01283) 790612 E-mail valwilkerson@aol.com

WILKES, Jonathan Peter. b 66. Leic Poly BA88. Ripon Coll Cuddesdon BTh96. **d** 96 **p** 97. C Hackney *Lon* 96-00; P-in-c Paddington St Pet from 00; P-in-c Paddington St Mary Magd from 04. *St Mary Magdalene Vicarage, 2 Rowington Close, London W2 5TF* Tel (020) 7289 2011

WILKES, Canon Robert Anthony. b 48. Trin Coll Ox BA70 MA73. Wycliffe Hall Ox 71. **d** 74 **p** 75. C Netherton *Liv* 74-77; V 77-81; Bp's Dom Chapl 81-85; CMS 85-98; Pakistan 85-86; Regional Sec Middle E and Pakistan 87-98; P-in-c Mossley Hill St Matt and St Jas *Liv* 98-05; TR Mossley Hill from 05; Hon Can Liv Cathl from 03. *The Vicarage, Rose Lane, Liverpool L18 8DB* Tel 0151-724 2650 E-mail wilkesmh@surfaid.org

WILKIE, Alan James. b 17. Chich Th Coll 39. **d** 42 **p** 43. C Wednesbury St Paul Wood Green *Lich* 42-44; C Porthill 44-52; C Stoke-upon-Trent 52-54; Chapl Stoke-on-Trent City Gen Hosp 52-54; Lic to Offic *Guildf* 54-65; Lic to Offic *Nor* 66-68; Hd Badingham Coll Leatherhead 54-65; Wymondham 65-68; V Lindale *Carl* 69-71; P-in-c Field Broughton 71; V Lindale w Field Broughton 71-85; rtd 85; Perm to Offic *Carl* 85-99 and from 02. *Fernlea, Beckermet CA21 2YF* Tel (01946) 841284

WILKIE, Michael John David. b 65. Oak Hill Th Coll BA90 Ex Univ PGCE94. SW Minl Tr Course 98. **d** 00 **p** 01. NSM Combe Martin, Berrynarbor, Lynton, Brendon etc *Ex* 00-05. *The Terrace, Parracombe, Barnstaple EX31 4PE* Tel (01548) 763584

WILKIN, Kenneth. b 54. Open Univ BA97 Dip Environment & Development97. S'wark Ord Course 86 Wilson Carlile Coll. **d** 88 **p** 89. C Wolverhampton *Lich* 88-92; V W Bromwich St Andr w Ch Ch 92-98; Dep Chapl HM Pris Pentonville 98-00; Chapl HM Pris Holloway from 00. *HM Prison Holloway, 1 Parkhurst Road, London N7 0NU* Tel (020) 7979 4561
E-mail kenneth.wilkin@hmps.gsi.gov.uk *or* kwilkin@aol.com

WILKIN, Paul John. b 56. Linc Th Coll 88. **d** 90 **p** 91. C Leavesden All SS *St Alb* 90-93; C Jersey St Brelade *Win* 93-97; V Squirrels Heath *Chelmsf* from 97. *The Vicarage, 36 Ardleigh Green Road, Hornchurch RM11 2LQ* Tel (01708) 446571
E-mail paulwilkin@iname.com

WILKIN, Rose Josephine. *See* HUDSON-WILKIN, Mrs Rose Josephine

WILKINS, Mrs Janice Joy. b 49. St D Coll Lamp 90. **d** 93 **p** 97. NSM Tredegar St Jas *Mon* 93-96; NSM Newbridge 96-97; C Mynyddislwyn 97-01; V Abercarn and Cwmcarn from 01; AD Bedwellty from 05. *The Vicarage, Twyn Road, Abercarn, Newport NP11 5GU* Tel (01495) 243919

WILKINS, Ralph Herbert. b 29. Lon Univ BD61. St Aug Coll Cant 72. **d** 73 **p** 74. C Epsom Common Ch Ch *Guildf* 73-76; C Haslemere 77-79; P-in-c Market Lavington and Easterton *Sarum* 79-82; V 82-90; P-in-c Puddletown and Tolpuddle 90-94; P-in-c Milborne St Andrew w Dewlish 92-94; P-in-c Piddletrenthide w Plush, Alton Pancras etc 92-94; rtd 94; Perm to Offic *Ab* 94-01. *The Mill, Marton, Welshpool SY21 8JY* Tel (01938) 580566

WILKINS, Miss Susan Stafford. b 47. Dur Univ BA. Sarum Th Coll. **dss** 82 **d** 87 **p** 94. Redlynch and Morgan's Vale *Sarum* 82-88; Hon Par Dn 87-88; Hon Par Dn Bemerton 88-90; Par Dn Hilperton w Whaddon and Staverton etc 90-94; TV Worle *B & W* 94-99; P-in-c Hallwood *Ches* 99-04; V from 04. *The Vicarage, 6 Kirkstone Crescent, Runcorn WA7 3JQ* Tel (01928) 713101 E-mail suewilkins@hallwoodlep.fsnet.co.uk

WILKINS, Vernon Gregory. b 53. Trin Coll Cam MA74 Ox Univ BA88. Wycliffe Hall Ox 86. **d** 89 **p** 90. C Boscombe St Jo *Win* 89-91; C Bursledon 91-94; V Ramsgate St Luke *Cant* 94-03; Dir Tr Bromley Chr Tr Cen Trust from 03. *29 Heathfield Road, Bromley BR1 3RN* Tel (020) 8464 5135
E-mail vernon@vgwilkins.freeserve.co.uk

WILKINSON, Adrian Mark. b 68. TCD BA90 MA94 BTh94 NUI HDipEd91. CITC 91. **d** 94 **p** 95. C Douglas Union w Frankfield *C, C & R* 94-97; I Dunboyne Union *M & K* 97-02; Chapl NUI 97-02; Min Can St Patr Cathl Dublin 97-02; I Rathmolyon w Castlerickard, Rathcore and Agher *M & K* 01-02; I Douglas Union w Frankfield *C, C & R* from 02. *The Rectory, Carrigaline Road, Douglas, Cork, Irish Republic* Tel (00353) (21) 489 1539 E-mail amwilk@indigo.ie

WILKINSON, Canon Alan Bassindale. b 31. St Cath Coll Cam BA54 MA58 PhD59 DD97. Coll of Resurr Mirfield 57. **d** 59 **p** 60. C Kilburn St Aug *Lon* 59-61; Chapl St Cath Coll Cam 61-67; V Barrow Gurney *B & W* 67-70; Asst Chapl and Lect St Matthias's Coll Bris 67-70; Prin Chich Th Coll 70-74; Can and Preb Chich Cathl *Chich* 70-74; Warden Verulam Ho 74-75; Dir of Aux Min Tr *St Alb* 74-75; Sen Lect Crewe and Alsager Coll of HE 75-78; Hon C Alsager St Mary *Ches* 76-78; Dioc Dir of Tr *Ripon* 78-84; P-in-c Thornthwaite w Thruscross and Darley 84-88; Hon Can Ripon Cathl 84-88; Perm to Offic *Portsm* from 88; Hon P Portsm Cathl from 88; Hon Dioc Th 93-01; Hon Chapl Portsm Cathl 94-01; rtd 96; Visiting Lect Portsm Univ 98-05. *17A High Street, Portsmouth PO1 2LP* Tel (023) 9273 6270

WILKINSON, Alice Margaret Marion. *See* BISHOP, Mrs Alice Margaret Marion

WILKINSON, Andrew Wilfrid. b 66. Nottm Univ BTh96 Lanc Univ MA99. Linc Th Coll 93. **d** 96 **p** 97. C Longridge *Blackb* 96-99; V Garstang St Helen and St Michaels-on-Wyre from 99; AD Garstang from 02; CF (TA) from 02. *The Vicarage, 6 Vicarage Lane, Churchtown, Preston PR3 0HW* Tel and fax (01995) 602294 E-mail areadean@tiscali.co.uk

WILKINSON (née PHILPOTT), Canon Barbara May. b 48. Leeds Univ BA69 CertEd70 MA90. N Ord Course 90. **d** 93 **p** 94. NSM Carleton and Lothersdale *Bradf* 93-96; C Steeton 96-00; Asst Chapl Airedale NHS Trust 96-01; Hd Chapl Services from 01; RD S Craven *Bradf* from 04; Hon Can Bradf Cathl from 04. *37 Aire Valley Drive, Bradley, Keighley BD20 9HY* Tel (01535) 636339

WILKINSON, Mrs Christine Margaret. b 52. Man Univ BA74 Neville's Cross Coll of Educn Dur PGCE75 Birm Univ MEd78. **d** 04 **p** 05. OLM Eythorne and Elvington w Waldershare etc *Cant* from 04. *4 The Glen, Shepherdswell, Dover CT15 7PF* Tel (01304) 831025 E-mail chriswilk.shep@virgin.net

WILKINSON, David Andrew. b 62. Edge Hill Coll of HE BA83. Oak Hill Th Coll BA85. **d** 88 **p** 89. C Upton (Overchurch) *Ches* 88-91; C Fulham St Matt *Lon* 91-94; V Duffield *Derby* 94-99; V Finchley St Paul and St Luke *Lon* 99-03. *Honeysuckle Cottage, 19 Church Street, Windermere LA23 1AQ* Tel (015394) 43069

WILKINSON, David Edward Paul. b 36. Univ of Wales (Swansea) BSc57. St Mich Coll Llan 57. **d** 59 **p** 60. C Brecon w Battle *S & B* 59-60; Min Can Brecon Cathl 60-66; R Llanelwedd w Llanfaredd, Cwmbach Llechryd etc 66-72; V Tycoch 72-74; Asst Master Churchmead Sch Datchet 75-82; TV Seacroft *Ripon* 82-01; rtd 01; Hon C Bishop Monkton and Burton Leonard *Ripon* from 01; Hon Min Can Ripon Cathl from 01. *The Vicarage, Knaresborough Road, Bishop Monkton, Harrogate HG3 3QQ* Tel (01765) 677372 Mobile 07909-961197
E-mail paulwilkinson4@aol.com

WILKINSON, Canon David James. b 45. St D Coll Lamp 65 Wycliffe Hall Ox 68. **d** 69 **p** 70. C Swansea St Thos and Kilvey *S & B* 69-73; C Clydach 73-76; R Llanbadarn Fawr, Llandegley and Llanfihangel etc 76-81; V Swansea St Nic 81-88; V Killay 88-94; V Ilston w Pennard from 94; RD W Gower from 99; Can Brecon Cathl 99-04; Prec from 04. *The Vicarage, 88 Pennard Road, Pennard, Swansea SA3 2AD* Tel and fax (01792) 232928

WILKINSON, Edward. b 55. Cranmer Hall Dur 86. **d** 88 **p** 89. C Bishopwearmouth St Nic *Dur* 88-92; P-in-c Newbottle 92-96; V from 96. *The Vicarage, Newbottle, Houghton le Spring DH4 4EP* Tel 0191-584 3244

WILKINSON, Edwin. b 29. Oak Hill Th Coll 53. **d** 56 **p** 57. C Blackb Ch Ch *Blackb* 56-58; C Cheltenham St Mark *Glouc* 58-61; V Tiverton St Geo *Ex* 61-66; V Rye Harbour *Chich* 66-73; V Camber and E Guldeford 73-79; V Westfield 79-87; V Bexhill St Steph 87-93; rtd 93; Perm to Offic *Chich* from 93. *51 Anderida Road, Eastbourne BN22 0PZ* Tel (01323) 503083

WILKINSON, Mrs Elizabeth Mary. b 65. St Edm Hall Ox MA91. NEOC 02. **d** 05. C Harlow Green and Lamesley *Dur* from 05. *The Rectory, 91 Old Durham Road, Gateshead NE8 4BS* Tel 0191-477 3990 E-mail libby.wilkinson@fish.co.uk

WILKINSON, Geoffrey. *See* WILKINSON, Roy Geoffrey

WILKINSON, Guy Alexander. b 48. Magd Coll Cam BA69. Ripon Coll Cuddesdon 85. **d** 87 **p** 88. C Coventry Caludon *Cov* 87-90; P-in-c Ockham w Hatchford *Guildf* 90-91; R 91-94; Bp's Dom Chapl 90-94; V Small Heath *Birm* 94-99; Adn Bradf 99-04. *12 Davenant Road, Oxford OX2 8BX* Tel (01865) 429171 Mobile 07932-652315 E-mail guy@gwilkinson.org.uk

WILKINSON, Miss Helen Mary. b 53. Homerton Coll Cam BEd76. Trin Coll Bris 02. **d** 04 **p** 05. C Newbury *Ox* from 04. *10 Braunfels Walk, Newbury RG14 5NQ* Tel (01635) 581456 Mobile 07790-262631
E-mail helen.wilkinson@st-nicolas-newbury.org

WILKINSON, James Daniel. b 73. Westmr Coll Ox BTh95. St Steph Ho Ox 97. **d** 99 **p** 00. C Wantage *Ox* 99-02; P-in-c S Hinksey from 02; Sec to Bp Ebbsfleet 02-04. *The Vicarage, 33 Vicarage Road, Oxford OX1 4RD* Tel (01865) 245879
E-mail frwilkinson@ukonline.co.uk

WILKINSON, John Andrew. b 59. Pemb Coll Ox BA83 MA87 St Jo Coll Dur BA86. Cranmer Hall Dur 84. **d** 87 **p** 88. C Broadheath *Ches* 87-91; TV Worthing Ch the King *Chich* 91-97; Chapl Chantilly *Eur* from 97. *7A avenue du Bouteiller, 60500 Chantilly, France* Tel (0033) (3) 44 57 52 00 *or* tel and fax 44 58 53 22 E-mail wilkstp@club-internet.fr

WILKINSON, John David. b 36. K Coll Lon AKC59. **d** 60 **p** 61. C Wythenshawe Wm Temple Ch CD *Man* 60-63; C Morley St Pet w Churwell *Wakef* 63-65; V Robert Town 65-75; V Battyeford 75-88; V Airedale w Fryston 88-98; P-in-c Cawthorne 98-04; rtd 04. *29 Pontefract Road, Ferry Bridge, Knottingley WF11 8PN* Tel (01977) 607250

WILKINSON, Canon John Donald. b 29. Mert Coll Ox BA54 MA56 Louvain Univ Belgium LTh59 Lon Univ PhD82 FSA80. Gen Th Sem (NY) Hon STD63 Cuddesdon Coll 54. **d** 56 **p** 57. C Stepney St Dunstan and All SS *Lon* 56-59; Jerusalem 61-63; Gen Ed USPG 63-69; Dean St Geo Coll Jerusalem 69-75; Can Jerusalem 73-75; P-in-c S Kensington H Trin w All SS *Lon* 75-78; Bp's Dir of Clergy Tr 75-79; Dir Br Sch of Archaeology Jerusalem 79-83; USA 83-91; NSM Kensington St Mary Abbots w St Geo *Lon* 91-94; rtd 94; Hon C St Marylebone St Cypr *Lon* 94-98; Perm to Offic from 98. *7 Tenniel Close, London W2 3LE* Tel and fax (020) 7229 9205

WILKINSON, Canon John Lawrence. b 43. Ch Coll Cam BA65 MA69 Birm Univ MLitt91. Qu Coll Birm DipTh68 Gen Th Sem (NY) STB69. **d** 69 **p** 70. C Braunstone *Leic* 69-71; C Hodge Hill *Birm* 71-74; P-in-c Aston St Jas 75-84; Tutor Qu Coll Birm 85-95; Hon C Birm St Geo *Birm* 86-95; V Kings Heath from 95; Hon Can Birm Cathl from 99. *All Saints' Vicarage, 2 Vicarage Road, Birmingham B14 7RA* Tel 0121-444 1207 E-mail jrwilkinson@dsl.pipex.com

WILKINSON, John Stoddart. b 47. Univ of Wales (Cardiff) CQSW83. St D Coll Lamp DipTh70. **d** 70 **p** 71. C Kells *Carl* 70-72; C Barrow St Geo w St Luke 72-74; Perm to Offic *Mon* 74-89; Sub-Chapl HM YOI Hewell Grange 89-90; Sub-Chapl HM Rem Cen Brockhill 89-90; rtd 02. *Seren y Mor, 11 Dunsany Park, Haverfordwest SA61 1UD* Tel (01437) 762364

WILKINSON, Jonathan Charles. b 61. Leeds Univ BA83. Wycliffe Hall Ox 85. **d** 87 **p** 88. C Plymouth St Andr w St Paul and St Geo *Ex* 87-90; C Oulton Broad *Nor* 90-93; V Hallwood *Ches* 93-99; TR Gateshead *Dur* from 99. *The Rectory, 91 Old Durham Road, Gateshead NE8 4BS* Tel 0191-477 3990 E-mail wilkinson@clara.net

WILKINSON, Mrs Joyce Aileen. b 29. BSc(Econ) MA. **d** 99 **p** 00. NSM Bredon w Bredon's Norton *Worc* 99-04; rtd 04; Perm to Offic *Worc* from 04. *Foxgloves, Back Lane, Bredon, Tewkesbury GL20 7LH* Tel (01684) 773389

WILKINSON, Miss Julia Mary. b 52. Cam Inst of Educn CertEd73 Open Univ BA85 Univ of Wales (Ban) BD89. Linc Th Coll 92. **d** 92 **p** 94. Par Dn High Wycombe *Ox* 92-94; C 94-96; TV 96-01; Bp's Adv for Women in Ord Min 97-01; P-in-c St Issey w St Petroc Minor *Truro* from 01; P-in-c St Merryn from 01; Co Dioc Dir of Ords from 01. *The Rectory, Glebe Crescent, St Issey, Wadebridge PL27 7HJ* Tel and fax (01841) 540314 E-mail revjulia@stpetroc.fsnet.co.uk

WILKINSON, Canon Keith Howard. b 48. Hull Univ BA70 FRSA94 MCT99. Westcott Ho Cam 74. **d** 76 **p** 77. C Pet St Jude *Pet* 76-79; Chapl Eton Coll 79-84; Perm to Offic *Pet* 82-94; Chapl Malvern Coll 84-89; Hd Master Berkhamsted Sch Herts 89-96; Lic to Offic *St Alb* 89-96; Hd Master K Sch Cant from 96; Hon Can Cant Cathl *Cant* from 96. *The King's School, Canterbury CT1 2ES* Tel (01227) 595501 E-mail headmaster@kings-school.co.uk

WILKINSON, The Ven Kenneth Samuel. b 31. TCD BA60 MA69. CITC 60. **d** 60 **p** 61. C Dublin St Michan w St Paul *D & G* 60-63; Min Can St Patr Cathl Dublin 62-67; C Dublin Ch Ch Leeson Park *D & G* 63-67; I Killegney *C & O* 67-70; I Enniscorthy w Clone, Clonmore, Monart etc 70-02; Preb Ferns Cathl 83-88; Adn Ferns 88-02; Dioc Dir of Ords 94-02; rtd 02. *149 Hazelwood, Old Coach Road, Gorey, Co Wexford, Irish Republic* Tel (00353) (55) 20784

WILKINSON, Margaret Anne. b 46. Lon Univ MB, BS70 MSc74 MRCPsych77. St Alb and Ox Min Course 95. **d** 98 **p** 99. NSM Heston *Lon* 98-01; Chapl HM YOI Feltham from 01. *HM Young Offender Institution, Bedfont Road, Feltham TW13 4ND* Tel (020) 8890 0061 *or* 8844 5325 E-mail maggie.wilkinson@hmps.gsi.gov.uk

WILKINSON, Miss Marlene Sandra. b 45. SRN71 Huddersfield Poly NDN86 Leeds Univ DipTh91 Sheff Univ Dip Bibl Studies 93. Trin Coll Bris IDC78. **dss** 78 **d** 93 **p** 94. Wrose *Bradf* 78-82; Chapl St Luke's Hosp Bradf 78-82; Past Tutor Aston Tr Scheme 79-81; W Yorkshire CECS 82-84; Westgate Common *Wakef* 84-86; E Ardsley 86-92; Wakef St Jo 92-94; NSM 93-94; TV Barrow St Geo w St Luke *Carl* 94-00; TV Darwen St Pet w Hoddlesden *Blackb* 00-02; rtd 03. *4 Hopefield Court, East Ardsley, Wakefield WF3 2LL* Tel (01924) 872825

WILKINSON, Mrs Mary Frances. b 52. St As Minl Tr Course 99. **d** 03 **p** 04. NSM Shotton *St As* from 03. *10 Appleby Drive, Hawarden, Deeside CH5 3HN* Tel (01244) 534036

WILKINSON, Michael Alan. b 27. Selw Coll Cam BA51. Westcott Ho Cam 52. **d** 53 **p** 54. C Swindon Ch Ch *Bris* 53-57; C Knowle St Barn 57-59; C Eltham St Jo *S'wark* 59-65; C Sydenham St Bart 65-77; Perm to Offic *Ex* 77-84; P-in-c Yealmpton 84-91; P-in-c Brixton 87-91; V Yealmpton and Brixton 91-97; RD Ivybridge 91-93; rtd 97; Perm to Offic *Ex* from 97. *The Old Forge, Kingston, Kingsbridge TQ7 4PT* Tel (01548) 810424

WILKINSON, Paul. b 51. Sarum & Wells Th Coll 75. **d** 78 **p** 79. C Allerton *Bradf* 78-80; C Baildon 80-83; V Hengoed w Gobowen *Lich* 83-90; V Potterne w Worton and Marston *Sarum* 90-03; Chapl Roundway Hosp Devizes 92-03; P-in-c Leckhampton St Pet *Glouc* from 03. *The Rectory, Church Road, Leckhampton, Cheltenham GL53 0QJ* Tel (01242) 513647 E-mail pwilkinson@vicarage79.fsnet.co.uk

WILKINSON, Paul Harold. b 40. Regents Th Coll BA95 CEng74 MIEE72. N Ord Course 04. **d** 04 **p** 05. NSM Wistaston *Ches* from 04. *4 Willaston Hall Gardens, Nantwich CW5 6NX* Tel (01270) 663551 E-mail wilkinsonph@btinternet.com

WILKINSON, Paul Martin. b 56. Brunel Univ BSc. Wycliffe Hall Ox 83. **d** 86 **p** 87. C Hinckley H Trin *Leic* 86-90; V Newbold on Avon *Cov* from 90. *The Vicarage, Main Street, Newbold, Rugby CV21 1HH* Tel (01788) 543055 Fax 542458 E-mail paul.wilkinson4@tesco.net

WILKINSON, Peter David Lloyd. b 67. Trin Coll Ox BA89 MA93. Ridley Hall Cam BA94 CTM95. **d** 95 **p** 96. C Brampton St Thos *Derby* 95-98; C Tunbridge Wells St Jo *Roch* 98-02; C Ox St Ebbe w H Trin and St Pet *Ox* from 02. *10 Lincoln Road, Oxford OX1 4TB* Tel (01865) 728885 E-mail pete@peteandjules.freeserve.co.uk

WILKINSON, Peter Howarth. b 32. St Pet Hall Ox BA54 MA58. Ridley Hall Cam 56. **d** 58 **p** 59. C Cheadle *Ches* 58-62; V Nettlebed *Ox* 62-68; rtd 68; Hon C Cheadle *Ches* 69-82. *12 Henley Grange, 81 Gatley Road, Cheadle SK8 1LX* Tel 0161-428 7699

WILKINSON, Robert. *See* WILKINSON, Walter Edward Robert

WILKINSON, Robert Ian. b 43. MIMunE73 MICE84 CEng73. Oak Hill NSM Course. **d** 88 **p** 89. NSM Hawkwell *Chelmsf* 88-89; NSM Thundersley 89-91; C New Thundersley 91-94; V Berechurch St Marg w St Mich from 94. *The Vicarage, 348 Mersea Road, Colchester CO2 8RA* Tel (01206) 576859 E-mail vicar@stmargcol.org.uk

WILKINSON, Robert John. b 66. Birkbeck Coll Lon BA98 Fitzw Coll Cam BA00 ACIB90. Westcott Ho Cam 98. **d** 01 **p** 02. C Southgate Ch Ch *Lon* 01-04; TV Wood Green St Mich w Bounds Green St Gabr etc from 04. *27 Collings Close, London N22 8RL* Tel (020) 8881 9386 Fax 8373 0465 E-mail robert.wilkinson@london.anglican.org

WILKINSON, Robert Matthew. b 21. TCD BA46. TCD Div Sch 47. **d** 47 **p** 48. C Limerick St Lawr w H Trin and St Jo *L & K* 47-49; C Arm St Mark *Arm* 49-51; I Mullavilly 51-55; I Derryloran 55-73; Can Arm Cathl 67-73; I Ballymore 73-87; Treas Arm Cathl 73-75; Chan 75-83; Prec 83-87; rtd 87. *60 Coleraine Road, Portrush BT56 8HN* Tel (028) 7082 2758

WILKINSON, Robert Samuel. b 52. Wycliffe Hall Ox DipMin94. **d** 94 **p** 95. C Boughton Monchelsea *Cant* 94-96; C Parkwood CD 95-96; C Plymouth St Andr and St Paul Stonehouse *Ex* 96-01; P-in-c Whimple, Talaton and Clyst St Lawr from 01. *The Rectory, Grove Road, Whimple, Exeter EX5 2TP* Tel (01404) 822521 E-mail rob@standrewschurch.org.uk

WILKINSON, Roger. b 46. K Coll Lon BA68 AKC68 AKC72. St Aug Coll Cant 72. **d** 73 **p** 74. C Lt Stanmore St Lawr *Lon* 73-76; Asst Chapl St Geo Hosp Lon 76-78; Chapl Hounslow and Spelthorne HA 78-88; TV Langley and Parkfield *Man* 88-89; C Shelf and Buttershaw St Aid *Bradf* 89-90; Chapl Asst Ipswich Hosp NHS Trust 90-94; C Fingringhoe w E Donyland and Abberton etc *Chelmsf* 94-01; P-in-c Greensted-juxta-Ongar w Stanford Rivers 01-04; P-in-c Stapleford Tawney w Theydon Mt 01-04; R Greensted-juxta-Ongar w Stanford Rivers etc from 04. *52 Epping Road, Toot Hill, Ongar CM5 9SQ* Tel (01992) 524005 E-mail rogerwilko@supanet.com

WILKINSON, Roy Geoffrey. b 42. Open Univ BSc93. Sarum Th Coll 67. **d** 70 **p** 71. C Belsize Park *Lon* 70-73; C Heston 73-75; C Hythe *Cant* 75-79; V Croydon Woodside 79-86; NSM Skegness and Winthorpe *Linc* 96-04; NSM Skegness Gp from 04; Asst Mental Health Chapl Linc Distr Healthcare NHS Trust 96-97; Mental Health Chapl from 97. *Witham Court EMI Unit, Fen Lane, North Hykeham, Lincoln LN6 8UZ* Tel (01522) 500690 *or* 851399

WILKINSON, Simon Evelyn. b 49. Nottm Univ BA74. Cuddesdon Coll 74. **d** 76 **p** 77. C Cheam *S'wark* 76-78; P-in-c Warlingham w Chelsham and Farleigh 78-83; Hd RS Radley Coll 83-89; R Bishop's Waltham and Upham *Portsm* 89-97; TR Shaston *Sarum* 97-03; P-in-c Amesbury from 03; RD Stonehenge from 03. *The Vicarage, Church Street, Amesbury, Salisbury SP4 7EU* Tel (01980) 623145 E-mail simon@amesburyabbey.freeserve.co.uk

WILKINSON, Walter Edward Robert. b 38. St Andr Univ MA60. Lon Coll of Div BD63 ALCD63. **d** 63 **p** 64. C High Wycombe *Ox* 63-70; PV, Succ and Sacr Roch Cathl *Roch* 70-73; P-in-c Asby w Ormside *Carl* 73-80; R Cherry Burton *York* 80-95; RD Beverley 88-94; P-in-c Grasmere *Carl* 95-03; rtd 03; Perm to Offic *Carl* from 03. *4 Heversham Gardens, Heversham, Milnthorpe LA7 7RA* Tel (01539) 564044 E-mail bob@carliol.clara.co.uk

WILKINSON, Canon Wilfred Badger. b 21. K Coll Lon BD50 AKC50. **d** 50 **p** 51. C Luton St Mary *St Alb* 50-53; C Gt Berkhamsted 53-57; C-in-c Wythenshawe Wm Temple Ch CD *Man* 57-65; R Clifton w Glapton *S'well* 65-71; TR Clifton 71-86; Hon Can S'well Minster 83-86; rtd 86; Perm to Offic *S'well* 86-04. *c/o Dr Mark Wilkinson, Barn House, 18B Chearsley Road, Long Crendon, Aylesbury HP18 9AW* Tel (01844) 201091

WILKS, Eric Percival. b 32. Wells Th Coll 67. **d** 68 **p** 69. C Fladbury w Throckmorton, Wyre Piddle and Moor *Worc* 68-70; Perm to Offic from 70. *4 Catherine Cottages, Droitwich Road, Hartlebury, Kidderminster DY10 4EL* Tel (01299) 251580

WILKS, Ernest Howard. b 26. Oak Hill Th Coll 64. **d** 66 **p** 67. C Slough *Ox* 66-69; R Gressenhall w Longham and Bittering Parva *Nor* 69-77; Area Sec CMS *St E* and *Nor* 77-83; P-in-c Deopham w Hackford *Nor* 83-84; P-in-c Morley 83-84; P-in-c Wicklewood and Crownthorpe 83-84; R Morley w Deopham, Hackford, Wicklewood etc 84-88; CMS Nigeria 89-91; rtd 91; Perm to Offic *Nor* from 91. *Corner Cottage, Carbrooke Road, Griston, Thetford IP25 6QE* Tel (01953) 881413

WILL, Nicholas James. b 53. Birm Univ LLB75. Qu Coll Birm 93. **d** 95 **p** 96. C Bridgnorth, Tasley, Astley Abbotts, etc *Heref* 95-00; R Raveningham Gp *Nor* from 00. *The Rectory, Church Road, Thurlton, Norwich NR14 6RN* Tel (01508) 548648

WILLANS, Jonathan Michael Arthur. b 60. QUB BD. CITC 83. **d** 85 **p** 86. C Larne and Inver *Conn* 85-88; R Hawick *Edin* 88-91; P-in-c Brockham Green *S'wark* from 91; P-in-c Leigh from 91. *The Vicarage, Clayhill Road, Leigh, Reigate RH2 8PD* Tel and fax (01306) 611224

WILLANS, William Richard Gore. b 48. Qu Coll Ox BA70 MA74 Ox Univ PGCE71. CITC 77. **d** 79 **p** 80. Canada 79-98; C Bonne Bay 79-80; P-in-c Bonne Bay N 80-82; R 82-87; R Thunder Bay St Thos 87-98; RD Thunder Bay 89-93 and 95-97; I Craigs w Dunaghy and Killagan *Conn* from 98. *Craigs Rectory, 95 Hillmount Road, Cullybackey, Ballymena BT42 1NZ* Tel (028) 2588 0248 *or* 2588 2225 E-mail willans@btinternet.com

WILLARD, John Fordham. b 38. K Coll Lon BD62 AKC62. **d** 63 **p** 64. C Balham Hill Ascension *S'wark* 63-67; C Leigh Park *Portsm* 67-73; C-in-c Leigh Park St Clare CD 73-75; R Bishop's Waltham 75-87; P-in-c Upham 78-79; R 79-87; V Dalston H Trin w St Phil *Lon* 87-97; P-in-c Haggerston All SS 90-97; P-in-c Fairford *Glouc* 97-98; V Fairford and Kempsford w Whelford 98-04; rtd 04; Perm to Offic *Glouc* from 05. *15 Highwood Avenue, Cheltenham GL53 0JJ* Tel (01242) 530051

WILLCOCK, Canon Richard William. b 39. Hertf Coll Ox BA62 MA66. Ripon Hall Ox 62. **d** 64 **p** 65. C Ashton St Mich *Man* 64-68; Bp's Dom Chapl 68-72; V Charlestown 72-75; Chapl Casterton Sch Lancs 75-80; V Bamford *Man* 80-92; R Framlingham w Saxtead *St E* 92-04; RD Loes 95-97; Warden of Readers 98-03; Hon Can St E Cathl 00-04; rtd 04. *High Green Cottage, Sandford, Appleby-in-Westmorland CA16 6NR* Tel (017683) 51021

WILLCOX, Canon Frederick John. b 29. Kelham Th Coll 49. **d** 54 **p** 55. C Tranmere St Paul *Ches* 54-56; Lic to Offic *S'well* 57-61; S Africa 62-70; P-in-c Derby St Andr w St Osmund *Derby* 70-74; V 74-80; V Netherton St Andr *Worc* 80-94; Hon Can Worc Cathl 91-94; rtd 94; Perm to Offic *Worc* from 94. *48 Meadow Croft, West Hagley, Stourbridge DY9 0LJ* Tel (01562) 887255

WILLCOX, Ralph Arthur. b 32. Westhill Coll Birm CertYS59 Cranfield Inst of Tech MSc80. St Alb Minl Tr Scheme 86. **d** 89 **p** 90. NSM Aspley Guise w Husborne Crawley and Ridgmont *St Alb* 89-92; Chapl HM Pris Bedf 92-99; Asst Chapl 99-02; Lic to Offic *St Alb* 92-03; rtd 02; Perm to Offic *St Alb* from 03. *5 Church Road, Woburn Sands, Milton Keynes MK17 8TE* Tel (01908) 582510

WILLCOX, Richard John Michael. b 39. Birm Univ BSc62 PhD67. Qu Coll Birm 78. **d** 80 **p** 81. C Boldmere *Birm* 80-83; V Edgbaston SS Mary and Ambrose 83-89; V Evercreech w Chesterblade and Milton Clevedon *B & W* 89-97; Dioc Development Rep 90-01; V Bridgwater H Trin 97-01; rtd 01. *The Briars, Ledbury Road, Wellington Heath, Ledbury HR8 1NB* Tel (01531) 636191 E-mail rswillcox@aol.com

WILLCOX, Canon Sydney Harold. b 36. Univ of Wales (Lamp) BA58. St Mich Coll Llan. **d** 60 **p** 61. C Pwllheli *Ban* 60-62; C Llandegfan w Beaumaris and Llanfaes 62-65; R Llanenddwyn 65-70; R Dolgellau, Llanfachreth, Brithdir etc 70-76; TR Ridgeway *Sarum* 76-86; RD Marlborough 81-86; TR Cockermouth w Embleton and Wythop *Carl* 86-94; RD Derwent 89-94; Hon Can Carl Cathl 91-94; TR Chalke Valley *Sarum* 94-01; rtd 02. *7 Hillingdon, Bridport DT6 3DH* Tel (01308) 459139

WILLESDEN, Area Bishop of. *See* BROADBENT, The Rt Revd Peter Alan

WILLETT, Canon Allen Gardiner. b 20. Bris Univ BA51 Lon Univ BD54. Clifton Th Coll 47. **d** 54 **p** 55. C Rawtenstall St Mary *Man* 54-57; Nigeria 57-58; Tutor Clifton Th Coll 58-60; C Wallington H Trin *S'wark* 60-62; Tutor All Nations Miss Coll Taplow 62-63; V Bedminster St Luke w St Silas *Bris* 63-68; V Galleywood Common *Chelmsf* 68-87; RD Chelmsf 81-86; Hon Can Chelmsf Cathl 85-87; rtd 87; Perm to Offic *Pet* 87-00; *Ely* 90-97; *Linc* 90-99; *Chelmsf* and *St E* from 01. *61 Ashdown Way, Ipswich IP3 8RL* Tel (01473) 423751 E-mail allenmary@willett61.freeserve.co.uk

WILLETT, Frank Edwin. b 45. Lon Univ DipTh68. Kelham Th Coll 64. **d** 68 **p** 69. C Oswestry H Trin *Lich* 68-71; C Bilston St Leon 71-74; USPG Coll of the Ascension Selly Oak 74-75; USPG 74-80; Zambia 75-80; V Curbar and Stoney Middleton *Derby* 80-88; Area Sec USPG *Derby* and *Leic* 88-91; V Chesterfield St Aug *Derby* 91-98; Chapl Walton Hosp 91-98; Ind Chapl *Derby* 98-03; P-in-c Brampton St Mark from 03; P-in-c Loundsley Green from 03. *The Vicarage, 15 St Mark's Road, Chesterfield S40 1DH* Tel (01246) 234015 E-mail f@willett85.freeserve.co.uk

WILLETT, Canon Geoffrey Thomas. b 38. Dur Univ BA59 MA82. Cranmer Hall Dur. **d** 62 **p** 63. C Widnes St Paul *Liv* 62-65; C Harborne Heath *Birm* 65-68; V Wakef St Andr and St Mary *Wakef* 68-75; V Hinckley H Trin *Leic* 75-89; TR 89; RD Sparkenhoe II 84-87; RD Sparkenhoe W 87-89; P-in-c Markfield 89-90; R 90-99; P-in-c Thornton, Bagworth and Stanton 96-99; R Markfield, Thornton, Bagworth and Stanton etc 99-04; RD Sparkenhoe E 91-99; Hon Can Leic Cathl 87-04; rtd 04; Perm to Offic *Derby* and *Leic* from 04. *22 Clifton Way, Burton-on-Trent DE15 9DW* Tel (01283) 548868

WILLETT, Canon John Ivon. b 40. Ch Ch Ox BA63 MA65. Chich Th Coll 61. **d** 63 **p** 64. C Leic St Andr *Leic* 63-66; C Bordesley St Alb *Birm* 66-72; Min Can, Prec and Sacr Pet Cathl *Pet* 72-82; R Uppingham w Ayston and Wardley w Belton 82-99; Can Pet Cathl 97-99; V Cantley *Sheff* from 99; AD Doncaster from 04. *St Wilfrid's Vicarage, 200 Cantley Lane, Doncaster DN4 6PA* Tel (01302) 535133

WILLETT, Stephen John. b 54. Ridley Hall Cam 88. **d** 90 **p** 91. C Chapeltown *Sheff* 90-94; V Hackenthorpe from 94. *The Vicarage, 63 Sheffield Road, Sheffield S12 4LR* Tel 0114-248 4486

WILLETTS, Alfred. b 15. **d** 62 **p** 63. C Canton St Jo *Llan* 62-65; V Afan Vale 65-67; R Man St Phil w St Mark *Man* 67-75; R Man Apostles 75-84; rtd 85; Perm to Offic *Ches* 85-91 and *Man* 85-97. *c/o Dr P Willetts, 25 Kings Way, Harrow HA1 1XT* Tel (020) 8427 0111

WILLETTS, Ms Mary Elizabeth Willetts. b 33. St Hild Coll Dur BA54 Hughes Hall Cam CertEd55. Cranmer Hall Dur 02. **d** 02 **p** 03. NSM Stockton-on-the-Forest w Holtby and Warthill *York* from 02. *Walnut Cottage, Warthill, York YO19 5XL* Tel (01904) 489874

WILLEY, David Geoffrey. b 53. Imp Coll Lon BSc74. Oak Hill Th Coll BA86. **d** 86 **p** 87. C Cromer *Nor* 86-90; R High Halstow w All Hallows and Hoo St Mary *Roch* 90-94; R Gravesend St Geo 94-02; TR N Farnborough *Guildf* from 02. *The Rectory, 66 Church Avenue, Farnborough GU14 7AP* Tel (01252) 544754 E-mail david.willey@btopenworld.com

WILLEY, Graham John. b 38. Moray Ord Course 91. **d** 93 **p** 94. NSM W Coast Jt Congregations *Mor* 93-99; NSM Stirling *St And* 99-03; rtd 03; Perm to Offic *St And* from 03. *The Cedars, Main Street, Killin FK21 8TN* Tel (01567) 820366

WILLIAMS, Alan Ronald Norman. b 60. RMN85. Linc Th Coll 95. **d** 95 **p** 96. C Malvern Link w Cowleigh *Worc* 95-99; TV from 03; V Risca *Mon* 99-03. *165 Leigh Sinton Road, Malvern WR14 1LB* Tel (01886) 833578 E-mail alan.r.williams@btinternet.com

WILLIAMS, Aled Jones. b 56. Univ of Wales (Ban) BA77 Univ of Wales (Cardiff) DipTh79. St Mich Coll Llan 77. **d** 79 **p** 80. C Conwy w Gyffin *Ban* 79-82; R Llanrug 82-86; R Machynlleth and Llanwrin 86-87; Member L'Arche Community 88-95; V Ynyscynhaearn w Penmorfa and Porthmadog 95-01; V Porthmadoc and Ynyscynhaearn and Dolbenmaen from 01. *The Vicarage, Ffordd Penamser, Porthmadog LL49 9PA* Tel (01766) 514951

WILLIAMS, Canon Aled Wyn. b 47. Univ of Wales (Abth) BA69. St Mich Coll Llan 69. **d** 71 **p** 72. C Llanelli *St D* 71-73; P-in-c Capel Colman w Llanfihangel Penbedw etc 73-74; V 74-81; V Llanddewi Brefi w Llanbadarn Odwyn 81-84; V Llanddewi Brefi w Llanbadarn Odwyn, Cellan etc 84-01; V Lampeter and Llanddewibrefi Gp from 01; RD Lampeter and Ultra-Aeron from 96; Can St D Cathl from 97. *Y Ficerdy Newydd, Maes y Llan, Guilsfield, Welshpool SY21 9NF* Tel (01974) 298937

WILLIAMS, Alexander Ernest. b 14. Fitzw Ho Cam BA35 MA46 Regent's Park Coll Ox 35. Coll of Resurr Mirfield 79. **d** 79 **p** 80. Hon C Carshalton Beeches *S'wark* 79-87; rtd 87; Perm to Offic *S'wark* from 87. *34 Marlborough Court, Wallington SM6 9PG* Tel (020) 8647 8446

WILLIAMS, Alfred Donald. b 26. St Aid Birkenhead 57. **d** 59 **p** 60. C Ordsall *S'well* 59-62; V Ladybrook 62-70; P-in-c Newark Ch Ch 70-71; R Gotham 72-88; P-in-c W Leake w Kingston-on-Soar and Ratcliffe-on-Soar 72-81; rtd 88; Perm to Offic *Bradf* from 88. *20 Grassington Road, Skipton BD23 1LL* Tel (01756) 794496

WILLIAMS, Miss Alison Lindsay. b 47. Univ of Wales (Abth) BA69 PGCE70. Wycliffe Hall Ox 00. **d** 00 **p** 01. C Stratton St Margaret w S Marston etc *Bris* 00-04; TV Chalke Valley *Sarum* from 04. *The Vicarage, Nunton, Salisbury SP5 4HP* Tel (01722) 330628 E-mail alisonlwilliams@fish.co.uk

WILLIAMS, Amanda Clare. *See* WILLIAMS-POTTER, Mrs Amanda Clare

WILLIAMS, Andrew Barrington. b 62. Ripon Coll Cuddesdon 96. **d** 98 **p** 99. C Oswaldtwistle Immanuel and All SS *Blackb* 98-01; C Whittle-le-Woods 01-02; P-in-c Hillock *Man* from 02. *St Andrew's Vicarage, Mersey Drive, Whitefield, Manchester M45 8LA* Tel 0161-766 1635 Fax 08712-421319 E-mail revandy.williams@btinternet.com

WILLIAMS, Andrew David. b 67. Univ of Wales (Lamp) BA91. Linc Th Coll 93. **d** 93 **p** 94. C Perry Street *Roch* 93-96; C Ealing St Pet Mt Park *Lon* 96-00; R Finchley St Mary from 00. *St Mary's Rectory, Rectory Close, London N3 1TS* Tel (020) 8346 4600 Fax 8343 3174 E-mail awstmary@dialstart.net

WILLIAMS, Andrew Gibson. b 31. Edin Univ MA57. Edin Th Coll 56. **d** 59 **p** 60. C Todmorden *Wakef* 59-61; C Clitheroe St Mary *Blackb* 61-63; V Burnley St Jas 63-65; CF (TA) 64-65; CF 65-71; R Winterslow *Sarum* 71-84; P-in-c Condover *Heref* 84-88; P-in-c Acton Burnell w Pitchford 84-88; P-in-c Frodesley 84-88; R Condover w Frodesley, Acton Burnell etc 88-90; R Whimple, Talaton and Clyst St Lawr *Ex* 90-94; rtd 94; Perm to Offic *Ex* from 94. *14 Sharps Court, Exmouth EX8 1DT* Tel (01395) 271014

WILLIAMS, Andrew Joseph. b 55. St Jo Coll Nottm BTh81. **d** 81 **p** 82. C Hollington St Leon *Chich* 81-84; C Sutton Coldfield H Trin *Birm* 84-87; Perm to Offic from 87; Chapl Blue Coat Comp Sch Walsall 91-01; Chapl St Elphin's Sch Matlock from 01; Lic to Offic *Derby* from 01. *St Elphin's School, Darley Dale, Matlock DE4 2HA* Tel (01629) 732314 *or* 735448 E-mail revandyw@aol.com

WILLIAMS, Andrew Thomas. b 66. Ex Univ LLB88 Solicitor 90. Trin Coll Bris BA00. **d** 00 **p** 01. C Whitchurch *Ex* 00-03; C Chorleywood St Andr *St Alb* from 03. *Wick Cottage, Quickley Lane, Chorleywood, Rickmansworth WD3 5AF*

WILLIAMS, Mrs Angela. b 50. Univ of Wales (Ban) BTh05. **d** 05. Min Can Ban Cathl and Dioc Children's Officer *Ban* from 05. *Creigle, 88 Lon Hedydd, Llanfairpwllgwyngyll LL61 5JY* Tel (01248) 712075

WILLIAMS, Mrs Anthea Elizabeth. b 50. Trevelyan Coll Dur BA71 Kent Univ MA97 Middx Univ MSc00. Linc Th Coll 72. **dss** 79 **d** 87 **p** 94. St Marylebone Ch Ch *Lon* 79-84; Maidstone St Martin *Cant* 84-91; Par Dn 87-91; Dn-in-c Rolvenden 91-94; P-in-c 94-04; P-in-c Newenden 01-04; Chapl E Kent NHS and Soc Care Partnership Trust 91-04; Asst Dir of Ords *Cant* 98-03; Perm to Offic *Cant* and *Roch* from 04. *2 Redwater Cottages, Cranbrook TN17 2LX* Tel (01580) 892191 Mobile 07810-306012 E-mail willtyd@aol.com

WILLIAMS, Anthony. **d** 03 **p** 04. NSM Iver *Ox* from 03. *4 Syke Ings, Iver SL0 9ET* Tel (01753) 653849

WILLIAMS, Anthony David. b 38. LRCP62 MRCS62 DRCOG65 Cert Family Planning 65 MRCGP68. S Dios Minl Tr Scheme 87. **d** 90 **p** 91. Hon C Jersey St Pet *Win* 90-92; NSM Jersey St Helier from 92. *Beau Vallon Ouest, Mont de la Rosier, St Saviour, Jersey JE2 7HF* Tel (01534) 863859 E-mail tonyw@jeresymail.co.uk

WILLIAMS, Anthony Francis. b 21. Trin Coll Ox BA49 MA53. Coll of Resurr Mirfield 49. **d** 51 **p** 52. C Paignton St Jo *Ex* 51-54; C Cov H Trin *Cov* 54-60; V Cov All SS 60-67; V Lindridge *Worc* 67-77; P-in-c Bluntisham w Earith *Ely* 77-79; R 79-88; rtd 88; Perm to Offic *Ely* from 88. *21 King's Hedges, St Ives PE27 3XU* Tel (01480) 467686

WILLIAMS, Canon Anthony Riley. b 36. Univ of Wales BA60. Chich Th Coll 57. **d** 59 **p** 60. C Llandinorwig *Ban* 59-61; C Llandegfan w Beaumaris and Llanfaes 61-64; R Ludchurch and Templeton *St D* 64-72; V Lamphey w Hodgeston 72-83; RD Castlemartin 75-83; V Llanelli 83-00; Can St D Cathl 86-00; Chan St D Cathl 93-00; Chapl Bryntirion Hosp Llanelli 90-94; Chapl Derwen NHS Trust W Wales 94-00; rtd 01. *66 Main Street, Pembroke SA71 4HH* Tel (01646) 685213

WILLIAMS, The Very Revd Arfon. b 58. Univ of Wales (Abth) BD83 Univ of Wales (Ban) MA84. Wycliffe Hall Ox 83. **d** 84 **p** 85. C Carmarthen St Dav *St D* 84-86; TV Aberystwyth 86-88; V Glanogwen *Ban* 88-94; C Ewhurst and Dir Oast Ho Retreat Cen *Chich* 95-98; Asst to RD Rye 95-98; Co-ord for Adult Educn (E Sussex Area) 97-98; I Jordanstown *Conn* 98-02; Adn Meirionnydd *Ban* 02-04; R Dolgellau w Llanfachreth and Brithdir etc 02-04; Dean Elphin and Ardagh *K, E & A* from 04; I Sligo w Knocknarea and Rosses Pt from 04. *The Deanery, Strandhill Road, Sligo, Irish Republic* Tel (00353) (71) 915 7993

WILLIAMS, Preb Arthur Edwin. b 33. Leeds Univ BA57. Coll of Resurr Mirfield 57. **d** 59 **p** 60. C Wednesfield St Thos *Lich* 59-62; C Codsall 62-65; V 83-98; V Coseley St Chad 65-73; R Kingswinford H Trin 73-81; TR Wordsley 81-83; RD Himley 77-83; Preb Lich Cathl 82-98; RD Penkridge 89-94; rtd 98; Perm to Offic *Heref* from 99 and *Lich* from 01. *2 Campbell Close, Bridgnorth WV16 5PD* Tel (01746) 761344

WILLIAMS, Barrie. b 33. Em Coll Cam BA54 MA58 Bris Univ MLitt71. Lambeth STh75 Ripon Hall Ox 62. **d** 63 **p** 64. C Penwortham St Mary *Blackb* 63-65; Hon C Salisbury St Martin *Sarum* 65-77; Chapl St Edw K and Martyr Cam *Ely* 77-84; Asst Chapl Trin Hall Cam 77-84; R Ashley w Weston by Welland and Sutton Bassett *Pet* 84-85; Asst Chapl St Hilda's Priory and Sch Whitby 85-97; rtd 98; Perm to Offic *York* from 98. *Flat 5, Grinkle Court, 9 Chubb Hill Road, Whitby YO21 1JU* Tel (01947) 600766

WILLIAMS, Benjamin Clive. b 24. Lon Univ BD59. Westcott Ho Cam 59. **d** 61 **p** 62. C Bury St Mark *Man* 61-63; C Christchurch *Win* 63-66; R Denton w S Heighton and Tarring Neville *Chich* 66-74; Dioc Stewardship Adv 74-81; P-in-c Clapham w Patching 76-81; V Ticehurst and Flimwell 81-89; rtd 89; Perm to Offic *Chich* from 89. *14 Lindfield Avenue, Seaford BN25 4DY* Tel (01323) 491019

WILLIAMS, Brian. *See* WILLIAMS, Herbert Brian

WILLIAMS, Brian. b 48. WMMTC. **d** 83 **p** 84. NSM Lich St Chad *Lich* 83-03; Asst Chapl Sandwell Health Care NHS Trust 98; Angl Chapl 98-99; Chapl Burton Hosps NHS Trust 99-03; Chapl R Bournemouth and Christchurch Hosps NHS Trust from 03. *Royal Bournemouth Hospital, Castle Lane East, Bournemouth BH7 7DW* Tel (01202) 704221 *or* 303626

WILLIAMS, Brian Frederick. b 55. Philippa Fawcett Coll CertEd77 BEd78. SEITE 98. **d** 01 **p** 02. NSM Folkestone St Mary and St Eanswythe *Cant* from 01. *79 Surrenden Road, Folkestone CT19 4EB* Tel (01303) 276242 E-mail brianwilliams@cheritonfolk.fsnet.co.uk

WILLIAMS, Brian Luke. b 54. AKC75. St Steph Ho Ox 76. **d** 77 **p** 78. C Kettering St Mary *Pet* 77-80; C Walsall St Gabr Fulbrook *Lich* 80-83; P-in-c Sneyd 83-85; V from 85; RD Stoke N 94-99. *Sneyd Vicarage, Hamil Road, Stoke-on-Trent ST6 1AP* Tel (01782) 825841 Fax as telephone

WILLIAMS, Bryan. **d** 01. OLM Fazeley *Lich* from 01. *47 Dama Road, Fazeley, Tamworth B78 3SU* Tel (01827) 289830

WILLIAMS, Ms Carol Jean Picknell. b 45. FCIPD89. Ox NSM Course 86. **d** 89 **p** 94. NSM High Wycombe *Ox* 89-97; P-in-c Penn 97-01; rtd 01; Perm to Offic *Heref* from 02. *Châtelaine House, Kinsham, Presteigne LD8 2HP* Tel (01544) 267067 E-mail caroljpwilliams@compuserve.com

WILLIAMS, Mrs Catherine Anne. b 65. Selw Coll Cam BA87 MA91. SEITE 98. **d** 00 **p** 01. C Chatham St Steph *Roch* 00-02; C Bishop's Cleeve *Glouc* from 03. *Abbey House, Church Street, Tewkesbury GL20 5SR* Tel (01684) 293333 Mobile 07966-709577 E-mail rev.catherine@virgin.net

WILLIAMS, Ms Catherine Lois. b 51. Swansea Coll of Educn CertEd74 Univ of Wales (Swansea) BEd80. St Mich Coll Llan. **d** 00 **p** 01. C Gorseinon *S & B* 00-02; C Cen Swansea 03; TV from 03. *Christ Church Vicarage, 226 Oystermouth Road, Swansea SA1 3UH* Tel (01792) 652606

WILLIAMS, Ms Catherine Mary (Kitty). b 56. OLM course 96. **d** 99 **p** 00. OLM Uttoxeter Area *Lich* 99-03; Chapl Blue Coat Comp Sch Walsall from 03. *58 Rowley Street, Walsall WS1 2AY* Tel (01922) 632970 E-mail rev.ian.williams@lineone.net

✠**WILLIAMS, The Rt Revd Cecil.** b 42. Punjab Univ MA(Ed)67 Peshawar Univ MA72. **d** 87 **p** 88 **c** 01. Pakistan 87-02; Asst Bp Peshawar 01-02; C Potternewton *Ripon* from 02. *8 Granton Road, Potternewton, Leeds LS7 3LZ* Tel 0113-262 6225 Mobile 07903-319014 E-mail cecilwilliams@amserve.net

WILLIAMS, Cecil Augustus Baldwin. b 09. TCD BA31 MA39. CITC 32. **d** 32 **p** 33. C Belfast St Mary Magd *Conn* 32-35; BCMS Kapoeta Sudan 35-39; I Schull *C, C & R* 40-49; Sec Ch of Ireland Jews' Soc 49-54; I Dublin St Luke *D & G* 54-71; BCMS Sec 56-63; I Crinken 71-81; rtd 81. *3 St John's Close, Portstewart BT55 7HJ* Tel (028) 7083 4249 E-mail cabwilliams@onetel.net

WILLIAMS, Canon Cecil Peter. b 41. TCD BA63 MA67 Lon Univ BD67 PhD86 Bris Univ MLitt77. Clifton Th Coll 64. **d** 67 **p** 68. C Maghull *Liv* 67-70; Lic to Offic *Bris* 70-91; Tutor Clifton Th Coll 70-72; Tutor Trin Coll Bris 72-91; Lib 73-81; Course Ldr 81-85; Vice-Prin 85-91; V Ecclesall *Sheff* from 91; Hon Can Sheff Cathl from 01. *The Vicarage, Ringinglow Road, Sheffield S11 7PQ* Tel 0114-236 0084 *or* 268 7574 Mobile 07801-353786 Fax 0870-137 1003 E-mail peter.williams@ecclesall.parishchurch.org.uk

WILLIAMS, Mrs Christine Mary. b 51. City Univ BSc72 Middx Univ BA05. NTMTC 02. **d** 05. NSM Pitsea w Nevendon *Chelmsf* from 05. *2 Foxleigh, Billericay CM12 9NS* Tel (01277) 654370 E-mail christine.mwilliams@btopenworld.com

WILLIAMS, Preb Clive Gregory. b 45. Trin Coll Bris 83. **d** 85 **p** 86. C Bedhampton *Portsm* 85-88; V Highley w Billingsley, Glazeley etc *Heref* from 88; RD Bridgnorth from 96; Preb Heref Cathl from 99. *The Vicarage, Church Street, Highley, Bridgnorth WV16 6NA* Tel (01746) 861612 E-mail highleyrectory@aol.com

WILLIAMS, The Ven Colin Henry. b 52. Pemb Coll Ox BA73 MA78. St Steph Ho Ox BA80. **d** 81 **p** 82. C Liv St Paul Stoneycroft *Liv* 81-84; TV Walton St Mary 84-89; Chapl Walton Hosp Liv 86-89; Bp's Dom Chapl *Blackb* 89-94; Chapl Whalley Abbey 89-94; V Poulton-le-Fylde 94-99; Adn Lancaster from 99. *St Michael's House, Hall Lane, St Michael's-on-Wyre, Preston PR3 0TQ* Tel (01995) 679242 Fax 679747 E-mail archdeacon.lancaster@ukonline.co.uk

WILLIAMS, David. b 19. **d** 66 **p** 67. Hon C Parkend *Glouc* 66-78; Hon C Coleford w Staunton 78-83; Perm to Offic from 83. *The Nook, Parkend Road, Bream, Lydney GL15 6JZ* Tel (01594) 562240

WILLIAMS, David. b 43. ACA65 FCA. K Coll Lon AKC69 BD69. **d** 70 **p** 71. C Walkden Moor *Man* 70-72; C Deane 72-75; V Horwich St Cath 75-81; Hon C Chorley All SS *Blackb* 84-86; P-in-c Weeton 86-87; V Singleton w Weeton 87-97; C Lancaster St Mary w St John and St Anne 98-00; Chapl HM Pris Lanc

Castle 98-00; rtd 00; Perm to Offic *Man* from 02. *153 Crompton Way, Bolton BL2 2SQ* Tel (01524) 382362 E-mail goodfornowt@aol.com

WILLIAMS, Canon David. b 49. BTh Dip Tech Mining. **d** 88 **p** 89. C Lurgan etc w Ballymachugh, Kildrumferton etc *K, E & A* 88-91; I Kinsale Union *C, C & R* from 91; Miss to Seafarers from 91; Can Cork and Cloyne Cathls *C, C & R* 95-97; Treas Cork Cathl from 97; Preb Tymothan St Patr Cathl Dublin from 97. *St Multose Rectory, Abbey Court, Kinsale, Co Cork, Irish Republic* Tel (00353) (21) 477 2220

WILLIAMS, David Alun. b 65. St Thos Hosp Lon MB, BS88. Wycliffe Hall Ox BTh94 All Nations Chr Coll MA98. **d** 94 **p** 95. C Ware Ch Ch *St Alb* 94-97; Crosslinks Kenya from 98; Perm to Offic *St Alb* 98-00. *PO Box 72584, Carlile College, Nairobi, Kenya* Tel (00254) (2) 715561

WILLIAMS, David Frank. b 48. S Dios Minl Tr Scheme 91. **d** 94 **p** 95. NSM Romsey *Win* from 94. *24 Feltham Close, Romsey SO51 8PB* Tel (01794) 524050 E-mail revdfw@talk21.com

WILLIAMS, David Gareth. b 58. Lon Univ BD81. Ripon Coll Cuddesdon 82. **d** 84 **p** 85. C Chandler's Ford *Win* 84-88; C Alton St Lawr 88-90; R Crawley and Littleton and Sparsholt w Lainston 90-97; P-in-c Andover w Foxcott from 97. *St Mary's Vicarage, Church Close, Andover SP10 1DP* Tel (01264) 350344 *or* 352729 E-mail david@twmpa.freeserve.co.uk

WILLIAMS, David Gerald Powell. b 35. St Mich Coll Llan DipTh62. **d** 62 **p** 63. C Canton St Jo *Llan* 62-64; Field Tr Officer Ch in Wales Prov Youth Coun 63-70; Prov Youth Chapl 65-70; V Treharris *Llan* 70-75; R Flemingston w Gileston and St Hilary 75-78; Warden of Ords 77-80; Dir Past Studies and Chapl St Mich Coll Llan 78-80; Sub-Warden 79-80; Dir Ch in Wales Publications and Communications 80-85; Prov Dir of Educn Ch in Wales 80-85; Dir of Miss Ch in Wales 85-87; Hon Can Llan Cathl *Llan* 84-93; V Pendoylan w Welsh St Donats 87-93; R Llandudno *Ban* 93-95; Press Officer to Abp of Wales 93-00; rtd 00. *Wentworth Lodge, 9 Tydraw Road, Penylan, Cardiff CF23 5HA* Tel (029) 2048 8598

WILLIAMS, Canon David Gordon. b 43. Selw Coll Cam BA65 MA69. Oak Hill Th Coll 66. **d** 68 **p** 69. C Maidstone St Luke *Cant* 68-71; C Rugby St Matt *Cov* 71-73; P-in-c Budbrooke 73-74; V 74-81; V Lenton *S'well* 81-87; TR Cheltenham St Mark *Glouc* 87-03; Hon Can Glouc Cathl 96-03; R Toodyay w Goomalling Australia from 03. *St Stephen's Church, PO Box 807, Toodyay, W Australia 6566* Tel (0061) (8) 9574 2203 E-mail revdwilliams@westnet.com.au

WILLIAMS, David Grant. b 61. Bris Univ BSocSc83. Wycliffe Hall Ox 86. **d** 89 **p** 90. C Ecclesall *Sheff* 89-92; V Dore 92-02; RD Ecclesall 97-02; V Win Ch Ch *Win* from 02. *Christ Church Vicarage, Sleepers Hill, Winchester SO22 4ND* Tel (01962) 862414 Mobile 07889-547095 E-mail vicarccwinch@aol.com

WILLIAMS, David Henry. b 33. Trin Coll Cam BA56 MA60 PhD77. St D Coll Lamp 67. **d** 69 **p** 70. C Monmouth *Mon* 69-70; Chapl St Woolos Cathl 70-71; P-in-c Six Bells 71-76; Libya 76-79; P-in-c Crumlin *Mon* 79-80; R Llanddewi Skirrid w Llanvetherine etc 80-83; Perm to Offic 83-87; Guest Master Caldey Abbey 83-87; V Buttington and Pool Quay *St As* 87-95; Chapl Warsaw *Eur* 95-97; rtd 97. *4 Clos-y-Drindod, Buarth Road, Aberystwyth SY23 1LR* Tel (01970) 612736 E-mail dh.williams@ukonline.co.uk

WILLIAMS, Canon David Humphrey. b 23. Em Coll Cam BA49 MA54. St Steph Ho Ox 49. **d** 51 **p** 52. C Daybrook *S'well* 51-55; C-in-c Bilborough St Jo Bapt CD 55-62; V Bilborough St Jo 62-63; RD Bulwell 70-88; P-in-c Bestwood Park 71-78; R Hucknall Torkard 63-71; TR 71-88; Hon Can S'well Minster 75-88; rtd 88; Perm to Offic *S'well* from 88. *12 Wollaton Paddocks, Nottingham NG8 2ED* Tel 0115-928 0639

WILLIAMS, David Ivan Ross. b 47. Imp Coll Lon BSc70 Leic Univ MSc72 ARCS70 FBIS. STETS 00. **d** 03 **p** 04. NSM Havant *Portsm* from 03. *9 St George's Road, Hayling Island PO11 0BS* Tel (023) 9246 7597 Mobile 07866-772025 E-mail david@dirw.demon.co.uk

WILLIAMS, David James. b 42. Chich Th Coll 67. **d** 70 **p** 71. C Charlton-by-Dover St Bart *Cant* 70-74; C Dorking w Ranmore *Guildf* 74-77; C Guildf H Trin w St Mary 77-78; P-in-c E Molesey St Paul 78-88; V Burpham 88-94; rtd 95. *1 Taleworth Close, Ashtead KT21 2PU* Tel (01372) 278056

WILLIAMS, David John. b 30. Open Univ BA79. St D Coll Lamp 64. **d** 66 **p** 67. C Mold *St As* 66-69; C Llanrhos 69-71; R Llangynhafal and Llanbedr Dyffryn Clwyd 71-86; P-in-c Llanychan 77-86; RD Dyffryn Clwyd 86-95; R Ruthin w Llanrhydd 86-95; rtd 95. *16 The Park, Ruthin LL15 1PW* Tel (01824) 705746

WILLIAMS, Canon David John. b 38. AKC62. **d** 63 **p** 64. C Benchill *Man* 63-66; C Heywood St Jas 66-69; V Leesfield 69-73; Chapl TS Arethusa 73-74; TV Southend St Jo w St Mark, All SS w St Fran etc *Chelmsf* 74-80; V Horndon on the Hill 80-93; RD Thurrock 83-92; P-in-c Rochford 93-02; RD Rochford 96-02; P-in-c Sutton w Shopland 98-02; Hon Can Chelmsf Cathl 99-02; rtd 02; Perm to Offic *Ripon* from 02. *29 Stonebeck Avenue, Harrogate HG1 2BN* Tel (01423) 522828

WILLIAMS, David John. b 43. Wadh Coll Ox BA64. St Jo Coll Nottm 73. **d** 75 **p** 76. C Newcastle w Butterton *Lich* 75-79; P-in-c Oulton 79-89; P-in-c Stone Ch Ch 84-89; V Stone Ch Ch and Oulton 89-96; P-in-c Ashley 96-04; P-in-c Mucklestone 96-04; R Ashley and Mucklestone from 04. *The Rectory, Charnes Road, Ashley, Market Drayton TF9 4LQ* Tel (01630) 672210

WILLIAMS, David John. b 52. N Ord Course 92. **d** 95 **p** 96. C Gt Crosby St Luke *Liv* 95-99; V W Derby St Jas 99-04; Chapl R Liverpool Children's NHS Trust from 99. *Alder Hey Children's Hospital, Eaton Road, Liverpool L12 2AP* Tel 0151-228 4811

WILLIAMS, Canon David Leslie. b 35. ALCD63. **d** 63 **p** 64. C Bexleyheath Ch Ch *Roch* 63-64; C Gt Faringdon w Lt Coxwell *Ox* 64-66; CMS 67-76; Uganda 67-73; C Shortlands *Roch* 73-74; Fiji 74-77; V Bromley H Trin *Roch* 77-86; R Meopham w Nurstead 86-96; RD Cobham 86-96; Chapl Thames Gateway NHS Trust 96-01; Hon Can Roch Cathl *Roch* 98-01. *107 Ploughmans Way, Gillingham ME8 8LT* Tel (01634) 372545

WILLIAMS, David Michael Rochfort. b 40. St Mich Coll Llan 62. **d** 65 **p** 66. C Pembroke Dock *St D* 65-68; Chapl Miss to Seamen and Ind Chapl 68-71; P-in-c Walwyn's Castle w Robeston W 68-70; R 70-71; Ind Chapl *Mon* 71-74; Hon Chapl St Woolos Cathl 71-74; V Blaenavon w Capel Newydd 74-77; Ind Chapl *St As* 77-88; V Whitford 81-87; V Ruabon 87-92; TR Cen Telford *Lich* 92-00; R Burton and Rosemarket *St D* 00-02; Chapl Miss to Seafarers Milford Haven 00-02; Southampton 02-05; rtd 05; Perm to Offic *Ox* from 05. *13 Sturt Road, Charlbury, Chipping Norton OX7 3SX* Tel (01608) 811284

WILLIAMS, David Norman. b 54. Lanc Univ BSc Leeds Univ BA. Coll of Resurr Mirfield. **d** 84 **p** 85. C Ireland Wood *Ripon* 84-87; C Beeston 87-91; V Cross Roads cum Lees *Bradf* 91-99; V Skipton Ch Ch from 99; P-in-c Carleton and Lothersdale from 03. *Christ Church Vicarage, Carleton Road, Skipton BD23 2BE* Tel (01756) 793612

WILLIAMS, David Paul. *See* HOWELL, David Paul

WILLIAMS, David Roger. b 49. Open Univ BA. St D Coll Lamp DipTh73. **d** 73 **p** 74. C Llansamlet *S & B* 73-76; C Oystermouth 76-79; V Aberedw w Llandeilo Graban and Llanbadarn etc 79-81; V Brynmawr 81-89; V Newport St Julian *Mon* from 89. *St Julian's Vicarage, 41 St Julians Avenue, Newport NP19 7JT* Tel (01633) 258046

WILLIAMS, Denise Laraine. b 50. Liv Univ TCert71. N Ord Course 00. **d** 03. C Padgate *Liv* from 03. *23 Kenilworth Drive, Padgate, Warrington WA1 3JT* Tel (01925) 831297 E-mail dwill001@fish.co.uk

WILLIAMS, Derek. b 27. Man Univ BSc49. St Deiniol's Hawarden 76. **d** 78 **p** 79. NSM Abergele *St As* 78-97; rtd 97; Perm to Offic *St As* from 97. *48 Eldon Drive, Abergele LL22 7DA* Tel (01745) 833479

WILLIAMS, Derek Ivor. **d** 05. OLM Chollerton w Birtley and Thockrington *Newc* from 05. *Buteland House, Bellingham, Hexham NE48 2EX* Tel (01434) 220389

WILLIAMS, Derek Lawrence. b 45. Tyndale Hall Bris 65. **d** 69 **p** 70. C Cant St Mary Bredin *Cant* 69-71; Gen Sec Inter-Coll Chr Fellowship 71-75; Lic to Offic *St Alb* 78-84 and *Bris* 85-92; Par and Miss Co-ord Northampton St Giles *Pet* 93-97; Dioc Millennium Officer 98-00; Communications Officer *Pet* 00-05 and *Eur* 02-05; Chapl to Bp Pet from 05; Hon C Brington w Whilton and Norton etc from 02. *The Rectory, Harlestone Road, Church Brampton, Northampton NN6 8AU* Tel (01604) 843881 Fax 843388 E-mail dl.williams@btopenworld.com

WILLIAMS, Derwyn Gavin. b 69. Trin Coll Cam BA89 MA93. Ripon Coll Cuddesdon. **d** 94 **p** 95. C Harpenden St Nic *St Alb* 94-97; Bp's Dom Chapl 97-00; R Sandy from 00. *The Rectory, High Street, Sandy SG19 1AQ* Tel (01767) 680512 E-mail rector@sandyparishchurch.org.uk

WILLIAMS, Diana Mary. b 36. Bris Univ CertEd56 Leeds Univ BSc57. Oak Hill Th Coll 86. **d** 87 **p** 94. C S Mymms K Chas *St Alb* 87-95; V 95-98; R Sandon, Wallington and Rushden w Clothall 98-04; RD Buntingford from 01; rtd 04. *7 Cockhall Close, Litlington, Royston SG8 0RB* Tel (01763) 853079 E-mail di.williams@btinternet.com

WILLIAMS, Ms Diane Patricia. b 53. Dur Univ CertEd74 Liv Univ DipRE83 Lanc Univ MA84. Cranmer Hall Dur 84. **dss** 86 **d** 87 **p** 94. Clubmoor *Liv* 86-90; Par Dn 87-90; Dioc Lay Tr Officer 90-96; Par Dn Everton St Geo 90-94; Assoc P 94-96; Chapl Lanc Univ *Blackb* 96-00; Chapl Edin Univ *Edin* from 00. *Chaplaincy Centre, The University of Edinburgh, 1 Bristo Square, Edinburgh EH8 9AL* Tel 0131-650 2596/5 Fax 650 9111 E-mail chaplain@ed.ac.uk

WILLIAMS, Diane Ruth. b 52. Hull Univ BA80. Linc Th Coll. **d** 94 **p** 95. C Stokesley *York* 94-98; TV Louth *Linc* from 98; Chapl Linc and Louth NHS Trust 98-01; Chapl United Lincs Hosps NHS Trust from 01. *The Vicarage, 24 Grosvenor Road, Louth LN11 0BB* Tel (01507) 604573

WILLIAMS, Donald. *See* WILLIAMS, Alfred Donald

WILLIAMS, Mrs Donna Ann. b 64. St Jo Coll Nottm BA00. **d** 00 **p** 01. C Denton St Lawr *Man* 00-03; P-in-c Droylsden St Martin from 03. *St Martin's Vicarage, Greenside Lane, Droylsden, Manchester M43 7QS* Tel 0161-370 9833 E-mail sweetpea@dwilliams11.freeserve.co.uk

WILLIAMS, Dorian George. b 26. Barrister-at-Law (Gray's Inn) 52. WMMTC 91. **d** 93 **p** 94. NSM Edvin Loach w Tedstone Delamere etc *Heref* 93-98; Perm to Offic from 98. *Howberry, Whitbourne, Worcester WR6 5RZ* Tel (01886) 821189

WILLIAMS, Dylan John. b 72. Univ of Wales (Ban) BTh97. Ripon Coll Cuddesdon 97. **d** 99 **p** 00. C Holyhead *Ban* 99-01; C Dolgellau w Llanfachreth and Brithdir etc 01-02; P-in-c Amlwch 02-03; R from 03. *The Rectory, Bull Bay Road, Amlwch LL68 9EA* Tel (01407) 830740 E-mail dylwilliams@lineone.net

WILLIAMS, Edward Ffoulkes (Peter). b 34. ALA65. Chich Th Coll 71. **d** 73 **p** 74. C Kidderminster St Geo *Worc* 73-78; TV Worc St Barn w Ch Ch 78-82; R Exhall w Wixford and V Temple Grafton w Binton *Cov* 82-00; rtd 00; Perm to Offic *Truro* from 00. *Penpons Cottage, Treviskey, Lanner, Redruth TR16 6AU* Tel (01209) 820230

WILLIAMS, Edward Heaton. b 18. St Aid Birkenhead 56. **d** 58 **p** 59. C Timperley *Ches* 58-62; V Macclesfield St Pet 62-66; Sec Dioc Miss Bd 63-67; R Wistaston 66-81; Dioc Bd for Miss and Unity 67-69; V Burton 81-85; rtd 85; Perm to Offic *Ox* 85-94 and *Pet* from 85. *4 Bowmens Lea, Aynho, Banbury OX17 3AG* Tel (01869) 810533

WILLIAMS, Prof Edward Sydney. b 23. FRCP FRCR K Coll Lon BSc PhD MB, BS MD AKC. Sarum & Wells Th Coll 84. **d** 87 **p** 88. NSM Bramley and Grafham *Guildf* 87-89; Hon C Shamley Green 89-94; Perm to Offic from 94. *Little Hollies, The Close, Wonersh, Guildford GU5 0PA* Tel (01483) 892591

WILLIAMS, Elfed Owain. b 24. Newc Univ DipAdEd74. St Deiniol's Hawarden 79. **d** 81 **p** 82. Hon C Whorlton *Newc* 81-82; Hon C Elham w Denton and Wootton *Cant* 82-86; R Barham w Bishopsbourne and Kingston 86-91; rtd 91; Perm to Offic *Newc* from 91. *Chusan, 31 Ryecroft Way, Wooler NE71 6DY* Tel (01668) 281253

WILLIAMS, Emlyn Cadwaladr. b 64. St Jo Coll Nottm 02. **d** 04 **p** 05. C Glanogwen w St Ann's w Llanllechid *Ban* from 04. *1 Vaynol Terrace, Deiniolen, Caernarfon LL55 3HW* Tel (01286) 870965 E-mail ecsaer@aol.com

WILLIAMS, Eric Rees. b 30. Roch Th Coll 60 St Deiniol's Hawarden 71. **d** 72 **p** 73. C Llanelli *St D* 72-75; P-in-c Tregaron 75-76; V 76-82; RD Lampeter and Ultra-Aeron 82-87; V Tregaron w Ystrad Meurig and Strata Florida 82-87; V St Dogmael's w Moylgrove and Monington 87-98; rtd 98. *Ty Elli, 1 Heol Derw, Cardigan SA43 1NH* Tel (01239) 612296

WILLIAMS, Evelyn Joyce. b 37. Cant Sch of Min 86. **d** 89 **p** 94. NSM Sittingbourne H Trin w Bobbing *Cant* from 89. *32 Rock Road, Sittingbourne ME10 1JF* Tel (01795) 470372

WILLIAMS, Frederick Errol. b 41. MBIM80. Sarum & Wells Th Coll 86. **d** 88 **p** 89. C Milton *Win* 88-91; P-in-c Chilbolton cum Wherwell 91-94; R from 94; RD Andover from 99. *The Rectory, Chilbolton, Stockbridge SO20 6BA* Tel (01264) 860258 E-mail errolsue69@aol.com

WILLIAMS, Gareth Wynn. b 67. St D Coll Lamp BA88 Hull Univ MA89. Westcott Ho Cam 89. **d** 91 **p** 92. C Mold *St As* 91-93; TV Hawarden 93-95; Ecum Chapl Glam Univ *Llan* 95-99; Lect Univ of Wales (Cardiff) 99-04; Dir Academic Studies St Mich Coll Llan 99-04; Vice-Prin 02-04; V Roath *Llan* from 04. *Roath Vicarage, Waterloo Road, Cardiff CF23 5AD* Tel (029) 2048 4808

WILLIAMS, Gavin John. b 61. Down Coll Cam BA84 Wycliffe Hall Ox BA88 Barrister-at-Law 85. **d** 89 **p** 90. C Muswell Hill St Jas w St Matt *Lon* 89-92; Asst Chapl Shrewsbury Sch 92-95; Chapl 95-02; Chapl Westmr Sch from 02. *Westminster School, Little Dean's Yard, London SW1P 3PF* Tel (020) 7963 1128 E-mail gavin.williams@westminster.org.uk

WILLIAMS, Geoffrey Thomas. b 35. Ox NSM Course 77. **d** 80 **p** 81. NSM Earley St Bart *Ox* 80-82; NSM Reading St Luke 82-85; C Wembley Park St Aug *Lon* 85-86; C-in-c S Kenton Annunciation CD 86-90; V Streatham Hill St Marg *S'wark* 90-03; rtd 03. *78 Park Court, Battersea Park Road, London SW11 4LE* Tel (020) 7498 8272

WILLIAMS, George Harold. b 20. Lon Univ BSc49. **d** 67 **p** 68. C Bishopsworth *Bris* 67-70; V Weston-super-Mare Ch Ch *B & W* 70-85; rtd 85; Perm to Offic *B & W* from 86. *15 Elmhurst Road, Hutton, Weston-super-Mare BS24 9RJ* Tel (01934) 813342

WILLIAMS, Preb George Maxwell Frazer. b 42. TCD BA65 MA69. Cuddesdon Coll 65. **d** 67 **p** 68. C Bolton St Jas w St Chrys *Bradf* 67-70; C Lich St Chad *Lich* 70-73; V Shawbury 73-79; P-in-c Moreton Corbet 73-79; V Willenhall H Trin 79-86; TR 86-88; V Penn from 88; Preb Lich Cathl from 96; RD Trysull from 02. *St Bartholomew's Vicarage, 68 Church Hill, Penn, Wolverhampton WV4 5JD* Tel (01902) 341399 *or* 576809

WILLIAMS, George Melvin (Kim). b 24. Worc Ord Coll 64. **d** 66 **p** 67. C Holdenhurst *Win* 66-70; V Yateley 70-75; V St Leonards and St Ives 75-90; rtd 90; Perm to Offic *Win* from 90. *20 Hillside Drive, Christchurch BH23 4RU* Tel (01202) 484930

WILLIAMS, George Ola. b 55. Bradf Univ PhD90 Waterloo Lutheran Univ MA83. St Jo Coll Nottm Cert Th & Min 94 MTh95. **d** 96 **p** 97. C Enfield St Jas *Lon* 96-00; V Allerton *Bradf* from 00. *The Vicarage, Ley Top Lane, Allerton, Bradford BD15 7LT* Tel (01274) 541948

WILLIAMS, Canon Giles Peter. b 54. Lon Univ BA77 MA78. Trin Coll Bris 80. **d** 82 **p** 83. C Reading Greyfriars *Ox* 82-85; Rwanda Miss 85-90; Mid-Africa Min (CMS) 90-94; Can Kigali Cathl Rwanda from 90; V Woking St Jo *Guildf* from 95. *The Vicarage, St John's Hill Road, Woking GU21 7RQ* Tel (01483) 761253 E-mail g@gilespw.plus.com *or* vicar@stjohnswoking.org.uk

WILLIAMS, Glyn. b 54. K Coll Lon BD77 AKC77. Ripon Coll Cuddesdon 77. **d** 78 **p** 79. C Coppenhall *Ches* 78-81; C Northampton St Alb *Pet* 81-82; TV Birkenhead Priory *Ches* 82-85; Chapl RAF 85-90 and from 96; Dep Chapl HM Pris Wandsworth 90-91; Chapl HM Pris Elmley 91-95. *Chaplaincy Services (RAF), HQ, Personnel and Training Command, RAF Innsworth, Gloucester GL3 1EZ* Tel (01452) 712612 ext 5164 Fax 510828

WILLIAMS, Graham Ivor. b 23. Jes Coll Ox BA48 MA48. Cuddesdon Coll 48. **d** 49 **p** 50. C Swansea St Mary and H Trin *S & B* 49-53; C Edgbaston St Bart *Birm* 53-55; R Nutfield *S'wark* from 55; rtd 05. *Tara, St Nicolas Lane, Shoreham-by-Sea BN43 5NH* Tel (01273) 462302 E-mail revgiw@hotmail.com

WILLIAMS, Graham Parry. b 46. Bp Burgess Hall Lamp 67 St D Coll Lamp DipTh70. **d** 70 **p** 71. C Ebbw Vale *Mon* 70-73; C Trevethin 73-74; V Nantyglo 74-76; Chapl RN 76-85; R Northlew w Ashbury *Ex* 85-87; R Bratton Clovelly w Germansweek 85-87; TV Pontypool *Mon* 88-90; C Skegness and Winthorpe *Linc* 90-91; V Sutton Bridge 91-94; P-in-c Witham Gp 94-97; P-in-c Ruskington 97-01; R 01-03; RD Lafford 02-03; P-in-c Ringstone in Aveland Gp from 03. *The Vicarage, 46A High Street, Morton, Bourne PE10 0NR* Tel (01778) 571474

WILLIAMS, Gwenllian. *See* GILES, Mrs Gwenllian

WILLIAMS, Gwilym Elfed. b 33. Univ of Wales (Lamp) BA53. St Mich Coll Llan 53. **d** 56 **p** 57. C Llandudno *Ban* 56-59; C Aberdare *Llan* 59-63; C Penarth All SS 63-65; R Eglwysilan 65-70; V Mountain Ash 70-81; V Llanblethian w Cowbridge and Llandough etc 81-93; P-in-c St Hilary 87-91; V Lisvane 93-00; rtd 00; Perm to Offic *Glouc* from 01. *2 Whitminster Lane, Frampton on Severn, Gloucester GL2 7HR* Tel (01452) 741442

WILLIAMS, Harry Abbott. b 19. Trin Coll Cam BA41 MA45. Cuddesdon Coll 41. **d** 43 **p** 44. C Pimlico St Barn *Lon* 43-45; C St Marylebone All SS 45-48; Chapl and Tutor Westcott Ho Cam 48-51; Fell and Lect Trin Coll Cam 51-69; Dean of Chpl and Tutor 58-69; CR from 72; Lic to Offic *Wakef* from 80; rtd 89. *House of the Resurrection, Stocks Bank Road, Mirfield WF14 0BN* Tel (01924) 494318

WILLIAMS, Haydn Clifford. b 32. Univ of Wales (Abth) BA54 DipEd55. EMMTC 89. **d** 95 **p** 99. NSM Anstey *Leic* 95-01; NSM Broom Leys 01-03; rtd 03; Perm to Offic *Leic* from 03. *38 Abbotts Oak Drive, Coalville LE67 4SA*

WILLIAMS, Preb Heather Marilyn. b 42. Oak Hill Th Coll 82. **dss** 85 **d** 87 **p** 94. Taunton Lyngford *B & W* 85-87; Hon C 87-89; C Worle 89-94; V Weston-super-Mare St Andr Bournville 94-03; Preb Wells Cathl 02-03; rtd 04. *2 Cliff Road, Worlebury, Weston-super-Mare BS22 9SF* Tel (01934) 420711 E-mail williams.heather@btinternet.com

WILLIAMS, Helena Maria Alija. *See* CERMAKOVA, Helena Maria Alija

WILLIAMS, Henry Gordon. b 33. JP83. St Aid Birkenhead 57. **d** 60 **p** 61. C Radcliffe St Mary *Man* 60-63; Australia from 63; rtd 99. *36 Onslow Street, PO Box 259, Northampton, W Australia 6535* Tel (0061) (8) 9934 1259 Fax 9934 1507 E-mail hgw@wn.com.au

WILLIAMS, The Ven Henry Leslie. b 19. Univ of Wales (Lamp) BA41. St Mich Coll Llan 41. **d** 43 **p** 44. C Aberdovey *Ban* 43-45; C Ban Cathl Par 45-48; Chapl RN 48-49; C Ches St Mary *Ches* 49-53; V Barnston 53-84; CF (TA) 54-62; RD Wirral N *Ches* 67-75; Hon Can Ches Cathl 72-75; Adn Ches 75-88; rtd 88; Perm to Offic *Ches* from 88. *1 Bartholomew Way, Chester CH4 7RJ* Tel (01244) 675296

WILLIAMS, Herbert Brian. b 18. BNC Ox BA39 MA48. Linc Th Coll 80. **d** 81 **p** 82. NSM Asterby Gp *Linc* 81-94; rtd 88; Perm to Offic *Linc* 94-97. *55 Upgate, Louth LN11 9HD* Tel (01507) 608093

WILLIAMS, Mrs Hilary Susan. b 45. STETS 99. **d** 02 **p** 03. NSM Shottermill *Guildf* from 02. *Stacey's Farm Cottage, Thursley Road, Elstead, Godalming GU8 6DG* Tel (01252) 703217 E-mail staceyfc@hotmail.com

WILLIAMS, Canon Howard. b 08. Univ of Wales BA29 MA32 St Jo Coll Cam MLitt45 ALCM27. St Steph Ho Ox 30. **d** 31 **p** 32. C Aberystwyth St Mich *St D* 31-36; Perm to Offic *Ely* 36-38; V Llan-non *St D* 38-49; Dioc Insp of Schs 40-50; Lect Univ of Wales 49-50; V Betws w Ammanford 49-57; V Llanelli 57-75; Chapl Llanelli Hosps 57-75; Can St D Cathl 60-75; Treas 73-75; rtd 75. *Cwm Eithin, 53 Maes Hendre, Waunfawr, Aberystwyth SY23 3PS* Tel (01970) 615311

WILLIAMS, Howell Mark. b 56. Univ of Wales (Cardiff) BD87. St Mich Coll Llan 84. **d** 87 **p** 88. C Swansea St Thos and Kilvey

S & B 87-89; TV Aberystwyth *St D* 89-93; V Hirwaun *Llan* 93-99; V Swansea St Pet *S & B* from 99. *St Peter's Vicarage, 59 Station Road, Fforestfach, Swansea SA5 5AU* Tel (01792) 581514 E-mail mark@swanseastpeters.freeserve.co.uk

WILLIAMS, Hugh Marshall. b 38. Lon Univ MB, BS62 Liv Univ MChOrth71 FRCS70. St Alb and Ox Min Course 95. **d** 97 **p** 98. NSM Lt Compton w Chastleton, Cornwell etc *Ox* 97-01; Team Min Chipping Norton from 01. *Wayside, Worcester Road, Salford, Chipping Norton OX7 5YJ* Tel (01608) 646933 Mobile 07889-343456 E-mail hmw@surfaid.org

WILLIAMS, Canon Hugh Martin. b 45. AKC73. St Aug Coll Cant 73. **d** 74 **p** 75. C Heston *Lon* 74-78; Chapl City Univ 78-84; PV Westmr Abbey 82-84; V Newquay *Truro* 84-93; V Christchurch *Win* from 93; Hon Can Win Cathl from 04. *The Priory Vicarage, Quay Road, Christchurch BH23 1BU* Tel (01202) 483102 E-mail hugh.m.williams@ukgateway.net

WILLIAMS, Hugh Wynford. b 16. Selw Coll Cam BA40 MA44. St D Coll Lamp BA38 St Mich Coll Llan 40. **d** 41 **p** 42. C Kirkburton *Wakef* 41-43; C Skipton H Trin *Bradf* 43-44; Perm to Offic *Bradf* 44-51 and *Pet* 51-74; Chapl Oundle Sch 54-74; R Tichmarsh *Pet* 74-88; P-in-c Clapton 77-88; rtd 88; Perm to Offic *Pet* from 88. *28 Church Street, Tichmarsh, Kettering NN14 3DB* Tel (01832) 734529

WILLIAMS, Ian Kenneth. b 44. MMS83 MBIM87 Nottm Univ DipAE92 MEd94. EMMTC 84. **d** 87 **p** 88. NSM Corby Glen *Linc* 87-98; R Ingoldsby 98-00; NSM Edenham w Witham on the Hill and Swinstead from 00. *65 High Street, Corby Glen, Grantham NG33 4LU* Tel (01476) 550595 E-mail ikw2@tutor.open.ac.uk

WILLIAMS, Ian Withers. b 43. Linc Th Coll 68. **d** 69 **p** 70. C Burney Lane *Birm* 69-72; C Cleobury Mortimer w Hopton Wafers *Heref* 72-75; P-in-c Coreley and Doddington 75-79; V Knowbury 75-79; V Lich Ch Ch *Lich* from 79. *Christ Church Vicarage, Christ Church Lane, Lichfield WS13 8AL* Tel (01543) 305526 Mobile 07711-260521 Fax (01543) 305527 E-mail ian@christchurchlichfield.co.uk

WILLIAMS, Ifan. b 24. St D Coll Lamp 54. **d** 56 **p** 57. C Llangefni w Tregaean *Ban* 56-60; R Llanfachreth 60-67; Dioc Youth Officer 62-65; Area Sec (Merioneth) USPG 63-89; P-in-c Brithdir and Bryncoedifor *Ban* 65-67; V Ffestiniog w Blaenau Ffestiniog 67-89; RD Ardudwy 80-89; rtd 89; Perm to Offic *Ban* from 89. *Cil-y-Coed, 6 Stad Penrallt, Llanystumdwy, Criccieth LL52 0SR* Tel (01766) 522978

WILLIAMS, Jack. b 26. Univ of Wales (Ban) BSc50. St Mich Coll Llan 50. **d** 52 **p** 53. C Buckley *St As* 52-55; C Llanrhos 55-59; V Bronnington and Bettisfield 59-61; C Ripponden *Wakef* 61-65; Chapl Rishworth Sch Ripponden 65-68; Hd Master 68-86; V Halifax St Jo *Wakef* 86-89; rtd 89; Perm to Offic *Ban* from 89. *2 Pont-y-Rhyd, Llangoed, Beaumaris LL58 8NU* Tel (01248) 490732

WILLIAMS, James Llanfair Warren. b 48. St Mich Coll Llan 92. **d** 92 **p** 93. C Pembroke Dock *St D* 92-93; C Pembroke Dock w Cosheston w Nash and Upton 93-95; V Cwmaman 95-98; Chapl Costa Blanca *Eur* 98-00; V Meifod w Llangynyw w Pont Robert w Pont Dolanog *St As* from 01. *The Vicarage, Meifod SY22 6DH* Tel (01938) 500231

WILLIAMS, James Nicholas Owen. b 39. MBE. CEng. S'wark Ord Course. **d** 82 **p** 83. C Petersfield w Sheet *Portsm* 82-86; TV Droitwich Spa *Worc* 86-88; R Church Lench w Rous Lench and Abbots Morton 88-94; V Milton *B & W* 94-04; RD Locking 99-04; rtd 04; Dioc Ecum Officer *B & W* from 04; Hon C Pill, Portbury and Easton-in-Gordano from 04. *151 Charlton Mead Drive, Brentry, Bristol BS10 6LP* Tel 0117-950 4152 E-mail jnowil@lineone.net

WILLIAMS, Janet Patricia. *See* FFRENCH, Mrs Janet Patricia

WILLIAMS, Jeffrey. *See* WILLIAMS, Robert Jeffrey Hopkin

WILLIAMS, Jeffrey. b 52. Llan Ord Course. **d** 03 **p** 04. NSM Cardiff St Mary and St Steph w St Dyfrig etc *Llan* from 03. *36 Dinas Street, Cardiff CF11 6QZ* Tel (029) 2038 2187 E-mail jeffreywilliams@ntlworld.com

WILLIAMS, Ms Jennifer Ruth. b 66. St Hugh's Coll Ox BA88 PGCE89 Man Univ MA00. Wycliffe Hall Ox 98 N Ord Course 00. **d** 00 **p** 01. C Heatons *Man* 00-04; Hon C Burnage St Marg 04-05; Lect Wycliffe Hall Ox from 05. *Wycliffe Hall, 54 Banbury Road, Oxford OX2 6PW* Tel (01865) 274200 E-mail jonjenni@fish.co.uk

WILLIAMS, Canon John. b 31. AKC56. **d** 57 **p** 58. C Cockerton *Dur* 57-60; C Camberwell St Geo *S'wark* 60-62; C Stockton St Chad *Dur* 62-65; V 65-68; R Longnewton 68-75; Soc Resp Officer 68-83; Hon Can Dur Cathl 80-83; Bp's Officer for Min *Lich* 83-96; Preb Lich Cathl 83-96; C Lich St Mary w St Mich 95-96; rtd 96; NSM Edin Ch Ch *Edin* from 97. *2 Fox Spring Rise, Edinburgh EH10 6NE* Tel and fax 0131-445 2983 E-mail jwilliams@quista.net *or* johnw@6a.org.uk

WILLIAMS, John Anthony. b 53. G&C Coll Cam BA75 MA79 St Jo Coll Dur BA83 PhD86. Cranmer Hall Dur 81. **d** 86 **p** 87. C Beverley Minster *York* 86-89; C Cloughton 89-90; P-in-c 90-93; Clergy Tr Officer E Riding 89-93; P-in-c Emley *Wakef* 93-98; Dioc Minl Tr Officer from 93; Min Scheme Officer from 98; Co-ord for Local Min from 02. *6 Stonecroft Gardens, Shepley, Huddersfield HD8 8EX* Tel and fax (01484) 608703 E-mail jwilwms@surefish.co.uk

WILLIAMS, John Barrie. b 38. Lon Univ DSS68 Univ of Wales (Cardiff) MSc77 DipEd80 PhD91. St Mich Coll Llan 89. **d** 87 **p** 88. NSM Newcastle *Llan* 87-89; C Port Talbot St Theodore 89; Perm to Offic from 89. *Shorncliffe, 11 Priory Oak, Bridgend CF31 2HY* Tel (01656) 660369

WILLIAMS, John Beattie. b 42. Univ of Wales BA66. Cuddesdon Coll 67. **d** 69 **p** 69. C St Helier *S'wark* 69-70; C Yeovil H Trin *B & W* 70-76; P-in-c Ebbesbourne Wake w Fifield Bavant and Alvediston *Sarum* 76-78; Chapl to the Deaf 76-78; Chapl to the Deaf *B & W* 78-83; TV Fareham H Trin *Portsm* 83-94; R W Wittering and Birdham w Itchenor *Chich* from 94. *The Rectory, Pound Road, West Wittering, Chichester PO20 8AJ* Tel (01243) 514057

WILLIAMS, John David Anthony. b 55. Open Univ BA98. St Steph Ho Ox 85. **d** 87 **p** 88. C Paignton St Jo *Ex* 87-90; C Heavitree w Ex St Paul 90-91; TV 91-01; P-in-c Exminster and Kenn from 01. *The Rectory, Milbury Lane, Exminster, Exeter EX6 8AD* Tel (01392) 824283 E-mail john.williams30@btinternet.com

WILLIAMS, John Francis Meyler. b 34. St Jo Coll Cam BA56 MA60. Sarum & Wells Th Coll 79. **d** 81 **p** 82. C Hadleigh w Layham and Shelley *St E* 81-84; P-in-c Parham w Hacheston 84-87; P-in-c Campsey Ashe and Marlesford 84-87; R Campsea Ashe w Marlesford, Parham and Hacheston 87-95; P-in-c Kedington 95-97; rtd 97; Chapl St Kath Convent Parmoor 97-98; Perm to Offic *Ox* 01-05. *Ashgrove, Smyth Street, Fishguard SA65 9LG* Tel (01348) 871971

WILLIAMS, John Francis Oliver. b 15. TCD BA40 MA43. **d** 40 **p** 41. C Shankill *C & O* 40-42; C Oldcastle *M & K* 42-44; P-in-c Clonfadfornan w Castletown 44-46; I Athboy w Girley and Kildalkey 46-54; Sec Ch of Ireland Jews' Soc 54-56; I Dublin Irishtown *D & G* 56-73; I Dalkey St Patr 73-82; Can Ch Ch Cathl Dublin 81-82; rtd 82. *Kerlogue Nursing Home, Rosslare Road, Wexford, Irish Republic* Tel (00353) (53) 70436

WILLIAMS, John Frederick Arthur. b 26. Lon Univ BSc50 Southn Univ PhD53. Ridley Hall Cam 63. **d** 65 **p** 66. C Cambridge H Sepulchre w All SS *Ely* 65-66; P-in-c Cambridge St Mark 66-67; V Portswood Ch Ch *Win* 67-90; Assoc V 90-93; C Win Ch Ch 93-96; rtd 96; Perm to Offic *Win* from 96. *120 Bellemoor Road, Southampton SO5 7QY* Tel (023) 8077 1482

WILLIAMS, John Gilbert. b 36. St Aid Birkenhead 64. **d** 67 **p** 68. C Bollington St Jo *Ches* 67-69; C Oxton 69-72; P-in-c Acton Beauchamp and Evesbatch 72-76; P-in-c Castle Frome *Heref* 72-76; P-in-c Bishop's Frome 72-76; R Kingsland 76-83; P-in-c Eardisland 77-83; P-in-c Aymestry and Leinthall Earles 82-83; R Cradley w Mathon and Storridge 83-94; R Norton St Philip w Hemington, Hardington etc *B & W* 94-01; rtd 01; Perm to Offic *St D* from 02. *Bronydd, Parc y Plas, Aberporth, Cardigan SA43 2BZ* Tel (01239) 810268 E-mail j.s@johngwilliams.fsnet.co.uk

WILLIAMS, Canon John Heard. b 35. Bris Univ BA58. Clifton Th Coll 59. **d** 59 **p** 60. C Tunbridge Wells Ch Ch *Roch* 59-65; V Forest Gate St Sav *Chelmsf* 65-75; P-in-c W Ham St Matt 72-75; TR Forest Gate St Sav w W Ham St Matt from 75; Hon Can Chelmsf Cathl from 82. *St Saviour's Rectory, Sidney Road, London E7 0EF* Tel (020) 8534 6109

WILLIAMS, Canon John James. b 20. TD61. Linc Coll Ox BA42 MA46. St Mich Coll Llan 42. **d** 44 **p** 45. C Rhosymedre *St As* 44-47; C Flint 47-50; CF 49-62; C Llanrhos *St As* 50-53; V Whixall *Lich* 53-57; V Prees 57-64; Sen CF (TA) 62-67; CF (TA) 67-68; V Powick *Worc* 64-85; Hon Can Worc Cathl 77-85; rtd 85; Perm to Offic *Worc* from 85. *9 St Nicholas's Road, Peopleton, Pershore WR10 2EN* Tel (01905) 840032

WILLIAMS, John Keith. b 63. Ridley Hall Cam 95. **d** 97 **p** 98. C Potters Bar *St Alb* 97-99; C Bishop's Stortford St Mich 99-01; P-in-c Bishop's Stortford from 01. *Holy Trinity Vicarage, 69 Havers Lane, Bishop's Stortford CM23 3PA* Tel (01279) 656546 E-mail holytrinitybs@hotmail.com

WILLIAMS, Prof John Mark Gruffydd. b 52. St Pet Coll Ox BA73 MSc76 MA77 DPhil79 Ox Univ DSc FBPsS84. EAMTC 86. **d** 89 **p** 90. NSM Girton *Ely* 89-91; Perm to Offic *Ban* 91-03; NSM Wheatley *Ox* from 03. *Hollyfield Cottage, 17 Bell Lane, Wheatley, Oxford OX33 1XY* Tel (01865) 422037 E-mail mark.williams@psychiatry.oxford.ac.uk

WILLIAMS, John Michael. b 44. MBASW Univ of Wales (Cardiff) CQSW74. St Deiniol's Hawarden 80. **d** 83 **p** 84. NSM Llanrhos *St As* 83-94; P-in-c Brynymaen w Trofarth 94-95; V 95-99; V Llanrhaeadr-yng-Nghinmeirch w Prion and Nantglyn from 99. *The Vicarage, Llanrhaeadr, Denbigh LL16 4NN* Tel (01745) 890250 E-mail dyfnog@btinternet.com

WILLIAMS, Canon John Peter Philip. b 49. Univ of Wales (Ban) DipTh70 Open Univ BA84. Chich Th Coll 71. **d** 72 **p** 73. C Abergele *St As* 72-77; R Henllan and Llannefydd 77-82; R Henllan and Llannefydd and Bylchau from 82; RD Denbigh from 98; Hon Can St As Cathl from 01. *The Rectory, Henllan, Denbigh LL16 5BB* Tel (01745) 812628

WILLIAMS, The Ven John Richard. b 48. Rhodes Univ BA68 K Coll Lon BD72 AKC72. **d** 73 **p** 74. S Africa 73-76; C Addington *Cant* 77-80; C Minster-in-Sheppey 80-86; R Temple Ewell w Lydden 86-90; V Hound *Win* 90-94; V Highcliffe w Hinton Admiral 94-03; RD Christchurch 98-03; Chapl Montreux w Gstaad *Eur* from 03; Adn Switzerland from 04. *St John's House, 92 avenue de Chillon, CH-1820 Territet, Montreux, Switzerland* Tel (0041) (21) 963 4354 Fax 963 4391 E-mail montreux@anglican.ch

WILLIAMS, John Roger. b 31. Bris Univ BA55 Lon Univ BD57. Tyndale Hall Bris 57. **d** 57 **p** 58. C Islington H Trin Cloudesley Square *Lon* 57-60; Travelling Sec IVF 60-64; V Selly Hill St Steph *Birm* 64-74; P-in-c Chilwell *S'well* 74-75; V 75-90; Dioc Tourism Officer 90-95; P-in-c Perlethorpe 90-95; P-in-c Norton Cuckney 90-95; rtd 95; Perm to Offic *Derby* from 95. *Derwent Lights, 4 Wyntor Avenue, Winster, Matlock DE4 2DU* Tel (01629) 650142

WILLIAMS, Canon John Roger. b 37. Westmr Coll Ox MTh97. Lich Th Coll 60. **d** 63 **p** 64. C Wem *Lich* 63-66; C Wolverhampton St Pet 66-69; R Pudleston w Hatf *Heref* 69-74; P-in-c Stoke Prior and Ford w Humber 69-74; P-in-c Docklow 69-74; V Fenton *Lich* 74-81; R Shipston-on-Stour w Honington and Idlicote *Cov* 81-92; RD Shipston 83-90; Hon Can Cov Cathl 90-00; R Lighthorne 92-00; V Chesterton 92-00; V Newbold Pacey w Moreton Morrell 92-00; P-in-c Denstone w Ellastone and Stanton *Lich* 00-05; Master St Jo Hosp Lich from 05. *The Master's House, St John's Hospital, St John Street, Lichfield WS13 6PB* Tel (01543) 251884 Fax 418062

WILLIAMS, John Strettle. b 44. MBE00. DipEd73 BA84. N Ord Course 77. **d** 80 **p** 81. NSM Liv St Paul Stoneycroft *Liv* 80-83; Chapl Cen Liv Coll of FE from 80; Hon C Liv Our Lady and St Nic w St Anne from 83; Chapl RNR 84-90; Chapl City Coll of FE Liv from 85; CF (TA) from 95. *28 Brook Street, Whiston, Prescot L35 5AP* Tel 0151-426 9598

WILLIAMS, John Trefor. b 23. Worc Ord Coll 65. **d** 67 **p** 68. C Paignton St Jo *Ex* 67-72; V Winkleigh 72-80; P-in-c Ashreigney 73-79; R 79-80; P-in-c Brushford 75-79; V 79-80; R Broadwoodkelly 79-80; P-in-c Berrynarbor 80-81; P-in-c Combe Martin 80-81; R Combe Martin and Berrynarbor 81-92; rtd 92; Perm to Offic *Ex* from 92. *97 Littleham Road, Exmouth EX8 2RA* Tel (01395) 264460

WILLIAMS, Jonathan Anthony. b 65. Wycliffe Hall Ox BTh95. **d** 98 **p** 99. C Denton Ch Ch *Man* 98-02; R Burnage St Marg from 02. *St Margaret's Rectory, 250 Burnage Lane, Manchester M19 1FL* Tel 0161-432 1844 E-mail jonjenni@fish.co.uk

WILLIAMS, Jonathan Lane. b 59. Dorset Inst of HE 85. STETS 96. **d** 99 **p** 00. NSM Moordown *Win* from 99. *28 Queen Mary Avenue, Moordown, Bournemouth BH9 1TS* Tel and fax (01202) 531630 Mobile 07977-444186 E-mail jonathan.williams7@ntlworld.com

WILLIAMS, Jonathan Simon. b 60. Univ of Wales (Cardiff) BSc81. Coll of Resurr Mirfield 83. **d** 86 **p** 87. C Gelligaer *Llan* 86-89; C Cwmbran *Mon* 89-90; TV 90-97; V Marshfield and Peterstone Wentloog etc 97-00; TR Bassaleg from 00; RD Bassaleg from 99. *The Vicarage, 1 Church View, Bassaleg, Newport NP10 8ND* Tel (01633) 893258 E-mail jonathan@williamsvicarage.freeserve.co.uk

WILLIAMS, Mrs Josephine Mary. b 47. Reading Univ BEd78 Hatfield Poly MEd87. St Alb and Ox Min Course 96. **d** 99 **p** 00. NSM Terriers *Ox* 99-02; Chapl HM YOI Aylesbury from 02. *HM Young Offender Institution, Bierton Road, Aylesbury HP20 1EH* Tel (01296) 444000 ext 4325

WILLIAMS, Miss Joy Margaret. b 30. Lon Univ BD69. Linc Th Coll 82. **dss** 83 **d** 87 **p** 94. Pershore w Pinvin, Wick and Birlingham *Worc* 83-87; Par Dn 87-88; Par Dn Dudley St Jo 88-90; rtd 90; Perm to Offic *Worc* from 90. *Pixie Cottage, 40 Ridge Street, Pershore WR10 1AT* Tel (01386) 556867

WILLIAMS, Julian Thomas. b 65. Clare Coll Cam BA87. Wycliffe Hall Ox BA90. **d** 91 **p** 92. Min Can St D Cathl *St D* 91-94; C St D Cathl 91-94; V Cil-y-Cwm and Ystrad-ffin w Rhandir-mwyn etc 94-00; R Nursling and Rownhams *Win* from 00. *The Vicarage, 27 Horns Drove, Rownhams, Southampton SO16 8AH* Tel (023) 8073 8293

WILLIAMS, Keith. b 37. St Jo Coll Nottm 83. **d** 85 **p** 86. C Holbeck *Ripon* 85-88; R Swillington 88-95; V Batley All SS *Wakef* 95-01; P-in-c Purlwell 95-00; rtd 01; Perm to Offic *Ripon* from 01. *17 Kirkfield Drive, Colton, Leeds LS15 9DR* Tel 0113-225 5754 Mobile 07808-832147 E-mail kwilliams000@btclick.com

WILLIAMS, Keith Douglas. b 41. EMMTC 86. **d** 89 **p** 90. NSM Netherfield w Colwick *S'well* from 89; NSM Gedling from 95; Chapl Notts Healthcare NHS Trust 93-03. *19 Eastholme Croft, Nottingham NG2 4DZ* Tel 0115-961 4850 E-mail keiwil@ntlworld.com

WILLIAMS, Keith Graham. b 38. Reading Univ MSc70 MRICS62. Cranmer Hall Dur. **d** 77 **p** 78. C Almondbury *Wakef* 77-81; C Chapelthorpe 81-82; V Ryhill 82-88; V E Ardsley 88-99; RD Wakef 96-99; rtd 03. *21 Cadogan Court, Grenville Road, Pevensey Bay, Pevensey BN24 6BS* Tel (01323) 764424

WILLIAMS, Kelvin George John. b 36. ALCD62. **d** 62 **p** 63. C Bath Abbey w St Jas *B & W* 62-65; CF (TA) 64-65 and 70-79; Chapl R Nat Hosp for Rheumatic Diseases Bath 64-65; CF 65-68; C Clevedon St Andr *B & W* 68-70; V Ston Easton w Farrington Gurney 70-74; P-in-c Bradford 74-75; R Bradford w Oake, Hillfarrance and Heathfield 75-76; NSM Puriton and Pawlett 89-91; V 92-02; NSM Bridgwater Deanery 91-92; rtd 02; Perm to Offic *B & W* 03-04; P-in-c Weston Zoyland w Chedzoy from 04. *Highlands, Knowleyards Road, Middlezoy, Bridgwater TA7 0NY* Tel (01823) 698413 E-mail kelvin@revwilliams.freeserve.co.uk

WILLIAMS, Kim. *See* WILLIAMS, George Melvin

WILLIAMS (née HANNAH), Mrs Kimberley Victoria. b 75. Bp Grosseteste Coll BSc98. Ripon Coll Cuddesdon BTh01. **d** 01 **p** 02. C Machynlleth w Llanwrin and Penegoes *Ban* 01-02; C Twrcelyn Deanery from 02. *The Rectory, Bull Bay Road, Amlwch LL68 9EA* Tel (01407) 831670 Fax as telephone E-mail kimwilliams@lineone.net

WILLIAMS, Lee Lawrence. b 75. St Steph Ho Ox 98. **d** 01 **p** 02. C Cowbridge *Llan* 01-04. *34 Queens Drive, Llantwit Fadre, Pontypridd CF83 2NT*

WILLIAMS, Lloyd. b 43. Oak Hill Th Coll 71. **d** 74 **p** 75. C Laisterdyke *Bradf* 74-77; C Hoole *Ches* 77-80; V Rawthorpe *Wakef* 80-84; HM Pris Leeds 84-85; Chapl HM Pris Cardiff 85-88; Chapl HM Pris Aldington 88-95; R Aldington w Bonnington and Bilsington *Cant* 88-95; RD N Lympne 94-95; P-in-c Tuen Mun Hong Kong 95-99; V Clayton *Bradf* 99-03; rtd 03; Perm to Offic *York* from 04. *Charters Garth, Hutton-le-Hole, York YO62 6UD* Tel (01751) 417032 Mobile 07866-604345 E-mail lloyd@healingtrust.fslife.co.uk

WILLIAMS, Lois. *See* WILLIAMS, Ms Catherine Lois

WILLIAMS, Mrs Louise Margaret. b 66. Lanc Univ BA87. St Jo Coll Nottm DPS91. **d** 91 **p** 94. Par Dn W Ham *Chelmsf* 91-94; C Harold Hill St Geo 94-95; NSM Southend St Sav Westcliff from 95; Chapl Asst Southend Health Care NHS Trust from 97. *St Saviour's Vicarage, 33 King's Road, Westcliff-on-Sea SS0 8LL* Tel (01702) 342920 E-mail stsaviorwest@aol.com

WILLIAMS, Malcolm Clive. b 50. Univ Coll Worc BA(Ed)04. Trin Coll Bris 74. **d** 04. NSM Amesbury *Sarum* from 04. *Solstice Farmhouse, 39 Holders Road, Amesbury, Salisbury SP4 7PH* Tel (01980) 625052 Mobile 07870-593505 E-mail williamsmc@btinternet.com

WILLIAMS, Mark. b 64. St Mich Coll Llan BTh94. **d** 97 **p** 98. C Mountain Ash *Llan* 97; C Mountain Ash and Miskin 97-99; C Neath w Llantwit 99-01; C Neath 01-02; V Skewen from 02. *Skewen Vicarage, 41 Hill Road, Neath Abbey, Neath SA10 7NP* Tel (01792) 814116

WILLIAMS, Mark. b 73. Pemb Coll Cam BA94 MA98 Ox Univ BA98 MA02. Ripon Coll Cuddesdon 95 Ven English Coll Rome 97. **d** 98 **p** 99. C Caerphilly *Llan* 98-00; V Walworth St Chris *S'wark* from 00; Warden Pemb Coll (Cam) Miss from 00; Dioc Voc Adv from 02. *45 Aldbridge Street, London SE17 2RG* Tel (020) 7701 4162 *or* 7703 3803 E-mail fr_mark@yahoo.com

WILLIAMS, Mark John. b 66. St Martin's Coll Lanc BA88 PGCE93. Cranmer Hall Dur 98. **d** 00 **p** 01. C Hockerill *St Alb* 00-03; TV Chipping Barnet from 03. *St Peter's Vicarage, Barnet Road, Barnet EN5 3JF* Tel (020) 8440 5797 E-mail mark.john.williams@lineone.net

WILLIAMS, Mark Naylor. b 28. CCC Cam BA52 MA56 CertEd. Ripon Hall Ox 58. **d** 59 **p** 60. C Dorchester *Ox* 59-65; R Gt and Lt Braxted *Chelmsf* 65-70; R E Kilbride *Glas* 70-74; R Norton *Sheff* 74-89; R Lt w Gt Ellingham w Rockland *Nor* 89-95; rtd 95; Perm to Offic *Chelmsf* from 95. *15 Olivia Drive, Leigh-on-Sea SS9 3EF* Tel (01702) 478734

WILLIAMS, Mark Robert. b 62. Spurgeon's Coll Lon BA83 Univ Coll of Swansea PGCE84. Ripon Coll Cuddesdon 99. **d** 01 **p** 02. C Wellington and Distr *B & W* 01-05; V Belmont *S'wark* from 05. *St John's Vicarage, Belmont Rise, Sutton SM2 6EA* Tel (020) 8642 2363 E-mail blots@lineone.net

WILLIAMS, The Ven Martin Inffeld. b 37. SS Coll Cam BA62 MA92. Chich Th Coll 62. **d** 64 **p** 65. C Greenford H Cross *Lon* 64-70; Tutor Chich Th Coll 70-75; Vice-Prin 75-77; V Roath St German *Llan* 77-92; Adn Margam 92-01; Adn Morgannwg 02-04; Treas Llan Cathl 92-04; V Penydarren 92-04; rtd 04. *29 Blackfriars Court, Brecon LD3 8LJ* Tel (01874) 622351

WILLIAMS, Martin Jonathan. b 63. Birm Univ BA84. Trin Coll Bris DipHE96. **d** 98 **p** 99. C Bisley and W End *Guildf* 98-01; C Gerrards Cross and Fulmer *Ox* from 01. *Willowbrook, 54 The Uplands, Gerrards Cross SL9 7JG* Tel (01753) 892571 Mobile 07974-010703 E-mail williamsmartinj@cs.com

WILLIAMS, Mary Edith. b 50. Darlington Tr Coll BEd73. Cranmer Hall Dur 00. **d** 02 **p** 03. C Filey *York* from 02. *16A Willow Close, Filey YO14 9NY* Tel (01723) 515439 E-mail brmewilliams@supanet.com

WILLIAMS, Mervyn Rees. b 28. Univ of Wales (Swansea) BA49 Lon Univ PGCE54. St Deiniol's Hawarden 68. **d** 72 **p** 73. NSM

Llangollen w Trevor and Llantysilio *St As* 72-94; rtd 94. *12 Wern Road, Llangollen LL20 8DU* Tel (01978) 860369

WILLIAMS, The Ven Meurig Llwyd. b 61. Univ of Wales (Abth) BA83 PGCE84 Univ of Wales (Cardiff) BD90. Westcott Ho Cam 90. **d** 92 **p** 93. C Holyhead w Rhoscolyn w Llanfair-yn-Neubwll *Ban* 92-95; P-in-c Denio w Abererch 95-96; V 96-99; V Cardiff Dewi Sant *Llan* 99-05; Adn Ban from 05. *The Archdeaconry, 1 Belmont Road, Bangor LL57 2LL* Tel (01248) 354360 E-mail mllwyd@aol.com

WILLIAMS, Michael. *See* WILLIAMS, David Michael Rochfort

WILLIAMS, Michael. b 70. Nottm Univ BA98. St Jo Coll Nottm 95. **d** 98 **p** 99. C Shifnal *Lich* 98-01; TV Stafford from 01. *St Bertelin's Vicarage, 36 Holmcroft Road, Stafford ST16 1JB* Tel (01785) 252874

WILLIAMS, Michael Dermot Andrew. b 57. Ex Univ BA86. Ripon Coll Cuddesdon 90. **d** 92 **p** 93. NSM Christow, Ashton, Trusham and Bridford *Ex* 92-97; NSM Marston w Elsfield *Ox* 97-99; Chief Exec Radcliffe Infirmary NHS Trust 97-99; V Shipton-under-Wychwood w Milton, Fifield etc *Ox* 99-02; RD Chipping Norton 01-02; Exec Dir Thames Valley HA 02-05; NSM Kennington 04-05; Chief Exec Taunton and Somerset NHS Trust from 05. *Taunton and Somerset Hospital, Musgrove Park, Taunton TA1 5DA* Tel (01823) 333444 E-mail williamsmda@btopenworld.com

WILLIAMS, Michael John. b 31. St Edm Hall Ox BA53 MA57. Wells Th Coll 53. **d** 55 **p** 56. C Wood Green St Mich *Lon* 55-59; C Bedminster St Aldhelm *Bris* 59-62; C Witney *Ox* 62-65; C Thatcham 66-70; Perm to Offic *Ex* 70-81; C Rainhill *Liv* 81-86; Chapl Whiston Hosp 83-86; rtd 86; Perm to Offic *Ex* from 86. *1 Bramble Lane, Crediton EX17 1DA* Tel (01363) 774005

WILLIAMS, Canon Michael Joseph. b 42. St Jo Coll Dur BA68. Bernard Gilpin Soc Dur 63 Cranmer Hall Dur 64. **d** 70 **p** 71. C Toxteth Park St Philemon *Liv* 70-75; TV Toxteth St Philemon w St Gabr 75-78; Dir Past Studies St Jo Coll Dur 78-88; Prin N Ord Course 89-99; Hon Can Liv Cathl *Liv* 92-99; P-in-c Bolton St Pet *Man* 99-04; V from 04; P-in-c Bolton St Phil from 04; Hon Can Man Cathl from 00; AD Bolton 02-05. *The Vicarage, Silverwell Street, Bolton BL1 1PS* Tel and fax (01204) 533847 E-mail vicar@boltonparishchurch.co.uk

WILLIAMS, Michael Robert John. b 41. Cranmer Hall Dur 67. **d** 70 **p** 71. C Middleton *Man* 70-73; C-in-c Blackley White Moss St Mark CD 73-79; R Blackley St Mark White Moss 79-86; R Gorton Em 86-96; R Gorton Em w St Jas from 96. *Emmanuel Rectory, 35 Blackwin Street, Manchester M12 5LD* Tel 0161-223 3510

WILLIAMS, Mrs Nia Catrin. b 69. Univ of Wales (Abth) DipTh94 Univ of Wales (Cardiff) BTh96. St As Minl Tr Course 97. **d** 98 **p** 99. C Llanrhos *St As* 98-02; C Colwyn Bay w Brynymaen from 02. *The Vicarage, 27 Walshaw Avenue, Colwyn Bay LL29 7UY*

WILLIAMS, Nicholas Jolyon. b 68. Univ of Wales (Swansea) BA89. Wycliffe Hall Ox BTh96. **d** 96 **p** 97. C Ditton *Roch* 96-99; C N Farnborough *Guildf* 99-05; P-in-c Tongham from 05. *The Vicarage, Poyle Road, Tongham, Farnham GU10 1DU* Tel (01252) 782224 E-mail nick@williams75.fsnet.co.uk

WILLIAMS, Nick. *See* WILLIAMS, James Nicholas Owen

WILLIAMS, Nigel Howard. b 63. Llys Fasi Agric Coll NCA81. St Mich Coll Llan DipTh95. **d** 95 **p** 96. C Denbigh and Nantglyn *St As* 95-97; P-in-c Llanrwst and Llanddoget and Capel Garmon 97-98; R 98-04; V Colwyn Bay w Brynymaen from 04; AD Rhos from 04. *The Vicarage, 27 Walshaw Avenue, Colwyn Bay LL29 7UY*

WILLIAMS, Norman Ernest. b 23. IEng FIEEE AMIEE Cardiff Coll of Tech HNC. Llan Dioc Tr Scheme 78. **d** 82 **p** 83. NSM Llanblethian w Cowbridge and Llandough etc *Llan* 82-93; rtd 93; Perm to Offic *Llan* from 93. *The Poplars, Southgate, Cowbridge CF71 7BD* Tel (01446) 772107 E-mail normanewilliams@compuserve.com

WILLIAMS, Norman Leigh. b 26. Open Univ BA86 Trin Coll Carmarthen 83. **d** 85 **p** 86. NSM Loughor *S & B* 85-96; NSM Adnry Gower 87-96; rtd 96. *Gorwydd Villa, 13 The Woodlands, Gowerton, Swansea SA4 3DP* Tel (01792) 874853

WILLIAMS, Olivia Hazel. b 55. Dun Laoghaire Inst CertEd98 TCD BTh01. CITC 98. **d** 01 **p** 02. C Greystones *D & G* from 01; Abp's Dom Chapl from 03. *192 Heathervue, Greystones, Co Wicklow, Irish Republic* Tel (00353) (1) 287 1336 E-mail curate.greystones@glendalough.anglican.org

WILLIAMS, Owen David. b 38. S'wark Ord Course 72. **d** 75 **p** 76. NSM Tatsfield *S'wark* 75-80; C Maidstone All SS w St Phil and H Trin *Cant* 80-81; C Maidstone All SS and St Phil w Tovil 81-82; V St Nicholas at Wade w Sarre and Chislet w Hoath 82-92; TV Bruton and Distr *B & W* 92-98; R Kirkby Fleetham w Langton on Swale and Scruton *Ripon* 98-03; rtd 03; P-in-c Walford and St John w Bishopswood, Goodrich etc *Heref* from 03. *The Vicarage, Walford, Ross-on-Wye HR9 5QP* Tel (01989) 562703

WILLIAMS, Paul Andrew. b 62. Oak Hill Th Coll BA91. **d** 91 **p** 92. C Ware Ch Ch *St Alb* 91-94; C Harold Wood *Chelmsf* 94-99; C Langham Place All So *Lon* from 99. *12 De Walden Street, London W1G 8RN* Tel (020) 7935 9811 *or* 7580 3522 E-mail paul.williams@allsouls.org

WILLIAMS, Paul Gavin. b 68. Grey Coll Dur BA89. Wycliffe Hall Ox MPhil93. **d** 92 **p** 93. C Muswell Hill St Jas w St Matt *Lon* 92-96; C Clifton Ch Ch w Em *Bris* 96-99; R Gerrards Cross and Fulmer *Ox* from 99. *The Rectory, Oxford Road, Gerrards Cross SL9 7DJ* Tel (01753) 883301 Fax 892177

WILLIAMS, Paul Rhys. b 58. St Andr Univ MTh82. Westcott Ho Cam 83. **d** 86 **p** 87. Asst Chapl Selw Coll Cam 86-87; C Chatham St Steph *Roch* 87-90; V Gillingham St Aug 90-95; Bp's Dom Chapl 95-03; Hon Can Roch Cathl 01-03; V Tewkesbury w Walton Cardiff and Twyning *Glouc* from 03. *Abbey House, Church Street, Tewkesbury GL20 5SR* Tel (01684) 293333 Fax 273113 E-mail vicar@tewkesburyabbey.org.uk

WILLIAMS, Paul Robert. b 66. Huddersfield Poly BA88. Wycliffe Hall Ox. **d** 99 **p** 00. C Roxeth *Lon* 99-03; C Harlow St Mary and St Hugh w St Jo the Bapt *Chelmsf* from 03. *134 East Park, Harlow CM17 0SA* Tel and fax (01279) 427357 E-mail paul-w@xalt.co.uk

WILLIAMS, Mrs Pauline Mary. b 52. Univ of Wales (Cardiff) BD96 Trin Coll Carmarthen PGCE97. St Mich Coll Llan 00. **d** 02 **p** 03. C Coity w Nolton *Llan* from 02. *2 Fenwick Drive, Brackla, Bridgend CF31 2LD* Tel (01656) 659749 Mobile 07974-652211 E-mail williamspm89@hotmail.com

WILLIAMS, Canon Peris Llewelyn. b 39. Univ of Wales (Lamp) BA59. Qu Coll Birm 59. **d** 62 **p** 63. C Upton Ascension *Ches* 62-65; C Davenham 65-68; C Grange St Andr 68-73; TV E Runcorn w Halton 73-74; V Backford 74-80; Youth Chapl 74-80; V Witton 80-86; V Hoylake 86-93; R Ches H Trin 93-02; Hon Can Ches Cathl 98-02; rtd 02; Perm to Offic *Ches* and *Lon* from 02. *Padarn, 65 Long Lane, Chester CH2 2PG* Tel (01244) 341305

WILLIAMS, Peter. *See* WILLIAMS, Canon Cecil Peter

WILLIAMS, Peter. *See* WILLIAMS, Edward Ffoulkes

WILLIAMS, Peter Charles. b 50. SW Minl Tr Course 98. **d** 01 **p** 02. OLM Landrake w St Erney and Botus Fleming *Truro* from 01. *5 North Road, Landrake, Saltash PL12 5EL* Tel (01752) 851260 E-mail peterfreda@5northroad.fsnet.co.uk

WILLIAMS, Peter Hurrell. b 34. Keble Coll Ox BA58 MA61. Tyndale Hall Bris 62. **d** 64 **p** 65. C Sparkbrook Ch Ch *Birm* 64-67; C Rushden St Pet 67-70; P-in-c Clapham Park All SS *S'wark* 70-78; R Stanford-le-Hope w Mucking *Chelmsf* 78-92; P-in-c Gt Oakley w Wix 92-96; R Gt Oakley w Wix and Wrabness 96-97; rtd 97; Perm to Offic *Chelmsf* from 01. *3 Hillcrest Close, Horndon-on-the-Hill, Stanford-le-Hope SS17 8LS* Tel (01375) 643697

WILLIAMS, Canon Peter John. b 55. Southn Univ BTh80 Univ of Wales (Swansea) DSS90. Chich Th Coll 76. **d** 80 **p** 81. C Chepstow *Mon* 80-84; C Morriston *S & B* 84-85; V Glantawe 85-88; R Reynoldston w Penrice and Llangennith from 73; Hon Can Brecon Cathl from 04; Dioc Soc Resp Officer from 88. *The Vicarage, Llangennith, Swansea SA3 1HU* Tel (01792) 386391

WILLIAMS, Peter Rodney. b 22. Chich Th Coll 60. **d** 62 **p** 63. C Seaford w Sutton *Chich* 62-65; P-in-c Wivelsfield 65-72; V Eastbourne St Jo 72-87; rtd 87; Perm to Offic *Chich* from 87. *33 Park Gates, Chiswick Place, Eastbourne BN21 4BD* Tel (01323) 723359

WILLIAMS, Philip Allan. b 48. Bris Univ BSc69 CertEd74. Trin Coll Bris 86. **d** 88 **p** 89. C Heref St Pet w St Owen and St Jas *Heref* 88-93; R Peterchurch w Vowchurch, Turnastone and Dorstone 93-96; P-in-c Holmer w Huntington 96-01; V from 01. *The Vicarage, Holmer, Hereford HR4 9RG* Tel (01432) 273200 E-mail revphil@holmer.supanet.com

WILLIAMS, Philip Andrew. b 64. Sheff Univ BA86. St Jo Coll Dur 88. **d** 90 **p** 91. C Hillsborough and Wadsley Bridge *Sheff* 90-94; C Lenton Abbey *S'well* 94-96; P-in-c 96-02; C Wollaton Park 94-96; V Porchester from 02; AD Gedling from 05. *St James's Vicarage, Marshall Hill Drive, Nottingham NG3 6FY* Tel 0115-960 6185 E-mail phil.stjames@virgin.net

WILLIAMS, Philip James. b 52. St Chad's Coll Dur BA73. Coll of Resurr Mirfield 74. **d** 76 **p** 77. C Stoke upon Trent *Lich* 76-80; TV 80; Chapl N Staffs Poly 80-84; TV Stoke-upon-Trent 80-84; R Shrewsbury St Giles w Sutton and Atcham from 84. *St Giles's Rectory, 127 Abbey Foregate, Shrewsbury SY2 6LY* Tel (01743) 356426 E-mail philipjwilliams@lineone.net

WILLIAMS, Ray. b 23. Birm City Tech Coll DipMechE41 Lon Univ DipEd46. St Aid Birkenhead 56. **d** 58 **p** 59. C Sparkhill St Jo *Birm* 58-60; Area Sec (Dios St Alb and Chelmsf) CMS 60-65; V Shenstone *Lich* 65-73; New Zealand from 73; Asst P Blenheim 73-78; V Wakefield and Tapawera 78-83; P-in-c Murchison 79-82; Asst P Nelson All SS 83-85; Asst P Havelock and the Sounds 92-96. *16 Limerick Grove, Ascot Park, Porirua 6006, New Zealand* Tel (0064) (4) 235 9912

WILLIAMS, Raymond Howel. b 27. St Jo Coll Cam BA49 MA51 Ball Coll Ox BLitt63. St Jo Coll Nottm 72 NW Ord Course 73. **d** 73 **p** 74. C Derby St Pet *Derby* 73-76; C Enfield Ch Ch Trent Park *Lon* 75-81; V S Mymms K Chas *St Alb* 81-94; NSM 94-95; rtd 94; Perm to Offic *St Alb* from 95. *7 Cockhall Close, Litlington, Royston SG8 0RB* Tel (01763) 853079

WILLIAMS, Rhys. *See* WILLIAMS, Thomas Rhys

WILLIAMS, Richard Dennis. b 57. LTCL79. Coll of Resurr Mirfield 79. **d** 82 **p** 83. C Roath *Llan* 82-85; C Penarth w Lavernock 85-88; V Abertillery *Mon* 88-95; V Tredunnoc and Llantrisant w Llanhennock etc 95-01; V Hay w Llanigon and Capel-y-Ffin *S & B* from 01. *19 Gypsy Castle Lane, Hay-on-Wye, Hereford HR3 1XX* Tel (01497) 820448

WILLIAMS, Richard Elwyn. b 57. Hull Univ BA79. Coll of Resurr Mirfield 79. **d** 81 **p** 82. C Altrincham St Geo *Ches* 81-84; C Stockport St Thos 84-85; C Stockport St Thos w St Pet 86; R Withington St Crispin *Man* 86-95; V Alveston *Cov* from 95; RD Fosse from 99. *The Vicarage, Alveston, Stratford-upon-Avon CV37 7QB* Tel (01789) 292777 E-mail rrickvic@aol.com

WILLIAMS, Canon Richard Glyndwr. b 18. St D Coll Lamp BA39 BD50. **d** 41 **p** 42. C Kidwelly *St D* 41-46; C Llandudno *Ban* 46-52; R Trefriw 52-55; V Llandinorwig 55-62; Sec Dioc Coun for Educn 58-62; Warden Ch Hostel Ban 62-70; Chapl Univ of Wales (Ban) *Ban* 62-70; Dir of Ords 62-70 and 84-86; Prec Ban Cathl 68-88; Can from 68; R Llanbeblig w Caernarfon 70-71; R Llanbeblig w Caernarfon and Betws Garmon etc 71-81; V Llandysilio 81-88; RD Tindaethwy 82-88; rtd 88; Perm to Offic *Ban* from 88. *Borth, 9 Cae Cil Melyn, Penrhosgarnedd, Bangor LL57 2ND* Tel (01248) 362883

WILLIAMS, Canon Richard Henry Lowe. b 31. Liv Univ BA52. K Coll (NS) BD64 Ridley Hall Cam 54. **d** 56 **p** 57. C Drypool St Andr and St Pet *York* 56-59; Canada 59-64; V Kirkdale St Athanasius *Liv* 64-68; R Much Woolton 68-79; R Croft w Southworth 79-89; Dioc Communications Officer 79-97; Hon Can Liv Cathl 88-97; R Wavertree St Mary 89-97; rtd 97; Perm to Offic *Liv* from 97. *16 Childwall Crescent, Liverpool L16 7PQ* Tel 0151-722 7962

WILLIAMS, Richard Huw. b 63. Bradf and Ilkley Coll BA85. St Jo Coll Nottm LTh88 DPS89. **d** 89 **p** 90. C Forest Gate St Edm *Chelmsf* 89-90; C Plaistow 90-92; C Canning Town St Matthias 92-96; V Southend St Sav Westcliff from 96. *St Saviour's Vicarage, 33 King's Road, Westcliff-on-Sea SS0 8LL* Tel (01702) 342920 E-mail stsaviourwest@aol.com

WILLIAMS, Richard Lawrence. b 62. Warw Univ BSc83 ACA87. Wycliffe Hall Ox 95. **d** 97 **p** 98. C Wallington H Trin *S'wark* 97-00; V Addiscombe St Mary Magd w St Martin from 00. *The Vicarage, Canning Road, Addiscombe CR0 6QD* Tel and fax (020) 8654 3459 *or* 8656 3457
E-mail richard@rlwilliams.fsnet.co.uk

WILLIAMS, Robert. b 49. **d** 97 **p** 98. C W Derby St Mary *Liv* 97-01; R Golborne from 01. *The Rectory, Church Street, Golborne, Warrington WA3 3TH* Tel (01942) 728305

WILLIAMS, Robert Edward. b 42. Ex Univ BA63. Lich Th Coll. **d** 65 **p** 66. C Wednesbury St Paul Wood Green *Lich* 65-67; C Whitchurch 67-69; P-in-c Whixall 69-72; P-in-c Edstaston 69-72; CF 72-91; R Cheriton w Tichborne and Beauworth *Win* 91-01; R Upper Itchen 01-02; rtd 02. *84 Portway, Warminster BA12 8QE*

WILLIAMS, Robert Edward. b 50. Univ of Wales (Ban) DipTh71. St Mich Coll Llan BD74 CertEd79. **d** 74 **p** 75. C Flint *St As* 74-77; Asst Chapl Sandbach Sch 79-80; Chapl and Hd RE 80-88; CF 88-05. *Address temp unknown*

WILLIAMS, Robert Ellis Greenleaf. b 12. St D Coll Lamp BA34 Lich Th Coll 34. **d** 36 **p** 37. C S Banbury *Ox* 36-39; Australia 39-54; R Croydon w Clopton *Ely* 54-58; V Tadlow w E Hatley 54-58; R Hatley 54-58; V Oldham St Ambrose *Man* 58-66; V Rochdale St Aid 66-75; TV Weston-super-Mare Cen Par *B & W* 75-78; P-in-c Castleton All So *Man* 78-80; rtd 80; Perm to Offic *Man* 81-96. *18 Barrowdale Drive, Rochdale OL11 3JZ* Tel (01706) 356582

WILLIAMS, Robert Jeffrey Hopkin. b 62. Univ of Wales (Abth) BA84 ALAM. Chich Th Coll BTh90. **d** 90 **p** 91. C Eastbourne St Mary *Chich* 90-94; R Upper St Leonards St Jo 94-02; V Twickenham St Mary *Lon* from 02. *37 Arragon Road, Twickenham TW1 3NG* Tel (020) 8892 2318

WILLIAMS, The Ven Robert John. b 51. Cartrefle Coll of Educn CertEd72 Univ of Wales (Ban) BEd73 MA92. St Mich Coll Llan BD76. **d** 76 **p** 77. C Swansea St Mary and H Trin *S & B* 76-78; Chapl Univ of Wales (Swansea) 78-84; Children's Adv 81-88; Asst Dir of Educn 81-88; Bp's Chapl for Th Educn 83-88; R Reynoldston w Penrice and Llangennith 84-88; R Denbigh and Nantglyn *St As* 88-94; V Sketty *S & B* 94-99; Dir of Ords 94-99; P-in-c Port Eynon w Rhosili and Llanddewi and Knelston 99-03; Can Brecon Cathl 95-00; Adn Gower from 00. *56 Pinewood Road, Uplands, Swansea SA2 0LT* Tel (01792) 297817

WILLIAMS, Roger. *See* WILLIAMS, David Roger

WILLIAMS, Roger. *See* WILLIAMS, Canon John Roger

WILLIAMS, Roger Anthony. b 54. Univ of Wales (Lamp) BA76. Bp Burgess Hall Lamp 72 Qu Coll Birm 76. **d** 78 **p** 79. C Llanelli *St D* 78-82; V Monkton 82-86; Chapl to the Deaf *B & W* 86-90; Chapl to the Deaf *Ox* from 90. *Denchworth House, Denchworth, Wantage OX12 0DX* Tel and Minicom (01235) 868442 Fax 867402 E-mail roger@williams24.freeserve.co.uk

WILLIAMS, Roger Stewart. b 54. Qu Coll Cam BA75 MA79. Wycliffe Hall Ox BA78 MA82. **d** 79 **p** 80. C Hamstead St Paul *Birm* 79-82; C Barking St Marg w St Patr *Chelmsf* 82-85; V Mildmay Grove St Jude and St Paul *Lon* 85-95; P-in-c Charles w Plymouth St Matthias *Ex* from 95; Chapl Plymouth Univ from 95. *The Vicarage, 6 St Lawrence Road, Plymouth PL4 6HN* Tel (01752) 665640 E-mail rswilliams@supanet.com

WILLIAMS, Roger Thomas. b 54. Man Univ BSc76 Birm Univ MSc78 PhD83 Pemb Coll Cam PGCE92. Ridley Hall Cam 00. **d** 02 **p** 03. C Cambridge St Martin *Ely* from 02; V Cambridge H Cross from 05. *Holy Cross Vicarage, 192 Peverell Road, Cambridge CB5 8RL* Tel (01223) 413343 Mobile 07751-601066 E-mail rogertw11@hotmail.com

WILLIAMS, Ronald Ernest Nathan. b 66. Univ of Sierra Leone BSc95. St Jo Coll Nottm MTh05. **d** 05. C Cowplain *Portsm* from 05. *24 Wincanton Way, Waterlooville PO7 8NW* Tel (023) 9225 7915 Mobile 07796-655225 E-mail ronnierenw@hotmail.com

WILLIAMS, Ronald Hywel. b 35. St D Coll Lamp BA62. **d** 63 **p** 64. C Machynlleth and Llanwrin *Ban* 63-66; C Llanaber 66-69; C Hawarden *St As* 69-73; R Llansantffraid Glan Conwy and Eglwysbach 73-77; V Rhosllannerchrugog 77-88; R Cilcain and Nannerch and Rhydymwyn 88-92; V Llanbadarn Fawr w Capel Bangor and Goginan *St D* 92-95; V Llanbadarn Fawr 95-00; RD Llanbadarn Fawr 94-00; rtd 00. *15 Maes y Garn, Bow Street SY24 5DS* Tel (01970) 820247

WILLIAMS (née TYDEMAN), Mrs Rosemary (Rose). b 47. Roehampton Inst TCert69. St Alb and Ox Min Course 97. **d** 00 **p** 01. NSM Walton H Trin *Ox* 00-03; NSM E and W Horndon w Lt Warley and Childerditch *Chelmsf* from 03. *The Rectory, 155 Thorndon Avenue, West Horndon, Brentwood CM13 3TR* Tel (01277) 811223 E-mail stevecgs@ukonline.co.uk

WILLIAMS, Ms Rowan Clare. b 67. K Coll Cam BA90 MA93 Jes Coll Cam BA05. Westcott Ho Cam 02. **d** 05. C Leic Resurr *Leic* from 05. *St Matthew's House, 25 Kamloops Crescent, Leicester LE1 2HX* Tel 0116-253 9158 Mobile 07919-861912

✠**WILLIAMS, The Most Revd and Rt Hon Rowan Douglas.** b 50. PC02. Ch Coll Cam BA71 MA75 Wadh Coll Ox DPhil75 DD89 Erlangen Hon DrTheol99 FBA90 Hon FGCM00. Coll of Resurr Mirfield 75. **d** 77 **p** 78 **c** 92. Tutor Westcott Ho Cam 77-80; Hon C Chesterton St Geo *Ely* 80-83; Lect Div Cam Univ 80-86; Dean Clare Coll Cam 84-86; Can Th Leic Cathl *Leic* 81-92; Lady Marg Prof Div Ox Univ 86-92; Can Res Ch Ch *Ox* 86-92; Bp Mon 92-02; Abp Wales 99-02; Abp Cant from 02. *Lambeth Palace, London SE1 7JU,* or *The Old Palace, Canterbury CT1 2EE* Tel (020) 7898 1200 *or* (01227) 459401 Fax (020) 7261 9836

WILLIAMS, Canon Roy. b 28. Lon Univ DipTh60. Ely Th Coll 58. **d** 60 **p** 61. C Daybrook *S'well* 60-63; V Bilborough St Jo 63-73; V Arnold 73-92; Hon Can S'well Minster 85-92; rtd 92; Perm to Offic *S'well* from 92. *10 Maris Drive, Burton Joyce, Nottingham NG14 5AJ* Tel 0115-931 2030

WILLIAMS (née CROSLAND), Mrs Sarah Rosita. b 50. St Mary's Coll Chelt CertEd71 BEd72. EAMTC CertHE03. **d** 03 **p** 04. C Warmley, Syston and Bitton *Bris* from 03. *25 Poplar Road, Warmley, Bristol BS30 5JX* Tel 0117-960 9969
E-mail sarah.williams@porfalas.plus.com

WILLIAMS, Canon Shamus Frank Charles. b 57. St Cath Coll Cam BA79 MA83. Ripon Coll Cuddesdon 81. **d** 84 **p** 85. C Swanage and Studland *Sarum* 84-87; C St Alb St Pet *St Alb* 87-90; TV Saffron Walden w Wendens Ambo and Littlebury *Chelmsf* 90-95; R Shingay Gp *Ely* from 95; RD Shingay from 97; Hon Can Ely Cathl from 05. *The Vicarage, Church Street, Guilden Morden, Royston SG8 0JD* Tel (01763) 853067

WILLIAMS, Stephen Clark. b 47. Univ of Wales (Cardiff) BSc(Econ)69 Warw Univ MSc70. Wycliffe Hall Ox DipMin93. **d** 93 **p** 94. C High Wycombe *Ox* 93-96; C Walton H Trin 96-97; TV 97-03; Acting TR 01-03; P-in-c E and W Horndon w Lt Warley and Childerditch *Chelmsf* from 03. *The Rectory, 155 Thorndon Avenue, West Horndon, Brentwood CM13 3TR* Tel (01277) 811223 E-mail stevecgs@ukonline.co.uk

WILLIAMS, Stephen Geoffrey. b 54. St Jo Coll Nottm BTh79 LTh79. **d** 79 **p** 80. C Skelmersdale St Paul *Liv* 79-81; C Burley *Ripon* 81-86. *24 Coronation Drive, Penketh, Warrington WA5 2DD* Tel (01925) 723599

WILLIAMS, Stephen Grant. b 51. K Coll Lon BD73 AKC73. **d** 75 **p** 76. C Paddington Ch Ch *Lon* 75-78; C Paddington St Jas 78-80; Chapl LSE 80-91; Chapl (Sen) Lon Univs from 91. *15 Wilmington Square, London WC1X 0ER* Tel (020) 7837 1782 *or* 7387 0670 Fax 7387 4373
E-mail chaplaincy@admin.lon.ac.uk

WILLIAMS, Stephen James. b 52. Lon Univ BSc73. Ridley Hall Cam 73. **d** 78 **p** 79. C Waltham Abbey *Chelmsf* 78-82; C Bedford St Paul *St Alb* 82-86; P-in-c Chalgrave 86-88; V Harlington from 86. *The Vicarage, Church Road, Harlington, Dunstable LU5 6LE* Tel (01525) 872413 Fax 753683
E-mail stephenwilliams@harlingtonchurch.org.uk

WILLIAMS, The Very Revd Stephen John. b 49. Univ of NSW BA73 DipEd73 Cam Univ BA77 MA81 Macquarie Univ (NSW) MA92. Ridley Hall Cam 75. **d** 78 **p** 79. Lect Th Bp Tucker Coll Uganda 78; C Brompton H Trin w Onslow Square St Paul *Lon* 79-82; Australia from 82; C Shenton Park St Matt

82-83; Chapl Blue Mountains Gr Sch 84-90; R W Lindfield 91-01; Dean Armidale from 02. *PO Box 749, Armidale, NSW, Australia 2350* Tel (0061) (2) 6772 2269 Fax 6772 0188

WILLIAMS, Stephen Lionel. b 48. St Kath Coll Liv CertEd73 Open Univ BA77. N Ord Course 93. **d** 96 **p** 97. NSM Hough Green St Basil and All SS *Liv* 96-99; C Padgate 99-02; V Walton St Jo from 02. *66 Roseworth Avenue, Liverpool L9 8HF* Tel 0151-525 3458

WILLIAMS, Stephen Stuart. b 60. Magd Coll Ox BA82 Dur Univ BA88. Cranmer Hall Dur 86. **d** 89 **p** 90. C W Derby Gd Shep *Liv* 89-93; Relig Affairs Producer BBC Radio Merseyside 92-00; TV Liv Our Lady and St Nic w St Anne *Liv* 93-01; P-in-c Prestwich St Gabr *Man* from 01; Bp's Dom Chapl 01-05; Interfaith Adv from 05. *St Gabriel's Vicarage, 8 Bishops Road, Prestwich, Manchester M25 0HT* Tel 0161-773 8839 *or* 792 2096 Mobile 07813-436170

WILLIAMS, Susan. b 50. Swansea Coll of Educn CertEd72. Ban Ord Course 94. **d** 97 **p** 98. NSM Criccieth w Treflys *Ban* 97-00; P-in-c 00-01; P-in-c Criccieth and Treflys w Llanystumdwy etc 01-02; R from 02. *Taleifion, High Street, Criccieth LL52 0RN* Tel (01766) 523222 *or* (01248) 354999 Fax 523183 E-mail rev.sue-williams@btopenworld.com

WILLIAMS, Ms Susan Jean. b 54. Chester Coll of HE MTh00 Lanc Univ MA02. N Ord Course 95. **d** 98 **p** 99. C Prescot *Liv* 98-01; Perm to Offic *Blackb* 01-02; C Scotforth 02-05; P-in-c Chipping and Whitewell from 05; Vice-Prin Carl and Blackb Dioc Tr Inst from 05. *The Vicarage, Garstang Road, Chipping, Preston PR3 2QH* Tel (01995) 61252 Mobile 07904-076864 E-mail rev_sue@lineone.net

WILLIAMS, Mrs Susan Merrilyn Marsh. b 62. Ban Ord Course 00. **d** 03 **p** 04. NSM Botwnnog w Bryncroes *Ban* from 03. *Tyddyn Mawr, Tudweiliog, Pwllheli LL53 8PB* Tel (01758) 770208 E-mail smw4tmawr@aol.com

WILLIAMS, Terence. b 36. Univ of Wales (Abth) BSc57 Univ of Wales (Cardiff) MA67 Aston Univ PhD71. Glouc Sch of Min 78. **d** 81 **p** 81. NSM Deerhurst, Apperley w Forthampton and Chaceley *Glouc* 81-87; NSM Tarrington w Stoke Edith, Aylton, Pixley etc *Heref* 87-88; P-in-c Upper and Lower Slaughter w Eyford and Naunton *Glouc* 88-91; P-in-c Redmarley D'Abitot, Bromesberrow w Pauntley etc 91-95; R 95-99; RD Forest N 95-99; rtd 99; Perm to Offic *Glouc* 99-02; P-in-c Hasfield w Tirley and Ashleworth 02-05. *Crudens Cottage, The Village, Ashleworth, Gloucester GL19 4HT* Tel (01452) 700644

WILLIAMS, Terence James. b 76. St Jo Coll Dur BA05. Cranmer Hall Dur 02. **d** 05. C Bolsover *Derby* from 05. *114 Horsehead Lane, Bolsover S44 6XH* Tel (01246) 828296 E-mail wterry774@aol.com

WILLIAMS, Terence John. b 36. Univ of Wales BSc62. St Deiniol's Hawarden 85. **d** 86 **p** 87. C Llangyfelach *S & B* 86-88; C Morriston 88-89; V Llanwrtyd w Llanddulas in Tir Abad etc 89-91; V Llanedi w Tycroes and Saron *St D* 91-00; rtd 01. *Coedmawr, 50 Swansea Road, Penllergaer, Swansea SA4 9AQ* Tel (01792) 892110

WILLIAMS, Thomas Bruce. b 41. Oak Hill Th Coll 74 DipPS76. **d** 76 **p** 77. C Liskeard w St Keyne and St Pinnock *Truro* 76-79; Australia from 79; rtd 99. *1 Thomas Street, Bendigo, Vic, Australia 3550* Tel (0061) (3) 5444 0485

WILLIAMS, Thomas Rhys. **d** 04 **p** 05. NSM Llandygai and Maes y Groes *Ban* from 04. *Groeslon, Talybont, Bangor LL57 3YG* Tel (01248) 372934

WILLIAMS, Timothy John. b 54. BEd83. Trin Coll Carmarthen. **d** 89 **p** 90. NSM Llansamlet *S & B* 89-97; P-in-c Bryngwyn and Newchurch and Llanbedr etc 97-01; V Aberedw w Llandeilo Graban and Llanbadarn etc from 01. *The Vicarage, Aberedw, Builth Wells LD2 3UW* Tel (01982) 560359

WILLIAMS, Timothy John. b 64. Kent Univ BA86. St Mich Coll Llan BD89. **d** 89 **p** 90. C Killay *S & B* 89-91; C Llwynderw 91-94; V Knighton and Norton 94-00; P-in-c Whitton w Pilleth w Cascob 99-00; V Killay from 00. *The Vicarage, Church Street, Knighton LD7 1AG* Tel (01547) 528566

WILLIAMS, Tom David. b 19. St D Coll Lamp BA41 St Mich Coll Llan 41. **d** 43 **p** 45. C Llanbeblig *Ban* 43-47; C Aberdovey 47-49; C Llanengan and Llangian 49; C Llandegai 49-53; R Llangybi w Llanarmon 53-60; V Llanidloes 60-75; P-in-c Llangurig 66-72; V 72-75; RD Arwystli 73-75; R Criccieth w Treflys 75-82; V Llanfihangel Ysgeifiog and Llanffinan etc 82-84; rtd 84; Perm to Offic *Ban* from 84. *Trefri Fach, Llangaffo, Gaerwen LL60 6LT* Tel (01248) 440687

WILLIAMS, Canon Trevor Russell. b 48. TCD BA71. St Jo Coll Nottm BA73. **d** 74 **p** 75. C Maidenhead St Andr and St Mary *Ox* 74-77; Asst Chapl QUB 78-80; Relig Broadcasting Producer BBC 81-88; I Newcastle *D & D* 88-93; Ldr Corrymeela Community 93-03; I Belfast H Trin and St Silas *Conn* from 03; Preb Rathmichael St Patr Cathl Dublin from 02. *The Rectory, 313 Ballysillan Road, Belfast BT14 6RD* Tel (028) 9071 3958 Mobile 07790-534498 E-mail belfast.holytrinity@connor.anglican.org

WILLIAMS, Canon Trevor Stanley Morlais. b 38. Jes Coll Ox BA63 Univ of E Africa MA67. Westcott Ho Cam BA67. **d** 67 **p** 68. C Clifton St Paul *Bris* 67-70; Asst Chapl Bris Univ 67-70; Chapl and Fell Trin Coll Ox 70-04; Hon Can Ch Ch *Ox* from 95; rtd 04. *13 Southmoore End, Oxford OX2 6RF* Tel (01865) 553975 E-mail trevor.williams@trinity.ox.ac.uk

WILLIAMS, Valerie Jane. b 53. **d** 03 **p** 04. OLM Merstham and Gatton *S'wark* from 03. *Merstham Lodge, Harps Oak Lane, Merstham, Redhill RH1 3AN* Tel (01737) 644850 E-mail valwilliams@vwilliams99.freeserve.co.uk

WILLIAMS, Vincent Handley. b 24. LRAM LLCM ARCM CertEd. St Deiniol's Hawarden 76. **d** 78 **p** 79. Hon C Barrow *Ches* 78-81; C Dodleston 81-83; V Lostock Gralam 83-90; rtd 90; Perm to Offic *Ches* from 90. *2 Springfield Close, Higher Kinnerton, Chester CH4 9BU* Tel (01244) 660983

WILLIAMS, Walter Haydn. b 31. Univ of Wales (Lamp) BA53 Selw Coll Cam BA55 MA60. St Mich Coll Llan 55. **d** 56 **p** 57. C Denbigh *St As* 56-58; V Choral St As Cathl 58-61; C St As 58-61; R Llanfyllin 61-68; V Northop 68-73; V Mold 73-86; RD Mold 79-86; Can St As Cathl 77-82; Prec 81-82; Preb and Chan 82-86; R Overton and Erbistock and Penley 86-94; Chmn Ch of Wales Liturg Cttee 86-94; rtd 94. *2 Park Lane, Craig y Don, Llandudno LL30 1PQ* Tel (01492) 877294

WILLIAMS, William David Brynmor. b 48. Univ of Wales (Swansea) DipTh71 Open Univ BA89. St D Coll Lamp 71. **d** 72 **p** 73. C Killay *S & B* 72-74; C Wokingham All SS *Ox* 74-75; CF 75-77; C Spilsby w Hundleby *Linc* 83-87; R Meppershall w Campton and Stondon *St Alb* 87-90; V Hemsby *Nor* 90-96; P-in-c Winterton w E and W Somerton and Horsey 94-96; rtd 96. *The Old School, 14 Weekley, Kettering NN16 9UW* Tel (01536) 417612

WILLIAMS, William John. b 23. Fitzw Ho Cam BA50 MA55. Wycliffe Hall Ox. **d** 54 **p** 55. V Cholsey *Ox* 69-73; rtd 88. *3 Lon-y-Bugail, Bridgend CF31 4UE* Tel (01656) 663453

WILLIAMS-HUNTER, Ian Roy. b 44. Trin Coll Bris 71. **d** 73 **p** 74. C Redhill H Trin *S'wark* 73-75; C Deane *Man* 76-80; R Hartshorne *Derby* 80-02; P-in-c Bretby w Newton Solney 01-02; R Hartshorne and Bretby from 02. *The Rectory, 74 Woodville Road, Hartshorne, Swadlincote DE11 7ET* Tel (01283) 217866

WILLIAMS-POTTER, Mrs Amanda Clare. b 69. Univ of Wales (Ban) BD90. Westcott Ho Cam 90. **d** 92 **p** 97. C Carmarthen St Dav *St D* 92-94; Chapl Trin Coll Carmarthen 94-99; V Llannon *St D* 99-01; TV Cwm Gwendraeth 01-05; Bp's Chapl and Communications Officer from 05; C Cynwil Elfed and Newchurch from 05. *11 Cwrt y Gloch, Peniel, Carmarthen SA32 7HW* E-mail mandy.williams-potter@barclays.net

WILLIAMSON, Alfred Michael. b 28. Kelham Th Coll 53. **d** 58 **p** 59. C Nottingham St Geo w St Jo *S'well* 58-64; SSM 60-64; V Kenwyn St Geo *Truro* 64-73; V St Agnes 73-87; Australia from 87; R Beverley and Brookton 87-93; rtd 93. *19 Lakeview Crescent, Forster, NSW, Australia 2428* Tel (0061) (2) 6554 2239 E-mail coomba@ozemail.com.au

WILLIAMSON, Andrew John. b 39. MRPharmS62. St Alb Minl Tr Scheme 82. **d** 85 **p** 86. NSM Oxhey All SS *St Alb* 85-88; NSM Bricket Wood 88-97; NSM Campbeltown *Arg* from 97. *Pier View Low Askomil, Campbeltown PA28 6EP* Tel (01586) 551478 Mobile 07970-708191 E-mail andrew@awilliamson.abelgratis.com

WILLIAMSON, Mrs Anne. b 57. **d** 04. NSM Blackheath St Jo *S'wark* from 04. *Address temp unknown*

WILLIAMSON, Canon Anthony William. b 33. OBE77 DL98. Trin Coll Ox BA56 MA60. Cuddesdon Coll 56. **d** 60 **p** 61. Hon C Cowley St Jas *Ox* 60-79; TV 79-89; Dir of Educn (Schs) 89-00; Hon Can Ch Ch 94-00; rtd 00. *9 The Goggs, Watlington OX49 5JX* Tel (01491) 612143 E-mail tony_williamson@lineone.net

WILLIAMSON, Barry. *See* WILLIAMSON, Peter Barry Martin

WILLIAMSON, Brian. *See* WILLIAMSON, John Brian Peter

WILLIAMSON, David Barry. b 56. St Jo Coll Nottm 80. **d** 83 **p** 84. C N Mymms *St Alb* 83-86; C Burley *Ripon* 86-92; Project Worker CECS 92-96; Youth and Children's Adv *B & W* 96-04; Dir Time For God from 04. *Time For God, 2 Chester House, Pages Lane, London N10 1PR* Tel (020) 8883 1504 Fax 8365 2471

WILLIAMSON, Desmond Carl. b 63. QUB BSc84 Westmr Coll Ox MTh03. Trin Coll Bris 03. **d** 05. C Portishead *B & W* from 05. *110 Brampton Way, Portishead, Bristol BS20 6YT* Tel (01275) 840596 E-mail des.williamson1@ntlworld.com

WILLIAMSON, Edward McDonald. b 42. CITC 67. **d** 69 **p** 70. C Limerick St Mary *L & K* 69-70; CF 70-73; C Penzance St Mary w St Paul *Truro* 73-76; V Mullion 76-81; rtd 81; Perm to Offic *Truro* from 81. *Hazelmere, The Commons, Mullion, Helston TR12 7HZ* Tel (01326) 240865

WILLIAMSON, Henry Lyttle (Ray). b 47. Lon Bible Coll DipTh91. BA02. **d** 95 **p** 96. P-in-c Edin St Marg *Edin* 96-02; P-in-c Edin St Salvador from 02. *44/9 Restalrig Drive, Edinburgh EH7 6JF* Tel 0131-652 0111 Mobile 07718-971914

WILLIAMSON, Ivan Alister. b 63. TCD BTh90 Ulster Univ HNC87. CITC 87. **d** 90 **p** 91. C Lisburn St Paul *Conn* 90-95; C Roxbourne St Andr *Lon* 95-99; Lect QUB from 95; Bp's C

Ematris w Rockcorry, Aghabog and Aughnamullan *Clogh* 99-01. *48 Willesden Park, Belfast BT9 5GY* Tel (028) 9066 0705

WILLIAMSON, Mrs Jennifer Irene. b 44. Glas Univ MA66 Sunderland Poly Dip Teaching79. NEOC 89. **d** 92 **p** 94. NSM Easby w Brompton on Swale and Bolton on Swale *Ripon* 92-95; P-in-c Gilling and Kirkby Ravensworth from 95. *The Vicarage, Gilling West, Richmond DL10 5JG* Tel (01748) 824466

WILLIAMSON, John. b 33. Bede Coll Dur. NEOC 81. **d** 84 **p** 85. NSM Beamish *Dur* 84-85; C Sedgefield 85-88; P-in-c Trimdon 88-89; V 89-94; rtd 94. *9 Beamish View, Stanley DH9 0XB* Tel (01207) 237380 E-mail john.williamson@durham.anglican.org

WILLIAMSON, John Brian Peter. b 30. Selw Coll Cam PhD55 CEng EurIng FIMechE FIEE FInstP FWeldI. WMMTC. **d** 84 **p** 87. NSM Malvern H Trin and St Jas *Worc* 84-94; Perm to Offic from 94. *Monkfield House, Newland, Malvern WR13 5BB* Tel (01905) 830522

WILLIAMSON, John Mark. b 43. Birm Univ BA65 Univ of Wales (Cardiff) MEd75 MA82 FCP87. St D Coll Lamp 67. **d** 67 **p** 68. C Shepton Mallet *B & W* 67-70; Hon C Dinder 70-71; Chapl Clifton Coll Bris 71-75; Lect Bris Ch Ch w St Ewen and All SS *Bris* 75-78; Chapl Bris Cathl 77-78; Perm to Offic *Pet* 78-84 and *B & W* 84-97. *Long Lane House, Cranford Avenue, Exmouth EX8 2HP* Tel (01395) 224910
E-mail mark@markwill.force9.co.uk

WILLIAMSON, Kathleen Lindsay. b 50. Leeds Univ Medical Sch MB, ChB74 Liv Univ BSc87. N Ord Course 00. **d** 03. NSM Stretton and Appleton Thorn *Ches* from 03. *39 Thirlmere Close, Frodsham WA6 7NA* Tel 07899-664068 (mobile)

WILLIAMSON, Michael. *See* WILLIAMSON, Alfred Michael

WILLIAMSON, Canon Michael John. b 39. ALCD63. **d** 64 **p** 65. C Pennington *Man* 64-67; C Higher Openshaw 67-69; P-in-c Man St Jerome w Ardwick St Silas 69-72; C-in-c Holts CD 72-77; R Droylsden St Mary 77-04; Hon Can Man Cathl 97-04; rtd 04. *49 Ennerdale Road, Tyldesley, Manchester M29 7AR* Tel (01942) 870274

WILLIAMSON, Olwen Joan. b 43. **d** 03 **p** 04. OLM Mortlake w E Sheen *S'wark* from 03. *25 Christchurch Road, London SW14 7AB* Tel and fax (020) 8876 7183
E-mail olwenontour@hotmail.com

WILLIAMSON, Paul Nicholas. b 55. Univ of Otago BTh79 Nottm Univ MPhil93. St Jo Coll Auckland 80. **d** 80 **p** 81. New Zealand 80-86 and from 88; C Selston *S'well* 86-88. *94 Hamilton Road, Hataitai, Wellington 3, New Zealand* Tel (0064) (4) 386 2140 *or* 386 3042 Fax 386 4231 E-mail allsaint@ihug.co.nz

WILLIAMSON, Peter Barry Martin. b 21. Wycliffe Hall Ox 61. **d** 62 **p** 63. C Billericay St Mary *Chelmsf* 62-68; V Bentley Common 68-77; V Lt Thurrock St Jo 77-86; rtd 86; Perm to Offic *St E* 86-99. *Corner Cottage, The Street, Kelsale, Saxmundham IP17 2PB* Tel (01728) 602963

WILLIAMSON, Ralph James. b 62. LSE BSc(Econ)84. Ripon Coll Cuddesdon BA89 MA97. **d** 90 **p** 91. C Southgate St Andr *Lon* 90-93; TV Ross w Brampton Abbotts, Bridstow, Peterstow etc *Heref* 93-97; Chapl Ch Ch Ox from 97. *Christ Church, Oxford OX1 1DP* Tel (01865) 276236

WILLIAMSON, Ray. *See* WILLIAMSON, Henry Lyttle

WILLIAMSON, Robert Harvey (Robin). b 45. DMA75. Dioc OLM tr scheme 99. **d** 02 **p** 03. OLM Maidstone St Luke *Cant* from 02. *Holly Bank, Bower Mount Road, Maidstone ME16 8AU* Tel (01622) 682959 E-mail robin.helen@tesco.net

WILLIAMSON, Robert John. b 55. K Coll Lon BA77. Coll of Resurr Mirfield 78. **d** 79 **p** 80. C Kirkby *Liv* 79-82; C Warrington St Elphin 82-84; P-in-c Burneside *Carl* 84-90; V Walney Is 90-00; V Darlington St Cuth *Dur* from 00. *The Vicarage, 26 Upsall Drive, Darlington DL3 8RB* Tel (01325) 358911

✠**WILLIAMSON, The Rt Revd Robert Kerr (Roy).** b 32. Kingston Univ DEd98. Oak Hill Th Coll 61. **d** 63 **p** 64 **c** 84. C Crowborough *Chich* 63-66; V Hyson Green *S'well* 66-72; V Nottingham St Ann w Em 72-76; V Bramcote 76-79; Adn Nottingham 78-84; Bp Bradf 84-91; Bp S'wark 91-98; rtd 98; Hon Asst Bp S'well from 98. *30 Sidney Road, Beeston, Nottingham NG9 1AN* Tel and fax 0115-925 4901
E-mail roywilliamson@waitrose.com

WILLIAMSON, Robin. *See* WILLIAMSON, Robert Harvey

WILLIAMSON, Roger Brian. b 38. Imp Coll Lon BSc59 MIEE61. St Steph Ho Ox 01. **d** 02 **p** 03. NSM Harting w Elsted and Treyford cum Didling *Chich* 02-05; P-in-c Stedham w Iping from 05. *The Rectory, The Street, Stedham, Midhurst GU29 0NQ* Tel (01730) 817570 Mobile 07767-266031
E-mail williamsonroger@aol.com

WILLIAMSON, Mrs Sheilagh Catherine. b 54. Dur Inst of Educn CertEd76 St Martin's Coll Lanc MA00. Carl and Blackb Dioc Tr Inst 97. **d** 00 **p** 01. C Darlington St Hilda and St Columba *Dur* 00-03; P-in-c from 03. *The Vicarage, 26 Upsall Drive, Darlington DL3 8RB* Tel (01325) 358911

WILLIAMSON, Canon Thomas George. b 33. AKC57. **d** 58 **p** 59. C Winshill *Derby* 58-61; C Hykeham *Linc* 61-64; V Brauncewell w Dunsby 64-78; R S w N Leasingham 64-78; RD Lafford 78-87; V Cranwell 78-80; R Leasingham 78-80; V Billinghay 80-87; V Gosberton 87-97; V Gosberton, Gosberton Clough and Quadring 97-98; Can and Preb Linc Cathl 94-98; rtd 98; Perm to Offic *Linc* 98-01. *10 Newton Way, Woolsthorpe, Grantham NG33 5NR* Tel (01476) 861749
E-mail thomas.williamson1@btinternet.com

WILLIE, Canon Andrew Robert. b 43. Bris Univ BA65 Fitzw Coll Cam BA73 MA77. Ridley Hall Cam 71. **d** 74 **p** 75. Chapl St Woolos Cathl *Mon* 74-79; Chapl St Woolos Hosp Newport 75-79; V Newbridge *Mon* 79-85; V Mathern and Mounton w St Pierre 85-98; Post-Ord Tr Officer 85-98; Warden of Readers from 91; V Newport St Mark from 98; Can St Woolos Cathl from 02. *The Vicarage, 7 Gold Tops, Newport NP20 4PH* Tel (01633) 263321

WILLINK, Simon Wakefield. b 29. Magd Coll Cam BA52 MA55. Cuddesdon Coll 52. **d** 54 **p** 55. C Thornbury *Glouc* 54-57; C Tetbury w Beverston 57-60; R Siddington w Preston 60-64; New Zealand 65-71; C Kelburn St Mich 65; V Takapau 65-70; Lic to Offic Waiapu 70-80; Perm to Offic *Ex* 90-92; Hon C Sidmouth, Woolbrook, Salcombe Regis, Sidbury etc from 92; rtd 95. *Coombe Cottage, Cotford, Sidbury, Sidmouth EX10 0SH* Tel (01395) 597545

WILLIS, Andrew Lyn. b 48. Univ of Wales (Lamp) BA73. **d** 74 **p** 75. C Swansea St Mary w H Trin and St Mark *S & B* 74-81; V Glasbury and Llowes 81-83; Chapl RAF 83-02; Perm to Offic *Ban* 83-96. *Address temp unknown*

WILLIS, Anthony David. b 40. Sarum & Wells Th Coll 87. **d** 89 **p** 90. C Ivybridge w Harford *Ex* 89-92; C Catherington and Clanfield *Portsm* 92-94; R Ellesborough, The Kimbles and Stoke Mandeville *Ox* from 94. *28A Risborough Road, Stoke Mandeville, Aylesbury HP22 5UT* Tel (01296) 612855

WILLIS, Canon Anthony John. b 38. MBE00. Univ of Wales (Lamp) BA62. Qu Coll Birm DipTh74. **d** 64 **p** 65. C Kidderminster St Jo *Worc* 64-68; C Dunstable *St Alb* 68-72; V Rubery *Birm* 72-80; R Salwarpe and Hindlip w Martin Hussingtree *Worc* 80-92; Chapl to Agric and Rural Life 85-03; Hon Can Worc Cathl 99-03; rtd 03; Perm to Offic *Worc* from 04. *1 Snowberry Avenue, Home Meadow, Worcester WR4 0JA* Tel (01905) 723509 E-mail jwillis@cofe-worcester.org.uk

WILLIS, Christopher Charles Billopp. b 32. MCIPD. Bps' Coll Cheshunt 57. **d** 59 **p** 60. C Golders Green St Alb *Lon* 59-61; C N Harrow St Alb 61-64; V Shaw and Whitley *Sarum* 64-69; Ind Chapl *Ex* 69-77; C Swimbridge 70-77; Lic to Offic 77-92; Chapl W Buckland Sch Barnstaple 77-92; rtd 97; Perm to Offic *Ex* from 97. *Rose Cottage, Chittlehampton, Umberleigh EX37 9PU* Tel (01769) 540289

WILLIS, David George. b 45. Oak Hill Th Coll BA79. **d** 79 **p** 80. C Wallington H Trin *S'wark* 79-84; V Ramsgate St Mark *Cant* 84-89; Hon C Woodnesborough w Worth and Staple 94-02; Hon C Eastry and Northbourne w Tilmanstone etc from 02. *75 Poulders Gardens, Sandwich CT13 0AJ* Tel (01304) 611959
E-mail davidandjane@poulders.freeserve.co.uk

WILLIS, Geoffrey Stephen Murrell. b 58. Sussex Univ BA80. Wycliffe Hall Ox 83. **d** 86 **p** 87. C Ashtead *Guildf* 86-89; Chapl Lee Abbey 89-94; Lic to Offic *Ex* 89-94; R Dunsfold *Guildf* 94-01; R Dunsfold and Hascombe from 01. *The Rectory, Church Green, Dunsfold, Godalming GU8 4LT* Tel (01483) 200207
E-mail geoffrey@rod.demon.co.uk

WILLIS, Hugh. b 39. Bris Univ BDS63 MGDSRCSEng82 FRSH87. LNSM course 97. **d** 98 **p** 99. OLM Charminster and Stinsford *Sarum* from 98. *Glebe Farmhouse, West Hill, Charminster, Dorchester DT2 9RD* Tel and fax (01305) 262940
E-mail tournai@aol.com

WILLIS, John. *See* WILLIS, Canon Anthony John

WILLIS, Joyce Muriel. b 42. CQSW73 Open Univ BA86. EAMTC 86. **d** 89 **p** 94. NSM Hadleigh *St E* 89-02; NSM Hadleigh, Layham and Shelley from 02. *26 Ramsey Road, Hadleigh, Ipswich IP7 6AN* Tel (01473) 823165
E-mail willisjm@lineone.net

WILLIS, Mrs Marilyn Lesley. b 47. EAMTC 99. **d** 02 **p** 03. NSM Irthlingborough *Pet* 02-05; NSM Markington w S Stainley and Bishop Thornton *Ripon* from 05. *The Vicarage, Westerns Lane, Harrogate HG3 3PB* Tel 07947-020044 (mobile)
E-mail willis_marilyn@hotmail.com

WILLIS, Mrs Patricia. b 50. RGN85 Brunel Univ BSc95 Ox Brookes Univ PGDE98. St Alb and Ox Min Course 96. **d** 99 **p** 00. C Warmley, Syston and Bitton *Bris* 99-03; V Hanham from 03. *The Vicarage, 30 Church Road, Bristol BS15 3AE* Tel and fax 0117-967 3580 Mobile 07932-654833
E-mail revpatwillis@aol.com

WILLIS, Peter Ambrose Duncan. b 34. Kelham Th Coll 55 Lich Th Coll 58. **d** 59 **p** 60. C Sevenoaks St Jo *Roch* 59-63; Trinidad and Tobago 63-68; P-in-c Diptford *Ex* 68-69; R 69-85; P-in-c N Huish 68-69; R 69-85; R Diptford, N Huish, Harberton and Harbertonford 85-96; rtd 99. *Sun Cottage, Church Street, Modbury, Ivybridge PL21 0QR* Tel (01548) 830541

WILLIS, The Very Revd Robert Andrew. b 47. Warw Univ BA68 Worc Coll Ox DipTh71. Cuddesdon Coll 70. **d** 72 **p** 73. C Shrewsbury St Chad *Lich* 72-75; V Choral Sarum Cathl *Sarum* 75-78; TR Tisbury 78-87; RD Chalke 82-87; V Sherborne w Castleton and Lillington 87-92; Can and Preb Sarum Cathl

88-92; RD Sherborne 91-92; Chapl Cranborne Chase Sch 78-92; Dean Heref 92-01; P-in-c Heref St Jo 92-01; Dean Cant from 01. *The Deanery, The Precincts, Canterbury CT1 2EP* Tel (01227) 865264 *or* 762862 E-mail dean@canterbury-cathedral.org

WILLIS, Mrs Rosemary Ann. b 39. LNSM course 89. **d** 93 **p** 96. OLM Fressingfield, Mendham etc *St E* from 93. *Priory House, Fressingfield, Eye IP21 5PH* Tel (01379) 586254

WILLIS, Thomas Charles. b 30. Bps' Coll Cheshunt 55. **d** 58 **p** 59. C Anlaby Common St Mark *York* 58-61; C Middlesbrough St Martin 61-63; V Kingston upon Hull St Paul w Sculcoates Ch Ch 63-69; P-in-c Sculcoates St Silas 67-69; V Sculcoates St Paul w Ch Ch and St Silas 69-80; V Bridlington H Trin and Sewerby w Marton 80-96; rtd 96; Perm to Offic *York* from 96. *23 Hillcrest Drive, Beverley HU17 7JL* Tel (01482) 888511

WILLMINGTON, John Martin Vanderlure. b 45. St D Coll Lamp BA69. St Steph Ho Ox 69. **d** 71 **p** 72. C Upper Teddington SS Pet and Paul *Lon* 71-75; C Kensington St Mary Abbots w St Geo 75-83; R Perivale 83-91; V Acton Green from 91. *206 St Alban's Avenue, London W4 5JU* Tel (020) 8994 5735 E-mail acton.green@london.anglican.org *or* vicar@actongreen.org

WILLMONT, Anthony Vernon. b 35. Lich Th Coll 62. **d** 63 **p** 64. C Yardley St Edburgha *Birm* 63-65; C Smethwick H Trin w St Alb 65-68; V Ropley w W Tisted *Win* 68-77; V Ipswich St Aug *St E* 77-84; R King's Worthy *Win* 84-90; R Headbourne Worthy 84-90; R Lapworth *Birm* 90-99; R Baddesley Clinton 90-99; P-in-c Thornton in Lonsdale w Burton in Lonsdale *Bradf* 99-02; rtd 02; Perm to Offic *Bradf* from 02. *9 Lowcroft, Butts Lane, Bentham, Lancaster LA2 2FD* Tel (01524) 261655

WILLMOTT, Robert Owen Noel. b 41. Lich Th Coll 65. **d** 68 **p** 69. C Perry Hill St Geo *S'wark* 68-71; C Denham *Ox* 71-76; P-in-c Tingewick w Water Stratford 76-77; P-in-c Radclive 76-77; R Tingewick w Water Stratford, Radclive etc 77-89; R Wingrave w Rowsham, Aston Abbotts and Cublington from 89; P-in-c Wing w Grove from 04. *The Rectory, Leighton Road, Wingrave, Aylesbury HP22 4PA* Tel (01296) 681623 E-mail wingravebob@yahoo.com

✠**WILLMOTT, The Rt Revd Trevor.** b 50. St Pet Coll Ox BA71 MA74. Westcott Ho Cam DipTh73. **d** 74 **p** 75 **c** 02. C Norton *St Alb* 74-77; Asst Chapl Oslo w Bergen, Trondheim and Stavanger *Eur* 78-79; Chapl Naples w Sorrento, Capri and Bari 79-83; R Ecton *Pet* 83-89; Warden Ecton Ho 83-89; Dioc Dir of Ords and Dir Post-Ord Tr *Pet* 86-97; Can Res, Prec and Sacr Pet Cathl 89-97; Adn Dur and Can Res Dur Cathl *Dur* 97-02; Suff Bp Basingstoke *Win* from 02. *Bishopswood End, Kingswood Rise, Four Marks, Alton GU34 5BD* Tel (01420) 562925 Fax 561251 E-mail trevor.willmott@dial.pipex.com

WILLOUGHBY, Francis Edward John. b 38. St Jo Coll Nottm. **d** 83 **p** 84. C Tonbridge SS Pet and Paul *Roch* 83-87; V Sutton at Hone 87-02; P-in-c Horton Kirby 00-02; rtd 03. *23 Mountjoy, Battle TN33 0EQ* Tel (01424) 775234

WILLOUGHBY, The Ven George Charles. b 20. TCD BA43 MA46. CITC Div Test 44. **d** 44 **p** 45. C Conwall *D & R* 44-47; C Derry Cathl 47-51; I Clooney 59-85; Dioc Dir of Ords 62-72; Adn Derry 79-85; rtd 85. *21 Tyler Avenue, Limavady BT49 0DT* Tel (028) 7776 5382

✠**WILLOUGHBY, The Rt Revd Noel Vincent.** b 26. TCD BA48 MA52. TCD Div Sch Div Test48. **d** 50 **p** 51 **c** 80. C Drumglass *Arm* 50-53; C Dublin St Cath *D & G* 53-55; C Bray Ch Ch 55-59; I Delgany 59-69; I Glenageary 69-80; Treas St Patr Cathl Dublin 77-80; Adn Dublin *D & G* 78-80; Bp C & O 80-97; rtd 97. *Dromingle, Belmont, Newtown Road, Wexford, Irish Republic* Tel (00353) (53) 20008

WILLOUGHBY, Canon Paul Moore. b 60. DipTh BA. **d** 86 **p** 87. C Dublin St Patr Cathl Gp *D & G* 86-90; C Glenageary 90-92; I Dublin Booterstown 92-94; I Kilmocomogue Union *C, C & R* from 94; Can Cork and Ross Cathls from 00. *The Rectory, Durrus, Bantry, Co Cork, Irish Republic* Tel (00353) (27) 61011 Fax 61608 E-mail bantry@cork.anglican.org

WILLOUGHBY, Mrs Serena Louise. b 72. Oak Hill Th Coll BA93. **d** 96 **p** 97. C St Paul's Cray St Barn *Roch* 96-99; C Hildenborough 99-00; C Tonbridge St Steph 03; Perm to Offic from 03. *88 Tonbridge Road, Hildenborough, Tonbridge TN11 9BT* Tel (01732) 832659 Mobile 07788-428010 E-mail johnser@20judd.fsnet.co.uk

WILLOWS, David Keith. b 70. St Jo Coll Dur BA90 K Coll Lon MA94 PhD99. Wycliffe Hall Ox. **d** 95 **p** 96. C Ox St Mary V w St Cross and St Pet *Ox* 95-97; Asst Chapl Oxon Mental Healthcare NHS Trust 97-00; P-in-c St Martin Ludgate *Lon* 00-01; Research Dir Paternoster Cen from 00. *104C Camden Street, London NW1 0HY* Tel (020) 7248 6233 E-mail david.willows@paternostercentre.com

WILLOWS, Michael John. b 35. Sarum & Wells Th Coll 70. **d** 72 **p** 73. C Pershore w Wick *Worc* 72-75; Ind Chapl 75-88; P-in-c Astley 75-81; P-in-c Hallow 81-85; V 85-88; V Wollaston 88-05; rtd 05. *Address temp unknown*

WILLOX, Peter. b 63. Sunderland Poly BSc85. St Jo Coll Dur 86. **d** 89 **p** 90. C Bradley *Wakef* 89-92; C Utley *Bradf* 92-95; TV Bingley All SS 95-02; C Ambleside w Brathay *Carl* from 02; Chapl St Martin's Coll from 02. *Hazeldene, Nook Lane, Ambleside LA22 9BJ* Tel (01539) 430303

WILLS, David. b 58. Oak Hill Th Coll DipHE94. **d** 94 **p** 95. C Chadwell *Chelmsf* 94-99; P-in-c Darlaston St Lawr *Lich* from 99; C Darlaston All SS from 99. *The Rectory, 1 Victoria Road, Darlaston, Wednesbury WS10 8AA* Tel 0121-526 2240

WILLS, David Ernest. b 37. St Jo Coll Cam BA58 MA62. Ridley Hall Cam 58. **d** 60 **p** 61. C Kenilworth St Jo *Cov* 60-63; C Northwood Em *Lon* 63-66; V Huyton St Geo *Liv* 66-73; V Littleover *Derby* 73-84; V Mossley Hill St Matt and St Jas *Liv* 84-97; TR Walbrook Epiphany *Derby* 97-02; RD Derby S 99-02; rtd 02; Perm to Offic *Derby* from 02. *90 Chesterfield Road, Holmewood, Chesterfield S42 5TE* Tel (01246) 856625

WILLS, Preb David Stuart Ralph. b 36. Chich Th Coll 64. **d** 66 **p** 67. C Bodmin *Truro* 66-70; V Bude Haven 70-78; TV Banbury *Ox* 78-83; Accredited Cllr from 81; V Launceston St Steph w St Thos *Truro* 83-88; P-in-c Kenwyn St Geo 88-93; V Truro St Geo and St Jo 93-96; Preb St Endellion 95-01; rtd 96. *Garden Cottage, Penwinnick Road, St Agnes TR5 0LA* Tel (01872) 553020 Mobile 07773-402109 Fax (01872) 553121 E-mail david.wills@cpt.cornwall.nhs.uk

WILLS, Ian Leslie. b 49. Wycliffe Hall Ox 77. **d** 80 **p** 81. C Henbury *Bris* 80; C Gtr Corsham 80-83; C Whitchurch 83-86; Chapl HM Rem Cen Pucklechurch 86-96; P-in-c Pucklechurch and Abson w Dyrham *Bris* 86-87; V Pucklechurch and Abson 87-99; V Soundwell from 99. *Soundwell Vicarage, 46 Sweets Road, Bristol BS15 1XQ* Tel 0117-967 1511 E-mail ian.wills@bristoldiocese.org

WILLS, Morley. b 35. Ex & Truro NSM Scheme. **d** 80 **p** 81. NSM St Enoder *Truro* 80-82; NSM Kenwyn St Geo 82-85; NSM Truro St Paul and St Clem 85-88; P-in-c Crantock from 89. *81 Vyvyan Drive, Quintrell Downs, Newquay TR8 4NF* Tel (01637) 872648

WILLS, Nicholas Richard. b 71. Birm Univ BA93. Cranmer Hall Dur. **d** 99 **p** 00. C Boldmere *Birm* 99-03; P-in-c Kettering St Andr *Pet* from 03. *St Andrew's Vicarage, Lindsay Street, Kettering NN16 8RG* Tel (01536) 513858 E-mail nickandbecky@nbwills.freeserve.co.uk

WILLSON, Andrew William. b 64. Oriel Coll Ox BA85 Nottm Univ BTh90 MA98. Linc Th Coll 87. **d** 90 **p** 91. C Northampton St Mary *Pet* 90-93; C Cov E *Cov* 93-96; Perm to Offic 96-01; Chapl Solihull Sixth Form Coll 98-01; Assoc Chapl Imp Coll *Lon* 01-03; Co-ord Chapl from 03; Assoc Chapl R Coll of Art 01-03; Co-ord Chapl from 03. *1 Porchester Gardens, London W2 3LA* Tel (020) 7229 6359 E-mail mary-andrew@clarkewillson.fsnet.co.uk

WILLSON, Stephen Geoffrey. b 63. Nottm Univ BTh90. St Jo Coll Nottm. **d** 90 **p** 91. C Newport St Andr *Mon* 90-92; C Risca 92-94; TV Cyncoed 94-96; Dioc Youth Chapl 94-99; Lay Past Asst 96-98; TV Cyncoed 98-01; TR from 01. *The Rectory, 256 Cyncoed Road, Cardiff CF23 6RU* Tel (029) 2075 2138

WILLSON, Stuart Leslie. b 61. Nottm Univ BA83. Sarum & Wells Th Coll 83. **d** 84 **p** 85. C Llandrindod w Cefnllys *S & B* 84-85; Chapl Angl Students Univ of Wales (Swansea) 85-88; C Llwynderw 85-88; Ind Chapl Gatwick Airport *Chich* 88-95; Nene Coll of HE Northn 95-98; Dir Fundraising and Communication CUF from 98. *1D Northstead Cottage, Northstead Road, London SW2 3JN* Tel (020) 8674 3146 E-mail stuart@willson.freeserve.co.uk

WILMAN, Arthur Garth. b 37. EAMTC 84. **d** 87 **p** 88. NSM Swavesey *Ely* 87-90; NSM Fen Drayton w Conington 87-90; NSM Hardwick 90-98; NSM Toft w Caldecote and Childerley 90-98; Perm to Offic from 98. *37 Prentice Close, Longstanton, Cambridge CB4 5DY* Tel (01954) 781400

WILMAN, Mrs Dorothy Ann Jane. b 38. Reading Univ BSc60 Lon Univ DipTh67. Westcott Ho Cam 89. **d** 90 **p** 94. NSM Toft w Caldecote and Childerley *Ely* 90-93; Dean's Asst Trin Hall Cam 92-98; Asst Chapl Cam St Edw *Ely* 93-98; P-in-c Hemingford Abbots 98-02; P-in-c Houghton w Wyton 98-02; rtd 02; Perm to Offic *Ely* from 02. *37 Prentice Close, Longstanton, Cambridge CB4 5DY* Tel (01954) 781400

WILMAN, Leslie Alan. b 37. Selw Coll Cam BA61 MA65. Ridley Hall Cam 61. **d** 63 **p** 64. C Skipton H Trin *Bradf* 63-67; C Guiseley 67-69; V Morton St Luke 69-79; R Swanton Morley w Worthing *Nor* 79-82; P-in-c E Bilney w Beetley 79-82; P-in-c Hoe 80-82; R Swanton Morley w Worthing, E Bilney, Beetley etc 82-89; R Swanton Morley w Beetley w E Bilney and Hoe 89-00; RD Brisley and Elmham 87-93; rtd 00; Perm to Offic *Nor* from 00. *Last House, Chapel Lane, Foulsham, Dereham NR20 5RA* Tel (01362) 684109

WILMER, John Watts. b 26. Lich Th Coll 56. **d** 58 **p** 59. C Wolverhampton Ch Ch *Lich* 58-60; C Fenton 60-63; V Dresden 63-76; TV Sutton St Jas and Wawne *York* 76-80; R Bishop Wilton w Full Sutton 80; P-in-c Kirby Underdale w Bugthorpe 80; R Bishop Wilton w Full Sutton, Kirby Underdale etc 80-87; V York St Hilda 87-91; rtd 92; Perm to Offic *York* from 92. *27 Hunters Way, Dringhouses, York YO24 1JL* Tel (01904) 709591

WILMOT, David Mark Baty. b 60. Liv Univ BA82. Sarum & Wells Th Coll 84. **d** 87 **p** 88. C Penrith w Newton Reigny and Plumpton Wall *Carl* 87-91; C St Alb St Pet *St Alb* 91-93; Chapl City Coll St Alb 92-93; V Milton *Lich* 93-01; RD Leek 96-01; V Windermere St Mary and Troutbeck *Carl* from 01. *St Mary's Vicarage, Ambleside Road, Windermere LA23 1BA* Tel (01539) 443032 E-mail dwilmot@fish.co.uk

WILMOT, Jonathan Anthony de Burgh. b 48. St Jo Coll Nottm LTh73 BTh74. **d** 74 **p** 75. C Cambridge St Martin *Ely* 74-77; Chapl Chantilly *Eur* 77-82; Asst Chapl Paris St Mich 80-82; Chapl Versailles 82-87; V Blackheath St Jo *S'wark* 88-95; V Reading Greyfriars *Ox* from 95. *Greyfriars Vicarage, 64 Friar Street, Reading RG1 1EH* Tel 0118-951 6707 E-mail jonathan.wilmot@greyfriars.org.uk

WILMOT, Stuart Leslie. b 42. Oak Hill Th Coll 64. **d** 68 **p** 69. C Spitalfields Ch Ch w All SS *Lon* 68-71; C Islington St Mary 71-74; P-in-c Brixton St Paul *S'wark* 75-81; R Mursley w Swanbourne and Lt Horwood *Ox* 81-91; P-in-c Bermondsey St Jas w Ch Ch *S'wark* 91-96; V 96-99; V Bermondsey St Jas w Ch Ch and St Crispin 99-02; P-in-c Bermondsey St Anne 91-93; P-in-c Bermondsey St Anne and St Aug 93-96; V 96-02; RD Bermondsey 96-00; rtd 02. *Amberlea, College, East Chinnock, Yeovil BA22 9DY*

✠**WILSON, The Rt Revd Alan Thomas Lawrence.** b 55. St Jo Coll Cam BA77 MA81 Ball Coll Ox DPhil89. Wycliffe Hall Ox 77. **d** 79 **p** 80 **c** 03. Hon C Eynsham *Ox* 79-81; C 81-82; C Caversham St Pet and Mapledurham etc 82-89; V Caversham St Jo 89-92; R Sandhurst 92-03; RD Sonning 98-03; Hon Can Ch Ch from 02; Area Bp Buckm from 03. *Sheridan, Grimms Hill, Great Missenden HP16 9BG* Tel (01494) 862173 Fax 890508 E-mail atwilson@macline.co.uk *or* bishopbucks@oxford.anglican.org

WILSON, Canon Alfred Michael Sykes. b 32. Jes Coll Cam BA56 MA61. Ridley Hall Cam 56. **d** 58 **p** 59. C Fulwood *Sheff* 58-63; V Gt Horton *Bradf* 63-69; R Rushden w Newton Bromswold *Pet* 69-76; RD Higham 75-83; P-in-c Rushden St Pet 75-77; R Rushden w Newton Bromswold 77-83; Can Pet Cathl 77-97; R Preston and Ridlington w Wing and Pilton 83-97; RD Rutland 85-95; rtd 97; Perm to Offic *Nor* from 98. *Swallow Cottage, 2 Little Lane, Blakeney, Holt NR25 7NH* Tel (01263) 740975

WILSON, Andrew. *See* WILSON, Canon James Andrew Christopher

WILSON, Canon Andrew Alan. b 47. Nottm Univ BA68. St Steph Ho Ox 68. **d** 71 **p** 72. C Streatham St Paul *S'wark* 71-75; TV Catford (Southend) and Downham 75-80; V Malden St Jas 80-89; Chapl Croydon Community Mental Health Unit 89-94; Chapl Bethlem and Maudsley NHS Trust Lon 94-99; Chapl S Lon and Maudsley NHS Trust from 99; Mental Health Chapl (Croydon) from 00; Hon Can S'wark Cathl *S'wark* from 05. *The Chaplaincy, Bethlem Royal Hospital, Monks Orchard Road, Beckenham BR3 3BX* Tel (020) 8776 4361

WILSON, Andrew Kenneth. b 62. Cert Journalism. Oak Hill Th Coll BA91. **d** 91 **p** 92. C Springfield H Trin *Chelmsf* 91-96; V Sidcup Ch Ch *Roch* from 96. *The Vicarage, 16 Christchurch Road, Sidcup DA15 7HE* Tel (020) 8308 0835 E-mail akw@fish.co.uk

WILSON, Andrew Marcus William. b 69. Ex Coll Ox BA91 CCC Cam BA93 K Coll Lon MA99. Westcott Ho Cam CTM94. **d** 94 **p** 95. C Forest Gate Em w Upton Cross *Chelmsf* 94-99; TV Poplar *Lon* from 99. *St Nicholas' Vicarage, Dee Street, London E14 0PT* Tel and fax (020) 7515 8405 *or* 7538 9198 E-mail andrewwilson@bigfoot.com

WILSON, Andrew Martin. b 60. Bris Univ BSc82 Univ Coll Chich BA04. Trin Coll Bris 97. **d** 99 **p** 00. C Broadwater St Mary *Chich* from 99. *26 Rectory Gardens, Worthing BN14 7TE* Tel (01903) 237685 E-mail andywilson@broadwaterparish.com

WILSON, Antony Charles. b 69. Em Coll Cam MA92 PGCE92. Wycliffe Hall Ox 01. **d** 03 **p** 04. C Bath Walcot *B & W* from 03. *5 The Linleys, Bath BA1 2XE* Tel (01225) 316572 E-mail curate@walcotchurch.org.uk

WILSON, Arthur Guy Ross. b 28. St Aid Birkenhead 58. **d** 59 **p** 60. C Bexley St Mary *Roch* 59-63; C Gravesend St Geo 63-66; C Belvedere All SS 66-70; V Brighton St Matthias *Chich* 70-77; V Bradf St Clem *Bradf* 77-84; Lic to Offic 84-87; C Baildon 87-88; V Skirwith, Ousby and Melmerby w Kirkland *Carl* 88-93; C Menston w Woodhead *Bradf* 93-96; Chapl High Royds Hosp Menston 93-96; rtd 96; Perm to Offic *Derby* 96-98; Hon C Tamworth *Lich* 98-03. *43 Borough Road, Tamworth B79 8AW* Tel (01827) 310224

WILSON, Ashley Peter. b 58. Edin Univ BSc81 BVM&S83 St Jo Coll Dur BA99. Cranmer Hall Dur 97. **d** 00 **p** 01. C Nunthorpe *York* 00-03; P-in-c Rounton w Welbury from 03. *St Oswald's House, West Rounton, Northallerton DL6 2LW* Tel (01609) 882401 E-mail ashley@dunelm.org.uk

WILSON, Mrs Barbara Anne. b 38. Brighton Poly BEd79. **d** 04. NSM Southwick *Chich* from 04. *10 Phoenix Crescent, Southwick, Brighton BN42 4HR* Tel (01273) 269771 Mobile 07814-655121 E-mail barbwilson@onetel.com

WILSON, Mrs Barbara Joyce. b 51. Carl and Blackb Dioc Tr Inst 98. **d** 01 **p** 02. OLM Leyland St Jo *Blackb* from 01. *43 Hall Lane, Leyland PR25 3YD* Tel (01772) 435340 E-mail barbara.j.wilson@btinternet.com

WILSON, Barry Frank. b 58. Man Metrop Univ BA89 MPhil94 MTh99 Keele Univ PGCE90. N Ord Course 94. **d** 97 **p** 98. C Stone St Mich w Aston St Sav *Lich* 97-99; Chapl St Mary and St Anne's Sch Abbots Bromley 00-04; V Betley *Lich* from 04; V Madeley from 04. *The Vicarage, Vicarage Lane, Madeley, Crewe CW3 9PQ* Tel (01782) 750205

WILSON, Barry Richard. b 46. WMMTC 88. **d** 91 **p** 92. NSM Leek and Meerbrook *Lich* 91-93; C Styvechale *Cov* 93-98; V Chesterton *Lich* from 98. *The Vicarage, Church Street, Chesterton, Newcastle ST5 7HJ* Tel (01782) 562479 E-mail barry-hazel@breathemail.net

WILSON, Bernard Martin. b 40. St Jo Coll Cam BA63 MA68 Lon Univ CertEd67. Ripon Hall Ox 72. **d** 73 **p** 74. C Bilton *Cov* 73-77; Dioc Development Officer *Birm* 78-83; Soc Resp Officer *Derby* 83-90; V Darley Abbey 83-90; Chapl Derbyshire R Infirmary 88-90; Educn Unit Dir Traidcraft Exchange 91; V Mickleover St Jo *Derby* 92-98; Adv to Bd of Miss and Soc Resp *Leic* 98-03; rtd 03. *74 Station Road, Wigston, Leicester LE18 2DJ* Tel 0116-288 1051

WILSON, Canon Cecil Henry. b 40. CITC 67. **d** 69 **p** 70. C Lurgan St Jo *D & D* 69-72; Min Can Dromore Cathl 72-75; Youth Sec CMS Ireland 75-80; N Regional Sec 80-87; Gen Sec from 87; Can Belf Cathl from 00. *20 Knockbreda Road, Belfast BT6 0JA* Tel (028) 9064 4011 *or* 9032 4581 Fax 9032 1756

WILSON, Charles Roy. b 30. Brasted Place Coll 56. St Aid Birkenhead 57. **d** 59 **p** 60. C Kirkdale St Paul N Shore *Liv* 59-62; C St Helens St Mark 62-66; V Wolverhampton St Matt *Lich* 66-74; V Ripley *Derby* 74-88; V Willington 88-95; V Findern 88-95; rtd 95; Perm to Offic *Derby* from 95. *Jubilate, 12 Oak Tree Close, Swanwick, Alfreton DE55 1FG* Tel (01773) 541822

WILSON (née BRAVERY), Mrs Christine Louise. b 58. STETS 94. **d** 97 **p** 98. NSM Henfield w Shermanbury and Woodmancote *Chich* 97-99; C 99-02; TV Hove from 02. *The Vicarage, 119 Holland Road, Hove BN3 1JS* Tel (01273) 721176 *or* 728895 E-mail revchristine@talk21.com

WILSON, Christopher Harry. b 59. Man Univ MusB80 Ox Univ MTh01. Wycliffe Hall Ox 88. **d** 91 **p** 92. C S Lafford *Linc* 91-95; P-in-c Billingborough 95-96; P-in-c Sempringham w Pointon and Birthorpe 95-96; P-in-c Horbling 95-96; P-in-c Aslackby and Dowsby 95-96; V Billingborough Gp 96-03; P-in-c Leamington Priors All SS *Cov* from 03; Jt P-in-c Leamington Spa H Trin and Old Milverton from 03. *Clive House, Kenilworth Road, Leamington Spa CV32 5TL* Tel (01926) 424016 Fax 337422 E-mail wilson@fish.co.uk *or* holy.trinity@btinternet.com

WILSON, Mrs Claire Frances. b 43. Hull Univ BA65. SW Minl Tr Course 85. **d** 87 **p** 94. Par Dn Belsize Park *Lon* 87-94; C 94-97; C Chingford SS Pet and Paul *Chelmsf* from 97. *Old Church House, Priory Avenue, London E4 8AA* Tel (020) 8529 0110

WILSON, Colin Edward. b 63. Ripon Coll Cuddesdon BTh94. **d** 94 **p** 95. C High Wycombe *Ox* 94-98; P-in-c Broadwell, Evenlode, Oddington and Adlestrop *Glouc* 98-00; P-in-c Westcote w Icomb and Bledington 98-00; R Broadwell, Evenlode, Oddington, Adlestrop etc 00-03. *10 rue du Moulin, Migron 17770, France* Tel (0033) (5) 46 92 08 55

WILSON, David. b 67. Univ of Northumbria at Newc BSc94 St Jo Coll Dur BA00. Cranmer Hall Dur 97. **d** 00 **p** 01. C Nantwich *Ches* 00-03; P-in-c Waverton from 03. *The Vicarage, Waverton, Chester CH3 7QN* Tel (01244) 335581 Mobile 07760-378085 E-mail dywilson@tinyworld.co.uk

WILSON, David Brian. b 47. QUB BA68. CITC 71. **d** 71 **p** 72. C Ballyholme *D & D* 71-74; C Guildf Ch Ch *Guildf* 74-78; I Arvagh w Carrigallen, Gowna and Columbkille *K, E & A* 78-81; R Clogherny w Seskinore and Drumnakilly *Arm* 81-95; I Caledon w Brantry from 95. *The Rectory, 36 Church Hill Road, Caledon BT68 4UY* Tel (028) 3756 8205

WILSON, Preb David Gordon. b 40. Man Univ BSc61 Clare Coll Cam BA63 MA68. Ridley Hall Cam 63. **d** 65 **p** 66. C Clapham Common St Barn *S'wark* 65-69; C Onslow Square St Paul *Lon* 69-73; V Leic H Apostles *Leic* 73-84; V Spring Grove St Mary *Lon* 84-05; P-in-c Isleworth St Fran 00-05; Chapl Brunel Univ 90-02; AD Hounslow 97-02; Preb St Paul's Cathl 02-05; rtd 05; Perm to Offic *Portsm* from 05. *8 Clover Close, Locks Heath, Southampton SO31 6SQ* Tel and fax (01489) 571426 E-mail david@gwilson20.freeserve.co.uk

WILSON, David Mark. b 53. Lon Univ BSc75. Wycliffe Hall Ox BA77 MA82. **d** 78 **p** 79. C Romford Gd Shep Collier Row *Chelmsf* 78-81; C Cheadle Hulme St Andr *Ches* 81-85; V Huntington and Chapl Bp's Blue Coat C of E High Sch 85-95; V Birkenhead Ch Ch *Ches* 95-04; V Over St Jo from 04. *St John's Vicarage, Delamere Street, Winsford CW7 2LY* Tel (01606) 594651 E-mail the.vicar@talk21.com

WILSON, Derrick. b 33. Oak Hill Th Coll 69. **d** 71 **p** 72. C Lurgan Ch the Redeemer *D & D* 71-74; C Willowfield 74-75; I 83-88; I Knocknamuckley 75-83; I Tullylish 88-98; rtd 98. *Hollycroft, 6 Thornhill Crescent, Tandragee, Craigavon BT62 2NZ* Tel (028) 3884 9900

WILSON, Mrs Dorothy Jean. b 35. St Mary's Coll Dur BA57 DipEd58 Newc Poly LLB78. NEOC 86. **d** 88 **p** 96. NSM Dur St Giles *Dur* 88-03; Perm to Offic *Newc* 88-96; Chapl Univ of Northumbria at Newc 94-96; Chapl N Dur Healthcare NHS Trust from 97; NSM Pittington, Shadforth and Sherburn *Dur* from 03. *The Chaplaincy, Dryburn Hospital, North Road, Durham DH1 5TW,* or *86 Gilesgate, Durham DH1 1HY* Tel 0191-333 2333 *or* 386 5016

WILSON, Edith Yvonne. b 43. St Martin's Coll Lanc MA98. Carl and Blackb Dioc Tr Inst 97. **d** 97 **p** 98. NSM Skerton St Chad *Blackb* 97-05; Perm to Offic from 05. *28 Roedean Avenue, Morecambe LA4 6SB* Tel (01524) 417097 E-mail yvonne@ywilson7.freeserve.co.uk

WILSON, Edward Thomas. b 48. Southn Univ BTh82. Chich Th Coll 78. **d** 82 **p** 83. C Cardiff St Jo *Llan* 82-86; V Aberavon H Trin 86-92; R St Nicholas w Bonvilston and St George-super-Ely from 92. *The Rectory, 8 Ger-y-Llan, St Nicholas, Cardiff CF5 6SY* Tel (01446) 760728

WILSON, Canon Erik. b 51. Lanc Univ BA72. Trin Coll Bris 83. **d** 85 **p** 86. C Linthorpe *York* 85-89; V Hull St Martin w Transfiguration 89-98; AD W Hull 96-98; V Linthorpe from 98; Can and Preb York Minster from 05. *St Barnabas' Vicarage, 8 The Crescent, Middlesbrough TS5 6SQ* Tel (01642) 817306 E-mail erik.wilson@ntlworld.com

WILSON, Frances Mary. b 61. Leeds Univ BA98. Westcott Ho Cam. **d** 00 **p** 01. C Rothwell *Ripon* 00-04; V Catterick from 04; Initial Reader Tr Officer from 04. *The Vicarage, High Green, Catterick, Richmond DL10 7LN* Tel (01748) 811462 E-mail mo.frances@tiscali.co.uk

WILSON, Francis. b 34. ACP67. Cuddesdon Coll 71. **d** 73 **p** 74. C Newc St Fran *Newc* 73-79; V Wallsend St Jo 79-99; rtd 99; Perm to Offic *Newc* from 99. *65 Bede Close, Holystone, Newcastle upon Tyne NE12 9SP* Tel 0191-270 0848

WILSON, Frederick John. b 25. Lon Univ BScEng45. Oak Hill Th Coll 68. **d** 70 **p** 71. C Wandsworth All SS *S'wark* 70-75; P-in-c Garsdon w Lea and Cleverton *Bris* 75-84; P-in-c Charlton w Brokenborough and Hankerton 80-84; Chapl Barn Fellowship Whatcombe Ho 84-87; C Corby Epiphany w St Jo *Pet* 87-92; rtd 92; Perm to Offic *Linc* 93-02 and *Pet* from 93. *2 Thorseby Close, Peterborough PE3 9QS* Tel (01733) 263386

WILSON, Geoffrey. *See* WILSON, Samuel Geoffrey

WILSON, Geoffrey. b 42. LNSM course 96. **d** 97 **p** 98. OLM Gunton St Pet *Nor* from 97. *7 Monet Square, Gunton, Lowestoft NR32 4LZ* Tel (01502) 564064

WILSON, Geoffrey Samuel Alan. b 46. TCD BA69 QUB DipEd70 TCD MA72. CITC BTh93. **d** 96 **p** 97. C Glendermott *D & R* 96-99; I Camus-juxta-Mourne from 99. *The Rectory, Newtown Street, Strabane BT82 8DW* Tel (028) 7188 2314 E-mail gsa.wilson@btopenworld.com

WILSON, George Thomas. b 47. Carl and Blackb Dioc Tr Inst 97. **d** 00 **p** 01. OLM Barrow St Paul *Carl* from 00. *21 Furness Park Road, Barrow-in-Furness LA14 5PH* Tel (01229) 820168

✠**WILSON, The Rt Revd Godfrey Edward Armstrong.** b 26. Linc Th Coll. **d** 54 **p** 55 **c** 80. C Sheff St Geo and St Steph *Sheff* 54-57; New Zealand from 58; C Masterton 58-59; V Aramoho 59-62; V St Pet Wellington 62-78; Min Tr Officer Waiapu Dio 78-80; Asst Bp Auckland 80-91; rtd 91. *30 Maryland Street, Point Chevalier, Auckland 1002, New Zealand* Tel (0064) (9) 846 4669

WILSON, Graham Whitelaw. b 46. Glas Sch of Art DA70 Leeds Univ CertEd77 Birm Univ MPhil00 Derby Univ DMin03. EMMTC. **d** 95 **p** 96. NSM Burbage w Aston Flamville *Leic* 95-97; C 97-01; C Fenn Lanes Gp 01-04; Perm to Offic from 04. *10 The Courtyard, Higham Lane, Stoke Golding, Nuneaton CV13 6EX* Tel (01455) 213598 E-mail gwwilson@btinternet.com

WILSON, Canon Harold. b 29. St Jo Coll Ox BA53 MA57. Ridley Hall Cam 57. **d** 59 **p** 60. C Leamington Priors St Mary *Cov* 59-61; C Walsgrave on Sowe 61-64; V Potters Green 64-67; Chapl Barcelona *Eur* 67-73; V Bursledon *Win* 73-83; RD Eastleigh 75-83; V Yateley 83-94; RD Odiham 85-88; Hon Can Win Cathl 87-94; rtd 94; Perm to Offic *Win* from 94. *11 Hill Meadow, Overton, Basingstoke RG25 3JD* Tel (01256) 771825

WILSON, Mrs Heather Clarissa. b 49. Hull Univ BA71 Leic Univ PGCE72. EAMTC 01. **d** 03 **p** 04. NSM Duston Team *Pet* from 03. *12 Ardens Grove, Rothersthorpe, Northampton NN7 3JJ* Tel (01604) 832200 Mobile 07702-033727 E-mail heather@wilson1214.freeserve.co.uk

WILSON, Hewitt. *See* WILSON, Canon John Hewitt

WILSON, Ian Andrew. b 57. Nottm Univ BTh89. Linc Th Coll 86. **d** 89 **p** 90. C Whitton and Thurleston w Akenham *St E* 89-93; P-in-c Elmsett w Aldham 93-02; R Elmsett w Aldham, Hintlesham, Chattisham etc 02; Chapl Woodbridge Sch from 03. *12 Moorfield Road, Woodbridge IP12 4JN* Tel (01394) 384573

WILSON, James. b 65. St Steph Ho Ox. **d** 01 **p** 02. C Whitchurch *Bris* 01-03; C Horfield St Greg 03-05; P-in-c from 05. *St Gregory's Vicarage, Filton Road, Horfield, Bristol BS7 0PD* Tel 0117-969 2839 E-mail revjameswilson@aol.com

WILSON, Canon James Andrew Christopher. b 48. Ex & Truro NSM Scheme. **d** 82 **p** 83. NSM Plymouth Crownhill Ascension *Ex* 82-83; NSM Yelverton 83-85; C Plymstock 85-87; R Lifton 87-92; R Kelly w Bradstone 87-92; V Broadwoodwidger 87-92; R Calstock *Truro* from 92; RD E Wivelshire from 00; Hon Can Truro Cathl from 04. *The Rectory, Sand Lane, Calstock PL18 9QX* Tel (01822) 832518 E-mail andrew.wilson@virgin.net

WILSON, James Charles. TCD BA82 MLL82 MA84 BD87. **d** 85 **p** 86. C Bangor Abbey *D & D* 85-88; C Dublin Rathfarnham *D & G* 88-91; I Desertcreat *Arm* 91-95; Bp's C Rathmolyon w Castlerickard, Rathcore and Agher *M & K* 95-00; Asst P Mullingar, Portnashangan, Moyliscar, Kilbixy etc 00-03; P-in-c Ardclinis and Tickmacrevan w Layde and Cushendun *Conn* 03-04; I Belfast St Mark from 04. *St Mark's Rectory, 119 Ligoniel Road, Belfast BT14 8DN* Tel (028) 9072 3151 E-mail ballysillan@aol.com

WILSON, James Kenneth. b 47. **d** 88 **p** 89. C Holyhead w Rhoscolyn w Llanfair-yn-Neubwll *Ban* 88-91; Chapl RAF from 91. *Chaplaincy Services (RAF), HQ, Personnel and Training Command, RAF Innsworth, Gloucester GL3 1EZ* Tel (01452) 712612 ext 5164 Fax 510828

WILSON, James Lewis. b 39. TCD BA62 HDipEd63 MA65 BD71. TCD Div Sch Div Test74. **d** 74 **p** 75. C Enniskillen *Clogh* 74-76; C Belfast St Matt *Conn* 76-79; I Killeshandra w Killegar *K, E & A* 79-81; I Derrylane 79-81; I Loughgilly w Clare *Arm* from 81. *The Rectory, 124 Gosford Road, Loughgilly, Armagh BT60 2DE* Tel (028) 3750 7265

WILSON, Lt Col James Phillip Maclean. b 31. RMA 52 MBIM75. Glouc Sch of Min 89. **d** 91 **p** 92. NSM Quinton w Marston Sicca *Glouc* 91-97; P-in-c 97-01. *The Old Bakery, Upper Quinton, Stratford-upon-Avon CV37 8SX* Tel (01789) 720224

WILSON, James Robert. b 36. CITC. **d** 66 **p** 67. C Ballywillan *Conn* 67-73; I Drummaul 73-79; I Drummaul w Duneane and Ballyscullion 79-01; Preb Conn Cathl 96; Treas 96-98; Chan 98-01; rtd 01. *90 Killycowan Road, Glarryford, Ballymena BT44 9HJ* Tel (028) 2568 5737

WILSON, Miss Jane Jennifer. b 43. Ch Ch Coll Cant TCert65 Open Univ BA84. Wycliffe Hall Ox 89. **d** 91 **p** 94. Par Dn Northwood Em *Lon* 91-94; C 94-98; TV Blythburgh w Reydon *St E* 98; TV Sole Bay 98-02; TR from 02; RD Halesworth from 01. *The Vicarage, Gardner Road, Southwold IP18 6HJ* Tel (01502) 722397 E-mail swoldjane@aol.com

WILSON, Mrs Janet Mary. b 44. Bedf Coll of Educn TCert66 SRN74. **d** 03 **p** 04. OLM S Croydon Em *S'wark* from 03. *Elmwood, 2 Weybourne Place, Sanderstead CR2 0RZ* Tel (020) 8657 2195 E-mail revjanwilson@blueyonder.co.uk

WILSON, Janet Mary. b 54. St Alb and Ox Min Course 02. **d** 05. C Oxhey All SS *St Alb* from 05. *14 The Hoe, Watford WD19 5AY* Tel (020) 8420 1047 E-mail janwilson@waitrose.com

WILSON, John Anthony. b 34. Linc Th Coll. **d** 83 **p** 84. C Nunthorpe *York* 83-85; V Whorlton w Carlton and Faceby 85-94; V E Coatham 94-99; rtd 99; Perm to Offic *York* from 00 and *Ripon* 00-03; P-in-c Kirkby Fleetham w Langton on Swale and Scruton *Ripon* 03-04; P-in-c Lower Swale from 04. *The Vicarage, 11 Meadow Drive, Scruton, Northallerton DL7 0QW* Tel (01609) 748245 E-mail johnjean.wilson@virgin.net

WILSON, Canon John Christopher Heathcote. b 13. Qu Coll Ox BA39 MA41. Cuddesdon Coll 40. **d** 41 **p** 42. C Bradf St Wilfrid Lidget Green *Bradf* 41-44; C Skipton H Trin 44-47; CF 47-50; V Kingston upon Hull St Nic *York* 50-59; V Kirk Ella 59-88; AD W Hull 72-79; Can and Preb York Minster 79-95; rtd 88; Perm to Offic *York* from 95. *14 Tremayne Avenue, Brough HU15 1BL* Tel (01482) 668481

WILSON, John Clifford. b 32. AKC56. **d** 57 **p** 58. C Bordesley St Andr *Birm* 57-59; C Kings Norton 59-61; Somalia and Aden 61-63; V Lydbrook *Glouc* 64-67; TV Bow w Bromley St Leon *Lon* 69-73; P-in-c Stepney St Pet w St Benet 73-80; P-in-c Long Marton w Dufton and w Milburn *Carl* 80-81; R 81-87; V Annesley Our Lady and All SS *S'well* 87-95; V Annesley w Newstead 95-97; rtd 97; Perm to Offic *Heref* from 98. *Cwm Well Cottage, Upper Cwm, Little Dewchurch, Hereford HR2 6PS* Tel (01432) 840559

WILSON, John Frederick. b 33. Qu Coll Birm 58. **d** 61 **p** 62. C Jarrow St Paul *Dur* 61-65; C Monkwearmouth All SS 65-68; Br Honduras 68-71; V Scunthorpe Resurr *Linc* 71-90; Chapl Divine Healing Miss Crowhurst 90-91; V Terrington St Clement *Ely* 91-99; rtd 99; Perm to Offic *Ely* from 99. *7 Oakleigh Crescent, Godmanchester, Huntingdon PE29 2JJ* Tel (01480) 392791

WILSON, Canon John Hamilton. b 29. St Chad's Coll Dur BA53. Sarum Th Coll 53. **d** 55 **p** 56. C W End *Win* 55-59; C Fishponds St Mary *Bris* 59-64; V Bedminster St Fran 64-73; RD Bedminster 68-73; R Horfield H Trin 73-96; Hon Can Bris Cathl 77-96; rtd 96; Perm to Offic *Bris* from 96. *2 West Croft, Bristol BS9 4PQ* Tel 0117-962 9204 Fax as telephone

WILSON, Canon John Hewitt. b 24. CB77. TCD BA46 Div Test47 MA61. **d** 47 **p** 48. C Dublin St Geo *D & G* 47-50; Chapl RAF 50-73; Chapl-in-Chief RAF 73-80; QHC 73-80; Can and Preb Linc Cathl *Linc* 74-80; R The Heyfords w Rousham and Somerton *Ox* 81-93; rtd 93. *Glencree, Philcote Street, Deddington, Banbury OX15 0TB* Tel (01869) 38903

WILSON, John Lake. b 34. Linc Th Coll 74. **d** 76 **p** 77. C N Lynn w St Marg and St Nic *Nor* 76-80; V Narborough w Narford 80-85; R Pentney St Mary Magd w W Bilney 80-85; V Lakenham St Mark 85-93; P-in-c Trowse 92-93; V Lakenham St Mark w Trowse 93-98; Chapl Whitlingham Hosp 93-98; rtd 98; Perm to Offic *Nor* from 98. *Slinmoor, Warham Road, Wells-next-the-Sea NR23 1NE* Tel (01328) 711035

WILSON, Joseph William Sidney. b 23. St Aid Birkenhead 62. **d** 64 **p** 65. C Gt Sankey *Liv* 64-66; Chapl Rotterdam w Schiedam etc *Eur* 67-68; C Birkdale St Jo *Liv* 68-71; V Eppleton *Dur* 71-78; V Riccall *York* 78-84; V Freckleton *Blackb* 84-87; rtd 87; Perm to Offic *Ches* from 87. *27 Sandy Lane, Wallasey CH45 3JY* Tel 0151-639 9083

WILSON, Miss Judith Anne. b 48. Keele Univ BA71 Leic Univ PGCE72. S Dios Minl Tr Scheme 92. **d** 95 **p** 96. NSM Slaugham *Chich* 95-96; Sub Chapl HM Pris Wandsworth 95-96; Chapl HM Pris and YOI Hollesley Bay 96-01; Chapl HM Pris Nor from 01; Bp's Adv for Women's Min *Nor* from 04. *HM Prison, Knox Road, Norwich NR1 4LU* Tel (01603) 437531 E-mail judith.wilson@virgin.net

WILSON, Julian John. b 64. Collingwood Coll Dur BSc85. N Ord Course 01. **d** 04 **p** 05. C Uttoxeter Area *Lich* from 04. *5 Beech Close, Uttoxeter ST14 7PY* Tel (01889) 567677 Mobile 07787-373117 E-mail juleswilson@fish.co.uk

WILSON, Mrs Kathleen. b 47. Bucks Coll of Educn BSc90 Ox Brookes Univ MBA93 RGN69. **d** 03 **p** 04. OLM Iver *Ox* from 03. *26 Wellesley Avenue, Iver SL0 9BN* Tel (01753) 652105 Mobile 07770-944054 Fax (01753) 654105 E-mail mail@katewilson.co.uk

WILSON, Kenneth. b 59. Selw Coll Cam BA82 MA82 Birm Univ MPhil95 MRICS84. S'wark Ord Course 86. **d** 89 **p** 90. C Walthamstow St Pet *Chelmsf* 89-92; TV Wolverhampton *Lich* 92-97; Perm to Offic from 00. *6 Westland Road, Wolverhampton WV3 9NY* Tel and fax (01902) 561485 E-mail kw@soulofindia.com

WILSON, Ms Lauretta Joy. b 64. Bath Univ BSc87 CertEd87. St Alb and Ox Min Course 02. **d** 05. C Boxmoor St Jo *St Alb* from 05. *23 Beechfield Road, Hemel Hempstead HP1 1PR* Tel (01442) 253102 E-mail lwilson@fish.co.uk

WILSON, Malcolm Richard Milburn. b 30. Edin Th Coll 57. **d** 59 **p** 60. C Dumbarton *Glas* 59-61; Miss P Chanda Nagpur India 62-63; C Dunfermline *St And* 63-65; R Newport-on-Tay and Tayport 65-70; R Baillieston *Glas* 70-74; R Milngavie and Bearsden 74-84; R Dalbeattie 84-88; R Gourock 88-94; rtd 94; Warrant Glas from 94. *20 Dougalston Gardens North, Milngavie, Glasgow G62 6HN* Tel 0141-956 4138

WILSON, Marjorie Jayne. *See* SHIPTON, Mrs Marjorie Jayne

WILSON, Mark Anthony John. b 56. TCD BA80. CITC 75. **d** 80 **p** 81. C Dublin Rathfarnham *D & G* 80-83; Bp's C Dublin Finglas 83-85; I Celbridge w Straffan and Newcastle-Lyons 85-88; CF 88-93; I Dundalk w Heynestown *Arm* 93-03; Chapl Adelaide and Meath Hosp Dublin from 04. *7 Newlands Park, Clondalkin, Dublin 22, Irish Republic* Tel (00353) 87-669 3215 (mobile)

WILSON, Canon Mark John Crichton. b 46. Clare Coll Cam BA67 MA70. Ridley Hall Cam 67. **d** 69 **p** 70. C Luton w E Hyde *St Alb* 69-72; C Ashtead *Guildf* 72-77; Chapl Epsom Coll 77-81; V Epsom Common Ch Ch *Guildf* 81-96; RD Epsom 87-91; Adn Dorking 96-05; Hon Can Guildf Cathl from 96; Warden Community of St Pet Woking from 03; Public Preacher *Guildf* from 05. *The Rectory, Parsonage Way, Frimley, Camberley GU16 8HZ* Tel (01276) 62820

WILSON, Martin. *See* WILSON, Bernard Martin

WILSON, Canon Mavis Kirby. b 42. Ex Univ BA64 Cam Univ CertEd71. S Dios Minl Tr Scheme 82. **dss** 84 **d** 87 **p** 94. Chessington *Guildf* 84-85; Epsom St Martin 85-86; Epsom Common Ch Ch 86-87; C 87-96; Dioc Adv in Miss, Evang, and Par Development 90-02; R Frimley from 02; Hon Can Guildf Cathl from 94. *The Rectory, Parsonage Way, Frimley, Camberley GU16 8HZ* Tel (01276) 23309 E-mail mavis@frimrec.fsnet.co.uk

WILSON, Mervyn Raynold Alwyn. b 33. Qu Coll Cam BA57 MA61. Ripon Hall Ox 57. **d** 59 **p** 60. C Rubery *Birm* 59-62; C Kings Norton 62-63; V Hamstead St Bernard 63-69; R Bermondsey St Mary w St Olave, St Jo etc *S'wark* 69-78; R Bulwick, Blatherwycke w Harringworth and Laxton *Pet* 78-03; rtd 03. *The Red Post House, Fivehead, Taunton TA3 6PX* Tel (01460) 281555 E-mail mervyn@ratilova.freeserve.co.uk

WILSON, The Very Revd Mervyn Robert. b 22. Bris Univ BA51 Lon Univ BD58. Tyndale Hall Bris 52. **d** 52 **p** 53. C Ballymacarrett St Patr *D & D* 52-56; C Donaghcloney 56-59; C Newtownards 59-61; I Ballyphilip w Ardquin 61-70; I Newry St Patr 70-92; Preb Dromore Cathl 83-85; Can Belf Cathl 85-89; Dean Dromore *D & D* 90-92; rtd 92. *31 Manor Drive, Lisburn BT28 1JH* Tel (028) 9266 6361

WILSON, Michael. *See* WILSON, Canon Alfred Michael Sykes

WILSON, Canon Michael. b 44. Liv Univ BA66 Fitzw Coll Cam BA68 MA73 De Montfort Univ MBA94. Westcott Ho Cam. **d** 69 **p** 70. C Worksop Priory *S'well* 69-71; C Gt Malvern St Mary *Worc* 71-75; V Leic St Anne *Leic* 75-85; TR Leic Ascension 85-88; Hon Can Leic Cathl 85-88; Can Res and Treas from 88. *39 Meadowcourt Road, Leicester LE2 2PD* Tel 0116-272 0041 Fax 272 2315 E-mail mwilson@leicester.anglican.org

WILSON, Neil. b 61. Newc Univ BA83. Ripon Coll Cuddesdon 85. **d** 88 **p** 89. C Wallsend St Luke *Newc* 88-91; C Monkseaton St Pet 91-93; V Earsdon and Backworth 93-04; P-in-c Newc St Jo from 04. *3 Crossway, Jesmond, Newcastle upon Tyne NE2 3QH* Tel 0191-212 0181 E-mail frneilwilson@aol.com

WILSON, Paul David. b 64. Cranmer Hall Dur 96. **d** 98 **p** 99. C Bramley and Ravenfield w Hooton Roberts etc *Sheff* 98-01; V Hatfield from 01. *The Vicarage, High Street, Hatfield, Doncaster DN7 6RS* Tel (01302) 840280

WILSON, Paul Edward. b 43. Ridley Hall Cam 81. **d** 83 **p** 84. C Brighstone and Brooke w Mottistone *Portsm* 83-86; C Shorwell w Kingston 83-86; TV Tring *St Alb* 86-90; P-in-c Renhold 90-91; Chapl HM Pris Bedf 90-91; V Buckfastleigh w Dean Prior *Ex* 91-96; P-in-c Stockland, Dalwood, Kilmington and Shute 96-00; TR Melbury *Sarum* 00-03; rtd 03; P-in-c Ashford Hill w Headley *Win* from 04. *The Vicarage, Ashford Hill, Thatcham RG19 8AZ* Tel (01635) 269180 E-mail revpwilson@ntlworld.com

WILSON, Paul Hugh. b 26. Glouc Sch of Min 80. **d** 83 **p** 84. NSM Much Birch w Lt Birch, Much Dewchurch etc *Heref* 83-86; C 86-92; rtd 92; Perm to Offic *Heref* from 92. *Cherry Lyn, Staunton-on-Wye, Hereford HR4 7LR* Tel (01981) 500231

WILSON, Paul Thomas Wardley. b 43. AKC67. St Aug Coll Cant. **d** 70 **p** 71. C Tokyngton St Mich *Lon* 70-74; Soc Community Worker *Roch* 74-81; Perm to Offic 81-90; Lic to Offic *Cant* 83-88; Sen Adv Coun for Soc Resp from 83; Chief Exec Carr Gomm Soc from 88. *Carr Gomm Society, 6-12 Tabard Street, London SE1 4JU* Tel (020) 7397 5300

WILSON, Peter Dennis. b 51. **d** 03 **p** 04. OLM Benwell *Newc* from 03. *34 Benwell Lane, Benwell, Newcastle upon Tyne NE15 6RR* Tel 0191-273 2856

WILSON, Peter John. b 43. CertEd76 BEd84. Linc Th Coll. **d** 71 **p** 72. C Stretford St Matt *Man* 71-73; C Rugby St Andr *Cov* 73-76; TV 86-92; Hon C Bilton 76-79; Asst Dir of Educn *Blackb* 79-81; P-in-c Accrington St Paul 79-81; Dioc Officer for Stewardship *Carl* 92-02; P-in-c Dacre 95-02; Hon Can Carl Cathl 98-02; R Stone St Mich and St Wulfad w Aston St Sav *Lich* from 02. *11 Farrier Close, Stone ST15 8XP* Tel (01785) 812747 E-mail ptrwln@lineone.net

WILSON, Peter Sheppard. b 39. TCD BA61. CITC Div Test 62. **d** 62 **p** 63. C Killowen *D & R* 62-68; C Portadown St Columba *Arm* 68-70; I Convoy w Monellan and Donaghmore *D & R* 70-78; V Castletown *S & M* 78-83; R Kilmacolm and Bridge of Weir *Glas* 83-85; I Camus-juxta-Bann *D & R* 85-92; Bp's Dom Chapl 90-92; I Maguiresbridge w Derrybrusk *Clogh* 92-05; Chapl to Bp Clogh 98-00; Can Clogh Cathl 03-05; rtd 05. *23 Rathean Avenue, Coleraine BT52 1JH*

WILSON, Quentin Harcourt. b 45. K Coll Lon AKC68 BD76 Cen Lancs Univ MA97 FTCL75. St Aug Coll Cant 69. **d** 70 **p** 71. C Is of Dogs Ch Ch and St Jo w St Luke *Lon* 70-72; C Muswell Hill St Jas 72-77; Succ and Sacr Ex Cathl *Ex* 77-81; Min Can Windsor 81-84; V Langho Billington *Blackb* 84-97; Chapl Brockhall Hosp Blackb 85-97; RD Whalley *Blackb* 89-95; P-in-c Burnley St Pet 97-98; R 98-02; rtd 02; Perm to Offic *York* from 03; Chapl Castle Howard from 03. *The Coach House, East Heslerton, Malton YO17 8RN* Tel (01944) 728060 E-mail qhwilson@btinternet.com

WILSON, Mrs Rachel Elizabeth. b 56. Keswick Hall Coll BEd79. N Ord Course 00. **d** 03 **p** 04. NSM Slaidburn *Bradf* from 03; NSM Long Preston w Tosside from 03. *The Vicarage, 7 Station Road, Long Preston, Skipton BD23 4NH* Tel (01729) 840513 E-mail rachel@revrwilson.demon.co.uk

WILSON, Richard Graham. b 67. Bris Univ BSc91 DipSW93. Trin Coll Bris BA01. **d** 01 **p** 02. C Wandsworth St Mich *S'wark* 01-05; TR Bath Twerton-on-Avon *B & W* from 05. *The Rectory, Watery Lane, Bath BA2 1RL* Tel (01225) 421438 E-mail richardandtory@tiscali.co.uk

WILSON, Robert Brian. b 29. AKC55. **d** 56 **p** 57. C Wortley de Leeds *Ripon* 56-60; C Chapel Allerton 60-63; V Hunslet Moor St Pet and St Cuth 63-70; V Bilton 70-80; V Gt and Lt Ouseburn w Marton cum Grafton 80-90; rtd 90; Perm to Offic *Ripon* from 01. *56 Church Avenue, Harrogate HG1 4HG* Tel (01423) 504398 E-mail branddyharrogate@aol.com

WILSON, Canon Robert Malcolm (Robin). b 35. St Andr Univ MA59. ALCD62. **d** 62 **p** 63. C Wallington H Trin *S'wark* 62-66; C Dur St Nic *Dur* 66-70; V Colchester St Pet *Chelmsf* 70-01; RD Colchester 93-98; Hon Can Chelmsf Cathl 94-01; rtd 01; Perm to Offic *St E* and *Chelmsf* from 01. *Hawthorns, Melton Road, Melton, Woodbridge IP12 1NH* Tel (01394) 383514

WILSON, Robert Stoker. b 39. Dur Univ BSc62. Oak Hill Th Coll 62. **d** 64 **p** 65. C High Elswick St Paul *Newc* 64-68; C Kirkheaton 68-70; Youth Chapl *Liv* 70-73; P-in-c S Shields

St Steph *Dur* 73-78; R 78-83; Youth Chapl 73-77; P-in-c S Shields St Aid 81-83; V Greenside 83-94; P-in-c Fatfield 94-98; P-in-c Coniscliffe 98-04; Dioc Adv for IT 98-04; rtd 04. *9 Augusta Close, Darlington DL1 3HT* Tel 07808-911928 (mobile) E-mail stoker.wilson@durham.anglican.org

WILSON, Canon Ronald. b 11. St Aid Birkenhead. **d** 51 **p** 52. C Lenton *S'well* 51-53; C Worksop St Anne 53-55; V Lenton Abbey 55-63; V Pinchbeck *Linc* 63-78; Can and Preb Linc Cathl 72-78; rtd 78; Perm to Offic *Ox* from 01. *14 Windermere Gardens, Linslade, Leighton Buzzard LU7 7QP* Tel (01525) 379676

WILSON, Mrs Rosamund Cynthia. b 54. Univ of Wales MSc94 MCSP75. Trin Coll Bris. **d** 01 **p** 02. NSM Stoke Bishop *Bris* 01-05; C Frenchay and Winterbourne Down from 05. *10 Druid Stoke Avenue, Bristol BS9 1DD* Tel 0117-330 1610 Fax 959 3645 Mobile 07855-998520 E-mail rosw@another.com

WILSON, Samuel Geoffrey. b 62. CITC BTh04. **d** 04. C Swanlinbar w Tomregan, Kinawley, Drumlane etc *K, E & A* from 04. *The Rectory, Swanlinbar, Co Cavan, Irish Republic* Tel (00353) (49) 952 1404 Mobile 86-832 2201 E-mail geoffwilson@utvinternet.com

WILSON, Simon Anthony. b 67. Portsm Poly BA88. Cranmer Hall Dur 96. **d** 99 **p** 00. NSM Barnham Broom *Nor* 99-00; NSM Barnham Broom and Upper Yare 00-02; NSM Hellesdon from 02; Chapl Norfolk Constabulary (Cen Area) from 05. *50 Wensum Valley Close, Norwich NR6 5DJ* Tel (01603) 483790 E-mail vswilson@fish.co.uk

WILSON, Stephen Charles. b 51. Newc Univ BA73 Cam Univ MA82. Westcott Ho Cam BA78. **d** 79 **p** 80. C Fulham All SS *Lon* 79-82; C W Hampstead St Jas 82-85; P-in-c Alexandra Park St Sav 85-93; V Preston next Faversham, Goodnestone and Graveney *Cant* from 93; Hon Min Can Cant Cathl from 98. *The Vicarage, Preston Lane, Faversham ME13 8LG* Tel (01795) 536801 E-mail scwilson@coolblue.eclipse.co.uk

WILSON, Stephen John. b 45. Bradf Univ BTech69. Trin Coll Bris DipHE92. **d** 92 **p** 93. C Marple All SS *Ches* 92-96; P-in-c Moulton 96-01; Chapl Mid Cheshire Hosps Trust 96-99; V Hyde St Geo *Ches* from 01; RD Mottram from 03. *The Vicarage, 85 Edna Street, Hyde SK14 1DR* Tel 0161-367 8787 E-mail hydes@fish.co.uk

WILSON, Stoker. *See* WILSON, Robert Stoker

WILSON, Stuart Arnold. b 47. NDA68. SW Minl Tr Course 94. **d** 97 **p** 98. NSM Okehampton w Inwardleigh, Bratton Clovelly etc *Ex* 97-02; TV from 02. *The Vicarage, Northlew, Okehampton EX20 3NJ* Tel (01409) 221714 E-mail revsawil@aol.com

WILSON, Susan Annette. b 60. Bath Univ BPharm81 PhD86 MRPharmS82. Westcott Ho Cam 98. **d** 00 **p** 01. C Newc St Geo *Newc* 00-03; Chapl Dame Allan's Schs Newc 02-03; TV Willington *Newc* from 03. *St Paul's Vicarage, 47 Norman Terrace, Wallsend NE28 6SP* Tel 0191-263 5409 E-mail susan.wilson@tinyworld.co.uk

WILSON, Miss Susan Elizabeth. b 52. Lady Spencer Chu Coll of Educn CertEd74 BEd75. WEMTC DipApTh99. **d** 99 **p** 00. NSM Saltford w Corston and Newton St Loe *B & W* from 99. *Glendale, 7 Leighton Road, Bath BA1 4NF* Tel (01225) 330587

WILSON, Thomas Irven. b 30. TCD BA51 Div Test 52 MA58. **d** 53 **p** 54. C Ballymena *Conn* 53-56; Chapl RAF 56-85; Asst Chapl-in-Chief 73-85; QHC from 80; rtd 85. *Rathclaren House, Kilbrittain, Co Cork, Irish Republic* Tel (00353) (23) 49689

WILSON, Canon Thomas Roderick. b 26. St Pet Hall Ox BA50 MA55. Sarum Th Coll 50. **d** 52 **p** 53. C Poulton-le-Sands *Blackb* 52-56; C Altham w Clayton le Moors 56-58; V Habergham Eaves H Trin 58-78; RD Burnley 70-78; Hon Can Blackb Cathl 75-89; V Bare 78-81; P-in-c Accrington St Jas 81-82; P-in-c Accrington St Paul 81-82; V Accrington St Jas w St Paul 82-89; rtd 89; Perm to Offic *Blackb* from 89. *33 Nook Terrace, Blackburn BB2 4SW* Tel (01254) 209390

WILSON, Timothy Charles. b 62. Oak Hill Th Coll BA90. **d** 90 **p** 91. C Highley *Heref* 90-94; C Margate H Trin *Cant* 94-98; P-in-c Margate St Phil 98-02; V 02-03; P-in-c Gt Chart from 03. *The Rectory, The Street, Great Chart, Ashford TN23 3AY* Tel (01233) 620371 E-mail tandcwilson@lineone.net

WILSON, Timothy John. b 58. St Pet Coll Ox MA80. Trin Coll Bris 81. **d** 83 **p** 84. C Gt Horton *Bradf* 83-86; C Handforth *Ches* 86-90; V Halifax All SS *Wakef* from 90. *All Saints' Vicarage, Greenroyd Avenue, Halifax HX3 0LP* Tel and fax (01422) 365805 E-mail wilsons@domini.org

WILSON (née NICHOLSON), Mrs Veronica Mary. b 66. Nene Coll Northampton BSc88 Chester Coll of HE PGCE90. Cranmer Hall Dur DMS99. **d** 99 **p** 00. C Barnham Broom *Nor* 99-00; C Barnham Broom and Upper Yare 00-02; C Hellesdon from 02. *50 Wensum Valley Close, Norwich NR6 5DJ* Tel (01603) 483790 E-mail vswilson@fish.co.uk

WILSON, Walter. b 33. Wm Temple Coll Rugby 55. **d** 59 **p** 60. C Sheff St Swithun *Sheff* 59-63; Ind Chapl 63-66; C Attercliffe 63-66; R Swallow w Cabourn *Linc* 66-72; Dioc Youth Officer *Heref* 72-77; Chapl Ipswich Sch 77-94; rtd 94; Perm to Offic *St E* 94-02. *Riverside Cottage, Mendlesham Green, Stowmarket IP14 5RF* Tel (01449) 766198

WILSON, William Adam. b 53. Sheff Univ BA74 St Jo Coll Dur BA84. Cranmer Hall Dur 82. **d** 85 **p** 86. C S Croydon Em *S'wark* 85-89; C Wandsworth All SS 89-93; Chapl Fontainebleau *Eur* 93-00; V S Lambeth St Steph *S'wark* from 00. *The Vicarage, St Stephen's Terrace, London SW8 1DH* Tel (020) 7564 1930 *or* 7735 8461 Fax (020) 7735 7171 E-mail vicar@ststephenssouthlambeth.org.uk

WILSON, William Gerard. b 42. St Chad's Coll Dur BA65 DipTh67. **d** 67 **p** 68. C Hollinwood *Man* 67-71; V Oldham St Jas 71-79; R Birch w Fallowfield 79-93; V Paddington St Jas *Lon* from 93; AD Westmr Paddington from 97. *St James's Vicarage Maisonette, 6 Gloucester Terrace, London W2 3DD* Tel (020) 7262 2410 *or* 7262 9976 Mobile 07976-363480 E-mail synaxis52@hotmail.com

WILSON, William John. b 25. CEng MIEE MRTvS. S Dios Minl Tr Scheme 79. **d** 82 **p** 83. NSM Weeke *Win* 82-88; NSM Win St Barn 89-95; Hon Chapl R Hants Co Hosp Win from 89; rtd 95; Perm to Offic *Win* from 95. *23 Buriton Road, Winchester SO22 6JE* Tel (01962) 881904

WILSON, Yvonne. *See* WILSON, Edith Yvonne

WILSON-BARKER, Mrs Carol Amanda. b 64. SW Minl Tr Course 00. **d** 03. C Godrevy *Truro* from 03. *Godrevy House, Penpol Avenue, Hayle TR27 4NQ* Tel (01736) 757259 E-mail carolw953@aol.com

WILSON-BROWN, Nigel Hugh. b 65. Goldsmiths' Coll Lon BSc87. Wycliffe Hall Ox DipMin95. **d** 97 **p** 98. C Wimbledon Em Ridgway Prop Chpl *S'wark* 97-00; Chapl K Sch Bruton from 00. *King's School, Plox, Bruton BA10 0ED* Tel (01749) 814200

WILTON, Albert Edward. b 10. St Paul's Coll Grahamstown 69. **d** 67 **p** 68. Rhodesia 67-68; S Africa 69-77; rtd 77; Perm to Offic *St E* 77-86; Perm to Offic *Chich* from 92. *College of St Barnabas, Blackberry Lane, Lingfield RH7 6NJ* Tel (01342) 870522

WILTON, Mrs Carlyn Zena. b 54. R Holloway Coll Lon BA75 Southn Univ PGCE76. SW Minl Tr Course 99. **d** 02 **p** 03. NSM Carbis Bay w Lelant *Truro* from 02. *Venton Ellway, 61 Queensway, Hayle TR27 4NL* Tel (01736) 752863 E-mail ventonellway@thefreeinternet.com

WILTON, Christopher. b 52. Lon Univ LLB75 Solicitor 79. NEOC 97. **d** 00 **p** 01. NSM Sherburn in Elmet w Saxton *York* from 00; P-in-c from 03. *The Vicarage, 2 Sir John's Lane, Sherburn in Elmet, Leeds LS25 6BJ* Tel (01977) 682122 Mobile 07968-268622 E-mail frwilton@aol.com

WILTON, Gary Ian. b 60. Bath Univ BSc83. Trin Coll Bris MA93 Wycliffe Hall Ox 85. **d** 88 **p** 89. C Clevedon St Andr and Ch Ch *B & W* 88-92; Lect Univ of the W of England, Bris 92-93; TV Bath Twerton-on-Avon *B & W* 93-97; Dir Studies and Lect Wilson Carlile Coll of Evang 98-04; Assoc Prin from 04. *3 Silverdale Croft, Sheffield S11 9JP* Tel 0114-236 9397 *or* 278 7020 Fax 279 5863 E-mail g.wilton@churcharmy.org.uk

WILTON (née ADAMS), Mrs Gillian Linda. b 57. SRN79 SCM81. Trin Coll Bris 82. **dss** 85 **d** 87 **p** 94. Easton H Trin w St Gabr and St Lawr and St Jude *Bris* 85-91; Par Dn 87-91; Regional Adv (SW) CMJ 91-97; Perm to Offic *B & W* 92-93; NSM Bath Twerton-on-Avon 93-97; Chapl Sheff Children's Hosp NHS Trust from 98. *3 Silverdale Croft, Sheffield S11 9JP* Tel 0114-236 9397 *or* 271 7000 E-mail gillian.wilton@sheffch-tr-trent.nhs.uk

WILTON, Glenn Warner Paul. b 33. Miami Univ Ohio BSc55 Catholic Univ of America 69 Univ of Washington Seattle MSW76. Pontifical Beda Coll Rome 66 Ch Div Sch of the Pacific (USA) 77. **d** 65 **p** 66. In RC Ch 65-72; NSM Seattle USA 77-81; Chapl Pastures Hosp Derby 82-88; Chapl St Martin's Hosp Cant 89-93; Chapl St Aug Hosp Cant 89-93; Chapl E Kent NHS and Soc Care Partnership Trust 93-03; rtd 03; Perm to Offic *Cant* from 03. *10 Lichfield Avenue, Canterbury CT1 3YA* Tel (01227) 454230 E-mail paul@wilton25.freeserve.co.uk

WILTON, Harry Owens. b 22. St Aid Birkenhead 43. **d** 46 **p** 47. C Edge Hill St Cypr *Liv* 46-49; C Kingston upon Hull H Trin *York* 49-51; Area Sec (NW England) CCCS 51-53; V Southport All So *Liv* 53-56; Perm to Offic *C, C & R* from 99. *Crantock, Mansfield's Land, Kinsale, Co Cork, Irish Republic* Tel (00353) (21) 477 3417 Fax 477 3418

WILTS, Archdeacon of. *See* WRAW, The Ven John Michael

WILTSE, Joseph August Jean Paul. b 41. Leeds Univ BA64. Coll of Resurr Mirfield 64. **d** 66 **p** 67. C Airedale w Fryston *Wakef* 66-70; Canada from 70. *6983 Richmond Street, Powell River BC, Canada, V8A 1H7*

WILTSHIRE, John Herbert Arthur. b 27. S'wark Ord Course 63. **d** 66 **p** 67. C Lee Gd Shep w St Pet *S'wark* 66-69; Min W Dulwich Em CD 69-79; R Coulsdon St Jo 79-93; rtd 93; Perm to Offic *Ches* from 93. *66 Meadow Lane, Willaston, Neston CH64 2TZ* Tel 0151-327 6668

WILTSHIRE, Robert Michael. b 50. WMMTC. **d** 89 **p** 90. NSM Droitwich Spa *Worc* 89-93; Asst Chapl HM Pris Wormwood Scrubs 93-94; Chapl HM Pris Standford Hill 94-97; Chapl HM Pris Whitemoor 97-99; Asst Chapl Gen of Pris from 99. *HM Prison Service Chaplaincy, Horseferry House, Dean Ryle Street, London SW1P 2AW* Tel (020) 7217 8667 Fax 7217 8980 E-mail robert.wiltshire@hmps.gsi.gov.uk

WIMBUSH, Canon Timothy. b 44. JP. St Steph Ho Ox. **d** 68 **p** 69. C Hobs Moat *Birm* 68-71; C W Wycombe *Ox* 71-76; R

Wykeham from 76; RD Deddington 86-00; Hon Can Ch Ch from 95. *The Rectory, Sibford Gower, Banbury OX15 5RW* Tel (01295) 780555

WIMMER, Michael John. b 41. Natal Univ BA64. Coll of Resurr Mirfield 65. **d** 67 **p** 68. S Africa 67-86; Miss to Seamen Canada from 86. *401 East Waterfront Road, Vancouver BC, Canada, V6A 4G9*

WIMSETT, Paul. b 58. Univ of Wales (Abth) BSc(Econ)79 Hull Univ MA86. St Jo Coll Nottm 82. **d** 85 **p** 86. C Nuneaton St Nic *Cov* 85-89; C Loughborough Em *Leic* 89-92; TV Totnes, Bridgetown and Berry Pomeroy etc *Ex* 92-99; V Chudleigh w Chudleigh Knighton and Trusham from 99. *The Vicarage, Parade, Chudleigh, Newton Abbot TQ13 0JF* Tel (01626) 853241 E-mail wimsett@tesco.net

WIMSHURST, Michael Alexander. b 33. St Jo Coll Ox BA58. Westcott Ho Cam 59. **d** 60 **p** 61. C Lewisham St Mary *S'wark* 60-65; India 66-70; V Battersea St Pet *S'wark* 71-73; V Battersea St Pet and St Paul 73-97; rtd 97; Perm to Offic *Cant* from 98. *50 Broad Street, Canterbury CT1 2LS* Tel (01227) 457889

WINBOLT LEWIS, Martin John. b 46. Fitzw Coll Cam BA69 MA72. St Jo Coll Nottm LTh75. **d** 75 **p** 76. C Highbury Ch Ch *Lon* 75-78; C Nottingham St Nic *S'well* 79-82; R Carlton Colville *Nor* 82-83; R Carlton Colville w Mutford and Rushmere 83-88; V Burley *Ripon* 88-96; Asst Chapl Pinderfields and Pontefract Hosps NHS Trust 96-99; Chapl 99-00; Lead Chapl 00-02; Lead Chapl Mid Yorks Hosps NHS Trust from 02. *27 Arncliffe Road, West Park, Leeds LS16 5AP* Tel (01924) 814677 Mobile 07929-538510 E-mail martin.winbolt-lewis@panp-tr.northy.nhs.uk

WINCH, Victor Edward. b 17. ACIB41 Selw Coll Cam BA47 MA52. Ridley Hall Cam. **d** 48 **p** 49. C Gt Baddow *Chelmsf* 48-50; SW Area Sec CPAS 50-54; V Hastings Em *Chich* 54-69; V Hastings St Mary in the Castle 54-69; Chapl Buchanan Hosp 59-69; V Kirdford 69-82; rtd 82; Perm to Offic *Heref* 83-97 and *Ex* from 97. *26 Gracey Court, Woodland Road, Broadclyst, Exeter EX5 3GA* Tel (01392) 469650

WINCHESTER, Gordon Law. b 50. DRSAMD71. Trin Coll Bris. **d** 82 **p** 83. C Cheadle *Ches* 82-84; Asst Chapl Amsterdam *Eur* 84-88; C Hove Bp Hannington Memorial Ch *Chich* 88-96; V Wandsworth All SS *S'wark* 96-04; P-in-c Ewhurst *Chich* 04-05; R from 05; P-in-c Bodiam 04-05; V from 05. *The Rectory, Ewhurst Green, Robertsbridge TN32 5TB* Tel (01580) 830268 E-mail gordon.winchester@virgin.net

WINCHESTER, Paul. b 44. St Pet Coll Ox BA66 MA70. Ridley Hall Cam 67. **d** 69 **p** 70. C Wednesfield Heath *Lich* 69-72; Perm to Offic *Sarum* 73-84; R Tushingham and Whitewell *Ches* 84-02; Perm to Offic *Ox* from 02. *12 The Pines, Faringdon SN7 8AU*

WINCHESTER, Paul Marc. b 53. Univ of Wales (Lamp) BA80 DipTh. St Mich Coll Llan 82. **d** 84 **p** 85. C Bedwellty *Mon* 84-86; C Chepstow 86-89; V Cwmcarn 89-93; V Fleur-de-Lis 93-98; R Bedwas and Rudry from 98. *The Rectory, Bryn Golea, Bedwas, Newport CF83 8AU* Tel (029) 2088 5220

WINCHESTER, Archdeacon of. *See* GUILLE, The Ven John Arthur

WINCHESTER, Bishop of. *See* SCOTT-JOYNT, The Rt Revd Michael Charles

WINCHESTER, Dean of. *See* TILL, The Very Revd Michael Stanley

WINDEBANK, Clive Leonard. b 41. New Coll Ox BA62 MA85. Ox NSM Course 75. **d** 78 **p** 79. Kuwait 78-83; NSM Brompton H Trin w Onslow Square St Paul *Lon* 83-84; NSM Basildon w Aldworth and Ashampstead *Ox* 85-88; NSM Streatley w Moulsford 88-00; NSM Wallingford from 00. *The Coombe House, The Coombe, Streatley, Reading RG8 9QL* Tel (01491) 872174

WINDER, John William. b 15. SS Coll Cam BA37 MA41. Ridley Hall Cam 37. **d** 39 **p** 40. C Huddersfield H Trin *Wakef* 39-43; C Sowerby Bridge w Norland 43-48; V Stainland 48-53; V Manningham St Paul *Bradf* 53-66; R Bolton by Bowland 66-81; rtd 81; Perm to Offic *Bradf* from 81. *2 Croft Rise, Menston, Ilkley LS29 6LU* Tel (01943) 872084

WINDIATE, Mary Elizabeth. *See* WEST, Mrs Mary Elizabeth

WINDLE, Mrs Catharine Elizabeth. b 72. Hatf Coll Dur BA95 Homerton Coll Cam PGCE96 St Jo Coll Nottm MTh02. Cranmer Hall Dur 00. **d** 03 **p** 04. C Hucknall Torkard *S'well* from 03. *149 Beardall Street, Hucknall, Nottingham NG15 7HA* Tel 0115-964 0683 E-mail mkt.windle@ntlworld.com

WINDLE, Christopher Rodney. b 45. Univ of Wales (Lamp) BA66. Qu Coll Birm DipTh68. **d** 70 **p** 71. C Lache cum Saltney *Ches* 70-73; C Stockton Heath 73-76; P-in-c Bredbury St Barn 76-83; V from 83. *St Barnabas' Vicarage, Osborne Street, Stockport SK6 2DA* Tel 0161-406 6569 E-mail kit@stbarnabasbredbury.co.uk

WINDLEY, Caroline Judith. b 62. Trent Poly BA84 CQSW84 Nottm Univ MA97. St Jo Coll Nottm MA96. **d** 97 **p** 98. C Kidderminster St Geo *Worc* 97-01; P-in-c Quarry Bank from 01; RD Kingswinford from 04. *The Vicarage, Maughan Street, Brierley Hill DY5 2DN* Tel (01384) 565480 E-mail cwindley@wfcsmail.com

WINDMILL, Roy Stanley. b 17. Sarum Th Coll. **d** 54 **p** 55. C Wells St Cuth w Coxley and Wookey Hole *B & W* 54-58; R Honiley *Cov* 58-64; PC Wroxall 58-64; V Meriden 64-66; C Cov H Trin 66-70; P-in-c Kineton 70-75; P-in-c Combroke w Compton Verney 70-75; C Wraxall *B & W* 76-78; P-in-c Holton 78-82; rtd 82; Perm to Offic *B & W* 82-97; Perm to Offic *Ex* 82-98. *21 Rectory Drive, Burnham-on-Sea TA8 2DT* Tel (01278) 782715

WINDON, Gary. b 62. N Staffs Poly BSc85. Qu Coll Birm 98. **d** 00 **p** 01. C Penn *Lich* 00-04; TV Radcliffe *Man* from 04. *The Rectory, Rectory Close, Radcliffe, Manchester N26 2PB* Tel 0161-723 2460 E-mail gary@windon.co.uk

WINDRIDGE, Michael Harry. b 47. Sarum & Wells Th Coll DCM93. **d** 93 **p** 94. C Hempnall *Nor* 93-96; NSM Twickenham St Mary *Lon* 96-97; Perm to Offic *Nor* from 98. *Fritton Cottage, The Common, Fritton, Norwich NR15 2QS* Tel (01508) 498577

WINDRIDGE, Peter William Roland. b 23. BScEng ACGI MIMechE. Sarum & Wells Th Coll 82. **d** 84 **p** 85. NSM Shirley St Jo *Cant* 84; NSM Shirley St Jo *S'wark* 85-86; NSM New Addington 86-95; rtd 95; Perm to Offic *S'wark* from 95. *83 Orchard Avenue, Croydon CR0 7NF* Tel (020) 8655 0872

WINDROSS, Preb Andrew. b 49. Univ of Wales (Ban) BA71. Cuddesdon Coll 71. **d** 74 **p** 75. C Wakef St Jo *Wakef* 74-78; C Bromley All Hallows *Lon* 78-83; V De Beauvoir Town St Pet 83-02; AD Hackney 89-94; Bp's Officer for Ordained Min Stepney Area from 02; Hon C S Hackney St Mich w Haggerston St Paul from 02; Preb St Paul's Cathl from 02. *31 Lavender Grove, London E8 3LU* Tel and fax (020) 7254 7440 E-mail andy.windross@london.anglican.org

WINDROSS, Anthony Michael. b 50. CCC Cam BA72 MA75 Birm Univ PGCE73. S Dios Minl Tr Scheme 90. **d** 93 **p** 94. NSM Eastbourne St Mary *Chich* 93-97; C E Grinstead St Swithun 97-99; V Sheringham *Nor* from 99. *The Vicarage, 10 North Street, Sheringham NR26 8LW* Tel (01263) 822089 E-mail amw@telinco.co.uk

WINDSLOW, Miss Kathryn Alison. b 62. Southn Univ BTh83 K Coll Lon MPhil01. Linc Th Coll 84. **dss** 86 **d** 87 **p** 94. Littlehampton and Wick *Chich* 86-89; Par Dn 87-89; Dn-in-c Scotton w Northorpe *Linc* 89-94; P-in-c 94-97; Asst Local Min Officer 89-97; Local Min Officer and Prin OLM Course 97-02; V Graffoe Gp from 02. *The Rectory, Vicarage Lane, Wellingore, Lincoln LN5 0JF* Tel (01522) 810246 E-mail graffoe.rector@tesco.net

WINDSOR, Graham. b 35. G&C Coll Cam BA57 MA64 PhD67 Lon Univ BD60. Clifton Th Coll 58 Trin Coll Bris 79. **d** 79 **p** 80. C Rainham *Chelmsf* 79-82; rtd 00. *Château du Viseney, Le Viseney Bersaillin, France 39800* E-mail graham_windsor@hotmail.com

WINDSOR, Julie Fiona. b 59. Ridley Hall Cam 98. **d** 00 **p** 01. C Chertsey *Guildf* 00-04; TV Papworth *Ely* from 04. *The Rectory, 1 Barons Way, Papworth Everard, Cambridge CB3 8QJ* Tel (01480) 830061 E-mail fiona.windsor@amserve.net

WINDSOR, Dean of. *See* CONNER, The Rt Revd David John

WINFIELD, Canon Flora Jane Louise. b 64. Univ of Wales (Lamp) BA85 FRSA98. Ripon Coll Cuddesdon 87. **d** 89 **p** 94. Par Dn Stantonbury and Willen *Ox* 89-92; Co Ecum Officer *Glouc* 92-94; Chapl Mansf Coll Ox 94-97; Local Unity Sec Coun for Chr Unity 97-02; CF (TA) from 97; Can Res Win Cathl *Win* 02-05; Asst Sec Gen World Conf of Relig for Peace from 05. *22 Hayes Court, Camberwell New Road, London SE5 0TQ* E-mail florence_crt@yahoo.co.uk

WINFIELD, Miss June Mary. b 29. Gilmore Ho 57. **dss** 66 **d** 87 **p** 94. Is of Dogs Ch Ch and St Jo w St Luke *Lon* 66-68; Bracknell *Ox* 68-74; Dean of Women's Min 74-80; St Marylebone w H Trin *Lon* 80-82; Ind Chapl 82-89; rtd 89; NSM Ealing St Steph Castle Hill *Lon* 89-97; Asst Dioc Dir Ords Willesden Area 94-97; Perm to Offic from 97. *25 Trinity Road, Marlow SL7 3AN* Tel (01628) 484317

WING, Mrs Julie. b 62. Teesside Univ BSc99. NEOC 02. **d** 05. C Sunderland St Chad *Dur* from 05. *12 Meadow Drive, East Herrington, Sunderland SR3 3RD* Tel 0191-522 5055 Mobile 07910-293936 E-mail julie_wing_1@hotmail.com

WING, Miss Myra Susan (Sue). b 45. Cranmer Hall Dur 92. **d** 94 **p** 95. C Appledore w Brookland, Fairfield, Brenzett etc *Cant* 94-98; Hon C Wittersham w Stone-in-Oxney and Ebony 95-98; V Grayshott *Guildf* from 98. *The Vicarage, 10 Vicarage Gardens, Grayshott, Hindhead GU26 6NH* Tel (01428) 604540 E-mail susan@wing63.fsnet.co.uk

WINGATE, Canon Andrew David Carlile. b 44. Worc Coll Ox BA66 MA71 MPhil68 Birm Univ PhD95. Linc Th Coll 70. **d** 72 **p** 73. C Halesowen *Worc* 72-75; Lect Tamilnadu Th Sem India 76-82; Prin WMMTC 82-90; Prin United Coll of Ascension Selly Oak 90-00; Hon Can Birm Cathl *Birm* 97-00; Dir Min and Tr *Leic* 00-03; Dir Interfaith Relns and Co-ord Lay Tr from 03; Can Th Leic Cathl from 00. *23 Roundhill Road, Leicester LE5 5RJ* Tel 0116-221 6146 *or* 273 6363 Mobile 07808-586259 E-mail andrew.wingate@leccofe.org

WINGATE, Canon David Hugh. b 22. Qu Coll Cam BA48 MA53. Qu Coll Birm 47. **d** 49 **p** 50. C Cov St Mary *Cov* 49-52; V

Wolston 52-56; V Cov All SS 56-60; R Patterdale *Carl* 60-66; Chapl United Leeds Hosp 66-71; Chapl Garlands Cumberland and Westmoreland Hosps 71-86; V Cotehill and Cumwhinton *Carl* 72-86; Hon Can Carl Cathl 85-86; rtd 87; Perm to Offic *Carl* from 87-01 and *Bradf* from 02. *1 Whiteley Croft Road, Otley LS21 3HT* Tel (01943) 463710

WINGFIELD, Christoper Laurence. b 57. Westmr Coll Ox BTh99. Ripon Coll Cuddesdon DipMin95. **d** 95 **p** 96. C Hadleigh w Layham and Shelley *St E* 95-98; C Hadleigh 98-99; P-in-c Melton 99-00; R 00-01; R Sproughton w Burstall, Copdock w Washbrook etc from 01. *The Rectory, Glebe Close, Sproughton, Ipswich IP8 3BQ* Tel (01473) 241078 Mobile 07703-814022
E-mail chris.wingfield@stedmundsbury.anglican.org

WINGFIELD, Eric John. b 16. Univ of Qld BA51. ACT ThL43 St Fran Coll Brisbane. **d** 44 **p** 44. Australia 44-57; C Westmr St Matt *Lon* 57-58; R Wadingham w Snitterby *Linc* 59-77; V Cowbit 77-78; P-in-c Moulton St Jas 77-78; P-in-c Weston 78; V Cowbit (united benefice) 78-81; rtd 81. *The College of St Barnabas, Blackberry Lane, Lingfield RH7 6NJ* Tel (01342) 870652

WINGFIELD DIGBY, Andrew Richard. b 50. Keble Coll Ox BA72. Wycliffe Hall Ox 74. **d** 77 **p** 78. C Cockfosters Ch Ch CD *Lon* 77-80; C Hadley Wood St Paul Prop Chpl 80-84; Dir Chrs in Sport 84-02; V Ox St Andr *Ox* from 02; Six Preacher Cant Cathl *Cant* from 97. *St Andrew's Vicarage, 46 Charlbury Road, Oxford OX2 6UX* Tel (01865) 311695 Mobile 07768-611232
E-mail andrew.wingfield.digby@standrewsoxford.org.uk

WINGFIELD DIGBY, The Very Revd Richard Shuttleworth. b 11. Ch Coll Cam BA35 MA39. Westcott Ho Cam 35. **d** 36 **p** 37. C Rugby St Andr *Cov* 36-46; CF (EC) 40-45; V Newmarket All SS *St E* 46-53; R Bury St Mary *Man* 53-66; RD Bury 62-66; Hon Can Man Cathl 65-66; Dean Pet 66-80; rtd 80; Perm to Offic *B & W* from 81. *Byways, Higher Holton, Wincanton BA9 8AP* Tel (01963) 32137

WINKETT, Canon Lucy Clare. b 68. Selw Coll Cam BA90 MA94 ARCM92. Qu Coll Birm BD94. **d** 95 **p** 96. C Lt Ilford St Mich *Chelmsf* 95-97; Min Can and Chapl St Paul's Cathl *Lon* 97-03; Can Res and Prec from 03. *1 Amen Court, London EC4M 7BU* Tel (020) 7236 3871 *or* 7248 1817
E-mail precentor@stpaulscathedral.org.uk

WINKS, Paul David. b 45. Ex Univ BA67. Cuddesdon Coll 68. **d** 70 **p** 71. C Rickerscote *Lich* 70-73; Chapl RAF 73-75; C Yate *Bris* 76-77; TV Yate New Town 77-83; P-in-c Leigh upon Mendip w Stoke St Michael *B & W* 83-84; V from 84. *The Vicarage, Leigh Street, Leigh upon Mendip, Radstock BA3 5QP* Tel (01373) 812559

WINN, Alan John. b 42. FRSA73. **d** 01 **p** 02. OLM Ringwould w Kingsdown *Cant* 01-04; OLM Ringwould w Kingsdown and Ripple etc from 05. *Chilterns, Back Street, Ringwould, Deal CT14 8HL* Tel (01304) 361030 E-mail revjohnwinn@aol.com

WINN, Mrs Jean Elizabeth. b 58. Man Univ BSc80. Wycliffe Hall Ox 85. **d** 88 **p** 98. C W Derby St Luke *Liv* 88-89; Perm to Offic 89-98; NSM Seaforth 98-02; NSM Anfield St Marg from 02. *St Margaret's Vicarage, Rocky Lane, Liverpool L6 4BA* Tel 0151-263 3118

WINN, Paul William James. b 44. Liv Univ BSc66. EMMTC 86. **d** 89 **p** 90. NSM Spalding St Paul *Linc* 89-98; Perm to Offic 98-00; P-in-c Cowbit 00-01; V from 01. *The Vicarage, 2 Small Drove, Weston, Spalding PE12 6HS* Tel (01406) 373630
E-mail paulwinn80@hotmail.com

WINN, Peter Anthony. b 60. Worc Coll Ox BA82 MA86. Wycliffe Hall Ox 83. **d** 86 **p** 87. C W Derby Gd Shep *Liv* 86-89; V Seaforth 89-02; P-in-c Anfield St Marg from 02. *St Margaret's Vicarage, Rocky Lane, Liverpool L6 4BA* Tel 0151-263 3118

WINN, Simon Reynolds. b 66. Bris Univ BA88. Trin Coll Bris 96. **d** 98 **p** 99. C Portswood Ch Ch *Win* 98-02; V Northolt W End St Jos *Lon* from 02. *St Joseph's Vicarage, 430 Yeading Lane, Northolt UB5 6JS* Tel (020) 8845 6161 *or* 8842 4766
E-mail simon.winn@ukgateway.net

WINNARD, Jack. b 30. Oak Hill Th Coll 79. **d** 81 **p** 82. C Skelmersdale St Paul *Liv* 81-84; C Goose Green 84-85; V Wigan St Barn Marsh Green 85-98; rtd 99; Perm to Offic *Liv* from 00. *Maranatha, 11 Beech Walk, Winstanley, Wigan WN3 6DH* Tel (01942) 222339

WINNINGTON-INGRAM, David Robert. b 59. Hertf Coll Ox BA82 MA85 K Coll Cam BA89. Westcott Ho Cam 87. **d** 90 **p** 91. C Bishop's Cleeve *Glouc* 90-94; TV Colyton, Southleigh, Offwell, Widworthy etc *Ex* 94-00; V S Brent and Rattery from 00. *The Vicarage, Firswood, South Brent TQ10 9AN* Tel (01364) 649070 *or* 72774 E-mail wis100acre.wood@virgin.net

WINSLADE, Richard Clive. b 69. Aston Tr Scheme 91 Linc Th Coll BTh93. **d** 96 **p** 97. C Waltham Cross *St Alb* 96-99; C Leavesden All SS 99-03; R Maulden from 03. *The Rectory, Clophill Road, Maulden, Bedford MK45 2AA* Tel and fax (01525) 403139 E-mail richardjo@rwinslade.fsnet.co.uk

WINSOR, Anthony Geoffrey. b 56. Nottm Univ BTh87 Middx Univ MA92 PhD97. Linc Th Coll 84. **d** 87. C Cobbold Road St Sav w St Mary *Lon* 87-88; Barnardo's CANDL Project 88-89. *2 The Bench, Ham Street, Richmond TW10 7HX* Tel (020) 8940 9978 E-mail tony.winsor@btinternet.com

WINSPER, Arthur William (Brother Benedict). b 46. Glas NSM Course 89. **d** 91 **p** 92. SSF from 70; NSM Barrowfield *Glas* 91-96; P-in-c St Aug Miss Penhalonga Zimbabwe 96-98; Perm to Offic *Worc* from 98. *Society of St Francis, Glasshampton, Shrawley, Worcester WR6 6TQ* Tel (01299) 896345

✠WINSTANLEY, The Rt Revd Alan Leslie. b 49. Nottm Univ BTh72. St Jo Coll Nottm 68 ALCD72. **d** 72 **p** 73 **c** 88. C Livesey *Blackb* 72-75; C Gt Sankey *Liv* 75-77; P-in-c Penketh 75-77; V 78-81; SAMS 81-93; Bp Bolivia and Peru 88-93; V Eastham *Ches* 94-03; Hon Asst Bp Ches 94-03; V Whittle-le-Woods *Blackb* from 03; Hon Asst Bp Blackb from 03. *The Vicarage, Preston Road, Whittle-le-Woods, Chorley PR6 7PS* Tel and fax (01257) 263306 E-mail bpalan.winstanley@ic24.net

WINSTANLEY, John Graham. b 47. K Coll Lon 67. **d** 71 **p** 72. C Wandsworth St Paul *S'wark* 71-74; Chapl Salford Univ *Man* 75-79; R Kersal Moor 79-87. *14 Lyndhurst Avenue, Prestwich, Manchester M25 0GF* Tel 0161-740 2715 Fax 720 6916
E-mail john@blots.co.uk

WINSTON, Canon Jeremy Hugh. b 54. Trin Coll Carmarthen BEd76 BA CertEd. St Steph Ho Ox 78. **d** 79 **p** 80. C Bassaleg *Mon* 79-83; Dioc Children's Adv 79-89; V Itton and St Arvans w Penterry and Kilgwrrwg etc 83-93; V Abergavenny St Mary w Llanwenarth Citra from 93; RD Abergavenny from 02; Can St Woolos Cathl from 02. *St Mary's Vicarage, Monk Street, Abergavenny NP7 5ND* Tel (01873) 853168
E-mail jeremy.winston@virgin.net

WINSTONE, Canon Peter John. b 30. Jes Coll Ox BA52 MA56. Ridley Hall Cam 53. **d** 55 **p** 56. C Bitterne *Win* 55-58; C Keighley *Bradf* 58-60; PC Fairweather Green 60-67; V Clapham 67-84; R Leathley w Farnley, Fewston and Blubberhouses 84-95; Hon Can Bradf Cathl 89-95; rtd 95; Perm to Offic *Worc* from 95. *7 Kingfisher Close, Worcester WR5 3RY* Tel (01905) 763114

WINTER, Anthony Cathcart. b 28. FCA. Ridley Hall Cam 54. **d** 56 **p** 57. C Childwall St Dav *Liv* 56-58; C Hackney St Jo *Lon* 58-63; V Newmarket All SS *St E* 63-73; Lic to Offic 74-81; Perm to Offic *Lon* 78-81 and 97-99; Hon C St Andr-by-the-Wardrobe w St Ann, Blackfriars 81-86; Hon C Smithfield St Bart Gt 86-95; Chapl S'wark Cathl *S'wark* from 99. *25 Bowater House, Golden Lane Estate, London EC1Y 0RJ* Tel (020) 7490 5765 Fax 7490 1064

WINTER, Dagmar. b 63. Heidelberg Univ DrTheol96. Herborn Th Sem 93. **d** 96 **p** 97. C Bromley St Mark *Roch* 96-99; C Hexham *Newc* from 99. *3 Dipton Close, Hexham NE46 1UG* Tel and fax (01434) 604935
E-mail dagmar@winternet.freeserve.co.uk

WINTER, Canon David Brian. b 29. K Coll Lon BA53 CertEd54. Oak Hill NSM Course. **d** 87 **p** 88. NSM Finchley St Paul and St Luke *Lon* 87-89; Hd of Relig Broadcasting BBC 87-89; Bp's Officer for Evang *Ox* 89-95; P-in-c Ducklington 89-95; Hon Can Ch Ch 95; rtd 95; Hon C Hermitage *Ox* 95-00; Perm to Offic 00-02; Hon C Dorchester 02-05. *4 Ilbury Court, 2A Wentworth Road, Oxford OX2 7TG* Tel (01865) 513551
E-mail david_winter@onetel.com

WINTER, Canon Dennis Graham St Leger. b 33. K Coll Lon BSc54 AKC54. Tyndale Hall Bris BD62. **d** 61 **p** 62. C Pennycross *Ex* 61-64; C Maidstone St Faith *Cant* 64-66; V Paddock Wood *Roch* 66-99; RD Tonbridge 89-95; RD Paddock Wood 95-99; Hon Can Roch Cathl 90-99; rtd 99; Perm to Offic *Newc* from 00. *4 Oaky Balks, Alnwick NE66 2QE* Tel (01665) 602658

WINTER, Ernest Philip. b 18. Bris Univ BA49 St Cath Coll Ox BLitt54 MA56. Worc Ord Coll 57. **d** 58 **p** 59. C Worc St Barn w Ch Ch *Worc* 58-61; V Reddal Hill St Luke 61-79; P-in-c Upper Arley 79-86; P-in-c Wribbenhall 81-83; rtd 86; Perm to Offic *Worc* from 86 and *Heref* from 87. *4 Summit Road, Clows Top, Kidderminster DY14 9HN* Tel (01299) 832342

WINTER, Mrs Fiona Helen. b 64. Sheff Univ BSc87. NEOC 97. **d** 00. NSM Gt Ayton w Easby and Newton in Cleveland *York* 00-02. *9 The Acres, Stokesley, Middlesbrough TS9 5QA* Tel (01642) 713146

WINTER, Jonathan Gay. b 37. Lon Inst of Educn DipEd84. AKC64. **d** 65 **p** 66. C W Dulwich All SS and Em *S'wark* 65-69; Asst Master Kidbrooke Sch 69-77; Norwood Sch 77-80; Dep Hd Lewisham Sch 80-89; Hon C Dulwich St Barn from 90; Chapl Dulwich Coll 95-98; Cllr from 98; Dean of MSE (Woolwich) 00-04. *160 Turney Road, London SE21 7JJ* Tel and fax (020) 7274 3060 Mobile 07811-529503
E-mail jonathanwinter@btinternet.com

WINTER, Nichola Jane. b 58. Trevelyan Coll Dur BA79. Dioc OLM tr scheme 99. **d** 02 **p** 03. OLM Aldeburgh w Hazlewood *St E* from 02. *Threeways, Donkey Lane, Friston, Saxmundham IP17 1PL* Tel (01728) 688979 E-mail njwinter@clara.co.uk

WINTER, Philip. *See* WINTER, Ernest Philip

WINTER, Raymond McMahon. b 23. Selw Coll Cam BA52 MA60 FSA73. Wycliffe Hall Ox 59. **d** 61 **p** 62. C Gaywood, Bawsey and Mintlyn *Nor* 61-64; P-in-c Horstead w Frettenham w Stanninghall 64-71; Youth Chapl and Warden Dioc Conf Ho 64-71; Chapl Loretto Sch Musselburgh 71-74; P-in-c

Latchingdon w Mundon and N Fambridge *Chelmsf* 74-75; P-in-c Brettenham w Rushford *Nor* 75-83; P-in-c Riddlesworth w Gasthorpe and Knettishall 76-83; P-in-c Garboldisham w Blo' Norton 77-83; Chapl Bedgebury Sch Kent 83-88; Hon C Kilndown *Cant* 83-87; Hon C Goudhurst w Kilndown 87-91; Warden Coll of St Barn Lingfield 88-94; rtd 91; Perm to Offic *Nor* 94-04. *27 Breydon Road, Norwich NR7 8EF* Tel (01602) 484889

WINTER, Stephen Christopher. b 55. Southn Univ BA76. Trin Coll Bris 85. **d** 88 **p** 89. C Birm St Luke *Birm* 88-92; TV Kings Norton 92-98; Ind Chapl *Worc* 98-04; Asst Dir Development (Discipleship) from 04; C Finstall from 04. *1 Marlborough Avenue, Bromsgrove B60 2PG* Tel (01527) 575737 *or* (01905) 732813 E-mail swinter@cofe-worcester.co.uk

WINTER, Thomas Andrew. b 24. Wadh Coll Ox BA51 MA63. Ely Th Coll 51. **d** 53 **p** 54. C Horninglow *Lich* 53-56; S Africa 56-83; R Woodston *Ely* 83-90; rtd 90; Perm to Offic *Ely* 90-97 and *Chich* from 90. *6 The Close, Shoreham-by-Sea BN43 5AH* Tel (01273) 452606

WINTERBOTTOM, Canon Ian Edmund. b 42. St Andr Univ MA66 Nottm Univ DipTh68. Linc Th Coll 66. **d** 68 **p** 69. C Blackb St Steph *Blackb* 68-71; C Wingerworth *Derby* 71-73; P-in-c Brimington 73-77; R 77-89; RD Bolsover and Staveley 86-93; R Pleasley 89-94; P-in-c Shirebrook 92-94; TR E Scarsdale 94-00; Hon Can Derby Cathl from 95; Prin Ind Chapl from 00. *The Vicarage, Barrow-on-Trent, Derby DE72 1HA* Tel (01332) 703350 E-mail ianwinterbottom@compuserve.com

WINTERBOURNE, George. b 20. ERD61. S'wark Ord Course 64. **d** 67 **p** 68. C Cove St Jo *Guildf* 67-71; Perm to Offic 72; Hon C Aldershot St Mich 73-78; Perm to Offic *B & W* 79-80; Lic to Offic 80-87; rtd 87; Perm to Offic *Glouc* 87-99. *4 Lawn Crescent, Shurdington, Cheltenham GL51 5UR* Tel (01242) 862671

WINTERBURN, Derek Neil. b 60. Bris Univ BSc82 Ox Univ BA85. Wycliffe Hall Ox 83. **d** 86 **p** 87. C Mildmay Grove St Jude and St Paul *Lon* 86-89; C Hackney Marsh 89-91; TV 91-96; V Hampton St Mary from 96. *St Mary's Vicarage, Church Street, Hampton TW12 2EB* Tel (020) 8979 3071 Fax 8941 7221 E-mail stmary@bigfoot.com *or* vicar@winterburn.me.uk

WINTERBURN, Maurice. b 14. Oak Hill Th Coll 61. **d** 62 **p** 63. C Bethnal Green St Jas Less *Lon* 62-65; C Ealing St Mary 65-68; V Stambermill *Worc* 68-79; P-in-c The Lye 74-79; rtd 79; Perm to Offic *Worc* from 79. *36 Whittingham Road, Halesowen B63 3TF* Tel 0121-550 0434

WINTLE, Anthony Robert. b 44. K Coll Lon 64. St Mich Coll Llan DipTh68. **d** 68 **p** 69. C Llandaff N *Llan* 68-70; C Baglan 70-75; V Treharris 75-86; V Treharris w Bedlinog 86-90; R St Fagans w Michaelston-super-Ely from 90. *The Rectory, Greenwood Lane, St Fagans, Cardiff CF5 6EL* Tel (029) 2056 5869

WINTLE, David Robert. b 56. Open Univ BA84. Qu Coll Birm 93. **d** 95 **p** 96. C Cov St Mary *Cov* 95-00; P-in-c Baginton w Bubbenhall and Ryton-on-Dunsmore from 00; P-in-c Baginton from 02. *The Vicarage, Church Road, Ryton on Dunsmore, Coventry CV8 3ET* Tel (024) 7630 1283 E-mail david@wintled.fsnet.co.uk

WINTLE, Graham. b 52. Bris Univ BSc73. Oak Hill Th Coll BA86. **d** 86 **p** 87. C Southgate *Chich* 86-89; C New Malden and Coombe *S'wark* 89-92; V Surbiton Hill Ch Ch from 92. *Christ Church Vicarage, 7 Christ Church Road, Surbiton KT5 8JJ* Tel (020) 8399 3444 *or* 8390 7215 E-mail gwintle@blueyonder.co.uk

WINTLE, Canon Ruth Elizabeth. b 31. Westf Coll Lon BA53 St Hugh's Coll Ox BA67 MA74. St Mich Ho Ox 63. **dss** 72 **d** 87 **p** 94. Tutor St Jo Coll Dur 72-74; Selection Sec ACCM 74-83; St Jo in Bedwardine *Worc* 83-87; Par Dn 87-94; Dir of Ords 84-92; Hon Can Worc Cathl 87-97; rtd 95; Bp's Adv on Women's Min *Worc* 95-97; Perm to Offic from 98. *Westwood, Claphill Lane, Rushwick, Worcester WR2 5TP* Tel (01905) 422841

WINTON, Alan Peter. b 58. Sheff Univ BA83 PhD87. Linc Th Coll 91. **d** 91 **p** 92. C Southgate Ch Ch *Lon* 91-95; P-in-c St Paul's Walden *St Alb* 95-99; Dioc CME Officer 95-02; R Welwyn w Ayot St Peter from 99. *The Rectory, 2 Ottway Walk, Welwyn AL6 9DS* Tel (01438) 714150 E-mail rector@welwyn.org.uk

WINTON, Ms Philippa Mary. b 56. St Jo Coll Nottm BA78 Trin Coll Bris. **dss** 83 **d** 87 **p** 94. Sheff St Jo *Sheff* 83-86; Sheff Gillcar St Silas 86-87; Chapl Asst R Hallamshire Hosp Sheff 87; Hon Par Dn Linc St Faith and St Martin w St Pet *Linc* 90-92; Chapl Asst W Middx Univ Hosp Isleworth 92-93; Perm to Offic *Lon* 93-95 and *St Alb* from 95. *The Rectory, 2 Ottway Walk, Welwyn AL6 9DS* Tel (01438) 714150

WINTON, Stanley Wootton. b 30. Sarum & Wells Th Coll 70. **d** 72 **p** 73. C Birkenhead St Jas w St Bede *Ches* 72-75; V 75-79; TR Ellesmere Port 79-88; Chapl Ellesmere Port and Manor Hosps 79-95; R Delamere *Ches* 88-95; rtd 95; Perm to Offic *Ches* from 95. *26 Wimborne Avenue, Thingwall, Wirral CH61 7UL* Tel 0151-648 0176

WINTOUR, Mrs Anne Elizabeth. b 52. **d** 03 **p** 04. OLM Melksham *Sarum* from 03. *Weavers House, 264 Sandridge Lane, Bromham, Chippenham SN15 2JW* Tel (01380) 850880 E-mail anniewintour@fsmail.net

WINWARD, Stuart James. b 36. Open Univ BA85. Lich Th Coll 65. **d** 68 **p** 69. C Lytham St Cuth *Blackb* 68-71; C Padiham 71-73; V Musbury 73-84; R Old Trafford St Hilda *Man* 84-89; V Davyhulme St Mary 89-98; rtd 98; Perm to Offic *Ches* from 99. *1 Walnut Grove, Sale M33 6AJ* Tel 0161-905 1039

WIPPELL, David Stanley. b 46. Univ of Qld BSc67 Selw Coll Cam BA77 MA. Westcott Ho Cam 76. **d** 78 **p** 79. C Wolvercote w Summertown *Ox* 78-80; Asst Chapl St Edw Sch Ox 78-00; Chapl from 00; Housemaster 85-97; Chapl St Hugh's Coll Ox 80-85. *St Edward's School, Woodstock Road, Oxford OX2 7NN* Tel (01865) 319271 Fax 319206 E-mail wippell@aol.com

WISBECH, Archdeacon of. *Vacant*

WISE, David Reginald. b 46. Glas Univ BSc68 QUB PhD74 LRAM67. Edin Th Coll 72. **d** 74 **p** 75. Chapl St Andr Cathl *Ab* 74-75; C Ayr *Glas* 75-78; R Airdrie 78-81; P-in-c Gartcosh 78-81; P-in-c Leic St Nic *Leic* 81-82; Chapl Leic Univ 81-89; TV Leic H Spirit 82-89; Chapl St Hilda's Priory and Sch Whitby 89-96; TV Louth *Linc* 96-98; V Mexborough *Sheff* from 98. *The Vicarage, Church Street, Mexborough S64 0ER* Tel (01709) 582321

WISE, Ms Pamela Margaret. b 51. CertEd73 BA79. Ripon Coll Cuddesdon 89. **d** 91 **p** 94. Par Dn Tokyngton St Mich *Lon* 91-94; C N Greenford All Hallows 94; C Bedford All SS *St Alb* 94-97; TV Hitchin 97-03; V Oxhey All SS from 03. *All Saints' Vicarage, Gosforth Lane, Watford WD19 7AX* Tel (020) 8421 5949 E-mail pamela.wise@gmail.com

WISE, Richard Edmund. b 67. Clare Coll Cam BA88 MusB89 LRAM91. Cranmer Hall Dur 01. **d** 03 **p** 04. C Stanmore *Win* from 03. *St Mark's House, Oliver's Battery Crescent, Winchester SO22 4EU* Tel (01962) 861970 E-mail rwise@fish.co.uk

WISEMAN, David John. b 51. Lon Univ BD80 Birm Univ Dip Islam87 Derby Univ MA99. Cranmer Hall Dur 77. **d** 80 **p** 81. C Bilston *Lich* 80-84; P-in-c W Bromwich St Phil 84-86; V 86-89; P-in-c Cheetham St Mark *Man* 89-94; Dioc Community Relns Officer 89-96; P-in-c Ashton H Trin 94-99; TR Ashton 00-03; Chapl Tameside Coll 94-03; Soc Resp Adv *Pet* from 03. *St Paul's Vicarage, 104 Semilong Road, Northampton NN2 6EX* Tel (01604) 710033 E-mail david@wiseman50.freeserve.co.uk

WISEMAN, John. b 56. Sarum & Wells Th Coll 80. **d** 83 **p** 84. C Swinton St Pet *Man* 83-87; C Swinton and Pendlebury 87-88; TV Atherton 88-93; V Bedford Leigh 93-02; V Lt Lever from 02. *The Vicarage, Market Street, Little Lever, Bolton BL3 1HH* Tel (01204) 700936

WISHART, Michael Leslie. b 45. St Mich Coll Llan 70. **d** 73 **p** 74. C Llangyfelach *S & B* 73-76; Chapl RN 76-80 and 85-96; V Beguildy and Heyope *S & B* 80-84; V Gowerton 84-85; Chapl RNR 80-85; R Dowlais *Llan* 97-04; R Bishops Lydeard w Bagborough and Cothelstone *B & W* from 04. *The Rectory, Church Street, Bishops Lydeard, Taunton TA4 3AT* Tel (01823) 432414 E-mail michael.wishart@btopenworld.com

WISKEN, Canon Brian Leonard. b 34. Dur Univ BA58. Linc Th Coll 58. **d** 60 **p** 61. C Lobley Hill *Dur* 60-63; C Ipswich All Hallows *St E* 63-65; P-in-c Scunthorpe All SS *Linc* 65-69; V 69-71; Dioc Stewardship Adv 70-75; R Panton w Wragby 71-75; V Langton by Wragby 71-75; R Cleethorpes 75-77; TR 77-89; V Linc St Nic w St Jo Newport 89-99; Can and Preb Linc Cathl 88-00; rtd 99; Perm to Offic *Nor* and *St E* from 99. *49 Gainsborough Drive, Lowestoft NR32 4NJ* Tel (01502) 512378 E-mail brian@wisken.fslife.co.uk

WISKEN, Robert Daniel. b 30. ACT. **d** 60 **p** 60. C N Rockhampton St Barn Australia 60; V N Rockhampton St Matt 61-63; V Winton *Man* 63-65; R Luddington w Hemington and Thurning *Pet* 65-69; P-in-c Clopton *St E* 66-69; V Ipswich All SS 69-73; V Sompting *Chich* 74-78; Org Sec (SW England) CECS 78-80; R Edmundbyers w Muggleswick *Dur* 80-83; R Wexham *Ox* 83-86; Australia 86-03 and from 04; rtd 95. *3/52 Bordeaux Parade, Mermaid Waters, Qld, Australia 4218* Tel (0061) (7) 5578 6754 E-mail rwisken@gc.quik.com.au

WITCHELL, David William. b 47. St Jo Coll Nottm BTh75 LTh75. **d** 75 **p** 76. C Northampton St Mary *Pet* 75-78; C Oakham w Hambleton and Egleton 78-81; C Oakham, Hambleton, Egleton, Braunston and Brooke 81-82; V Weedon Bec w Everdon 82-90; V Wellingborough St Barn 90-00; RD Wellingborough 98-00; P-in-c Paignton St Paul Preston *Ex* 00-02; V Paignton Ch Ch and Preston St Paul from 03; RD Torbay from 03. *St Paul's Vicarage, Locarno Avenue, Paignton TQ3 2DH* Tel (01803) 522872

WITCHELL, Derek William Frederick. b 49. Ox Poly DipArch78. St Alb and Ox Min Course 00. **d** 03 **p** 04. C Bloxham w Milcombe and S Newington *Ox* from 03. *121 Courtington Lane, Bloxham OX15 4HS* Tel (01295) 722273 Mobile 07745-867508 E-mail derek@witchell.psa-online.com

WITCHER, Ian. b 49. CertEd93 Lon Inst of Educn Lic97. **d** 97 **p** 98. NSM Shaston *Sarum* from 97. *7 Old Boundary Road, Shaftesbury SP7 8ND* Tel (01747) 854878

WITCOMBE, John Julian. b 59. Cam Univ MA84 Nottm Univ MPhil91. St Jo Coll Nottm BA83. **d** 84 **p** 85. C Birtley *Dur* 84-87; C Chilwell *S'well* 87-91; V Lodge Moor St Luke *Sheff* 91-95; TR Uxbridge *Lon* 95-98; Dean St Jo Coll Nottm 98-05;

Officer for Min *Glouc* from 05. *St Paul's Vicarage, 2 King Edward's Avenue, Gloucester GL1 5DA* Tel (01452) 523732

WITCOMBE, Michael David. b 53. Univ of Wales (Lamp) BA76. Qu Coll Birm 76. **d** 78 **p** 79. C Neath w Llantwit *Llan* 78-80; C Whitchurch 80-83; V Newcastle 83-02; P-in-c Ewenny 84-86; V Llanishen from 02. *The Vicarage, 2 The Rise, Llanishen, Cardiff CF14 0RA* Tel (029) 2075 2545

WITCOMBE, Ricarda Jane. b 64. Ch Coll Cam BA86 MA90. St Jo Coll Nottm MA(TS)99. **d** 01 **p** 02. C Wilford *S'well* 01-05; P-in-c Glouc St Paul *Glouc* from 05. *St Paul's Vicarage, 2 King Edward's Avenue, Gloucester GL1 5DA* Tel (01452) 523732 E-mail ricarda@ricarda.fsnet.co.uk

WITCOMBE, Simon Christopher. b 61. Dundee Univ MA83 PGCE84 Dur Univ BA90. St Jo Coll Dur 88. **d** 91 **p** 92. C Earlham St Anne *Nor* 91-95; Assoc P Skegness and Winthorpe *Linc* 95-98; Gen Preacher 95-98; R Woodhall Spa Gp from 98. *The Vicarage, Alverston Avenue, Woodhall Spa LN10 6SN* Tel (01526) 353856 E-mail witcombe@tinyonline.co.uk

WITHERIDGE, John Stephen. b 53. Kent Univ BA76 Ch Coll Cam BA78 MA82 FRSA98. Ridley Hall Cam 78. **d** 79 **p** 80. C Luton St Mary *St Alb* 79-82; Asst Chapl Marlborough Coll 82-84; Abp's Chapl *Cant* 84-87; Conduct Eton Coll 87-96; Hd Charterhouse Sch Godalming from 96; Perm to Offic *Guildf* from 96. *Charterhouse, Godalming, Surrey GU7 2DJ* Tel (01483) 291600 Fax 291647

WITHERS, Mrs Christine Mary. b 37. ALA60. Gilmore Ho DipRS81. **dss** 81 **d** 87 **p** 94. Chorleywood Ch Ch *St Alb* 81-86; Darley *Derby* 86-92; C 87-92; Chapl HM Pris Drake Hall 92-95; P-in-c Standon and Cotes Heath *Lich* 96-98; Perm to Offic *Heref* from 98; rtd 02. *St Mary's Close, Westbury, Shrewsbury SY5 9QX* Tel (01743) 885038

WITHERS, Geoffrey Edward. b 68. QUB BSc90 TCD BTh93. CITC 90. **d** 93 **p** 94. C Ballymena w Ballyclug *Conn* 93-97; I Monkstown 97-01; Chapl RAF from 01. *Chaplaincy Services (RAF), HQ, Personnel and Training Command, RAF Innsworth, Gloucester GL3 1EZ* Tel (01452) 712612 ext 5032 Fax 510828 E-mail stchap.dgcs@ptc.raf.mod.uk *or* gwithers@vodafone.net

WITHERS, Miss Gillian. b 58. Stranmillis Coll BEd80. St Jo Coll Nottm 94. **d** 97 **p** 98. NSM Mossley *Conn* 97-03; C Bangor St Comgall *D & D* from 03. *17 Grange Road, Bangor BT20 3QQ* Tel (028) 9127 4168 E-mail vicarofdibley44@hotmail.com

WITHERS, John Geoffrey. b 39. St Jo Coll Dur BA61 Birm Univ CertEd63 Reading Univ Dip Educn Guidance 70 CQSW72. SW Minl Tr Course 84. **d** 87 **p** 88. NSM Drewsteignton *Ex* 87-01; P-in-c 99-01; P-in-c Hittisleigh and Spreyton 99-01; P-in-c Chagford, Drewsteignton, Hittisleigh etc 01; C from 01; Sub Chapl HM Pris Ex from 96. *St Levan, Broomhill, Chagford, Newton Abbot TQ13 8DD* Tel (01647) 432340

WITHERS, Michael. b 41. TCD BA66 Edin Univ BD70 QUB MTh83 Birm Univ PGCE67. Union Th Sem (NY) STM71. **d** 71 **p** 73. C Seagoe *D & D* 71-77; C Seapatrick 77-80; I Belfast St Chris 80-89; I Movilla 89-96; rtd 96. *11 Earlswood Road, Belfast BT4 3DY* Tel (028) 9047 1037

WITHERS, Michael Selby. b 36. Sheff Univ BA61 PGCE62 Univ of Wales (Swansea) 75. St Alb and Ox Min Course 93. **d** 96 **p** 97. NSM Bletchley *Ox* 96-97; NSM Ellesborough, The Kimbles and Stoke Mandeville 97-01; NSM Risborough from 01. *Penjarrick House, Main Road, Lacey Green, Princes Risborough HP27 0QU* Tel (01844) 274424

WITHEY, Michael John. b 45. Open Univ BA80 Ox Univ MTh98. Oak Hill Th Coll 71. **d** 74 **p** 75. C St Alb St Paul *St Alb* 74-76; C Luton St Mary 77; C Luton St Fran 77-80; V Woodside w E Hyde 80-87; CF (TA) 83-87; Dioc Stewardship Adv *Ox* 87-89; Chapl HM YOI Onley 89-91; V Hengoed w Gobowen *Lich* 91-95; Chapl Robert Jones and Agnes Hunt Orthopaedic Hosp 91-95; P-in-c Chasetown *Lich* 95-00; V 00-02; V Stroud H Trin *Glouc* from 02; Chapl Cotswold and Vale Primary Care Trust from 02; Chapl Glos Partnership Trust from 02. *Holy Trinity Vicarage, 10 Bowbridge Lane, Stroud GL5 2JW* Tel (01453) 764551

WITHINGTON, Brian James. b 54. Sheff Poly CQSW76 Leic Univ MSc01. EAMTC 94. **d** 97 **p** 98. NSM Pet St Jo *Pet* 97-04; P-in-c Broughton w Loddington and Cransley etc from 04. *The Rectory, Gate Lane, Broughton, Kettering NN14 1ND* Tel (01536) 791373 E-mail brian.andco@virgin.net

WITHINGTON, George Kenneth. b 37. Birm Univ BA59. Wells Th Coll 59. **d** 61 **p** 62. C Hartcliffe St Andr CD *Bris* 61-65; V Swindon St Jo 65-73; V Cricklade w Latton 73-97; RD Cricklade 94-97; rtd 97; Perm to Offic *Heref* and *Worc* from 97. *19 Oak Drive, Colwall, Malvern WR13 6RA* Tel (01684) 540590

WITHINGTON, Canon Keith. b 32. Univ of Wales (Lamp) BA55. Qu Coll Birm 55. **d** 57 **p** 58. C Bournville *Birm* 57-61; V 61-00; RD Moseley 81-91; Hon Can Birm Cathl 83-00; rtd 00; Perm to Offic *Birm* and *Worc* from 00. *44 Dugard Way, Droitwich WR9 8UX* Tel (01905) 795847 E-mail kw1000@bushinternet.com

WITHINGTON, Paul Martin. b 60. Kent Univ BSc86. Trin Coll Bris 01. **d** 03. C Elworth and Warmingham *Ches* from 03. *80 Abbey Road, Sandbach CW11 3HB* Tel (01270) 764014

WITHNELL, Roderick David. b 55. Leic Univ Cert Th & Past Studies 89. EMMTC 86 Ridley Hall Cam 89. **d** 90 **p** 91. C Shenfield *Chelmsf* 90-94; C Woodleigh and Loddiswell *Ex* 94-95; TV Modbury, Bigbury, Ringmore w Kingston etc 95-00; Canada 00-01; TR Burrington, Chawleigh, Cheldon, Chulmleigh etc *Ex* from 01. *The Rectory, Chulmleigh EX18 7BY* Tel (01769) 580537

WITHY, John Daniel Forster. b 38. Bible Tr Inst Glas CertRK61 ALCD64. **d** 64 **p** 65. C Belfast St Aid *Conn* 64-68; Dir Chr Conf Cen Sion Mills from 68. *Zion House, 120 Melmont Road, Strabane BT82 9ET* Tel (028) 8165 8672

WITT, Bryan Douglas. b 52. St Mich Coll Llan BD84. **d** 84 **p** 85. C Betws w Ammanford *St D* 84-87; V Llanllwni 87-91; V Llangennech and Hendy 91-04; V St Clears w Llangynin and Llanddowror etc from 04. *The Vicarage, Bridge Street, St Clears, Carmarthen SA33 4EE* Tel (01994) 230266

WITTER, Mrs Tania Judy Ingram. b 37. Girton Coll Cam BA58 MA63. Oak Hill Th Coll 94. **d** 95 **p** 96. NSM Highbury Ch Ch w St Jo and St Sav *Lon* 95-03; Perm to Offic *Lon* and *Eur* from 03. *Viewpoint # 26, 30-32 Highbury Grove, London N5 2DL* Tel (020) 7226 6908 E-mail tania.witter@btinternet.com

WITTING, Anna Brynhild Marianne. b 48. Lund Univ Sweden MDiv72. **p** 72. Sweden 72-99, 01-03 and from 04; C Frodingham *Linc* 00-01; Bp's C Donagh w Tyholland and Errigal Truagh *Clogh* 03-04; Bp's C Ematris w Rockcorry, Aghabog and Aughnamullan 03-04. *Address temp unknown*

WITTS, Donald Roger. b 47. Cranmer Hall Dur 86. **d** 88 **p** 89. C Leyland St Ambrose *Blackb* 88-90; C Staines St Mary and St Pet *Lon* 90-93; Ind Missr *Man* 93-95; Dioc Communications Officer *Cant* 95-00; P-in-c Blean 95-01; P-in-c Birchington w Acol and Minnis Bay 01-03; V from 03. *All Saints' Vicarage, 15 Minnis Road, Birchington CT7 9SE* Tel (01843) 841117 E-mail don.witts@ukonline.co.uk

WITTS, Graham Robert. b 53. Newc Univ BEd Bris Univ MA01. Linc Th Coll 79. **d** 82 **p** 83. C Horncastle w Low Toynton *Linc* 82-85; TV Gt Grimsby St Mary and St Jas 85-89; TR Yelverton, Meavy, Sheepstor and Walkhampton *Ex* 89-93; C Glastonbury w Meare *B & W* 93-03; RD Glastonbury 00-03; V Burnham from 03. *The Vicarage, Rectory Road, Burnham-on-Sea TA8 2BZ* Tel (01278) 782991 E-mail thewittsonweb@hotmail.com

WOADDEN, Christopher Martyn. b 56. St Jo Coll Nottm LTh. **d** 87 **p** 88. C Mickleover All SS *Derby* 87-90; C Wirksworth w Alderwasley, Carsington etc 90-92; C Wirksworth 92; TV Gt and Lt Coates w Bradley *Linc* 92-98; V Holton-le-Clay and Tetney from 98. *The Vicarage, Church Walk, Holton-le-Clay, Grimsby DN36 5AN* Tel (01472) 824082

WOAN, Miss Susan Ann. b 52. Univ of Wales (Abth) BSc71 Ch Ch Coll Cant MA91 Rob Coll Cam BA95. Ridley Hall Cam 93. **d** 96 **p** 97. C Histon *Ely* 96-97; C Radipole and Melcombe Regis *Sarum* 97-00; Chapl Bournemouth and Poole Coll of FE *Win* 00-04; Hon C Bournemouth St Jo w St Mich 00-04; Vice-Prin Dioc Min Course *Nor* from 04. *2 Conesford Drive, Norwich NR1 2BB* Tel (01603) 622579 E-mail sue.woan@dial.pipex.com

WODEHOUSE, Armine Boyle. b 24. Oak Hill Th Coll 83. **d** 86 **p** 86. NSM Gt Parndon *Chelmsf* 86-92; Perm to Offic *Eur* 89-92; Chapl Menton 92-99; rtd 99; Perm to Offic *Lon* from 02. *Flat 12, 105 Onslow Square, London SW7 3LU* Tel (020) 7584 4845

WODEHOUSE, Carol Lylie. *See* KIMBERLEY, Countess of

WODEMAN, Cyril Peter Guy. b 28. Qu Coll Cam BA50 MA55 ARCO54 LRAM58 ARCM58. Cranmer Hall Dur 72. **d** 73 **p** 74. C Penwortham St Mary *Blackb* 73-77; V Burnley St Steph 77-85; V Hornby w Claughton 85-93; rtd 93; Perm to Offic *Blackb* and *Carl* from 93. *5 Harling Bank, Kirkby Lonsdale, Carnforth LA6 2DJ* Tel (01524) 272474

WOFFENDEN (née HANCOCK), Mrs Dorothy Myfanwy. b 41. N Ord Course 01. **d** 03. NSM Brinnington w Portwood *Ches* from 03. *8 Churchill Crescent, Marple, Stockport SK6 6HJ* Tel 0161-427 6839 E-mail dwoffenden@smartone.co.uk

WOLFE, Canon Michael Matheson. b 29. Pemb Coll Ox BA49 MA53. Cuddesdon Coll 51. **d** 53 **p** 54. C Moorfields *Bris* 53-57; P-in-c Fochabers *Mor* 57-58; Sub-Warden Aberlour Orphanage 58-59; V Southport St Paul *Liv* 59-65; V Upholland 65-73; TR 73-82; RD Ormskirk 78-82; RD Ormskirk and Hon Can Liv Cathl 78-82; Can Res Liv Cathl 82-96; Merseyside Ecum Officer 82-96; AD Toxteth and Wavertree 89-96; rtd 96; Perm to Offic *Liv* from 97; Hon Chapl Liv Cathl from 97. *23 Hunters Lane, Liverpool L15 8HL* Tel 0151-733 1541

WOLFENDEN, Peter Graham. b 40. St Pet Coll Ox BA63 MA66. Linc Th Coll 62. **d** 64 **p** 65. C Adlington *Blackb* 64-66; Asst Master Barton Peveril Gr Sch 66-69; Chapl Bp Wordsworth Sch Salisbury 69-72; Hon C Bishopstoke *Win* 66-72; Hon C Ponteland *Newc* 72-02; Hd Master Richard Coates Middle Sch Ponteland 78-01; Chapl Malta and Gozo *Eur* from 02. *Bishop's House, 75 Rodolphe Street, Sliema SLM14, Malta GC* Tel (00356) 2133 0575 Fax 2133 4677

WOLLASTON, Canon Barbara Kathleen. b 30. LSE BSc(Soc)64. Gilmore Ho 51. **d** 87 **p** 94. Dir Past Studies Qu Coll Birm 80-89; Dioc Dir of Ords *S'wark* 89-94; rtd 94. *21 Chapel Street, Wem, Shrewsbury SY4 5ER* Tel (01939) 232229

WOLLEY, John. BSc. **d** 85 **p** 86. Hon C Croydon St Aug *S'wark* 85-89; Perm to Offic *Linc* 89-01. *7 Royal Oak Court, Upgate, Louth LN11 9JA* Tel (01507) 601614

WOLLEY, Richard. b 33. Ox Univ MA. S Dios Minl Tr Scheme 82. **d** 85 **p** 86. NSM Brighton Resurr *Chich* 85-88; C 88-89; C Brighton St Geo w St Anne and St Mark 89-91; R Buxted and Hadlow Down 91-98; rtd 98. *35 Scarletts Close, Uckfield TN22 2BA* Tel (01825) 761042

WOLSTENCROFT, The Ven Alan. b 37. Cuddesdon Coll. **d** 69 **p** 70. C Halliwell St Thos *Man* 69-71; C Stand 71-73; V Wythenshawe St Martin 73-80; AD Withington 78-91; Chapl Wythenshawe Hosp Man 80-89; V Baguley *Man* 80-91; V Bolton St Pet 91-98; Hon Can Man Cathl 86-98; Can Res 98-04; Adn Man 98-04; rtd 04; Perm to Offic *Man* from 04. *The Bakehouse, 1 Latham Row, Horwich, Bolton BL6 6QZ* Tel and fax (01204) 469985 E-mail archdeaconalan@wolstencrofta.fsnet.co.uk

WOLSTENHULME, Arthur James. b 20. Leeds Univ BA42. Coll of Resurr Mirfield 42. **d** 44 **p** 46. C Tonge Moor *Man* 44-45; C Hollinwood 45-48; C Walsall St Mary and All SS Palfrey *Lich* 48-52; V Cov St Pet *Cov* 52-56; V New Bilton 56-66; R Kingsthorpe *Pet* 66-73; TR Kingsthorpe w Northampton St Dav 73-86; rtd 86; Perm to Offic *Pet* from 86. *2 Springbanks Way, Northampton NN4 0QA* Tel (01604) 766405 Fax as telephone

WOLVERHAMPTON, Area Bishop of. *See* BOURKE, The Rt Revd Michael Gay

WOLVERSON, Marc Ali Morad. b 68. Univ of Kansas BA91. Ripon Coll Cuddesdon 93. **d** 96 **p** 97. C Nantwich *Ches* 96-99; Baton Rouge St Luke USA 99-00; Assoc V Bramhall *Ches* 00-04; V High Lane from 04. *The Vicarage, 85 Buxton Road, High Lane, Stockport SK6 8DX* Tel (01663) 762627 E-mail frmarc@onetel.com

WOOD, Mrs Ann Rene. b 49. St Deiniol's Hawarden 87. **d** 90 **p** 94. Par Dn Bamber Bridge St Aid *Blackb* 90-93; C W Burnley All SS 93-95; V Marton Moss 95-00; Hon Can Blackb Cathl 98-00; R Whiston *Sheff* from 00; AD Rotherham from 04. *The Rectory, Doles Lane, Whiston, Rotherham S60 4JA* Tel (01709) 364430 E-mail ann.wood@ukonline.co.uk

WOOD (née BLACKBURN), Mrs Anne Dorothy. b 54. Keele Univ BA76 Huddersfield Univ DPSE89 Bradf Univ MSc90. N Ord Course 95. **d** 98 **p** 99. NSM Batley St Thos *Wakef* 98-00; Jt P-in-c Morley St Paul 01-02; C Bruntcliffe 01-02; C Morley 02-03; TV from 03. *St Paul's Vicarage, 2 Bridge Court, Morley, Leeds LS27 0BD* Tel 0113-238 1037 Mobile 07769-503147 E-mail anne.d.wood@talk21.com

WOOD, Anthony James. b 38. Kelham Th Coll 58. **d** 63 **p** 64. C Shrewsbury St Alkmund *Lich* 63; C Harlescott 63-66; C Porthill 66-70; P-in-c Priorslee 70-76; Chapl Telford Town Cen 73-76; V Barton-under-Needwood 76-97; V Barton under Needwood w Dunstall from 97; RD Tutbury from 02. *The Vicarage, 3 Church Lane, Barton under Needwood, Burton-on-Trent DE13 8HU* Tel (01283) 712359 E-mail tonywood@surefish.co.uk

WOOD, The Ven Arnold. b 18. Clifton Th Coll 66. **d** 65 **p** 66. C Kirkheaton *Wakef* 65-67; V Mount Pellon 67-73; R Lanreath *Truro* 73-81; V Pelynt 73-81; RD W Wivelshire 76-81; Lib Truro Cathl 81-88; Can Res Truro Cathl 81-88; Adn Cornwall 81-88; Warden Community of the Epiphany Truro 85-00; rtd 88; Perm to Offic *Truro* from 00 and *Wakef* from 03. *13 Groveville, Northedge Lane, Hipperholme, Halifax HX3 8LD* Tel (01422) 207014 E-mail awood.cobblers@virgin.net

WOOD, Barbara Ann. b 49. St Mich Coll Llan 00. **d** 02 **p** 03. C Glan Ely *Llan* from 02. *12 Mansell Avenue, Cardiff CF5 4TB* Tel (029) 2084 3242 E-mail babswood01@hotmail.com

WOOD, Barry. b 56. CQSW81 CYCW81 Open Univ BA87 Sheff Univ MMin01. St Steph Ho Ox 87. **d** 89 **p** 90. C Tranmere St Paul w St Luke *Ches* 89-92; TV Ches Team 92-94; P-in-c S Tawton and Belstone *Ex* 94-00; R 00-02; RD Okehampton 98-02; TR Wylye and Till Valley *Sarum* 02-03; rtd 03. *77 Slade Close, Ottery St Mary EX11 1SY* Tel (01404) 814953

WOOD, Beresford Donald Richard. b 32. Leeds Univ BA58. Cant Sch of Min 91. **d** 94 **p** 95. Chapl St Mary's Sch Westbrook from 94; NSM Folkestone St Mary and St Eanswythe *Cant* 94-02; Perm to Offic from 02. *St Katherine's Cottage, Pound Lane, Elham, Canterbury CT4 6TS* Tel (01303) 840817

WOOD, Canon Beryl Jean. b 54. Linc Th Coll 85. **d** 87 **p** 94. C Gaywood, Bawsey and Mintlyn *Nor* 87-92; C Gaywood 92-93; Asst Chapl Univ Hosp Nottm 93-95; R Shipdham w E and W Bradenham *Nor* from 95; RD Dereham in Mitford 00-03; Hon Can Nor Cathl from 05. *The Rectory, Church Close, Shipdham, Thetford IP25 7LX* Tel (01362) 820234

WOOD, Mrs Brenda. b 46. Eliz Gaskell Coll Man TCert67 Leeds Metrop Univ BEd94 Leeds Univ MA04. N Ord Course 00. **d** 03 **p** 04. NSM Kirkstall *Ripon* from 03. *18 Wentworth Crescent, Leeds LS17 7TW* Tel 0113-226 7991 E-mail bwood@ntlworld.com

WOOD, Canon Brian Frederick. b 31. Leeds Univ BA52. Coll of Resurr Mirfield 55. **d** 57 **p** 58. C Wigan St Anne *Liv* 57-60; C Elland *Wakef* 60-63; V Carlinghow 63-73; V Drighlington 73-94; RD Birstall 83-92; Hon Can Wakef Cathl 89-94; rtd 94; Perm to Offic *Bradf* and *Wakef* from 94. *10 Grove Road, Menston, Ilkley LS29 6JD* Tel (01943) 872820

WOOD, Ms Carolyn Marie Therese. b 57. Sussex Univ BA91. St Mich Coll Llan 02. **d** 04 **p** 05. C Monkton *St D* from 04. *The Vicarage, Lamphey, Pembroke Dock SA71 5NR* Tel (01646) 672899 Mobile 07956-051591 E-mail tuppywood@hotmail.com

WOOD, Catherine Rosemary. b 54. Melbourne Coll of Div 82 St Jo Coll Auckland 83. **d** 83 **p** 84. New Zealand 83-01; C Howick 83-87; C Auckland St Paul 88; P-in-c Mangere E 89-90; Co-ord Environmental Educn 90-95; N Fieldworker Chr World Service 96-01; Hon C Glen Eden 90-97; NSM Auckland Cathl 98-01; Perm to Offic *S'wark* 01-02; P-in-c Tatsfield from 02; C Limpsfield and Titsey 02-03; Min Limpsfield Chart St Andr CD from 03. *The Rectory, Ricketts Hill Road, Tatsfield, Westerham TN16 2NA* Tel (01959) 577289 Mobile 07960-088873 E-mail catswhiskers@ukonline.co.uk

WOOD, Christine Denise. b 48. EMMTC. **d** 05. NSM Clifton *S'well* from 05. *64 Henry Road, West Bridgford, Nottingham NG2 7ND* Tel 0115-982 5498

WOOD, Christopher William. b 44. Rhodes Univ BA66 Univ of S Africa BTh82. St Bede's Coll Umtata 79. **d** 80 **p** 82. S Africa 80-87; C Houghton Regis *St Alb* 87-00; C Milton *Portsm* 00-03; Perm to Offic *Lich* from 04. *27 Penton Walk, Stoke-on-Trent ST3 3DG* Tel (01782) 311779

WOOD, Canon Colin Arthur. b 41. CEng. S'wark Ord Course 86. **d** 89 **p** 90. C Tadworth *S'wark* 89-93; TV Morden from 93; Hon Can S'wark Cathl from 05. *49 Camborne Road, Morden SM4 4JL* Tel (020) 8542 2966 E-mail colinwood@stmartin49.freeserve.co.uk

WOOD, David Arthur. b 30. Man Univ BA51. Lich Th Coll 59. **d** 61 **p** 62. C Ashton Ch Ch *Man* 61-64; C Elton All SS 64-68; Dioc Youth Adv *Newc* 68-72; R Cramlington 72-73; TR 73-83; V Wylam 83-86; TV Egremont and Haile *Carl* 86-94; rtd 94; Perm to Offic *Carl* from 94. *6 John Street, Maryport CA15 6JT* Tel (01900) 816706

WOOD, David Christopher. b 52. Oak Hill Th Coll 89. **d** 91 **p** 92. C Kendal St Thos *Carl* 91-95; P-in-c Asby from 95; P-in-c Bolton and Crosby Ravensworth 95-05. *The Vicarage, Crosby Ravensworth, Penrith CA10 3JJ* Tel (01931) 715226 E-mail revdavidcwood@hotmail.com

WOOD, David John. b 48. Newc Univ BSc70 PGCE71 Open Univ MA91. Dioc OLM tr scheme 99. **d** 01 **p** 02. OLM Bedlington *Newc* from 01. *7 East Riggs, Bedlington NE22 5SH* Tel (01670) 825200 E-mail davwd50@hotmail.com

WOOD, David Michael. b 39. Chich Th Coll. **d** 82 **p** 83. C Epping St Jo *Chelmsf* 82-85; C Totton *Win* 85-88; V Southway *Ex* 88-97; P-in-c Black Torrington, Bradf w Cookbury etc 97-01; R 01-04; rtd 04; Perm to Offic *Portsm* from 04. *29 Alver Bridge View, Gosport PO12 2JB*

WOOD, Dennis William. b 28. Qu Mary Coll Lon BSc53 Glas Univ PhD57. NEOC 82. **d** 85 **p** 85. NSM Stanhope *Dur* 85-86; NSM Stanhope w Frosterley 86-94; NSM Eastgate w Rookhope 86-94; NSM Melrose *Edin* from 94. *Gordonlee, Ormiston Terrace, Melrose TD6 9SP* Tel (01896) 823835

WOOD, Donald. b 40. **d** 95 **p** 96. NSM Caldicot *Mon* 95-99; P-in-c Llangwm Uchaf and Llangwm Isaf w Gwernesney etc from 99. *The Rectory, Gwernesney, Usk NP15 1HF* Tel (01291) 672518

WOOD, Edward Berryman. b 33. Ely Th Coll 54. **d** 57 **p** 58. C Aldershot St Mich *Guildf* 57-60; C Worplesdon 60-62; V Littleport St Matt *Ely* 62-64; V Balham St Jo Bedf Hill *S'wark* 64-71; V New Eltham All SS 71-84; RD Eltham (Sub-Deanery) 79-82; P-in-c Woldingham 84-98; rtd 98; Perm to Offic *Chich* from 99. *5 The Mount, 45 Meads Road, Eastbourne BN20 7PX* Tel (01323) 730501

WOOD, Edward Francis. b 28. Chich Th Coll 56. **d** 58 **p** 59. C Newc St Fran *Newc* 58-62; C High Elswick St Phil 62-64; C Delaval 64-67; C-in-c Shiremoor CD 67-68; V Shiremoor and Dioc Broadcasting Adv 68-78; C Newc St Geo 78-82; C Newc Epiphany 82-93; rtd 93; Perm to Offic *Newc* from 93. *52 Albemarle Avenue, Newcastle upon Tyne NE2 3NQ* Tel 0191-284 5338 E-mail francis@fwood11.fsnet.co.uk

WOOD, Elaine Mary. *See* RICHARDSON, Elaine Mary

WOOD, Mrs Elizabeth Jane. b 51. Ch Ch Coll Cant DipEd73. NEOC 98. **d** 01 **p** 02. C Denton *Newc* 01-04; V N Sunderland from 04; V Beadnell from 04. *The Vicarage, South Lane, North Sunderland, Seahouses NE68 7TU* Tel (01665) 720202 E-mail jane.wood3@btopenworld.com

WOOD, Elizabeth Lucy. b 35. WMMTC 89. **d** 92 **p** 94. NSM Wellingborough St Mark *Pet* 92-95; P-in-c Stanwick w Hargrave 95-00; Perm to Offic from 00. *21 Meadow Way, Irthlingborough, Wellingborough NN9 5RS*

WOOD, Francis. *See* WOOD, Edward Francis

WOOD, Frederick Leonard. b 19. BEM59. Worc Ord Coll. **d** 64 **p** 65. C Paignton St Paul Preston *Ex* 64-68; V Charles w Plymouth St Matthias 68-81; rtd 82; Perm to Offic *B & W* 85-92 and *Ox* from 93. *Oaklands, 1 Windrush Heights, Sandhurst GU47 8ET* Tel (01344) 762368

WOOD, Geoffrey. b 33. Tyndale Hall Bris 56. **d** 61 **p** 62. C Tranmere St Cath *Ches* 61-64; C Newburn *Newc* 64-68; R Gt Smeaton w Appleton upon Wiske *Ripon* 69-79; P-in-c Cowton w Birkby 73-79; P-in-c Danby Wiske w Yafforth and Hutton Bonville 76-79; R Gt Smeaton w Appleton Wiske and Birkby etc 79-89; R Fressingfield, Mendham etc *St E* 92-98; rtd 98; Perm to Offic *Dur* 98-04. *Clova, 16 Main Street, Longniddry EH32 0NF*

WOOD, Geoffrey James. b 47. N Ord Course 88. **d** 91 **p** 92. C Stainton-in-Cleveland *York* 91-94; V Middlesbrough St Oswald 94-99; V Eskdaleside w Ugglebarnby and Sneaton from 99. *The Vicarage, 22 Eskdaleside, Sleights, Whitby YO22 5EP* Tel (01947) 810349 E-mail frgeoffwood@supanet.com

WOOD, George Albert. b 22. St Paul's Coll Grahamstown. **d** 54 **p** 55. S Africa 54-60 and 63-77; C Cheam *S'wark* 60-63; Area Sec USPG *Chich* from 78; TV Littlehampton and Wick *Chich* 86-88; rtd 88; Perm to Offic *Chich* from 88. *3 Orchard Gardens, Rustington, Littlehampton BN16 3HS* Tel (01903) 787746

WOOD, George Robert. b 26. Em Coll Cam BA52. Oak Hill Th Coll 52. **d** 53 **p** 54. C Denton Holme *Carl* 53-56; V Cambridge St Matt *Ely* 56-60; NW Area Sec CPAS 60-61; R Watermillock *Carl* 61-74; V Holme Eden 74-76; Chapl Lindley Lodge 76-78; C Kingston upon Hull H Trin *York* 78-80; V Chipping *Blackb* 80-81; P-in-c Whitewell 80-81; V Chipping and Whitewell 82-83; R Bunwell w Carleton Rode and Tibenham *Nor* 83-88; P-in-c Wray w Tatham Fells *Blackb* 88-89; rtd 89; Perm to Offic *Carl* 89-99. *11 Woodlands, Bridge Lane, Penrith CA11 8GW* Tel (01768) 210194

WOOD, Heather Dawn. b 69. Leeds Univ BA02. N Ord Course 03. **d** 05. C Morley *Wakef* from 05. *47 Margaret Close, Morley, Leeds LS27 8NF* Tel 0113-253 3637 Mobile 07766-575371

WOOD, Miss Helen Ruth. b 54. Bedf Coll Lon BA75. Glouc Sch of Min 87. **d** 91 **p** 94. NSM Up Hatherley *Glouc* 91-94; NSM Cheltenham Em w St Steph from 94; Asst Chapl Cheltenham Ladies' Coll from 91. *9 Southfield Manor Park, Sandy Lane, Charlton Kings, Cheltenham GL53 9DJ* Tel (01242) 242793

WOOD, Jane. *See* WOOD, Mrs Elizabeth Jane

WOOD, Mrs Jennifer Sarah. b 40. Sarum Dioc Tr Coll CertEd60. Oak Hill Th Coll DipHE94. **d** 94 **p** 95. C St Illogan *Truro* 94-98; R Heanton Punchardon w Marwood *Ex* from 98. *The Rectory, Heanton, Barnstaple EX31 4DG* Tel and fax (01271) 812249 E-mail sarah@heanton-marwood.freeserve.co.uk

WOOD, John. b 37. LNSM course 75. **d** 77 **p** 79. NSM Dunbar *Edin* from 77; NSM Haddington from 77. *7 Herdmanflatt, Haddington EH41 3LN* Tel (01620) 822838

WOOD, John Anthony Scriven. b 48. Leeds Univ BSc70. St Jo Coll Nottm 76. **d** 79 **p** 80. C Colwich *Lich* 79-82; C W Bridgford *S'well* 82-90; V Gamston and Bridgford 90-95; Chapl Kings Mill Cen NHS Trust 95-01; Chapl Sherwood Forest Hosps NHS Trust from 01. *The King's Mill Centre, Mansfield Road, Sutton in Ashfield NG17 4JL* Tel (01623) 622515 ext 4137 *or* 0115-982 0969

WOOD, John Arthur. b 23. Roch Th Coll 68. **d** 70 **p** 71. C Wetherby *Ripon* 70-71; P-in-c Sheff Arbourthorne *Sheff* 71-75; TV Sheff Manor 75-81; R Rodney Stoke w Draycott *B & W* 81-88; rtd 88; Perm to Offic *Sheff* from 88. *36 The Glen, Endcliffe Vale Road, Sheffield S10 3FN* Tel 0114-266 5173

WOOD, John Maurice. b 58. Qu Coll Cam BA80 MA83. Wycliffe Hall Ox BA87. **d** 87 **p** 88. C Northwood Em *Lon* 87-91; C Muswell Hill St Jas w St Matt 91-94; P-in-c S Tottenham St Ann 94-01; V from 01. *St Ann's Vicarage, South Grove, London N15 5QG* Tel and fax (020) 8800 3506 Mobile 07771-867359 E-mail johnwood@st-anns.fsnet.co.uk

WOOD, John Samuel. b 47. Lanchester Poly BSc69 Sheff Univ DipEd. Westcott Ho Cam 72. **d** 81 **p** 82. NSM Haverhill *St E* 81-83; C Whitton and Thurleston w Akenham 83-86; P-in-c Walsham le Willows 86-88; P-in-c Finningham w Westhorpe 86-88; R Walsham le Willows and Finningham w Westhorpe 88-94; Min Can St E Cathl 89-94; TR Whitstable *Cant* 94-02; Hon Min Can Cant Cathl 96-02; TR Swanage and Studland *Sarum* from 02. *The Rectory, 12 Church Hill, Swanage BH19 1HU* Tel (01929) 422916 E-mail john.s.wood@btinternet.com

WOOD, Keith. b 49. St Steph Ho Ox 76. **d** 78 **p** 79. C Bognor *Chich* 78-81; C Hangleton 81-83; R W Blatchington 83-87; V W Worthing St Jo 87-96; R Winchelsea and Icklesham 96-00; rtd 00. *12 Boveway Drive, Liskeard PL14 3UH* Tel (01579) 349080

WOOD, Canon Keith Ernest. b 33. Qu Coll Ox BA55 BCL56 DipTh57 MA70. Wycliffe Hall Ox 56. **d** 58 **p** 59. C Barking St Marg *Chelmsf* 58-61; Min Basildon St Andr ED 61-70; V Brampton Bierlow *Sheff* 70-82; R Grasmere *Carl* 82-94; RD Windermere 89-94; Hon Can Carl Cathl 91-94 and 98-01; Bp's Dom Chapl 94-01; rtd 01; Perm to Offic *Carl* from 01. *The Old Tower, Brackenburgh, Calthwaite CA11 9PW* Tel (01768) 894273 Fax 894019

WOOD, Laurence Henry. b 27. Kelham Th Coll 47. **d** 52 **p** 53. C Ravensthorpe *Wakef* 52-55; C Almondbury 55-58; V Linthwaite 58-64; R Bonsall and V Cromford *Derby* 64-70; V Longwood *Wakef* 70-76; V Liversedge 76-92; rtd 92; Perm to Offic *Wakef* from 92. *203 The Rock, Gillroyd Lane, Linthwaite, Huddersfield HD7 5SR* Tel (01484) 843499

WOOD, Mrs Lorna. b 43. EAMTC 85. **d** 88 **p** 94. NSM Sprowston *Nor* 88-90; NSM Sprowston w Beeston 90-95; P-in-c Nor St Helen 95-01; Chapl Gt Hosp Nor 95-99; NSM Coltishall w Gt Hautbois and Horstead *Nor* 01-04; Perm to Offic from 04. *39 Inman Road, Sprowston, Norwich NR7 8JT*

WOOD, Mark. *See* WOOD, The Rt Revd Stanley Mark

WOOD, Mark Robert. b 68. Trin Coll Ox BA89 ALCM83 ARCO89. STETS 02. **d** 05. NSM Mere w W Knoyle and Maiden Bradley *Sarum* from 05. *19 Church Street, Maiden Bradley, Warminster BA12 7HW* Tel (01985) 844456 Mobile 07795-254983 E-mail mrwood@lineone.net

WOOD, Martin. *See* WOOD, Canon Nicholas Martin

WOOD, Martin Robert. b 65. Birm Univ BSc86. Trin Coll Bris 98. **d** 00 **p** 01. C Wells St Cuth w Wookey Hole *B & W* 00-03; C Shepton Mallet w Doulting from 03. *35 Society Road, Shepton Mallet BA4 5GF* Tel (01749) 346991 E-mail mrwood@tesco.net

✠**WOOD, The Rt Revd Maurice Arthur Ponsonby.** b 16. DSC44. Qu Coll Cam BA38 MA42. Ridley Hall Cam 40. **d** 40 **p** 41 **c** 71. C Portman Square St Paul *Lon* 40-43; Chapl RNVR 43-47; Hon Chapl Commando Assn from 47; R Ox St Ebbe *Ox* 47-52; V Islington St Mary *Lon* 52-61; RD Islington 52-61; Prin Oak Hill Th Coll 61-71; Preb St Paul's Cathl *Lon* 69-71; Bp Nor 71-85; Chapl RNR from 71; rtd 85; Perm to Offic *Nor* from 85; Hon Asst Bp Lon from 85; Res P Englefield *Ox* 87-94; Hon Asst Bp Ox 89-94. *30 Stuart Court, High Street, Kibworth, Leicester LE8 0LR* Tel 0116-279 1194

WOOD, Michael Edmund. b 46. Dur Univ BA67 PGCE68. Coll of Resurr Mirfield 94. **d** 96 **p** 97. NSM Battyeford *Wakef* from 96; Asst Chapl Kirkwood Hospice Huddersfield 96-97; Chapl from 97. *9 Dorchester Road, Fixby, Huddersfield HD2 2JZ* Tel (01484) 536496 E-mail mike@revwood.freeserve.co.uk

WOOD, Michael Frank. b 55. Nottm Univ BCombStuds. Linc Th Coll. **d** 84 **p** 85. C Marton *Blackb* 84-88; TV Ribbleton 88-93; V Blackpool St Mary 93-00; P-in-c S Shore St Pet 98-00; RD Blackpool 96-00; TR Brighouse and Clifton *Wakef* from 00. *The Rectory, 56 Bracken Road, Brighouse HD6 2HXJ* Tel and fax (01484) 714032 E-mail fr-m-wood@brighouse71.fsnet.co.uk

WOOD, Mrs Michaela. b 67. **d** 01 **p** 02. NSM Sunbury *Lon* 01-04; NSM Whitton St Aug from 04. *The Vicarage, 1 Byechurch End, Teddington TW11 8PS* Tel (020) 8977 0054 E-mail michaelawood@aol.com

WOOD, Canon Nicholas Martin. b 51. AKC74. **d** 75 **p** 76. C E Ham w Upton Park St Alb *Chelmsf* 75-78; C Leyton St Luke 78-81; V Rush Green 81-91; Chapl Barking Tech Coll 81-91; TR Elland *Wakef* from 91; RD Brighouse and Elland from 96; Hon Can Wakef Cathl from 00. *Elland Rectory, 50 Victoria Road, Elland HX5 0QA* Tel and fax (01422) 256088 E-mail phyllmartin@aol.com

WOOD, Paul Dominic. b 52. R Agric Coll Cirencester DipAgr74 Tasmania Coll of Ad Educn DipEd80. Ridley Coll Melbourne BTh87. **d** 87 **p** 88. Australia 87-92 and from 95; C Newtown St Jas 87-89; C Launceston St Jo 89-91; TV Ifield *Chich* 92-95; P-in-c Lancefield w Romsey 96-97; I 97-00; R Mansfield from 01. *St John's Rectory, 43 Highett Street, PO Box 261, Mansfield, Vic, Australia 3722* Tel and fax (0061) (3) 5775 2036 E-mail qwoodies@bigpond.com

WOOD, Preb Peter Thomas. b 31. Clifton Th Coll 57. **d** 60 **p** 61. C Woodford Wells *Chelmsf* 60-63; SAMS 63-72; Chile 63-72; V Clevedon Ch Ch *B & W* 72-82; Chapl St Brandon's Sch Clevedon 72-82; Chapl Heref Gen Hosp 82-93; V Heref St Pet w St Owen and St Jas *Heref* 82-98; Police Chapl 86-98; RD Heref City 90-96; Preb Heref Cathl 91-98; P-in-c Chilton Cantelo, Ashington, Mudford, Rimpton etc *B & W* 98-01; Hon P-in-c from 01; rtd 01. *The Vicarage, Camel Street, Marston Magna, Yeovil BA22 8DD* Tel (01935) 850536 E-mail ptwood@breathemail.net

WOOD, Philip James. b 48. Bris Univ BSc69 Westmr Coll Ox MTh93. Oak Hill Th Coll 71. **d** 74 **p** 75. C Islington St Mary *Lon* 74-77; C Stapenhill w Cauldwell *Derby* 77-80; V Walthamstow St Luke *Chelmsf* 80-94; AD Waltham Forest 89-94; Can Chelmsf Cathl 93-94; NSM Hackney Wick St Mary of Eton w St Aug *Lon* 01-02; TV Becontree W *Chelmsf* from 02. *St Thomas's Vicarage, Burnside Road, Dagenham RM8 2JN* Tel (020) 8590 6190 E-mail phillip.wood@tiscali.co.uk

WOOD, Philip Norman. b 52. EMMTC 97. **d** 00 **p** 01. NSM Pleasley Hill *S'well* 00-04; NSM Mansfield St Aug 00-04; NSM Ladybrook 00-04; TV Newton Flotman, Swainsthorpe, Tasburgh, etc *Nor* from 04. *The New Rectory, The Street, Saxlingham Nethergate, Norwich NR15 1AJ* Tel (01508) 499869 Mobile 07961-524495 E-mail philyvonne@hotmail.com

WOOD, Ms Rachel Astrid. b 71. Birm Univ BA92 MA99. Qu Coll Birm BD98. **d** 99 **p** 00. C Attercliffe, Darnall and Tinsley *Sheff* 99-01; C Roundhay St Edm *Ripon* 01-04. *The Rectory, Church Close, Hartlepool TS24 0PW* E-mail raw@fish.co.uk

WOOD, Raymond John Lee. b 28. ACII55 ACIArb. Linc Th Coll 66. **d** 68 **p** 69. C Beaconsfield *Ox* 68-72; CF 70-72; V Wath-upon-Dearne w Adwick-upon-Dearne *Sheff* 72-77; R St Tudy w Michaelstow *Truro* 77-86; P-in-c St Mabyn 82-86; R St Tudy w St Mabyn and Michaelstow 86-95; Chapl Bodmin Fire Brigade from 91; rtd 95; Perm to Offic *Truro* from 96. *1 Wesley Chapel, Harewood Road, Calstock PL18 9QN* Tel (01822) 835918 E-mail rlwood@tesco.net

WOOD, Richard. *See* WOOD, Beresford Donald Richard

✠**WOOD, The Rt Revd Richard James.** b 20. Wells Th Coll 51. **d** 52 **p** 53 **c** 73. C Calne *Sarum* 52-55; S Africa 55-73; Namibia 73-77; Suff Bp Damaraland 73-77; V Kingston upon Hull St Mary *York* 77-79; Chapl Hull Coll of HE 77-79; Tanzania 79-85; rtd 85; Asst Bp York 79 and 85-99. *3 Plough Steep, Itchen Abbas, Winchester SO21 1BQ* Tel (01962) 779400 E-mail cwood20498@aol.com

WOOD, Roger Graham. b 49. K Coll Lon BD. Chich Th Coll 74. **d** 76 **p** 77. C Skipton H Trin *Bradf* 76-79; Dioc Youth Chapl 79-87; V Queensbury 87-96; P-in-c Langcliffe w Stainforth and Horton 96-01; V from 01. *The Vicarage, Stainforth, Settle BD24 9PG* Tel (01729) 823010

WOOD, Roger William. b 43. Leeds Univ BA65 MA67 Fitzw Coll Cam BA69 MA75. Westcott Ho Cam 67. **d** 70 **p** 71. C Bishop's Stortford St Mich *St Alb* 70-74; C Sundon w Streatley 75-79; V Streatley from 80. *17 Sundon Road, Streatley, Luton LU3 3PL* Tel (01582) 882780

WOOD, Ronald Ernest. b 49. Sarum & Wells Th Coll 79. **d** 81 **p** 82. C Weston-super-Mare Cen Par *B & W* 81-84; C Forest of Dean Ch Ch w English Bicknor *Glouc* 84-88; R Sixpenny Handley w Gussage St Andrew etc *Sarum* 88-05; P-in-c Seale, Puttenham and Wanborough *Guildf* from 05. *The Rectory, Elstead Road, Seale, Farnham GU10 1JA* Tel (01252) 783057 E-mail office@spw.org.uk

WOOD, Sarah. *See* WOOD, Mrs Jennifer Sarah

WOOD, Shane Grant Lindsay. b 60. Southn Univ BTh91. St Steph Ho Ox 95. **d** 97 **p** 98. C Parkstone St Pet w Branksea and St Osmund *Sarum* 97-00; V Teddington SS Pet and Paul and Fulwell *Lon* from 00. *The Vicarage, 1 Bychurch End, Teddington TW11 8PS* Tel (020) 8977 0054 *or* 8977 3330 E-mail shaneglwood@aol.com

WOOD, Stanley Charles. b 26. Glouc Th Course 80. **d** 83 **p** 84. NSM Lower Cam w Coaley *Glouc* 83-87; P-in-c Shipton Moyne w Westonbirt and Lasborough 87-91; rtd 92; Perm to Offic *Glouc* from 92. *8 The Vennings, Cam, Dursley GL11 5NQ* Tel (01453) 544873

✠**WOOD, The Rt Revd Stanley Mark.** b 19. Univ of Wales BA40. Coll of Resurr Mirfield 40. **d** 42 **p** 43 **c** 71. C Cardiff St Mary *Llan* 42-45; S Africa 45-55; S Rhodesia 55-65; Rhodesia 65-77; Can Mashonaland 61-65; Dean Salisbury 65-71; Bp Matabeleland 71-77; Asst Bp Heref 77-81; Preb Heref Cathl 77-87; Suff Bp Ludlow 81-87; Adn Ludlow 82-83; rtd 87; Perm to Offic *Llan* from 87. *College of St Barnabas, Blackberry Lane, Lingfield RH7 6NJ* Tel (01342) 871556 E-mail revmarkwood@onetel.com

WOOD, Stella Margaret. b 70. Trin Coll Ox BA91 MA DPhil95. STETS 95. **d** 97 **p** 98. NSM Mere w W Knoyle and Maiden Bradley *Sarum* from 97; Chapl Sherborne Sch for Girls from 00. *19 Church Street, Maiden Bradley, Warminster BA12 7HW* Tel (01985) 844456 E-mail mrwood@lineone.net

WOOD, Stuart Hughes. b 32. ACIB64. Guildf Dioc Min Course 93. **d** 95 **p** 96. OLM Camberley St Martin Old Dean *Guildf* 95-02; OLM Camberley St Paul 99-02; OLM Camberley St Mich Yorktown 99-02; rtd 02; Perm to Offic *Guildf* from 02. *42 Roundway, Camberley GU15 1NS* Tel (01276) 22115 E-mail stuart.wood1@tesco.net

WOOD, Sylvia Marian. *See* CHAPMAN, Canon Sylvia Marian

WOOD, Thomas Henry. Glassboro Coll (USA) BEcon84. St D Coll Lamp 57. **d** 60 **p** 61. C Pontnewynydd *Mon* 60-62; C Middlesbrough All SS *York* 64-69; C Fleetwood St Pet *Blackb* 69-73; V Ferndale *Llan* 73-77; C Sheff St Cecilia Parson Cross *Sheff* 88-93; V St Hilary Greenway *Mon* 93-01; rtd 01. *Brousse Pave, 50140 St Clement-Rancourdray, France*

WOOD, Timothy Robert. b 55. Dioc OLM tr scheme 99. **d** 02 **p** 03. OLM Maidstone St Paul *Cant* from 02. *7 The Hedges, Maidstone ME14 2JW* Tel (01622) 753982 E-mail jane_wood@lineone.net

✠**WOOD, The Rt Revd Wilfred Denniston.** b 36. KA00. Lambeth DipTh62 Gen Th Sem NY Hon DD86 FRSA93. Codrington Coll Barbados 57. **d** 61 **p** 62 **c** 85. C Hammersmith St Steph *Lon* 62-63; C Shepherd's Bush St Steph w St Thos 63-74; Bp's Chapl for Community Relns 67-74; V Catford St Laur *S'wark* 74-82; Hon Can S'wark Cathl 77-82; RD E Lewisham 77-82; Borough Dean S'wark 82-85; Adn S'wark 82-85; Suff Bp Croydon 85-91; Area Bp Croydon 91-02; rtd 02. *69 Pegwell Gardens, Christ Church, Barbados* Tel (001) (246) 420 1822 Fax 420 3426

WOOD, William George. b 31. Oak Hill Th Coll 61. **d** 63 **p** 64. C Woking St Jo *Guildf* 63-69; V Camberwell All SS *S'wark* 69-88; R Horne 88-97; P-in-c Outwood 88-97; rtd 97. *43 Kingston Way, Seaford BN25 4NG* Tel (01323) 490572

WOODALL, David Paul. b 59. Chester Coll of HE BTh03. N Ord Course 00. **d** 03 **p** 04. C Darwen St Pet w Hoddlesden *Blackb* from 03. *44 Minster Crescent, Darwen, Blackburn BB3 3PY* Tel and fax (01254) 703796

WOODALL, Reginald Homer. b 38. Univ of Wales DipTh59. St Mich Coll Llan 59. **d** 61 **p** 62. C Newtown w Llanllwchaiarn w Aberhafesp *St As* 61-65; C Rhosddu 65-66; C Hawarden 66-70; CF 70-74; C Thornton Heath St Jude *Cant* 74-77; TV Cannock *Lich* 77-79; TV Basildon St Martin w H Cross and Laindon etc *Chelmsf* 79-84; P-in-c Canning Town St Cedd 84-93; rtd 93. *64 Stephens Road, London E15 3JL*

WOODASON, Anthony Norman. b 37. SW Minl Tr Course 02. **d** 04 **p** 05. NSM Bovey Tracey St Jo w Heathfield *Ex* from 04. *5 St John's Cottages, Newton Road, Bovey Tracey, Newton Abbot TQ13 9BE* Tel (01626) 836509

WOODBRIDGE, Trevor Geoffrey. b 31. Lon Univ BSc52. ALCD57. **d** 58 **p** 59. C Bitterne *Win* 58-61; C Ilkeston St Mary *Derby* 61-65; Area Sec CMS *Ex* and *Truro* 65-81; SW Regional Sec 70-81; TV Clyst St George, Aylesbeare, Clyst Honiton etc *Ex* 82-84; V Aylesbeare, Rockbeare, Farringdon etc 85-95; rtd 95; Perm to Offic *Ex* from 95. *19 Marlborough Road, Exeter EX2 4TJ* Tel (01392) 491050

WOODCOCK, Carolyn. b 47. N Ord Course BTh98. **d** 98 **p** 99. NSM Laneside *Blackb* 98-00; Chapl HM Pris Lanc Castle from 00. *HM Prison Lancaster, The Castle, Lancaster LA1 1YL* Tel (01524) 385100

WOODCOCK, Edward Marsden. b 47. Hull Univ MSc01 Leeds Univ BA03. Coll of Resurr Mirfield 01. **d** 03 **p** 04. C Wrenthorpe *Wakef* from 03; C Alverthorpe from 03. *The Vicarage, St Paul's Drive, Alverthorpe, Wakefield WF2 0BT* Tel (01924) 371300 E-mail edward@thewoodcocks.plus.com

WOODCOCK, John Charles Gerard. b 31. Kelham Th Coll 52. **d** 56 **p** 57. SSM 56-88; S Africa 56-62 and 76-83; Lesotho 62-76; Chapl Bede Ho Staplehurst 83-87; C Auckland St Andr and St Anne *Dur* 87-88. *3 Helena Terrace, Cockton Hill, Bishop Auckland DL14 6BP* Tel (01388) 604956

WOODCOCK, Michael David. b 67. Avery Hill Coll BEd91. Wycliffe Hall Ox BTh96. **d** 96 **p** 97. C Orpington Ch Ch *Roch* 96-99; R Knockholt w Halstead from 99. *The Rectory, Church Road, Halstead, Sevenoaks TN14 7HQ* Tel (01959) 532133 E-mail meesh@fish.co.uk

WOODCOCK, Michael Paul. b 71. Univ of Greenwich BA93. St Jo Coll Nottm MA98 DipTM99. **d** 99 **p** 00. C Brinsley w Underwood *S'well* 99-02; C New Malden and Coombe *S'wark* from 02. *2 California Road, New Malden KT3 3RU* Tel (020) 8942 0544

WOODCOCK, Nicholas Ethelbert. b 46. Abps' Cert in Ch Music 74 FRSA90. Cant Sch of Min 80. **d** 90 **p** 91. Chief Exec and Co Sec Keston Coll Kent 89-92; NSM Clerkenwell H Redeemer w St Phil *Lon* 90-92; NSM Clerkenwell H Redeemer and St Mark 92-93; Chapl RN 93-01; Min Can, Prec and Sacr Ely Cathl *Ely* 01-03; R Lavenham w Preston *St E* from 03; Min Can St E Cathl from 03. *The Rectory, Church Street, Lavenham, Sudbury CO10 9SA* Tel and fax (01787) 247244 E-mail nick.woodcock@ukonline.co.uk

WOODERSON, Mrs Marguerite Ann. b 44. RGN SCM. Qu Coll Birm 86. **d** 89 **p** 94. Par Dn Stoneydelph St Martin CD *Lich* 89-90; Par Dn Glascote and Stonydelph 90-91; Par Dn Chasetown 91-94; C 94; C-in-c Chase Terrace St Jo Distr Ch 92-94; Chapl Naas Gen Hosp 94-98; I Celbridge w Straffan and Newcastle-Lyons *D & G* from 98. *The Rectory, 15 Spring Gardens, Naas, Co Kildare, Irish Republic* Tel and fax (00353) (45) 897206 Mobile 86-851 2557 E-mail annwooderson@eircom.net

WOODERSON, Michael George. b 39. Southn Univ BA61. Lon Coll of Div BD69. **d** 69 **p** 70. C Morden *S'wark* 69-73; C Aldridge *Lich* 73-81; V Chasetown 81-94; RD Lich 86-94; Preb Lich Cathl 89-94; P-in-c Hammerwich 91-94; I Naas w Kill and Rathmore *M & K* from 94. *The Rectory, 15 Spring Gardens, Naas, Co Kildare, Irish Republic* Tel and fax (00353) (45) 897206 E-mail mgwooderson@eircom.net

WOODGATE, Mrs Elizabeth Mary. b 66. W Sussex Inst of HE BEd87. St Jo Coll Nottm MTh02. **d** 02 **p** 04. C Crofton *Portsm* 02-03; C Lee-on-the-Solent from 03. *85 Seymour Road, Lee-on-the-Solent PO13 9EQ* Tel (01329) 668089 E-mail bethpoppy@hotmail.com

WOODGATES, Mrs Margaret. b 47. St D Coll Lamp BA67. WMMTC 00. **d** 03 **p** 04. NSM Redditch, The Ridge *Worc* 03-05; NSM Redditch Ch the K from 05. *18 Warwick Hall Gardens, Bromsgrove B60 2AU* Tel (01527) 577785 E-mail margaret.woody@tesco.net

WOODGER, John McRae. b 36. Tyndale Hall Bris 60. **d** 63 **p** 64. C Heref St Pet w St Owen *Heref* 63-66; C Macclesfield St Mich *Ches* 66-69; V Llangarron w Llangrove *Heref* 69-74; P-in-c Garway 70-74; R Church Stretton 74-84; Preb Heref Cathl 82-84; V Watford *St Alb* 84-01; rtd 01; Perm to Offic *Heref* from 01. *39 Bronte Drive, Ledbury HR8 2FZ* Tel (01531) 636745 E-mail woodger@fish.co.uk

WOODGER, John Page. b 30. Master Mariner 56 Lon Univ DipTh58. St Aid Birkenhead 56. **d** 59 **p** 60. C Kimberworth *Sheff* 59-62; Chapl HM Borstal Pollington 62-70; C Goole *Sheff* 62-63; V Balne 63-70; C Halesowen *Worc* 70-74; V Cookley

74-81; TV Droitwich 81-85; TV Bedminster *Bris* 85-93; rtd 93; Perm to Offic *Bris* 93-97 and *Worc* from 98. *1 Barbel Crescent, Worcester WR5 3QU* Tel (01905) 769065

WOODGER, Richard William. b 50. Sarum & Wells Th Coll 76. **d** 79 **p** 80. C Chessington *Guildf* 79-82; C Frimley 82-85; C Frimley Green 82-85; V N Holmwood 85-90; TR Headley All SS 90-98; TR Penrith w Newton Reigny and Plumpton Wall *Carl* from 98. *The Rectory, 3 Lamley Gardens, Graham Street, Penrith CA11 9LR* Tel (01768) 863000 *or* 862867 E-mail dickwoodger@yahoo.co.uk

WOODHALL, Peter. b 32. Edin Th Coll 57. **d** 60 **p** 61. C Carl St Barn *Carl* 60-63; Hon Chapl Estoril *Eur* 63-65; Chapl RN 66-82; TR Is of Scilly *Truro* 82-90; V Mithian w Mount Hawke 90-95; rtd 97. *Tregarth, 4 Peverell Road, Porthleven, Helston TR13 9DH*

WOODHAM, Richard Medley Swift. b 43. Master Mariner 70. S'wark Ord Course 71. **d** 73 **p** 74. C Gravesend St Aid *Roch* 73-75; C Chessington *Guildf* 75-78; Warden Dioc Conf Ho Horstead *Nor* 78-87; R Horstead 78-87; Youth Chapl 78-88; V Nor St Mary Magd w St Jas 87-91; TR Norwich Over-the-Water 91-98; P-in-c Lakenham St Jo 98-99; V Nor Lakenham St Jo and All SS and Tuckswood from 99; RD Nor E from 02. *The Vicarage, Harwood Road, Norwich NR1 2NG* Tel (01603) 625678 E-mail rich1w@aol.com

WOODHAMS, Raymond John. b 40. Garnett Coll Lon CertEd68 IEng. STETS 98. **d** 01. NSM E Blatchington *Chich* from 01. *The Long House, West Dean, Seaford BN25 4AL* Tel and fax (01323) 870432 E-mail raymondj.woodhams@virgin.net

WOODHAMS, Roy Owen. b 57. ARCM76 GRSM78 Lon Inst of Educn TCert79. Ripon Coll Cuddesdon 91. **d** 93 **p** 94. C Deal St Leon and St Rich and Sholden *Cant* 93-97; P-in-c Cherbury *Ox* 97-02; P-in-c Gainfield 99-02; R Cherbury w Gainfield 02-04; AD Vale of White Horse 01-04; V Fleet *Guildf* from 04. *The Vicarage, Branksomewood Road, Fleet GU51 4JU* Tel (01252) 616361

WOODHAMS, Mrs Sophie Harriet. b 27. Cranmer Hall Dur 66. **dss** 80 **d** 87. Raveningham *Nor* 80-81; Henleaze *Bris* 81-87; rtd 87. *12 Hanover House, Hyde Valley, Welwyn Garden City AL7 4DA* Tel (01707) 890944

WOODHEAD, Mrs Bernice. b 45. Man OLM Scheme 98. **d** 01 **p** 02. OLM Shore *Man* from 01; OLM Calderbrook from 01. *2 Mount Avenue, Littleborough OL15 9JP* Tel (01706) 379517

WOODHEAD, Christopher Godfrey. b 26. Pemb Coll Cam BA50 MA55. Ely Th Coll 50. **d** 52 **p** 53. C Barnsley St Edw *Wakef* 52-54; C Mill Hill St Mich *Lon* 54-58; C Sandridge *St Alb* 58-66; R Earl Stonham *St E* 66-72; V Hoo St Werburgh *Roch* 72-88; C Cheam *S'wark* 88-91; rtd 91; Perm to Offic *Cant* from 91. *4 Eastgate Close, Herne Bay CT6 7ER* Tel (01227) 374137

WOODHEAD, Miss Helen Mary. b 35. Bedf Coll Lon BA57. Westcott Ho Cam 86. **d** 87 **p** 94. Par Dn Daventry *Pet* 87-90; Asst Dioc Dir of Ords *Guildf* 90-00; C Godalming 90-95; C Worplesdon 95-00; rtd 00; Perm to Offic *Lich* from 00. *12 Barley Croft, Whittington, Lichfield WS14 9LY* Tel (01543) 432345

WOODHEAD, Michael. b 51. St Jo Coll Nottm 88. **d** 90 **p** 91. C Stannington *Sheff* 90-93; V Deepcar 93-01; TV Crookes St Thos 01-05; TR from 05. *79 Glebe Road, Sheffield S10 1FB* Tel 0114-268 3463

WOODHEAD, Mrs Sandra Buchanan. b 42. Man Poly BA82 Man Univ BD85. St Deiniol's Hawarden. **dss** 86 **d** 87 **p** 94. High Lane *Ches* 86-90; Hon Par Dn 87-90; C Brinnington w Portwood 91-94; V 94-00; R Withington St Paul *Man* from 00. *Withington Rectory, 491 Wilmslow Road, Manchester M20 4AW* Tel 0161-445 3781

WOODHEAD-KEITH-DIXON, James Addison. b 25. St Aid Birkenhead 44. **d** 48 **p** 49. C Upperby St Jo *Carl* 48-50; C Dalton-in-Furness 50-52; V Blawith w Lowick 52-59; V Lorton 59-80; Chapl Puerto de la Cruz Tenerife *Eur* 80-82; TV Bellingham/Otterburn Gp *Newc* 82-83; TR 83-91; TR N Tyne and Redesdale 91-92; rtd 92. *Culpee House, Creebridge, Newton Stewart DG8 6NR*

WOODHOUSE, Canon Alison Ruth. b 43. Bedf Coll of Educn CertEd64. Dalton Ho Bris 68. **dss** 79 **d** 87 **p** 94. Bayston Hill *Lich* 79-81; W Derby St Luke *Liv* 81-86; Burscough Bridge 86-95; Par Dn 87-94; C 94-95; V Formby St Luke from 95; AD Sefton from 00; Hon Can Liv Cathl from 02. *St Luke's Vicarage, St Luke's Church Road, Liverpool L37 2DF* Tel and fax (01704) 877655 E-mail arw@fish.co.uk

WOODHOUSE, The Ven Andrew Henry. b 23. DSC45. Qu Coll Ox BA48 MA49. Linc Th Coll 48. **d** 50 **p** 51. C Poplar All SS w St Frideswide *Lon* 50-56; V W Drayton 56-70; RD Hillingdon 67-70; Adn Ludlow *Heref* 70-82; R Wistanstow 70-82; P-in-c Acton Scott 70-73; Can Res Heref Cathl 82-91; Treas 82-85; Adn Heref 82-91; rtd 91; Perm to Offic *Guildf* from 91. *Orchard Cottage, Bracken Close, Woking GU22 7HD* Tel (01483) 760671

WOODHOUSE, Andrew Laurence. b 40. Leeds Univ NDD63 ATCL64 Nottm Univ DipEd72. NW Ord Course. **d** 82 **p** 83. NSM Bedale *Ripon* 82-02; NSM Bedale and Leeming from 03; P-in-c Thornton Watlass from 99. *The Rectory, Thornton Watlass, Ripon HG4 4AH* Tel (01677) 422737 Mobile 07720-670163

WOODHOUSE, The Ven Charles David Stewart. b 34. Kelham Th Coll 55. **d** 59 **p** 60. C Leeds Halton St Wilfrid *Ripon* 59-63; Youth Chapl *Liv* 63-66; Bermuda 66-69; Asst Gen Sec CEMS 69-70; Gen Sec 70-76; Bp's Dom Chapl *Ex* 76-81; R Ideford, Luton and Ashcombe 76-81; V Hindley St Pet *Liv* 81-92; Adn Warrington 81-01; Hon Can Liv Cathl 83-01; rtd 01; Perm to Offic *Liv* from 03. *9 Rob Lane, Newton-le-Willows WA12 0DR*

WOODHOUSE, David Edwin. b 45. Lon Univ BSc68. Cuddesdon Coll 68. **d** 71 **p** 72. C E Dulwich St Jo *S'wark* 71-74; Lic to Offic 74-77; Perm to Offic *Bris* 77-79; Lic to Offic 79-98. *Kingsbury Hall, The Green, Calne SN11 8DG* Tel (01249) 821521 Fax 817246 E-mail kingsburyhallcd@aol.com

WOODHOUSE, David Maurice. b 40. Lon Univ BA62. Clifton Th Coll 63. **d** 65 **p** 66. C Wellington w Eyton *Lich* 65-68; C Meole Brace 68-71; V Colwich 71-82; P-in-c Gt Haywood 78-82; R Clitheroe St Jas *Blackb* 82-88; Ellel Grange Chr Healing Cen 88-91; V The Lye and Stambermill *Worc* 91-99; Chapl Acorn Chr Foundn 99-02; Dioc Healing Adv *Guildf* 00-02; rtd 02. *1 Lilac Avenue, Penwortham, Preston PR1 9PB* Tel (01772) 742088 E-mail david.woodhouse@classicfm.net

WOODHOUSE, Hugh Frederic. b 12. TCD BA34 BD37 DD52. **d** 37 **p** 38. C Belfast St Donard *D & D* 37-39; C Bangor St Comgall 40-44; I Aghalee 44-46; I Newtownards 46-51; Prof Wycliffe Coll Toronto 51-54; Prin and Prof Angl Th Coll Vancouver 54-59; Prof Univ of K Coll Halifax 59-63; Regius Prof Div TCD 63-82; rtd 82. *4591 West 16th Avenue, Vancouver BC, Canada, V6R 3E8* Tel (001) (604) 224 4812

WOODHOUSE, Canon Keith Ian. b 33. K Coll Lon 54. **d** 58 **p** 59. C Stockton St Chad CD *Dur* 58-61; C Man St Aid *Man* 61-64; V Peterlee *Dur* 64-99; AD Easington 72-98; Hon Can Dur Cathl 79-99; rtd 99; Dioc Pensions and Widows Officer *Dur* from 00. *85 Baulkham Hills, Penshaw, Houghton le Spring DH4 7RZ* Tel and fax 0191-584 3977 E-mail keithianwoodhouse@excite.com

WOODHOUSE, Canon Patrick Henry Forbes. b 47. Ch Ch Ox BA69 MA81. St Jo Coll Nottm 69 Lon Coll of Div ALCD71 LTh71. **d** 72 **p** 73. C Birm St Martin *Birm* 72-74; C Whitchurch *Bris* 75-76; C Harpenden St Nic *St Alb* 76-80; Tanzania 80-81; Soc Resp Officer *Carl* 81-85; P-in-c Dean 81-85; Dir Soc Resp *Win* 85-90; V Chippenham St Andr w Tytherton Lucas *Bris* 90-00; Can Res and Prec Wells Cathl *B & W* from 00. *4 The Liberty, Wells BA5 2SU* Tel and fax (01749) 673188 E-mail pwoodhouse@liberty4.fsnet.co.uk

WOODHOUSE, Thomas Mark Bews. b 66. Cheltenham & Glouc Coll of HE BA98 Glos Univ MA05. Aston Tr Scheme 90 Westcott Ho Cam 92. **d** 95 **p** 96. C Cainscross w Selsley *Glouc* 95-98; V Hardwicke and Elmore w Longney from 98; P-in-c Wootton Bassett *Sarum* from 05. *The Vicarage, Glebe Road, Wootton Bassett, Swindon SN4 7DU* Tel (01793) 854302

WOODING JONES, Andrew David. b 61. Oak Hill Th Coll BA91. **d** 91 **p** 92. C Welling *Roch* 91-95; TV Crookes St Thos *Sheff* 95-00; Resident Dir Ashburnham Trust from 00; NSM Ashburnham w Penhurst *Chich* from 01. *Ashburnham Christian Trust, Ashburnham Place, Battle TN33 9NF* Tel (01424) 892244 Fax 894200 E-mail andrewwj@ashburnham.org.uk

WOODLEY, David James. b 38. K Coll Lon BD61 AKC61 Open Univ BA98. **d** 62 **p** 63. C Lancing St Jas *Chich* 62-64; C St Alb St Pet *St Alb* 64-67; Malaysia 67-70; Lic to Offic *Linc* 71-72; V Westoning w Tingrith *St Alb* 72-77; Asst Chapl HM Pris Wormwood Scrubs 77-78; Chapl HM Pris Cardiff 78-84; Chapl HM Rem Cen Risley 84-92; Chapl HM Pris Styal 92-98; rtd 98; Perm to Offic *Ches* from 98. *36 Brock Street, Macclesfield SK10 1DL* Tel (01625) 615222

WOODLEY, Canon John Francis Chapman. b 33. Univ of Wales (Lamp) BA58. Edin Th Coll 58. **d** 60 **p** 61. C Edin All SS *Edin* 60-65; Chapl St Andr Cathl *Ab* 65-67; Prec 67-71; R Glas St Oswald *Glas* 71-77; P-in-c Cumbernauld 77-93; Can St Mary's Cathl 82-99; CSG from 82; R Dalbeattie *Glas* 93-99; rtd 99; Hon Can St Mary's Cathl *Glas* from 99; Dioc Supernumerary from 99. *3 Highburgh Drive, Rutherglen, Glasgow G73 3RR* Tel 0141-647 3118 E-mail jfcwoodley@talk21.com

WOODLEY, The Ven Ronald John. b 25. Bps' Coll Cheshunt 50. **d** 53 **p** 54. C Middlesbrough St Martin *York* 53-58; C Whitby 58-61; C-in-c Middlesbrough Berwick Hills CD 61-66; V Middlesbrough Ascension 66-71; R Stokesley 71-85; RD Stokesley 77-85; Can and Preb York Minster 82-00; Adn Cleveland 85-91; rtd 91; Perm to Offic *Ripon* from 91 and *York* from 00. *2A Minster Court, York YO1 7JJ* Tel (01904) 679675

WOODLEY, Simon Andrew. b 66. Liv Univ BA88 Univ of Cen England in Birm 96. Ridley Hall Cam BTh00. **d** 00 **p** 01. C Birm St Martin w Bordesley St Andr *Birm* 00-04; TR Bemerton *Sarum* from 04. *St Michael's Rectory, St Michael's Road, Salisbury SP2 9EQ* Tel (01722) 333750

WOODMAN, Brian Baldwin. b 35. Leeds Univ BA57 PhD73. N Ord Course 84. **d** 87 **p** 88. C Guiseley w Esholt *Bradf* 87-90; TV Bingley All SS 90-94; P-in-c St Merryn *Truro* 94-00; rtd 00;

Perm to Offic *Truro* from 00. *Penty an Garth, Trevance, St Issey, Wadebridge PL27 7QF* Tel (01841) 541387

WOODMAN, Christopher James. b 65. Chich Th Coll BTh93. **d** 93 **p** 94. C Leigh-on-Sea St Marg *Chelmsf* 93-97; TV Canvey Is 97-00; TV Moulsecoomb *Chich* 00-03; C Brighton St Matthias from 03. *116 Brentwood Road, Brighton BN1 7ES* Tel (01273) 504382 E-mail cjw@btinternet.com

WOODMAN, Oliver Nigel. b 47. FCIPD. Sarum Th Coll 67. **d** 70 **p** 82. C Stepney St Dunstan and All SS *Lon* 70-71; NSM Ovingdean w Rottingdean and Woodingdean *Chich* 81-87; NSM Eastbourne St Sav and St Pet 88-93; Asst to RD Eastbourne 93-98; NSM Eastbourne St Sav and St Pet 98-01; NSM Stanmore *Win* from 02. *48 Old Kennels Lane, Winchester SO22 4JS* Tel (01962) 878937 E-mail oliver@seemp.co.uk *or* ojwoodman@ntlworld.com

WOODMAN, The Ven Peter Wilfred. b 36. Univ of Wales (Lamp) BA58. Wycliffe Hall Ox 58. **d** 60 **p** 61. C New Tredegar *Mon* 60-61; C Newport St Paul 61-64; C Llanfrechfa All SS 64-66; Abp of Wales's Messenger 66-67; V Llantilio Pertholey w Bettws Chpl etc *Mon* 67-74; V Bassaleg 74-90; Can St Woolos Cathl 84-01; V Caerwent w Dinham and Llanfair Discoed etc 90-96; Adn Mon 93-01; R Mamhilad and Llanfihangel Pontymoile 96-01; rtd 01. *Glaslyn, 40 Longhouse Barn, Penperlleni, Pontypool NP4 0BD* Tel (01873) 881322

WOODMANSEY, Michael Balfour. b 55. Leic Univ BSc. Ridley Hall Cam. **d** 83 **p** 84. C St Paul's Cray St Barn *Roch* 83-89; C S Shoebury *Chelmsf* 89-93; R Stifford 93-01; TR Heworth H Trin *York* from 01. *Heworth Rectory, Melrosegate, York YO31 0RP* Tel (01904) 422958 E-mail michael@mwoodmansey.freeserve.co.uk

WOODMORE, Mrs Dilys Mary. b 44. St Alb and Ox Min Course 98. **d** 01 **p** 02. NSM Dedworth *Ox* 01-04; NSM Burchetts Green from 04. *59 Terrington Hill, Marlow SL7 2RE* Tel (01628) 486274

WOODROFFE, Ian Gordon. b 46. Edin Th Coll 69. **d** 72 **p** 73. C Soham *Ely* 72-75; P-in-c Swaffham Bulbeck 75-80; Youth Chapl 75-80; V Cambridge St Jas 80-87; Chapl Mayday Univ Hosp Thornton Heath 87-94; Chapl Mayday Healthcare NHS Trust Thornton Heath 94-97; Staff Cllr Epsom and St Helier NHS Trust 97-02. *4 Station Road, Swaffham Bulbeck, Cambridge CB5 0NB* Tel (01223) 813122

WOODS, The Very Revd Alan Geoffrey. b 42. TD93. ACCA65 FCCA80. Sarum Th Coll 67. **d** 70 **p** 71. C Bedminster St Fran *Bris* 70-73; Youth Chapl 73-76; Warden Legge Ho Res Youth Cen 73-76; P-in-c Neston 76-79; TV Gtr Corsham 79-81; CF (TA) 80-94; P-in-c Charminster *Sarum* 81-83; V Charminster and Stinsford 83-90; RD Dorchester 85-90; Chapl Dorchester Hosps 86-87; V Calne and Blackland *Sarum* 90-96; RD Calne 90-96; Chapl St Mary's Sch Calne 90-96; Can and Preb Sarum Cathl *Sarum* 92-96; Sen Chapl Malta and Gozo *Eur* 96-03; Chan Malta Cathl 96-03; Dean Gib from 03; V Gen to Bp Eur 03-05; Adn Gib from 05. *The Deanery, Bomb House Lane, Gibraltar* Tel (00350) 78377 *or* 75745 Fax 78463 E-mail deangib@gibnet.gi

WOODS, Albert. b 12. St Paul's Coll Burgh St Chad's Coll Regina LTh47. **d** 41 **p** 42. Canada 41-50; C Huyton Quarry *Liv* 50-51; V Litherland St Andr 51-56; Chapl Whiston Co Hosp Prescot 50-51; CF (TA) 50-78; V Rainbow Hill St Barn *Worc* 56-61; P-in-c Tolladine 58-61; V Elmley Castle w Netherton and Bricklehampton 61-63; Dioc Adv on Chr Stewardship 58-63; Dir Chr Stewardship 63-66; V Hampton 66-71; V Upper w Nether Swell *Glouc* 71-78; rtd 78; Perm to Offic *Liv* 85-91 and *Worc* 91-02. *Fosbrooke House, 8 Clifton Drive, Lytham St Annes FY8 5RQ*

WOODS, Allan Campbell. b 32. MIEH59. Ox NSM Course 85. **d** 89 **p** 90. NSM W Wycombe w Bledlow Ridge, Bradenham and Radnage *Ox* 89-97; NSM Terriers 97-98; Perm to Offic from 98. *4 Pitcher's Cottages, Bennett End, Radnage, High Wycombe HP14 4EF* Tel (01494) 482083 E-mail allanwoods@email.msn.com

WOODS, Charles William. b 31. Lich Th Coll 55. **d** 58 **p** 59. C Hednesford *Lich* 58-62; V Wilnecote 62-67; V Basford 67-76; V Chasetown 76-81; P-in-c Donington 81-83; V 83-96; V Boningale 83-96; RD Shifnal 84-89; rtd 96; Perm to Offic *Lich* from 96. *17 Campion Drive, Telford TF2 7RH* Tel (01952) 677134

WOODS, Christopher Guy Alistair. b 35. Dur Univ BA60. Clifton Th Coll 60. **d** 62 **p** 63. C Rainham *Chelmsf* 62-65; C Edin St Thos *Edin* 65-69; Sec Spanish and Portuguese Ch Aid Soc 69-79; C Willesborough w Hinxhill *Cant* 74-80; P-in-c Murston w Bapchild and Tonge 80-87; R 87-90; R Gt Horkesley *Chelmsf* 90-98; RD Dedham and Tey 91-98; rtd 98; P-in-c Tenerife Sur *Eur* 99-00; Perm to Offic *Chelmsf* from 00. *Bluebonnet, Mill Lane, Bradfield, Manningtree CO11 2UT* Tel (01255) 870411

WOODS, Christopher Morrison. b 77. St Andr Univ MA00 TCD BTh04. CITC 01. **d** 04 **p** 05. C Dundela St Mark *D & D* from 04. *St Mark's Curatage, 29 Marmont Park, Belfast BT4 2GR* Tel and fax (028) 9076 1967 *or* tel 9065 4090 E-mail curate.dundela@down.anglican.org

WOODS, Canon Christopher Samuel. b 43. Cant Univ (NZ) BA. Qu Coll Birm 75. **d** 76 **p** 77. C Childwall All SS *Liv* 76-79; V Parr Mt 79-00; TV Parr 01-05; P-in-c St Helens St Helen from 05; AD St Helens from 00; Hon Can Liv Cathl from 03. *The Vicarage, 51A Rainford Road, St Helens WA10 6BZ* Tel (01744) 22067 E-mail csw@gasworksview.freeserve.co.uk

WOODS, David Arthur. b 28. Bris Univ BA52. Tyndale Hall Bris 48. **d** 53 **p** 54. C Camborne *Truro* 53-56; C Bromley Ch Ch *Roch* 56-58; V Tewkesbury H Trin *Glouc* 58-66; V Stapleford *S'well* 66-70; Miss to Seamen 70-93; Hon Chapl Miss to Seamen 70-93; V Fowey *Truro* 70-93; RD St Austell 80-88; rtd 93; Perm to Offic *Truro* from 93. *Linden, 7 Richmond Road, Pelynt, Looe PL13 2NH* Tel (01503) 220374

WOODS, David Benjamin. b 42. Linc Th Coll 88. **d** 90 **p** 91. C Louth *Linc* 90-93; P-in-c Ingoldmells w Addlethorpe 93-97; R 97-01; P-in-c Sutton Bridge from 01. *The Vicarage, 79 Bridge Road, Sutton Bridge, Spalding PE12 9SD* Tel (01406) 351503

WOODS, David Edward. b 36. City Univ FBCO61 FSMC61. SW Minl Tr Course 83 S Dios Minl Tr Scheme 94. **d** 95 **p** 96. NSM Bemerton *Sarum* 95-98; NSM Salisbury St Martin 98-00; NSM Laverstock 98-00; NSM Salisbury St Martin and Laverstock 00-05; Perm to Offic *Truro* from 05. *8 Tower Meadows, St Buryan, Penzance TR19 6AJ* Tel (01736) 811253

WOODS, Edward Christopher John. b 44. NUI BA67. CITC 66. **d** 67 **p** 68. C Drumglass *Arm* 67-70; C Belfast St Mark *Conn* 70-73; I Kilcolman *L & K* 73-78; I Portarlington w Cloneyhurke and Lea *M & K* 78-84; Chan Kildare Cathl 81-84; I Killiney Ballybrack *D & G* 85-92; I Dublin Rathfarnham from 93; Dir of Ords (Dub) from 98. *Rathfarnham Rectory, Rathfarnham, Terenure, Dublin 6W, Irish Republic* Tel and fax (00353) (1) 490 5543 E-mail anneted@gofree.indigo.ie

WOODS, Canon Eric John. b 51. Magd Coll Ox BA72 MA77 Trin Coll Cam BA77 MA83 FRSA94. Westcott Ho Cam 75. **d** 78 **p** 79. C Bris St Mary Redcliffe w Temple etc *Bris* 78-81; Hon C Clifton St Paul 81-83; Asst Chapl Bris Univ 81-83; V Wroughton 83-93; RD Wroughton 88-93; V Sherborne w Castleton and Lillington *Sarum* from 93; Chapl Sherborne Sch for Girls from 93; RD Sherborne *Sarum* 96-04; Can and Preb Sarum Cathl from 98; Chapl Dorset Community NHS Trust 93-00; Chapl SW Dorset Primary Care Trust from 01. *The Vicarage, Abbey Close, Sherborne DT9 3LQ* Tel (01935) 812452 Fax 812206 E-mail vicar@sherborneabbey.com

WOODS, Frederick James. b 45. Southn Univ BA66 MPhil74 Fitzw Coll Cam BA76 MA79. Ridley Hall Cam 74. **d** 77 **p** 78. C Stratford-on-Avon w Bishopton *Cov* 77-81; V Warminster Ch Ch *Sarum* 81-96; RD Heytesbury 95-96; TR Woodley *Ox* 96-01; V Colchester St Pet and St Botolph *Chelmsf* from 01. *St Peter's Vicarage, Balkerne Close, Colchester CO1 1NZ* Tel (01206) 572641 E-mail fredjwoods@hotmail.com

WOODS, Geoffrey Edward. b 49. Lon Univ BD70 K Coll Lon MA94. Tyndale Hall Bris 67. **d** 73 **p** 74. C Gipsy Hill Ch Ch *S'wark* 73-76; C Uphill *B & W* 76-79; R Swainswick w Langridge and Woolley 79-84; Perm to Offic *Bris* 84-96; NSM Colerne w N Wraxall from 96. *22 Watergates, Colerne, Chippenham SN14 8DR* Tel (01225) 743675

WOODS, Canon John Mawhinney. b 19. Edin Th Coll 55. **d** 58 **p** 59. C Kirkcaldy *St And* 58-60; R Walpole St Peter *Ely* 60-75; R Inverness St Andr *Mor* 75-80; Provost St Andr Cathl Inverness 75-80; Hon Can St Andr Cathl Inverness from 80; V The Suttons w Tydd *Linc* 80-85; rtd 85; Perm to Offic *Nor* from 85. *24 Queen Street, King's Lynn PE30 1HT* Tel (01553) 762569

WOODS, John William Ashburnham. b 22. Reading Univ BSc50. NW Ord Course 73 St Jo Coll Lusaka 69. **d** 71 **p** 74. Zambia 71-72; C Goole *Sheff* 73-75; P-in-c Firbeck w Letwell 75-76; R 76-82; P-in-c Woodsetts 75-76; V 76-82; Bp's Rural Adv 80-92; R Barnburgh w Melton on the Hill 82-92; RD Wath 86-92; rtd 92; NSM Birdsall w Langton *York* 93-96; P-in-c Settrington w N Grimston, Birdsall w Langton 96-98; Perm to Offic from 00. *The Vicarage, 2 Cromarty Cottages, Birdsall, Malton YO17 9NN* Tel (01944) 768374 E-mail revjwoods@btinternet.com

WOODS, Joseph Richard Vernon. b 31. Solicitor 57. Cuddesdon Coll 58. **d** 60 **p** 61. C Newc St Gabr *Newc* 60-63; Trinidad and Tobago 63-67; Chapl Long Grove Hosp Epsom 67-76; P-in-c Ewell St Fran *Guildf* 76-79; V 79-87; V Englefield Green 87-96; rtd 96; Perm to Offic *Win* from 97. *8 Wren Close, Christchurch BH23 4BD* Tel (01425) 270799

WOODS, Michael. b 57. Preston Poly DipMechE79. Ripon Coll Cuddesdon 99. **d** 01 **p** 02. C Bamber Bridge St Aid *Blackb* from 01. *6 Bluebell Way, Bamber Bridge, Preston PR5 6XQ* Tel (01772) 311073 E-mail woodsfamily@cuddesdon.fsnet.co.uk

WOODS, Canon Michael Spencer. b 44. K Coll Lon BD66 AKC66 Hull Univ DipMin88 Sheff Univ MMinTheol99. **d** 67 **p** 68. C Sprowston *Nor* 67-70; Malaysia 70-74; TV Hempnall *Nor* 74-79; TV Halesworth w Linstead, Chediston, Holton etc *St E* 79-85; TR Braunstone *Leic* 85-92; RD Sparkenhoe E 89-91; TR Gt Yarmouth *Nor* from 92; Hon Can Nor Cathl from 96. *The Rectory, 1 Osborne Avenue, Great Yarmouth NR30 4EE* Tel (01493) 850666 E-mail michael.woods@rjt.co.uk

WOODS, Canon Norman Harman. b 35. K Coll Lon BD62 AKC62. **d** 63 **p** 64. C Poplar All SS w St Frideswide *Lon* 63-68; C-in-c W Leigh CD *Portsm* 68-76; V Hythe *Cant* 76-01; RD Elham 83-89; Hon Can Cant Cathl 90-01; rtd 01; Perm to Offic *Cant* from 01. *36 Abbey Gardens, Canterbury CT2 7EU* Tel (01227) 470957 E-mail norman.woods@tesco.net

WOODS, Richard. *See* WOODS, Joseph Richard Vernon

WOODS, Richard Thomas Evelyn Brownrigg. b 51. St Steph Ho Ox 83. **d** 85 **p** 86. C Southgate Ch Ch *Lon* 85-88; C Northampton All SS w St Kath *Pet* 88-89; V Maybridge *Chich* 89-99; R Singleton from 99; V E Dean from 99; V W Dean from 99. *The Rectory, Singleton, Chichester PO18 0EZ* Tel and fax (01243) 811213 E-mail rector_singleton@hotmail.com

WOODS, Roger Andrew. b 60. Southn Univ BSc81. Oak Hill Th Coll DipHE97 BA01. **d** 98 **p** 99. C Audley *Lich* 98-02; TV Leek and Meerbrook from 02. *St Luke's Vicarage, Novi Lane, Leek ST13 6NR* Tel (01538) 386109

WOODS, Tanya Joy. b 73. CITC 99. **d** 02 **p** 03. NSM Killesher *K, E & A* from 02. *Cornacrea, Cavan Town, Irish Republic* Tel (00353) (49) 433 2188 *or* (42) 966 9229 Mobile 87-233 4534 Fax (42) 966 9119 E-mail tanya@roeoils.com

WOODS, Theodore Frank Spreull. b 37. Cam Univ BA58 DipEd80. Wells Th Coll 60. **d** 62 **p** 63. C Stocking Farm CD *Leic* 62-67; Papua New Guinea 67-77; V Knighton St Jo *Leic* 77-80; Australia from 80; Chapl Angl Ch Gr Sch Brisbane 80-88; Chapl Hillbrook Angl Sch from 89; rtd 03. *44 Merle Street, Carina, Qld, Australia 4152* Tel (0061) (7) 3398 4437 *or* 3354 3422 Fax 3354 1057

WOODS, Timothy James. b 52. Poly Cen Lon BA78 MSc79 Ex Univ MA96 ACIB75 PACTA88. Qu Coll Birm 81. **d** 83 **p** 84. C Brierley Hill *Lich* 83-86; C Stoneydelph St Martin CD 86-88; World Development Officer 86-88; Chr Aid Area Sec (SE Lon) 88-91; V Estover *Ex* 91-97; TR Brixham w Churston Ferrers and Kingswear 97-00; Dir Bd of Ch and Soc *Sarum* from 00; RD Salisbury from 05; Advocacy and Middle E Desk Officer USPG from 05. *The Vicarage, 14 Church Road, Laverstock, Salisbury SP1 1QX* Tel (01722) 349152 *or* (020) 7928 8681 E-mail timber.woods@surefish.co.uk

WOODS, Mrs Valerie Irene. b 44. Trin Coll Bris 82. **dss** 84 **d** 87 **p** 94. Coleford w Staunton *Glouc* 84-88; C 87-88; TD Bedminster *Bris* 88-94; TV 94-95; Chapl HM Rem Cen Pucklechurch 95-96; Chapl HM Pris Eastwood Park 96-00; V Wood End *Cov* from 01. *St Chad's Vicarage, Hillmorton Road, Coventry CV2 1FY* Tel (024) 7661 2909 E-mail val.woods@surefish.co.uk

WOODSFORD, Canon Andrew Norman. b 43. Nottm Univ BA65. Ridley Hall Cam 65. **d** 67 **p** 68. C Radcliffe-on-Trent *S'well* 67-70; P-in-c Ladybrook 70-73; P-in-c Barton in Fabis 73-81; P-in-c Thrumpton 73-81; R Gamston w Eaton and W Drayton 81-88; Chapl Bramcote Sch Notts 81-93; Warden of Readers *S'well* from 88; Hon Can S'well Minster from 93; RD Retford 93-00. *The Rectory, Gamston, Retford DN22 0QB* Tel (01777) 838706 E-mail woodsford@.msn.com

WOODSFORD, Martyn Paul. b 64. Oak Hill Th Coll 01. **d** 03 **p** 04. C Southover *Chich* from 03. *The Vicarage, Church Lane, Lewes BN7 2JA* Tel (01273) 474387 Mobile 07904-239842

WOODSIDE, David. b 60. St Jo Coll Dur BA81. Cranmer Hall Dur 87. **d** 90 **p** 91. C Stoke Newington St Mary *Lon* 90-92. *Address temp unknown*

WOODWARD, Andrew John. b 59. ACIB85. SEITE 96. **d** 99 **p** 00. NSM Weybridge *Guildf* 99-03; NSM St Botolph Aldgate w H Trin Minories *Lon* from 03; Perm to Offic *Guildf* from 03. *22 Moorholme, Woking GU22 7QZ* Tel (01483) 771331 E-mail thewoodys1@tiscali.co.uk

WOODWARD, Anthony John. b 50. Salford Univ BSc78. St Jo Coll Nottm 79. **d** 81 **p** 82. C Deane *Man* 81-84; CF 84-87; R Norris Bank *Man* 87-90; V Lostock St Thos and St Jo 92-96; Perm to Offic 96-01; C Halliwell 01-02; TV 02-04; P-in-c Chard and Distr *B & W* from 04. *The Vicarage, 2 Glebe Court, Forton Road, Chard TA20 2HJ* Tel (01460) 62320 *or* 67867 E-mail stmary@fish.co.uk

WOODWARD, Arthur Robert Harry (Bob). b 28. **d** 76 **p** 77. Rhodesia 76-80; Zimbabwe 80-87; Adn E Harare 82-87; R Wymington w Podington *St Alb* 87-97; RD Sharnbrook 89-97; rtd 97; Perm to Offic *Portsm* from 97. *9 Briarfield Gardens, Horndean, Waterlooville PO8 9HX* Tel (023) 9259 6983 E-mail woodward@bushinternet.com

WOODWARD, Clive Ian. b 49. City of Lon Poly BSc84. STETS 01. **d** 04 **p** 05. NSM Willingdon *Chich* from 04. *61 Rowan Avenue, Eastbourne BN22 0RX* Tel (01323) 509891 E-mail woodwards@surefish.co.uk

WOODWARD, Ian. b 44. OLM course 96. **d** 97 **p** 98. OLM Queen Thorne *Sarum* 97-99; Adv to Bd of Ch and Soc 97-00; NSM Wilton w Netherhampton and Fugglestone 00-02; R Bere Regis and Affpuddle w Turnerspuddle from 02. *The Vicarage, West Street, Bere Regis, Wareham BH20 7HQ* Tel (01929) 471262 Mobile 07973-318866 E-mail revianw@btinternet.com

WOODWARD, James Welford. b 61. K Coll Lon BD82 AKC82 Lambeth STh85 Birm Univ MPhil91 Open Univ PhD99. Westcott Ho Cam 83. **d** 85 **p** 86. C Consett *Dur* 85-87; Bp's Dom Chapl *Ox* 87-90; Chapl Qu Eliz Hosp Birm 90-96; Distr Chapl Co-ord S Birm HA 90-96; Chapl Manager Univ Hosp Birm NHS Trust 92-96; P-in-c Middleton *Birm* 96-98; P-in-c Wishaw 96-98; Bp's Adv on Health and Soc Care from 96; V Temple Balsall from 98; Master Foundn and Hosp of Lady Katherine Leveson from 98; Dir Leveson Cen for the Study of Ageing, Spirituality and Soc Policy from 00. *Temple House, Fen End Road, Knowle, Solihull B93 0AN* Tel (01564) 772415 Fax 778432 E-mail james.w.woodward@btinternet.com

WOODWARD, Canon John Clive. b 35. Univ of Wales (Lamp) BA56. St Jo Coll Dur 56. **d** 58 **p** 59. C Risca *Mon* 58-63; C Chepstow 63-66; V Ynysddu 66-74; V Newport Ch Ch 74-84; Can St Woolos Cathl 82-00; TR Cyncoed 84-00; rtd 00. *17 Carisbrooke Way, Cyncoed, Cardiff CF23 9HS* Tel (029) 2048 4448

WOODWARD, Mark Christian. b 73. Univ of Wales (Lamp) BA95 Trin Coll Carmarthen PGCE97. Trin Coll Bris MA02. **d** 02 **p** 03. C Egham *Guildf* from 02. *33 Grange Road, Egham TW20 9QP* Tel (01784) 434137 Mobile 07949-630031 E-mail mark@stjohnsegham.com

WOODWARD, Matthew Thomas. b 75. Brunel Univ BA97 K Coll Lon MA99 Anglia Poly Univ MA05. Westcott Ho Cam 99. **d** 01 **p** 02. C Hampstead St Jo *Lon* 01-05; P-in-c Pimlico St Sav from 05. *59 Aylesford Street, London SW1V 3RY* Tel (020) 7821 9865 Mobile 07971-573734 E-mail matthewwoodward@mac.com

WOODWARD, Maurice George. b 29. Selw Coll Cam BA56 MA58. Wells Th Coll 56. **d** 58 **p** 59. C Gedling *S'well* 58-61; Succ Leic Cathl *Leic* 61-64; Chapl Leic R Infirmary 62-64; CF (R of O) 63-94; V Barrow upon Soar *Leic* 64-77; Hon Chapl Leic Cathl 64-77; V Clare w Poslingford *St E* 77-85; P-in-c Stoke by Clare w Wixoe 84-85; R How Caple w Sollarshope, Sellack etc *Heref* 85-94; rtd 94; Perm to Offic *Glouc* 95-01; Hon C Northleach w Hampnett and Farmington etc from 01. *3 Bank Villas, West End, Northleach, Cheltenham GL54 3HG* Tel (01451) 860971

WOODWARD, Canon Peter Cavell. b 36. St Cath Coll Cam BA58 MA62. Bps' Coll Cheshunt 58. **d** 60 **p** 61. C Chingford St Anne *Chelmsf* 60-63; Madagascar 63-75; V Weedon Bec *Pet* 75-76; P-in-c Everdon 75-76; V Weedon Bec w Everdon 76-81; RD Daventry 79-81; Can Pet Cathl 81-02; V Brackley St Pet w St Jas 81-02; Chapl Brackley Cottage Hosp 81-02; RD Brackley 82-88; rtd 02; Perm to Offic *Pet* from 02. *7 Glastonbury Road, Northampton NN4 8BB* Tel (01604) 660679 E-mail pcwoodward@lineone.net

WOODWARD, Reginald Charles Huphnill. b 19. Lon Univ BA41 DipEd FRGS FRAS. Wells Th Coll 41. **d** 43 **p** 44. C Linc St Giles *Linc* 43-46; Succ St Mary's Cathl *Edin* 46-51; Hd Master St Mary's Cathl Choir Sch Edin 47-53; Lic to Offic *Linc* 53-95; Teacher K Sch Grantham 53-74; Hd Master K Lower Sch Grantham 74-79; rtd 79. *104 Harrowby Road, Grantham NG31 9DS* Tel (01476) 571912

WOODWARD, Richard Tharby. b 39. Man Univ BA60. Chich Th Coll 60. **d** 62 **p** 63. C Mansfield St Mark *S'well* 62-65; Chapl Liddon Ho Lon 65-69; C-in-c Beaconsfield St Mich CD *Ox* 69-76; TV Beaconsfield 76-94; rtd 94; Perm to Offic *Ox* 97-00. *10 Baring Crescent, Beaconsfield HP9 2NG* Tel (01494) 670690

WOODWARD, Robert. *See* WOODWARD, Arthur Robert Harry

WOODWARD, Roger David. b 38. WMMTC 87. **d** 90 **p** 91. C Castle Bromwich SS Mary and Marg *Birm* 90-93; C Kingstanding St Luke 93-04; C Kingstanding St Mark 93-04; rtd 04; Perm to Offic *Birm* from 04. *77 Bannersgate Road, Sutton Coldfield B73 6TY* Tel 0121-355 8497

WOODWARDS, David George. b 36. K Coll Lon BD62 MTh73. Oak Hill Th Coll 62. **d** 64 **p** 65. C Heworth H Trin *York* 64-66; Chapl St Pet Coll Kaduna Nigeria 67-71; V Edwardstone w Groton *St E* 72-82; RD Sudbury 81-88; R Glemsford 82-88; P-in-c Hartest w Boxted 85-86; P-in-c Stanstead w Shimplingthorne and Alpheton 85-86; P-in-c Lawshall 85-86; P-in-c Hartest w Boxted, Somerton and Stanstead 86-88; Hon Can St E Cathl 87-94; R Thorndon w Rishangles, Stoke Ash, Thwaite etc 88-94; RD Hartismere 88-93; rtd 98; Perm to Offic *St E* from 99 and *Chelmsf* from 03. *4 Cricketers Close, Sudbury CO10 2AL* Tel (01787) 374160 Fax 883312 E-mail tradrev@aol.com

WOOFF, Ms Erica Mielle. b 67. City Univ BSc90 Lon Inst of Educn MA95. SEITE 02. **d** 05. C Sydenham St Bart *S'wark* from 05. *St Bartholomew's Vicarage, 4 Westwood Hill, London SE26 6QR* E-mail ericauk@aol.com

WOOKEY, Mrs Frances Anne. b 52. ACII73. WEMTC 94. **d** 97 **p** 98. C Glouc St Jas and All SS *Glouc* 97-01; V Hanley Castle, Hanley Swan and Welland *Worc* from 01; RD Upton from 05. *The Vicarage, 5 Westmere, Hanley Swan, Worcester WR8 0DG* Tel (01684) 310321 E-mail fwookey@fides.demon.co.uk

WOOKEY, Stephen Mark. b 54. Em Coll Cam BA76 MA80. Wycliffe Hall Ox 77. **d** 80 **p** 81. C Enfield Ch Ch Trent Park *Lon*

80-84; Asst Chapl Paris St Mich *Eur* 84-87; C Langham Place All So *Lon* 87-96; R Moreton-in-Marsh w Batsford, Todenham etc *Glouc* from 96; RD Stow 99-04. *The Rectory, Bourton Road, Moreton-in-Marsh GL56 0BG* Tel (01608) 652680 E-mail stevewookey@mac.com

WOOLCOCK, Mrs Annette Elisabeth. b 56. Qu Coll Birm BTheol94. **d** 94 **p** 95. C Hethersett w Canteloff w Lt and Gt Melton *Nor* 94-96; C Stourport and Wilden *Worc* 96-00; P-in-c The Ampneys w Driffield and Poulton *Glouc* from 00. *The Rectory, Ampney Crucis, Cirencester GL7 5RY* Tel (01285) 851240

WOOLCOCK, Christine Ann. *See* FROUDE, Canon Christine Ann

WOOLCOCK, John. b 47. DipRK70 Open Univ BA82 BA86. Wm Temple Coll Rugby 69 Sarum & Wells Th Coll 70. **d** 72 **p** 73. C Kells *Carl* 72-76; C Barrow St Matt 76-78; R Distington 78-86; V Staveley w Kentmere 86-93; V Staveley, Ings and Kentmere 93; Soc Resp Officer 89-93; Hon Can Carl Cathl 91-93; TR Egremont and Haile from 93. *The Rectory, Grove Road, Egremont CA22 2LU* Tel (01946) 820268

WOOLCOCK, Mrs Olwen Sylvia. b 57. Birm Univ BA78. WEMTC 02. **d** 05. C Claines St Jo *Worc* from 05. *1 Tamarisk Close, Claines, Worcester WR3 7LE* Tel (01905) 758743 Mobile 07913-977579 E-mail olwen@woolcock.org

WOOLDRIDGE, Derek Robert. b 33. Nottm Univ BA57. Oak Hill Th Coll. **d** 59 **p** 60. C Chesterfield H Trin *Derby* 59-63; C Heworth w Peasholme St Cuth *York* 63-70; R York St Paul 70-00; rtd 01; Perm to Offic *York* from 01. *80 Grantham Drive, York YO26 4TZ* Tel (01904) 798393 E-mail drw@100york.freeserve.co.uk

WOOLDRIDGE, John Bellamy. b 27. Tyndale Hall Bris 54. **d** 56 **p** 57. C Norbury *Ches* 56-58; C Bramcote *S'well* 58-60; R Eccleston *Ches* 60-66; NW Area Sec CPAS 66-68; P-in-c Knutsford St Jo *Ches* 68-71; V Knutsford St Jo and Toft 71-79; V Gt Clacton *Chelmsf* 79-82; V Disley *Ches* 82-88; Min Buxton Trin Prop Chpl *Derby* 88-92; rtd 92; Perm to Offic *Derby* and *S'well* from 92. *227 Bramcote Lane, Nottingham NG8 2QL* Tel 0115-928 8332

WOOLHOUSE, Kenneth. b 38. BNC Ox BA61 MA65. Cuddesdon Coll 61. **d** 64 **p** 65. C Old Brumby *Linc* 64-67; W Germany 67-68; Chapl Cov Cathl *Cov* 68-75; C-in-c Hammersmith SS Mich and Geo White City Estate CD *Lon* 75-81; Dir Past Studies Chich Th Coll 81-86; P-in-c Birdham w W Itchenor *Chich* 81-86; Chapl W Sussex Inst of HE 86-95; TV N Lambeth *S'wark* 95-01; rtd 01; Perm to Offic *S'wark* from 01. *15 Tavistock Tower, Russell Place, London SE16 7PQ* Tel (020) 7237 8147

WOOLHOUSE, Miss Linda June. b 49. ACP76 CertEd70. WMMTC 85. **d** 88 **p** 94. Hon Par Dn Old Swinford Stourbridge *Worc* 88-92; Par Dn 93-94; Community Chapl 92-93; C Old Swinford Stourbridge 94-96; Black Country Urban Ind Miss *Lich* 96-01; Res Min W Bromwich All SS 96-01; V Pensnett *Worc* from 01. *St Mark's Vicarage, Vicarage Lane, Pensnett, Brierley Hill DY5 4JH* Tel and fax (01384) 262666 E-mail ljwstmark@nascr.net

WOOLLARD, David John. b 39. Leic Univ BSc62. Trin Coll Bris DipHE88. **d** 88 **p** 89. C Clifton *York* 88-91; C York St Luke 91-94; V Selby St Jas from 94; V Wistow 94-96. *St James's Vicarage, 14 Leeds Road, Selby YO8 4HX* Tel (01757) 702861

WOOLLASTON, Brian. b 53. CertEd76 DipTh83. St Paul's Coll Grahamstown 81. **d** 83 **p** 84. C Kington w Huntington, Old Radnor, Kinnerton etc *Heref* 88-89; C Tupsley 89-91; V Newbridge-on-Wye and Llanfihangel Brynpabuan etc *S & B* 91-98; CF 98-03; V Whiteshill and Randwick *Glouc* from 03. *The Vicarage, 98 Farmhill Lane, Stroud GL5 4DD* Tel (01453) 764757

WOOLLCOMBE (née DEARMER), Mrs Juliet. b 38. St Mary's Coll Dur BA60 Hughes Hall Cam DipEd61. Gilmore Course 74. **dss** 77 **d** 87 **p** 94. St Marylebone Ch Ch *Lon* 77-80; Dean of Women's Min (Lon Area) 87-89; Dn-in-c Upton Snodsbury and Broughton Hackett etc *Worc* 89-94; NSM Pershore w Pinvin, Wick and Birlingham 94-98; rtd 98; Perm to Offic *Worc* from 98. *19 Ashdale Avenue, Pershore WR10 1PL* Tel (01386) 556550 E-mail julietatashdale@talk21.com

✠**WOOLLCOMBE, The Rt Revd Kenneth John.** b 24. St Jo Coll Ox BA49 MA53 S Sewanee Univ STD63 Trin Coll Hartford (USA) Hon DD75. Westcott Ho Cam 49. **d** 51 **p** 52 **c** 71. C Gt Grimsby St Jas *Linc* 51-53; Fell Chapl and Lect St Jo Coll Ox 53-60; Tutor St Jo Coll Ox 56-60; USA 60-63; Prof Dogmatic Th Gen Th Sem NY 60-63; Prin Edin Th Coll 63-71; Can St Mary's Cathl *Edin* 63-71; Bp Ox 71-78; Asst Bp Lon 78-81; Can Res and Prec St Paul's Cathl 81-89; rtd 89; Asst Bp Worc from 89; Perm to Offic from 89. *19 Ashdale Avenue, Pershore WR10 1PL* Tel (01386) 556550

WOOLLEY, Canon Francis Bertram Hopkinson. b 43. Sarum & Wells Th Coll 75. **d** 78 **p** 79. C Halesowen *Worc* 78-81; TV Droitwich 81-86; TV Cambridge Ascension *Ely* 86-92; R Leverington 92-01; P-in-c Wisbech St Mary 92-98; P-in-c Southea w Murrow and Parson Drove 98-01; P-in-c Balsham 01-02; P-in-c W Wickham 01-02; P-in-c Weston Colville 01-02; P-in-c W Wratting 01-02; R Balsham, Weston Colville, W Wickham etc from 02; Hon Can Ely Cathl from 05. *The Rectory, 19 West Wratting Road, Balsham, Cambridge CB1 6DX* Tel (01223) 894010 E-mail francis.woolley@tesco.net

WOOLLEY, John Alexander. b 28. St Deiniol's Hawarden 61. **d** 63 **p** 64. C Garston *Liv* 63-65; C-in-c Gt Crosby St Luke 65-71; R Croft w Southworth 71-75; Chapl Cherry Knowle & Ryhope Hosps Sunderland 75-83; Chapl Cell Barnes Hosp St Alb 83-93; Chapl Hill End Hosp St Alb 83-93; rtd 93; NSM Niton *Portsm* 95-97; NSM Whitwell 95-97; NSM St Lawrence 95-97. *39 Falkland Road, Southport PR8 6LG*

WOOLLEY, Justine Clare. b 73. Plymouth Univ BSc95 SS Mary & Jo Coll Cheltenham PGCE98. Cranmer Hall Dur 03. **d** 05. C Dulverton and Brushford *B & W* from 05. *7 Valentines, Dulverton TA22 9ED* Tel (01398) 324051 Mobile 07863-345331 E-mail justine@surefish.co.uk

WOOLLEY, Miss Susan Margaret. b 41. Hockerill Coll of Educn TCert63. Dioc OLM tr scheme 97. **d** 00 **p** 01. NSM Catford (Southend) and Downham *S'wark* from 00. *195 Conisborough Crescent, London SE6 2SF* Tel (020) 8698 4437

WOOLMER, John Shirley Thursby. b 42. Wadh Coll Ox BA63 MA69. St Jo Coll Nottm 70. **d** 71 **p** 72. Asst Chapl Win Coll 72-75; C Ox St Aldate w H Trin *Ox* 75-82; R Shepton Mallet w Doulting *B & W* 82-02; Chapl Bath and West Community NHS Trust 97-01; Preb Wells Cathl *B & W* 00-02; NSM Leic H Trin w St Jo *Leic* from 02; Par Evang from 02. *Fig Tree Cottage, Hall Gates, Cropston, Leicester LE7 7GQ* Tel 0116-235 3569

WOOLMER, Kelvin Frederick. b 55. EAMTC 98. **d** 01 **p** 02. NSM Squirrels Heath *Chelmsf* from 01. *228 Pettits Lane North, Romford RM1 4PB* Tel (01708) 509913 *or* 782595 E-mail kelvinwoolmer@aol.com

WOOLNOUGH, Jeffrey Ralph. b 59. MCSD88. Coll of Resurr Mirfield 00. **d** 02 **p** 03. C Gt Ilford St Mary *Chelmsf* from 02. *5 Regent Gardens, Ilford IG3 8UL* Tel (020) 8597 7443 E-mail jwoolnough@hotmail.com

WOOLSTENHOLMES, Cyril Esmond. b 16. Bede Coll Dur BA37 MA41 DipTh38. **d** 39 **p** 40. C Leadgate *Dur* 39-44; C Darlington St Cuth 44-46; C W Hartlepool St Paul 46-50; V Tudhoe Grange 50-67; R Shadforth 67-82; rtd 82. *12 Wearside Drive, The Sands, Durham DH1 1LE* Tel 0191-384 3763

WOOLVEN, Ronald. b 36. Oak Hill Th Coll 60. **d** 63 **p** 64. C Romford Gd Shep Collier Row *Chelmsf* 63-68; C Widford 68-73; P-in-c Barling w Lt Wakering 73-84; V from 84. *154 Little Wakering Road, Great Wakering, Southend-on-Sea SS3 0JN* Tel (01702) 219200 E-mail r.woolven@btopenworld.com

WOOLVERIDGE, Gordon Hubert. b 27. Barrister-at-Law 52 CCC Cam BA51 MA55. S Dios Minl Tr Scheme 81. **d** 84 **p** 85. NSM St Edm the King w St Nic Acons etc *Lon* 84-85; NSM Chich St Paul and St Pet *Chich* 85-88; P-in-c Greatham w Empshott *Portsm* 88-90; P-in-c Hawkley w Prior's Dean 88-90; P-in-c Greatham w Empshott and Hawkley w Prior's Dean 90-92; rtd 92; Perm to Offic *Sarum* from 93. *Brook House, Winfrith Newburgh, Dorchester DT2 8JH* Tel (01305) 853633

WOOLWAY, Joanne. *See* GRENFELL, Joanne Woolway

WOOLWICH, Area Bishop of. *See* CHESSUN, The Rt Revd Christopher Thomas James

WOON, Edward Charles. b 43. SW Minl Tr Course 94. **d** 96 **p** 97. OLM Tuckingmill *Truro* 96-02; P-in-c from 02; TV Redruth w Lanner and Treleigh from 04. *All Saints' Vicarage, 35 Roskear, Camborne TR14 8DG* Tel (01209) 715910 Mobile 07974-431863 E-mail eddie.woon@btopenworld.com

WOOSTER, Patrick Charles Francis. b 38. Qu Coll Birm 63. **d** 65 **p** 66. C Chippenham St Andr w Tytherton Lucas *Bris* 65-70; C Cockington *Ex* 70-72; V Stone w Woodford *Glouc* 72-73; P-in-c Hill 72-73; V Stone w Woodford and Hill 73-99; rtd 99; Perm to Offic *Worc* from 99. *20 Hylton Road, Hampton, Evesham WR11 2QB* Tel (01386) 45907

WOOSTER, Mrs Ruth Mary. b 45. St Alb and Ox Min Course 95. **d** 98 **p** 99. OLM High Wycombe *Ox* from 98. *Homewood, 45 New Road, Sands, High Wycombe HP12 4LH* Tel (01494) 530087 E-mail ruth@woosies.freeserve.co.uk

WOOTTON, Philip Charles. b 63. Hatf Coll Dur BA85 Dur Inst of Educn PGCE86. Cranmer Hall Dur 98. **d** 00 **p** 01. C Meopham w Nurstead *Roch* 00-04; TV S Chatham H Trin from 04. *29 Keefe Close, Chatham ME5 9AG* Tel (01634) 660087 E-mail philwootton@supanet.com

WORCESTER, Archdeacon of. *See* TETLEY, The Ven Joy Dawn

WORCESTER, Bishop of. *See* SELBY, The Rt Revd Peter Stephen Maurice

WORCESTER, Dean of. *See* MARSHALL, The Very Revd Peter Jerome

WORDSWORTH, Jeremy Nathaniel. b 30. Clare Coll Cam BA54 MA58. Ridley Hall Cam 54. **d** 56 **p** 57. C Gt Baddow *Chelmsf* 56-59; Chapl Felsted Sch 59-63; Chapl Sherborne Sch 63-71; PV and Succ S'wark Cathl *S'wark* 71-73; P-in-c Stone *Worc* 73-77; V Malvern St Andr 77-82; V Combe Down w

Monkton Combe and S Stoke *B & W* 82-95; rtd 95. *4 The Glebe, Hinton Charterhouse, Bath BA2 7SB* Tel (01225) 722520 E-mail hintonwordys@ukonline.co.uk

WORDSWORTH, Paul. b 42. Birm Univ BA64 Hull Univ DipMin89. Wells Th Coll 64. **d** 66 **p** 67. C Anlaby St Pet *York* 66-71; C Marfleet 71-72; TV 72-77; V Sowerby 77-90; P-in-c Sessay 77-90; V York St Thos w St Maurice 90-01; Dioc Community Miss Project Ldr from 90; Abp's Miss Adv 96-00; Miss Strategy Development Officer from 01; Abp's Officer for Miss and Evang from 01. *12 Muncastergate, Heworth, York YO31 9LA* Tel (01904) 427035 Fax 427034

WORGAN, Maurice William. b 40. Ely Th Coll 62 Sarum Th Coll 64. **d** 65 **p** 66. C Cranbrook *Cant* 65-69; C Maidstone St Martin 69-72; P-in-c Stanford w Postling and Radegund 72-73; R Lyminge w Paddlesworth 72-73; R Lyminge w Paddlesworth, Stanford w Postling etc 73-88; V Cant St Dunstan w H Cross from 88. *St Dunstan's Vicarage, 5 Harkness Drive, Canterbury CT2 7RW* Tel (01227) 463654 Fax as telephone E-mail maurice@maurice-worgan.co.uk

WORKMAN, David Andrew. b 22. MICS49 AMBIM78 FBIM80. Arm Aux Min Course 87. **d** 90 **p** 91. C Dundalk w Heynestown *Arm* 90-97; rtd 97; Lic to Offic *Arm* from 97. *Dunbeag, Togher, Drogheda, Co Louth, Irish Republic* Tel (00353) (41) 685 2171

WORKMAN, John Lewis. b 26. St Deiniol's Hawarden 82. **d** 83 **p** 84. C Brecon St Mary and Battle w Llanddew *S & B* 83-86; Min Can Brecon Cathl 83-86; P-in-c Swansea St Luke 86-87; V 87-95; rtd 95. *12 Grove House, Clyne Close, Mayals, Swansea SA3 5HL* Tel (01792) 405674

WORLEDGE, Paul Robert. b 70. Hertf Coll Ox BA91 Lon Inst of Educn PGCE92. Oak Hill Th Coll BA00. **d** 00 **p** 01. C Boscombe St Jo *Win* 00-04; V Ramsgate St Luke *Cant* from 04. *St Luke's Vicarage, St Luke's Avenue, Ramsgate CT11 7JX* Tel (01843) 592562 E-mail worledge@bigfoot.com

WORLEY, William. b 37. TD89. Cranmer Hall Dur 69. **d** 72 **p** 73. C Consett *Dur* 72-76; V Seaton Carew 76-03; CF (TA) from 77; rtd 03. *5 Peakston Close, Hartlepool TS26 0PN*

WORMALD, Roy Henry. b 42. Chich Th Coll 64. **d** 67 **p** 68. C Walthamstow St Mich *Chelmsf* 67-69; C Cov St Thos *Cov* 69-72; C Cov St Jo 69-72; C Wood Green St Mich *Lon* 72-77; P-in-c Hanwell St Mellitus 77-80; V Hanwell St Mellitus w St Mark 80-95; C Hillingdon St Jo 95-99; R Kirkley St Pet and St Jo *Nor* from 99. *St Peter's Rectory, Rectory Road, Lowestoft NR33 0ED* Tel (01502) 502155

WORN, Nigel John. b 56. Sarum & Wells Th Coll. **d** 84 **p** 85. C Walworth St Jo *S'wark* 84-88; Succ S'wark Cathl 88-92; V Mitcham Ascension 92-01; RD Merton 97; V Kew from 01. *The Vicarage, 278 Kew Road, Kew, Richmond TW9 3EE* Tel (020) 8940 4616 E-mail nigel.worn@which.net

WORRALL, Frederick Rowland. b 27. **d** 86 **p** 87. NSM Chellaston *Derby* 86-93; NSM Barrow-on-Trent w Twyford and Swarkestone 94-97; Perm to Offic from 97. *37 St Peter's Road, Chellaston, Derby DE73 6UU* Tel (01332) 701890

WORRALL, Peter Henry. b 62. CA Tr Coll 85 WMMTC 93. **d** 95 **p** 96. C Bromsgrove St Jo *Worc* 95-99; P-in-c Hartlebury 99-04. *Address temp unknown*

WORRALL, Suzanne. *See* SHERIFF, Canon Suzanne

WORSDALL, John Robin. b 33. Dur Univ BA57. Linc Th Coll 62. **d** 63 **p** 64. C Manthorpe w Londonthorpe *Linc* 63-66; C Folkingham w Laughton 66-68; V New Bolingbroke w Carrington 68-74; P-in-c S Somercotes 74-80; V N Somercotes 74-80; P-in-c Stickney 80-82; P-in-c E Ville w Mid Ville 80-82; P-in-c Stickford 80-82; R Stickney Gp 82-98; rtd 98. *2 Streathers Court, Raunds, Wellingborough NN9 6DR* Tel (01933) 460078

WORSDELL, William Charles. b 35. AKC59. **d** 60 **p** 61. C Glouc St Aldate *Glouc* 60-66; V Devonport St Barn *Ex* 66-72; R Uplyme 72-77; R Withington and Compton Abdale w Haselton *Glouc* 77-87; V Badgeworth w Shurdington 87-95; rtd 95; Perm to Offic *Ex* 97-99; *Pet* 00-02; *St Alb* from 04. *Fairhaven, 13 Spriggs Close, Clapham, Bedford MK41 6GD* Tel (01234) 211990

WORSFOLD, Ms Caroline Jayne. b 61. St Steph Ho Ox. **d** 88 **p** 94. Chapl Asst Leic R Infirmary 88-90; C Sunderland Pennywell St Thos *Dur* 90-91; Sunderland HA Chapl 90-94; Chapl Priority Healthcare Wearside NHS Trust from 94. *Cherry Knowle Hospital, Ryhope, Sunderland SR2 0NB* Tel 0191-565 6256 ext 43370 *or* 522 7347

WORSFOLD, John. b 24. Keble Coll Ox BA50 MA50. Cuddesdon Coll 50. **d** 51 **p** 52. C Clapham H Spirit *S'wark* 51-62; C Richmond St Mary w St Matthias and St Jo 62-63; C Shirley St Geo *Cant* 63-80; C Croydon H Sav 80-84; C Croydon H Sav *S'wark* 85-89; rtd 90; Perm to Offic *S'wark* from 90. *26 Links Road, West Wickham BR4 0QW* Tel (020) 8777 7463

WORSFOLD, Richard Vernon. b 64. Ex Univ LLB86. Cranmer Hall Dur BA94. **d** 95 **p** 96. C Countesthorpe w Foston *Leic* 95-99; TV Bradgate Team 99-01; TR from 01. *The Vicarage, 15 Groby Road, Ratby, Leicester LE6 0LJ* Tel 0116-239 3009 E-mail rworsfold@btconnect.com *or* rworsfold@leicester.anglican.org

WORSLEY, Mrs Christine Anne. b 52. Hull Univ BA73 Bris Univ CertEd74 Birm Univ MPhil94. WMMTC 82. **dss** 84 **d** 87 **p** 94. Smethwick St Mary *Birm* 84-87; Par Dn Smethwick H Trin w St Alb 87-89; Par Dn Coventry Caludon *Cov* 89-91; Chapl Myton Hamlet Hospice 91-95; Tutor WMMTC 95-04; Minl and Adult Learning Officer *Ely* from 05. *2A Wisbech Road, Littleport, Ely CB6 1PR* Tel (01353) 861356 E-mail christine@worsleyc.fsnet.co.uk

WORSLEY, Howard John. b 61. Man Univ BA83 Leeds Univ PGCE85 Birm Univ PhD00. St Jo Coll Nottm MA93. **d** 93 **p** 94. C Huthwaite *S'well* 93-96; V Radford St Pet 96-01; Dir Studies St Jo Coll Nottm 02-04; Dir of Educn *S'well* from 04. *St Stephen's Vicarage, 18 Russell Road, Nottingham NG7 6HB* Tel 0115-978 7473 *or* (01636) 814504 E-mail hjworsley@aol.com *or* dde@southwell.anglican.org

WORSLEY, Malcolm. b 37. Carl Dioc Tr Inst 94. **d** 96 **p** 97. NSM Hawes Side *Blackb* 96-98 and 01-04; NSM Lt Thornton 98-01; rtd 04; Perm to Offic *Blackb* from 04. *14 Winslow Avenue, Carleton, Poulton-le-Fylde FY6 7PQ* Tel (01253) 882208 *or* 621859 Fax 751156 E-mail m_worsley@dial.pipex.com

WORSLEY, Richard John. b 52. Qu Coll Cam BA74 MA78 Univ of Wales CertEd76 Birm Univ MPhil91 Warwick Univ MA96. Qu Coll Birm DipTh79. **d** 80 **p** 81. C Styvechale *Cov* 80-84; V Smethwick H Trin w St Alb *Birm* 84-89; TV Coventry Caludon *Cov* 89-96; Hon C Binley 97-05. *2A Wisbech Road, Littleport, Ely CB6 1PR* Tel (01353) 861356

WORSLEY, Mrs Ruth Elizabeth. b 62. **d** 96 **p** 97. C Basford w Hyson Green *S'well* 96-99; C Hyson Green and Forest Fields 99-01; P-in-c from 01. *St Stephen's Vicarage, 18 Russell Road, Nottingham NG7 6HB* Tel 0115-978 7473 E-mail ruthworsley@aol.com

WORSNIP, Harry. b 29. Oldham Tech Coll HNC50. St Alb Minl Tr Scheme 89. **d** 92 **p** 93. NSM Arlesey w Astwick *St Alb* 92-96; NSM Goldington 96-99; Perm to Offic from 00. *28 Milburn Road, Bedford MK41 0NZ* Tel (01234) 266422

WORSSAM, Richard Mark. b 61. St Jo Coll Dur BA83 Selw Coll Cam BA92. Ridley Hall Cam CTM93. **d** 93 **p** 94. C Green Street Green and Pratts Bottom *Roch* 93-97; R Fawkham and Hartley from 97. *The Rectory, 3 St John's Lane, Hartley, Longfield DA3 8ET* Tel (01474) 703819

WORT, Gavin. b 78. K Alfred's Coll Win BTh99. Westcott Ho Cam 00. **d** 02 **p** 03. C Eastleigh *Win* from 02. *St Francis House, Nightingale Avenue, Eastleigh SO50 9JB* Tel (023) 8061 9949 E-mail gwort@hotmail.com

WORTH, Preb Frederick Stuart. b 30. Oak Hill Th Coll 60. **d** 62 **p** 63. C Okehampton w Inwardleigh *Ex* 62-68; R Dunkeswell and Dunkeswell Abbey 68-78; P-in-c Luppitt 69-72; P-in-c Upottery 72-76; V Sheldon 73-78; RD Honiton 77-84 and 86-90; R Uplyme 78-86; R Uplyme w Axmouth 86-00; Preb Ex Cathl 96-00; rtd 00; Perm to Offic *Ex* and *Sarum* from 00. *Yarrow, 3 Westcliff Road, Charmouth, Bridport DT6 6BG* Tel (01297) 560194

WORTHEN, Jeremy Frederick. b 65. Rob Coll Cam BA86 MPhil88 Toronto Univ PhD92. Ripon Coll Cuddesdon DipTh93 DipMin94. **d** 94 **p** 95. C Bromley SS Pet and Paul *Roch* 94-97; Tutor SEITE 97-05; Prin from 05. *SEITE, Ground Floor Offices, Sun Pier House, Medway Street, Chatham ME4 4HF* Tel (01634) 832299 E-mail j.f.worthen@kent.ac.uk

WORTHINGTON, George. b 35. AKC60. **d** 61 **p** 62. C Stockton St Pet *Dur* 61-65; C Poulton-le-Fylde *Blackb* 65-67; V Trawden 67-76; P-in-c Gressingham 76-78; P-in-c Arkholme 76-78; P-in-c Whittington 77-78; V Whittington w Arkholme and Gressingham 78-91; V Warton St Paul 91-00; rtd 00; Perm to Offic *Blackb* from 00 and *Carl* from 02. *4 Cavendish Gardens, Kirby Lonsdale, Carnforth LA6 3BW* Tel (01524) 271699

WORTHINGTON, Mark. b 55. Solicitor 80 Leeds Poly BA77. Cranmer Hall Dur 93. **d** 93 **p** 94. C Monkwearmouth St Andr *Dur* 93-96; C Chester le Street 96-00; V Harlow Green and Lamesley from 00. *The Vicarage, Lamesley, Gateshead NE11 0EU* Tel 0191-487 6490 E-mail mark.worthington@durham.anglican.org

WORTLEY, Prof John Trevor. b 34. Dur Univ BA57 MA60 DD86 Lon Univ PhD69 FRHistS. Edin Th Coll 57. **d** 59 **p** 60. C Huddersfield St Jo *Wakef* 59-64; Canada from 64; Prof Medical Hist Manitoba Univ from 69; Visiting Prof Sorbonne Univ from 99. *298 Yale Avenue, Winnipeg MB, Canada, R3M 0M1,* or *Manitoba University, Winnipeg MB, Canada, R3T 2N2* Tel (001) (204) 284 7554 *or* 474 9830 E-mail wortley@cc.umanitoba.ca

WORTLEY, Mrs Lyn Sharon. b 59. Open Univ BA94 Coll of Ripon & York St Jo MA98. N Ord Course 95. **d** 98 **p** 99. C Greasbrough *Sheff* 98-01; P-in-c Bramley and Ravenfield w Hooton Roberts etc 01-04; V Bramley from 04. *The Vicarage, 88 Main Street, Bramley, Rotherham S66 2SQ* Tel (01709) 702828 E-mail lyn@thewortleys.freeserve.co.uk

WORTON, David Reginald (Brother Paschal). b 56. St Steph Ho Ox 88. **d** 90 **p** 90. SSF from 77; NSM Anfield St Columba *Liv* 90-92; Zimbabwe 92-94; Asst P Harare Cathl 92-93; Asst P St Aug Miss Penhalonga 93-94; Lic to Offic *Newc* from 94. *The Friary, Alnmouth, Alnwick NE66 3NJ* Tel (01665) 830213

WOSTENHOLM, David Kenneth. b 56. Edin Univ BSc77 MB, ChB80 Southn Univ BTh88. Chich Th Coll 82. **d** 85 **p** 86. C Leytonstone St Marg w St Columba *Chelmsf* 85-90; V Brighton Annunciation *Chich* 90-01; TR Hove from 01; RD Hove from 03. *The Vicarage, Wilbury Road, Hove BN3 3PB* Tel (01273) 681341 E-mail david@glitterage.f9.co.uk

WOTHERSPOON, David Colin. b 36. Portsm Coll of Tech CEng65 MIMechE65. St Jo Coll Dur 76. **d** 78 **p** 79. C Blackb St Gabr *Blackb* 78-81; V Witton 81-90; Chapl Berne w Neuchâtel *Eur* 90-01; rtd 01; Perm to Offic *Blackb* from 01. *300 Pleckgate Road, Blackburn BB1 8QU* Tel (01254) 249743

WOTTON, David Ashley. b 44. Chich Th Coll 71. **d** 74 **p** 75. C Allington and Maidstone St Pet *Cant* 74-77; C Ham St Andr *S'wark* 78-79; Chapl HM Rem Cen Latchmere Ho 78-79; C Tattenham Corner and Burgh Heath *Guildf* 85-88; P-in-c E Molesey St Mary 88-93; R Headley w Box Hill from 93; Offg Chapl RAF from 93. *The Rectory, Headley, Epsom KT18 6LE* Tel (01372) 377327 E-mail dwotton@headley15.fsnet.co.uk

WRAGG, Christopher William. b 60. SEITE 97. **d** 00 **p** 01. C Gt Warley Ch Ch *Chelmsf* 00-01; C Warley Ch Ch and Gt Warley St Mary 01-04; TV Buckhurst Hill from 04. *10 Albert Road, Buckhurst Hill IG9 6EH* Tel (020) 8504 6698 Mobile 07714-507147 E-mail wragg@fish.co.uk

WRAGG, Peter Robert. b 46. Lon Univ BSc68. Sarum & Wells Th Coll 71. **d** 74 **p** 75. C Feltham *Lon* 74-79; TV Hackney 79-85; P-in-c Isleworth St Mary 85-94; V Feltham from 94. *The Vicarage, Cardinal Road, Feltham TW13 5AL* Tel (020) 8890 6681 *or* 8890 2011 E-mail pwragg@fish.co.uk

WRAIGHT, John Radford. b 38. St Chad's Coll Dur BA62 DipTh64. **d** 64 **p** 65. C Shildon *Dur* 64-67; C Newton Aycliffe 67-70; C Darlington St Jo 70-75; P-in-c Livingston LEP *Edin* 75-80; TV Carl H Trin and St Barn *Carl* 80-85; P-in-c Lindale w Field Broughton 85-95; R Middleton Tyas w Croft and Eryholme *Ripon* 95-03; rtd 03. *14 Colorado Grove, Darlington DL1 2YW* Tel (01325) 354613 E-mail j.r.wraight@amserve.net

WRAKE, John. b 28. RMA. Clifton Th Coll 56. **d** 59 **p** 60. C Gt Baddow *Chelmsf* 59-62; CF 62-66; V Tilton w Lowesby *Leic* 66-73; R Maresfield *Chich* 73-79; rtd 93. *Parkfield, Batts Ridge Road, Maresfield, Uckfield TN22 2HJ* Tel (01825) 762727

WRAPSON, Donald. b 36. St Aid Birkenhead 60. **d** 65 **p** 66. C Bacup St Sav *Man* 65-68; C Wolverhampton St Matt *Lich* 68-72; C Normanton *Derby* 72-78; V Dordon *Birm* 78-82; Chapl Birm Accident Hosp 82-92; Chapl Selly Oak Hosp Birm 82-92; Chapl Trauma Unit Birm Gen Hosp 92-95; Chapl S Birm Community Health NHS Trust 95-01; rtd 01; Perm to Offic *Birm* from 01 and *Worc* from 03. *37 Walkers Heath Road, Birmingham B38 0AB* Tel 0121-458 2995

WRATTEN, Martyn Stephen. b 34. AKC58 St Boniface Warminster 58. **d** 59 **p** 60. C Wandsworth Common St Mary *S'wark* 59-62; C Putney St Mary 62-65; C Pembury *Roch* 65-70; R Stone 70-76; Chapl Joyce Green Hosp Dartford 70-73; Stone Ho Hosp Kent 73-76; Hillcrest Hosp and Netherne Hosp Coulsdon 76-87; Hon C Netherne St Luke CD *S'wark* 76-87; V Gt Doddington *Pet* 87-88; V Gt Doddington and Wilby 88-95; Hon C N Petherton w Northmoor Green *B & W* 95-96; rtd 95; Perm to Offic *B & W* from 96. *1 Baymead Close, North Petherton, Bridgwater TA6 6QZ* Tel (01278) 662873

WRAW, The Ven John Michael. b 59. Linc Coll Ox BA81 Fitzw Ho Cam BA84. Ridley Hall Cam 82. **d** 85 **p** 86. C Bromyard *Heref* 85-88; TV Sheff Manor *Sheff* 88-92; V Clifton St Jas 92-01; P-in-c Wickersley 01-04; AD Rotherham 98-04; Hon Can Sheff Cathl 01-04; Adn Wilts *Sarum* from 04. *Southbroom House, London Road, Devizes SN10 1LT* Tel (01380) 729808 E-mail adwilts@salisbury.anglican.org

WRAY, Christopher. b 48. Hull Univ BA70 New Coll Ox DipTh73. Cuddesdon Coll 70. **d** 73 **p** 74. C Brighouse *Wakef* 73-76; C Almondbury 76-78; C Tong *Bradf* 78-80; V Ingleton w Chapel le Dale 80-86; R Brompton Regis w Upton and Skilgate *B & W* 86-91; V Yoxford and Peasenhall w Sibton *St E* 91-94; Perm to Offic *Carl* 94-97; R Brough w Stainmore, Musgrave and Warcop 97-02; R Walkingham Hill *Ripon* from 02. *The Rectory, Main Street, Staveley, Knaresborough HG5 9LD* Tel (01423) 340275

WRAY, Christopher Brownlow. b 46. Open Univ BA91. Oak Hill Th Coll 86. **d** 88 **p** 89. C Quidenham *Nor* 88-91; TV Chippenham St Paul w Hardenhuish etc *Bris* 91-97; P-in-c Chipping Sodbury and Old Sodbury *Glouc* from 97; P-in-c Horton and Lt Sodbury from 04. *The Vicarage, Horseshoe Lane, Chipping Sodbury, Bristol BS37 6ET* Tel (01454) 313159

WRAY, Karl. b 51. St And Coll Greystoke 72 Ian Ramsey Coll 74 Coll of Resurr Mirfield 75. **d** 78 **p** 79. C Salford St Phil w St Steph *Man* 78-83; CF 83-86 and 89-92; V Sculcoates St Paul w Ch Ch and St Silas *York* 86-89; V Carl St Luke Morton *Carl* from 92. *St Luke's Vicarage, Brownrigg Drive, Carlisle CA2 6PA* Tel and fax (01228) 515693 E-mail karl@wray6008.fsbusiness.co.uk

WRAY, Kenneth Martin. b 43. Linc Th Coll 72. **d** 75 **p** 76. C Shipley St Paul *Bradf* 75-79; V Edlington *Sheff* 79-85; V Nether Hoyland St Pet 85-97; V Up Hatherley *Glouc* 97-04. *5 Benall Avenue, Cheltenham GL51 6AF* Tel (01242) 236966 E-mail martin@wray111.fsnet.co.uk

WRAY, Martin John. b 51. St Steph Ho Ox 86. **d** 88 **p** 89. C E Boldon *Dur* 88-90; C Seaham w Seaham Harbour 90-92; P-in-c Chopwell 92-95; V 95-97; C Shildon 98-00; C Croxdale and Tudhoe 00-04; P-in-c from 04; C Spennymoor, Whitworth and Merrington from 04. *21 York Villas, Spennymoor DL16 6LP* Tel (01388) 818418

WRAY, Michael. b 49. Univ of Wales (Cardiff) BSc(Econ)77 Keele Univ PGCE78 RGN87. Ripon Coll Cuddesdon 80. **d** 82 **p** 83. C Blackpool St Steph *Blackb* 82-83; C Torrisholme 83-84; NSM Headington Quarry *Ox* 93-95; C Kennington *Cant* 95-99; CF (TA) 95-99; P-in-c Isham w Pytchley *Pet* 99-04; Chapl Rockingham Forest NHS Trust 99-01; Chapl Northants Healthcare NHS Trust 01-04; R Potterspury w Furtho and Yardley Gobion etc *Pet* from 04. *The Vicarage, 11 Church Lane, Potterspury, Towcester NN12 7PU* Tel (01908) 543990 E-mail revwray.aeiou@virgin.net

WRAYFORD, Geoffrey John. b 38. Ex Coll Ox BA61 MA65. Linc Th Coll 61. **d** 63 **p** 64. C Cirencester *Glouc* 63-69; Chapl Chelmsf Cathl *Chelmsf* 69-74; V 70-74; V Canvey Is 74-76; TR 76-80; P-in-c Woodlands *B & W* 80-88; V 89-92; P-in-c Frome St Jo 80-88; P-in-c Frome Ch Ch 80-85; P-in-c Frome St Mary 85-88; V Frome St Jo and St Mary 89-92; V Minehead 92-03; Chapl Taunton and Somerset NHS Trust 92-03; rtd 03. *Little Garth, Longmeadow Road, Lympstone, Exmouth EX8 5LF* Tel (01395) 267838 E-mail g.wrayford@breathemail.net

WREN, Ann. *See* WREN, Mrs Kathleen Ann

WREN, Christopher John. b 54. Dur Univ BEd76 MA85. St Steph Ho Ox 77. **d** 79 **p** 80. C Stockton St Pet *Dur* 79-82; C Newton Aycliffe 82-85; V Gateshead St Chad Bensham 85-91; TR Bensham 91-98; V Marton *Blackb* from 98. *St Paul's Vicarage, 55 Vicarage Lane, Marton, Blackpool FY4 4EF* Tel (01253) 762679 Fax 318791 E-mail wthenest@cs.com *or* wthenest@aol.com

WREN, Douglas Peter. b 59. Lanc Univ BA82. Trin Coll Bris BA88. **d** 88 **p** 89. C Nantwich *Ches* 88-91; C Chatham St Phil and St Jas *Roch* 91-94; R Kingsdown 94-02; R Speldhurst w Groombridge and Ashurst from 02. *The Rectory, Southfields, Speldhurst, Tunbridge Wells TN3 0PD* Tel (01892) 862821 E-mail douglas.wren@diocese-rochester.org

WREN, John Aubrey. b 46. St Chad's Coll Dur BA69 Sussex Univ MA92. Cuddesdon Coll 72. **d** 74 **p** 75. C Fenny Stratford and Water Eaton *Ox* 74-77; TV Brighton Resurr *Chich* 77-84; V Eastbourne St Andr 84-92; V Hove St Barn and St Agnes 92-96. *24 Marlborough Road, Lowestoft NR32 3BU* Tel (01502) 530243

WREN, Mrs Kathleen Ann. b 50. St Steph Ho Ox 83. **dss** 85 **d** 87. Gateshead St Cuth w St Paul *Dur* 85-86; Gateshead St Chad Bensham 86-91; Par Dn 87-91; Adv for Women's Min 90-98; Par Dn Bensham 91-94; C 94-98; Hon Can Dur Cathl 93-98; C Marton *Blackb* from 98. *St Paul's Vicarage, 55 Vicarage Lane, Marton, Blackpool FY4 4EF* Tel (01253) 762679 Fax 318791 E-mail wthenest@cs.com *or* wthenest@aol.com

WREN, Comdr Richard. b 35. S Dios Minl Tr Scheme 88. **d** 90 **p** 91. NSM Tisbury *Sarum* 90-01; TV 95-01; TV Nadder Valley from 01. *Gaston House, Tisbury, Salisbury SP3 6LG* Tel (01747) 870674 E-mail twowrens@tesco.net

WRENBURY, The Revd and Rt Hon Lord (John Burton Buckley). b 27. Solicitor 52 K Coll Cam BA48 MA48. S'wark Ord Course 87. **d** 90 **p** 91. NSM Brightling, Dallington, Mountfield etc *Chich* from 90. *Oldcastle, Dallington, Heathfield TN21 9JP* Tel (01435) 830400

WRENN, Peter Henry. b 34. Lon Univ BA56. Qu Coll Birm 58. **d** 60 **p** 61. C Dronfield *Derby* 60-64; C Hessle *York* 64-65; V Loscoe *Derby* 65-70; Asst Chapl Solihull Sch 71-77; Chapl 77-97; rtd 97; Perm to Offic *Birm* from 97. *63 Shakespeare Drive, Shirley, Solihull B90 2AN* Tel 0121-744 3941

WREXHAM, Archdeacon of. *See* SQUIRES, The Ven Malcolm

WRIGHT, Alan James. b 38. Chich Th Coll 63. **d** 66 **p** 67. C Edgehill St Dunstan *Liv* 66-69; Swaziland 69-71; P-in-c Seaforth *Liv* 71-76; V Taunton All SS *B & W* 76-95; rtd 99. *Bethel, Langford Lane, Norton Fitzwarren, Taunton TA2 6NZ* Tel (01823) 326558

WRIGHT, Alan Richard. b 31. LNSM course 95. **d** 96 **p** 97. OLM Quidenham Gp *Nor* 96-04; Perm to Offic from 04. *Upgate Farm, Carleton Rode, Norwich NR16 1NJ* Tel (01953) 860300

WRIGHT, Alan William. b 44. AMusTCL71 Hull Univ BA66 Bris Univ PGCE67. Local Minl Tr Course 87. **d** 95 **p** 96. OLM Barton upon Humber *Linc* from 95. *1 Birchdale, Barton-upon-Humber DN18 5ED* Tel (01652) 632364 E-mail wrightherewrightnow@hotmail.com

WRIGHT, Alfred John. b 22. Wycliffe Hall Ox 66. **d** 66 **p** 67. C Newbury St Jo *Ox* 66-71; V E Challow 71-91; Chapl Community of St Mary V Wantage 75-89; rtd 91; Perm to Offic *Ox* from 92. *3 Latton Close, Southmoor, Abingdon OX13 5AE* Tel (01865) 820625 E-mail sheba@eggconnect.net

WRIGHT, Andrew David Gibson. b 58. St Andr Univ MTheol81. Ridley Hall Cam. **d** 83 **p** 84. C W Derby Gd Shep *Liv* 83-86; C

Carl H Trin and St Barn *Carl* 86-88; V Wigan St Jas w St Thos *Liv* 88-91; Chapl St Edw Sch Ox 91-97; Ho Master from 97. *St Edward's School, Oxford OX2 7NN* Tel (01865) 319252 *or* 319204

WRIGHT, Anna Chang. b 55. **d** 02 **p** 03. OLM Blyth Valley *St E* from 02. *Rose End, Back Road, Wenhaston, Halesworth IP19 9DY* Tel (01502) 478411 E-mail awright@dircon.co.uk

WRIGHT, Miss Anne. b 39. Dalton Ho Bris 67. **dss** 76 **d** 87 **p** 94. BCMS Uganda 71-77; N Area Sec BCMS 78-88; Pudsey St Lawr and St Paul *Bradf* 82-88; Hon Par Dn 87-88; Par Dn Kingston upon Hull H Trin *York* 88-93; Hd of Min amongst Women CPAS 93-02; CPAS Consultant (W Midl) 96-02; Regional Consultant (Midl) 99-02; Perm to Offic *Cov* 93-04 and *York* from 04; rtd 02. *Oxenby, Whitby Road, Pickering YO18 7HL* Tel (01751) 472689 E-mail jacquelinewright@btopenworld.com

WRIGHT, Anthony. *See* WRIGHT, Derek Anthony

WRIGHT, Anthony John. b 47. ACA70 FCA77 Ex Univ MA98. Ripon Coll Cuddesdon 86. **d** 88 **p** 89. C Kidderminster St Mary and All SS w Trimpley etc *Worc* 88-91; P-in-c Offenham and Bretforton 91-96; R Backwell w Chelvey and Brockley *B & W* 96-02; RD Portishead 01-02; P-in-c Tetbury w Beverston *Glouc* 02-03; R from 03; P-in-c Shipton Moyne w Westonbirt and Lasborough 02-03; V Shipton Moyne from 03. *The Vicarage, 6 The Green, Tetbury GL8 8DN* Tel (01666) 502333 Fax 500893 E-mail sheba.wright@virgin.net

WRIGHT, Canon Anthony Robert. b 49. Lanchester Poly BA70. St Steph Ho Ox 70. **d** 73 **p** 74. C Amersham on the Hill *Ox* 73-76; C Reading St Giles 76-78; P-in-c Prestwood 78-84; P-in-c Wantage 84-87; V 87-92; RD Wantage 84-92; P-in-c W w E Hanney 88-91; V Portsea St Mary *Portsm* 92-98; Hon Can Portsm Cathl 96-98; R Westmr St Marg from 98; Chapl to Speaker of Ho of Commons from 98; Can Westmr Abbey from 98. *2 Little Cloister, London SW1P 3PL* Tel (020) 7654 4806 Fax 7654 4821 E-mail robert.wright@westminster-abbey.org

WRIGHT, Antony John. b 31. St Pet Coll Saltley CertEd53. Chan Sch Truro 76. **d** 79 **p** 80. NSM St Breoke *Truro* 79-84; TV Probus, Ladock and Grampound w Creed and St Erme 84-89; V Perranzabuloe 89-95; rtd 96; Perm to Offic *Truro* from 96. *Nansmoor Cottage, Hendrawna Lane, Bolingey, Perranporth TR6 0DF* Tel (01872) 572850

WRIGHT, Canon Barry Owen. b 38. S'wark Ord Course 66. **d** 69 **p** 70. C Plumstead Ascension *S'wark* 69-74; Hon C Welling 74-89; Hon Can S'wark Cathl 79-89; Sen Chapl W Midl Police *Birm* 89-93; Sen Chapl Metrop Police *Lon* from 93; V Mill Hill St Mich from 02. *St Michael's Vicarage, 9 Flower Lane, London NW7 2JA* Tel (020) 8959 1449 *or* 8358 1077 Fax 8906 1857 E-mail bwrg8@aol.com

WRIGHT, Preb Catherine Jane. b 62. Bris Univ BA84 MA92 PhD00 Selw Coll Cam BA96. Ridley Hall Cam 94. **d** 97 **p** 98. C Highworth w Sevenhampton and Inglesham etc *Bris* 97-00; Perm to Offic *Ex* 00-01; NSM Stoke St Gregory w Burrowbridge and Lyng *B & W* from 01; Dioc Voc Adv from 02; Assoc Dir of Ords from 02; Preb Wells Cathl from 05. *The Rectory, West Monkton, Taunton TA2 8QT* Tel (01823) 413380 E-mail cjwright@onetel.com

WRIGHT, Charles Frederick Peter. b 16. Qu Coll Ox BA39 MA42. Westcott Ho Cam 40. **d** 41 **p** 42. C Stocksbridge *Sheff* 41-43; C Goole 43-47; C Ecclesall 47-50; R Brown and Chilton Candover w Northington etc *Win* 50-54; V Long Sutton 54-61; V Welton *Linc* 61-69; Lect Linc Th Coll 61-63; Lic to Offic *Linc* 69-99; rtd 81. *9 Bromley College, London Road, Bromley BR1 1PE* Tel (020) 8460 9461

WRIGHT, Charles Kenneth (Ken). b 38. CEng73 MIMechE73 MBIM91. Sarum & Wells Th Coll DCM93. **d** 93 **p** 94. C Bridgwater St Mary, Chilton Trinity and Durleigh *B & W* 93-96; Chapl Workington *Carl* 96-03; C Camerton, Seaton and W Seaton 96-03; Chapl W Cumbria Health Care NHS Trust 96-01; Chapl N Cumbria Acute Hosps NHS Trust 01-03; rtd 03; Perm to Offic *Carl* from 03. *Naemair, 72 Ruskin Close, High Harrington, Workington CA14 4LS* Tel (01946) 833536 E-mail ckwright@fish.co.uk

WRIGHT, Christopher Joseph Herbert. b 47. St Cath Coll Cam BA69 MA73 PhD77. Ridley Hall Cam 75. **d** 77 **p** 78. C Tonbridge SS Pet and Paul *Roch* 77-81; Perm to Offic *St Alb* 82-01; BCMS India 83-88; Tutor and Dir Studies All Nations Chr Coll Ware 88-93; Prin from 93; Public Preacher *Lon* from 01. *All Nations Christian College, Easneye, Ware SG12 8LX* Tel (01920) 461243 Fax 462997

WRIGHT, Christopher Nigel. b 39. Kelham Th Coll 60. **d** 65 **p** 66. C Ellesmere Port *Ches* 65-69; C Latchford Ch Ch 69-72; C Gt Budworth 72-75; C Wigan St Andr *Liv* 75-76; V New Springs 77-82; C Dovecot 82-85; C Rainford 85-89; rtd 89; Perm to Offic *Liv* 89-01. *105 Ilfracombe Road, Sutton Leach, St Helens WA9 4NN* Tel (01744) 821199

WRIGHT, Clifford. *See* WRIGHT, The Rt Revd Royston Clifford

WRIGHT, Canon Clifford Nelson. b 35. K Coll Lon BD59 AKC59. **d** 60 **p** 61. C Stevenage *St Alb* 60-67; V Camberwell St Luke *S'wark* 67-81; RD Camberwell 75-80; Hon Can S'wark Cathl 79-80; TR Basingstoke *Win* 81-93; RD Basingstoke 84-93; Hon Can Win Cathl 89-00; R Win St Matt 93-00; rtd 00; Perm to Offic *Win* from 01. *1 Valley Dene, Dibden Purlieu, Southampton SO45 4NG* Tel (023) 8084 5898 E-mail cliffwright@waitrose.com

WRIGHT, David Evan Cross. b 35. K Coll Lon BD64 AKC64. **d** 65 **p** 66. C Morpeth *Newc* 65-69; C Benwell St Jas 69-70; C Bushey *St Alb* 70-74; V High Wych 74-77; R High Wych and Gilston w Eastwick 77-80; V St Alb St Mary Marshalswick 80-89; P-in-c Sandridge 87-89; R Lenham w Boughton Malherbe *Cant* 89-00; rtd 00; P-in-c Fuengirola St Andr *Eur* from 01; Perm to Offic *Chich* from 01. *Calle Paulino Uzcudun 16, 29640 Torreblanca, Fuengirola, Malaga, Spain* Tel (0034) (5) 247 2140 Fax as telephone

WRIGHT, David Henry. b 23. Keble Coll Ox BA48. St Steph Ho Ox 52. **d** 54 **p** 55. C Penton Street St Silas w All SS *Lon* 54-57; V Barnsbury St Clem 57-66; V Wandsworth St Anne *S'wark* 66-73; P-in-c Stanley *St And* 73-75; R Dunkeld 73-92; R Strathtay 75-92; rtd 92; Hon C Aberdeen St Marg *Ab* from 00. *28 Midstocket Mews, Aberdeen AB15 5FG* Tel (01224) 636554

WRIGHT, David William. b 63. Barrister 86 Liv Univ LLB85 Fitzw Coll Cam BA92 Cam Univ MA96 Univ of Wales (Cardiff) LLM99. Westcott Ho Cam 90. **d** 93 **p** 94. C Chorlton-cum-Hardy St Clem *Man* 93-97; P-in-c Donnington Wood *Lich* 97-99; V from 99. *The Vicarage, St George's Road, Donnington Wood, Telford TF2 7NJ* Tel and fax (01952) 604239 Mobile 07977-543735 E-mail david.wright@lichfield.anglican.org

WRIGHT, Denise Ann. b 42. **d** 98. Par Dn Machen *Mon* from 98. *56 St David's Drive, Machen, Newport CF83 8RH* Tel (029) 2088 5655

WRIGHT, Derek Anthony. b 35. ACP66 Lon Univ CertEd57. Cranmer Hall Dur 80. **d** 81 **p** 82. C Auckland St Andr and St Anne *Dur* 81-83; V Cornforth 83-87; P-in-c Thornley 87-88; R Gt and Lt Glemham, Blaxhall etc *St E* 88-90; V Evenwood *Dur* 90-93; P-in-c Satley and Tow Law 93-95; V 95-99; rtd 99. *39 Hilltop Road, Bearpark, Durham DH7 7TA*

WRIGHT, Edward Maurice Alexanderson. b 54. Wycliffe Hall Ox. **d** 88 **p** 91. C Maidstone St Luke *Cant* 88-93; R Cliffe at Hoo w Cooling *Roch* from 93. *St Helen's Rectory, Church Street, Cliffe, Rochester ME3 7PY* Tel (01634) 220220 E-mail emawright@talk21.com

WRIGHT, Edward Michael. b 37. St Cath Soc Ox BA61 MA65. Cuddesdon Coll DipTh63. **d** 64 **p** 65. C Willesden St Andr *Lon* 64-68; Bahamas 68-71; V Lewisham St Steph and St Mark *S'wark* 72-80; V Ox St Barn and St Paul *Ox* from 80. *St Barnabas' Vicarage, St Barnabas Street, Oxford OX2 6BG* Tel and fax (01865) 557530 E-mail michaelwright@cwcom.net

WRIGHT, Frank Albert. b 51. Portsm Univ MA02. Sarum & Wells Th Coll 80. **d** 83 **p** 84. C Buckingham *Ox* 83-86; C Newport Pagnell w Lathbury and Moulsoe 86-89; TV W Slough 89-95; TR 95-99; TR Fareham H Trin *Portsm* from 99; Dioc Interfaith Adv from 01. *The Rectory, 9 Brook Meadow, Fareham PO15 5JH* Tel and fax (01329) 280180 Fax 232688 E-mail wrightfa@fish.co.uk

WRIGHT, Frederic Ian. b 64. City Univ BSc85. Wycliffe Hall Ox BTh94. **d** 94 **p** 95. C Carl St Jo *Carl* 94-98; C Bassenthwaite, Isel and Setmurthy 98-02; TV Binsey from 02. *The Vicarage, Bassenthwaite, Keswick CA12 4QH* Tel (01768) 776198 E-mail iwright@fish.co.uk

WRIGHT, Frederick John. b 15. AKC42. **d** 42 **p** 43. C Brierley Hill *Lich* 42-45; C Walsall Pleck and Bescot 45-49; V W Bromwich Gd Shep 49-54; R Headless Cross *Worc* 54-67; R Romsley 67-80; rtd 80; Perm to Offic *Ely* from 97. *Rosevear, 3 Dury Lane, Colne, Huntingdon PE28 3NB* Tel (01487) 840518

WRIGHT, Graham. b 50. Oak Hill Th Coll 73. **d** 76 **p** 77. C Northampton St Giles *Pet* 76-79; C Man Resurr *Man* 79-82; V Barkingside St Laur *Chelmsf* 82-88; Chapl K Geo V Hosp Ilford 82-88; P-in-c Yoxford and Chapl Suffolk Constabulary *St E* 88-90; Perm to Offic *Linc* 03-05; Lic Preacher from 05. *47 Vinters Way, Butterwick, Boston PE22 0HB* Tel (01205) 761042 Mobile 07793-086887 E-mail rockinrev@bostonunited.wanadoo.co.uk

WRIGHT, Mrs Heather Margaret. b 47. EAMTC 93. **d** 96 **p** 97. NSM Heigham St Thos *Nor* 96-99; Hon Asst Dioc Chapl among Deaf and Deaf-blind People from 99; NSM Sprowston w Beeston from 03. *133 Moore Avenue, Norwich NR6 7LQ* Tel (01603) 301329 Fax and minicom as telephone

WRIGHT, Howard John Douglas. b 64. BA85. Trin Coll Bris BA94. **d** 96 **p** 97. C Ipswich St Matt *St E* 96-00; V Four Marks *Win* from 00. *The Vicarage, 22 Lymington Bottom, Four Marks, Alton GU34 5AA* Tel (01420) 563344 E-mail howardwright@xalt.co.uk

WRIGHT, Hugh Edward. b 57. BNC Ox BA79 MA87 Ex Univ CertEd81. Sarum & Wells Th Coll 85. **d** 87 **p** 88. C Hobs Moat *Birm* 87-90; C W Drayton *Lon* 90-92; V Oakfield St Jo *Portsm* from 92; RD E Wight 00-05. *St John's Vicarage, Victoria Crescent, Ryde PO33 1DQ* Tel (01983) 562863 E-mail hewright@stjohnsryde.freeserve.co.uk

WRIGHT, Ian. *See* WRIGHT, Frederic Ian

WRIGHT, Ian. b 65. SSC. Coll of Resurr Mirfield 97. **d** 99 **p** 00. C S Lafford *Linc* 99-01; C Hawley H Trin *Guildf* 01-03; Chapl Bonn w Cologne *Eur* from 03. *Altenrather Strasse 156, 53797 Lohmar, Germany* Tel (0049) (2246) 302565 Fax as telephone E-mail frianssc@t-online.de

WRIGHT, Mrs Jean. b 41. Man Univ BA63 CertEd64. Carl Dioc Tr Inst 88. **d** 91 **p** 94. NSM Kirkby Stephen w Mallerstang etc *Carl* from 91. *Mains View, Crosby Garrett, Kirkby Stephen CA17 4PR* Tel (01768) 371457

WRIGHT, John. *See* WRIGHT, Nicholas John

WRIGHT, John. *See* WRIGHT, Alfred John

WRIGHT, John. *See* WRIGHT, Anthony John

WRIGHT, John Alastair. b 30. FRSA72. Cranmer Hall Dur 62. **d** 64 **p** 65. C Thornton-le-Fylde *Blackb* 64-67; Miss to Seamen 67-72; V Darlington St Luke *Dur* 72-78; Community Chapl Darlington 78-89; rtd 89. *4 Grasmere, Agar Nook, Coalville LE67 4SH* Tel (01530) 837390

WRIGHT, John Douglas. b 42. Birm Univ BSc64 CertEd66. St Steph Ho Ox 69. **d** 69 **p** 70. C Swanley St Mary *Roch* 69-74; C Stockwell Green St Andr *S'wark* 74-79; V Leigh St Jo *Man* 79-82; P-in-c Whitehawk *Chich* from 82. *St Cuthman's Vicarage, 1 St Cuthman's Close, Whitehawk, Brighton BN2 5HW* Tel (01273) 699424 Mobile 07944-419007 E-mail jonwrightscuthmans@amserve.net

WRIGHT, Canon John Harold. b 36. ATCL Dur Univ BA58 ACertCM. Ely Th Coll 58. **d** 61 **p** 62. C Boston *Linc* 61-64; C Willesborough w Hinxhill *Cant* 64-68; V Westwell 68-75; R Eastwell w Boughton Aluph 68-75; V Rolvenden 75-84; R Cheriton 84-01; Hon Can Cant Cathl 97-01; rtd 01; Perm to Offic *Cant* from 01. *1 Cliff Road, Hythe CT21 5XA* Tel (01303) 265303

WRIGHT, Miss Julia Mary. b 64. Reading Univ BA88. Trin Coll Bris 96. **d** 98 **p** 99. C Woodley *Ox* 98-03; TV Aylesbury w Bierton and Hulcott 03-05; C Bernwode from 05. *4 Cubb Field, Aylesbury HP19 7SH* Tel (01296) 421326 E-mail jwrightstmary@aol.com

WRIGHT, Ken. *See* WRIGHT, Charles Kenneth

WRIGHT, Canon Kenneth William. b 13. Coll of Resurr Mirfield 37. **d** 39 **p** 40. C Clerkenwell H Redeemer w St Phil *Lon* 39-42; C Acton Green St Pet 42-45; C Boyne Hill *Ox* 45-50; V Stony Stratford St Mary 50-57; R Fenny Stratford 54-74; TR Fenny Stratford and Water Eaton 74-79; P-in-c Lt Brickhill 57-58; RD Bletchley 63-70; P-in-c Simpson w Woughton on the Green 69-72; RD Milton Keynes 70-72; Hon Can Ch Ch 70-79; rtd 80; Perm to Offic *S'well* 80-92. *St Katharine's House, Ormond Road, Wantage OX12 8EA* Tel (01235) 768030

WRIGHT, Canon Kenyon Edward. b 32. CBE99. Glas Univ MA53 Fitzw Coll Cam BA55 Serampore Coll MTh61 Edin Univ DLitt00. Wesley Ho Cam 53. **d** 71 **p** 71. In Meth Ch India 57-71; Dir Urban Min Cov Cathl *Cov* 71-81; Dir of Internat Min and Can Res 72-81; Public Preacher 72-74; Gen Sec Scottish Chs Coun 81-90; Dir Scottish Chs Ho Dunblane 81-90; Dir Kairos Trust 90-92; Hon C Glas H Cross *Glas* 91-92; rtd 92; P-in-c Glencarse *Bre* 94-00. *4 Katrine Crescent, Callander FK17 8JS* Tel and fax (01877) 330464 Mobile 07801-849941 E-mail kenyonwright@aol.com

WRIGHT, Lawrence Charles. b 57. Hull Univ MA94. EMMTC 93. **d** 96 **p** 96. Australia 96-98; C Penzance St Jo *Truro* 98-02; TV Penzance St Mary w St Paul and St Jo 02-04; Manager Relig Affairs Yarlswood Immigration and Detention Cen from 04; Lic to Offic *St Alb* from 04. *Yarlswood Detention Centre, Twinwood Road, Clapham, Bedford MK41 6HL* Tel (01234) 821000 E-mail lwright@fish.co.uk

WRIGHT, Leslie Vandernoll. b 24. Trin Hall Cam MA50. Ridley Hall Cam 49. **d** 51 **p** 52. C Aldershot H Trin *Guildf* 51-53; C Cambridge H Trin *Ely* 53-57; V Marston *Ox* 57-59; Asst Master Castle Ct Sch Parkstone 59-61; Asst Chapl Stowe Sch 61-64; Hd Master St Mich Prep Sch Five Oaks Jersey 64-66; Chapl Windlesham Ho Sch Sussex 66-68; Chapl Vevey *Eur* 68-73; Hd St Geo Sch Clarens 73-89; rtd 89; Chapl Lugano *Eur* 89-92. *18 avenue Schubert, Domine de Tournon, 83440 Montauroux, France* Tel (0033) (4) 94 47 6 43

WRIGHT, Mrs Louisa Mary (Lisa). b 33. S'wark Ord Course. **d** 87 **p** 94. NSM Streatham Hill St Marg *S'wark* 87-95; Hon C Streatham St Leon 95-02; rtd 02; Perm to Offic *S'wark* from 02. *19 Hillside Road, London SW2 3HL* Tel (020) 8671 8037

WRIGHT, Marion Jane. b 47. Whitelands Coll Lon CertEd69. Cranmer Hall Dur 73. **d** 00 **p** 02. NSM Scalby *York* from 00. *3 East Park Road, Scalby, Scarborough YO13 0PZ* Tel (01723) 350208 E-mail coda@fish.co.uk

WRIGHT, Martin. b 48. Avery Hill Coll BEd81 K Alfred's Coll Win CertEd69 LRAM76. St Alb and Ox Min Course 95. **d** 98 **p** 99. NSM St Alb St Mary Marshalswick *St Alb* 98-01; C Gt Berkhamsted 02-05; V Reigate St Mark *S'wark* from 05. *St Mark's Vicarage, 8 Alma Road, Reigate RH2 0DA* Tel (01737) 241161 Mobile 07774-923550 E-mail m.wright@c-of-e.freeserve.co.uk

WRIGHT, Canon Martin Neave. b 37. AKC61 Leic Univ DSRS67. St Boniface Warminster. **d** 62 **p** 63. C Corby St Columba *Pet* 62-65; Ind Chapl 65-71; Nigeria 71-75; P-in-c Honiley *Cov* 75-84; P-in-c Wroxall 75-84; Ind Chapl 75-84; Soc Resp Officer 84-96; Hon Can Cov Cathl 95-96; Bp's Chapl and Past Asst *B & W* 96-02; Preb Wells Cathl 96-02; Sub-Dean Wells 00-02; rtd 02. *2 Honiwell Close, Harbury, Leamington Spa CV33 9LY* Tel (01926) 613699

WRIGHT, Michael. *See* WRIGHT, Edward Michael

WRIGHT, Canon Michael. b 30. St Chad's Coll Dur BA55 DipTh56 De Montfort Univ MPhil04. **d** 56 **p** 57. C New Cleethorpes *Linc* 56-59; C Skegness 59-62; V Louth St Mich 62-73; R Stewton 62-73; R Warmsworth *Sheff* 73-86; Warden Dioc Readers' Assn 81-86; Hon Can Sheff Cathl 82-95; V Wath-upon-Dearne w Adwick-upon-Dearne 86-94; V Wath-upon-Dearne 94-95; RD Wath 92-95; rtd 95; Perm to Offic *Linc* from 95. *17 Ashfield Road, Sleaford NG34 7DZ* Tel (01529) 415698

WRIGHT, Michael Christopher. b 44. Leeds Univ BA65 CertEd67 MSc75 FRSA95. Wells Th Coll 65. **d** 67 **p** 68. C Dormanstown *York* 67-69; Perm to Offic *Linc* 69-88 and *Sheff* 71-95; Hd Master Eastmoor High Sch Wakef 84-87; Hd Master Carleton High Sch Pontefract 87-95; C-in-c St Edm Anchorage Lane CD *Sheff* 95-96; Chapl Doncaster R Infirmary and Montagu Hosp NHS Trust 95-01; Chapl Doncaster and Bassetlaw Hosps NHS Trust from 01. *Doncaster Royal Infirmary, Armthorpe Road, Doncaster DN2 5LT* Tel (01302) 366666 ext 3616 E-mail mcw@tcseuro.co.uk

WRIGHT, Michael George. b 52. WEMTC 01. **d** 04 **p** 05. NSM Woodchester and Brimscombe *Glouc* from 04. *The Trumpet, West End, Minchinhampton, Stroud GL6 9JA* Tel (01453) 883027 Mobile 07974-303527 E-mail thetrumpet.antiques@virgin.net

WRIGHT, Michael John. b 38. Dur Univ MA91 DipTM84 Cert Cllr Supervision 94. Chich Th Coll 59. **d** 62 **p** 63. C Yate *Glouc* 62-65; C Kirby Moorside w Gillamoor *York* 65-68; V 68-72; V Bransdale cum Farndale 68-72; V Kirkbymoorside w Gillamoor, Farndale etc 72-73; Dioc Communications Officer 72-74; V Ormesby 74-80; P-in-c Middlesbrough St Cuth 81-88; Perm to Offic 88-99; NSM W Acklam 91-97; Chapl Butterwick Hospice Stockton-on-Tees 97-99; Chapl S Dur Hospice Bp Auckland 97-99; rtd 03. *25 Thornfield Road, Middlesbrough TS5 5DD* Tel (01642) 816247 E-mail mjw@careatwork.fsnet.co.uk

WRIGHT, Nicholas John. b 65. Liv Univ BA87. Wycliffe Hall Ox 89. **d** 92 **p** 93. C Burley *Ripon* 92-95; C Brightside w Wincobank *Sheff* 95-97; TV Sheff Manor 97-03; Perm to Offic from 03. *22 Norfolk Road, Sheffield S2 2SX*

WRIGHT, Nicholas Mark. b 59. Loughb Univ BSc80. Qu Coll Birm 82. **d** 85 **p** 86. C Coney Hill *Glouc* 85-89; C Rotherham *Sheff* 89-91; TV Worc SE *Worc* 91-98; R Inkberrow w Cookhill and Kington w Dormston from 98. *The Vicarage, High Street, Inkberrow, Worcester WR7 4DU* Tel (01386) 792222 E-mail ncbjmswright@btinternet.com

✠**WRIGHT, The Rt Revd Nicholas Thomas.** b 48. Ex Coll Ox BA71 MA75 DPhil81 DD00. Wycliffe Hall Ox BA73. **d** 75 **p** 76 **c** 03. Fell Mert Coll Ox 75-78; Chapl 76-78; Chapl and Fell Down Coll Cam 78-81; Asst Prof NT Studies McGill Univ Montreal 81-86; Chapl and Fell Worc Coll Ox and Univ Lect Th 86-93; Dean Lich 93-99; Can Th Cov Cathl *Cov* 92-99; Lector Theologiae and Can Westmr Abbey 00-03; Bp Dur from 03. *Auckland Castle, Bishop Auckland DL14 7NR* Tel (01388) 602576 Fax 605264 E-mail bishop.of.durham@durham.anglican.org

WRIGHT, Ms Pamela Anne. b 45. Open Univ BSc00. St As Minl Tr Course 01. **d** 03 **p** 04. NSM Llanrhos *St As* from 03. *Brackenrigg, Bryn Pydew Road, Bryn Pydew, Llandudno Junction LL31 9JH* Tel (01492) 541552 Mobile 07850-180420 Fax (01492) 541652 E-mail pamscot45@aol.com

WRIGHT, Miss Pamela Jean. b 38. ALA63. NTMTC 02. **d** 03 **p** 04. NSM Harrow Trin St Mich *Lon* 03-05; NSM Wealdstone H Trin from 05. *71 Curzon Avenue, Stanmore HA7 2AL* Tel (020) 8863 0597 E-mail pamwright@tstmichaels.fsnet.co.uk

WRIGHT, Patricia. b 46. SRN68 DN68 DipHV69. S'wark Ord Course 80. **dss** 85 **d** 89. Chapl R Lon Hosp (Mile End) 83-89; Bethnal Green St Matt w St Jas the Gt *Lon* 85-87; St Botolph Aldgate w H Trin Minories 88-89; Hon C from 89. *8 Royal Mint Street, London E1 8LG* Tel (020) 7283 1670

WRIGHT, The Ven Paul. b 54. K Coll Lon BD78 AKC78 Heythrop Coll Lon MTh90. Ripon Coll Cuddesdon 78. **d** 79 **p** 80. C Beckenham St Geo *Roch* 79-83; Chapl Ch Sch Richmond 83-85; C Richmond St Mary w St Matthias and St Jo *S'wark* 83-85; V Gillingham St Aug *Roch* 85-90; R Crayford 90-99; RD Erith 93-97; V Sidcup St Jo 99-03; Hon Can Roch Cathl from 98; Adn Bromley and Bexley from 03. *The Archdeaconry, The Glebe, Chislehurst BR7 5PX* Tel (020) 8467 8743 Mobile 07811-147219 E-mail archdeacon.bromley@rochester.anglican.org

WRIGHT, Paul Stephen. b 66. Cen Lancs Univ BA88 Liv Univ MA96. Westcott Ho Cam 90. **d** 93 **p** 94. C Upholland *Liv* 93-96;

CF from 96. *c/o MOD Chaplains (Army)* Tel (01980) 615804 Fax 615800

WRIGHT, Peter. *See* WRIGHT, Charles Frederick Peter

WRIGHT, Canon Peter. b 35. K Coll Lon AKC61 Hull Univ MA86. St Boniface Warminster 61. **d** 62 **p** 63. C Goole *Sheff* 62-67; V Norton Woodseats St Chad 67-80; R Aston cum Aughton 80-84; P-in-c Ulley 80-84; Chapl Rotherham Priority Health Services NHS Trust 80-84; R Aston cum Aughton and Ulley *Sheff* 84-93; TR Aston cum Aughton w Swallownest, Todwick etc 93-00; RD Laughton 85-93; Chapter Clerk and Hon Can Sheff Cathl 92-00; rtd 00; Perm to Offic *Sheff* from 01. *40 Chancet Wood Drive, Sheffield S8 7TR* Tel and fax 0114-274 7218 E-mail allsaints.pw@talk21.com

WRIGHT, Peter Reginald. b 34. St Chad's Coll Dur BA60. Linc Th Coll 60. **d** 62 **p** 63. C Lt Ilford St Mich *Chelmsf* 62-65; C Billingham St Aid *Dur* 65-68; TV 68-71; TR 71-76; Chapl Portsm Poly *Portsm* 76-87; Sec Chapls in HE Gen Syn Bd of Educn 88-95; rtd 95; Perm to Offic *Portsm* from 95. *6 Garden Lane, Southsea PO5 3DP* Tel (023) 9273 6651

WRIGHT, Peter Westrope. b 24. Kelham Th Coll 43. **d** 48 **p** 49. C Pimlico St Barn *Lon* 48-50; C Sidley *Chich* 50-59; R E Blatchington 59-73; P-in-c Lewes St Mich 73-75; TV Lewes All SS, St Anne, St Mich and St Thos 75-84; TR 84-87; rtd 89; Perm to Offic *Chich* from 89. *17 South Street, Lewes BN7 2BT* Tel (01273) 473332

WRIGHT, Philip. b 32. G&C Coll Cam BA53 MA57. Wells Th Coll 56. **d** 57 **p** 58. C Barnard Castle *Dur* 57-60; C Heworth St Mary 60-64; V Tow Law 64-70; V Tanfield 70-78; V Gateshead Ch Ch 78-02; rtd 02. *Meldon, High Heworth Lane, Gateshead NE10 0PB* Tel 0191-469 2161

WRIGHT, Phillip. b 35. Kelham Th Coll 57 St Aid Birkenhead 59. **d** 61 **p** 62. C Goldthorpe *Sheff* 61-65; V Doncaster St Jude 65-71; V Kettering All SS *Pet* 71-82; V S Kirkby *Wakef* 82-94; rtd 98. *2 The Grove, Wickersley, Rotherham S66 2BP* Tel (01709) 543922 E-mail thegrove@onetel.com

WRIGHT, Robert. *See* WRIGHT, Canon Anthony Robert

WRIGHT, Robert Charles. b 31. Roch Th Coll 65. **d** 67 **p** 68. C Manston *Ripon* 67-70; C Moor Allerton 70-74; P-in-c Terrington St John *Ely* 74-79; P-in-c Walpole St Andrew 74-75; V Terrington St John 80-91; V Tilney St Lawrence 80-91; V Tilney All Saints 80-91; R Stiffkey and Cockthorpe w Morston, Langham etc *Nor* 91-96; rtd 96; Perm to Offic *Nor* from 96. *Glenfinnan, 83 Childs Way, Sheringham NR26 8TX* Tel (01263) 822535

WRIGHT, Robert Doogan. b 24. TCD BA46 MA. TCD Div Sch Div Test 47. **d** 47 **p** 48. C Carnmoney *Conn* 47-49; C Belfast St Jas 49-51; C Belfast St Matt 51-53; P-in-c Belfast Whiterock 53-57; I Magheragall 57-64; I Belfast St Mark 64-70; I Carrickfergus 70-82; Can Conn Cathl 79-86; I Killead w Gartree 82-86; Chan Conn Cathl 83-86; rtd 86. *123 Station Road, Greenisland, Carrickfergus BT38 8UN* Tel (028) 9086 2779

WRIGHT, Robert John. b 47. St Jo Coll Dur BA70. SEITE 00. **d** 03 **p** 04. NSM Notting Hill St Jo *Lon* from 03; NSM Notting Hill St Pet from 03. *93 Peel Street, London W8 7PB* Tel (020) 7221 4399 Mobile 07010-701332 Fax (020) 7460 2736 E-mail home@robert-wright.com *or* curate@stjohnsnottinghill.com

✠**WRIGHT, The Rt Revd Royston Clifford.** b 22. Univ of Wales BA42. St Steph Ho Ox 43. **d** 45 **p** 46 **c** 86. C Bedwas *Mon* 45-47; C Newport St Jo Bapt 47-49; C Walton St Mary *Liv* 49-51; Chapl RNVR 50-51; Chapl RN 51-68; V Blaenavon w Capel Newydd *Mon* 68-74; RD Pontypool 73-74; TR Ebbw Vale 74-77; Can St Woolos Cathl 74-77; Adn Mon 77-88; Adn Newport 77-86; Bp Mon 86-91; rtd 91; Lic to Offic *Mon* from 91. *23 Rupert Brooke Drive, Newport NP20 3HP* Tel (01633) 250770

WRIGHT (née PRECIOUS), Sally Joanne. b 75. Hatf Coll Dur BA97 Anglia Poly Univ MA03. Westcott Ho Cam 00. **d** 02 **p** 03. C Chich St Paul and Westhampnett *Chich* 02-05; Perm to Offic *S'wark* from 05. *St John's Vicarage, 10A Meeting House Lane, London SE15 2UN* Tel (020) 7635 5576 E-mail sallywright29@yahoo.co.uk

WRIGHT, Samuel. *See* WRIGHT, William Samuel

WRIGHT, Sarah Jane. b 64. Nottm Trent Univ BA99. Ripon Coll Cuddesdon 99. **d** 01 **p** 02. C Clarendon Park St Jo w Knighton St Mich *Leic* 01-03; C Leic Martyrs from 04. *50 Aberdale Road, Leicester LE2 6GA* Tel 0116-288 3191 Mobile 07790-342728 E-mail squeeks@hotmail.com

WRIGHT, Simon Christopher. b 44. AKC67. **d** 68 **p** 69. C Bitterne Park *Win* 68-72; C Kirkby *Liv* 72-74; V Wigan St Anne 74-79; Abp's Dom Chapl and Dioc Dir of Ords *York* 79-84; V W Acklam 84-00; RD Middlesbrough 87-98; Can and Preb York Minster 94-00; V Dartmouth and Dittisham *Ex* from 00. *The Vicarage, Northford Road, Dartmouth TQ6 9EP* Tel and fax (01803) 835543

WRIGHT, Stephen Irwin. b 58. Ex Coll Ox BA80 MA84 Selw Coll Cam BA85 MA90 Lanc Univ MA92 St Jo Coll Dur PhD97. Ridley Hall Cam 83. **d** 86 **p** 87. C Newbarns w Hawcoat *Carl* 86-90; C Burton and Holme 90-94; NSM Esh *Dur* 94-97; NSM Hamsteels 94-97; C Consett 97-98; Dir Coll of Preachers from 98; Perm to Offic *S'wark* from 99. *Spurgeon's College, 189 South Norwood Hill, London SE25 6DJ* Tel (020) 8653 0850 *or* 8768 0878 ext 233 Fax 8711 0959 E-mail s.wright@spurgeons.ac.uk

WRIGHT, Canon Stephen Mark. b 60. Keele Univ BA83. Trin Coll Bris 86. **d** 89 **p** 90. C Thorne *Sheff* 89-92; CMS from 92; Nigeria 93-98; Hon Can Asaba from 98; Chapl Ahmadi St Paul Kuwait 99-03; Chapl Dubai and Sharjah w N Emirates from 03. *PO Box 7415, Dubai, United Arab Emirates* Tel (00971) (4) 884 4904 E-mail stephenw@emirates.net.ae

WRIGHT, Stewart. *See* WRIGHT, William Charles Stewart

WRIGHT, Thomas. *See* WRIGHT, The Rt Revd Nicholas Thomas

WRIGHT, Thomas Stephen. b 31. Fitzw Ho Cam BA54 MA58. Bps' Coll Cheshunt 56. **d** 57 **p** 58. C Bishop's Stortford St Mich *St Alb* 57-61; C St E Cathl *St E* 61-64; R Hartest w Boxted 64-82; Chapl RAF 64-71; RD Sudbury *St E* 70-81; P-in-c Somerton 71-82; P-in-c Stansfield 82-91; V Denston w Stradishall and Stansfield 91-97; Min Can St E Cathl 82-97; rtd 98. *21 Manderville Road, Bury St Edmunds IP33 2BJ* Tel (01284) 765287

WRIGHT, Tim Stanley. b 63. Derby Coll of Educn BEd86. St Jo Coll Dur 89. **d** 92 **p** 93. C Eccleshill *Bradf* 92-96; TV Southend *Chelmsf* 96-00; V Boulton *Derby* from 00. *The Vicarage, 1 St Mary's Close, Alvaston, Derby DE24 0GF* Tel (01332) 572308 E-mail revboulton@tiscali.co.uk

WRIGHT, Timothy. b 63. NUU BSc85. Cranmer Hall Dur 86. **d** 89 **p** 90. C Bramcote *S'well* 89-93; I Glenavy w Tunny and Crumlin *Conn* 93-98; Chapl RAF from 98; Perm to Offic *Lich* from 01. *Chaplaincy Services (RAF), HQ, Personnel and Training Command, RAF Innsworth, Gloucester GL3 1EZ* Tel (01452) 712612 ext 5164 Fax 510828

WRIGHT, Timothy John. b 41. K Coll Lon BD63 AKC63. **d** 64 **p** 65. C Highfield *Ox* 64-68; Asst Chapl Worksop Coll Notts 68-71; Chapl Malvern Coll 71-77; Ho Master 77-86; Hd Master Jo Lyon Sch Harrow 86-01; rtd 01. *Beech House, Colwall Green, Malvern WR13 6DX* Tel (01684) 541102

WRIGHT, Timothy John. b 54. Nottm Univ BA76. Ripon Coll Cuddesdon 90. **d** 92 **p** 93. C Dawlish *Ex* 92-95; TV Teignmouth, Ideford w Luton, Ashcombe etc 95-01; Chapl Wycombe Abbey Sch from 01. *Wycombe Abbey School, Abbey Way, High Wycombe HP11 1PE* Tel (01494) 520381

WRIGHT, Toby Christopher. b 75. New Coll Ox BA98 MA01 Leeds Univ MA01. Coll of Resurr Mirfield 99. **d** 01 **p** 02. C Petersfield *Portsm* 01-04; P-in-c Peckham St Jo w St Andr *S'wark* from 04. *St John's Vicarage, 10A Meeting House Lane, London SE15 2UN* Tel (020) 7639 0084 E-mail priest@stjohnspeckham.org.uk

WRIGHT, Mrs Vyvienne Mary. b 35. S Dios Minl Tr Scheme 80. **dss** 83 **d** 87 **p** 94. Martock w Ash *B & W* 83-00; Hon C 87-00; Perm to Offic from 00. *36 Church Close, Martock TA12 6DS* Tel (01935) 823292

WRIGHT, William Charles Stewart. b 53. Ulster Poly BSc81. CITC BTh95. **d** 95 **p** 96. C Ballyholme *D & D* 95-98; I Conwal Union w Gartan *D & R* from 98. *Conwal Rectory, New Line Road, Letterkenny, Co Donegal, Irish Republic* Tel (00353) (74) 912 2573

WRIGHT, William Samuel. b 59. TCD BTh89 MA90. **d** 87 **p** 88. C Belfast St Aid *Conn* 87-91; Sec Dioc Bd of Miss 90-91; I Cleenish w Mullaghdun *Clogh* 91-99; I Lisburn Ch Ch Cathl *Conn* from 99; Can and Preb Conn Cathl from 01. *Cathedral Rectory, 2 Clonevin Park, Lisburn BT28 3BL* Tel (028) 9266 2865 *or* 9260 2400 E-mail sam@rector.fsnet.co.uk *or* cathedral@connor.anglican.org

WRIGHTSON, Bernard. b 25. CertEd50 Leeds Univ DipSC60 ACP65. Linc Th Coll 83. **d** 83 **p** 84. Hon C Alford w Rigsby *Linc* 83-86; Perm to Offic 86-89; NSM Mablethorpe w Trusthorpe 89-94; Perm to Offic from 94. *Pipits Acre, 64 Church Lane, Mablethorpe LN12 2NU* Tel (01507) 472394

WRIGLEY, George Garnett. b 50. St Cath Coll Cam BA71 Loughb Coll of Educn PGCE72. NTMTC 02. **d** 04 **p** 05. NSM Hounslow H Trin w St Paul *Lon* from 04. *63 Lionel Road, Brentford TW8 9QZ* Tel (020) 8232 8640 E-mail georgewrig@hotmail.com

WRISDALE, Jean May. b 40. LNSM course. **d** 90 **p** 94. OLM Fotherby *Linc* from 90. *The Meadows, Livesey Road, Ludborough, Grimsby DN36 5SQ* Tel (01472) 840474

WRIST-KNUDSEN, Svend Michael. b 61. Copenhagen Univ DipTh87. St Jo Coll Dur BA91. **d** 91 **p** 92. C Newton Aycliffe *Dur* 91-95; P-in-c Penzance St Jo *Truro* 95-97. *Address temp unknown*

WROE, Mark. b 69. Surrey Univ BA92. Ridley Hall Cam 94. **d** 96 **p** 97. C Chilvers Coton w Astley *Cov* 96-00; P-in-c Heworth St Alb *Dur* 00-03; V from 03. *The Vicarage, Coldwell Park Drive, Felling, Gateshead NE10 9BY* Tel 0191-438 1720 E-mail revdocwroe@supanet.com

WROE, Martin Daniel Edward. b 61. NTMTC. **d** 04 **p** 05. NSM Covent Garden St Paul *Lon* from 04. *45 Penn Road, London N7 9RE* Tel (020) 7607 6086 E-mail martinwroe@blueyonder.co.uk

WYARD, Peter Joseph. b 54. Pemb Coll Cam MA76 Sussex Univ MSc80 Brunel Univ MSc88. EAMTC 99. **d** 02 **p** 03. C Framlingham w Saxtead *St E* from 02. *17 Fulchers Field, Framlingham, Woodbridge IP13 9HT* Tel (01728) 622042 E-mail peter.wyard@btinternet.com

WYATT, Colin. b 27. Ex Coll Ox BA54 MA55 Lon Univ BD62. Tyndale Hall Bris 60. **d** 63 **p** 64. C Radipole *Sarum* 63-66; C Southborough St Pet *Roch* 66-67; V Tetsworth *Ox* 67-72; Lect Bible Tr Inst Glas 72-74; R Hurworth *Dur* 74-79; P-in-c Dinsdale w Sockburn 74-76; R 76-79; R Sadberge 79-84; R Bacton w Wyverstone and Cotton *St E* 84-92; rtd 92; Perm to Offic *Ripon* from 92. *20 Harrogate Road, Ripon HG4 1SR* Tel (01765) 606810

WYATT, Canon David Stanley Chadwick. b 36. Fitzw Ho Cam BA59 MA71. Ely Th Coll 59. **d** 61 **p** 62. C Rochdale *Man* 61-63; Bp's Dom Chapl 63-68; R Salford St Paul w Ch Ch from 68; Hon Can Man Cathl from 82; P-in-c Salford Ordsall St Clem 91-96; AD Salford 97. *St Paul's Church House, Broadwalk, Salford M6 5FX* Tel 0161-736 8868

WYATT, Peter John. b 38. Kelham Th Coll 58. **d** 64 **p** 65. C N Stoneham *Win* 64-68; C Brixham *Ex* 68-69; Dominica 69-75; Zambia 76-78; P-in-c Ettington *Cov* 78-79; V Butlers Marston and the Pillertons w Ettington 79-86; V Codnor and Loscoe *Derby* 86-91; Chapl for Deaf People 91-03; rtd 03. *16 Cae Melyn, Tregynon, Newtown SY16 3EF* Tel (01686) 650368

WYATT, Richard Norman. b 21. LVCM. **d** 84 **p** 85. C Puttenham and Wanborough *Guildf* 84-90; Perm to Offic *Chich* 91-93 and from 97; P-in-c Stedham w Iping 93-97; rtd 97; RD Midhurst *Chich* 98-99. *Trenethick, June Lane, Midhurst GU29 9EL* Tel (01730) 813447 E-mail normanwyatt@midhurst0.demon.co.uk

WYATT, Royston Dennis. b 36. FRICS67. Sarum & Wells Th Coll 74. **d** 77 **p** 78. NSM Canford Magna *Sarum* 77-82; V Abbotsbury, Portesham and Langton Herring 82-88; Dioc Missr *Linc* 88-95; R Welford w Weston *Glouc* 95-05; RD Campden 96-01; rtd 05. *78 Lower Meadow, Ilminster TA19 9DP* Tel (01460) 53996 E-mail revrdw@btinternet.com

WYATT (née OWEN), Mrs Susan Elizabeth. b 53. Bris Univ BSc75 Bath Univ PGCE78. EAMTC 97. **d** 00 **p** 01. Asst Dioc Adv in Miss and Evang *Ely* from 00; C Over from 00; C Long Stanton w St Mich from 02. *The Vicarage, High Street, Longstanton, Cambridge CB4 5BP* Tel (01954) 201853 *or* 204529 Mobile 07713-241261 E-mail sue.wyatt1@ntlworld.com *or* sue.wyatt@ely.anglican.org

WYATT, Trevor. b 60. Keele Univ BSc81. SEITE 97. **d** 00 **p** 01. NSM Wilmington *Roch* from 00. *216 Birchwood Road, Wilmington, Dartford DA2 7HA* Tel (01322) 666521 Mobile 07860-306746 E-mail trevor.wyatt@bt.com

WYBREW, Canon Hugh Malcolm. b 34. Qu Coll Ox BA58 MA. Linc Th Coll 59. **d** 60 **p** 61. C E Dulwich St Jo *S'wark* 60-64; Tutor St Steph Ho Ox 65-71; Chapl Bucharest *Eur* 71-73; V Pinner *Lon* 73-83; Sec Fellowship of SS Alb and Sergius 84-86; Dean Jerusalem 86-89; Hon Can Gib Cathl *Eur* from 89; V Ox St Mary Magd *Ox* 89-04; Hon Can Ch Ch 01-04; rtd 04. *96 Warwick Street, Oxford OX4 1SY* Tel (01865) 241355 E-mail hugh.wybrew@theology.ox.ac.uk

WYER, Keith George. b 45. St Paul's Cheltenham CertEd66 K Coll Lon BD71 AKC71. St Aug Coll Cant 71. **d** 72 **p** 73. C Moseley St Mary *Birm* 72-76; Chapl RNR 73-92; C Walsall *Lich* 76-77; Min Walsall St Martin 77-79; Chapl Colston's Sch Bris 79-86; Chapl Kelly Coll Tavistock 86-92; R Combe Martin and Berrynarbor *Ex* 92-95; TR Combe Martin, Berrynarbor, Lynton, Brendon etc from 96; RD Shirwell 95-01. *The Rectory, Rectory Road, Combe Martin, Ilfracombe EX34 0NS* Tel (01271) 883203 E-mail keith@kgw.eurobell.co.uk

WYKES, Peter. b 44. Lon Univ MB, BS68. Ban & St As Minl Tr Course 97. **d** 00 **p** 01. NSM Trefnant w Tremeirchion *St As* 00-01; NSM Cefn w Trefnant w Tremeirchion from 01. *Clattwm, 1 Plas Chambres Road, Denbigh LL16 5UP* Tel (01745) 730263

WYLAM, John. b 43. AKC66 FE TCert75. **d** 67 **p** 68. C Derby St Bart *Derby* 67-70; SSF 70-73; C Seaton Hirst *Newc* 74-77; V Byker St Silas 77-83; V Alwinton w Holystone and Alnham 83-98; R Chollerton w Birtley and Thockrington from 98. *The Vicarage, Chollerton, Hexham NE46 4TF* Tel (01434) 681721 E-mail johnwylam@btopenworld.com

WYLD, Kevin Andrew. b 58. St Cath Coll Ox BA79 MA85 Univ Coll Dur MSc83 Edin Univ BD85. Edin Th Coll 82. **d** 85 **p** 86. C Winlaton *Dur* 85-87; C Houghton le Spring 87-90; V Medomsley 90-95; V High Spen and Rowlands Gill 95-00; R Cen Florida St Rich USA from 00. *St Richard's Episcopal Church, 5151 Lake Howell Road, Winter Park, FL 32792, USA* Tel (001) (407) 671 4211 Fax 671 2028

WYLIE, Alan. b 47. Is of Man Tr Inst 88. **d** 92 **p** 93. NSM Douglas St Geo *S & M* 92-97; NSM Challoch *Glas* 97-00; P-in-c Motherwell from 00; P-in-c Wishaw from 00. *The Rectory, 14 Crawford Street, Motherwell ML1 3AD* Tel (01698) 249441 E-mail revawylie@fsmail.net

WYLIE, Clive George. b 64. QUB BSc86 TCD BTh90 MA93. CITC 97. **d** 90 **p** 91. C Drumglass w Moygashel *Arm* 90-93; I Tynan, Aghavilly and Middletown 93-98; Hon V Choral Arm Cathl 93-98; Team P Glas E End *Glas* from 98; Miss 21 Co-ord from 98. *451 Tollcross Road, Glasgow G31 4XY* Tel and fax 0141-556 7120 Mobile 07974-342851 E-mail mission21@glasgow.anglican.org

WYLIE, David Victor. b 61. ACA86 LSE BSc(Econ)82 Leeds Univ BA91. Coll of Resurr Mirfield 89. **d** 92 **p** 93. C Kilburn St Aug w St Jo *Lon* 92-95; C Heston 95-98; Chapl RN from 98. *Royal Naval Chaplaincy Service, Room 203, Victory Building, HM Naval Base, Portsmouth PO1 3LS* Tel (023) 9272 7903 Fax 9272 7111

WYLIE, Nigel Bruce. b 62. Trin Coll Bris 88. **d** 91 **p** 92. C Selly Park St Steph and St Wulstan *Birm* 91-94. *Address temp unknown*

WYLIE-SMITH, Ms Megan Judith. b 52. S'wark Ord Course 88. **d** 91 **p** 94. C Greenstead *Chelmsf* 91-94; C W Ham 94-97; TV Becontree S 97-01; rtd 01; Perm to Offic *Chelmsf* from 01. *67 Gordon Road, London E11 2RA* Tel (020) 8530 6434 E-mail megan@wylie-smith.freeserve.co.uk

WYNBURNE, John Paterson Barry. b 48. St Jo Coll Dur BA70. Wycliffe Coll Toronto MDiv72 Ridley Hall Cam 72. **d** 73 **p** 74. C Gt Stanmore *Lon* 73-76; Chapl Bucharest w Sofia *Eur* 76-77; C Dorking w Ranmore *Guildf* 77-80; V Send 80-88; V York Town St Mich 88-93; V Camberley St Mich Yorktown 93-95; TR Beaconsfield *Ox* from 95; AD Amersham from 04. *The Rectory, Wycombe End, Beaconsfield HP9 1NB* Tel (01494) 677058 *or* 673949 E-mail jwynburne@aol.com

WYNES, Michael John. b 33. AKC57. **d** 58 **p** 59. C Gt Berkhamsted *St Alb* 58-62; C Silverhill St Matt *Chich* 62-65; C Wilton *B & W* 65-68; R Berkley w Rodden 68-77; V Priddy 77-86; V Westbury sub Mendip w Easton 77-86; C Milton 86-93; rtd 93; Perm to Offic *B & W* from 95. *23A Fairways, Wells BA5 2DF* Tel (01749) 673778

WYNGARD, Canon Ernest Clive. b 30. Leeds Univ BA52. Coll of Resurr Mirfield 52. **d** 54 **p** 55. C Bishopwearmouth St Mich *Dur* 54-59; C Winlaton 59-61; V Castleside 61-67; V Beamish 67-80; RD Lanchester 74-80; V Dur St Giles 80-87; Hon Can Dur Cathl from 83; V Greatham 87-94; Master Greatham Hosp 87-94; rtd 94. *20 Chichester Close, Hartlepool TS25 2QT* Tel (01429) 297261

WYNN, Edward Laurence. b 65. Leeds Metrop Univ BSc96 Leeds Univ MA02 RGN88. N Ord Course 98. **d** 01 **p** 02. C Emley *Wakef* 01-04; C Flockton cum Denby Grange 01-04; Chapl RAF from 04. *Chaplaincy Services (RAF), HQ, Personnel and Training Command, RAF Innsworth, Gloucester GL3 1EZ* Tel (01452) 712612 ext 5164 Mobile 07714-062869 Fax (01452) 510828 E-mail eddie@wynn11.freeserve.co.uk

WYNN, Richard David. b 44. Univ Coll of Rhodesia & Nyasaland Inst of Educn TCert65. St Paul's Coll Grahamstown 86. **d** 88 **p** 89. S Africa 88-02; C Kirby-Hilton Ascension 88-91; R Ixopo St Jo 91-99; R Richmond-cum-Byrne St Mary 99-02; P-in-c Cinderford St Steph w Littledean *Glouc* from 02. *The Vicarage, St Annal's Road, Cinderford GL14 2AS* Tel and fax (01594) 822286 E-mail rswynn@cinderschurch.fsnet.co.uk

WYNN-EVANS, Canon James Naylor. b 34. Magd Coll Ox BA55 MA59. Linc Th Coll 57. **d** 59 **p** 60. C Goole *Sheff* 59-62; C Hatfield 62-63; Chapl HM Borstal Hatfield 62-67; C-in-c Dunscroft CD *Sheff* 63-67; Bp's Dom Chapl *Edin* 67-75; C Edin St Columba 67-69; R Edin St Marg 69-85; P-in-c Edin SS Phil and Jas 76-85; P-in-c Edin St Dav 85-97; Info Officer Scottish Episc Ch 97-99; Admin Chapl to Primus 97-01; Can St Mary's Cathl 86-95; Hon Can St Mary's Cathl from 98. *1 Gayfield Place, Edinburgh EH7 4AB* Tel 0131-556 1566 E-mail wynn-evans@supanet.com

WYNNE, Preb Alan John. b 46. St Luke's Coll Ex CertEd71. St Steph Ho Ox BA71 MA75. **d** 71 **p** 72. C Watford St Pet *St Alb* 71-74; Chapl Liddon Ho Lon 74-75; Chapl Abp Tenison's Sch Kennington 75-86; Hon C St Marylebone Annunciation Bryanston Street *Lon* 81-86; V Hoxton St Anne w St Columba 86-94; TR Poplar from 94; Preb St Paul's Cathl from 01; AD Tower Hamlets from 01. *Poplar Rectory, Newby Place, London E14 0EY* Tel and fax (020) 7987 3133 *or* tel 7538 9198 E-mail alan@poplar22.fsnet.co.uk

WYNNE, The Very Revd Frederick John Gordon. b 44. Chu Coll Cam BA66 MA70. CITC 81. **d** 84 **p** 85. C Dublin St Patr Cathl Gp *D & G* 84-86; C Romsey *Win* 86-89; R Broughton, Bossington, Houghton and Mottisfont 89-97; I Dunleckney w Nurney, Lorum and Kiltennel *C & O* from 97; Chan Ossory Cathl from 00; Chan Leighlin Cathl from 00; Dean Leighlin from 04. *The Rectory, Dunleckney, Muine Bheag, Co Carlow, Irish Republic* Tel (00353) (59) 972 1570

WYNNE, Preb Geoffrey. b 41. K Coll Lon BD64 AKC64 Lon Univ BSc(Soc)75 Heythrop Coll Lon MTh86. **d** 66 **p** 67. C Wolverhampton St Pet *Lich* 66-70; Chapl Wolv Poly 66-79; Sen Chapl 79-92; Sen Chapl Wolv Univ from 92; Dir of Ords 76-83; Preb Lich Cathl from 83; AD Wolverhampton from 03; Bp's Adv for Univ and HE Chapl from 04. *The Chaplain's House, 1 Compton Park, Wolverhampton WV3 9DU* Tel (01902) 712051 *or* 322904 E-mail g.wynne@wlv.ac.uk

WYNNE, Jean. **d** 02 **p** 03. NSM Mullingar, Portnashangan, Moyliscar, Kilbixy etc *M & K* from 02. *Ballinure House, Rathangan, Co Kildare, Irish Republic* Tel (00353) (46) 973 0098 Mobile 86-356 4590

WYNNE, Canon Ronald Charles. b 16. Selw Coll Cam BA38 MA42 Cape Town Univ MA79. Bp's Coll Calcutta 41. **d** 42 **p** 43. Ceylon 42-45; C Basingstoke *Win* 46-50; C Fleet *Guildf* 50-56; V Lockerley w E Dean *Win* 56-61; St Vincent 61-67; Botswana 68-82; rtd 82; Perm to Offic *Glouc* from 83. *19 Ricardo Road, Minchinhampton, Stroud GL6 9BY* Tel (01453) 883372

WYNNE, Trefor. b 35. St Mich Coll Llan 72. **d** 74 **p** 75. C Llangynwyd w Maesteg *Llan* 74-77; V Trealaw 77-83; R Llanbeulan w Llanfaelog and Tal-y-Llyn *Ban* 83-96; RD Llifon and Talybolion 93-96; rtd 96; Perm to Offic *Llan* from 96. *3 St John's Drive, Ton Pentre, Pentre CF41 7EU* Tel (01443) 433660

WYNNE-GREEN, Roy Rowland. b 36. SSC90 Westmr Coll Ox DipTh99. Chich Th Coll 67. **d** 70 **p** 71. C Fleetwood St Pet *Blackb* 70-73; C Cen Torquay *Ex* 73-75; Chapl SW Hosp and Chapl Asst St Thos Hosp Lon 75-85; Chapl R Surrey Co Hosp Guildf 85-94; Chapl R Surrey Co Hosp NHS Trust 94-01; Chapl Heathlands Mental Health Trust Surrey 94-98; Chapl Surrey Hants Borders NHS Trust 98-01; rtd 01; Perm to Offic *Guildf* from 02. *St Benedict's House, 6 Lawn Road, Guildford GU2 5DE* Tel (01483) 574582

WYNNE-JONES, Nicholas Winder. b 45. Jes Coll Ox BA67 MA72 Selw Coll Cam 71. Oak Hill Th Coll 69. **d** 72 **p** 73. C St Marylebone All So w SS Pet and Jo *Lon* 72-75; Chapl Stowe Sch 75-83; V Gt Clacton *Chelmsf* 83-95; V Beckenham Ch Ch *Roch* from 95; RD Beckenham 00-05. *Christ Church Vicarage, 18 Court Downs Road, Beckenham BR3 6LR* Tel (020) 8650 3847 Fax 8658 9532 E-mail vicar@ccb.org.uk

WYNTER, Michael Pallant. b 48. Ripon Coll Cuddesdon 93. **d** 95 **p** 96. C Hughenden *Ox* 95-98; P-in-c Norton sub Hamdon, W Chinnock, Chiselborough etc *B & W* 98-01; R 01-05; RD Ivelchester 01-04; Perm to Offic *Ox* from 05. *Pipers Cottage, Pipers Lane, Great Kingshill, High Wycombe HP15 6LW* Tel (01494) 714758

Y

YABBACOME, David Wallace. b 55. Bp Otter Coll BEd Linc Th Coll DipTh. **d** 83 **p** 84. C Egham Hythe *Guildf* 83-86; C Cen Telford *Lich* 86-87; TV 87-92; R Cheadle w Freehay 92-00; V Linc St Nic w St Jo Newport *Linc* from 00. *St Nicholas' Vicarage, 103 Newport, Lincoln LN1 3EE* Tel (01522) 525653 Mobile 07779-557541 E-mail revyabb@ntlworld.com

YABSLEY, Mrs Janet. b 42. St Alb Minl Tr Scheme 81. **dss** 84 **d** 87 **p** 94. Luton St Andr *St Alb* 84-87; NSM Luton St Aug Limbury 87-00; NSM Luton All SS w St Pet from 00. *11 Dale Road, Dunstable LU5 4PY* Tel (01582) 661480

YACOMENI, Peter Frederick. b 34. Worc Coll Ox BA58 MA61. Wycliffe Hall Ox 58. **d** 60 **p** 61. C New Malden and Coombe *S'wark* 60-64; C Bethnal Green St Jas Less *Lon* 64-68; V Barton Hill St Luke w Ch Ch *Bris* 68-75; V Bishopsworth 75-86; RD Bedminster 84-86; P-in-c Wick w Doynton 86-87; V Wick w Doynton and Dyrham 87-98; RD Bitton 95-98; Chapl Wilts and Swindon Healthcare NHS Trust from 98; rtd 98; Perm to Offic *Bris* from 98. *15 Orwell Close, Malmesbury SN16 9UB* Tel (01666) 826628

YALLOP, John. b 47. BA79. Oak Hill Th Coll 79. **d** 79 **p** 80. C Brinsworth w Catcliffe *Sheff* 79-81; C Heeley 81-83; C Pitsmoor Ch Ch 83-86; V Ellesmere St Pet 86-88; C Worksop St Jo *S'well* 90-94; P-in-c Cliftonville *Cant* 94-99. *75 Snowdon Avenue, Maidstone ME14 5NT* Tel (01622) 755774

YAM, David Tong Kho. *See* HAOKIP, David Tongkhoyam

YANGON, Bishop of. *See* SAN SI HTAY, The Most Revd Samuel

YAP, Thomas Fook Piau. b 75. Leeds Univ BA98 MA99. St Jo Coll Nottm MTh02. **d** 03 **p** 04. C Starbeck *Ripon* from 03. *41 Pearl Street, Harrogate HG1 4QW* Tel (01423) 889162 E-mail thomasyap@redeemed-one.fsnet.co.uk

YATES, Alan John Richard. b 38. Lon Univ LDS62. **d** 99 **p** 00. OLM Cley Hill Warminster *Sarum* from 99. *212 Pottle Street, Horningsham, Warminster BA12 7LX* Tel and fax (01985) 844374 Mobile 07970-864714 E-mail revrichardyates@lineone.net

YATES, Andrew Martin. b 55. St Chad's Coll Dur BA77. Linc Th Coll 78. **d** 80 **p** 81. C Brightside St Thos and St Marg *Sheff* 80-83; TV Haverhill w Withersfield, the Wrattings etc *St E* 84-90; Ind Chapl 84-90; R Aylesham w Adisham *Cant* 90-96; P-in-c Dudley St Aug Holly Hall *Worc* 96-03; Chapl Merry Hill Shopping Cen 96-03; P-in-c Lamorran and Merther *Truro* from 03; P-in-c St Michael Penkevil from 03; Dioc Soc Resp Officer from 03. *The Rectory, 18 Fore Street, Tregony, Truro TR2 5RN* Tel (01872) 530507 E-mail yatesasb@aol.com

YATES, Anthony Hugh. b 39. Univ of Wales BA62. Wycliffe Hall Ox 62. **d** 65 **p** 66. C Withington St Crispin *Man* 65-68; C Sheff St Cecilia Parson Cross *Sheff* 68-73; V Middlesbrough St Thos *York* 73-82; V Fenton *Lich* 82-95; V Kilburn St Aug w St Jo *Lon* from 95. *St Augustine's House, Kilburn Park Road, London NW6 5XB* Tel (020) 7624 1637 E-mail saint@augustine93.freeserve.co.uk

YATES (formerly WENSLEY), Mrs Beryl Kathleen. b 29. CertRK55. Selly Oak Coll 53. **dss** 76 **d** 87 **p** 94. Raynes Park St Sav *S'wark* 76-83; Chapl Asst St Geo Hosp Lon 83-89; Chapl Win HA 89-94; rtd 94. *15 Abbotts Ann Road, Winchester SO22 6ND* Tel (01962) 882854

YATES, Esther Christine. St As Minl Tr Course. **d** 05. NSM Newtown w Llanllwchaiarn w Aberhafesp *St As* from 05. *Gwawr y Grug, 7 Millfields, Milford, Newtown SY16 3JP* Tel (01686) 625559

YATES, Francis Edmund. b 49. Ox Univ BEd72 Sheff Univ MEd88. Linc Th Coll 95. **d** 95 **p** 96. C Chesterfield St Mary and All SS *Derby* 95-98; P-in-c Newlyn St Newlyn *Truro* 98-03; Dioc Adv for Schs and RE 98-03; P-in-c Tideswell *Derby* from 03. *The Vicarage, 6 Pursglove Drive, Tideswell, Buxton SK17 8PA* Tel (01298) 871317 E-mail fryates@msn.com

YATES, James Ainsworth. b 21. Bps' Coll Cheshunt 56. **d** 58 **p** 59. C Dunstable *St Alb* 58-60; V Shillington 60-79; V Upper Gravenhurst 62-72; R Lower Gravenhurst 62-72; RD Shefford 69-79; V Upper w Lower Gravenhurst 72-79; V Sandon and Wallington w Rushden 79; R Sandon, Wallington and Rushden w Clothall 79-87; rtd 87; Perm to Offic *St Alb* 87-00. *97 Grove Road, Hitchin SG5 1SQ* Tel (01462) 434959

YATES, Miss Joanna Mary. b 49. St Anne's Coll Ox BA71 MA74 K Coll Lon PGCE72. S'wark Ord Course 89. **d** 91 **p** 94. Promotions and Publications Officer Nat Soc 85-95; Chapl Ch Ho Westmr 91-95; C Regent's Park St Mark *Lon* 91-95; C Finchley St Mary 95-01; TV Leeds City *Ripon* from 01. *St Peter's Vicarage, 15 Parkside Green, Leeds LS6 4NY* Tel 0113-278 7449 *or* 256 2036 Mobile 07904-440152 Fax 0113-243 9731 E-mail precentor@lpch.freeserve.co.uk

✠YATES, The Rt Revd John. b 25. Jes Coll Cam BA49 MA52 Cheltenham & Glouc Coll of HE Hon DLitt92. Linc Th Coll 49. **d** 51 **p** 52 **c** 72. C Southgate Ch Ch *Lon* 51-54; Lic to Offic *Linc* 54-59; Tutor Linc Th Coll 54-59; Chapl 56-59; V Bottesford *Linc* 59-65; Prin Lich Th Coll 66-72; Preb Lich Cathl *Lich* 72; Lic to Offic 66-72; Suff Bp Whitby *York* 72-75; Bp Glouc 75-91; Bp at Lambeth (Hd of Staff) *Cant* 91-94; rtd 94; Hon Asst Bp Win from 94. *15 Abbotts Ann Road, Winchester SO22 6ND* Tel (01962) 882854

YATES, Keith Leonard. b 36. K Coll Lon BD AKC61 Nottm Univ MPhil79. Wells Th Coll. **d** 69 **p** 70. C Luton Ch Ch *St Alb* 69-73; Hon C Luton St Andr 73-76; R Grimoldby w Manby *Linc* 76-80; P-in-c Yarburgh 76-78; R 78-80; P-in-c Alvingham w N and S Cockerington 76-78; V 78-80; P-in-c Gt w Lt Carlton 77-78; R 78-80; Lect Sarum & Wells Th Coll 80-87; R Upper Chelsea H Trin w St Jude *Lon* 87-96; rtd 96; Perm to Offic *Sarum* from 97. *4 Redlands Lane, Broadwindsor, Beaminster DT8 3ST* Tel (01308) 868892

YATES, Kenneth. b 44. Leeds Univ CQSW80. Kelham Th Coll 65. **d** 70 **p** 71. C Leeds City *Ripon* 70-74; C Worksop Priory *S'well* 74-75; Hon C Bawtry w Austerfield 75-78; Hon C Cantley *Sheff* 80-83; Hon C Doncaster St Jude 83-86; Hon C Ashford St Matt *Lon* 86-88; TV Brighton Resurr *Chich* 88-95; R E Blatchington 95-04. *25 Carew Views, Carew Road, Eastbourne BN21 2JL* Tel (01323) 722002

YATES, Lindsay Anne. *See* ADAM, Mrs Lindsay Anne

YATES, Michael Anthony. b 48. Oak Hill Th Coll. **d** 82 **p** 83. C Hebburn St Jo *Dur* 82-85; C Sheldon *Birm* 85-87; V Lea Hall 87-92; TV Old Brampton and Loundsley Green *Derby* 92-98; V Loundsley Green 98-01; V Riddings and Ironville from 01. *The Vicarage, Vicarage Lane, Ironville, Nottingham NG16 5PT* Tel (01773) 602241

YATES, Michael Peter. b 47. JP91. Leeds Univ BA69 MA70 MPhil85 Sheff Univ DCouns95 Potchefstroom Univ PhD03. Coll of Resurr Mirfield 69. **d** 71 **p** 72. C Crewe St Andr *Ches* 71-76; V Wheelock 76-79; Chapl Rainhill Hosp Liv 79-89; Chapl Barnsley Distr Gen Hosp 89-94; Chapl Barnsley Distr Gen Hosp

NHS Trust from 94. *The Chaplain's Office, Barnsley Hospital, Gawber Road, Barnsley S75 2EP* Tel (01226) 730000 Fax 202859 E-mail peter.yates@bhnft.nhs.uk

YATES, Paul David. b 47. Sussex Univ BA73 DPhil80. Sarum & Wells Th Coll 88. **d** 91 **p** 92. NSM Lewes All SS, St Anne, St Mich and St Thos *Chich* 91-00; NSM Lewes St Mich and St Thos at Cliffe w All SS from 00. *17 St Swithun's Terrace, Lewes BN7 1UJ* Tel (01273) 473463

YATES, Peter Francis. b 47. Sheff Univ BA69 Nottm Univ DipTh71. Kelham Th Coll 69. **d** 74 **p** 75. C Mexborough *Sheff* 74-78; C Sevenoaks St Jo *Roch* 78-81; CSWG from 81; Lic to Offic *Chich* from 86. *The Monastery, Crawley Down, Crawley RH10 4LH* Tel (01342) 712074

YATES, Raymond Paul. b 55. Oak Hill Th Coll BA88. **d** 88 **p** 89. C Bootle St Mary w St Paul *Liv* 88-91; C Drypool *York* 91-92; TV 92-97; C Orpington All SS *Roch* 97-00; R Beeford w Frodingham and Foston *York* from 00; RD N Holderness from 02; Chapl HM Pris Hull 01-02. *The Rectory, 11 Glebe Gardens, Beeford, Driffield YO25 8BF* Tel (01262) 488042

YATES, Richard. *See* YATES, Alan John Richard

YATES, Ricky. *See* YATES, Warwick John

YATES, Canon Roger Alan. b 47. MRCP77 Trin Coll Cam BA68 MB71 BChir71 MA72 Bris Univ PhD75. N Ord Course 84. **d** 87 **p** 88. NSM Wilmslow *Ches* from 87; Hon Can Ches Cathl from 99. *3 Racecourse Park, Wilmslow SK9 5LU* Tel (01625) 520246 E-mail raycandoc@yahoo.co.uk

YATES, Mrs Rosamund. b 63. Rob Coll Cam BA84 MA88. Oak Hill Th Coll BA93. **d** 93. C Holloway St Mary Magd *Lon* 93-95; NSM Tervuren w Liège *Eur* 95-97; NSM W Ealing St Jo w St Jas *Lon* from 01. *14 Rosemont Road, London W3 9LR* Tel (020) 8993 6614 Mobile 07713-163756 E-mail rosyates@tiscali.co.uk

YATES, Mrs Sîan. b 57. Univ of Wales (Ban) Westmr Coll Ox MTh91. Linc Th Coll 78. **d** 80 **p** 94. C Risca *Mon* 80-83; Chapl Ch Hosp Horsham 83-85; TD Haverhill w Withersfield, the Wrattings etc *St E* 85-90; Dioc Youth Chapl *Cant* 90-93; Assoc Min Cant St Martin and St Paul 93-96; Educn Chapl *Worc* 96-03; P-in-c Dudley St Jas 96-03; P-in-c Dudley St Barn 01-02; P-in-c Tregony w St Cuby and Cornelly *Truro* from 03; Dioc Adv in RE from 03. *The Rectory, 18 Fore Street, Tregony, Truro TR2 5RN* Tel (01872) 530507 E-mail yatesasb@aol.com

YATES, Canon Timothy Edward. b 35. Magd Coll Cam BA59 MA62 Uppsala Univ DTh78. Ridley Hall Cam 58. **d** 60 **p** 61. C Tonbridge SS Pet and Paul *Roch* 60-63; Tutor St Jo Coll Dur 63-71; Warden Cranmer Hall Dur 71-79; P-in-c Darley w S Darley *Derby* 79-82; R Darley 82-90; Dioc Dir of Ords 85-95; Hon Can Derby Cathl 89-00; C Ashford w Sheldon and Longstone 90-00; rtd 00; Perm to Offic *Derby* from 01. *Holly House, South Church Street, Bakewell DE45 1FD* Tel (01629) 812686

YATES, Warwick John (Ricky). b 52. Univ of Wales (Lamp) BA78. Wycliffe Hall Ox 87. **d** 89 **p** 90. C Hoddesdon *St Alb* 89-93; R Finmere w Mixbury, Cottisford, Hardwick etc *Ox* 93-95; R Shelswell from 95. *The Rectory, Water Stratford Road, Finmere, Buckingham MK18 4AT* Tel (01280) 847184 Fax as telephone E-mail rickyyates@supanet.com

YATES, William Herbert. b 35. Man Univ BA59. Chich Th Coll 60. **d** 61 **p** 62. C Blackpool St Steph *Blackb* 61-65; C Wednesbury St Jo *Lich* 65-69; V Porthill 69-78; R Norton in the Moors 78-84; R Church Aston 84-00; rtd 00; Perm to Offic *Lich* from 01. *83 Stallington Road, Blythe Bridge, Stoke-on-Trent ST11 9PD* Tel (01782) 397182

YATES, Mrs Yvonne Louise. b 52. NEOC 01. **d** 04 **p** 05. NSM Kirkbymoorside w Gillamoor, Farndale etc *York* from 04. *Top Cottage, Newton-on-Rawcliffe, Pickering YO18 8QA* Tel (01751) 473455 Mobile 07760-226810 E-mail ylyates@btinternet.com

YATES-ROUND, Joseph Laurence John. b 25. S'wark Ord Course 75. **d** 76 **p** 77. NSM Tonbridge SS Pet and Paul *Roch* 76-83; Chapl Palma and Balearic Is w Ibiza etc *Eur* 83-90; rtd 90; Perm to Offic *Ches* from 90. *5 Willow Tree Grove, Rode Heath, Stoke-on-Trent ST7 3TE* Tel (01270) 883425

YEATS, Charles. b 56. Natal Univ BCom77 Witwatersrand Univ MBA79 Ball Coll Ox MA85 K Coll Lon MTh90 Dur Univ PhD99. Wycliffe Hall Ox 85. **d** 87 **p** 88. C Islington St Mary *Lon* 87-90; Research Fell Whitefield Inst Ox 90-92; Chapl and Fell Univ Coll Dur 92-00; Perm to Offic *Dur* from 00. *58 Archery Rise, Durham DH1 4LA* Tel 0191-384 0606

YEATS, Peter Derek. b 62. Leeds Univ BA84. Cranmer Hall Dur 85. **d** 87 **p** 88. C Tynemouth Cullercoats St Paul *Newc* 87-90; USPG 90-00; Miss to Seafarers Port Chapl Kobe Japan from 00. *USPG, Partnership House, 157 Waterloo Road, London SE1 8XA* Tel (020) 7928 8681 Fax 7928 2371

YELDHAM, Anthony Paul Richard. *See* KYRIAKIDES-YELDHAM, Anthony Paul Richard

YELLAND, Jeffrey Charles. b 46. CEng MIStructE72. STETS 98. **d** 01 **p** 02. NSM Effingham w Lt Bookham *Guildf* 01-04; NSM Dorking St Paul from 04. *32 Hookfield, Epsom KT19 8JG* Tel and fax (01372) 807096 Mobile 07802-781836 E-mail jeff.yelland@ntlworld.com *or* rev.jeff.yelland@ntlworld.com

YENDALL, John Edward Thomas. b 52. St Jo Coll Dur BA88. Cranmer Hall Dur 84. **d** 88 **p** 89. C Bangor *Ban* 88-90; C Botwnnog 90-91; R Trefdraeth w Aberffraw etc 91-01; RD Malltraeth 97-01; V Llanwddyn and Llanfihangel-yng-Nghwynfa etc *St As* from 01. *The Vicarage, Llanwddyn, Oswestry SY10 0LX* Tel (01691) 870663

YEO (née HARRISSON), Mrs Jennifer Marjorie. b 40. SRN62. Cant Sch of Min 87. **d** 90 **p** 97. NSM Kemsing w Woodlands *Roch* 90-91; Chapl Stone Ho Hosp Kent 90-91; NSM Totnes, Bridgetown and Berry Pomeroy etc *Ex* 95-97; NSM Ashprington, Cornworthy and Dittisham 97-98; Perm to Offic from 98. *Address temp unknown*

YEO, Richard Ellery. b 25. Ex Coll Ox MA49 DipEd49. Cant Sch of Min 86. **d** 89 **p** 90. NSM Broadstairs *Cant* 89-92; Perm to Offic *Ex* from 95. *Address temp unknown*

✠**YEOMAN, The Rt Revd David.** b 44. St Mich Coll Llan 66. **d** 70 **p** 71 **c** 04. C Cardiff St Jo *Llan* 70-72; C Caerphilly 72-76; V Ystrad Rhondda w Ynyscynon 76-81; V Mountain Ash 81-96; R Coity w Nolton 96-04; Can Llan Cathl from 00; Asst Bp Llan from 04; Adn Morgannwg from 04. *3 Denison Way, Cardiff CF5 4SF* Tel (029) 2059 8110 Mobile 07971-926631 E-mail david@calon.freeserve.co.uk

YEOMAN, Douglas. b 35. ACII63. **d** 77 **p** 78. NSM Edin St Martin *Edin* 77-96; NSM Edin St Luke 79-90; Chapl Edinburgh Healthcare NHS Trust 95-99; Chapl Lothian Primary Healthcare NHS Trust from 98; NSM Edin St Cuth *Edin* from 96. *6 Craiglockhart Crescent, Edinburgh EH14 1EY* Tel 0131-443 5449 E-mail dyeoman@tiscali.co.uk

YEOMAN, Miss Ruth Jane. b 60. Sheff Univ BSc82 MSc85 Dur Univ PGCE83. Ripon Coll Cuddesdon BA90 MA94. **d** 91 **p** 94. C Coleshill *Birm* 91-95; C Hodge Hill 95-01; Bp's Adv for Children's Work 95-01; L'Arche Lambeth Community 01-03; Perm to Offic *S'wark* 01-03 and *Birm* 03; V Menston w Woodhead *Bradf* from 03. *The Vicarage, 12 Fairfax Gardens, Menston, Ilkley LS29 6ET* Tel (01943) 877739 Mobile 07752-912646 E-mail ruthjyeoman@hotmail.com

YEOMANS, Robert John. b 44. AKC66. **d** 67 **p** 68. C Pontesbury I and II *Heref* 67-70; Asst Youth Officer *St Alb* 70-72; Project Officer (Dio St Alb) Gen Syn Bd of Educn 73-77; V Is of Dogs Ch Ch and St Jo w St Luke *Lon* 77-87; V Waterloo St Jo w St Andr *S'wark* 87-93; Chapl United Bris Healthcare NHS Trust 93-02; Chapl Ex Hospiscare from 02. *The White Barn, Maxworthy, Launceston PL15 8LY* Tel (01566) 781570 E-mail r.yeomans@hospiscare-devon.org.uk

YERBURGH, Canon David Savile. b 34. Magd Coll Cam BA57 MA61. Wells Th Coll 57. **d** 59 **p** 60. C Cirencester *Glouc* 59-63; C Bitterne Park *Win* 63-67; V Churchdown St Jo *Glouc* 67-74; RD Glouc N 73-74; V Charlton Kings St Mary 74-85; R Minchinhampton 85-95; Hon Can Glouc Cathl 86-95; rtd 95; Perm to Offic *Sarum* from 95. *2 Mill Race Close, Mill Road, Salisbury SP2 7RX* Tel (01722) 320064

YERBURGH, Peter Charles. b 31. Magd Coll Cam BA53 MA57. Wells Th Coll 53. **d** 55 **p** 56. C Southbroom *Sarum* 55-58; Chapl Wells Cathl Sch 58-71; Chapl Durlston Court Sch 71-91; rtd 91. *2 Mill Race Close, Mill Road, Salisbury SP2 7RX* Tel (01722) 327796

YERBURY, Gregory Howard. b 67. Trin Coll Bris BA93. St Jo Coll Nottm 94. **d** 96 **p** 97. C Crofton *Portsm* 96-00; P-in-c Bolton St Jo *Man* from 00; P-in-c Bolton Breightmet St Jas from 05. *St John's Vicarage, 7 Alford Close, Bolton BL2 6NR* Tel (01204) 389044 E-mail greg@stjohns.arbonne.co.uk

YEWDALL, Mrs Mary Doreen. b 23. Nottm Univ DipEd71 BTh85. EMMTC 76. **dss** 79 **d** 87 **p** 94. Kirkby in Ashfield St Thos *S'well* 79-81; Daybrook 81-87; Par Dn 87-89; rtd 89; Hon Par Dn Bilsthorpe *S'well* 89-91; Hon Par Dn Eakring 89-91; Hon Par Dn Winkburn 89-91; Hon Par Dn Maplebeck 89-91; NSM Norton juxta Malton *York* 92-95; NSM Whitwell w Crambe, Flaxton, Foston etc 95-98; Perm to Offic from 98. *West Croft, The Rise, Thornton Dale, Pickering YO18 7TG* Tel (01751) 477757

YIEND, Paul Martin. b 57. UEA BA80. St Jo Coll Nottm MA96. **d** 92 **p** 94. C Bushbury *Lich* 92-95; Asst Chapl Brussels *Eur* 99-00; P-in-c Charleroi 00-03; P-in-c Liège from 00. *rue Basse des Canes 11, 5300 Andenne, Belgium* Tel and fax (0032) (85) 844482 E-mail paul.yiend@skynet.be

YIN, Canon Roy Henry Bowyer. b 10. K Coll Cam BA32 MA36. Cuddesdon Coll 32. **d** 33 **p** 34. C Cambridge St Giles w St Pet *Ely* 33-37; Chapl K Coll Cam 33-37; Chapl Hurstpierpoint Coll 37-46; Ceylon 46-62; Singapore from 64; rtd 75; Hon Can Singapore from 80. *1 Khiang Guan Avenue, #04-04 Lincoln Lodge, Singapore 308380*

YODER, John Henry. b 36. California State Univ BA73. Ch Div Sch of Pacific MDiv76. **d** 76 **p** 77. USA 76-79 and from 80; C Wolverhampton *Lich* 79-80; rtd 99. *6233 West Washington Boulevard, Las Vegas, NV 89107, USA* E-mail johnhtrain2@gateway.net

✠**YONG, The Most Revd Datuk Ping Chung.** b 41. Memorial Univ Newfoundland BA68. Qu Coll Newfoundland LTh69. **d** 69 **p** 70 **c** 90. Malaysia 69-84 and from 90; P Sabah 69-77; Adn

Sabah 77-84; Chairman ACC 84-90; Bp Sabah from 90; Abp SE Asia from 00. *PO Box 10811, 88809 Kota Kinabalu, Sabah, Malaysia* Tel (0060) (88) 245846 *or* 249296 Fax 245942 E-mail pcyong@pc.jaring.my

YONGE, James Mohun (Brother Amos). b 47. Keele Univ BA71. WMMTC 91. **d** 94 **p** 95. SSF from 76. *Address temp unknown*

✠**YOON, The Rt Revd Paul Hwan.** b 38. **d** 67 **c** 87. Bp Taejon 87-02; Presiding Bp Korea 00-02; rtd 02. *PO Box 22, Taejon 300-600, Republic of Korea* Tel (0082) (42) 256 9987 Fax 255 8918

YORK, Canon Humphrey Bowmar. b 28. St Chad's Coll Dur BA54 Univ of Wales (Lamp) MA04. **d** 55 **p** 56. C Beamish *Dur* 55-57; C Tettenhall Regis *Lich* 57-62; P-in-c Lansallos w Pelynt *Truro* 62-63; R Lanreath 62-67; V Pelynt 63-67; P-in-c Lanlivery 67-74; P-in-c Luxulyan 67-74; P-in-c Lanlivery w Luxulyan 74-83; RD Bodmin 76-82; R Antony w Sheviock 83-93; Hon Can Truro Cathl 90-93; rtd 93; Perm to Offic *Truro* and *Sarum* from 93. *8 Huntingdon Street, Bradford-on-Avon BA15 1RF* E-mail canonhumphrey@tinyworld.co.uk

YORK, Archbishop of. *See* SENTAMU, The Most Revd and Rt Hon John Mugabi

YORK, Archdeacon of. *See* SEED, The Ven Richard Murray Crosland

YORK, Dean of. *See* JONES, The Very Revd Keith Brynmor

YORKE, John Andrew. b 47. Cranmer Hall Dur 70. **d** 73 **p** 74. C Spitalfields Ch Ch w All SS *Lon* 73-78; Canada 78-92; V Totland Bay *Portsm* from 92; V Thorley from 95. *The Vicarage, Alum Bay New Road, Totland Bay PO39 0ES* Tel (01983) 752031 E-mail andy.yorke@lineone.net

YORKE, The Very Revd Michael Leslie. b 39. Magd Coll Cam BA62 MA66. Cuddesdon Coll 62. **d** 64 **p** 65. C Croydon St Jo *Cant* 64-68; Succ Chelmsf Cathl *Chelmsf* 68-69; Prec and Chapl 69-73; Dep Dir Cathl Cen for Research and Tr 72-74; P-in-c Ashdon w Hadstock 74-76; R 76-78; Can Res Chelmsf Cathl 78-88; Vice-Provost 84-88; P-in-c N Lynn w St Marg and St Nic *Nor* 88-92; P-in-c King's Lynn St Marg w St Nic 92-94; Chmn Dioc Adv Bd for Min 90-94; Hon Can Nor Cathl 93-94; Provost Portsm 94-99; Dean Lich 99-04; rtd 04; Perm to Offic *Nor* from 04. *Westgate House, The Green, Burnham Market, King's Lynn PE31 8HD* Tel (01328) 738833

YORKSTONE, Peter. b 48. Loughb Univ BTech72. Oak Hill Th Coll 79. **d** 81 **p** 82. C Blackpool St Thos *Blackb* 81-85; V Copp 85-00; P-in-c Giggleswick and Rathmell w Wigglesworth *Bradf* from 00. *The Vicarage, Bankwell Road, Giggleswick, Settle BD24 0AP* Tel (01729) 822425 E-mail peter@pyorkstone.freeserve.co.uk

YOUATT, Jennifer Alison. *See* MONTGOMERY, Mrs Jennifer Alison

YOUDE, Paul Crosland. b 47. Birm Univ LLB68. WEMTC 93. **d** 96 **p** 97. NSM Cheltenham St Luke and St Jo *Glouc* 96-99; C Cirencester 99-03; P-in-c Lydney from 03. *5 Raglan Gardens, Lydney GL15 5GZ* Tel (01594) 842321 Fax as telephone E-mail paul@pyoude.freeserve.co.uk

YOUELL, Mrs Deborah Mary. b 57. STETS 01. **d** 04. NSM Cowplain *Portsm* from 04. *42 The Yews, Horndean, Waterlooville PO8 0BH* Tel (023) 9279 9946 E-mail deborah.youell@ntlworld.com

YOUENS, Edward. *See* MONTAGUE-YOUENS, Canon Hubert Edward

YOUINGS, Adrian. b 65. Ex Univ BSc86 Bath Univ PhD90. Wycliffe Hall Ox 93. **d** 96 **p** 97. C Dorking St Paul *Guildf* 96-99; C S Croydon Em *S'wark* 99-03; R Trull w Angersleigh *B & W* from 03. *The Rectory, Wild Oak Lane, Trull, Taunton TA3 7JT* Tel (01823) 253518

YOULD, Guy Martin. b 37. FSAScot75 Keble Coll Ox BA61 DipTh62 MA65 Magd Coll Ox BD68 Hull Univ PhD80. Lambeth STh75 St Steph Ho Ox 61. **d** 63 **p** 64. C Middlesbrough St Jo the Ev *York* 63-65; Chapl Magd Coll Ox 65-68; C Cowley St Jo *Ox* 65-68; Asst Chapl Radley Coll 68-71; C W Kirby St Bridget *Ches* 71-74; Chapl Loretto Sch Musselburgh 74; V Liscard St Mary w St Columba *Ches* 74-78; St Barn Coll Belair Australia 78-80; C Doncaster St Leon and St Jude *Sheff* 80-81; V Brodsworth w Hooton Pagnell, Frickley etc 81-87; Chapl St Mary's Sch Wantage 87-93; R Chapel Chorlton, Maer and Whitmore *Lich* 93-98; P-in-c Altarnon w Bolventor, Laneast and St Clether *Truro* 98-02; P-in-c Lezant 98-02; rtd 03; C Gt and Lt Torrington and Frithelstock *Ex* from 03. *St Giles' House, Little Torrington, Torrington EX38 8PS* Tel (01805) 622497

YOUNG, Andrew Charles. b 54. FIBMS83. N Ord Course 98. **d** 01 **p** 02. C Heywood *Man* 01-05; TV Eccles from 05. *St Paul's Vicarage, Egerton Road, Eccles, Manchester M30 9LR* Tel 0161-789 2420 E-mail andrew.young66@ntlworld.com

YOUNG, Andrew John. b 50. St Jo Coll Dur BA73. Westcott Ho Cam 73. **d** 75 **p** 89. C Nailsworth *Glouc* 75-76; NSM Yeovil w Kingston Pitney *B & W* 89-93; NSM Tintinhull w Chilthorne Domer, Yeovil Marsh etc from 93. *15 Cook Avenue, Chard TA20 2JR* Tel (01460) 62182

YOUNG, Miss Anne Patricia. b 44. Cov Coll of Educn CertEd66 Leeds Univ BEd76 Sheff Univ MEd82. N Ord Course 01. **d** 05. NSM Middlestown *Wakef* from 05. *58 The Crofts, Emley, Huddersfield HD8 9RU* Tel and fax (01924) 840738 Mobile 07906-835309 E-mail anne@ayoung94.fsbusiness.co.uk

YOUNG, Arthur. b 65. Belf Bible Coll BTh92. CITC 99. **d** 01 **p** 02. C Donaghadee *D & D* 01-04; I Tullylish from 04. *Tullylish Rectory, 100 Banbridge Road, Gilford, Craigavon BT63 6DL* Tel and fax (028) 3883 1298

YOUNG, Canon Brian Thomas. b 42. Linc Th Coll 67. **d** 70 **p** 71. C Monkseaton St Mary *Newc* 70-73; C Berwick H Trin 73-77; P-in-c Gt Broughton *Carl* 77-80; V Gt Broughton and Broughton Moor 80-83; V Chorley *Ches* 83-90; V Alderley Edge from 90; RD Knutsford from 96; Hon Can Ches Cathl from 97. *The Vicarage, Church Lane, Alderley Edge SK9 7UZ* Tel (01625) 583249 E-mail byoung@alderley.fserve.co.uk

YOUNG, Canon Charles John. b 24. GIMechE50 Open Univ BA98. Qu Coll Birm 52. **d** 55 **p** 56. C Dudley St Thos *Worc* 55-58; C Beeston *S'well* 58-61; V Lady Bay 61-66; R Kirkby in Ashfield 66-75; V Balderton 75-92; RD Newark 82-90; Hon Can S'well Minster 84-92; rtd 92; Bp's Chapl for Rtd Clergy *S'well* 92-04; Perm to Offic from 04. *9 The Paddocks, London Road, Newark NG24 1SS* Tel (01636) 613445

YOUNG, Christopher Terence. b 53. Cape Town Univ BA76 Univ of S Africa BTh80. St Bede's Coll Umtata 79. **d** 80 **p** 81. S Africa 80-86 and from 88; C Rainham *Chelmsf* 86-88. *11B Coniston Road, Rondebosch, 7700 South Africa* Tel (0027) (21) 685 6868 *or* 689 2087

✠**YOUNG, The Rt Revd Clive.** b 48. St Jo Coll Dur BA70. Ridley Hall Cam 70. **d** 72 **p** 73 **c** 99. C Neasden cum Kingsbury St Cath *Lon* 72-75; C Hammersmith St Paul 75-79; P-in-c Old Ford St Paul w St Steph 79-82; V Old Ford St Paul w St Steph and St Mark 82-92; AD Tower Hamlets 88-92; Adn Hackney 92-99; V St Andr Holborn 92-99; Suff Bp Dunwich *St E* from 99. *28 Westerfield Road, Ipswich IP4 2UJ* Tel (01473) 222276 Fax 210303 E-mail bishop.clive@stedmundsbury.anglican.org

YOUNG, Daniel George Harding. b 52. New Coll Ox BA73 MA83. Cranmer Hall Dur 77. **d** 80 **p** 81. C Bushbury *Lich* 80-83; Chapl Dean Close Sch Cheltenham 83-99; Perm to Offic *Win* from 01. *6 Tyfield, Sherborne St John, Basingstoke RG24 9HZ* Tel (01256) 850397 E-mail dan-young@tiscali.co.uk

YOUNG, David. b 37. NDTJ61 Open Univ PhD89. Ely Th Coll 61 Linc Th Coll 64 STh79. **d** 67 **p** 68. C Crofton *Wakef* 67-68; C Heckmondwike 68-71; V Stainland 71-76; R Patrington w Winestead *York* 76-80; Chapl Winestead Hosp 76-80; Gen Preacher *Linc* from 80; Chapl St Jo Hosp Linc 80-90; Chapl N Lincs Mental Health Unit 90-93; Chapl Linc Distr Healthcare NHS Trust 93-97; Dep Chapl from 98. *Westview, Aisthorpe, Lincoln LN1 2SG* Tel (01522) 730912

YOUNG, David Charles. b 44. Oriel Coll Ox BA66 MA70. S'wark Ord Course 74. **d** 77 **p** 78. C Harborne St Pet *Birm* 77-81; P-in-c Edgbaston St Germain 81-83; P-in-c Birm St Paul 83-85; Perm to Offic *St Alb* from 85; *Ox* 91-00. *18 Tamar Walk, Leighton Buzzard LU7 8DD* Tel (01525) 382881 E-mail david.young@dial.pipex.com

YOUNG, David John. b 43. Nottm Univ BA64 MPhil89 Lambeth STh87. Coll of Resurr Mirfield 64. **d** 66 **p** 67. C Warsop *S'well* 66-68; C Harworth 68-71; P-in-c Hackenthorpe Ch Ch *Derby* 71-73; TV Frecheville and Hackenthorpe 73-75; V Chaddesden St Phil 75-83; R Narborough and Huncote *Leic* 83-89; RD Guthlaxton I 87-90; Chapl Leic Univ 90-95; V Eyres Monsell 95-98; Perm to Offic 98-99; rtd 03. *57 Castle Fields, Leicester LE4 1AN* Tel 0116-236 5634

✠**YOUNG, The Rt Revd David Nigel de Lorentz.** b 31. CBE00. Ball Coll Ox BA54 MA58. Wycliffe Hall Ox 57. **d** 59 **p** 60 **c** 77. C Allerton *Liv* 59-62; C St Marylebone St Mark Hamilton Terrace *Lon* 62-63; CMS 63-67; Lect Man Univ 67-70; V Burwell *Ely* 70-75; Hon Can Ely Cathl 75-77; Adn Huntingdon 75-77; V Gt w Lt Gidding and Steeple Gidding 75-77; R Hemingford Abbots 77; Bp Ripon 77-99; rtd 99; Hon Asst Bp Bradf from 00. *Chapel House, Lawkland, Austwick, Lancaster LA2 8AT* Tel (01524) 251209

YOUNG, Derek John. b 42. St D Coll Lamp DipTh73. **d** 73 **p** 74. C Griffithstown *Mon* 73-76; C Ebbw Vale 76-77; V Penmaen 77-81; V Penmaen and Crumlin 81-87; Chapl Oakdale Hosp Gwent 83-87; V New Tredegar *Mon* 87-99; V Llanfihangel Crucorney w Oldcastle etc from 99. *The Vicarage, Llanfihangel Crucorney, Abergavenny NP7 8DH* Tel (01873) 890349

YOUNG, Desmond Terence. b 17. TCD BA40. **d** 41 **p** 42. C Hadfield *Derby* 41-44; C Derby St Werburgh 44-47; CF 47-55; I Fertagh *C & O* 55-62; I Inistioge w the Rower 62-74; P-in-c Thomastown 62-74; C Roundhay St Edm *Ripon* 74-77; V Leeds Gipton Epiphany 77-83; rtd 83; Perm to Offic *Guildf* 83-94. *c/o T D Young Esq, Carden House, Rectory Lane, Gedney, Spalding PE12 0BU*

YOUNG, George William. b 31. Lon Coll of Div ALCD55. **d** 56 **p** 57. C Everton Em *Liv* 56-58; C Halliwell St Pet *Man* 58-61; V Newburn *Newc* 61-67; P-in-c Tyler's Green *Ox* 67-69; V 69-80; Lic to Offic 80-84; Area Sec (W England) SAMS 80-84; Hon C Purley Ch Ch *S'wark* 84-87; V Beckenham St Jo *Roch* 87-92; rtd

92; Perm to Offic *S'wark* from 92. *9 Shortacres, High Street, Nutfield, Redhill RH1 4HJ* Tel (01737) 822363

YOUNG, Hilary Antoinette Francesca. b 57. **d** 01 **p** 02. NSM Thorne *Sheff* 01-03; C 03-05; V Wigan St Jas w St Thos *Liv* from 05. *97 Melrose Drive, Wigan WN3 6EG* Tel (01942) 225311 E-mail hyoung.youngvic@virgin.net

YOUNG, Hyacinth Loretta. b 49. NTMTC 95. **d** 98 **p** 99. NSM Harlesden All So *Lon* 98-00; TV Wembley Park from 00. *194 Windermere Avenue, Wembley HA9 8QT* Tel (020) 8908 2252 E-mail hyacinth512@aol.com

YOUNG, Iain Clavering. b 56. Newc Poly BA79. Coll of Resurr Mirfield 80. **d** 83 **p** 84. C Wallsend St Luke *Newc* 83-86; C Horton 86-87; V 87-92; V Friern Barnet St Pet le Poer *Lon* 92-95; C Holborn St Alb w Saffron Hill St Pet 96-97; P-in-c Hoxton H Trin w St Mary 97-02; V from 02; Chapl Moorfields Eye Hosp NHS Trust 97-03. *Holy Trinity Vicarage, 3 Bletchley Street, London N1 7QG* Tel (020) 7253 4796 E-mail iain.young@fish.co.uk

YOUNG, Jeremy Michael. b 54. Ch Coll Cam BA76 MA80 Lon Univ MTh94. Coll of Resurr Mirfield 78. **d** 80 **p** 81. C Whitworth w Spennymoor *Dur* 80-83; C Boxmoor St Jo *St Alb* 83-86; V Croxley Green St Oswald 86-94; Dir Past Studies CITC 94-99; Lic to Offic *D & G* 99-03. *Westerley House, Tellisford, Bath BA2 7RL* Tel (01373) 830920 E-mail jeremy_young@mac.com

YOUNG, John. *See* YOUNG, David John

YOUNG, Canon John David. b 37. DLC60 Lon Univ BD65 Sussex Univ MA77. Clifton Th Coll 62. **d** 65 **p** 66. C Plymouth St Jude *Ex* 65-68; Hd of RE Northgate Sch Ipswich 68-71; Chapl and Sen Lect Bp Otter Coll Chich 71-81; Chapl and Sen Lect W Sussex Inst of HE 77-81; Chapl and Sen Lect York St Jo Coll 81-87; C York St Paul *York* 87-88; Dioc Ev 88-02; Can and Preb York Minster 92-03; Miss Strategy Development Officer 00-02; rtd 02; Lic to Offic *York* from 02. *72 Middlethorpe Grove, York YO24 1JY* Tel and fax (01904) 704195 E-mail johnyoung@stpaulsyork.org.uk

YOUNG, John <u>Kenneth</u>. Edin Th Coll 62. **d** 64 **p** 65. C Gosforth All SS *Newc* 64-67; C Newc St Gabr 67-69; R Bowers Gifford *Chelmsf* 69-72; R Bowers Gifford w N Benfleet 72-75; P-in-c Kirkwhelpington *Newc* 75-79; P-in-c Kirkharle 77-79; P-in-c Kirkheaton 75-79; P-in-c Cambo 77-79; V Kirkwhelpington, Kirkharle, Kirkheaton and Cambo 79-82; V Gosforth St Nic 82-92; V Healey and Slaley 92-97; rtd 97; Perm to Offic *Newc* from 97. *20 Mitford Way, Dinnington, Newcastle upon Tyne NE13 7LW* Tel (01661) 821050

YOUNG, John Robert. b 43. SSM 63. **d** 68 **p** 69. Australia 68-72; C Ch Ch Cathl Darwin 68-70; C Murrumbeena 70-72; C Stocking Farm *Leic* 72-74; Australia from 74; P-in-c W Reservoir 75-78; I Montmorency 78-85; I E Burwood 85-96; R Warracknabeal from 96. *21 Regent Street, PO Box 78, Port Fairy, Vic, Australia 3284* Tel (0061) (3) 5568 1028 Fax as telephone

YOUNG, Canon Jonathan Frederick. b 25. Univ of Wales (Lamp) BA51 Birm Univ MA81. St Mich Coll Llan 51. **d** 53 **p** 54. C Roath St Martin *Llan* 53-59; Lic to Offic *Ox* 59-74; SSJE 62-71; Bp's Chapl for Community Relns *Birm* 71-74; Chapl Coun for Soc Resp 74-85; Hon Can Birm Cathl 84-85; USA from 85; rtd 90. *52 Harvard Road, Belmont, MA 02478, USA* Tel (001) (617) 484 9439 E-mail youngmj@aol.com

YOUNG, Canon Jonathan Priestland. b 44. AKC68. **d** 69 **p** 70. C Clapham H Trin *S'wark* 69-73; C Mitcham St Mark 73-74; V Godmanchester *Ely* 74-82; P-in-c Cambridge St Giles w St Pet 82; P-in-c Chesterton St Luke 82; TR Cambridge Ascension 82-01; Chapl St Jo Coll Sch Cam 88-93; P-in-c Ellington *Ely* 01-02; P-in-c Grafham 01-02; P-in-c Easton 01-02; P-in-c Spaldwick w Barham and Woolley 01-02; R E Leightonstone from 02; P-in-c Alconbury w Alconbury Weston from 04; P-in-c Buckworth from 04; Hon Can Ely Cathl from 01; RD Leightonstone 02-04. *The Rectory, Parson's Drive, Ellington, Huntingdon PE28 0AU* Tel and fax (01480) 891695

YOUNG, Miss Karen Heather. b 66. Nottm Univ BA01. Westcott Ho Cam 02. **d** 05. C Airedale w Fryston *Wakef* from 05. *St Peter's House, 3 Kendall Gardens, Castleford WF10 3NY* Tel (01977) 511598 Mobile 07747-602686 E-mail k.young2@zoom.co.uk

YOUNG, Kathleen Margaret. *See* BROWN, Canon Kathleen Margaret

YOUNG, Kenneth. *See* YOUNG, John Kenneth

YOUNG, Mark Gilbert Campbell. b 60. Mert Coll Ox BA88. Wycliffe Hall Ox 86. **d** 91 **p** 92. C Holborn St Geo w H Trin and St Bart *Lon* 91-95; C St Pancras w St Jas and Ch Ch 95-99; V W Hampstead Trin from 99; P-in-c W Hampstead St Cuth from 01. *Holy Trinity Vicarage, 1A Akenside Road, London NW3 5BS* Tel (020) 7794 2975 *or* 7435 0083 E-mail gil.trinity@virgin.net

YOUNG, Martin Edward. b 20. Oriel Coll Ox BA41 MA45. Cuddesdon Coll 41. **d** 43 **p** 44. C Newbury *Ox* 43-45; C Wymondham *Nor* 45-49; C Gt Berkhamsted *St Alb* 49-51; V Littlemore *Ox* 51-64; R Wootton w Quinton *Pet* 64-72; R Wootton w Quinton and Preston Deanery 72-78; V Welford w Sibbertoft 78-82; V Welford w Sibbertoft and Marston Trussell 82-88; rtd 88; Perm to Offic *Pet* from 88. *2 Knutsford Lane, Long Buckby, Northampton NN6 7RL* Tel (01327) 843929

YOUNG, Martin John. b 72. Univ Coll Lon BSc93. Oak Hill Th Coll BA01. **d** 01 **p** 02. C Heigham H Trin *Nor* from 01; P-in-c Nor St Andr from 05. *24 Carnoustie, Norwich NR4 6AY* Tel (01603) 4598821 E-mail martin@standrewsnorwich.org

YOUNG, Mrs Maureen. b 47. SEITE 02. **d** 04. NSM Roughey *Chich* from 04. *29 Badgers Close, Horsham RH12 5RU* Tel (01403) 263119 E-mail maureen@agra.org.uk

YOUNG, Norman Keith. b 35. EAMTC 85. **d** 87 **p** 88. C Burwell *Ely* 87-91; V Swaffham Bulbeck and Swaffham Prior w Reach 91-92; V Barnby Dun *Sheff* 92-05; Ind Chapl 92-05; AD Doncaster 98-04; rtd 05; P-in-c Aspull St Eliz *Liv* from 05. *97 Melrose Drive, Wigan WN3 6EG* Tel (01942) 225311 E-mail norman@youngvic.u-net.com

YOUNG, Peter John. b 26. Pemb Coll Cam BA49 MA54. Ridley Hall Cam 49. **d** 51 **p** 52. C Cheadle *Ches* 51-54; Malaya 54-63; Malaysia from 63; rtd 92. *247 Jalan 5/48, 46000 Petaling Jaya, Selangor, Malaysia* Tel (0060) (3) 7782 9269 Fax 7783 0849

YOUNG, Philip Anderson. b 53. St Jo Coll Dur BA75 Fitzw Coll Cam BA78 MA89. Ridley Hall Cam 75. **d** 78 **p** 79. C Surbiton St Andr and St Mark *S'wark* 78-80; NSM Aylsham *Nor* from 04. *48 Starling Close, Aylsham, Norwich NR11 6XG* Tel (01263) 732224 *or* tel and fax 735543 Mobile 07890-588295 E-mail philipyoung@btinternet.com

YOUNG, Canon Raymond Grant. b 11. MBE81. **d** 43 **p** 44. C Ince Ch Ch *Liv* 43-45; C Pemberton St Jo 46; Chapl to Deaf *Win* and *Portsm* 46-49; Perm to Offic *Portsm* 48-59; V Marchwood *Win* 59-70; Chapl to Deaf *Win* and *Portsm* 70-81; Hon Can Win Cathl *Win* 77-81; rtd 81; Perm to Offic *Win* 81-95. *c/o R Young Esq, 36 Cundell Way, Kings Worthy, Winchester SO23 7NP*

YOUNG, Richard Christian. b 65. Southn Univ LLB87 Solicitor 91. St Jo Coll Nottm 02. **d** 04 **p** 05. C Alperton *Lon* from 04. *19 Bowrons Avenue, Wembley HA0 4QS* Tel (020) 8902 5997 Mobile 07940-810390 E-mail richard@theyoungones.org.uk

YOUNG, Richard Michael. b 63. **d** 96 **p** 97. NSM Brunswick *Man* from 96. *2 Birch Grove, Rusholme, Manchester M14 5JY* Tel 0161-225 0884 Mobile 07778-817784 E-mail richard_young@3igroup.com

YOUNG, Stephen. b 33. St Edm Hall Ox MA61. St Jo Coll Nottm 75 ALCD77. **d** 77 **p** 78. C Crofton *Portsm* 77-81; C Rainham *Chelmsf* 81-87; V Ramsgate Ch Ch *Cant* 87-98; rtd 98; Perm to Offic *Cant* from 98. *9 Egerton Drive, Cliftonville, Margate CT9 9YE* Tel (01843) 223071

YOUNG, Stephen Edward. b 52. K Coll Lon BD73 AKC73 Ch Ch Coll Cant CertEd74 Open Univ PhD04. **d** 75 **p** 76. C Walton St Mary *Liv* 75-79; C St Marylebone All SS *Lon* 83; C Pimlico St Gabr 83-85; Chapl Whitelands Coll of HE *S'wark* 85-88; Asst Chapl St Paul's Sch Barnes 88-91; Chapl 91-02; P in O from 91; Hon C Pimlico St Mary Bourne Street *Lon* from 94; Chapl Dulwich Coll from 02. *Dulwich College, Dulwich Common, London SE21 7LD* Tel (020) 8693 3601 E-mail presby@btopenworld.com

YOUNG, Stuart Kincaid. b 59. **d** 95 **p** 96. C Letchworth St Paul w Willian *St Alb* 95-00; V Pucklechurch and Abson *Bris* from 00. *The Vicarage, Westerleigh Road, Pucklechurch, Bristol BS16 9RD* Tel 0117-937 2260 E-mail vicar@pucklechurchandabson.org.uk

YOUNG, William Maurice. b 32. St Jo Coll Nottm 80. **d** 81 **p** 82. C Harlescott *Lich* 81-84; V Hadley 84-94; rtd 94; Perm to Offic *Heref* from 94. *Old Chapel School, Newport Street, Clun, Craven Arms SY7 8JZ* Tel (01588) 640846

YOUNGER, Jeremy Andrew. b 46. Nottm Univ BA68 Bris Univ MA71. Wells Th Coll 68. **d** 70 **p** 71. C Basingstoke *Win* 70-74; C Harpenden St Nic *St Alb* 74-76; Dir Communications 77-81; Chapl Sarum & Wells Th Coll 77-81; V Clifton All SS w St Jo *Bris* 81-84; Relig Affairs Producer BBC Radio Nottm *S'well* 84-86; C Bow w Bromley St Leon *Lon* 86-88; Projects and Min Manager Westmr St Jas 89-93; Hon C St Marylebone All SS 89-93; New Zealand from 93. *1/102 Valley Road, Mount Eden, Aukland, New Zealand*

YOUNGSON, David Thoms. b 38. Cuddesdon Coll 71. **d** 73 **p** 74. C Norton St Mary *Dur* 73-76; C Hartlepool St Paul 76-79; P-in-c Stockton St Jo CD 79-84; V Stockton St Jo 84-86; V Owton Manor 86-90; rtd 90; Perm to Offic *Dur* 90-99. *35 Buxton Gardens, Billingham TS22 5AJ*

YULE, John David. b 49. G&C Coll Cam BA70 MA74 PhD76. Westcott Ho Cam 79. **d** 81 **p** 82. C Cherry Hinton St Andr *Ely* 81-84; C Almondbury w Farnley Tyas *Wakef* 84-87; V Swavesey *Ely* 87-95; V Fen Drayton w Conington 87-95; R Fen Drayton w Conington and Lolworth etc from 95. *The Vicarage, Honey Hill, Fen Drayton, Cambridge CB4 5SF* Tel (01954) 231903 Fax 204446 E-mail vicar@honeyhill.org

YULE, Robert White. b 49. FCMA81. St Jo Coll Nottm. **d** 88 **p** 89. C Wilford *S'well* 88-91; TV Bestwood 91-96; P-in-c Selston 96-98; V 98-00; C Watford St Pet *St Alb* from 00. *68 Tudor Avenue, Watford WD24 7NX* Tel (01923) 223510, 337002 *or* 337000 E-mail bob.yule@soulsurvivor.com

Z

ZACHAU, Eric. b 31. AKC57. **d** 58 **p** 59. C Bishopwearmouth St Mich *Dur* 58-62; C Ryhope 62-63; V Beadnell *Newc* 63-69; V Earsdon 69-81; V Bamburgh and Lucker 81-95; V Bamburgh and Beadnell 95-01; RD Bamburgh and Glendale 92-97; rtd 01; Perm to Offic *Newc* from 01. *4 Beadnell Hall, Beadnell, Chathill NE67 5AT* Tel (01665) 721802

ZAIDI-CROSSE, Philip Kenneth. **d** 05. NSM Erdington *Birm* from 05. *3 Watt Road, Birmingham B23 6ET*

ZAIR, Richard George. b 52. Newc Univ BSc74. Trin Coll Bris 75 St Jo Coll Dur 79. **d** 80 **p** 81. C Bishopsworth *Bris* 80-83; C New Malden and Coombe *S'wark* 83-91; Dir of Evang CPAS 91-99; Regional Dir from 99; Perm to Offic *Cov* from 91. *64 Kingsway, Leamington Spa CV31 3LE* Tel (01926) 424634 *or* 458458 Fax 458459 E-mail rzair@cpas.org.uk

ZAMMIT, Mark Timothy Paul. b 60. Aston Tr Scheme 90 Sarum & Wells Th Coll 94. **d** 94 **p** 95. C Bitterne Park *Win* 94-98; TV Shaston *Sarum* 98-03; TR from 03; RD Blackmore Vale from 01; Chapl Port Regis Prep Sch from 99. *The Vicarage, Bittles Green, Motcombe, Shaftesbury SP7 9NX* Tel and fax (01747) 851442 E-mail markzammit@beeb.net

ZANDSTRA-HOUGH, Wendy Lorraine. *See* HOUGH, Wendy Lorraine

ZANKER, Mrs Diana. b 39. Leeds Univ BA01 Edge Hill Coll of HE TCert59. N Ord Course 04. **d** 05. NSM Leeds St Aid *Ripon* from 05. *10 Mount Gardens, Leeds LS17 7QN* Tel 0113-267 5893 E-mail diana@zanker.org

ZAPHIRIOU, Paul Victor. b 49. Hamilton Coll (NY) BA73 INSEAD MBA74. Wycliffe Hall Ox 00. **d** 02 **p** 03. C Holborn St Geo w H Trin and St Bart *Lon* from 02. *18 Doughty Mews, London WC1N 2PF* Tel (020) 7404 4407 Mobile 07899-796409 E-mail paul.zaphiriou@sgtm.org *or* pzaphiriou@hotmail.com

ZAREK, Jennifer Hilary. b 51. Newnham Coll Cam BA72 MA76 Southn Univ MSc73 PhD78 Ox Univ BTh98 Garnett Coll Lon CertEd83. St Steph Ho Ox 95. **d** 97 **p** 98. C Caterham *S'wark* 97-00; V Hutton Cranswick w Skerne, Watton and Beswick *York* 00-05; rtd 05. *Horsedale House, Silver Street, Huggate, York YO42 1YB* E-mail jzarek@beeb.net

ZASS-OGILVIE, Ian David. b 38. MRICS72 FRICS80. AKC65 St Boniface Warminster 65. **d** 66 **p** 67. C Washington *Dur* 66-70; Bp's Soc and Ind Adv for N Dur 70-73; Hon C Newc St Jo *Newc* 73-75; V Tynemouth St Jo 75-78; Hon C St Marylebone St Mary *Lon* 78-81; V Bromley St Jo *Roch* 81-84; R Keith, Huntly and Aberchirder *Mor* 84-88; R Edin St Pet *Edin* 88-00; Dir Churches' Regional Commn in the NE *Newc & Dur* 00-05; rtd 05. *12 St Giles Close, Gilesgate, Durham DH1 1XH* Tel 0191-383 0887 E-mail idzo@ricsonline.org

ZEAL, Stanley Allan. b 33. Leeds Univ BA55. Coll of Resurr Mirfield. **d** 57 **p** 58. C Perry Hill St Geo *S'wark* 57-61; C Cobham *Guildf* 61-64; V Ash Vale 64-69; R Ash 64-69; Chapl Northfield Hosp Aldershot 69-98; V Aldershot St Mich *Guildf* 69-98; rtd 98. *68 Church Road, Seven Sisters, Neath SA10 9DT* Tel (01439) 700726

ZIETSMAN, Sheila. **d** 90 **p** 91. C Geashill w Killeigh and Ballycommon *M & K* 90-91; C Mullingar, Portnashangan, Moyliscar, Kilbixy etc 91-96; Chapl Wilson's Hosp Sch Multyfarnham 91-96; Chapl E Glendalough Sch from 96. *East Glendalough School, Station Road, Wicklow, Irish Republic* Tel (00353) (404) 69608 Fax 68180

ZIHNI, Andrew Stephen. b 77. Mert Coll Ox BA99. St Steph Ho Ox BA01. **d** 02 **p** 03. C Goldthorpe w Hickleton *Sheff* from 02. *Church House, 3 West Street, Goldthorpe, Rotherham S63 9JU* Tel (01709) 881468 Mobile 07967-390010 E-mail father_andrew_zihni@oratorium.zzn.com

ZIPFEL, Marilyn Ellen. b 48. Open Univ BA94 MA98 Goldsmiths' Coll Lon TCert70 LTCL97. Dioc OLM tr scheme 01. **d** 03 **p** 04. OLM Oulton Broad *Nor* from 03. *Rozel, Station Road, Lowestoft NR32 4QF* Tel (01502) 583825 Mobile 07818-093133 E-mail marilyn@rozelstrd.fsnet.co.uk

ZORAB, Mark Elston. b 53. FRICS77 MRAC75. Mon Dioc Tr Scheme 92. **d** 94. NSM Itton and St Arvans w Penterry and Kilgwrrwg etc *Mon* from 94. *Oak Cottage, Itton Road, Chepstow NP16 6BQ* Tel (01291) 626222 *or* 672138

ZOTOV, Mrs Carolyn Ann. b 47. Lady Mabel Coll CertEd68 Open Univ BA78 Nottm Univ Dip Special Educn 86. EMMTC 91. **d** 92 **p** 94. NSM Hykeham *Linc* 92-94; NSM Aisthorpe w Scampton w Thorpe le Fallows etc 94; C Ingham w Cammeringham w Fillingham 94-97; C Linc Minster Gp 97-01; rtd 01; Assoc P Nettleham *Linc* from 01. *Greenleaves, 1 The Drive, Church Lane, Lincoln LN2 1QR* Tel (01522) 525435 E-mail caz@greenleaves.fsnet.co.uk

ZUCCA, Peter Rennie. b 43. **d** 96 **p** 97. NSM Spotland *Man* 96-99; NSM Bamford from 99; NSM Rochdale St Geo w St Alb from 99. *19 Judith Street, Rochdale OL12 7HS* Tel (01706) 675830 *or* 346003

ZVIMBA, Josephat. b 60. SEITE. **d** 04. C W Norwood St Luke *S'wark* from 04. *12 Chestnut Road, London SE27 9LF* Tel (020) 8761 0068 E-mail janjosh@tiscali.co.uk

ZWALF, Willem Anthony Louis (Wim). b 46. AKC68. **d** 71 **p** 72. C Fulham St Etheldreda w St Clem *Lon* 71-74; Chapl City Univ 74-78; R Coalbrookdale, Iron-Bridge and Lt Wenlock *Heref* 78-90; V Wisbech SS Pet and Paul *Ely* from 90; P-in-c Wisbech St Aug 03-04; C from 04; RD Wisbech Lynn Marshland from 02. *The Vicarage, Love Lane, Wisbech PE13 1HP* Tel (01945) 583559 *or* 582508 Fax 466686 E-mail wimzwalf@aol.com

DEACONESSES

The biographies of women clergy are to be found in the preceding section.

BENNETT, Miss Doreen. b 29. St Mich Ho Ox 60. **dss** 79. Moreton *Ches* 79-80; Dewsbury Moor *Wakef* 80-86; Germany 86-91; rtd 89; Perm to Offic *Blackb* 95-02 and from 04. *27 Fosbrooke House, 8 Clifton Drive, Lytham St Annes FY8 5RQ* Tel (01253) 667008

BLACKBURN, Mary Paterson. b 16. St Chris Coll Blackheath 45 Wm Temple Coll Rugby 59. **dss** 76. Sawston *Ely* 74-78; rtd 78. *3 Stuart Court, High Street, Kibworth, Leicester LE8 0LR* Tel 0116-279 6324

BRIERLY, Margaret Ann. b 32. Dalton Ho Bris 54. **dss** 85. Wreningham *Nor* 85-86; Tetsworth, Adwell w S Weston, Lewknor etc *Ox* 86-95; rtd 95; Perm to Offic *Blackb* from 03. *13 Pinewood Avenue, Brookhouse, Lancaster LA2 9NU*

BUTLER, Miss Ann. b 41. St Mich Ho Ox 67 Dalton Ho Bris IDC69. **dss** 82. Bucknall and Bagnall *Lich* 82-87; Leyton St Mary w St Edw *Chelmsf* 89-97; Leyton St Mary w St Edw and St Luke 97-02; rtd 02. *40 Lichfield Street, Stone ST15 8NB* Tel (01785) 818160

BYATT, Margaret Nelly. b 18. Bedf Coll Lon BA40. Lon Bible Coll DipTh50 Gilmore Ho 59. **dss** 62. Chelsea St Luke *Lon* 60-63; St Helier *S'wark* 63-66; Lee Gd Shep w St Pet 66-78; rtd 78. *41 Woodlands, Overton, Basingstoke RG25 3HW* Tel (01256) 770347

COOPER, Janet Pamela. b 46. Glos Coll of Educn TCert67 Ox Poly CETD79. Trin Coll Bris DipHE83. **dss** 83. Patchway *Bris* 83-88; Perm to Offic *Glouc* 90-96. *Ephraim Cottage, Kington Mead Farm, Kington Road, Thornbury, Bristol BS35 1PQ* Tel (01454) 414230

DEE, Mary. b 21. St Chris Coll Blackheath 55. **dss** 64. Shottermill *Guildf* 63-66; Bishop's Waltham *Portsm* 66-72; Cumnor *Ox* 75-81; rtd 81. *Flat 4, 45 Oxford Avenue, Bournemouth BH6 5HT* Tel (01202) 424240

DOROTHY, Sister. *See* WARR, Sister Dorothy Lilian Patricia

DUCKERING, Alice Muriel. b 07. Gilmore Ho 43. **dss** 46. USPG 45-70; Kegworth *Leic* 71-77; rtd 77. *23 Stuart Court, High Street, Kibworth, Leicester LE8 0LR*

ESSAM, Susan Catherine. b 46. Southn Univ BA67 CertEd68. Linc Th Coll DipTh74. **dss** 80. Pershore w Pinvin, Wick and Birlingham *Worc* 78-82; CMS Nigeria from 83. *c/o Bishopscourt, PO Box 6283, Jos, Plateau State, Nigeria* Tel (00234) (73) 612221 E-mail jos@anglican.skannet.com.ng

EVANS (née CHERRETT), Mrs Diana. b 59. Somerville Coll Ox BA81 MA85 Warwick Univ CertEd96. St Steph Ho Ox 81. **dss** 84. Sherborne w Castleton and Lillington *Sarum* 84-88; Northampton St Paul *Pet* 93-98; Sec Dioc Adv Cttee from 94; Lic to Offic from 98. *The Rectory, London Road, Uppingham, Oakham LE15 9TJ* Tel (01572) 823381 E-mail diana.evans@peterborough-diocese.org.uk

FINDER, Miss Patricia Constance. b 30. Dalton Ho Bris 63. **dss** 79. Clapham St Jas *S'wark* 79-90; rtd 90. *5 Castle Gate, Ilkley LS29 8DF* Tel (01943) 607023

FISH, Margaret. b 18. St Mich Ho Ox 49. **dss** 77. Perm to Offic *Nor* 78-89. *35 Ashwell Court, Norwich NR5 9BS* Tel (01603) 746123

FROST, Constance Mary. b 09. Gilmore Ho 34. **dss** 37. Walworth St Jo *S'wark* 36-40; Fenton *Lich* 41-47; Gt Wyrley 47-49; Bilston 49-73; rtd 73; Perm to Offic *Chich* from 73. *17 Church Way, Worthing BN13 1HD* Tel (01903) 201596

GOUGH, Mrs Janet Ainley. b 46. SRN RSCN SCM Lon Univ CertRK73. Trin Coll Bris 70. **dss** 76. Leic H Apostles *Leic* 73-80; USA 80-81; Perm to Offic *Leic* 81-96. *410 Hinckley Road, Leicester LE3 0WA* Tel and fax 0116-285 4284

GRIERSON, Miss Janet. b 13. Westf Coll Lon BA34. Lambeth STh37 MA82 Greyladies Coll 34 K Coll Lon 34. **dss** 48. Vice-Prin Gilmore Ho 48-55; Prin 55-60; Lect Div St Mary's Coll Ban 62-63; Prin Lect RE Summerfield Coll Kidderminster 63-75; rtd 75; Perm to Offic *Worc* from 75. *8 Parkview, Abbey Road, Malvern WR14 3HG* Tel (01684) 569341

HAMBLY, Miss Winifred Kathleen. b 18. Lambeth DipTh55 Gilmore Ho 54. **dss** 55. Cricklewood St Pet *Lon* 55-78; Eastbourne St Mich *Chich* from 78. *4 Tutts Barn Court, Tutts Barn Lane, Eastbourne BN22 8XP* Tel (01323) 640735

HAMILTON, Miss Pamela Moorhead. b 43. SRN64 SCM66. Trin Coll Bris DipTh75. **dss** 77. Derby St Pet and Ch Ch w H Trin *Derby* 77-84; Bedworth *Cov* from 85; rtd 03. *10 William Street, Bedworth, Nuneaton CV12 9DS* Tel (024) 7649 1608

HARRIS, Audrey Margaret. *See* STOKES, Audrey Margaret

HARRISON, Mrs Ann. b 55. Ex Univ BSc77. Linc Th Coll DipHE81. **dss** 82. Acomb H Redeemer *York* 82-83; Lic to Offic *Wakef* 83-91. *The Vicarage, Church Hill, Easingwold, York YO61 3JT* Tel (01347) 821394

HEWITT, Miss Joyce Evelyn. b 30. SRN51 SCM55. St Mich Ho Ox IDC61. **dss** 67. Spitalfields Ch Ch w All SS *Lon* 67-70; CMJ 71-73; Canonbury St Steph *Lon* 73-75; Chorleywood RNIB Coll for Blind Girls 75-80; rtd 90. *38 Ashridge Court, Station Road, Newbury RG14 7LL* Tel (01635) 47829

HIDER, Ms Margaret Joyce Barbara. b 25. St Mich Ho Ox 52. **dss** 77. Bris H Cross Inns Court *Bris* 77-84; Uphill *B & W* 84-89; rtd 89; Perm to Offic *B & W* from 89. *Bethany, 8 Uphill Way, Weston-super-Mare BS23 4TH* Tel (01934) 414191

HINDE, Miss Mavis Mary. b 29. Lightfoot Ho Dur. **dss** 65. Hitchin St Mary *St Alb* 65-68; Ensbury *Sarum* 69-70; Portsea St Alb *Portsm* 70-76; Houghton Regis *St Alb* 77-85; Eaton Socon 85-94; rtd 94; Perm to Offic *Ely* from 94. *8 Burnt Close, Eynesbury, St Neots PE19 2LZ* Tel (01480) 218219

HORNBY-NORTHCOTE, Mrs Vivien Sheena. b 42. Birkbeck Coll Lon BA91 Warwick Univ MA96. Gilmore Course 74. **dss** 79. Mitcham St Olave *S'wark* 79-81; St Dunstan in the West *Lon* 82-86; St Marg Lothbury and St Steph Coleman Street etc 86; rtd 98. *3 Priory Mews, Sidney Street, Cheltenham GL52 6DJ* Tel (01242) 525659

HOWARD, Jean Elizabeth. b 37. Man Univ BA59 Univ of Wales (Cardiff) TDip61 Lon Univ DipTh BD86. St Mich Ho Ox 61. **dss** 82. Hanger Lane St Ann *Lon* 82-84; Dagenham *Chelmsf* 88-90; Perm to Offic from 90; rtd 97. *99 Kitchener Road, London E17 4LJ* Tel (020) 8527 0472

MacCORMACK, Mrs June Elizabeth. b 45. St Jo Coll Nottm 85. **dss** 86. Bieldside *Ab* from 86. *5 Overton Park, Dyce, Aberdeen AB21 7FT* Tel (01224) 722691 E-mail jadm1@aol.com

MOORE (née STOWE), Mrs Ann Jessica Margaret. b 41. St Mich Ho Ox. **dss** 87. Watford *St Alb* 87-88; Spitalfields Ch Ch w All SS *Lon* 88-89; rtd 89. *168 Thorpe Road, Kirby Cross, Frinton-on-Sea CO13 0NQ* Tel (01255) 851933

MOORHOUSE, Olga Marian. b 28. Dalton Ho Bris 54. **dss** 63. Wolverhampton St Matt *Lich* 62-68; Fazakerley Em *Liv* 68-70; Huyton St Geo 70-76; Blurton *Lich* 76-88; rtd 88. *37 Rosalind Grove, Wednesfield, Wolverhampton WV11 3RZ* Tel (01902) 630128

MORGAN, Beryl. b 19. Dalton Ho Bris 47. **dss** 77. Princess Marg Hosp Swindon 69-79; rtd 79. *Ty Clyd, 120 Beacons Park, Brecon LD3 9BP* Tel (01874) 622398

MULLER, Louise Irmgard. b 12. **dss** 64. Prestonville St Luke *Chich* 65-72; rtd 73; Perm to Offic *Chich* from 73. *24 Clifton Road, Worthing BN11 4DP* Tel (01903) 206541

NORTHCOTE, Vivien. *See* HORNBY-NORTHCOTE, Mrs Vivien Sheena

OBEE, Sister Monica May. b 37. **dss** 82. Radford *Cov* 82-97; rtd 97. *14 The Hill, Walsingham NR22 6DF* Tel (01328) 821033

OLIVER, Miss Kathleen Joyce. b 44. Man Univ BA65. N Ord Course 80. **dss** 83. Littleborough *Man* from 83. *Littleborough Christian Centre, 43 Todmorden Road, Littleborough OL15 9EA* Tel (01706) 376477 Fax 375520

OLPHIN, Miss Maureen Rose. b 30. Lon Univ BSc Sheff Univ DipEd Man Univ DipTh. **dss** 84. Sheff St Barn and St Mary *Sheff* 84-90; rtd 90. *41A Queen Street, Mosborough, Sheffield S20 5BP* Tel 0114-247 3009

PATRICK, Ruby Olivia. b 16. Gilmore Ho 69. **dss** 72. E Ham w Upton Park *Chelmsf* 72-74; Becontree St Elisabeth 74-75; Trinidad and Tobago 75-82; rtd 82. *41A New River Crescent, London N13 5RD* Tel (020) 8882 5146

PIERSON, Mrs Valerie Susan (Sue). b 44. TCert65. Trin Coll Bris 76. **dss** 79. Fulham St Matt *Lon* from 79. *48 Peterborough Road, London SW6 3EB* Tel (020) 7731 6544 Fax 7731 1858 E-mail sue@lancepierson.org

PLATT, Marjorie. b 18. Qu Coll Birm 76. **dss** 78. Hinckley St Mary *Leic* 78-91; Burbage w Aston Flamville 91-00; Perm to Offic from 00. *216 Brookside, Burbage, Hinckley LE10 2TW* Tel (01455) 233928

POLLARD, Shirley Ann. b 27. Wm Temple Coll Rugby 67 Cranmer Hall Dur 69. **dss** 84. Cramlington *Newc* 78-85; rtd 85; Perm to Offic *Worc* from 92. *22 The Cedars, Fernhill Heath, Worcester WR3 8RU* Tel (01905) 453792

PRICE, Mrs Patricia Kate Lunn. *See* SCHMIEGELOW, Patricia Kate Lunn

RAINEY, Miss Irene May. b 14. RSCN36 SCM38. Gilmore Ho 69. **dss** 72. Filton *Bris* 70-74; Crowthorne *Ox* 74-79; rtd 79; Perm to Offic *Ely* from 80. *12 Stevens Close, Cottenham, Cambridge CB4 8TT* Tel (01954) 251634

ROBINSON, Philippa. b 09. R Holloway Coll Lon BA31. **dss** 75. Branksome St Aldhelm *Sarum* 76-83; Lic to Offic from 83; Tutor Bp's Cert 84-86. *6 Lindum Court, Poole Road, Branksome BH12 1AS* Tel (01202) 769493

SAMPSON, Miss Hazel. b 35. Lightfoot Ho Dur 58. **dss** 64. Fenton *Lich* 64-67; Gt Wyrley 67-69; Chapl Asst Manor Hosp Walsall 69-76; Lich St Mary w St Mich 76-95; rtd 95; Perm to Offic *Lich* 95-03. *107 Walsall Road, Lichfield WS13 8DD* Tel (01543) 419664

SCHMIEGELOW, Patricia Kate Lunn. b 37. St Mich Ho Ox IDC65. **dss** 86. The Hague *Eur* 86-89; Perm to Offic *Glouc* from 90; Gen Sec ICS 92-97; rtd 97. *Waterside, Coln St Aldwyns, Cirencester GL7 5AJ* Tel (01285) 750218 Fax as telephone

SELWOOD, Miss Eveline Mary. b 34. **dss** 76. Huddersfield St Jo *Wakef* 76-79; King Cross 79-85; rtd 94; Perm to Offic *Wakef* from 94. *27 Alverthorpe Road, Wakefield WF2 9NW* Tel (01924) 378364

SILL, Grace Mary. b 11. St Chris Coll Blackheath 53. **dss** 62. Lawrence Weston *Bris* 55-63; Southmead Hosp Bris 63-77; rtd 77; Perm to Offic *Bris* 77-87. *10 Tyndale Court, Chertsey Road, Bristol BS6 6NF* Tel 0117-973 2903

SKINNER, Elizabeth Alice. b 53. **dss** 82. Bourne *Guildf* 82-84. *The Manse, 27 King's Road, Fleet GU13 9AF* Tel (01252) 615903

SPROSON, Doreen. b 31. St Mich Ho Ox IDC58. **dss** 70. Wandsworth St Mich *S'wark* 68-71; Women's Sec CMS 71-74; Goole *Sheff* 74-76; Kirby Muxloe *Leic* 76-77; Perm to Offic *S'wark* 85-97; rtd 91. *20 Huggens' College, College Road, Northfleet, Gravesend DA11 9LL* Tel (01474) 325262

STOKES, Audrey Margaret. b 39. Dalton Ho Bris 68. **dss** 82. Collier Row St Jas *Chelmsf* 82-85; Woking St Mary *Guildf* 85-95; rtd 95. *1 Greet Park Close, Southwell NG25 0EE*

STOWE, Ann Jessica Margaret. *See* MOORE, Mrs Ann Jessica Margaret

SYMES, Miss Annabel. b 41. AIMLS68. S Dios Minl Tr Scheme 79. **dss** 85. Chapl Asst Salisbury Health Care NHS Trust from 85; Barford St Martin, Dinton, Baverstock etc *Sarum* 89-01; Nadder Valley from 01. *7 Shaftesbury Road, Barford St Martin, Salisbury SP3 4BL* Tel (01722) 744110

TAYLOR, Muriel. b 28. CA Tr Coll 48. **dss** 76. Gateshead Fell *Dur* 76-86; Gateshead Harlow Green 86-88; rtd 88. *18 Beechwood Avenue, Gateshead NE9 6PP* Tel 0191-487 6902

THUMWOOD, Janet Elizabeth. b 30. STh60 DipRE61. Trin Coll Toronto 58. **dss** 62. Canada 62-63; Mile End Old Town H Trin *Lon* 63-65; CSF 66-77; rtd 90. *24 Ramsay Hall, 11-13 Byron Road, Worthing BN11 3HN* Tel (01903) 203586

TURNER, Miss Rosie (Poppy). b 22. St Mich Ho Ox 56. **dss** 61. Hornsey Rise St Mary *Lon* 61-62; Wealdstone H Trin 62-70; CMJ 71-72; CMS 73-74; Dss Ho Hindhead 74-76; Sutton Ch Ch *S'wark* 77-80; rtd 80. *Bungalow 16, Huggens' College, College Road, Northfleet, Gravesend DA11 9DL* Tel (01474) 357722

WARR, Sister Dorothy Lilian Patricia. b 14. Selly Oak Coll 38. **dss** 53. St Etheldreda's Children's Home Bedf 51-59; CSA from 53; Goldington *St Alb* 54-59; S'wark St Sav w All Hallows *S'wark* 59-65; St Mich Convalescent Home Westgate-on-Sea 65-74; rtd 75. *37 Spinners Court, Queen Street, Lancaster LA1 1RY* Tel (01524) 845613

WEBB, Sybil Janet. b 20. SRN42 SCM43. Gilmore Course 69. **dss** 77. Worthing St Geo *Chich* 77-80; rtd 80; Perm to Offic *Chich* from 80. *42 Ham Road, Worthing BN11 2QX* Tel (01903) 202997

WRIGHT, Edith Mary. b 22. St Hugh's Coll Ox MA46 DipEd46. Gilmore Ho STh58. **dss** 61. St Marylebone St Mary *Lon* 58-71; Lect Linc Th Coll 71-73; Oatlands *Guildf* 73-76; Roehampton H Trin *S'wark* 76-82; rtd 82. *26 Hazelwood Close, Harrow HA2 6HD* Tel 0181-863 7320

WRIGHT, Gloria Mary. b 40. **dss** 83. Smethwick St Matt w St Chad *Birm* 83-84; Tottenham H Trin *Lon* 84-86; rtd 00. *76 Barnards Hill, Marlow SL7 2NZ*

DIOCESAN, AREA, SUFFRAGAN AND ASSISTANT BISHOPS AND PROVINCIAL EPISCOPAL VISITORS IN ENGLAND, WALES, SCOTLAND AND IRELAND

BATH AND WELLS

Bishop of Bath and Wells	P B PRICE
Honorary Assistant Bishops	J R G NEALE
	W M D PERSSON
	R H M THIRD
	P E BARBER
	B ROGERSON
	R F SAINSBURY
Suffragan Bishop of Taunton	A J RADFORD

BIRMINGHAM

Bishop of Birmingham	*vacant*
Honorary Assistant Bishops	A P HALL
	A C DUMPER
	I K MOTTAHEDEH
	M W SINCLAIR
	M H D WHINNEY
Suffragan Bishop of Aston	J M AUSTIN

BLACKBURN

Bishop of Blackburn	N S READE
Honorary Assistant Bishops	M E VICKERS
	A L WINSTANLEY
Suffragan Bishop of Burnley	J W GODDARD
Suffragan Bishop of Lancaster	G S PEDLEY

BRADFORD

Bishop of Bradford	D C JAMES
Honorary Assistant Bishops	D M HOPE OF THORNES
	C O BUCHANAN
	M W JARRETT
	D N DE L YOUNG

BRISTOL

Bishop of Bristol	M A HILL
Honorary Assistant Bishops	J GIBBS
	J R G NEALE
	P ST G VAUGHAN
Suffragan Bishop of Swindon	L S RAYFIELD

CANTERBURY

Archbishop of Canterbury, Primate of All England and Metropolitan	R D WILLIAMS
Honorary Assistant Bishops	M F GEAR
	R D SAY
	A M A TURNBULL
Suffragan Bishop of Dover	S S VENNER
Suffragan Bishop of Maidstone	G A CRAY
Suffragan Bishop of Ebbsfleet (Provincial Episcopal Visitor)	A BURNHAM
Suffragan Bishop of Richborough (Provincial Episcopal Visitor)	K NEWTON

CARLISLE

Bishop of Carlisle	G G DOW
Honorary Assistant Bishops	G BATES
	A A K GRAHAM
	I M GRIGGS
	G L HACKER
	R M HARDY
	J H RICHARDSON
	J R SATTERTHWAITE
	G H THOMPSON
Suffragan Bishop of Penrith	J W S NEWCOME

CHELMSFORD

Bishop of Chelmsford	J W GLADWIN
Honorary Assistant Bishop	J M BALL
Area Bishop of Barking	D J L HAWKINS
Area Bishop of Bradwell	L A GREEN
Area Bishop of Colchester	C H MORGAN

CHESTER

Bishop of Chester	P R FORSTER
Honorary Assistant Bishops	W A PWAISIHO
	C F BAZLEY
	A D CHESTERS
Suffragan Bishop of Birkenhead	D A URQUHART
Suffragan Bishop of Stockport	W N STOCK

CHICHESTER

Bishop of Chichester	J W HIND
Honorary Assistant Bishops	C C LUXMOORE
	M GREEN
	M H ST J MADDOCKS
	M E ADIE
	R A JUPP
	M R J MANKTELOW
	M E MARSHALL
	D P WILCOX
Area Bishop of Horsham	L G URWIN
Area Bishop of Lewes	W P BENN

COVENTRY

Bishop of Coventry	C J BENNETTS
Honorary Assistant Bishop	D R J EVANS
Suffragan Bishop of Warwick	J R A STROYAN

DERBY

Bishop of Derby	A L J REDFERN
Honorary Assistant Bishop	R M C BEAK
Suffragan Bishop of Repton	D C HAWTIN

DURHAM

Bishop of Durham	N T WRIGHT
Honorary Assistant Bishop	S W SYKES
Suffragan Bishop of Jarrow	J L PRITCHARD

ELY

Bishop of Ely	A J RUSSELL
Honorary Assistant Bishops	I P M CUNDY
	S BARRINGTON-WARD
	P S DAWES
	J B TAYLOR
Suffragan Bishop of Huntingdon	J G INGE

EXETER

Bishop of Exeter	M L LANGRISH
Honorary Assistant Bishops	R F CARTWRIGHT
	I C DOCKER
	R S HAWKINS
	R D SILK
Suffragan Bishop of Crediton	R J S EVENS
Suffragan Bishop of Plymouth	*vacant*

GLOUCESTER

Bishop of Gloucester	M F PERHAM
Honorary Assistant Bishops	P J FIRTH
	J GIBBS
	M A MANN
	J R G NEALE
	E ST Q WALL
Suffragan Bishop of Tewkesbury	J S WENT

GUILDFORD

Bishop of Guildford	C J HILL
Suffragan Bishop of Dorking	I J BRACKLEY

HEREFORD

Bishop of Hereford	A M PRIDDIS
Suffragan Bishop of Ludlow	M W HOOPER

LEICESTER

Bishop of Leicester	T J STEVENS
Honorary Assistant Bishop	C J F SCOTT

LICHFIELD

Bishop of Lichfield	J M GLEDHILL
Honorary Assistant Bishops	R O BOWLBY
	D E BENTLEY
	I K MOTTAHEDEH
Area Bishop of Shrewsbury	A G C SMITH
Area Bishop of Stafford	A G MURSELL
Area Bishop of Wolverhampton	M G BOURKE

LINCOLN

Bishop of Lincoln	J C SAXBEE
Honorary Assistant Bishops	P B HARRIS
	J E BROWN
	D G SNELGROVE
	D TUSTIN
Suffragan Bishop of Grantham	*vacant*
Suffragan Bishop of Grimsby	D D J ROSSDALE

LIVERPOOL

Bishop of Liverpool	J S JONES
Honorary Assistant Bishops	J W ROXBURGH
	I C STUART
	M W JARRETT
Suffragan Bishop of Warrington	D W M JENNINGS

LONDON
Bishop of London — R J C CHARTRES
Honorary Assistant Bishops — D S ARDEN
M A BAUGHEN
E HOLLAND
M E MARSHALL
M A P WOOD
Area Bishop of Edmonton — P W WHEATLEY
Suffragan Bishop of Fulham — J C BROADHURST
Area Bishop of Kensington — M J COLCLOUGH
Area Bishop of Stepney — S J OLIVER
Area Bishop of Willesden — P A BROADBENT

MANCHESTER
Bishop of Manchester — N S MCCULLOCH
Suffragan Bishop of Hulme — S R LOWE
Suffragan Bishop of Middleton — M A O LEWIS
Suffragan Bishop of Bolton — D K GILLETT

NEWCASTLE
Bishop of Newcastle — J M WHARTON
Assistant Bishops — P RICHARDSON
K E GILL
J H RICHARDSON

NORWICH
Bishop of Norwich — G R JAMES
Honorary Assistant Bishops — E N DEVENPORT
A C FOOTTIT
R GARRARD
D LEAKE
M J MENIN
Suffragan Bishop of Lynn — J H LANGSTAFF
Suffragan Bishop of Thetford — D J ATKINSON

OXFORD
Bishop of Oxford — R D HARRIES
Honorary Assistant Bishops — A R M GORDON
S E VERNEY
A K CRAGG
K A ARNOLD
J F E BONE
W J D DOWN
J N JOHNSON
P J NOTT
F H A RICHMOND
Area Bishop of Buckingham — A T L WILSON
Area Bishop of Dorchester — C W FLETCHER
Area Bishop of Reading — S G COTTRELL

PETERBOROUGH
Bishop of Peterborough — I P M CUNDY
Honorary Assistant Bishops — J R FLACK
P F HULLAH
Suffragan Bishop of Brixworth — F WHITE

PORTSMOUTH
Bishop of Portsmouth — K W STEVENSON
Honorary Assistant Bishops — M E ADIE
H D HALSEY

RIPON AND LEEDS
Bishop of Ripon and Leeds — J R PACKER
Honorary Assistant Bishops — R EMMERSON
D E JENKINS
Suffragan Bishop of Knaresborough — J H BELL

ROCHESTER
Bishop of Rochester — M J NAZIR-ALI
Honorary Assistant Bishop — M F GEAR
Suffragan Bishop of Tonbridge — B C CASTLE

ST ALBANS
Bishop of St Albans — C W HERBERT
Honorary Assistant Bishops — D J FARMBROUGH
R J N SMITH
Suffragan Bishop of Bedford — R N INWOOD
Suffragan Bishop of Hertford — C R J FOSTER

ST EDMUNDSBURY AND IPSWICH
Bishop of St Edmundsbury and Ipswich — J H R LEWIS
Suffragan Bishop of Dunwich — C YOUNG

SALISBURY
Bishop of Salisbury — D S STANCLIFFE
Honorary Assistant Bishops — J K CAVELL
J D G KIRKHAM
Area Bishop of Ramsbury — P F HULLAH
Area Bishop of Sherborne — T M THORNTON

SHEFFIELD
Bishop of Sheffield — J NICHOLLS
Honorary Assistant Bishops — D M HALLATT
K H PILLAR
Suffragan Bishop of Doncaster — C G ASHTON

SODOR AND MAN
Bishop of Sodor and Man — G P KNOWLES

SOUTHWARK
Bishop of Southwark — T F BUTLER
Honorary Assistant Bishop — M D DOE
Area Bishop of Kingston-upon-Thames — R I CHEETHAM
Area Bishop of Woolwich — C T J CHESSUN
Area Bishop of Croydon — N BAINES

SOUTHWELL
Bishop of Southwell — G H CASSIDY
Honorary Assistant Bishops — R J MILNER
J T FINNEY
J W H FLAGG
R K WILLIAMSON
Suffragan Bishop of Sherwood — *vacant*

TRURO
Bishop of Truro — W IND
Suffragan Bishop of St Germans — R SCREECH

WAKEFIELD
Bishop of Wakefield — S G PLATTEN
Honorary Assistant Bishop — R A M GENDERS
Suffragan Bishop of Pontefract — A W ROBINSON

WINCHESTER
Bishop of Winchester — M C SCOTT-JOYNT
Honorary Assistant Bishops — H B DEHQANI-TAFTI
J A BAKER
E R BARNES
S H BURROWS
J DENNIS
C C W JAMES
L L REES
J YATES
Suffragan Bishop of Basingstoke — T WILLMOTT
Suffragan Bishop of Southampton — P R BUTLER

WORCESTER
Bishop of Worcester — P S M SELBY
Honorary Assistant Bishops — K J WOOLLCOMBE
C J MAYFIELD
J RUHUMULIZA
Suffragan Bishop of Dudley — D S WALKER

YORK
Archbishop of York, Primate of England and Metropolitan — J M SENTAMU
Honorary Assistant Bishops — C C BARKER
R G G FOLEY
D G GALLIFORD
M HENSHALL
N D JONES
D R LUNN
D J SMITH
Suffragan Bishop of Hull — R M C FRITH
Suffragan Bishop of Selby — M W WALLACE
Suffragan Bishop of Whitby — R S LADDS
Suffragan Bishop of Beverley (Provincial Episcopal Visitor) — M W JARRETT

GIBRALTAR IN EUROPE
Bishop of Gibraltar in Europe — D G ROWELL
Suffragan Bishop in Europe — D HAMID
Honorary Assistant Bishops — J W ROWTHORN
J G VOBBE
A W M WEEKES
D P DOS SDE PINA CABRAL
J R FLACK
R GARRARD
I HARLAND
P B HARRIS
E HOLLAND
C LOPEZ LOZANO
M R J MANKTELOW
A SANCHEZ
F P SARGEANT
D J SMITH
F L SOARES
J B TAYLOR
P W WHALON
H F DE WAAL

CHURCH IN WALES

ST ASAPH
Bishop of St Asaph — J S DAVIES

BANGOR
Bishop of Bangor — P A CROCKETT

ST DAVIDS
Bishop of St Davids — C N COOPER

LLANDAFF
Bishop of Llandaff — B C MORGAN
Assistant Bishop — D YEOMAN

MONMOUTH
Bishop of Monmouth — E W M WALKER

SWANSEA AND BRECON
Bishop of Swansea and Brecon — A E PIERCE
Honorary Assistant Bishops — LORD CAREY OF CLIFTON
J K OLIVER

SCOTTISH EPISCOPAL CHURCH

ABERDEEN AND ORKNEY
Bishop of Aberdeen and Orkney — A B CAMERON

ARGYLL AND THE ISLES
Bishop of Argyll and the Isles — A M SHAW

BRECHIN
Bishop of Brechin — J A C MANTLE

EDINBURGH
Bishop of Edinburgh — B A SMITH
Honorary Assistant Bishop

GLASGOW AND GALLOWAY
Bishop of Glasgow and Galloway — I JONES
Honorary Assistant Bishop — J M TAYLOR

MORAY, ROSS AND CAITHNESS
Bishop of Moray, Ross and Caithness — J M CROOK

ST ANDREWS, DUNKELD AND DUNBLANE
Bishop of St Andrews, Dunkeld and Dunblane — D R CHILLINGWORTH

CHURCH OF IRELAND

ARMAGH
Archbishop of Armagh and Primate of All Ireland and Metropolitan — R H A EAMES

CASHEL AND OSSORY
Bishop of Cashel and Ossory — P F BARRETT

CLOGHER
Bishop of Clogher — M G ST A JACKSON

CONNOR
Bishop of Connor — A E T HARPER

CORK, CLOYNE AND ROSS
Bishop of Cork, Cloyne and Ross — W P COLTON

DERRY AND RAPHOE
Bishop of Derry and Raphoe — K R GOOD

DOWN AND DROMORE
Bishop of Down and Dromore — H C MILLER

DUBLIN AND GLENDALOUGH
Archbishop of Dublin, Bishop of Glendalough, Primate of Ireland and Metropolitan — J R W NEILL

KILMORE, ELPHIN AND ARDAGH
Bishop of Kilmore, Elphin and Ardagh — K H CLARKE

LIMERICK AND KILLALOE
Bishop of Limerick and Killaloe — M H G MAYES

MEATH AND KILDARE
Bishop of Meath and Kildare — R L CLARKE

TUAM, KILLALA AND ACHONRY
Bishop of Tuam, Killala and Achonry — R C A HENDERSON

BISHOPS IN THE HOUSE OF LORDS

The Archbishops of Canterbury and York, and the Bishops of London, Durham and Winchester always have seats in the House of Lords. Twenty-one of the remaining Diocesan Bishops also sit in the Upper House, and they do so according to their dates of seniority. When a vacancy arises, it is filled by the senior Diocesan Bishop without a seat, and the vacated See is placed at the foot of the list of those awaiting seats. Translation of a Bishop from one See to another does not affect his right to sit in the House of Lords.

The Bishop of Sodor and Man and the Bishop of Gibraltar in Europe are not eligible to sit in the House of Lords, but the former has a seat in the Upper House of the Tynwald, Isle of Man.

ARCHBISHOPS

	Enthroned	Entered House of Lords
CANTERBURY	2003	2003
YORK	2005	2005

BISHOPS SITTING IN THE HOUSE OF LORDS

(as at 1 December 2005)

	Became Diocesan Bishop	Entered House of Lords
LONDON	1995	1996
DURHAM	2003	2003
WINCHESTER	1995	1996
OXFORD	1987	1993
SOUTHWARK	1991	1997
MANCHESTER	1992	1997
SALISBURY	1993	1998
ROCHESTER	1994	1999
CHELMSFORD	1994	1999
PORTSMOUTH	1995	1999
ST ALBANS	1995	1999
PETERBOROUGH	1996	2001
CHESTER	1996	2001
ST EDMUNDSBURY AND IPSWICH	1997	2002
TRURO	1997	2002
WORCESTER	1997	2002
NEWCASTLE	1997	2003
SHEFFIELD	1997	2003
COVENTRY	1998	2003
LIVERPOOL	1998	2003
LEICESTER	1999	2003
SOUTHWELL	1999	2004
NORWICH	1999	2004
EXETER	2000	2005

BISHOPS AWAITING SEATS IN THE HOUSE OF LORDS

(in order of seniority)

	Became Diocesan Bishop
RIPON AND LEEDS	2000
ELY	2000
CARLISLE	2000
CHICHESTER	2001
LINCOLN	2001
BATH AND WELLS	2002
BRADFORD	2002
WAKEFIELD	2003
BRISTOL	2003
LICHFIELD	2003
BLACKBURN	2004
HEREFORD	2004
GLOUCESTER	2004
GUILDFORD	2004
DERBY	2005
BIRMINGHAM	*vacant*

HISTORICAL SUCCESSION OF ARCHBISHOPS AND BISHOPS

In a number of dioceses, especially for the mediaeval period, the dating of some episcopal appointments is not known for certain. For ease of reference, the date of consecration is given when known, or, in the case of more modern appointments, the date of confirmation of election. More information on the dates of individual bishops can be found in the Royal Historical Society's *Handbook of British Chronology*.

ENGLAND

PROVINCE OF CANTERBURY

Canterbury

Description of arms. Azure, an archiepiscopal cross in pale or surmounted by a pall proper charged with four crosses patée fitchée sable.

597 Augustine
604 Laurentius
619 Mellitus
624 Justus
627 Honorius
655 Deusdedit
668 Theodorus
693 Berhtwald
731 Tatwine
735 Nothelm
740 Cuthbert
761 Bregowine
765 Jaenberht
793 Æthelheard
805 Wulfred
832 Feologild
833 Ceolnoth
870 Æthelred
890 Plegmund
914 Æthelhelm
923 Wulfhelm
942 Oda
959 Ælfsige
959 Byrhthelm
960 Dunstan
*c.*988 Athelgar
990 Sigeric Serio
995 Ælfric
1005 Ælfheah
1013 Lyfing [Ælfstan]
1020 Æthelnoth
1038 Eadsige
1051 Robert of Jumièges
1052 Stigand
1070 Lanfranc
1093 Anselm
1114 Ralph d'Escures
1123 William de Corbeil
1139 Theobald of Bec
1162 Thomas Becket
1174 Richard [of Dover]
1184 Baldwin
1193 Hubert Walter
1207 Stephen Langton
1229 Richard le Grant
1234 Edmund Rich
1245 Boniface of Savoy
1273 Robert Kilwardby
1279 John Pecham
1294 Robert Winchelsey
1313 Walter Reynolds
1328 Simon Mepham
1333 John Stratford
1349 Thomas Bradwardine
1349 Simon Islip
1366 Simon Langham
1368 William Whittlesey
1375 Simon Sudbury
1381 William Courtenay
1396 Thomas Arundel[1]
1398 Roger Walden
1414 Henry Chichele
1443 John Stafford
1452 John Kempe
1454 Thomas Bourgchier
1486 John Morton
1501 Henry Deane
1503 William Warham
1533 Thomas Cranmer
1556 Reginald Pole
1559 Matthew Parker
1576 Edmund Grindal
1583 John Whitgift
1604 Richard Bancroft
1611 George Abbot
1633 William Laud
1660 William Juxon
1663 Gilbert Sheldon
1678 William Sancroft
1691 John Tillotson
1695 Thomas Tenison
1716 William Wake
1737 John Potter
1747 Thomas Herring
1757 Matthew Hutton
1758 Thomas Secker
1768 Frederick Cornwallis
1783 John Moore
1805 Charles Manners Sutton
1828 William Howley
1848 John Bird Sumner
1862 Charles Thomas Longley
1868 Archibald Campbell Tait
1883 Edward White Benson
1896 Frederick Temple
1903 Randall Thomas Davidson
1928 Cosmo Gordon Lang
1942 William Temple
1945 Geoffrey Francis Fisher
1961 Arthur Michael Ramsey
1974 Frederick Donald Coggan
1980 Robert Alexander Kennedy Runcie
1991 George Leonard Carey
2002 Rowan Douglas Williams

London

Description of arms. Gules, two swords in saltire argent hilts and pommels or.

Theanus
Eluanus
Cadar
Obinus
Conanus
Palladius
Stephanus
Iltutus
Theodwinus
Theodredus
Hilarius
314 Restitutus
Guitelinus
Fastidius
Vodinus
Theonus
*c.*604 Mellitus
664 Cedd[2]
666 Wini
675 Eorcenwald
693 Waldhere
716 Ingwald
745 Ecgwulf
772 Wigheah
782 Eadbeorht
789 Eadgar
793 Coenwalh
796 Eadbald
798 Heathoberht
803 Osmund
*c.*811 Æthelnoth
824 Ceolberht
862 Deorwulf
898 Swithwulf
898 Heahstan
900 Wulfsige
*c.*926 Æthelweard
926 Leofstan
926 Theodred
— Wulfstan I
953 Brihthelm
959 Dunstan
964 Ælfstan
996 Wulfstan II
1004 Ælfhun
1014 Ælfwig

[1] On 19 October 1399 Boniface IX annulled Arundel's translation to St Andrew and confirmed him in the See of Canterbury.
[2] See vacant for a term of years.

1035 Ælfweard
1044 Robert of Jumièges
1051 William
1075 Hugh of Orival
1086 Maurice
1108 Richard de Belmeis
1128 Gilbert [the Universal]
1141 Robert de Sigillo
1152 Richard de Belmeis II
1163 Gilbert Foliot
1189 Richard Fitz Neal
1199 William of Ste-Mere-Eglise
1221 Eustace de Fauconberg
1229 Roger Niger
1244 Fulk Basset
1260 Henry Wingham
1263 Henry of Sandwich
1274 John Chishull
1280 Richard Gravesend
1306 Ralph Baldock
1313 Gilbert Segrave
1317 Richard Newport
1319 Stephen Gravesend
1338 Richard Bintworth
1340 Ralph Stratford
1355 Michael Northburgh
1362 Simon Sudbury
1375 William Courtenay
1382 Robert Braybrooke
1404 Roger Walden
1406 Nicholas Bubwith
1407 Richard Clifford
1421 John Kempe
1426 William Gray
1431 Robert Fitz-Hugh
1436 Robert Gilbert
1450 Thomas Kempe
1489 Richard Hill
1496 Thomas Savage
1502 William Warham
1504 William Barons [Barnes]
1506 Richard Fitz-James
1522 Cuthbert Tunstall [Tonstall]
1530 John Stokesley
1540 Edmund Bonner
1550 Nicholas Ridley
1553 Edmund Bonner (restored)
1559 Edmund Grindal
1570 Edwin Sandys
1577 John Aylmer
1595 Richard Fletcher
1597 Richard Bancroft
1604 Richard Vaughan
1607 Thomas Ravis
1610 George Abbot
1611 John King
1621 George Monteigne [Mountain]
1628 William Laud
1633 William Juxon
1660 Gilbert Sheldon
1663 Humfrey Henchman
1676 Henry Compton
1714 John Robinson
1723 Edmund Gibson
1748 Thomas Sherlock
1761 Thomas Hayter
1762 Richard Osbaldeston
1764 Richard Terrick
1778 Robert Lowth
1787 Beilby Porteus
1809 John Randolph
1813 William Howley
1828 Charles James Blomfield
1856 Archibald Campbell Tait
1869 John Jackson
1885 Frederick Temple
1897 Mandell Creighton
1901 Arthur Foley Winnington-Ingram
1939 Geoffrey Francis Fisher
1945 John William Charles Wand
1956 Henry Colville Montgomery Campbell
1961 Robert Wright Stopford
1973 Gerald Alexander Ellison
1981 Graham Douglas Leonard
1991 David Michael Hope
1995 Richard John Carew Chartres

†Westminster

1540 Thomas Thirlby

Winchester

Description of arms. Gules, two keys endorsed and conjoined at the bows in bend, the upper or, the lower argent, between which a sword in bend sinister of the third, hilt and pommel gold.

BISHOPS OF THE WEST SAXONS
634 Birinus
650 Ægilberht

BISHOPS OF WINCHESTER
660 Wine
670 Leutherius
676 Haedde
705 Daniel
744 Hunfrith
756 Cyneheard
778 Æthelheard
778 Ecbald
785 Dudd
*c.*785 Cyneberht
803 Eahlmund
814 Wigthegn
825 Herefrith[1]
838 Eadmund
*c.*838 Eadhun
839 Helmstan
852 Swithhun
867 Ealhferth
877 Tunberht
879 Denewulf
909 Frithestan
931 Byrnstan
934 Ælfheah I
951 Ælfsige I
960 Brihthelm
963 Æthelwold I
984 Ælfheah II
1006 Cenwulf
1006 Æthelwold II
*c.*1014 Ælfsige II
1032 Ælfwine
1043 Stigand
Ælfsige III?
1070 Walkelin
1107 William Giffard
1129 Henry of Blois
1174 Richard of Ilchester (Toclyve)
1189 Godfrey de Lucy
1205 Peter des Roches
1244 Will. de Raleigh
1260 Aymer de Valance [of Lusignan]
1262 John Gervaise
1268 Nicholas of Ely
1282 John of Pontoise
1305 Henry Merewell [or Woodlock]
1316 John Sandale
1320 Rigaud of Assier
1323 John Stratford
1333 Adam Orleton
1346 William Edendon [Edington]
1367 William of Wykeham
1404 Henry Beaufort
1447 William of Waynflete
1487 Peter Courtenay
1493 Thomas Langton
1501 Richard Fox
1529 Thomas Wolsey
1531 Stephen Gardiner (deposed)
1551 John Ponet [Poynet]
1553 Stephen Gardiner (restored)
1556 John White (deposed)
1561 Robert Horne
1580 John Watson
1584 Thomas Cowper [Cooper]
1595 William Wickham [Wykeham]
1596 William Day
1597 Thomas Bilson
1616 James Montague
1619 Lancelot Andrewes
1628 Richard Neile
1632 Walter Curll
1660 Brian Duppa
1662 George Morley
1684 Peter Mews
1707 Jonathan Trelawney
1721 Charles Trimnell
1723 Richard Willis
1734 Benjamin Hoadly
1761 John Thomas
1781 Brownlow North
1820 George Pretyman Tomline
1827 Charles Richard Sumner
1869 Samuel Wilberforce
1873 Edward Harold Browne
1891 Anthony Wilson Thorold
1895 Randall Thomas Davidson
1903 Herbert Edward Ryle
1911 Edward Stuart Talbot
1923 Frank Theodore Woods
1932 Cyril Forster Garbett
1942 Mervyn George Haigh
1952 Alwyn Terrell Petre Williams
1961 Sherard Falkner Allison
1975 John Vernon Taylor
1985 Colin Clement Walter James
1995 Michael Charles Scott-Joynt

Bath and Wells

Description of arms. Azure, a saltire per saltire quarterly counterchanged or and argent.

BISHOPS OF WELLS
909 Athelm
925 Wulfhelm I

† Indicates a diocese no longer extant, or united with another diocese.
[1] Never signed without Wigthegn.

928 Ælfheah
938 Wulfhelm II
956 Byrhthelm
974 Cyneweard
979 Sigegar
997 Ælfwine
999 Lyfing
1013 Æthelwine (ejected)
1013 Beorhtwine (deposed)
Æthelwine (restored)
Beorhtwine (restored)
1024 Brihtwig [also Merehwit]
1033 Duduc
1061 Gisa
1088 John of Tours [de Villula]

BISHOPS OF BATH
1090 John of Tours [de Villula]
1123 Godfrey
1136 Robert
1174 Reg. Fitz Jocelin
1192 Savaric FitzGeldewin

BATH AND GLASTONBURY
1206 Jocelin of Wells

BATH AND WELLS
1244 Roger of Salisbury
1248 William Bitton I
1265 Walter Giffard
1267 William Bitton II
1275 Robert Burnell
1293 William of March
1302 Walter Hasleshaw
1309 John Droxford
1329 Ralph of Shrewsbury
1364 John Barnet
1367 John Harewell
1386 Walter Skirlaw
1388 Ralph Erghum
1401 Henry Bowet
1407 Nicholas Bubwith
1425 John Stafford
1443 Thomas Beckington
1466 Robert Stillington
1492 Richard Fox
1495 Oliver King
1504 Adriano de Castello [di Corneto]
1518 Thomas Wolsey
1523 John Clerk
1541 William Knight
1548 William Barlow
1554 Gilbert Bourne
1560 Gilbert Berkeley
1584 Thomas Godwin
1593 John Still
1608 James Montague
1616 Arthur Lake
1626 William Laud
1628 Leonard Mawe
1629 Walter Curll
1632 William Piers
1670 Robert Creighton
1673 Peter Mews
1685 Thomas Ken (deposed)
1691 Richard Kidder
1704 George Hooper
1727 John Wynne
1743 Edward Willes
1774 Charles Moss
1802 Richard Beadon
1824 George Henry Law
1845 Richard Bagot
1854 Robert John Eden, Lord Auckland
1869 Arthur Charles Hervey
1894 George Wyndham Kennion
1921 St John Basil Wynne Wilson
1937 Francis Underhill
1943 John William Charles Wand
1946 Harold William Bradfield
1960 Edward Barry Henderson
1975 John Monier Bickersteth
1987 George Leonard Carey
1991 James Lawton Thompson
2002 Peter Bryan Price

Birmingham

Description of arms. Per pale indented or and gules, five roundels, two, two, and one, and in chief two crosses patée all counterchanged.

1905 Charles Gore
1911 Henry Russell Wakefield
1924 Ernest William Barnes
1953 John Leonard Wilson
1969 Laurence Ambrose Brown
1978 Hugh William Montefiore
1987 Mark Santer
2002 John Mugabi Sentamu

Bristol

Description of arms. Sable, three ducal coronets in pale or.

1542 Paul Bush
1554 John Holyman
1562 Richard Cheyney
1581 John Bullingham (held Gloucester and Bristol 1586–9)
1589 Richard Fletcher
[See vacant for ten years]
1603 John Thornborough
1617 Nicholas Felton
1619 Rowland Searchfield
1623 Robert Wright
1633 George Coke
1637 Robert Skinner
1642 Thomas Westfield
1644 Thomas Howell
1661 Gilbert Ironside
1672 Guy Carleton
1679 William Gulston
1684 John Lake
1685 Jonathan Trelawney
1689 Gilbert Ironside
1691 John Hall
1710 John Robinson
1714 George Smalridge
1719 Hugh Boulter
1724 William Bradshaw
1733 Charles Cecil
1735 Thomas Secker
1737 Thomas Gooch
1738 Joseph Butler
1750 John Conybeare
1756 John Hume
1758 Philip Yonge
1761 Thomas Newton
1782 Lewis Bagot
1783 Christopher Wilson
1792 Spencer Madan
1794 Henry Reginald Courtenay
1797 Ffolliott Herbert Walker Cornewall
1803 George Pelham
1807 John Luxmoore
1808 William Lort Mansel
1820 John Kaye
1827 Robert Gray
1834 Joseph Allen
[1836 to 1897 united with Gloucester]
1897 George Forrest Browne
1914 George Nickson
1933 Clifford Salisbury Woodward
1946 Frederick Arthur Cockin
1959 Oliver Stratford Tomkins
1976 Ernest John Tinsley
1985 Barry Rogerson
2003 Michael Arthur Hill

Chelmsford

Description of arms. Or, on a saltire gules a pastoral staff of the first and a sword argent, hilt and pommel gold.

1914 John Edwin Watts-Ditchfield
1923 Frederic Sumpter Guy Warman
1929 Henry Albert Wilson
1951 Sherard Falkner Allison
1962 John Gerhard Tiarks
1971 Albert John Trillo
1986 John Waine
1996 John Freeman Perry
2003 John Warren Gladwin

Chichester

Description of arms. Azure, our blessed Lord in judgement seated in His throne, His dexter hand upraised or, His sinister hand holding an open book proper, and issuant from His mouth a two-edged sword point to the sinister gules.

BISHOPS OF SELSEY
681 Wilfrid
716 Eadberht

731 Eolla
733 Sigga [Sigeferth]
765 Aaluberht
c.765 Oswald [Osa]
780 Gislhere
786 Tota
c.789 Wihthun
c.811 Æthelwulf
824 Cynered
845 Guthheard
900 Wighelm
909 Beornheah
931 Wulfhun
943 Ælfred
955 Daniel
956 Brihthelm
963 Eadhelm
980 Æthelgar
990 Ordbriht
1009 Ælfmaer
1032 Æthelric I
1039 Grimketel
1047 Heca
1058 Æthelric II
1070 Stigand

BISHOPS OF CHICHESTER
1075 Stigand
1088 Godfrey
1091 Ralph Luffa
1125 Seffrid I [d'Escures Pelochin]
1147 Hilary
1174 John Greenford
1180 Seffrid II
1204 Simon FitzRobert
1215 Richard Poore
1218 Ranulf of Wareham
1224 Ralph Nevill
1245 Richard Wich
1254 John Climping
1262 Stephen Bersted [or Pagham]
1288 Gilbert de St Leofard
1305 John Langton
1337 Robert Stratford
1362 William Lenn
1369 William Reade
1386 Thomas Rushock
1390 Richard Mitford
1396 Robert Waldby
1397 Robert Reade
1417 Stephen Patrington
1418 Henry de la Ware
1421 John Kempe
1421 Thomas Polton
1426 John Rickingale
1431 Simon Sydenham
1438 Richard Praty
1446 Adam de Moleyns
1450 Reginald Pecock
1459 John Arundel
1478 Edward Story
1504 Richard Fitz-James
1508 Robert Sherburne
1536 Richard Sampson
1543 George Day (deposed)
1552 John Scory
1553 George Day (restored)
1557 John Christopherson
1559 William Barlow
1570 Richard Curtis
1586 Thomas Bickley
1596 Anthony Watson
1605 Lancelot Andrewes
1609 Samuel Harsnett
1619 George Carleton
1628 Richard Montague
1638 Brian Duppa
1642 Henry King
1670 Peter Gunning
1675 Ralph Brideoake
1679 Guy Carleton
1685 John Lake
1689 Simon Patrick
1691 Robert Grove
1696 John Williams
1709 Thomas Manningham
1722 Thomas Bowers
1724 Edward Waddington
1731 Francis Hare
1740 Matthias Mawson
1754 William Ashburnham
1798 John Buckner
1824 Robert James Carr
1831 Edward Maltby
1836 William Otter
1840 Philip Nicholas Shuttleworth
1842 Ashurst Turner Gilbert
1870 Richard Durnford
1896 Ernest Roland Wilberforce
1908 Charles John Ridgeway
1919 Winfrid Oldfield Burrows
1929 George Kennedy Allen Bell
1958 Roger Plumpton Wilson
1974 Eric Waldram Kemp
2001 John William Hind

Coventry

Description of arms. Gules, within a bordure argent charged with eight torteaux, a cross potent quadrate of the second.

1918 Huyshe Wolcott Yeatman-Biggs
1922 Charles Lisle Carr
1931 Mervyn George Haigh
1943 Neville Vincent Gorton
1956 Cuthbert Killick Norman Bardsley
1976 John Gibbs
1985 Simon Barrington-Ward
1998 Colin James Bennetts

Derby

Description of arms. Purpure, a cross of St Chad argent beneath three fountains in chief.

1927 Edmund Courtenay Pearce
1936 Alfred Edward John Rawlinson
1959 Geoffrey Francis Allen
1969 Cyril William Johnston Bowles
1988 Peter Spencer Dawes
1995 Jonathan Sansbury Bailey
2005 Alastair Llewellyn John Redfern

Dorchester[1]

634 Birinus
650 Agilbert
c.660 Ætla
c.888 Ahlheard

Ely

Description of arms. Gules, three ducal coronets or.

1109 Hervey
1133 Nigel
1174 Geoffrey Ridel
1189 William Longchamp
1198 Eustace
1220 John of Fountains
1225 Geoffrey de Burgo
1229 Hugh of Northwold
1255 William of Kilkenny
1258 Hugh of Balsham
1286 John of Kirkby
1290 William of Louth
1299 Ralph Walpole
1303 Robert Orford
1310 John Ketton
1316 John Hotham
1337 Simon Montacute
1345 Thomas de Lisle
1362 Simon Langham
1367 John Barnet
1374 Thomas Arundel
1388 John Fordham
1426 Philip Morgan
1438 Lewis of Luxembourg
1444 Thomas Bourgchier
1454 William Grey
1479 John Morton
1486 John Alcock
1501 Richard Redman
1506 James Stanley
1515 Nicholas West
1534 Thomas Goodrich
1555 Thomas Thirlby
1559 Richard Cox
1600 Martin Heton
1609 Lancelot Andrewes
1619 Nicolas Felton
1628 John Buckeridge
1631 Francis White
1638 Matthew Wren
1667 Benjamin Laney
1675 Peter Gunning
1684 Francis Turner
1691 Simon Patrick
1707 John Moore
1714 William Fleetwood

[1] Originally a West Saxon, after Ahlheard's time a Mercian, bishopric. See transferred to Lincoln 1077.

1723 Thomas Greene
1738 Robert Butts
1748 Thomas Gooch
1754 Matthias Mawson
1771 Edmund Keene
1781 James Yorke
1808 Thomas Dampier
1812 Bowyer Edward Sparke
1836 Joseph Allen
1845 Thomas Turton
1864 Edward Harold Browne
1873 James Russell Woodford
1886 Alwyne Frederick Compton
1905 Frederick Henry Chase
1924 Leonard Jauncey White-Thomson
1934 Bernard Oliver Francis Heywood
1941 Harold Edward Wynn
1957 Noel Baring Hudson
1964 Edward James Keymer Roberts
1977 Peter Knight Walker
1990 Stephen Whitefield Sykes
2000 Anthony John Russell

Exeter

Description of arms. Gules, a sword erect in pale argent hilt or surmounted by two keys addorsed in saltire gold.

BISHOPS OF CORNWALL

870 Kenstec
893 Asser
931 Conan
950 Æthelge[ard]
*c.*955 Daniel
963 Wulfsige Comoere
990 Ealdred
1009 Æthelsige
1018 Buruhwold
1027 Lyfing, Bishop of Crediton Cornwall and Worcester
1046 Leofric, Bishop of Crediton and Cornwall
[See transferred to Exeter 1050]

BISHOPS OF CREDITON

909 Eadwulf
934 Æthelgar
953 Ælfwold I
973 Sideman
979 Ælfric
987 Ælfwold II
1008 Ælfwold III
1015 Eadnoth
1027 Lyfing
1046 Leofric[1]

BISHOPS OF EXETER

1050 Leofric
1072 Osbern Fitz-Osbern
1107 Will. Warelwast
1138 Robert Warelwast
1155 Robert II of Chichester
1161 Bartholomew
1186 John the Chanter
1194 Henry Marshall
1214 Simon of Apulia
1224 William Brewer
1245 Richard Blund
1258 Walter Bronescombe
1280 Peter Quinel [Wyvill]
1292 Thomas Bitton
1308 Walter Stapeldon
1327 James Berkeley
1328 John Grandisson
1370 Thomas Brantingham
1395 Edmund Stafford
1419 John Catterick
1420 Edmund Lacy
1458 George Nevill
1465 John Booth
1478 Peter Courtenay
1487 Richard Fox
1493 Oliver King
1496 Richard Redman
1502 John Arundel
1505 Hugh Oldham
1519 John Veysey (resigned)
1551 Miles Coverdale
1553 John Veysey (restored)
1555 James Turberville
1560 William Alley [or Allei]
1571 William Bradbridge
1579 John Woolton
1595 Gervase Babington
1598 William Cotton
1621 Valentine Carey
1627 Joseph Hall
1642 Ralph Brownrigg
1660 John Gauden
1662 Seth Ward
1667 Anthony Sparrow
1676 Thomas Lamplugh
1689 Jonathan Trelawney
1708 Offspring Blackall
1717 Lancelot Blackburn
1724 Stephen Weston
1742 Nicholas Claget
1747 George Lavington
1762 Frederick Keppel
1778 John Ross
1792 William Buller
1797 Henry Reginald Courtenay
1803 John Fisher
1807 George Pelham
1820 William Carey
1830 Christopher Bethell
1831 Henry Phillpotts
1869 Frederick Temple
1885 Edward Henry Bickersteth
1901 Herbert Edward Ryle
1903 Archibald Robertson
1916 Rupert Ernest William Gascoyne Cecil
1936 Charles Edward Curzon
1949 Robert Cecil Mortimer
1973 Eric Arthur John Mercer
1985 Geoffrey Hewlett Thompson
1999 Michael Laurence Langrish

Gibraltar in Europe

Description of arms. Argent, in base rising out of the waves of the sea a rock proper, thereon a lion guardant or supporting a passion cross erect gules, on a chief engrailed of the last a crosier in bend dexter and a key in bend sinister or surmounted by a Maltese cross argent fimbriated gold.

BISHOPS OF GIBRALTAR

1842 George Tomlinson
1863 Walter John Trower
1868 Charles Amyand Harris
1874 Charles Waldegrave Sandford
1904 William Edward Collins
1911 Henry Joseph Corbett Knight
1921 John Harold Greig
1927 Frederick Cyril Nugent Hicks
1933 Harold Jocelyn Buxton
1947 Cecil Douglas Horsley
1953 Frederick William Thomas Craske
1960 Stanley Albert Hallam Eley
1970 John Richard Satterthwaite[2]

BISHOPS OF GIBRALTAR IN EUROPE

1980 John Richard Satterthwaite
1993 John William Hind
2001 Douglas Geoffrey Rowell

Gloucester

Description of arms. Azure, two keys addorsed in saltire the wards upwards or.

1541 John Wakeman *alias* Wiche
1551 John Hooper
1554 James Brooks
1562 Richard Cheyney[3]
1581 John Bullingham[4]
1598 Godfrey Goldsborough
1605 Thomas Ravis
1607 Henry Parry
1611 Giles Thompson
1612 Miles Smith
1625 Godfrey Goodman
1661 William Nicolson

[1] Removed See from Crediton.
[2] Bishop of Fulham and Gibraltar from 1970 to 1980.
[3] Also Bishop of Bristol.
[4] Held Gloucester and Bristol 1581-9.

1672 John Pritchett
1681 Robert Frampton
1691 Edward Fowler
1715 Richard Willis
1721 Joseph Wilcocks
1731 Elias Sydall
1735 Martin Benson
1752 James Johnson
1760 William Warburton
1779 James Yorke
1781 Samuel Hallifax
1789 Richard Beadon
1802 George Isaac Huntingford
1815 Henry Ryder
1824 Christopher Bethell
1830 James Henry Monk
[1836 to 1897, united with Bristol]

BISHOPS OF GLOUCESTER AND BRISTOL

1836 James Henry Monk
1856 Charles Baring
1861 William Thomson
1863 Charles John Ellicott[1]

BISHOPS OF GLOUCESTER

1897 Charles John Ellicott
1905 Edgar Charles Sumner Gibson
1923 Arthur Cayley Headlam
1946 Clifford Salisbury Woodward
1954 Wilfred Marcus Askwith
1962 Basil Tudor Guy
1975 John Yates
1992 Peter John Ball
1993 David Edward Bentley
2004 Michael Francis Perham

Guildford

Description of arms. Gules, two keys conjoined wards outwards in bend, the uppermost or, the other argent, interposed between them in bend sinister a sword of the third, hilt and pommel gold, all within a bordure azure charged with ten wool-packs argent.

1927 John Harold Greig
1934 John Victor Macmillan
1949 Henry Colville Montgomery Campbell
1956 Ivor Stanley Watkins
1961 George Edmund Reindorp
1973 David Alan Brown
1983 Michael Edgar Adie
1994 John Warren Gladwin
2004 Christopher John Hill

[1] Gloucester only from 1897.

Hereford

Description of arms. Gules, three leopards' faces jessant-de-lis reversed or.

676 Putta
688 Tyrhtel
710 Torhthere
*c.*731 Wahistod
736 Cuthberht
741 Podda
*c.*758 Acca
*c.*770 Headda
777 Aldberht
786 Esne
*c.*788 Ceolmund
*c.*798 Utel
801 Wulfheard
824 Beonna
*c.*832 Eadwulf
*c.*839 Cuthwulf
866 Mucel
*c.*866 Deorlaf
888 Cynemund
890 EadBar
*c.*931 Tidhelm
940 Wulfhelm
*c.*940 Ælfric
971 Æthelwulf
1016 Æthelstan
1056 Leofgar
1056 Ealdred, Bishop of Hereford and Worcester
1060 Walter
1079 Robert Losinga
1096 Gerard
1107 Reinhelm
1115 Geoffrey de Clive
1121 Richard de Capella
1131 Robert de Bethune
1148 Gilbert Foliot
1163 Robert of Melun
1174 Robert Foliot
1186 William de Vere
1200 Giles de Braose
1216 Hugh of Mapenore
1219 Hugh Foliot
1234 Ralph Maidstone
1240 Peter d'Aigueblanche
1269 John Breton
1275 Thomas Cantilupe
1283 Richard Swinfeld
1317 Adam Orleton
1327 Thomas Chariton
1344 John Trilleck
1361 Lewis Charleton
1370 William Courtenay
1375 John Gilbert
1389 John Trefnant
1404 Robert Mascall
1417 Edmund Lacy
1420 Thomas Polton
1422 Thomas Spofford
1449 Richard Beauchamp
1451 Reginald Boulers
1453 John Stanbury
1474 Thomas Milling
1492 Edmund Audley
1502 Adriano de Castello [di Corneto]
1504 Richard Mayeu
1516 Charles Booth
1535 Edward Fox
1539 John Skip
1553 John Harley
1554 Robert Parfew or Wharton
1559 John Scory
1586 Herbert Westfaling
1603 Robert Bennett
1617 Francis Godwin
1634 Augustine Lindsell
1635 Matthew Wren
1635 Theophilus Field
1636 George Coke
1661 Nicolas Monk
1662 Herbert Croft
1691 Gilbert Ironside
1701 Humphrey Humphries
1713 Philip Bisse
1721 Benjamin Hoadly
1724 Henry Egerton
1746 James Beauclerk
1787 John Harley
1788 John Butler
1803 Ffolliott Herbert Walker Cornewall
1808 John Luxmoore
1815 George Isaac Huntingford
1832 Edward Grey
1837 Thomas Musgrave
1848 Renn Dickson Hampden
1868 James Atlay
1895 John Percival
1918 Herbert Hensley Henson
1920 Martin Linton Smith
1931 Charles Lisle Carr
1941 Richard Godfrey Parsons
1949 Tom Longworth
1961 Mark Allin Hodson
1974 John Richard Gordon Eastaugh
1990 John Keith Oliver
2004 Anthony Martin Priddis

Leicester

see also under Lincoln

Description of arms. Gules, a pierced cinquefoil ermine, in chief a lion passant guardant grasping in the dexter forepaw a cross crosslet fitchée or.

NEW FOUNDATION

1927 Cyril Charles Bowman Bardsley
1940 Guy Vernon Smith
1953 Ronald Ralph Williams
1979 Cecil Richard Rutt
1991 Thomas Frederick Butler
1999 Timothy John Stevens

Lichfield

Description of arms. Per pale gules and argent, a cross potent quadrate in the centre per pale argent and or between four crosses patée those to the dexter argent and those to the sinister gold.

BISHOPS OF MERCIA

656 Diuma[1]
658 Ceollach
659 Trumhere
662 Jaruman

BISHOPS OF LICHFIELD

669 Chad[2]
672 Winfrith
676 Seaxwulf
691 Headda[3]
731 Aldwine
737 Hwita
757 Hemele
765 Cuthfrith
769 Berhthun
779 Hygeberht[4]
801 Aldwulf
816 Herewine
818 Æthelwald
830 Hunberht
836 Cyneferth
845 Tunberht
869 Eadberht
883 Wulfred
900 Wigmund or Wilferth
915 Ælfwine
941 Wulfgar
949 Cynesige
964 Wynsige
975 Ælfheah
1004 Godwine
1020 Leofgar
1026 Brihtmaer
1039 Wulfsige
1053 Leofwine
1072 Peter

BISHOPS OF LICHFIELD, CHESTER, AND COVENTRY[5]

1075 Peter
1086 Robert de Limesey[5]
1121 Robert Peche
1129 Roger de Clinton
1149 Walter Durdent
1161 Richard Peche
1183 Gerard La Pucelle
1188 Hugh Nonant
1198 Geoffrey Muschamp
1215 William Cornhill
1224 Alex. Stavensby
1240 Hugh Pattishall
1246 Roger Weseham
1258 Roger Longespee
1296 Walter Langton
1322 Roger Northburgh
1360 Robert Stretton
1386 Walter Skirlaw
1386 Richard le Scrope
1398 John Burghill
1415 John Catterick
1420 William Heyworth
1447 William Booth
1452 Nicholas Close
1453 Reginald Boulers
1459 John Hales
1493 William Smith
1496 John Arundel
1503 Geoffrey Blyth
1534 Rowland Lee
1541 [Chester formed as a bishopric]
1543 Richard Sampson
1554 Ralph Baynes
1560 Thomas Bentham
1580 William Overton
1609 George Abbot
1610 Richard Neile
1614 John Overall
1619 Thomas Morton
1632 Robert Wright
1644 Accepted Frewen
1661 John Hackett
1671 Thomas Wood
1692 William Lloyd
1699 John Hough
1717 Edward Chandler
1731 Richard Smalbroke
1750 Fred. Cornwallis
1768 John Egerton
1771 Brownlow North
1775 Richard Hurd
1781 James Cornwallis [4th Earl Cornwallis]
1824 Henry Ryder
1836 [Coventry transferred to Worcester diocese]
1836 Samuel Butler
1840 James Bowstead
1843 John Lonsdale
1868 George Augustus Selwyn
1878 William Dalrymple Maclagan
1891 Augustus Legge
1913 John Augustine Kempthorne
1937 Edward Sydney Woods
1953 Arthur Stretton Reeve
1975 Kenneth John Fraser Skelton
1984 Keith Norman Sutton
2003 Jonathan Michael Gledhill

Lincoln

Description of arms. Gules, two lions passant guardant or, on a chief azure, the Virgin ducally crowned sitting on a throne issuant from the chief, on her dexter arm the infant Jesus, and in her sinister hand a sceptre all gold.

BISHOPS OF LINDSEY

634 Birinus
650 Agilbert
660 Aetlai
678 Eadhaed
680 Æthelwine
693 (?)Edgar
731 (?)Cyneberht
733 Alwig
750 Aldwulf
767 Ceolwulf
796 Eadwulf
839 Beorhtred
869 Burgheard
933 Ælfred
953 Leofwine
996 Sigefrith

BISHOPS OF LEICESTER

664 Wilfrid, translated from York
679 Cuthwine
691 Headda[6] (founder of Lichfield Cathedral 705–37)
727 Aldwine
737 Torhthelm
764 Eadberht
785 Unwona
803 Wernberht
816 Raethhun
840 Ealdred
844 Ceolred
874 [See of Leicester removed to Dorchester]

BISHOPS OF DORCHESTER

(after it became a Mercian See)
*c.*888 Ahlheard
900 Wigmund or Wilferth
909 Cenwulf
925 Wynsige
*c.*951 Osketel
953 Leofwine
975 Ælfnoth
979 Æscwig
1002 Ælfheln
1006 Eadnoth I
1016 Æthelric
1034 Eadnoth II

[1] Archbishop of the Mercians, the Lindisfari, and the Middle Angles.
[2] Bishop of the Mercians and the Lindisfari.
[3] Bishop of Lichfield and Leicester.
[4] Archbishop of Lichfield after 787.
[5] 1102 Robert de Limesey, Bishop of Lichfield, moved the See to Coventry. Succeeding Bishops are usually termed *of Coventry* until 1228. Then *Coventry and Lichfield* was the habitual title until the Reformation. *Chester* was used by some 12th-century Bishops, and popularly afterwards. After the Reformation *Lichfield and Coventry* was used until 1846.
[6] Bishop of Leicester and Lichfield.

1049 Ulf
1053 Wulfwig
1067 Remigius

BISHOPS OF LINCOLN

1072 Remigius
1094 Robert Bloett
1123 Alexander
1148 Robert de Chesney
1183 Walter de Coutances
1186 Hugh of Avalon
1203 William of Blois
1209 Hugh of Wells
1235 Robert Grosseteste
1254 Henry Lexington [Sutton]
1258 Richard Gravesend
1280 Oliver Sutton [Lexington]
1300 John Dalderby
1320 Henry Burghersh
1342 Thomas Bek
1347 John Gynewell
1363 John Bokyngham [Buckingham]
1398 Henry Beaufort
1405 Philip Repingdon
1420 Richard Fleming
1431 William Gray
1436 William Alnwick
1450 Marmaduke Lumley
1452 John Chedworth
1472 Thomas Rotherham [Scott]
1480 John Russell
1495 William Smith
1514 Thomas Wolsey
1514 William Atwater
1521 John Longland
1547 Henry Holbeach [Rands]
1552 John Taylor
1554 John White
1557 Thomas Watson
1560 Nicholas Bullingham
1571 Thomas Cooper
1584 William Wickham
1595 William Chaderton
1608 William Barlow
1614 Richard Neile
1617 George Monteigne [Mountain]
1621 John Williams
1642 Thomas Winniffe
1660 Robt. Sanderson
1663 Benjamin Laney
1667 William Fuller
1675 Thomas Barlow
1692 Thomas Tenison
1695 James Gardiner
1705 William Wake
1716 Edmund Gibson
1723 Richard Reynolds
1744 John Thomas
1761 John Green
1779 Thomas Thurlow
1787 George Pretyman [Pretyman Tomline after June 1803]
1820 George Pelham
1827 John Kaye
1853 John Jackson
1869 Christopher Wordsworth
1885 Edward King
1910 Edward Lee Hicks
1920 William Shuckburgh Swayne
1933 Frederick Cyril Nugent Hicks
1942 Henry Aylmer Skelton
1946 Leslie Owen
1947 Maurice Henry Harland
1956 Kenneth Riches
1975 Simon Wilton Phipps
1987 Robert Maynard Hardy
2001 John Charles Saxbee

Norwich

Description of arms. Azure, three labelled mitres or.

BISHOPS OF DUNWICH

631 Felix
648 Thomas
*c.*653 Berhtgils [Boniface]
*c.*670 Bisi
*c.*673 Æcce
693 Alric (?)
716 Eardred
731 Aldbeorht I
747 Æscwulf
747 Eardwulf
775 Cuthwine
775 Aldbeorht II
781 Ecglaf
781 Heardred
793 Ælfhun
798 Tidferth
824 Waermund[1]
825 Wilred
836 Husa
870 Æthelwold

BISHOPS OF ELMHAM

673 Beaduwine
706 Nothberht
*c.*731 Heathulac
736 Æthelfrith
758 Eanfrith
*c.*781 Æthelwulf
*c.*785 Alhheard
814 Sibba
824 Hunferth
824 Hunbeorht
836 Cunda[2]
*c.*933 Ælfred[3]
*c.*945 Æthelweald
956 Eadwulf
970 Ælfric I
974 Theodred I
982 Theodred II
997 Æthelstan
1001 Ælfgar
1021 Ælfwine
1038 Ælfric II
1039 Ælfric III
1043 Stigand[4]
1043 Grimketel[5]
1044 Stigand (restored)
1047 Æthelmaer

BISHOPS OF THETFORD

1070 Herfast
1086 William de Beaufai
1091 Herbert Losinga

BISHOPS OF NORWICH

1091 Herbert Losinga
1121 Everard of Montgomery
1146 William de Turbe
1175 John of Oxford
1200 John de Gray
1222 Pandulf Masca
1226 Thomas Blundeville
1239 William Raleigh
1245 Walter Suffield or Calthorp
1258 Simon Walton
1266 Roger Skerning
1278 William Middleton
1289 Ralph Walpole
1299 John Salmon
1325 [Robert de Baldock]
1325 William Ayermine
1337 Anthony Bek
1344 William of Norwich [Bateman]
1356 Thomas Percy
1370 Henry Spencer [Dispenser]
1407 Alexander Tottington
1413 Richard Courtenay
1416 John Wakeryng
1426 William Ainwick
1436 Thomas Brown
1446 Walter Lyhert [le Hart]
1472 James Goldwell
1499 Thomas Jane
1501 Richard Nykke
1536 William Reppes [Rugge]
1550 Thomas Thirlby
1554 John Hopton
1560 John Parkhurst
1575 Edmund Freke
1585 Edmund Scambler
1595 William Redman
1603 John Jegon
1618 John Overall
1619 Samuel Harsnett
1629 Francis White
1632 Richard Corbet
1635 Matthew Wren
1638 Richard Montagu
1641 Joseph Hall
1661 Edward Reynolds
1676 Antony Sparrow
1685 William Lloyd
1691 John Moore
1708 Charles Trimnell
1721 Thomas Green
1723 John Leng
1727 William Baker
1733 Robert Butts
1738 Thomas Gooch
1748 Samuel Lisle
1749 Thomas Hayter
1761 Philip Yonge
1783 Lewis Bagot
1790 George Horne
1792 Charles Manners Sutton
1805 Henry Bathurst
1837 Edward Stanley
1849 Samuel Hinds
1857 John Thomas Pelham
1893 John Sheepshanks
1910 Bertram Pollock
1942 Percy Mark Herbert
1959 William Launcelot Scott Fleming
1971 Maurice Arthur Ponsonby Wood

[1] Bishop of Dunwich or Elmham.
[2] Bishop of Elmham or Dunwich.
[3] Bishop of Elmham or Lindsey.
[4] Deposed before consecration.
[5] Bishop of Selsey and Elmham.

1985 Peter John Nott
1999 Graham Richard James

Oxford

Description of arms. Sable, a fess argent, in chief three demi-ladies couped at the waist heads affrontée proper crowned or arrayed and veiled of the second, in base an ox of the last, horned and hoofed gold, passing a ford barry wavy of six azure and argent.

1542 Robert King[1]
1558 [Thomas Goldwell]
1567 Hugh Curen [Curwen]
1589 John Underhill
1604 John Bridges
1619 John Howson
1628 Richard Corbet
1632 John Bancroft
1641 Robert Skinner
1663 William Paul
1665 Walter Blandford
1671 Nathaniel Crewe [Lord Crewe]
1674 Henry Compton
1676 John Fell
1686 Samuel Parker
1688 Timothy Hall
1690 John Hough
1699 William Talbot
1715 John Potter
1737 Thomas Secker
1758 John Hume
1766 Robert Lowth
1777 John Butler
1788 Edward Smallwell
1799 John Randolph
1807 Charles Moss
1812 William Jackson
1816 Edward Legge
1827 Charles Lloyd
1829 Richard Bagot
1845 Samuel Wilberforce
1870 John Fielder Mackarness
1889 William Stubbs
1901 Francis Paget
1911 Charles Gore
1919 Hubert Murray Burge
1925 Thomas Banks Strong
1937 Kenneth Escott Kirk
1955 Harry James Carpenter
1971 Kenneth John Woollcombe
1978 Patrick Campbell Rodger
1987 Richard Douglas Harries

Peterborough

Description of arms. Gules, two keys in saltire the wards upwards between four cross crosslets fitchée or.

1541 John Chamber
1557 David Pole
1561 Edmund Scambler
1585 Richard Howland
1601 Thomas Dove
1630 William Piers
1633 Augustine Lindsell
1634 Francis Dee
1639 John Towers
1660 Benjamin Laney
1663 Joseph Henshaw
1679 William Lloyd
1685 Thomas White
1691 Richard Cumberland
1718 White Kennett
1729 Robert Clavering
1747 John Thomas
1757 Richard Terrick
1764 Robert Lambe
1769 John Hinchliffe
1794 Spencer Madan
1813 John Parsons
1819 Herbert Marsh
1839 George Davys
1864 Francis Jeune
1868 William Connor Magee
1891 Mandell Creighton
1897 Edward Carr Glyn
1916 Frank Theodore Woods
1924 Cyril Charles Bowman Bardsley
1927 Claude Martin Blagden
1949 Spencer Stottisbury Gwatkin Leeson
1956 Robert Wright Stopford
1961 Cyril Eastaugh
1972 Douglas Russell Feaver
1984 William John Westwood
1996 Ian Patrick Martyn Cundy

Portsmouth

Description of arms. Per fess or and gules, in chief upon waves of the sea proper a lymphad sable, and in base two keys conjoined wards outwards in bend, the uppermost or, the other argent, interposed between them in bend sinister a sword also argent, hilt and pommel gold.

1927 Ernest Neville Lovett
1936 Frank Partridge
1942 William Louis Anderson
1949 William Launcelot Scott Fleming
1960 John Henry Lawrence Phillips
1975 Archibald Ronald McDonald Gordon
1985 Timothy John Bavin
1995 Kenneth William Stevenson

Rochester

Description of arms. Argent, on a saltire gules an escallop or.

604 Justus
624 Romanus
633 Paulinus
644 Ithamar
664 Damianus
669 Putta
676 Cwichelm
678 Gebmund
716 Tobias
727 Aldwulf
741 Dunn
747 Eardwulf
772 Diora
785 Waermund I
805 Beornmod
844 Tatnoth
868 Badenoth
868 Waermund II
868 Cuthwulf
880 Swithwulf
900 Ceolmund
*c.*926 Cyneferth
*c.*934 Burhric
949 Beorhtsige
955 [Daniel?] Rochester or Selsey
964 Ælfstan
995 Godwine I
1046 Godwine II
1058 Siward
1076 Arnost
1077 Gundulf
1108 Ralph d'Escures
1115 Ernulf
1125 John
1137 John II
1142 Ascelin
1148 Walter
1182 Waleran
1185 Gilbert Glanvill
1215 Benedict of Sausetun [Sawston]
1227 Henry Sandford
1238 Richard Wendene
1251 Lawrence of St Martin
1274 Walter Merton
1278 John Bradfield
1283 Thomas Ingoldsthorpe
1292 Thomas of Wouldham
1319 Hamo Hethe
1353 John Sheppey
1362 William of Whittlesey

[1] Bishop Rheon. *in partibus*. Of Oseney 1542-5. See transferred to Oxford 1545.

1364 Thomas Trilleck
1373 Thomas Brinton
1389 William Bottlesham [Bottisham]
1400 John Bottlesham
1404 Richard Young
1419 John Kempe
1422 John Langdon
1435 Thomas Brouns
1437 William Wells
1444 John Low
1468 Thomas Rotherham [otherwise Scott]
1472 John Alcock
1476 John Russell
1480 Edmund Audley
1493 Thomas Savage
1497 Richard Fitz-James
1504 John Fisher
1535 John Hilsey [Hildesleigh]
1540 Nicolas Heath
1544 Henry Holbeach
1547 Nicholas Ridley
1550 John Ponet [Poynet]
1551 John Scory
1554 Maurice Griffith
1560 Edmund Gheast [Guest]
1572 Edmund Freke
1576 John Piers
1578 John Young
1605 William Barlow
1608 Richard Neile
1611 John Buckeridge
1628 Walter Curil
1630 John Bowle
1638 John Warner
1666 John Dolben
1683 Francis Turner
1684 Thomas Sprat
1713 Francis Atterbury
1723 Samuel Bradford
1731 Joseph Wilcocks
1756 Zachary Pearce
1774 John Thomas
1793 Samuel Horsley
1802 Thomas Dampier
1809 Walker King
1827 Hugh Percy
1827 George Murray
1860 Joseph Cotton Wigram
1867 Thomas Legh Claughton
1877 Anthony Wilson Thorold
1891 Randall Thomas Davidson
1895 Edward Stuart Talbot
1905 John Reginald Harmer
1930 Martin Linton Smith
1940 Christopher Maude Chavasse
1961 Richard David Say
1988 Anthony Michael Arnold Turnbull
1994 Michael James Nazir-Ali

St Albans

Description of arms. Azure, a saltire or, overall a sword erect in pale proper, hilt and pommel gold, in chief a celestial crown of the same.

1877 Thomas Legh Claughton
1890 John Wogan Festing
1903 Edgar Jacob
1920 Michael Bolton Furse
1944 Philip Henry Loyd
1950 Edward Michael Gresford Jones
1970 Robert Alexander Kennedy Runcie
1980 John Bernard Taylor
1995 Christopher William Herbert

St Edmundsbury and Ipswich

Description of arms. Per pale gules and azure, between three ducal coronets a demi-lion passant guardant conjoined to the demi-hulk of an ancient ship or.

1914 Henry Bernard Hodgson
1921 Albert Augustus David
1923 Walter Godfrey Whittingham
1940 Richard Brook
1954 Arthur Harold Morris
1966 Leslie Wilfrid Brown
1978 John Waine
1986 John Dennis
1997 John Hubert Richard Lewis

Salisbury

Description of arms. Azure, our Lady crowned, holding in her dexter arm the infant Jesus, and in her sinister arm a sceptre all or, round both the heads circles of glory gold.

BISHOPS OF SHERBORNE

705 Ealdhelm
709 Forthhere
736 Hereweald
774 Æthelmod
793 Denefrith
801 Wigberht
825 Ealhstan
868 Heahmund
877 Æthelheah
889 Wulfsige I
900 Asser
c.909 Æthelweard
c.909 Waerstan
925 Æthelbald
925 Sigehelm
934 Ælfred
943 Wulfsige II
958 Ælfwold I
979 Æthelsige I
992 Wulfsige III
1002 Æthelric
1012 Æthelsige II
1017 Brihtwine I
1017 Ælfmaer
1023 Brihtwine II
1045 Ælfwold II
1058 Hereman, Bishop of Ramsbury

BISHOPS OF RAMSBURY

909 Æthelstan
927 Oda
949 Ælfric I
951 Osulf
970 Ælfstan
981 Wulfgar
986 Sigeric
993 Ælfric II
1005 Brihtwold
1045 Hereman[1]

BISHOPS OF SALISBURY

1078 Osmund Osmer
1107 Roger
1142 Jocelin de Bohun
1189 Hubert Walter
1194 Herbert Poore
1217 Richard Poore
1229 Robert Bingham
1247 William of York
1257 Giles of Bridport
1263 Walter de la Wyle
1274 Robert Wickhampton
1284 Walter Scammel
1287 Henry Brandeston
1289 William de la Corner
1292 Nicholas Longespee
1297 Simon of Ghent
1315 Roger de Mortival
1330 Robert Wyville
1375 Ralph Erghum
1388 John Waltham
1395 Richard Mitford
1407 Nicholas Bubwith
1407 Robert Hallum
1417 John Chaundler
1427 Robert Nevill
1438 William Aiscough
1450 Richard Beauchamp
1482 Lionel Woodville
1485 Thomas Langton
1494 John Blythe
1500 Henry Deane
1502 Edmund Audley
1525 Lorenzo Campeggio
1535 Nicholas Shaxton
1539 John Salcot [Capon]
1560 John Jewell
1571 Edmund Gheast [Guest]
1577 John Piers
1591 John Coldwell
1598 Henry Cotton
1615 Robert Abbot
1618 Martin Fotherby
1620 Robert Townson [Toulson]
1621 John Davenant
1641 Brian Duppa
1660 Humfrey Henchman
1663 John Earle
1665 Alexander Hyde
1667 Seth Ward
1689 Gilbert Burnet
1715 William Talbot
1721 Richard Wilis
1723 Benjamin Hoadly

[1] Ramsbury was added to Sherbourne in 1058 when Hereman became Bishop of Sherbourne. The See was moved to Salisbury in 1078.

1734 Thomas Sherlock
1748 John Gilbert
1757 John Thomas
1761 Robert Hay Drummond
1761 John Thomas
1766 John Hume
1782 Shute Barrington
1791 John Douglas
1807 John Fisher
1825 Thomas Burgess
1837 Edward Denison
1854 Walter Kerr Hamilton
1869 George Moberly
1885 John Wordsworth
1911 Frederic Edward Ridgeway
1921 St Clair George Alfred Donaldson
1936 Ernest Neville Lovett
1946 Geoffrey Charles Lester Lunt
1949 William Louis Anderson
1963 Joseph Edward Fison
1973 George Edmund Reindorp
1982 John Austin Baker
1993 David Staffurth Stancliffe

Southwark

Description of arms. Argent, eleven fusils in cross conjoined, seven in pale fesswise, four in fess palewise, in the dexter chief a mitre all gules.

1905 Edward Stuart Talbot
1911 Hubert Murray Burge
1919 Cyril Forster Garbett
1932 Richard Godfrey Parsons
1942 Bertram Fitzgerald Simpson
1959 Arthur Mervyn Stockwood
1980 Ronald Oliver Bowlby
1991 Robert Kerr Williamson
1998 Thomas Frederick Butler

Truro

Description of arms. Argent, on a saltire gules a sword and key or and in base a fleur-de-lis sable all within a bordure of the last charged with fifteen besants.

1877 Edward White Benson
1883 George Howard Wilkinson
1891 John Gott
1906 Charles William Stubbs
1912 Winfrid Oldfield Burrows
1919 Frederic Sumpter Guy Warman
1923 Walter Howard Frere
1935 Joseph Wellington Hunkin
1951 Edmund Robert Morgan
1960 John Maurice Key
1973 Graham Douglas Leonard
1981 Peter Mumford
1990 Michael Thomas Ball
1997 William Ind

Worcester

Description of arms. Argent, ten torteaux, four, three, two, and one.

680 Bosel
691 Oftfor
693 Ecgwine
718 Wilfrid I
745 Milred
775 Waermund
777 Tilhere
781 Heathured
798 Deneberht
822 Heahberht
845 Alhhun
873 Waerferth
915 Æthelhun
922 Wilferth II
929 Cenwald
957 Dunstan
961 Oswald
992 Ealdwulf
1002 Wulfstan I
1016 Leofsige
1027 Lyfing
1033 Brihtheah
1040 Æltric Puttoc, Bishop of York and Worcester
1041 Lyfing (restored)
1046 Ealdred Bishop of Hereford and Worcester 1056–60
1062 Wulfstan II
1096 Samson
1115 Theulf
1125 Simon
1151 John of Pagham
1158 Aldred
1164 Roger of Gloucester
1180 Baldwin
1186 William of Northolt
1191 Robert Fitz Ralph
1193 Henry de Sully
1196 John of Coutances
1200 Mauger
1214 Walter de Gray
1216 Silvester of Evesham
1218 William of Blois
1237 Walter Cantilupe
1266 Nicolas of Ely
1268 Godfrey Giffard
1302 William Gainsborough
1308 Walter Reynolds
1313 Walter Maidstone
1317 Thomas Cobham
1327 Adam Orleton
1334 Simon Montacute
1337 Thomas Hempnall
1339 Wulstan Bransford
1350 John Thoresby
1353 Reginald Brian
1362 John Barnet
1364 William of Whittlesey
1369 William Lenn
1375 Henry Wakefield
1396 Robert Tideman of Winchcomb
1401 Richard Clifford
1407 Thomas Peverel
1419 Philip Morgan
1426 Thomas Polton
1435 Thomas Bourgchier
1444 John Carpenter
1476 John Alcock
1487 Robert Morton
1497 Giovanni de' Gigli
1499 Silvestro de' Gigli
1521 Julius de Medici Guilio de Medici (administrator)
1523 Geronimo Ghinucci
1535 Hugh Latimer
1539 John Bell
1544 Nicholas Heath (deposed)
1552 John Hooper
1554 Nicholas Heath (restored)
1555 Richard Pates
1559 Edwin Sandys
1571 Nicholas Bullingham
1577 John Whitgift
1584 Edmund Freke
1593 Richard Fletcher
1596 Thomas Bilson
1597 Gervase Babington
1610 Henry Parry
1617 John Thornborough
1641 John Prideaux
1660 George Morley
1662 John Gauden
1662 John Earle
1663 Robert Skinner
1671 Walter Blandford
1675 James Fleetwood
1683 William Thomas
1689 Edward Stillingfleet
1699 William Lloyd
1717 John Hough
1743 Isaac Maddox
1759 James Johnson
1774 Brownlow North
1781 Richard Hurd
1808 Ffolliott Herbert Walker Cornewall
1831 Robert James Carr
1841 Henry Pepys
1861 Henry Philpott
1891 John James Stewart Perowne
1902 Charles Gore
1905 Huyshe Wolcott Yeatman-Biggs
1919 Ernest Harold Pearce
1931 Arthur William Thomson Perowne
1941 William Wilson Cash
1956 Lewis Mervyn Charles-Edwards
1971 Robert Wylmer Woods
1982 Philip Harold Ernest Goodrich
1997 Peter Stephen Maurice Selby

PROVINCE OF YORK

York

Description of arms. Gules, two keys in saltire argent, in chief a regal crown proper.

BISHOPS

314 Eborius
625 Paulinus
[Vacancy 633–64]
664 Cedda
664 Wilfrid I
678 Bosa (retired)
686 Bosa (restored)
691 Wilfrith (restored)
706 John of Beverley
718 Wilfrid II

ARCHBISHOPS

734 Egberht
767 Æthelberht
780 Eanbald I
796 Eanbald II
808 Wulfsige
837 Wigmund
854 Wulfhere
900 Æthelbald
*c.*928 Hrothweard
931 Wulfstan I
956 Osketel
971 Oswald
971 Edwald
992 Ealdwulf[1]
1003 Wulfstan II
1023 Ælfric Puttoc
1041 Æthelric
1051 Cynesige
1061 Ealdred
1070 Thomas I of Bayeux
1100 Gerard
1109 Thomas II
1119 Thurstan
1143 William Fitzherbert
1147 Henry Murdac
1153 William Fitzherbert (restored)
1154 Roger of Pont l'Eveque
1191 Geoffrey Plantagenet
1215 Walter de Gray
1256 Sewal de Bovill
1258 Godfrey Ludham [Kineton]
1266 Walter Giffard
1279 William Wickwane
1286 John Romanus [le Romeyn]
1298 Henry Newark
1300 Thomas Corbridge
1306 William Greenfield
1317 William Melton
1342 William de la Zouche
1352 John Thoresby
1374 Alexander Neville
1388 Thomas Arundel
1396 Robert Waldby
1398 Richard le Scrope
1407 Henry Bowet
1426 John Kempe
1452 William Booth
1464 George Nevill
1476 Lawrence Booth
1480 Thomas Rotherham [Scott]
1501 Thomas Savage
1508 Christopher Bainbridge
1514 Thomas Wolsey
1531 Edward Lee
1545 Robert Holgate
1555 Nicholas Heath
1561 Thomas Young
1570 Edmund Grindal
1577 Edwin Sandys
1589 John Piers
1595 Matthew Hutton
1606 Tobias Matthew
1628 George Monteigne [Mountain]
1629 Samuel Harsnett
1632 Richard Neile
1641 John Williams
1660 Accepted Frewen
1664 Richard Sterne
1683 John Dolben
1688 Thomas Lamplugh
1691 John Sharp
1714 William Dawes
1724 Lancelot Blackburn
1743 Thomas Herring
1747 Matthew Hutton
1757 John Gilben
1761 Roben Hay Drummond
1777 William Markham
1808 Edward Venables Vernon Harcourt
1847 Thomas Musgrave
1860 Charles Thomas Longley
1863 William Thomson
1891 William Connor Magee
1891 William Dalrymple Maclagan
1909 Cosmo Gordon Lang
1929 William Temple
1942 Cyril Forster Garbett
1956 Arthur Michael Ramsey
1961 Frederick Donald Coggan
1975 Stuart Yarworth Blanch
1983 John Stapylton Habgood
1995 David Michael Hope
2005 John Mugabi Sentamu

Durham

Description of arms. Azure, a cross or between four lions rampant argent.

BISHOPS OF LINDISFARNE[2]

635 Aidan
651 Finan
661 Colman
664 Tuda
[Complications involving Wilfrid and Chad]
681 Eata
685 Cuthberht
[Vacancy during which Wilfrid administered the See]
688 Eadberht
698 Eadfenh
731 Æthelweald
740 Cynewulf
781 Higbald
803 Ecgberht
821 Heathwred
830 Ecgred
845 Eanberht
854 Eardwulf

BISHOPS OF HEXHAM

664 Wilfrith
678 Eata
681 Tunberht
684 Cuthbert
685 Eata (restored)
687 John of Beverley
709 Acca
734 Frithoberht
767 Ahimund
781 Tilberht
789 Æthelberht
797 Heardred
800 Eanberht
813 Tidferth

BISHOPS OF CHESTER-LE-STREET[3]

899 Eardwulf
899 Cutheard
915 Tilred
925 Wigred
944 Uhtred
944 Seaxhelm
944 Ealdred
968 Ælfsige
990 Aldhun

BISHOPS OF DURHAM

990 Aldhun d. 1018
[See vacant 1018–1020]
1020 Edmund
*c.*1040 Eadred
1041 Æthelric
1056 Æthelwine
1071 Walcher
1081 William of Saint Calais
1099 Ralph [Ranulf] Flambard
1133 Geoffrey Rufus
1143 William of Sainte-Barbe
1153 Hugh of le Puiset
1197 Philip of Poitiers
1217 Richard Marsh
1228 Richard Poore
1241 Nicholas Farnham
1249 Walter Kirkham
1261 Robert Stichill
1274 Robert of Holy Island
1284 Anthony Bek
1311 Richard Kellaw

[1] Ealdwulf and Wulfstan II held the Sees of York and Worcester together, Ælfric Puttoc held both 1040-41 and Ealdred 1060-61.
[2] See transferred to Chester-le-Street 883.
[3] See transferred to Durham 995.

1318 Lewis de Beaumont
1333 Richard of Bury
1345 Thomas Hatfield
1382 John Fordham
1388 Walter Skirlaw
1406 Thomas Langley
1438 Robert Nevill
1457 Lawrence Booth
1476 William Dudley
1485 John Shirwood
1494 Richard Fox
1502 William Senhouse [Sever]
1507 Christopher Bainbridge
1509 Thomas Ruthall
1523 Thomas Wolsey
1530 Cuthbert Tunstall
1561 James Pilkington
1577 Richard Barnes
1589 Matthew Hutton
1595 Tobias Matthew
1606 William James
1617 Richard Neile
1628 George Monteigne [Mountain]
1628 John Howson
1632 Thomas Morton
1660 John Cosin
1674 Nathaniel Crew [Lord Crew]
1721 William Talbot
1730 Edward Chandler
1750 Joseph Butler
1752 Richard Trevor
1771 John Egerton
1787 Thomas Thurlow
1791 Shute Barrington
1826 William Van Mildert
1836 Edward Maltby
1856 Charles Thomas Longley
1860 Henry Montagu Villiers
1861 Charles Baring
1879 Joseph Barber Lightfoot
1890 Brooke Foss Westcott
1901 Handley Carr Glyn Moule
1920 Herbert Hensley Henson
1939 Alwyn Terrell Petre Williams
1952 Arthur Michael Ramsey
1956 Maurice Henry Harland
1966 Ian Thomas Ramsey
1973 John Stapylton Habgood
1984 David Edward Jenkins
1994 Anthony Michael Arnold Turnbull
2003 Nicholas Thomas Wright

Blackburn

Description of arms. Per fess gules and or, in chief two keys in saltire wards downwards argent, in base a rose of the first barbed and seeded proper.

1926 Percy Mark Herbert
1942 Wilfred Marcus Askwith
1954 Walter Hubert Baddeley
1960 Charles Robert Claxton
1972 Robert Arnold Schürhoff Martineau
1982 David Stewart Cross
1989 Alan David Chesters
2004 Nicholas Stewart Reade

Bradford

Description of arms. Azure, two keys in saltire or, in chief a woolpack proper corded gold.

1920 Arthur William Thomson Perowne
1931 Alfred Walter Frank Blunt
1956 Frederick Donald Coggan
1961 Clement George St Michael Parker
1972 Ross Sydney Hook
1981 Geoffrey John Paul
1984 Robert Kerr Williamson
1992 David James Smith
2002 David Charles James

Carlisle

Description of arms. Argent, on a cross sable a labelled mitre or.

1133 Æthelwulf
1203 Bernard
1219 Hugh of Beaulieu
1224 Walter Mauclerc
1247 Silvester Everdon
1255 Thomas Vipont
1258 Robert de Chause
1280 Ralph Ireton
1292 John of Halton
1325 John Ross
1332 John Kirkby
1353 Gilbert Welton
1363 Thomas Appleby
1396 Robert Reade
1397 Thomas Merks
1400 William Strickland
1420 Roger Whelpdale
1424 William Barrow
1430 Marmaduke Lumley
1450 Nicholas Close
1452 William Percy
1462 John Kingscote
1464 Richard le Scrope
1468 Edward Story
1478 Richard Bell
1496 William Senhouse [Sever]
1504 Roger Layburne
1508 John Penny
1521 John Kite
1537 Robert Aldrich
1556 Owen Oglethorpe
1561 John Best
1570 Richard Barnes
1577 John May
1598 Henry Robinson
1616 Robert Snowden
1621 Richard Milbourne
1624 Richard Senhouse
1626 Francis White
1629 Barnabas Potter
1642 James Ussher
1660 Richard Sterne
1664 Edward Rainbowe
1684 Thomas Smith
1702 William Nicolson
1718 Samuel Bradford
1723 John Waugh
1735 George Fleming
1747 Richard Osbaldeston
1762 Charles Lyttleton
1769 Edmund Law
1787 John Douglas
1791 Edward Venables Vernon [Harcourt]
1808 Samuel Goodenough
1827 Hugh Percy
1856 Henry Montagu Villiers
1860 Samuel Waldegrave
1869 Harvey Goodwin
1892 John Wareing Bardsley
1905 John William Diggle
1920 Henry Herbert Williams
1946 Thomas Bloomer
1966 Sydney Cyril Bulley
1972 Henry David Halsey
1989 Ian Harland
2000 Geoffrey Graham Dow

Chester

Description of arms. Gules, three labelled mitres or.

1541 John Bird
1554 George Cotes
1556 Cuthbert Scott
1561 William Downham
1579 William Chaderton
1595 Hugh Bellott
1597 Richard Vaughan
1604 George Lloyd
1616 Thomas Morton
1619 John Bridgeman
1660 Brian Walton
1662 Henry Ferne
1662 George Hall
1668 John Wilkins
1673 John Pearson
1686 Thomas Cartwright
1689 Nicolas Stratford
1708 William Dawes
1714 Francis Gastrell
1726 Samuel Peploe
1752 Edmund Keene
1771 William Markham
1777 Beilby Porteus
1788 William Cleaver
1800 Henry William Majendie

1810 Bowyer Edward Sparke
1812 George Henry Law
1824 Charles James Blomfield
1828 John Bird Sumner
1848 John Graham
1865 William Jacobson
1884 William Stubbs
1889 Francis John Jayne
1919 Henry Luke Paget
1932 Geoffrey Francis Fisher
1939 Douglas Henry Crick
1955 Gerald Alexander Ellison
1974 Hubert Victor Whitsey
1982 Michael Alfred Baughen
1996 Peter Robert Forster

Liverpool

Description of arms. Argent, an eagle with wings expanded sable, holding in its dexter claw an ancient inkhorn proper, around its head a nimbus or, a chief paly azure and gules, the dexter charged with an open book or, inscribed with the words 'Thy Word is Truth', the sinister charged with a lymphad gold.

1880 John Charles Ryle
1900 Francis James Chavasse
1923 Albert Augustus David
1944 Clifford Arthur Martin
1966 Stuart Yarworth Blanch
1975 David Stuart Sheppard
1998 James Stuart Jones

Manchester

Description of arms. Or, on a pale engrailed gules three mitres of the first, on a canton of the second three bendlets enhanced gold.

1848 James Prince Lee
1870 James Fraser
1886 James Moorhouse
1903 Edmund Arbuthnott Knox
1921 William Temple
1929 Frederic Sumpter Guy Warman
1947 William Derrick Lindsay Greer
1970 Patrick Campbell Rodger
1979 Stanley Eric Francis Booth-Clibborn

1993 Christopher John Mayfield
2002 Nigel Simeon McCulloch

Newcastle

Description of arms. Gules, a cross between four lions rampant or, on a chief gold three triple-towered castles of the first.

1882 Ernest Roland Wilberforce
1896 Edgar Jacob
1903 Arthur Thomas Lloyd
1907 Norman Dumenil John Straton
1915 Herbert Louis Wild
1927 Harold Ernest Bilbrough
1941 Noel Baring Hudson
1957 Hugh Edward Ashdown
1973 Ronald Oliver Bowlby
1981 Andrew Alexander Kenny Graham
1997 John Martin Wharton

Ripon and Leeds (Ripon until 1999)

Description of arms. Argent, on a saltire gules two keys wards upwards or, on a chief of the second a Holy Lamb proper.

*c.*678 Eadheath

NEW FOUNDATION

1836 Charles Thomas Longley
1857 Robert Bickersteth
1884 William Boyd Carpenter
1912 Thomas Wortley Drury
1920 Thomas Banks Strong
1926 Edward Arthur Burroughs
1935 Geoffrey Charles Lester Lunt
1946 George Armitage Chase
1959 John Richard Humpidge Moorman
1975 Stuart Hetley Price
1977 David Nigel de Lorentz Young
2000 John Richard Packer

Sheffield

Description of arms. Azure, a crosier in pale ensigned by a fleur-de-lis vert, between in fess a key surmounted by a sword in saltire to the dexter, and to the sinister eight arrows interlaced and banded saltirewise, all or.

1914 Leonard Hedley Burrows
1939 Leslie Stannard Hunter
1962 Francis John Taylor
1971 William Gordon Fallows
1980 David Ramsay Lunn
1997 John Nicholls

Sodor and Man[1]

Description of arms. Argent, upon a pedestal between two coronetted pillars the Virgin Mary with arms extended, in her dexter hand a church proper and in base upon an escutcheon, surmounted by a mitre, the arms of Man – viz. gules, three legs in armour conjoined at the thigh and flexed at the knee.

447 Germanus
Conindrius
Romulus
Machutus
Conanus
Contentus
Baldus
Malchus
Torkinus
Brendanus
[Before 1080 Roolwer]
William
Hamond
1113 Wimund
1151 John
1160 Gamaliel
Ragnald
Christian of Argyle
Michael
1203 Nicholas de Meaux
Nicholas II
1217 Reginald
1226 John
1229 Simon of Argyle
1252 Richard
1275 Mark of Galloway
1305 Alan
1321 Gilbert Maclelan
1329 Bernard de Linton

[1] Included in the province of York by Act of Parliament 1542. Prior to Richard Oldham there is some uncertainty as to several names and dates. From 1425 to 1553 there was an English and Scottish succession. It is not easy to say which claimant was Bishop either *de jure* or *de facto*.

1334 Thomas
1348 William Russell
1387 John Donegan
1387 Michael
1392 John Sproten
1402 Conrad
1402 Theodore Bloc
1429 Richard Messing Andrew
1435 John Seyre
1455 Thomas Burton
1458 Thomas Kirklam
1472 Angus
1478 Richard Oldham
1487 Hugh Blackleach
1513 Hugh Hesketh
1523 John Howden
1546 Henry Man
1556 Thomas Stanley
1570 John Salisbury
1576 John Meyrick
1600 George Lloyd
1605 John Philips
1634 William Forster
1635 Richard Parr
1661 Samuel Rutter
1663 Isaac Barrow
1671 Henry Bridgman
1683 John Lake
1685 Baptist Levinz
1698 Thomas Wilson
1755 Mark Hildesley
1773 Richard Richmond
1780 George Mason
1784 Claudius Crigan
1814 George Murray
1828 William Ward
1838 James Bowstead
1840 Henry Pepys
1841 Thomas Vowler Short
1847 Walter Augustus Shirley
1847 Robert John Eden
1854 Horatio Powys
1877 Rowley Hill
1887 John Wareing Bardsley
1892 Norman Dumenil John Straton
1907 Thomas Wortley Drury
1912 James Denton Thompson
1925 Charles Leonard Thornton-Duesbery
1928 William Stanton Jones
1943 John Ralph Strickland Taylor
1954 Benjamin Pollard
1966 George Eric Gordon
1974 Vernon Sampson Nicholls
1983 Arthur Henry Attwell
1989 Noël Debroy Jones
2003 Graeme Paul Knowles

Southwell

Description of arms. Sable, three fountains proper, on a chief or a pale azure, charged with a representation of the Virgin Mary seated bearing the Infant Christ or between a stag lodged proper and two staves raguly crossed vert.

1884 George Ridding
1904 Edwyn Hoskyns
1926 Bernard Oliver Francis Heywood
1928 Henry Mosley
1941 Frank Russell Barry
1964 Gordon David Savage
1970 John Denis Wakeling
1985 Michael Humphrey Dickens Whinney
1988 Patrick Burnet Harris
1999 George Henry Cassidy

Wakefield

Description of arms. Or, a fleur-de-lis azure, on a chief of the last three celestial crowns gold.

1888 William Walsham How
1897 George Rodney Eden
1928 James Buchanan Seaton
1938 Campbell Richard Hone
1946 Henry McGowan
1949 Roger Plumpton Wilson
1958 John Alexander Ramsbotham
1968 Eric Treacy
1977 Colin Clement Walter James
1985 David Michael Hope
1992 Nigel Simeon McCulloch
2003 Stephen George Platten

BISHOPS SUFFRAGAN IN ENGLAND

Aston (Birmingham)

1954 Clement George St Michael Parker
1962 David Brownfield Porter
1972 Mark Green
1982 Michael Humphrey Dickens Whinney
1985 Colin Ogilvie Buchanan
1989–92 *no appointment*
1992 John Michael Austin

Barking (Chelmsford)

[in St Albans diocese to 1914]

1901 Thomas Stevens
1919 James Theodore Inskip
1948 Hugh Rowlands Gough
1959 William Frank Percival Chadwick
1975 Albert James Adams
1983 James William Roxburgh
1991 Roger Frederick Sainsbury
2002 David John Leader Hawkins

Barrow-in-Furness (Carlisle)

1889 Henry Ware
1909 Campbell West-Watson
1926 Henry Sidney Pelham
1944 *in abeyance*

Basingstoke (Winchester)

1973 Colin Clement Walter James
1977 Michael Richard John Manktelow
1994 Douglas Geoffrey Rowell
2002 Trevor Willmott

Bedford (St Albans)

1537 John Hodgkins[1]
1560–1879 *in abeyance*
1879 William Walsham How[2]
1888 Robert Claudius Billing[3]
1898–1935 *in abeyance*
1935 James Lumsden Barkway
1939 Aylmer Skelton
1948 Claude Thomas Thellusson Wood
1953 Angus Campbell MacInnes
1957 Basil Tudor Guy
1963 Albert John Trillo
1968 John Tyrrell Holmes Hare
1977 Andrew Alexander Kenny Graham
1981 David John Farmbrough
1994 John Henry Richardson
2003 Richard Neil Inwood

Berwick (Durham)

1536 Thomas Sparke
1572 *in abeyance*

Beverley (York)

1889 Robert Jarratt Crosthwaite
1923–94 *in abeyance*
1994 John Scott Gaisford
2000 Martyn William Jarrett

Birkenhead (Chester)

1965 Eric Arthur John Mercer
1974 Ronald Brown
1993 Michael Laurence Langrish
2000 David Andrew Urquhart

Bolton (Manchester)

1984 David George Galliford
1991 David Bonser
1999 David Keith Gillett

Bradwell (Chelmsford)

1968 William Neville Welch

[1] Appointed for the diocese of London. [2] Appointed for the diocese of London.
[3] Appointed for the diocese of London, and retained title after resigning his suffragan duties in 1895.

1973 John Gibbs
1976 Charles Derek Bond
1993 Laurence Alexander Green

Bristol (Worcester)

1538 Henry Holbeach [Rands]
1542 *became diocesan see*

Brixworth (Peterborough)

1989 Paul Everard Barber
2002 Francis White

Buckingham (Oxford)

1914 Edward Domett Shaw
1921 Philip Herbert Eliot
1944 Robert Milton Hay
1960 Gordon David Savage
1964 George Christopher Cutts Pepys
1974 Simon Hedley Burrows
1994 Colin James Bennetts
1998 Michael Arthur Hill
2003 Alan Thomas Lawrence Wilson

Burnley (Blackburn)

[in Manchester diocese to 1926]

1901 Edwyn Hoskyns
1905 Alfred Pearson
1909 Henry Henn
1931 Edgar Priestley Swain
1950 Charles Keith Kipling Prosser
1955 George Edward Holderness
1970 Richard Charles Challinor Watson
1988 Ronald James Milner
1994 Martyn William Jarrett
2000 John William Goddard

Colchester (Chelmsford)

[in London diocese to 1845
in Rochester diocese to 1877
in St Albans diocese 1877–1914]

1536 William More
1541–91 *in abeyance*
1592 John Sterne
1608–1882 *in abeyance*
1882 Alfred Blomfield
1894 Henry Frank Johnson
1909 Robert Henry Whitcombe
1922 Thomas Alfred Chapman
1933 Charles Henry Ridsdale
1946 Frederick Dudley Vaughan Narborough
1966 Roderic Norman Coote
1988 Michael Edwin Vickers
1995 Edward Holland
2001 Christopher Heudebourck Morgan

Coventry (Worcester)

see also under Lichfield

1891 Henry Bond Bowlby
1894 Edmund Arbuthnott Knox
1903–18 *no appointment*
1918 *became diocesan see*

Crediton (Exeter)

1897 Robert Edward Trefusis
1930 William Frederick Surtees
1954 Wilfred Arthur Edmund Westall

1974 Philip John Pasterfield
1984 Peter Everard Coleman
1996 Richard Stephen Hawkins
2004 Robert John Scott Evens

Croydon (Southwark)

(in Canterbury diocese to 1985)

1904 Henry Horace Pereira
1924–30 *no appointment*
1930 Edward Sydney Woods
1937 William Louis Anderson
1942 Maurice Henry Harland
1947 Cuthbert Killick Norman Bardsley
1957 John Taylor Hughes
1977 Geoffrey Stuart Snell
1985 Wilfred Denniston Wood
2003 Nicholas Baines

Derby (Southwell)

1889 Edward Ash Were
1909 Charles Thomas Abraham
1927 *became diocesan see*

Doncaster (Sheffield)

1972 Stuart Hetley Price
1976 David Stewart Cross
1982 William Michael Dermot Persson
1993 Michael Frederick Gear
2000 Cyril Guy Ashton

Dorchester (Oxford)

see also under Dorchester (*diocesan see*) *and* Lincoln

1939 Gerald Burton Allen
1952 Kenneth Riches
1957 David Goodwin Loveday
1972 Peter Knight Walker
1979 Conrad John Eustace Meyer
1988 Anthony John Russell
2000 Colin William Fletcher

Dorking (Guildford)

[in Winchester diocese to 1927]

1905 Cecil Henry Boutflower
1909–68 *in abeyance*
1968 Kenneth Dawson Evans
1986 David Peter Wilcox
1996 Ian James Brackley

Dover (Canterbury)

1537 Richard Yngworth
1545 Richard Thornden
1557–69 *no appointment*
1569 Richard Rogers
1597–1870 *in abeyance*
1870 Edward Parry
1890 George Rodney Eden
1898 William Walsh
1916 Harold Ernest Bilbrough
1927 John Victor Macmillan
1935 Alfred Careywollaston Rose
1957 Lewis Evan Meredith
1964 Anthony Paul Tremlett
1980 Richard Henry McPhail Third
1992 John Richard Allan Llewellin
1999 Stephen Squires Venner

Dudley (Worcester)

1974 Michael Ashley Mann
1977 Anthony Charles Dumper

1993 Rupert William Noel Hoare
2000 David Stuart Walker

Dunwich (St Edmundsbury and Ipswich)

see also under Norwich

1934 Maxwell Homfray Maxwell-Gumbleton
1945 Clement Mallory Ricketts
1955 Thomas Herbert Cashmore
1967 David Rokeby Maddock
1977 William Johnston
1980 Eric Nash Devenport
1992 Jonathan Sansbury Bailey
1995 Timothy John Stevens
1999 Clive Young

Ebbsfleet (Canterbury)

1994 John Richards
1998 Michael Alan Houghton
2000 Andrew Burnham

Edmonton (London)

1970 Alan Francis Bright Rogers
1975 William John Westwood
1985 Brian John Masters
1999 Peter William Wheatley

Europe (Europe)

1980 Ambrose Walter Marcus Weekes
1986 Edward Holland
1995 Henry William Scriven
2002 David Hamid

Fulham (London)[1]

1926 Basil Staunton Batty
1947 William Marshall Selwyn
1949 George Ernest Ingle
1955 Robert Wright Stopford
1957 Roderic Norman Coote
1966 Alan Francis Bright Rogers
1970 John Richard Satterthwaite[2]
1980–1982 *no appointment*
1982 Brian John Masters
1985 Charles John Klyberg
1996 John Charles Broadhurst

Grantham (Lincoln)

1905 Welbore MacCarthy
1920 John Edward Hine
1930 Ernest Morell Blackie
1935 Arthur Ivan Greaves
1937 Algernon Augustus Markham
1949 Anthony Otter
1965 Ross Sydney Hook
1972 Dennis Gascoyne Hawker
1987 William Ind
1997 Alastair Lewellyn John Redfern

Grimsby (Lincoln)

1935 Ernest Morell Blackie
1937 Anhur Ivan Greaves
1958 Kenneth Healey
1966 Gerald Fitzmaurice Colin
1979 David Tustin
2000 David Douglas James Rossdale

Guildford (Winchester)

1874 John Sutton Utterton
1888 George Henry Sumner

[1] From 1926 to 1980 exercised the Bishop of London's extra-diocesan jurisdiction over chaplaincies in Northern and Central Europe. Since 1996 has assisted the Diocesan Bishop in all matters not delegated to the Areas, and in pastoral care of parishes operating under the London Plan.
[2] Bishop of Fulham and Gibraltar.

1909 John Hugh Granville Randolph
1927 *became diocesan see*

Hertford (St Albans)

1968 Albert John Trillo
1971 Hubert Victor Whitsey
1974 Peter Mumford
1982 Kenneth Harold Pillar
1990 Robin Jonathan Norman Smith
2001 Christopher Richard James Foster

Horsham (Chichester)

1968 Simon Wilton Phipps
1975 Ivor Colin Docker
1991 John William Hind
1993 Lindsay Goodall Urwin

Hull (York)

1538 Robert Sylvester (Pursglove)
1579–1891 *in abeyance*
1891 Richard Frederick Lefevre Blunt
1910 John Augustus Kempthome
1913 Francis Gurdon
1929–31 *no appointment*
1931 Bemard Oliver Francis Heywood
1934 Henry Townsend Vodden
1957 George Fredenck Townley
1965 Hubert Laurence Higgs
1977 Geoffrey John Paul
1981 Donald George Snelgrove
1994 James Stuart Jones
1998 Richard Michael Cockayne Frith

Hulme (Manchester)

1924 John Charles Hill
1930 Thomas Sherwood Jones
1945 Hugh Leycester Homby
1953 Kenneth Venner Ramsey
1975 David George Galliford
1984 Colin John Fraser Scott
1999 Stephen Richard Lowe

Huntingdon (Ely)

1966 Robert Arnold Schürhoff Martineau
1972 Eric St Quintin Wall
1980 William Gordon Roe
1997 John Robert Flack
2003 John Geoffrey Inge

Ipswich (Norwich)

1536 Thomas Manning[1]
?–1899 *in abeyance*[2]
1899 George Carnac Fisher
1906 Henry Luke Paget
1909 *no appointment*
1914 *became diocesan see with St Edmundsbury*

Islington (London)

1898 Charles Henry Turner
1923 *in abeyance*

Jarrow (Durham)

1906 George Nickson
1914 John Nathaniel Quirk
1924 Samuel Kirshbaum Knight
1932 James Geoffrey Gordon
1939 Leslie Owen
1944 David Colin Dunlop
1950 John Alexander Ramsbotham
1958 Mervyn Armstrong
1965 Alexander Kenneth Hamilton
1980 Michael Thomas Ball
1990 Alan Smithson
2002 John Lawrence Pritchard

Kensington (London)

1901 Frederic Edward Ridgeway
1911 John Primatt Maud
1932 Bertram Fitzgerald Simpson
1942 Henry Colville Montgomery Campbell
1949 Cyril Eastaugh
1962 Edward James Keymer Roberts
1964 Ronald Cedric Osbourne Goodchild
1981 Mark Santer
1987 John George Hughes
1994–96 *no appointment*
1996 Michael John Colclough

Kingston-upon-Thames (Southwark)

1905 Cecil Hook
1915 Samuel Mumford Taylor
1922 Percy Mark Herbert
1927 Frederick Ochterlony Taylor Hawkes
1952 William Percy Gilpin
1970 Hugh William Montefiore
1978 Keith Norman Sutton
1984 Peter Stephen Maurice Selby
1992 John Martin Wharton
1997 Peter Bryan Price
2002 Richard Ian Cheetham

Knaresborough (Ripon)

1905 Lucius Frederick Moses Bottomley Smith
1934 Paul Fulcrand Dalacour de Labilliere
1938 John Norman Bateman-Champain
1948 Henry Handley Vully de Candole
1965 John Howard Cruse
1972 Ralph Emmerson
1979 John Dennis
1986 Malcolm James Menin
1997 Frank Valentine Weston
2004 James Harold Bell

Lancaster (Blackburn)

1936 Benjamin Pollard
1955 Anthony Leigh Egerton Hoskyns-Abrahall
1975 Dennis Fountain Page
1985 Ian Harland
1990 John Nicholls
1998 Geoffrey Stephen Pedley

Leicester (Peterborough)

see also under Lichfield *and* Lincoln

1888 Francis Henry Thicknesse
1903 Lewis Clayton
1913 Norman MacLeod Lang
1927 *became diocesan see*

Lewes (Chichester)

1909 Leonard Hedley Burrows
1914 Herbert Edward Jones
1920 Henry Kemble Southwell
1926 Thomas William Cook
1929 William Champion Streatfield
1929 Hugh Maudsley Hordern
1946 Geoffrey Hodgson Warde
1959 James Herbert Lloyd Morrell
1977 Peter John Ball
1992 Ian Patrick Martyn Cundy
1997 Wallace Parke Benn

Ludlow (Hereford)

1981 Stanley Mark Wood
1987 Ian Macdonald Griggs
1994 John Charles Saxbee
2002 Michael Wrenford Hooper

Lynn (Norwich)

1963 William Somers Llewellyn
1972 William Aubrey Aitken
1986 David Edward Bentley
1994 David John Conner
1999 Anthony Charles Foottit

Maidstone (Canterbury)

1944 Leslie Owen
1946–56 *no appointment*
1956 Stanley Woodley Betts
1966–69 *no appointment*
1969 Geoffrey Lewis Tiarks
1976 Richard Henry McPhail Third
1980 Robert Maynard Hardy
1987 David James Smith
1992 Gavin Hunter Reid
2001 Graham Alan Cray

Malmesbury (Bristol)

1927 Ronald Erskine Ramsay
1946 Ivor Stanley Watkins
1956 Edward James Keymer Roberts
1962 Clifford Leofric Purdy Bishop
1973 Frederick Stephen Temple
1983 Peter James Firth
1994 *renamed* Swindon

Marlborough

1537 Thomas Morley (Bickley)[3]
*c*1561–1888 *in abeyance*
1888 Alfred Earle[4]
1919 *in abeyance*

Middleton (Manchester)

1927 Richard Godfrey Parsons
1932 Cecil Wilfred Wilson
1938 Arthur Fawssett Alston
1943 Edward Worsfold Mowll
1952 Frank Woods
1958 Robert Nelson

[1] Manning does not appear to have acted as a suffragan bishop in the diocese of Norwich.
[2] The date of Manning's death is not known.
[3] Appointed for the diocese of London.
[4] Appointed for the diocese of London, but retained the title while Dean of Exeter 1900-18.

1959 Edward Ralph Wickham
1982 Donald Alexander Tytler
1994 Stephen Squires Venner
1999 Michael Augustine Owen Lewis

Nottingham (Lincoln)

[in York diocese to 1837]

1567 Richard Barnes
1570–1870 *in abeyance*
1870 Henry Mackenzie
1877 Edward Trollope
1893 *in abeyance*

Penrith (Carlisle)

see also under Richmond

1537 John Bird[1]
1539–1888 *in abeyance*
1888 John James Pulleine[2]
1939 Grandage Edwards Powell
1944 Herbert Victor Turner
1959 Sydney Cyril Bulley
1967 Reginald Foskett
1970 William Edward Augustus Pugh
1979 George Lanyon Hacker
1994 Richard Garrard
2002 James William Scobie Newcome

Plymouth (Exeter)

1923 John Howard Bertram Masterman
1934 Francis Whitfield Daukes
1950 Norman Harry Clarke
1962 Wilfred Guy Sanderson
1972 Richard Fox Cartwright
1982 Kenneth Albert Newing
1988 Richard Stephen Hawkins
1996 John Henry Garton

Pontefract (Wakefield)

1931 Campbell Richard Hone
1939 Tom Longworth
1949 Arthur Harold Morris
1954 George William Clarkson
1961 Eric Treacy
1968 William Gordon Fallows
1971 Thomas Richard Hare
1993 John Thornley Finney
1998 David Charles James
2002 Anthony William Robinson

Ramsbury (Salisbury)

see also under Salisbury

1974 John Robert Geoffrey Neale
1989 Peter St George Vaughan
1999 Peter Fearnley Hullah

Reading (Oxford)

1889 James Leslie Randall
1909–42 *in abeyance*
1942 Arthur Groom Parham
1954 Eric Henry Knell
1972 Eric Wild
1982 Ronald Graham Gregory Foley
1989 John Frank Ewan Bone
1997 Edward William Murray Walker
2004 Stephen Geoffrey Cottrell

Repton (Derby)

1965 William Warren Hunt
1977 Stephen Edmund Verney
1986 Francis Henry Arthur Richmond
1999 David Christopher Hawtin

Richborough (Canterbury)

1995 Edwin Ronald Barnes
2002 Keith Newton

Richmond (Ripon)

1889 John James Pulleine[3]
1913 Francis Charles Kilner
1921 *in abeyance*

St Germans (Truro)

1905 John Rundle Cornish
1918–74 *in abeyance*
1974 Cecil Richard Rutt
1979 Reginald Lindsay Fisher
1985 John Richard Allan Llewellin
1993 Graham Richard James
2000 Royden Screech

Selby (York)

1939 Henry St John Stirling Woollcombe
1941 Carey Frederick Knyvett
1962 Douglas Noel Sargent
1972 Morris Henry St John Maddocks
1983 Clifford Conder Barker
1991 Humphrey Vincent Taylor
2003 Martin William Wallace

Shaftesbury (Salisbury)

[in Bristol diocese 1542–1836]

1539 John Bradley
? *in abeyance*[4]

Sheffield (York)

1901 John Nathaniel Quirk
1914 *became diocesan see*

Sherborne (Salisbury)

1925 Robert Crowther Abbott
1928 Gerald Burton Allen
1936 Harold Nickinson Rodgers
1947 John Maurice Key
1960 Victor Joseph Pike
1976 John Dudley Galtrey Kirkham
2001 Timothy Martin Thornton

Sherwood (Southwell)

1965 Kenneth George Thompson
1975 Harold Richard Darby
1989 Alan Wyndham Morgan

Shrewsbury (Lichfield)

1537 Lewis Thomas[5]
1561–1888 *in abeyance*
1888 Sir Lovelace Tomlinson Stamer
1905–40 *in abeyance*
1940 Eric Knightley Chetwode Hamilton

1944 Robert Leighton Hodson
1959 William Alonzo Parker
1970 Francis William Cocks
1980 Leslie Lloyd Rees
1987 John Dudley Davies
1994 David Marrison Hallatt
2001 Alan Gregory Clayton Smith

Southampton (Winchester)

1895 William Awdry
1896 George Carnac Fisher
1898 The Hon Arthur Temple Lyttelton
1903 James Macarthur
1921 Cecil Henry Boutflower
1933 Arthur Baillie Lumsdaine Karney
1943 Edmund Robert Morgan
1951 Kenneth Edward Norman Lamplugh
1972 John Kingsmill Cavell
1984 Edward David Cartwright
1989 John Freeman Perry
1996 Jonathan Michael Gledhill
2004 Paul Roger Butler

Southwark (Rochester)

1891 Huyshe Wolcott Yeatman-Biggs
1905 *became diocesan see*

Stafford (Lichfield)

1909 Edward Ash Were
1915 Lionel Payne Crawfurd
1934 Douglas Henry Crick
1938 Lemprière Durell Hammond
1958 Richard George Clitherow
1975 John Waine
1979 John Stevens Waller
1987 Michael Charles Scott-Joynt
1996 Christopher John Hill
2005 Alfred Gordon Mursell

Stepney (London)

1895 George Forrest Browne
1897 Arthur Foley Winnington-Ingram
1901 Cosmo Gordon Lang
1909 Henry Luke Paget
1919 Henry Mosley
1928 Charles Edward Curzon
1936 Robert Hamilton Moberly
1952 Joost de Blank
1957 Francis Evered Lunt
1968 Ernest Urban Trevor Huddleston
1978 James Lawton Thompson
1992 Richard John Carew Chartres
1996 John Mugabi Sentamu
2003 Stephen John Oliver

Stockport (Chester)

1949 Frank Jackson Okell
1951 David Henry Saunders Saunders-Davies
1965 Rupert Gordon Strutt
1984 Frank Pilkington Sargeant
1994 Geoffrey Martin Turner
2000 William Nigel Stock

[1] Appointed for the diocese of Lichfield.
[2] Appointed for the diocese of Ripon.
[3] His suffragan title was changed from Penrith to Richmond by Royal Warrant.
[4] The date of Bradley's death is not known.
[5] Not appointed for Lichfield, but probably for Llandaff.

Swindon (Bristol)

1994 Michael David Doe
2005 Lee Stephen Rayfield

Taunton (Bath and Wells)

1538 William Finch
1559–1911 *in abeyance*
1911 Charles Fane de Salis
1931 George Arthur Hollis
1945 Harry Thomas
1955 Mark Allin Hodson
1962 Francis Horner West
1977 Peter John Nott
1986 Nigel Simeon McCulloch
1992 John Hubert Richard Lewis
1997 William Allen Stewart
1998 Andrew John Radford

Tewkesbury (Gloucester)

1938 Augustine John Hodson
1955 Edward Barry Henderson
1960 Forbes Trevor Horan
1973 Thomas Carlyle Joseph Robert Hamish Deakin
1986 Geoffrey David Jeremy Walsh
1996 John Stewart Went

Thetford (Norwich)

see also under Norwich

1536 John Salisbury
1570–1894 *in abeyance*
1894 Arthur Thomas Lloyd
1903 John Philips Alcott Bowers
1926–45 *no appointment*
1945 John Walker Woodhouse
1953 Manin Patrick Grainge Leonard
1963 Eric William Bradley Cordingly
1977 Hugh Charles Blackburne
1981 Timothy Dudley-Smith
1992 Hugo Ferdinand de Waal
2001 David John Atkinson

Tonbridge (Rochester)

1959 Russell Berridge White
1968 Henry David Halsey
1973 Philip Harold Ernest Goodrich
1982 David Henry Bartleet
1993 Brian Arthur Smith
2002 Brian Colin Castle

Warrington (Liverpool)

1918 Martin Linton Smith
1920 Edwin Hone Kempson
1927 Herbert Gresford Jones
1946 Charles Robert Claxton
1960 Laurence Ambrose Brown
1970 John Monier Bickersteth
1976 Michael Henshall
1996 John Richard Packer
2000 David Wilfred Michael Jennings

Warwick (Coventry)

1980 Keith Appleby Arnold
1990 Clive Handford
1996 Anthony Martin Priddis
2005 John Ronald Angus Stroyan

Whalley (Blackburn)

[in Manchester diocese to 1926]

1909 Atherton Gwillym Rawstorne
1936 *in abeyance*

Whitby (York)

1923 Harry St John Stirling Woollcombe
1939 Harold Evelyn Hubbard
1947 Walter Hubert Baddeley
1954 Philip William Wheeldon
1961 George D'Oyly Snow
1972 John Yates
1976 Clifford Conder Barker
1983 Gordon Bates
1999 Robert Sidney Ladds

Willesden (London)

1911 William Willcox Perrin
1929 Guy Vernon Smith
1940 Henry Colville Montgomery Campbell
1942 Edward Michael Gresford Jones
1950 Gerald Alexander Ellison
1955 George Ernest Ingle
1964 Graham Douglas Leonard
1974 Geoffrey Hewlett Thompson
1985 Thomas Frederick Butler
1992 Geoffrey Graham Dow
2001 Peter Alan Broadbent

Wolverhampton (Lichfield)

1979 Barry Rogerson
1985 Christopher John Mayfield
1994 Michael Gay Bourke

Woolwich (Southwark)

1905 John Cox Leeke
1918 William Woodcock Hough
1932 Arthur Llewellyn Preston
1936 Leslie Hamilton Lang
1947 Robert William Stannard
1959 John Arthur Thomas Robinson
1969 David Stuart Sheppard
1975 Michael Eric Marshall
1984 Albert Peter Hall
1996 Colin Ogilvie Buchanan
2005 Christopher Thomas James Chessun

WALES

Archbishops of Wales

1920 Alfred George Edwards (St Asaph 1889–1934)
1934 Charles Alfred Howell Green (Bangor 1928–44)
1944 David Lewis Prosser (St Davids 1927–50)
1949 John Morgan (Llandaff 1939–57)
1957 Alfred Edwin Morris (Monmouth 1945–67)
1968 William Glyn Hughes Simon (Llandaff 1957–71)
1971 Gwilym Owen Williams (Bangor 1957–82)
1983 Derrick Greenslade Childs (Monmouth 1972–87)
1987 George Noakes (St Davids 1982–91)
1991 Alwyn Rice Jones (St Asaph 1982–99)
1999 Rowan Douglas Williams (Monmouth 1992–2002)
2003 Barry Cennydd Morgan (Llandaff 1999–)

Bangor[1]

Description of arms. Gules, a bend or guttée de poix between two mullets pierced argent.

c.550 Deiniol [Daniel]
c.775 Elfod [Elbodugen]
1092 Herve
[*Vacancy* 1109–20]
1120 David the Scot
1140 Maurice (Meurig)
[*Vacancy* 1161–77]
1177 Guy Rufus [Gwion Goch]
[*Vacancy c*1190–95]
1195 Alan [Alban]
1197 Robert of Shrewsbury
[*Vacancy* 1212–15]
1215 Cadwgan
1237 Richard
1267 Anian [or Einion]
1307 Gruflydd ab Iowerth
1309 Anian [Einion] Sais
1328 Matthew de Englefield
1357 Thomas de Ringstead
1366 Gervase de Castro
1371 Hywel ap Gronwy
1372 John Gilbert
1376 John Swaffham
1400 Richard Young
[*Vacancy c*1404–8]
1408 Benedict Nicolls
1418 William Barrow
1425 John Cliderow
1436 Thomas Cheriton
1448 John Stanbury
1453 James Blakedon
1465 Richard Edenham
1495 Henry Dean
1500 Thomas Pigot
1505 Thomas Penny
1509 Thomas Skevington
1534 John Salcot [or Capon]

[1] Very few of the names of the Celtic bishops have been preserved.

1539 John Bird
1542 Arthur Bulkeley
1555 William Glynn
1559 Rowland Meyrick
1566 Nicholas Robinson
1586 Hugh Bellot
1596 Richard Vaughan
1598 Henry Rowlands
1616 Lewis Bayly
1632 David Dolben
1634 Edmund Griffith
1637 William Roberts
1666 Robert Morgan
1673 Humphrey Lloyd
1689 Humphrey Humphreys
1702 John Evans
1716 Benjamin Hoadley
1721 Richard Reynolds
1723 William Baker
1728 Thomas Sherlock
1734 Charles Cecil
1738 Thomas Herring
1743 Matthew Hutton
1748 Zachary Pearce
1756 John Egerton
1769 John Ewer
1775 John Moore
1783 John Warren
1800 William Cleaver
1807 John Randolph
1809 Henry William Majendie
1830 Christopher Bethell
1859 James Colquhoun Campbell
1890 Daniel Lewis Lloyd
1899 Watkin Herbert Williams
1925 Daniel Davies
1928 Charles Alfred Howell Green (Archbishop of Wales 1934)
1944 David Edwardes Davies
1949 John Charles Jones
1957 Gwilym Owen Williams (Archbishop of Wales 1971)
1982 John Cledan Mears
1993 Barry Cennydd Morgan
1999 Francis James Saunders Davies
2004 Phillip Anthony Crockett

Llandaff[1]

Description of arms. Sable, two pastoral staves endorsed in saltire, the dexter or, the sinister argent. On a chief azure three labelled mitres or.

*c.*550 Teiliau
*c.*872 Cyfeiliag
*c.*880 Libiau
*c.*940 Marchlwys
982 Gwyzan
*c.*995 Bledri
1027 Joseph
1056 Herewald
1107 Urban
[*Vacancy of six years*]
1140 Uchtryd
1148 Nicolas ap Gwrgant
[*Vacancy of two years*]
1186 William Saltmarsh
1193 Henry of Abergavenny
1219 William of Goldcliff
1230 Elias of Radnor
1245 William de Burgh
1254 John de Ware
1257 William of Radnor
1266 Willam de Breuse [or Brus]
1297 John of Monmouth
1323 John of Eaglescliffe
1344 John Paschal
1361 Roger Cradock
1383 Thomas Rushook
1386 William Bottesham
1389 Edmund Bromfield
1393 Tideman de Winchcomb
1395 Andrew Barret
1396 John Burghill
1398 Thomas Peverel
1408 John de la Zouch [Fulford]
1425 John Wells
1441 Nicholas Ashby
1458 John Hunden
1476 John Smith
1478 John Marshall
1496 John Ingleby
1500 Miles Salley
1517 George de Athequa
1537 Robert Holdgate [or Holgate]
1545 Anthony Kitchin
1567 Hugh Jones
1575 William Blethin
1591 Gervase Babington
1595 William Morgan
1601 Francis Godwin
1618 George Carleton
1619 Theophilus Field
1627 William Murray
1640 Morgan Owen
1660 Hugh Lloyd
1667 Francis Davies
1675 William Lloyd
1679 William Beaw
1706 John Tyler
1725 Robert Clavering
1729 John Harris
1739 Matthias Mawson
1740 John Gilbert
1749 Edward Cressett
1755 Richard Newcome
1761 John Ewer
1769 Jonathan Shipley
1769 Shute Barrington
1782 Richard Watson
1816 Herbert Marsh
1819 William Van Mildert
1826 Charles Richard Sumner
1828 Edward Copleston
1849 Alfred Ollivant
1883 Richard Lewis
1905 Joshua Pritchard Hughes
1931 Timothy Rees
1939 John Morgan (Archbishop of Wales 1949)
1957 William Glyn Hughes Simon (Archbishop of Wales 1968)
1971 Eryl Stephen Thomas
1975 John Richard Worthington Poole-Hughes
1985 Roy Thomas Davies
1999 Barry Cennydd Morgan (Archbishop of Wales 2003)

Monmouth

Description of arms. Per pale azure and sable, two crosiers in satire or between in chief a besant charged with a lion passant guardant gules, in fess two fleurs-de-lis and in base a fleur-de-lis all of the third.

1921 Charles Alfred Howell Green
1928 Gilbert Cunningham Joyce
1940 Alfred Edwin Monahan
1945 Alfred Edwin Morris (Archbishop of Wales 1957)
1968 Eryl Stephen Thomas
1972 Derrick Greenslade Childs (Archbishop of Wales 1983)
1986 Royston Clifford Wright
1992 Rowan Douglas Williams (Archbishop of Wales 1999)
2003 Edward William Murray Walker

St Asaph[2]

Description of arms. Sable, two keys endorsed in saltire the wards upwards argent.

*c.*560 Kentigern
*c.*573 Asaph
1143 Gilbert
1152 Geoffrey of Monmouth
1154 Richard
1160 Godfrey
1175 Adam
1183 John I
1186 Reiner
1225 Abraham
1235 Hugh
1242 Hywel Ab Ednyfed
1249 Anian I [or Einion]
1267 John II
1268 Anian II
1293 Llywelyn de Bromfield
1315 Dafydd ap Bleddyn
1346 John Trevor I
1357 Llywelyn ap Madoc ab Ellis
1377 William de Spridlington
1382 Lawrence Child
1390 Alexander Bache
1395 John Trevor II
1411 Robert de Lancaster
1433 John Lowe
1444 Reginald Pecock

[1] The traditional list of bishops of the Celtic Church has little historical foundation. But the names of the following, prior to Urban, may be regarded as fairly trustworthy, though the dates are very uncertain.
[2] Prior to the Norman period there is considerable uncertainty as to names and dates.

1451 Thomas Bird *alias* Knight
1471 Richard Redman
1496 Michael Deacon
1500 Dafydd ab Iorwerth
1504 Dafydd ab Owain
1513 Edmund Birkhead
1518 Henry Standish
1536 Robert Warton [or Parfew]
1555 Thomas Goldwell
1560 Richard Davies
1561 Thomas Davies
1573 William Hughes
1601 William Morgan
1604 Richard Parry
1624 John Hanmer
1629 John Owen
1660 George Griffith
1667 Henry Glemham
1670 Isaac Barrow
1680 William Lloyd
1692 Edward Jones
1703 George Hooper
1704 William Beveridge
1708 Will. Fleetwood
1715 John Wynne
1727 Francis Hare
1732 Thomas Tanner
1736 Isaac Maddox
1744 Samuel Lisle
1748 Robert Hay Drummond
1761 Richard Newcome
1769 Jonathan Shipley
1789 Samuel Hallifax
1790 Lewis Bagot
1802 Samuel Horsley
1806 William Cleaver
1815 John Luxmore
1830 William Carey
1846 Thomas Vowler Short
1870 Joshua Hughes
1889 Alfred George Edwards (Archbishop of Wales 1920)
1934 William Thomas Havard
1950 David Daniel Bartlett
1971 Harold John Charles
1982 Alwyn Rice Jones (Archbishop of Wales 1991–99)
1999 John Stewart Davies

St Davids[1]

Description of arms. Sable, on a cross or five cinquefoils of the first.

*c.*601 David
*c.*606 Cynog
831 Sadyrnfyw
Meurig
*c.*840 Novis
?Idwal
*c.*906 Asser
Llunwerth
944 Eneuris
*c.*961 Rhydderch
*c.*999 Morgeneu
1023 Morgeneu
1023 Erwyn
1039 Tramerin
1061 Joseph
1061 Bleddud
1072 Sulien
1078 Abraham
1080 Sulien
1085 Wilfrid
1115 Bernard
1148 David Fitz-Gerald
1176 Peter de Leia
1203 Geoffrey de Henlaw
1215 Gervase [Iorwerth]
1231 Anselm le Gras
1248 Thomas le Waleys
1256 Richard de Carew
1280 Thomas Bek
1296 David Martin
1328 Henry Gower
1347 John Thoresby
1350 Reginald Brian
1352 Thomas Fastolf
1362 Adam Houghton
1389 John Gilbert
1397 Guy de Mohne
1408 Henry Chichele
1414 John Catterick
1415 Stephen Patrington
1418 Benedict Nichols
1434 Thomas Rodburn [Rudborne]
1442 William Lindwood
1447 John Langton
1447 John de la Bere
1460 Robert Tully
1482 Richard Martin
1483 Thomas Langton
1485 Hugh Pavy
1496 John Morgan [Young]
1505 Robert Sherborn
1509 Edward Vaughan
1523 Richard Rawlins
1536 William Barlow
1548 Robert Ferrar
1554 Henry Morgan
1560 Thomas Young
1561 Richard Davies
1582 Marmaduke Middleton
1594 Anthony Rudd
1615 Richard Milbourne
1621 William Laud
1627 Theophilus Field
1636 Roger Mainwaring
1660 William Lucy
1678 William Thomas
1683 Laurence Womock
1686 John Lloyd
1687 Thomas Watson
[*Vacancy* 1699–1705]
1705 George Bull
1710 Philip Bisse
1713 Adam Ottley
1724 Richard Smallbrooke
1731 Elias Sydall
1732 Nicholas Claggett
1743 Edward Willes
1744 Richard Trevor
1753 Anthony Ellis
1761 Samuel Squire
1766 Robert Lowth
1766 Charles Moss
1774 James Yorke
1779 John Warren
1783 Edward Smallwell
1788 Samuel Horsley
1794 William Stewart
1801 George Murray
1803 Thomas Burgess
1825 John Banks Jenkinson
1840 Connop Thirlwall
1874 William Basil Tickell Jones
1897 John Owen
1927 David Lewis Prosser (Archbishop of Wales 1944)
1950 William Thomas Havard
1956 John Richards Richards
1971 Eric Matthias Roberts
1982 George Noakes (Archbishop of Wales 1987)
1991 John Ivor Rees
1996 David Huw Jones
2002 Carl Norman Cooper

Swansea and Brecon

Description of arms. Per fess azure and or, in chief surmounting a catherine wheel issuant an eagle rising regardant of the second and in base a fleur-de-lis of the first.

1923 Edward Latham Bevan
1934 John Morgan
1939 Edward William Williamson
1953 William Glyn Hughes Simon
1958 John James Absalom Thomas
1976 Benjamin Noel Young Vaughan
1988 Dewi Morris Bridges
1999 Anthony Edward Pierce

Provincial Assistant Bishops

1996 David Thomas

[1] The following names occur in early records though the dates given cannot always be reconciled.

SCOTLAND

Sources: Bp Dowden's *The Bishops of Scotland* (Glasgow 1912), for all the sees up to the Reformation, and for Aberdeen and Moray to the present time.

For bishops after the Reformation (and for a few of the earliest ones before Queen Margaret) – Grub, *Ecclesiastical History of Scotland* (Edinburgh 1861, 4 Vols.) and Bp Keith and Bp Russel, *Scottish Bishops* (2nd ed. Edinburgh 1824).

Scottish episcopal elections became subject immediately to Roman confirmation in 1192. The subordination of the Scottish Church to York became less direct in 1165, and its independence was recognized in a bill of Celestine III in 1192. St Andrews was raised to metropolitan rank on 17 August 1472 and the Archbishop became primate of all Scotland with the same legative rights as the Archbishop of Canterbury on 27 March 1487.

The dates in the margin are those of the consecration or translation to the particular see of the bishops named; or in the case of bishops elect, who are not known to have been consecrated, they are those of the election; or in the case of titular bishops, of the date of their appointment.

The date of the death has been given where there was a long interregnum, or where there is dislocation (as at the Reformation and at the Revolution), or for some special reason to make the history intelligible.

The extra information in the list of College Bishops is given for the reason just stated.

St Andrews

St Andrews, Dunkeld and Dunblane

Description of arms. Quarterly, 1st azure, a saltire argent (for the See of St Andrews); 2nd per fess sable and vert, an open book proper in base, fore-edges and binding or, a dove argent, her wings displayed in chief perching thereon and holding in her beak a spray of olive of the second (for the See of Dunkeld); 3rd chevronny or and gules, a saltire engrailed azure, charged at the fess point with a crescent inverted argent (for the See of Dunblane); 4th azure, a saltire argent supported in front of and by St Andrew enhaloed or and vested pupure with mantle vert, and in base a crescent inverted of the second (for the See of St Andrews).

906 Cellach I
915(?) Fothad I
955 Malisius I
963 Maelbridge
970 Cellach II
996(?) Malasius II
(?) Malmore
1025 Alwyn
1028 Maelduin
1055 Tuthald or Tuadal
1059 Fothad II
1077 to 1107 { Gregory (elect)
Catharas (elect)
Edmarus (elect)
Godricus (elect) }
1109 Turgot
1120 Eadmer (elect)
1127 Robert
1159 Waldeve (elect)
1160 Ernald
1165 Richard
1178 Hugh
1180 John the Scot
1198 Roger de Beaumon
1202 William Malveisin
1238 Geoffrey (elect)
1240 David de Bernham
1253 Robert de Stuteville (elect)
1254 Abel de Golin
1255 Gamelin
1273 William Wischard
1280 William Fraser
1298 William de Lamberton
1328 James Bennet
1342 William de Laundels
1385 Stephen de Pay (elect)
1386(?) Walter Trayl
1388 Alexander de Neville
1398 Thomas de Arundel
1401 Thomas Stewart (elect)
1402 Walter de Danielston (elect)
1403(?) Gilbert Greenlaw
1403 Henry Wardlaw
1408 John Trevor
1440 James Kennedy

ARCHBISHOPS

1465 Patrick Graham
1478 William Scheves
1497 James Stewart (elect)
1504 Alexander Stewart (elect)
1513 John Hepburn (elect)
1513 Innocenzo Cibo (elect)
1514 Andrew Forman
1522 James Betoun
1538 David Betoun [coadjutor]
1547 John Hamilton
1551 Gavin Hamilton [coadjutor] died 1571
1572 John Douglas (titular)
1576 Patrick Adamson (titular) died 1592
1611 George Gladstanes
1615 John Spottiswoode, died 1639
1661 James Sharp
1679 Alexander Burnet
1684 Arthur Rose, died 1704

BISHOPS OF FIFE

[1704–26 See vacant]
1726 James Rose
1733 Robert Keith
1743 Robert White
1761 Henry Edgar

BISHOPS OF ST ANDREWS

1842 Patrick Torry
1853 Charles Wordsworth
1893 George Howard Wilkinson
1908 Charles Edward Plumb
1931 Edward Thomas Scott Reid
1938 James Lumsden Barkway
1949 Arnold Brian Burrowes
1955 John William Alexander Howe
1969 Michael Geoffrey Hare Duke
1995 Michael Harry George Henley
2005 David Robert Chillingworth

†Dunkeld

849(?) Tuathal
865(?) Flaithbertach
1114 Cormac
1147 Gregory
1170 Richard I
1178 Walter de Bidun (elect)
1183(?) John I, the Scot
1203 Richard II, de Prebenda
1212(?) John II, de Leycester
1214(?) Hugh de Sigillo
1229 Matthew Scot (elect)
1229 Gilbert
1236(?) Geoffrey de Liberatione
1252 Richard III, of Inverkeithing
1273(?) Robert de Stuteville
1283(?) Hugh de Strivelin [Stirling] (elect)
1283 William
1288 Matthew de Crambeth
1309 John de Leek (elect)
1312 William Sinclair
1337 Malcolm de Innerpeffray (elect)
1344 Richard de Pilmor
1347 Robert de Den (elect)
1347(?) Duncan de Strathearn
1355 John Luce
1370 John de Carrick (elect)
1371(?) Michael de Monymusk
1377(?) Andrew Umfray (elect)
1379 John de Peblys [? of Peebles]
1379 Robert de Derling
1390(?) Nicholas Duffield
1391 Robert Sinclair
1398(?) Robert de Cardeny
1430 William Gunwardby
1437 Donald MacNaughton (elect)
1438 James Kennedy
1440(?) Thomas Livingston
1440 Alexander de Lawedre [Lauder] (elect)
1442 James de Brois [Brewhous]
1447 William Turnbull (elect)
1448 John Ralston
1452(?) Thomas Lauder
1476 James Livingston
1483 Alexander Inglis (elect)
1484 George Brown
1515 Andrew Stewart (elect)
1516 Gavin Dougias
1524 Robert Cockburn
1526(?) George Crichton
1546 John Hamilton
1552 Robert Crichton
1572 James Paton (titular)
1585 Peter Rollock (titular)
1607 James Nicolson (titular)
1611(?) Alexander Lindsay (deposed 1638)
1662 George Haliburton

† Indicates a diocese no longer extant, or united with another diocese.

1665 Henry Guthrie
1677 William Lindsay
1679 Andrew Bruce
1686 John Hamilton
1717 Thomas Rattray
1743 John Alexander
1776(?) Charles Rose
1792 Jonathan Watson
1808 Patrick Torry
1842 Held with St Andrews

†Dunblane

1162 Laurence
c.1180 Symon
1196 W[illelmus]
1198 Jonathan
1215 Abraham
1225 Ralph (elect)
1227 Osbert
1233 Clement
1259 Robert de Prebenda
1284 William I
1296 Alpin
1301 Nicholas
1307 Nicholas de Balmyle
1318(?) Roger de Balnebrich (elect)
1322 Maurice
c.1347 William II
c.1361 Walter de Coventre
c.1372 Andrew
c.1380 Dougal
1403(?) Finlay or Dermoch
1419 William Stephen
1430 Michael Ochiltree
1447(?) Robert Lauder
1468 John Hepburn
1487 James Chisolm
1527 William Chisolm I
1561 William Chisom II [coadjutor]
1575 Andrew Graham (titular)
1611 George Graham
1616 Adam Bellenden
1636 James Wedderburn
1661 Robert Leighton
1673 James Ramsay
1684 Robert Douglas
[1716–31 See vacant]
1731 John Gillan
1735 Robert White
1744 Thomas Ogilvie (elect)
1774 Charles Rose, died 1791
1776 Held with Dunkeld

Edinburgh

Description of arms. Azure, a saltire and, in chief, a labelled mitre argent.

1634 William Forbes
1634 David Lindsay
1662 George Wishart
1672 Alexander Young
1679 John Paterson
1687 Alexander Rose
1720 John Fullarton
1727 Arthur Millar
1727 Andrew Lumsden
1733 David Freebairn
[1739–76 See vacant]
1776 William Falconer
1787 William Abernethy Drummond
1806 Daniel Sandford
1830 James Walker
1841 Charles Hughes Terrot
1872 Henry Cotterill
1886 John Dowden
1910 George Henry Somerset Walpole
1929 Harry Seymour Reid
1939 Ernest Denny Logie Danson
1947 Kenneth Charles Harman Warner
1961 Kenneth Moir Carey
1975 Alastair Iain Macdonald Haggart
1986 Richard Frederick Holloway
2001 Brian Arthur Smith

Aberdeen

Aberdeen and Orkney

Description of arms. Azure, parted per pale: dexter, a chevron round embattled on its upper edge between a fleur-de-lis argent ensigned of an open crown or in dexter chief, and in base a bishop proper, attired of the second, mitred and holding in his sinister hand a pastoral staff of the third, his dexter hand raised in benediction over three children gules issuant from a cauldron of the third; sinister, an open boat or, an anchor argent pendant from its prow, issuant therefrom a saint proper, attired of the third, enhaloed and holding in his sinister hand a pastoral staff of the second; over all and issuant from the chief a sunburst or, the central ray projected along the palar line to the base.

BISHOPS AT MURTHLAC

(?) Beyn [Beanus]
(?) Donort
(?) Cormac

BISHOPS AT ABERDEEN

1132 Nechtan
c.1150 Edward
c.1172 Matthew
c.1201 John
c.1208 Adam de Kalder
1228 Matthew Scot (elect)
1230 Gilbert de Strivelyn
1240 Radulf de Lamley
1247 Peter de Ramsey
1258 Richard de Pottun
1272 Hugh de Bennum
1282 Henry le Chene
1329 Walter Herok (elect)
1329 Alexander I, de Kyninmund
1344 William de Deyn
1351 John de Rate
1356 Alexander II, de Kyninmund
1380 Adam de Tynyngham
1391 Gilbert de Grenlaw
1422 Henry de Lychton [Leighton]
c.1441 Ingram de Lindsay
1458 Thomas Spens
1480 Robert Blackadder (elect)
1488 William Elphinstone
1515 Robert Forman (elect)
1516 Alexander Gordon
1519 Gavin Dunbar
1529 George Learmonth [coadjutor]
1533 William Stewart
1547 William Gordon
1577 David Cunningham (elect)
1611 Peter Blackburn
1616 Alexander Forbes
1618 Patrick Forbes of Corse
1635 Adam Bellenden [Bannatyne]
1662 David Mitchell
1663 Alexander Burnet
1664 Patrick Scougal
1682 George Halyburton
[1715–21 See vacant]
1721 Archibald Campbell
1724 James Gadderar
1733 William Dunbar
1746 Andrew Gerard
1768 Robert Kilgour
1786 John Skinner
1816 William Skinner
1857 Thomas George Spink Suther
1883 Arthur Gascoigne Douglas
1906 Rowland Ellis
1912 Anthony Mitchell
1917 Frederic Llewellyn Deane
1943 Herbert William Hall
1956 Edward Frederick Easson
1973 Ian Forbes Begg
1978 Frederick Charles Darwent
1992 Andrew Bruce Cameron

†Orkney

1035 Henry
1050 Turolf
1072 John I
1072 Adalbert
1073 Radulf
1102 William I, 'the Old'
1108 Roger
1114 Radulf Novell
1168(?) William II
1188(?) Bjarni
1224 Jofreyrr
1248 Henry I
1270 Peter
1286 Dolgfinn
1310 William III
c.1369 William IV
c.1384 Robert Sinclair
1384(?) John
1394 Henry II
1396(?) John Pak
1407 Alexander Vaus (elect)
1415 William Stephenson
1420 Thomas Tulloch
1461 William Tulloch
1477 Andrew Painter
1500 Edward Stewart
1524 John Benston [coadjutor]
1526(?) Robert Maxwell
1541 Robert Reid
1559 Adam Bothwell
1611 James Law
1615 George Graham
1639 Robert Barron (elect)
1661 Thomas Sydserf
1664 Andrew Honeyman

1677 Murdo Mackenzie
1688 Andrew Bruce, See afterwards administered with Caithness
1857 Held with Aberdeen

Brechin

Description of arms. Or, three piles in point purpure.

1153(?) Samson
1178 Turpin
1202 Radulf
1215 Hugh
1218 Gregory
1246 Albin
1269(?) William de Crachin (elect)
1275 William Comyn
1296 Nicholas
1298 John de Kyninmund
1328 Adam de Moravia
1350 Philip Wilde
1351 Patrick de Locrys [Leuchars]
1383 Stephen de Cellario
1411 Walter Forrester
1426 John de Crannach
1455 George Schoriswood
1464 Patrick Graham
1465 John Balfour
1489 William Meldrum
1523 John Hepburn
1557 Donald Campbell (elect)
1565(?) John Sinclair (elect)
1566 Alexander Campbell (titular)
1610 Andrew Lamb
1619 David Lindsay
1634 Thomas Sydserf
1635 Walter Whitford
1662 David Strachan
1672 Robert Laurie
1678 George Haliburton
1682 Robert Douglas
1684 Alexander Cairncross
1684 James Drummond
1695–1709 Held with Edinburgh
1709 John Falconar
1724 Robert Norrie
1726 John Ochterlonie
1742 James Rait
1778 George Innes
1787 William Abernethy Drummond
1788 John Strachan
1810 George Gleig
1840 David Moir
1847 Alexander Penrose Forbes
1876 Hugh Willoughby Jermyn
1904 Walter John Forbes Robberds
1935 Kenneth Donald Mackenzie
1944 Eric Graham
1959 John Chappell Sprott
1975 Lawrence Edward Luscombe
1990 Robert Taylor Halliday
1997 Neville Chamberlain
2005 John Ambrose Cyril Mantle

Moray

Moray, Ross and Caithness

Description of arms. Party per fess and in chief per pale: 1 or, two lions combatant gules, pulling at a cushion of the last issuant from a crescent azure, on a chief wavy of the third three mullets argent (for the See of Moray); 2 argent, a bishop standing in the sinister vested purpure, mitred and holding in his sinister hand a crosier or and pointing with the dexter hand to a saint affontée, his hands clasped on this breast proper, habited gules, above his head a halo of the third (for the See of Ross); 3 azure, issuant from an antique boat or, a demi-bishop proper vested argent, his mitre and pastoral staff in hand sinister of the second, accompanied by two demi-angels, one in the dexter and the other in the sinister chief holding open books proper, their wings addorsed, also of the second (for the See of Caithness).

1114 Gregory
1153(?) William
1164 Felix
1172 Simon de Tonei
1187 Richard de Lincoln
1203 Brice de Douglas
1224(?) Andrew de Moravia
1244(?) Simon
1251 Radulf de Leycester (elect)
1253 Archibald
1299 David de Moravia
1326 John de Pilmor
1363 Alexander Bur
1397 William de Spyny
1407 John de Innes
1415 Henry Leighton
1422 Columba de Dunbar
1437 John de Winchester
1460(?) James Stewart
1463 David Stewart
1477 William de Tulloch
1487 Andrew Stewart
1501(?) Andrew Forman
1516(?) James Hepburn
1525 Robert Shaw
1532(?) Alexander Stewart
1538(?) Patrick Hepburn
1574 George Douglas
1611 Alexander Douglas
1623 John Guthrie
1662 Murdo Mackenzie
1677 James Aitken
1680 Colin Falconer
1687 Alexander Rose
1688 William Hay
1707 Held with Edinburgh
1725 Held with Aberdeen
1727 William Dunbar
1737 George Hay (elect)
1742 William Falconar
1777 Arthur Petrie
1787 Andrew Macfarlane
1798 Alexander Jolly
1838 Held with Ross
1851 Robert Eden
1886 James Butler Knill Kelly
1904 Arthur John Maclean
1943 Piers Holt Wilson
1953 Duncan Macinnes
1970 George Minshull Sessford
1994 Gregor Macgregor
1999 John Michael Crook

†Ross

1131(?) Macbeth
1150(?) Simon
1161 Gregory
1195 Reginald
1213 Andrew de Moravia (elect)
1215(?) Robert I
1250 Robert II
1272 Matthew
1275(?) Robert II de Fyvin
1295(?) Adam de Derlingtun (elect)
1297(?) Thomas de Dundee
1325 Roger
1351 Alexander Stewart
1372 Alexander de Kylwos
1398(?) Alexander de Waghorn
1418 Thomas Lyell (elect) Griffin Yonge (elect)
1420 John Bulloch
1441(?) Andrew de Munro (elect)
1441(?) Thomas Tulloch
1464(?) Henry Cockburn
1478 John Wodman
1481 William Elphinstone (elect)
1483 Thomas Hay
1492 John Guthrie
1498 John Frisel [Fraser]
c.1507 Robert Cockburn
1525 James Hay
c.1539 Robert Cairncross
1552 David Painter
1561(?) Henry Sinclair
1566 John Lesley
1575 Alexander Hepburn
1611 David Lindsay
1613 Patrick Lindsay
1633 John Maxwell
1662 John Paterson
1679 Alexander Young
1684 James Ramsay
1696 See vacant or held with Caithness until 1727
1727 Held with Moray
1742 Held with Caithness
1762 Robert Forbes
1777 Held with Moray
1819 David Low
1851 Held with Moray

†Caithness

c.1146 Andrew
c.1187 John
1214 Adam
1223(?) Gilbert de Moravia
1250(?) William
1263 Walter de Baltrodin
1273(?) Nicholas (elect)
1275 Archibald Herok
1278 Richard (elect)
1279(?) Hervey de Dundee (elect)
1282 Alan de St Edmund
1295 John or James (elect)
1296 Adam de Derlingtun
1297 Andrew
1306 Fercard Belegaumbe
1328(?) David
1341 Alan de Moravia

1343 Thomas de Fingask
1370 Malcolm de Dumbrek
1381 Alexander Man
1414 Alexander Vaus
1425 John de Crannach
1428 Robert Strabrok
1446 John Innes
1448 William Mudy
1478(?) Prospero Camogli de Medici
1484(?) John Sinclair (elect)
1502 Andrew Stewart I
1517(?) Andrew Stewart II
1542 Robert Stewart (elect)
1600 George Gledstanes (elect)
1611 Alexander Forbes
1616 John Abernethy
1662 Patrick Forbes
1680 Andrew Wood
[1695 See vacant]
1731 Robert Keith
1741 Wm. Falconas
1762 Held with Ross
[1742 See Vacant]
1777 Held with Moray

Glasgow

Glasgow and Galloway

Description of arms. Party per pale: dexter, vert, a fess wavy argent charged with a bar wavy azure between a representation of St Mungo issuant from the fess proper, habited or, his dexter hand raised in benediction and in his sinister hand a Celtic cross of the same in chief, in nombril point a salmon proper and in base an annulet of the fourth; sinister, argent a representation of St Ninian standing full-faced proper, clothed in a pontifical robe purpure, on his head a mitre and in his dexter hand a crosier or.

550(?) Kentigern or Mungo (no record of his successors)
1114(?) (Michael)
1118(?) John
1147 Herbert
1164 Ingram
1175 Jocelin
1199 Hugh de Roxburgh (elect)
1200 William Malveisin
1202 Florence (elect)
1208 Walter de St Albans
1233 William de Bondington
1259 Nicholas de Moffat (elect)
1259 John de Cheam
1268 Nicholas de Moffat (elect)
1271 William Wischard (elect)
1273 Robert Wischard
1317 Stephen de Donydouer (elect)
1318 John de Eglescliffe
1323 John de Lindsay
1337 John Wischard
1339 William Rae
1367 Walter Wardlaw
1388 Matthew de Glendonwyn
1391 John Framisden (titular)
1408 William Lauder
1427 John Cameron
1447 James de Brois [Brewhouse]
1448 William Turnbull
1456 Andrew de Durrisdeer
1475 John Laing
1483 George Carmichael (elect)

ARCHBISHOPS

1483 Robert Blackadder (Archbishop 9 Jan 1492)
1509 James Betoun I
1525 Gavin Dunbar
1551 Alexander Gordon
1552 James Betoun II (restored 1587)
1571 John Porterfield (titular)
1573 James Boyd (titular)
1581 Robert Montgomery (titular)
1585 William Erskine (titular)
1610 John Spottiswoode
1615 James Law
1633 Patrick Lindsay
1661 Andrew Fairfoul
1664 Alexander Burnet (restored 1674)
1671 Robert Leighton, died 1684 (resigned 1674)
1679 Arthur Rose
1684 Alexander Cairncross, died 1701
1687 John Paterson,[1] died 1708
[1708 Vacant]

BISHOPS

1731 Alexander Duncan, died 1733
[1733 Vacant]
1787 Held with Edinburgh
1805 William Abernethy Drummond
1809–37 Held with Edinburgh
1837 Michael Russell
1848 Walter John Trower
1859 William Scott Wilson
1888 William Thomas Harrison
1904 Archibald Ean Campbell
1921 Edward Thomas Scott Reid
1931 John Russell Darbyshire
1938 John Charles Halland How
1952 Francis Hamilton Moncreiff
1974 Frederick Goldie
1981 Derek Alec Rawcliffe
1991 John Mitchell Taylor
1998 Idris Jones

†Galloway or Candida Casa or Whithorn[2]

Ninian, died 432(?)
(?) Octa
681 Trumwine
731 Penthelm, died 735(?)
735 Frithowald, died 764
763 Pehtwine, died 776
777 Ethelbert
791 Beadwulf
1140 Gilla-Aldan
1154 Christian
1189 John
1214 Walter
1235 Odo Ydonc (elect)
1235 Gilbert
1255 Henry
1294 Thomas de Kircudbright [de Daltoun]
1327 Simon de Wedale
1355 Michael Malconhalgh
1359(?) Thomas Macdowell (elect)
1359 Thomas
1364 Adam de Lanark
(?) David Douglas, died 1373
(?) James Carron (resigned 1373)
1378 Ingram de Kethnis (elect)
1379 Oswald
1380 Thomas de Rossy
(?) Francis Ramsay, died 1402
1406 Elisaeus Adougan
1414(?) Gilbert Cavan (elect)
1415 Thomas de Butil
1422 Alexander Vaus
1451 Thomas Spens
1457(?) Thomas Vaus (elect)
1459 Ninian Spot
1482(?) George Vaus
1508(?) James Betoun (elect)
1509(?) David Arnot
1526 Henry Wemyss
1541(?) Andrew Dury
1559(?) Alexander Gordon
1610 Gavin Hamilton
1612(?) William Couper
1619 Andrew Lamb
1635 Thomas Sydserf
1661 James Hamilton
1675 John Paterson
1679 Arthur Rose
1680 James Aitken
1688 John Gordon, died 1726
1697 Held with Edinburgh
1837 Held with Glasgow

Argyll or Lismore

Argyll and The Isles

Description of arms. Azure, two crosiers in saltire and in chief a mitre or.

1193 Harald
1240 William
1253 Alan
1268 Laurence de Erganis
1300 Andrew
1342 Angusde Ergadia (elect)
1344 Martinde Ergaill
1387 John Dugaldi
1397(?) Bean Johannis
1420(?) Finlay de Albany
1428 George Lauder
1476 Robert Colquhoun
1504 David Hamilton
1532 Robert Montgomery
1539(?) William Cunningham (elect)
1553(?) James Hamilton (elect)
1580 Neil Campbell (titular)
1611 John Campbell (titular)

[1] After the deposition of John Paterson at the Revolution the See ceased to be Archiepiscopal.
[2] The traditional founder of the See is St Ninian, but nothing authentic is known of the bishops prior to the accession of Gilla-Aldan between 1133 and 1140.

1613 Andrew Boyd
1637 James Fairlie
1662 David Fletcher
1665 John Young (elect)
1666 William Scroggie
1675 Arthur Rose
1679 Colin Falconer
1680 Hector Maclean
1688 Alexander Monro (elect)
Held with Ross
1847 Alexander Ewing
1874 George Mackarness
1883 James Robert Alexander Chinnery-Haldane
1907 Kenneth Mackenzie
1942 Thomas Hannay
1963 Richard Knyvet Wimbush
1977 George Kennedy Buchanan Henderson
1993 Douglas MacLean Cameron
2004 Alexander Martin Shaw

†The Isles

900 Patrick
1080 Roolwer
1080 William
1095 Hamundr
1138 Wimund
1152 John I
1152(?) Ragnald
1154 Gamaliel
1170 Christian
1194 Michael
1210 Nicholas I
1219 Nicholas II of Meaux
1226(?) Reginald
1226 Simon
1249 Laurence (elect)
1253 Richard
1275 Gilbert (elect)
1275 Mark
1305 Alan
1324 Gilbert Maclelan
1328 Bernard de Linton
1331 Thomas de Rossy
1349 William Russell
1374 John Donkan
1387 Michael
1392 John Sproten (Man) (titular)
1402(?) Conrad (Man) (titular)
1402(?) Theodore Bloc (Man) (titular)
1410 Richard Messing (Man)
1422 Michael Anchire
1425(?) John Burgherlinus (Man)
1428 Angus I
1441(?) John Hectoris [McCachane] Macgilleon
1472 Angus II
1487 John Campbell
1511 George Hepburn
1514 John Campbell (elect)
1530(?) Ferchar MacEachan (elect)
1550(?) Roderick Maclean
1553(?) Alexander Gordon
1567 John Carswell (titular)
1573 John Campbell
1605 Andrew Knox
1619 Thomas Knox
1628 John Leslie
1634 Neil Campbell
1662 Robert Wallace
1677 Andrew Wood
1680 Archibald Graham [or McIlvernock]
Held with Orkney and Caithness
1819 Held with Argyll

College Bishops, Consecrated without Sees

1705 John Sage, died 1711
1705 John Fullarton (Edinburgh 1720), died 1727
1709 Henry Christie, died 1718
1709 John Falconar (Fife 1720), died 1723
1711 Archibald Campbell (Aberdeen 1721), died 1744
1712 James Gadderar (Aberdeen 1725, Moray 1725), died 1733
1718 Arthur Millar (Edinburgh 1727), died 1727
1718 William Irvine, died 1725
1722 Andrew Cant, died 1730
1722 David Freebairn (Edinburgh 1733)
1726 John Ochterlonie (Brechin 1731), died 1742
1726 James Ross (Fife 1731), died 1733
1727 John Gillan (Dunblane 1731), died 1735
1727 David Ranken, died 1728

Bishops who have held the Office of Primus

1704 Alexander Rose (Edinburgh 1704–20)
1720 John Fullarton (Edinburgh 1720–27)
1727 Arthur Millar (Edinburgh 1727)
1727 Andrew Lumsden (Edinburgh 1727–33)
1731 David Freebairn (Edinburgh 1733–39)
1738 Thomas Rattray (Dunkeld 1727–43)
1743 Robert Keith (Caithness 1731–41)
1757 Robert White (Dunblane 1735–43, St Andrews 1743–61)
1762 William Falconar (Orkney and Caithness 1741–62)
1782 Robert Kilgour (Aberdeen 1768–86)
1788 John Skinner (Aberdeen 1786–1816)
1816 George Gleig (Brechin 1810–40)
1837 James Walker (Edinburgh 1880–41)
1841 William Skinner (Aberdeen 1816–57)
1857 Charles Hughes Terrot (Edinburgh 1841–72)
1862 Robert Eden (Moray, Ross, and Caithness 1851–86)
1886 Hugh Willoughby Jermyn (Brechin 1875–1903)
1901 James Butler Knill Kelly (Moray, Ross, and Caithness 1886–1904)
1904 George Howard Wilkinson (St Andrews, Dunkeld, and Dunblane 1893–1907)
1908 Walter John Forbes Robberds (Brechin 1904–34)
1935 Arthur John Maclean (Moray, Ross, and Caithness 1904–43)
1943 Ernest Denny Logie Danson (Edinburgh 1939–46)
1946 John Charles Halland How (Glasgow and Galloway 1938–52)
1952 Thomas Hannay (Argyll and The Isles 1942–62)
1962 Francis Hamilton Moncreiff (Glasgow and Galloway 1952–74)
1974 Richard Knyvet Wimbush (Argyll and The Isles 1963–77)
1977 Alastair Iain Macdonald Haggart (Edinburgh 1975–85)
1985 Lawrence Edward Luscombe (Brechin 1975–90)
1990 George Kennedy Buchanan Henderson (Argyll and The Isles 1977–92)
1992 Richard Frederick Holloway (Edinburgh 1986–2000)
2000 Andrew Bruce Cameron (Aberdeen 1992–)

IRELAND

PROVINCE OF ARMAGH

†Achonry

BISHOPS

c.558 Cathfuidh
1152 Mael Ruanaid ua Ruadain
1159 Gille na Naehm O Ruadain [Gelasius]
1208 Clemens O Sniadaig
1220 Connmach O Torpaig [Carus]
1226 Gilla Isu O Cleirig [Gelasius]
1237 Tomas O Ruadhan
1238 Oengus O Clumain [Elias]
1251 Tomas O Maicin
1266 Tomas O Miadachain [Dionysus]
1286 Benedict O Bracain
1312 David of Kilheny
1348 David II
1348 Nicol Alias Muircheartach O hEadhra
1374 William Andrew
1385 Simon
c.1390 Tomas mac Muirgheasa MacDonn-chadha
1401 Brian mac Seaain O hEadhra
1410 Maghnus O h Eadhra
1424 Donatus
1424 Richard Belmer
1436 Tadhg O Dalaigh
1442 James Blakedon
1449 Cornelius O Mochain
1463 Brian O hEasdhra [Benedictus]
1470 Nicholas Forden
1475 Robert Wellys
1484 Thomas fitzRichard
1484 Tomas O Conghalain
1489 John Bustamente
1492 Thomas Ford
1508 Eugenius O Flannagain
1522 Cormac O Snighe
1547 Thomas O Fihilly
1562 Eugene O'Harte
1613 Miler Magrath (with Cashel)
United to Killala 1622

†Annadown

BISHOPS

1189 Conn ua Mellaig [Concors]
1202 Murchad ua Flaithbertaig
1242 Tomas O Mellaig
1251 Conchobar [Concors]
1283 John de Ufford
1308 Gilbert O Tigernaig
1323 Jacobus O Cethernaig
1326 Robert Petit
1328 Albertus
1329 Tomas O Mellaig
1359 Dionysius
1393 Johannes
1394 Henry Trillow
1402 John Bryt
1408 John Wynn
1421 John Boner [Camere]
1425 Seean Mac Braddaigh
1428 Seamus O Lonnghargain
1431 Donatus O Madagain
1446 Thomas Salscot
1450 Redmund Bermingham
1458 Thomas Barrett
1496 Francis Brunand
1540 John Moore
United to Tuam c.1555

†Ardagh

454 Mel
c.670 Erard
874 Faelghus
Cele 1048
1152 Mac Raith ua Morain
1172 Gilla Crist O hEothaig [Christianus]
O'Tirlenain 1187
ua hEislinnen
Annud O Muiredaig 1216
1217 Robert
1224 M.
1228 Loseph mac Teichthechain
1229 Mac Raith Mac Serraig
1232 Gilla Isu mac in Scelaige O Tormaid [Gelasius]
1232 Iocelinus
1238 Brendan Mac Teichthechain
1256 Milo of Dunstable
1290 Matha O'h-Eothaig [Mattheus]
1323 Robert Wirsop (did not get possession)
1324 Mac Eoaighseoan
1347 Eoghan O Ferghail [Audovenus]
1368 William Mac Carmaic
1373 Cairbre O'Ferghail [Charles]
1373 John Aubrey
1392 Henry Nony (did not get possession)
1396 Comedinus Mac Bradaigh [Gilbert]
1400 Adam Leyns
1419 Conchobar O'Ferghail [Cornelius]
1425 Risdeard O'Ferghail
[1444 O'Murtry, not consecrated resigned]
1445 Cormac Mac Shamhradhain
1462 Seaan O'Ferghail
1467 Donatus O'Ferghail
1482 William O'Ferghail
1517 Ruaidri O'Maoileoin
1517 Rory O'Mallone [Roger O Melleine]
1541 Richard O'Ferrall
1553 Patrick MacMahon
[1572 John Garvey, not consecrated]
1583 Lysach O'Ferrall
1604 Robert Draper
1613 Thomas Moigne
1679 William Bedell
1633 John Richardson
1661 Robert Maxwell
1673 Francis Marsh
1682 William Sheridan
1692 Ulysses Burgh
1604–33, 1661–92 and 1692–1751 Held by the Bishops of Kilmore
1751–1839 Held by the Archbishops of Tuam
United to Kilmore 1839

Armagh

Description of arms. Azure, an archiepiscopal staff in pale argent ensigned with a cross pattée or, surmounted by a pall argent fimbriated and fringed or, charged with four crosses pattées-fitchées sable.

BISHOPS

444 Patrick
Benignus 467
Jarlath 481
Cormac 497
Dubthach 513
Ailill I 526
Ailill II 536
David O'Faranan 551
Carlaen 588
MacLaisre 623
–640 Thomian MacRonan
Segeni 688
Suibhne 730
–732 Congusa
Affinth 794
–811 Nundha
–818 Artri
835 Forannan
Mael Patraic I 862
Fethgna 875
Cathasach MacRobartach 883
Mochta 893
900 Maelaithghin
Cellach
Mael Ciarain 915
Joseph 936
Mael Patraic II 936
Cathasach MacDolgen 966
Maelmiure 994
Airindach 1000
Maeltuile 1032
1032 Hugh O'Ferris
Mael Patraic III 1096
1099 Caincomrac O'Boyle

ARCHBISHOPS

1105 Cellach mac Aeda meic Mael Isu [Celsus]
1132 Mael maedoc Ua Morgair [Malachais]
1137 Gilla Meic Liac mac Diarmata meic Ruaidri [Gelasius]
1174 Conchobar O Conchaille [Concors]

† Indicates a diocese no longer extant, or united with another diocese.

1175 Gille in Coimhedh O Caran [Gilbertus]
1180 Tomaltach O Conchobair [Thomas]
1184 Mael Isu Ua Cerbaill [Malachias]
1202 Echdonn mac Gilla Uidir [Eugenius]
1217 Lucas Neterville
1227 Donatus O Fidabra
1240 Albert Suebeer of Cologne
1247 Reginald
1258 Abraham O'Conallain
1261 Mael Patraic O Scannail
1270 Nicol Mac Mael Isu
1303 Michael MacLochlainn (not confirmed)
1304 Dionysius (not confirmed)
1306 John Taaffe
1307 Walter Jorz
1311 Roland Jorz
1324 Stephen Segrave
1334 David Mag Oireachtaigh
1347 Richard FitzRalph
1362 Milo Sweetman
1383 John Colton
1404 Nicholas Fleming
1418 John Swayne
1439 John Prene
1444 John Mey
1457 John Bole [Bull]
1471 John Foxhalls or Foxholes
1475 Edmund Connesburgh
1480 Ottaviano Spinelli [de Palatio]
1513 John Kite
1521 George Cromer
1543 George Dowdall
1552 Hugh Goodacre
1553 George Dowdall (again)
[1560 Donat MacTeague, not recognized by the Crown, 1562]
1563 Adam Loftus
1568 Thomas Lancaster
1584 John Long
1589 John Garvey
1595 Henry Ussher
1613 Christopher Hampton
1625 James Ussher
[Interregnum 1656–61]
1661 John Bramhall
1663 James Margetson
1679 Michael Boyle
1703 Narcissus Marsh
1714 Thomas Lindsay
1724 Hugh Boulter
1742 John Hoadly
1747 George Stone
1765 Richard Robinson [afterwards Baron Rokeby]
1795 William Newcome
1800 William Stuart
1822 John George Beresford
United to Clogher 1850–86
1862 Marcus Gervais Beresford
1886 Robert Bentknox
1893 Robert Samuel Gregg
1896 William Alexander
1911 John Baptist Crozier
1920 Charles Frederick D'Arcy
1938 John Godfrey FitzMaurice Day
1939 John Allen Fitzgerald Gregg
1959 James McCann
1969 George Otto Simms
1980 John Ward Armstrong
1986 Robert Henry Alexander Eames

Clogher

Description of arms. Azure, a bishop seated in full pontificals proper, in the act of benediction, and holding his pastoral staff in the left hand.

*c.*493 MacCarthinn or Ferdachrioch
Ailill 869
1135 Cinaeth O Baigill
1135 Gilla Crist O Morgair [Christianus] (moved his see to Louth)

BISHOPS OF LOUTH

1135 Gilla Crist O Morgair [Christianus]
1138 Aed O Ceallaide [Edanus]
1178 Mael Isu O Cerbaill [Malachias]
1187 Gilla Crist O Mucaran [Christinus]
1194 Mael Isu Ua Mael Chiarain
1197 Gilla Tigernaig Mac Gilla Ronain [Thomas]

BISHOPS OF CLOGHER

1218 Donatus O Fidabra
1228 Nehemias
1245 David O Bracain
1268 Michael Mac an tSair
1287 Matthew Mac Cathasaigh I
–1310 Henricus
1316 Gelasius O Banain
1320 Nicholas Mac Cathasaigh
1356 Brian Mac Cathmaoil [Bernard]
1362 Matthew Mac Cathasaigh II
— Aodh O hEothaigh [*alias* O Neill]
1373 John O Corcrain [Wurzburg]
1390 Art Mac Cathmhail
1433 Piaras Mag Uidhir [Petrus]
1450 Rossa mac Tomais Oig Mag Uidhir [Rogerius]
1475 Florence Woolley
[1484 Niall mac Seamuis Mac Mathghamna]
1484 John Edmund de Courci
1494 Seamus Mac Pilip Mac Mathghamna
1500 Andreas
1502 Nehemias O Cluainin
1504 Giolla Padraig O Conalaigh [Patrick]
1505 Eoghan Mac Cathmhail [Eugenius]
1517 Padraig O Cuilin
1535 Aodh O Cearbhalain [Odo]
1517 Patrick O'Cullen
1535 Hugh O'Carolan
1570 Miler Magrath
1605 George Montgomery
1621 James Spottiswood
1645 Henry Jones
1661 John Leslie
1671 Robert Leslie
1672 Roger Boyle
1691 Richard Tennison
1697 St George Ashe
1717 John Stearne
1745 Robert Clayton
1758 John Garnett
1782 John Hotham
1796 William Foster
1797 John Porter
1819 John George Beresford
1820 Percy Jocelyn
1822 Robert Ponsonby Tottenham Luftus
United to Armagh 1850–86
1886 Charles Maurice Stack
1903 Charles Frederick D'Arcy
1908 Maurice Day
1923 James MacManaway
1944 Richard Tyner
1958 Alan Alexander Buchanan
1970 Richard Patrick Crosland Hanson
1973 Robert William Heavener
1980 Gordon McMullan
1986 Brian Desmond Anthony Hannon
2002 Michael Geoffrey St Aubyn Jackson

Connor

Description of arms. Azure, a lamb passant supporting with the dexter foreleg a staff proper flying therefrom a pennant argent charged with a saltire gules between three cross crosslets or; on a chief of the last two crosiers in saltire of the first.

506 Oengus MacNessa 514
Lughadh 543
640 Dimma Dubh [the Black]
Duchonna the Pious 725
Cunnen or Cuinden 1038
Flann O'Sculu 1117
1124 Mael Maedoc Ua Morgair [Malachias]
–1152 MaelPatraic O'Banain
1172 Nehemias
1178 Reginaldus
1226 Eustacius
1242 Adam
1245 Isaac de Newcastle-on-Tyne
1258 William de Portroyal
1261 William de Hay [or la Haye]
1263 Robert de Flanders
1275 Peter de Dunach
1293 Johannes
1320 Richard
1321 James de Couplith
1323 John de Eglecliff
1323 Robert Wirsop
1324 Jacabus O Cethernaig
1353 William Mercier
1374 Paulus
1389 Johannes
[1420 Seaan O Luachrain, not consecrated]

1423 Eoghan O'Domhnaill
1429 Domhnall O'Meraich
1431 John Fossade [Festade]
1459 Patricius
1459 Simon Elvington
United to Down 1441
1945 Charles King Irwin
1956 Robert Cyril Hamilton Glover Elliott
1969 Arthur Hamilton Butler
1981 William John McCappin
1987 Samuel Greenfield Poyntz
1995 James Edward Moore
2002 Alan Edwin Thomas Harper

Derry

Derry and Raphoe

Description of arms. Party per pale: dexter gules, two swords in saltire proper, the hilts in base or, and on a chief azure a harp or stringed argent (for the See of Derry); sinister ermine, a chief per pale azure and or, the first charged with a sun in splendour of the last, the second with a cross pattée gules (for the See of Raphoe).

Caencomhrac 927
–937 Finachta MacKellach
–949 Mael Finnen

BISHOPS OF MAGHERA

(Where the See was in the twelfth and the thirteenth centuries)
1107 Mael Coluim O Brolchain
— Mael Brigte O Brolchain
1152 O Gormgaile Muiredach O Cobthaig [Mauricius]
1173 Amhlaim O Muirethaig
1185 Fogartach O Cerballain [Florentius]
c.1230 Gilla in Coimhded O Cerballain [Germanus]
c.1280 Fogartach O Cerballain II [Florentius]

BISHOPS OF DERRY

(Where the See was resettled)
1295 Enri Mac Airechtaig [O'Reghly] [of Ardagh]
1297 Gofraid MacLochlainn [Godfrey]
1316 Aed O Neill [Odo]
1319 Michael Mac Lochlainn [Maurice]
1349 Simon
1391 Johannes
1391 John Dongan
1394 Seoan O Mochain
1398 Aodh [Hugo]
1401 Seoan O Flannabhra
1415 Domhnall Mac Cathmhail
1419 Domhnall O Mearaich
1429 Eoghan O Domhnaill [Eugenius]
1433 John Oguguin
[1456 John Bole, appointment not completed, translated to Armagh]
1458 Bartholomew O Flannagain
c.1464 Johannes
1467 Nicholas Weston
1485 Domhnall O Fallamhain
1501 Seamus mac Pilip Mac Mathghamna [MacMahon]
1520 Ruaidhri O Domhnaill
1520 Rory O'Donnell
1554 Eugene O'Doherty
1568 F. [doubtful authority]
1569 Redmond O'Gallagher
[1603 Denis Campbell, not consecrated]
1605 George Montgomery
1610 Brutus Babington
[1611 Christopher Hampton, consecrated]
1613 John Tanner
1617 George Downham
1634 John Bramhall
1661 George Wild
1666 Robert Mossom
1680 Michael Ward
1681 Ezekiel Hopkins
1691 William King
1703 Charles Hickman
1714 John Hartstonge
1717 St George Ashe
1718 William Nicolson
1727 Henry Downes
1735 Thomas Rundle
1743 Carew Reynell
1745 George Stone
1747 William Barnard
1768 Frederick Augustus Hervey [afterwards Earl of Bristol]
1803 William Knox
1831 Richard Ponsonby
Raphoe united to Derry from 1834
1853 William Higgin
1867 William Alexander
1896 George Alexander Chadwick (resigned)
1916 Joseph Irvine Peacocke
1945 Robert M'Neil Boyd
1958 Charles John Tyndall
1970 Cuthbert Irvine Peacocke
1975 Robert Henry Alexander Eames
1980 James Mehaffey
2002 Kenneth Raymond Good

Down

Down and Dromore

Description of arms. Quarterly, 1 and 4 azure, two keys endorsed in saltire the wards in chief or, surmounted in the fess point by a lamb passant proper (for the See of Down); 2 and 3 Argent, two keys endorsed in saltire the wards in chief gules, surmounted by an open book in fess proper between two crosses pattées-fitchées in pale sable (for the See of Dromore).

Fergus 584
Suibhne 825
Graithene 956
Finghin 964
Flaithbertach 1043
MaelKevin 1086
— Mael Muire 1117
Oengus Ua Gormain 1123
— [Anonymous]
c.1124 Mael Maedoc O Morgair [Malachias]
1152 Mael Isu mac in Chleirig Chuirr [Malachias]
1175 Gilla Domangairt Mac Cormaic
c.1176 Echmilid [Malachias]
c.1202 Radulfus
1224 Thomas
1251 Randulphus
1258 Reginaldus
1265 Thomas Lydel
1277 Nicholas le Blund
1305 Thomas Ketel
1314 Thomas Bright
1328 John of Baliconingham
1329 Ralph of Kilmessan
1353 Richard Calf I
1365 Robert of Aketon
1367 William White
1369 Richard Calf [II]
1386 John Ross
1394 John Dongan
1413 John Cely [or Sely]
1445 Ralph Alderle

BISHOPS OF DOWN AND CONNOR

1441 John Fossard
1447 Thomas Pollard
1451 Richard Wolsey
1456 Thomas Knight
1469 Tadhg O Muirgheasa [Thaddaeus]
1489 Tiberio Ugolino
1520 Robert Blyth
1542 Eugene Magennis
1565 James MacCawell
1569 John Merriman
1572 Hugh Allen
1593 Edward Edgeworth
1596 John Charden
1602 Roben Humpston
1607 John Todd (resigned)
1612 James Dundas
1613 Robert Echlin
1635 Henry Leslie
1661 Jeremy Taylor
1667 Roger Boyle
1672 Thomas Hacket
1694 Samuel Foley
1695 Edward Walkington
1699 Edward Smyth
1721 Francis Hutchinson
1739 Carew Reynell
1743 John Ryder
1752 John Whitcombe
1752 Robert Downes
1753 Arthur Smyth
1765 James Traill
1784 William Dickson
1804 Nathaniel Alexander
1823 Richard Mant

BISHOPS OF DOWN, CONNOR AND DROMORE

1849 Robert Bent Knox
1886 William Reeves
1892 Thomas James Welland
1907 John Baptist Crozier
1911 Charles Frederick D'Arcy

1919 Charles Thornton Primrose Grierson
1934 John Frederick McNeice
1942 Charles King Irwin

BISHOPS OF DOWN AND DROMORE

1945 William Shaw Kerr
1955 Frederick Julian Mitchell
1970 George Alderson Quin
1980 Robert Henry Alexander Eames
1986 Gordon McMullan
1997 Harold Creeth Miller

†Dromore

Mael Brighde 974
Riagan 1101
1197 Ua Ruanada
1227 Geraldus
1245 Andreas
1284 Tigernach I
1290 Gervasius
— Tigernach II
1309 Florentius Mac Donnocain
1351 Anonymous
1366 Milo
1369 Christophorus Cornelius 1382
1382 John O'Lannoy
1398 Thomas Orwell
1400 John Waltham
1402 Roger Appleby
1408 Richard Payl
1410 Marcus
1411 John Chourles
1414 Seaan O Ruanadha
1419 Nicholas Wartre
1429 Thomas Rackelf
1431 William
1431 David Chirbury
1450 Thomas Scrope [Bradley]
1450 Thomas Radcliff
1456 Donatus O h-Anluain [Ohendua]
1457 Richard Messing
1463 William Egremond
— Aonghus [Aeneas] 1476
1476 Robert Kirke
1480 Yvo Guillen
1483 George Braua
1511 Tadhg O Raghallaigh [Thaddeus]
1536 Quintin O Quigley [Cogley]
1539 Roger McHugh
1540 Arthur Magennis
1607 John Todd
[1613 John Tanner, not consecrated]
1613 Theophilus Buckworth
1661 Robert Leslie
1661 Jeremy Taylor (administered the diocese)
1667 George Rust
1671 Essex Digby
1683 Capel Wiseman
1695 Tobias Pullein
1713 John Stearne
1717 Ralph Lambert
1727 Charles Cobbe
1732 Henry Maule
1744 Thomas Fletcher
1745 Jemmett Browne
1745 George Marlay
1763 John Oswald
1763 Edward Young
1765 Henry Maxwell
1766 William Newcome
1775 James Hawkins
1780 William de la Poer Beresford
1782 Thomas Percy
1811 George Hall
1812 John Leslie
1819 James Saurin
United to Down since 1842

†Elphin

Domnall mac Flannacain Ua Dubhthaig 1136
Muiredach O Dubhthaig 1150
1152 Mael Isu O Connachtain
Flannacan O Dubhthaig 1168
*c.*1177 Tomaltach mac Aeda Ua Conchobhair [Thomas]
*c.*1180 Florint Ua Riacain Ui Maelrvanaid
1206 Ardgar O Conchobhair
1226 Dionysius O Mordha
*c.*1230 Alanus
1231 Donnchad mac Fingein O Conchobhair [Dionysius Donatus]
1245 Eoin O Mugroin
1247 Tomaltach macToirrdelbaig O Conchobhair [Thomas]
1260 Mael Sechlainn O Conchobhair [Milo]
1262 Tomas mac Fergail mac Diarmata
1266 Muiris O Conchobhair
[1285 Amiaim O Tommaltaig, not consecrated]
1285 Gilla Isu mac in Liathana O Conchobhair
1297 Maelsechlainn mac Briain [Malachias]
1303 Donnchad O Flannacain, [Donatus]
1307 Cathal O Conchobhair
1310 Mael Sechlainn Mac Aedha
1313 Lurint O Lachtnain [Laurence]
1326 Sean O Finnachta
1355 Carolus
1357 Gregory O Mochain
1372 Thomas Barrett
1383 Seoan O Mochain
1407 Seaan O Grada
1405 Gerald Caneton
1412 Thomas Colby
1418 Robert Fosten
1421 Edmund Barrett
1427 Johannes
1429 Laurence O Beolain
1429 William O hEidighean
1448 Conchobhar O Maolalaidh
1458 Nicholas O Flanagan
1487 Hugo Arward
1492 Rlocard mac Briain O gCuanach
1499 George Brana
1501 Cornelius O Flannagain
1508 Christopher Fisher
1525 John Maxey
1539 William Maginn 1541(?)
1539 Gabriel de Sancto Serio
1541 Conach or Con O'Negall or O'Shyagall
1552 Roland Burke [de Burgo]
1582 Thomas Chester
1583 John Lynch
1611 Edward King
1639 Henry Tilson
1661 John Parker
1667 John Hodson
1691 Simon Digby
1720 Henry Downes
1724 Theophilus Bolton
1730 Robert Howard
1740 Edward Synge
1762 William Gore
1772 Jemmett Browne
1775 Charles Dodgson
1795 John Law
1810 Power le Poer Trench
1819 John Leslie 1854
United to Kilmore and Ardagh on the death of Bishop Beresford in 1841, when Bishop Leslie became Bishop of the united dioceses.

†Killala

Muiredach
Kellach
O Maolfogmair I 1137
O Maolfogmair II 1151
Imar O Ruaidhin 1176
1179 O Maolfogmair III
1199 Domnall Ua Becdha
1207 Cormac O'Tarpy
O'Kelly 1214
1226 Aengus O Maolfogmair [Elias]
Gille Cellaig O Ruaidhin
1253 Seoan O Laidlg
1281 Donnchad O Flaithbertaig [Donatus]
1307 John Tankard
Sean O Flaithim 1343
1344 James Bermingham
1347 William O DusucBhda
1351 Robert Elyot
1381 Thomas Lodowys
1383 Conchobar O Coineoil [Cornelius]
1390 Thomas Horwell [Orwell]
1400 Thomas Barrett
1403 Muircheartach Cleirach mac Donnchadha O DusucBhda
Connor O'Connell 1423
1427 Fergal Mac Martain
1431 Thaddaeus Mac Creagh
1432 Brian O Coneoil
1447 Robert Barrett
1452 Ruaidhri Bairead [Barrett]
1453 Thomas
1459 Richard Viel
Miler O'Connell
1461 Donatus O Conchobhair
1470 Tomas Bairead [Barrett]
1487 John de Tuderto [Seaan O Caissin]
1500 Thomas Clerke
1508 Malachias O Clumhain
1513 Risdeard Bairead
1545 Redmond O'Gallagher
1570 Donat O'Gallagher
1580 John O'Casey
1592 Owen O'Conor
1613 Miler Magrath
Achonry united to Killala 1622
1623 Archibald Hamilton
1630 Archibald Adair (deposed, but subsequently restored)
164? John Maxwell
1661 Henry Hall
1664 Thomas Bayly
1671 Thomas Otway
1680 John Smith
1681 William Smyth
1682 Richard Tennison
1691 William Lloyd
1717 Henry Downes
1720 Charles Cobbe
1727 Robert Howard
1730 Robert Clayton
173? Mordecai Cary
175? Richard Robinson [afterwards Baron Rokeby]
1759 Samuel Hutchinson

1781 William Cecil Pery
1784 William Preston
1787 John Law
1795 John Porter
1798 Joseph Stock
1810 James Verschoyle
United to Tuam since 1834

Kilmore

Kilmore, Elphin and Ardagh

Description of arms. Argent, on a cross azure a pastoral staff enfiling a mitre, all or (for the See of Kilmore). Sable, two pastoral staves in saltire or, in base a lamb couchant, argent (for the See of Elphin). Or, a cross gules between four trefoils slipped vert, on a chief sable, a key erect of the first (for the See of Ardagh).

— Aed Ua Finn 1136
— Muirchenach Ua Maelmoeherge 1149
1152 Tuathal Ua Connachtaig [Thadeus]
1202 Mi Ua Dobailen
— Flann O Connachtaig [Florentius] 1231
1237 Congalach Mac Idneoil
1251 Simon O Ruairc
1286 Mauricius
— Matha Mac Duibne 1314
1320 Padraig O Cridecain
— Conchobhar Mac Conshnamha [Ford] 1355
1356 Richard O Raghilligh
1373 Johannes
1388 Thomas Rushook
1392 Sean O Raghilligh I [John]
1398 Nicol Mac Bradaigh
1401 Sean O'Raghilligh II
1407 John Stokes
1409 David O'Fairchellaigh
1422 Domhnall O Gabhann
1445 Aindrias Mac Bradaigh
1455 Fear Sithe Mag Dhuibhne
1465 Sean O Raghilligh II
1476 Cormac Mag Shamhradhain
1480 Tomas MacBradaigh
1512 Diarmaid O Raghilligh
1530 Edmund Nugent
1540 Sean Mac Bradaigh
1585 John Garvey
1604 Robert Draper
1613 Thomas Moigne
1629 William Bedell
1643 Robert Maxwell
1673 Francis Marsh
1682 William Sheridan
1693 William Smyth
1699 Edward Wetenhall
1715 Timothy Godwin
1727 Josiah Hott
1742 Joseph Story
1757 John Cradock
1772 Denison Cumberland
1775 George Lewis Jones
1790 William Foster
1796 Charles Broderick
1802 George de la Poer Beresford
Ardagh united to Kilmore 1839
Elphin united to Kilmore 1841
1841 John Leslie
1854 Marcus Gervais Beresford
1862 Hamilton Verschoyle
1870 Charles Leslie
1870 Thomas Carson
1874 John Richard Darley
1884 Samuel Shone
1897 Alfred George Elliott
1915 William Richard Moore
1930 Arthur William Barton
1939 Albert Edward Hughes
1950 Frederick Julian Mitchell
1956 Charles John Tyndall
1959 Edward Francis Butler Moore
1981 William Gilbert Wilson
1993 Michael Hugh Gunton Mayes
2001 Kenneth Harbert Clarke

†Mayo

Gerald 732
Muiredach [or Murray]
Mcinracht 732
Aidan 773
1172 Gilla Isu Ua Mailin
Cele O Dubhthaig 1210
1210 ?Patricius
1428 William Prendergast
1430 Nicholas 'Wogmay'
1439 Odo O h-Uiginn
1432 Martin Campania
1457 Simon de Duren
1493 John Bel
1541 Eugenius Macan Brehon
United to Tuam 1559

†Raphoe

Sean O Gairedain
Donell O Garvan
Felemy O Syda
Oengus O'Lappin 959
1150 Muiredhach O'Cofley
1156 Gille in Coimhded Ua Carain [Gilbertus]
— Anonymous
1204 Mael Isu Ua Doirig
— Anonymous
1253 Mael Padraig O Scannail [Patricius]
1263 John de Alneto
1265 Cairpre O Scuapa
1275 Fergal O Firghil [Florentius]
1306 Enri Mac-in-Chrossain [Henricus]
1319 Tomas Mac Carmaic Ui Domhnaill
1363 Padraig Mac Maonghail
1367 Conchobar Mac Carmaic Ui Domhnaill [Cornelius]
1397 Seoan MacMenmain
1400 Eoin MacCarmaic [Johannes]
–1413 Anthony
–1414 Robert Rubire
1416 John McCormic
1420 Lochlainn O Gallchobhair I [Laurentius]
1440 Cornelius Mac Giolla Brighde
1443 Lochlainn O Gallchobhair II [Laurentius]
1479 John de Rogeriis
1482 Meanma Mac Carmail [Menclaus Mac Carmacain]
1514 Conn O Cathain [Cornelius]
1534 Eamonn O Gallchobhair
1547 Arthur o'Gallagher
1563 Donnell Magonigle [or McCongail]
[1603 Denis Campbell, not consecrated]
1605 George Montgomery
1611 Andrew Knox
1633 John Leslie
1661 Robert Leslie
1671 Ezekiel Hopkins
1682 William Smyth
1693 Alexander Cairncross
1701 Robert Huntington
1702 John Pooley
1713 Thomas Lindsay
1714 Edward Synge
1716 Nicholas Forster
1744 William Barnard
1747 Philip Twysden
1753 Robert Downes
1763 John Oswald
1780 James Hawkins
1807 John George Beresford
1819 William Magee
1822 William Bissett
United to Derry since 1834

Tuam

Tuam, Killala and Achonry

Description of arms. Azure beneath a triple architectural canopy three figures, in the centre the Blessed Virgin Mary holding in her arms the Holy Child, between, on the dexter the figure of a bishop (St Jarlath) in pontificalibus and in the act of benediction, and, on the sinister St John supporting with his left arm a lamb argent, each in proper vestments or, the hands, feet, and faces proper.

BISHOPS

Murrough O'Nioc 1032
Hugh O'Hessian 1085
Cathusach Ua Conaill 1117
O Clerig 1137
Muiredach Ua Dubhthaig 1150

ARCHBISHOPS

1152 Aed Ua h-Oisin [Edanus]
1167 Cadhla Ua Dubhthaig [Catholicus]
1202 Felix Ua Ruanada
1236 Mael Muire O Lachtain [Marianus]
1250 Flann Mac Flainn [Florentius]
[1256 James O'Laghtnan, not confirmed or consecrated]
1257 Walter de Salerno
1258 Tomaltach O Conchobair [Thomas]
1286 Stephen de Fulbourn
1289 William de Bermingham
1312 Mael Sechlainn Mac Aeda
1348 Tomas MacCerbhaill [MacCarwill]
1364 Eoin O Grada
1372 Gregory O Mochain I

1384 Gregory O Mochain II
1387 William O Cormacain
1393 Muirchertach mac Pilb O Cellaigh
1410 John Babingle
1411 Cornelius
1430 John Bermingham [Winfield]
1438 Tomas mac Muirchearthaigh O Cellaigh
1441 John de Burgo
1452 Donatus O Muiredaigh
1485 William Seoighe [Joyce]
1503 Philip Pinson
1506 Muiris O Fithcheallaigh
1514 Tomas O Maolalaidh
1537 Christopher Bodkin
1573 William O'Mullally [or Lealy]
Annadown united to Tuam c.1555
Mayo united to Tuam 1559
1595 Nehemiah Donnellan
1609 William O'Donnell [or Daniel]
1629 Randolph or Ralph Barlow
1638 Richard Boyle
1645 John Maxwell
1661 Samuel Pullen
1667 John Parker
1679 John Vesey
1716 Edward Synge
1742 Josiah Hort
1752 John Ryder
1775 Jemmett Browne
1782 Joseph Dean Bourke [afterwards Earl of Mayo]
1794 William Beresford [afterwards Baron Decies]
1819 Power le Poer Trench
Killala united to Tuam from 1834

BISHOPS

1839 Thomas Plunket [afterwards Baron Plunket]
1867 Charles Brodrick Bernard
1890 James O'Sullivan
1913 Benjamin John Plunket
1920 Arthur Edwin Ross
1923 John Ort
1928 John Mason Harden
1932 William Hardy Holmes
1939 John Winthrop Crozier
1958 Arthur Hamilton Butler
1970 John Coote Duggan
1986 John Robert Winder Neill
1998 Richard Crosbie Aitken Henderson

PROVINCE OF DUBLIN

†Ardfert

BISHOPS

Anmchad O h-Anmchada 1117
1152 Mael Brenain Ua Ronain
Gilla Mac Aiblen O'Anmehadha 1166
Domnall O Connairche 1193
1200 David Ua Duibdithrib
Anonymous 1217
1218 John
1218 Gilbertus
1237 Brendan
1253 Christianus
1257 Philippus
1265 Johannes
1286 Nicolaus
1288 Nicol O Samradain
1336 Ailin O hEichthighirn
1331 Edmund of Caermaerthen
1348 John de Valle
1372 Cornelius O Tigernach
1380 William Bull
1411 Nicholas FitzMaurice
1404 Nicholas Ball
1405 Tomas O Ceallaigh
1409 John Attilburgh [Artilburch]
1450 Maurice Stack
1452 Maurice O Conchobhair
1461 John Stack
1461 John Pigge
1473 Philip Stack
1495 John FitzGerald
[See vacant in 1534]
1536 James FitzMaurice
1588 Nicholas Kenan
1600 John Crosbie
1622 John Steere
1628 William Steere
1641 Thomas Fulwar
United to Limerick 1661

†Ardmore

1153 Eugenius
Incorporated with Lismore 1192

Cashel

Cashel, Waterford, Lismore, Ossory, Ferns and Leighlin

Description of arms. Gules, two keys addorsed in saltire the wards in chief, or.

BISHOPS

Cormac MacCuillenan 908
Donnell O'Heney 1096 *or* 1098

ARCHBISHOPS

*c.*1111 Mael los Ua h-Ainmire
Mael losa Ua Fogludha [Mauricius] 1131
Domnall Ua Conaing 1137
Gilla Naomh O'Marty 1149
–1152 Donat O'Lonergan I
–*c.*1160 M.
1172 Domnall O h-Ualla-chain [Donatus]
1186 Muirghes O h-Enna [Matheus]
*c.*1208 Donnchad Ua Longargain I [Donatus]
1216 Donnchad Ua Longargain II [Donatus]
1224 Mairin O Briain [Marianus]
1238 David mac Ceallaig [O'Kelly]
1254 David Mac Cearbaill [Mac Carwill]
1290 Stiamna O Bracain
1303 Maurice Mac Cearbaill
1317 William FitzJohn
1327 Seoan Mac Cerbaill
1329 Walter le Rede
1332 Eoin O Grada
1346 Radulphus O Cellaigh [Kelly]
1362 George Roche [de Rupe]
1365 Tomas Mac Cearbhaill
1374 Philip of Torrington
1382 Michael
1384 Peter Hackett
1406 Richard O Hedian
1442 John Cantwell I
1452 John Cantwell II
1484 David Creagh
1504 Maurice FitzGerald
1525 Edmund Butler
1553 Roland Baron or FitzGerald
1567 James MacCawell
Emly united to Cashel 1569
1571 Miler Magrath (Bishop of Cashel and Waterford from 1582)
1623 Malcolm Hamilton
1630 Archibald Hamilton
1661 Thomas Fulwar
1667 Thomas Price
[See vacant 1685–91]
1691 Narcissus Marsh
1694 William Palliser
[1727 William Nicolson, not enthroned]
1727 Timothy Goodwin
1730 Theophilus Bolton
1744 Arthur Price
1752 John Whitcombe
1754 Michael Cox
1779 Charles Agar
1801 Charles Brodrick
1822 Richard Laurence
Waterford and Lismore united to Cashel from 1833; on the death of Abp Laurence in 1838 the province was united to Dublin and the see ceased to be an Archbishopric

BISHOPS

1839 Stephen Creagh Sandes
1843 Robert Daly
1872 Maurice FitzGerald Day
1900 Henry Stewart O'Hara
1919 Robert Miller
1931 John Frederick McNeice
1935 Thomas Arnold Harvey
1958 William Cecil De Pauley

1968 John Ward Armstrong
Ossory united to Cashel 1977
1980 Noel Vincent Willoughby
1997 John Robert Winder Neill
2003 Peter Francis Barrett

†Clonfert

Moena, or Moynean, or Moeinend 572
Cummin the Tall 662
Ceannfaeladh 807
Laithbheartach 822
Ruthnel or Ruthme 826
Cormac MacEdain 922
Ciaran O'Gabbla 953
Cathal 963
Eochu 1031
O'Corcoran 1095
Muiredach Ua h-Enlainge 1117
Gille Patraic Ua Ailcinned 1149
*c.*1152 Petrus Ua Mordha
1172 Mail Isu mac in Baird
1179 Celechair Ua h-Armedaig
Muirchertach Ua'Maeluidir 1187
Domnall Ua Finn 1195
Muirchertach Ua Carmacain 1204
1205 Mael Brigte Ua hErurain
1224 Cormac O Luimlin [Carus]
1248 Thomas
1259 Tomas mac Domnaill Moire O Cellaig
1266 Johannes de Alatre
1296 Robert
*c.*1302 John
1308 Gregorius O Brocaig
1320 Robert Le Petit
1322 Seoan O Leaain
1347 Tomas mac Gilbert O Cellaigh I
1378 Muircheartach mac Pilib O Cellaigh [Maurice]
1393 William O Cormacain
1398 David Corre
1398 Enri O Conmaigh
1405 Tomasi O Cellaigh II
1410 Cobhthach O Madagain
1438 Seaan O hEidin
1441 John White
1447 Conchobhar O Maolalaidh
1448 Cornelius O Cuinnlis
1463 Matthaeus Mag Raith
1508 David de Burgo
1509 Dionysius O'Mordha
1534 Roland de Burgo
1536 Richard Nangle
1580 Hugh
1582 Stephen Kirwan
1602 Roland Lynch
1627 Robert Dawson
1644 William Baily
1665 Edward Wolley
1691 William FitzGerald
1722 Theophilus Bolton
1724 Arthur Price
1730 Edward Synye
1732 Mordecai Cary
1716 John Whitcombe
1752 Arthur Smyth
1753 William Carmichael
1758 William Gote
1762 John Oswald
1763 Denison Cumberland
1772 Walter Cope
1782 John Law
1787 Richard Marlay
1795 Charles Broderick
1796 Hugh Hamilton
1798 Matthew Young
1801 George de la l'oer Beresford
1802 Nathaniel Alexander
1804 Christopher Butson
United to Killaloe since 1834

†Clonmacnoise

–663 Baitan O'Cormac
–839 Joseph [of Rossmore]
Maclodhar 890
Cairbre Crom 904
Loingsech 919
–940 Donough I
–953 Donough II
–966 Cormae O Cillin
Maenach 971
Conaing O'Cosgraigh 998
Male Poil 1001
Flaithbertach 1038
Celechar 1067
O'Mallaen 1093
Christian Aherne 1104
?1111 Domnall mac Flannacain Ua Dubthaig
1152 Muirchertach Ua Maeluidir
Cathal Ua Maeileoin 1207
*c.*1207 Muirchertach Ua Muiricen
1214 Aed O Maeileoin I
1227 Aed O Maeileoin II [Elias]
1236 Thomas Fitzpatrick
1252 Tomas O Cuinn
1280 Anonymous
1282 Gilbert (not consecrated)
1290 William O Dubhthaig
1298 William O Finnein
1303 Domnall O Braein
1324 Lughaid O Dalaigh
1337 Henricus
1349 Simon
1369 Richard [Braybroke]
1371 Hugo
1388 Philippus O Maoil
1389 Milo Corr
1397 O'Gallagher
1397 Philip Nangle
1423 David Prendergast
1426 Cormac Mac Cochlain [Cornelius]
1444 Sean O Dalaigh
1449 Thomas
1458 Robertus
1458 William
1459 John
1487 Walter Blake
1509 Tomas O Maolalaidh
1516 Quintin O h-Uiginn
1539 Richard O'Hogan
1539 Florence Kirwan
1556 Peter Wall [Wale]
United to Meath 1569

†Cloyne

Reachtaidh 887
1148 Gilla na Naem O Muirchertaig [Nehemias]
Ua Dubcroin 1159
Ua Flannacain 1167
1177 Matthaeus Ua Mongaig
1201 Laurence Ua Suilleabain
1205 C.
1281 Luke
*c.*1224 Florence
1226 Daniel
1237 David mac Cellaig [O'Kelly]
1240 Ailinn O Suilleabain
1247 Daniel
1265 Reginaldus
1275 Alan O Longain
1284 Nicholas of Effingham
1323 Maurice O Solchain
1333 John Brid
1351 John Whitekot
1363 John Swaffham
1376 Richard Wye
1394 Gerard Caneton
1413 Adam Payn
United to Cork 1418–1638
1638 George Synge
1661–78 Held by the Bishops of Cork
1679 Patrick Sheridan
1683 Edward Jones
1693 William Palliser
1694 Tobias Pullein
1695 St George Ashe
1697 John Pooley
1702 Charles Crow
1726 Henry Maule
1732 Edward Synge
1734 George Berkeley
1753 James Stopford
1759 Robert Johnson
1767 Frederick Augustus Hervery
1768 Charles Agar
1780 George Chinnery
1781 Richard Woodward
1794 William Bennett
1820 Charles Mongan Warhurton
1826 John Brinkley
United to Cork on the death of Bp Brinkley in 1835

Cork

Cork, Cloyne and Ross

Description of arms. Argent, on a plain cross, the ends pattée, gules, a pastoral staff, surmounted on a mitre, or (for the See of Cork). Azure, a mitre proper labelled or, between three crosses pattées-fitchées argent (for the See of Cloyne). No arms are borne for the See of Ross.

Donnell 876
Soer Bhreatach 892
DusucBhdhurn O'Stefam 959
Cathmogh 969
Mugron O'Mutan 1057
1138 Gregory
? Ua Menngorain 1147
1148 Gilla Aedha Ua Maigin
1174 [Gregorius] O h-Aedha [O Hea]
*c.*1182 Reginaldus I
1187 Aicher
1192 Murchad Ua h-Aedha
Anonymous 1214
1215 Mairin Ua Briain [Marianus]
1225 Gilbertus
1248 Laurentius
1265 William of Jerpoint
1267 Reginaldus
1277 Robert Mac Donnchada
1302 Seoan Mac Cearbaill [Mac Carwill]
1321 Philip of Slane

1327 Walter le Rede
1330 John of Ballyconingham
1347 John Roche
1359 Gerald de Barri
1396 Roger Ellesmere
1406 Richard Kynmoure
1409 Patrick Fox
1409 Milo fitzJohn
1425 John Paston
1418 Adam Payn
1429 Jordan Purcell
1463 Gerald FitzGerald
1472 William Roche (Coadjutor)
1490 Tadhg Mac Carthaigh
1499 John FitzEdmund FitzGerald
1499 Patrick Cant
1523 John Benet
1536 Dominic Tyrre [Tirrey]
1562 Roger Skiddy
1570 Richard Dyxon
1572 Matthew Sheyn
Ross united to Cork 1583
1583 William Lyon
1618 John Boyle
1620 Richard Boyle
1638 William Chappell
1661 Michael Boyle
1663 Edward Synge
1679 Edward Wetenhall
1699 Dive Downes
1710 Peter Browne
1735 Robert Clayton
1745 Jemmett Browne
1772 Isaac Mann
1789 Euseby Cleaver
1789 William Foster
1790 William Bennet
1794 Thomas Stopford
1805 John George Beresford
1807 Thomas St Laurence
1831 Samuel Kyle
Cloyne united to Cork from 1835
1848 James Wilson
1857 William FitzGerald
1862 John Gregg
1878 Robert Samuel Gregg
1894 William Edward Meade
1912 Charles Benjamin Dowse
1933 William Edward Flewett
1938 Robert Thomas Hearn
1952 George Otto Sims
1957 Richard Gordon Perdue
1978 Samuel Greenfield Poyntz
1988 Robert Alexander Warke
1999 William Paul Colton

Dublin

Dublin and Glendalough

Description of arms. Azure, an episcopal staff argent, ensigned with a cross pattée or, surmounted by a pallium of the second edged and fringed or, charged with five crosses formée fitchée, sable.

BISHOPS

Sinhail 790
c.1028 Dunan [Donatus]
1074 Gilla Patraic
1085 Donngus
1096 Samuel Ua'h-Aingliu

ARCHBISHOPS

1121 Grene [Gregorius]
1162 Lorcan Ua'Tuathail [Laurentius]
1182 John Cumin
1213 Henry de Loundres
Glendalough united to Dublin
1230 Luke
125? Fulk de Sandford
1279 John de Derlington
1286 John de Sandford
1295 Thomas de Chadworth
1296 William de Hotham
1299 Richard de Ferings
[1307 Richard de Havering, not consecrated]
1311 John de Leche
1317 Alexander de Bicknor
1349 John de St Paul
1363 Thomas Minot
1376 Robert de Wikeford
1391 Robert Waldeby
1396 Richard Northalis
1397 Thomas Cranley
1418 Richard Talbot
1451 Michael Tregury
1472 John Walton
1484 Walter Fitzsimons
1512 William Rokeby
1521 Hugh Inge
1529 John Alan
1535 George Browne
1555 Hugh Curwin
1567 Adam Loftus
1605 Thomas Jones
1619 Lancelot Bulkeley
1661 James Margetson
1663 Michael Boyle
1679 John Parker
1682 Francis Marsh
1694 Narcissus Marsh
1703 William King
1730 John Hoadly
1743 Charles Cobbe
1765 William Carmichael
1766 Arthur Smyth
1772 John Cradock
1779 Robert Fowler
1801 Charles Agar [Earl of Normanton]
1809 Euseby Cleaver
1820 John George Beresford
1822 William Magee
1831 Richard Whately
Kildare united to Dublin 1846
1864 Richard Chenevix Trench (resigned)
1885 William Conyngham [Lord Plunket]
1897 Joseph Ferguson Peacocke
1915 John Henry Bernard
1919 Charles Frederick D'Arcy
1920 John Allen Fitzgerald Gregg
1939 Arthur William Barton
1956 George Otto Simms
1969 Alan Alexander Buchanan
1977 Henry Robert McAdoo
1985 Donald Arthur Richard Caird
1996 Walton Newcome Francis Empey
2002 John Robert Winder Neill

†Emly

Raidghil 881
Ua Ruaich 953
Faelan 980
MaelFinan 1030
Diarmait Ua Flainnchua 1114
1152 Gilla in Choimhded Ua h-Ardmhail Mael Isu Ua Laigenain 1163
1172 Ua Meic Stia
1177 Charles O'Buacalla
1177 Isaac O'Hamery
1192 Ragnall Ua Flainnchua
1205 M.
1209 William
1212 Henry
1227 John Collingham
1238 Daniel
1238 Christianus
1251 Gilbert O'Doverty
1266 Florence or Laurence O'hAirt
1272 Matthew MacGormain
1275 David O Cossaig
1286 William de Clifford
1306 Thomas Cantock [Quantock]
1309 William Roughead
1335 Richard le Walleys
1353 John Esmond
1363 David Penlyn [Foynlyn]
1363 William
1405 Nicholas Ball
1421 John Rishberry
1422 Robert Windell
1428 Thomas de Burgo
1428 Robert Portland
1445 Cornelius O Cuinnlis
1444 Robert
1448 Cornelius O Maolalaidh
1449 William O Hetigan
1476 Pilib O Cathail
1494 Donatus Mac Briain
1498 Cinneidigh Mac Briain
1507 Tomas O hUrthaille
1543 Angus O'Hernan
1551 Raymond de Burgo
United to Cashel 1569
Transferred to Limerick 1976

†Ferns

–598 Edar [or Maedoc or Hugh]
Maeldogair 676
Coman 678
Diratus 693
Cillenius 715
Cairbre O'Kearney 1095
Ceallach Ua Colmain 1117
Mael Eoin Ua Dunacain 1125
Ua Cattain 1135
1178 Loseph Ua h-Aeda
1186 Ailbe Ua Maelmuaid [Albinus]
1224 John of St John
1254 Geoffrey of St John
1258 Hugh of Lamport
1283 Richard of Northampton
1304 Simon of Evesham
1305 Robert Walrand
1312 Adam of Northampton
1347 Hugh de Saltu [of Leixlip]
1347 Geoffrey Grandfeld
1349 John Esmond
1350 William Charnells
1363 Thomas Dene
1400 Patrick Barret
1418 Robert Whittey
1453 Tadhg O Beirn
1457 John Purcell I
1479 Laurence Nevill
1505 Edmund Comerford

1510 Nicholas Comyn
1519 John Purcell II
1539 Alexander Devereux
1566 John Devereux
1582 Hugh Allen
Leighlin united to Ferns 1597
1600 Robert Grave
1601 Nicholas Statford
1605 Thomas Ram
1635 George Andrews
1661 Robert Price
1667 Richard Boyle
1683 Narcissus Marsh
1691 Bartholomew Vigors
1722 Josiah Hort
1727 John Hoadly
1730 Arthur Price
1734 Edward Synge
1740 George Stone
1743 William Cottrell
1744 Robert Downes
1752 John Garnet
1758 William Carmichael
1758 Thomas Salmon
1759 Richard Robinson
1761 Charles Jackson
1765 Edward Young
1772 Joseph Deane Bourke
1782 Walter Cope
1787 William Preston
1789 Euseby Cleaver
1809 Percy Jocelyn
1820 Robert Ponsonby Tottenham Loftus
1822 Thomas Elrington
United to Ossory 1835

†Glendalough

Dairchell 678
Eterscel 814
Dungal 904
Cormac 927
Nuadha 920 [or Neva]
Gilda Na Naomh *c.*1080
Cormac O'Mail 1101
Aed Ua Modain 1126
1140 Anonymous
1152 Gilla na Naem
1157 Cinaed O Ronain [Celestinus]
1176 Maelcallann Ua Cleirchen [Malchus]
1186 Macrobius
1192 William Piro
1214 Robert de Bedford
United to Dublin
After the union with Dublin some rival bishops appear
*c.*1216 Bricheus
1468 John
1475 Michael
1481 Denis White John 1494
1494 Ivo Ruffi
1495 John
1500 Francis Fitzjohn of Corduba

†Iniscattery (Scattery Island)

861 Aidan
959 Cinaeda O'Chommind
973 Scandlam O'Lenz
O'Bruil 1069
O'Bruil II 1081
Dermot O Lennain 1119
Aed Ua Bechain I 1188
Cearbhal Ua'h-Enna [Carolus] 1193
1360 Tomas Mac Mathghamhna
1392 John Donkan
1414 Richard Belmer
Dionysius 1447
1447 John Grene
Incorporated with Limerick

†Kells

Mael Finnen 968
*c.*1152 Tuathal Ua Connachtarg
1185 Anonymous
1202 M. Ua Dobailen
Incorporated with Meath

†Kildare

Conlaedh 520
Hugh [or Hed] the Black 639
Maeldoborcon 709
Eutigern 762
Lomthiull 787
Snedbran 787
Tuatchar 834
Orthanach 840
Aedgene Britt 864
Macnghal 870
Lachtnan 875
Suibhne 881
Scannal 885
Lergus 888
Mael Findan 950
Annchadh 981
Murrough McFlan 986
1030 MaelMartain
MaelBrighde 1042
Finn 1085
MaelBrighde O Brolchan 1097
Hugh [Heremon] 1100
Ferdomnach 1101
Cormac O Cathassaig 1146
Ua Duibhin 1148
1152 Finn mac Mael Muire Mac Cianain
Fin mac Gussain Ua Gormain
1161 Malachias Ua Brain
1177 Nehemias
1206 Cornelius Mac Fealain
1223 Ralph of Bristol
1233 John of Taunton
1258 Simon of Kilkenny
1280 Nicholas Cusack
1300 Walter Calf [de Veel]
1333 Richard Houlot
1352 Thomas Giffard
1366 Robert of Aketon [Acton]
1404 John Madock
1431 William fitzEdward
1449 Geoffrey Hereford
1456 John Bole [Bull]
1464 Richard Lang
1474 David Cone
1475 James Wall
William Barret
1480 Edward Lane
1526 Thomas Dillon
1529 Walter Wellesley
1540 William Miagh
1550 Thomas Lancaster
1555 Thomas Leverous
1560 Alexander Craik
1564 Robert Daly
1583 Daniel Neylan
1604 William Pilsworth
1636 Robert Ussher
1644 William Golborne
1661 Thomas Price
1667 Ambrose Jones
1679 Anthony Dopping
1682 William Moreton
1705 Welbore Ellis
1731 Charles Cobbe
1743 George Stone
1745 Thomas Fletcher
1761 Richard Robinson
1765 Charles Jackson
1790 George Lewis Jones
1804 Charles Lindsay
United to Dublin after the death of Bp Lindsay in 1846
1976 Separated from Dublin and united to Meath

†Kilfenora

1172 Anonymous
1205 F.
1224 Johannes
1254 Christianus
Anonymous 1264
1266 Mauricius
1273 Florentius O Tigernaig
1281 Congalach [O Lochlainn]
1291 G.
1299 Simon O Cuirrin
1303 Maurice O Briain
1323 Risdeard O Lochlainn
*c.*1355 Dionysius
1372 Henricus
Cornelius
1390 Patricius
1421 Feidhlimidh mac Mathghamhna O Lochlainn [Florentius]
1433 Fearghal
1434 Dionysius O Connmhaigh
1447 John Greni
1476 [? Denis] O Tombaigh
1491 Muircheartach mac Murchadha O Briain [Mauricius]
1514 Maurice O'Kelly
1541 John O'Neylan
–1585 Daniel, bishop-elect
1606 Bernard Adams [with Limerick q.v.]
1617 John Steere
1622 William Murray
[1628 Richard Betts, not consecrated]
1630 James Heygate
1638 Robert Sibthorp
1661–1741 Held by the Archbishops of Tuam
1742–52 Held by the Bishop of Clonfert
United to Killaloe 1752

†Killaloe

BISHOPS

O'Gerruidher 1054
Domnall Ua hEnna 1098
Mael Muire O Dunain 1117
Domnall Ua Conaing 1131
Domnall Ua Longargain 1137
Tadg Ua Longargain 1161
Donnchad mac Diarmata Ua Briain 1164
1179 Constantin mac Toirrdelbaig Ua Briain
1194 Diarmait Ua Conaing
1201 Conchobhar Ua h-Enna [Cornelius]
1217 Robert Travers
1221 Domnall Ua h-Enna [Donatus]
1231 Domnall O Cenneitig [Donatus]

1253 Isoc O Cormacain [Isaac]
1268 Mathgamain O h-Ocain [O Hogan]
1281 Maurice O h-Ocain
1299 David Mac Mathghamna [Mac Mahon]
1317 Tomas O Cormacain I
1323 Brian O Cosgraig
1326 David Mac Briain [David of Emly]
?1326 Natus O Heime
1343 Tomas O h-Ogain
1355 Tomas O Cormacain II
1389 Mathghamain Mag Raith
1400 Donatus Mag Raith
1409 Robert Mulfield
1418 Eugenius O Faolain
1423 Thadeus Mag Raith I
1429 Seamus O Lonnghargain
1443 Donnchadh mac Toirdhealbhaigh O Briain
1460 Thadeus Mag Raith II
1463 Matthaeus O Griobhtha
1483 Toirdhealbhach mac Mathghamhna O Briain [Theodoricus]
1523 Thadeus
1526 Seamus O Cuirrin
1546 Cornelius O Dea
1554 Turlough [or Terence] O'Brien II
1570 Maurice [or Murtagh] O'Brien-Arra
1613 John Rider
1633 Lewis Jones
1647 Edward Parry
1661 Edward Worth
1669 Daniel Wytter
1675 John Roan
1693 Henry Ryder
1696 Thomas Lindsay
1713 Thomas Vesey
1714 Nicholas Forster
1716 Charles Carr
1740 Joseph Story
1742 John Ryder
1743 Jemmet Browne
1745 Richard Chenevix
1746 Nicholas Synge
Kilfenora united to Killaloe 1752
1771 Robert Fowler
1779 George Chinnery
1780 Thomas Barnard
1794 William Knox
1803 Charles Dalrymple Lindsay
1804 Nathaniel Alexander
1804 Robert Ponsonby Tottenham Loftus
1820 Richard Mant
1823 Alexander Arbuthnot
1828 Richard Ponsonby
1831 Edmund Knox [with Clonfert]
Clonfert united to Killaloe 1834
Kilmacduagh united to Killaloe 1834
1834 Christopher Butson
1836 Stephen Crengh Sandes
1839 Ludlow Tonson [afterwards Baron Riversdale]
1862 William FitzGerald
1884 William Bennet Chester
1893 Frederick Richards Wynne
1897 Mervyn Archdall
1912 Charles Benjamin Dowse
1913 Thomas Sterling Berry (resigned)
1924 Henry Edmund Patton
1943 Robert M'Neil Boyd
1945 Hedley Webster
1953 Richard Gordon Perdue
1957 Henry Arthur Stanistreet
1972 Edwin Owen
1976 United to Limerick

†Kilmacduagh

? Ua Cleirig 1137
Imar Ua Ruaidin 1176
Rugnad O'Rowan 1178
1179 Mac Gilla Cellaig Ua Ruaidin
1206 Ua Cellaig
Mael Muire O Connmaig 1224
1227 Aed [Odo]
Conchobhar O Muiredaig 1247
1248 Gilla Cellaig O Ruaidin [Gilbertus]
1249 David yFredrakern
1254 Mauricius O Leaain
1284 David O Setachain
1290 Luirint O Lachtnain [Laurentius]
1307 Lucas
1326 Johannes
1360 Nicol O Leaain
1394 Gregory O Leaain
1405 Enri O Connmhaigh
1409 Dionysius
1409 Eugene O Faolain
1418 Diarmaid O Donnchadha
1419 Nicol O Duibhghiolla
1419 Seaan O Connmhaigh
1441 Dionysius O Donnchadha
1479 Cornelius O Mullony
1503 Matthaeus O Briain
1533 Christopher Bodkin
1573 Stephen O'Kirwan
[1584 Thomas Burke, not consecrated]
1587 Roland Lynch
1627–1836 Held in commendam by the Bishops of Clonfert
United to Killaloe since 1834

†Leighlin

–633 Laserian or Molaise
–865 Mainchin
–940 Conella McDonegan Daniel 969
Cleitic O'Muinic 1050
c.1096 Ferdomnac
Mael Eoin Ua Dunacain 1125
Sluaigedach Ua Cathain 1145
1152 Dungal O Caellaide
1192 Johannes
1197 Johannes
1202 Herlewin
1217 Richard [Fleming]
1228 William le Chauniver
1252 Thomas
1275 Nicholas Chever
1309 Maurice de Blanchville
1321 Meiler le Poer
1344 Radulphus O Ceallaigh
1349 Thomas of Brakenberg
1360 Johannes
1362 William (not consecrated)
1363 John Young
1371 Philip FitzPeter
1385 John Griffin
1398 Thomas Peverell
1400 Richard Bocomb
1419 John Mulgan
1432 Thomas Fleming
— Diarmaid 1464
1464 Milo Roche
1490 Nicholas Magwyr
1513 Thomas Halsey
1524 Mauricius O Deoradhain
1527 Matthew Sanders
1550 Robert Travers
1555 Thomas O'Fihelly
1567 Donnell or Daniel Cavanagh
1589 Richard Meredith
United to Ferns since 1597 on the death of Bp Meredith

Limerick

Limerick, Ardfert, Aghadoe, Killaloe, Kilfenora, Clonfert, Kilmacduagh and Emly

Description of arms. Azure two keys addorsed in saltire the wards upwards; in the dexter chief a crosier paleways, in the sinister a mitre, all or.

–1106 Gilli alias Gilla Espaic
1140 Patricius
1150 Erolb [? = Harold]
1152 Torgesius
1179 Brictius
1203 Donnchad Ua'Briain [Donatus]
1207 Geoffrey
–1215 Edmund
1223 Hubert de Burgo
1252 Robert de Emly or Neil
1273 Gerald [or Miles] de Mareshall
1302 Robert de Dundonald
1312 Eustace de Aqua or de l'Eau
1336 Maurice de Rochfort
1354 Stephen Lawless
1360 Stephen Wall [de Valle]
1369 Peter Curragh
1399 Bernardus O Conchobhair
1400 Conchobhar O Deadhaidh
1426 John Mothel (resigned)
Iniscattery incorporated with Limerick
1456 Thomas Leger
1458 William Russel, *alias* Creagh
1463 Thomas Arthur
[1486 Richard Stakpoll, not consecrated]
1486 John Dunowe
1489 John O'Phelan [Folan]
1524 Sean O Cuinn
1551 William Casey
1557 Hugh de Lacey or Lees (deposed)
1571 William Casey
1594 John Thornburgh
1604 Bernard Adams
1626 Francis Gough
1634 George Webb
1643 Robert Sibthorp
Ardfert united to Limerick 1661
1661 Edward Synge
1664 William Fuller
1667 Francis Marsh
1673 John Vesey
1679 Simon Digby
1692 Nathaniel Wilson
1695 Thomas Smyth
1725 William Burscough
1755 James Leslie
1771 James Averill

1772 William Gore
1784 William Cecil Pery
1794 Thomas Barnard
1806 Charles Morgan Warburton
1820 Thomas Elrington
1823 John Jebb
1834 Edmund Knox
1849 William Higgin
1854 Henry Griffin
1866 Charles Graves
1899 Thomas Bunbury
1907 Raymond D'Audemra Orpen
1921 Harry Vere White
1934 Charles King Irwin
1942 Evelyn Charles Hodges
1961 Robert Wyse Jackson
1970 Donald Arthur Richard Caird
Killaloe united to Limerick 1976
Emly transferred to Limerick 1976
1976 Edwin Owen
1981 Walton Newcome Francis Empey
1985 Edward Flewett Darling
2000 Michael Hugh Gunton Mayes

†Lismore

Ronan 764
Cormac MacCuillenan 918
–999 Cinneda O'Chonmind
Niall mac Meic Aedacain 1113
Ua Daightig 1119
1121 Mael Isu Ua h-Ainmere
Mael Muire Ua Loingsig 1150
1151 Gilla Crist Ua Connairche [Christianus]
1179 Felix
Ardmore incorporated with Lismore 1192
1203 Malachias, O'Heda or O'Danus
1216 Thomas
1219 Robert of Bedford
1228 Griffin Christopher
1248 Ailinn O Suilleabain
1253 Thomas
1270 John Roche
1280 Richard Corre
1309 William Fleming
1310 R.
1322 John Leynagh
1356 Roger Cradock, provision annulled
1358 Thomas le Reve
United to Waterford 1363

Meath

Meath and Kildare

Description of arms. Sable three mitres argent, two, and one.

BISHOPS OF THE SEE OF CLONARD

Senach 588
–640 Colman 654
DusucBhduin O'Phelan 718
Tole 738
–778 Fulartach 779
Clothcu 796
Clemens 826
Cormac MacSuibhne
Cumsuth 858
Suarlech 870
Ruman MacCathasaid 922
Colman MacAilild 926
Tuathal O'Dubhamaigh 1028

BISHOPS OF MEATH

1096 Mael Muire Ua Dunain
1128 Eochaid O Cellaig
1151 Etru Ua Miadacain [Eleuzerius]
1177 Echtigern mac Mael Chiarain [Eugenius]
1192 Simon Rochfort
(The See was transferred from Clonard to Newtown near Trim, 1202)
Kells incorporated with Meath
1224 Donan De [Deodatus] (not consecrated)
1227 Ralph Petit
1231 Richard de la Corner
1253 Geoffrey Cusack
1255 Hugo de Taghmon
1283 Walter de Fulburn
1287 Thomas St Leger
1322 Seoan Mac Cerbaill [John MacCarwill]
1327 William de Paul
1350 William St Leger
1353 Nicholas [Allen]
1369 Stephen de Valle [Wall]
1380 William Andrew
1385 Alexander Petit [or de Balscot]
1401 Robert Montayne
1412 Edward Dantesey
[1430 Thomas Scurlog, apparently not consecrated]
1430 William Hadsor
1435 William Silk
1450 Edmund Ouldhall
1460 William Shirwood
1483 John Payne
1507 William Rokeby
1512 Hugh Inge
1523 Richard Wilson
1529 Edward Staples
1554 William Walsh
1563 Hugh Brady
Clonmacnoise united to Meath 1569
1584 Thomas Jones
1605 Roger Dod
1612 George Montgomery
1621 James Usher
1625 Anthony Martin
[Interregnum 1650–61]
1661 Henry Leslie
1661 Henry Jones
1682 Anthony Dopping
1697 Richard Tennison
1705 William Moreton
1716 John Evans
1724 Henry Downes
1727 Ralph Lambert
1732 Welbore Ellis
1734 Arthur Price
1744 Henry Maule
1758 William Carmichael
1765 Richard Pococke
1765 Arthur Smyth
1766 Henry Maxwell
1798 Thomas Lewis O'Beirne
1823 Nathaniel Alexander
1840 Charles Dickinson
1842 Edward Stopford
1850 Thomas Stewart Townsend
1852 James Henderson Singer
1866 Samuel Butcher
1876 William Conyngham [Lord Plunket]
1885 Charles Parsons Reichel
1894 Joseph Ferguson Peacocke
1897 James Bennett Keene
1919 Benjamin John Plunket
1926 Thomas Gibson George Collins
1927 John Orr
1938 William Hardy Holmes
1945 James McCann
1959 Robert Bonsall Pike
Kildare united to Meath 1976
1976 Donald Arthur Richard Caird
1985 Walton Newcome Francis Empey
1996 Richard Lionel Clarke

†Ossory

Dermot 973
1152 Domnall Ua Fogartaig
1180 Felix Ua Duib Slaine
1202 Hugo de Rous [Hugo Rufus]
1220 Peter Mauveisin
1231 William of Kilkenny
1233 Walter de Brackley
1245 Geoffrey de Turville
1251 Hugh de Mapilton
1260 Geoffrey St Leger
1287 Roger of Wexford
1289 Michael d'Exeter
1303 William FitzJohn
1317 Richard Ledred
1361 John de Tatenhale
1366 William
— John of Oxford
1371 Alexander Petit [de Balscot]
1387 Richard Northalis
1396 Thomas Peverell
1399 John Waltham
1400 John Griffin
1400 John
1401 Roger Appleby
1402 John Waltham
1407 Thomas Snell
1417 Patrick Foxe
1421 Dionysius O Deadhaidh
1427 Thomas Barry
1460 David Hacket
1479 Seaan O hEidigheain
1487 Oliver Cantwell
1528 Milo Baron [or FitzGerald]
1553 John Bale
1554 John Tonory
1567 Christopher Gaffney
1577 Nicholas Walsh
1586 John Horsfall
1610 Richard Deane
1613 Jonas Wheeler
1641 Griffith Williams
1672 John Parry
1678 Benjamin Parry
1678 Michael Ward
1680 Thomas Otway
1693 John Hartstonge
1714 Thomas Vesey
1731 Edward Tennison
1736 Charles Este
1741 Anthony Dopping
1743 Michael Cox
1754 Edward Maurice
1755 Richard Pococke
1765 Charles Dodgson
1775 William Newcome

1779 John Hotham
1782 William Heresford
1795 Thomas Lewis O'Beirne
1799 Hugh Hamilton
1806 John Kearney
1813 Robert Fowler
Ferns united to Ossory 1835
1842 James Thomas O'Brien
1874 Robert Samuel Gregg
1878 William Fakenham Walsh
1897 John Baptist Crozier
1907 Charles Frederick D'Arcy
1911 John Henry Bernard
1915 John Allen Fitzgerald Gregg
1920 John Godfrey FitzMaurice Day
1938 Ford Tichbourne
1940 John Percy Phair
1962 Henry Robert McAdoo
United to Cashel 1977

†Ross

Nechtan MacNechtain 1160
Isaac O'Cowen 1161
O'Carroll 1168
1177 Benedictus
1192 Mauricius
1198 Daniel
1224 Fineen O Clothna [Florentius]
*c.*1250 Malachy
1254 Mauricius
1269 Walter O Mithigein
1275 Peter O h-Uallachain [? Patrick]
1291 Laurentius
1310 Matthaeus O Finn
1331 Laurentius O h-Uallachain
1336 Dionysius
1379 Bernard O Conchobhair
1399 Peter Curragh
1400 Thadeus O Ceallaigh
1401 Mac Raith O hEidirsgeoil [Macrobius]
1402 Stephen Brown
1403 Matthew
1418 Walter Formay
1424 John Bloxworth
1426 Conchobhar Mac Fhaolchadha [Cornelius]
Maurice Brown 1431
1431 Walter of Leicester
1434 Richard Clerk
1448 Domhnall O Donnobhain
John 1460
1460 Robert Colynson
–1464 Thomas
1464 John Hornse *alias* Skipton
1473 Aodh O hEidirsgeoil [Odo]
1482 Tadhg Mac Carthaigh
1494 John Edmund Courci
1517 Seaan O Muirthile
1519 Tadgh O Raghallaigh [Thaddeus]
1523 Bonaventura
1526 Diarmaid Mac Carthaigh
1544 Dermot McDonnell
1551 John
1554 Maurice O'Fihelly
1559 Maurice O'Hea
1561 Thomas O'Herlihy
1582 William Lyon [with Cork and Cloyne after 1581]
United to Cork 1583

†Waterford

1096 Mael lus Ua h-Ainmere
1152 Toistius
1175 Augustinus Ua Selbaig
Anonymous 1199
1200 Robert I
1204 David the Welshman
1210 Robert II [Breathnach]
1223 William Wace
1227 Walter
1232 Stephen
1250 Henry
1252 Philip
1255 Walter de Southwell
1274 Stephen de Fulbourn
1286 Walter de Fulbourn
1308 Matthew
1323 Nicholas Welifed
1338 Richard Francis
1349 Robert Elyot
1350 Roger Cradock
Lismore united to Waterford 1363
1363 Thomas le Reve
1394 Robert Read
1396 Thomas Sparklord
1397 John Deping
1400 Thomas Snell
1407 Roger of Appleby (*see under* Ossory)
1409 John Geese
1414 Thomas Colby
1421 John Geese
1426 Richard Cantwell
1446 Robert Poer
1473 Richard Martin
1475 John Bulcomb
1480 Nicol O hAonghusa
1483 Thomas Purcell
1519 Nicholas Comyn
1551 Patrick Walsh
1579 Marmaduke Middleton
1582 Miler Magrath (Bishop of Cashel and Waterford)
1589 Thomas Wetherhead [or Walley]
1592 Miler Magrath
1608 John Lancaster
1619 Michael Boyle
1636 John Atherton
1641 Archibald Adair
1661 George Baker
1666 Hugh Gore
1691 Nathaniel Foy
1708 Thomas Mills
1740 Charles Este
1746 Richard Chenevix
1779 William Newcome
1795 Richard Marlay
1802 Power le Poer Trench
1810 Joseph Stock
1813 Richard Bourke
United to Cashel under Church Temporalities Act 1833

CATHEDRALS

CHURCH OF ENGLAND

(BATH AND) WELLS (St Andrew) Dean J M CLARKE, **Cans Res** P H F WOODHOUSE, R I BOWMAN-EADIE, THE VEN P D MAURICE, **Sub-Dean** N A SULLIVAN, **PV** A J KEEP
BIRMINGHAM (St Philip) Dean *vacant*, **Can Res** G O'NEILL, P HOWELL-JONES
BLACKBURN (St Mary) Dean C J ARMSTRONG, **Cans Res** A D HINDLEY, A CLITHEROW, C M CHIVERS
BRADFORD (St Peter) Dean *vacant*, **Can Th** K N MEDHURST
BRISTOL (Holy Trinity) Dean R W GRIMLEY, **Cans Res** P F JOHNSON, D R HOLT, B D CLOVER
CANTERBURY (Christ) Dean R A WILLIS, **Cans Res** R ST J J MARSH, THE VEN P A S EVANS, E F CONDRY, D C EDWARDS **Prec** J J FROST
CARLISLE (Holy Trinity) Dean M C BOYLING, **Cans Res** D W V WESTON, THE VEN D THOMSON, D H JENKINS
CHELMSFORD (St Mary, St Peter and St Cedd) Dean P S M JUDD, **Cans Res** A W A KNOWLES, W R KING, G L TUNBRIDGE
CHESTER (Christ and Blessed Virgin Mary) Dean G F MCPHATE, **Cans Res** T J DENNIS, C P BURKETT, J M HUNT, C W HUMPHRIES, **Can Th** L C A ALEXANDER, **Min Can** L DIXON
CHICHESTER (Holy Trinity) Dean N A FRAYLING, **Cans Res** J F FORD, P C KEFFORD, P G ATKINSON, **PV** D NASON, **Chapl** S J DAVIES
COVENTRY (St Michael) Dean J D IRVINE, **Cans Res** S A BEAKE, J P WELBY, A M DAFFERN, **Succ** D H ROBINSON
DERBY (All Saints) Dean M KITCHEN, **Cans Res** B V GAUGE, N J HENSHALL, E J JONES, **Can Th** A BROWN, **Chapl** C J HODDER
DURHAM (Christ and Blessed Virgin Mary) Dean M SADGROVE, **Cans Res** D W BROWN, D J KENNEDY, THE VEN S D CONWAY, R BROWN, **Min Can** G M MYERS, **Chapl** C C COULING
ELY (Holy Trinity) Dean M J CHANDLER, **Cans Res** P M SILLS, A L HARGRAVE, C P PRITCHARD
EXETER (St Peter) Dean C J MEYRICK, **Cans Res** THE VEN R T GILPIN, D J ISON, N COLLINGS, C F TURNER, M J RYLANDS
GLOUCESTER (St Peter and Holy Trinity) Dean N A S BURY, **Cans Res** N C HEAVISIDES, D M HOYLE, G S BRIDGEWATER, C S M THOMSON
GUILDFORD (Holy Spirit) Dean V A STOCK, **Cans Res** M F PALMER, N J THISTLETHWAITE, J H FROST
HEREFORD (Blessed Virgin Mary and St Ethelbert) Dean M E TAVINOR, **Cans Res** V HAMER, A PIPER, M J COLMER
LEICESTER (St Martin) Dean V F FAULL, **Cans Res** M WILSON, J B NAYLOR, S A FOSTER, **Chapl** J S PARKIN
LICHFIELD (Blessed Virgin Mary and St Chad) Dean A J DORBER, **Cans Res** A N BARNARD, C W TAYLOR, C F LILEY, **Dean's V** P LOCKETT, **Chan's V** P L HOLLIDAY
LINCOLN (Blessed Virgin Mary) Dean A F KNIGHT, **Cans Res** A H NUGENT, G J KIRK, M F WEST, **PV** A C BUXTON
LIVERPOOL (Christ) Dean R W N HOARE, **Cans Res** A B HAWLEY, E T FORWARD, **Chapl** J C LYNN
LONDON (St Paul) Dean J H MOSES, **Cans Res** P J W BUCKLER, E J NEWELL, M C WARNER, L C WINKETT **Min Cans** S A REYNOLDS, C E ROBSON, L J BURGESS
MANCHESTER (St Mary, St Denys and St George) Dean *vacant*, **Cans Res** P DENBY, R P GAMBLE, R A G SHANKS, A E HOLLINGHURST
NEWCASTLE (St Nicholas) Dean C C DALLISTON, **Cans Res** P R STRANGE, THE VEN G V MILLER, D J ELKINGTON
NORWICH (Holy Trinity) Dean G C M SMITH, **Cans Res** C J OFFER, M A KITCHENER, R CAPPER, **Prec** J M HASELOCK, **Chapl** A R LONG
OXFORD (Christ Church) Dean C A LEWIS, **Cans Res** O M T O'DONOVAN, J S K WARD, M M PARRY, THE VERY REVD N G COULTON, G L PATTISON, THE VEN J R H HUBBARD, **Prec** M E BIDE
PETERBOROUGH (St Peter, St Paul and St Andrew) Dean M BUNKER, **Cans Res** J W BAKER, R B RUDDOCK
PORTSMOUTH (St Thomas of Canterbury) Dean D C BRINDLEY, **Cans Res** D T ISAAC, M A TRISTRAM, N J ASH, P A W JONES
RIPON (AND LEEDS) (St Peter and St Wilfrid) Dean J A R METHUEN, **Cans Res** M R GLANVILLE-SMITH, K PUNSHON, **Min Can** P M DRIVER
ROCHESTER (Christ and Blessed Virgin Mary) Dean A NEWMAN, **Cans Res** P H D'A LOCK, R C GODSALL, P J HESKETH
ST ALBANS (St Alban) Dean J P H JOHN, **Cans Res** M C SANSOM, I R LANE, S D LAKE, R R WHEELER, D L STAMPS, **Prec** B T HUISH, **Chapl** S W CRADDUCK, **Assoc Min** D C FITZGERALD CLARK
ST EDMUNDSBURY (St James) Dean J E ATWELL, **Cans Res** A J TODD, P BARHAM, M H J HAMPEL
SALISBURY (Blessed Virgin Mary) Dean J OSBORNE, **Cans Res** D J C DAVIES, D M K DURSTON, E C PROBERT, M P J BONNEY
SHEFFIELD (St Peter and St Paul) Dean P E BRADLEY, **Cans Res** A P SHACKERLEY, N S HOWE, H I J SUCH, **Can Th** M W PERCY
SODOR AND MAN (St German) Dean THE BISHOP, **Can Prec** B H KELLY
SOUTHWARK (St Saviour and St Mary Overie) Dean C B SLEE, **Cans Res** B A SAUNDERS, A P NUNN, M A HART, J E STEEN, **Succ** J A D BUXTON
SOUTHWELL (Blessed Virgin Mary) Dean D LEANING, **Cans Res** J D JONES, N J COATES, **PV** M L SHACKLEY
TRURO (St Mary) Dean *vacant*, **Cans Res** P R GAY, P A A WALKER, R C BUSH
WAKEFIELD (All Saints) Dean G P NAIRN-BRIGGS, **Cans Res** R E GAGE, I M GASKELL, A W ROBINSON, P VANNOZZI, **Can Missr** J R HOLMES
WINCHESTER (Holy Trinity, St Peter, St Paul and St Swithun) Dean M S TILL, **Cans Res** C STEWART, J A GUILLE, K E ANDERSON, R G A RIEM
WORCESTER (Christ and Blessed Virgin Mary) Dean P J MARSHALL, **Cans Res** THE VEN J D TETLEY, A L PETTERSEN, D J STANTON, **Min Cans** M R DORSETT, C M MANSHIP
YORK (St Peter) Dean K B JONES, **Cans Res** G H WEBSTER, J L DRAPER, J J FLETCHER

Collegiate Churches

WESTMINSTER ABBEY
ST GEORGE'S CHAPEL, WINDSOR *See Royal Peculiars, p. 965.*

Diocese in Europe

GIBRALTAR (Holy Trinity) Dean A G WOODS
MALTA Valletta (St Paul) Pro-Cathedral T O MENDEL
BRUSSELS (Holy Trinity) Pro-Cathedral Chan R N INNES

CHURCH IN WALES

BANGOR (St Deiniol) **Dean** A J HAWKINS, **Can Res** J W DANIELS, **Min Cans** R J K ELLIS, A WILLIAMS
LLANDAFF (St Peter and St Paul) **Dean** J T LEWIS, **Can** G W A HOLCOMBE, **Hon Chapl** M J PRICE
MONMOUTH Newport (St Woolos) **Dean** R D FENWICK, **Min Cans** G P HOWELL, M SOADY
ST ASAPH (St Asaph) **Dean** C N L POTTER, **Can Res** M K R STALLARD, **Prec** H J LLOYD, **PV** A C SULLY, **Chapl** V C ROWLANDS
ST DAVIDS (St David and St Andrew) **Dean** J W EVANS, **Min Can** R P DAVIES, **Chapl** J S BENNETT
(SWANSEA AND) BRECON (St John the Evangelist) **Dean** J D E DAVIES, **Min Can** R J B TAYLOR

SCOTTISH EPISCOPAL CHURCH

For the members of the chapter the *Scottish Episcopal Church Directory* should be consulted.

Aberdeen and Orkney
ABERDEEN (St Andrew) **Provost** R E KILGOUR

Argyll and The Isles
OBAN (St John) **Provost** N D MACCALLUM
CUMBRAE (Holy Spirit) Cathedral of The Isles **Provost** A M SHAW *Bishop of Argyll and The Isles*

Brechin
DUNDEE (St Paul) **Provost** M A F BYRNE

Edinburgh
EDINBURGH (St Mary) **Provost** G J T FORBES

Glasgow and Galloway
GLASGOW (St Mary) **Provost** P J DINES

Moray, Ross and Caithness
INVERNESS (St Andrew) **Provost** A R GORDON

St Andrews, Dunkeld and Dunblane
PERTH (St Ninian) **Provost** H B FARQUHARSON

CHURCH OF IRELAND

Most cathedrals are parish churches, and the dean is usually, but not always, the incumbent. For the members of the chapter the *Church of Ireland Directory* should be consulted. The name of the dean is given, together with those of other clergy holding full-time appointments.

NATIONAL CATHEDRAL OF ST PATRICK, Dublin **Dean** R B MACCARTHY, **Dean's V** C W MULLEN
CATHEDRAL OF ST ANNE, Belfast R S J H MCKELVEY (St Anne's is a cathedral of the dioceses of Down and Dromore and of Connor)

Province of Armagh

Armagh
ARMAGH (St Patrick) H CASSIDY, **V Choral** G M KINGSTON

Clogher
CLOGHER (St Macartan) R C THOMPSON
ENNISKILLEN (St Macartin) R C THOMPSON *Dean of Clogher*

Derry and Raphoe
DERRY (St Columb) W W MORTON
RAPHOE (St Eunan) J HAY

Down and Dromore
DOWN (Holy and Undivided Trinity) J F DINNEN
DROMORE (Christ the Redeemer) S H LOWRY

Connor
LISBURN (Christ) *(Dean of Connor)* J F A BOND, **I** W S WRIGHT

Kilmore, Elphin and Ardagh
KILMORE (St Fethlimidh) *vacant*
SLIGO (St Mary and St John the Baptist) A WILLIAMS

Tuam, Killala and Achonry
TUAM (St Mary) A J GRIMASON
KILLALA (St Patrick) S M PATTERSON

Province of Dublin

Dublin and Glendalough
DUBLIN (Holy Trinity) Christ Church R D HARMAN

Meath and Kildare
TRIM (St Patrick) R W JONES *Dean of Clonmacnoise*
KILDARE (St Brigid) R K TOWNLEY

Cashel and Ossory
CASHEL (St John the Baptist) P J KNOWLES
WATERFORD (Blessed Trinity) Christ Church T R LESTER
LISMORE (St Carthage) W BEARE
KILKENNY (St Canice) N N LYNAS *Dean of Ossory*
LEIGHLIN (St Laserian) F J G WYNNE
FERNS (St Edan) L D A FORREST

Cork, Cloyne and Ross
CORK (St Fin Barre) M A J BURROWS
CLOYNE (St Colman) A G MARLEY
ROSS (St Fachtna) C L PETERS

Limerick and Killaloe
LIMERICK (St Mary) J M G SIRR
KILLALOE (St Flannan) S R WHITE

ROYAL PECULIARS, CLERGY OF THE QUEEN'S HOUSEHOLD, ETC.

Royal Peculiars

Description of arms. Azure the reputed arms of Edward the Confessor, viz. a cross patonce between five martlets or, on a chief of the same, between two double roses of Lancaster and York, barbed and seeded proper, a pale charged with the Royal arms (viz. Quarterly of France and England).

Collegiate Church of St Peter Westminster (Westminster Abbey) **Dean** A W CARR, **Cans** A R WRIGHT, N SAGOVSKY, R P REISS, **Prec** D T MORGAN, **PVs** J G PEDLAR, R G HOLLOWAY, P A E CHESTER, P J COWELL, P F BRADSHAW, T H MORDECAI, P MCGEARY, D A PETERS, A R BODDY, A C COLES, J M GOODALL, B D FENTON

Description of arms. The arms of the Order of the Garter, viz. Argent, a St George's Cross gules. The shield is encircled by the blue Garter with its motto.

Queen's Free Chapel of St George Windsor Castle (St George's Chapel) **Dean** THE RT REVD D J CONNER, **Cans** J A WHITE, L F P GUNNER, J A OVENDEN, H E FINLAY, **Min Can** G S P C NAPIER

The Queen's Household

Royal Almonry

High Almoner THE RT REVD N S MCCULLOCH (Bishop of Manchester)
Sub-Almoner W J BOOTH

The College of Chaplains

Clerk of the Closet THE RT REVD C J HILL (Bishop of Guildford)

Deputy Clerk of the Closet W J BOOTH

Chaplains to The Queen

J D A ADAMS	R T COOPER	J W R MOWLL
D L BARTLES-SMITH	A S CRAIG	W A NOBLETT
M J BENTON	A G DEUCHAR	B C OSBORNE
R A BOWDEN	C M FARRINGTON	J A OVENDEN
R V BRAZIER	D FLEMING	J C PRIESTLEY
D J BURGESS	G R HALL	C W J SAMUELS
J V BYRNE	R A J HILL	W S SCOTT
P N CALVERT	G I KOVOOR	C M SMITH
R A CHAPMAN	W A MATTHEWS	E G STEPHENSON
G A CHESTERMAN	M E MINGINS	J SYKES
R S CLARKE	G MOFFAT	P H J THORNEYCROFT

Extra Chaplains to The Queen

A D CAESAR	J G M W MURPHY	J R W STOTT
E A JAMES	J P ROBSON	E J G WARD

Chapels Royal

Dean of the Chapels Royal THE BISHOP OF LONDON
Sub-Dean of the Chapels Royal W J BOOTH
Priests in Ordinary R D E BOLTON, P R THOMAS, S E YOUNG
Deputy Priests in Ordinary P R C ABRAM, A H MEAD, D R MULLINER, M D OAKLEY
Domestic Chaplain, Buckingham Palace W J BOOTH
Domestic Chaplain, Windsor Castle THE DEAN OF WINDSOR
Domestic Chaplain, Sandringham J B V RIVIERE
Chaplain, Royal Chapel, Windsor Great Park J A OVENDEN
Chaplain, Hampton Court Palace D R MULLINER
Chaplain, HM Tower of London P R C ABRAM

The Queen's Chapel of the Savoy

Chaplain W S SCOTT

Royal Memorial Chapel, Sandhurst

Chaplain S ROBBINS

Royal Foundation of St Katharine in Ratcliffe

Master R F SWAN

DIOCESAN OFFICES

CHURCH OF ENGLAND

BATH AND WELLS	Diocesan Office, The Old Deanery, Wells BA5 2UG Tel (01749) 670777 Fax 674240 E-mail general@bathwells.anglican.org Web www.bathwells.anglican.org
BIRMINGHAM	Diocesan Office, 175 Harborne Park Road, Birmingham B17 0BH Tel 0121–426 0400 Fax 428 1114 E-mail reception@birmingham.anglican.org Web www.birmingham.anglican.org
BLACKBURN	Church House, Cathedral Close, Blackburn BB1 5AA Tel (01254) 503070 Fax 667309 E-mail diocese@blackburn.anglican.org Web www.blackburn.anglican.org
BRADFORD	Kadugli House, Elmsley Street, Steeton, Keighley BD20 6SE Tel (01535) 650555 Fax 650550 Web www.bradford.anglican.org
BRISTOL	Diocesan Church House, 23 Great George Street, Bristol BS1 5QZ Tel 0117–906 0100 Fax 925 0460 E-mail any.name@bristoldiocese.org Web www.bristol.anglican.org
CANTERBURY	Diocesan House, Lady Wootton's Green, Canterbury CT1 1NQ Tel (01227) 459401 Fax 450964 E-mail reception@diocant.org Web www.canterbury.anglican.org
CARLISLE	Church House, West Walls, Carlisle CA3 8UE Tel (01228) 522573 Fax 815400 E-mail enquiries@carlislediocese.org.uk Web www.carlisle.anglican.org.uk
CHELMSFORD	Diocesan Office, 53 New Street, Chelmsford CM1 1AT Tel (01245) 294400 Fax 294477 E-mail mail@chelmsford.anglican.org Web www.chelmsford.anglican.org
CHESTER	Church House, Lower Lane, Aldford, Chester CH3 6HP Tel (01244) 620444 Fax 620456 E-mail churchhouse@chester.anglican.org Web www.chester.anglican.org
CHICHESTER	Diocesan Church House, 211 New Church Road, Hove BN3 4ED Tel (01273) 421021 Fax 421041 E-mail admin@diochi.org.uk Web www.diochi.org.uk
COVENTRY	Cathedral and Diocesan Offices, 1 Hill Top, Coventry CV1 5AB Tel (024) 7652 1200 Fax 7652 1330 E-mail isobel.chapman@covcofe.org Web www.coventry.anglican.org
DERBY	Derby Church House, Full Street, Derby DE1 3DR Tel (01332) 388650 Fax 292969 E-mail finance@derby.anglican.org Web www.derby.anglican.org
DURHAM	Diocesan Office, Auckland Castle, Market Place, Bishop Auckland DL14 7QJ Tel (01388) 604515 Fax 603695 E-mail diocesan.secretary@durham.anglican.org Web www.durham.anglican.org
ELY	Diocesan Office, Bishop Woodford House, Barton Road, Ely CB7 4DX Tel (01353) 652701 Fax 652745 E-mail d.secretary@office.ely.anglican.org Web www.ely.anglican.org
EUROPE	Diocesan Office, 14 Tufton Street, London SW1P 3QZ Tel (020) 7898 1155 Fax 7898 1166 E-mail diocesan.office@europe.c-of-e.org.uk Web www.europe.anglican.org
EXETER	Diocesan House, Palace Gate, Exeter EX1 1HX Tel (01392) 272686 Fax 499594 E-mail admin@exeter.anglican.org Web www.exeter.anglican.org
GLOUCESTER	Church House, College Green, Gloucester GL1 2LY Tel (01452) 410022 Fax 308324 E-mail church.house@glosdioc.org.uk Web www.glosdioc.org.uk

GUILDFORD	Diocesan House, Quarry Street, Guildford GU1 3XG Tel (01483) 571826 Fax 790333 E-mail reception.diocese@guildford.org.uk Web www.guildford.anglican.org
HEREFORD	Diocesan Office, The Palace, Hereford HR4 9BL Tel (01432) 373300 Fax 352952 E-mail diooffice@hereford.anglican.org Web www.hereford.anglican.org
LEICESTER	Church House, 3–5 St Martin's East, Leicester LE1 5FX Tel 0116–248 7400 Fax 253 2889 E-mail churchhouse@leccofe.org Web www.leicester.anglican.org
LICHFIELD	St Mary's House, The Close, Lichfield WS13 7LD Tel (01543) 306030 Fax 306039 E-mail info@lichfield.anglican.org Web www.lichfield.anglican.org
LINCOLN	Diocesan Office, Church House, Lincoln LN2 1PU Tel (01522) 529241 Fax 512717 E-mail administration@lincoln.anglican.org Web www.lincoln.anglican.org
LIVERPOOL	Church House, 1 Hanover Street, Liverpool L1 3DW Tel 0151–709 9722 Fax 709 2885 Web www.liverpool.anglican.org
LONDON	Diocesan House, 36 Causton Street, London SW1P 4AU Tel (020) 7932 1100 Fax 7932 1112 E-mail keith.robinson@london.anglican.org Web www.london.anglican.org
MANCHESTER	Diocesan Church House, 90 Deansgate, Manchester M3 2GJ Tel 0161–828 1400 Fax 828 1480 E-mail manchesterdbf@manchester.anglican.org Web www.manchester.anglican.org
NEWCASTLE	Church House, St John's Terrace, North Shields NE29 6HS Tel 0191–270 4100 Fax 270 4101 E-mail church_house@newcastle.anglican.org Web www.newcastle.anglican.org
NORWICH	Diocesan House, 109 Dereham Road, Easton, Norwich NR9 5ES Tel (01603) 880853 Fax 881083 E-mail diocesanhouse@norwich.anglican.org Web www.norwich.anglican.org
OXFORD	Diocesan Church House, North Hinksey Lane, Botley, Oxford OX2 0NB Tel (01865) 208200 Fax 790470 E-mail diosec@oxford.anglican.org Web www.oxford.anglican.org
PETERBOROUGH	The Palace, Peterborough PE1 1YB Tel (01733) 887000 Fax 555271 E-mail office@peterborough-diocese.org.uk Web www.peterborough-diocese.org.uk
PORTSMOUTH	Cathedral House, St Thomas's Street, Portsmouth PO1 2HA Tel (023) 9282 5731 Fax 9229 3423 E-mail admin@portsmouth.anglican.org Web www.portsmouth.anglican.org
RIPON AND LEEDS	Ripon and Leeds Diocesan Office, St Mary's Street, Leeds LS9 7DP Tel 0113–200 0540 Fax 249 1129 E-mail philipa@riponleeds-diocese.org.uk Web www.ripon.anglican.org
ROCHESTER	St Nicholas' Church, Boley Hill, Rochester ME1 1SL Tel (01634) 830333 Fax 829463 E-mail dio.off@rochester.anglican.org Web www.rochester.anglican.org
ST ALBANS	Holywell Lodge, 41 Holywell Hill, St Albans AL1 1HE Tel (01727) 854532 Fax 844469 E-mail mail@stalbans.anglican.org Web www.stalbans.anglican.org
ST EDMUNDSBURY AND IPSWICH	St Nicholas Centre, 4 Cutler Street, Ipswich IP1 1UQ Tel (01473) 298500 Fax 298501 E-mail dbf@stedmundsbury.anglican.org Web www.stedmundsbury.anglican.org
SALISBURY	Church House, Crane Street, Salisbury SP1 2QB Tel (01722) 411922 Fax 411990 E-mail enquiries@salisbury.anglican.org Web www.salisbury.anglican.org
SHEFFIELD	Diocesan Church House, 95/99 Effingham Street, Rotherham S65 1BL Tel (01709) 309100 Fax 512550 E-mail reception@sheffield.anglican.org Web www.sheffield.anglican.org

SODOR AND MAN	Holly Cottage, Ballaughton Meadows, Douglas IM2 1JG Tel (01624) 626994 Fax as telephone E-mail dsec-sodor@mcb.net Web www.sodorman.anglican.org
SOUTHWARK	Trinity House, 4 Chapel Court, Borough High Street, London SE1 1HW Tel (020) 7939 9400 Fax 7939 9468 E-mail trinity@southwark.anglican.org Web www.southwark.anglican.org
SOUTHWELL	Dunham House, 8 Westgate, Southwell NG25 0JL Tel (01636) 814331 Fax 815084 E-mail mail@southwell.anglican.org Web www.southwell.anglican.org
TRURO	Diocesan House, Kenwyn, Truro TR1 1JQ Tel (01872) 274351 Fax 222510 E-mail info@truro.anglican.org Web www.truro.anglican.org
WAKEFIELD	Church House, 1 South Parade, Wakefield WF1 1LP Tel (01924) 371802 Fax 364834 E-mail church.house@wakefield.anglican.org
WINCHESTER	Church House, 9 The Close, Winchester SO23 9LS Tel (01962) 844644 Fax 841815 E-mail chsewinchester@winchester.anglican.org Web www.winchester.anglican.org
WORCESTER	The Old Palace, Deansway, Worcester WR1 2JE Tel (01905) 20537 Fax 612302 Web www.cofe-worcester.org.uk
YORK	Diocesan House, Aviator Court, Clifton Moor, York YO30 4WJ Tel (01904) 699500 Fax 699501 E-mail yorkdbf@yorkdiocese.org Web www.dioceseofyork.org.uk

CHURCH IN WALES

BANGOR	Diocesan Centre, Cathedral Close, Bangor LL57 1RL Tel (01248) 354999 Fax 353882
LLANDAFF	Llandaff Diocesan Board of Finance, Heol Fair, Llandaff, Cardiff CF5 2EE Tel (029) 2057 8899 Fax 2057 6198
MONMOUTH	Diocesan Office, 64 Caerau Road, Newport NP9 4HJ Tel (01633) 267490 Fax 265586
ST ASAPH	St Asaph Diocesan Board of Finance, High Street, St Asaph LL17 0RD Tel (01745) 582245 Fax 583556
ST DAVIDS	Diocesan Office, Abergwili, Carmarthen SA31 2JG Tel (01267) 236145 Fax 223046
SWANSEA AND BRECON	Swansea and Brecon Diocesan Board of Finance Ltd, Swansea and Brecon Diocesan Centre, Cathedral Close, Brecon LD3 9DP Tel (01874) 623716 Fax as telephone

SCOTTISH EPISCOPAL CHURCH

ABERDEEN AND ORKNEY	Diocesan Centre, 39 King's Crescent, Aberdeen AB24 3HP Tel (01224) 636653 Fax 636186
ARGYLL AND THE ISLES	The Pines, Ardconnel Road, Oban, Argyll PA34 5DR Tel (01631) 566912 Fax as telephone E-mail office@argyll.anglican.org
BRECHIN	The Bishop's Room, St Paul's Cathedral, 1 High Street, Dundee DD1 1TD Tel (01382) 229230 (mornings only) Fax 203446
EDINBURGH	Diocesan Centre, 21A Grosvenor Crescent, Edinburgh EH12 5EL Tel 0131–538 7033 Fax 538 7088
GLASGOW AND GALLOWAY	Diocesan Office, 5 St Vincent Place, Glasgow G1 2DH Tel 0141–221 5720 *or* 221 2694 Fax 221 7014
MORAY AND CAITHNESS	Diocesan Office, 11 Kenneth Street, Inverness IV3 5NR Tel (01463) 226255 (mornings only) Fax as telephone
ST ANDREWS, DUNKELD AND DUNBLANE	Perth Diocesan Centre, 28A Balhousie Street, Perth PH1 5HJ Tel (01738) 443173 Fax 443174

CHURCH OF IRELAND

PROVINCE OF ARMAGH

ARMAGH	Church House, 46 Abbey Street, Armagh BT61 7DZ Tel (028) 3752 2858 Fax 3751 0596
CLOGHER	The Deanery, 10 Augher Road, Clogher BT76 0AD Tel (028) 8554 8235 Fax as telephone E-mail dean@clogher.anglican.org
CONNOR	Diocesan Office, Church of Ireland House, 61/67 Donegall Street, Belfast BT1 2QH Tel (028) 9032 2268 *or* 9032 3188 Fax 9032 1635
DERRY AND RAPHOE	Diocesan Office, London Street, Londonderry BT48 6RQ Tel (028) 7126 2440 Fax 7137 2100
DOWN AND DROMORE	Diocesan Office, Church of Ireland House, 61/67 Donegall Street, Belfast BT1 2QH Tel (028) 9032 2268 *or* 9032 3188 Fax 9032 1635
KILMORE	Kilmore Diocesan Office, Whitestar Complex, Market Street, Cootehill, Co Cavan, Irish Republic Tel (00353) (49) 555 9954 Fax 555 9957 E-mail secretary@kilmore.anglican.org
ELPHIN AND ARDAGH	Calry Rectory, The Mall, Sligo, Irish Republic
TUAM, KILLALA AND ACHONRY	Stonehall House, Ballisodare, Co Sligo, Irish Republic Tel (00353) (71) 67280 Fax 30264 E-mail hsherlock@iolfree.ie

PROVINCE OF DUBLIN

CASHEL AND OSSORY	Diocesan Office, St Canice's Library, Kilkenny, Irish Republic Tel (00353) (56) 61910 *or* 27248 Fax 51813 E-mail dco@cashel.anglican.org
CORK, CLOYNE AND ROSS	St Nicholas House, 14 Cove Street, Cork, Irish Republic Tel (00353) (21) 427 2262 Fax 496 8467 E-mail office@cork.anglican.org
DUBLIN AND GLENDALOUGH	Diocesan Office, Church of Ireland House, Church Avenue, Rathmines, Dublin 6, Irish Republic Tel (00353) (1) 496 6981 Fax 497 2865 E-mail office@dublin.anglican.org
LIMERICK, KILLALOE AND ARDFERT	St Cronan's Rectory, Roscrea, Co Tipperary, Irish Republic Tel (00353) (505) 21725 Fax 21993 E-mail condell@iol.ie
MEATH AND KILDARE	Meath and Kildare Diocesan Centre, Moyglare, Maynooth, Co Kildare, Irish Republic Tel (00353) (1) 629 2163 Fax 629 2153 E-mail diomeath@iol.ie *or* office@meath.anglican.org

ARCHDEACONRIES, DEANERIES AND RURAL/AREA DEANS OF THE CHURCH OF ENGLAND AND THE CHURCH IN WALES

The numbers given to the deaneries below correspond to those given in the benefice entries in the combined benefice and church index for England (p. 978) and for Wales (p. 1156). Where an archdeacony comes within the jurisdiction of a suffragan or area bishop under an established scheme, the respective bishop is indicated.

Some dioceses use the title Area Dean.

CHURCH OF ENGLAND

BATH AND WELLS

ARCHDEACONRY OF WELLS

1. AXBRIDGE M P LEE
2. BRUTON S LOW
3. CARY S LOW
4. FROME R D M MARTIN
5. GLASTONBURY JURISDICTION W B GRAHAM
6. IVELCHESTER T J FARMILOE
7. YEOVIL I G HUGHES
8. SHEPTON MALLET D R OSBORNE

ARCHDEACONRY OF BATH

9. BATH P J WHITWORTH
10. CHEW MAGNA J P KNOTT
11. LOCKING M J SLADE
12. MIDSOMER NORTON C P J TURNER
13. PORTISHEAD I M HUBBARD

ARCHDEACONRY OF TAUNTON

14. SEDGEMOOR P MARTIN
15. CREWKERNE AND ILMINSTER N P M WHINNEY
16. EXMOOR J M THOROGOOD
17. QUANTOCK P DENISON
18. TAUNTON A L SMITH
19. TONE A D NORRIS

BIRMINGHAM

ARCHDEACONRY OF BIRMINGHAM

1. BIRMINGHAM CITY CENTRE A G LENOX-CONYNGHAM
2. EDGBASTON S G THORBURN
3. HANDSWORTH A M WEAVER
4. KINGS NORTON R S FIELDSON
5. MOSELEY N A HAND
6. SHIRLEY Q D WARBRICK
7. WARLEY M R DUNK

ARCHDEACONRY OF ASTON

8. ASTON C M FEAK
9. COLESHILL S T MAYES
10. POLESWORTH S J BANKS
11. SOLIHULL M J PARKER
12. SUTTON COLDFIELD D N MILLER
13. YARDLEY AND BORDESLEY P H SMITH

BLACKBURN

ARCHDEACONRY OF BLACKBURN

1. ACCRINGTON T R SMITH
2. BLACKBURN AND DARWEN A RAYNES
3. BURNLEY L LAYCOCK
4. CHORLEY M J EVERITT
5. LEYLAND C J NELSON
6. PENDLE A W RINDL
7. WHALLEY J W HARTLEY

ARCHDEACONRY OF LANCASTER

8. BLACKPOOL S J COX
9. GARSTANG A W WILKINSON
10. KIRKHAM G I HIRST
11. LANCASTER P S G HUDD
12. POULTON P R F CLEMENCE
13. PRESTON C J ENTWISTLE
14. TUNSTALL T J L MAIDMENT

BRADFORD

ARCHDEACONRY OF BRADFORD

1. AIREDALE D R JACKSON
2. BOWLING AND HORTON P M BILTON
3. CALVERLEY P G WALKER
4. OTLEY P Q TUDGE

ARCHDEACONRY OF CRAVEN

5. BOWLAND D W MEWIS
6. EWECROSS A W FELL
7. SKIPTON P A TURNER
8. SOUTH CRAVEN B M WILKINSON

BRISTOL

ARCHDEACONRY OF BRISTOL

1. BRISTOL SOUTH R V HEADING
2. BRISTOL WEST P W ROWE
3. CITY DEANERY J J HASLER

ARCHDEACONRY OF MALMESBURY

4. CHIPPENHAM S C TATTON-BROWN
5. KINGSWOOD AND SOUTH GLOUCESTERSHIRE V J HOWLETT
6. NORTH WILTSHIRE B RAVEN
7. SWINDON M A JOHNSON

CANTERBURY

ARCHDEACONRY OF CANTERBURY

1. EAST BRIDGE D J ROPER
2. WEST BRIDGE J S RICHARDSON
3. CANTERBURY S W JONES
4. DOVER S J BOWRING
5. ELHAM A G BUCKLEY
6. OSPRINGE A C OEHRING
7. RECULVER P D SALES
8. SANDWICH J M A ROBERTS
9. THANET A J HOUSTON

ARCHDEACONRY OF MAIDSTONE

10. ASHFORD S E MCLACHLAN
11. CRANBROOK P T MACKENZIE
12. ROMNEY S J A HARDY
13. MAIDSTONE K M GORHAM
14. NORTH DOWNS R M GILL
15. SITTINGBOURNE J W STREETING
16. TENTERDEN C F SMITH

CARLISLE

ARCHDEACONRY OF CARLISLE

1. APPLEBY J A H CLEGG
2. BRAMPTON C J MORRIS
3. CARLISLE J R LIBBY
4. PENRITH D M FOWLER

ARCHDEACONRY OF WEST CUMBERLAND

5. CALDER A D EDWARDS
6. DERWENT B ROTHWELL
7. SOLWAY B ROWE

ARCHDEACONRY OF WESTMORLAND AND FURNESS

8. BARROW P E MANN
9. FURNESS G WEMYSS
10. KENDAL N L DAVIES
11. WINDERMERE W R F COKE

CHELMSFORD

ARCHDEACONRY OF WEST HAM
(BISHOP OF BARKING)

1. BARKING AND DAGENHAM R K GAYLER
2. HAVERING J B PARSONS
3. NEWHAM A R EASTER
4. REDBRIDGE G M TARRY
5. WALTHAM FOREST P A REILY

ARCHDEACONRY OF SOUTHEND
(BISHOP OF BRADWELL)

6. BASILDON E W COCKETT
7. BRENTWOOD R B WHITE
8. CHELMSFORD NORTH C J ELLIOTT
9. CHELMSFORD SOUTH M G BLYTH
10. HADLEIGH R H S EASTOE
11. MALDON AND DENGIE E H BEAVAN
12. ROCHFORD C W COUSINS
13. SOUTHEND-ON-SEA M J HARRIS
14. THURROCK D R TOMLINSON

ARCHDEACONRY OF COLCHESTER
(BISHOP OF COLCHESTER)

15. BRAINTREE P A NEED
16. COLCHESTER S CARTER
17. DEDHAM AND TEY C HORSEMAN
18. DUNMOW L BOND
19. HINCKFORD J F BLORE
20. HARWICH A COLEBROOKE
21. NEWPORT AND STANSTED C BISHOP
22. SAFFRON WALDEN D J GREEN
23. ST OSYTH W B METCALFE
24. WITHAM J M HALL

ARCHDEACONRY OF HARLOW
(BISHOP OF BARKING)

25. EPPING FOREST G CONNOR
26. HARLOW D C KIRKWOOD
27. ONGAR B J PYKE

CHESTER

ARCHDEACONRY OF CHESTER

1. BIRKENHEAD D WALKER
2. CHESTER R C TOAN
3. FRODSHAM R J GILPIN
4. GREAT BUDWORTH E C HALL
5. MALPAS L R THOMAS
6. MIDDLEWICH I G BISHOP
7. WALLASEY A J MANNINGS
8. WIRRAL NORTH G P BENSON
9. WIRRAL SOUTH H J ALDRIDGE

ARCHDEACONRY OF MACCLESFIELD

10. BOWDON J SUTTON
11. CONGLETON J C CUTTELL
12. KNUTSFORD B T YOUNG
13. MACCLESFIELD E W L DAVIES
14. MOTTRAM S J WILSON
15. NANTWICH G D GEDDES
16. CHADKIRK T R PARKER
17. CHEADLE H B EALES
18. STOCKPORT A J BELL

CHICHESTER

ARCHDEACONRY OF CHICHESTER

1. ARUNDEL AND BOGNOR K D RICHARDS
2. BRIGHTON N E D MILMINE
3. CHICHESTER D L PARKER
4. HOVE D K WOSTENHOLM
5. WORTHING J K GAVIGAN

ARCHDEACONRY OF HORSHAM

6. CUCKFIELD I N CHANDLER
7. EAST GRINSTEAD C EVERETT-ALLEN
8. HORSHAM R C JACKSON
9. HURST C J COLLISON
10. MIDHURST A T CUNNINGTON
11. PETWORTH D S POLLARD
12. STORRINGTON P B WELCH
13. WESTBOURNE J J HOLLIMAN

ARCHDEACONRY OF LEWES AND HASTINGS

14. BATTLE AND BEXHILL *Vacant*
15. DALLINGTON M D REDHOUSE
16. EASTBOURNE G T RIDEOUT
17. HASTINGS C H KEY
18. LEWES AND SEAFORD C H ATHERSTONE
19. ROTHERFIELD J R JAMES
20. RYE H M MOSELEY
21. UCKFIELD *Vacant*

COVENTRY

ARCHDEACONRY OF COVENTRY

1. COVENTRY EAST R W HARE
2. COVENTRY NORTH R E WALKER
3. COVENTRY SOUTH M Q BRATTON
4. KENILWORTH R W E AWRE
5. NUNEATON D JONES
6. RUGBY E C LYONS

ARCHDEACONRY OF WARWICK

7. ALCESTER D A HALL
8. FOSSE R E WILLIAMS
9. SHIPSTON D A KNIGHT
10. SOUTHAM D R PATTERSON
11. WARWICK AND LEAMINGTON T M H BOYNS

DERBY

ARCHDEACONRY OF CHESTERFIELD

1. ALFRETON G M KNOX
2. BAKEWELL AND EYAM C A THROWER
3. BOLSOVER AND STAVELEY W T HICKS
4. BUXTON J O GOLDSMITH
5. CHESTERFIELD N V JOHNSON
6. GLOSSOP D J MURDOCH
7. WIRKSWORTH R E QUARTON

ARCHDEACONRY OF DERBY

8. ASHBOURNE C D HARRISON
9. DERBY NORTH R J ELGAR
10. DERBY SOUTH P R SANDFORD
11. DUFFIELD D PERKINS
12. HEANOR C L HUGHES
13. EREWASH I E GOODING
14. LONGFORD A G MURPHIE
15. MELBOURNE M G ALEXANDER
16. REPTON D J HORSFALL

DURHAM

ARCHDEACONRY OF DURHAM

1. DURHAM D J BELL
2. EASINGTON A MILNE
3. HARTLEPOOL M R GILBERTSON
4. LANCHESTER M JACKSON
5. SEDGEFIELD K LUMSDON

ARCHDEACONRY OF AUCKLAND

6. AUCKLAND N P VINE
7. BARNARD CASTLE A J HARDING
8. DARLINGTON J R DOBSON
9. STANHOPE P A GREENHALGH
10. STOCKTON T J D OLLIER

ARCHDEACONRY OF SUNDERLAND

11. CHESTER-LE-STREET *Vacant*
12. GATESHEAD D M JOHNSON
13. GATESHEAD WEST K TEASDALE
14. HOUGHTON LE SPRING I G WALLIS
15. JARROW W E BRAVINER
16. WEARMOUTH K A WALTON

ELY

ARCHDEACONRY OF ELY

1. BOURN C A COLLINS
2. CAMBRIDGE D P E REINDORP
3. FORDHAM AND QUY S G F EARL
4. LINTON C A SINDALL
5. NORTH STOWE N I MOIR
6. SHELFORD M R GOATER
7. SHINGAY S F C WILLIAMS

ARCHDEACONRY OF HUNTINGDON AND WISBECH

8. HUNTINGDON M A GUITE
9. ST IVES R A DARMODY
10. ST NEOTS R H W ARGUILE
11. YAXLEY R LONGFOOT
12. ELY F E G BRAMPTON
13. FINCHAM AND FELTWELL D J KIGHTLEY
14. MARCH P BAXANDALL
15. WISBECH LYNN MARSHLAND W A L ZWALF

EXETER

ARCHDEACONRY OF EXETER

1. AYLESBEARE R W C JEFFERY
2. CADBURY S G C SMITH
3. CHRISTIANITY A WHITE
4. CULLOMPTON D L D ROBOTTOM
5. HONITON J B HEDGES
6. KENN G K MAYER
7. OTTERY D H JAMES
8. TIVERTON D M FLETCHER

ARCHDEACONRY OF TOTNES

9. MORETON *Vacant*
10. NEWTON ABBOT AND IPPLEPEN C H BENSON
11. OKEHAMPTON A E GEERING
12. TORBAY D W WITCHELL
13. TOTNES S E ROBERTS
14. WOODLEIGH T W BRIGHTON

ARCHDEACONRY OF BARNSTAPLE

15. BARNSTAPLE M D D JONES
16. HARTLAND A J RICHARDSON
17. HOLSWORTHY R B DORRINGTON
18. SHIRWELL P BOWERS
19. SOUTH MOLTON J HANNA
20. TORRINGTON *Vacant*

ARCHDEACONRY OF PLYMOUTH

21. IVYBRIDGE D ARNOTT
22. PLYMOUTH DEVONPORT R M SIGRIST
23. PLYMOUTH MOORSIDE T R J DICKENS
24. PLYMOUTH SUTTON N H P MCKINNEL
25. TAVISTOCK S G MAY

GLOUCESTER

ARCHDEACONRY OF GLOUCESTER

1. BISLEY B C E COKER
2. DURSLEY W J BOON
3. FOREST NORTH R J SEAMAN
4. FOREST SOUTH R J M GROSVENOR
5. GLOUCESTER CITY G D OSBORNE
6. GLOUCESTER NORTH R J A MITCHELL
7. HAWKESBURY D E S PRIMROSE
8. STONEHOUSE C D SUTCH

ARCHDEACONRY OF CHELTENHAM

9. CHELTENHAM S S GREGORY
10. CAMPDEN D E VINCE
11. CIRENCESTER M A M ST JOHN-CHANNELL
12. FAIRFORD B C ATKINSON
13. NORTHLEACH *Vacant*
14. STOW *Vacant*
15. TEWKESBURY AND WINCHCOMBE I F CALDER

GUILDFORD

ARCHDEACONRY OF SURREY

1. ALDERSHOT I M SCOTT-THOMPSON
2. CRANLEIGH J N E BUNDOCK
3. FARNHAM J T L STILL
4. GODALMING N JONES
5. GUILDFORD C J MATTHEWS
6. SURREY HEATH B NICOLE

ARCHDEACONRY OF DORKING

7. DORKING A D J COE
8. EMLY W A J ALLBERRY
9. EPSOM S A WILCOCKSON
10. LEATHERHEAD J P CRESSWELL
11. RUNNYMEDE R HAY
12. WOKING N J AIKEN

HEREFORD

ARCHDEACONRY OF HEREFORD

1. ABBEYDORE J F BUTTERWORTH
2. BROMYARD C I FLETCHER
3. HEREFORD CITY B P CHAVE
4. HEREFORD RURAL D J BOWEN
5. KINGTON AND WEOBLEY P TARLING
6. LEDBURY M D VOCKINS
7. LEOMINSTER J T MIDDLEMISS
8. ROSS AND ARCHENFIELD J B HUNNISETT

ARCHDEACONRY OF LUDLOW

9. BRIDGNORTH C G WILLIAMS
10. CLUN FOREST R T SHAW
11. CONDOVER G H EARNEY
12. LUDLOW A G SEABROOK
13. PONTESBURY P D HARRATT
14. TELFORD SEVERN GORGE M A KINNA

LEICESTER

ARCHDEACONRY OF LEICESTER

1. CHRISTIANITY (LEICESTER) NORTH M E LAMBERT
2. CHRISTIANITY (LEICESTER) SOUTH J C BURCH
3. FRAMLAND (Melton) H M FLINT
4. GARTREE FIRST DEANERY (Harborough) I W Y GEMMELL
5. GARTREE SECOND DEANERY (Wigston) M F RUSK
6. GOSCOTE J F WELLINGTON

ARCHDEACONRY OF LOUGHBOROUGH

7. AKELEY EAST (Loughborough) D M F NEWMAN
8. AKELEY SOUTH (Coalville) *Vacant*
9. AKELEY WEST (Ashby) A J BURGESS
10. GUTHLAXTON K W BAKER
11. SPARKENHOE EAST J E SHARPE
12. SPARKENHOE WEST (Hinckley and Bosworth) M J NORMAN

LICHFIELD

ARCHDEACONRY OF LICHFIELD

1. LICHFIELD J W ALLAN
2. PENKRIDGE P H J THORNEYCROFT
3. RUGELEY T THAKE
4. TAMWORTH I H MURRAY

ARCHDEACONRY OF STOKE-ON-TRENT

5. ALSTONFIELD A J BURTON
6. CHEADLE L R PRICE
7. ECCLESHALL N A CLEMAS
8. LEEK M F LEIGH
9. NEWCASTLE W G H GARDINER
10. STAFFORD M R METCALF
11. STOKE NORTH W E SLATER
12. STOKE M K ELLOR
13. TRENTHAM B J BREWER
14. TUTBURY A J WOOD
15. UTTOXETER E G WHITTAKER

ARCHDEACONRY OF SALOP

16. EDGMOND AND SHIFNAL D J BUTTERFIELD
17. ELLESMERE J C VERNON
18. HODNET M G W HAYES
19. OSWESTRY D R NORTH
20. SHREWSBURY K T ROBERTS
21. TELFORD V C SWEET
22. WEM AND WHITCHURCH A R RIDLEY
23. WROCKWARDINE G HORNER

ARCHDEACONRY OF WALSALL

24. TRYSULL G M F WILLIAMS
25. WALSALL J C HILL
26. WEDNESBURY R E INGLESBY
27. WEST BROMWICH M A SMALLMAN
28. WOLVERHAMPTON M R GILBERT

LINCOLN

ARCHDEACONRY OF STOW

1. AXHOLME, ISLE OF M P COONEY
2. CORRINGHAM R PROSSER
3. LAWRES *Vacant*
4. MANLAKE M P COONEY
5. WEST WOLD I ROBINSON
6. YARBOROUGH C H LILLEY

ARCHDEACONRY OF LINDSEY

7. BOLINGBROKE P F COATES
8. CALCEWAITHE AND CANDLESHOE T STEELE
9. GRIMSBY AND CLEETHORPES P M MULLINS
10. HAVERSTOE I R SHELTON
11. HORNCASTLE M E BURSON-THOMAS
12. LOUTHESK S D HOLDAWAY

ARCHDEACONRY OF LINCOLN

13. AVELAND AND NESS WITH STAMFORD N RUSSELL
14. BELTISLOE A T HAWES
15. CHRISTIANITY T W THOMPSON
16. ELLOE EAST G J WICKSTEAD
17. ELLOE WEST T R BARKER
18. GRAFFOE R S EYRE
19. GRANTHAM P HOPKINS
20. HOLLAND EAST M A R COOPER
21. HOLLAND WEST A M HUGHES
22. LAFFORD P J MANDER
23. LOVEDEN A J MEGAHEY

LIVERPOOL

ARCHDEACONRY OF LIVERPOOL

1. BOOTLE N A WELLS
2. HUYTON G S PEARSON
3. LIVERPOOL NORTH H CORBETT
4. LIVERPOOL SOUTH G J BUTLAND
5. SEFTON A R WOODHOUSE
6. TOXTETH AND WAVERTREE J M MATTHEWS
7. WALTON R S BRIDSON
8. WEST DERBY J R I WIKELEY

ARCHDEACONRY OF WARRINGTON

9. NORTH MEOLS C POPE
10. ST HELENS C S WOODS
11. ORMSKIRK D G TOWLER
12. WARRINGTON S P ATTWATER
13. WIDNES G C ELSMORE
14. WIGAN EAST D W LONG
15. WIGAN WEST C HURST
16. WINWICK R G LEWIS

LONDON

ARCHDEACONRY OF LONDON

1. THE CITY J D M PATON

ARCHDEACONRY OF CHARING CROSS

2. WESTMINSTER PADDINGTON W G WILSON
3. WESTMINSTER ST MARGARET *Vacant*
4. WESTMINSTER ST MARYLEBONE L A MOSES

ARCHDEACONRY OF HACKNEY
(BISHOP OF STEPNEY)

5. HACKNEY I HARPER
6. ISLINGTON D SILVESTER
7. TOWER HAMLETS A J WYNNE

ARCHDEACONRY OF MIDDLESEX
(BISHOP OF KENSINGTON)

8. CHELSEA R A GILLION
9. HAMMERSMITH AND FULHAM S J WELCH
10. HAMPTON A J WATSON
11. HOUNSLOW D J SIMPSON
12. KENSINGTON H D J RAYMENT-PICKARD
13. SPELTHORNE R J COSH

ARCHDEACONRY OF HAMPSTEAD
(BISHOP OF EDMONTON)

14. BARNET, CENTRAL N T W TAYLOR
15. BARNET, WEST J E I HAWKINS
16. CAMDEN, NORTH (Hampstead) P J GALLOWAY
17. CAMDEN, SOUTH (Holborn and St Pancras) R N ARNOLD
18. ENFIELD J M PAUL
19. HARINGEY, EAST L J MILLER
20. HARINGEY, WEST G B SEABROOK

ARCHDEACONRY OF NORTHOLT
(BISHOP OF WILLESDEN)

21. BRENT P W STONE
22. EALING A R CORSIE
23. HARROW D M TALBOT
24. HILLINGDON O J FIELD

MANCHESTER

ARCHDEACONRY OF MANCHESTER

1. ARDWICK M THOMPSON
2. ECCLES M R AINSWORTH
3. HEATON L S IRELAND
4. HULME R A J HILL
5. MANCHESTER, NORTH M D ASHCROFT
6. SALFORD S A JONES
7. STRETFORD C C BROWN
8. WITHINGTON R M GOVENDER

ARCHDEACONRY OF BOLTON

9. BOLTON C A BRACEGIRDLE
10. BURY I M ROGERSON
11. DEANE R C COOPER
12. FARNWORTH B HARTLEY
13. LEIGH W BALDWIN
14. RADCLIFFE AND PRESTWICH C J C HEWITT
15. ROSSENDALE W L OLIVER
16. WALMSLEY A J LINDOP

ARCHDEACONRY OF ROCHDALE

17. ASHTON-UNDER-LYNE P R DIXON
18. HEYWOOD AND MIDDLETON N J FEIST
19. OLDHAM P B MCEVITT
20. ROCHDALE I C THOMPSON
21. SADDLEWORTH R W HAWKINS
22. TANDLE R MORRIS

NEWCASTLE

ARCHDEACONRY OF NORTHUMBERLAND

1. BEDLINGTON P J BRYARS
2. BELLINGHAM C S PRICE
3. CORBRIDGE M NELSON
4. HEXHAM R BEST
5. NEWCASTLE CENTRAL J C WIDDOWS
6. NEWCASTLE EAST M J WEBB
7. NEWCASTLE WEST M J JACKSON
8. TYNEMOUTH J A ROBERTSON

ARCHDEACONRY OF LINDISFARNE

9. ALNWICK B COWEN
10. BAMBURGH AND GLENDALE A J HUGHES
11. MORPETH R H MCLEAN
12. NORHAM A S ADAMSON

NORWICH

ARCHDEACONRY OF NORWICH

1. NORWICH EAST R M S WOODHAM
2. NORWICH NORTH *Vacant*
3. NORWICH SOUTH N J H GARRARD

ARCHDEACONRY OF NORFOLK

4. BLOFIELD *Vacant*
5. DEPWADE H D POTTS
6. GREAT YARMOUTH M G KICHENSIDE
7. HUMBLEYARD A J BRADDOCK
8. LODDON P M KNIGHT
9. LOTHINGLAND J B SIMPSON
10. REDENHALL J B SCOTT
11. THETFORD AND ROCKLAND M AISBITT
12. ST BENET AT WAXHAM AND TUNSTEAD A D PARSONS

ARCHDEACONRY OF LYNN

13. BRECKLAND S J SMITH
14. BRISLEY AND ELMHAM B R A COLE
15. BURNHAM AND WALSINGHAM J CHARLES
16. HEACHAM AND RISING L H CAMPBELL
17. DEREHAM IN MITFORD R AMES-LEWIS
18. HOLT H C STOKER
19. INGWORTH R D BRANSON
20. LYNN I C WHITTLE
21. REPPS A H J LANE
22. SPARHAM M D W PADDISON

OXFORD

ARCHDEACONRY OF OXFORD

1. ASTON AND CUDDESDON A R HAWKEN
2. BICESTER AND ISLIP P J BALL
3. CHIPPING NORTON S J A WESTON
4. COWLEY E B BARDWELL
5. DEDDINGTON B L M PHILLIPS
6. HENLEY D R B CARTER
7. OXFORD J A ELLIS
8. WITNEY R K BILLINGS
9. WOODSTOCK R J HUMPHREYS

ARCHDEACONRY OF BERKSHIRE (BISHOP OF READING)

10. ABINGDON J N COOPER
11. BRACKNELL N A PARISH
12. BRADFIELD J M H LOVERIDGE
13. MAIDENHEAD AND WINDSOR T A SCOTT
14. NEWBURY N T MOFFATT
15. READING B SHENTON
16. SONNING D P HODGSON
17. VALE OF WHITE HORSE *Vacant*
18. WALLINGFORD E G CLEMENTS
19. WANTAGE J L SALTER

ARCHDEACONRY OF BUCKINGHAM

20. AMERSHAM J P B WYNBURNE
21. AYLESBURY *Vacant*
22. BUCKINGHAM K P ASHBY
23. BURNHAM AND SLOUGH D K MIELL
24. CLAYDON D A HISCOCK
25. MILTON KEYNES A J MARRIOTT
26. MURSLEY C J DYER
27. NEWPORT I J PUSEY
28. WENDOVER M C DEARNLEY
29. WYCOMBE *Vacant*

PETERBOROUGH

ARCHDEACONRY OF NORTHAMPTON

1. BRACKLEY T C OAKLEY
2. BRIXWORTH C R EVANS
3. DAVENTRY O R PAGE
4. NORTHAMPTON S P ADAMS
5. TOWCESTER M J BURTON
6. WELLINGBOROUGH M C W WEBBER
7. WOOTTON R B STAINER

ARCHDEACONRY OF OAKHAM

8. BARNACK P J C CLEMENTS
9. CORBY J M COLLINS
10. HIGHAM G L BROCKHOUSE
11. KETTERING R T COOK
12. OUNDLE R J ORMSTON
13. PETERBOROUGH G J STEELE
14. RUTLAND S J EVANS

PORTSMOUTH

ARCHDEACONRY OF THE MEON

1. BISHOP'S WALTHAM P H KELLY
2. FAREHAM W C DAY
3. GOSPORT I G BOOTH
4. PETERSFIELD S A WEEDEN

ARCHDEACONRY OF PORTSDOWN

5. HAVANT P H MOORE
6. PORTSMOUTH J V BYRNE

ARCHDEACONRY OF ISLE OF WIGHT

7. WIGHT, EAST G E MORRIS
8. WIGHT, WEST R J EMBLIN

RIPON AND LEEDS

ARCHDEACONRY OF RICHMOND

1. HARROGATE P D G HOOPER
2. RICHMOND P S MIDWOOD
3. RIPON D J CLEEVES
4. WENSLEY D G PATON-WILLIAMS

ARCHDEACONRY OF LEEDS

5. ALLERTON S C COWLING
6. ARMLEY T W LIPSCOMB
7. HEADINGLEY C R CORNWELL
8. WHITKIRK J SYKES

ROCHESTER

ARCHDEACONRY OF ROCHESTER

1. COBHAM J E TIPP
2. DARTFORD D B KITLEY
3. GILLINGHAM A T VOUSDEN
4. GRAVESEND V J LAWRENCE
5. ROCHESTER P T KERR
6. STROOD J F SOUTHWARD

ARCHDEACONRY OF TONBRIDGE

7. MALLING J R TERRANOVA
8. PADDOCK WOOD C J REED
9. SEVENOAKS P E FRANCIS
10. SHOREHAM S M RAMSARAN
11. TONBRIDGE L W G KEVIS
12. TUNBRIDGE WELLS J P STEWART

ARCHDEACONRY OF BROMLEY AND BEXLEY

13. BECKENHAM M E PORTER
14. BROMLEY S D BURTON-JONES
15. ERITH F D JAKEMAN
16. ORPINGTON A A MUSTOE
17. SIDCUP D HILDRED

ST ALBANS

ARCHDEACONRY OF ST ALBANS

1. ALDENHAM V C ORAM
2. BERKHAMSTED D J ABBOTT
3. HEMEL HEMPSTEAD P J COTTON
4. HITCHIN J N LUSCOMBE
5. RICKMANSWORTH T J MARSHALL
6. ST ALBANS D RIDGEWAY
7. WATFORD G R WARREN
8. WHEATHAMPSTEAD C M FARRINGTON

ARCHDEACONRY OF BEDFORD

9. AMPTHILL N JEFFERY
10. BEDFORD C M DENT
11. BIGGLESWADE V W BEYNON
12. DUNSTABLE M E GRANT
13. ELSTOW N P MORRELL
14. LUTON R C H FRANKLIN
15. SHARNBROOK I M MCINTOSH
16. SHEFFORD M J VENABLES

ARCHDEACONRY OF HERTFORD

17. BARNET R F WATSON
18. BISHOP'S STORTFORD R A V MARCHAND
19. BUNTINGFORD D M WILLIAMS
20. CHESHUNT C J SELBY
21. WELWYN HATFIELD R E PYKE
22. HERTFORD AND WARE P M HIGHAM
23. STEVENAGE G B WHITE

ST EDMUNDSBURY AND IPSWICH

ARCHDEACONRY OF IPSWICH

1. BOSMERE *Vacant*
2. COLNEYS G L GRANT
3. HADLEIGH D A C STRANACK
4. IPSWICH P K TOWNLEY
5. SAMFORD S J SWAIN
6. STOWMARKET B B BILSTON
7. WOODBRIDGE P C E STENTIFORD

ARCHDEACONRY OF SUDBURY

8. CLARE E J BETTS
9. IXWORTH I HOOPER
10. LAVENHAM M C THROWER
11. MILDENHALL S PETTITT
12. SUDBURY L R PIZZEY
13. THINGOE G J WEBB

ARCHDEACONRY OF SUFFOLK

14. BECCLES AND SOUTH ELMHAM P J NELSON
15. HALESWORTH J J WILSON
16. HARTISMERE R H AXFORD
17. HOXNE D W FINCH
18. LOES G W OWEN
19. SAXMUNDHAM R F WEBB

SALISBURY

ARCHDEACONRY OF SHERBORNE

1. DORCHESTER P C LAMBERT
2. LYME BAY A J ASHWELL
3. SHERBORNE H G PEARSON
4. WEYMOUTH R H FRANKLIN

ARCHDEACONRY OF DORSET

5. BLACKMORE VALE M T P ZAMMIT
6. MILTON AND BLANDFORD S F EVERETT
7. POOLE N J C LLOYD
8. PURBECK R J NAYLOR
9. WIMBORNE J E HOLBROOK

ARCHDEACONRY OF SARUM

10. ALDERBURY A P JEANS
11. CHALKE H I J SOUTHERN
12. SALISBURY P J D HAWKSWORTH
13. STONEHENGE S E WILKINSON

ARCHDEACONRY OF WILTS

14. BRADFORD D G SMITH
15. CALNE M J FLIGHT
16. DEVIZES J RECORD
17. HEYTESBURY P RICHARDSON
18. MARLBOROUGH S RAILTON
19. PEWSEY N A LEIGH-HUNT

SHEFFIELD

ARCHDEACONRY OF SHEFFIELD AND ROTHERHAM

1. ATTERCLIFFE A PATTERSON
2. ECCLESALL J C SULLIVAN
3. ECCLESFIELD E MITCHELL
4. HALLAM P R TOWNSEND
5. LAUGHTON D C BLISS
6. ROTHERHAM A R WOOD

ARCHDEACONRY OF DONCASTER

7. ADWICK-LE-STREET M WIGGLESWORTH
8. DONCASTER J I WILLETT
9. DONCASTER, WEST A J GILBERT
10. SNAITH AND HATFIELD C ROBERTS
11. TANKERSLEY N P HOLMES
12. WATH A J DELVES

SODOR AND MAN

ARCHDEACONRY OF SODOR AND MAN

1. CASTLETOWN AND PEEL G M BREFFITT
2. DOUGLAS D WHITWORTH
3. RAMSEY D J GREEN

SOUTHWARK

ARCHDEACONRY OF LEWISHAM
(BISHOP OF WOOLWICH)

1. CHARLTON M D MARSHALL
2. DEPTFORD W G CORNECK
3. ELTHAM AND MOTTINGHAM M R HARRISON
4. LEWISHAM, EAST P D BUTLER
5. LEWISHAM, WEST M J KINGSTON
6. PLUMSTEAD H D OWEN

ARCHDEACONRY OF SOUTHWARK
(BISHOP OF WOOLWICH)

7. BERMONDSEY A M DOYLE
8. CAMBERWELL J D JELLEY
9. DULWICH D L GWILLIAMS
10. SOUTHWARK AND NEWINGTON G W GODDARD

ARCHDEACONRY OF LAMBETH
(BISHOP OF KINGSTON)

11. BRIXTON M H CLARK
12. CLAPHAM P J ROSE-CASEMORE
13. LAMBETH C R TRUSS
14. MERTON D R M MONTEITH
15. STREATHAM R J TITLEY

ARCHDEACONRY OF WANDSWORTH
(BISHOP OF KINGSTON)

16. BATTERSEA G M VEVERS
17. KINGSTON K W SCOTT
18. RICHMOND AND BARNES C PALMER
19. TOOTING G G HOWARD
20. WANDSWORTH H D TOLLER

ARCHDEACONRY OF CROYDON

21. CROYDON ADDINGTON A H R QUINN
22. CROYDON CENTRAL C J L BOSWELL
23. CROYDON SOUTH C F SPURWAY
24. CROYDON NORTH C E BLANKENSHIP
25. SUTTON C WHEATON

ARCHDEACONRY OF REIGATE
(BISHOP OF CROYDON)

26. CATERHAM A D MIDDLETON
27. GODSTONE D F G BUTLIN
28. REIGATE *Vacant*

SOUTHWELL

ARCHDEACONRY OF NEWARK

1. BAWTRY J N GREEN
2. MANSFIELD G K KNOTT
3. NEWARK A I TUCKER
4. NEWSTEAD A N EVANS
5. RETFORD A C ST J WALKER
6. WORKSOP M C ALVEY

ARCHDEACONRY OF NOTTINGHAM

7. BEESTON J P SMITHURST
8. EAST BINGHAM D L HARPER
9. WEST BINGHAM S D SILVESTER
10. GEDLING P A WILLIAMS
12. NOTTINGHAM NORTH C J RATTENBERRY
13. NOTTINGHAM CENTRAL S F MORRIS
14. NOTTINGHAM WEST A R HOWE
15. SOUTHWELL M S TANNER

TRURO

ARCHDEACONRY OF CORNWALL

1. ST AUSTELL K P ARTHUR
2. CARNMARTH NORTH E J M HOGAN
3. CARNMARTH SOUTH J HARRIS
4. KERRIER D J STEVENS
5. PENWITH A J WADE
6. POWDER I H MORRIS
7. PYDAR C M MALKINSON

ARCHDEACONRY OF BODMIN

8. STRATTON R C W DICKENSON
9. TRIGG MAJOR G PENGELLY
10. TRIGG MINOR AND BODMIN S L BRYAN
11. WIVELSHIRE, EAST J A C WILSON
12. WIVELSHIRE, WEST G LONSDALE

WAKEFIELD

ARCHDEACONRY OF HALIFAX

1. ALMONDBURY J AUSTIN
2. BRIGHOUSE AND ELLAND N M WOOD
3. CALDER VALLEY P N CALVERT
4. HALIFAX J VICKERMAN
5. HUDDERSFIELD R M F CROMPTON
6. KIRKBURTON G F WHITCROFT

ARCHDEACONRY OF PONTEFRACT

7. BARNSLEY A BRISCOE
8. BIRSTALL D E CRAIG-WILD
9. CHEVET J F WHITE
10. DEWSBURY L C DEW
11. PONTEFRACT M DAVIES
12. WAKEFIELD A S MACPHERSON

WINCHESTER

ARCHDEACONRY OF WINCHESTER

1. ALRESFORD J G CRUICKSHANK
2. ALTON J M CAMPBELL
3. ANDOVER F E WILLIAMS
4. BASINGSTOKE C L HAWKINS
5. ODIHAM R A EWBANK
6. WHITCHURCH M S KENNING
7. WINCHESTER N P SEAL

ARCHDEACONRY OF BOURNEMOUTH

8. BOURNEMOUTH R D PETERS
9. CHRISTCHURCH D M WEBSTER
10. EASTLEIGH P A VARGESON
11. LYNDHURST J D CURTIS
12. ROMSEY D B KINGTON
13. SOUTHAMPTON N BOAKES

ARCHDEACONRY OF THE CHANNEL ISLANDS

14. GUERNSEY K P MELLOR
15. JERSEY R F KEY

WORCESTER

ARCHDEACONRY OF WORCESTER

1. EVESHAM R N ARMITAGE
2. MALVERN M J A BARR
3. MARTLEY AND WORCESTER WEST C PULLIN
4. PERSHORE M T C BAYNES
5. UPTON F A WOOKEY
6. WORCESTER EAST R G JONES

ARCHDEACONRY OF DUDLEY

7. BROMSGROVE D ROGERS
8. DROITWICH A J FULLER
9. DUDLEY H C HANKE
10. KINGSWINFORD C J WINDLEY
11. KIDDERMINSTER N J W BARKER
12. STOURBRIDGE S M FALSHAW
13. STOURPORT B GILBERT

YORK

ARCHDEACONRY OF YORK
(BISHOP OF SELBY)

1. AINSTY, NEW R P BURTON
2. DERWENT R M KIRKMAN
3. EASINGWOLD J HARRISON
4. SELBY D H REYNOLDS
5. SOUTH WOLD V P HEWETSON
6. SOUTHERN RYEDALE N N JONES
7. YORK, CITY OF C W M BALDOCK

ARCHDEACONRY OF EAST RIDING
(BISHOP OF HULL)

8. BEVERLEY D W HOSKIN
9. BRIDLINGTON J A WARDLE
10. HARTHILL M TEARE
11. HOLDERNESS, NORTH R P YATES
12. HOLDERNESS, SOUTH R HOWARD
13. HOWDEN P G FAULKNER
14. HULL D A WALKER
15. SCARBOROUGH M P DUNNING

ARCHDEACONRY OF CLEVELAND
(BISHOP OF WHITBY)

16. GUISBOROUGH J C WEETMAN
17. HELMSLEY J D PURDY
18. MIDDLESBROUGH D G HODGSON
19. MOWBRAY R F ROWLING
20. PICKERING F J A HEWITT
21. STOKESLEY W J FORD
22. WHITBY D S MACKENZIE

CHURCH IN WALES

ST ASAPH

ARCHDEACONRY OF ST ASAPH

1. ST ASAPH R W ROWLAND
2. DENBIGH J P P WILLIAMS
3. DYFFRYN CLWYD J B DAVIES
4. HOLYWELL G H TRIMBY
5. LLANRWST *Vacant*
6. RHOS N H WILLIAMS

ARCHDEACONRY OF MONTGOMERY

7. CEDEWAIN A T W REYNOLDS
8. CAEREINION D E B FRANCIS
9. LLANFYLLIN C F CARTER
10. POOL R L BROWN

ARCHDEACONRY OF WREXHAM

11. BANGOR ISYCOED A W A COPPING
12. GRESFORD *Vacant*
13. HAWARDEN M K SNELLGROVE
14. LLANGOLLEN J S EVANS
15. MINERA J G CANHAM
16. MOLD C I DAY
17. PENLLYN AND EDEIRNION S J ROBERTS
18. WREXHAM G O MARSHALL

BANGOR

ARCHDEACONRY OF BANGOR

1. ARFON R F DONALDSON
2. ARLLECHWEDD P R JONES
3. LLIFON AND TALYBOLION T BONNET
4. MALLTRAETH *Vacant*
5. OGWEN L J PERRY
6. TINDAETHWY R L NEWALL
7. TWRCELYN G W EDWARDS

ARCHDEACONRY OF MEIRIONNYDD

8. ARDUDWY R A BEACON
9. ARWYSTLI R P PITCHER
10. CYFEILIOG AND MAWDDWY E W ROWLANDS
11. LLYN AND EIFIONYDD A JONES
12. YSTUMANER N D ADAMS

ST DAVIDS

ARCHDEACONRY OF ST DAVIDS

1. CASTLEMARTIN V F MILLGATE
2. DAUGLEDDAU G D GWYTHER
3. DEWISLAND AND FISHGUARD R GRIFFITHS
4. NARBERTH M BUTLER
5. ROOSE D M WIGHT

ARCHDEACONRY OF CARDIGAN

6. CEMAIS AND SUB-AERON E L THOMAS
7. EMLYN E ROBERTS
8. GLYN AERON C L BOLTON
9. LAMPETER AND ULTRA-AERON A W WILLIAMS
10. LLANBADARN FAWR D B THOMAS

ARCHDEACONRY OF CARMARTHEN

11. CARMARTHEN S E JONES
12. CYDWELI J H A JAMES
13. DYFFRYN AMAN J H GRAVELL
14. LLANGADOG AND LLANDEILO B T RICE
15. ST CLEARS J GAINER

LLANDAFF

ARCHDEACONRY OF LLANDAFF

1. CAERPHILLY A H STEVENS
2. CARDIFF A RABJOHNS
3. LLANDAFF S LISK
4. LLANTWIT MAJOR AND COWBRIDGE P M LEONARD
5. PENARTH AND BARRY *Vacant*

ARCHDEACONRY OF MARGAM

6. BRIDGEND M KOMOR
7. MARGAM P R MASSON
8. NEATH S J RYAN

ARCHDEACONRY OF MORGANNWG

9. CYNON VALLEY R E DAVIES
10. MERTHYR TYDFIL M J DAVIES
11. PONTYPRIDD M K JONES
12. RHONDDA R G LLOYD

MONMOUTH

ARCHDEACONRY OF MONMOUTH

1. ABERGAVENNY J H WINSTON
2. CHEPSTOW *Vacant*
3. MONMOUTH J P W REES
4. NETHERWENT J E L WHITE
5. RAGLAN-USK T G CLEMENT

ARCHDEACONRY OF NEWPORT

6. BASSALEG J S WILLIAMS
7. BEDWELLTY J J WILKINS
8. BLAENAU GWENT M J BEASLEY
9. NEWPORT A J EDWARDS
10. PONTYPOOL B R PIPPEN

SWANSEA AND BRECON

ARCHDEACONRY OF BRECON

1. BRECON B H JOHN
2. BUILTH N D HALL
3. CRICKHOWELL K RICHARDS
4. HAY R T EDWARDS
5. MAELIENYDD L A MARSHALL

ARCHDEACONRY OF GOWER

6. CLYNE G E BENNETT
7. CWMTAWE G TURNER
8. WEST GOWER D J WILKINSON
9. LLWCHWR D H E MOSFORD
10. PENDERI T H JONES
11. SWANSEA H V PARSELL

ENGLISH BENEFICES AND CHURCHES

An index of benefices, conventional districts, local ecumenical projects, and proprietary chapels (shown in bold type), together with entries for churches and other licensed places of worship listed on the Parish Index of the Central Board of Finance. Where the church name is the same as that of the benefice (or as that of the place whose name forms the beginning of the benefice name), the church entry is omitted. Church dedications are indicated in brackets.

The benefice entry gives the full legal name, followed by the diocese, its deanery number (p. 970), the patron(s), and the name(s) and appointment(s) of clergy serving there (if there ane none, the telephone number of the parsonage house is given). The following are the main abbreviations used; for others see the full list of abbreviations.

C	Curate	**P**	Patron(s)
C-in-c	Curate-in-charge	**P-in-c**	Priest-in-charge
Dn-in-c	Deacon-in-charge	**Par Dn**	Parish Deacon
Dss	Deaconess	**R**	Rector
Hon C	Honorary Curate	**TM**	Team Minister
Hon Par Dn	Honorary Parish Deacon	**TR**	Team Rector
Min	Minister	**TV**	Team Vicar
NSM	Non-stipendiary Minister	**V**	Vicar

Listed below are the elements in place names which are not normally treated as substantive in the index:

CENTRAL	**HIGHER**	**MUCH**	**OVER**
EAST	**LITTLE**	**NETHER**	**SOUTH**
GREAT	**LOW**	**NEW**	**THE**
GREATER	**LOWER**	**NORTH**	**UPPER**
HIGH	**MIDDLE**	**OLD**	**WEST**

Thus WEST WIMBLEDON (Christ Church) appears as **WIMBLEDON, WEST (Christ Church)** and CENTRAL TELFORD as **TELFORD, CENTRAL**. The only exception occurs where the second element of the place name is a common noun thus, NEW LANE remains as **NEW LANE**, and WEST TOWN as **WEST TOWN**.

AB KETTLEBY (St James) and Holwell w Asfordby *Leic 3* **P** *DBP, MMCET and V Rothley (jt)* **R** M J SHEPHERD

ABBAS and Templecombe w Horsington *B & W 2* **P** *Bp and Ch Trust Fund (jt)* **R** A J SYMONDS

ABBERLEY (St Mary) *see* Shrawley, Witley, Astley and Abberley *Worc*

ABBERLEY (St Michael) *as above*

ABBERTON (St Andrew) *see* Fingringhoe w E Donyland and Abberton etc *Chelmsf*

ABBERTON (St Edburga), The Flyfords, Naunton Beauchamp and Bishampton w Throckmorton *Worc 4* **P** *Bp and Croome Estate Trustees (1 turn), and Ld Chan (1 turn)* **R** A W BENNETT

ABBESS RODING (St Edmund King and Martyr) *see* S Rodings *Chelmsf*

ABBEY CHAPEL (St Mary) *see* Annesley w Newstead *S'well*

ABBEY HEY (St George) *Man 1* **P** *Bp* **P-in-c** S SCHOFIELD, **C** S O'ROURKE

ABBEY HULTON (St John) *see* Bucknall *Lich*

ABBEY WOOD (St Michael and All Angels) *S'wark 3* **P** *Bp* **V** D A SHERRATT, **NSM** D C ROBINSON

ABBEY WOOD (William Temple) *see* Thamesmead *S'wark*

ABBEYDALE *see* Sheff St Pet Abbeydale *Sheff*

ABBEYDALE (St John the Evangelist) *Sheff 2* **P** *Mrs C Longworth, Sir Samuel Roberts Bt, K B Jones, and J A Goodwin Esq* **V** V J FILER

ABBEYDORE (St Mary) *see* Ewyas Harold w Dulas, Kenderchurch etc *Heref*

ABBEYSTEAD (Christ Church) *see* Dolphinholme w Quernmore and Over Wyresdale *Blackb*

ABBOTS BICKINGTON (St James) *see* Bradworthy, Sutcombe, Putford etc *Ex*

ABBOTS BROMLEY (St Nicholas) w Blithfield *Lich 3* **P** *Bp and D&C (jt)* **P-in-c** S C DAVIS

ABBOTS LANGLEY (St Lawrence) *St Alb 7* **P** *Bp* **V** B K ANDREWS, **C** A R MATTHEWS

ABBOTS LEIGH (Holy Trinity) w Leigh Woods *Bris 2* **P** *Bp* **P-in-c** D J SMITH

ABBOTS MORTON (St Peter) *see* Church Lench w Rous Lench and Abbots Morton etc *Worc*

ABBOTS RIPTON (St Andrew) w Wood Walton *Ely 8* **P** *Lord de Ramsey (2 turns), D&C (1 turn)* **P-in-c** E B ATLING

ABBOTSBURY (St Mary) *see* Highweek and Teigngrace *Ex*

ABBOTSBURY (St Nicholas), Portesham and Langton Herring *Sarum 4* **P** *The Hon C A Townshend and Bp (alt)* **P-in-c** P S THOMAS

ABBOTSHAM (St Helen) *see* Parkham, Alwington, Buckland Brewer etc *Ex*

ABBOTSKERSWELL (Blessed Virgin Mary) *Ex 10* **P** *Ld Chan* **P-in-c** P A WHITE, **Hon C** J C WHITE

ABBOTSLEY (St Margaret) *see* Gt Gransden and Abbotsley and Lt Gransden etc *Ely*

ABBOTSWOOD (St Nicholas Family Centre) *see* Yate New Town *Bris*

ABBOTTS ANN (St Mary) and Upper Clatford and Goodworth Clatford *Win 3* **P** *Exors T P de Paravicini Esq and Bp (jt)* **R** D N A BROAD, **NSM** N J JUDD

ABDON (St Margaret) *Heref 12* **P** *Bp* **R** I E GIBBS

ABENHALL (St Michael) w Mitcheldean *Glouc 3* **P** *DBP* **R** R G STURMAN

ABERFORD (St Ricarius) *see* Aberford w Micklefield *York*

ABERFORD (St Ricarius) w Micklefield *York 4* **P** *Abp and Oriel Coll Ox (jt)* **V** *vacant* 0113-286 2154

ABINGDON (Christ Church) (St Helen) (St Michael and All Angels) (St Nicolas) *Ox 10* **P** *Patr Bd* **TR** M A J GOODE, **TV** P M DOLL, T C DAVIS, **C** D R P WIGNALL, D J ARCHER, **Hon C** P W L WALKER, **NSM** T W HEWES, L HODGES

ABINGER (St James) cum Coldharbour *Guildf 7* **P** *Ch Patr Trust and J P M H Evelyn Esq (alt)* **R** A N BERRY

ABINGTON (St Peter and St Paul) *Pet 4* **P** *Bp* **R** S P ADAMS, **C** S C GARDNER

ABINGTON, GREAT (St Mary the Virgin) w LITTLE (St Mary) *Ely 4* **P** *MMCET* **P-in-c** J B MYNORS

ABINGTON PIGOTTS (St Michael and All Angels) *see* Shingay Gp *Ely*

ABNEY (Mission Room) *see* Hope, Castleton and Bradwell *Derby*

ABRAM (St John) *Liv 14* **P** *R Wigan* **V** J L STEVENTON

ABRIDGE (Holy Trinity) *see* Lambourne w Abridge and Stapleford Abbotts *Chelmsf*

ABSON (St James the Great) *see* Pucklechurch and Abson *Bris*

ABTHORPE (St John the Baptist) *see* Silverstone and Abthorpe w Slapton etc *Pet*

ACASTER MALBIS (Holy Trinity) *York 1* **P** *R A G Raimes Esq* **V** C I COATES

ACASTER SELBY (St John) *see* Appleton Roebuck w Acaster Selby *York*

ACCRINGTON Christ Church *Blackb 1* **P** *Bp and V S Shore H Trin (jt)* **V** K LOGAN

ACCRINGTON Christ the King (St James) (St Paul) (St Andrew) (St Peter) (St Clement) (St Mary Magdalen) *Blackb 1* **P** *Patr Bd* **TR** A D LYON, **TV** S D MANSFIELD, L W CARSON-FEATHAM

ACCRINGTON (St John) w Huncoat St Augustine *Blackb 1* **P** *Bp and V Accrington St Jas w St Paul (jt)* **V** I H ROBERTSON

ACKLAM (St John the Baptist) *see* W Buckrose *York*

ACKLAM, WEST (St Mary) *York 18* **P** *Trustees* **V** J H HEARN, **C** D APPLEBY

ACKLETON (Mission Room) *see* Worfield *Heref*

ACKLINGTON (St John the Divine) *see* Warkworth and Acklington *Newc*

ACKWORTH (All Saints) (St Cuthbert) *Wakef 11* **P** *Duchy of Lanc* **R** P HARTLEY, **NSM** J S MONTGOMERY

ACLE (St Edmund) w Fishley; North Burlingham; Beighton w Moulton *Nor 4* **P** *Bp and Ch Soc Trust (jt)* **R** D M BOND

ACOCKS GREEN (St Mary) *Birm 13* **P** *Trustees* **P-in-c** A T BULLOCK

ACOL (St Mildred) *see* Birchington w Acol and Minnis Bay *Cant*
ACOMB (Holy Redeemer) *York 7* **P** *The Crown* **V** M A HAND
ACOMB (St Stephen) *York 7* **P** *Trustees* **V** D J ERRIDGE, **C** P A HORSLEY, **NSM** C M A RUTT
ACOMB MOOR (James the Deacon) *York 7* **P** *Abp* **V** A A HORSMAN
ACRISE (St Martin) *see* Hawkinge w Acrise and Swingfield *Cant*
ACTON (All Saints) w Great Waldingfield *St E 12* **P** *Bp* **V** J W S FIELDGATE
ACTON (St Mary) *Lon 22* **P** *Bp* **R** J F FOX, **C** D H K HILBORN, **NSM** P M SMEDLEY
ACTON (St Mary) and Worleston, Church Minshull and Wettenhall *Ches 15* **P** *Bp, V Over St Chad, and R C Roundell Esq (jt)* **V** D P BROCKBANK
ACTON, EAST (St Dunstan w St Thomas) *Lon 22* **P** *Bp* **V** N J BLANDFORD-BAKER
ACTON, NORTH (St Gabriel) *Lon 22* **P** *Bp* **V** K A ROBUS
ACTON, WEST (St Martin) *Lon 22* **P** *Bp* **V** N P HENDERSON, **Hon C** A GRIFFITHS
ACTON BEAUCHAMP (St Giles) and Evesbatch w Stanford Bishop *Heref 2* **P** *Bp and MMCET (alt)* **P-in-c** J A DAVIES
ACTON BURNELL (St Mary) *see* Condover w Frodesley, Acton Burnell etc *Heref*
ACTON GREEN (St Alban) *see* Oak Tree Angl Fellowship *Lon*
ACTON GREEN (St Peter) (All Saints) *Lon 22* **P** *Bp* **V** J M V WILLMINGTON
ACTON ROUND (St Mary) *Heref 9* **P** *DBP* **Hon C** H J PATTERSON
ACTON SCOTT (St Margaret) *Heref 11* **P** *DBP* **P-in-c** M L COPE
ACTON TRUSSELL (St James) *see* Penkridge Team *Lich*
ACTON TURVILLE (St Mary) *see* Boxwell, Leighterton, Didmarton, Oldbury etc *Glouc*
ADBASTON (St Michael and All Angels), High Offley, Knightley, Norbury and Woodseaves *Lich 7* **P** *Bp* **R** P M FREEMAN, **NSM** D HOLLINGS
ADDERBURY (St Mary) w Milton *Ox 5* **P** *New Coll Ox* **V** S W FLETCHER, **OLM** S NEWBY
ADDERLEY (St Peter), Ash, Calverhall, Ightfield and Moreton Say *Lich 18* **P** *C C Corbet Esq, A E H Heber-Percy Esq, T C Heywood-Lonsdale Esq, and R Whitchurch (jt)* **R** R J ANDERS
ADDINGHAM (St Michael) *see* Cross Fell Gp *Carl*
ADDINGHAM (St Peter) *Bradf 4* **P** *J R Thompson-Ashby Esq* **R** A R TAWN
ADDINGTON (St Margaret) *see* Birling, Addington, Ryarsh and Trottiscliffe *Roch*
ADDINGTON (St Mary) *see* Winslow w Gt Horwood and Addington *Ox*
ADDINGTON (St Mary) *S'wark 22* **P** *Abp* **V** J M MALES, **C** Y FRANCIS
ADDINGTON, GREAT (All Saints) w LITTLE (St Mary the Virgin) and Woodford *Pet 10* **P** *Bp and DBP (alt)* **R** *vacant* (01832) 733087
ADDINGTON, NEW (St Edward) *S'wark 22* **P** *Bp* **V** M POWELL, **NSM** E ILORI
ADDISCOMBE (St Mary Magdalene) *S'wark 23* **P** *Trustees* **V** R L WILLIAMS, **C** M T POWLEY, **NSM** A H BARRON
ADDISCOMBE (St Mildred) *S'wark 23* **P** *Bp* **P-in-c** H J MARSHALL, **OLM** M KING
ADDLESTONE (St Augustine) (St Paul) *Guildf 11* **P** *Bp* **V** R HAY, **C** A D UWADIAE, **Hon C** S A BRASSIL, **OLM** A G BARDELL
ADDLETHORPE (St Nicholas) *see* Skegness Gp *Linc*
ADEL (St John the Baptist) *Ripon 7* **P** *Brig R G Lewthwaite, D R Lewthwaite Esq, and J V Lewthwaite Esq (jt)* **R** T C GILL
ADEYFIELD (St Barnabas) *see* Hemel Hempstead *St Alb*
ADFORTON (St Andrew) *see* Wigmore Abbey *Heref*
ADISHAM (Holy Innocents) *see* Aylesham w Adisham *Cant*
ADLESTROP (St Mary Magdalene) *see* Broadwell, Evenlode, Oddington, Adlestrop etc *Glouc*
ADLINGFLEET (All Saints) *see* The Marshland *Sheff*
ADLINGTON (St John's Mission Church) *see* Prestbury *Ches*
ADLINGTON (St Paul) *Blackb 4* **P** *Bp* **V** D F C MORGAN
ADSTOCK (St Cecilia) *see* Lenborough *Ox*
ADSTONE (All Saints) *see* Blakesley w Adstone and Maidford etc *Pet*
ADSWOOD (St Gabriel's Mission Church) *see* Stockport SW *Ches*
ADVENT (St Adwena) *see* Lanteglos by Camelford w Advent *Truro*
ADWELL (St Mary) *see* Thame *Ox*
ADWICK-LE-STREET (St Laurence) w Skelbrooke *Sheff 7* **P** *Mrs P N Fullerton and Bp (alt)* **R** P A INGRAM
ADWICK-UPON-DEARNE (St John the Baptist) *see* Barnburgh w Melton on the Hill etc *Sheff*
AFFPUDDLE (St Lawrence) *see* Bere Regis and Affpuddle w Turnerspuddle *Sarum*
AIGBURTH (St Anne) *Liv 4* **P** *Trustees* **V** G G AMEY
AIKTON (St Andrew) *see* Barony of Burgh *Carl*
AINDERBY STEEPLE (St Helen) *see* Lower Swale *Ripon*
AINSDALE (St John) *Liv 9* **P** *R Walton, Bp, and Adn (jt)* **V** A OVEREND
AINSTABLE (St Michael and All Angels) *see* Inglewood Gp *Carl*
AINSWORTH (Christ Church) *Man 14* **P** *Bp* **P-in-c** D B GRIFFITHS, **NSM** C T HAYDEN
AINTREE (St Giles) w St Peter *Liv 7* **P** *Bp* **V** B A WALLES
AIREDALE (Holy Cross) w Fryston *Wakef 11* **P** *Bp* **V** J W KNILL-JONES, **C** K H YOUNG
AIRMYN (St David), Hook and Rawcliffe *Sheff 10* **P** *Bp and Ch Soc Trust (jt)* **V** G HOLLINGSWORTH
AISHOLT (All Saints), Enmore, Goathurst, Nether Stowey, Over Stowey and Spaxton w Charlynch *B & W 17* **P** *Bp, D&C Windsor, MMCET, and Ch Trust Fund Trust (jt)* **R** P DENISON, **C** H O WATKINS
AISLABY (St Margaret) *see* Whitby w Aislaby and Ruswarp *York*
AISTHORPE (St Peter) w Scampton w Thorpe le Fallows w Brattleby *Linc 3* **P** *DBP and J M Wright Esq (jt)* **R** *vacant*
AKELEY (St James) *see* N Buckingham *Ox*
AKEMAN *Ox 2* **P** *New Coll and Ch Ch (1 turn), Qu Coll, St Jo Coll, and Period and Country Houses Ltd (1 turn)* **R** D F WALKER, **NSM** D R KABOLEH
ALBERBURY (St Michael and All Angels) w Cardeston *Heref 13* **P** *Bp and Sir Michael Leighton Bt (alt)* **V** *vacant*
ALBOURNE (St Bartholomew) w Sayers Common and Twineham *Chich 9* **P** *Bp (2 turns), Ex Coll Ox (1 turn)* **R** D M SWYER
ALBRIGHTON (St John the Baptist) *see* Leaton and Albrighton w Battlefield *Lich*
ALBRIGHTON (St Mary Magdalene) *Lich 16* **P** *Haberdashers' Co and Ch Hosp Horsham (alt)* **V** R B BALKWILL
ALBURGH (All Saints) *see* Earsham w Alburgh and Denton *Nor*
ALBURY (St Helen) Tiddington *see* Wheatley *Ox*
ALBURY (St Mary) *see* Lt Hadham w Albury *St Alb*
ALBURY (St Peter and St Paul) *see* Shere, Albury and Chilworth *Guildf*
ALBY (St Ethelbert) *see* Erpingham w Calthorpe, Ingworth, Aldborough etc *Nor*
ALCESTER (St Nicholas) and Arrow w Oversley and Weethley *Cov 7* **P** *Marquess of Hertf* **R** D C CAPRON, **NSM** R F DOBELL
ALCISTON (not known) *see* Berwick w Selmeston and Alciston *Chich*
ALCOMBE (St Michael the Archangel) *B & W 16* **P** *Bp* **V** S STUCKES
ALCONBURY (St Peter and St Paul) w Alconbury Weston *Ely 8* **P** *D&C Westmr* **P-in-c** J P YOUNG, **NSM** M J HARE
ALDBOROUGH (St Andrew) w Boroughbridge and Roecliffe *Ripon 3* **P** *D&C York and Bp (alt)* **V** P J SMITH, **C** C J HEWLETT
ALDBOROUGH (St Mary) *see* Erpingham w Calthorpe, Ingworth, Aldborough etc *Nor*
ALDBOROUGH HATCH (St Peter) *Chelmsf 4* **P** *The Crown* **V** C NICHOLSON
ALDBOURNE (St Michael) *see* Whitton *Sarum*
ALDBROUGH (St Bartholomew) and Mappleton w Goxhill and Withernwick *York 11* **P** *Ld Chan, Abp, and Adn E Riding (by turn)* **P-in-c** J R RICE-OXLEY
ALDBROUGH (St Paul) *see* Forcett and Aldbrough and Melsonby *Ripon*
ALDBURY (St John the Baptist) *see* Tring *St Alb*
ALDE RIVER *see* Sternfield, Benhall, Snape etc *St E*
ALDEBURGH (St Peter and St Paul) w Hazlewood *St E 19* **P** *Mrs A C V Wentworth* **V** N J HARTLEY, **OLM** N J WINTER
ALDEBY (St Mary) *see* Raveningham Gp *Nor*
ALDENHAM (St John the Baptist), Radlett and Shenley *St Alb 1* **P** *Patr Bd* **TR** W J HOGG, **TV** R A FLETCHER, V C ORAM, **NSM** M TAYLOR, V M HARVEY
ALDERBROOK (St Richard) *see* Crowborough *Chich*
ALDERBURY (St Mary the Virgin) *see* Clarendon *Sarum*
ALDERCAR (St John) *see* Langley Mill *Derby*
ALDERFORD (St John the Baptist) *see* Wensum Benefice *Nor*
ALDERHOLT (St James) *Sarum 9* **P** *DBP* **V** P J MARTIN
ALDERLEY (St Kenelm) *see* Wotton-under-Edge w Ozleworth, N Nibley etc *Glouc*

ALDERLEY (St Mary) w Birtles *Ches 12* **P** *Trustees and Bp (alt)* **R** W G BOWNESS
ALDERLEY EDGE (St Philip) *Ches 12* **P** *Trustees* **V** B T YOUNG, **NSM** L C A ALEXANDER
ALDERMASTON (St Mary the Virgin) w Wasing and Brimpton *Ox 12* **P** *Bp, DBP, Sir William Mount Bt, and Worc Coll Ox (jt)* **P-in-c** P G STEELE, **NSM** D FOOTE, J K WEBSTER, C PYNN, E M OKE
ALDERMINSTER (St Mary and Holy Cross) and Halford *Cov 9* **P** *Bp and SMF (jt)* **P-in-c** A J ADAMS, **Hon C** D R J EVANS
ALDERNEY (St Anne) *Win 14* **P** *The Crown* **V** S M MASTERS
ALDERSBROOK (St Gabriel) *Chelmsf 4* **P** *DBP* **V** P H SMITH
ALDERSHOT (Holy Trinity) *Guildf 1* **P** *CPAS* **V** G P H NEWTON
ALDERSHOT (St Augustine) *Guildf 1* **P** *Bp* **V** K M HODGES, **OLM** J W A HARVEY
ALDERSHOT (St Michael the Archangel) (Ascension) *Guildf 1* **P** *Bp* **V** J A MARTIN, **C** A J K MACKENZIE, **NSM** N C FORD
ALDERSLEY (Christ the King) *see* Tettenhall Regis *Lich*
ALDERTON (St Andrew) *see* Wilford Peninsula *St E*
ALDERTON (St Giles) *see* Sherston Magna, Easton Grey, Luckington etc *Bris*
ALDERTON (St Margaret) *see* Blisworth and Stoke Bruerne w Grafton Regis etc *Pet*
ALDERTON (St Margaret of Antioch) *see* Winchcombe *Glouc*
ALDERWASLEY (All Saints) *see* Wirksworth *Derby*
ALDFIELD (St Lawrence) *see* Fountains Gp *Ripon*
ALDFORD (St John the Baptist) and Bruera *Ches 5* **P** *Duke of Westmr and D&C (alt)* **R** *vacant* (01244) 620281
ALDHAM (St Margaret and St Catherine) *see* Marks Tey and Aldham *Chelmsf*
ALDHAM (St Mary) *see* Elmsett w Aldham, Hintlesham, Chattisham etc *St E*
ALDINGBOURNE (St Mary the Virgin), Barnham and Eastergate *Chich 1* **P** *Bp and D&C (jt)* **R** S P HOLLAND, **NSM** C R S HARDING
ALDINGHAM (St Cuthbert) and Dendron and Rampside and Urswick *Carl 9* **P** *Prime Min (1 turn), V Dalton-in-Furness and Resident Landowners of Urswick (1 turn)* **R** C R HONOUR, **NSM** M WEBSTER
ALDINGTON (St Martin) w Bonnington and Bilsington and Lympne w West Hythe *Cant 12* **P** *Abp* **P-in-c** R A LOVE
ALDRIDGE (St Mary the Virgin) (St Thomas) *Lich 25* **P** *MMCET* **R** R J CORNFIELD, **C** R G TAYLOR, M C JONES, **OLM** S E QUIBELL
ALDRINGHAM (St Andrew) w Thorpe, Knodishall w Buxlow and Friston *St E 19* **P** *Mrs A C V Wentworth, Ch Patr Trust, and Ch Soc Trust (by turn)* **R** C E BROOKS
ALDRINGTON (St Leonard) *Chich 4* **P** *Bp* **TR** S J TERRY
ALDSWORTH (St Bartholomew) *see* Sherborne, Windrush, the Barringtons etc *Glouc*
ALDWARK (St Stephen) *see* Alne *York*
ALDWICK (St Richard) *Chich 1* **P** *Bp* **V** L C J NAGEL, **NSM** A B VENESS
ALDWINCLE (St Peter) w Thorpe Achurch and Pilton w Wadenhoe and Stoke Doyle *Pet 12* **P** *Soc Merchant Venturers Bris (2 turns), G C Capron Esq (1 turn), and Wadenhoe Trust (1 turn)* **R** *vacant* (01832) 720613
ALDWORTH (St Mary the Virgin) *see* Basildon w Aldworth and Ashampstead *Ox*
ALEXANDRA PARK (St Andrew) *Lon 20* **P** *Bp* **V** A F PYBUS
ALFINGTON (St James and St Anne) *see* Ottery St Mary, Alfington, W Hill, Tipton etc *Ex*
ALFOLD (St Nicholas) and Loxwood *Guildf 2* **P** *Bp and CPAS (jt)* **R** J R J BURLEY
ALFORD (All Saints) *see* Six Pilgrims *B & W*
ALFORD (St Wilfrid) w Rigsby *Linc 8* **P** *Bp* **V** R H IRESON
ALFRED JEWEL *B & W 14* **P** *D&C Windsor (4 turns), Bp (2 turns), Sir Benjamin Slade Bt (1 turn)* **R** S M ROSE, **C** M H CLEMENTS
ALFRETON (St Martin) *Derby 1* **P** *Bp* **NSM** A M V ROOME
ALFRICK (St Mary Magdalene) and Lulsley and Suckley and Leigh and Bransford *Worc 3* **P** *Prime Min and Bp (alt)* **P-in-c** A B BULLOCK
ALFRISTON (St Andrew) w Lullington, Litlington and West Dean *Chich 18* **P** *Ld Chan (3 turns), R A Brown Esq (1 turn), and Duke of Devonshire (1 turn)* **R** F J FOX-WILSON
ALGARKIRK (St Peter and St Paul) *see* Sutterton, Fosdyke, Algarkirk and Wigtoft *Linc*
ALHAMPTON (Mission Church) *see* Fosse Trinity *B & W*
ALKBOROUGH (St John the Baptist) *Linc 4* **P** *Em Coll Cam and Bp (alt)* **V** A F PLEDGER
ALKERTON (St Michael and All Angels) *see* Ironstone *Ox*
ALKHAM (St Anthony) w Capel le Ferne and Hougham *Cant 4* **P** *Abp* **V** *vacant* (01303) 244119
ALKMONTON (St John), Cubley, Marston, Montgomery and Yeaveley *Derby 14* **P** *Bp (3 turns), V Shirley (1 turn)* **R** *vacant* (01335) 330680
ALL CANNINGS (All Saints) *see* Bishop's Cannings, All Cannings etc *Sarum*
ALL SAINTS *see* Highertown and Baldhu *Truro*
ALL SAINTS (All Saints) *see* Axminster, Chardstock, All Saints etc *Ex*
ALL STRETTON (St Michael and All Angels) *see* Church Stretton *Heref*
ALLENDALE (St Cuthbert) w Whitfield *Newc 4* **P** *Viscount Allendale and J C Blackett-Ord Esq (alt)* **R** *vacant* (01434) 683336
ALLENS CROSS (St Bartholomew) *Birm 4* **P** *Bp* **V** D W JAMES
ALLENS GREEN (Mission Church) *see* High Wych and Gilston w Eastwick *St Alb*
ALLEN'S ROUGH (Worship Centre) *see* Willenhall H Trin *Lich*
ALLENSMORE (St Andrew) *see* Kingstone w Clehonger, Eaton Bishop etc *Heref*
ALLENTON (St Edmund) and Shelton Lock *Derby 15* **P** *Bp* **V** M J FENTON
ALLER (St Andrew) *see* Langport Area Chs *B & W*
ALLERSTON (St John) *see* Thornton Dale w Allerston, Ebberston etc *York*
ALLERTHORPE (St Botolph) *see* Barmby Moor Gp *York*
ALLERTON (All Hallows) *see* Mossley Hill *Liv*
ALLERTON (not known) *see* Mark w Allerton *B & W*
ALLERTON (St Peter) (St Francis of Assisi) *Bradf 1* **P** *Bp* **V** G O WILLIAMS
ALLERTON BYWATER (St Mary) *see* Kippax w Allerton Bywater *Ripon*
ALLESLEY (All Saints) *Cov 2* **P** *J R W Thomson-Bree Esq* **R** R N TREW
ALLESLEY PARK (St Christopher) and Whoberley *Cov 3* **P** *Bp* **V** G L PRINGLE, **C** D M FARMER
ALLESTREE (St Edmund King and Martyr) *Derby 11* **P** *Bp* **V** *vacant* (01332) 557396
ALLESTREE (St Nicholas) *Derby 11* **P** *Bp* **V** W F BATES, **NSM** J M NEEDLE
ALLHALLOWS (All Saints) *see* Binsey *Carl*
ALLINGTON (St John the Baptist) *see* Bourne Valley *Sarum*
ALLINGTON (St Nicholas) and Maidstone St Peter *Cant 13* **P** *Abp* **R** J E PERRYMAN
ALLINGTON (St Swithin) *see* Bridport *Sarum*
ALLINGTON, EAST (St Andrew) *see* Modbury, Bigbury, Ringmore w Kingston etc *Ex*
ALLINGTON, WEST (Holy Trinity) *see* Saxonwell *Linc*
ALLITHWAITE (St Mary) *see* Cartmel Peninsula *Carl*
ALLONBY (Christ Church), Cross Canonby and Dearham *Carl 7* **P** *TR Solway Plain, D&C, and Bp (jt)* **V** M E DAY, **NSM** S M MCKENDREY, M FOGG
ALMELEY (St Mary) *see* Eardisley w Bollingham, Willersley, Brilley etc *Heref*
ALMER (St Mary) *see* Red Post *Sarum*
ALMONDBURY (St Michael and St Helen) (St Mary) (All Hallows) w Farnley Tyas *Wakef 1* **P** *DBP* **TV** A J SMITH, **NSM** M J BUTTERWORTH
ALMONDSBURY (St Mary the Virgin) and Olveston *Bris 2* **P** *Bp and D&C (jt)* **V** P W ROWE
ALNE (St Mary) *York 3* **P** *CPAS and MMCET (alt)* **NSM** R WADSWORTH
ALNE, GREAT (St Mary Magdalene) *see* Kinwarton w Gt Alne and Haselor *Cov*
ALNHAM (St Michael and All Angels) *see* Upper Coquetdale *Newc*
ALNMOUTH (St John the Baptist) *see* Lesbury w Alnmouth *Newc*
ALNWICK (St Michael and St Paul) *Newc 9* **P** *Duke of Northd* **C** S J H WHITE
ALPERTON (St James) *Lon 21* **P** *CPAS* **V** J B ROOT, **C** R C YOUNG, **Hon C** D B WADLAND, **NSM** A S JACOB
ALPHAMSTONE (not known) *see* N Hinckford *Chelmsf*
ALPHETON (St Peter and St Paul) *see* Chadbrook *St E*
ALPHINGTON (St Michael and All Angels) *Ex 3* **P** *DBP* **P-in-c** S L BESSENT, **C** N C MILFORD
ALRESFORD (St Andrew) *Chelmsf 23* **P** *Bp* **P-in-c** C J A HARVEY
ALRESFORD, NEW (St John the Baptist) w Ovington and Itchen Stoke *Win 1* **P** *Bp* **R** P H N COLLINS, **NSM** J A BROWNING
ALRESFORD, OLD (St Mary) and Bighton *Win 1* **P** *Bp* **P-in-c** R D TOMKINSON
ALREWAS (All Saints) *Lich 1* **P** *Bp* **V** J W ALLAN, **NSM** P A L MADDOCK, V A WILKERSON

ALSAGER (Christ Church) *Ches 11* **P** *Bp* **V** J E VARTY
ALSAGER (St Mary Magdalene) (St Patrick's Mission Church) *Ches 11* **P** *Bp* **V** R J ISHERWOOD, **NSM** C S SEDDON
ALSAGERS BANK (St John) *Lich 9* **P** *Bp* **V** P G HOUGH
ALSOP-EN-LE-DALE (St Michael and All Angels) *see* Fenny Bentley, Thorpe, Tissington, Parwich etc *Derby*
ALSTON MOOR (St Augustine) *Newc 4* **P** *Bp* **R** J C HARDY
ALSTONE (St Margaret) *see* Overbury w Teddington, Alstone etc *Worc*
ALSTONFIELD (St Peter), Butterton, Ilam, Warslow w Elkstone and Wetton *Lich 5* **P** *Bp, DBP, V Mayfield, and Sir Peter Walker-Okeover Bt (jt)* **V** M E JACKSON, **NSM** E H CAMPBELL
ALSWEAR (not known) *see* Bishopsnympton, Rose Ash, Mariansleigh etc *Ex*
ALTARNON (St Nonna) w Bolventor, Laneast and St Clether *Truro 9* **P** *Bp, D&C, and SMF (jt)* **P-in-c** B STAMFORD
ALTCAR (St Michael and All Angels) and Hightown *Liv 5* **P** *Bp* **V** J C BAKER, **NSM** D C M TAYLOR
ALTHAM (St James) w Clayton le Moors *Blackb 1* **P** *DBP and Trustees (alt)* **V** J TRANTER
ALTHORNE (St Andrew) *see* Creeksea w Althorne, Latchingdon and N Fambridge *Chelmsf*
ALTHORPE (St Oswald) *see* Belton Gp *Linc*
ALTOFTS (St Mary Magdalene) *Wakef 9* **P** *Meynall Ingram Trustees* **V** K RYDER-WEST
ALTON (All Saints) *Win 2* **P** *Bp* **P-in-c** P A BARLOW
ALTON (St Lawrence) *Win 2* **P** *D&C* **P-in-c** P G H DOORES, **C** K E HUTCHINSON
ALTON (St Peter) w Bradley-le-Moors and Oakamoor w Cotton *Lich 6* **P** *Earl of Shrewsbury and Talbot, DBP, and R Cheadle (jt)* **V** M L E LAST
ALTON BARNES (St Mary the Virgin) *see* Pewsey and Swanborough *Sarum*
ALTON COMMON (Mission Room) *see* Alton w Bradley-le-Moors and Oakamoor w Cotton *Lich*
ALTON PANCRAS (St Pancras) *see* Piddle Valley, Hilton, Cheselbourne etc *Sarum*
ALTRINCHAM (St George) *Ches 10* **P** *V Bowdon* **V** B R MCCONNELL, **C** E R COSTIGAN, **NSM** M A JONES
ALTRINCHAM (St John the Evangelist) *Ches 10* **P** *Bp* **V** *vacant* 0161-928 3236
ALVANLEY (St John the Evangelist) *Ches 3* **P** *Bp* **P-in-c** J GLEAVES
ALVASTON (St Michael and All Angels) *Derby 15* **P** *PCC* **V** C J C FRITH, **C** V J CUTHBERT
ALVECHURCH (St Lawrence) *Worc 7* **P** *Bp* **R** D H MARTIN
ALVEDISTON (St Mary) *see* Chalke Valley *Sarum*
ALVELEY (St Mary the Virgin) and Quatt *Heref 9* **P** *J W H Thompson Esq and Lady Labouchere (jt)* **R** N P ARMSTRONG
ALVERDISCOTT (All Saints) *see* Newton Tracey, Horwood, Alverdiscott etc *Ex*
ALVERSTOKE (St Faith) (St Francis) (St Mary) *Portsm 3* **P** *Bp* **R** E A GOODYER, **C** J H TABOR, **NSM** R A FORSE
ALVERSTONE (Church Hall) *see* Brading w Yaverland *Portsm*
ALVERTHORPE (St Paul) *Wakef 12* **P** *Bp* **P-in-c** P WHITTINGHAM, **C** E M WOODCOCK
ALVESCOT (St Peter) *see* Shill Valley and Broadshire *Ox*
ALVESTON (St Helen) and Littleton-on-Severn w Elberton *Bris 2* **P** *Bp and D&C (jt)* **V** D J POLE
ALVESTON (St James) *Cov 8* **P** *R Hampton Lucy w Charlecote and Loxley* **V** R E WILLIAMS
ALVINGHAM (St Adelwold) *see* Mid Marsh Gp *Linc*
ALVINGTON (St Andrew) *see* Woolaston w Alvington and Aylburton *Glouc*
ALVINGTON, WEST (All Saints) *see* Thurlestone, S Milton, W Alvington etc *Ex*
ALWALTON (St Andrew) *see* The Ortons, Alwalton and Chesterton *Ely*
ALWINGTON (St Andrew) *see* Parkham, Alwington, Buckland Brewer etc *Ex*
ALWINTON (St Michael and All Angels) *see* Upper Coquetdale *Newc*
ALWOODLEY (St Barnabas) *see* Moor Allerton *Ripon*
AMBERGATE (St Anne) and Heage *Derby 11* **P** *V Duffield and Exors M A T Johnson Esq* **P-in-c** R J I PAGET
AMBERLEY (Holy Trinity) *Glouc 8* **P** *DBP* **P-in-c** M O TUCKER, **NSM** A V M MORRIS
AMBERLEY (no dedication) *see* Marden w Amberley and Wisteston *Heref*
AMBERLEY (St Michael) w North Stoke and Parham, Wiggonholt and Greatham *Chich 12* **P** *Bp and Parham Estate Trustees (jt)* **P-in-c** D S FARRANT
AMBLE (St Cuthbert) *Newc 9* **P** *Bp* **V** G HARWOOD
AMBLECOTE (Holy Trinity) *Worc 12* **P** *Bp* **V** P TONGUE
AMBLESIDE (St Mary) w Brathay *Carl 11* **P** *DBP* **V** W R F COKE, **C** P WILLOX
AMBROSDEN (St Mary the Virgin) *see* Ray Valley *Ox*
AMCOTTS (St Mark) *see* Belton Gp *Linc*
AMERSHAM (St Mary the Virgin) *Ox 20* **P** *Capt F Tyrwhitt Drake* **R** T J L HARPER, **NSM** D C CARR, C E CROISDALE-APPLEBY
AMERSHAM ON THE HILL (St Michael and All Angels) *Ox 20* **P** *Bp* **P-in-c** D M GLOVER, **C** J-S S GALLANT, **NSM** P R BINNS
AMESBURY (St Mary and St Melor) *Sarum 13* **P** *D&C Windsor* **P-in-c** S E WILKINSON, **C** S M LANGDON, **NSM** M C WILLIAMS
AMINGTON (St Editha) *Birm 10* **P** *Bp* **V** M A HARRIS
AMOTHERBY (St Helen) *see* The Street Par *York*
AMPFIELD (St Mark) *see* Hursley and Ampfield *Win*
AMPLEFORTH (St Hilda) w Oswaldkirk, Gilling East and Stonegrave *York 17* **P** *Abp, Trin Coll Cam, and Prime Min (by turn)* **V** W M CARTWRIGHT
AMPNEYS (St Mary) (St Peter) (Holy Rood) w Driffield and Poulton, The *Glouc 12* **P** *Bp and Col Sir Piers Bengough (jt)* **P-in-c** A E WOOLCOCK
AMPORT (St Mary), Grateley, Monxton and Quarley *Win 3* **P** *D&C Chich, Exors T P de Paravicini Esq, Mrs C E Land, Bp, and R Foundn of St Kath (jt)* **P-in-c** C F PETTET
AMPTHILL (St Andrew) w Millbrook and Steppingley *St Alb 9* **P** *Ld Chan* **R** M J TRODDEN
AMPTON (St Peter) *see* Blackbourne *St E*
AMWELL, GREAT (St John the Baptist) w St Margaret's and Stanstead Abbots *St Alb 22* **P** *Bp, Peache Trustees, and Haileybury Coll (jt)* **V** E A DONALDSON, **Hon C** M G H LACKEY
AMWELL, LITTLE (Holy Trinity) *St Alb 22* **P** *Ch Patr Trust* **V** *vacant* (01992) 589140
ANCASTER (St Martin) *see* Ancaster Wilsford Gp *Linc*
ANCASTER WILSFORD Group, The *Linc 23* **P** *Bp (2 turns), DBP (1 turn), and Mrs G V Hoare (1 turn)* **R** *vacant* (01400) 230398
ANCHORSHOLME (All Saints) *Blackb 8* **P** *Bp, V Bispham, and Ch Soc Trust (jt)* **V** P R NUNN, **C** J W TROOD
ANCOATS (All Souls) *see* Manchester Gd Shep and St Barn *Man*
ANCROFT (St Anne) *see* Lowick and Kyloe w Ancroft *Newc*
ANDERBY (St Andrew) *see* Sutton, Huttoft and Anderby *Linc*
ANDOVER (St Mary the Virgin) (St Thomas) w Foxcott *Win 3* **P** *St Mary's Coll Win* **P-in-c** D G WILLIAMS, **C** J M BENTALL
ANDOVER, WEST (St Michael and All Angels) *Win 3* **P** *Bp* **P-in-c** C B RANKINE, **NSM** J A TAYLOR
ANDREAS (St Andrew) *S & M 3* **P** *The Crown* **P-in-c** G F BARKER
ANDREAS (St Jude Chapelry) *S & M 3* **P** *R Andreas* **V** *vacant*
ANERLEY Christ Church *Roch 13* **P** *CPAS* **V** M E PORTER
ANERLEY (St Paul) *Roch 13* **P** *Ch Patr Trust* **V** M M JONES
ANFIELD (St Columba) *Liv 7* **P** *Bp* **V** R S BRIDSON, **NSM** K L MILLER
ANFIELD (St Margaret) *Liv 3* **P** *Bp* **P-in-c** P A WINN, **NSM** J E WINN
ANGELL TOWN (St John the Evangelist) *S'wark 11* **P** *Bp* **V** M H CLARK
ANGERSLEIGH (St Michael) *see* Trull w Angersleigh *B & W*
ANGLESEY Group, The *Ely 3* **P** *Trin Coll Cam, D&C, and Bp (jt)* **V** D H LEWIS, **NSM** D J KETTLE
ANGMERING (St Margaret) *Chich 1* **P** *J F P Somerset Esq and Ch Patr Trust (jt)* **R** M J STANDEN, **C** B J REDDING
ANKER PARISHES *see* Wolvey w Burton Hastings, Copston Magna etc *Cov*
ANLABY (St Peter) *York 14* **P** *Trustees* **V** N D BARNES
ANLABY COMMON (St Mark) Hull *York 14* **P** *Abp* **P-in-c** D J W BATH
ANMER (St Mary) *see* Dersingham w Anmer and Shernborne *Nor*
ANNESLEY (Our Lady and All Saints) w Newstead *S'well 4* **P** *Exors Major R P Chaworth-Musters* **P-in-c** E A TURNER-LOISEL, **NSM** P H JONES
ANNFIELD PLAIN (St Aidan) *see* Collierley w Annfield Plain *Dur*
ANNSCROFT (Christ Church) *see* Longden and Annscroft w Pulverbatch *Heref*
ANSFORD (St Andrew) *see* Castle Cary w Ansford *B & W*
ANSLEY (St Lawrence) and Arley *Cov 5* **P** *Ch Patr Trust, N W H Sylvester Esq, and A C D'O Ransom Esq (jt)* **R** P B ALLAN
ANSLOW (Holy Trinity) *Lich 14* **P** *MMCET* **V** I R WHITEHEAD

ANSTEY (St George) *see* Hormead, Wyddial, Anstey, Brent Pelham etc *St Alb*
ANSTEY (St Mary) *Leic 11* **P** *R Thurcaston* **R** S J D FOSTER
ANSTEY, EAST (St Michael) *see* Bishopsnympton, Rose Ash, Mariansleigh etc *Ex*
ANSTEY, WEST (St Petrock) *as above*
ANSTON (St James) *Sheff 5* **P** *Bp* **V** P J COGHLAN
ANSTY (St James) *see* Bulkington w Shilton and Ansty *Cov*
ANSTY (St James) *see* Nadder Valley *Sarum*
ANSTY (St John) *see* Cuckfield *Chich*
ANTINGHAM (St Mary) *see* Trunch *Nor*
ANTONY (St James the Great) w Sheviock *Truro 11* **P** *Bp and Col Sir John Carew-Pole Bt (alt)* **P-in-c** B A ANDERSON
ANTROBUS (St Mark), Aston by Sutton, Little Leigh and Lower Whitley *Ches 4* **P** *Bp, V Gt Budworth, Lord Daresbury, and B H Talbot Esq (jt)* **V** D J JOHNSON
ANWICK (St Edith) *see* Kirkby Laythorpe *Linc*
APETHORPE (St Leonard) *Pet 12* **P** *Lord Brassey* **V** *vacant*
APLEY (St Andrew) *see* Bardney *Linc*
APPERLEY (Holy Trinity) *see* Deerhurst and Apperley w Forthampton etc *Glouc*
APPLEBY Group, The *Leic 9* **P** *DBP, MMCET, Bp, and Ld Chan (by turn)* **NSM** S C POLASHEK, L S BIRTWISTLE
APPLEBY (St Bartholomew) *see* Winterton Gp *Linc*
APPLEBY (St Lawrence) *Carl 1* **P** *D&C and Bp (jt)* **P-in-c** J A H CLEGG, **C** R J SANER-HAIGH, **NSM** R A COLLINSON
APPLEBY MAGNA (St Michael and All Angels) *see* Appleby Gp *Leic*
APPLEDORE (St Mary) *see* Bideford, Northam, Westward Ho!, Appledore etc *Ex*
APPLEDORE (St Peter and St Paul) w Brookland and Fairfield and Brenzett w Snargate *Cant 12* **P** *Abp* **P-in-c** N R GALLAGHER, **C** A A DUGUID, **NSM** S J BODY, K FAZZANI
APPLEDRAM (St Mary the Virgin) *Chich 3* **P** *D&C* **P-in-c** C A ASHLEY
APPLEFORD (St Peter and St Paul) *see* Sutton Courtenay w Appleford *Ox*
APPLESHAW (St Peter) Kimpton, Thruxton, Fyfield and Shipton Bellinger *Win 3* **P** *Bp (1 turn), and Bp, D&C, and M H Routh Esq (1 turn)* **R** I J TOMLINSON, **NSM** A E MCKENZIE, B A TIMS
APPLETHWAITE (St Mary) *see* Windermere St Mary and Troutbeck *Carl*
APPLETON (All Saints) *see* The Street Par *York*
APPLETON (St Lawrence) *Ox 10* **P** *Magd Coll Ox* **P-in-c** R G PENMAN
APPLETON (St Mary Magdalene) *see* Stockton Heath *Ches*
APPLETON-LE-MOORS (Christ Church) *see* Lastingham w Appleton-le-Moors, Rosedale etc *York*
APPLETON ROEBUCK (All Saints) w Acaster Selby *York 1* **P** *Abp* **V** *vacant* (01904) 744327
APPLETON THORN (St Cross) *see* Stretton and Appleton Thorn *Ches*
APPLETON WISKE (St Mary) *see* E Richmond *Ripon*
APPLETREEWICK (St John the Baptist) *see* Burnsall w Rylstone *Bradf*
APPLEY BRIDGE (All Saints) *Blackb 4* **P** *Bp* **V** I J J DEWAR
APSLEY END (St Mary) *see* Chambersbury *St Alb*
APULDRAM (St Mary the Virgin) *see* Appledram *Chich*
ARBORFIELD (St Bartholomew) w Barkham *Ox 16* **P** *DBP* **R** E P BICKERSTETH, **C** T J SILK, L J O PARKER
ARBORY (St Columba) *S & M 1* **P** *The Crown* **NSM** C L BARRY
ARBOURTHORNE (St Paul) and Norfolk Park *Sheff 1* **P** *Bp and V Sheffield (jt)* **V** J T HODGES
ARDELEY (St Lawrence) *St Alb 19* **P** *D&C St Paul's* **V** *vacant*
ARDINGLY (St Peter) *Chich 6* **P** *MMCET* **R** S A K ALLABY, **NSM** P N MORGAN
ARDINGTON (Holy Trinity) *see* Wantage Downs *Ox*
ARDLEIGH (St Mary the Virgin) and Bromleys, The *Chelmsf 20* **P** *Ld Chan (2 turns), CR (1 turn), Wadh Coll Ox (1 turn)* **R** N SPICER
ARDLEIGH GREEN (All Saints) *see* Squirrels Heath *Chelmsf*
ARDLEY (St Mary) *see* Cherwell Valley *Ox*
ARDSLEY (Christ Church) *Sheff 12* **P** *R Darfield* **V** R G R EVANS
ARDSLEY, EAST (St Gabriel) (St Michael) *Wakef 12* **P** *E C S J G Brudenell Esq* **V** A R ROWE, **NSM** K R M CAMPBELL
ARDSLEY, WEST (St Mary) *Wakef 8* **P** *E C S J G Brudenell Esq* **V** B A J BARRACLOUGH
ARDWICK (St Benedict) *see* Longsight St Luke *Man*
ARDWICK (St Jerome and St Silas) *see* Manchester Gd Shep and St Barn *Man*
ARELEY KINGS (St Bartholomew) *Worc 13* **P** *R Martley* **R** M TURNER
ARKENDALE (St Bartholomew) *see* Walkingham Hill *Ripon*
ARKENGARTHDALE (St Mary) *see* Swaledale *Ripon*
ARKESDEN (St Mary the Virgin) *see* Clavering and Langley w Arkesden etc *Chelmsf*
ARKHOLME (St John the Baptist) *see* Hornby w Claughton and Whittington etc *Blackb*
ARKLEY (St Peter) *see* Chipping Barnet *St Alb*
ARKSEY (All Saints) *Sheff 7* **P** *DBP* **P-in-c** S P DICKINSON
ARLECDON (St Michael) *see* Crosslacon *Carl*
ARLESEY (St Andrew) (St Peter) w Astwick *St Alb 16* **P** *DBP* **V** S D EDWARDS
ARLEY (St Michael) *see* Ansley and Arley *Cov*
ARLEY (St Wilfred) *as above*
ARLEY, UPPER (St Peter) *see* Kidderminster St Mary and All SS w Trimpley etc *Worc*
ARLINGHAM (St Mary the Virgin) *see* Frampton on Severn, Arlingham, Saul etc *Glouc*
ARLINGTON (St James) *see* Shirwell, Loxhore, Kentisbury, Arlington, etc *Ex*
ARLINGTON (St Pancras), Folkington and Wilmington *Chich 18* **P** *Bp Lon, Mrs S J Harcourt-Smith, and Duke of Devonshire (by turn)* **P-in-c** I E MORRISON
ARMATHWAITE (Christ and St Mary) *see* Inglewood Gp *Carl*
ARMINGHALL (St Mary) *see* Stoke H Cross w Dunston, Arminghall etc *Nor*
ARMITAGE (Holy Trinity) (St John the Baptist) *Lich 3* **P** *Bp* **R** D R H THOMAS
ARMITAGE BRIDGE (St Paul) *see* Em TM *Wakef*
ARMLEY (St Bartholomew) w New Wortley *Ripon 6* **P** *Bp, DBP, and Hyndman Trustees (jt)* **V** T W LIPSCOMB
ARMLEY, UPPER (Christ Church) *Ripon 6* **P** *Ch Patr Trust* **V** A G KAYE, **C** R J DIMERY, R J TWITTY
ARMLEY HEIGHTS (Church of the Ascension) *see* Upper Armley *Ripon*
ARMTHORPE (St Leonard and St Mary) *Sheff 8* **P** *Bp* **R** R LANDALL
ARNCLIFFE (St Oswald) *see* Kettlewell w Conistone, Hubberholme etc *Bradf*
ARNE (St Nicholas) *see* Wareham *Sarum*
ARNESBY (St Peter) w Shearsby and Bruntingthorpe *Leic 10* **P** *Bp* **P-in-c** B STANTON
ARNOLD (Emmanuel) *see* Bestwood Em w St Mark *S'well*
ARNOLD (St Mary) *S'well 10* **P** *Bp* **V** K L SHILL, **C** J L BLATHERWICK
ARNSIDE (St James) *Carl 10* **P** *Bp* **V** D P COOPER, **NSM** P A HENDERSON, **OLM** J S BROCKBANK
ARRETON (St George) *Portsm 7* **P** *Bp* **V** P H FORD
ARRINGTON (St Nicholas) *see* Orwell Gp *Ely*
ARROW (Holy Trinity) *see* Alcester and Arrow w Oversley and Weethley *Cov*
ARTHINGTON (St Peter) *see* Lower Wharfedale *Ripon*
ARTHINGWORTH (St Andrew) and Harrington w Oxendon and East Farndon *Pet 2* **P** *St Jo Coll Ox (2 turns), E G Nugee Esq (2 turns), and Bp (1 turn)* **R** *vacant*
ARTHURET (St Michael and All Angels) *Carl 2* **P** *Sir James Graham Bt* **P-in-c** E C ROBINSON
ARUNDEL (St Nicholas) w Tortington and South Stoke *Chich 1* **P** *Bp (2 turns), Duke of Norfolk (1 turn)* **V** K D RICHARDS, **NSM** A-M CROSSE
ASBY (St Peter) *Carl 1* **P** *Bp* **P-in-c** D C WOOD
ASCENSION Team Ministry, The *Leic 1* **P** *Patr Bd* **TR** G J JOHNSON, **TV** V J JUPP
ASCOT, NORTH (St Mary and St John) *see* Ascot Heath *Ox*
ASCOT, SOUTH (All Souls) *Ox 11* **P** *Bp* **V** D S JONES, **NSM** S J JONES
ASCOT HEATH (All Saints) *Ox 11* **P** *Bp* **P-in-c** A P LURY, **C** L J TRAINOR, **NSM** G H WIGGINS, A B COOPER
ASCOTT UNDER WYCHWOOD (Holy Trinity) *Ox 3* **P** *Bp* **P-in-c** M E J ABREY **Hon C** M B CRAMERI
ASFORDBY (All Saints) *see* Ab Kettleby and Holwell w Asfordby *Leic*
ASGARBY (St Andrew) *see* Kirkby Laythorpe *Linc*
ASH (Christ Church) *see* Adderley, Ash, Calverhall, Ightfield etc *Lich*
ASH (Holy Trinity) *see* Martock w Ash *B & W*
ASH (St Nicholas) w Westmarsh *Cant 1* **P** *Abp* **V** J SWEATMAN
ASH (St Peter) *Guildf 1* **P** *Win Coll* **R** K R M BRISTOW
ASH (St Peter and St Paul) *Roch 1* **P** *J R A B Scott Esq* **R** J A PEAL
ASH (Thomas Chapel) *see* Sampford Peverell, Uplowman, Holcombe Rogus etc *Ex*

ASH PRIORS (Holy Trinity) *see* Lydeard St Lawrence w Brompton Ralph etc *B & W*
ASH VALE (St Mary) *Guildf 1* **P** *Bp* **P-in-c** C M BRENNAND, **NSM** S M R CUMMING-LATTEY
ASHAMPSTEAD (St Clement) *see* Basildon w Aldworth and Ashampstead *Ox*
ASHBOCKING (All Saints) *see* Clopton w Otley, Swilland and Ashbocking *St E*
ASHBOURNE (St John the Baptist) *Derby 8* **P** *Wright Trustees* **V** *vacant*
ASHBOURNE (St Oswald) w Mapleton *Derby 8* **P** *Bp* **C** J M WHITE
ASHBRITTLE (St John the Baptist) *see* Wellington and Distr *B & W*
ASHBURNHAM (St Peter) w Penhurst *Chich 14* **P** *Ashburnham Chr Trust* **P-in-c** S R TALBOT, **NSM** A D WOODING JONES
ASHBURTON (St Andrew) w Buckland in the Moor and Bickington *Ex 9* **P** *D&C* **V** P W DARBY
ASHBURY (St Mary the Virgin) *see* Shrivenham and Ashbury *Ox*
ASHBY (St Catherine) *see* Bottesford w Ashby *Linc*
ASHBY (St Mary) *see* Somerleyton, Ashby, Fritton, Herringfleet etc *Nor*
ASHBY (St Mary) *see* Thurton *Nor*
ASHBY (St Paul) *see* Bottesford w Ashby *Linc*
ASHBY, WEST (All Saints) *see* Hemingby *Linc*
ASHBY-BY-PARTNEY (St Helen) *see* Partney Gp *Linc*
ASHBY-CUM-FENBY (St Peter) *see* Laceby and Ravendale Gp *Linc*
ASHBY DE LA LAUNDE (St Hibald) *see* Digby Gp *Linc*
ASHBY-DE-LA-ZOUCH (Holy Trinity) (St Helen) and Breedon on the Hill *Leic 9* **P** *Patr Bd* **TR** B A ROBERTSON, **TV** T L PHILLIPS, **C** D S TYLER, **NSM** J W A DAWSON, D FLOWER
ASHBY FOLVILLE (St Mary) *see* S Croxton Gp *Leic*
ASHBY MAGNA (St Mary) *see* Willoughby Waterleys, Peatling Magna etc *Leic*
ASHBY PARVA (St Peter) *see* Leire w Ashby Parva and Dunton Bassett *Leic*
ASHBY PUERORUM (St Andrew) *see* Greetham w Ashby Puerorum *Linc*
ASHBY ST LEDGERS (St Mary) *see* Daventry, Ashby St Ledgers, Braunston etc *Pet*
ASHCHURCH (St Nicholas) *Glouc 15* **P** *K Storey Esq* **R** R E ROBERTS
ASHCOMBE (St Nectan) *see* Teignmouth, Ideford w Luton, Ashcombe etc *Ex*
ASHCOTT (All Saints) *see* Shapwick w Ashcott and Burtle *B & W*
ASHDON (All Saints) *see* Saffron Walden w Wendens Ambo, Littlebury etc *Chelmsf*
ASHE (Holy Trinity and St Andrew) *see* N Waltham and Steventon, Ashe and Deane *Win*
ASHEN (St Augustine) *see* Ridgewell w Ashen, Birdbrook and Sturmer *Chelmsf*
ASHENDON (St Mary) *see* Bernwode *Ox*
ASHFIELD, GREAT (All Saints) *see* Badwell and Walsham *St E*
ASHFIELD CUM THORPE (St Mary) *see* Earl Soham w Cretingham and Ashfield *St E*
ASHFORD (St Hilda) *Lon 13* **P** *Bp* **V** C A ROGERS
ASHFORD (St Mary the Virgin) *Cant 10* **P** *Abp* **P-in-c** C G PREECE, **C** R F KENYON
ASHFORD (St Matthew) *Lon 13* **P** *Ld Chan* **V** R E HORTON
ASHFORD (St Peter) *see* Barnstaple *Ex*
ASHFORD, SOUTH (Christ Church) *Cant 10* **P** *Abp* **P-in-c** A D KIRKWOOD
ASHFORD, SOUTH (St Francis of Assisi) *Cant 10* **P** *Abp* **P-in-c** I L GARRETT, **NSM** C J GARRETT
ASHFORD BOWDLER (St Andrew) *see* Ludlow, Ludford, Ashford Carbonell etc *Heref*
ASHFORD CARBONELL (St Mary) *as above*
ASHFORD COMMON (St Benedict) *see* Upper Sunbury St Sav *Lon*
ASHFORD HILL (St Paul) w Headley *Win 6* **P** *V Kingsclere* **P-in-c** P E WILSON
ASHFORD IN THE WATER (Holy Trinity) w Sheldon and Great Longstone *Derby 2* **P** *V Bakewell* **V** C A THROWER
ASHILL (Blessed Virgin Mary) *see* Ilminster and Distr *B & W*
ASHILL (St Nicholas) w Saham Toney *Nor 13* **P** *Bp and New Coll Ox (alt)* **P-in-c** J E ATKINS
ASHILL (St Stephen) *see* Cullompton, Willand, Uffculme, Kentisbeare etc *Ex*
ASHINGDON (St Andrew) w South Fambridge *Chelmsf 12* **P** *CCC Cam* **P-in-c** T F CLAY, **NSM** S ADAMS
ASHINGTON (Holy Sepulchre) *Newc 11* **P** *Bp* **V** E J NOBLE, **NSM** L BEADLE
ASHINGTON (St Matthew) *see* Canford Magna *Sarum*
ASHINGTON (St Peter and St Paul), Washington and Wiston w Buncton *Chich 12* **P** *Bp and R H Goring Esq (alt)* **R** *vacant* (01903) 893878
ASHINGTON (St Vincent) *see* Chilton Cantelo, Ashington, Mudford, Rimpton etc *B & W*
ASHLEWORTH (St Bartholomew) *see* Hasfield w Tirley and Ashleworth *Glouc*
ASHLEY (St Elizabeth) *see* Hale and Ashley *Ches*
ASHLEY (St James), Crudwell, Hankerton, Long Newnton and Oaksey *Bris 6* **P** *Trustees* **R** B RAVEN
ASHLEY (St John the Baptist) and Mucklestone *Lich 7* **P** *Meynell Ch Trustees and Mrs F F Friend (jt)* **R** D J WILLIAMS
ASHLEY (St Mary the Virgin) *see* Stoke Albany w Wilbarston and Ashley etc *Pet*
ASHLEY (St Mary) w Silverley *Ely 4* **P** *Bp and DBP (alt)* **R** C A SINDALL, **Hon C** L M BROUGHTON
ASHLEY (St Peter) *see* Milton *Win*
ASHLEY (St Peter and St Paul) *see* Somborne w Ashley *Win*
ASHLEY GREEN (St John the Evangelist) *see* Gt Chesham *Ox*
ASHMANHAUGH (St Swithin), Barton Turf, Beeston St Laurence, Horning, Irstead and Neatishead *Nor 12* **P** *Bp and Sir Ronald Preston Bt (jt)* **R** S A ELLISON, **NSM** J S PEEL
ASHMANSWORTH (St James) *see* Highclere and Ashmansworth w Crux Easton *Win*
ASHMORE (St Nicholas) *see* Iwerne Valley *Sarum*
ASHMORE PARK (St Alban) *see* Wednesfield *Lich*
ASHOVER (All Saints) and Brackenfield w Wessington *Derby 5* **P** *Exors Revd J J C Nodder, Duke of Devonshire, V Crich and S Wingfield, and DBF (jt)* **R** R G LAWRENCE, **NSM** R SMITH
ASHOW (Assumption of Our Lady) *see* Stoneleigh w Ashow *Cov*
ASHPERTON (St Bartholomew) *see* Ledbury *Heref*
ASHPRINGTON (St David) *see* Totnes w Bridgetown, Berry Pomeroy etc *Ex*
ASHREIGNEY (St James) *Ex 20* **P** *DBP* **R** P J NORMAN
ASHTEAD (St George) (St Giles) *Guildf 10* **P** *Bp* **R** R J KITELEY, **C** J R JONES, S J F THOMAS, **OLM** P R DAWSON, R M N HOOKER, J M WATTS
ASHTON (Annunciation) *see* Breage w Germoe and Godolphin *Truro*
ASHTON (Holy Trinity) (St James) (St Michael and All Angels) (St Gabriel) (Queen Victoria Memorial Church) *Man 17* **P** *Patr Bd* **TR** R FARNWORTH, **TV** H T NICOL, J H FARNWORTH, A S MITCHELL
ASHTON (St John the Baptist) *see* Christow, Ashton and Bridford *Ex*
ASHTON (St Michael and All Angels) *see* Roade and Ashton w Hartwell *Pet*
ASHTON, WEST (St John) *see* Trowbridge St Thos and W Ashton *Sarum*
ASHTON GATE (St Francis) *see* Bedminster *Bris*
ASHTON HAYES (St John the Evangelist) *Ches 2* **P** *Keble Coll Ox* **P-in-c** B R K PERKES
ASHTON-IN-MAKERFIELD (Holy Trinity) *Liv 15* **P** *Bp* **R** D R ABBOTT
ASHTON-IN-MAKERFIELD (St Thomas) *Liv 15* **P** *R Ashton-in-Makerfield H Trin* **V** M E GREENWOOD, **C** D A HAYES
ASHTON KEYNES (Holy Cross), Leigh and Minety *Bris 6* **P** *Bp* **V** P E H SELLEY
ASHTON-ON-RIBBLE (St Andrew) *Blackb 13* **P** *Trustees* **V** C J ENTWISTLE
ASHTON-ON-RIBBLE (St Michael and All Angels) w Preston St Mark *Blackb 13* **P** *Bp* **P-in-c** R W BUNDAY, **OLM** D L CAREY
ASHTON UNDER HILL (St Barbara) *see* Overbury w Teddington, Alstone etc *Worc*
ASHTON-UNDER-LYNE (Christ Church) *Man 17* **P** *Bp* **V** J S HOLLAND, **C** N G SMEETON, E A JUMP
ASHTON-UNDER-LYNE (St Peter) *Man 17* **P** *R Ashton-under-Lyne St Mich* **P-in-c** H T NICOL
ASHTON-UPON-MERSEY (St Martin) *Ches 10* **P** *SMF* **R** R J E CLACK, **NSM** D R LAW
ASHTON-UPON-MERSEY (St Mary Magdalene) *Ches 10* **P** *Trustees* **V** G J SKINNER, **C** J D SHARPLES, S B RANKIN
ASHURST (St James) *Chich 12* **P** *MMCET* **R** P M RAMPTON
ASHURST (St Martin of Tours) *see* Speldhurst w Groombridge and Ashurst *Roch*
ASHURST WOOD (St Dunstan) *see* Forest Row *Chich*

ASHWATER (St Peter ad Vincula), Halwill, Beaworthy, Clawton and Tetcott w Luffincott *Ex 17* **P** *Ld Chan (1 turn), Major L J Melhuish, Lt-Col Sir John Molesworth-St Aubyn Bt, and Bp (jt) (2 turns)* **R** D K MAY
ASHWELL (St Mary) *see* Cottesmore and Barrow w Ashwell and Burley *Pet*
ASHWELL (St Mary the Virgin) w Hinxworth and Newnham *St Alb 19* **P** *Bp, R Smyth Esq, and N J A Farr Esq (jt) (1 turn), Bp (3 turns)* **R** *vacant* (01462) 742277
ASHWELLTHORPE (All Saints), Forncett, Fundenhall, Hapton, Tacolneston and Wreningham *Nor 7* **P** *Bp, Keble Coll Ox, Ch Coll Cam, and MMCET (by turn)* **V** C W J STYLES
ASHWICK (St James) w Oakhill and Binegar *B & W 8* **P** *Bp* **P-in-c** R W WIDDOWSON
ASHWICKEN (All Saints) *see* Gayton, Gayton Thorpe, E Walton, E Winch etc *Nor*
ASHWORTH (St James) *see* Norden w Ashworth *Man*
ASKAM (Church Centre) *see* Dalton-in-Furness and Ireleth-with-Askam *Carl*
ASKAM (St Peter) *as above*
ASKERN (St Peter) *Sheff 7* **P** *Bp* **V** M WIGGLESWORTH
ASKERSWELL (St Michael), Loders and Powerstock *Sarum 2* **P** *Ld Chan, Lady Laskey, Bp, and D&C (by turn)* **P-in-c** M N A JONES
ASKHAM (St Nicholas) *see* E Markham w Askham, Headon w Upton and Grove *S'well*
ASKHAM (St Peter) *see* Lowther and Askham and Clifton and Brougham *Carl*
ASKHAM BRYAN (St Nicholas) *York 1* **P** *Abp* **P-in-c** D S COOK
ASKHAM RICHARD (St Mary) *see* Healaugh w Wighill, Bilbrough and Askham Richard *York*
ASKRIGG (St Oswald) w Stallingbusk *Ripon 4* **P** *V Aysgarth* **P-in-c** A B CHAPMAN
ASLACKBY (St James) *see* Billingborough Gp *Linc*
ASLACTON (St Michael) *see* Bunwell, Carleton Rode, Tibenham, Gt Moulton etc *Nor*
ASLOCKTON (St Thomas) *see* Whatton w Aslockton, Hawksworth, Scarrington etc *S'well*
ASPALL (St Mary of Grace) *see* Debenham and Helmingham *St E*
ASPATRIA (St Kentigern) w Hayton and Gilcrux *Carl 7* **P** *Bp* **V** M MCBRIDE
ASPENDEN (St Mary), Buntingford and Westmill *St Alb 19* **P** *CPAS, MCET, and K Coll Lon (jt)* **R** N J RICHARDS, **NSM** G HOWDLE
ASPLEY (St Margaret) *S'well 14* **P** *Trustees* **P-in-c** J G HUTCHINSON
ASPLEY GUISE (St Botolph) w Husborne Crawley and Ridgmont *St Alb 9* **P** *Ld Chan (1 turn), Trustees Bedf Estates (1 turn), and Bp (2 turns)* **R** G BRADSHAW
ASPULL (St Elizabeth) *Liv 14* **P** *Trustees* **P-in-c** N K YOUNG, **OLM** M L PERRIN
ASSINGTON (St Edmund) *see* Bures w Assington and Lt Cornard *St E*
ASTBURY (St Mary) and Smallwood *Ches 11* **P** *Sir Richard Baker Wilbraham Bt* **R** J C CUTTELL, **C** R J KEMP
ASTERBY Group, The *Linc 11* **P** *Bp, DBP, J N Heneage Esq, F Smith Esq, and Mrs J Fox (jt)* **R** I D MCGRATH
ASTHALL (St Nicholas) *see* Burford w Fulbrook, Taynton, Asthall etc *Ox*
ASTLEY (St Mary the Virgin) *see* Chilvers Coton w Astley *Cov*
ASTLEY (St Mary), Clive, Grinshill and Hadnall *Lich 22* **P** *D R B Thompson Esq* **P-in-c** R R HAARHOFF
ASTLEY (St Peter) *see* Shrawley, Witley, Astley and Abberley *Worc*
ASTLEY (St Stephen) *Man 13* **P** *V Leigh St Mary* **P-in-c** R J CARMYLLIE, **OLM** A J DAND
ASTLEY ABBOTTS (St Calixtus) *see* Bridgnorth, Tasley, Astley Abbotts, etc *Heref*
ASTLEY BRIDGE (St Paul) *Man 16* **P** *The Crown* **V** A J LINDOP, **C** M A FRASER
ASTON (St Giles) *see* Wigmore Abbey *Heref*
ASTON (St Mary) *see* Woore and Norton in Hales *Lich*
ASTON (St Mary) *see* Stevenage St Mary Shephall w Aston *St Alb*
ASTON (St Peter) *see* Antrobus, Aston by Sutton, Lt Leigh etc *Ches*
ASTON (St Saviour) *see* Stone St Mich and St Wulfad w Aston St Sav *Lich*
ASTON, LITTLE (St Peter) *Lich 1* **P** *Patr Bd* **V** P MOON
ASTON, NORTH (St Mary the Virgin) *see* Steeple Aston w N Aston and Tackley *Ox*
ASTON ABBOTS (St James the Great) *see* Wingrave w Rowsham, Aston Abbotts and Cublington *Ox*
ASTON BOTTERELL (St Michael and All Angels) *see* Ditton Priors w Neenton, Burwarton etc *Heref*
ASTON CANTLOW (St John the Baptist) and Wilmcote w Billesley *Cov 7* **P** *SMF* **P-in-c** D B ADDLEY
ASTON CLINTON (St Michael and All Angels) w Buckland and Drayton Beauchamp *Ox 28* **P** *Exors Major S W Jenney, Jes Coll Ox, and Bp (by turn)* **R** A W BENNETT, **C** E J MOXLEY
ASTON CUM AUGHTON (All Saints) w Swallownest and Ulley *Sheff 5* **P** *Bp* **TV** J M HOFFMANN, **C** J D PARKER
ASTON EYRE (not known) *see* Morville w Aston Eyre *Heref*
ASTON FLAMVILLE (St Peter) *see* Burbage w Aston Flamville *Leic*
ASTON INGHAM (St John the Baptist) *see* Ross *Heref*
ASTON JUXTA BIRMINGHAM (St James) *Birm 8* **P** *V Aston* **V** *vacant* 0121-327 3230
ASTON JUXTA BIRMINGHAM (St Peter and St Paul) *Birm 8* **P** *Aston Trustees* **V** A J JOLLEY, **C** J A ARNOLD
ASTON LE WALLS (St Leonard) *see* Byfield w Boddington and Aston le Walls *Pet*
ASTON ON TRENT (All Saints), Elvaston, Weston on Trent and Shardlow *Derby 15* **P** *Bp, Earl of Harrington, and DBP (by turn)* **R** A LUKE
ASTON ROWANT (St Peter and St Paul) *see* Chinnor, Sydenham, Aston Rowant and Crowell *Ox*
ASTON SANDFORD (St Michael and All Angels) *see* Haddenham w Cuddington, Kingsey etc *Ox*
ASTON SOMERVILLE (St Mary) *see* Winchcombe *Glouc*
ASTON-SUB-EDGE (St Andrew) *see* Mickleton, Willersey, Saintbury etc *Glouc*
ASTON TIRROLD (St Michael) *see* S w N Moreton, Aston Tirrold and Aston Upthorpe *Ox*
ASTON UPTHORPE (All Saints) *as above*
ASTWELL Group of Parishes, The *Pet 1* **P** *Bp, Worc Coll Ox, Ox Univ, Mert Coll Ox, DBP, and Jes Coll Ox (jt)* **R** W T ADAMS, **NSM** D E MICKLETHWAITE
ASTWICK (St Guthlac) *see* Arlesey w Astwick *St Alb*
ASTWOOD (St Peter) *see* Sherington w Chicheley, N Crawley, Astwood etc *Ox*
ASTWOOD BANK (St Matthias and St George) *see* Redditch Ch the K *Worc*
ASWARBY (St Denys) *see* S Lafford *Linc*
ASWARDBY (St Helen) *see* Partney Gp *Linc*
ATCHAM (St Eata) *see* Shrewsbury St Giles w Sutton and Atcham *Lich*
ATHELINGTON (St Peter) *see* Stradbroke, Horham, Athelington and Redlingfield *St E*
ATHERINGTON (St Mary) *see* Newton Tracey, Horwood, Alverdiscott etc *Ex*
ATHERSLEY (St Helen) *Wakef 7* **P** *Bp* **V** R H MARSHALL, **C** L BENNETT, **OLM** J M CROSSLAND
ATHERSTONE (St Mary) *Cov 5* **P** *V Mancetter* **V** P I HARRIS
ATHERTON (St John the Baptist) (St George) (St Philip) and Hindsford w Howe Bridge *Man 13* **P** *DBP* **TR** R W BUCKLEY, **TV** W BALDWIN, K BAINES, **C** A STANTON, **OLM** D SIMPSON
ATLOW (St Philip and St James) *see* Hulland, Atlow, Kniveton, Bradley and Hognaston *Derby*
ATTENBOROUGH (St Mary the Virgin) *S'well 7* **P** *CPAS* **P-in-c** S M HEMSLEY HALLS, **NSM** J P SMITHURST
ATTERCLIFFE (Hill Top Chapel) *see* Nine o'Clock Community *Sheff*
ATTERCLIFFE (St Alban) and Darnall *Sheff 1* **P** *Bp, Dean Sheff, and Sheff Ch Burgesses Trust (jt)* **V** M L FUDGER
ATTLEBOROUGH (Assumption of the Blessed Virgin Mary) w Besthorpe *Nor 11* **P** *CR and Mrs S P J Scully (jt)* **R** M AISBITT, **OLM** J I MAY
ATTLEBOROUGH (Holy Trinity) *Cov 5* **P** *V Nuneaton* **V** C JONES
ATTLEBRIDGE (St Andrew) *see* Wensum Benefice *Nor*
ATWICK (St Lawrence) *see* Hornsea w Atwick *York*
ATWORTH (St Michael and All Angels) w Shaw and Whitley *Sarum 14* **P** *D&C Bris and R Melksham (alt)* **P-in-c** G R J FORCE-JONES
AUBOURN (St Peter) *see* Bassingham Gp *Linc*
AUCKLAND (St Andrew) (St Anne) *Dur 6* **P** *Bp* **V** N P VINE, **C** K M BROOKE
AUCKLAND (St Helen) *Dur 6* **P** *Bp* **V** R I MCTEER
AUCKLAND (St Peter) *Dur 6* **P** *The Crown* **V** P K LEE
AUCKLEY (St Saviour) *see* Finningley w Auckley *S'well*
AUDENSHAW (St Hilda) *Man 17* **P** *Bp* **V** J H KERSHAW
AUDENSHAW (St Stephen) *Man 17* **P** *Bp* **V** P R DIXON
AUDLEM (St James the Great) *Ches 15* **P** *Bp* **P-in-c** H F CHANTRY
AUDLEY (St James the Great) *Lich 9* **P** *Ch Soc Trust* **V** P T W DAVIES, **C** J R OAKLEY

AUGHTON (All Saints) *see* Bubwith w Skipwith *York*
AUGHTON (Christ Church) *Liv 11* **P** *R Aughton St Mich* **V** R MOUGHTIN, **C** M S FOLLIN
AUGHTON (St Michael) *Liv 11* **P** *Bp* **R** M P ADAMS
AUGHTON (St Saviour) *see* Halton w Aughton *Blackb*
AUKBOROUGH (St John the Baptist) *see* Alkborough *Linc*
AUKBOROUGH (St John the Baptist) *as above*
AULT HUCKNALL (St John the Baptist) and Scarcliffe *Derby 3* **P** *Bp and Duke of Devonshire (alt)* **V** A L BELL
AUNSBY (St Thomas of Canterbury) *see* S Lafford *Linc*
AUST (not known) *see* Almondsbury and Olveston *Bris*
AUSTERFIELD (St Helen) *see* Bawtry w Austerfield and Misson *S'well*
AUSTREY (St Nicholas) and Warton (Holy Trinity) *Birm 10* **P** *Ld Chan and V Polesworth St Editha (alt)* **P-in-c** S J BANKS, **C** A E MANN
AUSTWICK (Epiphany) *see* Clapham-with-Keasden and Austwick *Bradf*
AVEBURY (St James) *see* Upper Kennet *Sarum*
AVELEY (St Michael) and Purfleet *Chelmsf 14* **P** *Bp* **P-in-c** V J ROCKALL, **C** A J HUDSON
AVENING (Holy Cross) w Cherington *Glouc 11* **P** *E A Tarlton Esq (1 turn), D&C (2 turns)* **NSM** C CARTER
AVERHAM (St Michael and All Angels) w Kelham *S'well 3* **P** *DBP* **R** *vacant*
AVETON GIFFORD (St Andrew) *see* Modbury, Bigbury, Ringmore w Kingston etc *Ex*
AVINGTON (St Mary) *see* Itchen Valley *Win*
AVON DASSETT (St Peter and St Clare) w Farnborough and Fenny Compton *Cov 8* **P** *G V L Holbech Esq and Mrs A D Seyfried (jt), CCC Ox, and Bp(alt)* **R** D P PYM
AVON-SWIFT Group *see* Gilmorton, Peatling Parva, Kimcote etc *Leic*
AVON VALLEY *Sarum 13* **P** *Bp (3 turns), MOD (2 turns), and Ch Hosp (1 turn)* **P-in-c** C G FOX
AVONMOUTH (St Andrew) *see* Lawrence Weston and Avonmouth *Bris*
AWBRIDGE (All Saints) *see* Michelmersh and Awbridge and Braishfield etc *Win*
AWLISCOMBE (St Michael and All Angels) *see* Honiton, Gittisham, Combe Raleigh, Monkton etc *Ex*
AWRE (St Andrew) *see* Newnham w Awre and Blakeney *Glouc*
AWSWORTH (St Peter) *see* Trowell, Awsworth and Cossall *S'well*
AXBRIDGE (St John the Baptist) w Shipham and Rowberrow *B & W 1* **P** *Bp and D&C (alt)* **NSM** P R ROGERS
AXFORD (St Michael) *see* Whitton *Sarum*
AXMINSTER (St Mary), Chardstock, All Saints, Combpyne w Rousdon and Membury *Ex 5* **P** *Bp* **TR** J H GOOD
AXMOUTH (St Michael) *see* Uplyme w Axmouth *Ex*
AYCLIFFE (Church Centre) *see* Dover St Mary *Cant*
AYCLIFFE, GREAT (St Andrew) (St Clare) and Chilton *Dur 5* **P** *Patr Bd* **TR** L POTTER, **TV** R C DAVIES, **C** M E ANDERSON
AYLBURTON (St Mary) *see* Woolaston w Alvington and Aylburton *Glouc*
AYLBURTON COMMON (Mission Church) *see* Lydney *Glouc*
AYLESBEARE (Blessed Virgin Mary), Rockbeare, Farringdon, Clyst Honiton and Sowton *Ex 1* **P** *Bp and D&C (jt)* **V** *vacant* (01404) 822569
AYLESBURY (Holy Trinity) *see* Walton H Trin *Ox*
AYLESBURY (St Mary the Virgin) w Bierton and Hulcott *Ox 21* **P** *Bp and Patr Bd (jt)* **TR** T J HIGGINS
AYLESBY (St Lawrence) *see* Keelby Gp *Linc*
AYLESFORD (St Peter and St Paul) *Roch 7* **P** *D&C* **V** S C TILLOTSON, **NSM** C M HAYDON
AYLESHAM (St Peter) w Adisham *Cant 1* **P** *Abp* **P-in-c** A P SADLER, **Hon C** H D CONNOLL, **NSM** D N J HALE
AYLESTONE (St Andrew) w St James *Leic 2* **P** *Bp* **R** A RACE
AYLESTONE PARK (Church of the Nativity) Conventional District *Leic 2* **NSM** A T HELM
AYLMERTON (St John the Baptist); Runton; Beeston Regis; Gresham *Nor 21* **P** *Bp and Guild of All So (2 turns), Duchy of Lanc (1 turn)* **R** S J HOTCHEN
AYLSHAM (St Michael) *Nor 19* **P** *D&C Cant* **V** R D BRANSON, **NSM** P A YOUNG
AYLTON (not known) *see* Ledbury *Heref*
AYMESTREY (St John the Baptist and St Alkmund) *see* Kingsland w Eardisland, Aymestrey etc *Heref*
AYNHO (St Michael) and Croughton w Evenley and Farthinghoe and Hinton-in-the-Hedges w Steane *Pet 1* **P** *Bp (2 turns), Mrs E A J Cartwright-Hignett (1 turn), Magd Coll Ox (1 turn), and Ld Chan (1 turn)* **R** P A M GOMPERTZ
AYOT ST LAWRENCE (St Lawrence) *see* Kimpton w Ayot St Lawrence *St Alb*
AYOT ST PETER (St Peter) *see* Welwyn *St Alb*
AYSGARTH (St Andrew) and Bolton cum Redmire *Ripon 4* **P** *R Wensley and Trin Coll Cam (jt)* **V** S C WHITEHOUSE, **C** M RIMMER, **Hon C** J H RICHARDSON
AYSTON (St Mary the Virgin) *see* Uppingham w Ayston and Wardley w Belton *Pet*
AYTHORPE RODING (St Mary) *see* Gt Canfield w High Roding and Aythorpe Roding *Chelmsf*
AYTON, EAST (St John the Baptist) *York 15* **P** *Abp* **P-in-c** R C WALSER
AYTON, GREAT (All Saints) (Christ Church) w Easby and Newton in Cleveland *York 21* **P** *Abp* **V** P H PEVERELL, **NSM** G S JAQUES
BABBACOMBE (All Saints) *Ex 12* **P** *V St Marychurch* **P-in-c** S N WAKELY
BABCARY (Holy Cross) *see* Six Pilgrims *B & W*
BABRAHAM (St Peter) *Ely 6* **P** *H R T Adeane Esq* **P-in-c** G KENDALL
BABWORTH (All Saints) w Sutton-cum-Lound and Scofton w Osberton *S'well 5* **P** *Bp, G M T Foljambe Esq, and Sir John Whitaker Bt (jt)* **R** H R SMITH
BACKFORD (St Oswald) and Capenhurst *Ches 9* **P** *Bp* **R** S M SOUTHGATE
BACKWELL (St Andrew) w Chelvey and Brockley *B & W 13* **P** *DBP* **R** S J HILL, **C** P A OLLIVE
BACKWORTH (St John) *see* Earsdon and Backworth *Newc*
BACONSTHORPE (St Mary) *see* Barningham w Matlaske w Baconsthorpe etc *Nor*
BACTON (St Andrew) w Edingthorpe w Witton and Ridlington *Nor 12* **P** *Duchy of Lanc (1 turn), Bp and Earl of Kimberley (1 turn)* **C** S D EARIS, R A HINES, **OLM** R M SEEL
BACTON (St Faith) *see* Ewyas Harold w Dulas, Kenderchurch etc *Heref*
BACTON (St Mary the Virgin) w Wyverstone, Cotton and Old Newton, and Wickham Skeith *St E 6* **P** *Patr Bd (2 turns), Ld Chan (1 turn)* **R** R W JACK
BACUP (Christ Church) (St John the Evangelist) (St Saviour) and Stacksteads *Man 15* **P** *Patr Bd* **V** G WHITTAKER, **NSM** P S J HEDWORTH, **OLM** D ALLEN
BADBY (St Mary) w Newham and Charwelton w Fawsley and Preston Capes *Pet 3* **P** *Bp* **R** M D PETITT
BADDESLEY, NORTH (All Saints' Mission Church) *see* Chilworth w N Baddesley *Win*
BADDESLEY, NORTH (St John the Baptist) *as above*
BADDESLEY, SOUTH (St Mary the Virgin) *see* Boldre w S Baddesley *Win*
BADDESLEY CLINTON (St Michael) *Birm 6* **P** *T W Ferrers-Walker Esq* **R** M J MORGAN
BADDESLEY ENSOR (St Nicholas) w Grendon *Birm 10* **P** *Bp, V Polesworth, and PCC (jt)* **V** K HODSON
BADDILEY (St Michael) and Wrenbury w Burleydam *Ches 15* **P** *V Acton and Bp (alt)* **V** P J PARRY, **NSM** R M HARRISON
BADDOW, GREAT (Meadgate Church Centre) (St Mary the Virgin) (St Paul) *Chelmsf 9* **P** *Patr Bd* **TR** A D MCGREGOR, **TV** M A FARAH, T V ROBERTS, **Hon C** R C MATTHEWS, **NSM** P F ROBERTS, G R HAMBORG
BADDOW, LITTLE (St Mary the Virgin) *Chelmsf 9* **P** *Bp* **Hon C** C A MCCAFFERTY
BADGER (St Giles) *see* Beckbury, Badger, Kemberton, Ryton, Stockton etc *Lich*
BADGEWORTH (Holy Trinity), Shurdington and Witcombe w Bentham *Glouc 6* **P** *Bp and F D Hicks Beach Esq (jt)* **P-in-c** R J A MITCHELL, **NSM** M A WILESMITH, **OLM** M J THOMPSON
BADGWORTH (St Congar) *see* Crook Peak *B & W*
BADINGHAM (St John the Baptist) w Bruisyard, Cransford and Dennington w Rendham and Sweffling *St E 18* **P** *R C Rous Esq, DBP, and CPAS (jt)* **R** J P T OLANCZUK
BADLESMERE (St Leonard) *see* Selling w Throwley, Sheldwich w Badlesmere etc *Cant*
BADMINTON (St Michael and All Angels) *see* Boxwell, Leighterton, Didmarton, Oldbury etc *Glouc*
BADMINTON, LITTLE (St Michael and All Angels) *as above*
BADSEY (St James) w Aldington and Offenham and Bretforton *Worc 1* **P** *Bp and Ch Ch Ox (jt)* **V** R L COURT
BADSHOT LEA (St George) *see* Hale w Badshot Lea *Guildf*
BADSWORTH (St Mary the Virgin) *Wakef 11* **P** *DBP* **R** D MATHERS
BADWELL (St Mary) and Walsham *St E 9* **P** *Bp, DBP, R M Martineau Esq, and Soc of the Faith (jt)* **R** M G CLARKE
BAG ENDERBY (St Margaret) *see* S Ormsby Gp *Linc*
BAGBOROUGH (St Pancras) *see* Bishops Lydeard w Bagborough and Cothelstone *B & W*
BAGBY (St Mary) *see* Thirkleby w Kilburn and Bagby *York*

BAGENDON (St Margaret) *see* Stratton, N Cerney, Baunton and Bagendon *Glouc*
BAGINTON (St John the Baptist) w Bubbenhall and Ryton-on-Dunsmore *Cov 6* **P** *D&C (2 turns), Bp (1 turn), Lord Leigh and Bp (1 turn)* **P-in-c** D R WINTLE
BAGNALL (St Chad) w Endon *Lich 8* **P** *R Leek and Meerbrook and A D Owen Esq (jt)* **V** A J BETTS
BAGSHOT (Good Shepherd) *see* Savernake *Sarum*
BAGSHOT (St Anne) *Guildf 6* **P** *Ld Chan* **V** S F BRIAN
BAGULEY (St John the Divine) Brooklands *Man 8* **P** *Bp and A W Hargreaves Esq (jt)* **V** I MCVEETY, **NSM** E SHORT
BAGWORTH (The Holy Rood) *see* Markfield, Thornton, Bagworth and Stanton etc *Leic*
BAILDON (St John the Evangelist) (St Hugh Mission Church) (St James) *Bradf 1* **P** *S H K Butcher Esq* **V** J D NOWELL, **C** J M WATERMAN, **NSM** K N MEDHURST
BAINTON (St Andrew) *see* Woldsburn *York*
BAINTON (St Mary) *see* Barnack w Ufford and Bainton *Pet*
BAKEWELL (All Saints) *Derby 2* **P** *D&C Lich* **V** E R URQUHART, **NSM** L E ELLSWORTH
BALBY (St John the Evangelist) *Sheff 9* **P** *Bp* **V** B J INSTON
BALCOMBE (St Mary) *Chich 6* **P** *P A D Secretan Esq* **R** M S MALKINSON
BALDERSBY (St James) *see* Topcliffe, Baldersby w Dishforth, Dalton etc *York*
BALDERSTONE (St Leonard) *Blackb 7* **P** *V Blackb* **P-in-c** J R GARRARD
BALDERSTONE (St Mary) *see* S Rochdale *Man*
BALDERTON (St Giles) and Barnby-in-the-Willows *S'well 3* **P** *Bp and Ld Chan (alt)* **V** A I TUCKER, **C** D C NJUGUNA
BALDHU (St Michael) *see* Highertown and Baldhu *Truro*
BALDOCK (St Mary the Virgin) w Bygrave and Weston *St Alb 19* **P** *Patr Bd* **TR** A P HOLFORD, **TV** S TETZLAFF
BALDWIN (St Luke) *see* Marown *S & M*
BALE (All Saints) *see* Stiffkey and Bale *Nor*
BALHAM (St Mary and St John the Divine) *S'wark 19* **P** *Bp and Keble Coll Ox (jt)* **V** D A NICHOLSON, **NSM** K W BISHOP, **OLM** R E SERBUTT
BALHAM HILL (Ascension) *S'wark 19* **P** *Bp* **V** S J HANCE, **C** N J GROARKE, **NSM** D V PENNIECOOKE
BALKWELL (St Peter) *Newc 8* **P** *Bp* **V** *vacant* 0191-257 0952 *or* 258 3380
BALLAM (St Matthew) *see* Ribby cum Wrea and Weeton *Blackb*
BALLAUGH (St Mary) (St Mary Old Church) *S & M 3* **P** *The Crown* **R** C D ROGERS
BALLIDON (All Saints) *see* Wirksworth *Derby*
BALLINGER (St Mary Mission Hall) *see* Gt Missenden w Ballinger and Lt Hampden *Ox*
BALLINGHAM (St Dubricius) *see* Heref S Wye *Heref*
BALSALL COMMON (St Peter) *Birm 11* **P** *Bp* **V** *vacant* (01676) 532721
BALSALL HEATH (St Barnabas) *see* Sparkbrook St Agatha w Balsall Heath St Barn *Birm*
BALSALL HEATH (St Paul) *Birm 5* **P** *Bp* **P-in-c** C A GRYLLS
BALSCOTE (St Mary Magdalene) *see* Ironstone *Ox*
BALSHAM (Holy Trinity), Weston Colville, W Wickham and W Wratting *Ely 4* **P** *Bp, D&C, and Charterhouse (jt)* **R** F B H WOOLLEY, **Hon C** K W T W JOHNSON, **NSM** M C BANNER
BALTERLEY (All Saints' Memorial Church) *see* Barthomley *Ches*
BALTONSBOROUGH (St Dunstan) w Butleigh, West Bradley and West Pennard *B & W 5* **P** *Bp* **V** B A M GILLETT, **NSM** C M DONKERSLEY
BAMBER BRIDGE (St Aidan) *Blackb 5* **P** *Bp* **C** M WOODS
BAMBER BRIDGE (St Saviour) *Blackb 5* **P** *V Blackb* **P-in-c** G HALSALL
BAMBURGH (St Aidan) *Newc 10* **P** *Exors Lady Armstrong* **V** E M MCLEAN
BAMFORD (St John the Baptist) *see* Hathersage w Bamford and Derwent *Derby*
BAMFORD (St Michael) *Man 20* **P** *Bp* **P-in-c** P D GULLY, **NSM** P R ZUCCA
BAMFURLONG (Good Shepherd) *see* Abram *Liv*
BAMPTON (Holy Trinity) (St James) (St Mary) w Clanfield *Ox 8* **P** *Bp, DBP, St Jo Coll Ox, D&C Ex, and B Babington-Smith Esq (jt)* **V** D J LLOYD
BAMPTON (St Michael and All Angels), Morebath, Clayhanger and Petton *Ex 8* **P** *DBP and D&C (jt)* **P-in-c** A J STONE
BAMPTON (St Patrick) *see* Shap w Swindale and Bampton w Mardale *Carl*
BAMPTON ASTON (St James) *see* Bampton w Clanfield *Ox*
BAMPTON LEW (Holy Trinity) *as above*
BAMPTON PROPER (St Mary) *as above*
BANBURY (St Francis) *Ox 5* **P** *Bp* **V** *vacant* (01295) 275449
BANBURY (St Hugh) *Ox 5* **P** *Bp* **V** D JACKSON
BANBURY (St Leonard) *Ox 5* **P** *Bp* **P-in-c** M R CHARMLEY
BANBURY (St Mary) *Ox 5* **P** *Bp* **P-in-c** J E CHAPMAN, **NSM** H L ADEY HUISH
BANBURY (St Paul) *Ox 5* **P** *Bp* **P-in-c** E N COOMBS
BANHAM (St Mary) *see* Quidenham Gp *Nor*
BANKFOOT (St Matthew) *Bradf 2* **P** *Bp* **V** A I G SNOWDEN
BANKS (St Stephen's Church within the School) Conventional District *Liv 9* **Min** R J GIBBS
BANNINGHAM (St Botolph) *see* King's Beck *Nor*
BANSFIELD *St E 8* **P** *DBP, Mrs G S M Slater, and Ld Chan (by turn)* **R** I M FINN
BANSTEAD (All Saints) *Guildf 9* **P** *Bp* **V** D N CHANCE, **Hon C** E P I WESTBROOK
BANWELL (St Andrew) *B & W 11* **P** *D&C Bris* **V** D R G LOCKYER
BAPCHILD (St Lawrence) *see* Murston w Bapchild and Tonge *Cant*
BAR HILL (not known) *Ely 5* **P** *Bp* **P-in-c** G J RENISON
BARBON (St Bartholomew) *see* Kirkby Lonsdale *Carl*
BARBOURNE (St Stephen) *Worc 6* **P** *Bp* **V** S W CURRIE, **C** T A DAVIES
BARBROOK (St Bartholomew) *see* Combe Martin, Berrynarbor, Lynton, Brendon etc *Ex*
BARBY (St Mary) w Kilsby *Pet 3* **P** *Bp* **R** P M DE LA P BERESFORD
BARCHESTON (St Martin) *Cov 9* **P** *Bp* **P-in-c** R K SMITH, **C** H C W PARBURY
BARCOMBE (St Francis) (St Mary the Virgin) *Chich 18* **P** *Ld Chan* **R** J W HOLLINGSWORTH, **NSM** R A MOORE
BARDFIELD, GREAT (St Mary the Virgin) and LITTLE (St Katherine) *Chelmsf 18* **P** *Ch Union Trust* **P-in-c** R W F BEAKEN
BARDFIELD SALING (St Peter and St Paul) *see* Stebbing and Lindsell w Gt and Lt Saling *Chelmsf*
BARDNEY (St Laurence) *Linc 11* **P** *DBP (1 turn), Bp (2 turns), and St Jo Coll Cam (1 turn)* **R** J M PRATT
BARDON HILL (St Peter) *see* Coalville and Bardon Hill *Leic*
BARDSEA (Holy Trinity) *see* Pennington and Lindal w Marton and Bardsea *Carl*
BARDSEY (All Hallows) *Ripon 5* **P** *G L Fox Esq* **V** R J PEARSON
BARDSLEY (Holy Trinity) *Man 17* **P** *Wm Hulme Trustees* **V** G D GARRETT, **NSM** A D GRANT, **OLM** E M LOWE
BARDWELL (St Peter and St Paul) *see* Blackbourne *St E*
BARE (St Christopher) *Blackb 11* **P** *Bp* **V** D L HEAP
BARFORD (St Botolph) *see* Barnham Broom and Upper Yare *Nor*
BARFORD (St John) *see* Deddington w Barford, Clifton and Hempton *Ox*
BARFORD (St Martin) *see* Nadder Valley *Sarum*
BARFORD (St Michael) *see* Deddington w Barford, Clifton and Hempton *Ox*
BARFORD (St Peter) w Wasperton and Sherbourne *Cov 8* **P** *Major J M Mills, R Hampton Lucy, and Lady Jeryl Smith-Ryland (jt)* **P-in-c** D C JESSETT
BARFORD, GREAT (All Saints) *see* Blunham, Gt Barford, Roxton and Tempsford etc *St Alb*
BARFREYSTONE (St Nicholas) *see* Eythorne and Elvington w Waldershare etc *Cant*
BARHAM (St Giles) *see* E Leightonstone *Ely*
BARHAM (St John the Baptist) w Bishopsbourne and Kingston *Cant 1* **P** *Abp* **R** D J ROPER, **C** A S ARDLEY, **NSM** E R G HOPTHROW
BARHAM (St Mary) *see* Claydon and Barham *St E*
BARHOLME (St Martin) *see* Uffington Gp *Linc*
BARKBY (St Mary) *see* Syston *Leic*
BARKESTONE (St Peter and St Paul) *see* Vale of Belvoir Par *Leic*
BARKHAM (St James) *see* Arborfield w Barkham *Ox*
BARKING (St Erkenwald) *Chelmsf 1* **P** *Bp* **V** C N POOLEY
BARKING (St Margaret) (St Patrick) *Chelmsf 1* **P** *Patr Bd* **TV** G M BARLEY, J D PEARSON, **C** J A H EVENS
BARKING (St Mary) *see* Ringshall w Battisford, Barking w Darmsden etc *St E*
BARKINGSIDE (Holy Trinity) *Chelmsf 4* **P** *V Gt Ilford* **V** E A J CARGILL THOMPSON
BARKINGSIDE (St Cedd) *Chelmsf 4* **P** *Bp* **V** S G O O OLUKANMI, **NSM** M FLINTOFT-CHAPMAN, M CHAPMAN
BARKINGSIDE (St Francis of Assisi) *Chelmsf 4* **P** *Bp* **V** M JENNINGS
BARKINGSIDE (St George) *Chelmsf 4* **P** *Bp* **V** B J WALLIS

BARKINGSIDE (St Laurence) *Chelmsf 4* **P** *Bp* **V** *vacant* (020) 8518 3113
BARKISLAND (Christ Church) w West Scammonden *Wakef 4* **P** *V Halifax* **V** D F HANDLEY
BARKSTON (St Nicholas) and Hough Group, The *Linc 23* **P** *Sir Oliver Thorold Bt; the Revd J R H Thorold and J R Thorold Esq; Lord Brownlow; and Sir Lyonel Tollemache Bt (by turn)* **R** A J FIDDYMENT, **NSM** S J HADLEY
BARKSTON ASH (Holy Trinity) *see* Sherburn in Elmet w Saxton *York*
BARKWAY (St Mary Magdalene), Reed and Buckland w Barley *St Alb 19* **P** *The Crown and DBP (alt)* **R** *vacant* (01763) 848077
BARKWITH Group, The *Linc 5* **P** *D&C, J N Heneage Esq, K Coll Lon, and DBP (by turn)* **R** *vacant* (01673) 858291
BARKWITH, EAST (St Mary) *see* Barkwith Gp *Linc*
BARLASTON (St John the Baptist) *Lich 13* **P** *Countess of Sutherland* **P-in-c** W H SMITH
BARLAVINGTON (St Mary), Burton w Coates and Sutton w Bignor *Chich 11* **P** *Lord Egremont and Miss J B Courtauld (jt)* **P-in-c** W ELLIOT
BARLBOROUGH (St James) and Renishaw *Derby 3* **P** *Prime Min and Sir Reresby Sitwell Bt (alt)* **R** J PINDER-PACKARD
BARLBY (All Saints) w Riccall *York 2* **P** *Abp and V Hemingbrough (jt)* **V** I J FOX, **NSM** F LOFTUS, A D ROBINSON
BARLESTONE (St Giles) *Leic 12* **P** *Bp* **P-in-c** G M DALLOW
BARLEY (St Margaret of Antioch) *see* Barkway, Reed and Buckland w Barley *St Alb*
BARLING (All Saints) w Little Wakering *Chelmsf 12* **P** *D&C St Paul's and Bp (alt)* **V** R WOOLVEN
BARLING MAGNA (All Saints) *see* Barling w Lt Wakering *Chelmsf*
BARLINGS (St Edward) *Linc 3* **P** *DBP* **V** R G SPAIGHT
BARLOW (not known) *see* Brayton *York*
BARLOW, GREAT (St Lawrence) *Derby 5* **P** *TR Staveley and Barrow Hill* **P-in-c** A P KAUNHOVEN
BARLOW MOOR (Emmanuel) *see* Didsbury St Jas and Em *Man*
BARMBY MARSH (St Helen) *see* Howden *York*
BARMBY MOOR Group, The (St Catherine) *York 5* **P** *Abp (1 turn), Abp and Trustees Duke of Norfolk's Settlement Everingham Fund (2 turns)* **V** V P HEWETSON, **NSM** J H DAWKINS
BARMING (St Margaret of Antioch) w West Barming *Roch 7* **P** *Ld Chan* **R** N S MCGREGOR
BARMING HEATH (St Andrew) *Cant 13* **P** *Abp* **V** B REED
BARMSTON (All Saints) *see* Skipsea w Ulrome and Barmston w Fraisthorpe *York*
BARNACK (St John the Baptist) w Ufford and Bainton *Pet 8* **P** *Bp and St Jo Coll Cam (alt)* **R** *vacant* (01780) 740234
BARNACRE (All Saints) *see* Scorton and Barnacre and Calder Vale *Blackb*
BARNARD CASTLE (St Mary) w Whorlton *Dur 7* **P** *Trin Coll Cam* **V** A J HARDING
BARNARDISTON (All Saints) *see* Stourhead *St E*
BARNBURGH (St Peter) w Melton on the Hill and Aldwick-upon-Dearne *Sheff 12* **P** *Ld Chan (2 turns), Bp (1 turn)* **P-in-c** V D CLARKE
BARNBY (St John the Baptist) *see* Worlingham w Barnby and N Cove *St E*
BARNBY, EAST (Mission Chapel) *see* Hinderwell, Roxby and Staithes etc *York*
BARNBY DUN (St Peter and St Paul) *Sheff 8* **P** *Bp* **P-in-c** J M FODEN
BARNBY IN THE WILLOWS (All Saints) *see* Balderton and Barnby-in-the-Willows *S'well*
BARNEHURST (St Martin) *Roch 15* **P** *Bp* **V** O MURPHY
BARNES Team Ministry, The (St Mary) (Holy Trinity) (St Michael and All Angels) *S'wark 18* **P** *Patr Bd* **TR** R N F COLLINS, **TV** P W HOLLAND, **Hon C** G W HOLMES, L R F COLLINS
BARNET (Christ Church) *see* S Mimms Ch Ch *Lon*
BARNET (St John the Baptist) *see* Chipping Barnet *St Alb*
BARNET (St Stephen) *as above*
BARNET, EAST (St Mary the Virgin) *St Alb 17* **P** *The Crown* **R** R F WATSON
BARNET, NEW (St James) *St Alb 17* **P** *Ch Patr Trust* **V** B R PENFOLD
BARNET VALE (St Mark) *see* Chipping Barnet *St Alb*
BARNETBY LE WOLD (St Barnabas) *see* N Wolds Gp *Linc*
BARNEY (St Mary), Fulmodeston w Croxton, Hindringham, Thursford, Great and Little Snoring w Kettlestone and Pensthorpe *Nor 15* **P** *Lord Hastings, St Jo Coll Cam, D&C, DBP, and CCC Cam (by turn)* **R** J MUGGLETON
BARNHAM (St Gregory) *see* Blackbourne *St E*
BARNHAM (St Mary) *see* Aldingbourne, Barnham and Eastergate *Chich*
BARNHAM BROOM (St Peter and St Paul) and Upper Yare *Nor 17* **P** *Patr Bd* **TR** D K ALEXANDER, **OLM** R A JACKSON
BARNINGHAM (St Andrew) *see* Stanton, Hopton, Market Weston, Barningham etc *St E*
BARNINGHAM (St Mary the Virgin) w Matlaske w Baconsthorpe w Plumstead w Hempstead *Nor 18* **P** *Duchy of Lanc (1 turn), Lady Mott-Radclyffe, CPAS, and D&C (jt) (1 turn)* **R** *vacant* (01263) 577420
BARNINGHAM (St Michael and All Angels) w Hutton Magna and Wycliffe *Ripon 2* **P** *Bp and V Gilling and Kirkby Ravensworth (jt)* **R** C H COWPER
BARNINGHAM, LITTLE (St Andrew), Blickling, Edgefield, Itteringham w Mannington, Oulton w Irmingland, Saxthorpe w Corpusty and Wickmere w Wolterton *Nor 19* **P** *Bp, Lord Walpole, SMF, MMCET (2 turns), and Pemb Coll Cam (1 turn)* **R** *vacant* (01263) 584262
BARNINGHAM WINTER (St Mary the Virgin) *see* Barningham w Matlaske w Baconsthorpe etc *Nor*
BARNOLDBY LE BECK (St Helen) *Linc 10* **P** *Ld Chan* **R** I R SHELTON, **NSM** A HUNDLEBY
BARNOLDSWICK (Holy Trinity) (St Mary le Gill) w Bracewell *Bradf 7* **P** *Bp* **V** J R LANCASTER
BARNSBURY (St Andrew) *Lon 6* **P** *Patr Bd* **TR** M W LEARMOUTH, **TV** M L J SAUNDERS, **C** M FLETCHER
BARNSLEY Old Town (St Paul) *see* Barnsley St Mary *Wakef*
BARNSLEY (St Edward the Confessor) *Wakef 7* **P** *Bp* **V** *vacant* (01226) 201616
BARNSLEY (St George's Parish Church Centre) *Wakef 7* **P** *Bp* **V** D P J MUNBY
BARNSLEY (St Mary) *see* Bibury w Winson and Barnsley *Glouc*
BARNSLEY (St Mary) *Wakef 7* **P** *Bp* **R** I E WILDEY
BARNSLEY (St Peter and St John the Baptist) *Wakef 7* **P** *Bp* **V** A BRISCOE
BARNSTAPLE (St Peter and St Mary Magdalene) (Holy Trinity) *Ex 15* **P** *Patr Bd (4 turns), Ld Chan (1 turn)* **TR** V ROSS, **TV** J P BENSON, G CHAVE-COX, M J PEARSON, M D D JONES, K A ELLIOTT, **C** J H CRUTCHLEY
BARNSTON (Christ Church) *Ches 8* **P** *Bp* **V** G P BENSON, **C** P D BASKERVILLE, **NSM** I G URQUHART
BARNSTON (St Andrew) *see* Gt Dunmow and Barnston *Chelmsf*
BARNSTONE (St Mary Mission Room) *see* Cropwell Bishop w Colston Bassett, Granby etc *S'well*
BARNT GREEN (St Andrew) *see* Cofton Hackett w Barnt Green *Birm*
BARNTON (Christ Church) *Ches 4* **P** *Bp* **V** P NEWMAN
BARNWELL (All Saints) (St Andrew) w Tichmarsh, Thurning and Clapton *Pet 12* **P** *Soc of Merchant Venturers, MMCET, Em Coll Cam, and DBP (by turn)* **R** *vacant* (01832) 272374
BARNWOOD (St Lawrence) *Glouc 5* **P** *D&C* **V** R C COATES, **NSM** A D HAYMAN
BARONY OF BURGH, The (St Michael) *Carl 3* **P** *Patr Bd* **R** G M HART, **C** S J FYFE, **NSM** E A BLACK
BARR, GREAT (St Margaret) *Lich 25* **P** *M D S Farnham* **V** M C RUTTER, **Hon C** T W WARD
BARRINGTON (All Saints) *see* Orwell Gp *Ely*
BARRINGTON (Blessed Virgin Mary) *see* Ilminster and Distr *B & W*
BARRINGTON, GREAT (St Mary) *see* Sherborne, Windrush, the Barringtons etc *Glouc*
BARRINGTON, LITTLE (St Peter) *as above*
BARROW (All Saints) *St E 13* **P** *Ld Chan (1 turn), Mrs E C Gordon-Lennox, the Russell-Cooke Trust Co and Bp (1 turn), and St Jo Coll Cam (1 turn)* **V** P N MACLEOD-MILLER, **NSM** S A LONG
BARROW and Goxhill *Linc 6* **P** *Ld Chan* **V** J C GIRTCHEN
BARROW (St Bartholomew) *Ches 2* **P** *D Okell Esq* **P-in-c** E J TURNER
BARROW (St Giles) *see* Broseley w Benthall, Jackfield, Linley etc *Heref*
BARROW, NORTH (St Nicholas) *see* Six Pilgrims *B & W*
BARROW, SOUTH (St Peter) *as above*
BARROW GURNEY (Blessed Virgin Mary and St Edward King and Martyr) *B & W 13* **P** *Major M A Gibbs* **P-in-c** A SARGENT, **NSM** V L BARLEY
BARROW HILL (St Andrew) *see* Staveley and Barrow Hill *Derby*
BARROW-IN-FURNESS (St Aidan) *see* S Barrow *Carl*
BARROW-IN-FURNESS (St George) *as above*
BARROW-IN-FURNESS (St James the Great) *Carl 8* **P** *DBP* **P-in-c** S A EVASON

BARROW-IN-FURNESS (St John the Evangelist) *Carl 8* **P** *DBP* **P-in-c** M D HERVEY
BARROW-IN-FURNESS (St Luke) *see* S Barrow *Carl*
BARROW-IN-FURNESS (St Mark) *Carl 8* **P** *Bp* **V** I K HOOK, **C** E POW
BARROW-IN-FURNESS (St Mary the Virgin) *see* Walney Is *Carl*
BARROW-IN-FURNESS (St Matthew) *Carl 8* **P** *Patr Bd* **TV** M A EDWARDS
BARROW IN FURNESS (St Paul) *Carl 8* **P** *Simeon's Trustees* **R** D H PRICE, **C** G J WESTON, **OLM** G T WILSON
BARROW-ON-HUMBER (Holy Trinity) *see* Barrow and Goxhill *Linc*
BARROW-ON-TRENT (St Wilfrid) *see* Ticknall, Smisby and Stanton by Bridge etc *Derby*
BARROW UPON SOAR (Holy Trinity) w Walton le Wolds *Leic 7* **P** *St Jo Coll Cam and DBP (jt)* **P-in-c** J WHITTAKER, **Hon C** W ROBSON, **NSM** T E EDMONDS
BARROWBY (All Saints) and Gonerby, Great *Linc 19* **P** *R Grantham, and Duke of Devonshire (by turn)* **R** P HOPKINS, **C** M E MASSEY
BARROWDEN (St Peter) and Wakerley w South Luffenham and Morcott w Duddington and Tixover *Pet 8* **P** *Burghley Ho Preservation Trust, P W Rowley Esq, and Bp (3 turns), Ball Coll Ox (1 turn)* **R** P J C CLEMENTS
BARROWFORD (St Thomas) and Newchurch-in-Pendle *Blackb 6* **P** *Ld Chan and trustees (alt)* **V** J M HALLOWS
BARSHAM (Holy Trinity) *see* Wainford *St E*
BARSHAM, EAST (All Saints) *see* Walsingham, Houghton and Barsham *Nor*
BARSHAM, NORTH (All Saints) *as above*
BARSHAM, WEST (The Assumption of the Blessed Virgin Mary) *as above*
BARSTON (St Swithin) *Birm 11* **P** *MMCET* **V** *vacant* (01564) 776 844
BARTHOMLEY (St Bertoline) *Ches 11* **P** *Lord O'Neill* **P-in-c** D C SPEEDY
BARTLEY (Mission Church) *see* Copythorne *Win*
BARTLEY GREEN (St Michael and All Angels) *Birm 2* **P** *Bp* **V** C E MANSLEY, **C** S H MARSHALL, **NSM** B M A ROBERTS
BARTLOW (St Mary) *see* Linton *Ely*
BARTON (St Cuthbert w St Mary) *see* E Richmond *Ripon*
BARTON (St Lawrence) *see* Fellside Team *Blackb*
BARTON (St Mark's Chapel) w Peel Green (St Michael and All Angels) (St Catherine) *Man 2* **P** *Bp and TR Eccles* **P-in-c** B LAMB
BARTON (St Martin) *see* Torquay St Martin Barton *Ex*
BARTON (St Michael), Pooley Bridge and Martindale *Carl 4* **P** *Bp and Earl of Lonsdale (jt)* **V** *vacant* (01768) 486220
BARTON (St Paul) *Portsm 8* **P** *R Whippingham* **V** P E PIMENTEL
BARTON (St Peter) *Ely 1* **P** *Ld Chan* **P-in-c** C A COLLINS
BARTON, GREAT (Holy Innocents) *St E 13* **P** *Sir Michael Bunbury Bt* **P-in-c** A R GATES
BARTON BENDISH (St Andrew) w Beachamwell and Shingham *Ely 13* **P** *Bp and DBP (alt)* **P-in-c** D J POMERY, **Hon C** A G F VILLER
BARTON HARTSHORN (St James) *see* Swan *Ox*
BARTON HILL (St Luke w Ch Ch) and Moorfields St Matthew *Bris 3* **P** *Bp, CPAS, and V Bris St Phil and St Jacob w Em (jt)* **P-in-c** D HOLMYARD
BARTON IN FABIS (St George) *S'well 9* **P** *Ld Chan* **P-in-c** S W OSMAN
BARTON-LE-CLEY (St Nicholas) w Higham Gobion and Hexton *St Alb 9* **P** *The Crown (3 turns), Mrs F A A Cooper (1 turn)* **R** G H NEWTON, **NSM** M M PARRETT
BARTON-LE-STREET (St Michael) *see* The Street Par *York*
BARTON MILLS (St Mary) *see* Mildenhall *St E*
BARTON-ON-THE-HEATH (St Lawrence) *see* Long Compton, Whichford and Barton-on-the-Heath *Cov*
BARTON SEAGRAVE (St Botolph) w Warkton *Pet 11* **P** *Ch Soc Trust (2 turns), Duke of Buccleuch (1 turn)* **R** J M PERRIS, **C** S G MCKENZIE
BARTON ST DAVID (St David) *see* Wheathill Priory Gp *B & W*
BARTON STACEY (All Saints) *see* Lower Dever Valley *Win*
BARTON TURF (St Michael) *see* Ashmanhaugh, Barton Turf etc *Nor*
BARTON UNDER NEEDWOOD (St James) w Dunstall *Lich 14* **P** *Bp and Sir Rupert Hardy Bt (jt)* **V** A J WOOD
BARTON UPON HUMBER (St Mary) *Linc 6* **P** *Bp* **P-in-c** D P ROWETT, **OLM** A W WRIGHT
BARTON UPON IRWELL (St Catherine) *see* Barton w Peel Green *Man*
BARWELL (St Mary) w Potters Marston and Stapleton *Leic 12* **P** *R J W Titley Esq* **R** A C DEEGAN
BARWICK (St Mary Magdalene) *see* Yeovil H Trin w Barwick *B & W*
BARWICK IN ELMET (All Saints) *Ripon 8* **P** *Duchy of Lanc* **R** B H G JAMES
BASCHURCH (All Saints) and Weston Lullingfield w Hordley *Lich 17* **P** *Ch Patr Trust and Bp (jt)* **R** M P HOBBS
BASCOTE HEATH (Chapel) *see* Radford Semele *Cov*
BASEGREEN (St Peter) *see* Gleadless *Sheff*
BASFORD (St Aidan) *S'well 12* **P** *Bp* **V** *vacant* 0115-960 5427
BASFORD (St Leodegarius) *S'well 12* **P** *Bp* **NSM** A C DE ALWIS
BASFORD (St Mark) *Lich 9* **P** *Bp* **NSM** F P DUNN
BASFORD, NEW (St Augustine) *see* Basford St Leodegarius *S'well*
BASHLEY (St John) *see* Milton *Win*
BASILDON (St Andrew) (Holy Cross) *Chelmsf 6* **P** *Bp* **V** J R CARR
BASILDON (St Martin of Tours) *Chelmsf 6* **P** *Bp* **R** E E MCCAFFERTY, **NSM** I J E SWIFT
BASILDON (St Stephen) w Aldworth and Ashampstead *Ox 12* **P** *St Jo Coll Cam, Simeon's Trustees, and DBF (by turn)* **P-in-c** A F HOGARTH, **NSM** C F VERE NICOLL, **OLM** A KIGGELL
BASING (St Mary) *Win 4* **P** *Magd Coll Ox* **V** A S BISHOP
BASINGSTOKE (All Saints) (St Michael) *Win 4* **P** *Patr Bd* **TR** J M STOKER, **TV** S P V CADE, M A PHILLIPS, A BOTHAM, **C** A J WAY, **NSM** E A GEORGE
BASINGSTOKE Brighton Hill (Christ the King) *see* Basingstoke *Win*
BASINGSTOKE Popley (Bethlehem Chapel) *as above*
BASINGSTOKE South Ham (St Peter) *as above*
BASLOW (St Anne) w Curbar and Stoney Middleton *Derby 2* **P** *Duke of Devonshire and V Hathersage (jt)* **V** G R ORCHARD
BASSENTHWAITE (St Bega) *see* Binsey *Carl*
BASSENTHWAITE (St John) *as above*
BASSETT (St Michael and All Angels) *see* N Stoneham *Win*
BASSETT GREEN (St Christopher) *as above*
BASSINGBOURN (St Peter and St Paul) *Ely 7* **P** *D&C Westmr* **P-in-c** D C R MCFADYEN
BASSINGHAM Group, The (St Michael and All Angels) *Linc 18* **P** *Lady Jean Nevile, CCC Ox, Lord Middleton, Bp, and W R S Brown Esq (jt)* **P-in-c** N J BUCK, **NSM** R E TAYLOR
BASSINGTHORPE (St Thomas à Becket) *see* Ingoldsby *Linc*
BASTON (St John the Baptist) *see* Ness Gp *Linc*
BASWICH or Berkswich (Holy Trinity) *Lich 10* **P** *Bp* **V** P A GRAYSMITH, **NSM** J BISHOP, J J DAVIS
BATCOMBE (Blessed Virgin Mary) *see* Bruton and Distr *B & W*
BATCOMBE (St Mary) *see* Wriggle Valley *Sarum*
BATH Abbey (St Peter and St Paul) w St James *B & W 9* **P** *Simeon's Trustees* **R** T E MASON, **C** D M DEWES, T C OSMOND
BATH Bathwick (St John the Baptist) (Blessed Virgin Mary) *B & W 9* **P** *Bp* **R** D J PROTHERO, **C** S J P FISHER
BATH (Christ Church) Proprietary Chapel *B & W 11* **P** *R Walcot* **Min** A A J CLARIDGE, **NSM** C R BURROWS
BATH (Holy Trinity) *B & W 9* **P** *SMF* **R** G OAKES
BATH Odd Down (St Philip and St James) w Combe Hay *B & W 9* **P** *Simeon's Trustees* **V** A BAIN, **NSM** M JOYCE
BATH (St Barnabas) w Englishcombe *B & W 9* **P** *Bp* **V** D J BURLEIGH, **NSM** A M GREEN
BATH (St Bartholomew) *B & W 9* **P** *Simeon's Trustees* **V** I R LEWIS
BATH (St Luke) *B & W 9* **P** *Simeon's Trustees* **V** D F PERRYMAN, **C** J M TAYLOR
BATH (St Mary Magdalene) Holloway, Extra-parochial Chapelry *B & W 11* **P** *Bath Municipal Charities for Ld Chan* **Min** W G BURMAN
BATH (St Michael) w St Paul *B & W 9* **P** *CPAS* **R** M C LLOYD WILLIAMS, **NSM** H J LATTY
BATH (St Saviour) w Swainswick and Woolley *B & W 9* **P** *Ch Patr Trust and Or Coll Ox (jt)* **R** M J NORMAN, **NSM** J R BULLAMORE
BATH (St Stephen) *see* Charlcombe w Bath St Steph *B & W*
BATH Twerton-on-Avon (Ascension) (St Michael) *B & W 9* **P** *Patr Bd* **TR** R G WILSON, **TV** E C BROWN, R J PIMM
BATH Walcot (St Andrew) (St Swithin) *B & W 9* **P** *Simeon's Trustees* **R** H KOPSCH, **C** A C WILSON
BATH Weston (All Saints) w North Stoke and Langridge *B & W 9* **P** *Ld Chan* **R** P J WHITWORTH, **C** M J WATKINS, **NSM** J N RAWLINSON, P J NORMAN
BATH Weston (St John the Evangelist) (Emmanuel) w Kelston *B & W 9* **P** *Ld Chan* **R** C R GARRETT
BATH Widcombe (St Matthew) (St Thomas à Becket) *B & W 9* **P** *Simeon's Trustees* **V** *vacant* (01225) 464918

BATHAMPTON (St Nicholas) w Claverton *B & W 9* **P** *D&C Bris and Personal Reps R L D Skrine Esq (jt)* **R** P BURDEN
BATHEALTON (St Bartholomew) *see* Wellington and Distr *B & W*
BATHEASTON (St John the Baptist) (St Catherine) *B & W 9* **P** *Ch Ch Ox* **V** A J FRY
BATHFORD (St Swithun) *B & W 9* **P** *D&C Bris* **V** T C LING
BATHWICK (Blessed Virgin Mary) *see* Bath Bathwick *B & W*
BATHWICK (St John the Baptist) *as above*
BATLEY (All Saints) and Purlwell *Wakef 10* **P** *E C S J G Brudenell Esq, Trustees D Stubley Esq, and Bp (jt)* **V** A P JOHNSON
BATLEY (St Thomas) *Wakef 10* **P** *V Batley* **V** P L BENSON
BATLEY CARR (Holy Trinity) *see* Dewsbury *Wakef*
BATSFORD (St Mary) *see* Moreton-in-Marsh w Batsford, Todenham etc *Glouc*
BATTERSEA (Christ Church and St Stephen) *S'wark 16* **P** *Bp and V Battersea St Mary (alt)* **V** P CLARK
BATTERSEA (St George) *see* Battersea Fields *S'wark*
BATTERSEA (St Luke) *S'wark 16* **P** *Bp* **V** J M SHEPHERD, **C** R HOLY, **Hon C** J A BAKER, **OLM** J DEVERILL
BATTERSEA (St Mary) *S'wark 16* **P** *Earl Spencer* **V** J P KENNINGTON, **C** L M M FERNANDEZ-VICENTE
BATTERSEA (St Michael) Wandsworth Common *S'wark 16* **P** *V Battersea St Mary* **P-in-c** A H STEVENS
BATTERSEA (St Peter) (St Paul) *S'wark 16* **P** *V Battersea St Mary* **P-in-c** P J S PERKIN
BATTERSEA (St Philip w St Bartholomew) *see* Lavender Hill Ascension etc *S'wark*
BATTERSEA FIELDS (St Saviour) (All Saints) (St George) *S'wark 16* **P** *Bp, CPAS, and Ch Patr Trust (jt)* **V** G M VEVERS, **C** S E MULLALLY, D D PREMRAJ, D C PREMRAJ
BATTERSEA PARK (All Saints) *see* Battersea Fields *S'wark*
BATTERSEA PARK (St Saviour) *as above*
BATTERSEA RISE (St Mark) *S'wark 16* **P** *V Battersea St Mary* **V** P J S PERKIN, **C** T J J MAYFIELD, **NSM** D A LARLEE
BATTISFORD (St Mary) *see* Ringshall w Battisford, Barking w Darmsden etc *St E*
BATTLE (Church of the Ascension) (St Mary the Virgin) *Chich 14* **P** *The Crown* **V** J J W EDMONDSON
BATTLE HILL (Good Shepherd) *see* Willington *Newc*
BATTLESDEN (St Peter and All Saints) *see* Woburn w Eversholt, Milton Bryan, Battlesden etc *St Alb*
BATTYEFORD (Christ the King) *Wakef 10* **P** *V Mirfield* **V** R A CLEMENTS, **Hon C** R E WHITNALL, **NSM** M E WOOD
BAUGHURST (St Stephen) and Ramsdell and Wolverton w Ewhurst and Hannington *Win 4* **P** *Ld Chan, Duke of Wellington, and Bp (by turn)* **R** A E BARTON
BAULKING (St Nicholas) *see* Uffington, Shellingford, Woolstone and Baulking *Ox*
BAUMBER (St Swithin) *see* Hemingby *Linc*
BAUNTON (St Mary Magdalene) *see* Stratton, N Cerney, Baunton and Bagendon *Glouc*
BAVERSTOCK (St Editha) *see* Nadder Valley *Sarum*
BAWBURGH (St Mary and St Walstan) *see* Easton, Colton, Marlingford and Bawburgh *Nor*
BAWDESWELL (All Saints) *see* Lyng, Sparham, Elsing, Bylaugh, Bawdeswell etc *Nor*
BAWDRIP (St Michael and All Angels) *see* Woolavington w Cossington and Bawdrip *B & W*
BAWDSEY (St Mary) *see* Wilford Peninsula *St E*
BAWTRY (St Nicholas) w Austerfield and Misson *S'well 1* **P** *Bp* **V** J N GREEN
BAXENDEN (St John) *Blackb 1* **P** *Bp* **V** S LEES, **C** R W MARKS
BAXTERGATE (St Ninian) *see* Whitby w Aislaby and Ruswarp *York*
BAXTERLEY (not known) w Hurley and Wood End and Merevale w Bentley *Birm 10* **P** *Ld Chan (1 turn), Bp and Sir William Dugdale Bt (1 turn)* **R** J E GASPER
BAYDON (St Nicholas) *see* Whitton *Sarum*
BAYFORD (Mission Room) *see* Charlton Musgrove, Cucklington and Stoke Trister *B & W*
BAYFORD (St Mary) *see* Lt Berkhamsted and Bayford, Essendon etc *St Alb*
BAYLHAM (St Peter) *see* Gt and Lt Blakenham w Baylham and Nettlestead *St E*
BAYSTON HILL (Christ Church) *Lich 20* **P** *V Shrewsbury H Trin w St Julian* **V** R M GOLDENBERG, **C** A G STONE
BAYSWATER (St Matthew) *Lon 2* **P** *Exors Dame Jewell Magnus-Allcroft* **V** G M EVANS
BAYTON (St Bartholomew) *see* Mamble w Bayton, Rock w Heightington etc *Worc*
BEACHAMPTON (Assumption of the Blessed Virgin Mary) *see* Buckingham *Ox*
BEACHAMWELL (St Mary) *see* Barton Bendish w Beachamwell and Shingham *Ely*
BEACON Parishes *see* Painswick, Sheepscombe, Cranham, The Edge etc *Glouc*
BEACONSFIELD (St Mary and All Saints) (St Michael and All Angels) *Ox 20* **P** *Patr Bd* **TR** J P B WYNBURNE, **TV** R A CADDELL, **C** R J GRAYSON, **NSM** R P SPICER, P J HOLMES, C T T ROGERS
BEADLAM (St Hilda) *see* Kirkdale w Harome, Nunnington and Pockley *York*
BEADNELL (St Ebba) *Newc 10* **P** *Newc Dioc Soc* **V** E J WOOD
BEAFORD (All Saints) *see* Newton Tracey, Horwood, Alverdiscott etc *Ex*
BEALINGS, GREAT (St Mary) and LITTLE (All Saints) w Playford and Culpho *St E 7* **P** *Lord Cranworth (1 turn), Bp (3 turns)* **P-in-c** P C E STENTIFORD
BEAMINSTER AREA (St Mary of the Annunciation) *Sarum 2* **P** *Patr Bd* **TR** K L MASTERS, **TV** P C AVES
BEAMISH (St Andrew) *see* Ch the K *Dur*
BEARD (St James the Less) *see* New Mills *Derby*
BEARLEY (St Mary the Virgin) *see* Snitterfield w Bearley *Cov*
BEARPARK (St Edmund) *see* Dur N *Dur*
BEARSTED (Holy Cross) w Thurnham *Cant 14* **P** *Abp* **V** J CORBYN, **C** C J RYALLS
BEARWOOD (St Catherine) *Ox 16* **P** *Bp* **R** H D ETCHES
BEARWOOD (St Mary the Virgin) *Birm 7* **P** *V Smethwick* **V** A H PERRY, **NSM** L GRANNER
BEAUCHAMP RODING (St Botolph) *see* S Rodings *Chelmsf*
BEAUDESERT (St Nicholas) and Henley-in-Arden w Ullenhall *Cov 7* **P** *MMCET, Bp, and High Bailiff of Henley-in-Arden (jt)* **R** J F GANJAVI
BEAULIEU (Blessed Virgin and Holy Child) and Exbury and East Boldre *Win 11* **P** *Bp and Lord Montagu of Beaulieu (jt)* **V** D T P ABERNETHY
BEAUMONT CUM MOZE (St Leonard and St Mary) *see* Tendring and Lt Bentley w Beaumont cum Moze *Chelmsf*
BEAUMONT LEYS (Christ the King) *Leic 2* **P** *Bp* **P-in-c** A K FORD
BEAUWORTH (St James) *see* Upper Itchen *Win*
BEAUXFIELD (St Peter) *see* Whitfield w Guston *Cant*
BEAWORTHY (St Alban) *see* Ashwater, Halwill, Beaworthy, Clawton etc *Ex*
BEBINGTON (St Andrew) *Ches 8* **P** *M C Saunders-Griffiths Esq* **R** S L JAMES, **C** S J BURMESTER, N J C TUCKER
BEBINGTON, HIGHER (Christ Church) *Ches 8* **P** *C J C Saunders-Griffiths Esq* **V** A E SAMUELS, **C** A J NICOLLS
BECCLES (St Michael the Archangel) (St Luke's Church Centre) *St E 14* **P** *Patr Bd* **P-in-c** J N BEAUCHAMP, **C** B E DAVIS
BECK ROW (St John) *see* Mildenhall *St E*
BECKBURY (St Milburga), Badger, Kemberton, Ryton, Stockton and Sutton Maddock *Lich 16* **P** *Lord Hamilton of Dalzell, Or Coll Ox, and MMCET (2 turns), Ld Chan (1 turn)* **R** D F CHANTREY
BECKENHAM (Christ Church) *Roch 13* **P** *Ch Trust Fund Trust* **V** N W WYNNE-JONES, **Hon C** J T ANSCOMBE
BECKENHAM (Holy Trinity) *see* Penge Lane H Trin *Roch*
BECKENHAM (St Barnabas) *Roch 13* **P** *Keble Coll Ox* **V** S J HEANS
BECKENHAM (St George) *Roch 13* **P** *Bp* **R** M J HANCOCK, **C** D D HARRISON
BECKENHAM (St James) Elmers End *Roch 13* **P** *Bp* **V** L C CARBERRY
BECKENHAM (St John the Baptist) Eden Park *Roch 13* **P** *Ch Trust Fund Trust, Bp and Adn Bromley (jt)* **V** N LANG
BECKENHAM (St Michael and All Angels) w St Augustine *Roch 13* **P** *SMF and Bp (jt)* **V** C M SMITH
BECKENHAM, NEW (St Paul) *Roch 13* **P** *Bp* **V** B W ROWLAND, **Hon C** N E BAINES
BECKERMET (St Bridget) (St Bridget Old Church) (St John) w Ponsonby *Carl 5* **P** *Bp, Adn W Cumberland, P Stanley Esq, and PCCs of Beckermet St Jo and St Bridget (jt)* **V** *vacant* (01946) 841327
BECKFORD (St John the Baptist) *see* Overbury w Teddington, Alstone etc *Worc*
BECKHAM, WEST (St Helen and All Saints) *see* Weybourne Gp *Nor*
BECKINGHAM (All Saints) *see* Brant Broughton and Beckingham *Linc*
BECKINGHAM (All Saints) w Walkeringham and Gringley-on-the-Hill *S'well 1* **P** *Bp and Ld Chan (alt)* **V** *vacant* (01427) 848266

BECKINGTON (St George) w Standerwick, Berkley, Rodden, Lullington and Orchardleigh *B & W 4* **P** *Bp (3 turns), Ch Soc Trust (1 turn), and Exors A Duckworth Esq* **P-in-c** T M GOULDSTONE
BECKLEY (All Saints) and Peasmarsh *Chich 20* **P** *Univ Coll Ox and SS Coll Cam (alt)* **R** C F HOPKINS
BECKLEY (Assumption of the Blessed Virgin Mary) *see* Wheatley *Ox*
BECKTON (St Mark) *Chelmsf 3* **P** *Bp* **V** *vacant* (020) 7476 0618
BECKWITHSHAW (St Michael and All Angels) *see* Pannal w Beckwithshaw *Ripon*
BECONTREE (St Elisabeth) *Chelmsf 1* **P** *Bp* **V** N JOHN
BECONTREE (St George) *Chelmsf 1* **P** *Bp* **V** S L SMALLWOOD
BECONTREE (St Mary) *Chelmsf 1* **P** *CPAS* **V** R HERBERT, **C** J P CROOS
BECONTREE SOUTH (St Alban) (St John the Divine) (St Martin) *Chelmsf 1* **P** *Patr Bd* **TR** G A CLARKE, **TV** J SAXTON, **NSM** B M HULL
BECONTREE WEST (St Cedd) (St Thomas) *Chelmsf 1* **P** *DBP* **TR** S A LAW, **TV** T D HULL, P J WOOD
BEDALE (St Gregory) and Leeming *Ripon 4* **P** *Sir Henry Beresford-Peirse Bt and R Kirklington w Burnestonetc (jt)* **R** D G PATON-WILLIAMS, **C** J BALL, **NSM** A L WOODHOUSE
BEDDINGHAM (St Andrew) *see* Glynde, W Firle and Beddingham *Chich*
BEDDINGTON (St Francis' Church Hall) *see* S Beddington St Mich *S'wark*
BEDDINGTON (St Mary) *S'wark 25* **P** *Lady Nairne* **R** *vacant* (020) 8647 1973
BEDDINGTON, SOUTH (St Michael and All Angels) *S'wark 25* **P** *Bp* **V** P I D GRANT, **Hon C** D WALFORD
BEDFIELD (St Nicholas) *see* Worlingworth, Southolt, Tannington, Bedfield etc *St E*
BEDFONT, EAST (St Mary the Virgin) *Lon 11* **P** *Ld Chan* **V** G D G PRICE
BEDFORD (All Saints) *St Alb 10* **P** *Bp* **P-in-c** J M MACLEOD
BEDFORD (Christ Church) *St Alb 10* **P** *Bp* **V** R C HIBBERT, **C** T S ROBB
BEDFORD (St Andrew) *St Alb 10* **P** *Ld Chan* **V** C M DENT, **C** P E F CUDBY, **Hon C** J A ROWLANDS, **NSM** M D ROBINSON
BEDFORD (St John the Baptist) (St Leonard) *St Alb 10* **P** *MMCET* **R** N COOPER
BEDFORD (St Mark) *St Alb 10* **P** *Bp* **V** C ROYDEN, **C** J W CROSSLEY, **NSM** G R CAPPLEMAN, P J LITTLEFORD
BEDFORD (St Martin) *St Alb 10* **P** *Bp* **P-in-c** R S STOKES
BEDFORD (St Michael and All Angels) *see* Elstow *St Alb*
BEDFORD (St Paul) *St Alb 10* **P** *Bp* **V** J G PEDLAR
BEDFORD (St Peter de Merton) w St Cuthbert *St Alb 10* **P** *Ld Chan* **Hon C** A S BURROW
BEDFORD LEIGH (St Thomas) (All Saints' Mission) *Man 13* **P** *V Leigh St Mary* **V** A M HIRST
BEDFORD PARK (St Michael and All Angels) *Lon 11* **P** *Bp* **V** K J MORRIS, **C** N V STANLEY, **NSM** G MORGAN
BEDGROVE (Holy Spirit) *Ox 21* **P** *DBP* **P-in-c** L P R MEERING
BEDHAMPTON (St Nicholas's Mission Church) (St Thomas) *Portsm 5* **P** *Bp* **R** J A RISDON, **C** C W MACLAY
BEDINGFIELD (St Mary) *see* Eye *St E*
BEDINGHAM (St Andrew) *see* Hempnall *Nor*
BEDLINGTON (St Cuthbert) *Newc 1* **P** *D&C Dur* **OLM** D J WOOD
BEDMINSTER (St Aldhelm) (St Paul) *Bris 1* **P** *Bp* **TR** R V HEADING, **TV** M F JEFFERY, C J PEARCE
BEDMINSTER (St Michael and All Angels) *Bris 1* **P** *Bp* **V** D S MOSS
BEDMINSTER DOWN (St Oswald) *see* Bishopsworth and Bedminster Down *Bris*
BEDMONT (Ascension) *see* Abbots Langley *St Alb*
BEDNALL (All Saints) *see* Penkridge Team *Lich*
BEDSTONE (St Mary) *see* Clungunford w Clunbury and Clunton, Bedstone etc *Heref*
BEDWORTH (All Saints) *Cov 5* **P** *Patr Bd* **TV** T E BENNETT, **Dss** P M HAMILTON
BEDWYN, GREAT (St Mary) *see* Savernake *Sarum*
BEDWYN, LITTLE (St Michael) *as above*
BEECH (St Peter) *see* Alton St Lawr *Win*
BEECH, HIGH (Holy Innocents) *see* Waltham H Cross *Chelmsf*
BEECH HILL (St Anne) *see* Wigan St Anne *Liv*
BEECH HILL (St Mary the Virgin) *see* Loddon Reach *Ox*
BEECHDALE ESTATE (St Chad) *see* Blakenall Heath *Lich*
BEECHINGSTOKE (St Stephen) *see* Pewsey and Swanborough *Sarum*
BEEDING (St Peter) and Bramber w Botolphs *Chich 12* **P** *Bp* **R** T J N L'ESTRANGE
BEEDING, LOWER (Holy Trinity) (St John the Evangelist) *Chich 8* **P** *Bp* **P-in-c** S GALLAGHER
BEEDON (St Nicholas) and Peasemore w West Ilsley and Farnborough *Ox 14* **P** *Bp* **P-in-c** J P TOWNEND, **Hon C** T MAINES, **NSM** D F BROWN
BEEFORD (St Leonard) w Frodingham and Foston *York 11* **P** *Abp and Ch Soc Trust (jt)* **R** R P YATES
BEELEY (St Anne) and Edensor *Derby 2* **P** *Duke of Devonshire* **P-in-c** J D SLYFIELD
BEELSBY (St Andrew) *see* Laceby and Ravendale Gp *Linc*
BEENHAM VALENCE (St Mary) *see* Woolhampton w Midgham and Beenham Valance *Ox*
BEER (St Michael) *see* Seaton and Beer *Ex*
BEER HACKETT (St Michael) *see* Bradford Abbas and Thornford w Beer Hackett *Sarum*
BEERCROCOMBE (St James) *see* Beercrocombe w Curry Mallet, Hatch Beauchamp etc *B & W*
BEERCROCOMBE (St James) w Curry Mallet, Hatch Beauchamp, Orchard Portman, Staple Fitzpaine, Stoke St Mary w Thurlbear and West Hatch *B & W 18* **P** *Bp, Ch Trust Fund Trust, and D&C (4 turns), Duchy of Cornwall (1 turn)* **R** *vacant* (01823) 480220
BEESANDS (St Andrew) *see* Stokenham w Sherford and Beesands, and Slapton *Ex*
BEESBY (St Andrew) *see* Saleby w Beesby and Maltby *Linc*
BEESTON (St Andrew) *see* Sprowston w Beeston *Nor*
BEESTON (St John the Baptist) *S'well 7* **P** *Duke of Devonshire* **V** G B BARRODALE, **C** A J CARTWRIGHT
BEESTON (St Mary the Virgin) *Ripon 6* **P** *Patr Bd* **TV** R BROOKE, **P-in-c** W A D BERRYMAN
BEESTON HILL (Holy Spirit) and Hunslet Moor St Peter w St Cuthbert *Ripon 6* **P** *Bp and TR Leeds City (jt)* **V** R W SHAW
BEESTON NEXT MILEHAM (St Mary the Virgin) *see* Litcham w Kempston, E and W Lexham, Mileham etc *Nor*
BEESTON REGIS (All Saints) *see* Aylmerton, Runton, Beeston Regis and Gresham *Nor*
BEESTON RYLANDS (St Mary) *see* Beeston *S'well*
BEESTON ST LAURENCE (St Laurence) *see* Ashmanhaugh, Barton Turf etc *Nor*
BEETHAM (St Michael and All Angels) *Carl 10* **P** *Bp* **V** *vacant* (01539) 562216
BEETLEY (St Mary) *see* Swanton Morley w Beetley w E Bilney and Hoe *Nor*
BEGBROKE (St Michael) *see* Blenheim *Ox*
BEIGHTON (All Saints) *see* Acle w Fishley, N Burlingham, Beighton w Moulton *Nor*
BEIGHTON (St Mary the Virgin) *Sheff 1* **P** *Bp* **V** M J CAMERON
BEKESBOURNE (St Peter) *see* Patrixbourne w Bridge and Bekesbourne *Cant*
BELAUGH (St Peter) *see* Wroxham w Hoveton and Belaugh *Nor*
BELBROUGHTON (Holy Trinity) w Fairfield and Clent *Worc 12* **P** *Ld Chan and St Jo Coll Ox (alt)* **R** B J MAPLEY
BELCHALWELL (St Aldheim) *see* Hazelbury Bryan and the Hillside Par *Sarum*
BELCHAMP (St Paul and St Andrew) *see* N Hinckford *Chelmsf*
BELCHAMP OTTEN (St Ethelbert and All Saints) *as above*
BELCHAMP WALTER (St Mary the Virgin) *as above*
BELCHFORD (St Peter and St Paul) *Linc 11* **P** *Ld Chan* **R** *vacant*
BELFIELD (St Ann) *Man 20* **P** *Bp* **V** C G KETLEY
BELFORD (St Mary) and Lucker *Newc 10* **P** *V Bamburgh and Beadnell and Bp (alt)* **V** A J HUGHES
BELGRAVE (St Gabriel) *see* Leic Resurr *Leic*
BELGRAVE (St Michael and All Angels) *as above*
BELGRAVE (St Paul) *see* Wilnecote *Lich*
BELGRAVE (St Peter) *see* Leic Resurr *Leic*
BELHUS PARK (All Saints) *see* S Ockendon and Belhus Park *Chelmsf*
BELLE GREEN (Mission) *see* Ince Ch Ch *Liv*
BELLE ISLE (St John and St Barnabas) *see* Leeds Belle Is St Jo and St Barn *Ripon*
BELLEAU (St John the Baptist) *see* Legbourne and Wold Marsh *Linc*
BELLERBY (St John) *see* Leyburn w Bellerby *Ripon*
BELLFIELD (St Mark) *see* Sutton St Jas and Wawne *York*
BELLINGDON (St John the Evangelist) *see* Gt Chesham *Ox*
BELLINGHAM (St Cuthbert) *see* N Tyne and Redesdale *Newc*
BELLINGHAM (St Dunstan) *S'wark 4* **P** *Bp* **V** P D BUTLER, **C** A P DAVISON, **NSM** D L RILEY
BELMONT (St Anselm) *Lon 23* **P** *Bp* **V** I BRADY

BELMONT (St John) *S'wark 25* **P** *R Cheam* **V** M R WILLIAMS
BELMONT (St Mary Magdalene) *Dur 1* **P** *The Crown* **C** J L MOBERLY
BELMONT (St Peter) *see* Turton Moorland Min *Man*
BELPER (Christ Church) (St Faith's Mission Church) w Turnditch *Derby 11* **P** *Bp* **V** D PERKINS
BELPER (St Peter) *Derby 11* **P** *V Duffield* **V** R M PARSONS, **C** D E KERR, C L TUPLING
BELSIZE PARK (St Peter) *Lon 16* **P** *D&C Westmr* **V** J P F HARRIS, **Hon C** D R BURY
BELSTEAD (St Mary the Virgin) *see* Sproughton w Burstall, Copdock w Washbrook etc *St E*
BELSTONE (St Mary) *see* S Tawton and Belstone *Ex*
BELTINGHAM (St Cuthbert) *see* Haydon Bridge and Beltingham w Henshaw *Newc*
BELTON (All Saints) and Burgh Castle *Nor 6* **P** *Bp and Ld Chan (alt)* **R** J J QUINN
BELTON Group, The (All Saints) *Linc 1* **P** *Bp and Prime Min (alt)* **V** T D BUCKLEY
BELTON (St John the Baptist) *see* Kegworth, Hathern, Long Whatton, Diseworth etc *Leic*
BELTON (St Peter) *see* Uppingham w Ayston and Wardley w Belton *Pet*
BELTON (St Peter and St Paul) *see* Barkston and Hough Gp *Linc*
BELVEDERE (All Saints) *Roch 15* **P** *DBP* **V** C A TERRY
BELVEDERE (St Augustine) *Roch 15* **P** *Bp* **P-in-c** C W JONES
BEMBRIDGE (Holy Trinity) (St Luke's Mission Church) *Portsm 7* **P** *V Brading* **V** A P MENNISS
BEMERTON (St Andrew) (St John the Evangelist) (St Michael and All Angels) *Sarum 12* **P** *Prime Min (2 turns) and Bp (1 turn)* **TR** S A WOODLEY, **NSM** P D NEWTON, P A CLEGG
BEMPTON (St Michael) w Flamborough, Reighton w Speeton *York 9* **P** *Patr Bd* **V** P J PIKE
BEN RHYDDING (St John the Evangelist) *Bradf 4* **P** *V Ilkey* **V** B GREGORY, **NSM** H LEALMAN
BENCHILL (St Luke the Physician) *see* Wythenshawe *Man*
BENEFIELD (St Mary the Virgin) *see* Oundle w Ashton and Benefield w Glapthorn *Pet*
BENENDEN (St George and St Margaret) *Cant 16* **P** *Abp* **V** C F SMITH, **NSM** R M VAN WENGEN
BENFIELDSIDE (St Cuthbert) *Dur 4* **P** *Bp* **V** M JACKSON, **NSM** I W WAUGH
BENFLEET, SOUTH (St Mary the Virgin) *Chelmsf 10* **P** *D&C Westmr* **V** M E GALLOWAY
BENGEO (Holy Trinity) (St Leonard) and Christ Church *St Alb 22* **P** *R M A Smith Esq* **R** *vacant* (01992) 504997
BENGEWORTH (St Peter) *Worc 1* **P** *Bp* **V** B D COLLINS
BENHALL (St Mary) *see* Sternfield, Benhall, Snape etc *St E*
BENHILTON (All Saints) *S'wark 25* **P** *Bp* **V** M A J OADES
BENINGTON (All Saints) *see* Freiston, Butterwick w Bennington, and Leverton *Linc*
BENINGTON (St Peter) w Walkern *St Alb 23* **P** *Trustees Ripon Coll Ox and K Coll Cam (alt), and Bp* **P-in-c** R H TOTTERDELL, **NSM** J A PAGE
BENNETTS END (St Benedict) *see* Chambersbury *St Alb*
BENNIWORTH (St Julian) *see* Asterby Gp *Linc*
BENSHAM (St Chad) *Dur 12* **P** *Bp* **TV** M R PALMER, B M C BROGGIO
BENSINGTON (St Helen) *see* Benson *Ox*
BENSON (St Helen) *Ox 1* **P** *Ch Ch Ox* **V** A R HAWKEN, **OLM** J K TRAVIS
BENTHALL (St Bartholomew) *see* Broseley w Benthall, Jackfield, Linley etc *Heref*
BENTHAM (St John the Baptist) (St Margaret) *Bradf 6* **P** *Bp* **R** N B THOMAS
BENTILEE (St Stephen) *see* Bucknall *Lich*
BENTLEY (Emmanuel) *Lich 28* **P** *Bp, Mrs H G Jenkins, and A D Owen Esq (jt)* **P-in-c** B PRENTICE, **C** S L HOUGH
BENTLEY (St Mary) *see* Sproughton w Burstall, Copdock w Washbrook etc *St E*
BENTLEY (St Mary) and Binsted *Win 2* **P** *Adn Surrey and D&C (jt)* **R** J M CAMPBELL
BENTLEY (St Peter) *Sheff 7* **P** *Bp* **V** D R FOUNTAIN
BENTLEY (St Peter) *see* Rowley w Skidby *York*
BENTLEY, GREAT (St Mary the Virgin) and Frating w Thorrington *Chelmsf 23* **P** *St Jo Coll Cam and Bp (alt)* **R** W B METCALFE
BENTLEY, LITTLE (St Mary) *see* Tendring and Lt Bentley w Beaumont cum Moze *Chelmsf*
BENTLEY, LOWER (St Mary) *see* Redditch H Trin *Worc*
BENTLEY, NEW (St Philip and St James) *Sheff 7* **P** *Bp* **V** S P DICKINSON
BENTLEY COMMON (St Paul), Kelvedon Hatch and Navestock *Chelmsf 7* **P** *Bp* **R** R A L ROSE
BENTLEY HEATH (St James) *see* Dorridge *Birm*
BENTWORTH (St Mary), Lasham, Medstead and Shalden *Win 2* **P** *J L Jervoise Esq and Ld Chan (alt)* **R** B R G FLENLEY
BENWELL Team, The (St James) (St John) (Venerable Bede) *Newc 7* **P** *Bp* **TR** A PATTISON, **TV** C R PICKFORD, **OLM** P D WILSON
BEOLEY (St Leonard) (St Andrew's Church Centre) *Worc 7* **P** *Patr Bd* **V** D ROGERS, **C** L D MACHELL
BEPTON (St Mary) *see* Cocking, Bepton and W Lavington *Chich*
BERDEN (St Nicholas) *see* Manuden w Berden and Quendon w Rickling *Chelmsf*
BERE ALSTON (Holy Trinity) *see* Bere Ferrers *Ex*
BERE FERRERS (St Andrew) *Ex 25* **P** *DBP* **R** N C LAW
BERE REGIS (St John the Baptist) and Affpuddle w Turnerspuddle *Sarum 6* **P** *Ball Coll Ox (2 turns), Bp (1 turn)* **R** I WOODWARD
BERECHURCH (St Margaret w St Michael) *Chelmsf 16* **P** *Bp* **V** R I WILKINSON
BERGH APTON (St Peter and St Paul) *see* Thurton *Nor*
BERGHOLT, EAST (St Mary the Virgin) and Brantham *St E 5* **P** *Em Coll Cam* **R** S J SWAIN, **C** L OOSTERHOF, **OLM** D W SEARLE
BERGHOLT, WEST (St Mary the Virgin) and Great Horkesley *Chelmsf 17* **P** *Bp and Ball Coll Ox (alt)* **R** C HORSEMAN
BERINSFIELD (St Mary and St Berin) *see* Dorchester *Ox*
BERKELEY (St Mary the Virgin) w Wick, Breadstone, Newport, Stone, Woodford and Hill *Glouc 2* **P** *Bp, Berkeley Will Trustees, and Mrs J D Jenner-Fust (jt)* **NSM** R P CHIDLAW
BERKHAMSTED, GREAT (All Saints) (St Peter) *St Alb 2* **P** *Bp* **NSM** L GEOGHEGAN
BERKHAMSTED, LITTLE (St Andrew) and Bayford, Essendon and Ponsbourne *St Alb 22* **P** *Marquess of Salisbury (2 turns), CPAS (1 turn), and Bp (1 turn)* **P-in-c** P M HIGHAM, **NSM** J D COPE
BERKHAMSYTCH (St Mary and St John) *see* Ipstones w Berkhamsytch and Onecote w Bradnop *Lich*
BERKLEY (Blessed Virgin Mary) *see* Beckington w Standerwick, Berkley, Rodden etc *B & W*
BERKSWELL (St John the Baptist) *Cov 4* **P** *Trustees Col C J H Wheatley* **P-in-c** P P HUGHES
BERKSWICH (Holy Trinity) *see* Baswich *Lich*
BERMONDSEY (St Anne) and St Augustine *S'wark 7* **P** *Bp and F W Smith Esq (alt)* **V** S J R HARTLEY
BERMONDSEY (St Hugh) Charterhouse Mission Conventional District *S'wark 5* **C-in-c** B A SAUNDERS, **C** J G CAVALCANTI
BERMONDSEY (St James w Christ Church) and St Crispin *S'wark 7* **P** *The Crown, Bp, and R Bermondsey St Mary (by turn)* **V** S J R HARTLEY, **OLM** W F GARLICK, S C CATTON
BERMONDSEY (St Katharine) w St Bartholomew *S'wark 7* **P** *Bp and R Rotherhithe St Mary w All SS (jt)* **V** L M WANJIE
BERMONDSEY (St Mary Magdalen w St Olave, St John and St Luke) *S'wark 7* **P** *Ch Patr Soc (2 turns), Ld Chan (1 turn), and Bp (1 turn)* **R** C D MOORE, **OLM** P E HOPPER
BERNEY, GREAT (St John) *see* Langdon Hills *Chelmsf*
BERNWODE *Ox 21* **P** *Bp, CPAS, Earl Temple of Stowe, and Sir Henry Aubrey-Fletcher Bt (jt)* **R** C D STIRLING, **C** J M WRIGHT
BERRICK SALOME (St Helen) *see* Chalgrove w Berrick Salome *Ox*
BERRINGTON (All Saints) *see* Wenlock *Heref*
BERROW (Blessed Virgin Mary) and Breane *B & W 1* **P** *Adn Wells* **R** S F LACY
BERROW (St Faith) w Pendock, Eldersfield, Hollybush and Birtsmorton *Worc 5* **P** *Bp, D&C, and Exors Sir Berwick Lechmere Bt (jt)* **R** M A ROGERS
BERRY POMEROY (St Mary) *see* Totnes w Bridgetown, Berry Pomeroy etc *Ex*
BERRYNARBOR (St Peter) *see* Combe Martin, Berrynarbor, Lynton, Brendon etc *Ex*
BERSTED, NORTH (Holy Cross) *Chich 1* **P** *Abp* **P-in-c** J C QUIGLEY
BERSTED, SOUTH (St Mary Magdalene) w NORTH (St Peter) *Chich 1* **P** *Abp* **P-in-c** D H THORNLEY
BERWICK (Holy Trinity) (St Mary) *Newc 12* **P** *Bp (2 turns), D&C Dur (1 turn)* **V** A HUGHES
BERWICK (St John) *see* Chalke Valley *Sarum*
BERWICK (St Michael and All Angels) w Selmeston and Alciston *Chich 18* **P** *Miss I M Newson and Mrs A Fitzherbert (1 turn), D&C (1 turn)* **P-in-c** P M BLEE
BERWICK PARK (Good Shepherd) *see* Wood Green St Mich w Bounds Green St Gabr etc *Lon*

BERWICK ST JAMES (St James) *see* Wylye and Till Valley *Sarum*
BESFORD (St Peter's Chapelry) *see* Defford w Besford *Worc*
BESSACARR, WEST (St Francis of Assisi) *Sheff 8* **P** *Bp* **V** C S W VAN D'ARQUE
BESSELSLEIGH (St Lawrence) *Ox 10* **P** *Ox Ch Trust* **P-in-c** R G PENMAN
BESSINGBY (St Magnus) (St Mark) *York 9* **P** *G W J H Wright Esq* **V** *vacant*
BESSINGHAM (St Mary) *see* Roughton and Felbrigg, Metton, Sustead etc *Nor*
BESTHORPE (All Saints) *see* Attleborough w Besthorpe *Nor*
BESTHORPE (Holy Trinity) *see* Collingham w S Scarle and Besthorpe and Girton *S'well*
BESTWOOD (Emmanuel) (St Mark) *S'well 12* **P** *Bp and Ch Patr Trust (jt)* **V** P A HUXTABLE, **C** J R PRANCE
BESTWOOD (St Matthew on the Hill) (St Philip) *S'well 12* **P** *Bp and Ch Patr Trust (jt)* **V** E A MORRIS
BESTWOOD/RISE PARK Local Ecumenical Project *S'well 9 vacant*
BESTWOOD PARK (no dedication) w Rise Park *S'well 12* **P** *Bp and Ch Patr Trust (jt)* **V** A P ISON, **NSM** B J NEILL
BESWICK (St Margaret) *see* Hutton Cranswick w Skerne, Watton and Beswick *York*
BETCHWORTH (St Michael and All Angels) *S'wark 27* **P** *D&C Windsor* **V** S J BAILEY, **OLM** P A VIGERS
BETHERSDEN (St Margaret) w High Halden *Cant 16* **P** *Abp* **V** D W FLEWKER
BETHESDA (Shared Church) *see* Hallwood *Ches*
BETHNAL GREEN (St Barnabas) *Lon 7* **P** *D&C Cant* **V** B C RALPH, **NSM** M G WEBB
BETHNAL GREEN (St James the Less) *Lon 7* **P** *CPAS* **V** R MONTGOMERY
BETHNAL GREEN (St John) *see* St Jo on Bethnal Green *Lon*
BETHNAL GREEN (St Matthew w St James the Great) *Lon 7* **P** *Bp* **R** K J SCULLY, **C** E R BUSH, **Hon C** H LODER
BETHNAL GREEN (St Peter) (St Thomas) *Lon 7* **P** *City Corp* **P-in-c** J E BLACKBURN
BETLEY (St Margaret) *Lich 9* **P** *DBP* **V** B F WILSON, **NSM** S W JOHNSON, **OLM** P LANE
BETTISCOMBE (St Stephen) *see* Golden Cap Team *Sarum*
BETTON STRANGE (St Margaret) *see* Wenlock *Heref*
BETTWS-Y-CRWYN (St Mary) *see* Clun w Bettws-y-Crwyn and Newcastle *Heref*
BEVENDEAN (Holy Nativity) *see* Moulsecoomb *Chich*
BEVERLEY (St Mary) *York 8* **P** *Abp* **V** D W HOSKIN
BEVERLEY (St Nicholas) *York 8* **P** *Abp* **V** J A EVANS, **C** R J W LONG, **NSM** R MERRYWEATHER
BEVERLEY MINSTER (St John and St Martin) *York 8* **P** *Simeon's Trustees* **V** D C BAILEY, **C** N J Q DRAYSON, R C CAREW
BEVERSTON (St Mary the Virgin) *see* Tetbury w Beverston *Glouc*
BEWBUSH (Community Centre) *see* Ifield *Chich*
BEWCASTLE (St Cuthbert), Stapleton and Kirklinton w Hethersgill *Carl 2* **P** *Bp, D&C, and DBP (jt)* **R** A T BARTLAM
BEWDLEY (St Anne) *see* Ribbesford w Bewdley and Dowles *Worc*
BEWERLEY GRANGE (Chapel) *see* Upper Nidderdale *Ripon*
BEWHOLME (St John the Baptist) *see* Sigglesthorne w Nunkeeling and Bewholme *York*
BEWICK, OLD (Holy Trinity) *see* Glendale Gp *Newc*
BEXHILL (All Saints) *see* Sidley *Chich*
BEXHILL (St Augustine) *Chich 14* **P** *Bp* **V** R COATES, **Hon C** P A FROSTICK
BEXHILL (St Barnabas) *Chich 14* **P** *Bp* **V** C I PRITCHARD
BEXHILL (St Mark) *Chich 14* **P** *Bp* **R** J J FRAIS
BEXHILL (St Peter) (St Michael) (Good Shepherd) (St Andrew) *Chich 14* **P** *Bp* **TR** E F P BRYANT, **TV** D J KING, **C** M A BRYDON, **NSM** O M WERRETT
BEXHILL (St Stephen) *Chich 14* **P** *Bp* **V** D R FROST
BEXLEY (St John the Evangelist) *Roch 17* **P** *The Crown* **V** V J LAMONT, **C** J A DONNELLY
BEXLEY (St Mary) *Roch 17* **P** *Bp* **V** C E POTTER
BEXLEYHEATH (Christ Church) *Roch 15* **P** *Bp* **V** F D JAKEMAN, **C** J A FLETCHER, R M JOHNSON
BEXLEYHEATH (St Peter) *Roch 15* **P** *Bp* **V** M H C LUMGAIR
BEXWELL (St Mary) *see* Denver and Ryston w Roxham and W Dereham etc *Ely*
BEYTON (All Saints) *see* Rougham, Beyton w Hessett and Rushbrooke *St E*
BIBURY (St Mary) w Winson and Barnsley *Glouc 12* **P** *Bp and W H Wykeham-Musgrave Esq (alt)* **P-in-c** J H MAIS
BICESTER (St Edburg) w Bucknell, Caversfield and Launton *Ox 2* **P** *Patr Bd* **TR** P J BALL, **TV** M MULLINS, D W BOUSKILL, **C** R C WEBBLEY, C A BOYCE, **NSM** R B ATKINS
BICKENHILL (St Peter) *Birm 11* **P** *Birm Dioc Trustees* **P-in-c** K CLARINGBULL
BICKER (St Swithin) *Linc 21* **P** *D&C* **V** *vacant*
BICKERSHAW (St James and St Elizabeth) *Liv 14* **P** *Bp* **V** J L STEVENTON
BICKERSTAFFE Four Lane Ends (not known) *see* Bickerstaffe and Melling *Liv*
BICKERSTAFFE (Holy Trinity) and Melling *Liv 11* **P** *Earl of Derby and R Halsall (jt)* **V** P TAYLOR
BICKERTON (Holy Trinity), Bickley, Harthill and Burwardsley *Ches 5* **P** *Bp, Adn Ches, DBP, Dowager Marchioness of Cholmondeley, and A G Barbour Esq (jt)* **V** L R THOMAS, **NSM** R J DIGGLE
BICKINGTON (St Andrew) *see* Fremington *Ex*
BICKINGTON (St Mary the Virgin) *see* Ashburton w Buckland in the Moor and Bickington *Ex*
BICKINGTON, HIGH (St Mary) *see* Newton Tracey, Horwood, Alverdiscott etc *Ex*
BICKLEIGH Roborough (St Mary the Virgin) and Shaugh Prior *Ex 21* **P** *Patr Bd* **TR** R J CARLTON
BICKLEIGH (St Mary) *see* Silverton, Butterleigh, Bickleigh and Cadeleigh *Ex*
BICKLEIGH DOWN (School) *see* Bickleigh and Shaugh Prior *Ex*
BICKLEY (St George) *Roch 14* **P** *SMF* **V** D A S HERBERT, **Hon C** B W SHARPE
BICKLEY (St Wenefrede) *see* Bickerton, Bickley, Harthill and Burwardsley *Ches*
BICKNACRE (St Andrew) *see* Woodham Ferrers and Bicknacre *Chelmsf*
BICKNOLLER (St George) *see* Quantock Towers *B & W*
BICKNOR (St James) *see* Bredgar w Bicknor and Frinsted w Wormshill etc *Cant*
BICTON (Holy Trinity), Montford w Shrawardine and Fitz *Lich 20* **P** *Earl of Powis, N E E Stephens Esq, and J G O Wingfield Esq (jt)* **P-in-c** M R GODSON
BICTON (St Mary) *see* E Budleigh w Bicton and Otterton *Ex*
BIDBOROUGH (St Lawrence) *see* Southborough St Pet w Ch Ch and St Matt etc *Roch*
BIDDENDEN (All Saints) and Smarden *Cant 16* **P** *Abp* **R** P G COX, **Hon C** P A ANDERSON, **NSM** J A MUXLOW
BIDDENHAM (St James) *St Alb 10* **P** *Bp* **Hon C** G SMITH
BIDDESTONE (St Nicholas) *see* By Brook *Bris*
BIDDISHAM (St John the Baptist) *see* Crook Peak *B & W*
BIDDLESDEN (St Margaret) *see* W Buckingham *Ox*
BIDDULPH (St Lawrence) *Lich 8* **P** *MMCET* **V** M S J CANNAM, **C** R J TRETHEWEY
BIDDULPH MOOR (Christ Church) *Lich 8* **P** *MMCET* **P-in-c** J A DAWSWELL
BIDEFORD (St Mary) (St Peter East the Water), Northam, Westward Ho!, Appledore, Weare Giffard, Littleham, Landcross and Monkleigh *Ex 16* **P** *Patr Bd* **TR** M EDSON, **TV** P J DOBBIN, R J FROST, J EWINGTON, **C** S M ANTHONY, **NSM** A GLOVER
BIDFORD-ON-AVON (St Laurence) *Cov 7* **P** *Bp* **V** D A HALL, **NSM** S M HENWOOD
BIDSTON (St Oswald) *Ches 1* **P** *Bp* **V** R E IVESON
BIELBY (St Giles) *see* Holme and Seaton Ross Gp *York*
BIERLEY (St John the Evangelist) *Bradf 2* **P** *DBP* **V** K S TROMANS
BIERLEY, EAST (St Luke) *see* Birkenshaw w Hunsworth *Wakef*
BIERTON (St James the Great) *see* Aylesbury w Bierton and Hulcott *Ox*
BIGBURY (St Lawrence) *see* Modbury, Bigbury, Ringmore w Kingston etc *Ex*
BIGBY (All Saints) *see* N Wolds Gp *Linc*
BIGGIN (St Thomas) *see* Hartington, Biggin and Earl Sterndale *Derby*
BIGGIN HILL (St Mark) *Roch 14* **P** *Bp* **V** C W KITCHENER, **NSM** E C KITCHENER
BIGGLESWADE (St Andrew) *St Alb 11* **P** *Bp* **V** W H THACKRAY, **C** F M ARNOLD
BIGHTON (All Saints) *see* Old Alresford and Bighton *Win*
BIGNOR (Holy Cross) *see* Barlavington, Burton w Coates, Sutton and Bignor *Chich*
BIGRIGG (St John) *see* Egremont and Haile *Carl*
BILBOROUGH (St John the Baptist) *S'well 14* **P** *Bp* **P-in-c** J E D CAVE, **C** J E LAMB
BILBOROUGH (St Martin) w Strelley *S'well 14* **P** *SMF* **P-in-c** J E D CAVE, **C** J E LAMB
BILBROOK (Holy Cross) and Coven *Lich 2* **P** *Bp* **V** D C BAKER

BILBROUGH (St James) *see* Healaugh w Wighill, Bilbrough and Askham Richard *York*

BILDESTON (St Mary Magdalene) w Wattisham and Lindsey, Whatfield w Semer, Nedging and Naughton *St E 3* **P** *Abp, Bp, CPAS, Jes Coll Cam, and Reformation Ch Trust (jt)* **R** *vacant* (01473) 822100

BILHAM *Sheff 12* **P** *Bp, Major W Warde-Aldam, W G A Warde-Norbury Esq, and Mrs S Grant-Dalton (jt)* **P-in-c** C D LETHBRIDGE

BILLERICAY (Christ Church) (Emmanuel) (St John the Divine) (St Mary Magdalen) and Little Burstead *Chelmsf 6* **P** *Bp* **TR** E W COCKETT, **TV** P F HINCKLEY, D BARLOW, **C** A COPELAND

BILLESDON (St John the Baptist) *see* Church Langton cum Tur Langton etc *Leic*

BILLESLEY COMMON (Holy Cross) *Birm 5* **P** *Bp* **V** G L HODKINSON, **NSM** S H SHEWRING, R C EVANS

BILLING, GREAT (St Andrew) w LITTLE (All Saints) *Pet 4* **P** *BNC Ox and Bp (alt)* **R** S R PALMER, **C** M J NEWITT, **NSM** J H CRAIG PECK

BILLINGBOROUGH Group, The (St Andrew) *Linc 13* **P** *Prime Min (2 turns), Bp and St Jo Coll Dur (1 turn)* **P-in-c** A K E SORENSEN, **OLM** J G SPREADBURY

BILLINGE (St Aidan) *Liv 15* **P** *R Wigan* **V** S C PRATT

BILLINGFORD (St Leonard) *see* Scole, Brockdish, Billingford, Thorpe Abbots etc *Nor*

BILLINGFORD (St Peter) *see* N Elmham w Billingford and Worthing *Nor*

BILLINGHAM (St Aidan) *Dur 10* **P** *D&C* **P-in-c** S J LIDDLE

BILLINGHAM (St Cuthbert) *Dur 10* **P** *D&C* **V** R I SMITH, **NSM** M A VIGOR

BILLINGHAM (St Luke) *Dur 10* **P** *D&C* **V** T P PARKER

BILLINGHAM (St Mary Magdalene) *Dur 10* **P** *D&C* **V** *vacant*

BILLINGHAM (St Mary Magdalene) *see* Grindon, Stillington and Wolviston *Dur*

BILLINGHAY (St Michael) *see* Carr Dyke Gp *Linc*

BILLINGSHURST (St Mary the Virgin) *Chich 8* **P** *Bp* **V** *vacant* (01403) 786540 *or* 782332

BILLINGSLEY (St Mary) *see* Highley w Billingsley, Glazeley etc *Heref*

BILLINGTON (St Michael and All Angels) *see* Leighton Buzzard w Eggington, Hockliffe etc *St Alb*

BILLOCKBY (All Saints) *see* S Trin Broads *Nor*

BILLY MILL (St Aidan) *see* Cullercoats St Geo *Newc*

BILNEY, EAST (St Mary) *see* Swanton Morley w Beetley w E Bilney and Hoe *Nor*

BILSBORROW (St Hilda) *see* Fellside Team *Blackb*

BILSBY (Holy Trinity) w Farlesthorpe *Linc 8* **P** *Bp* **V** R H IRESON

BILSDALE MIDCABLE (St John) *see* Upper Ryedale *York*

BILSDALE PRIORY (St Hilda) *see* Ingleby Greenhow w Bilsdale Priory, Kildale etc *York*

BILSINGTON (St Peter and St Paul) *see* Aldington w Bonnington and Bilsington etc *Cant*

BILSON (Mission Church) *see* Cinderford St Steph w Littledean *Glouc*

BILSTHORPE (St Margaret) *S'well 15* **P** *DBP* **P-in-c** E F CULLY, **C** J R CHAMBERS, **NSM** M A GROVES

BILSTON (St Leonard) (St Chad) (St Mary the Virgin) *Lich 28* **P** *Patr Bd* **TR** C D C THORPE, **TV** M R GILBERT, B M LEACH, **C** J L WATERFIELD, **OLM** C E DAVIES

BILTON (St John the Evangelist) and St Luke *Ripon 1* **P** *Bp* **TR** L BENTLEY, **C** P T ASKEW, D J MCCLINTOCK, **NSM** G P CORNISH

BILTON (St Mark) *Cov 6* **P** *N M Assheton Esq* **P-in-c** T D COCKELL, **C** L J BLAY

BILTON, NEW (St Oswald) *Cov 6* **P** *Dioc Trustees* **P-in-c** G J HARDWICK

BILTON-IN-AINSTY (St Helen) *see* Tockwith and Bilton w Bickerton *York*

BILTON IN HOLDERNESS (St Peter) *York 12* **P** *Abp* **V** R J E MAJOR

BINBROOK Group, The (St Mary) *Linc 10* **P** *Ld Chan, DBP and G F Sleight Esq (alt)* **R** T J WALKER

BINCOMBE (Holy Trinity) w Broadwey, Upwey and Buckland Ripers *Sarum 4* **P** *G&C Coll Cam (2 turns), Miss M B F Frampton (1 turn), and Bp (1 turn)* **R** R A C SIMMONS

BINEGAR (Holy Trinity) *see* Ashwick w Oakhill and Binegar *B & W*

BINFIELD (All Saints) (St Mark) *Ox 11* **P** *Ld Chan* **R** W J MEYER, **OLM** M THIRLWELL

BINGFIELD (St Mary) *see* St Oswald in Lee w Bingfield *Newc*

BINGHAM (St Mary and All Saints) *S'well 8* **P** *The Crown* **R** D L HARPER, **NSM** L FOOT

BINGLEY (All Saints) *Bradf 1* **P** *Bp* **TV** H FIELDEN, **P-in-c** D R JACKSON

BINGLEY (Holy Trinity) *Bradf 1* **P** *Bp* **V** A J CLARKE, **C** C J ANDREW, **NSM** J JACKSON

BINHAM (St Mary) *see* Stiffkey and Bale *Nor*

BINLEY (St Bartholomew) *Cov 1* **P** *Bp* **V** E E JONES

BINLEY WOODS Local Ecumenical Project *Cov 1* **Min** J CHEVERTON

BINSEY (St Margaret) *see* Ox St Thos w St Frideswide and Binsey *Ox*

BINSEY Team Ministry *Carl 7* **P** *Patr Bd* **TR** S P WALKER, **TV** F I WRIGHT, **C** J M FEARNLEY

BINSTEAD (Holy Cross) *Portsm 7* **P** *Bp* **R** N R WALLACE, **NSM** K R ADLAM

BINSTED (Holy Cross) *see* Bentley and Binsted *Win*

BINSTED (St Mary) *see* Walberton w Binsted *Chich*

BINTON (St Peter) *see* Temple Grafton w Binton *Cov*

BINTREE (St Swithin) *see* Twyford, Guist, Bintree, Themelthorpe etc *Nor*

BIRCH (St James) w Fallowfield *Man 4* **P** *Bp* **R** W G RAINES

BIRCH (St Mary) *see* Rhodes *Man*

BIRCH-IN-RUSHOLME (St Agnes) w Longsight St John w St Cyprian *Man 1* **P** *Prime Min and Bp (alt)* **P-in-c** S M EDWARDS

BIRCHAM, GREAT (St Mary the Virgin) *see* Docking, the Birchams, Stanhoe and Sedgeford *Nor*

BIRCHAM NEWTON (All Saints) *as above*

BIRCHANGER (St Mary the Virgin) *see* Stansted Mountfitchet w Birchanger and Farnham *Chelmsf*

BIRCHENCLIFFE (St Philip the Apostle) *Wakef 5* **P** *V Lindley* **P-in-c** J A LAWSON

BIRCHES HEAD (St Matthew) *see* Hanley H Ev *Lich*

BIRCHFIELD (Holy Trinity) *Birm 3* **P** *Bp* **V** D J G BOWEN

BIRCHILLS, THE (St Andrew) *see* Walsall St Andr *Lich*

BIRCHIN COPPICE (St Peter) *see* Kidderminster St Jo and H Innocents *Worc*

BIRCHINGTON (All Saints) w Acol and Minnis Bay *Cant 9* **P** *Abp* **V** D R WITTS

BIRCHMOOR (St John) *see* Polesworth *Birm*

BIRCHOVER (St Michael) *see* Youlgreave, Middleton, Stanton-in-Peak etc *Derby*

BIRCHWOOD (Mission Church) *see* Blackdown *B & W*

BIRCHWOOD (St Luke) *Linc 15* **P** *Bp* **V** J B PAVEY, **C** L E TURNER

BIRCHWOOD (Transfiguration) *Liv 12* **P** *Bp, Adn, and R Warrington (jt)* **V** R C HARDCASTLE

BIRCLE (St John the Baptist) *Man 10* **P** *R Middleton St Leon* **V** A R BROCKBANK, **NSM** D ALTHAM

BIRDBROOK (St Augustine) *see* Ridgewell w Ashen, Birdbrook and Sturmer *Chelmsf*

BIRDHAM (St James) *see* W Wittering and Birdham w Itchenor *Chich*

BIRDINGBURY (St Leonards) *see* Leam Valley *Cov*

BIRDLIP (St Mary in Hamlet) *see* Brimpsfield w Birdlip, Syde, Daglingworth etc *Glouc*

BIRDSALL (St Mary) *see* W Buckrose *York*

BIRKBY (St Peter) *see* E Richmond *Ripon*

BIRKDALE (St James) *Liv 9* **P** *Trustees* **V** J S BELLAMY

BIRKDALE (St John) *Liv 9* **P** *Trustees* **V** P C CATON

BIRKDALE (St Peter) *Liv 9* **P** *Trustees* **P-in-c** C POPE, **OLM** S CALVELEY, E LOXHAM

BIRKENHEAD (Christ Church) *Ches 1* **P** *Bp* **V** *vacant* 0151-652 5647 *or* 652 3990

BIRKENHEAD (St James) w St Bede *Ches 1* **P** *Trustees* **V** D A LAMB, **C** C J COVERLEY

BIRKENHEAD (St Winifred) Welsh Church *Ches 1 vacant*

BIRKENHEAD PRIORY (Christ the King) *Ches 1* **P** *Bp, Simeon's Trustees, and Ch Patr Trust (jt)* **TR** D WALKER, **TV** D J AYLING

BIRKENSHAW (St Paul) w Hunsworth *Wakef 8* **P** *V Birstall* **V** S MITCHELL, **NSM** D S ANDREW, **OLM** R DAVIDSON

BIRKIN (St Mary) *see* Haddlesey w Hambleton and Birkin *York*

BIRLEY (St Peter) *see* Canon Pyon w King's Pyon, Birley and Wellington *Heref*

BIRLING (All Saints), Addington, Ryarsh and Trottiscliffe *Roch 7* **P** *Bp* **R** J B CROSS

BIRLING, LOWER (Christ Church) *see* Snodland All SS w Ch Ch *Roch*

BIRLINGHAM (St James the Great) *see* Pershore w Pinvin, Wick and Birlingham *Worc*

BIRMINGHAM (Bishop Latimer w All Saints) *Birm 3* **P** *St Martin's Trustees* **R** R F BASHFORD

BIRMINGHAM (St George) *Birm 8* **P** *St Martin's Trustees* **P-in-c** R K JOHNSON

BIRMINGHAM (St John the Evangelist) *see* Ladywood St Jo and St Pet *Birm*
BIRMINGHAM (St Luke) *Birm 1* **P** *Trustees* **V** A G LENOX-CONYNGHAM
BIRMINGHAM (St Martin-in-the-Bull-Ring) w Bordesley St Andrew *Birm 1* **P** *St Martin's Trustees* **C** I D GOW, J E DOUGLAS, A KAMBLE, **NSM** F J BERRY
BIRMINGHAM (St Paul) *Birm 1* **P** *St Martin's Trustees* **V** T F PYKE, **C** G P LANHAM, **NSM** P M JONES
BIRSTALL (St James the Greater) and Wanlip *Leic 6* **P** *Bp and C A Palmer-Tomkinson Esq (jt)* **P-in-c** J D G SHAKESPEARE
BIRSTALL (St Peter) *Wakef 8* **P** *Bp* **V** P J KNIGHT
BIRSTWITH (St James) *see* Hampsthwaite and Killinghall and Birstwith *Ripon*
BIRTLES (St Catherine) *see* Alderley w Birtles *Ches*
BIRTLEY (St Giles) *see* Chollerton w Birtley and Thockrington *Newc*
BIRTLEY (St John the Evangelist) *Dur 11* **P** *R Chester le Street* **V** E G LLOYD
BIRTSMORTON (St Peter and St Paul) *see* Berrow w Pendock, Eldersfield, Hollybush etc *Worc*
BISBROOKE (St John the Baptist) *see* Lyddington w Stoke Dry and Seaton etc *Pet*
BISCATHORPE (St Helen) *see* Asterby Gp *Linc*
BISCOT (Holy Trinity) *St Alb 14* **P** *Bp* **V** T B SINGH
BISHAM (All Saints) *see* Gt Marlow w Marlow Bottom, Lt Marlow and Bisham *Ox*
BISHAMPTON (St James) *see* Abberton, The Flyfords, Naunton Beauchamp etc *Worc*
BISHOP AUCKLAND (St Andrew) (St Anne) *see* Auckland St Andr and St Anne *Dur*
BISHOP AUCKLAND (St Peter) *see* Auckland St Pet *Dur*
BISHOP AUCKLAND Woodhouse Close Area of Ecumenical Experiment (Conventional District) *Dur 10* **C-in-c** V T FENTON
BISHOP BURTON (All Saints) w Walkington *York 8* **P** *Abp and DBP (alt)* **R** D G KIRBY
BISHOP CAUNDLE (not known) *see* The Caundles w Folke and Holwell *Sarum*
BISHOP MIDDLEHAM (St Michael) *see* Upper Skerne *Dur*
BISHOP MONKTON (St John the Baptist) *see* Ripon Cathl *Ripon*
BISHOP NORTON (St Peter), Waddingham and Snitterby *Linc 6* **P** *Bp and The Crown (alt)* **R** *vacant* (01673) 818551
BISHOP SUTTON (Holy Trinity) and Stanton Drew and Stowey *B & W 10* **P** *Bp and Adn Bath (alt)* **V** J HIGGINS
BISHOP THORNTON (St John the Evangelist) *see* Markington w S Stainley and Bishop Thornton *Ripon*
BISHOP WILTON (St Edith) *see* Garrowby Hill *York*
BISHOPDALE (Mission Room) *see* Aysgarth and Bolton cum Redmire *Ripon*
BISHOPHILL JUNIOR (St Mary) *see* York St Clem w St Mary Bishophill *York*
BISHOPHILL SENIOR (St Clement w St Mary) *as above*
BISHOP'S CANNINGS (St Mary the Virgin), All Cannings and Etchilhampton *Sarum 16* **P** *DBP* **P-in-c** S ATTWATER, **OLM** E S BAILEY
BISHOP'S CASTLE (St John the Baptist) w Mainstone, Lydbury North and Edgton *Heref 10* **P** *Earl of Powis (3 turns), Ld Chan (1 turn), and Mrs R E Bell (1 turn)* **P-in-c** P D A COLLINS, **C** D C HOARE
BISHOP'S CLEEVE (St Michael and All Angels) *Glouc 15* **P** *DBP* **R** I F CALDER, **C** A J ROBINSON, C A WILLIAMS
BISHOP'S FROME (St Mary the Virgin) w Castle Frome and Fromes Hill *Heref 2* **P** *Bp* **P-in-c** J A DAVIES
BISHOPS GREEN (Community Church) *see* Burghclere w Newtown and Ecchinswell w Sydmonton *Win*
BISHOP'S HATFIELD (St Etheldreda) (St John) (St Michael and All Angels) (St Luke) *St Alb 21* **P** *Marquess of Salisbury* **TR** R E PYKE, **TV** P L SEGRAVE-PRIDE, P D SWINN, **C** V A HATHAWAY, **NSM** S E MARSH
BISHOP'S HULL (St John the Evangelist) *see* Taunton St Jo *B & W*
BISHOPS HULL (St Peter and St Paul) *B & W 18* **P** *Adn Taunton* **V** S TUCKER
BISHOP'S ITCHINGTON (St Michael) *Cov 10* **P** *Bp* **P-in-c** M C GREEN
BISHOP'S LAVINGTON (All Saints) *see* The Lavingtons, Cheverells, and Easterton *Sarum*
BISHOPS LYDEARD (Blessed Virgin Mary) w Bagborough and Cothelstone *B & W 18* **P** *D&C (3 turns), Ms P M G Mitford (1 turn)* **R** M L WISHART
BISHOPS NORTON (St John the Evangelist) *see* Twigworth, Down Hatherley, Norton, The Leigh etc *Glouc*
BISHOP'S STORTFORD (Holy Trinity) *St Alb 18* **P** *Bp* **P-in-c** J K WILLIAMS
BISHOP'S STORTFORD (St Michael) *St Alb 18* **P** *Bp* **V** R A V MARCHAND, **C** D M JORDAN, **NSM** D C HINGE, J E KNIGHT
BISHOP'S SUTTON (St Nicholas) and Ropley and West Tisted *Win 1* **P** *Peache Trustees* **R** R J SUCH
BISHOP'S TACHBROOK (St Chad) *Cov 11* **P** *Bp* **P-in-c** K M ROBERTS, **NSM** R C PANTLING
BISHOPS TAWTON (St John the Baptist) *see* Barnstaple *Ex*
BISHOP'S WALTHAM (St Peter) *Portsm 1* **P** *Bp* **R** A G DAVIS, **C** J M HEMMINGS
BISHOP'S WOOD (St Mary) *see* Hartlebury *Worc*
BISHOPSBOURNE (St Mary) *see* Barham w Bishopsbourne and Kingston *Cant*
BISHOPSNYMPTON (St Mary the Virgin), Rose Ash, Mariansleigh, Molland, Knowstone, East Anstey and West Anstey *Ex 19* **P** *DBP* **P-in-c** A C JONES
BISHOPSTEIGNTON (St John the Baptist) *see* Teignmouth, Ideford w Luton, Ashcombe etc *Ex*
BISHOPSTOKE (St Mary) (St Paul) *Win 10* **P** *Bp* **R** D J COTTRILL
BISHOPSTON (Church of the Good Shepherd) *see* Bishopston and St Andrews *Bris*
BISHOPSTON (St Michael and All Angels) *as above*
BISHOPSTON (St Michael and All Angels) (Church of the Good Shepherd) and St Andrews *Bris 3* **P** *Patr Bd* **TR** P R BAILEY, **TV** R J BURBRIDGE, **NSM** B J PULLAN, V LEE
BISHOPSTONE (St Andrew) *Chich 18* **P** *Bp Lon* **NSM** M E SITWELL
BISHOPSTONE (St John the Baptist) *see* Chalke Valley *Sarum*
BISHOPSTONE (St Lawrence) *see* Credenhill w Brinsop and Wormsley etc *Heref*
BISHOPSTONE (St Mary the Virgin) *see* Lyddington and Wanborough and Bishopstone etc *Bris*
BISHOPSTROW (St Aldhelm) and Boreham *Sarum 17* **P** *DBP* **R** D R A BRETT
BISHOPSWOOD (All Saints) *see* Walford and St John w Bishopswood, Goodrich etc *Heref*
BISHOPSWOOD (St John the Evangelist) *Lich 2* **P** *V Brewood* **V** C B BURGESS, **NSM** M J COULTER
BISHOPSWORTH (St Peter) and Bedminster Down *Bris 1* **P** *Bp* **TR** T R J GODDEN, **TV** J M LEWIS, **NSM** E P WHERLOCK, R A LANE
BISHOPTHORPE (St Andrew) *York 1* **P** *Abp* **V** C I COATES
BISHOPTON (St Peter) w Great Stainton *Dur 10* **P** *Ld Chan* **V** D M BROOKE
BISHOPWEARMOUTH (Good Shepherd) *Dur 16* **P** *Bp* **P-in-c** B SKELTON
BISHOPWEARMOUTH (St Gabriel) *Dur 16* **P** *V Sunderland* **V** A THORP, **NSM** H M THORP, J P TALBOT
BISHOPWEARMOUTH (St Luke Pallion) *see* Millfield St Mark and Pallion St Luke *Dur*
BISHOPWEARMOUTH (St Mary) *see* Millfield St Mary *Dur*
BISHOPWEARMOUTH (St Nicholas) (Christ Church) *Dur 16* **P** *Bp* **V** N B WARNER
BISLEY (All Saints), Chalford, France Lynch, and Oakridge *Glouc 1* **P** *Bp and Adn Glouc (1 turn), and Ld Chan (1 turn)* **V** S G RICHARDS, **C** A GUY
BISLEY (St John the Baptist) and West End (Holy Trinity) *Guildf 6* **P** *Bp* **R** A J ARMITT, **C** K B NICHOLLS, **NSM** D H ROBINSON
BISPHAM (All Hallows) *Blackb 8* **P** *Ch Soc Trust* **R** S J COX, **C** D O'BRIEN
BISTERNE (St Paul) *see* Ringwood *Win*
BITCHFIELD (St Mary Magdalene) *see* Ingoldsby *Linc*
BITTADON (St Peter) *see* Ilfracombe, Lee, Woolacombe, Bittadon etc *Ex*
BITTERING PARVA (St Peter and St Paul) *see* Gressenhall w Longham w Wendling etc *Nor*
BITTERLEY (St Mary) w Middleton, Stoke St Milborough w The Heath and Hopton Cangeford, Clee St Margaret and Cold Weston *Heref 12* **P** *Bp, DBP, Walcott Trustees, and Miss M F Rouse-Boughton (jt)* **R** A G SEABROOK
BITTERNE (Holy Saviour) *Win 13* **P** *Bp* **P-in-c** S P E MOURANT, **C** A G H GAY, E L TALBOT
BITTERNE PARK (All Hallows) (Ascension) *Win 13* **P** *Bp* **V** S J CHAPMAN, **C** P BRADBURY
BITTESWELL (St Mary) *see* Lutterworth w Cotesbach and Bitteswell *Leic*
BITTON (St Mary) *see* Warmley, Syston and Bitton *Bris*
BIX (St James) *see* Nettlebed w Bix, Highmoor, Pishill etc *Ox*
BLABY (All Saints) *Leic 10* **P** *Bp* **P-in-c** J G GIBBINS
BLACK BOURTON (St Mary the Virgin) *see* Shill Valley and Broadshire *Ox*
BLACK NOTLEY (St Peter and St Paul) *Chelmsf 15* **P** *St Jo Coll Cam* **R** A G MORRISON

BLACK TORRINGTON (St Mary), Bradford w Cookbury, Thornbury and Highampton *Ex 17* **P** *DBP* **R** *vacant* (01409) 231279
BLACKAWTON (St Michael) *see* Stoke Fleming, Blackawton and Strete *Ex*
BLACKBIRD LEYS (Holy Family) *Ox 4* **P** *Bp* **V** D T N PARRY, **NSM** E P MUKHOLI
BLACKBOURNE *St E 9* **P** *Patr Bd* **TR** P M OLIVER, **TV** E S FOGDEN, **OLM** D A NEUPERT, S M NUTT, J F WALKER
BLACKBROOK (St Paul) *see* Parr *Liv*
BLACKBURN (Christ Church w St Matthew) *Blackb 2* **P** *Bp* **V** A RAYNES
BLACKBURN Christ the King (St Luke) (St Mark) *Blackb 2* **P** *Bp and V Blackb (jt)* **V** F E GREEN
BLACKBURN (St Andrew) *see* Livesey *Blackb*
BLACKBURN (St Barnabas) *Blackb 2* **P** *Bp* **V** H H DANIEL
BLACKBURN (St Francis) (St Aidan) *Blackb 2* **P** *Bp* **V** D G KENNEDY
BLACKBURN (St Gabriel) *Blackb 2* **P** *Bp* **P-in-c** G THOMAS, **C** A D THOMPSON
BLACKBURN (St James) *Blackb 2* **P** *Bp* **P-in-c** S TRANTER
BLACKBURN (St Luke) *see* Blackb Christ the King *Blackb*
BLACKBURN (St Michael and All Angels) (Holy Trinity Worship Centre) w St John the Evangelist *Blackb 2* **P** *V Blackb* **P-in-c** C R SCHAEFER, **C** C W HILL, **NSM** M FISH
BLACKBURN (St Silas) *Blackb 2* **P** *Trustees* **P-in-c** A F RANSON
BLACKBURN (St Stephen) *Blackb 2* **P** *Trustees* **P-in-c** S TRANTER
BLACKBURN St Thomas (St Jude) *Blackb 2* **P** *Bp and Trustees (alt)* **V** C R SCHAEFER, **C** C W HILL, **NSM** M FISH
BLACKBURN The Redeemer (St Bartholomew) (The Saviour) *Blackb 2* **P** *Bp and CPAS (jt)* **V** R A H MARSHALL
BLACKDOWN Benefice, The *B & W 18* **P** *DBP (4 turns), Pitminster PCC and Corfe PCC (1 turn)* **NSM** D GODDARD
BLACKDOWN (Holy Trinity) *see* Beaminster Area *Sarum*
BLACKFEN (Good Shepherd) *see* Lamorbey H Redeemer *Roch*
BLACKFORD (Holy Trinity) *see* Wedmore w Theale and Blackford *B & W*
BLACKFORD (St John the Baptist) *see* Rockcliffe and Blackford *Carl*
BLACKFORD (St Michael) *see* Camelot Par *B & W*
BLACKFORDBY (St Margaret) and Woodville *Leic 9* **P** *Bp* **V** T S G VALE
BLACKHALL (St Andrew), Castle Eden and Monkhesleden *Dur 2* **P** *Bp* **R** G LIDDLE
BLACKHAM (All Saints) *see* Withyham St Mich *Chich*
BLACKHEATH (All Saints) *S'wark 4* **P** *V Lewisham St Mary* **V** N W S CRANFIELD, **OLM** T W CHATTERTON
BLACKHEATH (Ascension) *S'wark 4* **P** *V Lewisham St Mary* **NSM** E R NEWNHAM
BLACKHEATH (St John the Evangelist) *S'wark 3* **P** *CPAS* **V** M D MARSHALL, **C** P S DOEL, **NSM** A M BESWETHERICK, N C WHEELER, A WILLIAMSON
BLACKHEATH (St Martin) *see* Wonersh w Blackheath *Guildf*
BLACKHEATH (St Paul) *Birm 7* **P** *Bp* **V** M J SERMON, **C** M S PRASADAM
BLACKHEATH PARK (St Michael and All Angels) *S'wark 3* **P** *Bp* **V** A R CHRISTIE, **C** M R CURTIS, **NSM** A SCOTT, M J CALLAGHAN
BLACKLAND (St Peter) *see* Calne and Blackland *Sarum*
BLACKLANDS Hastings (Christchurch and St Andrew) *Chich 17* **P** *Ch Patr Trust* **V** D F FENTIMAN
BLACKLEY (Holy Trinity) *Man 5* **P** *Bp* **R** P A STAMP
BLACKLEY (St Andrew) *Man 5* **P** *Bp* **P-in-c** I D THOMPSON
BLACKLEY (St Mark) White Moss *Man 5* **P** *D&C* **P-in-c** I C J GORTON
BLACKLEY (St Paul) *Man 5* **P** *Bp* **P-in-c** J L CLEGG
BLACKLEY (St Peter) *Man 5* **P** *D&C* **P-in-c** H M EVANS
BLACKMOOR (St Matthew) and Whitehill *Portsm 4* **P** *Earl of Selborne* **V** *vacant* (01420) 473548
BLACKMORE (St Laurence) and Stondon Massey *Chelmsf 27* **P** *Bp* **V** I E CRAWFORD, **C** A WHITAKER
BLACKPOOL (Christ Church w All Saints) (St Andrew) *Blackb 8* **P** *Bp and Trustees (jt)* **V** P J WARREN, **C** S KEARNEY
BLACKPOOL (Holy Cross) South Shore *Blackb 8* **P** *Bp* **V** S EDWARDS, **C** H E MURPHY
BLACKPOOL (Holy Trinity) *see* S Shore H Trin *Blackb*
BLACKPOOL (St John) *Blackb 8* **P** *Trustees* **V** M A MANLEY, **C** S A PURVIS
BLACKPOOL (St Mark) *Blackb 8* **P** *CPAS* **V** S E BROOK
BLACKPOOL (St Mary) South Shore *Blackb 8* **P** *Bp* **V** C G LORD
BLACKPOOL (St Michael and All Angels) *Blackb 8* **P** *Bp* **V** N J HEALE
BLACKPOOL (St Paul) Marton *see* Marton *Blackb*
BLACKPOOL (St Paul's Worship Centre) *Blackb 8* **P** *Trustees* **V** J E SHAW
BLACKPOOL (St Peter) *see* S Shore St Pet *Blackb*
BLACKPOOL (St Stephen on the Cliffs) *Blackb 8* **P** *Bp, R Bispham All Hallows, and Ch Wardens (jt)* **V** A G SAGE
BLACKPOOL (St Thomas) *Blackb 8* **P** *CPAS* **V** G A FISHER, **C** P J NESBITT, **NSM** J FISHER
BLACKPOOL (St Wilfrid) Mereside *Blackb 8* **P** *Bp* **V** P H HUDSON
BLACKROD (St Catherine) (Scot Lane School) *Man 11* **P** *V Bolton-le-Moors St Pet* **V** R C COOPER, **OLM** C MCCABE, H K SHARP
BLACKTOFT (Holy Trinity) *see* Howden *York*
BLACKWATER (St Barnabas) *see* Arreton *Portsm*
BLACKWELL (All Saints) and Salutation *Dur 8* **P** *Bp* **V** J R DOBSON
BLACKWELL (St Catherine) *see* The Lickey *Birm*
BLACKWELL (St Werburgh) w Tibshelf *Derby 1* **P** *Bp and MMCET (jt)* **V** J CRANE
BLACON (Holy Trinity) *see* Ches H Trin *Ches*
BLADON (St Martin) *see* Blenheim *Ox*
BLAGDON (St Andrew) w Compton Martin and Ubley *B & W 10* **P** *Bp and Sir John Wills Bt (jt)* **R** V E S GOODMAN
BLAGREAVES (St Andrew) *Derby 10* **P** *Bp, Churchwardens, and CPAS (jt)* **V** P G BYSOUTH
BLAISDON (St Michael and All Angels) *see* Westbury-on-Severn w Flaxley, Blaisdon etc *Glouc*
BLAKEDOWN (St James the Great) *see* Churchill-in-Halfshire w Blakedown and Broome *Worc*
BLAKEMERE (St Leonard) *see* Cusop w Blakemere, Bredwardine w Brobury etc *Heref*
BLAKENALL HEATH (Christ Church) *Lich 25* **P** *Patr Bd* **TV** B D SIMS, **C** J D DEAKIN
BLAKENEY (All Saints) *see* Newnham w Awre and Blakeney *Glouc*
BLAKENEY (St Nicholas w St Mary and St Thomas) w Cley, Wiveton, Glandford and Letheringsett *Nor 18* **P** *Bp and Keble Coll Ox (jt)* **R** P G F NORWOOD, **NSM** J M FAWCETT
BLAKENHALL (St Luke) *see* Wolverhampton St Luke *Lich*
BLAKENHAM, GREAT (St Mary) and LITTLE (St Mary) w Baylham and Nettlestead *St E 1* **P** *Bp and MMCET (jt)* **R** *vacant* (01473) 623840
BLAKESLEY (St Mary) w Adstone and Maidford and Farthingstone *Pet 5* **P** *Sons of Clergy Corp, Bp, Hertf Coll Ox, and Capt R Grant-Renwick (by turn)* **P-in-c** J T P HALL
BLANCHLAND (St Mary's Abbey) w Hunstanworth and Edmundbyers and Muggleswick *Newc 3* **P** *D E Scott-Harden Esq, Lord Crewe's Trustees and D&C (alt)* **P-in-c** D J IRVINE, **NSM** J LYNCH
BLANDFORD FORUM (St Peter and St Paul) and Langton Long *Sarum 6* **P** *Bp* **R** T STOREY, **C** M COURT
BLANDFORD ST MARY (St Mary) *see* Spetisbury w Charlton Marshall etc *Sarum*
BLANKNEY (St Oswald) *see* Metheringham w Blankney and Dunston *Linc*
BLASTON (St Giles) *see* Six Saints circa Holt *Leic*
BLATCHINGTON, EAST (St John the Evangelist) (St Peter) *Chich 18* **P** *Bp* **P-in-c** B R COOK, **NSM** R J WOODHAMS, R A WARD
BLATCHINGTON, WEST (St Peter) *Chich 4* **P** *Bp* **R** R T A FARROW
BLAXHALL (St Peter) *see* Sternfield, Benhall, Snape etc *St E*
BLAYDON (St Cuthbert) and Swalwell *Dur 13* **P** *Bp* **R** H DITCHBURN
BLEADON (St Peter and St Paul) *B & W 11* **P** *Guild of All So* **R** D T PARKINSON
BLEAN (St Cosmus and St Damian) *Cant 3* **P** *Master of Eastbridge Hosp* **P-in-c** D M H HAYES, **OLM** G S J H WHITTLESEA
BLEASBY (St Mary) *see* Thurgarton w Hoveringham and Bleasby etc *S'well*
BLEASDALE (St Eadmor) *see* Fellside Team *Blackb*
BLEATARN (Chapel of Ease) *see* Brough w Stainmore, Musgrave and Warcop *Carl*
BLEDINGTON (St Leonard) *see* Broadwell, Evenlode, Oddington, Adlestrop etc *Glouc*
BLEDLOW (Holy Trinity) *see* Risborough *Ox*
BLEDLOW RIDGE (St Paul) *see* W Wycombe w Bledlow Ridge, Bradenham and Radnage *Ox*
BLENDON (St James the Great) *Roch 17* **P** *The Crown* **V** A KEELER

BLENDWORTH (Holy Trinity) w Chalton w Idsworth *Portsm 5* **P** *Bp* **P-in-c** R I P COUTTS, **NSM** R A DONALD
BLENHEIM *Ox 9* **P** *Patr Bd* **TR** R J HUMPHREYS, **TV** A PARKINSON, **C** S C HENSON, **NSM** C A W SANDERS
BLETCHINGDON (St Giles) *see* Akeman *Ox*
BLETCHINGLEY (St Andrew) (St Mary) *S'wark 26* **P** *Em Coll Cam* **P-in-c** P MOSELING
BLETCHLEY (St Mary) *Ox 25* **P** *DBP* **P-in-c** M J ARCHER, **C** C BUTT, J M A ADAMS
BLETCHLEY, NORTH (Whaddon Way Church) Conventional District *Ox 25 vacant* (01908) 75370
BLETSOE (St Mary) *see* Riseley w Bletsoe *St Alb*
BLEWBURY (St Michael and All Angels), Hagbourne and Upton *Ox 18* **P** *Bp* **R** E G CLEMENTS, **C** R J E DEWHURST, **OLM** L G BUTLER
BLICKLING (St Andrew) *see* Lt Barningham, Blickling, Edgefield etc *Nor*
BLIDWORTH (St Mary of the Purification) w Rainworth *S'well 2* **P** *DBP and Ld Chan (alt)* **V** R GOODHAND, **NSM** B A ALLSOP
BLIDWORTH, NEW (St Andrew) *see* Blidworth w Rainworth *S'well*
BLINDLEY HEATH (St John the Evangelist) *see* Godstone and Blindley Heath *S'wark*
BLISLAND (St Protus and St Hyacinth) w St Breward *Truro 10* **P** *SMF and D&C (alt)* **R** *vacant* (01208) 850869
BLISWORTH (St John the Baptist) and Stoke Bruerne w Grafton Regis and Alderton *Pet 5* **P** *BNC Ox and MMCET (2 turns), Ld Chan (1 turn)* **R** R MELLOR
BLITHFIELD (St Leonard) *see* Abbots Bromley w Blithfield *Lich*
BLO' NORTON (St Andrew) *see* Guiltcross *Nor*
BLOCKLEY (St Peter and St Paul) w Aston Magna and Bourton on the Hill *Glouc 10* **P** *Lord Dulverton and DBP (jt)* **P-in-c** G L HUMPHRIES
BLOFIELD (St Andrew) w Hemblington *Nor 4* **P** *G&C Coll Cam* **P-in-c** P J UNSWORTH
BLOOMSBURY (St George) w Woburn Square (Christ Church) *Lon 17* **P** *Ld Chan* **R** P A BUTLER, **Hon C** R I T JARRETT
BLORE RAY (St Bartholomew) *see* Calton, Cauldon, Grindon, Waterfall etc *Lich*
BLOXHAM (Our Lady of Bloxham) w Milcombe and South Newington *Ox 5* **P** *Ex Coll Ox and Eton Coll (jt)* **C** D W F WITCHELL
BLOXHOLME (St Mary) *see* Digby Gp *Linc*
BLOXWICH (All Saints) (Holy Ascension) *Lich 25* **P** *Patr Bd* **TR** S C RAWLING, **TV** M H HAWKSWORTH, K A LOWTHER
BLOXWORTH (St Andrew) *see* Red Post *Sarum*
BLUBBERHOUSES (St Andrew) *see* Leathley w Farnley, Fewston and Blubberhouses *Bradf*
BLUCHER (St Cuthbert) *see* Newburn *Newc*
BLUE BELL HILL (St Alban) *see* S Chatham H Trin *Roch*
BLUNDELLSANDS (St Michael) *Liv 5* **P** *Trustees* **P-in-c** M C FREEMAN
BLUNDELLSANDS (St Nicholas) *Liv 5* **P** *Trustees* **V** C M M THORNBOROUGH
BLUNDESTON (St Mary) *see* Somerleyton, Ashby, Fritton, Herringfleet etc *Nor*
BLUNHAM (St Edmund King and Martyr and St James), Great Barford, Roxton and Tempsford w Little Barford *St Alb 11* **P** *Prime Min, Trin Coll Cam (2 turns), and Ball Coll Ox (by turn)* **R** B EBELING, **NSM** D C QUIN
BLUNSDON (St Andrew) *see* N Swindon St Andr *Bris*
BLUNTISHAM (St Mary) cum Earith w Colne and Woodhurst *Ely 9* **P** *Ch Ch Ox* **R** C BACKHOUSE
BLURTON (St Bartholomew) (St Alban) *Lich 13* **P** *Bp* **V** P J MOCKFORD, **C** B A A LAWAL, D A HEWITSON, **OLM** H T ADAMS, L J WALKER
BLYBOROUGH (St Alkmund) *see* Glentworth Gp *Linc*
BLYFORD (All Saints) *see* Blyth Valley *St E*
BLYMHILL (St Mary) w Weston-under-Lizard *Lich 2* **P** *W H C Montgomery Esq, Sir Brooke Boothby Bt, and Viscount Boyne (jt)* **P-in-c** G J THOMPSON, **NSM** M G SIMS
BLYTH (St Cuthbert) *Newc 1* **P** *Bp* **V** R D TAYLOR
BLYTH (St Mary) *Newc 1* **P** *Bp* **V** *vacant* (01670) 353417
BLYTH (St Mary and St Martin) and Scrooby w Ranskill *S'well 1* **P** *Bp and Trin Coll Cam (jt)* **V** R A SPRAY
BLYTH VALLEY Team Ministry, The *St E 15* **P** *Patr Bd* **TR** E L RENNARD, **TV** A B NORTON, **C** I B BYRNE, **OLM** A G DEERING, J E A BAILEY, M T JOEL, T SAVEGE, A C WRIGHT
BLYTHBURGH (Holy Trinity) *see* Sole Bay *St E*
BLYTON (St Martin) *see* Corringham and Blyton Gp *Linc*
BOARHUNT (St Nicholas) *see* Southwick w Boarhunt *Portsm*
BOARSTALL (St James) *see* Bernwode *Ox*
BOBBING (St Bartholomew) *see* Sittingbourne H Trin w Bobbing *Cant*
BOBBINGTON (Holy Cross) *see* Smestow Vale *Lich*
BOBBINGWORTH (St Germain) *see* Fyfield, Moreton w Bobbingworth etc *Chelmsf*
BOCKING (St Mary) *Chelmsf 15* **P** *Abp Cant* **R** P A NEED
BOCKING (St Peter) *Chelmsf 15* **P** *Abp Cant* **V** T C DIAPER
BOCKLETON (St Michael) *see* Leominster *Heref*
BOCONNOC (not known) *see* Lostwithiel, St Winnow w St Nectan's Chpl etc *Truro*
BODDINGTON (St John the Baptist) *see* Byfield w Boddington and Aston le Walls *Pet*
BODDINGTON (St Mary Magdalene) *see* Twigworth, Down Hatherley, Norton, The Leigh etc *Glouc*
BODENHAM (St Michael and All Angels) w Hope-under-Dinmore, Felton and Preston Wynne *Heref 4* **P** *Bp* **P-in-c** H M SHORT
BODHAM (All Saints) *see* Weybourne Gp *Nor*
BODIAM (St Giles) *Chich 20* **P** *All So Coll Ox* **V** G L WINCHESTER
BODICOTE (St John the Baptist) *Ox 5* **P** *New Coll Ox* **V** B L M PHILLIPS, **OLM** B C GARDNER
BODINNICK (St John) *see* Lanteglos by Fowey *Truro*
BODLE STREET GREEN (St John the Evangelist) *see* Warbleton and Bodle Street Green *Chich*
BODMIN (St Leonard) (St Petroc) w Lanhydrock and Lanivet *Truro 10* **P** *DBP* **TR** G G C MINORS, **C** A B SHAW, M F GODFREY, **Hon C** J MARSHALL, **NSM** F B J COOMBES, C F CLEMOW
BODNEY (St Mary) *see* Hilborough w Bodney *Nor*
BOGNOR (St Wilfrid) *Chich 1* **P** *Abp* **V** *vacant* (01243) 821965
BOLAM (St Andrew) *see* Heighington *Dur*
BOLAM (St Andrew) w Whalton and Hartburn w Meldon *Newc 11* **P** *Ld Chan (2 turns), J I K Walker Esq (1 turn), and D&C Dur (1 turn)* **R** M A G BRYCE
BOLAS MAGNA (St John the Baptist) *see* Tibberton w Bolas Magna and Waters Upton *Lich*
BOLDMERE (St Michael) *Birm 12* **P** *Birm Dioc Trustees* **C** E G A DAVIS
BOLDON (St Nicholas) *Dur 15* **P** *Bp* **P-in-c** S BUYERS
BOLDON, EAST (St George) *Dur 15* **P** *Bp* **V** E G STEPHENSON, **NSM** M R DEVINE
BOLDRE (St John the Baptist) w South Baddesley *Win 11* **P** *Bp and Lord Teynham (jt)* **V** C I WALTON
BOLDRE, EAST (St Paul) *see* Beaulieu and Exbury and E Boldre *Win*
BOLDRON (Mission Room) *see* Startforth and Bowes and Rokeby w Brignall *Ripon*
BOLE (St Martin) *see* N Wheatley, W Burton, Bole, Saundby, Sturton etc *S'well*
BOLINGBROKE (St Peter and St Paul) *see* Marden Hill Gp *Linc*
BOLINGBROKE, NEW (St Peter) *see* Sibsey w Frithville *Linc*
BOLLINGHAM (St Silas) *see* Eardisley w Bollingham, Willersley, Brilley etc *Heref*
BOLLINGTON (Holy Trinity) *see* Rostherne w Bollington *Ches*
BOLLINGTON (St John the Baptist) *see* Bollington St Jo *Ches*
BOLLINGTON (St John the Baptist) *Ches 13* **P** *V Prestbury* **V** S R MARSH
BOLLINGTON CROSS (St Oswald) *see* Bollington St Jo *Ches*
BOLNEY (St Mary Magdalene) *Chich 6* **P** *K Coll Lon* **V** *vacant* (01444) 881301
BOLNHURST (St Dunstan) *see* Keysoe w Bolnhurst and Lt Staughton *St Alb*
BOLSOVER (St Mary and St Laurence) *Derby 3* **P** *Bp* **V** W T HICKS, **C** T J WILLIAMS
BOLSTERSTONE (St Mary) *Sheff 3* **P** *R B Rimington Wilson Esq* **V** K J BARNARD, **C** C E BARNARD
BOLTBY (Holy Trinity) *see* Felixkirk w Boltby *York*
BOLTON (All Saints) *see* Binsey *Carl*
BOLTON (All Saints) *Carl 1* **P** *V Morland w Thrimby etc* **P-in-c** S D RUDKIN
BOLTON Breightmet (St James) *Man 16* **P** *The Crown* **P-in-c** G H YERBURY, **NSM** A PIERCE, **OLM** E P ABRAHAM
BOLTON Chapel (unknown) *see* Whittingham and Edlingham w Bolton Chapel *Newc*
BOLTON (St Chad) *see* Tonge Fold *Man*
BOLTON (St James w St Chrysostom) *Bradf 3* **P** *Bp* **V** D J SWALES, **C** C B LLOYD
BOLTON (St John the Evangelist) Top o' th' Moss *Man 16* **P** *The Crown* **P-in-c** G H YERBURY

BOLTON (St Matthew w St Barnabas) *see* Halliwell *Man*
BOLTON (St Paul) *as above*
BOLTON (St Thomas the Apostle) *as above*
BOLTON ABBEY (St Mary and St Cuthbert) *Bradf 7* **P** *Duke of Devonshire* **R** J S WARD
BOLTON BY BOWLAND (St Peter and St Paul) w Grindleton *Bradf 5* **P** *Bp and V Hurst Green and Mitton (jt)* **R** D W MEWIS
BOLTON LE MOORS (St Bede) *Man 11* **P** *Bp* **P-in-c** W P BREW
BOLTON LE MOORS (St Paul) (Emmanuel) *Man 9* **P** *Patr Bd* **P-in-c** R J HORROCKS, **C** J A M BARNETT
BOLTON LE MOORS (St Peter) *Man 9* **P** *Bp* **V** M J WILLIAMS, **C** D A PLUMMER, **NSM** K G C NEWPORT
BOLTON LE MOORS (St Philip) *Man 9* **P** *Bp and Hulme Trustees (alt)* **P-in-c** M J WILLIAMS, **NSM** R E IDDON
BOLTON LE MOORS (St Simon and St Jude) *Man 9* **P** *Trustees* **P-in-c** G BUSH
BOLTON-LE-SANDS (Holy Trinity) *Blackb 14* **P** *Bp* **V** T J L MAIDMENT, **NSM** B C JONES, L MACLUSKIE
BOLTON ON SWALE (St Mary) *see* Easby w Skeeby and Brompton on Swale etc *Ripon*
BOLTON PERCY (All Saints) *York 1* **P** *Abp* **P-in-c** F A R MINAY
BOLTON-UPON-DEARNE (St Andrew the Apostle) *Sheff 12* **P** *Meynall Ch Trust* **V** D G STAFFORD
BOLTONS, THE *see* W Brompton St Mary w St Pet *Lon*
BOLVENTOR (Holy Trinity) *see* Altarnon w Bolventor, Laneast and St Clether *Truro*
BOMERE HEATH (Mission Room) *see* Leaton and Albrighton w Battlefield *Lich*
BONBY (St Andrew) *Linc 6* **P** *DBP* **V** G A PLUMB
BONCHURCH (St Boniface) (St Boniface Old Church) *Portsm 7* **P** *Ch Patr Trust* **R** *vacant*
BONDLEIGH (St James the Apostle) *see* N Tawton, Bondleigh, Sampford Courtenay etc *Ex*
BONEY HAY *see* Chase Terrace *Lich*
BONINGALE (St Chad) *Lich 16* **P** *MMCET* **P-in-c** R B BALKWILL
BONNINGTON (St Rumwold) *see* Aldington w Bonnington and Bilsington etc *Cant*
BONSALL (St James the Apostle) *see* Wirksworth *Derby*
BOOKER (St Birinus' Mission Church) *see* High Wycombe *Ox*
BOOKHAM, GREAT (St Nicolas) *Guildf 10* **P** *Bp* **R** P R FLEMING, **C** A E EVANS
BOOKHAM, LITTLE (not known) *see* Effingham w Lt Bookham *Guildf*
BOONGATE (St Mary) *see* Pet St Mary Boongate *Pet*
BOOSBECK (St Aidan) w Moorsholm *York 16* **P** *Abp* **V** E R NORRIS
BOOTHBY GRAFFOE (St Andrew) *see* Graffoe Gp *Linc*
BOOTHBY PAGNELL (St Andrew) *see* Ingoldsby *Linc*
BOOTHSTOWN (St Andrew's Church Institute) *see* Worsley *Man*
BOOTLE (Christ Church) *Liv 1* **P** *Bp* **V** T RICH
BOOTLE (St Andrew) (St Leonard) (St Mary w St Paul) (St Matthew) (St Thomas) *Liv 1* **P** *Patr Bd* **TR** R J DRIVER, **TV** J C M BISSEX
BOOTLE (St Michael and All Angels), Corney, Whicham and Whitbeck *Carl 5* **P** *Earl of Lonsdale* **R** *vacant* (01229) 718223
BORASTON (not known) *see* Burford I *Heref*
BORDEN (St Peter and St Paul) *Cant 15* **P** *SMF* **P-in-c** J H G LEWIS
BORDERLINK PARISHES *see* Cusop w Blakemere, Bredwardine w Brobury etc *Heref*
BORDESLEY (St Alban and St Patrick) *see* Highgate *Birm*
BORDESLEY (St Benedict) *Birm 13* **P** *Keble Coll Ox* **C** R J PRESTON, **NSM** P L CADOGAN
BORDESLEY GREEN (St Paul) *Birm 13* **P** *The Crown* **V** *vacant* 0121-772 0418
BORDON (St Mark) *Guildf 3* **P** *Bp* **V** D J SCOTT-BROMLEY
BOREHAM (St Andrew) *Chelmsf 9* **P** *Bp* **P-in-c** A J ROSE
BOREHAM (St John the Evangelist) *see* Bishopstrow and Boreham *Sarum*
BOREHAMWOOD (All Saints) *see* Elstree and Borehamwood *St Alb*
BOREHAMWOOD (Holy Cross) *as above*
BOREHAMWOOD (St Michael and All Angels) *as above*
BORLEY (not known) *see* N Hinckford *Chelmsf*
BOROUGH GREEN (Good Shepherd) *Roch 10* **P** *Bp* **V** A J POWELL
BOROUGHBRIDGE (St James) *see* Aldborough w Boroughbridge and Roecliffe *Ripon*
BORROWASH (St Stephen's Chapel) *see* Ockbrook *Derby*
BORROWDALE (St Andrew) *see* Thornthwaite cum Braithwaite, Newlands etc *Carl*
BORSTAL (St Matthew) *Roch 5* **P** *V Rochester St Marg* **P-in-c** J E G DASH
BORWICK (St Mary) *see* Warton St Oswald w Yealand Conyers *Blackb*
BOSBURY (Holy Trinity) *see* Ledbury *Heref*
BOSCASTLE w Davidstow *Truro 10* **P** *Duchy of Cornwall (1 turn), DBP (2 turns)* **P-in-c** C MUSSER
BOSCOMBE (St Andrew) *see* Bourne Valley *Sarum*
BOSCOMBE (St Andrew) *Win 8* **P** *Bp* **V** N A CARTER
BOSCOMBE (St John the Evangelist) *Win 8* **P** *Peache Trustees* **V** R P KHAKHRIA, **C** P J TAYLOR
BOSCOPPA *Truro 1* **P** *Prime Min* **P-in-c** K P ARTHUR
BOSHAM (Holy Trinity) *Chich 13* **P** *Bp* **V** T J INMAN, **NSM** J V EMERSON
BOSLEY (St Mary the Virgin) and North Rode (St Michael) w Wincle (St Michael) and Wildboarclough (St Saviour) *Ches 13* **P** *Bp, V Prestbury, and Earl of Derby (jt)* **V** V BREED
BOSSALL (St Botolph) *see* Sand Hutton *York*
BOSSINGTON (St James) *see* Broughton, Bossington, Houghton and Mottisfont *Win*
BOSTALL HEATH (St Andrew) *Roch 15* **P** *DBP* **V** S SHOOTER
BOSTON (Holy Trinity) *see* Skirbeck H Trin *Linc*
BOSTON (St Botolph) (St Christopher) *Linc 20* **P** *Bp* **V** R L WHITEHEAD, **C** P N MARSHALL, R K R COLES
BOSTON (St Nicholas) *see* Skirbeck St Nic *Linc*
BOSTON (St Thomas) *see* Skirbeck Quarter *Linc*
BOSTON SPA (St Mary) *York 1* **P** *Ch Ch Ox* **V** P E BRISTOW, **NSM** S H MENZIES
BOSWORTH (St Peter) and Sheepy Group *Leic 12* **P** *Patr Bd (2 turns), Ld Chan (1 turn)* **TR** J F PLANT, **TV** B CAMPBELL, A S REED, **NSM** A C HOLDSTOCK, G R JACKSON
BOTCHERBY (St Andrew) *see* Carl St Aid and Ch Ch *Carl*
BOTESDALE (St Botolph) *see* Redgrave cum Botesdale w Rickinghall *St E*
BOTHAL (St Andrew) and Pegswood w Longhirst *Newc 11* **P** *Bp* **R** *vacant* (01670) 510793
BOTHAMSALL (Our Lady and St Peter) *see* Elkesley w Bothamsall *S'well*
BOTHENHAMPTON (Holy Trinity) *see* Bridport *Sarum*
BOTLEY (All Saints) *Portsm 1* **P** *Bp* **C** G M W KEITH, **NSM** E A GROVES
BOTLEY (St Peter and St Paul) *see* N Hinksey and Wytham *Ox*
BOTLEYS AND LYNE (Holy Trinity) *see* Chertsey, Lyne and Longcross *Guildf*
BOTOLPHS (St Botolph) *see* Beeding and Bramber w Botolphs *Chich*
BOTTESFORD (St Mary the Virgin) *see* Vale of Belvoir Par *Leic*
BOTTESFORD (St Peter) w Ashby *Linc 4* **P** *Patr Bd* **TR** P J LILEY, **TV** G M LINES
BOTTISHAM (Holy Trinity) *see* Anglesey Gp *Ely*
BOTUS FLEMING (St Mary) *see* Landrake w St Erney and Botus Fleming *Truro*
BOUGHTON (All Saints) *Ely 13* **P** *Bp* **R** *vacant*
BOUGHTON (St John the Baptist) *see* Pitsford w Boughton *Pet*
BOUGHTON (St Matthew) *see* Ollerton w Boughton *S'well*
BOUGHTON ALUPH (All Saints) *see* Westwell, Hothfield, Eastwell and Boughton Aluph *Cant*
BOUGHTON ALUPH (St Christopher) *as above*
BOUGHTON MALHERBE (St Nicholas) *see* Len Valley *Cant*
BOUGHTON MONCHELSEA (St Augustine) (St Peter) *Cant 14* **P** *Abp* **V** R G DAVIS, **OLM** Y D SALMON
BOUGHTON UNDER BLEAN (St Barnabas) (St Peter and St Paul) w Dunkirk and Hernhill *Cant 6* **P** *Abp* **V** J W R MOWLL
BOULGE (St Michael) w Burgh, Grundisburgh and Hasketon *St E 7* **P** *Bp and DBP (jt)* **P-in-c** H C SANDERS
BOULMER (St Andrew) *see* Longhoughton w Howick *Newc*
BOULTHAM (Holy Cross) (St Helen) *Linc 15* **P** *DBP* **R** D J OSBOURNE, **C** C M THACKER
BOULTON (St Mary the Virgin) *Derby 15* **P** *Bp* **V** T S WRIGHT, **C** D BISHOP
BOUNDSTONE (Mission Church) *see* Wrecclesham *Guildf*
BOURN (St Helena and St Mary) *see* Papworth *Ely*
BOURNE (St Peter and St Paul) *Linc 13* **P** *DBP* **V** C J ATKINSON
BOURNE, The (St Thomas) and Tilford *Guildf 3* **P** *Bp and Adn Surrey (alt)* **V** J T L STILL, **C** V E BURROWS, **Hon C** J W BELL, **NSM** J D A ADAMS, M E JACKSON
BOURNE, LOWER (St Martin) *see* The Bourne and Tilford *Guildf*

BOURNE END (St John) *see* Sunnyside w Bourne End *St Alb*
BOURNE END (St Mark) *see* Hedsor and Bourne End *Ox*
BOURNE STREET (St Mary) *see* Pimlico St Mary Bourne Street *Lon*
BOURNE VALLEY *Sarum 10* **P** *Patr Bd* **TV** S S BURNS, **C** R V GOODBODY, **NSM** T E GOODBODY
BOURNEMOUTH (All Saints) *see* Pokesdown All SS *Win*
BOURNEMOUTH (Christ Church) *see* Westbourne Ch Ch Prop Chpl *Win*
BOURNEMOUTH (Holy Epiphany) *Win 8* **P** *Bp* **V** K V BATT, **NSM** D S THOMPSON
BOURNEMOUTH (St Alban) *Win 8* **P** *Bp* **P-in-c** R L NASH
BOURNEMOUTH (St Ambrose) *Win 8* **P** *Bp* **P-in-c** G J WHEELER
BOURNEMOUTH (St Andrew) Bennett Road *Win 8* **P** *Trustees* **V** G M ROBERTS
BOURNEMOUTH (St Augustine) *Win 8* **P** *Bp* **P-in-c** J J RICHARDSON
BOURNEMOUTH (St Barnabas) Queen's Park *see* Holdenhurst and Iford *Win*
BOURNEMOUTH (St Christopher) *see* Southbourne St Chris *Win*
BOURNEMOUTH (St Clement) *Win 8* **P** *DBP* **V** *vacant* (01202) 392851
BOURNEMOUTH (St Francis) *Win 8* **P** *CR* **V** P G BERRETT
BOURNEMOUTH (St James) *see* Pokesdown St Jas *Win*
BOURNEMOUTH (St John) (St Michael and All Angels) *Win 8* **P** *Bp and S R Willcox Esq (jt)* **P-in-c** R D BALDOCK
BOURNEMOUTH (St John the Evangelist) *see* Boscombe St Jo *Win*
BOURNEMOUTH (St Luke) *Win 8* **P** *Bp* **V** S HOLMES
BOURNEMOUTH (St Peter) (St Stephen) w St Swithun and Holy Trinity *Win 8* **P** *Patr Bd* **TR** J J RICHARDSON, **TV** R C N HARGER, **Hon C** B G APPS
BOURNVILLE (St Andrew) *see* Weston-super-Mare St Andr Bournville *B & W*
BOURNVILLE (St Francis) *Birm 5* **P** *Bp* **V** P G BABINGTON, **NSM** J M ADAMS, E L BREUILLY
BOURTON (Holy Trinity) *see* Wenlock *Heref*
BOURTON (St George) *see* Upper Stour *Sarum*
BOURTON (St James) *see* Shrivenham and Ashbury *Ox*
BOURTON (St Peter) w Frankton and Stretton on Dunsmore w Princethorpe *Cov 6* **P** *Bp (2 turns), Simeon's Trustees (1 turn), and Mrs J H Shaw-Fox (1 turn)* **P-in-c** C B POLLARD, **NSM** B C CLUTTON
BOURTON, GREAT (All Saints) *see* Shires' Edge *Ox*
BOURTON ON THE HILL (St Lawrence) *see* Blockley w Aston Magna and Bourton on the Hill *Glouc*
BOURTON-ON-THE-WATER (St Lawrence) w Clapton and The Rissingtons *Glouc 14* **P** *Wadh Coll Ox, DBP and C T R Wingfield Esq, and Ld Chan (by turn)* **R** E N P TUFNELL, **OLM** T LOCKWOOD
BOVEY, NORTH (St John the Baptist) *see* Moretonhampstead, Manaton, N Bovey and Lustleigh *Ex*
BOVEY TRACEY (St John the Evangelist) w Heathfield *Ex 9* **P** *Guild of All So* **NSM** A N WOODASON
BOVEY TRACEY (St Peter and St Paul and St Thomas of Canterbury) w Hennock *Ex 9* **P** *Prime Min (2 turns), MMCET (1 turn)* **V** W G HAMILTON, **Hon C** J E SPENCER
BOVINGDON (St Lawrence) *St Alb 5* **P** *Ch Soc Trust* **V** T J MARSHALL
BOW (All Hallows) *see* Bromley by Bow All Hallows *Lon*
BOW (St Bartholomew) w Broad Nymet *Ex 2* **P** *DBP* **R** *vacant* (01363) 82566
BOW (St Mary) w Bromley (St Leonard) *Lon 7* **P** *Bp* **R** G W GARNER, **NSM** D F WAXHAM
BOW BRICKHILL (All Saints) *see* Brickhills and Stoke Hammond *Ox*
BOW COMMON (St Paul) *Lon 7* **P** *Bp* **V** D G ROSS, **NSM** D S WEBB
BOWBROOK NORTH: Feckenham and Hanbury and Stock and Bradley *Worc 8* **P** *Bp and D&C (jt)* **R** A J FULLER
BOWBROOK SOUTH: Crowle w Bredicot and Hadzor w Oddingley and Tibberton and Himbleton and Huddington *Worc 8* **P** *Bp, D&C, R J G Berkeley Esq, and J F Bennett Esq (jt)* **R** W D S WELLS
BOWBURN (Christ the King) *see* Cassop cum Quarrington *Dur*
BOWDEN, GREAT (St Peter and St Paul) w Welham, Glooston and Cranoe and Stonton Wyville *Leic 4* **P** *Bp, E Brudenell Esq, and MMCET (jt)* **R** I W Y GEMMELL, **C** S K BURNS
BOWDEN, LITTLE (St Hugh) *see* Market Harborough and The Transfiguration etc *Leic*
BOWDEN, LITTLE (St Nicholas) *as above*
BOWDEN HILL (St Anne) *see* Gtr Corsham and Lacock *Bris*
BOWDON (St Luke) (St Mary the Virgin) *Ches 10* **P** *Bp* **V** K E HINE
BOWERCHALKE (Holy Trinity) *see* Chalke Valley *Sarum*
BOWERS GIFFORD (St John) (St Margaret) w North Benfleet *Chelmsf 6* **P** *Em Coll Cam and Brig R H C Bryhers CBE (alt)* **NSM** R WIFFEN
BOWES (St Giles) *see* Startforth and Bowes and Rokeby w Brignall *Ripon*
BOWES PARK (St Michael-at-Bowes) *see* Wood Green St Mich w Bounds Green St Gabr etc *Lon*
BOWLEE (St Thomas) *see* Rhodes *Man*
BOWLING (St John) *Bradf 2* **P** *V Bradford* **V** H K ASTIN, **C** J SALMON
BOWLING (St Stephen) *Bradf 2* **P** *CPAS* **P-in-c** J W HINTON
BOWNESS-ON-SOLWAY (St Michael), Kirkbride and Newton Arlosh *Carl 3* **P** *Earl of Lonsdale (2 turns), V Holme Cultram (1 turn)* **R** R P BLACKETT
BOWTHORPE (St Michael) *Nor 3* **P** *Bp and CPAS (jt)* **V** *vacant* (01603) 747871
BOX (St Barnabas) *see* Minchinhampton *Glouc*
BOX (St Thomas à Becket) w Hazlebury and Ditteridge *Bris 4* **P** *Bp* **R** R J SNOW, **NSM** J AYERS
BOX HILL (St Andrew) *see* Headley w Box Hill *Guildf*
BOX RIVER *see* Boxford, Edwardstone, Groton etc *St E*
BOXFORD (St Andrew) *see* Welford w Wickham and Gt Shefford, Boxford etc *Ox*
BOXFORD (St Mary), Edwardstone, Groton, Little Waldingfield and Newton *St E 12* **P** *DBP and The Hon Thomas Lindsay (1 turn), Ld Chan (2 turns), Peterho Cam (1 turn)* **R** D W MATTHEWS, **NSM** B WATLING
BOXGROVE (St Mary and St Blaise) *Chich 3* **P** *Duke of Richmond and Gordon* **P-in-c** I M FORRESTER
BOXLEY (St Mary the Virgin and All Saints) w Detling *Cant 14* **P** *Abp* **P-in-c** R G GAMBLE, **NSM** E A ATTAWAY
BOXMOOR (St John the Evangelist) *St Alb 3* **P** *Bp* **V** J S REVELEY, **C** L J WILSON, **NSM** G A J ADAM
BOXTED (Holy Trinity) *see* Glemsford, Hartest w Boxted, Somerton etc *St E*
BOXTED (St Peter) *see* Langham w Boxted *Chelmsf*
BOXWELL (St Mary the Virgin), Leighterton, Didmarton, Oldbury-on-the-Hill, Sopworth, Badminton w Little Badminton, Acton Turville, Hawkesbury, Westonbirt and Lasborough *Glouc 7* **P** *Duke of Beaufort, J A Hutley Esq, and Westonbirt Sch (jt)* **R** N C J MULHOLLAND, **Hon C** J GREEN, **NSM** G H EDWARDS, H K NICHOLS, E M NICHOLS
BOXWORTH (St Peter) *see* Papworth *Ely*
BOYATT WOOD (St Peter) *Win 10* **P** *Bp* **V** P M GILKS, **NSM** V A CORCORAN
BOYLESTONE (St John the Baptist), Church Broughton, Dalbury, Longford, Long Lane, Radbourne, Sutton on the Hill and Trusley *Derby 14* **P** *Patr Bd* **R** P M BISHOP
BOYNE HILL (All Saints) *Ox 13* **P** *Bp* **NSM** R E BRAGG
BOYNTON (St Andrew) *see* Rudston w Boynton, Carnaby and Kilham *York*
BOYTHORPE (St Francis) *see* Chesterfield St Aug *Derby*
BOYTON (Holy Name), North Tamerton, Werrington w St Giles-in-the-Heath and Virginstow *Truro 9* **P** *Duke of Cornwall, MMCET, Ld Chan, and R Williams Esq (by turn)* **P-in-c** K WAKEFIELD
BOYTON (St Andrew) *see* Wilford Peninsula *St E*
BOYTON (St Mary the Virgin) *see* Upper Wylye Valley *Sarum*
BOZEAT (St Mary) w Easton Maudit *Pet 6* **P** *Bp and Marquess of Northn (alt)* **P-in-c** A I MORTON
BRABOURNE (St Mary the Blessed Virgin) *see* Smeeth w Monks Horton and Stowting and Brabourne *Cant*
BRACEBOROUGH (St Margaret) *see* Uffington Gp *Linc*
BRACEBRIDGE (All Saints) *Linc 15* **P** *Mrs B M Ellison-Lendrum* **V** J D DUCKETT, **OLM** S E KIDDLE
BRACEBRIDGE HEATH (St John the Evangelist) *Linc 15* **P** *Bp* **V** H C MIDDLETON
BRACEBY (St Margaret) *see* Sapperton w Braceby *Linc*
BRACEWELL (St Michael) *see* Barnoldswick w Bracewell *Bradf*
BRACKENFIELD (Holy Trinity) *see* Ashover and Brackenfield w Wessington *Derby*
BRACKLEY (St Peter w St James) *Pet 1* **P** *Bp* **V** N J GANDY, **C** C MORGAN-CROMAR
BRACKNELL (Holy Trinity) *Ox 11* **P** *Bp* **TR** D R OSBORN, **TV** C BLUNDELL, J M HARRIS, **C** C M ACKFORD, **Hon C** M G CLARKE, P M BESTLEY
BRACON ASH (St Nicholas) *see* Mulbarton w Bracon Ash, Hethel and Flordon *Nor*
BRADBOURNE (All Saints) *see* Wirksworth *Derby*
BRADDAN (St Brendan) *S & M 2* **P** *Bp* **V** P S FREAR
BRADDEN (St Michael) *see* Greens Norton w Bradden and Lichborough *Pet*

BRADELEY (St Mary and All Saints), Church Eaton and Moreton *Lich 10* **P** *Bp and V Gnosall (jt)* **R** *vacant* (01785) 823091
BRADENHAM (St Botolph) *see* W Wycombe w Bledlow Ridge, Bradenham and Radnage *Ox*
BRADENHAM, WEST (St Andrew) *see* Shipdham w E and W Bradenham *Nor*
BRADENSTOKE (St Mary) *see* Lyneham w Bradenstoke *Sarum*
BRADFIELD (St Andrew) and Stanford Dingley *Ox 12* **P** *Ch Soc Trust* **P-in-c** E MARQUEZ, **NSM** R C OBIN, **OLM** R S GREEN
BRADFIELD (St Giles) *see* Trunch *Nor*
BRADFIELD (St Lawrence) *see* Mistley w Manningtree and Bradfield *Chelmsf*
BRADFIELD (St Nicholas) *Sheff 3* **P** *V Ecclesfield* **R** T M PAGE
BRADFIELD COMBUST (All Saints) *see* St Edm Way *St E*
BRADFIELD ST CLARE (St Clare), Bradfield St George w Little Whelnetham, Cockfield, Felsham and Gedding *St E 10* **P** *St Jo Coll Cam (1 turn), Bp and Lt-Col J G Aldous (1 turn)* **R** S G HILL, **C** R W JAMES
BRADFIELD ST GEORGE (St George) *see* Bradfield St Clare, Bradfield St George etc *St E*
BRADFORD (All Saints) *see* Black Torrington, Bradf w Cookbury etc *Ex*
BRADFORD (St Augustine) Undercliffe *Bradf 3* **P** *V Bradf* **V** D J POOLE, **C** A BOWERMAN
BRADFORD (St Clement) *Bradf 3* **P** *Bp (2 turns) and Trustees (1 turn)* **V** J E BAVINGTON
BRADFORD (St Giles) w Oake, Hillfarrance and Heathfield *B & W 19* **P** *Bp and M V Spurway Esq (jt)* **P-in-c** A NORRIS, **NSM** D G AGER
BRADFORD (St Martin) *see* Heaton St Martin *Bradf*
BRADFORD (St Oswald) *see* Lt Horton *Bradf*
BRADFORD (St Saviour) *see* Fairweather Green *Bradf*
BRADFORD (St Stephen) *see* Bowling St Steph *Bradf*
BRADFORD (St Wilfrid) (St Columba w St Andrew) *Bradf 2* **P** *Bp* **V** P M BILTON, **NSM** G A BRIGHOUSE
BRADFORD, WEST (St Catherine) *see* Waddington *Bradf*
BRADFORD ABBAS (St Mary the Virgin) and Thornford w Beer Hackett *Sarum 3* **P** *J K Wingfield Digby Esq and Win Coll (alt)* **R** J A EVANS
BRADFORD-ON-AVON (Christ Church) *Sarum 14* **P** *V Bradf H Trin* **P-in-c** R M LOWRIE, **C** T G RAE SMITH, **NSM** B F CHAPMAN
BRADFORD-ON-AVON (Holy Trinity) *Sarum 14* **P** *D&C* **V** W A MATTHEWS, **NSM** A A ONIONS
BRADFORD ON TONE (St Giles) *see* Bradford w Oake, Hillfarrance and Heathfield *B & W*
BRADFORD PEVERELL (Church of the Assumption), Stratton, Frampton and Sydling St Nicholas *Sarum 1* **P** *Win Coll and Bp (alt)* **R** K J SCOTT, **OLM** P A STEAR
BRADGATE TEAM, The - Ratby cum Groby w Newton Linford *Leic 11* **P** *Patr Bd* **TR** R V WORSFOLD, **TV** L D CORKE
BRADING (St Mary the Virgin) w Yaverland *Portsm 7* **P** *Hon Mrs I S T Monck and Trin Coll Cam (jt)* **R** D J B ABINGTON
BRADLEY (All Saints) *see* Hulland, Atlow, Kniveton, Bradley and Hognaston *Derby*
BRADLEY (All Saints) *see* The Candover Valley *Win*
BRADLEY (St George) *see* Gt and Lt Coates w Bradley *Linc*
BRADLEY (St John the Baptist) *see* Bowbrook N *Worc*
BRADLEY (St Martin) *Lich 28* **P** *Baldwin Pugh Trustees* **V** R M WALKER
BRADLEY (St Mary) *see* Cononley w Bradley *Bradf*
BRADLEY (St Thomas) *Wakef 5* **P** *Bp* **V** D R WARD
BRADLEY, GREAT (St Mary the Virgin) *see* Stourhead *St E*
BRADLEY, LITTLE (All Saints) *as above*
BRADLEY, NORTH (St Nicholas), Southwick and Heywood *Sarum 14* **P** *Win Coll* **V** J R PARKER, **OLM** A R J LONGDON
BRADLEY, WEST (not known) *see* Baltonsborough w Butleigh, W Bradley etc *B & W*
BRADLEY-LE-MOORS (St Leonard) *see* Alton w Bradley-le-Moors and Oakamoor w Cotton *Lich*
BRADLEY STOKE (Christ the King) *see* Stoke Gifford *Bris*
BRADLEY STOKE NORTH (Holy Trinity) Conventional District *Bris 5* **C-in-c** P J PETERSON
BRADMORE (Mission Room) *see* Keyworth and Stanton-on-the-Wolds and Bunny etc *S'well*
BRADNINCH (St Denis) and Clyst Hydon *Ex 4* **P** *D&C and D&C Windsor (jt)* **R** D L D ROBOTTOM
BRADNOP (Mission Church) *see* Ipstones w Berkhamsytch and Onecote w Bradnop *Lich*
BRADOC (Blessed Virgin Mary) *see* Lanreath, Pelynt and Bradoc *Truro*
BRADPOLE (Holy Trinity) *see* Bridport *Sarum*
BRADSHAW (St John the Evangelist) and Holmfield *Wakef 4* **P** *Bp* **V** A DICK
BRADSHAW (St Maxentius) *see* Turton Moorland Min *Man*
BRADWELL (Holy Trinity) *see* Cressing w Stisted and Bradwell etc *Chelmsf*
BRADWELL (St Barnabas) *see* Hope, Castleton and Bradwell *Derby*
BRADWELL (St Barnabas) *see* Wolstanton *Lich*
BRADWELL (St Laurence and Methodist United) *see* Stantonbury and Willen *Ox*
BRADWELL (St Nicholas) *Nor 6* **P** *Bp* **R** R J TUCK, **NSM** C A POWLES, S D UPTON, C M UPTON
BRADWELL, NEW (St James) *see* Stantonbury and Willen *Ox*
BRADWELL ON SEA (St Thomas) (St Peter-on-the-Wall) *Chelmsf 11* **P** *Bp* **R** *vacant* (01621) 776203
BRADWORTHY (St John the Baptist), Sutcombe, Putford, Abbots Bickington and Bulkworthy *Ex 17* **P** *Prime Min and Bp (alt)* **R** R B DORRINGTON
BRAFFERTON (St Peter) w Pilmoor, Myton-on-Swale and Thormanby *York 3* **P** *Abp and Prof Sir Anthony Milnes Coates Bt (jt)* **V** *vacant* (01423) 360244
BRAFIELD ON THE GREEN (St Laurence) *see* Cogenhoe and Gt and Lt Houghton w Brafield *Pet*
BRAILES (St George) *Cov 9* **P** *D&C* **V** N J MORGAN, **NSM** J W ROLFE
BRAILSFORD (All Saints) w Shirley and Osmaston w Edlaston *Derby 8* **P** *Bp, Earl Ferrers, and Sir Peter Walker-Okeover Bt (by turn)* **R** I ALDERSLEY, **NSM** C L JOHNSON
BRAINTREE (St Michael) *Chelmsf 15* **P** *Ch Trust Fund Trust* **V** C O MASON, **C** M J PETERS
BRAINTREE (St Paul) *Chelmsf 15* **P** *Ch Trust Fund Trust* **V** R W SEWELL
BRAISHFIELD (All Saints) *see* Michelmersh and Awbridge and Braishfield etc *Win*
BRAITHWAITE (St Herbert) *see* Thornthwaite cum Braithwaite, Newlands etc *Carl*
BRAITHWELL (St James) *see* Ravenfield, Hooton Roberts and Braithwell *Sheff*
BRAMBER (St Nicholas) *see* Beeding and Bramber w Botolphs *Chich*
BRAMBLETON (not known) *see* The Bourne and Tilford *Guildf*
BRAMCOTE (St Michael and All Angels) *S'well 7* **P** *CPAS* **V** N C STYLES, **C** J J MILSON
BRAMDEAN (St Simon and St Jude) *see* Upper Itchen *Win*
BRAMDEAN COMMON (Church in the Wood) *as above*
BRAMERTON (St Peter) *see* Rockland St Mary w Hellington, Bramerton etc *Nor*
BRAMFIELD (St Andrew) *see* Blyth Valley *St E*
BRAMFIELD (St Andrew), Stapleford, Waterford and Watton-at-Stone *St Alb 22* **P** *R M A Smith Esq (3 turns), Grocers' Co (1 turn)* **R** B D S FAIRBANK, **NSM** R A MARTIN
BRAMFORD (St Mary the Virgin) *St E 1* **P** *D&C Cant* **P-in-c** R J DEDMAN
BRAMHALL (St Michael and All Angels) (Hall Chapel) *Ches 17* **P** *Trustees* **V** R J GILLINGS, **NSM** P HARDMAN
BRAMHAM (All Saints) *York 1* **P** *G Lane Fox Esq* **P-in-c** H N LAWRANCE
BRAMHOPE (St Giles) *Ripon 7* **P** *Trustees* **V** D M ROBINSON
BRAMLEY (Holy Trinity) and Grafham *Guildf 2* **P** *Ld Chan* **V** J N E BUNDOCK, **NSM** R J HEYES
BRAMLEY (St Francis) *Sheff 6* **P** *Bp and Sir Philip Naylor-Leyland Bt (jt)* **V** L S WORTLEY, **NSM** A PRICE
BRAMLEY (St James) *Win 4* **P** *Qu Coll Ox* **V** R C TOOGOOD
BRAMLEY (St Peter) *Ripon 6* **P** *DBP* **TR** I T RODLEY, **TV** J UPTON
BRAMPFORD SPEKE (St Peter) *see* Thorverton, Cadbury, Upton Pyne etc *Ex*
BRAMPTON (St Mark) *Derby 5* **P** *Bp* **P-in-c** F E WILLETT
BRAMPTON (St Martin) *see* Eden, Gelt and Irthing *Carl*
BRAMPTON (St Mary Magdalene) *Ely 8* **P** *Bp* **R** M R GREENFIELD, **NSM** S A WATTS
BRAMPTON (St Peter) *see* Buxton w Oxnead, Lammas and Brampton *Nor*
BRAMPTON (St Peter) *see* Hundred River *St E*
BRAMPTON (St Thomas the Martyr) *Derby 5* **P** *Bp* **P-in-c** D P MOUNCER
BRAMPTON, OLD (St Peter and St Paul) (Cutthorpe Institute) *Derby 5* **P** *Bp* **P-in-c** A P KAUNHOVEN
BRAMPTON ABBOTTS (St Michael) *see* Ross *Heref*
BRAMPTON ASH (St Mary) *see* Desborough, Brampton Ash, Dingley and Braybrooke *Pet*

BRAMPTON BIERLOW (Christ Church) *Sheff 12* **P** *V Wath-upon-Dearne* **P-in-c** P E BOLD

BRAMPTON BRYAN (St Barnabas) *see* Wigmore Abbey *Heref*

BRAMSHALL (St Laurence) *see* Uttoxeter Area *Lich*

BRAMSHAW (St Peter) and Landford w Plaitford *Sarum 10* **P** *Bp and D&C (alt)* **P-in-c** D G BACON, **OLM** P J WHITMARSH

BRAMSHILL (Mission Church) *see* Yateley and Eversley *Win*

BRAMSHOTT (St Mary the Virgin) and Liphook *Portsm 4* **P** *Qu Coll Ox* **R** S A WEEDEN, **C** A I FORDYCE

BRANCASTER (St Mary the Virgin) *see* Hunstanton St Mary w Ringstead Parva etc *Nor*

BRANCEPETH (St Brandon) *Dur 1* **P** *Bp* **R** *vacant* 0191-378 0503 or 374 4407

BRANCEPETH, NEW (St Catherine) *see* Brandon and Ushaw Moor *Dur*

BRANDESBURTON (St Mary) and Leven w Catwick *York 11* **P** *St Jo Coll Cam, Exors Sir Henry Strickland-Constable Bt, and Simeon's Trustees (jt)* **R** B S DIXON

BRANDESTON (All Saints) w Kettleburgh and Easton *St E 18* **P** *J Austin Esq, Capt J L Round-Turner, and MMCET (jt)* **P-in-c** P G VELLACOTT

BRANDLESHOLME (St Francis House Chapel) *see* Elton All SS *Man*

BRANDON (Chapel) *see* Barkston and Hough Gp *Linc*

BRANDON (St John the Evangelist) and Ushaw Moor *Dur 1* **P** *R Brancepeth* **V** D B GODSELL, **C** P BROWN

BRANDON (St Peter) and Santon Downham w Elveden and Lakenheath *St E 11* **P** *Ld Chan (1 turn), Bp, M F Carter Esq, Earl of Iveagh, and D&C Ely (2 turns)* **R** R N LEACH, **NSM** P W TAMS, **OLM** A S I BUTTREY

BRANDON PARVA (All Saints) *see* Barnham Broom and Upper Yare *Nor*

BRANDSBY (All Saints) *see* Crayke w Brandsby and Yearsley *York*

BRANDWOOD (St Bede) *Birm 5* **P** *Bp* **V** A M DELMEGE, **NSM** R J REYNOLDS

BRANKSEA ISLAND (St Mary) *see* Parkstone St Pet and St Osmund w Branksea *Sarum*

BRANKSOME (St Aldhelm) (St Francis) *Sarum 7* **P** *Bp* **V** S R BATTY, **NSM** I M DOWLEN

BRANKSOME (St Clement) (St Barnabas) *Sarum 8* **P** *MMCET* **V** J G V FOSTER, **C** S C L DIMES

BRANKSOME PARK (All Saints) *Sarum 7* **P** *MMCET* **V** C M DAY

BRANSCOMBE (St Winifred) *see* Colyton, Musbury, Southleigh and Branscombe *Ex*

BRANSDALE (St Nicholas) *see* Kirkbymoorside w Gillamoor, Farndale etc *York*

BRANSFORD (St John the Baptist) *see* Alfrick, Lulsley, Suckley, Leigh and Bransford *Worc*

BRANSGORE (St Mary the Virgin) *Win 9* **P** *P W J Jesson Esq* **P-in-c** P A RICKMAN

BRANSHOLME (St John) *see* Sutton St Jas and Wawne *York*

BRANSTON (All Saints) w Nocton and Potterhanworth *Linc 18* **P** *Stowe Sch (2 turns), Ld Chan (1 turn), and Nocton Ltd (1 turn)* **R** D F REAGON

BRANSTON (St Saviour) w Tatenhill *Lich 14* **P** *Bp and Simeon's Trustees (jt)* **V** A R HUMPHRIES

BRANSTON BY BELVOIR (St Guthlac) *see* High Framland Par *Leic*

BRANT BROUGHTON (St Helen) and Beckingham *Linc 23* **P** *Bp and Sir Richard Sutton Bt (alt)* **R** A J MEGAHEY

BRANT ROAD (Church Centre) *see* Bracebridge *Linc*

BRANTHAM (St Michael and All Angels) *see* E Bergholt and Brantham *St E*

BRANTINGHAM (All Saints) *see* Elloughton and Brough w Brantingham *York*

BRANXTON (St Paul) *Newc 12* **P** *Abp* **P-in-c** M J GILLHAM, **Hon C** J W SHEWAN, **NSM** C MYLNE

BRASSINGTON (St James) *see* Wirksworth *Derby*

BRASTED (St Martin) *Roch 9* **P** *Abp* **P-in-c** P C STEPHENS

BRATHAY (Holy Trinity) *see* Ambleside w Brathay *Carl*

BRATOFT (St Peter and St Paul) w Irby-in-the-Marsh *Linc 8* **P** *Bp* **R** T STEELE

BRATTLEBY (St Cuthbert) *see* Aisthorpe w Scampton w Thorpe le Fallows etc *Linc*

BRATTON (St James the Great) (Oratory), Edington and Imber, Erlestoke and Coulston *Sarum 16* **P** *Bp and V Westbury (jt)* **R** G SOUTHGATE

BRATTON CLOVELLY (St Mary the Virgin) *see* Okehampton w Inwardleigh, Bratton Clovelly etc *Ex*

BRATTON FLEMING (St Peter) *see* Shirwell, Loxhore, Kentisbury, Arlington, etc *Ex*

BRATTON ST MAUR (St Nicholas) *see* Bruton and Distr *B & W*

BRAUGHING (St Mary the Virgin) w Furneux Pelham and Stocking Pelham *St Alb 18* **P** *Bp and Lord Hamilton (alt)* **P-in-c** J M GOSNEY

BRAUNSTON (All Saints) *see* Daventry, Ashby St Ledgers, Braunston etc *Pet*

BRAUNSTON (All Saints) *see* Oakham, Hambleton, Egleton, Braunston and Brooke *Pet*

BRAUNSTONE (St Crispin) *Leic 11* **P** *Bp* **P-in-c** S R STEVENSON, **NSM** F M KNIGHT

BRAUNSTONE PARK (St Peter) Conventional District *Leic 2* **C-in-c** J C BURCH, **C** R R SOUTER

BRAUNTON (St Brannock) *Ex 15* **P** *Bp* **Hon C** L A BUTTLE

BRAXTED, GREAT (All Saints) *see* Tolleshunt Knights w Tiptree and Gt Braxted *Chelmsf*

BRAXTED, LITTLE (St Nicholas) *see* Wickham Bishops w Lt Braxted *Chelmsf*

BRAY (St Michael) and Braywood *Ox 13* **P** *Bp* **V** G D REPATH

BRAY, HIGH (All Saints) *see* S Molton w Nymet St George, High Bray etc *Ex*

BRAYBROOKE (All Saints) *see* Desborough, Brampton Ash, Dingley and Braybrooke *Pet*

BRAYDESTON (St Michael) *see* Brundall w Braydeston and Postwick *Nor*

BRAYTON (St Wilfrid) *York 4* **P** *Abp* **TR** D H REYNOLDS

BREADSALL (All Saints) *Derby 9* **P** *Miss A I M Harpur-Crewe* **P-in-c** N E WATSON, **NSM** D M MORRISON

BREADSTONE (St Michael and All Angels) *see* Berkeley w Wick, Breadstone, Newport, Stone etc *Glouc*

BREAGE (St Breaca) w Germoe and Godolphin *Truro 4* **P** *Bp and Ld Chan (alt)* **P-in-c** P A STEVENS

BREAM (St James) *Glouc 4* **P** *Bp* **V** A G KENDALL

BREAMORE (St Mary) *see* Fordingbridge and Breamore and Hale etc *Win*

BREAN (St Bridget) *see* Berrow and Breane *B & W*

BREARTON (St John the Baptist) *see* Knaresborough *Ripon*

BREASTON (St Michael) *see* Wilne and Draycott w Breaston *Derby*

BRECKLES (St Margaret) *see* Caston, Griston, Merton, Thompson etc *Nor*

BREDBURY (St Barnabas) *Ches 16* **P** *V Bredbury St Mark* **V** C R WINDLE

BREDBURY (St Mark) *Ches 16* **P** *Bp* **V** A R GARNER, **C** N J HAIGH

BREDE (St George) w Udimore *Chich 20* **P** *Bp and Mrs M E Crook (alt)* **R** D G LLOYD-JAMES

BREDENBURY (St Andrew) w Grendon Bishop and Wacton, Edwyn Ralph, Collington, Thornbury, Pencombe and Marston Stannett and Little Cowarne *Heref 2* **P** *DBP, V Bromyard, and Lt-Col H H Barneby (jt)* **R** C I FLETCHER

BREDFIELD (St Andrew) *see* Woodbridge St Jo and Bredfield *St E*

BREDGAR (St John the Baptist) w Bicknor and Frinsted w Wormshill and Milsted *Cant 15* **P** *Abp, Lord Kingsdown, M Nightingale Esq, and S McCandlish Esq (jt)* **P-in-c** J L SMITH

BREDHURST (St Peter) *see* S Gillingham *Roch*

BREDICOT (St James the Less) *see* Bowbrook S *Worc*

BREDON (St Giles) w Bredon's Norton *Worc 4* **P** *Bp* **R** M T C BAYNES

BREDON'S NORTON (not known) *see* Bredon w Bredon's Norton *Worc*

BREDWARDINE (St Andrew) *see* Cusop w Blakemere, Bredwardine w Brobury etc *Heref*

BREDY, LITTLE (St Michael and All Angels) *see* Bride Valley *Sarum*

BREEDON-ON-THE-HILL (St Mary and St Hardulph) *see* Ashby-de-la-Zouch and Breedon on the Hill *Leic*

BREIGHTMET (St James) *see* Bolton Breightmet St Jas *Man*

BREIGHTMET Top o' th' Moss (St John the Evangelist) *see* Bolton St Jo *Man*

BREINTON (St Michael) (Mission Hall) *Heref 3* **P** *Bp* **V** R NORTH

BREMHILL (St Martin) *see* Derry Hill w Bremhill and Foxham *Sarum*

BRENCHLEY (All Saints) *Roch 8* **P** *D&C Cant* **V** R C PAGET

BRENDON (St Brendon) *see* Combe Martin, Berrynarbor, Lynton, Brendon etc *Ex*

BRENT, EAST (The Blessed Virgin Mary) *see* Brent Knoll, E Brent and Lympsham *B & W*

BRENT, SOUTH (St Petroc) and Rattery *Ex 13* **P** *Bp and Sir Rivers Carew Bt (jt)* **V** D R WINNINGTON-INGRAM, **Hon C** D G H HAMBLIN

BRENT ELEIGH (St Mary) *see* Monks Eleigh w Chelsworth and Brent Eleigh etc *St E*

BRENT KNOLL (St Michael) and East Brent and Lympsham *B & W 1* **P** *Adn Wells (1 turn), Bp (2 turns)* **R** M P LEE, **NSM** S A BOYD
BRENT PELHAM (St Mary the Virgin) *see* Hormead, Wyddial, Anstey, Brent Pelham etc *St Alb*
BRENT TOR (Christ Church) *see* Peter Tavy, Mary Tavy, Lydford and Brent Tor *Ex*
BRENT TOR (St Michael) *as above*
BRENTFORD (St Paul w St Lawrence and St George) (St Faith) *Lon 11* **P** *Bp* **TR** D J SIMPSON, **TV** R C HOAD, **C** A L BROOKER
BRENTRY (St Mark) *see* Henbury *Bris*
BRENTS and Davington w Oare and Luddenham, The *Cant 6* **P** *Abp and Ld Chan (alt)* **P-in-c** A C OEHRING
BRENTWOOD (St George the Martyr) *Chelmsf 7* **P** *DBP* **V** G F JENKINS
BRENTWOOD (St Thomas) *Chelmsf 7* **P** *DBP* **P-in-c** R B WHITE, **C** E J TOMLINSON
BRENZETT (St Eanswith) *see* Appledore w Brookland, Fairfield, Brenzett etc *Cant*
BRERETON (St Michael) *Lich 3* **P** *R Rugeley* **P-in-c** W H HEATH
BRERETON (St Oswald) w Swettenham *Ches 11* **P** *DBP and MMCET (jt)* **P-in-c** C M KEMP
BRESSINGHAM (St John the Baptist) w North and South Lopham and Fersfield *Nor 10* **P** *R D A Woode Esq, MMCET, and St Jo Coll Cam (by turn)* **P-in-c** R J MELLOWSHIP
BRETBY (St Wystan) *see* Hartshorne and Bretby *Derby*
BRETFORTON (St Leonard) *see* Badsey w Aldington and Offenham and Bretforton *Worc*
BRETHERTON (St John the Baptist) *see* Croston and Bretherton *Blackb*
BRETTENHAM (St Andrew) *see* E w W Harling, Bridgham w Roudham, Larling etc *Nor*
BRETTENHAM (St Mary) *see* Rattlesden w Thorpe Morieux, Brettenham etc *St E*
BRETTON (Holy Spirit) *see* Pet H Spirit Bretton *Pet*
BRETTON PARK (St Bartholomew) *see* Woolley *Wakef*
BREWHAM, SOUTH (St John the Baptist) *see* Bruton and Distr *B & W*
BREWOOD (St Mary and St Chad) *Lich 2* **P** *Bp* **V** C B BURGESS, **NSM** M J COULTER
BRICETT, GREAT (St Mary and St Lawrence) *see* Ringshall w Battisford, Barking w Darmsden etc *St E*
BRICKENDON (Holy Cross and St Alban) *see* Lt Berkhamsted and Bayford, Essendon etc *St Alb*
BRICKET WOOD (St Luke) *St Alb 1* **P** *CPAS* **V** M RAJKOVIC
BRICKHILL, GREAT (St Mary) *see* Brickhills and Stoke Hammond *Ox*
BRICKHILL, LITTLE (St Mary Magdalene) *as above*
BRICKHILL, NORTH (St Mark) *see* Bedf St Mark *St Alb*
BRICKHILLS and Stoke Hammond, The *Ox 26* **P** *Bp, Major Sir Philip Pauncefort-Duncombe Bt, St Edw Sch Ox, and Cam Univ (jt)* **R** J WALLER
BRICKLEHAMPTON (St Michael) *see* Elmley Castle w Bricklehampton and Combertons *Worc*
BRIDE (St Bridget) *see* Kirkbride *S & M*
BRIDE VALLEY *Sarum 2* **P** *Patr Bd* **TR** R A D'V THORN, **TV** A J ASHWELL
BRIDEKIRK (St Bridget) *Carl 6* **P** *Trustees* **V** *vacant* (01900) 826557
BRIDESTOWE (St Bridget) *see* Okehampton w Inwardleigh, Bratton Clovelly etc *Ex*
BRIDFORD (St Thomas à Becket) *see* Christow, Ashton and Bridford *Ex*
BRIDGE (St Peter) *see* Patrixbourne w Bridge and Bekesbourne *Cant*
BRIDGE SOLLARS (St Andrew) *see* Credenhill w Brinsop and Wormsley etc *Heref*
BRIDGEMARY (St Matthew) *Portsm 3* **P** *Bp* **V** J W DRAPER, **C** J W FRANKS
BRIDGERULE (St Bridget) *see* Pyworthy, Pancrasweek and Bridgerule *Ex*
BRIDGETOWN (St John the Evangelist) *see* Totnes w Bridgetown, Berry Pomeroy etc *Ex*
BRIDGFORD, EAST (St Peter) and Kneeton *S'well 8* **P** *Magd Coll Ox (2 turns), C G Neale Esq (1 turn)* **R** A HAYDOCK
BRIDGFORD, WEST (St Giles) (St Luke) *S'well 9* **P** *Waddington Trustees* **R** S J L CANSDALE, **C** J H CURRAN
BRIDGHAM (St Mary) *see* E w W Harling, Bridgham w Roudham, Larling etc *Nor*
BRIDGNORTH (St Mary Magdalene) (St Leonard) (St James), Tasley, Astley Abbotts, Oldbury and Quatford *Heref 9* **P** *DBP (3 turns) and Ld Chan (1 turn)* **TR** A A ROBERTS, **TV** M J KNEEN, **OLM** A ROGERS, T O'BRIEN
BRIDGWATER (Holy Trinity) *B & W 14* **P** *Bp* **V** *vacant* (01278) 422610
BRIDGWATER (St Francis of Assisi) *B & W 14* **P** *Bp* **P-in-c** B D JOY
BRIDGWATER (St John the Baptist) *B & W 14* **P** *Bp* **P-in-c** G M KIRK
BRIDGWATER (St Mary) and Chilton Trinity and Durleigh *B & W 14* **P** *Ld Chan* **V** C J P CHADWICK, **C** J M MUNNS
BRIDLINGTON (Emmanuel) *York 9* **P** *Trustees* **V** J J L HAY, **C** G O MITCHELL
BRIDLINGTON (Holy Trinity) and Sewerby w Marton *York 9* **P** *Abp* **V** D J MATHER
BRIDLINGTON (St Mary's Priory Church) *York 9* **P** *Simeon's Trustees* **R** J A WARDLE, **C** P LAMB
BRIDLINGTON QUAY (Christ Church) *York 9* **P** *R Bridlington Priory* **V** J G COUPER
BRIDPORT (St Mary) *Sarum 2* **P** *Patr Bd (2 turns) and Ld Chan (1 turn)* **TR** T N STUBBS, **TV** M A ALLCHIN, S GUISE, **C** A STALEY, **OLM** D E CAMPLING
BRIDSTOW (St Bridget) *see* Ross *Heref*
BRIERCLIFFE (St James) *Blackb 3* **P** *Hulme Trustees* **V** R D WATTS, **C** H HORNBY, **NSM** R D SHOOTER
BRIERFIELD (St Luke) *Blackb 6* **P** *Bp* **V** E A SAVILLE
BRIERLEY (St Paul) *see* Grimethorpe w Brierley *Wakef*
BRIERLEY HILL (St Michael) (St Paul) *Worc 10* **P** *TR Wordsley* **R** *vacant* (01384) 78146
BRIGG (St John the Evangelist), Wrawby and Cadney cum Howsham *Linc 6* **P** *Bp* **V** *vacant* (01652) 653989
BRIGHAM (St Bridget) *Carl 7* **P** *Earl of Lonsdale* **V** *vacant* (01900) 825383
BRIGHOUSE (St Martin) (St Chad) and Clifton *Wakef 2* **P** *Bp* **TR** M F WOOD, **TV** S J LORD, **NSM** C FOX
BRIGHSTONE (St Mary the Virgin) and Brooke w Mottistone *Portsm 8* **P** *Bp (2 turns), D&C St Paul's (1 turn)* **R** T W EADY
BRIGHTLING (St Thomas of Canterbury), Dallington, Mountfield and Netherfield *Chich 15* **P** *Bp, Adn Lewes and Hastings, H C Grissell Esq, Mrs A Egerton, and Mrs L A Fraser (jt)* **R** S BAKER, **NSM** J B B WRENBURY
BRIGHTLINGSEA (All Saints) (St James) *Chelmsf 23* **P** *Ld Chan* **NSM** J H LE SEVE
BRIGHTON (Annunciation) *Chich 2* **P** *Wagner Trustees* **P-in-c** S F FOSTER
BRIGHTON (Good Shepherd) Preston *Chich 2* **P** *Bp* **P-in-c** N L BIDDLE, **NSM** S J DATE
BRIGHTON (Resurrection) (St Alban) (St Luke) (St Martin w St Wilfrid) *Chich 2* **P** *Patr Bd* **TR** B L BRANDIE
BRIGHTON (St Bartholomew) *Chich 2* **P** *Wagner Trustees* **V** V W HOUSE
BRIGHTON (St Cuthman) *see* Whitehawk *Chich*
BRIGHTON (St George w St Anne and St Mark) *Chich 2* **P** *Bp and V Brighton (jt)* **V** A H MANSON-BRAILSFORD, **C** C J F BARBER
BRIGHTON (St John) *see* Preston St Jo w Brighton St Aug and St Sav *Chich*
BRIGHTON (St Mary the Virgin) *see* Kemp Town St Mary *Chich*
BRIGHTON (St Matthias) *Chich 2* **P** *V Preston* **P-in-c** E J POLLARD, **C** C J WOODMAN, **Hon C** B S TYLER
BRIGHTON (St Michael and All Angels) *Chich 2* **P** *V Brighton* **V** R S FAYERS, **C** B A NORTH, **NSM** D G HEWETSON
BRIGHTON (St Nicholas) *Chich 2* **P** *Bp* **NSM** J A EGAR
BRIGHTON (St Paul) *Chich 2* **P** *Wagner Trustees* **NSM** J N BALDRY
BRIGHTON (St Peter) (Chapel Royal) *Chich 2* **P** *Bp* **P-in-c** D J BIGGS, **NSM** J NEWSON
BRIGHTON, NEW (All Saints) *see* Wallasey St Nic w All SS *Ches*
BRIGHTON, NEW (St James) (Emmanuel) *Ches 7* **P** *Bp* **V** F R CAIN, **C** M LEWIS
BRIGHTSIDE (St Thomas and St Margaret) w Wincobank *Sheff 3* **P** *The Crown and Sheff Ch Burgesses (alt)* **V** M V GILBERT
BRIGHTWALTON (All Saints) w Catmore, Leckhampstead, Chaddleworth and Fawley *Ox 14* **P** *Bp, P L Wroughton Esq, and D&C Westmr (jt)* **P-in-c** J P TOWNEND, **Hon C** T MAINES, **NSM** D F BROWN
BRIGHTWELL (St Agatha) *see* Wallingford *Ox*
BRIGHTWELL (St John the Baptist) *see* Martlesham w Brightwell *St E*
BRIGHTWELL BALDWIN (St Bartholomew) *see* Ewelme, Brightwell Baldwin, Cuxham w Easington *Ox*
BRIGNALL (St Mary) *see* Startforth and Bowes and Rokeby w Brignall *Ripon*
BRIGSLEY (St Helen) *see* Laceby and Ravendale Gp *Linc*

BRIGSTOCK (St Andrew) w Stanion and Lowick and Sudborough *Pet 9* **P** *Bp (2 turns), L G Stopford Sackville Esq (1 turn)* **R** H R WATSON
BRILL (All Saints) *see* Bernwode *Ox*
BRILLEY (St Mary) *see* Eardisley w Bollingham, Willersley, Brilley etc *Heref*
BRIMFIELD (St Michael) *see* Leominster *Heref*
BRIMINGTON (St Michael) *Derby 3* **P** *V Chesterfield* **R** M SHAW
BRIMPSFIELD (St Michael) w Birdlip, Syde, Daglingworth, The Duntisbournes, Winstone, Miserden and Edgeworth *Glouc 11* **P** *Ld Chan (1 turn), Bp, DBP, Major M N T H Wills and CCC Ox (1 turn)* **R** J E JESSOP, **NSM** J R HOBBS
BRIMPTON (St Peter) *see* Aldermaston w Wasing and Brimpton *Ox*
BRIMSCOMBE (Holy Trinity) *see* Woodchester and Brimscombe *Glouc*
BRINDLE (St James) *Blackb 4* **P** *Trustees* **P-in-c** M H CANNON
BRINGHURST (St Nicholas) *see* Six Saints circa Holt *Leic*
BRINGTON (All Saints) w Molesworth and Old Weston *Ely 8* **P** *Bp* **P-in-c** C M FURLONG
BRINGTON (St Mary w St John) w Whilton and Norton and Church Brampton w Chapel Brampton and Harlestone and East Haddon and Holdenby *Pet 2* **P** *Patr Bd (5 turns), Prime Min (1 turn)* **R** C GOBLE, **Hon C** D L WILLIAMS
BRININGHAM (St Maurice) *see* Brinton, Briningham, Hunworth, Stody etc *Nor*
BRINKBURN (not known) *see* Longframlington w Brinkburn *Newc*
BRINKHILL (St Philip) *see* S Ormsby Gp *Linc*
BRINKLEY (St Mary) *see* Raddesley Gp *Ely*
BRINKLOW (St John the Baptist) *Cov 6* **P** *Ld Chan* **P-in-c** C A GARROD
BRINKWORTH (St Michael and All Angels) w Dauntsey *Bris 6* **P** *Bp* **R** D ORMSTON
BRINNINGTON (St Luke) w Portwood St Paul *Ches 18* **P** *Bp* **V** R ATTLEY, **NSM** D M WOFFENDEN
BRINSCALL (St Luke) *see* Heapey St Barnabas and Withnell St Paul *Blackb*
BRINSLEY (St James the Great) w Underwood *S'well 4* **P** *Bp* **P-in-c** R B MURRAY
BRINSOP (St George) *see* Credenhill w Brinsop and Wormsley etc *Heref*
BRINSWORTH (St Andrew) *see* Rivers Team *Sheff*
BRINTON (St Andrew), Briningham, Hunworth, Stody, Swanton Novers and Thornage *Nor 18* **P** *J S Howlett Esq, Lord Hastings, and DBP (by turn)* **P-in-c** R J MARSDEN
BRISLEY (St Bartholomew) *see* Upper Wensum Village Gp *Nor*
BRISLINGTON (St Anne) *Bris 1* **P** *Bp* **V** S A HAWKINS, **NSM** J F HOUSE
BRISLINGTON (St Christopher) (St Cuthbert) *Bris 1* **P** *Bp and Simeon's Trustees (jt)* **V** N HAWKINS
BRISLINGTON (St Luke) *Bris 1* **P** *Bp* **V** H F THOMAS, **C** G E ANDERSON
BRISTOL (Christ the Servant) Stockwood *Bris 1* **P** *Bp* **V** D G OWEN
BRISTOL Lockleaze (St Mary Magdalene w St Francis) *Bris 3* **P** *Bp* **V** J J HASLER
BRISTOL St Aidan w St George *Bris 3* **P** *Bp and SMF* **P-in-c** J K NICHOLSON
BRISTOL (St Andrew) Hartcliffe *Bris 1* **P** *Bp* **V** R H MARTIN, **C** J A LOW
BRISTOL (St Andrew w St Bartholomew) *see* Bishopston and St Andrews *Bris*
BRISTOL (St Anne w St Mark and St Thomas) *see* Eastville St Anne w St Mark and St Thos *Bris*
BRISTOL (St Leonard) Redfield *see* E Bris St Ambrose and St Leon *Bris*
BRISTOL (St Mary the Virgin) Redcliffe w Temple and Bedminster St John the Baptist *Bris 1* **P** *Bp* **NSM** W C BEAVER
BRISTOL (St Matthew and St Nathanael) (St Katharine) *Bris 3* **P** *Bp and CPAS (jt)* **V** R V BRAZIER
BRISTOL St Paul's (St Agnes) *Bris 3* **P** *Ld Chan and Patr Bd (alt)* **TR** D C SELF, **C** C L JONES, **NSM** P BARTLE-JENKINS
BRISTOL (St Philip and St Jacob w Emmanuel) *Bris 3* **P** *Trustees* **V** M M WIDDECOMBE
BRISTOL, The City of (Christ Church w St George) (St James w St Peter) (St Stephen w St James and St John the Baptist) *Bris 3* **P** *Ld Chan (1 turn), Trustees (2 turns)* **R** *vacant* 0117-942 7546
BRISTOL, EAST (St Aidan) *see* Bristol St Aid w St Geo *Bris*
BRISTOL, EAST (St Ambrose) (St Leonard) *Bris 3* **P** *Bp* **V** R D JAMES
BRISTOL, EAST (St George) *see* Bristol St Aid w St Geo *Bris*
BRISTON (All Saints) w Burgh Parva and Melton Constable *Nor 18* **P** *Bp and Lord Hastings (jt)* **P-in-c** J G SYKES
BRITFORD (St Peter) *see* Chalke Valley *Sarum*
BRITWELL SALOME (St Nicholas) *see* Icknield *Ox*
BRIXHAM (St Mary) (All Saints) w Churston Ferrers and Kingswear *Ex 12* **P** *The Crown* **TR** A S ALLEN, **TV** A M BURDEN, D F LAMBERT
BRIXTON (St Mary) *see* Yealmpton and Brixton *Ex*
BRIXTON (St Matthew) (St Jude) *S'wark 11* **P** *Abp and Ch Soc Trust (jt)* **V** S M SICHEL
BRIXTON (St Paul) *S'wark 11* **P** *Ch Soc Trust* **P-in-c** J M MCLAREN
BRIXTON, NORTH (Christ Church) *see* Brixton Road Ch Ch *S'wark*
BRIXTON DEVERILL (St Michael) *see* Cley Hill Warminster *Sarum*
BRIXTON HILL (St Saviour) *S'wark 11* **P** *Ch Soc Trust* **V** *vacant* (020) 8674 6914
BRIXTON ROAD (Christ Church) *S'wark 11* **P** *CPAS* **V** D J B HAZLEHURST, **C** M R MALLETT
BRIXWORTH (All Saints) w Holcot *Pet 2* **P** *Bp* **V** A J WATKINS
BRIZE NORTON (St Britius) and Carterton *Ox 8* **P** *Patr Bd* **TR** R K BILLINGS, **TV** A R TURNER
BROAD BLUNSDON (St Leonard) *see* Broad Blunsdon *Bris*
BROAD BLUNSDON (St Leonard) *Bris 7* **P** *Bp* **P-in-c** R C WARD
BROAD CAMPDEN (St Michael and All Angels) *see* Chipping Campden w Ebrington *Glouc*
BROAD HINTON (St Peter ad Vincula) *see* Upper Kennet *Sarum*
BROAD LANE (Licensed Room) *see* Wybunbury w Doddington *Ches*
BROAD OAK (St George) *see* Heathfield *Chich*
BROAD TOWN (Christ Church), Clyffe Pypard, Hilmarton and Tockenham *Sarum 15* **P** *Ld Chan, DBP, and Prime Min (by turns)* **R** M J FLIGHT
BROADBOTTOM (St Mary Magdalene) *see* Mottram in Longdendale *Ches*
BROADBRIDGE HEATH (St John) *see* Horsham *Chich*
BROADCHALKE (All Saints) *see* Chalke Valley *Sarum*
BROADCLYST (St John the Baptist) *see* Pinhoe and Broadclyst *Ex*
BROADFIELD (Christ the Lord) *see* Southgate *Chich*
BROADHEATH (Christ Church) *see* Worc St Clem and Lower Broadheath *Worc*
BROADHEATH (St Alban) *Ches 10* **P** *Bp* **V** J BEANEY
BROADHEMBURY (St Andrew the Apostle and Martyr), Payhembury and Plymtree *Ex 7* **P** *W Drewe Esq, Ex Coll Ox, and Or Coll Ox (by turn)* **R** A M ROBERTS
BROADHEMPSTON (St Peter and St Paul), Woodland, Staverton w Landscove and Littlehempston *Ex 13* **P** *Prime Min (1 turn), D&C and Bp (1 turn)* **R** N R C PEARKES
BROADMAYNE (St Martin) *see* Watercombe *Sarum*
BROADOAK (St Paul) *see* Symondsbury *Sarum*
BROADSTAIRS (Holy Trinity) *Cant 9* **P** *V St Peter-in-Thanet* **R** M W HAYTON
BROADSTAIRS (St Andrew) *see* St Peter-in-Thanet *Cant*
BROADSTONE (not known) *see* Diddlebury w Munslow, Holdgate and Tugford *Heref*
BROADSTONE (St John the Baptist) *Sarum 7* **P** *Bp* **V** M FREDRIKSEN, **NSM** G A J SMITH
BROADWAS (St Mary Magdalene) *see* Martley and Wichenford, Knightwick etc *Worc*
BROADWATER (St Mary) (St Stephen) *Chich 5* **P** *Patr Bd* **TR** J BERRY, **TV** W M TSANG, D A STEVENSON, **C** A M WILSON, R J EDWARDS
BROADWATER DOWN *see* Tunbridge Wells St Mark *Roch*
BROADWATERS (St Oswald) *see* Kidderminster St Mary and All SS w Trimpley etc *Worc*
BROADWAY (St Aldhem and St Eadburga) *see* Ilminster and Distr *B & W*
BROADWAY (St Eadburgha) (St Michael and All Angels) w Wickhamford *Worc 1* **P** *Peache Trustees and Ch Ch Ox (jt)* **V** T M MASON
BROADWELL (Good Shepherd) *see* Coleford w Staunton *Glouc*
BROADWELL (St Paul), Evenlode, Oddington, Adlestrop and Westcote w Icomb and Bledington *Glouc 14* **P** *Bp, Ch Soc Trust, Lord Leigh and DBP (1 turn), and Ch Ch Ox and D&C Worc (1 turn)* **R** R J RENDALL, **Hon C** B P DE W GOODWIN HUDSON
BROADWELL (St Peter and St Paul) *see* Shill Valley and Broadshire *Ox*

BROADWEY (St Nicholas) *see* Bincombe w Broadwey, Upwey and Buckland Ripers *Sarum*
BROADWINDSOR (St John the Baptist) *see* Beaminster Area *Sarum*
BROADWOODKELLY (All Saints) *Ex 20* **P** *DBP* **R** P J NORMAN
BROADWOODWIDGER (St Nicholas) *see* Lifton, Broadwoodwidger, Stowford etc *Ex*
BROCKDISH (St Peter and St Paul) *see* Scole, Brockdish, Billingford, Thorpe Abbots etc *Nor*
BROCKENHURST (St Nicholas) (St Saviour) *Win 11* **P** *E J F Morant Esq* **V** F R CUMBERLEGE, **Hon C** R DROWN
BROCKHALL (St Peter and St Paul) *see* Heyford w Stowe Nine Churches and Flore etc *Pet*
BROCKHAM GREEN (Christ Church) *S'wark 27* **P** *Hon J L Hamilton* **P-in-c** J M A WILLANS, **OLM** F G LEHANEY
BROCKHAMPTON (All Saints) *see* Fownhope w Mordiford, Brockhampton etc *Heref*
BROCKHAMPTON (Chapel) *see* Bromyard *Heref*
BROCKHOLES (St George) *see* Honley *Wakef*
BROCKLESBY PARK (All Saints) *Linc 6* **P** *Earl of Yarborough* **V** *vacant* (01469) 560641
BROCKLEY (St Andrew) *see* Horringer *St E*
BROCKLEY HILL (St Saviour) *S'wark 5* **P** *V Forest Hill Ch Ch* **V** A S PEBERDY, **OLM** R G TURPIN
BROCKMOOR (St John) *Worc 10* **P** *Prime Min* **P-in-c** G E P NATHANIEL, **NSM** B I PRITCHETT
BROCKWORTH (St George) *Glouc 6* **P** *DBP* **P-in-c** D A GILL
BROCTON (All Saints) *see* Baswich *Lich*
BRODSWORTH (St Michael and All Angels) *see* Bilham *Sheff*
BROKENBOROUGH (St John the Baptist) *see* Malmesbury w Westport and Brokenborough *Bris*
BROKERS WOOD (All Saints) *see* White Horse *Sarum*
BROMBOROUGH (St Barnabas) *Ches 9* **P** *D&C* **C** I M ARCH
BROME (St Mary) *see* N Hartismere *St E*
BROMESWELL (St Edmund) *see* Wilford Peninsula *St E*
BROMFIELD (St Mary the Virgin) *see* Culmington w Onibury, Bromfield etc *Heref*
BROMFIELD (St Mungo) *see* Solway Plain *Carl*
BROMFORD FIRS (not Known) *see* Hodge Hill *Birm*
BROMHAM (St Nicholas) *see* Rowde and Bromham *Sarum*
BROMHAM (St Owen) w Oakley and Stagsden *St Alb 13* **P** *Bp* **V** A C M TWEEDY, **NSM** D J HARPHAM
BROMLEY (Christ Church) *Roch 14* **P** *CPAS* **V** I J BROOMFIELD, **C** N R T HISCOCKS
BROMLEY (Holy Trinity Mission Church) *see* Pensnett *Worc*
BROMLEY (St Andrew) *Roch 14* **P** *Bp* **V** H A ATHERTON, **NSM** E J DAVIS, A M KING
BROMLEY (St John the Evangelist) *Roch 14* **P** *Bp* **V** H P C BROADBENT
BROMLEY (St Mark) *Roch 14* **P** *V Bromley SS Pet & Paul* **V** S C VARNEY, **C** N J TEVERSON
BROMLEY (St Mary) *see* Plaistow St Mary *Roch*
BROMLEY (St Peter and St Paul) *Roch 14* **P** *Bp* **V** M M CAMP, **C** A M NEWMAN
BROMLEY, GREAT (St George) *see* Ardleigh and The Bromleys *Chelmsf*
BROMLEY BY BOW (All Hallows) *Lon 7* **P** *Bp and Grocers' Co (jt)* **R** *vacant*
BROMLEY COMMON (Holy Trinity) *Roch 14* **P** *The Crown* **V** R BRISTOW, **NSM** G E COLLETT
BROMLEY COMMON (St Augustine) *Roch 14* **P** *Bp* **V** E H HESELWOOD
BROMLEY COMMON (St Luke) *Roch 14* **P** *Bp* **V** M G P INSLEY
BROMLEY CROSS (St Andrew's Mission Church) *see* Turton Moorland Min *Man*
BROMPTON (Holy Trinity) w Onslow Square St Paul *Lon 8* **P** *Bp and MMCET (jt)* **V** J A K MILLAR, **C** N G P GUMBEL, R M COATES, P W COWLEY, N K LEE, A N EMERTON, J MARCH, A K KEIGHLEY, J R HAITH
BROMPTON (St Thomas) w Deighton *York 19* **P** *D&C Dur* **V** M S SNOWBALL
BROMPTON, NEW (St Luke) *Roch 3* **P** *Bp* **P-in-c** R L FEATHERSTONE
BROMPTON, WEST (St Mary) (St Peter) *Lon 8* **P** *Bp* **NSM** V J THOMAS
BROMPTON BY SAWDON (All Saints) w Hutton Buscel, Snainton and Wykeham *York 20* **P** *Viscountess Downe (1 turn), Sir Philip Naylor-Leyland (Bt) (1 turn), Abp (2 turns)* **V** P E JARAM
BROMPTON ON SWALE (St Paul) *see* Easby w Skeeby and Brompton on Swale etc *Ripon*
BROMPTON RALPH (The Blessed Virgin Mary) *see* Lydeard St Lawrence w Brompton Ralph etc *B & W*
BROMPTON REGIS (Blessed Virgin Mary) w Upton and Skilgate *B & W 16* **P** *Bp, Em Coll Cam, and Keble Coll Ox (jt)* **P-in-c** B J RUMBOLD
BROMSBERROW (St Mary the Virgin) *see* Redmarley D'Abitot, Bromesberrow, Pauntley etc *Glouc*
BROMSGROVE (All Saints) *Worc 7* **P** *V Bromsgrove St Jo* **V** W MOORE, **NSM** F J MANT
BROMSGROVE (St John the Baptist) *Worc 7* **P** *D&C* **V** N G MARNS, **NSM** M C T B JONES
BROMWICH, WEST (All Saints) (St Mary Magdalene) *Lich 27* **P** *Bp* **V** A J SMITH, **C** P J SELLICK, **OLM** A M BIRD, E A BROWN
BROMWICH, WEST (Good Shepherd w St John) *Lich 27* **P** *Bp* **V** P O OKECHI, **C** M A SMALLMAN, **NSM** M BEDEAU
BROMWICH, WEST (Holy Trinity) *Lich 27* **P** *Peache Trustees* **P-in-c** M A SMALLMAN
BROMWICH, WEST (St Andrew) (Christ Church) *Lich 27* **P** *Bp and V W Bromwich All SS (jt)* **V** M J CLARIDGE
BROMWICH, WEST (St Francis of Assisi) *Lich 27* **P** *Bp* **V** R A FARRELL
BROMWICH, WEST (St James) (St Paul) *Lich 27* **P** *Bp and V Tipton St Martin and St Paul* **V** P G ASHBY, **C** D HART
BROMWICH, WEST (St Peter) *Lich 27* **P** *Bp* **V** *vacant* 0121-525 5147
BROMWICH, WEST (St Philip) *Lich 27* **P** *Bp* **V** R C DESON
BROMYARD (St Peter) *Heref 2* **P** *Bp* **V** G T G SYKES, **C** F M BINDING, **NSM** C M SYKES, D B HYETT, C A STOKES
BROMYARD DOWNS (Mission Church) *see* Bromyard *Heref*
BRONDESBURY (Christ Church) (St Laurence) *Lon 21* **P** *Ld Chan* **R** D E NENO
BRONDESBURY St Anne w Kilburn (Holy Trinity) *Lon 21* **P** *Bp and Ch Patr Soc (alt)* **V** F B CAPIE, **NSM** L C F HILLEL
BROOK (St Mary) *see* Wye w Brook *Cant*
BROOKE (St Mary the Virgin) *see* Brighstone and Brooke w Mottistone *Portsm*
BROOKE (St Peter) *see* Oakham, Hambleton, Egleton, Braunston and Brooke *Pet*
BROOKE (St Peter), Kirstead, Mundham w Seething and Thwaite *Nor 5* **P** *G&C Coll Cam, Gt Hosp and Countess Ferrers, and Ld Chan (by turn)* **R** J H ROBSON
BROOKE STREET (St Alban the Martyr) *see* Holborn St Alb w Saffron Hill St Pet *Lon*
BROOKEND (Mission Room) *see* Sharpness, Purton, Brookend and Slimbridge *Glouc*
BROOKFIELD (St Anne), Highgate Rise *Lon 17* **P** *Bp* **V** A J B MELDRUM
BROOKFIELD (St Margaret) *York 21* **P** *Abp* **V** R W SMITH, **NSM** M TONGE
BROOKFIELD (St Mary) *Lon 17* **P** *Bp* **V** C G POPE
BROOKHOUSE (St Paul) *see* Caton w Littledale *Blackb*
BROOKHURST (St Peter's Chapel) *see* Eastham *Ches*
BROOKING (St Barnabas) *see* Totnes w Bridgetown, Berry Pomeroy etc *Ex*
BROOKLAND (St Augustine) *see* Appledore w Brookland, Fairfield, Brenzett etc *Cant*
BROOKLANDS *see* Baguley *Man*
BROOKMANS PARK (St Michael) *see* N Mymms *St Alb*
BROOKSBY (St Michael and All Angels) *see* Upper Wreake *Leic*
BROOKSIDE (Pastoral Centre) *see* Cen Telford *Lich*
BROOKWOOD (St Saviour) *see* Knaphill w Brookwood *Guildf*
BROOM (St Matthew) *see* Bidford-on-Avon *Cov*
BROOM LEYS (St David) *Leic 8* **P** *Bp* **V** J W STEVENSON, **NSM** J P DREW
BROOM VALLEY (St Barnabas) *see* Rotherham *Sheff*
BROOME (St Michael) *see* Ditchingham, Hedenham and Broome *Nor*
BROOME (St Peter) *see* Churchill-in-Halfshire w Blakedown and Broome *Worc*
BROOMFIELD (St Margaret) *see* Hollingbourne and Hucking w Leeds and Broomfield *Cant*
BROOMFIELD (St Mary and All Saints) *see* Kingston St Mary w Broomfield etc *B & W*
BROOMFIELD (St Mary w St Leonard) *Chelmsf 8* **P** *Bp* **V** P E BALL
BROOMFLEET (St Mary) *see* S Cave and Ellerker w Broomfleet *York*
BROOMHILL (St Mark) *see* Sheff St Mark Broomhill *Sheff*
BROSELEY (All Saints) w Benthall, Jackfield, Linley, Willey and Barrow *Heref 14* **P** *Patr Bd* **R** M A KINNA, **NSM** B D SHINTON
BROTHERTOFT Group, The (Christ Church) (St Gilbert of Sempringham) *Linc 21* **P** *Bp (2 turns), V Algarkirk (1 turn)* **V** *vacant* (01205) 280267

BROTHERTON (St Edward the Confessor) *Wakef 11* **P** *D&C York* **P-in-c** P J WALKER
BROTTON PARVA (St Margaret) *York 16* **P** *Abp* **R** G R DREWERY
BROUGH (All Saints) *see* Elloughton and Brough w Brantingham *York*
BROUGH (St Michael) w Stainmore, Musgrave and Warcop *Carl 1* **P** *Bp (2 turns) and Lord Hothfield (1 turn)* **P-in-c** B G MAGORRIAN
BROUGHAM (St Wilfrid Chapel) *see* Lowther and Askham and Clifton and Brougham *Carl*
BROUGHTON (All Saints) *see* Warboys w Broughton and Bury w Wistow *Ely*
BROUGHTON (All Saints), Marton and Thornton *Bradf 7* **P** *Ch Ch Ox and Exors Dame Harriet Nelson (jt)* **P-in-c** N A TURNER, **C** P A TURNER
BROUGHTON (St Andrew) w Loddington and Cransley and Thorpe Malsor *Pet 11* **P** *Ld Chan (1 turn), Bp (2 turns), and Keble Coll Ox (1 turn)* **P-in-c** B J WITHINGTON, **NSM** A R G DUTTON
BROUGHTON (St James) (St Clement and St Matthias) (St John the Baptist) *Man 6* **P** *Patr Bd* **TR** H R F MARTIN, **TV** I C FELLOWS, **OLM** J S CORRIE
BROUGHTON (St John the Baptist) *Blackb 13* **P** *Trustees* **V** S FOX, **C** R C HOLLIS
BROUGHTON (St Mary) *Lich 22* **P** *D R B Thompson Esq* **P-in-c** D T W PRICE, **NSM** T D SMITH
BROUGHTON (St Mary) *Linc 6* **P** *MMCET* **R** J W COTTON
BROUGHTON (St Mary Magdalene) (Holy Innocents) and Duddon *Carl 9* **P** *V Millom, Lt-Col D A S Pennefather, and Ch Patr Trust (by turn)* **P-in-c** A P ADAMS
BROUGHTON (St Mary the Virgin) *see* Wykeham *Ox*
BROUGHTON (St Mary) w Bossington and Houghton and Mottisfont *Win 12* **P** *Ld Chan (1 turn), Mr and Mrs R G L Pugh, A Humbert Esq and Miss R A Humbert (jt) (2 turns)* **R** R A CORNE
BROUGHTON (St Peter) w Croxton and Cotes Heath w Standon *Lich 7* **P** *Bp, V Eccleshall, and T A J Hall Esq (jt)* **P-in-c** M F WALKER
BROUGHTON, GREAT (Christ Church) and Broughton Moor *Carl 7* **P** *Bp* **P-in-c** D R KING
BROUGHTON, LOWER (Ascension) *Man 6* **P** *Trustees* **R** *vacant* 0161-834 4370
BROUGHTON, NETHER (St Mary the Virgin) *see* Old Dalby, Nether Broughton, Saxelbye etc *Leic*
BROUGHTON, UPPER (St Luke) *see* Hickling w Kinoulton and Broughton Sulney *S'well*
BROUGHTON ASTLEY (St Mary) and Croft w Stoney Stanton *Leic 10* **P** *Patr Bd* **TR** D T SHAW, **C** E M WALLACE
BROUGHTON GIFFORD (St Mary the Virgin), Great Chalfield and Holt St Katharine *Sarum 14* **P** *D&C Bris (3 turns), Ld Chan (2 turns), and R C Floyd Esq (1 turn)* **R** R G HART, **OLM** E A FIELDEN
BROUGHTON HACKETT (St Leonard) *see* Peopleton and White Ladies Aston w Churchill etc *Worc*
BROUGHTON IN FURNESS (St Mary Magdalene) *see* Broughton and Duddon *Carl*
BROUGHTON MILLS (Holy Innocents) *as above*
BROUGHTON MOOR (St Columba) *see* Gt Broughton and Broughton Moor *Carl*
BROUGHTON POGGS (St Peter) *see* Shill Valley and Broadshire *Ox*
BROWN CANDOVER (St Peter) *see* The Candover Valley *Win*
BROWN EDGE (St Anne) *Lich 8* **P** *Bp* **P-in-c** R J S GRIGSON
BROWNHILL (St Saviour) *Wakef 8* **P** *V Batley* **V** P N A SENIOR, **C** D INGHAM
BROWNHILLS (St James) *see* Ogley Hay *Lich*
BROWNSOVER (Christ Church) *Cov 6* **P** *Bp* **V** E C LYONS
BROWNSWOOD PARK (St John the Evangelist) *Lon 5* **P** *City Corp* **P-in-c** J D CLARK, **C** M J HAWKES, S J SNYDER, **NSM** S BISASO-SEKITOLEKO
BROXBOURNE (St Augustine) w Wormley *St Alb 20* **P** *Bp and Peache Trustees (jt)* **P-in-c** I J TOMKINS
BROXHOLME (All Saints) *see* Saxilby Gp *Linc*
BROXTED (St Mary the Virgin) w Chickney and Tilty and Great and Little Easton *Chelmsf 18* **P** *Mrs F Spurrier (2 turns), DBP (1 turn), and MMCET (1 turn)* **R** G C GREENSLADE
BROXTOWE (St Martha) *S'well 14* **P** *Bp* **P-in-c** P J NOTT
BRUERA (St Mary) *see* Aldford and Bruera *Ches*
BRUISYARD (St Peter) *see* Badingham w Bruisyard, Cransford etc *St E*
BRUMBY (St Hugh) (All Saints) *Linc 4* **P** *Bp* **TV** D M BROWN, **C** T A REDFEARN, **OLM** A K PEAT
BRUNDALL (St Lawrence) w Braydeston and Postwick *Nor 4* **P** *Bp and MMCET (jt)* **R** R M BAKER
BRUNDISH (St Lawrence) *see* Laxfield, Cratfield, Wilby and Brundish *St E*
BRUNSTEAD (St Peter) *see* Stalham, E Ruston, Brunstead, Sutton and Ingham *Nor*
BRUNSWICK (Christ Church) *Man 4* **P** *Ch Soc Trust* **R** S J T GATENBY, **C** C A MULLINS, **NSM** R M YOUNG
BRUNSWICK (St Cuthbert) *see* Ch the King *Newc*
BRUNTCLIFFE (St Andrew) *see* Morley *Wakef*
BRUNTINGTHORPE (St Mary) *see* Arnesby w Shearsby and Bruntingthorpe *Leic*
BRUNTON PARK (St Aidan) *see* Ch the King *Newc*
BRUSHFORD (St Mary the Virgin) *Ex 20* **P** *D&C* **V** P J NORMAN
BRUSHFORD (St Nicholas) *see* Dulverton and Brushford *B & W*
BRUTON (Blessed Virgin Mary) and District *B & W 2* **P** *Patr Bd* **C** M B BROWN, **NSM** A C PARFITT
BRYANSTON SQUARE (St Mary) w St Marylebone (St Mark) *Lon 4* **P** *The Crown* **R** J P T PETERS, **C** B J KISSELL, W R VAN DER HART
BRYANSTON STREET (Annunciation) *see* St Marylebone Annunciation Bryanston Street *Lon*
BRYHER (All Saints) *see* Is of Scilly *Truro*
BRYMPTON (St Andrew) *see* Odcombe, Brympton, Lufton and Montacute *B & W*
BRYN (St Chad) *see* Clun w Bettws-y-Crwyn and Newcastle *Heref*
BRYN (St Peter) *Liv 15* **P** *Bp* **V** D J HOOTON
BUBBENHALL (St Giles) *see* Baginton w Bubbenhall and Ryton-on-Dunsmore *Cov*
BUBWITH (All Saints) w Skipwith *York 2* **P** *Abp and D&C, and Ld Chan (alt)* **P-in-c** J M OLIVER
BUCKDEN (St Mary) w the Offords *Ely 10* **P** *Bp and Ld Chan (alt)* **R** M E SMITH
BUCKENHAM, NEW (St Martin) *see* Quidenham Gp *Nor*
BUCKENHAM, OLD (All Saints) *as above*
BUCKERELL (St Mary and St Giles) *see* Feniton, Buckerell and Escot *Ex*
BUCKFAST SANCTUARY (not known) *see* Buckfastleigh w Dean Prior *Ex*
BUCKFASTLEIGH (Holy Trinity) (St Luke's Mission) w Dean Prior *Ex 13* **P** *D&C (2 turns), DBP (1 turn)* **V** D J ROWLAND, **NSM** J N C IRWIN
BUCKHORN WESTON (St John the Baptist) *see* Stour Vale *Sarum*
BUCKHURST HILL (St Elisabeth) (St John the Baptist) (St Stephen) *Chelmsf 25* **P** *Patr Bd* **TR** I D FARLEY, **TV** C W WRAGG, **C** C J BRIXTON
BUCKINGHAM (St Peter and St Paul) *Ox 22* **P** *Bp, Adn Buckm, Mrs S A J Doulton, G&C Coll Cam, New Coll Ox, and Exors R J Dalziel Smith Esq (jt)* **R** K P ASHBY, **NSM** P D DERBYSHIRE, J F KING
BUCKINGHAM, NORTH *Ox 22* **P** *Ch Soc Trust, Mrs J M Williams, and D J Robarts Esq (by turn)* **P-in-c** J A TALING, **OLM** J A PRICE
BUCKINGHAM, WEST *Ox 22* **P** *Bp, D&C Westmr, G Purefoy Esq, and R L Randall Esq (1 turn), New Coll Ox (1 turn), and DBP (1 turn)* **P-in-c** E A SIMPSON
BUCKLAND (All Saints) *see* Aston Clinton w Buckland and Drayton Beauchamp *Ox*
BUCKLAND (St Mary the Virgin) *see* Cherbury w Gainfield *Ox*
BUCKLAND (St Mary the Virgin) *S'wark 27* **P** *All So Coll Ox* **R** S J BAILEY, **OLM** P A VIGERS
BUCKLAND (St Michael) *see* Winchcombe *Glouc*
BUCKLAND, EAST (St Michael) *see* S Molton w Nymet St George, High Bray etc *Ex*
BUCKLAND, WEST (Blessed Virgin Mary) *see* Wellington and Distr *B & W*
BUCKLAND, WEST (St Peter) *see* Swimbridge w W Buckland and Landkey *Ex*
BUCKLAND BREWER (St Mary and St Benedict) *see* Parkham, Alwington, Buckland Brewer etc *Ex*
BUCKLAND DINHAM (St Michael and All Angels) *see* Mells w Buckland Dinham, Elm, Whatley etc *B & W*
BUCKLAND FILLEIGH (St Mary and Holy Trinity) *see* Shebbear, Buckland Filleigh, Sheepwash etc *Ex*
BUCKLAND IN DOVER (St Andrew) w Buckland Valley (St Nicholas) *Cant 4* **P** *Abp* **R** T FOREMAN
BUCKLAND IN THE MOOR (St Peter) *see* Ashburton w Buckland in the Moor and Bickington *Ex*
BUCKLAND MONACHORUM (St Andrew) *Ex 25* **P** *Bp* **V** G M COTTER
BUCKLAND NEWTON (Holy Rood), Cerne Abbas, Godmanstone and Minterne Magna *Sarum 1* **P** *Adn*

Sherborne, Lord Digby, D H C Batten Esq, G E H Gallia Esq, and Col J L Yeatman (jt) **V** K S CURNOCK
BUCKLAND RIPERS (St Nicholas) *see* Bincombe w Broadwey, Upwey and Buckland Ripers *Sarum*
BUCKLAND ST MARY (Blessed Virgin Mary) *see* Blackdown *B & W*
BUCKLAND TOUT SAINTS (St Peter) *see* Charleton w Buckland Tout Saints etc *Ex*
BUCKLAND VALLEY (St Nicholas) *see* Buckland in Dover w Buckland Valley *Cant*
BUCKLEBURY (St Mary) w Marlston *Ox 12* **P** *C J Pratt Esq* **P-in-c** E MARQUEZ, **C** D M CHATTELL, **NSM** R C OBIN
BUCKLEBURY, UPPER (All Saints) *see* Bucklebury w Marlston *Ox*
BUCKLERS HARD (St Mary) *see* Beaulieu and Exbury and E Boldre *Win*
BUCKLESHAM (St Mary) *see* Nacton and Levington w Bucklesham and Foxhall *St E*
BUCKMINSTER (St John the Baptist) *see* S Framland *Leic*
BUCKNALL (St Margaret) *see* Woodhall Spa Gp *Linc*
BUCKNALL Team Ministry, The (St Mary the Virgin) *Lich 12* **P** *Patr Bd* **TR** M K ELLOR, **TV** M N STEPHENS, W E DUDLEY
BUCKNELL (St Mary) w Chapel Lawn, Llanfair Waterdine and Stowe *Heref 10* **P** *Earl of Powis, Grocers' Co, and J Coltman Rogers Esq (jt)* **V** E TAVERNOR
BUCKNELL (St Peter) *see* Bicester w Bucknell, Caversfield and Launton *Ox*
BUCKROSE, WEST *York 6* **P** *Ld Chan (1 turn), Lord Middleton and Abp (3 turns)* **P-in-c** M D B SINCLAIR
BUCKROSE CARRS *York 6* **P** *Prime Min, Major G R H Cholmley, Sir Philip Naylor-Leyland Bt, and D&C (by turn)* **R** C J HAYES, **NSM** J M DUKE
BUCKS MILLS (St Anne) *see* Parkham, Alwington, Buckland Brewer etc *Ex*
BUCKWORTH (All Saints) *Ely 8* **P** *Bp* **P-in-c** J P YOUNG, **NSM** M J HARE
BUDBROOKE (St Michael) *Cov 4* **P** *MMCET* **P-in-c** A D BRADLEY
BUDE HAVEN (St Michael and All Angels) and Marhamchurch *Truro 8* **P** *Bp and PCC (jt)* **R** C M SCOTT, **OLM** P JUDSON
BUDLEIGH, EAST (All Saints) w Bicton and Otterton *Ex 1* **P** *Lord Clinton* **P-in-c** J S CACKETT
BUDLEIGH SALTERTON (St Peter) *Ex 1* **P** *Lord Clinton* **V** R S J CHARLES
BUDOCK (St Budock) *Truro 3* **P** *Bp* **V** G K BENNETT
BUDWORTH, GREAT (St Mary and All Saints) *Ches 4* **P** *Ch Ch Ox* **V** A G BROWN
BUDWORTH, LITTLE (St Peter) *see* Whitegate w Lt Budworth *Ches*
BUGBROOKE (St Michael and All Angels) w Rothersthorpe *Pet 3* **P** *Exors E W Harrison (2 turns), DBP (1 turn)* **R** *vacant* (01604) 830373
BUGLAWTON (St John the Evangelist) *see* Congleton *Ches*
BUGTHORPE (St Andrew) *see* Garrowby Hill *York*
BUILDWAS (Holy Trinity) *see* Wrockwardine Deanery *Lich*
BULCOTE (Holy Trinity) *see* Burton Joyce w Bulcote and Stoke Bardolph *S'well*
BULFORD (St Leonard) *see* Avon Valley *Sarum*
BULKELEY (All Saints) *see* Bickerton, Bickley, Harthill and Burwardsley *Ches*
BULKINGTON (Christ Church) *see* Seend, Bulkington and Poulshot *Sarum*
BULKINGTON (St James) w Shilton and Ansty *Cov 5* **P** *Ld Chan* **V** A J WADSWORTH, **NSM** N W STEVENS
BULKWORTHY (St Michael) *see* Bradworthy, Sutcombe, Putford etc *Ex*
BULLEY (St Michael and All Angels) *see* Huntley and Longhope, Churcham and Bulley *Glouc*
BULLINGHOPE, UPPER (St Peter) *see* Heref S Wye *Heref*
BULLINGTON (St Michael and All Angels) *see* Lower Dever Valley *Win*
BULMER (St Andrew) *see* N Hinckford *Chelmsf*
BULMER (St Martin) *see* Howardian Gp *York*
BULPHAN (St Mary the Virgin) *see* Orsett and Bulphan and Horndon on the Hill *Chelmsf*
BULWELL (St John the Divine) *S'well 12* **P** *Bp* **P-in-c** D GRAY
BULWELL (St Mary the Virgin and All Souls) *S'well 12* **P** *Bp* **R** C GALE
BULWICK (St Nicholas) and Blatherwycke w Harringworth and Laxton *Pet 8* **P** *G T G Conant Esq (3 turns), F & A George Ltd (1 turn)* **NSM** J A PORTLOCK
BUNBURY (St Boniface) and Tilstone Fearnall *Ches 5* **P** *Haberdashers' Co* **V** R J GATES, **NSM** J STEPHENSON
BUNCTON (All Saints) *see* Ashington, Washington and Wiston w Buncton *Chich*
BUNGAY (Holy Trinity) w St Mary *St E 14* **P** *DBP* **V** I S MORGAN, **OLM** R C B ALLEN
BUNNY (St Mary the Virgin) *see* Keyworth and Stanton-on-the-Wolds and Bunny etc *S'well*
BUNWELL (St Michael and All Angels), Carleton Rode, Tibenham, Great Moulton and Aslacton *Nor 5* **P** *Bp and DBP (alt)* **R** H D POTTS
BURBAGE (All Saints) *see* Savernake *Sarum*
BURBAGE (Christ Church) *see* Buxton w Burbage and King Sterndale *Derby*
BURBAGE (St Catherine) w Aston Flamville *Leic 12* **P** *Ball Coll Ox* **R** F D JENNINGS, **C** A QUIGLEY, **NSM** A M ADAMS, R STEPHEN
BURCHETTS GREEN *Ox 13* **P** *DBP and Bp (jt)* **V** T A SCOTT, **NSM** D M WOODMORE
BURES (St Mary the Virgin) w Assington and Lt Cornard *St E 12* **P** *DBP and Bp (jt)* **V** R L C KING, **C** D K WAKEFIELD, **NSM** K M KING, **OLM** J L GOYMOUR
BURFORD First Portion *Heref 12* **P** *DBP, Bp Birm, Bp, and J J C Caldwell Esq (jt)* **R** *vacant*
BURFORD Second Portion (St Mary) w Greete and Hope Bagot *Heref 12* **P** *DBP* **R** *vacant*
BURFORD (St John the Baptist) w Fulbrook, Taynton, Asthall, Swinbrook and Widford *Ox 8* **P** *Bp and Capt D Mackinnon (jt)* **V** R M COOMBS, **C** S P ALLEN
BURFORD Third Portion (St Mary) w Little Hereford *Heref 12* **P** *DBP and Bp Birm (jt)* **R** *vacant*
BURGATE (St Mary) *see* N Hartismere *St E*
BURGESS HILL (St Andrew) *Chich 9* **P** *Bp* **V** I G PRIOR, **C** S C M MCLARNON
BURGESS HILL (St Edward) *Chich 9* **P** *Bp Chich, Bp Horsham, and R Clayton w Keymer (jt)* **V** T L PESKETT, **NSM** S S MACCARTHY
BURGESS HILL (St John the Evangelist) *Chich 9* **P** *Bp Chich, Bp Horsham, and R Clayton w Keymer (jt)* **V** M C KNOWLES
BURGH (St Botolph) *see* Boulge w Burgh, Grundisburgh and Hasketon *St E*
BURGH (St Margaret and St Mary) *see* S Trin Broads *Nor*
BURGH (St Peter) *see* Raveningham Gp *Nor*
BURGH-BY-SANDS (St Michael) *see* Barony of Burgh *Carl*
BURGH CASTLE (St Peter and St Paul) *see* Belton and Burgh Castle *Nor*
BURGH HEATH (St Mary the Virgin) *see* Howell Hill w Burgh Heath *Guildf*
BURGH LE MARSH (St Peter and St Paul) *Linc 8* **P** *Bp* **V** T STEELE
BURGH-NEXT-AYLSHAM (St Mary) *see* Marsham w Burgh-next-Aylsham *Nor*
BURGH-ON-BAIN (St Helen) *see* Asterby Gp *Linc*
BURGH PARVA (St Mary) *see* Briston w Burgh Parva and Melton Constable *Nor*
BURGHCLERE (Ascension) (All Saints) w Newtown and Ecchinswell w Sydmonton *Win 6* **P** *Earl of Carnarvon* **R** D G BARTHOLOMEW
BURGHFIELD (St Mary the Virgin) *Ox 12* **P** *Earl of Shrewsbury* **P-in-c** J M H LOVERIDGE
BURGHILL (St Mary the Virgin) *Heref 4* **P** *DBP* **V** J W R MORRISON, **NSM** E S V VERWEY
BURGHWALLIS (St Helen) and Campsall *Sheff 7* **P** *Bp (2 turns), Mrs E H I Ellison-Anne (1 turn)* **R** M G JOHNSON
BURHAM (Methodist Church) and Wouldham *Roch 5* **P** *Bp and Ld Chan (alt)* **P-in-c** E M R WALKER
BURITON (St Mary the Virgin) *Portsm 4* **P** *Bp* **R** W G HARRIS-EVANS, **NSM** D R TOWNSEND
BURLESCOMBE (St Mary) *see* Sampford Peverell, Uplowman, Holcombe Rogus etc *Ex*
BURLEY (St Matthias) *Ripon 7* **P** *G M Bedford Esq, J C Yeadon Esq, E Beety Esq, Mrs M E Dunham, and Mrs L M Rawse (jt)* **V** K TROUT
BURLEY IN WHARFEDALE (St Mary the Virgin) *Bradf 4* **P** *Bp* **V** M BURLEY
BURLEY VILLE (St John the Baptist) *Win 9* **P** *V Ringwood* **P-in-c** D M WEBSTER
BURLEYDAM (St Mary and St Michael) *see* Baddiley and Wrenbury w Burleydam *Ches*
BURLINGHAM (St Andrew) *see* Acle w Fishley, N Burlingham, Beighton w Moulton *Nor*
BURLINGHAM (St Edmund King and Martyr) w Lingwood, Strumpshaw w Hassingham and Buckenham *Nor 4* **P** *Ch Soc Trust, MMCET, and Bp (jt)* **P-in-c** V M ELPHICK
BURLTON (St Anne) *see* Loppington w Newtown *Lich*
BURMANTOFTS (St Stephen and St Agnes) *Ripon 5* **P** *Ch Trust Fund Trust* **P-in-c** M HARPER
BURMARSH (All Saints) *see* Dymchurch w Burmarsh and Newchurch *Cant*

BURMINGTON (St Nicholas and St Barnabas) *see* Wolford w Burmington *Cov*
BURNAGE (St Margaret) *Man 3* **P** *Bp* **R** J A WILLIAMS
BURNAGE (St Nicholas) *Man 8* **P** *Trustees* **P-in-c** P D ROLFE
BURNBY (St Giles) *York 5* **P** *Trustees* **NSM** S D JONES
BURNESIDE (St Oswald) *Carl 10* **P** *J A Cropper Esq, Mrs E Bingham, and Mrs B Baines (jt)* **V** N L DAVIES, **NSM** M MASHITER, **Hon Par Dn** J L TYRER
BURNESTON (St Lambert) *see* Kirklington w Burneston and Wath and Pickhill *Ripon*
BURNETT (St Michael) *see* Keynsham *B & W*
BURNEY LANE (Christ Church) *Birm 13* **P** *Bp* **V** P H SMITH, **C** P N WARMAN
BURNHAM (St Andrew) *B & W 1* **P** *D&C* **V** G R WITTS
BURNHAM (St Mary the Virgin) *Chelmsf 11* **P** *N D Beckett Esq and Walsingham Coll Trust (jt)* **V** E H BEAVAN
BURNHAM (St Peter) w Dropmore, Hitcham and Taplow *Ox 23* **P** *Patr Bd* **TV** A C DIBDEN, T R HEWSON, O J GRAHAM, **C** G J LOVELL, **NSM** G M EDEN, R R HEWSON, **OLM** N PLANT
BURNHAM DEEPDALE (St Mary) *see* Hunstanton St Mary w Ringstead Parva etc *Nor*
BURNHAM NORTON (St Margaret) *see* Burnham Gp of Par *Nor*
BURNHAM-ON-CROUCH (St Mary the Virgin) *see* Burnham *Chelmsf*
BURNHAM-ON-SEA (St Andrew) *as above*
BURNHAM OVERY (St Clement) *see* Burnham Gp of Par *Nor*
BURNHAM THORPE (All Saints) *as above*
BURNHAM ULPH (All Saints) *as above*
BURNHAM WESTGATE (St Mary), Burnham Norton, Burnham Overy, Burnham Thorpe, and Burnham Sutton w Ulph (The Burnham Group of Parishes) *Nor 15* **P** *Ch Coll Cam (1 turn), Ld Chan (2 turns), and DBP (1 turn)* **P-in-c** J CHARLES
BURNLEY (St Andrew) w St Margaret and Burnley St James *Blackb 3* **P** *Prime Min and R Burnley St Pet (alt)* **V** P R HAPGOOD-STRICKLAND, **C** D J LLOYD
BURNLEY (St Catherine) (St Alban) and St Paul *Blackb 3* **P** *R Burnley* **V** R T D PARKER, **C** S SMITH
BURNLEY (St Cuthbert) *Blackb 3* **P** *R Burnley* **P-in-c** I C WATTS
BURNLEY (St Mark) *Blackb 3* **P** *Bp* **V** J G HAIGH
BURNLEY (St Matthew the Apostle) Habergham Eaves w Holy Trinity *Blackb 3* **P** *R Burnley* **V** I S MOSSLEY
BURNLEY (St Peter) *Blackb 3* **P** *Bp* **R** T A G BILL
BURNLEY (St Stephen) *Blackb 3* **P** *R Burnley* **V** P V F CHEW
BURNLEY, WEST (All Saints) *Blackb 3* **P** *Bp and R Burnley (jt)* **V** P K HARRISON, **C** I R BENGE
BURNMOOR (St Barnabas) *Dur 14* **P** *Lord Lambton* **P-in-c** N A CHAMBERLAIN
BURNOPFIELD (St James) *Dur 4* **P** *Bp* **V** R G BIRCHALL
BURNSALL (St Wilfrid) w Rylstone *Bradf 7* **P** *Exors Earl of Craven and CPAS (jt)* **P-in-c** A J CHRICH, **C** A HODGE
BURNT OAK (St Alphage) *see* Hendon St Alphage *Lon*
BURNT YATES (St Andrew) *see* Ripley *Ripon*
BURNTWOOD (Christ Church) *Lich 1* **P** *D&C* **V** D A WEAVER, **OLM** C J LATIMER
BURPHAM (St Luke) Guildford *Guildf 5* **P** *Bp* **V** C J MATTHEWS, **C** J H MCCABE, P M S ROSS-MCCABE, **NSM** C E REDDIN
BURPHAM (St Mary the Virgin) *Chich 1* **P** *D&C* **P-in-c** E J RICHARDSON
BURRADON (Good Shepherd) *see* Weetslade *Newc*
BURRILL (Mission Church) *see* Bedale and Leeming *Ripon*
BURRINGTON (Holy Trinity) and Churchill *B & W 11* **P** *D&C Bris and Burrington PCC (jt)* **V** J C ABDY
BURRINGTON (Holy Trinity), Chawleigh, Cheldon, Chulmleigh, Meshaw, Thelbridge, Wembworthy, Witheridge and the Worlingtons *Ex 19* **P** *Patr Bd* **TR** R D WITHNELL, **TV** J HANNA, **C** J ROBERTS
BURRINGTON (St George) *see* Wigmore Abbey *Heref*
BURROUGH GREEN (St Augustine of Canterbury) *see* Raddesley Gp *Ely*
BURROUGH HILL Parishes, The: Burrough on the Hill, Great Dalby, Little Dalby, Pickwell and Somerby *Leic 3* **P** *Bp, DBP, and Mrs M Burdett Fisher (jt)* **P-in-c** A J HAMPTON
BURROUGH ON THE HILL (St Mary the Virgin) *see* Burrough Hill Pars *Leic*
BURROWBRIDGE (St Michael) *see* Stoke St Gregory w Burrowbridge and Lyng *B & W*
BURRSVILLE (St Mark) *see* Gt Clacton *Chelmsf*
BURSCOUGH BRIDGE (St John) (St Andrew) (St Cyprian) *Liv 11* **P** *V Ormskirk* **V** N R SHORT, **C** S A GLYNN, **OLM** B ABRAHAM
BURSDON MOOR (St Martin) *see* Parkham, Alwington, Buckland Brewer etc *Ex*
BURSEA (Chapel) *see* Holme and Seaton Ross Gp *York*
BURSLEDON Pilands Wood (St Paul) *see* Bursledon *Win*
BURSLEDON (St Leonard) *Win 10* **P** *Bp* **V** P A VARGESON, **C** J PAWSON
BURSLEM (St John the Baptist) (St Paul) *Lich 11* **P** *Bp and MMCET (jt)* **R** C R JOHNSON
BURSLEM (St Werburgh) *Lich 11* **P** *Bp* **V** K L ROUND
BURSTALL (St Mary the Virgin) *see* Sproughton w Burstall, Copdock w Washbrook etc *St E*
BURSTEAD, GREAT (St Mary Magdalene) *Chelmsf 6* **P** *Bp* **V** S SWIFT, **NSM** J M BARHAM
BURSTEAD, LITTLE (St Mary) *see* Billericay and Lt Burstead *Chelmsf*
BURSTOCK (St Andrew) *see* Beaminster Area *Sarum*
BURSTON (St Mary) *see* Winfarthing w Shelfanger w Burston w Gissing etc *Nor*
BURSTON (St Rufin) *see* Mid Trent *Lich*
BURSTOW (St Bartholomew) w Horne *S'wark 27* **P** *Ld Chan and Bp (alt)* **R** C E GALE
BURSTWICK (All Saints) w Thorngumbald *York 12* **P** *Abp* **V** A J BURDON, **NSM** P M BURDON
BURTLE (St Philip and St James) *see* Shapwick w Ashcott and Burtle *B & W*
BURTON (All Saints) w Christ Church *Lich 14* **P** *CPAS and Ch Soc Trust (jt)* **V** N R IRONS, **C** G N CROWE
BURTON (St James) and Holme *Carl 10* **P** *Simeon's Trustees* **P-in-c** P G BAXENDALE
BURTON (St Luke) and Sopley *Win 9* **P** *Bp and D&C Cant (alt)* **P-in-c** M C SURMAN
BURTON (St Nicholas) and Shotwick *Ches 9* **P** *D&C (1 turn) and St Jo Hosp Lich (2 turns)* **V** H J ALDRIDGE
BURTON w COATES (St Agatha) *see* Barlavington, Burton w Coates, Sutton and Bignor *Chich*
BURTON AGNES (St Martin) w Harpham and Lowthorpe w Ruston Parva *York 10* **P** *Ld Chan (2 turns), Sir Charles Legard Bt (1 turn)* **P-in-c** A J E KIDD
BURTON BRADSTOCK (St Mary) *see* Bride Valley *Sarum*
BURTON BY LINCOLN (St Vincent) *Linc 2* **P** *Lord Monson* **R** *vacant*
BURTON COGGLES (St Thomas à Becket) *see* Ingoldsby *Linc*
BURTON DASSETT (All Saints) *Cov 8* **P** *Bp* **V** P T FRANCIS
BURTON FLEMING (St Cuthbert) w Fordon, Grindale and Wold Newton *York 9* **P** *Abp and MMCET (jt)* **P-in-c** S V COPE, **Hon C** W R KILFORD
BURTON GREEN (Chapel of Ease) *see* Kenilworth St Nic *Cov*
BURTON HASTINGS (St Botolph) *see* Wolvey w Burton Hastings, Copston Magna etc *Cov*
BURTON IN LONSDALE (All Saints) *see* Thornton in Lonsdale w Burton in Lonsdale *Bradf*
BURTON JOYCE (St Helen) w Bulcote and Stoke Bardolph *S'well 10* **P** *MMCET* **V** J A FISHER, **NSM** E C KIRK, F J M COTTON-BETTRIDGE
BURTON LATIMER (St Mary the Virgin) *Pet 11* **P** *Bp* **R** Q D CHANDLER
BURTON LAZARS (St James) *see* Melton Mowbray *Leic*
BURTON LEONARD (St Leonard) *see* Ripon Cathl *Ripon*
BURTON-ON-TRENT (All Saints) *see* Burton All SS w Ch Ch *Lich*
BURTON-ON-TRENT (St Aidan) *see* Shobnall *Lich*
BURTON-ON-TRENT (St Chad) *Lich 14* **P** *Bp* **V** M P SKILLINGS, **OLM** H FERGUSON-STUART, P J ORTON
BURTON-ON-TRENT (St Modwen) (St Paul) *Lich 14* **P** *Bp and Lord Burton (jt)* **P-in-c** P A FARTHING
BURTON OVERY (St Andrew) *see* Glen Magna cum Stretton Magna etc *Leic*
BURTON PEDWARDINE (St Andrew and the Blessed Virgin Mary and St Nicholas) *see* Helpringham w Hale *Linc*
BURTON PIDSEA (St Peter) and Humbleton w Elsternwick *York 12* **P** *Ld Chan and D&C (alt)* **V** J L CAMPBELL
BURTON UPON STATHER (St Andrew) *see* Flixborough w Burton upon Stather *Linc*
BURTONWOOD (St Michael) *Liv 16* **P** *R Warrington* **V** R S NAYLOR
BURWARDSLEY (St John) *see* Bickerton, Bickley, Harthill and Burwardsley *Ches*
BURWASH (St Bartholomew) *Chich 14* **P** *BNC Ox* **P-in-c** S M FRANCE
BURWASH WEALD (St Philip) *Chich 15* **P** *Bp* **P-in-c** J C HAWKINS
BURWELL (St Andrew) (St Mary) w Reach *Ely 3* **P** *DBP* **V** S G F EARL, **NSM** G SMITH
BURY (Christ the King) *Man 10* **P** *Patr Bd* **P-in-c** K M TRIVASSE

BURY (Holy Cross) *see* Warboys w Broughton and Bury w Wistow *Ely*
BURY (Holy Trinity) *Man 10* **P** *Patr Bd* **V** *vacant* 0161-764 2006
BURY (St John the Evangelist) w Houghton and Coldwaltham and Hardham *Chich 11* **P** *Pemb Coll Ox, D&C, and Col Sir Brian Barttelot Bt (jt)* **V** D A TWINLEY, **NSM** C S STRIDE
BURY (St John w St Mark) *Man 10* **P** *R Bury St Mary* **V** I J STAMP, **C** J F J O'DWYER, **OLM** P SANDERSON, E A BINNS
BURY (St Mary the Virgin) *Man 10* **P** *Earl of Derby* **R** J C FINDON
BURY St Paul *Man 10* **P** *Trustees* **V** *vacant* 0161-761 6991
BURY (St Peter) *Man 10* **P** *R Bury St Mary* **V** F E F WARD, **NSM** J M SMITH
BURY (St Stephen) *see* Elton St Steph *Man*
BURY, NEW (St James) *Man 12* **P** *Bp* **TR** B HARTLEY, **TV** P D GULLY, **C** G KENNEDY, **OLM** D N BIRD, A COMBER, N A COWELL
BURY ST EDMUNDS (All Saints) (St John the Evangelist) (St George) *St E 13* **P** *Patr Bd* **TR** G J WEBB, **TV** J M N HUNT, **C** M R FARRELL, **NSM** A J REDMAN
BURY ST EDMUNDS (Cathedral of St James) District *St E 13* **V** *vacant*
BURY ST EDMUNDS (Christ Church) Moreton Hall *St E 13* **P** *Bp, V Bury St Edm St Jas, and V Bury St Edm St Mary (jt)* **V** J L ALDERTON-FORD, **NSM** N T CORWIN
BURY ST EDMUNDS (St Mary) (St Peter's District Church) *St E 13* **P** *Hyndman Trustees* **V** M D ROGERS, **OLM** D T CROFTS, W J SUNDERLAND, G A BROWN
BURYTHORPE (All Saints) *see* W Buckrose *York*
BUSBRIDGE (St John the Baptist) and Hambledon *Guildf 4* **P** *Patr Bd* **R** C J TRICKEY, **C** S J COUVELA, **NSM** M P W SPENCER, **OLM** A SPENCER
BUSCOT (St Mary) *see* Gt Coxwell w Buscot, Coleshill etc *Ox*
BUSH END (St John the Evangelist) *see* Hatfield Broad Oak and Bush End *Chelmsf*
BUSH HILL PARK (St Mark) *Lon 18* **P** *Bp* **V** P C ATHERTON, **NSM** S E HEARD
BUSH HILL PARK (St Stephen) *Lon 18* **P** *V Edmonton All SS* **V** R J ANNIS
BUSHBURY (St Mary) *Lich 28* **P** *Patr Bd* **TR** P H SMITH
BUSHEY (Holy Trinity) (St James) (St Paul) *St Alb 1* **P** *Bp* **R** G E W BUCKLER, **C** T S MOORE
BUSHEY HEATH (St Peter) *St Alb 1* **P** *Bp* **V** S P SEATON
BUSHLEY (St Peter) *see* Longdon, Castlemorton, Bushley, Queenhill etc *Worc*
BUSHMEAD (Christ Church) *St Alb 14* **P** *Bp* **V** S P DUST
BUSSAGE (St Michael and All Angels) *Glouc 1* **P** *Bp* **V** H J VAN DER LINDE
BUTCOMBE (St Michael and All Angels) *see* Wrington w Butcombe *B & W*
BUTLEIGH (St Leonard) *see* Baltonsborough w Butleigh, W Bradley etc *B & W*
BUTLERS MARSTON (St Peter and St Paul) and the Pillertons w Ettington *Cov 9* **P** *Ch Ch Ox (1 turn), Bp, Major and Mrs J E Shirley, and Miss M L P Shirley (1 turn), and Mr and Mrs G Howell (1 turn)* **P-in-c** A J ADAMS, **Hon C** D R J EVANS
BUTLEY (St John the Baptist) *see* Wilford Peninsula *St E*
BUTTERCRAMBE (St John the Evangelist) *see* Sand Hutton *York*
BUTTERLEIGH (St Matthew) *see* Silverton, Butterleigh, Bickleigh and Cadeleigh *Ex*
BUTTERMERE (St James) *see* Lorton and Loweswater w Buttermere *Carl*
BUTTERMERE (St James the Great) *see* Savernake *Sarum*
BUTTERSHAW (St Aidan) *see* Shelf w Buttershaw St Aid *Bradf*
BUTTERSHAW (St Paul) *Bradf 2* **P** *Bp* **V** D J GRIFFITHS, **C** S A GRIFFITHS
BUTTERTON (St Bartholomew) *see* Alstonfield, Butterton, Ilam etc *Lich*
BUTTERTON (St Thomas) *see* Newcastle w Butterton *Lich*
BUTTERWICK (Mission Chapel) *see* The Street Par *York*
BUTTERWICK (St Andrew) *see* Freiston, Butterwick w Bennington, and Leverton *Linc*
BUTTERWICK (St Nicholas) *see* Langtoft w Foxholes, Butterwick, Cottam etc *York*
BUTTERWICK, EAST (St Andrew) *see* Messingham *Linc*
BUTTERWICK, WEST (St Mary the Virgin) *see* Epworth Gp *Linc*
BUTTSBURY (St Mary) *see* Margaretting w Mountnessing and Buttsbury *Chelmsf*
BUXHALL (St Mary) *see* Gt Finborough w Onehouse, Harleston, Buxhall etc *St E*
BUXTED (St Margaret the Queen) (St Mary) and Hadlow Down *Chich 21* **P** *Abp, Bp, and Wagner Trustees (jt)* **P-in-c** J W A CHALLIS
BUXTON (St Andrew) w Oxnead, Lammas and Brampton *Nor 19* **P** *Bp* **P-in-c** C S R WALTER
BUXTON (St Anne) (St John the Baptist) (St Mary the Virgin) w Burbage and King Sterndale *Derby 4* **P** *Patr Bd* **TR** J F HUDGHTON, **TV** A H COX
BUXTON (Trinity Chapel) Proprietary Chapel *Derby 4* **C-in-c** R MARSDEN
BUXWORTH (St James) *see* Hayfield and Chinley w Buxworth *Derby*
BY BROOK *Bris 4* **P** *Patr Bd* **TR** A C ASHCROFT, **TV** W D L HAWLEY
BYERS GREEN (St Peter) *Dur 6* **P** *Bp* **P-in-c** W SCOTT
BYFIELD (Holy Cross) w Boddington and Aston le Walls *Pet 1* **P** *Bp, CCC Ox, and Em Coll Cam (by turn)* **R** L L RANDALL
BYFLEET (St Mary) *Guildf 12* **P** *Ld Chan* **R** *vacant* (01932) 342374
BYFLEET, WEST (St John) *Guildf 12* **P** *Bp* **V** A B ELKINS, **NSM** J K ELKINS
BYFORD (St John the Baptist) *see* Letton w Staunton, Byford, Mansel Gamage etc *Heref*
BYGRAVE (St Margaret of Antioch) *see* Baldock w Bygrave and Weston *St Alb*
BYKER (St Anthony) *Newc 6* **P** *Bp* **V** *vacant* 0191-265 1605
BYKER St Mark and Walkergate (St Oswald) *Newc 6* **P** *Bp and Ch Trust Fund Trust (jt)* **V** K MOULDER
BYKER (St Martin) Newcastle upon Tyne *Newc 6* **P** *Bp* **P-in-c** P J A ROBINSON
BYKER (St Michael w St Lawrence) *Newc 6* **P** *Bp* **P-in-c** P J A ROBINSON
BYKER (St Silas) *Newc 6* **P** *Bp* **P-in-c** S A FAULKNER, **NSM** A F TAYLOR
BYLAND, OLD (All Saints) *see* Upper Ryedale *York*
BYLAUGH (St Mary) *see* Lyng, Sparham, Elsing, Bylaugh, Bawdeswell etc *Nor*
BYLEY CUM LEES (St John the Evangelist) *see* Middlewich w Byley *Ches*
BYRNESS (St Francis) *see* N Tyne and Redesdale *Newc*
BYTHAM, LITTLE (St Medardus) *see* Castle Bytham w Creeton *Linc*
BYTHORN (St Lawrence) *see* Keyston and Bythorn *Ely*
BYTON (St Mary) *see* Pembridge w Moor Court, Shobdon, Staunton etc *Heref*
BYWELL (St Peter) *Newc 3* **P** *Adn Northd* **V** T EMMETT
BYWORTH (St Francis) *see* Farnham *Guildf*
CABLE STREET (St Mary) *see* St Geo-in-the-East St Mary *Lon*
CABOURN (St Nicholas) *see* Swallow *Linc*
CADBURY (St Michael and All Angels) *see* Thorverton, Cadbury, Upton Pyne etc *Ex*
CADBURY, NORTH (St Michael the Archangel) *see* Camelot Par *B & W*
CADBURY, SOUTH (St Thomas à Becket) *as above*
CADDINGTON (All Saints) *St Alb 14* **P** *D&C St Paul's* **V** A J D SMITH
CADEBY (All Saints) *see* Bosworth and Sheepy Gp *Leic*
CADELEIGH (St Bartholomew) *see* Silverton, Butterleigh, Bickleigh and Cadeleigh *Ex*
CADGWITH (St Mary) *see* St Ruan w St Grade and Landewednack *Truro*
CADISHEAD (St Mary the Virgin) *Man 2* **P** *Bp* **P-in-c** J R R TALLON
CADMORE END (St Mary le Moor) *see* Lane End w Cadmore End *Ox*
CADNEY (All Saints) *see* Brigg, Wrawby and Cadney cum Howsham *Linc*
CADOGAN SQUARE (St Simon Zelotes) *see* Upper Chelsea *Lon*
CAERHAYS (St Michael) *see* St Goran w Caerhays *Truro*
CAGE GREEN (Church Hall) *see* Tonbridge SS Pet and Paul *Roch*
CAINSCROSS (St Matthew) w Selsley *Glouc 8* **P** *Bp and Sir Charles Marling Bt (alt)* **V** C D SUTCH, **C** H B TERRY
CAISTER NEXT YARMOUTH (Holy Trinity) (St Edmund) *Nor 6* **P** *SMF* **R** T C THOMPSON
CAISTOR Group, The (St Peter and St Paul) *Linc 5* **P** *Bp and D&C (jt)* **V** I ROBINSON, **Hon C** S W ANDREW
CAISTOR ST EDMUNDS (St Edmund) *see* Stoke H Cross w Dunston, Arminghall etc *Nor*
CALBOURNE (All Saints) w Newtown *Portsm 8* **P** *Bp* **V** D J BEVINGTON, **NSM** M O'DONNELL
CALCOT (St Birinus) *Ox 15* **P** *Magd Coll Ox* **V** A D BARNES

CALDBECK (St Mungo) (Fellside), Castle Sowerby and Sebergham *Carl 3* **P** *Bp and D&C (alt)* **R** S K PRIOR, **C** R E HIND, **NSM** K M ASHBRIDGE
CALDECOTE (All Saints), Northill and Old Warden *St Alb 11* **P** *Grocers' Co (2 turns), R O Shuttleworth Remembrance Trust (1 turn)* **V** F COLEMAN
CALDECOTE (St Michael and All Angels) *see* Toft w Caldecote and Childerley *Ely*
CALDECOTE (St Theobald and St Chad) *see* Weddington and Caldecote *Cov*
CALDECOTT (St John the Evangelist) *see* Lyddington w Stoke Dry and Seaton etc *Pet*
CALDER GROVE (St John the Divine) *see* Chapelthorpe *Wakef*
CALDER VALE (Mission) *see* Scorton and Barnacre and Calder Vale *Blackb*
CALDER VALE (St John the Evangelist) *as above*
CALDERBROOK (St James the Great) *Man 20* **P** *Bp* **P-in-c** M S THORP, **OLM** B WOODHEAD
CALDMORE (St Michael and All Angels) w All Saints Palfrey *Lich 25* **P** *Bp* **V** F R MILLER, **C** T R H COYNE
CALDWELL (Chapel) *see* Forcett and Aldbrough and Melsonby *Ripon*
CALDWELL (St Giles) *see* Stapenhill w Cauldwell *Derby*
CALDY (Church of the Resurrection and All Saints) *see* W Kirby St Bridget *Ches*
CALEDONIAN ROAD (All Saints Hall) *see* Barnsbury *Lon*
CALIFORNIA (St Mary and St John) *Ox 16* **P** *DBP* **P-in-c** C R EDWARDS, **NSM** H M WAKELING, J R EDWARDS
CALLINGTON (St Mary) *see* S Hill w Callington *Truro*
CALLOW END (St James) *see* Powick and Guarlford and Madresfield w Newland *Worc*
CALMORE (St Anne) *see* Totton *Win*
CALNE (Holy Trinity) (St Mary the Virgin) and Blackland *Sarum 15* **P** *Bp* **V** R A KENWAY, **C** P A BROMILEY
CALOW (St Peter) and Sutton cum Duckmanton *Derby 3* **P** *Bp and V Chesterfield (jt)* **R** M H CHAMPNEYS
CALSHOT (St George) *see* Fawley *Win*
CALSTOCK (St Andrew) *Truro 11* **P** *Duchy of Cornwall* **R** J A C WILSON, **NSM** R MUNRO, L S SCOTT
CALSTONE WELLINGTON (St Mary the Virgin) *see* Oldbury *Sarum*
CALTHORPE (Our Lady w St Margaret) *see* Erpingham w Calthorpe, Ingworth, Aldborough etc *Nor*
CALTHWAITE (All Saints) *see* Inglewood Gp *Carl*
CALTON (St Mary the Virgin), Cauldon, Grindon, Waterfall and Blore Ray w Okeover *Lich 5* **P** *Bp and Sir Peter Walker-Okeover Bt (jt)* **R** A J BURTON
CALUDON *see* Coventry Caludon *Cov*
CALVELEY CHURCH (not known) *see* Bunbury and Tilstone Fearnall *Ches*
CALVERHALL or CORRA (Holy Trinity) *see* Adderley, Ash, Calverhall, Ightfield etc *Lich*
CALVERLEIGH (St Mary the Virgin) *see* Washfield, Stoodleigh, Withleigh etc *Ex*
CALVERLEY (St Wilfrid) *Bradf 3* **P** *Bp* **V** J H WALKER
CALVERTON (All Saints) *Ox 25* **P** *DBP* **R** R NORTHING, **C** G A PINNOCK
CALVERTON (St Wilfrid) *S'well 15* **P** *Bp* **V** P HEMSTOCK, **C** J E DRAYCOTT, **NSM** M N TAYLOR
CAM (St George) w Stinchcombe *Glouc 2* **P** *Bp* **V** J S KNEE, **NSM** S J FISHER
CAM, LOWER (St Bartholomew) w Coaley *Glouc 2* **P** *Bp* **V** I A ROBB
CAM VALE *B & W 3* **P** *Bp and DBP (2 turns), CPAS, MMCET and Revd G Bennett (1 turn)* **R** M J M PERRY
CAMBER (St Thomas) *see* Rye *Chich*
CAMBERLEY (St Martin) Old Dean *Guildf 6* **P** *Bp* **V** P A DOBSON
CAMBERLEY (St Mary) *Guildf 6* **P** *Bp* **V** M J WAINWRIGHT, **OLM** R WALKER
CAMBERLEY (St Michael) Yorktown *Guildf 6* **P** *Bp* **V** B NICOLE, **Hon C** R S CROSSLEY, **NSM** S BOWIE
CAMBERLEY (St Paul) (St Mary) *Guildf 6* **P** *Bp* **V** M CHESTER, **C** G H L WATTS, **NSM** S A L WATTS, **OLM** S H STEPHENS
CAMBERLEY HEATHERSIDE (Community Centre) *Guildf 6* **P** *Bp* **V** P J DYKES
CAMBERWELL (All Saints) Blenheim Grove *S'wark 8* **P** *Ch Trust Fund Trust* **V** F I L ORR-EWING, **C** J A NICKOLS
CAMBERWELL (Christ Church) *S'wark 8* **P** *Trustees* **V** H R BALFOUR
CAMBERWELL (St George) *S'wark 8* **P** *Bp and Trin Coll Cam (jt)* **V** N J ELDER, **C** W N PAXTON, **OLM** M JOHN
CAMBERWELL (St Giles) (St Matthew) *S'wark 8* **P** *Bp* **V** N P GEORGE, **C** C J THOMPSON, **Hon C** M E TODD, **OLM** P A ALDEN, I L RUSSELL
CAMBERWELL (St Luke) *S'wark 8* **P** *Bp* **V** J D JELLEY
CAMBERWELL (St Michael and All Angels w All Souls w Emmanuel) *S'wark 10* **P** *DBP* **V** P VOWLES
CAMBERWELL (St Philip) and St Mark *S'wark 7* **P** *The Crown* **V** *vacant* (020) 7237 3239
CAMBO (Holy Trinity) *see* Kirkwhelpington, Kirkharle, Kirkheaton and Cambo *Newc*
CAMBOIS St Peter (St Andrew's Mission Church) and Sleekburn *Newc 1* **P** *D&C* **V** J BLAKESLEY
CAMBORNE (St Martin and St Meriadoc) *Truro 2* **P** *Ch Soc Trust* **R** W R STUART-WHITE, **C** O STEVENS, **NSM** D E HARVEY
CAMBRIDGE Ascension (St Giles) (St Luke the Evangelist) (St Augustine of Canterbury) (All Souls Chapel) *Ely 2* **P** *Bp* **TR** P A KING, **C** K R PEACOCK, **NSM** O R SPENCER-THOMAS
CAMBRIDGE (Holy Cross) *Ely 2* **P** *Bp* **V** R T WILLIAMS, **NSM** A C RIGELSFORD
CAMBRIDGE (Holy Sepulchre) (St Andrew the Great) *Ely 2* **P** *PCC* **V** M H ASHTON, **C** G R WALTER, F L PRICE
CAMBRIDGE (Holy Trinity) *Ely 2* **P** *D&C and Peache Trustees (jt)* **V** R A CHARKHAM, **C** B J DE LA T DE BERRY, **NSM** C M BENNETT-REES
CAMBRIDGE (St Andrew the Less) (Christ Church) *Ely 2* **P** *Ch Trust Fund Trust* **P-in-c** S N MIDGLEY
CAMBRIDGE (St Barnabas) *Ely 2* **P** *V Cam St Paul* **V** N M LADD, **C** C S BROOKES
CAMBRIDGE (St Benedict) *Ely 2* **P** *CCC Cam* **V** R S DOUBLE, **NSM** D P FORD
CAMBRIDGE (St Botolph) *Ely 2* **P** *Qu Coll Cam* **P-in-c** W HORBURY, **NSM** M J WIDDESS
CAMBRIDGE (St Clement) *Ely 2* **P** *Jes Coll Cam* **V** *vacant*
CAMBRIDGE (St Edward King and Martyr) Proprietary Chapel *Ely 2*, F N WATTS **NSM** M J RAMSHAW
CAMBRIDGE (St James) *Ely 2* **P** *Bp* **V** D G DEBOYS
CAMBRIDGE (St John the Evangelist) *see* Cherry Hinton St Jo *Ely*
CAMBRIDGE (St Mark) *Ely 2* **P** *DBP* **Hon C** M M G ROBERTS
CAMBRIDGE (St Martin) (St Thomas) *Ely 2* **P** *V Cam St Paul* **V** S O LEEKE, **C** R T WILLIAMS
CAMBRIDGE (St Mary the Great) w St Michael *Ely 2* **P** *Trin Coll Cam* **V** J R E BINNS, **C** J A LOEWE, **NSM** R K DUERR
CAMBRIDGE (St Mary the Less) *Ely 2* **P** *Peterho Cam* **V** R A H GREANY, **Hon C** I M THOMPSON, **NSM** M A BISHOP
CAMBRIDGE (St Matthew) *Ely 2* **P** *V Cam St Andr the Less* **V** E P J FOSTER
CAMBRIDGE (St Paul) *Ely 2* **P** *Ch Trust Fund Trust* **V** M S BECKETT, **NSM** C J ROSE
CAMBRIDGE (St Philip) (St Stephen) *Ely 2* **P** *Ch Trust Fund Trust* **V** S TAYLOR, **NSM** R A HIGGINSON
CAMDEN SQUARE (St Paul) *see* Old St Pancras *Lon*
CAMDEN TOWN (St Michael) *as above*
CAMEL, WEST (All Saints) *see* Cam Vale *B & W*
CAMELFORD (St Julitta) *see* Lanteglos by Camelford w Advent *Truro*
CAMELFORD (St Thomas of Canterbury) *as above*
CAMELOT Parishes, The *B & W 3* **P** *Patr Bd* **R** J E G ANGLE, **Hon C** R J BAWTREE, **NSM** R A HOSKINS
CAMELSDALE (St Paul) *see* Lynchmere and Camelsdale *Chich*
CAMERTON (St Peter) w Dunkerton, Foxcote and Shoscombe *B & W 12* **P** *Bp* **P-in-c** K G X TINGAY
CAMERTON (St Peter), Seaton and West Seaton *Carl 7* **P** *D&C and Ch Trust Fund Trust (jt)* **V** I GRAINGER
CAMMERINGHAM (St Michael) *see* Ingham w Cammeringham w Fillingham *Linc*
CAMP HILL (St Mary and St John) w Galley Common *Cov 5* **P** *Bp* **V** S D SNEATH
CAMPBELL ROOMS (not known) *see* Parr *Liv*
CAMPSALL (St Mary Magdalene) *see* Burghwallis and Campsall *Sheff*
CAMPSEA ASHE (St John the Baptist) w Marlesford, Parham and Hacheston *St E 18* **P** *Prime Min, Ch Soc Trust, and J S Schreiber Esq (by turn)* **R** H V EDWARDS
CAMPTON (All Saints), Clophill and Haynes *St Alb 16* **P** *Bp and Ball Coll Ox (alt)* **R** M J VENABLES
CANDLESBY (St Benedict) *see* Partney Gp *Linc*
CANDOVER VALLEY, The *Win 1* **P** *D&C and Lord Ashburton (jt)* **P-in-c** D J KEIGHLEY
CANEWDON (St Nicholas) w Paglesham *Chelmsf 12* **P** *D&C Westmr and Hyndman Trustees (jt)* **P-in-c** T F CLAY
CANFIELD, GREAT (St Mary) w High Roding and Aythorpe

Roding *Chelmsf 18* **P** *A Sainthill Esq, Ch Soc Trust, and Bp (by turn)* **R** *vacant* (01279) 870760
CANFIELD, LITTLE (All Saints) *see* Takeley w Lt Canfield *Chelmsf*
CANFORD CLIFFS (Transfiguration) and Sandbanks *Sarum 7* **P** *Bp* **V** J C OAKES
CANFORD HEATH (St Paul) *see* Oakdale *Sarum*
CANFORD MAGNA (Bearwood) (The Lantern) *Sarum 9* **P** *Patr Bd* **TR** P H LAWRENCE, **TV** G BOLAND, **NSM** A SIMPSON, D A PHILLIPS, M G COATES, A A GEE, **OLM** C CLARK, A J CORKE, B S PROBERT
CANLEY (St Stephen) *Cov 3* **P** *Bp* **V** A NEWTON
CANNING TOWN (St Matthias) *see* Plaistow and N Canning Town *Chelmsf*
CANNINGTON (Blessed Virgin Mary), Otterhampton, Combwich and Stockland *B & W 14* **P** *Bp* **R** P MARTIN
CANNOCK (St Luke) *Lich 3* **P** *Patr Bd* **TR** A R OSBORNE, **TV** K M BUCK, D E HEBBLEWHITE, R I O'CONNOR, P O HART, **C** H THAKE, L M HARRIS, **NSM** L J FARRINGTON, **OLM** D J SUNLEY
CANON FROME (St James) *see* Ledbury *Heref*
CANON PYON (St Lawrence) w King's Pyon, Birley and Wellington *Heref 7* **P** *Bp, Ch Union, and D&C (jt)* **V** M C CLUETT
CANONBURY (St Stephen) *Lon 6* **P** *V Islington St Mary* **V** D J P MOORE, **NSM** M E EVANS
CANTERBURY (All Saints) *Cant 3* **P** *Abp* **P-in-c** S W JONES, **NSM** M J STACE
CANTERBURY (St Dunstan w Holy Cross) *Cant 3* **P** *Abp* **V** M W WORGAN
CANTERBURY (St Martin) (St Paul) *Cant 3* **P** *Abp* **R** N M HALL
CANTERBURY (St Mary Bredin) *Cant 3* **P** *Simeon's Trustees* **V** A T C PEMBERTON, **C** M R SEARLE
CANTERBURY (St Peter w St Alphege) (St Mildred) and St Margaret w St Mary de Castro *Cant 3* **P** *The Crown* **R** D M H HAYES, **Hon C** P E S DAVIE, **OLM** I W J TAYLOR
CANTERBURY (St Stephen) *see* Hackington *Cant*
CANTLEY (St Margaret) *see* Freethorpe, Wickhampton, Halvergate etc *Nor*
CANTLEY (St Wilfrid) *Sheff 8* **P** *Guild of All So* **V** J I WILLETT
CANTLEY, NEW (St Hugh of Lincoln) *Sheff 8* **P** *Guild of All So* **V** A P ARNOLD
CANTRIL FARM (St Jude) *see* Stockbridge Village *Liv*
CANVEY ISLAND (St Anne) (St Katherine's Worship Centre) (St Nicholas) *Chelmsf 10* **P** *Bp and Patr Bd (jt)* **TR** D ST C TUDOR, **TV** M E WEST, J M ALLWRIGHT, **NSM** B E WEST
CANWELL (St Mary, St Giles and All Saints) *Lich 4* **P** *Bp* **V** H J BAKER
CANWICK (All Saints) *see* Washingborough w Heighington and Canwick *Linc*
CAPEL (St John the Baptist) *see* Surrey Weald *Guildf*
CAPEL (St Thomas à Becket) *see* Tudeley cum Capel w Five Oak Green *Roch*
CAPEL LE FERNE (St Radigund) *see* Alkham w Capel le Ferne and Hougham *Cant*
CAPEL ST MARY (St Mary) w Little Wenham and Great Wenham *St E 5* **P** *Bp and SMF (jt)* **P-in-c** D B SINGLETON
CAPENHURST (Holy Trinity) *see* Backford and Capenhurst *Ches*
CAPESTHORNE (Holy Trinity) w Siddington and Marton *Ches 13* **P** *W A B Davenport Esq* **P-in-c** P O MOULTON
CAR COLSTON (St Mary) w Screveton *S'well 8* **P** *H S Blagg Esq* **P-in-c** D G WAKEFIELD
CARBIS BAY (St Anta and All Saints) w Lelant (St Uny) *Truro 5* **P** *Bp* **P-in-c** P A PULLEN, **NSM** C Z WILTON
CARBROOKE (St Peter and St Paul) *see* Watton w Carbrooke and Ovington *Nor*
CARBURTON (St Giles) *see* Worksop Priory *S'well*
CARDESTON (St Michael) *see* Alberbury w Cardeston *Heref*
CARDINGTON (St James) *Heref 11* **P** *Rt Hon Sir Frederick Corfield* **P-in-c** J GROVES
CARDINGTON (St Mary) *see* Elstow *St Alb*
CARDYNHAM (St Mewbud) *see* St Neot and Warleggan w Cardynham *Truro*
CAREBY (St Stephen) *see* Castle Bytham w Creeton *Linc*
CARHAM (St Cuthbert) *see* Cornhill w Carham *Newc*
CARHAMPTON (St John the Baptist) *see* Dunster, Carhampton and Withycombe w Rodhuish *B & W*
CARHARRACK (St Piran's Mission Church) *see* Chacewater w St Day and Carharrack *Truro*
CARISBROOKE (St John the Baptist) *see* Newport St Jo *Portsm*
CARISBROOKE (St Mary the Virgin) *Portsm 8* **P** *Qu Coll Ox* **V** M A J EXELL
CARISBROOKE St Nicholas in the Castle *Portsm 8* **P** *Qu Coll Ox* **V** M A J EXELL
CARLBY (St Stephen) *see* Ryhall w Essendine and Carlby *Pet*
CARLECOATES (St Anne) *see* Penistone and Thurlstone *Wakef*
CARLETON (St Chad) *see* Poulton Carleton and Singleton *Blackb*
CARLETON (St Mary the Virgin) and Lothersdale *Bradf 7* **P** *Ch Ch Ox* **P-in-c** D N WILLIAMS
CARLETON (St Michael) and E Hardwick *Wakef 11* **P** *V Pontefract and Cawood Trustees (jt)* **V** S A STACEY
CARLETON (St Peter) *see* Rockland St Mary w Hellington, Bramerton etc *Nor*
CARLETON, EAST (St Mary) *see* Swardeston w E Carleton, Intwood, Keswick etc *Nor*
CARLETON IN CRAVEN *see* Carleton and Lothersdale *Bradf*
CARLETON RODE (All Saints) *see* Bunwell, Carleton Rode, Tibenham, Gt Moulton etc *Nor*
CARLIN HOW (St Helen) *see* Loftus and Carlin How w Skinningrove *York*
CARLINGHOW (St John the Evangelist) *see* Staincliffe and Carlinghow *Wakef*
CARLISLE Belah (St Mark) *see* Stanwix *Carl*
CARLISLE (Holy Trinity) (St Barnabas) *Carl 3* **P** *Patr Bd* **TR** H J CARTER, **C** E M C HANCOCK, G A TUBBS
CARLISLE (St Aidan) and Christ Church *Carl 3* **P** *Bp* **V** R J OAKLEY
CARLISLE (St Cuthbert) *Carl 3* **P** *D&C* **P-in-c** R D PRATT
CARLISLE (St Herbert) w St Stephen *Carl 3* **P** *Bp* **P-in-c** A JONES
CARLISLE (St James) *see* Denton Holme *Carl*
CARLISLE (St John the Evangelist) *Carl 3* **P** *CPAS* **V** S DONALD, **C** A V WEST
CARLISLE (St Luke) Morton *Carl 3* **P** *Bp* **V** K WRAY
CARLISLE (St Michael) *see* Stanwix *Carl*
CARLISLE, SOUTH Team Ministry (St John the Baptist) (St Elisabeth) *Carl 3* **P** *Patr Bd* **TR** T J HYSLOP, **TV** S L WICKS, **C** C G Y HYSLOP, **NSM** P J IRWIN
CARLTON (St Aidan) *see* Helmsley *York*
CARLTON (St Andrew) *see* Nailstone and Carlton w Shackerstone *Leic*
CARLTON (St Bartholomew) *see* Guiseley w Esholt *Bradf*
CARLTON (St Botolph) *see* Whorlton w Carlton and Faceby *York*
CARLTON (St John the Baptist) *S'well 10* **P** *Bp* **V** A M LUCKCUCK
CARLTON (St John the Evangelist) *Wakef 7* **P** *DBP* **P-in-c** J L HUDSON
CARLTON (St Mary) *see* Harrold and Carlton w Chellington *St Alb*
CARLTON (St Peter) *see* Raddesley Gp *Ely*
CARLTON (St Peter) *see* Saxmundham w Kelsale cum Carlton *St E*
CARLTON, EAST (St Peter) *see* Gretton w Rockingham and Cottingham w E Carlton *Pet*
CARLTON, GREAT (St John the Baptist) *see* Mid Marsh Gp *Linc*
CARLTON, NORTH (St Luke) w SOUTH (St John the Baptist) *Linc 3* **P** *Lord Monson* **V** *vacant*
CARLTON BY SNAITH (St Mary) and Drax *York 4* **P** *Abp and Ch Trust Fund Trust (jt)* **P-in-c** J H MDUMULLA
CARLTON COLVILLE (St Peter) and Mutford *Nor 9* **P** *Simeon's Trustees and G&C Coll Cam (jt)* **V** J S BISHOP
CARLTON CURLIEU (St Mary the Virgin) *see* Glen Magna cum Stretton Magna etc *Leic*
CARLTON FOREHOE (St Mary) *see* Barnham Broom and Upper Yare *Nor*
CARLTON HUSTHWAITE (St Mary) *see* Coxwold and Husthwaite *York*
CARLTON-IN-LINDRICK (St John the Evangelist) and Langold w Oldcotes *S'well 6* **P** *Bp and Ld Chan (alt)* **R** S E CLARK, **C** R C HINSLEY
CARLTON-IN-THE-WILLOWS (St Paul) *S'well 10* **P** *MMCET* **R** B HALL
CARLTON-LE-MOORLAND (St Mary) *see* Bassingham Gp *Linc*
CARLTON MINIOTT (St Lawrence) *see* Thirsk *York*
CARLTON-ON-TRENT (St Mary) *see* Sutton w Carlton and Normanton upon Trent etc *S'well*
CARLTON SCROOP (St Nicholas) *see* Caythorpe *Linc*
CARNABY (St John the Baptist) *see* Rudston w Boynton, Carnaby and Kilham *York*
CARNFORTH (Christ Church) *Blackb 14* **P** *Bp* **V** S L JONES, **C** P S BURCH

CARNFORTH (Holy Trinity) *see* Bolton-le-Sands *Blackb*
CARPENTER'S ARMS, The *see* Deal, The Carpenter's Arms *Cant*
CARR CLOUGH (St Andrew) *see* Kersal Moor *Man*
CARR DYKE GROUP, The *Linc 22* **P** *Sir Philip Naylor-Leyland Bt and Ld Chan (alt)* **V** M K NICHOLAS
CARR MILL (St David) *Liv 10* **P** *V St Helens St Mark and Bp (jt)* **V** T THOMAS
CARRINGTON (St John the Evangelist) *S'well 12* **P** *Bp* **V** J M MACGILLIVRAY, **C** E J R MARTIN
CARRINGTON (St Paul) *see* Sibsey w Frithville *Linc*
CARSHALTON (All Saints) *S'wark 25* **P** *Bp* **R** J C THEWLIS
CARSHALTON BEECHES (Good Shepherd) *S'wark 25* **P** *Bp* **V** C WHEATON, **NSM** T A BRYAN, **OLM** P C M TURRELL
CARSINGTON (St Margaret) *see* Wirksworth *Derby*
CARTERTON (St John the Evangelist) *see* Brize Norton and Carterton *Ox*
CARTMEL FELL (St Anthony) *Carl 10* **P** *Bp* **V** *vacant*
CARTMEL PENINSULA Team Ministry, The (St Mary and St Michael) *Carl 11* **P** *Patr Bd* **TR** I G COOMBER, **TV** J E CROSSLEY, R A LATHAM, R W BAILEY, **C** R J CROSSLEY, **NSM** A BAKER, D S SIMON
CASSINGTON (St Peter) *see* Eynsham and Cassington *Ox*
CASSOP CUM QUARRINTON *Dur 5* **P** *Bp* **V** J THOMPSON
CASTERTON (Holy Trinity) *see* Kirkby Lonsdale *Carl*
CASTERTON, GREAT (St Peter and St Paul) and LITTLE (All Saints) w Pickworth and Tickencote *Pet 8* **P** *Burghley Ho Preservation Trust (2 turns), Lord Chesham (1 turn), and Bp (1 turn)* **R** P STREET, **NSM** J M SAUNDERS
CASTLE ACRE (St James) *see* Castleacre, Newton, Westacre and Southacre *Nor*
CASTLE ASHBY (St Mary Magdalene) *see* Yardley Hastings, Denton and Grendon etc *Pet*
CASTLE BOLTON (St Oswald) *see* Aysgarth and Bolton cum Redmire *Ripon*
CASTLE BROMWICH (St Clement) *Birm 9* **P** *Bp* **V** W J SANDS
CASTLE BROMWICH (St Mary and St Margaret) *Birm 9* **P** *Earl of Bradf* **R** M A SEARS
CASTLE BYTHAM (St James) w Creeton *Linc 14* **P** *D&C, Bp, Ld Chan, and DBP (by turn)* **R** *vacant* (01780) 410166
CASTLE CAMPS (All Saints) *see* Linton *Ely*
CASTLE CARROCK (St Peter) *see* Eden, Gelt and Irthing *Carl*
CASTLE CARY (All Saints) w Ansford *B & W 3* **P** *Bp* **V** J G PESCOD, **C** A HILLIER, **NSM** J R F KIRLEW
CASTLE CHURCH (St Mary) *Lich 10* **P** *Bp* **V** J T H PYE
CASTLE COMBE (St Andrew) *see* By Brook *Bris*
CASTLE DONINGTON (St Edward the King and Martyr) and Lockington cum Hemington *Leic 7* **P** *Lady Gretton and C H C Coaker Esq (jt)* **V** A Q MICKLETHWAITE
CASTLE EATON (St Mary the Virgin) *see* Meysey Hampton w Marston Meysey and Castle Eaton *Glouc*
CASTLE EDEN (St James) *see* Blackhall, Castle Eden and Monkhesleden *Dur*
CASTLE FROME (St Michael) *see* Bishop's Frome w Castle Frome and Fromes Hill *Heref*
CASTLE HEDINGHAM (St Nicholas) *see* Sible Hedingham w Castle Hedingham *Chelmsf*
CASTLE HILL (St Philip) *see* Hindley All SS *Liv*
CASTLE RISING (St Lawrence) *Nor 16* **P** *G Howard Esq* **P-in-c** J B V RIVIERE
CASTLE SOWERBY (St Kentigern) *see* Caldbeck, Castle Sowerby and Sebergham *Carl*
CASTLE TOWN (St Thomas and St Andrew) *Lich 10* **P** *Hyndman Trustees* **P-in-c** P W THOMAS
CASTLE VALE (St Cuthbert of Lindisfarne) *Birm 12* **P** *Bp* **V** D N MILLER, **NSM** R M SHEPPARD
CASTLE VIEW ESTATE (St Francis) *see* Langley Marish *Ox*
CASTLEACRE (St James), Newton-by-Castleacre, Westacre and Southacre *Nor 13* **P** *Bp, Earl of Leicester, and Capt H Birkbeck (jt)* **P-in-c** S R NAIRN
CASTLECROFT (The Good Shepherd) *see* Tettenhall Wood and Perton *Lich*
CASTLEFIELDS (All Saints and St Michael) *see* Shrewsbury All SS w St Mich *Lich*
CASTLEFORD (St Michael and All Angels) *see* Smawthorpe St Mich *Wakef*
CASTLEFORD Team Parish (All Saints) *Wakef 11* **P** *Duchy of Lanc and Bp (alt)* **TR** S BINDOFF, **C** M J A CARPENTER, **OLM** D WHEATLEY
CASTLEMORTON (St Gregory) *see* Longdon, Castlemorton, Bushley, Queenhill etc *Worc*
CASTLESIDE (St John the Evangelist) *Dur 4* **P** *Bp* **P-in-c** J V HALLETT
CASTLETHORPE (St Simon and St Jude) *see* Hanslope w Castlethorpe *Ox*
CASTLETON (St Edmund) *see* Hope, Castleton and Bradwell *Derby*
CASTLETON (St Mary Magdalene) *see* Sherborne w Castleton and Lillington *Sarum*
CASTLETON (St Michael and St George) *see* Danby *York*
CASTLETON MOOR (St Martin) *Man 18* **P** *Bp* **V** I E BUTTERWORTH, **C** G C DOBBS, **NSM** C G GULLY
CASTLETOWN (St Mary) *S & M 1* **P** *Bp* **NSM** J R GULLAND
CASTON (St Cross), Griston, Merton, Thompson, Stow Bedon, Breckles and Great Hockham *Nor 13* **P** *Bp and DBP (jt)* **R** *vacant* (01953) 483222
CASTOR (St Kyneburgha) w Sutton and Upton w Marholm *Pet 13* **P** *Sir Stephen Hastings (2 turns), Mrs V S V Gunnery (1 turn)* **R** W S D BURKE
CATCLIFFE (St Mary) *see* Rivers Team *Sheff*
CATCOTT (St Peter) *see* W Poldens *B & W*
CATERHAM (St Mary the Virgin) (St Laurence) (St Paul) (St John the Evangelist) *S'wark 26* **P** *Bp* **TV** G P REEVES, J GARTON, C A BRADSHAW, **NSM** F M BALDWIN, A-M GARTON, S J ELLISON
CATESBY (St Mary) *see* Daventry, Ashby St Ledgers, Braunston etc *Pet*
CATFIELD (All Saints) *see* Ludham, Potter Heigham, Hickling and Catfield *Nor*
CATFORD (St Andrew) *S'wark 4* **P** *Bp* **V** R B JORDAN
CATFORD (St John) and Downham *S'wark 4* **P** *Bp* **TV** M B HUSTON, **NSM** F M NEAL, S M WOOLLEY
CATFORD (St Laurence) *S'wark 4* **P** *Bp* **V** C F PICKSTONE
CATHERINGTON (All Saints) and Clanfield *Portsm 5* **P** *Bp* **V** G B HILL, **C** J F O'SHAUGHNESSY, **NSM** M S HOLLOWAY, A C L JOHNSON, A M GOTHARD
CATHERSTON LEWESTON (St Mary) *see* Golden Cap Team *Sarum*
CATON (St Paul) w Littledale *Blackb 11* **P** *V Lanc* **P-in-c** G A POLLITT
CATSFIELD (St Laurence) and Crowhurst *Chich 14* **P** *Bp and J P Papillon (alt)* **R** J W BESWICK
CATSHILL (Christ Church) and Dodford *Worc 7* **P** *Bp* **V** C P SMITH
CATTERICK (St Anne) *Ripon 2* **P** *Bp* **V** F M WILSON
CATTHORPE (St Thomas) *see* Gilmorton, Peatling Parva, Kimcote etc *Leic*
CATTISTOCK (St Peter and St Paul) *see* Melbury *Sarum*
CATTON (All Saints) *see* Stamford Bridge Gp *York*
CATTON (St Nicholas and the Blessed Virgin Mary) *see* Walton-on-Trent w Croxall, Rosliston etc *Derby*
CATTON, NEW (Christ Church) *Nor 2* **P** *Bp* **V** K G CROCKER, **OLM** J EASTON
CATTON, NEW (St Luke) w St Augustine *Nor 2* **P** *Bp, D&C, and CPAS (jt)* **V** N I VESEY
CATTON, OLD (St Margaret) *Nor 2* **P** *D&C* **V** S J BETTS, **C** A J FULFORD, **OLM** T I PATIENT
CATWICK (St Michael) *see* Brandesburton and Leven w Catwick *York*
CATWORTH, GREAT *see* Catworth Magna *Ely*
CATWORTH MAGNA (St Leonard) *Ely 8* **P** *BNC Ox* **P-in-c** S P MEWS, **NSM** J RAWLINSON
CAULDON (St Mary and St Laurence) *see* Calton, Cauldon, Grindon, Waterfall etc *Lich*
CAUNDLE MARSH (St Peter and St Paul) *see* The Caundles w Folke and Holwell *Sarum*
CAUNDLES w Folke and Holwell, The *Sarum 3* **P** *J K Wingfield Digby Esq, Bp, and D&C (jt)* **P-in-c** J H P HAMILTON
CAUNTON (St Andrew) *see* Norwell w Ossington, Cromwell and Caunton *S'well*
CAUSEWAY HEAD (St Paul) *see* Solway Plain *Carl*
CAUTLEY (St Mark) *see* Sedbergh, Cautley and Garsdale *Bradf*
CAVENDISH (St Mary) *see* Stour Valley *St E*
CAVENHAM (St Andrew) *see* Mildenhall *St E*
CAVERSFIELD (St Laurence) *see* Bicester w Bucknell, Caversfield and Launton *Ox*
CAVERSHAM (Park Church) *see* Emmer Green w Caversham Park *Ox*
CAVERSHAM (St Andrew) *Ox 15* **P** *Bp* **V** K KINNAIRD
CAVERSHAM (St John the Baptist) *Ox 15* **P** *Bp* **V** P A DALLAWAY
CAVERSHAM (St Peter) and Mapledurham *Ox 15* **P** *Eton Coll and Ch Ch Ox (jt)* **R** R J KINGSBURY, **C** H F SERJEANT, **NSM** A F THORESEN, **OLM** K F KNEE-ROBINSON
CAVERSHAM HEIGHTS (St Andrew) *see* Caversham St Andr *Ox*
CAVERSHAM PARK Local Ecumenical Project *Ox 15 vacant*

CAVERSWALL (St Peter) and Weston Coyney w Dilhorne *Lich 6* **P** *D&C* **V** S J OSBOURNE
CAWOOD (All Saints) w Ryther and Wistow *York 4* **P** *Abp and Ld Chan (alt)* **P-in-c** I M W ELLERY
CAWSAND (St Andrew's Mission Church) *see* Maker w Rame *Truro*
CAWSTON (St Agnes) w Booton and Brandiston, Haveringland andHeydon *Nor 19* **P** *Pemb Coll Cam (3 turns), DBP (1 turn)* **P-in-c** T W HARRIS
CAWTHORNE (All Saints) *Wakef 7* **P** *S W Fraser Esq* **P-in-c** W R PLIMMER, **NSM** J E DAYKIN
CAXTON (St Andrew) *see* Papworth *Ely*
CAYNHAM (St Mary) *see* Ludlow, Ludford, Ashford Carbonell etc *Heref*
CAYTHORPE (St Aidan) *see* Lowdham w Caythorpe, and Gunthorpe *S'well*
CAYTHORPE (St Vincent) *Linc 23* **P** *Bp, J F Fane Esq, and S J Packe-Drury-Lowe Esq (by turn)* **P-in-c** J FRESHNEY, **NSM** B HANCOCK
CAYTON (St John the Baptist) w Eastfield *York 15* **P** *Abp* **V** A CAMPBELL-WILSON
CENTRAL *see under substantive place names*
CERNE ABBAS (St Mary) *see* Buckland Newton, Cerne Abbas, Godmanstone etc *Sarum*
CERNEY, NORTH (All Saints) *see* Stratton, N Cerney, Baunton and Bagendon *Glouc*
CERNEY, SOUTH (All Hallows) w Cerney Wick and Down Ampney *Glouc 12* **P** *Bp and Ch Ch Ox (alt)* **V** J R CALVERT, **OLM** R H GEORGE
CERNEY WICK (Holy Trinity) *see* S Cerney w Cerney Wick and Down Ampney *Glouc*
CHACELEY (St John the Baptist) *see* Deerhurst and Apperley w Forthampton etc *Glouc*
CHACEWATER (St Paul) w St Day and Carharrack *Truro 2* **P** *D&C and R Kenwyn w St Allen (jt)* **V** A S GOUGH, **NSM** I D T LITTLE
CHACOMBE (St Peter and St Paul) *see* Chenderit *Pet*
CHADBROOK *St E 12* **P** *Bp and DBP (jt)* **R** I M G FRIARS
CHADDERTON (Christ Church) (St Saviour) *Man 22* **P** *Trustees* **V** *vacant* 0161-624 2326
CHADDERTON (Emmanuel) (St George) *Man 22* **P** *Trustees* **V** *vacant* 0161-681 1310
CHADDERTON (St Mark) *Man 22* **P** *The Crown* **V** A COOKE
CHADDERTON (St Matthew) (St Luke) *Man 22* **P** *Bp and Prime Min (alt)* **OLM** J TAYLOR, R W A REECE
CHADDESDEN (St Mary) *Derby 9* **P** *MMCET* **V** W A STILLWELL
CHADDESDEN (St Philip) *Derby 9* **P** *Bp* **V** J M PAGE
CHADDESLEY CORBETT (St Cassian) and Stone *Worc 11* **P** *Ld Chan* **V** J A COX
CHADDLEWORTH (St Andrew) *see* Brightwalton w Catmore, Leckhampstead etc *Ox*
CHADKIRK (St Chad) *Ches 16* **P** *R Stockport St Mary* **V** T D BARLOW, **C** T R PARKER, **NSM** J BEAUMONT
CHADLINGTON (St Nicholas) *see* Chase *Ox*
CHADSMOOR (St Aidan) *see* Cannock *Lich*
CHADSMOOR (St Chad) *as above*
CHADWELL (Emmanuel) (St Mary) *Chelmsf 14* **P** *Ch Soc Trust* **R** N T B DEANE, **C** J T D M WEISSERHORN
CHADWELL HEATH (St Chad) *Chelmsf 1* **P** *Vs Dagenham and Ilford (alt)* **V** P A CARR
CHAFFCOMBE (St Michael and All Angels) *see* Chard and Distr *B & W*
CHAGFORD (St Michael), Drewsteignton, Hittisleigh, Spreyton, Gidleigh, and Throwleigh *Ex 11* **P** *Bp, Guild of All So, Personal reps Sir George Hayter-Hames, and Exors B Drew Esq* **R** A E GEERING, **C** J G WITHERS
CHAILEY (St Peter) *Chich 21* **P** *J P B Tillard Esq* **R** G A LAY
CHALBURY (All Saints) *see* Horton, Chalbury, Hinton Martel and Holt St Jas *Sarum*
CHALDON (St Peter and St Paul) *see* Caterham *S'wark*
CHALDON HERRING (St Nicholas) *see* The Lulworths, Winfrith Newburgh and Chaldon *Sarum*
CHALE (St Andrew) *Portsm 8* **P** *Keble Coll Ox* **R** J W RUSSELL, **Hon C** M R HODGE, **NSM** L F HUMPHRYS
CHALFIELD, GREAT (All Saints) *see* Broughton Gifford, Gt Chalfield and Holt *Sarum*
CHALFONT, LITTLE (St George) *see* Chenies and Lt Chalfont, Latimer and Flaunden *Ox*
CHALFONT ST GILES (St Giles) *Ox 20* **P** *Bp* **P-in-c** T A STACEY, **NSM** A L J THOMPSON, M T BLEAKLEY
CHALFONT ST PETER (St Peter) *Ox 20* **P** *St Jo Coll Ox* **P-in-c** C H OVERTON, **C** M R EWBANK, **OLM** W GRAHAM
CHALFORD (Christ Church) *see* Bisley, Chalford, France Lynch, and Oakridge *Glouc*
CHALGRAVE (All Saints) *see* Toddington and Chalgrave *St Alb*
CHALGROVE (St Mary) w Berrick Salome *Ox 1* **P** *Ch Ch Ox* **V** I G H COHEN, **NSM** J A ARNOLD
CHALK (St Mary) *Roch 4* **P** *R Milton* **V** N I BOURNE
CHALKE VALLEY (Team Ministry) *Sarum 11* **P** *Bp, DBP, and K Coll Cam (by turn)* **TR** D E HENLEY, **TV** R C REDDING, A L WILLIAMS, **NSM** S W T COLE, K D N ROSSLYN SMITH
CHALLACOMBE (Holy Trinity) *see* Shirwell, Loxhore, Kentisbury, Arlington, etc *Ex*
CHALLOCK (St Cosmas and St Damian) *see* Chilham w Challock and Molash *Cant*
CHALLOW, EAST (St Nicolas) *see* Hanney, Denchworth and E Challow *Ox*
CHALLOW, WEST (St Laurence) *see* Ridgeway *Ox*
CHALTON (St Michael and All Angels) *see* Blendworth w Chalton w Idsworth *Portsm*
CHALVEY (St Peter) *see* Upton cum Chalvey *Ox*
CHALVINGTON (St Bartholomew) *see* Laughton w Ripe and Chalvington *Chich*
CHAMBERSBURY Hemel Hempstead (Holy Trinity) (St Mary) (St Benedict) *St Alb 3* **P** *DBP* **TR** D M LAWSON, **TV** S G CUTMORE, J C NEALE, **Hon C** D A BUTLER, **NSM** C BAYNES
CHANDLER'S FORD (St Boniface) (St Martin in the Wood) *Win 10* **P** *Bp* **V** M HARLEY, **C** J S KRONENBERG, F C GIBBS
CHANTRY (Holy Trinity) *see* Mells w Buckland Dinham, Elm, Whatley etc *B & W*
CHAPEL ALLERTON (St Matthew) *Ripon 5* **P** *V Leeds St Pet* **C** M D BENNET
CHAPEL CHORLTON (St Laurence), Maer and Whitmore *Lich 7* **P** *Bp and G Cavenagh-Mainwaring Esq (jt)* **R** N A CLEMAS
CHAPEL-EN-LE-FRITH (St Thomas à Becket) *Derby 4* **P** *PCC* **V** N R BRALESFORD
CHAPEL GREEN (St Oswald) *see* Lt Horton *Bradf*
CHAPEL HOUSE (Holy Nativity) *Newc 7* **P** *Bp* **P-in-c** W RIGBY, **NSM** A E MARR, **OLM** D P MARR, R AYRE
CHAPEL LAWN (St Mary) *see* Bucknell w Chapel Lawn, Llanfair Waterdine etc *Heref*
CHAPEL LE DALE (St Leonard) *see* Ingleton w Chapel le Dale *Bradf*
CHAPEL PLAISTER (not known) *see* Box w Hazlebury and Ditteridge *Bris*
CHAPEL ST LEONARDS (St Leonard) w Hogsthorpe *Linc 8* **P** *V Willoughby St Helen* **V** *vacant* (01754) 872666
CHAPELTHORPE (St James) *Wakef 9* **P** *V Sandal* **V** J F WHITE
CHAPELTOWN (St John the Baptist) *Sheff 3* **P** *Bp* **V** R A STORDY
CHAPMANSLADE (St Philip and St James) *see* Cley Hill Warminster *Sarum*
CHAPPEL (St Barnabas) *see* Gt and Lt Tey w Wakes Colne and Chappel *Chelmsf*
CHARBOROUGH (St Mary) *see* Red Post *Sarum*
CHARD (Blessed Virgin Mary) and District *B & W 15* **P** *Patr Bd* **TV** C FURNESS, **P-in-c** A J WOODWARD, **NSM** A T BOYLAND
CHARDSTOCK (All Saints) *see* Axminster, Chardstock, All Saints etc *Ex*
CHARDSTOCK (St Andrew) *as above*
CHARFIELD (St John) and Kingswood *Glouc 7* **P** *Bp, DBP and R W Neeld Esq (jt)* **R** R C PESTELL
CHARFORD (St Andrew) *see* Bromsgrove St Jo *Worc*
CHARING (St Peter and St Paul) w Charing Heath (Holy Trinity) and Little Chart *Cant 10* **P** *Abp and D&C (jt)* **V** B CHALMERS, **OLM** P G COX
CHARLBURY (St Mary the Virgin) w Shorthampton *Ox 3* **P** *St Jo Coll Ox* **V** J K FRENCH
CHARLCOMBE (Blessed Virgin Mary) w Bath (St Stephen) *B & W 9* **P** *DBP and Simeon's Trustees (jt)* **P-in-c** J W LLOYD, **C** C L O'NEILL
CHARLECOTE (St Leonard) *see* Hampton Lucy w Charlecote and Loxley *Cov*
CHARLES (St John the Baptist) *see* S Molton w Nymet St George, High Bray etc *Ex*
CHARLES w Plymouth St Matthias *Ex 24* **P** *Ch Patr Trust* **P-in-c** R S WILLIAMS
CHARLESTOWN (St George) *see* Pendleton *Man*
CHARLESTOWN (St Paul) *Truro 1* **P** *The Crown* **V** J C GREATBATCH, **Hon C** A D J JAGO
CHARLESTOWN (St Thomas the Apostle) *see* Southowram and Claremount *Wakef*
CHARLESWORTH (St John the Evangelist) and Dinting Vale *Derby 6* **P** *The Crown (2 turns), Bp (1 turn)* **NSM** S M MCLEOD, R G ALLARD, C A PRICE

CHARLETON (St Mary) w Buckland Tout Saints, East Portlemouth, South Pool and Chivelstone *Ex 14* **P** *Ld Chan (2 turns), E Roberts Esq, S Tyler Esq and N Tyler Esq (1 turn), Bp (1 turn), and DBP (1 turn)* **R** T W BRIGHTON
CHARLTON (All Saints) *see* Chalke Valley *Sarum*
CHARLTON (Holy Trinity) *see* Wantage *Ox*
CHARLTON (St John) *see* Fladbury w Wyre Piddle and Moor etc *Worc*
CHARLTON (St John the Baptist) *see* Garsdon, Lea and Cleverton and Charlton *Bris*
CHARLTON (St John the Baptist) *see* The Donheads *Sarum*
CHARLTON (St Luke w Holy Trinity) (St Richard) (St Thomas) *S'wark 1* **P** *Bp and Viscount Gough (jt)* **R** J G HESKINS, **C** P G JORDAN, **Hon C** J P LEE, J A CONALTY, **NSM** M R HOUSE
CHARLTON (St Peter) *see* Upavon w Rushall and Charlton *Sarum*
CHARLTON (St Thomas the Apostle) *see* Andover w Foxcott *Win*
CHARLTON, SOUTH (St James) *see* Glendale Gp *Newc*
CHARLTON ABBOTS (St Martin) *see* Sevenhampton w Charlton Abbots, Hawling etc *Glouc*
CHARLTON ADAM (St Peter and St Paul) *see* Somerton w Compton Dundon, the Charltons etc *B & W*
CHARLTON HORETHORNE (St Peter and St Paul) *see* Henstridge and Charlton Horethorne w Stowell *B & W*
CHARLTON-IN-DOVER (St Peter and St Paul) *Cant 4* **P** *Keble Coll Ox* **P-in-c** S J BOWRING, **C** C S JOHNSON
CHARLTON KINGS (Holy Apostles) *Glouc 9* **P** *R Cheltenham* **P-in-c** R J PATERSON
CHARLTON KINGS (St Mary) *Glouc 9* **P** *Bp* **V** M GARLAND, **C** K C FLEMING
CHARLTON MACKRELL (Blessed Virgin Mary) *see* Somerton w Compton Dundon, the Charltons etc *B & W*
CHARLTON MARSHALL (St Mary the Virgin) *see* Spetisbury w Charlton Marshall etc *Sarum*
CHARLTON MUSGROVE (St John) (St Stephen), Cucklington and Stoke Trister *B & W 2* **P** *Bp* **R** *vacant* (01963) 33233
CHARLTON ON OTMOOR (St Mary) *see* Ray Valley *Ox*
CHARLWOOD (St Nicholas) *S'wark 27* **P** *DBP* **R** W G CAMPEN
CHARMINSTER (St Mary the Virgin) and Stinsford *Sarum 1* **P** *The Hon C A Townshend and Bp (alt)* **V** P J SMITH, **OLM** H WILLIS
CHARMOUTH (St Andrew) *see* Golden Cap Team *Sarum*
CHARNEY BASSETT (St Peter) *see* Cherbury w Gainfield *Ox*
CHARNOCK RICHARD (Christ Church) *Blackb 4* **P** *DBF* **P-in-c** N J P HAYTON
CHARSFIELD w Debach (St Peter), Monewden, Hoo, Dallinghoo and Letheringham *St E 18* **P** *MMCET and CPAS, Ld Chan, and Ch Patr Trust (by turn)* **P-in-c** B A MOCKFORD
CHART, GREAT (St Mary) *Cant 10* **P** *Abp* **P-in-c** T C WILSON, **NSM** J CRAY
CHART, LITTLE (St Mary) *see* Charing w Charing Heath and Lt Chart *Cant*
CHART SUTTON (St Michael) *see* Sutton Valence w E Sutton and Chart Sutton *Cant*
CHARTERHOUSE-ON-MENDIP (St Hugh) *see* Blagdon w Compton Martin and Ubley *B & W*
CHARTHAM (St Mary) *Cant 2* **P** *Abp* **R** C C BARLOW
CHARWELTON (Holy Trinity) *see* Badby w Newham and Charwelton w Fawsley etc *Pet*
CHASE *Ox 3* **P** *Bp and D&C Ch Ch (jt)* **V** M E J ABREY, **Hon C** M B CRAMERI
CHASE *Sarum 7* **P** *Bp, Adn Dorset, Ch Soc Trust, Pemb Coll Cam, Univ Coll Ox, J P C Bourke Esq (4 turns), Ld Chan (1 turn)* **R** M J FOSTER, **Hon C** W H G JOHNSTONE, **NSM** W G EDWARDS, **OLM** S J EVANS
CHASE TERRACE (St John) *Lich 1* **P** *Bp* **V** D B LEAKE, **OLM** D POOLE
CHASETOWN (St Anne) *Lich 1* **P** *V Burntwood* **V** D J DITCH, **OLM** R V BAGLEY
CHASETOWN (St John) *see* Chase Terrace *Lich*
CHASTLETON (St Mary the Virgin) *see* Chipping Norton *Ox*
CHATBURN (Christ Church) and Downham *Blackb 7* **P** *Hulme Trustees and Lord Clitheroe (jt)* **P-in-c** R NICHOLSON
CHATHAM (Christ the King) *see* Prince's Park CD *Roch*
CHATHAM (St Mary and St John) *Roch 5* **P** *D&C* **P-in-c** B P ADAMS
CHATHAM (St Paul w All Saints) *Roch 5* **P** *Bp* **V** B T KNAPP, **C** R A KNAPP, **NSM** S M BROOKS
CHATHAM (St Philip and St James) *Roch 5* **P** *Ch Soc Trust* **V** G J ACKERLEY, **C** E N CLOUSTON, **NSM** S C SPENCER
CHATHAM (St Stephen) *Roch 5* **P** *Bp* **V** P J HESKETH, **NSM** S R DUTTON
CHATHAM, SOUTH Holy Trinity (St William) (St Alban) (St David) *Roch 5* **P** *Bp* **TR** M ILYAS, **TV** J S CURRIE, P C WOOTTON
CHATTERIS (St Peter and St Paul) *Ely 14* **P** *G&C Coll Cam* **V** J M THOMSON, **C** W L THOMSON
CHATTISHAM (All Saints and St Margaret) *see* Elmsett w Aldham, Hintlesham, Chattisham etc *St E*
CHATTON (Holy Cross) *see* Glendale Gp *Newc*
CHAULDEN (St Stephen) *see* Hemel Hempstead *St Alb*
CHAVEY DOWN (St Martin) *see* Winkfield and Cranbourne *Ox*
CHAWLEIGH (St James) *see* Burrington, Chawleigh, Cheldon, Chulmleigh etc *Ex*
CHAWTON (St Nicholas) *see* Northanger *Win*
CHEADLE (All Hallows) (St Philip's Mission Church) *Ches 17* **P** *R Cheadle* **V** *vacant* 0161-428 9071 *or* 428 2804
CHEADLE (St Cuthbert) (St Mary) *Ches 17* **P** *Ch Soc Trust* **R** R S MUNRO, **C** J E M NEWMAN, J T P BEAUCHAMP, **NSM** N C HALL, D G WHITEHOUSE
CHEADLE (St Giles) w Freehay *Lich 6* **P** *DBP* **R** I C THURSTON
CHEADLE HEATH (St Augustine) *Ches 18* **P** *Bp* **P-in-c** H SCARISBRICK
CHEADLE HULME (All Saints) *Ches 17* **P** *Bp* **V** H B EALES, **C** D A PARKER
CHEADLE HULME (Emmanuel) Conventional District *Ches 17* **C-in-c** R G IVESON
CHEADLE HULME (St Andrew) *Ches 17* **P** *R Cheadle* **V** D W GUEST
CHEAM (St Dunstan) (St Alban the Martyr) (St Oswald) *S'wark 25* **P** *St Jo Coll Ox* **R** C A FRENCH, **C** G P THOMPSON, R T LAWSON, **OLM** D W F BRICE, P C GOODRIDGE
CHEAM COMMON (St Philip) *see* Worcester Park Ch Ch w St Phil *S'wark*
CHEARSLEY (St Nicholas) *see* Long Crendon w Chearsley and Nether Winchendon *Ox*
CHEBSEY (All Saints), Ellenhall and Seighford-with-Creswell *Lich 7* **P** *D&C, Trustees Earl of Lich, Personal Reps Major C Eld, and Qu Eliz Grant Trustees (jt)* **P-in-c** A HETHERINGTON
CHECKENDON (St Peter and St Paul) *see* Langtree *Ox*
CHECKLEY (Mission Room) *see* Fownhope w Mordiford, Brockhampton etc *Heref*
CHECKLEY (St Mary and All Saints) *see* Uttoxeter Area *Lich*
CHEDBURGH (All Saints) *see* Chevington w Hargrave, Chedburgh w Depden etc *St E*
CHEDDAR (St Andrew) *B & W 1* **P** *D&C* **V** V L DALEY, **NSM** R D H BURSELL
CHEDDINGTON (St Giles) w Mentmore and Marsworth *Ox 26* **P** *Bp and Earl of Rosebery (jt)* **R** R A HALE, **OLM** M HANCE
CHEDDLETON (St Edward the Confessor) *Lich 8* **P** *Bp* **V** M F LEIGH, **NSM** P A BECKETT
CHEDDON FITZPAINE (The Blessed Virgin Mary) *see* Kingston St Mary w Broomfield etc *B & W*
CHEDGRAVE (All Saints) *see* Loddon, Sisland, Chedgrave, Hardley and Langley *Nor*
CHEDISTON (St Mary) *see* Blyth Valley *St E*
CHEDWORTH (St Andrew), Yanworth and Stowell, Coln Rogers and Coln St Denys *Glouc 13* **P** *Ld Chan (2 turns), Qu Coll Ox (1 turn)* **P-in-c** D G MITCHELL
CHEDZOY (The Blessed Virgin Mary) *see* Weston Zoyland w Chedzoy *B & W*
CHEETHAM (St John the Evangelist) *Man 5* **P** *Patr Bd* **P-in-c** D J A BURTON, **C** S D MORGAN
CHEETHAM (St Mark) *see* Lower Crumpsall w Cheetham St Mark *Man*
CHELBOROUGH, EAST (St James) *see* Melbury *Sarum*
CHELBOROUGH, WEST (St Andrew) *as above*
CHELDON (St Mary) *see* Burrington, Chawleigh, Cheldon, Chulmleigh etc *Ex*
CHELFORD (St John the Evangelist) w Lower Withington *Ches 12* **P** *J M Dixon Esq* **V** I SPARKS
CHELL (St Michael) *Lich 11* **P** *Patr Bd* **TR** J REID, **TV** S S PRATT
CHELL HEATH (Saviour) *see* Chell *Lich*
CHELLASTON (St Peter) *Derby 15* **P** *Bp* **V** P SWALES, **C** A R GILES
CHELLS (St Hugh) *see* Stevenage St Hugh and St Jo *St Alb*
CHELLS (St John) *as above*
CHELMARSH (St Peter) *see* Highley w Billingsley, Glazeley etc *Heref*
CHELMONDISTON (St Andrew) and Erwarton w Harkstead *St E 5* **P** *Ld Chan (1 turn), Bp (2 turns)* **R** *vacant* (01473) 780214

CHELMORTON AND FLAGG (St John the Baptist) *see* Taddington, Chelmorton and Flagg, and Monyash *Derby*
CHELMSFORD (All Saints) (St Michael's Church Centre) *Chelmsf 8* **P** *Bp* **V** M A HALL
CHELMSFORD (Ascension) *Chelmsf 8* **P** *Bp* **V** I L MORRIS
CHELMSFORD (St Andrew) *Chelmsf 8* **P** *Bp* **P-in-c** P H GREENLAND
CHELMSLEY WOOD (St Andrew) *Birm 9* **P** *Bp* **R** J M FATHERS
CHELSEA (All Saints) (Old Church) *Lon 8* **P** *R Chelsea St Luke and Earl Cadogan (jt)* **V** *vacant* (020) 7352 5627
CHELSEA (St John w St Andrew) (St John) *Lon 8* **P** *CPAS and Lon Coll of Div (jt)* **V** J R M COOK
CHELSEA (St Luke) (Christ Church) *Lon 8* **P** *Earl Cadogan* **R** C C KEVILL-DAVIES, **C** J B MOFFATT
CHELSEA, UPPER (Holy Trinity) (St Jude) *Lon 8* **P** *Earl Cadogan* **R** M E MARSHALL
CHELSEA, UPPER (St Saviour) (St Simon Zelotes) *Lon 8* **P** *R Upper Chelsea H Trin w St Jude and Hyndman's Trustees (jt)* **V** R A GILLION
CHELSFIELD (St Martin of Tours) *Roch 16* **P** *All So Coll Ox* **R** L G VIRGO
CHELSHAM (St Christopher) *see* Warlingham w Chelsham and Farleigh *S'wark*
CHELSHAM (St Leonard) *as above*
CHELSTON (St Peter) *see* Cockington *Ex*
CHELSWORTH (All Saints) *see* Monks Eleigh w Chelsworth and Brent Eleigh etc *St E*
CHELTENHAM (All Saints) *see* Prestbury and All SS *Glouc*
CHELTENHAM (Christ Church) *Glouc 9* **P** *Simeon's Trustees* **V** T J E MAYFIELD, **C** L FLEWKER-BARKER
CHELTENHAM (Emmanuel) (St Stephen) *Glouc 9* **P** *Bp* **P-in-c** P H NAYLOR, **NSM** H R WOOD, B E TORODE
CHELTENHAM (St Luke and St John) *Glouc 9* **P** *R Cheltenham and Simeon's Trustees (alt)* **V** *vacant* (01242) 513940
CHELTENHAM (St Mark) (St Barnabas) (St Aidan) (Emmanuel) *Glouc 9* **P** *Patr Bd* **TR** P HARRIS, **TV** P D SMITH, M ALLEN, **NSM** J M RODWELL, R I MERCHANT, **OLM** B E HORNE, M L D HORNE
CHELTENHAM (St Mary) (St Matthew) (St Paul) (Holy Trinity) *Glouc 9* **P** *Patr Bd* **TV** M R BAILEY, **P-in-c** A J M DOW, **C** K J HITCHMAN, D M WHEATLEY
CHELTENHAM (St Michael) *Glouc 9* **P** *Bp* **V** D I LAWRENCE
CHELTENHAM (St Peter) *Glouc 9* **P** *DBP* **P-in-c** S W ELDRIDGE, **NSM** M J FRENCH
CHELTENHAM, WEST Team Ministry *see* Cheltenham St Mark *Glouc*
CHELVESTON (St John the Baptist) *see* Higham Ferrers w Chelveston *Pet*
CHELVEY (St Bridget) *see* Backwell w Chelvey and Brockley *B & W*
CHELWOOD (St Leonard) *see* Publow w Pensford, Compton Dando and Chelwood *B & W*
CHELWOOD GATE (not known) *see* Danehill *Chich*
CHENDERIT *Pet 1* **P** *Bp and BNC Ox (2 turns), and Ld Chan (1 turn)* **R** D P RANDELL, **NSM** S J GOUNDREY-SMITH
CHENIES (St Michael) and Little Chalfont, Latimer and Flaunden *Ox 23* **P** *Bedf Estates Trustees and Lord Chesham (jt)* **P-in-c** D G ALLSOP, **Hon C** M F PAYNE
CHEQUERBENT (St Thomas) *see* Westhoughton and Wingates *Man*
CHEQUERFIELD (St Mary) *see* Pontefract St Giles *Wakef*
CHERBURY w Gainfield *Ox 17* **P** *Bp, DBP, Jes Coll, Oriel Coll, and Worc Coll Ox (jt)* **R** S A WELCH, **NSM** J HANCE
CHERHILL (St James the Great) *see* Oldbury *Sarum*
CHERINGTON (St John the Baptist) w Stourton *Cov 9* **P** *Bp* **P-in-c** R K SMITH, **C** H C W PARBURY
CHERINGTON (St Nicholas) *see* Avening w Cherington *Glouc*
CHERITON (All Souls) w Newington *Cant 5* **P** *Abp* **V** A G RICHARDS
CHERITON (St Martin) *Cant 5* **P** *Abp* **R** H C JONES
CHERITON (St Michael and All Angels) *see* Upper Itchen *Win*
CHERITON, NORTH (St John the Baptist) *see* Camelot Par *B & W*
CHERITON BISHOP (St Mary) *see* Tedburn St Mary, Whitestone, Oldridge etc *Ex*
CHERITON FITZPAINE (St Matthew) *see* N Creedy *Ex*
CHERRY BURTON (St Michael) *York 8* **P** *Mrs P J Burton* **P-in-c** M J WESTBY
CHERRY HINTON (St Andrew) *Ely 2* **P** *Peterho Cam* **V** B J LINNEY, **C** J L MEADER
CHERRY HINTON (St John the Evangelist) *Ely 2* **P** *Bp* **V** D P E REINDORP, **Hon C** P S HESLAM, **NSM** A C W TILBY
CHERRY WILLINGHAM (St Peter and St Paul) *see* S Lawres Gp *Linc*
CHERTSEY (St Peter w All Saints), Lyne and Longcross *Guildf 11* **P** *Bp and Haberdashers' Co (jt)* **V** T J HILLIER, **C** S BRUNN, **NSM** M WALKER
CHERWELL VALLEY *Ox 2* **P** *Patr Bd* **TR** P E HUNT
CHESELBORNE (St Martin) *see* Piddle Valley, Hilton, Cheselbourne etc *Sarum*
CHESHAM, GREAT (Christ Church) (Emmanuel) (St Mary the Virgin) *Ox 20* **P** *Patr Bd* **TR** R J SALISBURY, **TV** R S HARRIS, J M SHEPHERD, **C** P T J CHADDER
CHESHAM BOIS (St Leonard) *Ox 20* **P** *Peache Trustees* **P-in-c** P H DAVIES, **NSM** D J BUTLER, C CLARE
CHESHUNT (St Mary the Virgin) *St Alb 20* **P** *Marquess of Salisbury* **V** B M BLACKSHAW, **C** A J M MACHAM, M C H JONES
CHESSINGTON (St Mary the Virgin) *Guildf 9* **P** *Mert Coll Ox* **V** P M FLYNN
CHESTER (Christ Church) *Ches 2* **P** *Bp* **P-in-c** R C TOAN, **C** A D BUCHANAN
CHESTER (Holy Trinity without the Walls) *Ches 2* **P** *Bp* **R** J A STONE, **NSM** P B BARROW
CHESTER (St Barnabas) *see* Ches St Pet w St Jo *Ches*
CHESTER (St Mary on the Hill) *Ches 2* **P** *Duke of Westmr* **R** C W J SAMUELS
CHESTER St Oswald (St Thomas of Canterbury) *Ches 2* **P** *D&C* **V** P WALSH
CHESTER (St Paul) *Ches 2* **P** *R Ches* **V** S T PENDLEBURY
CHESTER (St Peter) (St John the Baptist) *Ches 2* **P** *Bp and Duke of Westminster (jt)* **V** *vacant*
CHESTER GREEN (St Paul) *see* Derby St Paul *Derby*
CHESTER LE STREET (St Mary and St Cuthbert) *Dur 11* **P** *St Jo Coll Dur* **R** K H DUNNE, **C** P J W TYREUS, K A PRZYWALA, A ANDERSON
CHESTER SQUARE (St Michael) (St Philip) *Lon 3* **P** *Duke of Westmr* **V** C C MARNHAM, **NSM** A P CHEATLE
CHESTERBLADE (The Blessed Virgin Mary) *see* Evercreech w Chesterblade and Milton Clevedon *B & W*
CHESTERFIELD (Holy Trinity) (Christ Church) *Derby 5* **P** *CPAS* **P-in-c** C J W JACKSON, **C** B M HOLBROOK
CHESTERFIELD (St Augustine) *Derby 5* **P** *Bp* **V** *vacant* (01246) 273942
CHESTERFIELD (St Mary and All Saints) *Derby 5* **P** *Bp* **V** M R KNIGHT
CHESTERFORD, GREAT (All Saints) w LITTLE (St Mary the Virgin) *Chelmsf 22* **P** *Bp* **V** A KEMP
CHESTERTON (Good Shepherd) *Ely 2* **P** *Bp* **V** A R MCKEARNEY, **C** S ROTHWELL
CHESTERTON (Holy Trinity) (St Chad) *Lich 9* **P** *Prime Min* **V** B R WILSON, **C** K A THOMAS
CHESTERTON (St Andrew) *Ely 2* **P** *Trin Coll Cam* **V** J T D GARDOM, **C** H E DAWES, **NSM** D H PEYTON JONES
CHESTERTON (St George) *Ely 2* **P** *Bp* **NSM** R NICHOLLS
CHESTERTON (St Giles) *Cov 8* **P** *Lady Willoughby de Broke* **V** G J BURRELL, **C** R C FLOATE
CHESTERTON (St Lawrence) *see* Cirencester *Glouc*
CHESTERTON (St Michael) *see* The Ortons, Alwalton and Chesterton *Ely*
CHESTERTON, GREAT (St Mary) *see* Akeman *Ox*
CHESWARDINE (St Swithun), Childs Ercall, Hales, Hinstock, Sambrook and Stoke on Tern *Lich 18* **P** *Patr Bd* **TR** J M STAGG, **NSM** B R NASH-WILLIAMS, L CHAPMAN
CHET VALLEY, The *see* Loddon, Sisland, Chedgrave, Hardley and Langley *Nor*
CHETNOLE (St Peter) *see* Wriggle Valley *Sarum*
CHETTISHAM (St Michael and All Angels) *see* Ely *Ely*
CHETTLE (St Mary) *see* Chase *Sarum*
CHETTON (St Giles) *see* Ditton Priors w Neenton, Burwarton etc *Heref*
CHETWODE (St Mary and St Nicholas) *see* Swan *Ox*
CHETWYND (St Michael and All Angels) *see* Newport w Longford, Chetwynd and Forton *Lich*
CHEVELEY (St Mary) *Ely 4* **P** *DBP and Mrs D A Bowlby (alt)* **R** C A SINDALL, **Hon C** L M BROUGHTON
CHEVENING (St Botolph) *Roch 9* **P** *Abp* **R** C F JOHNSON
CHEVERELL, GREAT (St Peter) *see* The Lavingtons, Cheverells, and Easterton *Sarum*
CHEVERELL, LITTLE (St Peter) *as above*
CHEVINGTON (All Saints) w Hargrave, Chedburgh w Depden, Rede and Hawkedon *St E 8* **P** *Guild of All So (1 turn), Ld Chan (2 turns), Bp and DBP (1 turn)* **P-in-c** G DARVILL
CHEVINGTON (St John the Divine) *Newc 9* **P** *Bp* **P-in-c** E M DIXON, **Hon C** F L BROOKS
CHEVITHORNE (St Thomas) *see* Tiverton St Pet and Chevithorne w Cove *Ex*

CHEW MAGNA (St Andrew) w Dundry and Norton Malreward *B & W 10* **P** *Bp* **R** C R M ROBERTS, **C** J R EASTELL, **NSM** E HICKS
CHEW STOKE (St Andrew) w Nempnett Thrubwell *B & W 10* **P** *Bp and SMF (jt)* **P-in-c** C R M ROBERTS, **C** J R EASTELL
CHEWTON (Mission Church) *see* Keynsham *B & W*
CHEWTON MENDIP (St Mary Magdalene) w Ston Easton, Litton and Emborough *B & W 8* **P** *Earl Waldegrave (2 turns), Bp (1 turn)* **P-in-c** J F M MILES
CHEYLESMORE (Christ Church) *Cov 3* **P** *Ch Trust Fund Trust* **V** F P SELDON
CHICHELEY (St Laurence) *see* Sherington w Chicheley, N Crawley, Astwood etc *Ox*
CHICHESTER (St Pancras and St John) *Chich 3* **P** *Simeon's Trustees (2 turns), St Jo Chpl Trustees (1 turn)* **R** R B M GRIFFITHS
CHICHESTER (St Paul) and Westhampnett St Peter *Chich 3* **P** *Bp and D&C (jt)* **R** R W HUNT, **C** J W F THEODOSIUS, F P A MASCARENHAS, **Hon C** M G STONE
CHICHESTER (St Wilfrid) *Chich 3* **P** *Bp* **P-in-c** P S J RITCHIE
CHICKERELL (St Mary) w Fleet *Sarum 4* **P** *Bp* **P-in-c** R J PRESS, **C** V A THURTELL
CHICKLADE (All Saints) *see* Nadder Valley *Sarum*
CHIDDINGFOLD (St Mary) *Guildf 4* **P** *Ld Chan* **R** S A BROUGH, **OLM** G M WELFORD
CHIDDINGLY (not known) w East Hoathly *Chich 21* **P** *Bp* **P-in-c** P A HODGINS
CHIDDINGSTONE (St Mary) w Chiddingstone Causeway *Roch 11* **P** *Abp and Bp (jt)* **P-in-c** I D HARRISON
CHIDDINGSTONE CAUSEWAY (St Luke) *see* Chiddingstone w Chiddingstone Causeway *Roch*
CHIDEOCK (St Giles) *see* Golden Cap Team *Sarum*
CHIDHAM (St Mary) *Chich 13* **P** *Bp* **P-in-c** D C PAIN
CHIEVELEY (St Mary the Virgin) w Winterbourne and Oare *Ox 14* **P** *Adn Berks* **P-in-c** J P TOOGOOD
CHIGNAL SMEALEY (St Nicholas) *see* The Chignals w Mashbury *Chelmsf*
CHIGNALS w Mashbury, The *Chelmsf 8* **P** *CPAS (2 turns), Bp (1 turn)* **R** *vacant*
CHIGWELL (St Mary) (St Winifred) and Chigwell Row *Chelmsf 25* **P** *The Crown and Patr Bd (alt)* **TR** P J TRENDALL, **TV** A J NEALE, A SMITH
CHIGWELL ROW (All Saints) *see* Chigwell and Chigwell Row *Chelmsf*
CHILBOLTON (St Mary) cum Wherwell *Win 3* **P** *Bp and Marquess of Camden (alt)* **R** F E WILLIAMS
CHILCOMB (St Andrew) *see* Win All SS w Chilcomb and Chesil *Win*
CHILCOMBE (not known) *see* Bride Valley *Sarum*
CHILCOMPTON (St John the Baptist) w Downside and Stratton on the Fosse *B & W 12* **P** *Bp, MMCET, and V Midsomer Norton (jt)* **P-in-c** C D NORTH
CHILCOTE (St Matthew's Chapel) *see* Clifton Campville w Edingale and Harlaston *Lich*
CHILDE OKEFORD (St Nicholas) *see* Okeford *Sarum*
CHILDERDITCH (All Saints and St Faith) *see* E and W Horndon w Lt Warley and Childerditch *Chelmsf*
CHILDREY (St Mary the Virgin) *see* Ridgeway *Ox*
CHILDS ERCALL (St Michael and All Angels) *see* Cheswardine, Childs Ercall, Hales, Hinstock etc *Lich*
CHILDS HILL (All Saints) *see* Hendon All SS Childs Hill *Lon*
CHILDSWYCKHAM (St Mary the Virgin) *see* Winchcombe *Glouc*
CHILDWALL (All Saints) *Liv 4* **P** *Bp* **C** E J DURHAM
CHILDWALL (St David) *Liv 4* **P** *Bp* **V** S W C GOUGH, **NSM** G R NISBET
CHILDWALL VALLEY (St Mark) *see* Gateacre *Liv*
CHILDWICK (St Mary) *see* St Alb St Mich *St Alb*
CHILFROME (Holy Trinity) *see* Melbury *Sarum*
CHILHAM (St Mary) w Challock and Molash *Cant 2* **P** *Abp and Viscount Massereene and Ferrard (jt)* **V** C R DUNCAN
CHILLENDEN (All Saints) *see* Nonington w Wymynswold and Goodnestone etc *Cant*
CHILLESFORD (St Peter) *see* Wilford Peninsula *St E*
CHILLINGHAM (St Peter) *see* Glendale Gp *Newc*
CHILLINGTON (St James) *see* Ilminster and Distr *B & W*
CHILMARK (St Margaret of Antioch) *see* Nadder Valley *Sarum*
CHILTHORNE DOMER (Blessed Virgin Mary) *see* Tintinhull w Chilthorne Domer, Yeovil Marsh etc *B & W*
CHILTINGTON, EAST (not known) *see* Plumpton w E Chiltington cum Novington *Chich*
CHILTINGTON, WEST (St Mary) *Chich 12* **P** *Bp* **R** K G O'DONNELL
CHILTON (All Saints) *see* Harwell w Chilton *Ox*
CHILTON (St Aidan) *see* Gt Aycliffe and Chilton *Dur*
CHILTON (St Mary) *see* Bernwode *Ox*
CHILTON CANTELO (St James) w Ashington, Mudford, Rimpton and Marston Magna *B & W 7* **P** *DBP and D&C, D&C Bris, and Bp Lon (by turn)* **P-in-c** P T WOOD
CHILTON FOLIAT (St Mary) *see* Whitton *Sarum*
CHILTON MOOR (St Andrew) *Dur 14* **P** *Bp* **V** P D DAVEY
CHILTON POLDEN (St Edward) *see* W Poldens *B & W*
CHILTON TRINITY (Holy Trinity) *see* Bridgwater St Mary, Chilton Trinity and Durleigh *B & W*
CHILVERS COTON (All Saints) w Astley *Cov 5* **P** *Viscount Daventry* **V** P BROWN
CHILWELL (Christ Church) *S'well 7* **P** *CPAS* **C** G A O JESSON, **NSM** L HEPTINSTALL
CHILWORTH (St Denys) w North Baddesley *Win 12* **P** *Mrs P M A T Chamberlayne-Macdonald* **V** P B C SALISBURY, **C** P S SHERWOOD
CHILWORTH (St Thomas) *see* Shere, Albury and Chilworth *Guildf*
CHINEHAM (Christ Church) *Win 4* **P** *Bp* **V** I R BENTLEY, **C** P J J PLYMING
CHINESE CONGREGATION *see* St Martin-in-the-Fields *Lon*
CHINGFORD (All Saints) (St Peter and St Paul) *Chelmsf 5* **P** *Bp* **R** T W PAGE, **C** C F WILSON, T J HIDE, D V COLLINS
CHINGFORD (St Anne) *Chelmsf 5* **P** *Bp* **V** *vacant* (020) 8529 4740
CHINGFORD (St Edmund) *Chelmsf 5* **P** *Bp* **V** C L OWENS
CHINLEY (St Mary) *see* Hayfield and Chinley w Buxworth *Derby*
CHINNOCK, EAST (Blessed Virgin Mary) *see* W Coker w Hardington Mandeville, E Chinnock etc *B & W*
CHINNOCK, MIDDLE (St Margaret) *see* Norton sub Hamdon, W Chinnock, Chiselborough etc *B & W*
CHINNOCK, WEST (Blessed Virgin Mary) *as above*
CHINNOR (St Andrew), Sydenham, Aston Rowant and Crowell *Ox 1* **P** *Bp, DBP, and Peache Trustees (jt)* **R** M L LANGE-SMITH, **OLM** J M DEVAL, S Q HUTTON
CHIPPENHAM (St Andrew) w Tytherton Lucas *Bris 4* **P** *Ch Ch Ox* **V** S C TATTON-BROWN
CHIPPENHAM (St Margaret) *Ely 3* **P** *Mrs A Crawley* **NSM** M G BANYARD
CHIPPENHAM (St Paul) w Hardenhuish and Langley Burrell *Bris 4* **P** *Patr Bd* **TR** S J TYNDALL, **TV** J K S DENNISTON
CHIPPENHAM (St Peter) *Bris 4* **P** *Bp* **V** A D FENSOME, **C** M F HERBERT
CHIPPERFIELD (St Paul) *see* Sarratt and Chipperfield *St Alb*
CHIPPING (St Bartholomew) and Whitewell (St Michael) *Blackb 7* **P** *Bp and Hulme Trustees (jt)* **P-in-c** S J WILLIAMS
CHIPPING BARNET (St John the Baptist) (St Mark) (St Stephen) *St Alb 17* **P** *Prime Min (2 turns) and Bp (1 turn)* **TR** S H SPEERS, **TV** M J WILLIAMS, **C** M J A LINDSAY
CHIPPING CAMPDEN (St James) w Ebrington *Glouc 10* **P** *Peache Trustees (1 turn), Earl of Harrowby (2 turns)* **P-in-c** D C M COOK, **NSM** M J ABSOLON
CHIPPING NORTON (St Mary the Virgin) *Ox 3* **P** *Patr Bd* **TR** S J A WESTON, **TV** T A CANNON, **NSM** S A HAYES, H M WILLIAMS, J FIELDEN
CHIPPING ONGAR (St Martin) w Shelley *Chelmsf 27* **P** *Guild of All So and Keble Coll Ox* **R** B J PYKE, **NSM** G FRITH
CHIPPING SODBURY (St John the Baptist) and Old Sodbury *Glouc 7* **P** *D&C Worc* **P-in-c** C B WRAY, **C** H RUNDLE
CHIPPING WARDEN (St Peter and St Paul) *see* Culworth w Sulgrave and Thorpe Mandeville etc *Pet*
CHIPSTABLE (All Saints) *see* Wiveliscombe w Chipstable, Huish Champflower etc *B & W*
CHIPSTEAD (Good Shepherd) *see* Chevening *Roch*
CHIPSTEAD (St Margaret of Antioch) *S'wark 27* **P** *Abp* **P-in-c** P J BATEMAN, **OLM** J N WATES
CHIRBURY (St Michael) *Heref 13* **P** *Sir David Wakeman Bt and Bp (alt)* **V** P D HARRATT
CHIRTON (St John the Baptist) *see* Redhorn *Sarum*
CHISELBOROUGH (St Peter and St Paul) *see* Norton sub Hamdon, W Chinnock, Chiselborough etc *B & W*
CHISHILL, GREAT (St Swithun) *see* Heydon, Gt and Lt Chishill, Chrishall etc *Chelmsf*
CHISHILL, LITTLE (St Nicholas) *as above*
CHISLEDON (Holy Cross) *see* Ridgeway *Sarum*
CHISLEHURST (Annunciation) *Roch 14* **P** *Keble Coll* **V** W B BEER
CHISLEHURST (Christ Church) *Roch 14* **P** *CPAS* **V** J M ADAMS, **C** T J MILLS
CHISLEHURST (St Nicholas) *Roch 14* **P** *Bp* **C** J N WHATTON, **NSM** J B HURN

CHISLET (St Mary the Virgin) *see* St Nicholas at Wade w Sarre and Chislet w Hoath *Cant*
CHISWICK (St Michael) *Lon 11* **P** *V St Martin-in-the-Fields* **P-in-c** N C FINCHAM
CHISWICK (St Michael and All Angels) *see* Bedford Park *Lon*
CHISWICK (St Nicholas w St Mary Magdalene) *Lon 11* **P** *D&C St Paul's* **V** P A TUFT
CHISWICK (St Paul) Grove Park *Lon 11* **P** *V Chiswick* **V** M C RILEY
CHITHURST (St Mary) *see* Rogate w Terwick and Trotton w Chithurst *Chich*
CHITTERNE (All Saints and St Mary) *see* Wylye and Till Valley *Sarum*
CHITTERNE (St Mary) *as above*
CHITTLEHAMHOLT (St John) *see* S Molton w Nymet St George, High Bray etc *Ex*
CHITTLEHAMPTON (St Hieritha) *as above*
CHITTS HILL (St Cuthbert) *Lon 19* **P** *CPAS* **V** D M DALEY
CHIVELSTONE (St Sylvester) *see* Charleton w Buckland Tout Saints etc *Ex*
CHOBHAM (St Lawrence) w Valley End *Guildf 6* **P** *Bp and Brig R W Acworth (alt)* **V** A BODY, **OLM** C J BEDFORD
CHOLDERTON (St Nicholas) *see* Bourne Valley *Sarum*
CHOLESBURY (St Lawrence) *see* Hawridge w Cholesbury and St Leonard *Ox*
CHOLLERTON w Birtley and Thockrington *Newc 2* **P** *Mrs P I Enderby (2 turns), Newc Dioc Soc (1 turn)* **R** J WYLAM, **OLM** D I WILLIAMS
CHOLSEY (St Mary) and Moulsford *Ox 18* **P** *Ld Chan and Bp (alt)* **V** A M PETIT, **OLM** V M L GIBBONS
CHOPPARDS (Mission Room) *see* Upper Holme Valley *Wakef*
CHOPPINGTON (St Paul the Apostle) *Newc 1* **P** *D&C* **V** J J T THOMPSON
CHOPWELL (St John the Evangelist) *Dur 13* **P** *Bp* **P-in-c** P R MURRAY
CHORLEY (All Saints) *Blackb 4* **P** *Bp* **V** E N STRASZAK
CHORLEY (St George) *Blackb 4* **P** *R Chorley* **V** K BARRETT
CHORLEY (St James) *Blackb 4* **P** *R Chorley* **V** K HOWLES
CHORLEY (St Laurence) *Blackb 4* **P** *Bp* **R** J R CREE, **C** T R WEBBER
CHORLEY (St Peter) *Blackb 4* **P** *R Chorley* **V** L T ATHERTON
CHORLEY (St Philip) *see* Alderley Edge *Ches*
CHORLEYWOOD (Christ Church) *St Alb 5* **P** *CPAS* **V** G A COLLINS, **C** P MANUEL
CHORLEYWOOD (St Andrew) *St Alb 5* **P** *Bp* **V** M W G STIBBE, **C** A T WILLIAMS, **Hon C** M S MCCRUM
CHORLTON-CUM-HARDY (St Clement) (St Barnabas) *Man 4* **P** *D&C* **R** H J BARBER, **C** I M DELINGER
CHORLTON-CUM-HARDY (St Werburgh) *Man 4* **P** *Bp* **OLM** M J CLEALL-HILL
CHRISHALL (Holy Trinity) *see* Heydon, Gt and Lt Chishill, Chrishall etc *Chelmsf*
CHRIST THE KING comprising the parishes of Tanfield, Stanley and South Moor *Dur 4* **P** *Bp (4 turns), Prime Min (1 turn)* **TR** A JOHNSTON, **TV** G J SIMMONS, I GROSU
CHRIST THE KING in the Diocese of Newcastle *Newc 5* **P** *Patr Bd* **TR** R K KENNEDY, **TV** M S JONES
CHRISTCHURCH (Christ Church) and Manea and Welney *Ely 14* **P** *Bp and R T Townley Esq (jt)* **R** *vacant* (01354) 638379
CHRISTCHURCH (Holy Trinity) *Win 9* **P** *Bp* **V** H M WILLIAMS, **C** J E F JASPER, A HAWTHORNE, **NSM** A M SMITH
CHRISTCHURCH Stourvale (St George) *see* Christchurch *Win*
CHRISTIAN MALFORD (All Saints) *see* Draycot *Bris*
CHRISTLETON (St James) *Ches 2* **P** *Bp* **R** K P LEE
CHRISTON (Blessed Virgin Mary) *see* Crook Peak *B & W*
CHRISTOW (St James), Ashton and Bridford *Ex 6* **P** *SMF, MMCET, Viscount Exmouth, Bp, and E A Beard Esq (jt)* **P-in-c** G K MAYER
CHUDLEIGH (St Mary and St Martin) w Chudleigh Knighton and Trusham *Ex 9* **P** *Patr Bd* **V** P WIMSETT
CHUDLEIGH KNIGHTON (St Paul) *see* Chudleigh w Chudleigh Knighton and Trusham *Ex*
CHULMLEIGH (St Mary Magdalene) *see* Burrington, Chawleigh, Cheldon, Chulmleigh etc *Ex*
CHURCH ASTON (St Andrew) *Lich 16* **P** *R Edgmond* **P-in-c** J C COWBURN
CHURCH BRAMPTON (St Botolph) *see* Brington w Whilton and Norton etc *Pet*
CHURCH BROUGHTON (St Michael) *see* Boylestone, Church Broughton, Dalbury, etc *Derby*
CHURCH CONISTON (St Andrew) *Carl 9* **P** *Peache Trustees* **P-in-c** M R EAST
CHURCH EATON (St Editha) *see* Bradeley, Church Eaton and Moreton *Lich*
CHURCH HONEYBOURNE (St Ecgwyn) *see* Pebworth, Dorsington, Honeybourne etc *Glouc*
CHURCH HULME (St Luke) *Ches 11* **P** *V Sandbach* **V** P MASON
CHURCH IN THE WOOD *see* Hollington St Leon *Chich*
CHURCH KIRK (St James) *Blackb 1* **P** *Hulme Trustees* **R** N A ASHTON
CHURCH KNOWLE (St Peter) *see* Corfe Castle, Church Knowle, Kimmeridge etc *Sarum*
CHURCH LANGLEY (Church and Community Centre) *Chelmsf 26* **P** *V Harlow* **V** T J VOLTZENLOGEL
CHURCH LANGTON (St Peter) cum Tur Langton, Thorpe Langton and Shangton, Billesdon cum Goadby and Rolleston and Skeffington *Leic 4* **P** *Bp, E Brudenell Esq, and MMCET (jt)* **R** B M KNIGHT, **NSM** A J ROBERTS
CHURCH LAWFORD (St Peter) *see* Wolston and Church Lawford *Cov*
CHURCH LAWTON (All Saints) *Ches 11* **P** *Mrs I L Lawton* **R** G L JOYCE
CHURCH LENCH (All Saints) w Rous Lench and Abbots Morton and Harvington *Worc 1* **P** *Bp and D&C (jt)* **R** R J G THORNILEY
CHURCH MINSHULL (St Bartholomew) *see* Acton and Worleston, Church Minshull etc *Ches*
CHURCH OAKLEY (St Leonard) *see* Oakley w Wootton St Lawrence *Win*
CHURCH PREEN (St John the Baptist) *see* Wenlock *Heref*
CHURCH STRETTON (St Laurence) *Heref 11* **P** *Ch Patr Trust* **R** J G STONES, **NSM** A J HUGHES
CHURCHAM (St Andrew) *see* Huntley and Longhope, Churcham and Bulley *Glouc*
CHURCHDOWN (St Andrew) (St Bartholomew) *Glouc 6* **P** *D&C* **V** J G PERKIN, **C** M A BALFOUR
CHURCHDOWN (St John the Evangelist) and Innsworth *Glouc 6* **P** *Bp* **V** K I MORGAN, **C** A MORRIS
CHURCHILL (All Saints) *see* Chipping Norton *Ox*
CHURCHILL (St John the Baptist) *see* Burrington and Churchill *B & W*
CHURCHILL-IN-HALFSHIRE (St James) w Blakedown and Broome *Worc 12* **P** *Viscount Cobham and N A Bourne Esq (alt)* **R** N J DAVIS
CHURCHOVER (Holy Trinity) w Willey *Cov 6* **P** *Bp* **P-in-c** C A GARROD, **Hon C** C S HARPER
CHURCHSTANTON (St Peter and St Paul) *see* Blackdown *B & W*
CHURCHSTOKE (St Nicholas) w Hyssington and Sarn *Heref 10* **P** *The Crown (1 turn), Earl of Powis (2 turns)* **NSM** I R BALL
CHURCHSTOW (St Mary) *see* Thurlestone, S Milton, W Alvington etc *Ex*
CHURCHTOWN (St Helen) *see* Garstang St Helen and St Michaels-on-Wyre *Blackb*
CHURSTON FERRERS (St Mary the Vigin) *see* Brixham w Churston Ferrers and Kingswear *Ex*
CHURT (St John the Evangelist) and Hindhead *Guildf 3* **P** *Adn Surrey* **V** D WILBRAHAM, **C** S R JELLEY, **NSM** J D STRAIN
CHURWELL (All Saints) *see* Morley *Wakef*
CHUTE (St Nicholas) *see* Savernake *Sarum*
CHYNGTON (St Luke) *see* Seaford w Sutton *Chich*
CINDERFORD (St John the Evangelist) *Glouc 4* **P** *The Crown* **V** J W HOLDER
CINDERFORD (St Stephen) w Littledean *Glouc 4* **P** *Ch Patr Trust* **P-in-c** R D WYNN
CINDERHILL (Christ Church) *S'well 14* **P** *Bp* **C** L P B O'BOYLE
CINNAMON BROW (Resurrection) *Liv 12* **P** *Bp, Adn, and R Warrington (jt)* **V** S W ELSTOB
CIPPENHAM (St Andrew) *see* W Slough *Ox*
CIRENCESTER (St John the Baptist) *Glouc 11* **P** *Bp* **V** M A M ST JOHN-CHANNELL, **C** C A MCCLURE, W G HEATHCOTE, **NSM** J A GARDNER, R M FRANKLIN
CLACTON, GREAT (St John the Baptist) *Chelmsf 23* **P** *Ch Patr Trust* **V** G D A THORBURN
CLACTON, LITTLE (St James) *see* Weeley and Lt Clacton *Chelmsf*
CLACTON-ON-SEA (St Christopher) (St James) *Chelmsf 23* **P** *Bp* **V** A P D SPOONER, **C** A R BREWERTON
CLACTON-ON-SEA (St Paul) *Chelmsf 23* **P** *Ch Patr Trust* **V** D J TITLEY, **NSM** D W HART
CLAINES (St George w St Mary Magdalene) *see* Worc St Geo w St Mary Magd *Worc*
CLAINES (St John the Baptist) *Worc 6* **P** *Bp* **V** S M AGNEW, **C** O S WOOLCOCK

CLANDON, EAST (St Thomas of Canterbury) and WEST (St Peter and St Paul) *Guildf 5* **P** *Earl of Onslow and Bp (alt)* **R** B L PREECE, **NSM** D M MACMILLAN
CLANFIELD (St James) *see* Catherington and Clanfield *Portsm*
CLANFIELD (St Stephen) *see* Bampton w Clanfield *Ox*
CLANNABOROUGH (St Petrock) *see* N Creedy *Ex*
CLAPHAM (Christ Church) (St John the Evangelist) *S'wark 12* **P** *Bp* **V** P J ROSE-CASEMORE, **NSM** S PEAKE
CLAPHAM (Holy Spirit) *S'wark 12* **P** *Bp* **V** J A BLUNDEN, **Hon C** R F VICKERY, **NSM** R A BURGE-THOMAS
CLAPHAM (Holy Trinity) (St Peter) *S'wark 12* **P** *DBP* **V** D O ISHERWOOD, **NSM** C A CLARKE, M P STRANGE
CLAPHAM (St James) *S'wark 12* **P** *CPAS* **V** C A COTTON, **Hon C** J MARSHALL
CLAPHAM (St Mary the Virgin) *see* Findon w Clapham and Patching *Chich*
CLAPHAM (St Paul) *S'wark 12* **P** *Bp* **V** D L MATTHEWS
CLAPHAM (St Thomas of Canterbury) *St Alb 13* **P** *MMCET* **V** S J LILEY
CLAPHAM COMMON (St Barnabas) *S'wark 16* **P** *Ch Trust Fund Trust* **V** D PAGE
CLAPHAM PARK (All Saints) *S'wark 12* **P** *CPAS* **V** *vacant* (020) 8678 6020
CLAPHAM PARK (St Stephen) *S'wark 13* **P** *Trustees* **V** S P GATES, **C** P M PULLINGER, **OLM** E B T PAYNE
CLAPHAM-WITH-KEASDEN (St James) and Austwick *Bradf 6* **P** *Bp* **V** I F GREENHALGH
CLAPTON (St James) *see* Bourton-on-the-Water w Clapton etc *Glouc*
CLAPTON (St James) *Lon 5* **P** *Bp* **V** R BROWN
CLAPTON (St Peter) *see* Barnwell w Tichmarsh, Thurning and Clapton *Pet*
CLAPTON, UPPER (St Matthew) *Lon 5* **P** *D&C Cant* **V** *vacant* (020) 8806 2430
CLARBOROUGH (St John the Baptist) w Hayton *S'well 5* **P** *Bp* **P-in-c** M W BRIGGS
CLARE (St Peter and St Paul) *see* Stour Valley *St E*
CLAREMOUNT (St Thomas the Apostle) *see* Southowram and Claremount *Wakef*
CLARENCE GATE GARDENS (St Cyprian) *see* St Marylebone St Cypr *Lon*
CLARENDON (Team Ministry) *Sarum 11* **P** *Team Coun* **TR** M A WARD, **TV** N H S BERSWEDEN, **Hon C** L M CATER, **NSM** D L SANDERS, **OLM** A M COCHRANE
CLARENDON PARK (St John the Baptist) *see* Emmaus Par Team *Leic*
CLATFORD, UPPER (All Saints) *see* Abbotts Ann and Upper and Goodworth Clatford *Win*
CLATWORTHY (St Mary Magdalene) *see* Wiveliscombe w Chipstable, Huish Champflower etc *B & W*
CLAUGHTON VILLAGE (St Bede) *see* Birkenhead St Jas w St Bede *Ches*
CLAVERDON (St Michael and All Angels) w Preston Bagot *Cov 7* **P** *Bp* **P-in-c** L G MORTIMER
CLAVERHAM (St Barnabas) *see* Yatton Moor *B & W*
CLAVERING (St Mary and St Clement) and Langley w Arkesden and Wicken Bonhunt *Chelmsf 21* **P** *Ch Hosp and Keble Coll Ox (jt)* **V** D S MCGUFFIE
CLAVERLEY (All Saints) w Tuckhill *Heref 9* **P** *Bp and E M A Thompson Esq (jt)* **V** S H CAWDELL, **NSM** S H L CAWDELL
CLAVERTON (Blessed Virgin Mary) *see* Bathampton w Claverton *B & W*
CLAVERTON DOWN (St Hugh) *as above*
CLAWTON (St Leonard) *see* Ashwater, Halwill, Beaworthy, Clawton etc *Ex*
CLAXBY (St Mary) *see* Walesby *Linc*
CLAXTON (St Andrew) *see* Rockland St Mary w Hellington, Bramerton etc *Nor*
CLAY CROSS (St Bartholomew) *see* N Wingfield, Clay Cross and Pilsley *Derby*
CLAY HILL (St John the Baptist) (St Luke) *Lon 18* **P** *V Enfield St Andr and Bp (jt)* **V** L S DRAKE
CLAYBROOKE (St Peter) cum Wibtoft and Frolesworth *Leic 10* **P** *The Crown and Adn Loughb (by turn)* **R** J M BRADSHAW
CLAYDON and Barham *St E 1* **P** *G R Drury Esq* **P-in-c** T W BROADBENT, **NSM** S M EVANS, **OLM** C B AUSTIN, J V ABLETT
CLAYDON (St James the Great) *see* Shires' Edge *Ox*
CLAYDONS, The (St Mary) (All Saints) *Ox 24* **P** *Sir Ralph Verney Bt* **P-in-c** R D HOLDER
CLAYGATE (Holy Trinity) *Guildf 8* **P** *Ch Patr Trust* **V** J T HENDERSON, **C** D M KING, **NSM** L M MORGAN
CLAYHANGER (Holy Trinity Worship Centre) *see* Ogley Hay *Lich*
CLAYHANGER (St Peter) *see* Bampton, Morebath, Clayhanger and Petton *Ex*
CLAYHIDON (St Andrew) *see* Hemyock w Culm Davy, Clayhidon and Culmstock *Ex*
CLAYPOLE (St Peter) *Linc 23* **P** *DBP (2 turns), The Revd J R H Thorold and J R Thorold Esq (1 turn)* **R** G MUNN, **NSM** C C MUNN
CLAYTON (St Cross w St Paul) *see* Man Clayton St Cross w St Paul *Man*
CLAYTON (St James the Great) *Lich 9* **P** *Bp* **V** N M EDWARDS
CLAYTON (St John the Baptist) *Bradf 2* **P** *V Bradf* **V** K O DUNNETT, **NSM** P COLES
CLAYTON (St John the Baptist) w Keymer *Chich 9* **P** *BNC Ox* **C** D H HUMPHREY
CLAYTON BROOK (Community Church) *see* Whittle-le-Woods *Blackb*
CLAYTON LE MOORS (All Saints) *see* Altham w Clayton le Moors *Blackb*
CLAYTON LE MOORS (St James) *as above*
CLAYTON WEST w HIGH HOYLAND (All Saints) *see* High Hoyland, Scissett and Clayton W *Wakef*
CLAYWORTH (St Peter) *see* Everton and Mattersey w Clayworth *S'well*
CLEADON (All Saints) *Dur 15* **P** *R Whitburn* **V** R A NIXON
CLEADON PARK (St Mark and St Cuthbert) *Dur 15* **P** *Bp* **V** R J A ALDERSON
CLEARWELL (St Peter) *see* Newland and Redbrook w Clearwell *Glouc*
CLEASBY (St Peter) *see* E Richmond *Ripon*
CLEATOR (St Leonard) *see* Crosslacon *Carl*
CLEATOR MOOR (St John) *as above*
CLECKHEATON (St John the Evangelist) *Wakef 8* **P** *V Birstall* **V** J BARKER
CLECKHEATON (St Luke) (Whitechapel) *Wakef 8* **P** *Bp and Sir Martin Wilson (jt)* **P-in-c** M A MCLEAN, **NSM** R M CAVE
CLEDFORD (Mission Room) *see* Middlewich w Byley *Ches*
CLEE, NEW (St John the Evangelist) (St Stephen) *Linc 9* **P** *Bp* **V** J W ELLIS
CLEE, OLD (Holy Trinity and St Mary the Virgin) *Linc 9* **P** *Bp* **V** D I WALKER
CLEE HILL (St Peter's Mission Room) *see* Wigmore Abbey *Heref*
CLEE ST MARGARET (St Margaret) *see* Bitterley w Middleton, Stoke St Milborough etc *Heref*
CLEETHORPE (Christ Church) *see* Clee *Linc*
CLEETHORPES St Aidan *Linc 9* **P** *Bp* **V** *vacant* (01472) 692989
CLEETHORPES (St Francis) Conventional District *Linc 9* **C-in-c** T STOTT
CLEETHORPES (St Peter) *Linc 9* **P** *Bp* **NSM** D H WEBSTER
CLEETON (St Mary) *see* Stottesdon w Farlow, Cleeton St Mary etc *Heref*
CLEEVE (Holy Trinity) *see* Yatton Moor *B & W*
CLEEVE, OLD (St Andrew), Leighland and Treborough *B & W 16* **P** *Selw Coll Cam (2 turns), Personal Reps G R Wolseley Esq (1 turn)* **P-in-c** J HENNING
CLEEVE HILL (St Peter) *see* Bishop's Cleeve *Glouc*
CLEEVE PRIOR (St Andrew) and The Littletons *Worc 1* **P** *D&C and Ch Ch Ox (alt)* **V** D R EVANS
CLEHONGER (All Saints) *see* Kingstone w Clehonger, Eaton Bishop etc *Heref*
CLENCHWARTON (St Margaret) and West Lynn *Ely 15* **P** *DBP* **R** A J DAVEY
CLENT (St Leonard) *see* Belbroughton w Fairfield and Clent *Worc*
CLEOBURY MORTIMER (St Mary the Virgin) w Hopton Wafers, Neen Sollars and Milson, Neen Savage w Kinlet *Heref 12* **P** *Patr Bd (2 turns), Ld Chan (1 turn)* **R** W A BUCK, **C** N S PATTERSON, **NSM** M H DABORN
CLEOBURY NORTH (St Peter and St Paul) *see* Ditton Priors w Neenton, Burwarton etc *Heref*
CLERKENWELL (Our Most Holy Redeemer) *Lon 6* **P** *Trustees* **V** P A BAGOTT, **C** R M MACKLEY
CLERKENWELL (St James and St John) (St Peter) *Lon 6* **P** *Ch Patr Trust and PCC (jt)* **V** A J BAUGHEN
CLERKENWELL (St Mark) *Lon 6* **P** *City Corp* **V** P A BAGOTT, **C** R M MACKLEY
CLEVEDON (St Andrew) (Christ Church) (St Peter) *B & W 13* **P** *Simeon's Trustees (1 turn), Ld Chan (2 turns)* **V** T J BAILLIE, **C** C J JENNINGS
CLEVEDON (St John the Evangelist) *B & W 13* **P** *SMF* **V** D S M SMITH, **C** N W M LEGGETT
CLEVEDON, EAST (All Saints) w Clapton in Gordano, Walton Clevedon, Walton in Gordano and Weston in Gordano *B & W 13*

P *Bp and SMF (jt)* **R** N A HECTOR, **C** P F SMITH, I M ROBERTSON
CLEVELEYS (St Andrew) *Blackb 12* **P** *Trustees* **V** D E REEVES
CLEWER (St Andrew) *Ox 13* **P** *Eton Coll* **P-in-c** L M BROWN
CLEWER (St Stephen) *see* New Windsor *Ox*
CLEY (St Margaret) *see* Blakeney w Cley, Wiveton, Glandford etc *Nor*
CLEY HILL Warminster (Team Ministry) *Sarum 17* **P** *Patr Bd* **TR** A G WATTS, **TV** N PAYNE, **C** W P M HUGHES, **NSM** C J OWEN, **OLM** A M WADSWORTH, A J R YATES
CLIBURN (St Cuthbert) *see* Morland, Thrimby, Gt Strickland and Cliburn *Carl*
CLIDDESDEN (St Leonard) and Ellisfield w Farleigh Wallop and Dummer *Win 1* **P** *Earl of Portsm and DBP (jt)* **P-in-c** C PARNELL-HOPKINSON
CLIFFE (St Andrew) *see* Hemingbrough *York*
CLIFFE, SOUTH (St John) *see* N Cave w Cliffe *York*
CLIFFE AT HOO (St Helen) w Cooling *Roch 6* **P** *D&C* **R** E M A WRIGHT
CLIFFE VALE (St Stephen) *see* Hartshill *Lich*
CLIFFORD (St Luke) *York 1* **P** *G Lane-Fox Esq* **P-in-c** H N LAWRANCE
CLIFFORD (St Mary the Virgin) *see* Cusop w Blakemere, Bredwardine w Brobury etc *Heref*
CLIFFORD CHAMBERS (St Helen) *see* Stratford-upon-Avon, Luddington etc *Cov*
CLIFFORDS MESNE (St Peter) *see* Newent and Gorsley w Cliffords Mesne *Glouc*
CLIFFSEND (St Mary the Virgin) *see* St Laur in Thanet *Cant*
CLIFTON (All Saints) and Southill *St Alb 16* **P** *Bp and C E S Whitbread Esq (jt)* **NSM** C T TOPLEY
CLIFTON (All Saints w St John) *Bris 2* **P** *Bp* **P-in-c** R D HOYAL, **Hon C** J H J PATRICK, **NSM** R DURBIN
CLIFTON (Christ Church w Emmanuel) *Bris 2* **P** *Simeon's Trustees* **C** M C CAIN, L WALTON
CLIFTON (Holy Trinity) *Derby 8* **P** *Mrs M F Stanton, T W Clowes Esq, and V Ashbourne (by turn)* **P-in-c** H J DOBBIN
CLIFTON (Holy Trinity) (St Francis) (St Mary the Virgin) *S'well 9* **P** *DBP* **TR** S JARRATT, **C** R H DAVEY, **NSM** C D WOOD
CLIFTON (Holy Trinity, St Andrew the Less and St Peter) *Bris 2* **P** *Simeon's Trustees* **V** B J DUCKETT, **NSM** I A BAILEY
CLIFTON (Mission Church) *see* Conisbrough *Sheff*
CLIFTON (St Anne) (St Thomas) *Man 2* **P** *Bp* **V** J R BAXENDALE, **OLM** M SOFIELD
CLIFTON (St Cuthbert) *see* Lowther and Askham and Clifton and Brougham *Carl*
CLIFTON (St James) *Sheff 6* **P** *Bp* **V** J H RICHARDSON
CLIFTON (St John the Evangelist) *see* Lund *Blackb*
CLIFTON (St John the Evangelist) *see* Brighouse and Clifton *Wakef*
CLIFTON (St Luke) *Carl 4* **P** *R Workington* **P-in-c** K KITCHIN
CLIFTON (St Paul) *see* Cotham St Sav w St Mary and Clifton St Paul *Bris*
CLIFTON (St Philip and St James) *York 7* **P** *Trustees* **V** D O CASSWELL, **C** R J FACER, R A HIRST
CLIFTON, NORTH (St George) *see* Harby w Thorney and N and S Clifton *S'well*
CLIFTON CAMPVILLE (St Andrew) w Edingale and Harlaston *Lich 4* **P** *Bp and Major F C Pipe-Wolferstan (jt)* **R** A L WHEALE, **Hon C** C M J IBALL
CLIFTON HAMPDEN (St Michael and All Angels) *see* Dorchester *Ox*
CLIFTON-ON-TEME (St Kenelm), Lower Sapey and the Shelsleys *Worc 3* **P** *Bp and A F Evans Esq (jt)* **R** *vacant* (01886) 812483
CLIFTON REYNES (St Mary the Virgin) *see* Lavendon w Cold Brayfield, Clifton Reynes etc *Ox*
CLIFTON UPON DUNSMORE (St Mary) and Newton *Cov 6* **P** *H A F W Boughton Leigh Esq* **P-in-c** P R GOULD
CLIFTONVILLE (St Paul) *Cant 9* **P** *Ch Patr Trust* **P-in-c** P L S ELLISDON
CLIPPESBY (St Peter) *see* Martham and Repps with Bastwick, Thurne etc *Nor*
CLIPSHAM (St Mary) *see* Greetham and Thistleton w Stretton and Clipsham *Pet*
CLIPSTON (All Saints) w Naseby and Haselbech w Kelmarsh *Pet 2* **P** *Ch Coll Cam, DBP, Mrs M F Harris, Exors Miss C V Lancaster (by turn)* **R** D W FAULKS
CLIPSTONE (All Saints) *S'well 2* **P** *Bp* **P-in-c** M J GARRATT
CLITHEROE (St James) *Blackb 7* **P** *Trustees* **R** M W L PICKETT
CLITHEROE (St Mary Magdalene) *Blackb 7* **P** *J R Peel Esq* **V** P H DEARDEN, **NSM** P W SHEPHERD
CLITHEROE (St Paul) Low Moor *Blackb 7* **P** *Bp* **V** R NICHOLSON
CLIVE (All Saints) *see* Astley, Clive, Grinshill and Hadnall *Lich*
CLIVE VALE (All Souls) *see* Hastings All So *Chich*
CLODOCK (St Clydog) and Longtown w Craswall, Llanveynoe, St Margaret's, Michaelchurch Escley and Newton *Heref 1* **P** *DBP (2 turns), MMCET (1 turn)* **V** F E RODGERS
CLOFORD (St Mary) *see* Nunney and Witham Friary, Marston Bigot etc *B & W*
CLOPHILL (St Mary the Virgin) *see* Campton, Clophill and Haynes *St Alb*
CLOPTON (St Mary) w Otley, Swilland and Ashbocking *St E 7* **P** *Ld Chan and Bp (alt)* **P-in-c** J N RAPLEY
CLOSWORTH (All Saints) *see* E Coker w Sutton Bingham and Closworth *B & W*
CLOTHALL (St Mary Virgin) *see* Sandon, Wallington and Rushden w Clothall *St Alb*
CLOUGHTON (St Mary) and Burniston w Ravenscar and Staintondale *York 15* **P** *Abp* **P-in-c** E KITCHING
CLOVELLY (All Saints) *see* Parkham, Alwington, Buckland Brewer etc *Ex*
CLOVELLY (St Peter) *as above*
CLOWNE (St John the Baptist) *Derby 3* **P** *Ld Chan* **R** *vacant* (01246) 810387
CLOWS TOP (Mission Room) *see* Mamble w Bayton, Rock w Heightington etc *Worc*
CLUBMOOR (St Andrew) *Liv 8* **P** *Bp* **V** S MCGANITY, **C** M A HINDLEY, **OLM** S J JAMIESON
CLUMBER PARK (St Mary the Virgin) *see* Worksop Priory *S'well*
CLUN (St George) w Bettws-y-Crwyn and Newcastle *Heref 10* **P** *Earl of Powis* **V** R T SHAW
CLUNBURY (St Swithin) *see* Clungunford w Clunbury and Clunton, Bedstone etc *Heref*
CLUNGUNFORD (St Cuthbert) w Clunbury and Clunton, Bedstone and Hopton Castle *Heref 10* **P** *Earl of Powis, Mrs S B Rocke, M S C Brown Esq, and Sir Hugh Ripley Bt (jt)* **R** S B BELL
CLUNTON (St Mary) *see* Clungunford w Clunbury and Clunton, Bedstone etc *Heref*
CLUTTON (St Augustine of Hippo) w Cameley *B & W 10* **P** *Earl of Warw (2 turns), Exors J P Hippisley Esq (1 turn)* **P-in-c** A D THORNE
CLYFFE PYPARD (St Peter) *see* Broad Town, Clyffe Pypard, Hilmarton etc *Sarum*
CLYMPING (St Mary the Virgin) and Yapton w Ford *Chich 1* **P** *Bp (2 turns), Ld Chan (1 turn)* **R** R H HAYES, **NSM** P WALLIS
CLYST HONITON (St Michael and All Angels) *see* Aylesbeare, Rockbeare, Farringdon etc *Ex*
CLYST HYDON (St Andrew) *see* Bradninch and Clyst Hydon *Ex*
CLYST ST GEORGE (St George) *see* Clyst St Mary, Clyst St George etc *Ex*
CLYST ST LAWRENCE (St Lawrence) *see* Whimple, Talaton and Clyst St Lawr *Ex*
CLYST ST MARY (St Mary), Clyst St George and Woodbury Salterton *Ex 1* **P** *Lord Wraxall, D&C, and S Radcliffe (jt)* **R** G L ROWE
COALBROOKDALE (Holy Trinity), Iron-Bridge and Little Wenlock *Heref 14* **P** *Bp, Lord Forester, V Madeley, and V Much Wenlock (jt)* **R** S H CARTER, **NSM** J M EDWARDS, P M JORDAN
COALEY (St Bartholomew) *see* Lower Cam w Coaley *Glouc*
COALPIT HEATH (St Saviour) *Bris 5* **P** *Bp* **V** C P LUNT
COALVILLE (Christ Church) and Bardon Hill *Leic 8* **P** *Simeon's Trustees and R Hugglescote (jt)* **V** T L RINGLAND
COATES (Holy Trinity) *see* Whittlesey, Pondersbridge and Coates *Ely*
COATES (St Edith) *see* Stow Gp *Linc*
COATES (St Matthew) *see* Kemble, Poole Keynes, Somerford Keynes etc *Glouc*
COATES, GREAT (St Nicholas) and LITTLE (Bishop Edward King Church) (St Michael) w Bradley *Linc 9* **P** *Patr Bd* **TR** P M MULLINS, **TV** J L VEREKER
COATES, NORTH (St Nicholas) *see* The North-Chapel Parishes *Linc*
COATHAM (Christ Church) and Dormanstown *York 16* **P** *Trustees* **V** B HARRISON
COBBOLD ROAD (St Saviour) (St Mary) *Lon 9* **P** *Bp* **V** D J WHEELER
COBERLEY (St Giles), Cowley, Colesbourne and Elkstone *Glouc 11* **P** *H W G Elwes Esq (2 turns), Ld Chan (1 turn), and W/Cdr H T Price (1 turn)* **R** *vacant* (01242) 870232

COBHAM Sole Street (St Mary's Church Room) *see* Cobham w Luddesdowne and Dode *Roch*
COBHAM (St Andrew) (St John the Divine) and Stoke D'Abernon *Guildf 10* **P** *D C H Combe Esq and K Coll Cam (jt)* **R** E R JENKINS, **C** S R MASON, **OLM** P G VICKERS
COBHAM (St Mary Magdalene) w Luddesdowne and Dode *Roch 1* **P** *Earl of Darnley and CPAS (alt)* **P-in-c** C D COLLINS, **NSM** A E BEETY
COBO (St Matthew) *see* Guernsey St Matt *Win*
COBRIDGE (Christ Church) *see* Hanley H Ev *Lich*
COCKAYNE HATLEY (St John the Baptist) *see* Potton w Sutton and Cockayne Hatley *St Alb*
COCKERHAM (St Michael) w Winmarleigh St Luke and Glasson Christ Church *Blackb 11* **P** *Bp (2 turns), Trustees (1 turn)* **V** M B ROBERTS
COCKERINGTON, SOUTH (St Leonard) *see* Mid Marsh Gp *Linc*
COCKERMOUTH (All Saints) (Christ Church) w Embleton and Wythop *Carl 6* **P** *Patr Bd* **TR** W E SANDERS, **TV** C GODDARD, **C** A N ROCKEY, **NSM** M GODDARD
COCKERNHOE (St Hugh) *see* Luton St Fran *St Alb*
COCKERTON (St Mary) *Dur 8* **P** *Bp* **V** R J WALLACE, **C** O L ERIKSSON
COCKFIELD (St Mary) *Dur 7* **P** *Bp* **P-in-c** F J GRIEVE
COCKFIELD (St Peter) *see* Bradfield St Clare, Bradfield St George etc *St E*
COCKFOSTERS (Christ Church) Trent Park *see* Enfield Ch Ch Trent Park *Lon*
COCKING (not known), Bepton and West Lavington *Chich 10* **P** *Ld Chan, and Bp, Rathbone Trust Co and Cowdray Trust (alt)* **P-in-c** C J BRADLEY
COCKINGTON (St George and St Mary) (St Matthew) *Ex 12* **P** *Bp* **V** A K F MACEY
COCKLEY CLEY (All Saints) w Gooderstone *Nor 13* **P** *Bp* **P-in-c** D J HANWELL
COCKSHUTT (St Simon and St Jude) *see* Petton w Cockshutt, Welshampton and Lyneal etc *Lich*
COCKYARD (Church Hall) *see* Chapel-en-le-Frith *Derby*
CODDENHAM (St Mary) w Gosbeck and Hemingstone w Henley *St E 1* **P** *Pemb Coll Cam (2 turns), Lord de Saumarez (1 turn)* **P-in-c** T P HALL, **OLM** H NORRIS
CODDINGTON (All Saints) *see* Colwall w Upper Colwall and Coddington *Heref*
CODDINGTON (All Saints) and Winthorpe and Langford w Holme *S'well 3* **P** *Keble Coll Ox and Bp (jt)* **R** *vacant* (01636) 704768
CODDINGTON (St Mary) *see* Farndon and Coddington *Ches*
CODFORD (St Mary) *see* Upper Wylye Valley *Sarum*
CODFORD (St Peter) *as above*
CODICOTE (St Giles) *St Alb 21* **P** *Abp* **V** L J BIGGS, **NSM** S V BECK
CODNOR (St James) *Derby 12* **P** *The Crown* **V** M M MOOKERJI, **P-in-c** D N GOUGH
CODSALL (St Nicholas) *Lich 2* **P** *Bp and Lady Wrottesley (jt)* **V** A P HARPER, **NSM** M A O FOX
CODSALL WOOD (St Peter) *see* Codsall *Lich*
COFFEEHALL (Community Church) *see* Woughton *Ox*
COFFINSWELL (St Bartholomew) *see* Kingskerswell w Coffinswell *Ex*
COFTON (St Mary) *see* Kenton, Mamhead, Powderham, Cofton and Starcross *Ex*
COFTON HACKETT (St Michael) w Barnt Green *Birm 4* **P** *Bp* **V** R S FIELDSON
COGENHOE (St Peter) and Great Houghton and Little Houghton w Brafield on the Green *Pet 7* **P** *C G V Davidge Esq, Mrs A C Usher, Magd Coll Ox, and DBP (jt)* **R** R B STAINER
COGGES (St Mary) and South Leigh *Ox 8* **P** *Bp and Payne Trustees (jt)* **V** A J SWEENEY, **C** J E HOWSON, P A JOYCE, M F KEEN, **NSM** T P EDGE
COGGESHALL (St Peter ad Vincula) w Markshall *Chelmsf 17* **P** *Bp (2 turns), SMF (1 turn)* **V** P C BANKS, **NSM** W J L HOWES
COGGESHALL, LITTLE (St Nicholas) *see* Coggeshall w Markshall *Chelmsf*
COKER, EAST (St Michael and All Angels) w Sutton Bingham and Closworth *B & W 7* **P** *D&C Ex* **P-in-c** R M BURT
COKER, WEST (St Martin of Tours) w Hardington Mandeville, East Chinnock and Pendomer *B & W 7* **P** *MMCET and Ox Chs Trust, and DBP (alt)* **R** R C P TERRELL
COLATON RALEIGH (St John the Baptist) *see* Ottery St Mary, Alfington, W Hill, Tipton etc *Ex*
COLBURN (St Cuthbert) *see* Hipswell *Ripon*
COLBURY (Christ Church) *Win 11* **P** *Mrs A V Barker-Mill* **P-in-c** T M JOHNS
COLBY (Belle Abbey Church) *see* Arbory *S & M*
COLBY (St Giles) *see* King's Beck *Nor*
COLCHESTER (Christ Church w St Mary at the Walls) *Chelmsf 16* **P** *Bp* **R** P R NORRINGTON
COLCHESTER (St Anne) *see* Greenstead w Colchester St Anne *Chelmsf*
COLCHESTER (St Barnabas) Old Heath *Chelmsf 16* **P** *Bp* **V** R E TILLBROOK
COLCHESTER (St James) *see* Colchester St Jas and St Paul w All SS etc *Chelmsf*
COLCHESTER (St James) and St Paul w All Saints, St Nicholas and St Runwald *Chelmsf 16* **P** *Bp* **R** P S WALKER, **C** T W J STATHER
COLCHESTER (St John the Evangelist) *Chelmsf 16* **P** *Adn Colchester* **V** R P FULLER, **C** P J COOK, **NSM** P H ADAMS
COLCHESTER (St Michael) Myland *Chelmsf 16* **P** *Ball Coll Ox* **R** G A CATCHPOLE, **C** R G GIBBS
COLCHESTER (St Peter) (St Botolph) *Chelmsf 16* **P** *Bp and Simeon's Trustees (jt)* **V** F J WOODS, **C** A FINCH
COLCHESTER (St Stephen) *see* Colchester, New Town and The Hythe *Chelmsf*
COLCHESTER, New Town and The Hythe (St Stephen, St Mary Magdalen and St Leonard) *Chelmsf 16* **P** *Ball Coll Ox (2 turns), Ld Chan (1 turn)* **R** I A HILTON, **NSM** S A LOXTON
COLD ASH (St Mark) *see* Hermitage *Ox*
COLD ASHBY (St Denys) *see* Guilsborough w Hollowell and Cold Ashby *Pet*
COLD ASHTON (Holy Trinity) *see* Marshfield w Cold Ashton and Tormarton etc *Bris*
COLD ASTON (St Andrew) *see* Northleach w Hampnett and Farmington etc *Glouc*
COLD BRAYFIELD (St Mary) *see* Lavendon w Cold Brayfield, Clifton Reynes etc *Ox*
COLD HIGHAM (St Luke) *see* Pattishall w Cold Higham and Gayton w Tiffield *Pet*
COLD KIRBY (St Michael) *see* Upper Ryedale *York*
COLD NORTON (St Stephen) *see* Purleigh, Cold Norton and Stow Maries *Chelmsf*
COLD OVERTON (St John the Baptist) *see* Whatborough Gp *Leic*
COLD SALPERTON (All Saints) *see* Sevenhampton w Charlton Abbots, Hawling etc *Glouc*
COLDEAN (St Mary Magdalene) *see* Moulsecoomb *Chich*
COLDEN (Holy Trinity) *Win 10* **P** *V Twyford* **V** A C MILLAR
COLDHAM (St Etheldreda) *see* Elm and Friday Bridge w Coldham *Ely*
COLDHARBOUR (Christ Church) *see* Abinger cum Coldharbour *Guildf*
COLDHARBOUR (St Alban Mission Church) *see* Mottingham St Andr *S'wark*
COLDHURST (Holy Trinity) *see* Oldham *Man*
COLDRED (St Pancras) *see* Eythorne and Elvington w Waldershare etc *Cant*
COLDRIDGE (St Matthew) *see* N Creedy *Ex*
COLDWALTHAM (St Giles) *see* Bury w Houghton and Coldwaltham and Hardham *Chich*
COLEBROOKE (St Andrew) *Ex 2* **P** *D&C* **V** *vacant*
COLEBY (All Saints) *see* Graffoe Gp *Linc*
COLEFORD (Holy Trinity) w Holcombe *B & W 12* **P** *Bp and V Kilmersdon (jt)* **P-in-c** V BONHAM
COLEFORD (St John the Evangelist) w Staunton *Glouc 4* **P** *Bp* **Hon C** P J COX, **NSM** A W WEARMOUTH
COLEGATE (St George) *see* Nor St Geo Colegate *Nor*
COLEHILL (St Michael and All Angels) *Sarum 9* **P** *Wimborne Minster Sch* **V** J W GOODALL
COLEMAN'S HATCH (Holy Trinity) *see* Hartfield w Coleman's Hatch *Chich*
COLEORTON (St Mary the Virgin) *see* Ashby-de-la-Zouch and Breedon on the Hill *Leic*
COLERNE (St John the Baptist) w North Wraxall *Bris 4* **P** *New Coll and Oriel Coll Ox (alt)* **NSM** G E WOODS
COLESBOURNE (St James) *see* Coberley, Cowley, Colesbourne and Elkstone *Glouc*
COLESHILL (All Saints) *see* Amersham *Ox*
COLESHILL (All Saints) *see* Gt Coxwell w Buscot, Coleshill etc *Ox*
COLESHILL (St Peter and St Paul) *Birm 9* **P** *J K Wingfield Digby Esq* **P-in-c** R N PARKER
COLEY Norwood Green (St George) *see* Coley *Wakef*
COLEY (St John the Baptist) *Wakef 2* **P** *V Halifax* **V** M K MADELEY, **Hon C** R C DOWSON
COLGATE (St Saviour) *see* Rusper w Colgate *Chich*
COLINDALE (St Matthias) *Lon 15* **P** *Bp* **V** M R POOLE
COLKIRK (St Mary) *see* Upper Wensum Village Gp *Nor*

COLLATON (St Mary the Virgin) *see* Stoke Gabriel and Collaton *Ex*
COLLIER ROW (Ascension) *see* Romford Ascension Collier Row *Chelmsf*
COLLIER ROW (Good Shepherd) *see* Romford Gd Shep Collier Row *Chelmsf*
COLLIER ROW (St James) and Havering-atte-Bower *Chelmsf 2* **P** *CPAS and Bp (jt)* **V** R J GARNETT
COLLIER STREET (St Margaret) *see* Yalding w Collier Street *Roch*
COLLIERLEY (St Thomas) w Annfield Plain *Dur 4* **P** *Bp and The Crown (alt)* **V** G H LAWES
COLLIERS END (St Mary) *see* High Cross *St Alb*
COLLIERS WOOD (Christ Church) *S'wark 14* **P** *Bp* **P-in-c** S A ROBERTS, **NSM** M J HANCOCK
COLLINGBOURNE DUCIS (St Andrew) *see* Savernake *Sarum*
COLLINGBOURNE KINGSTON (St Mary) *as above*
COLLINGHAM (All Saints) (St John the Baptist) w South Scarle and Besthorpe and Girton *S'well 3* **P** *Ld Chan and D&C Pet (alt)* **P-in-c** W D MILNER
COLLINGHAM (St Oswald) w Harewood *Ripon 1* **P** *Earl of Harewood and G H H Wheler Esq (jt)* **P-in-c** M PALLIS
COLLINGTON (St Mary) *see* Bredenbury w Grendon Bishop and Wacton etc *Heref*
COLLINGTREE (St Columba) w Courteenhall and Milton Malsor *Pet 7* **P** *Major Sir Hereward Wake Bt, G Phipps-Walker Esq, and Hyndman Trustees (by turn)* **P-in-c** T J JOHNSON, **C** C H FF NOBBS
COLLYHURST (The Saviour) *Man 5* **P** *Bp and Trustees (jt)* **OLM** M B ROGERS
COLLYWESTON (St Andrew) *see* Ketton, Collyweston, Easton-on-the-Hill etc *Pet*
COLMWORTH (St Denys) *see* Wilden w Colmworth and Ravensden *St Alb*
COLN ROGERS (St Andrew) *see* Chedworth, Yanworth and Stowell, Coln Rogers etc *Glouc*
COLN ST ALDWYNS (St John the Baptist), Hatherop, Quenington, Eastleach and Southrop *Glouc 12* **P** *Earl St Aldwyn, D&C, Wadh Coll Ox, and DBP (jt)* **V** A M ROSS, **NSM** C J FINLAY
COLN ST DENYS (St James the Great) *see* Chedworth, Yanworth and Stowell, Coln Rogers etc *Glouc*
COLNBROOK (St Thomas) *see* Riverside *Ox*
COLNE (Christ Church) (Holy Trinity) (St Bartholomew) and Villages *Blackb 6* **P** *Patr Bd* **TR** M L HARTLEY, **TV** A W RINDL, **C** M F SIBANDA, **NSM** K ALLEN, R L ALLEN
COLNE (St Helen) *see* Bluntisham cum Earith w Colne and Woodhurst *Ely*
COLNE, THE UPPER, Parishes of Great Yeldham, Little Yeldham, Stambourne, Tilbury-juxta-Clare and Toppesfield *Chelmsf 19* **P** *Prime Min, Ld Chan, Bp, Duchy of Lancaster, and Trustees of the late Miss W M N Brett (by turn)* **R** K G HOLLOWAY
COLNE ENGAINE (St Andrew) *see* Halstead Area *Chelmsf*
COLNEY (St Andrew) *see* Cringleford and Colney *Nor*
COLNEY (St Peter) *see* London Colney St Pet *St Alb*
COLNEY HEATH (St Mark) *St Alb 21* **P** *Trustees* **V** H J SPANNER
COLSTERWORTH Group, The (St John the Baptist) *Linc 14* **P** *Bp (2 turns), Mrs R S McCorquodale, The Revd J R H Thorold and J R Thorold Esq (1 turn)* **OLM** P C HOLLINGSHEAD
COLSTON BASSETT (St John the Divine) *see* Cropwell Bishop w Colston Bassett, Granby etc *S'well*
COLTISHALL (St John the Baptist) w Great Hautbois and Horstead *Nor 19* **P** *D&C and K Coll Cam (jt)* **R** *vacant* (01603) 737255
COLTON (Holy Trinity) *see* Egton-cum-Newland and Lowick and Colton *Carl*
COLTON (St Andrew) *see* Easton, Colton, Marlingford and Bawburgh *Nor*
COLTON (St Mary the Virgin) *see* Colton, Colwich and Gt Haywood *Lich*
COLTON (St Michael and All Angels), Colwich and Great Haywood *Lich 3* **P** *Bp and Earl of Lichfield's Trustees (jt)* **P-in-c** S C DAVIS, **C** J LEONARDI, G STATON, **NSM** M A DAVYS
COLTON (St Paul) *see* Bolton Percy *York*
COLWALL (St Crispin's Chapel) (St James the Great) w Upper Colwall (Good Shepherd) and Coddington *Heref 6* **P** *Bp* **R** C N H ATTWOOD, **NSM** A C LANYON-HOGG
COLWALL, UPPER (Good Shepherd) *see* Colwall w Upper Colwall and Coddington *Heref*
COLWICK (St John the Baptist) *S'well 10* **P** *DBP* **P-in-c** R B CHAPMAN
COLYFORD (St Michael) *see* Colyton, Musbury, Southleigh and Branscombe *Ex*
COLYTON (St Andrew), Musbury, Southleigh and Branscombe *Ex 5* **P** *D&C* **R** N J EDWARDS, **C** P A STAPLE
COMBE (St Swithin) *see* W Woodhay w Enborne, Hampstead Marshall etc *Ox*
COMBE DOWN (Holy Trinity) (St Andrew) w Monkton Combe and South Stoke *B & W 9* **P** *R Bath, Ox Chs Trust, and Comdr H R Salmer (jt)* **V** P J LANGHAM
COMBE FLOREY (St Peter and St Paul) *see* Lydeard St Lawrence w Brompton Ralph etc *B & W*
COMBE HAY (not known) *see* Bath Odd Down w Combe Hay *B & W*
COMBE LONGA (St Laurence) *see* Stonesfield w Combe Longa *Ox*
COMBE MARTIN (St Peter ad Vincula), Berrynarbor, Lynton, Brendon, Countisbury, Parracombe, Martinhoe and Trentishoe *Ex 18* **P** *Patr Bd* **TR** K G WYER, **TV** P A JARVIS
COMBE PYNE (St Mary the Virgin) *see* Axminster, Chardstock, All Saints etc *Ex*
COMBE RALEIGH (St Nicholas) *see* Honiton, Gittisham, Combe Raleigh, Monkton etc *Ex*
COMBE ST NICHOLAS (St Nicholas) w Wambrook *B & W 15* **P** *Bp and T V D Eames Esq (jt)* **V** P REGAN
COMBEINTEIGNHEAD (All Saints) *see* Shaldon, Stokeinteignhead, Combeinteignhead etc *Ex*
COMBERFORD (St Mary and St George) *see* Wigginton *Lich*
COMBERTON (St Mary) *Ely 1* **P** *Jes Coll Cam* **P-in-c** M P M BOOKER
COMBERTON, GREAT (St Michael) *see* Elmley Castle w Bricklehampton and Combertons *Worc*
COMBERTON, LITTLE (St Peter) *as above*
COMBROKE (St Mary and St Margaret) w Compton Verney *Cov 8* **P** *Bp* **V** C A HOST
COMBS (St Mary) and Little Finborough *St E 6* **P** *Bp and Pemb Coll Ox (jt)* **P-in-c** J C ROSS
COMBWICH (St Peter) *see* Cannington, Otterhampton, Combwich and Stockland *B & W*
COMER GARDENS (St David) *see* Worc St Clem and Lower Broadheath *Worc*
COMMONDALE (St Peter) *see* Danby *York*
COMPSTALL (St Paul) *see* Werneth *Ches*
COMPTON (All Saints) and Otterbourne *Win 7* **P** *Bp and Mrs P M A T Chamberlayne-Macdonald (jt)* **P-in-c** P D BAIRD
COMPTON (St Mary) *see* Farnham *Guildf*
COMPTON (St Mary and St Nicholas) *see* Hermitage *Ox*
COMPTON (St Mary), the Mardens, Stoughton and Racton *Chich 13* **P** *Bp Lon (1 turn), Bp (2 turns)* **P-in-c** A N STAMP
COMPTON (St Nicholas) w Shackleford and Peper Harow *Guildf 4* **P** *Bp and Major J R More-Molyneux (jt)* **R** J M FELLOWS, **NSM** J J SWANTON
COMPTON, LITTLE (St Denys) *see* Chipping Norton *Ox*
COMPTON, NETHER (St Nicholas) *see* Queen Thorne *Sarum*
COMPTON, OVER (St Michael) *as above*
COMPTON ABBAS (St Mary the Virgin) *see* Shaston *Sarum*
COMPTON ABDALE (St Oswald) *see* Northleach w Hampnett and Farmington etc *Glouc*
COMPTON BASSETT (St Swithin) *see* Oldbury *Sarum*
COMPTON BEAUCHAMP (St Swithun) *see* Shrivenham and Ashbury *Ox*
COMPTON BISHOP (St Andrew) *see* Crook Peak *B & W*
COMPTON CHAMBERLAYNE (St Michael) *see* Fovant, Sutton Mandeville and Teffont Evias etc *Sarum*
COMPTON DANDO (Blessed Virgin Mary) *see* Publow w Pensford, Compton Dando and Chelwood *B & W*
COMPTON DUNDON (St Andrew) *see* Somerton w Compton Dundon, the Charltons etc *B & W*
COMPTON GREENFIELD (All Saints) *see* Pilning w Compton Greenfield *Bris*
COMPTON MARTIN (St Michael) *see* Blagdon w Compton Martin and Ubley *B & W*
COMPTON PAUNCEFOOT (Blessed Virgin Mary) *see* Camelot Par *B & W*
COMPTON VALENCE (St Thomas à Beckett) *see* The Winterbournes and Compton Valence *Sarum*
CONDICOTE (St Nicholas) *see* Stow on the Wold, Condicote and The Swells *Glouc*
CONDOVER (St Andrew and St Mary) w Frodesley, Acton Burnell and Pitchford *Heref 11* **P** *Bp, Revd E W Serjeantson, and Mrs C R Colthurst (jt)* **R** J C W ROSE, **NSM** M G GILLIONS
CONEY HILL (St Oswald) *Glouc 5* **P** *The Crown* **V** L HOLLAND
CONEY WESTON (St Mary) *see* Stanton, Hopton, Market Weston, Barningham etc *St E*

CONEYSTHORPE (Chapel) *see* The Street Par *York*

CONGERSTONE (St Mary the Virgin) *see* Bosworth and Sheepy Gp *Leic*

CONGHAM (St Andrew) *see* Grimston, Congham and Roydon *Nor*

CONGLETON (St James) *Ches 11* **P** *Bp* **V** R N W ELBOURNE

CONGLETON (St John the Evangelist) (St Peter) (St Stephen) *Ches 11* **P** *Patr Bd* **TV** M L EAMAN

CONGRESBURY (St Andrew) w Puxton and Hewish St Ann *B & W 11* **P** *MMCET* **V** M J THOMSON, **C** V A COLE

CONINGSBY (St Michael) w Tattershall *Linc 11* **P** *DBP and Baroness Willoughby de Eresby (alt)* **R** J R MOORE, **OLM** M DONE

CONINGTON (St Mary) *see* Fen Drayton w Conington and Lolworth etc *Ely*

CONISBROUGH (St Peter) *Sheff 9* **P** *Bp* **V** A C GRIFFITHS

CONISCLIFFE (St Edwin) *Dur 8* **P** *Bp* **P-in-c** J R DOBSON

CONISHOLME (St Peter) *see* Somercotes and Grainthorpe w Conisholme *Linc*

CONISTON (St Andrew) *see* Church Coniston *Carl*

CONISTON COLD (St Peter) *see* Kirkby-in-Malhamdale w Coniston Cold *Bradf*

CONISTONE (St Mary) *see* Kettlewell w Conistone, Hubberholme etc *Bradf*

CONONLEY (St John the Evangelist) w Bradley *Bradf 8* **P** *Bp* **V** J C PEET

CONSETT (Christ Church) *Dur 4* **P** *Bp* **P-in-c** P SINCLAIR, **C** S BENNETT

CONSTABLE LEE (St Paul) *Man 15* **P** *CPAS* **P-in-c** G D PARKIN

CONSTANTINE (St Constantine) *Truro 4* **P** *D&C* **P-in-c** D J STEVENS

COOKBURY (St John the Baptist and the Seven Maccabees) *see* Black Torrington, Bradf w Cookbury etc *Ex*

COOKHAMS, The (Holy Trinity) (St John the Baptist) *Ox 13* **P** *Mrs E U Rogers* **V** M D SMITH, **C** R GREEN, **Hon C** A W WELLING, **OLM** T J ROBINSON

COOKHILL (St Paul) *see* Inkberrow w Cookhill and Kington w Dormston *Worc*

COOKLEY (St Michael and All Angels) *see* Heveningham *St E*

COOKLEY (St Peter) *see* Wolverley and Cookley *Worc*

COOKRIDGE (Holy Trinity) *Ripon 7* **P** *R Adel* **V** J F HAMILTON

COOMBE (Christ Church) *see* New Malden and Coombe *S'wark*

COOMBE BISSET (St Michael and All Angels) *see* Chalke Valley *Sarum*

COOMBES (not known) *see* Lancing w Coombes *Chich*

COOMBS WOOD (St Ambrose) *see* Blackheath *Birm*

COOPERSALE (St Alban) *see* Epping Distr *Chelmsf*

COPDOCK (St Peter) *see* Sproughton w Burstall, Copdock w Washbrook etc *St E*

COPFORD (St Michael and All Angels) w Easthorpe and Messing w Inworth *Chelmsf 24* **P** *Ld Chan, Duchy of Lanc, and DBP (by turn)* **R** C J GARLAND

COPGROVE (St Michael) *see* Walkingham Hill *Ripon*

COPLE (All Saints), Moggerhanger and Willington *St Alb 11* **P** *Bp (2 turns), Ch Ch Ox (1 turn)* **V** L KLIMAS

COPLESTON CENTRE *see* Peckham St Sav *S'wark*

COPLEY *Wakef 4* **P** *V Halifax* **V** *vacant* (01422) 652964

COPMANTHORPE (St Giles) *York 1* **P** *R Micklegate H Trin* **V** D S COOK

COPNOR (St Alban) *see* Portsea St Alb *Portsm*

COPNOR (St Cuthbert) *see* Portsea St Cuth *Portsm*

COPP (St Anne) w Inskip *Blackb 9* **P** *V Garstang St Helen and St Michaels-on-Wyre* **V** D GASKELL

COPPENHALL (All Saints and St Paul) *see* Crewe All SS and St Paul *Ches*

COPPENHALL (St Laurence) *see* Penkridge Team *Lich*

COPPENHALL (St Michael) *Ches 15* **P** *Bp* **R** C H RAZZALL

COPPULL (not known) *Blackb 4* **P** *R Standish* **V** J HUDSON

COPPULL (St John) *Blackb 4* **P** *R Standish* **P-in-c** A FISHWICK

COPSTON MAGNA (St John) *see* Wolvey w Burton Hastings, Copston Magna etc *Cov*

COPT OAK (St Peter) *see* Markfield, Thornton, Bagworth and Stanton etc *Leic*

COPTHORNE (St John the Evangelist) *Chich 7* **P** *Bp* **V** A M CUTTING, **NSM** P SMITH

COPYTHORNE (St Mary) *Win 11* **P** *Bp Liv* **P-in-c** N P JACOB

COQUETDALE, UPPER *Newc 9* **P** *Duchy of Lanc (2 turns), Ld Chan (1 turn), and Duke of Northumberland (1 turn)* **R** J R GLOVER, **NSM** P M LEAR

CORBRIDGE (St Andrew) w Halton and Newton Hall *Newc 3* **P** *D&C Carl* **V** M J MORPHY, **NSM** J KINNAIRD

CORBY (Epiphany) (St John the Baptist) *Pet 9* **P** *E Brudenell Esq* **P-in-c** M J ASQUITH

CORBY (St Columba and the Northern Saints) *Pet 9* **P** *Bp* **P-in-c** R J LEE

CORBY (St Peter and St Andrew) (Kingswood Church) *Pet 9* **P** *Bp* **V** M A CRAGGS

CORBY GLEN (St John the Evangelist) *Linc 14* **P** *Ld Chan (2 turns), Sir Simon Benton Jones Bt (1 turn)* **P-in-c** M A E BARTON

CORELEY (St Peter) and Doddington *Heref 12* **P** *DBP and Mrs R C Woodward (jt)* **R** *vacant* (01584) 890129

CORFE (St Nicholas) *see* Blackdown *B & W*

CORFE CASTLE (St Edward the Martyr), Church Knowle, Kimmeridge Steeple w Tyneham *Sarum 8* **P** *Major M J A Bond and Major J C Mansel (jt)* **P-in-c** I JACKSON

CORFE MULLEN (St Hubert) *Sarum 9* **P** *Bp* **R** P S WALKER, **NSM** J POTTS

CORHAMPTON (not known) *see* Meonstoke w Corhampton cum Exton *Portsm*

CORLEY (not known) *see* Fillongley and Corley *Cov*

CORNARD, GREAT (St Andrew) *St E 12* **P** *Bp* **OLM** L BANNISTER

CORNARD, LITTLE (All Saints) *see* Bures w Assington and Lt Cornard *St E*

CORNELLY (St Cornelius) *see* Tregony w St Cuby and Cornelly *Truro*

CORNEY (St John the Baptist) *see* Bootle, Corney, Whicham and Whitbeck *Carl*

CORNFORTH (Holy Trinity) *Dur 5* **P** *Bp* **P-in-c** K LUMSDON, **C** D GARRATT

CORNHILL (St Helen) w Carham *Newc 12* **P** *Abp (2 turns), E M Straker-Smith Esq (1 turn)* **P-in-c** M J GILLHAM, **Hon C** J W SHEWAN, **NSM** C MYLNE

CORNHOLME (St Michael and All Angels) and Walsden *Wakef 3* **P** *Bp and DBP (jt)* **OLM** I M GREENMAN

CORNISH HALL END (St John the Evangelist) *see* Finchingfield and Cornish Hall End etc *Chelmsf*

CORNWELL (St Peter) *see* Chipping Norton *Ox*

CORNWOOD (St Michael and All Angels) *Ex 21* **P** *Bp* **P-in-c** F G DENMAN

CORNWORTHY (St Peter) *see* Totnes w Bridgetown, Berry Pomeroy etc *Ex*

CORONATION SQUARE (St Aidan) *see* Cheltenham St Mark *Glouc*

CORRA (Holy Trinity) *see* Adderley, Ash, Calverhall, Ightfield etc *Lich*

CORRINGHAM (St John the Evangelist) (St Mary the Virgin) *Chelmsf 14* **P** *SMF* **P-in-c** D ROLLINS

CORRINGHAM (St Lawrence) and Blyton Group, The *Linc 2* **P** *Ld Chan (2 turns), Bp (1 turn), Meynell Ch Trustees (1 turn)* **V** *vacant* (01427) 628216

CORSCOMBE (St Mary the Virgin) *see* Melbury *Sarum*

CORSE (St Margaret) *see* Hartpury w Corse and Staunton *Glouc*

CORSENSIDE (All Saints) *see* N Tyne and Redesdale *Newc*

CORSENSIDE (St Cuthbert) *as above*

CORSHAM, GREATER (St Bartholomew) and Lacock *Bris 4* **P** *Patr Bd* **TR** R G CLIFTON, **TV** S A V WHEELER

CORSLEY (St Mary the Virgin) *see* Cley Hill Warminster *Sarum*

CORSLEY (St Mary the Virgin) *as above*

CORSTON (All Saints) *see* Saltford w Corston and Newton St Loe *B & W*

CORSTON (All Saints) *see* Gt Somerford, Lt Somerford, Seagry, Corston etc *Bris*

CORTON (St Bartholomew) *see* Hopton w Corton *Nor*

CORTON (St Bartholomew) *see* Abbotsbury, Portesham and Langton Herring *Sarum*

CORTON DENHAM (St Andrew) *see* Cam Vale *B & W*

CORYTON (St Andrew) *see* Milton Abbot, Dunterton, Lamerton etc *Ex*

COSBY (St Michael and All Angels) *Leic 10* **P** *Bp* **P-in-c** P J HARBORD, **NSM** P L BAILEY

COSELEY (Christ Church) (St Cuthbert) *Worc 10* **P** *Bp* **V** H M HUMPHREY, **C** S G AXTELL

COSELEY (St Chad) *Worc 10* **P** *Bp* **V** A HOWES

COSGROVE (St Peter and St Paul) *see* Potterspury w Furtho and Yardley Gobion etc *Pet*

COSHAM (St Philip) *Portsm 6* **P** *Bp* **V** *vacant* (023) 9232 6179

COSSALL (St Catherine) *see* Trowell, Awsworth and Cossall *S'well*

COSSINGTON (All Saints) *see* Sileby, Cossington and Seagrave *Leic*

COSSINGTON (Blessed Virgin Mary) *see* Woolavington w Cossington and Bawdrip *B & W*

COSTESSEY (St Edmund) *Nor 3* **P** *Gt Hosp Nor* **V** N J S PARRY
COSTESSEY, NEW (St Helen) *see* Costessey *Nor*
COSTOCK (St Giles) *see* E and W Leake, Stanford-on-Soar, Rempstone etc *S'well*
COSTON (St Andrew) *see* S Framland *Leic*
COTEBROOKE (St John and Holy Cross) *see* Tarporley *Ches*
COTEHELE HOUSE (Chapel) *see* Calstock *Truro*
COTEHILL (St John the Evangelist) *see* Scotby and Cotehill w Cumwhinton *Carl*
COTES HEATH (St James) *see* Broughton w Croxton and Cotes Heath w Standon *Lich*
COTESBACH (St Mary) *see* Lutterworth w Cotesbach and Bitteswell *Leic*
COTGRAVE (All Saints) *S'well 8* **P** *DBP* **R** P D S MASSEY
COTHAM (St Saviour w St Mary) and Clifton St Paul *Bris 3* **P** *Bp* **R** P J ROBERTS, **C** S J TAYLOR, **Hon C** B W SILVERMAN
COTHELSTONE (St Thomas of Canterbury) *see* Bishops Lydeard w Bagborough and Cothelstone *B & W*
COTHERIDGE (St Leonard) *see* Martley and Wichenford, Knightwick etc *Worc*
COTHERSTONE (St Cuthbert) *see* Romaldkirk w Laithkirk *Ripon*
COTLEIGH (St Michael and All Angels) *see* Offwell, Northleigh, Farway, Cotleigh etc *Ex*
COTMANHAY (Christ Church) *Derby 13* **P** *Bp* **V** P J DAVEY
COTON (St Peter) *Ely 1* **P** *St Cath Coll Cam* **P-in-c** C A COLLINS
COTON-IN-THE-ELMS (St Mary) *see* Seale and Lullington w Coton in the Elms *Derby*
COTTENHAM (All Saints) *Ely 5* **P** *Bp* **R** M J HORE, **NSM** D F SANDERS
COTTERED (St John the Baptist) w Broadfield and Throcking *St Alb 19* **P** *Bp* **R** *vacant* (01763) 281218
COTTERIDGE (St Agnes) *Birm 4* **P** *R Kings Norton* **V** M W BLOOD, **NSM** R R COLLINS
COTTERSTOCK (St Andrew) *see* Warmington, Tansor and Cotterstock etc *Pet*
COTTESBROOKE (All Saints) w Great Creaton and Thornby *Pet 2* **P** *Bp (2 turns), MacDonald-Buchanan Trustees (1 turn)* **P-in-c** B LEE, J M TARRANT
COTTESMORE (St Nicholas) and Barrow w Ashwell and Burley *Pet 14* **P** *E R Hanbury Esq, Viscount Downe, and DBP (by turn)* **C** L T FRANCIS-DEHQANI, M H W ROGERS
COTTIMORE (St John) *see* Walton-on-Thames *Guildf*
COTTINGHAM (St Mary) *York 14* **P** *Abp* **R** P A SMITH, **C** S Y AMOAKO-ADU
COTTINGHAM (St Mary Magdalene) *see* Gretton w Rockingham and Cottingham w E Carlton *Pet*
COTTINGLEY (St Michael and All Angels) *Bradf 1* **P** *Bp* **V** S J PINNINGTON
COTTINGWITH, EAST (St Mary) *see* Elvington w Sutton on Derwent and E Cottingwith *York*
COTTISFORD (St Mary the Virgin) *see* Shelswell *Ox*
COTTON (St Andrew) *see* Bacton w Wyverstone, Cotton and Old Newton etc *St E*
COTTON (St John the Baptist) *see* Alton w Bradley-le-Moors and Oakamoor w Cotton *Lich*
COTTON MILL (St Julian) *see* St Alb St Steph *St Alb*
COUGHTON (St Peter) *Cov 7* **P** *Bp* **V** *vacant*
COULSDON (St Andrew) *S'wark 24* **P** *Bp* **P-in-c** V L SIMS
COULSDON (St John) *S'wark 24* **P** *Abp* **R** P C ROBERTS, **C** S P STOCKS
COULSTON, EAST (St Thomas of Canterbury) *see* Bratton, Edington and Imber, Erlestoke etc *Sarum*
COUND (St Peter) *see* Wenlock *Heref*
COUNDON (St James) and Eldon *Dur 6* **P** *Bp and Prime Min (alt)* **P-in-c** G NICHOLSON
COUNTESS WEAR (St Luke) *Ex 3* **P** *V Topsham* **V** P J S CROCKETT
COUNTESTHORPE (St Andrew) w Foston *Leic 10* **P** *DBP and Bp (alt)* **V** A W JOHNSON, **C** A BRADFORD, **NSM** M D GILLESPIE
COUNTISBURY (St John the Evangelist) *see* Combe Martin, Berrynarbor, Lynton, Brendon etc *Ex*
COURTEENHALL (St Peter and St Paul) *see* Collingtree w Courteenhall and Milton Malsor *Pet*
COVE (St John the Baptist) (St Christopher) *Guildf 1* **P** *Bp* **TR** I M SCOTT-THOMPSON, **TV** J HILLMAN, S J STEWART, **OLM** G H THOMAS
COVEHITHE (St Andrew) *see* Sole Bay *St E*
COVEN (St Paul) *see* Bilbrook and Coven *Lich*
COVEN HEATH (Mission Church) *see* Bushbury *Lich*
COVENEY (St Peter ad Vincula) *Ely 12* **P** *Bp* **P-in-c** M T COOPER
COVENHAM (Annunciation of the Blessed Virgin Mary) *see* Fotherby *Linc*
COVENT GARDEN (St Paul) *Lon 3* **P** *Bp* **NSM** M A KENNY, M D E WROE
COVENTRY Caludon *Cov 1* **P** *Bp and Ld Chan (alt)* **TR** J M FRANCIS, **TV** C LUNGA, R W HARE, D T PETTIFOR, **NSM** P J H SMITH
COVENTRY Holbrooks (St Luke) *see* Holbrooks *Cov*
COVENTRY (Holy Trinity) *Cov 2* **P** *Ld Chan* **V** G K SINCLAIR, **C** H E A JOHNSTON, **NSM** A M IRVINE
COVENTRY (St Francis of Assisi) North Radford *Cov 2* **P** *Bp* **V** T C BROOKE
COVENTRY (St George) *Cov 2* **P** *Bp* **V** L N JANICKER
COVENTRY (St John the Baptist) *Cov 2* **P** *Trustees* **R** P N SUCH
COVENTRY (St Mary Magdalen) *Cov 3* **P** *Bp* **V** C H KNOWLES
COVENTRY (St Nicholas) *see* Radford *Cov*
COVENTRY EAST (St Anne and All Saints) (St Margaret) (St Peter) *Cov 1* **P** *Patr Bd* **TR** C M GREGORY, **TV** L D JOHNSON, L A HUMPHREYS, **C** N TIPPLE, P F HARTOPP
COVERACK (St Peter) *see* St Keverne *Truro*
COVERDALE (St Botolph) *see* Middleham w Coverdale and E Witton etc *Ripon*
COVINGHAM (St Paul) *see* Swindon Dorcan *Bris*
COVINGTON (All Saints) *Ely 8* **P** *Sir Stephen Hastings* **P-in-c** S P MEWS, **NSM** J RAWLINSON
COWARNE, LITTLE (not known) *see* Bredenbury w Grendon Bishop and Wacton etc *Heref*
COWARNE, MUCH (St Mary the Virgin) *see* Stoke Lacy, Moreton Jeffries w Much Cowarne etc *Heref*
COWBIT (St Mary) *Linc 17* **P** *Ld Chan and DBP (alt)* **V** P W J WINN
COWCLIFFE (St Hilda) *see* N Huddersfield *Wakef*
COWDEN (St Mary Magdalene) w Hammerwood *Chich 7* **P** *Ch Soc Trust* **R** *vacant* (01342) 850221
COWES (Holy Trinity) (St Mary the Virgin) *Portsm 8* **P** *Trustees and V Carisbrooke St Mary (jt)* **V** R J EMBLIN, **NSM** K H G MORRIS
COWES (St Faith) *Portsm 8* **P** *Bp* **C** A-L ALDER, **NSM** R S NETHERWAY
COWES, EAST (St James) *see* Whippingham w E Cowes *Portsm*
COWESBY (St Michael) *York 19* **P** *Abp* **P-in-c** P R A R HOARE, **NSM** E A HOARE
COWFOLD (St Peter) *Chich 9* **P** *Bp Lon* **V** G L DRIVER
COWGATE (St Peter) *Newc 7* **P** *Bp* **V** J BEBBINGTON
COWGILL (St John the Evangelist) *see* Dent w Cowgill *Bradf*
COWICK (Holy Trinity) *see* Gt Snaith *Sheff*
COWLAM (St Mary) *see* Waggoners *York*
COWLEIGH (St Peter) *see* Malvern Link w Cowleigh *Worc*
COWLEY (St James) (St Francis) *Ox 4* **P** *Patr Bd* **TR** S W M HARTLEY, **NSM** E M SPENCE
COWLEY (St John) (St Alban) (St Bartholomew) (St Mary and St John) *Ox 4* **P** *St Steph Ho Ox* **V** A J A ROMANIS, **C** J J HERAPATH, **NSM** K H LAMDIN, M E A MCALISTER, L R DENNY
COWLEY (St Laurence) *Lon 24* **P** *Bp* **R** S M HARDWICKE
COWLEY (St Mary) *see* Coberley, Cowley, Colesbourne and Elkstone *Glouc*
COWLEY CHAPEL (St Antony) *see* Thorverton, Cadbury, Upton Pyne etc *Ex*
COWLING (Holy Trinity) *Bradf 8* **P** *Bp* **P-in-c** J R PRICE
COWLINGE (St Margaret) *see* Bansfield *St E*
COWPEN (St Benedict) *see* Horton *Newc*
COWPLAIN (St Wilfrid) *Portsm 5* **P** *Bp* **V** P H MOORE, **C** R E N WILLIAMS, **NSM** D M YOUELL
COWTON, EAST (All Saints) *see* E Richmond *Ripon*
COWTON, SOUTH (St Luke's Pastoral Centre) *as above*
COX GREEN (Good Shepherd) *Ox 13* **P** *Bp* **P-in-c** J R HICKS
COXFORD Group, The *see* E w W Rudham, Helhoughton etc *Nor*
COXHEATH (Holy Trinity), East Farleigh, Hunton, Linton and West Farleigh *Roch 7* **P** *Ld Chan (1 turn), Abp, Lord Cornwallis, and D&C (1 turn)* **C** R A BIERBAUM, **NSM** D W JONES
COXHOE (St Mary) *see* Kelloe and Coxhoe *Dur*
COXLEY (Christ Church) w Godney, Henton and Wookey *B & W 8* **P** *Bp* **P-in-c** A SYER
COXWELL, GREAT (St Giles) w Buscot, Coleshill and Eaton Hastings *Ox 17* **P** *Bp and Lord Faringdon (jt)* **P-in-c** J H NODDINGS, **NSM** C E CROISDALE-APPLEBY
COXWELL, LITTLE (St Mary) *see* Gt Faringdon w Lt Coxwell *Ox*
COXWOLD (St Michael) and Husthwaite *York 3* **P** *Abp* **P-in-c** I B KITCHEN, **NSM** N L CHAPMAN

CRABBS CROSS (St Peter) *see* Redditch Ch the K *Worc*
CRADLEY (St James) w Mathon and Storridge *Heref 6* **P** *Bp and D&C Westmr (jt)* **R** S R ASHTON, **NSM** M D VOCKINS
CRADLEY (St Katherine's Mission Church) *see* Halas *Worc*
CRADLEY (St Peter) *as above*
CRADLEY HEATH (St Luke) *see* Reddal Hill St Luke *Worc*
CRAGG VALE (St John the Baptist in the Wilderness) *see* Erringden *Wakef*
CRAKEHALL (St Gregory) *Ripon 4* **P** *Sir Henry Beresford-Peirse Bt* **V** D J CHRISTIE
CRAMBE (St Michael) *see* Whitwell w Crambe, Flaxton and Foston *York*
CRAMLINGTON (St Nicholas) *Newc 1* **P** *Bp* **TR** J A MACNAUGHTON, **TV** R G BATEMAN, H L SAVAGE, **OLM** S M WARD
CRAMPMOOR (St Swithun) *see* Romsey *Win*
CRANBORNE (St Mary and St Bartholomew) w Boveridge, Edmondsham, Wimborne St Giles and Woodlands *Sarum 9* **P** *Viscount Cranborne, Earl of Shaftesbury, and Mrs J E Smith (jt)* **R** D J PASKINS
CRANBOURNE (St Peter) *see* Winkfield and Cranbourne *Ox*
CRANBROOK (St Dunstan) *Cant 11* **P** *Abp* **V** M J BURRELL, **NSM** S M COX
CRANFIELD (St Peter and St Paul) and Hulcote w Salford *St Alb 13* **P** *MMCET* **R** H K SYMES-THOMPSON
CRANFORD (Holy Angels) (St Dunstan) *Lon 11* **P** *R J G Berkeley Esq and Sir Hugo Huntington-Whiteley Bt (jt)* **R** L T IRVINE-CAPEL
CRANFORD (St John the Baptist) w Grafton Underwood and Twywell *Pet 11* **P** *Boughton Estates, DBP, and Sir John Robinson Bt (by turn)* **R** D H P FOOT
CRANHAM (All Saints) *Chelmsf 2* **P** *St Jo Coll Ox* **NSM** G K ARBER
CRANHAM (St James the Great) *see* Painswick, Sheepscombe, Cranham, The Edge etc *Glouc*
CRANHAM PARK Moor Lane (not known) *see* Cranham Park *Chelmsf*
CRANHAM PARK (St Luke) *Chelmsf 2* **P** *Bp* **V** J F DUNNETT, **C** L C J DUCKETT, A C WARD
CRANLEIGH (St Nicolas) *Guildf 2* **P** *Bp* **R** N P NICHOLSON, **C** J M BRIDGES
CRANMER Group *see* Whatton w Aslockton, Hawksworth, Scarrington etc *S'well*
CRANMORE, WEST (St Bartholomew) *see* Shepton Mallet w Doulting *B & W*
CRANOE (St Michael) *see* Gt Bowden w Welham, Glooston and Cranoe etc *Leic*
CRANSFORD (St Peter) *see* Badingham w Bruisyard, Cransford etc *St E*
CRANSLEY (St Andrew) *see* Broughton w Loddington and Cransley etc *Pet*
CRANTOCK (St Carantoc) *Truro 7* **P** *SMF* **P-in-c** M WILLS
CRANWELL (St Andrew) *Linc 22* **P** *DBP* **P-in-c** A J LITTLEWOOD
CRANWICH (St Mary) *Nor 13* **P** *CPAS* **P-in-c** P M FARROW
CRANWORTH (St Mary the Virgin) *see* Barnham Broom and Upper Yare *Nor*
CRASSWALL (St Mary) *see* Clodock and Longtown w Craswall, Llanveynoe etc *Heref*
CRASTER (Mission Church) *see* Embleton w Rennington and Rock *Newc*
CRATFIELD (St Mary) *see* Laxfield, Cratfield, Wilby and Brundish *St E*
CRATHORNE (All Saints) *York 21* **P** *Lord Crathorne, Hon David Dugdale, and J Southern Esq (jt)* **P-in-c** P KITCHING
CRAWCROOK (Church of the Holy Spirit) *see* Greenside *Dur*
CRAWFORD (District Church) *see* Upholland *Liv*
CRAWLEY (St John the Baptist) *Chich 7* **P** *Bp* **TR** M D LILES, **TV** F J M POLE, L M HELLMUTH, **C** J M BALDWIN, **NSM** C D WATKINS
CRAWLEY (St Mary) and Littleton and Sparsholt w Lainston *Win 7* **P** *Ld Chan and DBP (alt)* **R** J MONTAGUE, **C** S DAVIES
CRAWLEY, NORTH (St Firmin) *see* Sherington w Chicheley, N Crawley, Astwood etc *Ox*
CRAWLEY DOWN (All Saints) *Chich 7* **P** *R Worth* **V** A J HALE
CRAWSHAWBOOTH (St John) *see* Goodshaw and Crawshawbooth *Man*
CRAY (St Barnabas) *see* St Paul's Cray St Barn *Roch*
CRAY (St Mary and St Paulinus) *see* St Mary Cray and St Paul's Cray *Roch*
CRAY, NORTH (St James) *see* Footscray w N Cray *Roch*
CRAYFORD (St Paulinus) *Roch 15* **P** *Bp* **R** A K LANE, **C** J A EVANS
CRAYKE (St Cuthbert) w Brandsby and Yearsley *York 3* **P** *The Crown and Abp (alt)* **P-in-c** I B KITCHEN
CRAZIES HILL (Mission Room) *see* Wargrave w Knowl Hill *Ox*
CREAKE, NORTH (St Mary) and SOUTH (St Mary) w Waterden, Syderstone w Barmer and Sculthorpe *Nor 15* **P** *Bp, Earl Spencer, Earl of Leicester, Guild of All So, J Labouchere Esq, Mrs M E Russell, and DBP (jt)* **R** A M THOMSON
CREATON, GREAT (St Michael and All Angels) *see* Cottesbrooke w Gt Creaton and Thornby *Pet*
CREDENHILL (St Mary) Brinsop and Wormsley, Mansel Lacy and Yazor, Kenchester, Bridge Sollers and Bishopstone *Heref 4* **P** *R M Ecroyd Esq, Major D J C Davenport and Bp (3 turns), Ld Chan (1 turn)* **P-in-c** A C E KNIGHT, **NSM** A C DEANE
CREDITON (Holy Cross) (St Lawrence) Shobrooke and Sandford w Upton Hellions *Ex 2* **P** *12 Govs of Crediton Ch* **R** N GUTHRIE, **C** K M ROBERTS, W P JACKSON
CREECH ST MICHAEL (St Michael) *B & W 18* **P** *MMCET* **V** D G MANNING
CREED (St Crida) *see* Probus, Ladock and Grampound w Creed and St Erme *Truro*
CREEDY, NORTH: Cheriton Fitzpaine, Woolfardisworthy, Kennerley, Washford Pyne, Puddington, Poughill, Stockleigh English, Morchard Bishop, Stockleigh Pomeroy, Down St Mary, Clannaborough, Lapford, Nymet Rowland, and Coldridge *Ex 2* **P** *Ld Chan (1 turn), Patr Bd (5 turns)* **TV** S G C SMITH, M A HALL, **NSM** J E LUCAS
CREEKMOOR (Christ Church) *see* Oakdale *Sarum*
CREEKSEA (All Saints) w Althorne and Latchingdon w North Fambridge *Chelmsf 11* **P** *Bp, Abp and Ld Chan (by turn)* **V** S A ROBERTSON, **NSM** V M WADMAN
CREETING (St Peter) *see* Creeting St Mary, Creeting St Peter etc *St E*
CREETING ST MARY (St Mary), Creeting St Peter and Earl Stonham w Stonham Parva *St E 1* **P** *DBP (2 turns), Pemb Coll Cam (1 turn)* **P-in-c** C M EVERETT, **NSM** M G WAINWRIGHT
CREETON (St Peter) *see* Castle Bytham w Creeton *Linc*
CREGNEISH (St Peter) *see* Rushen *S & M*
CRESSAGE (Christ Church) *see* Wenlock *Heref*
CRESSBROOK (St John the Evangelist) *see* Tideswell *Derby*
CRESSING (All Saints) w Stisted and Bradwell-juxt-Coggeshall and Pattiswick *Chelmsf 15* **P** *Bp, Exors Mrs D E G Keen, and Abp (by turn)* **R** J R CORBYN
CRESSINGHAM, GREAT (St Michael) and LITTLE (St Andrew), w Threxton *Nor 13* **P** *Bp and Sec of State for Defence* **C** D J HANWELL
CRESSWELL (St Bartholomew) and Lynemouth *Newc 11* **P** *Bp* **P-in-c** A E SIMPSON
CRESWELL (St Mary Magdalene) *see* Elmton *Derby*
CRETINGHAM (St Peter) *see* Earl Soham w Cretingham and Ashfield *St E*
CREWE (All Saints and St Paul) *Ches 15* **P** *Bp* **V** M SAVILLE
CREWE (Christ Church) (St Peter) *Ches 15* **P** *Bp* **V** W C W FOSS
CREWE (St Andrew w St John the Baptist) *Ches 15* **P** *Bp* **V** W J BAKER
CREWE (St Barnabas) *Ches 15* **P** *Bp* **V** R D POWELL
CREWE GREEN (St Michael and All Angels) *see* Haslington w Crewe Green *Ches*
CREWKERNE (St Bartholomew) w Wayford *B & W 15* **P** *Ld Chan* **R** M C GALLAGHER, **C** A G ELLACOTT, **NSM** M E GOODLAND
CREWTON (St Peter) *see* Boulton *Derby*
CRICH (St Mary) and South Wingfield *Derby 1* **P** *Ch Trust Fund Trust and Duke of Devonshire (jt)* **V** P D BROOKS, **C** T A DAVIS, A J HORLOCK, **NSM** J W GRAY
CRICK (St Margaret) and Yelvertoft w Clay Coton and Lilbourne *Pet 2* **P** *MMCET and St Jo Coll Ox (jt)* **P-in-c** D M LAKE
CRICKET MALHERBIE (St Mary Magdalene) *see* Chard and Distr *B & W*
CRICKET ST THOMAS (St Thomas) *as above*
CRICKLADE (St Sampson) w Latton *Bris 6* **P** *D&C, Bp, and Hon P N Eliot (by turn)* **P-in-c** J A S ASHBY
CRICKLEWOOD (St Gabriel) and St Michael *Lon 21* **P** *Bp* **V** J E MORRIS, **C** J M ITUMU
CRICKLEWOOD (St Peter) *Lon 15* **P** *Bp* **V** P D RABIN
CRIFTINS (St Matthew) w Dudleston and Welsh Frankton *Lich 17* **P** *Bp and V Ellesmere (jt)* **P-in-c** A C NETHERWOOD
CRIMPLESHAM (St Mary) *see* Downham Market and Crimplesham w Stradsett *Ely*
CRINGLEFORD (St Peter) and Colney *Nor 7* **P** *Exors E H Barclay Esq and Gt Hosp Nor (alt)* **R** A J BRADDOCK, **NSM** G R EVEREST

CROCKENHILL (All Souls) *Roch 2* **P** *Bp* **P-in-c** C CROOK

CROCKERNWELL (Holy Trinity) *see* Tedburn St Mary, Whitestone, Oldridge etc *Ex*

CROCKHAM HILL (Holy Trinity) *Roch 11* **P** *J St A Warde Esq* **P-in-c** S A J MITCHELL, **C** R JONES

CROFT (All Saints) *see* The Wainfleet Gp *Linc*

CROFT (Christ Church) *see* Newchurch w Croft *Liv*

CROFT (St Michael and All Angels) *see* Leominster *Heref*

CROFT (St Michael and All Angels) *see* Broughton Astley and Croft w Stoney Stanton *Leic*

CROFT (St Peter) *see* E Richmond *Ripon*

CROFTON (All Saints) *Wakef 9* **P** *Duchy of Lanc* **P-in-c** L J COLLYER, **NSM** H WALKER, **OLM** A JORDAN

CROFTON (Holy Rood) (St Edmund) *Portsm 2* **P** *Bp* **V** S P GIRLING, **C** D MEDWAY, **NSM** C R PRESTIDGE

CROFTON (St Paul) *Roch 16* **P** *V Orpington* **V** B A ABAYOMI-COLE

CROFTON PARK (St Hilda w St Cyprian) *S'wark 5* **P** *V Lewisham St Mary* **V** S G BATES

CROGLIN (St John the Baptist) *Carl 2* **P** *D&C* **P-in-c** C A RANDALL, **C** K S CAPELIN-JONES

CROMER (St Peter and St Paul) *Nor 21* **P** *CPAS* **V** D E COURT, **C** J R PORTER

CROMFORD (St Mary) *see* Matlock Bath and Cromford *Derby*

CROMHALL (St Andrew), Tortworth, Tytherington, Falfield and Rockhampton *Glouc 7* **P** *Bp, R Thornbury and Oldbury etc, Adn, and J Leigh Esq (1 turn), Earl of Ducie, Oriel Coll Ox, and MMCET (1 turn)* **R** P M LYES-WILSDON, **Hon C** R D WALKER

CROMPTON, EAST (St James) *Man 22* **P** *Bp* **C** M D CARLISLE

CROMPTON, HIGH (St Mary) *Man 22* **P** *Bp* **P-in-c** A BUTLER

CROMPTON FOLD (St Saviour) *see* E Crompton *Man*

CROMWELL (St Giles) *see* Norwell w Ossington, Cromwell and Caunton *S'well*

CRONDALL (All Saints) and Ewshot *Guildf 3* **P** *Bp* **V** P M RICH, **NSM** B D BURBIDGE

CROOK (St Catherine) *Carl 10* **P** *CPAS* **V** *vacant*

CROOK (St Catherine) *Dur 9* **P** *R Brancepeth* **R** *vacant* (01388) 764024

CROOK PEAK *B & W 1* **P** *Ld Chan, Bp, Bp Lon, and R M Dod Esq (by turn)* **P-in-c** K R BROWN

CROOKES (St Thomas) *Sheff 4* **P** *Patr Bd* **TR** M WOODHEAD, **TV** A F MACLAURIN, **NSM** R J G HOPKINS

CROOKES (St Timothy) *Sheff 4* **P** *Sheff Ch Burgesses* **V** P R TOWNSEND

CROOKHAM (Christ Church) *Guildf 1* **P** *V Crondall and Ewshot* **V** M S NICHOLLS

CROOKHORN (Good Shepherd) *Portsm 5* **P** *Simeon's Trustees* **V** A M RIMMER

CROPREDY (St Mary the Virgin) *see* Shires' Edge *Ox*

CROPTHORNE (St Michael) *see* Fladbury w Wyre Piddle and Moor etc *Worc*

CROPTON (St Gregory) *see* Lastingham w Appleton-le-Moors, Rosedale etc *York*

CROPWELL BISHOP (St Giles) w Colston Bassett, Granby w Elton, Langar cum Barnstone and Tythby w Cropwell Butler *S'well 8* **P** *CPAS and Bp, Ld Chan (alt)* **C** C T DOLBY

CROSBY (St George) (St Michael) *Linc 4* **P** *Sir Reginald Sheffield Bt* **V** J W THACKER

CROSBY, GREAT (All Saints) *Liv 5* **P** *R Sefton, Bp, V St Luke, and CPAS (jt)* **P-in-c** M C FREEMAN

CROSBY, GREAT (St Faith) and Waterloo Park St Mary the Virgin *Liv 1* **P** *St Chad's Coll Dur and Trustees (jt)* **V** N G KELLEY, **Hon C** D A SMITH, **NSM** M WATERS

CROSBY, GREAT (St Luke) *Liv 5* **P** *R Sefton* **P-in-c** P H SPIERS, **OLM** B A CHAMBERS

CROSBY GARRETT (St Andrew) *see* Kirkby Stephen w Mallerstang etc *Carl*

CROSBY-ON-EDEN (St John the Evangelist) *see* Eden, Gelt and Irthing *Carl*

CROSBY RAVENSWORTH (St Lawrence) *Carl 1* **P** *DBP* **P-in-c** S D RUDKIN

CROSCOMBE (Blessed Virgin Mary) *see* Pilton w Croscombe, N Wootton and Dinder *B & W*

CROSLAND, SOUTH (Holy Trinity) *see* Em TM *Wakef*

CROSLAND MOOR (St Barnabas) *Wakef 5* **P** *Bp* **V** M STOREY

CROSS CANONBY (St John the Evangelist) *see* Allonby, Cross Canonby and Dearham *Carl*

CROSS FELL Group, The *Carl 4* **P** *D&C (2 turns) and DBP (1 turn)* **V** R A MOATT, **OLM** E M FROGGATT

CROSS GREEN (St Hilda) *see* Hunslet w Cross Green *Ripon*

CROSS GREEN (St Saviour) *see* Leeds Richmond Hill *Ripon*

CROSS HEATH (St Michael and All Angels) *Lich 9* **P** *Bp* **P-in-c** N B JAMIESON-HARVEY

CROSS IN HAND (St Bartholomew) *see* Waldron *Chich*

CROSS ROADS cum Lees (St James) *Bradf 8* **P** *Bp* **P-in-c** E M CANNON

CROSS STONE (St Paul) *see* Todmorden *Wakef*

CROSS TOWN (St Cross) *see* Knutsford St Cross *Ches*

CROSSCRAKE (St Thomas) *Carl 10* **P** *V Heversham and Milnthorpe* **P-in-c** N L DAVIES, **NSM** T G WILCOCK

CROSSENS (St John) *see* N Meols *Liv*

CROSSFLATTS (St Aidan) *see* Bingley All SS *Bradf*

CROSSLACON Team Ministry *Carl 5* **P** *Patr Bd* **TR** W A MCCAFFERTY, **TV** A M GRANGE

CROSSPOOL (St Columba) *Sheff 4* **P** *Bp* **V** E HOPE, **NSM** L A FURBEY

CROSTHWAITE (St Kentigern) Keswick *Carl 6* **P** *Bp* **V** A S E PENNY

CROSTHWAITE (St Mary) Kendal *Carl 10* **P** *DBP* **V** *vacant* (01539) 568276

CROSTON (St Michael and All Angels) and Bretherton *Blackb 4* **P** *M G Rawstorne Esq* **R** R J BRUNSWICK, **NSM** A J M WATKINSON

CROSTWICK (St Peter) *see* Spixworth w Crostwick and Frettenham *Nor*

CROSTWIGHT (All Saints) *see* Smallburgh w Dilham w Honing and Crostwight *Nor*

CROUCH END HILL (Christ Church) *see* Hornsey Ch Ch *Lon*

CROUGHTON (All Saints) *see* Aynho and Croughton w Evenley etc *Pet*

CROWAN (St Crewenna) and Treslothan *Truro 2* **P** *D L C Roberts Esq and Mrs W A Pendarves (jt)* **V** P DOUGLASS, **C** M L PASCOE

CROWBOROUGH (All Saints) *Chich 19* **P** *Ld Chan* **V** A C J CORNES, **C** J P FRITH, **NSM** J A HOBBS

CROWBOROUGH (St John the Evangelist) *Chich 19* **P** *Guild of All So* **P-in-c** P A NAYLOR

CROWCOMBE (Holy Ghost) *see* Quantock Towers *B & W*

CROWELL (Nativity of the Blessed Virgin Mary) *see* Chinnor, Sydenham, Aston Rowant and Crowell *Ox*

CROWFIELD (All Saints) w Stonham Aspal and Mickfield *St E 1* **P** *DBP, Bp, and Lord de Saumarez (alt)* **P-in-c** T P HALL, **OLM** H NORRIS

CROWHURST (St George) *see* Catsfield and Crowhurst *Chich*

CROWHURST (St George) *see* Lingfield and Crowhurst *S'wark*

CROWLAND (St Mary and St Bartholomew and St Guthlac) *Linc 17* **P** *Earl of Normanton* **R** *vacant* (01733) 210499

CROWLE Group, The (St Oswald) *Linc 1* **P** *Bp (2 turns), Prime Min (1 turn)* **V** D SCHOFIELD

CROWLE (St John the Baptist) *see* Bowbrook S *Worc*

CROWMARSH GIFFORD (St Mary Magdalene) *see* Wallingford *Ox*

CROWN EAST AND RUSHWICK (St Thomas) *see* Worc Dines Green St Mich and Crown E, Rushwick *Worc*

CROWNHILL (Ascension) *see* Plymouth Crownhill Ascension *Ex*

CROWTHORNE (St John the Baptist) *Ox 16* **P** *Bp* **V** *vacant* (01344) 772413

CROWTON (Christ Church) *see* Norley, Crowton and Kingsley *Ches*

CROXALL-CUM-OAKLEY (St John the Baptist) *see* Walton-on-Trent w Croxall, Rosliston etc *Derby*

CROXBY (All Saints) *see* Swallow *Linc*

CROXDALE (St Bartholomew) and Tudhoe *Dur 6* **P** *D&C* **P-in-c** M J WRAY

CROXDEN (St Giles) *see* Rocester and Croxden w Hollington *Lich*

CROXLEY GREEN (All Saints) *St Alb 5* **P** *V Rickmansworth* **V** L G-H LEE

CROXLEY GREEN (St Oswald) *St Alb 5* **P** *Bp* **V** A C WALTON, **NSM** C M CLARK

CROXTETH (St Paul) *Liv 8* **P** *R W Derby and Bp (jt)* **V** I G BROOKS

CROXTETH PARK (St Cuthbert) *Liv 8* **P** *Bp* **V** D R LESLIE

CROXTON (All Saints) *see* Thetford *Nor*

CROXTON Group, The SOUTH (St John the Baptist) *Leic 3* **P** *DBP, Ch Soc Trust, and MMCET (jt)* **R** D A G G DOLMAN

CROXTON (St James) *see* Papworth *Ely*

CROXTON (St John the Evangelist) *Linc 6* **P** *Ld Chan* **R** *vacant*

CROXTON (St Paul) *see* Broughton w Croxton and Cotes Heath w Standon *Lich*

CROXTON KERRIAL (St Botolph and St John the Baptist) *see* High Framland Par *Leic*

CROYDE (St Mary Magdalene) *see* Georgeham *Ex*
CROYDON (All Saints) *see* Orwell Gp *Ely*
CROYDON (Christ Church) Broad Green *S'wark 23* **P** *Simeon's Trustees* **V** W MUNCEY, **OLM** J K EYNON, K H VEEN
CROYDON (Holy Saviour) *S'wark 25* **P** *Bp* **V** X SOOSAINAYAGAM, **NSM** P L GIBBS
CROYDON (St Andrew) *S'wark 23* **P** *Trustees* **P-in-c** K L W SYLVIA
CROYDON (St Augustine) *S'wark 23* **P** *Bp* **P-in-c** S J KNOWERS, **NSM** S C RAYNER
CROYDON (St John the Baptist) *S'wark 23* **P** *Abp* **V** C J L BOSWELL, **C** T J JEFFREYS, K E ASTON
CROYDON (St Mary Magdalene) *see* Addiscombe St Mary Magd w St Martin *S'wark*
CROYDON (St Matthew) *S'wark 23* **P** *V Croydon* **V** P J BROWN
CROYDON (St Michael and All Angels w St James) *S'wark 23* **P** *Trustees* **V** D P MINCHEW
CROYDON (St Peter) *S'wark 23* **P** *V Croydon* **V** S J KNOWERS, **NSM** S C RAYNER
CROYDON Woodside (St Luke) *S'wark 25* **P** *Bp* **P-in-c** N C GOLDING
CROYDON, SOUTH (Emmanuel) *S'wark 24* **P** *Ch Trust Fund Trust* **V** T A MAPSTONE, **C** H M DURANT, S L FENBY, **NSM** D J RICHARDSON, **OLM** J M WILSON
CROYDON, SOUTH (St Augustine) *see* Croydon St Aug *S'wark*
CROYLAND (St Mary and St Bartholomew and St Guthlac) *see* Crowland *Linc*
CRUDGINGTON (St Mary Mission Church) *see* Wrockwardine Deanery *Lich*
CRUDWELL (All Saints) *see* Ashley, Crudwell, Hankerton, Long Newnton etc *Bris*
CRUMPSALL (St Matthew w St Mary) *Man 5* **P** *Bp* **R** *vacant* 0161-795 4376
CRUMPSALL, LOWER (St Thomas) w Cheetham St Mark *Man 5* **P** *Bp* **P-in-c** N J ANDREWES
CRUNDALE (St Mary the Blessed Virgin) w Godmersham *Cant 2* **P** *Abp* **P-in-c** I G CAMPBELL
CRUWYS MORCHARD (Holy Cross) *see* Washfield, Stoodleigh, Withleigh etc *Ex*
CRUX EASTON (St Michael and All Angels) *see* Highclere and Ashmansworth w Crux Easton *Win*
CUBBINGTON (St Mary) *Cov 11* **P** *Bp* **V** K LINDOP
CUBERT (St Cubert) *Truro 7* **P** *DBP* **V** P E TIDMARSH
CUBLEY (St Andrew) *see* Alkmonton, Cubley, Marston, Montgomery etc *Derby*
CUBLINGTON (St Nicholas) *see* Wingrave w Rowsham, Aston Abbotts and Cublington *Ox*
CUCKFIELD (Holy Trinity) *Chich 6* **P** *Bp* **V** N G WETHERALL, **NSM** J SEDGLEY
CUCKLINGTON (St Lawrence) *see* Charlton Musgrove, Cucklington and Stoke Trister *B & W*
CUDDESDON (All Saints) *see* Wheatley *Ox*
CUDDINGTON (St Mary) *Guildf 9* **P** *Bp* **P-in-c** R G HARVEY, **NSM** S P AYLING
CUDDINGTON (St Nicholas) *see* Haddenham w Cuddington, Kingsey etc *Ox*
CUDHAM (St Peter and St Paul) and Downe *Roch 16* **P** *Ch Soc Trust and Bp (jt)* **V** T R HATWELL, **NSM** N K HINTON
CUDWORTH (St John) *Wakef 7* **P** *Bp* **V** D NICHOLSON, **NSM** S C TRAVES
CUDWORTH (St Michael) *see* Ilminster and Distr *B & W*
CUFFLEY (St Andrew) *see* Northaw and Cuffley *St Alb*
CULBONE (St Beuno) *see* Oare w Culbone *B & W*
CULFORD (St Mary) *see* Lark Valley *St E*
CULGAITH (All Saints) *see* Cross Fell Gp *Carl*
CULHAM (St Paul) *see* Dorchester *Ox*
CULLERCOATS (St George) *Newc 8* **P** *Patr Bd* **TR** M SLACK, **TV** A J CAVANAGH, **NSM** A B BEESTON
CULLERCOATS (St Paul) *see* Tynemouth Cullercoats St Paul *Newc*
CULLINGWORTH (St John the Evangelist) *Bradf 8* **P** *Bp* **P-in-c** D P HALLIDAY
CULLOMPTON (St Andrew) (Langford Chapel), Willand, Uffculme, Kentisbeare, and Blackborough *Ex 4* **P** *Patr Bd* **TR** P J SOURBUT, **TV** K HORSFALL, A R DODDS, **C** A E NORMAN-WALKER, **NSM** L M BARLEY
CULM DAVY (St Mary's Chapel) *see* Hemyock w Culm Davy, Clayhidon and Culmstock *Ex*
CULM VALLEY *see* Cullompton, Willand, Uffculme, Kentisbeare etc *Ex*
CULMINGTON (All Saints) w Onibury, Bromfield and Stanton Lacy *Heref 12* **P** *O T M Rogers-Coltman (1 turn), Earl of Plymouth (2 turns)* **P-in-c** M J STEWART
CULMSTOCK (All Saints) *see* Hemyock w Culm Davy, Clayhidon and Culmstock *Ex*
CULPHO (St Botolph) *see* Gt and Lt Bealings w Playford and Culpho *St E*
CULWORTH (St Mary the Virgin) w Sulgrave and Thorpe Mandeville and Chipping Warden w Edgcote and Moreton Pinkney *Pet 1* **P** *T M Sergison-Brooke Esq, DBP, D L P Humfrey Esq, Ch Patr Trust, and Oriel Coll Ox (jt)* **R** C H R WHITEMAN
CUMBERWORTH (St Helen) *see* Sutton, Huttoft and Anderby *Linc*
CUMBERWORTH (St Nicholas), Denby and Denby Dale *Wakef 6* **P** *Bp and V Penistone (jt)* **P-in-c** T L ROBINS
CUMDIVOCK (St John) *see* Dalston w Cumdivock, Raughton Head and Wreay *Carl*
CUMMERSDALE (St James) *see* Denton Holme *Carl*
CUMNOR (St Michael) *Ox 10* **P** *St Pet Coll Ox* **V** C B GARDNER, **NSM** B M WEBB, D WENHAM
CUMREW (St Mary the Virgin) *see* Eden, Gelt and Irthing *Carl*
CUMWHINTON (St John's Hall) *see* Scotby and Cotehill w Cumwhinton *Carl*
CUMWHITTON (St Mary the Virgin) *see* Eden, Gelt and Irthing *Carl*
CUNDALL (St Mary and All Saints) *see* Kirby-on-the-Moor, Cundall w Norton-le-Clay etc *Ripon*
CURBAR (All Saints) *see* Baslow w Curbar and Stoney Middleton *Derby*
CURBRIDGE (St Barnabas) *see* Sarisbury *Portsm*
CURBRIDGE (St John the Baptist) *see* Witney *Ox*
CURDRIDGE (St Peter) *Portsm 1* **P** *D&C Win* **C** G M W KEITH, **NSM** E A GROVES
CURDWORTH (St Nicholas and St Peter ad Vincula) (St George) *Birm 12* **P** *Bp and Lord Norton (jt)* **P-in-c** M I RHODES
CURRY, NORTH (St Peter and St Paul) *B & W 18* **P** *D&C* **V** C H TOWNSHEND
CURRY MALLET (All Saints) *see* Beercrocombe w Curry Mallet, Hatch Beauchamp etc *B & W*
CURRY RIVEL (St Andrew) w Fivehead and Swell *B & W 15* **P** *D&C Bris (1 turn), P G H Speke Esq (2 turns)* **R** J M LANGDOWN
CURY (St Corentine) and Gunwalloe w St Mawgan-in-Meneage *Truro 4* **P** *Bp* **P-in-c** E B L BROWNING, **C** G C SCOTT
CUSOP (St Mary) w Blakemere, Bredwardine w Brobury, Clifford, Dorstone, Hardwicke, Moccas and Preston-on-Wye *Heref 1* **P** *Bp, D&C, CPAS, MMCET, P M I S Trumper Esq, S Penoyre Esq, and Mrs P Chester-Master (jt)* **R** R M JAMES, **Hon C** S F BARNES, **OLM** C P STUTZ, R R DAVIES-JAMES
CUTCOMBE (St John the Evangelist) *see* Exton and Winsford and Cutcombe w Luxborough *B & W*
CUTSDEAN (St James) *see* The Guitings, Cutsdean, Farmcote etc *Glouc*
CUXHAM (Holy Rood) *see* Ewelme, Brightwell Baldwin, Cuxham w Easington *Ox*
CUXTON (St Michael and All Angels) and Halling *Roch 6* **P** *Bp and D&C (jt)* **R** R I KNIGHT
CUXWOLD (St Nicholas) *see* Swallow *Linc*
CWM HEAD (St Michael) *see* Wistanstow *Heref*
DACRE (Holy Trinity) w Hartwith and Darley w Thornthwaite *Ripon 3* **P** *Bp, D&C, V Masham and Healey, and Mrs K A Dunbar (jt)* **P-in-c** M S EVANS
DACRE (St Andrew) *Carl 4* **P** *Trustees* **V** *vacant* (01768) 63179
DADLINGTON (St James) *see* Fenn Lanes Gp *Leic*
DAGENHAM (St Martin) *see* Becontree S *Chelmsf*
DAGENHAM (St Peter and St Paul) *Chelmsf 1* **P** *Ch Soc Trust* **V** R M REITH, **C** S J HANNA
DAGLINGWORTH (Holy Rood) *see* Brimpsfield w Birdlip, Syde, Daglingworth etc *Glouc*
DAGNALL (All Saints) *see* Kensworth, Studham and Whipsnade *St Alb*
DAISY HILL (St James) *Man 11* **P** *Bp* **V** R COWARD
DALBURY (All Saints) *see* Boylestone, Church Broughton, Dalbury, etc *Derby*
DALBY (St James) *see* Patrick *S & M*
DALBY (St Lawrence and Blessed Edward King) *see* Partney Gp *Linc*
DALBY (St Peter) *see* Howardian Gp *York*
DALBY, GREAT (St Swithun) *see* Burrough Hill Pars *Leic*
DALBY, LITTLE (St James) *as above*
DALBY, OLD (St John the Baptist), Nether Broughton, Saxelbye w Shoby, Grimston and Wartnaby *Leic 3* **P** *Bp, MMCET, V Rothley, and Personal Reps K J M Madocks-Wright Esq (jt)* **V** J S HOPEWELL

DALE ABBEY (All Saints) *see* Stanton-by-Dale w Dale Abbey and Risley *Derby*
DALE HEAD (St James) *see* Long Preston w Tosside *Bradf*
DALHAM (St Mary), Gazeley, Higham, Kentford and Moulton *St E 11* **P** *Bp (2 turns), Ch Coll Cam (1 turn), C E L Philipps Esq (1 turn), and D W Barclay Esq (1 turn)* **V** S J MITCHELL
DALLAM (St Mark) *Liv 12* **P** *R Warrington and Bp (jt)* **V** P J MARSHALL
DALLINGHOO (St Mary) *see* Charsfield w Debach, Monewden, Hoo etc *St E*
DALLINGTON (St Giles) *see* Brightling, Dallington, Mountfield etc *Chich*
DALLINGTON (St Mary) *Pet 7* **P** *Earl Spencer* **V** A E PANTON
DALLOWGILL (St Peter) *see* Fountains Gp *Ripon*
DALSTON (Holy Trinity) w St Philip and Haggerston All Saints *Lon 5* **P** *Ld Chan and Bp (alt)* **V** R J HUDSON-WILKIN
DALSTON (St Mark w St Bartholomew) *Lon 5* **P** *Ch Patr Trust* **V** R W WALL
DALSTON (St Michael) w Cumdivock, Raughton Head and Wreay *Carl 3* **P** *Bp, DBP, and D&C (jt)* **V** S P CARTER, **C** C J TAYLOR, **NSM** H R CARTER
DALTON (Holy Trinity) *see* Newburn *Newc*
DALTON (Holy Trinity) *Sheff 6* **P** *Bp* **V** M INESON
DALTON (St James) *see* Gilling and Kirkby Ravensworth *Ripon*
DALTON (St John the Evangelist) *see* Topcliffe, Baldersby w Dishforth, Dalton etc *York*
DALTON (St Michael and All Angels) *Liv 11* **P** *Bp* **V** T C BARTON
DALTON, NORTH (All Saints) *see* Woldsburn *York*
DALTON, SOUTH *see* Dalton le Dale and New Seaham *Dur*
DALTON HOLME (St Mary) *see* Etton w Dalton Holme *York*
DALTON-IN-FURNESS (St Mary) and Ireleth-with-Askam *Carl 9* **P** *Bp* **V** A MITCHELL
DALTON LE DALE (St Andrew) and New Seaham *Dur 2* **P** *Bp and D&C (alt)* **V** *vacant* 0191-581 3270
DALWOOD (St Peter) *see* Kilmington, Stockland, Dalwood, Yarcombe etc *Ex*
DAMERHAM (St George) *see* W Downland *Sarum*
DANBURY (St John the Baptist) *Chelmsf 9* **P** *Lord Fitzwalter* **P-in-c** M G BLYTH, **C** D S GILMORE
DANBY (St Hilda) *York 22* **P** *Viscountess Downe* **V** M J HAZELTON
DANBY WISKE (not known) *see* E Richmond *Ripon*
DANEHILL (All Saints) *Chich 21* **P** *Ch Soc Trust* **P-in-c** D M HALL
DANESMOOR (St Barnabas) *see* N Wingfield, Clay Cross and Pilsley *Derby*
DARBY END (St Peter) *Worc 9* **P** *Bp* **P-in-c** W J A BARNES
DARBY GREEN (St Barnabas) *Win 5* **P** *Bp* **V** *vacant* (01252) 877817
DARENTH (St Margaret) *Roch 2* **P** *D&C* **V** *vacant* (01322) 227153
DARESBURY (All Saints) *Ches 4* **P** *D G Greenhall Esq* **V** D R FELIX
DARFIELD (All Saints) *Sheff 12* **P** *MMCET* **R** N M REDEYOFF
DARLASTON (All Saints) *Lich 26* **P** *Simeon's Trustees* **P-in-c** N D PERKINSON, **C** D WILLS, R E INGLESBY
DARLASTON (St Lawrence) *Lich 26* **P** *Bp and Simeon's Trustees (jt)* **P-in-c** D WILLS, **C** R E INGLESBY
DARLEY (Christ Church) *see* Dacre w Hartwith and Darley w Thornthwaite *Ripon*
DARLEY (St Helen) *Derby 7* **P** *Bp* **R** R E QUARTON
DARLEY, SOUTH (St Mary the Virgin), Elton and Winster *Derby 7* **P** *Bp and DBF (jt)* **P-in-c** R E QUARTON
DARLEY ABBEY (St Matthew) *Derby 11* **P** *DBP* **NSM** J CALDWELL
DARLINGSCOTT (St George) *see* Tredington and Darlingscott w Newbold on Stour *Cov*
DARLINGTON (All Saints) *see* Blackwell All SS and Salutation *Dur*
DARLINGTON (Holy Trinity) *Dur 8* **P** *Adn Dur* **V** R C WARDALE, **NSM** L G PEALL
DARLINGTON (St Cuthbert) *Dur 8* **P** *Lord Barnard* **V** R J WILLIAMSON, **NSM** P M SINCLAIR
DARLINGTON St Hilda and (St Columba) *Dur 8* **P** *Bp* **P-in-c** S C WILLIAMSON
DARLINGTON (St James) *Dur 8* **P** *The Crown* **V** I L GRIEVES
DARLINGTON (St Mark) w St Paul *Dur 8* **P** *Bp and St Jo Coll Dur* **V** P A BAKER
DARLINGTON (St Matthew) and St Luke *Dur 8* **P** *Bp* **V** B HOLMES
DARLINGTON, EAST (St John) (St Herbert) *Dur 8* **P** *The Crown* **TR** M L DENT, **TV** C M BLAKESLEY
DARLTON (St Giles) *see* Dunham w Darlton, Ragnall, Fledborough etc *S'well*
DARNALL (Church of Christ) *see* Attercliffe and Darnall *Sheff*
DARRINGTON (St Luke and All Saints) *see* Went Valley *Wakef*
DARSHAM (All Saints) *St E 19* **P** *Exors Earl of Stradbroke* **V** R J GINN, **C** H W TURNER, **OLM** S A WARNE, A B BAYMAN, E M COLE
DARTFORD (Christ Church) *Roch 2* **P** *V Dartford H Trin* **V** D B KITLEY, **C** A R ANGEL
DARTFORD (Holy Trinity) *Roch 2* **P** *Bp* **V** M J HENWOOD
DARTFORD (St Alban) *Roch 2* **P** *V Dartford H Trin* **V** *vacant* (01322) 224052
DARTFORD (St Edmund the King and Martyr) *Roch 2* **P** *Bp* **V** R P CALLAGHAN, **C** S C BREWER
DARTINGTON (Old St Mary's Church Tower) *see* Totnes w Bridgetown, Berry Pomeroy etc *Ex*
DARTINGTON (St Mary) *as above*
DARTMOUTH (St Petrox) (St Saviour) and Dittisham *Ex 13* **P** *Sir John Seale Bt, DBP, and Bp (jt)* **V** S C WRIGHT, **C** M D MACEY
DARTMOUTH PARK (St Mary) *see* Brookfield St Mary *Lon*
DARTON (All Saints) *Wakef 7* **P** *Bp* **V** W R PLIMMER
DARWEN (St Barnabas) *Blackb 2* **P** *Bp* **V** L R COLLINSON
DARWEN (St Cuthbert) w Tockholes St Stephen *Blackb 2* **P** *Bp* **P-in-c** D G MOORE, **C** L S KENYON
DARWEN (St Peter) w Hoddlesden St Paul *Blackb 2* **P** *V Blackburn and DBP (jt)* **TV** G R MUMFORD, **P-in-c** A HOLLIDAY, **C** D P WOODALL
DARWEN, LOWER (St James) *Blackb 2* **P** *V Blackb* **P-in-c** G M DYER, **OLM** J R H CRAWFORD
DARWEN, OVER (St James) *Blackb 2* **P** *V Blackb* **P-in-c** T N DYER, **OLM** M E CROOK
DASSETT MAGNA (All Saints) *see* Burton Dassett *Cov*
DATCHET (St Mary the Virgin) *see* Riverside *Ox*
DATCHWORTH (All Saints) *see* Welwyn *St Alb*
DAUBHILL (St George the Martyr) *Man 9* **P** *Trustees* **V** *vacant* (01204) 61067
DAUNTSEY (St James Great) *see* Brinkworth w Dauntsey *Bris*
DAVENHAM (St Wilfrid) *Ches 6* **P** *Bp* **P-in-c** M C R CRIPPS, **C** A Q GREENHOUGH, **Hon C** M W WALTERS
DAVENTRY (Holy Cross), Ashby St Ledgers, Braunston, Catesby, Hellidon, Staverton and Welton *Pet 3* **P** *Patr Bd* **TR** O R PAGE, **TV** C P ROSE-CASEMORE, A SLATER, E M COWLEY, **C** P L DAVIS
DAVIDSTOW (St David) *see* Boscastle w Davidstow *Truro*
DAVINGTON (St Mary Magdalene) *see* The Brents and Davington w Oare and Luddenham *Cant*
DAVYHULME (Christ Church) *Man 7* **P** *Bp* **P-in-c** R J HILL
DAVYHULME (St Mary) *Man 7* **P** *Bp* **P-in-c** C S FORD
DAWDON (St Hild and St Helen) *Dur 2* **P** *Bp* **V** J C G POLLOCK
DAWLEY (Holy Trinity) *see* Cen Telford *Lich*
DAWLEY (St Jerome) *Lon 24* **P** *Hyndman Trustees* **P-in-c** I W JONES
DAWLISH (St Gregory) *Ex 6* **P** *D&C* **P-in-c** J P BIRD, **C** C S PEER
DAWLISH WARREN (Church Hall) *see* Kenton, Mamhead, Powderham, Cofton and Starcross *Ex*
DAYBROOK (St Paul) *S'well 12* **P** *Bp* **V** C J RATTENBERRY, **C** D E ANDERTON, **NSM** R SHAW
DAYLESFORD (St Peter) *see* Chipping Norton *Ox*
DE BEAUVOIR TOWN (St Peter) *Lon 5* **P** *Bp* **V** J F PORTER-PRYCE, **C** K S REEVES, **Hon C** C J BRICE, **NSM** D GERRANS
DEAL (St Andrew) *Cant 8* **P** *Abp* **P-in-c** C M D LINDLAR
DEAL (St George the Martyr) *Cant 8* **P** *Abp* **V** C G SPENCER, **C** S PORTER
DEAL (St Leonard) (St Richard) and Sholden w Great Mongeham *Cant 8* **P** *Abp* **R** G D KENDREW, **C** G F SMALL, **OLM** P J HAMBROOK
DEAL The Carpenter's Arms (extra-parochial place) *Cant 8 vacant*
DEAN (All Hallows) *see* The Stodden Churches *St Alb*
DEAN (St Oswald) *Carl 6* **P** *Trustees the late A R Sherwen Esq and R Workington (jt)* **P-in-c** K KITCHIN
DEAN, EAST (St Simon and St Jude) w Friston and Jevington *Chich 16* **P** *Duke of Devonshire (1 turn), D&C (2 turns)* **P-in-c** I K SMALE
DEAN, EAST (St Winifred) *see* Lockerley and E Dean w E and W Tytherley *Win*
DEAN, WEST (All Saints) *see* Alfriston w Lullington, Litlington and W Dean *Chich*

DEAN, WEST (St Mary) *see* Clarendon *Sarum*
DEAN COURT (St Andrew) *see* Cumnor *Ox*
DEAN FOREST (Christ Church) *see* Forest of Dean Ch Ch w English Bicknor *Glouc*
DEAN FOREST (Holy Trinity) *Glouc 4* **P** *The Crown* **V** A N JAMES
DEAN FOREST (St Paul) *see* Parkend and Viney Hill *Glouc*
DEAN PRIOR (St George the Martyr) *see* Buckfastleigh w Dean Prior *Ex*
DEANE (All Saints) *see* N Waltham and Steventon, Ashe and Deane *Win*
DEANE (St Mary the Virgin) *Man 11* **P** *Patr Bd* **TR** I G MAINEY, **TV** P ELLIS, **OLM** J M DAVIES
DEANSHANGER (Holy Trinity) *see* Passenham *Pet*
DEARHAM (St Mungo) *see* Allonby, Cross Canonby and Dearham *Carl*
DEARNLEY (St Andrew) *Man 20* **P** *Bp* **P-in-c** P F DAVEY
DEBDEN (St Mary the Virgin) and Wimbish w Thunderley *Chelmsf 22* **P** *Bp* **R** A K GAIR
DEBENHAM (St Mary Magdalene) and Helmingham *St E 18* **P** *Ld Chan, Lord Henniker, MMCET, Bp, and Lord Tollemache (by turn)* **R** G E NOBLE, **OLM** P A R WILKES, J E BUFTON
DEDDINGTON (St Peter and St Paul) Barford, Clifton and Hempton *Ox 5* **P** *D&C Windsor and Bp (jt)* **V** H R B WHITE
DEDHAM (St Mary the Virgin) *Chelmsf 17* **P** *Duchy of Lanc and Lectureship Trustees (alt)* **V** G G MOATE
DEDWORTH (All Saints) *Ox 13* **P** *Bp* **P-in-c** L M BROWN
DEEPCAR (St John the Evangelist) *Sheff 3* **P** *Bp* **V** J P RAFFAY, **NSM** T S GREGORY, K J CROOKES
DEEPING, WEST (St Andrew) *see* Uffington Gp *Linc*
DEEPING ST JAMES (St James) *Linc 13* **P** *Burghley Ho Preservation Trust* **V** M WARRICK, **NSM** S M C MARSHALL
DEEPING ST NICHOLAS (St Nicholas) *see* Spalding St Jo w Deeping St Nicholas *Linc*
DEEPLISH (St Luke) *see* S Rochdale *Man*
DEERHURST (St Mary) and Apperley w Forthampton, Chaceley, Tredington, Stoke Orchard and Hardwicke *Glouc 15* **P** *Bp, V Longdon, and J S Yorke Esq (jt)* **V** D BOWERS
DEFFORD (St James) w Besford *Worc 4* **P** *D&C Westmr* **NSM** F B KINGS
DEIGHTON (All Saints) *see* Brompton w Deighton *York*
DELABOLE (St John the Evangelist) *see* St Teath *Truro*
DELAMERE (St Peter) *Ches 6* **P** *The Crown* **P-in-c** B R K PERKES
DELAVAL (Our Lady) *Newc 1* **P** *Lord Hastings* **V** P J BRYARS, **OLM** D R ORMESHER, A K HAYE
DEMBLEBY (St Lucia) *see* S Lafford *Linc*
DENABY, OLD (Mission Church) *see* Mexborough *Sheff*
DENABY MAIN (All Saints) *Sheff 7* **P** *Bp* **V** R C DAVIES
DENBURY (St Mary the Virgin) *see* Ipplepen, Torbryan and Denbury *Ex*
DENBY (St John the Evangelist) *see* Cumberworth, Denby and Denby Dale *Wakef*
DENBY (St Mary the Virgin) *see* Horsley and Denby *Derby*
DENBY DALE (Holy Trinity) *see* Cumberworth, Denby and Denby Dale *Wakef*
DENCHWORTH (St James) *see* Hanney, Denchworth and E Challow *Ox*
DENDRON (St Matthew) *see* Aldingham, Dendron, Rampside and Urswick *Carl*
DENESIDE (All Saints) *see* Seaham *Dur*
DENFORD (Holy Trinity) w Ringstead *Pet 10* **P** *L Stopford-Sackville Esq* **V** *vacant* (01933) 624627
DENGIE (St James) w Asheldham *Chelmsf 11* **P** *Bp* **R** *vacant*
DENHAM (St John the Baptist) *see* Hoxne w Denham, Syleham and Wingfield *St E*
DENHAM (St Mark) (St Mary the Virgin) *Ox 20* **P** *L J Way Esq* **R** J A HIRST
DENHAM (St Mary) *see* Barrow *St E*
DENHAM, NEW (St Francis) *see* Denham *Ox*
DENHOLME *Bradf 8* **P** *Bp* **P-in-c** R J BROOKS, **NSM** M M MOWER
DENMARK PARK (St Saviour) *see* Peckham St Sav *S'wark*
DENMEAD (All Saints) *Portsm 5* **P** *Ld Chan* **NSM** S M EDWARDS
DENNINGTON (St Mary) *see* Badingham w Bruisyard, Cransford etc *St E*
DENSHAW (Christ Church) *Man 21* **P** *Bp* **V** S C L CLAYTON
DENSTON (St Nicholas) *see* Bansfield *St E*
DENSTONE (All Saints) w Ellastone and Stanton *Lich 15* **P** *Bp and Col Sir Walter Bromley-Davenport (jt)* **V** *vacant* (01889) 590263
DENT (St Andrew) w Cowgill *Bradf 6* **P** *Bp and Sidesmen of Dent (alt)* **V** P J BOYLES
DENTON (Christ Church) *Man 17* **P** *Bp* **P-in-c** D J COX
DENTON Dane Bank (St George) *see* Denton Ch Ch *Man*
DENTON (Holy Spirit) *Newc 7* **P** *Bp* **V** W S GRIFFITH, **NSM** P H PEARSON
DENTON (St Andrew) *see* Harlaxton Gp *Linc*
DENTON (St Helen) *see* Weston w Denton *Bradf*
DENTON (St Lawrence) *Man 17* **P** *Earl of Wilton* **R** R CASSIDY
DENTON (St Leonard) w South Heighton and Tarring Neville *Chich 18* **P** *MMCET and Bp (alt)* **R** N A MANNING
DENTON (St Margaret) *see* Yardley Hastings, Denton and Grendon etc *Pet*
DENTON (St Mary) *see* Earsham w Alburgh and Denton *Nor*
DENTON (St Mary Magdalene) *see* Elham w Denton and Wootton *Cant*
DENTON, NETHER (St Cuthbert) *see* Lanercost, Walton, Gilsland and Nether Denton *Carl*
DENTON HOLME (St James) *Carl 3* **P** *Trustees* **V** J R LIBBY, **C** I K D HARDCASTLE
DENVER (St Mary) and Ryston w Roxham and West Dereham and Bexwell *Ely 13* **P** *G&C Coll Cam and Bp (jt)* **R** J M T M GRUNDY
DENVILLE (Christchurch Centre) *see* Havant *Portsm*
DEOPHAM (St Andrew) *see* High Oak, Hingham and Scoulton w Wood Rising *Nor*
DEPDEN (St Mary the Virgin) *see* Chevington w Hargrave, Chedburgh w Depden etc *St E*
DEPTFORD Brockley (St Peter) *S'wark 3* **P** *Bp* **V** C M E G TOURNAY
DEPTFORD (St John) (Holy Trinity) *S'wark 3* **P** *Peache Trustees and Ch Trust Fund Trust (jt)* **P-in-c** C S BAINBRIDGE, **C** M T PRIOR, E T PRIOR, **OLM** P K M SOER
DEPTFORD (St Nicholas) (St Luke) *S'wark 3* **P** *MMCET, Peache Trustees, and CPAS (jt)* **V** W G CORNECK
DEPTFORD (St Paul) *S'wark 3* **P** *Bp* **R** P W FELLOWS, **OLM** P J HUDSON
DERBY (St Alkmund and St Werburgh) *Derby 9* **P** *Simeon's Trustees* **V** J M WHITE, **C** D G HONOUR
DERBY (St Andrew w St Osmund) *Derby 10* **P** *Bp* **V** D C MACDONALD, **NSM** R HOWORTH, M J MORGAN
DERBY (St Anne) (St John the Evangelist) *Derby 9* **P** *Bp* **V** C M G BRINKWORTH, **NSM** R L BOYLE
DERBY (St Augustine) *see* Walbrook Epiphany *Derby*
DERBY (St Barnabas) *Derby 9* **P** *Bp* **V** R J ELGAR, **NSM** A L MARTIN
DERBY (St Bartholomew) *Derby 10* **P** *Bp* **P-in-c** M J R WHITING
DERBY (St Luke) *Derby 9* **P** *Bp* **V** G W SILLIS
DERBY (St Mark) *Derby 9* **P** *Bp* **Hon C** M R FUTERS
DERBY (St Paul) *Derby 9* **P** *Bp* **NSM** S M JAMES
DERBY (St Peter and Christ Church w Holy Trinity) *Derby 10* **P** *CPAS* **C** P M TAYLOR
DERBY (St Thomas) *see* Walbrook Epiphany *Derby*
DERBY, WEST (Good Shepherd) *Liv 8* **P** *Bp and R W Derby (jt)* **P-in-c** J DAVIES
DERBY, WEST (St James) *Liv 8* **P** *Trustees* **P-in-c** J R I WIKELEY
DERBY, WEST (St John) *Liv 8* **P** *Trustees* **V** T P E NENER, **C** T B SHERRING, **Hon C** M S O B FISHER
DERBY, WEST (St Luke) *Liv 2* **P** *Bp* **P-in-c** S NICHOLSON, **C** K E WHARTON
DERBY, WEST (St Mary) *Liv 8* **P** *Bp* **V** J R I WIKELEY, **C** G H CAPON, J E BOWEN
DERBYHAVEN (Chapel) *see* Malew *S & M*
DERBYSHIRE HILL (St Philip) *see* Parr *Liv*
DEREHAM, EAST (St Nicholas) and Scarning *Nor 17* **P** *Ld Chan* **TR** R AMES-LEWIS, **TV** B A HILL
DEREHAM, WEST (St Andrew) *see* Denver and Ryston w Roxham and W Dereham etc *Ely*
DERRINGHAM BANK (Ascension) (St Thomas) *York 14* **P** *Abp* **V** S J WHALEY, **NSM** R D WAITE
DERRINGTON (St Matthew), Haughton and Ranton *Lich 10* **P** *Bp, Mrs M N Nutt, and Trustees Earl of Lichfield (jt)* **R** *vacant* (01785) 780181
DERRY Hill (Christ Church) w Bremhill and Foxham *Sarum 15* **P** *Prime Min and V Calne and Blackland* **V** D C FROST, **NSM** J W SCOTT
DERSINGHAM (St Nicholas) w Anmer and Shernborne *Nor 16* **P** *Ld Chan* **R** *vacant* (01485) 540214
DESBOROUGH (St Giles), Brampton Ash, Dingley and Braybrooke *Pet 11* **P** *Bp, Earl Spencer, and DBP (by turn)* **R** M P TANNER, **C** M Y GARBUTT, **NSM** N M CLARKE
DESFORD (St Martin) and Peckleton w Tooley *Leic 11* **P** *Ld Chan* **R** R G SHARPE
DETHICK (St John the Baptist) *see* Tansley, Dethick, Lea and Holloway *Derby*

DETLING (St Martin) *see* Boxley w Detling *Cant*
DEVER VALLEY, LOWER *Win 7* **P** *Bp and D&C (jt)* **R** C FINCH
DEVIZES (St John) (St Mary) *Sarum 16* **P** *Ld Chan* **P-in-c** J RECORD
DEVIZES (St Peter) *Sarum 16* **P** *Bp* **P-in-c** P J MOSS
DEVONPORT (St Aubyn) *Ex 22* **P** *The Crown and R Stoke Damerel (alt)* **P-in-c** D J NIXON
DEVONPORT (St Bartholomew) *Ex 22* **P** *Bp* **V** R M SIGRIST
DEVONPORT (St Boniface) *see* Devonport St Boniface and St Phil *Ex*
DEVONPORT (St Boniface) (St Philip) *Ex 22* **P** *Bp* **TR** P J LOW, **C** D R DAVIS
DEVONPORT (St Budeaux) *Ex 22* **P** *V Plymouth St Andr w St Paul and St Geo* **V** S J BEACH
DEVONPORT (St Mark) Ford *Ex 22* **P** *Trustees* **V** A E APPLEGARTH
DEVONPORT (St Michael) (St Barnabas) *Ex 22* **P** *Bp and R Stoke Damerel (jt)* **P-in-c** T J BUCKLEY
DEVONPORT (St Thomas) *see* N Keyham *Ex*
DEVONPORT, NORTH *see* Devonport St Boniface and St Phil *Ex*
DEVORAN (St John the Evangelist and St Petroc) *Truro 6* **P** *Bp* **P-in-c** D R CARRIVICK
DEWCHURCH, LITTLE (St David) *see* Heref S Wye *Heref*
DEWCHURCH, MUCH (St David) *see* Much Birch w Lt Birch, Much Dewchurch etc *Heref*
DEWLISH (All Saints) *see* Puddletown, Tolpuddle and Milborne w Dewlish *Sarum*
DEWSALL (St Michael) *see* Heref S Wye *Heref*
DEWSBURY (All Saints) (St Mark) (St Matthew and St John the Baptist) *Wakef 11* **P** *Bp, Adn Pontefract, RD Dewsbury, and Lay Chmn Dewsbury Deanery Syn (jt)* **TR** K PARTINGTON, **TV** P A CRABB, V R SMITH, **C** K ROBERTSON
DEWSBURY (St Matthew and St John the Baptist) *see* Dewsbury *Wakef*
DEWSBURY (All Saints) *as above*
DEWSBURY (St Mark) *as above*
DEWSBURY MOOR (St John the Evangelist) *as above*
DHOON (Christ Church) *see* Maughold *S & M*
DIBDEN (All Saints) *Win 11* **P** *MMCET* **C** G A TYTE
DIBDEN PURLIEU (St Andrew) *see* Dibden *Win*
DICKER, UPPER (Holy Trinity) *see* Hellingly and Upper Dicker *Chich*
DICKLEBURGH (All Saints) and The Pulhams *Nor 10* **P** *Ld Chan (1 turn), Patr Bd (2 turns), Prime Min (1 turn)* **R** J B SCOTT, **NSM** N W STEER, **OLM** P D SCHWIER
DIDBROOK (St George) *see* Winchcombe *Glouc*
DIDCOT (All Saints) *Ox 18* **P** *BNC Ox* **P-in-c** A M COLEBY, **NSM** A J EDWARDS
DIDCOT (St Peter) *Ox 18* **P** *Bp* **P-in-c** E J CARTER, **NSM** P A GORDON
DIDDINGTON (St Laurence) *see* The Paxtons w Diddington *Ely*
DIDDLEBURY (St Peter) w Munslow, Holdgate and Tugford *Heref 12* **P** *Bp (3 turns), D&C (1 turn)* **R** I E GIBBS
DIDLINGTON (St Michael) *Nor 13* **P** *CPAS* **V** *vacant*
DIDMARTON (St Lawrence) *see* Boxwell, Leighterton, Didmarton, Oldbury etc *Glouc*
DIDSBURY (Christ Church) Barlow Moor Road *Man 8* **P** *Trustees* **P-in-c** R M GOVENDER, **C** S L BENNETT, J F HOLLYWELL
DIDSBURY (St James) (Emmanuel) *Man 8* **P** *Patr Bd* **TR** D M HUGHES, **TV** N J BUNDOCK, **C** C J PARK
DIGBY GROUP, The (St Thomas of Canterbury) *Linc 22* **P** *Mrs H E Gillatt, Ld Chan, and DBP (by turn)* **P-in-c** J A BLANCHARD
DIGMOOR (Christ the Servant) *see* Upholland *Liv*
DIGSWELL (St John the Evangelist) (Christ the King) and Panshanger *St Alb 21* **P** *Patr Bd* **TV** S SHAHZAD, S Q MOORE, **P-in-c** C GARNER, **NSM** K E SUCKLING
DILHAM (St Nicholas) *see* Smallburgh w Dilham w Honing and Crostwight *Nor*
DILHORNE (All Saints) *see* Caverswall and Weston Coyney w Dilhorne *Lich*
DILSTON (St Mary Magdalene) *see* Corbridge w Halton and Newton Hall *Newc*
DILTON or LEIGH (Holy Saviour) *see* White Horse *Sarum*
DILTON MARSH (Holy Trinity) *as above*
DILWYN AND STRETFORD (St Mary the Virgin) *see* Leominster *Heref*
DINDER (St Michael and All Angels) *see* Pilton w Croscombe, N Wootton and Dinder *B & W*
DINEDOR (St Andrew) *see* Heref S Wye *Heref*
DINES GREEN (St Michael) *see* Worc Dines Green St Mich and Crown E, Rushwick *Worc*
DINGLEY (All Saints) *see* Desborough, Brampton Ash, Dingley and Braybrooke *Pet*
DINNINGTON (St Leonard) w Laughton-en-le-Morthen and Throapham *Sheff 5* **P** *Bp and J C Athorpe Esq (jt)* **R** J E BOLTON
DINNINGTON (St Matthew) *see* Ch the King *Newc*
DINNINGTON (St Nicholas) *see* Merriott w Hinton, Dinnington and Lopen *B & W*
DINSDALE (St John the Baptist) w Sockburn *Dur 8* **P** *D&C and Sherburn Hosp (alt)* **R** M D M FERGUSON
DINTING VALE (Holy Trinity) *see* Charlesworth and Dinting Vale *Derby*
DINTON (St Mary) *see* Nadder Valley *Sarum*
DINTON (St Peter and St Paul) *see* Stone w Dinton and Hartwell *Ox*
DIPTFORD (St Mary the Virgin), North Huish, Harberton, Harbertonford, Halwell and Moreleigh *Ex 13* **P** *Bp and D&C (jt)* **R** J C OUGH, **C** H G POLLOCK, **Hon C** J E SPENCE, B PETTY
DIPTON (St John the Evangelist) and Leadgate *Dur 4* **P** *Bp* **V** D G HERON, **NSM** W S JACKSON
DISCOED (St Michael) *see* Presteigne w Discoed, Kinsham, Lingen and Knill *Heref*
DISEWORTH (St Michael and All Angels) *see* Kegworth, Hathern, Long Whatton, Diseworth etc *Leic*
DISHLEY (All Saints) *see* Thorpe Acre w Dishley *Leic*
DISLEY (St Mary the Virgin) *Ches 16* **P** *Lord Newton* **V** P S DANIEL
DISS Heywood (St James the Great) *see* Diss *Nor*
DISS (St Mary) *Nor 10* **P** *Bp* **R** A C BILLETT, **C** S M OAKLAND
DISTINGTON (Holy Spirit) *Carl 7* **P** *Earl of Lonsdale* **R** *vacant* (01946) 830384
DITCHINGHAM (St Mary), Hedenham and Broome *Nor 5* **P** *Countess Ferrers and Bp (jt)* **R** I R BENTLEY
DITCHLING (St Margaret) *Chich 9* **P** *Bp* **V** J S CLARKE
DITTERIDGE (St Christopher) *see* Box w Hazlebury and Ditteridge *Bris*
DITTISHAM (St George) *see* Dartmouth and Dittisham *Ex*
DITTON (St Basil and All Saints) *see* Hough Green St Basil and All SS *Liv*
DITTON (St Michael) (St Thomas) *Liv 13* **P** *Bp* **V** P R SKIRROW, **OLM** J I CLARKE, D STRATFORD, L MOSS
DITTON (St Peter ad Vincula) *Roch 7* **P** *Ch Trust Fund Trust* **R** J R TERRANOVA, **NSM** P M PAYNE
DITTON PRIORS (St John the Baptist) w Neenton, Burwarton, Cleobury North, Aston Botterell, Wheathill and Loughton and Chetton *Heref 9* **P** *Bp, Princess Josephine zu Loewenstein, and Exors Viscount Boyne (jt)* **P-in-c** J N ROWLAND
DIXTON (St Peter) *Heref 8* **P** *DBP* **P-in-c** K V CECIL, **NSM** J S TUNNICLIFFE
DOBCROSS (Holy Trinity) *see* Saddleworth *Man*
DOBWALLS (St Peter) *see* Liskeard and St Keyne *Truro*
DOCCOMBE (Chapel) *see* Moretonhampstead, Manaton, N Bovey and Lustleigh *Ex*
DOCK (Mission Church) *see* Immingham *Linc*
DOCKENFIELD (Church of the Good Shepherd) *see* Rowledge and Frensham *Guildf*
DOCKING (St Mary), the Birchams, Stanhoe and Sedgeford *Nor 16* **P** *Bp, D&C, and Mrs A J Ralli (3 turns), The Crown (1 turn)* **V** A J BUTCHER
DOCKLOW (St Bartholomew) *see* Leominster *Heref*
DODBROOKE (St Thomas à Beckett) *see* Kingsbridge and Dodbrooke *Ex*
DODDERHILL (St Augustine) *see* Droitwich Spa *Worc*
DODDINGHURST (All Saints) *Chelmsf 7* **P** *Bp* **P-in-c** O F TRELLIS
DODDINGTON (All Saints) *see* Quantoxhead *B & W*
DODDINGTON (St John) *see* Wybunbury w Doddington *Ches*
DODDINGTON (St John the Baptist) *see* Coreley and Doddington *Heref*
DODDINGTON (St John the Baptist), Newnham and Wychling *Cant 6* **P** *Abp, Adn, and Exors Sir John Croft Bt (jt)* **P-in-c** G BAISLEY
DODDINGTON (St Mary and St Michael) *see* Glendale Gp *Newc*
DODDINGTON (St Mary) w Benwick and Wimblington *Ely 14* **P** *Bp, St Jo Coll Dur, and R Raynar Esq (jt)* **R** G COGGINS
DODDINGTON (St Peter) *see* Skellingthorpe w Doddington *Linc*
DODDINGTON, GREAT (St Nicholas) and Wilby *Pet 6* **P** *Exors Lt-Col H C M Stockdale and Ld Chan (alt)* **P-in-c** C J PEARSON
DODDISCOMBSLEIGH (St Michael) *see* Tedburn St Mary, Whitestone, Oldridge etc *Ex*

DODFORD (Holy Trinity and St Mary) *see* Catshill and Dodford *Worc*
DODFORD (St Mary the Virgin) *see* Weedon Bec w Everdon and Dodford *Pet*
DODLESTON (St Mary) *Ches 2* **P** *D&C* **P-in-c** J A KENDALL
DODWORTH (St John the Baptist) *Wakef 7* **P** *V Silkstone* **V** S P RACE
DOGMERSFIELD (All Saints) *see* Hartley Wintney, Elvetham, Winchfield etc *Win*
DOGSTHORPE (Christ the Carpenter) *see* Pet Ch Carpenter *Pet*
DOLPHINHOLME (St Mark) w Quernmore and Over Wyresdale *Blackb 11* **P** *Bp and V Lanc (jt)* **V** R TAYLOR
DOLTON (St Edmund King and Martyr) *Ex 20* **P** *Ch Soc Trust* **P-in-c** A S GRAESSER, **NSM** D J URSELL
DONCASTER Holy Trinity *Sheff 8* **P** *SMF* **V** *vacant* (01302) 349684
DONCASTER Intake (All Saints) *Sheff 8* **P** *Bp* **V** L M WELLS
DONCASTER (St George) (St Edmund's Church Centre) *Sheff 8* **P** *Bp* **V** C M SMITH
DONCASTER (St James) *Sheff 9* **P** *Hyndman's Trustees* **V** A MURRAY, **C** J LEVERTON
DONCASTER (St Jude) *Sheff 9* **P** *Bp* **V** A J GILBERT, **C** N BOWLER
DONCASTER (St Leonard and St Jude) *Sheff 7* **P** *The Crown* **V** N J PAY
DONCASTER (St Mary) *Sheff 8* **P** *Hyndman's Trustees* **V** M S A TANNER
DONHEAD ST ANDREW (St Andrew) *see* The Donheads *Sarum*
DONHEAD ST MARY (St Mary the Virgin) *as above*
DONHEADS, The *Sarum 11* **P** *DBP and New Coll Ox (alt)* **P-in-c** T C CURRY
DONINGTON (St Cuthbert) *Lich 16* **P** *MMCET* **P-in-c** J B HALL
DONINGTON (St Mary and the Holy Rood) *Linc 21* **P** *Simeon's Trustees* **V** *vacant* (01775) 822355
DONINGTON-ON-BAIN (St Andrew) *see* Asterby Gp *Linc*
DONISTHORPE (St John) and Moira w Stretton-en-le-Field *Leic 9* **P** *Ch Soc Trust (1 turn), and Bp (3 turns)* **V** A J BURGESS
DONNINGTON (St George) *Chich 3* **P** *Bp* **P-in-c** C R BEARD
DONNINGTON WOOD (St Matthew) *Lich 21* **P** *Bp* **V** D W WRIGHT
DONNISON (School) *see* Sunderland *Dur*
DONYATT (The Blessed Virgin Mary) *see* Ilminster and Distr *B & W*
DONYLAND, EAST (St Lawrence) *see* Fingringhoe w E Donyland and Abberton etc *Chelmsf*
DORCHESTER (St George) (St Mary the Virgin) (St Peter, Holy Trinity and All Saints) *Sarum 1* **P** *Patr Bd (3 turns), Ld Chan (1 turn)* **TR** P C LAMBERT, **TV** D L DENNIS, R A BETTS, **C** D J SMITH, **NSM** G TURNOCK
DORCHESTER (St Peter and St Paul) *Ox 1* **P** *Patr Bd* **TR** S E BOOYS, **TV** N A R HAWKES, S D MILLAR, E W D TILDESLEY, **NSM** R M GODFREY
DORDON (St Leonard) *Birm 10* **P** *V Polesworth* **P-in-c** V J HICKS
DORE (Christ Church) *Sheff 2* **P** *Sir Philip Naylor-Leyland Bt* **V** M J HUNTER
DORKING (St Martin) w Ranmore *Guildf 7* **P** *Bp* **V** R M CATTLEY, **OLM** L J TROMBETTI, S V PEACE
DORKING (St Paul) *Guildf 7* **P** *Ch Patr Trust* **V** P D BRYER, **C** A S JOHNSON, **NSM** J C YELLAND
DORMANSLAND (St John) *S'wark 26* **P** *Bp* **V** G PADDICK
DORMANSTOWN (All Saints) *see* Coatham and Dormanstown *York*
DORMINGTON (St Peter) *see* Fownhope w Mordiford, Brockhampton etc *Heref*
DORMSTON (St Nicholas) *see* Inkberrow w Cookhill and Kington w Dormston *Worc*
DORNEY (St James the Less) *see* Riverside *Ox*
DORRIDGE (St Philip) *Birm 6* **P** *Bp* **V** *vacant* (01564) 772472 *or* 775652
DORRINGTON (St Edward) w Leebotwood, Longnor, Stapleton, Smethcote and Woolstaston *Heref 11* **P** *DBP and J J C Coldwell Esq (jt)* **R** R S PAYNE
DORRINGTON (St James) *see* Digby Gp *Linc*
DORSINGTON (St Peter) *see* Pebworth, Dorsington, Honeybourne etc *Glouc*
DORSTONE (St Faith) *see* Cusop w Blakemere, Bredwardine w Brobury etc *Heref*
DORTON (St John the Baptist) *see* Bernwode *Ox*
DOSTHILL (St Paul) *Birm 10* **P** *Bp* **V** A W MOORE
DOTTERY (St Saviour) *see* Askerswell, Loders and Powerstock *Sarum*
DOUGLAS (All Saints) (St Thomas the Apostle) *S & M 2* **P** *Bp* **V** E T PETTENGELL, **C** M RAILTON-CROWDER, **OLM** S A FERRIS
DOUGLAS (Christ Church) *Blackb 4* **P** *Bp* **V** B E HARDING
DOUGLAS (St George) *S & M 2* **P** *Bp* **V** B SMITH, **NSM** R HARPER
DOUGLAS (St Matthew the Apostle) *S & M 2* **P** *Bp* **V** D WHITWORTH
DOUGLAS (St Ninian) *S & M 2* **P** *CPAS* **V** B DARBYSHIRE, **NSM** G B QUINN
DOUGLAS-IN-PARBOLD (Christ Church) *see* Douglas *Blackb*
DOULTING (St Aldhelm) *see* Shepton Mallet w Doulting *B & W*
DOVE HOLES (St Paul) *see* Wormhill, Peak Forest w Peak Dale and Dove Holes *Derby*
DOVECOT (Holy Spirit) *Liv 2* **P** *Bp* **V** J R STOTT
DOVER Buckland Valley (St Nicholas) *see* Buckland in Dover w Buckland Valley *Cant*
DOVER (St Martin) *Cant 4* **P** *CPAS* **V** K G GARRETT, **OLM** P M DAY
DOVER (St Mary the Virgin) *Cant 4* **P** *Abp, Ld Warden of Cinque Ports, and Ld Lt of Kent (jt)* **V** D G RIDLEY, **NSM** P A GODFREY
DOVER (St Peter and St Paul) *see* Charlton-in-Dover *Cant*
DOVERCOURT (All Saints) *see* Harwich Peninsula *Chelmsf*
DOVERDALE (St Mary) *see* Ombersley w Doverdale *Worc*
DOVERIDGE (St Cuthbert), Scropton, Sudbury and Somersal Herbert *Derby 14* **P** *Duke of Devonshire* **P-in-c** J J VICKERSTAFF, **NSM** P R JONES
DOWDESWELL (St Michael) *see* Sevenhampton w Charlton Abbots, Hawling etc *Glouc*
DOWLAND (St Peter) *see* Iddesleigh w Dowland *Ex*
DOWLES Button Oak (St Andrew) *see* Ribbesford w Bewdley and Dowles *Worc*
DOWLISHWAKE (St Andrew) *see* Ilminster and Distr *B & W*
DOWN, East (St John the Baptist) *see* Shirwell, Loxhore, Kentisbury, Arlington, etc *Ex*
DOWN AMPNEY (All Saints) *see* S Cerney w Cerney Wick and Down Ampney *Glouc*
DOWN HATHERLEY (St Mary and Corpus Christi) *see* Twigworth, Down Hatherley, Norton, The Leigh etc *Glouc*
DOWN ST MARY (St Mary the Virgin) *see* N Creedy *Ex*
DOWNDERRY (St Nicholas) *see* St Germans *Truro*
DOWNE (St Mary Magdalene) *see* Cudham and Downe *Roch*
DOWNEND (Christ Church) (Church Centre) *Bris 5* **P** *Peache Trustees* **P-in-c** J L VICKERY, **C** M A C ANDREWS, R J WIDDECOMBE
DOWNHAM (St Barnabas) *S'wark 4* **P** *Bp* **V** J D S FRENCH
DOWNHAM (St Leonard) *see* Chatburn and Downham *Blackb*
DOWNHAM (St Leonard) *Ely 12* **P** *Bp* **R** *vacant* (01353) 699337
DOWNHAM (St Luke) *see* Catford (Southend) and Downham *S'wark*
DOWNHAM (St Margaret) w South Hanningfield *Chelmsf 9* **P** *Bp* **R** *vacant* (01268) 710370
DOWNHAM, NORTH (St Mark) *see* Catford (Southend) and Downham *S'wark*
DOWNHAM MARKET (St Edmund) and Crimplesham w Stradsett *Ely 13* **P** *Bp* **R** J W MATHER
DOWNHEAD (All Saints) *see* Leigh upon Mendip w Stoke St Michael *B & W*
DOWNHOLME (St Michael and All Angels) *see* Richmond w Hudswell and Downholme and Marske *Ripon*
DOWNLEY (St James the Great) *see* High Wycombe *Ox*
DOWNS BARN and NEAT HILL (Community Church) *see* Stantonbury and Willen *Ox*
DOWNSHIRE HILL (St John) *see* Hampstead St Jo Downshire Hill Prop Chpl *Lon*
DOWNSIDE (St Michael's Chapel) *see* E Horsley and Ockham w Hatchford and Downside *Guildf*
DOWNSWAY (All Souls Worship Centre) *see* Southwick *Chich*
DOWNTON (St Giles) *see* Wigmore Abbey *Heref*
DOWNTON (St Lawrence) *Sarum 10* **P** *Win Coll* **P-in-c** F H GIMSON
DOWSBY (St Andrew) *see* Billingborough Gp *Linc*
DOXEY (St Thomas and St Andrew) *see* Castle Town *Lich*
DOXFORD (St Wilfrid) *Dur 16* **P** *Bp* **P-in-c** J MORGAN
DOYNTON (Holy Trinity) *see* Wick w Doynton and Dyrham *Bris*
DRAKES BROUGHTON (St Barnabas) *see* Stoulton w Drake's Broughton and Pirton etc *Worc*
DRAUGHTON (St Augustine) *see* Skipton H Trin *Bradf*

DRAUGHTON (St Catherine) *see* Maidwell w Draughton, Lamport w Faxton *Pet*
DRAX (St Peter and St Paul) *see* Carlton and Drax *York*
DRAYCOT *Bris 6* **P** *Bp, D&C Sarum, and R W Neeld Esq (jt)* **P-in-c** G W HEWITT
DRAYCOTT (St Mary) *see* Wilne and Draycott w Breaston *Derby*
DRAYCOTT (St Peter) *see* Rodney Stoke w Draycott *B & W*
DRAYCOTT IN THE CLAY (St Augustine) *see* Hanbury w Newborough and Rangemore *Lich*
DRAYCOTT-LE-MOORS (St Margaret) w Forsbrook *Lich 6* **P** *Bp* **C** N M RUSSELL
DRAYTON (Iron Mission Room) *see* Chaddesley Corbett and Stone *Worc*
DRAYTON (St Catherine) *see* Langport Area Chs *B & W*
DRAYTON (St Leonard and St Catherine) *see* Dorchester *Ox*
DRAYTON (St Margaret) w Felthorpe *Nor 2* **P** *Bp* **P-in-c** D WELLS
DRAYTON (St Peter) *see* Ironstone *Ox*
DRAYTON (St Peter) Berks *Ox 10* **P** *Bp* **P-in-c** J I MIDWINTER
DRAYTON, EAST (St Peter) *see* Dunham w Darlton, Ragnall, Fledborough etc *S'well*
DRAYTON, LITTLE (Christ Church) *Lich 18* **P** *V Drayton in Hales* **P-in-c** J H K NORTON
DRAYTON, WEST (St Martin) *Lon 24* **P** *Bp* **V** O J FIELD, **C** L R HILLIER
DRAYTON, WEST (St Paul) *see* Gamston w Eaton and W Drayton *S'well*
DRAYTON BASSETT (St Peter) *Lich 4* **P** *Bp* **R** H J BAKER, **Hon C** M R F MACLACHLAN
DRAYTON-BEAUCHAMP (St Mary the Virgin) *see* Aston Clinton w Buckland and Drayton Beauchamp *Ox*
DRAYTON IN HALES (St Mary) *Lich 18* **P** *C C Corbet Esq* **P-in-c** M G W HAYES, **C** J F SHOESMITH
DRAYTON PARSLOW (Holy Trinity) *see* Stewkley w Soulbury and Drayton Parslow *Ox*
DRESDEN (Resurrection) *Lich 12* **P** *V Blurton* **P-in-c** P J MOCKFORD
DREWSTEIGNTON (Holy Trinity) *see* Chagford, Drewsteignton, Hittisleigh etc *Ex*
DRIFFIELD (St Mary) *see* The Ampneys w Driffield and Poulton *Glouc*
DRIFFIELD, GREAT (All Saints) and LITTLE (St Peter) *York 10* **P** *Abp* **V** M R G SMITH, **NSM** D T PHILLIPS
DRIGG (St Peter) *see* Seascale and Drigg *Carl*
DRIGHLINGTON (St Paul) *Wakef 8* **P** *Bp* **P-in-c** S M ASKEY
DRIMPTON (St Mary) *see* Beaminster Area *Sarum*
DRINGHOUSES (St Edward the Confessor) *York 7* **P** *Abp* **V** C W M BALDOCK, **NSM** S M COLLIER
DRINKSTONE (All Saints) *see* Woolpit w Drinkstone *St E*
DROITWICH SPA (St Andrew w St Mary de Witton) (St Nicholas) (St Peter) (St Richard) *Worc 8* **P** *Bp* **TR** S K BANYARD, **TV** D A CHAPLIN, **C** J RUHUMULIZA, **NSM** R HOLDEN
DRONFIELD (St John the Baptist) w Holmesfield *Derby 5* **P** *Ld Chan* **TR** B GREEN, **TV** C D I REES, W R EARDLEY, **NSM** R DOVE
DROPMORE (St Anne) *see* Burnham w Dropmore, Hitcham and Taplow *Ox*
DROXFORD (St Mary and All Saints) *Portsm 1* **P** *Bp* **P-in-c** J F FOLEY, **NSM** K V HOWES
DROYLSDEN (St Andrew) *Man 17* **P** *Bp* **OLM** J A HEMSWORTH
DROYLSDEN (St Martin) *Man 17* **P** *Bp* **P-in-c** D A WILLIAMS
DROYLSDEN (St Mary) (St John) *Man 17* **P** *Bp* **P-in-c** A M BAILIE
DRY DODDINGTON (St James) *see* Claypole *Linc*
DRY DRAYTON (St Peter and St Paul) *Ely 1* **P** *MMCET* **P-in-c** C A COLLINS
DRY SANDFORD (St Helen) *see* Wootton and Dry Sandford *Ox*
DRYBROOK (Holy Trinity) *see* Dean Forest H Trin *Glouc*
DRYPOOL (St Columba) (St John) *York 14* **P** *Patr Bd* **TR** W B G MATHER, **TV** M I BENNETT
DUCKLINGTON (St Bartholomew) *Ox 8* **P** *DBP* **P-in-c** R J EDY
DUCKMANTON (St Peter and St Paul) *see* Calow and Sutton cum Duckmanton *Derby*
DUDDENHOE END (The Hamlet Church) *see* Heydon, Gt and Lt Chishill, Chrishall etc *Chelmsf*
DUDDESTON (St Matthew) *see* Nechells *Birm*
DUDDINGTON (St Mary) *see* Barrowden and Wakerley w S Luffenham etc *Pet*
DUDDON (St Peter) *see* Tarvin *Ches*
DUDLESTON (St Mary) *see* Criftins w Dudleston and Welsh Frankton *Lich*
DUDLEY (St Andrew) *see* Netherton St Andr *Worc*
DUDLEY (St Augustine) Holly Hall *Worc 9* **P** *V Dudley* **P-in-c** C M BROWNE
DUDLEY (St Barnabas) *Worc 9* **P** *Bp* **P-in-c** A N ATTWOOD
DUDLEY (St Edmund King and Martyr) *Worc 9* **P** *V Dudley* **P-in-c** G S JOHNSTON
DUDLEY (St Francis) *Worc 9* **P** *Bp* **P-in-c** G S JOHNSTON
DUDLEY (St James the Great) Eve Hill *Worc 9* **P** *V Dudley* **P-in-c** A ST L J WICKENS
DUDLEY (St John) Kate's Hill *Worc 9* **P** *V Dudley* **V** *vacant* (01384) 253807
DUDLEY (St Paul) *see* Weetslade *Newc*
DUDLEY (St Thomas and St Luke) *Worc 9* **P** *Bp* **P-in-c** A N ATTWOOD
DUDLEY WOOD (St John) *Worc 9* **P** *V Netherton* **P-in-c** J A OLIVER
DUFFIELD (St Alkmund) and Little Eaton *Derby 11* **P** *Patr Bd* **V** M A PICKLES, **C** R C J HOPKINS
DUFTON (St Cuthbert) *see* Long Marton w Dufton and w Milburn *Carl*
DUKINFIELD (St John) (St Alban Mission Church) *Ches 14* **P** *R Stockport St Mary* **V** T J HAYES
DUKINFIELD (St Mark) (St Luke) *Ches 14* **P** *Bp* **V** *vacant* 0161-330 2783
DULAS (St Michael) *see* Ewyas Harold w Dulas, Kenderchurch etc *Heref*
DULCOTE (All Saints) *see* Wells St Cuth w Wookey Hole *B & W*
DULLINGHAM (St Mary) *see* Raddesley Gp *Ely*
DULOE (St Cuby), Herodsfoot, Morval and St Pinnock *Truro 12* **P** *Ld Chan, Ch Soc Trust, and Ball Coll Ox (by turn)* **NSM** G LONSDALE
DULVERTON (All Saints) and Brushford *B & W 16* **P** *D&C and Bp (jt)* **R** J M THOROGOOD, **C** J C WOOLLEY
DULWICH (St Barnabas) *S'wark 9* **P** *Bp* **V** D L GWILLIAMS, **C** H N GILBERT, **Hon C** J H JONES, J G WINTER
DULWICH (St Clement) St Peter *S'wark 9* **P** *Bp* **V** M E A COULTER
DULWICH, EAST (St John the Evangelist) *S'wark 9* **P** *Ripon Coll Cuddesdon* **V** C L J RICHARDSON, **C** R C ANDREWS, **Hon C** R A SHAW, J M W SEDGWICK, **OLM** A CLARKE
DULWICH, NORTH (St Faith) *S'wark 9* **P** *Bp* **V** H W DAWES
DULWICH, SOUTH (St Stephen) *S'wark 9* **P** *Dulwich Coll* **C** E J OGLESBY
DULWICH, WEST (All Saints) *S'wark 15* **P** *Bp* **V** R J TITLEY, **OLM** R J SHAFTO
DULWICH, WEST (Emmanuel) *S'wark 15* **P** *Bp* **V** K G A ANSAH, **OLM** H O KIMBER
DUMBLETON (St Peter) *see* Winchcombe *Glouc*
DUMMER (All Saints) *see* Cliddesden and Ellisfield w Farleigh Wallop etc *Win*
DUNCHIDEOCK (St Michael and All Angels) and Shillingford St George w Ide *Ex 6* **P** *D&C and Mrs J M Michelmore (alt)* **P-in-c** G K MAYER
DUNCHURCH (St Peter) *Cov 6* **P** *Bp* **V** E M DYKE
DUNCTON (Holy Trinity) *Chich 11* **P** *Lord Egremont* **P-in-c** R A STAVELEY-WADHAM
DUNDRY (St Michael) *see* Chew Magna w Dundry and Norton Malreward *B & W*
DUNGEON HILL *Sarum 3* **P** *DBP and N G Halsey Esq (jt)* **P-in-c** J H P HAMILTON
DUNHAM, GREAT (St Andrew) and LITTLE (St Margaret), w Great and Little Fransham and Sporle *Nor 14* **P** *Hertf Coll Ox, Ch Soc Trust, Magd Coll Cam, and DBP (by turn)* **P-in-c** B R A COLE, **C** S J SMITH
DUNHAM MASSEY (St Margaret) (St Mark) (All Saints) *Ches 10* **P** *J G Turnbull Esq* **V** J J E SUTTON
DUNHAM-ON-THE-HILL (St Luke) *see* Helsby and Dunham-on-the-Hill *Ches*
DUNHAM-ON-TRENT (St Oswald) w Darlton, Ragnall, Fledborough and East Drayton *S'well 5* **P** *Bp (2 turns), D&C York (1 turn)* **P-in-c** J H LITTLE
DUNHOLME (St Chad) *see* Welton and Dunholme w Scothern *Linc*
DUNKERTON (All Saints) *see* Camerton w Dunkerton, Foxcote and Shoscombe *B & W*
DUNKESWELL (Holy Trinity) (St Nicholas), Luppitt, Sheldon and Upottery *Ex 5* **P** *MMCET, Bp, and D&C (jt)* **V** N J WALL
DUNMOW, GREAT (St Mary the Virgin) and Barnston *Chelmsf 18* **P** *Ld Chan (2 turns), CPAS (1 turn)* **R** D S AINGE, **C** M N JAMES, **NSM** R DREW

DUNMOW, LITTLE (St Mary the Virgin) *see* Felsted and Lt Dunmow *Chelmsf*
DUNNINGTON (not known) *see* Salford Priors *Cov*
DUNNINGTON (St Nicholas) *see* Beeford w Frodingham and Foston *York*
DUNNINGTON (St Nicholas) *York 2* **P** *Abp* **R** M W SEARLE, **NSM** L E LUDKIN
DUNS TEW (St Mary Magdalene) *see* Westcote Barton w Steeple Barton, Duns Tew etc *Ox*
DUNSBY (All Saints) *see* Ringstone in Aveland Gp *Linc*
DUNSCROFT (St Edwin) *Sheff 10* **P** *Bp* **V** A WATSON
DUNSDEN (All Saints) *see* Shiplake w Dunsden and Harpsden *Ox*
DUNSFOLD (St Mary and All Saints) and Hascombe *Guildf 2* **P** *Bp and SMF (jt)* **R** G S M WILLIS
DUNSFORD (St Mary) *see* Tedburn St Mary, Whitestone, Oldridge etc *Ex*
DUNSFORTH (St Mary) *see* Aldborough w Boroughbridge and Roecliffe *Ripon*
DUNSLAND (Mission Church) *see* Ashwater, Halwill, Beaworthy, Clawton etc *Ex*
DUNSLEY (Mission Room) *see* Whitby w Aislaby and Ruswarp *York*
DUNSMORE (Chapel of the Ressurection) *see* Ellesborough, The Kimbles and Stoke Mandeville *Ox*
DUNSOP BRIDGE (St George) *see* Slaidburn *Bradf*
DUNSTABLE (St Augustine of Canterbury) (St Fremund the Martyr) (St Peter) *St Alb 12* **P** *Bp* **TR** R J ANDREWS, **TV** N D JONES, **NSM** M BREWSTER
DUNSTALL (St Mary) *see* Barton under Needwood w Dunstall *Lich*
DUNSTAN (St Leonard) *see* Penkridge Team *Lich*
DUNSTAN (St Peter) *see* Metheringham w Blankney and Dunston *Linc*
DUNSTER (St George), Carhampton and Withycombe w Rodhuish *B & W 16* **P** *Bp* **R** M P GRANTHAM
DUNSTON (Church House) *see* Newbold w Dunston *Derby*
DUNSTON (St Nicholas) w (Christ Church) *Dur 13* **P** *Bp* **V** K TEASDALE, **C** D ATKINSON
DUNSTON (St Remigius) *see* Stoke H Cross w Dunston, Arminghall etc *Nor*
DUNSWELL (St Faith's Mission Church) *see* Hull St Jo Newland *York*
DUNTERTON (All Saints) *see* Milton Abbot, Dunterton, Lamerton etc *Ex*
DUNTISBOURNE ABBOTS (St Peter) *see* Brimpsfield w Birdlip, Syde, Daglingworth etc *Glouc*
DUNTISBOURNE ROUS (St Michael and All Angels) *as above*
DUNTON (St Martin) *see* Schorne *Ox*
DUNTON (St Mary Magdalene) w Wrestlingworth and Eyeworth *St Alb 11* **P** *Ld Chan and DBP (alt)* **R** A MANNING
DUNTON BASSETT (All Saints) *see* Leire w Ashby Parva and Dunton Bassett *Leic*
DUNWICH (St James) *see* Westleton w Dunwich *St E*
DURHAM (St Giles) *Dur 1* **P** *D&C* **V** R I DAVISON
DURHAM (St Margaret of Antioch) and Neville's Cross St John *Dur 1* **P** *D&C* **R** D C GLOVER, **NSM** S C BARTON
DURHAM (St Nicholas) *Dur 1* **P** *CPAS* **V** D R HANSON, **C** A R BALDOCK, R F T MURPHY, **NSM** D V DAY, P S JOHNSON
DURHAM (St Oswald King and Martyr) *Dur 1* **P** *D&C* **P-in-c** P Z KASHOURIS, **NSM** K S BRUCE
DURHAM NORTH (St Cuthbert) *Dur 1* **P** *Patr Bd* **TR** D J BELL, **TV** J THORNS, S J BAMBER, **C** R KALUS, **NSM** O R OMOLE
DURLEIGH (not known) *see* Bridgwater St Mary, Chilton Trinity and Durleigh *B & W*
DURLEY (Holy Cross) *Portsm 1* **P** *Ld Chan* **C** G M W KEITH, **NSM** E A GROVES
DURNFORD (St Andrew) *see* Woodford Valley *Sarum*
DURRINGTON (All Saints) *Sarum 13* **P** *D&C Win* **R** P H TAMPLIN, **NSM** R A BUSSEY
DURRINGTON (St Symphorian) *Chich 5* **P** *Bp* **V** N A TAYLOR, **C** R E BENNETT
DURSLEY (St James the Great) *Glouc 2* **P** *Bp* **R** J C G BROMLEY, **C** T D HEANEY, **NSM** I N GARDNER
DURSTON (St John the Baptist) *see* Alfred Jewel *B & W*
DURWESTON (St Nicholas) *see* Pimperne, Stourpaine, Durweston and Bryanston *Sarum*
DUSTON Team, The (St Francis) (St Luke) *Pet 7* **P** *Bp* **TR** N PURVEY-TYRER, **TV** A W BAINES, S J M READING, **NSM** H C WILSON
DUSTON, NEW (Mission Church) *see* Duston Team *Pet*
DUTTON (Licensed Room) *see* Antrobus, Aston by Sutton, Lt Leigh etc *Ches*
DUXFORD (St Peter) w St John *Ely 6* **P** *Bp* **P-in-c** A T SCHOFIELD
DYMCHURCH (St Peter and St Paul) w Burmarsh and Newchurch *Cant 12* **P** *Abp* **P-in-c** M N DALE, **NSM** P B SNARE
DYMOCK (St Mary the Virgin) *see* Redmarley D'Abitot, Bromesberrow, Pauntley etc *Glouc*
DYRHAM (St Peter) *see* Wick w Doynton and Dyrham *Bris*
EAGLE (All Saints) *see* Swinderby *Linc*
EAKRING (St Andrew) *S'well 15* **P** *DBP* **P-in-c** E F CULLY, **C** J R CHAMBERS
EALING (All Saints) *Lon 22* **P** *Bp* **V** N P HENDERSON, **C** D J BRAMMER, **Hon C** A GRIFFITHS
EALING (Ascension) *see* Hanger Hill Ascension and W Twyford St Mary *Lon*
EALING (Christ the Saviour) *Lon 22* **P** *Bp* **V** A F DAVIS, **C** R D E JONES
EALING (St Barnabas) *Lon 22* **P** *Bp* **V** N D R NICHOLLS
EALING (St Mary) *Lon 22* **P** *Bp* **V** S D PAYNTER, **C** A L POULSON, **NSM** M P J DEL RIO
EALING (St Paul) *Lon 22* **P** *Bp* **V** M P MELLUISH, **NSM** R L M ECKHARD
EALING (St Peter) Mount Park *Lon 22* **P** *Bp* **V** M POWELL, **NSM** M J JOACHIM, J O A CHOUFAR
EALING (St Stephen) Castle Hill *Lon 22* **P** *D&C St Paul's* **V** J E CLARK
EALING, WEST (St John) w St James *Lon 22* **P** *Bp* **V** W R DONALDSON, **TV** D E SMITH, **C** S K HOBBS, **NSM** R YATES
EALING COMMON (St Matthew) *Lon 22* **P** *Bp* **V** P G WATKINS
EARBY (All Saints) *Bradf 7* **P** *Bp* **V** R C WALLACE, **C** T J RISHTON
EARDISLAND (St Mary the Virgin) *see* Kingsland w Eardisland, Aymestrey etc *Heref*
EARDISLEY (St Mary Magdalene) w Bollingham, Willersley, Brilley, Michaelchurch, Whitney, Winforton, Almeley and Kinnersley *Heref 5* **P** *Patr Bd* **R** M J SMALL
EARL SHILTON (St Simon and St Jude) w Elmesthorpe *Leic 12* **P** *Bp* **V** G GITTINGS
EARL SOHAM (St Mary) w Cretingham and Ashfield cum Thorpe *St E 18* **P** *Lord Henniker, Ld Chan, and Wadh Coll Ox (by turn)* **P-in-c** H C SANDERS
EARL STERNDALE (St Michael and All Angels) *see* Hartington, Biggin and Earl Sterndale *Derby*
EARL STONHAM (St Mary) *see* Creeting St Mary, Creeting St Peter etc *St E*
EARLESFIELD (The Epiphany) *see* Grantham, Earlesfield *Linc*
EARLESTOWN (St John the Baptist) *Liv 16* **P** *R Wargrave* **V** *vacant* (01925) 224771
EARLEY (St Nicolas) *Ox 15* **P** *DBP* **V** D F TYNDALL, **NSM** D L H WEBSTER
EARLEY (St Peter) *Ox 15* **P** *DBP* **V** R R D SPEARS, **C** R E RUTHERFORD
EARLEY Trinity *Ox 15* **P** *DBP* **V** *vacant* 0118-986 8615
EARLEY, LOWER Trinity Church Local Ecumenical Project *Ox 15 vacant*
EARLHAM (St Anne) *Nor 3* **P** *Bp* **P-in-c** P C BAKER
EARLHAM (St Elizabeth) *Nor 3* **P** *Bp* **P-in-c** E M CONSTANTINE, **OLM** R M A HOUGHTON
EARLHAM (St Mary) *Nor 3* **P** *Trustees* **P-in-c** P C BAKER
EARLS BARTON (All Saints) *Pet 6* **P** *DBP* **V** M C W WEBBER
EARLS COLNE (St Andrew) *see* Halstead Area *Chelmsf*
EARL'S COURT (St Cuthbert) (St Matthias) *Lon 12* **P** *Trustees* **V** J VINE
EARL'S COURT (St Philip) *see* Kensington St Phil Earl's Court *Lon*
EARLS CROOME (St Nicholas) *see* Upton-on-Severn, Ripple, Earls Croome etc *Worc*
EARL'S HEATON *see* Dewsbury *Wakef*
EARL'S HEATON (St Peter) *as above*
EARLSDON (St Barbara) *Cov 3* **P** *Bp* **V** H J WILD
EARLSFIELD (St Andrew) *S'wark 20* **P** *Bp* **V** J BROWN, **NSM** V A HACKETT
EARLSFIELD (St John the Divine) *S'wark 20* **P** *Bp* **V** C E ROBERTS
EARLY (St Bartholomew) *see* Reading St Luke w St Bart *Ox*
EARNLEY (not known) and East Wittering *Chich 3* **P** *Bp (2 turns), Bp Lon (1 turn)* **P-in-c** S J DAVIES
EARNSHAW BRIDGE (St John) *see* Leyland St Jo *Blackb*
EARSDON (St Alban) and Backworth *Newc 8* **P** *Bp* **V** J A FRANCE
EARSHAM (All Saints) w Alburgh and Denton *Nor 10* **P** *Abp,*

J M Meade Esq, and St Jo Coll Cam (by turn) **R** I R BENTLEY, **OLM** B L CRAMP, S L CRAMP
EARSWICK, NEW (St Andrew) *see* Huntington *York*
EARTHAM (St Margaret) *see* Slindon, Eartham and Madehurst *Chich*
EASBY (Chapel) *see* Gt Ayton w Easby and Newton in Cleveland *York*
EASBY (St Agatha) w Skeeby and Brompton on Swale and Bolton on Swale *Ripon 2* **P** *Bp* **V** R M WIGRAM
EASEBOURNE (St Mary) *Chich 10* **P** *Rathbone Trust Co and Cowdray Trust (jt)* **V** D B WELSMAN, **NSM** A M HALLIWELL
EASINGTON (All Saints) w Liverton *York 16* **P** *Ld Chan* **R** P F LANGFORD
EASINGTON (All Saints) w Skeffling, Kilnsea and Holmpton *York 12* **P** *Ld Chan* **R** W J G HEALE
EASINGTON (St Hugh) *see* Banbury St Hugh *Ox*
EASINGTON (St Mary), Easington Colliery and South Hetton *Dur 2* **P** *Bp* **R** B E CLOSE
EASINGTON (St Peter) *see* Ewelme, Brightwell Baldwin, Cuxham w Easington *Ox*
EASINGTON COLLIERY (The Ascension) *see* Easington, Easington Colliery and S Hetton *Dur*
EASINGWOLD (St John the Baptist and All Saints) w Raskelf *York 3* **P** *Abp* **V** J HARRISON
EAST *see also under substantive place name*
EAST DEAN (All Saints) *Chich 13* **P** *Bp* **V** R T E B WOODS
EAST FERRY (St Mary the Virgin) *see* Scotter w E Ferry *Linc*
EAST HAM (St Bartholomew) (St Mary Magdalene) w Upton Park *Chelmsf 3* **P** *Patr Bd* **TV** Q B D PEPPIATT, J FREEMAN, **C** L A GOLDSMITH, **NSM** J D HALLIDAY
EAST HAM (St George and St Ethelbert) *Chelmsf 3* **P** *Bp* **V** D T HAOKIP
EAST HAM (St Paul) *Chelmsf 3* **P** *Ch Patr Trust* **C** A M BAKER
EAST LANE (St Mary) *see* W Horsley *Guildf*
EAST MARSHLAND *Ely 15* **P** *Bp and MMCET (1 turn), Pemb Coll Cam (2 turns), Prime Min (1 turn), and Ld Chan (1 turn)* **V** *vacant*
EAST ORCHARD (St Thomas) *see* Shaston *Sarum*
EAST WINCH (All Saints) *see* Gayton, Gayton Thorpe, E Walton, E Winch etc *Nor*
EASTBOURNE (All Saints) *Chich 16* **P** *Trustees* **V** W R LOVATT, **C** J M PACKMAN
EASTBOURNE (All Souls) *Chich 16* **P** *Ch Soc Trust* **V** N H GREEN, **C** P-J GUY
EASTBOURNE (Christ Church) *Chich 16* **P** *V Eastbourne* **V** N P CHATFIELD
EASTBOURNE Haven *see* Haven CD *Chich*
EASTBOURNE (Holy Trinity) *Chich 16* **P** *V Eastbourne* **V** J A CHEESEMAN, **C** J G HOBSON
EASTBOURNE (St Andrew) *Chich 16* **P** *Bp* **V** A F STONE, **C** A J LANE
EASTBOURNE St Elizabeth (Church Hall) *Chich 16* **P** *Bp* **P-in-c** D J GILLARD
EASTBOURNE (St John) Meads *Chich 16* **P** *Trustees* **V** G T DAINTREE, **NSM** K C ENGLAND
EASTBOURNE (St Mary) *Chich 16* **P** *Bp* **V** C R LANSDALE, **C** D P WALLIS, **NSM** B J KING
EASTBOURNE (St Michael and All Angels) Ocklynge *Chich 16* **P** *V Eastbourne* **V** J R HOUGHTON, **Dss** W K HAMBLY
EASTBOURNE (St Philip) *Chich 16* **P** *Bp* **V** *vacant* (01323) 732381
EASTBOURNE (St Richard of Chichester) *see* Langney *Chich*
EASTBOURNE (St Saviour and St Peter) *Chich 16* **P** *Keble Coll Ox* **V** J T GUNN
EASTBURY (St James the Great) and East Garston *Ox 14* **P** *Bp and Ch Ch Ox (alt)* **P-in-c** A W CUMBERLIDGE
EASTCHURCH (All Saints) w Leysdown and Harty *Cant 15* **P** *Abp and Keble Coll Ox (jt)* **R** F R SEARLE
EASTCOMBE (St Augustine) *see* Bussage *Glouc*
EASTCOTE (St Lawrence) *Lon 24* **P** *Bp* **V** S DANDO
EASTER, HIGH (St Mary the Virgin) and Good Easter w Margaret Roding *Chelmsf 18* **P** *Bp Lon, Trustees R K Shepherd Esq, and D&C St Paul's (by turn)* **R** *vacant* (01245) 231429
EASTERGATE (St George) *see* Aldingbourne, Barnham and Eastergate *Chich*
EASTERN GREEN (St Andrew) *Cov 3* **P** *R Allesley* **P-in-c** G P SMITH
EASTERTON (St Barnabas) *see* The Lavingtons, Cheverells, and Easterton *Sarum*
EASTFIELD (Holy Nativity) *see* Cayton w Eastfield *York*
EASTGATE (All Saints) *see* Upper Weardale *Dur*
EASTHAM (St Mary the Blessed Virgin) (St Peter's Chapel) (Chapel of the Holy Spirit) *Ches 9* **P** *D&C* **V** E A GLOVER
EASTHAM (St Peter and St Paul) *see* Teme Valley S *Worc*
EASTHAMPSTEAD (St Michael and St Mary Magdalene) *Ox 11* **P** *Ch Ch Ox* **R** G S COLE, **C** B L PEARSON, A S MARSHALL, E L ANTOINE
EASTHOPE (St Peter) *see* Wenlock *Heref*
EASTHORPE (St Mary the Virgin) *see* Copford w Easthorpe and Messing w Inworth *Chelmsf*
EASTINGTON (St Michael and All Angels), Frocester, Haresfield, Moreton Valence, Standish and Whitminster *Glouc 8* **P** *Bp and Col Sir Piers Bengough (1 turn), DBP and Exors Lady Mary Cooper (1 turn)* **R** R J R AMYS
EASTLEACH (St Andrew) *see* Coln St Aldwyns, Hatherop, Quenington etc *Glouc*
EASTLEIGH (All Saints) *Win 10* **P** *Bp* **V** R P DAVIES, **C** G WORT
EASTLEIGH Nightingale Avenue (St Francis) *see* Eastleigh *Win*
EASTLING (St Mary) w Ospringe and Stalisfield w Otterden *Cant 6* **P** *The Crown* **P-in-c** P A FENTON, **OLM** A M CHEESEMAN
EASTMOORS (St Mary Magdalene) *see* Helmsley *York*
EASTNEY (St Margaret) *Portsm 6* **P** *Bp* **V** *vacant* (023) 9273 1316
EASTNOR (St John the Baptist) *see* Ledbury *Heref*
EASTOFT (St Bartholomew) *see* The Marshland *Sheff*
EASTOKE (St Andrew) *see* Hayling Is St Andr *Portsm*
EASTON (All Hallows) *Bris 3* **P** *R Bris St Steph* **P-in-c** R D HOYAL
EASTON (All Saints) *see* Brandeston w Kettleburgh and Easton *St E*
EASTON (Holy Trinity w St Gabriel and St Lawrence and St Jude) *Bris 3* **P** *Trustees* **V** *vacant* 0117-955 4255
EASTON (St Mary) *see* Itchen Valley *Win*
EASTON (St Paul) *see* Westbury sub Mendip w Easton *B & W*
EASTON (St Peter) *see* E Leightonstone *Ely*
EASTON (St Peter), Colton, Marlingford and Bawburgh *Nor 17* **P** *Bp, D&C, Adn, and Sir Edward Evans-Lombe (jt)* **P-in-c** A H REYNOLDS
EASTON, GREAT (St Andrew) *see* Six Saints circa Holt *Leic*
EASTON, GREAT (St John and St Giles) *see* Broxted w Chickney and Tilty etc *Chelmsf*
EASTON, LITTLE (not known) *as above*
EASTON GREY (not known) *see* Sherston Magna, Easton Grey, Luckington etc *Bris*
EASTON IN GORDANO (St George) *see* Pill, Portbury and Easton-in-Gordano *B & W*
EASTON MAUDIT (St Peter and St Paul) *see* Bozeat w Easton Maudit *Pet*
EASTON NESTON (St Mary) *see* Towcester w Easton Neston *Pet*
EASTON ON THE HILL (All Saints) *see* Ketton, Collyweston, Easton-on-the-Hill etc *Pet*
EASTON ROYAL (Holy Trinity) *see* Pewsey and Swanborough *Sarum*
EASTOVER (St John the Baptist) *see* Bridgwater St Jo *B & W*
EASTRINGTON (St Michael) *see* Howden *York*
EASTROP (St Mary) *Win 4* **P** *CPAS* **R** C L HAWKINS, **C** C D E MOLL, **NSM** C E WEST
EASTRY (St Mary Blessed Virgin) and Northbourne w Tilmanstone and Betteshanger w Ham *Cant 8* **P** *Abp and Lord Northbourne (jt)* **R** F KENT, **Hon C** D G WILLIS, **OLM** J A PILCHER
EASTTHORPE (St Paul) and Upper Hopton *Wakef 10* **P** *V Mirfield* **P-in-c** P J CRAIG-WILD
EASTVILLE (St Anne w St Mark and St Thomas) *Bris 3* **P** *Bp* **V** P J HAYWARD
EASTVILLE (St Paul) *see* Stickney Gp *Linc*
EASTWELL (St Michael) *see* Scalford w Wycombe and Chadwell etc *Leic*
EASTWICK (St Botolph) *see* High Wych and Gilston w Eastwick *St Alb*
EASTWOOD (St David) *Chelmsf 10* **P** *Bp* **V** P D JOYCE
EASTWOOD (St Laurence and All Saints) *Chelmsf 10* **P** *Ld Chan* **V** N L RANSOM
EASTWOOD (St Mary) *S'well 4* **P** *J N Plumptre Esq* **R** E A C CARDWELL, **C** R S TAYLOR
EATON (All Saints) *see* Gamston w Eaton and W Drayton *S'well*
EATON (Christ Church) and Hulme Walfield *Ches 11* **P** *Bp and R Astbury (alt)* **V** *vacant* (01260) 279863
EATON (Christ Church) (St Andrew) *Nor 3* **P** *D&C* **V** A BEARDSMORE
EATON (St Denys) *see* Scalford w Wycombe and Chadwell etc *Leic*
EATON (St Thomas) *see* Tarporley *Ches*
EATON, LITTLE (St Paul) *see* Duffield and Lt Eaton *Derby*
EATON BISHOP (St Michael and All Angels) *see* Kingstone w Clehonger, Eaton Bishop etc *Heref*

EATON BRAY (St Mary the Virgin) w Edlesborough *St Alb 12* **P** *DBP* **V** M E GRANT
EATON HASTINGS (St Michael and All Angels) *see* Gt Coxwell w Buscot, Coleshill etc *Ox*
EATON SOCON (St Mary) *St Alb 11* **P** *E W Harper Esq* **V** K P FITZGIBBON
EATON SQUARE (St Peter) *see* Pimlico St Pet w Westmr Ch Ch *Lon*
EATON-UNDER-HEYWOOD (St Edith) *see* Hope Bowdler w Eaton-under-Heywood *Heref*
EBBERSTON (St Mary) *see* Thornton Dale w Allerston, Ebberston etc *York*
EBBESBOURNE WAKE (St John the Baptist) *see* Chalke Valley *Sarum*
EBCHESTER (St Ebba) *Dur 4* **P** *Bp* **R** *vacant* (01207) 563348
EBERNOE (Holy Trinity) *see* N Chapel w Ebernoe *Chich*
EBONY (St Mary the Virgin) *see* Wittersham w Stone-in-Oxney and Ebony *Cant*
EBREY WOOD (Mission Chapel) *see* Wrockwardine Deanery *Lich*
EBRINGTON (St Eadburgha) *see* Chipping Campden w Ebrington *Glouc*
ECCHINSWELL (St Lawrence) *see* Burghclere w Newtown and Ecchinswell w Sydmonton *Win*
ECCLES (St Mary the Virgin) *see* Quidenham Gp *Nor*
ECCLES (St Mary the Virgin) (St Andrew) *Man 2* **P** *Ld Ch (1 turn), Patr Bd (2 turns)* **TR** E A CROFTON, **TV** C M PAINTER, A C YOUNG, **C** A-L CRITCHLOW
ECCLESALL (St Gabriel) *see* Greystones *Sheff*
ECCLESALL BIERLOW (All Saints) *Sheff 2* **P** *Dean* **V** C P WILLIAMS, **NSM** S A P HUNTER
ECCLESFIELD (St Mary the Virgin) *Sheff 3* **P** *DBF* **V** P I IMPEY, **C** A B WALTON
ECCLESFIELD (St Paul) *see* Sheff St Paul *Sheff*
ECCLESHALL (Holy Trinity) *Lich 7* **P** *Bp* **V** J H GRAHAM
ECCLESHILL (St Luke) *Bradf 3* **P** *V Bradf* **V** J P HARTLEY
ECCLESTON (Christ Church) *Liv 10* **P** *F Webster Esq, Lord Blanch, Canon J A Lawton, Revd D G Mellors, and Bp (jt)* **V** C D HENDRICKSE, **OLM** B PARKER, D E ANDERTON
ECCLESTON (St Luke) *Liv 10* **P** *Trustees* **V** P G DAY
ECCLESTON (St Mary the Virgin) *Blackb 4* **P** *DBP* **R** I M TEMPLETON
ECCLESTON (St Mary the Virgin) and Pulford *Ches 2* **P** *Duke of Westmr* **R** *vacant* (01244) 674703
ECCLESTON (St Thomas) *Liv 10* **P** *Bp* **P-in-c** P H BURMAN
ECCLESTON, GREAT *see* Copp w Inskip *Blackb*
ECCLESTON PARK (St James) *Liv 10* **P** *Bp* **V** J H WELCH
ECKINGTON (Holy Trinity) *Worc 4* **P** *D&C Westmr* **NSM** F B KINGS
ECKINGTON (St Peter and St Paul) and Ridgeway *Derby 3* **P** *The Crown and Patr Bd (alt)* **R** N R HARVEY
ECKINGTON, UPPER (St Luke) *see* Eckington and Ridgeway *Derby*
ECTON (St Mary Magdalene) *Pet 6* **P** *The Crown* **P-in-c** J A PARKIN
EDALE (Holy and Undivided Trinity) *Derby 2* **P** *Rep Landowners* **P-in-c** A J G MURRAY-LESLIE
EDBURTON (St Andrew) *see* Poynings w Edburton, Newtimber and Pyecombe *Chich*
EDEN, Gelt and Irthing Team Ministry, The *Carl 2* **P** *Patr Bd* **TV** C J LAXON, **C** N J H REEVES, **NSM** D B MILLS, **OLM** E GOUGH
EDEN PARK (St John the Baptist) *see* Beckenham St Jo *Roch*
EDENBRIDGE (St Peter and St Paul) *Roch 11* **P** *Bp* **V** S A J MITCHELL, **C** R JONES
EDENFIELD (not known) and Stubbins *Man 10* **P** *Bp* **P-in-c** I M ROGERSON, **C** J ARCUS
EDENHALL (St Cuthbert) *see* Cross Fell Gp *Carl*
EDENHAM (St Michael) w Witham on the Hill and Swinstead *Linc 14* **P** *Baroness Willoughby de Eresby, Ld Chan, and Bp (by turn)* **V** A T HAWES, **NSM** I K WILLIAMS
EDENSOR (St Paul) *Lich 12* **P** *Prime Min* **P-in-c** G O STONE
EDENSOR (St Peter) *see* Beeley and Edensor *Derby*
EDGBASTON (St Augustine) *Birm 2* **P** *Bp* **V** M R E TOMLINSON
EDGBASTON (St Bartholomew) *Birm 2* **P** *Sir Euan Anstruther-Gough-Calthorpe Bt* **V** *vacant* 0121-454 0070
EDGBASTON (St George w St Michael) (St Michael's Hall) *Birm 2* **P** *Sir Euan Anstruther-Gough-Calthorpe Bt* **V** S G THORBURN
EDGBASTON (St Germain) *Birm 2* **P** *Trustees* **V** H A SCRIVEN, **C** S J WATKINS
EDGBASTON (St Mary and St Ambrose) *Birm 5* **P** *Bp and Sir Euan Anstruther-Gough-Calthorpe Bt (jt)* **P-in-c** C A GRYLLS
EDGCOTE (St James) *see* Culworth w Sulgrave and Thorpe Mandeville etc *Pet*
EDGCOTT (St Michael) *see* Swan *Ox*
EDGE, THE (St John the Baptist) *see* Painswick, Sheepscombe, Cranham, The Edge etc *Glouc*
EDGE HILL (St Cyprian) (St Mary) *Liv 3* **P** *Simeon's Trustees and Bp (jt)* **V** D A LEWIS, **C** J E WARHURST
EDGE HILL (St Dunstan) *see* St Luke in the City *Liv*
EDGE HILL (St Mary) *see* Edge Hill St Cypr w St Mary *Liv*
EDGEFIELD (School Room) *see* Worsley *Man*
EDGEFIELD (St Peter and St Paul) *see* Lt Barningham, Blickling, Edgefield etc *Nor*
EDGELEY (St Mark) *see* Stockport SW *Ches*
EDGELEY (St Matthew) *see* Stockport St Matt *Ches*
EDGESIDE (St Anne) *see* Rossendale Middle Valley *Man*
EDGEWORTH (St Mary) *see* Brimpsfield w Birdlip, Syde, Daglingworth etc *Glouc*
EDGMOND (St Peter) w Kynnersley and Preston Wealdmoors *Lich 16* **P** *Bp, Adn Salop, Chan Lich, MMCET, and Preston Trust Homes Trustees (jt)* **R** W E WARD, **C** M C V NASH-WILLIAMS
EDGTON (St Michael the Archangel) *see* Bishop's Castle w Mainstone, Lydbury N etc *Heref*
EDGWARE (St Alphage) *see* Hendon St Alphage *Lon*
EDGWARE (St Andrew) (St Margaret) (St Peter) *Lon 15* **P** *MMCET* **TR** M D CLARK, **TV** R T BODLE, **C** P T COOPER
EDINGALE (Holy Trinity) *see* Clifton Campville w Edingale and Harlaston *Lich*
EDINGLEY (St Giles) w Halam *S'well 14* **P** *Bp* **P-in-c** D LEANING
EDINGTHORPE (All Saints) *see* Bacton w Edingthorpe w Witton and Ridlington *Nor*
EDINGTON (St George) *see* W Poldens *B & W*
EDINGTON (St Mary, St Katharine and All Saints) *see* Bratton, Edington and Imber, Erlestoke etc *Sarum*
EDITH WESTON (St Mary) w North Luffenham and Lyndon w Manton *Pet 14* **P** *Baroness Willoughby de Eresby, Sir John Conant Bt, and Em Coll Cam (by turn)* **R** *vacant* (01780) 720931
EDITHMEAD (Mission) *see* Burnham *B & W*
EDLASTON (St James) *see* Brailsford w Shirley and Osmaston w Edlaston *Derby*
EDLINGHAM (St John the Baptist w Bolton Chapel) *see* Whittingham and Edlingham w Bolton Chapel *Newc*
EDLINGTON (St Helen) *see* Hemingby *Linc*
EDLINGTON (St John the Baptist) *Sheff 9* **P** *Bp* **V** W J STOKOE
EDMONDSHAM (St Nicholas) *see* Cranborne w Boveridge, Edmondsham etc *Sarum*
EDMONTON (All Saints) (St Michael) *Lon 18* **P** *D&C St Paul's* **V** B G KYRIACOU, **NSM** J E MARKBY
EDMONTON (St Aldhelm) *Lon 18* **P** *V Edmonton All SS* **V** D R BOLSTER
EDMONTON (St Alphege) *Lon 18* **P** *Bp* **V** R C KNOWLING, **C** S P J CLARK, D W HYETT
EDMONTON (St Mary w St John) (St Mary's Centre) *Lon 18* **P** *D&C St Paul's* **C** S J OWEN
EDMONTON (St Matthew) *see* Ponders End St Matt *Lon*
EDMONTON (St Peter w St Martin) *Lon 18* **P** *Bp* **V** B M SMITH
EDMUNDBYERS (St Edmund) *see* Blanchland w Hunstanworth and Edmundbyers etc *Newc*
EDSTASTON (St Mary the Virgin) *see* Tilstock, Edstaston and Whixall *Lich*
EDSTON (St Michael) *see* Kirby Misperton w Normanby, Edston and Salton *York*
EDVIN LOACH (St Mary) w Tedstone Delamere, Tedstone Wafer, Upper Sapey, Wolferlow and Whitbourne *Heref 2* **P** *Bp, BNC Ox, Sir Francis Winnington Bt, and D P Barneby Esq (jt)* **P-in-c** D P HOWELL
EDWALTON (Holy Rood) *S'well 8* **P** *Exors Major R P Chaworth-Musters* **V** D C BIGNELL, **NSM** P A EDWARDS
EDWARDSTONE (St Mary the Virgin) *see* Boxford, Edwardstone, Groton etc *St E*
EDWINSTOWE (St Mary) *S'well 6* **P** *Earl Manvers' Trustees* **P-in-c** A D LITTLEWOOD, **C** N J CARNALL
EDWYN RALPH (St Michael) *see* Bredenbury w Grendon Bishop and Wacton etc *Heref*
EFFINGHAM (St Lawrence) w Little Bookham *Guildf 10* **P** *Keble Coll Ox* **V** *vacant* (01372) 458314
EFFORD (St Paul) *see* Plymouth Em, St Paul Efford and St Aug *Ex*
EGDEAN (St Bartholomew) *Chich 11* **P** *Bp* **R** D S POLLARD
EGERTON (St James) w Pluckley *Cant 10* **P** *Abp* **C** D E FAWCETT

EGG BUCKLAND (St Edward) *Ex 23* **P** *Ld Chan* **V** T R J DICKENS
EGGESFORD (All Saints) *see* Burrington, Chawleigh, Cheldon, Chulmleigh etc *Ex*
EGGINTON (St Michael) *see* Leighton Buzzard w Eggington, Hockliffe etc *St Alb*
EGGINTON (St Wilfrid) *see* Etwall w Egginton *Derby*
EGGLESCLIFFE (St John the Baptist) *Dur 10* **P** *Bp* **R** T J D OLLIER
EGGLESTON (Holy Trinity) *Dur 7* **P** *The Crown* **P-in-c** A S G PIKE
EGHAM (St John the Baptist) *Guildf 11* **P** *Ch Soc Trust* **C** M C WOODWARD, **Hon C** J H GOODING
EGHAM HYTHE (St Paul) *Guildf 11* **P** *Bp* **V** G D KING, **NSM** S M LOVEDAY
EGLETON (St Edmund) *see* Oakham, Hambleton, Egleton, Braunston and Brooke *Pet*
EGLINGHAM (St Maurice) *see* Glendale Gp *Newc*
EGLOSHAYLE (St Petroc) *see* St Breoke and Egloshayle *Truro*
EGLOSKERRY (St Petrock and St Keri), North Petherwin, Tremaine and Tresmere *Truro 9* **P** *Duchy of Cornwall and Bp (alt)* **V** G PENGELLY
EGMANTON (Our Lady of Egmanton) *S'well 3* **P** *SMF* **V** C C LEVY
EGREMONT (St Mary and St Michael) and Haile *Carl 5* **P** *Patr Bd* **TR** J WOOLCOCK, **NSM** B J JEAPES, L V FULKER
EGTON (St Hilda) *see* Middle Esk Moor *York*
EGTON-CUM-NEWLAND (St Mary the Virgin) and Lowick and Colton *Carl 9* **P** *Patr Bd* **V** G WEMYSS
EIGHT ASH GREEN (All Saints) *see* Fordham *Chelmsf*
EIGHTON BANKS (St Thomas) *Dur 12* **P** *Bp* **P-in-c** R L FERGUSON
ELBERTON (St John) *see* Alveston and Littleton-on-Severn w Elberton *Bris*
ELBURTON (St Matthew) *Ex 24* **P** *CPAS* **V** R C H THOMAS
ELDENE (not known) *see* Swindon Dorcan *Bris*
ELDERSFIELD (St John the Baptist) *see* Berrow w Pendock, Eldersfield, Hollybush etc *Worc*
ELDON (St Mark) *see* Coundon and Eldon *Dur*
ELDWICK (St Lawrence) *see* Bingley All SS *Bradf*
ELFORD (St Peter) *Lich 4* **P** *Bp* **P-in-c** A L WHEALE, **Hon C** J R FAGAN
ELHAM (St Mary the Virgin) w Denton and Wootton *Cant 5* **P** *Abp and Mert Coll Ox (jt)* **V** J V H RUSSELL
ELING (St Mary) *see* Totton *Win*
ELING, NORTH (St Mary) *see* Copythorne *Win*
ELKESLEY (St Giles) w Bothamsall *S'well 5* **P** *SMF* **P-in-c** C F ANDREWS
ELKINGTON, SOUTH (All Saints) *see* Louth *Linc*
ELKSTONE (St John the Baptist) *see* Alstonfield, Butterton, Ilam etc *Lich*
ELKSTONE (St John the Evangelist) *see* Coberley, Cowley, Colesbourne and Elkstone *Glouc*
ELLACOMBE (Christ Church) *see* Torquay St Jo and Ellacombe *Ex*
ELLAND (All Saints) (St Mary the Virgin) *Wakef 2* **P** *Bp, Adn Halifax, and V Halifax (jt)* **TR** N M WOOD, **TV** D BURROWS
ELLASTONE (St Peter) *see* Denstone w Ellastone and Stanton *Lich*
ELLEL (St John the Evangelist) w Shireshead *Blackb 11* **P** *V Cockerham w Winmarleigh and Glasson* **V** E W GRAY
ELLENBROOK (St Mary's Chapel) *see* Worsley *Man*
ELLENHALL (St Mary) *see* Chebsey, Ellenhall and Seighford-with-Creswell *Lich*
ELLERBURN (St Hilda) *see* Thornton Dale w Allerston, Ebberston etc *York*
ELLERBY (St James) *see* Skirlaugh w Long Riston, Rise and Swine *York*
ELLERKER (not known) *see* S Cave and Ellerker w Broomfleet *York*
ELLESBOROUGH (St Peter and St Paul), The Kimbles and Stoke Mandeville *Ox 28* **P** *Chequers Trustees, The Hon I Hope-Morley, and D&C Linc (by turn)* **R** A D WILLIS, **NSM** D J FREEMAN
ELLESMERE (St Mary) *Lich 17* **P** *Bp* **V** P J EDGE, **Hon C** M W H GRAY
ELLESMERE (St Peter) *Sheff 3* **P** *Bp* **V** *vacant* 0114-276 2555
ELLESMERE PORT *Ches 9* **P** *Bp* **TR** G B MCGUINNESS, **TV** N R KING, **Hon C** R A WIFFEN, **NSM** G J WELCH
ELLINGHAM (St Mary) *see* Gillingham w Geldeston, Stockton, Ellingham etc *Nor*
ELLINGHAM (St Mary and All Saints) and Harbridge and Hyde w Ibsley *Win 9* **P** *Earl of Normanton and Keble Coll Ox (jt)* **V** M L RICHES
ELLINGHAM (St Maurice) *Newc 10* **P** *D&C Dur* **V** E M MCLEAN
ELLINGHAM, GREAT (St James), LITTLE (St Peter), Rockland All Saints, Rockland St Peter and Shropham w Snetterton *Nor 11* **P** *Bp, Major E H C Garnier, and CCC Cam (jt)* **P-in-c** K J REEVE
ELLINGTON (All Saints) *see* E Leightonstone *Ely*
ELLISFIELD (St Martin) *see* Cliddesden and Ellisfield w Farleigh Wallop etc *Win*
ELLISTOWN (St Christopher) *see* Hugglescote w Donington, Ellistown and Snibston *Leic*
ELLOUGHTON (St Mary) and Brough w Brantingham *York 13* **P** *Abp and D&C Dur (jt)* **V** P CUBITT
ELM (All Saints) and Friday Bridge w Coldham *Ely 15* **P** *Bp* **P-in-c** D L MASON, **Hon C** J E PHILLIPS
ELM (St Mary Magdalene) *see* Mells w Buckland Dinham, Elm, Whatley etc *B & W*
ELM PARK (St Nicholas) Hornchurch *Chelmsf 2* **P** *Bp* **V** R W FINCH, **NSM** R MORTON
ELMBRIDGE (St Mary) *see* Elmley Lovett w Hampton Lovett and Elmbridge etc *Worc*
ELMDON (St Nicholas) *see* Heydon, Gt and Lt Chishill, Chrishall etc *Chelmsf*
ELMDON (St Nicholas) (St Stephen's Church Centre) (St Nicholas' Hall) *Birm 11* **P** *Ch Trust Fund Trust* **R** P R CARTER, **NSM** C L CARTER
ELMDON HEATH (St Francis of Assisi) *see* Solihull *Birm*
ELMERS END (St James) *see* Beckenham St Jas *Roch*
ELMESTHORPE (St Mary) *see* Earl Shilton w Elmesthorpe *Leic*
ELMHAM, NORTH (St Mary) w Billingford and Worthing *Nor 14* **P** *Bp (1 turn), Viscount Coke (2 turns), and G & C Coll Cam (1 turn)* **P-in-c** D SIXSMITH
ELMHAM, SOUTH (St Cross) (St James) (St Margaret) (St Peter) (St Michael and All Angels) and Ilketshall *St E 14* **P** *Bp (3 turns), Ld Chan (1 turn), and Duke of Norfolk (1 turn)* **R** R H P THORNBURGH, **NSM** C S LEE
ELMHURST (Mission Room) *see* Lich St Chad *Lich*
ELMLEY *see* Emley *Wakef*
ELMLEY CASTLE (St Mary) w Bricklehampton and the Combertons *Worc 4* **P** *Bp* **R** T J HENDERSON
ELMLEY LOVETT (St Michael) w Hampton Lovett and Elmbridge w Rushdock *Worc 8* **P** *Bp and Ch Coll Cam (alt)* **P-in-c** J READER
ELMORE (St John the Baptist) *see* Hardwicke and Elmore w Longney *Glouc*
ELMSALL, NORTH (St Margaret) *see* Badsworth *Wakef*
ELMSALL, SOUTH (St Mary the Virgin) *Wakef 11* **P** *Bp* **V** P M WITTS, **NSM** A J EARL
ELMSETT (St Peter) w Aldham, Hintlesham, Chattisham and Kersey *St E 3* **P** *Bp, MMCET, and St Chad's Coll Dur (jt)* **R** J M SIMPSON
ELMSTEAD (St Anne and St Laurence) *Chelmsf 20* **P** *Jes Coll Cam* **P-in-c** M H GREEN
ELMSTED (St James the Great) w Hastingleigh *Cant 2* **P** *Abp* **P-in-c** D W J HOUSTON
ELMSTONE (not known) *see* Wingham w Elmstone and Preston w Stourmouth *Cant*
ELMSTONE HARDWICKE (St Mary Magdalene) *see* Swindon w Uckington and Elmstone Hardwicke *Glouc*
ELMSWELL (St John) *St E 10* **P** *MMCET* **R** M I MCNAMARA
ELMTON (St Peter) *Derby 3* **P** *Bp* **V** D J HULL
ELSDON (St Cuthbert) *see* N Tyne and Redesdale *Newc*
ELSECAR (Holy Trinity) *Sheff 11* **P** *Sir Philip Naylor-Leyland Bt* **V** *vacant* (01226) 742149
ELSENHAM (St Mary the Virgin) *see* Henham and Elsenham w Ugley *Chelmsf*
ELSFIELD (St Thomas of Canterbury) *see* Marston w Elsfield *Ox*
ELSHAM (All Saints) *see* N Wolds Gp *Linc*
ELSING (St Mary) *see* Lyng, Sparham, Elsing, Bylaugh, Bawdeswell etc *Nor*
ELSON (St Thomas) *Portsm 3* **P** *DBP* **P-in-c** S P RUNDELL, **NSM** M A HAY
ELSTEAD (St James) *Guildf 4* **P** *Adn Surrey* **R** W D LANG
ELSTED (St Paul) *see* Harting w Elsted and Treyford cum Didling *Chich*
ELSTERNWICK (St Laurence) *see* Burton Pidsea and Humbleton w Elsternwick *York*
ELSTON (All Saints) w Elston Chapelry *S'well 3* **P** *J C S Darwin Esq* **P-in-c** D HOLLIS
ELSTOW (St Mary and St Helena) *St Alb 13* **P** *Patr Bd* **TR** J R CROCKER, **TV** S T SMITH

ELSTREE (St Nicholas) and Borehamwood *St Alb 1* **P** *Patr Bd (3 turns), Ld Chan (1 turn)* **TR** T G WARR, **TV** R C A LESLIE, A-M L RENSHAW, K J SAYERS
ELSWICK, HIGH (St Paul) *Newc 7* **P** *Trustees* **P-in-c** G R CURRY
ELSWICK, HIGH (St Philip) *see* Newc St Phil and St Aug and St Matt w St Mary *Newc*
ELSWICK, LOW (St Stephen) *Newc 7* **P** *Ch Soc Trust* **V** G R CURRY
ELSWORTH (Holy Trinity) *see* Papworth *Ely*
ELTHAM (Holy Trinity) *S'wark 3* **P** *Bp* **V** M R HARRISON, **NSM** T N ALEXANDER-YATES
ELTHAM (St Barnabas) *S'wark 3* **P** *Bp* **P-in-c** S COOK, **Hon C** G E STEVENSON, **NSM** S E BLACKALL, **OLM** W J DAVID
ELTHAM (St John the Baptist) *S'wark 3* **P** *DBP* **V** J E NEAL
ELTHAM (St Saviour) *S'wark 3* **P** *Bp* **P-in-c** W J SAUNDERS, **NSM** K J GRANT
ELTHAM, NEW (All Saints) *S'wark 3* **P** *Bp* **V** J WADSWORTH, **OLM** G S LYONS
ELTHAM PARK (St Luke) *S'wark 3* **P** *Bp* **P-in-c** E CRANMER, **Hon C** P A KEOGH, **NSM** I NASH, **OLM** R J NORBURY
ELTISLEY (St Pandionia and St John the Baptist) *see* Papworth *Ely*
ELTON (All Saints) *see* S Darley, Elton and Winster *Derby*
ELTON All Saints *Man 10* **P** *R Bury St Mary* **P-in-c** S MILLINGTON, **Hon C** P J BEDDINGTON
ELTON (All Saints) w Stibbington and Water Newton *Ely 11* **P** *Sir Peter Proby Bt, Sir Philip Naylor-Leyland Bt, and Keble Coll Ox (jt)* **R** *vacant* (01832) 280222
ELTON (St John) *Dur 10* **P** *St Chad Coll Dur* **V** M M GILLEY, **NSM** P CLAYTON
ELTON (St Mary the Virgin) *see* Wigmore Abbey *Heref*
ELTON (St Stephen) *Man 10* **P** *V Elton All SS* **P-in-c** S D HARROP, **OLM** A M BULCOCK
ELTON-ON-THE-HILL (St Michael) *see* Cropwell Bishop w Colston Bassett, Granby etc *S'well*
ELVASTON (St Bartholomew) *see* Aston on Trent, Elvaston, Weston on Trent etc *Derby*
ELVEDEN (St Andrew and St Patrick) *see* Brandon and Santon Downham w Elveden etc *St E*
ELVETHAM HEATH Local Ecumenical Project *Guildf 1* **Min** D G M PRICE
ELVINGTON (Holy Trinity) w Sutton on Derwent and East Cottingwith *York 2* **P** *Lt Col J Darlington* **C** M C PARKIN
ELWICK HALL (St Peter) *see* Hart w Elwick Hall *Dur*
ELWORTH (St Peter) and Warmingham *Ches 11* **P** *V Sandbach, Q H Crewe Esq and J C Crewe Esq (alt)* **R** D J PAGE, **C** P M WITHINGTON
ELY (Holy Trinity w St Mary) (St Peter) *Ely 12* **P** *Patr Bd* **TR** F J KILNER, **TV** J R SANSOM, **C** A C PARTRIDGE, **Hon C** M J M HUGHES, **NSM** V J KILNER, E A HUBBARD
EMBERTON (All Saints) *see* Lamp *Ox*
EMBLETON (Holy Trinity) w Rennington and Rock *Newc 9* **P** *Mert Coll Ox* **V** J M MOUNTNEY
EMBLETON (St Cuthbert) *see* Cockermouth w Embleton and Wythop *Carl*
EMBROOK (Community of St Nicholas) *see* Wokingham St Paul *Ox*
EMBSAY (St Mary the Virgin) w Eastby *Bradf 7* **P** *R Skipton H Trin* **P-in-c** A P BOTWRIGHT, **C** J W DANIELS
EMERY DOWN (Christ Church) *see* Lyndhurst and Emery Down and Minstead *Win*
EMLEY (St Michael the Archangel) *Wakef 6* **P** *Lord Savile* **P-in-c** C E BULLIMORE, **C** H M HODGSON, **OLM** L BROOKES
EMMANUEL Team Ministry, The *Wakef 1* **P** *Patr Bd* **NSM** D KENT
EMMAUS Parish Team, The *Leic 2* **P** *Bp* **R** D C WHITE, **C** L D BRABIN-SMITH, **NSM** J N N ANAND
EMMER GREEN (St Barnabas) w Caversham Park *Ox 15* **P** *Bp and Ch Ch Ox (jt)* **R** D E CHANDLER, **OLM** M L DIMMICK
EMNETH (St Edmund) and Marshland St James *Ely 15* **P** *Bp* **V** D L MASON
EMPINGHAM (St Peter) and Exton w Horn w Whitwell *Pet 14* **P** *Bp and Earl of Gainsborough (alt)* **C** P STREET
EMPSHOTT (Holy Rood) *see* Greatham w Empshott and Hawkley w Prior's Dean *Portsm*
EMSCOTE (All Saints) *see* Warwick *Cov*
EMSWORTH (St James) *see* Warblington w Emsworth *Portsm*
ENBORNE (St Michael and All Angels) *see* W Woodhay w Enborne, Hampstead Marshall etc *Ox*
ENDCLIFFE (St Augustine) *Sheff 2* **P** *Ch Burgesses* **P-in-c** J C SULLIVAN, **NSM** I W DRAFFAN
ENDERBY (St John the Baptist) w Lubbesthorpe and Thurlaston *Leic 10* **P** *Bp and F B Drummond Esq* **P-in-c** S J DAVIES
ENDON (St Luke) *see* Bagnall w Endon *Lich*
ENFIELD (Christ Church) Trent Park *Lon 18* **P** *Ch Trust Fund Trust* **V** R D JAMES, **C** S L ALEXANDER, A J WADSWORTH
ENFIELD (St Andrew) *Lon 18* **P** *Trin Coll Cam* **V** M M EDGE, **Hon C** O R COPE
ENFIELD (St George) *Lon 18* **P** *Bp* **V** C J FULLER
ENFIELD (St James) (St Barnabas) *Lon 18* **P** *V Enfield* **V** S LEADER
ENFIELD (St John the Baptist) *see* Clay Hill St Jo and St Luke *Lon*
ENFIELD (St Luke) *as above*
ENFIELD (St Mark) *see* Bush Hill Park St Mark *Lon*
ENFIELD (St Matthew) *see* Ponders End St Matt *Lon*
ENFIELD (St Michael and All Angels) *Lon 18* **P** *V Enfield* **P-in-c** A J F MANSFIELD
ENFIELD (St Peter and St Paul) *Lon 18* **P** *Bp* **V** J C VAUGHAN
ENFIELD (St Stephen) *see* Bush Hill Park St Steph *Lon*
ENFIELD CHASE (St Mary Magdalene) *Lon 18* **P** *Bp* **V** G J GILES, **NSM** J W FISH
ENFORD (All Saints) *see* Avon Valley *Sarum*
ENGLEFIELD (St Mark) *see* Theale and Englefield *Ox*
ENGLEFIELD GREEN (St Jude) *Guildf 11* **P** *Bp* **V** L C SMITH
ENGLISH BICKNOR (St Mary) *see* Forest of Dean Ch Ch w English Bicknor *Glouc*
ENGLISHCOMBE (St Peter) *see* Bath St Barn w Englishcombe *B & W*
ENHAM ALAMEIN (St George) *see* Knight's Enham and Smannell w Enham Alamein *Win*
ENMORE (St Michael) *see* Aisholt, Enmore, Goathurst, Nether Stowey etc *B & W*
ENMORE GREEN (St John the Evangelist) *see* Shaston *Sarum*
ENNERDALE (St Mary) *see* Lamplugh w Ennerdale *Carl*
ENSBURY PARK (St Thomas) *Sarum 7* **P** *Bp* **V** S A EVANS
ENSTONE (St Kenelm) *see* Chase *Ox*
ENVILLE (St Mary the Virgin) *see* Kinver and Enville *Lich*
EPPERSTONE (Holy Cross) *S'well 15* **P** *Bp, Ld Chan, and C P L Francklin Esq (by turn)* **R** M J BROCK, **C** J E DRAYCOTT, **NSM** M N TAYLOR
EPPING District (All Saints) (St John the Baptist) *Chelmsf 25* **P** *Patr Bd* **TR** G CONNOR, **TV** C F J BARD, **C** B C MORRISON, C SMITH
EPPLETON and Hetton le Hole *Dur 14* **P** *Prime Min and Bp (alt)* **C** J M PERKINS, K L WASSALL
EPSOM (St Barnabas) *Guildf 9* **P** *Bp* **V** M C PRESTON, **NSM** S H BULL
EPSOM (St Martin) (St Stephen on the Downs) *Guildf 9* **P** *Bp* **V** S J TALBOTT, **C** C S BOURNE, **NSM** C A CASE
EPSOM COMMON (Christ Church) *Guildf 9* **P** *Bp* **V** A J FACEY, **C** D M AYRES
EPWELL (St Anne) *see* Wykeham *Ox*
EPWORTH Group, The (St Andrew) *Linc 1* **P** *Prime Min (2 turns), Ld Chan (1 turn)* **R** J D BROWN
ERCALL, HIGH (St Michael and All Angels) *see* Wrockwardine Deanery *Lich*
ERDINGTON Team Ministry, The (St Barnabas) (St Chad) *Birm 8* **P** *Patr Bd* **TR** P R SPENCER, **TV** N M A TRAYNOR, **NSM** E M BLAIR-CHAPPELL, P K ZAIDI-CROSSE
ERIDGE GREEN (Holy Trinity) *see* Frant w Eridge *Chich*
ERISWELL (St Laurence and St Peter) *see* Mildenhall *St E*
ERITH (Christ Church) *Roch 15* **P** *Bp* **V** J DRAYCOTT
ERITH (St John the Baptist) *Roch 15* **P** *Bp* **P-in-c** R J IRETON
ERITH (St Paul) Northumberland Heath *Roch 15* **P** *CPAS* **V** *vacant* (01322) 332809
ERLESTOKE (Holy Saviour) *see* Bratton, Edington and Imber, Erlestoke etc *Sarum*
ERMINE (St John) *see* Linc St Jo *Linc*
ERMINGTON (St Peter and St Paul) and Ugborough *Ex 21* **P** *Prime Min (1 turn), Bp and Grocers' Co (3 turns)* **V** N M HUNT
ERNESETTLE (St Aidan) *Ex 22* **P** *Bp* **P-in-c** G J SMITH
ERPINGHAM (St Mary) w Calthorpe, Ingworth, Aldborough, Thurgarton and Alby w Thwaite *Nor 19* **P** *Bp, Lord Walpole, Gt Hosp Nor, Mrs S M Lilly, and DBP (by turn)* **R** B T FAULKNER, **NSM** J W SMITH
ERRINGDEN *Wakef 3* **P** *Bp and V Halifax (jt)* **V** J T ALLISON, **NSM** A MAUDE
ERWARTON (St Mary the Virgin) *see* Chelmondiston and Erwarton w Harkstead *St E*
ERYHOLME (St Mary) *see* E Richmond *Ripon*
ESCOMB (no dedication) *Dur 6* **P** *Bp* **V** N P DENHAM
ESCOT (St Philip and St James) *see* Feniton, Buckerell and Escot *Ex*

ESCRICK (St Helen) and Stillingfleet w Naburn *York 2* **P** *Abp, D&C, and N C Forbes Adam Esq (jt)* **R** R M KIRKMAN
ESH (St Michael and All Angels) *Dur 1* **P** *Prime Min* **V** M J PEERS, **C** T E HUBBLE
ESHER (Christ Church) (St George) *Guildf 8* **P** *Wadh Coll Ox* **R** W A J ALLBERRY
ESHOLT (St Paul) *see* Guiseley w Esholt *Bradf*
ESK MOOR, MIDDLE *York 22* **P** *Abp* **V** D C KING
ESKDALE (St Catherine) (St Bega's Mission), Irton, Muncaster and Waberthwaite *Carl 5* **P** *Bp, Adn W Cumberland, Mrs P Gordon-Duff-Pennington, and P Stanley Esq (jt)* **P-in-c** A C BAKER, **NSM** I M HALL
ESKDALESIDE (St John) w Ugglebarnby and Sneaton *York 22* **P** *Abp* **V** G J WOOD
ESSENDINE (St Mary the Virgin) *see* Ryhall w Essendine and Carlby *Pet*
ESSENDON (St Mary the Virgin) *see* Lt Berkhamsted and Bayford, Essendon etc *St Alb*
ESSINGTON (St John the Evangelist) *Lich 2* **P** *Bp, R Bushbury, R Wednesfield, and Simeon's Trustees (jt)* **V** N S ATKINS
ESTON (Christ Church) w Normanby *York 18* **P** *Abp* **TR** J G BLAKELEY, **TV** D N H CHISLETT
ESTOVER (Christ Church) *Ex 23* **P** *Bp* **P-in-c** T R J DICKENS
ETAL (St Mary the Virgin) *see* Ford and Etal *Newc*
ETCHILHAMPTON (St Andrew) *see* Bishop's Cannings, All Cannings etc *Sarum*
ETCHING HILL (The Holy Spirit) *see* Rugeley *Lich*
ETCHINGHAM (Assumption and St Nicholas) *Chich 15* **P** *Bp* **R** R DIXON
ETHERLEY (St Cuthbert) *Dur 6* **P** *Bp* **R** N P DENHAM
ETON (St John the Evangelist) *see* Riverside *Ox*
ETON WICK (St John the Baptist) *as above*
ETTINGSHALL (Holy Trinity) *Lich 28* **P** *Bp* **V** A J JONES
ETTINGTON (Holy Trinity and St Thomas of Canterbury) *see* Butlers Marston and the Pillertons w Ettington *Cov*
ETTON (St Mary) w Dalton Holme *York 8* **P** *Lord Hotham* **P-in-c** R C THORP
ETTON (St Stephen) w Helpston and Maxey *Pet 13* **P** *Sir Stephen Hastings (2 turns), D&C (1 turn)* **R** *vacant* (01733) 253456
ETWALL (St Helen) w Egginton *Derby 14* **P** *Bp, Sir Henry Every Bt, Major J W Chandos-Pole, and DBP (by turn)* **R** S L RAYNER, **NSM** P A SHORT
EUSTON (St Genevieve) *see* Blackbourne *St E*
EUXTON (not known) *Blackb 4* **P** *Bp* **V** J G RILEY
EVE HILL (St James the Great) *see* Dudley St Jas *Worc*
EVEDON (St Mary) *see* Kirkby Laythorpe *Linc*
EVENLEY (St George) *see* Aynho and Croughton w Evenley etc *Pet*
EVENLODE (St Edward King and Martyr) *see* Broadwell, Evenlode, Oddington, Adlestrop etc *Glouc*
EVENWOOD (St Paul) *Dur 7* **P** *Bp* **P-in-c** K STEVENTON
EVERCREECH (St Peter) w Chesterblade and Milton Clevedon *B & W 2* **P** *DBP* **P-in-c** P N RAPSEY
EVERDON (St Mary) *see* Weedon Bec w Everdon and Dodford *Pet*
EVERINGHAM (St Everilda) *see* Holme and Seaton Ross Gp *York*
EVERSDEN, GREAT (St Mary) *see* Haslingfield w Harlton and Gt and Lt Eversden *Ely*
EVERSDEN, LITTLE (St Helen) *as above*
EVERSHOLT (St John the Baptist) *see* Woburn w Eversholt, Milton Bryan, Battlesden etc *St Alb*
EVERSHOT (St Osmund) *see* Melbury *Sarum*
EVERSLEY (St Mary) *see* Yateley and Eversley *Win*
EVERTON (Holy Trinity) and Mattersey w Clayworth *S'well 1* **P** *Ld Chan (2 turns), Bp (2 turns)* **R** *vacant* (01777) 817364
EVERTON (St George) *Liv 3* **P** *Bp* **NSM** I D CASSIDY
EVERTON (St Mary) *see* Gamlingay and Everton *Ely*
EVERTON (St Mary) *see* Milford *Win*
EVERTON (St Peter) (St John Chrysostom) (Emmanuel) *Liv 3* **P** *Patr Bd* **R** H CORBETT, **C** D H STATTER
EVESBATCH (St Andrew) *see* Acton Beauchamp and Evesbatch w Stanford Bishop *Heref*
EVESHAM (All Saints w St Lawrence) w Norton and Lenchwick *Worc 1* **P** *Bp and D&C (jt)* **V** R N ARMITAGE, **NSM** C W PARR
EVINGTON (St Denys) *Leic 1* **P** *Bp* **V** S B HEYGATE, **C** J IQBAL
EVINGTON (St Stephen) *see* Twigworth, Down Hatherley, Norton, The Leigh etc *Glouc*
EVINGTON, NORTH (St Stephen) *Leic 1* **P** *Bp* **P-in-c** I ST C RICHARDS, **NSM** L M HUGHES
EWELL (St Francis of Assisi) Ruxley Lane *Guildf 9* **P** *Bp* **V** S G THOMAS, **NSM** I A JACOBSON
EWELL (St Mary the Virgin) *Guildf 9* **P** *Bp* **V** W R HANFORD
EWELL, WEST (All Saints) *Guildf 9* **P** *Bp* **V** *vacant* (020) 8393 4357
EWELME (St Mary the Virgin), Brightwell Baldwin, Cuxham w Easington *Ox 1* **P** *F D Wright Esq and Mert Coll Ox, Prime Min (alt)* **R** M W GARNER
EWERBY (St Andrew) *see* Kirkby Laythorpe *Linc*
EWHURST (St James the Great) *Chich 20* **P** *K Coll Cam* **R** G L WINCHESTER
EWHURST (St Peter and St Paul) *Guildf 2* **P** *Ld Chan* **R** D A MINNS
EWOOD (St Bartholomew) *see* Blackb Redeemer *Blackb*
EWSHOT (St Mary the Virgin) *see* Crondall and Ewshot *Guildf*
EWYAS HAROLD (St Michael and All Angels) w Dulas, Kenderchurch, Abbeydore, Bacton, Kentchurch, Llangua, Rowlestone, Llancillo, Walterstone, Kilpeck, St Devereux and Wormbridge *Heref 1* **P** *Patr Bd* **P-in-c** J F BUTTERWORTH
EXBOURNE (St Mary the Virgin) *see* Hatherleigh, Meeth, Exbourne and Jacobstowe *Ex*
EXBURY (St Katherine) *see* Beaulieu and Exbury and E Boldre *Win*
EXE, WEST (St Paul) *see* Tiverton St Geo and St Paul *Ex*
EXE VALLEY *see* Washfield, Stoodleigh, Withleigh etc *Ex*
EXETER (St David) (St Michael and All Angels) *Ex 3* **P** *D&C* **V** J M HENTON, **C** J M D HUGHES, **Hon C** P A LEE
EXETER (St James) *Ex 3* **P** *D&C* **R** H H D PRYSE
EXETER (St Leonard w Holy Trinity) *Ex 3* **P** *CPAS* **R** D R HARRIS, **C** J P A ELVIN, D P AP G MEIRION-JONES
EXETER (St Mark) (St Matthew) (St Sidwell) *Ex 3* **P** *Bp and D&C (jt)* **R** S CROFT
EXETER (St Mary Steps) *see* Heavitree and St Mary Steps *Ex*
EXETER (St Paul) *as above*
EXETER (St Thomas the Apostle) (Emmanuel) (St Andrew) (St Philip) *Ex 3* **P** *Bp* **TR** A WHITE, **TV** D B M GILL, C P BARRETT, **C** G A M RAWLINGS
EXETER, CENTRAL (St Martin) (St Mary Arches) (St Olave) (St Pancras) (St Petrock) (St Stephen) *Ex 3* **P** *Patr Bd* **NSM** A A HALL
EXFORD (St Mary Magdalene), Exmoor, Hawkridge and Withypool *B & W 16* **P** *Bp (1 turn), Peterho Cam (2 turns)* **P-in-c** J K L POWELL
EXHALL (St Giles) *Cov 5* **P** *Bp* **V** W M SMITH, **C** L A MUDD
EXHALL (St Giles) w Wixford *Cov 7* **P** *Bp* **P-in-c** S R TASH, **NSM** L E DAVIES
EXMINSTER (St Martin) and Kenn *Ex 6* **P** *Mrs M P L Bate and 12 Govs of Crediton Ch (jt)* **P-in-c** J D A WILLIAMS
EXMOOR (St Luke) *see* Exford, Exmoor, Hawkridge and Withypool *B & W*
EXMOUTH (All Saints) *see* Withycombe Raleigh *Ex*
EXMOUTH (Holy Trinity) *see* Littleham w Exmouth *Ex*
EXMOUTH (St Andrew) *as above*
EXMOUTH (St John in the Wilderness) *see* Withycombe Raleigh *Ex*
EXMOUTH (St John the Evangelist) *as above*
EXMOUTH (St Saviour) *see* Littleham w Exmouth *Ex*
EXNING (St Agnes) *see* Newmarket St Mary w Exning St Agnes *St E*
EXNING (St Martin) (St Philip) w Landwade *St E 11* **P** *D&C Cant* **V** S PETTITT, **NSM** C T MCCARTY
EXTON (St Andrew) *see* Lympstone and Woodbury w Exton *Ex*
EXTON (St Peter and St Paul) *see* Empingham and Exton w Horn w Whitwell *Pet*
EXTON (St Peter and St Paul) *see* Meonstoke w Corhampton cum Exton *Portsm*
EXTON (St Peter) and Winsford and Cutcombe w Luxborough *B & W 16* **P** *Ld Chan (2 turns), Em Coll Cam (1 turn), and G A Warren Esq and D M Warren Esq (1 turn)* **R** T M STAPLES
EXWICK (St Andrew) *Ex 3* **P** *Lord Wraxall* **P-in-c** M S HART
EYAM (St Lawrence) *Derby 2* **P** *Earl Temple* **P-in-c** A S MONTGOMERIE
EYDON (St Nicholas) *see* Woodford Halse w Eydon *Pet*
EYE (St Matthew) *Pet 13* **P** *Bp* **V** *vacant* (01733) 222334
EYE (St Peter and St Paul) *see* Leominster *Heref*
EYE (St Peter and St Paul) *St E 16* **P** *Bp, SMF, and Lt Comdr G C Marshall (jt)* **R** A M MITCHAM
EYEWORTH (All Saints) *see* Dunton w Wrestlingworth and Eyeworth *St Alb*
EYKE (All Saints) *see* Wilford Peninsula *St E*
EYNESBURY (St Mary) *Ely 10* **P** *Bp* **R** T J MCCABE
EYNSFORD (St Martin) w Farningham and Lullingstone *Roch 10* **P** *D&C* **R** N H TAYLOR, **NSM** C H SALMON
EYNSHAM (St Leonard) and Cassington *Ox 9* **P** *Wycliffe Hall Ox and Ch Ch Ox (alt)* **V** I R BENTLEY, **NSM** A C ATHERSTONE, **OLM** J A UNDERWOOD, R ASTON

EYPE (St Peter) *see* Symondsbury *Sarum*
EYRES MONSELL (St Hugh) *Leic 2* **P** *Bp* **V** D H P BROWN
EYTHORNE (St Peter and St Paul) and Elvington w Waldershare and Barfreystone w Sherdswell and Coldred *Cant 4* **P** *Abp, St Jo Coll Ox, and Earl of Guilford (jt)* **R** A L WAY, **C** H M BURN, **OLM** C M WILKINSON
EYTON (All Saints) *see* Leominster *Heref*
EYTON (St Catherine) *see* Wellington, All SS w Eyton *Lich*
FACCOMBE (St Barnabas) *see* Hurstbourne Tarrant, Faccombe, Vernham Dean etc *Win*
FACEBY (St Mary Magdalene) *see* Whorlton w Carlton and Faceby *York*
FACIT (St John the Evangelist) *see* Whitworth w Facit *Man*
FACIT (St Michael the Archangel) *as above*
FAILAND (St Bartholomew) *see* Wraxall *B & W*
FAILSWORTH (Holy Family) *Man 19* **P** *Bp* **P-in-c** P B MCEVITT
FAILSWORTH (Holy Trinity) *Man 19* **P** *The Crown* **R** *vacant* 0161-682 7901
FAILSWORTH (St John) (St John the Evangelist) *Man 19* **P** *Bp* **R** A J MATTHEWS
FAIR OAK (St Thomas) *Win 10* **P** *Bp* **V** D S SNUGGS, **C** W M PIDGEON
FAIRBURN (St James) *see* Ledsham w Fairburn *York*
FAIRFIELD (St John the Divine) *Liv 3* **P** *MMCET* **V** A W PORTER
FAIRFIELD (St Mark) *see* Belbroughton w Fairfield and Clent *Worc*
FAIRFIELD (St Matthew) *Linc 9* **P** *Bp* **V** *vacant* (01472) 821183
FAIRFIELD (St Peter) *Derby 4* **P** *Ch Govs* **P-in-c** D J COOPER
FAIRFIELD (St Thomas à Becket) *see* Appledore w Brookland, Fairfield, Brenzett etc *Cant*
FAIRFORD (St Mary the Virgin) and Kempsford w Whelford *Glouc 12* **P** *D&C, Bp, and Mercers' Co (jt)* **P-in-c** B C ATKINSON, **C** D M ACKERMAN
FAIRHAVEN (St Paul) *Blackb 10* **P** *J C Hilton Esq* **V** G ROUSE
FAIRLIGHT, Guestling and Pett *Chich 20* **P** *Patr Bd* **R** B E CROSBY, **Hon C** H E PATTEN
FAIRSEAT (Holy Innocents) *see* Stansted w Fairseat and Vigo *Roch*
FAIRSTEAD (St Mary) w Terling and White Notley w Faulkbourne *Chelmsf 24* **P** *Bp, Exors Lord Rayleigh, and C W O Parker Esq (by turn)* **R** J M HALL
FAIRWARP (Christ Church) *Chich 21* **P** *Bp* **P-in-c** M COXHEAD, **NSM** S J MORGAN
FAIRWEATHER GREEN (St Saviour) *Bradf 1* **P** *Bp* **V** P J CLEMENT
FAKENHAM (St Peter and St Paul) w Alethorpe *Nor 15* **P** *Trin Coll Cam* **R** A C BELL
FAKENHAM MAGNA (St Peter) *see* Blackbourne *St E*
FALCONWOOD (Bishop Ridley Church) *Roch 15* **P** *Bp* **V** I F DURNDELL
FALDINGWORTH (All Saints) *see* Middle Rasen Gp *Linc*
FALFIELD (St George) *see* Cromhall, Tortworth, Tytherington, Falfield etc *Glouc*
FALINGE (St Edmund) *see* Rochdale *Man*
FALKENHAM (St Ethelbert) *see* Kirton w Falkenham *St E*
FALLOWFIELD (St Crispin) *see* Withington St Crispin *Man*
FALMER (St Laurence) *see* Stanmer w Falmer *Chich*
FALMOUTH (All Saints) *Truro 3* **P** *Bp* **P-in-c** S R F DRAKELEY
FALMOUTH (King Charles the Martyr) *Truro 3* **P** *Bp* **P-in-c** S J TUDGEY
FALSTONE (St Peter) *see* N Tyne and Redesdale *Newc*
FAMBRIDGE, NORTH (Holy Trinity) *see* Creeksea w Althorne, Latchingdon and N Fambridge *Chelmsf*
FAMBRIDGE, SOUTH (All Saints) *see* Ashingdon w S Fambridge *Chelmsf*
FANGFOSS (St Martin) *see* Barmby Moor Gp *York*
FAR FOREST (Holy Trinity) *see* Mamble w Bayton, Rock w Heightington etc *Worc*
FAR HEADINGLEY St Chad (St Oswald) *Ripon 7* **P** *Lord Grimthorpe* **V** B M OVEREND, **C** A CLAYTON
FARCET HAMPTON (St Mary) *Ely 11* **P** *Bp and Em Coll Cam (jt)* **V** D W SPENCER
FAREHAM (Holy Trinity) (St Columba) *Portsm 2* **P** *Bp* **TR** F A WRIGHT, **TV** J N J C DUSSEK, **C** M F PYE, **Hon C** A P BURR, **NSM** D M JACKSON, S MARTIN, G J S SNAPE
FAREHAM (St John the Evangelist) *Portsm 2* **P** *CPAS* **V** P D HALL
FAREHAM (St Peter and St Paul) *Portsm 2* **P** *Bp* **V** A W MARKS
FAREWELL (St Bartholomew) *Lich 1* **P** *MMCET* **P-in-c** M J BUTT, **NSM** M R AUSTIN, **OLM** J R ANDREWS
FARFORTH (St Peter) *see* S Ormsby Gp *Linc*
FARINGDON, GREAT (All Saints) w Little Coxwell *Ox 17* **P** *Simeon's Trustees* **P-in-c** C J DRAPER
FARINGDON, LITTLE (St Margaret of England) *see* Shill Valley and Broadshire *Ox*
FARINGTON MOSS (St Paul) *Blackb 5* **P** *V Penwortham* **P-in-c** P D HALLETT, **NSM** F KENDALL
FARLAM (St Thomas à Becket) *see* Eden, Gelt and Irthing *Carl*
FARLEIGH (St Mary) *see* Warlingham w Chelsham and Farleigh *S'wark*
FARLEIGH, EAST (not known) *see* Coxheath, E Farleigh, Hunton, Linton etc *Roch*
FARLEIGH, WEST (All Saints) *as above*
FARLEIGH HUNGERFORD (St Leonard) *see* Hardington Vale *B & W*
FARLEIGH WALLOP (St Andrew) *see* Cliddesden and Ellisfield w Farleigh Wallop etc *Win*
FARLESTHORPE (St Andrew) *see* Bilsby w Farlesthorpe *Linc*
FARLEY (All Saints) *see* Clarendon *Sarum*
FARLEY CHAMBERLAYNE (St John) *see* Michelmersh and Awbridge and Braishfield etc *Win*
FARLEY GREEN (St Michael) *see* Shere, Albury and Chilworth *Guildf*
FARLEY HILL (St John the Baptist) *St Alb 14* **P** *Bp* **V** R E MERRY
FARLEY HILL (St John the Evangelist) *see* Loddon Reach *Ox*
FARLINGTON (St Andrew) (Church of the Resurrection) *Portsm 6* **P** *Mrs S J Wynter-Bee and E G Nugee Esq (jt)* **R** S B SUMMERS, **NSM** G A STEADMAN
FARLINGTON (St Leonard) *see* Sheriff Hutton, Farlington, Stillington etc *York*
FARLOW (St Giles) *see* Stottesdon w Farlow, Cleeton St Mary etc *Heref*
FARMBOROUGH (All Saints) and Marksbury and Stanton Prior *B & W 10* **P** *MMCET (3 turns), Duchy of Cornwall (1 turn), and DBF (1 turn)* **R** J P KNOTT, **Hon C** J J HARRIES
FARMCOTE (St Faith) *see* The Guitings, Cutsdean, Farmcote etc *Glouc*
FARMINGTON (St Peter) *see* Northleach w Hampnett and Farmington etc *Glouc*
FARMOOR (St Mary) *see* Cumnor *Ox*
FARNBOROUGH (All Saints) *see* Beedon and Peasemore w W Ilsley and Farnborough *Ox*
FARNBOROUGH (St Botolph) *see* Avon Dassett w Farnborough and Fenny Compton *Cov*
FARNBOROUGH (St Giles) (St Nicholas) *Roch 16* **P** *Em Coll Cam* **R** M J HUGHES, **C** M HIRST
FARNBOROUGH, NORTH (St Peter) (Good Shepherd) *Guildf 1* **P** *Patr Bd* **TR** D G WILLEY, **TV** N L SHARP, **C** J C HUNT, **NSM** S J CRABTREE, C F HOLT, **OLM** M JAMES
FARNBOROUGH, SOUTH (St Mark) *Guildf 1* **P** *Bp* **V** I C HEDGES
FARNCOMBE (St John the Evangelist) *Guildf 4* **P** *Bp* **R** M BLAKE
FARNDALE (St Mary) *see* Kirkbymoorside w Gillamoor, Farndale etc *York*
FARNDON (St Chad) and Coddington *Ches 5* **P** *Duke of Westmr and D&C (jt)* **V** D A BOYD
FARNDON (St Peter) w Thorpe, Hawton and Cotham *S'well 3* **P** *Ld Chan* **R** J B QUARRELL
FARNDON, EAST (St John the Baptist) *see* Arthingworth, Harrington w Oxendon and E Farndon *Pet*
FARNHAM (St Andrew) *Guildf 3* **P** *Bp* **R** A K TUCK, **NSM** J M LIEVESLEY
FARNHAM (St Laurence) *see* Chase *Sarum*
FARNHAM (St Mary) *see* Sternfield, Benhall, Snape etc *St E*
FARNHAM (St Mary the Virgin) *see* Stansted Mountfitchet w Birchanger and Farnham *Chelmsf*
FARNHAM (St Oswald) *see* Walkingham Hill *Ripon*
FARNHAM COMMON (St John the Evangelist) *see* Farnham Royal w Hedgerley *Ox*
FARNHAM ROYAL (St Mary the Virgin) w Hedgerley *Ox 23* **P** *Bp and Eton Coll (jt)* **P-in-c** G H SAUNDERS, **NSM** S F BEDWELL, **OLM** G J BRIGGS
FARNHAM ROYAL SOUTH (St Michael) *see* W Slough *Ox*
FARNINGHAM (St Peter and St Paul) *see* Eynsford w Farningham and Lullingstone *Roch*
FARNLEY (All Saints) *see* Leathley w Farnley, Fewston and Blubberhouses *Bradf*
FARNLEY (St Michael) *Ripon 6* **P** *Bp* **R** D GRASBY, **Hon C** D H RANDOLPH-HORN
FARNLEY, NEW (St James) *see* Farnley *Ripon*

FARNLEY TYAS (St Lucias) *see* Almondbury w Farnley Tyas *Wakef*
FARNSFIELD (St Michael) *S'well 15* **P** *Bp* **P-in-c** E F CULLY, **C** J R CHAMBERS, **NSM** M A GROVES
FARNWORTH (St George) *see* New Bury *Man*
FARNWORTH (St Luke) (Bold Mission) (Cronton Mission) *Liv 13* **P** *V Prescot St Mary* **V** H M MORBY, **C** P MAKIN
FARNWORTH, EAST (All Saints) (St John) (St Peter) (St Thomas) and Kearsley *Man 12* **P** *Bp (2 turns), Ld Chan (1 turn)* **TR** C E VANN, **TV** C NIGHTINGALE, **NSM** J H M AINSWORTH, **OLM** P S CASTLE
FARRINGDON (All Saints) *see* Northanger *Win*
FARRINGDON (St Petrock and St Barnabas) *see* Aylesbeare, Rockbeare, Farringdon etc *Ex*
FARRINGTON GURNEY (St John the Baptist) *B & W 12* **P** *Bp* **V** J G EDWARDS
FARSLEY (St John the Evangelist) *Bradf 3* **P** *V Calverley* **V** J N WHITE
FARTHINGHOE (St Michael and All Angels) *see* Aynho and Croughton w Evenley etc *Pet*
FARTHINGSTONE (St Mary the Virgin) *see* Blakesley w Adstone and Maidford etc *Pet*
FARWAY (St Michael and All Angels) *see* Offwell, Northleigh, Farway, Cotleigh etc *Ex*
FATFIELD (St George) *Dur 11* **P** *Lord Lambton* **P-in-c** B P S VALLIS
FAULKBOURNE (St Germanus) *see* Fairstead w Terling and White Notley etc *Chelmsf*
FAULS (Holy Emmanuel) *Lich 22* **P** *V Prees* **P-in-c** D F B BALDWIN, **Hon C** H S WATSON
FAVELL, WEST (Emmanuel) *see* Northampton Em *Pet*
FAVERSHAM (St Mary of Charity) *Cant 6* **P** *D&C* **P-in-c** A C OEHRING, **Hon C** R V PARRETT, **NSM** C B CLAPPERTON
FAWDON (St Mary the Virgin) *Newc 5* **P** *Bp* **P-in-c** P INGHAM
FAWKENHURST *Cant 10* **P** *DBP* **R** *vacant*
FAWKHAM (St Mary) and Hartley *Roch 1* **P** *Bp and D&C (jt)* **R** R M WORSSAM
FAWLEY (All Saints) *Win 11* **P** *Bp* **R** B P JAMES, **C** S VAN DER TOORN
FAWLEY (St Mary) *see* Brightwalton w Catmore, Leckhampstead etc *Ox*
FAWLEY (St Mary the Virgin) *see* Hambleden Valley *Ox*
FAWSLEY (St Mary the Virgin) *see* Badby w Newham and Charwelton w Fawsley etc *Pet*
FAZAKERLEY (Emmanuel) (St Paul) *Liv 7* **P** *Patr Bd* **TR** W FORSTER, **TV** M SIMMONS
FAZAKERLEY (St Nathanael) *see* Walton-on-the-Hill *Liv*
FAZELEY (St Paul) (St Barnabas) *Lich 4* **P** *Bp* **V** H J BAKER, **OLM** S ROWLEY, B WILLIAMS
FEATHERSTONE (All Saints) *Wakef 11* **P** *Ch Ch Ox* **V** N CLEWS, **C** M R MATTHEWS
FEATHERSTONE (School Chapel) *see* Haltwhistle and Greenhead *Newc*
FECKENHAM (St John the Baptist) *see* Bowbrook N *Worc*
FEERING (All Saints) *see* Kelvedon and Feering *Chelmsf*
FELBRIDGE (St John) *S'wark 26* **P** *DBP* **V** S G BOWEN
FELBRIGG (St Margaret) *see* Roughton and Felbrigg, Metton, Sustead etc *Nor*
FELIXKIRK (St Felix) w Boltby *York 19* **P** *Abp* **P-in-c** P R A R HOARE, **NSM** E A HOARE
FELIXSTOWE (St John the Baptist) (St Edmund) *St E 2* **P** *Bp* **P-in-c** D C LOWE, **C** G J S HAYHOE
FELIXSTOWE (St Peter and St Paul) (St Andrew) (St Nicholas) *St E 2* **P** *Ch Trust Fund Trust* **P-in-c** J L ASTON, **OLM** H STALKER
FELKIRK (St Peter) *Wakef 11* **P** *Bp* **C** R HARRIS
FELLING (Christ Church) *Dur 12* **P** *CPAS* **V** T J DAVIDSON
FELLISCLIFFE (Mission Church) *see* Hampsthwaite and Killinghall and Birstwith *Ripon*
FELLSIDE TEAM, The *Blackb 9* **P** *Patr Bd* **TR** T D WILBY, **TV** J W FINCH, **NSM** M A SHERDLEY
FELMERSHAM (St Mary) *St Alb 15* **P** *Bp* **P-in-c** R A EVENS, **NSM** D G MASON
FELMINGHAM (St Andrew) *see* King's Beck *Nor*
FELPHAM (St Mary the Virgin) *Chich 1* **P** *D&C* **C** T THORP
FELSHAM (St Peter) *see* Bradfield St Clare, Bradfield St George etc *St E*
FELSTED (Holy Cross) and Little Dunmow *Chelmsf 18* **P** *CPAS* **V** *vacant* (01371) 820242
FELTHAM (Christ Church) (St Dunstan) *Lon 11* **P** *Bp* **V** P R WRAGG
FELTHORPE (St Margaret) *see* Drayton w Felthorpe *Nor*
FELTON (St Katharine and the Noble Army of Martyrs) *see* Winford w Felton Common Hill *B & W*
FELTON (St Michael and All Angels) *Newc 9* **P** *Bp* **V** *vacant* (01670) 787263
FELTON (St Michael the Archangel) *see* Bodenham w Hope-under-Dinmore, Felton etc *Heref*
FELTON, WEST (St Michael) *Lich 19* **P** *Bp* **P-in-c** D R NORTH, **Hon C** B R W HAYES
FELTWELL (St Mary) and Methwold *Ely 13* **P** *Bp* **R** D J KIGHTLEY
FEN DITTON (Holy Cross) (St Mary Magdalene) (St Mary the Virgin) *Ely 3* **P** *Bp* **P-in-c** M C BOWERS
FEN DRAYTON (St Mary the Virgin) w Conington and Lolworth and Swavesey *Ely 5* **P** *The Crown, Jes Coll Cam, SMF, and Ch Coll Cam (by turn)* **R** J D YULE
FENCE-IN-PENDLE (St Anne) and Higham *Blackb 6* **P** *Bp and Ld Chan (alt)* **V** R J ADAMS
FENCOTE (St Andrew) *see* Lower Swale *Ripon*
FENHAM (Holy Cross) *see* Newc H Cross *Newc*
FENHAM (St James and St Basil) *Newc 7* **P** *Bp* **V** J M DOTCHIN, **C** L CHAPMAN
FENISCLIFFE (St Francis) *see* Blackb St Fran and St Aid *Blackb*
FENISCOWLES (Immanuel) *Blackb 2* **P** *V Blackb* **P-in-c** P A DAVISON
FENITON (St Andrew), Buckerell and Escot *Ex 7* **P** *DBP, D&C and J M Kennaway Esq (jt)* **R** *vacant* (01404) 850253
FENN LANES Group, The *Leic 12* **P** *Bp, D&C, and Lord O'Neill (jt)* **R** S J WICKS
FENNY BENTLEY (St Edmund King and Martyr), Thorpe, Tissington, Parwich and Alsop-en-le-Dale *Derby 8* **P** *Bp, D A G Shields Esq, and Sir Richard FitzHerbert Bt (jt)* **R** C D HARRISON
FENNY DRAYTON (St Michael and All Angels) *see* Fenn Lanes Gp *Leic*
FENNY STRATFORD (St Martin) *Ox 25* **P** *Bp* **V** V J A BULLOCK, **NSM** I W THOMAS
FENSTANTON (St Peter and St Paul) *Ely 8* **P** *Bp* **V** M A GUITE
FENTON (All Saints) *see* Claypole *Linc*
FENTON (Christ Church) *Lich 12* **P** *R Stoke-on-Trent* **V** D A CAMERON
FENWICK and MOSS (St John) *see* Fishlake w Sykehouse and Kirk Bramwith etc *Sheff*
FEOCK (St Feock) *Truro 6* **P** *Bp* **P-in-c** P A A WALKER, **NSM** B J HESELTINE
FERHAM PARK (St Paul) *see* Masbrough *Sheff*
FERNDOWN (St Mary) *see* Hampreston *Sarum*
FERNHAM (St John the Evangelist) *see* Shrivenham and Ashbury *Ox*
FERNHURST (St Margaret) *Chich 10* **P** *Rathbone Trust Co and Cowdray Trust (jt)* **V** A R G ROAKE
FERNILEE (Holy Trinity) *see* Whaley Bridge *Ches*
FERRIBY, NORTH (All Saints) *York 14* **P** *H Trin Hull and Distr Ch Patr Soc Ltd* **V** *vacant* (01482) 631306
FERRIBY, SOUTH (St Nicholas) *Linc 6* **P** *Bp* **R** G A PLUMB
FERRING (St Andrew) *Chich 5* **P** *D&C* **V** T S STRATFORD
FERRYBRIDGE (St Andrew) *Wakef 11* **P** *D&C York* **P-in-c** P J WALKER
FERRYHILL (St Luke) (St Martha and St Mary) *Dur 5* **P** *D&C* **V** K LUMSDON, **C** D GARRATT
FERSFIELD (St Andrew) *see* Bressingham w N and S Lopham and Fersfield *Nor*
FETCHAM (St Mary) *Guildf 10* **P** *Bp* **R** P H BOUGHTON, **NSM** E M V BOUGHTON
FEWSTON (St Michael and St Lawrence) *see* Leathley w Farnley, Fewston and Blubberhouses *Bradf*
FIDDINGTON (St Martin) *see* Stogursey w Fiddington *B & W*
FIELD BROUGHTON (St Peter) *see* Cartmel Peninsula *Carl*
FIELD DALLING (St Andrew) *see* Stiffkey and Bale *Nor*
FIFEHEAD MAGDALEN (St Mary Magdalene) *see* Stour Vale *Sarum*
FIFEHEAD NEVILLE (All Saints) *see* Hazelbury Bryan and the Hillside Par *Sarum*
FIFIELD (St John the Baptist) *see* Shipton-under-Wychwood w Milton, Fifield etc *Ox*
FIFIELD BAVANT (St Martin) *see* Chalke Valley *Sarum*
FIGHELDEAN (St Michael and All Angels) *see* Avon Valley *Sarum*
FILBY (All Saints) *see* S Trin Broads *Nor*
FILEY (St John) (St Oswald) *York 15* **P** *PCC* **C** M E WILLIAMS
FILKINS (St Peter) *see* Shill Valley and Broadshire *Ox*
FILLEIGH (St Paul) *see* S Molton w Nymet St George, High Bray etc *Ex*
FILLINGHAM (St Andrew) *see* Ingham w Cammeringham w Fillingham *Linc*

FILLONGLEY (St Mary and All Saints) and Corley *Cov 5* **P** *Bp and Ch Soc Trust (jt)* **V** N J CLARKE, **NSM** J CLOSE
FILTON (St Gregory) *see* Horfield St Greg *Bris*
FILTON (St Peter) *Bris 5* **P** *Bp* **R** B R ARMAN, **NSM** M E DESMOND
FIMBER (St Mary) *see* Waggoners *York*
FINBOROUGH, GREAT (St Andrew) w Onehouse, Harleston, Buxhall and Shelland *St E 6* **P** *Bp* **P-in-c** L LLEWELLYN-MACDUFF
FINBOROUGH, LITTLE (St Mary) *see* Combs and Lt Finborough *St E*
FINCHAM (St Martin) *Ely 13* **P** *Bp* **P-in-c** D J POMERY, **Hon C** A G F VILLER
FINCHAMPSTEAD (St James) *Ox 16* **P** *DBP* **P-in-c** R J WARDEN
FINCHFIELD (St Thomas) *see* Tettenhall Wood and Perton *Lich*
FINCHINGFIELD (St John the Baptist) and Cornish Hall End and Wethersfield w Shalford *Chelmsf 15* **P** *Mrs E M Bishop and Bp (alt)* **V** *vacant* (01371) 810309
FINCHLEY (Christ Church) *Lon 14* **P** *Ch Patr Trust* **V** T D ATKINS
FINCHLEY (Holy Trinity) *Lon 16* **P** *Bp* **V** L B HILL
FINCHLEY (St Barnabas) *see* Woodside Park St Barn *Lon*
FINCHLEY (St Mary) *Lon 14* **P** *Bp* **R** A D WILLIAMS, **NSM** J KRAFT
FINCHLEY (St Paul) (St Luke) *Lon 14* **P** *Simeon Trustees and Ch Patr Trust (jt)* **V** N R PYE
FINCHLEY, EAST (All Saints) *Lon 14* **P** *Bp* **V** C R HARDY
FINDERN (All Saints) *Derby 16* **P** *Bp* **V** S A STARKEY
FINDON (St John the Baptist) w Clapham and Patching *Chich 5* **P** *Abp, Bp, and J E P Somerset Esq (jt)* **V** S J GURR
FINDON VALLEY (All Saints) *Chich 5* **P** *Bp* **V** G J WHITING
FINEDON (St Mary the Virgin) *Pet 10* **P** *Bp* **V** J HUMPHRIES
FINGEST (St Bartholomew) *see* Hambleden Valley *Ox*
FINGHALL (St Andrew) *see* Spennithorne w Finghall and Hauxwell *Ripon*
FINGRINGHOE (St Andrew) w East Donyland and Abberton w Langenhoe *Chelmsf 16* **P** *Bp (3 turns), Ld Chan (1 turn)* **R** R J MARTIN
FINHAM (St Martin in the Fields) *Cov 3* **P** *Bp* **V** P WATKINS, **C** A J EVANS
FINMERE (St Michael) *see* Shelswell *Ox*
FINNINGHAM (St Bartholomew) *see* Badwell and Walsham *St E*
FINNINGLEY (Holy Trinity and St Oswald) w Auckley *S'well 1* **P** *DBP* **P-in-c** D OTTEWELL
FINSBURY (St Clement) (St Barnabas) (St Matthew) *Lon 5* **P** *D&C St Paul's* **V** D E ALLEN
FINSBURY PARK (St Thomas) *Lon 6* **P** *Abp* **V** S R COLES, **NSM** V R ATTA-BAFFOE, B E F PEARSON
FINSTALL (St Godwald) *Worc 7* **P** *V Stoke Prior* **V** P A ALLSOPP, **C** S C WINTER
FINSTHWAITE (St Peter) *see* Leven Valley *Carl*
FINSTOCK (Holy Trinity) *see* Ramsden, Finstock and Fawler, Leafield etc *Ox*
FIR TREE (St Mary the Virgin) *see* Howden-le-Wear and Hunwick *Dur*
FIR VALE (St Cuthbert) *see* Sheff St Cuth *Sheff*
FIRBANK (St John the Evangelist), Howgill and Killington *Bradf 6* **P** *Ld Chan and V Sedbergh (alt)* **Hon C** A W FELL
FIRBECK (St Martin) w Letwell *Sheff 5* **P** *Bp* **R** A P FEREDAY
FIRLE, WEST (St Peter) *see* Glynde, W Firle and Beddingham *Chich*
FIRSBY (St Andrew) *see* Spilsby Gp *Linc*
FIRSWOOD (St Hilda) and Gorse Hill *Man 7* **P** *Prime Min* **P-in-c** T R MALKIN
FISH HALL (Mission Church) *see* Tonbridge SS Pet and Paul *Roch*
FISHBOURNE, NEW (St Peter and St Mary) *Chich 3* **P** *Ld Chan* **R** C A ASHLEY
FISHBURN (St Catherine) *see* Upper Skerne *Dur*
FISHERMEAD (Trinity Church) *see* Woughton *Ox*
FISHERTON ANGER (St Paul) *Sarum 12* **P** *Ch Patr Trust* **R** A S W CULLIS, **C** J D BIRCHALL
FISHLAKE (St Cuthbert) w Sykehouse and Kirk Bramwith w Fenwick and Moss *Sheff 10* **P** *Duchy of Lanc (1 turn), D&C Dur (2 turns), and Bp (1 turn)* **R** E S ATHERFOLD, **NSM** J E ROBINSON
FISHLEY (St Mary) *see* Acle w Fishley, N Burlingham, Beighton w Moulton *Nor*
FISHPOND (St John the Baptist) *see* Golden Cap Team *Sarum*
FISHPONDS (All Saints) *Bris 3* **P** *Bp* **V** *vacant* 0117-965 4143
FISHPONDS (St John) *Bris 3* **P** *Bp* **V** *vacant* 0117-965 4130
FISHPONDS (St Mary) *Bris 3* **P** *Bp* **V** R G MINSON
FISHTOFT (St Guthlac) *Linc 20* **P** *DBP* **R** M A R COOPER
FISKERTON (St Clement) *see* S Lawres Gp *Linc*
FITTLETON (All Saints) *see* Avon Valley *Sarum*
FITTLEWORTH (St Mary the Virgin) *see* Stopham and Fittleworth *Chich*
FITTON HILL (St Cuthbert) *see* Bardsley *Man*
FITZ (St Peter and St Paul) *see* Bicton, Montford w Shrawardine and Fitz *Lich*
FITZHEAD (St James) *see* Milverton w Halse and Fitzhead *B & W*
FITZWILLIAM (St Maurice) *see* Kinsley w Wragby *Wakef*
FIVE ASHES (Church of the Good Shepherd) *see* Mayfield *Chich*
FIVE OAK GREEN (St Luke) *see* Tudeley cum Capel w Five Oak Green *Roch*
FIVEHEAD (St Martin) *see* Curry Rivel w Fivehead and Swell *B & W*
FIXBY (St Francis) *see* N Huddersfield *Wakef*
FLACKWELL HEATH (Christ Church) *Ox 29* **P** *DBP* **V** C D BULL, **C** G FOSTER, **OLM** M H COURTNEY
FLADBURY (St John the Baptist) w Wyre Piddle and Moor and Cropthorne w Charlton *Worc 4* **P** *Bp and D&C (jt)* **R** C N VON BENZON, **C** J H GREEN, S J OLIVER
FLAGG (School Mission Room) *see* Taddington, Chelmorton and Flagg, and Monyash *Derby*
FLAMBOROUGH (St Oswald) *see* Bempton w Flamborough, Reighton w Speeton *York*
FLAMSTEAD (St Leonard) *St Alb 8* **P** *Univ Coll Ox* **P-in-c** J F H GREEN
FLAUNDEN (St Mary Magdalene) *see* Chenies and Lt Chalfont, Latimer and Flaunden *Ox*
FLAWBOROUGH (St Peter) *see* Staunton w Flawborough *S'well*
FLAX BOURTON (St Michael and All Angels) *B & W 13* **P** *Lord Wraxall* **P-in-c** A SARGENT, **NSM** V L BARLEY
FLAXLEY (St Mary the Virgin) *see* Westbury-on-Severn w Flaxley, Blaisdon etc *Glouc*
FLAXTON (St Lawrence) *see* Whitwell w Crambe, Flaxton and Foston *York*
FLECKNEY (St Nicholas) *see* Wistow *Leic*
FLECKNOE (St Mark) *see* Leam Valley *Cov*
FLEET (All Saints) (St Philip and St James) *Guildf 1* **P** *Bp* **V** R O WOODHAMS, **C** R M ROBERTS
FLEET (Holy Trinity) *see* Chickerell w Fleet *Sarum*
FLEET (Old Church) *as above*
FLEET (St Mary Magdalene) w Gedney *Linc 16* **P** *The Crown and DBP (alt)* **R** D F BRATLEY
FLEETWOOD (St David) *Blackb 12* **P** *Bp and Meynell Trustees (jt)* **V** E K SILLIS
FLEETWOOD (St Nicholas) *Blackb 12* **P** *Bp and Meynell Trustees (jt)* **V** P J BENFIELD, **C** E A ALP
FLEETWOOD (St Peter) *Blackb 12* **P** *Meynell Trustees* **V** A J GWILLIM
FLEGG COASTAL Benefice, The: Hemsby, Winterton, East and West Somerton and Horsey *Nor 6* **P** *Bp, D&C, SMF, and Major R A Ferrier (jt)* **R** M G KICHENSIDE, **NSM** A T CADMORE
FLEMPTON (St Catherine of Alexandria) *see* Lark Valley *St E*
FLETCHAMSTEAD (St James) *Cov 3* **P** *Bp* **V** S R BURCH, **C** M A HEADING
FLETCHING (St Mary and St Andrew) *Chich 21* **P** *Abp* **V** *vacant* (01825) 722498
FLETTON (St Margaret) *Ely 11* **P** *Sir Stephen Hastings* **P-in-c** W P L GAMMON
FLIMBY (St Nicholas) *see* Maryport, Netherton and Flimby *Carl*
FLIMWELL (St Augustine of Canterbury) *see* Ticehurst and Flimwell *Chich*
FLINTHAM (St Augustine of Canterbury) *S'well 8* **P** *M T Hildyard Esq* **P-in-c** D G WAKEFIELD
FLITCHAM (St Mary the Virgin) *see* Sandringham w W Newton and Appleton etc *Nor*
FLITTON (St John the Baptist) *see* Silsoe, Pulloxhill and Flitton *St Alb*
FLITWICK (St Andrew) (St Peter and St Paul) *St Alb 9* **P** *DBP* **V** M F J BRADLEY
FLIXBOROUGH (All Saints) w Burton upon Stather *Linc 4* **P** *Sir Reginald Sheffield Bt* **V** P W DADD
FLIXTON (St John) *Man 7* **P** *Bp* **V** K J MASSEY, **OLM** R W GREEN, B R CORKE, J N EDGE
FLIXTON (St Mary) *see* S Elmham and Ilketshall *St E*
FLIXTON (St Michael) *Man 7* **P** *Bp* **P-in-c** S J SMITH, **OLM** A H CLEPHANE
FLOCKTON (St James the Great) cum Denby Grange *Wakef 6* **P** *R Carter's Trustees* **P-in-c** C E BULLIMORE, **C** H M HODGSON, **OLM** L BROOKES

FLOOKBURGH (St John the Baptist) *see* Cartmel Peninsula *Carl*
FLORDON (St Michael) *see* Mulbarton w Bracon Ash, Hethel and Flordon *Nor*
FLORE (All Saints) *see* Heyford w Stowe Nine Churches and Flore etc *Pet*
FLOWTON (St Mary) *see* Somersham w Flowton and Offton w Willisham *St E*
FLUSHING (St Peter) *see* Mylor w Flushing *Truro*
FLYFORD FLAVELL (St Peter) *see* Abberton, The Flyfords, Naunton Beauchamp etc *Worc*
FOBBING (St Michael) *Chelmsf 14* **P** *The Crown* **P-in-c** D ROLLINS
FOLESHILL (St Laurence) *Cov 2* **P** *Ld Chan* **V** M R CLEVELAND
FOLESHILL (St Paul) *Cov 2* **P** *Ld Chan* **V** A J CANNING
FOLEY PARK (Holy Innocents) *see* Kidderminster St Jo and H Innocents *Worc*
FOLKE (St Lawrence) *see* The Caundles w Folke and Holwell *Sarum*
FOLKESTONE (Holy Trinity w Christ Church) *Cant 5* **P** *Abp* **V** J C TAPPER, **C** S K C RICHARDSON, **OLM** J A ROBERTSON
FOLKESTONE (St Augustine) Conventional District *Cant 5 vacant* (01303) 245807
FOLKESTONE (St Augustine) (St Mary and St Eanswythe) *Cant 5* **P** *Abp* **V** D J ADLINGTON, **NSM** B F WILLIAMS
FOLKESTONE (St George) *see* Sandgate St Paul w Folkestone St Geo *Cant*
FOLKESTONE (St John the Baptist) *see* Foord St Jo *Cant*
FOLKESTONE (St Peter) *Cant 5* **P** *Trustees* **P-in-c** S F BOULD
FOLKESTONE (St Saviour) *Cant 5* **P** *Abp* **P-in-c** B M LLEWELLYN
FOLKESWORTH (St Helen) *see* Stilton w Denton and Caldecote etc *Ely*
FOLKINGHAM (St Andrew) *see* S Lafford *Linc*
FOLKINGTON (St Peter ad Vincula) *see* Arlington, Folkington and Wilmington *Chich*
FOLKTON (St John) *see* Willerby w Ganton and Folkton *York*
FOLLIFOOT (St Joseph and St James) *see* Spofforth w Kirk Deighton *Ripon*
FONTHILL BISHOP (All Saints) *see* Nadder Valley *Sarum*
FONTHILL GIFFORD (Holy Trinity) *as above*
FONTMELL MAGNA (St Andrew) *see* Iwerne Valley *Sarum*
FOOLOW (St Hugh) *see* Eyam *Derby*
FOORD (St John the Baptist) *Cant 5* **P** *CPAS* **V** A G BUCKLEY, **C** R P GRINSELL
FOOTSCRAY (All Saints) w North Cray *Roch 17* **P** *Bp and Ld Chan (alt)* **R** A C UPHILL
FORCETT (St Cuthbert) and Aldbrough and Melsonby *Ripon 2* **P** *DBP and Univ Coll Ox (alt)* **P-in-c** S R HAWORTH
FORD (St Andrew) *see* Clymping and Yapton w Ford *Chich*
FORD (St John of Jerusalem) *see* Leominster *Heref*
FORD (St John the Evangelist) *see* Colerne w N Wraxall *Bris*
FORD (St Mark) *see* Devonport St Mark Ford *Ex*
FORD (St Michael) *Heref 13* **P** *Bp* **V** *vacant* (01743) 850254
FORD (St Michael and All Angels) and Etal *Newc 12* **P** *Lord Joicey* **R** V T DICKINSON
FORD END (St John the Evangelist) *see* Gt Waltham w Ford End *Chelmsf*
FORDCOMBE (St Peter) *see* Penshurst and Fordcombe *Roch*
FORDHAM (All Saints) *Chelmsf 17* **P** *Reformation Ch Trust, Ball Coll Ox (alt)* **R** M R J NEVILLE, **C** A SAVILLE, **NSM** E J A SAVILLE
FORDHAM (St Peter and St Mary Magdalene) *Ely 3* **P** *Jes Coll Cam* **V** A HASELHURST, **NSM** P M DEBENHAM
FORDHOUSES (St James) *see* Bushbury *Lich*
FORDINGBRIDGE (St Mary) and Breamore and Hale with the Charfords *Win 9* **P** *Patr Bd* **TV** S T HORNE, **Hon C** M L ASHTON, P D ASHTON, P F MURPHY
FORDON (St James) *see* Burton Fleming w Fordon, Grindale etc *York*
FOREBRIDGE (St Paul) *see* Stafford St Paul Forebridge *Lich*
FOREMARK (St Saviour) and Repton w Newton Solney *Derby 16* **P** *Bp and DBP (jt)* **P-in-c** P S PAINE
FOREST (St Stephen) *see* Rainow w Saltersford and Forest *Ches*
FOREST GATE (All Saints) (St Edmund) *Chelmsf 3* **P** *Bp* **P-in-c** B K SHIPSIDES, **C** N A B MATLOOB
FOREST GATE (Emmanuel w St Peter) Upton Cross *Chelmsf 3* **P** *Bp* **V** P J MOSSOP
FOREST GATE (St James) *see* Stratford St Jo w Ch Ch and St Jas *Chelmsf*
FOREST GATE (St Mark) *Chelmsf 3* **P** *Ch Patr Trust* **V** P J STOW
FOREST GATE (St Saviour) w West Ham St Matthew *Chelmsf 3* **P** *Patr Bd* **TR** J H WILLIAMS, **TV** M OKELLO
FOREST GREEN (Holy Trinity) *see* Ockley, Okewood and Forest Green *Guildf*
FOREST HILL (Christ Church) *see* Perry Hill St Geo w Ch Ch and St Paul *S'wark*
FOREST HILL (St Augustine) Honor Oak Park *S'wark 5* **P** *Bp* **P-in-c** S A LASKEY, **NSM** S R SCOTT
FOREST HILL (St Nicholas) *see* Wheatley *Ox*
FOREST HILL (St Paul) *see* Perry Hill St Geo w Ch Ch and St Paul *S'wark*
FOREST-IN-TEESDALE (St Mary the Virgin) *see* Middleton-in-Teesdale w Forest and Frith *Dur*
FOREST OF DEAN (Christ Church) w English Bicknor *Glouc 4* **P** *The Crown (3 turns), SMF (1 turn)* **P-in-c** V K TURNER
FOREST OF DEAN (Holy Trinity) *see* Dean Forest H Trin *Glouc*
FOREST ROW (Holy Trinity) *Chich 7* **P** *V E Grinstead* **V** N H LAMB, **NSM** D A TIDSWELL
FOREST TOWN (St Alban) *S'well 2* **P** *Bp* **P-in-c** P J STEAD
FORESTSIDE (Christ Church) *see* Stansted *Chich*
FORMBY (Holy Trinity) *Liv 5* **P** *Trustees* **V** K E JONES
FORMBY (St Luke) *Liv 5* **P** *Bp* **V** A R WOODHOUSE
FORMBY (St Peter) *Liv 5* **P** *R Walton* **V** P W ORMROD
FORNCETT (St Peter) *see* Ashwellthorpe, Forncett, Fundenhall, Hapton etc *Nor*
FORNCETT END (St Edmund) *as above*
FORNHAM ALL SAINTS (All Saints) *see* Lark Valley *St E*
FORNHAM ST MARTIN (St Martin) *as above*
FORRABURY (St Symphorian) *see* Boscastle w Davidstow *Truro*
FORSBROOK (St Peter) *see* Draycott-le-Moors w Forsbrook *Lich*
FORTHAMPTON (St Mary) *see* Deerhurst and Apperley w Forthampton etc *Glouc*
FORTON (All Saints) *see* Newport w Longford, Chetwynd and Forton *Lich*
FORTON (St James) *see* Ellel w Shireshead *Blackb*
FORTON (St John the Evangelist) *Portsm 3* **P** *DBP* **P-in-c** B E WARD
FORTY HILL (Jesus Church) *Lon 18* **P** *V Enfield* **V** J E TOWNSEND, **NSM** M MOSELEY
FOSDYKE (All Saints) *see* Sutterton, Fosdyke, Algarkirk and Wigtoft *Linc*
FOSSE TRINITY *B & W 8* **P** *Bp and Canon D S Salter (jt)* **P-in-c** J M D SWAYNE
FOSTON (All Saints) *see* Whitwell w Crambe, Flaxton and Foston *York*
FOSTON (St Bartholomew) *see* Countesthorpe w Foston *Leic*
FOSTON (St Peter) *see* Saxonwell *Linc*
FOSTON-ON-THE-WOLDS (St Andrew) *see* Beeford w Frodingham and Foston *York*
FOTHERBY (St Mary) *Linc 12* **P** *Ld Chan (1 turn), DBP, MMCET and G F Sleight Esq (1 turn), and Bp (1 turn)* **P-in-c** K M TOMLIN, **OLM** J M WRISDALE
FOTHERINGHAY (St Mary and All Saints) *see* Warmington, Tansor and Cotterstock etc *Pet*
FOULDEN (All Saints) *see* Oxborough w Foulden and Caldecote *Nor*
FOULNESS (St Mary the Virgin) *see* Gt Wakering w Foulness *Chelmsf*
FOULRIDGE (St Michael and All Angels) *see* Colne and Villages *Blackb*
FOULSHAM (Holy Innocents) Hindolveston and Guestwick *Nor 22* **P** *Lord Hastings, Mrs M E E Bulwer-Long and D&C (alt)* **P-in-c** D SIXSMITH
FOUNTAINS Group, The *Ripon 3* **P** *D&C* **R** R SELLERS, **C** C A CAMPLING
FOUR ELMS (St Paul) *see* Hever, Four Elms and Mark Beech *Roch*
FOUR MARKS (Good Shepherd) *Win 2* **P** *Bp* **V** H J D WRIGHT, **C** T J FLETCHER
FOUR OAKS (All Saints) *Birm 12* **P** *Bp* **V** T C PLATTS, **C** C A PAILING
FOURSTONES (St Aidan) *see* Warden w Newbrough *Newc*
FOVANT (St George), Sutton Mandeville and Teffont Evias w Teffont Magna and Compton Chamberlayne *Sarum 11* **P** *Reformation Ch Trust, Bp, and Ch Soc Trust (jt)* **R** J C EADE
FOWEY (St Fimbarrus) *Truro 1* **P** *Ch Soc Trust* **P-in-c** P DE GREY-WARTER
FOWLMERE (St Mary), Foxton, Shepreth and Thriplow *Ely 7* **P** *Bp* **R** C P STRONG, **NSM** S O FALASCHI-RAY
FOWNHOPE (St Mary) w Mordiford, Brockhampton and Fawley and Woolhope *Heref 4* **P** *D&C (4 turns), and Major R J Hereford (1 turn)* **R** W R PRIDIE, **NSM** M M DEES

FOXCOTE (St James the Less) *see* Camerton w Dunkerton, Foxcote and Shoscombe *B & W*
FOXDALE (St Paul) *S & M 1* **P** *The Crown and Bp (alt)* **V** G M BREFFITT
FOXEARTH (St Peter and St Paul) *see* N Hinckford *Chelmsf*
FOXHAM (St John the Baptist) *see* Derry Hill w Bremhill and Foxham *Sarum*
FOXHILL (Chapel) *see* Frodsham *Ches*
FOXHOLE (St Boniface) *see* Paignton St Jo *Ex*
FOXHOLES (St Mary) *see* Langtoft w Foxholes, Butterwick, Cottam etc *York*
FOXLEY (not known) *see* Sherston Magna, Easton Grey, Luckington etc *Bris*
FOXLEY (St Thomas) *see* Lyng, Sparham, Elsing, Bylaugh, Bawdeswell etc *Nor*
FOXT (St Mark the Evangelist) *see* Kingsley and Foxt-w-Whiston *Lich*
FOXTON (St Andrew) w Gumley and Laughton *Leic 4* **P** *Bp Leic and D&C Linc (alt)* **P-in-c** I L JOHNSON
FOXTON (St Laurence) *see* Fowlmere, Foxton, Shepreth and Thriplow *Ely*
FOY (St Mary) *see* How Caple w Sollarshope, Sellack etc *Heref*
FRADLEY (St Stephen) *see* Alrewas *Lich*
FRADSWELL (St James the Less) *see* Mid Trent *Lich*
FRAISTHORPE (St Edmund King and Martyr) *see* Skipsea w Ulrome and Barmston w Fraisthorpe *York*
FRAMFIELD (St Thomas à Becket) *Chich 21* **P** *Mrs E R Wix* **V** E G DORE
FRAMILODE (St Peter) *see* Frampton on Severn, Arlingham, Saul etc *Glouc*
FRAMINGHAM EARL (St Andrew) *see* Poringland *Nor*
FRAMINGHAM PIGOT (St Andrew) *see* Thurton *Nor*
FRAMLAND Parishes, The HIGH *Leic 3* **P** *Duke of Rutland and Sir Lyonel Tollemache Bt (jt)* **P-in-c** P L BOTTING
FRAMLAND, SOUTH *Leic 3* **P** *Ld Chan, Duke of Rutland, Lady Gretton, and Sir Lyonel Tollemache Bt (by turn)* **R** M R SAMUEL
FRAMLINGHAM (St Michael) w Saxtead *St E 18* **P** *Pemb Coll Cam* **P-in-c** G W OWEN, **C** P J WYARD
FRAMPTON (St Mary) *see* Bradford Peverell, Stratton, Frampton etc *Sarum*
FRAMPTON (St Mary) (St Michael) *Linc 21* **P** *Trustees* **V** A M HUGHES
FRAMPTON COTTERELL (St Peter) *Bris 5* **P** *SMF* **P-in-c** S E RUSHTON, **NSM** J D TAILBY
FRAMPTON MANSELL (St Luke) *see* Kemble, Poole Keynes, Somerford Keynes etc *Glouc*
FRAMPTON ON SEVERN (St Mary), Arlingham, Saul, Fretherne and Framilode *Glouc 8* **P** *DBP, V Standish w Haresfield etc, Brig Sir Jeffrey Darell Bt, and Bp (jt)* **V** P CHEESMAN
FRAMSDEN (St Mary) *see* Debenham and Helmingham *St E*
FRAMWELLGATE MOOR (St Aidan) *see* Dur N *Dur*
FRANCE LYNCH (St John the Baptist) *see* Bisley, Chalford, France Lynch, and Oakridge *Glouc*
FRANCHE (St Barnabas) *see* Kidderminster St Mary and All SS w Trimpley etc *Worc*
FRANKBY (St John the Divine) w Greasby St Nicholas *Ches 8* **P** *D&C* **V** K P OWEN, **C** E H CLARKE
FRANKLEY (St Leonard) *Birm 4* **P** *Bp* **R** M T DENNY
FRANKTON (St Nicholas) *see* Bourton w Frankton and Stretton on Dunsmore etc *Cov*
FRANSHAM, GREAT (All Saints) *see* Gt and Lt Dunham w Gt and Lt Fransham and Sporle *Nor*
FRANSHAM, LITTLE (St Mary) *as above*
FRANT (St Alban) w Eridge *Chich 19* **P** *Bp and Marquess of Abergavenny (jt)* **R** A J TURNER
FREASLEY (St Mary) *see* Dordon *Birm*
FRECHEVILLE (St Cyprian) *Sheff 2* **P** *Bp* **R** M J GILLINGHAM
FRECKENHAM (St Andrew) *see* Mildenhall *St E*
FRECKLETON (Holy Trinity) *Blackb 10* **P** *Bp* **P-in-c** J E C PERCIVAL, **NSM** T B SCHOLZ
FREEBY (St Mary) *see* Melton Mowbray *Leic*
FREEHAY (St Chad) *see* Cheadle w Freehay *Lich*
FREELAND (St Mary the Virgin) *see* Hanborough and Freeland *Ox*
FREEMANTLE (Christ Church) *Win 13* **P** *Bp* **NSM** J B WALTERS
FREETHORPE (All Saints), Wickhampton, Halvergate w Tunstall, Reedham, Cantley and Limpenhoe w Southwood *Nor 4* **P** *Patr Bd* **R** C R DUXBURY
FREEZYWATER (St George) *see* Enfield St Geo *Lon*
FREISTON (St James), Butterwick w Bennington, and Leverton *Linc 20* **P** *Ld Chan and Bp (alt)* **R** *vacant* (01205) 760550
FREMINGTON (St Peter) *Ex 15* **P** *MMCET* **V** P H HOCKEY
FRENCHAY (St John the Baptist) and Winterbourne Down *Bris 5* **P** *St Jo Coll Ox and SMF (jt)* **P-in-c** D C CHEDZEY, **C** R C WILSON, **NSM** M R J EVANS
FRENSHAM (St Mary the Virgin) *see* Rowledge and Frensham *Guildf*
FRESHFORD (St Peter) w Limpley Stoke and Hinton Charterhouse *B & W 9* **P** *Simeon's Trustees and V Norton St Phil (jt)* **R** *vacant* (01225) 723135
FRESHWATER (All Saints) (St Agnes) *Portsm 8* **P** *St Jo Coll Cam* **R** M E C WHATSON, **NSM** D K BELLAMY, G M HURT
FRESSINGFIELD (St Peter and St Paul), Mendham, Metfield, Weybread and Withersdale *St E 17* **P** *Bp, Em Coll Cam, Ch Soc Trust, and SMF (jt)* **P-in-c** D W FINCH, **NSM** P A SCHWIER, **OLM** R A WILLIS
FRESTON (St Peter) *see* Holbrook, Stutton, Freston, Woolverstone etc *St E*
FRETHERNE (St Mary the Virgin) *see* Frampton on Severn, Arlingham, Saul etc *Glouc*
FRETTENHAM (St Swithin) *see* Spixworth w Crostwick and Frettenham *Nor*
FRIAR PARK (St Francis of Assisi) *see* W Bromwich St Fran *Lich*
FRIARMERE (St Thomas) *see* Saddleworth *Man*
FRICKLEY (All Saints) *see* Bilham *Sheff*
FRIDAY BRIDGE (St Mark) *see* Elm and Friday Bridge w Coldham *Ely*
FRIDAYTHORPE (St Mary) *see* Waggoners *York*
FRIERN BARNET (All Saints) *Lon 14* **P** *Bp* **V** A V BENJAMIN
FRIERN BARNET (St James the Great) (St John the Evangelist) *Lon 14* **P** *D&C St Paul's* **R** P A WALMSLEY-MCLEOD
FRIERN BARNET (St Peter le Poer) *Lon 14* **P** *D&C St Paul's* **P-in-c** B W BRIDGEWOOD
FRIESTHORPE (St Peter) *see* Middle Rasen Gp *Linc*
FRIETH (St John the Baptist) *see* Hambleden Valley *Ox*
FRIEZLAND (Christ Church) *see* Saddleworth *Man*
FRILSHAM (St Frideswide) *see* Hermitage *Ox*
FRIMLEY (St Francis) (St Peter) *Guildf 6* **P** *R Ash* **R** M K WILSON, **C** W K PUGH, I P BRENNAND
FRIMLEY GREEN (St Andrew) and Mytchett *Guildf 6* **P** *Bp* **V** S EDWARDS
FRINDSBURY (All Saints) w Upnor and Chattenden *Roch 6* **P** *Bp* **C** D G S JOHNSTON
FRING (All Saints) *see* Snettisham w Ingoldisthorpe and Fring *Nor*
FRINGFORD (St Michael) *see* Shelswell *Ox*
FRINSTED (St Dunstan) *see* Bredgar w Bicknor and Frinsted w Wormshill etc *Cant*
FRINTON (St Mary Magdalene) (St Mary the Virgin Old Church) *Chelmsf 23* **P** *CPAS* **R** A D ROSE
FRISBY-ON-THE-WREAKE (St Thomas of Canterbury) *see* Upper Wreake *Leic*
FRISKNEY (All Saints) *Linc 8* **P** *Bp* **V** *vacant* (01754) 820418
FRISTON (St Mary Magdalene) *see* Aldringham w Thorpe, Knodishall w Buxlow etc *St E*
FRISTON (St Mary the Virgin) *see* E Dean w Friston and Jevington *Chich*
FRITCHLEY (Mission Room) *see* Crich and S Wingfield *Derby*
FRITHELSTOCK (St Mary and St Gregory) *see* Gt and Lt Torrington and Frithelstock *Ex*
FRITHVILLE (St Peter) *see* Sibsey w Frithville *Linc*
FRITTENDEN (St Mary) *see* Sissinghurst w Frittenden *Cant*
FRITTON (St Catherine) *see* Hempnall *Nor*
FRITTON (St Edmund) *see* Somerleyton, Ashby, Fritton, Herringfleet etc *Nor*
FRITWELL (St Olave) *see* Cherwell Valley *Ox*
FRIZINGHALL (St Margaret) *Bradf 1* **P** *Bp* **P-in-c** S P HACKING
FRIZINGTON (St Paul) *see* Crosslacon *Carl*
FROCESTER (St Andrew) *see* Eastington, Frocester, Haresfield etc *Glouc*
FRODESLEY (St Mark) *see* Condover w Frodesley, Acton Burnell etc *Heref*
FRODINGHAM (St Lawrence) *Linc 4* **P** *Lord St Oswald* **V** M P COONEY, **C** R M LATHAM, **NSM** M DUNFORD
FRODINGHAM, NORTH (St Elgin) *see* Beeford w Frodingham and Foston *York*
FRODSHAM (St Lawrence) *Ches 3* **P** *Ch Ch Ox* **V** M H MILLS
FROGMORE (Holy Trinity) *St Alb 1* **P** *CPAS* **V** D R HEATH-WHYTE, **NSM** N A WARD
FROLESWORTH (St Nicholas) *see* Claybrooke cum Wibtoft and Frolesworth *Leic*
FROME (Christ Church) *B & W 4* **P** *Bp* **P-in-c** N A MAXTED
FROME (Holy Trinity) *B & W 4* **P** *Bp* **V** R D M MARTIN, **C** W H H LANE

FROME (St John the Baptist) *B & W 4* **P** *DBP* **V** C ALSBURY
FROME (St Mary the Virgin) *B & W 4* **P** *Bp* **V** D R BARGE
FROME ST QUINTON (St Mary) *see* Melbury *Sarum*
FROME VAUCHURCH (St Mary) *as above*
FROMES HILL (St Matthew) *see* Bishop's Frome w Castle Frome and Fromes Hill *Heref*
FROSTENDEN (All Saints) *see* Sole Bay *St E*
FROSTERLEY (St Michael and All Angels) *see* Upper Weardale *Dur*
FROXFIELD (All Saints) *see* Whitton *Sarum*
FROXFIELD (St Peter) *see* Steep and Froxfield w Privett *Portsm*
FROXFIELD (St Peter on the Green) *as above*
FROYLE (Assumption of the Blessed Virgin Mary) and Holybourne *Win 2* **P** *Guild of All So and D&C (jt)* **V** J S CROFT
FRYERNING (St Mary the Virgin) *see* Ingatestone w Fryerning *Chelmsf*
FRYSTON (St Peter) *see* Airedale w Fryston *Wakef*
FUGGLESTONE (St Peter) *see* Wilton w Netherhampton and Fugglestone *Sarum*
FULBECK (St Nicholas) *see* Caythorpe *Linc*
FULBOURN (St Vigor w All Saints) *Ely 3* **P** *St Jo Coll Cam* **R** R E JONES
FULBROOK (St Gabriel) *see* Walsall St Gabr Fulbrook *Lich*
FULBROOK (St James the Great) *see* Burford w Fulbrook, Taynton, Asthall etc *Ox*
FULFORD (St Oswald) *York 7* **P** *Abp* **V** D J GOODHEW, **C** S FOSTER
FULFORD-IN-STONE (St Nicholas) w Hilderstone *Lich 13* **P** *D&C* **P-in-c** P D DAKIN, **NSM** C E DAKIN
FULHAM (All Saints) *Lon 9* **P** *Bp* **V** J P HAWES, **C** E A MORSE, **NSM** L A PERRY
FULHAM (Christ Church) *Lon 9* **P** *CPAS* **V** S C R LEES, **C** R P MALONE
FULHAM (St Alban) (St Augustine) *Lon 9* **P** *Bp and City Corp (jt)* **P-in-c** G R KNIGHT
FULHAM (St Andrew) Fulham Fields *Lon 9* **P** *Bp* **P-in-c** G R KNIGHT
FULHAM (St Dionis) Parson's Green *Lon 9* **P** *Bp* **V** *vacant* (020) 7736 2585 *or* 7731 1376
FULHAM (St Etheldreda) (St Clement) *Lon 9* **P** *Bp* **P-in-c** J F H HENLEY
FULHAM (St Mary) North End *Lon 9* **P** *Ch Soc Trust* **V** R W CURL
FULHAM (St Matthew) *Lon 9* **P** *Ch Patr Trust* **V** G Q D PIPER, **Dss** V S PIERSON
FULHAM (St Peter) *Lon 9* **P** *Bp* **P-in-c** J F GANGA
FULKING (Good Shepherd) *see* Poynings w Edburton, Newtimber and Pyecombe *Chich*
FULL SUTTON (St Mary) *see* Garrowby Hill *York*
FULLETBY (St Andrew) *Linc 11* **P** *Keble Coll Ox* **V** *vacant*
FULMER (St James) *see* Gerrards Cross and Fulmer *Ox*
FULMODESTON (Christ Church) *see* Barney, Fulmodeston w Croxton, Hindringham etc *Nor*
FULSHAW (St Anne) *see* Wilmslow *Ches*
FULSTOW (St Laurence) *see* Fotherby *Linc*
FULWOOD (Christ Church) *Blackb 13* **P** *V Lanc* **V** B R MCCONKEY
FULWOOD (Christ Church) *Sheff 4* **P** *CPAS* **C** J P CLARKE
FULWOOD Lodge Moor (St Luke) *see* Lodge Moor St Luke *Sheff*
FULWOOD (St Cuthbert) *see* Preston St Cuth *Blackb*
FUNDENHALL (St Nicholas) *see* Ashwellthorpe, Forncett, Fundenhall, Hapton etc *Nor*
FUNTINGTON (St Mary) and Sennicotts *Chich 13* **P** *Bp* **V** J J HOLLIMAN
FUNTLEY (St Francis) *see* Fareham SS Pet and Paul *Portsm*
FURNACE GREEN (St Andrew) *see* Southgate *Chich*
FURNESS VALE (St John) *see* Disley *Ches*
FURNEUX PELHAM (St Mary the Virgin) *see* Braughing w Furneux Pelham and Stocking Pelham *St Alb*
FURNHAM (Good Shepherd) *see* Chard and Distr *B & W*
FURTHO (St Bartholomew) *see* Potterspury w Furtho and Yardley Gobion etc *Pet*
FURZE PLATT (St Peter) *Ox 13* **P** *Bp* **Hon C** A C A PARRY, **NSM** J R G HYDE
FURZEBANK (Worship Centre) *see* Willenhall H Trin *Lich*
FURZEDOWN (St Paul) *see* Streatham St Paul *S'wark*
FURZTON (not known) *see* Watling Valley *Ox*
FYFIELD (St Nicholas) *see* Upper Kennet *Sarum*
FYFIELD (St Nicholas) *see* Appleshaw, Kimpton, Thruxton, Fyfield etc *Win*
FYFIELD (St Nicholas) w Tubney and Kingston Bagpuize *Ox 10* **P** *St Jo Coll Ox* **V** K J TRIPLOW
FYFIELD (St Nicholas), Moreton w Bobbingworth and Willingale w Shellow and Berners Roding *Chelmsf 27* **P** *Ld Chan, St Jo Coll Cam, MMCET, and Major G N Capel-Cure (by turn)* **R** G J WILCOX
FYLINGDALES (St Stephen) and Hawsker cum Stainsacre *York 22* **P** *Abp* **P-in-c** D W SMITH
GADDESBY (St Luke) *see* S Croxton Gp *Leic*
GADDESDEN, GREAT (St John the Baptist) and LITTLE (St Peter and St Paul) *St Alb 2* **P** *N G Halsey Esq and Bp (jt)* **R** *vacant* (01442) 252672
GADEBRIDGE (St Peter) *see* Hemel Hempstead *St Alb*
GAINFORD (St Mary) *Dur 7* **P** *Trin Coll Cam* **P-in-c** M ALDERSON
GAINSBOROUGH (All Saints) (St George) and Morton *Linc 2* **P** *Bp* **TR** N A THORNLEY, **C** A C SMITH, **OLM** J S THOROLD, F A JEFFRIES
GALLEY COMMON (St Peter) *see* Camp Hill w Galley Common *Cov*
GALLEYWOOD (Junior School Worship Centre) *see* Galleywood Common *Chelmsf*
GALLEYWOOD COMMON (St Michael and All Angels) *Chelmsf 9* **P** *CPAS* **V** A T GRIFFITHS
GALMINGTON (St Michael) *see* Wilton *B & W*
GALMPTON (Chapel of The Good Shepherd) *see* Brixham w Churston Ferrers and Kingswear *Ex*
GAMESLEY (Bishop Geoffrey Allen Church and County Centre) *see* Charlesworth and Dinting Vale *Derby*
GAMLINGAY (St Mary the Virgin) and Everton *Ely 10* **P** *Bp, Clare Coll Cam, and Down Coll Cam (by turn)* **R** C J-B HAMMOND
GAMLINGAY HEATH (St Sylvester) *see* Gamlingay and Everton *Ely*
GAMSTON and Bridgford *S'well 5* **P** *DBP* **V** S D SILVESTER, **C** R R BUSHYAGER
GAMSTON (St Peter) w Eaton and West Drayton *S'well 5* **P** *D&C York and Bp (alt)* **R** C F ANDREWS
GANAREW (St Swithin) *see* Llangarron w Llangrove, Whitchurch and Ganarew *Heref*
GANTON (St Nicholas) *see* Willerby w Ganton and Folkton *York*
GARBOLDISHAM (St John the Baptist) *see* Guiltcross *Nor*
GARFORD (St Luke) *see* Marcham w Garford *Ox*
GARFORTH (St Mary the Virgin) *Ripon 8* **P** *DBP* **R** R G N PLANT
GARGRAVE (St Andrew) *Bradf 5* **P** *Bp* **P-in-c** R C GEDDES
GARRETTS GREEN (St Thomas) *Birm 9* **P** *Bp* **P-in-c** B S CASTLE
GARRIGILL (St John) *see* Alston Moor *Newc*
GARROWBY HILL *York 5* **P** *Ld Chan (1 turn), Abp, D&C, and Earl of Halifax (3 turns)* **R** J C FINNEMORE
GARSDALE (St John the Baptist) *see* Sedbergh, Cautley and Garsdale *Bradf*
GARSDON (All Saints), Lea and Cleverton and Charlton *Bris 6* **P** *Ch Soc Trust and Bp (jt)* **R** R K EAST
GARSINGTON (St Mary) *see* Wheatley *Ox*
GARSTANG (St Helen) Churchtown and St Michaels-on-Wyre *Blackb 9* **P** *Dr I R H Jackson and R P Hornby Esq (jt)* **V** A W WILKINSON, **NSM** C M WHALLEY
GARSTANG (St Thomas) *Blackb 9* **P** *V Churchtown St Helen* **V** M A GISBOURNE, **NSM** A J ROBERTS
GARSTON (St Michael) *Liv 4* **P** *Trustees* **P-in-c** R L METCALF
GARSTON, EAST (All Saints) *see* Eastbury and E Garston *Ox*
GARSWOOD (St Andrew) *see* Ashton-in-Makerfield H Trin *Liv*
GARTHORPE (St Mary) *see* Crowle Gp *Linc*
GARTON IN HOLDERNESS (St Michael) *see* Roos and Garton w Tunstall, Grimston and Hilston *York*
GARTON-ON-THE-WOLDS (St Michael and All Angels) *see* Woldsburn *York*
GARVESTON (St Margaret) *see* Barnham Broom and Upper Yare *Nor*
GARWAY (St Michael) *see* St Weonards w Orcop, Garway, Tretire etc *Heref*
GASTARD (St John the Baptist) *see* Gtr Corsham and Lacock *Bris*
GATCOMBE (St Olave) *Portsm 8* **P** *Qu Coll Ox* **R** J W RUSSELL, **Hon C** M R HODGE, **NSM** L F HUMPHRYS
GATE BURTON (St Helen) *see* Lea Gp *Linc*
GATE HELMSLEY (St Mary) *see* Sand Hutton *York*
GATEACRE (St Stephen) *Liv 4* **P** *Bp* **TR** P H JANVIER, **TV** J L MCKELVEY, M NORRIS, **C** R K LYALL
GATEFORTH (St Mary's Mission Room) *see* Haddlesey w Hambleton and Birkin *York*
GATELEY (St Helen) *see* Upper Wensum Village Gp *Nor*

GATESHEAD Lobley Hill (All Saints) *see* Hillside *Dur*
GATESHEAD (St Chad) *see* Bensham *Dur*
GATESHEAD (St Edmund's Chapel w Holy Trinity) (Venerable Bede) *Dur 12* **P** *Bp and The Crown (alt)* **TR** J C WILKINSON, **TV** D M JOHNSON, **NSM** E CARR
GATESHEAD (St George) *Dur 12* **P** *Trustees* **V** E M T UNDERHILL
GATESHEAD (St Helen) *Dur 12* **P** *Bp* **V** B M HARRISON
GATESHEAD (St Ninian) Harlow Green *see* Harlow Green and Lamesley *Dur*
GATESHEAD FELL (St John) *Dur 12* **P** *Bp* **R** D J TULLY
GATLEY (St James) *Ches 17* **P** *R Stockport St Thos* **V** D S FISHER
GATTEN (St Paul) *Portsm 7* **P** *Ch Patr Trust* **V** P G ALLEN
GATTON (St Andrew) *see* Merstham and Gatton *S'wark*
GAULBY (St Peter) *Leic 5* **P** *Ch Soc Trust* **V** A F B CHEESMAN
GAUTBY (All Saints) *see* Bardney *Linc*
GAWBER (St Thomas) *Wakef 7* **P** *V Darton* **V** A PRITCHETT
GAWCOTT (Holy Trinity) *see* Lenborough *Ox*
GAWSWORTH (St James) *Ches 13* **P** *T R R Richards Esq* **R** W A PWAISIHO
GAYDON (St Giles) w Chadshunt *Cov 8* **P** *Bp* **V** P T FRANCIS
GAYHURST (St Peter) w Ravenstone, Stoke Goldington and Weston Underwood *Ox 27* **P** *Bp and Lord Hesketh (jt)* **R** A E D MURDOCH
GAYTON (St Mary) *see* Pattishall w Cold Higham and Gayton w Tiffield *Pet*
GAYTON (St Nicholas), Gayton Thorpe, East Walton, East Winch w West Bilney, Ashwicken w Leziate and Bawsey *Nor 20* **P** *Bp, Capt H Birkbeck, and W O Lancaster Esq (jt)* **R** I C WHITTLE
GAYTON (St Peter) *see* Mid Trent *Lich*
GAYTON LE WOLD (St Peter) *see* Asterby Gp *Linc*
GAYTON THORPE (St Mary) *see* Gayton, Gayton Thorpe, E Walton, E Winch etc *Nor*
GAYWOOD (St Faith) King's Lynn *Nor 20* **P** *Patr Bd* **TR** S M THEAKSTON, **C** L A HUMPHREYS, K L BRANT, **OLM** H E BERRY
GAZELEY (All Saints) *see* Dalham, Gazeley, Higham, Kentford and Moulton *St E*
GEDDING (St Mary the Virgin) *see* Bradfield St Clare, Bradfield St George etc *St E*
GEDDINGTON (St Mary Magdalene) w Weekley *Pet 11* **P** *Boughton Estates* **P-in-c** F G GODBER
GEDLING (All Hallows) *S'well 10* **P** *DBP* **R** D J STOTER, **C** S A BAYLIS, **NSM** K D WILLIAMS
GEDNEY (St Mary Magdalene) *see* Fleet w Gedney *Linc*
GEDNEY DROVE END (Christ Church) *see* Lutton w Gedney Drove End, Dawsmere *Linc*
GEDNEY HILL (Holy Trinity) (St Polycarp) *Linc 16* **P** *Bp* **V** R J MORRISON
GEE CROSS (Holy Trinity) (St Philip's Mission Room) *Ches 14* **P** *V Werneth* **V** G D OSGOOD
GELDESTON (St Michael) *see* Gillingham w Geldeston, Stockton, Ellingham etc *Nor*
GENTLESHAW (Christ Church) *Lich 1* **P** *MMCET* **P-in-c** M J BUTT, **NSM** M R AUSTIN
GEORGEHAM (St George) *Ex 15* **P** *MMCET* **P-in-c** B STRANGE
GERMAN (St German) *S & M 1* **P** *Bp* **V** B H KELLY
GERMAN (St John the Baptist) *S & M 1* **P** *Bp* **V** G M BREFFITT
GERMANSWEEK (St German) *see* Okehampton w Inwardleigh, Bratton Clovelly etc *Ex*
GERMOE (St Germoe) *see* Breage w Germoe and Godolphin *Truro*
GERRANS (St Gerran) w St Anthony-in-Roseland and Philleigh *Truro 6* **P** *Bp and MMCET (jt)* **P-in-c** D G ROBINS, **NSM** J SHARPLES
GERRARDS CROSS (St James) and Fulmer *Ox 20* **P** *Bp and Simeon's Trustees (jt)* **R** P G WILLIAMS, **C** M J WILLIAMS, **NSM** M R L BEEBEE
GESTINGTHORPE (St Mary) *see* Knights and Hospitallers Par *Chelmsf*
GIDDING, GREAT (St Michael) w LITTLE (St John) and Steeple Gidding *Ely 8* **P** *Sir Stephen Hastings and Bp (alt)* **P-in-c** C M FURLONG
GIDEA PARK (St Michael) *Chelmsf 2* **P** *Bp* **V** M A H FINCH
GIDLEIGH (Holy Trinity) *see* Chagford, Drewsteignton, Hittisleigh etc *Ex*
GIGGETTY LANE (The Venerable Bede) *see* Smestow Vale *Lich*
GIGGLESWICK (St Alkelda) and Rathmell w Wigglesworth *Bradf 5* **P** *Bp and Ch Trust Fund Trust (jt)* **P-in-c** P YORKSTONE
GILCRUX (St Mary) *see* Aspatria w Hayton and Gilcrux *Carl*
GILDERSOME (St Peter) *Wakef 8* **P** *V Batley* **V** A F LAWSON, **C** S DYE
GILLAMOOR (St Aidan) *see* Kirkbymoorside w Gillamoor, Farndale etc *York*
GILLING (St Agatha) and Kirkby Ravensworth *Ripon 2* **P** *Bp and A C P Wharton Esq (jt)* **P-in-c** J I WILLIAMSON
GILLING EAST (Holy Cross) *see* Ampleforth w Oswaldkirk, Gilling E etc *York*
GILLINGHAM (Holy Trinity) *Roch 3* **P** *Bp* **V** G E TOVAR, **NSM** H J CONNELL
GILLINGHAM (St Augustine) *Roch 3* **P** *Bp* **V** C J VAN STRAATEN, **NSM** P MATTHIAS
GILLINGHAM (St Barnabas) *Roch 3* **P** *Bp* **V** K B BEST
GILLINGHAM (St Luke) *see* New Brompton St Luke *Roch*
GILLINGHAM (St Mark) *Roch 3* **P** *Hyndman Trustees* **V** J M SAUNDERS, **C** J FINDLAY
GILLINGHAM (St Mary Magdalene) *Roch 3* **P** *DBP* **V** K R HAYES
GILLINGHAM (St Mary the Virgin) and Milton-on-Stour *Sarum 5* **P** *Bp* **V** A G GILL, **NSM** J R HEDGES
GILLINGHAM (St Mary) w Geldeston w Stockton w Ellingham St Mary and Kirby Cane *Nor 8* **P** *Ld Chan (1 turn), Bp, MMCET and Ch Trust Fund Trust (1 turn)* **P-in-c** W M C BESTELINK
GILLINGHAM, SOUTH (St Matthew) *Roch 3* **P** *Patr Bd* **TR** C M BUTT, **TV** R A LEE, A D JENKINS, **NSM** A L LEE, G R LEWIS
GILLOW HEATH (Mission Room) *see* Biddulph *Lich*
GILMORTON (All Saints), Peatling Parva, Kimcote cum Walton, North Kilworth, South Kilworth, Misterton, Swinford, Catthorpe, Shawell and Stanford *Leic 10* **P** *Patr Bd (5 turns), Ld Chan (1 turn)* **TR** K W BAKER, **TV** J D CURTIS, **NSM** G MARTIN
GILSLAND (St Mary Magdalene) *see* Lanercost, Walton, Gilsland and Nether Denton *Carl*
GILSTEAD (St Wilfrid) *see* Bingley H Trin *Bradf*
GILSTON (St Mary) *see* High Wych and Gilston w Eastwick *St Alb*
GIMINGHAM (All Saints) *see* Trunch *Nor*
GIPPING (Chapel of St Nicholas) *see* Haughley w Wetherden and Stowupland *St E*
GIPSY HILL (Christ Church) *S'wark 15* **P** *CPAS* **V** A P RUMSEY, **C** N R KIRK, **NSM** B ALLEN
GIPTON (Church of the Epiphany) *see* Leeds Gipton Epiphany *Ripon*
GIRLINGTON (St Philip) *Bradf 1* **P** *Simeon's Trustees* **V** A A TOOBY
GIRTON (St Andrew) *Ely 5* **P** *Ld Chan* **P-in-c** W J ADAM
GIRTON (St Cecilia) *see* Collingham w S Scarle and Besthorpe and Girton *S'well*
GISBURN (St Mary the Virgin) *Bradf 5* **P** *Bp* **P-in-c** E A KYTE, **Hon C** K J PHILLIPS
GISLEHAM (Holy Trinity) *see* Kessingland, Gisleham and Rushmere *Nor*
GISLINGHAM (St Mary) *see* S Hartismere *St E*
GISSING (St Mary the Virgin) *see* Winfarthing w Shelfanger w Burston w Gissing etc *Nor*
GITTISHAM (St Michael) *see* Honiton, Gittisham, Combe Raleigh, Monkton etc *Ex*
GIVENDALE, GREAT (St Ethelberga) *see* Pocklington and Owsthorpe and Kilnwick Percy etc *York*
GLAISDALE (St Thomas) *see* Middle Esk Moor *York*
GLANDFORD (St Martin) *see* Blakeney w Cley, Wiveton, Glandford etc *Nor*
GLANTON (St Peter) *see* Whittingham and Edlingham w Bolton Chapel *Newc*
GLAPTHORN (St Leonard) *see* Oundle w Ashton and Benefield w Glapthorn *Pet*
GLAPWELL (St Andrew) *see* Ault Hucknall and Scarcliffe *Derby*
GLASCOTE (St George) and Stonydelph *Lich 4* **P** *Patr Bd* **TR** I H MURRAY, **TV** D S MCDONOUGH, **C** E A LANDER, **OLM** M R LE-WORTHY, D BURGESS, R LOCKWOOD, P D FAULTLESS, K R LINDSAY-SMITH
GLASCOTE HEATH (St Peter) *see* Glascote and Stonydelph *Lich*
GLASSHOUGHTON (St Paul) *see* Castleford *Wakef*
GLASSON (Christ Church) *see* Cockerham w Winmarleigh and Glasson *Blackb*
GLASTON (St Andrew) *see* Lyddington w Stoke Dry and Seaton etc *Pet*
GLASTONBURY (St John the Baptist) (St Benedict) w Meare *B & W 5* **P** *Bp* **P-in-c** M D MARSH, **C** J P LAWRENCE, **Hon C** M B MUDIE, **NSM** S L GRAHAM

GLATTON (St Nicholas) *see* Sawtry and Glatton *Ely*
GLAZEBURY (All Saints) w Hollinfare *Liv 16* **P** *Bp and R Warrington (jt)* **R** R G LEWIS, **C** P L GRAY
GLAZELEY (St Bartholomew) *see* Highley w Billingsley, Glazeley etc *Heref*
GLEADLESS (Christ Church) *Sheff 1* **P** *DBP* **TR** H A JOWETT, **TV** M CAUNT, **NSM** S D HOLDAWAY
GLEADLESS VALLEY (Holy Cross) *see* Heeley and Gleadless Valley *Sheff*
GLEMHAM, GREAT (All Saints) *see* Sternfield, Benhall, Snape etc *St E*
GLEMHAM, LITTLE (St Andrew) *as above*
GLEMSFORD (St Mary the Virgin), Hartest w Boxted, Somerton and Stanstead (Glem Valley United Benefice) *St E 12* **P** *Bp, Prime Min, and Ch Soc Trust (by turn)* **R** P J PRIGG
GLEN AULDYN (Mission Church) *see* Lezayre *S & M*
GLEN GROUP, The *Linc 17* **P** *Bp* **V** M A HARVEY
GLEN MAGNA (St Cuthbert) cum Stretton Magna w Carlton Curlieu and Burton Overy *Leic 5* **P** *Bp, Dr A Llewelyn, and Sir Geoffrey Palmer Bt (jt)* **V** *vacant* 0116-259 2238
GLEN PARVA and South Wigston *Leic 5* **P** *Bp* **V** P DAY
GLENDALE Group, The *Newc 10* **P** *Patr Bd (4 turns), Ld Chan (1 turn)* **TR** R B S BURSTON, **TV** B C HURST, G R KELSEY
GLENFIELD (St Peter) *Leic 11* **P** *Bp* **R** J E SHARPE, **C** O A ADAMS
GLENHOLT (St Anne) *see* Bickleigh and Shaugh Prior *Ex*
GLENTHAM (St Peter) *see* Owmby Gp *Linc*
GLENTWORTH Group, The (St Michael) *Linc 2* **P** *Bp, MMCET, and Ch Soc Trust (jt)* **V** M DAWSON
GLINTON (St Benedict) *see* Peakirk w Glinton and Northborough *Pet*
GLODWICK (St Mark w Christ Church) *Man 19* **P** *Bp* **V** A R HEYES
GLOOSTON (St John the Baptist) *see* Gt Bowden w Welham, Glooston and Cranoe etc *Leic*
GLOSSOP (All Saints) *Derby 6* **P** *Patr Bd* **P-in-c** M F LOVELESS
GLOUCESTER (St Aldate) Finlay Road *Glouc 5* **P** *Bp* **P-in-c** K C JONES
GLOUCESTER (St Barnabas) *see* Tuffley *Glouc*
GLOUCESTER (St Catharine) *Glouc 5* **P** *Bp* **V** G D OSBORNE, **C** J S J GROVES
GLOUCESTER (St George) w Whaddon *Glouc 5* **P** *Bp* **V** J A B PADDOCK, **C** F A WALTERS
GLOUCESTER (St James and All Saints) *Glouc 5* **P** *Bp* **P-in-c** R C SIMPSON, **NSM** J M HOWARD
GLOUCESTER (St Mark) (St Mary de Crypt) (St John the Baptist) (Christ Church) (St Mary de Lode and St Nicholas) *Glouc 5* **P** *D&C (1 turn), Bp (3 turns), Ld Chan (1 turn)* **R** J L MARSHALL
GLOUCESTER (St Michael) *see* Tuffley *Glouc*
GLOUCESTER (St Oswald) *see* Coney Hill *Glouc*
GLOUCESTER (St Paul) *Glouc 5* **P** *Bp* **P-in-c** R J WITCOMBE, **NSM** J R MURPHY
GLOUCESTER (St Stephen) *Glouc 5* **P** *Bp* **P-in-c** J A L B CATERER
GLOUCESTER DOCKS Mariners' Church Proprietary Chapel *Glouc 5* **P** *Ch Soc Trust vacant*
GLOUCESTER ROAD (St Stephen) *see* S Kensington St Steph *Lon*
GLUSBURN (All Saints) *see* Sutton *Bradf*
GLYMPTON (St Mary) *see* Wootton w Glympton and Kiddington *Ox*
GLYNDE (St Mary), West Firle and Beddingham *Chich 18* **P** *Bp and D&C Windsor (alt)* **P-in-c** P C OWEN-JONES
GNOSALL (St Lawrence) *Lich 7* **P** *Bp* **V** C M CASE, **C** C M PLANT
GOADBY (St John the Baptist) *see* Church Langton cum Tur Langton etc *Leic*
GOADBY MARWOOD (St Denys) *see* Scalford w Wycombe and Chadwell etc *Leic*
GOATHILL (St Peter) *see* Milborne Port w Goathill *B & W*
GOATHLAND (St Mary) *see* Middle Esk Moor *York*
GOATHURST (St Edward the King and Martyr) *see* Aisholt, Enmore, Goathurst, Nether Stowey etc *B & W*
GOBOWEN (All Saints) *see* Hengoed w Gobowen *Lich*
GOBOWEN ROAD (Mission Room) *see* Oswestry *Lich*
GODALMING (St Peter and St Paul) *Guildf 4* **P** *Bp* **TR** F J ASHE, **TV** I P BUSSELL, **NSM** M E HOBROUGH, J E J WETHERALL, **OLM** D S MACE, R HARVIE
GODINGTON (Holy Trinity) *see* Shelswell *Ox*
GODLEY cum Newton Green (St John the Baptist) *Ches 14* **P** *R Cheadle* **V** *vacant* 0161-368 2159
GODMANCHESTER (St Mary) *Ely 8* **P** *D&C Westmr* **C** A M BARRETT
GODMANSTONE (Holy Trinity) *see* Buckland Newton, Cerne Abbas, Godmanstone etc *Sarum*
GODMERSHAM (St Lawrence the Martyr) *see* Crundale w Godmersham *Cant*
GODREVY *Truro 5* **P** *Patr Bd* **TR** A T NEAL, **TV** L T ATTWOOD, **C** C A WILSON-BARKER, **NSM** R E WICKREMASINGHE, P C JOHNSON
GODSHILL (All Saints) *Portsm 7* **P** *Guild of All So* **V** J M RYDER, **NSM** M M K KAY
GODSHILL (St Giles) *see* Fordingbridge and Breamore and Hale etc *Win*
GODSTONE (St Nicholas) and Blindley Heath *S'wark 27* **P** *Bp and C K G Hoare Esq (jt)* **R** R E WATTS, **OLM** D G E HARDING
GOFF'S OAK (St James) *St Alb 20* **P** *V Cheshunt* **V** J W BRIDSTRUP
GOLBORNE (St Thomas) *Liv 16* **P** *Bp* **R** R WILLIAMS
GOLCAR (St John the Evangelist) *Wakef 5* **P** *V Huddersfield* **V** R M F CROMPTON
GOLDEN CAP TEAM (Team Ministry) *Sarum 2* **P** *Patr Bd* **TR** R H FAIRBROTHER, **TV** J A L HARRISSON, A-M L STUART, **NSM** T E C SHARPE, F A KEEGAN
GOLDEN GREEN (Mission) *see* Hadlow *Roch*
GOLDEN VALLEY (St Matthias) *see* Riddings and Ironville *Derby*
GOLDENHILL (St John the Evangelist) *Lich 11* **P** *Bp* **P-in-c** K P SCOTT
GOLDERS GREEN (St Alban the Martyr and St Michael) *Lon 15* **P** *Bp* **V** T E A PARK
GOLDHANGER (St Peter) *see* Gt Totham and Lt Totham w Goldhanger *Chelmsf*
GOLDINGTON (St Mary the Virgin) *St Alb 10* **P** *Bp* **V** R L HOWLETT, **C** J M CAPPLEMAN
GOLDS HILL (St Paul) *see* W Bromwich St Jas w St Paul *Lich*
GOLDSBOROUGH (St Mary) *see* Knaresborough *Ripon*
GOLDSWORTH PARK (St Andrew) *Guildf 12* **P** *Bp* **V** R J N COOK, **C** J L BLAIR, C J BLAIR, **NSM** C A HARRISON, **OLM** P R B DONAGHY
GOLDTHORPE (St John the Evangelist and St Mary Magdalene) w Hickleton *Sheff 12* **P** *CR (2 turns), Earl of Halifax (1 turn)* **V** A J DELVES, **C** A S ZIHNI
GOMERSAL (St Mary) *Wakef 8* **P** *Bp* **P-in-c** J C BARNES
GONALSTON (St Laurence) *S'well 15* **P** *C P L Francklin Esq, Bp, and Ld Chan (by turn)* **R** M J BROCK, **C** J E DRAYCOTT, **NSM** M N TAYLOR
GONERBY, GREAT (St Sebastian) *see* Barrowby and Gt Gonerby *Linc*
GOOD EASTER (St Andrew) *see* High and Gd Easter w Margaret Roding *Chelmsf*
GOOD SHEPHERD TEAM MINISTRY, The *Carl 4* **P** *Patr Bd* **TR** M A HOUSTON, **TV** H M K BRETT YOUNG
GOODERSTONE (St George) *see* Cockley Cley w Gooderstone *Nor*
GOODLEIGH (St Gregory) *see* Barnstaple *Ex*
GOODMANHAM (All Saints) *York 5* **P** *Abp* **R** L C MUNT
GOODMAYES (All Saints) *Chelmsf 4* **P** *Hyndman Trustees* **V** C R KEATING
GOODMAYES (St Paul) *Chelmsf 4* **P** *Bp* **V** B J RUTT-FIELD
GOODNESTONE (Holy Cross) *see* Nonington w Wymynswold and Goodnestone etc *Cant*
GOODRICH (St Giles) *see* Walford and St John w Bishopswood, Goodrich etc *Heref*
GOODRINGTON (St George) *Ex 12* **P** *Bp* **P-in-c** G H MAUDE
GOODSHAW (St Mary and All Saints) and Crawshawbooth *Man 15* **P** *Bp and Wm Hulme Trustees (jt)* **P-in-c** W L OLIVER
GOODWORTH CLATFORD (St Peter) *see* Abbotts Ann and Upper and Goodworth Clatford *Win*
GOOLE (St John the Evangelist) (St Mary) (Mariners' Club and Chapel) *Sheff 10* **P** *Bp* **V** J M STRIDE
GOOSE GREEN (St Paul) *Liv 15* **P** *Bp* **V** K BOLTON
GOOSEY (All Saints) *see* Stanford in the Vale w Goosey and Hatford *Ox*
GOOSNARGH (St Mary the Virgin) *see* Fellside Team *Blackb*
GOOSTREY (St Luke) *Ches 11* **P** *V Sandbach* **P-in-c** D R OTTLEY, **NSM** A SARGEANT
GORAN HAVEN (St Just) *see* St Goran w Caerhays *Truro*
GORDON HILL (St Michael and All Angels) *see* Enfield St Mich *Lon*
GOREFIELD (St Paul) *see* Wisbech St Mary and Guyhirn w Ring's End etc *Ely*
GORING (St Thomas of Canterbury) w South Stoke *Ox 6* **P** *Ch Ch Ox* **P-in-c** M K BLAMEY, **C** H A CAMPBELL, **NSM** E J DOWDING

GORING-BY-SEA (St Mary) (St Laurence) *Chich 4* **P** *Bp* **V** A TREMLETT, **C** D A BURT, **NSM** P MATTHEWS
GORLESTON (St Andrew) *Nor 6* **P** *Ch Trust Fund Trust* **V** A P WARD, **C** M K SIMM, A NAISH, **NSM** H F WARD, **OLM** D A N WAITE
GORLESTON (St Mary Magdalene) *Nor 6* **P** *Bp and Ch Trust Fund Trust (jt)* **V** *vacant* (01493) 661741
GORNAL (St Peter) and Sedgley *Worc 10* **P** *Patr Bd* **TR** S R BUCKLEY, **TV** M K BATE, **C** S K RENSHAW
GORNAL, LOWER (St James the Great) *Worc 10* **P** *Bp* **V** J W MOTT
GORSLEY (Christ Church) *see* Newent and Gorsley w Cliffords Mesne *Glouc*
GORTON (Emmanuel) (St James) *Man 1* **P** *Bp and D&C (jt)* **R** M R J WILLIAMS, **OLM** D C GRAY
GORTON (St Philip) *Man 1* **P** *The Crown* **P-in-c** S SCHOFIELD, **C** S O'ROURKE
GOSBECK (St Mary) *see* Coddenham w Gosbeck and Hemingstone w Henley *St E*
GOSBERTON (St Peter and St Paul), Gosberton Clough and Quadring *Linc 17* **P** *Bp and D&C (jt)* **V** J W FURST
GOSBERTON CLOUGH (St Gilbert and St Hugh) *see* Gosberton, Gosberton Clough and Quadring *Linc*
GOSCOTE, EAST (St Hilda) *see* Syston *Leic*
GOSFIELD (St Katherine) *see* Halstead Area *Chelmsf*
GOSFORTH (All Saints) *Newc 5* **P** *Bp* **V** R B HILL, **C** G G B TINDALE, **NSM** R B BIRNIE
GOSFORTH (St Hugh) *Newc 5* **P** *Bp* **P-in-c** P KENNEY, **NSM** A D MCCARTAN
GOSFORTH (St Mary) w Nether Wasdale and Wasdale Head *Carl 5* **P** *Bp, Earl of Lonsdale, V St Bees, and PCCs (jt)* **R** *vacant* (01946) 725251
GOSFORTH (St Nicholas) *Newc 5* **P** *Bp* **V** P J CUNNINGHAM, **NSM** M C DOUGLASS
GOSFORTH, NORTH (St Columba) *see* Ch the King *Newc*
GOSFORTH VALLEY (St Andrew) *see* Dronfield w Holmesfield *Derby*
GOSPEL END (St Barnabas) *see* Gornal and Sedgley *Worc*
GOSPEL LANE (St Michael) *Birm 6* **P** *Bp* **P-in-c** R M WHARTON
GOSPEL OAK (All Hallows) *see* Hampstead St Steph w All Hallows *Lon*
GOSPEL OAK (St Martin) *see* Kentish Town St Martin w St Andr *Lon*
GOSPORT (Christ Church) *Portsm 3* **P** *Bp* **V** I G BOOTH
GOSPORT (Holy Trinity) *Portsm 3* **P** *DBP* **V** I G BOOTH
GOSSOPS GREEN (St Alban) *see* Ifield *Chich*
GOTHAM (St Lawrence) *S'well 9* **P** *Bp* **P-in-c** S W OSMAN
GOUDHURST (St Mary the Virgin) w Kilndown *Cant 11* **P** *Abp and Prime Min (alt)* **V** P T MACKENZIE
GOULCEBY (All Saints) *see* Asterby Gp *Linc*
GOXHILL (All Saints) *see* Barrow and Goxhill *Linc*
GOXHILL (St Giles) *see* Aldbrough, Mappleton w Goxhill and Withernwick *York*
GRADE (St Grada and the Holy Cross) *see* St Ruan w St Grade and Landewednack *Truro*
GRAFFHAM (St Giles) w Woolavington *Chich 11* **P** *Bp* **P-in-c** P M GILBERT
GRAFFOE Group *Linc 18* **P** *Ch Coll Cam, D&C and DBP, Viscountess Chaplin, Oriel Coll Ox, and Mrs P N Fullerton (by turn)* **V** K A WINDSLOW, **C** C E SACKLEY
GRAFHAM (All Saints) *see* E Leightonstone *Ely*
GRAFHAM (St Andrew) *see* Bramley and Grafham *Guildf*
GRAFTON, EAST (St Nicholas) *see* Savernake *Sarum*
GRAFTON FLYFORD (St John the Baptist) *see* Abberton, The Flyfords, Naunton Beauchamp etc *Worc*
GRAFTON REGIS (St Mary) *see* Blisworth and Stoke Bruerne w Grafton Regis etc *Pet*
GRAFTON UNDERWOOD (St James the Apostle) *see* Cranford w Grafton Underwood and Twywell *Pet*
GRAHAME PARK (St Augustine) Conventional District *Lon 15* **C-in-c** D C BATLEY-GLADDEN
GRAIN (St James) w Stoke *Roch 6* **P** *DBP* **V** *vacant* (01634) 270263
GRAINSBY (St Nicholas) *see* The North-Chapel Parishes *Linc*
GRAINTHORPE (St Clement) *see* Somercotes and Grainthorpe w Conisholme *Linc*
GRAMPOUND (St Nun) *see* Probus, Ladock and Grampound w Creed and St Erme *Truro*
GRAMPOUND ROAD Mission Church *as above*
GRANBOROUGH (St John the Baptist) *see* Schorne *Ox*
GRANBY (All Saints) *see* Cropwell Bishop w Colston Bassett, Granby etc *S'well*
GRANDBOROUGH (St Peter) *see* Leam Valley *Cov*
GRANGE (Holy Trinity) *see* Thornthwaite cum Braithwaite, Newlands etc *Carl*
GRANGE (St Andrew) *Ches 3* **P** *Bp* **P-in-c** U R ONUNWA
GRANGE FELL (not known) *see* Cartmel Peninsula *Carl*
GRANGE MOOR (St Bartholomew) *see* Kirkheaton *Wakef*
GRANGE-OVER-SANDS (St Paul) *see* Cartmel Peninsula *Carl*
GRANGE PARK (St Peter) *Lon 18* **P** *Bp* **V** E G GREER
GRANGE VILLA (St Columba) *see* W Pelton *Dur*
GRANGETOWN (St Aidan) *Dur 16* **P** *V Ryhope* **V** C COLLINS
GRANGETOWN (St Hilda of Whitby) *York 18* **P** *Abp* **V** I M GRAHAM
GRANSDEN, GREAT (St Bartholomew) and Abbotsley and Lt Gransden and Waresley *Ely 10* **P** *Pemb Coll Cam (1 turn), Clare Coll Cam (2 turns), and Ball Coll Ox (1 turn)* **R** *vacant* (01767) 677227
GRANSDEN, LITTLE (St Peter and St Paul) *see* Gt Gransden and Abbotsley and Lt Gransden etc *Ely*
GRANTCHESTER (St Andrew and St Mary) *Ely 6* **P** *CCC Cam* **P-in-c** K F M FISHER
GRANTHAM Earlesfield *Linc 19* **P** *Bp* **V** S G ROWLAND
GRANTHAM Harrowby w Londonthorpe *Linc 19* **P** *Bp* **P-in-c** C P BOLAND
GRANTHAM Manthorpe *Linc 19* **P** *Bp* **P-in-c** J C BRUCE
GRANTHAM (St Anne) New Somerby and St John Spitalgate *Linc 19* **P** *Bp and R Grantham (jt)* **V** F H LONG
GRANTHAM (St John the Evangelist) *see* Grantham, Manthorpe *Linc*
GRANTHAM (St Wulfram) *Linc 19* **P** *Bp* **R** C P ANDREWS, **C** V L SIMS, **NSM** J T FARLEY, J M ROWLAND
GRANTHAM (The Ascension) *see* Grantham, Harrowby w Londonthorpe *Linc*
GRANTHAM (The Epiphany) *see* Grantham, Earlesfield *Linc*
GRANVILLES WOOTTON (St Mary the Virgin) *see* Dungeon Hill *Sarum*
GRAPPENHALL (St Wilfrid) *Ches 4* **P** *P G Greenall Esq* **R** M B KELLY
GRASBY (All Saints) *see* Caistor Gp *Linc*
GRASMERE (St Oswald) *Carl 11* **P** *Qu Coll Ox* **R** C J BUTLAND
GRASSENDALE (St Mary) *Liv 4* **P** *Trustees* **V** *vacant* 0151-427 1474
GRATELEY (St Leonard) *see* Amport, Grateley, Monxton and Quarley *Win*
GRATWICH (St Mary the Virgin) *see* Uttoxeter Area *Lich*
GRAVELEY (St Botolph) *see* Papworth *Ely*
GRAVELEY (St Mary) *see* Stevenage St Nic and Graveley *St Alb*
GRAVELLY HILL (All Saints) *Birm 8* **P** *Bp* **V** G R MENSINGH, **C** R F PAILING
GRAVENEY (All Saints) *see* Preston next Faversham, Goodnestone and Graveney *Cant*
GRAVENHURST (St Giles), Shillington and Stondon *St Alb 16* **P** *Bp* **V** S J WHEATLEY, **NSM** L A JONES
GRAVESEND (Holy Family) w Ifield *Roch 4* **P** *Bp and Lt-Col F B Edmeades (jt)* **R** J L FIELD
GRAVESEND (St Aidan) *Roch 4* **P** *Bp* **V** P G RICH, **NSM** J P LITTLEWOOD
GRAVESEND (St George) *Roch 4* **P** *Bp* **R** R A D STURT
GRAVESEND (St Mary) *Roch 4* **P** *R Gravesend* **V** R OATES, **NSM** P J BARNES
GRAYINGHAM (St Radegunda) *Linc 6* **P** *Bp* **R** S J FOSTER
GRAYRIGG (St John the Evangelist), Old Hutton and New Hutton *Carl 10* **P** *V Kendal* **V** *vacant* (01539) 824272
GRAYS NORTH (St John the Evangelist) *Chelmsf 14* **P** *Bp* **V** D R TOMLINSON, **NSM** J C TOMLINSON
GRAYS THURROCK (St Peter and St Paul) *Chelmsf 14* **P** *DBP* **TR** J C HASSELL, **TV** L H LEE, A J GOWING-CUMBER, **C** M E WHITFORD, S H GIBBS, **NSM** J K EDWARDS
GRAYSHOTT (St Luke) *Guildf 3* **P** *Bp* **V** M S WING
GRAYSWOOD (All Saints) *see* Haslemere and Grayswood *Guildf*
GRAYTHWAITE (Mission Room) *see* Hawkshead and Low Wray w Sawrey and Rusland etc *Carl*
GRAZELEY (Holy Trinity) *see* Loddon Reach *Ox*
GREASBROUGH (St Mary) *Sheff 6* **P** *Sir Philip Naylor-Leyland Bt* **V** K E TONES
GREASBY (St Nicholas) *see* Frankby w Greasby *Ches*
GREASLEY (St Mary) *S'well 4* **P** *Bp* **P-in-c** D A MARVIN
GREAT *see also under substantive place name*
GREAT CAMBRIDGE ROAD (St John the Baptist and St James) *Lon 19* **P** *D&C St Paul's* **V** P B LYONS
GREAT GLEN (St Cuthbert) *see* Glen Magna cum Stretton Magna etc *Leic*
GREAT MOOR (St Saviour) *see* Stockport St Sav *Ches*
GREATER *see also under substantive place name*
GREATFORD (St Thomas à Becket) *see* Uffington Gp *Linc*
GREATHAM (not known) *see* Amberley w N Stoke and Parham, Wiggonholt etc *Chich*

GREATHAM (St John the Baptist) *Dur 3* **P** *Trustees* **P-in-c** R A COLLINS
GREATHAM w Empshott and Hawkley w Prior's Dean *Portsm 4* **P** *DBP* **R** D H HEATLEY, **NSM** D C STICKLAND
GREATSTONE (St Peter) *see* Lydd *Cant*
GREATWORTH (St Peter) *see* Chenderit *Pet*
GREAVE FOLD (Holy Innocents) *see* Chadkirk *Ches*
GREEN HAMMERTON (St Thomas) *see* Gt and Lt Ouseburn w Marton cum Grafton etc *Ripon*
GREEN HAWORTH (St Clement) *see* Accrington Ch the King *Blackb*
GREEN HEATH (St Saviour) *see* Hednesford *Lich*
GREEN STREET GREEN (St Mary) and Pratts Bottom *Roch 16* **P** *Bp* **V** K A CARPANI, **C** P J AVANN
GREEN VALE (Holy Trinity) *see* Stockton H Trin *Dur*
GREENFIELD *see* Bridgwater H Trin *B & W*
GREENFIELD (St Mary) *see* Saddleworth *Man*
GREENFIELDS (United Church) *see* Shrewsbury St Geo w Greenfields *Lich*
GREENFORD (Holy Cross) (St Edward the Confessor) *Lon 22* **P** *K Coll Cam* **R** N RICHARDSON, **NSM** W R HEPPER
GREENFORD, NORTH (All Hallows) *Lon 22* **P** *Bp* **P-in-c** P F HEAZELL, **NSM** D C DAVIS
GREENGATES (St John the Evangelist) *Bradf 3* **P** *D&C* **V** *vacant* (01274) 613111
GREENHAM (St Mary the Virgin) *Ox 14* **P** *Bp* **V** J P H CLARKE
GREENHAM (St Peter) *see* Wellington and Distr *B & W*
GREENHEAD (St Cuthbert) *see* Haltwhistle and Greenhead *Newc*
GREENHILL (St John the Baptist) *Lon 23* **P** *Bp, Adn, and V Harrow St Mary (jt)* **V** R A WAKELING
GREENHILL (St Peter) *Sheff 2* **P** *Bp* **V** L C JENKINS
GREENHITHE (St Mary) *Roch 2* **P** *Ch Soc Trust and Canon T L Livermore (jt)* **R** R D BARRON
GREENHOW HILL (St Mary) *see* Upper Nidderdale *Ripon*
GREENLANDS (St Anne) *Blackb 8* **P** *Bp and V Blackpool St Steph (jt)* **V** A M BARTLETT
GREENLANDS (St John the Evangelist) *see* Ipsley *Worc*
GREENS NORTON (St Bartholomew) w Bradden and Lichborough *Pet 5* **P** *J E Grant-Ives Esq (1 turn), The Crown (3 turns), and Melanesian Miss Trust (1 turn)* **P-in-c** J F A M KNIGHT
GREENSIDE (St John) *Dur 13* **P** *R Ryton w Hedgefield* **V** C W DEVONISH
GREENSTEAD (St Andrew) (St Edmund's Church Hall) (St Matthew) w Colchester St Anne *Chelmsf 16* **P** *Patr Bd and Ld Chan (alt)* **TR** B S RAWLINGS, **TV** A M PARKER, **C** R M ROBERTS
GREENSTEAD GREEN (St James Apostle) *see* Halstead Area *Chelmsf*
GREENSTED-JUXTA-ONGAR (St Andrew) w Stanford Rivers and Stapleford Tawney w Theydon Mount *Chelmsf 27* **P** *Bp Lon and DBP (1 turn), and Duchy of Lanc (1 turn)* **R** R WILKINSON
GREENWICH (St Alfege) *S'wark 3* **P** *The Crown* **C** D C WALSH, **Hon C** S J DAVIES
GREENWICH, EAST (Christ Church) (St Andrew w St Michael) (St George) *S'wark 3* **P** *Patr Bd* **TR** M N A TORRY, **TV** D P CLACEY
GREETE (St James) *see* Burford II w Greete and Hope Bagot *Heref*
GREETHAM (All Saints) w Ashby Puerorum *Linc 11* **P** *D&C* **R** M E BURSON-THOMAS, **C** A C V HARVEY, **NSM** A C FORD
GREETHAM (St Mary the Virgin) and Thistleton w Stretton and Clipsham *Pet 14* **P** *Bp and Sir David Davenport-Handley (alt)* **P-in-c** M H W ROGERS
GREETLAND (St Thomas) and West Vale *Wakef 2* **P** *V Halifax* **V** S GOTT
GREETWELL (All Saints) *see* S Lawres Gp *Linc*
GREINTON (St Michael and All Angels) *B & W 5* **P** *Bp* **P-in-c** W B GRAHAM
GRENDON (All Saints) *see* Baddesley Ensor w Grendon *Birm*
GRENDON (St Mary) *see* Yardley Hastings, Denton and Grendon etc *Pet*
GRENDON BISHOP (St John the Baptist) *see* Bredenbury w Grendon Bishop and Wacton etc *Heref*
GRENDON UNDERWOOD (St Leonard) *see* Swan *Ox*
GRENOSIDE (St Mark) *Sheff 3* **P** *Bp and V Ecclesfield (jt)* **V** M J CAREY
GRESHAM (All Saints) *see* Aylmerton, Runton, Beeston Regis and Gresham *Nor*
GRESLEY (St George and St Mary) *Derby 16* **P** *Simeon's Trustees* **P-in-c** D T PERRETT, **C** J A BURGESS
GRESSENHALL (Assumption of the Blessed Virgin Mary) w Longham w Wendling and Bittering Parva *Nor 14* **P** *Ld Chan (1 turn), CPAS (2 turns)* **R** J E BELHAM, **NSM** K D BLOGG
GRESSINGHAM (St John the Evangelist) *see* Hornby w Claughton and Whittington etc *Blackb*
GRETTON (Christ Church) *see* Winchcombe *Glouc*
GRETTON (St James the Great) w Rockingham and Cottingham w East Carlton *Pet 9* **P** *Bp, Comdr L M M Saunders Watson, Sir Geoffrey Palmer Bt, and BNC Ox (jt)* **V** *vacant* (01536) 770237
GREWELTHORPE (St James) *see* Fountains Gp *Ripon*
GREYSTOKE (St Andrew) *see* Gd Shep TM *Carl*
GREYSTONES (St Gabriel) *Sheff 2* **P** *Dean* **V** P W BECKLEY
GREYWELL (St Mary) *see* Newnham w Nately Scures w Mapledurwell etc *Win*
GRIMEHILLS (St Mary) *see* Darwen St Barn *Blackb*
GRIMETHORPE (St Luke) w Brierley *Wakef 7* **P** *Bp* **V** P D NEEDHAM
GRIMLEY (St Bartholomew) *see* Hallow and Grimley w Holt *Worc*
GRIMOLDBY (St Edith) *see* Mid Marsh Gp *Linc*
GRIMSARGH (St Michael) *Blackb 13* **P** *R Preston* **V** G R LOXHAM
GRIMSBURY (St Leonard) *see* Banbury St Leon *Ox*
GRIMSBY (St Augustine of Hippo) *Linc 9* **P** *TR Gt Grimsby SS Mary and Jas* **V** S W JONES
GRIMSBY, GREAT (St Andrew w St Luke and All Saints) *Linc 9* **P** *Bp* **P-in-c** T H ATKINSON
GRIMSBY, GREAT (St Mary and St James) (St Hugh) (St Mark) (St Martin) *Linc 9* **P** *Bp* **TR** M O HUNTER, **C** D J SUDRON, T R BARDELL, **NSM** J MCMANN
GRIMSBY, LITTLE (St Edith) *see* Fotherby *Linc*
GRIMSBY WEST *see* Gt and Lt Coates w Bradley *Linc*
GRIMSTEAD, EAST (Holy Trinity) *see* Clarendon *Sarum*
GRIMSTEAD, WEST (St John) *as above*
GRIMSTON (St Botolph), Congham and Roydon *Nor 20* **P** *Qu Coll Cam, Bp, and G Howard Esq (jt)* **R** W A HOWARD
GRIMSTON (St John the Baptist) *see* Old Dalby, Nether Broughton, Saxelbye etc *Leic*
GRIMSTON, NORTH (St Nicholas) *see* W Buckrose *York*
GRINDALE (St Nicholas) *see* Burton Fleming w Fordon, Grindale etc *York*
GRINDLEFORD (St Helen) *see* Eyam *Derby*
GRINDLETON (St Ambrose) *see* Bolton by Bowland w Grindleton *Bradf*
GRINDON (All Saints) *see* Calton, Cauldon, Grindon, Waterfall etc *Lich*
GRINDON (St James), Stillington and Wolviston *Dur 10* **P** *Bp (2 turns), D&C (1 turn)* **R** D M BROOKE
GRINDON (St Oswald) *see* Sunderland Pennywell St Thos *Dur*
GRINGLEY-ON-THE-HILL (St Peter and St Paul) *see* Beckingham w Walkeringham and Gringley *S'well*
GRINSDALE (St Kentigern) *see* Barony of Burgh *Carl*
GRINSHILL (All Saints) *see* Astley, Clive, Grinshill and Hadnall *Lich*
GRINSTEAD, EAST (St Mary the Virgin) *Chich 7* **P** *Bp* **V** G BOND, **NSM** J GAYFORD
GRINSTEAD, EAST (St Swithun) *Chich 7* **P** *Bp* **V** C EVERETT-ALLEN, **C** R J S CATCHPOLE, **NSM** J K PEATY
GRINSTEAD, WEST (St George) *Chich 8* **P** *Bp* **R** W E M HARRIS
GRINTON (St Andrew) *see* Swaledale *Ripon*
GRISTHORPE (St Thomas) *see* Filey *York*
GRISTON (St Peter and St Paul) *see* Caston, Griston, Merton, Thompson etc *Nor*
GRITTLETON (St Mary the Virgin) *see* By Brook *Bris*
GRIZEBECK (The Good Shepherd) *see* Kirkby Ireleth *Carl*
GROBY (St Philip and St James) *see* Bradgate Team *Leic*
GROOMBRIDGE (St John the Evangelist) *see* Speldhurst w Groombridge and Ashurst *Roch*
GROOMBRIDGE, NEW (St Thomas) *Chich 19* **P** *R Withyham* **P-in-c** A B GREEN
GROSMONT (St Matthew) *see* Middle Esk Moor *York*
GROSVENOR CHAPEL (no dedication) Chapel of Ease in the parish of Hanover Square St George w St Mark *Lon 3* **C-in-c** S J HOBBS, **Hon C** S D DEWEY, **NSM** J M HICKS
GROTON (St Bartholomew) *see* Boxford, Edwardstone, Groton etc *St E*
GROVE (St Helen) *see* E Markham w Askham, Headon w Upton and Grove *S'well*
GROVE (St John the Baptist) *Ox 19* **P** *D&C Windsor* **V** J C ROBERTSON
GROVE GREEN (St John) Local Ecumenical Project *Cant 15* **C-in-c** O HARRISON
GROVE PARK (St Augustine) *see* Lee St Aug *S'wark*
GROVEHILL (Resurrection) *see* Hemel Hempstead *St Alb*

GRUNDISBURGH (St Mary the Virgin) *see* Boulge w Burgh, Grundisburgh and Hasketon *St E*
GUARLFORD (St Mary) *see* Powick and Guarlford and Madresfield w Newland *Worc*
GUERNSEY (Holy Trinity) *Win 14* **P** *Trustees* **V** G C A STOREY
GUERNSEY L'Islet (St Mary) *see* Guernsey St Sampson *Win*
GUERNSEY (St Andrew de la Pommeraye) *Win 14* **P** *The Crown* **R** C R SMITH
GUERNSEY (St John the Evangelist) *Win 14* **P** *Trustees* **V** A T SHARP, **NSM** J LE BILLON
GUERNSEY (St Marguerite de la Foret) *Win 14* **P** *The Crown* **NSM** L S LE VASSEUR
GUERNSEY (St Martin) *Win 14* **P** *The Crown* **R** M R KEIRLE, **NSM** R G BELLINGER
GUERNSEY (St Matthew) *Win 14* **P** *R Ste Marie du Castel* **V** C E SELIM
GUERNSEY (St Michel du Valle) *Win 14* **P** *The Crown* **R** K C NORTHOVER
GUERNSEY (St Peter Port) *Win 14* **P** *The Crown* **R** K P MELLOR
GUERNSEY (St Philippe de Torteval) *Win 14* **P** *The Crown* **R** M A STRIKE
GUERNSEY (St Pierre du Bois) *Win 14* **P** *The Crown* **R** M A STRIKE
GUERNSEY (St Sampson) *Win 14* **P** *The Crown* **R** J C SYKES
GUERNSEY (St Saviour) (Chapel of St Apolline) *Win 14* **P** *The Crown* **R** W A PRESCOTT, **NSM** L S LE VASSEUR
GUERNSEY (St Stephen) *Win 14* **P** *R St Peter Port* **V** *vacant* (01481) 720268
GUERNSEY (Ste Marie du Castel) *Win 14* **P** *The Crown* **R** C E SELIM
GUESTLING (St Lawrence) *see* Fairlight, Guestling and Pett *Chich*
GUESTWICK (St Peter) *see* Foulsham w Hindolveston and Guestwick *Nor*
GUILDEN MORDEN (St Mary) *see* Shingay Gp *Ely*
GUILDEN SUTTON (St John the Baptist) *see* Plemstall w Guilden Sutton *Ches*
GUILDFORD (All Saints) *Guildf 5* **P** *Bp* **V** B L MESSHAM, **NSM** R D S SANDERS
GUILDFORD (Christ Church) (St Martha-on-the-Hill) *Guildf 5* **P** *Simeon's Trustees and Duke Northd (jt)* **V** S R SANDERS, **C** E J OLSWORTH-PETER, **NSM** R D S SANDERS
GUILDFORD (Holy Spirit) *see* Burpham *Guildf*
GUILDFORD (Holy Trinity) (St Mary the Virgin) (St Michael) *Guildf 5* **P** *Bp* **R** R L COTTON, **C** A E DIXON, **OLM** B D ROBERTS
GUILDFORD (St Clare) *see* Westborough *Guildf*
GUILDFORD (St Francis) *as above*
GUILDFORD (St Luke) *see* Burpham *Guildf*
GUILDFORD (St Nicolas) *Guildf 5* **P** *Bp* **R** A H NORMAN
GUILDFORD (St Saviour) *Guildf 5* **P** *Simeon's Trustees* **R** D J BRACEWELL, **C** S G HOLLAND, **NSM** A C WHEELER, P J LEVELL
GUILSBOROUGH (St Ethelreda) w Hollowell and Cold Ashby *Pet 2* **P** *J L Lowther Esq (2 turns) and Bp (1 turn)* **P-in-c** J M TARRANT
GUILTCROSS *Nor 11* **P** *Bp, Mrs C Noel, Exors C P B Goldson, and DBP (jt)* **P-in-c** C J DAVIDSON, **Hon C** M J BULL
GUISBOROUGH (St Nicholas) *York 16* **P** *Abp* **R** P L BISHOP, **C** M JACKSON
GUISELEY (St Oswald King and Martyr) w Esholt *Bradf 4* **P** *Patr Bd* **TR** G B ATHERTON, **TV** C NORMAN
GUIST (St Andrew) *see* Twyford, Guist, Bintree, Themelthorpe etc *Nor*
GUITING POWER (St Michael) *see* The Guitings, Cutsdean, Farmcote etc *Glouc*
GUITINGS, Cutsdean, Farmcote, Upper and Lower Slaughter w Eyford and Naunton, The *Glouc 14* **P** *Bp, Ch Ch Ox, Guiting Manor Amenity Trust, and F E B Witts Esq (jt)* **R** G L SIMPSON, **NSM** H J GARDNER
GULDEFORD, EAST (St Mary) *see* Rye *Chich*
GULVAL (St Gulval) and Madron *Truro 5* **P** *Ld Chan and Bp (jt)* **P-in-c** D J PHIPPS, **OLM** P A T HORDER
GULWORTHY (St Paul) *see* Tavistock and Gulworthy *Ex*
GUMLEY (St Helen) *see* Foxton w Gumley and Laughton *Leic*
GUNBY (St Nicholas) *see* Witham Gp *Linc*
GUNBY (St Peter) *see* Welton-le-Marsh w Gunby *Linc*
GUNHOUSE (St Barnabas) *see* Trentside E *Linc*
GUNN CHAPEL (Holy Name) *see* Swimbridge w W Buckland and Landkey *Ex*
GUNNERTON (St Christopher) *see* Chollerton w Birtley and Thockrington *Newc*
GUNNESS (St Barnabas) *see* Trentside E *Linc*
GUNNISLAKE (St Anne) *see* Calstock *Truro*
GUNTHORPE (St John the Baptist) *see* Lowdham w Caythorpe, and Gunthorpe *S'well*
GUNTHORPE (St Mary) *see* Stiffkey and Bale *Nor*
GUNTON St Peter (St Benedict) *Nor 9* **P** *CPAS* **R** J A FAIRBAIRN, **OLM** G WILSON
GUNWALLOE (St Winwalloe) *see* Cury and Gunwalloe w Mawgan *Truro*
GURNARD (All Saints) *Portsm 8* **P** *Bp* **V** G E MORRIS, **NSM** D M NETHERWAY
GUSSAGE (St Andrew) *see* Sixpenny Handley w Gussage St Andrew etc *Sarum*
GUSSAGE ALL SAINTS (All Saints) *see* Chase *Sarum*
GUSSAGE ST MICHAEL (St Michael) *as above*
GUSTARD WOOD (St Peter) *see* Wheathampstead *St Alb*
GUSTON (St Martin of Tours) *see* Whitfield w Guston *Cant*
GWEEK (Mission Church) *see* Constantine *Truro*
GWENNAP (St Weneppa) *see* St Stythians w Perranarworthal and Gwennap *Truro*
GWINEAR (St Winnear) *see* Godrevy *Truro*
GWITHIAN (St Gwithian) *as above*
HABBERLEY (St Mary) *Heref 13* **P** *Bp* **R** A N TOOP, **NSM** M-L TOOP
HABERGHAM (All Saints) *see* W Burnley All SS *Blackb*
HABERGHAM EAVES (St Matthew the Apostle) *see* Burnley St Matt w H Trin *Blackb*
HABROUGH Group, The (St Margaret) *Linc 10* **P** *DBP* **P-in-c** M W PAGE-CHESTNEY, **NSM** S V PAGE-CHESTNEY
HABTON, GREAT (St Chad) *see* Kirby Misperton w Normanby, Edston and Salton *York*
HACCOMBE (St Blaise) *see* Shaldon, Stokeinteignhead, Combeinteignhead etc *Ex*
HACCONBY (St Andrew) *see* Ringstone in Aveland Gp *Linc*
HACHESTON (St Andrew) *see* Campsea Ashe w Marlesford, Parham and Hacheston *St E*
HACKBRIDGE and Beddington Corner (All Saints) *S'wark 25* **P** *Bp* **P-in-c** A O ROLAND
HACKENTHORPE (Christ Church) *Sheff 2* **P** *Bp* **V** S J WILLETT, **C** P R ALLEN
HACKFORD (St Mary the Virgin) *see* High Oak, Hingham and Scoulton w Wood Rising *Nor*
HACKINGTON (St Stephen) *Cant 3* **P** *Adn Cant* **R** J G LEWIS-ANTHONY, **Hon C** S C E LAIRD
HACKNESS (St Peter) w Harwood Dale *York 15* **P** *Lord Derwent* **V** *vacant* (01723) 882224
HACKNEY Mount Pleasant Lane (St Matthew) *see* Upper Clapton St Matt *Lon*
HACKNEY (St James) *see* Clapton St Jas *Lon*
HACKNEY (St John) *see* St John-at-Hackney *Lon*
HACKNEY (St Luke) Homerton Terrace *see* Homerton St Luke *Lon*
HACKNEY (St Thomas) *see* Stamford Hill St Thos *Lon*
HACKNEY, OVER (Mission Room) *see* Darley *Derby*
HACKNEY, SOUTH (St John of Jerusalem) (Christ Church) *Lon 5* **P** *Lord Amherst* **R** N R J FUNNELL, **C** S M CONNELL
HACKNEY, SOUTH (St Michael and All Angels) London Fields w Haggerston (St Paul) *Lon 5* **P** *R S Hackney St Jo w Ch Ch* **V** A N EVERETT, **Hon C** A WINDROSS
HACKNEY, WEST St Barnabas (St Paul) *Lon 5* **P** *Bp* **R** W D N WEIR
HACKNEY MARSH (All Souls) *Lon 5* **P** *Patr Bd* **TR** D J SAVILLE, **TV** G L CLAYDON, J A G POPP, **NSM** T A HALEY
HACKNEY WICK (St Mary of Eton) (St Augustine) *Lon 5* **P** *Eton Coll* **C** A R L PIGGOT
HACKTHORN (St Michael and All Angels) *see* Owmby Gp *Linc*
HADDENHAM (Holy Trinity) *Ely 12* **P** *Adn Ely* **V** F E G BRAMPTON
HADDENHAM (St Mary the Virgin) w Cuddington, Kingsey and Aston Sandford *Ox 21* **P** *D&C Roch* **V** A C DENHAM, **OLM** J A RACE
HADDESLEY (St John the Baptist) *see* Haddlesey w Hambleton and Birkin *York*
HADDISCOE (St Mary) *see* Raveningham Gp *Nor*
HADDLESEY w Hambleton and Birkin *York 4* **P** *Abp and Simeon's Trustees (jt)* **P-in-c** S J MURRAY
HADDON (St Mary) *see* Stilton w Denton and Caldecote etc *Ely*
HADDON, EAST (St Mary the Virgin) *see* Brington w Whilton and Norton etc *Pet*
HADDON, OVER (St Anne) *see* Bakewell *Derby*
HADDON, WEST (All Saints) w Winwick and Ravensthorpe *Pet 2* **P** *DBP* **P-in-c** C R EVANS, **C** A M LORD
HADFIELD (St Andrew) *Derby 6* **P** *Bp* **V** G C GRIFFITHS, **NSM** J R ROSEDALE

HADHAM, LITTLE (St Cecilia) w Albury *St Alb 18* **P** *Bp Lon* **R** *vacant* (01279) 771361
HADHAM, MUCH (St Andrew) *St Alb 18* **P** *Bp Lon* **P-in-c** C D BOULTON
HADLEIGH (St Barnabas) *Chelmsf 10* **P** *Bp* **V** S J HOLMES
HADLEIGH (St James the Less) *Chelmsf 10* **P** *Dr P W M Copeman* **R** M J KETLEY
HADLEIGH (St Mary), Layham and Shelley *St E 3* **P** *St Jo Coll Cam and Abp (alt)* **V** D A C STRANACK, **C** E A MORRIS, **NSM** J M WILLIS
HADLEY (Holy Trinity) *Lich 21* **P** *Bp, Adn Salop, V Wrockwardine, R Kynnersley, and V Wellington w Eyton (jt)* **V** V C SWEET, **C** T B BLOOR
HADLEY WOOD (St Paul) Proprietary Chapel *Lon 18* **Min** R MACKAY
HADLOW (St Mary) *Roch 8* **P** *Exors Miss I N King* **V** G A SMITH
HADLOW DOWN (St Mark) *see* Buxted and Hadlow Down *Chich*
HADNALL (St Mary Magdalene) *see* Astley, Clive, Grinshill and Hadnall *Lich*
HADSTOCK (St Botolph) *see* Saffron Walden w Wendens Ambo, Littlebury etc *Chelmsf*
HADZOR w Oddingley (St James) *see* Bowbrook S *Worc*
HAGBOURNE (St Andrew) *see* Blewbury, Hagbourne and Upton *Ox*
HAGGERSTON (St Chad) *Lon 5* **P** *The Crown* **V** J J WESTCOTT
HAGLEY (St John the Baptist) *Worc 12* **P** *Viscount Cobham* **R** R J C NEWTON
HAGLEY, WEST (St Saviour) *see* Hagley *Worc*
HAGNABY (St Andrew) *see* Marden Hill Gp *Linc*
HAGWORTHINGHAM (Holy Trinity) *as above*
HAIGH (St David) *Liv 14* **P** *R Wigan* **V** *vacant* (01942) 831255
HAIL WESTON (St Nicholas) *see* Gt Staughton w Hail Weston w Southoe *Ely*
HAILE (not known) *see* Egremont and Haile *Carl*
HAILES (Chapel) *see* Winchcombe *Glouc*
HAILEY (St John the Evangelist) *see* Witney *Ox*
HAILSHAM (St Mary) *Chich 15* **P** *Ch Soc Trust* **V** D J BOURNE
HAINAULT (St Paul) *Chelmsf 4* **P** *Bp* **V** C S T CANT
HAINFORD (All Saints) *see* Hevingham w Hainford and Stratton Strawless *Nor*
HAINTON (St Mary) *see* Barkwith Gp *Linc*
HALA (St Paul's Centre) *see* Scotforth *Blackb*
HALAM (St Michael) *see* Edingley w Halam *S'well*
HALAS *Worc 9* **P** *Patr Bd* **TR** J C EVEREST, **TV** A D PETTIT, R S HALL, G A BYRNE
HALBERTON (St Andrew) *see* Sampford Peverell, Uplowman, Holcombe Rogus etc *Ex*
HALCON *see* Taunton All SS *B & W*
HALDEN, HIGH (St Mary the Virgin) *see* Bethersden w High Halden *Cant*
HALDENS (Christ the King) *see* Digswell and Panshanger *St Alb*
HALDON *see* Teignmouth, Ideford w Luton, Ashcombe etc *Ex*
HALE (St David) *see* Timperley *Ches*
HALE (St John the Evangelist) w Badshot Lea *Guildf 3* **P** *Patr Bd* **TR** J J PAGE, **TV** D HENLEY
HALE (St Mary) *Liv 13* **P** *Trustees* **P-in-c** J M COLLIER
HALE (St Mary) *see* Fordingbridge and Breamore and Hale etc *Win*
HALE (St Peter) and Ashley *Ches 10* **P** *V Bowdon* **V** M J ROBINSON, **C** C BULL, **NSM** C E HOLMES
HALE, GREAT (St John the Baptist) *see* Helpringham w Hale *Linc*
HALE, UPPER (St Mark) *see* Hale w Badshot Lea *Guildf*
HALE BARNS (All Saints) w Ringway *Ches 10* **P** *Bp* **V** R M HINTON
HALEBANK (St Mary Mission) *see* Hale *Liv*
HALES (St Mary) *see* Cheswardine, Childs Ercall, Hales, Hinstock etc *Lich*
HALESOWEN (St John the Baptist) *see* Halas *Worc*
HALESWORTH (St Mary) *see* Blyth Valley *St E*
HALEWOOD (St Nicholas) (St Mary) *Liv 4* **P** *Bp* **TR** A D J JEWELL, **TV** S ERRINGTON, **NSM** C CRITCHLEY
HALEY HILL (All Souls) *see* Halifax All So and St Aug *Wakef*
HALFORD (Our Blessed Lady) *see* Alderminster and Halford *Cov*
HALFORD (St Thomas) *see* Sibdon Carwood w Halford *Heref*
HALFWAY (St Peter) *see* Minster-in-Sheppey *Cant*
HALIFAX (All Saints) *Wakef 4* **P** *Ch Trust Fund Trust* **V** T J WILSON, **NSM** J C K FREEBORN
HALIFAX (All Souls) (St Augustine) *Wakef 4* **P** *Simeon's Trustees and local trustees (jt)* **V** D J CHILLMAN, **C** T TURNER
HALIFAX (Holy Trinity) (St Jude) *Wakef 4* **P** *Bp, V Halifax, and trustees (jt)* **V** M C RUSSELL, **NSM** M RUSSELL
HALIFAX (St Anne-in-the-Grove) *see* Southowram and Claremount *Wakef*
HALIFAX (St Hilda) *Wakef 4* **P** *Bp* **P-in-c** P F MILLWARD
HALIFAX (St John the Baptist) *Wakef 4* **P** *The Crown* **V** W A WILBY, **C** L A CHEETHAM
HALL GREEN (Church of the Ascension) *Birm 6* **P** *Bp, V Yardley, and Vice-Chmn of PCC (jt)* **V** D J SENIOR
HALL GREEN (St Peter) *Birm 6* **P** *Bp* **V** M W STEPHENSON, **C** F J JOHNSON
HALL STREET (St Andrew) *see* Stockport St Mary *Ches*
HALLAM, WEST (St Wilfred) and Mapperley w Stanley *Derby 13* **P** *Bp* **R** S I D WHITE, **C** M I JACQUES, **NSM** P J OWEN-JONES
HALLATON (St Michael and All Angels) w Horninghold and Allexton; Tugby; East Norton; and Slawston *Leic 4* **P** *Bp, DBP, and E Brudenell Esq (jt)* **R** D M FISHER
HALLING (St John the Baptist) *see* Cuxton and Halling *Roch*
HALLINGBURY, GREAT (St Giles) (St Andrew) and LITTLE (St Mary the Virgin) *Chelmsf 26* **P** *Bp and Charterhouse (jt)* **P-in-c** M CHAPMAN
HALLIWELL (St Luke) *Man 9* **P** *MMCET* **P-in-c** A S CORNES, **C** S M DNISTRIANSKYJ, **OLM** L ALLMARK
HALLIWELL (St Margaret) *Man 9* **P** *Trustees* **P-in-c** D J FRENCH
HALLIWELL (St Matthew w St Barnabas) (St Paul) (St Thomas the Apostle) *Man 9* **P** *Patr Bd* **C** S H FOSTER-CLARK, **NSM** M A J TAYLOR, **OLM** J M SHEPHERD
HALLIWELL (St Peter) (Barrow Bridge Mission) (St Andrew's Mission Church) *Man 9* **P** *Trustees* **V** P D HARDINGHAM, **C** R F OLDFIELD, **NSM** C WATSON
HALLOUGHTON (St James) *see* Thurgarton w Hoveringham and Bleasby etc *S'well*
HALLOW (St Philip and St James) and Grimley w Holt *Worc 3* **P** *Bp* **R** R N LATHAM, **NSM** D C L EVE
HALLWOOD (St Mark) *Ches 3* **P** *DBP* **V** S S WILKINS
HALSALL (St Cuthbert) *Liv 11* **P** *Brig D H Blundell-Hollinshead-Blundell* **P-in-c** P L ROBINSON
HALSE (Mission Church) *see* Brackley St Pet w St Jas *Pet*
HALSE (St James) *see* Milverton w Halse and Fitzhead *B & W*
HALSETOWN (St John's in the Fields) *Truro 5* **P** *D&C* **P-in-c** A N COUCH, **C** C H CLEMENTS
HALSHAM (All Saints) *see* Keyingham w Ottringham, Halsham and Sunk Is *York*
HALSTEAD (St Margaret) *see* Knockholt w Halstead *Roch*
HALSTEAD AREA Team Ministry, The (St Andrew) *Chelmsf 19* **P** *Patr Bd* **TR** J F BLORE, **TV** V J BROOKS, G B T BAYLISS, **C** J S RIDGE
HALSTOCK (St Mary) *see* Melbury *Sarum*
HALSTOW, HIGH (St Margaret) (All Hallows) and Hoo St Mary *Roch 6* **P** *MMCET and Ch Soc Trust (jt)* **R** S G GWILT
HALSTOW, LOWER (St Margaret) *see* Upchurch w Lower Halstow *Cant*
HALTER DEVIL (Mission Room) *see* Mugginton and Kedleston *Derby*
HALTON (St Mary) *Ches 3* **P** *Bp* **V** M G GREENSTREET
HALTON (St Michael and All Angels) *see* Wendover and Halton *Ox*
HALTON (St Oswald and St Cuthbert and King Alfwald) *see* Corbridge w Halton and Newton Hall *Newc*
HALTON (St Wilfred) w Aughton *Blackb 14* **P** *Exors of R T Sanderson Esq* **P-in-c** D RAITT
HALTON (St Wilfrid) *see* Leeds Halton St Wilfrid *Ripon*
HALTON, EAST (St Peter) *see* Habrough Gp *Linc*
HALTON, WEST (St Etheldreda) *see* Alkborough *Linc*
HALTON HOLGATE (St Andrew) *see* Spilsby Gp *Linc*
HALTON QUAY (St Indract's Chapel) *see* St Dominic, Landulph and St Mellion w Pillaton *Truro*
HALTON WEST (Mission Church) *see* Hellifield *Bradf*
HALTWHISTLE (Holy Cross) and Greenhead *Newc 4* **P** *Bp* **V** R BEST
HALVERGATE (St Peter and St Paul) *see* Freethorpe, Wickhampton, Halvergate etc *Nor*
HALWELL (St Leonard) *see* Diptford, N Huish, Harberton, Harbertonford etc *Ex*
HALWILL (St Peter and St James) *see* Ashwater, Halwill, Beaworthy, Clawton etc *Ex*
HAM (All Saints) *see* Savernake *Sarum*
HAM (St Andrew) *S'wark 17* **P** *K Coll Cam* **V** S BROCKLEHURST, **NSM** F M FORWARD

HAM (St Barnabas Mission Church) *see* Combe St Nicholas w Wambrook *B & W*
HAM (St James the Less) *see* Plymouth St Jas Ham *Ex*
HAM (St Richard) *S'wark 18* **P** *Bp* **V** P J H DUNN, **OLM** J R WEBB
HAMBLE LE RICE (St Andrew) *Win 10* **P** *St Mary's Coll Win* **V** J W TRAVERS
HAMBLEDEN VALLEY (St Mary the Virgin) *Ox 29* **P** *Bp, Viscount Hambleden, and Miss M Mackenzie (jt)* **R** W M MACNAUGHTON, **C** A E BLOOR, **NSM** M A C GAYNOR
HAMBLEDON (St Peter) *see* Busbridge and Hambledon *Guildf*
HAMBLEDON (St Peter and St Paul) *Portsm 1* **P** *Ld Chan* **P-in-c** R H G BRAND
HAMBLETON (St Andrew) *see* Oakham, Hambleton, Egleton, Braunston and Brooke *Pet*
HAMBLETON (St Mary) *see* Haddlesey w Hambleton and Birkin *York*
HAMBLETON (The Blessed Virgin Mary) *see* Waterside Par *Blackb*
HAMBRIDGE (St James the Less) *see* Kingsbury Episcopi w E Lambrook, Hambridge etc *B & W*
HAMER (All Saints) *Man 20* **P** *Bp* **V** *vacant* (01706) 355591
HAMERINGHAM (All Saints) w Scrafield and Winceby *Linc 11* **P** *DBP* **P-in-c** A J BOYD, **OLM** K A BUSH
HAMERTON (All Saints) *Ely 8* **P** *G R Petherick Esq* **R** *vacant*
HAMILTON Conventional District *Leic 1* **C-in-c** P C WHITE
HAMILTON TERRACE (St Mark) *see* St Marylebone St Mark Hamilton Terrace *Lon*
HAMMER (St Michael) *see* Lynchmere and Camelsdale *Chich*
HAMMERFIELD (St Francis of Assisi) *see* Boxmoor St Jo *St Alb*
HAMMERSMITH (Holy Innocents) (St John the Evangelist) *Lon 9* **P** *Bp* **P-in-c** D W G MATTHEWS, **NSM** A H MEAD, S R G MCDOWELL
HAMMERSMITH (St Luke) *Lon 9* **P** *Bp* **P-in-c** I C ROGERS
HAMMERSMITH (St Matthew) *Lon 9* **P** *Trustees* **V** G H CHIPLIN
HAMMERSMITH (St Michael and St George) White City Estate Conventional District *Lon 9 vacant* (020) 8743 7100
HAMMERSMITH (St Paul) *Lon 9* **P** *Bp* **P-in-c** S G DOWNHAM, **C** T J STILWELL, **NSM** P E BATES
HAMMERSMITH (St Peter) *Lon 9* **P** *Bp* **P-in-c** S J WELCH, **C** I M STONE
HAMMERSMITH (St Saviour) *see* Cobbold Road St Sav w St Mary *Lon*
HAMMERSMITH (St Simon) *Lon 9* **P** *Simeon's Trustees* **V** C J COLLINGTON, **C** S M ARNOLD
HAMMERSMITH, NORTH (St Katherine) *Lon 9* **P** *Bp* **P-in-c** J TATE
HAMMERWICH (St John the Baptist) *Lich 1* **P** *Hammerwich Ch Lands Trustees* **P-in-c** M J BUTT, **NSM** M R AUSTIN
HAMMERWOOD (St Stephen) *see* Cowden w Hammerwood *Chich*
HAMMOON (St Paul) *see* Okeford *Sarum*
HAMNISH (St Dubricius and All Saints) *see* Leominster *Heref*
HAMPDEN, GREAT (St Mary Magdalene) *see* Prestwood and Gt Hampden *Ox*
HAMPDEN, LITTLE (not known) *see* Gt Missenden w Ballinger and Lt Hampden *Ox*
HAMPDEN PARK (St Mary-in-the-Park) *Chich 16* **P** *Bp* **V** R L TREE
HAMPNETT (St George) *see* Northleach w Hampnett and Farmington etc *Glouc*
HAMPRESTON (All Saints) *Sarum 9* **P** *Patr Bd* **TR** R G L LUTHER, **TV** L S CLOW
HAMPSTEAD Belsize Park (St Peter) *see* Belsize Park *Lon*
HAMPSTEAD (Christ Church) *Lon 16* **P** *Trustees* **V** P D CONRAD
HAMPSTEAD (Emmanuel) West End *Lon 16* **P** *Trustees* **V** P J GALLOWAY
HAMPSTEAD (St James) *see* Kilburn St Mary w All So and W Hampstead St Jas *Lon*
HAMPSTEAD (St John) *Lon 16* **P** *DBP* **V** S R TUCKER, **C** T J BELL, S F L EYNSTONE
HAMPSTEAD (St John) Downshire Hill Proprietary Chapel *Lon 16* **Min** J G L GOULD
HAMPSTEAD St Stephen w (All Hallows) *Lon 16* **P** *DBP and D&C Cant (jt)* **V** D N C HOULDING
HAMPSTEAD, SOUTH (St Saviour) *Lon 16* **P** *V Hampstead St Jo* **V** *vacant* (020) 7722 4621
HAMPSTEAD, WEST (Holy Trinity) *Lon 16* **P** *MMCET* **V** M G C YOUNG
HAMPSTEAD, WEST (St Cuthbert) *Lon 16* **P** *Ch Trust Fund Trust* **P-in-c** M G C YOUNG, **NSM** D W JOHN
HAMPSTEAD, WEST (St Luke) *Lon 16* **P** *CPAS* **V** A C TRESIDDER
HAMPSTEAD GARDEN SUBURB (St Jude on the Hill) *Lon 15* **P** *Bp* **V** A R G WALKER
HAMPSTEAD NORREYS (St Mary) *see* Hermitage *Ox*
HAMPSTHWAITE (St Thomas à Becket) and Killinghall and Birstwith *Ripon 1* **P** *Mrs S J Finn, Sir James Aykroyd Bt, Sir Thomas Ingilby Bt, and Bp (jt)* **V** G A F HINCHCLIFFE
HAMPTON (All Saints) *Lon 10* **P** *Ld Chan* **V** W D F VANSTONE
HAMPTON (St Andrew) *see* Herne Bay Ch Ch *Cant*
HAMPTON (St Andrew) w Sedgeberrow and Hinton-on-the-Green *Worc 1* **P** *Ch Ch Ox, D&C Worc, and Laslett's Charity (jt)* **R** J R N J BOMYER
HAMPTON (St Mary the Virgin) *Lon 10* **P** *The Crown* **V** D N WINTERBURN, **Hon C** G CLARKSON
HAMPTON, GREAT AND LITTLE (St Andrew) *see* Hampton w Sedgeberrow and Hinton-on-the-Green *Worc*
HAMPTON BISHOP (St Andrew) *see* Tupsley w Hampton Bishop *Heref*
HAMPTON GAY (St Giles) *see* Akeman *Ox*
HAMPTON HILL (St James) *Lon 10* **P** *V Hampton St Mary* **V** B LEATHARD, **C** J A GITTOES, **NSM** B STEWART
HAMPTON IN ARDEN (St Mary and St Bartholomew) *Birm 11* **P** *Guild of All So* **P-in-c** K CLARINGBULL
HAMPTON LOVETT (St Mary and All Saints) *see* Elmley Lovett w Hampton Lovett and Elmbridge etc *Worc*
HAMPTON LUCY (St Peter ad Vincula) w Charlecote and Loxley *Cov 8* **P** *Sir Edmund Fairfax-Lucy Bt (3 turns), Col A M H Gregory-Hood (1 turn)* **P-in-c** S A EDMONDS
HAMPTON POYLE (St Mary the Virgin) *see* Kidlington w Hampton Poyle *Ox*
HAMPTON WICK (St John the Baptist) *see* Teddington St Mark and Hampton Wick St Jo *Lon*
HAMSEY (St Peter) *Chich 18* **P** *Bp* **P-in-c** D BASTIDE
HAMSTALL RIDWARE (St Michael and All Angels) *see* The Ridwares and Kings Bromley *Lich*
HAMSTEAD (St Bernard) *Birm 3* **P** *Bp* **P-in-c** H HINGLEY
HAMSTEAD (St Paul) *Birm 3* **P** *Bp* **V** A M WEAVER, **C** A F M GOODMAN
HAMSTEAD MARSHALL (St Mary) *see* W Woodhay w Enborne, Hampstead Marshall etc *Ox*
HAMSTEELS (St John the Baptist) *Dur 1* **P** *The Crown* **V** M J PEERS, **C** T E HUBBLE
HAMSTERLEY (St James) and Witton-le-Wear *Dur 6* **P** *Bp and The Crown (alt)* **V** N P DENHAM
HAMWORTHY (St Gabriel) (St Michael) *Sarum 7* **P** *MMCET* **P-in-c** S D GODDARD
HANBOROUGH (St Peter and St Paul) and Freeland *Ox 9* **P** *St Jo Coll Ox* **R** T J N NAISH
HANBURY (St Mary the Virgin) *see* Bowbrook N *Worc*
HANBURY (St Werburgh) w Newborough and Rangemore *Lich 14* **P** *DBP and Lord Burton (jt)* **V** *vacant* (01283) 813357
HANCHURCH (Chapel of Ease) *see* Trentham *Lich*
HANDCROSS (All Saints) *see* Slaugham *Chich*
HANDFORTH (St Chad) *Ches 17* **P** *R Cheadle* **V** P F REYNOLDS, **C** A F WEIGHTMAN
HANDLEY (All Saints) *see* Tattenhall and Handley *Ches*
HANDLEY (St John the Baptist) *see* Eckington and Ridgeway *Derby*
HANDLEY (St Mark) *see* N Wingfield, Clay Cross and Pilsley *Derby*
HANDSACRE (St Luke) *see* Armitage *Lich*
HANDSWORTH (St Andrew) *Birm 3* **P** *Bp* **V** P R FRENCH, **C** J AUSTEN
HANDSWORTH (St James) *Birm 3* **P** *Bp* **V** P J HIBBERT, **NSM** M FARR
HANDSWORTH (St Mary) *Sheff 1* **P** *DBP* **R** I HOLLIN
HANDSWORTH (St Mary) (Epiphany) *Birm 3* **P** *Bp* **R** B A HALL
HANDSWORTH (St Michael) (St Peter) *Birm 3* **P** *Bp* **P-in-c** I E PHILLIP
HANDSWORTH WOODHOUSE (St James) *see* Woodhouse St Jas *Sheff*
HANFORD (St Matthias) *Lich 13* **P** *Bp* **V** N A DI CASTIGLIONE, **C** R M D ORAM
HANGER HILL (Ascension) and West Twyford *Lon 22* **P** *Bp and DBP (jt)* **V** S J REED, **Hon C** L B SMILLIE
HANGER LANE (St Ann) *see* S Tottenham St Ann *Lon*
HANGING HEATON (St Paul) *Wakef 10* **P** *R Dewsbury* **P-in-c** C A GILL
HANGLETON (St Helen) (St Richard) *Chich 4* **P** *Bp* **P-in-c** K G PERKINTON
HANHAM (Christ Church) (St George) *Bris 5* **P** *Bp* **V** P WILLIS

HANKERTON (Holy Cross) *see* Ashley, Crudwell, Hankerton, Long Newnton etc *Bris*
HANLEY (All Saints) *see* Stoke-upon-Trent *Lich*
HANLEY Holy Evangelists (St Luke) *Lich 11* **P** *Bp* **TR** K R HAYWOOD, **TV** P R CLARK, G E CHARLES, **C** G R ETHERTON
HANLEY (St Chad) *see* Hanley H Ev *Lich*
HANLEY CASTLE (St Mary), Hanley Swan and Welland *Worc 5* **P** *Ld Chan and Exors Sir Berwick Lechmere Bt (alt)* **V** F A WOOKEY
HANLEY CHILD (St Michael and All Angels) *see* Teme Valley S *Worc*
HANLEY SWAN (St Gabriel) *see* Hanley Castle, Hanley Swan and Welland *Worc*
HANLEY WILLIAM (All Saints) *see* Teme Valley S *Worc*
HANNAH (St Andrew) cum Hagnaby w Markby *Linc 8* **P** *Bp and Mrs A M Johnson (alt)* **R** R H IRESON
HANNEY (St James the Great), Denchworth and East Challow *Ox 19* **P** *Bp (2 turns), Worc Coll Ox (1 turn)* **V** A HOGG, **NSM** S N JAMES
HANNINGFIELD, EAST (All Saints) *Chelmsf 9* **P** *CPAS* **P-in-c** K R PLAISTER
HANNINGFIELD, WEST (St Mary and St Edward) *Chelmsf 9* **P** *DBP* **P-in-c** R V GOODWIN
HANNINGTON (All Saints) *see* Baughurst, Ramsdell, Wolverton w Ewhurst etc *Win*
HANNINGTON (St John the Baptist) *see* Highworth w Sevenhampton and Inglesham etc *Bris*
HANNINGTON (St Peter and St Paul) *see* Walgrave w Hannington and Wold and Scaldwell *Pet*
HANOVER SQUARE (St George) *Lon 3* **P** *Bp* **C** S J HOBBS
HANSLOPE (St James the Great) w Castlethorpe *Ox 27* **P** *Bp* **P-in-c** G E ECCLESTONE
HANWELL (St Mary) (St Christopher) *Lon 22* **P** *Bp* **R** M R GRAYSHON, **C** E J MOODY
HANWELL (St Mellitus w St Mark) *Lon 22* **P** *Bp* **P-in-c** J O HEREWARD, **C** D H CHAPMAN
HANWELL (St Peter) *see* Ironstone *Ox*
HANWELL (St Thomas) *Lon 22* **P** *The Crown* **V** P A ANDREWS
HANWOOD, GREAT (St Thomas) *Heref 13* **P** *Lt-Col H de Grey-Warter* **R** M G WHITTOCK
HANWORTH (All Saints) *Lon 11* **P** *Bp* **V** L T MCKENNA, **NSM** J M TEED
HANWORTH (St Bartholomew) *see* Roughton and Felbrigg, Metton, Sustead etc *Nor*
HANWORTH (St George) *Lon 11* **P** *Lee Abbey Trust* **P-in-c** P S WILLIAMSON
HANWORTH (St Richard of Chichester) *Lon 11* **P** *Bp* **V** A JACKSON
HAPPISBURGH (St Mary the Virgin), Walcott, Hempstead w Eccles and Sea Palling w Waxham *Nor 12* **P** *Bp (3 turns), K Coll Cam (2 turns), E C Evans-Lombe Esq and Bp (1 turn)* **R** R A HINES, **C** S K BARTER, **OLM** E M MELLERUP, R M SEEL
HAPTON (St Margaret) *see* Padiham w Hapton and Padiham Green *Blackb*
HAPTON (St Margaret) *see* Ashwellthorpe, Forncett, Fundenhall, Hapton etc *Nor*
HARBERTON (St Andrew) *see* Diptford, N Huish, Harberton, Harbertonford etc *Ex*
HARBERTONFORD (St Peter) *as above*
HARBLEDOWN (St Michael and All Angels) *Cant 3* **P** *Abp* **R** M A MORRIS
HARBORNE (St Faith and St Laurence) *Birm 2* **P** *Bp* **V** *vacant* 0121-427 2410
HARBORNE (St Peter) *Birm 2* **P** *Bp* **V** C J EVANS
HARBORNE HEATH (St John the Baptist) *Birm 2* **P** *Ch Soc Trust* **V** J P HUGHES, **C** J E GRIER, R J BEWLEY
HARBOROUGH MAGNA (All Saints) *Cov 6* **P** *A H F W Boughton-Leigh Esq* **P-in-c** C A GARROD
HARBRIDGE (All Saints) *see* Ellingham and Harbridge and Hyde w Ibsley *Win*
HARBURY (All Saints) and Ladbroke *Cov 10* **P** *Bp* **R** P R BROWN
HARBY (All Saints) w Thorney and North and South Clifton *S'well 3* **P** *Ld Chan and Bp (alt)* **P-in-c** K B POTTER
HARBY (St Mary the Virgin) *see* Vale of Belvoir Par *Leic*
HARDEN (St Saviour) and Wilsden *Bradf 8* **P** *Bp, Adn, V Bradf, and R Bingley Esq (jt)* **P-in-c** R J BROOKS, **NSM** M M MOWER
HARDENHUISH (St Nicholas) *see* Chippenham St Paul w Hardenhuish etc *Bris*
HARDHAM (St Botolph) *see* Bury w Houghton and Coldwaltham and Hardham *Chich*
HARDINGHAM (St George) *see* Barnham Broom and Upper Yare *Nor*
HARDINGSTONE (St Edmund) and Horton and Piddington *Pet 7* **P** *Bp* **V** B H STEVENS
HARDINGTON MANDEVILLE (Blessed Virgin Mary) *see* W Coker w Hardington Mandeville, E Chinnock etc *B & W*
HARDINGTON VALE *B & W 4* **P** *Bp and J B Owen-Jones Esq (jt)* **R** N A DONE, **NSM** H A SCARR, B L DAVIES
HARDLEY (St Margaret) *see* Loddon, Sisland, Chedgrave, Hardley and Langley *Nor*
HARDMEAD (St Mary) *see* Sherington w Chicheley, N Crawley, Astwood etc *Ox*
HARDRAW (St Mary and St John) *see* Hawes and Hardraw *Ripon*
HARDRES, LOWER (St Mary) *see* Petham and Waltham w Lower Hardres etc *Cant*
HARDRES, UPPER (St Peter and St Paul) *as above*
HARDSTOFT (St Peter) *see* Ault Hucknall and Scarcliffe *Derby*
HARDWICK (St James) *see* Stockton St Jas *Dur*
HARDWICK (St Leonard) *see* Mears Ashby and Hardwick and Sywell etc *Pet*
HARDWICK (St Margaret) *see* Hempnall *Nor*
HARDWICK (St Mary) *Ely 1* **P** *Bp* **P-in-c** K J BROWNING
HARDWICK, EAST (St Stephen) *see* Carleton and E Hardwick *Wakef*
HARDWICK-CUM-TUSMORE (St Mary) *see* Shelswell *Ox*
HARDWICKE (Holy Trinity) *see* Cusop w Blakemere, Bredwardine w Brobury etc *Heref*
HARDWICKE (St Mary the Virgin) *see* Schorne *Ox*
HARDWICKE (St Nicholas) and Elmore w Longney *Glouc 8* **P** *Adn Glouc and Ld Chan (alt)* **V** T M B WOODHOUSE, **NSM** V J KERNER
HAREBY (St Peter and St Paul) *see* Marden Hill Gp *Linc*
HAREFIELD (St Mary the Virgin) *Lon 24* **P** *The Hon J E F Newdegate* **V** A J R GANDON, **NSM** A F ILSLEY
HAREHILLS (St Aidan) *see* Leeds St Aid *Ripon*
HAREHILLS (St Cyprian and St James) *see* Leeds St Cypr Harehills *Ripon*
HARESCOMBE (St John the Baptist) *see* Painswick, Sheepscombe, Cranham, The Edge etc *Glouc*
HARESFIELD (St Peter) *see* Eastington, Frocester, Haresfield etc *Glouc*
HAREWOOD (Methodist Chapel) *see* Collingham w Harewood *Ripon*
HARFORD (St Petroc) *see* Ivybridge w Harford *Ex*
HARGRAVE (All Saints) *see* Stanwick w Hargrave *Pet*
HARGRAVE (St Edmund King and Martyr) *see* Chevington w Hargrave, Chedburgh w Depden etc *St E*
HARGRAVE (St Peter) *Ches 5* **P** *Bp* **V** *vacant* (01829) 781378
HARKSTEAD (St Mary) *see* Chelmondiston and Erwarton w Harkstead *St E*
HARLASTON (St Matthew) *see* Clifton Campville w Edingale and Harlaston *Lich*
HARLAXTON Group, The (St Mary and St Peter) *Linc 19* **P** *Bp, DBP, Sir Richard Welby Bt, D&C, and Duke of Rutland (jt)* **P-in-c** G P POND
HARLESCOTT (Holy Spirit) (Emmanuel) *Lich 20* **P** *Bp* **P-in-c** M H SALMON, **NSM** D W G UFFINDELL, **OLM** W L STONEHOLD
HARLESDEN (All Souls) *Lon 21* **P** *The Crown* **V** M D MOORHEAD
HARLESDEN (St Mark) *see* Kensal Rise St Mark and St Martin *Lon*
HARLESTON (St Augustine) *see* Gt Finborough w Onehouse, Harleston, Buxhall etc *St E*
HARLESTON (St John the Baptist) *see* Redenhall, Harleston, Wortwell and Needham *Nor*
HARLESTONE (St Andrew) *see* Brington w Whilton and Norton etc *Pet*
HARLEY (St Mary) *see* Wenlock *Heref*
HARLING, EAST (St Peter and St Paul) w West, Bridgham w Roudham, Larling, Brettenham and Rushford *Nor 11* **P** *Ld Chan (1 turn), DBP, Sir Robin Nugent Bt, C D F Musker Esq, Major E H C Garnier, and Exors Sir John Musker (3 turns)* **OLM** L J FRY, V I SHELDRAKE
HARLINGTON (Christ Church) Waltham Avenue Conventional District *Lon 24* **C-in-c** I W JONES, **C** D M CARTER
HARLINGTON (St Mary the Virgin) *St Alb 9* **P** *Bp* **V** S J WILLIAMS
HARLINGTON (St Peter and St Paul) *Lon 24* **P** *Bp* **P-in-c** M E SMITH
HARLOW (St Mary and St Hugh w St John the Baptist) *Chelmsf 26* **P** *Simeon's Trustees and Bp (alt)* **C** P R WILLIAMS, **NSM** J C MOURANT
HARLOW (St Mary Magdalene) *Chelmsf 26* **P** *V Harlow St Mary and St Hugh etc* **V** C P M PATTERSON

HARLOW Town Centre (St Paul) w Little Parndon *Chelmsf 26* **P** *Patr Bd* **TR** D C KIRKWOOD, **TV** A E MELANIPHY, **C** M J T JOSS
HARLOW GREEN (St Ninian) and Lamesley *Dur 12* **P** *Bp* **V** M WORTHINGTON, **C** E M WILKINSON
HARLOW HILL (All Saints) *see* Low Harrogate St Mary *Ripon*
HARLSEY, EAST (St Oswald) *see* Osmotherley w Harlsey and Ingleby Arncliffe *York*
HARLTON (Assumption of the Blessed Virgin Mary) *see* Haslingfield w Harlton and Gt and Lt Eversden *Ely*
HARMANSWATER (St Paul) *see* Bracknell *Ox*
HARMER HILL (St Andrew) *see* Myddle *Lich*
HARMONDSWORTH (St Mary the Virgin) *Lon 24* **P** *DBP* **P-in-c** P G J HUGHES
HARMSTON (All Saints) *see* Graffoe Gp *Linc*
HARNHAM (St George) (All Saints) *Sarum 12* **P** *Bp (1 turn), V Britford (2 turns)* **V** D P SCRACE, **NSM** J G POPPLETON
HARNHILL (St Michael and All Angels) *see* The Ampneys w Driffield and Poulton *Glouc*
HAROLD HILL (St George) *Chelmsf 2* **P** *Bp* **V** P A BROWN, **C** J KASOZI NSAMBA
HAROLD HILL (St Paul) *Chelmsf 2* **P** *Bp* **V** R D MOUL
HAROLD WOOD (St Peter) *Chelmsf 2* **P** *New Coll Ox* **V** D P BANTING, **C** J R TERRY, T M CROOK
HAROME (St Saviour) *see* Kirkdale w Harome, Nunnington and Pockley *York*
HARPENDEN (St John the Baptist) *St Alb 8* **P** *DBP* **V** J P SMITH, **NSM** J E H WHITE, M MONK
HARPENDEN (St Nicholas) (All Saints) *St Alb 8* **P** *Ld Chan* **R** C D FUTCHER, **C** E F INALL, J E PAVYER
HARPFORD (St Gregory the Great) *see* Ottery St Mary, Alfington, W Hill, Tipton etc *Ex*
HARPHAM (St John of Beverley) *see* Burton Agnes w Harpham and Lowthorpe etc *York*
HARPLEY (St Lawrence) *see* Gt w Lt Massingham, Harpley, Rougham etc *Nor*
HARPOLE (All Saints) *see* Kislingbury and Harpole *Pet*
HARPSDEN (St Margaret) *see* Shiplake w Dunsden and Harpsden *Ox*
HARPSWELL (St Chad) *see* Glentworth Gp *Linc*
HARPTREE, EAST (St Laurence) w WEST (Blessed Virgin Mary) and Hinton Blewett *B & W 10* **P** *Duchy of Cornwall* **P-in-c** T J DAPLYN
HARPUR HILL (St James) *see* Buxton w Burbage and King Sterndale *Derby*
HARPURHEY cum Moston (Christ Church) *Man 5* **P** *Bp, Dean, K Greenwood Esq, Ms A Greenhalgh, and V Morley Esq (jt)* **R** M D ASHCROFT
HARPURHEY (St Stephen) *Man 5* **P** *Bp* **R** M D ASHCROFT
HARRABY (St Elisabeth) *see* S Carl TM *Carl*
HARRIETSHAM (St John the Baptist) *see* Len Valley *Cant*
HARRINGAY (St Paul) *Lon 19* **P** *Bp* **V** R P P MARTIN
HARRINGTON (St Mary) *Carl 7* **P** *Mrs E H S Thornely* **R** J S DIXON
HARRINGTON (St Mary) *see* S Ormsby Gp *Linc*
HARRINGTON (St Peter and St Paul) *see* Arthingworth, Harrington w Oxendon and E Farndon *Pet*
HARRINGWORTH (St John the Baptist) *see* Bulwick, Blatherwycke w Harringworth and Laxton *Pet*
HARROGATE (St Mark) *Ripon 1* **P** *Peache Trustees* **V** P D G HOOPER, **C** J LOGAN, **Hon C** A M C DUNN
HARROGATE (St Wilfrid) *Ripon 1* **P** *Bp* **TR** M C R SOWERBY, **TV** J ARENS, **NSM** T J BUCKINGHAM
HARROGATE, HIGH (Christ Church) *Ripon 1* **P** *Bp* **V** J E COLSTON, **C** J P RHODES, **NSM** C M SEDGEWICK
HARROGATE, HIGH (St Peter) *Ripon 1* **P** *Ch Patr Trust* **V** A M SHEPHERD, **NSM** T J HURREN
HARROGATE, LOW (St Mary) *Ripon 4* **P** *Peache Trustees* **V** M W SOAR
HARROLD (St Peter and All Saints) and Carlton w Chellington *St Alb 15* **P** *Bp* **P-in-c** J BURROWS
HARROW (Church of the Holy Spirit) *see* Kenton *Lon*
HARROW (Holy Trinity) *see* Wealdstone H Trin *Lon*
HARROW (St John the Baptist) *see* Greenhill St Jo *Lon*
HARROW (St Peter) *see* Roxeth *Lon*
HARROW, NORTH (St Alban) *Lon 23* **P** *Bp* **V** J A FOSTER, **Hon C** D S ARDEN, D J TUCK, **NSM** P BAGULEY
HARROW, SOUTH (St Paul) *Lon 23* **P** *R St Bride Fleet Street w Bridewell and Trin Gough Square* **V** A J HULME, **NSM** J I HULME
HARROW GREEN (Holy Trinity and St Augustine of Hippo) *see* Leytonstone H Trin Harrow Green *Chelmsf*
HARROW ON THE HILL (St Mary) *Lon 23* **P** *Bp, Adn, and Hd Master Harrow Sch (jt)* **V** T J GOSDEN
HARROW WEALD (All Saints) *Lon 23* **P** *Bp, Adn, V Harrow St Mary, and R Bushey (jt)* **V** T HANDLEY MACMATH
HARROW WEALD (St Michael and All Angels) *Lon 23* **P** *Bp* **V** G E HEWLETT
HARROWBARROW (All Saints) *see* Calstock *Truro*
HARROWBY (The Ascension) *see* Grantham, Harrowby w Londonthorpe *Linc*
HARROWDEN, GREAT (All Saints) w LITTLE (St Mary the Virgin) and Orlingbury *Pet 6* **P** *Sir Stephen Hastings and Bp (alt)* **P-in-c** S P DOMMETT
HARSTON (All Saints) w Hauxton and Newton *Ely 6* **P** *Bp (2 turns), D&C (1 turn)* **P-in-c** P A WAINWRIGHT, **NSM** R G HOWELLS
HARSTON (St Michael and All Angels) *see* High Framland Par *Leic*
HARSWELL (St Peter) *see* Holme and Seaton Ross Gp *York*
HART (St Mary Magdalene) w Elwick Hall *Dur 3* **P** *Bp and DBP (alt)* **V** J E LUND, **NSM** A STAINSBY
HART COMMON (not known) *see* Westhoughton and Wingates *Man*
HARTBURN (All Saints) *see* Stockton St Pet *Dur*
HARTBURN (St Andrew) *see* Bolam w Whalton and Hartburn w Meldon *Newc*
HARTCLIFFE (St Andrew) *see* Bris St Andr Hartcliffe *Bris*
HARTEST (All Saints) *see* Glemsford, Hartest w Boxted, Somerton etc *St E*
HARTFIELD (St Mary) w Coleman's Hatch *Chich 19* **P** *Bp and Earl De la Warr (jt)* **R** P E P BRICE, **NSM** N T LEVISEUR
HARTFORD (All Saints) *see* Huntingdon *Ely*
HARTFORD (St John the Baptist) *Ches 6* **P** *Ch Soc Trust* **V** M I A SMITH, **C** D J HYNDMAN, **NSM** G AGAR
HARTHILL (All Hallows) and Thorpe Salvin *Sheff 5* **P** *Bp* **P-in-c** P L CHAMBERS
HARTING (St Mary and St Gabriel) w Elsted and Treyford cum Didling *Chich 10* **P** *Bp* **R** D R C GIBBONS, **P-in-c** M J LANE
HARTINGTON (St Giles), Biggin and Earl Sterndale *Derby 4* **P** *Duke of Devonshire* **P-in-c** J O GOLDSMITH
HARTISMERE, NORTH *St E 16* **P** *MMCET, K Coll Cam, Bp, and DBP (jt)* **R** R H AXFORD, **NSM** C R AXFORD
HARTISMERE, SOUTH *St E 16* **P** *Bp, Comdr F P Brooke-Popham, MMCET, Ch Soc Trust, SMF, and Lord Henniker (jt)* **R** D E CLAYDEN, **C** J K B FOWLER
HARTLAND (St Nectan) *see* Parkham, Alwington, Buckland Brewer etc *Ex*
HARTLAND COAST *as above*
HARTLEBURY (St James) *Worc 13* **P** *Bp* **P-in-c** A P WHITE
HARTLEPOOL (Holy Trinity) (St Mark's Centre) *Dur 3* **P** *Bp* **V** J L SMITH
HARTLEPOOL (St Aidan) (St Columba) *Dur 3* **P** *Bp* **V** A D WHIPP
HARTLEPOOL (St Hilda) *Dur 3* **P** *Bp* **P-in-c** J GOODE
HARTLEPOOL (St Luke) *Dur 3* **P** *Bp* **V** M R JUDSON, **C** P W JUDSON
HARTLEPOOL (St Oswald) *Dur 3* **P** *Bp* **V** G BUTTERY
HARTLEPOOL (St Paul) *Dur 3* **P** *Bp* **V** R E MASSHEDAR
HARTLEY (All Saints) *see* Fawkham and Hartley *Roch*
HARTLEY, NEW (St Michael and All Angels) *see* Delaval *Newc*
HARTLEY BROOK (Mission Hall) *see* Becontree St Mary *Chelmsf*
HARTLEY MAUDITT (St Leonard) *see* Northanger *Win*
HARTLEY WESPALL (St Mary) *see* Sherfield-on-Loddon and Stratfield Saye etc *Win*
HARTLEY WINTNEY (St John the Evangelist), Elvetham, Winchfield and Dogmersfield *Win 5* **P** *Bp and Sir Euan Anstruther-Gough-Calthorpe Bt (jt)* **V** R A EWBANK, **C** B G DEANS
HARTLIP (St Michael and All Angels) *see* Newington w Hartlip and Stockbury *Cant*
HARTOFT (Mission Room) *see* Lastingham w Appleton-le-Moors, Rosedale etc *York*
HARTON (St Peter) (St Lawrence) *Dur 15* **P** *D&C* **V** R O DICK, **C** C A DICK
HARTPLAIN (not known) *Portsm 5* **P** *DBP* **P-in-c** T E JESSIMAN
HARTPURY (St Mary the Virgin) w Corse and Staunton *Glouc 6* **P** *Bp (2 turns), DBP (1 turn)* **P-in-c** J G EVANS, **NSM** P A HAMER
HARTSHEAD (St Peter) *see* Roberttown w Hartshead *Wakef*
HARTSHILL (Holy Trinity) *Cov 5* **P** *V Mancetter* **P-in-c** L P BEARD
HARTSHILL (Holy Trinity) *Lich 12* **P** *Bp* **V** *vacant* (01782) 616965
HARTSHORNE (St Peter) and Bretby *Derby 16* **P** *Bp and MMCET (jt)* **R** I R WILLIAMS-HUNTER
HARTWELL (St John the Baptist) *see* Roade and Ashton w Hartwell *Pet*

HARTWITH (St Jude) *see* Dacre w Hartwith and Darley w Thornthwaite *Ripon*
HARTY (St Thomas Apostle) *see* Eastchurch w Leysdown and Harty *Cant*
HARVINGTON (St James) *see* Church Lench w Rous Lench and Abbots Morton etc *Worc*
HARWELL (St Matthew) w Chilton *Ox 18* **P** *DBP and CPAS (jt)* **R** C J STOTT, **NSM** J V BARTON
HARWICH PENINSULA, The (St Nicholas) *Chelmsf 20* **P** *Patr Bd* **TR** S HARDIE, **TV** E B E LAMMENS, **C** S M WHITE
HARWOOD (Christ Church) *Man 16* **P** *DBP* **V** A R HAZLEHURST, **OLM** H MOLLOY, M J FROST
HARWOOD, GREAT (St Bartholomew) *Blackb 7* **P** *V Blackb* **V** J HEIL, **C** L MCGREGOR
HARWOOD, GREAT (St John) *Blackb 7* **P** *Bp and V Gt Harwood St Bart (jt)* **P-in-c** J HEIL, **C** L MCGREGOR
HARWOOD DALE (St Margaret) *see* Hackness w Harwood Dale *York*
HARWORTH (All Saints) *S'well 1* **P** *Sir John Whitaker Bt* **V** D L ANDERSON
HASBURY (St Margaret) *see* Halas *Worc*
HASCOMBE (St Peter) *see* Dunsfold and Hascombe *Guildf*
HASELBECH (St Michael) *see* Clipston w Naseby and Haselbech w Kelmarsh *Pet*
HASELBURY PLUCKNETT (St Michael and All Angels), Misterton and North Perrott *B & W 15* **P** *Ld Chan (2 turns), Bp (2 turns), and H W F Hoskyns Esq (1 turn)* **P-in-c** J M FREE
HASELEY (St Mary) *see* Hatton w Haseley, Rowington w Lowsonford etc *Cov*
HASELEY, GREAT (St Peter) *see* Gt w Lt Milton and Gt Haseley *Ox*
HASELOR (St Mary and All Saints) *see* Kinwarton w Gt Alne and Haselor *Cov*
HASELTON (St Andrew) *see* Northleach w Hampnett and Farmington etc *Glouc*
HASFIELD (St Mary) w Tirley and Ashleworth *Glouc 6* **P** *W G F Meath-Baker Esq, Ld Chan, and Bp (by turn)* **R** *vacant*
HASKETON (St Andrew) *see* Boulge w Burgh, Grundisburgh and Hasketon *St E*
HASLAND (St Paul) *Derby 5* **P** *V Chesterfield* **R** M R AINSCOUGH
HASLEMERE (St Bartholomew) (St Christopher) and Grayswood *Guildf 4* **P** *Ld Chan* **R** N JONES, **C** M L PLAYLE, **NSM** B A STEELE-PERKINS
HASLINGDEN (St James) w Grane and Stonefold *Blackb 1* **P** *Bp and Hulme Trustees (jt)* **V** T R SMITH
HASLINGDEN (St Peter) *see* Laneside *Blackb*
HASLINGDEN (St Thomas) *see* Musbury *Blackb*
HASLINGFIELD (All Saints) w Harlton and Great and Little Eversden *Ely 1* **P** *Qu Coll Cam, Ld Chan, Jes Coll Cam (by turn)* **R** *vacant* (01223) 870285
HASLINGTON (St Matthew) w Crewe Green St Michael *Ches 15* **P** *Bp* **V** S A LAWSON
HASSALL GREEN (St Philip) *see* Sandbach Heath w Wheelock *Ches*
HASSINGHAM (St Mary) *see* Burlingham St Edmund w Lingwood, Strumpshaw etc *Nor*
HASTINGLEIGH (St Mary the Virgin) *see* Elmsted w Hastingleigh *Cant*
HASTINGS (All Souls) Clive Vale *Chich 17* **P** *R Upper St Leon* **V** *vacant* (01424) 421445
HASTINGS (Christ Church and St Andrew) *see* Blacklands Hastings Ch Ch and St Andr *Chich*
HASTINGS (Emmanuel and St Mary in the Castle) *Chich 17* **P** *MMCET and Hyndman Trustees (alt)* **V** P J COEKIN
HASTINGS (Holy Trinity) *Chich 17* **P** *Bp* **V** C TOLWORTHY, **C** R J MORTIMER, **NSM** P J DOODES
HASTINGS (St Clement) (All Saints) *Chich 17* **P** *Bp* **P-in-c** B R HOBBS
HASTINGS (St Peter and St Paul) *see* Hollington St Jo *Chich*
HASWELL (St Paul), Shotton and Thornley *Dur 2* **P** *Bp* **V** D BODDY
HATCH, WEST (St Andrew) *see* Beercrocombe w Curry Mallet, Hatch Beauchamp etc *B & W*
HATCH BEAUCHAMP (St John the Baptist) *as above*
HATCH END (St Anselm) *Lon 23* **P** *Bp* **V** C PEARCE, **NSM** D P BANISTER
HATCH WARREN (Church Hall) Conventional District *Win 4 vacant*
HATCHAM (St Catherine) *S'wark 3* **P** *Haberdashers' Co* **V** F J MAKAMBWE, **OLM** A C OBIORA
HATCHAM (St James) (St George) (St Michael) *S'wark 3* **P** *Ch Patr Soc* **NSM** E BOGLE
HATCHAM PARK (All Saints) *S'wark 3* **P** *Hyndman Trustees (2 turns), Haberdashers' Co (1 turn)* **V** O J BEAMENT, **OLM** J FRANCIS
HATCLIFFE (St Mary) *see* Laceby and Ravendale Gp *Linc*
HATFIELD *see* Bp's Hatfield *St Alb*
HATFIELD (St Lawrence) *Sheff 10* **P** *Bp* **V** P D WILSON, **C** M E GREGORY, **NSM** G BECKETT
HATFIELD (St Leonard) *see* Leominster *Heref*
HATFIELD BROAD OAK (St Mary the Virgin) and Bush End *Chelmsf 26* **P** *Bp* **P-in-c** C A HAWKINS
HATFIELD HEATH (Holy Trinity) and Sheering *Chelmsf 26* **P** *Ch Ch Ox and V Hatfield Broad Oak (alt)* **R** T J POTTER, **NSM** B L SURTEES
HATFIELD HYDE (St Mary Magdalene) *St Alb 21* **P** *Marquess of Salisbury* **P-in-c** D L MUNCHIN, **C** G J RICHARDSON
HATFIELD PEVEREL (St Andrew) w Ulting *Chelmsf 24* **P** *Bp* **V** S R NORTHFIELD
HATFIELD REGIS *see* Hatfield Broad Oak and Bush End *Chelmsf*
HATHERDEN (Christ Church) w Tangley and Weyhill and Penton Mewsey *Win 3* **P** *Bp and Qu Coll Ox (jt)* **V** R E WHETTINGSTEEL
HATHERLEIGH (St John the Baptist) Meeth, Exbourne and Jacobstowe *Ex 11* **P** *CPAS, Lord Clinton, DBP, and Keble Coll Ox (jt)* **P-in-c** R A L WELBY
HATHERN (St Peter and St Paul) *see* Kegworth, Hathern, Long Whatton, Diseworth etc *Leic*
HATHEROP (St Nicholas) *see* Coln St Aldwyns, Hatherop, Quenington etc *Glouc*
HATHERSAGE (St Michael and All Angels) w Bamford and Derwent *Derby 2* **P** *Duke of Devonshire and A C H Barnes Esq (jt)* **R** D C PICKERING
HATHERTON (St Saviour) *Lich 3* **P** *A R W Littleton Esq* **V** A R OSBORNE
HATLEY ST GEORGE (St George) *see* Gamlingay and Everton *Ely*
HATTERS LANE (St Andrew) *see* High Wycombe *Ox*
HATTERSLEY (St Barnabas) *Ches 14* **P** *Bp* **V** D A AKKER
HATTON (All Saints) *Derby 14* **P** *Bp and N J M Spurrier Esq (jt)* **C** H GUEST
HATTON (Chapel of Ease) *see* E Bedfont *Lon*
HATTON (Holy Trinity) w Haseley, Rowington w Lowsonford and Honiley and Wroxall *Cov 4* **P** *Bp* **R** K J MOBBERLEY, **NSM** S MOBBERLEY
HATTON (St Stephen) *see* Hemingby *Linc*
HAUGH (St Leonard) *see* S Ormsby Gp *Linc*
HAUGHLEY (St Mary the Virgin) w Wetherden and Stowupland *St E 6* **P** *Ld Chan, Bp, and DBP (by turn)* **V** D J PARMENTER, **NSM** A M BAIRD, **OLM** D WEBB
HAUGHTON (Mission Room) *see* Bunbury and Tilstone Fearnall *Ches*
HAUGHTON (St Anne) *Man 17* **P** *DBP* **P-in-c** J M PRESTWOOD, **NSM** P A CLARK
HAUGHTON (St Chad) *see* W Felton *Lich*
HAUGHTON (St Giles) *see* Derrington, Haughton and Ranton *Lich*
HAUGHTON (St Mary the Virgin) *Man 17* **P** *Bp* **R** M J DOWLAND
HAUGHTON LE SKERNE (St Andrew) *Dur 8* **P** *Bp* **R** D J BRYAN, **C** D M KEEN, R A HATFIELD
HAUTBOIS, GREAT (Holy Trinity) *see* Coltishall w Gt Hautbois and Horstead *Nor*
HAUXTON (St Edmund) *see* Harston w Hauxton and Newton *Ely*
HAUXWELL (St Oswald) *see* Spennithorne w Finghall and Hauxwell *Ripon*
HAVANT (St Faith) *Portsm 5* **P** *Bp* **R** D A GIBBONS, **C** C E KEAY, **NSM** D I R WILLIAMS
HAVEN Conventional District *Chich 16* **C-in-c** A W WEAVER
HAVENSTREET (St Peter) *Portsm 7* **P** *SMF* **V** N R WALLACE, **NSM** K R ADLAM
HAVERHILL (St Mary the Virgin) w Withersfield *St E 8* **P** *Bp* **V** E J BETTS
HAVERIGG (St Luke) *see* Millom *Carl*
HAVERING-ATTE-BOWER (St John) *see* Collier Row St Jas and Havering-atte-Bower *Chelmsf*
HAVERINGLAND (St Peter) *see* Cawston w Booton and Brandiston etc *Nor*
HAVERSHAM (St Mary) *see* Lamp *Ox*
HAVERSTOCK HILL (Holy Trinity) *see* Kentish Town St Silas and H Trin w St Barn *Lon*
HAVERTHWAITE (St Anne) *see* Leven Valley *Carl*
HAWES (St Margaret) and Hardraw *Ripon 4* **P** *Bp, V Aysgarth and Bolton cum Redmire, Mrs R Metcalfe, and W H Willan Esq (jt)* **V** W M SIMMS

HAWES SIDE (St Christopher) and Marton Moss St Nicholas *Blackb 8* **P** *Bp* **V** G PIPER, **C** D A ARNOLD
HAWKCHURCH (St John the Baptist) *see* Golden Cap Team *Sarum*
HAWKEDON (St Mary) *see* Chevington w Hargrave, Chedburgh w Depden etc *St E*
HAWKESBURY (St Mary) *see* Boxwell, Leighterton, Didmarton, Oldbury etc *Glouc*
HAWKHURST (St Laurance) *Cant 11* **P** *Ch Ch Ox* **V** R G DREYER
HAWKINGE (St Luke) w Acrise and Swingfield *Cant 5* **P** *Abp* **R** S F WARDELL, **NSM** R A BIRCH
HAWKLEY (St Peter and St Paul) *see* Greatham w Empshott and Hawkley w Prior's Dean *Portsm*
HAWKRIDGE (St Giles) *see* Exford, Exmoor, Hawkridge and Withypool *B & W*
HAWKSHAW LANE (St Mary) *Man 10* **P** *F Whowell Esq* **P-in-c** J G ARMSTRONG, **C** P H SUMSION
HAWKSHEAD (St Michael and All Angels) and Low Wray w Sawrey and Rusland and Satterthwaite *Carl 11* **P** *Bp* **V** A S PYE
HAWKSWOOD (Emmanuel) Conventional District *Chich 15* **C-in-c** S J E TOMALIN
HAWKSWORTH (St Mary and All Saints) *see* Whatton w Aslockton, Hawksworth, Scarrington etc *S'well*
HAWKSWORTH WOOD (St Mary) *Ripon 7* **P** *Patrons Leeds St Pet* **V** A J PEARSON
HAWKWELL (Emmanuel) (St Mary the Virgin) *Chelmsf 12* **P** *CPAS* **R** P A CORRIE, **C** P S HAMILTON
HAWKWOOD (St Francis) *see* Chingford SS Pet and Paul *Chelmsf*
HAWLEY (Holy Trinity) *Guildf 1* **P** *Keble Coll Ox* **V** M W NEALE, **C** E SKUBLICS
HAWLEY, SOUTH (All Saints) *see* Hawley H Trin *Guildf*
HAWLING (St Edward) *see* Sevenhampton w Charlton Abbots, Hawling etc *Glouc*
HAWNBY (All Saints) *see* Upper Ryedale *York*
HAWORTH (St Michael and All Angels) *Bradf 8* **P** *V Bradf and Haworth Ch Lands Trust (jt)* **R** J A SAVAGE
HAWRIDGE (St Mary) w Cholesbury and St Leonard *Ox 28* **P** *Bp, Chpl Trust, and Neale's Charity (jt)* **P-in-c** D J BURGESS, **NSM** I CORNISH
HAWSKER (All Saints) *see* Fylingdales and Hawsker cum Stainsacre *York*
HAWSTEAD (All Saints) *see* St Edm Way *St E*
HAWTHORN (St Michael and All Angels) and Murton *Dur 2* **P** *D&C and I Pemberton Esq (alt)* **R** A MILNE
HAWTON (All Saints) *see* Farndon w Thorpe, Hawton and Cotham *S'well*
HAXBY (St Mary) w Wigginton *York 7* **P** *Abp and Ld Chan (alt)* **TR** M GREEN, **TV** B L GANT
HAXEY (St Nicholas) *Linc 1* **P** *Ld Chan* **V** vacant (01427) 752351
HAY MILL (St Cyprian) *see* Yardley St Cypr Hay Mill *Birm*
HAYDOCK (St James) *Liv 16* **P** *R Ashton-in-Makerfield* **V** R MIDDLETON, **C** R W HART, **NSM** G J HARDMAN
HAYDOCK (St Mark) *Liv 10* **P** *MMCET* **V** P POTTER, **C** R S WHITE, M G COCKAYNE
HAYDON BRIDGE (St Cuthbert) and Beltingham w Henshaw *Newc 4* **P** *Bp and V Haltwhistle and Greenhead (jt)* **V** J E HAMPSON
HAYDON WICK (St John) *Bris 7* **P** *CPAS* **V** R W ADAMS
HAYES (St Anselm) *Lon 24* **P** *Bp* **P-in-c** P L DE S HOMEWOOD
HAYES (St Edmund of Canterbury) *Lon 24* **P** *Bp* **V** R M REEVE, **NSM** S J LAFFORD
HAYES (St Mary) *Lon 24* **P** *Keble Coll Ox* **R** P L DE S HOMEWOOD
HAYES (St Mary the Virgin) *Roch 14* **P** *D&C* **R** G D GRAHAM, **NSM** M HALLAM
HAYES, NORTH (St Nicholas) *Lon 24* **P** *Bp and Keble Coll Ox (jt)* **V** A K SILLIS
HAYFIELD (St Matthew) and Chinley w Buxworth *Derby 6* **P** *Bp and Resident Freeholders (jt)* **V** H A EDGERTON
HAYLE (St Elwyn) *see* Godrevy *Truro*
HAYLING, NORTH (St Peter) *Portsm 5* **P** *DBP* **V** A C LEONARD, **NSM** H V HAWKES
HAYLING, SOUTH (St Mary) *Portsm 5* **P** *DBP* **V** P M J GINEVER, **NSM** C MEATYARD, P K PAYNE
HAYLING ISLAND (St Andrew) Eastoke *Portsm 5* **P** *DBP* **V** A C LEONARD, **NSM** H V HAWKES
HAYNES (Mission Room) *see* Campton, Clophill and Haynes *St Alb*
HAYNES (St Mary) *as above*
HAYTON (St James) *see* Aspatria w Hayton and Gilcrux *Carl*
HAYTON (St Martin) *see* Shiptonthorpe and Hayton *York*
HAYTON (St Mary Magdalene) *see* Eden, Gelt and Irthing *Carl*
HAYTON (St Peter) *see* Clarborough w Hayton *S'well*
HAYWARDS HEATH (St Richard) *Chich 6* **P** *Bp* **V** I N CHANDLER, **C** J F TWISLETON, **Hon C** L D POODHUN
HAYWARDS HEATH (St Wilfrid) (Church of the Ascension) (Church of the Good Shepherd) (Church of the Presentation) *Chich 6* **P** *Bp* **TR** R C W SMITH, **TV** T J STEAD, D F COOMBES
HAYWOOD, GREAT (St Stephen) *see* Colton, Colwich and Gt Haywood *Lich*
HAZELBURY BRYAN (St Mary and St James) and the Hillside Parishes *Sarum 5* **P** *Duke of Northd (2 turns), M J Scott-Williams Esq, G A L-F Pitt-Rivers Esq, Exors F N Kent Esq, and Bp (1 turn each)* **P-in-c** D JONES
HAZELWELL (St Mary Magdalen) *Birm 5* **P** *Bp* **V** A C PRIESTLEY
HAZELWOOD (St John the Evangelist), Holbrook and Milford *Derby 11* **P** *Bp and DBP (jt)* **V** R J HARRIS
HAZLEMERE (Holy Trinity) *Ox 29* **P** *Peache Trustees* **V** P C COLLIER, **C** W F MASON, J M WIGRAM, R G WIGRAM, **NSM** A W GARRATT
HEACHAM (St Mary) *Nor 16* **P** *Bp* **V** P B FOREMAN
HEADBOURNE WORTHY (St Swithun) *Win 7* **P** *Univ Coll Ox and Lord Northbrook (alt)* **R** A W GORDON
HEADCORN (St Peter and St Paul) *Cant 11* **P** *Abp* **V** B E LANGMAN
HEADINGLEY (St Chad) *see* Far Headingley St Chad *Ripon*
HEADINGLEY (St Michael and All Angels) *Ripon 7* **P** *V Leeds St Pet* **NSM** D W PEAT
HEADINGLEY (St Oswald) *see* Far Headingley St Chad *Ripon*
HEADINGTON (St Andrew) *Ox 4* **P** *Keble Coll Ox* **V** W M BREWIN
HEADINGTON (St Mary) *Ox 4* **P** *Bp* **P-in-c** J W SEWELL, **Hon C** S C BULLOCK
HEADINGTON QUARRY (Holy Trinity) *Ox 4* **P** *Bp* **P-in-c** T D HONEY, **C** L J GREEN
HEADLESS CROSS (St Luke) *see* Redditch Ch the K *Worc*
HEADLEY (All Saints) *Guildf 3* **P** *Qu Coll Ox* **V** H M SEMPLE
HEADLEY (St Mary the Virgin) w Box Hill (St Andrew) *Guildf 9* **P** *Bp* **R** D A WOTTON
HEADLEY (St Peter) *see* Ashford Hill w Headley *Win*
HEADON (St Peter) *see* E Markham w Askham, Headon w Upton and Grove *S'well*
HEADSTONE (St George) *Lon 23* **P** *Bp* **V** S R KEEBLE
HEAGE (St Luke) *see* Ambergate and Heage *Derby*
HEALAUGH (St John the Baptist) w Wighill, Bilbrough and Askham Richard *York 1* **P** *Abp (3 turns), A G Wailes Fairburn Esq (1 turn)* **P-in-c** J A RENDALL, **NSM** B H FRAY
HEALD GREEN (St Catherine) *Ches 17* **P** *Bp* **V** G D C LANE, **C** G W LAMB, **NSM** S C JOHNSON
HEALEY (Christ Church) *Man 20* **P** *Bp* **P-in-c** L O RUDEN
HEALEY (St John) *Newc 3* **P** *V Bywell St Pet* **P-in-c** D J IRVINE, **NSM** J LYNCH
HEALEY (St Paul) *see* Masham and Healey *Ripon*
HEALEY (War Memorial Mission) *see* S Ossett *Wakef*
HEALING (St Peter and St Paul) *see* Keelby Gp *Linc*
HEAMOOR (St Thomas) *see* Gulval and Madron *Truro*
HEANOR (St Laurence) *Derby 12* **P** *Wright Trustees* **P-in-c** D J PATTIMORE, **C** J W BYATT, **NSM** K PATTIMORE
HEANTON PUNCHARDON (St Augustine) w Marwood *Ex 15* **P** *CPAS (3 turns), St Jo Coll Cam (1 turn)* **R** J S WOOD, **C** S N PAINTING
HEAP BRIDGE (St Thomas and St George) *see* Bury Ch King *Man*
HEAPEY (St Barnabas) and Withnell *Blackb 4* **P** *V Leyland* **V** K HOWARD
HEAPHAM (All Saints) *see* Lea Gp *Linc*
HEATH (All Saints) *Derby 5* **P** *Duke of Devonshire and Simeon's Trustees (jt)* **V** A LOVE, **NSM** M GUEST
HEATH (Mission Church) *see* Uttoxeter Area *Lich*
HEATH, LITTLE (Christ Church) *St Alb 17* **P** *Ch Patr Trust* **V** I D BROWN, **NSM** R H WIKNER
HEATH, THE (not known) *see* Bitterley w Middleton, Stoke St Milborough etc *Heref*
HEATH AND REACH (St Leonard) *St Alb 12* **P** *V Leighton Buzzard* **V** G A NEALE
HEATH HAYES (St John) *see* Cannock *Lich*
HEATH TOWN (Holy Trinity) *see* Wednesfield Heath *Lich*
HEATHER (St John the Baptist) *see* Ibstock w Heather *Leic*
HEATHERLANDS (St John) *Sarum 7* **P** *MMCET* **V** G A G LOUGHLIN, **C** T F GOMM
HEATHERYCLEUGH (St Thomas) *see* Upper Weardale *Dur*
HEATHFIELD (All Saints) *Chich 15* **P** *Bp* **V** G C PICKERING
HEATHFIELD (St Catherine) *see* Bovey Tracey St Jo w Heathfield *Ex*
HEATHFIELD (St John the Baptist) *see* Bradford w Oake, Hillfarrance and Heathfield *B & W*

HEATHFIELD (St Richard) *Chich 15* **P** *Bp* **V** R S CRITTALL
HEATON (Christ Church) *Man 9* **P** *R Deane St Mary* **V** C A BRACEGIRDLE, **NSM** M E MAYOH
HEATON (St Barnabas) *Bradf 1* **P** *Trustees* **V** R S ANDERSON
HEATON (St Gabriel) *see* Newc St Gabr *Newc*
HEATON (St Martin) *Bradf 1* **P** *Bp* **V** A J BURNISTON
HEATON, HIGH (St Francis) *see* Newc St Fran *Newc*
HEATON CHAPEL (St Thomas) *see* Heatons *Man*
HEATON MERSEY (St John the Baptist) *as above*
HEATON MOOR (St Paul) *as above*
HEATON NORRIS (Christ w All Saints) *as above*
HEATON REDDISH (St Mary) *Man 3* **P** *Trustees* **R** W J MCKAE
HEATONS *Man 3* **P** *Patr Bd (4 turns), Prime Min (1 turn)* **TR** M H MAXWELL, **TV** M C MARSHALL, P G STANNARD, R I MECHANIC, **C** G C SMITH, **OLM** H J TATE
HEAVITREE (St Michael and All Angels) (St Lawrence) (St Loye) and St Mary Steps *Ex 3* **P** *Patr Bd* **TR** M S HART, **TV** J F SEWARD, L M BATE, **C** C J FLETCHER, P R MORRELL
HEBBURN (St Cuthbert) (St Oswald) *Dur 15* **P** *Prime Min and TR Jarrow (alt)* **V** J B HUNT
HEBBURN (St John) *Dur 15* **P** *Bp* **P-in-c** D T OSMAN, **C** B UNWIN
HEBDEN (St Peter) *see* Linton in Craven *Bradf*
HEBDEN BRIDGE (St James) and Heptonstall *Wakef 3* **P** *V Halifax* **V** H PASK
HEBRON (St Cuthbert) *see* Longhorsley and Hebron *Newc*
HECK (St John the Baptist) *see* Gt Snaith *Sheff*
HECKFIELD (St Michael) w Mattingley and Rotherwick *Win 5* **P** *New Coll Ox (2 turns), Bp (1 turn)* **V** *vacant* 0118-932 6385
HECKINGTON (St Andrew) *Linc 22* **P** *Bp* **P-in-c** D F BOUTLE
HECKMONDWIKE (All Souls) (St James) *Wakef 8* **P** *V Birstall* **P-in-c** S J PITCHER, **C** D E CRAIG-WILD
HEDDINGTON (St Andrew) *see* Oldbury *Sarum*
HEDDON-ON-THE-WALL (St Andrew) *Newc 3* **P** *Ld Chan* **P-in-c** K M EMERY
HEDENHAM (St Peter) *see* Ditchingham, Hedenham and Broome *Nor*
HEDGE END (St John the Evangelist) *Win 10* **P** *Bp* **V** C J BANNISTER, **NSM** S E LITJENS
HEDGE END (St Luke) *Win 10* **P** *Bp* **V** M R POWIS
HEDGERLEY (St Mary the Virgin) *see* Farnham Royal w Hedgerley *Ox*
HEDNESFORD (St Peter) *Lich 3* **P** *Bp* **V** D A BUCK, **C** K M BUCK
HEDON (St Augustine) w Paull *York 12* **P** *Abp* **V** I R HOWITT, **NSM** C WALL
HEDSOR (St Nicholas) and Bourne End *Ox 29* **P** *Bp* **P-in-c** A P TREW
HEDWORTH (St Nicholas) *Dur 15* **P** *The Crown* **P-in-c** J S BAIN, **C** J E HOWES, **Hon C** D M DUKE
HEELEY (Christ Church) and Gleadless Valley *Sheff 1* **P** *DBP and Prime Min (alt)* **TR** A PATTERSON
HEENE (St Botolph) *Chich 5* **P** *D&C* **R** P R ROBERTS, **C** C G H KASSELL
HEIGHAM (Holy Trinity) *Nor 3* **P** *Ch Trust Fund Trust* **R** A M STRANGE, **C** M J YOUNG, P R RODD
HEIGHAM (St Barnabas) (St Bartholomew) *Nor 3* **P** *Bp* **P-in-c** E HUTCHEON
HEIGHAM (St Thomas) *Nor 3* **P** *Bp* **V** N J H GARRARD, **C** D ROGERS
HEIGHINGTON (not known) *see* Washingborough w Heighington and Canwick *Linc*
HEIGHINGTON (St Michael) *Dur 8* **P** *D&C* **V** P H E THOMAS
HEIGHTINGTON (St Giles) *see* Mamble w Bayton, Rock w Heightington etc *Worc*
HELFORD (St Paul's Mission Church) *see* Manaccan w St Anthony-in-Meneage and St Martin *Truro*
HELHOUGHTON (All Saints) *see* E w W Rudham, Helhoughton etc *Nor*
HELIDON (St John the Baptist) *see* Daventry, Ashby St Ledgers, Braunston etc *Pet*
HELIONS BUMPSTEAD (St Andrew) *see* Steeple Bumpstead and Helions Bumpstead *Chelmsf*
HELLAND (St Helena) *Truro 10* **P** *MMCET* **R** *vacant*
HELLESDON (St Mary) (St Paul and St Michael) *Nor 2* **P** *Bp* **V** P E GRIFFITHS, **C** V M WILSON, **NSM** S A WILSON, **OLM** E O JONES-BLACKETT
HELLIFIELD (St Aidan) *Bradf 5* **P** *Ch Ch Ox* **P-in-c** E A KYTE, **Hon C** K J PHILLIPS
HELLINGLY (St Peter and St Paul) and Upper Dicker *Chich 15* **P** *Abp and Bp (jt)* **V** C M HILL
HELMDON (St Mary Magdalene) *see* Astwell Gp *Pet*
HELME (Christ Church) *see* Meltham *Wakef*
HELMINGHAM (St Mary) *see* Debenham and Helmingham *St E*
HELMSHORE (St Thomas) *see* Musbury *Blackb*
HELMSLEY (All Saints) *York 17* **P** *Lord Feversham* **V** D J WILBOURNE
HELMSLEY, UPPER (St Peter) *see* Sand Hutton *York*
HELPERTHORPE (St Peter) *see* Weaverthorpe w Helperthorpe, Luttons Ambo etc *York*
HELPRINGHAM (St Andrew) w Hale *Linc 22* **P** *Ld Chan (2 turns), D&C (1 turn), DBP (1 turn), and the Rt Revd A C Foottit (1 turn)* **P-in-c** S SAMUEL
HELPSTON (St Botolph) *see* Etton w Helpston and Maxey *Pet*
HELSBY (St Paul) and Dunham-on-the-Hill *Ches 3* **P** *Bp* **V** *vacant* (01928) 722151
HELSINGTON (St John the Baptist) *Carl 10* **P** *V Kendal H Trin* **V** *vacant*
HELSTON (St Michael) and Wendron *Truro 4* **P** *Patr Bd* **TR** D G MILLER, **OLM** D NOAKES
HEMBLINGTON (All Saints) *see* Blofield w Hemblington *Nor*
HEMEL HEMPSTEAD (Holy Trinity) Leverstock Green *see* Chambersbury *St Alb*
HEMEL HEMPSTEAD (St Benedict) Bennetts End *as above*
HEMEL HEMPSTEAD (St Mary) *St Alb 3* **P** *Ld Chan* **TR** P J COTTON, **TV** G R PATCHELL, S R ALLEN, S R J FRENCH, D J MIDDLEBROOK, **NSM** T J BARTON, D SPINK
HEMEL HEMPSTEAD (St Mary) Apsley End *see* Chambersbury *St Alb*
HEMINGBROUGH (St Mary the Virgin) *York 2* **P** *Abp* **P-in-c** M A PASKETT
HEMINGBY (St Margaret) *Linc 11* **P** *Bp (2 turns), Ld Chan (2 turns), and DBP (1 turn)* **R** *vacant*
HEMINGFORD ABBOTS (St Margaret of Antioch) *Ely 8* **P** *Lord Hemingford* **P-in-c** P H CUNLIFFE
HEMINGFORD GREY (St James) *Ely 8* **P** *Mrs G A Scott* **V** P H CUNLIFFE
HEMINGSTONE (St Gregory) *see* Coddenham w Gosbeck and Hemingstone w Henley *St E*
HEMINGTON (St Peter and St Paul) *see* Polebrook and Lutton w Hemington and Luddington *Pet*
HEMINGTON (The Blessed Virgin Mary) *see* Hardington Vale *B & W*
HEMLEY (All Saints) *see* Waldringfield w Hemley and Newbourn *St E*
HEMLINGTON (St Timothy) *York 21* **P** *Abp* **V** A HOWARD
HEMPNALL (St Margaret) *Nor 5* **P** *Ld Chan (1 turn), Patr Bd (5 turns)* **TR** C M MAHONY, **TV** E N BILLETT
HEMPSTEAD (All Saints) *see* Barningham w Matlaske w Baconsthorpe etc *Nor*
HEMPSTEAD (All Saints) *see* S Gillingham *Roch*
HEMPSTEAD (St Andrew) *see* The Sampfords and Radwinter w Hempstead *Chelmsf*
HEMPSTEAD (St Andrew) *see* Happisburgh, Walcott, Hempstead w Eccles etc *Nor*
HEMPSTED (St Swithun) *Glouc 5* **P** *Bp* **P-in-c** A M BUTLER
HEMPTON (Holy Trinity) and Pudding Norton *Nor 15* **P** *The Crown* **P-in-c** P J NORTH
HEMPTON (St John the Evangelist) *see* Deddington w Barford, Clifton and Hempton *Ox*
HEMSBY (St Mary) *see* Flegg Coastal Benefice *Nor*
HEMSWELL (All Saints) *see* Glentworth Gp *Linc*
HEMSWORTH (St Helen) *Wakef 11* **P** *Bp* **R** M DAVIES
HEMYOCK (St Mary) w Culm Davy, Clayhidon and Culmstock *Ex 4* **P** *DBP, SMF, and D&C (jt)* **P-in-c** D C SHERWOOD
HENBURY (St Mary the Virgin) *Bris 2* **P** *Lord Middleton (1 turn), Bp (3 turns)* **V** D P LLOYD
HENBURY (St Thomas) *Ches 13* **P** *Bp* **V** D S HARRISON
HENDFORD (Holy Trinity) *see* Yeovil H Trin w Barwick *B & W*
HENDFORD (St Mary the Virgin and All Saints) *as above*
HENDON (All Saints) Childs Hill *Lon 15* **P** *Bp* **V** J P WAINWRIGHT
HENDON (St Alphage) *Lon 15* **P** *Bp* **V** H D MOORE, **C** J F CASTER
HENDON (St Ignatius) *Dur 16* **P** *Bp* **R** A C JONES
HENDON (St Mary) (Christ Church) *Lon 15* **P** *Bp* **V** T G CLEMENT, **NSM** R G CORP
HENDON (St Paul) Mill Hill *Lon 15* **P** *Bp* **V** A J SHAW, **C** J E LOWE
HENDON, WEST (St John) *Lon 15* **P** *Bp* **V** J E I HAWKINS, **C** W A WHITCOMBE
HENDRED, EAST (St Augustine of Canterbury) *see* Wantage Downs *Ox*

HENDRED, WEST (Holy Trinity) *as above*
HENFIELD (St Peter) w Shermanbury and Woodmancote *Chich 9* **P** *Bp* **V** C J COLLISON, **C** J H GOULSTON
HENGOED w Gobowen *Lich 19* **P** *R Selattyn* **P-in-c** A R BAILEY
HENGROVE (Christ Church) *Bris 1* **P** *Bp and Simeon's Trustees (alt)* **V** *vacant* (01275) 832346
HENHAM (St Mary the Virgin) and Elsenham w Ugley *Chelmsf 21* **P** *Ch Hosp, Ch Soc Trust, and Bp (jt)* **P-in-c** R W FARR, **C** J P RICHARDSON
HENLEAZE (St Peter) *Bris 2* **P** *Bp* **V** C M PILGRIM
HENLEY on Thames w Remenham *Ox 6* **P** *Bp and Jes Coll Ox (jt)* **R** M R GRIFFITHS, **C** E LOZADA-UZURIAGA
HENLEY (St Peter) *see* Coddenham w Gosbeck and Hemingstone w Henley *St E*
HENLEY IN ARDEN (St John the Baptist) *see* Beaudesert and Henley-in-Arden w Ullenhall *Cov*
HENLEY-ON-THAMES (Holy Trinity) *Ox 6* **P** *R Rotherfield Greys St Nich* **V** D R B CARTER
HENLOW (St Mary the Virgin) and Langford *St Alb 16* **P** *Ld Chan* **V** J MORLEY
HENNOCK (St Mary) *see* Bovey Tracey SS Pet, Paul and Thos w Hennock *Ex*
HENNY, GREAT (St Mary) *see* N Hinckford *Chelmsf*
HENSALL (St Paul) *see* Gt Snaith *Sheff*
HENSHAW (All Hallows) *see* Haydon Bridge and Beltingham w Henshaw *Newc*
HENSINGHAM (St John) (Keekle Mission) *Carl 5* **P** *Trustees* **V** F T PEARSON
HENSTEAD (St Mary) *see* Sole Bay *St E*
HENSTRIDGE (St Nicholas) and Charlton Horethorne w Stowell *B & W 2* **P** *Bp (2 turns), K S D Wingfield Digby Esq (1 turn)* **R** P HALLETT
HENTLAND (St Dubricius) *see* How Caple w Sollarshope, Sellack etc *Heref*
HENTON (Christ Church) *see* Coxley w Godney, Henton and Wookey *B & W*
HEPPLE (Christ Church) *see* Upper Coquetdale *Newc*
HEPTONSTALL (St Thomas à Becket and St Thomas the Apostle) *see* Hebden Bridge and Heptonstall *Wakef*
HEPWORTH (Holy Trinity) *see* Upper Holme Valley *Wakef*
HEPWORTH (St Peter) w Hinderclay, Wattisfield and Thelnetham *St E 9* **P** *Bp, K Coll Cam, MMCET, and P J Holt-Wilson Esq (jt)* **R** J W FULTON
HEREFORD (All Saints) (St Barnabas Church Centre) *Heref 3* **P** *D&C Windsor* **P-in-c** A P MOTTRAM
HEREFORD (Holy Trinity) *Heref 3* **P** *Bp* **V** R NORTH
HEREFORD (St Francis) *see* Heref S Wye *Heref*
HEREFORD (St John the Baptist) *Heref 3* **P** *D&C* **V** *vacant*
HEREFORD (St Martin) *see* Heref S Wye *Heref*
HEREFORD (St Paul) *see* Tupsley w Hampton Bishop *Heref*
HEREFORD (St Peter w St Owen) (St James) *Heref 3* **P** *Simeon's Trustees* **P-in-c** P TOWNER, **C** J J MERCER, **NSM** P W MASSEY, **OLM** S A ELSON
HEREFORD, LITTLE (St Mary Magdalene) *see* Burford III w Lt Heref *Heref*
HEREFORD, WEST Team Ministry (St Nicholas) *Heref 3* **P** *Ld Chan* **TR** R NORTH, **TV** B P CHAVE, **C** V J TAIT, **NSM** S GREEN, I A TERRY
HEREFORD SOUTH WYE (St Francis) (St Martin) *Heref 3* **P** *Patr Bd* **TR** P G HADDLETON, **TV** M JOHNSON, **C** R C GREEN, **OLM** C R EVANS
HERMITAGE (Holy Trinity) *Ox 14* **P** *Patr Bd* **TR** J K COOMBS, **TV** A H LYNN
HERMITAGE (St Mary) *see* Wriggle Valley *Sarum*
HERNE (St Martin) *Cant 7* **P** *Abp* **V** S M LANGDON-DAVIES, **OLM** J L HADLOW, J A BAKER
HERNE BAY (Christ Church) (St Andrew's Church and Centre) *Cant 7* **P** *Simeon's Trustees* **V** A W EVERETT, **C** C R HARTLEY
HERNE BAY (St Bartholomew) *see* Reculver and Herne Bay St Bart *Cant*
HERNE HILL (St Paul) (St Saviour) *S'wark 9* **P** *Bp and Simeon's Trustees (jt)* **V** C T BARKER, **C** S POWNALL
HERNER (Chapel) *see* Barnstaple *Ex*
HERNHILL (St Michael) *see* Boughton under Blean w Dunkirk and Hernhill *Cant*
HERODSFOOT (All Saints) *see* Duloe, Herodsfoot, Morval and St Pinnock *Truro*
HERONSGATE (St John the Evangelist) *see* Mill End and Heronsgate w W Hyde *St Alb*
HERRIARD (St Mary) w Winslade and Long Sutton and South Warnborough and Tunworth and Upton Grey and Weston Patrick *Win 5* **P** *Bp, Qu Coll Ox, St Jo Coll Ox, Exors Viscount Camrose, and J L Jervoise Esq (jt)* **P-in-c** P W DYSON, **NSM** J E LEESE
HERRINGFLEET (St Margaret) *see* Somerleyton, Ashby, Fritton, Herringfleet etc *Nor*
HERRINGSWELL (St Ethelbert) *see* Mildenhall *St E*
HERRINGTHORPE (St Cuthbert) *Sheff 6* **P** *Bp* **V** J TRICKETT
HERRINGTON, Penshaw and Shiney Row *Dur 14* **P** *Bp and Prime Min (alt)* **R** P M HOOD, **NSM** M S GOURLEY
HERSHAM (St Peter) *Guildf 8* **P** *Bp* **V** N J WHITEHEAD, **NSM** J W ANDREW
HERSTMONCEUX (All Saints) and Wartling *Chich 15* **P** *Bp* **P-in-c** S L PANTER MARSHALL, **NSM** M E C TALBOT
HERSTON (St Mark) *see* Swanage and Studland *Sarum*
HERTFORD (All Saints) *St Alb 22* **P** *Ld Chan and Marquess Townshend (alt)* **V** W ST J KEMM
HERTFORD (St Andrew) *St Alb 22* **P** *Duchy of Lanc* **NSM** W J CHURCH
HERTFORD HEATH (Holy Trinity) *see* Lt Amwell *St Alb*
HERTINGFORDBURY (St Mary) *St Alb 22* **P** *The Crown* **P-in-c** R A CARUANA
HESKET-IN-THE-FOREST (St Mary the Virgin) *see* Inglewood Gp *Carl*
HESKETH (All Saints) w Becconsall *Blackb 5* **P** *Trustees* **R** R PLANT
HESLERTON, EAST (St Andrew) *see* Buckrose Carrs *York*
HESLERTON, WEST (All Saints) *as above*
HESLINGTON (St Paul) *York 2* **P** *Abp* **V** N E ECKERSLEY
HESSAY (St John the Baptist) *see* Rufforth w Moor Monkton and Hessay *York*
HESSENFORD (St Anne) *see* St Germans *Truro*
HESSETT (St Ethelbert) *see* Rougham, Beyton w Hessett and Rushbrooke *St E*
HESSLE (All Saints) *York 14* **P** *Ld Chan* **C** K L BURGESS
HESTER WAY LANE (St Silas) *see* Cheltenham St Mark *Glouc*
HESTON (All Saints) (St Leonard) *Lon 11* **P** *Bp* **V** R CRANKSHAW
HESWALL (Church of the Good Shepherd) (St Peter) *Ches 8* **P** *W A B Davenport Esq* **R** J R GIBBS, **C** C M HELM, S M MANSFIELD
HETHE (St Edmund King and Martyr and St George) *see* Shelswell *Ox*
HETHEL (All Saints) *see* Mulbarton w Bracon Ash, Hethel and Flordon *Nor*
HETHERSETT (St Remigius) w Canteloff w Little Melton and Great Melton *Nor 7* **P** *G&C Coll Cam, E C Evans-Lombe Esq, and Em Coll Cam (by turn)* **R** D B LAMMAS, **NSM** J C MALLETT, **OLM** M KERSLAKE
HETHERSGILL (St Mary) *see* Bewcastle, Stapleton and Kirklinton etc *Carl*
HETTON, SOUTH (Holy Trinity) *see* Easington, Easington Colliery and S Hetton *Dur*
HEVENINGHAM (St Margaret) w Ubbeston, Huntingfield and Cookley *St E 15* **P** *Capt the Revd J S Peel* **P-in-c** K R HAGAN
HEVER (St Peter), Four Elms and Mark Beech *Roch 11* **P** *Bp and C Talbot Esq (jt)* **P-in-c** M G GRIBBLE, **NSM** W J IZOD
HEVERSHAM (St Peter) and Milnthorpe *Carl 10* **P** *Trin Coll Cam* **V** J C HANCOCK, **NSM** R RUTTER
HEVINGHAM (St Mary and St Botolph) w Hainford and Stratton Strawless *Nor 19* **P** *Bp and Sir Thomas Beevor Bt (jt)* **P-in-c** C J ENGELSEN
HEWELSFIELD (St Mary Magdalene) *see* St Briavels w Hewelsfield *Glouc*
HEWISH (Good Shepherd) *see* Crewkerne w Wayford *B & W*
HEWORTH (Christ Church) *York 7* **P** *Ch Trust Fund Trust* **V** T MCDONOUGH, **NSM** M D P NOKES, P MOORE
HEWORTH (Holy Trinity) (St Wulstan) *York 7* **P** *Patr Bd* **TR** M B WOODMANSEY
HEWORTH (St Alban) *Dur 12* **P** *V Heworth St Mary* **V** M WROE, **C** S M WHITE
HEWORTH (St Mary) *Dur 12* **P** *Bp* **V** V SHEDDEN, **NSM** D M SNOWBALL
HEXHAM (St Andrew) *Newc 4* **P** *Mercers' Co and Viscount Allendale (alt)* **R** G B USHER, **C** D WINTER
HEXTABLE (St Peter) *see* Swanley St Paul *Roch*
HEXTHORPE (St Jude) *see* Doncaster St Jude *Sheff*
HEXTON (St Faith) *see* Barton-le-Cley w Higham Gobion and Hexton *St Alb*
HEY (St John the Baptist) *Man 21* **P** *R Aston-under-Lyne St Mich* **P-in-c** R W HAWKINS, **C** D R PENNY
HEYBRIDGE (St Andrew) (St George) w Langford *Chelmsf 11* **P** *D&C St Paul's and Lord Byron (alt)* **V** S E MANLEY
HEYBROOK BAY (Holy Nativity) *see* Wembury *Ex*
HEYDON (Holy Trinity), Great Chishill and Little Chishill, Chrishall, Elmdon w Wenden Lofts and Strethall *Chelmsf 22* **P** *Patr Bd* **R** J G SIMMONS

HEYDON (St Peter and St Paul) *see* Cawston w Booton and Brandiston etc *Nor*
HEYDOUR (St Michael and All Angels) *see* Ancaster Wilsford Gp *Linc*
HEYFORD (St Peter and St Paul) w Stowe Nine Churches and Flore w Brockhall *Pet 3* **P** *The Revd S Hope, Ch Ch Ox, DPB and Bp (by turn)* **R** A SLATER
HEYFORD, LOWER (St Mary) *see* Cherwell Valley *Ox*
HEYFORD, UPPER (St Mary) *as above*
HEYHOUSES (St Nicholas) *see* Sabden and Pendleton *Blackb*
HEYHOUSES ON SEA (St Anne) *see* St Annes St Anne *Blackb*
HEYSHAM (St Peter) (St Andrew) (St James) *Blackb 11* **P** *C E C Royds Esq* **R** D A TICKNER
HEYSHOTT (St James) *Chich 10* **P** *Bp* **P-in-c** C BOXLEY
HEYSIDE (St Mark) *Man 22* **P** *Trustees* **V** R MORRIS, **NSM** S E WARD
HEYTESBURY (St Peter and St Paul) *see* Upper Wylye Valley *Sarum*
HEYTHROP (St Nicholas) *see* Chase *Ox*
HEYWOOD (All Souls) (St Luke) (St Margaret) *Man 18* **P** *Patr Bd* **TR** G TURNER, **TV** M E READ, **OLM** A BROWN, I TAYLOR, R A J MILLER, I WARRINGTON
HEYWOOD (St James) *Man 18* **P** *Bp* **P-in-c** L J READING
HIBALDSTOW (St Hibald) *see* Scawby, Redbourne and Hibaldstow *Linc*
HICKLETON (St Wilfrid) *see* Goldthorpe w Hickleton *Sheff*
HICKLING (St Luke) w Kinoulton and Broughton Sulney (Upper Broughton) *S'well 8* **P** *Prime Min, Qu Coll Cam, and Bp (by turn)* **R** S B FAHIE
HICKLING (St Mary) *see* Ludham, Potter Heigham, Hickling and Catfield *Nor*
HIGH *see also under substantive place name*
HIGH CROSS (St John the Evangelist) *St Alb 22* **P** *DBP* **V** H J SHARMAN
HIGH GREEN (St Saviour) *see* Mortomley St Sav High Green *Sheff*
HIGH HAM (St Andrew) *see* Langport Area Chs *B & W*
HIGH LANE (St Thomas) *Ches 16* **P** *R Stockport* **V** M A M WOLVERSON
HIGH OAK, Hingham and Scoulton w Wood Rising *Nor 7* **P** *Patr Bd* **OLM** P J TRETT, S A HOLT, B K FURNESS
HIGHAM (St John the Evangelist) *see* Fence-in-Pendle and Higham *Blackb*
HIGHAM (St John the Evangelist) and Merston *Roch 6* **P** *St Jo Coll Cam* **V** J F SOUTHWARD
HIGHAM (St Mary), Holton St Mary, Raydon and Stratford St Mary *St E 3* **P** *Duchy of Lanc, Reformation Ch Trust, and Mrs S E F Holden* **R** C A GARRARD
HIGHAM FERRERS (St Mary the Virgin) w Chelveston *Pet 10* **P** *Bp* **V** G L BROCKHOUSE, **NSM** P R NEEDLE
HIGHAM GOBION (St Margaret) *see* Barton-le-Cley w Higham Gobion and Hexton *St Alb*
HIGHAM GREEN (St Stephen) *see* Dalham, Gazeley, Higham, Kentford and Moulton *St E*
HIGHAM HILL (St Andrew) *see* Walthamstow St Andr *Chelmsf*
HIGHAM-ON-THE-HILL (St Peter) *see* Fenn Lanes Gp *Leic*
HIGHAMPTON (Holy Cross) *see* Black Torrington, Bradf w Cookbury etc *Ex*
HIGHAMS PARK (All Saints) Hale End *Chelmsf 5* **P** *Bp* **V** C A MCGHIE
HIGHBRIDGE (St John the Evangelist) *B & W 1* **P** *Bp* **V** R P LODGE
HIGHBROOK (All Saints) and West Hoathly *Chich 6* **P** *Ld Chan* **V** A C CARR
HIGHBURY (Christ Church) (St John) (St Saviour) *Lon 6* **P** *Ch Trust Fund Trust and Islington Ch Trust (jt)* **V** J D BREWSTER, **C** F J GREEN
HIGHBURY NEW PARK (St Augustine) *Lon 6* **P** *Trustees* **V** C T MAIN
HIGHCLERE (St Michael and All Angels) and Ashmansworth w Crux Easton *Win 6* **P** *Earl of Carnarvon* **R** T F HORSINGTON
HIGHCLIFFE (St Mark) w Hinton Admiral *Win 9* **P** *Sir George Tapps-Gervis-Meyrick Bt and Bp (alt)* **V** G K TAYLOR, **C** J H WATSON
HIGHER *see also under substantive place name*
HIGHER FOLD Leigh (St Matthew) *see* Bedford Leigh *Man*
HIGHERTOWN (All Saints) and Baldhu *Truro 6* **P** *Bp and Viscount Falmouth (alt)* **V** G W SMYTH, **NSM** A J STEVENSON
HIGHFIELD (All Saints) *Ox 4* **P** *Bp* **V** J E COCKE
HIGHFIELD (Christ Church) *see* Portswood Ch Ch *Win*
HIGHFIELD (St Catherine) *see* New Bury *Man*
HIGHFIELD (St Mary) *see* Sheff St Mary Bramall Lane *Sheff*
HIGHFIELD (St Matthew) *Liv 15* **P** *Trustees* **V** R L PEARSON
HIGHFIELD (St Paul) *see* Hemel Hempstead *St Alb*
HIGHGATE (All Saints) *Lon 20* **P** *Bp* **P-in-c** P STORR VENTER
HIGHGATE (St Alban and St Patrick) *Birm 13* **P** *Keble Coll Ox* **P-in-c** J A HERVE
HIGHGATE (St Augustine) *Lon 20* **P** *Bp* **P-in-c** P F M GOFF
HIGHGATE (St Michael) *Lon 20* **P** *Bp* **V** J D TRIGG, **C** N J LITTLE, E M WEST
HIGHGATE CENTRE *see* Bredbury St Barn *Ches*
HIGHGATE RISE (St Anne) *see* Brookfield St Anne, Highgate Rise *Lon*
HIGHLEY (St Mary) w Billingsley, Glazeley and Deuxhill and Chelmarsh *Heref 9* **P** *MMCET* **V** C G WILLIAMS
HIGHMORE (St Paul) *see* Nettlebed w Bix, Highmoor, Pishill etc *Ox*
HIGHNAM (Holy Innocents), Lassington, Rudford, Tibberton and Taynton *Glouc 3* **P** *D&C, T J Fenton Esq, and A E Woolley (jt)* **R** M S RILEY, **Hon C** G N CRAGO, **OLM** G R W PARFITT
HIGHTERS HEATH (Immanuel) *Birm 5* **P** *Bp* **V** E I PITTS
HIGHTOWN (All Saints) *see* Castleford *Wakef*
HIGHTOWN (St Barnabas) *see* Liversedge w Hightown *Wakef*
HIGHTOWN (St Stephen) *see* Altcar and Hightown *Liv*
HIGHWEEK (All Saints) (St Mary) and Teigngrace *Ex 10* **P** *Bp* **R** C R KNOTT
HIGHWORTH (St Michael) w Sevenhampton and Inglesham and Hannington *Bris 7* **P** *Bp (4 turns), Mrs M G Hussey-Freke (1 turn)* **V** G D SOWDEN, **C** R C WARD, S J RUSHTON
HILBOROUGH (All Saints) w Bodney *Nor 13* **P** *DBP* **C** D J HANWELL
HILDENBOROUGH (St John the Evangelist) *Roch 11* **P** *V Tonbridge* **V** J C CHANDLER, **C** P MEIER, **NSM** E M TOY
HILDERSHAM (Holy Trinity) *Ely 4* **P** *Trustees* **P-in-c** J B MYNORS
HILDERSTONE (Christ Church) *see* Fulford w Hilderstone *Lich*
HILFIELD (St Nicholas) *see* Wriggle Valley *Sarum*
HILGAY (All Saints) *Ely 13* **P** *Hertf Coll Ox* **R** D J EVANS
HILL (St James) *Birm 12* **P** *Bp* **C** P OGILVIE
HILL (St Michael) *see* Berkeley w Wick, Breadstone, Newport, Stone etc *Glouc*
HILL CROOME (St Mary) *see* Upton-on-Severn, Ripple, Earls Croome etc *Worc*
HILL TOP (Mission Room) *see* Greasley *S'well*
HILL TOP (St James) *see* W Bromwich St Jas w St Paul *Lich*
HILLESDEN (All Saints) *see* Lenborough *Ox*
HILLESLEY (St Giles) *see* Wickwar, Rangeworthy and Hillesley *Glouc*
HILLFARRANCE (Holy Cross) *see* Bradford w Oake, Hillfarrance and Heathfield *B & W*
HILLINGDON (All Saints) *Lon 24* **P** *Bp* **V** P C HULLYER
HILLINGDON (St John the Baptist) *Lon 24* **P** *Bp* **V** R W HARRISON, **C** E M MOORE-BICK, **NSM** G PINNELL, W F WHITE
HILLINGTON (St Mary the Virgin) *Nor 16* **P** *E W Dawnay Esq* **P-in-c** J B V RIVIERE
HILLMORTON (St John the Baptist) *Cov 6* **P** *Bp and TR Rugby* **V** A P HAINES
HILLOCK (St Andrew) *Man 14* **P** *Bp and R Stand All SS* **P-in-c** A B WILLIAMS
HILLSBOROUGH and Wadsley Bridge (Christ Church) *Sheff 4* **P** *Ch Patr Trust* **V** J E COUSANS
HILLSIDE Lobley Hill and Marley Hill *Dur 13* **P** *Bp and Prime Min (alt)* **V** R K HOPPER
HILLTOP (Mission Room) *see* Bagnall w Endon *Lich*
HILMARTON (St Lawrence) *see* Broad Town, Clyffe Pypard, Hilmarton etc *Sarum*
HILPERTON (St Michael and All Angels) w Whaddon and Staverton w Hilperton Marsh *Sarum 14* **P** *R Trowbridge St Jas and Viscount Long (alt)* **P-in-c** R J H MAGILL, **C** S A BALL
HILPERTON MARSH (St Mary Magdalen) *see* Hilperton w Whaddon and Staverton etc *Sarum*
HILSTON (St Margaret) *see* Roos and Garton w Tunstall, Grimston and Hilston *York*
HILTON (All Saints) *see* Piddle Valley, Hilton, Cheselbourne etc *Sarum*
HILTON (St Mary Magdalene) *Ely 8* **P** *Bp* **V** M A GUITE
HILTON (St Peter) *see* Stainton w Hilton *York*
HILTON w Marston-on-Dove *Derby 14* **P** *N J M Spurrier Esq* **V** A G MURPHIE, **NSM** S K MATSON DE LAURIER
HIMBLETON (St Mary Magdalen) *see* Bowbrook S *Worc*
HIMLEY (St Michael and All Angels) *see* Smestow Vale *Lich*
HINCASTER (Mission Room) *see* Heversham and Milnthorpe *Carl*

HINCHLEY WOOD (St Christopher) *Guildf 8* **P** *Bp* **V** T A DONNELLY
HINCKFORD, NORTH *Chelmsf 19* **P** *Patr Bd (4 turns), Ld Chan (1 turn)* **TR** E G BUCHANAN, **TV** M H KING, **C** B A SAMPSON
HINCKLEY (Assumption of St Mary the Virgin) (St Francis) (St Paul) *Leic 12* **P** *Bp* **V** B DAVIS
HINCKLEY (Holy Trinity) (St John the Evangelist) *Leic 12* **P** *DBP* **TR** J C MCGINLEY, **TV** T J WARD, **C** P J HUBBARD
HINDERCLAY (St Mary) *see* Hepworth, Hinderclay, Wattisfield and Thelnetham *St E*
HINDERWELL (St Hilda), Roxby and Staithes w Lythe, Ugthorpe and Sandsend *York 22* **P** *Abp* **R** *vacant* (01947) 840249
HINDHEAD (St Alban) *see* Churt and Hindhead *Guildf*
HINDLEY (All Saints) *Liv 14* **P** *R Wigan* **V** J TAYLOR
HINDLEY (St Peter) *Liv 14* **P** *St Pet Coll Ox* **V** S A MATHER, **NSM** C A CLOSE
HINDLEY GREEN (St John) *Liv 14* **P** *Bp* **V** M J SHERWIN
HINDOLVESTON (St George) *see* Foulsham w Hindolveston and Guestwick *Nor*
HINDON (St John the Baptist) *see* Nadder Valley *Sarum*
HINDRINGHAM (St Martin) *see* Barney, Fulmodeston w Croxton, Hindringham etc *Nor*
HINGHAM (St Andrew) *see* High Oak, Hingham and Scoulton w Wood Rising *Nor*
HINKSEY, NEW (St John the Evangelist) *see* S Hinksey *Ox*
HINKSEY, NORTH (St Lawrence) and Wytham *Ox 7* **P** *Bp* **P-in-c** A RUSTELL, **Hon C** P J BUDD, **NSM** R M HILL
HINKSEY, SOUTH (St Lawrence) *Ox 7* **P** *Bp* **P-in-c** J D WILKINSON, **Hon C** B SINGH
HINSTOCK (St Oswald) *see* Cheswardine, Childs Ercall, Hales, Hinstock etc *Lich*
HINTLESHAM (St Nicholas) *see* Elmsett w Aldham, Hintlesham, Chattisham etc *St E*
HINTON ADMIRAL (St Michael and All Angels) *see* Highcliffe w Hinton Admiral *Win*
HINTON AMPNER (All Saints) *see* Upper Itchen *Win*
HINTON BLEWETT (St Margaret) *see* E w W Harptree and Hinton Blewett *B & W*
HINTON CHARTERHOUSE (St John the Baptist) *see* Freshford, Limpley Stoke and Hinton Charterhouse *B & W*
HINTON-IN-THE-HEDGES (Holy Trinity) *see* Aynho and Croughton w Evenley etc *Pet*
HINTON MARTEL (St John the Evangelist) *see* Horton, Chalbury, Hinton Martel and Holt St Jas *Sarum*
HINTON-ON-THE-GREEN (St Peter) *see* Hampton w Sedgeberrow and Hinton-on-the-Green *Worc*
HINTON PARVA (St Swithun) *see* Lyddington and Wanborough and Bishopstone etc *Bris*
HINTON ST GEORGE (St George) *see* Merriott w Hinton, Dinnington and Lopen *B & W*
HINTON ST MARY (St Mary) *see* Sturminster Newton, Hinton St Mary and Lydlinch *Sarum*
HINTON WALDRIST (St Margaret) *see* Cherbury w Gainfield *Ox*
HINTS (St Bartholomew) *Lich 1* **P** *Personal Reps A E Jones Esq* **V** J H MARTIN
HINXHILL (St Mary) *see* Mersham w Hinxhill and Sellindge *Cant*
HINXTON (St Mary and St John) *Ely 6* **P** *Jes Coll Cam* **P-in-c** A T SCHOFIELD
HINXWORTH (St Nicholas) *see* Ashwell w Hinxworth and Newnham *St Alb*
HIPSWELL (St John the Evangelist) *Ripon 2* **P** *Bp* **V** E A VARLEY, **NSM** M J VICKERS
HISTON (St Andrew) *Ely 5* **P** *MMCET* **C** K A HODGINS, **NSM** J M GLOVER
HITCHAM (All Saints) *see* Rattlesden w Thorpe Morieux, Brettenham etc *St E*
HITCHAM (St Mary) *see* Burnham w Dropmore, Hitcham and Taplow *Ox*
HITCHIN (Holy Saviour) (St Faith) (St Mark) (St Mary) *St Alb 4* **P** *Patr Bd* **TR** M A H RODEN, **TV** J FOX, J F MAINWARING, **C** C C M SABEY-CORKINDALE
HITTISLEIGH (St Andrew) *see* Chagford, Drewsteignton, Hittisleigh etc *Ex*
HIXON (St Peter) *see* Mid Trent *Lich*
HOAR CROSS (Holy Angels) w Newchurch *Lich 14* **P** *Bp and Meynell Ch Trustees* **V** *vacant*
HOARWITHY (St Catherine) *see* How Caple w Sollarshope, Sellack etc *Heref*
HOATH (Holy Cross) *see* St Nicholas at Wade w Sarre and Chislet w Hoath *Cant*
HOATHLY, EAST (not known) *see* Chiddingly w E Hoathly *Chich*
HOATHLY, WEST (St Margaret) *see* Highbrook and W Hoathly *Chich*
HOBS MOAT (St Mary) *Birm 11* **P** *Bp* **V** D A LEAHY
HOBY (All Saints) *see* Upper Wreake *Leic*
HOCKERILL (All Saints) *St Alb 18* **P** *Bp Lon* **P-in-c** K I GOSS, **C** M A MILLER
HOCKERING (St Michael), Honingham, East Tuddenham and North Tuddenham *Nor 17* **P** *J V Berney Esq (1 turn), DBP (2 turns)* **P-in-c** G R KEGG
HOCKERTON (St Nicholas) *see* Kirklington w Hockerton *S'well*
HOCKHAM, GREAT (Holy Trinity) *see* Caston, Griston, Merton, Thompson etc *Nor*
HOCKLEY (St Matthew) *see* Wilnecote *Lich*
HOCKLEY (St Paul) *see* Birm St Paul *Birm*
HOCKLEY (St Peter and St Paul) *Chelmsf 12* **P** *Wadh Coll Ox* **V** *vacant* (01702) 203668
HOCKLIFFE (St Nicholas) *see* Leighton Buzzard w Eggington, Hockliffe etc *St Alb*
HOCKWOLD (St James) w Wilton *Ely 13* **P** *G&C Coll Cam* **R** S BETSON
HOCKWORTHY (St Simon and St Jude) *see* Sampford Peverell, Uplowman, Holcombe Rogus etc *Ex*
HODDESDON (St Catherine and St Paul) *St Alb 20* **P** *Peache Trustees* **P-in-c** J P BROOKS, **C** M A REYNOLDS, **NSM** D A MOORE BROOKS
HODDESDON (St Cuthbert) *see* Rye Park St Cuth *St Alb*
HODDLESDEN (St Paul) *see* Darwen St Pet w Hoddlesden *Blackb*
HODGE HILL (St Philip and St James) *Birm 9* **P** *Bp* **TR** *vacant* 0121-747 2094 *or* 747 9262
HODNET (St Luke) w Weston under Redcastle *Lich 18* **P** *A E H Heber-Percy Esq* **P-in-c** C P BEECH
HODTHORPE (St Martin) *see* Whitwell *Derby*
HOE (St Andrew) *see* Swanton Morley w Beetley w E Bilney and Hoe *Nor*
HOE, WEST (St Michael) *see* Plymouth St Andr and St Paul Stonehouse *Ex*
HOE BENHAM (not known) *see* Welford w Wickham and Gt Shefford, Boxford etc *Ox*
HOGGESTON (Holy Cross) *see* Schorne *Ox*
HOGHTON (Holy Trinity) *Blackb 5* **P** *V Leyland* **P-in-c** D C DICKINSON
HOGNASTON (St Bartholomew) *see* Hulland, Atlow, Kniveton, Bradley and Hognaston *Derby*
HOGSTHORPE (St Mary) *see* Chapel St Leonards w Hogsthorpe *Linc*
HOLBEACH (All Saints) *Linc 16* **P** *Bp* **V** G J WICKSTEAD, **C** J M DUNKLING
HOLBEACH FEN (St John) *Linc 16* **P** *Bp* **V** *vacant*
HOLBEACH MARSH (St Luke) (St Mark) (St Martin) *Linc 16* **P** *V Holbeach* **P-in-c** M J NOTLEY
HOLBECK (St Luke the Evangelist) *Ripon 6* **P** *Bp, V Leeds St Pet, and Meynell Ch Trust (jt)* **P-in-c** C BUTLER
HOLBETON (All Saints) *Ex 21* **P** *The Crown* **P-in-c** T R DEACON
HOLBORN (St Alban the Martyr) w Saffron Hill St Peter *Lon 17* **P** *D&C St Paul's* **V** H LEVETT, **Hon C** A C LEE
HOLBORN (St George the Martyr) Queen Square (Holy Trinity) (St Bartholomew) Grays Inn Road *Lon 17* **P** *Ch Soc Trust* **P-in-c** J H VALENTINE, **C** P V ZAPHIRIOU
HOLBORN (St Giles-in-the-Fields) *see* St Giles-in-the-Fields *Lon*
HOLBROOK (All Saints), Stutton, Freston, Woolverstone and Wherstead *St E 5* **P** *Patr Bd* **R** N S TODD
HOLBROOK (St Michael) *see* Hazelwood, Holbrook and Milford *Derby*
HOLBROOK ROAD (St Swithin) *see* Belper *Derby*
HOLBROOKS (St Luke) *Cov 2* **P** *Bp* **V** C DUNKLEY, **C** P CALVERT
HOLBURY (Good Shepherd) *see* Fawley *Win*
HOLCOMBE (Emmanuel) (Canon Lewis Hall) *Man 10* **P** *R Bury St Mary* **P-in-c** J G ARMSTRONG, **C** P H SUMSION, **OLM** R W AIREY
HOLCOMBE (St Andrew) *see* Coleford w Holcombe *B & W*
HOLCOMBE (St George) *see* Dawlish *Ex*
HOLCOMBE BURNELL (St John the Baptist) *see* Tedburn St Mary, Whitestone, Oldridge etc *Ex*
HOLCOMBE ROGUS (All Saints) *see* Sampford Peverell, Uplowman, Holcombe Rogus etc *Ex*
HOLCOT (St Mary and All Saints) *see* Brixworth w Holcot *Pet*
HOLDENHURST (St John the Evangelist) and Iford *Win 8* **P** *Bp* **V** A L MCPHERSON, **C** T J BATESON, **NSM** N M BENCE, J M SEARE
HOLDGATE (Holy Trinity) *see* Diddlebury w Munslow, Holdgate and Tugford *Heref*

HOLFORD (St Mary the Virgin) *see* Quantoxhead *B & W*
HOLGATE (St Paul) *see* York St Paul *York*
HOLKHAM (St Withiburga) w Egmere w Warham, Wells-next-the-Sea and Wighton *Nor 15* **P** *Viscount Coke (2 turns), M J Beddard Esq (2 turns), and D&C(1 turn)* **R** A V DOUGLAS
HOLLACOMBE (St Petroc) *see* Holsworthy w Hollacombe and Milton Damerel *Ex*
HOLLAND, GREAT (All Saints) *see* Kirby-le-Soken w Gt Holland *Chelmsf*
HOLLAND, NEW (Christ Church) *see* Barrow and Goxhill *Linc*
HOLLAND FEN (All Saints) *see* Brothertoft Gp *Linc*
HOLLAND-ON-SEA (St Bartholomew) *Chelmsf 23* **P** *Ch Patr Trust* **V** J W TURNER
HOLLAND ROAD (St John the Baptist) *see* Kensington St Jo *Lon*
HOLLESLEY (All Saints) *see* Wilford Peninsula *St E*
HOLLINFARE (St Helen) *see* Glazebury w Hollinfare *Liv*
HOLLINGBOURNE (All Saints) and Hucking w Leeds and Broomfield *Cant 14* **P** *Abp* **P-in-c** R M GILL, **C** N FRY, **OLM** N A DABBS
HOLLINGDEAN (St Richard) *see* Brighton St Matthias *Chich*
HOLLINGTON (St John the Evangelist) *see* Rocester and Croxden w Hollington *Lich*
HOLLINGTON (St John the Evangelist) (St Peter and St Paul) *Chich 17* **P** *Ch Patr Trust* **V** C D REDKNAP, **NSM** M HINKLEY
HOLLINGTON (St Leonard) (St Anne) *Chich 17* **P** *E G Brabazon Esq* **R** J G KENNEDY, **C** L A HARDING
HOLLINGWOOD (St Francis) *see* Staveley and Barrow Hill *Derby*
HOLLINGWORTH (St Hilda) *see* Milnrow *Man*
HOLLINGWORTH (St Mary) w Tintwistle *Ches 14* **P** *Patr Bd* **V** R A K LAW
HOLLINSWOOD (not known) *see* Cen Telford *Lich*
HOLLINWOOD (St Margaret) and Limeside *Man 19* **P** *Bp and V Prestwich (jt)* **V** D HAWTHORN
HOLLOWAY (Emmanuel) *see* Tollington *Lon*
HOLLOWAY Hanley Road (St Saviour) *as above*
HOLLOWAY (St Francis of Assisi) *see* W Holloway St Luke *Lon*
HOLLOWAY (St Mary Magdalene) *Lon 6* **P** *Bp and V Islington St Mary (jt)* **C** J K RUST
HOLLOWAY, UPPER (All Saints) *see* Tufnell Park St Geo and All SS *Lon*
HOLLOWAY, UPPER (St Andrew) (St John) (St Mary) (St Peter) *Lon 6* **P** *Patr Bd* **TR** S J W COX, **TV** R J POWELL, W K DORGU, **C** J B MURRAY, **NSM** P J R RAJKUMAR
HOLLOWAY, WEST (St Luke) *Lon 6* **P** *Lon Coll Div Trustees* **V** D W TOMLINSON
HOLLOWELL (St James) *see* Guilsborough w Hollowell and Cold Ashby *Pet*
HOLLY HALL (St Augustine) *see* Dudley St Aug Holly Hall *Worc*
HOLLY HILL (Church Centre) *see* Frankley *Birm*
HOLLYBUSH (All Saints) *see* Berrow w Pendock, Eldersfield, Hollybush etc *Worc*
HOLLYM (St Nicholas) *see* Patrington w Hollym, Welwick and Winestead *York*
HOLMBRIDGE (St David) *see* Upper Holme Valley *Wakef*
HOLMBURY ST MARY (St Mary the Virgin) *see* Wotton and Holmbury St Mary *Guildf*
HOLMCROFT (St Bertelin) *see* Stafford *Lich*
HOLME (All Saints) and Seaton Ross Group, The *York 5* **P** *St Jo Coll Cam and Ld Chan (alt)* **R** N T B STRAFFORD, **NSM** J H ANDERSON
HOLME (Holy Trinity) *see* Burton and Holme *Carl*
HOLME (St Giles) *see* Yaxley and Holme w Conington *Ely*
HOLME (St Giles) *see* Coddington and Winthorpe and Langford w Holme *S'well*
HOLME, EAST (St John the Evangelist) *see* Wareham *Sarum*
HOLME CULTRAM (St Cuthbert) *see* Solway Plain *Carl*
HOLME CULTRAM (St Mary) *as above*
HOLME EDEN (St Paul) and Wetheral w Warwick *Carl 2* **P** *D&C and DBP (jt)* **R** C A RANDALL, **C** K S CAPELIN-JONES, **NSM** P TIPLADY
HOLME HALE (St Andrew) *see* Necton, Holme Hale w N and S Pickenham *Nor*
HOLME-IN-CLIVIGER (St John) w Worsthorne *Blackb 3* **P** *Patr Bd* **V** L LAYCOCK
HOLME-NEXT-THE-SEA (St Mary) *see* Hunstanton St Mary w Ringstead Parva etc *Nor*
HOLME-ON-SPALDING-MOOR (All Saints) *see* Holme and Seaton Ross Gp *York*
HOLME-ON-SPALDING-MOOR (Old School Mission Room) *as above*
HOLME PIERREPONT (St Edmund King and Martyr) *see* Radcliffe-on-Trent and Shelford etc *S'well*
HOLME RUNCTON (St James) w South Runcton and Wallington *Ely 13* **P** *Bp* **R** J C W NOLAN
HOLME VALLEY, The UPPER *Wakef 6* **P** *Patr Bd* **TR** J S ROBERTSHAW, **TV** K GRIFFIN, G A BANKS, **NSM** M D ELLERTON, **OLM** G B BAMFORD
HOLME WOOD (St Christopher) *see* Tong *Bradf*
HOLMER (St Bartholomew) (St Mary) w Huntington *Heref 3* **P** *D&C* **V** P A WILLIAMS
HOLMER GREEN (Christ Church) *see* Penn Street *Ox*
HOLMES CHAPEL (St Luke) *see* Church Hulme *Ches*
HOLMESDALE (St Philip) *see* Dronfield w Holmesfield *Derby*
HOLMESFIELD (St Swithin) *as above*
HOLMEWOOD (St Alban Mission) *see* Heath *Derby*
HOLMFIELD (St Andrew) *see* Bradshaw and Holmfield *Wakef*
HOLMFIRTH (Holy Trinity) *see* Upper Holme Valley *Wakef*
HOLMPTON (St Nicholas) *see* Easington w Skeffling, Kilnsea and Holmpton *York*
HOLMSIDE (St John the Evangelist) *Dur 4* **P** *The Crown* **P-in-c** P WATERHOUSE
HOLMWOOD (St Mary Magdalene) *see* Surrey Weald *Guildf*
HOLMWOOD, NORTH (St John the Evangelist) *Guildf 12* **P** *Bp* **P-in-c** C A CORRY, **NSM** A M J HAVILAND
HOLNE (St Mary the Virgin) *see* Widecombe-in-the-Moor, Leusdon, Princetown etc *Ex*
HOLNEST (Church of the Assumption) *see* Dungeon Hill *Sarum*
HOLSWORTHY (St Peter and St Paul) w Hollacombe and Milton Damerel *Ex 17* **P** *DBP and Mrs F M Palmer (jt)* **R** R M REYNOLDS
HOLT (St Andrew) w High Kelling *Nor 18* **P** *St Jo Coll Cam* **R** H C STOKER, **NSM** J H DAVIES
HOLT (St James) *see* Horton, Chalbury, Hinton Martel and Holt St Jas *Sarum*
HOLT (St Katharine) *see* Broughton Gifford, Gt Chalfield and Holt *Sarum*
HOLT (St Martin) *see* Hallow and Grimley w Holt *Worc*
HOLTBY (Holy Trinity) *see* Stockton-on-the-Forest w Holtby and Warthill *York*
HOLTON (St Bartholomew) *see* Wheatley *Ox*
HOLTON (St Nicholas) *see* Camelot Par *B & W*
HOLTON (St Peter) *see* Blyth Valley *St E*
HOLTON-CUM-BECKERING (All Saints) *see* Wragby Gp *Linc*
HOLTON-LE-CLAY (St Peter) and Tetney *Linc 10* **P** *Ld Chan (2 turns), Bp (1 turn)* **V** C M WOADDEN
HOLTON-LE-MOOR (St Luke) *see* Kelsey Gp *Linc*
HOLTON ST MARY (St Mary) *see* Higham, Holton St Mary, Raydon and Stratford *St E*
HOLTS (St Hugh) Conventional District *Man 18 vacant* 0161-620 1646
HOLTSPUR (St Thomas) *see* Beaconsfield *Ox*
HOLTYE (St Peter) *see* Cowden w Hammerwood *Chich*
HOLWELL (St Laurence) *see* The Caundles w Folke and Holwell *Sarum*
HOLWELL (St Leonard) *see* Ab Kettleby and Holwell w Asfordby *Leic*
HOLWELL (St Mary the Virgin) *see* Shill Valley and Broadshire *Ox*
HOLWELL (St Peter), Ickleford and Pirton *St Alb 4* **P** *Bp and D&C Ely (jt)* **R** J A S PAYNE COOK, **NSM** M S HOLFORD
HOLWORTH (St Catherine by the Sea) *see* Watercombe *Sarum*
HOLY ISLAND (St Mary the Virgin) *Newc 12* **P** *Bp* **V** R J KIRKPATRICK
HOLYBOURNE (Holy Rood) *see* Froyle and Holybourne *Win*
HOLYMOORSIDE (St Peter) *see* Brampton St Thos *Derby*
HOLYSTONE (St Mary the Virgin) *see* Upper Coquetdale *Newc*
HOLYWELL (St Cross) *see* Ox St Mary V w St Cross and St Pet *Ox*
HOLYWELL (St John the Baptist) w Needingworth *Ely 9* **P** *Bp* **P-in-c** E J G STRICKLAND
HOLYWELL (St Mary) *see* Seghill *Newc*
HOMERSFIELD (St Mary) *see* S Elmham and Ilketshall *St E*
HOMERTON (Christ Church on the Mead) *see* Hackney Marsh *Lon*
HOMERTON (St Barnabas w St Paul) *as above*
HOMERTON (St Luke) *Lon 5* **P** *St Olave Hart Street Trustees* **V** I HARPER
HOMINGTON (St Mary the Virgin) *see* Chalke Valley *Sarum*
HONEYCHURCH (St Mary) *see* N Tawton, Bondleigh, Sampford Courtenay etc *Ex*

HONICKNOWLE (St Francis) *Ex 23* **P** *Ld Chan*
V P J MORGAN
HONILEY (St John the Baptist) *see* Hatton w Haseley, Rowington w Lowsonford etc *Cov*
HONING (St Peter and St Paul) *see* Smallburgh w Dilham w Honing and Crostwight *Nor*
HONINGHAM (St Andrew) *see* Hockering, Honingham, E and N Tuddenham *Nor*
HONINGTON (All Saints) *see* Shipston-on-Stour w Honington and Idlicote *Cov*
HONINGTON (All Saints) *see* Blackbourne *St E*
HONINGTON (St Wilfred) *see* Barkston and Hough Gp *Linc*
HONITON (St Michael) (St Paul), Gittisham, Combe Raleigh, Monkton and Awliscombe *Ex 5* **P** *DBP* **TR** J B HEDGES, **TV** A P SHEATH, **C** A E J POLLINGTON, **Hon C** R C H SAUNDERS
HONLEY (St Mary) *Wakef 1* **P** *R Almondbury*
V D K BARNES, **C** D L SMITH
HOO (All Hallows) *see* High Halstow w All Hallows and Hoo St Mary *Roch*
HOO (St Andrew and St Eustachius) *see* Charsfield w Debach, Monewden, Hoo etc *St E*
HOO (St Werburgh) *Roch 6* **P** *D&C* **V** A B HARDING
HOOBROOK (St Cecilia) *see* Kidderminster St Geo *Worc*
HOOE (St John the Evangelist) *see* Plymstock and Hooe *Ex*
HOOE (St Oswald) *Chich 14* **P** *Bp* **V** S R EARL
HOOK (St John the Evangelist) *Win 5* **P** *Bp* **R** N S VIGERS
HOOK (St Mary the Virgin) *see* Airmyn, Hook and Rawcliffe *Sheff*
HOOK (St Mary) w Warsash *Portsm 2* **P** *Bp* **V** A P NORRIS, **NSM** S J MORGAN
HOOK (St Paul) *S'wark 17* **P** *The Crown*
V C P HOLLINGSHURST, **OLM** D E HEATHER
HOOK COMMON (Good Shepherd) *see* Upton-on-Severn, Ripple, Earls Croome etc *Worc*
HOOK NORTON (St Peter) w Great Rollright, Swerford and Wigginton *Ox 3* **P** *Bp, DBP, BNC Ox, and Jes Coll Ox (jt)* **R** J ACREMAN, **Hon C** C G TURNER, **NSM** W CUNNINGHAM
HOOKE (St Giles) *see* Beaminster Area *Sarum*
HOOLE (All Saints) *Ches 2* **P** *Simeon's Trustees*
V R J KIRKLAND, **NSM** R ACKROYD
HOOLE (St Michael) *Blackb 5* **P** *Reps of Mrs E A Dunne and Mrs D Downes (jt)* **P-in-c** S P HUGHES
HOOLEY (Mission Hall) *see* Redhill St Jo *S'wark*
HOOTON (St Paul) *Ches 9* **P** *Trustees* **V** D G SARGENT
HOOTON PAGNELL (All Saints) *see* Bilham *Sheff*
HOOTON ROBERTS (St John) *see* Ravenfield, Hooton Roberts and Braithwell *Sheff*
HOPE (Holy Trinity) w Shelve *Heref 13* **P** *New Coll Ox (3 turns), J J C Coldwell Esq (1 turn)* **P-in-c** A KNIGHT, **NSM** M-L TOOP
HOPE (St James) *Man 6* **P** *Trustees* **V** D SHARPLES
HOPE (St Peter), Castleton and Bradwell *Derby 2* **P** *Bp and D&C Lich (jt)* **P-in-c** I A DAVIS
HOPE BAGOT (St John the Baptist) *see* Burford II w Greete and Hope Bagot *Heref*
HOPE BOWDLER (St Andrew) w Eaton-under-Heywood *Heref 11* **P** *DBP, Bp Birm, and Mrs R Bell (jt)*
P-in-c J GROVES
HOPE COVE (St Clements) *see* Salcombe and Malborough w S Huish *Ex*
HOPE MANSEL (St Michael) *see* Ross *Heref*
HOPE-UNDER-DINMORE (St Mary the Virgin) *see* Bodenham w Hope-under-Dinmore, Felton etc *Heref*
HOPESAY (St Mary the Virgin) *see* Hopesay *Heref*
HOPESAY (St Mary the Virgin) *Heref 10* **P** *Earl of Powis (3 turns), Mrs R E Bell (1 turn)* **P-in-c** R T SHAW
HOPTON (All Saints) *see* Stanton, Hopton, Market Weston, Barningham etc *St E*
HOPTON (St Peter) *see* Mid Trent *Lich*
HOPTON w Corton *Nor 9* **P** *Ld Chan and D&C (alt)*
V R A KEY
HOPTON, UPPER (St John the Evangelist) *see* Eastthorpe and Upper Hopton *Wakef*
HOPTON CASTLE (St Edward) *see* Clungunford w Clunbury and Clunton, Bedstone etc *Heref*
HOPTON WAFERS (St Michael and All Angels) *see* Cleobury Mortimer w Hopton Wafers etc *Heref*
HOPWAS (St Chad) *see* Tamworth *Lich*
HOPWOOD (St John) *see* Heywood *Man*
HORAM (Christ Church) (St James) *Chich 15* **P** *Bp*
V M D REDHOUSE
HORBLING (St Andrew) *see* Billingborough Gp *Linc*
HORBURY (St Peter and St Leonard) w Horbury Bridge (St John) *Wakef 12* **P** *Dean* **V** P TWISLETON, **NSM** J M PARTON
HORBURY JUNCTION (St Mary) *Wakef 12* **P** *DBP*
P-in-c A S MACPHERSON, **NSM** M D WALKER
HORDEN (St Mary) *Dur 2* **P** *Bp* **P-in-c** K SMITH
HORDLE (All Saints) *Win 11* **P** *Bp* **V** M G ANDERSON, **C** J E GRAINGER-SMITH, **NSM** A C PETTS
HORDLEY (St Mary the Virgin) *see* Baschurch and Weston Lullingfield w Hordley *Lich*
HORFIELD (Holy Trinity) *Bris 3* **P** *Bp* **P-in-c** J S F HADLEY, **C** E L L BAUGHAN
HORFIELD (St Gregory) *Bris 3* **P** *Bp* **P-in-c** J WILSON
HORHAM (St Mary) *see* Stradbroke, Horham, Athelington and Redlingfield *St E*
HORKESLEY, GREAT (All Saints) *see* W Bergholt and Gt Horkesley *Chelmsf*
HORKESLEY, GREAT (St John) *as above*
HORKESLEY, LITTLE (St Peter and St Paul) *see* Wormingford, Mt Bures and Lt Horkesley *Chelmsf*
HORKSTOW (St Maurice) *Linc 6* **P** *DBP* **V** G A PLUMB
HORLEY (St Bartholomew) (St Francis) (St Wilfrid) *S'wark 27* **P** *Patr Bd* **TV** S A HOLLOWAY, **P-in-c** S P DAVIE
HORLEY (St Etheldreda) *see* Ironstone *Ox*
HORLEY ROW (St Wilfrid) *see* Horley *S'wark*
HORMEAD (St Nicholas), Wyddial, Anstey, Brent Pelham and Meesden *St Alb 19* **P** *St Jo Coll Cam, Ch Coll Cam, and Bp (by turn)* **P-in-c** C L KIMBERLEY
HORN HILL (St Paul) *see* Chalfont St Peter *Ox*
HORN PARK (St Francis) *see* Eltham St Jo *S'wark*
HORNBLOTTON (St Peter) *see* Six Pilgrims *B & W*
HORNBY (St Margaret) w Claughton and Whittington w Arkhome and Gressingham *Blackb 14* **P** *Patr Bd*
V I H RENNIE, **NSM** S E EVANS
HORNBY (St Mary) *Ripon 4* **P** *D&C York* **V** D J CHRISTIE
HORNCASTLE (St Mary the Virgin) w Low Toynton *Linc 11* **P** *Bp (2 turns), Baroness Wiloughby de Eresby (1 turn)*
V M E BURSON-THOMAS, **C** A C V HARVEY, **NSM** J F PARKIN, A C FORD
HORNCHURCH Elm Park (St Nicholas) *see* Elm Park St Nic Hornchurch *Chelmsf*
HORNCHURCH (Holy Cross) *Chelmsf 2* **P** *Bp and New Coll Ox (alt)* **P-in-c** J B PARSONS
HORNCHURCH (St Andrew) (St George) (St Matthew and St John) *Chelmsf 2* **P** *New Coll Ox* **V** H R DIBBENS, **C** V N ARNOLD, M UDDIN, D W PARROTT, **NSM** S M PAPWORTH
HORNCHURCH, SOUTH (St John and St Matthew) *Chelmsf 2* **P** *MMCET* **V** R LOVE, **C** K S TURNER, **NSM** K D NORRIS
HORNDALE (St Francis) *see* Gt Aycliffe and Chilton *Dur*
HORNDON EAST (St Francis) and West Horndon w Little Warley and Childerditch *Chelmsf 7* **P** *Sir Antony Browne's Sch and Bp (by turn)* **P-in-c** S C WILLIAMS, **NSM** R WILLIAMS
HORNDON ON THE HILL (St Peter and St Paul) *see* Orsett and Bulphan and Horndon on the Hill *Chelmsf*
HORNE (St Mary) *see* Burstow w Horne *S'wark*
HORNING (St Benedict) *see* Ashmanhaugh, Barton Turf etc *Nor*
HORNINGHOLD (St Peter) *see* Hallaton w Horninghold and Allexton, Tugby etc *Leic*
HORNINGLOW (St John the Divine) *Lich 14* **P** *Trustees*
V M R FREEMAN, **C** I NEWTON
HORNINGSEA (St Peter) *Ely 3* **P** *St Jo Coll Cam*
P-in-c M C BOWERS
HORNINGSHAM (St John the Baptist) *see* Cley Hill Warminster *Sarum*
HORNINGTOFT (St Edmund) *see* Upper Wensum Village Gp *Nor*
HORNSEA (St Nicholas) w Atwick *York 11* **P** *Ld Chan*
V J R RICE-OXLEY
HORNSEY (Christ Church) *Lon 20* **P** *Bp* **V** D O AGBELUSI
HORNSEY (Holy Innocents) *Lon 20* **P** *Bp* **P-in-c** T D PIKE, **C** P J HENDERSON
HORNSEY (St Mary) (St George) *Lon 20* **P** *Bp*
R G B SEABROOK, **C** S TAYLOR, **Hon C** E NICOL, **NSM** C L FRANSELLA
HORNSEY RISE (St Mary) *see* Upper Holloway *Lon*
HORNTON (St John the Baptist) *see* Ironstone *Ox*
HORRABRIDGE (St John the Baptist) *see* Sampford Spiney w Horrabridge *Ex*
HORRINGER (St Leonard) *St E 13* **P** *Bp and DBP (jt)*
R C F TODD
HORSEHEATH (All Saints) *see* Linton *Ely*
HORSELL (St Mary the Virgin) *Guildf 12* **P** *Bp* **V** R JONES, **C** C A COSLETT, **NSM** B ASHLEY
HORSENDON (St Michael and All Angels) *see* Risborough *Ox*
HORSEY (All Saints) *see* Flegg Coastal Benefice *Nor*
HORSFORD (All Saints) and Horsham w Newton St Faith *Nor 2* **P** *Bp* **V** *vacant* (01603) 893537

HORSFORTH (St Margaret) *Ripon 7* **P** *Bp* **V** R E HAYES, **C** D L STEVENS
HORSHAM (Holy Trinity) (St Leonard) (St Mary the Virgin) (St Peter in the Causeway) *Chich 8* **P** *Patr Bd* **TR** D E E TANSILL, **TV** W E L SOUTER, M J BROADLEY, A G LOW, P J APTED, **C** K D LITTLEJOHN, **Hon C** E V WHEELER, **NSM** B SINTON
HORSHAM ST FAITH (St Mary and Andrew) *see* Horsford and Horsham w Newton St Faith *Nor*
HORSINGTON (All Saints) *see* Woodhall Spa Gp *Linc*
HORSINGTON (St John the Baptist) *see* Abbas and Templecombe w Horsington *B & W*
HORSLEY (Holy Trinity) *see* N Tyne and Redesdale *Newc*
HORSLEY (St Clement) and Denby *Derby 12* **P** *Bp and Mrs L B Palmer (jt)* **V** K W HORLESTON, **NSM** D C BEECH
HORSLEY (St Martin) *see* Nailsworth w Shortwood, Horsley etc *Glouc*
HORSLEY, EAST (St Martin) and Ockham w Hatchford and Downside *Guildf 10* **P** *D&C Cant and Bp (jt)* **R** B J PARADISE, **OLM** E A BURKE
HORSLEY, WEST (St Mary) *Guildf 10* **P** *Col A R N Weston* **R** A DELANEY
HORSLEY HILL (St Lawrence the Martyr) South Shields *Dur 15* **P** *D&C* **V** *vacant* 0191-456 1747
HORSLEY WOODHOUSE (St Susanna) *see* Morley w Smalley and Horsley Woodhouse *Derby*
HORSMONDEN (St Margaret) *Roch 8* **P** *Bp* **P-in-c** R J STEVEN
HORSPATH (St Giles) *see* Wheatley *Ox*
HORSTEAD (All Saints) *see* Coltishall w Gt Hautbois and Horstead *Nor*
HORSTED, LITTLE (St Michael and All Angels) *Chich 21* **P** *Rt Revd P J Ball* **R** B H WILCOX, **NSM** C HOWARTH
HORSTED KEYNES (St Giles) *Chich 6* **P** *Bp* **R** T D RAWDON-MOGG
HORTON (St James the Elder) and Little Sodbury *Glouc 7* **P** *Duke of Beaufort (1 turn), CPAS (2 turns)* **P-in-c** C B WRAY, **NSM** G H EDWARDS
HORTON (St Mary Magdalene) *see* Hardingstone and Horton and Piddington *Pet*
HORTON (St Mary the Virgin) *Newc 1* **P** *V Woodhorn w Newbiggin* **V** B T B BELL
HORTON (St Michael and All Angels) *see* Riverside *Ox*
HORTON (St Michael), Lonsdon and Rushton Spencer *Lich 8* **P** *Bp and R Leek and Meerbrook (jt)* **V** E J TOMLINSON
HORTON (St Peter) *see* Ilminster and Distr *B & W*
HORTON (St Wolfrida), Chalbury, Hinton Martel and Holt St James *Sarum 9* **P** *Earl of Shaftesbury and Qu Eliz Free Gr Sch (jt)* **V** *vacant* (01258) 840256
HORTON, GREAT (St John the Evangelist) *Bradf 2* **P** *V Bradf* **V** N G JONES, **NSM** L J SLOW, I SLATER
HORTON, LITTLE (All Saints) (St Oswald) *Bradf 2* **P** *Bp and J F Bardsley Esq (jt)* **V** A S TREASURE, **C** J W HINTON, **NSM** M M MALEK
HORTON-CUM-STUDLEY (St Barnabas) *see* Wheatley *Ox*
HORTON-IN-RIBBLESDALE (St Oswald) *see* Langcliffe w Stainforth and Horton *Bradf*
HORTON KIRBY (St Mary) and Sutton-at-Hone *Roch 2* **P** *Bp and D&C (jt)* **V** F C PAPANTONIOU
HORWICH (Holy Trinity) (St Catherine) (St Elizabeth) and Rivington *Man 11* **P** *Patr Bd* **TR** S FLETCHER, **TV** G C BURROWS, M C BEHREND, P E BERRY, **OLM** T LITHERLAND
HORWOOD (St Michael) *see* Newton Tracey, Horwood, Alverdiscott etc *Ex*
HORWOOD, GREAT (St James) *see* Winslow w Gt Horwood and Addington *Ox*
HORWOOD, LITTLE (St Nicholas) *see* Newton Longville and Mursley w Swanbourne etc *Ox*
HOSE (St Michael) *see* Vale of Belvoir Par *Leic*
HOTHAM (St Oswald) *York 13* **P** *Ld Chan* **P-in-c** C H GOULDER
HOTHFIELD (St Margaret) *see* Westwell, Hothfield, Eastwell and Boughton Aluph *Cant*
HOUGH GREEN (St Basil and All Saints) *Liv 13* **P** *Bp* **V** G C ELSMORE
HOUGH-ON-THE-HILL (All Saints) *see* Barkston and Hough Gp *Linc*
HOUGHAM (All Saints) *as above*
HOUGHAM (St Laurence) *see* Alkham w Capel le Ferne and Hougham *Cant*
HOUGHTON (All Saints) *see* Broughton, Bossington, Houghton and Mottisfont *Win*
HOUGHTON (St Giles) *see* Walsingham, Houghton and Barsham *Nor*
HOUGHTON (St John the Evangelist) (St Peter) *Carl 3* **P** *Trustees* **V** S N AUSTEN, **C** C G TINKER
HOUGHTON (St Martin) *see* E w W Rudham, Helhoughton etc *Nor*
HOUGHTON (St Mary) w Wyton *Ely 8* **P** *Bp* **P-in-c** E B ATLING
HOUGHTON (St Nicholas) *see* Bury w Houghton and Coldwaltham and Hardham *Chich*
HOUGHTON, GREAT (St Mary) *see* Cogenhoe and Gt and Lt Houghton w Brafield *Pet*
HOUGHTON, GREAT (St Michael and All Angels) Conventional District *Sheff 12 vacant*
HOUGHTON, LITTLE (St Mary the Blessed Virgin) *see* Cogenhoe and Gt and Lt Houghton w Brafield *Pet*
HOUGHTON, NEW (Christ Church) *see* E Scarsdale *Derby*
HOUGHTON CONQUEST (All Saints) *see* Wilshamstead and Houghton Conquest *St Alb*
HOUGHTON LE SPRING (St Michael and All Angels) *Dur 14* **P** *Bp* **R** I G WALLIS, **C** K L WASSALL
HOUGHTON-ON-THE-HILL (St Catharine) Keyham and Hungarton *Leic 5* **P** *Bp* **P-in-c** P M HOLLINGSWORTH
HOUGHTON REGIS (All Saints) (St Thomas) *St Alb 12* **P** *DBP* **V** B C D WHEELHOUSE, **C** S HALSTEAD
HOUND (St Edward the Confessor) (St Mary the Virgin) *Win 10* **P** *St Mary's Coll Win* **V** R W GOODHEW
HOUNSLOW (Holy Trinity) (St Paul) *Lon 11* **P** *Bp* **V** O C M ROSS, **C** A PETRINE, **NSM** G G WRIGLEY, P CLEMENT, N LAWRENCE
HOUNSLOW (St Stephen) *Lon 11* **P** *Bp* **V** R L RAMSDEN
HOUNSLOW WEST (Good Shepherd) *Lon 11* **P** *Bp* **V** K A BUCKLER, **Hon C** P R TOPHAM
HOVE (All Saints) (St Andrew Old Church) (St John the Baptist) (Holy Trinity) *Chich 4* **P** *Bp* **TR** D K WOSTENHOLM, **TV** C L WILSON, C G SPINKS, **C** P S J DOICK, **NSM** S UNDERDOWN
HOVE (Bishop Hannington Memorial Church) (Holy Cross) *Chich 4* **P** *Trustees* **P-in-c** P R MOON, **C** J B ERLEBACH, J DUDLEY-SMITH
HOVE (St Barnabas) and St Agnes *Chich 4* **P** *Bp and V Hove (alt)* **V** A R REED, **NSM** T J MACDONALD
HOVE St Patrick *Chich 4* **P** *Bp, V Hove, and V Brighton (jt)* **V** A B SHARPE
HOVE (St Philip) *see* Aldrington *Chich*
HOVERINGHAM (St Michael) *see* Thurgarton w Hoveringham and Bleasby etc *S'well*
HOVETON (St John) *see* Wroxham w Hoveton and Belaugh *Nor*
HOVETON (St Peter) *as above*
HOVINGHAM (All Saints) *see* The Street Par *York*
HOW CAPLE (St Andrew and St Mary) w Sollarshope, Sellack, Kings Caple, Foy, Hentland and Hoarwithy *Heref 8* **P** *Bp, D&C, and Brig A F L Clive (jt)* **R** *vacant* (01432) 840485
HOWARDIAN GROUP, The *York 6* **P** *Abp and Hon S B G Howard (jt)* **R** *vacant* (01653) 648226
HOWDEN Team Ministry, The (St Peter) *York 13* **P** *Abp (4 turns), Ld Chan (1 turn)* **TV** M S POSKITT
HOWDEN-LE-WEAR and Hunwick *Dur 9* **P** *Bp and V Auckland St Andr (alt)* **V** S IRWIN
HOWE (St Mary the Virgin) *see* Poringland *Nor*
HOWE BRIDGE (St Michael and All Angels) *see* Atherton and Hindsford w Howe Bridge *Man*
HOWELL (St Oswald) *see* Heckington *Linc*
HOWELL HILL (St Paul) w Burgh Heath *Guildf 9* **P** *Bp* **V** S A WILCOCKSON, **C** I M BLAKE, **NSM** B W RICHARDS, **OLM** S C FACCINI
HOWGILL (Holy Trinity) *see* Firbank, Howgill and Killington *Bradf*
HOWICK (St Michael and All Angels) *see* Longhoughton w Howick *Newc*
HOWLE HILL (St John the Evangelist) *see* Walford and St John w Bishopswood, Goodrich etc *Heref*
HOWSHAM (St John) *see* Sand Hutton *York*
HOXNE (St Peter and St Paul) w Denham, Syleham and Wingfield *St E 17* **P** *Bp and DBP (jt)* **R** A R LOWE
HOXTON (Holy Trinity) (St Mary) *Lon 5* **P** *Bp* **V** I C YOUNG
HOXTON (St Anne) (St Columba) *Lon 5* **P** *The Crown* **P-in-c** I C CZERNIAWSKA EDGCUMBE
HOXTON (St John the Baptist) w Ch Ch *Lon 5* **P** *Haberdashers' Co and Adn (jt)* **V** A I KEECH, **NSM** S C EJIAKU
HOYLAKE (Holy Trinity and St Hildeburgh) *Ches 8* **P** *Bp* **V** A HEZEL, **Hon C** D K CHESTER
HOYLAND (St Peter) (St Andrew) *Sheff 11* **P** *Bp and Sir Stephen Hastings (jt)* **V** N P HOLMES
HOYLAND, HIGH (All Saints), Scissett and Clayton West *Wakef 6* **P** *Bp* **R** *vacant* (01484) 862321

HOYLANDSWAINE (St John the Evangelist) and Silkstone w Stainborough *Wakef 7* **P** *Bp* **V** S A MOOR
HUBBERHOLME (St Michael and All Angels) *see* Kettlewell w Conistone, Hubberholme etc *Bradf*
HUCCABY (St Raphael) *see* Widecombe-in-the-Moor, Leusdon, Princetown etc *Ex*
HUCCLECOTE (St Philip and St James) *Glouc 5* **P** *Bp* **V** M R BURKE, **C** E C AMYES, G E AMYES
HUCKING (St Margaret) *see* Hollingbourne and Hucking w Leeds and Broomfield *Cant*
HUCKLOW, GREAT (Mission Room) *see* Hope, Castleton and Bradwell *Derby*
HUCKNALL TORKARD (St Mary Magdalene) (St Peter and St Paul) (St John's Mission Church) *S'well 4* **P** *Bp* **TR** L A CHURCH, **TV** P COMPTON, S W BATTEN, **C** C E WINDLE
HUDDERSFIELD All Saints (St Thomas) *Wakef 5* **P** *DBP* **V** *vacant* (01484) 530814
HUDDERSFIELD (Holy Trinity) *Wakef 5* **P** *Simeon's Trustees* **P-in-c** C C PRENTIS, **C** J M LAWSON, **NSM** R C SWINDELL, P T WILCOCK
HUDDERSFIELD (St John the Evangelist) *see* N Huddersfield *Wakef*
HUDDERSFIELD (St Peter) *Wakef 5* **P** *DBP* **V** C OGLE, **C** M R POLLARD
HUDDERSFIELD, NORTH (St Cuthbert) *Wakef 5* **P** *DBP* **TR** M J LOWLES, **TV** M R UMPLEBY
HUDDINGTON (St James) *see* Bowbrook S *Worc*
HUDSWELL (St Michael and All Angels) *see* Richmond w Hudswell and Downholme and Marske *Ripon*
HUGGATE (St Mary) *see* Nunburnholme and Warter and Huggate *York*
HUGGLESCOTE (St John the Baptist) w Donington, Ellistown and Snibston *Leic 8* **P** *Bp* **TR** J E HALL, **TV** V T GOODMAN
HUGHENDEN (St Michael) *Ox 29* **P** *DBP* **V** S N CRONK, **NSM** F J FRIEND
HUGHLEY (St John the Baptist) *see* Wenlock *Heref*
HUISH (St James the Less) *see* Shebbear, Buckland Filleigh, Sheepwash etc *Ex*
HUISH (St Nicholas) *see* Pewsey and Swanborough *Sarum*
HUISH, SOUTH (Holy Trinity) *see* Salcombe and Malborough w S Huish *Ex*
HUISH CHAMPFLOWER (St Peter) *see* Wiveliscombe w Chipstable, Huish Champflower etc *B & W*
HUISH EPISCOPI (Blessed Virgin Mary) *see* Langport Area Chs *B & W*
HULCOTE (St Nicholas) *see* Cranfield and Hulcote w Salford *St Alb*
HULCOTT (All Saints) *see* Aylesbury w Bierton and Hulcott *Ox*
HULL (Ascension) *see* Derringham Bank *York*
HULL (Holy Apostles) *see* Kingston upon Hull H Trin *York*
HULL (Most Holy and Undivided Trinity) *as above*
HULL (St Aidan) Southcoates *see* Kingston upon Hull St Aid Southcoates *York*
HULL (St Alban) *see* Kingston upon Hull St Alb *York*
HULL (St Cuthbert) *York 14* **P** *Abp* **V** A M LAIRD
HULL (St George) *see* Marfleet *York*
HULL (St Giles) *as above*
HULL (St Hilda) *as above*
HULL (St John) Newland *York 14* **P** *Abp* **V** M TINKER, **C** L J MCMUNN, N J BUTTERY, M C BRAILSFORD
HULL (St John the Baptist) *see* Newington w Dairycoates *York*
HULL (St Martin) w The Transfiguration *York 14* **P** *Abp* **V** S R J ELLIOTT
HULL (St Mary) Sculcoates *York 14* **P** *V Sculcoates* **P-in-c** J G LEEMAN
HULL (St Mary the Virgin) Lowgate *see* Kingston upon Hull St Mary *York*
HULL (St Matthew w St Barnabas) *see* Kingston upon Hull St Matt w St Barn *York*
HULL (St Nicholas) *see* Kingston upon Hull St Nic *York*
HULL (St Paul) *see* Sculcoates *York*
HULL (St Philip) *see* Marfleet *York*
HULL (St Stephen) *see* Sculcoates *York*
HULL (St Thomas) *see* Derringham Bank *York*
HULL, NORTH (St Michael and All Angels) *York 14* **P** *Abp* **V** D A WALKER, **C** M J LEIGH
HULLAND (Christ Church), Atlow, Kniveton, Bradley and Hognaston *Derby 8* **P** *Patr Bd* **R** C A MITCHELL
HULLAVINGTON (St Mary Magdalene), Norton and Stanton St Quintin *Bris 6* **P** *Bp, Eton Coll, and R W Neeld Esq (jt)* **R** A EVANS
HULLBRIDGE (St Thomas of Canterbury) *Chelmsf 12* **P** *Bp* **V** W H REED
HULME (Ascension) *Man 4* **P** *Trustees* **R** A J SERVANT, **C** K FLOOD
HULME WALFIELD (St Michael) *see* Eaton and Hulme Walfield *Ches*
HULTON, LITTLE (St John the Baptist) *see* Walkden and Lt Hulton *Man*
HULTON, OVER (St Andrew) *see* Deane *Man*
HUMBER (St Mary the Virgin) *see* Leominster *Heref*
HUMBERSTON (St Peter) *Linc 10* **P** *Bp* **V** B V EAST
HUMBERSTONE (St Mary) *see* Ascension TM *Leic*
HUMBERSTONE, NEW (St Barnabas) *see* Leic Presentation *Leic*
HUMBLE, WEST (St Michael) *see* Leatherhead and Mickleham *Guildf*
HUMBLETON (St Peter) *see* Burton Pidsea and Humbleton w Elsternwick *York*
HUMPHREY PARK (St Clement) *see* Urmston *Man*
HUMSHAUGH (St Peter) w Simonburn and Wark *Newc 2* **P** *Bp* **R** J M THOMPSON
HUNCOAT (St Augustine) *see* Accrington St Jo w Huncoat *Blackb*
HUNCOTE (St James the Greater) *see* Narborough and Huncote *Leic*
HUNDLEBY (St Mary) *see* Spilsby Gp *Linc*
HUNDON (All Saints) *see* Stour Valley *St E*
HUNDRED RIVER Benefice, The *St E 14* **P** *DBP, Shadingfield Properties Ltd, Bp, Miss to Seamen, and F D L Barnes Esq (by turn)* **R** P J NELSON, **OLM** J M LOFTUS, S K NEAL
HUNGARTON (St John the Baptist) *see* Houghton-on-the-Hill, Keyham and Hungarton *Leic*
HUNGERFORD (St Lawrence) and Denford *Ox 14* **P** *D&C Windsor* **V** A W SAWYER
HUNMANBY (All Saints) w Muston *York 15* **P** *MMCET* **V** J W R HATTAN, **NSM** M R SHAW
HUNNINGHAM (St Margaret) *Cov 10* **P** *Ld Chan* **P-in-c** J T H BRITTON, **C** D R PATTERSON
HUNSDON (St Dunstan) (St Francis) w Widford and Wareside *St Alb 22* **P** *DBP* **R** J RISBY
HUNSINGORE (St John the Baptist) *see* Lower Nidderdale *Ripon*
HUNSLET (St Mary the Virgin) w Cross Green *Ripon 6* **P** *Keble Coll Ox, Bp and TR Leeds City (jt)* **V** P ANDERTON
HUNSLET MOOR (St Peter's Christian Community Centre) *see* Beeston Hill and Hunslet Moor *Ripon*
HUNSLEY (St Peter) *see* Rowley w Skidby *York*
HUNSTANTON (St Edmund) w Ringstead *Nor 16* **P** *H Le Strange Esq* **V** J S BLOOMFIELD
HUNSTANTON (St Mary) w Ringstead Parva, Holme-next-the-Sea, Thornham, Brancaster, Burnham Deepdale and Titchwell *Nor 16* **P** *Bp, Exors of the late H le Strange Esq, and Exors of the late H S N Simms-Adams Esq (jt)* **R** L H CAMPBELL, **NSM** R L EASEMAN
HUNSTANWORTH (St James) *see* Blanchland w Hunstanworth and Edmundbyers etc *Newc*
HUNSTON (St Leodegar) *see* N Mundham w Hunston and Merston *Chich*
HUNSTON (St Michael) *see* Badwell and Walsham *St E*
HUNTINGDON (All Saints w St John the Baptist) (St Barnabas) (St Mary) *Ely 8* **P** *Bp* **TR** A J MILTON, **TV** J M SAVAGE, **C** N E DEVENISH, **Hon C** M D KETTLE
HUNTINGFIELD (St Mary) *see* Heveningham *St E*
HUNTINGTON (All Saints) *York 7* **P** *Patr Bd* **TR** K J DAVIES, **TV** F R SCOTT
HUNTINGTON (St Luke) *Ches 2* **P** *Bp* **V** I J HUTCHINGS
HUNTINGTON (St Mary Magdalene) *see* Holmer w Huntington *Heref*
HUNTINGTON (St Thomas) *see* Cannock *Lich*
HUNTINGTON (St Thomas à Becket) *see* Kington w Huntington, Old Radnor, Kinnerton etc *Heref*
HUNTLEY (St John the Baptist) and Longhope, Churcham and Bulley *Glouc 3* **P** *Bp and D&C (jt)* **R** M E THOMPSON
HUNTON (St James) *see* Lower Dever Valley *Win*
HUNTON (St Mary) *see* Coxheath, E Farleigh, Hunton, Linton etc *Roch*
HUNTS CROSS (St Hilda) *Liv 4* **P** *Bp* **V** *vacant* 0151-486 1220
HUNTSHAM (All Saints) *see* Sampford Peverell, Uplowman, Holcombe Rogus etc *Ex*
HUNTSHAW (St Mary Magdalene) *see* Newton Tracey, Horwood, Alverdiscott etc *Ex*
HUNTSPILL (St Peter and All Hallows) *B & W 1* **P** *Ball Coll Ox* **R** G M WALSH
HUNWICK (St Paul) *see* Howden-le-Wear and Hunwick *Dur*
HUNWORTH (St Lawrence) *see* Brinton, Briningham, Hunworth, Stody etc *Nor*

HURDSFIELD (Holy Trinity) *Ches 13* **P** *Hyndman Trustees* **V** I M RUMSEY, **NSM** M J OWENS
HURLEY (Resurrection) *see* Baxterley w Hurley and Wood End and Merevale etc *Birm*
HURLEY (St Mary the Virgin) *see* Burchetts Green *Ox*
HURSLEY (All Saints) and Ampfield *Win 12* **P** *T H Faber Esq and Lord Lifford (jt)* **V** R B EDWARDS, **NSM** L M ROBERTSON
HURST *see* Fawkenhurst *Cant*
HURST (St John the Evangelist) *Man 17* **P** *The Crown* **V** A L OWENS, **OLM** A G LEES
HURST (St Nicholas) *Ox 16* **P** *Bp* **Hon C** C SMITH
HURST GREEN (Holy Trinity) *Chich 15* **P** *Bp* **V** R DIXON
HURST GREEN (St John the Evangelist) *S'wark 26* **P** *Bp* **V** D F G BUTLIN, **NSM** M J SELLER
HURST GREEN (St John the Evangelist) and Mitton *Bradf 5* **P** *Bp and J E R Aspinall Esq (jt)* **P-in-c** S G RIDLEY
HURSTBOURNE PRIORS (St Andrew), Longparish, St Mary Bourne and Woodcott *Win 6* **P** *Bp and J C Woodcock Esq (jt)* **V** M A COPPEN, **NSM** N M HARRISON, D M MARSDEN
HURSTBOURNE TARRANT (St Peter) and Faccombe and Vernham Dean and Linkenholt *Win 3* **P** *Bp* **V** A T R GOODE, **NSM** P A MILLS
HURSTPIERPOINT (Holy Trinity) (St George) *Chich 9* **P** *Hurstpierpoint Coll* **R** J B A JOYCE
HURSTWOOD, HIGH (Holy Trinity) *Chich 21* **P** *Abp* **P-in-c** M COXHEAD
HURWORTH (All Saints) *Dur 8* **P** *Ch Soc Trust* **R** M D M FERGUSON
HUSBANDS BOSWORTH (All Saints) w Mowsley and Knaptoft and Theddingworth *Leic 4* **P** *DBP (2 turns), Bp (1 turn)* **P-in-c** B STANTON
HUSBORNE CRAWLEY (St Mary Magdalene or St James) *see* Aspley Guise w Husborne Crawley and Ridgmont *St Alb*
HUSTHWAITE (St Nicholas) *see* Coxwold and Husthwaite *York*
HUTHWAITE (All Saints) *S'well 4* **P** *V Sutton-in-Ashfield* **P-in-c** C A K MAIDEN, **NSM** J L ALLEN
HUTTOFT (St Margaret) *see* Sutton, Huttoft and Anderby *Linc*
HUTTON (All Saints) (St Peter) *Chelmsf 7* **P** *D&C St Paul's* **R** R WALLACE, **C** B C WALLACE
HUTTON (Blessed Virgin Mary) *B & W 11* **P** *DBP* **R** B N STEVENSON
HUTTON, NEW (St Stephen) *see* Grayrigg, Old Hutton and New Hutton *Carl*
HUTTON, OLD (St John the Evangelist) *as above*
HUTTON BONVILLE (St Laurence) *see* E Richmond *Ripon*
HUTTON BUSCEL (St Matthew) *see* Brompton by Sawdon w Hutton Buscel, Snainton etc *York*
HUTTON CRANSWICK (St Peter) w Skerne, Watton and Beswick *York 10* **P** *Abp* **V** *vacant* (01377) 270402
HUTTON HENRY (St Francis) *see* Wheatley Hill and Wingate w Hutton Henry *Dur*
HUTTON-IN-THE-FOREST (St James) *see* Inglewood Gp *Carl*
HUTTON-LE-HOLE (St Chad) *see* Lastingham w Appleton-le-Moors, Rosedale etc *York*
HUTTON MAGNA (St Mary) *see* Barningham w Hutton Magna and Wycliffe *Ripon*
HUTTON ROOF (St John the Divine) *see* Kirkby Lonsdale *Carl*
HUTTON RUDBY (All Saints) *see* Rudby in Cleveland w Middleton *York*
HUTTONS AMBO (St Margaret) *see* Howardian Gp *York*
HUXHAM (St Mary the Virgin) *see* Stoke Canon, Poltimore w Huxham and Rewe etc *Ex*
HUXLEY (St Andrew) *see* Hargrave *Ches*
HUYTON (St George) *Liv 2* **P** *Bp* **C** D A GREEN
HUYTON (St Michael) *Liv 2* **P** *Earl of Derby* **V** J A STANLEY
HUYTON QUARRY (St Gabriel) *Liv 2* **P** *V Huyton St Mich* **V** M K ROGERS
HYDE (Holy Ascension) *see* Ellingham and Harbridge and Hyde w Ibsley *Win*
HYDE (Holy Trinity) Gee Cross *see* Gee Cross *Ches*
HYDE (St George) *Ches 14* **P** *R Stockport St Mary* **V** S J WILSON, **C** A BROWN, J BROWN
HYDE (St John the Baptist) Godley cum Newton Green *see* Godley cum Newton Green *Ches*
HYDE (St Mary) Newton in Mottram *see* Newton in Mottram *Ches*
HYDE (St Stephen) Newton Flowery Field *see* Newton Flowery Field *Ches*
HYDE (St Thomas) *Ches 14* **P** *Bp* **P-in-c** P O BENNISON
HYDE, EAST (Holy Trinity) *see* Woodside w E Hyde *St Alb*
HYDE, WEST (St Thomas) *see* Mill End and Heronsgate w W Hyde *St Alb*
HYDE HEATH (Mission Church) *see* Lt Missenden *Ox*
HYDE PARK CRESCENT (St John) *see* Paddington St Jo w St Mich *Lon*
HYDNEYE, THE (St Peter) *Chich 16* **P** *Bp* **V** C R GORING, **NSM** J MANN
HYKEHAM (All Saints) (St Hugh) (St Michael and All Angels) *Linc 18* **P** *Ld Chan and Bp (alt)* **TR** R S EYRE, **C** C M TURNER, **NSM** G F REID
HYLTON, SOUTH (St Mary) *Dur 16* **P** *Bp* **V** J E RUSCOE
HYSON GREEN (St Stephen) and Forest Fields *S'well 12* **P** *CPAS* **P-in-c** R E WORSLEY, **C** G J BURTON, C J COOKE
HYSSINGTON (St Etheldreda) *see* Churchstoke w Hyssington and Sarn *Heref*
HYTHE Butts Ash (St Anne) *see* Hythe *Win*
HYTHE (St John the Baptist) *Win 11* **P** *Bp* **V** E J WETHERELL
HYTHE (St Leonard) (St Michael and All Angels) *Cant 5* **P** *R Saltwood* **V** B BARNES, **C** E M RICHARDSON
HYTHE, WEST (St Mary) *see* Aldington w Bonnington and Bilsington etc *Cant*
IBBERTON (St Eustace) *see* Hazelbury Bryan and the Hillside Par *Sarum*
IBSTOCK (St Denys) w Heather *Leic 8* **P** *Bp and MMCET (jt)* **R** R A WHITE
IBSTONE (St Nicholas) *see* Stokenchurch and Ibstone *Ox*
ICKBURGH (St Peter) w Langford *Nor 13* **P** *Bp* **P-in-c** P M FARROW
ICKENHAM (St Giles) *Lon 24* **P** *Eton Coll* **R** A M GUTHRIE, **NSM** K R TOMBS
ICKFORD (St Nicholas) *see* Worminghall w Ickford, Oakley and Shabbington *Ox*
ICKHAM (St John the Evangelist) *see* Littlebourne and Ickham w Wickhambreaux etc *Cant*
ICKLEFORD (St Katherine) *see* Holwell, Ickleford and Pirton *St Alb*
ICKLESHAM (St Nicolas) *see* Winchelsea and Icklesham *Chich*
ICKLETON (St Mary Magdalene) *Ely 6* **P** *Ld Chan* **P-in-c** A T SCHOFIELD
ICKLINGHAM (All Saints w St James) *see* Mildenhall *St E*
ICKNIELD *Ox 1* **P** *Ld Chan (1 turn), Ch Ch Ox (1 turn), Bp and Earl of Macclesfield (1 turn)* **R** C I EVANS, **C** S O GRIFFITHS, **NSM** A M PATERSON
ICOMB (St Mary) *see* Broadwell, Evenlode, Oddington, Adlestrop etc *Glouc*
IDBURY (St Nicholas) *see* Shipton-under-Wychwood w Milton, Fifield etc *Ox*
IDDESLEIGH (St James) w Dowland *Ex 20* **P** *Bp* **P-in-c** A S GRAESSER
IDE (St Ida) *see* Dunchideock and Shillingford St George w Ide *Ex*
IDE HILL (St Mary the Virgin) *see* Sundridge w Ide Hill and Toys Hill *Roch*
IDEFORD (St Mary the Virgin) *see* Teignmouth, Ideford w Luton, Ashcombe etc *Ex*
IDEN (All Saints) *see* Rye *Chich*
IDLE (Holy Trinity) *Bradf 3* **P** *V Calverley* **V** D A JOHNSON
IDLICOTE (St James the Great) *see* Shipston-on-Stour w Honington and Idlicote *Cov*
IDRIDGEHAY (St James) *see* Wirksworth *Derby*
IDSWORTH (St Hubert) *see* Blendworth w Chalton w Idsworth *Portsm*
IFFLEY (St Mary the Virgin) *Ox 4* **P** *Ch Ch Ox* **V** R J R LEA, **NSM** D D HANNAH
IFIELD (St Margaret) *Chich 7* **P** *Bp* **TR** L W DOOLAN, **TV** D G STANIFORD, **C** H C JEVONS, **NSM** D M GOODWIN, M P HANSON
IFIELD (St Margaret) *see* Gravesend H Family w Ifield *Roch*
IFORD (St Nicholas) w Kingston and Rodmell *Chich 18* **P** *Bp* **V** G M DAW
IFORD (St Saviour) *see* Holdenhurst and Iford *Win*
IGHTFIELD (St John the Baptist) *see* Adderley, Ash, Calverhall, Ightfield etc *Lich*
IGHTHAM (St Peter) *Roch 10* **P** *C B Winnifrith Esq* **P-in-c** P D MCGRATH
IKEN (St Botolph) *see* Wilford Peninsula *St E*
ILAM (Holy Cross) *see* Alstonfield, Butterton, Ilam etc *Lich*
ILCHESTER (St Mary Major) w Northover, Limington, Yeovilton and Podimore *B & W 6* **P** *Bp Lon (7 turns), Bp (1 turn), and Wadh Coll Ox (1 turn)* **R** C F H SUTCLIFFE
ILDERTON (St Michael) *see* Glendale Gp *Newc*
ILFORD, GREAT (St Alban) *Chelmsf 4* **P** *Bp* **V** D I MILNES
ILFORD, GREAT (St Andrew) *Chelmsf 4* **P** *Bp* **V** R A D ENEVER, **NSM** J W ENEVER

ILFORD, GREAT (St John the Evangelist) *Chelmsf 4* **P** *Bp* **V** G M TARRY, **C** E A GUEST, **NSM** A C OKWUOSA
ILFORD, GREAT (St Luke) *Chelmsf 4* **P** *Bp* **P-in-c** J BROWN, **Hon C** A W M RITCHIE
ILFORD, GREAT (St Margaret of Antioch) (St Clement) *Chelmsf 4* **P** *Patr Bd* **V** S G PUGH
ILFORD, GREAT (St Mary) *Chelmsf 4* **P** *V Gt Ilford* **V** J G F KESTER, **C** J R WOOLNOUGH
ILFORD, LITTLE (St Barnabas) *Chelmsf 3* **P** *Bp* **P-in-c** J A RAMSAY
ILFORD, LITTLE (St Michael and All Angels) *Chelmsf 3* **P** *Hertf Coll Ox* **R** B J LEWIS, **C** J R BULLOCK, K L A FARRELL
ILFRACOMBE (Holy Trinity) (St Peter), Lee, Woolacombe, Bittadon and Mortehoe *Ex 15* **P** *Patr Bd* **TR** N JACKSON-STEVENS, **TV** G A B KING-SMITH
ILFRACOMBE (St Philip and St James) w West Down *Ex 15* **P** *Bp and Ch Trust Fund Trust (jt)* **P-in-c** J J CLARK
ILKESTON (Holy Trinity) *Derby 13* **P** *Bp* **V** A M COLE
ILKESTON (St John the Evangelist) *Derby 13* **P** *V Ilkeston St Mary* **C** A J FISHER
ILKESTON (St Mary the Virgin) *Derby 13* **P** *Bp* **V** A J BROWN, **C** D FERGUS, **NSM** G L HALLIDAY
ILKETSHALL ST ANDREW (St Andrew) *see* Wainford *St E*
ILKETSHALL ST JOHN (St John the Baptist) *see* S Elmham and Ilketshall *St E*
ILKETSHALL ST LAWRENCE (St Lawrence) *as above*
ILKETSHALL ST MARGARET (St Margaret) *as above*
ILKLEY (All Saints) *Bradf 4* **P** *Hyndman Trustees* **V** P Q TUDGE
ILKLEY (St Margaret) *Bradf 4* **P** *CR* **P-in-c** D M HOPE OFTHORNES, **NSM** A G BROWN, R G KELLETT
ILLINGWORTH (St Mary) *Wakef 4* **P** *V Halifax* **V** *vacant* (01422) 244322 *or* 246668
ILLOGAN (St Illogan) *see* St Illogan *Truro*
ILLSTON (St Michael and All Angels) *see* Gaulby *Leic*
ILMER (St Peter) *see* Risborough *Ox*
ILMINGTON (St Mary) and Stretton-on-Fosse and Ditchford w Preston-on-Stour w Whitchurch and Atherstone-on-Stour *Cov 9* **P** *Bp, MMCET, and Ms C A Alston-Roberts-West (jt)* **R** B MERRINGTON
ILMINSTER (Blessed Virgin Mary) and District *B & W 15* **P** *Patr Bd* **TR** A R WALLACE, **TV** A F TATHAM, G A WADE, **C** E J SCOTT, **NSM** N P M WHINNEY
ILSINGTON (St Michael) *Ex 9* **P** *D&C Windsor* **V** *vacant* (01364) 661245
ILSLEY, EAST (St Mary) *see* Hermitage *Ox*
ILSLEY, WEST (All Saints) *see* Beedon and Peasemore w W Ilsley and Farnborough *Ox*
ILTON (St Peter) *see* Ilminster and Distr *B & W*
IMMINGHAM (St Andrew) *Linc 10* **P** *DBP* **P-in-c** M W PAGE-CHESTNEY, **NSM** S V PAGE-CHESTNEY
IMPINGTON (St Andrew) *Ely 5* **P** *Adn Ely* **C** K A HODGINS, **NSM** J M GLOVER
INCE (St James) *see* Thornton-le-Moors w Ince and Elton *Ches*
INCE IN MAKERFIELD (Christ Church) (St Christopher) *Liv 14* **P** *Simeon's Trustees* **C** L RILEY
INCE IN MAKERFIELD (St Mary) *Liv 14* **P** *Simeon's Trustees* **V** D W LONG
INDIAN QUEEN (St Francis) *see* St Enoder *Truro*
INGATESTONE (St Edmund and St Mary) w Fryerning *Chelmsf 7* **P** *Bp and Wadh Coll Ox (jt)* **V** P SHERRING, **NSM** S E CRUSE
INGESTRE (St Mary the Virgin) *see* Stafford St Jo and Tixall w Ingestre *Lich*
INGHAM (All Saints) w Cammeringham w Fillingham *Linc 3* **P** *Bp and Ball Coll Ox (jt)* **V** *vacant* (01522) 730519
INGHAM (Holy Trinity) *see* Stalham, E Ruston, Brunstead, Sutton and Ingham *Nor*
INGHAM (St Bartholomew) *see* Blackbourne *St E*
INGLEBY ARNCLIFFE (All Saints) *see* Osmotherley w Harlsey and Ingleby Arncliffe *York*
INGLEBY BARWICK (St Francis) *York 21* **P** *Abp* **V** D S WATSON, **C** P E SEYMOUR
INGLEBY GREENHOW (St Andrew) w Bilsdale Priory, Kildale and Westerdale *York 21* **P** *Abp, Adn Cleveland, Bp Whitby, Viscount de l'Isle, R G Beckett Esq, and A H W Sutcliffe Esq (jt)* **V** *vacant* (01642) 723947
INGLETON (St John the Evangelist) *Dur 8* **P** *Lord Barnard* **P-in-c** K STEVENTON, **NSM** D J ELLEANOR
INGLETON (St Mary the Virgin) w Chapel le Dale *Bradf 6* **P** *Bp* **V** C H ELLIS
INGLEWOOD Group, The *Carl 4* **P** *Bp, D&C, CCC Ox, and E P Ecroyd Esq (jt)* **R** E M SMITH, **C** R C PATTINSON, **NSM** J J H SMITH
INGOL (St Margaret) *Blackb 13* **P** *Bp* **V** M S HATTON
INGOLDISTHORPE (St Michael) *see* Snettisham w Ingoldisthorpe and Fring *Nor*
INGOLDMELLS (St Peter and St Paul) *see* Skegness Gp *Linc*
INGOLDSBY (St Bartholomew) *Linc 14* **P** *Ch Coll Cam, Sir Lyonel Tollemache Bt, D&C, Bp, and DBP (by turn)* **OLM** I R WALTERS
INGRAM (St Michael) *see* Glendale Gp *Newc*
INGRAVE (St Nicholas) (St Stephen) *Chelmsf 7* **P** *Bp and Ch Patr Trust (jt)* **V** A P PARSONS
INGRAVE (St Stephen) Conventional District *Chelmsf 7* **NSM** J A SEDANO
INGROW (St John the Evangelist) cum Hainworth *Bradf 8* **P** *Bp* **V** C H KIRKE
INGS (St Anne) *see* Staveley, Ings and Kentmere *Carl*
INGWORTH (St Lawrence) *see* Erpingham w Calthorpe, Ingworth, Aldborough etc *Nor*
INHAM NOOK (St Barnabas) *see* Chilwell *S'well*
INKBERROW (St Peter) w Cookhill and Kington w Dormston *Worc 1* **P** *Bp* **R** N M WRIGHT, **C** D GEORGE
INKERSALL (St Columba) *see* Staveley and Barrow Hill *Derby*
INKPEN (St Michael) *see* W Woodhay w Enborne, Hampstead Marshall etc *Ox*
INNS COURT (Holy Cross) *Bris 1* **P** *Bris Ch Trustees* **V** *vacant* 0117-966 4123
INSKIP (St Peter) *see* Copp w Inskip *Blackb*
INSTOW (All Saints Chapel) (St John the Baptist) *Ex 16* **P** *Christie Trustees* **P-in-c** C A C COOPER
INTAKE (All Saints) *see* Doncaster Intake *Sheff*
INTWOOD (All Saints) *see* Swardeston w E Carleton, Intwood, Keswick etc *Nor*
INWARDLEIGH (St Petroc) *see* Okehampton w Inwardleigh, Bratton Clovelly etc *Ex*
INWORTH (All Saints) *see* Copford w Easthorpe and Messing w Inworth *Chelmsf*
IPING (St Mary) *see* Stedham w Iping *Chich*
IPPLEPEN (St Andrew), Torbryan and Denbury *Ex 10* **P** *D&C Windsor and SMF (jt)* **V** I C EGLIN
IPSDEN (St Mary the Virgin) *see* Langtree *Ox*
IPSLEY (St Peter) *Worc 7* **P** *Patr Bd* **TR** W BROWN, **TV** A J KELSO, A E J TOSTEVIN, **NSM** J W DAVEY, C WAUDBY
IPSTONES (St Leonard) w Berkhamsytch and Onecote w Bradnop *Lich 6* **P** *Bp and R Leek and Meerbrook (jt)* **V** C M SCARGILL, **OLM** M J EVANS
IPSWICH (All Hallows) *St E 4* **P** *Bp* **V** R F TOBIN, **OLM** S J POTTER
IPSWICH (All Saints) *St E 4* **P** *Bp* **V** A G WILCOX
IPSWICH (St Andrew) *St E 4* **P** *Bp* **V** S R LLOYD
IPSWICH (St Augustine of Hippo) *St E 4* **P** *Bp* **V** L F SIMPKINS, **C** P A SHULER
IPSWICH (St Bartholomew) *St E 4* **P** *Bp* **V** P J CARTER
IPSWICH (St Helen) (Holy Trinity) (St Clement w St Luke) *St E 4* **P** *Ch Patr Trust* **R** P R DALTRY, **C** C D KEYS
IPSWICH (St John the Baptist) *St E 4* **P** *Simeon's Trustees* **V** K WHITE, **C** D J MIDDLETON, **NSM** M GREEN, **OLM** L G THORPE
IPSWICH (St Margaret) *St E 4* **P** *Simeon's Trustees* **V** D CUTTS
IPSWICH (St Mary at Stoke) (St Peter) (St Francis) (St Clare's Church Centre) *St E 4* **P** *Bp* **TR** I D J MORGAN, **TV** C G G EVERETT, M S G MORGAN
IPSWICH (St Mary at the Elms) *St E 4* **P** *PCC* **P-in-c** J H DOSSOR
IPSWICH (St Mary-le-Tower) (St Nicholas) *St E 4* **P** *Bp (3 turns), Ch Patr Trust (1 turn)* **V** P K TOWNLEY, **NSM** D J WARNES
IPSWICH (St Matthew) *St E 4* **P** *Ld Chan* **P-in-c** N S ATKINS, **C** J I SEARS
IPSWICH (St Thomas) *St E 4* **P** *Bp* **V** P BOURNER, **OLM** B F ROSE
IRBY (St Chad's Mission Church) *see* Thurstaston *Ches*
IRBY-IN-THE-MARSH (All Saints) *see* Bratoft w Irby-in-the-Marsh *Linc*
IRBY ON HUMBER (St Andrew) *see* Laceby and Ravendale Gp *Linc*
IRCHESTER (St Katharine) *Pet 10* **P** *Bp* **V** J SIMMONS
IRCHESTER, LITTLE (St John) *see* Irchester *Pet*
IREBY (St James) *see* Binsey *Carl*
IRELAND WOOD (St Paul) *Ripon 7* **P** *R Adel* **V** C R CORNWELL, **C** R J COX
IRLAM (St John the Baptist) *Man 2* **P** *Trustees* **OLM** J DODD, J STEPHENS
IRNHAM (St Andrew) *see* Corby Glen *Linc*
IRON ACTON (St James the Less) *Bris 5* **P** *Ch Ch Ox* **P-in-c** S E RUSHTON, **NSM** J D TAILBY

IRON-BRIDGE (St Luke) *see* Coalbrookdale, Iron-Bridge and Lt Wenlock *Heref*
IRONSTONE: Drayton, Hanwell, Horley, Hornton, Shenington w Alkerton, and Wroxton w Balscote *Ox 5* **P** *Ld Chan (1 turn), Bp, Earl De la Warr, and DBP (1 turn)* **R** R J CHARD, **NSM** P C SMITH
IRONVILLE (Christ Church) *see* Riddings and Ironville *Derby*
IRSTEAD (St Michael) *see* Ashmanhaugh, Barton Turf etc *Nor*
IRTHINGTON (St Kentigern) *see* Eden, Gelt and Irthing *Carl*
IRTHLINGBOROUGH (St Peter) *Pet 10* **P** *Sir Stephen Hastings* **R** J R WESTWOOD
IRTON (St Paul) *see* Eskdale, Irton, Muncaster and Waberthwaite *Carl*
ISEL (St Michael) *see* Binsey *Carl*
ISFIELD (St Margaret) *Chich 21* **P** *Abp* **R** B H WILCOX, **Hon C** B K MELBOURNE, **NSM** C HOWARTH
ISHAM (St Peter) w Pytchley *Pet 11* **P** *Bp* **P-in-c** S P DOMMETT
ISLE ABBOTTS (Blessed Virgin Mary) *see* Ilminster and Distr *B & W*
ISLE BREWERS (All Saints) *as above*
ISLE OF DOGS (Christ Church and St John) (St Luke) *Lon 7* **P** *Bp* **V** M A SEELEY
ISLEHAM (St Andrew) *Ely 3* **P** *Ld Chan* **V** *vacant*
ISLES OF SCILLY: St Mary's, St Agnes, St Martin's, Bryher and Tresco *Truro 5* **P** *Duchy of Cornwall* **R** J C OULD
ISLEWORTH (All Saints) *Lon 11* **P** *D&C Windsor* **V** *vacant* (020) 8560 6662
ISLEWORTH (St Francis of Assisi) *Lon 11* **P** *Bp* **NSM** L P SMITH, S P THOMPSON
ISLEWORTH (St John the Baptist) *Lon 11* **P** *V Isleworth All SS* **P-in-c** P R MYLES
ISLEWORTH (St Luke) *see* Spring Grove St Mary *Lon*
ISLEWORTH (St Mary) Osterley Road *as above*
ISLEWORTH (St Mary the Virgin) *see* Hounslow H Trin w St Paul *Lon*
ISLEY WALTON (All Saints) *see* Ashby-de-la-Zouch and Breedon on the Hill *Leic*
ISLINGTON (St James the Apostle) (St Peter) *Lon 6* **P** *Bp* **V** E H JONES
ISLINGTON (St Jude and St Paul) *see* Mildmay Grove St Jude and St Paul *Lon*
ISLINGTON (St Mary) *Lon 6* **P** *CPAS* **V** G R KINGS, **Hon C** E W LOVERIDGE
ISLINGTON (St Mary Magdalene) *see* Holloway St Mary Magd *Lon*
ISLIP (St Nicholas) *see* Ray Valley *Ox*
ISLIP (St Nicholas) *Pet 10* **P** *L G Stopford-Sackville Esq* **R** *vacant*
ISTEAD RISE (St Barnabas) *Roch 4* **P** *Bp* **V** V C SHORT
ITCHEN ABBAS (St John the Baptist) *see* Itchen Valley *Win*
ITCHEN VALLEY, The *Win 1* **P** *Ld Chan* **R** J G CRUICKSHANK
ITCHENOR, WEST (St Nicholas) *see* W Wittering and Birdham w Itchenor *Chich*
ITCHINGFIELD (St Nicholas) w Slinfold *Chich 7* **P** *Bp* **R** D M BEAL
IVEGILL (Christ Church) *see* Inglewood Gp *Carl*
IVER (St Peter) *Ox 23* **P** *Trustees* **V** B A SKINNER, **C** A D R HOLMES, **NSM** A M WILLIAMS, **OLM** K WILSON
IVER HEATH (St Margaret) *Ox 23* **P** *Trustees* **P-in-c** W P G HAZLEWOOD
IVINGHOE (St Mary the Virgin) w Pitstone and Slapton *Ox 26* **P** *Bp and Ch Ch Ox (jt)* **P-in-c** T E DOYLE
IVINGTON (St John) *see* Leominster *Heref*
IVY HATCH (not known) *see* Ightham *Roch*
IVY ROW (Mission Room) *see* Roos and Garton w Tunstall, Grimston and Hilston *York*
IVYBRIDGE (St John the Evangelist) w Harford *Ex 21* **P** *Bp* **V** C H OSBORNE, **C** M J W BENTON-EVANS, **NSM** H L STAINER
IVYCHURCH (St George) *see* St Mary's Bay w St Mary-in-the-Marsh etc *Cant*
IWADE (All Saints) *Cant 15* **P** *Adn Maidstone* **P-in-c** J P LEFROY
IWERNE COURTNEY (St Mary) *see* Iwerne Valley *Sarum*
IWERNE MINSTER (St Mary) *as above*
IWERNE VALLEY *Sarum 7* **P** *D&C Windsor, DBP, G A L F Pitt-Rivers Esq, and A C L Sturge Esq (jt)* **V** S F EVERETT, **NSM** J H SIMMONS
IXWORTH (St Mary) *see* Blackbourne *St E*
IXWORTH THORPE (All Saints) *as above*
JACKFIELD (St Mary) *see* Broseley w Benthall, Jackfield, Linley etc *Heref*
JACOBSTOW (St James) *see* St Gennys, Jacobstow w Warbstow and Treneglos *Truro*
JACOBSTOWE (St James) *see* Hatherleigh, Meeth, Exbourne and Jacobstowe *Ex*
JARROW (St John the Baptist) (St Mark) (St Paul) (St Peter) *Dur 15* **P** *Bp* **TR** W E BRAVINER, **TV** G W OPPERMAN, J S CURRY, **C** B JONES, **NSM** A RAINE
JARROW GRANGE (Christ Church) *Dur 15* **P** *Lord Northbourne* **P-in-c** D T OSMAN, **C** B UNWIN
JARVIS BROOK (St Michael and All Angels) *Chich 19* **P** *Bp* **NSM** P K BURNETT
JERSEY (All Saints) *Win 15* **P** *R St Helier, Bp, and The Crown (by turn)* **V** G J HOUGHTON, **NSM** G L BAUDAINS
JERSEY Gouray (St Martin) *Win 15* **P** *Bp and The Crown (alt)* **Hon C** L W MATTHEWS
JERSEY Greve d'Azette (St Nicholas) *see* Jersey St Clem *Win*
JERSEY (Holy Trinity) *Win 15* **P** *The Crown* **R** A KEOGH
JERSEY Millbrook (St Matthew) *Win 15* **P** *The Crown* **P-in-c** P J WARREN
JERSEY (St Andrew) *Win 15* **P** *Dean of Jersey* **V** M S TAYLOR
JERSEY (St Brelade) (Communicare Chapel) (St Aubin) *Win 15* **P** *The Crown* **R** M F W BOND, **Par Dn** J M GURDON, **NSM** G GREEN, **Hon Par Dn** J A DAVY
JERSEY (St Clement) *Win 15* **P** *The Crown* **R** D M SHAW
JERSEY (St Helier) *Win 15* **P** *The Crown* **P-in-c** R F KEY, **C** C PRICE, **NSM** A D WILLIAMS
JERSEY (St James) *Win 15* **P** *Bp* **V** D R D JONES, **NSM** A F PEARCE
JERSEY (St John) *Win 15* **P** *The Crown* **R** A J THEWLIS
JERSEY (St Lawrence) *Win 15* **P** *The Crown* **P-in-c** P J WARREN
JERSEY (St Luke) *Win 15* **P** *Bp and The Crown (alt)* **V** D R D JONES, **NSM** A F PEARCE
JERSEY (St Mark) *Win 15* **P** *Bp* **V** C I BUCKLEY
JERSEY (St Martin) *Win 15* **P** *The Crown* **R** L J TURNER
JERSEY (St Mary) *Win 15* **P** *The Crown* **R** D R D JONES, **NSM** A F PEARCE
JERSEY (St Ouen) (St George) *Win 15* **P** *The Crown* **R** J P HARKIN
JERSEY (St Paul) Proprietary Chapel *Win 15* **Min** P J BROOKS
JERSEY (St Peter) *Win 15* **P** *The Crown* **R** M R POOLTON
JERSEY (St Saviour) *Win 15* **P** *The Crown* **R** A C SWINDELL, **NSM** J J ILTON
JERSEY (St Simon) *Win 15* **P** *R St Helier, Bp, and The Crown (by turn)* **V** G J HOUGHTON, **NSM** G L BAUDAINS
JERSEY DE GROUVILLE (St Martin) (St Peter la Roque) *Win 15* **P** *The Crown* **R** *vacant* (01534) 853073
JESMOND (Clayton Memorial Church) *Newc 5* **P** *Trustees* **V** D R J HOLLOWAY, **C** J J S PRYKE, **Hon C** A F MUNDEN
JESMOND (Holy Trinity) *Newc 5* **P** *Trustees* **P-in-c** R L SIMPSON, **NSM** C SMITH
JESMOND (St George) *see* Newc St Geo *Newc*
JESMOND (St Hilda) *see* Newc St Hilda *Newc*
JEVINGTON (St Andrew) *see* E Dean w Friston and Jevington *Chich*
JOYDENS WOOD (St Barnabas) *Roch 17* **P** *Bp* **V** G C DAY
JURBY (St Patrick) *S & M 3* **P** *Bp* **P-in-c** G F BARKER
KATE'S HILL (St John) *see* Dudley St Jo *Worc*
KEA (All Hallows) (Old Church) *Truro 6* **P** *V St Clement* **V** *vacant* (01872) 272850
KEAL, EAST (St Helen) *see* Marden Hill Gp *Linc*
KEAL, WEST (St Helen) *as above*
KEARSLEY MOOR (St Stephen) *Man 6* **P** *R E Farnworth and Kearsley* **V** K F WAINWRIGHT
KEASDEN (St Matthew) *see* Clapham-with-Keasden and Austwick *Bradf*
KEDDINGTON (St Margaret) *see* Louth *Linc*
KEDINGTON (St Peter and St Paul) *see* Stourhead *St E*
KEEDWELL HILL (Ascension) *see* Long Ashton *B & W*
KEELBY Group, The (St Bartholomew) *Linc 10* **P** *J E Spilman Esq and DBP (1 turn), Bp (1 turn)* **R** *vacant* (01469) 560251
KEELE (St John the Baptist) *Lich 9* **P** *T H G Howard-Sneyd Esq* **V** S A ANSELL, **NSM** S W JOHNSON
KEEVIL (St Leonard) *see* Steeple Ashton w Semington and Keevil *Sarum*
KEGWORTH (St Andrew), Hathern, Long Whatton, Diseworth, Belton and Osgathorpe *Leic 7* **P** *Patr Bd* **TR** N O TUFFNELL, **TV** A M PRINCE
KEIGHLEY (All Saints) *Bradf 8* **P** *Bp and R Keighley St Andr* **P-in-c** J L PRITCHARD
KEIGHLEY (St Andrew) *Bradf 8* **P** *Bp* **P-in-c** P J MOTT
KEINTON MANDEVILLE (St Mary Magdalene) *see* Wheathill Priory Gp *B & W*
KELBROOK (St Mary) *Bradf 7* **P** *Bp* **P-in-c** R C WALLACE, **C** T J RISHTON
KELBY (St Andrew) *see* Ancaster Wilsford Gp *Linc*

KELHAM (St Wilfrid) *see* Averham w Kelham *S'well*
KELLAWAYS (St Giles) *see* Draycot *Bris*
KELLET, NETHER (St Mark) *see* Bolton-le-Sands *Blackb*
KELLET, OVER (St Cuthbert) *Blackb 14* **P** *Reformation Ch Trust* **V** K CLAPHAM
KELLING (St Mary) *see* Weybourne Gp *Nor*
KELLINGTON (St Edmund) *see* Knottingley and Kellington w Whitley *Wakef*
KELLOE (St Helen) and Coxhoe *Dur 5* **P** *Bp* **V** M J COOKE
KELLS (St Peter) *Carl 5* **P** *Bp* **P-in-c** J D KELLY, **OLM** A J BANKS
KELLY (St Mary the Virgin) *see* Lifton, Broadwoodwidger, Stowford etc *Ex*
KELMARSH (St Denys) *see* Clipston w Naseby and Haselbech w Kelmarsh *Pet*
KELMSCOTT (St George) *see* Shill Valley and Broadshire *Ox*
KELSALE (St Peter) *see* Saxmundham w Kelsale cum Carlton *St E*
KELSALL (St Philip) *Ches 2* **P** *V Tarvin* **P-in-c** I P ENTICOTT
KELSEY Group, The *Linc 5* **P** *Bp (3 turns), J M B Young Esq and S B Young Esq (1 turn)* **R** P J GREEN
KELSEY, NORTH (All Hallows) *see* Kelsey Gp *Linc*
KELSEY, SOUTH (St Mary) *as above*
KELSHALL (St Faith) *see* Therfield w Kelshall *St Alb*
KELSTERN (St Faith) *see* Binbrook Gp *Linc*
KELSTON (St Nicholas) *see* Bath Weston St Jo w Kelston *B & W*
KELVEDON (St Mary the Virgin) and Feering *Chelmsf 24* **P** *Bp* **V** D S REYNISH
KELVEDON HATCH (St Nicholas) *see* Bentley Common, Kelvedon Hatch and Navestock *Chelmsf*
KEMBERTON (St Andrew) *see* Beckbury, Badger, Kemberton, Ryton, Stockton etc *Lich*
KEMBLE (All Saints), Poole Keynes, Somerford Keynes w Sharncote, Coates, Rodmarton and Sapperton w Frampton Mansell *Glouc 11* **P** *Bp, Lord Bathurst, Mrs L R Rank, Guild of All So, and DBP (2 turns), Duchy of Lanc (1 turn)* **R** C K RACE, **Hon C** R A BOWDEN
KEMERTON (St Nicholas) *see* Woolstone w Gotherington and Oxenton etc *Glouc*
KEMP TOWN (St Mary) *Chich 2* **P** *Bp, Mrs R A Hinton, A C R Elliott Esq, T J Elliott Esq, and the Revd Canon D H McKittrick (jt)* **V** N J MASON
KEMPSEY (St Mary the Virgin) and Severn Stoke w Croome d'Abitot *Worc 5* **P** *D&C and Croome Estate Trustees (alt)* **R** P R HOLZAPFEL
KEMPSFORD (St Mary) *see* Fairford and Kempsford w Whelford *Glouc*
KEMPSHOTT (St Mark) *Win 4* **P** *Bp* **V** D J STRATHIE, **C** A J WALKER
KEMPSTON (All Saints) *St Alb 10* **P** *Bp* **V** D J P ISIORHO, **NSM** G A WEBB
KEMPSTON (Transfiguration) *St Alb 10* **P** *Bp* **NSM** V E HOLLIS
KEMSING (St Mary the Virgin) w Woodlands *Roch 10* **P** *DBP* **V** J N ASHWORTH
KENARDINGTON (St Mary) *see* Orlestone w Snave and Ruckinge w Warehorne etc *Cant*
KENCHESTER (St Michael) *see* Credenhill w Brinsop and Wormsley etc *Heref*
KENCOT (St George) *see* Shill Valley and Broadshire *Ox*
KENDAL (Holy Trinity) (All Hallows Chapel) *Carl 10* **P** *Trin Coll Cam* **V** R METCALFE, **NSM** P SMITH
KENDAL (St George) *Carl 10* **P** *V Kendal H Trin* **V** A R BILLINGS, **C** B LOCK, **OLM** J F RADLEY
KENDAL (St Thomas) *Carl 10* **P** *CPAS* **V** T R MONTGOMERY, **C** T S MAY, **NSM** S R WEATHERILL
KENDERCHURCH (St Mary) *see* Ewyas Harold w Dulas, Kenderchurch etc *Heref*
KENDRAY (St Andrew) *Sheff 12* **P** *V Ardsley* **P-in-c** R G R EVANS
KENILWORTH (St John) *Cov 4* **P** *Simeon's Trustees* **P-in-c** D CONNOLLY, **OLM** J M MULLANEY
KENILWORTH (St Nicholas) (St Barnabas) *Cov 4* **P** *Ld Chan* **V** R W E AWRE, **C** C R GROOCOCK
KENLEY (All Saints) *S'wark 24* **P** *Abp* **V** R C HAGON, **NSM** S C CONWAY, D C HADLEY
KENLEY (St John the Baptist) *see* Wenlock *Heref*
KENN (St Andrew) *see* Exminster and Kenn *Ex*
KENN (St John the Evangelist) *see* Yatton Moor *B & W*
KENN, NORTH *see* Tedburn St Mary, Whitestone, Oldridge etc *Ex*
KENNERLEIGH (St John the Baptist) *see* N Creedy *Ex*
KENNET, EAST (Christ Church) *see* Upper Kennet *Sarum*
KENNET, UPPER *Sarum 18* **P** *Bp* **R** C A DAVIES
KENNETT (St Nicholas) *Ely 3* **P** *Mrs M F de Packh* **P-in-c** A HASELHURST, **NSM** P M DEBENHAM
KENNINGHALL (St Mary) *see* Guiltcross *Nor*
KENNINGTON (St John the Divine w St James the Apostle) *S'wark 11* **P** *Ripon Coll Cuddesdon and Bp (jt)* **V** D M BRADSHAW, **C** L P DARRANT
KENNINGTON (St Mark) *S'wark 13* **P** *Abp* **V** R D DE BERRY, **C** C P BAKER
KENNINGTON (St Mary) *Cant 10* **P** *Abp* **P-in-c** Y L MURPHY
KENNINGTON (St Swithun) *Ox 10* **P** *Bp* **V** T SMITH
KENNINGTON CROSS (St Anselm) *see* N Lambeth *S'wark*
KENNINGTON PARK (St Agnes) *S'wark 10* **P** *Trustees* **V** C I PEARSON
KENNY HILL (St James) *see* Mildenhall *St E*
KENSAL GREEN (St John) *Lon 2* **P** *Bp* **V** R D BEAL
KENSAL RISE Team Ministry, The (St Mark) (St Martin) *Lon 21* **P** *Patr Bd* **TR** P W STONE, **TV** G P NOYCE, **C** P D HILLAS, **Hon C** E J BARRATT
KENSAL TOWN (St Thomas) (St Andrew) (St Philip) *Lon 12* **P** *Hyndman Trustees* **V** D FLETCHER
KENSINGTON (St Barnabas) *Lon 12* **P** *V Kensington St Mary Abbots w St Geo and Ch Ch* **V** T M HUMPHREY, **C** M C MACDONALD, **NSM** S K GREEN
KENSINGTON (St Clement) *see* Notting Dale St Clem w St Mark and St Jas *Lon*
KENSINGTON (St Helen) (Holy Trinity) *Lon 12* **P** *Bp* **V** J C TERRY, **C** I P DOWSETT
KENSINGTON (St James) *see* Notting Dale St Clem w St Mark and St Jas *Lon*
KENSINGTON (St John the Baptist) *Lon 12* **P** *Trustees* **V** G F BRIGHT, **NSM** A E SPEAKMAN
KENSINGTON (St Mary Abbots) w St George (Christ Church) *Lon 12* **P** *Bp* **V** G W CRAIG, **C** A G C PEARSON, W J M GIBBS, M G FULLER
KENSINGTON (St Philip) Earl's Court *Lon 12* **P** *Bp* **V** *vacant* (020) 7602 5025 *or* 7373 4847
KENSINGTON, NORTH (St Michael and All Angels) *see* Notting Hill St Mich and Ch Ch *Lon*
KENSINGTON, SOUTH (Holy Trinity w All Saints) *Lon 3* **P** *D&C Westmr* **P-in-c** J A CAVE BERGQUIST
KENSINGTON, SOUTH (St Augustine) *Lon 12* **P** *Keble Coll Ox* **V** *vacant* (020) 7584 6622 *or* 7581 1877
KENSINGTON, SOUTH (St Jude) *Lon 8* **P** *Sir Laurence Magnus Bt* **P-in-c** T A GILLUM
KENSINGTON, SOUTH (St Luke) *Lon 8* **P** *Ch Patr Trust* **V** W R HEALD
KENSINGTON, SOUTH (St Stephen) *Lon 12* **P** *Guild of All So* **V** R F BUSHAU
KENSINGTON, WEST (St Andrew) *see* Fulham St Andr Fulham Fields *Lon*
KENSINGTON, WEST (St Mary) *see* Fulham St Mary N End *Lon*
KENSINGTON, WEST (St Mary) The Boltons *see* W Brompton St Mary w St Pet *Lon*
KENSWORTH (St Mary the Virgin), Studham and Whipsnade *St Alb 12* **P** *Ld Chan and D&C St Paul's (alt)* **V** N Y LENTHALL
KENT TOWN *see* E Molesey St Paul *Guildf*
KENTCHURCH (St Mary) *see* Ewyas Harold w Dulas, Kenderchurch etc *Heref*
KENTFORD (St Mary) *see* Dalham, Gazeley, Higham, Kentford and Moulton *St E*
KENTISBEARE (St Mary) *see* Cullompton, Willand, Uffculme, Kentisbeare etc *Ex*
KENTISBURY (St Thomas) *see* Shirwell, Loxhore, Kentisbury, Arlington, etc *Ex*
KENTISH TOWN (St Benet and All Saints) (St Luke) *Lon 17* **P** *Prime Min and D&C St Paul's (alt)* **V** R N ARNOLD
KENTISH TOWN (St Martin) (St Andrew) *Lon 17* **P** *Exors Dame Jewell Magnus-Allcroft* **V** J A HAYWARD
KENTISH TOWN (St Silas) and (Holy Trinity) w St Barnabas *Lon 17* **P** *Bp and D&C St Paul's (jt)* **V** G C ROWLANDS
KENTMERE (St Cuthbert) *see* Staveley, Ings and Kentmere *Carl*
KENTON (All Saints) *see* Debenham and Helmingham *St E*
KENTON (All Saints), Mamhead, Powderham, Cofton and Starcross *Ex 6* **P** *Earl of Devon, D&C Ex, D&C Sarum, and SMF (jt)* **C** R RANN, **Hon C** P DAWKES
KENTON (Ascension) *Newc 5* **P** *Bp* **P-in-c** A C RUSSELL
KENTON (St Mary the Virgin) *Lon 23* **P** *Bp* **V** D J SHERWOOD
KENTON, SOUTH (Annunciation) *see* Wembley Park *Lon*
KENWYN (St Keyne) w St Allen *Truro 6* **P** *Bp* **R** P D SAYLE, **OLM** R W HUMPHRIES

KERESLEY (St Thomas) and Coundon *Cov 2* **P** *Bp* **V** P A WALKER, **C** R E WALKER
KERESLEY END (Church of the Ascension) *see* Keresley and Coundon *Cov*
KERRIDGE (Holy Trinity) *see* Bollington St Jo *Ches*
KERSAL, LOWER (St Aidan) *Man 6* **P** *Bp* **P-in-c** M K J SMITH
KERSAL MOOR (St Paul) *Man 6* **P** *Trustees* **R** L K BATTYE, **C** A J BARNSHAW
KERSEY (St Mary) *see* Elmsett w Aldham, Hintlesham, Chattisham etc *St E*
KERSWELL GREEN (St John the Baptist) *see* Kempsey and Severn Stoke w Croome d'Abitot *Worc*
KESGRAVE (All Saints) *St E 4* **P** *Bp* **V** R SPITTLE
KESSINGLAND (St Edmund), Gisleham and Rushmere *Nor 9* **P** *Ld Chan (1 turns) and Bp (2 turns)* **R** S J COLLIER
KESTON (not known) (St Audrey) *Roch 14* **P** *D&C* **R** D F SPRINGTHORPE
KESWICK (All Saints) *see* Swardeston w E Carleton, Intwood, Keswick etc *Nor*
KESWICK (St John) *Carl 6* **P** *Trustees* **V** *vacant* (01768) 772130
KESWICK, EAST (St Mary Magdalene) *see* Bardsey *Ripon*
KETLEY (St Mary the Virgin) *see* Cen Telford *Lich*
KETTERING (All Saints) *Pet 11* **P** *SMF* **V** R T COOK
KETTERING (Christ the King) *Pet 11* **P** *R Barton Seagrave w Warkton* **V** S M BENOY, **C** M C PEREIRA
KETTERING (St Andrew) *Pet 11* **P** *Bp* **P-in-c** N R WILLS
KETTERING (St Mary the Virgin) (St John the Evangelist) *Pet 11* **P** *SMF* **V** S J RAINE
KETTERING (St Peter and St Paul) (St Michael and All Angels) *Pet 11* **P** *Comdr L M M Saunders Watson* **P-in-c** D M J BARRINGTON, **C** R A HILL, J J E ROWLEY
KETTERINGHAM (St Peter) *see* Swardeston w E Carleton, Intwood, Keswick etc *Nor*
KETTLEBASTON (St Mary) *see* Monks Eleigh w Chelsworth and Brent Eleigh etc *St E*
KETTLEBROOK (St Andrew) *see* Tamworth *Lich*
KETTLEBURGH (St Andrew) *see* Brandeston w Kettleburgh and Easton *St E*
KETTLENESS (St John the Baptist) *see* Hinderwell, Roxby and Staithes etc *York*
KETTLESTONE (All Saints) *see* Barney, Fulmodeston w Croxton, Hindringham etc *Nor*
KETTLETHORPE (St Peter and St Paul) *see* Saxilby Gp *Linc*
KETTLEWELL (St Mary) w Conistone, Hubberholme and Arncliff w Halton Gill *Bradf 7* **P** *Bp, Mrs A M Harries and W R G Bell Esq (jt)* **V** M A HESLOP
KETTON (St Mary the Virgin), Collyweston, Easton-on-the-Hill, Tinwell and Wittering *Pet 8* **P** *Burghley Ho Preservation Trust, Bp, and Ld Chan (by turn)* **R** D G EVERETT, **NSM** R J BATES
KEW (St Anne) *S'wark 18* **P** *The Crown* **V** N J WORN
KEW (St Francis of Assisi) *Liv 9* **P** *Bp, Adn Warrington, and V Southport All SS and All So (jt)* **V** A P J GALBRAITH
KEW (St Philip and All Saints) (St Luke) *S'wark 18* **P** *Bp* **V** P W HART, **NSM** E D LONGFELLOW
KEWSTOKE (St Paul) w Wick St Lawrence *B & W 11* **P** *Ld Chan* **V** N A SCHEMANOFF
KEXBY (St Paul) w Wilberfoss *York 5* **P** *Viscount de Vesci and Lord Egremont (alt)* **V** (020) 7898 1610
KEYHAM (All Saints) *see* Houghton-on-the-Hill, Keyham and Hungarton *Leic*
KEYHAM, NORTH (St Thomas) *Ex 22* **P** *Bp* **V** *vacant* (01752) 51102
KEYINGHAM (St Nicholas) w Ottringham, Halsham and Sunk Island *York 12* **P** *Abp (3 turns), DBP (1 turn)* **R** R HOWARD
KEYMER (St Cosmas and St Damian) *see* Clayton w Keymer *Chich*
KEYMER (St Francis of Assisi) *as above*
KEYNSHAM (St Francis) (St John the Baptist) *B & W 10* **P** *Patr Bd* **TR** J F SAMWAYS, **TV** A D JUDGE, A-M C BIRD, **C** S K GREATOREX, **NSM** M A SNOOK
KEYSOE (St Mary the Virgin) w Bolnhurst and Little Staughton *St Alb 15* **P** *CCC Ox (1 turn), Bp (2 turns)* **V** *vacant* (01234) 708251
KEYSTON (St John the Baptist) and Bythorn *Ely 8* **P** *Sir Stephen Hastings (2 turns), Bp (1 turn)* **P-in-c** S P MEWS, **NSM** J RAWLINSON
KEYWORTH (St Mary Magdalene) and Stanton-on-the-Wolds and Bunny w Bradmore *S'well 8* **P** *Bp and Ld Chan (alt)* **NSM** T H KIRKMAN, S M OLDROYD
KIBWORTH (St Wilfrid) and Smeeton Westerby and Saddington *Leic 5* **P** *Mert Coll Ox and Bp (jt)* **R** S M LEE, **NSM** M B W COOK
KIDBROOKE (St James) (Holy Spirit) *S'wark 3* **P** *Patr Bd* **R** K W HITCH, **NSM** K F SITCH
KIDBROOKE (St Nicholas) *S'wark 1* **P** *Bp and Simeon's Trustees (jt)* **V** T M LINKENS
KIDDERMINSTER (St George) (St Chad) (St John the Baptist Church Hall) *Worc 11* **P** *Patr Bd* **TR** N J W BARKER, **TV** H A BURTON
KIDDERMINSTER (St John the Baptist) (Holy Innocents) *Worc 11* **P** *Patr Bd* **TR** H F GODDARD, **TV** J R STEWART
KIDDERMINSTER (St Mary and All Saints) w Trimpley, Franche, Broadwaters and Upper Arley *Worc 11* **P** *Bp* **TR** D O BELL, **TV** F H HAWORTH, **C** A A GOODMAN, **NSM** C L ALLEN
KIDDERMINSTER WEST *see* Kidderminster St Jo and H Innocents *Worc*
KIDDINGTON (St Nicholas) *see* Wootton w Glympton and Kiddington *Ox*
KIDLINGTON (St Mary the Virgin) w Hampton Poyle *Ox 7* **P** *Patr Bd* **TR** J A ELLIS, **C** J P ST JOHN NICOLLE, **NSM** J A TURNER
KIDLINGTON, SOUTH (St John the Baptist) *see* Kidlington w Hampton Poyle *Ox*
KIDMORE END (St John the Baptist) *see* Rotherfield Peppard and Kidmore End etc *Ox*
KIDSGROVE (St Thomas) *Lich 9* **P** *MMCET* **V** I BAKER
KILBURN (Mission Room) *see* Horsley and Denby *Derby*
KILBURN (St Augustine) (St John) *Lon 2* **P** *SMF* **V** A H YATES, **C** D R HUMPHREYS
KILBURN (St Mary) *see* Thirkleby w Kilburn and Bagby *York*
KILBURN (St Mary w All Souls) Priory Road and W Hampstead St James *Lon 16* **P** *Bp, Ch Patr Trust, and trustees (jt)* **V** A D CAIN, **NSM** M W SPEEKS, A FRITZE-SHANKS
KILBURN, WEST (St Luke) (St Simon) (St Jude) *Lon 2* **P** *CPAS* **P-in-c** A G THOM, **C** J P TRIFFITT, J F BARRY, **NSM** B A ENWUCHOLA
KILBY (St Mary Magdalene) *see* Wistow *Leic*
KILDALE (St Cuthbert) *see* Ingleby Greenhow w Bilsdale Priory, Kildale etc *York*
KILDWICK (St Andrew) *Bradf 8* **P** *Ch Ch Ox* **V** R A R FIGG
KILHAM (All Saints) *see* Rudston w Boynton, Carnaby and Kilham *York*
KILKHAMPTON (St James the Great) w Morwenstow *Truro 8* **P** *DBP and Bp (jt)* **R** P J ABELL
KILLAMARSH (St Giles) *Derby 3* **P** *The Crown* **R** R J BRADSHAW
KILLERTON (Holy Evangelist) *see* Pinhoe and Broadclyst *Ex*
KILLINGHALL (St Thomas the Apostle) *see* Hampsthwaite and Killinghall and Birstwith *Ripon*
KILLINGHOLME, NORTH AND SOUTH (St Denys) *see* Habrough Gp *Linc*
KILLINGTON (All Saints) *see* Firbank, Howgill and Killington *Bradf*
KILLINGWORTH (St John) *Newc 1* **P** *V Longbenton St Bart* **V** M L MALLESON, **C** P S MCCONNELL
KILMERSDON (St Peter and St Paul) w Babington *B & W 12* **P** *Lord Hylton* **R** C P J TURNER
KILMESTON (St Andrew) *see* Upper Itchen *Win*
KILMINGTON (St Giles) *see* Kilmington, Stockland, Dalwood, Yarcombe etc *Ex*
KILMINGTON (St Giles), Stockland, Dalwood, Yarcombe and Shute *Ex 5* **P** *Bp and D&C (2 turns), Prime Min (1 turn)* **V** N H FREATHY, **NSM** L A MILLS
KILMINGTON (St Mary the Virgin) *see* Upper Stour *Sarum*
KILNDOWN (Christ Church) *see* Goudhurst w Kilndown *Cant*
KILNGREEN (Diggle Mission Church) *see* Saddleworth *Man*
KILNHURST (St Thomas) *Sheff 12* **P** *Ld Chan* **V** N H ELLIOTT, **C** D E BARNSLEY
KILNWICK (All Saints) *see* Woldsburn *York*
KILNWICK PERCY (St Helen) *see* Pocklington and Owsthorpe and Kilnwick Percy etc *York*
KILPECK (St Mary and St David) *see* Ewyas Harold w Dulas, Kenderchurch etc *Heref*
KILSBY (St Faith) *see* Barby w Kilsby *Pet*
KILVERSTONE (St Andrew) *see* Thetford *Nor*
KILVINGTON (St Mary) *S'well 3* **P** *E G Staunton Esq* **P-in-c** D HOLLIS
KILVINGTON, SOUTH (St Wilfrid) *see* Thirsk *York*
KILWORTH, NORTH (St Andrew) *see* Gilmorton, Peatling Parva, Kimcote etc *Leic*
KILWORTH, SOUTH (St Nicholas) *as above*
KIMBERLEY (Holy Trinity) *S'well 7* **P** *Bp* **R** D W WILDE
KIMBERLEY (St Peter) *see* Barnham Broom and Upper Yare *Nor*
KIMBERWORTH (St Thomas) (St Mark) *Sheff 6* **P** *Bp* **V** *vacant* (01709) 554441
KIMBERWORTH PARK (St John) *Sheff 6* **P** *Bp* **V** S G MILLWOOD

KIMBLE, GREAT (St Nicholas) *see* Ellesborough, The Kimbles and Stoke Mandeville *Ox*
KIMBLE, LITTLE (All Saints) *as above*
KIMBLESWORTH (St Philip and St James) *see* Dur N *Dur*
KIMBOLTON (St Andrew) *Ely 8* **P** *Trustees Duke of Manchester* **V** R A FROST
KIMBOLTON (St James the Great) *see* Leominster *Heref*
KIMCOTE (All Saints) *see* Gilmorton, Peatling Parva, Kimcote etc *Leic*
KIMMERIDGE (St Nicholas of Myra) *see* Corfe Castle, Church Knowle, Kimmeridge etc *Sarum*
KIMPTON (St Peter and St Paul) *see* Appleshaw, Kimpton, Thruxton, Fyfield etc *Win*
KIMPTON (St Peter and St Paul) w Ayot St Lawrence *St Alb 8* **P** *Bp* **P-in-c** K A BUCKLER
KINETON (St Peter) *Cov 8* **P** *Lady Willoughby de Broke* **V** C A HOST
KING CROSS (St Paul) *Wakef 4* **P** *Bp* **V** J VICKERMAN
KING STERNDALE (Christ Church) *see* Buxton w Burbage and King Sterndale *Derby*
KINGHAM (St Andrew) *see* Chipping Norton *Ox*
KINGMOOR (St Peter) *see* Houghton *Carl*
KING'S BECK *Nor 12* **P** *Bp, D&C, P H C Barber Esq, and J T D Shaw Esq (jt)* **R** S A SMITH
KINGS BROMLEY (All Saints) *see* The Ridwares and Kings Bromley *Lich*
KING'S CAPLE (St John the Baptist) *see* How Caple w Sollarshope, Sellack etc *Heref*
KING'S CLIFFE (All Saints) *Pet 8* **P** *Bp* **P-in-c** P J DAVIES
KINGS HEATH (All Saints) *Birm 5* **P** *V Moseley St Mary* **V** J L WILKINSON, **C** R G MORTON
KINGS HEATH (St Augustine) *Pet 7* **P** *Bp* **V** L MATHIAS
KING'S HILL (St Andrew) *see* Wednesbury St Bart *Lich*
KINGS LANGLEY (All Saints) *St Alb 2* **P** *Abp* **V** P R STEARN, **NSM** C THORP
KING'S LYNN (All Saints) *see* S Lynn *Nor*
KING'S LYNN (St John the Evangelist) *Nor 20* **P** *Bp* **P-in-c** S C STOKES
KING'S LYNN (St Margaret) (St Edmund) w St Nicholas *Nor 20* **P** *D&C* **R** C J IVORY, **C** M C JACKSON
KING'S LYNN (St Peter) *see* Clenchwarton and W Lynn *Ely*
KING'S NORTON (St John the Baptist) *see* Gaulby *Leic*
KINGS NORTON (St Nicolas) *Birm 4* **P** *Patr Bd* **TR** R J MORRIS, **TV** H M FLACK, D R GOULD, **NSM** J B CROOKS
KING'S PYON (St Mary the Virgin) *see* Canon Pyon w King's Pyon, Birley and Wellington *Heref*
KINGS RIPTON (St Peter) *Ely 8* **P** *Lord de Ramsey* **P-in-c** E B ATLING
KING'S SOMBORNE *see* Somborne w Ashley *Win*
KING'S STANLEY (St George) *see* The Stanleys *Glouc*
KING'S SUTTON (St Peter and St Paul) and Newbottle and Charlton *Pet 1* **P** *SMF and Lady Townsend (jt)* **P-in-c** M R H BELLAMY
KING'S WALDEN (St Mary) and Offley w Lilley *St Alb 4* **P** *Sir Thomas Pilkington Bt (2 turns), St Jo Coll Cam (1 turn), D K C Salusbury-Hughes Esq and Mrs P A L McGrath (2 turns)* **V** *vacant* (01438) 871278
KING'S WORTHY (St Mary) (St Mary's Chapel) *Win 7* **P** *Univ Coll Ox and Lord Northbrook (alt)* **R** A W GORDON
KINGSBRIDGE (St Edmund the King and Martyr) and Dodbrooke *Ex 14* **P** *Bp* **R** C C ROBINS
KINGSBURY (Holy Innocents) *Lon 21* **P** *D&C St Paul's* **V** C F MORTON, **NSM** A J HOPKINS
KINGSBURY (St Andrew) *Lon 21* **P** *The Crown* **V** J T SMITH
KINGSBURY (St Peter and St Paul) *Birm 10* **P** *Bp* **P-in-c** J E GASPER
KINGSBURY EPISCOPI (St Martin) w East Lambrook, Hambridge and Earnshill *B & W 15* **P** *Bp (2 turns), D&C (1 turn)* **V** D A BURTON, A R ELWOOD
KINGSCLERE (St Mary) *Win 6* **P** *Bp* **P-in-c** L R THIRTLE
KINGSCLERE WOODLANDS (St Paul) *see* Ashford Hill w Headley *Win*
KINGSCOTE (St John the Baptist) *see* Nailsworth w Shortwood, Horsley etc *Glouc*
KINGSDON (All Saints) *see* Somerton w Compton Dundon, the Charltons etc *B & W*
KINGSDOWN (St Edmund the King and Martyr) *Roch 10* **P** *D&C* **R** J M B THURLOW
KINGSDOWN (St John the Evangelist) *see* Ringwould w Kingsdown and Ripple etc *Cant*
KINGSEY (St Nicholas) *see* Haddenham w Cuddington, Kingsey etc *Ox*
KINGSHURST (St Barnabas) *Birm 9* **P** *Bp* **V** F C EVANS, **C** W E G CARTER
KINGSKERSWELL (St Mary) w Coffinswell *Ex 10* **P** *V St Marychurch* **V** J F LEONARD
KINGSLAND (St Michael and All Angels) w Eardisland, Aymestrey and Leinthall Earles *Heref 7* **P** *DBP (2 turns), Ld Chan (1 turn)* **R** N J TYSON
KINGSLEY (All Saints) *see* Northanger *Win*
KINGSLEY (St John the Evangelist) *see* Norley, Crowton and Kingsley *Ches*
KINGSLEY (St Werburgh) and Foxt-with-Whiston *Lich 6* **P** *Mrs N A Faulkner* **R** L R PRICE
KINGSLEY MOOR (St John the Baptist) *see* Kingsley and Foxt-w-Whiston *Lich*
KINGSNORTH (St Michael and All Angels) and Shadoxhurst *Cant 10* **P** *Abp* **P-in-c** S E MCLACHLAN, **NSM** M P JONES
KINGSNYMPTON (St James) *see* S Molton w Nymet St George, High Bray etc *Ex*
KINGSTAG (not known) *see* Sturminster Newton, Hinton St Mary and Lydlinch *Sarum*
KINGSTANDING (St Luke) *Birm 3* **P** *Bp* **V** D J A SMITH, **C** L B VARQUEZ, P E JONES
KINGSTANDING (St Mark) *Birm 3* **P** *Bp* **V** D S COSSLETT
KINGSTEIGNTON (St Michael) *Ex 10* **P** *Bp* **V** C H BENSON, **NSM** R W BAMBERG
KINGSTHORPE (St John the Baptist) w Northampton St David *Pet 4* **P** *Patr Bd* **TR** J T SHORT, **TV** M A TAYLOR, E M REW
KINGSTON (All Saints and St Andrew) *see* Papworth *Ely*
KINGSTON (St Giles) *see* Barham w Bishopsbourne and Kingston *Cant*
KINGSTON (St James) *see* Modbury, Bigbury, Ringmore w Kingston etc *Ex*
KINGSTON (St James) *see* Shorwell w Kingston *Portsm*
KINGSTON (St James), Langton Matravers and Worth Matravers *Sarum 8* **P** *Bp, D E Scott Esq, and R Swanage and Studland (jt)* **P-in-c** J MALINS
KINGSTON (St Pancras) *see* Iford w Kingston and Rodmell *Chich*
KINGSTON (St Winifred) and Ratcliffe-on-Soar *S'well 9* **P** *D&C* **P-in-c** S W OSMAN
KINGSTON BAGPUIZE (St John the Baptist) *see* Fyfield w Tubney and Kingston Bagpuize *Ox*
KINGSTON BUCI (St Julian) *Chich 4* **P** *Lord Egremont* **R** D M REEVE
KINGSTON DEVERILL (St Mary) *see* Cley Hill Warminster *Sarum*
KINGSTON HILL (St Paul) *S'wark 17* **P** *DBP* **V** S C COUPLAND, **NSM** F M M DE QUIDT
KINGSTON LACY (St Stephen) *see* Sturminster Marshall, Kingston Lacy and Shapwick *Sarum*
KINGSTON LISLE (St John the Baptist) *see* Ridgeway *Ox*
KINGSTON PARK (not known) *Newc 5* **P** *Bp* **V** R C MILLS
KINGSTON SEYMOUR (All Saints) *see* Yatton Moor *B & W*
KINGSTON ST MARY (Blessed Virgin Mary) Broomfield and Cheddon Fitzpaine *B & W 18* **P** *D&C Bris and Bp (alt)* **R** R J EDWARDS, **NSM** M M T DOBLE, A E FULTON
KINGSTON UPON HULL (Ascension) *see* Derringham Bank *York*
KINGSTON UPON HULL (Most Holy and Undivided Trinity) *York 14* **P** *H Trin Hull & Distr Ch Patr Soc Ltd* **V** J O FORRESTER, **C** P J BALL, M E BALL
KINGSTON UPON HULL (St Aidan) Southcoates *York 14* **P** *Simeon's Trustees* **V** M A FRYER, **C** L J MCWILLIAMS
KINGSTON UPON HULL (St Alban) *York 14* **P** *Abp* **V** *vacant* (01482) 446639
KINGSTON UPON HULL (St Cuthbert) *see* Hull St Cuth *York*
KINGSTON UPON HULL (St John the Baptist) *see* Newington w Dairycoates *York*
KINGSTON UPON HULL (St Martin) *see* Hull St Martin w Transfiguration *York*
KINGSTON UPON HULL (St Mary) Sculcoates *see* Hull St Mary Sculcoates *York*
KINGSTON UPON HULL (St Mary the Virgin) *York 14* **P** *Abp* **P-in-c** P A BURKITT
KINGSTON UPON HULL (St Matthew w St Barnabas) *York 14* **P** *V Hull H Trin* **V** J A BAGSHAWE
KINGSTON UPON HULL (St Nicholas) *York 14* **P** *Abp* **P-in-c** M R B HILLS, **C** T A COTSON
KINGSTON UPON HULL (St Paul) *see* Sculcoates *York*
KINGSTON UPON HULL (St Stephen) *as above*
KINGSTON UPON HULL (St Thomas) *see* Derringham Bank *York*
KINGSTON UPON THAMES (All Saints) (St John the Evangelist) *S'wark 17* **P** *K Coll Cam* **C** A M SHILSON-THOMAS, **NSM** S A CRAGG, R P RITCHIE
KINGSTON UPON THAMES (St Luke) *S'wark 17* **P** *Bp* **V** M G HISLOP

KINGSTON VALE (St John the Baptist) *S'wark 17* **P** *Bp* **P-in-c** A R BECK
KINGSTONE (St John and All Saints) *see* Ilminster and Distr *B & W*
KINGSTONE (St John the Baptist) *see* Uttoxeter Area *Lich*
KINGSTONE (St Michael and All Angels) w Clehonger, Eaton Bishop, Allensmore and Thruxton *Heref 1* **P** *Bp (2 turns), Prime Min (1 turn)* **P-in-c** J W MORRISH
KINGSWEAR (St Thomas of Canterbury) *see* Brixham w Churston Ferrers and Kingswear *Ex*
KINGSWINFORD (St Mary) *Worc 10* **P** *Patr Bd* **TR** J S LUNGLEY, **TV** D J HOSKIN
KINGSWOOD (Church of the Ascension) (Holy Trinity) *Bris 5* **P** *Patr Bd* **TR** P G HUZZEY, **TV** A J HEAGERTY, **C** C J H BLOCKLEY, **NSM** T M TAYLOR
KINGSWOOD (St Andrew) *S'wark 27* **P** *Bp and R&S Ch Trust (jt)* **P-in-c** G A BARBER, **NSM** A G F BOWYER
KINGSWOOD (St Mary the Virgin) *see* Charfield and Kingswood *Glouc*
KINGSWOOD, LOWER (Wisdom of God) *see* Kingswood *S'wark*
KINGTON (St James) *see* Inkberrow w Cookhill and Kington w Dormston *Worc*
KINGTON (St Mary) w Huntington, Old Radnor, Kinnerton and Titley *Heref 5* **P** *Patr Bd* **R** P TARLING, **C** A F EVANS, **NSM** P J BUCKINGHAM
KINGTON, WEST (St Mary the Virgin) *see* By Brook *Bris*
KINGTON LANGLEY (St Peter) *see* Draycot *Bris*
KINGTON MAGNA (All Saints) *see* Stour Vale *Sarum*
KINGTON ST MICHAEL (St Michael) *Bris 4* **P** *Patr Bd* **V** *vacant*
KINGWESTON (All Saints) *see* Wheathill Priory Gp *B & W*
KINLET (St John the Baptist) *see* Cleobury Mortimer w Hopton Wafers etc *Heref*
KINNERLEY (St Mary) w Melverley and Knockin w Maesbrook *Lich 19* **P** *W H C Montgomery Esq, Sir Brooke Boothby Bt, and Viscount Boyne (jt)* **P-in-c** R A L MOWAT, **OLM** P L WEST
KINNERSLEY (St James) *see* Eardisley w Bollingham, Willersley, Brilley etc *Heref*
KINNERTON (St Mary the Virgin) *see* Kington w Huntington, Old Radnor, Kinnerton etc *Heref*
KINNERTON, HIGHER (All Saints) *see* Dodleston *Ches*
KINNINVIE (Mission Room) *see* Barnard Castle w Whorlton *Dur*
KINOULTON (St Luke) *see* Hickling w Kinoulton and Broughton Sulney *S'well*
KINSBOURNE GREEN (St Mary) *see* Harpenden St Nic *St Alb*
KINSHAM (All Saints) *see* Presteigne w Discoed, Kinsham, Lingen and Knill *Heref*
KINSLEY (Resurrection) w Wragby *Wakef 11* **P** *Bp and Lord St Oswald (jt)* **V** J HADJIOANNOU, **C** R HARRIS, **NSM** S J BAKER, R H BAILEY
KINSON (St Andrew) (St Philip) *Sarum 7* **P** *Patr Bd* **TR** R G SAUNDERS, **TV** M J A HOWARD, **C** J D ANDERSON, G R NEAL, **NSM** L G NORTON, D ROBERTS, **OLM** B J KENT
KINTBURY (St Mary the Virgin) w Avington *Ox 14* **P** *DBP (2 turns), Bp (1 turn)* **V** *vacant* (01488) 658243
KINVER (St Peter) and Enville *Lich 24* **P** *Bp, Mrs A D Williams, and DBP (jt)* **R** D J BLACKBURN, **Hon C** M MORRIS, **NSM** E B DAVIES, R A LAWLEY
KINWARTON (St Mary the Virgin) w Great Alne and Haselor *Cov 7* **P** *Bp* **R** *vacant* (01789) 488344
KIPPAX (St Mary the Virgin) w Allerton Bywater *Ripon 8* **P** *Bp* **TR** W P B CARLIN, **TV** J SYKES, **C** M C CRABTREE
KIPPINGTON (St Mary) *Roch 9* **P** *DBP* **V** S R JONES
KIRBY, WEST (St Andrew) *Ches 8* **P** *D&C* **P-in-c** D M DIXON
KIRBY, WEST (St Bridget) *Ches 8* **P** *D&C* **R** R D CLARKE, **C** M COWAN
KIRBY BEDON (St Andrew) *see* Rockland St Mary w Hellington, Bramerton etc *Nor*
KIRBY BELLARS (St Peter) *see* Upper Wreake *Leic*
KIRBY CANE (All Saints) *see* Gillingham w Geldeston, Stockton, Ellingham etc *Nor*
KIRBY GRINDALYTHE (St Andrew) *see* Weaverthorpe w Helperthorpe, Luttons Ambo etc *York*
KIRBY KNOWLE (St Wilfrid) *York 19* **P** *Abp* **P-in-c** P R A R HOARE, **NSM** E A HOARE
KIRBY-LE-SOKEN (St Michael) w Great Holland *Chelmsf 23* **P** *Bp and CPAS (jt)* **R** P L COLEY
KIRBY MISPERTON (St Laurence) w Normanby, Edston and Salton *York 20* **P** *Lady Clarissa Collin, Abp, and St Jo Coll Cam (by turn)* **R** J M E COOPER
KIRBY MUXLOE (St Bartholomew) *Leic 11* **P** *Bp* **TV** A M MCCULLOUGH
KIRBY-ON-THE-MOOR (All Saints), Cundall w Norton-le-Clay and Skelton-cum-Newby *Ripon 3* **P** *Bp, Sir Arthur Collins, and R E J Compton Esq (jt)* **V** J N O HORTON
KIRBY SIGSTON (St Lawrence) *see* Northallerton w Kirby Sigston *York*
KIRBY UNDERDALE (All Saints) *see* Garrowby Hill *York*
KIRBY WISKE (St John the Baptist) *see* Lower Swale *Ripon*
KIRDFORD (St John the Baptist) *Chich 11* **P** *Lord Egremont* **V** S C KERSLEY
KIRK ARBORY (St Columba) *see* Arbory *S & M*
KIRK BRAMWITH (St Mary) *see* Fishlake w Sykehouse and Kirk Bramwith etc *Sheff*
KIRK DEIGHTON (All Saints) *see* Spofforth w Kirk Deighton *Ripon*
KIRK ELLA (St Andrew) and Willerby *York 14* **P** *Patr Bd* **TR** J S JUCKES, **TV** A M SAVAGE, **C** P J SOWERBUTTS
KIRK FENTON (St Mary) w Kirkby Wharfe and Ulleskelfe *York 1* **P** *Abp, J Fielden Esq, and T E Fielden Esq (jt)* **V** R A CLEGG
KIRK HALLAM (All Saints) *Derby 13* **P** *Bp* **V** M J DOBBS
KIRK HAMMERTON (St John the Baptist) *see* Lower Nidderdale *Ripon*
KIRK IRETON (Holy Trinity) *see* Wirksworth *Derby*
KIRK LANGLEY (St Michael) *Derby 11* **P** *G Meynell Esq and J M Clark-Maxwell Esq (alt)* **P-in-c** S I MITCHELL
KIRK MAUGHOLD (St Maughold) *see* Maughold *S & M*
KIRK ONCHAN (St Peter) *see* Onchan *S & M*
KIRK PATRICK (Holy Trinity) *see* Patrick *S & M*
KIRK SANDALL and Edenthorpe (Good Shepherd) *Sheff 8* **P** *Ld Chan* **R** J H MARTIN
KIRK SANTON (St Sanctain) *see* Santan *S & M*
KIRK SMEATON (St Peter) *see* Went Valley *Wakef*
KIRKANDREWS ON EDEN (St Mary) *see* Barony of Burgh *Carl*
KIRKANDREWS ON ESK (St Andrew) *see* Nicholforest and Kirkandrews on Esk *Carl*
KIRKBAMPTON (St Peter) *see* Barony of Burgh *Carl*
KIRKBRIDE (St Bride) *see* Bowness-on-Solway, Kirkbride and Newton Arlosh *Carl*
KIRKBRIDE (St Bridget) *S & M 3* **P** *The Crown* **R** P J UPTON-JONES
KIRKBURN (St Mary) *see* Woldsburn *York*
KIRKBURTON (All Hallows) *Wakef 6* **P** *Bp* **V** G S HODGSON
KIRKBY (St Andrew) *see* Kelsey Gp *Linc*
KIRKBY (St Chad) (St Mark) (St Martin) (St Andrew) *Liv 7* **P** *Patr Bd* **TR** T R STRATFORD, **TV** A J HEBER, J D FAGAN, R TAGUE
KIRKBY, SOUTH (All Saints) *Wakef 11* **P** *Guild of All So* **V** T H KAYE
KIRKBY FLEETHAM (St Mary) *see* Lower Swale *Ripon*
KIRKBY GREEN (Holy Cross) *see* Digby Gp *Linc*
KIRKBY IN ASHFIELD (St Thomas) *S'well 4* **P** *Bp* **V** M EVANS
KIRKBY IN ASHFIELD (St Wilfrid) *S'well 4* **P** *Bp* **R** *vacant* (01623) 753790
KIRKBY-IN-CLEVELAND (St Augustine) *York 21* **P** *Abp* **V** *vacant*
KIRKBY-IN-MALHAMDALE (St Michael the Archangel) w Coniston Cold *Bradf 5* **P** *Bp and D&C (jt)* **P-in-c** F M I'ANSON
KIRKBY IRELETH (St Cuthbert) *Carl 9* **P** *D&C York* **V** G MURFET
KIRKBY KNOWLE (St Wilfrid) *see* Kirby Knowle *York*
KIRKBY LAYTHORPE (St Denys) *Linc 22* **P** *Bp and DBP (alt)* **R** *vacant* (01529) 304804
KIRKBY LONSDALE (St Mary the Virgin) Team Ministry *Carl 10* **P** *Patr Bd* **TR** G W BETTRIDGE, **TV** A WHITTAKER, **C** S A LUNN, **NSM** P S ATKINSON, G BATES, **OLM** D A PRESTON
KIRKBY MALHAM (St Michael the Archangel) *see* Kirkby-in-Malhamdale w Coniston Cold *Bradf*
KIRKBY MALLORY (All Saints) *see* Newbold de Verdun and Kirkby Mallory *Leic*
KIRKBY MALZEARD (St Andrew) *see* Fountains Gp *Ripon*
KIRKBY-ON-BAIN (St Mary) *see* Thornton Gp *Linc*
KIRKBY OVERBLOW (All Saints) *see* Lower Wharfedale *Ripon*
KIRKBY RAVENSWORTH (St Peter and St Felix) *see* Gilling and Kirkby Ravensworth *Ripon*
KIRKBY STEPHEN (not known) w Mallerstang and Crosby Garrett w Soulby *Carl 1* **P** *Bp, Earl of Lonsdale, and Lord Hothfield (jt)* **R** R P PAUL, **NSM** J WRIGHT
KIRKBY THORE (St Michael) w Temple Sowerby and Newbiggin *Carl 1* **P** *Lord Hothfield (3 turns), Major and Mrs*

Sawrey-Cookson (1 turn) **P-in-c** S D RUDKIN, **NSM** K B RICHARDSON
KIRKBY UNDERWOOD (St Mary and All Saints) *see* Ringstone in Aveland Gp *Linc*
KIRKBY WHARFE (St John the Baptist) *see* Kirk Fenton w Kirkby Wharfe and Ulleskelfe *York*
KIRKBY WOODHOUSE (St John the Evangelist) *S'well 4* **P** *Bp* **V** M J MACDONALD
KIRKBYMOORSIDE (All Saints) w Gillamoor, Farndale and Bransdale *York 17* **P** *Countess Feversham* **V** J D PURDY, **NSM** Y L YATES
KIRKDALE (St Athanaseus with St Mary) *Liv 3* **P** *Simeon's Trustees* **V** *vacant* 0151-933 6860
KIRKDALE (St Gregory) w Harome, Nunnington and Pockley *York 17* **P** *Abp, Adn Cleveland, and Lady Clarissa Collin (2 turns), Ox Univ (1 turn)* **V** J M WARDEN
KIRKDALE (St Lawrence) *Liv 3* **P** *CPAS* **V** M GRIFFIN, **OLM** J D GARNER
KIRKDALE (St Paul) *see* Bootle *Liv*
KIRKHAM (St Michael) *Blackb 10* **P** *Ch Ch Ox* **V** J K BROCKBANK
KIRKHAUGH (Holy Paraclete) *see* Alston Moor *Newc*
KIRKHEATON (St Bartholomew) *see* Kirkwhelpington, Kirkharle, Kirkheaton and Cambo *Newc*
KIRKHEATON (St John the Baptist) *Wakef 1* **P** *Ch Trust Fund Trust* **NSM** R J STEEL, **OLM** B R SHORT
KIRKHOLT (St Thomas) *Man 20* **P** *Bp* **V** *vacant* (01706) 645962
KIRKLAND (Mission Church) *see* Lamplugh w Ennerdale *Carl*
KIRKLAND (St Lawrence) *see* Cross Fell Gp *Carl*
KIRKLEATHAM (St Cuthbert) (St Hilda) *York 16* **P** *Abp* **V** C GREENWELL, **C** L M SHIPP, **NSM** M E GARDNER
KIRKLEVINGTON (St Martin) *York 21* **P** *Abp* **P-in-c** M D ALLSOPP
KIRKLEY (St Peter and St John) *Nor 9* **P** *Bp and DBP (jt)* **R** R H WORMALD
KIRKLINGTON (St Michael) w Burneston and Wath and Pickhill *Ripon 4* **P** *Ch Soc Trust, Mrs M St B Anderson, G W Prior-Wandesforde Esq, and DBP (jt)* **P-in-c** J NELSON
KIRKLINGTON (St Swithin) w Hockerton *S'well 15* **P** *Bp* **P-in-c** E F CULLY, **C** J R CHAMBERS
KIRKLINTON (St Cuthbert) *see* Bewcastle, Stapleton and Kirklinton etc *Carl*
KIRKNEWTON (St Gregory) *see* Glendale Gp *Newc*
KIRKOSWALD (St Oswald), Renwick, Great Salkeld and Lazonby *Carl 4* **P** *Bp* **R** D M FOWLER
KIRKSTALL (St Stephen) *Ripon 7* **P** *Patrons Leeds St Pet* **V** C A JAMES, **NSM** B WOOD
KIRKSTEAD (St Leonard) *see* Woodhall Spa Gp *Linc*
KIRKTHORPE (St Peter) *see* Warmfield *Wakef*
KIRKWHELPINGTON (St Bartholomew) w Kirkharle, Kirkheaton and Cambo *Newc 11* **P** *Ld Chan (2 turns), J P P Anderson Esq (1 turn), and Bp (1 turn)* **V** *vacant* (01830) 540260
KIRMINGTON (St Helen) *see* Brocklesby Park *Linc*
KIRMOND-LE-MIRE (St Martin) *see* Walesby *Linc*
KIRSTEAD (St Margaret) *see* Brooke, Kirstead, Mundham w Seething and Thwaite *Nor*
KIRTLING (All Saints) *Ely 4* **P** *Mrs D A Bowlby and Countess Ellesmere (alt)* **V** C A SINDALL, **Hon C** L M BROUGHTON
KIRTLINGTON (St Mary the Virgin) *see* Akeman *Ox*
KIRTON (Holy Trinity) *S'well 3* **P** *SMF* **R** C C LEVY
KIRTON (St Mary and St Martin) w Falkenham *St E 2* **P** *Ld Chan* **P-in-c** G L GRANT
KIRTON HOLME (Christ Church) *see* Brothertoft Gp *Linc*
KIRTON IN HOLLAND (St Peter and St Paul) *Linc 21* **P** *Mercers' Co* **P-in-c** D A CARNEY
KIRTON IN LINDSEY (St Andrew) w Manton *Linc 6* **P** *Bp* **R** S J FOSTER
KISLINGBURY (St Luke) and Harpole *Pet 3* **P** *Bp and Sir Stephen Hastings (alt)* **R** *vacant* (01604) 830322
KITT GREEN (St Francis of Assisi) *see* Pemberton St Fran Kitt Green *Liv*
KITTISFORD (St Nicholas) *see* Wellington and Distr *B & W*
KLIVE (Blessed Virgin Mary) *see* Quantoxhead *B & W*
KNAITH (St Mary) *see* Lea Gp *Linc*
KNAPHILL (Holy Trinity) w Brookwood *Guildf 12* **P** *CPAS* **V** N D GREW
KNAPTON (St Peter) *see* Trunch *Nor*
KNAPWELL (All Saints) *see* Papworth *Ely*
KNARESBOROUGH (Holy Trinity) (St John the Baptist) *Ripon 1* **P** *Bp and Earl of Harewood (jt)* **TR** A C BETTS, **TV** A CALLAN-TRAVIS, **NSM** D LOXLEY
KNARESDALE (St Jude) *see* Alston Moor *Newc*
KNEBWORTH (St Martin) (St Mary the Virgin and St Thomas of Canterbury) *St Alb 23* **P** *Hon D A Fromanteel* **R** J T PYE
KNEESALL w Laxton and Wellow *S'well 3* **P** *DBP and Bp (jt)* **P-in-c** D R MOORE
KNEETON (St Helen) *see* E Bridgford and Kneeton *S'well*
KNIGHTLEY (Christ Church) *see* Adbaston, High Offley, Knightley, Norbury etc *Lich*
KNIGHTON (St Mary Magdalene) (St Guthlac) *Leic 2* **P** *Bp* **V** C D ALLEN, **C** H E DEARNLEY, J M SHARP, **NSM** M R SEDEN, R J BONNEY
KNIGHTON (Village Hall) *see* Ashley and Mucklestone *Lich*
KNIGHTON, WEST (St Peter) *see* Watercombe *Sarum*
KNIGHTON-ON-TEME (St Michael and All Angels) *see* Teme Valley N *Worc*
KNIGHTS AND HOSPITALLERS PARISHES, The *Chelmsf 19* **P** *Hosp of St Jo of Jerusalem, Bp, and Earl of Verulam (jt)* **V** J E DONALDSON
KNIGHT'S ENHAM (St Michael and All Angels) (St Paul's Church Centre) and Smannell w Enham Alamein *Win 3* **P** *Bp* **R** B L COX, **C** B ROSTILL, **Hon C** A JARDINE
KNIGHTSBRIDGE (St Paul) Wilton Place *see* Wilton Place St Paul *Lon*
KNILL (St Michael and All Angels) *see* Presteigne w Discoed, Kinsham, Lingen and Knill *Heref*
KNIPTON (All Saints) *see* High Framland Par *Leic*
KNIVETON (St Michael and All Angels) *see* Hulland, Atlow, Kniveton, Bradley and Hognaston *Derby*
KNOCKHOLT (St Katharine) w Halstead *Roch 9* **P** *D&C* **R** M D WOODCOCK, **NSM** H V THOMAS
KNOCKIN (St Mary) *see* Kinnerley w Melverley and Knockin w Maesbrook *Lich*
KNODISHALL (St Lawrence) *see* Aldringham w Thorpe, Knodishall w Buxlow etc *St E*
KNOOK (St Margaret) *see* Upper Wylye Valley *Sarum*
KNOSSINGTON (St Peter) *see* Whatborough Gp *Leic*
KNOTTING (St Margaret) *see* Sharnbrook and Knotting w Souldrop *St Alb*
KNOTTINGLEY (St Botolph) and Kellington w Whitley *Wakef 11* **P** *Patr Bd* **TR** C A FLATTERS, **TV** C D WHITE
KNOTTY ASH (St John) *Liv 2* **P** *R W Derby* **V** J G M ROOKE
KNOWBURY (St Paul) w Clee Hill *Heref 12* **P** *Bp* **V** *vacant*
KNOWBURY (St Peter's Mission Room) Clee Hill *see* Wigmore Abbey *Heref*
KNOWL HILL (St Peter) *see* Wargrave w Knowl Hill *Ox*
KNOWLE (Holy Nativity) *Bris 1* **P** *Bp* **V** J M BROWN
KNOWLE (Mission Room) *see* Coreley and Doddington *Heref*
KNOWLE (St Barnabas) *Bris 1* **P** *Bp* **V** A G PALMER
KNOWLE (St Boniface) *see* Crediton, Shobrooke and Sandford etc *Ex*
KNOWLE (St John) *see* E Budleigh w Bicton and Otterton *Ex*
KNOWLE (St John the Baptist) (St Lawrence and St Anne) *Birm 11* **P** *Bp* **V** M J PARKER, **C** J R LEACH, S L TILLETT
KNOWLE (St Martin) *Bris 1* **P** *Bp* **V** R WARD
KNOWLE, WEST (Holy Cross) *see* Inns Court H Cross *Bris*
KNOWSLEY (St Mary) *Liv 2* **P** *Earl of Derby* **V** C DOWDLE, **NSM** S C LEDBETTER
KNOWSTONE (St Peter) *see* Bishopsnympton, Rose Ash, Mariansleigh etc *Ex*
KNOYLE, EAST (St Mary the Virgin), Semley and Sedgehill *Sarum 11* **P** *Bp and Ch Ch Ox* **OLM** L J LANE
KNOYLE, WEST (St Mary the Virgin) *see* Mere w W Knoyle and Maiden Bradley *Sarum*
KNUTSFORD (St Cross) Cross Town *Ches 12* **P** *Mrs J Singer* **V** A T M TOLLEFSEN
KNUTSFORD (St John the Baptist) and Toft *Ches 12* **P** *Bp (3 turns), Mrs L M Anderson (1 turn)* **V** N T ATKINSON, **C** P W HIGHTON
KNUTTON (St Mary) *Lich 9* **P** *Sir Beville Stanier Bt and T H G Howard-Sneyd Esq (alt)* **V** P G HOUGH
KNUZDEN (St Oswald) *Blackb 2* **P** *Bp* **V** M A MORRIS
KNYPERSLEY (St John the Evangelist) *Lich 8* **P** *CPAS* **V** J A DAWSWELL
KYME, NORTH (St Luke) *see* Kirkby Laythorpe *Linc*
KYME, SOUTH (St Mary and All Saints) *as above*
KYNNERSLEY (St Chad) *see* Edgmond w Kynnersley and Preston Wealdmoors *Lich*
KYRE WYARD (St Mary) *see* Teme Valley S *Worc*
LACEBY (St Margaret) and Ravendale Group, The *Linc 10* **P** *D Parkinson Settled Estates, Ridley Hall Cam, and Earl of Yarborough (jt), Bp, and Ld Chan (by turn)* **P-in-c** P M TOMPKINS
LACEY GREEN (Church Hall) *see* Wilmslow *Ches*
LACEY GREEN (St John the Evangelist) *see* Risborough *Ox*
LACH DENNIS (All Saints) *see* Lostock Gralam *Ches*
LACHE (St Mark) cum Saltney *Ches 2* **P** *Bp* **V** T G N GREEN, **C** S CHESTERS, A P WATTS

LACKFORD (St Lawrence) *see* Lark Valley *St E*
LACOCK (St Cyriac) *see* Gtr Corsham and Lacock *Bris*
LADBROKE (All Saints) *see* Harbury and Ladbroke *Cov*
LADBROKE GROVE (St Michael and All Angels) *see* Notting Hill St Mich and Ch Ch *Lon*
LADDINGFORD (St Mary) *see* Yalding w Collier Street *Roch*
LADOCK (St Ladoca) *see* Probus, Ladock and Grampound w Creed and St Erme *Truro*
LADY BAY (All Hallows) *S'well 9* **P** *Bp* **V** R W BRECKLES
LADYBARN (St Chad) *Man 8* **P** *Bp* **R** D K PRYCE
LADYBROOK (St Mary the Virgin) *S'well 2* **P** *Bp* **P-in-c** R C THOMPSON
LADYWOOD (St John the Evangelist) (St Peter) *Birm 2* **P** *Trustees* **V** R J TETLOW, **C** J M MASON
LAFFORD, SOUTH *Linc 22* **P** *G Heathcote Esq, Bp, J Wilson Esq, D&C, DBP, N Playne Esq, Sir Bruno Welby Bt, and Lady Willoughby de Eresby (by turn)* **P-in-c** C P ROBERTSON
LAINDON (St Martin of Tours) *see* Basildon St Martin *Chelmsf*
LAINDON (St Nicholas) w Dunton *Chelmsf 6* **P** *Bp* **R** N C PAUL
LAIRA (St Augustine) *see* Plymouth Em, St Paul Efford and St Aug *Ex*
LAIRA (St Mary the Virgin) *see* Plymouth St Simon and St Mary *Ex*
LAISTERDYKE (St Mary) *Bradf 3* **P** *Simeon's Trustees* **V** P DEO
LAITHKIRK (not known) *see* Romaldkirk w Laithkirk *Ripon*
LAKE (Good Shepherd) *Portsm 7* **P** *Bp* **V** R M SMITH, **NSM** B M DOWNER
LAKENHAM (St Alban) *see* Nor Lakenham St Alb and St Mark *Nor*
LAKENHAM (St John the Baptist and All Saints) *see* Nor Lakenham St Jo and All SS and Tuckswood *Nor*
LAKENHAM (St Mark) *see* Nor Lakenham St Alb and St Mark *Nor*
LAKENHEATH (St Mary) *see* Brandon and Santon Downham w Elveden etc *St E*
LALEHAM (All Saints) *Lon 13* **P** *Earl of Lucan* **V** P R BROWN
LAMARSH (Holy Innocents) *see* N Hinckford *Chelmsf*
LAMBERHURST (St Mary) and Matfield *Roch 8* **P** *D&C and V Brenchley (jt)* **V** D M BOURNE
LAMBETH (St Andrew) *see* Waterloo St Jo w St Andr *S'wark*
LAMBETH (St John the Evangelist) *as above*
LAMBETH, NORTH (St Anselm) (St Mary's Mission) (St Peter) *S'wark 13* **P** *The Crown (1 turn), Patr Bd (2 turns)* **TR** A R AAGAARD, **TV** W ROEST, **NSM** M A K HILBORN
LAMBETH, SOUTH (St Anne and All Saints) *S'wark 13* **P** *Abp and Bp* **V** A B NEWBY
LAMBETH, SOUTH (St Stephen) *S'wark 13* **P** *CPAS* **V** W A WILSON
LAMBLEY (Holy Trinity) *S'well 10* **P** *Revd W J Gull* **P-in-c** K A PAYNE
LAMBLEY (St Mary and St Patrick) *see* Alston Moor *Newc*
LAMBOURN (St Michael and All Angels) *Ox 14* **P** *Bp* **P-in-c** A W CUMBERLIDGE
LAMBOURNE (St Mary and All Saints) w Abridge and Stapleford Abbotts *Chelmsf 25* **P** *CCC Cam and Ld Chan (alt)* **P-in-c** G W ELLIS
LAMBROOK, EAST (St James) *see* Kingsbury Episcopi w E Lambrook, Hambridge etc *B & W*
LAMERTON (St Peter) *see* Milton Abbot, Dunterton, Lamerton etc *Ex*
LAMESLEY (St Andrew) *see* Harlow Green and Lamesley *Dur*
LAMMAS (St Andrew) *see* Buxton w Oxnead, Lammas and Brampton *Nor*
LAMORBEY (Holy Redeemer) *Roch 17* **P** *Bp* **V** N I KERR
LAMORBEY (Holy Trinity) *Roch 17* **P** *Mrs H K L Whittow* **V** G W DAVIES
LAMORRAN (Holy Trinity) and Merther *Truro 6* **P** *Viscount Falmouth* **P-in-c** A M YATES
LAMP *Ox 27* **P** *CPAS* **P-in-c** I J PUSEY, **OLM** H J LOWNDES
LAMPLUGH (St Michael) w Ennerdale *Carl 5* **P** *Trustees* **R** *vacant* (01946) 861310
LAMPORT (All Saints) *see* Maidwell w Draughton, Lamport w Faxton *Pet*
LAMYATT (St Mary and St John) *see* Bruton and Distr *B & W*
LANCASTER (Christ Church) (Christ Church Worship Centre) *Blackb 11* **P** *V Lanc and Trustees (alt)* **V** P S G HUDD, **NSM** B K HARDING
LANCASTER (St Chad) *see* Skerton St Chad *Blackb*
LANCASTER (St Luke) *see* Skerton St Luke *Blackb*
LANCASTER (St Mary) w St John and St Anne *Blackb 11* **P** *Trustees* **V** P B CAVANAGH, **C** P J PAYTON, S MCMAHON
LANCASTER (St Paul) *see* Scotforth *Blackb*
LANCASTER (St Thomas) *Blackb 11* **P** *CPAS* **V** P G GUINNESS, **C** S J C CORLEY, D A PEATMAN
LANCHESTER (All Saints) *Dur 4* **P** *Ld Chan* **V** P WATERHOUSE, **C** H M BARTON
LANCING (St James the Less) w Coombes *Chich 5* **P** *Bp Lon* **R** R G RUSSELL, **C** B J MINTON
LANCING (St Michael and All Angels) *Chich 5* **P** *Bp* **V** B G CARTER
LANDBEACH (All Saints) *Ely 5* **P** *CCC Cam* **R** N I MOIR
LANDCROSS (Holy Trinity) *see* Bideford, Northam, Westward Ho!, Appledore etc *Ex*
LANDEWEDNACK (St Wynwallow) *see* St Ruan w St Grade and Landewednack *Truro*
LANDFORD (St Andrew) *see* Bramshaw and Landford w Plaitford *Sarum*
LANDKEY (St Paul) *see* Swimbridge w W Buckland and Landkey *Ex*
LANDRAKE (St Michael) w St Erney and Botus Fleming *Truro 11* **P** *Bp and MMCET (jt)* **V** M GRIFFITHS, **OLM** P C WILLIAMS
LANDSCOVE (St Matthew) *see* Broadhempston, Woodland, Staverton etc *Ex*
LANDULPH (St Leonard and St Dilpe) *see* St Dominic, Landulph and St Mellion w Pillaton *Truro*
LANDYWOOD (St Andrew) *see* Gt Wyrley *Lich*
LANE END (Holy Trinity) w Cadmore End *Ox 29* **P** *Bp* **V** R H JENNINGS
LANEAST (St Sidwell and St Gulvat) *see* Altarnon w Bolventor, Laneast and St Clether *Truro*
LANEHAM (St Peter) *see* Rampton w Laneham, Treswell, Cottam and Stokeham *S'well*
LANERCOST (St Mary Magdalene), Walton, Gilsland and Nether Denton *Carl 2* **P** *Bp, Adn, and the Hon P C W Howard (jt)* **R** C J MORRIS, **NSM** J T RICHARDSON
LANESIDE (St Peter) *Blackb 1* **P** *V Haslingden St Jas* **V** S C BROWN
LANGAR (St Andrew) *see* Cropwell Bishop w Colston Bassett, Granby etc *S'well*
LANGCLIFFE (St John the Evangelist) w Stainforth and Horton-in-Ribblesdale *Bradf 5* **P** *Bp, Adn Craven, W R G Bell Esq, N Caton Esq, and Churchwardens of Horton-in-Ribblesdale (jt)* **V** R G WOOD
LANGDALE (Holy Trinity) (Mission Chapel) *Carl 11* **P** *R Grasmere* **P-in-c** W R F COKE, **NSM** A J FOLKS
LANGDALE END (St Peter) *see* Brompton by Sawdon w Hutton Buscel, Snainton etc *York*
LANGDON, EAST (St Augustine) *see* St Margarets-at-Cliffe w Westcliffe etc *Cant*
LANGDON, WEST (St Mary the Virgin) *as above*
LANGDON HILLS (St Mary and All Saints) *Chelmsf 6* **P** *D&C St Paul's* **R** C E HOPKINSON, **C** M A SHAW
LANGFORD (Blessed Virgin Mary) *see* Burrington and Churchill *B & W*
LANGFORD (St Andrew) *see* Henlow and Langford *St Alb*
LANGFORD (St Bartholomew) *see* Coddington and Winthorpe and Langford w Holme *S'well*
LANGFORD (St Giles) *see* Heybridge w Langford *Chelmsf*
LANGFORD (St Matthew) *see* Shill Valley and Broadshire *Ox*
LANGFORD, LITTLE (St Nicholas of Mira) *see* Wylye and Till Valley *Sarum*
LANGFORD BUDVILLE (St Peter) *see* Wellington and Distr *B & W*
LANGHAM (St George) *see* Stour Vale *Sarum*
LANGHAM (St Mary the Virgin) *see* Badwell and Walsham *St E*
LANGHAM (St Mary the Virgin) w Boxted *Chelmsf 17* **P** *Bp and Duchy of Lanc (alt)* **P-in-c** T M BULL
LANGHAM (St Peter and St Paul) *Pet 14* **P** *Bp* **P-in-c** L T FRANCIS-DEHQANI
LANGHAM EPISCOPI (St Andrew and St Mary) *see* Stiffkey and Bale *Nor*
LANGHAM PLACE (All Souls) *Lon 4* **P** *The Crown* **R** H PALMER, **C** P A WILLIAMS, R A HIGGINS, M N PRENTICE, P BLACKHAM, R I TICE, **Hon C** J R W STOTT, **NSM** M R E REEVES
LANGHO BILLINGTON (St Leonard) *Blackb 7* **P** *V Blackb* **P-in-c** D NOBLET
LANGLEY (All Saints and Martyrs) and Parkfield *Man 18* **P** *Patr Bd* **TR** P H MILLER, **TV** A I GALLAGHER, **C** L P LONGDEN
LANGLEY (St Francis) *see* Fawley *Win*
LANGLEY (St John) *Birm 7* **P** *Bp* **P-in-c** J R BARNETT, **C** A D BARRETT, **NSM** A E HANNY

LANGLEY (St John the Evangelist) *see* Clavering and Langley w Arkesden etc *Chelmsf*
LANGLEY (St Mary) *see* Otham w Langley *Cant*
LANGLEY (St Mary the Virgin) *see* Wolverton w Norton Lindsey and Langley *Cov*
LANGLEY (St Michael) *see* Loddon, Sisland, Chedgrave, Hardley and Langley *Nor*
LANGLEY (St Michael and All Angels) *Birm 7* **P** *The Crown* **P-in-c** J R BARNETT, **C** A D BARRETT, **NSM** A E HANNY
LANGLEY BURRELL (St Peter) *see* Chippenham St Paul w Hardenhuish etc *Bris*
LANGLEY GREEN (St Leonard) *see* Ifield *Chich*
LANGLEY MARISH (St Mary the Virgin) *Ox 23* **P** *Patr Bd* **TV** B H RUSSELL, C HANSON
LANGLEY MARSH (St Luke Mission Church) *see* Wiveliscombe w Chipstable, Huish Champflower etc *B & W*
LANGLEY MILL (St Andrew) *Derby 12* **P** *V Heanor* **P-in-c** C L HUGHES
LANGLEY PARK (All Saints) *Dur 1* **P** *Prime Min* **V** M J PEERS, **C** T E HUBBLE
LANGLEY PARK (St Peter's Church Hall) *see* Beckenham St Barn *Roch*
LANGLEY STREET (Mission Room) *see* Derby St Barn *Derby*
LANGLEYBURY (St Paul) *St Alb 7* **P** *D W A Loyd Esq* **P-in-c** D L ELLSON
LANGNEY (St Richard of Chichester) *Chich 16* **P** *Bp* **V** D ASHTON
LANGOLD (St Luke) *see* Carlton-in-Lindrick and Langold w Oldcotes *S'well*
LANGPORT Area Churches, The *B & W 6* **P** *Patr Bd* **TR** H W ELLIS, **TV** L F WHATLEY, **NSM** M CUMMINGS
LANGRICK (St Margaret of Scotland) *see* Brothertoft Gp *Linc*
LANGRIDGE (St Mary Magdalene) *see* Bath Weston All SS w N Stoke and Langridge *B & W*
LANGRISH (St John the Evangelist) *Portsm 4* **P** *Bp* **V** T E LOUDEN
LANGSTONE (St Nicholas) *see* Havant *Portsm*
LANGTOFT (St Michael) *see* Ness Gp *Linc*
LANGTOFT (St Peter) w Foxholes, Butterwick, Cottam and Thwing *York 10* **P** *Abp and Keble Coll Ox (2 turns), Ld Chan (1 turn)* **P-in-c** R SELWOOD, **NSM** C A ACONLEY
LANGTON (St Andrew) *see* W Buckrose *York*
LANGTON (St Margaret) *see* Woodhall Spa Gp *Linc*
LANGTON (St Peter) *as above*
LANGTON, GREAT (St Wilfrid) *see* Lower Swale *Ripon*
LANGTON, GREAT (The Good Shepherd) *as above*
LANGTON BY PARTNEY (St Peter and St Paul) *see* Partney Gp *Linc*
LANGTON-BY-WRAGBY (St Giles) *see* Wragby Gp *Linc*
LANGTON GREEN (All Saints) *Roch 12* **P** *R Speldhurst* **V** M J GENTRY, **NSM** P J ATTWOOD
LANGTON HERRING (St Peter) *see* Abbotsbury, Portesham and Langton Herring *Sarum*
LANGTON LONG (All Saints) *see* Blandford Forum and Langton Long *Sarum*
LANGTON MATRAVERS (St George) *see* Kingston, Langton Matravers and Worth Matravers *Sarum*
LANGTON ON SWALE (St Wilfrid) *see* Lower Swale *Ripon*
LANGTREE *Ox 6* **P** *Patr Bd* **TR** K G DAVIES, **TV** N E MOSS, **Hon C** J L EVANS, **NSM** A M LINTON, P J R STEDDON
LANGTREE (All Saints) *see* Shebbear, Buckland Filleigh, Sheepwash etc *Ex*
LANGWATHBY (St Peter) *see* Cross Fell Gp *Carl*
LANGWITH, UPPER (Holy Cross) *see* E Scarsdale *Derby*
LANGWORTH (St Hugh) *see* Barlings *Linc*
LANHYDROCK (St Hydrock) *see* Bodmin w Lanhydrock and Lanivet *Truro*
LANIVET (St Ia) *as above*
LANLIVERY (St Brevita) w Luxulyan *Truro 10* **P** *Bp (1 turn), Adn Bodmin (1 turn), and DBP (2 turns)* **P-in-c** F M BOWERS, **C** S D MICHAEL
LANNER (Christ Church) *see* Redruth w Lanner and Treleigh *Truro*
LANREATH (St Marnarck), Pelynt and Bradoc *Truro 12* **P** *A D G Fortescue Esq, J B Kitson Esq, and H M Parker Esq (jt)* **C** L J SMITH, F C STEVENS
LANSALLOS (St Ildierna) *Truro 12* **P** *DBP and W Gundry-Mills Esq (alt)* **P-in-c** L A H COURTNEY
LANSDOWN (St Stephen) *see* Charlcombe w Bath St Steph *B & W*
LANSDOWNE ROAD (St Mary the Virgin) *see* Tottenham St Mary *Lon*
LANTEGLOS BY CAMELFORD (St Julitta) w Advent *Truro 10* **P** *Duchy of Cornwall* **P-in-c** B J BERRIMAN
LANTEGLOS BY FOWEY (St Wyllow) *Truro 12* **P** *D&C* **P-in-c** L A H COURTNEY
LAPAL (St Peter) *see* Halas *Worc*
LAPFORD (St Thomas of Canterbury) *see* N Creedy *Ex*
LAPLEY (All Saints) w Wheaton Aston *Lich 2* **P** *Keble Coll Ox* **V** G J THOMPSON, **OLM** G P ELLIS
LAPWORTH (St Mary the Virgin) *Birm 6* **P** *Mert Coll Ox* **R** M J MORGAN
LARCHFIELD (St George) *see* Boyne Hill *Ox*
LARK VALLEY Benefice, The *St E 13* **P** *R W Gough Esq (1 turn), Bp (2 turns)* **R** D P BURRELL, **NSM** E M ELLIOTT
LARKFIELD (Holy Trinity) *Roch 7* **P** *DBP* **V** D J WALKER
LARLING (St Ethelbert) *see* E w W Harling, Bridgham w Roudham, Larling etc *Nor*
LASBOROUGH (St Mary) *see* Boxwell, Leighterton, Didmarton, Oldbury etc *Glouc*
LASHAM (St Mary) *see* Bentworth, Lasham, Medstead and Shalden *Win*
LASHBROOK (Mission Room) *see* Shiplake w Dunsden and Harpsden *Ox*
LASTINGHAM (St Mary) w Appleton-le-Moors, Rosedale and Cropton *York 17* **P** *Abp (2 turns), Ld Chan (1 turn)* **V** A S FERGUSON
LATCHFORD (Christ Church) *Ches 4* **P** *R Grappenhall* **V** J L GOODE
LATCHFORD (St James) (St Hilda) *Ches 4* **P** *R Grappenhall* **V** J T MCNAUGHTAN-OWEN, **C** J E HARRIES
LATCHINGDON (Christ Church) *see* Creeksea w Althorne, Latchingdon and N Fambridge *Chelmsf*
LATHBURY (All Saints) *see* Newport Pagnell w Lathbury and Moulsoe *Ox*
LATHOM PARK (St John) *see* Ormskirk *Liv*
LATIMER (St Mary Magdalene) *see* Chenies and Lt Chalfont, Latimer and Flaunden *Ox*
LATTON (St John the Baptist) *see* Cricklade w Latton *Bris*
LAUGHTON (All Saints) *see* Corringham and Blyton Gp *Linc*
LAUGHTON (All Saints) w Ripe and Chalvington *Chich 18* **P** *Bp (2 turns), Hertf Coll Ox (1 turn)* **R** D M FAREY
LAUGHTON (St Luke) *see* Foxton w Gumley and Laughton *Leic*
LAUGHTON-EN-LE-MORTHEN (All Saints) *see* Dinnington w Laughton and Throapham *Sheff*
LAUNCELLS (St Andrew and St Swithin) *see* Stratton and Launcells *Truro*
LAUNCESTON (St Mary Magdalene) (St Thomas the Apostle) (St Stephen) *Truro 9* **P** *Patr Bd* **P-in-c** D A E MICHAELS, **C** C R CARLYON
LAUNTON (Assumption of the Blessed Virgin Mary) *see* Bicester w Bucknell, Caversfield and Launton *Ox*
LAVANT (St Mary) (St Nicholas) *Chich 3* **P** *Earl of March and Kinrara* **R** D L PARKER
LAVENDER HILL (The Ascension) and Battersea St Philip w St Bartholomew *S'wark 16* **P** *Bp and Keble Coll Ox (jt)* **V** P C B ALLEN
LAVENDON (St Michael) w Cold Brayfield, Clifton Reynes and Newton Blossomville *Ox 27* **P** *T V Sutthery Esq, The Revd S F Hamill-Stewart, Exors M E Farrer Esq, and Bp (jt)* **P-in-c** C E CERRATTI, **C** J A TOMKINS
LAVENHAM (St Peter and St Paul) w Preston *St E 10* **P** *G&C Coll Cam, and Em Coll Cam (by turn)* **R** N E WOODCOCK
LAVENHAM (St Peter and St Paul) *see* Lavenham w Preston *St E*
LAVER, HIGH (All Saints) w Magdalen Laver and Little Laver and Matching *Chelmsf 27* **P** *Bp* **R** P T C MASHEDER
LAVER, LITTLE (St Mary the Virgin) *see* High Laver w Magdalen Laver and Lt Laver etc *Chelmsf*
LAVERSTOCK (St Andrew) *see* Salisbury St Martin and Laverstock *Sarum*
LAVERSTOKE (St Mary) *see* Overton w Laverstoke and Freefolk *Win*
LAVERTON (The Blessed Virgin Mary) *see* Hardington Vale *B & W*
LAVINGTON, WEST (St Mary Magdalene) *see* Cocking, Bepton and W Lavington *Chich*
LAVINGTONS, Cheverells, and Easterton, The *Sarum 16* **P** *Bp and Ch Ch Ox (jt)* **R** H W B STEPHENS, **NSM** P A STROWGER, **OLM** A L COCKING
LAWFORD (St Mary) *Chelmsf 20* **P** *St Jo Coll Cam* **R** P C M PRESTNEY, **NSM** P W MANN
LAWHITTON (St Michael) *see* Lezant w Lawhitton and S Petherwin w Trewen *Truro*
LAWLEY (St John the Evangelist) *see* Cen Telford *Lich*
LAWRENCE WESTON (St Peter) and Avonmouth *Bris 2* **P** *Bp* **V** *vacant* 0117-982 5863

LAWRES Group, The SOUTH *Linc 3* **P** *D&C Linc, D&C Pet, and Mercers' Co (jt)* **P-in-c** C TODD
LAWSHALL (All Saints) *see* St Edm Way *St E*
LAWTON (All Saints) *see* Church Lawton *Ches*
LAWTON MOOR (St Michael and All Angels) *Man 8* **P** *Bp* **P-in-c** J S A LAW, **OLM** I V SMITH
LAXEY (Christ Church) *S & M 2* **P** *Bp* **V** W H MARTIN, **OLM** J E GUILFORD
LAXFIELD (All Saints), Cratfield, Wilby and Brundish *St E 17* **P** *Patr Bd* **R** F O NEWTON
LAXTON (All Saints) *see* Bulwick, Blatherwycke w Harringworth and Laxton *Pet*
LAXTON (St Michael) *see* Kneesall w Laxton and Wellow *S'well*
LAXTON (St Peter) *see* Howden *York*
LAYER BRETON (St Mary the Virgin) *see* Layer de la Haye and Layer Breton w Birch etc *Chelmsf*
LAYER DE LA HAYE (St John the Baptist) and Layer Breton w Birch and Layer Marney *Chelmsf 24* **P** *Bp, Col J G Round, and N S Charrington Esq (by turn)* **R** M H CLARKE
LAYER MARNEY (St Mary the Virgin) *see* Layer de la Haye and Layer Breton w Birch etc *Chelmsf*
LAYHAM (St Andrew) *see* Hadleigh, Layham and Shelley *St E*
LAYSTON W BUNTINGFORD (St Peter) *see* Aspenden, Buntingford and Westmill *St Alb*
LAYTON (St Mark) *see* Blackpool St Mark *Blackb*
LAYTON, EAST (Christ Church) *see* Forcett and Aldbrough and Melsonby *Ripon*
LAZONBY (St Nicholas) *see* Kirkoswald, Renwick, Gt Salkeld and Lazonby *Carl*
LEA Group, The (St Helen) *Linc 2* **P** *Bp, DBP, and Exors Lt Col J E W G Sandars (jt)* **R** P WAIN, **NSM** L Y LUCAS
LEA (St Christopher) (St Barnabas) *Blackb 13* **P** *Bp* **V** D J THOMPSON
LEA (St Giles) *see* Garsdon, Lea and Cleverton and Charlton *Bris*
LEA, THE (St John the Baptist) *see* Ross *Heref*
LEA AND HOLLOWAY (Christ Church) *see* Tansley, Dethick, Lea and Holloway *Derby*
LEA CROSS (St Anne) *see* Pontesbury I and II *Heref*
LEA HALL (St Richard) *Birm 9* **P** *Bp* **V** P M BRACHER
LEA MARSTON (St John the Baptist) *see* The Whitacres and Shustoke *Birm*
LEADEN RODING (St Michael) *see* S Rodings *Chelmsf*
LEADENHAM (St Swithin) *Linc 23* **P** *P R Reeve Esq* **R** A J MEGAHEY
LEADGATE (St Ives) *see* Dipton and Leadgate *Dur*
LEAFIELD (St Michael and All Angels) *see* Ramsden, Finstock and Fawler, Leafield etc *Ox*
LEAGRAVE (St Luke) *St Alb 14* **P** *Bp* **V** S PURVIS, **C** S MARTIN
LEAHOLM (St James's Chapel) *see* Middle Esk Moor *York*
LEAKE (St Mary) w Over and Nether Silton and Kepwick *York 19* **P** *Abp* **P-in-c** P R A R HOARE, **NSM** E A HOARE
LEAKE, EAST (St Mary), WEST (St Helena), Stanford-on-Soar, Rempstone and Costock *S'well 9* **P** *Bp, DBP, Lord Belper, and SS Coll Cam (jt)* **R** G C HETHERINGTON, **NSM** M R ESSEX
LEAKE, NEW (St Jude) *see* Stickney Gp *Linc*
LEAKE, OLD (St Mary) w Wrangle *Linc 20* **P** *Bp and DBP (alt)* **Hon C** J F GLEADALL
LEAM LANE (St Andrew) *Dur 12* **P** *Bp* **V** *vacant* 0191-469 3257
LEAM VALLEY *Cov 6* **P** *Bp (2 turns), Mrs H M O Lodder (1 turn)* **NSM** W T G GRIFFITHS
LEAMINGTON, SOUTH (St John the Baptist) *Cov 11* **P** *Bp* **V** D W LAWSON
LEAMINGTON HASTINGS (All Saints) *see* Leam Valley *Cov*
LEAMINGTON PRIORS (All Saints) *Cov 11* **P** *Bp* **P-in-c** C H WILSON, **NSM** A MORRIS, D HISCOX
LEAMINGTON PRIORS (St Mary) *Cov 11* **P** *Ch Patr Trust* **V** M RODHAM, **C** A M ATTWOOD
LEAMINGTON PRIORS (St Paul) *Cov 11* **P** *Ch Patr Trust* **V** J N JEE, **C** M P J KING, **Hon C** J S TILLEY
LEAMINGTON SPA (Holy Trinity) and Old Milverton *Cov 11* **P** *Bp and M Heber-Percy Esq (jt)* **C** K LINDOP, C H WILSON, **NSM** F A SMITH, A MORRIS, D HISCOX
LEAMINGTON SPA (St Mark New Milverton) *see* New Milverton *Cov*
LEAMORE (St Aidan) *see* Blakenall Heath *Lich*
LEASINGHAM (St Andrew) *Linc 22* **P** *DBP* **P-in-c** A J LITTLEWOOD
LEASOWE (St Chad) *Ches 7* **P** *Bp* **P-in-c** M F TURNBULL
LEATHERHEAD (All Saints) (St Mary and St Nicholas) and Mickleham *Guildf 10* **P** *Bp Guildf and D&C Roch (jt)* **R** D J EATON, **C** B J MARTIN, **NSM** D A IRELAND
LEATHLEY (St Oswald) w Farnley, Fewston and Blubberhouses *Bradf 4* **P** *Bp and G N le G Horton-Fawkes Esq* **P-in-c** S J WHARTON, **NSM** M F CLEVERLEY, T H BAXTER
LEATON (Holy Trinity) and Albrighton w Battlefield *Lich 20* **P** *Mrs J M Jagger* **P-in-c** N C M SALTER
LEAVELAND (St Laurence) *see* Selling w Throwley, Sheldwich w Badlesmere etc *Cant*
LEAVENHEATH (St Matthew) *see* Stoke by Nayland w Leavenheath and Polstead *St E*
LEAVENING (not known) *see* W Buckrose *York*
LEAVESDEN (All Saints) *St Alb 7* **P** *Bp* **V** P R S BOLTON, **C** J M M SPREADBURY, C N DRURY, **NSM** A R ROSS
LECHLADE (St Lawrence) *Glouc 12* **P** *Em Coll Cam* **P-in-c** C P BRYAN
LECK (St Peter) *see* E Lonsdale *Blackb*
LECKFORD (St Nicholas) *see* Stockbridge and Longstock and Leckford *Win*
LECKHAMPSTEAD (Assumption of the Blessed Virgin Mary) *see* N Buckingham *Ox*
LECKHAMPSTEAD (St James) *see* Brightwalton w Catmore, Leckhampstead etc *Ox*
LECKHAMPTON (St Christopher) *see* Leckhampton SS Phil and Jas w Cheltenham St Jas *Glouc*
LECKHAMPTON (St Peter) *Glouc 9* **P** *Bp* **P-in-c** P WILKINSON, **NSM** F M BAYNE
LECKHAMPTON (St Philip and St James) w Cheltenham (St James) *Glouc 9* **P** *Bp* **V** P L CHICKEN, **NSM** J C HORAN
LECONFIELD (St Catherine) *see* Lockington and Lund and Scorborough w Leconfield *York*
LEDBURY Team Ministry, The (St Michael and All Angels) (St Katherine's Chapel *Heref 6* **P** *Patr Bd* **TV** H J MAYELL, S STRUTT, **C** C E MUNDELL, **NSM** E C REED, E N SEABRIGHT, **OLM** J L SCHOLEFIELD
LEDGEMOOR (Mission Room) *see* Canon Pyon w King's Pyon, Birley and Wellington *Heref*
LEDSHAM (All Saints) w Fairburn *York 4* **P** *G H H Wheler Esq* **V** W F R BATSON
LEDSTON LUCK (Mission Church) *see* Ledsham w Fairburn *York*
LEE (Good Shepherd) (St Peter) *S'wark 4* **P** *R Lee St Marg* **V** R D BAINBRIDGE, **C** A E HOAD, **NSM** J E CROUCHER
LEE (St Augustine) Grove Park *S'wark 4* **P** *Bp* **V** G A BERRIMAN
LEE (St Margaret) *S'wark 4* **P** *Ld Chan* **R** D S GATLIFFE, **C** J MIDDLEMISS, **Hon C** E E W MARTIN, **NSM** J K BURKITT-GRAY
LEE (St Matthew) *see* Ilfracombe, Lee, Woolacombe, Bittadon etc *Ex*
LEE (St Mildred) Burnt Ash Hill *S'wark 4* **P** *Bp* **NSM** S E KNIGHT
LEE (St Oswald) *see* St Oswald in Lee w Bingfield *Newc*
LEE, THE (St John the Baptist) *Ox 28* **P** *Bp* **P-in-c** D J BURGESS, **NSM** I CORNISH
LEE BROCKHURST (St Peter) *Lich 22* **P** *Lord Barnard* **P-in-c** C S COOKE
LEE MOOR (Mission Church) *see* Bickleigh and Shaugh Prior *Ex*
LEE-ON-THE-SOLENT (St Faith) *Portsm 3* **P** *Bp* **V** P A SUTTON, **C** E M WOODGATE
LEEBOTWOOD (St Mary) *see* Dorrington w Leebotwood, Longnor, Stapleton etc *Heref*
LEEDS (All Hallows) *Ripon 7* **P** *Bp and DBP (jt)* **V** R G GASTON
LEEDS (All Saints) w Osmondthorpe *Ripon 8* **P** *Bp* **V** A M GUBBINS
LEEDS (All Souls) *Ripon 7* **P** *V Leeds St Pet, Simeon's Trustees, and DBP (jt)* **V** D B EMMOTT
LEEDS Belle Isle (St John and St Barnabas) *Ripon 6* **P** *Bp* **V** I W RUTHERFORD, **C** P M MEADOWS
LEEDS (Emmanuel) *see* Leeds St Geo *Ripon*
LEEDS Gipton (Church of the Epiphany) *Ripon 5* **P** *Bp* **P-in-c** J E HEIGHTON
LEEDS Halton (St Wilfrid) *Ripon 8* **P** *Bp* **V** M D G HEATHER
LEEDS (Parish Church) *see* Leeds City *Ripon*
LEEDS Richmond Hill (St Saviour) *Ripon 6* **P** *Bp and Keble Coll Ox (jt)* **V** *vacant* 0113-248 0971
LEEDS (St Aidan) *Ripon 5* **P** *V Leeds St Pet* **V** A L TAYLOR, **C** A T C MYERS, **NSM** C T RAWLINS, D ZANKER
LEEDS (St Cyprian and St James) Harehills *Ripon 5* **P** *Bp* **P-in-c** M HARPER
LEEDS (St Edmund King and Martyr) *see* Roundhay St Edm *Ripon*
LEEDS (St George) *Ripon 7* **P** *Simeon's Trustees* **TR** J J CLARK, **TV** J A M BARNETT

LEEDS (St John the Evangelist) *see* Roundhay St Jo *Ripon*
LEEDS (St Nicholas) *see* Hollingbourne and Hucking w Leeds and Broomfield *Cant*
LEEDS (St Paul) *see* Ireland Wood *Ripon*
LEEDS (St Wilfrid) *Ripon 5* **P** *Bp* **V** J HILTON
LEEDS CITY (St Peter) (Holy Trinity) *Ripon 5* **P** *DBP* **TR** A F BUNDOCK, **TV** J M YATES, C V TAYLOR, **NSM** S J ROBINSON
LEEDSTOWN (St James's Mission Church) *see* Crowan and Treslothan *Truro*
LEEK (All Saints) (St Edward the Confessor) (St John the Evangelist) (St Luke) (St Paul) and Meerbrook *Lich 8* **P** *Patr Bd* **TR** M J PARKER, **TV** C R PETERS, R A WOODS, **C** E J FAIRLESS
LEEK WOOTTON (All Saints) *Cov 4* **P** *Lord Leigh* **P-in-c** B W PEARSON
LEEMING (St John the Baptist) *see* Bedale and Leeming *Ripon*
LEEMING BAR (St Augustine) *as above*
LEES HILL (Mission Hall) *see* Lanercost, Walton, Gilsland and Nether Denton *Carl*
LEESFIELD Knoll's Lane (St Agnes) *see* Leesfield *Man*
LEESFIELD (St Thomas) *Man 19* **P** *Bp* **C** K L SMEETON, **OLM** R FARRAR
LEFTWICH (Farm of the Good Shepherd) *see* Davenham *Ches*
LEGBOURNE (All Saints) and Wold Marsh *Linc 12* **P** *Ld Chan (1 turn), Bp, Viscountess Chaplin, Ch Trust Fund Trust, D&C, and DBP (1 turn), Duchy of Lanc (1 turn)* **V** *vacant* (01507) 602231
LEGBURTHWAITE (Mission Church) *see* St John's-in-the-Vale, Threlkeld and Wythburn *Carl*
LEGH, HIGH (St John) *see* Over Tabley and High Legh *Ches*
LEGSBY (St Thomas) *Linc 5* **P** *Bp* **V** M J CARTWRIGHT
LEICESTER (Holy Apostles) (St Oswald) *Leic 2* **P** *DBP and Ridley Hall Cam (jt)* **P-in-c** P R BERRY
LEICESTER (Holy Spirit) (St Andrew) (St Nicholas) *Leic 2* **P** *Bp* **TV** E MATTHEWS-LOYDALL, D L CAWLEY, **C** J B NAYLOR
LEICESTER (Holy Trinity w St John the Divine) *Leic 2* **P** *Peache Trustees* **V** R W MORGAN, **C** T L PHILLIPS, **NSM** A J MORGAN, J S T WOOLMER
LEICESTER (Martyrs) *Leic 2* **P** *Bp* **V** A P HOBSON, **C** A M ROCHE, D J CUNDILL, **Hon C** S J WRIGHT
LEICESTER Presentation of Christ (St Barnabas) (St Peter) (St Saviour) *Leic 1* **P** *Bp* **TR** P J BRINDLE, **TV** R N WHITTINGHAM, **C** C M KING
LEICESTER Resurrection (St Alban) *Leic 1* **P** *Bp* **TR** M E LAMBERT, **C** R C WILLIAMS, S A A ANAND
LEICESTER (St Aidan) *Leic 2* **P** *Bp* **V** *vacant* 0116-287 2342
LEICESTER (St Alban) *see* Leic Resurr *Leic*
LEICESTER (St Anne) *Leic 2* **P** *Bp* **P-in-c** C R OXLEY, **NSM** P J OXLEY
LEICESTER (St Chad) *Leic 1* **P** *Bp* **P-in-c** P J BRINDLE
LEICESTER (St Christopher) *Leic 2* **P** *MMCET* **V** A TELFORD
LEICESTER (St James the Greater) *Leic 2* **P** *Bp* **V** G RICHERBY, **NSM** M R BATTISON
LEICESTER (St John the Baptist) *see* Emmaus Par Team *Leic*
LEICESTER St Leonard Conventional District *Leic 2* **C-in-c** R W MORGAN
LEICESTER (St Mary de Castro) *Leic 2* **P** *Bp* **V** D L CAWLEY, **NSM** S P WARD
LEICESTER St Paul *Leic 2* **P** *Bp* **V** *vacant* 0116-262 8062
LEICESTER (St Philip) *Leic 1* **P** *Adn Leic, V Evington, V Leic H Trin, G A Cooling Esq, and A S Price Esq (jt)* **P-in-c** D P JOHNSON
LEICESTER (St Stephen) *see* N Evington *Leic*
LEICESTER (St Theodore of Canterbury) *Leic 1* **P** *Bp* **V** J J LEONARD
LEICESTER, The Abbey (St Augustine) (St Margaret and All Saints) *Leic 2* **P** *Bp* **C** J B NAYLOR
LEICESTER FOREST EAST (St Andrew) *see* Kirby Muxloe *Leic*
LEIGH (All Saints) *see* Ashton Keynes, Leigh and Minety *Bris*
LEIGH (All Saints) *see* Uttoxeter Area *Lich*
LEIGH (All Saints' Mission) *see* Bedford Leigh *Man*
LEIGH (Holy Saviour) *see* White Horse *Sarum*
LEIGH or Wimborne (St John the Evangelist) *see* New Borough and Leigh *Sarum*
LEIGH (St Andrew) *see* Wriggle Valley *Sarum*
LEIGH (St Bartholomew) *S'wark 27* **P** *N J Charrington Esq* **P-in-c** J M A WILLANS, **OLM** F G LEHANEY
LEIGH (St Catherine) *see* Twigworth, Down Hatherley, Norton, The Leigh etc *Glouc*
LEIGH (St Clement) *Chelmsf 10* **P** *Bp* **R** K R HAVEY
LEIGH (St Edburga) *see* Alfrick, Lulsley, Suckley, Leigh and Bransford *Worc*
LEIGH (St John the Evangelist) *Man 13* **P** *Bp* **V** *vacant* (01942) 672868
LEIGH (St Mary) *Roch 11* **P** *Ch Trust Fund Trust* **P-in-c** L W G KEVIS, **NSM** F A HASKETT
LEIGH (St Mary the Virgin) *Man 13* **P** *Bp* **P-in-c** A CUNNINGHAM, **C** K R CARMYLLIE
LEIGH, LITTLE (St Michael and All Angels) *see* Antrobus, Aston by Sutton, Lt Leigh etc *Ches*
LEIGH, NORTH (St Mary) *Ox 9* **P** *Ld Chan* **P-in-c** S G KIRKHAM
LEIGH, SOUTH (St James the Great) *see* Cogges and S Leigh *Ox*
LEIGH, WEST (St Alban) *Portsm 5* **P** *Bp* **P-in-c** P A SMITH
LEIGH-ON-SEA (St Aidan) the Fairway *Chelmsf 10* **P** *Bp* **V** T BARNES
LEIGH-ON-SEA (St James) *Chelmsf 10* **P** *Bp* **V** W G BULLOCH, **Hon Par Dn** E J A INGRAM
LEIGH-ON-SEA (St Margaret) *Chelmsf 10* **P** *Bp* **V** R H S EASTOE, **C** A R FENBY
LEIGH PARK (St Francis) *Portsm 5* **P** *Bp* **V** J G P JEFFERY, **C** J M B HONNOR, **NSM** M S HARPER, W P KENNEDY
LEIGH UPON MENDIP (St Giles) w Stoke St Michael *B & W 4* **P** *DBP and V Doulting (jt)* **V** P D WINKS
LEIGH WOODS (St Mary the Virgin) *see* Abbots Leigh w Leigh Woods *Bris*
LEIGHLAND (St Giles) *see* Old Cleeve, Leighland and Treborough *B & W*
LEIGHS, GREAT (St Mary the Virgin) and LITTLE (St John) and Little Waltham *Chelmsf 8* **P** *Linc Coll Ox, Reformation Ch Trust, and Ex Coll Ox (jt)* **R** C J ELLIOTT, **C** D P RITCHIE, **NSM** C I HAMPTON
LEIGHTERTON (St Andrew) *see* Boxwell, Leighterton, Didmarton, Oldbury etc *Glouc*
LEIGHTON (Holy Trinity) *see* Trelystan *Heref*
LEIGHTON (St Mary) *see* Wrockwardine Deanery *Lich*
LEIGHTON BROMSWOLD (St Mary) *Ely 8* **P** *Bp* **P-in-c** C M FURLONG
LEIGHTON BUZZARD (All Saints) w Eggington, Hockliffe and Billington *St Alb 12* **P** *Bp* **V** G FELLOWS, **C** A E CRAWFORD, P D ANDREWS
LEIGHTON-CUM-MINSHULL VERNON (St Peter) *Ches 15* **P** *Bp* **V** G D GEDDES, **NSM** A S FOSTER
LEIGHTONSTONE, EAST *Ely 8* **P** *Bp (2 turns), Peterho Cam (1 turn)* **R** J P YOUNG, **NSM** M J HARE
LEINTHALL EARLES (St Andrew) *see* Kingsland w Eardisland, Aymestrey etc *Heref*
LEINTHALL STARKES (St Mary Magdalene) *see* Wigmore Abbey *Heref*
LEINTWARDINE (St Andrew) Adforton *as above*
LEINTWARDINE (St Mary Magdalene) *as above*
LEIRE (St Peter) w Ashby Parva and Dunton Bassett *Leic 10* **P** *Ball Coll Ox, Exors Major T G F Paget, and Adn Loughb (by turn)* **R** D J TURNER
LEISTON (St Margaret) *St E 19* **P** *Ch Hosp* **P-in-c** M E PERCIVAL, **OLM** R ELLIS
LELANT (St Uny) *see* Carbis Bay w Lelant *Truro*
LEMINGTON, LOWER (St Leonard) *see* Moreton-in-Marsh w Batsford, Todenham etc *Glouc*
LEMSFORD (St John the Evangelist) *St Alb 21* **P** *Lord Brocket* **P-in-c** E C CARDALE
LEN VALLEY, The *Cant 14* **P** *Abp, All So Coll Ox, Viscount Chilston, and Lord Cornwallis (jt)* **R** D A IRVINE, **C** F NAYLOR
LENBOROUGH *Ox 22* **P** *Ch Ch Ox, Cam Univ, and New Coll Ox (2 turns), Ld Chan (1 turn)* **P-in-c** T P GIBBONS, **OLM** J J SHIELDS
LENHAM (St Mary) *see* Len Valley *Cant*
LENTON (Holy Trinity) (Priory Church of St Anthony) *S'well 14* **P** *CPAS* **V** M L KIRKBRIDE, **NSM** J D LEEMING
LENTON (St Peter) *see* Ingoldsby *Linc*
LENTON ABBEY (St Barnabas) *S'well 14* **P** *CPAS* **P-in-c** V L FLANAGAN
LENWADE (All Saints) *see* Wensum Benefice *Nor*
LEOMINSTER (St Peter and St Paul) *Heref 7* **P** *Patr Bd* **TR** P J SWAIN, **TV** G L JONES, J T MIDDLEMISS, M T TOWNSEND, **C** P J SANDERS, **NSM** P J PRIVETT, R T AYERS-HARRIS, **OLM** P C REES, P SMITH, C P REES
LEONARD STANLEY (St Swithun) *see* The Stanleys *Glouc*
LEPTON (St John) *Wakef 6* **P** *R Kirkheaton* **V** G F WHITCROFT
LESBURY (St Mary) w Alnmouth *Newc 9* **P** *Dioc Soc* **V** B COWEN
LESNEWTH (St Michael and All Angels) *see* Boscastle w Davidstow *Truro*
LESSINGHAM (All Saints) *see* Happisburgh, Walcott, Hempstead w Eccles etc *Nor*

LETCHWORTH (St Mary the Virgin) (St Michael) *St Alb 4* **P** *Guild of All So* **R** P BENNETT
LETCHWORTH (St Paul) w Willian *St Alb 4* **P** *Bp* **V** A M LOVEGROVE, **C** C D LAWRENCE, **NSM** M P DACK, A J FERRIS
LETCOMBE BASSETT (St Michael and All Angels) *see* Ridgeway *Ox*
LETCOMBE REGIS (St Andrew) *as above*
LETHERINGHAM (St Mary) *see* Charsfield w Debach, Monewden, Hoo etc *St E*
LETHERINGSETT (St Andrew) *see* Blakeney w Cley, Wiveton, Glandford etc *Nor*
LETTON (St John the Baptist) w Staunton, Byford, Mansel Gamage and Monnington *Heref 5* **P** *Sir John Cotterell Bt (2 turns), Exors Mrs Dew (1 turn), Ch Ch Ox (3 turns), and DBP (1 turn)* **R** R D KING
LETWELL (St Peter) *see* Firbeck w Letwell *Sheff*
LEUSDON (St John the Baptist) *see* Widecombe-in-the-Moor, Leusdon, Princetown etc *Ex*
LEVEDALE (Mission Church) *see* Penkridge Team *Lich*
LEVEN (Holy Trinity) *see* Brandesburton and Leven w Catwick *York*
LEVEN VALLEY *Carl 11* **P** *Mrs C M Chaplin, V Colton, and Bp (jt)* **P-in-c** D G GODDARD
LEVENS (St John the Evangelist) *Carl 10* **P** *Trustees* **V** *vacant* (01539) 560233
LEVENSHULME (St Andrew) (St Peter) *Man 3* **P** *Bp and trustees (jt)* **R** L S IRELAND, **C** L A IRELAND, **OLM** F G KERR
LEVENSHULME (St Mark) *Man 3* **P** *Bp* **P-in-c** L S IRELAND
LEVER, GREAT (St Michael w St Bartholomew) *Man 12* **P** *Bp* **P-in-c** B HARTLEY
LEVER, LITTLE (St Matthew) *Man 12* **P** *V Bolton-le-Moors St Pet* **V** J WISEMAN, **NSM** I C ANTHONY
LEVER BRIDGE (St Stephen and All Martyrs) *Man 9* **P** *The Crown* **P-in-c** B SAGAR
LEVERINGTON (St Leonard), Newton and Tydd St Giles *Ely 15* **P** *Bp* **R** S K GARDNER
LEVERSTOCK GREEN (Holy Trinity) *see* Chambersbury *St Alb*
LEVERTON (St Helena) *see* Freiston, Butterwick w Bennington, and Leverton *Linc*
LEVERTON, NORTH and SOUTH (St Martin) (All Saints) *S'well 5* **P** *Bp* **P-in-c** M J LEATON, **NSM** I CARTER, F E M FERRITER
LEVINGTON (St Peter) *see* Nacton and Levington w Bucklesham and Foxhall *St E*
LEVISHAM (St John the Baptist) *see* Pickering w Lockton and Levisham *York*
LEWANNICK (St Martin) *see* North Hill and Lewannick *Truro*
LEWES (St Anne) *Chich 18* **P** *Bp and SMF (jt), and Ld Chan* **R** P R C HAMILTON MANON, **NSM** J R LOWERSON
LEWES (St John sub Castro) *Chich 18* **P** *Bp* **R** M J SULLY
LEWES (St John the Baptist) *see* Southover *Chich*
LEWES (St Mary) *see* Lewes St Anne *Chich*
LEWES (St Michael) (St Thomas at Cliffe) w All Saints *Chich 18* **P** *Bp and SMF (jt), and Ld Chan* **R** C K CHANNER, **NSM** P D YATES
LEWISHAM (St Mary) *S'wark 4* **P** *Earl of Dartmouth* **V** D GARLICK
LEWISHAM (St Stephen) and St Mark *S'wark 4* **P** *Keble Coll Ox* **V** G KIRK, **Hon C** F D GARDOM
LEWISHAM (St Swithun) Hither Green *S'wark 4* **P** *V Lewisham St Mary* **V** R DANIELL
LEWKNOR (St Margaret) *see* Thame *Ox*
LEWSEY (St Hugh) *see* Luton Lewsey St Hugh *St Alb*
LEWTRENCHARD (St Peter) *see* Lifton, Broadwoodwidger, Stowford etc *Ex*
LEXDEN (St Leonard) *Chelmsf 16* **P** *Bp* **R** S CARTER
LEXHAM, EAST (St Andrew) *see* Litcham w Kempston, E and W Lexham, Mileham etc *Nor*
LEXHAM, WEST (St Nicholas) *as above*
LEYBOURNE (St Peter and St Paul) *Roch 7* **P** *Major Sir David Hawley Bt* **R** C D DENCH
LEYBURN (St Matthew) w Bellerby *Ripon 4* **P** *Lord Bolton and Mrs M E Scragg (alt)* **P-in-c** C R HUGGETT
LEYFIELDS (St Francis) *see* Tamworth *Lich*
LEYLAND (St Ambrose) *Blackb 5* **P** *V Leyland* **V** P C BATTERSBY
LEYLAND (St Andrew) *Blackb 5* **P** *CPAS* **V** D R A GIBB, **C** M L SIMPSON
LEYLAND (St James) *Blackb 5* **P** *Sir Henry Farington Bt* **NSM** M H PENMAN, **OLM** P A BELSHAW
LEYLAND (St John) *Blackb 5* **P** *V Leyland St Andr and CPAS (jt)* **V** A MCHAFFIE, **OLM** B J WILSON
LEYSTERS (St Andrew) *see* Leominster *Heref*
LEYTON (All Saints) *Chelmsf 5* **P** *V St Mary's Leyton* **V** M I HOLMDEN
LEYTON (Christ Church) *Chelmsf 5* **P** *Ch Trust Fund Trust* **V** M E BURKILL, **C** D N GIBBS
LEYTON (Emmanuel) *Chelmsf 5* **P** *Bp* **V** A ADEMOLA
LEYTON (St Catherine) (St Paul) *Chelmsf 5* **P** *V Leyton St Mary w St Edw* **V** P A REILY, **C** R C ASHLEY
LEYTON (St Mary w St Edward) and St Luke *Chelmsf 5* **P** *Simeon's Trustees* **V** *vacant* (020) 8539 7882
LEYTONSTONE (Holy Trinity) Harrow Green *Chelmsf 5* **P** *Bp* **V** I HARKER
LEYTONSTONE (St Andrew) *Chelmsf 5* **P** *Bp* **P-in-c** D J DALAIS
LEYTONSTONE (St John the Baptist) *Chelmsf 5* **P** *Bp* **V** R J DRAPER, **NSM** R A WHITE, K E ROBINSON
LEYTONSTONE (St Margaret w St Columba) *Chelmsf 5* **P** *Bp* **V** R W C PAGE
LEZANT (St Briochus) *see* Stoke Climsland *Truro*
LEZANT (St Briochus) w Lawhitton and South Petherwin w Trewen *Truro 9* **P** *Bp and Ox Univ (jt)* **P-in-c** C J D PROBERT, **C** G PENGELLY
LEZAYRE (Holy Trinity) *S & M 3* **P** *The Crown* **P-in-c** G F BARKER
LEZAYRE (St Olave) Ramsey *S & M 3* **P** *The Crown and Bp (alt)* **V** P J UPTON-JONES
LICHBOROUGH (St Martin) *see* Greens Norton w Bradden and Lichborough *Pet*
LICHFIELD (Christ Church) *Lich 1* **P** *Bp* **V** I W WILLIAMS
LICHFIELD (St Chad) *Lich 1* **P** *D&C* **R** R D BULL, **NSM** E A WALL, **OLM** J HEELEY
LICHFIELD (St John's Hospital) Proprietary Chapel *Lich 1* **P** *Bp*, **Master** J R WILLIAMS
LICHFIELD (St Michael) (St Mary) and Wall St John *Lich 1* **P** *D&C* **R** D K BEEDON, **C** M D GELDARD, C POLHILL, **NSM** J ANKETELL, C J BAKER
LICKEY, THE (Holy Trinity) *Birm 4* **P** *V Bromsgrove* **V** P D SWAN, **NSM** C P G BARKER
LIDEN (St Timothy) *see* Swindon Dorcan *Bris*
LIDGET GREEN (St Wilfrid) *see* Bradf St Wilfrid w St Columba *Bradf*
LIDLINGTON (St Margaret) *see* Marston Morteyne w Lidlington *St Alb*
LIFTON (St Mary), Broadwoodwidger, Stowford, Lewtrenchard, Thrushelton and Kelly w Bradstone *Ex 25* **P** *Bp, Mrs A M Baring-Gould Almond, W F Kelly Esq, and J B Wollocombe Esq (jt)* **V** A S PAGETT, **C** J W HUNWICKE
LIGHTBOWNE (St Luke) *Man 5* **P** *D&C* **P-in-c** P A STAMP, **Hon C** J G O'CONNOR
LIGHTCLIFFE (St Matthew) *Wakef 2* **P** *V Halifax* **V** *vacant* (01422) 202424
LIGHTHORNE (St Laurence) *Cov 8* **P** *Lady Willoughby de Broke* **R** G J BURRELL, **C** R C FLOATE
LIGHTWATER (All Saints) *Guildf 6* **P** *Ld Chan and Bp (alt)* **V** M D SHELDON, **OLM** R D BROWNING
LILBOURNE (All Saints) *see* Crick and Yelvertoft w Clay Coton and Lilbourne *Pet*
LILLESHALL (St John the Evangelist) (St Michael and All Angels), Muxton and Sheriffhales *Lich 16* **P** *Bp* **V** D J BUTTERFIELD, **OLM** J EVANS
LILLEY (St Peter) *see* King's Walden and Offley w Lilley *St Alb*
LILLINGSTONE DAYRELL (St Nicholas) *see* N Buckingham *Ox*
LILLINGSTONE LOVELL (Assumption of the Blessed Virgin Mary) *as above*
LILLINGTON (St Martin) *see* Sherborne w Castleton and Lillington *Sarum*
LILLINGTON (St Mary Magdalene) *Cov 11* **P** *Bp* **V** T M H BOYNS, **C** J S MCCOACH
LILLIPUT (Holy Angels) *Sarum 7* **P** *Bp* **P-in-c** I J MAYO
LIMBER, GREAT (St Peter) *see* Brocklesby Park *Linc*
LIMEHOUSE (St Anne) (St Peter) *Lon 7* **P** *BNC Ox* **R** G L WARREN, **C** M C C NODDER
LIMESIDE (St Chad) *see* Hollinwood and Limeside *Man*
LIMINGTON (The Blessed Virgin Mary) *see* Ilchester w Northover, Limington, Yeovilton etc *B & W*
LIMPENHOE (St Botolph) *see* Freethorpe, Wickhampton, Halvergate etc *Nor*
LIMPLEY STOKE (St Mary) *see* Freshford, Limpley Stoke and Hinton Charterhouse *B & W*
LIMPSFIELD (St Peter) and Titsey *S'wark 26* **P** *Bp* **R** N H THOMPSON, **OLM** R P RAINBIRD
LIMPSFIELD CHART (St Andrew) Conventional District *S'wark 26* **Min** C R WOOD
LINBY (St Michael) w Papplewick *S'well 4* **P** *T W A Cundy Esq* **R** K H TURNER

LINCH (St Luke) *see* Lynch w Iping Marsh and Milland *Chich*

LINCHMERE (St Peter) *see* Lynchmere and Camelsdale *Chich*

LINCOLN (All Saints) *Linc 15* **P** *Bp* **V** *vacant* (01522) 803572

LINCOLN Minster Group, The (St Mary Magdalene) (St Michael on the Mount) (St Peter in Eastgate) *Linc 15* **P** *Adn Linc, D&C, and Bp (by turn)* **P-in-c** E M C BOWES-SMITH

LINCOLN (St Botolph by Bargate) *Linc 15* **P** *Bp* **P-in-c** T W THOMPSON, **C** N P MORROW

LINCOLN (St Faith) (St Martin) (St Peter-at-Arches) *Linc 15* **P** *Bp* **P-in-c** L C ACKLAM, **C** H P GEISOW

LINCOLN (St George) Swallowbeck *Linc 15* **P** *Bp and V Skellingthorpe (jt)* **V** I G SILK, **OLM** S A BROWN

LINCOLN (St Giles) *Linc 15* **P** *Bp* **V** M J O'CONNELL

LINCOLN (St John the Baptist) (St John the Evangelist) *Linc 15* **P** *Bp* **V** S A HOY

LINCOLN (St Mary-le-Wigford) (St Benedict) (St Mark) *Linc 15* **P** *Bp* **V** *vacant* (01522) 29364

LINCOLN (St Nicholas) (St John) Newport *Linc 15* **P** *Bp and D&C (alt)* **V** D W YABBACOME, **C** R J GODDARD

LINCOLN (St Peter-at-Gowts) (St Andrew) *Linc 15* **P** *Bp* **P-in-c** T W THOMPSON, **C** N P MORROW

LINCOLN (St Swithin) *Linc 15* **P** *Bp* **P-in-c** D EDGAR

LINDAL IN MARTON (St Peter) *see* Pennington and Lindal w Marton and Bardsea *Carl*

LINDALE (St Paul) *see* Cartmel Peninsula *Carl*

LINDFIELD (All Saints) *Chich 6* **P** *Ch Soc Trust* **V** D J CLARKE, **C** J N A HOBBS

LINDLEY (St Stephen) *Wakef 5* **P** *V Huddersfield* **V** *vacant* (01484) 650996

LINDOW (St John) *Ches 12* **P** *Bp* **V** S R GALES

LINDRIDGE (St Lawrence) *see* Teme Valley N *Worc*

LINDSELL (St Mary the Virgin) *see* Stebbing and Lindsell w Gt and Lt Saling *Chelmsf*

LINDSEY (St Peter) *see* Bildeston w Wattisham and Lindsey, Whatfield etc *St E*

LINFORD (St Francis) *see* E and W Tilbury and Linford *Chelmsf*

LINFORD, GREAT (St Andrew) *see* Stantonbury and Willen *Ox*

LINFORD, LITTLE (St Leonard) *see* Lamp *Ox*

LINGDALE (Mission Room) *see* Boosbeck w Moorsholm *York*

LINGEN (St Michael and All Angels) *see* Presteigne w Discoed, Kinsham, Lingen and Knill *Heref*

LINGFIELD (St Peter and St Paul) and Crowhurst *S'wark 26* **P** *Bp* **V** S M GENDALL

LINGWOOD (St Peter) *see* Burlingham St Edmund w Lingwood, Strumpshaw etc *Nor*

LINKENHOLT (St Peter) *see* Hurstbourne Tarrant, Faccombe, Vernham Dean etc *Win*

LINKINHORNE (St Mellor) *Truro 12* **P** *DBP* **P-in-c** A R INGLEBY, **C** E V A FOOT

LINLEY (St Leonard) *see* Broseley w Benthall, Jackfield, Linley etc *Heref*

LINLEY GREEN (not known) *see* Acton Beauchamp and Evesbatch w Stanford Bishop *Heref*

LINSLADE (St Barnabas) (St Mary) *Ox 26* **P** *Bp* **P-in-c** C J DYER, **OLM** W JONES

LINSTEAD PARVA (St Margaret) *see* Blyth Valley *St E*

LINTHORPE (St Barnabas) *York 18* **P** *Abp* **V** E WILSON, **C** N M HEATON, **NSM** R A MORRIS

LINTHWAITE (Christ Church) *Wakef 5* **P** *R Almondbury* **V** T MORLEY

LINTON (Christ Church) *see* Walton-on-Trent w Croxall, Rosliston etc *Derby*

LINTON (St Aidan) *see* Ashington *Newc*

LINTON (St Mary) *Ely 4* **P** *Patr Bd* **TR** M O M MILLS-POWELL, **NSM** G E C RIDGWELL

LINTON (St Mary the Virgin) *see* Ross *Heref*

LINTON (St Nicholas) *see* Coxheath, E Farleigh, Hunton, Linton etc *Roch*

LINTON IN CRAVEN (St Michael) *Bradf 7* **P** *D&C* **R** A J CHRICH, **C** A HODGE, T G WHARTON

LINWOOD (St Cornelius) *Linc 5* **P** *MMCET* **R** M J CARTWRIGHT

LIPHOOK (Church Centre) *see* Bramshott and Liphook *Portsm*

LISCARD Resurrection (St Mary w St Columba) *Ches 7* **P** *Bp* **V** A J MANNINGS

LISCARD (St Thomas) *Ches 7* **P** *Bp* **P-in-c** R T NELSON

LISKEARD (St Martin) and St Keyne *Truro 12* **P** *Simeon's Trustees* **P-in-c** A R INGLEBY

LISS (St Mary) (St Peter) (St Saviour) *Portsm 4* **P** *Bp* **R** J R PINDER, **C** D A STROUD, **NSM** W N MALLAS

LISSET (St James of Compostella) *see* Beeford w Frodingham and Foston *York*

LISSINGTON (St John the Baptist) *see* Lissington *Linc*

LISSINGTON (St John the Baptist) *Linc 5* **P** *D&C York* **V** M J CARTWRIGHT

LISTON (not known) *see* N Hinckford *Chelmsf*

LITCHAM (All Saints) w Kempston, East and West Lexham, Mileham, Beeston-next-Mileham, Stanfield, Tittleshall and Godwick *Nor 14* **P** *Bp, Earl of Leic, Ch Soc Tr, DBP, Mrs E M Olesen, and N W D Foster Esq (jt)* **P-in-c** J B BOSTON

LITCHFIELD (St James the Less) *see* Whitchurch w Tufton and Litchfield *Win*

LITHERLAND (St Andrew) *see* Bootle *Liv*

LITHERLAND (St John and St James) *see* Orrell Hey St Jo and St Jas *Liv*

LITHERLAND (St Paul) Hatton Hill *Liv 1* **P** *Bp* **V** J W WHITLEY

LITHERLAND (St Philip) *Liv 1* **P** *Trustees* **V** D A PARRY, **C** J L C DUFF

LITLINGTON (St Catherine) *see* Shingay Gp *Ely*

LITLINGTON (St Michael the Archangel) *see* Alfriston w Lullington, Litlington and W Dean *Chich*

LITTLE *see also under substantive place name*

LITTLE BIRCH (St Mary) *see* Much Birch w Lt Birch, Much Dewchurch etc *Heref*

LITTLE COMMON *see* Bexhill St Mark *Chich*

LITTLE DART Team Ministry *see* Burrington, Chawleigh, Cheldon, Chulmleigh etc *Ex*

LITTLEBOROUGH (Holy Trinity) *Man 20* **P** *TR Rochdale* **P-in-c** I C THOMPSON, **Dss** K J OLIVER

LITTLEBOURNE (St Vincent) and Ickham w Wickhambreaux and Stodmarsh *Cant 1* **P** *Abp, D&C, Ch Trust Fund Trust, and Adn Cant (jt)* **R** A J ALLAN

LITTLEBURY (Holy Trinity) *see* Saffron Walden w Wendens Ambo, Littlebury etc *Chelmsf*

LITTLEBURY GREEN (St Peter) *as above*

LITTLEDEAN (St Ethelbert) *see* Cinderford St Steph w Littledean *Glouc*

LITTLEHAM (St Margaret) w Exmouth *Ex 1* **P** *Patr Bd* **TR** I C MORTER, **TV** I W MACKENZIE, **NSM** I H BLYDE

LITTLEHAM (St Swithin) *see* Bideford, Northam, Westward Ho!, Appledore etc *Ex*

LITTLEHAMPTON (St James) (St Mary) and Wick *Chich 1* **P** *Bp* **TR** R J CASWELL, **TV** J S A HUDSON, **C** S R MERRIMAN, **NSM** E A CARVER, P P SEDLMAYR

LITTLEHEMPSTON (St John the Baptist) *see* Broadhempston, Woodland, Staverton etc *Ex*

LITTLEMOOR (St Francis of Assisi) *see* Preston w Sutton Poyntz and Osmington w Poxwell *Sarum*

LITTLEMORE (St Mary the Virgin and St Nicholas) *Ox 4* **P** *Or Coll Ox* **P-in-c** B G SCHUNEMANN, **C** M C M ARMITSTEAD, **Hon C** S A COAKLEY, **NSM** J B MUDDIMAN, T J MORGAN

LITTLEOVER (St Peter) *Derby 10* **P** *PCC* **V** J A SEARLE

LITTLEPORT (St George) *Ely 12* **P** *Bp* **V** R H MASKELL, **C** T M DIXON

LITTLETON (St Catherine of Alexandria) *see* Crawley and Littleton and Sparsholt w Lainston *Win*

LITTLETON (St Mary Magdalene) *Lon 13* **P** *C W L Barratt Esq* **P-in-c** P G MCAVOY

LITTLETON, HIGH (Holy Trinity) *B & W 12* **P** *Hyndman Trustees* **V** S TRICKETT

LITTLETON, NORTH (St Nicholas) *see* Cleeve Prior and The Littletons *Worc*

LITTLETON, SOUTH (St Michael the Archangel) *as above*

LITTLETON DREW (All Saints) *see* By Brook *Bris*

LITTLETON-ON-SEVERN (St Mary of Malmesbury) *see* Alveston and Littleton-on-Severn w Elberton *Bris*

LITTLEWICK (St John the Evangelist) *see* Burchetts Green *Ox*

LITTLEWICK (St Thomas) *see* Horsell *Guildf*

LITTLEWORTH (Holy Ascension) *see* Cherbury w Gainfield *Ox*

LITTON (Christ Church) *see* Tideswell *Derby*

LITTON (St Mary the Virgin) *see* Chewton Mendip w Ston Easton, Litton etc *B & W*

LITTON CHENEY (St Mary) *see* Bride Valley *Sarum*

LIVERMERE, GREAT (St Peter) *see* Blackbourne *St E*

LIVERPOOL (All Souls) Springwood *Liv 4* **P** *The Crown* **P-in-c** A J COLMER

LIVERPOOL (Christ Church) Norris Green *Liv 8* **P** *Bp* **P-in-c** H A BENNETT

LIVERPOOL (Our Lady and St Nicholas w St Anne) *Liv 3* **P** *Patr Bd* **TV** D E EMMOTT, **P-in-c** S D BROOKES, **Hon C** J S WILLIAMS

LIVERPOOL (St Anne) *see* Stanley *Liv*

LIVERPOOL (St Christopher) Norris Green *Liv 8* **P** *Bp* **P-in-c** J M COLEMAN

LIVERPOOL (St Luke in the City) (St Bride w St Saviour) (St Michael in the City) (St Stephen w St Catherine) *Liv 6* **P** *Patr Bd* **TV** M J FRY, **OLM** A Y CHEUNG
LIVERPOOL (St Paul) Stoneycroft *Liv 8* **P** *St Chad's Coll Dur* **P-in-c** M C DAVIES
LIVERPOOL (St Philip w St David) *Liv 3* **P** *Bp* **P-in-c** J A GARNETT
LIVERSEDGE (Christ Church) w Hightown *Wakef 8* **P** *Bp and V Birstall (jt)* **C** D E CRAIG-WILD, S J PITCHER, **NSM** S M HOLT
LIVERTON (St Michael) *see* Easington w Liverton *York*
LIVERTON MINES (St Hilda) *as above*
LIVESEY (St Andrew) *Blackb 2* **P** *Trustees* **P-in-c** J P MILTON-THOMPSON
LLANCILLO (St Peter) *see* Ewyas Harold w Dulas, Kenderchurch etc *Heref*
LLANDINABO (St Junabius) *see* Much Birch w Lt Birch, Much Dewchurch etc *Heref*
LLANFAIR WATERDINE (St Mary) *see* Bucknell w Chapel Lawn, Llanfair Waterdine etc *Heref*
LLANGARRON (St Deinst) w Llangrove, Whitchurch and Ganarew *Heref 8* **P** *Bp, DBP, and D&C (jt)* **P-in-c** M A KELK
LLANGROVE (Christ Church) *see* Llangarron w Llangrove, Whitchurch and Ganarew *Heref*
LLANGUA (St James) *see* Ewyas Harold w Dulas, Kenderchurch etc *Heref*
LLANVEYNOE (St Beuno and St Peter) *see* Clodock and Longtown w Craswall, Llanveynoe etc *Heref*
LLANWARNE (Christ Church) *see* Much Birch w Lt Birch, Much Dewchurch etc *Heref*
LLANYBLODWEL (St Michael) and Trefonen *Lich 19* **P** *Bp and Earl of Powis (jt)* **P-in-c** C W PENN, **C** E OSMAN
LLANYMYNECH (St Agatha) *Lich 19* **P** *Bp* **P-in-c** C W PENN
LOBLEY HILL (All Saints) *see* Hillside *Dur*
LOCKERLEY (St John) and East Dean w East and West Tytherley *Win 12* **P** *DBP (1 turn), H B G Dalgety Esq (2 turns)* **V** J M PITKIN
LOCKING (St Augustine) *B & W 11* **P** *MMCET* **P-in-c** C J S TURNER
LOCKING CASTLE (no church) Conventional District *B & W 11* **C-in-c** J BOLTON
LOCKINGE (All Saints) *see* Wantage Downs *Ox*
LOCKINGE, WEST (All Souls) *as above*
LOCKINGTON (St Mary) and Lund and Scorborough w Leconfield *York 8* **P** *Abp* **R** P MOATE
LOCKINGTON (St Nicholas) *see* Castle Donington and Lockington cum Hemington *Leic*
LOCKLEAZE (St Mary Magdalene w St Francis) *see* Bris Lockleaze St Mary Magd w St Fran *Bris*
LOCKS HEATH (St John the Baptist) *Portsm 2* **P** *Bp* **V** P D INGRAMS, **NSM** P A BOGGUST
LOCKTON (St Giles) *see* Pickering w Lockton and Levisham *York*
LODDINGTON (St Leonard) *see* Broughton w Loddington and Cransley etc *Pet*
LODDINGTON (St Michael and All Angels) *Leic 3* **P** *Bp* **P-in-c** T J BLEWETT
LODDISWELL (St Michael and All Angels) *see* Modbury, Bigbury, Ringmore w Kingston etc *Ex*
LODDON (Holy Trinity), Sisland, Chedgrave, Hardley and Langley *Nor 8* **P** *Bp, E G Gilbert Esq, Gt Hosp, and Sir Christopher Beauchamp Bt (jt)* **V** N W R EVANS, **C** L E RICKETTS, **OLM** J EVANS
LODDON REACH *Ox 15* **P** *Patr Bd* **NSM** M M DEVINE, C J LESLIE
LODE (St James) *see* Anglesey Gp *Ely*
LODERS (St Mary Magdalene) *see* Askerswell, Loders and Powerstock *Sarum*
LODGE, THE (St John) *see* Weston Rhyn and Selattyn *Lich*
LODGE MOOR (St Luke) *Sheff 4* **P** *CPAS* **V** J D STRIDE, **C** S T STEWART
LODSWORTH (St Peter) *see* Lurgashall, Lodsworth and Selham *Chich*
LOFTHOUSE (Christ Church) *Ripon 8* **P** *DBP* **V** V G UTTLEY
LOFTUS-IN-CLEVELAND (St Leonard) and Carlin How w Skinningrove *York 16* **P** *Ld Chan (2 turns), Abp (1 turn)* **R** T J WHITWELL
LOLWORTH (All Saints) *see* Fen Drayton w Conington and Lolworth etc *Ely*
LONAN (All Saints) *S & M 2* **P** *The Crown* **V** W H MARTIN, **OLM** J E GUILFORD
LONDESBOROUGH (All Saints) *York 5* **P** *Mrs P R Rowlands* **NSM** S D JONES

LONDON, LITTLE (St Stephen) *see* Bramley *Win*
LONDON CITY CHURCHES:
All Hallows Berkynchirche-by-the-Tower w St Dunstan-in-the-East *Lon 1* **P** *Abp* **V** B M D OLIVIER, **C** D DRISCOLL, **Hon C** G R DE MELLO
St Andrew-by-the-Wardrobe w St Ann, Blackfriars *Lon 1* **P** *PCC and Mercers' Co (jt)* **R** A H F GRIFFIN, **Hon C** E R NORMAN, **NSM** D HITCHCOCK, E GRIFFITHS
St Bartholomew the Great, Smithfield *Lon 1* **P** *D&C Westmr* **R** M R DUDLEY, **NSM** C T OLADUJI
St Bartholomew the Less, Smithfield Gate *Lon 1* **P** *St Bart's Hosp* **V** P J COWELL, **NSM** N J GOULDING, B RHODES
St Botolph Aldgate w Holy Trinity Minories *Lon 1* **P** *Bp* **V** B J LEE, **Hon C** P WRIGHT, **NSM** J PEIRCE, A J WOODWARD
St Botolph without Bishopgate *Lon 1* **P** *D&C St Paul's* **P-in-c** J D M PATON, **Hon C** H J M TURNER
St Bride Fleet Street w Bridewell and Trinity Gough Square *Lon 1* **P** *D&C Westmr* **R** D G MEARA, **NSM** G M PITCHER
St Clement Eastcheap w St Martin Orgar *Lon 1* **P** *D&C St Paul's* **P-in-c** K H GIBBONS, **Hon C** M B KIDDLE
St Edmund the King and St Mary Woolnoth w St Nicholas Acons, All Hallows Lombard Street, St Benet Gracechurch, St Leonard Eastcheap, St Dionis Backchurch and St Mary Woolchurch, Haw *Lon 1* **P** *The Crown (3 turns), D&C Cant (1 turn), Bp (1 turn), and Abp (1 turn)* **R** A S WALKER
St Giles Cripplegate w St Bartholomew Moor Lane and St Alphage London Wall and St Luke Old Street w St Mary Charterhouse and St Paul Clerkenwell *Lon 1* **P** *D&C St Paul's* **R** K M RUMENS
St Helen, Bishopsgate w St Andrew Undershaft and St Ethelburga, Bishopsgate and St Martin Outwich and St Mary Axe *Lon 1* **P** *Merchant Taylors' Co* **R** W T TAYLOR, **C** N D BEYNON, B C COOPER, A JONES, L GATISS, S M C DOWDY, M R O'DONOGHUE, J P DE COSTOBADIE, C W D SKRINE, M J FULLER
St James Garlickhythe w St Michael Queenhithe and Holy Trinity-the-Less *Lon 1* **P** *D&C St Paul's* **R** A H F GRIFFIN, **Hon C** E R NORMAN, **NSM** D HITCHCOCK, E GRIFFITHS
St Magnus the Martyr w St Margaret New Fish Street and St Michael Crooked Lane *Lon 1* **P** *DBP* **P-in-c** J P WARNER
St Margaret Lothbury and St Stephen Coleman Street w St Christopher-le-Stocks, St Bartholomew-by-the-Exchange, St Olave Old Jewry, St Martin Pomeroy, St Mildred Poultry and St Mary Colechurch *Lon 1* **P** *Simeon's Trustees* **R** W J H CROSSLEY, **NSM** B W RICKARDS
St Mary at Hill w St Andrew Hubbard, St George Botolph Lane and St Botolph by Billingsgate *Lon 1* **P** *Ball Coll Ox (2 turns), PCC (1 turn), and Abp (1 turn)* **R** B A C KIRK-DUNCAN
St Mary le Bow w St Pancras Soper Lane, All Hallows Honey Lane, All Hallows Bread Street, St John the Evangelist Watling Street, St Augustine w St Faith under St Paul's and St Mildred Bread Street w St Margaret Moyses *Lon 1* **P** *Grocers' Co (1 turn), Abp (2 turns)* **R** G R BUSH
St Michael Cornhill w St Peter le Poer and St Benet Fink *Lon 1* **P** *Drapers' Co* **P-in-c** P J MULLEN
St Olave Hart Street w All Hallows Staining and St Catherine Coleman *Lon 1* **P** *Trustees* **R** *vacant* (020) 7488 4318 *or* 7702 0244
St Peter Cornhill *Lon 1* **P** *City Corp* **R** W T TAYLOR
St Sepulchre w Christ Church Greyfriars and St Leonard Foster Lane *Lon 1* **P** *St Jo Coll Ox* **P-in-c** P J MULLEN
St Stephen Walbrook and St Swithun London Stone w St Benet Sherehog and St Mary Bothaw w St Laurence Pountney *Lon 1* **P** *Grocers' Co and Magd Coll Cam (alt)* **P-in-c** P A DELANEY
St Vedast w St Michael-le-Querne, St Matthew Friday Street, St Peter Cheap, St Alban Wood Street, St Olave Silver Street, St Michael Wood Street, St Mary Staining, St Anne and St Agnes and St John Zachary Gresham Street *Lon 1* **P** *D&C St Paul's* **P-in-c** J D M PATON
LONDON COLNEY (St Peter) *St Alb 1* **P** *Bp* **V** L FAWNS
LONDON DOCKS (St Peter) w Wapping St John *Lon 7* **P** *Bp* **R** T E JONES
LONDON GUILD CHURCHES:
All Hallows London Wall *Lon 1* **P** *Ld Chan* **V** G B HEWITT
St Andrew Holborn *Lon 1* **P** *Bp* **V** L DENNEN, **NSM** W C BEAVER
St Benet Paul's Wharf *Lon 1* **P** *Bp* **V** *vacant* (020) 7723 3104 *or* 7489 8754
St Botolph without Aldersgate *Lon 1* **P** *Bp* **P-in-c** S M C DOWDY
St Dunstan in the West *Lon 1* **P** *Abp* **P-in-c** W D F GULLIFORD
St Katharine Cree *Lon 1* **P** *Bp* **V** *vacant* (020) 7283 5733
St Lawrence Jewry *Lon 1* **P** *City Corp* **V** D J BURGESS

St Margaret Pattens *Lon 1* **P** *Ld Chan* **P-in-c** A G C PEARSON
St Martin Ludgate *Lon 1* **P** *D&C St Paul's* **P-in-c** A J MORLEY
St Mary Abchurch *Lon 1* **P** *CCC Cam* **P-in-c** J P WARNER
St Mary Aldermary *Lon 1* **P** *The Crown and Ld Chan (alt)* **P-in-c** J R MOTHERSOLE
St Michael Paternoster Royal *Lon 1* **P** *Bp* **V** R J CHRISTIANSON, **Hon C** K PETERS
LONDONDERRY (St Mark) (Holy Trinity) *Birm 7* **P** *Bp* **P-in-c** J R BARNETT, **C** A D BARRETT, **NSM** A E HANNY
LONDONTHORPE (St John the Baptist) *see* Grantham, Harrowby w Londonthorpe *Linc*
LONG ASHTON (All Saints) *B & W 13* **P** *Bp* **V** *vacant* (01275) 393109
LONG BENNINGTON (St Swithin) *see* Saxonwell *Linc*
LONG BENTON (St Bartholomew) *Newc 6* **P** *Ball Coll Ox* **V** P S RAMSDEN, **C** A E STARKIE
LONG BENTON (St Mary Magdalene) *Newc 6* **P** *Ball Coll Ox* **V** D M GRAY
LONG BREDY (St Peter) *see* Bride Valley *Sarum*
LONG BUCKBY (St Lawrence) w Watford *Pet 2* **P** *Bp and Ld Chan (alt)* **V** C R EVANS, **C** A M LORD
LONG BURTON (St James) *see* Dungeon Hill *Sarum*
LONG CLAWSON (St Remigius) *see* Vale of Belvoir Par *Leic*
LONG COMPTON (St Peter and St Paul), Whichford and Barton-on-the-Heath *Cov 9* **P** *Bp, Trin Coll Ox, and Ch Ch Ox (by turn)* **P-in-c** R K SMITH, **C** H C W PARBURY
LONG CRENDON (St Mary the Virgin) w Chearsley and Nether Winchendon *Ox 21* **P** *Bp and R V Spencer-Bernard Esq (jt)* **V** R JACKSON
LONG DITTON (St Mary) *Guildf 8* **P** *Bp S'wark* **R** S A COOPER
LONG EATON (St John) *Derby 13* **P** *Bp* **V** *vacant* 0115-973 4819
LONG EATON (St Laurence) *Derby 13* **P** *Bp* **V** S D ELLIS, **C** C D KINCH
LONG HANBOROUGH (Christ Church) *see* Hanborough and Freeland *Ox*
LONG ITCHINGTON (Holy Trinity) and Marton *Cov 10* **P** *Bp* **P-in-c** J T H BRITTON, **C** D R PATTERSON
LONG LANE (Christ Church) *see* Boylestone, Church Broughton, Dalbury, etc *Derby*
LONG LOAD (Christ Church) *see* Langport Area Chs *B & W*
LONG MARSTON (All Saints) *see* Tring *St Alb*
LONG MARSTON (All Saints) *York 1* **P** *Col E C York* **R** J A RENDALL, **NSM** B H FRAY
LONG MARTON (St Margaret and St James) w Dufton and w Milburn *Carl 1* **P** *Lord Hothfield* **P-in-c** M S LANGLEY, **NSM** J COX
LONG MELFORD (Holy Trinity) *see* Chadbrook *St E*
LONG MELFORD (St Catherine) *as above*
LONG NEWNTON (Holy Trinity) *see* Ashley, Crudwell, Hankerton, Long Newnton etc *Bris*
LONG PRESTON (St Mary the Virgin) w Tosside *Bradf 5* **P** *D&C Ch Ch Ox and V Gisburn (alt)* **P-in-c** M R RUSSELL-SMITH, **NSM** R E WILSON
LONG RISTON (St Margaret) *see* Skirlaugh w Long Riston, Rise and Swine *York*
LONG STANTON (All Saints) w St Michael *Ely 5* **P** *Magd Coll Cam and Bp (alt)* **P-in-c** M E RABY, **C** S E WYATT
LONG STANTON (St Michael and All Angels) *see* Wenlock *Heref*
LONG SUTTON (All Saints) *see* Herriard w Winslade and Long Sutton etc *Win*
LONG SUTTON (Holy Trinity) *see* Langport Area Chs *B & W*
LONG SUTTON (St Mary) *see* Sutton St Mary *Linc*
LONG WHATTON (All Saints) *see* Kegworth, Hathern, Long Whatton, Diseworth etc *Leic*
LONG WITTENHAM (St Mary the Virgin) *see* Dorchester *Ox*
LONGBOROUGH (St James) *see* Moreton-in-Marsh w Batsford, Todenham etc *Glouc*
LONGBRIDGE (St John the Baptist) *Birm 4* **P** *Bp* **V** C J CORKE, **C** J L C SHAW
LONGBRIDGE DEVERILL (St Peter and St Paul) *see* Cley Hill Warminster *Sarum*
LONGCOT (St Mary the Virgin) *see* Shrivenham and Ashbury *Ox*
LONGDEN (St Ruthen) and Annscroft w Pulverbatch *Heref 13* **P** *Bp and MMCET (jt)* **R** M G WHITTOCK, **NSM** J J WADDINGTON-FEATHER, **OLM** O S DAWSON-CAMPBELL, A M TAYLOR
LONGDON (St James) *Lich 1* **P** *Bp* **P-in-c** M W JEFFERSON
LONGDON (St Mary), Castlemorton, Bushley, Queenhill w Holdfast *Worc 5* **P** *Bp, D&C Westmr, and Soc of the Faith (jt)* **V** C A MOSS
LONGDON-UPON-TERN (St Bartholomew) *see* Wrockwardine Deanery *Lich*
LONGFIELD (Mission Room) (St Mary Magdalene) *Roch 1* **P** *Ld Chan* **R** K C BARNES
LONGFLEET (St Mary) *Sarum 7* **P** *MMCET* **V** A N PERRY, **C** P J TAYLOR
LONGFORD (St Chad) *see* Boylestone, Church Broughton, Dalbury, etc *Derby*
LONGFORD (St Thomas) *Cov 2* **P** *Bp* **V** G BUCKBY
LONGFRAMLINGTON (St Mary the Virgin) w Brinkburn *Newc 9* **P** *Bp* **V** *vacant* (01665) 570272
LONGHAM (St Andrew and St Peter) *see* Gressenhall w Longham w Wendling etc *Nor*
LONGHILL (St Margaret) *see* Sutton St Mich *York*
LONGHIRST (St John the Evangelist) *see* Bothal and Pegswood w Longhirst *Newc*
LONGHOPE (All Saints) *see* Huntley and Longhope, Churcham and Bulley *Glouc*
LONGHORSLEY (St Helen) and Hebron *Newc 11* **P** *Ld Chan* **P-in-c** M D TETLEY, **OLM** R M DORANS
LONGHOUGHTON (St Peter and St Paul) (including Boulmer) w Howick *Newc 9* **P** *Duke of Northd and Bp (alt)* **V** B COWEN
LONGLEVENS (Holy Trinity) *see* Wotton St Mary *Glouc*
LONGNEWTON (St Mary) *see* Preston-on-Tees and Longnewton *Dur*
LONGNEY (St Lawrence) *see* Hardwicke and Elmore w Longney *Glouc*
LONGNOR (St Bartholomew), Quarnford and Sheen *Lich 5* **P** *Bp, V Alstonfield, and DBP (jt)* **V** D C NICOL
LONGNOR (St Mary) *see* Dorrington w Leebotwood, Longnor, Stapleton etc *Heref*
LONGPARISH (St Nicholas) *see* Hurstbourne Priors, Longparish etc *Win*
LONGRIDGE (St Lawrence) (St Paul) *Blackb 13* **P** *Trustees* **V** S M AIKEN, **C** K D THOMASSON
LONGSDON (St Chad) *see* Horton, Lonsdon and Rushton Spencer *Lich*
LONGSIGHT (St Luke) *Man 1* **P** *D&C and Trustees (jt)* **R** P N CLARK, **C** C A E DOWDING
LONGSLEDDALE (St Mary) *see* Skelsmergh w Selside and Longsleddale *Carl*
LONGSOLE (Mission Room) *see* Barming *Roch*
LONGSTOCK (St Mary) *see* Stockbridge and Longstock and Leckford *Win*
LONGSTONE, GREAT (St Giles) *see* Ashford w Sheldon and Longstone *Derby*
LONGSTOWE (St Mary) *see* Papworth *Ely*
LONGTHORPE (St Botolph) *Pet 13* **P** *Sir Stephen Hastings* **P-in-c** W S CROFT, **NSM** B G HOWITT
LONGTON (St Andrew) *Blackb 5* **P** *A F Rawstorne Esq* **V** A PARKINSON
LONGTON (St James and St John) *Lich 12* **P** *Bp* **R** S F JONES
LONGTON (St Mark) *see* Edensor *Lich*
LONGTON (St Mary and St Chad) *Lich 12* **P** *Bp* **V** P LOCKETT
LONGTON, NEW (All Saints) *Blackb 5* **P** *Bp* **V** D M ROGERS
LONGWELL GREEN (All Saints) *Bris 5* **P** *Bp* **V** D J A ADAMS
LONGWOOD (St Mark) *Wakef 5* **P** *V Huddersfield* **V** J A HUNT
LONGWORTH (St Mary) *see* Cherbury w Gainfield *Ox*
LONSDALE, EAST *Blackb 14* **P** *Patr Bd* **V** R N HAMBLIN, **Hon C** R HANNAFORD
LOOE, WEST (St Nicholas) *see* St Martin w Looe *Truro*
LOOSE (All Saints) *Cant 13* **P** *Abp* **V** L S TOWNEND, **NSM** C H THOM
LOPEN (All Saints) *see* Merriott w Hinton, Dinnington and Lopen *B & W*
LOPHAM NORTH (St Nicholas) *see* Bressingham w N and S Lopham and Fersfield *Nor*
LOPHAM SOUTH (St Andrew) *as above*
LOPPINGTON (St Michael and All Angels) w Newtown *Lich 22* **P** *Bp and R Wem (jt)* **P-in-c** D T W PRICE, **NSM** T D SMITH, **OLM** A EVANS
LORD'S HILL Local Ecumenical Project *Win 13* **P** *Bp* **V** D F CAVEEN
LORTON (St Cuthbert) and Loweswater w Buttermere *Carl 6* **P** *Bp and Earl of Lonsdale (alt)* **P-in-c** M JENKINSON
LOSCOE (St Luke) *Derby 12* **P** *Bp* **P-in-c** D N GOUGH
LOSTOCK (St Thomas and St John) *Man 11* **P** *Bp and TR Deane St Mary the Virgin (jt)* **V** W P BREW, **C** S M FORREST-REDFERN
LOSTOCK GRALAM (St John the Evangelist) *Ches 6* **P** *V Witton* **V** *vacant* (01606) 43806
LOSTOCK HALL (St James) *Blackb 5* **P** *Bp* **V** P D HALLETT, **NSM** D A BAINES, F KENDALL

LOSTWITHIEL (St Bartholomew), St Winnow w St Nectan's Chapel, St Veep and Boconnoc *Truro 10* **P** *D&C and A D G Fortescue Esq (jt)* **R** F C STEVENS, **C** A J MUNRO-SMITH, **Hon C** F E STUBBINGS
LOTHERSDALE (Christ Church) *see* Carleton and Lothersdale *Bradf*
LOTHERTON (St James) *see* Aberford w Micklefield *York*
LOTTISHAM (The Blessed Virgin Mary) *see* Baltonsborough w Butleigh, W Bradley etc *B & W*
LOUDWATER (St Peter) *Ox 21* **P** *MMCET* **V** T G BUTLIN
LOUGHBOROUGH (All Saints) *see* Thorpe Acre w Dishley *Leic*
LOUGHBOROUGH (All Saints) w Holy Trinity *Leic 7* **P** *Bp and Em Coll Cam (jt)* **R** S A CHERRY
LOUGHBOROUGH (Emmanuel) (St Mary in Charnwood) *Leic 7* **P** *Patr Bd* **TR** D M F NEWMAN, **TV** S E FIELD, **C** B L HILL, S J HILL, **NSM** H M NEWMAN
LOUGHBOROUGH (Good Shepherd) *Leic 7* **P** *Bp* **V** E K WHITLEY, **NSM** R J WHITLEY
LOUGHBOROUGH (St Peter) *Leic 7* **P** *Bp* **V** *vacant* (01509) 263047
LOUGHTON (All Saints) *see* Watling Valley *Ox*
LOUGHTON (not known) *see* Ditton Priors w Neenton, Burwarton etc *Heref*
LOUGHTON (St John the Baptist) (St Gabriel) (St Nicholas) *Chelmsf 25* **P** *Patr Bd* **TV** S J BREWSTER, M F BALL, **Hon C** C P COLLINGWOOD
LOUGHTON (St Mary the Virgin) *Chelmsf 25* **P** *Bp* **R** A COMFORT
LOUGHTON (St Michael and All Angels) *Chelmsf 25* **P** *Bp* **V** *vacant* (020) 8508 1489
LOUND (St Anne) *see* Babworth w Sutton-cum-Lound and Scofton etc *S'well*
LOUND (St John the Baptist) *see* Somerleyton, Ashby, Fritton, Herringfleet etc *Nor*
LOUNDSLEY GREEN (Church of the Ascension) *Derby 5* **P** *Bp* **P-in-c** F E WILLETT, **NSM** R E SMITH
LOUTH (Holy Trinity) (St James) (St Michael) *Linc 12* **P** *Patr Bd* **TR** S D HOLDAWAY, **TV** A P WICKENS, D R WILLIAMS, **C** R G HOLDEN, **OLM** R W MANSFIELD
LOVERSALL (St Katherine) *see* Wadworth w Loversall *Sheff*
LOVINGTON (St Thomas à Becket) *see* Six Pilgrims *B & W*
LOW *see also under substantive place name*
LOW FELL (St Helen) *see* Gateshead St Helen *Dur*
LOW HAM (Chapel) *see* Langport Area Chs *B & W*
LOW HILL (Good Shepherd) *see* Bushbury *Lich*
LOW MOOR (Holy Trinity) *Bradf 2* **P** *Bp and V Bradf (jt)* **P-in-c** S R EVANS
LOW VALLEY (St Matthew) *see* Darfield *Sheff*
LOWDHAM (St Mary the Virgin) w Caythorpe, and Gunthorpe *S'well 10* **P** *Bp* **V** C A TAINTON
LOWER *see also under substantive place name*
LOWER MANOR (St Andrew) *see* Sheff Manor *Sheff*
LOWESBY (All Saints) *see* Whatborough Gp *Leic*
LOWESTOFT (Christ Church) *Nor 9* **P** *CPAS* **V** M C PAYNE, **C** P C W JACKSON
LOWESTOFT (Good Shepherd) *see* Lowestoft St Marg *Nor*
LOWESTOFT (St Andrew) *Nor 9* **P** *Ch Patr Tr* **V** M A MCCAGHREY
LOWESTOFT (St Margaret) *Nor 9* **P** *Patr Bd* **TR** J B SIMPSON, **C** D E PENNY, **OLM** S M E WETTON
LOWESWATER (St Bartholomew) *see* Lorton and Loweswater w Buttermere *Carl*
LOWFIELD HEATH (St Michael) *see* Crawley *Chich*
LOWGATE (St Mary) *see* Hexham *Newc*
LOWGATE (St Mary the Virgin) *see* Kingston upon Hull St Mary *York*
LOWICK (St John the Baptist) and Kyloe w Ancroft *Newc 12* **P** *D&C Dur (2 turns), Bp (1 turn)* **V** V T DICKINSON
LOWICK (St Luke) *see* Egton-cum-Newland and Lowick and Colton *Carl*
LOWICK (St Peter) *see* Brigstock w Stanion and Lowick and Sudborough *Pet*
LOWSONFORD (St Luke) *see* Hatton w Haseley, Rowington w Lowsonford etc *Cov*
LOWTHER (St Michael) and Askham and Clifton and Brougham *Carl 1* **P** *Earl of Lonsdale* **R** D J RADCLIFFE
LOWTHORPE (St Martin) *see* Burton Agnes w Harpham and Lowthorpe etc *York*
LOWTON (St Luke) *Liv 16* **P** *Bp* **R** *vacant* (01942) 728434
LOWTON (St Mary) *Liv 16* **P** *Bp* **P-in-c** W J STALKER
LOXBEARE (St Michael and All Angels) *see* Washfield, Stoodleigh, Withleigh etc *Ex*
LOXHORE (St Michael and All Angels) *see* Shirwell, Loxhore, Kentisbury, Arlington, etc *Ex*
LOXLEY (St Nicholas) *see* Hampton Lucy w Charlecote and Loxley *Cov*
LOXTON (St Andrew) *see* Crook Peak *B & W*
LOXWOOD (St John the Baptist) *see* Alfold and Loxwood *Guildf*
LOZELLS (St Paul and St Silas) *Birm 8* **P** *Aston Patr Trust* **P-in-c** J PRASADAM
LUBENHAM (All Saints) *see* Market Harborough and The Transfiguration etc *Leic*
LUCCOMBE (The Blessed Virgin Mary) *see* Selworthy, Timberscombe, Wootton Courtenay etc *B & W*
LUCKER (St Hilda) *see* Belford and Lucker *Newc*
LUCKINGTON (St Mary) *see* Sherston Magna, Easton Grey, Luckington etc *Bris*
LUDBOROUGH (St Mary) *see* Fotherby *Linc*
LUDDENDEN (St Mary) w Luddenden Foot *Wakef 3* **P** *Bp and V Halifax (alt)* **P-in-c** B PEDLEY
LUDDESDOWN (St Peter and St Paul) *see* Cobham w Luddesdowne and Dode *Roch*
LUDDINGTON (All Saints) *see* Stratford-upon-Avon, Luddington etc *Cov*
LUDDINGTON (St Margaret) *see* Polebrook and Lutton w Hemington and Luddington *Pet*
LUDDINGTON (St Oswald) *see* Crowle Gp *Linc*
LUDFORD (St Giles) *see* Ludlow, Ludford, Ashford Carbonell etc *Heref*
LUDFORD MAGNA (St Mary) *see* Binbrook Gp *Linc*
LUDGERSHALL (St James) *see* Tidworth, Ludgershall and Faberstown *Sarum*
LUDGERSHALL (St Mary the Virgin) *see* Bernwode *Ox*
LUDGVAN (St Ludgvan and St Paul), Marazion, St Hilary and Perranuthnoe *Truro 5* **P** *D&C, Lord St Levan, and H M Parker Esq (jt)* **R** A J WADE, **NSM** A K WATSON, L E M HALL
LUDHAM (St Catherine), Potter Heigham, Hickling and Catfield *Nor 12* **P** *Bp and G M H Mills Esq (jt)* **V** N H KHAMBATTA, **OLM** D M NICHOLSON
LUDLOW (St Laurence) (St John), Ludford, Ashford Carbonell, Ashford Bowdler, Caynham and Richards Castle *Heref 12* **P** *Patr Bd* **TR** B L CURNEW, **TV** R A GREEN, **C** A M BARGE
LUFFENHAM, NORTH (St John the Baptist) *see* Edith Weston w N Luffenham and Lyndon w Manton *Pet*
LUFFENHAM, SOUTH (St Mary the Virgin) *see* Barrowden and Wakerley w S Luffenham etc *Pet*
LUFTON (St Peter and St Paul) *see* Odcombe, Brympton, Lufton and Montacute *B & W*
LUGWARDINE (St Peter) w Bartestree, Weston Beggard and Dormington *Heref 4* **P** *D&C (3 turns), and A T Foley Esq (1 turn)* **V** D J BOWEN
LULLINGSTONE (St Botolph) *see* Eynsford w Farningham and Lullingstone *Roch*
LULLINGTON (All Saints) *see* Beckington w Standerwick, Berkley, Rodden etc *B & W*
LULLINGTON (All Saints) *see* Seale and Lullington w Coton in the Elms *Derby*
LULLINGTON (not known) *see* Alfriston w Lullington, Litlington and W Dean *Chich*
LULWORTHS, (St Andrew) (Holy Trinity) Winfrith Newburgh and Chaldon, The *Sarum 8* **P** *Bp (3 turns), Col Sir Joseph Weld (1 turn)* **P-in-c** R J NAYLOR
LUMLEY (Christ Church) *Dur 11* **P** *Bp* **V** *vacant* 0191-388 2228
LUND (All Saints) *see* Lockington and Lund and Scorborough w Leconfield *York*
LUND (St John the Evangelist) *Blackb 10* **P** *Ch Ch Ox* **V** G D ALLEN
LUNDWOOD (St Mary Magdalene) *Wakef 7* **P** *Bp* **P-in-c** J C MCCASKILL, **NSM** S C TRAVES
LUNDY ISLAND (St Helen) Extra-Parochial Place *Ex 15* **P-in-c** P J F GOODEY
LUPPITT (St Mary) *see* Dunkeswell, Luppitt, Sheldon and Upottery *Ex*
LUPSET (St George) *Wakef 12* **P** *Bp* **P-in-c** P M MAGUIRE, **C** J M WARE
LUPTON (All Saints) *see* Kirkby Lonsdale *Carl*
LURGASHALL (St Laurence), Lodsworth and Selham *Chich 11* **P** *Rathbone Trust Co and Cowdray Trust, and Lord Egremont (alt)* **R** J A LUSTED
LUSBY (St Peter) *see* Marden Hill Gp *Linc*
LUSTLEIGH (St John the Baptist) *see* Moretonhampstead, Manaton, N Bovey and Lustleigh *Ex*
LUTON (All Saints) (St Peter) *St Alb 14* **P** *Bp* **V** R C H FRANKLIN, **C** C K PERERA, **NSM** J YABSLEY
LUTON (Christ Church) *Roch 5* **P** *R Chatham* **R** *vacant* (01634) 843780
LUTON (Christ Church) *see* Bushmead *St Alb*
LUTON (Holy Cross) *see* Marsh Farm *St Alb*

LUTON Lewsey (St Hugh) *St Alb 14* **P** *Bp* **V** P J LAW, **C** H D BARNES, **NSM** C A PULLINGER
LUTON Limbury (St Augustine of Canterbury) *St Alb 14* **P** *Bp* **V** G R CALVERT
LUTON (St Andrew) *St Alb 14* **P** *Bp* **V** G A FINLAYSON
LUTON (St Anne) *St Alb 14* **P** *Peache Trustees, Bp, and V Luton (jt)* **V** P C BUDGELL
LUTON (St Christopher) Round Green *St Alb 14* **P** *Bp* **NSM** J M COX
LUTON (St Francis) *St Alb 14* **P** *Peache Trustees, Bp, and V Luton (jt)* **V** M C NEWBON, **C** C J ADAMS
LUTON (St John) *see* Teignmouth, Ideford w Luton, Ashcombe etc *Ex*
LUTON (St Mary) *St Alb 14* **P** *Peache Trustees* **V** N P J BELL, **NSM** C A MOSS
LUTON (St Matthew) High Town *St Alb 14* **P** *Ch Patr Trust* **V** M J PRITCHARD
LUTON (St Paul) *St Alb 14* **P** *Peache Trustees* **V** A SELLERS
LUTON (St Saviour) *St Alb 14* **P** *Bp* **V** D H GOODBURN, **NSM** D C ANDERSON
LUTTERWORTH (St Mary) w Cotesbach and Bitteswell *Leic 10* **P** *Prime Min (3 turns), Ld Chan (1 turn), and Ch Hosp (1 turn)* **R** M H W COUSSENS, **C** M J IRELAND
LUTTON (St Nicholas) w Gedney Drove End, Dawsmere *Linc 16* **P** *The Crown, Ld Chan, and V Long Sutton (by turn)* **P-in-c** M J NOTLEY
LUTTON (St Peter) *see* Polebrook and Lutton w Hemington and Luddington *Pet*
LUTTONS AMBO (St Mary) *see* Weaverthorpe w Helperthorpe, Luttons Ambo etc *York*
LUXBOROUGH (Blessed Virgin Mary) *see* Exton and Winsford and Cutcombe w Luxborough *B & W*
LUXULYAN (St Cyrus and St Julietta) *see* Lanlivery w Luxulyan *Truro*
LYDBROOK (Holy Jesus) *Glouc 4* **P** *Bp* **V** *vacant* (01594) 860225
LYDBURY NORTH (St Michael and All Angels) *see* Bishop's Castle w Mainstone, Lydbury N etc *Heref*
LYDD (All Saints) *Cant 12* **P** *Abp* **P-in-c** S J A HARDY, **OLM** L A HARDY
LYDDEN (St Mary the Virgin) *see* Temple Ewell w Lydden *Cant*
LYDDINGTON (All Saints) and Wanborough and Bishopstone w Hinton Parva *Bris 7* **P** *Bp and Ld Chan (alt)* **V** J R CARDWELL
LYDDINGTON (St Andrew) w Stoke Dry and Seaton w Caldecott and Glaston and Blisbrooke *Pet 14* **P** *Bp, Burghley Ho Preservation Trust, R E M Elborne Esq, and Peterho Cam (jt)* **P-in-c** J E BAXTER, **NSM** J A PORTLOCK
LYDEARD ST LAWRENCE (St Lawrence) w Brompton Ralph, Combe Florey, Ash Priors and Tolland *B & W 19* **P** *Ld Chan (2 turns), W H J Hancock Esq (2 turns), and MMCET (1 turn)* **P-in-c** M B ARMSTRONG
LYDFORD (St Petrock) *see* Peter Tavy, Mary Tavy, Lydford and Brent Tor *Ex*
LYDFORD ON FOSSE (St Peter) *see* Wheathill Priory Gp *B & W*
LYDGATE (St Anne) *see* Saddleworth *Man*
LYDGATE (St Mary) *see* Bansfield *St E*
LYDHAM (Holy Trinity) *see* Wentnor w Ratlinghope, Myndtown, Norbury etc *Heref*
LYDIARD MILLICENT (All Saints) *see* W Swindon and the Lydiards *Bris*
LYDIARD TREGOZE (St Mary) *as above*
LYDIATE and Downholland (St Thomas) *Liv 11* **P** *R Halsall* **V** P L ROBINSON
LYDLINCH (St Thomas à Beckett) *see* Sturminster Newton, Hinton St Mary and Lydlinch *Sarum*
LYDNEY (St Mary the Virgin) *Glouc 4* **P** *Ld Chan* **P-in-c** P C YOUDE, **NSM** M D MILLER, **OLM** A JONES
LYE, THE (Christchurch) and Stambermill *Worc 12* **P** *Bp and CPAS (alt)* **P-in-c** S M FALSHAW, **NSM** C A KENT
LYFORD (St Mary) *see* Cherbury w Gainfield *Ox*
LYME REGIS (St Michael the Archangel) *see* Golden Cap Team *Sarum*
LYMINGE (St Mary and St Ethelburga) w Paddlesworth and Stanford w Postling and Radegund *Cant 5* **P** *Abp* **R** P N ASHMAN, **OLM** V M ASHMAN
LYMINGTON (St Thomas the Apostle) *Win 11* **P** *Bp* **V** *vacant* (01590) 673847
LYMINGTON Woodside (All Saints) *see* Lymington *Win*
LYMINSTER (St Mary Magdalene) *Chich 1* **P** *Eton Coll on nomination of BNC Ox* **V** J E SLEGG
LYMM (St Mary the Virgin) *Ches 4* **P** *Bp* **R** K MAUDSLEY
LYMPNE (St Stephen) *see* Aldington w Bonnington and Bilsington etc *Cant*
LYMPSHAM (St Christopher) *see* Brent Knoll, E Brent and Lympsham *B & W*
LYMPSTONE (Nativity of the Blessed Virgin Mary) and Woodbury w Exton *Ex 1* **P** *SMF and D&C (jt)* **R** J CLAPHAM
LYNCH (St Luke) w Iping Marsh and Milland *Chich 10* **P** *Rathbone Trust Co, Cowdray Trust and Bp (jt)* **P-in-c** J A L HULBERT
LYNCHMERE (St Peter) and Camelsdale *Chich 10* **P** *Prime Min* **V** W J MUSSON
LYNCOMBE (St Bartholomew) *see* Bath St Bart *B & W*
LYNDHURST (St Michael) and Emery Down and Minstead *Win 11* **P** *Bp and P J P Green Esq (jt)* **V** *vacant* (023) 8028 2154
LYNDON (St Martin) *see* Edith Weston w N Luffenham and Lyndon w Manton *Pet*
LYNEAL (St John the Evangelist) *see* Petton w Cockshutt, Welshampton and Lyneal etc *Lich*
LYNEHAM (St Michael) w Bradenstoke *Sarum 15* **P** *Ld Chan* **P-in-c** A P R FLETCHER
LYNEMOUTH (St Aidan) *see* Cresswell and Lynemouth *Newc*
LYNESACK (St John the Evangelist) *Dur 7* **P** *Bp* **P-in-c** F J GRIEVE
LYNG (St Bartholomew) *see* Stoke St Gregory w Burrowbridge and Lyng *B & W*
LYNG (St Margaret), Sparham, Elsing, Bylaugh, Bawdeswell and Foxley *Nor 22* **P** *DBP, Sir Edward Evans-Lombe, and Bp (by turn)* **R** D N HEAD, **OLM** T B CANDELAND
LYNGFORD (St Peter) *see* Taunton Lyngford *B & W*
LYNMOUTH (St John the Baptist) *see* Combe Martin, Berrynarbor, Lynton, Brendon etc *Ex*
LYNN, NORTH (St Edmund) *see* King's Lynn St Marg w St Nic *Nor*
LYNN, SOUTH (All Saints) *Nor 20* **P** *Bp* **R** P KINSEY
LYNN, WEST (St Peter) *see* Clenchwarton and W Lynn *Ely*
LYNSTED (St Peter and St Paul) *see* Teynham w Lynsted and Kingsdown *Cant*
LYNTON (St Mary the Virgin) *see* Combe Martin, Berrynarbor, Lynton, Brendon etc *Ex*
LYONS (St Michael and All Angels) *Dur 14* **P** *The Crown* **C** K L WASSALL
LYONSDOWN (Holy Trinity) *St Alb 17* **P** *Ch Patr Trust* **V** C W G DOBBIE
LYONSHALL (St Michael and All Angels) *see* Pembridge w Moor Court, Shobdon, Staunton etc *Heref*
LYSTON (not known) *see* N Hinckford *Chelmsf*
LYTCHETT MATRAVERS (St Mary the Virgin) *Sarum 6* **P** *DBP* **P-in-c** P J A HASTINGS
LYTCHETT MINSTER (not known) *Sarum 7* **P** *Bp* **P-in-c** J H T DE GARIS, **C** S CROSS, **OLM** H D PAGE-CLARK
LYTHAM (St Cuthbert) *Blackb 10* **P** *DBP* **V** G I HIRST
LYTHAM (St John the Divine) *Blackb 10* **P** *J C Hilton Esq* **P-in-c** T J COOPER
LYTHAM ST ANNE (St Margaret of Antioch) *see* St Annes St Marg *Blackb*
LYTHAM ST ANNE (St Thomas) *see* St Annes St Thos *Blackb*
LYTHAM ST ANNES (St Anne) *see* St Annes St Anne *Blackb*
LYTHAM ST ANNES (St Paul) *see* Fairhaven *Blackb*
LYTHE (St Oswald) *see* Hinderwell, Roxby and Staithes etc *York*
MABE (St Laudus) *Truro 3* **P** *Bp* **P-in-c** J SAVAGE
MABLETHORPE (St Mary) w Trusthorpe *Linc 8* **P** *Bp Lon (2 turns), Bp Linc (1 turn)* **P-in-c** L T WHITFIELD
MACCLESFIELD (Holy Trinity) *see* Hurdsfield *Ches*
MACCLESFIELD (St John the Evangelist) *Ches 13* **P** *Bp* **V** D TAYLOR
MACCLESFIELD (St Paul) *Ches 13* **P** *Bp* **V** J C TEAR
MACCLESFIELD Team Parish, The (All Saints) (Christ Church) (St Michael and All Angels) (St Peter) (St Barnabas) *Ches 13* **P** *Patr Bd* **TR** G C TURNER, **TV** R J DOULTON, D L MOCK, **C** M W DOUGLAS
MACKWORTH (All Saints) *Derby 11* **P** *J M Clark-Maxwell Esq* **P-in-c** S I MITCHELL
MACKWORTH (St Francis) *Derby 9* **P** *Bp* **P-in-c** J R PHILLIPS
MADEHURST (St Mary Magdalene) *see* Slindon, Eartham and Madehurst *Chich*
MADELEY (All Saints) *Lich 9* **P** *J C Crewe Esq* **V** B F WILSON, **NSM** S W JOHNSON
MADELEY (St Michael) *Heref 14* **P** *Patr Bd* **TR** H J MORRIS, **TV** P W H ACHURCH, **C** R T M J DUCKETT, **NSM** R FREEMAN
MADINGLEY (St Mary Magdalene) *Ely 5* **P** *Bp* **V** *vacant*
MADLEY (Nativity of the Blessed Virgin Mary) w Tyberton, Peterchurch, Vowchurch and Turnastone *Heref 1* **P** *Bp and*

D&C (jt) **R** T R N JONES, **NSM** F M HANCOCK, B A CHILLINGTON, J M DINNEN
MADRESFIELD (St Mary) *see* Powick and Guarlford and Madresfield w Newland *Worc*
MADRON (St Maddern) *see* Gulval and Madron *Truro*
MAER (St Peter) *see* Chapel Chorlton, Maer and Whitmore *Lich*
MAESBROOK (St John) *see* Kinnerley w Melverley and Knockin w Maesbrook *Lich*
MAESBURY (St John the Baptist) *Lich 19* **P** *Bp* **P-in-c** R H MARTIN
MAGDALEN LAVER (St Mary Magdalen) *see* High Laver w Magdalen Laver and Lt Laver etc *Chelmsf*
MAGHAM DOWN (St Mark) *see* Hailsham *Chich*
MAGHULL (St Andrew) (St James) (St Peter) *Liv 11* **P** *Patr Bd* **TR** M J DUERDEN, **TV** S M LEATHLEY, **C** C DORAN
MAIDA VALE (St Peter) *see* Paddington St Pet *Lon*
MAIDA VALE (St Saviour) *see* Paddington St Sav *Lon*
MAIDEN BRADLEY (All Saints) *see* Mere w W Knoyle and Maiden Bradley *Sarum*
MAIDEN NEWTON (St Mary) *see* Melbury *Sarum*
MAIDENHEAD (All Saints) *see* Boyne Hill *Ox*
MAIDENHEAD (St Andrew and St Mary Magdalene) *Ox 13* **P** *Peache Trustees* **P-in-c** W M C STILEMAN, **C** N WATKINSON, **Hon C** R P TAYLOR
MAIDENHEAD (St Luke) *Ox 13* **P** *Bp* **P-in-c** J R HOLROYD
MAIDENHEAD (St Peter) *see* Furze Platt *Ox*
MAIDFORD (St Peter and St Paul) *see* Blakesley w Adstone and Maidford etc *Pet*
MAIDS MORETON (St Edmund) *see* N Buckingham *Ox*
MAIDSTONE (All Saints) (St Philip) w St Stephen Tovil *Cant 13* **P** *Abp* **V** C J MORGAN-JONES, **NSM** P S DOE
MAIDSTONE Barming Heath (St Andrew) *see* Barming Heath *Cant*
MAIDSTONE (St Faith) *Cant 13* **P** *Abp* **V** I H CROFTS
MAIDSTONE (St Luke the Evangelist) *Cant 13* **P** *Trustees* **V** E D DELVE, **OLM** R H WILLIAMSON
MAIDSTONE (St Martin) *Cant 13* **P** *Abp* **P-in-c** C A TOMKINS, **C** S M BIMSON
MAIDSTONE (St Michael and All Angels) *Cant 13* **P** *Abp* **V** P J GIBBONS
MAIDSTONE (St Paul) *Cant 13* **P** *Abp* **P-in-c** K M GORHAM, **NSM** J E MAYHEW, **OLM** T R WOOD
MAIDWELL (St Mary) w Draughton and Lamport w Faxton *Pet 2* **P** *Bp (3 turns), Sir Ian Isham Bt (1 turn)* **R** *vacant*
MAINSTONE (St John the Baptist) *see* Bishop's Castle w Mainstone, Lydbury N etc *Heref*
MAISEMORE (St Giles) *Glouc 6* **P** *Bp* **P-in-c** J G EVANS
MAKER (St Mary and St Julian) w Rame *Truro 11* **P** *The Crown and Earl of Mount Edgcumbe (jt)* **R** R A DOYLE
MALBOROUGH (All Saints) *see* Salcombe and Malborough w S Huish *Ex*
MALDEN (St James) *S'wark 17* **P** *Bp* **V** P E THROWER, **NSM** A HARDY, **OLM** C PIGGOTT
MALDEN (St John) *S'wark 17* **P** *Mert Coll Ox* **V** K W SCOTT, **NSM** M D BROOME
MALDEN, NEW (Christ Church) (St John the Divine) and Coombe *S'wark 17* **P** *CPAS* **V** J S DOWNEY, **C** M P WOODCOCK, S J KUHRT, **NSM** I R L PRIOR
MALDON (All Saints w St Peter) *Chelmsf 11* **P** *Bp* **V** D J ATKINS, **NSM** R J R HUMPHRIES
MALDON (St Mary) w Mundon *Chelmsf 11* **P** *D&C Westmr* **R** A M A MCINTOSH
MALEW Ballasalla (St Mary the Virgin) *see* Malew *S & M*
MALEW (St Mark) (St Moluag or St Lupus) *S & M 1* **P** *The Crown* **V** M F ROBERTS
MALIN BRIDGE (St Polycarp) *Sheff 4* **P** *Bp* **V** *vacant* 0114-234 3450
MALINS LEE (St Leonard) *see* Cen Telford *Lich*
MALLERSTANG (St Mary) *see* Kirkby Stephen w Mallerstang etc *Carl*
MALLING, EAST (St James) *Roch 7* **P** *D&C* **P-in-c** J D BROWN
MALLING, SOUTH (St Michael) *Chich 18* **P** *MMCET* **V** *vacant* (01273) 474387
MALLING, WEST (St Mary) w Offham *Roch 7* **P** *Ld Chan and DBP (alt)* **V** R B STEVENSON, **C** S N MOUSIR-HARRISON
MALMESBURY (St Peter and St Paul) w Westport and Brokenborough *Bris 6* **P** *Ch Trust Fund Trust* **P-in-c** N J ARCHER, **NSM** M J NOAH
MALPAS (St Andrew) *see* Truro St Paul and St Clem *Truro*
MALPAS (St Oswald) and Threapwood *Ches 5* **P** *DBF* **R** T ETHERIDGE
MALTBY (St Bartholomew) (Ascension) (Venerable Bede) *Sheff 5* **P** *Bp* **TR** J E CURTIS, **TV** P F TURNBULL
MALTON, NEW (St Michael) *York 6* **P** *Sir Philip Naylor-Leyland Bt* **V** N N JONES
MALTON, OLD (St Mary the Virgin) *York 6* **P** *Sir Philip Naylor-Leyland Bt* **V** J C MANCHESTER
MALVERN (Holy Trinity) (St James) *Worc 2* **P** *Bp and D&C Westmr (jt)* **V** W D NICHOL, **NSM** R HERBERT
MALVERN (St Andrew) and Malvern Wells and Wyche *Worc 2* **P** *Bp* **V** P W FINCH, **C** I S MCFARLANE
MALVERN, GREAT (Christchurch) *Worc 2* **P** *Bp* **V** P FURBER
MALVERN, GREAT (St Mary and St Michael) *Worc 2* **P** *Bp* **V** M J A BARR, **C** I J SPENCER, **NSM** M E BARR
MALVERN, LITTLE (St Giles) *Worc 2* **P** *Exors T M Berington Esq* **P-in-c** E G KNOWLES
MALVERN, WEST (St James) *see* Malvern H Trin and St Jas *Worc*
MALVERN LINK (Church of the Ascension) (St Matthias) w Cowleigh *Worc 2* **P** *Patr Bd* **TV** A R N WILLIAMS, **NSM** J M FURBER, M J NOBLES
MAMBLE (St John the Baptist) w Bayton, Rock w Heightington w Far Forest *Worc 4* **P** *Ld Chan and R Ribbesford w Bewdley etc (alt)* **V** S G F OWENS
MAMHEAD (St Thomas the Apostle) *see* Kenton, Mamhead, Powderham, Cofton and Starcross *Ex*
MANACCAN (St Manaccus and St Dunstan) w St Anthony-in-Meneage and St Martin-in-Meneage *Truro 4* **P** *Ld Chan* **P-in-c** E B L BROWNING
MANATON (St Winifred) *see* Moretonhampstead, Manaton, N Bovey and Lustleigh *Ex*
MANBY (St Mary) *see* Mid Marsh Gp *Linc*
MANCETTER (St Peter) *Cov 5* **P** *Ch Patr Trust* **V** A S MAIRS
MANCHESTER (Apostles) w Miles Platting *Man 1* **P** *DBP* **P-in-c** P B ROUCH
MANCHESTER (Church of the Resurrection) *see* Manchester Gd Shep and St Barn *Man*
MANCHESTER Clayton (St Cross w St Paul) *Man 1* **P** *Bp* **P-in-c** M THOMPSON
MANCHESTER Good Shepherd (St Barnabas) (Church of the Resurrection) *Man 1* **P** *Prime Min and Trustees (alt)* **R** T S R CHOW
MANCHESTER (St Ann) *Man 4* **P** *Bp* **R** R A J HILL, **C** G R RAINES
MANCHESTER (St John Chrysostom) Victoria Park *Man 1* **P** *Bp* **P-in-c** I D GOMERSALL, **NSM** E J DISLEY
MANCHESTER (St Werburgh) *see* Chorlton-cum-Hardy St Werburgh *Man*
MANEA (St Nicholas) *see* Christchurch and Manea and Welney *Ely*
MANEY (St Peter) *Birm 12* **P** *Bp* **V** P T FISHER
MANFIELD (All Saints) *see* E Richmond *Ripon*
MANGOTSFIELD (St James) *Bris 5* **P** *Peache Trustees* **P-in-c** S A ABBOTT, **NSM** V A ABBOTT
MANLEY (St John the Evangelist) *see* Alvanley *Ches*
MANNINGFORD BRUCE (St Peter) *see* Pewsey and Swanborough *Sarum*
MANNINGHAM (St Paul and St Jude) *Bradf 1* **P** *Patr Bd* **TR** G MOFFAT, **TV** A A JOHN
MANNINGS HEATH (Church of the Good Shepherd) *see* Nuthurst and Mannings Heath *Chich*
MANOR PARK (St Barnabas) *see* Lt Ilford St Barn *Chelmsf*
MANOR PARK (St John the Baptist) *see* W Slough *Ox*
MANOR PARK (St John the Evangelist) *see* Lt Ilford St Mich *Chelmsf*
MANOR PARK (St Mary the Virgin) *as above*
MANOR PARK (St Michael and All Angels) *as above*
MANOR PARK (William Temple) *see* Sheff Manor *Sheff*
MANSEL LACY (St Michael) *see* Credenhill w Brinsop and Wormsley etc *Heref*
MANSERGH (St Peter) *see* Kirkby Lonsdale *Carl*
MANSFIELD Oak Tree Lane *S'well 2* **P** *DBP* **P-in-c** P A CHAPMAN
MANSFIELD (St Augustine) *S'well 2* **P** *Bp* **P-in-c** G E HOLLOWAY
MANSFIELD (St John the Evangelist) *S'well 2* **P** *Bp* **P-in-c** G K KNOTT, **C** O J BALOGUN
MANSFIELD (St Lawrence) *S'well 2* **P** *Bp* **P-in-c** K K BARRON
MANSFIELD (St Mark) *S'well 2* **P** *Bp* **P-in-c** G J BUTLER
MANSFIELD (St Peter and St Paul) *S'well 2* **P** *Bp* **P-in-c** D J FUDGER, **NSM** J DEWHIRST
MANSFIELD WOODHOUSE (St Edmund King and Martyr) *S'well 2* **P** *Bp* **V** R A SCRIVENER, **C** C L DAWSON
MANSTON (St Catherine) *see* St Laur in Thanet *Cant*

MANSTON (St James) *Ripon 8* **P** *R Barwick in Elmet* **V** G STOTT

MANSTON (St Nicholas) *see* Okeford *Sarum*

MANTHORPE (St John the Evangelist) *see* Grantham, Manthorpe *Linc*

MANTON (St Mary the Virgin) *see* Edith Weston w N Luffenham and Lyndon w Manton *Pet*

MANUDEN (St Mary the Virgin) w Berden and Quendon w Rickling *Chelmsf 21* **P** *Bp, DBP and Ch Hosp (jt)* **P-in-c** C BISHOP

MAPERTON (St Peter and St Paul) *see* Camelot Par *B & W*

MAPLEBECK (St Radegund) *S'well 15* **P** *Sir Philip Naylor-Leyland Bt* **P-in-c** E F CULLY, **C** J R CHAMBERS

MAPLEDURHAM (St Margaret) *see* Caversham and Mapledurham *Ox*

MAPLEDURWELL (St Mary) *see* Newnham w Nately Scures w Mapledurwell etc *Win*

MAPLESTEAD, GREAT (St Giles) *see* Knights and Hospitallers Par *Chelmsf*

MAPLESTEAD, LITTLE (St John) *as above*

MAPPERLEY (Holy Trinity) *see* W Hallam and Mapperley w Stanley *Derby*

MAPPERLEY (St Jude) *see* Nottingham St Jude *S'well*

MAPPLEBOROUGH GREEN (Holy Ascension) *see* Studley *Cov*

MAPPLETON (All Saints) *see* Aldbrough, Mappleton w Goxhill and Withernwick *York*

MAPPLETON (St Mary) *see* Ashbourne w Mapleton *Derby*

MAPPOWDER (St Peter and St Paul) *see* Hazelbury Bryan and the Hillside Par *Sarum*

MARAZION (All Saints) *see* Ludgvan, Marazion, St Hilary and Perranuthnoe *Truro*

MARBURY (St Michael) *Ches 5* **P** *Bp* **P-in-c** M S SEARLE

MARCH (St John) *Ely 14* **P** *Bp* **R** *vacant* (01354) 653525

MARCH (St Mary) *Ely 14* **P** *Bp* **R** A CHANDLER

MARCH (St Peter) *Ely 14* **P** *Bp* **R** A CHANDLER

MARCH (St Wendreda) *Ely 14* **P** *MMCET* **R** P BAXANDALL

MARCHAM (All Saints) w Garford *Ox 10* **P** *Ch Ch Ox* **P-in-c** E S SHIRRAS, **NSM** P S SHIRRAS

MARCHINGTON (St Peter) *see* Uttoxeter Area *Lich*

MARCHINGTON WOODLANDS (St John) *as above*

MARCHWOOD (St John) *Win 11* **P** *Bp* **R** J D CURTIS, **NSM** W WHITFIELD

MARCLE, LITTLE (St Michael and All Angels) *see* Ledbury *Heref*

MARDEN (All Saints) *see* Redhorn *Sarum*

MARDEN (St Hilda) *see* Cullercoats St Geo *Newc*

MARDEN (St Mary the Virgin) w Amberley and Wisteston *Heref 4* **P** *D&C* **P-in-c** H M SHORT

MARDEN (St Michael and All Angels) *Cant 11* **P** *Abp* **V** J M ROBERTSON

MARDEN, EAST (St Peter) *see* Compton, the Mardens, Stoughton and Racton *Chich*

MARDEN, NORTH (St Mary) *as above*

MARDEN ASH (St James) *see* High Ongar w Norton Mandeville *Chelmsf*

MARDEN HILL Group, The *Linc 7* **P** *Bp (2 turns), B Eley Esq & DBP, Baroness Willoughby, Duchy of Lanc, J Pain Esq & M Dudley Hewitt Esq, A Lee Esq (1 each)* **R** A M SULLIVAN

MAREHAM-LE-FEN (St Helen) and Revesby *Linc 11* **P** *Bp and Mrs A D Lee (alt)* **P-in-c** A J BOYD, **OLM** K A BUSH

MAREHAM ON THE HILL (All Saints) *Linc 11* **P** *Bp* **P-in-c** A J BOYD, **OLM** K A BUSH

MARESFIELD (St Bartholomew) *Chich 21* **P** *Ch Trust Fund Trust* **R** M D S GREIG

MARFLEET (St Giles) (St George) (St Hilda) (St Philip) *York 14* **P** *Patr Bd* **TR** S SHERIFF, **TV** O J LAMBERT

MARGARET MARSH (St Margaret) *see* Shaston *Sarum*

MARGARET RODING (St Margaret) *see* High and Gd Easter w Margaret Roding *Chelmsf*

MARGARET STREET (All Saints) *see* St Marylebone All SS *Lon*

MARGARETTING (St Margaret) w Mountnessing and Buttsbury *Chelmsf 7* **P** *Bp* **P-in-c** F M DRAKE

MARGATE (All Saints) *Cant 9* **P** *Abp* **P-in-c** J W RICHARDSON, **NSM** P R RUSSELL

MARGATE (Holy Trinity) *Cant 9* **P** *Ch Patr Trust* **V** A J HOUSTON, **C** K M THORPE, J E T STRICKLAND, R F VENN

MARGATE (St John the Baptist in Thanet) *Cant 9* **P** *Abp* **V** B P SHARP, **C** M JACQUES, **OLM** J F TULLY

MARGATE (St Paul) *see* Cliftonville *Cant*

MARGATE (St Philip) Northdown Park *Cant 9* **P** *Ch Patr Trust* **V** S GAY

MARHAM (Holy Trinity) *Ely 13* **P** *St Jo Coll Cam* **P-in-c** D J POMERY, **Hon C** A G F VILLER

MARHAMCHURCH (St Marwenne) *see* Bude Haven and Marhamchurch *Truro*

MARHOLM (St Mary the Virgin) *see* Castor w Sutton and Upton w Marholm *Pet*

MARIANSLEIGH (St Mary) *see* Bishopsnympton, Rose Ash, Mariansleigh etc *Ex*

MARISHES, THE (St Francis) *see* Pickering w Lockton and Levisham *York*

MARK (Holy Cross) w Allerton *B & W 1* **P** *Bp and D&C (jt)* **P-in-c** C NELMES

MARK BEECH (Holy Trinity) *see* Hever, Four Elms and Mark Beech *Roch*

MARK CROSS (St Mark) *see* Rotherfield w Mark Cross *Chich*

MARKBY (St Peter) *see* Hannah cum Hagnaby w Markby *Linc*

MARKET BOSWORTH (St Peter) *see* Bosworth and Sheepy Gp *Leic*

MARKET DEEPING (St Guthlac) *Linc 13* **P** *Ld Chan* **R** P BRENT

MARKET DRAYTON (St Mary) *see* Drayton in Hales *Lich*

MARKET HARBOROUGH (St Dionysius) (The Transfiguration) - Little Bowden w Lubenham *Leic 4* **P** *Patr Bd* **V** C J E MOODY, **TV** E J SEWELL, **C** P J MESSAM, **NSM** J C DUDLEY

MARKET LAVINGTON (St Mary of the Assumption) *see* The Lavingtons, Cheverells, and Easterton *Sarum*

MARKET OVERTON (St Peter and St Paul) *see* Teigh w Whissendine and Market Overton *Pet*

MARKET RASEN (St Thomas the Apostle) *Linc 5* **P** *Ld Chan* **V** M J CARTWRIGHT

MARKET STAINTON (St Michael and All Angels) *see* Asterby Gp *Linc*

MARKET WEIGHTON (All Saints) *York 5* **P** *Abp* **V** L C MUNT

MARKET WESTON (St Mary) *see* Stanton, Hopton, Market Weston, Barningham etc *St E*

MARKFIELD (St Michael), Thornton, Bagworth and Stanton, and Copt Oak *Leic 11* **P** *MMCET* **R** S J NICHOLLS, **NSM** J A DOWNS

MARKHAM, EAST (St John the Baptist) w Askham, Headon w Upton and Grove *S'well 5* **P** *Grove Settled Estate Trustees and SMF (jt)* **R** J H LITTLE

MARKHAM CLINTON (All Saints) *see* Tuxford w Weston and Markham Clinton *S'well*

MARKINGTON (St Michael) w South Stainley and Bishop Thornton *Ripon 3* **P** *Bp, D&C, Sir Thomas Ingilby Bt and N A Hudleston Esq (jt) (by turn)* **NSM** M L WILLIS

MARKS GATE (St Mark) Chadwell Heath *Chelmsf 1* **P** *Bp* **V** R K GAYLER

MARKS TEY (St Andrew) and Aldham *Chelmsf 17* **P** *CPAS and MMCET (jt)* **R** R T MORGAN

MARKSBURY (St Peter) *see* Farmborough, Marksbury and Stanton Prior *B & W*

MARKYATE STREET (St John the Baptist) *St Alb 8* **P** *Bp* **P-in-c** J F H GREEN

MARLBOROUGH (St Mary the Virgin) *Sarum 18* **P** *Patr Bd* **TR** A G STUDDERT-KENNEDY, **TV** L M BUSFIELD, **C** S L C REIDE, **OLM** D P MAURICE

MARLBROOK (St Luke) *see* Catshill and Dodford *Worc*

MARLBROOK Team Ministry, The *see* Bath Twerton-on-Avon *B & W*

MARLDON (St John the Baptist) *see* Totnes w Bridgetown, Berry Pomeroy etc *Ex*

MARLESFORD (St Andrew) *see* Campsea Ashe w Marlesford, Parham and Hacheston *St E*

MARLEY HILL (St Cuthbert) *see* Hillside *Dur*

MARLINGFORD (Assumption of the Blessed Virgin Mary) *see* Easton, Colton, Marlingford and Bawburgh *Nor*

MARLOW, GREAT (All Saints) w Marlow Bottom, Little Marlow and Bisham *Ox 29* **P** *Patr Bd* **TR** N J MOLONY, **TV** D MUNOZ-TRIVINO, S E IRWIN, **NSM** G L C SMITH

MARLOW, LITTLE (St John the Baptist) *see* Gt Marlow w Marlow Bottom, Lt Marlow and Bisham *Ox*

MARLOW BOTTOM (St Mary the Virgin) *as above*

MARLPIT HILL (St Paulinus) *see* Edenbridge *Roch*

MARLPOOL (All Saints) *Derby 12* **P** *V Heanor* **V** K PADLEY

MARLSTON (St Mary) *see* Bucklebury w Marlston *Ox*

MARNHULL (St Gregory) *Sarum 5* **P** *DBF* **P-in-c** R D G WEYMAN, **C** M J TREGENZA, **OLM** M J FICKE

MAROWN (Old Parish Church) (St Runius) *S & M 2* **P** *The Crown* **V** I DAVIES

MARPLE (All Saints) *Ches 16* **P** *R Stockport St Mary* **V** I R PARKINSON, **C** S M M WALKER, **NSM** B J LOWE, C M BLODWELL

MARPLE, LOW (St Martin) *Ches 16* **P** *Keble Coll Ox* **V** J H CAM

MARR (St Helen) *see* Bilham *Sheff*

MARSDEN (St Bartholomew) *Wakef 5* **P** *R Almondbury* **P-in-c** G CLAY
MARSDEN, GREAT (St John's Church Centre) w Nelson St Philip *Blackb 6* **P** *Prime Min and Bp (alt)* **V** J D DAGLISH
MARSDEN, LITTLE (St Paul) w Nelson St Mary *Blackb 6* **P** *Bp* **P-in-c** A PIERCE-JONES
MARSH (St George) *see* Lancaster St Mary w St John and St Anne *Blackb*
MARSH (St James chapel) *see* Huddersfield H Trin *Wakef*
MARSH BALDON (St Peter) *see* Dorchester *Ox*
MARSH FARM (Holy Cross) *St Alb 14* **P** *Bp* **V** J R BELITHER
MARSH GIBBON (St Mary the Virgin) *see* Swan *Ox*
MARSHAM (All Saints) w Burgh-next-Aylsham *Nor 19* **P** *Bp, Mercers' Co, and J M Roberts Esq (jt)* **P-in-c** C S R WALTER
MARSHCHAPEL (St Mary the Virgin) *see* The North-Chapel Parishes *Linc*
MARSHFIELD (St Mary the Virgin) w Cold Ashton and Tormarton w West Littleton *Bris 4* **P** *New Coll Ox and Bp (alt)* **V** S M DREW
MARSHLAND, The *Sheff 10* **P** *Ld Chan and Bp (alt)* **V** J P L WHALLEY
MARSHWOOD (St Mary) *see* Golden Cap Team *Sarum*
MARSKE (St Edmund King and Martyr) *see* Richmond w Hudswell and Downholme and Marske *Ripon*
MARSKE, NEW (St Thomas) *York 16* **P** *Abp* **P-in-c** R E HARRISON
MARSKE IN CLEVELAND (St Mark) *York 16* **P** *Trustees* **V** D H LAMBERT
MARSTON (St Alban) *see* Stafford *Lich*
MARSTON (St Leonard) *as above*
MARSTON (St Mary) *see* Barkston and Hough Gp *Linc*
MARSTON (St Nicholas) w Elsfield *Ox 4* **P** *Bp and D&C (jt)* **V** A R PRICE, **NSM** A C HOLMES
MARSTON, NEW (St Michael and All Angels) *Ox 4* **P** *Bp* **V** E B BARDWELL, **NSM** R I S RYCRAFT
MARSTON, NORTH (Assumption of the Blessed Virgin Mary) *see* Schorne *Ox*
MARSTON, SOUTH (St Mary Magdalene) *see* Stratton St Margaret w S Marston etc *Bris*
MARSTON BIGOT (St Leonard) *see* Nunney and Witham Friary, Marston Bigot etc *B & W*
MARSTON GREEN (St Leonard) *Birm 9* **P** *Birm Dioc Trustees* **V** R V ALLEN
MARSTON MAGNA (Blessed Virgin Mary) *see* Chilton Cantelo, Ashington, Mudford, Rimpton etc *B & W*
MARSTON MEYSEY (St James) *see* Meysey Hampton w Marston Meysey and Castle Eaton *Glouc*
MARSTON MONTGOMERY (St Giles) *see* Alkmonton, Cubley, Marston, Montgomery etc *Derby*
MARSTON MORTEYNE (St Mary the Virgin) w Lidlington *St Alb 13* **P** *Bp and St Jo Coll Cam (alt)* **R** R L HOWLETT
MARSTON ON DOVE (St Mary) *see* Hilton w Marston-on-Dove *Derby*
MARSTON SICCA (St James the Great) *see* Pebworth, Dorsington, Honeybourne etc *Glouc*
MARSTON ST LAWRENCE (St Lawrence) *see* Chenderit *Pet*
MARSTON TRUSSELL (St Nicholas) *see* Welford w Sibbertoft and Marston Trussell *Pet*
MARSTOW (St Matthew) *see* Walford and St John w Bishopswood, Goodrich etc *Heref*
MARSWORTH (All Saints) *see* Cheddington w Mentmore and Marsworth *Ox*
MARTHALL (All Saints) *Ches 12* **P** *DBP* **P-in-c** S HAWKINS
MARTHAM (St Mary) and Repps with Bastwick, Thurne and Clippesby *Nor 6* **P** *Bp, D&C, DBP and K Edw VI Gr Sch (jt)* **P-in-c** J A CRAFER
MARTIN (All Saints) *see* W Downland *Sarum*
MARTIN (Holy Trinity) *see* Carr Dyke Gp *Linc*
MARTIN (St Michael) *see* Thornton Gp *Linc*
MARTIN HUSSINGTREE (St Michael) *see* Salwarpe and Hindlip w Martin Hussingtree *Worc*
MARTINDALE (Old Church) *see* Barton, Pooley Bridge and Martindale *Carl*
MARTINDALE (St Peter) *as above*
MARTINHOE (St Martin) *see* Combe Martin, Berrynarbor, Lynton, Brendon etc *Ex*
MARTLESHAM (St Mary the Virgin) w Brightwell *St E 2* **P** *Bp* **P-in-c** I S NAYLOR, **OLM** H L COOKE, E J CORKER
MARTLEY (St Peter) and Wichenford, Knightwick and Doddenham, Broadwas and Cotheridge *Worc 3* **P** *D&C (2 turns), Bp (1 turn)* **P-in-c** D R SHERWIN, **C** R M BARLOW, **NSM** J M WHITTAKER
MARTOCK (All Saints) w Ash *B & W 6* **P** *Bp* **V** T J FARMILOE, **NSM** M I MACCORMACK
MARTON (Room) *see* Middleton, Newton and Sinnington *York*
MARTON (St Esprit) *see* Long Itchington and Marton *Cov*
MARTON (St James) *see* Capesthorne w Siddington and Marton *Ches*
MARTON (St Margaret of Antioch) *see* Lea Gp *Linc*
MARTON (St Mark) *Heref 13* **P** *V Chirbury* **V** P D HARRATT
MARTON (St Mary) *see* Sheriff Hutton, Farlington, Stillington etc *York*
MARTON (St Paul) *Blackb 8* **P** *V Poulton-le-Fylde* **V** C J WREN, **C** H G SNOOK, K A WREN
MARTON CUM GRAFTON (Christ Church) *see* Gt and Lt Ouseburn w Marton cum Grafton etc *Ripon*
MARTON-IN-CHIRBURY (St Mark) *see* Marton *Heref*
MARTON-IN-CLEVELAND (St Cuthbert) *York 18* **P** *Abp* **V** M J PROCTOR, **C** J APPLEBY
MARTON IN CRAVEN (St Peter) *see* Broughton, Marton and Thornton *Bradf*
MARTON MOSS (St Nicholas) *see* Hawes Side and Marton Moss *Blackb*
MARTYR WORTHY (St Swithun) *see* Itchen Valley *Win*
MARWOOD (St Michael and All Angels) *see* Heanton Punchardon w Marwood *Ex*
MARY TAVY (St Mary) *see* Peter Tavy, Mary Tavy, Lydford and Brent Tor *Ex*
MARYFIELD (St Philip and St James) *see* Antony w Sheviock *Truro*
MARYLEBONE ROAD (St Marylebone) *see* St Marylebone w H Trin *Lon*
MARYPORT (St Mary) (Christ Church), Netherton and Flimby *Carl 7* **P** *Patr Bd* **TR** D C BICKERSTETH, **TV** K S ELLIS, **NSM** I FEARON
MARYSTOWE (St Mary the Virgin) *see* Milton Abbot, Dunterton, Lamerton etc *Ex*
MASBROUGH (St Paul) *Sheff 6* **P** *Bp and Ld Chan (alt)* **V** T H CASWELL
MASHAM (St Mary the Virgin) and Healey *Ripon 3* **P** *Trin Coll Cam* **V** D J CLEEVES
MASSINGHAM, GREAT (St Mary) and LITTLE (St Andrew), Harpley, Rougham, Weasenham and Wellingham *Nor 14* **P** *Bp, Earl of Leicester, Mrs P M Brereton, T F North Esq, and DBP (jt)* **R** J M NOCKELS
MASTIN MOOR (St Paul) *see* Staveley and Barrow Hill *Derby*
MATCHBOROUGH (Christ Church) *see* Ipsley *Worc*
MATCHING (St Mary) *see* High Laver w Magdalen Laver and Lt Laver etc *Chelmsf*
MATCHING GREEN (St Edmund) *as above*
MATFEN (Holy Trinity) *see* Stamfordham w Matfen *Newc*
MATFIELD (St Luke) *see* Lamberhurst and Matfield *Roch*
MATHON (St John the Baptist) *see* Cradley w Mathon and Storridge *Heref*
MATLASKE (St Peter) *see* Barningham w Matlaske w Baconsthorpe etc *Nor*
MATLOCK (St Giles) (St John the Baptist) *Derby 7* **P** *Bp* **P-in-c** B M CROWTHER-ALWYN
MATLOCK BANK (All Saints) *Derby 7* **P** *Bp* **P-in-c** R B READE
MATLOCK BATH (Holy Trinity) and Cromford *Derby 7* **P** *Ch Trust Fund Trust* **V** J CURRIN, **NSM** J E STANTON
MATSON (St Katherine) *Glouc 5* **P** *D&C* **R** J A PARSONS, **C** D R SMITH
MATTERDALE (not known) *see* Gd Shep TM *Carl*
MATTERSEY (All Saints) *see* Everton and Mattersey w Clayworth *S'well*
MATTINGLEY (not known) *see* Heckfield w Mattingley and Rotherwick *Win*
MATTISHALL (All Saints) w Mattishall Burgh, Welborne and Yaxham *Nor 17* **P** *G&C Coll Cam and Bp (alt)* **P-in-c** G R KEGG, **C** L FREMMER, **NSM** G KEGG, **OLM** S E THURGILL, G R ROOTHAM
MATTISHALL BURGH (St Peter) *see* Mattishall w Mattishall Burgh, Welborne etc *Nor*
MAUGHOLD (St Maughold) *S & M 3* **P** *The Crown* **V** D J GREEN, **NSM** E C B CORLETT, I C FAULDS
MAULDEN (St Mary) *St Alb 9* **P** *Bp* **R** R C WINSLADE
MAUNBY (St Michael) *see* Lower Swale *Ripon*
MAUTBY (St Peter and St Paul) *see* S Trin Broads *Nor*
MAVESYN RIDWARE (St Nicholas) *see* The Ridwares and Kings Bromley *Lich*
MAVIS ENDERBY (St Michael) *see* Marden Hill Gp *Linc*
MAWDESLEY (St Peter) *Blackb 4* **P** *R Croston* **R** D J REYNOLDS
MAWGAN (St Mawgan) *see* Cury and Gunwalloe w Mawgan *Truro*
MAWNAN (St Mawnan) (St Michael) *Truro 3* **P** *Bp* **P-in-c** G K BENNETT, **C** C R PINCHBECK
MAXEY (St Peter) *see* Etton w Helpston and Maxey *Pet*

MAXSTOKE (St Michael and All Angels) *Birm 9* **P** *Lord Leigh* **P-in-c** R N PARKER
MAY HILL (All Saints) *see* Huntley and Longhope, Churcham and Bulley *Glouc*
MAYBRIDGE (St Richard) *Chich 5* **P** *Bp* **C** J K GAVIGAN
MAYBUSH Redbridge (All Saints) *see* Southampton Maybush St Pet *Win*
MAYBUSH (St Peter) *as above*
MAYFAIR (Christ Church) extra-parochial place *Lon 3* **P** *Bp* **C** J P DE COSTOBADIE
MAYFIELD (St Dunstan) *Chich 15* **P** *Keble Coll Ox* **V** N J PRIOR, **Hon C** J P CAPERON
MAYFIELD (St John the Baptist) *Lich 15* **P** *Ch Soc Trust* **V** *vacant* (01335) 342855
MAYFORD (Emmanuel) *see* Woking St Jo *Guildf*
MAYLAND (St Barnabas) (St Barnabas Family Centre) *Chelmsf 11* **P** *Bp* **P-in-c** L BLANEY
MEANWOOD (Holy Trinity) *Ripon 7* **P** *Bp* **V** R M WIGGEN
MEARE (Blessed Virgin Mary and All Saints) *see* Glastonbury w Meare *B & W*
MEARS ASHBY (All Saints) and Hardwick and Sywell w Overstone *Pet 6* **P** *Duchy of Cornwall (2 turns), Bracegirdle Trustees (1 turn),and Mrs C K Edmiston (1 turn)* **P-in-c** D C BEET
MEASHAM (St Lawrence) *Leic 9* **P** *CPAS* **V** *vacant* (01530) 270354
MEAVY (St Peter) *see* Yelverton, Meavy, Sheepstor and Walkhampton *Ex*
MEDBOURNE (St Giles) *see* Six Saints circa Holt *Leic*
MEDMENHAM (St Peter and St Paul) *see* Hambleden Valley *Ox*
MEDOMSLEY (St Mary Magdalene) *Dur 4* **P** *Bp* **V** *vacant* (01207) 560289
MEDSTEAD (St Andrew) *see* Bentworth, Lasham, Medstead and Shalden *Win*
MEERBROOK (St Matthew) *see* Leek and Meerbrook *Lich*
MEESDEN (St Mary) *see* Hormead, Wyddial, Anstey, Brent Pelham etc *St Alb*
MEETH (St Michael and All Angels) *see* Hatherleigh, Meeth, Exbourne and Jacobstowe *Ex*
MEIR (Holy Trinity) *Lich 6* **P** *Bp* **P-in-c** J S FOULDS, **OLM** M M ALLBUTT
MEIR HEATH (St Francis of Assisi) and Normacot *Lich 12* **P** *Bp and DBP (jt)* **V** P F BLANCH, **C** T J HARVEY
MEIR PARK (St Clare) *see* Meir Heath and Normacot *Lich*
MELBECKS (Holy Trinity) *see* Swaledale *Ripon*
MELBOURN (All Saints) *Ely 7* **P** *D&C* **V** A D O'BRIEN, **NSM** M L PRICE
MELBOURNE (St Michael) *Derby 15* **P** *Bp* **V** J H DAVIES, **NSM** A J FLINTHAM
MELBOURNE (St Monica) *see* Barmby Moor Gp *York*
MELBURY (St Mary the Virgin) (St Osmund) *Sarum 3* **P** *Patr Bd* **TR** I BROWN, **TV** G F PERRYMAN
MELBURY ABBAS (St Thomas) *see* Shaston *Sarum*
MELBURY BUBB (St Mary the Virgin) *see* Melbury *Sarum*
MELBURY OSMUND (St Osmund) *as above*
MELCHBOURNE (St Mary Magdalene) *see* The Stodden Churches *St Alb*
MELCOMBE HORSEY (St Andrew) *see* Piddle Valley, Hilton, Cheselbourne etc *Sarum*
MELDON (St John the Evangelist) *see* Bolam w Whalton and Hartburn w Meldon *Newc*
MELDRETH (Holy Trinity) *Ely 7* **P** *D&C* **V** A D O'BRIEN, **NSM** M L PRICE
MELKSHAM (St Barnabas) (St Michael and All Angels) *Sarum 14* **P** *DBP* **TR** D G SMITH, **TV** M G KUHRT, **C** C C NERY, **NSM** J DARLING, **OLM** A E WINTOUR
MELKSHAM FOREST (St Andrew) *see* Melksham *Sarum*
MELLING (St Thomas) *see* Bickerstaffe and Melling *Liv*
MELLING (St Wilfrid) *see* E Lonsdale *Blackb*
MELLIS (St Mary the Virgin) *see* S Hartismere *St E*
MELLOR (St Mary) *Blackb 7* **P** *V Blackb* **V** J P HUDSON
MELLOR (St Thomas) *Derby 6* **P** *Bp* **V** P J JENNER
MELLS (St Andrew) w Buckland Dinham, Elm, Whatley, Vobster and Chantry *B & W 4* **P** *DBP (2 turns), Bp (1 turns)* **P-in-c** M E WEYMONT
MELMERBY (St John the Baptist) *see* Cross Fell Gp *Carl*
MELPLASH (Christ Church) *see* Beaminster Area *Sarum*
MELSONBY (St James the Great) *see* Forcett and Aldbrough and Melsonby *Ripon*
MELTHAM Christ the King (St Bartholomew) (St James) *Wakef 1* **P** *Simeon's Trustees, R Almondbury w Farnley Tyas, and Bp (jt)* **V** J AUSTIN, **NSM** P ROLLS, S W DIXON, **OLM** J H HELLIWELL, J F RADCLIFFE
MELTHAM (St Bartholomew) *see* Meltham *Wakef*
MELTHAM MILLS (St James) *as above*
MELTON (St Andrew) and Ufford *St E 7* **P** *D&C Ely (3 turns), and T R E Blois-Brooke Esq (1 turn)* **R** *vacant* (01394) 380279
MELTON, GREAT (All Saints) *see* Hethersett w Canteloff w Lt and Gt Melton *Nor*
MELTON, HIGH (St James) *see* Barnburgh w Melton on the Hill etc *Sheff*
MELTON, LITTLE (All Saints) *see* Hethersett w Canteloff w Lt and Gt Melton *Nor*
MELTON, WEST (St Cuthbert) *see* Brampton Bierlow *Sheff*
MELTON CONSTABLE (St Peter) *see* Briston w Burgh Parva and Melton Constable *Nor*
MELTON MOWBRAY (St Mary) *Leic 3* **P** *Patr Bd* **TR** C A G JENKIN, **TV** P N GROVES, S A PATERSON
MELTON ROSS (Ascension) *see* Brocklesby Park *Linc*
MELVERLEY (St Peter) *see* Kinnerley w Melverley and Knockin w Maesbrook *Lich*
MEMBURY (St John the Baptist) *see* Axminster, Chardstock, All Saints etc *Ex*
MENDHAM (All Saints) *see* Fressingfield, Mendham etc *St E*
MENDLESHAM (St Mary) *St E 6* **P** *SMF* **V** P T GRAY
MENHENIOT (St Lalluwy and St Antoninus) *Truro 12* **P** *Ex Coll Ox* **P-in-c** P J CONWAY
MENITH WOOD (Chapel) *see* Teme Valley N *Worc*
MENSTON (St John the Divine) w Woodhead *Bradf 4* **P** *Bp* **V** R J YEOMAN
MENTMORE (St Mary the Virgin) *see* Cheddington w Mentmore and Marsworth *Ox*
MEOLE BRACE (Holy Trinity) *Lich 20* **P** *J K Bather Esq* **V** K T ROBERTS, **C** S A KELLY, **NSM** A M ROBERTS
MEOLS, GREAT (St John the Baptist) *Ches 8* **P** *Bp* **V** *vacant* 0151-632 1661
MEOLS, NORTH Team Ministry, The (St Cuthbert) *Liv 9* **P** *Patr Bd* **TR** P C GREEN, **C** M J TAYLOR
MEON, EAST (All Saints) *Portsm 4* **P** *Ld Chan* **V** T E LOUDEN
MEON, WEST (St John the Evangelist) and Warnford *Portsm 4* **P** *Bp and DBP (alt)* **P-in-c** C J HEADLEY
MEONSTOKE (St Andrew) w Corhampton cum Exton *Portsm 1* **P** *Bp* **P-in-c** J F FOLEY, **NSM** K V HOWES
MEOPHAM (St John the Baptist) w Nurstead *Roch 1* **P** *D&C and Lt-Col F B Edmeades (jt)* **R** S H DUNN, **C** A H CARR
MEPAL (St Mary) *see* Witcham w Mepal *Ely*
MEPPERSHALL (St Mary the Virgin) and Shefford *St Alb 16* **P** *Bp and St Jo Coll Cam (alt)* **V** J A HARPER
MERE (St Michael the Archangel) w West Knoyle and Maiden Bradley *Sarum 17* **P** *Bp* **V** D J J R LINAKER, **C** J PERRETT, **NSM** S M WOOD, M R WOOD
MERESIDE (St Wilfrid) *see* Blackpool St Wilfrid *Blackb*
MEREVALE (St Mary the Virgin) *see* Baxterley w Hurley and Wood End and Merevale etc *Birm*
MEREWORTH (St Lawrence) w West Peckham *Roch 7* **P** *Viscount Falmouth and D&C (alt)* **R** R N MCCONACHIE, **C** S N MOUSIR-HARRISON
MERIDEN (St Laurence) *Cov 4* **P** *Chapter Cov Cathl* **R** M H DAWKINS
MERRINGTON (St John the Evangelist) *see* Spennymoor, Whitworth and Merrington *Dur*
MERRIOTT (All Saints) w Hinton, Dinnington and Lopen *B & W 15* **P** *D&C Bris (2 turns), Bp (1 turn)* **R** V N JAMES
MERROW (St John the Evangelist) *Guildf 5* **P** *Earl of Onslow* **R** A P HODGETTS, **C** H C ORCHARD, **OLM** D E C MATTHEWS
MERRY HILL (St Joseph of Arimathea) *see* Penn Fields *Lich*
MERRYMEET (St Mary) *see* Menheniot *Truro*
MERSEA, WEST (St Peter and St Paul) w East (St Edmund) *Chelmsf 16* **P** *Bp and The Crown (alt)* **R** S C NORTON, **Hon C** M BROSNAN, **NSM** J R PANTRY
MERSHAM (St John the Baptist) w Hinxhill and Sellindge *Cant 10* **P** *Abp* **P-in-c** J W TIPPING, **NSM** R L LE ROSSIGNOL
MERSTHAM (St Katharine) (Epiphany) and Gatton *S'wark 27* **P** *Abp* **P-in-c** J E SMITH, **C** C E LATHAM, **OLM** V J WILLIAMS
MERSTHAM, SOUTH (All Saints) *S'wark 27* **P** *Bp* **P-in-c** M S RANDALL
MERSTON (St Giles) *see* N Mundham w Hunston and Merston *Chich*
MERTON (All Saints) *see* Shebbear, Buckland Filleigh, Sheepwash etc *Ex*
MERTON (St James) *S'wark 14* **P** *Bp and V Merton St Mary (jt)* **V** G N OWEN
MERTON (St John the Divine) *S'wark 14* **P** *Bp and V Merton St Mary (jt)* **V** S A ROBERTS
MERTON (St Mary) *S'wark 14* **P** *Bp* **V** T G LEARY, **OLM** J F HILLIER
MERTON (St Peter) *see* Caston, Griston, Merton, Thompson etc *Nor*

MERTON (St Swithun) *see* Ray Valley *Ox*
MESHAW (St John) *see* Burrington, Chawleigh, Cheldon, Chulmleigh etc *Ex*
MESSING (All Saints) *see* Copford w Easthorpe and Messing w Inworth *Chelmsf*
MESSINGHAM (Holy Trinity) *Linc 4* **P** *Bp* **V** G D MASSEY
MESTY CROFT (St Luke) *see* Wednesbury St Paul Wood Green *Lich*
METFIELD (St John the Baptist) *see* Fressingfield, Mendham etc *St E*
METHERINGHAM (St Wilfred) w Blankney and Dunston *Linc 18* **P** *Bp (2 turns), Br Field Products Ltd (1 turn)* **V** *vacant* (01526) 321115
METHLEY (St Oswald) w Mickletown *Ripon 8* **P** *Bp (3 turns), Duchy of Lanc (1 turn)* **Hon C** M C E BOOTES
METHWOLD (St George) *see* Feltwell and Methwold *Ely*
METTINGHAM (All Saints) *see* Wainford *St E*
METTON (St Andrew) *see* Roughton and Felbrigg, Metton, Sustead etc *Nor*
MEVAGISSEY (St Peter) *see* St Mewan w Mevagissey and St Ewe *Truro*
MEXBOROUGH (St John the Baptist) *Sheff 12* **P** *Adn York* **V** D R WISE
MEYSEY HAMPTON (St Mary) w Marston Meysey and Castle Eaton *Glouc 12* **P** *Ch Soc Trust* **R** *vacant* (01285) 851249
MICHAEL (St Michael and All Angels) *S & M 3* **P** *The Crown* **V** *vacant*
MICHAELCHURCH ESCLEY (St Michael) *see* Clodock and Longtown w Craswall, Llanveynoe etc *Heref*
MICHAELSTOW (St Michael) *see* St Tudy w St Mabyn and Michaelstow *Truro*
MICHELDEVER (St Mary) and East Stratton, Woodmancote and Popham *Win 7* **P** *Lord Northbrook (3 turns), Bp (2 turns)* **P-in-c** S A FOSTER
MICHELMERSH (Our Lady) and Awbridge and Braishfield and Farley Chamberlayne and Timsbury *Win 12* **P** *Bp* **R** D B KINGTON, **NSM** S P HEATHER
MICKLEGATE (Holy Trinity) *see* York H Trin Micklegate *York*
MICKLEHAM (St Michael) *see* Leatherhead and Mickleham *Guildf*
MICKLEHURST (All Saints) *Ches 14* **P** *Bp* **P-in-c** R C BOWERS
MICKLEOVER (All Saints) *Derby 10* **P** *MMCET* **V** A W WARD, **C** C G PEARSON
MICKLEOVER (St John) *Derby 10* **P** *Bp* **V** J R HENSON, **NSM** M A PRIDDIN
MICKLETON (St Lawrence), Willersey, Saintbury, Weston-sub-Edge and Aston-sub-Edge *Glouc 10* **P** *Bp, Lt Col J H Gibbon, Viscount Sandon (1 turn), Ld Chan (1 turn)* **R** D E VINCE, **Hon C** J A DAVIES
MICKLEY (St George) *Newc 3* **P** *Bp* **P-in-c** T EMMETT
MICKLEY (St John the Evangelist) *see* Fountains Gp *Ripon*
MID MARSH Group, The *Linc 12* **P** *Rear Admiral G P D Hall, Bp, D&C, and Lord Deramore (by turn)* **OLM** L W CARROLL, J R SELFE
MID TRENT *Lich 10* **P** *Patr Bd* **TR** J H STERLING, **TV** P H MYERS
MIDDLE *see also under substantive place name*
MIDDLE RASEN Group, The *Linc 5* **P** *Bp, Charterhouse, and DBP (jt)* **R** P C PATRICK
MIDDLEHAM (St Mary and St Alkelda) w Coverdale and East Witton and Thornton Steward *Ripon 4* **P** *Bp, R Craven-Smith-Milnes Esq, and W R Burdon Esq (jt)* **R** B A GIBLIN
MIDDLESBROUGH (All Saints) *York 18* **P** *Abp* **V** G HOLLAND, **C** S L NICHOLSON
MIDDLESBROUGH (Ascension) *York 18* **P** *Abp* **V** D G HODGSON, **C** A GAUNT
MIDDLESBROUGH (Holy Trinity) *see* N Ormesby *York*
MIDDLESBROUGH (St Agnes) *York 18* **P** *Abp* **V** P J MOTHERSDALE
MIDDLESBROUGH (St Barnabas) *see* Linthorpe *York*
MIDDLESBROUGH (St Chad) *York 18* **P** *Abp* **V** C L BRERETON
MIDDLESBROUGH (St Columba w St Paul) *York 18* **P** *Abp* **P-in-c** S COOPER, **NSM** P M KRONBERGS
MIDDLESBROUGH (St John the Evangelist) *York 18* **P** *Abp* **P-in-c** S COOPER
MIDDLESBROUGH (St Martin of Tours) (St Cuthbert) *York 18* **P** *Abp* **V** D JAGO
MIDDLESBROUGH (St Oswald) *York 18* **P** *Abp* **V** S RICHARDSON, **NSM** W A DEWING
MIDDLESBROUGH (St Thomas) *York 18* **P** *Abp* **V** P W SKINNER
MIDDLESMOOR (St Chad) *see* Upper Nidderdale *Ripon*
MIDDLESTOWN (St Luke) *Wakef 12* **P** *R Thornhill* **V** H C BAKER, **NSM** A P YOUNG
MIDDLETON (All Saints) *see* N Hinckford *Chelmsf*
MIDDLETON (Holy Ghost) *see* Kirkby Lonsdale *Carl*
MIDDLETON (Holy Trinity) *see* Bitterley w Middleton, Stoke St Milborough etc *Heref*
MIDDLETON (Holy Trinity) *Heref 13* **P** *V Chirbury* **P-in-c** P D HARRATT
MIDDLETON (Holy Trinity) *see* Middleton cum Fordley and Theberton w Eastbridge *St E*
MIDDLETON (St Andrew), Newton and Sinnington *York 20* **P** *Abp (2 turns), Simeon's Trustees (1 turn)* **R** A M F REED
MIDDLETON (St Cross) *Ripon 6* **P** *DBP* **P-in-c** C BARRETT, **NSM** J H TURNER
MIDDLETON (St George) (St Laurence) *Dur 8* **P** *Bp* **R** P S D NEVILLE
MIDDLETON (St John the Baptist) *Birm 12* **P** *Bp* **P-in-c** M I RHODES
MIDDLETON (St Leonard) (St Margaret) w Thornham *Man 18* **P** *Bp* **TR** N J FEIST, **TV** C FALLONE, **OLM** F JACKSON, S L SPENCER
MIDDLETON (St Mary) *see* W Winch w Setchey, N Runcton and Middleton *Nor*
MIDDLETON (St Mary the Virgin) *Ripon 6* **P** *V Rothwell* **V** R L A PATERSON, **C** C BANDAWE
MIDDLETON (St Michael and All Angels) *see* Youlgreave, Middleton, Stanton-in-Peak etc *Derby*
MIDDLETON (St Nicholas) *Chich 1* **P** *D&C* **V** W T MARSTON
MIDDLETON-BY-WIRKSWORTH (Holy Trinity) *see* Wirksworth *Derby*
MIDDLETON CHENEY (All Saints) *see* Chenderit *Pet*
MIDDLETON CUM FORDLEY (Holy Trinity) and Theberton w Eastbridge *St E 19* **P** *Prime Min and Ch Patr Trust (alt)* **P-in-c** R J GINN, **C** H W TURNER, **OLM** S A WARNE, A B BAYMAN, E M COLE
MIDDLETON-IN-CHIRBY (Holy Trinity) *see* Middleton *Heref*
MIDDLETON-IN-TEESDALE (St Mary the Virgin) w Forest and Frith *Dur 7* **P** *Lord Barnard and The Crown (alt)* **P-in-c** A S G PIKE
MIDDLETON JUNCTION (St Gabriel) *Man 18* **P** *Bp* **V** I B COOK
MIDDLETON ON LEVEN (St Cuthbert) *see* Rudby in Cleveland w Middleton *York*
MIDDLETON-ON-THE-HILL (St Mary the Virgin) *see* Leominster *Heref*
MIDDLETON-ON-THE-WOLDS (St Andrew) *see* Woldsburn *York*
MIDDLETON SCRIVEN (St John the Baptist) *see* Stottesdon w Farlow, Cleeton St Mary etc *Heref*
MIDDLETON STONEY (All Saints) *see* Akeman *Ox*
MIDDLETON TYAS (St Michael and All Angels) *see* E Richmond *Ripon*
MIDDLETOWN (St John the Baptist) *see* Gt Wollaston *Heref*
MIDDLEWICH (St Michael and All Angels) w Byley *Ches 6* **P** *Bp* **V** I G BISHOP, **C** L BUTLER, **NSM** B W JOBBER
MIDDLEZOY (Holy Cross) and Othery and Moorlinch *B & W 5* **P** *Bp Worc (1 turn), Bp (2 turns)* **P-in-c** M PETERS
MIDGHAM (St Matthew) *see* Woolhampton w Midgham and Beenham Valance *Ox*
MIDHOPE (St James) *see* Penistone and Thurlstone *Wakef*
MIDHURST (St Mary Magdalene and St Denis) *Chich 10* **P** *Rathbone Trust Co and Cowdray Trust (jt)* **V** A T CUNNINGTON
MIDSOMER NORTON (St John the Baptist) w Clandown *B & W 12* **P** *Ch Ch Ox* **V** C G CHIPLIN
MIDVILLE (St Peter) *see* Stickney Gp *Linc*
MILBER (St Luke) *Ex 10* **P** *Bp* **V** J E POTTER
MILBORNE (St Andrew) *see* Puddletown, Tolpuddle and Milborne w Dewlish *Sarum*
MILBORNE PORT (St John the Evangelist) w Goathill *B & W 2* **P** *Mrs J E Smith (2 turns), Trustees (1 turn)* **V** J W B PERRY
MILBORNE WICK (Mission Church) *see* Milborne Port w Goathill *B & W*
MILBOURNE (Holy Saviour) *see* Ponteland *Newc*
MILBURN (St Cuthbert) *see* Long Marton w Dufton and w Milburn *Carl*
MILCOMBE (St Laurence) *see* Bloxham w Milcombe and S Newington *Ox*
MILDEN (St Peter) *see* Monks Eleigh w Chelsworth and Brent Eleigh etc *St E*
MILDENHALL (St John the Baptist) *see* Marlborough *Sarum*
MILDENHALL (St Mary) *St E 11* **P** *Patr Bd (2 turns), Bp (1 turn)* **TV** A W SPENCER, I COOPER, S M HODGES, **OLM** H B MULLIN, M E RUSTED, B J STEDMAN
MILDMAY GROVE (St Jude and St Paul) *Lon 6* **P** *Islington Ch Trust* **V** D SILVESTER, **C** J S SWIFT, **NSM** A SHEERAN

MILE CROSS (St Catherine) *see* Horsford and Horsham w Newton St Faith *Nor*
MILE CROSS (St Catherine) *Nor 2* **P** *Dr J P English, Canon G F Bridger, Revd K W Habershon, and Revd H Palmer (jt)* **V** P D MACKAY, **C** V A FERNANDEZ
MILE END (Holy Trinity) *Lon 7* **P** *Bp and Grocers' Co (jt)* **V** J M PEET
MILE END Old Town (St Paul) *see* Bow Common *Lon*
MILE OAK (The Good Shepherd) *see* Portslade Gd Shep *Chich*
MILEHAM (St John the Baptist) *see* Litcham w Kempston, E and W Lexham, Mileham etc *Nor*
MILES PLATTING (St Cuthbert) *see* Man Apostles w Miles Platting *Man*
MILFORD (Holy Trinity) *see* Hazelwood, Holbrook and Milford *Derby*
MILFORD (St John the Evangelist) *Guildf 4* **P** *V Witley* **V** D J MUSKETT
MILFORD, SOUTH (St Mary the Virgin) *see* Monk Fryston and S Milford *York*
MILFORD-ON-SEA (All Saints) *Win 11* **P** *Bp* **V** D J FURNESS
MILKWALL (St Luke) *see* Coleford w Staunton *Glouc*
MILL END (St Peter) and Heronsgate w West Hyde *St Alb 5* **P** *Bp and V Rickmansworth* **V** M R NICHOLLS, **C** A R LING
MILL HILL (John Keble Church) *Lon 15* **P** *Bp* **V** O R OSMOND, **NSM** I GODFREY
MILL HILL (St Michael and All Angels) *Lon 15* **P** *Bp* **V** B O WRIGHT
MILL HILL (St Paul) *see* Hendon St Paul Mill Hill *Lon*
MILLAND (St Luke) *see* Lynch w Iping Marsh and Milland *Chich*
MILLBROOK (All Saints) *see* St John w Millbrook *Truro*
MILLBROOK (Christ the King) *see* Kettering Ch the King *Pet*
MILLBROOK (Holy Trinity) *Win 13* **P** *Bp* **P-in-c** W F P PERRY
MILLBROOK Regents Park (St Clement) *see* Millbrook *Win*
MILLBROOK (St James) *Ches 14* **P** *Bp, V Stalybridge St Paul, and Mrs E Bissill (jt)* **P-in-c** A M DI CHIARA, **NSM** B J SWORD
MILLBROOK (St Michael and All Angels) *see* Ampthill w Millbrook and Steppingley *St Alb*
MILLERS DALE (St Anne) *see* Tideswell *Derby*
MILLFIELD (St Mark) and Pallion St Luke *Dur 16* **P** *Bp* **V** *vacant* 0191-565 6372
MILLFIELD (St Mary) *Dur 16* **P** *The Crown* **V** B SKELTON
MILLHOUSES (Holy Trinity) *Sheff 2* **P** *Bp* **V** P A INGRAM, **NSM** J LEE
MILLHOUSES (St Oswald) *see* Sheff St Oswald *Sheff*
MILLINGTON (St Margaret) *see* Pocklington and Owsthorpe and Kilnwick Percy etc *York*
MILLOM Holburn Hill (Mission) *see* Millom *Carl*
MILLOM (Holy Trinity) (St George) *Carl 9* **P** *Bp and Trustees (jt)* **P-in-c** R K S BRACEGIRDLE
MILNROW (St James) *Man 20* **P** *TR Rochdale* **V** R R USHER
MILNSHAW (St Mary Magdalen) *see* Accrington Ch the King *Blackb*
MILNTHORPE (St Thomas) *see* Heversham and Milnthorpe *Carl*
MILSON (St George) *see* Cleobury Mortimer w Hopton Wafers etc *Heref*
MILSTED (St Mary and the Holy Cross) *see* Bredgar w Bicknor and Frinsted w Wormshill etc *Cant*
MILSTON (St Mary) *see* Avon Valley *Sarum*
MILTON (All Saints) *Ely 5* **P** *K Coll Cam* **R** D J CHAMBERLIN
MILTON (St Blaise) *see* Steventon w Milton *Ox*
MILTON (St James) (St Andrew's Church Centre) (St Patrick) *Portsm 6* **P** *V Portsea St Mary* **V** H O ALBY, **C** N CHUMU MUTUKU
MILTON (St John the Evangelist) *see* Adderbury w Milton *Ox*
MILTON (St Mary Magdalene) *Win 9* **P** *V Milford* **R** A H BAILEY, **C** H M GRIFFISS, W H M LEMMEY
MILTON (St Peter) w St Jude *B & W 11* **P** *Ld Chan* **V** G P EALES, **NSM** G PUTNAM
MILTON (St Philip and St James) *Lich 8* **P** *Bp* **V** D W WATKIN
MILTON (St Simon and St Jude) *see* Gillingham and Milton-on-Stour *Sarum*
MILTON, GREAT (St Mary the Virgin) w Little (St James) and Great Haseley *Ox 1* **P** *Bp and D&C Windsor (jt)* **R** V L STORY
MILTON, SOUTH (All Saints) *see* Thurlestone, S Milton, W Alvington etc *Ex*
MILTON ABBAS (St James the Great) *see* Winterborne Valley and Milton Abbas *Sarum*
MILTON ABBOT (St Constantine), Dunterton, Lamerton, Sydenham Damerel, Marystowe and Coryton *Ex 25* **P** *Bp, Bedford Estates, J W Tremayne Esq, Mrs E J Bullock, P T L Newman Esq (jt)* **V** G J STANTON
MILTON BRYAN (St Peter) *see* Woburn w Eversholt, Milton Bryan, Battlesden etc *St Alb*
MILTON CLEVEDON (St James) *see* Evercreech w Chesterblade and Milton Clevedon *B & W*
MILTON COMBE (Holy Spirit) *see* Buckland Monachorum *Ex*
MILTON DAMEREL (Holy Trinity) *see* Holsworthy w Hollacombe and Milton Damerel *Ex*
MILTON ERNEST (All Saints), Pavenham and Thurleigh *St Alb 15* **P** *Bp (2 turns), Lord Luke (1 turn)* **V** N A MCINTOSH, **C** I M MCINTOSH
MILTON KEYNES (Christ the Cornerstone) *Ox 25* **P** *Bp* **C** B J HOLLINS
MILTON KEYNES VILLAGE (All Saints) *see* Walton Milton Keynes *Ox*
MILTON LILBOURNE (St Peter) *see* Pewsey and Swanborough *Sarum*
MILTON MALSOR (Holy Cross) *see* Collingtree w Courteenhall and Milton Malsor *Pet*
MILTON NEXT GRAVESEND (Christ Church) *Roch 4* **P** *Bp* **V** J S KING, **Hon C** A P WIBROE
MILTON NEXT GRAVESEND (St Peter and St Paul) w Denton *Roch 4* **P** *Bp* **R** V J LAWRENCE
MILTON NEXT SITTINGBOURNE (Holy Trinity) *Cant 15* **P** *D&C* **V** G H GREEN
MILTON REGIS (Holy Trinity) *see* Milton next Sittingbourne *Cant*
MILTON REGIS (St Mary) *see* Sittingbourne St Mary and St Mich *Cant*
MILTON-UNDER-WYCHWOOD (St Simon and St Jude) *see* Shipton-under-Wychwood w Milton, Fifield etc *Ox*
MILVERTON (St Michael) w Halse and Fitzhead *B & W 19* **P** *Adn Taunton (4 turns), Bp and V Wiveliscombe (1 turn)* **R** A D NORRIS
MILVERTON, NEW (St Mark) *Cov 11* **P** *CPAS* **V** A MORT
MILVERTON, OLD (St James) *see* Leamington Spa H Trin and Old Milverton *Cov*
MILWICH (All Saints) *see* Mid Trent *Lich*
MIMMS *see also* MYMMS
MIMMS, SOUTH (Christ Church) *Lon 14* **P** *Ch Patr Trust* **V** N T W TAYLOR, **C** K G M HILTON-TURVEY, **NSM** P W LIDDELOW
MINCHINHAMPTON (Holy Trinity) *Glouc 8* **P** *Bp* **R** M J D IRVING, **NSM** J A JAMES, J WALDEN
MINEHEAD (St Andrew) (St Michael) (St Peter) *B & W 16* **P** *Lt-Col G W F Luttrell and Bp (jt)* **V** S D LLOYD, **C** E D H LEAF
MINETY (St Leonard) *see* Ashton Keynes, Leigh and Minety *Bris*
MININGSBY WITH EAST KIRKBY (St Nicholas) *see* Marden Hill Gp *Linc*
MINLEY (St Andrew) *Guildf 1* **P** *Bp* **V** M W NEALE
MINNIS BAY (St Thomas) *see* Birchington w Acol and Minnis Bay *Cant*
MINSKIP (Mission Room) *see* Aldborough w Boroughbridge and Roecliffe *Ripon*
MINSTEAD (All Saints) *see* Lyndhurst and Emery Down and Minstead *Win*
MINSTER (St Mary the Virgin) w Monkton *Cant 9* **P** *Abp* **P-in-c** R R COLES
MINSTER (St Merteriana) *see* Boscastle w Davidstow *Truro*
MINSTER-IN-SHEPPEY (St Mary and St Sexburga) *Cant 15* **P** *Ch Patr Trust* **V** G H SPENCER, **NSM** J G KNELL, S A BIRCH
MINSTER LOVELL (St Kenelm) *Ox 8* **P** *Eton Coll and Ch Ch Ox (jt)* **V** A W D GABB-JONES
MINSTERLEY (Holy Trinity) *Heref 13* **P** *DBP and Bp (alt)* **V** A N TOOP, **NSM** M-L TOOP
MINSTERWORTH (St Peter) *see* Westbury-on-Severn w Flaxley, Blaisdon etc *Glouc*
MINTERNE MAGNA (St Andrew) *see* Buckland Newton, Cerne Abbas, Godmanstone etc *Sarum*
MINTING (St Andrew) *see* Bardney *Linc*
MIREHOUSE (St Andrew) *Carl 5* **P** *Bp* **V** *vacant* (01946) 693565
MIRFIELD (St Mary) *Wakef 10* **P** *Bp* **V** P J CRAIG-WILD, **C** S J BUCHANAN, **NSM** H C BUTLER, **OLM** A B POLLARD
MISERDEN (St Andrew) *see* Brimpsfield w Birdlip, Syde, Daglingworth etc *Glouc*
MISSENDEN, GREAT (St Peter and St Paul) w Ballinger and Little Hampden *Ox 28* **P** *Bp* **P-in-c** R E HARPER

MISSENDEN, LITTLE (St John the Baptist) *Ox 28* **P** *Earl Howe* **P-in-c** J V SIMPSON
MISSION (St John the Baptist) *see* Bawtry w Austerfield and Misson *S'well*
MISTERTON (All Saints) and West Stockwith *S'well 1* **P** *D&C York and Bp (alt)* **NSM** J D HENSON
MISTERTON (St Leonard) *see* Haselbury Plucknett, Misterton and N Perrott *B & W*
MISTERTON (St Leonard) *see* Gilmorton, Peatling Parva, Kimcote etc *Leic*
MISTLEY (St Mary and St Michael) w Manningtree and Bradfield *Chelmsf 20* **P** *DBP and Bp (jt)* **R** A COLEBROOKE, **NSM** J R BRIEN
MITCHAM (Ascension) Pollards Hill *S'wark 14* **P** *Bp* **V** J M THOMAS, **NSM** J E ROBERTS
MITCHAM (Christ Church) *see* Colliers Wood Ch Ch *S'wark*
MITCHAM (St Barnabas) *S'wark 14* **P** *Bp* **V** A J PRICE, **NSM** A M BUDDEN
MITCHAM (St Mark) *S'wark 14* **P** *Bp* **V** S H COULSON, **C** D A J MADDOX, **NSM** H NEALE
MITCHAM (St Olave) *S'wark 14* **P** *The Crown* **V** P G ENSOR
MITCHAM (St Peter and St Paul) *S'wark 14* **P** *Keble Coll Ox* **V** J C ANSELL
MITCHELDEAN (St Michael and All Angels) *see* Abenhall w Mitcheldean *Glouc*
MITFORD (St Mary Magdalene) *Newc 11* **P** *Brig E C Mitford* **V** D F MAYHEW, **OLM** J ROWLEY
MITHIAN (St Peter) *see* St Agnes and Mithian w Mount Hawke *Truro*
MITTON (All Hallows) *see* Hurst Green and Mitton *Bradf*
MIXBURY (All Saints) *see* Shelswell *Ox*
MIXENDEN (Holy Nativity) *Wakef 4* **P** *Bp* **P-in-c** D E FLETCHER
MOBBERLEY (St Wilfrid) *Ches 12* **P** *Bp* **R** I BLAY
MOCCAS (St Michael and All Angels) *see* Cusop w Blakemere, Bredwardine w Brobury etc *Heref*
MODBURY (St George), Bigbury, Ringmore w Kingston, Aveton Gifford, Woodleigh, Loddiswell and Allington, East *Ex 14* **P** *Patr Bd* **TR** N A BARKER, **TV** M L JEFFERIES, **C** J A ELLIOTT
MODDERSHALL (All Saints) *see* Stone Ch Ch and Oulton *Lich*
MOGGERHANGER (St John the Evangelist) *see* Cople, Moggerhanger and Willington *St Alb*
MOIRA (St Hilda) *see* Donisthorpe and Moira w Stretton-en-le-Field *Leic*
MOLASH (St Peter) *see* Chilham w Challock and Molash *Cant*
MOLDGREEN (Christ Church) and Rawthorpe St James *Wakef 1* **P** *R Kirkheaton and DBP (jt)* **V** V POLLARD
MOLESCROFT (St Leonard) *see* Beverley Minster *York*
MOLESEY, EAST (St Mary) *Guildf 8* **P** *Bp* **V** *vacant* (020) 8979 1441
MOLESEY, EAST (St Paul) *Guildf 8* **P** *Bp* **P-in-c** A D MILTON, **OLM** C J C KIRK
MOLESEY, WEST (St Peter) *Guildf 8* **P** *Canon W K Perry-Gore* **P-in-c** P A TAILBY
MOLESWORTH (St Peter) *see* Brington w Molesworth and Old Weston *Ely*
MOLLAND (St Mary) *see* Bishopsnympton, Rose Ash, Mariansleigh etc *Ex*
MOLLINGTON (All Saints) *see* Shires' Edge *Ox*
MOLTON, NORTH (All Saints) *see* S Molton w Nymet St George, High Bray etc *Ex*
MOLTON, SOUTH (St Mary Magdalene) w Nymet St George, High Bray, Charles, Filleigh, East Buckland, Warkleigh, Satterleigh, Chittlehamholt, Kingsnympton, Romansleigh, North Molton, Twitchen and Chittlehampton *Ex 19* **P** *DBP* **TV** D W T RUDMAN, C A J DAVIS, **C** C G ROBINSON, **NSM** C M G POUNCEY
MONEWDEN (St Mary) *see* Charsfield w Debach, Monewden, Hoo etc *St E*
MONGEHAM, GREAT (St Martin) *see* Deal St Leon w St Rich and Sholden etc *Cant*
MONK BRETTON (St Paul) *Wakef 7* **P** *V Royston* **P-in-c** R H MARSHALL, **C** L BENNETT, **OLM** J M CROSSLAND
MONK FRYSTON (St Wilfrid of Ripon) and South Milford *York 4* **P** *Ld Chan and Abp (alt)* **P-in-c** S JUKES
MONK SHERBORNE (All Saints) *see* The Sherbornes w Pamber *Win*
MONK SOHAM (St Peter) *see* Worlingworth, Southolt, Tannington, Bedfield etc *St E*
MONKEN HADLEY (St Mary the Virgin) *Lon 14* **P** *N A Dove Esq* **R** D J NASH, **NSM** J D LINTHICUM
MONKHOPTON (St Peter) *see* Upton Cressett w Monk Hopton *Heref*
MONKLAND (All Saints) *see* Leominster *Heref*
MONKLEIGH (St George) *see* Bideford, Northam, Westward Ho!, Appledore etc *Ex*
MONKMOOR (St Peter) *see* Shrewsbury H Cross *Lich*
MONKOKEHAMPTON (All Saints) *Ex 20* **P** *Bp* **P-in-c** A S GRAESSER
MONKS COPPENHALL (Christ Church) *see* Crewe Ch Ch and St Pet *Ches*
MONKS ELEIGH (St Peter) w Chelsworth and Brent Eleigh w Milden and Kettlebaston *St E 10* **P** *Bp, Guild of All So, Ld Chan (2 turns), and M J Hawkins Esq* **R** B J FINDLAY
MONKS HORTON (St Peter) *see* Smeeth w Monks Horton and Stowting and Brabourne *Cant*
MONKS KIRBY (St Editha) w Pailton and Stretton-under-Fosse *Cov 6* **P** *Trin Coll Cam* **P-in-c** C A GARROD
MONKS RISBOROUGH (St Dunstan) *see* Risborough *Ox*
MONKSEATON (St Mary) *Newc 8* **P** *Bp* **V** R P GREENWOOD
MONKSEATON (St Peter) *Newc 8* **P** *Bp* **V** J A ROBERTSON, **C** A J ELDER, **NSM** L E GARDHAM
MONKSILVER (All Saints) *see* Quantock Towers *B & W*
MONKTON (St Mary Magdalene) *see* Minster w Monkton *Cant*
MONKTON, WEST (St Augustine) *B & W 18* **P** *Bp* **P-in-c** G J BOUCHER
MONKTON COMBE (St Michael) *see* Combe Down w Monkton Combe and S Stoke *B & W*
MONKTON FARLEIGH (St Peter), South Wraxall and Winsley *Sarum 14* **P** *D&C Bris (2 turns), Bp (1 turn)* **NSM** M A CLARK
MONKTON WYLD (St Andrew) *see* Golden Cap Team *Sarum*
MONKWEARMOUTH (All Saints) (St Andrew) (St Peter) *Dur 16* **P** *Bp* **TR** I G STOCKTON, **TV** S G HILL, **C** J R MCMANNERS, **NSM** K J BAGNALL
MONKWOOD (Mission Church) *see* Bishop's Sutton and Ropley and W Tisted *Win*
MONNINGTON-ON-WYE (St Mary) *see* Letton w Staunton, Byford, Mansel Gamage etc *Heref*
MONTACUTE (St Catherine of Alexandria) *see* Odcombe, Brympton, Lufton and Montacute *B & W*
MONTFORD (St Chad) *see* Bicton, Montford w Shrawardine and Fitz *Lich*
MONTON (St Paul) *see* Eccles *Man*
MONXTON (St Mary) *see* Amport, Grateley, Monxton and Quarley *Win*
MONYASH (St Leonard) *see* Taddington, Chelmorton and Flagg, and Monyash *Derby*
MOOR (St Thomas) *see* Fladbury w Wyre Piddle and Moor etc *Worc*
MOOR ALLERTON (St John the Evangelist) (St Stephen) *Ripon 5* **P** *Patr Bd* **TR** C P DOBBIN, **TV** N D BEER, P H AINSWORTH, **NSM** J E SHAW, I RATHBONE
MOOR COURT (St Mary) *see* Pembridge w Moor Court, Shobdon, Staunton etc *Heref*
MOOR GRANGE (St Andrew) *see* Hawksworth Wood *Ripon*
MOOR MILNER (Church Institute) *see* Daresbury *Ches*
MOOR MONKTON (All Saints) *see* Rufforth w Moor Monkton and Hessay *York*
MOORBRIDGE LANE (St Luke) *see* Stapleford *S'well*
MOORCOURT (St Mary) *see* Pembridge w Moor Court, Shobdon, Staunton etc *Heref*
MOORDOWN (St John the Baptist) *Win 8* **P** *Bp* **V** W A SWAIN, **NSM** J L WILLIAMS
MOORENDS (St Wilfrith) *Sheff 10* **P** *Bp* **V** R B PARKER
MOORHOUSE (Chantry Chapel) *see* Kneesall w Laxton and Wellow *S'well*
MOORHOUSES (St Lawrence) *see* Mareham-le-Fen and Revesby *Linc*
MOORLAND TEAM *see* Widecombe-in-the-Moor, Leusdon, Princetown etc *Ex*
MOORLINCH (Blessed Virgin Mary) *see* Middlezoy and Othery and Moorlinch *B & W*
MOORSHOLM (St Mary) *see* Boosbeck w Moorsholm *York*
MOORSIDE (St Thomas) *see* Oldham Moorside *Man*
MOORSIDE (St Wilfrid) *see* Doxford St Wilfrid *Dur*
MOORTOWN (St Stephen) *see* Moor Allerton *Ripon*
MORBORNE (All Saints) *see* Stilton w Denton and Caldecote etc *Ely*
MORCHARD BISHOP (St Mary) *see* N Creedy *Ex*
MORCOTT (St Mary the Virgin) *see* Barrowden and Wakerley w S Luffenham etc *Pet*
MORDEN (Emmanuel Church Hall) (St George) (St Lawrence) (St Martin) *S'wark 14* **P** *Patr Bd* **TR** R F SKINNER, **TV** C A WOOD, A L FLOWERDAY, J C BRIGHTWELL, **OLM** J D GODDARD

MORDEN (St Mary) *see* Red Post *Sarum*
MORDIFORD (Holy Rood) *see* Fownhope w Mordiford, Brockhampton etc *Heref*
MORE (St Peter) *see* Wentnor w Ratlinghope, Myndtown, Norbury etc *Heref*
MOREBATH (St George) *see* Bampton, Morebath, Clayhanger and Petton *Ex*
MORECAMBE (Holy Trinity) *see* Poulton-le-Sands w Morecambe St Laur *Blackb*
MORECAMBE (St Andrew) *see* Heysham *Blackb*
MORECAMBE (St Barnabas) *Blackb 11* **P** *R Poulton-le-Sands* **V** G J HUMPHRYES
MORECAMBE (St Christopher) *see* Bare *Blackb*
MORECAMBE (St James) *see* Heysham *Blackb*
MORECAMBE (St John) *see* Sandylands *Blackb*
MORECAMBE (St Peter) *see* Heysham *Blackb*
MORECAMBE (The Ascension) *see* Torrisholme *Blackb*
MORELEIGH (All Saints) *see* Diptford, N Huish, Harberton, Harbertonford etc *Ex*
MORESBY (St Bridget) *Carl 5* **P** *Earl of Lonsdale* **R** A D EDWARDS
MORESBY PARKS (Mission Church) *see* Moresby *Carl*
MORESTEAD (not known) *see* Twyford and Owslebury and Morestead *Win*
MORETON (Christ Church) *Ches 8* **P** *Simeon's Trustees* **R** G J COUSINS, **C** S W J REA
MORETON (St Mary) *see* Fyfield, Moreton w Bobbingworth etc *Chelmsf*
MORETON (St Mary) *see* Bradeley, Church Eaton and Moreton *Lich*
MORETON (St Nicholas) and Woodsford w Tincleton *Sarum 1* **P** *Hon Mrs M A Bartenk and Miss M B F Frampton (alt)* **R** J A BIRDSEYE, **C** M R B DURRANT
MORETON, SOUTH (St John the Baptist) w North (All Saints), Aston Tirrold and Aston Upthorpe *Ox 18* **P** *Adn Berks, Hertf Coll Ox, and Magd Coll Ox (jt)* **R** C J WALKER
MORETON CORBET (St Bartholomew) *Lich 22* **P** *C C Corbet Esq* **R** D J HUMPHRIES
MORETON HALL (Christ Church) *see* Bury St Edmunds Ch Ch *St E*
MORETON-IN-MARSH (St David) w Batsford, Todenham, Lower Lemiington and Longborough w Sezincote *Glouc 14* **P** *Bp and Lord Dulverton (1 turn), and Bp, Lord Dulverton, Lord Leigh, and Mrs S Peake (1 turn)* **R** S M WOOKEY, **C** S P REES
MORETON JEFFRIES (St Peter and St Paul) *see* Stoke Lacy, Moreton Jeffries w Much Cowarne etc *Heref*
MORETON MORRELL (Holy Cross) *see* Newbold Pacey w Moreton Morrell *Cov*
MORETON-ON-LUGG (St Andrew) *see* Pipe-cum-Lyde and Moreton-on-Lugg *Heref*
MORETON PINKNEY (St Mary the Virgin) *see* Culworth w Sulgrave and Thorpe Mandeville etc *Pet*
MORETON SAY (St Margaret of Antioch) *see* Adderley, Ash, Calverhall, Ightfield etc *Lich*
MORETON VALENCE (St Stephen) *see* Eastington, Frocester, Haresfield etc *Glouc*
MORETONHAMPSTEAD (St Andrew), Manaton, North Bovey and Lustleigh *Ex 9* **P** *Bp and DBP (jt)* **R** I A HELLYER
MORGAN'S VALE (St Birinus) *see* Redlynch and Morgan's Vale *Sarum*
MORLAND (St Lawrence), Thrimby, Gt Strickland and Cliburn *Carl 1* **P** *Lord Hothfield and D&C (jt)* **V** S D RUDKIN
MORLEY (St Botolph) *see* High Oak, Hingham and Scoulton w Wood Rising *Nor*
MORLEY (St Matthew) w Smalley and Horsley Woodhouse *Derby 12* **P** *Bp* **R** C HENSON, **NSM** E S BERRY
MORLEY (St Peter) *see* High Oak, Hingham and Scoulton w Wood Rising *Nor*
MORLEY (St Peter) (St Paul) *Wakef 8* **P** *Patr Bd* **TR** M R EAREY, **TV** M M DYE, A D WOOD, **C** H D WOOD
MORNINGTHORPE (St John the Baptist) *see* Hempnall *Nor*
MORPETH (St Aidan) (St James) (St Mary the Virgin) *Newc 11* **P** *Bp* **R** R H MCLEAN, **C** J C PARK, J J BECKWITH, **NSM** M O CHESTER
MORRIS GREEN (St Bede) *see* Bolton St Bede *Man*
MORSTON (All Saints) *see* Stiffkey and Bale *Nor*
MORTEHOE (St Mary Magdalene) *see* Ilfracombe, Lee, Woolacombe, Bittadon etc *Ex*
MORTIMER COMMON (St John) *see* Stratfield Mortimer and Mortimer W End etc *Ox*
MORTIMER WEST END (St Saviour) *as above*
MORTLAKE (St Mary) w East Sheen *S'wark 18* **P** *Patr Bd* **TR** F A JACKSON, **TV** E H LEE, C PALMER, **C** M D A ROPER, **Hon C** P D KING, **OLM** O J WILLIAMSON
MORTOMLEY (St Saviour) High Green *Sheff 3* **P** *Bp* **V** E MITCHELL
MORTON (Holy Cross) and Stonebroom w Shirland *Derby 1* **P** *Bp, St Jo Coll Cam, Adn Chesterfield, and trustees (by turn)* **R** C A DYER, **C** J C BAINES
MORTON (St Denis) *see* Rolleston w Fiskerton, Morton and Upton *S'well*
MORTON (St John the Baptist) *see* Ringstone in Aveland Gp *Linc*
MORTON (St Luke) *Bradf 8* **P** *Bp* **P-in-c** P RUGEN
MORTON (St Paul) *see* Gainsborough and Morton *Linc*
MORTON (St Philip and St James) *Lich 19* **P** *Ld Chan* **P-in-c** C W PENN
MORTON BAGOT (Holy Trinity) *see* Spernall, Morton Bagot and Oldberrow *Cov*
MORVAH (St Bridget of Sweden) *see* Pendeen w Morvah *Truro*
MORVAL (St Wenna) *see* Duloe, Herodsfoot, Morval and St Pinnock *Truro*
MORVILLE (St Gregory) w Aston Eyre *Heref 9* **P** *DBP* **Hon C** H J PATTERSON
MORWENSTOW (St John the Baptist) *see* Kilkhampton w Morwenstow *Truro*
MOSBROUGH (St Mark) *Sheff 1* **P** *Bp* **V** D AKRILL
MOSELEY (St Agnes) *Birm 5* **P** *V Moseley St Mary* **V** P H ANSELL
MOSELEY (St Anne) *Birm 5* **P** *V Moseley St Mary* **P-in-c** A BRADBROOK, **C** R A DONOVAN
MOSELEY (St Mary) *Birm 5* **P** *Bp* **V** A BRADBROOK, **C** R A DONOVAN, P M HANSELL, **Hon C** A J DUNNING, **NSM** J A GRIFFIN
MOSLEY COMMON (St John) *Man 13* **P** *Bp* **P-in-c** J J HARTLEY
MOSS BANK (Mission Church) *see* Carr Mill *Liv*
MOSS SIDE (Christ Church) *Man 4* **P** *Trustees* **P-in-c** S D A KILLWICK
MOSS SIDE (St James w St Clement) *see* Whalley Range St Edm and Moss Side etc *Man*
MOSSER (St Philip) (Michael's Chapel) *Carl 6* **P** *Bp* **P-in-c** K KITCHIN
MOSSLEY (Holy Trinity) *see* Congleton *Ches*
MOSSLEY (St George) *Man 17* **P** *R Ashton-under-Lyne St Mich* **V** R J LINDSAY, **OLM** P PHILLIPS
MOSSLEY ESTATE (St Thomas Church) *see* Bloxwich *Lich*
MOSSLEY HILL (St Barnabas) (St Matthew and St James) *Liv 4* **P** *Patr Bd* **TR** R A WILKES, **TV** G J BUTLAND
MOSSWOOD (St Barnabas) *see* Cannock *Lich*
MOSTERTON (St Mary) *see* Beaminster Area *Sarum*
MOSTON (St Chad) *Man 5* **P** *Bp* **P-in-c** I C J GORTON, **OLM** I L SMITH
MOSTON (St John) Ashley Lane *Man 5* **P** *Bp* **R** *vacant* 0161-205 4967
MOSTON (St Luke) *see* Lightbowne *Man*
MOSTON (St Mary) *Man 5* **P** *D&C* **P-in-c** M R M CALLADINE, **NSM** J E CALLADINE, **OLM** G L CORNISH
MOTCOMBE (St Mary) *see* Shaston *Sarum*
MOTSPUR PARK (Holy Cross) *S'wark 14* **P** *Bp* **V** R S TAYLOR
MOTTINGHAM (St Andrew) (St Alban Mission Church) *S'wark 3* **P** *Bp* **NSM** D WARREN
MOTTINGHAM (St Edward the Confessor) *S'wark 3* **P** *Bp* **V** M J JACKSON
MOTTISFONT (St Andrew) *see* Broughton, Bossington, Houghton and Mottisfont *Win*
MOTTISTONE (St Peter and St Paul) *see* Brighstone and Brooke w Mottistone *Portsm*
MOTTRAM IN LONGDENDALE (St Michael) *Ches 14* **P** *Bp* **V** P G BURROWS
MOULSECOOMB (St Andrew) *Chich 2* **P** *Bp* **C** R C GOULDTHORPE
MOULSFORD (St John the Baptist) *see* Cholsey and Moulsford *Ox*
MOULSHAM (St John the Evangelist) *Chelmsf 9* **P** *Dean* **V** K R MAGEE, **NSM** S M SOUTHEE
MOULSHAM (St Luke) *Chelmsf 9* **P** *Bp* **V** S M CHAPMAN, **NSM** S E IVES
MOULSOE (The Assumption of the Blessed Virgin Mary) *see* Newport Pagnell w Lathbury and Moulsoe *Ox*
MOULTON (All Saints) (St James) (Mission Room) *Linc 17* **P** *DBP* **V** *vacant* (01406) 370791
MOULTON (Mission Church) *see* E Richmond *Ripon*
MOULTON (St Peter) *see* Dalham, Gazeley, Higham, Kentford and Moulton *St E*
MOULTON (St Peter and St Paul) *Pet 4* **P** *Ch Soc Trust* **V** P H BRECKWOLDT, **C** E F Q PENNINGTON
MOULTON (St Stephen the Martyr) *Ches 6* **P** *R Davenham* **P-in-c** A Q GREENHOUGH

MOULTON, GREAT (St Michael) *see* Bunwell, Carleton Rode, Tibenham, Gt Moulton etc *Nor*
MOUNT BURES (St John) *see* Wormingford, Mt Bures and Lt Horkesley *Chelmsf*
MOUNT HAWKE (St John the Baptist) *see* St Agnes and Mithian w Mount Hawke *Truro*
MOUNT PELLON (Christ Church) *Wakef 4* **P** *Bp* **V** J HELLEWELL
MOUNTFIELD (All Saints) *see* Brightling, Dallington, Mountfield etc *Chich*
MOUNTNESSING (St Giles) *see* Margaretting w Mountnessing and Buttsbury *Chelmsf*
MOUNTSORREL (Christ Church) (St Peter) *Leic 7* **P** *CPAS and Bp* **P-in-c** K C EMMETT
MOW COP (St Luke's Mission Church) *see* Odd Rode *Ches*
MOW COP (St Thomas) *Lich 11* **P** *Prime Min* **P-in-c** J C WATERS
MOWSLEY (St Nicholas) *see* Husbands Bosworth w Mowsley and Knaptoft etc *Leic*
MOXLEY (All Saints) *Lich 26* **P** *Prime Min* **P-in-c** R E INGLESBY, **OLM** A J DUCKWORTH
MUCH *see also under substantive place name*
MUCH BIRCH (St Mary and St Thomas à Becket) w Little Birch, Much Dewchurch, Llanwarne and Llandinabo *Heref 8* **P** *A W Twiston-Davies Esq (1 turn), Bp (3 turns), and Ld Chan (1 turn)* **P-in-c** K B GARLICK
MUCH MARCLE (St Bartholomew) *see* Ledbury *Heref*
MUCHELNEY (St Peter and St Paul) *see* Langport Area Chs *B & W*
MUCKLESTONE (St Mary) *see* Ashley and Mucklestone *Lich*
MUDEFORD (All Saints) *see* Christchurch *Win*
MUDFORD (Blessed Virgin Mary) *see* Chilton Cantelo, Ashington, Mudford, Rimpton etc *B & W*
MUGGINTON (All Saints) and Kedleston *Derby 11* **P** *Major J W Chandos-Pole* **P-in-c** S I MITCHELL
MUGGLESWICK (All Saints) *see* Blanchland w Hunstanworth and Edmundbyers etc *Newc*
MUKER (St Mary) *see* Swaledale *Ripon*
MULBARTON (St Mary Magdalene) w Bracon Ash, Hethel and Flordon *Nor 7* **P** *R T Berney Esq (1 turn), Mrs R M Watkinson (2 turns), DBP (1 turn), and Ld Chan (1 turn)* **R** J W STUBENBORD
MULLION (St Mellanus) *Truro 4* **P** *Bp* **P-in-c** G C SCOTT
MUMBY (St Thomas of Canterbury) *see* Willoughby *Linc*
MUNCASTER (St Michael) *see* Eskdale, Irton, Muncaster and Waberthwaite *Carl*
MUNDENS, The (All Saints) w Sacombe *St Alb 22* **P** *Ch Trust Fund Trust, K Coll Cam, and R M Abel Smith Esq (jt)* **P-in-c** A E DAVIE
MUNDESLEY (All Saints) *see* Trunch *Nor*
MUNDFORD (St Leonard) w Lynford *Nor 13* **P** *Ch Patr Trust* **P-in-c** P M FARROW
MUNDHAM (St Peter) *see* Brooke, Kirstead, Mundham w Seething and Thwaite *Nor*
MUNDHAM, NORTH (St Stephen) w Hunston and Merston *Chich 3* **P** *St Jo Coll Cam* **R** V C DE R MALAN
MUNGRISDALE (St Kentigern) *see* Gd Shep TM *Carl*
MUNSLEY (St Bartholomew) *see* Ledbury *Heref*
MUNSLOW (St Michael) *see* Diddlebury w Munslow, Holdgate and Tugford *Heref*
MUNSTER SQUARE (Christ Church) (St Mary Magdalene) *Lon 17* **P** *Bp* **V** S J GRIGG, **C** P H-S CHO
MUNSTONE (Church Room) *see* Holmer w Huntington *Heref*
MURCOTT (Mission Room) *see* Ray Valley *Ox*
MURROW (Corpus Christi) *see* Wisbech St Mary and Guyhirn w Ring's End etc *Ely*
MURSLEY (St Mary the Virgin) *see* Newton Longville and Mursley w Swanbourne etc *Ox*
MURSTON (All Saints) w Bapchild and Tonge *Cant 15* **P** *Abp and St Jo Coll Cam (jt)* **R** B A SHERSBY
MURTON (Holy Trinity) *see* Hawthorn and Murton *Dur*
MURTON (St James) *see* Osbaldwick w Murton *York*
MURTON (St John the Baptist) *see* Appleby *Carl*
MUSBURY (St Michael) *see* Colyton, Musbury, Southleigh and Branscombe *Ex*
MUSBURY (St Thomas) *Blackb 1* **P** *The Crown* **V** W N PRICE
MUSGRAVE (St Theobald) *see* Brough w Stainmore, Musgrave and Warcop *Carl*
MUSKHAM, NORTH (St Wilfrid) and SOUTH (St Wilfrid) *S'well 3* **P** *Ld Chan* **V** *vacant* (01636) 702655
MUSTON (All Saints) *see* Hunmanby w Muston *York*
MUSTON (St John the Baptist) *see* Vale of Belvoir Par *Leic*
MUSWELL HILL (St James) (St Matthew) *Lon 20* **P** *Bp and CPAS (jt)* **V** D A ROSS, **C** P H SUDELL, J P ARANZULLA, A R F B GAGE, **NSM** H C HENDRY, J R LENTON
MUTFORD (St Andrew) *see* Carlton Colville and Mutford *Nor*
MYDDELTON SQUARE (St Mark) *see* Clerkenwell St Mark *Lon*
MYDDLE (St Peter) *Lich 22* **P** *Bp* **P-in-c** D T W PRICE, **NSM** T D SMITH
MYLAND (St Michael) *see* Colchester St Mich Myland *Chelmsf*
MYLOR (St Mylor) w Flushing *Truro 3* **P** *Bp* **V** J C JAMES
MYLOR BRIDGE (All Saints) *see* Mylor w Flushing *Truro*
MYMMS, NORTH (St Mary) (St Michael) *St Alb 21* **P** *Bp* **P-in-c** S E DAVENPORT
MYMMS, SOUTH (King Charles the Martyr) *see* Potters Bar K Chas *St Alb*
MYMMS, SOUTH (St Giles) and Ridge *St Alb 17* **P** *DBP* **P-in-c** B M TIPPING
MYNDTOWN (St John the Baptist) *see* Wentnor w Ratlinghope, Myndtown, Norbury etc *Heref*
MYTHOLMROYD (St Michael) *see* Erringden *Wakef*
MYTON ON SWALE (St Mary) *see* Brafferton w Pilmoor, Myton-on-Swale etc *York*
NABB (Mission Church) *see* Oakengates and Wrockwardine Wood *Lich*
NABURN (St Matthew) *see* Escrick and Stillingfleet w Naburn *York*
NACKINGTON (St Mary) *see* Petham and Waltham w Lower Hardres etc *Cant*
NACTON (St Martin) and Levington w Bucklesham and Foxhall *St E 2* **P** *DBP* **R** G L GRANT, **OLM** D E N KING
NADDER VALLEY *Sarum 11* **P** *Patr Bd (4 turns), Ld Chan (1 turn)* **TR** H I J SOUTHERN, **TV** J M STAPLES, **C** C A FAIRCLOUGH, S M SYMONS, **NSM** R WREN, M A SHALLCROSS, **Dss** A SYMES
NAFFERTON (All Saints) w Wansford *York 10* **P** *Abp* **P-in-c** P J ARTLEY
NAILSEA (Christ Church) w Tickenham *B & W 13* **P** *CPAS (3 turns), Ld Chan (1 turn)* **R** A Q H WHEELER, **C** S C AIREY
NAILSEA (Holy Trinity) *B & W 13* **P** *MMCET* **R** K J BOULLIER, **C** R H SMITH, J R BACKHOUSE
NAILSTONE (All Saints) and Carlton w Shackerstone *Leic 12* **P** *The Crown and DBP (alt)* **P-in-c** J F PLANT
NAILSWORTH (St George) w Shortwood, Horsley and Newington Bapath w Kingscote *Glouc 8* **P** *Bp* **V** S J EARLEY, **Hon C** J GREEN
NANPANTAN (St Mary in Charnwood) *see* Loughborough Em and St Mary in Charnwood *Leic*
NANPEAN (St George) *see* St Stephen in Brannel *Truro*
NANSTALLION (St Stephen's Mission Room) *see* Bodmin w Lanhydrock and Lanivet *Truro*
NANTWICH (St Mary) *Ches 15* **P** *Q H Crewe Esq and J C Crewe Esq (jt)* **R** P T CHANTRY, **C** S J CLAPHAM
NAPTON-ON-THE-HILL (St Lawrence), Lower Shuckburgh and Stockton *Cov 10* **P** *Ld Chan (2 turns), Sir Rupert Shuckburgh Bt (1 turn), and New Coll Ox (2 turns)* **P-in-c** M L D GREIG, **C** P A LILLICRAP
NARBOROUGH (All Saints) and Huncote *Leic 10* **P** *SMF* **R** N J BURTON
NARBOROUGH (All Saints) w Narford and Pentney *Nor 13* **P** *Bp* **R** S R NAIRN
NARFORD (St Mary) *see* Narborough w Narford and Pentney *Nor*
NASEBY (All Saints) *see* Clipston w Naseby and Haselbech w Kelmarsh *Pet*
NASH (All Saints) *see* Buckingham *Ox*
NASH (St John the Baptist) *see* Burford I *Heref*
NASSINGTON (St Mary the Virgin and All Saints) w Yarwell and Woodnewton *Pet 12* **P** *Lord Brassey and Bp (alt)* **V** R A LOVELESS
NATELY SCURES (St Swithun) *see* Newnham w Nately Scures w Mapledurwell etc *Win*
NATLAND (St Mark) *Carl 10* **P** *V Kendal H Trin* **P-in-c** T S EVANS, **NSM** M P JAYNE, M J DEW
NAUGHTON (St Mary) *see* Bildeston w Wattisham and Lindsey, Whatfield etc *St E*
NAUNTON (St Andrew) *see* The Guitings, Cutsdean, Farmcote etc *Glouc*
NAUNTON BEAUCHAMP (St Bartholomew) *see* Abberton, The Flyfords, Naunton Beauchamp etc *Worc*
NAVENBY (St Peter) *see* Graffoe Gp *Linc*
NAVESTOCK (St Thomas) *see* Bentley Common, Kelvedon Hatch and Navestock *Chelmsf*
NAWTON (St Hilda) *see* Kirkdale w Harome, Nunnington and Pockley *York*
NAYLAND (St James) w Wiston *St E 3* **P** *Ld Chan (2 turns) and DBP (1 turn)* **P-in-c** C A GRAY
NAYLAND DRIVE (Church Centre) *see* Clacton St Jas *Chelmsf*

NAZEING (All Saints) (St Giles) *Chelmsf 26* **P** *Ld Chan* **P-in-c** C P PENNINGTON, **NSM** D RICKETTS
NEASDEN (St Catherine w St Paul) *Lon 21* **P** *Bp and D&C St Paul's (jt)* **V** E E GAUNT
NEATISHEAD (St Peter) *see* Ashmanhaugh, Barton Turf etc *Nor*
NECHELLS (St Matthew) *Birm 8* **P** *Bp and V Aston-juxta-Birm (jt)* **V** *vacant* 0121-359 6965
NECTON (All Saints), Holme Hale w Pickenham, North and South *Nor 13* **P** *Major-Gen R S Broke, Ch Soc Trust, MMCET and S Pickenham Estate Co Ltd (jt)* **R** P J TAYLOR
NEDGING (St Mary) *see* Bildeston w Wattisham and Lindsey, Whatfield etc *St E*
NEEDHAM (St Peter) *see* Redenhall, Harleston, Wortwell and Needham *Nor*
NEEDHAM MARKET (St John the Baptist) w Badley *St E 1* **P** *PCC* **P-in-c** P R DALTRY
NEEN SAVAGE (St Mary) *see* Cleobury Mortimer w Hopton Wafers etc *Heref*
NEEN SOLLARS (All Saints) *as above*
NEENTON (All Saints) *see* Ditton Priors w Neenton, Burwarton etc *Heref*
NEITHROP (St Paul) *see* Banbury St Paul *Ox*
NELSON (St Bede) *Blackb 6* **P** *Bp* **P-in-c** A PIERCE-JONES
NELSON (St John the Evangelist) *see* Gt Marsden w Nelson St Phil *Blackb*
NELSON (St Mary) *see* Lt Marsden w Nelson St Mary *Blackb*
NELSON (St Paul) *as above*
NELSON (St Philip) *see* Gt Marsden w Nelson St Phil *Blackb*
NEMPNETT THRUBWELL (The Blessed Virgin Mary) *see* Chew Stoke w Nempnett Thrubwell *B & W*
NENTHEAD (St John) *see* Alston Moor *Newc*
NESS Group, The *Linc 13* **P** *Ld Chan (1 turn), Bp and DBP (2 turns)* **V** J M BEADLE
NESS, GREAT (St Andrew) *see* Ruyton XI Towns w Gt and Lt Ness *Lich*
NESS, LITTLE (St Martin) *as above*
NESTON (St Mary and St Helen) *Ches 9* **P** *D&C* **V** R H N ROBB, **C** G A ROSSITER, **NSM** A C G LEACH
NESTON (St Phillip and St James) *see* Gtr Corsham and Lacock *Bris*
NESTON, LITTLE (St Michael and All Angels) *see* Neston *Ches*
NETHER *see also under substantive place name*
NETHER HALL (St Elizabeth) *see* Scraptoft *Leic*
NETHERAVON (All Saints) *see* Avon Valley *Sarum*
NETHERBURY (St Mary) *see* Beaminster Area *Sarum*
NETHEREXE (St John the Baptist) *see* Stoke Canon, Poltimore w Huxham and Rewe etc *Ex*
NETHERFIELD (St George) *S'well 10* **P** *DBP* **P-in-c** R B CHAPMAN
NETHERFIELD (St John the Baptist) *see* Brightling, Dallington, Mountfield etc *Chich*
NETHERHAMPTON (St Katherine) *see* Wilton w Netherhampton and Fugglestone *Sarum*
NETHERLEY (Christ Church) *see* Gateacre *Liv*
NETHERNE (St Luke) *see* Merstham and Gatton *S'wark*
NETHERSEAL (St Peter) *see* Seale and Lullington w Coton in the Elms *Derby*
NETHERTHONG (All Saints) *see* Upper Holme Valley *Wakef*
NETHERTHORPE (St Bartholomew) *see* Sheff St Bart *Sheff*
NETHERTHORPE (St Stephen) *Sheff 4* **P** *Ch Patr Trust and Sheff Ch Burgesses Trust (jt)* **V** P J BATCHFORD
NETHERTON (All Souls) *see* Maryport, Netherton and Flimby *Carl*
NETHERTON (St Andrew) *see* Middlestown *Wakef*
NETHERTON (St Andrew) *Worc 9* **P** *V Dudley* **P-in-c** W J A BARNES
NETHERTON (St Oswald) *Liv 1* **P** *Bp* **V** N A WELLS, **C** D F LARKEY
NETHERWITTON (St Giles) *see* Nether Witton *Newc*
NETLEY ABBEY *see* Hound *Win*
NETLEY MARSH (St Matthew) *see* Totton *Win*
NETTLEBED (St Bartholomew) w Bix, Highmoor, Pishill and Rotherfield Greys *Ox 6* **P** *DBP, Earl of Macclesfield, Ch Patr Trust, and Trin Coll Ox (jt)* **R** B J BAILEY, **NSM** R W M BOWDER, **OLM** E F LAKEY
NETTLECOMBE (Blessed Virgin Mary) *see* Quantock Towers *B & W*
NETTLEDEN (Ashridge Chapel) *see* Potten End w Nettleden *St Alb*
NETTLEDEN (St Lawrence) *as above*
NETTLEHAM (All Saints) *Linc 3* **P** *Bp* **NSM** C A ZOTOV
NETTLESTEAD (St Mary) *see* Gt and Lt Blakenham w Baylham and Nettlestead *St E*
NETTLESTEAD (St Mary the Virgin) *see* E Peckham and Nettlestead *Roch*
NETTLETON (St John the Baptist) *see* Swallow *Linc*
NETTLETON (St Mary) *see* By Brook *Bris*
NEVENDON (St Peter) *see* Pitsea w Nevendon *Chelmsf*
NEVILLE'S CROSS (St John) *see* Dur St Marg and Neville's Cross St Jo *Dur*
NEW *see also under substantive place name*
NEW BOROUGH and Leigh (St John the Evangelist) *Sarum 9* **P** *Ch Soc Trust* **V** R J A TULLOCH, **C** R E R DEMERY
NEW BUILDINGS (Beacon Church) *see* Crediton, Shobrooke and Sandford etc *Ex*
NEW FERRY (St Mark) *Ches 8* **P** *R Bebington* **NSM** A D DRURY
NEW HAW (All Saints) *Guildf 11* **P** *Bp* **V** R J GOSTELOW, **OLM** J J PHILLIPS
NEW MILL (Christ Church) *see* Upper Holme Valley *Wakef*
NEW MILLS (St George) (St James the Less) *Derby 6* **P** *V Glossop* **V** D J MURDOCH
NEW PARKS (St Aidan) *see* Leic St Aid *Leic*
NEW SPRINGS (St John the Baptist) and Whelley St Stephen *Liv 14* **P** *Bp* **V** D J ROSCOE
NEW TOWN (St George w St Michael) *see* Edgbaston St Geo *Birm*
NEWALL GREEN (St Francis of Assisi) *see* Wythenshawe *Man*
NEWARK-UPON-TRENT (St Mary Magdalene) (St Augustine's Mission) (Christ Church) (St Leonard) *S'well 3* **P** *The Crown* **TR** V J ENEVER, **TV** D F OLNEY, P HUTCHINSON
NEWBALD (St Nicholas) *York 13* **P** *Abp* **P-in-c** M R BUSHBY
NEWBARNS (St Paul) *see* Barrow St Paul *Carl*
NEWBIGGIN (St Edmund) *see* Kirkby Thore w Temple Sowerby and Newbiggin *Carl*
NEWBIGGIN-BY-THE-SEA (St Bartholomew) *see* Woodhorn w Newbiggin *Newc*
NEWBIGGIN HALL (St Wilfrid) *Newc 7* **P** *Bp* **V** P D MCLEOD
NEWBOLD (St John the Evangelist) w Dunston *Derby 5* **P** *R Chesterfield* **V** N V JOHNSON, **C** J C MILNES
NEWBOLD (St Peter) *see* S Rochdale *Man*
NEWBOLD DE VERDUN (St James) and Kirkby Mallory *Leic 12* **P** *Bp and Trin Coll Ox (jt)* **R** *vacant* (01455) 822528
NEWBOLD ON AVON (St Botolph) *Cov 6* **P** *H A F W Boughton Leigh Esq* **V** P M WILKINSON
NEWBOLD ON STOUR (St David) *see* Tredington and Darlingscott w Newbold on Stour *Cov*
NEWBOLD PACEY (St George) w Moreton Morrell *Cov 8* **P** *Qu Coll Ox and Lt-Col J E Little (alt)* **V** G J BURRELL, **C** R C FLOATE
NEWBOROUGH (All Saints) *see* Hanbury w Newborough and Rangemore *Lich*
NEWBOROUGH (St Bartholomew) *Pet 13* **P** *The Crown* **V** *vacant* (01733) 810682
NEWBOTTLE (St James) *see* King's Sutton and Newbottle and Charlton *Pet*
NEWBOTTLE (St Matthew) *Dur 14* **P** *Bp* **V** E WILKINSON
NEWBOURN (St Mary) *see* Waldringfield w Hemley and Newbourn *St E*
NEWBROUGH (St Peter) *see* Warden w Newbrough *Newc*
NEWBURGH (Christ Church) w Westhead *Liv 11* **P** *Bp and V Ormskirk (jt)* **V** D G TOWLER, **NSM** D M BURROWS, **OLM** J SEPHTON
NEWBURN (St Michael and All Angels) *Newc 7* **P** *MMCET* **V** J R SINCLAIR, **C** S MCCORMACK, **OLM** M P LEDGER
NEWBURY (St John the Evangelist) (St Nicholas and St Mary) *Ox 14* **P** *Bp* **TR** D A STONE, **TV** B DAGNALL, J C WALL, **C** E Q HOBBS, H M WILKINSON, **NSM** B J PRITCHARD
NEWBY (St Mark) *York 15* **P** *Abp* **V** M SPENCELEY
NEWCASTLE (Christ Church) (St Ann) *Newc 5* **P** *Bp* **V** C M SAVAGE
NEWCASTLE (St Andrew) (St Luke) *Newc 5* **P** *Bp and V Newcastle (jt)* **P-in-c** G EVANS
NEWCASTLE (St John the Evangelist) *see* Clun w Bettws-y-Crwyn and Newcastle *Heref*
NEWCASTLE (St Philip) and St Augustine and (St Matthew w St Mary) *Newc 7* **P** *Bp* **V** R G S DEADMAN
NEWCASTLE UNDER LYME (St George) *Lich 9* **P** *R Newcastle w Butterton* **P-in-c** W E J MASH
NEWCASTLE UNDER LYME (St Giles) w Butterton *Lich 9* **P** *Simeon's Trustees* **P-in-c** A F CREBER, **OLM** M A TAYLOR, J WARHAM
NEWCASTLE UNDER LYME (St Paul) *Lich 9* **P** *Trustees* **P-in-c** L O FRANKLIN
NEWCASTLE UPON TYNE (Christ Church) *see* Walker *Newc*
NEWCASTLE UPON TYNE Christ the King *see* Ch the King *Newc*
NEWCASTLE UPON TYNE (Clayton Memorial Church) *see* Jesmond Clayton Memorial *Newc*

NEWCASTLE UPON TYNE (Holy Cross) *Newc 7* **P** *Bp* **V** A W MARKS, **C** J E APPLEBY
NEWCASTLE UPON TYNE (Holy Trinity) *see* Jesmond H Trin *Newc*
NEWCASTLE UPON TYNE (St Anthony) *see* Byker St Ant *Newc*
NEWCASTLE UPON TYNE (St Barnabas and St Jude) *Newc 5* **P** *V Jesmond Clayton Memorial and CPAS (alt)* **P-in-c** R L SIMPSON, **NSM** C SMITH
NEWCASTLE UPON TYNE (St Francis) High Heaton *Newc 6* **P** *Bp* **V** C J CLINCH, **C** J P HAGGER
NEWCASTLE UPON TYNE (St Gabriel) Heaton *Newc 6* **P** *Bp* **V** M J WEBB, **C** M THRELFALL-HOLMES
NEWCASTLE UPON TYNE (St George) *Newc 5* **P** *Bp* **V** F R DEXTER, **C** I H FLINTOFT, **NSM** L B VASEY-SAUNDERS
NEWCASTLE UPON TYNE (St Hilda) *Newc 5* **P** *Bp* **V** *vacant*
NEWCASTLE UPON TYNE (St James and St Basil) *see* Fenham St Jas and St Basil *Newc*
NEWCASTLE UPON TYNE (St John the Baptist) *Newc 5* **P** *V Newc* **P-in-c** N WILSON
NEWCASTLE UPON TYNE (St Margaret) *see* Scotswood *Newc*
NEWCASTLE UPON TYNE (St Martin) *see* Byker St Martin *Newc*
NEWCASTLE UPON TYNE (St Michael w St Lawrence) *see* Byker St Mich w St Lawr *Newc*
NEWCASTLE UPON TYNE (St Oswald) *see* Byker St Mark and Walkergate St Oswald *Newc*
NEWCASTLE UPON TYNE (St Paul) *see* High Elswick St Paul *Newc*
NEWCASTLE UPON TYNE (St Silas) *see* Byker St Silas *Newc*
NEWCASTLE UPON TYNE (St Stephen) *see* Low Elswick *Newc*
NEWCASTLE UPON TYNE (St Thomas) Proprietary Chapel *Newc 5* **P** *Trustees of St Thos Chpl Charity* **C-in-c** J C WIDDOWS
NEWCASTLE UPON TYNE, WEST Benwell *see* Benwell *Newc*
NEWCHAPEL (St James the Apostle) *Lich 11* **P** *CPAS* **V** W E SLATER
NEWCHURCH (All Saints) *Portsm 7* **P** *Bp* **V** P H FORD
NEWCHURCH (not known) w Croft *Liv 16* **P** *Bp* **R** C J STAFFORD, **OLM** B SMART
NEWCHURCH (St Nicholas w St John) *see* Rossendale Middle Valley *Man*
NEWCHURCH (St Peter and St Paul) *see* Dymchurch w Burmarsh and Newchurch *Cant*
NEWCHURCH-IN-PENDLE (St Mary) *see* Barrowford and Newchurch-in-Pendle *Blackb*
NEWDIGATE (St Peter) *see* Surrey Weald *Guildf*
NEWENDEN (St Peter) *see* Sandhurst w Newenden *Cant*
NEWENT (St Mary the Virgin) and Gorsley w Cliffords Mesne *Glouc 3* **P** *Bp* **NSM** R G CHIVERS
NEWHALL (St John) *Derby 16* **P** *Bp* **V** R G HOLLINGS
NEWHAVEN (St Michael) *Chich 18* **P** *Ch Patr Trust* **R** M M MILLER, **NSM** H E HOWELL
NEWHEY (St Thomas) *Man 20* **P** *Bp* **NSM** G W LINDLEY
NEWICK (St Mary) *Chich 21* **P** *Ch Soc Trust* **R** P P FRANCIS
NEWINGTON (St Christopher) *see* St Laur in Thanet *Cant*
NEWINGTON (St Giles) *see* Dorchester *Ox*
NEWINGTON (St John the Baptist) w Dairycoates St Mary and St Peter *York 14* **P** *Abp* **P-in-c** M R B HILLS
NEWINGTON (St Martin) *see* Hull St Martin w Transfiguration *York*
NEWINGTON (St Mary) *S'wark 10* **P** *Bp* **R** A P DODD
NEWINGTON (St Mary the Virgin) w Hartlip and Stockbury *Cant 15* **P** *Abp* **P-in-c** W J HORNSBY, **NSM** E A COX
NEWINGTON (St Nicholas) *see* Cheriton All So w Newington *Cant*
NEWINGTON (St Paul) *S'wark 10* **P** *Bp* **V** G D SHAW
NEWINGTON, SOUTH (St Peter ad Vincula) *see* Bloxham w Milcombe and S Newington *Ox*
NEWLAND (All Saints) and Redbrook w Clearwell *Glouc 4* **P** *Bp* **NSM** M M HALE
NEWLAND (St John) *see* Hull St Jo Newland *York*
NEWLAND (St Lawrence) *see* St Lawrence *Chelmsf*
NEWLANDS (not known) *see* Thornthwaite cum Braithwaite, Newlands etc *Carl*
NEWLAY LANE (St Margaret's Church Hall) *see* Bramley *Ripon*
NEWLYN (St Newlyn) *Truro 5* **P** *Bp* **P-in-c** P A ROBSON
NEWLYN (St Peter) *Truro 5* **P** *Bp* **V** R L STRANGE
NEWMARKET (All Saints) *St E 11* **P** *Bp* **V** M E OSBORNE
NEWMARKET (St Mary the Virgin) w Exning St Agnes *St E 11* **P** *Bp and DBP (alt)* **R** E J NEWEY
NEWNHAM (St Mark) *see* Cambridge St Mark *Ely*
NEWNHAM (St Michael and All Angels) *see* Badby w Newham and Charwelton w Fawsley etc *Pet*
NEWNHAM (St Nicholas) w Nately Scures w Mapledurwell w Up Nateley w Greywell *Win 5* **P** *Bp and Qu Coll Ox (jt)* **P-in-c** P W DYSON, **C** M R M JAGGS
NEWNHAM (St Peter and St Paul) *see* Doddington, Newnham and Wychling *Cant*
NEWNHAM (St Peter) w Awre and Blakeney *Glouc 3* **P** *Haberdashers' Co and Bp (alt)* **V** R J SEAMAN
NEWNHAM (St Vincent) *see* Ashwell w Hinxworth and Newnham *St Alb*
NEWNTON, NORTH (St James) *see* Pewsey and Swanborough *Sarum*
NEWPORT (St John the Baptist) *see* Barnstaple *Ex*
NEWPORT (St John the Baptist) *Portsm 8* **P** *Ch Patr Trust* **V** S C PALMER, **NSM** R J WHATLEY
NEWPORT (St Mary the Virgin) and Widdington *Chelmsf 21* **P** *Bp* **V** R J GRIFFITHS, **NSM** A P WANT
NEWPORT (St Nicholas) w Longford, Chetwynd and Forton *Lich 16* **P** *Bp* **R** *vacant* (01952) 810089
NEWPORT (St Stephen) *see* Howden *York*
NEWPORT (St Thomas) *Portsm 8* **P** *Bp* **V** S C PALMER
NEWPORT PAGNELL (St Luke) w Lathbury and Moulsoe *Ox 27* **P** *Bp, Ch Ch Ox, and Lord Carrington (jt)* **R** J H LEWIS, **C** L M CORNWELL, **OLM** G M BELL
NEWQUAY (St Michael) *Truro 7* **P** *Bp* **V** M J ADAMS, **C** R W BARBER
NEWSHAM (St Bede) *Newc 1* **P** *Bp* **V** J R PRINGLE
NEWSHOLME (St John) *see* Oakworth *Bradf*
NEWSOME (St John the Evangelist) *see* Em TM *Wakef*
NEWSTEAD (St Mary the Virgin) *see* Annesley w Newstead *S'well*
NEWTIMBER (St John the Evangelist) *see* Poynings w Edburton, Newtimber and Pyecombe *Chich*
NEWTON (Church Hall) *see* Blackwell w Tibshelf *Derby*
NEWTON (Good Shepherd) *see* Clifton upon Dunsmore and Newton *Cov*
NEWTON (Mission Church) *see* Embleton w Rennington and Rock *Newc*
NEWTON (St Botolph) *see* S Lafford *Linc*
NEWTON (St John the Baptist) *see* Clodock and Longtown w Craswall, Llanveynoe etc *Heref*
NEWTON (St Luke) *see* Bp's Hatfield *St Alb*
NEWTON (St Margaret) *see* Harston w Hauxton and Newton *Ely*
NEWTON (St Michael and All Angels) *Ches 8* **P** *R W Kirby St Bridget* **V** D POTTER
NEWTON (St Oswald) *see* Gt Ayton w Easby and Newton in Cleveland *York*
NEWTON (St Petrock) *see* Shebbear, Buckland Filleigh, Sheepwash etc *Ex*
NEWTON, NORTH (St Peter) *see* Alfred Jewel *B & W*
NEWTON, OLD (St Mary) *see* Bacton w Wyverstone, Cotton and Old Newton etc *St E*
NEWTON, SOUTH (St Andrew) *see* Wylye and Till Valley *Sarum*
NEWTON, WEST (St Peter and St Paul) *see* Sandringham w W Newton and Appleton etc *Nor*
NEWTON ABBOT *see* Highweek and Teigngrace *Ex*
NEWTON ABBOT (St Michael) *see* Wolborough and Ogwell *Ex*
NEWTON ABBOT (St Paul) *as above*
NEWTON ARLOSH (St John the Evangelist) *see* Bowness-on-Solway, Kirkbride and Newton Arlosh *Carl*
NEWTON AYCLIFFE (St Clare) *see* Gt Aycliffe and Chilton *Dur*
NEWTON BLOSSOMVILLE (St Nicolas) *see* Lavendon w Cold Brayfield, Clifton Reynes etc *Ox*
NEWTON BROMSWOLD (St Peter) *see* Rushden St Mary w Newton Bromswold *Pet*
NEWTON-BY-CASTLE-ACRE (All Saints) *see* Castleacre, Newton, Westacre and Southacre *Nor*
NEWTON BY TOFT (St Michael) *see* Middle Rasen Gp *Linc*
NEWTON CAP (St Paul) *see* Auckland St Andr and St Anne *Dur*
NEWTON FERRERS (Holy Cross) w Revelstoke *Ex 21* **P** *Bp and Comdr P E Yonge* **R** T R DEACON
NEWTON FLOTMAN (St Mary the Virgin), Swainsthorpe, Tasburgh, Tharston, Saxlingham Nethergate and Shotesham *Nor 5* **P** *Patr Bd* **TR** S A GAZE, **TV** P N WOOD, **OLM** J A L COOPER
NEWTON FLOWERY FIELD (St Stephen) *Ches 14* **P** *Bp* **P-in-c** P O BENNISON
NEWTON GREEN (All Saints) *see* Boxford, Edwardstone, Groton etc *St E*

NEWTON HALL (All Saints) *see* Dur N *Dur*
NEWTON HARCOURT (St Luke) *see* Wistow *Leic*
NEWTON HEATH (All Saints) *Man 5* **P** *Prime Min and D&C (alt)* **P-in-c** K F A GABBADON
NEWTON IN MAKERFIELD (Emmanuel) *Liv 16* **P** *Bp* **P-in-c** L MCCLUSKEY
NEWTON IN MAKERFIELD (St Peter) *Liv 16* **P** *Lord Newton* **NSM** F M A LOVETT
NEWTON IN MOTTRAM (St Mary) *Ches 14* **P** *V Mottram* **P-in-c** R J LAMEY
NEWTON IN THE ISLE (St James) *see* Leverington, Newton and Tydd St Giles *Ely*
NEWTON KYME (St Andrew) *see* Tadcaster w Newton Kyme *York*
NEWTON-LE-WILLOWS (All Saints) *Liv 16* **P** *Bp* **V** D HALL
NEWTON LINFORD (All Saints) *see* Bradgate Team *Leic*
NEWTON LONGVILLE (St Faith) and Mursley w Swanbourne and Little Horwood *Ox 26* **P** *Ch Patr Trust, Lord Cottesloe, Ch Soc Trust, and New Coll Ox (jt)* **R** J M KINCHIN-SMITH, **C** L J HOLT
NEWTON ON OUSE (All Saints) *see* Skelton w Shipton and Newton on Ouse *York*
NEWTON-ON-RAWCLIFFE (St John) *see* Middleton, Newton and Sinnington *York*
NEWTON-ON-TRENT (St Peter) *see* Saxilby Gp *Linc*
NEWTON POPPLEFORD (St Luke) *see* Ottery St Mary, Alfington, W Hill, Tipton etc *Ex*
NEWTON PURCELL (St Michael) *see* Shelswell *Ox*
NEWTON REGIS (St Mary) w Seckington and Shuttington *Birm 10* **P** *Birm Dioc Trustees and Mrs E V G Inge-Innes-Lillingston (alt)* **R** *vacant* (01827) 830254
NEWTON REIGNY (St John) *see* Penrith w Newton Reigny and Plumpton Wall *Carl*
NEWTON SOLNEY (St Mary the Virgin) *see* Foremark and Repton w Newton Solney *Derby*
NEWTON ST CYRES (St Cyr and St Julitta) *see* Thorverton, Cadbury, Upton Pyne etc *Ex*
NEWTON ST LOE (Holy Trinity) *see* Saltford w Corston and Newton St Loe *B & W*
NEWTON TONY (St Andrew) *see* Bourne Valley *Sarum*
NEWTON TRACEY (St Thomas à Becket), Horwood, Alverdiscott, Huntshaw, Yarnscombe, Tawstock, Atherington, High Bickington, Roborough, St Giles in the Wood and Beaford *Ex 20* **P** *Ld Chan (1 turn), Patr Bd (3 turns)* **TR** K D MATHERS, **TV** J C CARVOSSO, S L THORP
NEWTON VALENCE (St Mary) *see* Northanger *Win*
NEWTOWN (Holy Spirit) *see* Calbourne w Newtown *Portsm*
NEWTOWN (Holy Trinity) *see* Soberton w Newtown *Portsm*
NEWTOWN (King Charles the Martyr) *see* Loppington w Newtown *Lich*
NEWTOWN (St Mark) *see* Pemberton St Mark Newtown *Liv*
NEWTOWN (St Mary the Virgin) *see* Hungerford and Denford *Ox*
NEWTOWN (St Mary the Virgin and St John the Baptist) *see* Burghclere w Newtown and Ecchinswell w Sydmonton *Win*
NEWTOWN (St Paul) *see* Longnor, Quarnford and Sheen *Lich*
NIBLEY, NORTH (St Martin) *see* Wotton-under-Edge w Ozleworth, N Nibley etc *Glouc*
NICHOLFOREST (St Nicholas) and Kirkandrews on Esk *Carl 2* **P** *Bp, Sir Charles Graham Bt, and PCC (jt)* **P-in-c** E C ROBINSON
NIDD (St Paul and St Margaret) *Ripon 1* **P** *Viscount Mountgarret and R Knaresborough (alt)* **V** *vacant* (01423) 770060
NIDDERDALE, LOWER *Ripon 3* **P** *Trustees K Bell Esq, DBP, and C J Dent Esq (jt)* **R** M P SPURGEON
NIDDERDALE, UPPER *Ripon 3* **P** *D&C and V Masham and Healey (jt)* **V** P L DUNBAR, **NSM** T C KEIGHLEY
NINE O'CLOCK COMMUNITY at Hill Top Chapel, The (extra-parochial place) *Sheff 1*, M L FUDGER
NINEBANKS (St Mark) *see* Allendale w Whitfield *Newc*
NINEFIELDS (St Lawrence School Worship Centre) *see* Waltham H Cross *Chelmsf*
NINFIELD (St Mary the Virgin) *Chich 14* **P** *D&C Cant* **R** S R EARL
NITON (St John the Baptist) *Portsm 7* **P** *Qu Coll Ox* **R** S E LLOYD
NOAK HILL (St Thomas) *see* Harold Hill St Geo *Chelmsf*
NOCTON (All Saints) *see* Branston w Nocton and Potterhanworth *Linc*
NOEL PARK (St Mark) *Lon 19* **P** *Bp* **V** R R ROBINSON
NOKE (St Giles) *see* Ray Valley *Ox*
NONINGTON (St Mary the Virgin) w Wymynswold and Goodnestone w Chillenden and Knowlton *Cant 1* **P** *Abp and Lord Fitzwalter (jt)* **C** D J ROPER, A P SADLER, **Hon C** H D CONNOLL, **NSM** D N J HALE
NORBITON (St Peter) *S'wark 17* **P** *V Kingston All SS* **V** P A HOLMES
NORBURY (All Saints) *see* Wentnor w Ratlinghope, Myndtown, Norbury etc *Heref*
NORBURY (St Mary and St Barlok) w Snelston *Derby 8* **P** *Mrs M F Stanton, L A Clowes Esq, and V Ashbourne (by turn)* **P-in-c** H J DOBBIN
NORBURY (St Oswald) *S'wark 25* **P** *Bp* **P-in-c** C J MORGAN, **Hon C** M K WATTS
NORBURY (St Peter) *see* Adbaston, High Offley, Knightley, Norbury etc *Lich*
NORBURY (St Philip) *S'wark 25* **P** *Bp* **V** P L WASHINGTON
NORBURY (St Stephen) and Thornton Heath *S'wark 25* **P** *Bp* **V** A L NICKSON, **C** A M A GBEBIKAN, **OLM** J B FORBES
NORBURY (St Thomas) *Ches 16* **P** *Lord Newton* **V** W F M COLLINS, **C** D D STAFFORD, R H GREEN
NORDEN (St Paul) w Ashworth *Man 20* **P** *Bp* **V** S C A MAY
NORFOLK PARK (St Leonard) *see* Arbourthorne and Norfolk Park *Sheff*
NORHAM (St Cuthbert) and Duddo *Newc 12* **P** *D&C (1 turn), D&C Dur (2 turns)* **V** M J GILLHAM, **Hon C** J W SHEWAN, **NSM** C MYLNE
NORK (St Paul) *Guildf 9* **P** *The Crown* **V** P J BROOKS
NORLAND (St Luke) *see* Sowerby Bridge w Norland *Wakef*
NORLANDS (St James) *see* Notting Dale St Clem w St Mark and St Jas *Lon*
NORLEY (St John the Evangelist), Crowton and Kingsley *Ches 3* **P** *Bp, V Frodsham, and V Weaverham (jt)* **V** R J GILPIN, **C** J E PEARCE
NORMACOT (Holy Evangelists) *see* Meir Heath and Normacot *Lich*
NORMANBY (St Andrew) *see* Kirby Misperton w Normanby, Edston and Salton *York*
NORMANBY (St George) *see* Eston w Normanby *York*
NORMANBY-LE-WOLD (St Peter) *see* Walesby *Linc*
NORMANTON (All Saints) *Wakef 9* **P** *Trin Coll Cam* **V** D M GILKES
NORMANTON (St Giles) *Derby 10* **P** *CPAS* **V** N A A BARBER, **C** S R GRIFFITHS
NORMANTON, SOUTH (St Michael) *Derby 1* **P** *MMCET* **P-in-c** S M POTTER
NORMANTON-LE-HEATH (Holy Trinity) *see* Packington w Normanton-le-Heath *Leic*
NORMANTON-ON-SOAR (St James) *see* Sutton Bonington w Normanton-on-Soar *S'well*
NORMANTON-ON-TRENT (St Matthew) *see* Sutton w Carlton and Normanton upon Trent etc *S'well*
NORRIS BANK (St Martin) *see* Heatons *Man*
NORRIS GREEN (Christ Church) *see* Liv Ch Ch Norris Green *Liv*
NORRIS GREEN (St Christopher) *see* Liv St Chris Norris Green *Liv*
NORRISTHORPE (All Souls) *see* Heckmondwike *Wakef*
NORTH *see also under substantive place name*
NORTH BURY Team Ministry *see* Bury St Edmunds All SS w St Jo and St Geo *St E*
NORTH CAVE (All Saints) w Cliffe *York 13* **P** *C H J Carver Esq* **P-in-c** C H GOULDER
NORTH-CHAPEL Parishes, The *Linc 10* **P** *The Revd J M Ashley, Mrs M F Davis, R H C Haigh Esq, and Trustees (1 turn), and Duchy of Lanc (1 turn)* **R** R K EMM
NORTH CHAPEL (St Michael) w Ebernoe *Chich 11* **P** *Lord Egremont* **R** *vacant* (01428) 707373
NORTH COVE (St Botolph) *see* Worlingham w Barnby and N Cove *St E*
NORTH DEVON COAST *see* Combe Martin, Berrynarbor, Lynton, Brendon etc *Ex*
NORTH END (Ascension) *see* Portsea Ascension *Portsm*
NORTH END (Chapel of Ease) *see* Burton Dassett *Cov*
NORTH END (St Francis) *see* Portsea N End St Mark *Portsm*
NORTH END (St Mark) *as above*
NORTH END (St Nicholas) *as above*
NORTH HILL (St Torney) and Lewannick *Truro 9* **P** *Ld Chan and DBP (alt)* **P-in-c** C J D PROBERT
NORTH SHIELDS (Christ Church) *see* N Shields *Newc*
NORTH SHIELDS (St Augustine) (Christ Church) *Newc 5* **P** *Patr Bd* **TR** S H CONNOLLY, **C** E A BLAND
NORTH SHORE (St Paul's Worship Centre) *see* Blackpool St Paul *Blackb*
NORTHALLERTON (All Saints) w Kirby Sigston *York 19* **P** *D&C Dur* **V** H G SMITH
NORTHAM (St Margaret) *see* Bideford, Northam, Westward Ho!, Appledore etc *Ex*
NORTHAMPTON (All Saints w St Katharine) (St Peter) *Pet 4* **P** *Bp and R Foundn of St Kath (jt)* **R** S H M GODFREY

NORTHAMPTON (Christ Church) *Pet 4* **P** *Bp* **V** J D V EVANS
NORTHAMPTON (Emmanuel) *Pet 4* **P** *DBP* **TR** M A H JOHNSON, **TV** H M JEFFERY
NORTHAMPTON (Holy Sepulchre w St Andrew and St Lawrence) *Pet 4* **P** *Bp* **P-in-c** M W J HILLS
NORTHAMPTON (Holy Trinity) (St Paul) *Pet 4* **P** *Bp* **V** A C MCGOWAN
NORTHAMPTON (St Alban the Martyr) (Glorious Ascension) *Pet 4* **P** *Bp* **V** I R LOWELL, **NSM** A M MARCH
NORTHAMPTON (St Benedict) *Pet 7* **P** *Bp* **V** *vacant* (01604) 768624
NORTHAMPTON (St David) *see* Kingsthorpe w Northampton St Dav *Pet*
NORTHAMPTON (St Giles) *Pet 4* **P** *Simeon's Trustees* **V** D R BIRD, **C** L A F ALLWOOD
NORTHAMPTON (St James) *Pet 4* **P** *Bp* **P-in-c** P E NIXON
NORTHAMPTON (St Mary the Virgin) *Pet 4* **P** *Bp* **V** I S HOLDSWORTH
NORTHAMPTON (St Matthew) *Pet 4* **P** *DBP* **V** N M SETTERFIELD, **NSM** G C RUMBOLD
NORTHAMPTON (St Michael and All Angels w St Edmund) *Pet 4* **P** *Bp* **V** M W J HILLS, **NSM** P D MUNCH
NORTHAMPTON (St Peter) *see* Northampton All SS w St Kath and St Pet *Pet*
NORTHANGER Benefice, The *Win 2* **P** *Bp (1 turn), D&C (1 turn), Bp, Earl of Selborne and Sir James Scott Bt (1 turn)* **R** A J PEARS
NORTHAW (St Thomas of Canterbury) and Cuffley *St Alb 20* **P** *Mrs S Peasley* **V** M T BEER, **NSM** J M BEER
NORTHBOROUGH (St Andrew) *see* Peakirk w Glinton and Northborough *Pet*
NORTHBOURNE (St Augustine) *see* Eastry and Northbourne w Tilmanstone etc *Cant*
NORTHCHURCH (St Mary) and Wigginton *St Alb 2* **P** *Duchy of Cornwall and Bp (alt)* **P-in-c** J A GORDON
NORTHCOURT (Christ Church) *see* Abingdon *Ox*
NORTHDOWN PARK (St Philip) *see* Margate St Phil *Cant*
NORTHENDEN (St Wilfrid) *Man 8* **P** *Bp* **R** G S FORSTER
NORTHFIELD (St Laurence) *Birm 4* **P** *Keble Coll Ox* **R** R I WARREN
NORTHFLEET (All Saints) *see* Perry Street *Roch*
NORTHFLEET (St Botolph) and Rosherville *Roch 4* **P** *Patr Bd and Prime Min (alt)* **TR** A C SMITH, **TV** J PERUMBALATH
NORTHGATE (St Elizabeth) *see* Crawley *Chich*
NORTHIAM (St Mary) *Chich 20* **P** *MMCET* **R** R H WHITE
NORTHILL (St Mary the Virgin) *see* Caldecote, Northill and Old Warden *St Alb*
NORTHINGTON (St John the Evangelist) *see* The Candover Valley *Win*
NORTHLEACH (St Peter and St Paul) w Hampnett and Farmington, Cold Aston w Notgrove and Turkdean, and Compton Abdale w Haselton *Glouc 13* **P** *Bp (2 turns), Ld Chan (1 turn)* **Hon C** M G WOODWARD
NORTHLEIGH (St Giles) *see* Offwell, Northleigh, Farway, Cotleigh etc *Ex*
NORTHLEW (St Thomas of Canterbury) *see* Okehampton w Inwardleigh, Bratton Clovelly etc *Ex*
NORTHMOOR (St Denys) *see* Lower Windrush *Ox*
NORTHMOOR GREEN (St Peter and St John) *see* Alfred Jewel *B & W*
NORTHOLT (St Joseph) W End *Lon 22* **P** *DBP* **V** S R WINN, **C** E BLATCHLEY
NORTHOLT (St Mary) (St Hugh) (St Richard) *Lon 22* **P** *BNC Ox* **P-in-c** G S THOMAS, **C** J B CHAPMAN
NORTHOLT PARK (St Barnabas) *Lon 22* **P** *Bp* **V** P D HILLAS, **NSM** G P TUFFIN
NORTHORPE (St John the Baptist) *see* Scotton w Northorpe *Linc*
NORTHOWRAM (St Matthew) *Wakef 2* **P** *Bp* **V** P A HOLMES
NORTHREPPS (St Mary) *see* Overstrand, Northrepps, Sidestrand etc *Nor*
NORTHUMBERLAND HEATH (St Paul) *see* Erith St Paul *Roch*
NORTHWICH (St Helen) *see* Witton *Ches*
NORTHWICH (St Luke) (Holy Trinity) *Ches 6* **P** *Bp* **V** S HUGHES
NORTHWOLD (St Andrew) and Wretton w Stoke Ferry and Whittington *Ely 13* **P** *Ld Chan (1 turn), Bp and Ch Patr Trust (1 turn)* **R** *vacant* (01366) 501075
NORTHWOOD (Emmanuel) *Lon 23* **P** *Ch Trust Fund Trust* **V** D M TALBOT, **C** S G HOWELL, N M COULTHARD, **NSM** P D O GREENE, D F HOYLE
NORTHWOOD (Holy Trinity) *see* Hanley H Ev *Lich*
NORTHWOOD (Holy Trinity) *Lon 23* **P** *Trustees* **V** R C BARTLETT
NORTHWOOD Pinner Road (St Edmund the King) *see* Northwood Hills St Edm *Lon*
NORTHWOOD (St John the Baptist) *Portsm 8* **P** *Bp* **R** G E MORRIS, **NSM** D M NETHERWAY
NORTHWOOD (St Mark) *see* Kirkby *Liv*
NORTHWOOD GREEN (Mission Church) *see* Westbury-on-Severn w Flaxley, Blaisdon etc *Glouc*
NORTHWOOD HILLS (St Edmund the King) *Lon 23* **P** *Bp* **V** B L DRIVER
NORTON (All Saints) *see* Hullavington, Norton and Stanton St Quintin *Bris*
NORTON (All Saints) *see* Brington w Whilton and Norton etc *Pet*
NORTON (St Andrew) *see* Pakenham w Norton and Tostock *St E*
NORTON (St Berteline and St Christopher) *Ches 3* **P** *DBP* **V** S J ARTUS
NORTON (St Egwin) *see* Evesham w Norton and Lenchwick *Worc*
NORTON (St George) (St Nicholas) *St Alb 4* **P** *Bp* **V** J N LUSCOMBE, **C** M-A B TISDALE, **Hon C** R M LAMPARD
NORTON (St James) *Sheff 2* **P** *CCC Cam* **R** M N R BOWIE, **C** M H E HEALEY
NORTON (St James) *see* Stoulton w Drake's Broughton and Pirton etc *Worc*
NORTON (St Mary) *Cant 6* **P** *Ld Chan* **P-in-c** G BAISLEY
NORTON (St Mary) *see* Twigworth, Down Hatherley, Norton, The Leigh etc *Glouc*
NORTON (St Mary the Virgin) *Dur 10* **P** *Bp* **V** N R SHAVE, **C** B L K SHERLOCK
NORTON (St Michael and All Angels) *Dur 10* **P** *V Norton St Mary* **V** M G T GOBBETT
NORTON (St Michael and All Angels) *see* Stourbridge St Mich Norton *Worc*
NORTON (St Peter) *see* Norton juxta Malton *York*
NORTON, EAST (All Saints) *see* Hallaton w Horninghold and Allexton, Tugby etc *Leic*
NORTON, OVER (St James) *see* Chipping Norton *Ox*
NORTON BAVANT (All Saints) *see* Upper Wylye Valley *Sarum*
NORTON BRIDGE (St Luke) *see* Chebsey, Ellenhall and Seighford-with-Creswell *Lich*
NORTON CANES (St James) *Lich 3* **P** *Bp* **R** N L HIBBINS
NORTON CANON (St Nicholas) *see* Weobley w Sarnesfield and Norton Canon *Heref*
NORTON CUCKNEY (St Mary) *S'well 6* **P** *Lady Alexandra Cavendish Bentinck* **P-in-c** S A CASH
NORTON DISNEY (St Peter) *see* Bassingham Gp *Linc*
NORTON FITZWARREN (All Saints) *see* Staplegrove w Norton Fitzwarren *B & W*
NORTON IN HALES (St Chad) *see* Woore and Norton in Hales *Lich*
NORTON IN THE MOORS (St Bartholomew) *Lich 8* **P** *Walsingham Coll Trust Assn* **R** P W DAVEY
NORTON JUXTA MALTON (St Peter) *York 6* **P** *Abp* **V** C W ANKERS
NORTON JUXTA TWYCROSS (Holy Trinity) *see* Appleby Gp *Leic*
NORTON LE MOORS *see* Norton in the Moors *Lich*
NORTON LEES (St Paul) *Sheff 2* **P** *R Norton* **V** P M BROWN
NORTON LINDSEY (Holy Trinity) *see* Wolverton w Norton Lindsey and Langley *Cov*
NORTON MALREWARD (Holy Trinity) *see* Chew Magna w Dundry and Norton Malreward *B & W*
NORTON MANDEVILLE (All Saints) *see* High Ongar w Norton Mandeville *Chelmsf*
NORTON ST PHILIP (St Philip and St James) *see* Hardington Vale *B & W*
NORTON SUB HAMDON (Blessed Virgin Mary) w West Chinnock, Chiselborough and Middle Chinnock *B & W 6* **P** *Bp* **P-in-c** P J THOMAS
NORTON SUBCOURSE (St Mary) *see* Raveningham Gp *Nor*
NORTON WOODSEATS (St Chad) *see* Woodseats St Chad *Sheff*
NORTON WOODSEATS (St Paul) *see* Norton Lees St Paul *Sheff*
NORWELL (St Laurence), w Ossington, Cromwell and Caunton *S'well 3* **P** *Bp, SMF, and Mrs P Goedhuis (jt)* **P-in-c** S DIXON
NORWICH (Christ Church) *see* Eaton *Nor*
NORWICH (Christ Church) *see* New Catton Ch Ch *Nor*
NORWICH Heartsease (St Francis) *Nor 1* **P** *Bp* **P-in-c** P L HOWARD
NORWICH (Holy Trinity) *see* Heigham H Trin *Nor*

NORWICH Lakenham (St Alban) (St Mark) *Nor 1* **P** *D&C* **V** S E WEST-LINDELL
NORWICH (St Andrew) *see* Eaton *Nor*
NORWICH (St Andrew) *Nor 1* **P** *PCC* **P-in-c** M J YOUNG
NORWICH (St Anne) *see* Earlham St Anne *Nor*
NORWICH (St Barnabas) *see* Heigham St Barn w St Bart *Nor*
NORWICH (St Catherine) *see* Mile Cross *Nor*
NORWICH (St Elizabeth) *see* Earlham St Eliz *Nor*
NORWICH (St Francis) *see* Nor Heartsease St Fran *Nor*
NORWICH (St George) Colegate *Nor 1* **P** *D&C* **P-in-c** P MCFADYEN
NORWICH (St George) Tombland *Nor 1* **P** *Bp* **P-in-c** J C MINNS, **OLM** M E DIFFEY
NORWICH (St Giles) *Nor 1* **P** *Ld Chan and Bp (alt)* **P-in-c** D T THORNTON
NORWICH (St Helen) *Nor 1* **P** *Gt Hosp Nor* **P-in-c** M M LIGHT
NORWICH (St John the Baptist) Timberhill w Norwich St Julian *Nor 1* **P** *Bp, Guild of All So, and D&C (jt)* **R** M D SMITH, **Hon C** T S P PHELAN
NORWICH (St Julian) *see* Nor St Jo w St Julian *Nor*
NORWICH (St Luke) *see* New Catton St Luke w St Aug *Nor*
NORWICH (St Mary) *see* Earlham St Mary *Nor*
NORWICH (St Mary in the Marsh) *Nor 1* **P** *D&C* **P-in-c** R CAPPER
NORWICH (St Mary Magdalene) w St James *Nor 2* **P** *D&C* **V** A TYLER, **NSM** C J A BELCHER, **OLM** J SPENCER
NORWICH (St Matthew) *see* Thorpe St Matt *Nor*
NORWICH (St Michael) *see* Bowthorpe *Nor*
NORWICH (St Peter Mancroft) (St John Maddermarket) *Nor 1* **P** *PCC* **R** P W NOKES, **C** J E A MUSTARD, **Hon C** H R G COOKE
NORWICH (St Stephen) *Nor 1* **P** *D&C* **P-in-c** H R G COOKE
NORWICH (St Thomas) *see* Heigham St Thos *Nor*
NORWICH, Lakenham (St John the Baptist and All Saints) and Tuckswood St Paul *Nor 1* **P** *Bp and D&C (jt)* **V** R M S WOODHAM, **C** K P B LOVESEY
NORWOOD (St Leonard) *see* Sheff St Leon Norwood *Sheff*
NORWOOD (St Mary the Virgin) *Lon 23* **P** *SMF* **P-in-c** L LAWRENCE
NORWOOD, SOUTH (Holy Innocents) *S'wark 25* **P** *Bp* **P-in-c** N J COLEMAN
NORWOOD, SOUTH (St Alban the Martyr) *S'wark 25* **P** *Bp* **P-in-c** C E BLANKENSHIP, **Hon C** J R HALL
NORWOOD, SOUTH (St Mark) *S'wark 25* **P** *Bp* **P-in-c** T W HURCOMBE
NORWOOD, UPPER (All Saints) *S'wark 25* **P** *V Croydon* **P-in-c** L S A MARSH
NORWOOD, UPPER (St John) *S'wark 25* **P** *Bp* **P-in-c** B A MASON
NORWOOD, WEST (St Luke) *S'wark 15* **P** *Abp* **V** L I WICKINGS, **C** J ZVIMBA
NOTGROVE (St Bartholomew) *see* Northleach w Hampnett and Farmington etc *Glouc*
NOTTING DALE (St Clement) (St Mark) and Norlands St James *Lon 12* **P** *Bp* **V** H D J RAYMENT-PICKARD, **C** M J DEED
NOTTING HILL (All Saints) (St Columb) *Lon 12* **P** *SMF* **V** J K BROWNSELL, **NSM** R E DUGUID
NOTTING HILL (St John) *Lon 12* **P** *Bp* **V** W H TAYLOR, **NSM** R J WRIGHT
NOTTING HILL (St Michael and All Angels) (Christ Church) (St Francis) *Lon 12* **P** *Trustees* **V** A B ANDREWS
NOTTING HILL (St Peter) *Lon 12* **P** *Bp* **V** M K HARGREAVES, **C** A C COLPUS, **NSM** R J WRIGHT
NOTTINGHAM (St Andrew) *S'well 13* **P** *Peache Trustees* **V** R M CLARK
NOTTINGHAM (St Ann w Emmanuel) *S'well 13* **P** *Trustees* **V** J P NEILL
NOTTINGHAM (St George w St John the Baptist) *S'well 13* **P** *Bp* **V** *vacant* 0115-986 4881
NOTTINGHAM (St Jude) *S'well 13* **P** *CPAS* **P-in-c** G F HADFIELD, **C** J M KIRKHAM
NOTTINGHAM (St Mary the Virgin) and St Catharine *S'well 13* **P** *Bp* **P-in-c** A G DEUCHAR, **C** S F MORRIS
NOTTINGHAM (St Nicholas) *S'well 13* **P** *CPAS* **R** T HATTON, **C** S I V MASON, **NSM** A R HASKEY, F P R J CONNELL
NOTTINGHAM (St Peter w St James) (All Saints) *S'well 13* **P** *Bp and trustees (jt)* **R** A G DEUCHAR, **C** D MCCOULOUGH, C LITTLE
NOTTINGHAM (St Saviour) *S'well 13* **P** *CPAS* **V** G E JONES, **NSM** A R HASKEY
NOTTINGHAM (St Stephen) *see* Hyson Green and Forest Fields *S'well*
NOWTON (St Peter) *see* St Edm Way *St E*
NUFFIELD (Holy Trinity) *Ox 6* **P** *MMCET* **R** J F SHEARER
NUN MONKTON (St Mary) *see* Lower Nidderdale *Ripon*
NUNBURNHOLME (St James) and Warter and Huggate *York 5* **P** *Abp* **NSM** S D JONES
NUNEATON (St Mary) *Cov 5* **P** *V Nuneaton* **V** G A WELSBY
NUNEATON (St Nicolas) *Cov 5* **P** *The Crown* **V** D JONES, **NSM** D WATERTON
NUNHEAD (St Antony) (St Silas) *S'wark 8* **P** *Bp* **V** C A M BRADDICK-SOUTHGATE
NUNNEY (All Saints) and Witham Friary, Marston Bigot, Wanstrow and Cloford *B & W 4* **P** *Bp, SMF, and C N Clarke Esq and Duke of Somerset (jt)* **R** J K HODDER
NUNNINGTON (All Saints) *see* Kirkdale w Harome, Nunnington and Pockley *York*
NUNTHORPE (St Mary the Virgin) (St Mary's Church Hall) *York 21* **P** *Abp* **V** G K HENWOOD, **C** A AMELIA
NUNTON (St Andrew) *see* Chalke Valley *Sarum*
NURSLING (St Boniface) and Rownhams *Win 12* **P** *Bp* **R** J T WILLIAMS
NURSTEAD (St Mildred) *see* Meopham w Nurstead *Roch*
NUTBOURNE (St Wilfrid) *see* Chidham *Chich*
NUTFIELD (St Peter and St Paul) *S'wark 27* **P** *Jes Coll Ox* **R** G I WILLIAMS
NUTFIELD, LOWER *see* S Nutfield w Outwood *S'wark*
NUTFIELD, SOUTH (Christ Church) w Outwood *S'wark 27* **P** *Bp and Ch Patr Trust (jt)* **V** T G KEMP, **NSM** M L PUDNEY
NUTHALL (St Patrick) *S'well 7* **P** *Bp* **P-in-c** J HENDERSON, **NSM** E B GAMBLE
NUTHURST (St Andrew) and Mannings Heath *Chich 8* **P** *Bp Lon* **R** D EVANS
NUTLEY (St James the Less) *Chich 21* **P** *R Maresfield* **P-in-c** M D S GREIG
NYMET (St George) *see* S Molton w Nymet St George, High Bray etc *Ex*
NYMET ROWLAND (St Bartholomew) *see* N Creedy *Ex*
NYMET TRACEY (St Bartholomew) *see* Bow w Broad Nymet *Ex*
NYMPSFIELD (St Bartholomew) *see* Uley w Owlpen and Nympsfield *Glouc*
NYNEHEAD (All Saints) *see* Wellington and Distr *B & W*
OADBY (St Paul) (St Peter) *Leic 5* **P** *Bp* **TR** M F RUSK, **TV** S J HARVEY, **C** M C FLAHERTY, **NSM** H M BENCE
OAK TREE ANGLICAN FELLOWSHIP, The *Lon 22* **Min** M R ALDRIDGE
OAKAMOOR (Holy Trinity) *see* Alton w Bradley-le-Moors and Oakamoor w Cotton *Lich*
OAKDALE (St George) *Sarum 7* **P** *Bp* **TV** M G OATES, **P-in-c** A C MACROW-WOOD, **C** J E AUDIBERT
OAKE (St Bartholomew) *see* Bradford w Oake, Hillfarrance and Heathfield *B & W*
OAKENGATES (Holy Trinity) and Wrockwardine Wood *Lich 21* **P** *Bp* **R** M C STAFFORD
OAKENROD (St George w St Alban) *see* Rochdale St Geo w St Alb *Man*
OAKENSHAW (Church of the Good Shepherd) *see* Willington and Sunnybrow *Dur*
OAKENSHAW (St Andrew) cum Woodlands *Bradf 2* **P** *Bp* **P-in-c** G PERCIVAL
OAKFIELD (St John the Baptist) *Portsm 7* **P** *V St Helens* **V** H E WRIGHT
OAKFORD (St Peter) *see* Washfield, Stoodleigh, Withleigh etc *Ex*
OAKHAM (All Saints) w Hambleton and Egleton and Braunston w Brooke *Pet 14* **P** *Dr E R Hanbury (1 turn), D&C Linc (2 turns)* **P-in-c** L T FRANCIS-DEHQANI, **C** J RIDLEY, G ANGELL
OAKHANGER (St Luke's Mission Church) *see* Alsager Ch Ch *Ches*
OAKHANGER (St Mary Magdalene) *see* Northanger *Win*
OAKHILL (All Saints) *see* Ashwick w Oakhill and Binegar *B & W*
OAKHILL Eastwood View (shared church) *see* Clifton St Jas *Sheff*
OAKINGTON (St Andrew) *Ely 5* **P** *Qu Coll Cam* **V** J C ALEXANDER
OAKLEY (St Leonard) w Wootton St Lawrence *Win 4* **P** *Qu Coll Ox and D&C (alt)* **R** B W NICHOLSON, **NSM** C A VAUGHAN
OAKLEY (St Mary) *see* Worminghall w Ickford, Oakley and Shabbington *Ox*
OAKLEY (St Mary) *see* Bromham w Oakley and Stagsden *St Alb*
OAKLEY (St Nicholas) *see* N Hartismere *St E*

OAKLEY, EAST (St John) *see* Oakley w Wootton St Lawrence *Win*
OAKLEY, GREAT (All Saints) w Wix and Wrabness *Chelmsf 20* **P** *Ld Chan, Ch Patr Trust, and St Jo Coll Cam (by turn)* **P-in-c** E H G FISHER
OAKLEY, GREAT (St Michael) and LITTLE (St Peter) *Pet 9* **P** *H W G de Capell Brooke Esq and Boughton Estates Ltd (alt)* **V** *vacant*
OAKLEY SQUARE (St Matthew) *see* Old St Pancras *Lon*
OAKMOOR *see* Bishopsnympton, Rose Ash, Mariansleigh etc *Ex*
OAKRIDGE (St Bartholomew) *see* Bisley, Chalford, France Lynch, and Oakridge *Glouc*
OAKS IN CHARNWOOD (St James the Greater) *see* Shepshed and Oaks in Charnwood *Leic*
OAKSEY (All Saints) *see* Ashley, Crudwell, Hankerton, Long Newnton etc *Bris*
OAKWOOD (no dedication) *Derby 9* **P** *Bp and MMCET (jt)* **P-in-c** P T WALLER
OAKWOOD (St Thomas) *Lon 18* **P** *Bp* **V** C J P HOBBS, **Hon C** J E ROBSON
OAKWORTH (Christ Church) *Bradf 8* **P** *Bp* **V** T G ALLEN
OARE (Blessed Virgin Mary) w Culbone *B & W 16* **P** *Bp* **P-in-c** C D BURKE
OARE (Holy Trinity) *see* Pewsey and Swanborough *Sarum*
OARE (St Bartholomew) *see* Chieveley w Winterbourne and Oare *Ox*
OARE (St Peter) *see* The Brents and Davington w Oare and Luddenham *Cant*
OATLANDS (St Mary) *Guildf 8* **P** *Bp* **V** *vacant* (01932) 847963
OBORNE (St Cuthbert) *see* Queen Thorne *Sarum*
OCCOLD (St Michael) *see* Eye *St E*
OCKBROOK (All Saints) *Derby 13* **P** *Lt-Col T H Pares* **V** T M SUMPTER, **C** A C M PETTY, **NSM** J D BISHOP
OCKENDON, NORTH (St Mary Magdalene) *Chelmsf 2* **P** *Bp* **P-in-c** M E MILLARD
OCKENDON, SOUTH (St Nicholas) and Belhus Park *Chelmsf 14* **P** *Bp and Guild of All So (jt)* **R** B G DUCKWORTH, **C** J PAULRAJ
OCKER HILL (St Mark) *Lich 26* **P** *Bp* **V** A R BOYD-WILLIAMS
OCKFORD RIDGE (St Mark) *see* Godalming *Guildf*
OCKHAM (All Saints) *see* E Horsley and Ockham w Hatchford and Downside *Guildf*
OCKLEY (St Margaret), Okewood and Forest Green *Guildf 7* **P** *Bp and J P M H Evelyn Esq (alt)* **R** R R MCALLEN
OCLE PYCHARD (St James the Great) *see* Stoke Lacy, Moreton Jeffries w Much Cowarne etc *Heref*
ODCOMBE (St Peter and St Paul), Brympton, Lufton and Montacute *B & W 7* **P** *Ch Ch Ox (4 turns), C E B Clive-Ponsonby-Fane Esq (1 turn)* **R** J F JENKINS
ODD DOWN (St Philip and St James) *see* Bath Odd Down w Combe Hay *B & W*
ODD RODE (All Saints) *Ches 11* **P** *R Astbury* **R** T R EVANS, **Hon C** S H GILBERT
ODDINGLEY (St James) *see* Bowbrook S *Worc*
ODDINGTON (Holy Ascension) *see* Broadwell, Evenlode, Oddington, Adlestrop etc *Glouc*
ODDINGTON (St Andrew) *see* Ray Valley *Ox*
ODDINGTON (St Nicholas) *see* Broadwell, Evenlode, Oddington, Adlestrop etc *Glouc*
ODELL (All Saints) *St Alb 15* **P** *Lord Luke* **R** *vacant* (01234) 720234
ODIHAM (All Saints) *Win 5* **P** *Bp* **P-in-c** M C S BEVER
ODSTOCK (St Mary) *see* Chalke Valley *Sarum*
OFFCHURCH (St Gregory) *Cov 10* **P** *Bp* **P-in-c** J T H BRITTON, **C** D R PATTERSON
OFFENHAM (St Mary and St Milburgh) *see* Badsey w Aldington and Offenham and Bretforton *Worc*
OFFERTON (St Alban) (St John) *Ches 18* **P** *Bp* **V** R E READ, **C** C A JONES
OFFHAM (Old St Peter) *see* Hamsey *Chich*
OFFHAM (St Michael) *see* W Malling w Offham *Roch*
OFFLEY (St Mary Magdalene) *see* King's Walden and Offley w Lilley *St Alb*
OFFLEY, HIGH (St Mary the Virgin) *see* Adbaston, High Offley, Knightley, Norbury etc *Lich*
OFFLEY HAY (Mission Church) *see* Eccleshall *Lich*
OFFORD D'ARCY w OFFORD CLUNY (All Saints) *see* Buckden w the Offords *Ely*
OFFTON (St Mary) *see* Somersham w Flowton and Offton w Willisham *St E*
OFFWELL (St Mary the Virgin), Northleigh, Farway, Cotleigh and Widworthy *Ex 5* **P** *Trustees, R T Marker Esq, Cotleigh PCC, and Bp (jt)* **NSM** S J HOUGHTON
OGBOURNE (St Andrew) *see* Ridgeway *Sarum*
OGBOURNE (St George) *as above*
OGLEY HAY (St James) *Lich 1* **P** *Bp* **V** C N THOMAS, **C** P KELLY, E SNOWDEN
OGWELL (St Bartholomew) *see* Wolborough and Ogwell *Ex*
OKEFORD Benefice, The *Sarum 6* **P** *G A L-F Pitt-Rivers Esq and DBP (alt)* **R** P J RAHILLY, **NSM** S S MUFFETT, **OLM** D J MARL
OKEFORD FITZPAINE (St Andrew) *see* Okeford *Sarum*
OKEHAMPTON (All Saints) (St James) w Inwardleigh; Bratton Clovelly w Germansweek; Northlew w Ashbury; and Bridestowe and Sourton *Ex 11* **P** *Patr Bd* **TR** S W COOK, **TV** S A WILSON, **C** J M THOMAS, A PARSONS
OKEWOOD (St John the Baptist) *see* Ockley, Okewood and Forest Green *Guildf*
OLD *see also under substantive place name*
OLD FORD (St Paul) (St Mark) *Lon 7* **P** *Hyndman Trustees and CPAS (jt)* **V** P J BOARDMAN
OLD HEATH (St Barnabas) *see* Colchester St Barn *Chelmsf*
OLD HILL (Holy Trinity) *Worc 9* **P** *Ch Soc Trust* **V** J M HANCOCK
OLD LANE (Mission Church) *see* Bloxwich *Lich*
OLD WIVES LEES (Mission Church) *see* Chilham w Challock and Molash *Cant*
OLDBERROW (St Mary) *see* Spernall, Morton Bagot and Oldberrow *Cov*
OLDBROOK (Community Church) *see* Woughton *Ox*
OLDBURY *Sarum 15* **P** *Bp, CPAS, Marquis of Lansdowne, and C E R Money-Kyrle Esq (jt)* **R** *vacant* (01380) 850640
OLDBURY (Christ Church) *Birm 7* **P** *Bp* **P-in-c** J R BARNETT, **C** A D BARRETT, **NSM** A E HANNY
OLDBURY (St Nicholas) *see* Bridgnorth, Tasley, Astley Abbotts, etc *Heref*
OLDBURY-ON-SEVERN (St Arilda) *see* Thornbury and Oldbury-on-Severn w Shepperdine *Glouc*
OLDCOTES (St Mark's Mission Church) *see* Carlton-in-Lindrick and Langold w Oldcotes *S'well*
OLDHAM Moorside (St Thomas) *Man 21* **P** *Trustees* **V** J H GRAY
OLDHAM (St Andrew) (St Mary w St Peter) *Man 19* **P** *Patr Bd* **TV** D C MEYER
OLDHAM (St Barnabas) *Man 19* **P** *The Crown* **P-in-c** D OATES
OLDHAM (St Chad) *see* Hollinwood and Limeside *Man*
OLDHAM (St James) (St Ambrose) *Man 19* **P** *Bp and R Prestwich (jt)* **V** P PLUMPTON
OLDHAM (St Paul) *Man 19* **P** *Bp* **P-in-c** E M POPE, **Hon C** D J QUARMBY
OLDHAM (St Stephen and All Martyrs) Lower Moor *Man 19* **P** *Bp* **V** *vacant* 0161-678 9565
OLDHURST (St Peter) *see* Somersham w Pidley and Oldhurst *Ely*
OLDLAND (St Anne) *Bris 5* **P** *Bp* **V** A J M SPEAR
OLDRIDGE (St Thomas) *see* Tedburn St Mary, Whitestone, Oldridge etc *Ex*
OLDSWINFORD (St Mary) *see* Old Swinford Stourbridge *Worc*
OLIVER'S BATTERY (St Mark) *see* Stanmore *Win*
OLLERTON (St Giles) (St Paulinus) w Boughton *S'well 6* **P** *Ld Chan and Bp (alt)* **P-in-c** R A KIRTON
OLNEY (St Peter and St Paul) *Ox 27* **P** *Bp* **P-in-c** P S DAVIES, **OLM** V M REVELEY
OLTON (St Margaret) *Birm 11* **P** *Bp and V Bickenhill (jt)* **V** N I JONES
OLVESTON (St Mary of Malmesbury) *see* Almondsbury and Olveston *Bris*
OMBERSLEY (St Andrew) w Doverdale *Worc 8* **P** *Bp and Lord Sandys (alt)* **P-in-c** S P KERR
ONCHAN (St Peter) *S & M 2* **P** *The Crown* **V** A M CONVERY
ONECOTE (St Luke) *see* Ipstones w Berkhamsytch and Onecote w Bradnop *Lich*
ONEHOUSE (St John the Baptist) *see* Gt Finborough w Onehouse, Harleston, Buxhall etc *St E*
ONGAR, HIGH (St Mary the Virgin) w Norton Mandeville *Chelmsf 27* **P** *Ch Soc Trust* **R** C R DUXBURY, **NSM** A N HITCHING
ONIBURY (St Michael and All Angels) *see* Culmington w Onibury, Bromfield etc *Heref*
ONSLOW VILLAGE (All Saints) *see* Guildf All SS *Guildf*
OPENSHAW (St Barnabas) *see* Manchester Gd Shep and St Barn *Man*
OPENSHAW, HIGHER (St Clement) *Man 1* **P** *Trustees* **P-in-c** C J R HOWITZ
OPENWOODGATE (St Mark) *see* Belper *Derby*
ORBY (All Saints) *Linc 8* **P** *Bp* **V** T STEELE
ORCHARD (Community Centre) *see* Egglescliffe *Dur*

ORCHARD PARK (St Michael and All Angels) *see* N Hull St Mich *York*
ORCHARD PORTMAN (St Michael) *see* Beercrocombe w Curry Mallet, Hatch Beauchamp etc *B & W*
ORCHARD WAY (St Barnabas) *see* Cheltenham St Mark *Glouc*
ORCHARDLEIGH (Blessed Virgin Mary) *see* Beckington w Standerwick, Berkley, Rodden etc *B & W*
ORCHESTON (St Mary) *see* Wylye and Till Valley *Sarum*
ORCOP (St John the Baptist) *see* St Weonards w Orcop, Garway, Tretire etc *Heref*
ORDSALL (All Hallows) *S'well 5* **P** *Bp* **P-in-c** P S BAGSHAW
ORDSALL (St Clement) and Salford Quays *Man 6* **P** *Bp* **R** R A ROSS
ORE (Christ Church) *Chich 17* **P** *Simeon's Trustees* **P-in-c** R P C ELVERSON
ORE (St Helen) (St Barnabas) *Chich 17* **P** *Simeon's Trustees* **R** C H KEY, **C** N G BURTON
ORESTON (Church of the Good Shepherd) *see* Plymstock and Hooe *Ex*
ORFORD (St Andrew) *Liv 12* **P** *Bp* **V** M RAYNOR
ORFORD (St Bartholomew) *see* Wilford Peninsula *St E*
ORFORD (St Margaret) *Liv 12* **P** *Bp* **V** J W REED
ORLESTONE (St Mary) w Snave and Ruckinge w Warehorne and Kenardington *Cant 12* **P** *Ld Chan and Abp (alt)* **R** T R WHATELEY, **NSM** P A CLARK, **OLM** P L M FOGDEN
ORLETON (St George) *see* Leominster *Heref*
ORLINGBURY (St Mary) *see* Gt w Lt Harrowden and Orlingbury *Pet*
ORMESBY (St Cuthbert) *York 18* **P** *Abp* **V** R BROWN
ORMESBY, NORTH (Holy Trinity) *York 18* **P** *Abp* **V** D P BLACK
ORMESBY ST MARGARET (St Margaret) w Scratby, Ormesby St Michael and Rollesby *Nor 6* **P** *Bp, D&C, DBP and R J H Tacon Esq (jt)* **P-in-c** N R SPENCER
ORMESBY ST MICHAEL (St Michael) *see* Ormesby St Marg w Scratby, Ormesby St Mich etc *Nor*
ORMSBY Group, The South (St Leonard) *Linc 7* **P** *A J Massingberd-Mundy Esq, Sir Thomas Ingilby Bt, Mert Coll Ox, Bp, and DBP (jt)* **P-in-c** C HILLIAM
ORMSGILL (St Francis) *see* Barrow St Matt *Carl*
ORMSIDE (St James) *Carl 1* **P** *Bp and D&C (jt)* **P-in-c** J A H CLEGG, **NSM** R A COLLINSON
ORMSKIRK (St Peter and St Paul) *Liv 11* **P** *Earl of Derby* **V** C H JONES, **C** A A HOUSLEY
ORPINGTON (All Saints) *Roch 16* **P** *D&C* **V** A A MUSTOE, **C** P A SPREADBRIDGE, **NSM** Y R MARCUSSEN
ORPINGTON (Christ Church) *Roch 16* **P** *Ch Trust Fund Trust, Bp, and V Orpington (jt)* **V** J P COLWILL
ORPINGTON (St Andrew) *Roch 16* **P** *Bp* **P-in-c** M T SKINNER
ORRELL (St Luke) *Liv 15* **P** *Bp* **V** P G WHITTINGTON, **Hon C** F S FAIRBAIRN
ORRELL HEY (St John and St James) *Liv 1* **P** *CPAS* **V** R J G PANTER, **C** M D COATES
ORSETT (St Giles and All Saints) and Bulphan and Horndon on the Hill *Chelmsf 14* **P** *Bp and D&C St Paul's (jt)* **P-in-c** E W HANSON, **NSM** S R BLAKE
ORSTON (St Mary) *see* Whatton w Aslockton, Hawksworth, Scarrington etc *S'well*
ORTON (All Saints) and Tebay w Ravenstonedale and Newbiggin-on-Lune *Carl 1* **P** *Bp and Ravenstonedale Trustees (1 turn), Resident Landowners (1 turn)* **R** A I DALTON
ORTON, GREAT (St Giles) *see* Barony of Burgh *Carl*
ORTON GOLDHAY (St John) *see* The Ortons, Alwalton and Chesterton *Ely*
ORTON LONGUEVILLE (Holy Trinity) *as above*
ORTON MALBORNE (not known) *as above*
ORTON-ON-THE-HILL (St Edith of Polesworth) *see* Bosworth and Sheepy Gp *Leic*
ORTON WATERVILLE (St Mary) *see* The Ortons, Alwalton and Chesterton *Ely*
ORTONS, Alwalton and Chesterton, The *Ely 11* **P** *Patr Bd* **TV** R A HAMILTON, M J INGHAM, I A PULLINGER, **NSM** S GRIFFITH
ORWELL Group, The (St Andrew) *Ely 7* **P** *Bp, DBP, and Trin Coll Cam (jt)* **R** N A BRICE
ORWELL Team Ministry *see* Walton and Trimley *St E*
OSBALDWICK (St Thomas) w Murton *York 2* **P** *Abp* **V** A CLEMENTS
OSBOURNBY (St Peter and St Paul) *see* S Lafford *Linc*
OSCOTT, OLD (All Saints) *see* Kingstanding St Mark *Birm*
OSGATHORPE (St Mary the Virgin) *see* Kegworth, Hathern, Long Whatton, Diseworth etc *Leic*
OSMASTON (St Martin) *see* Brailsford w Shirley and Osmaston w Edlaston *Derby*
OSMINGTON (St Osmond) *see* Preston w Sutton Poyntz and Osmington w Poxwell *Sarum*
OSMONDTHORPE (St Philip) *see* Leeds All SS w Osmondthorpe *Ripon*
OSMOTHERLEY (St Peter) w Harlsey and Ingleby Arncliffe *York 19* **P** *J B Barnard Esq (1 turn), Ld Chan (2 turns)* **V** A H DODD, **NSM** G L MORLEY
OSMOTHERLY (St John) *see* Ulverston St Mary w H Trin *Carl*
OSPRINGE (St Peter and St Paul) *see* Eastling w Ospringe and Stalisfield w Otterden *Cant*
OSSETT (Holy and Undivided Trinity) and Gawthorpe *Wakef 10* **P** *Bp and R Dewsbury (jt)* **V** P D MAYBURY
OSSETT, SOUTH (Christ Church) *Wakef 10* **P** *Bp* **P-in-c** J HARRIS, **OLM** B R ASQUITH
OSSINGTON (Holy Rood) *see* Norwell w Ossington, Cromwell and Caunton *S'well*
OSTERLEY ROAD (St Mary) *see* Spring Grove St Mary *Lon*
OSWALDKIRK (St Oswald) *see* Ampleforth w Oswaldkirk, Gilling E etc *York*
OSWALDTWISTLE (Immanuel) (All Saints) *Blackb 1* **P** *Trustees* **V** P W WATSON
OSWALDTWISTLE (St Paul) *Blackb 1* **P** *Trustees* **V** M D RATCLIFFE
OSWESTRY (Holy Trinity) *Lich 19* **P** *Bp* **P-in-c** P T DARLINGTON
OSWESTRY (St Oswald) *Lich 19* **P** *Earl of Powis* **V** D B CROWHURST
OTFORD (St Bartholomew) *Roch 10* **P** *D&C Westmr* **V** P M HOPKINS
OTFORD LANE (Mission Hall) *see* Knockholt w Halstead *Roch*
OTHAM (St Nicholas) w Langley *Cant 14* **P** *Abp and CPAS (jt)* **R** A W SEWELL
OTHERY (St Michael) *see* Middlezoy and Othery and Moorlinch *B & W*
OTLEY (All Saints) *Bradf 4* **P** *Bp* **V** G C BUTTANSHAW, **C** J ROGERS
OTLEY (St Mary) *see* Clopton w Otley, Swilland and Ashbocking *St E*
OTTER VALE *see* Ottery St Mary, Alfington, W Hill, Tipton etc *Ex*
OTTERBOURNE (St Matthew) *see* Compton and Otterbourne *Win*
OTTERBURN (St John the Evangelist) *see* N Tyne and Redesdale *Newc*
OTTERFORD (St Leonard) *see* Blackdown *B & W*
OTTERHAM (St Denis) *see* Boscastle w Davidstow *Truro*
OTTERINGTON, NORTH (St Michael and All Angels) *see* The Thorntons and The Otteringtons *York*
OTTERINGTON, SOUTH (St Andrew) *as above*
OTTERSHAW (Christ Church) *Guildf 11* **P** *Bp* **V** *vacant*
OTTERTON (St Michael) *see* E Budleigh w Bicton and Otterton *Ex*
OTTERY ST MARY (St Mary the Virgin), Alfington, West Hill, Tipton St John, Venn Ottery, Newton Poppleford, Harpford and Colaton Raleigh *Ex 7* **P** *Patr Bd* **TR** S G FRANKLIN, **TV** M WARD, **NSM** K J BRIMACOMBE
OTTRINGHAM (St Wilfrid) *see* Keyingham w Ottringham, Halsham and Sunk Is *York*
OUGHTIBRIDGE (Ascension) *Sheff 3* **P** *V Wadsley* **V** J F E MANN
OUGHTRINGTON (St Peter) *Ches 10* **P** *Bp* **R** E M BURGESS
OULTON (St John the Evangelist) *see* Stone Ch Ch and Oulton *Lich*
OULTON (St John) w Woodlesford *Ripon 8* **P** *Bp* **P-in-c** C J TRUMAN
OULTON (St Michael) *Nor 9* **P** *Ch Soc Trust* **R** A R PRITCHARD, **NSM** C S PRITCHARD
OULTON (St Peter and St Paul) *see* Lt Barningham, Blickling, Edgefield etc *Nor*
OULTON BROAD (St Mark) (St Luke the Evangelist) *Nor 9* **P** *Simeon's Trustees* **OLM** M E ZIPFEL
OUNDLE (St Peter) w Ashton and Benefield w Glapthorn *Pet 12* **P** *Bp and Mrs G S Watts-Russell (jt)* **R** R J ORMSTON, **C** D L SMITH, **NSM** E A WALLER
OUSBY (St Luke) *see* Cross Fell Gp *Carl*
OUSDEN (St Peter) *see* Bansfield *St E*
OUSEBURN, GREAT (St Mary) and LITTLE (Holy Trinity) w Marton cum Grafton and Whixley w Green Hammerton *Ripon 3* **P** *Bp, R Knaresborough and DBP (3 turns), St Jo Coll Cam (1 turn)* **NSM** M SAUNDERS
OUT RAWCLIFFE (St John the Evangelist) *see* Waterside Par *Blackb*
OUTLANE (St Mary Magdalene) *see* Stainland w Outlane *Wakef*

OUTWELL (St Clement) *Ely 15* **P** *Bp* **R** A F JESSON
OUTWOOD (St John) *see* S Nutfield w Outwood *S'wark*
OUTWOOD (St Mary Magdalene) *Wakef 12* **P** *V Stanley* **V** J W BUTTERWORTH
OUTWOOD COMMON (St John the Divine) *see* Billericay and Lt Burstead *Chelmsf*
OVAL WAY (All Saints) *see* Chalfont St Peter *Ox*
OVENDEN (St George) *Wakef 4* **P** *V Halifax* **V** D J ROBERTSON, **NSM** P A PICKARD, G ROPER
OVENDEN (St John the Evangelist) *see* Bradshaw and Holmfield *Wakef*
OVER *see also under substantive place name*
OVER (St Chad) *Ches 6* **P** *Bp* **V** A L D FRIEND
OVER (St John the Evangelist) *Ches 6* **P** *Lord Delamere and W R Cullimore Esq (jt)* **V** D M WILSON
OVER (St Mary) *Ely 5* **P** *Trin Coll Cam* **P-in-c** M E RABY, **C** S E WYATT
OVERBURY (St Faith) w Teddington, Alstone and Little Washbourne w Beckford and Ashton under Hill *Worc 4* **P** *D&C and MMCET (jt)* **V** J M MOORE, **C** M A SCHUTTE
OVERCHURCH (St Mary) *see* Upton (Overchurch) *Ches*
OVERPOOL (St Francis) *see* Ellesmere Port *Ches*
OVERSEAL (St Matthew) *see* Seale and Lullington w Coton in the Elms *Derby*
OVERSTONE (St Nicholas) *see* Mears Ashby and Hardwick and Sywell etc *Pet*
OVERSTRAND (St Martin), Northrepps, Sidestrand and Trimingham *Nor 21* **P** *Duchy of Lanc, DBP, and Bp (by turn)* **R** M L LANGAN
OVERTON (St Helen) *Blackb 11* **P** *V Lanc* **P-in-c** D E NEWTON
OVERTON (St Mary) w Laverstoke and Freefolk *Win 6* **P** *Bp* **R** N P CUMMING, **C** K J TAYLOR
OVERTON (St Michael and All Angels) *see* Upper Kennet *Sarum*
OVING (All Saints) *see* Schorne *Ox*
OVING (St Andrew) *see* Tangmere and Oving *Chich*
OVINGDEAN (St Wulfran) *Chich 2* **P** *SMF* **P-in-c** A D MAYES, **C** M WICKENS
OVINGHAM (St Mary the Virgin) *Newc 3* **P** *Bp* **P-in-c** M NELSON
OVINGTON (St John the Evangelist) *see* Watton w Carbrooke and Ovington *Nor*
OVINGTON (St Mary) *see* N Hinckford *Chelmsf*
OVINGTON (St Peter) *see* New Alresford w Ovington and Itchen Stoke *Win*
OWERMOIGNE (St Michael) *see* Watercombe *Sarum*
OWERSBY, NORTH (St Martin) *see* Kelsey Gp *Linc*
OWLERTON (St John the Baptist) *Sheff 4* **P** *Ch Patr Trust* **V** N A DAWSON, **C** C J TRUMAN
OWLPEN (Holy Cross) *see* Uley w Owlpen and Nympsfield *Glouc*
OWLSMOOR (St George) *Ox 16* **P** *Bp* **P-in-c** R G BURGESS
OWLSWICK (Chapel) *see* Risborough *Ox*
OWMBY Group, The (St Peter and St Paul) *Linc 3* **P** *Duchy of Lanc, Bp and D&C, Bp and Mrs S Hutton, and Mrs B K Cracroft-Eley (by turn)* **R** P D GODDEN
OWSLEBURY (St Andrew) *see* Twyford and Owslebury and Morestead *Win*
OWSTON (All Saints) *Sheff 7* **P** *DBP* **V** M MOSSMAN
OWSTON (St Andrew) *see* Whatborough Gp *Leic*
OWSTON (St Martin) *Linc 1* **P** *The Crown* **V** *vacant*
OWTHORNE (St Matthew) and Rimswell w Withernsea *York 12* **P** *Ld Chan and Abp (alt)* **P-in-c** W J G HEALE
OWTHORPE (St Margaret) *S'well 8* **P** *Trustees Sir Rupert Bromley Bt* **P-in-c** P D S MASSEY
OWTON MANOR (St James) *Dur 3* **P** *Bp* **V** S J LOCKE
OXBOROUGH (St John the Evangelist) w Foulden and Caldecote *Nor 13* **P** *G&C Coll Cam* **C** D J HANWELL
OXCLOSE (not known) *Dur 11* **P** *R Washington, TR Usworth, and V Fatfield (jt)* **P-in-c** S E KENT
OXENDON (St Helen) *see* Arthingworth, Harrington w Oxendon and E Farndon *Pet*
OXENHALL (St Anne) *see* Redmarley D'Abitot, Bromesberrow, Pauntley etc *Glouc*
OXENHOPE (St Mary the Virgin) *Bradf 8* **P** *Bp* **P-in-c** D J BRIERLEY
OXENTON *see* Woolstone w Gotherington and Oxenton etc *Glouc*
OXFORD Canning Crescent (St Luke) *see* Ox St Matt *Ox*
OXFORD (St Aldate) *Ox 7* **P** *Simeon's Trustees* **R** C ST G CLEVERLY, **C** S C R PONSONBY, M H B REES, H A AZER
OXFORD (St Andrew) *Ox 7* **P** *Trustees* **V** A R WINGFIELD DIGBY, **C** A S ATKINS, T M GARRETT, **Hon C** E A GODDARD, **NSM** R M CUNNINGHAM
OXFORD (St Barnabas and St Paul) *Ox 7* **P** *Keble Coll Ox* **V** E M WRIGHT, **NSM** D W MASON, M I LETTERS
OXFORD (St Clement) *Ox 4* **P** *Ox Ch Trust* **R** J B GILLINGHAM, **C** J BROWN, **NSM** V M SINTON
OXFORD (St Ebbe w Holy Trinity and St Peter-le-Bailey) *Ox 7* **P** *Ox Ch Trust* **R** V E ROBERTS, **C** P D L WILKINSON, J P BIDGOOD
OXFORD (St Giles) (St Philip) (St James) (St Margaret) *Ox 7* **P** *St Jo Coll Ox* **V** A W H BUNCH, **C** G SIMPSON, **NSM** M SCREECH
OXFORD (St Mary Magdalene) *Ox 7* **P** *Ch Ch Ox* **P-in-c** P J GROVES
OXFORD (St Mary the Virgin) (St Cross *or* Holywell) (St Peter in the East) *Ox 7* **P** *Or Coll Ox and Mert Coll Ox (jt)* **V** B W MOUNTFORD, **C** H A HARRIS, **NSM** C BANNISTER-PARKER
OXFORD (St Matthew) *Ox 7* **P** *Ox Ch Trust* **P-in-c** S J HELLYER, **NSM** T BRADSHAW
OXFORD (St Michael at the North Gate w St Martin and All Saints) *Ox 7* **P** *Linc Coll Ox* **P-in-c** J C H M LEE, **Hon C** G D WESTHAVER
OXFORD (St Thomas the Martyr) (St Frideswide) and Binsey *Ox 7* **P** *Ch Ch Ox* **P-in-c** T H C MEYRICK
OXHEY (All Saints) *St Alb 7* **P** *Bp* **V** P M WISE, **C** J M WILSON
OXHEY (St Matthew) *St Alb 7* **P** *DBP* **V** D M SHEPHERD
OXHILL (St Lawrence) *see* Tysoe w Oxhill and Whatcote *Cov*
OXLEY (Epiphany) *Lich 28* **P** *Bp* **V** P S HAWKINS
OXNEAD (St Michael & all Angels) *see* Buxton w Oxnead, Lammas and Brampton *Nor*
OXSHOTT (St Andrew) *Guildf 10* **P** *Bp* **V** J P CRESSWELL, **NSM** V PITT
OXSPRING (St Aidan) *see* Penistone and Thurlstone *Wakef*
OXTED (St Mary) and Tandridge *S'wark 24* **P** *Bp* **R** A J MAYER, **OLM** D C WEIGHTMAN
OXTON (St Peter and St Paul) *S'well 15* **P** *Ld Chan, Bp, and C P L Francklin Esq (by turn)* **V** M J BROCK, **C** J E DRAYCOTT, **NSM** M N TAYLOR
OXTON (St Saviour) *Ches 1* **P** *DBP* **V** I A DAVENPORT, **C** N C M FEAVER
PACKINGTON (Holy Rood) w Normanton-le-Heath *Leic 9* **P** *MMCET and The Crown (alt)* **V** *vacant* (01530) 412215
PACKWOOD (St Giles) w Hockley Heath *Birm 6* **P** *Bp and M R Parkes Esq (alt)* **V** Q D WARBRICK
PADBURY (St Mary the Virgin) *see* Lenborough *Ox*
PADDINGTON (Emmanuel) Harrow Road *Lon 2* **P** *Hyndman Trustees* **P-in-c** A G THOM, **C** J F BARRY, J P TRIFFITT
PADDINGTON (St David's Welsh Church) Extra-Parochial Place *Lon 2 vacant*
PADDINGTON (St James) *Lon 2* **P** *Bp* **V** W G WILSON, **C** M H HARRISON, **Hon C** W H BAYNES, **NSM** R RAJ-SINGH
PADDINGTON (St John the Evangelist) (St Michael and All Angels) *Lon 2* **P** *DBP* **V** S D MASON, **C** D J O KEARLEY-HEYWOOD, **Hon C** M S PUDGE
PADDINGTON (St Luke the Evangelist) *see* W Kilburn St Luke w St Simon and St Jude *Lon*
PADDINGTON (St Mary) *Lon 2* **P** *Bp* **P-in-c** G S BRADLEY, **NSM** M GIBSON
PADDINGTON (St Mary Magdalene) *Lon 2* **P** *Keble Coll Ox* **P-in-c** J P WILKES, G S BRADLEY, **NSM** M GIBSON
PADDINGTON (St Peter) *Lon 2* **P** *Ch Patr Trust* **P-in-c** J P WILKES, **NSM** F W WARD
PADDINGTON (St Saviour) *Lon 2* **P** *Bp* **V** G S BRADLEY, **NSM** F E BLACKMORE, M GIBSON, J BROWNING, A W WAKEHAM-DAWSON
PADDINGTON (St Stephen w St Luke) *Lon 2* **P** *Bp* **V** J R ALLCOCK
PADDINGTON GREEN (St Mary) *see* Paddington St Mary *Lon*
PADDLESWORTH (St Oswald) *see* Lyminge w Paddlesworth, Stanford w Postling etc *Cant*
PADDOCK WOOD (St Andrew) *Roch 8* **P** *D&C Cant* **V** C J DOBSON, **C** C F GILBERT
PADGATE (Christ Church) *Liv 12* **P** *Bp, Adn, and R Warrington (jt)* **V** S P ATTWATER, **C** D L WILLIAMS
PADIHAM (St Leonard) w Hapton and Padiham Green *Blackb 3* **P** *Bp* **V** M A JONES
PADSTOW (St Petrock) *Truro 7* **P** *C R Prideaux Brune Esq* **V** C M MALKINSON
PADWORTH (St John the Baptist) *see* Stratfield Mortimer and Mortimer W End etc *Ox*
PAGANHILL (Holy Spirit) *see* Whiteshill and Randwick *Glouc*
PAGHAM (St Thomas à Becket) *Chich 1* **P** *Abp* **V** K SMITH
PAGLESHAM (St Peter) *see* Canewdon w Paglesham *Chelmsf*
PAIGNTON (Christ Church) and Preston St Paul *Ex 12* **P** *Bp*

and Peache Trustees (jt) **V** D W WITCHELL, **C** M A BAKER, **NSM** E P LEWIS
PAIGNTON (St John the Baptist) (St Andrew) (St Boniface) *Ex 12* **P** *DBP* **V** B R TUBBS, **C** M J P CAIN, P HASTROP
PAILTON (St Denis) *see* Monks Kirby w Pailton and Stretton-under-Fosse *Cov*
PAINSWICK (St Mary the Virgin), Sheepscombe, Cranham, The Edge, Pitchcombe, Harescombe and Brookthorpe *Glouc 1* **P** *Bp, D&C, Mrs N Owen (1 turn), and Ld Chan (1 turn)* **V** J LONGUET-HIGGINS, **NSM** I C GOBEY, H M SAMMON, **OLM** D W NEWELL
PAKEFIELD (All Saints and St Margaret) *Nor 9* **P** *Ch Patr Trust* **R** R J K BAKER, **C** C P PARSONS
PAKENHAM (St Mary) w Norton and Tostock *St E 9* **P** *Bp and Peterho Cam (jt)* **R** I HOOPER, **NSM** J R LONGE
PALGRAVE (St Peter) *see* N Hartismere *St E*
PALLION (St Luke) *see* Millfield St Mark and Pallion St Luke *Dur*
PALMARSH (Holy Cross) *see* Hythe *Cant*
PALMERS GREEN (St John the Evangelist) *Lon 18* **P** *V Southgate Ch Ch* **V** *vacant* (020) 8886 1348
PALTERTON (St Luke's Mission Room) *see* E Scarsdale *Derby*
PAMBER (St Mary and St John the Baptist) *see* The Sherbornes w Pamber *Win*
PAMBER HEATH (St Luke) *see* Tadley S and Silchester *Win*
PAMPISFORD (St John the Baptist) *Ely 6* **P** *Mrs B A Killander* **V** *vacant*
PANCRASWEEK (St Pancras) *see* Pyworthy, Pancrasweek and Bridgerule *Ex*
PANFIELD (St Mary the Virgin) and Rayne *Chelmsf 15* **P** *Bp and DBP (alt)* **R** P J MEADER
PANGBOURNE (St James the Less) w Tidmarsh and Sulham *Ox 12* **P** *Bp, Ch Soc Trust, and Mrs I E Moon (jt)* **R** J W STAPLES
PANNAL (St Robert of Knaresborough) w Beckwithshaw *Ripon 1* **P** *Bp and Peache Trustees (jt)* **V** N C SINCLAIR
PANSHANGER (United Church) Conventional District *St Alb 7 vacant*
PAPCASTLE (Mission Church) *see* Bridekirk *Carl*
PAPPLEWICK (St James) *see* Linby w Papplewick *S'well*
PAPWORTH (St Peter) *Ely 1* **P** *Patr Bd* **TR** J C B PEMBERTON, **TV** J F WINDSOR, A C MCCOLLUM, **C** A N M CLARKE, **NSM** P C M SCOTT
PAR (St Mary the Virgin) (Good Shepherd) *Truro 1* **P** *The Crown* **P-in-c** I M TUCKER
PARHAM (St Mary the Virgin) *see* Campsea Ashe w Marlesford, Parham and Hacheston *St E*
PARHAM (St Peter) *see* Amberley w N Stoke and Parham, Wiggonholt etc *Chich*
PARK BARN (St Clare) *see* Westborough *Guildf*
PARKEND (St Paul) and Viney Hill *Glouc 4* **P** *Bp and Univ Coll Ox (jt)* **V** P A BRUNT
PARKESTON (St Paul) *see* Harwich Peninsula *Chelmsf*
PARKFIELD (Holy Trinity) *see* Langley and Parkfield *Man*
PARKGATE (St Thomas) *see* Neston *Ches*
PARKHAM (St James), Alwington, Buckland Brewer, Abbotsham, Hartland, Welcombe, Clovelly, Woolfardisworthy West and Buck Mills *Ex 16* **P** *Patr Bd (4 turns), Crown (1 turn)* **TR** P J F GOODEY, **TV** A J RICHARDSON, **C** R P HANSFORD, C W J HODGETTS, **NSM** D BAKER
PARKSTONE (Good Shepherd) *see* Heatherlands St Jo *Sarum*
PARKSTONE (St Barnabas) *see* Branksome St Clem *Sarum*
PARKSTONE (St Clement) *as above*
PARKSTONE (St John) *see* Heatherlands St Jo *Sarum*
PARKSTONE (St Luke) *Sarum 7* **P** *Ch Trust Fund Trust* **V** C M STRAIN
PARKSTONE (St Peter) and St Osmund w Branksea St Mary *Sarum 7* **P** *Patr Bd* **R** N J C LLOYD, **C** S P CHAMBERS, **NSM** J P M MARTIN, D J NEWMAN, **OLM** P SOUTHGATE, R BAYLDON
PARKWOOD (Christ Church) Conventional District *Cant 15* **C-in-c** M A MCLAUGHLIN
PARLAUNT ROAD (Christ the Worker) *see* Langley Marish *Ox*
PARLEY, WEST (All Saints) (St Mark) *Sarum 9* **P** *P E E Prideaux-Brune Esq* **R** E C BOOTH
PARNDON, GREAT (St Mary) *Chelmsf 26* **P** *Patr Bd* **TV** J M RAGAN, M D BENNET
PARNDON, LITTLE (St Mary) *see* Harlow Town Cen w Lt Parndon *Chelmsf*
PARR (St Peter) (St Paul) (St Philip) (Holy Trinity) *Liv 10* **P** *Patr Bd* **TR** J L ROBERTS, **TV** J MARSDEN, **C** S R I HARDY, **OLM** A KIRKHAM, I A WHITAKER, M E TAYLOR, H MCCANN
PARR MOUNT (Holy Trinity) *see* Parr *Liv*
PARRACOMBE (Christ Church) *see* Combe Martin, Berrynarbor, Lynton, Brendon etc *Ex*
PARSON CROSS (St Bernard) *see* Southey Green St Bernard CD *Sheff*
PARSON CROSS (St Cecilia) *see* Sheff St Cecilia Parson Cross *Sheff*
PARSON'S GREEN (St Dionis) *see* Fulham St Dionis Parson's Green *Lon*
PARTINGTON (St Mary) and Carrington *Ches 10* **P** *Bp and V Bowdon (alt)* **V** P H GEDDES
PARTNEY Group, The (St Nicholas) *Linc 7* **P** *Bp and DBP, Baroness Willoughby de Eresby, Mrs E M V Drake, and Mrs D E P Douglas (by turn)* **R** R J BENSON
PARTRIDGE GREEN (St Michael and All Angels) *see* W Grinstead *Chich*
PARWICH (St Peter) *see* Fenny Bentley, Thorpe, Tissington, Parwich etc *Derby*
PASSENHAM (St Guthlac) *Pet 5* **P** *MMCET* **R** C J MURRAY
PASTON (All Saints) *Pet 13* **P** *Bp* **R** G M JESSOP, **NSM** R F WATKINSON
PASTON (St Margaret) *see* Trunch *Nor*
PATCHAM (All Saints) *Chich 2* **P** *MMCET* **V** N E D MILMINE, **C** J A T RUSSELL, S MATTAPALLY, **NSM** M PHILIP
PATCHAM, SOUTH (Christ the King) *Chich 2* **P** *Bp* **NSM** J W M COLLINS
PATCHING (St John the Divine) *see* Findon w Clapham and Patching *Chich*
PATCHWAY (St Chad) *Bris 5* **P** *Trustees* **V** D R BYRNE
PATELEY BRIDGE (St Cuthbert) *see* Upper Nidderdale *Ripon*
PATRICK (Holy Trinity) *S & M 1* **P** *Bp* **V** G M BREFFITT
PATRICK BROMPTON (St Patrick) and Hunton *Ripon 4* **P** *Bp* **V** D J CHRISTIE
PATRICROFT (Christ Church) *see* Eccles *Man*
PATRINGTON (St Patrick) w Hollym, Welwick and Winestead *York 12* **P** *DBP, Ld Chan, and CPAS (by turn)* **P-in-c** D R HARRIS
PATRIXBOURNE (St Mary) w Bridge and Bekesbourne *Cant 1* **P** *Abp* **P-in-c** P J FILMER
PATTERDALE (St Patrick) *see* Gd Shep TM *Carl*
PATTINGHAM (St Chad) w Patshull *Lich 24* **P** *Bp and Lady Kwiatkowska (jt)* **P-in-c** J E DAIMOND
PATTISHALL (Holy Cross) w Cold Higham and Gayton w Tiffield *Pet 5* **P** *Bp, SS Coll Cam, and SMF (jt)* **R** P J BROADBENT
PAUL (St Pol de Lion) *Truro 5* **P** *Ld Chan* **V** G J HANSFORD
PAULERSPURY (St James the Apostle) *see* Silverstone and Abthorpe w Slapton etc *Pet*
PAULL (St Andrew and St Mary) *see* Hedon w Paull *York*
PAULSGROVE (St Michael and All Angels) *Portsm 6* **P** *Bp* **V** G R WADDINGTON
PAULTON (Holy Trinity) *B & W 12* **P** *Bp and R Chewton Mendip (alt)* **V** J G EDWARDS
PAUNTLEY (St John the Evangelist) *see* Redmarley D'Abitot, Bromesberrow, Pauntley etc *Glouc*
PAVENHAM (St Peter) *see* Milton Ernest, Pavenham and Thurleigh *St Alb*
PAWLETT (St John the Baptist) *see* Puriton and Pawlett *B & W*
PAXFORD (Mission Church) *see* Blockley w Aston Magna and Bourton on the Hill *Glouc*
PAXTONS, The (Holy Trinity) (St James) w Diddington *Ely 10* **P** *D&C Linc (2 turns) and E G W Thornhill Esq (1 turn)* **V** *vacant* (01480) 214280 *or* 475085
PAYHEMBURY (St Mary the Virgin) *see* Broadhembury, Payhembury and Plymtree *Ex*
PEACEHAVEN (Ascension) and Telscombe Cliffs *Chich 18* **P** *Bp* **V** D A HIDER, **C** D L N GUTSELL
PEAK DALE (Holy Trinity) *see* Wormhill, Peak Forest w Peak Dale and Dove Holes *Derby*
PEAK FOREST (St Charles the King and Martyr) *as above*
PEAKIRK (St Pega) w Glinton and Northborough *Pet 13* **P** *D&C* **R** *vacant* (01733) 252265
PEAR TREE (Jesus Chapel) *see* Southampton St Mary Extra *Win*
PEASE POTTAGE (Ascension) *see* Slaugham *Chich*
PEASEDOWN ST JOHN (St John the Baptist) w Wellow *B & W 12* **P** *Bp and R H Horton-Fawkes Esq (jt)* **P-in-c** M G STREET
PEASEMORE (St Barnabas) *see* Beedon and Peasemore w W Ilsley and Farnborough *Ox*
PEASENHALL (St Michael) *see* Yoxford, Peasenhall and Sibton *St E*
PEASE'S WEST (St George) *see* Crook *Dur*
PEASLAKE (St Mark) *see* Shere, Albury and Chilworth *Guildf*
PEASLEY CROSS (Mission Hall) *see* Parr *Liv*

PEASMARSH (St Michael) *see* Shalford *Guildf*
PEASMARSH (St Peter and St Paul) *see* Beckley and Peasmarsh *Chich*
PEATLING MAGNA (All Saints) *see* Willoughby Waterleys, Peatling Magna etc *Leic*
PEATLING PARVA (St Andrew) *see* Gilmorton, Peatling Parva, Kimcote etc *Leic*
PEBMARSH (St John the Baptist) *see* Knights and Hospitallers Par *Chelmsf*
PEBWORTH (St Peter), Dorsington, Honeybourne and Marston Sicca *Glouc 10* **P** *Bp* **R** C G MATTOCK
PECKHAM (St John w St Andrew) *S'wark 8* **P** *Bp* **P-in-c** T C WRIGHT
PECKHAM (St Luke) *see* Camberwell St Luke *S'wark*
PECKHAM (St Mary Magdalene) (St Paul) *S'wark 8* **P** *Ch Patr Soc* **V** *vacant* (020) 7639 4596
PECKHAM (St Saviour) *S'wark 9* **P** *Bp* **V** W C HEATLEY, **NSM** C DAVIES
PECKHAM, EAST (Holy Trinity) and Nettlestead *Roch 8* **P** *St Pet Coll Ox and D&C Cant (jt)* **R** A H CARR, **NSM** S M MORRELL
PECKHAM, WEST (St Dunstan) *see* Mereworth w W Peckham *Roch*
PECKLETON (St Mary Magdalene) *see* Desford and Peckleton w Tooley *Leic*
PEDLINGE (Estate Chapel) *see* Saltwood *Cant*
PEDMORE (St Peter) *Worc 12* **P** *Oldswinford Hosp* **R** A L HAZLEWOOD, **C** T E FFRENCH
PEEL (St Paul) *see* Walkden and Lt Hulton *Man*
PEEL GREEN (St Catherine) *see* Barton w Peel Green *Man*
PEEL GREEN (St Michael and All Angels) *as above*
PEGSWOOD (St Margaret) *see* Bothal and Pegswood w Longhirst *Newc*
PELDON (St Mary) w Great and Little Wigborough *Chelmsf 16* **P** *Ch Soc Trust and T Wheatley-Hubbard Esq* **P-in-c** S C NORTON, **Hon C** M BROSNAN
PELSALL (St Michael and All Angels) *Lich 25* **P** *Bp* **V** C A ST A RAMSAY
PELTON (Holy Trinity) *Dur 16* **P** *R Chester le Street* **P-in-c** J LINTERN, **C** L F NOWEN
PELTON, WEST (St Paul) *Dur 11* **P** *Bp* **P-in-c** J LINTERN, **C** L F NOWEN
PELYNT (St Nun) *see* Lanreath, Pelynt and Bradoc *Truro*
PEMBERTON (St Francis of Assisi) Kitt Green *Liv 15* **P** *R Wigan and Bp (jt)* **P-in-c** R HARVEY
PEMBERTON (St John) *Liv 15* **P** *R Wigan* **V** C B OXENFORTH
PEMBERTON (St Mark) Newtown *Liv 15* **P** *Duke of Sutherland, Bp, and R Pemberton St Jo (jt)* **V** D V ROUCH, **OLM** S Y FULFORD, E TAULTY
PEMBRIDGE (St Mary the Virgin) w Moor Court, Shobdon, Staunton-on-Arrow, Byton and Lyonshall *Heref 5* **P** *Ld Chan (1 turn), Patr Bd (4 turns)* **R** J M READ
PEMBURY (St Peter) *Roch 8* **P** *Ch Ch Ox* **NSM** H A HUGHES
PEN SELWOOD (St Michael) *B & W 2* **P** *Bp* **R** S LOW, **C** S J TANCOCK
PENCOMBE (St John) *see* Bredenbury w Grendon Bishop and Wacton etc *Heref*
PENCOYD (St Denys) *see* St Weonards w Orcop, Garway, Tretire etc *Heref*
PENCOYS (St Andrew) *see* Redruth w Lanner and Treleigh *Truro*
PENDEEN (St John the Baptist) w Morvah *Truro 5* **P** *R A H Aitken Esq and C W M Aitken Esq (jt)* **V** A ROWELL
PENDEFORD (St Paul) *see* Tettenhall Regis *Lich*
PENDLEBURY (St Augustine) *see* Swinton and Pendlebury *Man*
PENDLEBURY (St John) *Man 6* **P** *Trustees* **P-in-c** S K TIMMINS, **OLM** V TYLDESLEY
PENDLETON (All Saints) *see* Sabden and Pendleton *Blackb*
PENDLETON (St Ambrose) (St Thomas) *Man 6* **P** *Patr Bd* **TR** M N HAWORTH, **TV** M K J SMITH, J C BRADING, **C** A W BENNETT, **Hon C** D J H KEYTE, **OLM** J I WHITTINGHAM
PENDOCK CROSS (Holy Redeemer) *see* Berrow w Pendock, Eldersfield, Hollybush etc *Worc*
PENDOMER (St Roch) *see* W Coker w Hardington Mandeville, E Chinnock etc *B & W*
PENGE (Christ Church w Holy Trinity) *see* Anerley *Roch*
PENGE (St John the Evangelist) *Roch 13* **P** *Simeon's Trustees* **V** P R M VENABLES
PENGE (St Paul) *see* Anerley St Paul *Roch*
PENGE LANE (Holy Trinity) *Roch 13* **P** *CPAS* **P-in-c** N G READ
PENHILL (St Peter) *Bris 7* **P** *Bp* **V** S WATERS, **C** C A WATERS
PENHURST (St Michael the Archangel) *see* Ashburnham w Penhurst *Chich*
PENISTONE (St John the Baptist) and Thurlstone *Wakef 7* **P** *Bp* **TV** D J HOPKIN
PENKETH (St Paul) *Liv 12* **P** *Bp* **V** P W HOCKLEY
PENKEVIL (St Michael) *see* St Michael Penkevil *Truro*
PENKHULL (St Thomas) *Lich 12* **P** *R Stoke-on-Trent* **V** I MAITIN
PENKRIDGE Team, The (St Michael and All Angels) *Lich 2* **P** *Patr Bd* **TV** C G HEATH, **C** L C STARRS
PENN (Holy Trinity) and Tylers Green *Ox 20* **P** *Earl Howe* **V** M D BISSET, **NSM** A M CAW
PENN (St Bartholomew) (St Anne) *Lich 24* **P** *Bp* **V** G M F WILLIAMS
PENN FIELDS St Philip (St Aidan) *Lich 24* **P** *Ch Trust Fund Trust* **V** J S OAKLEY, **C** P J CANSDALE
PENN STREET (Holy Trinity) *Ox 20* **P** *Earl Howe* **P-in-c** M J BOYES, **NSM** C E L SMITH
PENNARD, EAST (All Saints) *see* Fosse Trinity *B & W*
PENNARD, WEST (St Nicholas) *see* Baltonsborough w Butleigh, W Bradley etc *B & W*
PENNINGTON (Christ Church) *Man 13* **P** *Trustees* **C** E D COCKSHAW, **OLM** E J WHITE, J HARNEY
PENNINGTON (St Mark) *Win 11* **P** *V Milford* **V** P H RENYARD
PENNINGTON (St Michael and the Holy Angels) and Lindal w Marton and Bardsea *Carl 9* **P** *Bp and DBP (jt)* **V** D E WEBSTER, **NSM** M WEBSTER
PENNYCROSS (St Pancras) *Ex 22* **P** *CPAS* **V** A M M PARKER
PENNYWELL (St Thomas) *see* Sunderland Pennywell St Thos *Dur*
PENPONDS (Holy Trinity) *Truro 2* **P** *The Crown* **P-in-c** P DOUGLASS, **C** M L PASCOE
PENRITH (Christ Church) (St Andrew) w Newton Reigny and Plumpton Wall *Carl 4* **P** *Bp* **TR** R W WOODGER, **TV** A P HUTCHINSON, **C** C N CASEY, A M E OSMASTON
PENRUDDOCK (All Saints) *see* Gd Shep TM *Carl*
PENSAX (St James the Great) *see* Teme Valley N *Worc*
PENSBY (St Michael and All Angels) *see* Barnston *Ches*
PENSHAW (All Saints) *see* Herrington, Penshaw and Shiney Row *Dur*
PENSHURST (St John the Baptist) and Fordcombe *Roch 12* **P** *Viscount De L'Isle* **P-in-c** T E HOLME
PENSILVA (St John) *see* St Ive and Pensilva w Quethiock *Truro*
PENSNETT (St Mark) *Worc 10* **P** *Bp* **V** L J WOOLHOUSE, **C** S J MAINWARING
PENTEWAN (All Saints) *see* St Austell *Truro*
PENTLOW (St George and St Gregory) *see* N Hinckford *Chelmsf*
PENTNEY (St Mary Magdalene) *see* Narborough w Narford and Pentney *Nor*
PENTON MEWSEY (Holy Trinity) *see* Hatherden w Tangley, Weyhill and Penton Mewsey *Win*
PENTONVILLE (St Silas w All Saints) (St James) *Lon 6* **P** *Bp* **V** S RICHARDS
PENTRICH (St Matthew) *see* Swanwick and Pentrich *Derby*
PENTRIDGE (St Rumbold) *see* Sixpenny Handley w Gussage St Andrew etc *Sarum*
PENWERRIS (St Michael and All Angels) (Holy Spirit) *Truro 3* **P** *V St Gluvias* **V** D S SMITH
PENWORTHAM (St Leonard) *Blackb 5* **P** *Bp* **V** J N MANSFIELD, **NSM** J V SCOTT
PENWORTHAM (St Mary) *Blackb 5* **P** *Miss A M Rawstorne* **V** C J NELSON, **C** A J LOGAN
PENZANCE (St Mary) (St Paul) (St John the Baptist) *Truro 5* **P** *Bp* **TR** K R OWEN, **C** C R PERRY, **NSM** N W MARTIN, J COTTON, J A MILLAR
PEOPLETON (St Nicholas) and White Ladies Aston w Churchill and Spetchley and Upton Snodsbury and Broughton Hackett *Worc 4* **P** *Bp, Croom Estate Trustees, and Major R J G Berkley (1 turn), and Ld Chan (1 turn)* **R** S M EAST
PEOVER, OVER (St Lawrence) w Lower Peover (St Oswald) *Ches 12* **P** *DBP and Man Univ (jt)* **V** P J LLOYD
PEPER HAROW (St Nicholas) *see* Compton w Shackleford and Peper Harow *Guildf*
PEPLOW (The Epiphany) *see* Hodnet w Weston under Redcastle *Lich*
PERIVALE (St Mary w St Nicholas) *Lon 22* **P** *Trustees* **P-in-c** A R CORSIE, **NSM** V A AITKEN
PERLETHORPE (St John the Evangelist) *S'well 6* **P** *Earl Manvers' Trustees* **P-in-c** A D LITTLEWOOD
PERRANARWORTHAL (St Piran) *see* St Stythians w Perranarworthal and Gwennap *Truro*

PERRANPORTH (St Michael's Mission Church) *see* Perranzabuloe *Truro*
PERRANUTHNOE (St Michael and St Piran) *see* Ludgvan, Marazion, St Hilary and Perranuthnoe *Truro*
PERRANZABULOE (St Piran) *Truro 7* **P** *D&C* **P-in-c** J C E ANDREW, **NSM** P M NIXON
PERROTT, NORTH (St Martin) *see* Haselbury Plucknett, Misterton and N Perrott *B & W*
PERROTT, SOUTH (St Mary) *see* Beaminster Area *Sarum*
PERRY BARR (St John the Evangelist) *Birm 3* **P** *Bp and trustees (jt)* **V** C S JONES
PERRY BEECHES (St Matthew) *Birm 3* **P** *St Martin's Trustees* **V** S P M MACKENZIE
PERRY COMMON (St Martin) *Birm 8* **P** *Bp* **V** C M FEAK
PERRY GREEN (St Thomas) *see* Much Hadham *St Alb*
PERRY HILL (St George) (Christ Church) (St Paul) *S'wark 5* **P** *D&C and Earl of Dartmouth (1 turn), Bp and Earl of Darmouth (1 turn)* **V** J R W ACKLAND, **C** L C VINCER, **NSM** T G BURMAN, A D W DUPUY
PERRY STREET (All Saints) *Roch 4* **P** *Bp* **V** P E WAKELIN, **C** J E MOWBRAY
PERSHORE (Holy Cross) w Pinvin, Wick and Birlingham *Worc 4* **P** *Patr Bd* **V** K I CRAWFORD, **NSM** D C OWEN
PERTENHALL (St Peter) *see* The Stodden Churches *St Alb*
PETER TAVY (St Peter), Mary Tavy, Lydford and Brent Tor *Ex 25* **P** *Guild of All So and Bp (1 turn), Duchy of Cornwall (1 turn)* **R** I SYKES, **Hon C** R D ORMSBY, **NSM** G STILL
PETERBOROUGH (All Saints) *Pet 13* **P** *Bp* **V** D J T MILLER
PETERBOROUGH (Christ the Carpenter) *Pet 13* **P** *Bp* **V** N E FRY, **C** C R IEVINS, **NSM** P V IEVINS
PETERBOROUGH (Holy Spirit) Bretton *Pet 13* **P** *Bp* **V** P M HAWKINS
PETERBOROUGH (St John the Baptist) (Mission Church) *Pet 13* **P** *Bp* **V** G J STEELE, **C** I D HOUGHTON
PETERBOROUGH (St Jude) *Pet 13* **P** *Bp* **V** G J KEATING
PETERBOROUGH (St Mark) and St Barnabas *Pet 13* **P** *Bp* **P-in-c** J J PRICE
PETERBOROUGH (St Mary) Boongate *Pet 13* **P** *D&C* **P-in-c** S A WALKER, **NSM** C D MASON
PETERBOROUGH (St Paul) *Pet 13* **P** *Bp* **V** P R LARCOMBE
PETERCHURCH (St Peter) *see* Madley w Tyberton, Peterchurch, Vowchurch etc *Heref*
PETERLEE (St Cuthbert) *Dur 2* **P** *Bp* **V** P M TEMPLEMAN, **C** D R H MCGOWAN, **NSM** A J TEMPLEMAN
PETERSFIELD (St Peter) *Portsm 4* **P** *Bp* **V** W G HARRIS-EVANS
PETERSHAM (All Saints) (St Peter) *S'wark 18* **P** *Bp* **P-in-c** F R BENTLEY
PETERSMARLAND (St Peter) *see* Shebbear, Buckland Filleigh, Sheepwash etc *Ex*
PETERSTOW (St Peter) *see* Ross *Heref*
PETHAM (All Saints) and Waltham w Lower Hardres and Nackington w Upper Hardres and Stelling *Cant 2* **P** *Abp, St Jo Coll Ox, and Trustees Lord Tomlin (jt)* **P-in-c** D W J HOUSTON
PETHERTON, NORTH (St Mary the Virgin) *see* Alfred Jewel *B & W*
PETHERTON, SOUTH (St Peter and St Paul) w the Seavingtons *B & W 15* **P** *D&C* **R** D J M JASPER
PETHERWIN, NORTH (St Paternus) *see* Egloskerry, N Petherwin, Tremaine and Tresmere *Truro*
PETROCKSTOWE (St Petrock) *see* Shebbear, Buckland Filleigh, Sheepwash etc *Ex*
PETT (St Mary and St Peter) *see* Fairlight, Guestling and Pett *Chich*
PETT LEVEL (St Nicholas) *as above*
PETTAUGH (St Catherine) *see* Debenham and Helmingham *St E*
PETTISTREE (St Peter and St Paul) *see* Wickham Market w Pettistree *St E*
PETTON (not known) w Cockshutt, Welshampton and Lyneal w Colemere *Lich 17* **P** *Bp and R K Mainwaring Esq (jt)* **P-in-c** J C VERNON
PETTON (St Petrock) *see* Bampton, Morebath, Clayhanger and Petton *Ex*
PETTS WOOD (St Francis) *Roch 16* **P** *Bp* **V** O C G HIGGS
PETWORTH (St Mary) *Chich 11* **P** *Lord Egremont* **R** D S POLLARD
PEVENSEY (St Nicholas) (St Wilfred) *Chich 16* **P** *Bp* **V** A C H CHRISTIAN
PEWSEY (St John the Baptist) and Swanborough Team Ministry, The *Sarum 19* **P** *Patr Bd* **TR** H G HOSKINS, **TV** V S ROWE, **OLM** G E R OSBORNE
PHEASEY (St Chad) *Lich 25* **P** *DBP* **P-in-c** K S NJENGA
PHILADELPHIA (St Thomas) Extra-Parochial Place *Sheff 4* **Min** A F MACLAURIN, A J D E ABSALOM
PHILBEACH GARDENS (St Cuthbert) *see* Earl's Court St Cuth w St Matthias *Lon*
PHILLACK (St Felicitas) *see* Godrevy *Truro*
PHILLEIGH (St Philleigh) *see* Gerrans w St Anthony-in-Roseland and Philleigh *Truro*
PICCADILLY (St James) *see* Westmr St Jas *Lon*
PICKENHAM, NORTH (St Andrew) *see* Necton, Holme Hale w N and S Pickenham *Nor*
PICKENHAM, SOUTH (All Saints) *as above*
PICKERING (St Peter and St Paul) w Lockton and Levisham *York 20* **P** *Abp* **V** F J A HEWITT, **NSM** L GROVE
PICKHILL (All Saints) *see* Kirklington w Burneston and Wath and Pickhill *Ripon*
PICKWELL (All Saints) *see* Burrough Hill Pars *Leic*
PICKWORTH (All Saints) *see* Gt and Lt Casterton w Pickworth and Tickencote *Pet*
PICKWORTH (St Andrew) *see* S Lafford *Linc*
PICTON (St Hilary) *see* Kirklevington *York*
PIDDINGHOE (St John) *Chich 18* **P** *Bp and Gorham Trustees (jt)* **V** D A HIDER, **C** D L N GUTSELL
PIDDINGTON (St John the Baptist) *see* Hardingstone and Horton and Piddington *Pet*
PIDDINGTON (St Nicholas) *see* Ray Valley *Ox*
PIDDLE, NORTH (St Michael) *see* Abberton, The Flyfords, Naunton Beauchamp etc *Worc*
PIDDLE VALLEY, Hilton, Cheselbourne and Melcombe Horsey, The *Sarum 1* **P** *Bp, Eton Coll, G A L F Pitt-Rivers Esq, D&C Sarum, and D&C Win (by turn)* **V** J M BAILEY, **NSM** H J P EXON
PIDDLEHINTON (St Mary the Virgin) *see* Piddle Valley, Hilton, Cheselbourne etc *Sarum*
PIDDLETRENTHIDE (All Saints) *as above*
PIDLEY CUM FENTON (All Saints) *see* Somersham w Pidley and Oldhurst *Ely*
PIERCEBRIDGE (St Mary) *see* Coniscliffe *Dur*
PILHAM (All Saints) *see* Corringham and Blyton Gp *Linc*
PILL (Christ Church), Portbury and Easton-in-Gordano *B & W 13* **P** *Bp* **V** R H M LEGG, **Hon C** J N O WILLIAMS
PILLATON (St Modwen) *see* Penkridge Team *Lich*
PILLATON (St Odolph) *see* St Dominic, Landulph and St Mellion w Pillaton *Truro*
PILLERTON HERSEY (St Mary) *see* Butlers Marston and the Pillertons w Ettington *Cov*
PILLEY (Mission Church) *see* Tankersley, Thurgoland and Wortley *Sheff*
PILLEY (St Nicholas) *see* Boldre w S Baddesley *Win*
PILLING (St John the Baptist) *see* Stalmine w Pilling *Blackb*
PILNING (St Peter) w Compton Greenfield *Bris 2* **P** *Bp* **V** B TOPALIAN
PILSLEY (St Mary the Virgin) *see* N Wingfield, Clay Cross and Pilsley *Derby*
PILTON (All Saints) *see* Aldwincle w Thorpe Achurch, Pilton, Wadenhoe etc *Pet*
PILTON (St John the Baptist) w Croscombe, North Wootton and Dinder *B & W 8* **P** *Bp and Peache Trustees (jt)* **R** D R OSBORNE, **C** E J THOMSON
PILTON (St Mary the Virgin) *see* Barnstaple *Ex*
PILTON (St Nicholas) *see* Preston and Ridlington w Wing and Pilton *Pet*
PIMLICO Bourne Street (St Mary) *see* Pimlico St Mary Bourne Street *Lon*
PIMLICO (St Barnabas) *Lon 3* **P** *Bp* **P-in-c** A C COLES, **Hon C** E S J EWER
PIMLICO (St Gabriel) *Lon 3* **P** *Bp* **V** D W SKEOCH, **NSM** W D PATTINSON
PIMLICO (St James the Less) *see* Westminster St Jas the Less *Lon*
PIMLICO (St Mary) Bourne Street *Lon 3* **P** *Trustees* **P-in-c** A C COLES, **Hon C** S E YOUNG, E S J EWER, **NSM** S N LEAMY
PIMLICO (St Peter) w Westminster Christ Church *Lon 3* **P** *Bp* **V** D B TILLYER, **C** L M RODRIGUEZ, **NSM** A R CHIDWICK
PIMLICO (St Saviour) *Lon 3* **P** *Bp* **P-in-c** M T WOODWARD
PIMPERNE (St Peter), Stourpaine, Durweston and Bryanston *Sarum 6* **P** *DBP (2 turns), D&C (1 turn)* **R** S P COULTER, **NSM** J W WHITTLE
PIN GREEN (All Saints) *see* Stevenage All SS Pin Green *St Alb*
PINCHBECK (St Mary) *see* Glen Gp *Linc*
PINCHBECK, WEST (St Bartholomew) *as above*
PINHOE (St Michael and All Angels) (Hall) and Broadclyst *Ex 1* **P** *Patr Bd* **TR** A J MORTIMER
PINNER (St Anselm) *see* Hatch End St Anselm *Lon*
PINNER (St John the Baptist) *Lon 23* **P** *V Harrow* **V** S J POTHEN, **Hon C** M S NATTRASS
PINNER VIEW (St George) *see* Headstone St Geo *Lon*

PINVIN (St Nicholas) *see* Pershore w Pinvin, Wick and Birlingham *Worc*
PINXTON (St Helen) (Church Hall) *Derby 1* **P** *Bp* **R** L G C E HARRIS
PIPE-CUM-LYDE (St Peter) and Moreton-on-Lugg *Heref 4* **P** *Bp, Soc of the Faith, and D&C (by turn)* **P-in-c** J W R MORRISON, **NSM** E S V VERWEY
PIPEWELL (St Mary) *see* Rothwell w Orton, Rushton w Glendon and Pipewell *Pet*
PIRBRIGHT (St Michael and All Angels) *Guildf 12* **P** *Ld Chan* **P-in-c** V K LUCAS
PIRNOUGH (All Hallows) *see* Ditchingham, Hedenham and Broome *Nor*
PIRTON (St Mary) *see* Holwell, Ickleford and Pirton *St Alb*
PIRTON (St Peter) *see* Stoulton w Drake's Broughton and Pirton etc *Worc*
PISHILL (not known) *see* Nettlebed w Bix, Highmoor, Pishill etc *Ox*
PITCHCOMBE (St John the Baptist) *see* Painswick, Sheepscombe, Cranham, The Edge etc *Glouc*
PITCHFORD (St Michael and All Angels) *see* Condover w Frodesley, Acton Burnell etc *Heref*
PITCOMBE (St Leonard) *see* Bruton and Distr *B & W*
PITMINSTER (St Mary and St Andrew) *see* Blackdown *B & W*
PITNEY (St John the Baptist) *see* Langport Area Chs *B & W*
PITSEA (St Gabriel) w Nevendon *Chelmsf 6* **P** *Bp* **P-in-c** D A DEER, **NSM** C M WILLIAMS
PITSFORD (All Saints) w Boughton *Pet 2* **P** *Bp* **R** S TROTT
PITSMOOR (Christ Church) *Sheff 3* **P** *Ch Patr Trust* **V** M J SNOW
PITTINGTON (St Laurence), Shadforth and Sherburn *Dur 1* **P** *D&C* **P-in-c** R I DAVISON, **NSM** E TARREN, D J WILSON, M THRUSH
PITTON (St Peter) *see* Clarendon *Sarum*
PITTVILLE (All Saints) *see* Prestbury and All SS *Glouc*
PIXHAM (St Mary the Virgin) *see* Dorking w Ranmore *Guildf*
PIXLEY (St Andrew) *see* Ledbury *Heref*
PLAISTOW (Holy Trinity) *see* Kirdford *Chich*
PLAISTOW (St Martin) (St Mary) (St Philip and St James) and North Canning Town *Chelmsf 3* **P** *Patr Bd* **TR** S D MASON, **TV** E O ADOYO
PLAISTOW (St Mary) *Roch 14* **P** *Bp* **V** S D BURTON-JONES, **Hon C** R B HANDFORTH
PLAISTOW The Divine Compassion *see* Plaistow and N Canning Town *Chelmsf*
PLAITFORD (St Peter) *see* Bramshaw and Landford w Plaitford *Sarum*
PLAS NEWTON (St Michael) *Ches 2* **P** *Simeon's Trustees* **V** R C TOAN, **C** J E JEPSON
PLATT (St Mary the Virgin) *Roch 10* **P** *Bp* **V** *vacant* (01732) 885482
PLATT BRIDGE (St Nathaniel) *Liv 14* **P** *Bp* **V** K D CRINKS
PLATT'S HEATH (St Edmund) *see* Len Valley *Cant*
PLAXTOL (not known) *see* Shipbourne w Plaxtol *Roch*
PLAYDEN (St Michael) *see* Rye *Chich*
PLAYFORD (St Mary) *see* Gt and Lt Bealings w Playford and Culpho *St E*
PLEASLEY (St Michael) *see* E Scarsdale *Derby*
PLEASLEY HILL (St Barnabas) *S'well 2* **P** *Bp* **P-in-c** G E HOLLOWAY
PLEASLEY VALE (St Chad) *see* Mansfield Woodhouse *S'well*
PLEMSTALL (St Peter) w Guilden Sutton *Ches 2* **P** *Capt P Egerton Warburton* **V** M HART
PLESHEY (Holy Trinity) *Chelmsf 8* **P** *Bp* **P-in-c** S F COUGHTREY, **NSM** B M H MAIN
PLUCKLEY (St Mary) *see* Egerton w Pluckley *Cant*
PLUCKLEY (St Nicholas) *as above*
PLUMBLAND (St Cuthbert) *see* Binsey *Carl*
PLUMPTON (All Saints) (St Michael and All Angels) w East Chiltington cum Novington *Chich 18* **P** *Ld Chan* **R** G D BROSTER
PLUMPTON (St John the Baptist) *see* Astwell Gp *Pet*
PLUMPTON WALL (St John the Evangelist) *see* Penrith w Newton Reigny and Plumpton Wall *Carl*
PLUMSTEAD (All Saints) Shooters Hill *S'wark 3* **P** *CPAS* **V** H D OWEN
PLUMSTEAD (Ascension) *S'wark 3* **P** *Bp* **V** C R WELHAM
PLUMSTEAD (St John the Baptist) w St James and St Paul *S'wark 3* **P** *Simeon's Trustees and CPAS (alt)* **V** P J ROGERS
PLUMSTEAD (St Mark and St Margaret) *S'wark 3* **P** *DBP* **V** R W JAMES
PLUMSTEAD (St Michael) *see* Barningham w Matlaske w Baconsthorpe etc *Nor*
PLUMSTEAD (St Nicholas) *S'wark 3* **P** *V Plumstead St Mark w St Marg* **V** A G STEVENS
PLUMSTEAD, GREAT (St Mary) and LITTLE (St Gervase and Protase) w Thorpe End and Witton *Nor 4* **P** *Bp and D&C (jt)* **R** M M KINGSTON
PLUMTREE (St Mary) *S'well 8* **P** *DBP* **P-in-c** M H WAINWRIGHT
PLUNGAR (St Helen) *see* Vale of Belvoir Par *Leic*
PLYMOUTH Crownhill (Ascension) *Ex 23* **P** *Bp* **V** P HANCOCK, **C** J A THOMPSON-VEAR
PLYMOUTH Emmanuel, St Paul Efford and St Augustine *Ex 24* **P** *Patr Bd* **TR** K F FREEMAN, **TV** J M BARRETT, **C** S M PAYNE
PLYMOUTH (St Andrew) and St Paul Stonehouse *Ex 24* **P** *Patr Bd* **TR** N H P MCKINNEL, **TV** M T BAILEY, **C** J D G NASH
PLYMOUTH (St Augustine) *see* Plymouth Em, St Paul Efford and St Aug *Ex*
PLYMOUTH (St Gabriel) Peverell *Ex 24* **P** *Bp* **V** J J STARK
PLYMOUTH (St James the Less) Ham *Ex 22* **P** *Keble Coll Ox* **V** T M S MORLEY
PLYMOUTH (St John the Evangelist) *see* Sutton on Plym *Ex*
PLYMOUTH (St Jude) *Ex 24* **P** *Trustees* **V** *vacant* (01752) 661232
PLYMOUTH (St Mary the Virgin) *see* Plymouth St Simon and St Mary *Ex*
PLYMOUTH (St Matthias) *see* Charles w Plymouth St Matthias *Ex*
PLYMOUTH (St Pancras) *see* Pennycross *Ex*
PLYMOUTH (St Peter) (All Saints) *Ex 22* **P** *Keble Coll Ox* **V** S PHILPOTT
PLYMOUTH (St Simon) and St Mary Laira *Ex 24* **P** *Bp and St Simon Trustees (jt)* **V** S P PICKERING
PLYMPTON (St Mary the Blessed Virgin) *Ex 23* **P** *Bp* **V** M M CAMERON, **C** H T BARNES, R W BECK, **NSM** M BRIMICOMBE
PLYMPTON (St Maurice) *Ex 23* **P** *D&C Windsor* **P-in-c** J P MASON
PLYMSTOCK (St Mary and All Saints) and Hooe *Ex 24* **P** *Patr Bd* **TR** D J WALLER, **TV** I K PROVOST, J J SPEAR, **NSM** M P HINKS, C A BRODRIBB
PLYMTREE (St John the Baptist) *see* Broadhembury, Payhembury and Plymtree *Ex*
POCKLEY (St John the Baptist) *see* Kirkdale w Harome, Nunnington and Pockley *York*
POCKLINGTON (All Saints) and Owsthorpe and Kilnwick Percy w Great Givendale and Millington *York 5* **P** *Abp* **R** C J SIMMONS, **C** S MITCHELL
PODIMORE (St Peter) *see* Ilchester w Northover, Limington, Yeovilton etc *B & W*
PODINGTON (St Mary the Virgin) *see* Wymington w Podington *St Alb*
POINT CLEAR (Mission) *see* St Osyth *Chelmsf*
POINTON (Christ Church) *see* Billingborough Gp *Linc*
POKESDOWN (All Saints) *Win 8* **P** *V Christchurch* **P-in-c** K P ARKELL, **NSM** N S LEGRAND
POKESDOWN (St James) *Win 8* **P** *Bp* **P-in-c** R L VERNON, **NSM** P M SCHOLLAR
POLDENS, WEST *B & W 5* **P** *Bp* **P-in-c** W B GRAHAM
POLEBROOK (All Saints) and Lutton w Hemington and Luddington *Pet 12* **P** *Bp, Sir Stephen Hastings, and DBP (by turn)* **R** *vacant* (01832) 274941
POLEGATE (St John) *Chich 16* **P** *Bp* **V** M W LUCAS, **NSM** R A HERKES
POLEGATE (St Wilfrid) *see* Lower Willingdon St Wilfrid CD *Chich*
POLESWORTH (St Editha) *Birm 10* **P** *Ld Chan* **V** P A WELLS
POLING (St Nicholas) *Chich 1* **P** *Bp* **V** J E SLEGG
POLLINGTON (St John the Baptist) *see* Gt Snaith *Sheff*
POLPERRO (St John the Baptist) *see* Talland *Truro*
POLRUAN (St Saviour) *see* Lanteglos by Fowey *Truro*
POLSTEAD (St Mary) *see* Stoke by Nayland w Leavenheath and Polstead *St E*
POLTIMORE (St Mary the Virgin) *see* Stoke Canon, Poltimore w Huxham and Rewe etc *Ex*
PONDERS END (St Matthew) *Lon 18* **P** *V Enfield* **P-in-c** R C KNOWLING, **C** S P J CLARK, D W HYETT
PONDERSBRIDGE (St Thomas) *see* Whittlesey, Pondersbridge and Coates *Ely*
PONSANOOTH (St Michael and All Angels) *see* Mabe *Truro*
PONSBOURNE (St Mary) *see* Lt Berkhamsted and Bayford, Essendon etc *St Alb*
PONSONBY (not known) *see* Beckermet St Jo and St Bridget w Ponsonby *Carl*
PONTEFRACT (All Saints) *Wakef 11* **P** *Bp* **P-in-c** V IWANUSCHAK

PONTEFRACT (St Giles) (St Mary) *Wakef 11* **P** *Bp* **V** R G COOPER
PONTELAND (St Mary the Virgin) *Newc 7* **P** *Mert Coll Ox* **V** M J JACKSON, **C** T M FERGUSON, **NSM** C L BROWN
PONTESBURY First and Second Portions (St George) *Heref 13* **P** *St Chad's Coll Dur* **R** D B HEWLETT
PONTON, GREAT (Holy Cross) *see* Colsterworth Gp *Linc*
PONTON, LITTLE (St Guthlac) *as above*
POOL (St Wilfrid) *see* Lower Wharfedale *Ripon*
POOLBROOK (St Andrew) *see* Malvern St Andr and Malvern Wells and Wyche *Worc*
POOLE (St James w St Paul) *Sarum 7* **P** *Ch Soc Trust and J H Cordle Esq (jt)* **R** R H G MASON, **NSM** C E SUGDEN
POOLE KEYNES (St Michael and All Angels) *see* Kemble, Poole Keynes, Somerford Keynes etc *Glouc*
POOLEY BRIDGE (St Paul) *see* Barton, Pooley Bridge and Martindale *Carl*
POOLSBROOK (St Alban) *see* Staveley and Barrow Hill *Derby*
POORTON, NORTH (St Mary Magdalene) *see* Askerswell, Loders and Powerstock *Sarum*
POPLAR (All Saints) *Lon 7* **P** *Patr Bd* **TR** A J WYNNE, **TV** A M W WILSON, **C** I E VIBERT, **NSM** T J DUNCAN, J C SHELDON
POPPLETON, NETHER (St Everilda) w Upper (All Saints) *York 1* **P** *Abp* **NSM** M C S FOSSETT
POPPLETON ROAD (Mission Room) *see* York St Paul *York*
PORCHESTER (St James) *S'well 10* **P** *Bp* **V** P A WILLIAMS, **C** J C MONEY
PORINGLAND (All Saints) *Nor 8* **P** *Bp, BNC Ox, J D Alston Esq, and G H Hastings Esq (3 turns) and DBP (1 turn)* **R** R H PARSONAGE
PORLOCK (St Dubricius) w Stoke Pero *B & W 16* **P** *Ld Chan* **R** B E PRIORY
PORLOCK WEIR (St Nicholas) *see* Porlock w Stoke Pero *B & W*
PORT ERIN (St Catherine) *see* Rushen *S & M*
PORT ISAAC (St Peter) *see* St Endellion w Port Isaac and St Kew *Truro*
PORT ST MARY (St Mary) *see* Rushen *S & M*
PORTBURY (Blessed Virgin Mary) *see* Pill, Portbury and Easton-in-Gordano *B & W*
PORTCHESTER (St Mary) *Portsm 2* **P** *J R Thistlethwaite Esq* **V** M S COOPER
PORTESHAM (St Peter) *see* Abbotsbury, Portesham and Langton Herring *Sarum*
PORTHILL (St Andrew) *see* Wolstanton *Lich*
PORTHLEVEN (St Bartholomew) w Sithney *Truro 4* **P** *Bp* **P-in-c** H PUGH
PORTHPEAN (St Levan) *see* St Austell *Truro*
PORTINSCALE (Mission) *see* Crosthwaite Keswick *Carl*
PORTISHEAD (St Peter) *B & W 13* **P** *Patr Bd* **TR** A C TAYLOR, **TV** S M J CROSSMAN, C L LAWS, **C** D C WILLIAMSON
PORTKELLIS (St Christopher) *see* Helston and Wendron *Truro*
PORTLAND (All Saints w St Peter) *Sarum 4* **P** *Bp* **P-in-c** N A MCKINTY, **OLM** M E CADE
PORTLAND (St John) *Sarum 4* **P** *Hyndman Trustees* **P-in-c** D D BOTTERILL
PORTLEMOUTH, EAST (St Winwaloe Onocaus) *see* Charleton w Buckland Tout Saints etc *Ex*
PORTLOE (All Saints) *see* Veryan w Ruan Lanihorne *Truro*
PORTMAN SQUARE (St Paul) *see* Langham Place All So *Lon*
PORTON (St Nicholas) *see* Bourne Valley *Sarum*
PORTREATH (St Mary) *see* St Illogan *Truro*
PORTSDOWN (Christ Church) *Portsm 5* **P** *Simeon's Trustees* **V** P J NORTON, **NSM** S G PHILLIPS
PORTSEA (All Saints) *Portsm 6* **P** *V Portsea St Mary and Bp (jt)* **P-in-c** L FOX, **NSM** M E TILLMAN, F M GATES
PORTSEA North End (St Mark) *Portsm 6* **P** *V Portsea St Mary* **P-in-c** M S KING, **C** C J POWELL, **NSM** S K WHITELOCK, R LOVEMAN
PORTSEA (St Alban) *Portsm 6* **P** *Bp* **P-in-c** R P CALDER
PORTSEA (St Cuthbert) *Portsm 6* **P** *Bp* **V** D M POWER, **NSM** J POWER, N J POULTON
PORTSEA (St George) *Portsm 6* **P** *Bp* **P-in-c** K B GREEN, **NSM** F M GATES
PORTSEA (St Luke) *Portsm 6* **P** *Ch Patr Trust* **P-in-c** C D TOWNER, **C** A G BRIDGEN
PORTSEA (St Mary) (St Faith and St Barnabas) (St Wilfrid) *Portsm 6* **P** *Win Coll* **V** R C WHITE, **C** C E HETHERINGTON, M J STEADMAN, **NSM** F M GATES
PORTSEA (St Saviour) *Portsm 6* **P** *Bp* **P-in-c** R P CALDER
PORTSEA (The Ascension) *Portsm 6* **P** *Bp* **P-in-c** R F ROBINSON
PORTSLADE (Good Shepherd) *Chich 4* **P** *Bp* **V** P D CLEGG
PORTSLADE (St Nicolas) (St Andrew) *Chich 4* **P** *Bp* **V** R H RUSHFORTH
PORTSWOOD (Christ Church) *Win 13* **P** *Bp* **V** G J ARCHER, **C** M W LEFROY
PORTSWOOD (St Denys) *Win 13* **P** *Bp* **C** K J RANDALL
POSBURY (St Francis Proprietary Chapel) *see* Crediton, Shobrooke and Sandford etc *Ex*
POSLINGFORD (St Mary) *see* Stour Valley *St E*
POSTBRIDGE (St Gabriel) *see* Widecombe-in-the-Moor, Leusdon, Princetown etc *Ex*
POSTLEBURY *see* Nunney and Witham Friary, Marston Bigot etc *B & W*
POSTLING (St Mary and St Radegund) *see* Lyminge w Paddlesworth, Stanford w Postling etc *Cant*
POSTWICK (All Saints) *see* Brundall w Braydeston and Postwick *Nor*
POTT SHRIGLEY (St Christopher) *Ches 13* **P** *MMCET* **P-in-c** J BUCKLEY
POTTEN END (Holy Trinity) w Nettleden *St Alb 2* **P** *Bp* **V** J V M KIRKBY
POTTER HEIGHAM (St Nicholas) *see* Ludham, Potter Heigham, Hickling and Catfield *Nor*
POTTERHANWORTH (St Andrew) *see* Branston w Nocton and Potterhanworth *Linc*
POTTERNE (St Mary the Virgin) w Worton and Marston *Sarum 16* **P** *Bp* **V** D J HOWARD, **OLM** R Y COULSON, J A HAYNES
POTTERNEWTON (St Martin) *Ripon 5* **P** *Trustees* **V** J R W SILLER, **C** C WILLIAMS
POTTERS BAR (King Charles the Martyr) *St Alb 17* **P** *Bp Lon* **P-in-c** M J BURNS
POTTERS BAR (St Mary and All Saints) *St Alb 17* **P** *Bp Lon* **V** P J BEVAN, **NSM** G J RANDALL
POTTERS GREEN (St Philip Deacon) *Cov 1* **P** *Ld Chan* **P-in-c** C GALE
POTTERS MARSTON (St Mary) *see* Barwell w Potters Marston and Stapleton *Leic*
POTTERSPURY (St Nicholas) w Furtho and Yardley Gobion w Cosgrove and Wicken *Pet 5* **P** *D&C, Jes Coll Ox, and Soc Merchant Venturers Bris (jt)* **R** M WRAY
POTTO (St Mary) *see* Whorlton w Carlton and Faceby *York*
POTTON (St Mary the Virgin) w Sutton and Cockayne Hatley *St Alb 11* **P** *The Crown (3 turns), St Jo Coll Ox (1 turn)* **R** V W BEYNON, **NSM** D L SMITH, J S HUMPHRIES
POUGHILL (St Michael and All Angels) *see* N Creedy *Ex*
POUGHILL (St Olaf King and Martyr) *Truro 8* **P** *Ch Soc Trust* **V** P A WHYBROW
POULNER (St John) *see* Ringwood *Win*
POULSHOT (St Peter) *see* Seend, Bulkington and Poulshot *Sarum*
POULTON (St Luke) *Ches 7* **P** *Bp* **P-in-c** A J MAUNDER
POULTON (St Michael and All Angels) *see* The Ampneys w Driffield and Poulton *Glouc*
POULTON CARLETON (St Chad) and Singleton *Blackb 12* **P** *DBP and Exors R Dumbreck Esq (jt)* **V** M P KEIGHLEY, **C** R NICHOLSON
POULTON LANCELYN (Holy Trinity) *Ches 8* **P** *R Bebington* **V** R K WILES, **NSM** P J GASKELL
POULTON-LE-FYLDE (St Chad) *see* Poulton Carleton and Singleton *Blackb*
POULTON-LE-SANDS (Holy Trinity) w Morecambe St Laurence *Blackb 11* **P** *V Lanc* **R** G S INGRAM, **OLM** A CUNLIFFE
POUND HILL (St Barnabas) *see* Worth *Chich*
POUNDSBRIDGE (Chapel) *see* Penshurst and Fordcombe *Roch*
POUNDSTOCK (St Winwaloe) *see* Week St Mary w Poundstock and Whitstone *Truro*
POWDERHAM (St Clement Bishop and Martyr) *see* Kenton, Mamhead, Powderham, Cofton and Starcross *Ex*
POWERSTOCK (St Mary the Virgin) *see* Askerswell, Loders and Powerstock *Sarum*
POWICK (St Peter) and Guarlford and Madresfield w Newland *Worc 2* **P** *Bp, Lady Rosalind Morrison, and Croome Estate Trustees (jt)* **R** *vacant* (01905) 830270
POYNINGS (Holy Trinity) w Edburton, Newtimber and Pyecombe *Chich 9* **P** *Ld Chan (1 turn), Bp and Abp (1 turn)* **R** *vacant* (01273) 857375
POYNTINGTON (All Saints) *see* Queen Thorne *Sarum*
POYNTON (St George) *Ches 17* **P** *Bp* **V** R I MCLAREN, **NSM** F T COOKE
POYNTON, HIGHER (St Martin) *see* Poynton *Ches*
PRADOE (extra-parochial place) *Lich 19* **Min** G C JONES
PRATTS BOTTOM (All Souls) *see* Green Street Green and Pratts Bottom *Roch*

PREES (St Chad) *Lich 22* **P** *Bp* **P-in-c** D F B BALDWIN, **Hon C** H S WATSON
PREESALL (St Oswald) *see* Waterside Par *Blackb*
PRENTON (St Stephen) *Ches 1* **P** *Bp* **V** E W LAUTENBACH
PRENTON DELL (St Alban) *see* Prenton *Ches*
PRESCOT (St Mary) (St Paul) *Liv 2* **P** *K Coll Cam* **V** J A TAYLOR, **C** P G ANDERSON, **OLM** J D ROSE
PRESHUTE (St George) *see* Marlborough *Sarum*
PRESTBURY (St Mary) (St Nicholas) and All Saints *Glouc 9* **P** *Patr Bd* **TR** S S GREGORY, **TV** M G COZENS, **C** G D BAYLISS, **Hon C** P R ILES, **OLM** P T BROWN
PRESTBURY (St Peter) *Ches 13* **P** *Ms C J C B Legh* **V** D ASHWORTH
PRESTEIGNE (St Andrew) w Discoed, Kinsham, Lingen and Knill *Heref 5* **P** *Patr Bd* **R** S HOLLINGHURST
PRESTLEIGH (St James Mission Church) *see* Shepton Mallet w Doulting *B & W*
PRESTOLEE (Holy Trinity) *see* Ringley w Prestolee *Man*
PRESTON Acregate Lane (Mission) *see* Preston Risen Lord *Blackb*
PRESTON (All Saints) *Blackb 13* **P** *Trustees* **V** *vacant* (01772) 700672
PRESTON (All Saints) *see* Siddington w Preston *Glouc*
PRESTON (All Saints) and Sproatley in Holderness *York 12* **P** *Abp* **C** P M BURDON
PRESTON (Church of the Ascension) *see* Wembley Park *Lon*
PRESTON (Emmanuel) *Blackb 13* **P** *R Preston* **V** S JOHNSON
PRESTON (Good Shepherd) *see* Brighton Gd Shep Preston *Chich*
PRESTON (St Alban) *see* Brighton Resurr *Chich*
PRESTON (St Andrew) w Sutton Poyntz and Osmington w Poxwell *Sarum 4* **P** *Patr Bd* **TR** T R WEST, **TV** L S DOBBINS, **C** A W STEPHENS
PRESTON (St Cuthbert) *Blackb 13* **P** *Bp* **V** C E HALLIWELL, **C** A R GILCHRIST
PRESTON (St John) (St George the Martyr) (Christ the King Chapel) *Blackb 13* **P** *DBP* **R** *vacant* (01772) 252528
PRESTON (St John the Baptist) *see* Redmarley D'Abitot, Bromesberrow, Pauntley etc *Glouc*
PRESTON (St John) w Brighton St Augustine and St Saviour *Chich 2* **P** *Bp* **P-in-c** A V BOWMAN, **C** C M CHAMBERS
PRESTON St Jude w St Paul *Blackb 13* **P** *Bp and V Preston St John* **P-in-c** G W NELSON
PRESTON (St Luke) (St Oswald) *Blackb 13* **P** *Bp and Simeon's Trustees (jt)* **P-in-c** G W NELSON
PRESTON (St Mark) *see* Ashton-on-Ribble St Mich w Preston St Mark *Blackb*
PRESTON (St Martin) *see* King's Walden and Offley w Lilley *St Alb*
PRESTON (St Mary the Virgin) *see* Lavenham w Preston *St E*
PRESTON (St Matthias) *see* Brighton St Matthias *Chich*
PRESTON (St Mildred) *see* Wingham w Elmstone and Preston w Stourmouth *Cant*
PRESTON (St Paul) *see* Paignton Ch Ch and Preston St Paul *Ex*
PRESTON (St Peter and St Paul) and Ridlington w Wing and Pilton *Pet 14* **P** *Bp, Baroness Willoughby de Eresby, and DBP (jt)* **P-in-c** P A SPENCE
PRESTON (St Stephen) *Blackb 13* **P** *Bp* **V** J N FIELDER
PRESTON The Risen Lord (St Matthew) (St Hilda) (St James's church hall) *Blackb 13* **P** *Patr Bd* **TR** P N TYERS, **TV** P A HARDACRE
PRESTON, EAST (St Mary) w Kingston *Chich 1* **P** *D&C* **V** J H LYON
PRESTON, GREAT (St Aidan) *see* Kippax w Allerton Bywater *Ripon*
PRESTON BAGOT (All Saints) *see* Claverdon w Preston Bagot *Cov*
PRESTON BISSET (St John the Baptist) *see* Swan *Ox*
PRESTON BROOK (St Faith) *see* Daresbury *Ches*
PRESTON CAPES (St Peter and St Paul) *see* Badby w Newham and Charwelton w Fawsley etc *Pet*
PRESTON NEXT FAVERSHAM (St Catherine) w Goodnestone and Graveney *Cant 6* **P** *Abp* **V** S C WILSON, **C** A C OEHRING
PRESTON ON STOUR (St Mary) *see* Ilmington w Stretton-on-Fosse etc *Cov*
PRESTON-ON-TEES (All Saints) and Longnewton *Dur 10* **P** *Bp* **V** A J FARISH, **NSM** D G HAMMOND, P CLAYTON
PRESTON-ON-WYE (St Lawrence) *see* Cusop w Blakemere, Bredwardine w Brobury etc *Heref*
PRESTON PATRICK (St Patrick) *see* Kirkby Lonsdale *Carl*
PRESTON PLUCKNETT (St James the Great) (St Peter) *B & W 7* **P** *Bp (2 turns), Mrs S W Rawlins (1 turn)* **V** A PERRIS
PRESTON UNDER SCARR (St Margaret) *see* Wensley *Ripon*
PRESTON WEALDMOORS (St Lawrence) *see* Edgmond w Kynnersley and Preston Wealdmoors *Lich*
PRESTON WYNNE (Holy Trinity) *see* Bodenham w Hope-under-Dinmore, Felton etc *Heref*
PRESTONVILLE (St Luke) *Chich 2* **P** *CPAS* **P-in-c** A W KILPATRICK
PRESTWICH (St Gabriel) *Man 14* **P** *Bp* **P-in-c** S S WILLIAMS
PRESTWICH (St Hilda) *Man 14* **P** *Trustees* **V** *vacant* 0161-773 1642
PRESTWICH (St Margaret) (St George) *Man 14* **P** *R Prestwich St Mary* **V** M ASHWORTH
PRESTWICH (St Mary the Virgin) *Man 14* **P** *Trustees* **P-in-c** B M HACKETT, **C** J D POSTON
PRESTWOLD (St Andrew) *see* Wymeswold and Prestwold w Hoton *Leic*
PRESTWOOD (Holy Trinity) and Great Hampden *Ox 28* **P** *Bp and Hon I H Hope-Morley (jt)* **P-in-c** M MOWFORTH, **OLM** K WATTERS
PRICKWILLOW (St Peter) *see* Ely *Ely*
PRIDDY (St Lawrence) *B & W 1* **P** *Bp* **V** E A MACPHERSON
PRIESTWOOD (St Andrew) *see* Bracknell *Ox*
PRIMROSE HILL (Holy Trinity) *see* Lydney *Glouc*
PRIMROSE HILL (St Mary the Virgin) w Avenue Road (St Paul) *Lon 16* **P** *Trustees* **V** R R ATWELL, **C** P S NICHOLSON, **NSM** J H ROOSE-EVANS, L L DEAN
PRINCE ALBERT ROAD (St Mark) *see* Regent's Park St Mark *Lon*
PRINCE CONSORT ROAD (Holy Trinity) *see* S Kensington H Trin w All SS *Lon*
PRINCE'S PARK (Christ the King) Conventional District *Roch 5* **Min** K G FOOT
PRINCES RISBOROUGH (St Mary) *see* Risborough *Ox*
PRINCETOWN (St Michael and All Angels) *see* Widecombe-in-the-Moor, Leusdon, Princetown etc *Ex*
PRIOR'S DEAN (not known) *see* Greatham w Empshott and Hawkley w Prior's Dean *Portsm*
PRIORS HARDWICK (St Mary the Virgin) w Priors Marston and Wormleighton *Cov 10* **P** *Earl Spencer* **P-in-c** G D MORRIS
PRIORS LEE (St Peter) (St Georges) *Lich 21* **P** *Bp and V Shifnal (jt)* **V** P G F LAWLEY
PRIORS MARSTON (St Leonard) *see* Priors Hardwick, Priors Marston and Wormleighton *Cov*
PRIORS PARK (Mission Hall) *see* Tewkesbury w Walton Cardiff and Twyning *Glouc*
PRISTON (St Luke) *see* Timsbury and Priston *B & W*
PRITTLEWELL (All Saints) *see* Southend *Chelmsf*
PRITTLEWELL (St Luke) *Chelmsf 13* **P** *Bp* **V** M J HALSALL
PRITTLEWELL (St Mary the Virgin) *Chelmsf 13* **P** *Bp* **V** R A MASON, **C** D C STANDEN, **NSM** F M SMITH
PRITTLEWELL (St Peter) w Westcliff St Cedd and the Saints of Essex *Chelmsf 13* **P** *Bp* **V** G R STEEL, **NSM** C ROBINSON
PRITTLEWELL (St Stephen) *Chelmsf 13* **P** *Bp* **P-in-c** C S BALDWIN
PROBUS (St Probus and St Grace), Ladock and Grampound w Creed and St Erme *Truro 6* **P** *DBP* **TR** I H MORRIS, **TV** D H DIXON, **Hon C** M E RICHARDS
PRUDHOE (St Mary Magdalene) *Newc 3* **P** *Dioc Soc* **P-in-c** C H HOPE, **OLM** D WEETMAN
PSALTER LANE (St Andrew) *Sheff 2* **P** *Trustees* **V** N P A JOWETT
PUBLOW (All Saints) w Pensford, Compton Dando and Chelwood *B & W 10* **P** *Bp* **P-in-c** G CALWAY, **NSM** S M E STEVENS
PUCKINGTON (St Andrew) *see* Ilminster and Distr *B & W*
PUCKLECHURCH (St Thomas à Becket) and Abson *Bris 5* **P** *D&C* **V** S K YOUNG
PUDDINGTON (St Thomas à Becket) *see* N Creedy *Ex*
PUDDLETOWN (St Mary the Virgin), Tolpuddle and Milborne w Dewlish *Sarum 1* **P** *Bp, Ch Ch Ox, Viscount Rothermere, and trustees (jt)* **NSM** S J GODFREY
PUDLESTON (St Peter) *see* Leominster *Heref*
PUDSEY (St James the Great) *see* Woodhall *Bradf*
PUDSEY (St Lawrence and St Paul) *Bradf 3* **P** *Bp and V Calverley (jt)* **V** P N AYERS, **C** A J GREIFF
PULBOROUGH (St Mary) *Chich 12* **P** *Lord Egremont* **R** P B WELCH
PULFORD (St Mary the Virgin) *see* Eccleston and Pulford *Ches*
PULHAM (St Thomas à Beckett) *see* Dungeon Hill *Sarum*
PULHAM MARKET (St Mary Magdalene) *see* Dickleburgh and The Pulhams *Nor*
PULHAM ST MARY (St Mary the Virgin) *as above*
PULLOXHILL (St James the Apostle) *see* Silsoe, Pulloxhill and Flitton *St Alb*

PULVERBATCH (St Edith) *see* Longden and Annscroft w Pulverbatch *Heref*
PUNCKNOWLE (St Mary the Blessed Virgin) *see* Bride Valley *Sarum*
PUNNETS TOWN (St Peter) *see* Heathfield *Chich*
PURBROOK (St John the Baptist) *Portsm 5* **P** *Bp* **P-in-c** K R SCHMIDT, **Hon C** C R ABBOTT, **NSM** M M SHERWIN
PUREWELL (St John) *see* Christchurch *Win*
PURFLEET (St Stephen) *see* Aveley and Purfleet *Chelmsf*
PURITON (St Michael and All Angels) and Pawlett *B & W 14* **P** *Ld Chan (1 turn), D&C Windsor (2 turns)* **V** D J L MACGEOCH
PURLEIGH (All Saints), Cold Norton and Stow Maries *Chelmsf 11* **P** *Charterhouse, Or Coll Ox, and Bp (jt)* **P-in-c** J E BLAND
PURLEY (Christ Church) *S'wark 24* **P** *Bp* **V** C R TREFUSIS, **C** M D FITTER, **OLM** S P BISHOP
PURLEY (St Barnabas) *S'wark 24* **P** *Bp* **P-in-c** R C HAGON
PURLEY (St Mark) Woodcote *S'wark 24* **P** *Bp* **P-in-c** J W S PATON
PURLEY (St Mary the Virgin) *Ox 12* **P** *Ld Chan* **R** R B HOWELL, **NSM** J ROTHERY, **OLM** A MACKIE
PURLEY (St Swithun) *S'wark 24* **P** *Bp* **P-in-c** J W S PATON
PURLWELL (St Andrew) *see* Batley All SS and Purlwell *Wakef*
PURSE CAUNDLE (St Peter) *see* The Caundles w Folke and Holwell *Sarum*
PURSTON (St Thomas) cum South Featherstone *Wakef 11* **P** *Bp* **P-in-c** N CLEWS, **C** M R MATTHEWS
PURTON (St John) *see* Sharpness, Purton, Brookend and Slimbridge *Glouc*
PURTON (St Mary) *Bris 7* **P** *Bp* **P-in-c** J HASLAM, **C** M H HASLAM
PUSEY (All Saints) *see* Cherbury w Gainfield *Ox*
PUTFORD (St Stephen) *see* Bradworthy, Sutcombe, Putford etc *Ex*
PUTLEY (not known) *see* Ledbury *Heref*
PUTNEY (St Margaret) *S'wark 20* **P** *Bp* **V** W F WARREN, **C** A BRODIE, **NSM** P J MILLIGAN
PUTNEY (St Mary) (All Saints) *S'wark 20* **P** *Patr Bd* **TR** G A FRASER, **TV** D E REES, **C** R M SEWELL, **NSM** T J E MARWOOD
PUTTENHAM (St John the Baptist) *see* Seale, Puttenham and Wanborough *Guildf*
PUTTENHAM (St Mary) *see* Tring *St Alb*
PYE NEST (St James) *see* King Cross *Wakef*
PYECOMBE (Transfiguration) *see* Poynings w Edburton, Newtimber and Pyecombe *Chich*
PYLLE (St Thomas à Becket) *see* Fosse Trinity *B & W*
PYPE HAYES (St Mary the Virgin) *see* Erdington *Birm*
PYRFORD (Church of the Good Shepherd) *see* Wisley w Pyrford *Guildf*
PYRFORD (St Nicholas) *as above*
PYRTON (St Mary) *see* Icknield *Ox*
PYTCHLEY (All Saints) *see* Isham w Pytchley *Pet*
PYWORTHY (St Swithun), Pancrasweek and Bridgerule *Ex 17* **P** *DBP* **P-in-c** L R D RYDER
QUADRING (St Margaret) *see* Gosberton, Gosberton Clough and Quadring *Linc*
QUAINTON (Holy Cross and St Mary) *see* Schorne *Ox*
QUANTOCK TOWERS, The *B & W 17* **P** *Bp, D&C Windsor, and D&C Wells (jt)* **R** E B SAVIGEAR
QUANTOXHEAD (Blessed Virgin Mary) (St Ethelreda) *B & W 17* **P** *Bp, Lady Gass, and Lt-Col W Luttrell (jt)* **R** J D A STEVENS, **NSM** P CUFF, S L CAMPBELL, D D BRIMSON
QUARLEY (St Michael and All Angels) *see* Amport, Grateley, Monxton and Quarley *Win*
QUARNDON (St Paul) *Derby 11* **P** *Exors Viscount Scarsdale* **P-in-c** W F BATES
QUARNFORD (St Paul) *see* Longnor, Quarnford and Sheen *Lich*
QUARRENDON ESTATE (St Peter) *see* Aylesbury w Bierton and Hulcott *Ox*
QUARRINGTON (St Botolph) w Old Sleaford *Linc 22* **P** *Bp* **P-in-c** P J MANDER, **C** A J HIGGINSON
QUARRY BANK (Christ Church) *Worc 10* **P** *Prime Min* **P-in-c** C J WINDLEY, **C** N A POPHAM
QUARRY HILL (St Mary) *see* Leeds City *Ripon*
QUATFORD (St Mary Magdalene) *see* Bridgnorth, Tasley, Astley Abbotts, etc *Heref*
QUATT (St Andrew) *see* Alveley and Quatt *Heref*
QUEDGELEY (St James) *Glouc 5* **P** *Bp* **V** G J B STICKLAND
QUEEN CAMEL (St Barnabas) *see* Cam Vale *B & W*
QUEEN CHARLTON (St Margaret) *see* Keynsham *B & W*
QUEEN THORNE *Sarum 3* **P** *Bp, The Revd J M P Goodden, J K Wingfield Digby Esq, and MMCET (jt)* **R** H G PEARSON, **OLM** P M SHERWIN, E MARTIN
QUEENBOROUGH (Holy Trinity) *Cant 15* **P** *Abp* **P-in-c** J W STREETING
QUEENHILL (St Nicholas) *see* Longdon, Castlemorton, Bushley, Queenhill etc *Worc*
QUEEN'S GATE (St Augustine) *see* S Kensington St Aug *Lon*
QUEEN'S PARK (St Barnabas) *see* Holdenhurst and Iford *Win*
QUEENSBURY (All Saints) *Lon 23* **P** *The Crown* **V** R M HILLS, **NSM** P A JONES
QUEENSBURY (Holy Trinity) *Bradf 2* **P** *Bp* **V** P A HEDGE
QUENDON (not known) *see* Manuden w Berden and Quendon w Rickling *Chelmsf*
QUENIBOROUGH (St Mary) *see* Syston *Leic*
QUENINGTON (St Swithun) *see* Coln St Aldwyns, Hatherop, Quenington etc *Glouc*
QUERNMORE (St Peter) *see* Dolphinholme w Quernmore and Over Wyresdale *Blackb*
QUETHIOCK (St Hugh) *see* St Ive and Pensilva w Quethiock *Truro*
QUIDENHAM Group, The (St Andrew) *Nor 11* **P** *Ld Chan (1 turn), Bp, Sir Thomas Beevor Bt, Major E H C Garnier, Trustees, and New Buckenham PCC (3 turns)* **R** C J DAVIDSON, **C** N P KINSELLA
QUINTET Group of Parishes *see* Cranborne w Boveridge, Edmondsham etc *Sarum*
QUINTON and PRESTON DEANERY (St John the Baptist) *see* Wootton w Quinton and Preston Deanery *Pet*
QUINTON (St Swithin) and Welford w Weston *Glouc 10* **P** *DBP and D&C Worc (jt)* **NSM** J Y CARMAN
QUINTON, THE (Christ Church) *Birm 2* **P** *Bp* **C** S C CARTER, R L HUGHES
QUINTON ROAD WEST (St Boniface) *Birm 2* **P** *Bp* **C** J P FFRENCH
QUORN (St Bartholomew) *see* Quorndon *Leic*
QUORNDON (St Bartholomew) *Leic 7* **P** *Bp* **V** D H BOWLER
QUY (St Mary) *see* Anglesey Gp *Ely*
RACKENFORD (All Saints) *see* Washfield, Stoodleigh, Withleigh etc *Ex*
RACKHEATH (Holy Trinity) and Salhouse *Nor 4* **P** *Bp* **P-in-c** R J SUTTON
RACTON (St Peter) *see* Compton, the Mardens, Stoughton and Racton *Chich*
RADBOURNE (St Andrew) *see* Boylestone, Church Broughton, Dalbury, etc *Derby*
RADCLIFFE (St Andrew) Black Lane *Man 14* **P** *R Radcliffe St Mary* **V** P N W GRAYSHON, **OLM** J BESWICK
RADCLIFFE (St Mary) (St Thomas and St John) (St Philip Mission Church) *Man 14* **P** *Patr Bd* **TR** C J C HEWITT, **TV** G WINDON, **NSM** M TRIVASSE
RADCLIFFE-ON-TRENT (St Mary) and Shelford w Holme Pierrepont and Adbolton *S'well 8* **P** *DBP (2 turns), Ld Chan (1 turn)* **R** N WESTON
RADCLIVE (St John the Evangelist) *see* Buckingham *Ox*
RADDESLEY Group of Parishes, The *Ely 4* **P** *E H Vestey Esq, Mrs B O Killander, Mrs B A Taylor, F R Egerton Esq, Exors C L Thomas (5 turns), St Jo Coll Cam (1 turn)* **R** D J COCKERELL
RADDINGTON (St Michael) *see* Wiveliscombe w Chipstable, Huish Champflower etc *B & W*
RADDON *see* Thorverton, Cadbury, Upton Pyne etc *Ex*
RADFORD (All Souls) w Christ Church and St Michael *S'well 13* **P** *Bp* **V** *vacant* 0115-978 5364
RADFORD (St Nicholas) *Cov 2* **P** *Bp* **V** G J MARCER
RADFORD (St Peter) *S'well 13* **P** *Bp* **P-in-c** D EDINBOROUGH
RADFORD, NORTH (St Francis of Assisi) *see* Cov St Fran N Radford *Cov*
RADFORD SEMELE (St Nicholas) *Cov 10* **P** *Bp* **P-in-c** M C GREEN
RADIPOLE (Emmanuel) (St Adhelm) (St Ann) and Melcombe Regis *Sarum 4* **P** *Patr Bd* **TR** K I HOBBS, **TV** T J GREENSLADE, P J SALMON, **C** D P HARKNETT, **NSM** P E LEGG
RADLETT (Christ Church) *see* Aldenham, Radlett and Shenley *St Alb*
RADLETT (St John) *as above*
RADLEY (St James the Great) and Sunningwell *Ox 10* **P** *Radley Coll and DBP (by turn)* **P-in-c** P J MCKELLEN
RADNAGE (St Mary) *see* W Wycombe w Bledlow Ridge, Bradenham and Radnage *Ox*
RADNOR, OLD (St Stephen) *see* Kington w Huntington, Old Radnor, Kinnerton etc *Heref*
RADSTOCK (St Nicholas) w Writhlington *B & W 12* **P** *Bp* **R** C P J TURNER
RADSTONE (St Lawrence) *see* Astwell Gp *Pet*

RADWAY (St Peter) *see* Warmington w Shotteswell and Radway w Ratley *Cov*
RADWELL (All Saints) *see* Stotfold and Radwell *St Alb*
RADWINTER (St Mary the Virgin) *see* The Sampfords and Radwinter w Hempstead *Chelmsf*
RAGDALE (All Saints) *see* Upper Wreake *Leic*
RAINBOW HILL (St Barnabas) *see* Worc St Barn w Ch Ch *Worc*
RAINFORD (All Saints) *Liv 11* **P** *V Prescot* **V** F R N MICHELL
RAINHAM (St Helen and St Giles) w Wennington *Chelmsf 2* **P** *MMCET* **C** R A DESICS
RAINHAM (St Margaret) *Roch 3* **P** *Bp* **V** A T VOUSDEN, **C** S M PATTLE
RAINHILL (St Ann) *Liv 10* **P** *Trustees* **V** N P ANDERSON
RAINOW (Holy Trinity) w Saltersford and Forest *Ches 13* **P** *Bp* **P-in-c** S D RATHBONE
RAINTON (not known) *see* Topcliffe, Baldersby w Dishforth, Dalton etc *York*
RAINTON, EAST (St Cuthbert) *Dur 14* **P** *D&C* **P-in-c** M L BECK
RAINTON, WEST (St Mary) *Dur 14* **P** *Bp* **P-in-c** M L BECK
RAINWORTH (St Simon and St Jude) *see* Blidworth w Rainworth *S'well*
RAITHBY (Holy Trinity) *see* Spilsby Gp *Linc*
RAITHBY (St Peter) *see* Legbourne and Wold Marsh *Linc*
RAME (St Germanus) *see* Maker w Rame *Truro*
RAMPISHAM (St Michael and All Angels) *see* Melbury *Sarum*
RAMPSIDE (St Michael) *see* Aldingham, Dendron, Rampside and Urswick *Carl*
RAMPTON (All Saints) *Ely 5* **P** *Bp* **R** G E TURNER
RAMPTON (All Saints) w Laneham, Treswell, Cottam and Stokeham *S'well 5* **P** *D&C York and The Crown (alt)* **P-in-c** M J LEATON, **NSM** F E M FERRITER
RAMSBOTTOM (St Andrew) *Man 10* **P** *Bp* **V** I M ROGERSON, **NSM** J W DAVIES
RAMSBOTTOM (St John) (St Paul) *Man 10* **P** *Prime Min and Bp (alt)* **V** J ARCUS
RAMSBURY (Holy Cross) *see* Whitton *Sarum*
RAMSDELL (Christ Church) *see* Baughurst, Ramsdell, Wolverton w Ewhurst etc *Win*
RAMSDEN (Church of Unity) *see* Orpington All SS *Roch*
RAMSDEN (St James), Finstock and Fawler, Leafield w Wychwood and Wilcote *Ox 3* **P** *Bp, V Charlbury, and Sir Mark Norman Bt (jt)* **V** J F KNOWLES, **NSM** B FORD, S C JONES
RAMSDEN BELLHOUSE (St Mary the Virgin) *see* Ramsden Crays w Ramsden Bellhouse *Chelmsf*
RAMSDEN CRAYS w Ramsden Bellhouse *Chelmsf 6* **P** *Reformation Ch Trust* **P-in-c** S HARDIE
RAMSDEN HEATH (St John) *see* Downham w S Hanningfield *Chelmsf*
RAMSEY (St Michael) *see* Harwich Peninsula *Chelmsf*
RAMSEY, NORTH (St Olave) *see* Lezayre St Olave Ramsey *S & M*
RAMSEY, SOUTH (St Paul) *S & M 3* **P** *Bp* **V** N D GREENWOOD, **OLM** B EVANS-SMITH
RAMSEY ST MARY'S (St Mary) *see* The Ramseys and Upwood *Ely*
RAMSEYS (St Thomas à Becket) (St Mary) and Upwood, The *Ely 9* **P** *Patr Bd* **TR** R A DARMODY, **C** S R SIMCOX
RAMSGATE (Christ Church) *Cant 9* **P** *Ch Patr Trust* **V** P F TIZZARD
RAMSGATE (Holy Trinity) (St George) *Cant 9* **P** *Abp* **R** P A ADAMS
RAMSGATE (St Luke) *Cant 9* **P** *CPAS* **V** P R WORLEDGE
RAMSGATE (St Mark) *Cant 9* **P** *CPAS* **V** C G SKINGLEY
RAMSGILL (St Mary) *see* Upper Nidderdale *Ripon*
RAMSHOLT (All Saints) *see* Wilford Peninsula *St E*
RANBY (St German) *see* Asterby Gp *Linc*
RANBY (St Martin) *see* Babworth w Sutton-cum-Lound and Scofton etc *S'well*
RAND (St Oswald) *see* Wragby Gp *Linc*
RANDWICK (St John the Baptist) *see* Whiteshill and Randwick *Glouc*
RANGEMORE (All Saints) *see* Hanbury w Newborough and Rangemore *Lich*
RANGEWORTHY (Holy Trinity) *see* Wickwar, Rangeworthy and Hillesley *Glouc*
RANMOOR (St John the Evangelist) *Sheff 4* **P** *Trustees* **V** D C KNIGHT, **C** F M ECCLESTON
RANMORE (St Barnabas) *see* Dorking w Ranmore *Guildf*
RANSKILL (St Barnabas) *see* Blyth and Scrooby w Ranskill *S'well*
RANTON (All Saints) *see* Derrington, Haughton and Ranton *Lich*
RANWORTH (St Helen) w Panxworth, Woodbastwick, South Walsham and Upton *Nor 4* **P** *Bp, Qu Coll Cam, and J Cator Esq (jt)* **R** P MCFADYEN
RASEN, WEST (All Saints) *see* Middle Rasen Gp *Linc*
RASHCLIFFE (St Stephen) *see* Em TM *Wakef*
RASKELF (St Mary) *see* Easingwold w Raskelf *York*
RASTRICK (St John the Divine) *Wakef 2* **P** *Bp* **P-in-c** J R BROADHURST
RASTRICK (St Matthew) *Wakef 2* **P** *V Halifax* **V** T L SWINHOE
RATBY (St Philip and St James) *see* Bradgate Team *Leic*
RATCLIFFE CULEY (All Saints) *see* Bosworth and Sheepy Gp *Leic*
RATCLIFFE-ON-SOAR (Holy Trinity) *see* Kingston and Ratcliffe-on-Soar *S'well*
RATCLIFFE ON THE WREAKE (St Botolph) *see* Syston *Leic*
RATHMELL (Holy Trinity) *see* Giggleswick and Rathmell w Wigglesworth *Bradf*
RATLEY (St Peter ad Vincula) *see* Warmington w Shotteswell and Radway w Ratley *Cov*
RATLINGHOPE (St Margaret) *see* Wentnor w Ratlinghope, Myndtown, Norbury etc *Heref*
RATTERY (Blessed Virgin Mary) *see* S Brent and Rattery *Ex*
RATTLESDEN (St Nicholas) w Thorpe Morieux, Brettenham and Hitcham *St E 10* **P** *Bp (3 turns), Ld Chan (1 turn)* **R** *vacant* (01449) 737993
RAUCEBY, NORTH (St Peter) *see* Ancaster Wilsford Gp *Linc*
RAUGHTON HEAD (All Saints) *see* Dalston w Cumdivock, Raughton Head and Wreay *Carl*
RAUNDS (St Peter) *Pet 10* **P** *Bp* **P-in-c** S M BELL
RAVENDALE, EAST (St Martin) *see* Laceby and Ravendale Gp *Linc*
RAVENFIELD (St James), Hooton Roberts and Braithwell *Sheff 6* **P** *Bp and Sir Philip Naylor-Leyland Bt (jt)* **V** M GREENLAND
RAVENGLASS (Mission Room) *see* Eskdale, Irton, Muncaster and Waberthwaite *Carl*
RAVENHEAD (St John) *see* Parr *Liv*
RAVENHEAD (St John the Evangelist) *Liv 10* **P** *V St Helens* **V** E R DORAN
RAVENINGHAM Group, The (St Andrew) *Nor 8* **P** *Bp, Adn Nor, Sir Nicholas Bacon Bt, Major C A Boycott, D&C, K Coll Cam, and DBP (jt)* **R** N J WILL
RAVENSCAR (St Hilda) *see* Cloughton and Burniston w Ravenscar etc *York*
RAVENSDEN (All Saints) *see* Wilden w Colmworth and Ravensden *St Alb*
RAVENSHEAD (St Peter) *S'well 4* **P** *Bp* **V** *vacant* (01623) 405203
RAVENSTHORPE (St Denys) *see* W Haddon w Winwick and Ravensthorpe *Pet*
RAVENSTHORPE (St Saviour) and Thornhill Lees w Savile Town *Wakef 10* **P** *Bp and V Mirfield (jt)* **V** N L STIMPSON
RAVENSTONE (All Saints) *see* Gayhurst w Ravenstone, Stoke Goldington etc *Ox*
RAVENSTONE (St Michael and All Angels) and Swannington *Leic 8* **P** *Ld Chan and V Whitwick (alt)* **R** *vacant* (01530) 839802
RAVENSTONEDALE (St Oswald) *see* Orton and Tebay w Ravenstonedale etc *Carl*
RAWCLIFFE (St James) *see* Airmyn, Hook and Rawcliffe *Sheff*
RAWCLIFFE (St Mark) *see* Clifton *York*
RAWCLIFFE BRIDGE (St Philip) *see* Airmyn, Hook and Rawcliffe *Sheff*
RAWDON (St Peter) *Bradf 4* **P** *Trustees* **V** C M MORRIS
RAWMARSH (St Mary the Virgin) w Parkgate *Sheff 6* **P** *Ld Chan* **R** J T BIRBECK
RAWMARSH (St Nicolas) *see* Ryecroft St Nic *Sheff*
RAWNSLEY (St Michael) *see* Hednesford *Lich*
RAWRETH (St Nicholas) w Rettendon *Chelmsf 12* **P** *Ld Chan and Pemb Coll Cam (alt)* **P-in-c** L C STEWARD
RAWTENSTALL (St Mary) *Man 15* **P** *CPAS* **V** G D PARKIN
RAWTHORPE (St James) *see* Moldgreen and Rawthorpe *Wakef*
RAY VALLEY, The *Ox 2* **P** *Trustees, Ex Coll Ox, and Piddington PCC (1 turn), D&C Westmr, Qu Coll Ox, and Walsingham Coll Trust Assn Ltd (1 turn)* **P-in-c** M P CARNEY, **C** S D LOCKETT, **NSM** D A R SODADASI
RAYDON (St Mary) *see* Higham, Holton St Mary, Raydon and Stratford *St E*
RAYLEIGH (Holy Trinity) (St Michael) *Chelmsf 12* **P** *Patr Bd* **TR** M J LODGE, **TV** J H E ROSKELLY
RAYNE (All Saints) *see* Panfield and Rayne *Chelmsf*
RAYNES PARK (St Saviour) *S'wark 14* **P** *Bp* **P-in-c** M O BLACKMAN

RAYNHAM, EAST (St Mary) *see* E w W Rudham, Helhoughton etc *Nor*
RAYNHAM, SOUTH (St Martin) *as above*
REACH (St Ethelreda and the Holy Trinity) *see* Burwell w Reach *Ely*
READ IN WHALLEY (St John the Evangelist) *Blackb 7* **P** *V Whalley* **V** A SOWERBUTTS
READING (All Saints) *Ox 15* **P** *Bp* **V** R H EVERETT
READING (Christ Church) *Ox 15* **P** *Bp* **V** D M WEST
READING Greyfriars (St James) *Ox 15* **P** *Ch Trust Fund Trust* **V** J A DE B WILMOT, **C** P J ANDREW, J M WESTALL
READING (Holy Trinity) *Ox 15* **P** *SMF* **V** D A PETERS, **C** C L CARD-REYNOLDS
READING (St Agnes w St Paul) (St Barnabas) *Ox 15* **P** *Bp* **R** R V ORR, **C** D M REID
READING (St Giles w St Saviour) *Ox 15* **P** *Bp* **R** M J G MELROSE
READING (St John the Evangelist and St Stephen) *Ox 15* **P** *Simeon's Trustees* **V** A R VIGARS, **NSM** S KNIGHT, A M MARSHALL, N H BENSON
READING (St Luke) (St Bartholomew) *Ox 15* **P** *Bp and V Reading St Giles (alt)* **V** N J HARDCASTLE, **C** R CHRISTOPHER, **NSM** B D E BLACKMAN, C F BLACKMAN
READING (St Mark) *Ox 15* **P** *Bp* **V** D A PETERS, **C** C L CARD-REYNOLDS
READING (St Mary the Virgin) (St Laurence) *Ox 15* **P** *Bp* **R** B SHENTON, **C** C I RUSSELL, **NSM** R M LITTLE
READING (St Matthew) *Ox 15* **P** *Bp* **P-in-c** J HUDSON, **NSM** P G GROSSE
REAPSMOOR (St John) *see* Longnor, Quarnford and Sheen *Lich*
REARSBY (St Michael and All Angels) *see* Syston *Leic*
RECULVER (St Mary the Virgin) and Herne Bay St Bartholomew *Cant 7* **P** *Abp* **V** R L HAWKES, **NSM** E A HAWKES, **OLM** B R NICHOLSON
RED HOUSE (St Cuthbert) *see* N Wearside *Dur*
RED POST *Sarum 6* **P** *Mrs V M Chattey, H W Plunkett-Ernle-Erle-Drax Esq, and Bp (by turn)* **P-in-c** J E WARING
REDBOURN (St Mary) *St Alb 8* **P** *Earl of Verulam* **V** D J SWAN
REDBROOK (St Saviour) *see* Newland and Redbrook w Clearwell *Glouc*
REDCAR (St Peter) *York 16* **P** *Trustees* **V** J C WEETMAN, **C** J C COWAN, **NSM** J S WATSON
REDCLIFFE BAY (St Nicholas) *see* Portishead *B & W*
REDCLIFFE WAY (St Mary the Virgin) *see* Bris St Mary Redcliffe w Temple etc *Bris*
REDDAL HILL (St Luke) *Worc 9* **P** *The Crown* **P-in-c** H C HANKE, **C** S R MITCHELL
REDDISH (St Elisabeth) *Man 3* **P** *Bp* **R** N D HAWLEY, **C** M J APPLEBY, **OLM** R C CRAVEN, H E EVANS
REDDISH (St Mary) *see* Heaton Reddish *Man*
REDDISH, NORTH (St Agnes) *Man 3* **P** *The Crown* **P-in-c** C E LARSEN
REDDITCH Christ the King *Worc 7* **P** *Patr Bd* **TR** M F BARTLETT, **TV** M DEW, P G HARRISON, **NSM** M WOODGATES
REDDITCH Holy Trinity *Worc 7* **P** *Patr Bd* **TR** A J SMITH, **TV** G DEW, **C** P A BARFORD
REDDITCH (St George) *see* Redditch H Trin *Worc*
REDDITCH (St Stephen) *as above*
REDE (All Saints) *see* Chevington w Hargrave, Chedburgh w Depden etc *St E*
REDENHALL (Assumption of the Blessed Virgin Mary), Harleston, Wortwell and Needham *Nor 10* **P** *Bp* **R** P MORRIS, **OLM** C HUDSON
REDFIELD (St Leonard) *see* E Bris St Ambrose and St Leon *Bris*
REDGRAVE cum Botesdale St Mary w Rickinghall *St E 16* **P** *P J H Wilson Esq* **R** C R NORBURN
REDHILL (Christ Church) *see* Wrington w Butcombe *B & W*
REDHILL (Holy Trinity) *S'wark 27* **P** *Simeon's Trustees* **V** G J JENKINS, **C** M J HOUGH, **NSM** H J COWAN
REDHILL (St John the Evangelist) (Meadvale Hall) *S'wark 27* **P** *Bp* **V** N J CALVER, **NSM** P H BRADSHAW
REDHILL (St Matthew) *S'wark 27* **P** *Bp* **V** A N TREDENNICK, **C** J F PERCIVAL
REDHORN *Sarum 16* **P** *Patr Bd* **TR** M B COLE, **TV** G D BAKER, **NSM** E P LORT-PHILLIPS
REDISHAM (St Peter) *see* Wainford *St E*
REDLAND (not known) *Bris 3* **P** *Ch Trust Fund Trust* **P-in-c** R P SYMMONS, **NSM** M K GOODMAN
REDLINGFIELD (St Andrew) *see* Stradbroke, Horham, Athelington and Redlingfield *St E*
REDLYNCH (St Mary) and Morgan's Vale *Sarum 10* **P** *DBF and V Downton (alt)* **P-in-c** F H GIMSON, **Hon C** L A LUNN
REDLYNCH (St Peter) *see* Bruton and Distr *B & W*
REDMARLEY D'ABITOT (St Bartholomew), Bromesberrow, Pauntley, Upleadon, Oxenhall, Dymock, Donnington, Kempley and Preston *Glouc 3* **P** *Pemb Coll Ox, Bp, R D Marcon Esq, and Miss C Daniel (jt)* **R** P PHILLIPS, **Hon C** J B LUMBY, **NSM** A W PERRY, P NEWING, **OLM** V G CHESTER
REDMARSHALL (St Cuthbert) *Dur 10* **P** *The Crown* **R** D M BROOKE
REDMILE (St Peter) *see* Vale of Belvoir Par *Leic*
REDMIRE (St Mary) *see* Aysgarth and Bolton cum Redmire *Ripon*
REDNAL (St Stephen the Martyr) *Birm 4* **P** *Bp* **V** P W THOMAS
REDRUTH (St Andrew) (St Euny) w Lanner and Treleigh *Truro 2* **P** *DBP* **TV** E C WOON
REED (St Mary) *see* Barkway, Reed and Buckland w Barley *St Alb*
REEDHAM (St John the Baptist) *see* Freethorpe, Wickhampton, Halvergate etc *Nor*
REEPHAM (St Mary) and Hackford w Whitwell and Kerdiston, Thurning w Wood Dalling and Salle *Nor 22* **P** *Bp, CCC Cam, Pemb Coll Cam, Trin Coll Cam, and Ch Soc Trust (jt)* **R** M D W PADDISON
REEPHAM (St Peter and St Paul) *see* S Lawres Gp *Linc*
REGENT'S PARK (Christ Church) *see* Munster Square Ch Ch and St Mary Magd *Lon*
REGENT'S PARK (St Mark) *Lon 16* **P** *D&C St Paul's* **V** P G BAKER, **Hon C** R F MCLAREN, D J H JONES
REGIL (St James Mission Church) *see* Winford w Felton Common Hill *B & W*
REIGATE (St Luke) w Doversgreen St Peter *S'wark 27* **P** *Bp* **P-in-c** M J H FOX
REIGATE (St Mark) *S'wark 27* **P** *Bp* **V** M WRIGHT
REIGATE (St Mary Magdalene) *S'wark 27* **P** *Trustees* **C** G E MCWATT, **NSM** D G O ROBINSON
REIGATE (St Peter) Conventional District *S'wark 26 vacant*
REIGATE (St Philip) *S'wark 27* **P** *Bp* **P-in-c** J P SCOTT, **OLM** E STANGHAN
REIGATE HEATH (not known) *see* Reigate St Mary *S'wark*
REIGHTON (St Peter) *see* Bempton w Flamborough, Reighton w Speeton *York*
REKENDYKE (St Jude) *Dur 15* **P** *The Crown and D&C* **V** A J BEALING, **C** P R BEALING
REMENHAM (St Nicholas) *see* Henley w Remenham *Ox*
REMPSTONE (All Saints) *see* E and W Leake, Stanford-on-Soar, Rempstone etc *S'well*
RENDCOMB (St Peter) *Glouc 11* **P** *Major M T N H Wills* **P-in-c** C D JEFFERSON
RENDHAM (St Michael) *see* Badingham w Bruisyard, Cransford etc *St E*
RENDLESHAM (St Gregory the Great) *see* Wilford Peninsula *St E*
RENHOLD (All Saints) *St Alb 10* **P** *MMCET* **P-in-c** C D BRADLEY
RENISHAW (St Matthew) *see* Barlborough and Renishaw *Derby*
RENNINGTON (All Saints) *see* Embleton w Rennington and Rock *Newc*
RENWICK (All Saints) *see* Kirkoswald, Renwick, Gt Salkeld and Lazonby *Carl*
REPPS (St Peter) *see* Martham and Repps with Bastwick, Thurne etc *Nor*
REPTON (St Wystan) *see* Foremark and Repton w Newton Solney *Derby*
RESTON, NORTH (St Edith) *see* Legbourne and Wold Marsh *Linc*
RETFORD (St Michael the Archangel) (St Saviour) (St Swithin) *S'well 5* **P** *Patr Bd* **TR** A C ST J WALKER, **TV** M A STAFFORD, **C** J STEPHENSON
RETTENDON (All Saints) *see* Rawreth w Rettendon *Chelmsf*
REVELSTOKE (St Peter) *see* Newton Ferrers w Revelstoke *Ex*
REVESBY (St Lawrence) *see* Mareham-le-Fen and Revesby *Linc*
REWE (St Mary the Virgin) *see* Stoke Canon, Poltimore w Huxham and Rewe etc *Ex*
REYDON (St Margaret) *see* Sole Bay *St E*
REYMERSTON (St Peter) *see* Barnham Broom and Upper Yare *Nor*
RHODES (All Saints) (St Thomas) *Man 18* **P** *R Middleton* **V** C A PELL, **OLM** A BROXTON
RHYDYCROESAU (Christ Church) *Lich 19* **P** *Bp* **R** D B CROWHURST
RIBBESFORD (St Leonard) w Bewdley and Dowles *Worc 11* **P** *E J Winnington-Ingram Esq* **R** K N JAMES, **Hon C** G D MORPHY

RIBBLETON (St Mary Magdalene) (St Anne's Church Centre) (Ascension) *Blackb 13* **P** *Patr Bd* **TR** N L STIMPSON, **TV** T B ENSOR, **C** D M OVERTON
RIBBY CUM WREA (St Nicholas) and Weeton St Michael *Blackb 10* **P** *V Kirkham* **V** J WIXON
RIBCHESTER (St Wilfred) w Stidd *Blackb 13* **P** *Bp* **R** J FRANCIS
RIBSTON, LITTLE (St Helen) *see* Spofforth w Kirk Deighton *Ripon*
RIBY (St Edmund) *see* Keelby Gp *Linc*
RICCALL (St Mary) *see* Barlby w Riccall *York*
RICHARDS CASTLE (All Saints) *see* Ludlow, Ludford, Ashford Carbonell etc *Heref*
RICHMOND (Holy Trinity and Christ Church) *S'wark 18* **P** *CPAS* **V** T H PATTERSON, **C** J C WATSON, **NSM** J F HARTERINK
RICHMOND (St Luke) *see* Kew St Phil and All SS w St Luke *S'wark*
RICHMOND (St Mary Magdalene) (St Matthias) (St John the Divine) *S'wark 18* **P** *K Coll Cam* **TR** M C J REINDORP, **TV** C F IRVINE, P J ASHWIN-SIEJKOWSKI, **NSM** N T SUMMERS, R C CARNEGIE
RICHMOND (St Mary w Holy Trinity) w Hudswell and Downholme and Marske *Ripon 2* **P** *Bp* **R** R T COOPER, **C** J E KEARTON, J K BALL
RICHMOND, EAST *Ripon 2* **P** *Patr Bd* **TR** A L GLASBY, **TV** D T LEWIS, **C** A J NICHOLSON, **NSM** G SMITH
RICHMOND HILL (All Saints) *see* Leeds All SS w Osmondthorpe *Ripon*
RICHMOND HILL (St Hilda) *see* Hunslet w Cross Green *Ripon*
RICHMOND HILL (St Saviour) *see* Leeds Richmond Hill *Ripon*
RICKERSCOTE (St Peter) *Lich 10* **P** *Bp and V Stafford St Paul (jt)* **NSM** G P BOTT
RICKINGHALL (St Mary) *see* Redgrave cum Botesdale w Rickinghall *St E*
RICKLING (All Saints) *see* Manuden w Berden and Quendon w Rickling *Chelmsf*
RICKMANSWORTH (St Mary the Virgin) *St Alb 5* **P** *Bp* **V** S R MEPHAM, **NSM** A P L SHAW
RIDDINGS (Holy Spirit) *see* Bottesford w Ashby *Linc*
RIDDINGS (St James) and Ironville *Derby 1* **P** *Wright Trustees and V Alfreton (jt)* **V** M A YATES
RIDDLESDEN (St Mary the Virgin) *Bradf 8* **P** *Bp* **P-in-c** P RUGEN
RIDDLESDOWN (St James) *S'wark 24* **P** *Bp* **P-in-c** C F SPURWAY, **C** F M LONG, **NSM** D J ROWLAND
RIDDLESWORTH (St Peter) *see* Guiltcross *Nor*
RIDGE (St Margaret) *see* S Mymms and Ridge *St Alb*
RIDGE, The *see* Redditch H Trin *Worc*
RIDGEWAY *Ox 19* **P** *DBP, CCC Ox, and Qu Coll Ox (jt)* **R** A WADGE
RIDGEWAY *Sarum 18* **P** *Patr Bd* **P-in-c** R R POWELL
RIDGEWAY (St John the Evangelist) *see* Eckington and Ridgeway *Derby*
RIDGEWELL (St Laurence) w Ashen, Birdbrook and Sturmer *Chelmsf 19* **P** *Duchy of Lanc, Bp, and DBP (by turn)* **R** M D HEWITT
RIDGMONT (All Saints) *see* Aspley Guise w Husborne Crawley and Ridgmont *St Alb*
RIDING MILL (St James) *Newc 3* **P** *Viscount Allendale* **P-in-c** C G LEWIS
RIDLEY (St Peter) *Roch 1* **P** *J R A B Scott Esq* **R** J A PEAL
RIDLINGTON (St Mary Magdalene and St Andrew) *see* Preston and Ridlington w Wing and Pilton *Pet*
RIDLINGTON (St Peter) *see* Bacton w Edingthorpe w Witton and Ridlington *Nor*
RIDWARES and Kings Bromley, The *Lich 1* **P** *Bp, Lord Leigh, and D&C (jt)* **P-in-c** T J LEYLAND, **C** J G LISTER, **NSM** D J SHERIDAN
RIEVAULX (St Mary) *see* Helmsley *York*
RIGSBY (St James) *see* Alford w Rigsby *Linc*
RIGTON, NORTH (St John) *see* Lower Wharfedale *Ripon*
RILLINGTON (St Andrew) *see* Buckrose Carrs *York*
RIMPTON (The Blessed Virgin Mary) *see* Chilton Cantelo, Ashington, Mudford, Rimpton etc *B & W*
RIMSWELL (St Mary) *see* Owthorne and Rimswell w Withernsea *York*
RINGLAND (St Peter) *see* Wensum Benefice *Nor*
RINGLEY (St Saviour) w Prestolee *Man 12* **P** *R Prestwich St Mary* **P-in-c** A ROACHE
RINGMER (St Mary the Virgin) *Chich 18* **P** *Abp* **V** W R PRATT, **C** A W N S CANE
RINGMORE (All Hallows) *see* Modbury, Bigbury, Ringmore w Kingston etc *Ex*
RINGSFIELD (All Saints) *see* Wainford *St E*
RINGSHALL (St Catherine) w Battisford, Barking w Darmsden and Great Bricett *St E 1* **P** *Bp, Ch Patr Trust, and J C W de la Bere Esq (jt)* **P-in-c** L E FLETCHER
RINGSTEAD (Nativity of the Blessed Virgin Mary) *see* Denford w Ringstead *Pet*
RINGSTEAD (St Andrew) *see* Hunstanton St Edm w Ringstead *Nor*
RINGSTONE IN AVELAND Group, The *Linc 13* **P** *Bp (2 turns), Baroness Willoughby de Eresby and Charterhouse (1 turn)* **P-in-c** G P WILLIAMS
RINGWAY Hale Barns (All Saints) *see* Hale Barns w Ringway *Ches*
RINGWOOD (St Peter and St Paul) *Win 9* **P** *K Coll Cam* **V** J R TURPIN, **C** J R EVANS
RINGWOULD (St Nicholas) w Kingsdown and Ripple w Sutton by Dover *Cant 8* **P** *Abp, Ch Patr Trust, and R S C Monins Esq (jt)* **R** S A FALLOWS, **OLM** P J HAMBROOK, A J WINN
RIPE (St John the Baptist) *see* Laughton w Ripe and Chalvington *Chich*
RIPLEY (All Saints) *Derby 12* **P** *Wright Trustees* **V** A C EDMUNDS, **C** J V TAYLOR, **NSM** C J GRAHAM
RIPLEY (All Saints) *Ripon 3* **P** *Sir Thomas Ingilby Bt* **P-in-c** S J BROWN
RIPLEY (St Mary) *Guildf 12* **P** *Bp* **V** C J ELSON
RIPON (Holy Trinity) *Ripon 3* **P** *Simeon's Trustees* **V** D MANN, **NSM** J A MONTGOMERY
RIPPINGALE (St Andrew) *see* Ringstone in Aveland Gp *Linc*
RIPPLE (St Mary) *see* Upton-on-Severn, Ripple, Earls Croome etc *Worc*
RIPPLE (St Mary the Virgin) *see* Ringwould w Kingsdown and Ripple etc *Cant*
RIPPONDEN (St Bartholomew) *Wakef 4* **P** *Bp and V Halifax (jt)* **V** D F HANDLEY, **Hon C** N SALT, **NSM** M JAMES
RISBOROUGH *Ox 21* **P** *Ld Chan (2 turns), Patr Bd (1 turn)* **TR** P F B FISKE, **TV** D E CRITCHELL, A F MEYNELL, **C** L M GIBBONS, **NSM** D R DEWICK, M S WITHERS, **OLM** M J SPENCE
RISBY (St Giles) *see* Barrow *St E*
RISE (All Saints) *see* Skirlaugh w Long Riston, Rise and Swine *York*
RISE PARK *see* Bestwood Park w Rise Park *S'well*
RISEHOLME (St Mary) *see* Nettleham *Linc*
RISELEY (All Saints) w Bletsoe *St Alb 15* **P** *MMCET* **V** *vacant* (01234) 708234
RISHTON (St Peter and St Paul) *Blackb 7* **P** *Trustees* **V** *vacant* (01254) 886191
RISHWORTH (St John) *see* Ripponden *Wakef*
RISLEY (All Saints) *see* Stanton-by-Dale w Dale Abbey and Risley *Derby*
RISSINGTON, GREAT (St John the Baptist) *see* Bourton-on-the-Water w Clapton etc *Glouc*
RISSINGTON, LITTLE (St Peter) *as above*
RITCHINGS PARK (St Leonard) *see* Iver *Ox*
RIVENHALL (St Mary the Virgin and All Saints) *Chelmsf 24* **P** *DBP* **R** *vacant* (01376) 511161
RIVER (St Peter and St Paul) *Cant 4* **P** *Abp* **R** S J BOWRING
RIVERHEAD (St Mary) w Dunton Green *Roch 9* **P** *R Sevenoaks and Bp (jt)* **V** P E FRANCIS
RIVERS Team Ministry, The *Sheff 6* **P** *Patr Bd* **TR** D M BENT, **TV** A T ISAACSON, M J LUNT, **C** S J GARDNER
RIVERSIDE: Colnbrook, Datchet, Dorney, Eton, Eton Wick, Horton, Wraysbury *Ox 23* **P** *Patr Bd* **TV** P A REYNOLDS, C S P DOUGLAS LANE, P W ABRAHAMS, **OLM** C DEAMER
RIVINGTON (not known) *see* Horwich and Rivington *Man*
ROADE (St Mary the Virgin) and Ashton w Hartwell *Pet 5* **P** *Ld Chan and Bp (alt)* **V** M J BURTON
ROADHEAD Kinkry Hill (Mission Room) *see* Bewcastle, Stapleton and Kirklinton etc *Carl*
ROADWATER (St Luke) *see* Old Cleeve, Leighland and Treborough *B & W*
ROBERTSBRIDGE (Mission Room) *see* Salehurst *Chich*
ROBERTTOWN (All Saints) w Hartshead *Wakef 8* **P** *V Birstall and TR Dewsbury (jt)* **P-in-c** D E CRAIG-WILD, **C** S J PITCHER, M J BULLIMORE
ROBOROUGH *see* Bickleigh and Shaugh Prior *Ex*
ROBOROUGH (St Peter) *see* Newton Tracey, Horwood, Alverdiscott etc *Ex*
ROBY (St Bartholomew) *Liv 2* **P** *Bp* **V** G S PEARSON, **C** G PINNINGTON
ROCESTER (St Michael) and Croxden w Hollington *Lich 15* **P** *Bp and Trustees (jt)* **V** E G WHITTAKER
ROCHDALE (St Chad) (St John the Divine) *Man 20* **P** *Bp* **TR** D B FOSS, **TV** D FINNEY, **NSM** I G KAY

ROCHDALE (St George w St Alban) *Man 20* **P** *Bp* **P-in-c** P D GULLY, **NSM** P R ZUCCA
ROCHDALE, SOUTH (St Mary) (St Luke) (St Peter) *Man 20* **P** *Patr Bd* **TR** J FARADAY, **TV** P J MAGUMBA, **C** F ADMAN
ROCHE (St Gomonda of the Rock) and Withiel *Truro 1* **P** *Bp and DBP (jt)* **NSM** E C DEELEY
ROCHESTER (St Justus) *Roch 5* **P** *Bp* **V** P T KERR
ROCHESTER (St Margaret) (St Peter's Parish Centre) *Roch 5* **P** *Bp and D&C (jt)* **V** G S COLVILLE
ROCHESTER ROW (St Stephen) *see* Westmr St Steph w St Jo *Lon*
ROCHFORD (St Andrew) *Chelmsf 12* **P** *Bp* **P-in-c** C W COUSINS, **NSM** J M HILL, L SAPWELL
ROCHFORD (St Michael) *see* Teme Valley S *Worc*
ROCK (St Peter and St Paul) *see* Mamble w Bayton, Rock w Heightington etc *Worc*
ROCK (St Philip and St James) *see* Embleton w Rennington and Rock *Newc*
ROCK FERRY (St Peter) *Ches 1* **P** *Bp* **V** P M FROGGATT
ROCKBEARE (St Mary w St Andrew) *see* Aylesbeare, Rockbeare, Farringdon etc *Ex*
ROCKBOURNE (St Andrew) *see* W Downland *Sarum*
ROCKCLIFFE (St Mary the Virgin) and Blackford *Carl 2* **P** *D&C* **P-in-c** J J VAN DEN BERG
ROCKHAMPTON (St Oswald) *see* Cromhall, Tortworth, Tytherington, Falfield etc *Glouc*
ROCKINGHAM (St Leonard) *see* Gretton w Rockingham and Cottingham w E Carlton *Pet*
ROCKLAND (All Saints) *see* Gt and Lt Ellingham, Rockland and Shropham etc *Nor*
ROCKLAND (St Peter) *as above*
ROCKLAND ST MARY (St Mary) with Hellington, Bramerton, Surlingham, Claxton, Carleton St Peter and Kirby Bedon w Whitlingham *Nor 8* **P** *Bp, Adn Nor, MMCET, and BNC Ox (jt)* **P-in-c** J B SHAW, **OLM** G D SAUNDERS, M ANSELL
RODBOROUGH (St Mary Magdalene) *Glouc 8* **P** *Bp* **R** *vacant* (01453) 764399
RODBOURNE (Holy Rood) *see* Gt Somerford, Lt Somerford, Seagry, Corston etc *Bris*
RODBOURNE CHENEY (St Mary) *Bris 7* **P** *CPAS* **R** N D J LINES
RODDEN (All Saints) *see* Beckington w Standerwick, Berkley, Rodden etc *B & W*
RODE, NORTH (St Michael) *see* Bosley and N Rode w Wincle and Wildboarclough *Ches*
RODE HEATH (Good Shepherd) *see* Odd Rode *Ches*
RODHUISH (St Bartholomew) *see* Dunster, Carhampton and Withycombe w Rodhuish *B & W*
RODING, HIGH (All Saints) *see* Gt Canfield w High Roding and Aythorpe Roding *Chelmsf*
RODING, HIGH (Mission Hall) *as above*
RODINGS, SOUTH *Chelmsf 18* **P** *Ld Chan, Bp, and Viscount Gough (by turn)* **R** T J PIGREM
RODINGTON (St George) *see* Wrockwardine Deanery *Lich*
RODLEY (Ecumenical Centre) *see* Bramley *Ripon*
RODLEY (Mission Church) *see* Westbury-on-Severn w Flaxley, Blaisdon etc *Glouc*
RODMARTON (St Peter) Conventional District *Glouc 11* **C-in-c** S G EMSON
RODMELL (St Peter) *see* Iford w Kingston and Rodmell *Chich*
RODMERSHAM (St Nicholas) *see* Tunstall w Rodmersham *Cant*
RODNEY STOKE (St Leonard) w Draycott *B & W 1* **P** *Bp* **P-in-c** S G PRICE
ROEHAMPTON (Holy Trinity) *S'wark 20* **P** *Bp* **V** J A MCKINNEY
ROFFEY (All Saints) *see* Roughey *Chich*
ROGATE (St Bartholomew) w Terwick and Trotton w Chithurst *Chich 10* **P** *Ld Chan* **R** E M DOYLE
ROGERS LANE (St Andrew's Chapel) *see* Stoke Poges *Ox*
ROKEBY (St Mary) *see* Startforth and Bowes and Rokeby w Brignall *Ripon*
ROKER (St Aidan) *see* Monkwearmouth *Dur*
ROLLESBY (St George) *see* Ormesby St Marg w Scratby, Ormesby St Mich etc *Nor*
ROLLESBY (St George) w Burgh w Billockby w Ashby w Oby, Thurne and Clippesby *Nor 6* **P** *Bp, R J H Tacon Esq, and DBP (jt)* **R** *vacant* (01493) 740323
ROLLESTON (Holy Trinity) w Fiskerton, Morton and Upton *S'well 15* **P** *Ld Chan* **P-in-c** S SPENCER
ROLLESTON (St John the Baptist) *see* Church Langton cum Tur Langton etc *Leic*
ROLLESTON (St Mary) *Lich 14* **P** *MMCET* **R** I R WHITEHEAD
ROLLRIGHT, GREAT (St Andrew) *see* Hook Norton w Gt Rollright, Swerford etc *Ox*
ROLLRIGHT, LITTLE (St Phillip) *see* Chipping Norton *Ox*
ROLVENDEN (St Mary the Virgin) *Cant 16* **P** *Abp* **P-in-c** J T M DESROSIERS
ROMALDKIRK (St Romald) w Laithkirk *Ripon 2* **P** *Bp and Earl of Strathmore's Trustees (alt)* **R** P S MIDWOOD
ROMANBY (St James) *see* Northallerton w Kirby Sigston *York*
ROMANSLEIGH (St Rumon) *see* S Molton w Nymet St George, High Bray etc *Ex*
ROMFORD (Ascension) Collier Row *Chelmsf 2* **P** *Trustees* **V** G P LAUT, **NSM** A BAXTER
ROMFORD (Good Shepherd) Collier Row *Chelmsf 2* **P** *CPAS* **V** R C SAMME, **C** H PRADELLA, **NSM** C A HILLS
ROMFORD (St Alban) *Chelmsf 2* **P** *Bp* **V** R S P HINGLEY
ROMFORD (St Andrew) (St Agnes) *Chelmsf 2* **P** *New Coll Ox* **R** R G FRIENDSHIP
ROMFORD (St Augustine) Rush Green *see* Rush Green *Chelmsf*
ROMFORD (St Edward the Confessor) *Chelmsf 2* **P** *New Coll Ox* **V** S J WAINE, **C** M K LAWRENCE, B C DENNIS, **NSM** A D PERRY
ROMFORD (St John the Divine) *Chelmsf 2* **P** *Bp* **P-in-c** S J WAINE
ROMILEY (St Chad) *see* Chadkirk *Ches*
ROMNEY, NEW (St Nicholas) w OLD (St Clement) and Midley *Cant 12* **P** *Abp* **P-in-c** M N DALE
ROMSEY (St Mary and St Ethelflaeda) *Win 12* **P** *Bp* **V** N C JONES, **C** T C HARLING, **NSM** D F WILLIAMS, B G TAPHOUSE
ROMSLEY (Mission Room) *see* Halas *Worc*
ROMSLEY (St Kenelm) *as above*
ROOKERY, THE (St Saviour) *see* Mow Cop *Lich*
ROOKHOPE (St John the Evangelist) *see* Upper Weardale *Dur*
ROOS (All Saints) and Garton in Holderness w Tunstall, Grimston and Hilston *York 12* **P** *Abp (1 turn), SMF (2 turns)* **P-in-c** G M SMETHURST
ROOSE (St Perran) *see* S Barrow *Carl*
ROPLEY (St Peter) *see* Bishop's Sutton and Ropley and W Tisted *Win*
ROPSLEY (St Peter) *Linc 14* **P** *Bp* **R** *vacant*
ROSE ASH (St Peter) *see* Bishopsnympton, Rose Ash, Mariansleigh etc *Ex*
ROSEDALE (St Lawrence) *see* Lastingham w Appleton-le-Moors, Rosedale etc *York*
ROSHERVILLE (St Mark) *see* Northfleet and Rosherville *Roch*
ROSLEY (Holy Trinity) *see* Westward, Rosley-w-Woodside and Welton *Carl*
ROSLISTON (St Mary) *see* Walton-on-Trent w Croxall, Rosliston etc *Derby*
ROSS Team Ministry, The (St Mary the Virgin) *Heref 8* **P** *DBP* **TR** J B HUNNISETT, **TV** A M GRIGOR, S J GEACH, **C** S J JONES
ROSSENDALE (St Anne) (St Nicholas w St John) Middle Valley *Man 15* **P** *Patr Bd* **TR** R BEVAN, **TV** S A DAVIES
ROSSENDALE (St Peter) *see* Laneside *Blackb*
ROSSENDALE (St Thomas) *see* Musbury *Blackb*
ROSSINGTON (St Michael) *Sheff 9* **P** *Bp* **R** A J LACEY, **C** A LAMB
ROSSINGTON, NEW (St Luke) *Sheff 9* **P** *Bp* **V** J P CARLISLE
ROSTHERNE (St Mary) w Bollington *Ches 12* **P** *C L S Cornwall-Legh Esq* **V** N D ROGERS
ROTHBURY (All Saints) *see* Upper Coquetdale *Newc*
ROTHERBY (All Saints) *see* Upper Wreake *Leic*
ROTHERFIELD (St Denys) w Mark Cross *Chich 19* **P** *Bp, Adn Lewes and Hastings, and Ch Patr Trust (jt)* **R** N F MASON
ROTHERFIELD GREYS (Holy Trinity) *see* Henley H Trin *Ox*
ROTHERFIELD GREYS (St Nicholas) *see* Nettlebed w Bix, Highmoor, Pishill etc *Ox*
ROTHERFIELD PEPPARD (All Saints) and Kidmore End and Sonning Common *Ox 6* **P** *Bp and Jes Coll Ox (jt)* **R** G D FOULIS BROWN, **Hon C** A B OLSEN, **NSM** H J WARWICK
ROTHERHAM (All Saints) *Sheff 6* **P** *Bp* **V** J E M SINCLAIR, **C** N R RAO
ROTHERHAM (St Paul) Ferham Park *see* Masbrough *Sheff*
ROTHERHITHE (Holy Trinity) *S'wark 7* **P** *R Rotherhithe St Mary* **V** A M DOYLE
ROTHERHITHE (St Katharine) *see* Bermondsey St Kath w St Bart *S'wark*
ROTHERHITHE (St Mary) w All Saints *S'wark 7* **P** *Clare Coll Cam* **R** C E N RICHARDS
ROTHERSTHORPE (St Peter and St Paul) *see* Bugbrooke w Rothersthorpe *Pet*
ROTHERWICK (not known) *see* Heckfield w Mattingley and Rotherwick *Win*

ROTHLEY (St Mary the Virgin and St John the Baptist) *Leic 6* **P** *MMCET* **V** R M GLADSTONE
ROTHWELL (Holy Trinity) *Ripon 8* **P** *Bp* **V** P R CRESSALL, **NSM** G W SELLERS
ROTHWELL (Holy Trinity) w Orton and Rushton w Glendon and Pipewell *Pet 11* **P** *Hosp of Jes (1 turn), Bp (2 turns), J Hipwell Esq (1 turn), and Mert Coll Ox (1 turn)* **R** G I BURGON, **NSM** R W SMITH
ROTHWELL (St Mary the Virgin) *see* Swallow *Linc*
ROTTINGDEAN (St Margaret) *Chich 2* **P** *Bp* **V** M P MORGAN
ROUGH CLOSE (St Matthew) *see* Meir Heath and Normacot *Lich*
ROUGH COMMON (St Gabriel) *see* Harbledown *Cant*
ROUGH HAY (St Christopher) *see* Darlaston St Lawr *Lich*
ROUGH HILLS (St Martin) *Lich 28* **P** *Bp* **V** J C OAKES
ROUGHAM (St Mary) *see* Gt w Lt Massingham, Harpley, Rougham etc *Nor*
ROUGHAM (St Mary), Beyton w Hessett and Rushbrooke *St E 10* **P** *Bp, MMCET (2 turns), and Ld Chan* **R** N CUTLER, **OLM** G B RENDLE
ROUGHEY or Roffey (All Saints) *Chich 8* **P** *Bp* **V** K R C AGNEW, **NSM** M YOUNG
ROUGHTON (St Margaret) *see* Thornton Gp *Linc*
ROUGHTON (St Mary) and Felbrigg, Metton, Sustead, Bessingham and Gunton w Hanworth *Nor 21* **P** *Bp and Exors G Whately Esq (jt)* **P-in-c** E C BAILEY, **OLM** M F THODAY
ROUGHTOWN (St John the Baptist) *Man 17* **P** *Bp* **P-in-c** G D ROBINSON
ROUNDHAY (St Edmund King and Martyr) *Ripon 5* **P** *Bp* **V** S C COWLING, **C** L J ASHTON, **NSM** S L LANCASTER
ROUNDHAY (St John the Evangelist) *Ripon 5* **P** *DBF* **P-in-c** C H CHEESEMAN
ROUNDS GREEN (St James) *Birm 7* **P** *V Langley* **P-in-c** P NYATSANZA
ROUNDSHAW (St Paul) Conventional District *S'wark 24 vacant*
ROUNDSWELL Conventional District *Ex 15* **C-in-c** K A ELLIOTT
ROUNTON, WEST (St Oswald) and East (St Laurence) w Welbury *York 19* **P** *Ld Chan* **P-in-c** A P WILSON
ROUS LENCH (St Peter) *see* Church Lench w Rous Lench and Abbots Morton etc *Worc*
ROUSHAM (St Leonard and St James) *Ox 2* **P** *C Cottrell-Dormer Esq* **V** *vacant*
ROUTH (All Saints) *York 8* **P** *Ch Soc Trust and Reformation Ch Trust (jt)* **P-in-c** D C BAILEY
ROWBARTON (St Andrew) *see* Taunton St Andr *B & W*
ROWBERROW (St Michael and All Angels) *see* Axbridge w Shipham and Rowberrow *B & W*
ROWDE (St Matthew) and Bromham *Sarum 16* **P** *DBP and S Spicer Esq (jt)* **R** J R J HISCOX
ROWENFIELD (Emmanuel) *see* Cheltenham St Mark *Glouc*
ROWINGTON (St Lawrence) *see* Hatton w Haseley, Rowington w Lowsonford etc *Cov*
ROWLAND LUBBOCK (Memorial Hall) *see* E Horsley and Ockham w Hatchford and Downside *Guildf*
ROWLANDS CASTLE (St John the Baptist) *Portsm 5* **P** *Bp* **P-in-c** D J LLOYD
ROWLANDS GILL (St Barnabas) *see* High Spen and Rowlands Gill *Dur*
ROWLEDGE (St James) and Frensham *Guildf 3* **P** *Adn Surrey and Ld Chan (alt)* **V** C J RICHARDSON, **Hon C** C D SEMPER, **NSM** N L DAVIES
ROWLESTONE (St Peter) *see* Ewyas Harold w Dulas, Kenderchurch etc *Heref*
ROWLEY (St Peter) w Skidby *York 8* **P** *Abp and N A C Hildyard Esq (jt)* **P-in-c** A BAILEY
ROWLEY REGIS (St Giles) *Birm 7* **P** *Ld Chan* **V** J B NIGHTINGALE, **C** P R G HINTON
ROWNER (St Mary the Virgin) *Portsm 3* **P** *R J F Prideaux-Brune Esq* **R** J W DRAPER, **C** J W FRANKS
ROWNEY GREEN (Mission Chapel) *see* Alvechurch *Worc*
ROWNHAMS (St John the Evangelist) *see* Nursling and Rownhams *Win*
ROWSLEY (St Katherine) *Derby 2* **P** *Duke of Rutland* **V** *vacant* (01629) 733296
ROWSTON (St Clement) *see* Digby Gp *Linc*
ROWTON (All Hallows) *see* Wrockwardine Deanery *Lich*
ROXBOURNE (St Andrew) *Lon 23* **P** *Bp* **V** C M RABLEN
ROXBY (St Mary) *see* Winterton Gp *Linc*
ROXBY (St Nicholas) *see* Hinderwell, Roxby and Staithes etc *York*
ROXETH (Christ Church) *Lon 23* **P** *Patr Bd* **TR** M S PHILPS, **TV** P S MACKENZIE, **C** S M NEWBOLD, **NSM** F A MEADOWS, B C COLLINS, R M ROGERS
ROXHOLME *see* Leasingham *Linc*
ROXTON (St Mary Magdalene) *see* Blunham, Gt Barford, Roxton and Tempsford etc *St Alb*
ROXWELL (St Michael and All Angels) *Chelmsf 8* **P** *New Coll Ox* **P-in-c** B R HOBSON
ROYDON (All Saints) *see* Grimston, Congham and Roydon *Nor*
ROYDON (St Peter) *Chelmsf 26* **P** *Earl Cowley* **P-in-c** C P PENNINGTON, **NSM** D RICKETTS
ROYDON (St Remigius) *Nor 10* **P** *DBP* **P-in-c** R J MELLOWSHIP
ROYSTON (St John the Baptist) *St Alb 19* **P** *Bp* **V** L D HARMAN, **C** A A LAUCKNER, **NSM** J H FIDLER
ROYSTON (St John the Baptist) *Wakef 7* **P** *Bp* **V** J L HUDSON, **C** J A BOOTH
ROYTON (St Anne) Longsight *Man 22* **P** *Bp* **P-in-c** K L JUSTICE, **OLM** D J HALFORD
ROYTON (St Paul) *Man 22* **P** *R Prestwich St Mary* **V** D BOOTH, **C** P HUTCHINS
RUAN LANIHORNE (St Rumon) *see* Veryan w Ruan Lanihorne *Truro*
RUAN MINOR (St Rumon) *see* St Ruan w St Grade and Landewednack *Truro*
RUARDEAN (St John the Baptist) *Glouc 4* **P** *Bp* **R** C T DAVIES, **OLM** W J CAMMELL
RUBERY (St Chad) *Birm 4* **P** *The Crown* **V** *vacant* 0121-453 3255
RUCKINGE (St Mary Magdalene) *see* Orlestone w Snave and Ruckinge w Warehorne etc *Cant*
RUCKLAND (St Olave) *see* S Ormsby Gp *Linc*
RUDBY IN CLEVELAND (All Saints) w Middleton *York 21* **P** *Abp* **V** D F LICKESS
RUDDINGTON (St Peter) *S'well 9* **P** *Simeon's Trustees* **V** *vacant* 0115-921 1505
RUDFORD (St Mary the Virgin) *see* Highnam, Lassington, Rudford, Tibberton etc *Glouc*
RUDGWICK (Holy Trinity) *Chich 8* **P** *Ld Chan* **V** R C JACKSON
RUDHAM, EAST and WEST (St Mary), Helhoughton, Houghton-next-Harpley, The Raynhams, Tatterford, and Tattersett *Nor 15* **P** *Bp, The Most Revd G D Hand, Marquess of Cholmondeley, and Marquess Townshend (jt)* **R** E L BUNDOCK
RUDHEATH (Licensed Room) *see* Witton *Ches*
RUDSTON (All Saints) w Boynton, Carnaby and Kilham *York 9* **P** *Ld Chan (1 turn), Abp (3 turns)* **V** S V COPE
RUFFORD (St Mary the Virgin) *Blackb 5* **P** *Bp* **R** J D BURNS
RUFFORTH (All Saints) w Moor Monkton and Hessay *York 1* **P** *MMCET and Abp (alt)* **R** J A RENDALL, **NSM** B H FRAY
RUGBY (Christ Church) *see* Brownsover *Cov*
RUGBY (St Andrew) (St George) (St John) (St Peter) (St Philip) *Cov 6* **P** *Bp* **TR** M H F BEACH, **TV** C C TURNER, O SIMON, **NSM** H F COCKELL
RUGBY (St Matthew) *Cov 6* **P** *Ch Trust Fund Trust* **V** M P SAXBY, **C** D A BROWN
RUGELEY (St Augustine) (Good Shepherd) *Lich 3* **P** *Patr Bd* **TR** M J NEWMAN, **TV** C M MASON, **NSM** C BEATSON, **OLM** J L BRITTLE
RUISHTON (St George) w Thornfalcon *B & W 18* **P** *Bp and Dr W R Chisholm-Batten (alt)* **V** *vacant* (01823) 442269
RUISLIP (St Martin) *Lon 24* **P** *D&C Windsor* **V** S EVANS, **C** M J S MCAULAY, **NSM** M A BEDFORD, S C SIMPKINS
RUISLIP (St Mary) *Lon 24* **P** *Bp* **V** N G T WHEELER
RUISLIP MANOR (St Paul) *Lon 24* **P** *Bp* **V** A C BALL, **NSM** B C ALLEN
RUMBURGH (St Michael and All Angels and St Felix) *see* S Elmham and Ilketshall *St E*
RUNCORN (All Saints) *Ches 3* **P** *Ch Ch Ox* **P-in-c** J H A HAYES, **NSM** M A HAYES
RUNCORN (Holy Trinity) *Ches 3* **P** *Bp* **P-in-c** J H A HAYES, **NSM** M A HAYES
RUNCORN (St John the Evangelist) Weston *Ches 3* **P** *Bp* **P-in-c** E M GARDNER
RUNCORN (St Michael and All Angels) *Ches 3* **P** *Bp* **P-in-c** V L SCHOFIELD
RUNCTON, NORTH (All Saints) *see* W Winch w Setchey, N Runcton and Middleton *Nor*
RUNCTON, SOUTH (St Andrew) *see* Holme Runcton w S Runcton and Wallington *Ely*
RUNCTON HOLME (St James) *as above*
RUNHALL (All Saints) *see* Barnham Broom and Upper Yare *Nor*
RUNHAM (St Peter and St Paul) *see* S Trin Broads *Nor*
RUNNINGTON (St Peter and St Paul) *see* Wellington and Distr *B & W*

RUNTON (Holy Trinity) *see* Aylmerton, Runton, Beeston Regis and Gresham *Nor*
RUNTON, EAST (St Andrew) *as above*
RUNWELL (St Mary) *see* Wickford and Runwell *Chelmsf*
RUSCOMBE (St James the Great) and Twyford *Ox 16* **P** *Bp* **P-in-c** S C HOWARD, **Hon C** T J DAKIN, **NSM** S DAKIN
RUSH GREEN (St Augustine) Romford *Chelmsf 2* **P** *Bp* **V** M D HOWSE
RUSHALL (Christ the King) (St Michael the Archangel) *Lich 25* **P** *Sir Andrew Buchanan Bt and H C S Buchanan Esq (jt)* **V** C R SUCH
RUSHALL (St Mary) *see* Dickleburgh and The Pulhams *Nor*
RUSHALL (St Matthew) *see* Upavon w Rushall and Charlton *Sarum*
RUSHBROOKE (St Nicholas) *see* Rougham, Beyton w Hessett and Rushbrooke *St E*
RUSHBURY (St Peter) *Heref 11* **P** *Bp Birm* **P-in-c** J GROVES
RUSHDEN (St Mary) *see* Sandon, Wallington and Rushden w Clothall *St Alb*
RUSHDEN (St Mary) w Newton Bromswold *Pet 10* **P** *CPAS* **R** B J MORRISON, **C** P R EVANS, **NSM** E J TYE
RUSHDEN (St Peter) *Pet 10* **P** *CPAS* **P-in-c** D J K WALLER
RUSHEN Christ Church (Holy Trinity) *S & M 1* **P** *The Crown* **V** N J COLE
RUSHEY MEAD (St Theodore of Canterbury) *see* Leic St Theodore *Leic*
RUSHFORD (St John the Evangelist) *see* E w W Harling, Bridgham w Roudham, Larling etc *Nor*
RUSHLAKE GREEN (Little St Mary) *see* Warbleton and Bodle Street Green *Chich*
RUSHMERE (St Andrew) *St E 4* **P** *Bp* **V** B WAKELING
RUSHMERE (St Michael) *see* Kessingland, Gisleham and Rushmere *Nor*
RUSHMOOR (St Francis) *see* Churt and Hindhead *Guildf*
RUSHOCK (St Michael) *see* Elmley Lovett w Hampton Lovett and Elmbridge etc *Worc*
RUSHOLME (Holy Trinity) *Man 4* **P** *CPAS* **R** A PORTER, **C** P R HORLOCK, **NSM** D A CLARK
RUSHTON (All Saints) *see* Rothwell w Orton, Rushton w Glendon and Pipewell *Pet*
RUSHTON SPENCER *see* Horton, Lonsdon and Rushton Spencer *Lich*
RUSKIN PARK (St Saviour) *see* Herne Hill *S'wark*
RUSKINGTON (All Saints) *Linc 22* **P** *DBP* **P-in-c** C PENNOCK
RUSLAND (St Paul) *see* Hawkshead and Low Wray w Sawrey and Rusland etc *Carl*
RUSPER (St Mary Magdalene) w Colgate *Chich 8* **P** *Mrs E C Calvert and Bp (alt)* **R** N A FLINT
RUSTHALL (St Paul) (St Paul's Mission Church) *Roch 12* **P** *R Speldhurst* **V** R E WHYTE
RUSTINGTON (St Peter and St Paul) *Chich 1* **P** *Bp* **V** Z E ALLEN
RUSTON, SOUTH *see* Tunstead w Sco' Ruston *Nor*
RUSTON PARVA (St Nicholas) *see* Burton Agnes w Harpham and Lowthorpe etc *York*
RUSWARP (St Bartholomew) *see* Whitby w Aislaby and Ruswarp *York*
RUYTON XI TOWNS (St John the Baptist) w Great Ness and Little Ness *Lich 17* **P** *Bp and Guild of All So (jt) and Ld Chan (alt)* **P-in-c** L FOSTER, **OLM** J M BAKER
RYAL (All Saints) *see* Stamfordham w Matfen *Newc*
RYARSH (St Martin) *see* Birling, Addington, Ryarsh and Trottiscliffe *Roch*
RYBURGH, GREAT (St Andrew) *see* Upper Wensum Village Gp *Nor*
RYDAL (St Mary) *Carl 11* **P** *Bp* **V** C J BUTLAND
RYDE (All Saints) *Portsm 7* **P** *Bp* **V** J F REDVERS HARRIS, **NSM** E W BUTCHER, T I CARD
RYDE (Holy Trinity) *Portsm 7* **P** *Bp* **V** M F JONES
RYDE (St James) Proprietary Chapel *Portsm 7* **P** *Ch Soc Trust* **C-in-c** J H A LEGGETT
RYDE (St John the Baptist) *see* Oakfield St Jo *Portsm*
RYE (St Mary the Virgin) *Chich 20* **P** *Patr Bd* **TR** H M MOSELEY, **TV** P CLARK, **NSM** L E MURDOCH, J G DAVENPORT
RYE HARBOUR (Holy Spirit) *see* Rye *Chich*
RYE PARK (St Cuthbert) *St Alb 20* **P** *DBP* **P-in-c** A F BURFORD
RYECROFT (St Nicolas) Rawmarsh *Sheff 6* **P** *Bp* **V** T A PARKINSON
RYEDALE, UPPER *York 17* **P** *Abp, Adn Cleveland, Sir Richard Beckett Bt, and Sir George Wombwell Bt (jt)* **P-in-c** D COLEMAN
RYHALL (St John the Evangelist) w Essendine and Carlby *Pet 8* **P** *Burghley Ho Preservation Trust* **V** P J MCKEE
RYHILL (St James) *Wakef 9* **P** *Bp* **P-in-c** P A BOSTOCK
RYHOPE (St Paul) *Dur 16* **P** *Bp* **V** *vacant* 0191-521 0238
RYLSTONE (St Peter) *see* Burnsall w Rylstone *Bradf*
RYME INTRINSECA (St Hypolytus) *see* Wriggle Valley *Sarum*
RYPE (St John the Baptist) *see* Laughton w Ripe and Chalvington *Chich*
RYSTON (St Michael) *see* Denver and Ryston w Roxham and W Dereham etc *Ely*
RYTHER (All Saints) *see* Cawood w Ryther and Wistow *York*
RYTON (Holy Cross) *Dur 13* **P** *Bp* **R** T L JAMIESON
RYTON (Mission Chapel) *see* Condover w Frodesley, Acton Burnell etc *Heref*
RYTON (St Andrew) *see* Beckbury, Badger, Kemberton, Ryton, Stockton etc *Lich*
RYTON ON DUNSMORE (St Leonard) *see* Baginton w Bubbenhall and Ryton-on-Dunsmore *Cov*
SABDEN (St Nicholas) and Pendleton-in-Whalley (All Saints) *Blackb 7* **P** *Bp and Trustees (jt)* **P-in-c** T VAUGHAN
SACKLETON (St George the Martyr) *see* The Street Par *York*
SACOMBE (St Catherine) *see* The Mundens w Sacombe *St Alb*
SACRISTON (St Peter) *see* Dur N *Dur*
SADBERGE (St Andrew) *Dur 8* **P** *Bp* **R** P S D NEVILLE
SADDINGTON (St Helen) *see* Kibworth and Smeeton Westerby and Saddington *Leic*
SADDLEWORTH (St Chad) *Man 21* **P** *Patr Bd* **TR** S F BRANDES, **TV** J R BROCKLEHURST, W NESBITT, **Hon C** G K TIBBO, **NSM** A KERR, R WHYBORN, S A HARRISON, **OLM** G B ADAMS, D RHODES
SAFFRON WALDEN (St Mary) w Wendens Ambo, Littlebury, Ashdon and Hadstock *Chelmsf 22* **P** *Patr Bd* **TR** D J GREEN, **TV** M THOMPSON, **C** L P BATSON, **NSM** M J B LOVEGROVE, H M DAVEY, C P WARREN
SAHAM TONEY (St George) *see* Ashill w Saham Toney *Nor*
ST AGNES (St Agnes) *see* Is of Scilly *Truro*
ST AGNES (St Agnes) and Mithian w Mount Hawke *Truro 6* **P** *Bp and D&C (alt)* **V** A G BASHFORTH, **C** P G WIGNALL, **NSM** H L SAMSON
ST ALBANS (Christ Church) *St Alb 6* **P** *Trustees* **V** J M FOLLETT
ST ALBANS (St Luke) *St Alb 6* **P** *DBP* **V** M A SLATER
ST ALBANS (St Mary) Marshalswick *St Alb 6* **P** *Bp* **V** C M DAVEY, **NSM** A J T HINKSMAN
ST ALBANS (St Michael) *St Alb 6* **P** *Earl of Verulam* **V** T M BEAUMONT, **NSM** J A HAYTON
ST ALBANS (St Paul) *St Alb 6* **P** *V St Alb St Pet* **V** A R HURLE, **C** J L W HOOKWAY, **Hon C** G M ABBOTT, **NSM** L M HURLE
ST ALBANS (St Peter) *St Alb 6* **P** *The Crown* **V** D J BRENTNALL
ST ALBANS (St Saviour) *St Alb 6* **P** *Bp* **V** P R WADSWORTH, **NSM** M R MUGAN
ST ALBANS (St Stephen) *St Alb 6* **P** *J N W Dudley Esq* **V** D RIDGEWAY, **C** R C PYKE, **NSM** G I KEIR
ST ALLEN (St Alleyne) *see* Kenwyn w St Allen *Truro*
ST ANNES-ON-THE-SEA (St Anne) Heyhouses *Blackb 10* **P** *J C Hilton Esq* **V** D M PORTER, **C** K J FENTON
ST ANNES-ON-THE-SEA (St Margaret of Antioch) *Blackb 10* **P** *Bp* **V** A R HODGSON
ST ANNES-ON-THE-SEA (St Thomas) *Blackb 10* **P** *J C Hilton Esq* **V** P D LAW-JONES
ST ANTHONY-IN-MENEAGE (St Anthony) *see* Manaccan w St Anthony-in-Meneage and St Martin *Truro*
ST AUSTELL (Holy Trinity) *Truro 1* **P** *The Crown* **V** D P WHITE, **C** P H BAMBER
ST BEES (St Mary and St Bega) *Carl 5* **P** *Trustees* **V** P R BRYAN
ST BLAZEY (St Blaise) *Truro 1* **P** *Bp* **V** F M BOWERS, **C** S D MICHAEL
ST BREOKE (St Breoke) and Egloshayle in Wadebridge *Truro 10* **P** *Bp and DBP (jt)* **P-in-c** T COTTON, **NSM** V R FLEMING
ST BREWARD (St Breward) *see* Blisland w St Breward *Truro*
ST BRIAVELS (St Mary the Virgin) w Hewelsfield *Glouc 4* **P** *D&C Heref* **P-in-c** R J M GROSVENOR, **C** N R BROMFIELD
ST BUDEAUX *see* Devonport St Budeaux *Ex*
ST BURYAN (St Buriana), St Levan and Sennen *Truro 5* **P** *Duchy of Cornwall* **OLM** C M JAGO
ST CLEER (St Clarus) *Truro 12* **P** *Ld Chan* **P-in-c** K LANYON JONES
ST CLEMENT (St Clement) *see* Truro St Paul and St Clem *Truro*
ST CLEMENT DANES *see* St Mary le Strand w St Clem Danes *Lon*
ST CLETHER (St Clederus) *see* Altarnon w Bolventor, Laneast and St Clether *Truro*

ST COLAN (St Colan) *see* St Columb Minor and St Colan *Truro*
ST COLUMB MAJOR (St Columba) w St Wenn *Truro 7* **P** *Bp* **P-in-c** F T SURRIDGE
ST COLUMB MINOR (St Columba) and St Colan *Truro 7* **P** *Bp* **P-in-c** C C MCQUILLEN-WRIGHT
ST DECUMANS (St Decuman) *B & W 17* **P** *Bp* **V** D C IRESON
ST DENNIS (St Denys) *Truro 1* **P** *Bp* **P-in-c** T J RUSS
ST DEVEREUX (St Dubricius) *see* Ewyas Harold w Dulas, Kenderchurch etc *Heref*
ST DOMINIC (St Dominica), Landulph and St Mellion w Pillaton *Truro 11* **P** *D&C and Trustees Major J Coryton, Duchy of Cornwall, and SMF (by turn)* **R** P R J LAMB
ST EDMUND WAY *St E 10* **P** *Bp, Mrs J Oakes, and Lord de Saumarez* **R** M C THROWER, **C** R W JAMES
ST EDMUNDS Anchorage Lane Conventional District *Sheff 7* **C-in-c** M J ROWBERRY
ST ENDELLION (St Endelienta) w Port Isaac and St Kew *Truro 10* **P** *Bp* **R** M G BARTLETT, **NSM** J POLLINGER
ST ENODER (St Enoder) *Truro 7* **P** *Bp* **P-in-c** P A ROBSON, **OLM** J PRATT
ST ENODOC (St Enodoc) *see* St Minver *Truro*
ST ERME (St Hermes) *see* Probus, Ladock and Grampound w Creed and St Erme *Truro*
ST ERNEY (St Erney) *see* Landrake w St Erney and Botus Fleming *Truro*
ST ERTH (St Erth) *see* Godrevy *Truro*
ST ERVAN (St Ervan) *see* St Mawgan w St Ervan and St Eval *Truro*
ST EVAL (St Uvelas) *as above*
ST EWE (All Saints) *see* St Mewan w Mevagissey and St Ewe *Truro*
ST GENNYS (St Gennys), Jacobstow w Warbstow and Treneglos *Truro 8* **P** *Bp and Earl of St Germans (jt)* **P-in-c** R C W DICKENSON
ST GEORGE-IN-THE-EAST (St Mary) *Lon 7* **P** *Bp* **V** P MCGEARY
ST GEORGE-IN-THE-EAST w St Paul *Lon 7* **P** *Bp* **R** *vacant* (020) 7481 1345
ST GEORGES (St George) *see* Priors Lee and St Georges *Lich*
ST GERMANS (St Germans of Auxerre) *Truro 11* **P** *D&C Windsor* **P-in-c** A I JOHNSTON, **OLM** J M LOBB
ST GILES-IN-THE-FIELDS *Lon 3* **P** *Bp* **R** W M JACOB, **C** J E DAVIES
ST GILES-IN-THE-HEATH (St Giles) *see* Boyton, N Tamerton, Werrington etc *Truro*
ST GILES IN THE WOOD (St Giles) *see* Newton Tracey, Horwood, Alverdiscott etc *Ex*
ST GLUVIAS (St Gluvias) *Truro 3* **P** *Bp* **V** J HARRIS
ST GORAN (St Goranus) w Caerhays *Truro 1* **P** *Bp* **P-in-c** D J ALLAN
ST HELENS (St Helen) (Barton Street Mission) (St Andrew) *Liv 10* **P** *Trustees* **TV** C R SMITH, **P-in-c** C S WOODS, **C** V E HUGHES
ST HELENS (St Helen) (St Catherine by the Green) *Portsm 7* **P** *Bp* **V** M M STRANGE
ST HELENS (St Mark) *Liv 10* **P** *Trustees* **V** A J HASLAM
ST HELENS (St Matthew) Thatto Heath *Liv 10* **P** *Bp* **V** P D RATTIGAN
ST HELIER (St Peter) (Bishop Andrewes Church) *S'wark 25* **P** *Bp* **P-in-c** D M WEBB, **OLM** L V WELLS
ST HILARY (St Hilary) *see* Ludgvan, Marazion, St Hilary and Perranuthnoe *Truro*
ST ILLOGAN (St Illogan) *Truro 2* **P** *Ch Soc Trust* **R** M J KIPPAX, **C** M J FIRBANK, Y M HOBSON, **NSM** P I TREMELLING
ST IPPOLYTS (St Ippolyts) *St Alb 4* **P** *Bp* **P-in-c** I S TATTUM
ST ISSEY (St Issey) w St Petroc Minor *Truro 7* **P** *Keble Coll Ox* **P-in-c** J M WILKINSON
ST IVE (St Ive) and Pensilva w Quethiock *Truro 12* **P** *Bp (1 turn), The Crown (2 turns)* **C** P J CONWAY, K LANYON JONES
ST IVES (All Saints) *Ely 9* **P** *Guild of All So* **V** J S PULLEN
ST IVES (St Ia the Virgin) *Truro 5* **P** *V Lelant* **V** A N COUCH, **C** M A J DAVIES
ST JOHN (St John the Baptist) w Millbrook *Truro 11* **P** *Bp and Col Sir John Carew-Pole Bt (alt)* **P-in-c** T E THOMAS
ST JOHN-AT-HACKNEY *Lon 5* **P** *Bp, Adn, and Lord Amherst of Hackney (jt)* **V** J S PRIDMORE, **NSM** J M KING
ST JOHN IN BEDWARDINE (St John the Baptist) *Worc 3* **P** *D&C* **V** C PULLIN, **C** D J ARNOLD
ST JOHN IN WEARDALE (St John the Baptist) *see* Upper Weardale *Dur*
ST JOHN LEE (St John of Beverley) *Newc 4* **P** *Viscount Allendale* **R** R C CUTLER, **NSM** A R CURRIE
ST JOHN ON BETHNAL GREEN *Lon 7* **P** *Patr Bd* **TR** A J E GREEN, **NSM** R R R O'CALLAGHAN
ST JOHN'S-IN-THE-VALE (St John), St Mary's Threlkeld and Wythburn *Carl 6* **P** *Bp, Adn, V Crosthwaite, and Earl of Londsale (jt)* **R** B ROTHWELL
ST JOHN'S WOOD (St John) *Lon 4* **P** *Bp* **V** A K BERGQUIST, **C** G A D PLATTEN
ST JOHN'S WOOD (St Mark) *see* St Marylebone St Mark Hamilton Terrace *Lon*
ST JULIOT (St Julitta) *see* Boscastle w Davidstow *Truro*
ST JUST IN PENWITH (St Just) *Truro 5* **P** *Ld Chan* **V** S W LEACH
ST JUST-IN-ROSELAND (St Just) and St Mawes *Truro 6* **P** *A M J Galsworthy Esq* **P-in-c** J G SLEE
ST KEVERNE (St Keverne) *Truro 4* **P** *CPAS* **P-in-c** T ST J HAWKINS, **C** L A H COURTNEY
ST KEW (St James the Great) *see* St Endellion w Port Isaac and St Kew *Truro*
ST KEYNE (St Keyna) *see* Liskeard and St Keyne *Truro*
ST LAURENCE in the Isle of Thanet (St Laurence) *Cant 9* **P** *Patr Bd* **TR** S IRELAND, **TV** G B GRIFFITHS, **NSM** D VAN K VANNERLEY
ST LAWRENCE (Old Church) (St Lawrence) *Portsm 7* **P** *Bp* **P-in-c** M M SLATTERY
ST LAWRENCE (St Lawrence) *Chelmsf 10* **P** *Bp* **R** *vacant*
ST LEONARD (St Leonard) *see* Hawridge w Cholesbury and St Leonard *Ox*
ST LEONARDS and St Ives (All Saints) *Win 9* **P** *Bp* **V** D L GRACE
ST LEONARDS (Christ Church and St Mary Magdalen) *Chich 17* **P** *Bp and Trustees (jt)* **P-in-c** R A JUPP, **C** A J HOMER, **NSM** R G RALPH
ST LEONARDS, UPPER (St John the Evangelist) *Chich 17* **P** *Trustees* **R** A J PERRY
ST LEONARDS-ON-SEA (St Ethelburga) *Chich 17* **P** *Hyndman Trustees* **P-in-c** M J MILLS, **C** V G DOIDGE
ST LEONARDS-ON-SEA (St Leonard) *Chich 17* **P** *Hyndman Trustees* **P-in-c** M J MILLS, **Hon C** W D BOULTON
ST LEONARDS-ON-SEA (St Matthew) *see* Silverhill St Matt *Chich*
ST LEONARDS-ON-SEA (St Peter and St Paul) *Chich 17* **P** *Bp* **V** A P-A BROWN
ST LEVAN (St Levan) *see* St Buryan, St Levan and Sennen *Truro*
ST MABYN (St Mabena) *see* St Tudy w St Mabyn and Michaelstow *Truro*
ST MARGARET'S (St Margaret) *see* Clodock and Longtown w Craswall, Llanveynoe etc *Heref*
ST MARGARETS-AT-CLIFFE (St Margaret of Antioch) w Westcliffe and East Langdon w West Langdon *Cant 4* **P** *Abp* **V** A M DURKIN
ST MARGARET'S-ON-THAMES (All Souls) *Lon 11* **P** *Bp* **P-in-c** R S FRANK
ST MARTHA-ON-THE-HILL (St Martha) *see* Guildf Ch Ch w St Martha-on-the-Hill *Guildf*
ST MARTIN (St Martin) w Looe St Nicholas *Truro 12* **P** *Bp and Revd W M M Picken (jt)* **R** B A MCQUILLEN, **OLM** M A TUBBS
ST MARTIN-IN-MENEAGE (St Martin) *see* Manaccan w St Anthony-in-Meneage and St Martin *Truro*
ST MARTIN-IN-THE-FIELDS *Lon 3* **P** *Bp* **V** N R HOLTAM, **C** E L GRIFFITHS, R J LAIN-PRIESTLEY, E M V RUSSELL, **NSM** A HURST
ST MARTIN'S (St Martin) *Lich 19* **P** *Lord Trevor* **V** W J WEBB
ST MARTIN'S (St Martin) *see* Is of Scilly *Truro*
ST MARY ABBOTS *see* Kensington St Mary Abbots w St Geo *Lon*
ST MARY-AT-LATTON Harlow *Chelmsf 26* **P** *J L H Arkwright Esq* **V** S CONLON, **C** N R TAYLOR
ST MARY BOURNE (St Peter) *see* Hurstbourne Priors, Longparish etc *Win*
ST MARY CRAY and St Paul's (St Paulinus) Cray *Roch 16* **P** *Bp* **V** S R BIGGS
ST MARY LE STRAND w St Clement Danes *Lon 3* **P** *Ld Chan and Burley Ho Preservation Trust (alt)* **R** W D F GULLIFORD, **Hon C** J F A FARRANT
ST MARYCHURCH (St Mary the Virgin) *Ex 12* **P** *D&C* **V** D LASHBROOKE, **C** R T SILK
ST MARYLEBONE (All Saints) *Lon 4* **P** *Bp* **V** L A MOSES, **C** I D AQUILINA, **Hon C** J B GASKELL
ST MARYLEBONE (All Souls) *see* Langham Place All So *Lon*
ST MARYLEBONE (Annunciation) Bryanston Street *Lon 4* **P** *Bp* **V** M W BURGESS
ST MARYLEBONE (St Cyprian) *Lon 4* **P** *Bp* **P-in-c** C R GOWER, **Hon C** S B CATHIE

ST MARYLEBONE (St Mark) Hamilton Terrace *Lon 4* **P** *The Crown* **V** J A BARRIE
ST MARYLEBONE (St Mark w St Luke) *see* Bryanston Square St Mary w St Marylebone St Mark *Lon*
ST MARYLEBONE (St Marylebone) (Holy Trinity) *Lon 4* **P** *The Crown* **R** C R GOWER, **Hon C** S B CATHIE, **NSM** R C D MACKENNA
ST MARYLEBONE (St Paul) *Lon 4* **P** *Prime Min* **R** G M BUCKLE
ST MARYLEBONE (St Peter) *see* Langham Place All So *Lon*
ST MARY'S (St Mary) *see* Is of Scilly *Truro*
ST MARY'S BAY (All Saints) w St Mary-in-the-Marsh (St Mary the Virgin) and Ivychurch *Cant 12* **P** *Abp* **P-in-c** M N DALE
ST MAWES (St Mawes) *see* St Just-in-Roseland and St Mawes *Truro*
ST MAWGAN (St Mawgan) w St Ervan and St Eval *Truro 7* **P** *D&C and Bp (alt)* **P-in-c** G F SHIELD
ST MELLION (St Melanus) *see* St Dominic, Landulph and St Mellion w Pillaton *Truro*
ST MERRYN (St Merryn) *Truro 7* **P** *Bp* **P-in-c** J M WILKINSON
ST MEWAN (St Mewan) w Mevagissey and St Ewe *Truro 1* **P** *Bp, DBP, Penrice Ho (St Austell) Ltd, and A M J Galsworthy Esq (jt)* **R** M L BARRETT
ST MICHAEL PENKEVIL (St Michael) *Truro 6* **P** *Viscount Falmouth* **P-in-c** A M YATES
ST MICHAEL ROCK (St Michael) *see* St Minver *Truro*
ST MICHAELCHURCH (St Michael) *see* Alfred Jewel *B & W*
ST MICHAELS-ON-WYRE (St Michael) *see* Garstang St Helen and St Michaels-on-Wyre *Blackb*
ST MINVER (St Menefreda) *Truro 10* **P** *DBP* **P-in-c** R F LAW
ST NECTAN (St Nectan) *see* Lostwithiel, St Winnow w St Nectan's Chpl etc *Truro*
ST NEOT (St Neot) and Warleggan w Cardynham *Truro 12* **P** *R G Grylls Esq (2 turns), J Coode Esq (1 turn), and DBP (1 turn)* **R** A C R BALFOUR
ST NEOTS (St Mary) *Ely 10* **P** *P W Rowley Esq* **V** R H W ARGUILE, **C** M E MARSHALL, **Hon C** T R HENTHORNE
ST NEWLYN EAST (St Newlina) *see* Newlyn St Newlyn *Truro*
ST NICHOLAS (St Nicholas) *see* Shaldon, Stokeinteignhead, Combeinteignhead etc *Ex*
ST NICHOLAS AT WADE (St Nicholas) w Sarre and Chislet w Hoath *Cant 7* **P** *Abp* **P-in-c** R R COLES, **Hon C** P J RICHMOND, **NSM** R D PLANT
ST OSWALD IN LEE w Bingfield (St Mary) *Newc 2* **P** *Bp* **P-in-c** C S PRICE, **NSM** C F BULL
ST OSYTH (St Peter and St Paul) *Chelmsf 23* **P** *Bp* **V** M J FLOWERDEW
ST PANCRAS (Holy Cross) (St Jude) (St Peter) *Lon 17* **P** *Bp* **P-in-c** P W LEWIS, **NSM** R W NORWOOD
ST PANCRAS (Holy Trinity) *see* Kentish Town St Silas and H Trin w St Barn *Lon*
ST PANCRAS (Old Church) *Lon 17* **P** *Patr Bd* **TR** N P WHEELER, **TV** R J WICKHAM, **C** B BATSTONE, **NSM** J I ELSTON
ST PANCRAS (St Martin) *see* Kentish Town St Martin w St Andr *Lon*
ST PANCRAS (St Pancras) (St James) (Christ Church) *Lon 17* **P** *D&C St Paul's* **V** P H W HAWKINS, **C** E V DANDO, **Hon C** R I T JARRETT
ST PAUL'S CRAY (St Barnabas) *Roch 16* **P** *CPAS* **Hon C** J E RAWLING
ST PAUL'S WALDEN (All Saints) *St Alb 4* **P** *D&C St Paul's* **P-in-c** D M DEWEY
ST PETER in the Isle of Thanet (St Peter the Apostle) (St Andrew) *Cant 9* **P** *Abp* **V** B P MOORE, **C** J A F TAYLOR, **NSM** J A CHATER
ST PETER-UPON-CORNHILL *see* St Pet Cornhill *Lon*
ST PETER'S HOUSE (extra-parochial place) *Man 1 vacant*
ST PETROC MINOR (St Petroc) *see* St Issey w St Petroc Minor *Truro*
ST PINNOCK (St Pinnock) *see* Duloe, Herodsfoot, Morval and St Pinnock *Truro*
ST RUAN w St Grade and Landewednack *Truro 4* **P** *CPAS and A F Vyvyan-Robinson Esq (jt)* **P-in-c** W COLE
ST SAMPSON (St Sampson) *Truro 1* **P** *Bp* **P-in-c** P DE GREY-WARTER
ST STEPHEN IN BRANNEL (not known) *Truro 1* **P** *Capt J D G Fortescue* **P-in-c** E J WESTERMANN-CHILDS
ST STEPHENS (St Stephen) *see* Saltash *Truro*
ST STYTHIANS w Perranarworthal and Gwennap *Truro 2* **P** *Viscount Falmouth (2 turns), D&C (1 turn)* **V** E J M HOGAN, **OLM** L R T BARTER
ST TEATH (St Teatha) *Truro 10* **P** *Bp* **P-in-c** S L BRYAN
ST TUDY (St Tudy) w St Mabyn and Michaelstow *Truro 10* **P** *Ch Ch Ox, Viscount Falmouth, and Duchy of Cornwall (by turn)* **P-in-c** M L MILLSON
ST VEEP (St Cyricius) *see* Lostwithiel, St Winnow w St Nectan's Chpl etc *Truro*
ST WENN (St Wenna) *see* St Columb Major w St Wenn *Truro*
ST WEONARDS (St Weonard) w Orcop, Garway, Tretire, Michaelchurch, Pencoyd, Welsh Newton and Llanrothal *Heref 8* **P** *Bp, D&C, and MMCET (jt)* **P-in-c** E C GODDARD, **NSM** A CHAPLIN
ST WINNOW (St Winnow) *see* Lostwithiel, St Winnow w St Nectan's Chpl etc *Truro*
SAINTBURY (St Nicholas) *see* Mickleton, Willersey, Saintbury etc *Glouc*
SALCOMBE (Holy Trinity) and Malborough w South Huish *Ex 14* **P** *Keble Coll Ox and D&C Sarum (jt)* **V** R A OWEN, **C** A L HOWMAN, **Hon C** M J H HOWELL
SALCOMBE REGIS (St Mary and St Peter) *see* Sidmouth, Woolbrook, Salcombe Regis, Sidbury etc *Ex*
SALCOT VIRLEY (St Mary the Virgin) *see* Tollesbury w Salcot Virley *Chelmsf*
SALE (St Anne) (St Francis's Church Hall) *Ches 10* **P** *DBP* **V** J R HEATON, **C** M B COX
SALE (St Paul) *Ches 10* **P** *Trustees* **V** T SHEPHERD
SALEBY (St Margaret) w Beesby and Maltby *Linc 8* **P** *Bp and DBP (jt)* **R** R H IRESON
SALEHURST (St Mary) *Chich 15* **P** *Bp* **V** J B LAMBOURNE
SALESBURY (St Peter) *Blackb 7* **P** *V Blackb* **V** J W HARTLEY
SALFORD (Sacred Trinity) (St Philip) *Man 6* **P** *D&C Man and Sir Josslyn Gore-Booth Bt (jt)* **P-in-c** A I SALMON
SALFORD (St Ambrose) *see* Pendleton *Man*
SALFORD (St Clement) Ordsall *see* Ordsall and Salford Quays *Man*
SALFORD (St Ignatius and Stowell Memorial) *as above*
SALFORD (St Mary) *see* Chipping Norton *Ox*
SALFORD (St Mary) *see* Cranfield and Hulcote w Salford *St Alb*
SALFORD (St Paul w Christ Church) *Man 6* **P** *The Crown and Trustees (alt)* **R** D S C WYATT
SALFORD PRIORS (St Matthew) *Cov 7* **P** *Peache Trustees* **P-in-c** S R TASH, **NSM** L E DAVIES
SALFORDS (Christ the King) *S'wark 27* **P** *Bp* **V** S M CAPLE, **NSM** F PLUMMER
SALHOUSE (All Saints) *see* Rackheath and Salhouse *Nor*
SALING, GREAT (St James) *see* Stebbing and Lindsell w Gt and Lt Saling *Chelmsf*
SALING, LITTLE (St Peter and St Paul) *as above*
SALISBURY (St Francis) and St Lawrence Stratford sub Castle *Sarum 12* **P** *Bp (3 turns), D&C (1 turn)* **V** P F D TAYLOR
SALISBURY (St Mark) *Sarum 12* **P** *Bp* **V** P J D HAWKSWORTH, **C** D F R STOKES, **NSM** T A FISHER, **OLM** J P OFFER
SALISBURY (St Martin) and Laverstock *Sarum 13* **P** *D&C and Bp (alt)* **R** K ROBINSON
SALISBURY (St Paul) *see* Fisherton Anger *Sarum*
SALISBURY (St Thomas and St Edmund) *Sarum 12* **P** *Bp and D&C (alt)* **R** J C HATTON, **NSM** J A TAYLOR
SALKELD, GREAT (St Cuthbert) *see* Kirkoswald, Renwick, Gt Salkeld and Lazonby *Carl*
SALLE (St Peter and St Paul) *see* Reepham, Hackford w Whitwell, Kerdiston etc *Nor*
SALT (St James the Great) *see* Mid Trent *Lich*
SALTASH (St Nicholas and St Faith) *Truro 11* **P** *Patr Bd* **TR** R E B MAYNARD, **TV** A BUTLER, **NSM** P M SELLIX, D BURROWS
SALTBURN-BY-THE-SEA (Emmanuel) *York 16* **P** *Abp, Adn Cleveland, Marquis of Zetland, Mrs M Brignall, and Mrs S L Vernon (jt)* **V** G W DONEGAN-CROSS
SALTBY (St Peter) *see* High Framland Par *Leic*
SALTDEAN (St Nicholas) *Chich 2* **P** *Bp* **P-in-c** G J BUTTERWORTH
SALTER STREET (St Patrick) and Shirley *Birm 6* **P** *Patr Bd* **TR** M G B C CADDY, **TV** N LO POLITO, J M KNAPP
SALTERHEBBLE (All Saints) *see* Halifax All SS *Wakef*
SALTERSFORD (St John the Baptist) *see* Rainow w Saltersford and Forest *Ches*
SALTFLEETBY (St Peter) *Linc 12* **P** *Or Coll Ox, Bp, and MMCET (jt)* **V** *vacant* (01507) 338074
SALTFORD (Blessed Virgin Mary) w Corston and Newton St Loe *B & W 10* **P** *DBP (2 turns), Duchy of Cornwall (1 turn)* **R** G R W HALL, **C** T J K BELL, **NSM** S E WILSON
SALTHOUSE (St Nicholas) *see* Weybourne Gp *Nor*
SALTLEY (St Saviour) and Shaw Hill, Alum Rock *Birm 13* **P** *Bp and Trustees (jt)* **P-in-c** A H TOWNSEND

SALTNEY FERRY (St Matthew) *see* Lache cum Saltney *Ches*
SALTON (St John of Beverley) *see* Kirby Misperton w Normanby, Edston and Salton *York*
SALTWOOD (St Peter and St Paul) *Cant 5* **P** *Abp* **R** R I MARTIN
SALVINGTON (St Peter) *see* Durrington *Chich*
SALWARPE (St Michael) and Hindlip w Martin Hussingtree *Worc 8* **P** *Bp, D&C, and Exors Lady Hindlip (by turn)* **P-in-c** I R PETRIE, **NSM** J M JAMES
SALWAY ASH (Holy Trinity) *see* Beaminster Area *Sarum*
SAMBOURNE (Mission Church) *see* Coughton *Cov*
SAMBROOK (St Luke) *see* Cheswardine, Childs Ercall, Hales, Hinstock etc *Lich*
SAMFORD, NORTH *see* Sproughton w Burstall, Copdock w Washbrook etc *St E*
SAMLESBURY (St Leonard the Less) *see* Walton-le-Dale St Leon w Samlesbury St Leon *Blackb*
SAMPFORD, GREAT (St Michael) *see* The Sampfords and Radwinter w Hempstead *Chelmsf*
SAMPFORD, LITTLE (St Mary) *as above*
SAMPFORD ARUNDEL (Holy Cross) *see* Wellington and Distr *B & W*
SAMPFORD BRETT (St George) *see* Quantock Towers *B & W*
SAMPFORD COURTENAY (St Andrew) *see* N Tawton, Bondleigh, Sampford Courtenay etc *Ex*
SAMPFORD PEVERELL (St John the Baptist), Uplowman, Holcombe Rogus, Hockworthy, Burlescombe, Huntsham and Halberton w Ash Thomas *Ex 4* **P** *Patr Bd* **TV** K G GALE, **C** R J CLOETE, **NSM** H M BAYS
SAMPFORD SPINEY (St Mary) w Horrabridge *Ex 25* **P** *D&C Windsor* **P-in-c** W G LLOYD
SAMPFORDS, The (St Michael) (St Mary) and Radwinter with Hempstead *Chelmsf 22* **P** *Guild of All So, New Coll Ox, and Keble Coll Ox (jt)* **P-in-c** G M MANN
SANCREED (St Creden) *Truro 5* **P** *D&C* **V** S W LEACH
SANCTON (All Saints) *York 5* **P** *Abp* **V** L C MUNT
SAND HILL (Church of the Good Shepherd) *see* N Farnborough *Guildf*
SAND HUTTON (St Leonard) *see* Thirsk *York*
SAND HUTTON (St Mary) *York 6* **P** *Abp (2 turns), D&C Dur (1 turn)* **V** J W VALENTINE, **NSM** R C BENSON
SANDAL (St Catherine) *Wakef 9* **P** *V Sandal Magna* **V** M P CROFT, **C** N LEFROY-OWEN
SANDAL MAGNA (St Helen) *Wakef 9* **P** *Peache Trustees* **V** R G MARTIN
SANDBACH (St Mary) *Ches 11* **P** *DBP* **V** D R BUCKLEY, **NSM** H RUGMAN
SANDBACH HEATH (St John the Evangelist) w Wheelock *Ches 11* **P** *V Sandbach* **V** J A BACON, **NSM** P F DE J GOGGIN
SANDBANKS (St Nicolas) *see* Canford Cliffs and Sandbanks *Sarum*
SANDERSTEAD (All Saints) (St Anthony) (St Edmund the King and Martyr) *S'wark 24* **P** *DBP* **TV** S F ATKINSON-JONES, **P-in-c** S BUTLER, **C** C J CHILD, **Hon C** R RATCLIFFE, **NSM** D M GAMBLE
SANDERSTEAD (St Mary) *S'wark 24* **P** *Bp* **P-in-c** J J BOWER
SANDFORD (All Saints) *see* Burrington and Churchill *B & W*
SANDFORD (St Martin) *see* Westcote Barton w Steeple Barton, Duns Tew etc *Ox*
SANDFORD (St Martin) *see* Wareham *Sarum*
SANDFORD (St Swithin) *see* Crediton, Shobrooke and Sandford etc *Ex*
SANDFORD-ON-THAMES (St Andrew) *Ox 4* **P** *DBP* **P-in-c** R C MORGAN, **NSM** L M S COOK
SANDFORD ORCAS (St Nicholas) *see* Queen Thorne *Sarum*
SANDGATE (St Paul) w Folkestone (St George) *Cant 5* **P** *Abp and Ld Chan (alt)* **P-in-c** J C TAPPER, **C** S K C RICHARDSON
SANDHURST (St Lawrence) *see* Twigworth, Down Hatherley, Norton, The Leigh etc *Glouc*
SANDHURST (St Michael and All Angels) *Ox 16* **P** *Bp* **P-in-c** J A CASTLE, **NSM** J W WHITE
SANDHURST (St Nicholas) (Mission Church) w Newenden *Cant 16* **P** *Abp* **P-in-c** C F SMITH, **NSM** R M VAN WENGEN
SANDHURST, LOWER (St Mary) *see* Sandhurst *Ox*
SANDIACRE (St Giles) *Derby 13* **P** *Ld Chan* **R** W B COONEY, **NSM** K W G JOHNSON
SANDIWAY (St John the Evangelist) *Ches 6* **P** *Bp* **V** *vacant* (01606) 883815
SANDLEHEATH (St Aldhelm) *see* Fordingbridge and Breamore and Hale etc *Win*
SANDON (All Saints) *see* Mid Trent *Lich*
SANDON (All Saints), Wallington and Rushden w Clothall *St Alb 19* **P** *Duchy of Lanc (1 turn), Marquess of Salisbury (1 turn), and Bp (2 turns)* **NSM** L E SUMMERS
SANDON (St Andrew) *Chelmsf 9* **P** *Qu Coll Cam* **P-in-c** K R PLAISTER
SANDOWN (Christ Church) *Portsm 7* **P** *Ch Patr Trust* **V** *vacant* (01983) 402548
SANDOWN, LOWER (St John the Evangelist) *Portsm 7* **P** *Bp* **V** *vacant*
SANDRIDGE (St Leonard) *St Alb 8* **P** *Earl Spencer* **P-in-c** V G CATO
SANDRINGHAM (St Mary Magdalene) w West Newton and Appleton, Wolferton w Babingley and Flitcham *Nor 16* **P** *The Crown* **R** J B V RIVIERE
SANDS (Church of the Good Shepherd) *see* Seale, Puttenham and Wanborough *Guildf*
SANDS (St Mary and St George) *see* High Wycombe *Ox*
SANDSEND (St Mary) *see* Hinderwell, Roxby and Staithes etc *York*
SANDSFIELD *see* Carl H Trin and St Barn *Carl*
SANDWELL (St Philip) *see* W Bromwich St Phil *Lich*
SANDWICH (St Clement) *Cant 8* **P** *Adn Cant* **R** J M A ROBERTS, **NSM** J C ROBERTS
SANDY (St Swithun) *St Alb 11* **P** *Lord Pym* **R** D G WILLIAMS, **C** S C HILLMAN
SANDY LANE (St Mary and St Nicholas) *see* Rowde and Bromham *Sarum*
SANDYLANDS (St John) *Blackb 11* **P** *Bp* **V** J G REEVES
SANKEY, GREAT (St Mary) *Liv 12* **P** *Lord Lilford* **V** M BUCKLEY
SANTAN (St Sanctain) *S & M 1* **P** *The Crown* **V** *vacant*
SANTON DOWNHAM (St Mary the Virgin) *see* Brandon and Santon Downham w Elveden etc *St E*
SAPCOTE (All Saints) and Sharnford w Wigston Parva *Leic 12* **P** *Ld Chan and DBP (alt)* **R** M J NORMAN
SAPEY, UPPER (St Michael) *see* Edvin Loach w Tedstone Delamere etc *Heref*
SAPPERTON (St Kenelm) *see* Kemble, Poole Keynes, Somerford Keynes etc *Glouc*
SAPPERTON (St Nicholas) w Braceby *Linc 14* **P** *Bp (1 turn), Sir Richard Welby Bt (3 turns)* **R** *vacant*
SARISBURY (St Paul) *Portsm 2* **P** *V Titchfield* **V** A J MATHESON, **Par Dn** J EVANS
SARK (St Peter) *Win 14* **P** *Le Seigneur de Sercq* **P-in-c** K P MELLOR, **C** G L LEWORTHY
SARN (Holy Trinity) *see* Churchstoke w Hyssington and Sarn *Heref*
SARNESFIELD (St Mary) *see* Weobley w Sarnesfield and Norton Canon *Heref*
SARRATT (Holy Cross) and Chipperfield *St Alb 5* **P** *Churchwardens and DBP (jt)* **R** J A STEVENS
SATLEY (St Cuthbert), Stanley and Tow Law *Dur 9* **P** *Bp, Ld Chan, and R Brancepeth (by turn)* **V** *vacant* (01388) 730335
SATTERTHWAITE (All Saints) *see* Hawkshead and Low Wray w Sawrey and Rusland etc *Carl*
SAUGHALL, GREAT (All Saints) *Ches 9* **P** *Bp* **P-in-c** J B HARRIS
SAUL (St James the Great) *see* Frampton on Severn, Arlingham, Saul etc *Glouc*
SAUNDERTON (St Mary and St Nicholas) *see* Risborough *Ox*
SAUNTON (St Anne) *see* Braunton *Ex*
SAUSTHORPE (St Andrew) *see* Partney Gp *Linc*
SAVERNAKE (St Katharine) *Sarum 19* **P** *Patr Bd* **TR** N A LEIGH-HUNT, **TV** M EDWARDS, R L N HARRISON, **C** R W GRAHAM, **NSM** A J DEBOO, L A DYTHAM
SAW MILLS (St Mary) *see* Ambergate and Heage *Derby*
SAWBRIDGEWORTH (Great St Mary) *St Alb 18* **P** *Bp* **V** R F SIBSON, **C** D J SNOWBALL
SAWLEY (All Saints) (St Mary) *Derby 13* **P** *D&C Lich* **R** P HENRY
SAWLEY (St Michael) *see* Fountains Gp *Ripon*
SAWREY (St Peter) *see* Hawkshead and Low Wray w Sawrey and Rusland etc *Carl*
SAWSTON (St Mary) *Ely 6* **P** *SMF* **V** G KENDALL
SAWTRY (All Saints) and Glatton *Ely 11* **P** *Duke of Devonshire* **R** P M GRIFFITH
SAXBY (St Helen) *see* Owmby Gp *Linc*
SAXBY (St Peter) *see* S Framland *Leic*
SAXBY ALL SAINTS (All Saints) *Linc 6* **P** *R H H Barton Esq* **R** G A PLUMB
SAXELBYE (St Peter) *see* Old Dalby, Nether Broughton, Saxelbye etc *Leic*
SAXHAM, GREAT (St Andrew) *see* Barrow *St E*
SAXHAM, LITTLE (St Nicholas) *as above*
SAXILBY Group, The (St Botolph) *Linc 2* **P** *Bp and DBP (jt)* **R** R PROSSER, **NSM** S PROSSER
SAXLINGHAM (St Margaret) *see* Stiffkey and Bale *Nor*
SAXLINGHAM NETHERGATE (St Mary) *see* Newton Flotman, Swainsthorpe, Tasburgh, etc *Nor*

SAXMUNDHAM (St John the Baptist) w Kelsale cum Carlton *St E 19* **P** *Patr Bd* **R** R F WEBB, **NSM** B L WEBB
SAXONWELL *Linc 19* **P** *Duchy of Lanc (2 turns), Ld Chan (1 turn)* **OLM** C W B SOWDEN
SAXTEAD (All Saints) *see* Framlingham w Saxtead *St E*
SAXTHORPE (St Andrew) *see* Lt Barningham, Blickling, Edgefield etc *Nor*
SAXTON (All Saints) *see* Sherburn in Elmet w Saxton *York*
SAYERS COMMON (Christ Church) *see* Albourne w Sayers Common and Twineham *Chich*
SCALBY (St Laurence) *York 15* **P** *Abp* **NSM** M J WRIGHT
SCALDWELL (St Peter and St Paul) *see* Walgrave w Hannington and Wold and Scaldwell *Pet*
SCALEBY (All Saints) *see* Eden, Gelt and Irthing *Carl*
SCALFORD (St Egelwin) w Wycombe and Chadwell; Waltham-on-the-Wolds; Stonesby; Goadby Marwood; Eastwell; and Eaton *Leic 3* **P** *Lady Gretton, Ld Chan, Duke of Rutland, Bp, and Sir Lyonel Tollemache Bt (by turn)* **R** B A STARK
SCAMMONDEN, WEST (St Bartholomew) *see* Barkisland w W Scammonden *Wakef*
SCAMPSTON (St Martin) *see* Buckrose Carrs *York*
SCAMPTON (St John the Baptist) *see* Aisthorpe w Scampton w Thorpe le Fallows etc *Linc*
SCARBOROUGH (St Columba) *York 15* **P** *Abp* **P-in-c** K D JACKSON, **NSM** D B CROUCH
SCARBOROUGH (St James w Holy Trinity) *York 15* **P** *Abp and CPAS (jt)* **P-in-c** P W WHITE
SCARBOROUGH (St Luke) *York 15* **P** *Abp* **V** *vacant* (01723) 372831
SCARBOROUGH (St Mark) *see* Newby *York*
SCARBOROUGH (St Martin) *York 15* **P** *Trustees* **V** A J MILLS, **C** D R MOORE, **NSM** R G C COSTIN
SCARBOROUGH (St Mary) w Christ Church and (Holy Apostles) *York 15* **P** *Abp* **V** M P DUNNING, **C** R J WALKER
SCARBOROUGH (St Saviour w All Saints) *York 15* **P** *Abp* **V** A J MILLS, **NSM** G G A WARING
SCARCLIFFE (St Leonard) *see* Ault Hucknall and Scarcliffe *Derby*
SCARISBRICK (St Mark) (Good Shepherd) *Liv 11* **P** *V Ormskirk* **NSM** L N LAWRINSON
SCARLE, NORTH (All Saints) *see* Swinderby *Linc*
SCARLE, SOUTH (St Helena) *see* Collingham w S Scarle and Besthorpe and Girton *S'well*
SCARNING (St Peter and St Paul) *see* E Dereham and Scarning *Nor*
SCARRINGTON (St John of Beverley) *see* Whatton w Aslockton, Hawksworth, Scarrington etc *S'well*
SCARSDALE, EAST *Derby 3* **P** *Patr Bd* **TR** J W HARGREAVES, **TV** B DALE
SCARTHO (St Giles) *Linc 9* **P** *Jes Coll Ox* **R** I R S WALKER, **C** C F EDWARDS
SCAWBY (St Hibald), Redbourne and Hibaldstow *Linc 6* **P** *T M S Nelthorpe Esq (2 turns), Bp (1 turn), and Duke of St Alb (1 turn)* **V** C H LILLEY, **C** A R BARBER
SCAWTHORPE (St Luke) *see* Doncaster St Leon and St Jude *Sheff*
SCAWTON (St Mary) *see* Upper Ryedale *York*
SCAYNES HILL (St Augustine) *Chich 6* **P** *Bp* **P-in-c** M J T PAYNE
SCHOLES (St Philip) *see* Barwick in Elmet *Ripon*
SCHOLES (St Philip and St James) *Wakef 8* **P** *Bp* **P-in-c** M A MCLEAN, **Hon C** A G SWALLOW, **NSM** R M CAVE
SCHORNE *Ox 24* **P** *Patr Bd (2 turns), Ld Chan (1 turn)* **TV** A T BELL, **P-in-c** D J MEAKIN, **NSM** M D W PARTRIDGE, E A WELTERS
SCILLY *see* Is of Scilly *Truro*
SCISSETT (St Augustine) *see* High Hoyland, Scissett and Clayton W *Wakef*
SCOFTON (St John the Evangelist) *see* Babworth w Sutton-cum-Lound and Scofton etc *S'well*
SCOLE (St Andrew) w Brockdish, Billingford, Thorpe Abbots and Thorpe Parva *Nor 10* **P** *Bp, Ex Coll Ox, MMCET, Adn Norfolk, and Exors Lady Mann (jt)* **P-in-c** T W RIESS
SCOPWICK (Holy Cross) *see* Digby Gp *Linc*
SCORBOROUGH (St Leonard) *see* Lockington and Lund and Scorborough w Leconfield *York*
SCORTON (St Peter) and Barnacre All Saints and Calder Vale St John the Evangelist *Blackb 9* **P** *Bp, V Lanc St Mary w St Jo and St Anne, and Mrs V O Shepherd-Cross (jt)* **V** *vacant* (01524) 791229
SCOT WILLOUGHBY (St Andrew) *see* S Lafford *Linc*
SCOTBY (All Saints) and Cotehill w Cumwhinton *Carl 2* **P** *Trustees (2 turns), Prime Min (1 turn)* **P-in-c** G M CREGEEN, **C** T D HERBERT
SCOTFORTH (St Paul) *Blackb 11* **P** *Rt Revd J Nicholls* **V** M G SMITH, **C** I C TODD
SCOTHERN (St Germain) *see* Welton and Dunholme w Scothern *Linc*
SCOTSWOOD (St Margaret) *Newc 7* **P** *Bp* **P-in-c** C H KNIGHTS
SCOTTER (St Peter) w East Ferry *Linc 4* **P** *Bp* **R** O G FOLKARD
SCOTTON (St Genewys) w Northorpe *Linc 4* **P** *Ld Chan* **R** O G FOLKARD, **OLM** W KEAST, D L LANGFORD
SCOTTON (St Thomas) *see* Walkingham Hill *Ripon*
SCOTTOW (All Saints) *see* Worstead, Westwick, Sloley, Swanton Abbot etc *Nor*
SCOULTON (Holy Trinity) *see* High Oak, Hingham and Scoulton w Wood Rising *Nor*
SCRAMBLESBY (St Martin) *see* Asterby Gp *Linc*
SCRAPTOFT (All Saints) *Leic 1* **P** *Bp, Dr M J A Sharp, and DBP (jt)* **V** M J COURT, **NSM** A J POOLE
SCRAYINGHAM (St Peter and St Paul) *see* Stamford Bridge Gp *York*
SCREDINGTON (St Andrew) *see* Helpringham w Hale *Linc*
SCREMBY (St Peter and St Paul) *see* Partney Gp *Linc*
SCREMERSTON (St Peter) *Newc 12* **P** *Bp* **P-in-c** A S ADAMSON, **NSM** S J HARRISON
SCREVETON (St Wilfrid) *see* Car Colston w Screveton *S'well*
SCRIVELSBY (St Benedict) *see* Thornton Gp *Linc*
SCROOBY (St Wilfrid) *see* Blyth and Scrooby w Ranskill *S'well*
SCROPTON (St Paul) *see* Doveridge, Scropton, Sudbury etc *Derby*
SCRUTON (St Radegund) *see* Lower Swale *Ripon*
SCULCOATES (St Mary) *see* Hull St Mary Sculcoates *York*
SCULCOATES (St Paul) (St Stephen) *York 14* **P** *Abp and V Hull H Trin (1 turn), Ld Chan (1 turn)* **P-in-c** P A BURKITT
SCULTHORPE (St Mary and All Saints) *see* N and S Creake w Waterden, Syderstone etc *Nor*
SCUNTHORPE (All Saints) *see* Brumby *Linc*
SCUNTHORPE (The Resurrection) *see* Trentside E *Linc*
SEA MILLS (St Edyth) *Bris 2* **P** *Bp* **V** D A IZZARD, **C** E J HUXLEY
SEA PALLING (St Margaret) *see* Happisburgh, Walcott, Hempstead w Eccles etc *Nor*
SEA VIEW (St Peter) *Portsm 7* **P** *Bp* **V** M M STRANGE
SEABOROUGH (St John) *see* Beaminster Area *Sarum*
SEABROOK (Mission Hall) *see* Cheriton *Cant*
SEACOMBE (St Paul) *Ches 7* **P** *Trustees* **P-in-c** I HUGHES
SEACROFT (St James) (Church of the Ascension) (St Richard) *Ripon 8* **P** *DBF* **TV** T M TUNLEY, M P BENWELL, C MACLAREN, R H JAMIESON
SEAFORD (St Leonard) w Sutton *Chich 18* **P** *Ld Chan* **V** C H ATHERSTONE, **C** P J OWEN, C DOHERTY
SEAFORTH (St Thomas) *see* Bootle *Liv*
SEAGRAVE (All Saints) *see* Sileby, Cossington and Seagrave *Leic*
SEAGRY (St Mary the Virgin) *see* Gt Somerford, Lt Somerford, Seagry, Corston etc *Bris*
SEAHAM (St Mary the Virgin) *Dur 2* **P** *Bp* **V** *vacant* 0191-581 3385
SEAHAM, NEW (Christ Church) *see* Dalton le Dale and New Seaham *Dur*
SEAHAM HARBOUR (St John) *Dur 2* **P** *Bp* **V** J C G POLLOCK
SEAL (St Lawrence) *Roch 9* **P** *Bp* **P-in-c** M D COOKE
SEAL (St Peter and St Paul) *Roch 9* **P** *DBP* **V** K C BLACKBURN
SEALE (St Lawrence), Puttenham and Wanborough *Guildf 4* **P** *Adn Surrey, C R I Perkins Esq, and Ld Chan (by turn)* **P-in-c** R E WOOD
SEALE (St Peter) (St Matthew) and Lullington w Coton in the Elms *Derby 16* **P** *Bp, R D Nielson Esq, and C W Worthington Esq (jt)* **R** *vacant* (01283) 761179
SEAMER (St Martin) *York 15* **P** *Abp* **NSM** T JORDAN
SEAMER IN CLEVELAND (St Martin) *see* Stokesley w Seamer *York*
SEARBY (St Nicholas) *see* Caistor Gp *Linc*
SEASALTER (St Alphege) *see* Whitstable *Cant*
SEASCALE (St Cuthbert) and Drigg *Carl 5* **P** *DBP* **V** *vacant* (01946) 728217
SEATHWAITE (Holy Trinity) *see* Broughton and Duddon *Carl*
SEATON (All Hallows) *see* Lyddington w Stoke Dry and Seaton etc *Pet*
SEATON (St Gregory) and Beer *Ex 5* **P** *Lord Clinton and D&C (jt)* **V** N T SCHOFIELD, **C** A THORNE, **NSM** J S OLLIER
SEATON (St Paul) *see* Camerton, Seaton and W Seaton *Carl*
SEATON, WEST (Holy Trinity) *as above*
SEATON CAREW (Holy Trinity) *Dur 3* **P** *Bp* **P-in-c** P T ALLINSON

SEATON HIRST (St John) (St Andrew) *Newc 11* **P** *Bp* **TR** D P PALMER
SEATON ROSS (St Edmund) *see* Holme and Seaton Ross Gp *York*
SEATON SLUICE (St Paul) *see* Delaval *Newc*
SEAVIEW *see* Sea View *Portsm*
SEAVINGTON (St Michael and St Mary) *see* S Petherton w the Seavingtons *B & W*
SEBERGHAM (St Mary) *see* Caldbeck, Castle Sowerby and Sebergham *Carl*
SECKINGTON (All Saints) *see* Newton Regis w Seckington and Shuttington *Birm*
SEDBERGH (St Andrew), Cautley and Garsdale *Bradf 6* **P** *Trin Coll Cam* **V** A W FELL
SEDGEBERROW (St Mary the Virgin) *see* Hampton w Sedgeberrow and Hinton-on-the-Green *Worc*
SEDGEBROOK (St Lawrence) *see* Saxonwell *Linc*
SEDGEFIELD (St Edmund) *see* Upper Skerne *Dur*
SEDGEHILL (St Katherine) *see* E Knoyle, Semley and Sedgehill *Sarum*
SEDGFORD (St Mary) *see* Docking, the Birchams, Stanhoe and Sedgeford *Nor*
SEDGLEY (All Saints) *see* Gornal and Sedgley *Worc*
SEDGLEY (St Mary the Virgin) *Worc 10* **P** *Bp and V Sedgley All SS (jt)* **V** E SMITH, **NSM** T WESTWOOD
SEDLESCOMBE (St John the Baptist) w Whatlington *Chich 14* **P** *Ld Chan and Bp (alt)* **P-in-c** J J W EDMONDSON, **NSM** S D HUGGINS
SEEND (Holy Cross), Bulkington and Poulshot *Sarum 16* **P** *D&C (2 turns), Bp (1 turn)* **V** S J PEARCE
SEER GREEN (Holy Trinity) and Jordans *Ox 20* **P** *Bp* **P-in-c** F C CONANT
SEETHING (St Margaret) *see* Brooke, Kirstead, Mundham w Seething and Thwaite *Nor*
SEFTON (St Helen) and Thornton *Liv 5* **P** *Bp* **R** I C COWELL
SEFTON PARK (Christ Church) *see* Toxteth Park Ch Ch and St Mich w St Andr *Liv*
SEGHILL (Holy Trinity) *Newc 1* **P** *The Crown* **V** I G FALCONER
SEIGHFORD (St Chad) *see* Chebsey, Ellenhall and Seighford-with-Creswell *Lich*
SELATTYN (St Mary) *see* Weston Rhyn and Selattyn *Lich*
SELBORNE (St Mary) *see* Northanger *Win*
SELBY (St James the Apostle) *York 4* **P** *Simeon's Trustees* **V** D J WOOLLARD
SELBY ABBEY (St Mary and St Germain) (St Richard) *York 4* **P** *Abp* **V** K M JUKES, **C** G K WARDELL, **NSM** R N WAINWRIGHT
SELHAM (St James) *see* Lurgashall, Lodsworth and Selham *Chich*
SELLACK (St Tysilio) *see* How Caple w Sollarshope, Sellack etc *Heref*
SELLINDGE (St Mary the Virgin) *see* Mersham w Hinxhill and Sellindge *Cant*
SELLING (St Mary the Virgin) w Throwley and Sheldwich w Badlesmere and Leaveland *Cant 6* **P** *Abp and D&C (jt)* **P-in-c** J M MASON, **NSM** M JOHNSON, A SKINNER
SELLY OAK (St Mary) *Birm 2* **P** *Bp* **V** M V ROBERTS, **NSM** S A IZZARD
SELLY PARK Christ Church (St Stephen's Centre) *Birm 5* **P** *Trustees* **P-in-c** N A HAND
SELLY PARK (St Stephen) (St Wulstan) *Birm 5* **P** *Trustees* **V** C B HOBBS
SELMESTON (St Mary) *see* Berwick w Selmeston and Alciston *Chich*
SELSDON (St John) (St Francis) *S'wark 22* **P** *Bp* **P-in-c** I S BROTHWOOD, **NSM** K HOLT
SELSEY (St Peter) *Chich 3* **P** *Bp* **R** J C T HARRINGTON
SELSIDE (St Thomas) *see* Skelsmergh w Selside and Longsleddale *Carl*
SELSLEY (All Saints) *see* Cainscross w Selsley *Glouc*
SELSTON (St Helen) *S'well 4* **P** *Wright Trustees* **V** *vacant* (01773) 810247
SELWORTHY (All Saints), Timberscombe, Wootton Courtenay and Luccombe *B & W 16* **P** *Bp* **R** R MANN, **Hon C** S R B HUMPHREYS
SEMER (All Saints) *see* Bildeston w Wattisham and Lindsey, Whatfield etc *St E*
SEMINGTON (St George) *see* Steeple Ashton w Semington and Keevil *Sarum*
SEMLEY (St Leonard) *see* E Knoyle, Semley and Sedgehill *Sarum*
SEMPRINGHAM (St Andrew) *see* Billingborough Gp *Linc*
SEND (St Mary the Virgin) *Guildf 12* **P** *Bp* **P-in-c** A J SHUTT
SENNEN (St Sennen) *see* St Buryan, St Levan and Sennen *Truro*
SENNICOTTS (St Mary) *see* Funtington and Sennicotts *Chich*
SESSAY (St Cuthbert) *York 19* **P** *Viscountess Downe* **R** *vacant*
SETCHEY (St Mary) *see* W Winch w Setchey, N Runcton and Middleton *Nor*
SETMURTHY (St Barnabas) *see* Binsey *Carl*
SETTLE (Holy Ascension) *Bradf 5* **P** *Trustees* **V** *vacant* (01729) 822288
SETTRINGTON (All Saints) *see* W Buckrose *York*
SEVEN KINGS *see* Gt Ilford St Jo *Chelmsf*
SEVENHAMPTON (St Andrew) w Charlton Abbots, Hawling and Whittington, Dowdeswell and Andoversford w The Shiptons and Cold Salperton, and Withington *Glouc 13* **P** *Bp, MMCET, T W Bailey Esq, E M Bailey Esq, and Mrs J A Stringer (1 turn); Bp, MMCET, and Mrs L E Evans (1 turn)* **P-in-c** J A BECKETT, **C** A J AXON
SEVENHAMPTON (St James) *see* Highworth w Sevenhampton and Inglesham etc *Bris*
SEVENOAKS (St John the Baptist) *Roch 9* **P** *Guild of All So* **V** R WARD, **C** M R NORTH
SEVENOAKS (St Luke) *Roch 9* **P** *Bp* **V** R CHAVNER
SEVENOAKS (St Nicholas) *Roch 9* **P** *Trustees* **R** A M MACLEAY, **C** J M DENT, A D MCCLELLAN, **Hon C** N N HENSHAW, D G MILTON-THOMPSON
SEVENOAKS WEALD (St George) *Roch 9* **P** *R Sevenoaks* **V** *vacant* (01732) 463291
SEVERN BEACH (St Nicholas) *see* Pilning w Compton Greenfield *Bris*
SEVERN STOKE (St Dennis) *see* Kempsey and Severn Stoke w Croome d'Abitot *Worc*
SEVERNSIDE Group of Parishes, The *see* Frampton on Severn, Arlingham, Saul etc *Glouc*
SEVINGTON (St Mary) *Cant 10* **P** *Ch Soc Trust* **P-in-c** J W TIPPING
SEWARDS END (not known) *see* Saffron Walden w Wendens Ambo, Littlebury etc *Chelmsf*
SEWERBY (St John) *see* Bridlington H Trin and Sewerby w Marton *York*
SEWSTERN (Holy Trinity) *see* S Framland *Leic*
SHABBINGTON (St Mary Magdalene) *see* Worminghall w Ickford, Oakley and Shabbington *Ox*
SHACKERSTONE (St Peter) *see* Nailstone and Carlton w Shackerstone *Leic*
SHACKLEFORD (St Mary the Virgin) *see* Compton w Shackleford and Peper Harow *Guildf*
SHADFORTH (St Cuthbert) *see* Pittington, Shadforth and Sherburn *Dur*
SHADINGFIELD (St John the Baptist) *see* Hundred River *St E*
SHADOXHURST (St Peter and St Paul) *see* Kingsnorth and Shadoxhurst *Cant*
SHADWELL (St Paul) *Ripon 5* **P** *V Thorner* **V** H A THOMPSON
SHADWELL (St Paul) w Ratcliffe St James *Lon 7* **P** *Bp* **P-in-c** R C THORPE, **C** J P B BARNES
SHAFTESBURY (St James) *see* Shaston *Sarum*
SHAFTESBURY (St Peter) *as above*
SHAFTON (St Hugh) *see* Felkirk *Wakef*
SHALBOURNE (St Michael and All Angels) *see* Savernake *Sarum*
SHALDEN (St Peter and St Paul) *see* Bentworth, Lasham, Medstead and Shalden *Win*
SHALDON (St Nicholas) (St Peter), Stokeinteignhead, Combeinteignhead and Haccombe *Ex 10* **P** *SMF and Sir Rivers Carew Bt (jt)* **R** G S RICHARDSON, **C** J BUTLER
SHALFLEET (St Michael the Archangel) *Portsm 8* **P** *Ld Chan* **V** D J BEVINGTON, **NSM** M O'DONNELL
SHALFORD (St Andrew) *see* Finchingfield and Cornish Hall End etc *Chelmsf*
SHALFORD (St Mary the Virgin) *Guildf 5* **P** *Ld Chan* **V** J J CRUSE
SHALSTONE (St Edward the Confessor) *see* W Buckingham *Ox*
SHAMLEY GREEN (Christ Church) *Guildf 2* **P** *Bp* **V** *vacant* (01483) 892030
SHANGTON (St Nicholas) *see* Church Langton cum Tur Langton etc *Leic*
SHANKLIN (St Blasius) *Portsm 7* **P** *Bp* **P-in-c** A W SWANBOROUGH
SHANKLIN (St Paul) *see* Gatten St Paul *Portsm*
SHANKLIN (St Saviour on the Cliff) *Portsm 7* **P** *Bp* **V** R M SMITH, **NSM** B M DOWNER
SHAP (St Michael) w Swindale and Bampton w Mardale *Carl 1* **P** *Earl of Lonsdale* **P-in-c** C MARSDEN

SHAPWICK (Blessed Virgin Mary) w Ashcott and Burtle *B & W 5* **P** *Lord Vestey (2 turns), Bp (1 turn)* **P-in-c** J P ROWE
SHAPWICK (St Bartholomew) *see* Sturminster Marshall, Kingston Lacy and Shapwick *Sarum*
SHARD END (All Saints) *Birm 9* **P** *Keble Coll Ox* **P-in-c** A J CLUCAS
SHARDLOW (St James) *see* Aston on Trent, Elvaston, Weston on Trent etc *Derby*
SHARESHILL (St Luke and St Mary the Virgin) *Lich 2* **P** *Bp* **P-in-c** P H J THORNEYCROFT, **Hon C** R J BELLAMY
SHARLSTON (St Luke) *Wakef 9* **P** *Bp* **P-in-c** P A BOSTOCK
SHARNBROOK (St Peter) and Knotting w Souldrop *St Alb 15* **P** *Bp* **P-in-c** R A EVENS, **NSM** D G MASON
SHARNFORD (St Helen) *see* Sapcote and Sharnford w Wigston Parva *Leic*
SHARPNESS (St Andrew), Purton, Brookend and Slimbridge *Glouc 2* **P** *Magd Coll Ox and Bp (alt)* **R** W J BOON, **NSM** J A D'ESTERRE
SHARRINGTON (All Saints) *see* Stiffkey and Bale *Nor*
SHARROW (St Andrew) *see* Psalter Lane St Andr *Sheff*
SHASTON *Sarum 5* **P** *Patr Bd* **TR** M T P ZAMMIT, **TV** A C HEYWOOD, C A THOMAS, **NSM** I WITCHER, M E HARDING, U M GRAY
SHAUGH PRIOR (St Edward) *see* Bickleigh and Shaugh Prior *Ex*
SHAVINGTON (St Mark) *see* Weston *Ches*
SHAW (Christchurch) *see* Atworth w Shaw and Whitley *Sarum*
SHAW (Holy Trinity) *Man 22* **P** *R Prestwich St Mary* **P-in-c** R R WATSON
SHAW (St Mary) cum Donnington *Ox 14* **P** *DBP* **R** B TAYLOR, **C** E K FORBES STONE
SHAW HILL (St Mary and St John) *see* Saltley and Shaw Hill *Birm*
SHAWBURY (St Mary the Virgin) *Lich 22* **P** *C C Corbet Esq* **V** D J HUMPHRIES
SHAWELL (All Saints) *see* Gilmorton, Peatling Parva, Kimcote etc *Leic*
SHEARSBY (St Mary Magdalene) *see* Arnesby w Shearsby and Bruntingthorpe *Leic*
SHEBBEAR (St Michael), Buckland Filleigh, Sheepwash, Langtree, Newton St Petrock, Petrockstowe, Petersmarland, Merton and Huish *Ex 20* **P** *Ld Chan (1 turn), Patr Bd (2 turns)* **TV** C C R MERIVALE, **P-in-c** M J WARREN
SHEDFIELD (St John the Baptist) *Portsm 1* **P** *DBP* **P-in-c** S C HENDERSON, **NSM** B R MCHUGH, J BELOE
SHEEN (St Luke) *see* Longnor, Quarnford and Sheen *Lich*
SHEEN, EAST (All Saints) *see* Mortlake w E Sheen *S'wark*
SHEEN, EAST (Christ Church) *as above*
SHEEPSCOMBE (St John the Evangelist) *see* Painswick, Sheepscombe, Cranham, The Edge etc *Glouc*
SHEEPSTOR (St Leonard) *see* Yelverton, Meavy, Sheepstor and Walkhampton *Ex*
SHEEPWASH (St Lawrence) *see* Shebbear, Buckland Filleigh, Sheepwash etc *Ex*
SHEEPY (All Saints) *see* Bosworth and Sheepy Gp *Leic*
SHEERING (St Mary the Virgin) *see* Hatfield Heath and Sheering *Chelmsf*
SHEERNESS (Holy Trinity w St Paul) *Cant 15* **P** *V Minster-in-Sheppey* **V** J W STREETING, **C** V E HAYNES
SHEERWATER (St Michael and All Angels) *see* Woodham *Guildf*
SHEET (St Mary Magdalene) *Portsm 4* **P** *Bp* **V** R M E DEWING
SHEFFIELD (St Aidan w St Luke) *see* Sheff Manor *Sheff*
SHEFFIELD (St Andrew) *see* Psalter Lane St Andr *Sheff*
SHEFFIELD (St Bartholomew) *Sheff 4* **P** *Ch Patr Trust and Sheff Ch Burgesses Trust (jt)* **P-in-c** P W WEST
SHEFFIELD (St Catherine of Siena) Richmond Road *Sheff 1* **P** *The Crown* **V** H LOXLEY
SHEFFIELD (St Cecilia) Parson Cross *Sheff 3* **P** *Bp* **V** W J STOKOE
SHEFFIELD (St Cuthbert) *Sheff 3* **P** *Ch Burgesses* **V** I JENNINGS, **C** L RIDLEY
SHEFFIELD (St John the Evangelist) *Sheff 1* **P** *Ch Burgesses* **V** C H STEBBING
SHEFFIELD (St Leonard) Norwood *Sheff 3* **P** *Bp* **V** I K DUFFIELD, **C** T E FOUGNER, **NSM** J DALEY
SHEFFIELD (St Mark) Broomhill *Sheff 4* **P** *Ch Burgesses* **V** A ALKER, **C** S E HOBLEY
SHEFFIELD (St Mary) Bramall Lane *Sheff 2* **P** *Ch Burgesses and Dean (alt)* **V** J C SULLIVAN, **C** P J BATCHFORD, M J BAYLEY, **NSM** G C D DUNCAN
SHEFFIELD (St Matthew) Carver Street *Sheff 2* **P** *Bp and Sheff Ch Burgess Trust (jt)* **V** S M GRIFFITHS
SHEFFIELD (St Oswald) *Sheff 2* **P** *Ch Burgesses* **P-in-c** B R COLEMAN
SHEFFIELD (St Paul) *see* Arbourthorne and Norfolk Park *Sheff*
SHEFFIELD (St Paul) Wordsworth Avenue *Sheff 3* **P** *DBP* **P-in-c** I SMITH
SHEFFIELD St Peter Abbeydale *Sheff 2* **P** *Ch Burgesses* **P-in-c** B R COLEMAN, **C** I N C LOTHIAN
SHEFFIELD MANOR (St Swithun) *Sheff 1* **P** *Patr Bd* **Jt P-in-c** J C GRENFELL, J W GRENFELL
SHEFFIELD PARK (St John the Evangelist) *see* Sheff St Jo *Sheff*
SHEFFORD (St Michael) *see* Meppershall and Shefford *St Alb*
SHEFFORD, GREAT (St Mary) *see* Welford w Wickham and Gt Shefford, Boxford etc *Ox*
SHEINTON (St Peter and St Paul) *see* Wenlock *Heref*
SHELDON (St Giles) *Birm 9* **P** *J K Wingfield Digby Esq* **R** B A L CAMP
SHELDON (St James the Greater) *see* Dunkeswell, Luppitt, Sheldon and Upottery *Ex*
SHELDON (St Michael and All Angels) *see* Ashford w Sheldon and Longstone *Derby*
SHELDWICH (St James) *see* Selling w Throwley, Sheldwich w Badlesmere etc *Cant*
SHELF (St Michael and All Angels) w Buttershaw St Aidan *Bradf 2* **P** *Bp* **TR** M I GASKELL, **TV** S E W SHRINE
SHELFANGER (All Saints) *see* Winfarthing w Shelfanger w Burston w Gissing etc *Nor*
SHELFIELD (St Mark) *see* Walsall Wood *Lich*
SHELFORD (St Peter and St Paul) *see* Radcliffe-on-Trent and Shelford etc *S'well*
SHELFORD, GREAT (St Mary) *Ely 6* **P** *Bp* **P-in-c** M R GOATER, **NSM** M P WARD
SHELFORD, LITTLE (All Saints) *Ely 6* **P** *Bp* **R** S J SCOTT, **C** T M CHAPMAN
SHELLAND (King Charles the Martyr) *see* Gt Finborough w Onehouse, Harleston, Buxhall etc *St E*
SHELLEY (All Saints) *see* Hadleigh, Layham and Shelley *St E*
SHELLEY (Emmanuel) and Shepley *Wakef 6* **P** *V Kirkburton* **P-in-c** J R JONES
SHELLEY (St Peter) *see* Chipping Ongar w Shelley *Chelmsf*
SHELLINGFORD (St Faith) *see* Uffington, Shellingford, Woolstone and Baulking *Ox*
SHELSLEY BEAUCHAMP (All Saints) *see* Clifton-on-Teme, Lower Sapey and the Shelsleys *Worc*
SHELSLEY WALSH (St Andrew) *as above*
SHELSWELL *Ox 2* **P** *Ld Chan (1 turn) and Ch Ch Ox, CCC Ox, Baroness von Maltzahn, and R J Vallings Esq (1 turn)* **R** W J YATES, **NSM** S L BUSHELL, K FERGUSON, **OLM** M G WHITE
SHELTHORPE (Good Shepherd) *see* Loughb Gd Shep *Leic*
SHELTON (Christ Church) and Oxon *Lich 20* **P** *V Shrewsbury St Chad w St Mary* **P-in-c** S CADDY, **OLM** M I FEARNSIDE
SHELTON (St Mark) *see* Hanley H Ev *Lich*
SHELTON (St Mary) *see* Hempnall *Nor*
SHELTON (St Mary) *see* The Stodden Churches *St Alb*
SHELTON (St Mary and All Saints) *S'well 3* **P** *Bp* **P-in-c** D HOLLIS
SHELVE (All Saints) *see* Hope w Shelve *Heref*
SHENFIELD (St Mary the Virgin) *Chelmsf 7* **P** *Personal Reps R H Courage* **R** P G BRETT, **NSM** E A LOCKHART
SHENINGTON (Holy Trinity) *see* Ironstone *Ox*
SHENLEY (St Martin) *see* Aldenham, Radlett and Shenley *St Alb*
SHENLEY (St Mary) *see* Watling Valley *Ox*
SHENLEY GREEN (St David) *Birm 4* **P** *Bp* **V** N A P EVANS
SHENSTONE (St John the Baptist) *Lich 1* **P** *MMCET* **P-in-c** R W BAILEY, **NSM** J B ASTON
SHENTON (St John the Evangelist) *see* Bosworth and Sheepy Gp *Leic*
SHEPHERD'S BUSH (St Luke) Uxbridge Road *see* Hammersmith St Luke *Lon*
SHEPHERD'S BUSH (St Simon) *see* Hammersmith St Simon *Lon*
SHEPHERD'S BUSH (St Stephen) (St Thomas) *Lon 9* **P** *Bp* **C** S E ARCHER, **NSM** A CLARRIDGE
SHEPLEY (St Paul) *see* Shelley and Shepley *Wakef*
SHEPPERDINE (Chapel) *see* Thornbury and Oldbury-on-Severn w Shepperdine *Glouc*
SHEPPERTON (St Nicholas) *Lon 13* **P** *Bp* **R** C J SWIFT, **NSM** H S L NICHOLSON
SHEPRETH (All Saints) *see* Fowlmere, Foxton, Shepreth and Thriplow *Ely*
SHEPSHED (St Botolph) and Oaks in Charnwood *Leic 7* **P** *DBP and Lord Crawshaw (jt)* **V** C M HEBDEN, **C** G R TURNER-CALLIS

SHEPTON BEAUCHAMP (St Michael) *see* Ilminster and Distr *B & W*
SHEPTON MALLET (St Peter and St Paul) w Doulting *B & W 8* **P** *Duchy of Cornwall and Bp (alt)* **R** E J SMITH, **C** M R WOOD, **NSM** R F REAKES
SHEPTON MONTAGUE (St Peter) *see* Bruton and Distr *B & W*
SHEPWELL GREEN (St Matthias) *see* Willenhall St Giles *Lich*
SHERBORNE (Abbey Church of St Mary) (All Souls) (St Paul) w Castleton and Lillington *Sarum 3* **P** *J K Wingfield Digby Esq* **V** E J WOODS, **C** A J B MONDS, J R SWINDELLS, **NSM** D J DUNNING, **OLM** B PHILLIPS
SHERBORNE (St Mary Magdalene), Windrush, the Barringtons and Aldsworth *Glouc 13* **P** *C T R Wingfield Esq, Ch Ch Ox, and DBP (by turn)* **P-in-c** M SELWOOD
SHERBORNES (St Andrew) (Vyne Chapel) w Pamber, The *Win 4* **P** *Bp and Qu Coll Ox (jt)* **R** J N HAMILTON
SHERBOURNE (All Saints) *see* Barford w Wasperton and Sherbourne *Cov*
SHERBURN (St Mary) *see* Pittington, Shadforth and Sherburn *Dur*
SHERBURN (St Hilda) *see* Buckrose Carrs *York*
SHERBURN IN ELMET (All Saints) w Saxton *York 4* **P** *Abp* **V** C I COATES, **NSM** C WILTON
SHERE (St James), Albury and Chilworth *Guildf 2* **P** *Bp, Mrs H Bray, Duke of Northd, W F P Hugonin Esq, and the Hon M W Ridley (jt)* **R** C A E LAWRENCE, **C** C J GRUNDY, **NSM** K B HOBBS, **OLM** J A POTTER
SHEREFORD (St Nicholas) *see* Upper Wensum Village Gp *Nor*
SHERFIELD ENGLISH (St Leonard) *see* E w W Wellow and Sherfield English *Win*
SHERFIELD-ON-LODDON (St Leonard) and Stratfield Saye w Hartley Wespall w Stratfield Turgis *Win 4* **P** *Bp, Duke of Wellington, and D&C Windsor (jt)* **R** R W POLITT
SHERFORD (St Martin) *see* Stokenham w Sherford and Beesands, and Slapton *Ex*
SHERIFF HUTTON (St Helen and the Holy Cross), Farlington, Stillington and Marton w Moxby *York 3* **P** *Abp (3 turns), DBP (1 turn)* **P-in-c** C C ELLIS
SHERIFFHALES (St Mary) *see* Lilleshall, Muxton and Sheriffhales *Lich*
SHERINGHAM (St Peter) *Nor 21* **P** *Bp* **V** A M WINDROSS
SHERINGHAM, UPPER (All Saints) *see* Weybourne Gp *Nor*
SHERINGTON (St Laud) w Chicheley, North Crawley, Astwood and Hardmead *Ox 27* **P** *Bp (2 turns), MMCET (1 turn), and Major J G B Chester (1 turn)* **R** M C STANTON-SARINGER
SHERMANBURY (St Giles) *see* Henfield w Shermanbury and Woodmancote *Chich*
SHERNBOURNE (St Peter and St Paul) *see* Dersingham w Anmer and Shernborne *Nor*
SHERRARDS GREEN (St Mary the Virgin) *see* Gt Malvern Ch Ch *Worc*
SHERRINGTON (St Cosmo and St Damian) *see* Upper Wylye Valley *Sarum*
SHERSTON MAGNA (Holy Cross), Easton Grey, Luckington, Alderton and Foxley w Bremilham *Bris 6* **P** *D&C, Bp, Adn Swindon and Lord Lilford (jt)* **V** M H ROSS
SHERWOOD (St Martin) *S'well 12* **P** *Bp* **V** S J GRIFFITHS, **C** M F SHOULER
SHERWOOD PARK (St Philip) *see* Tunbridge Wells St Phil *Roch*
SHEVINGTON (St Anne) *Blackb 4* **P** *R Standish* **V** P I DENNISON
SHEVIOCK (Blessed Virgin Mary) *see* Antony w Sheviock *Truro*
SHIFFORD (St Mary) *see* Bampton w Clanfield *Ox*
SHIFNAL (St Andrew) *Lich 16* **P** *R I Legge Esq* **P-in-c** G C FOWELL, **C** J A MCWHIRTER
SHILBOTEL (St James) *see* Shilbottle *Newc*
SHILBOTTLE (St James) *Newc 9* **P** *Dioc Soc* **P-in-c** E M DIXON
SHILDON (St John) *Dur 6* **P** *Bp* **V** *vacant* (01388) 772122
SHILL VALLEY and Broadshire *Ox 8* **P** *J Heyworth Esq, Mrs P Allen, and Ch Ch Ox (1 turn), Ch Soc Tr, F R Goodenough Esq, and D F Goodenough Esq (1 turn)* **R** H C MACINNES, **Hon C** J M MOUNT, **NSM** L N USHER-WILSON, E J JOHNSON
SHILLING OKEFORD (Holy Rood) *see* Okeford *Sarum*
SHILLINGFORD (St George) *see* Dunchideock and Shillingford St George w Ide *Ex*
SHILLINGSTONE (Holy Rood) *see* Okeford *Sarum*
SHILLINGTON (All Saints) *see* Gravenhurst, Shillington and Stondon *St Alb*
SHILTON (Holy Rood) *see* Shill Valley and Broadshire *Ox*
SHILTON (St Andrew) *see* Bulkington w Shilton and Ansty *Cov*
SHIMPLINGTHORNE (St George) *see* Chadbrook *St E*
SHINCLIFFE (St Mary the Virgin) *Dur 1* **P** *D&C* **P-in-c** S M SANDHAM
SHINEY ROW (St Oswald) *see* Herrington, Penshaw and Shiney Row *Dur*
SHINFIELD (St Mary) *see* Loddon Reach *Ox*
SHINGAY Group of Parishes, The *Ely 7* **P** *Bp, Mrs E E Sclater, Ch Patr Trust, Down Coll Cam, New CollOx, and Jes Coll Cam (jt)* **R** S F C WILLIAMS, **NSM** D R GINGRICH
SHIPBOURNE (St Giles) w Plaxtol *Roch 10* **P** *Bp and Sir Edward Cazalet* **R** S M RAMSARAN
SHIPDHAM (All Saints) w East and West Bradenham *Nor 17* **P** *Bp* **R** B J WOOD, **OLM** D FOTHERBY
SHIPHAM (St Leonard) *see* Axbridge w Shipham and Rowberrow *B & W*
SHIPHAY COLLATON (St John the Baptist) *Ex 12* **P** *Bp* **V** C E DEACON
SHIPLAKE (St Peter and St Paul) w Dunsden and Harpsden *Ox 6* **P** *All So Coll Ox, D&C Windsor, and DBP (jt)* **R** M R C PRICE, **NSM** S M COUSINS
SHIPLEY (St Mary the Virgin) *Chich 8* **P** *C R Burrell Esq* **P-in-c** P A SINTON
SHIPLEY (St Paul) *Bradf 1* **P** *Simeon's Trustees* **V** C R PENFOLD
SHIPLEY (St Peter) *Bradf 1* **P** *V Shipley St Paul* **V** J C RAINER, **C** N MCCATHIE
SHIPPON (St Mary Magdalene) *Ox 10* **P** *Bp* **NSM** P E SEAMAN
SHIPSTON-ON-STOUR (St Edmund) w Honington and Idlicote *Cov 9* **P** *Jes Coll Ox, D&C Worc, Bp (jt)* **P-in-c** D R THURBURN-HUELIN
SHIPTON (Holy Evangelist) *see* Skelton w Shipton and Newton on Ouse *York*
SHIPTON (St James) *see* Wenlock *Heref*
SHIPTON BELLINGER (St Peter) *see* Appleshaw, Kimpton, Thruxton, Fyfield etc *Win*
SHIPTON GORGE (St Martin) *see* Bride Valley *Sarum*
SHIPTON MOYNE (St John the Baptist) *Glouc 11* **P** *DBP* **V** A J WRIGHT
SHIPTON OLIFFE (St Oswald) *see* Sevenhampton w Charlton Abbots, Hawling etc *Glouc*
SHIPTON ON CHERWELL (Holy Cross) *see* Blenheim *Ox*
SHIPTON-UNDER-WYCHWOOD (St Mary) w Milton-under-Wychwood, Fifield and Idbury *Ox 3* **P** *Bp* **V** W M CALLAN, **OLM** A T HARTLEY
SHIPTONTHORPE (All Saints) and Hayton *York 5* **P** *Abp* **NSM** S D JONES
SHIREBROOK (Holy Trinity) *see* E Scarsdale *Derby*
SHIREGREEN (St Hilda) *Sheff 3* **P** *Bp* **P-in-c** A NASCIMENTO COOK
SHIREGREEN (St James and St Christopher) *Sheff 3* **P** *Dean* **P-in-c** A NASCIMENTO COOK, **C** A H MORGAN
SHIREHAMPTON (St Mary) *Bris 2* **P** *Bp* **P-in-c** C A FROUDE, **C** A W E SCHUMAN
SHIREMOOR (St Mark) *Newc 8* **P** *Bp* **V** P M SCOTT
SHIREOAKS (St Luke) *S'well 6* **P** *Bp* **V** *vacant* (01909) 486537
SHIRES' EDGE *Ox 5* **P** *Bp* **V** P FREETH, **OLM** L M ALCOCK
SHIRLAND (St Leonard) *see* Morton and Stonebroom w Shirland *Derby*
SHIRLEY (Christ the King) *see* Salter Street and Shirley *Birm*
SHIRLEY (St George) *S'wark 22* **P** *Bp* **V** D J FROST, **OLM** C JONES
SHIRLEY (St James) (St John) *Win 13* **P** *Ch Patr Trust* **V** D P HAZLEWOOD, **C** N R SMART
SHIRLEY (St James the Great) *see* Salter Street and Shirley *Birm*
SHIRLEY (St John) *S'wark 22* **P** *Bp* **V** A H R QUINN, **Hon C** A C COLLIER
SHIRLEY (St John the Divine) *see* Salter Street and Shirley *Birm*
SHIRLEY (St Luke) *as above*
SHIRLEY (St Mary Magdalene) *as above*
SHIRLEY (St Michael) *see* Brailsford w Shirley and Osmaston w Edlaston *Derby*
SHIRLEY WARREN (St Jude) *see* Southampton St Jude *Win*
SHIRWELL (St Peter), Loxhore, Kentisbury, Arlington, East Down, Bratton Fleming, Challacombe and Stoke Rivers *Ex 18* **P** *Patr Bd* **TR** L E AUSTIN, **TV** C J HUDSPITH
SHOBDON (St John the Evangelist) *see* Pembridge w Moor Court, Shobdon, Staunton etc *Heref*
SHOBNALL (St Aidan) *Lich 14* **P** *Bp* **V** *vacant* (01283) 845130

SHOBROOKE (St Swithin) *see* Crediton, Shobrooke and Sandford etc *Ex*
SHOCKLACH (St Edith) *see* Tilston and Shocklach *Ches*
SHOEBURY, NORTH (St Mary the Virgin) *Chelmsf 13* **P** *Ld Chan* **V** I ST J FISHER
SHOEBURY, SOUTH (St Andrew) (St Peter) *Chelmsf 13* **P** *Hyndman Trustees* **R** J R D KEMP
SHOLDEN (St Nicholas) *see* Deal St Leon w St Rich and Sholden etc *Cant*
SHOLING (St Francis of Assisi) (St Mary) *Win 13* **P** *Bp* **V** B J HARTNELL, **C** S M STEVENS
SHOOTERS HILL (All Saints) *see* Plumstead All SS *S'wark*
SHOOTERS HILL (Christ Church) *S'wark 3* **P** *Bp* **V** N C WHITTLE, **NSM** J N PHILPOTT-HOWARD
SHORE (St Barnabas) *Man 20* **P** *D&C* **P-in-c** M S THORP, **OLM** B WOODHEAD
SHOREDITCH (All Saints) Haggerston Road *see* Dalston H Trin w St Phil and Haggerston All SS *Lon*
SHOREDITCH (St Anne) Hoxton Street *see* Hoxton St Anne w St Columba *Lon*
SHOREDITCH (St Leonard) w St Michael *Lon 5* **P** *Bp and Adn (jt)* **V** P R TURP
SHOREHAM (St Giles) *see* Kingston Buci *Chich*
SHOREHAM (St Peter and St Paul) *Roch 10* **P** *D&C Westmr* **P-in-c** R A FREEMAN
SHOREHAM, NEW (St Mary de Haura) *Chich 4* **P** *Bp* **V** V STANDING, **C** R WARHURST
SHOREHAM, OLD (St Nicolas) *Chich 4* **P** *Bp* **V** V STANDING, **C** R WARHURST
SHOREHAM BEACH (Good Shepherd) *Chich 4* **P** *Bp* **V** Q M RONCHETTI
SHORNE (St Peter and St Paul) *Roch 4* **P** *D&C* **V** P E LONGBOTTOM
SHORT HEATH (Holy Trinity) *see* Willenhall H Trin *Lich*
SHORT HEATH (St Margaret) *Birm 8* **P** *Bp* **V** T D HILL-BROWN, **C** R M ROGERS
SHORTHAMPTON (All Saints) *see* Charlbury w Shorthampton *Ox*
SHORTLANDS (All Saints' Community Church) *see* Bromley SS Pet and Paul *Roch*
SHORTLANDS (St Mary) *Roch 13* **P** *Bp* **V** P MILLER
SHORTWOOD (All Saints) *see* Nailsworth w Shortwood, Horsley etc *Glouc*
SHORWELL (St Peter) w Kingston *Portsm 8* **P** *Bp* **V** J W RUSSELL, **Hon C** M R HODGE, **NSM** L F HUMPHRYS
SHOSCOMBE (St Julian) *see* Camerton w Dunkerton, Foxcote and Shoscombe *B & W*
SHOTESHAM (All Saints w St Mary) *see* Newton Flotman, Swainsthorpe, Tasburgh, etc *Nor*
SHOTLEY (St John) *Newc 3* **P** *Lord Crewe's Trustees* **P-in-c** T J ATKINS
SHOTLEY (St Mary) *St E 5* **P** *Bp* **P-in-c** P THORN, **OLM** T J CROSBIE
SHOTTERMILL (St Stephen) *Guildf 4* **P** *Adn Surrey* **V** A J GREADY, **NSM** H S WILLIAMS
SHOTTERY (St Andrew) *Cov 8* **P** *Bp* **V** J R WARREN
SHOTTESBROOKE (St John the Baptist) *see* White Waltham w Shottesbrooke *Ox*
SHOTTESWELL (St Lawrence) *see* Warmington w Shotteswell and Radway w Ratley *Cov*
SHOTTISHAM (St Margaret) *see* Wilford Peninsula *St E*
SHOTTLE (St Lawrence) *see* Hazelwood, Holbrook and Milford *Derby*
SHOTTON (St Saviour) *see* Haswell, Shotton and Thornley *Dur*
SHOTWICK (St Michael) *see* Burton and Shotwick *Ches*
SHOULDHAM (All Saints) *Ely 13* **P** *Bp* **P-in-c** D J POMERY, **Hon C** A G F VILLER
SHOULDHAM THORPE (St Mary) *Ely 13* **P** *Bp* **P-in-c** D J POMERY, **Hon C** A G F VILLER
SHRAWARDINE (St Mary) *see* Bicton, Montford w Shrawardine and Fitz *Lich*
SHRAWLEY (St Mary), Witley, Astley and Abberley *Worc 13* **P** *Bp and Guild of All So (jt)* **R** A NORKETT
SHRED (Mission Church) *see* Slaithwaite w E Scammonden *Wakef*
SHREWSBURY (All Saints and St Michael) *Lich 20* **P** *Bp* **V** D F MAWSON
SHREWSBURY (Christ Church) *see* Shelton and Oxon *Lich*
SHREWSBURY (Holy Cross) (St Peter) *Lich 20* **P** *Bp* **V** C S SIMS, **C** C M ORME
SHREWSBURY (Holy Trinity) (St Julian) *Lich 20* **P** *Bp and Ch Patr Trust (jt)* **P-in-c** R D SPENCER
SHREWSBURY (St Alkmund) *Lich 20* **P** *Bp* **Hon C** R HAYES
SHREWSBURY (St Chad) w St Mary *Lich 20* **P** *Bp* **P-in-c** M W THOMAS, **C** R P MCKENZIE
SHREWSBURY (St George of Cappadocia) w Greenfields United Church *Lich 20* **P** *V Shrewsbury St Chad* **V** P F BARNES, **C** P R-M DE G GOWER
SHREWSBURY (St Giles) w Sutton and Atcham *Lich 20* **P** *Bp and R L Burton Esq (jt)* **R** P J WILLIAMS
SHREWTON (St Mary) *see* Wylye and Till Valley *Sarum*
SHRIVENHAM (St Andrew) and Ashbury *Ox 17* **P** *Ld Chan* **V** R M A HANCOCK, **NSM** M R STARR
SHROPHAM (St Peter) *see* Gt and Lt Ellingham, Rockland and Shropham etc *Nor*
SHROTON (St Mary) *see* Iwerne Valley *Sarum*
SHRUB END (All Saints) (St Cedd) *Chelmsf 16* **P** *Bp* **V** N A W DAVIS, **C** S E A MILES
SHUCKBURGH, LOWER (St John the Baptist) *see* Napton-on-the-Hill, Lower Shuckburgh etc *Cov*
SHUDY CAMPS (St Mary) *see* Linton *Ely*
SHURDINGTON (St Paul) *see* Badgeworth, Shurdington and Witcombe w Bentham *Glouc*
SHUSTOKE (St Cuthbert) *see* The Whitacres and Shustoke *Birm*
SHUTE (St Michael) *see* Kilmington, Stockland, Dalwood, Yarcombe etc *Ex*
SHUTFORD (St Martin) *see* Wykeham *Ox*
SHUTTINGTON (St Matthew) *see* Newton Regis w Seckington and Shuttington *Birm*
SHUTTLEWOOD (St Laurence Mission Church) *see* Bolsover *Derby*
SHUTTLEWORTH (St John) *see* Ramsbottom St Jo and St Paul *Man*
SIBBERTOFT (St Helen) *see* Welford w Sibbertoft and Marston Trussell *Pet*
SIBDON CARWOOD (St Michael) w Halford *Heref 11* **P** *Bp and R Holden (alt)* **P-in-c** M L COPE
SIBERTSWOLD (St Andrew) *see* Eythorne and Elvington w Waldershare etc *Cant*
SIBFORD (Holy Trinity) *see* Wykeham *Ox*
SIBLE HEDINGHAM (St Peter) w Castle Hedingham *Chelmsf 19* **P** *Bp, and Hon T R Lindsay (alt)* **R** D N KELLY
SIBSEY (St Margaret) w Frithville *Linc 20* **P** *Ld Chan* **V** W G PAGE, **NSM** J M MORTON
SIBSON (St Botolph) *see* Bosworth and Sheepy Gp *Leic*
SIBTHORPE (St Peter) *S'well 3* **P** *Bp* **P-in-c** D HOLLIS
SIBTON (St Peter) *see* Yoxford, Peasenhall and Sibton *St E*
SICKLINGHALL (St Peter) *see* Lower Wharfedale *Ripon*
SID VALLEY *see* Sidmouth, Woolbrook, Salcombe Regis, Sidbury etc *Ex*
SIDBURY (Holy Trinity) *see* Stottesdon w Farlow, Cleeton St Mary etc *Heref*
SIDBURY (St Giles and St Peter) *see* Sidmouth, Woolbrook, Salcombe Regis, Sidbury etc *Ex*
SIDCUP (Christ Church) Longland *Roch 17* **P** *Ch Trust Fund Trust* **V** A K WILSON
SIDCUP (St Andrew) *Roch 17* **P** *Bp* **V** D HILDRED
SIDCUP (St John the Evangelist) *Roch 17* **P** *D&C* **V** S SEALY
SIDDAL (St Mark) *Wakef 4* **P** *Ch Trust Fund Trust* **P-in-c** C SMITH
SIDDINGTON (All Saints) *see* Capesthorne w Siddington and Marton *Ches*
SIDDINGTON (St Peter) w Preston *Glouc 11* **P** *Ld Chan and R T G Chester-Master Esq (alt)* **P-in-c** J R CALVERT, **NSM** N F LUCKETT
SIDESTRAND (St Michael) *see* Overstrand, Northrepps, Sidestrand etc *Nor*
SIDFORD (St Peter) *see* Sidmouth, Woolbrook, Salcombe Regis, Sidbury etc *Ex*
SIDLESHAM (St Mary the Virgin) *Chich 3* **P** *Bp* **P-in-c** A K JENKINS
SIDLEY (All Saints) *Chich 14* **P** *R Bexhill* **V** T G BUXTON
SIDLOW BRIDGE (Emmanuel) *S'wark 27* **P** *DBP* **R** W G CAMPEN
SIDMOUTH (St Nicholas w St Giles), Woolbrook, Salcombe Regis, Sidbury w Sidford, and All Saints Sidmouth *Ex 7* **P** *Patr Bd* **TR** D H JAMES, **TV** R G PECKHAM, R D TRUMPER, **Hon C** S W WILLINK
SIGGLESTHORNE (St Lawrence) w Nunkeeling and Bewholme *York 11* **P** *Prime Min* **R** *vacant* (01964) 533033
SILCHESTER (St Mary) *see* Tadley S and Silchester *Win*
SILCHESTER COMMON (Mission Church) *as above*
SILEBY (St Mary), Cossington and Seagrave *Leic 6* **P** *Patr Bd* **R** *vacant* (01509) 812493
SILK WILLOUGHBY (St Denis) *Linc 22* **P** *Sir Lyonel Tollemache Bt* **P-in-c** P J MANDER, **C** A J HIGGINSON
SILKSTONE (All Saints) *see* Hoylandswaine and Silkstone w Stainborough *Wakef*
SILKSTONE COMMON (Mission Room) *as above*
SILKSWORTH (St Matthew) *Dur 16* **P** *Bp* **V** R G E BRADSHAW

SILLOTH (Christ Church) *see* Solway Plain *Carl*
SILSDEN (St James) *Bradf 8* **P** *Bp, Adn Craven, and Trustees (jt)* **V** J P GREENWOOD, **C** J MEDHURST
SILSOE (St James), Pulloxhill and Flitton *St Alb 9* **P** *Ball Coll Ox and Bp (alt)* **V** S C HOLROYD
SILTON (St Nicholas) *Sarum 5* **P** *DBP* **R** *vacant*
SILTON, NETHER (All Saints) *see* Leake w Over and Nether Silton and Kepwick *York*
SILTON, OVER (St Mary) *as above*
SILVER END (St Francis) *see* Rivenhall *Chelmsf*
SILVERDALE (St John) *Blackb 14* **P** *V Warton* **P-in-c** P K WARREN, **NSM** J NOVELL
SILVERDALE (St Luke) *Lich 9* **P** *T H G Howard-Sneyd Esq* **V** S A ANSELL, **NSM** S W JOHNSON
SILVERHILL (St Matthew) *Chich 17* **P** *Simeon's Trustees* **R** M S COE, **C** A D PICKERING
SILVERSTONE (St Michael) and Abthorpe w Slapton and Whittlebury and Paulerspury *Pet 5* **P** *T L Langton-Lockton Esq, Leeson's Trustees, and New Coll Ox (3 turns), Prime Min (2 turns)* **R** B M SMITH, **C** P A REID
SILVERTON (St Mary), Butterleigh, Bickleigh and Cadeleigh *Ex 8* **P** *Bp and Sir Rivers Carew Bt* **R** A H MACDONALD, **NSM** C JENKINS
SILVINGTON (St Michael) *see* Stottesdon w Farlow, Cleeton St Mary etc *Heref*
SIMONBURN (St Mungo) *see* Humshaugh w Simonburn and Wark *Newc*
SIMONSTONE (St Peter) *see* Padiham w Hapton and Padiham Green *Blackb*
SIMPSON (St Thomas) *see* Woughton *Ox*
SINFIN (St Stephen) *Derby 10* **P** *CPAS* **P-in-c** P R SANDFORD
SINFIN MOOR (not known) *Derby 10* **P** *Bp* **V** *vacant* (01332) 760016
SINGLETON (Blessed Virgin Mary) *Chich 13* **P** *Bp* **R** R T E B WOODS
SINGLETON (St Anne) *see* Poulton Carleton and Singleton *Blackb*
SINNINGTON (All Saints) *see* Middleton, Newton and Sinnington *York*
SISLAND (St Mary) *see* Loddon, Sisland, Chedgrave, Hardley and Langley *Nor*
SISSINGHURST (Holy Trinity) w Frittenden *Cant 11* **P** *CPAS* **V** A E NORRIS
SITHNEY (St Sithney) *see* Porthleven w Sithney *Truro*
SITTINGBOURNE (Holy Trinity) w Bobbing *Cant 15* **P** *Abp* **P-in-c** M J RESCH, **NSM** E J WILLIAMS
SITTINGBOURNE (St Mary) (St Michael) *Cant 15* **P** *Abp and D&C (jt)* **V** N FINLAY, **C** B C LANE
SITTINGBOURNE (St Peter and St Paul) *see* Borden *Cant*
SIX HILLS (Mission) *see* Old Dalby, Nether Broughton, Saxelbye etc *Leic*
SIX MILE BOTTOM (St George) *see* Lt Wilbraham *Ely*
SIX PILGRIMS, The *B & W 3* **P** *Ch Soc Trust, D&C, DBF, and Bp (by turn)* **P-in-c** P T CRAIG
SIX SAINTS circa Holt: Bringhurst, Great Easton, Medbourne cum Holt, Stockerston and Blaston *Leic 4* **P** *D&C Pet and Adn Leic (2 turns), St Jo Coll Cam (1 turn)* **R** S J BISHOP
SIXHILLS (All Saints) *see* Barkwith Gp *Linc*
SIXPENNY HANDLEY (St Mary) w Gussage St Andrew and Pentridge *Sarum 6* **P** *D&C Windsor and Earl of Shaftesbury (alt)* **NSM** W M GRIFFITH
SKEEBY (St Agatha's District Church) *see* Easby w Skeeby and Brompton on Swale etc *Ripon*
SKEFFINGTON (St Thomas à Beckett) *see* Church Langton cum Tur Langton etc *Leic*
SKEFFLING (St Helen) *see* Easington w Skeffling, Kilnsea and Holmpton *York*
SKEGBY (St Andrew) w Teversal *S'well 4* **P** *DBP and Ld Chan (alt)* **R** R KELLETT, **C** S J TREDWELL
SKEGNESS Group, The (St Clement) (St Matthew) *Linc 8* **P** *Bp and DBP (2 turns), and Ld Chan (1 turn)* **R** C M FRANCE, **C** L BOND, **NSM** R G WILKINSON
SKELBROOKE (St Michael and All Angels) *see* Adwick-le-Street w Skelbrooke *Sheff*
SKELLINGTHORPE (St Lawrence) w Doddington *Linc 18* **P** *MMCET* **R** R G BILLINGHURST
SKELLOW (St Michael and All Angels) *see* Owston *Sheff*
SKELMANTHORPE (St Aidan) *Wakef 6* **P** *Bp* **P-in-c** P D REYNOLDS
SKELMERSDALE (Church at the Centre) *Liv 11* **P** *Bp* **P-in-c** G E GREENWOOD
SKELMERSDALE (St Paul) *Liv 11* **P** *V Ormskirk* **V** G E GREENWOOD, **C** S JONES
SKELSMERGH (St John the Baptist) w Selside and Longsleddale *Carl 10* **P** *V Kendal H Trin and DBP (alt)* **V** R D J DEW
SKELTON (All Saints) w Upleatham *York 16* **P** *Abp* **R** G J PACEY
SKELTON (St Giles) w Shipton and Newton on Ouse *York 3* **P** *Abp* **R** E W A CRAGG
SKELTON (St Michael) *see* Inglewood Gp *Carl*
SKELTON-CUM-NEWBY (St Helen's Old Church) *see* Kirby-on-the-Moor, Cundall w Norton-le-Clay etc *Ripon*
SKENDLEBY (St Peter and St Paul) *see* Partney Gp *Linc*
SKERNE (St Leonard) *see* Hutton Cranswick w Skerne, Watton and Beswick *York*
SKERNE, UPPER *Dur 5* **P** *Ld Chan (1 turn), Patr Bd (2 turns)* **NSM** J A ROGERS
SKERTON (St Chad) *Blackb 11* **P** *Bp* **V** R S WADEY
SKERTON (St Luke) *Blackb 11* **P** *Trustees* **V** G LEWIS
SKEYTON (All Saints) *see* King's Beck *Nor*
SKIDBY (St Michael) *see* Rowley w Skidby *York*
SKILGATE (St John the Baptist) *see* Brompton Regis w Upton and Skilgate *B & W*
SKILLINGTON (St James) *see* Colsterworth Gp *Linc*
SKIPSEA (All Saints) w Ulrome and Barmston w Fraisthorpe *York 9* **P** *Abp, The Hon S E Cunliffe-Lister, Trustees A Potter and D Potter, Mrs R Potter, and P Roworth Esq (jt)* **P-in-c** J J L HAY
SKIPTON (Christ Church) *Bradf 7* **P** *R Skipton H Trin* **V** D N WILLIAMS, **C** A J FERNELEY
SKIPTON (Holy Trinity) *Bradf 7* **P** *Ch Ch Ox* **R** A P BOTWRIGHT
SKIPTON ON SWALE (St John) *see* Topcliffe, Baldersby w Dishforth, Dalton etc *York*
SKIPWITH (St Helen) *see* Bubwith w Skipwith *York*
SKIRBECK (Holy Trinity) *Linc 20* **P** *Trustees* **V** S P DOWSON
SKIRBECK (St Nicholas) *Linc 20* **P** *DBP* **R** P V NOBLE
SKIRBECK QUARTER (St Thomas) *Linc 20* **P** *DBP* **V** *vacant* (01205) 367380
SKIRLAUGH (St Augustine) w Long Riston, Rise and Swine *York 11* **P** *Abp, Abp and Baroness de Stempel, and Ld Chan (by turn)* **V** D W PERRY
SKIRPENBECK (St Mary) *see* Garrowby Hill *York*
SKIRWITH (St John the Evangelist) *see* Cross Fell Gp *Carl*
SLAD (Holy Trinity) *see* Stroud and Uplands w Slad *Glouc*
SLADE GREEN (St Augustine) *Roch 15* **P** *Bp* **V** *vacant* (01322) 337085
SLAIDBURN (St Andrew) *Bradf 5* **P** *Ch Soc Trust* **P-in-c** M R RUSSELL-SMITH, **NSM** R E WILSON
SLAITHWAITE (St James) w East Scammonden *Wakef 5* **P** *V Huddersfield* **V** C R TOWNSEND
SLALEY (St Mary the Virgin) *Newc 3* **P** *Bp* **P-in-c** D J IRVINE, **NSM** J LYNCH
SLAPTON (Holy Cross) *see* Ivinghoe w Pitstone and Slapton *Ox*
SLAPTON (St Botolph) *see* Silverstone and Abthorpe w Slapton etc *Pet*
SLAPTON (St James the Great) *see* Stokenham w Sherford and Beesands, and Slapton *Ex*
SLAUGHAM (St Mary) *Chich 6* **P** *Mrs D M Irwin-Clark* **R** G D SIMMONS, **Hon C** K W HABERSHON
SLAUGHTER, LOWER (St Mary) *see* The Guitings, Cutsdean, Farmcote etc *Glouc*
SLAUGHTER, UPPER (St Peter) *as above*
SLAUGHTERFORD (St Nicholas) *see* By Brook *Bris*
SLAWSTON (All Saints) *see* Hallaton w Horninghold and Allexton, Tugby etc *Leic*
SLEAFORD, NEW (St Denys) *Linc 22* **P** *Bp* **P-in-c** J A PATRICK
SLEDMERE (St Mary) *see* Waggoners *York*
SLEEKBURN (St John) *see* Cambois and Sleekburn *Newc*
SLEIGHTS (St John) *see* Eskdaleside w Ugglebarnby and Sneaton *York*
SLIMBRIDGE (St John the Evangelist) *see* Sharpness, Purton, Brookend and Slimbridge *Glouc*
SLINDON (St Chad) *see* Eccleshall *Lich*
SLINDON (St Mary), Eartham and Madehurst *Chich 1* **P** *Bp, D&C, and Mrs J Izard (jt)* **P-in-c** S M CONSTABLE
SLINFOLD (St Peter) *see* Itchingfield w Slinfold *Chich*
SLINGSBY (All Saints) *see* The Street Par *York*
SLIPTON (St John the Baptist) *Pet 11* **P** *L G Stopford Sackville Esq* **P-in-c** D H P FOOT
SLITTING MILL (St John the Baptist) *see* Rugeley *Lich*
SLOANE STREET (Holy Trinity) *see* Upper Chelsea H Trin w St Jude *Lon*
SLOLEY (St Bartholomew) *see* Worstead, Westwick, Sloley, Swanton Abbot etc *Nor*
SLOUGH (St Paul) (Christ Church) *Ox 23* **P** *Trustees* **V** M C COTTERELL

SLOUGH, WEST *Ox 23* **P** *Patr Bd* **TV** J S W CHORLTON, J S G COTMAN, S SMITH
SLYNE (St Luke) w Hest *Blackb 14* **P** *Bp* **P-in-c** P A BICKNELL
SMALL HEATH (All Saints) *Birm 13* **P** *Patr Bd* **V** B A I SMART
SMALLBRIDGE (St John the Baptist) and Wardle *Man 20* **P** *Bp* **P-in-c** A J HOWELL
SMALLBURGH (St Peter) w Dilham w Honing and Crostwight *Nor 12* **P** *Bp, T R Cubitt Esq, and J C Wickman Esq (jt)* **P-in-c** D R ANDERSON, **C** P J G BARNES-CLAY
SMALLEY (St John the Baptist) *see* Morley w Smalley and Horsley Woodhouse *Derby*
SMALLFIELD (Church Room) *see* Burstow w Horne *S'wark*
SMALLHYTHE (St John the Baptist) *see* Tenterden St Mildred w Smallhythe *Cant*
SMALLTHORNE (St Saviour) *Lich 11* **P** *R Norton in the Moors* **V** R J S GRIGSON
SMALLWOOD (St John the Baptist) *see* Astbury and Smallwood *Ches*
SMANNELL (Christ Church) *see* Knight's Enham and Smannell w Enham Alamein *Win*
SMARDEN (St Michael) *see* Biddenden and Smarden *Cant*
SMAWTHORPE (St Michael and All Angels) *Wakef 11* **P** *Bp* **V** E I CHETWYND
SMEATON, GREAT (St Eloy) *see* E Richmond *Ripon*
SMEETH (St Mary) w Monks Horton and Stowting and Brabourne *Cant 10* **P** *Abp* **V** *vacant* (01303) 812697
SMEETON WESTERBY (Christ Church) *see* Kibworth and Smeeton Westerby and Saddington *Leic*
SMESTOW VALE TEAM *Lich 24* **P** *Patr Bd* **TR** A P BROWN, **TV** M INMAN, P J REGAN, **Hon C** D J BELCHER
SMETHCOTT (St Michael) *see* Dorrington w Leebotwood, Longnor, Stapleton etc *Heref*
SMETHWICK (Old Church) *Birm 7* **P** *Dorothy Parkes Trustees* **V** R M PRYCE
SMETHWICK (Resurrection) (St Stephen and St Michael) *Birm 7* **P** *Bp* **V** J D R COX
SMETHWICK (St Mary the Virgin) *see* Bearwood *Birm*
SMETHWICK (St Matthew w St Chad) *Birm 7* **P** *Bp and V Smethwick (alt)* **V** P E NICHOLSON
SMISBY (St James) *see* Ticknall, Smisby and Stanton by Bridge etc *Derby*
SMITHILLS HALL (Chapel) *see* Halliwell St Pet *Man*
SMORRALL LANE (St Andrew) *see* Bedworth *Cov*
SNAILBEACH (St Luke) *see* Minsterley *Heref*
SNAILWELL (St Peter) *Ely 3* **P** *Mrs A Crawley* **R** *vacant*
SNAINTON (St Stephen) *see* Brompton by Sawdon w Hutton Buscel, Snainton etc *York*
SNAITH (St Laurence Priory) *see* Gt Snaith *Sheff*
SNAITH, GREAT (Holy Trinity) (St John the Baptist) (St Paul) *Sheff 10* **P** *Bp* **TR** C ROBERTS
SNAPE (St John the Baptist) *see* Sternfield, Benhall, Snape etc *St E*
SNAPE CASTLE (Chapel of St Mary) *see* W Tanfield and Well w Snape and N Stainley *Ripon*
SNARESTONE (St Bartholomew) *see* Appleby Gp *Leic*
SNARGATE (St Dunstan) *see* Appledore w Brookland, Fairfield, Brenzett etc *Cant*
SNEAD (St Mary the Virgin) *see* Wentnor w Ratlinghope, Myndtown, Norbury etc *Heref*
SNEATON (St Hilda) *see* Eskdaleside w Ugglebarnby and Sneaton *York*
SNEINTON (St Christopher) w St Philip *S'well 13* **P** *CPAS and Trustees (alt)* **P-in-c** A M SMYTHE, **NSM** A R HASKEY
SNEINTON (St Cyprian) *S'well 13* **P** *Bp* **P-in-c** K H BALL
SNEINTON (St Stephen) w St Matthias *S'well 13* **P** *Bp and SMF (jt)* **V** M G CROOK
SNELLAND (All Saints) *see* Wragby Gp *Linc*
SNELSTON (St Peter) *see* Norbury w Snelston *Derby*
SNETTISHAM (St Mary) w Ingoldisthorpe and Fring *Nor 16* **P** *Bp, CPAS, and D&C (jt)* **R** G H SUART
SNEYD (Holy Trinity) *Lich 11* **P** *Bp* **V** B L WILLIAMS
SNEYD GREEN (St Andrew) *Lich 11* **P** *Bp* **V** G R DAVIES
SNIBSTON (St James) *see* Hugglescote w Donington, Ellistown and Snibston *Leic*
SNITTERBY (St Nicholas) *see* Bishop Norton, Wadingham and Snitterby *Linc*
SNITTERFIELD (St James the Great) w Bearley *Cov 7* **P** *Bp and V Wootton Wawen* **P-in-c** R LIVINGSTON
SNODLAND (All Saints) (Christ Church) *Roch 1* **P** *Bp and CPAS (jt)* **R** J E TIPP, **C** E J NORTHERN
SNORING, GREAT (St Mary) *see* Barney, Fulmodeston w Croxton, Hindringham etc *Nor*
SNORING, LITTLE (St Andrew) *as above*
SNOWDEN HILL Chapel Farm (not known) *see* Penistone and Thurlstone *Wakef*
SNOWSHILL (St Barnabas) *see* Winchcombe *Glouc*
SOBERTON (St Peter) w Newtown *Portsm 1* **P** *Bp* **P-in-c** S H HOLT
SOCKBURN (All Saints) *see* Dinsdale w Sockburn *Dur*
SODBURY, LITTLE (St Adeline) *see* Horton and Lt Sodbury *Glouc*
SODBURY, OLD (St John the Baptist) *see* Chipping Sodbury and Old Sodbury *Glouc*
SOHAM (St Andrew) and Wicken *Ely 3* **P** *Pemb Coll Cam (1 turn), Pemb Coll Cam and Ch Patr Trust (jt) (1 turn)* **V** T M ALBAN-JONES, **C** E B GREEN
SOHO (St Anne) (St Thomas) (St Peter) *Lon 3* **P** *R Westmr St Jas* **R** C M HERBERT, **NSM** J S FRANCIS, R S F BUCKLEY
SOLE BAY Team Ministry, The *St E 15* **P** *Patr Bd* **TR** J J WILSON, **TV** D A EATON, L J PAYNE, S W J WARD, J E EATON, **C** C M HALLETT, **OLM** B R FISHER
SOLIHULL (Catherine de Barnes) (St Alphege) (St Helen) (St Michael) *Birm 11* **P** *Patr Bd* **TR** T W PILKINGTON, **TV** P J TAYLOR, M A JONES, **C** S A RICHARDS, **NSM** R J MURRAY
SOLLARS HOPE (St Michael) *see* How Caple w Sollarshope, Sellack etc *Heref*
SOLWAY PLAIN *Carl 7* **P** *Patr Bd* **TR** J M S FALKNER, **TV** A BYROM, **C** P M F STREATFEILD, **Hon C** P N HAYWARD, **NSM** D TEMBEY, M I STUDHOLME
SOMBORNE w Ashley *Win 12* **P** *Bp* **P-in-c** R V STAPLETON
SOMERBY (All Saints) *see* Burrough Hill Pars *Leic*
SOMERBY (St Margaret) *see* N Wolds Gp *Linc*
SOMERBY, NEW (St Anne) *see* Grantham St Anne New Somerby and Spitalgate *Linc*
SOMERBY, OLD (St Mary Magdalene) *Linc 14* **P** *Baroness Willoughby de Eresby* **R** *vacant*
SOMERCOTES and Grainthorpe w Conisholme *Linc 12* **P** *Duchy of Lanc (2 turns), Magd Coll Cam and Bp (1 turn)* **R** M K DAVIES
SOMERCOTES (St Thomas) *Derby 1* **P** *Bp* **V** G M KNOX
SOMERCOTES, NORTH (St Mary) *see* Somercotes and Grainthorpe w Conisholme *Linc*
SOMERFORD (All Saints) *see* Astbury and Smallwood *Ches*
SOMERFORD (St Mary) *see* Christchurch *Win*
SOMERFORD, GREAT (St Peter and St Paul), Little Somerford, Seagry and Corston w Rodbourne *Bris 6* **P** *Bp, MMCET, and Ex Coll Ox (jt) (3 turns), Ld Chan (2 turns)* **R** J E G OSWALD
SOMERFORD, LITTLE (St John the Baptist) *see* Gt Somerford, Lt Somerford, Seagry, Corston etc *Bris*
SOMERFORD KEYNES (All Saints) *see* Kemble, Poole Keynes, Somerford Keynes etc *Glouc*
SOMERLEYTON (St Mary), Ashby, Fritton, Herringfleet, Blundeston and Lound *Nor 9* **P** *Lord Somerleyton and SMF (jt)* **R** R A E KENT, **NSM** L HOBBS
SOMERS TOWN (St Mary the Virgin) *see* Old St Pancras *Lon*
SOMERSAL HERBERT (St Peter) *see* Doveridge, Scropton, Sudbury etc *Derby*
SOMERSBY (St Margaret) *see* S Ormsby Gp *Linc*
SOMERSHAM (St John the Baptist) w Pidley and Oldhurst *Ely 9* **P** *Bp* **R** C S BARTER
SOMERSHAM (St Mary) w Flowton and Offton w Willisham *St E 1* **P** *Bp and MMCET (jt)* **P-in-c** L E FLETCHER
SOMERTON (St James) *see* Cherwell Valley *Ox*
SOMERTON (St Margaret) *see* Glemsford, Hartest w Boxted, Somerton etc *St E*
SOMERTON (St Michael and All Angels) w Compton Dundon, the Charltons and Kingsdon *B & W 6* **P** *Bp Lon (1 turn), Bp (2 turns), and DBP (1 turn)* **C** K J HILL
SOMERTON, WEST (St Mary) *see* Flegg Coastal Benefice *Nor*
SOMPTING (St Mary the Virgin) (St Peter) *Chich 5* **P** *OStJ* **V** E K HOWARD
SONNING (St Andrew) (St Patrick) *Ox 16* **P** *Bp* **V** C G CLARKE, **Hon C** M D C FORRER
SONNING COMMON (Christ the King) *see* Rotherfield Peppard and Kidmore End etc *Ox*
SOOKHOLME (St Augustine) *see* Warsop *S'well*
SOOTHILL (St Luke) *see* Hanging Heaton *Wakef*
SOPLEY (St Michael and All Angels) *see* Burton and Sopley *Win*
SOPWORTH (St Mary the Virgin) *see* Boxwell, Leighterton, Didmarton, Oldbury etc *Glouc*
SOTHERTON (St Andrew) *see* Sole Bay *St E*
SOTTERLEY (St Margaret) *see* Hundred River *St E*
SOTWELL (St James) *see* Wallingford *Ox*
SOUDLEY (St Michael) *see* Cinderford St Jo *Glouc*

SOULBURY (All Saints) *see* Stewkley w Soulbury and Drayton Parslow *Ox*
SOULDERN (Annunciation of the Blessed Virgin Mary) *see* Cherwell Valley *Ox*
SOULDROP (All Saints) *see* Sharnbrook and Knotting w Souldrop *St Alb*
SOUNDWELL (St Stephen) *Bris 5* **P** *Bp* **V** I L WILLS, **C** S J PULLIN
SOURTON (St Thomas of Canterbury) *see* Okehampton w Inwardleigh, Bratton Clovelly etc *Ex*
SOUTH *see also under substantive place name*
SOUTH BANK (St John) *York 18* **P** *Abp* **P-in-c** D G HODGSON, **Hon C** C D E WHEAT
SOUTH BARROW Team Ministry, The *Carl 8* **P** *Bp* **TR** P E MANN, **TV** C E FARRER, E J NATTRASS, **NSM** H GRAINGER
SOUTH CAVE (All Saints) and Ellerker w Broomfleet *York 13* **P** *CPAS and D&C Dur (jt)* **V** P G FAULKNER, **NSM** P R DRAPER
SOUTH COVE (St Lawrence) *see* Sole Bay *St E*
SOUTH HILL (St Sampson) w Callington *Truro 11* **P** *PCC* **R** P R SHARPE, **NSM** B R JENNINGS, **OLM** P A RAYNHAM
SOUTH MOOR (St George) *see* Ch the K *Dur*
SOUTH PARK (St Luke) *see* Reigate St Luke w Doversgreen *S'wark*
SOUTH POOL (St Nicholas and St Cyriac) *see* Charleton w Buckland Tout Saints etc *Ex*
SOUTH SHIELDS (All Saints) (St Mary w St Martin) *Dur 15* **P** *Patr Bd* **TR** J D MILLER, **TV** D R D MASLEN
SOUTH SHIELDS St Aidan (St Stephen) The Lawe *Dur 15* **P** *Bp and D&C* **R** R SHAW
SOUTH SHIELDS (St Hilda) w St Thomas *Dur 15* **P** *D&C* **V** R L BURR
SOUTH SHIELDS (St Lawrence the Martyr) *see* Horsley Hill St Lawr *Dur*
SOUTH SHIELDS (St Simon) *Dur 15* **P** *The Crown* **P-in-c** J E HOWES
SOUTH SHORE (Holy Trinity) *Blackb 8* **P** *J C Hilton Esq* **P-in-c** R P W CARTMELL, **NSM** M H WARD
SOUTH SHORE (St Peter) *Blackb 8* **P** *Bp* **P-in-c** S EDWARDS
SOUTH TRINITY BROADS Benefice, The: Filby, Thrigby, Mautby, Stokesby, Runham and Burgh w Billockby *Nor 6* **P** *Bp, Adn Nor, DBP, Mrs Z K Cognetti, R T Daniel Esq, and I F M Lucas Esq (jt)* **P-in-c** C A LE PREVOST
SOUTHACRE (St George) *see* Castleacre, Newton, Westacre and Southacre *Nor*
SOUTHALL (Christ the Redeemer) *Lon 22* **P** *Bp* **V** N J ORCHARD
SOUTHALL (Emmanuel) Conventional District *Lon 22* **C-in-c** A SEN
SOUTHALL (Holy Trinity) *Lon 22* **P** *Ch Patr Trust* **P-in-c** M F BOLLEY
SOUTHALL (St George) *Lon 22* **P** *D&C St Paul's* **P-in-c** C RAMSAY
SOUTHALL GREEN (St John) *Lon 22* **P** *Ch Patr Trust* **P-in-c** M A POULSON, **Hon C** D J C BOOKLESS
SOUTHAM (Ascension) *see* Bishop's Cleeve *Glouc*
SOUTHAM (St James) *Cov 10* **P** *The Crown* **P-in-c** J E ARMSTRONG
SOUTHAMPTON (Christ Church) Portswood *see* Portswood Ch Ch *Win*
SOUTHAMPTON City Centre (St Mary) (St Michael) *Win 13* **P** *Bp* **TR** I L JOHNSON, **TV** S P HALL, T E DAYKIN, **NSM** P R HAND
SOUTHAMPTON (Holy Trinity) *see* Weston *Win*
SOUTHAMPTON Maybush (St Peter) *Win 13* **P** *Bp* **V** N BOAKES, **C** F M G HALL, S M PITKIN
SOUTHAMPTON (St Alban) *see* Swaythling *Win*
SOUTHAMPTON (St Barnabas) *Win 13* **P** *Bp* **V** B J FRY
SOUTHAMPTON (St Denys) Portswood *see* Portswood St Denys *Win*
SOUTHAMPTON (St Jude) Warren Road *Win 13* **P** *Bp* **P-in-c** N BOAKES
SOUTHAMPTON (St Mark) *Win 13* **P** *Ch Patr Trust* **V** G MARCH
SOUTHAMPTON (St Mary Extra) *Win 13* **P** *Bp* **V** P G FIRMIN
SOUTHAMPTON Thornhill (St Christopher) *Win 13* **P** *Bp* **V** G P ANNAS
SOUTHAMPTON Winkle Street (St Julian) *see* Southampton (City Cen) *Win*
SOUTHBERGH (St Andrew) *see* Barnham Broom and Upper Yare *Nor*
SOUTHBOROUGH (St Peter) (Christ Church) (St Matthew) and Bidborough *Roch 12* **P** *Patr Bd* **TR** G E HOVENDEN, **TV** C B WICKS, S A HILLS, **C** N A CHANDRAN
SOUTHBOROUGH (St Thomas) *Roch 12* **P** *Bp* **P-in-c** A M HORTON
SOUTHBOURNE (All Saints) *see* Pokesdown All SS *Win*
SOUTHBOURNE (St Christopher) *Win 8* **P** *Bp* **NSM** N S LEGRAND
SOUTHBOURNE (St John the Evangelist) w West Thorney *Chich 13* **P** *Bp* **V** C R JENKINS, **NSM** S BEAVIS
SOUTHBOURNE (St Katharine) (St Nicholas) *Win 8* **P** *Bp* **V** J C WHITE
SOUTHBROOM (St James) *Sarum 16* **P** *D&C* **P-in-c** C M TEBBUTT, **NSM** T V F PAPE
SOUTHCHURCH (Christ Church) *Chelmsf 13* **P** *Bp* **V** M J HARRIS, **C** J A NOLES
SOUTHCHURCH (Holy Trinity) *Chelmsf 13* **P** *Abp Cant* **R** M A BALLARD, **C** L S HURRY
SOUTHCOATES (St Aidan) *see* Kingston upon Hull St Aid Southcoates *York*
SOUTHCOURT (Good Shepherd) *see* Walton H Trin *Ox*
SOUTHDENE (St Martin) *see* Kirkby *Liv*
SOUTHEA (Emmanuel) *see* Wisbech St Mary and Guyhirn w Ring's End etc *Ely*
SOUTHEASE (St Peter) *Chich 18* **P** *Bp and Gorham Trustees (jt)* **V** D A HIDER, **C** D L N GUTSELL
SOUTHEND (St John the Baptist) (St Mark) (All Saints) (St Alban) *Chelmsf 13* **P** *Patr Bd* **TR** S M BURDETT, **TV** R H CADMAN, P A ROBERTS, **NSM** S SAYERS, P E OWEN
SOUTHEND (St Peter) *see* Bradfield and Stanford Dingley *Ox*
SOUTHEND-ON-SEA (St Saviour) Westcliff *Chelmsf 13* **P** *Bp, Adn Southend, and Churchwardens (jt)* **V** R H WILLIAMS, **NSM** L M WILLIAMS
SOUTHERY (St Mary) *Ely 13* **P** *Guild of All So* **R** D J EVANS
SOUTHEY GREEN (St Bernard) Conventional District *Sheff 3* **C-in-c** R GOMERSALL
SOUTHFIELDS (St Barnabas) *S'wark 20* **P** *Bp* **NSM** P A SEABROOK
SOUTHFIELDS (St Michael and All Angels) *see* Wandsworth St Mich *S'wark*
SOUTHFLEET (St Nicholas) *Roch 4* **P** *CPAS* **NSM** J C STONE
SOUTHGATE (Christ Church) *Lon 18* **P** *V Edmonton All SS* **V** P J E JACKSON
SOUTHGATE Local Ecumenical Project *St E 13* **Min** D C MARSHALL
SOUTHGATE (Shared Church) *see* Grange St Andr *Ches*
SOUTHGATE (St Andrew) *Lon 18* **P** *Bp* **V** *vacant* (020) 8886 7523 *or* 8866 5223
SOUTHGATE (St Mary) *Chich 7* **P** *Patr Bd* **TR** J M MORTIMER, **TV** R E POOLE, S D K TAYLOR, G R HOCKEN, **C** K J LEWIS
SOUTHGATE, NEW (St Paul) *Lon 14* **P** *V Southgate Ch Ch* **V** M C ELLIOTT SMITH
SOUTHILL (All Saints) *see* Clifton and Southill *St Alb*
SOUTHLAKE (St James's Church Centre) *see* Woodley *Ox*
SOUTHLEIGH (St Lawrence) *see* Colyton, Musbury, Southleigh and Branscombe *Ex*
SOUTHMEAD (St Stephen) *Bris 2* **P** *Bp* **V** J C HALL
SOUTHMINSTER (St Leonard) *Chelmsf 11* **P** *Govs Charterhouse* **V** G S ANDERSON, **NSM** V J BUTLER
SOUTHOE (St Leonard) *see* Gt Staughton w Hail Weston w Southoe *Ely*
SOUTHOVER (St John the Baptist) *Chich 18* **P** *CPAS* **R** S J DAUGHTERY, **C** M P WOODSFORD
SOUTHOWRAM (St Anne-in-the-Grove) and Claremount *Wakef 4* **P** *V Halifax* **V** G S JAMIESON
SOUTHPORT (All Saints) (All Souls) *Liv 9* **P** *Trustees* **C** A J EDWARDS, T P JARDINE
SOUTHPORT (Christ Church) *Liv 9* **P** *Trustees* **V** S T REID
SOUTHPORT (Emmanuel) *Liv 9* **P** *PCC* **V** C POPE, **C** D J PRESCOTT
SOUTHPORT (Holy Trinity) *Liv 9* **P** *Trustees* **V** R G GARNER
SOUTHPORT (St Luke) *Liv 9* **P** *V Southport H Trin* **P-in-c** I R SHACKLETON, **NSM** D H MARSTON
SOUTHPORT (St Philip) (St Paul) *Liv 9* **P** *V Southport Ch Ch and Trustees (jt)* **V** A J EDWARDS
SOUTHPORT (St Simon and St Jude) *Liv 9* **P** *Trustees* **V** T P JARDINE
SOUTHREPPS (St James) *see* Trunch *Nor*
SOUTHREY (St John the Divine) *see* Bardney *Linc*
SOUTHROP (St Peter) *see* Coln St Aldwyns, Hatherop, Quenington etc *Glouc*
SOUTHSEA (Holy Spirit) *Portsm 6* **P** *Bp* **V** M D B LEWIS
SOUTHSEA (St Jude) *Portsm 6* **P** *Trustees* **V** J V BYRNE, **C** M N RODEL
SOUTHSEA (St Luke) *see* Portsea St Luke *Portsm*
SOUTHSEA (St Peter) *Portsm 6* **P** *Bp* **P-in-c** C D TOWNER

SOUTHSEA (St Simon) *Portsm 6* **P** *Ch Patr Trust* **V** M F HOLLAND, **NSM** P A O'GORMAN
SOUTHTOWN (St Mary) *see* Gt Yarmouth *Nor*
SOUTHWARK (Christ Church) *S'wark 10* **P** *Marshall's Charity* **R** T C N SCOTT
SOUTHWARK (Holy Trinity w St Matthew) *S'wark 10* **P** *Bp* **R** N A MCKINNON
SOUTHWARK (St George the Martyr) (St Alphege) (St Jude) *S'wark 10* **P** *Lon Corp (1 turn), Ld Chan (4 turns), Walsingham Coll Trust Assn (1 turn)* **R** A S LUCAS, **Hon C** M DURRAN, **NSM** D SWABY, **OLM** D PAPE
SOUTHWARK (St Hugh) *see* Bermondsey St Hugh CD *S'wark*
SOUTHWATER (Holy Innocents) *Chich 8* **P** *V Horsham* **V** *vacant* (01403) 730229
SOUTHWAY (Holy Spirit) *Ex 23* **P** *Ld Chan* **C** P IRETON, **NSM** M J FAIRALL
SOUTHWELL (Holy Trinity) *S'well 15* **P** *CPAS* **V** M S TANNER, **NSM** D L ROBBINS
SOUTHWELL (St Andrew) *see* Portland All SS w St Pet *Sarum*
SOUTHWICK (Holy Trinity) *see* N Wearside *Dur*
SOUTHWICK (St Columba) *as above*
SOUTHWICK (St James) w Boarhunt *Portsm 1* **P** *R Thistlewayte Esq* **P-in-c** R L GREEN
SOUTHWICK (St Mary the Virgin) *see* Warmington, Tansor and Cotterstock etc *Pet*
SOUTHWICK (St Michael and All Angels) (St Peter) *Chich 4* **P** *Bp and Ld Chan (alt)* **P-in-c** R D HARRIS, **C** C ALLEN, D A GUEST, **NSM** B A WILSON
SOUTHWICK (St Thomas) *see* N Bradley, Southwick and Heywood *Sarum*
SOUTHWOLD (St Edmund King and Martyr) *see* Sole Bay *St E*
SOUTHWOOD (Mission Church) *see* Evercreech w Chesterblade and Milton Clevedon *B & W*
SOWERBY (St Mary) (St Peter) *Wakef 3* **P** *DBP* **P-in-c** K L S TURNER, **NSM** C J WARDMAN
SOWERBY (St Oswald) *York 19* **P** *Abp* **V** *vacant* (01845) 523546
SOWERBY BRIDGE (Christ Church) w Norland *Wakef 4* **P** *V Halifax* **V** P B STOODLEY, **NSM** L ENNIS
SOWTON (St Michael and All Angels) *see* Aylesbeare, Rockbeare, Farringdon etc *Ex*
SPALDING (St John the Baptist) w Deeping St Nicholas *Linc 17* **P** *Bp* **V** P S J GARLAND
SPALDING (St Mary and St Nicholas) *Linc 17* **P** *Feoffees* **V** T R BARKER, **C** R J SEAL, A C COX
SPALDING (St Paul) *Linc 17* **P** *Bp and V Spalding (jt)* **P-in-c** D C MAYLOR
SPALDWICK (St James) *see* E Leightonstone *Ely*
SPARHAM (St Mary) *see* Lyng, Sparham, Elsing, Bylaugh, Bawdeswell etc *Nor*
SPARKBROOK (Christ Church) *Birm 13* **P** *Aston Trustees* **C** H HOWARTH
SPARKBROOK (Emmanuel) *see* Sparkhill w Greet and Sparkbrook *Birm*
SPARKBROOK (St Agatha) w Balsall Heath St Barnabas *Birm 13* **P** *Bp* **V** J A HERVE
SPARKFORD (St Mary Magdalene) *see* Cam Vale *B & W*
SPARKHILL (St John the Evangelist) (St Bede and Emmanuel) w Greet St Bede and Sparkbrook *Birm 13* **P** *Dioc Trustees and Aston Trustees (alt)* **V** J A SELF, **C** A A UNDERWOOD
SPARKWELL (All Saints) *Ex 21* **P** *D&C Windsor* **V** F G DENMAN
SPARROW HALL (St George) *see* Fazakerley Em *Liv*
SPARSHOLT (Holy Cross) *see* Ridgeway *Ox*
SPARSHOLT (St Stephen) *see* Crawley and Littleton and Sparsholt w Lainston *Win*
SPAXTON (St Margaret) *see* Aisholt, Enmore, Goathurst, Nether Stowey etc *B & W*
SPEEN (St Mary the Virgin) *see* Newbury *Ox*
SPEETON (St Leonard) *see* Bempton w Flamborough, Reighton w Speeton *York*
SPEKE (St Aidan) (All Saints) *Liv 4* **P** *Bp* **TR** C I KIDD
SPELDHURST (St Mary the Virgin) w Groombridge and Ashurst *Roch 12* **P** *DBP* **R** D P WREN
SPELSBURY (All Saints) *see* Chase *Ox*
SPEN, HIGH (St Patrick) and Rowlands Gill *Dur 13* **P** *Bp* **P-in-c** S W HEWITT
SPENCER BENEFICE *see* Brington w Whilton and Norton etc *Pet*
SPENCER PERCIVAL MEMORIAL CHURCH *see* Ealing All SS *Lon*
SPENCERS WOOD (St Michael and All Angels) *see* Loddon Reach *Ox*
SPENNITHORNE (St Michael) w Finghall and Hauxwell *Ripon 4* **P** *R J Dalton Esq and M C AWyvill Esq (alt)* **P-in-c** W J HULSE
SPENNYMOOR (St Paul), Whitworth and Merrington *Dur 6* **P** *D&C* **V** L E GOUGH, **C** G NORMAN, M J WRAY, W SCOTT
SPERNALL, Morton Bagot and Oldberrow *Cov 7* **P** *Mrs J M Pinney and Bp (alt)* **R** *vacant* (01527) 892372
SPETISBURY (St John the Baptist) w Charlton Marshall and Blandford St Mary *Sarum 6* **P** *Worc Coll Ox (1 turn), Bp (2 turns)* **R** S F TREEBY
SPEXHALL (St Peter) *see* Blyth Valley *St E*
SPILSBY Group, The (St James) *Linc 7* **P** *Baroness Willoughby de Eresby (3 turns), Mrs J M Fox-Robinson (1 turn), and Bp (1 turn)* **P-in-c** P F COATES
SPITAL (St Agnes) *see* New Windsor *Ox*
SPITAL (St Leonard's Mission Room) *see* Chesterfield St Mary and All SS *Derby*
SPITALFIELDS (Christ Church w All Saints) *Lon 7* **P** *MMCET* **R** A RIDER, **NSM** S M HARTLEY
SPITALGATE (St John the Evangelist) *see* Grantham St Anne New Somerby and Spitalgate *Linc*
SPITTAL (St John) *Newc 12* **P** *Bp and Mercers' Co (alt)* **P-in-c** A S ADAMSON, **NSM** S J HARRISON
SPIXWORTH (St Peter) w Crostwick and Frettenham *Nor 2* **P** *Bp, Ch Soc Trust, and DBP (jt)* **R** *vacant* (01603) 898258
SPOFFORTH (All Saints) w Kirk Deighton *Ripon 1* **P** *Bp* **P-in-c** J C TREW
SPONDON (St Werburgh) *Derby 9* **P** *Mrs L B Palmer* **V** R J ANDREWS
SPORLE (St Mary) *see* Gt and Lt Dunham w Gt and Lt Fransham and Sporle *Nor*
SPOTLAND (St Clement) *Man 20* **P** *Bp* **V** L CONNOLLY, **NSM** G D MANCO
SPRATTON (St Andrew) *Pet 2* **P** *Bp* **V** B LEE
SPREYTON (St Michael) *see* Chagford, Drewsteignton, Hittisleigh etc *Ex*
SPRIDLINGTON (St Hilary) *see* Owmby Gp *Linc*
SPRIGG'S ALLEY (Mission Room) *see* Chinnor, Sydenham, Aston Rowant and Crowell *Ox*
SPRING GROVE (St Mary) *Lon 11* **P** *Ch Patr Trust* **Hon C** M A WARMAN
SPRING PARK (All Saints) *S'wark 22* **P** *Bp* **V** Y V CLARKE
SPRINGFIELD (All Saints) *Chelmsf 8* **P** *Air Cdre N S Paynter* **R** R J BROWN, **NSM** J MANN
SPRINGFIELD (Holy Trinity) *Chelmsf 8* **P** *Simeon's Trustees* **V** T W BALL
SPRINGFIELD (St Christopher) *Birm 5* **P** *Trustees* **P-in-c** T M HOWARTH
SPRINGFIELD Wallington *see* Wallington Springfield Ch *S'wark*
SPRINGFIELD, EAST (Church of Our Saviour) (not known) *Chelmsf 8* **P** *Bp* **P-in-c** A MACKENZIE
SPRINGFIELD, NORTH (St Augustine of Canterbury) *Chelmsf 8* **P** *Bp* **P-in-c** J V ANDERSON
SPRINGFIELDS (St Stephen) *see* Wolverhampton St Steph *Lich*
SPRINGTHORPE (St George and St Laurence) *see* Corringham and Blyton Gp *Linc*
SPRINGWELL (St Mary the Virgin) *see* Sunderland St Mary and St Pet *Dur*
SPRINGWOOD (All Souls) *see* Liv All So Springwood *Liv*
SPROATLEY (St Swithin) *see* Preston and Sproatley in Holderness *York*
SPROTBROUGH (St Mary the Virgin) *Sheff 7* **P** *Bp* **R** J M RICHARDS, **C** K FARROW
SPROUGHTON (All Saints) w Burstall, Copdock w Washbrook and Belstead and Bentley w Tattingstone *St E 5* **P** *Patr Bd* **R** C L WINGFIELD, **OLM** D W MEHEN
SPROWSTON (St Cuthbert) (St Mary and St Margaret) w Beeston *Nor 2* **P** *D&C* **R** J D BENNETT, **C** G M BRIDGES, **NSM** H M WRIGHT, M S WHITAKER
SPROXTON (St Bartholomew) *see* High Framland Par *Leic*
SPROXTON (St Chad) *see* Helmsley *York*
SQUIRRELS HEATH (All Saints) *Chelmsf 2* **P** *Bp* **V** P J WILKIN, **NSM** K F WOOLMER
STADHAMPTON (St John the Baptist) *see* Dorchester *Ox*
STAFFHURST WOOD (St Silvan) *see* Limpsfield and Titsey *S'wark*
STAFFORD (Christ Church) (St Chad) (St Mary) *Lich 10* **P** *Patr Bd* **TR** P J JEFFERIES, **TV** M WILLIAMS, **C** C CARSON, **NSM** M J FISHER, **OLM** B BUTTERY
STAFFORD (St John the Baptist) and Tixall w Ingestre *Lich 10* **P** *Bp and Earl of Shrewsbury and Talbot (jt)* **C** J E EVANS
STAFFORD (St Paul) Forebridge *Lich 10* **P** *V Castle Ch* **V** M R METCALF
STAFFORD (St Thomas and St Andrew) Doxey *see* Castle Town *Lich*

STAFFORD, WEST (St Andrew) *see* Dorchester *Sarum*
STAGSDEN (St Leonard) *see* Bromham w Oakley and Stagsden *St Alb*
STAGSHAW CHAPEL (St Aidan) *see* St John Lee *Newc*
STAINBY (St Peter) *see* Witham Gp *Linc*
STAINCLIFFE (Christ Church) and Carlinghow *Wakef 10* **P** *V Brownhill and V Batley (jt)* **V** *vacant* (01924) 473343
STAINCROSS (St John the Evangelist) *Wakef 7* **P** *Bp* **V** J K BUTTERWORTH
STAINDROP (St Mary) *Dur 7* **P** *Lord Barnard* **P-in-c** K STEVENTON
STAINES (Christ Church) *Lon 13* **P** *Bp* **P-in-c** R J COSH, **C** D J ESHUN, D J MAHER
STAINES (St Mary) (St Peter) *Lon 13* **P** *Ld Chan* **P-in-c** R J COSH, **C** J R A SAMPSON
STAINFIELD (St Andrew) *see* Bardney *Linc*
STAINFORTH (St Mary) *Sheff 10* **P** *Bp* **V** A W ALLINGTON
STAINFORTH (St Peter) *see* Langcliffe w Stainforth and Horton *Bradf*
STAINING (St Luke Mission Church) *see* Blackpool St Mich *Blackb*
STAINLAND (St Andrew) w Outlane *Wakef 2* **P** *V Halifax* **V** R A CHAPMAN
STAINLEY, NORTH (St Mary the Virgin) *see* W Tanfield and Well w Snape and N Stainley *Ripon*
STAINLEY, SOUTH (St Wilfrid) *see* Markington w S Stainley and Bishop Thornton *Ripon*
STAINMORE (St Stephen) *see* Brough w Stainmore, Musgrave and Warcop *Carl*
STAINTON (St Peter w St Paul) w Hilton *York 21* **P** *Abp (2 turns), DBP (1 turn)* **P-in-c** W J FORD
STAINTON (St Winifred) *see* Tickhill w Stainton *Sheff*
STAINTON, GREAT (All Saints) *see* Bishopton w Gt Stainton *Dur*
STAINTON BY LANGWORTH (St John the Baptist) *see* Barlings *Linc*
STAINTON DALE (St John the Baptist) *see* Cloughton and Burniston w Ravenscar etc *York*
STAINTON LE VALE (St Andrew) *see* Walesby *Linc*
STAITHES (St Peter) *see* Hinderwell, Roxby and Staithes etc *York*
STAKEFORD (Holy Family) *see* Choppington *Newc*
STALBRIDGE (St Mary) and Stock *Sarum 5* **P** *CCC Cam (4 turns), Col J L Yeatman (1 turn)* **R** W T RIDDING
STALHAM (St Mary), East Ruston, Brunstead, Sutton and Ingham *Nor 12* **P** *Bp, DBP and Mrs S F Baker (jt)* **R** D R ANDERSON, **OLM** R H JACKSON, G D BIRD
STALISFIELD (St Mary) *see* Eastling w Ospringe and Stalisfield w Otterden *Cant*
STALLING BUSK (St Matthew) *see* Askrigg w Stallingbusk *Ripon*
STALLINGBOROUGH (St Peter and St Paul) *see* Keelby Gp *Linc*
STALMINE (St James) w Pilling St John the Baptist *Blackb 9* **P** *Bp, V Lanc St Mary, Mrs C B Mason-Hornby, and H D H Elletson Esq (jt)* **V** G BILLINGTON, **OLM** D A DICKINSON, C PRITCHARD
STALYBRIDGE (Holy Trinity and Christ Church) *Ches 14* **P** *Trustees* **V** C A BELL
STALYBRIDGE (St George) *Man 17* **P** *Lord Deramore and R Ashton-under-Lyne St Mich (jt)* **V** I K STUBBS, **NSM** R FOX, **OLM** P BRIERLEY
STALYBRIDGE (St Paul) *Ches 14* **P** *Trustees* **P-in-c** R H LAWRY
STAMBOURNE (St Peter and St Thomas Becket) *see* Upper Colne *Chelmsf*
STAMBRIDGE (St Mary and All Saints) *Chelmsf 12* **P** *Ld Chan (1 turn), Charterhouse (3 turns)* **P-in-c** C W COUSINS
STAMFORD (All Saints) w St John the Baptist *Linc 13* **P** *Ld Chan and Burghley Ho Preservation Trust (alt)* **V** N RUSSELL, **C** C R DIXON, **Hon C** D M BOND
STAMFORD (Christ Church) *Linc 13* **P** *Bp* **P-in-c** R J MACKRILL
STAMFORD (St George) (St Paul) *Linc 13* **P** *Burghley Ho Preservation Trust* **R** M A N TAYLOR, **C** M P L SHEA
STAMFORD (St Mary) (St Martin) *Linc 13* **P** *Burghley Ho Preservation Trust* **R** *vacant* (01780) 51424
STAMFORD BRIDGE Group of Parishes, The (St John the Baptist) *York 5* **P** *Lord Egremont (2 turns), Prime Min (1 turn)* **P-in-c** D R WESTMORELAND
STAMFORD HILL (St Bartholomew) *Lon 19* **P** *The Crown* **V** R N S LEECE
STAMFORD HILL (St Thomas) *Lon 19* **P** *R Hackney* **V** M J BROWN, **C** S L GREEN
STAMFORDHAM (St Mary the Virgin) w Matfen *Newc 3* **P** *Ld Chan* **V** *vacant* (01661) 886456
STANBRIDGE (St John the Baptist) *see* Totternhoe, Stanbridge and Tilsworth *St Alb*
STANBURY (Mission Church) *see* Haworth *Bradf*
STAND (All Saints) *Man 14* **P** *Earl of Wilton* **R** A J HARDY
STANDISH (St Nicholas) *see* Eastington, Frocester, Haresfield etc *Glouc*
STANDISH (St Wilfrid) *Blackb 4* **P** *Bp* **R** M J EVERITT, **C** B J WARD, S G PRITCHARD
STANDLAKE (St Giles) *see* Lower Windrush *Ox*
STANDON (All Saints) *see* Broughton w Croxton and Cotes Heath w Standon *Lich*
STANDON (St Mary) *St Alb 18* **P** *Ch Fund Trust Fund* **V** *vacant* (01920) 821390
STANFIELD (St Margaret) *see* Litcham w Kempston, E and W Lexham, Mileham etc *Nor*
STANFORD (All Saints) *see* Lyminge w Paddlesworth, Stanford w Postling etc *Cant*
STANFORD (All Saints) *Nor 13* **P** *Bp* **V** *vacant*
STANFORD (St Nicholas) *see* Gilmorton, Peatling Parva, Kimcote etc *Leic*
STANFORD BISHOP (St James) *see* Acton Beauchamp and Evesbatch w Stanford Bishop *Heref*
STANFORD DINGLEY (St Denys) *see* Bradfield and Stanford Dingley *Ox*
STANFORD IN THE VALE (St Denys) w Goosey and Hatford *Ox 17* **P** *D&C Westmr (3 turns), Simeon's Trustees (2 turns)* **V** M T WENHAM
STANFORD-LE-HOPE (St Margaret) w Mucking *Chelmsf 14* **P** *MMCET* **R** J A K GUEST, **C** J WHITE
STANFORD-ON-SOAR (St John the Baptist) *see* E and W Leake, Stanford-on-Soar, Rempstone etc *S'well*
STANFORD-ON-TEME (St Mary) *see* Teme Valley N *Worc*
STANFORD RIVERS (St Margaret) *see* Greensted-juxta-Ongar w Stanford Rivers etc *Chelmsf*
STANGROUND (St John the Baptist) (St Michael and All Angels) *Ely 11* **P** *Em Coll Cam* **V** *vacant* (01733) 890552
STANHOE (All Saints) *see* Docking, the Birchams, Stanhoe and Sedgeford *Nor*
STANHOPE (St Thomas) *see* Upper Weardale *Dur*
STANION (St Peter) *see* Brigstock w Stanion and Lowick and Sudborough *Pet*
STANLEY (All Saints) *see* W Hallam and Mapperley w Stanley *Derby*
STANLEY (St Agnes) *see* Bagnall w Endon *Lich*
STANLEY (St Andrew) *see* W Hallam and Mapperley w Stanley *Derby*
STANLEY (St Anne) *Liv 8* **P** *R W Derby* **V** M C DAVIES, **C** M A READ
STANLEY (St Peter) *Wakef 12* **P** *Dean* **V** W E HENDERSON, **NSM** J KILSBY
STANLEY (St Thomas) *see* Satley, Stanley and Tow Law *Dur*
STANLEY, SOUTH (St Stephen) *see* Ch the K *Dur*
STANLEY PONTLARGE (Chapel) *see* Winchcombe *Glouc*
STANLEYS, The *Glouc 8* **P** *Mrs L Y K Fisher and Jes Coll Cam (jt)* **P-in-c** S P PHILLIPSON-MASTERS
STANMER (not known) w Falmer *Chich 2* **P** *Bp* **P-in-c** A N ROBINSON
STANMORE (St Luke) *Win 7* **P** *Bp* **V** M R GARDNER, **C** R E WISE, **NSM** O N WOODMAN
STANMORE, GREAT (St John the Evangelist) *Lon 23* **P** *R O Bernays Esq* **R** A J CHRISTIAN, **C** H A STEWART
STANMORE, LITTLE (St Lawrence) *Lon 23* **P** *Bp* **R** P M REECE
STANNEY (St Andrew) *see* Ellesmere Port *Ches*
STANNINGFIELD (St Nicholas) *see* St Edm Way *St E*
STANNINGLEY (St Thomas) *Ripon 6* **P** *V Leeds St Pet* **R** D M GREEN, **C** I J WHITE
STANNINGTON (Christ Church) *Sheff 4* **P** *Bp* **V** P W WEST
STANNINGTON (St Mary the Virgin) *Newc 1* **P** *Bp* **P-in-c** C R GOUGH
STANSFIELD (All Saints) *see* Bansfield *St E*
STANSTEAD (St James) *see* Glemsford, Hartest w Boxted, Somerton etc *St E*
STANSTEAD ABBOTS (St Andrew) *see* Gt Amwell w St Margaret's and Stanstead Abbots *St Alb*
STANSTEAD ST MARGARET (St Mary the Virgin) *as above*
STANSTED (St Mary) w Fairseat and Vigo *Roch 10* **P** *Bp* **R** C J L NOBLE
STANSTED (St Paul) (Christ Church) *Chich 13* **P** *Stansted Park Foundation* **P-in-c** A N STAMP
STANSTED MOUNTFITCHET (St John) w Birchanger and Farnham *Chelmsf 21* **P** *Bp, New Coll Ox, and Mrs L A Murphy (jt)* **R** A SPURR, **NSM** C M CURRER

STANTON (All Saints), Hopton, Market Weston, Barningham and Coney Weston *St E 9* **P** *Ld Chan (2 turns) and Bp (1 turn)* **R** M J HANSEN, **C** D H MESSER
STANTON (St Gabriel) *see* Golden Cap Team *Sarum*
STANTON (St Mary) *see* Denstone w Ellastone and Stanton *Lich*
STANTON (St Mary and All Saints) *see* Markfield, Thornton, Bagworth and Stanton etc *Leic*
STANTON (St Michael and All Angels) *see* Winchcombe *Glouc*
STANTON BY BRIDGE (St Michael) *see* Ticknall, Smisby and Stanton by Bridge etc *Derby*
STANTON-BY-DALE (St Michael and All Angels) w Dale Abbey and Risley *Derby 13* **P** *Bp* **R** I E GOODING
STANTON DREW (Blessed Virgin Mary) *see* Bishop Sutton and Stanton Drew and Stowey *B & W*
STANTON FITZWARREN (St Leonard) *see* Stratton St Margaret w S Marston etc *Bris*
STANTON HARCOURT (St Michael) *see* Lower Windrush *Ox*
STANTON HILL (All Saints) *see* Skegby w Teversal *S'well*
STANTON-IN-PEAK (Holy Trinity) *see* Youlgreave, Middleton, Stanton-in-Peak etc *Derby*
STANTON LACY (Hayton Bent Hall) *see* Culmington w Onibury, Bromfield etc *Heref*
STANTON LACY (St Peter) *as above*
STANTON ON HINE HEATH (St Andrew) *Lich 22* **P** *Sir Beville Stanier Bt* **V** D J HUMPHRIES
STANTON-ON-THE-WOLDS (All Saints) *see* Keyworth and Stanton-on-the-Wolds and Bunny etc *S'well*
STANTON PRIOR (St Lawrence) *see* Farmborough, Marksbury and Stanton Prior *B & W*
STANTON ST BERNARD (All Saints) *see* Pewsey and Swanborough *Sarum*
STANTON ST JOHN (St John the Baptist) *see* Wheatley *Ox*
STANTON ST QUINTIN (St Giles) *see* Hullavington, Norton and Stanton St Quintin *Bris*
STANTONBURY (Christ Church) and Willen *Ox 25* **P** *Patr Bd* **TV** A R B JOWITT, C E COLLINGE, P S BALLANTINE, P A SMITH, **OLM** J B ROSE
STANWAY (St Albright) (St Andrew) *Chelmsf 17* **P** *Magd Coll Ox* **R** P R MCLAREN-COOK, **NSM** A C BUSHELL
STANWAY (St Peter) *see* Winchcombe *Glouc*
STANWELL (St Mary the Virgin) *Lon 13* **P** *Ld Chan* **V** W P STAFFORD-WHITTAKER
STANWICK (St Laurence) w Hargrave *Pet 10* **P** *Ld Chan (2 turns), Bp (1 turn)* **P-in-c** S M BELL
STANWIX (St Michael) *Carl 3* **P** *Bp* **V** B G PHILLIPS
STAPEHILL (All Saints) *see* Hampreston *Sarum*
STAPENHILL (Immanuel) *Derby 16* **P** *Ch Soc Trust* **V** B S P LEATHERS
STAPENHILL (St Peter) w Cauldwell *Derby 16* **P** *Ch Soc Trust* **P-in-c** M ANDREYEV
STAPLE (St James) *see* Woodnesborough w Worth and Staple *Cant*
STAPLE FITZPAINE (St Peter) *see* Beercrocombe w Curry Mallet, Hatch Beauchamp etc *B & W*
STAPLE TYE (St James) *see* Gt Parndon *Chelmsf*
STAPLECROSS (St Mark) *see* Ewhurst *Chich*
STAPLEFIELD COMMON (St Mark) *Chich 6* **P** *V Cuckfield* **P-in-c** M C PEARSON
STAPLEFORD (All Saints) *see* Bassingham Gp *Linc*
STAPLEFORD (St Andrew) *Ely 6* **P** *D&C* **P-in-c** J L R ECHOLS
STAPLEFORD (St Andrew's Mission Church) (St Helen) (St Luke) *S'well 7* **P** *CPAS* **V** W N CRAFT, **NSM** J M JESSON
STAPLEFORD (St Mary) *see* Bramfield, Stapleford, Waterford etc *St Alb*
STAPLEFORD (St Mary) *see* Wylye and Till Valley *Sarum*
STAPLEFORD ABBOTTS (St Mary) *see* Lambourne w Abridge and Stapleford Abbotts *Chelmsf*
STAPLEFORD TAWNEY (St Mary the Virgin) *see* Greensted-juxta-Ongar w Stanford Rivers etc *Chelmsf*
STAPLEGROVE (St John) w Norton Fitzwarren *B & W 18* **P** *Bp and MMCET (jt)* **R** M S KIVETT
STAPLEHURST (All Saints) *Cant 11* **P** *St Jo Coll Cam* **R** G M CALVER, **C** J C N MACKENZIE, **NSM** P OSLER
STAPLETON (Holy Trinity) *Bris 3* **P** *Bp* **R** *vacant* 0117-958 3858
STAPLETON (St John) *see* Dorrington w Leebotwood, Longnor, Stapleton etc *Heref*
STAPLETON (St Martin) *see* Barwell w Potters Marston and Stapleton *Leic*
STAPLETON (St Mary) *see* Bewcastle, Stapleton and Kirklinton etc *Carl*
STARBECK (St Andrew) *Ripon 1* **P** *V Harrogate Ch Ch* **V** F S K WAINAINA, **C** T F P YAP
STARCROSS (St Paul) *see* Kenton, Mamhead, Powderham, Cofton and Starcross *Ex*
STARSTON (St Margaret) *see* Dickleburgh and The Pulhams *Nor*
STARTFORTH (Holy Trinity) and Bowes and Rokeby w Brignall *Ripon 2* **P** *Ld Chan (1 turn), Bp, Earl of Lonsdale and Lords of the Manor of Bowes (2 turns)* **NSM** K R STABLES
STATFOLD (St Matthew) *see* Clifton Campville w Edingale and Harlaston *Lich*
STATHERN (St Guthlac) *see* Vale of Belvoir Par *Leic*
STAUGHTON, GREAT (St Andrew) w Hail Weston w Southoe *Ely 10* **P** *Mert Coll Ox and St Jo Coll Ox (alt)* **R** J I CLARKE
STAUGHTON, LITTLE (All Saints) *see* Keysoe w Bolnhurst and Lt Staughton *St Alb*
STAUNTON (All Saints) *see* Coleford w Staunton *Glouc*
STAUNTON (St James) *see* Hartpury w Corse and Staunton *Glouc*
STAUNTON (St Mary) w Flawborough *S'well 3* **P** *E G Staunton Esq* **P-in-c** D HOLLIS
STAUNTON HAROLD (Holy Trinity) *see* Ashby-de-la-Zouch and Breedon on the Hill *Leic*
STAUNTON-ON-ARROW (St Peter) *see* Pembridge w Moor Court, Shobdon, Staunton etc *Heref*
STAUNTON-ON-WYE (St Mary the Virgin) *see* Letton w Staunton, Byford, Mansel Gamage etc *Heref*
STAVELEY (All Saints) *see* Walkingham Hill *Ripon*
STAVELEY (St James), Ings and Kentmere *Carl 10* **P** *V Kendal H Trin* **V** G WATSON
STAVELEY (St John the Baptist) and Barrow Hill *Derby 3* **P** *Bp, Adn Chesterfield, and Duke of Devonshire (jt)* **TR** W A BUTT
STAVELEY IN CARTMEL (St Mary) *see* Leven Valley *Carl*
STAVERTON (St Catherine) *see* Twigworth, Down Hatherley, Norton, The Leigh etc *Glouc*
STAVERTON (St Mary the Virgin) *see* Daventry, Ashby St Ledgers, Braunston etc *Pet*
STAVERTON (St Paul) *see* Hilperton w Whaddon and Staverton etc *Sarum*
STAVERTON (St Paul de Leon) *see* Broadhempston, Woodland, Staverton etc *Ex*
STAWELL (St Francis) *see* Middlezoy and Othery and Moorlinch *B & W*
STAWLEY (St Michael and All Angels) *see* Wellington and Distr *B & W*
STEANE (St Peter) *see* Aynho and Croughton w Evenley etc *Pet*
STEART BAY (St Andrew) *see* Cannington, Otterhampton, Combwich and Stockland *B & W*
STEBBING (St Mary the Virgin) and Lindsell w Great and Little (Bardfield) Saling *Chelmsf 18* **P** *Bp* **V** B SNELLING, **NSM** S C BAZLINTON
STECHFORD (All Saints) (St Andrew) *Birm 13* **P** *St Pet Coll Ox* **V** *vacant* 0121-783 2463
STEDHAM (St James) w Iping *Chich 10* **P** *Bp* **P-in-c** R B WILLIAMSON
STEEP (All Saints) and Froxfield w Privett *Portsm 4* **P** *Ld Chan and Magd Coll Cam (alt)* **V** P A KENNEDY
STEEPING, GREAT (All Saints) *see* Spilsby Gp *Linc*
STEEPING, LITTLE (St Andrew) *as above*
STEEPLE (St Lawrence and All Saints) *Chelmsf 11* **P** *Bp* **P-in-c** L BLANEY
STEEPLE (St Michael and All Angels) *see* Corfe Castle, Church Knowle, Kimmeridge etc *Sarum*
STEEPLE ASHTON (St Mary the Virgin) w Semington and Keevil *Sarum 14* **P** *D&C Win (1 turn), Magd Coll Cam (3 turns)* **V** *vacant* (01380) 870344
STEEPLE ASTON (St Peter and St Paul) w North Aston and Tackley *Ox 9* **P** *BNC Ox, St Jo Coll Ox, and Exors Lt-Col A D Taylor (jt)* **R** S A M'CAW
STEEPLE BARTON (St Mary) *see* Westcote Barton w Steeple Barton, Duns Tew etc *Ox*
STEEPLE BUMPSTEAD (St Mary) and Helions Bumpstead *Chelmsf 19* **P** *Ld Chan* **P-in-c** S M GRIFFITHS
STEEPLE CLAYDON (St Michael) *see* The Claydons *Ox*
STEEPLE LANGFORD (All Saints) *see* Wylye and Till Valley *Sarum*
STEEPLE MORDEN (St Peter and St Paul) *see* Shingay Gp *Ely*
STEETLY (All Saints) *see* Whitwell *Derby*
STEETON (St Stephen) *Bradf 8* **P** *V Kildwick* **V** M E PINNOCK
STELLA (St Cuthbert) *see* Blaydon and Swalwell *Dur*
STELLING (St Mary) *see* Petham and Waltham w Lower Hardres etc *Cant*
STENIGOT (St Nicholas) *see* Asterby Gp *Linc*

STEPNEY (St Dunstan and All Saints) *Lon 7* **P** *Bp* **R** C M BURKE, **C** M J HALL, S J PATCH, **Hon C** G G WHITE
STEPPINGLEY (St Lawrence) *see* Ampthill w Millbrook and Steppingley *St Alb*
STERNFIELD (St Mary Magdalene), Benhall, Snape, Great Glemhamham and Little Glemham, Blaxhall w Stratford St Andrew and Farnham *St E 19* **P** *Earl of Guilford, Major P W Hope-Cobbold, DBP, CPAS, Miss S F R Heycock-Hollond, and Exors Mrs A C V Wentworth (jt)* **C** B J SLATTER, **OLM** R E R ALDERSON
STERT (St James) *see* Redhorn *Sarum*
STETCHWORTH (St Peter) *see* Raddesley Gp *Ely*
STEVENAGE (All Saints) Pin Green *St Alb 23* **P** *Bp* **P-in-c** M J LEVERTON, **NSM** E W FAURE WALKER
STEVENAGE (Holy Trinity) *St Alb 23* **P** *Bp* **P-in-c** G J TICKNER, **C** Y R PENTELOW, **NSM** A MARINER, A J GILES
STEVENAGE (St Andrew and St George) *St Alb 23* **P** *Bp* **R** M BARNSLEY
STEVENAGE (St Hugh) (St John) Chells *St Alb 23* **P** *Bp* **V** J D CAMPBELL, **C** C M HINA
STEVENAGE (St Mary) Shephall w Aston *St Alb 23* **P** *Bp* **V** G B WHITE, **C** R J RILEY-BRALEY
STEVENAGE (St Nicholas) and Graveley *St Alb 23* **P** *Bp* **V** D E DOWLING
STEVENAGE (St Peter) Broadwater *St Alb 23* **P** *Bp* **V** D H HAGUE, **NSM** S M HUDSPITH
STEVENTON (St Michael and All Angels) w Milton *Ox 10* **P** *Ch Ch Ox and D&C Westmr (jt)* **P-in-c** C J PATCHING
STEVENTON (St Nicholas) *see* N Waltham and Steventon, Ashe and Deane *Win*
STEVINGTON (Church Room) (St Mary the Virgin) *St Alb 15* **P** *Bp* **P-in-c** D H C HUNTER
STEWARDS LANE (St Thomas) *see* Ditton St Mich w St Thos *Liv*
STEWKLEY (St Michael and All Angels) w Soulbury and Drayton Parslow *Ox 26* **P** *Bp, Earl of Rosebery, and MMCET (jt)* **P-in-c** M MORTON, **NSM** J D HIBBARD, **OLM** P LYMBERY
STEWTON (St Andrew) *see* Louth *Linc*
STEYNING (St Andrew) *Chich 12* **P** *MMCET* **V** P M RAMPTON
STIBBARD (All Saints) *see* Twyford, Guist, Bintree, Themelthorpe etc *Nor*
STIBBINGTON (St John the Baptist) *see* Elton w Stibbington and Water Newton *Ely*
STICKER (St Mark's Mission Church) *see* St Mewan w Mevagissey and St Ewe *Truro*
STICKFORD (St Helen) *see* Stickney Gp *Linc*
STICKLEPATH (St Mary) *see* S Tawton and Belstone *Ex*
STICKLEPATH (St Paul) *see* Barnstaple *Ex*
STICKNEY Group, The (St Luke) *Linc 7* **P** *DBP, Ld Chan, and Bp (by turn)* **R** *vacant* (01205) 480049
STIDD (St Saviour) *see* Ribchester w Stidd *Blackb*
STIFFKEY (St John and St Mary) and Bale *Nor 18* **P** *MMCET, Bp, DBP, Keble Coll Ox, and Sir Euan Hamilton Anstruther-Gough-Calthorpe Bt (jt)* **R** *vacant* (01328) 830246
STIFFORD (St Cedd) (St Mary) *Chelmsf 14* **P** *Bp* **R** A R B HIGGS
STIFFORD, SOUTH (St Mary the Virgin) *see* Grays Thurrock *Chelmsf*
STILLINGFLEET (St Helen) *see* Escrick and Stillingfleet w Naburn *York*
STILLINGTON (St John) *see* Grindon, Stillington and Wolviston *Dur*
STILLINGTON (St Nicholas) *see* Sheriff Hutton, Farlington, Stillington etc *York*
STILTON (St Mary Magdalene) w Denton and Caldectoe and Folkesworth w Morborne and Haddon *Ely 11* **P** *Mrs H R Horne and Bp, Ld Chan (alt)* **R** R LONGFOOT
STINCHCOMBE (St Cyr) *see* Cam w Stinchcombe *Glouc*
STINSFORD (St Michael) *see* Charminster and Stinsford *Sarum*
STIRCHLEY (All Saints) *see* Cen Telford *Lich*
STIRCHLEY (Ascension) *Birm 5* **P** *R Kings Norton* **V** S L HUCKLE
STISTED (All Saints) *see* Cressing w Stisted and Bradwell etc *Chelmsf*
STITHIANS (St Stythians) *see* St Stythians w Perranarworthal and Gwennap *Truro*
STIXWOULD (St Peter) *see* Woodhall Spa Gp *Linc*
STOAK (St Lawrence) *see* Ellesmere Port *Ches*
STOCK (St Barnabas) *see* Stalbridge and Stock *Sarum*
STOCK HARVARD (All Saints) *Chelmsf 9* **P** *Guild of All So* **R** N D L DE KEYSER
STOCKBRIDGE (Old St Peter) (St Peter) and Longstock and Leckford *Win 12* **P** *Bp and St Jo Coll Ox (jt)* **R** G C G TRASLER
STOCKBRIDGE VILLAGE (St Jude) *Liv 2* **P** *Bp and R W Derby (jt)* **V** E D O'NEILL
STOCKBURY (St Mary Magdalene) *see* Newington w Hartlip and Stockbury *Cant*
STOCKCROSS (St John) *see* Welford w Wickham and Gt Shefford, Boxford etc *Ox*
STOCKERSTON (St Peter) *see* Six Saints circa Holt *Leic*
STOCKING FARM (St Luke) *Leic 1* **P** *Bp* **V** P WATSON
STOCKING PELHAM (St Mary) *see* Braughing w Furneux Pelham and Stocking Pelham *St Alb*
STOCKINGFORD (St Paul) *Cov 5* **P** *V Nuneaton* **V** M F VINCENT
STOCKLAND (St Mary Magdalene) *see* Cannington, Otterhampton, Combwich and Stockland *B & W*
STOCKLAND (St Michael and All Angels) *see* Kilmington, Stockland, Dalwood, Yarcombe etc *Ex*
STOCKLAND GREEN (St Mark) *Birm 8* **P** *The Crown* **V** S W POWELL
STOCKLEIGH ENGLISH (St Mary the Virgin) *see* N Creedy *Ex*
STOCKLEIGH POMEROY (St Mary the Virgin) *as above*
STOCKLINCH (St Mary Magdalene) *see* Ilminster and Distr *B & W*
STOCKPORT South West (St George) (St Mark) (St Gabriel) *Ches 18* **P** *Patr Bd* **TR** A J BELL, **TV** E J H LANE, D T BREWSTER, **C** R J LAMEY
STOCKPORT (St Augustine) *see* Cheadle Heath *Ches*
STOCKPORT (St Martin) *see* Heatons *Man*
STOCKPORT (St Mary) *Ches 18* **P** *G&C Coll Cam* **R** R P SCOONES
STOCKPORT (St Matthew) *Ches 18* **P** *Bp* **P-in-c** B E STATHAM
STOCKPORT (St Saviour) *Ches 18* **P** *Trustees* **V** D V COOKSON
STOCKPORT (St Thomas) (St Peter) *Ches 18* **P** *Bp and Soc of the Faith (jt)* **R** K D N KENRICK, **Hon C** K R BROOKES
STOCKSBRIDGE (St Matthias) *Sheff 3* **P** *Bp* **V** *vacant* 0114-288 6964
STOCKSFIELD (St John) *see* Bywell *Newc*
STOCKTON (Holy Trinity) *Dur 10* **P** *Bp* **P-in-c** S J GILES
STOCKTON (St Andrew) *see* Teme Valley N *Worc*
STOCKTON (St Chad) *Dur 10* **P** *Bp* **P-in-c** N R SHAVE, **C** B L K SHERLOCK, **NSM** E WALKER
STOCKTON (St Chad) *see* Beckbury, Badger, Kemberton, Ryton, Stockton etc *Lich*
STOCKTON (St John the Baptist) *see* Wylye and Till Valley *Sarum*
STOCKTON (St Mark) *Dur 10* **P** *Bp* **V** M M GILLEY
STOCKTON (St Michael and All Angels) *see* Napton-on-the-Hill, Lower Shuckburgh etc *Cov*
STOCKTON (St Michael and All Angels) *see* Gillingham w Geldeston, Stockton, Ellingham etc *Nor*
STOCKTON HEATH (St Thomas) *Ches 4* **P** *P G Greenall Esq* **V** M L RIDLEY
STOCKTON-ON-TEES (St Chad) *see* Stockton St Chad *Dur*
STOCKTON ON TEES (St James) *Dur 10* **P** *Bp* **V** D J STEPHENSON
STOCKTON-ON-TEES (St John the Baptist) *Dur 10* **P** *Bp* **V** D J STEPHENSON, **C** D J BAGE
STOCKTON-ON-TEES (St Mark) *see* Stockton St Mark *Dur*
STOCKTON-ON-TEES (St Paul) *Dur 10* **P** *The Crown* **P-in-c** D W ROSAMOND
STOCKTON-ON-TEES (St Peter) *Dur 10* **P** *Bp* **V** P D ASHDOWN, **NSM** N G BENZIES
STOCKTON-ON-TEES (St Thomas) *Dur 10* **P** *Bp* **V** A FEATHERSTONE
STOCKTON-ON-THE-FOREST (Holy Trinity) w Holtby and Warthill *York 2* **P** *Abp* **NSM** M E W WILLETTS
STOCKWELL (St Andrew) (St Michael) *S'wark 11* **P** *Bp* **V** A R GRANT, **NSM** F A COUCH, **OLM** I A BOWMAN
STOCKWITH, EAST (St Peter) *see* Corringham and Blyton Gp *Linc*
STOCKWITH, WEST (St Mary the Virgin) *see* Misterton and W Stockwith *S'well*
STOCKWOOD (Christ the Servant) *see* Bris Ch the Servant Stockwood *Bris*
STODDEN Churches, The *St Alb 15* **P** *MMCET and DBP (alt)* **R** J C BROOKSHAW
STODMARSH (St Mary) *see* Littlebourne and Ickham w Wickhambreaux etc *Cant*
STODY (St Mary) *see* Brinton, Briningham, Hunworth, Stody etc *Nor*
STOGUMBER (Blessed Virgin Mary) *see* Quantock Towers *B & W*

STOGURSEY (St Andrew) w Fiddington *B & W 17* **P** *Eton Coll and DBP (alt)* **P-in-c** J T TYLER
STOKE (St Mary and St Andrew) *see* Colsterworth Gp *Linc*
STOKE (St Michael) *see* Coventry Caludon *Cov*
STOKE (St Peter and St Paul) *see* Grain w Stoke *Roch*
STOKE, EAST (St Oswald) w Syerston *S'well 3* **P** *Bp* **P-in-c** D HOLLIS
STOKE, NORTH (St Martin) *see* Bath Weston All SS w N Stoke and Langridge *B & W*
STOKE, NORTH (St Mary the Virgin) *see* Langtree *Ox*
STOKE, SOUTH (St Andrew) *see* Goring w S Stoke *Ox*
STOKE, SOUTH (St James the Great) *see* Combe Down w Monkton Combe and S Stoke *B & W*
STOKE, SOUTH (St Leonard) *see* Arundel w Tortington and S Stoke *Chich*
STOKE, WEST (St Andrew) *Chich 13* **P** *Bp* **R** J J HOLLIMAN
STOKE ABBOTT (St Mary) *see* Beaminster Area *Sarum*
STOKE ALBANY (St Botolph) w Wilbarston and Ashley w Weston-by-Welland and Sutton Bassett *Pet 9* **P** *Comdr L M M Saunders-Watson (2 turns), Bp (1 turn), DBP (1 turn)* **P-in-c** S L HUGHES
STOKE ALDERMOOR (St Catherine) *see* Coventry Caludon *Cov*
STOKE ASH (All Saints) *see* S Hartismere *St E*
STOKE BARDOLPH (St Luke) *see* Burton Joyce w Bulcote and Stoke Bardolph *S'well*
STOKE BISHOP (St Mary Magdalene) *Bris 2* **P** *Bp* **V** D J R RITCHIE
STOKE BLISS (St Peter) *see* Teme Valley S *Worc*
STOKE BRUERNE (St Mary the Virgin) *see* Blisworth and Stoke Bruerne w Grafton Regis etc *Pet*
STOKE BY CLARE (St John the Baptist) *see* Stour Valley *St E*
STOKE BY NAYLAND (St Mary) w Leavenheath and Polstead *St E 3* **P** *Mrs S E F Holden and St Jo Coll Ox (alt)* **R** M J A TILLETT, **NSM** J T FOWLER, **OLM** V ARMSTRONG
STOKE CANON (St Mary Magdalene), Poltimore w Huxham and Rewe w Netherexe *Ex 2* **P** *D&C, Lady Stucley, and Bp (by turn)* **C** J H LISTER
STOKE CHARITY (St Mary and St Michael) *see* Lower Dever Valley *Win*
STOKE CLIMSLAND (not known) *Truro 12* **P** *Bp and Duchy of Cornwall (alt)* **P-in-c** A R INGLEBY, **C** E V A FOOT
STOKE D'ABERNON (St Mary the Virgin) *see* Cobham and Stoke D'Abernon *Guildf*
STOKE DAMEREL (St Andrew w St Luke) *Ex 22* **P** *Trustees Lord St Levan* **P-in-c** D J NIXON
STOKE DOYLE (St Rumbold) *see* Aldwincle w Thorpe Achurch, Pilton, Wadenhoe etc *Pet*
STOKE DRY (St Andrew) *see* Lyddington w Stoke Dry and Seaton etc *Pet*
STOKE EDITH (St Mary) *see* Ledbury *Heref*
STOKE FLEMING (St Peter), Blackawton and Strete *Ex 14* **P** *Bp and BDP (jt)* **V** J H BELL
STOKE GABRIEL (St Gabriel) and Collaton *Ex 13* **P** *Bp* **V** D A TREBY
STOKE GIFFORD (St Michael) *Bris 5* **P** *Bp* **TR** D C R WIDDOWS, **TV** T G E WEBBER, **C** E M SAMMONS, **NSM** J C BRADLEY, P D VROLIJK
STOKE GOLDING (St Margaret) *see* Fenn Lanes Gp *Leic*
STOKE GOLDINGTON (St Peter) *see* Gayhurst w Ravenstone, Stoke Goldington etc *Ox*
STOKE HAMMOND (St Luke) *see* Brickhills and Stoke Hammond *Ox*
STOKE HEATH (St Alban) *see* Cov E *Cov*
STOKE HILL (St Peter) *Guildf 5* **P** *Bp* **OLM** B J RICH
STOKE HOLY CROSS (Holy Cross) w Dunston, Arminghall and Caistor St Edmunds w Markshall *Nor 8* **P** *D&C and Mrs D Pott (jt)* **R** R J BUNN
STOKE LACY (St Peter and St Paul) and Moreton Jeffries w Much Cowarne, Ocle Pychard and Ullingswick *Heref 2* **P** *D&C, Bp Birm, P H G Morgan Esq, and Bp (by turn)* **P-in-c** J A DAVIES, G T G SYKES, **NSM** C M SYKES
STOKE LYNE (St Peter) *see* Shelswell *Ox*
STOKE MANDEVILLE (St Mary the Virgin) *see* Ellesborough, The Kimbles and Stoke Mandeville *Ox*
STOKE NEWINGTON (St Andrew) *Lon 5* **P** *Bp* **V** R K BALLANTINE
STOKE NEWINGTON St Faith (St Matthias) and All Saints *Lon 5* **P** *City Corp* **V** *vacant* (020) 7254 5063
STOKE NEWINGTON (St John the Evangelist) *see* Brownswood Park *Lon*
STOKE NEWINGTON (St Mary) (Old Parish Church) *Lon 5* **P** *Bp* **R** J D CLARK, **C** M J HAWKES, S J SNYDER
STOKE NEWINGTON (St Olave) *Lon 5* **P** *Ld Chan* **V** V A ROBERTS
STOKE NEWINGTON COMMON (St Michael and All Angels) *Lon 5* **P** *Bp* **V** S J A FARRER
STOKE-NEXT-GUILDFORD (St John the Evangelist) *Guildf 5* **P** *Simeon's Trustees* **NSM** R J PECK
STOKE-ON-TRENT *see* Stoke-upon-Trent *Lich*
STOKE ORCHARD (St James the Great) *see* Deerhurst and Apperley w Forthampton etc *Glouc*
STOKE PARK (St Peter) *see* Ipswich St Mary at Stoke w St Pet and St Fran *St E*
STOKE PERO (not known) *see* Porlock w Stoke Pero *B & W*
STOKE POGES (St Giles) *Ox 23* **P** *Ch Ch Ox* **P-in-c** H N L LATHAM
STOKE PRIOR (St Luke) *see* Leominster *Heref*
STOKE PRIOR (St Michael), Wychbold and Upton Warren *Worc 8* **P** *Bp and D&C (alt)* **R** R H ANTELL
STOKE RIVERS (St Bartholomew) *see* Shirwell, Loxhore, Kentisbury, Arlington, etc *Ex*
STOKE ROW (St John the Evangelist) *see* Langtree *Ox*
STOKE ST GREGORY (St Gregory) w Burrowbridge and Lyng *B & W 18* **P** *D&C (2 turns), R O Meade-King Esq (1 turn)* **P-in-c** G TREASURE, **NSM** C J WRIGHT
STOKE ST MARY (St Mary) *see* Beercrocombe w Curry Mallet, Hatch Beauchamp etc *B & W*
STOKE ST MICHAEL (St Michael) *see* Leigh upon Mendip w Stoke St Michael *B & W*
STOKE ST MILBOROUGH (St Milburgha) *see* Bitterley w Middleton, Stoke St Milborough etc *Heref*
STOKE SUB HAMDON (Blessed Virgin Mary) (All Saints Mission Church) *B & W 6* **P** *Ch Patr Trust* **P-in-c** P KERTON-JOHNSON
STOKE TALMAGE (St Mary Magdalene) *see* Thame *Ox*
STOKE TRISTER (St Andrew) *see* Charlton Musgrove, Cucklington and Stoke Trister *B & W*
STOKE UPON TERN (St Peter) *see* Cheswardine, Childs Ercall, Hales, Hinstock etc *Lich*
STOKE-UPON-TRENT (St Peter-ad-Vincula) (St Paul) *Lich 12* **P** *Bp* **TR** D P LINGWOOD, **TV** P R SEARLE, P M SHELTON, **NSM** L M A TIDESWELL, **OLM** P M LOCKLEY
STOKEHAM (St Peter) *see* Rampton w Laneham, Treswell, Cottam and Stokeham *S'well*
STOKEINTEIGNHEAD (St Andrew) *see* Shaldon, Stokeinteignhead, Combeinteignhead etc *Ex*
STOKENCHURCH (St Peter and St Paul) and Ibstone *Ox 29* **P** *Bp* **P-in-c** R A FRANCE
STOKENHAM (St Michael and All Angels) w Sherford and Beesands, and Slapton *Ex 14* **P** *Prime Min* **R** R M HARDING
STOKESAY (St Christopher) (St John the Baptist) *Heref 11* **P** *T P D La Touche Esq* **P-in-c** M L COPE
STOKESBY (St Andrew) *see* S Trin Broads *Nor*
STOKESLEY (St Peter and St Paul) w Seamer *York 21* **P** *Abp* **R** M D A DYKES, **C** A PHILLIPSON
STOLFORD (St Peter) *see* Stogursey w Fiddington *B & W*
STON EASTON (Blessed Virgin Mary) *see* Chewton Mendip w Ston Easton, Litton etc *B & W*
STONDON (All Saints) *see* Gravenhurst, Shillington and Stondon *St Alb*
STONDON MASSEY (St Peter and St Paul) *see* Blackmore and Stondon Massey *Chelmsf*
STONE (All Saints) *see* Berkeley w Wick, Breadstone, Newport, Stone etc *Glouc*
STONE (Christ Church) and Oulton-with-Moddershall *Lich 13* **P** *Simeon's Trustees* **V** P H C KINGMAN
STONE near Dartford (St Mary) *Roch 2* **P** *Bp* **R** K W CLARK
STONE (St John the Baptist) w Dinton and Hartwell *Ox 21* **P** *Bp and Grocers' Co (jt)* **R** D J COOKE
STONE (St Mary the Virgin) *see* Chaddesley Corbett and Stone *Worc*
STONE (St Michael and St Wulfad) w Aston (St Saviour) *Lich 13* **P** *Bp* **R** P J WILSON
STONE CROSS (St Luke) w Langney, North *Chich 16* **P** *Bp* **V** J D VINE
STONE-IN-OXNEY (St Mary the Virgin) *see* Wittersham w Stone-in-Oxney and Ebony *Cant*
STONE QUARRY (St Luke) *see* E Grinstead St Swithun *Chich*
STONEBRIDGE (St Michael and All Angels) *Lon 21* **P** *Bp* **V** R L SMITH
STONEBROOM (St Peter) *see* Morton and Stonebroom w Shirland *Derby*
STONEGATE (St Peter) *Chich 19* **P** *E J B Hardcastle Esq and Mrs C J J Reid (jt)* **P-in-c** J R JAMES, **C** C D LAWRENCE, **NSM** R G ALFORD
STONEGRAVE (Holy Trinity) *see* Ampleforth w Oswaldkirk, Gilling E etc *York*
STONEHAM, NORTH (St Nicholas) (All Saints) *Win 10* **P** *R H W Fleming Esq* **R** J E OWEN, **NSM** C A DAY
STONEHAM, SOUTH (St Mary) *see* Swaythling *Win*

STONEHOUSE (St Cyr) *Glouc 8* **P** *The Crown* **P-in-c** C S MINCHIN
STONEHOUSE (St Paul) *see* Plymouth St Andr and St Paul Stonehouse *Ex*
STONELEIGH (St John the Baptist) *Guildf 9* **P** *Bp* **P-in-c** R A KING, **OLM** I GRACE
STONELEIGH (St Mary the Virgin) w Ashow *Cov 4* **P** *Lord Leigh and Bp (jt)* **P-in-c** V L BALDWIN, **NSM** D JOHNSON
STONESBY (St Peter) *see* Scalford w Wycombe and Chadwell etc *Leic*
STONESFIELD (St James the Great) w Combe Longa *Ox 9* **P** *Duke of Marlborough* **R** G J H B VAN DER WEEGEN
STONEY MIDDLETON (St Martin) *see* Baslow w Curbar and Stoney Middleton *Derby*
STONEY STANTON (St Michael) *see* Broughton Astley and Croft w Stoney Stanton *Leic*
STONEYCROFT (All Saints) *Liv 8* **P** *Bp* **V** S W C GOUGH
STONEYCROFT (St Paul) *see* Liv St Paul Stoneycroft *Liv*
STONEYDELPH (St Martin in the Delph) *see* Glascote and Stonydelph *Lich*
STONHAM ASPAL (St Mary and St Lambert) *see* Crowfield w Stonham Aspal and Mickfield *St E*
STONHAM PARVA (St Mary) *see* Creeting St Mary, Creeting St Peter etc *St E*
STONNALL (St Peter) *Lich 1* **P** *V Shenstone* **P-in-c** R W BAILEY, **NSM** J B ASTON, J FORRESTER
STONTON WYVILLE (St Denys) *see* Gt Bowden w Welham, Glooston and Cranoe etc *Leic*
STONY STRATFORD (St Mary and St Giles) *Ox 25* **P** *Bp* **V** R NORTHING, **C** G A PINNOCK
STOODLEIGH (St Margaret) *see* Washfield, Stoodleigh, Withleigh etc *Ex*
STOPHAM (St Mary the Virgin) and Fittleworth *Chich 11* **P** *D&C and Col Sir Brian Barttelot Bt (jt)* **R** A I SMYTH
STOPSLEY (St Thomas) *St Alb 14* **P** *Bp* **V** D G ALEXANDER
STORRIDGE (St John the Baptist) *see* Cradley w Mathon and Storridge *Heref*
STORRINGTON (St Mary) *Chich 12* **P** *Keble Coll Ox* **R** J M ACHESON, **Hon C** S J TURRELL, **NSM** T C HOLLAND
STORTH (All Saints Mission) *see* Arnside *Carl*
STOTFOLD (St Mary the Virgin) and Radwell *St Alb 16* **P** *Bp* **V** P M QUINT
STOTTESDON (St Mary) w Farlow, Cleeton St Mary, Silvington, Sidbury and Middleton Scriven *Heref 9* **P** *Bp* **R** W J BROMLEY
STOUGHTON (Emmanuel) *Guildf 5* **P** *Simeon's Trustees* **V** F SCAMMELL, **C** L J W BAIN
STOUGHTON (St Mary) *see* Compton, the Mardens, Stoughton and Racton *Chich*
STOUGHTON (St Mary and All Saints) *see* Thurnby w Stoughton *Leic*
STOULTON (St Edmund) w Drake's Broughton and Pirton and Norton *Worc 4* **P** *Croome Estate Trustees, D&C, and Bp (jt)* **R** D G SLOGGETT
STOUR, EAST (Christ Church) *see* Stour Vale *Sarum*
STOUR, UPPER *Sarum 17* **P** *Exors H P R Hoare (1 turn), Bp (2 turns), and Bourton Chpl Trustees (1 turn)* **R** C A R MOORSOM
STOUR, WEST (St Mary) *see* Stour Vale *Sarum*
STOUR PROVOST (St Michael and All Angels) *as above*
STOUR ROW (All Saints) *as above*
STOUR VALE *Sarum 5* **P** *Bp* **V** J E SALTER, **NSM** G J MUGRIDGE
STOUR VALLEY, The *St E 8* **P** *DBP, Jes Coll Cam, Lady Loch, and Duchy of Lanc (by turn)* **R** W J A RANKIN, **Hon C** A R GEORGE, **NSM** G GREEN
STOURBRIDGE (St John the Evangelist) *see* Old Swinford Stourbridge *Worc*
STOURBRIDGE (St Mary) *as above*
STOURBRIDGE (St Michael and All Angels) Norton *Worc 12* **P** *Bp* **V** E BUTT
STOURBRIDGE (St Thomas) *Worc 12* **P** *Bp* **P-in-c** R V CURTIS
STOURHEAD *St E 8* **P** *E H Vestey Esq, St Chad's Coll Dur, Ridley Hall Cam, and Walsingham Coll Trust (jt)* **V** J E ELEY, **NSM** S A BAREHAM
STOURPAINE (Holy Trinity) *see* Pimperne, Stourpaine, Durweston and Bryanston *Sarum*
STOURPORT-ON-SEVERN (St Michael and All Angels) and Wilden *Worc 13* **P** *Earl Baldwin of Bewdley and V Kidderminster St Mary and AllSS (jt)* **V** B GILBERT, **C** J E SPECK
STOURTON (St Peter) *see* Kinver and Enville *Lich*
STOURTON (St Peter) *see* Upper Stour *Sarum*
STOURTON CAUNDLE (St Peter) *see* The Caundles w Folke and Holwell *Sarum*
STOVEN (St Margaret) *see* Hundred River *St E*
STOW Group, The (St Mary the Virgin) *Linc 2* **P** *Bp and DBP (jt)* **P-in-c** M A WHITEHEAD
STOW, WEST (St Mary) *see* Lark Valley *St E*
STOW BARDOLPH (Holy Trinity) *see* Wimbotsham w Stow Bardolph and Stow Bridge etc *Ely*
STOW BEDON (St Botolph) *see* Caston, Griston, Merton, Thompson etc *Nor*
STOW BRIDGE Mission (St Peter) *see* Wimbotsham w Stow Bardolph and Stow Bridge etc *Ely*
STOW LONGA (St Botolph) *Ely 8* **P** *Bp* **V** R A FROST
STOW MARIES (St Mary and St Margaret) *see* Purleigh, Cold Norton and Stow Maries *Chelmsf*
STOW ON THE WOLD (St Edward), Condicote and The Swells *Glouc 14* **P** *DBP and Ch Ch Ox (jt)* **R** D C FRANCIS
STOWE (Assumption of St Mary the Virgin) *Ox 22* **P** *Stowe Sch* **P-in-c** R M BUNDOCK
STOWE (St Michael and All Angels) *see* Bucknell w Chapel Lawn, Llanfair Waterdine etc *Heref*
STOWE, UPPER (St James) *see* Heyford w Stowe Nine Churches and Flore etc *Pet*
STOWE BY CHARTLEY (St John the Baptist) *see* Mid Trent *Lich*
STOWE NINE CHURCHES (St Michael) *see* Heyford w Stowe Nine Churches and Flore etc *Pet*
STOWELL (St Leonard) *see* Chedworth, Yanworth and Stowell, Coln Rogers etc *Glouc*
STOWELL (St Mary Magdalene) *see* Henstridge and Charlton Horethorne w Stowell *B & W*
STOWEY (St Nicholas and Blessed Virgin Mary) *see* Bishop Sutton and Stanton Drew and Stowey *B & W*
STOWEY, NETHER (Blessed Virgin Mary) *see* Aisholt, Enmore, Goathurst, Nether Stowey etc *B & W*
STOWEY, OVER (St Peter and St Paul) *as above*
STOWFORD (St John) *see* Lifton, Broadwoodwidger, Stowford etc *Ex*
STOWLANGTOFT (St George) *see* Badwell and Walsham *St E*
STOWMARKET (St Peter and St Mary) *St E 6* **P** *Ch Patr Trust* **P-in-c** M W EDEN, **OLM** R M STRETCH, R F GILBERT
STOWTING (St Mary the Virgin) *see* Smeeth w Monks Horton and Stowting and Brabourne *Cant*
STOWUPLAND (Holy Trinity) *see* Haughley w Wetherden and Stowupland *St E*
STRADBROKE (All Saints) w Horham, Athelington and Redlingfield *St E 17* **P** *Bp (3 turns), Lt-Comdr G C Marshall (1 turn), and Dr G I Soden (1 turn)* **R** D J STREETER
STRADISHALL (St Margaret) *see* Bansfield *St E*
STRADSETT (St Mary) *see* Downham Market and Crimplesham w Stradsett *Ely*
STRAGGLETHORPE (St Michael) *see* Brant Broughton and Beckingham *Linc*
STRAITS, The (St Andrew) *see* Gornal and Sedgley *Worc*
STRAMSHALL (St Michael and All Angels) *see* Uttoxeter Area *Lich*
STRANTON (All Saints) *Dur 3* **P** *St Jo Coll Dur* **V** M R GILBERTSON, **C** M P DUNSTAN, **NSM** A J CRAIG
STRATFIELD MORTIMER (St Mary) and Mortimer West End w Padworth *Ox 12* **P** *Eton Coll, Ld Chan, and Englefield Estate Trust Corp (by turn)* **V** P CHAPLIN, **NSM** C G LEA, J L STRAW
STRATFIELD SAYE (St Mary) *see* Sherfield-on-Loddon and Stratfield Saye etc *Win*
STRATFORD (St John the Evangelist w Christ Church) and St James *Chelmsf 3* **P** *V W Ham* **V** D A RICHARDS, **C** J T MADDERN, **NSM** J V MEADWAY
STRATFORD NEW TOWN (St Paul) *Chelmsf 3* **P** *Ch Patr Trust* **V** *vacant* (020) 8534 4243
STRATFORD ST MARY (St Mary) *see* Higham, Holton St Mary, Raydon and Stratford *St E*
STRATFORD SUB CASTLE (St Lawrence) *see* Salisbury St Fran and Stratford sub Castle *Sarum*
STRATFORD-UPON-AVON (Holy Trinity), Luddington and Clifford Chambers *Cov 8* **P** *Bp* **R** M C W GORICK, **C** L J FARMER, P J M ANGIER
STRATTON (St Andrew) and Launcells *Truro 8* **P** *Duchy of Cornwall and CPAS (alt)* **V** R N STRANACK
STRATTON (St Mary) (St Michael) and Wacton *Nor 5* **P** *G&C Coll Cam, DBP, and New Coll Ox (by turn)* **R** J A NASH
STRATTON (St Mary the Virgin) *see* Bradford Peverell, Stratton, Frampton etc *Sarum*
STRATTON (St Peter), North Cerney, Baunton and Bagendon *Glouc 11* **P** *Mrs P M Chester Master, Jes Coll Ox, Univ Coll Ox (jt)* **R** P F QUINNELL, **NSM** D H S LEESON
STRATTON, EAST (All Saints) *see* Micheldever and E Stratton, Woodmancote etc *Win*
STRATTON, UPPER (St Philip) *Bris 7* **P** *Bp* **V** C A STONE

STRATTON AUDLEY (St Mary and St Edburga) *see* Shelswell *Ox*
STRATTON ON THE FOSSE (St Vigor) *see* Chilcompton w Downside and Stratton on the Fosse *B & W*
STRATTON ST MARGARET (St Margaret) w South Marston and Stanton Fitzwarren *Bris 7* **P** *Patr Bd* **TR** T D HAWKINGS, **TV** G K BAKKER, **Hon C** R J BURSTON, **NSM** J J BAKKER
STRATTON STRAWLESS (St Margaret) *see* Hevingham w Hainford and Stratton Strawless *Nor*
STREAT (not known) w Westmeston *Chich 9* **P** *Woodard Schs* **P-in-c** J R TAYLOR
STREATHAM (Christ Church) *S'wark 15* **P** *R Streatham St Leon* **V** S TRICKLEBANK, **NSM** R J S ALLEN
STREATHAM (Immanuel) (St Andrew) *S'wark 15* **P** *Bp, Hyndman Trustees, and R Streatham St Leon (jt)* **V** E M SHEARCROFT, **NSM** W E AIRD
STREATHAM (St Leonard) *S'wark 15* **P** *Bp* **R** J R WILCOX, **NSM** M E HAWES
STREATHAM (St Paul) *S'wark 19* **P** *Bp* **V** A J R DRIVER, **Hon C** J M DRIVER
STREATHAM (St Peter) *S'wark 15* **P** *St Steph Ho Ox* **V** P D ANDREWS, **Hon C** S T MEYER
STREATHAM (St Thomas) *see* Telford Park St Thos *S'wark*
STREATHAM, WEST (St James) *S'wark 19* **P** *CPAS* **V** G G HOWARD, **C** T M MULRYNE, **OLM** S D WHITE
STREATHAM HILL (St Margaret the Queen) *S'wark 15* **P** *Bp* **V** S TRICKLEBANK, **NSM** R J S ALLEN
STREATHAM PARK (St Alban) *S'wark 19* **P** *Ch Soc Trust* **V** M S RICHEUX
STREATHAM VALE (Holy Redeemer) *S'wark 15* **P** *CPAS* **V** I H GILMOUR
STREATLEY (St Margaret) *St Alb 14* **P** *Bp* **V** R W WOOD
STREATLEY (St Mary) *Ox 18* **P** *Bp* **P-in-c** E R M POLOMSKI, **Hon C** J P MACKNEY
STREET (Holy Trinity) (Mission Church) w Walton *B & W 5* **P** *DBP* **R** F J GREED, **Hon C** D N HATREY
STREET Parishes, The *York 6* **P** *Patr Bd* **R** B S BOWES, **NSM** P H BOWES
STREETLY (All Saints) *Lich 25* **P** *Bp* **V** S A CHAPMAN
STRELLEY (All Saints) *see* Bilborough w Strelley *S'well*
STRENSALL (St Mary the Virgin) *York 3* **P** *Abp* **V** M HARRISON, **NSM** J A PALMER
STRETE (St Michael) *see* Stoke Fleming, Blackawton and Strete *Ex*
STRETFORD (All Saints) *Man 7* **P** *Bp* **P-in-c** R S THEWSEY
STRETFORD (St Bride) *see* Old Trafford St Bride *Man*
STRETFORD (St Matthew) *Man 7* **P** *D&C* **P-in-c** D T THOMAS, **C** R MANN
STRETFORD (St Peter) *see* Firswood and Gorse Hill *Man*
STRETHALL (St Mary the Virgin) *see* Heydon, Gt and Lt Chishill, Chrishall etc *Chelmsf*
STRETHAM (St James) *see* Ely *Ely*
STRETTON (St John) *see* Penkridge Team *Lich*
STRETTON (St Mary) w Claymills *Lich 14* **P** *Baroness Gretton* **NSM** D V WARNER
STRETTON (St Matthew) and Appleton Thorn *Ches 4* **P** *Mrs P F du Bois Grantham and Dr S P L du Bois Davidson (jt)* **V** E C HALL, **C** G H BUCHAN, H S HOUSTON, **NSM** K L WILLIAMSON
STRETTON (St Nicholas) *see* Greetham and Thistleton w Stretton and Clipsham *Pet*
STRETTON, LITTLE (All Saints) *see* Church Stretton *Heref*
STRETTON GRANDISON (St Laurence) *see* Ledbury *Heref*
STRETTON MAGNA (St Giles) *see* Glen Magna cum Stretton Magna etc *Leic*
STRETTON ON DUNSMORE (All Saints) *see* Bourton w Frankton and Stretton on Dunsmore etc *Cov*
STRETTON ON DUNSMORE (Mission Church) *as above*
STRETTON ON FOSSE (St Peter) *see* Ilmington w Stretton-on-Fosse etc *Cov*
STRETTON PARVA (St John the Baptist) *see* Gaulby *Leic*
STRETTON SUGWAS (St Mary Magdalene) *Heref 4* **P** *DBP* **R** J W R MORRISON, **NSM** E S V VERWEY
STRICKLAND, GREAT (St Barnabas) *see* Morland, Thrimby, Gt Strickland and Cliburn *Carl*
STRINES (St Paul) *see* Marple All SS *Ches*
STRINGSTON (not known) *see* Quantoxhead *B & W*
STRIXTON (St John the Baptist) *see* Wollaston and Strixton *Pet*
STROOD (St Francis) *Roch 6* **P** *Bp* **V** H DAUBNEY
STROOD (St Nicholas) w St Mary *Roch 6* **P** *Bp and D&C (jt)* **V** D W GREEN, **C** G V HERBERT
STROUD (Holy Trinity) (St Alban Mission Church) *Glouc 1* **P** *Bp* **V** M J WITHEY
STROUD (Mission Church) *see* Steep and Froxfield w Privett *Portsm*
STROUD (St Laurence) and Uplands w Slad *Glouc 1* **P** *Bp* **V** B C E COKER
STROUD GREEN (Holy Trinity) *Lon 20* **P** *Bp* **P-in-c** P J HENDERSON, **C** T D PIKE
STROXTON (All Saints) *see* Harlaxton Gp *Linc*
STRUBBY (St Oswald) *see* Legbourne and Wold Marsh *Linc*
STRUMPSHAW (St Peter) *see* Burlingham St Edmund w Lingwood, Strumpshaw etc *Nor*
STUBBINGS (St James the Less) *see* Burchetts Green *Ox*
STUBBINGTON (St Edmund) *see* Crofton *Portsm*
STUBBINS (St Philip) *see* Edenfield and Stubbins *Man*
STUBBS CROSS (St Francis) *see* Kingsnorth and Shadoxhurst *Cant*
STUBSHAW CROSS (St Luke) *see* Ashton-in-Makerfield St Thos *Liv*
STUBTON (St Martin) *see* Claypole *Linc*
STUDHAM (St Mary the Virgin) *see* Kensworth, Studham and Whipsnade *St Alb*
STUDLAND (St Nicholas) *see* Swanage and Studland *Sarum*
STUDLEY (Nativity of the Blessed Virgin Mary) *Cov 7* **P** *DBP* **V** R W DEIMEL, **NSM** M M DEIMEL
STUDLEY (St John the Evangelist) *Sarum 14* **P** *R Trowbridge St Jas* **P-in-c** P N BARNES
STUKELEY, GREAT (St Bartholomew) w Little (St Martin) *Ely 8* **P** *SMF and Bp (jt)* **P-in-c** A J MILTON, **C** J M SAVAGE
STUKELEY MEADOWS Local Ecumenical Project *Ely 9 vacant*
STUNTNEY (Holy Cross) *see* Ely *Ely*
STURMER (St Mary) *see* Ridgewell w Ashen, Birdbrook and Sturmer *Chelmsf*
STURMINSTER MARSHALL (St Mary), Kingston Lacy and Shapwick *Sarum 9* **P** *Eton Coll and Nat Trust (alt)* **V** A C STEWART-SYKES
STURMINSTER NEWTON (St Mary), Hinton St Mary and Lydlinch *Sarum 5* **P** *Col J L Yeatman (1 turn), G A L F Pitt-Rivers Esq (3 turns), V Iwerne Valley (1 turn)* **V** D R R SEYMOUR
STURRY (St Nicholas) w Fordwich and Westbere w Hersden *Cant 3* **P** *Abp, Ld Chan, and St Aug Foundn Cant (by turn)* **R** P A CORNISH, **OLM** P C J FREEMAN
STURTON (St Hugh) *see* Stow Gp *Linc*
STURTON, GREAT (All Saints) *see* Hemingby *Linc*
STURTON-LE-STEEPLE (St Peter and St Paul) *see* N Wheatley, W Burton, Bole, Saundby, Sturton etc *S'well*
STUSTON (All Saints) *see* N Hartismere *St E*
STUTTON (St Aidan) *see* Tadcaster w Newton Kyme *York*
STUTTON (St Peter) *see* Holbrook, Stutton, Freston, Woolverstone etc *St E*
STYVECHALE (St James) *Cov 3* **P** *Col A M H Gregory-Hood* **V** J K MILLS, **OLM** C M NEWBORN, A PRETT
SUCKLEY (St John the Baptist) *see* Alfrick, Lulsley, Suckley, Leigh and Bransford *Worc*
SUDBOROUGH (All Saints) *see* Brigstock w Stanion and Lowick and Sudborough *Pet*
SUDBOURNE (All Saints) *see* Wilford Peninsula *St E*
SUDBROOKE (St Edward) *see* Barlings *Linc*
SUDBURY (All Saints) *see* Doveridge, Scropton, Sudbury etc *Derby*
SUDBURY (All Saints) w Ballingdon and Brundon *St E 12* **P** *Simeon's Trustees* **P-in-c** S D GILL
SUDBURY (St Andrew) *Lon 21* **P** *Bp* **V** F M-L SCROGGIE, **NSM** L P NORTH
SUDBURY (St Gregory) St Peter and Chilton *St E 12* **P** *Bp (3 turns), Ch Soc Trust (1 turn)* **R** L R PIZZEY
SUDDEN (St Aidan) *Man 20* **P** *Bp* **V** G C DOBBS
SUDELEY MANOR (St Mary) *see* Winchcombe *Glouc*
SUFFIELD (St Margaret) *see* King's Beck *Nor*
SUFFIELD PARK (St Martin) *see* Cromer *Nor*
SUFFOLK HEIGHTS *see* Chevington w Hargrave, Chedburgh w Depden etc *St E*
SUGLEY (Holy Saviour) *Newc 7* **P** *Bp* **V** S T ROBSON
SULBY (St Stephen's Chapel) *see* Lezayre *S & M*
SULGRAVE (St James the Less) *see* Culworth w Sulgrave and Thorpe Mandeville etc *Pet*
SULHAM (St Nicholas) *see* Pangbourne w Tidmarsh and Sulham *Ox*
SULHAMSTEAD ABBOTS (St Mary) and Bannister w Ufton Nervet *Ox 12* **P** *Qu Coll Ox and Or Coll Ox (alt)* **P-in-c** P L DEWEY
SULLINGTON (St Mary) and Thakeham w Warminghurst *Chich 12* **P** *Bp and DBP (alt)* **R** P MESSENGER
SUMMERFIELD (Christ Church) (Cavendish Road Hall) *Birm 2* **P** *R Birm St Martin w Bordesley* **V** J B KNIGHT

SUMMERFIELD (St John's Chapel) *see* Hartlebury *Worc*
SUMMERSDALE (St Michael) *see* Chich St Paul and Westhampnett *Chich*
SUMMERSTOWN (St Mary) *S'wark 19* **P** *Ch Soc Trust* **V** R J RYAN
SUMMERTOWN (St Michael and All Angels) *see* Wolvercote w Summertown *Ox*
SUNBURY, UPPER (St Saviour) *Lon 13* **P** *V Sunbury* **P-in-c** D R MCDOUGALL, **C** A J SACHS
SUNBURY-ON-THAMES (St Mary) *Lon 13* **P** *D&C St Paul's* **V** P S DAVIES
SUNDERLAND Pennywell (St Thomas) *Dur 16* **P** *Bp* **C** G W MILLER
SUNDERLAND (St Bede) Town End Farm *see* N Wearside *Dur*
SUNDERLAND (St Chad) *Dur 16* **P** *Bp* **V** J D CHADD, **C** J WING, **NSM** P THOMPSON
SUNDERLAND (St Cuthbert) Red House *see* N Wearside *Dur*
SUNDERLAND (St Mary the Virgin) (St Peter) *Dur 16* **P** *Bp* **V** K A WALTON, **C** G W MILLER
SUNDERLAND (St Michael) *Dur 16* **P** *Bp* **TR** S R TAYLOR, **TV** S D HAZLETT, **C** S A A FAGBEMI, **NSM** J M M FRANCIS
SUNDERLAND, NORTH (St Paul) *Newc 10* **P** *Lord Crewe's Trustees* **V** E J WOOD
SUNDERLAND POINT (Mission Church) *see* Overton *Blackb*
SUNDON (St Mary) *St Alb 14* **P** *Bp* **P-in-c** Y M SMEJKAL
SUNDRIDGE (St Mary) w Ide Hill and Toys Hill *Roch 9* **P** *Abp* **R** D J E ATTWOOD, **NSM** A M BOYLE
SUNNINGDALE (Holy Trinity) *Ox 11* **P** *Bp* **V** H D UFFINDELL, **NSM** A M GRIGGS
SUNNINGHILL (St Michael and All Angels) *Ox 11* **P** *St Jo Coll Cam* **V** K RAMSAY
SUNNINGWELL (St Leonard) *see* Radley and Sunningwell *Ox*
SUNNYSIDE (St Barnabas) *see* E Grinstead St Swithun *Chich*
SUNNYSIDE (St Michael and All Angels) w Bourne End *St Alb 2* **P** *CPAS* **V** D J ABBOTT, **C** B C GRAY, **NSM** R CLARKSON
SURBITON (St Andrew) (St Mark) *S'wark 17* **P** *Bp* **V** J H TIDY, **C** V A CORY, **Hon C** T BRAUN, **NSM** G M AYERST
SURBITON (St Matthew) *S'wark 17* **P** *CPAS* **V** S A HONES, **C** C S LAKER, **OLM** V CUTHBERT
SURBITON HILL (Christ Church) *S'wark 17* **P** *Ch Soc Trust and Trustees (jt)* **V** G WINTLE, **C** D A BAKER, A M BOUSFIELD, **NSM** D J BENDELL
SURFLEET (St Lawrence) *see* Glen Gp *Linc*
SURLINGHAM (St Mary) *see* Rockland St Mary w Hellington, Bramerton etc *Nor*
SURREY WEALD *Guildf 7* **P** *Patr Bd (1 turn), Ld Chan (2 turns)* **TR** A D J COE, **TV** B STEADMAN-ALLEN, **NSM** J R BAXTER
SUSSEX GARDENS (St James) *see* Paddington St Jas *Lon*
SUSTEAD (St Peter and St Paul) *see* Roughton and Felbrigg, Metton, Sustead etc *Nor*
SUTCOMBE (St Andrew) *see* Bradworthy, Sutcombe, Putford etc *Ex*
SUTTERBY (not known) *see* Partney Gp *Linc*
SUTTERTON (St Mary), Fosdyke, Algarkirk and Wigtoft *Linc 21* **P** *Prime Min (1 turn), Bp and DBP (1 turn)* **R** *vacant* (01205) 460285
SUTTON (All Saints) *see* Potton w Sutton and Cockayne Hatley *St Alb*
SUTTON (All Saints) *see* Wilford Peninsula *St E*
SUTTON (All Saints) w Shopland *Chelmsf 12* **P** *SMF* **P-in-c** C W COUSINS
SUTTON (Christ Church) *S'wark 25* **P** *R Sutton St Nic* **V** C E GALE
SUTTON (Mission Room) *see* Felixkirk w Boltby *York*
SUTTON (St Andrew) *Ely 12* **P** *D&C* **V** J M AMEY, **NSM** M L BRADBURY
SUTTON (St Barnabas' Mission Church) *see* Macclesfield Team Par *Ches*
SUTTON (St Clement), Huttoft and Anderby *Linc 8* **P** *Bp (2 turns), Magd Coll Cam (1 turn)* **R** L ST J R AITKEN
SUTTON (St James) *Ches 13* **P** *Trustees* **V** E W L DAVIES
SUTTON (St James) and Wawne *York 14* **P** *Patr Bd* **TV** C FISHER-BAILEY, H H NESBITT, P COPLEY, **C** R J GANNEY
SUTTON (St John the Baptist) *see* Barlavington, Burton w Coates, Sutton and Bignor *Chich*
SUTTON (St Mary) *see* Calow and Sutton cum Duckmanton *Derby*
SUTTON (St Michael) *see* Stalham, E Ruston, Brunstead, Sutton and Ingham *Nor*
SUTTON (St Michael and All Angels) *see* Castor w Sutton and Upton w Marholm *Pet*
SUTTON (St Nicholas) *S'wark 25* **P** *Hertf Coll Ox* **R** S J H GOATCHER
SUTTON (St Nicholas) (All Saints) (St Michael and All Angels) *Liv 10* **P** *Patr Bd* **TR** C B SPITTLE, **C** J DUCK
SUTTON (St Thomas) *Bradf 8* **P** *Ch Ch Ox* **V** M COWGILL
SUTTON w Carlton and Normanton upon Trent and Marnham *S'well 3* **P** *Bp* **P-in-c** S DIXON
SUTTON, EAST (St Peter and St Paul) *see* Sutton Valence w E Sutton and Chart Sutton *Cant*
SUTTON, GREAT (St John the Evangelist) *Ches 9* **P** *V Eastham* **V** *vacant* 0151-339 9916
SUTTON, NORTH *see* Plymouth Em, St Paul Efford and St Aug *Ex*
SUTTON AT HONE (St John the Baptist) *see* Horton Kirby and Sutton-at-Hone *Roch*
SUTTON BASSETT (All Saints) *see* Stoke Albany w Wilbarston and Ashley etc *Pet*
SUTTON BENGER (All Saints) *see* Draycot *Bris*
SUTTON BONINGTON (St Michael) (St Anne) w Normanton-on-Soar *S'well 9* **P** *Bp* **P-in-c** J E PALMER
SUTTON BRIDGE (St Matthew) *Linc 16* **P** *Bp* **P-in-c** D B WOODS
SUTTON BY DOVER (St Peter and St Paul) *see* Ringwould w Kingsdown and Ripple etc *Cant*
SUTTON CHENEY (St James) *see* Bosworth and Sheepy Gp *Leic*
SUTTON COLDFIELD (Holy Trinity) *Birm 12* **P** *Bp* **C** B A ROBERTSON
SUTTON COLDFIELD (St Chad) *Birm 12* **P** *Bp* **V** W J ROUTH
SUTTON COLDFIELD (St Columba) *Birm 12* **P** *Bp* **V** R P TUCKER
SUTTON COURTENAY (All Saints) w Appleford *Ox 10* **P** *D&C Windsor* **P-in-c** H G KENDRICK
SUTTON-CUM-LOUND (St Bartholomew) *see* Babworth w Sutton-cum-Lound and Scofton etc *S'well*
SUTTON GREEN (All Souls) *see* Woking St Pet *Guildf*
SUTTON HILL (Pastoral Centre) *see* Madeley *Heref*
SUTTON IN ASHFIELD (St Mary Magdalene) *S'well 4* **P** *Bp* **P-in-c** A N EVANS, **C** S CADDY
SUTTON IN ASHFIELD St Michael and All Angels *S'well 4* **P** *Bp* **P-in-c** T MITCHELL
SUTTON IN HOLDERNESS (St Michael) *York 14* **P** *Abp* **V** M A JEAVONS, **NSM** P J NELSON
SUTTON LE MARSH (St Clement) *see* Sutton, Huttoft and Anderby *Linc*
SUTTON MADDOCK (St Mary) *see* Beckbury, Badger, Kemberton, Ryton, Stockton etc *Lich*
SUTTON MANDEVILLE (All Saints) *see* Fovant, Sutton Mandeville and Teffont Evias etc *Sarum*
SUTTON MONTIS (Holy Trinity) *see* Cam Vale *B & W*
SUTTON NEW TOWN (St Barnabas) *S'wark 25* **P** *Bp* **P-in-c** V A DAVIES
SUTTON ON DERWENT (St Michael) *see* Elvington w Sutton on Derwent and E Cottingwith *York*
SUTTON ON PLYM (St John the Evangelist) *Ex 24* **P** *Keble Coll Ox* **V** B R LAY
SUTTON-ON-SEA (St Clement) *see* Sutton, Huttoft and Anderby *Linc*
SUTTON ON THE FOREST (All Hallows) *York 3* **P** *Ld Chan* **P-in-c** S K NIGHTINGALE
SUTTON ON THE HILL (St Michael) *see* Boylestone, Church Broughton, Dalbury, etc *Derby*
SUTTON-ON-TRENT (All Saints) *see* Sutton w Carlton and Normanton upon Trent etc *S'well*
SUTTON PARK (St Andrew) *see* Sutton St Jas and Wawne *York*
SUTTON ST EDMUND (St Edmund King and Martyr) *see* The Suttons w Tydd *Linc*
SUTTON ST JAMES (St James) *as above*
SUTTON ST MARY (otherwise known as Long Sutton) (St Mary) *Linc 16* **P** *Lady McGeoch* **P-in-c** J P E SIBLEY
SUTTON ST MICHAEL (St Michael) *see* Sutton St Nicholas w Sutton St Michael *Heref*
SUTTON ST NICHOLAS *see* Lutton w Gedney Drove End, Dawsmere *Linc*
SUTTON ST NICHOLAS (St Nicholas) w Sutton St Michael *Heref 4* **P** *Bp* **P-in-c** H M SHORT
SUTTON UNDER BRAILES (St Thomas à Becket) *Cov 9* **P** *Bp* **R** N J MORGAN, **NSM** J W ROLFE
SUTTON VALENCE (St Mary the Virgin) w East Sutton and Chart Sutton *Cant 14* **P** *Abp York* **V** D R BARKER
SUTTON VENY (St John the Evangelist) *see* Upper Wylye Valley *Sarum*

SUTTON WALDRON (St Bartholomew) *see* Iwerne Valley *Sarum*
SUTTONS w Tydd, The *Linc 16* **P** *Ld Chan (1 turn), V Long Sutton (2 turns)* **V** *vacant* (01945) 440457
SWABY (St Nicholas) *see* Legbourne and Wold Marsh *Linc*
SWADLINCOTE (Emmanuel) *Derby 16* **P** *V Gresley* **V** D J HORSFALL
SWAFFHAM (St Peter and St Paul) *Nor 13* **P** *Bp* **V** S J SMITH, **C** P G BLAMIRE
SWAFFHAM BULBECK (St Mary) *see* Anglesey Gp *Ely*
SWAFFHAM PRIOR (St Mary) *as above*
SWAFIELD (St Nicholas) *see* Trunch *Nor*
SWAINSTHORPE (St Peter) *see* Newton Flotman, Swainsthorpe, Tasburgh, etc *Nor*
SWAINSWICK (Blessed Virgin Mary) *see* Bath St Sav w Swainswick and Woolley *B & W*
SWALCLIFFE (St Peter and St Paul) *see* Wykeham *Ox*
SWALE, LOWER *Ripon 4* **P** *D&C York, Duke of Northumberland, and Bp (jt)* **R** R J GLOVER, **P-in-c** J A WILSON
SWALECLIFFE (St John the Baptist) *see* Whitstable *Cant*
SWALEDALE *Ripon 2* **P** *Bp* **V** *vacant* (01748) 884706
SWALLOW (Holy Trinity) *Linc 5* **P** *The Revd J R H Thorold and J R Thorold Esq (jt), DBP, Bp, and Earl of Yarborough (by turn)* **P-in-c** L M MAGNUSSON
SWALLOWBECK (St George) *see* Linc St Geo Swallowbeck *Linc*
SWALLOWCLIFFE (St Peter) *see* Nadder Valley *Sarum*
SWALLOWFIELD (All Saints) *see* Loddon Reach *Ox*
SWALWELL (Holy Trinity) *see* Blaydon and Swalwell *Dur*
SWAN *Ox 24* **P** *Patr Bd* **TR** D A HISCOCK
SWANAGE (All Saints) (St Mary the Virgin) and Studland *Sarum 8* **P** *Patr Bd* **TR** J S WOOD, **TV** W H N WATTS, **OLM** A C HIGGINS
SWANBOURNE (St Swithun) *see* Newton Longville and Mursley w Swanbourne etc *Ox*
SWANLAND (St Barnabas) *York 14* **P** *H Trin Hull and Distr Ch Patr Soc Ltd* **V** R H O HILL
SWANLEY (St Mary) *Roch 2* **P** *Guild of All So* **V** M R BRUNDLE, **C** J T MCCLUSKEY
SWANLEY (St Paul) *Roch 2* **P** *Merchant Taylors' Co* **V** A D PROCTER
SWANMORE (St Barnabas) *Portsm 1* **P** *DBP* **P-in-c** P H KELLY, **NSM** M M MORT, M J MORFILL
SWANMORE (St Michael and All Angels) *Portsm 7* **P** *SMF* **V** M F JONES
SWANNINGTON (St George) *see* Ravenstone and Swannington *Leic*
SWANNINGTON (St Margaret) *see* Wensum Benefice *Nor*
SWANSCOMBE (St Peter and St Paul) *Roch 4* **P** *DBP* **R** D SCOTT
SWANTON ABBOT (St Michael) *see* Worstead, Westwick, Sloley, Swanton Abbot etc *Nor*
SWANTON MORLEY (All Saints) w Beetley w East Bilney and Hoe *Nor 14* **P** *G&C Coll Cam, Ld Chan, and DBP (by turn)* **P-in-c** R AMES-LEWIS
SWANTON NOVERS (St Edmund) *see* Brinton, Briningham, Hunworth, Stody etc *Nor*
SWANWICK (St Andrew) and Pentrich *Derby 1* **P** *Wright Trustees and Duke of Devonshire (alt)* **V** T B JOHNSON
SWANWICK (St Barnabas) *see* Sarisbury *Portsm*
SWARBY (St Mary and All Saints) *see* S Lafford *Linc*
SWARCLIFFE (St Luke) *see* Seacroft *Ripon*
SWARDESTON (St Mary the Virgin) w East Carleton, Intwood, Keswick and Ketteringham *Nor 7* **P** *Bp, DBP, and Miss M B Unthank (jt)* **P-in-c** P D BURR
SWARKESTONE (St James) *see* Ticknall, Smisby and Stanton by Bridge etc *Derby*
SWARTHMORE (Mission Church) *see* Pennington and Lindal w Marton and Bardsea *Carl*
SWATON (St Michael) *see* Helpringham w Hale *Linc*
SWAVESEY (St Andrew) *see* Fen Drayton w Conington and Lolworth etc *Ely*
SWAY (St Luke) *Win 11* **P** *Bp* **V** *vacant* (01590) 682358
SWAYFIELD (St Nicholas) *see* Corby Glen *Linc*
SWAYTHLING (St Mary South Stoneham w St Alban the Martyr) *Win 13* **P** *Bp and TR Southn City Cen (jt)* **V** G J PHILBRICK, **C** V A MAUNDER, **NSM** V J LAWRENCE
SWEFFLING (St Mary) *see* Badingham w Bruisyard, Cransford etc *St E*
SWELL (St Catherine) *see* Curry Rivel w Fivehead and Swell *B & W*
SWELL, LOWER (St Mary) *see* Stow on the Wold, Condicote and The Swells *Glouc*
SWELL, UPPER (St Mary) *as above*
SWEPSTONE (St Peter) *see* Appleby Gp *Leic*
SWERFORD (St Mary) *see* Hook Norton w Gt Rollright, Swerford etc *Ox*
SWETTENHAM (St Peter) *see* Brereton w Swettenham *Ches*
SWILLAND (St Mary) *see* Clopton w Otley, Swilland and Ashbocking *St E*
SWILLINGTON (St Mary) *Ripon 8* **P** *Bp* **R** *vacant* 0113-286 0172
SWIMBRIDGE (St James the Apostle) w West Buckland and Landkey *Ex 18* **P** *Bp and Trustees Earl Fortescue (jt)* **R** P BOWERS, **NSM** G F SQUIRE
SWINBROOK (St Mary) *see* Burford w Fulbrook, Taynton, Asthall etc *Ox*
SWINDERBY (All Saints) *Linc 18* **P** *Bp, Ld Chan, E M K Kirk Esq, and D&C (by turn)* **V** G C GOALBY, **NSM** J T ROOKE
SWINDON (All Saints) (St Barnabas) *Bris 7* **P** *Bp* **V** A R STEVENSON, **C** A M OVERTON-BENGE, M L BORLEY
SWINDON (Christ Church) (St Mary) *Bris 7* **P** *Ld Chan* **V** S M STEVENETTE, **C** E V QUIBELL
SWINDON Dorcan *Bris 7* **P** *Bp* **TR** A B KNAPP
SWINDON New Town (St Mark) (St Adhelm) (St Luke) (St Saviour) *Bris 7* **P** *Patr Bd* **TR** D B MCCONKEY, **TV** L A PINFIELD
SWINDON (St Andrew) (St John the Baptist) *Bris 7* **P** *Ld Chan* **TR** R J BURLES, **C** M T BEATON
SWINDON (St Augustine) *Bris 7* **P** *Bp* **C** A M OVERTON-BENGE, M L BORLEY
SWINDON (St John the Evangelist) *see* Smestow Vale *Lich*
SWINDON (St Lawrence) w Uckington and Elmstone Hardwicke *Glouc 9* **P** *Bp* **P-in-c** D R EADY
SWINDON (St Peter) *see* Penhill *Bris*
SWINDON, NORTH (St Andrew) *Bris 7* **P** *Bp* **V** R F I CRAM
SWINDON, WEST and the Lydiards *Bris 7* **P** *Patr Bd* **TR** S J SKINNER, **TV** P M KNIGHT, **Hon C** J M SKINNER
SWINE (St Mary) *see* Skirlaugh w Long Riston, Rise and Swine *York*
SWINEFLEET (St Margaret) *see* The Marshland *Sheff*
SWINESHEAD (St Mary) *Linc 21* **P** *Bp* **V** *vacant* (01205) 820271
SWINESHEAD (St Nicholas) *see* The Stodden Churches *St Alb*
SWINFORD (All Saints) *see* Gilmorton, Peatling Parva, Kimcote etc *Leic*
SWINFORD, OLD Stourbridge (St Mary) *Worc 12* **P** *Bp* **R** G S CROSS, **C** J M DOORES
SWINHOPE (St Helen) *see* Binbrook Gp *Linc*
SWINNOW (Christ the Saviour) *see* Stanningley St Thos *Ripon*
SWINSTEAD (St Mary) *see* Edenham w Witham on the Hill and Swinstead *Linc*
SWINTON (Holy Rood) *Man 2* **P** *TR Swinton and Pendlebury* **P-in-c** C C CLAPHAM
SWINTON (St Margaret) *Sheff 12* **P** *Sir Philip Naylor-Leyland Bt* **V** C J BARLEY
SWINTON (St Peter) and Pendlebury *Man 2* **P** *Patr Bd* **TV** I A HALL, J R SIEMENS, **C** A L WAUDE
SWITHLAND (St Leonard) *see* Woodhouse, Woodhouse Eaves and Swithland *Leic*
SWYNCOMBE (St Botolph) *see* Icknield *Ox*
SWYNNERTON (St Mary) and Tittensor *Lich 13* **P** *Bp and Simeon's Trustees (jt)* **R** B J BREWER
SWYRE (Holy Trinity) *see* Bride Valley *Sarum*
SYDE (St Mary) *see* Brimpsfield w Birdlip, Syde, Daglingworth etc *Glouc*
SYDENHAM (All Saints) *S'wark 5* **P** *V Sydenham St Bart* **P-in-c** P H SMITH, **NSM** R W POTTIER
SYDENHAM (Holy Trinity) *S'wark 5* **P** *Simeon's Trustees* **P-in-c** S A LASKEY, **NSM** S R SCOTT, **OLM** V J SHIRLEY
SYDENHAM (St Bartholomew) *S'wark 5* **P** *Earl of Dartmouth* **V** M J KINGSTON, **C** E M WOOFF
SYDENHAM (St Mary) *see* Chinnor, Sydenham, Aston Rowant and Crowell *Ox*
SYDENHAM (St Philip) *S'wark 5* **P** *V Sydenham St Bart* **V** P W TIERNAN
SYDENHAM, LOWER (St Michael and All Angels) Bell Green *S'wark 5* **P** *Bp* **V** S M BURNETT
SYDENHAM DAMEREL (St Mary) *see* Milton Abbot, Dunterton, Lamerton etc *Ex*
SYDERSTONE (St Mary) *see* N and S Creake w Waterden, Syderstone etc *Nor*
SYDLING (St Nicholas) *see* Bradford Peverell, Stratton, Frampton etc *Sarum*
SYERSTON (All Saints) *see* E Stoke w Syerston *S'well*
SYKEHOUSE (Holy Trinity) *see* Fishlake w Sykehouse and Kirk Bramwith etc *Sheff*
SYLEHAM (St Mary) *see* Hoxne w Denham, Syleham and Wingfield *St E*

SYMONDS GREEN (Christ the King) *see* Stevenage H Trin *St Alb*
SYMONDSBURY (St John the Baptist) *Sarum 2* **P** *Bp* **P-in-c** A J ASHWELL
SYRESHAM (St James) *see* Astwell Gp *Pet*
SYSTON (St Mary) *see* Barkston and Hough Gp *Linc*
SYSTON Team Ministry, The (St Peter and St Paul) *Leic 6* **P** *Patr Bd* **TR** J F WELLINGTON, **TV** K F SHEPHERD, J F AMBROSE, **C** S M COOPER
SYSTON (St Anne) *see* Warmley, Syston and Bitton *Bris*
SYSTONBY (not known) *see* Melton Mowbray *Leic*
SYWELL (St Peter and St Paul) *see* Mears Ashby and Hardwick and Sywell etc *Pet*
TABLEY, OVER (St Paul) and High Legh *Ches 12* **P** *Bp and Mrs P H Langford-Brooke (1 turn), C L S Cornwall-Legh Esq (1 turn)* **V** M R CAVANAGH
TACKLEY (St Nicholas) *see* Steeple Aston w N Aston and Tackley *Ox*
TACOLNESTON (All Saints) *see* Ashwellthorpe, Forncett, Fundenhall, Hapton etc *Nor*
TADCASTER (St Mary) w Newton Kyme *York 1* **P** *Abp* **V** R P BURTON, **C** M D LAYNESMITH
TADDINGTON (St Michael), Chelmorton and Flagg, and Monyash *Derby 4* **P** *V Bakewell* **P-in-c** J O GOLDSMITH, **NSM** M L GOLDSMITH, J S FOUNTAIN
TADDIPORT (St Mary Magdalene) *see* Gt and Lt Torrington and Frithelstock *Ex*
TADLEY, NORTH (St Mary) *Win 4* **P** *Bp* **V** B J NORRIS, **NSM** S G ARMSTRONG
TADLEY SOUTH (St Peter) (St Paul) and Silchester *Win 4* **P** *Duke of Wellington and Bp (alt)* **R** P D COOPER, **Hon C** A W H ASHDOWN, **NSM** P V BROWN
TADLOW (St Giles) *see* Shingay Gp *Ely*
TADMARTON (St Nicholas) *see* Wykeham *Ox*
TADWORTH (Good Shepherd) *S'wark 27* **P** *V Kingswood St Andr* **P-in-c** M W ELFRED, **C** S A C FOUNTAIN, **OLM** A S BLAIN
TAKELEY (Holy Trinity) w Little Canfield *Chelmsf 18* **P** *Bp and Ch Coll Cam* **R** L BOND, **NSM** C M HAWKES
TALATON (St James the Apostle) *see* Whimple, Talaton and Clyst St Lawr *Ex*
TALBOT VILLAGE (St Mark) *Sarum 7* **P** *Trustees* **V** C J F RUTLEDGE, **C** P M TRIMMER, **NSM** J BURKE
TALKE O' THE HILL (St Martin) *Lich 9* **P** *V Audley* **P-in-c** P D HOWARD
TALKIN (not known) *see* Eden, Gelt and Irthing *Carl*
TALLAND (St Tallan) *Truro 12* **P** *DBP and W Gundry-Mills Esq (alt)* **P-in-c** L J SMITH
TALLINGTON (St Laurence) *see* Uffington Gp *Linc*
TAMERTON, NORTH (St Denis) *see* Boyton, N Tamerton, Werrington etc *Truro*
TAMERTON FOLIOT (St Mary) *Ex 23* **P** *Ld Chan* **P-in-c** D B M GILL
TAMWORTH (St Editha) *Lich 4* **P** *Bp* **V** A BARRETT, **C** V M C VAN DEN BERGH, **Hon C** P J ENDALL, **NSM** M J PACEY
TANDRIDGE (St Peter) *see* Oxted and Tandridge *S'wark*
TANFIELD (St Margaret of Antioch) *see* Ch the K *Dur*
TANFIELD, WEST (St Nicholas) and Well w Snape and North Stainley *Ripon 3* **P** *Bp and Mrs M E Bourne-Arton (alt)* **R** M DE LA P BERESFORD-PEIRSE
TANGLEY (St Thomas of Canterbury) *see* Hatherden w Tangley, Weyhill and Penton Mewsey *Win*
TANGMERE (St Andrew) and Oving *Chich 3* **P** *Bp and Duke of Richmond (jt)* **R** *vacant* (01243) 785089
TANHOUSE The Oaks (Conventional District) *Liv 11* **Min** W D PETTY
TANKERSLEY (St Peter), Thurgoland and Wortley *Sheff 11* **P** *Dowager Countess of Wharncliffe, Sir Philip Naylor-Leyland Bt, and V Silkstone (jt)* **R** K J E HALE
TANNINGTON (St Ethelbert) *see* Worlingworth, Southolt, Tannington, Bedfield etc *St E*
TANSLEY (Holy Trinity), Dethick, Lea and Holloway *Derby 7* **P** *Bp, V Crich, and DBF (jt)* **R** *vacant* (01629) 534275
TANSOR (St Mary) *see* Warmington, Tansor and Cotterstock etc *Pet*
TANWORTH (St Mary Magdalene) *Birm 6* **P** *F D Muntz Esq* **V** T J HARMER
TAPLOW (St Nicholas) *see* Burnham w Dropmore, Hitcham and Taplow *Ox*
TARDEBIGGE (St Bartholomew) *see* Redditch H Trin *Worc*
TARLETON (Holy Trinity) *Blackb 5* **P** *St Pet Coll Ox* **P-in-c** N E DAVIS, **Hon C** T TAYLOR
TARLTON (St Osmund) *see* Rodmarton CD *Glouc*
TARPORLEY (St Helen) *Ches 5* **P** *Bp (4 turns), D&C (1 turn), and Sir John Grey Regerton Bt (1 turn)* **R** G L COOKSON
TARRANT GUNVILLE (St Mary) *see* Chase *Sarum*
TARRANT HINTON (St Mary) *as above*
TARRANT KEYNSTON (All Saints) *as above*
TARRANT MONKTON (All Saints) *as above*
TARRANT RUSHTON (St Mary) *as above*
TARRING, WEST (St Andrew) *Chich 5* **P** *Abp* **R** W E JERVIS
TARRING NEVILLE (St Mary) *see* Denton w S Heighton and Tarring Neville *Chich*
TARRINGTON (St Philip and St James) *see* Ledbury *Heref*
TARVIN (St Andrew) *Ches 2* **P** *Bp* **V** D R HERBERT, **NSM** M R MARR
TAS VALLEY *see* Newton Flotman, Swainsthorpe, Tasburgh, etc *Nor*
TASBURGH (St Mary) *as above*
TASLEY (St Peter and St Paul) *see* Bridgnorth, Tasley, Astley Abbotts, etc *Heref*
TATENHILL (St Michael and All Angels) *see* Branston w Tatenhill *Lich*
TATHAM (St James the Less) *see* E Lonsdale *Blackb*
TATHAM FELLS (Good Shepherd) *as above*
TATHWELL (St Vedast) *see* Legbourne and Wold Marsh *Linc*
TATSFIELD (St Mary) *S'wark 26* **P** *Bp* **P-in-c** C R WOOD
TATTENHALL (St Alban) and Handley *Ches 5* **P** *Bp and D&C (jt)* **P-in-c** L MUTETE
TATTENHAM CORNER (St Mark) *Guildf 9* **P** *Bp* **V** R J WHITTLE
TATTENHOE (St Giles) *see* Watling Valley *Ox*
TATTERFORD (St Margaret) *see* E w W Rudham, Helhoughton etc *Nor*
TATTERSETT (All Saints and St Andrew) *as above*
TATTERSHALL (Holy Trinity) *see* Coningsby w Tattershall *Linc*
TATTINGSTONE (St Mary) *see* Sproughton w Burstall, Copdock w Washbrook etc *St E*
TATWORTH (St John the Evangelist) *see* Chard and Distr *B & W*
TAUNTON (All Saints) *B & W 18* **P** *Bp* **V** D C W FAYLE
TAUNTON (Holy Trinity) *B & W 18* **P** *Bp* **V** J B V LAURENCE, **Hon C** J J STRATTON
TAUNTON (St Andrew) *B & W 18* **P** *Bp* **V** J SMITH, **C** J R MORRIS
TAUNTON (St James) *B & W 18* **P** *Simeon's Trustees* **V** *vacant* (01823) 333194
TAUNTON (St John the Evangelist) *B & W 18* **P** *Bp* **P-in-c** D ROBERTS
TAUNTON (St Mary Magdalene) *B & W 18* **P** *Ch Patr Trust* **P-in-c** R G CORKE, **Hon C** D E CAVAGHAN
TAUNTON (St Peter) Lyngford *B & W 18* **P** *Bp* **V** A L SMITH
TAVERHAM (St Edmund) *Nor 2* **P** *Bp* **V** D W JACKSON
TAVISTOCK (St Eustachius) and Gulworthy (St Paul) *Ex 25* **P** *Bp* **V** J E F RAWLINGS, **C** J M ABECASSIS
TAW VALLEY *see* Barnstaple *Ex*
TAWSTOCK (St Peter) *see* Newton Tracey, Horwood, Alverdiscott etc *Ex*
TAWTON, NORTH (St Peter), Bondleigh, Sampford Courtenay and Honeychurch *Ex 11* **P** *MMCET, K Coll Cam, and D&C (jt)* **R** R W B ARDILL
TAWTON, SOUTH (St Andrew) and Belstone *Ex 11* **P** *D&C Windsor and Bp (jt)* **R** M D THAYER
TAYNTON (St John the Evangelist) *see* Burford w Fulbrook, Taynton, Asthall etc *Ox*
TAYNTON (St Laurence) *see* Highnam, Lassington, Rudford, Tibberton etc *Glouc*
TEALBY (All Saints) *see* Walesby *Linc*
TEAN, UPPER (Christ Church) *Lich 6* **P** *R Checkley* **P-in-c** M R H TURNER, **Hon C** E C LAST
TEBAY (St James) *see* Orton and Tebay w Ravenstonedale etc *Carl*
TEDBURN ST MARY (St Mary), Whitestone, Oldridge, Holcombe Burnell, Dunsford, Doddiscombsleigh and Cheriton Bishop *Ex 6* **P** *Patr Bd* **P-in-c** J M S HOLLAND, **C** A C RYLANDS
TEDDINGTON (St Mark) and Hampton Wick (St John the Baptist) *Lon 11* **P** *Bp* **V** D P LUND, **NSM** V F FRAY
TEDDINGTON (St Mary) (St Alban the Martyr) *Lon 10* **P** *Bp* **V** J M CLEAVER
TEDDINGTON (St Nicholas) *see* Overbury w Teddington, Alstone etc *Worc*
TEDDINGTON (St Peter and St Paul) and Fulwell St Michael and St George *Lon 10* **P** *Bp* **V** S G L WOOD, **Hon C** P R TOPHAM
TEDSTONE DELAMERE (St James) *see* Edvin Loach w Tedstone Delamere etc *Heref*
TEDSTONE WAFER (St Mary) *as above*

TEFFONT EVIAS (St Michael) *see* Fovant, Sutton Mandeville and Teffont Evias etc *Sarum*
TEFFONT MAGNA (St Edward) *as above*
TEIGH (Holy Trinity) Whissendine and Market Overton *Pet 14* **P** *Bp and Lady Gretton (alt)* **P-in-c** J B J SAUNDERS, **C** L T FRANCIS-DEHQANI
TEIGNGRACE (St Peter and St Paul) *see* Highweek and Teigngrace *Ex*
TEIGNMOUTH (St James) (St Michael the Archangel), Ideford w Luton, Ashcombe and Bishopsteignton *Ex 6* **P** *Patr Bd* **TR** P G LUFF, **TV** S P WEST, **C** C M S LUFF, A M HOFBAUER
TELFORD, CENTRAL: Dawley, Lawley, Malinslee, Stirchley, Brookside and Hollinswood *Lich 21* **P** *Patr Bd (3 turns), The Crown (1 turn)* **TV** M A PETERS, E C PHILLIPS
TELFORD PARK (St Thomas) *S'wark 15* **P** *Trustees* **P-in-c** S P GATES
TELLISFORD (All Saints) *see* Hardington Vale *B & W*
TELSCOMBE VILLAGE (St Laurence) *Chich 18* **P** *Bp and Gorham Trustees (jt)* **V** D A HIDER
TEME VALLEY, LOWER *see* Martley and Wichenford, Knightwick etc *Worc*
TEME VALLEY NORTH: Knighton-on-Teme, Lindridge, Pensax, Menith Wood, Stanford-on-Teme and Stockton *Worc 13* **P** *Bp and D&C (alt)* **R** L S GRACE
TEME VALLEY SOUTH: Eastham, Rochford, Stoke Bliss, Hanley Child, Hanley William and Kyre Wyard *Worc 13* **P** *Ld Chan, Bp, and Mrs M M Miles (by turn)* **R** A M SHARPE
TEMPLE (St Catherine) *see* Blisland w St Breward *Truro*
TEMPLE BALSALL (St Mary) *Birm 11* **P** *Lady Leveson Hosp* **V** J W WOODWARD
TEMPLE BRUER (St John the Baptist) *see* Graffoe Gp *Linc*
TEMPLE CLOUD (St Barnabas) *see* Clutton w Cameley *B & W*
TEMPLE EWELL (St Peter and St Paul) w Lydden *Cant 4* **P** *Abp* **R** P CHRISTIAN
TEMPLE GRAFTON (St Andrew) w Binton *Cov 7* **P** *Dioc Trustees* **P-in-c** S R TASH, **NSM** L E DAVIES
TEMPLE GUITING (St Mary) *see* The Guitings, Cutsdean, Farmcote etc *Glouc*
TEMPLE HIRST (St John the Baptist) *see* Haddlesey w Hambleton and Birkin *York*
TEMPLE NORMANTON (St James the Apostle) *Derby 5* **P** *Bp* **V** M R AINSCOUGH
TEMPLE SOWERBY (St James) *see* Kirkby Thore w Temple Sowerby and Newbiggin *Carl*
TEMPLECOMBE (Blessed Virgin Mary) *see* Abbas and Templecombe w Horsington *B & W*
TEMPLETON (St Margaret) *see* Washfield, Stoodleigh, Withleigh etc *Ex*
TEMPSFORD (St Peter) *see* Blunham, Gt Barford, Roxton and Tempsford etc *St Alb*
TEN MILE BANK (St Mark) *see* Hilgay *Ely*
TENBURY (St Mary) *Heref 12* **P** *The Revd F J Evans* **TR** A N JEVONS, **TV** C A LORDING, **NSM** S FOSTER
TENBURY (St Michael and All Angels) *Heref 12* **P** *St Mich Coll* **V** *vacant* (01584) 810702
TENDRING (St Edmund King and Martyr) and Little Bentley w Beaufort cum Moze *Chelmsf 20* **P** *Em Coll Cam, DBP, and Ball Coll Ox (by turn)* **R** D W A KING
TENTERDEN (St Michael and All Angels) *Cant 16* **P** *Abp* **P-in-c** J K BUTTERWORTH
TENTERDEN (St Mildred) w Smallhythe *Cant 16* **P** *D&C* **V** D G TRUSTRAM, **NSM** M ROYLANCE
TERLING (All Saints) *see* Fairstead w Terling and White Notley etc *Chelmsf*
TERRIERS (St Francis) *Ox 29* **P** *V High Wycombe* **V** A W DICKINSON
TERRINGTON (All Saints) *see* Howardian Gp *York*
TERRINGTON ST CLEMENT (St Clement) *Ely 15* **P** *The Crown* **V** R J SLIPPER
TERRINGTON ST JOHN (St John) *see* E Marshland *Ely*
TERWICK (St Peter) *see* Rogate w Terwick and Trotton w Chithurst *Chich*
TESTON (St Peter and St Paul) *see* Wateringbury and Teston *Roch*
TESTWOOD (St Winfrid) *see* Totton *Win*
TETBURY (St Mary the Virgin) w Beverston *Glouc 11* **P** *Mrs J C B Joynson (5 turns), The Crown (1 turn)* **R** A J WRIGHT, **C** J A JACK
TETCOTT (Holy Cross) *see* Ashwater, Halwill, Beaworthy, Clawton etc *Ex*
TETFORD (St Mary) *see* S Ormsby Gp *Linc*
TETNEY (St Peter and St Paul) *see* The North-Chapel Parishes *Linc*
TETSWORTH (St Giles) *see* Thame *Ox*
TETTENHALL REGIS (St Michael and All Angels) *Lich 24* **P** *Patr Bd* **TR** D E NEWSOME, **TV** M R KINDER, **C** E RATHBONE, **OLM** J LLOYD
TETTENHALL WOOD (Christ Church) and Perton *Lich 24* **P** *Patr Bd* **TR** K M ELBOURNE, **C** L M DOWNS, **OLM** P A P SNAPE, C A HARLEY
TEVERSAL (St Katherine) *see* Skegby w Teversal *S'well*
TEVERSHAM (All Saints) *Ely 3* **P** *Bp* **P-in-c** M C BOWERS, **C** J L MEADER
TEW, GREAT (St Michael and All Angels) w Little (St John the Evangelist) *Ox 3* **P** *Bp and J M Johnston Esq (jt)* **V** *vacant*
TEWIN (St Peter) *see* Welwyn *St Alb*
TEWKESBURY (Holy Trinity) *Glouc 15* **P** *Ch Soc Trust* **V** *vacant* (01684) 293233
TEWKESBURY (St Mary the Virgin) w Walton Cardiff and Twyning *Glouc 15* **P** *Ld Chan (2 turns) and Ch Ch Ox (1 turn)* **V** P R WILLIAMS, **C** J J PERKINS, A P BISHOP, **NSM** C E WHITNEY
TEY, GREAT (St Barnabas) and LITTLE (St James the Less) w Wakes Colne and Chappel *Chelmsf 17* **P** *Bp, DBP, PCC Chappel and Ch Patr Trust (jt)* **R** J RICHARDSON
TEYNHAM (St Mary) (Primary School Worship Centre) w Lynsted and Kingsdown *Cant 6* **P** *Adn Cant* **P-in-c** M A GOOCH
THAKEHAM (St Mary) *see* Sullington and Thakeham w Warminghurst *Chich*
THAME (All Saints) (St Mary the Virgin) *Ox 1* **P** *Patr Bd* **TR** N R STUART-LEE, **TV** S F L BRIGNALL, I D MOUNTFORD, **Hon C** K A A WESTON, J H FIELDSEND, S H BAYNES, R COPPING, **NSM** J E M HULETT
THAMES DITTON (St Nicholas) *Guildf 8* **P** *K Coll Cam* **V** J A SILK, **NSM** M J HUSSEY
THAMES VIEW (Christ Church) *see* Barking St Marg w St Patr *Chelmsf*
THAMESMEAD (Church of the Cross) (St Paul's Ecumenical Centre) (William Temple) *S'wark 3* **P** *Bp* **TR** B THORLEY, **TV** P ORGAN, S R BOXALL, **Hon C** F J KING
THANET (St Andrew) *see* St Peter-in-Thanet *Cant*
THANET (St Laurence) *see* St Laur in Thanet *Cant*
THANET (St Peter the Apostle) *see* St Peter-in-Thanet *Cant*
THANINGTON (St Nicholas) (St Faith's Mission Church) *Cant 3* **P** *Abp* **P-in-c** I AVEYARD
THARSTON (St Mary) *see* Newton Flotman, Swainsthorpe, Tasburgh, etc *Nor*
THATCHAM (St Mary) *Ox 14* **P** *Patr Bd* **TR** N T MOFFATT, **C** P T JARVIS, D SCURR, **OLM** M E FONTAINE
THATTO HEATH (St Matthew) *see* St Helens St Matt Thatto Heath *Liv*
THAXTED (St John the Baptist, Our Lady and St Laurence) *Chelmsf 22* **P** *Bp* **V** R M TAYLOR
THE *see also under substantive place name*
THEALE (Christ Church) *see* Wedmore w Theale and Blackford *B & W*
THEALE (Holy Trinity) and Englefield *Ox 12* **P** *Magd Coll Ox and Englefield Est Trust (jt)* **P-in-c** G N BORROWDALE, **Hon C** B R SPENCE
THEBERTON (St Peter) *see* Middleton cum Fordley and Theberton w Eastbridge *St E*
THEDDINGWORTH (All Saints) *see* Husbands Bosworth w Mowsley and Knaptoft etc *Leic*
THEDDLETHORPE (St Helen) *Linc 12* **P** *Baroness Willoughby de Eresby (2 turns), Bp (1 turn)* **R** *vacant*
THELBRIDGE (St David) *see* Burrington, Chawleigh, Cheldon, Chulmleigh etc *Ex*
THELNETHAM (St Nicholas) *see* Hepworth, Hinderclay, Wattisfield and Thelnetham *St E*
THELVETON (St Andrew) *see* Dickleburgh and The Pulhams *Nor*
THELWALL (All Saints) *Ches 4* **P** *Keble Coll Ox* **V** D J BLACK
THEMELTHORPE (St Andrew) *see* Twyford, Guist, Bintree, Themelthorpe etc *Nor*
THENFORD (St Mary the Virgin) *see* Chenderit *Pet*
THERFIELD (St Mary the Virgin) w Kelshall *St Alb 19* **P** *Ld Chan and D&C St Paul's (alt)* **R** R M MORGAN
THETFORD (St Cuthbert) (St Peter) *Nor 11* **P** *Patr Bd* **TV** S D GRIFFITHS, **C** J FRENCH, **Hon C** B R HOGWOOD
THETFORD, LITTLE (St George) *see* Ely *Ely*
THEYDON BOIS (St Mary) *Chelmsf 25* **P** *M G E N Buxton Esq* **V** C J TRAVERS, **NSM** A M CANNELL
THEYDON GARNON (All Saints) *see* Epping Distr *Chelmsf*
THEYDON MOUNT (St Michael) *see* Greensted-juxta-Ongar w Stanford Rivers etc *Chelmsf*
THIMBLEBY (St Margaret) *see* Thornton Gp *Linc*

THIRKLEBY (All Saints) w Kilburn and Bagby *York 19* **P** *Abp* **P-in-c** R W DAVILL
THIRSK (St Mary) *York 19* **P** *Abp* **TR** R F ROWLING, **C** N W R BIRD, E M BAXTER, **NSM** S R BAXTER
THISTLETON (St Nicholas) *see* Greetham and Thistleton w Stretton and Clipsham *Pet*
THIXENDALE (St Mary) *see* Waggoners *York*
THOCKRINGTON (St Aidan) *see* Chollerton w Birtley and Thockrington *Newc*
THOMPSON (St Martin) *see* Caston, Griston, Merton, Thompson etc *Nor*
THONGSBRIDGE (St Andrew) *see* Upper Holme Valley *Wakef*
THORESBY, NORTH (St Helen) *see* The North-Chapel Parishes *Linc*
THORESBY, SOUTH (St Andrew) *see* Legbourne and Wold Marsh *Linc*
THORESWAY (St Mary) *see* Swallow *Linc*
THORGANBY (All Saints) *see* Binbrook Gp *Linc*
THORGANBY (St Helen) *see* Wheldrake w Thorganby *York*
THORINGTON (St Peter) *see* Blyth Valley *St E*
THORLEY (St James the Great) *St Alb 18* **P** *Bp* **R** R H V PAYNE, **C** C A KOSLA, **NSM** A L KOSLA
THORLEY (St Swithun) *Portsm 8* **P** *Bp* **V** J A YORKE
THORMANBY (St Mary Magdalene) *see* Brafferton w Pilmoor, Myton-on-Swale etc *York*
THORNABY, NORTH (St Luke) (St Paul) *York 18* **P** *Abp* **V** H C HOPKINS, **NSM** N PETTY
THORNABY, SOUTH (St Mark) (St Peter ad Vincula) *York 18* **P** *Abp* **V** M L CATHERALL
THORNAGE (All Saints) *see* Brinton, Briningham, Hunworth, Stody etc *Nor*
THORNBOROUGH (St Mary) *see* Buckingham *Ox*
THORNBURY (St Anna) *see* Bredenbury w Grendon Bishop and Wacton etc *Heref*
THORNBURY (St Margaret) *Bradf 3* **P** *Vs Bradf, Calverley, and Laisterdyke (jt)* **V** P C HACKWOOD
THORNBURY (St Mary) (St Paul) and Oldbury-on-Severn w Shepperdine *Glouc 7* **P** *Ch Ch Ox* **V** D E S PRIMROSE, **C** S C BISHOP, **NSM** J T BROOKS, **OLM** G L HILL
THORNBURY (St Peter) *see* Black Torrington, Bradf w Cookbury etc *Ex*
THORNBY (St Helen) *see* Cottesbrooke w Gt Creaton and Thornby *Pet*
THORNCOMBE (The Blessed Virgin Mary) *see* Chard and Distr *B & W*
THORNDON (All Saints) *see* S Hartismere *St E*
THORNE (St Nicholas) *Sheff 10* **P** *Bp* **V** P J BOULTON-LEA
THORNE COFFIN (St Andrew) *see* Tintinhull w Chilthorne Domer, Yeovil Marsh etc *B & W*
THORNE ST MARGARET (St Margaret) *see* Wellington and Distr *B & W*
THORNER (St Peter) *Ripon 8* **P** *Earl of Mexborough* **P-in-c** J D W KING, **NSM** A B HAIGH
THORNES (St James) w Christ Church *Wakef 12* **P** *DBP* **P-in-c** P M MAGUIRE, **C** J M WARE
THORNEY (St Helen) *see* Harby w Thorney and N and S Clifton *S'well*
THORNEY, WEST (St Nicholas) *see* Southbourne w W Thorney *Chich*
THORNEY ABBEY (St Mary and St Botolph) *Ely 15* **P** *Bp* **P-in-c** R P FLINDALL
THORNEY CLOSE (St Peter) *see* Sunderland St Mary and St Pet *Dur*
THORNEY HILL (All Saints) *see* Bransgore *Win*
THORNEYBURN (St Aidan) *see* N Tyne and Redesdale *Newc*
THORNFALCON (Holy Cross) *see* Ruishton w Thornfalcon *B & W*
THORNFORD (St Mary Magdalene) *see* Bradford Abbas and Thornford w Beer Hackett *Sarum*
THORNGUMBALD (St Mary) *see* Burstwick w Thorngumbald *York*
THORNHAM (All Saints) *see* Hunstanton St Mary w Ringstead Parva etc *Nor*
THORNHAM (St James) *Man 22* **P** *Bp* **V** P N BARRATT
THORNHAM (St John) *see* Middleton w Thornham *Man*
THORNHAM MAGNA (St Mary Magdalene) *see* S Hartismere *St E*
THORNHAM PARVA (St Mary) *as above*
THORNHAUGH (St Andrew) and Wansford *Pet 8* **P** *Bp* **P-in-c** T R CHRISTIE
THORNHILL (Mission Church) *see* Beckermet St Jo and St Bridget w Ponsonby *Carl*
THORNHILL (St Christopher) *see* Southampton Thornhill St Chris *Win*
THORNHILL (St Michael and All Angels) and Whitley Lower *Wakef 10* **P** *Lord Savile* **R** L C DEW, **C** G M JOHNSON, **OLM** N F WEBB
THORNHILL LEES (Holy Innocents w St Mary) *see* Ravensthorpe and Thornhill Lees w Savile Town *Wakef*
THORNLEY (St Bartholomew) *see* Wolsingham and Thornley *Dur*
THORNTHWAITE (St Mary the Virgin) cum Braithwaite, Newlands and Borrowdale w Grange *Carl 6* **P** *V Keswick St Jo (1 turn), V Crosthwaite (2 turns)* **P-in-c** P H VIVASH, **NSM** C FORD
THORNTHWAITE (St Saviour) *see* Dacre w Hartwith and Darley w Thornthwaite *Ripon*
THORNTON Group, The (St Wilfrid) *Linc 11* **P** *R H Spurrier Esq, Bp, SMF, and Lt Col J L M Dymoke (2 turns), Ld Chan (1 turn)* **R** *vacant* (01507) 525832
THORNTON (St Frideswyde) *see* Sefton and Thornton *Liv*
THORNTON (St James) *Bradf 1* **P** *V Bradf* **V** W GREEN, **C** C E SHEDD
THORNTON (St Michael) *see* Barmby Moor Gp *York*
THORNTON (St Peter) *see* Markfield, Thornton, Bagworth and Stanton etc *Leic*
THORNTON, LITTLE (St John) *Blackb 12* **P** *Bp* **V** P R F CLEMENCE
THORNTON CURTIS (St Laurence) *see* Ulceby Gp *Linc*
THORNTON DALE (All Saints) w Allerston, Ebberston, Ellerburn and Wilton *York 20* **P** *Mrs E M Morgan (1 turn), Abp (3 turns)* **R** *vacant* (01751) 474244
THORNTON HEATH (St Jude w St Aidan) *S'wark 25* **P** *Bp* **P-in-c** N K NTEGE
THORNTON HEATH (St Paul) *S'wark 25* **P** *The Crown* **V** M P N JEWITT
THORNTON HOUGH (All Saints) *Ches 9* **P** *Simeon's Trustees* **P-in-c** D M SEBER
THORNTON IN CRAVEN (St Mary) *see* Broughton, Marton and Thornton *Bradf*
THORNTON IN LONSDALE (St Oswald) w Burton in Lonsdale *Bradf 6* **P** *Bp* **P-in-c** C M LOW
THORNTON LE FEN (St Peter) *see* Brothertoft Gp *Linc*
THORNTON-LE-FYLDE (Christ Church) *Blackb 12* **P** *Trustees* **V** A W FROUD, **C** D J BURY
THORNTON-LE-MOOR (All Saints) *see* Kelsey Gp *Linc*
THORNTON-LE-MOORS (St Mary) w Ince and Elton *Ches 3* **P** *Bp* **P-in-c** K W DAVEY
THORNTON LE STREET (St Leonard) *see* The Thorntons and The Otteringtons *York*
THORNTON RUST (Mission Room) *see* Aysgarth and Bolton cum Redmire *Ripon*
THORNTON STEWARD (St Oswald) *see* Middleham w Coverdale and E Witton etc *Ripon*
THORNTON WATLASS (St Mary the Virgin) *Ripon 4* **P** *Bp and D S Dodsworth Esq (jt)* **P-in-c** A L WOODHOUSE
THORNTONS and The Otteringtons, The *York 19* **P** *Ch Ch Ox, Linc Coll Ox, and Abp (by turn)* **P-in-c** S N FISHER, **NSM** A FISHER
THOROTON (St Helena) *see* Whatton w Aslockton, Hawksworth, Scarrington etc *S'well*
THORP ARCH (All Saints) w Walton *York 1* **P** *G H H Wheler Esq and G Lane Fox Esq (alt)* **P-in-c** P E BRISTOW
THORPE (St Andrew) (Good Shepherd) *Nor 1* **P** *Trustees W J Birkbeck Esq* **C** J A HAWKINS
Thorpe (St Laurence) *see* Farndon w Thorpe, Hawton and Cotham *S'well*
THORPE (St Leonard) *see* Fenny Bentley, Thorpe, Tissington, Parwich etc *Derby*
THORPE (St Mary) *Guildf 11* **P** *Keble Coll Ox* **V** M J HEREWARD-ROTHWELL
THORPE (St Matthew) *Nor 1* **P** *R Thorpe St Andr* **V** G R DRAKE, **C** A M BEANE
THORPE (St Peter) *see* The Wainfleet Gp *Linc*
THORPE ABBOTS (All Saints) *see* Scole, Brockdish, Billingford, Thorpe Abbots etc *Nor*
THORPE ACHURCH (St John the Baptist) *see* Aldwincle w Thorpe Achurch, Pilton, Wadenhoe etc *Pet*
THORPE ACRE w Dishley (All Saints) *Leic 7* **P** *Bp* **V** A R LEIGHTON, **NSM** S LEIGHTON, E T SKINNER
THORPE ARNOLD (St Mary the Virgin) *see* Melton Mowbray *Leic*
THORPE AUDIN (Mission Room) *see* Badsworth *Wakef*
THORPE BASSETT (All Saints) *see* Buckrose Carrs *York*
THORPE BAY (St Augustine) *Chelmsf 13* **P** *Bp* **V** R E FARRELL, **C** R J MAGOR
THORPE CONSTANTINE (St Constantine) *Lich 4* **P** *Mrs E V G Inge-Innes* **P-in-c** A L WHEALE

THORPE EDGE (St John the Divine) *Bradf 3* **P** *Vs Bradf, Calverley, and Idle (jt)* **V** *vacant* (01274) 613246
THORPE END (St David) *see* Gt and Lt Plumstead w Thorpe End and Witton *Nor*
THORPE EPISCOPI (St Andrew) *see* Thorpe *Nor*
THORPE HESLEY (Holy Trinity) *Sheff 6* **P** *Sir Philip Naylor-Leyland Bt* **V** J F HARDY
THORPE LANGTON (St Leonard) *see* Church Langton cum Tur Langton etc *Leic*
THORPE-LE-SOKEN (St Michael) *Chelmsf 23* **P** *Bp* **P-in-c** J C DOWDING
THORPE MALSOR (All Saints) *see* Broughton w Loddington and Cransley etc *Pet*
THORPE MANDEVILLE (St John the Baptist) *see* Culworth w Sulgrave and Thorpe Mandeville etc *Pet*
THORPE MARKET (St Margaret) *see* Trunch *Nor*
THORPE MORIEUX (St Mary the Virgin) *see* Rattlesden w Thorpe Morieux, Brettenham etc *St E*
THORPE-NEXT-HADDISCOE (St Matthias) *see* Raveningham Gp *Nor*
THORPE-ON-THE-HILL (St Michael) *see* Swinderby *Linc*
THORPE SALVIN (St Peter) *see* Harthill and Thorpe Salvin *Sheff*
THORPE SATCHVILLE (St Michael and All Angels) *see* S Croxton Gp *Leic*
THORPE WILLOUGHBY (St Francis of Assisi) *see* Brayton *York*
THORRINGTON (St Mary Magdalene) *see* Gt Bentley and Frating w Thorrington *Chelmsf*
THORVERTON (St Thomas of Canterbury), Cadbury, Upton Pyne, Brampford Speke and Newton St Cyres *Ex 2* **P** *Ld Chan (1 turn), Patr Bd (3 turns)* **P-in-c** D J DETTMER, **C** R A POTTER
THRANDESTON (St Margaret) *see* N Hartismere *St E*
THRAPSTON (St James) *Pet 10* **P** *Ld Chan* **R** G D R BELL, **NSM** P K NIEMIEC
THREAPWOOD (St John) *see* Malpas and Threapwood *Ches*
THRECKINGHAM (St Peter) *see* S Lafford *Linc*
THREE LEGGED CROSS (All Saints) *see* Verwood *Sarum*
THREE RIVERS GROUP, The *see* Chippenham *Ely*
THRELKELD (St Mary) *see* St John's-in-the-Vale, Threlkeld and Wythburn *Carl*
THREXTON (All Saints) *see* Gt and Lt Cressingham w Threxton *Nor*
THRIGBY (St Mary) *see* S Trin Broads *Nor*
THRIMBY (St Mary) *see* Morland, Thrimby, Gt Strickland and Cliburn *Carl*
THRINGSTONE (St Andrew) *Leic 8* **P** *Duchy of Lanc* **NSM** J A BIRD
THRIPLOW (St George) *see* Fowlmere, Foxton, Shepreth and Thriplow *Ely*
THROCKING (Holy Trinity) *see* Cottered w Broadfield and Throcking *St Alb*
THROCKLEY (St Mary the Virgin) *see* Newburn *Newc*
THROCKMORTON (Chapelry) *see* Abberton, The Flyfords, Naunton Beauchamp etc *Worc*
THROOP (St Paul) *Win 8* **P** *Ch Soc Trust* **V** R D PETERS, **C** J R CHARLES
THROPTON (St Andrew) *see* Upper Coquetdale *Newc*
THROWLEIGH (St Mary the Virgin) *see* Chagford, Drewsteignton, Hittisleigh etc *Ex*
THROWLEY (St Michael and All Angels) *see* Selling w Throwley, Sheldwich w Badlesmere etc *Cant*
THRUMPTON (All Saints) *S'well 9* **P** *Mrs M Gottlieb* **P-in-c** S W OSMAN
THRUSCROSS (no dedication) *see* Dacre w Hartwith and Darley w Thornthwaite *Ripon*
THRUSHELTON (St George) *see* Lifton, Broadwoodwidger, Stowford etc *Ex*
THRUSSINGTON (Holy Trinity) *see* Syston *Leic*
THRUXTON (St Bartholomew) *see* Kingstone w Clehonger, Eaton Bishop etc *Heref*
THRUXTON (St Peter and St Paul) *see* Appleshaw, Kimpton, Thruxton, Fyfield etc *Win*
THRYBERGH (St Leonard) *Sheff 6* **P** *Mrs P N Fullerton* **R** *vacant* (01709) 850336
THUNDERSLEY (St Michael and All Angels) (St Peter) *Chelmsf 10* **P** *Bp* **R** M E STURROCK, **C** A M E DOLLERY
THUNDERSLEY, NEW (St George) *Chelmsf 10* **P** *Bp* **V** A J ROSE, **C** S J JERMY
THUNDRIDGE (St Mary) *St Alb 22* **P** *Bp* **V** H J SHARMAN
THURCASTON (All Saints) w Cropston *Leic 11* **P** *Em Coll Cam* **R** D F BREWIN
THURCROFT (St Simon and St Jude) *Sheff 5* **P** *Bp* **V** P HUNTER
THURGARTON (St Peter) w Hoveringham and Bleasby w Halloughton *S'well 15* **P** *Ld Chan and Trin Coll Cam (alt)* **V** A P DE BERRY
THURGOLAND (Holy Trinity) *see* Tankersley, Thurgoland and Wortley *Sheff*
THURLASTON (All Saints) *see* Enderby w Lubbesthorpe and Thurlaston *Leic*
THURLASTON (St Edmund) *see* Dunchurch *Cov*
THURLBY (St Firmin) *see* Ness Gp *Linc*
THURLBY (St Germain) *see* Bassingham Gp *Linc*
THURLEIGH (St Peter) *see* Milton Ernest, Pavenham and Thurleigh *St Alb*
THURLESTON (All Saints), South Milton, West Alvington and Churchstow *Ex 14* **P** *Bp Ex and D&C Sarum (jt)* **R** A M GIRLING, **C** W J T HAMILTON
THURLOW, GREAT (All Saints) *see* Stourhead *St E*
THURLOW, LITTLE (St Peter) *as above*
THURLOXTON (St Giles) *see* Alfred Jewel *B & W*
THURLSTONE (St Saviour) *see* Penistone and Thurlstone *Wakef*
THURLTON (All Saints) *see* Raveningham Gp *Nor*
THURMASTON (St Michael and All Angels) *Leic 6* **P** *Bp* **V** T R MARTIN, **NSM** I M HILL
THURNBY (St Luke) w Stoughton *Leic 5* **P** *MMCET* **V** G W DUNSETH, **C** S J WALTON
THURNBY LODGE (Christ Church) *see* Ascension TM *Leic*
THURNE (St Edmund) *see* Martham and Repps with Bastwick, Thurne etc *Nor*
THURNHAM (St Mary the Virgin) *see* Bearsted w Thurnham *Cant*
THURNING (St Andrew) *see* Reepham, Hackford w Whitwell, Kerdiston etc *Nor*
THURNING (St James the Great) *see* Barnwell w Tichmarsh, Thurning and Clapton *Pet*
THURNSCOE (St Helen) *Sheff 12* **P** *Sir Philip Naylor Leyland Bt* **P-in-c** M P THOMPSON
THURNSCOE (St Hilda) *Sheff 12* **P** *Bp* **V** M P THOMPSON
THURROCK, LITTLE (St John the Evangelist) *see* Grays North *Chelmsf*
THURROCK, LITTLE (St Mary the Virgin) *see* Grays Thurrock *Chelmsf*
THURROCK, WEST (Church Centre) *as above*
THURSBY (St Andrew) *Carl 3* **P** *D&C* **P-in-c** N L ROBINSON
THURSFORD (St Andrew) *see* Barney, Fulmodeston w Croxton, Hindringham etc *Nor*
THURSLEY (St Michael and All Angels) *Guildf 4* **P** *V Witley* **V** W D LANG
THURSTASTON (St Bartholomew) *Ches 8* **P** *D&C* **R** D E WATSON, **NSM** M FLETCHER
THURSTON (St Peter) *St E 9* **P** *Bp* **V** D M B MATHERS
THURSTONLAND (St Thomas) *see* Upper Holme Valley *Wakef*
THURTON (St Ethelbert) w Ashby St Mary, Bergh Apton w Yelverton and Framingham Pigot *Nor 8* **P** *Bp and Major J H Thursby, Bp and MMCET, and Ld Chan (by turn)* **R** P M KNIGHT, **C** W J SHAW, **NSM** R J M COLLIER, **OLM** L G ALLIES
THUXTON (St Paul) *see* Barnham Broom and Upper Yare *Nor*
THWAITE (All Saints) *see* Erpingham w Calthorpe, Ingworth, Aldborough etc *Nor*
THWAITE (St George) *see* S Hartismere *St E*
THWAITE (St Mary) *see* Brooke, Kirstead, Mundham w Seething and Thwaite *Nor*
THWAITES (St Anne) *see* Millom *Carl*
THWAITES BROW (St Barnabas) *Bradf 8* **P** *DBP* **V** *vacant* (01535) 602830
THWING (All Saints) *see* Langtoft w Foxholes, Butterwick, Cottam etc *York*
TIBBERTON (All Saints) w Bolas Magna and Waters Upton *Lich 16* **P** *R Edgmond w Kynnersley etc, MMCET, and A B Davies Esq (jt)* **P-in-c** W E WARD
TIBBERTON (Holy Trinity) *see* Highnam, Lassington, Rudford, Tibberton etc *Glouc*
TIBBERTON (St Peter ad Vincula) *see* Bowbrook S *Worc*
TIBENHAM (All Saints) *see* Bunwell, Carleton Rode, Tibenham, Gt Moulton etc *Nor*
TIBSHELF (St John the Baptist) *see* Blackwell w Tibshelf *Derby*
TICEHURST (St Mary) and Flimwell *Chich 19* **P** *Bp, J A Sellick Esq, and K M H Millar Esq (jt)* **V** W M SIMPSON
TICHBORNE (St Andrew) *see* Upper Itchen *Win*
TICHMARSH (St Mary the Virgin) *see* Barnwell w Tichmarsh, Thurning and Clapton *Pet*
TICKENCOTE (St Peter) *see* Gt and Lt Casterton w Pickworth and Tickencote *Pet*
TICKENHAM (St Quiricus and St Julietta) *see* Nailsea Ch Ch w Tickenham *B & W*

TICKHILL (St Mary) w Stainton *Sheff 9* **P** *Bp* **V** G TAYLOR
TICKNALL (St George), Smisby and Stanton by Bridge, Barrow on Trent w Twyford and Swarkestone *Derby 15* **P** *Bp, Exors Miss A I M Harpur-Crewe, and Repton Sch (jt)* **V** M G ALEXANDER
TICKTON (St Paul) *see* Beverley Minster *York*
TIDCOMBE (St Michael) *see* Savernake *Sarum*
TIDDINGTON *see* Wheatley *Ox*
TIDDINGTON (St Peter) *see* Alveston *Cov*
TIDEBROOK (St John the Baptist) *Chich 19* **P** *V Wadhurst and V Mayfield (alt)* **V** J R JAMES, **C** C D LAWRENCE
TIDEFORD (St Luke) *see* St Germans *Truro*
TIDENHAM (St Mary) w Beachley and Lancaut *Glouc 4* **P** *Bp* **V** R J M GROSVENOR, **C** N R BROMFIELD
TIDENHAM CHASE (St Michael and All Angels) *see* Tidenham w Beachley and Lancaut *Glouc*
TIDESWELL (St John the Baptist) *Derby 4* **P** *D&C Lich* **P-in-c** F E YATES
TIDMARSH (St Laurence) *see* Pangbourne w Tidmarsh and Sulham *Ox*
TIDMINGTON (not known) *see* Shipston-on-Stour w Honington and Idlicote *Cov*
TIDWORTH (Holy Trinity), Ludgershall and Faberstown *Sarum 13* **P** *Ld Chan and DBP (alt)* **R** M R FREEMAN
TIFFIELD (St John the Baptist) *see* Pattishall w Cold Higham and Gayton w Tiffield *Pet*
TILBROOK (All Saints) *Ely 8* **P** *SMF* **P-in-c** S P MEWS, **NSM** J RAWLINSON
TILBURY, EAST (St Katherine) and West Tilbury and Linford *Chelmsf 14* **P** *Ld Chan* **R** W L WHITFORD
TILBURY DOCKS (St John the Baptist) *Chelmsf 14* **P** *Bp* **V** T M CODLING
TILBURY-JUXTA-CLARE (St Margaret) *see* Upper Colne *Chelmsf*
TILE CROSS (St Peter) *Birm 9* **P** *Bp* **V** B S CASTLE, **NSM** M MACLACHLAN
TILE HILL (St Oswald) *Cov 3* **P** *Bp* **V** B REGAN
TILEHURST (St Catherine of Siena) *Ox 15* **P** *Magd Coll Ox* **P-in-c** D R SMITH
TILEHURST (St George) *Ox 15* **P** *Bp* **V** A J CARLILL, **NSM** M J OKE
TILEHURST (St Mary Magdalen) *Ox 15* **P** *Bp* **P-in-c** A J CARLILL, **NSM** M J OKE
TILEHURST (St Michael) *Ox 15* **P** *Magd Coll Ox* **R** F W DAWSON
TILFORD (All Saints) *see* The Bourne and Tilford *Guildf*
TILGATE (Holy Trinity) *see* Southgate *Chich*
TILLINGHAM (St Nicholas) *Chelmsf 11* **P** *D&C St Paul's* **P-in-c** L R SMITH
TILLINGTON (All Hallows) *Chich 11* **P** *Lord Egremont* **P-in-c** R A STAVELEY-WADHAM
TILMANSTONE (St Andrew) *see* Eastry and Northbourne w Tilmanstone etc *Cant*
TILNEY ALL SAINTS (All Saints) *see* E Marshland *Ely*
TILNEY ST LAWRENCE (St Lawrence) *as above*
TILSHEAD (St Thomas à Becket) *see* Wylye and Till Valley *Sarum*
TILSTOCK (Christ Church), Edstaston and Whixall *Lich 22* **P** *V Prees, R Wem, and R Whitchurch (jt)* **V** D F B BALDWIN, **OLM** S E ARMSTRONG
TILSTON (St Mary) and Shocklach *Ches 5* **P** *Bp* **P-in-c** P A SMITH, **NSM** M M SMITH
TILSTONE FEARNALL (St Jude) *see* Bunbury and Tilstone Fearnall *Ches*
TILSWORTH (All Saints) *see* Totternhoe, Stanbridge and Tilsworth *St Alb*
TILTON ON THE HILL (St Peter) *see* Whatborough Gp *Leic*
TILTY (St Mary the Virgin) *see* Broxted w Chickney and Tilty etc *Chelmsf*
TIMBERHILL (St John the Baptist) *see* Nor St Jo w St Julian *Nor*
TIMBERLAND (St Andrew) *see* Carr Dyke Gp *Linc*
TIMBERSCOMBE (St Petroc) *see* Selworthy, Timberscombe, Wootton Courtenay etc *B & W*
TIMPERLEY (Christ Church) (Holy Cross) *Ches 10* **P** *Trustees* **V** J SUTTON, **C** B E SHARP, V W HYDON
TIMSBURY (Blessed Virgin Mary) and Priston *B & W 12* **P** *Ball Coll Ox (3 turns), R W Lovegrove Esq (1 turn)* **P-in-c** C S HARE
TIMSBURY (St Andrew) *see* Michelmersh and Awbridge and Braishfield etc *Win*
TIMWORTH (St Andrew) *see* Lark Valley *St E*
TINCLETON (St John the Evangelist) *see* Moreton and Woodsford w Tincleton *Sarum*
TINDALE (Mission Church) *see* Lanercost, Walton, Gilsland and Nether Denton *Carl*
TINGEWICK (St Mary Magdalene) *see* W Buckingham *Ox*
TINGRITH (St Nicholas) *see* Westoning w Tingrith *St Alb*
TINSLEY (St Lawrence) *see* Rivers Team *Sheff*
TINTAGEL (St Materiana) *Truro 10* **P** *D&C Windsor* **P-in-c** D J RAKE
TINTINHULL (St Margaret) w Chilthorne Domer, Yeovil Marsh and Thorne Coffin *B & W 7* **P** *Guild of All So* **P-in-c** S J HARTREE, **NSM** A J YOUNG
TINTWISTLE (Christ Church) *see* Hollingworth w Tintwistle *Ches*
TINWELL (All Saints) *see* Ketton, Collyweston, Easton-on-the-Hill etc *Pet*
TIPTOE (St Andrew) *see* Hordle *Win*
TIPTON Great Bridge (St Luke) *see* Tipton St Martin and St Paul *Lich*
TIPTON (St John) *see* Ottery St Mary, Alfington, W Hill, Tipton etc *Ex*
TIPTON (St John the Evangelist) *Lich 26* **P** *V W Bromwich St Jas* **V** B W PIERCE
TIPTON (St Mark) *see* Ocker Hill *Lich*
TIPTON (St Martin) (St Paul) *Lich 26* **P** *MMCET* **V** J F DUNN
TIPTON (St Matthew) *Lich 26* **P** *Simeon's Trustees* **V** C E HOWARD
TIPTREE (St Luke) *see* Tolleshunt Knights w Tiptree and Gt Braxted *Chelmsf*
TIRLEY (St Michael) *see* Hasfield w Tirley and Ashleworth *Glouc*
TISBURY (St John the Baptist) *see* Nadder Valley *Sarum*
TISMANS COMMON (St John the Baptist) *see* Rudgwick *Chich*
TISSINGTON (St Mary) *see* Fenny Bentley, Thorpe, Tissington, Parwich etc *Derby*
TISTED, EAST w Colemore (St James) *see* Northanger *Win*
TISTED, WEST (St Mary Magdalene) *see* Bishop's Sutton and Ropley and W Tisted *Win*
TITCHFIELD (St Peter) *Portsm 2* **P** *D&C Win* **V** W C DAY, **NSM** L E SNAPE
TITCHWELL (St Mary) *see* Hunstanton St Mary w Ringstead Parva etc *Nor*
TITLEY (St Peter) *see* Kington w Huntington, Old Radnor, Kinnerton etc *Heref*
TITTENSOR (St Luke) *see* Swynnerton and Tittensor *Lich*
TITTLESHALL (St Mary) *see* Litcham w Kempston, E and W Lexham, Mileham etc *Nor*
TIVERTON (St Andrew) *Ex 8* **P** *Bp* **P-in-c** D M FLETCHER
TIVERTON (St George) (St Paul) *Ex 8* **P** *MMCET and Peache Trustees (jt)* **V** M J PARTRIDGE, **C** M J CLARK, **NSM** D A LYDDON
TIVERTON (St Peter) and Chevithorne w Cove *Ex 8* **P** *Peache Trustees (3 turns), Ld Chan (1 turn)* **P-in-c** R J GORDON
TIVETSHALL (St Mary and St Margaret) *see* Winfarthing w Shelfanger w Burston w Gissing etc *Nor*
TIVIDALE (St Michael the Archangel) (Holy Cross) (St Augustine) *Lich 26* **P** *Bp* **V** C R MARSHALL
TIVINGTON (St Leonard) *see* Selworthy, Timberscombe, Wootton Courtenay etc *B & W*
TIXALL (St John the Baptist) *see* Stafford St Jo and Tixall w Ingestre *Lich*
TIXOVER (St Luke) *see* Barrowden and Wakerley w S Luffenham etc *Pet*
TOCKENHAM (St Giles) *see* Broad Town, Clyffe Pypard, Hilmarton etc *Sarum*
TOCKHOLES (St Stephen) *see* Darwen St Cuth w Tockholes St Steph *Blackb*
TOCKWITH (Epiphany) and Bilton w Bickerton *York 1* **P** *Abp and D&C (jt)* **P-in-c** J A RENDALL, **NSM** B H FRAY
TODBER (St Andrew) *see* Stour Vale *Sarum*
TODDINGTON (St Andrew) *see* Winchcombe *Glouc*
TODDINGTON (St George of England) and Chalgrave *St Alb 12* **P** *Bp and DBP (jt)* **R** N T MACNEILL
TODENHAM (St Thomas of Canterbury) *see* Moreton-in-Marsh w Batsford, Todenham etc *Glouc*
TODMORDEN (St Mary) (Christ Church) *Wakef 3* **P** *Bp* **V** P N CALVERT, **C** T A IBBOTSON
TODWICK (St Peter and St Paul) *Sheff 5* **P** *Bp* **V** D C BLISS
TOFT (St Andrew) w Caldecote and Childerley *Ely 1* **P** *Ch Coll Cam* **P-in-c** M P M BOOKER, **NSM** M J REISS
TOFT (St John the Evangelist) *see* Knutsford St Jo and Toft *Ches*
TOFT MONKS (St Margaret) *see* Raveningham Gp *Nor*
TOFTREES (All Saints) *Nor 15* **P** *Marquess Townshend* **V** *vacant*
TOFTS, WEST and Buckenham Parva *Nor 13* **P** *Guild of All So* **R** *vacant*

TOKYNGTON (St Michael) *Lon 21* **P** *Bp* **V** P J HARNDEN
TOLLADINE (Christ Church) *see* Worc St Barn w Ch Ch *Worc*
TOLLAND (St John the Baptist) *see* Lydeard St Lawrence w Brompton Ralph etc *B & W*
TOLLARD ROYAL (St Peter ad Vincula) *see* Chase *Sarum*
TOLLER FRATRUM (St Basil) *see* Melbury *Sarum*
TOLLER LANE St Chad *Bradf 1* **P** *Keble Coll Ox* **V** S R CROWE
TOLLER PORCORUM (St Andrew) *see* Beaminster Area *Sarum*
TOLLER WHELME (St John) *see* Melbury *Sarum*
TOLLERTON (St Michael) *see* Alne *York*
TOLLERTON (St Peter) *S'well 8* **P** *Ld Chan* **P-in-c** M H WAINWRIGHT
TOLLESBURY (St Mary) w Salcot Virley *Chelmsf 24* **P** *Bp (1 turn), Ex Coll Ox (3 turns)* **V** K M B LOVELL
TOLLESHUNT D'ARCY (St Nicholas) and Tolleshunt Major *Chelmsf 24* **P** *Mrs E A Comerford and MMCET (jt)* **V** P R SOUTHERN
TOLLESHUNT KNIGHTS w Tiptree and Great Braxted *Chelmsf 24* **P** *Bp (2 turns), Ld Chan (2 turns), and CCC Cam (1 turn)* **R** M FLETCHER, **NSM** R M HATCHETT
TOLLESHUNT MAJOR (St Nicholas) *see* Tolleshunt D'Arcy and Tolleshunt Major *Chelmsf*
TOLLINGTON (St Mark) *Lon 6* **P** *Patr Bd* **TV** T L WAMBUNYA, **P-in-c** J A K MILLAR, **C** P J R BELLENGER, **NSM** E MCCARTNEY
TOLPUDDLE (St John the Evangelist) *see* Puddletown, Tolpuddle and Milborne w Dewlish *Sarum*
TOLWORTH (Emmanuel) *see* Surbiton Hill Ch Ch *S'wark*
TOLWORTH (St George) *see* Surbiton St Matt *S'wark*
TONBRIDGE (St Peter and St Paul) (St Saviour) *Roch 11* **P** *Mabledon Trust* **V** S J G SEAMER, **C** G CLARKE, G TOWNSEND
TONBRIDGE (St Stephen) (St Eanswythe Mission Church) *Roch 11* **P** *CPAS* **V** M BARKER
TONG (St Bartholomew) *Lich 16* **P** *Bp* **V** J B HALL
TONG (St James) *Bradf 3* **P** *CR* **TR** C G N DEY, **C** C S HOWSON
TONGE (St Giles) *see* Murston w Bapchild and Tonge *Cant*
TONGE (St Michael) w Alkrington *Man 18* **P** *R Middleton St Leon* **V** G F JOYCE
TONGE FOLD (St Chad) *Man 9* **P** *Bp and Wm Hulme Trustees (alt)* **V** A J BUTTERWORTH, **OLM** S P MCGREGOR
TONGE MOOR (St Augustine) (St Aidan) *Man 16* **P** *Keble Coll Ox* **V** D A DAVIES, **Hon C** J M DRUMMOND
TONGHAM (St Paul) *Guildf 1* **P** *Adn Surrey* **P-in-c** N J WILLIAMS
TONWELL (St Mary the Virgin) *see* Bengeo *St Alb*
TOOT BALDON (St Lawrence) *see* Dorchester *Ox*
TOOTING (All Saints) *S'wark 19* **P** *Bp* **V** S D METZNER, **OLM** G R WALLER
TOOTING, UPPER (Holy Trinity) (St Augustine) *S'wark 19* **P** *Bp and R Streatham St Leon (jt)* **V** H M GREAR, **NSM** B E NICHOLS
TOOTING GRAVENEY (St Nicholas) *S'wark 19* **P** *MMCET* **R** C J DAVIS, **NSM** R A S THOMSON
TOP VALLEY (St Philip) *see* Bestwood St Matt w St Phil *S'well*
TOPCLIFFE (St Columba), Baldersby w Dishforth, Dalton and Skipton on Swale *York 19* **P** *Abp, Viscountess Downe, and D&C (jt)* **V** C M HADDON-REECE
TOPCROFT (St Margaret) *see* Hempnall *Nor*
TOPPESFIELD (St Margaret) *see* Upper Colne *Chelmsf*
TOPSHAM (St Margaret) *Ex 1* **P** *D&C* **V** R W C JEFFERY
TORBRYAN (Holy Trinity) *see* Ipplepen, Torbryan and Denbury *Ex*
TORKSEY (St Peter) *see* Stow Gp *Linc*
TORMARTON (St Mary Magdalene) *see* Marshfield w Cold Ashton and Tormarton etc *Bris*
TORPENHOW (St Michael and all Angels) *see* Binsey *Carl*
TORPOINT (St James) *Truro 11* **P** *R Antony* **P-in-c** B A ANDERSON, **C** J JOHNSON
TORQUAY (St John) and Ellacombe *Ex 12* **P** *Ch Patr Trust and Bp (jt)* **V** *vacant* (01803) 293441
TORQUAY (St Luke) *Ex 12* **P** *D&C* **P-in-c** C J BAKER
TORQUAY (St Martin) Barton *Ex 12* **P** *V St Marychurch* **V** G CHAPMAN
TORQUAY (St Mary Magdalene) *see* Upton *Ex*
TORQUAY (St Matthias) (St Mark) (Holy Trinity) *Ex 12* **P** *Ch Patr Trust, Bp and Torwood Trustees (jt)* **R** G R PERCY
TORRE (All Saints) *Ex 12* **P** *Bp* **P-in-c** R W SHAMBROOK
TORRIDGE ESTUARY *see* Bideford, Northam, Westward Ho, Appledore etc *Ex*
TORRINGTON, EAST (St Michael) *see* Barkwith Gp *Linc*
TORRINGTON, GREAT (St Michael), Little Torrington and Frithelstock *Ex 20* **P** *Ch Ch Ox (8 turns), Lord Clinton (1 turn), J de C Stevens-Guille Esq (1 turn)* **V** J D HUMMERSTONE, **C** G M YOULD, **Hon C** J C ALLEN
TORRINGTON, LITTLE (St Giles) *see* Gt and Lt Torrington and Frithelstock *Ex*
TORRINGTON, WEST (St Michael) *see* Barkwith Gp *Linc*
TORRISHOLME (Ascension) *Blackb 11* **P** *Bp* **V** P ENNION, **C** T H DAVIS
TORTWORTH (St Leonard) *see* Cromhall, Tortworth, Tytherington, Falfield etc *Glouc*
TORVER (St Luke) *Carl 9* **P** *Peache Trustees* **P-in-c** M R EAST
TOSELAND (St Michael) *see* Papworth *Ely*
TOSSIDE (St Bartholomew) *see* Long Preston w Tosside *Bradf*
TOSTOCK (St Andrew) *see* Pakenham w Norton and Tostock *St E*
TOTHAM, GREAT (St Peter) and Little Totham w Goldhanger *Chelmsf 24* **P** *Bp and Ld Chan (alt)* **R** M J HATCHETT
TOTHAM, LITTLE (All Saints) *see* Gt Totham and Lt Totham w Goldhanger *Chelmsf*
TOTLAND BAY (Christ Church) *Portsm 8* **P** *Ch Patr Trust* **V** J A YORKE
TOTLEY (All Saints) *Sheff 2* **P** *Bp* **V** D G RHODES
TOTNES (St Mary) w Bridgetown, Berry Pomeroy, Dartington, Marldon, Ashprington and Cornworthy *Ex 13* **P** *Patr Bd* **TV** N G BATCOCK, P C BELLENES, S E ROBERTS
TOTON (St Peter) *S'well 7* **P** *CPAS* **V** P W GIBBS, **C** H ROBINSON
TOTTENHAM (All Hallows) *Lon 19* **P** *D&C St Paul's* **V** R B PEARSON
TOTTENHAM (Holy Trinity) *Lon 19* **P** *Bp* **V** O A FAGBEMI
TOTTENHAM (St Bartholomew) *see* Stamford Hill St Bart *Lon*
TOTTENHAM (St Benet Fink) *Lon 19* **P** *D&C St Paul's* **V** M A DAVENPORT
TOTTENHAM (St Cuthbert) *see* Chitts Hill St Cuth *Lon*
TOTTENHAM (St Mary the Virgin) *Lon 19* **P** *Bp* **V** L J MILLER, **C** A C NEWCOMBE
TOTTENHAM (St Paul) *Lon 19* **P** *V Tottenham All Hallows* **V** A K DANGERFIELD, **C** C J DICKSON, **NSM** M A HAYNES
TOTTENHAM (St Philip the Apostle) *Lon 19* **P** *Bp* **P-in-c** K EVANS
TOTTENHAM, SOUTH (St Ann) *Lon 19* **P** *D&C St Paul's* **V** J M WOOD, **NSM** J A KING
TOTTENHILL (St Botolph) w Wormegay *Ely 13* **P** *Bp* **V** J C W NOLAN
TOTTERIDGE (St Andrew) *St Alb 17* **P** *R Hatfield* **V** C P HUITSON
TOTTERNHOE (St Giles), Stanbridge and Tilsworth *St Alb 12* **P** *Bp* **V** D J R SPICER
TOTTINGTON (St Anne) *Man 10* **P** *R Bury St Mary* **V** H W BEARN
TOTTON *Win 11* **P** *Bp* **TR** M N PREVETT, **TV** J K OLIVER, C M ROWBERRY, J R REEVE, **NSM** M B WHITE
TOW LAW (St Philip and St James) *see* Satley, Stanley and Tow Law *Dur*
TOWCESTER (St Lawrence) w Easton Neston *Pet 5* **P** *Bp and Lord Hesketh (alt)* **P-in-c** A C BRYER, **C** N M WARWICK
TOWEDNACK (St Tewinock) *Truro 5* **P** *Bp* **P-in-c** J M PILGRIM
TOWER CHAPEL (St Nicholas) *see* Whitehaven *Carl*
TOWERSEY (St Catherine) *see* Thame *Ox*
TOWN END FARM (St Bede) *see* N Wearside *Dur*
TOWNEND (St Paul) *see* Morley *Wakef*
TOWNSTAL (St Clement) *see* Dartmouth and Dittisham *Ex*
TOXTETH (St Bede) (St Clement) *Liv 6* **P** *Simeon's Trustees and Trustees (jt)* **V** *vacant* 0151-709 9880
TOXTETH (St Cyprian w Christ Church) *see* Edge Hill St Cypr w St Mary *Liv*
TOXTETH (St Margaret) *Liv 6* **P** *St Chad's Coll Dur* **V** R GALLAGHER
TOXTETH (St Philemon) (St Gabriel) St Cleopas *Liv 6* **P** *Patr Bd* **TV** R V STOCK, M R STANFORD, **P-in-c** D G GAVIN, **C** P HANOVA
TOXTETH PARK (Christ Church) (St Michael-in-the-Hamlet) (St Andrew) *Liv 6* **P** *Simeon's Trustees and Trustees (jt)* **V** *vacant* 0151-727 2601
TOXTETH PARK (St Agnes and St Pancras) *Liv 6* **P** *St Chad's Coll Dur* **P-in-c** J C D COOK, **C** L M DANIELS
TOYNTON, HIGH (St John the Baptist) *Linc 11* **P** *Bp* **V** M E BURSON-THOMAS, **C** A C V HARVEY, **NSM** J F PARKIN, A C FORD
TOYNTON ALL SAINTS (All Saints) *see* Marden Hill Gp *Linc*
TOYNTON ST PETER (St Peter) *as above*
TOYS HILL (Hall) *see* Hever, Four Elms and Mark Beech *Roch*
TRAFALGAR SQUARE (St Martin-in-the-Fields) *see* St Martin-in-the-Fields *Lon*

TRAFFORD, OLD (St Bride) *Man 7* **P** *Trustees* **R** P J RAWLINGS, **C** G W BRIGGS, **OLM** V M ECCLES, O H SAMUEL
TRAFFORD, OLD (St Hilda) *see* Firswood and Gorse Hill *Man*
TRAFFORD, OLD (St John the Evangelist) *Man 7* **P** *The Crown* **R** D I WHEELER
TRANMERE (St Catherine) *Ches 1* **P** *R Bebington* **P-in-c** D L MOORE
TRANMERE (St Paul w St Luke) *Ches 1* **P** *Bp* **V** J M CHESWORTH
TRANMERE PARK (St Peter's Hall) *see* Guiseley w Esholt *Bradf*
TRAWDEN (St Mary the Virgin) *see* Colne and Villages *Blackb*
TREALES (Christ Church) *see* Wesham and Treales *Blackb*
TREBOROUGH (St Peter) *see* Old Cleeve, Leighland and Treborough *B & W*
TREDINGTON (St Gregory) and Darlingscott w Newbold on Stour *Cov 9* **P** *Jes Coll Ox* **P-in-c** A J ADAMS
TREDINGTON (St John the Baptist) *see* Deerhurst and Apperley w Forthampton etc *Glouc*
TREETON (St Helen) *see* Rivers Team *Sheff*
TREFONEN (All Saints) *see* Llanyblodwel and Trefonen *Lich*
TREGADILLET (St Mary's Mission) *see* Launceston *Truro*
TREGONY (not known) w St Cuby and Cornelly *Truro 6* **P** *Bp* **P-in-c** S YATES
TREKNOW (Holy Family) *see* Tintagel *Truro*
TRELEIGH (St Stephen) *see* Redruth w Lanner and Treleigh *Truro*
TRELYSTAN (St Mary the Virgin) *Heref 13* **P** *Bp* **V** P D HARRATT
TREMAINE (St Winwalo) *see* Egloskerry, N Petherwin, Tremaine and Tresmere *Truro*
TRENDLEWOOD *see* Nailsea H Trin *B & W*
TRENEGLOS (St Gregory) *see* St Gennys, Jacobstow w Warbstow and Treneglos *Truro*
TRENT (St Andrew) *see* Queen Thorne *Sarum*
TRENT PARK (Christ Church) *see* Enfield Ch Ch Trent Park *Lon*
TRENT VALE (St John the Evangelist) *Lich 12* **P** *R Stoke-on-Trent* **C** P M JELF
TRENTHAM (St Mary and All Saints) *Lich 13* **P** *CPAS* **V** N A DI CASTIGLIONE, **C** R M D ORAM
TRENTISHOE (St Peter) *see* Combe Martin, Berrynarbor, Lynton, Brendon etc *Ex*
TRENTSIDE EAST *Linc 4* **P** *Bp Linc (2 turns), Bp Lon (1 turn)* **R** D J BEVERLEY
TRESCO (St Nicholas) *see* Is of Scilly *Truro*
TRESHAM (not known) *see* Wotton-under-Edge w Ozleworth, N Nibley etc *Glouc*
TRESILLIAN (no dedication) *see* Lamorran and Merther *Truro*
TRESLOTHAN (St John the Evangelist) *see* Crowan and Treslothan *Truro*
TRESMERE (St Nicholas) *see* Egloskerry, N Petherwin, Tremaine and Tresmere *Truro*
TRESWELL (St John the Baptist) *see* Rampton w Laneham, Treswell, Cottam and Stokeham *S'well*
TRETHEVY (St Piran) *see* Tintagel *Truro*
TRETIRE (St Mary) *see* St Weonards w Orcop, Garway, Tretire etc *Heref*
TREVALGA (St Petroc) *see* Boscastle w Davidstow *Truro*
TREVENSON (St Illogan) *see* St Illogan *Truro*
TREVERBYN (St Peter) *Truro 1* **P** *The Crown* **P-in-c** K P ARTHUR, **OLM** L N P HORE
TREVONE (St Saviour) *see* Padstow *Truro*
TREWEN (St Michael) *see* Lezant w Lawhitton and S Petherwin w Trewen *Truro*
TREYFORD CUM DIDLING (St Andrew) *see* Harting w Elsted and Treyford cum Didling *Chich*
TRIMDON (St Mary Magdalene) *see* Upper Skerne *Dur*
TRIMDON GRANGE (St Alban) *as above*
TRIMDON STATION (St Paul) *as above*
TRIMINGHAM (St John the Baptist) *see* Overstrand, Northrepps, Sidestrand etc *Nor*
TRIMLEY (St Martin) *see* Walton and Trimley *St E*
TRIMLEY (St Mary the Virgin) *as above*
TRIMPLEY (Holy Trinity) *see* Kidderminster St Mary and All SS w Trimpley etc *Worc*
TRING (St Martha) (St Peter and St Paul) (St Mary) *St Alb 2* **P** *Bp* **TR** F J C MERCURIO, **TV** H BELLIS, **Hon C** J E K RIDGWAY, **NSM** M S H MACDONALD
TROSTON (St Mary the Virgin) *see* Blackbourne *St E*
TROTTISCLIFFE (St Peter and St Paul) *see* Birling, Addington, Ryarsh and Trottiscliffe *Roch*
TROTTON (St George) *see* Rogate w Terwick and Trotton w Chithurst *Chich*
TROUTBECK (Jesus Church) *see* Windermere St Mary and Troutbeck *Carl*
TROWBRIDGE (Holy Trinity) *Sarum 14* **P** *Patr Bd* **P-in-c** S E HUTTON, **NSM** E A GIFFORD
TROWBRIDGE (St James) *Sarum 14* **P** *Ch Patr Trust* **R** C F BROWN
TROWBRIDGE (St Thomas) and West Ashton *Sarum 14* **P** *CPAS* **P-in-c** J A COUTTS
TROWELL (St Helen) *see* Trowell, Awsworth and Cossall *S'well*
TROWELL (St Helen), Awsworth and Cossall *S'well 7* **P** *Bp and Lord Middleton (jt)* **NSM** J WHYSALL, D C LESTER, P C WHITEHEAD
TROWSE (St Andrew) *Nor 1* **P** *D&C* **P-in-c** M D B LONG
TRULL (All Saints) w Angersleigh *B & W 18* **P** *DBP and M V Spurway Esq (jt)* **R** A YOUINGS, **Hon C** G C BOWYER
TRUMPINGTON (St Mary and St Michael) *Ely 2* **P** *Trin Coll Cam* **V** T AMBROSE
TRUNCH (St Botolph) *Nor 21* **P** *Duchy of Lanc (3 turns), Patr Bd (1 turn)* **TR** R C H KEY, **TV** D W BARTLETT, **NSM** R H MACPHEE
TRURO (St George the Martyr) (St John the Evangelist) *Truro 6* **P** *Prime Min and V Kenwyn St Cuby (alt)* **P-in-c** C D EPPS, **NSM** R F NICHOLLS
TRURO (St Mary's Cathedral and Parish Church) *Truro 6* **P** *The Crown* **R** *vacant* (01872) 79873
TRURO (St Paul) (St Clement) *Truro 6* **P** *Bp* **P-in-c** C D EPPS, **NSM** R F NICHOLLS
TRUSHAM (St Michael and All Angels) *see* Chudleigh w Chudleigh Knighton and Trusham *Ex*
TRUSLEY (All Saints) *see* Boylestone, Church Broughton, Dalbury, etc *Derby*
TRUSTHORPE (St Peter) *see* Mablethorpe w Trusthorpe *Linc*
TRYSULL (All Saints) *see* Smestow Vale *Lich*
TRYTHALL (Mission Church) *see* Gulval and Madron *Truro*
TUBNEY (St Lawrence) *see* Fyfield w Tubney and Kingston Bagpuize *Ox*
TUCKHILL (Holy Innocents) *see* Claverley w Tuckhill *Heref*
TUCKINGMILL (All Saints) *Truro 2* **P** *Bp* **P-in-c** E C WOON
TUCKSWOOD (St Paul) *see* Nor Lakenham St Jo and All SS and Tuckswood *Nor*
TUDDENHAM (St Martin) *see* Westerfield and Tuddenham w Witnesham *St E*
TUDDENHAM (St Mary) *see* Mildenhall *St E*
TUDDENHAM, EAST (All Saints) *see* Hockering, Honingham, E and N Tuddenham *Nor*
TUDDENHAM, NORTH (St Mary the Virgin) *as above*
TUDELEY (All Saints) cum Capel w Five Oak Green *Roch 11* **P** *Bp* **P-in-c** J G A IVE, **C** P F IVE
TUDHOE (St David) *see* Croxdale and Tudhoe *Dur*
TUDHOE GRANGE (St Andrew) *Dur 6* **P** *Bp* **V** N D BAKER
TUEBROOK (St John) *see* W Derby St Jo *Liv*
TUFFLEY (St Barnabas) *Glouc 5* **P** *Bp* **V** M SHARLAND, **NSM** A W GAGE, R F JEWELL
TUFNELL PARK (St George and All Saints) *Lon 6* **P** *Trustees and CPAS (jt)* **P-in-c** M L TOOGOOD, **NSM** M C DONEY
TUFNELL PARK (St Mary) *see* Brookfield St Mary *Lon*
TUFTON (St Mary) *see* Whitchurch w Tufton and Litchfield *Win*
TUGBY (St Thomas à Becket) *see* Hallaton w Horninghold and Allexton, Tugby etc *Leic*
TUGFORD (St Catherine) *see* Diddlebury w Munslow, Holdgate and Tugford *Heref*
TULSE HILL (Holy Trinity and St Matthias) *S'wark 12* **P** *Simeon's Trustees and Peache Trustees (jt)* **V** B A MUSK, **NSM** D C FRETT, **OLM** L ADENEKAN
TUNBRIDGE WELLS (Holy Trinity w Christ Church) *Roch 12* **P** *Mabledon Trust and CPAS (jt)* **V** J W BANNER
TUNBRIDGE WELLS (King Charles the Martyr) *Roch 12* **P** *Trustees* **V** R E AVERY
TUNBRIDGE WELLS (St Barnabas) *Roch 12* **P** *Guild of All So* **V** K E MACNAB
TUNBRIDGE WELLS (St James) *Roch 12* **P** *Ch Trust Fund Trust* **V** J P STEWART, **C** K L ROSSLYN-SMITH
TUNBRIDGE WELLS (St John) *Roch 12* **P** *CPAS and V Tunbridge Wells H Trin (jt)* **V** G R WALTER, **C** S J GOODBODY, M MASON
TUNBRIDGE WELLS (St Luke) *Roch 12* **P** *Five Trustees* **V** J A WHEELER
TUNBRIDGE WELLS (St Mark) Broadwater Down *Roch 12* **P** *Bp Chich* **V** B C H FORTNUM, **C** S C FERRIS
TUNBRIDGE WELLS (St Peter) Windmill Fields *Roch 12* **P** *Trustees and CPAS (jt)* **V** M P WARREN
TUNBRIDGE WELLS (St Philip) *Roch 12* **P** *Ch Trust Fund Trust* **V** B S SENIOR

TUNSTALL (All Saints) *see* Roos and Garton w Tunstall, Grimston and Hilston *York*
TUNSTALL (Christ Church) *Lich 11* **P** *Bp* **V** A D BUIK
TUNSTALL (Holy Trinity) *see* Catterick *Ripon*
TUNSTALL (St John the Baptist) *see* E Lonsdale *Blackb*
TUNSTALL (St John the Baptist) w Rodmersham *Cant 15* **P** *D&C and G L Doubleday Esq (jt)* **R** D MATTHIAE
TUNSTALL (St Michael and All Angels) *see* Wilford Peninsula *St E*
TUNSTEAD (Holy Trinity) *see* Bacup and Stacksteads *Man*
TUNSTEAD (St Mary) w Sco' Ruston *Nor 12* **P** *Bp* **P-in-c** A R LONG
TUNWORTH (All Saints) *see* Herriard w Winslade and Long Sutton etc *Win*
TUPSLEY (St Paul) w Hampton Bishop *Heref 3* **P** *Bp* **V** J D REESE, **C** C L DYSON
TUPTON (St John) *see* N Wingfield, Clay Cross and Pilsley *Derby*
TUR LANGTON (St Andrew) *see* Church Langton cum Tur Langton etc *Leic*
TURKDEAN (All Saints) *see* Northleach w Hampnett and Farmington etc *Glouc*
TURNASTONE (St Mary Magdalene) *see* Madley w Tyberton, Peterchurch, Vowchurch etc *Heref*
TURNDITCH (All Saints) *see* Belper Ch Ch w Turnditch *Derby*
TURNERS HILL (St Leonard) *Chich 7* **P** *Bp* **P-in-c** D M JARMY, **NSM** G M W PARRY
TURNFORD (St Clement) Conventional District *St Alb 6* **Min** C J SELBY
TURNHAM GREEN (Christ Church) *Lon 11* **P** *Bp* **V** J E DAINTY, **C** A J DENNISS
TURNWORTH (St Mary) *see* Winterborne Valley and Milton Abbas *Sarum*
TURTON MOORLAND MINISTRY (St Anne) (St James) *Man 16* **P** *Patr Bd* **TR** D M DUNN, **TV** M R SHORT, J MCGRATH, **NSM** D R JONES, K THOMAS, **OLM** S HAWORTH, L TAYLOR, A J HESLOP
TURVEY (All Saints) *St Alb 15* **P** *Mrs P K C Hanbury* **P-in-c** J A SPRAY
TURVILLE (St Mary) *see* Hambleden Valley *Ox*
TURWESTON (Assumption of the Blessed Virgin Mary) *see* W Buckingham *Ox*
TUSHINGHAM (St Chad) and Whitewell (St Mary) *Ches 5* **P** *MMCET* **P-in-c** M S SEARLE
TUTBURY (St Mary the Virgin) *Lich 14* **P** *Duchy of Lancaster* **V** *vacant* (01283) 813127
TUTSHILL (St Luke) *see* Tidenham w Beachley and Lancaut *Glouc*
TUTTINGTON (St Peter and St Paul) *see* King's Beck *Nor*
TUXFORD (St Nicholas) w Weston and Markham Clinton *S'well 3* **P** *Ld Chan and Bp (alt)* **P-in-c** E A THOMAS
TWEEDMOUTH (St Bartholomew) *Newc 12* **P** *D&C Dur* **V** A S ADAMSON, **OLM** K R COULTER
TWERTON-ON-AVON *see* Bath Twerton-on-Avon *B & W*
TWICKENHAM (All Hallows) *Lon 10* **P** *D&C St Paul's* **V** *vacant* (020) 8892 1322
TWICKENHAM (All Saints) *Lon 10* **P** *Bp* **V** P L BUSTIN
TWICKENHAM (St Mary the Virgin) *Lon 10* **P** *D&C Windsor* **V** R J H WILLIAMS, **Hon C** J T MARTIN, D J ELLIOTT
TWICKENHAM, EAST (St Stephen) (St Paul) *Lon 10* **P** *CPAS* **V** A J WATSON, **C** R L PENISTAN, A N BEAVIS, L A J TAYLOR
TWICKENHAM COMMON (Holy Trinity) *Lon 10* **P** *Bp* **V** M S STARKEY
TWIGWORTH (St Matthew), Down Hatherley, Norton, The Leigh, Evington, Sandhurst and Staverton w Boddington *Glouc 6* **P** *Ld Chan (1 turn), Bp Glouc and D&C Bris (1 turn)* **V** J F WARD, **NSM** O C BARRACLOUGH, R M BRYANT
TWINEHAM (St Peter) *see* Albourne w Sayers Common and Twineham *Chich*
TWINSTEAD (St John the Evangelist) *see* N Hinckford *Chelmsf*
TWITCHEN (St Peter) *see* S Molton w Nymet St George, High Bray etc *Ex*
TWO GATES (St Peter) *see* Wilnecote *Lich*
TWO MILE ASH (not known) *see* Watling Valley *Ox*
TWO MILE HILL (St Michael) *Bris 3* **P** *Prime Min* **V** S ALLMAN
TWO RIVERS *see* Newton Tracey, Horwood, Alverdiscott etc *Ex*
TWYCROSS (St James) *see* Bosworth and Sheepy Gp *Leic*
TWYFORD (Assumption of the Blessed Virgin Mary) *see* Swan *Ox*
TWYFORD (St Andrew) *see* Ticknall, Smisby and Stanton by Bridge etc *Derby*
TWYFORD (St Andrew) *see* S Croxton Gp *Leic*
TWYFORD (St Mary) and Owslebury and Morestead *Win 7* **P** *Em Coll Cam and Bp (alt)* **P-in-c** M D BAILEY, **NSM** M I JACKSON
TWYFORD (St Mary the Virgin) *see* Ruscombe and Twyford *Ox*
TWYFORD (St Nicholas), Guist, Bintree, Themelthorpe, Wood Norton and Stibbard *Nor 22* **P** *Bp and Mrs H M Cook (2 turns), DBP (1 turn)* **R** A K GREENHOUGH
TWYNING (St Mary Magdalene) *see* Tewkesbury w Walton Cardiff and Twyning *Glouc*
TWYWELL (St Nicholas) *see* Cranford w Grafton Underwood and Twywell *Pet*
TYBERTON (St Mary) *see* Madley w Tyberton, Peterchurch, Vowchurch etc *Heref*
TYDD (St Mary) *see* The Suttons w Tydd *Linc*
TYDD ST GILES (St Giles) *see* Leverington, Newton and Tydd St Giles *Ely*
TYE GREEN (St Barnabas) *see* Fairstead w Terling and White Notley etc *Chelmsf*
TYE GREEN (St Stephen) w St Andrew Netteswell *Chelmsf 26* **P** *J L H Arkwright Esq* **R** A V WATSON, **C** S L ELMAN
TYLDESLEY (St George) w Shakerley *Man 13* **P** *Bp* **P-in-c** C J STRATON
TYLER HILL (St Francis) *see* Hackington *Cant*
TYLERS GREEN (St Margaret) *see* Penn and Tylers Green *Ox*
TYLER'S HILL (St George) *see* Gt Chesham *Ox*
TYNE, NORTH and Redesdale Team *Newc 2* **P** *Patr Bd* **TR** W R LARGE, **TV** M J PENFOLD, **Hon C** B M JONES, **OLM** R VIRDEN
TYNEMOUTH Balkwell (St Peter) *see* Balkwell *Newc*
TYNEMOUTH Cullercoats (St Paul) *Newc 8* **P** *Dioc Soc* **V** G F GILCHRIST, **C** D W CARBERRY
TYNEMOUTH Shiremoor (St Mark) *see* Shiremoor *Newc*
TYNEMOUTH (St John Percy) *Newc 8* **P** *Dioc Soc* **P-in-c** H B GILL
TYNEMOUTH PRIORY (Holy Saviour) *Newc 8* **P** *Dioc Soc* **Hon C** T MOAT
TYNINGS LANE (St Mary's Mission Church) *see* Aldridge *Lich*
TYRINGHAM (St Peter) *see* Lamp *Ox*
TYRLEY (Mission Room) *see* Drayton in Hales *Lich*
TYSELEY (St Edmund) *Birm 13* **P** *The Crown* **V** *vacant* 0121-777 2433
TYSOE (Assumption of the Blessed Virgin Mary) w Oxhill and Whatcote *Cov 9* **P** *Marquess of Northampton and DBP (jt)* **V** D A KNIGHT
TYTHBY (Holy Trinity) *see* Cropwell Bishop w Colston Bassett, Granby etc *S'well*
TYTHERINGTON (St James) *see* Cromhall, Tortworth, Tytherington, Falfield etc *Glouc*
TYTHERINGTON (St James) *see* Upper Wylye Valley *Sarum*
TYTHERLEY, EAST (St Peter) *see* Lockerley and E Dean w E and W Tytherley *Win*
TYTHERLEY, WEST (St Peter) *as above*
TYTHERTON KELLAWAYS (St Giles) *see* Draycot *Bris*
TYTHERTON LUCAS (St Nicholas) *see* Chippenham St Andr w Tytherton Lucas *Bris*
TYWARDREATH (St Andrew) w Tregaminion *Truro 1* **P** *DBP* **P-in-c** F M BOWERS, **C** S D MICHAEL
UBLEY (St Bartholomew) *see* Blagdon w Compton Martin and Ubley *B & W*
UCKFIELD (Holy Cross) (St Saviour) *Chich 21* **P** *Abp* **R** B H WILCOX, **C** P K H LO, **NSM** C HOWARTH
UDIMORE (St Mary) *see* Brede w Udimore *Chich*
UFFCULME (St Mary the Virgin) *see* Cullompton, Willand, Uffculme, Kentisbeare etc *Ex*
UFFINGTON Group, The (St Michael and All Angels) *Linc 13* **P** *Ld Chan (2 turns), Bp (2 turns), D&C (1 turn)* **R** C R KENNEDY
UFFINGTON (Holy Trinity) *see* Wrockwardine Deanery *Lich*
UFFINGTON (St Mary), Shellingford, Woolstone and Baulking *Ox 17* **P** *Bp (2 turns), J J Twynam Esq (1 turn)* **P-in-c** R S MARTIN
UFFORD (Assumption of the Blessed Virgin Mary) *see* Melton and Ufford *St E*
UFFORD (St Andrew) *see* Barnack w Ufford and Bainton *Pet*
UFTON (St Michael and All Angels) *Cov 10* **P** *Bp* **P-in-c** J E ARMSTRONG
UGBOROUGH (St Peter) *see* Ermington and Ugborough *Ex*
UGGESHALL (St Mary) *see* Sole Bay *St E*
UGGLEBARNBY (All Saints) *see* Eskdaleside w Ugglebarnby and Sneaton *York*
UGLEY (St Peter) *see* Henham and Elsenham w Ugley *Chelmsf*
UGTHORPE (Christ Church) *see* Hinderwell, Roxby and Staithes etc *York*

ULCEBY (All Saints) *see* Willoughby *Linc*
ULCEBY Group, The (St Nicholas) *Linc 6* **P** *Ld Chan* **V** *vacant* (01469) 588239
ULCOMBE (All Saints) *see* Len Valley *Cant*
ULDALE (St James) *see* Binsey *Carl*
ULEY (St Giles) w Owlpen and Nympsfield *Glouc 2* **P** *Ld Chan* **P-in-c** N H TUCKER
ULGHAM (St John the Baptist) *Newc 11* **P** *Bp* **P-in-c** A E HARRISON
ULLENHALL (St Mary the Virgin) *see* Beaudesert and Henley-in-Arden w Ullenhall *Cov*
ULLESKELFE (St Saviour) *see* Kirk Fenton w Kirkby Wharfe and Ulleskelfe *York*
ULLEY (Holy Trinity) *see* Aston cum Aughton w Swallownest and Ulley *Sheff*
ULLINGSWICK (St Luke) *see* Stoke Lacy, Moreton Jeffries w Much Cowarne etc *Heref*
ULPHA (St John) *see* Broughton and Duddon *Carl*
ULROME (St Andrew) *see* Skipsea w Ulrome and Barmston w Fraisthorpe *York*
ULTING (All Saints) *see* Hatfield Peverel w Ulting *Chelmsf*
ULVERSTON (St Mary w Holy Trinity) (St Jude) *Carl 9* **P** *Peache Trustees* **R** A C BING, **C** P J DORLING
UMBERLEIGH (Church of the Good Shepherd) *see* S Molton w Nymet St George, High Bray etc *Ex*
UNDERBARROW (All Saints) *Carl 10* **P** *V Kendal H Trin* **V** *vacant*
UNDERRIVER (St Margaret) *Roch 9* **P** *Bp* **P-in-c** M D COOKE
UNDERSKIDDAW (Parish Room) *see* Crosthwaite Keswick *Carl*
UNDERWOOD (St Michael and All Angels) *see* Brinsley w Underwood *S'well*
UNSTONE (St Mary) *see* Dronfield w Holmesfield *Derby*
UNSWORTH (St George) *Man 14* **P** *R Prestwich St Mary* **V** R E MALLINSON
UP HATHERLEY (St Philip and St James) *Glouc 9* **P** *Soc of the Faith* **V** R I T-A RAVEN, **C** D G HUMPHRIES
UP MARDEN (St Michael) *see* Compton, the Mardens, Stoughton and Racton *Chich*
UP NATELY (St Stephen) *see* Newnham w Nately Scures w Mapledurwell etc *Win*
UP WALTHAM (St Mary the Virgin) *Chich 11* **P** *Lord Egremont* **P-in-c** R A STAVELEY-WADHAM
UPAVON (St Mary the Virgin) w Rushall and Charlton *Sarum 19* **P** *Mert Coll Ox, Ld Chan, and Ch Ch Ox (by turn)* **P-in-c** H L GIBBONS
UPCHURCH (St Mary the Virgin) w Lower Halstow *Cant 15* **P** *D&C* **V** J P LEFROY, **NSM** R W PARTRIDGE, **OLM** J DAVIS
UPHAM (All Saints) (Blessed Mary of Upham) *Portsm 1* **P** *Ld Chan* **R** A G DAVIS, **C** J M HEMMINGS
UPHILL (St Nicholas) (St Barnabas Mission Church) *B & W 11* **P** *Patr Bd* **TR** E W MCLEOD, **TV** A W G CHALKLEY, **NSM** P W TULLETT
UPHOLLAND (St Thomas the Martyr) *Liv 11* **P** *Patr Bd* **TR** P D D BRADLEY, **TV** A DILWORTH, **C** J A BALL
UPLANDS (All Saints) *see* Stroud and Uplands w Slad *Glouc*
UPLEADON (St Mary the Virgin) *see* Redmarley D'Abitot, Bromesberrow, Pauntley etc *Glouc*
UPLOWMAN (St Peter) *see* Sampford Peverell, Uplowman, Holcombe Rogus etc *Ex*
UPLYME (St Peter and St Paul) w Axmouth *Ex 5* **P** *CPAS and Hyndman Trustees (jt)* **R** J S WHITE
UPMINSTER (St Laurence) *Chelmsf 2* **P** *The Revd W R Holden* **R** C J MANN, **C** G J BOWEN
UPNOR (St Philip and St James) *see* Frindsbury w Upnor and Chattenden *Roch*
UPOTTERY (St Mary the Virgin) *see* Dunkeswell, Luppitt, Sheldon and Upottery *Ex*
UPPER *see also under substantive place name*
UPPER ITCHEN *Win 1* **P** *Prime Min (2 turns), D&C (1 turn)* **R** G A HENDY, **Hon C** R J GUYMER
UPPERBY (St John the Baptist) *see* S Carl TM *Carl*
UPPERTHONG (St John the Evangelist) *see* Upper Holme Valley *Wakef*
UPPINGHAM (St Peter and St Paul) w Ayston and Wardley w Belton *Pet 14* **P** *Bp* **R** S J EVANS, **C** P R H EDWARDS
UPPINGTON (Holy Trinity) *see* Wrockwardine Deanery *Lich*
UPSHIRE (St Thomas) *see* Waltham H Cross *Chelmsf*
UPTON (All Saints) *see* Lea Gp *Linc*
UPTON (Holy Ascension) *Ches 2* **P** *Duke of Westmr* **V** G H CONWAY
UPTON (St Dunstan) *see* Lytchett Minster *Sarum*
UPTON (St James) *see* Brompton Regis w Upton and Skilgate *B & W*
UPTON (St John the Baptist) *see* Castor w Sutton and Upton w Marholm *Pet*
UPTON (St Laurence) *see* Upton cum Chalvey *Ox*
UPTON (St Margaret) *see* Ranworth w Panxworth, Woodbastwick etc *Nor*
UPTON (St Margaret) and Copmanford *Ely 8* **P** *Bp* **V** *vacant*
UPTON (St Mary) *Ches 8* **P** *Simeon's Trustees* **V** R J SHIMWELL, **C** M C BAKER, **NSM** P J NICKSON, M J DALY
UPTON (St Mary Magdalene) *Ex 12* **P** *Simeon's Trustees and Ch Patr Trust (alt)* **P-in-c** M A BAKER, **NSM** J H GARNER
UPTON (St Mary the Virgin) *see* Blewbury, Hagbourne and Upton *Ox*
UPTON (St Peter and St Paul) *see* Rolleston w Fiskerton, Morton and Upton *S'well*
UPTON BISHOP (St John the Baptist) *see* Ross *Heref*
UPTON CRESSETT w Monk Hopton *Heref 9* **P** *DBP and Miss E A Bird (alt)* **Hon C** H J PATTERSON
UPTON CROSS (St Paul) *see* Linkinhorne *Truro*
UPTON CUM CHALVEY (St Mary) *Ox 23* **P** *Bp* **TR** D K MIELL, **TV** D E WEST, **C** C H OOSTRA
UPTON GREY (St Mary) *see* Herriard w Winslade and Long Sutton etc *Win*
UPTON HELLIONS (St Mary the Virgin) *see* Crediton, Shobrooke and Sandford etc *Ex*
UPTON LOVELL (St Augustine of Canterbury) *see* Upper Wylye Valley *Sarum*
UPTON MAGNA (St Lucia) *see* Wrockwardine Deanery *Lich*
UPTON NOBLE (St Mary Magdalene) *see* Bruton and Distr *B & W*
UPTON-ON-SEVERN (St Peter and St Paul), Ripple, Earls Croome w Hill Croome and Strensham *Worc 5* **P** *Bp (2 turns), Mrs A J Hyde-Smith and Mrs A L Wynne (1 turn)* **R** C G HARDWICK, **NSM** J A FRASER
UPTON PARK (St Alban) *see* E Ham w Upton Park St Alb *Chelmsf*
UPTON PRIORY (Church of the Resurrection) *Ches 13* **P** *Bp* **V** J H FIFE
UPTON PYNE (Our Lady) *see* Thorverton, Cadbury, Upton Pyne etc *Ex*
UPTON SCUDAMORE (St Mary the Virgin) *see* Cley Hill Warminster *Sarum*
UPTON SNODSBURY (St Kenelm) *see* Peopleton and White Ladies Aston w Churchill etc *Worc*
UPTON ST LEONARDS (St Leonard) *Glouc 5* **P** *Bp* **P-in-c** P R LECKEY
UPTON WARREN (St Michael) *see* Stoke Prior, Wychbold and Upton Warren *Worc*
UPWELL (St Peter) *Ely 15* **P** *R T Townley Esq* **R** A F JESSON
UPWELL CHRISTCHURCH (Christ Church) *see* Christchurch and Manea and Welney *Ely*
UPWEY (St Laurence) *see* Bincombe w Broadwey, Upwey and Buckland Ripers *Sarum*
UPWOOD (St Peter) *see* The Ramseys and Upwood *Ely*
URCHFONT (St Michael and All Angels) *see* Redhorn *Sarum*
URMSTON (St Clement) *Man 7* **P** *Bp* **P-in-c** C C BROWN, **C** K J STANTON, **OLM** C E FAULKNER
URSWICK (St Mary the Virgin and St Michael) *see* Aldingham, Dendron, Rampside and Urswick *Carl*
USHAW MOOR (St Luke) *see* Dur N *Dur*
USSELBY (St Margaret) *see* Kelsey Gp *Linc*
USWORTH (Holy Trinity) (St Michael and All Angels) *Dur 11* **P** *Patr Bd* **TR** A MELTON, **TV** P T HARRISON
UTKINTON (St Paul) *see* Tarporley *Ches*
UTLEY (St Mark) *Bradf 8* **P** *Bp and R Keighley St Andr (jt)* **V** D WALMSLEY, **C** R B RADLEY
UTTERBY (St Andrew) *see* Fotherby *Linc*
UTTOXETER AREA (St Mary the Virgin) *Lich 15* **P** *Patr Bd* **TR** D V EVANS, **TV** D C STONE, E C GARRETT, **C** J J WILSON, **OLM** I M SMITH, C W DALE, C H BROWN, J S LANDER
UXBRIDGE (St Andrew) (St Margaret) (St Peter) *Lon 24* **P** *Bp* **TR** A F SHEARD, **TV** S W COOPER, **C** J A HUGHMAN
VALE OF BELVOIR Parishes *Leic 3* **P** *Patr Bd (2 turns), Ld Chan (1 turn)* **TV** R D STAPLEFORD, **C** S P J BURNHAM
VALLEY END (St Saviour) *see* Chobham w Valley End *Guildf*
VALLEY PARK (St Francis) *Win 10* **P** *Bp* **V** P F HUTCHINSON
VANGE (St Chad) *Chelmsf 6* **P** *MMCET* **R** *vacant* (01268) 553248
VAUXHALL (St Peter) *see* N Lambeth *S'wark*
VENN OTTERY (St Gregory) *see* Ottery St Mary, Alfington, W Hill, Tipton etc *Ex*
VENTA Group, The *see* Stoke H Cross w Dunston, Arminghall etc *Nor*
VENTNOR (Holy Trinity) *Portsm 7* **P** *Bp* **V** *vacant*

VENTNOR (St Alban) *see* Godshill *Portsm*
VENTNOR (St Catherine) *Portsm 7* **P** *Ch Patr Trust* **V** *vacant* (01983) 854367
VERNHAM DEAN (St Mary the Virgin) *see* Hurstbourne Tarrant, Faccombe, Vernham Dean etc *Win*
VERWOOD (St Michael and All Angels) *Sarum 9* **P** *Bp* **V** A J M SINCLAIR, **C** A J W ROWLAND, P A KEMP, **NSM** P E MILES, **OLM** N F MOULAND, P M BASAVARAJ
VERYAN (St Symphorian) w Ruan Lanihorne *Truro 6* **P** *D&C and DBP (jt)* **P-in-c** C J BUDDEN
VICTORIA DOCKS (Ascension) *Chelmsf 3* **P** *Bp* **V** J A W BRICE
VICTORIA DOCKS St Luke *Chelmsf 3* **P** *Ld Chan* **V** D P WADE, **NSM** G J ANAN
VICTORIA PARK (St John Chrysostom) *see* Man Victoria Park *Man*
VICTORIA PARK (St Mark) *see* Old Ford St Paul and St Mark *Lon*
VIGO (Village Hall) *see* Stansted w Fairseat and Vigo *Roch*
VINEY HILL (All Saints) *see* Parkend and Viney Hill *Glouc*
VIRGINIA WATER (Christ Church) *Guildf 11* **P** *Simeon's Trustees* **V** S R SIZER, **C** J T HUGHES
VIRGINSTOW (St Bridget) *see* Boyton, N Tamerton, Werrington etc *Truro*
VOWCHURCH (St Bartholomew) *see* Madley w Tyberton, Peterchurch, Vowchurch etc *Heref*
WABERTHWAITE (St John) *see* Eskdale, Irton, Muncaster and Waberthwaite *Carl*
WACTON (All Saints) *see* Stratton St Mary w Stratton St Michael etc *Nor*
WADDESDON (St Michael and All Angels) *see* Schorne *Ox*
WADDINGHAM (St Mary and St Peter) *see* Bishop Norton, Wadingham and Snitterby *Linc*
WADDINGTON (St Helen) *Bradf 5* **P** *E C Parker Esq* **P-in-c** S G RIDLEY
WADDINGTON (St Michael) *Linc 18* **P** *Linc Coll Ox* **R** R J G PARKER
WADDON (St George) *see* Croydon St Jo *S'wark*
WADEBRIDGE *see* St Breoke and Egloshayle *Truro*
WADENHOE (St Michael and All Angels) *see* Aldwincle w Thorpe Achurch, Pilton, Wadenhoe etc *Pet*
WADHURST (St Peter and St Paul) *Chich 19* **P** *J M Hardcastle Esq and M R Toynbee Esq (jt)* **V** J R JAMES, **C** C D LAWRENCE, **NSM** R G ALFORD
WADINGHAM (St Mary and St Peter) *see* Bishop Norton, Wadingham and Snitterby *Linc*
WADSHELF (Mission Room) *see* Old Brampton *Derby*
WADSLEY (no dedication) *Sheff 4* **P** *Ch Patr Trust* **V** G J HUTCHISON
WADWORTH (St John the Baptist) w Loversall *Sheff 9* **P** *V Doncaster and DBP (alt)* **V** R W IVELL
WAGGONERS *York 10* **P** *Abp and Sir Tatton Sykes Bt, and Ld Chan (alt)* **V** M TEARE, **NSM** I D MACKARILL
WAINCLIFFE (St David) *see* Beeston *Ripon*
WAINFLEET (All Saints) *see* The Wainfleet Gp *Linc*
WAINFLEET Group, The (All Saints) (St Mary) (St Michael) *Linc 8* **P** *Ld Chan, Bp and T E Pitts Esq (alt)* **R** R D HACKING
WAINFLEET (St Mary) *see* The Wainfleet Gp *Linc*
WAINFLEET (St Michael) *as above*
WAINFORD *St E 14* **P** *Bp, Mrs B I T Suckling, CPAS, Magd Coll Cam, and Ch Soc Trust (jt)* **R** A T HINDLEY, **OLM** J F W BUCHANAN, N H SIMISTER
WAITHE (St Martin) *see* The North-Chapel Parishes *Linc*
WAKEFIELD (St Andrew and St Mary) (St Swithun) *Wakef 12* **P** *Peache Trustees* **P-in-c** K S BURKE
WAKEFIELD (St John the Baptist) *Wakef 12* **P** *Dean* **V** P M DOWLING, **Hon C** R B GRAINGER
WAKEFIELD (St Mary) Chantry Bridge *see* Wakef Cathl *Wakef*
WAKEFIELD (St Michael the Archangel) *see* Westgate Common *Wakef*
WAKERING, GREAT (St Nicholas) w Foulness *Chelmsf 13* **P** *Bp* **P-in-c** W C FREWIN
WAKERING, LITTLE (St Mary the Virgin) *see* Barling w Lt Wakering *Chelmsf*
WAKERLEY (St John the Baptist) *see* Barrowden and Wakerley w S Luffenham etc *Pet*
WAKES COLNE (All Saints) *see* Gt and Lt Tey w Wakes Colne and Chappel *Chelmsf*
WALBERSWICK (St Andrew) *see* Sole Bay *St E*
WALBERTON (St Mary) w Binsted *Chich 21* **P** *Bp* **V** T J C WARD
WALBROOK Epiphany *Derby 10* **P** *Patr Bd* **TR** A J FITCH, **TV** A J WARD, **NSM** A J CLARK
WALCOT *see* Bath Walcot *B & W*
WALCOT (All Saints) *see* Happisburgh, Walcott, Hempstead w Eccles etc *Nor*
WALCOT (St Nicholas) *see* S Lafford *Linc*
WALCOT (St Oswald) *see* Carr Dyke Gp *Linc*
WALDEN, LITTLE (St John) *see* Saffron Walden w Wendens Ambo, Littlebury etc *Chelmsf*
WALDERSLADE (St William) *see* S Chatham H Trin *Roch*
WALDINGFIELD, GREAT (St Lawrence) *see* Acton w Gt Waldingfield *St E*
WALDINGFIELD, LITTLE (St Lawrence) *see* Boxford, Edwardstone, Groton etc *St E*
WALDITCH (St Mary) *see* Bridport *Sarum*
WALDRINGFIELD (All Saints) w Hemley and Newbourn *St E 2* **P** *Canon T Waller and Revd A H N Waller, Ld Chan, and Mrs S E F Holden (by turn)* **R** J P WALLER
WALDRON (All Saints) *Chich 15* **P** *Ex Coll Ox* **P-in-c** J SHERWIN
WALES (St John the Baptist) *Sheff 5* **P** *Bp* **V** G SCHOFIELD
WALESBY (St Edmund) *S'well 3* **P** *DBP* **V** C C LEVY
WALESBY (St Mary and All Saints) *Linc 5* **P** *Bp, DBP, and C Drakes Esq (jt)* **R** J H P CARR, **OLM** E TURNER
WALFORD (St Michael and All Angels) and St John, w Bishopswood, Goodrich, Marstow and Welsh Bicknor *Heref 8* **P** *Bp and Ld Chan (alt)* **P-in-c** O D WILLIAMS
WALGRAVE (St Peter) w Hannington and Wold and Scaldwell *Pet 2* **P** *Bp (2 turns), BNC Ox (1 turn)* **P-in-c** K A I JONGMAN
WALHAM GREEN (St John) (St James) *Lon 9* **P** *Bp* **P-in-c** M W OSBORNE, **NSM** J C HUNTER
WALKDEN (St Paul) and Little Hulton *Man 12* **P** *Patr Bd* **TR** S C EDWARDS, **TV** C H PHARAOH, **OLM** K HOPWOOD OWEN, M SURREY
WALKER (Christ Church) *Newc 6* **P** *Bp* **V** K HUNT, **C** J LANCASTER
WALKERGATE (St Oswald) *see* Byker St Mark and Walkergate St Oswald *Newc*
WALKERINGHAM (St Mary Magdalene) *see* Beckingham w Walkeringham and Gringley *S'well*
WALKERN (St Mary the Virgin) *see* Benington w Walkern *St Alb*
WALKHAMPTON (St Mary the Virgin) *see* Yelverton, Meavy, Sheepstor and Walkhampton *Ex*
WALKINGHAM HILL *Ripon 1* **P** *Bp, DBP, R Knaresborough, MMCET, and Major Sir Arthur Collins (jt)* **R** C WRAY
WALKINGTON (All Hallows) *see* Bishop Burton w Walkington *York*
WALKLEY (St Mary) *Sheff 4* **P** *Bp* **P-in-c** M A FITZGERALD
WALL (St George) *see* St Oswald in Lee w Bingfield *Newc*
WALL (St John the Baptist) *see* Lich St Mich w St Mary and Wall *Lich*
WALL HEATH (Ascension) *see* Kingswinford St Mary *Worc*
WALLASEY (St Hilary) *Ches 7* **P** *Bp* **R** P L ROBINSON, **C** K J HODGSON, **NSM** D N CHESTERS
WALLASEY (St Nicholas) (All Saints) *Ches 7* **P** *Bp and DBP (jt)* **V** J J STAPLES
WALLINGFORD (St Mary le More w All Hallows) (St Leonard) *Ox 18* **P** *Bp* **TR** D RICE, **TV** G CHATFIELD, **Hon C** J K SPENCE, A F CHATFIELD
WALLINGTON (Holy Trinity) (St Patrick) *S'wark 25* **P** *Ch Soc Trust* **V** S D COE, **C** M C BREADMORE
WALLINGTON (Springfield Church) Extra-Parochial Place *S'wark 25* **Min** W COOKSON
WALLINGTON (St Mary) *see* Sandon, Wallington and Rushden w Clothall *St Alb*
WALLINGTON (St Michael and All Angels) *see* S Beddington St Mich *S'wark*
WALLINGTON (St Paul) *see* Roundshaw St Paul CD *S'wark*
WALLISDOWN (St Saviour) *see* Talbot Village *Sarum*
WALLOP, NETHER (St Andrew) *see* Over Wallop w Nether Wallop *Win*
WALLOP, OVER (St Peter) w Nether Wallop *Win 3* **P** *D&C York and Earl of Portsm (alt)* **P-in-c** F P MATTHEWS
WALLSEND (St John the Evangelist) *Newc 8* **P** *Bp* **P-in-c** C R BATES
WALLSEND (St Peter) (St Luke) *Newc 8* **P** *Bp* **R** M C VINE
WALMER (St Mary) (St Saviour) (Blessed Virgin Mary) *Cant 8* **P** *Abp* **V** *vacant* (01304) 374645
WALMERSLEY (Christ Church) *Man 10* **P** *Trustees* **NSM** D ALTHAM
WALMGATE (St Denys) *see* York St Denys *York*
WALMLEY (St John the Evangelist) *Birm 12* **P** *Trustess* **V** S P CORBETT, **C** M J HAMMOND
WALMSLEY (Christ Church) *see* Turton Moorland Min *Man*
WALNEY ISLAND (St Mary the Virgin) *Carl 8* **P** *V Dalton-in-Furness* **V** J D HODGKINSON, **C** M PEAT

WALPOLE (St Mary the Virgin) *see* Blyth Valley *St E*
WALPOLE ST PETER (St Peter and St Paul) w Walpole St Andrew *Ely 15* **P** *The Crown and DBP (alt)* **P-in-c** M CHESHER
WALSALL (Annunciation of Our Lady) *see* Walsall St Gabr Fulbrook *Lich*
WALSALL (St Andrew) *Lich 25* **P** *Bp* **P-in-c** M LIDDELL
WALSALL (St Gabriel) Fulbrook *Lich 25* **P** *Bp* **V** T R H COYNE, **NSM** W H POULTNEY
WALSALL (St Matthew) (St Luke) (St Martin) *Lich 25* **P** *Patr Bd* **TR** C T GIBSON, **TV** A P L SMITH, M C IRELAND, **C** D N ASH, B N WHITMORE, P J WILCOX, **NSM** D N H STOKES-HARRISON, F M TYSON, L F SAMUEL
WALSALL (St Michael and All Angels) *see* Caldmore w Palfrey *Lich*
WALSALL St Paul *Lich 25* **P** *R Walsall* **P-in-c** P J WILCOX, **C** J NIGHTINGALE, A P L SMITH, C T GIBSON, B N WHITMORE, **NSM** R W JORDAN, P J W LEES, F M TYSON
WALSALL (St Peter) *Lich 25* **P** *R Walsall* **V** S R KIRBY
WALSALL THE PLECK (St John) and Bescot *Lich 25* **P** *V Walsall* **V** B N WHITMORE, **C** P SHEPHERD, A P L SMITH, C T GIBSON, P J WILCOX, **NSM** F M TYSON
WALSALL WOOD (St John) (St Mark) *Lich 25* **P** *R Walsall* **V** N J CARTER, **C** J C HILL, **NSM** C SILVESTER
WALSDEN (St Peter) *see* Cornholme and Walsden *Wakef*
WALSGRAVE ON SOWE (St Mary) *Cov 1* **P** *Ld Chan* **V** M TYLER, **NSM** F E TYLER
WALSHAM, NORTH (St Nicholas) w Antingham *Nor 12* **P** *Bp* **V** S D EARIS, **C** M P DENT, **NSM** V A WATTS, **OLM** N J M PATERSON
WALSHAM, SOUTH (St Mary) *see* Ranworth w Panxworth, Woodbastwick etc *Nor*
WALSHAM LE WILLOWS (St Mary) *see* Badwell and Walsham *St E*
WALSHAW (Christ Church) *Man 10* **P** *Simeon's Trustees* **V** S FOSTER, **OLM** I J HALSALL
WALSINGHAM (St Mary and All Saints) (St Peter), Houghton and Barsham *Nor 15* **P** *J Gurney Esq and Capt J D A Keith (jt)* **V** N BANKS
WALSOKEN (All Saints) *Ely 15* **P** *DBP* **R** A R LANDALL
WALTERSTONE (St Mary) *see* Ewyas Harold w Dulas, Kenderchurch etc *Heref*
WALTHAM (All Saints) *Linc 10* **P** *The Crown* **R** I R SHELTON
WALTHAM (Holy Cross) *Chelmsf 25* **P** *Patr Bd* **TR** M D WEBSTER, **TV** J PEARCE, J M SMITH, **C** S M DAY, **NSM** T I SCOTT, D E CROOK
WALTHAM (St Bartholomew) *see* Petham and Waltham w Lower Hardres etc *Cant*
WALTHAM, GREAT (St Mary and St Lawrence) w Ford End *Chelmsf 8* **P** *Trin Coll Ox* **NSM** P PENNELL
WALTHAM, LITTLE (St Martin) *see* Gt and Lt Leighs and Lt Waltham *Chelmsf*
WALTHAM, NEW (St Matthew) *Linc 10* **P** *The Crown* **V** M E THORNE
WALTHAM, NORTH (St Michael) and Steventon, Ashe and Deane *Win 6* **P** *DBP* **R** M S KENNING, **NSM** C S READER
WALTHAM ABBEY (Holy Cross) *see* Waltham H Cross *Chelmsf*
WALTHAM CROSS (Christ Church) *St Alb 20* **P** *V Cheshunt* **V** *vacant* (01992) 633243
WALTHAM ON THE WOLDS (St Mary Magdalene) *see* Scalford w Wycombe and Chadwell etc *Leic*
WALTHAM ST LAWRENCE (St Lawrence) *Ox 13* **P** *Lord Braybrooke* **NSM** R E NUNN
WALTHAMSTOW (St Andrew) *Chelmsf 5* **P** *Bp* **V** M R J LAND
WALTHAMSTOW (St Barnabas and St James the Great) *Chelmsf 5* **P** *Bp* **V** A D COUCHMAN
WALTHAMSTOW (St Gabriel) (St Luke) (St Mary) (St Stephen) *Chelmsf 5* **P** *Patr Bd* **TV** N J ANSTEY, A M KENNEDY, **C** D J WELCH, A D CANT
WALTHAMSTOW (St John) *Chelmsf 5* **P** *TR Walthamstow* **V** A J BISHOP
WALTHAMSTOW (St Michael and All Angels) *Chelmsf 5* **P** *Bp* **V** J C RAVENSDALE
WALTHAMSTOW (St Peter-in-the-Forest) *Chelmsf 5* **P** *Bp* **V** S M P SAXBY, **Hon C** E C M K JONES, **NSM** W S ROBINS
WALTHAMSTOW (St Saviour) *Chelmsf 5* **P** *Bp* **V** D A WALLER, **C** S HEWITT-HORSMAN
WALTON (Holy Trinity) *see* Street w Walton *B & W*
WALTON (Holy Trinity) *Ox 21* **P** *Patr Bd and DBP (jt)* **TV** L P R MEERING, D A LAWTON, **P-in-c** A K E BLYTH, **C** W E GILL
WALTON Milton Keynes *Ox 25* **P** *Patr Bd* **TR** D LUNN, **TV** S JACKSON
WALTON (not known) *see* Gilmorton, Peatling Parva, Kimcote etc *Leic*
WALTON (St John) *see* Brampton St Thos *Derby*
WALTON (St John) *Derby 5* **P** *Bp* **V** A C BROOM, **C** L SHEMILT
WALTON (St John the Evangelist) *Ches 4* **P** *P G Greenall Esq* **P-in-c** J E HARRIES
WALTON (St Mary) *see* Lanercost, Walton, Gilsland and Nether Denton *Carl*
WALTON (St Mary) (St Philip) and Trimley *St E 2* **P** *Patr Bd (2 turns), Ld Chan (1 turn)* **TR** R G CORKE, **TV** T R J WELLS, P R GARBETT, **C** P S HARRIS, **OLM** I W BARLEY, A C BARLEY
WALTON (St Paul) *see* Sandal St Helen *Wakef*
WALTON (St Peter) *see* Thorp Arch w Walton *York*
WALTON (St Thomas) *see* Baswich *Lich*
WALTON, EAST (St Mary) *see* Gayton, Gayton Thorpe, E Walton, E Winch etc *Nor*
WALTON, HIGHER (All Saints) *Blackb 5* **P** *V Blackb* **V** S J HUNT
WALTON, WEST (St Mary) *Ely 15* **P** *Ld Chan* **P-in-c** M CHESHER
WALTON BRECK (Christ Church) (Holy Trinity) *Liv 3* **P** *Simeon's Trustees* **V** E J FLEMING, **NSM** A D STOTT
WALTON CLEVEDON (St Mary) *see* E Clevedon w Clapton in Gordano etc *B & W*
WALTON D'EIVILLE (St James) *Cov 8* **P** *Sir Richard Hamilton Bt* **P-in-c** C E MIER
WALTON IN GORDANO (St Paul) *see* E Clevedon w Clapton in Gordano etc *B & W*
WALTON-LE-DALE (St Leonard) w Samlesbury St Leonard the Less *Blackb 5* **P** *V Blackb St Mary and St Paul* **V** R MCCULLOUGH
WALTON LE SOKEN (All Saints) (St George) *Chelmsf 23* **P** *Bp* **V** S SANDERSON
WALTON LE WOLDS (St Mary) *see* Barrow upon Soar w Walton le Wolds *Leic*
WALTON-ON-THAMES (St Mary) *Guildf 8* **P** *Bp* **OLM** G L HORREX, L K KAYE-BESLEY
WALTON ON THE HILL (St John) *Liv 7* **P** *Bp, Adn, and R Walton (jt)* **V** S L WILLIAMS
WALTON ON THE HILL (St Luke) *Liv 7* **P** *Bp* **V** H E ROSS
WALTON-ON-THE-HILL (St Mary) (St Aidan) *Liv 5* **P** *Bp* **TR** T M LATHAM, **TV** J FLETCHER, T H ALLEN
WALTON-ON-THE-HILL (St Peter) *Guildf 9* **P** *Bp* **P-in-c** M E MARSH
WALTON-ON-TRENT (St Lawrence) w Croxall, Rosliston w Linton and Castle Gresley *Derby 16* **P** *Bp and R D Nielson Esq (jt)* **R** L A DE POMERAI, **NSM** D I M DE POMERAI
WALTON STREET (St Saviour) *see* Upper Chelsea *Lon*
WALWORTH (St Christopher) *S'wark 10* **P** *Bp and Pemb Coll Miss* **V** M WILLIAMS
WALWORTH (St John w the Lady Margaret) *S'wark 10* **P** *Bp* **V** J F WALKER, **C** D J LAMBERT
WALWORTH (St Peter) *S'wark 10* **P** *Bp* **TR** G W GODDARD, **NSM** I G THOMPSON, **OLM** A J WILD, S L SAUNDERS
WAMBROOK (Blessed Virgin Mary) *see* Combe St Nicholas w Wambrook *B & W*
WANBOROUGH (St Andrew) *see* Lyddington and Wanborough and Bishopstone etc *Bris*
WANBOROUGH (St Bartholomew) *see* Seale, Puttenham and Wanborough *Guildf*
WANDSWORTH (All Saints) (Holy Trinity) *S'wark 20* **P** *Ch Soc Trust* **P-in-c** G S PRIOR, **C** A V CINNAMOND
WANDSWORTH (St Anne) *S'wark 20* **P** *Bp* **V** G P JEANES
WANDSWORTH (St Faith) *S'wark 20* **P** *Bp* **P-in-c** G P JEANES
WANDSWORTH (St Michael and All Angels) Southfields *S'wark 20* **P** *Ch Soc Trust* **P-in-c** S MELLUISH, **NSM** R J COLLINS, N OSBORNE, **OLM** P A KURK
WANDSWORTH (St Paul) Wimbledon Park *S'wark 20* **P** *Bp* **V** H D TOLLER, **Hon C** E M TOLLER, **NSM** A J TOWNSEND
WANDSWORTH (St Stephen) *S'wark 20* **P** *CPAS* **V** S MELLUISH, **C** D P J MELDRUM, **NSM** R J COLLINS, **OLM** P A KURK
WANDSWORTH COMMON (St Mary Magdalene) *S'wark 19* **P** *Bp* **V** K PARKES, **NSM** C WILES
WANDSWORTH COMMON (St Michael) *see* Battersea St Mich *S'wark*
WANGFORD (St Peter) *see* Sole Bay *St E*
WANLIP (Our Lady and St Nicholas) *see* Birstall and Wanlip *Leic*
WANSFORD (St Mary) *see* Nafferton w Wansford *York*
WANSFORD (St Mary the Virgin) *see* Thornhaugh and Wansford *Pet*

WANSTEAD (Holy Trinity) Hermon Hill *Chelmsf 4* **P** *Bp* **V** R E HAMPSON
WANSTEAD (St Mary) (Christ Church) *Chelmsf 4* **P** *Bp* **R** R W SPRINGETT, **C** P R THOMAS
WANSTROW (Blessed Virgin Mary) *see* Nunney and Witham Friary, Marston Bigot etc *B & W*
WANTAGE (St Peter and St Paul) *Ox 19* **P** *D&C Windsor* **V** J L SALTER, **C** N J CHEESEMAN
WANTAGE DOWNS *Ox 19* **P** *Bp, CCC Ox, and C L Loyd Esq (jt)* **R** R E BALL, **NSM** D J PAGE
WANTISDEN (St John the Baptist) *see* Wilford Peninsula *St E*
WANTSUM GROUP *see* St Nicholas at Wade w Sarre and Chislet w Hoath *Cant*
WAPLEY (St Peter) *see* Yate New Town *Bris*
WAPPENBURY (St John the Baptist) w Weston under Wetherley *Cov 10* **P** *Bp* **P-in-c** J T H BRITTON, **C** D R PATTERSON
WAPPENHAM (St Mary the Virgin) *see* Astwell Gp *Pet*
WARBLETON (St Mary) and Bodle Street Green *Chich 15* **P** *Revd E S Haviland* **P-in-c** R J R PAICE
WARBLINGTON (St Thomas à Becket) w Emsworth *Portsm 5* **P** *Bp and J H Norris Esq (alt)* **R** S P SAYERS, **C** T P KENNAR
WARBOROUGH (St Lawrence) *Ox 1* **P** *CCC Ox* **V** S E BOOYS
WARBOYS (St Mary Magdelene) w Broughton and Bury w Wistow *Ely 9* **P** *Bp and Ch Soc Trust (jt)* **R** P R DOWMAN, **C** S P KINDER, **NSM** D J KINDER
WARBSTOW (St Werburgh) *see* St Gennys, Jacobstow w Warbstow and Treneglos *Truro*
WARBURTON (St Werburgh) *Ches 10* **P** *Hon M L W Flower* **P-in-c** E M BURGESS
WARCOP (St Columba) *see* Brough w Stainmore, Musgrave and Warcop *Carl*
WARD END (Christ Church) *see* Burney Lane *Birm*
WARD END (St Margaret) *Birm 13* **P** *Aston Trustees* **V** *vacant* 0121-327 0555
WARDEN (St Michael and All Angels) w Newbrough *Newc 4* **P** *Bp* **V** R C CUTLER, **NSM** A R CURRIE
WARDEN, OLD (St Leonard) *see* Caldecote, Northill and Old Warden *St Alb*
WARDINGTON (St Mary Magdalene) *see* Shires' Edge *Ox*
WARDLEWORTH (St Mary w St James) *see* Rochdale *Man*
WARDLEY (All Saints) *see* Swinton and Pendlebury *Man*
WARDLEY (St Botolph) *see* Uppingham w Ayston and Wardley w Belton *Pet*
WARDLOW (Good Shepherd) *see* Ashford w Sheldon and Longstone *Derby*
WARE (Christ Church) *St Alb 22* **P** *CPAS* **V** D J PROUD, **C** N PLEDGER
WARE (St Mary the Virgin) *St Alb 22* **P** *Trin Coll Cam* **V** D PEEL, **NSM** M S E M BEAZLEY, P A VOSS
WAREHAM (Lady St Mary) (St Martin) *Sarum 8* **P** *Patr Bd* **TR** W G BLAKEY, **TV** P S SIMESTER, **C** H K JAMESON
WAREHORNE (St Matthew) *see* Orlestone w Snave and Ruckinge w Warehorne etc *Cant*
WARESIDE (Holy Trinity) *see* Hunsdon w Widford and Wareside *St Alb*
WARESLEY (St James) *see* Gt Gransden and Abbotsley and Lt Gransden etc *Ely*
WARFIELD (St Michael the Archangel) *Ox 11* **P** *DBP* **V** B H MEARDON, **C** B H BEECROFT, **Hon C** B J WEAVER, **NSM** C M BEECROFT
WARGRAVE (St Mary the Virgin) w Knowl Hill *Ox 16* **P** *Lord Remnant* **V** J W RATINGS, **NSM** P A GORDON, D J THOMAS
WARHAM (All Saints) *see* Holkham w Egmere w Warham, Wells and Wighton *Nor*
WARK (St Michael) *see* Humshaugh w Simonburn and Wark *Newc*
WARKLEIGH (St John) *see* S Molton w Nymet St George, High Bray etc *Ex*
WARKTON (St Edmund King and Martyr) *see* Barton Seagrave w Warkton *Pet*
WARKWORTH (St Lawrence) and Acklington *Newc 9* **P** *Bp and Duke of Northd (alt)* **V** J M BREARLEY
WARKWORTH (St Mary the Virgin) *see* Chenderit *Pet*
WARLEGGAN (St Bartholomew) *see* St Neot and Warleggan w Cardynham *Truro*
WARLEY (Christ Church) and Gt Warley St Mary *Chelmsf 7* **P** *Bp and Hon G C D Jeffreys (jt)* **V** C D GOLDSMITH
WARLEY (St John the Evangelist) *Wakef 4* **P** *V Halifax* **V** A J STREET, **NSM** J S BRADBERRY
WARLEY, GREAT (St Mary the Virgin) *see* Warley Ch Ch and Gt Warley St Mary *Chelmsf*
WARLEY, LITTLE (St Peter) *see* E and W Horndon w Lt Warley and Childerditch *Chelmsf*
WARLEY WOODS (St Hilda) *Birm 7* **P** *Bp* **V** M R DUNK
WARLINGHAM (All Saints) w Chelsham and Farleigh *S'wark 25* **P** *Patr Bd* **TR** A D MIDDLETON, **TV** A E HEFFERNAN, **Hon C** J H STEVENS
WARMFIELD (St Peter) *Wakef 9* **P** *Oley Trustees Clare Coll Cam* **P-in-c** L J COLLYER
WARMINGHAM (St Leonard) *see* Elworth and Warmingham *Ches*
WARMINGTON (St Mary the Blessed Virgin), Tansor and Cotterstock and Fotheringhay and Southwick *Pet 12* **P** *Bp and D&C Linc (alt)* **V** B V ROGERS
WARMINGTON (St Michael) w Shotteswell and Radway w Ratley *Cov 8* **P** *Bp* **R** C A LAMB
WARMINSTER (Christ Church) *Sarum 17* **P** *R Warminster St Denys etc* **P-in-c** P W HUNTER, **C** T SMITH, **OLM** L A S MATHEW
WARMINSTER (St Denys) *see* Cley Hill Warminster *Sarum*
WARMLEY (St Barnabas), Syston and Bitton *Bris 5* **P** *Bp* **R** P H DENYER, **C** S R WILLIAMS, **Hon C** J E NORMAN, **NSM** C A COSTER
WARMSWORTH (St Peter) *Sheff 9* **P** *Bp* **R** S F BOND
WARMWELL (Holy Trinity) *see* Watercombe *Sarum*
WARNBOROUGH, SOUTH (St Andrew) *see* Herriard w Winslade and Long Sutton etc *Win*
WARNDON (St Nicholas) *Worc 6* **P** *Bp* **P-in-c** D P RYAN
WARNDON (St Wulstan) *see* Worc St Wulstan *Worc*
WARNERS END (St Alban) *see* Hemel Hempstead *St Alb*
WARNFORD (Our Lady) *see* W Meon and Warnford *Portsm*
WARNHAM (St Margaret) *Chich 8* **P** *J C Lucas Esq* **V** C H LOVELESS
WARNINGLID (St Andrew) *see* Slaugham *Chich*
WARREN PARK (St Clare) *Portsm 5* **P** *Bp* **V** J G P JEFFERY, **C** J M B HONNOR, **NSM** M S HARPER
WARREN ROW (St Paul) *see* Wargrave w Knowl Hill *Ox*
WARRINGTON (Holy Trinity) *Liv 12* **P** *R Warrington* **V** I D ELLIOTT
WARRINGTON (St Ann) *see* Warrington St Ann *Liv*
WARRINGTON (St Ann) *Liv 12* **P** *Simeon's Trustees* **V** S R PARISH, **OLM** P LOVATT, M M MCDONNELL, J M WEAVER
WARRINGTON (St Barnabas) Bank Quay *Liv 12* **P** *R Warrington and Bp (jt)* **V** K L F TIMMIS
WARRINGTON (St Elphin) (St John) *Liv 12* **P** *Lord Lilford* **R** M S FINLAY, **C** C N PERRINS
WARSLOW (St Lawrence) *see* Alstonfield, Butterton, Ilam etc *Lich*
WARSOP (St Peter and St Paul) *S'well 2* **P** *Trustees* **R** K HERROD, **C** M J CANTRILL
WARTER (St James) *see* Nunburnholme and Warter and Huggate *York*
WARTHILL (St Mary) *see* Stockton-on-the-Forest w Holtby and Warthill *York*
WARTLING (St Mary Magdalene) *see* Herstmonceux and Wartling *Chich*
WARTNABY (St Michael) *see* Old Dalby, Nether Broughton, Saxelbye etc *Leic*
WARTON (Holy Trinity) *see* Austrey and Warton *Birm*
WARTON (St Oswald or Holy Trinity) w Yealand Conyers *Blackb 14* **P** *Bp* **V** J M HALL
WARTON (St Paul) *Blackb 10* **P** *Ch Ch Ox* **V** P FORD
WARWICK (St Leonard) *see* Holme Eden and Wetheral w Warwick *Carl*
WARWICK Team, The New (St Mary) (St Nicholas) (St Paul) *Cov 11* **P** *Ld Chan and Patr Bd (alt)* **TR** V S ROBERTS, **TV** R C GARRATT, A W J FITZMAURICE, J HEARN
WARWICK SQUARE (St Gabriel) *see* Pimlico St Gabr *Lon*
WASDALE, NETHER (St Michael) *see* Gosforth w Nether Wasdale and Wasdale Head *Carl*
WASDALE HEAD (not known) *as above*
WASH COMMON (St George) *see* Newbury *Ox*
WASHBOURNE, GREAT (St Mary) *see* Winchcombe *Glouc*
WASHFIELD (St Mary the Virgin), Stoodleigh, Withleigh, Calverleigh, Oakford, Templeton, Loxbeare, Rackenford, and Cruwys Morchard *Ex 8* **P** *Patr Bd* **TV** G B BELL, **C** B P LUCK, **NSM** J C W ROBERTS
WASHFORD (St Mary) *see* Old Cleeve, Leighland and Treborough *B & W*
WASHFORD PYNE (St Peter) *see* N Creedy *Ex*
WASHINGBOROUGH (St John) w Heighington and Canwick *Linc 18* **P** *DBP and Mercers' Co (jt)* **R** S JONES-CRABTREE
WASHINGTON (Holy Trinity) *Dur 11* **P** *Bp* **C** D J BELL
WASHINGTON (St Mary) *see* Ashington, Washington and Wiston w Buncton *Chich*
WASHWOOD HEATH (St Mark) *Birm 13* **P** *V Saltley* **P-in-c** A H TOWNSEND
WASING (St Nicholas) *see* Aldermaston w Wasing and Brimpton *Ox*

WASKERLEY (St Andrew) *see* Blanchland w Hunstanworth and Edmundbyers etc *Newc*
WASPERTON (St John the Baptist) *see* Barford w Wasperton and Sherbourne *Cov*
WASS (St Thomas) *see* Coxwold and Husthwaite *York*
WATCHET (Holy Cross Chapel) *see* St Decumans *B & W*
WATCHET (St Decuman) *as above*
WATCHFIELD (St Thomas's Chapel) *see* Shrivenham and Ashbury *Ox*
WATER EATON (St Frideswide) *Ox 25* **P** *Bp* **P-in-c** A J MARRIOTT
WATER NEWTON (St Remigius) *see* Elton w Stibbington and Water Newton *Ely*
WATER ORTON (St Peter and St Paul) *Birm 9* **P** *Patr Bd* **V** S T MAYES, **NSM** M S WALTON
WATER STRATFORD (St Giles) *see* W Buckingham *Ox*
WATERBEACH (St John) *Ely 5* **P** *Bp* **V** N I MOIR, **NSM** P M THORN
WATERCOMBE *Sarum 1* **P** *M Cree Esq (1 turn), MMCET (2 turns), and Sir Robert Williams Bt (1 turn)* **R** J M COATES, **C** M R B DURRANT
WATERDEN (All Saints) *see* N and S Creake w Waterden, Syderstone etc *Nor*
WATERFALL (St James and St Bartholomew) *see* Calton, Cauldon, Grindon, Waterfall etc *Lich*
WATERFOOT (St James the Great) *Man 15* **P** *Trustees* **V** *vacant*
WATERFORD (St Michael and All Angels) *see* Bramfield, Stapleford, Waterford etc *St Alb*
WATERHEAD (Holy Trinity) *Man 21* **P** *The Crown* **C** D R PENNY
WATERHOUSES (St Paul) *Dur 1* **P** *R Brancepeth Esq* **V** M J PEERS, **C** T E HUBBLE
WATERINGBURY (St John the Baptist) and Teston *Roch 7* **P** *D&C and Peache Trustees (jt)* **P-in-c** J D BROWN
WATERLOO (Christ Church) (St John) *Liv 1* **P** *Trustees and Simeon's Trustees (jt)* **V** G J CUFF, **NSM** D A MCDOUGALL, **OLM** A L BROOKS
WATERLOO (St John the Evangelist) (St Andrew) *S'wark 13* **P** *Abp and CPAS (jt)* **V** C R TRUSS, **C** J L KUSTNER, **NSM** A M WARNER, **OLM** D PAPE, G S N KAZIRO
WATERLOO PARK (St Mary the Virgin) *see* Gt Crosby St Faith and Waterloo Park St Mary *Liv*
WATERLOOVILLE (St George the Martyr) *Portsm 5* **P** *Bp* **V** M J SHEFFIELD
WATERMILLOCK (All Saints) *see* Gd Shep TM *Carl*
WATERMOOR (Holy Trinity) *see* Cirencester *Glouc*
WATERPERRY (St Mary the Virgin) *see* Wheatley *Ox*
WATERS UPTON (St Michael) *see* Tibberton w Bolas Magna and Waters Upton *Lich*
WATERSIDE PARISHES of Hambleton, Out Rawcliffe and Preesall *Blackb 9* **P** *Bp, V Kirkham, and V Garstang St Helen etc (jt)* **V** S B GREY, **OLM** D BANKS
WATERSTOCK (St Leonard) *see* Wheatley *Ox*
WATERTHORPE (Emmanuel) *see* Mosbrough *Sheff*
WATFORD (Christ Church) (St Mark) *St Alb 7* **P** *Bp, V Watford, and Churchwardens (jt)* **V** R C LEWIS, **C** A J HARTROPP, **NSM** A G HOGG
WATFORD (St Andrew) *St Alb 7* **P** *Bp and Churchwardens (jt)* **V** G R WARREN, **NSM** S M TALBOTT
WATFORD (St John) *St Alb 7* **P** *Bp* **V** J B A COPE
WATFORD St Luke *St Alb 7* **P** *Bp, Adn St Alb, V Watford, and Ch Trust Fund Trust (jt)* **V** J KIDDLE, **C** P J STEVENSON, **NSM** I C PANKHURST
WATFORD (St Mary) *St Alb 7* **P** *Ch Trust Fund Trust* **V** J A ALDIS, **C** W D HUNTER SMART, J C JOBLING
WATFORD (St Michael and All Angels) *St Alb 7* **P** *Bp* **V** J B BROWN, **C** E C MACFARLANE
WATFORD (St Peter) *St Alb 7* **P** *Bp* **V** C P COTTEE, **C** R W YULE, **NSM** A D T GORTON
WATFORD (St Peter and St Paul) *see* Long Buckby w Watford *Pet*
WATH (St Mary) *see* Kirklington w Burneston and Wath and Pickhill *Ripon*
WATH BROW (Mission Church) *see* Crosslacon *Carl*
WATH-UPON-DEARNE (All Saints) *Sheff 12* **P** *Ch Ch Ox* **V** T E LEACH
WATLING VALLEY, Milton Keynes (not known) *Ox 25* **P** *Patr Bd* **TV** M J MORRIS, T NORWOOD, **C** P HARDY
WATLINGTON (St Leonard) *see* Icknield *Ox*
WATLINGTON (St Peter and St Paul) *Ely 13* **P** *Bp* **R** J C W NOLAN
WATTISFIELD (St Margaret) *see* Hepworth, Hinderclay, Wattisfield and Thelnetham *St E*
WATTLESBOROUGH (St Margaret) *see* Alberbury w Cardeston *Heref*
WATTON (St Mary) *see* Hutton Cranswick w Skerne, Watton and Beswick *York*
WATTON (St Mary) w Carbrooke and Ovington *Nor 13* **P** *Ld Chan (3 turns), Cam Univ (1 turn), and SMF (2 turns)* **P-in-c** M J TALBOT, **OLM** T B C WESTON
WATTON AT STONE (St Mary and St Andrew) *see* Bramfield, Stapleford, Waterford etc *St Alb*
WAVENDON (Assumption of the Blessed Virgin Mary) *see* Walton Milton Keynes *Ox*
WAVERTON (Christ Church) *see* Solway Plain *Carl*
WAVERTON (St Peter) *Ches 5* **P** *Bp* **P-in-c** D WILSON
WAVERTREE (Holy Trinity) *Liv 6* **P** *Bp* **R** J EASTWOOD, **NSM** L B BRUCE, J PHILLIPS
WAVERTREE (St Bridget) (St Thomas) *Liv 6* **P** *Simeon's Trustees and R Wavertree H Trin (jt)* **V** W J SANDERS
WAVERTREE (St Mary) *Liv 6* **P** *Bp* **R** J M MATTHEWS
WAWNE (St Peter) *see* Sutton St Jas and Wawne *York*
WAXHAM, GREAT (St John) *see* Happisburgh, Walcott, Hempstead w Eccles etc *Nor*
WAYFORD (St Michael and All Angels) *see* Crewkerne w Wayford *B & W*
WAYLAND Group, The *see* Caston, Griston, Merton, Thompson etc *Nor*
WEALD (St George) *see* Sevenoaks Weald *Roch*
WEALD, NORTH Bassett (St Andrew) *Chelmsf 27* **P** *Bp* **V** T C THORPE
WEALD, SOUTH (St Peter) *Chelmsf 7* **P** *Bp* **V** I H JORYSZ, **NSM** M K SEAMAN
WEALDSTONE (Holy Trinity) *Lon 23* **P** *Bp* **V** T M MALONEY, **NSM** F E MALONEY, P J WRIGHT
WEAR (St Luke) *see* Countess Wear *Ex*
WEARDALE, UPPER *Dur 9* **P** *Bp (5 turns), Duchy of Lancaster (1 turn), and Ld Chan (1 turn)* **R** P A GREENHALGH, **C** R P C BROWN
WEARE (St Gregory) *see* Crook Peak *B & W*
WEARE GIFFARD (Holy Trinity) *see* Bideford, Northam, Westward Ho!, Appledore etc *Ex*
WEARSIDE, NORTH *Dur 16* **P** *Patr Bd* **TR** G DRIVER, **TV** J W POULTER, **NSM** D RAINE
WEASENHAM (All Saints) *see* Gt w Lt Massingham, Harpley, Rougham etc *Nor*
WEASENHAM (St Peter) *as above*
WEASTE (St Luke w All Saints) *Man 6* **P** *Bp and V Eccles (jt)* **V** K M ARCHER
WEAVERHAM (St Mary the Virgin) *Ches 6* **P** *Bp* **V** *vacant* (01606) 852110
WEAVERTHORPE (St Andrew) w Helperthorpe, Luttons Ambo and Kirby Grindalythe w Wharram *York 6* **P** *Abp and D&C (jt)* **P-in-c** C J HAYES, **NSM** D F BAYLEY
WEBHEATH (St Philip) *see* Redditch H Trin *Worc*
WEDDINGTON (St James) and Caldecote *Cov 5* **P** *Bp* **C** B J JACQUES
WEDMORE (St Mary) w Theale and Blackford *B & W 1* **P** *Bp* **V** E M CROSS, **NSM** G E C FENTON
WEDNESBURY (St Bartholomew) *Lich 26* **P** *Bp* **V** M S BRIDGEN
WEDNESBURY (St James and St John) *Lich 26* **P** *Trustees* **R** K A PALMER, **NSM** R C GILBERT
WEDNESBURY (St Paul) Wood Green *Lich 26* **P** *Bp* **V** G WARREN
WEDNESFIELD (St Gregory) *Lich 28* **P** *Bp* **V** *vacant* (01902) 731677
WEDNESFIELD (St Thomas) (St Augustine and St Chad) (St Alban) *Lich 28* **P** *Patr Bd* **TR** J D POINTS, **TV** H L DUCKETT, **C** G W WARD, **NSM** P CARDWELL, J FORD
WEDNESFIELD HEATH (Holy Trinity) *Lich 28* **P** *CPAS* **V** D A VESTERGAARD
WEEDON (School Chapel) *see* Schorne *Ox*
WEEDON BEC (St Peter and St Paul) w Everdon and Dodford *Pet 3* **P** *Bp* **V** H E RAYMENT
WEEDON LOIS (St Mary and St Peter) *see* Astwell Gp *Pet*
WEEFORD (St Mary the Virgin) *see* Whittington w Weeford *Lich*
WEEK ST MARY (St Mary the Virgin) w Poundstock and Whitstone *Truro 8* **P** *SS Coll Cam, Walsingham Coll, and Guild of All So (jt)* **P-in-c** R C W DICKENSON, **C** G A DOUGLAS
WEEKE *see* Win St Matt *Win*
WEEKLEY (St Mary the Virgin) *see* Geddington w Weekley *Pet*
WEELEY (St Andrew) and Little Clacton *Chelmsf 23* **P** *Bp and BNC Ox (alt)* **R** D M NEWMAN
WEETHLEY (St James) *see* Alcester and Arrow w Oversley and Weethley *Cov*
WEETING (St Mary) *Ely 13* **P** *G&C Coll Cam* **R** S BETSON

WEETON (St Barnabas) *see* Lower Wharfedale *Ripon*
WEETON (St Michael) *see* Ribby cum Wrea and Weeton *Blackb*
WEETSLADE (St Paul) *Newc 1* **P** *Bp* **V** A MAUGHAN
WELBORNE (All Saints) *see* Mattishall w Mattishall Burgh, Welborne etc *Nor*
WELBOURN (St Chad) *Linc 23* **P** *Hyndman Trustees* **R** A J MEGAHEY
WELBURN (St John the Evangelist) *see* Howardian Gp *York*
WELBURY (St Leonard) *see* Rounton w Welbury *York*
WELBY (not known) *see* Melton Mowbray *Leic*
WELBY (St Bartholemew) *see* Ancaster Wilsford Gp *Linc*
WELCOMBE (St Nectan) *see* Parkham, Alwington, Buckland Brewer etc *Ex*
WELDON (St Mary the Virgin) w Deene *Pet 9* **P** *DBP and E Brudenell Esq (jt)* **P-in-c** J M COLLINS
WELFORD (St Gregory) w Wickham and Great Shefford, Boxford and Stockcross *Ox 14* **P** *Bp and BNC Ox (jt)* **R** N C SANDS
WELFORD (St Mary the Virgin) w Sibbertoft and Marston Trussell *Pet 2* **P** *Bp* **V** *vacant* (01858) 575252
WELFORD (St Peter) *see* Quinton and Welford w Weston *Glouc*
WELHAM (St Andrew) *see* Gt Bowden w Welham, Glooston and Cranoe etc *Leic*
WELL (St Margaret) *Linc 8* **P** *Bp* **R** R H IRESON
WELL (St Michael) *see* W Tanfield and Well w Snape and N Stainley *Ripon*
WELL HILL (Mission) *see* Chelsfield *Roch*
WELLAND (St James) *see* Hanley Castle, Hanley Swan and Welland *Worc*
WELLESBOURNE (St Peter) *Cov 8* **P** *Ld Chan* **P-in-c** C E MIER
WELLING (St John the Evangelist) *Roch 15* **P** *Bp* **V** A J D FOOT, **C** M R F SAUNDERS
WELLING (St Mary the Virgin) *S'wark 3* **P** *Bp* **V** L C GALE
WELLINGBOROUGH (All Hallows) *Pet 6* **P** *Exors Major E C S Byng-Maddick* **V** A READER-MOORE, **C** J D NAUDE
WELLINGBOROUGH (All Saints) *Pet 6* **P** *V Wellingborough* **V** A M LYNETT, **C** M R BASS
WELLINGBOROUGH (St Andrew) *Pet 6* **P** *Bp* **V** C M UPTON
WELLINGBOROUGH (St Barnabas) *Pet 6* **P** *Bp* **V** J P LEADER
WELLINGBOROUGH (St Mark) *Pet 6* **P** *Bp* **V** A CUTHBERTSON
WELLINGBOROUGH (St Mary the Virgin) *Pet 6* **P** *Guild of All So* **V** R J T FARMER
WELLINGHAM (St Andrew) *see* Gt w Lt Massingham, Harpley, Rougham etc *Nor*
WELLINGORE (All Saints) *see* Graffoe Gp *Linc*
WELLINGTON (All Saints) (St John the Baptist) and District *B & W 19* **P** *Patr Bd* **TR** C M S RANDALL, **TV** C F E ROWLEY, **C** J M ANDERSON-MACKENZIE, C I BRIERLEY, **NSM** J M HARRISON
WELLINGTON (All Saints) w Eyton (St Catherine) *Lich 21* **P** *Ch Trust Fund Trust* **V** M E POTTER, **C** C D BOURNE, **OLM** R A KIRBY
WELLINGTON (Christ Church) *Lich 21* **P** *V Wellington w Eyton* **P-in-c** V C SWEET, **NSM** P R WALKER
WELLINGTON (St Margaret of Antioch) *see* Canon Pyon w King's Pyon, Birley and Wellington *Heref*
WELLINGTON HEATH (Christ Church) *see* Ledbury *Heref*
WELLOW (St Julian the Hospitaller) *see* Peasedown St John w Wellow *B & W*
WELLOW (St Swithun) *see* Kneesall w Laxton and Wellow *S'well*
WELLOW, EAST w WEST (St Margaret) and Sherfield English *Win 12* **P** *Bp and CPAS (jt)* **V** G R BIGGS
WELLS (St Cuthbert) w Wookey Hole *B & W 8* **P** *D&C* **V** P G P FARRELL
WELLS (St Thomas) w Horrington *B & W 8* **P** *D&C* **V** C T TOOKEY
WELLS-NEXT-THE-SEA (St Nicholas) *see* Holkham w Egmere w Warham, Wells and Wighton *Nor*
WELNEY (St Mary) *see* Christchurch and Manea and Welney *Ely*
WELSH BICKNOR (St Margaret) *see* Walford and St John w Bishopswood, Goodrich etc *Heref*
WELSH FRANKTON (St Andrew) *see* Criftins w Dudleston and Welsh Frankton *Lich*
WELSH NEWTON (St Mary the Virgin) *see* St Weonards w Orcop, Garway, Tretire etc *Heref*
WELSH NEWTON COMMON (St Faith) *as above*
WELSHAMPTON (St Michael) *see* Petton w Cockshutt, Welshampton and Lyneal etc *Lich*
WELTON (St Helen) w Melton *York 14* **P** *DBP* **P-in-c** E E BIELBY, **NSM** A A V SCHRIMSHAW
WELTON (St James) *see* Westward, Rosley-w-Woodside and Welton *Carl*
WELTON (St Martin) *see* Daventry, Ashby St Ledgers, Braunston etc *Pet*
WELTON (St Mary) and Dunholme w Scothern *Linc 3* **P** *Bp and DBP (jt)* **V** G S DARLISON, **OLM** J M JOHNSON
WELTON-LE-MARSH (St Martin) w Gunby *Linc 8* **P** *J M Montgomery-Massingberd Esq* **R** T STEELE
WELTON-LE-WOLD (St Martin) *see* Louth *Linc*
WELWICK (St Mary) *see* Patrington w Hollym, Welwick and Winestead *York*
WELWYN Team Ministry, The (St Mary the Virgin) (St Michael) *St Alb 21* **P** *Patr Bd* **NSM** A O CHRISTIAN-IWUAGWU
WELWYN GARDEN CITY (St Francis of Assisi) *St Alb 21* **P** *Bp* **V** P A LOUIS, **C** J GRAY
WEM (St Peter and St Paul) *Lich 22* **P** *Lord Barnard* **P-in-c** C S COOKE
WEMBDON (St George) *B & W 14* **P** *Ch Soc Trust* **V** J S BARKS
WEMBLEY (St Augustine) *see* Wembley Park *Lon*
WEMBLEY (St John the Evangelist) *Lon 21* **P** *Ch Patr Trust* **V** F ADU-BOACHIE
WEMBLEY, NORTH (St Cuthbert) *Lon 21* **P** *Bp* **V** F G MCDERMOTT
WEMBLEY PARK (Church of the Ascension) (St Augustine) (Annunciation) *Lon 21* **P** *Bp* **TR** M J CATTERICK, **TV** T F CRITCHLOW, H L YOUNG, **Hon C** J M WARNER
WEMBURY (St Werburgh) *Ex 21* **P** *D&C Windsor* **V** T FREEMAN
WEMBWORTHY (St Michael) *see* Burrington, Chawleigh, Cheldon, Chulmleigh etc *Ex*
WENDENS AMBO (St Mary the Virgin) *see* Saffron Walden w Wendens Ambo, Littlebury etc *Chelmsf*
WENDLEBURY (St Giles) *see* Akeman *Ox*
WENDLING (St Peter and St Paul) *see* Gressenhall w Longham w Wendling etc *Nor*
WENDOVER (St Agnes's Chapel) *see* Wendover and Halton *Ox*
WENDOVER (St Mary) *as above*
WENDOVER (St Mary) (St Agnes's Chapel) and Halton *Ox 28* **P** *Ld Chan* **R** M C DEARNLEY, **C** E L COLEY, **NSM** B J ROBERTS
WENDRON(St Wendron) *see* Helston and Wendron *Truro*
WENDY (All Saints) *see* Shingay Gp *Ely*
WENHAM, GREAT (St John) *see* Capel St Mary w Lt and Gt Wenham *St E*
WENHASTON (St Peter) *see* Blyth Valley *St E*
WENLOCK *Heref 11* **P** *Patr Bd* **TR** S A LOWE, **TV** M J SMALL
WENLOCK, LITTLE (St Lawrence) *see* Coalbrookdale, Iron-Bridge and Lt Wenlock *Heref*
WENLOCK, MUCH (Holy Trinity) *see* Wenlock *Heref*
WENNINGTON (St Mary and St Peter) *see* Rainham w Wennington *Chelmsf*
WENSLEY (Holy Trinity) *Ripon 4* **P** *Lord Bolton* **R** *vacant* (01969) 263736
WENSUM Benefice, The *Nor 22* **P** *New Coll Ox, Margaret Lady Prince-Smith, Bp, and D&C (jt)* **R** L S TILLETT
WENSUM VILLAGE Group, UPPER *Nor 15* **P** *Marquess Townshend, the Revd C S P Douglas Lane, Ch Coll Cam, and DBP (jt)* **R** P S INMAN
WENT VALLEY *Wakef 11* **P** *Bp, Earl of Rosse, and Sir Philip Naylor-Leyland Bt (jt)* **V** A T JUDD
WENTBRIDGE (St John) *see* Went Valley *Wakef*
WENTNOR (St Michael and All Angels) w Ratlinghope, Myndtown, Norbury, More, Lydham and Snead *Heref 10* **P** *Ch Ch Ox (4 turns) and J J C Coldwell Esq (1 turn)* **R** N F M MORRIS
WENTWORTH (Harley Mission Church) (Holy Trinity) *Sheff 12* **P** *Sir Philip Naylor-Leyland Bt* **V** R IMPEY
WENTWORTH (St Peter) *see* Witchford w Wentworth *Ely*
WEOBLEY (St Peter and St Paul) w Sarnesfield and Norton Canon *Heref 5* **P** *Bp (2 turns), R A Marshall Esq (1 turn)* **V** R D KING
WEOLEY CASTLE (St Gabriel) *Birm 2* **P** *Bp* **V** M D CASTLE, **NSM** H A G HOUGHTON
WEREHAM (St Margaret) *Ely 13* **P** *Bp* **V** *vacant*
WERNETH (St Paul) *Ches 16* **P** *DBP* **P-in-c** R J BROOKE, **NSM** W S ATKINSON
WERNETH (St Thomas) *Man 19* **P** *Bp* **P-in-c** F A O D DAWSON
WERRINGTON (St John the Baptist w Emmanuel) *Pet 13* **P** *Bp* **V** G H ROGERS, **C** P E MARSH

WERRINGTON (St Martin of Tours) *see* Boyton, N Tamerton, Werrington etc *Truro*
WERRINGTON (St Philip) *Lich 6* **P** *V Caverswall* **V** J L HUMPHREYS, **NSM** I T COPELAND
WESHAM (Christ Church) and Treales *Blackb 10* **P** *V Kirkham* **V** P W BENNETT
WESSINGTON (Christ Church) *see* Ashover and Brackenfield w Wessington *Derby*
WEST *see also under substantive place name*
WEST BAY (St John) *see* Bridport *Sarum*
WEST DEAN (St Andrew) *Chich 13* **P** *D&C* **V** R T E B WOODS
WEST DOWN (St Calixtus) *see* Ilfracombe SS Phil and Jas w W Down *Ex*
WEST END (Holy Trinity) *see* Bisley and W End *Guildf*
WEST END (St George) *see* Esher *Guildf*
WEST END (St James) *Win 10* **P** *Bp* **V** B L PICKETT, **C** A J TARPER, **NSM** J E PICKETT
WEST END (St John the Evangelist) *see* High Wycombe *Ox*
WEST GREEN (Christ Church w St Peter) *Lon 19* **P** *Bp* **P-in-c** R P P MARTIN
WEST GREEN (St Peter) *see* Crawley *Chich*
WEST HAM (All Saints) *Chelmsf 3* **P** *The Crown* **V** U E E J SCHARF
WEST HAM (St Matthew) *see* Forest Gate St Sav w W Ham St Matt *Chelmsf*
WEST HEATH (St Anne) *Birm 4* **P** *Bp* **P-in-c** J G TSIPOURAS
WEST HILL (St Michael the Archangel) *see* Ottery St Mary, Alfington, W Hill, Tipton etc *Ex*
WEST MOORS (St Mary the Virgin) *Sarum 9* **P** *Bp* **V** *vacant* (01202) 893197
WEST NEWTON (St Matthew) *see* Solway Plain *Carl*
WEST ORCHARD (St Luke) *see* Shaston *Sarum*
WEST ROW (St Peter) *see* Mildenhall *St E*
WEST WINCH (St Mary) w Setchey, North Runcton and Middleton *Nor 20* **P** *H N D Gurney Esq (1 turn) and Ld Chan (2 turns)* **R** J F RYAN
WESTACRE (All Saints) *see* Castleacre, Newton, Westacre and Southacre *Nor*
WESTBERE (All Saints) *see* Sturry w Fordwich and Westbere w Hersden *Cant*
WESTBOROUGH (All Saints) *see* Claypole *Linc*
WESTBOROUGH (St Clare) (St Francis) *Guildf 5* **P** *Bp* **TR** C G POTTER, **TV** J BOULTON-REYNOLDS, **NSM** S J CAVALIER
WESTBOURNE (Christ Church) Proprietary Chapel *Win 8* **Min** A D M PAINE
WESTBOURNE (St John the Baptist) *Chich 13* **P** *Bp* **R** R J WELLS
WESTBROOK (All Saints) *see* Margate All SS *Cant*
WESTBROOK (St James) Hood Manor *Liv 12* **P** *Bp, R Warrington, and V Gt Sankey (jt)* **V** S W BOYD
WESTBROOK (St Philip) Old Hall and Callands *Liv 12* **P** *Bp and R Warrington (jt)* **V** M X THORPE, **C** A KENNEDY
WESTBURY (All Saints) *see* White Horse *Sarum*
WESTBURY (St Augustine) *see* W Buckingham *Ox*
WESTBURY (St Mary) *Heref 13* **P** *Bp* **R** C B BULL
WESTBURY-ON-SEVERN (St Peter and St Paul) w Flaxley, Blaisdon and Minsterworth *Glouc 3* **P** *Bp, D&C Heref, and Sir Thomas Crawley-Boevey Bt (jt)* **V** C A EDMONDS, **NSM** S L HOBBS
WESTBURY-ON-TRYM (Holy Trinity) *Bris 2* **P** *SMF* **V** A H HART, **C** T R CRANSHAW
WESTBURY-ON-TRYM (St Alban) *Bris 2* **P** *Bp* **NSM** R Q GREATREX
WESTBURY PARK (St Alban) *see* Westbury-on-Trym St Alb *Bris*
WESTBURY SUB MENDIP (St Lawrence) w Easton *B & W 1* **P** *Bp* **V** E A MACPHERSON
WESTCLIFF (Church of Reconciliation) *see* Brumby *Linc*
WESTCLIFF (St Alban) *see* Southend *Chelmsf*
WESTCLIFF (St Andrew) *Chelmsf 13* **P** *Bp* **V** S F KIMBER
WESTCLIFF (St Cedd and the Saints of Essex) *see* Prittlewell w Westcliff *Chelmsf*
WESTCLIFF (St Michael and All Angels) *Chelmsf 13* **P** *Bp* **V** P C NICHOLSON
WESTCLIFF (St Saviour) *see* Southend St Sav Westcliff *Chelmsf*
WESTCLIFFE (St Peter) *see* St Margarets-at-Cliffe w Westcliffe etc *Cant*
WESTCOMBE PARK (St George) *see* E Greenwich *S'wark*
WESTCOTE (St Mary the Virgin) *see* Broadwell, Evenlode, Oddington, Adlestrop etc *Glouc*
WESTCOTE BARTON (St Edward the Confessor) w Steeple Barton, Duns Tew and Sandford St Martin *Ox 9* **P** *Duke of Marlborough, Exors Mrs Rittson-Thomas, DBP, D C D Webb Esq, and Bp (jt)* **R** G R ARTHUR, **NSM** R CHAND
WESTCOTT (Holy Trinity) *Guildf 7* **P** *Bp* **P-in-c** A C JONAS
WESTCOTT (St Mary) *see* Schorne *Ox*
WESTDENE (The Ascension) *see* Patcham *Chich*
WESTERDALE (Christ Church) *see* Ingleby Greenhow w Bilsdale Priory, Kildale etc *York*
WESTERFIELD (St Mary Magdalene) and Tuddenham w Witnesham *St E 4* **P** *Bp, Peterho Cam, and DBP (alt)* **P-in-c** S H COWLEY, **OLM** M J MORTON
WESTERHAM (St Mary the Virgin) *Roch 9* **P** *J St A Warde Esq* **V** P S MCVEAGH
WESTERLEIGH (St James the Great) *see* Yate New Town *Bris*
WESTERN DOWNLAND *Sarum 11* **P** *Hyndman Trustees, A N Hanbury Esq, and W J Purvis Esq (jt)* **R** L M PLAYER
WESTFIELD (St Andrew) *see* Barnham Broom and Upper Yare *Nor*
WESTFIELD (St John the Baptist) *Chich 20* **P** *Bp* **V** E N L FRANCE
WESTFIELD (St Mark) *see* Woking St Pet *Guildf*
WESTFIELD (St Mary) *Carl 7* **P** *Bp* **V** A M ARMSTRONG, **C** C R SHAW, **NSM** M T STILWELL
WESTFIELD (St Peter) *B & W 12* **P** *Bp* **V** J B THICKE
WESTGATE (St Andrew) *see* Upper Weardale *Dur*
WESTGATE (St James) *Cant 9* **P** *Abp* **P-in-c** R T BASHFORD
WESTGATE (St Martin of Tours) *see* Torrisholme *Blackb*
WESTGATE COMMON (St Michael the Archangel) *Wakef 12* **P** *V Alverthorpe* **V** A S MACPHERSON, **NSM** C M FOGG
WESTGATE-ON-SEA (St Saviour) *Cant 9* **P** *Abp* **P-in-c** J W RICHARDSON, **NSM** P R RUSSELL
WESTHALL (St Andrew) *see* Hundred River *St E*
WESTHAM (St Mary) *Chich 16* **P** *Duke of Devonshire* **V** G J BARRETT
WESTHAMPNETT (St Peter) *see* Chich St Paul and Westhampnett *Chich*
WESTHEAD (St James) *see* Newburgh w Westhead *Liv*
WESTHIDE (St Bartholomew) *see* Withington w Westhide *Heref*
WESTHOPE (Mission Room) *see* Canon Pyon w King's Pyon, Birley and Wellington *Heref*
WESTHORPE (St Margaret) *see* Badwell and Walsham *St E*
WESTHOUGHTON (St Bartholomew) and Wingates *Man 11* **P** *Patr Bd* **TR** G A LAWSON, **TV** R JACKSON, **NSM** G J SMETHURST, **OLM** V A RADFORD
WESTHOUGHTON (St James) *see* Daisy Hill *Man*
WESTHOUSES (St Saviour) *see* Blackwell w Tibshelf *Derby*
WESTLANDS (St Andrew) *Lich 9* **P** *Simeon's Trustees* **V** W G H GARDINER
WESTLEIGH (St Paul) *Man 13* **P** *V Leigh St Mary* **V** T D HARGREAVES-STEAD
WESTLEIGH (St Peter) *Ex 16* **P** *D&C* **P-in-c** C A C COOPER
WESTLEIGH (St Peter) *Man 13* **P** *Bp, Dioc Chan, and V Leigh St Mary (jt)* **P-in-c** S POLLARD, **NSM** D VICKERS
WESTLETON (St Peter) w Dunwich *St E 19* **P** *Ch Patr Trust (2 turns), Shadingfield Properties Ltd (1 turn)* **V** R J GINN, **C** H W TURNER, **OLM** S A WARNE, A B BAYMAN, E M COLE
WESTLEY (St Mary) *see* Horringer *St E*
WESTLEY WATERLESS (St Mary the less) *see* Raddesley Gp *Ely*
WESTMEADS (St Michael and All Angels) *see* Aldwick *Chich*
WESTMESTON (St Martin) *see* Streat w Westmeston *Chich*
WESTMILL (St Mary the Virgin) *see* Aspenden, Buntingford and Westmill *St Alb*
WESTMINSTER Hanover Square (St George) *see* Hanover Square St Geo *Lon*
WESTMINSTER (St James) Piccadilly *Lon 3* **P** *Bp (2 turns), Ld Chan (1 turn)* **R** C J W HEDLEY, **NSM** H W J VALENTINE
WESTMINSTER (St James the Less) *Lon 3* **P** *D&C Westmr* **V** R P DORMANDY, **C** N E D SCHIBILD, **NSM** W M CHOW
WESTMINSTER (St Mary le Strand) *see* St Mary le Strand w St Clem Danes *Lon*
WESTMINSTER (St Matthew) *Lon 3* **P** *D&C Westmr* **V** P A E CHESTER, **Hon C** R CRAWFORD, **NSM** P L HANAWAY, I J MOBSBY
WESTMINSTER (St Michael) *see* Ches Square St Mich w St Phil *Lon*
WESTMINSTER (St Saviour) *see* Pimlico St Sav *Lon*
WESTMINSTER (St Stephen) w St John *Lon 3* **P** *The Crown* **V** P P WELSH, **C** J HOGAN
WESTOE, SOUTH (St Michael and All Angels) *Dur 15* **P** *Bp* **P-in-c** P J A KENNEDY
WESTON (All Saints) *see* Bath Weston All SS w N Stoke and Langridge *B & W*
WESTON (All Saints) *Ches 15* **P** *Bp* **V** S R MITCHELL, **C** A C HOWARD
WESTON (All Saints) *see* Quinton and Welford w Weston *Glouc*

WESTON (All Saints) *Guildf 8* **P** *Bp* **V** J V PERCIVAL
WESTON (All Saints) *see* Tuxford w Weston and Markham Clinton *S'well*
WESTON (All Saints) w Denton *Bradf 4* **P** *Lt-Col H V Dawson and C Wyvill Esq (jt)* **P-in-c** S J WHARTON, **NSM** T H BAXTER
WESTON (Emmanuel) *see* Bath Weston St Jo w Kelston *B & W*
WESTON (Holy Trinity) *see* Baldock w Bygrave and Weston *St Alb*
WESTON (Holy Trinity) *Win 13* **P** *Bp* **V** R A BURNINGHAM
WESTON (St John the Evangelist) *see* Bath Weston St Jo w Kelston *B & W*
WESTON (St John the Evangelist) *see* Runcorn St Jo Weston *Ches*
WESTON (St Mary) *see* Cowbit *Linc*
WESTON (St Peter) *see* Hundred River *St E*
WESTON, OLD (St Swithun) *see* Brington w Molesworth and Old Weston *Ely*
WESTON, SOUTH (St Lawrence) *see* Thame *Ox*
WESTON BAMPFLYDE (Holy Cross) *see* Cam Vale *B & W*
WESTON BEGGARD (St John the Baptist) *see* Lugwardine w Bartestree, Weston Beggard etc *Heref*
WESTON BY WELLAND (St Mary) *see* Stoke Albany w Wilbarston and Ashley etc *Pet*
WESTON COLVILLE (St Mary) *see* Balsham, Weston Colville, W Wickham etc *Ely*
WESTON COYNEY (St Andrew) *see* Caverswall and Weston Coyney w Dilhorne *Lich*
WESTON ESTATE CHURCH (not known) *see* Otley *Bradf*
WESTON FAVELL (St Peter) *Pet 4* **P** *DBP* **R** C W WAKE, **C** J R KIMBER
WESTON HILLS (St John the Evangelist) *see* Cowbit *Linc*
WESTON IN GORDANO (St Peter and St Paul) *see* E Clevedon w Clapton in Gordano etc *B & W*
WESTON LONGVILLE (All Saints) *see* Wensum Benefice *Nor*
WESTON LULLINGFIELD (Holy Trinity) *see* Baschurch and Weston Lullingfield w Hordley *Lich*
WESTON MILL (St Philip) *see* Devonport St Boniface and St Phil *Ex*
WESTON-ON-THE-GREEN (St Mary) *see* Akeman *Ox*
WESTON ON TRENT (St Mary the Virgin) *see* Aston on Trent, Elvaston, Weston on Trent etc *Derby*
WESTON PATRICK (St Lawrence) *see* Herriard w Winslade and Long Sutton etc *Win*
WESTON POINT (Christ Church) *see* Runcorn St Jo Weston *Ches*
WESTON RHYN (St John) and Selattyn *Lich 19* **P** *Bp and Mrs A F Hamilton-Hill (jt)* **C** A R BAILEY
WESTON-SUB-EDGE (St Lawrence) *see* Mickleton, Willersey, Saintbury etc *Glouc*
WESTON SUPER MARE (All Saints) and St Saviour *B & W 11* **P** *Bp* **V** P G CLARKE
WESTON-SUPER-MARE (Christ Church) *B & W 11* **P** *Trustees* **V** G W HOBDEN
WESTON SUPER MARE (Emmanuel) *B & W 11* **P** *Trustees* **V** *vacant* (01934) 621046
WESTON-SUPER-MARE (St Andrew) Bournville *B & W 11* **P** *Bp* **V** F M B GUTTRIDGE
WESTON SUPER MARE (St John the Baptist) *B & W 11* **P** *Bp and Trustees (jt)* **R** R J TAYLOR
WESTON-SUPER-MARE (St Paul) *B & W 11* **P** *Bp* **V** P H DAVIES, **C** A M ALDEN
WESTON TURVILLE (St Mary the Virgin) *Ox 28* **P** *All So Coll Ox* **P-in-c** D N WALES, **NSM** S E FELLOWS
WESTON-UNDER-LIZARD (St Andrew) *see* Blymhill w Weston-under-Lizard *Lich*
WESTON-UNDER-PENYARD (St Lawrence) *see* Ross *Heref*
WESTON UNDER REDCASTLE (St Luke) *see* Hodnet w Weston under Redcastle *Lich*
WESTON UNDER WETHERLEY (St Michael) *see* Wappenbury w Weston under Wetherley *Cov*
WESTON UNDERWOOD (St Laurence) *see* Gayhurst w Ravenstone, Stoke Goldington etc *Ox*
WESTON UPON TRENT (St Andrew) *see* Mid Trent *Lich*
WESTON ZOYLAND (Blessed Virgin Mary) w Chedzoy *B & W 14* **P** *Bp* **P-in-c** K G J WILLIAMS
WESTONING (St Mary Magdalene) w Tingrith *St Alb 9* **P** *Ld Chan* **NSM** N L WASHINGTON
WESTOW (St Mary) *see* W Buckrose *York*
WESTWARD (St Hilda), Rosley-with-Woodside and Welton *Carl 3* **P** *D&C* **P-in-c** N L ROBINSON
WESTWARD HO! (Holy Trinity) *see* Bideford, Northam, Westward Ho!, Appledore etc *Ex*
WESTWAY (St Katherine) *see* N Hammersmith St Kath *Lon*
WESTWELL (St Mary) *see* Shill Valley and Broadshire *Ox*
WESTWELL (St Mary) w Hothfield and Eastwell w Boughton Aluph *Cant 10* **P** *Abp and Lord Hothfield (jt)* **P-in-c** L J HAMMOND, **C** J S RICHARDSON
WESTWICK (St Botolph) *see* Worstead, Westwick, Sloley, Swanton Abbot etc *Nor*
WESTWOOD (Mission Church) *see* Golcar *Wakef*
WESTWOOD (St John the Baptist) *Cov 3* **P** *Bp* **V** P FINDLEY
WESTWOOD (St Mary) Jacksdale *see* Selston *S'well*
WESTWOOD (St Mary the Virgin) and Wingfield *Sarum 14* **P** *D&C Bris, CPAS, and Bp (jt)* **R** R M LOWRIE, **C** T G RAE SMITH
WESTWOOD, LOW (Christ Church) *see* Ebchester *Dur*
WETHERAL (Holy Trinity and St Constantine) *see* Holme Eden and Wetheral w Warwick *Carl*
WETHERBY (St James) *Ripon 1* **P** *Bp* **P-in-c** M A CROSS
WETHERDEN (St Mary the Virgin) *see* Haughley w Wetherden and Stowupland *St E*
WETHERINGSETT (All Saints) *see* S Hartismere *St E*
WETHERSFIELD (St Mary Magdalene) *see* Finchingfield and Cornish Hall End etc *Chelmsf*
WETLEY ROCKS (St John the Baptist) *Lich 8* **P** *Bp* **P-in-c** S E GOODWIN
WETTENHALL (St David) *see* Acton and Worleston, Church Minshull etc *Ches*
WETTON (St Margaret) *see* Alstonfield, Butterton, Ilam etc *Lich*
WETWANG (St Nicholas) *see* Waggoners *York*
WEXHAM (St Mary) *Ox 23* **P** *Ld Chan* **P-in-c** R M DONOVAN
WEYBOURNE (All Saints), Upper Sheringham, Kelling, Salthouse, Bodham and East and West Beckham (The Weybourne Group) *Nor 18* **P** *Bp (2 turns), Sir Charles Mott-Radclyffe (1 turn), D&C (1 turn), and Lord Walpole (1 turn)* **P-in-c** N C H VARNON
WEYBREAD (St Andrew) *see* Fressingfield, Mendham etc *St E*
WEYBRIDGE (St James) *Guildf 8* **P** *Ld Chan* **R** B D PROTHERO, **C** J RATTUE, **OLM** H E KEMPSTER
WEYHILL (St Michael and All Angels) *see* Hatherden w Tangley, Weyhill and Penton Mewsey *Win*
WEYMOUTH (Holy Trinity) (St Nicholas) *Sarum 4* **P** *Bp* **V** R H FRANKLIN, **C** D B EVANS, **NSM** A J WHITTOCK, **OLM** A DUNN
WEYMOUTH (St Edmund) *Sarum 4* **P** *R Wyke Regis* **P-in-c** P S THOMAS
WEYMOUTH (St John) *see* Radipole and Melcombe Regis *Sarum*
WEYMOUTH (St Mary) *as above*
WEYMOUTH (St Paul) *Sarum 4* **P** *Bp* **V** R M HARPER
WHADDON (St Margaret) *see* Glouc St Geo w Whaddon *Glouc*
WHADDON (St Mary) *Ely 7* **P** *D&C Windsor* **P-in-c** D C R MCFADYEN
WHADDON (St Mary) *see* Buckingham *Ox*
WHADDON (St Mary) *see* Clarendon *Sarum*
WHADDON (St Mary the Virgin) *see* Hilperton w Whaddon and Staverton etc *Sarum*
WHALEY BRIDGE (St James) *Ches 16* **P** *Bp and Bp Derby (alt)* **R** A M SPEEDY
WHALEY THORNS (St Luke) *see* E Scarsdale *Derby*
WHALLEY (St Mary and All Saints) *Blackb 7* **P** *Hulme Trustees* **V** C STERRY, **NSM** J E HOLT
WHALLEY RANGE (St Edmund) and Moss Side St James w St Clement *Man 4* **P** *Bp and Simeon's Trustees (jt)* **R** S R BULLOCK, **C** G S EVANS
WHALLEY RANGE (St Margaret) *Man 4* **P** *Trustees* **P-in-c** R G BOULTER
WHALTON (St Mary Magdalene) *see* Bolam w Whalton and Hartburn w Meldon *Newc*
WHAPLODE (St Mary) *Linc 16* **P** *Ld Chan* **V** *vacant* (01406) 370318
WHAPLODE DROVE (St John the Baptist) *Linc 16* **P** *Feoffees* **V** R J MORRISON
WHARFEDALE, LOWER *Ripon 1* **P** *Bp, V Otley, and W G C Sheepshanks Esq (jt)* **R** S W LEWIS, **Hon C** J E BASSETT
WHARNCLIFFE SIDE (not known) *see* Oughtibridge *Sheff*
WHARRAM (St Mary) *see* Weaverthorpe w Helperthorpe, Luttons Ambo etc *York*
WHARTON (Christ Church) *Ches 6* **P** *R Davenham* **V** T D HANSON, **NSM** R W FORRESTER
WHATBOROUGH Group of Parishes, The *Leic 4* **P** *Bp* **V** H R BROAD
WHATCOTE (St Peter) *see* Tysoe w Oxhill and Whatcote *Cov*
WHATFIELD (St Margaret) *see* Bildeston w Wattisham and Lindsey, Whatfield etc *St E*

WHATLEY (St George) *see* Mells w Buckland Dinham, Elm, Whatley etc *B & W*
WHATLINGTON (St Mary Magdalene) *see* Sedlescombe w Whatlington *Chich*
WHATSTANDWELL (Mission Room) *see* Crich and S Wingfield *Derby*
WHATTON (St John of Beverley) w Aslockton, Hawksworth, Scarrington, Orston and Thoroton *S'well 8* **P** *Trustees* **V** R A WALTON, **NSM** P C CONNELL
WHEATACRE (All Saints) *see* Raveningham Gp *Nor*
WHEATCROFT (St Michael and All Angels) *see* Scarborough St Martin *York*
WHEATFIELD (St Andrew) *see* Thame *Ox*
WHEATHAMPSTEAD (St Helen) *St Alb 8* **P** *Bp* **R** A P C DOYE, **NSM** M H KING
WHEATHILL (Holy Trinity) *see* Ditton Priors w Neenton, Burwarton etc *Heref*
WHEATHILL PRIORY Group of Parishes, The *B & W 3* **P** *Ch Soc Trust and J H Cordle Esq (1 turn), A J Whitehead Esq (2 turns), Bp (1 turn), and Mrs E J Burden (1 turn)* **R** P N LITTLEWOOD
WHEATLEY (St Mary) *see* Doncaster St Mary *Sheff*
WHEATLEY (St Mary the Virgin) *Ox 1* **P** *Patr Bd* **TR** J V J G WATSON, **TV** W D BRIERLEY, R M COWLES, **C** H M HARTLEY, **NSM** J EDMONDS-SEAL, C N KING, M D CHAPMAN, J M G WILLIAMS, **OLM** B E KNIGHT
WHEATLEY, NORTH (St Peter and St Paul) and West Burton w Bole and Saundby and Sturton w Littleborough *S'well 5* **P** *Lord Middleton and G M T Foljambe Esq (alt)* **R** M W BRIGGS
WHEATLEY HILL (All Saints) and Wingate w Hutton Henry *Dur 2* **P** *Bp* **V** M J VAIZEY
WHEATLEY HILLS (St Aidan) *Sheff 8* **P** *Bp* **V** D J GOSS
WHEATLEY PARK (St Paul) *Sheff 8* **P** *Bp* **V** N A SOPHIANOU
WHEATON ASTON (St Mary) *see* Lapley w Wheaton Aston *Lich*
WHEELOCK (Christ Church) *see* Sandbach Heath w Wheelock *Ches*
WHELDRAKE (St Helen) w Thorganby *York 2* **P** *Abp and Sir Mervyn Dunnington-Jefferson Bt (jt)* **NSM** P A BURGESS
WHELFORD (St Anne) *see* Fairford and Kempsford w Whelford *Glouc*
WHELLEY (St Stephen) *see* New Springs and Whelley *Liv*
WHELNETHAM, GREAT (St Thomas à Becket) *see* St Edm Way *St E*
WHELNETHAM, LITTLE (St Mary) *see* Bradfield St Clare, Bradfield St George etc *St E*
WHELPLEY HILL (St Michael and All Angels) *see* Gt Chesham *Ox*
WHENBY (St Martin) *see* Howardian Gp *York*
WHEPSTEAD (St Petronilla) *see* Horringer *St E*
WHERSTEAD (St Mary) *see* Holbrook, Stutton, Freston, Woolverstone etc *St E*
WHERWELL (St Peter and Holy Cross) *see* Chilbolton cum Wherwell *Win*
WHETSTONE (St John the Apostle) *Lon 14* **P** *Bp* **V** K MITCHELL
WHETSTONE (St Peter) *Leic 10* **P** *Bp* **P-in-c** P J HARBORD, **NSM** P L BAILEY
WHICHAM (St Mary) *see* Bootle, Corney, Whicham and Whitbeck *Carl*
WHICHFORD (St Michael) *see* Long Compton, Whichford and Barton-on-the-Heath *Cov*
WHICKHAM (St Mary the Virgin) *Dur 13* **P** *Ld Chan* **P-in-c** B J ABBOTT, **C** D E CHADWICK
WHILTON (St Andrew) *see* Brington w Whilton and Norton etc *Pet*
WHIMPLE (St Mary), Talaton and Clyst St Lawrence *Ex 7* **P** *DBP, D&C and MMCET (jt)* **P-in-c** R S WILKINSON
WHINBURGH (St Mary) *see* Barnham Broom and Upper Yare *Nor*
WHINMOOR (St Paul) *see* Seacroft *Ripon*
WHINNEY HILL (St Peter) *see* Thrybergh *Sheff*
WHIPPINGHAM (St Mildred) w East Cowes *Portsm 8* **P** *Ld Chan* **R** J HALL
WHIPSNADE (St Mary Magdalene) *see* Kensworth, Studham and Whipsnade *St Alb*
WHIPTON (St Boniface) *Ex 3* **P** *Bp* **V** P K FITZPATRICK
WHISSENDINE (St Andrew) *see* Teigh w Whissendine and Market Overton *Pet*
WHISSONSETT (St Mary) *see* Upper Wensum Village Gp *Nor*
WHISTON (St Mary Magdalene) *Sheff 6* **P** *Bp* **R** A R WOOD, **C** G J OWEN
WHISTON (St Mary the Virgin) *see* Yardley Hastings, Denton and Grendon etc *Pet*
WHISTON (St Mildred) *see* Kingsley and Foxt-w-Whiston *Lich*
WHISTON (St Nicholas) *Liv 2* **P** *V Prescot* **V** A J TELFER
WHITACRE, NETHER (St Giles) *see* The Whitacres and Shustoke *Birm*
WHITACRE, OVER (St Leonard) *as above*
WHITACRES and Shustoke, The *Birm 9* **P** *J K Wingfield Digby Esq (1 turn), Bp (2 turns), and Ld Chan (1 turn)* **R** D MAWBEY
WHITBECK (St Mary) *see* Bootle, Corney, Whicham and Whitbeck *Carl*
WHITBOURNE (Bringsty Iron Church) *see* Edvin Loach w Tedstone Delamere etc *Heref*
WHITBOURNE (St John the Baptist) *as above*
WHITBURN (no dedication) *Dur 16* **P** *Bp* **R** K R SMITH
WHITBY (St Hilda) (St John) (St Mary) w Aislaby and Ruswarp *York 22* **P** *Abp* **TR** D W SMITH, **TV** T M LEATHLEY, **C** A R F BATTEY
WHITBY (St Thomas) *see* Ellesmere Port *Ches*
WHITBY ROAD (St Michael) *see* W Slough *Ox*
WHITCHURCH (All Hallows) w Tufton and Litchfield *Win 6* **P** *Bp* **V** K J INGLIS
WHITCHURCH (St Alkmund) *Lich 22* **P** *Bp* **R** A R RIDLEY
WHITCHURCH (St Andrew) *Ex 25* **P** *Bp* **V** S G MAY, **C** D J PARR, **NSM** M L DONNE
WHITCHURCH (St Augustine) (St Nicholas) *Bris 1* **P** *Bp* **V** *vacant* (01275) 832380
WHITCHURCH (St Dubricius) *see* Llangarron w Llangrove, Whitchurch and Ganarew *Heref*
WHITCHURCH (St John the Evangelist) *see* Schorne *Ox*
WHITCHURCH (St Lawrence) *see* Lt Stanmore St Lawr *Lon*
WHITCHURCH (St Mary the Virgin) *see* Ilmington w Stretton-on-Fosse etc *Cov*
WHITCHURCH (St Mary the Virgin) *see* Langtree *Ox*
WHITCHURCH CANONICORUM (St Candida and Holy Cross) *see* Golden Cap Team *Sarum*
WHITCHURCH HILL (St John the Baptist) *see* Langtree *Ox*
WHITE COLNE (St Andrew) *see* Halstead Area *Chelmsf*
WHITE HORSE, The *Sarum 17* **P** *Bp* **TR** P RICHARDSON, **TV** G F HUGHES, **C** S F DEACON, **NSM** M A DAVIES, P J MCEUNE
WHITE LADIES ASTON (St John) *see* Peopleton and White Ladies Aston w Churchill etc *Worc*
WHITE MOSS (St Mark) *see* Blackley St Mark White Moss *Man*
WHITE NOTLEY (St Etheldreda) *see* Fairstead w Terling and White Notley etc *Chelmsf*
WHITE RODING (St Martin) *see* S Rodings *Chelmsf*
WHITE WALTHAM (St Mary the Virgin) w Shottesbrooke *Ox 13* **P** *Sir John Smith* **P-in-c** D N ANDREW
WHITE WELL (St Mary) *see* St Paul's Walden *St Alb*
WHITECHAPEL (St James) *see* Fellside Team *Blackb*
WHITEFIELD (St Andrew) *see* Hillock *Man*
WHITEGATE (St Mary) w Little Budworth *Ches 6* **P** *Bp, Lord Delamere and W R Cullimore Esq (alt)* **V** L P EDEN
WHITEHALL (St Ambrose) *see* E Bris St Ambrose and St Leon *Bris*
WHITEHALL PARK (St Andrew) *see* Upper Holloway *Lon*
WHITEHAVEN (St James) *Carl 5* **P** *Patr Bd* **TR** J L BANNISTER, **TV** M COWAN
WHITEHAWK (St Cuthman) *Chich 2* **P** *Bp* **P-in-c** J D WRIGHT, **NSM** D R S PORTER
WHITEHILLS (St Mark) *see* Kingsthorpe w Northampton St Dav *Pet*
WHITELACKINGTON (The Blessed Virgin Mary) *see* Ilminster and Distr *B & W*
WHITELEAS (St Mary w St Martin) *see* S Shields All SS *Dur*
WHITELEY Conventional District *Portsm 2* **C-in-c** B J DUGMORE
WHITEPARISH (All Saints) *see* Clarendon *Sarum*
WHITESHILL (St Paul) and Randwick *Glouc 1* **P** *Bp* **V** B WOOLLASTON, **OLM** D H COLE
WHITESTAUNTON (St Andrew) *B & W 15* **P** *Personal Reps Gp Capt N W D Marwood-Elton* **R** P REGAN
WHITESTONE (St Catherine) *see* Tedburn St Mary, Whitestone, Oldridge etc *Ex*
WHITESTONE PATHFINDER (St John the Evangelist) *as above*
WHITEWELL (St Mary) *see* Tushingham and Whitewell *Ches*
WHITEWELL (St Michael) *see* Chipping and Whitewell *Blackb*
WHITFIELD (Holy Trinity) *see* Allendale w Whitfield *Newc*
WHITFIELD (St James) (St Luke) *Derby 6* **P** *Bp* **V** C COOPER, **C** T P CLARK
WHITFIELD (St John) *see* Allendale w Whitfield *Newc*
WHITFIELD (St John the Evangelist) *see* Astwell Gp *Pet*
WHITFIELD (St Peter) w Guston *Cant 4* **P** *Abp and D&C (alt)* **P-in-c** B E WAY

WHITFORD (St Mary at the Cross) *see* Kilmington, Stockland, Dalwood, Yarcombe etc *Ex*
WHITGIFT (St Mary Magdalene) *see* The Marshland *Sheff*
WHITGREAVE (St John the Evangelist) *see* Stafford *Lich*
WHITKIRK (St Mary) *Ripon 8* **P** *Meynell Trustees* **V** I C BLACK, **C** K HANSON
WHITLEIGH (St Chad) *Ex 23* **P** *Bp* **V** *vacant* (01752) 773547
WHITLEY (Christ Church) *see* Reading Ch Ch *Ox*
WHITLEY (St Helen) *Newc 4* **P** *Bp* **V** A J PATTERSON
WHITLEY (St James) *Cov 1* **P** *Bp* **NSM** P A STOTE
WHITLEY, LOWER or NETHER (St Luke) *see* Antrobus, Aston by Sutton, Lt Leigh etc *Ches*
WHITLEY BRIDGE (All Saints) *see* Knottingley and Kellington w Whitley *Wakef*
WHITLEY LOWER (St Mary and St Michael) *see* Thornhill and Whitley Lower *Wakef*
WHITMINSTER (St Andrew) *see* Eastington, Frocester, Haresfield etc *Glouc*
WHITMORE (St Mary and All Saints) *see* Chapel Chorlton, Maer and Whitmore *Lich*
WHITNASH (St Margaret) *Cov 11* **P** *Lord Leigh* **R** R W S SUFFERN, **OLM** I D KENNEDY, S D BATE
WHITNEY (St Peter and St Paul) *see* Eardisley w Bollingham, Willersley, Brilley etc *Heref*
WHITSBURY (St Leonard) *see* W Downland *Sarum*
WHITSTABLE (All Saints) (St Alphage) (St Andrew) (St Peter) *Cant 7* **P** *DBP* **TR** S J CONEYS, **TV** P D SALES, A J EVANS, A BIENFAIT, **C** S N ROSCOE, **Hon C** J M J OUTEN
WHITSTONE (St Anne) *see* Week St Mary w Poundstock and Whitstone *Truro*
WHITTINGHAM (St Bartholomew) and Edlingham w Bolton Chapel *Newc 9* **P** *D&C Carl and D&C Dur (alt)* **V** M D CATLING
WHITTINGTON (Christ Church) *see* Northwold and Wretton w Stoke Ferry etc *Ely*
WHITTINGTON (St Bartholomew) *Derby 5* **P** *Bp* **P-in-c** J V LEWIS
WHITTINGTON (St Bartholomew) *see* Sevenhampton w Charlton Abbots, Hawling etc *Glouc*
WHITTINGTON (St Giles) w Weeford *Lich 1* **P** *Bp* **V** J H MARTIN, **Hon C** C M J IBALL
WHITTINGTON (St John the Baptist) *Lich 19* **P** *Mrs P Hamilton Hill* **R** D R NORTH
WHITTINGTON (St Michael the Archangel) *see* Hornby w Claughton and Whittington etc *Blackb*
WHITTINGTON (St Philip and St James) *see* Worc SE *Worc*
WHITTINGTON, NEW (St Barnabas) *Derby 5* **P** *Bp* **P-in-c** J V LEWIS
WHITTLE-LE-WOODS (St John the Evangelist) *Blackb 4* **P** *V Leyland* **V** A L WINSTANLEY
WHITTLEBURY (St Mary) *see* Silverstone and Abthorpe w Slapton etc *Pet*
WHITTLESEY (St Andrew) (St Mary), Pondersbridge and Coates *Ely 14* **P** *Ld Chan (2 turns), Patr Bd (1 turn)* **TR** N A WHITEHOUSE, **TV** G STEVENS
WHITTLESFORD Local Ecumenical Project *Ely 7 vacant*
WHITTLESFORD (St Mary and St Andrew) *Ely 6* **P** *Jes Coll Cam* **V** *vacant* (01223) 833382
WHITTON *Sarum 18* **P** *Patr Bd* **TR** J R H RAILTON, **TV** S RAILTON, **OLM** J PROUT
WHITTON (St Augustine of Canterbury) *Lon 10* **P** *Bp* **V** I L PHILLIPS, **NSM** M WOOD
WHITTON (St John the Baptist) *see* Alkborough *Linc*
WHITTON (St Mary) *see* Burford II w Greete and Hope Bagot *Heref*
WHITTON (St Mary and St Botolph) and Thurleston w Akenham *St E 4* **P** *Bp (2 turns), Exors G K Drury Esq (1 turn)* **P-in-c** A S DOTCHIN, **NSM** M N C SOKANOVIC
WHITTON (St Philip and St James) *Lon 10* **P** *V Twickenham St Mary* **V** J V MOWBRAY, **NSM** M E GREENWOOD
WHITTONSTALL (St Philip and St James) *Newc 3* **P** *D&C* **P-in-c** D J IRVINE, **NSM** J LYNCH
WHITWELL (St John the Evangelist) w Crambe, Flaxton and Foston *York 6* **P** *Abp and D&C Dur (jt)* **NSM** R C BENSON
WHITWELL (St Lawrence) *Derby 3* **P** *Bp* **R** *vacant* (01909) 720220
WHITWELL (St Mary) *see* St Paul's Walden *St Alb*
WHITWELL (St Mary and St Rhadegunde) *Portsm 7* **P** *Bp* **V** S E LLOYD
WHITWELL (St Michael and All Angels) *see* Reepham, Hackford w Whitwell, Kerdiston etc *Nor*
WHITWELL (St Michael and All Angels) *see* Empingham and Exton w Horn w Whitwell *Pet*
WHITWICK (St John the Baptist) *Leic 8* **P** *Duchy of Lanc* **V** D I CHARNOCK
WHITWOOD (All Saints) *see* Castleford *Wakef*
WHITWORTH (not known) *see* Spennymoor, Whitworth and Merrington *Dur*
WHITWORTH (not known) *see* St Pet Ho *Man*
WHITWORTH (St Bartholomew) w Facit *Man 20* **P** *Bp and Keble Coll Ox (jt)* **V** J A READ
WHIXALL (St Mary) *see* Tilstock, Edstaston and Whixall *Lich*
WHIXLEY (Ascension) *see* Gt and Lt Ouseburn w Marton cum Grafton etc *Ripon*
WHORLTON (Holy Cross Old Church) w Carlton and Faceby *York 21* **P** *Mrs A P F Kynge* **V** L M SHIPP
WHORLTON (St John the Evangelist) *Newc 7* **P** *Bp* **V** A D BOWDEN
WHORLTON (St Mary) *see* Barnard Castle w Whorlton *Dur*
WHYKE (St George) w Rumboldswhyke St Mary and Portfield All Saints *Chich 3* **P** *Bp* **R** P R SEAMAN, **Hon C** J RHODES-WRIGLEY, **NSM** B M WATERS
WHYTELEAFE (St Luke) *see* Caterham *S'wark*
WIBTOFT (Assumption of Our Lady) *see* Claybrooke cum Wibtoft and Frolesworth *Leic*
WICHENFORD (St Lawrence) *see* Martley and Wichenford, Knightwick etc *Worc*
WICK (All Saints) *see* Littlehampton and Wick *Chich*
WICK (St Bartholomew) w Doynton and Dyrham *Bris 5* **P** *Simeon's Trustees, Ld Chan, and M H W Blaythwayt Esq (by turn)* **V** V J HOWLETT
WICK (St Mary) *see* Pershore w Pinvin, Wick and Birlingham *Worc*
WICK ST LAWRENCE (St Lawrence) *see* Kewstoke w Wick St Lawrence *B & W*
WICKEN (St John the Evangelist) *see* Potterspury w Furtho and Yardley Gobion etc *Pet*
WICKEN (St Laurence) *see* Soham and Wicken *Ely*
WICKEN BONHUNT (St Margaret) *see* Clavering and Langley w Arkesden etc *Chelmsf*
WICKENBY (St Peter and St Laurence) *see* Wragby Gp *Linc*
WICKERSLEY (St Alban) *Sheff 6* **P** *DBP* **R** P J HUGHES
WICKFORD (St Andrew) (St Catherine) and Runwell *Chelmsf 6* **P** *Patr Bd* **TR** P G KEARNS, **TV** J H DELFGOU, A T FRANKLAND, **C** P K TRATHEN
WICKHAM (St Nicholas) *Portsm 1* **P** *Sir Richard Rashleigh Bt* **R** R A A HIRST
WICKHAM (St Swithun) *see* Welford w Wickham and Gt Shefford, Boxford etc *Ox*
WICKHAM, EAST (St Michael the Archangel) *S'wark 3* **P** *D&C* **V** M HUME, **Hon C** C HEARD, **NSM** M W SMITH, **OLM** I THOMAS
WICKHAM, WEST (St Francis) (St Mary of Nazareth) *S'wark 21* **P** *Bp* **V** M R MCKINNEY, **C** G C SOUPPOURIS
WICKHAM, WEST (St John) *S'wark 22* **P** *Bp* **V** T D GILES
WICKHAM, WEST (St Mary) *see* Balsham, Weston Colville, W Wickham etc *Ely*
WICKHAM BISHOPS (St Bartholomew) w Little Braxted *Chelmsf 24* **P** *Bp (3 turns), CCC Cam (1 turn)* **C** E A LAW
WICKHAM MARKET (All Saints) w Pettistree *St E 18* **P** *Ch Trust Fund Trust and Ld Chan (alt)* **P-in-c** J F ELDRIDGE
WICKHAM SKEITH (St Andrew) *see* Bacton w Wyverstone, Cotton and Old Newton etc *St E*
WICKHAM ST PAUL (St Paul and All Saints) *see* N Hinckford *Chelmsf*
WICKHAMBREAUX (St Andrew) *see* Littlebourne and Ickham w Wickhambreaux etc *Cant*
WICKHAMBROOK (All Saints) *see* Bansfield *St E*
WICKHAMFORD (St John the Baptist) *see* Broadway w Wickhamford *Worc*
WICKHAMPTON (St Andrew) *see* Freethorpe, Wickhampton, Halvergate etc *Nor*
WICKLEWOOD (All Saints) *see* High Oak, Hingham and Scoulton w Wood Rising *Nor*
WICKMERE (St Andrew) *see* Lt Barningham, Blickling, Edgefield etc *Nor*
WICKWAR (Holy Trinity), Rangeworthy and Hillesley *Glouc 7* **P** *Bp and Earl of Ducie (jt)* **R** D J RUSSELL
WIDCOMBE *see* Bath Widcombe *B & W*
WIDDINGTON (St Mary) *see* Newport and Widdington *Chelmsf*
WIDDRINGTON (Holy Trinity) *Newc 11* **P** *Bp* **P-in-c** A E HARRISON
WIDDRINGTON STATION (St Mary) *see* Ulgham *Newc*
WIDECOMBE-IN-THE-MOOR (St Pancras), Leusdon, Princetown, Postbridge, Huccaby and Holne *Ex 9* **P** *Duchy of Cornwall (1 turn), Patr Bd (2 turns)* **P-in-c** P W DARBY, **C** M N ALLSO, C E COOPER
WIDEMOUTH BAY (Our Lady and St Anne) *see* Week St Mary w Poundstock and Whitstone *Truro*

WIDFORD (St John the Baptist) *see* Hunsdon w Widford and Wareside *St Alb*
WIDFORD (St Mary) (Holy Spirit) *Chelmsf 9* **P** *CPAS* **R** D R W ROBBINS
WIDFORD (St Oswald) *see* Burford w Fulbrook, Taynton, Asthall etc *Ox*
WIDLEY w Wymering *Portsm 6* **P** *E G Nugee Esq* **V** M L HILL-TOUT, **NSM** L C DENNESS
WIDMER END (Good Shepherd) *see* Hazlemere *Ox*
WIDMERPOOL (St Peter) *see* Willoughby-on-the-Wolds w Wysall and Widmerpool *S'well*
WIDNES (St Ambrose) *Liv 13* **P** *Trustees* **V** J P LEFFLER
WIDNES (St John) *Liv 13* **P** *Bp and V Farnworth (jt)* **V** D J GAIT
WIDNES (St Mary) (St Paul) *Liv 13* **P** *Bp* **C** R JONES
WIDWORTHY (St Cuthbert) *see* Offwell, Northleigh, Farway, Cotleigh etc *Ex*
WIELD (St James) *Win 2* **P** *Ld Chan* **P-in-c** D J KEIGHLEY
WIGAN (All Saints) *Liv 14* **P** *Bp* **P-in-c** R J HUTCHINSON
WIGAN (St Andrew) *Liv 15* **P** *R Wigan* **V** C HURST
WIGAN (St Anne) *Liv 15* **P** *Bp* **V** *vacant* (01942) 241930
WIGAN (St Barnabas) Marsh Green *Liv 15* **P** *V Pemberton St Mark Newtown and Bp (jt)* **P-in-c** D V ROUCH
WIGAN (St Catherine) *Liv 14* **P** *R Wigan* **P-in-c** G J BIRCH
WIGAN (St George) *Liv 14* **P** *R Wigan* **P-in-c** R J HUTCHINSON
WIGAN (St James) (St Thomas) *Liv 15* **P** *R Wigan and Bp (jt)* **V** H A F YOUNG
WIGAN (St John the Baptist) New Springs *see* New Springs and Whelley *Liv*
WIGAN (St Michael and All Angels) *Liv 15* **P** *R Wigan* **V** *vacant* (01942) 233465
WIGAN (St Stephen) Whelley *see* New Springs and Whelley *Liv*
WIGBOROUGH, GREAT (St Stephen) *see* Peldon w Gt and Lt Wigborough *Chelmsf*
WIGBOROUGH, LITTLE (St Nicholas) *as above*
WIGGATON (St Edward the Confessor) *see* Ottery St Mary, Alfington, W Hill, Tipton etc *Ex*
WIGGENHALL ST GERMANS (St Mary the Virgin) *see* E Marshland *Ely*
WIGGENHALL ST MARY (St Mary Magdalene) *as above*
WIGGINTON (St Bartholomew) *see* Northchurch and Wigginton *St Alb*
WIGGINTON (St Giles) *see* Hook Norton w Gt Rollright, Swerford etc *Ox*
WIGGINTON (St Leonard) (St James) *Lich 4* **P** *V Tamworth* **P-in-c** I R CARDINAL, **NSM** R DAVIES
WIGGINTON (St Mary and St Nicholas) *see* Haxby w Wigginton *York*
WIGGLESWORTH (School) *see* Giggleswick and Rathmell w Wigglesworth *Bradf*
WIGGONHOLT (not known) *see* Amberley w N Stoke and Parham, Wiggonholt etc *Chich*
WIGHILL (All Saints) *see* Healaugh w Wighill, Bilbrough and Askham Richard *York*
WIGHTON (All Saints) *see* Holkham w Egmere w Warham, Wells and Wighton *Nor*
WIGMORE (St James the Apostle) *see* Wigmore Abbey *Heref*
WIGMORE ABBEY *Heref 7* **P** *Trustees* **R** S J TURNER
WIGSLEY *see* Harby w Thorney and N and S Clifton *S'well*
WIGSTON, SOUTH (St Thomas) *see* Glen Parva and S Wigston *Leic*
WIGSTON MAGNA (All Saints) (St Wistan) *Leic 5* **P** *Haberdashers' Co* **P-in-c** L R CURTIS, **C** P E GIBSON
WIGSTON PARVA (St Mary the Virgin) *see* Sapcote and Sharnford w Wigston Parva *Leic*
WIGTOFT (St Peter and St Paul) *see* Sutterton, Fosdyke, Algarkirk and Wigtoft *Linc*
WIGTON (St Mary) *Carl 3* **P** *Bp* **V** G P RAVALDE
WIKE (School Room) *see* Bardsey *Ripon*
WILBARSTON (All Saints) *see* Stoke Albany w Wilbarston and Ashley etc *Pet*
WILBERFOSS (St John the Baptist) *see* Kexby w Wilberfoss *York*
WILBRAHAM, GREAT (St Nicholas) *Ely 3* **P** *DBP* **V** R E JONES
WILBRAHAM, LITTLE (St John) *Ely 3* **P** *CCC Cam* **R** R E JONES
WILBURTON (St Peter) *Ely 12* **P** *Adn Ely* **V** F E G BRAMPTON
WILBURY (St Thomas) *St Alb 4* **P** *Bp* **V** B E C PATE
WILBY (All Saints) *see* Quidenham Gp *Nor*
WILBY (St Mary) *see* Laxfield, Cratfield, Wilby and Brundish *St E*
WILBY (St Mary the Virgin) *see* Gt Doddington and Wilby *Pet*
WILCOT (Holy Cross) *see* Pewsey and Swanborough *Sarum*
WILCOTE (St Peter) *see* Ramsden, Finstock and Fawler, Leafield etc *Ox*
WILDBOARCLOUGH (St Saviour) *see* Bosley and N Rode w Wincle and Wildboarclough *Ches*
WILDEN (All Saints) *see* Stourport and Wilden *Worc*
WILDEN (St Nicholas) w Colmworth and Ravensden *St Alb 15* **P** *Ld Chan, Bp, and DBP (by turn)* **R** S MORTON, **Hon C** C M LOOKER
WILFORD (St Wilfrid) *S'well 9* **P** *Lt Col Peter Clifton* **P-in-c** D B ROWE, **C** R K F BUSHYAGER
WILFORD HILL (St Paul) *S'well 9* **P** *DBP* **V** G J PIGOTT, **NSM** S D HIPPISLEY-COX
WILFORD PENINSULA, The *St E 7* **P** *Patr Bd* **TV** C MACDONALD, G P CLEMENT, P T S KERLEY, **OLM** J M ANDREWS
WILKSBY (All Saints) *see* Mareham-le-Fen and Revesby *Linc*
WILLAND (St Mary the Virgin) *see* Cullompton, Willand, Uffculme, Kentisbeare etc *Ex*
WILLASTON (Christ Church) *Ches 9* **P** *DBF* **V** R W DENT
WILLASTON (St Luke) *see* Wistaston *Ches*
WILLEN (St Mary Magdalene) *see* Stantonbury and Willen *Ox*
WILLENHALL (Holy Trinity) *Lich 28* **P** *Patr Bd* **TR** B PRENTICE, **TV** M R SHEARD, M S HATHORNE, M R SHEARD, **C** I R M POOLE, **NSM** C A HATHORNE
WILLENHALL (St Anne) *Lich 28* **P** *Mrs L Grant-Wilson* **V** *vacant* (01902) 606516
WILLENHALL (St Giles) *Lich 28* **P** *Trustees* **V** K H JOHNSON
WILLENHALL (St John the Divine) *Cov 1* **P** *V Cov H Trin* **V** K R SCOTT
WILLENHALL (St Stephen) *Lich 28* **P** *Bp* **V** G E T BENNETT
WILLERBY (St Luke) *see* Kirk Ella and Willerby *York*
WILLERBY (St Peter) w Ganton and Folkton *York 15* **P** *M H Wrigley Esq, MMCET, and the Revd C G Day (by turn)* **P-in-c** K G F HOLDING
WILLERSEY (St Peter) *see* Mickleton, Willersey, Saintbury etc *Glouc*
WILLESBOROUGH (St Mary the Virgin) *Cant 10* **P** *D&C* **P-in-c** A K MCNICOL, **NSM** L J SCHRYVER
WILLESDEN (St Mark) *see* Kensal Rise St Mark and St Martin *Lon*
WILLESDEN (St Martin) *as above*
WILLESDEN (St Mary) *Lon 21* **P** *D&C St Paul's* **V** D C CLUES, **NSM** H R F O'GARRO
WILLESDEN (St Matthew) *Lon 21* **P** *Bp* **V** A F HILL
WILLESDEN (St Michael and All Angels) *see* Stonebridge St Mich *Lon*
WILLESDEN GREEN (St Andrew) (St Francis of Assisi) *Lon 21* **P** *Bp* **V** P S ANDERSON
WILLEY (St Leonard) *see* Churchover w Willey *Cov*
WILLIAN (All Saints) *see* Letchworth St Paul w Willian *St Alb*
WILLINGALE (St Christopher) *see* Fyfield, Moreton w Bobbingworth etc *Chelmsf*
WILLINGDON (St Mary the Virgin) *Chich 16* **P** *D&C* **V** M G ONIONS, **C** D S MILES, **NSM** C I WOODWARD
WILLINGDON, LOWER (St Wilfrid) Conventional District *Chich 16* **C-in-c** A M TUCKER
WILLINGHAM (St Mary and All Saints) *Ely 5* **P** *Bp* **R** G E TURNER
WILLINGHAM, NORTH (St Thomas) *see* Walesby *Linc*
WILLINGHAM, SOUTH (St Martin) *see* Barkwith Gp *Linc*
WILLINGHAM BY STOW (St Helen) *see* Stow Gp *Linc*
WILLINGTON (St Lawrence) *see* Cople, Moggerhanger and Willington *St Alb*
WILLINGTON (St Michael) *Derby 16* **P** *CPAS* **V** S A STARKEY
WILLINGTON (St Stephen) and Sunnybrow *Dur 9* **P** *R Brancepeth* **R** P GRUNDY
WILLINGTON Team, The (Good Shepherd) (St Mary the Virgin) (St Paul) *Newc 8* **P** *Prime Min* **TR** R D HINDLEY, **TV** R A STONE, S A WILSON, **NSM** S HAMIL
WILLINGTON QUAY (St Paul) *see* Willington *Newc*
WILLISHAM (St Mary) *see* Somersham w Flowton and Offton w Willisham *St E*
WILLITON (St Peter) *B & W 17* **P** *V Watchet* **V** R J ALLEN
WILLOUGHBY (St Helen) *Linc 8* **P** *Baroness Willoughby de Eresby, Ball Coll Ox, and Bp (jt)* **R** D C ROBINSON
WILLOUGHBY (St Nicholas) *see* Leam Valley *Cov*
WILLOUGHBY-ON-THE-WOLDS (St Mary and All Saints) w Wysall and Widerpool *S'well 8* **P** *MMCET* **P-in-c** M A SKIDMORE
WILLOUGHBY WATERLEYS (St Mary), Peatling Magna and Ashby Magna *Leic 10* **P** *Bp* **R** *vacant* (01455) 209406

WILLOUGHTON (St Andrew) *see* Glentworth Gp *Linc*
WILMCOTE (St Andrew) *see* Aston Cantlow and Wilmcote w Billesley *Cov*
WILMINGTON (St Mary and St Peter) *see* Arlington, Folkington and Wilmington *Chich*
WILMINGTON (St Michael) *Roch 2* **P** *D&C* **V** R ARDING, **Hon C** P J IVESON, **NSM** T WYATT
WILMSLOW (St Bartholomew) *Ches 12* **P** *Bp* **R** A G SPARHAM, **C** S G TALBOT, **NSM** R A YATES, C J LEES
WILNE (St Chad) and Draycott w Breaston *Derby 13* **P** *Bp* **R** C J SMEDLEY
WILNECOTE (Holy Trinity) *Lich 4* **P** *V Tamworth* **V** M J G BINNEY, **C** S M ROSSETER, **OLM** C J ROBINSON
WILSDEN (St Matthew) *see* Harden and Wilsden *Bradf*
WILSFORD (St Mary) *see* Ancaster Wilsford Gp *Linc*
WILSFORD (St Michael) *see* Woodford Valley *Sarum*
WILSFORD (St Nicholas) *see* Redhorn *Sarum*
WILSHAMSTEAD (All Saints) and Houghton Conquest *St Alb 13* **P** *St Jo Coll Cam and Bp (alt)* **V** S J TOZE, **NSM** R C WHITE
WILSHAW (St Mary) *see* Meltham *Wakef*
WILSILL (St Michael and All Angels) *see* Upper Nidderdale *Ripon*
WILSTHORPE (St Faith) *see* Uffington Gp *Linc*
WILSTONE (St Cross) *see* Tring *St Alb*
WILTON (St Cuthbert) *York 16* **P** *Abp* **P-in-c** R E HARRISON
WILTON (St George) *B & W 18* **P** *Mrs E C Cutbush* **TR** N J TAYLOR, **TV** C SNELL, **NSM** C F CRAGGS, J A JEFFERY
WILTON (St George) *see* Thornton Dale w Allerston, Ebberston etc *York*
WILTON (St Mary and St Nicholas) w Netherhampton and Fugglestone *Sarum 12* **P** *Earl of Pembroke* **R** B R COOPER, **C** L J SWEET, **NSM** G SPENCER, S P J PORTER
WILTON PLACE (St Paul) *Lon 3* **P** *Bp* **V** A G GYLE, **C** A M MOORE, **NSM** N DAWSON
WIMBISH (All Saints) *see* Debden and Wimbish w Thunderley *Chelmsf*
WIMBLEDON (Emmanuel) Ridgway Proprietary Chapel *S'wark 12* **Min** J J M FLETCHER, **C** R A R WEEKES, P R DAWSON, **Hon C** D L JOHNSON, **NSM** R J COEKIN
WIMBLEDON (St Luke) *see* Wimbledon Park St Luke *S'wark*
WIMBLEDON (St Mary) (St Matthew) (St Mark) (St John the Baptist) *S'wark 14* **P** *Patr Bd* **TR** C J DAVIES, **TV** S G LEE, **C** G M PAWSON, **NSM** H A JOHNSON, C JACKSON, R G STEVENS
WIMBLEDON, SOUTH (All Saints) *S'wark 14* **P** *Bp* **P-in-c** M O BLACKMAN
WIMBLEDON, SOUTH (Holy Trinity and St Peter) *S'wark 14* **P** *Bp and TR Wimbledon (jt)* **P-in-c** D R M MONTEITH, **Hon C** J B EASTON-CROUCH
WIMBLEDON, SOUTH (St Andrew) *S'wark 14* **P** *Bp* **V** A D WAKEFIELD
WIMBLEDON, WEST (Christ Church) *S'wark 14* **P** *TR Wimbledon* **V** R P LANE
WIMBLEDON PARK (St Luke) *S'wark 14* **P** *Simeon's Trustees* **V** S D N VIBERT
WIMBLEDON PARK (St Paul) *see* Wandsworth St Paul *S'wark*
WIMBLINGTON (St Peter) *see* Doddington w Benwick and Wimblington *Ely*
WIMBORNE (St John the Evangelist) *see* New Borough and Leigh *Sarum*
WIMBORNE MINSTER (St Cuthberga) *Sarum 9* **P** *Qu Eliz Free Gr Sch* **R** J E HOLBROOK, **C** P SEABROOK, **NSM** B GIBSON
WIMBORNE ST GILES (St Giles) *see* Cranborne w Boveridge, Edmondsham etc *Sarum*
WIMBOTSHAM (St Mary) w Stow Bardolph and Stow Bridge w Nordelph *Ely 13* **P** *Bp* **R** *vacant* (01366) 385713
WIMPOLE (St Andrew) *see* Orwell Gp *Ely*
WINCANTON (St Peter and St Paul) *B & W 2* **P** *D&C* **R** S LOW, **C** S J TANCOCK
WINCHAM (St Andrew) *see* Lostock Gralam *Ches*
WINCHCOMBE (St Peter) *Glouc 15* **P** *Patr Bd* **TR** P J PARTINGTON, **TV** J A NEWCOMBE, N M ARTHY, **C** M M LUDLOW, **NSM** B P LUDLOW, C G POOLE
WINCHELSEA (St Thomas) (St Richard) and Icklesham *Chich 20* **P** *Bp and Guild of All So (jt)* **R** H A S COCKS, **Hon C** A H M COX
WINCHENDON, NETHER (St Nicholas) *see* Long Crendon w Chearsley and Nether Winchendon *Ox*
WINCHENDON, OVER (St Mary Magdalene) *see* Schorne *Ox*
WINCHESTER (All Saints), Chilcomb St Andrew and Chesil St Peter *Win 7* **P** *Bp and Ld Chan (alt)* **R** C BASTON, **NSM** T E HEMMING
WINCHESTER (Christ Church) *Win 7* **P** *Simeon's Trustees* **V** D G WILLIAMS, **C** H C SCAMMAN, J L SCAMMAN, **NSM** B R WAKELIN
WINCHESTER (Holy Trinity) *see* Winnall *Win*
WINCHESTER (St Barnabas) *Win 7* **P** *Bp* **P-in-c** T H ROBERTS, **NSM** A M DAVIES
WINCHESTER (St Cross Hospital w St Faith) *Win 7* **P** *Bp*, R C SWEET **P-in-c** J BATES
WINCHESTER (St John the Baptist w St Martin Winnall) *see* Winnall *Win*
WINCHESTER (St Lawrence and St Maurice) (St Swithun-upon-Kingsgate) *Win 7* **P** *Ld Chan* **R** D V SCOTT
WINCHESTER (St Luke) *see* Stanmore *Win*
WINCHESTER St Matthew (St Paul's Mission Church) *Win 7* **P** *Bp* **P-in-c** N P SEAL, **NSM** N W BIRKETT
WINCHESTER HYDE (St Bartholomew) *Win 7* **P** *Ld Chan* **P-in-c** M R STARR
WINCHFIELD (St Mary the Virgin) *see* Hartley Wintney, Elvetham, Winchfield etc *Win*
WINCHMORE HILL (Holy Trinity) *Lon 18* **P** *V Winchmore Hill St Paul* **V** C M GRAY, **Hon C** J D CORNISH
WINCHMORE HILL (St Andrew) *see* Amersham *Ox*
WINCHMORE HILL (St Paul) *Lon 18* **P** *V Edmonton* **V** J M PAUL, **C** S F CLIFFORD, **Hon C** C M MORTON
WINCLE (St Michael) *see* Bosley and N Rode w Wincle and Wildboarclough *Ches*
WINCOBANK (St Thomas) *see* Brightside w Wincobank *Sheff*
WINDERMERE (St Martin) and St John *Carl 11* **P** *Bp and Trustees (jt)* **R** J J RICHARDS, **C** S C BICKERSTETH
WINDERMERE (St Mary) Applethwaite and Troutbeck *Carl 11* **P** *Bp* **V** D M B WILMOT
WINDHILL (Christ Church) *Bradf 1* **P** *Bp* **NSM** M J ALLISON
WINDLESHAM (St John the Baptist) *Guildf 6* **P** *Ld Chan* **R** P W MICKLETHWAITE, **NSM** K M DYKES, **OLM** J A LEWIS
WINDRUSH (St Peter) *see* Sherborne, Windrush, the Barringtons etc *Glouc*
WINDRUSH, LOWER *Ox 8* **P** *Bp, DBP, St Jo Coll Ox, D&C Ex, and B Babington-Smith Esq (jt)* **R** S E SHARP
WINDSOR, NEW (Holy Trinity) (St John the Baptist w All Saints) *Ox 13* **P** *Ld Chan* **TV** M J BARNES, **P-in-c** A L SWIFT, **Hon C** D I DADSWELL, **OLM** J M QUICK
WINDSOR, OLD (St Luke's Mission Room) (St Peter and St Andrew) *Ox 13* **P** *Ld Chan* **V** N J POCOCK
WINESTEAD (St German) *see* Patrington w Hollym, Welwick and Winestead *York*
WINFARTHING (St Mary) w Shelfanger w Burston w Gissing and Tivetshall *Nor 10* **P** *Ld Chan, Bp, and DBP (jt), Hertf Coll Ox (alt)* **R** D F MILLS
WINFORD (Blessed Virgin Mary and St Peter) w Felton Common Hill *B & W 10* **P** *Worc Coll Ox and Mrs H D Pullman (jt)* **R** P M HAND
WINFORTON (St Michael and All Angels) *see* Eardisley w Bollingham, Willersley, Brilley etc *Heref*
WINFRITH NEWBURGH (St Christopher) *see* The Lulworths, Winfrith Newburgh and Chaldon *Sarum*
WING (St Peter and St Paul) *see* Preston and Ridlington w Wing and Pilton *Pet*
WING w Grove (All Saints) *Ox 26* **P** *Bp* **P-in-c** R O N WILLMOTT, **OLM** S TUNNICLIFFE
WINGATE GRANGE (Holy Trinity) *see* Wheatley Hill and Wingate w Hutton Henry *Dur*
WINGATES (St John the Evangelist) *see* Westhoughton and Wingates *Man*
WINGERWORTH (All Saints) *Derby 5* **P** *Bp* **R** R M WATTS, **C** M P SMITH
WINGFIELD (St Andrew) *see* Hoxne w Denham, Syleham and Wingfield *St E*
WINGFIELD (St Mary) *see* Westwood and Wingfield *Sarum*
WINGFIELD, NORTH (St Lawrence), Clay Cross and Pilsley *Derby 5* **P** *Bp* **TR** C E BERESFORD, **TV** L S LIVERSIDGE, M J BARNES, **C** C R BURROWS
WINGFIELD, SOUTH (All Saints) *see* Crich and S Wingfield *Derby*
WINGHAM (St Mary the Virgin) w Elmstone and Preston w Stourmouth *Cant 1* **P** *Lord Fitzwalter and D&C (alt)* **V** M R GRIFFIN
WINGRAVE (St Peter and St Paul) w Rowsham, Aston Abbotts and Cublington *Ox 26* **P** *Bp and Linc Coll Ox (jt)* **R** R O N WILLMOTT, **OLM** S TUNNICLIFFE
WINKBURN (St John of Jerusalem) *S'well 15* **P** *Bp* **P-in-c** E F CULLY, **C** J R CHAMBERS
WINKFIELD (St Mary the Virgin) and Cranbourne *Ox 11* **P** *Bp* **V** R W NEILL, **NSM** I N JAMES
WINKLEBURY (Good Shepherd) *Win 4* **P** *MMCET* **NSM** R P BOWSKILL

WINKLEIGH (All Saints) *Ex 20* **P** *D&C* **V** P J NORMAN
WINKSLEY (St Cuthbert and St Oswald) *see* Fountains Gp *Ripon*
WINLATON (St Paul) *Dur 13* **P** *Bp* **P-in-c** G W R HARPER
WINMARLEIGH (St Luke) *see* Cockerham w Winmarleigh and Glasson *Blackb*
WINNALL (Holy Trinity) (St John the Baptist w St Martin) *Win 7* **P** *Bp* **R** R J H TEARE
WINNERSH (St Mary the Virgin) *see* Hurst *Ox*
WINSCOMBE (St James) *B & W 11* **P** *D&C* **V** M J SLADE
WINSFORD (St Mary Magdalene) *see* Exton and Winsford and Cutcombe w Luxborough *B & W*
WINSHAM (St Stephen) *see* Chard and Distr *B & W*
WINSHILL (St Mark) *Derby 16* **P** *Lady H M Gretton and Baroness Gretton (jt)* **V** M M MOOKERJI
WINSLEY (St Nicholas) *see* Monkton Farleigh, S Wraxall and Winsley *Sarum*
WINSLOW (St Laurence) w Great Horwood and Addington *Ox 24* **P** *Ld Chan (3 turns), New Coll Ox (2 turns), and DBP (1 turn)* **R** A A WHALLEY, **NSM** G E BALL
WINSON (St Michael) *see* Bibury w Winson and Barnsley *Glouc*
WINSTER (Holy Trinity) *Carl 10* **P** *V Kendal H Trin* **V** *vacant*
WINSTER (St John the Baptist) *see* S Darley, Elton and Winster *Derby*
WINSTON (St Andrew) *Dur 7* **P** *Bp* **P-in-c** M ALDERSON
WINSTON (St Andrew) *see* Debenham and Helmingham *St E*
WINSTONE (St Bartholomew) *see* Brimpsfield w Birdlip, Syde, Daglingworth etc *Glouc*
WINTERBORNE CLENSTON (St Nicholas) *see* Winterborne Valley and Milton Abbas *Sarum*
WINTERBORNE HOUGHTON (St Andrew) *as above*
WINTERBORNE STICKLAND (St Mary) *as above*
WINTERBORNE VALLEY and Milton Abbas, The *Sarum 6* **P** *Bp (3 turns) and P D H Chichester Esq (1 turn)* **V** R N HUNGERFORD
WINTERBORNE WHITECHURCH (St Mary) *see* Winterborne Valley and Milton Abbas *Sarum*
WINTERBOURNE (St James) *see* Chieveley w Winterbourne and Oare *Ox*
WINTERBOURNE (St Michael the Archangel) *Bris 5* **P** *St Jo Coll Ox* **R** E I BAILEY, **Hon C** W J DEIGHTON
WINTERBOURNE ABBAS (St Mary) *see* The Winterbournes and Compton Valence *Sarum*
WINTERBOURNE BASSETT (St Katharine) *see* Upper Kennet *Sarum*
WINTERBOURNE DOWN (All Saints) *see* Frenchay and Winterbourne Down *Bris*
WINTERBOURNE EARLS (St Michael and All Angels) *see* Bourne Valley *Sarum*
WINTERBOURNE GUNNER (St Mary) *as above*
WINTERBOURNE KINGSTON (St Nicholas) *see* Red Post *Sarum*
WINTERBOURNE MONKTON (St Mary Magdalene) *see* Upper Kennet *Sarum*
WINTERBOURNE MONKTON (St Simon and St Jude) *see* Dorchester *Sarum*
WINTERBOURNE ST MARTIN (St Martin) *see* The Winterbournes and Compton Valence *Sarum*
WINTERBOURNE STEEPLETON (St Michael) *as above*
WINTERBOURNE STOKE (St Peter) *see* Wylye and Till Valley *Sarum*
WINTERBOURNE ZELSTONE (St Mary) *see* Red Post *Sarum*
WINTERBOURNES and Compton Valence, The *Sarum 1* **P** *Adn Sherborne, Linc Coll Ox, and Sir Robert Williams Bt (by turn)* **P-in-c** R L BASSETT, **NSM** M C MILES
WINTERBURN (Chapel of Ease) *see* Gargrave *Bradf*
WINTERINGHAM (All Saints) *see* Alkborough *Linc*
WINTERSLOW (All Saints) *see* Clarendon *Sarum*
WINTERSLOW (St John) *as above*
WINTERTON Group, The (All Saints) *Linc 4* **P** *Lord St Oswald, Bp, and Exors Capt J G G P Elwes (jt)* **V** A C NUNN, **OLM** J J WHITEHEAD
WINTERTON (Holy Trinity and All Saints) *see* Flegg Coastal Benefice *Nor*
WINTHORPE (All Saints) *see* Coddington and Winthorpe and Langford w Holme *S'well*
WINTHORPE (St Mary) *see* Skegness Gp *Linc*
WINTON (St Mary Magdalene) *Man 2* **P** *Trustees* **V** D R SUTTON
WINTRINGHAM (St Peter) *see* Buckrose Carrs *York*
WINWICK (All Saints) *Ely 8* **P** *Bp* **P-in-c** C M FURLONG
WINWICK (St Michael and All Angels) *see* W Haddon w Winwick and Ravensthorpe *Pet*
WINWICK (St Oswald) *Liv 16* **P** *Bp* **R** R G LEWIS
WIRKSWORTH (St Mary) *Derby 7* **P** *Bp* **TR** D C TRUBY, **TV** G MANLEY, **C** S J LUMBY, **NSM** K J ORFORD
WISBECH (St Augustine) *Ely 15* **P** *Bp* **P-in-c** N K GARDNER, **C** T J K CONLIN, W A L ZWALF
WISBECH (St Peter and St Paul) *Ely 15* **P** *Bp* **V** W A L ZWALF, **C** T J K CONLIN, N K GARDNER
WISBECH ST MARY (St Mary) and Guyhirn w Ring's End and Gorefield and Southea w Murrow and Parson Drove *Ely 15* **P** *Bp* **V** C HURST
WISBOROUGH GREEN (St Peter ad Vincula) *Chich 11* **P** *Bp Lon* **P-in-c** S F E NEWHAM
WISHAW (St Chad) *Birm 12* **P** *Bp* **P-in-c** M I RHODES
WISHFORD, GREAT (St Giles) *see* Wylye and Till Valley *Sarum*
WISLEY (not known) w Pyrford *Guildf 12* **P** *Bp* **R** N J AIKEN, **C** N J LAMBERT, **OLM** C D GIBSON
WISSETT (St Andrew) *see* Blyth Valley *St E*
WISSINGTON (St Mary the Virgin) *see* Nayland w Wiston *St E*
WISTANSTOW (Holy Trinity) *Heref 11* **P** *Bp* **R** *vacant* (01588) 672067
WISTASTON (St Mary) *Ches 15* **P** *Trustees* **R** W J WHITE, **NSM** P H WILKINSON, K H SAMBROOK
WISTON (St Mary) *see* Ashington, Washington and Wiston w Buncton *Chich*
WISTOW (All Saints) *see* Cawood w Ryther and Wistow *York*
WISTOW (St John the Baptist) *see* Warboys w Broughton and Bury w Wistow *Ely*
WISTOW (St Wistan) *Leic 5* **P** *Bp and The Hon Ann Brooks (jt)* **V** P J O'REILLY
WITCHAM (St Martin) w Mepal *Ely 12* **P** *D&C* **R** J M AMEY, **NSM** M L BRADBURY
WITCHAMPTON (St Mary and St Cuthberga and All Saints), Stanbridge and Long Crichel w More Crichel *Sarum 9* **P** *Hon Mrs M A S E Marten* **P-in-c** J E HOLBROOK
WITCHFORD (St Andrew) w Wentworth *Ely 12* **P** *D&C* **P-in-c** A E H HULT
WITCHINGHAM GREAT (St Mary) *see* Wensum Benefice *Nor*
WITCOMBE, GREAT (St Mary) *see* Badgeworth, Shurdington and Witcombe w Bentham *Glouc*
WITHAM Group, The *Linc 14* **P** *Sir Lyonel Tollemache Bt, The Revd J R H Thorold, J R Thorold Esq, and Bp (jt)* **R** N S F ALLDRIT
WITHAM (St Nicholas) *Chelmsf 24* **P** *Patr Bd* **TR** J M SUDDARDS, **TV** S F GARWOOD, **C** P A JOHNSON
WITHAM, NORTH (St Mary) *see* Witham Gp *Linc*
WITHAM, SOUTH (St John the Baptist) *as above*
WITHAM FRIARY (Blessed Virgin Mary and St John the Baptist and All Saints) *see* Nunney and Witham Friary, Marston Bigot etc *B*
WITHAM-ON-THE-HILL (St Andrew) *see* Edenham w Witham on the Hill and Swinstead *Linc*
WITHCALL (St Martin) *see* Legbourne and Wold Marsh *Linc*
WITHERIDGE (St John the Baptist) *see* Burrington, Chawleigh, Cheldon, Chulmleigh etc *Ex*
WITHERLEY (St Peter) *see* Fenn Lanes Gp *Leic*
WITHERNSEA (St Nicholas) *see* Owthorne and Rimswell w Withernsea *York*
WITHERNWICK (St Alban) *see* Aldbrough, Mappleton w Goxhill and Withernwick *York*
WITHERSDALE (St Mary Magdalene) *see* Fressingfield, Mendham etc *St E*
WITHERSFIELD (St Mary the Virgin) *see* Haverhill w Withersfield *St E*
WITHERSLACK (St Paul) *Carl 10* **P** *DBP* **V** *vacant*
WITHIEL (St Clement) *see* Roche and Withiel *Truro*
WITHIEL FLOREY (St Mary Magdalene) *see* Brompton Regis w Upton and Skilgate *B & W*
WITHINGTON (St Christopher) *Man 8* **P** *The Crown* **P-in-c** R M GOVENDER, **C** S L BENNETT, J F HOLLYWELL
WITHINGTON (St Crispin) *Man 4* **P** *Bp* **P-in-c** P C S DAVIES
WITHINGTON (St John the Baptist) *see* Wrockwardine Deanery *Lich*
WITHINGTON (St Michael and All Angels) *see* Northleach w Hampnett and Farmington etc *Glouc*
WITHINGTON (St Paul) *Man 8* **P** *Trustees* **R** S B WOODHEAD
WITHINGTON (St Peter) w Westhide *Heref 4* **P** *Bp* **P-in-c** D J BOWEN
WITHINGTON, LOWER (St Peter) *see* Chelford w Lower Withington *Ches*

WITHLEIGH (St Catherine) *see* Washfield, Stoodleigh, Withleigh etc *Ex*
WITHNELL (St Paul) *see* Heapey St Barnabas and Withnell St Paul *Blackb*
WITHYBROOK (All Saints) *see* Wolvey w Burton Hastings, Copston Magna etc *Cov*
WITHYCOMBE (St Nicholas) *see* Dunster, Carhampton and Withycombe w Rodhuish *B & W*
WITHYCOMBE RALEIGH (St John the Evangelist) (St John in the Wilderness) (All Saints) *Ex 1* **P** *Patr Bd* **TR** F A OSWIN, **TV** S J HOYLE, T C SMYTH
WITHYHAM (St John the Evangelist) *see* Crowborough St Jo *Chich*
WITHYHAM (St Michael and All Angels) *Chich 19* **P** *Earl De la Warr* **R** *vacant* (01892) 770241
WITHYPOOL (St Andrew) *see* Exford, Exmoor, Hawkridge and Withypool *B & W*
WITHYWOOD (shared church) *Bris 1* **P** *Bp* **V** J M CARPENTER
WITLEY (All Saints) *Guildf 4* **P** *Bp* **V** B M SHAND
WITLEY, GREAT (St Michael) *see* Shrawley, Witley, Astley and Abberley *Worc*
WITLEY, LITTLE (St Michael) *as above*
WITNESHAM (St Mary) *see* Westerfield and Tuddenham w Witnesham *St E*
WITNEY (St Mary the Virgin) (Holy Trinity) *Ox 8* **P** *Patr Bd* **TR** I C COOPER, **TV** D R CHILDS, **Hon C** J H COOK, **OLM** C TITCOMB
WITTENHAM, LITTLE (St Peter) *see* Dorchester *Ox*
WITTERING (All Saints) *see* Ketton, Collyweston, Easton-on-the-Hill etc *Pet*
WITTERING, EAST (St Anne) *see* Earnley and E Wittering *Chich*
WITTERING, WEST (St Peter and St Paul) and Birdham w Itchenor *Chich 3* **P** *Bp* **R** J B WILLIAMS, **Hon C** C J HANKINS, **NSM** B F HOLBEN, J M MOULD
WITTERSHAM (St John the Baptist) w Stone-in-Oxney and Ebony *Cant 12* **P** *Abp* **P-in-c** S M HALMSHAW
WITTON (St Helen) *Ches 6* **P** *Bp* **V** P C O DAWSON
WITTON (St Margaret) *see* Bacton w Edingthorpe w Witton and Ridlington *Nor*
WITTON (St Margaret) *see* Gt and Lt Plumstead w Thorpe End and Witton *Nor*
WITTON (St Mark) *see* Blackb Christ the King *Blackb*
WITTON, EAST (St John the Evangelist) *see* Middleham w Coverdale and E Witton etc *Ripon*
WITTON, NETHER (St Giles) *Newc 11* **P** *Ld Chan* **V** M A G BRYCE
WITTON, WEST (St Bartholomew) *Ripon 4* **P** *Lord Bolton* **V** *vacant*
WITTON GILBERT (St Michael and All Angels) *see* Dur N *Dur*
WITTON LE WEAR (St Philip and St James) *see* Hamsterley and Witton-le-Wear *Dur*
WITTON PARK (St Paul) *Dur 6* **P** *Bp* **V** N P DENHAM
WIVELISCOMBE (St Andrew) w Chipstable, Huish Champflower and Clatworthy *B & W 19* **P** *Bp and A H Trollope-Bellew Esq (jt)* **R** G A OWEN, **Hon C** A C ARMSTRONG, **NSM** S M GREEN
WIVELSFIELD (St Peter and St John the Baptist) *Chich 6* **P** *DBP* **V** C R BREEDS
WIVENHOE (St Mary) *Chelmsf 16* **P** *Bp* **R** D G THOMAS, **NSM** B HADFIELD
WIVERTON GROUP *see* Cropwell Bishop w Colston Bassett, Granby etc *S'well*
WIVETON (St Mary) *see* Blakeney w Cley, Wiveton, Glandford etc *Nor*
WIX (St Mary the Virgin) *see* Gt Oakley w Wix and Wrabness *Chelmsf*
WIXFORD (St Milburga) *see* Exhall w Wixford *Cov*
WIXOE (St Leonard) *see* Stour Valley *St E*
WOBURN (St Mary) w Eversholt, Milton Bryan, Battlesden and Pottesgrove *St Alb 9* **P** *Bedf Estates Trustees* **P-in-c** S W NUTH
WOBURN SANDS (St Michael) *St Alb 9* **P** *Bp* **V** N JEFFERY, **NSM** N J PARKINSON
WOBURN SQUARE (Christ Church) *see* Bloomsbury St Geo w Woburn Square Ch Ch *Lon*
WOKING (Christ Church) *Guildf 12* **P** *Ridley Hall Cam* **V** P J HARWOOD, **C** C SIMONS, **NSM** M S SMITH, **OLM** J A M VICKERS
WOKING (St John the Baptist) *Guildf 12* **P** *V Woking St Pet* **V** G P WILLIAMS, **Hon C** P D PEARSON, **OLM** R G BENNETT
WOKING (St Mary of Bethany) *Guildf 12* **P** *V Woking Ch Ch* **V** S R BEAK
WOKING (St Paul) *Guildf 12* **P** *Ridley Hall Cam* **V** J HUNTER
WOKING (St Peter) *Guildf 12* **P** *Patr Bd* **TR** B J GRIMSTER, **TV** I D TWEEDIE-SMITH, **OLM** M W MOORSE
WOKING, SOUTH Team Ministry *see* Woking St Pet *Guildf*
WOKINGHAM (All Saints) *Ox 16* **P** *Bp* **R** D P HODGSON, **C** P H COWAN, **NSM** C R JAMES, A E KEMP
WOKINGHAM (St Paul) *Ox 16* **P** *DBP* **P-in-c** J R CONNELL, **NSM** R G HOLMES
WOKINGHAM (St Sebastian) *Ox 16* **P** *Bp* **V** A P MARSDEN, **C** P PARKS, **NSM** E C FUDGE
WOLBOROUGH (St Mary) and Ogwell *Ex 10* **P** *Earl of Devon and Bp (jt)* **R** R C CHAMBERLAIN, **C** G A MILFORD, **NSM** A M WELLS, M J FLETCHER
WOLD (St Andrew) *see* Walgrave w Hannington and Wold and Scaldwell *Pet*
WOLD NEWTON (All Saints) *see* Binbrook Gp *Linc*
WOLD NEWTON (All Saints) *see* Burton Fleming w Fordon, Grindale etc *York*
WOLDINGHAM (St Agatha) *see* Caterham *S'wark*
WOLDINGHAM (St Paul) *as above*
WOLDS, NORTH Group *Linc 6* **P** *Bp, DBP, and D&C (jt)* **V** M A BATTY
WOLDSBURN *York 10* **P** *Abp, St Jo Coll Ox, and A J Page Esq (1 turn), and Ld Chan (1 turn)* **R** J TALLANT
WOLFERLOW (St Andrew) *see* Edvin Loach w Tedstone Delamere etc *Heref*
WOLFERTON (St Peter) *see* Sandringham w W Newton and Appleton etc *Nor*
WOLFORD (St Michael and All Angels) w Burmington *Cov 9* **P** *Mert Coll Ox* **P-in-c** R K SMITH, **C** H C W PARBURY
WOLLASTON (St James) *Worc 12* **P** *Bp* **V** *vacant* (01384) 395674
WOLLASTON (St Mary) and Strixton *Pet 6* **P** *Bp* **P-in-c** A I MORTON
WOLLASTON, GREAT (All Saints) (St John the Baptist) *Heref 13* **P** *Bp* **V** C B BULL
WOLLATON (St Leonard) *S'well 14* **P** *Lord Middleton* **R** J J LEPINE, **C** A J MADDOCKS, **NSM** P D C BROWN, R A SHOCK
WOLLATON PARK (St Mary) *S'well 14* **P** *CPAS* **V** A R HOWE, **NSM** P W WENHAM
WOLLESCOTE (St Andrew) *Worc 12* **P** *Bp* **V** R A BROADBENT
WOLSINGHAM (St Mary and St Stephen) and Thornley *Dur 9* **P** *Bp* **R** M GOODALL
WOLSTANTON (St Margaret) *Lich 9* **P** *Bp* **TR** J P EADES, **TV** R M MCINTYRE
WOLSTON (St Margaret) and Church Lawford *Cov 6* **P** *DBP (2 turns), Bp (1 turn)* **V** T J PULLEN
WOLVERCOTE (St Peter) w Summertown *Ox 7* **P** *Patr Bd* **P-in-c** J M RUSHTON, **C** M A BUTCHERS, **NSM** W L A PRYOR, V P BRIDGES
WOLVERHAMPTON Pond Lane (Mission Hall) *see* Wolverhampton St Luke *Lich*
WOLVERHAMPTON (St Andrew) *Lich 28* **P** *Bp* **V** J L SMITH, **NSM** T B FYFFE
WOLVERHAMPTON (St Jude) *Lich 28* **P** *CPAS* **V** R E CARTER, **C** R J MOY, **OLM** I J SAUNDERS
WOLVERHAMPTON (St Luke) Blakenhall *Lich 28* **P** *Trustees* **V** R J ESPIN-BRADLEY, **C** J N ROBBIE
WOLVERHAMPTON (St Martin) *see* Rough Hills *Lich*
WOLVERHAMPTON (St Matthew) *Lich 28* **P** *Baldwin Pugh Trustees* **V** D GHOSH, **OLM** D G WATKIN
WOLVERHAMPTON (St Stephen) *Lich 28* **P** *Bp* **P-in-c** J C OAKES, **Hon C** M JEAVONS
WOLVERHAMPTON, CENTRAL (St Chad) (St John's in the Square) (St Mark's Centre) (St Peter) *Lich 28* **P** *Patr Bd* **TR** D W FRITH, **TV** M Y CLAYTON, O SMITH, **C** J M PERRY, L K COLLINS, **OLM** E W BROOKES
WOLVERLEY (St John the Baptist) and Cookley *Worc 11* **P** *D&C and Bp (jt)* **V** G SHILVOCK
WOLVERTON (Holy Trinity) (St George the Martyr) *Ox 25* **P** *Bp* **R** J M TRIGG
WOLVERTON (St Katherine) *see* Baughurst, Ramsdell, Wolverton w Ewhurst etc *Win*
WOLVERTON (St Mary the Virgin) w Norton Lindsey and Langley *Cov 7* **P** *Bp* **P-in-c** R LIVINGSTON
WOLVEY (St John the Baptist) w Burton Hastings, Copston Magna and Withybrook *Cov 5* **P** *Bp* **V** T J COLLING
WOLVISTON (St Peter) *see* Grindon, Stillington and Wolviston *Dur*
WOMBOURNE (St Benedict) *see* Smestow Vale *Lich*
WOMBRIDGE (St Mary and St Leonard) *Lich 21* **P** *W J Charlton Meyrick Esq* **P-in-c** K S EVANS
WOMBWELL (St Mary) (St George) *Sheff 12* **P** *Trin Coll Cam* **R** A MAUCHAN, **C** T C KEIGHTLEY

WOMERSLEY (St Martin) *see* Went Valley *Wakef*
WONERSH (St John the Baptist) w Blackheath *Guildf 2* **P** *Selw Coll Cam* **V** J R WATTLEY, **OLM** K N BATESON
WONSTON (Holy Trinity) *see* Lower Dever Valley *Win*
WONSTON, SOUTH (St Margaret) Conventional District *Win 7* **Min** S A FOSTER
WOOBURN (St Paul) *Ox 29* **P** *Bp* **P-in-c** M J WALLINGTON, **NSM** R A PAYNE
WOOD DALLING (St Andrew) *see* Reepham, Hackford w Whitwell, Kerdiston etc *Nor*
WOOD DITTON (St Mary) w Saxon Street *Ely 4* **P** *Duke of Sutherland* **V** C A SINDALL, **Hon C** L M BROUGHTON
WOOD END (St Chad) *Cov 1* **P** *Ld Chan* **V** V I WOODS
WOOD END (St Michael and All Angels) *see* Baxterley w Hurley and Wood End and Merevale etc *Birm*
WOOD GREEN (St Michael) w Bounds Green (St Gabriel) (St Michael-at-Bowes) *Lon 19* **P** *Patr Bd* **TR** C W COPPEN, **TV** R J WILKINSON
WOOD GREEN (St Paul) *see* Wednesbury St Paul Wood Green *Lich*
WOOD NORTON (All Saints) *see* Twyford, Guist, Bintree, Themelthorpe etc *Nor*
WOOD STREET (St Alban) *see* Worplesdon *Guildf*
WOODBASTWICK (St Fabian and St Sebastian) *see* Ranworth w Panxworth, Woodbastwick etc *Nor*
WOODBERRY DOWN (St Olave) *see* Stoke Newington St Olave *Lon*
WOODBOROUGH (St Mary Magdalene) *see* Pewsey and Swanborough *Sarum*
WOODBOROUGH (St Swithun) *S'well 10* **P** *Bp* **P-in-c** M J BROCK, **NSM** M N TAYLOR
WOODBRIDGE (St John the Evangelist) and Bredfield *St E 7* **P** *Ch Patr Trust (3 turns), and Ld Chan (1 turn)* **V** D GARDNER
WOODBRIDGE (St Mary the Virgin) *St E 7* **P** *Bp* **R** K S MCCORMACK, **C** A S G PLATTEN
WOODBURY (Holy Cross) *see* Axminster, Chardstock, All Saints etc *Ex*
WOODBURY (St Swithun) *see* Lympstone and Woodbury w Exton *Ex*
WOODBURY SALTERTON (Holy Trinity) *see* Clyst St Mary, Clyst St George etc *Ex*
WOODCHESTER (St Mary) and Brimscombe *Glouc 8* **P** *Simeon's Trustees* **R** S A BOWEN, **NSM** D E STODDART, M G WRIGHT
WOODCHURCH (All Saints) *Cant 10* **P** *Abp* **P-in-c** D M MADZIMURE
WOODCHURCH (Holy Cross) *Ches 1* **P** *DBP* **R** M A DAVIS
WOODCOTE (St Leonard) *see* Langtree *Ox*
WOODCOTE (St Mark) *see* Purley St Mark *S'wark*
WOODCOTE (St Peter) *see* Lilleshall, Muxton and Sheriffhales *Lich*
WOODCOTT (St James) *see* Hurstbourne Priors, Longparish etc *Win*
WOODDITTON (St Mary) *see* Wood Ditton w Saxon Street *Ely*
WOODEATON (Holy Rood) *see* Ray Valley *Ox*
WOODFORD (Christ Church) *Ches 12* **P** *W A B Davenport Esq* **P-in-c** J G KNOWLES
WOODFORD (St Barnabas) *Chelmsf 4* **P** *Bp* **V** A CROSS
WOODFORD (St Mary the Virgin) *see* Gt w Lt Addington and Woodford *Pet*
WOODFORD (St Mary w St Philip and St James) *Chelmsf 4* **P** *Bp* **R** G R SMITH, **C** C A HAWKINS
WOODFORD, SOUTH (Holy Trinity) Hermon Hill *see* Wanstead H Trin Hermon Hill *Chelmsf*
WOODFORD BRIDGE (St Paul) *Chelmsf 4* **P** *R Woodford* **V** J H SPRINGBETT, **NSM** I K MONKS
WOODFORD HALSE (St Mary the Virgin) w Eydon *Pet 1* **P** *Ld Chan (2 turns), Bp (1 turn)* **V** T C OAKLEY
WOODFORD VALLEY (All Saints) *Sarum 13* **P** *Bp* **P-in-c** A C PHILP, **NSM** P POWELL
WOODFORD WELLS (All Saints) (St Andrew) *Chelmsf 4* **P** *Trustees* **V** P G HARCOURT, **C** S MARSHALL, S P CLARKE, M D PORTER, **NSM** D J BLACKLEDGE
WOODGATE VALLEY Conventional District *Birm 2 vacant*
WOODGATE VALLEY (St Francis) *see* Bartley Green *Birm*
WOODGREEN (St Boniface) *see* Fordingbridge and Breamore and Hale etc *Win*
WOODHALL (St James the Great) *Bradf 3* **P** *Bp* **V** F M SHAW
WOODHALL, OLD *see* Woodhall Spa Gp *Linc*
WOODHALL SPA Group *Linc 11* **P** *Bp and DBP (jt)* **R** S C WITCOMBE, **C** M A RAVEN
WOODHAM (All Saints) *Guildf 12* **P** *Bp* **V** I W FORBES, **C** P P LEONARD, **OLM** S V TASSELL
WOODHAM (St Elizabeth of Hungary) *see* Gt Aycliffe and Chilton *Dur*
WOODHAM FERRERS (St Mary) and Bicknacre *Chelmsf 9* **P** *Lord Fitzwalter* **P-in-c** M J COTTEE
WOODHAM FERRERS, SOUTH (Holy Trinity) (St Mary) *Chelmsf 9* **P** *Bp* **P-in-c** P HAWORTH
WOODHAM MORTIMER (St Margaret) w Hazeleigh *Chelmsf 11* **P** *Bp* **P-in-c** B C R JOHNSON
WOODHAM WALTER (St Michael) *Chelmsf 11* **P** *Ch Soc Trust* **R** *vacant*
WOODHAY, EAST (St Martin) and Woolton Hill *Win 6* **P** *Bp* **R** C DALE
WOODHAY, WEST (St Laurence) w Enborne, Hampstead Marshall, Inkpen and Combe *Ox 14* **P** *Bp, D&C Windsor, and J R Henderson Esq (jt)* **R** J F RAMSBOTTOM, **NSM** I J BLYTH
WOODHORN w Newbiggin *Newc 11* **P** *Bp* **P-in-c** J M GRIEVE, **OLM** F WALTON
WOODHOUSE (Christ Church) *Wakef 5* **P** *Bp* **V** *vacant* (01484) 542163
WOODHOUSE (St James) *Sheff 1* **P** *Bp* **V** S BARBER
WOODHOUSE (St Mark) and Wrangthorn *Ripon 7* **P** *DBP* **V** D A CALDER
WOODHOUSE (St Mary in the Elms), Woodhouse Eaves and Swithland *Leic 7* **P** *Ld Chan and DBP (alt)* **R** R A HORTON, **NSM** P SHERIDAN
WOODHOUSE CLOSE (not known) *see* Bishop Auckland Woodhouse Close CD *Dur*
WOODHOUSE EAVES (St Paul) *see* Woodhouse, Woodhouse Eaves and Swithland *Leic*
WOODHOUSE MILL (St James) *see* Woodhouse St Jas *Sheff*
WOODHOUSE PARK (Wm Temple Church) *see* Wythenshawe *Man*
WOODHOUSES (not known) *see* Bardsley *Man*
WOODHOUSES (St John the Divine) *see* Dunham Massey St Marg and St Mark *Ches*
WOODHURST (St John the Baptist) *see* Bluntisham cum Earith w Colne and Woodhurst *Ely*
WOODINGDEAN (Holy Cross) *Chich 2* **P** *Bp* **V** R A BROMFIELD
WOODKIRK (St Mary) *see* W Ardsley *Wakef*
WOODLAND (St John the Baptist) *see* Broadhempston, Woodland, Staverton etc *Ex*
WOODLAND (St John the Evangelist) *see* Broughton and Duddon *Carl*
WOODLAND (St Mary) *see* Lynesack *Dur*
WOODLANDS (All Saints) *Sheff 7* **P** *Bp* **V** S J GARDNER
WOODLANDS (Ascension) *see* Cranborne w Boveridge, Edmondsham etc *Sarum*
WOODLANDS (Mission Chapel) *see* W Meon and Warnford *Portsm*
WOODLANDS (St Katherine) *B & W 4* **P** *DBP* **V** C ALSBURY
WOODLANDS (St Mary) *see* Kemsing w Woodlands *Roch*
WOODLANDS (St Stephen) *see* Welford w Wickham and Gt Shefford, Boxford etc *Ox*
WOODLEIGH (St Mary the Virgin) *see* Modbury, Bigbury, Ringmore w Kingston etc *Ex*
WOODLEY (St John the Evangelist) *Ox 15* **P** *DBP* **TR** A P DOUGLAS, **TV** M A E ASTIN, J P HONOUR, **C** C J REID, **NSM** T R ASTIN, **OLM** S L COMERFORD
WOODMANCOTE (Mission Church) *see* Westbourne *Chich*
WOODMANCOTE (St James) *see* Micheldever and E Stratton, Woodmancote etc *Win*
WOODMANCOTE (St Mark) *see* Dursley *Glouc*
WOODMANCOTE (St Peter) *see* Henfield w Shermanbury and Woodmancote *Chich*
WOODMANSEY (St Peter) *see* Beverley Minster *York*
WOODMANSTERNE (St Peter) *S'wark 28* **P** *Ld Chan* **R** *vacant* (01737) 352849
WOODNESBOROUGH (St Mary the Blessed Virgin) w Worth and Staple *Cant 8* **P** *Abp* **P-in-c** N M GENDERS, **C** J M A ROBERTS, **NSM** R STEVENSON
WOODNEWTON (St Mary) *see* Nassington w Yarwell and Woodnewton *Pet*
WOODPLUMPTON (St Anne) *Blackb 9* **P** *V St Michael's-on-Wyre* **V** D P A FEENEY
WOODRISING (St Nicholas) *see* High Oak, Hingham and Scoulton w Wood Rising *Nor*
WOODSEATS (St Chad) *Sheff 2* **P** *Bp* **V** M J PORTER
WOODSETTS (St George) *Sheff 5* **P** *Bp* **V** A P FEREDAY
WOODSFORD (St John the Baptist) *see* Moreton and Woodsford w Tincleton *Sarum*
WOODSIDE (St Andrew) w East Hyde *St Alb 14* **P** *D&C St Paul's* **P-in-c** J DANIEL
WOODSIDE (St James) *Ripon 7* **P** *Bp* **V** C PUCKRIN

WOODSIDE (St Luke) *see* Croydon Woodside *S'wark*
WOODSIDE GREEN (St Andrew) *see* Gt Hallingbury and Lt Hallingbury *Chelmsf*
WOODSIDE PARK (St Barnabas) *Lon 14* **P** *Ch Patr Trust* **V** J S H COLES, **C** H D KENDAL, R G MORTON, S T KIRBY
WOODSTOCK (St Mary Magdalene) *see* Blenheim *Ox*
WOODSTON (St Augustine of Canterbury) (Mission Church) *Ely 11* **P** *Bp* **R** W P L GAMMON
WOODTHORPE (St Mark) *S'well 10* **P** *Bp* **V** P J THOMAS
WOODTHORPE (St Peter) *see* Staveley and Barrow Hill *Derby*
WOODTON (All Saints) *see* Hempnall *Nor*
WOODVILLE (St Stephen) *see* Blackfordby and Woodville *Leic*
WOOKEY (St Matthew) *see* Coxley w Godney, Henton and Wookey *B & W*
WOOKEY HOLE (St Mary Magdalene) *see* Wells St Cuth w Wookey Hole *B & W*
WOOL (Holy Rood) and East Stoke *Sarum 8* **P** *Bp (3 turns), Keble Coll Ox (1 turn)* **OLM** J A HILL
WOOLACOMBE (St Sabinus) *see* Ilfracombe, Lee, Woolacombe, Bittadon etc *Ex*
WOOLASTON (St Andrew) w Alvington and Aylburton *Glouc 4* **P** *DBP and Ld Chan (by turn)* **R** J E TAYLOR
WOOLAVINGTON (Blessed Virgin Mary) w Cossington and Bawdrip *B & W 14* **P** *D&C Windsor and J A Church Esq (alt)* **V** *vacant* (01278) 683408
WOOLBEDING (All Hallows) *Chich 10* **P** *Rathbone Trust Co and Cowdray Trust (jt)* **R** A T CUNNINGTON
WOOLBROOK (St Francis of Assisi) *see* Sidmouth, Woolbrook, Salcombe Regis, Sidbury etc *Ex*
WOOLER (St Mary) *see* Glendale Gp *Newc*
WOOLFARDISWORTHY (Holy Trinity) *see* Parkham, Alwington, Buckland Brewer etc *Ex*
WOOLFARDISWORTHY EAST (St Mary) *see* N Creedy *Ex*
WOOLFOLD (St James) *Man 10* **P** *R Bury St Mary* **P-in-c** S EDWARDS
WOOLHAMPTON (St Peter) w Midgham and Beenham Valance *Ox 12* **P** *Bp, Keble Coll Ox, and CPAS (jt)* **P-in-c** P G STEELE, **NSM** E M OKE, J K WEBSTER, D FOOTE, C PYNN
WOOLHOPE (St George) *see* Fownhope w Mordiford, Brockhampton etc *Heref*
WOOLLAND (not known) *see* Hazelbury Bryan and the Hillside Par *Sarum*
WOOLLEY (All Saints) *see* Bath St Sav w Swainswick and Woolley *B & W*
WOOLLEY (St Mary) *see* E Leightonstone *Ely*
WOOLLEY (St Peter) *Wakef 9* **P** *Bp* **P-in-c** S P KELLY
WOOLMER GREEN (St Michael) *see* Welwyn *St Alb*
WOOLPIT (Blessed Virgin Mary) w Drinkstone *St E 10* **P** *Bp and A Harvie-Clark Esq (alt)* **R** *vacant* (01359) 242244
WOOLSTASTON (St Michael and All Angels) *see* Dorrington w Leebotwood, Longnor, Stapleton etc *Heref*
WOOLSTHORPE (St James) *see* Harlaxton Gp *Linc*
WOOLSTON (Ascension) *Liv 12* **P** *Bp, Adn, and R Warrington (jt)* **V** B F DRYDEN
WOOLSTON (St Mark) *Win 13* **P** *Bp* **V** M J A NEWTON, **NSM** A R BEVIS
WOOLSTONE (All Saints) *see* Uffington, Shellingford, Woolstone and Baulking *Ox*
WOOLSTONE (not known) *see* Woughton *Ox*
WOOLSTONE (St Martin) w Gotherington and Oxenton, and Kemerton *Glouc 15* **P** *DBP and Croome Estate* **P-in-c** J WILBY
WOOLTON, MUCH (St Peter) *Liv 4* **P** *Bp* **R** C J CROOKS, **C** A N PEEK
WOOLTON HILL (St Thomas) *see* E Woodhay and Woolton Hill *Win*
WOOLVERSTONE (St Michael) *see* Holbrook, Stutton, Freston, Woolverstone etc *St E*
WOOLVERTON (St Lawrence) *see* Hardington Vale *B & W*
WOOLWICH (St Mary Magdelene and St Andrew) (St Michael and All Angels) *S'wark 3* **P** *Bp and Keble Coll Ox (jt)* **R** J VAN DER VALK
WOOLWICH (St Thomas) *see* Charlton *S'wark*
WOOLWICH, NORTH (St John) w Silvertown *Chelmsf 3* **P** *Bp and Lon Corp (alt)* **P-in-c** P M BUR
WOONTON (Mission Room) *see* Eardisley w Bollingham, Willersley, Brilley etc *Heref*
WOORE (St Leonard) and Norton in Hales *Lich 18* **P** *Bp and CPAS (jt)* **P-in-c** A B LEIGHTON
WOOSEHILL (Community Church) *see* Bearwood *Ox*
WOOTTON (St Andrew) *see* Ulceby Gp *Linc*
WOOTTON (St Edmund) *Portsm 8* **P** *DBP* **P-in-c** K F ABBOTT
WOOTTON (St George the Martyr) w Quinton and Preston Deanery *Pet 7* **P** *Ex Coll Ox and Bp (alt)* **R** D SCHOLEY
WOOTTON (St Martin) *see* Elham w Denton and Wootton *Cant*
WOOTTON (St Mary the Virgin) *St Alb 13* **P** *MMCET* **V** P M ACKROYD
WOOTTON (St Mary) w Glympton and Kiddington *Ox 9* **P** *New Coll Ox (2 turns), Bp (1 turn), and Exors E W Towler Esq (1 turn)* **P-in-c** E E S JONES
WOOTTON (St Peter) and Dry Sandford *Ox 10* **P** *Bp and Ox Churches Trust (jt)* **V** J N COOPER, **C** P N TOVEY
WOOTTON, NORTH (All Saints) w SOUTH (St Mary) *Nor 20* **P** *Ld Chan and G Howard Esq (alt)* **R** B R OAKE, **OLM** D TATE, L ASHBY
WOOTTON, NORTH (St Peter) *see* Pilton w Croscombe, N Wootton and Dinder *B & W*
WOOTTON BASSETT (St Bartholomew and All Saints) *Sarum 15* **P** *DBP* **P-in-c** T M B WOODHOUSE, **Hon C** B W HORLOCK
WOOTTON BRIDGE (St Mark) *see* Wootton *Portsm*
WOOTTON COURTENAY (All Saints) *see* Selworthy, Timberscombe, Wootton Courtenay etc *B & W*
WOOTTON FITZPAINE (not known) *see* Golden Cap Team *Sarum*
WOOTTON RIVERS (St Andrew) *see* Pewsey and Swanborough *Sarum*
WOOTTON ST LAWRENCE (St Lawrence) *see* Oakley w Wootton St Lawrence *Win*
WOOTTON WAWEN (St Peter) *Cov 7* **P** *K Coll Cam* **P-in-c** L G MORTIMER
WORCESTER Dines Green (St Michael), and Crown East, Rushwick *Worc 3* **P** *Bp and D&C (jt)* **V** R CHARLES
WORCESTER (St Andrew and All Saints w St Helen) *see* Worc City St Paul and Old St Martin etc *Worc*
WORCESTER (St Barnabas) (Christ Church) *Worc 6* **P** *Bp* **TR** R G JONES, **TV** N A MPUNZI, **C** D C J BALLARD
WORCESTER (St Clement) and Lower Broadheath *Worc 3* **P** *Bp and D&C (jt)* **V** S L BLOOMER
WORCESTER (St George w St Mary Magdalene) *Worc 6* **P** *Bp and V Claines (alt)* **V** *vacant* (01905) 613267
WORCESTER (St John in Bedwardine) *see* St Jo in Bedwardine *Worc*
WORCESTER (St Martin in the Cornmarket) *see* Worc City St Paul and Old St Martin etc *Worc*
WORCESTER (St Nicholas) *see* Warndon St Nic *Worc*
WORCESTER (St Stephen) *see* Barbourne *Worc*
WORCESTER (St Wulstan) *Worc 6* **P** *Bp* **V** D MELVILLE, **NSM** S A NALL
WORCESTER CITY (St Paul) (Old St Martin w St Swithun) (St Nicholas and All Saints) *Worc 6* **P** *Bp and D&C (jt)* **P-in-c** I PEARSON, **C** P D J SWANN
WORCESTER PARK (Christ Church w St Philip) *S'wark 25* **P** *R Cheam* **V** C E ELVEY
WORCESTER SOUTH EAST (St Martin w St Peter) (St Mark in the Cherry Orchard) (Holy Trinity w St Matthew) *Worc 6* **P** *Patr Bd* **TR** K A BOYCE, **TV** J HOUSE, J E FOX, P E JONES, **C** K SALTWELL, **NSM** A M WHERRY
WORDSLEY (Holy Trinity) *Worc 10* **P** *Patr Bd* **TV** C T ROGERSON, C WATKINS, **NSM** G HODGSON
WORFIELD (St Peter) *Heref 9* **P** *Trustees of the late J R S Greenshields Esq* **P-in-c** M E THOMPSON, **OLM** S C MONDON
WORKINGTON (St John) *Carl 7* **P** *R Workington* **V** J M COOK
WORKINGTON (St Michael) *Carl 7* **P** *Mrs E H S Thornely* **R** B ROWE, **C** S G SANDHAM
WORKSOP (St Anne) *S'well 6* **P** *Bp* **P-in-c** S A CASH
WORKSOP (St John the Evangelist) (Christchurch Centre) *S'well 6* **P** *CPAS* **V** N R HOGG, **C** M C ALVEY
WORKSOP (St Paul) *S'well 6* **P** *Bp* **V** B C B BROWN
WORKSOP PRIORY (St Mary and St Cuthbert) *S'well 6* **P** *St Steph Ho Ox* **V** A R WAGSTAFF, **C** S LUMBY
WORLABY (St Clement) *Linc 6* **P** *DBP* **V** G A PLUMB
WORLDHAM, EAST (St Mary the Virgin) *see* Northanger *Win*
WORLDHAM, WEST (St Nicholas) *as above*
WORLE (St Martin) (St Mark's Church Centre) *B & W 11* **P** *Ld Chan* **TR** N KENT, **TV** C D BLAKE, M D H FRANKUM
WORLESTON (St Oswald) *see* Acton and Worleston, Church Minshull etc *Ches*
WORLINGHAM (All Saints) w Barnby and North Cove *St E 14* **P** *Ld Chan* **R** S M ELLIS
WORLINGTON (All Saints) *see* Mildenhall *St E*
WORLINGTON, EAST (St Mary) *see* Burrington, Chawleigh, Cheldon, Chulmleigh etc *Ex*
WORLINGTON, WEST (St Mary) *as above*
WORLINGWORTH (St Mary) w Southolt, Tannington, Bedfield

and Monk Soham *St E 17* **P** *Lord Henniker, R C Rous Esq and Bp, and DBP (by turn)* **R** *vacant* (01728) 768102
WORMBRIDGE (St Peter) *see* Ewyas Harold w Dulas, Kenderchurch etc *Heref*
WORMEGAY (St Michael and All Angels and Holy Cross) *see* Tottenhill w Wormegay *Ely*
WORMHILL (St Margaret) and Peak Forest w Peak Dale and Dove Holes *Derby 4* **P** *Bp and Duke of Devonshire (jt)* **P-in-c** D J PHYPERS
WORMINGFORD (St Andrew), Mount Bures and Little Horkesley *Chelmsf 17* **P** *J J Tufnell Esq, Mrs F Reynolds, and Keble Coll Ox (jt)* **P-in-c** H HEATH
WORMINGHALL (St Peter and St Paul) w Ickford, Oakley and Shabbington *Ox 21* **P** *Bp and Guild of All So (jt)* **P-in-c** L M WILFORD, **NSM** D A R WALLACE
WORMINGTON (St Katharine) *see* Winchcombe *Glouc*
WORMLEIGHTON (St Peter) *see* Priors Hardwick, Priors Marston and Wormleighton *Cov*
WORMLEY (Church Room) *see* Broxbourne w Wormley *St Alb*
WORMLEY (St Laurence) *as above*
WORMSHILL (St Giles) *see* Bredgar w Bicknor and Frinsted w Wormshill etc *Cant*
WORPLESDON (St Mary the Virgin) *Guildf 5* **P** *Eton Coll* **R** A W BRYANT, **Hon C** A S LEAK, **NSM** J A ROBINSON, **OLM** M E KIRBY, A J WELCH
WORSALL, HIGH AND LOW (All Saints) *York 21* **P** *Abp (3 turns), V Northallerton (1 turn)* **P-in-c** M D ALLSOPP
WORSBROUGH (St Mary) *Sheff 11* **P** *DBP* **NSM** C KELLEHER
WORSBROUGH (St Thomas) (St James) *Sheff 11* **P** *Bp and The Crown (alt)* **V** G R HOLMES
WORSBROUGH COMMON (St Luke) *Sheff 11* **P** *Bp* **V** *vacant* (01226) 282619
WORSLEY (St Mark) *Man 2* **P** *Bp* **TR** M R AINSWORTH, **TV** P BRODY
WORSLEY MESNES (not known) *see* Wigan St Jas w St Thos *Liv*
WORSTEAD (St Mary), Westwick, Sloley, Swanton Abbot and Scottow *Nor 12* **P** *DBP, J T D Shaw Esq, D&C, and Bp (by turn)* **R** A R LONG
WORSTHORNE (St John the Evangelist) *see* Holme-in-Cliviger w Worsthorne *Blackb*
WORTH (St Nicholas) *Chich 7* **P** *DBP* **TV** V T LEONARD, **P-in-c** R A STIDOLPH, **NSM** A F STICKLEY
WORTH (St Peter and St Paul) *see* Woodnesborough w Worth and Staple *Cant*
WORTH MATRAVERS (St Aldhelm) *see* Kingston, Langton Matravers and Worth Matravers *Sarum*
WORTH MATRAVERS (St Nicholas) *as above*
WORTHAM (St Mary the Virgin) *see* N Hartismere *St E*
WORTHEN (All Saints) *Heref 13* **P** *New Coll Ox (8 turns), J J C Coldwell Esq (1 turn), I Chirbury (1 turn)* **P-in-c** A KNIGHT
WORTHING Christ the King (Christ Church) (Holy Trinity) (St Matthew) *Chich 5* **P** *Patr Bd* **TV** E J CHITHAM, **NSM** M E PARGETER, M E PARISH
WORTHING (St Andrew) *Chich 5* **P** *Keble Coll Ox* **P-in-c** M J GUDGEON
WORTHING (St George) (Emmanuel) *Chich 5* **P** *Ch Soc Trust* **V** D E A MARROW
WORTHING (St Margaret) *see* N Elmham w Billingford and Worthing *Nor*
WORTHING, WEST (St John the Divine) *Chich 5* **P** *Bp* **V** J K T ELDRIDGE
WORTHINGTON (St Matthew) *see* Ashby-de-la-Zouch and Breedon on the Hill *Leic*
WORTING (St Thomas of Canterbury) *Win 4* **P** *MMCET* **R** C J M VAUGHAN
WORTLEY (St Leonard) *see* Tankersley, Thurgoland and Wortley *Sheff*
WORTLEY, NEW (St Mary's Parish Centre) *see* Armley w New Wortley *Ripon*
WORTLEY DE LEEDS (St John the Evangelist) *Ripon 6* **P** *Trustees* **V** K A P DOWLING
WORTON (Christ Church) *see* Potterne w Worton and Marston *Sarum*
WORTON, NETHER (St James) *see* Over w Nether Worton *Ox*
WORTON, OVER (Holy Trinity) w Nether Worton *Ox 5* **P** *Exors J B Schuster Esq* **R** *vacant*
WOTTON (St John the Evangelist) and Holmbury St Mary *Guildf 7* **P** *Bp and J P M H Evelyn Esq (jt)* **NSM** P J ROBSON
WOTTON ST MARY WITHOUT (Holy Trinity) *Glouc 5* **P** *Bp* **V** T J G NEWCOMBE, **C** T E CLAMMER
WOTTON-UNDER-EDGE (St Mary the Virgin) w Ozleworth, N Nibley and Alderley *Glouc 2* **P** *Ch Ch Ox and Bp (jt)* **V** J A C MAY, **C** A J MARKEY
WOTTON UNDERWOOD (All Saints) *see* Bernwode *Ox*
WOUGHTON *Ox 25* **P** *Patr Bd* **TV** K F MCGARAHAN, D C BARNES, **NSM** D J RUDIGER
WOUGHTON-ON-THE-GREEN (St Mary) *see* Woughton *Ox*
WOULDHAM (All Saints) *see* Burham and Wouldham *Roch*
WRABNESS (All Saints) *see* Gt Oakley w Wix and Wrabness *Chelmsf*
WRAGBY Group, The (All Saints) *Linc 11* **P** *Bp, MMCET, and DBP (jt)* **R** M N HOLDEN
WRAGBY (St Michael and Our Lady) *see* Kinsley w Wragby *Wakef*
WRAMPLINGHAM (St Peter and St Paul) *see* Barnham Broom and Upper Yare *Nor*
WRANGBROOK (St Michael) *see* Badsworth *Wakef*
WRANGLE (St Mary and St Nicholas) *see* Old Leake w Wrangle *Linc*
WRANGTHORN (St Augustine of Hippo) *see* Woodhouse and Wrangthorn *Ripon*
WRATTING, GREAT (St Mary) *see* Stourhead *St E*
WRATTING, LITTLE (St Mary) *as above*
WRATTING, WEST (St Andrew) *see* Balsham, Weston Colville, W Wickham etc *Ely*
WRAWBY (St Mary the Virgin) *see* Brigg, Wrawby and Cadney cum Howsham *Linc*
WRAXALL (All Saints) *B & W 13* **P** *Trustees* **P-in-c** R C LUNN
WRAXALL (St Mary) *see* Melbury *Sarum*
WRAXALL, NORTH (St James) *see* Colerne w N Wraxall *Bris*
WRAXALL, SOUTH (St James) *see* Monkton Farleigh, S Wraxall and Winsley *Sarum*
WRAY (Holy Trinity) *see* E Lonsdale *Blackb*
WRAY, LOW (St Margaret) *see* Hawkshead and Low Wray w Sawrey and Rusland etc *Carl*
WRAYSBURY (St Andrew) *see* Riverside *Ox*
WREAKE, UPPER *Leic 3* **P** *Bp and DBP (jt)* **V** H M FLINT
WREAY (St Mary) *see* Dalston w Cumdivock, Raughton Head and Wreay *Carl*
WRECCLESHAM (St Peter) *Guildf 3* **P** *Bp* **V** A E GELL
WRENBURY (St Margaret) *see* Baddiley and Wrenbury w Burleydam *Ches*
WRENINGHAM (All Saints) *see* Ashwellthorpe, Forncett, Fundenhall, Hapton etc *Nor*
WRENTHAM (St Nicholas) *see* Sole Bay *St E*
WRENTHORPE (St Anne) *Wakef 12* **P** *Bp* **V** P WHITTINGHAM, **C** E M WOODCOCK
WRESSLE (St John of Beverly) *see* Howden *York*
WRESTLINGWORTH (St Peter) *see* Dunton w Wrestlingworth and Eyeworth *St Alb*
WRETHAM (St Ethelbert) *see* Thetford *Nor*
WRETTON (All Saints) *see* Northwold and Wretton w Stoke Ferry etc *Ely*
WRIBBENHALL (All Saints) *Worc 11* **P** *V Kidderminster* **P-in-c** H HUGHES
WRIGGLE VALLEY, The *Sarum 3* **P** *Duchy of Cornwall (1 turn), Bp (3 turns)* **R** P J RINGER
WRIGHTINGTON (St James the Great) *Blackb 4* **P** *Bp* **V** R TOWNLEY
WRINGTON (All Saints) w Butcombe *B & W 11* **P** *SMF* **R** N R MADDOCK
WRITTLE (All Saints) w Highwood *Chelmsf 8* **P** *New Coll Ox* **V** D M JONES, **NSM** M J ASTON
WROCKWARDINE, The Deanery of (St Peter) *Lich 23* **P** *Patr Bd* **TR** G HORNER, **TV** P H CAWTHORNE, G S GOODWIN, **C** C H DEAKIN
WROCKWARDINE WOOD (Holy Trinity) *see* Oakengates and Wrockwardine Wood *Lich*
WROOT (St Pancras) *see* Epworth Gp *Linc*
WROSE (St Cuthbert) *Bradf 3* **P** *The Crown* **V** P G WALKER, **C** S IRVINE
WROTHAM (St George) *Roch 10* **P** *D&C* **P-in-c** B E HURD
WROUGHTON (St John the Baptist) *Bris 7* **P** *Bp* **V** M A JOHNSON, **C** R M BENNETTS
WROXALL (St John the Evangelist) *Portsm 7* **P** *Bp* **Hon C** A E FAULKNER
WROXALL (St Leonard) *see* Hatton w Haseley, Rowington w Lowsonford etc *Cov*
WROXETER (St Mary) *see* Wrockwardine Deanery *Lich*
WROXHAM (St Mary) w Hoveton St John w Hoveton St Peter and Belaugh *Nor 12* **P** *Bp* **R** A D PARSONS, **OLM** J DODD
WROXTON (All Saints) *see* Ironstone *Ox*
WYBERTON (St Leodegar) *Linc 21* **P** *DBP* **R** A M HUGHES
WYBUNBURY (St Chad) w Doddington (St John) *Ches 15* **P** *Bp and Sir Evelyn Broughton Bt (jt)* **V** A A LONG

WYCH, HIGH (St James) and Gilston w Eastwick *St Alb 18* **P** *V Sawbridgeworth (2 turns), P T S Bowlby Esq (1 turn)* **P-in-c** R B REYNOLDS
WYCHBOLD (St Mary de Wyche) *see* Stoke Prior, Wychbold and Upton Warren *Worc*
WYCHE (All Saints) *see* Malvern St Andr and Malvern Wells and Wyche *Worc*
WYCHLING (St Margaret) *see* Doddington, Newnham and Wychling *Cant*
WYCHNOR (St Leonard) *Lich 1* **P** *Personal Reps W H Harrison Esq* **V** J W ALLAN, **NSM** P A L MADDOCK, V A WILKERSON
WYCK RISSINGTON (St Laurence) *see* Bourton-on-the-Water w Clapton etc *Glouc*
WYCLIFFE (St Mary) *see* Barningham w Hutton Magna and Wycliffe *Ripon*
WYCOMBE, HIGH (All Saints) *Ox 29* **P** *Patr Bd* **TR** D A PICKEN, **TV** M S GURR, S A WHITMORE, N R TOTTLE, S A SIMPSON, D B FOSTER, **NSM** P VINEY, J D ARTHUR, E S CARR, **OLM** M A JACKSON, R M WOOSTER
WYCOMBE, WEST (St Laurence) (St Paul) w Bledlow Ridge, Bradenham and Radnage *Ox 29* **P** *Bp, DBP, Peache Trustees, and Sir Francis Dashwood Bt (jt)* **P-in-c** N J LACEY, **NSM** V J BEAUMONT, L J RICHARDSON, **OLM** E NICHOLSON
WYCOMBE AND CHADWELL (St Mary) *see* Scalford w Wycombe and Chadwell etc *Leic*
WYCOMBE LANE (St Mary) *see* Wooburn *Ox*
WYCOMBE MARSH (St Anne and St Peter) *see* High Wycombe *Ox*
WYDDIAL (St Giles) *see* Hormead, Wyddial, Anstey, Brent Pelham etc *St Alb*
WYE (St Gregory and St Martin) w Brook *Cant 2* **P** *Abp* **V** J S RICHARDSON, **C** S H LILLICRAP, **NSM** L C CLEVELAND
WYE, SOUTH Team Ministry *see* Heref S Wye *Heref*
WYESHAM (St James) *see* Dixton *Heref*
WYFORDBY (St Mary) *see* S Framland *Leic*
WYKE *see* Win St Matt *Win*
WYKE (Holy Trinity) *see* Bruton and Distr *B & W*
WYKE (St Mark) *Guildf 5* **P** *Bp* **V** P A GODFREY
WYKE (St Mary the Virgin) *Bradf 2* **P** *Bp* **P-in-c** F SUDWORTH
WYKE REGIS (All Saints) *Sarum 4* **P** *D&C* **R** K A HUGO
WYKEHAM (All Saints) *see* Brompton by Sawdon w Hutton Buscel, Snainton etc *York*
WYKEHAM: Broughton w North Newington, Epwell w Sibford, Shutford, Swalcliffe, and Tadmarton *Ox 5* **P** *New Coll, Worc Coll, and Lord Saye and Sele (jt)* **R** T WIMBUSH, **NSM** K WALKLATE
WYKEN (Church of Risen Christ) *see* Coventry Caludon *Cov*
WYKEN (Holy Cross) *as above*
WYKEN (St Mary Magdalene) *as above*
WYLAM (St Oswin) *Newc 3* **P** *Bp* **P-in-c** D E CANT
WYLDE GREEN (Emmanuel) *Birm 12* **P** *Bp* **V** R E CRANE
WYLYE (St Mary the Virgin) *see* Wylye and Till Valley *Sarum*
WYLYE AND TILL VALLEY *Sarum 13* **P** *Patr Bd (2 turns), Ld Chan (1 turn)* **TR** D M K DURSTON, **TV** H R L BONSEY, S ARMITAGE, **NSM** L E HALLIDAY, **OLM** R D D HENDERSON, V M GARRARD
WYLYE VALLEY TEAM, UPPER *Sarum 17* **P** *Patr Bd (5 turns), Ld Chan (1 turn)* **TR** J H TOMLINSON, **C** H BEGLEY, **OLM** A E BENNETT-SHAW, D M HAMMOND
WYMERING (St Peter and St Paul) *see* Widley w Wymering *Portsm*
WYMESWOLD (St Mary) and Prestwold w Hoton *Leic 7* **P** *S J Packe-Drury-Lowe Esq and Bp (by turn)* **Hon C** W ROBSON
WYMINGTON (St Lawrence) w Podington *St Alb 15* **P** *R M Orlebar Esq (1 turn), DBP (3 turns)* **R** *vacant* (01933) 313069
WYMONDHAM (St Mary and St Thomas) *Nor 7* **P** *Bp* **V** M W SMITH, **C** R W NICHOLS, M R EASTWOOD
WYMONDHAM (St Peter) *see* S Framland *Leic*
WYMONDLEY, GREAT (St Mary the Virgin) and LITTLE (St Mary the Virgin) *St Alb 4* **P** *Bp and MMCET (jt)* **P-in-c** I S TATTUM
WYMYNSWOLD (St Margaret) *see* Nonington w Wymynswold and Goodnestone etc *Cant*
WYNYARD PARK (Chapel) *see* Grindon, Stillington and Wolviston *Dur*
WYRE PIDDLE (St Anne) *see* Fladbury w Wyre Piddle and Moor etc *Worc*
WYRESDALE, OVER (Christ Church) *see* Dolphinholme w Quernmore and Over Wyresdale *Blackb*
WYRLEY, GREAT (St Mark) *Lich 3* **P** *R Cannock* **V** R P OAKLEY, **C** A M JONES, R A WESTWOOD, **OLM** M J PRICE
WYSALL (Holy Trinity) *see* Willoughby-on-the-Wolds w Wysall and Widmerpool *S'well*
WYTHALL (no church) *Birm 6* **P** *R Kings Norton* **V** M J GODFREY
WYTHAM (All Saints) *see* N Hinksey and Wytham *Ox*
WYTHBURN (not known) *see* St John's-in-the-Vale, Threlkeld and Wythburn *Carl*
WYTHENSHAWE Lawton Moor (St Michael and All Angels) *see* Lawton Moor *Man*
WYTHENSHAWE (St Francis of Assisi) (St Luke) (St Martin) (St Richard of Chichester) (William Temple Church) *Man 8* **P** *Patr Bd* **TR** G BABB, **TV** A J HODGSON, A PILKINGTON, S E HERBERT, **C** J D HUGHES, S L MILLER, **NSM** O E MARLOW
WYTHER (Venerable Bede) *Ripon 6* **P** *Bp* **V** G W COOPER
WYTHOP (St Margaret) *see* Cockermouth w Embleton and Wythop *Carl*
WYVERSTONE (St George) *see* Bacton w Wyverstone, Cotton and Old Newton etc *St E*
WYVILL (St Catherine) *see* Harlaxton Gp *Linc*
YAFFORTH (All Saints) *see* Lower Swale *Ripon*
YALDING (St Peter and St Paul) w Collier Street *Roch 8* **P** *Ld Chan* **V** C J REED
YANWORTH (St Michael) *see* Chedworth, Yanworth and Stowell, Coln Rogers etc *Glouc*
YAPHAM (St Martin) *see* Barmby Moor Gp *York*
YAPTON (St Mary) *see* Clymping and Yapton w Ford *Chich*
YARCOMBE (St John the Baptist) *see* Kilmington, Stockland, Dalwood, Yarcombe etc *Ex*
YARDLEY (St Cyprian) Hay Mill *Birm 13* **P** *Bp* **P-in-c** A P JOHNSON
YARDLEY (St Edburgha) *Birm 13* **P** *St Pet Coll Ox* **P-in-c** J A OMOYAJOWO, **C** G R SMITH
YARDLEY (St Lawrence) *see* Ardeley *St Alb*
YARDLEY, SOUTH (St Michael and All Angels) *Birm 13* **P** *Bp* **V** C G GRAHAM, **NSM** G R PIKE
YARDLEY GOBION (St Leonard) *see* Potterspury w Furtho and Yardley Gobion etc *Pet*
YARDLEY HASTINGS (St Andrew), Denton and Grendon w Castle Ashby and Whiston *Pet 7* **P** *Marquess of Northampton and Bp (alt)* **R** D L SPOKES
YARDLEY WOOD (Christ Church) *Birm 5* **P** *Bp* **V** J G RICHARDS
YARKHILL (St John the Baptist) *see* Ledbury *Heref*
YARLINGTON (Blessed Virgin Mary) *see* Camelot Par *B & W*
YARM (St Mary Magdalene) *York 21* **P** *Abp* **R** B C GURD, **C** J C ROUNDTREE
YARMOUTH (St James) *Portsm 8* **P** *Keble Coll Ox* **R** M E C WHATSON, **NSM** D K BELLAMY, G M HURT
YARMOUTH, GREAT (St John) (St Nicholas) (St Paul) (St Luke) (St Mary) *Nor 6* **P** *Patr Bd* **TR** M S WOODS, **TV** M I KNOWLES, R J KNOWLES, **OLM** A W BOWLES
YARNFIELD (Mission Room St Barnabas) *see* Swynnerton and Tittensor *Lich*
YARNSCOMBE (St Andrew) *see* Newton Tracey, Horwood, Alverdiscott etc *Ex*
YARNTON (St Bartholomew) *see* Blenheim *Ox*
YARPOLE (St Leonard) *see* Leominster *Heref*
YARWELL (St Mary Magdalene) *see* Nassington w Yarwell and Woodnewton *Pet*
YATE New Town (St Mary) *Bris 5* **P** *Bp* **TR** D B HARREX, **TV** I P MACFARLANE, T ASHWORTH, **Hon C** D T R WILCOX, V ASHWORTH, **NSM** C D VEREY
YATELEY (St Peter) and Eversley *Win 5* **P** *Bp* **C** I S WHITHAM, M W SAUNDERS
YATESBURY (All Saints) *see* Oldbury *Sarum*
YATTENDON (St Peter and St Paul) *see* Hermitage *Ox*
YATTON (All Saints) *see* Ledbury *Heref*
YATTON KEYNELL (St Margaret) *see* By Brook *Bris*
YATTON MOOR (Blessed Virgin Mary) *B & W 13* **P** *DBF* **TR** I M HUBBARD, **TV** C J HORDER, J C ANDREWS, **C** W M MITCHELL, **NSM** C M HORSEMAN, C R LLEWELYN-EVANS
YAVERLAND (St John the Baptist) *see* Brading w Yaverland *Portsm*
YAXHAM (St Peter) *see* Mattishall w Mattishall Burgh, Welborne etc *Nor*
YAXLEY (St Mary the Virgin) *see* S Hartismere *St E*
YAXLEY (St Peter) and Holme w Conington *Ely 11* **P** *Ld Chan (2 turns), J H B Heathcote Esq (1 turn)* **V** I M COWLEY, **C** L E CLELAND
YEADON (St Andrew) *Bradf 4* **P** *Bp* **P-in-c** P J SUTCLIFFE
YEADON (St John the Evangelist) *Bradf 4* **P** *R Guiseley w Esholt* **P-in-c** R M WALKER, **NSM** J L SMITH
YEALAND CONYERS (St John the Evangelist) *see* Warton St Oswald w Yealand Conyers *Blackb*

YEALMPTON (St Bartholomew) and Brixton *Ex 21* **P** *D&C Windsor and Bp (jt)* **V** D ARNOTT
YEARSLEY (Holy Trinity) *see* Crayke w Brandsby and Yearsley *York*
YEAVELEY (Holy Trinity) *see* Alkmonton, Cubley, Marston, Montgomery etc *Derby*
YEDINGHAM (St John the Baptist) *see* Buckrose Carrs *York*
YELDEN (St Mary) *see* The Stodden Churches *St Alb*
YELDHAM, GREAT (St Andrew) *see* Upper Colne *Chelmsf*
YELDHAM, LITTLE (St John the Baptist) *as above*
YELFORD (St Nicholas and St Swithin) *see* Lower Windrush *Ox*
YELLING (Holy Cross) *see* Papworth *Ely*
YELVERTOFT (All Saints) *see* Crick and Yelvertoft w Clay Coton and Lilbourne *Pet*
YELVERTON (St Mary) *see* Thurton *Nor*
YELVERTON (St Paul), Meavy, Sheepstor and Walkhampton *Ex 25* **P** *Patr Bd* **TR** R H TEBBS, **NSM** J W M WEIR, M SALMON, N S SHUTT
YEOFORD CHAPEL (Holy Trinity) *see* Crediton, Shobrooke and Sandford etc *Ex*
YEOVIL (Holy Trinity) w Barwick *B & W 7* **P** *Ms Y L Bennett and Ms R S Mullen (1 turn), The Crown (3 turns)* **R** T J COOK, **C** D R GENT
YEOVIL (St Andrew) (St John the Baptist) w Kingston Pitney *B & W 7* **P** *Mrs S W Rawlins (3 turns), DBP (1 turn)* **R** I G HUGHES, **C** M R CAMPBELL
YEOVIL (St James the Great) *see* Preston Plucknett *B & W*
YEOVIL (St Michael and All Angels) *B & W 7* **P** *Bp* **V** M D ELLIS, **NSM** C Y JONES
YEOVIL (St Peter) *see* Preston Plucknett *B & W*
YEOVIL MARSH (All Saints) *see* Tintinhull w Chilthorne Domer, Yeovil Marsh etc *B & W*
YETMINSTER (St Andrew) *see* Wriggle Valley *Sarum*
YIEWSLEY (St Matthew) *Lon 24* **P** *V Hillingdon* **V** S A GROOM, **NSM** J SHEFFIELD
YOCKLETON (Holy Trinity) *Heref 13* **P** *Bp* **R** C B BULL
YORK Acomb (St Aidan) *see* Acomb St Steph *York*
YORK (All Saints) *see* Huntington *York*
YORK (All Saints) North Street *York 7* **P** *D&C* **P-in-c** A A HORSMAN
YORK (All Saints) Pavement w St Crux and St Michael Spurriergate *York 7* **P** *Abp* **P-in-c** S R STANLEY, **NSM** A P HUGHES
YORK (Christ Church) *see* Heworth Ch Ch *York*
YORK (Holy Redeemer) *see* Acomb H Redeemer *York*
YORK (Holy Trinity) *see* Heworth H Trin *York*
YORK (Holy Trinity) Micklegate *York 7* **P** *D&C* **R** R M C SEED
YORK (James the Deacon) *see* Acomb Moor *York*
YORK (St Barnabas) *York 7* **P** *CPAS* **P-in-c** K BURNETT-HALL
YORK (St Chad) *York 7* **P** *Abp* **P-in-c** S R STANLEY, **NSM** D C E SIMPSON
YORK (St Clement w St Mary) Bishophill *York 7* **P** *Abp and D&C (jt)* **R** A STOKER
YORK (St Denys) *York 7* **P** *Abp* **P-in-c** S R STANLEY, **NSM** A P HUGHES
YORK (St Edward the Confessor) *see* Dringhouses *York*
YORK (St Helen) Stonegate w (St Martin) Coney Street *York 7* **P** *Abp* **V** A C HODGE, **NSM** S A WHITTINGTON, S A NORTON
YORK (St Hilda) *York 7* **P** *Abp* **V** A P G MORGAN
YORK (St Lawrence w St Nicholas) *York 7* **P** *D&C* **P-in-c** J RICHARDSON
YORK (St Luke) *York 7* **P** *Abp* **P-in-c** S C BENFORD
YORK (St Martin-cum-Gregory) *see* York H Trin Micklegate *York*
YORK (St Michael-le-Belfrey) (St Cuthbert) *York 7* **P** *Abp* **V** R W SIMPSON, **C** I G BIRKINSHAW, R V JACKSON, A M LAMB, **NSM** W J ROBERTS
YORK (St Olave w St Giles) *York 7* **P** *Abp* **V** A C HODGE, **NSM** S A WHITTINGTON, S A NORTON
YORK (St Oswald) *see* Fulford *York*
YORK (St Paul) Holgate Road *York 7* **P** *CPAS* **R** J M A LEE, **NSM** U L SIMPSON
YORK (St Philip and St James) *see* Clifton *York*
YORK (St Stephen) *see* Acomb St Steph *York*
YORK (St Thomas w St Maurice) *York 7* **P** *Abp* **P-in-c** S A WHITTINGTON
YORK (St Wulstan) *see* Heworth H Trin *York*
YORKLEY, LOWER (St Luke's Church Centre) *see* Parkend and Viney Hill *Glouc*
YORKTOWN (St Michael) *see* Camberley St Mich Yorktown *Guildf*
YOULGREAVE (All Saints), Middleton, Stanton-in-Peak and Birchover *Derby 2* **P** *Duke of Devonshire and N B B Davie-Thornhill Esq (jt)* **P-in-c** O J POST
YOXALL (St Peter) *Lich 1* **P** *Bp* **P-in-c** J G LISTER
YOXFORD (St Peter), Peasenhall and Sibton *St E 19* **P** *Bp (1 turn), J K A Brooke Esq and CPAS (1 turn)* **P-in-c** R J GINN, **C** H W TURNER, **OLM** S A WARNE, A B BAYMAN, E M COLE
ZEAL, SOUTH (St Mary) *see* S Tawton and Belstone *Ex*
ZEAL MONACHORUM (St Peter) *Ex 2* **P** *DBP* **R** *vacant*
ZEALS (St Martin) *see* Upper Stour *Sarum*
ZENNOR (St Senera) *Truro 5* **P** *Bp* **P-in-c** J M PILGRIM

WELSH BENEFICES AND CHURCHES

An index of benefices of the Church in Wales (shown in bold type), together with entries for churches and other licensed places of worship. Where the church name is the same as the benefice (or the first place name in the benefice), the church entry is omitted. Church dedications are indicated in brackets.

The benefice entry gives the full legal name, followed by the diocese, its deanery number (p. 952), and the name(s) and appointment(s) of the clergy serving there (if there are none, the telephone number of the parsonage house is given). The following are the main abbreviations used; for others see the full list of abbreviations.

C	Curate	**P-in-c**	Priest-in-charge
C-in-c	Curate-in-charge	**Par Dn**	Parish Deacon
Dn-in-c	Deacon-in-charge	**R**	Rector
Dss	Deaconess	**TM**	Team Minister
Hon C	Honorary Curate	**TR**	Team Rector
Hon Par Dn	Honorary Parish Deacon	**TV**	Team Vicar
NSM	Non-stipendiary Minister	**V**	Vicar

ABBEY CWMHIR (St Mary the Virgin) *see* Llanbadarn Fawr, Llandegley and Llanfihangel etc *S & B*

ABER (St Bodfan) *see* Llanfairfechan w Aber *Ban*

ABERAERON (Holy Trinity) *see* Henfynyw w Aberaeron and Llanddewi Aberarth etc *St D*

ABERAMAN (St Margaret) and Abercwmboi w Cwmaman *Llan 9* **V** D C WAY

ABERAVON (St Mary) (St Paul) (Holy Trinity) *Llan 7* **TR** S P KIRK, **TV** J J JENKINS, **C** M R D THOMAS

ABERBARGOED (St Peter) *see* Bedwellty *Mon*

ABERBEEG (Christchurch) *see* Llanhilleth *Mon*

ABERCANAID (St Peter) *Llan 10* **P-in-c** G G FOSTER

ABERCARN and Cwmcarn *Mon 7* **V** J J WILKINS, **NSM** M REDWOOD

ABERCRAF (St David) *see* Cwmtawe Uchaf *S & B*

ABERCWMBOI *see* Aberaman and Abercwmboi w Cwmaman *Llan*

ABERCYNON (St Donat) (St Gwynno) *Llan 9* **V** *vacant* (01443) 740207

ABERDARE (St Fagan) *Llan 9* **V** P J BENNETT

ABERDARE (St John the Baptist) (St Elvan) (St Matthew) (St John the Evangelist) *Llan 9* **V** R E DAVIES

ABERDARON (St Hywyn) w Rhiw and Llanfaelrhys w Llangwnnadl and Penllech *Ban 11* **R** E D DAVIES

ABERDYFI (St Peter) *see* Llanegryn w Aberdyfi w Tywyn *Ban*

ABEREDW (St Cewydd) w Llandeilo Graban and Llanbadarn-y-Garreg w Crickadarn and Gwenddwr *S & B 2* **V** T J WILLIAMS, **NSM** P J MORRIS

ABERERCH (St Cawrdaf) *see* Denio w Abererch *Ban*

ABERFFRAW (St Beuno) *see* Trefdraeth w Aberffraw, Llangadwaladr etc *Ban*

ABERGAVENNY (Holy Trinity) (Christ Church) *Mon 1* **OLM** C R WALTERS

ABERGAVENNY (St Mary) (Christchurch) w Llanwenarth Citra *Mon 1* **V** J H WINSTON, **Par Dn** M C G LANE

ABERGELE (St Michael) (St David) *St As 6* **V** S T GRIFFITHS

ABERGORLECH (St David) *see* Brechfa w Abergorlech etc *St D*

ABERGWILI (St David) w Llanfihangel-uwch-Gwili and Capel-y-Groes *St D 11* **V** L L RICHARDSON

ABERGWYNFI (St Thomas) *see* Glyncorrwg and Upper Afan Valley *Llan*

ABERGWYNGREGYN (St Bodfan) *see* Llanfairfechan w Aber *Ban*

ABERGYNOLWYN *see* Llanegryn w Aberdyfi w Tywyn *Ban*

ABERHAFESP (St Gwynog) *see* Newtown w Llanllwchaiarn w Aberhafesp *St As*

ABERKENFIG (St John) *see* Llansantffraid, Bettws and Aberkenfig *Llan*

ABERNANT (St Lucia) *see* Tre-lech a'r Betws w Abernant and Llanwinio *St D*

ABERNANT (St Matthew) *see* Aberdare *Llan*

ABERPERGWM (St Cadoc) *see* Vale of Neath *Llan*

ABERPORTH (St Cynwyl) w Tremain w Blaenporth and Betws Ifan *St D 6* **R** *vacant* (01239) 810556

ABERSYCHAN and Garndiffaith *Mon 10* **P-in-c** J A V FLORANCE

ABERTILLERY (St Michael) w Cwmtillery w Six Bells *Mon 8* **C** P W S KING

ABERTYSSWG (St Paul) *see* New Tredegar *Mon*

ABERYSKIR (St Mary and St Cynidr) *see* Trallwng w Bettws Penpont w Aberyskir etc *S & B*

ABERYSTWYTH (St Michael) (Holy Trinity) (St Mary) (St Anne) *St D 10* **TR** S R BELL, **TV** I H AVESON, A F HERRICK

AFAN VALE *see* Glyncorrwg and Upper Afan Valley *Llan*

ALLTMAWR (St Mauritius) *see* Builth and Llanddewi'r Cwm w Llangynog etc *S & B*

ALLTWEN (St John the Baptist) *see* Cilybebyll *Llan*

AMBLESTON (St Mary) *see* Spittal w Trefgarn and Ambleston w St Dogwells *St D*

AMLWCH (St Eleth) (St Peter) (St Gwenllwyfo) (St Eilian) *Ban 7* **R** D J WILLIAMS

AMMANFORD (All Saints) *see* Betws w Ammanford *St D*

AMMANFORD (St Michael) *as above*

AMROTH (St Elidyr) *see* St Issell's and Amroth *St D*

ANGLE (St Mary) *see* Monkton *St D*

ARTHOG (St Catherine) w Fairbourne w Llangelynnin w Rhoslefain *Ban 12* **P-in-c** D C BRYANT

BAGILLT (St Mary) (St Peter) *St As 4* **V** B TAYLOR

BAGLAN (St Catherine) (St Baglan) *Llan 7* **V** D W LEWIS

BALA (Christ Church) *St As 17* **R** N W ROBERTS

BANGOR (Cathedral of St Deiniol) (St Mary) (Eglwys y Groes) (St James) (St David) (St Peter) *Ban 5* **R** A J HAWKINS, **TV** L J PERRY, S H JONES, A W COLEMAN, **NSM** C A OWEN

BANGOR MONACHORUM (St Dunawd), Worthenbury and Marchwiel *St As 11* **R** A W A COPPING

BANGOR TEIFI (St David) *see* Llandysul w Bangor Teifi w Henllan etc *St D*

BARGOED (St Gwladys) and Deri w Brithdir *Llan 1* **V** A P BOOKLESS

BARMOUTH *see* Llanaber w Caerdeon *Ban*

BARRY (All Saints) (St John w St Baruc) *Llan 5* **R** J G D OEPPEN

BARRY (St Paul) *see* Merthyr Dyfan *Llan*

BASSALEG (St Basil) *Mon 6* **TR** J S WILLIAMS, **TV** P D CROCKER, **NSM** R P MULCAHY, **OLM** G M JAMES

BATTLE (St Cynog) *see* Trallwng w Bettws Penpont w Aberyskir etc *S & B*

BEAUFORT (St Andrew) *see* Ebbw Vale *Mon*

BEAUFORT (St David) *as above*

BEAUMARIS (St Mary and St Nicholas) (St Catherine) (St Seiriol) (St Cawrdaf) (St Michael) *Ban 6* **R** N FAIRLAMB

BEDDGELERT (St Mary) *see* Penrhyndeudraeth w Llanfrothen w Beddgelert *Ban*

BEDLINOG (St Cadoc) *see* Treharris, Trelewis and Bedlinog *Llan*

BEDLINOG (St Mary) *as above*

BEDWAS (St Barrwg) and Rudry *Mon 6* **R** P M WINCHESTER

BEDWELLTY (St Sannan) *Mon 7* **V** J M T CARLYON, **Par Dn** K HEMMINGS

BEGELLY (St Mary) w Ludchurch and Crunwere *St D 4* **R** D G BATE

BEGUILDY (St Michael and All Angels) *see* Beguildy and Heyope and Llangynllo and Bleddfa *S & B*

BEGUILDY (St Michael and All Angels) (St Peter) and Heyope and Llangynllo and Bleddfa *S & B 5* **P-in-c** R HART

BENLLECH (St Andrew) *see* Llanfair Mathafarn Eithaf w Llanbedrgoch *Ban*

BERRIEW (St Beuno) *St As 10* **V** J B THELWELL, **NSM** F M ROBARTS

BERSE (Parish Church) *see* Broughton and Berse *St As*

BETTISFIELD (St John the Baptist) *see* Hanmer, Bronington, Bettisfield, Tallarn Green *St As*

BETTWS *see* Trallwng w Bettws Penpont w Aberyskir etc *S & B*

BETTWS (St David) *see* Llansantffraid, Bettws and Aberkenfig *Llan*

BETTWS (St David) *Mon 9* **R** *vacant* (01633) 855193

BETTWS CHAPEL *see* Llantilio Pertholey w Bettws Chpl etc *Mon*

BETTWS DISSERTH (St Mary) *see* Colwyn *S & B*

BETTWS NEWYDD (not known) w Trostrey and Kemeys Commander and Llanfihangel Gobion w Llanfair Kilgeddin *Mon 5* **R** T G CLEMENT

BETWS (Holy Trinity) *see* Glasbury and Llowes w Clyro and Betws *S & B*

BETWS (St David) w Ammanford *St D 13* **V** D BOWEN, **C** P H DAVIES
BETWS BLEDRWS (St Bledrws or St Michael) *St D 9* **R** *vacant*
BETWS CEDEWAIN (St Beuno) and Tregynon and Llanwyddelan *St As 7* **V** G K MARSHALL
BETWS GARMON (St Garmon) *see* Llanbeblig w Caernarfon and Betws Garmon etc *Ban*
BETWS GWERFUL GOCH (St Mary) w Llangwm, Gwyddelwern and Llawrybetws *St As 17* **NSM** D EVANS
BETWS LEUCU (St Lucia) *see* Llangeitho and Blaenpennal w Betws Leucu etc *St D*
BETWS-Y-COED (St Mary) and Capel Curig w Penmachno w Dolwyddelan *Ban 2* **P-in-c** K L JONES
BETWS-YN-RHOS (St Michael) w Petryal *St As 6* **R** J R MATTHIAS
BEULAH *see* Llanwrtyd w Llanddulas in Tir Abad etc *S & B*
BIRCHGROVE (St John) *see* Llansamlet *S & B*
BISHOPSTON (St Teilo) *S & B 8* **R** *vacant* (01441) 282140
BISHTON (St Cadwaladr) *Mon 4* **V** B M W STARES, **NSM** D E COLLINGBOURNE
BISTRE (Emmanuel) (All Saints) (St Cecilia) *St As 13* **V** M W HILL, **C** A ANTHAPURUSHA
BLACKWOOD (St Margaret) *Mon 7* **V** D JONES
BLAENAU FFESTINIOG (St David) *see* Ffestiniog w Blaenau Ffestiniog *Ban*
BLAENAVON (St Peter) w Capel Newydd *Mon 10* **V** J S BRAY
BLAENCELYN (St David) *see* Llangrannog w Llandysiliogogo w Penbryn *St D*
BLAENGARW (St James) *see* Llangeinor and the Garw Valley *Llan*
BLAENGWRACH (St Mary) *see* Vale of Neath *Llan*
BLAENLLECHAU (St Thomas) *see* Rhondda Fach Uchaf *Llan*
BLAENPENNAL (St David) *see* Llangeitho and Blaenpennal w Betws Leucu etc *St D*
BLAENPORTH (St David) *see* Aberporth w Tremain w Blaenporth and Betws Ifan *St D*
BLAINA (St Peter) and Nantyglo *Mon 8* **R** R L HEWETT, **Par Dn** C MORGAN
BLEDDFA (St Mary Magdalene) *see* Beguildy and Heyope and Llangynllo and Bleddfa *S & B*
BLETHERSTON (St Mary) *see* Llawhaden w Bletherston and Llanycefn *St D*
BODEDERN (St Edern) w Llanfaethlu *Ban 3* **R** *vacant* (01407) 730142
BODELYWDDAN (St Margaret) *St As 1* **V** G B HUGHES, **C** P A RIMMER
BODEWRYD (St Mary) *see* Llanfechell w Bodewryd w Rhosbeirio etc *Ban*
BODFARI (St Stephen) *see* Caerwys and Bodfari *St As*
BODWROG (St Twrog) *see* Llandrygarn w Bodwrog and Heneglwys etc *Ban*
BONTDDU *see* Llanaber w Caerdeon *Ban*
BONVILSTON (St Mary) *see* St Nicholas w Bonvilston and St George-super-Ely *Llan*
BONYMAEN (St Margaret) *see* Glantawe *S & B*
BORTH (St Matthew) and Eglwys-fach w Llangynfelyn *St D 10* **V** G A DAVIES
BOSHERSTON (St Michael) *see* Monkton *St D*
BOTWNNOG (St Beuno) w Bryncroes (St Mary) *Ban 11* **R** P D JAMES, **C** J E GOURDIE, **NSM** S M M WILLIAMS
BOUGHROOD (St Cynog) *see* Llandefalle and Llyswen w Boughrood etc *S & B*
BOULSTON *see* Slebech and Uzmaston w Boulston *St D*
BRAWDY (St David) *see* Dewisland *St D*
BRECHFA (St Teilo) w Abergorlech and Llanfihangel Rhos-y-corn *St D 14* **P-in-c** G A SYKES
BRECON (Cathedral of St John the Evangelist) (St Mary) w Llanddew *S & B 1* **V** J D E DAVIES
BRECON (St David) w Llanspyddid and Llanilltyd *S & B 1* **V** D E THOMAS
BRIDELL (St David) *see* Cilgerran w Bridell and Llantwyd *St D*
BRIDGEND (St Illtud) *see* Newcastle *Llan*
BRIDGEND (St Mary) *see* Coity w Nolton *Llan*
BRIGHTON, NEW (St James) *see* Mold *St As*
BRITHDIR (St David) *see* Bargoed and Deri w Brithdir *Llan*
BRITHDIR (St Mark) *see* Dolgellau w Llanfachreth and Brithdir etc *Ban*
BRITHDIR (St Mary) *see* Llanrhaeadr-ym-Mochnant etc *St As*
BRITON FERRY (St Clement) *see* Llansawel, Briton Ferry *Llan*
BRO DDYFI UCHAF *Ban 10* **NSM** R P BARNES
BRONGWYN (St Mary) *see* Newcastle Emlyn w Llandyfriog etc *St D*
BRONINGTON (Holy Trinity) *see* Hanmer, Bronington, Bettisfield, Tallarn Green *St As*
BRONLLYS (St Mary) w Llanfilo *S & B 4* **V** A J R THOMAS
BRONWYDD (St Celynnin) *see* Llanpumsaint w Llanllawddog *St D*
BROUGHTON (St Mary) *see* Hawarden *St As*
BROUGHTON (St Paul) (St Peter) and Berse *St As 15* **V** J G AYLWARD
BRYMBO (St Alban) (St Mary) and Southsea *St As 15* **P-in-c** N W CARTER
BRYN (St Tydfil) *see* Llangynwyd w Maesteg *Llan*
BRYNAMAN (St Catherine) w Cwmllynfell *St D 13* **V** A TEALE
BRYNCETHIN *see* Llansantffraid, Bettws and Aberkenfig *Llan*
BRYNCOEDIFOR (St Paul) *see* Dolgellau w Llanfachreth and Brithdir etc *Ban*
BRYNCROES (St Mary) *see* Botwnnog w Bryncroes *Ban*
BRYNEGLWYS (St Tysilio) *St As 17* **P-in-c** H FENTON
BRYNFORD (St Michael) *see* Gorsedd w Brynford, Ysgeifiog and Whitford *St As*
BRYNGWRAN *see* Valley w Llechylched and Caergeiliog *Ban*
BRYNGWYN (St Mary) *see* Newcastle Emlyn w Llandyfriog etc *St D*
BRYNGWYN (St Michael) and Newchurch and Llanbedr Painscastle and Llanddewi Fach *S & B 2* **NSM** H J FISHER
BRYNGWYN (St Peter) *see* Raglan w Llandenny and Bryngwyn *Mon*
BRYNMAWR (St Mary the Virgin) *S & B 3* **V** R T GREY
BRYNNA *see* Llanharan w Peterston-super-Montem *Llan*
BRYNYMAEN (Christ Church) *see* Colwyn Bay w Brynymaen *St As*
BUCKHOLT *see* Penallt and Trellech *Mon*
BUCKHOLT (St John the Baptist) *see* Monmouth w Overmonnow etc *Mon*
BUCKLEY (St Matthew) (Good Shepherd) *St As 13* **V** A M TILTMAN
BUILTH (St Mary) and Llanddewi'r Cwm w Llangynog and Maesmynis and Llanynys and Alltmawr *S & B 2* **V** N D HALL
BULWARK (St Christopher) *see* Chepstow *Mon*
BURRY PORT (St Mary) and Pwll *St D 12* **V** G D HARRIES
BURTON (St Mary) and Rosemarket *St D 5* **P-in-c** C C BARNES
BUTE TOWN (St Aidan) *see* Pontlottyn w Fochriw *Llan*
BUTTINGTON (All Saints) *see* Guilsfield w Buttington *St As*
BWLCH (All Saints) *see* Llyn Safaddan *S & B*
BWLCHGWYN (Christ Church) and Minera *St As 15* **V** J G CANHAM
BWLCHYCIBAU (Christ Church) *see* Llanfyllin and Bwlchycibau *St As*
BYLCHAU (St Thomas) *see* Henllan and Llannefydd and Bylchau *St As*
CADOXTON-JUXTA-BARRY (St Cadoc) (St Mary) *Llan 5* **R** J M HUGHES
CADOXTON-JUXTA-NEATH (St Catwg) *Llan 8* **V** N LEA, **NSM** C GALSWORTHY
CAERAU (St Cynfelin) (St Peter) *Llan 7* **V** K ANDREWS
CAERAU w Ely (St David) (St Timothy) *Llan 3* **V** N CAHILL, **C** M GIBBON
CAERDEON (St Philip) *see* Llanaber w Caerdeon *Ban*
CAEREITHIN (St Teilo) *S & B 10* **V** *vacant* (01792) 583646
CAERFALLWCH (St Paul) *see* Halkyn w Caerfallwch w Rhesycae *St As*
CAERGEILIOG *see* Valley w Llechylched and Caergeiliog *Ban*
CAERGYBI *see* Holyhead *Ban*
CAERHUN (St Mary) w Llangelynin w Llanbedr-y-Cennin *Ban 2* **V** W BYNON
CAERLEON (St Cadoc) w Llanhennock *Mon 9* **V** A J EDWARDS, **C** B N B MUSINDI, **NSM** E HILLS
CAERLEON-ULTRA-PONTEM (Holy Spirit) *see* Newport Ch Ch *Mon*
CAERNARFON (St Mary) *see* Llanbeblig w Caernarfon and Betws Garmon etc *Ban*
CAERPHILLY (St Martin) (St Catherine) (St Andrew) *Llan 1* **R** M J SHORT, **C** A J DAVIES, D O TREHARNE
CAERSWS (St Mary) *see* Llanwnnog and Caersws w Carno *Ban*
CAERWENT (St Stephen and St Tathan) w Dinham and Llanfair Discoed and Shirenewton w Newchurch *Mon 2* **V** H TRENCHARD, **NSM** E N M DAVIES
CAERWYS (St Michael) and Bodfari *St As 2* **R** J T EVANS, **NSM** G L HUGHES
CALDICOT (St Mary) *Mon 4* **TR** L HARRISON, **C** D C BOUTFLOWER, W C INGLE-GILLIS
CALLWEN (St John the Baptist) *see* Cwmtawe Uchaf *S & B*
CAMROSE (St Ishmael) *St D 5* **P-in-c** C W BOWEN

CANTON Cardiff (St Luke) *Llan 2* **TR** M R PREECE, **TV** R N PARRY, **C** C W COLES, J DURLEY
CANTON (St Catherine) *Llan 2* **V** *vacant* (029) 2038 2796
CANTON (St John) *Llan 2* **R** *vacant*
CANTREF (St Mary) *see* Llanfrynach and Cantref w Llanhamlach *S & B*
CAPEL (Dewi Sant) *see* Llansadwrn w Llanwrda and Manordeilo *St D*
CAPEL BANGOR (Church) *see* Elerch w Penrhyncoch w Capel Bangor and Goginan *St D*
CAPEL COELBREN (Capel Coelbren) *see* Cwmtawe Uchaf *S & B*
CAPEL COLMAN (St Colman) *see* Maenordeifi and Capel Colman w Llanfihangel etc *St D*
CAPEL CYNON (St Cynon) *see* Llanarth and Capel Cynon w Talgarreg etc *St D*
CAPEL DEWI (St David) *see* Llanfihangel-ar-arth w Capel Dewi *St D*
CAPEL GARMON *see* Llanrwst and Llanddoget and Capel Garmon *St As*
CAPEL IFAN (St John the Baptist) *see* Cwm Gwendraeth *St D*
CAPEL LLANILLTERNE (St Ellteyrn) *see* Pentyrch w Capel Llanillterne *Llan*
CAPEL MAIR *see* Llangeler w Pen-Boyr *St D*
CAPEL NEWYDD (St Paul) *see* Blaenavon w Capel Newydd *Mon*
CAPEL TYGWYDD *see* Maenordeifi and Capel Colman w Llanfihangel etc *St D*
CAPEL-Y-FFIN (St Mary) *see* Hay w Llanigon and Capel-y-Ffin *S & B*
CAPEL-Y-GROES *see* Abergwili w Llanfihangel-uwch-Gwili etc *St D*
CARDIFF (Christ Church) Roath Park *Llan 2* **V** E E DAVIES
CARDIFF (Dewi Sant) *Llan 2* **V** *vacant* (029) 2075 1418
CARDIFF (St Luke) *see* Canton Cardiff *Llan*
CARDIFF (St Mary) (St Stephen) w Cardiff (St Dyfrig and St Samson) *Llan 2* **V** G J FRANCIS, **C** B ANDREWS, **NSM** J WILLIAMS
CARDIFF, CENTRAL (St Andrew and St Teilo) (St John the Baptist) (St James the Great) (St Michael) *Llan 2* **TR** J K KIMBER, **TV** J WIGLEY
CARDIGAN (St Mary) w Mwnt and Y Ferwig w Llangoedmor *St D 6* **V** J POWELL, **C** J R THOMAS
CAREW (St Mary) *St D 1* **TR** V F MILLGATE, A J DAVIES, **TV** R A GORDON, **C** V L GARDNER
CARMARTHEN (St David) (Christ Church) *St D 11* **V** P H B THOMAS, **C** J E GOUPILLON
CARMARTHEN (St Peter) (St John the Evangelist) *St D 11* **V** W A STRANGE, **C** A R JOHNSON, **NSM** M K THORLEY, L CHAMBERS
CARMEL (Eglwys Fair) *see* Gors-las *St D*
CARNHEDRYN *see* Dewisland *St D*
CARNO (St John) *see* Llanwnnog and Caersws w Carno *Ban*
CARROG (St Ffraid) *see* Corwen w Llangar, Glyndyfrdwy etc *St As*
CASCOB (St Michael) *see* Knighton, Norton, Whitton, Pilleth and Cascob *S & B*
CASTELL DWYRAN *see* Llanfallteg w Castell Dwyran *St D*
CASTELLAN *see* Maenordeifi and Capel Colman w Llanfihangel etc *St D*
CASTLE BYTHE *see* Letterston w Llanfair Nant-y-Gof etc *St D*
CASTLE CAEREINION (St Garmon) *see* Welshpool w Castle Caereinion *St As*
CASTLEMARTIN (St Michael and All Angels) *see* Monkton *St D*
CATBROOK (St John the Baptist) *see* Penallt and Trellech *Mon*
CATHEDINE (St Michael) *see* Llyn Safaddan *S & B*
CEFN (St Mary) (All Saints) w Trefnant w Tremeirchion *St As 2* **R** S D GREEN, **NSM** P WYKES
CEFN COED (St John the Baptist) w Vaynor *S & B 1* **V** B H JOHN
CEFN CRIBWR (St Colman) *see* Kenfig Hill *Llan*
CEFN FOREST (St Thomas) *see* Fleur-de-Lis *Mon*
CEFN HENGOED (St Anne) *see* Gelligaer *Llan*
CEFN PENNAR (St Illtyd) *see* Mountain Ash and Miskin *Llan*
CEFNLLYS (St Michael) *see* Llandrindod w Cefnllys and Disserth *S & B*
CEIRCHIOG (St David) *see* Valley w Llechylched and Caergeiliog *Ban*
CELLAN (All Saints) *see* Lampeter and Llanddewibrefi Gp *St D*
CEMAES *see* Llanfechell w Bodewryd w Rhosbeirio etc *Ban*
CEMAIS (St Tydecho) *see* Bro Ddyfi Uchaf *Ban*
CENARTH (St Llawddog) *see* Maenordeifi and Capel Colman w Llanfihangel etc *St D*
CERRIGCEINWEN (St Ceinwen) *see* Trefdraeth w Aberffraw, Llangadwaladr etc *Ban*
CERRIGYDRUDION (St Mary Magdalene) w Llanfihangel Glyn Myfyr, Pentrefoelas and Ysbyty Ifan *St As 17* **V** S BRUSH
CHEPSTOW (St Mary) *Mon 2* **V** C J BLANCHARD, **C** D R MILTON
CHERITON *see* Monkton *St D*
CHERITON (St Cadoc) *see* Llanrhidian w Llanmadoc and Cheriton *S & B*
CHIRK (St Mary) *St As 14* **V** A J REES
CIL-Y-CWM (St Michael) and Ystrad-ffin w Rhandirmwyn Llanfair-ar-y-Bryn *St D 14* **P-in-c** R B MORGAN
CILCAIN (St Mary) and Nannerch and Rhydymwyn *St As 16* **NSM** B HARVEY
CILCENNIN (Holy Trinity) *see* Llanfihangel Ystrad and Cilcennin w Trefilan etc *St D*
CILFYNYDD (St Luke) *see* Pontypridd St Matt and Cilfynydd w Llanwynno *Llan*
CILGERRAN (St Llawddog) w Bridell and Llantwyd *St D 6* **R** E L THOMAS
CILGWYN (St Mary) *see* Newport w Cilgwyn and Dinas w Llanllawer *St D*
CILIAU AERON (St Michael) *see* Llanerch Aeron w Ciliau Aeron and Dihewyd etc *St D*
CILYBEBYLL (St John the Evangelist) *Llan 8* **R** M PERRY
CLARBESTON (St Martin of Tours) *see* Wiston w Walton E and Clarbeston *St D*
CLOCAENOG (St Foddhyd) *see* Llanfwrog and Clocaenog and Gyffylliog *St As*
CLUNDERWEN (St David) *see* Whitland w Cyffig and Henllan Amgoed etc *St D*
CLYDACH (St John the Evangelist) (St Mary) (St Michael) *S & B 7* **V** T J HEWITT
CLYDACH VALE (St Thomas) *see* Tonypandy w Clydach Vale *Llan*
CLYDAU (St Clydai) w Egremont and LLanglydwen w Cilymaenllwyd and LLanfyrnach *St D 15* **V** E A HOWELLS
CLYNNOG FAWR (St Beuno) *see* Llanaelhaearn w Clynnog Fawr *Ban*
CLYRO (St Michael and All Angels) *see* Glasbury and Llowes w Clyro and Betws *S & B*
CLYTHA *see* Llanddewi Rhydderch w Llangattock-juxta-Usk etc *Mon*
COCKETT (St Peter) *see* Swansea St Pet *S & B*
COEDKERNEW *see* Marshfield and Peterstone Wentloog etc *Mon*
COEDYPAEN (Christchurch) *see* Llangybi and Coedypaen w Llanbadoc *Mon*
COETMOR *see* Glanogwen w St Ann's w Llanllechid *Ban*
COITY (St Mary) w Nolton *Llan 6* **R** M KOMOR, **C** P M WILLIAMS, R T PITMAN
COLVA (St David) *see* New Radnor and Llanfihangel Nantmelan etc *S & B*
COLWINSTON (St Michael) w Llandow and Llysworney *Llan 4* **R** P M LEONARD
COLWYN *S & B 2* **P-in-c** J BILLAM
COLWYN (St Catherine) (St John the Baptist) *St As 6* **P-in-c** J P ATACK
COLWYN BAY (St Paul) (St Andrew) (St David) w Brynymaen *St As 6* **V** N H WILLIAMS, **P-in-c** M JONES, **C** M W A CHADWICK, N C WILLIAMS, S D GRANT
COMINS COCH *see* Llanbadarn Fawr *St D*
CONNAH'S QUAY (St Mark) (St David's Mission Church) *St As 16* **V** P H VARAH, **C** R EVANS
CONWY (St Mary and All Saints) w Gyffin *Ban 2* **V** P R JONES
CORRIS (Holy Trinity) *see* Pennal w Corris and Esgairgeiliog *Ban*
CORWEN (St Mael and St Sulien) w Llangar, Glyndyfrdwy and Llansantffraid Glyn Dyfrdwy *St As 17* **V** *vacant*
COSHESTON (St Michael) *see* Carew *St D*
COWBRIDGE (Holy Cross) *Llan 4* **TR** D G BELCHER, **TV** D Y L HELLARD, **C** D K SHEEN, **NSM** R H SPENCER
COYCHURCH (St Crallo), Llangan and St Mary Hill *Llan 6* **R** R S EVANS
COYTREAHEN (St Thomas) *see* Llansantffraid, Bettws and Aberkenfig *Llan*
CRAI (St Ilid) *see* Defynnog, Llandilo'r Fan, Llanulid, Llywel etc *S & B*
CREGRINA (St David) *see* Colwyn *S & B*
CRIBYN (St Silin) *see* Llanfihangel Ystrad and Cilcennin w Trefilan etc *St D*
CRICCIETH (St Catherine) and Treflys w Llanystumdwy w Llangybi and Llanarmon *Ban 11* **R** S WILLIAMS
CRICKADARN (St Mary) *see* Aberedw w Llandeilo Graban and Llanbadarn etc *S & B*

CRICKHOWELL (St Edmund) w Cwmdu and Tretower *S & B 3* **V** B LETSON
CRIGGION (St Michael) *see* Llandysilio and Penrhos and Llandrinio etc *St As*
CRINDAU (All Saints) *see* Newport All SS *Mon*
CRINOW (St Teilo) *see* Narberth w Mounton w Robeston Wathen and Crinow *St D*
CROESCEILIOG (St Mary) *see* Cwmbran *Mon*
CROESERW (St Clare) *see* Glyncorrwg and Upper Afan Valley *Llan*
CROSS HANDS (St Anne) *see* Gors-las *St D*
CROSS INN (Holy Trinity) *see* Llanllwchaearn and Llanina *St D*
CROSS KEYS (St Catherine) *see* Risca *Mon*
CROSSGATES *see* Llanbadarn Fawr, Llandegley and Llanfihangel etc *S & B*
CRUGYBYDDAR (St Peter) *see* Beguildy and Heyope and Llangynllo and Bleddfa *S & B*
CRUMLIN (St Mary) *see* Newbridge w Crumlin *Mon*
CRUNWERE (St Elidyr) *see* Begelly w Ludchurch and Crunwere *St D*
CRYNANT (Chapel of Ease) *see* Dulais Valley *Llan*
CRYNANT (St Margaret) *as above*
CWM (St Mael and St Sulien) *see* Dyserth and Trelawnyd and Cwm *St As*
CWM (St Paul) *see* Ebbw Vale *Mon*
CWM-COCH (St Mark) *see* Llandybie *St D*
CWM GWENDRAETH *St D 12* **TR** S R THOMAS, **TV** B MCNIVEN
CWM OGWR (St John the Baptist) *Llan 6* **P-in-c** K W LAKE
CWMAFAN (St Michael) *Llan 7* **P-in-c** H M O'SHEA
CWMAMAN (Christ Church) *St D 13* **V** *vacant* (01269) 822107
CWMAMAN (St Joseph) *see* Aberaman and Abercwmboi w Cwmaman *Llan*
CWMANN (St James) *see* Pencarreg and Llanycrwys *St D*
CWMAVON (St Michael) *see* Cwmafan *Llan*
CWMBACH (St Mary Magdalene) *Llan 9* **V** B H SHARP
CWMBACH LLECHRYD (St John the Divine) *see* Upper Wye *S & B*
CWMBRAN (St Gabriel) *Mon 10* **TR** M J PHILLIPS, **TV** D RICHARDS, G R EVANS, L C HALL, **OLM** G M PROSSER
CWMBWRLA (St Luke) *see* Swansea St Luke *S & B*
CWMCARN (St John the Evangelist) *see* Abercarn and Cwmcarn *Mon*
CWMCARVAN (St Clement) *see* Rockfield and Dingestow Gp *Mon*
CWMDARE (St Luke) *see* Aberdare St Fagan *Llan*
CWMDDAUDDWR (St Winifred) (St Bride) w St Harmon's and Llanwrthwl *S & B 5* **P-in-c** P BROOKS, **NSM** G TYLER
CWMDU (St Michael the Archangel) *see* Crickhowell w Cwmdu and Tretower *S & B*
CWMDUAD (St Alban) *see* Cynwil Elfed and Newchurch *St D*
CWMFFRWD (St Anne) *see* Llangunnor w Cwmffrwd *St D*
CWMFFRWDOER (All Saints) *see* Pontypool *Mon*
CWMLLYNFELL (St Margaret) *see* Brynaman w Cwmllynfell *St D*
CWMPARC (St George) *Llan 12* **V** B TAYLOR
CWMTAWE UCHAF *S & B 7* **P-in-c** A J BROOKFIELD
CWMTILLERY (St Paul) *see* Abertillery w Cwmtillery w Six Bells *Mon*
CWMYOY (St Martin) *see* Llanfihangel Crucorney w Oldcastle etc *Mon*
CWRT-HENRI (St Mary) *see* Llangathen w Llanfihangel Cilfargen etc *St D*
CYDWELI (St Mary) (St Teilo) and Llandyfaelog *St D 12* **V** J H A JAMES, **NSM** A R MORLEY-JONES
CYFFIG (St Cyffig) *see* Whitland w Cyffig and Henllan Amgoed etc *St D*
CYMAU (All Saints) *see* Llanfynydd *St As*
CYMMER (St John the Evangelist) and Porth *Llan 12* **V** R G LLOYD
CYMMER AFAN (St John the Evangelist) *see* Glyncorrwg and Upper Afan Valley *Llan*
CYNCOED (All Saints) (St Edeyrn) *Mon 6* **TR** S G WILLSON, **TV** S G CARBY, C M LAWSON-JONES
CYNOG HONDDU *S & B 1* **P-in-c** J D E DAVIES
CYNWIL ELFED (St Cynwyl) and Newchurch *St D 11* **V** A W EVANS, **C** A C WILLIAMS-POTTER
CYNWYL GAEO (St Cynwyl) w Llansawel and Talley *St D 14* **V** J S PENBERTHY
DAFEN (St Michael and All Angels) *St D 12* **V** D M C DAVIES
DALE (St James) and St Brides w Marloes *St D 5* **V** D M WIGHT, **NSM** S H WIGHT
DAROWEN (St Tudur) *see* Bro Ddyfi Uchaf *Ban*
DEFYNNOG (St Cynog) and Llandilo'r Fan and Llanulid and Llywel and Traean-glas *S & B 1* **V** M P WILDING
DEGANWY (All Saints) *see* Llanrhos *St As*
DENBIGH (St Mary) (St Marcella) (St David) *St As 2* **R** J P SMITH, **C** J M BAKER
DENIO (St Peter) w Abererch *Ban 11* **V** J M A GRIFFITHS
DERI (St Peter) *see* Bargoed and Deri w Brithdir *Llan*
DERWEN (St Mary) *see* Llanfair DC, Derwen, Llanelidan and Efenechtyd *St As*
DEVAUDEN (St James) *see* Itton and St Arvans w Penterry and Kilgwrrwg etc *Mon*
DEWISLAND (Cathedral of St David and St Andrew) *St D 3* **TR** J W EVANS, **TV** R P DAVIES, D J R LEAN, J S BENNETT, **NSM** M I PLANT
DIHEWYD (St Vitalis) *see* Llanerch Aeron w Ciliau Aeron and Dihewyd etc *St D*
DINAS (Mission) and Penygraig w Williamstown *Llan 12* **V** C R LEWIS-JENKINS
DINAS (St Brynach) *see* Newport w Cilgwyn and Dinas w Llanllawer *St D*
DINGESTOW (St Dingad) *see* Rockfield and Dingestow Gp *Mon*
DINHAM *see* Caerwent w Dinham and Llanfair Discoed etc *Mon*
DINMAEL (St Catherine) *see* Betws Gwerful Goch w Llangwm, Gwyddelwern etc *St As*
DISSERTH (St Cewydd) *see* Llandrindod w Cefnllys and Disserth *S & B*
DOLBENMAEN (St Mary) *see* Porthmadoc and Ynyscynhaearn and Dolbenmaen *Ban*
DOLFOR (St Paul) *see* Kerry and Llanmerewig and Dolfor *St As*
DOLGARROG (St Mary) *see* Caerhun w Llangelynin w Llanbedr-y-Cennin *Ban*
DOLGELLAU (St Mary) w Llanfachreth and Brithdir and Bryncoedifor and Llanelltud *Ban 12* **R** R B D REES, **C** V R HANCOCK
DOLWYDDELAN (St Gwyddelan) *see* Betws-y-Coed and Capel Curig w Penmachno etc *Ban*
DOWLAIS (St John the Baptist) (Christ Church) and Penydarren *Llan 10* **R** M A R HILL
DULAIS VALLEY *Llan 8* **V** S BARNES
DWYGYFYLCHI or Penmaenmawr (St Gwynin) (St Seiriol) (St David) *Ban 2* **V** D M OUTRAM
DYFFRYN *see* Llanenddwyn w Llanddwywe, Llanbedr w Llandanwg *Ban*
DYFFRYN (St Matthew) *Llan 8* **V** S J BODYCOMBE, **NSM** E S HARRIS
DYFFRYN HONDDU (St Cynog) *see* Cynog Honddu *S & B*
DYSERTH (St Bridget) (St Michael) (St Mael and St Sulien) and Trelawnyd and Cwm *St As 1* **V** R W ROWLAND
EBBW VALE (Christchurch) (St John the Baptist) *Mon 8* **TR** G J WAGGETT, **TV** P J ABBOTT, **C** J A CARTER
EDERN (St Edern) *see* Nefyn w Tudweiliog w Llandudwen w Edern *Ban*
EFENECHTYD (St Michael) *see* Llanfair DC, Derwen, Llanelidan and Efenechtyd *St As*
EGLWYS-FACH (St Michael) *see* Borth and Eglwys-fach w Llangynfelyn *St D*
EGLWYS FAIR GLYN-TAF *see* Whitland w Cyffig and Henllan Amgoed etc *St D*
EGLWYS GYMYN (St Margaret) *see* Pendine w Llanmiloe and Eglwys Gymyn w Marros *St D*
EGLWYS NEWYDD *see* Ysbyty Cynfyn w Llantrisant and Eglwys Newydd *St D*
EGLWYS OEN DUW *see* Llanwrtyd w Llanddulas in Tir Abad etc *S & B*
EGLWYSBREWIS (St Brewis) *see* Llantwit Major *Llan*
EGLWYSFACH *see* Llansantffraid Glan Conwy and Eglwysbach *St As*
EGLWYSILAN (St Ilan) *Llan 1* **R** A H STEVENS, **NSM** S G BROWN
EGLWYSRHOS (St Eleri and St Mary) *see* Llanrhos *St As*
EGLWYSWEN (St Michael) *see* Nevern and Y Beifil w Eglwyswrw and Meline etc *St D*
EGLWYSWRW (St Cristiolus) *as above*
ELERCH (St Peter) w Penrhyncoch w Capel Bangor and Goginan *St D 10* **V** J P LIVINGSTONE
ELY (St David) *see* Caerau w Ely *Llan*
ELY (St Timothy) *as above*
ERBISTOCK (St Hilary) *see* Overton and Erbistock and Penley *St As*
ESCLUSHAM (Holy Trinity) *St As 15* **V** P T ALLSWORTH
ESGAIRGEILIOG *see* Pennal w Corris and Esgairgeiliog *Ban*
EVANCOYD (St Peter) *see* New Radnor and Llanfihangel Nantmelan etc *S & B*
EWENNY (St Michael) w St Brides Major *Llan 6* **V** *vacant* (01656) 880108

EYTON (St Deiniol) *see* Bangor Monachorum, Worthenbury and Marchwiel *St As*
FAIRBOURNE (St Cynon) *see* Arthog w Fairbourne w Llangelynnin w Rhoslefain *Ban*
FAIRHILL *see* Cwmbran *Mon*
FAIRWATER (St Peter) *Llan 3* **V** C P SUTTON
FAIRWATER (St Peter) *see* Cwmbran *Mon*
FAWR *see* Llandeilo Fawr and Taliaris *St D*
FELIN-FOEL (Holy Trinity) *see* Llanelli *St D*
FELIN-GWM (St John) *see* Llanegwad w Llanfynydd *St D*
FELINDRE (St Barnabas) *see* Llangeler w Pen-Boyr *St D*
FERNDALE (St Dunstan) *see* Rhondda Fach Uchaf *Llan*
FERRYSIDE (St Thomas) *see* St Ishmael's w Llan-saint and Ferryside *St D*
FFESTINIOG (St Michael) w Blaenau Ffestiniog *Ban 8* **V** *vacant* (01341) 247207
FFYNNONGROEW (All Saints) *St As 4* **V** *vacant*
FISHGUARD (St Mary) w Llanychar and Pontfaen w Morfil and Llanychlwydog *St D 3* **V** D A T MACGREGOR
FLEMINGSTON (St Michael) *see* Cowbridge *Llan*
FLEUR-DE-LIS (St David) *Mon 7* **C** T MORGAN
FLINT (St Mary) (St Thomas) (St David) *St As 4* **R** M W FEARN, **NSM** M M GRAHAM
FOCHRIW (St Mary and St Andrew) *see* Pontlottyn w Fochriw *Llan*
FORD (Church) *see* Nolton w Roch and St Lawrence w Ford etc *St D*
FORDEN (St Michael) *see* Montgomery and Forden and Llandyssil *St As*
FREYSTROP (St Justinian) *see* Llangwm w Freystrop and Johnston *St D*
FRON (Mission Church) *see* Berriew *St As*
FRONCYSYLLTE (St David) *see* Chirk *St As*
FRONGOCH *see* Bala *St As*
FURNACE (Mission Church) *see* Llanelli *St D*
GABALFA (St Mark) (Highfields Centre and Mynachdy Institute) *Llan 2* **V** R M CAPPER, **C** M A PRINCE, **NSM** R H ALDIS
GAERWEN *see* Llanfihangel Ysgeifiog w Llangristiolus etc *Ban*
GARNDIFFAITH (St John the Evangelist) *see* Abersychan and Garndiffaith *Mon*
GARTHBEIBIO (St Tydecho) w Llanerfyl w Llangadfan *St As 8* **V** D E B FRANCIS
GARTHBRENGY (St David) *see* Cynog Honddu *S & B*
GARTHELI (St Gartheli) *see* Llangeitho and Blaenpennal w Betws Leucu etc *St D*
GAUFRON (St David) *see* Rhayader and Nantmel *S & B*
GELLIGAER (St Catwg) (St Margaret) (St Anne) *Llan 1* **R** D K WATERS
GILESTON (St Giles) *see* Llantwit Major *Llan*
GILFACH GOCH (St Barnabas) *see* Tonyrefail w Gilfach Goch *Llan*
GILVACH (St Margaret) *see* Gelligaer *Llan*
GLADWESTRY (St Mary) *see* New Radnor and Llanfihangel Nantmelan etc *S & B*
GLAIS (St Paul) *see* Llansamlet *S & B*
GLAN ELY (Resurrection) *Llan 3* **V** S LISK, **C** B A WOOD
GLANAMAN (St Margaret) *see* Cwmaman *St D*
GLANGWRYNE (Mission Church) *see* Llangenni and Llanbedr Ystrad Yw w Patricio *S & B*
GLANOGWEN (Christ Church) w St Ann's w Llanllechid *Ban 5* **C** E C WILLIAMS
GLANTAWE (St Margaret) (St Peter) *S & B 11* **V** C P G DICKSON
GLASBURY (St Peter) (All Saints) and Llowes w Clyro and Betws *S & B 4* **P-in-c** H E BAKER
GLASCOED (St Michael) *see* Mamhilad w Monkswood and Glascoed Chapel *Mon*
GLASCOMBE (St David) *see* Colwyn *S & B*
GLYN *see* Brecon St David w Llanspyddid and Llanilltyd *S & B*
GLYNCOCH (All Saints' Church Centre) *see* Pontypridd St Matt and Cilfynydd w Llanwynno *Llan*
GLYNCORRWG (St John the Baptist) (St Clare) (St Thomas) and Upper Afan Valley *Llan 7* **P-in-c** C E LASKEY
GLYNDYFRDWY (St Thomas) *see* Corwen w Llangar, Glyndyfrdwy etc *St As*
GLYNTAFF (St Mary) *Llan 11* **V** K D LERRY
GOETRE (St Peter) w Llanover *Mon 5* **R** P F COLEMAN
GOGINAN (Church) *see* Elerch w Penrhyncoch w Capel Bangor and Goginan *St D*
GOLDCLIFFE (St Mary Magdalen) *see* Magor *Mon*
GOODWICK (St Peter) *see* Llanwnda, Goodwick w Manorowen and Llanstinan *St D*
GORS-LAS (St Lleian) *St D 13* **V** M L REES, **NSM** J B JONES
GORSEDD (St Paul) w Brynford, Ysgeifiog and Whitford *St As 4* **V** S CAWLEY, **Par Dn** S M MORIARTY
GORSEINON (St Catherine) *S & B 9* **V** D H E MOSFORD, **C** R M HAWKEN, **NSM** W G G JAMES
GOVILON (Christchurch) w Llanfoist w Llanelen *Mon 1* **R** A F PYE, **NSM** D W F ROSSITER, L J DEROSAIRE
GOWER, SOUTH WEST *S & B 8* **P-in-c** J W GRIFFIN
GOWERTON (St John the Evangelist) *S & B 9* **P-in-c** T J WHETTLETON
GRAIG (St John) *see* Rhydyfelin w Graig *Llan*
GRANDSTON (St Catherine) *see* Mathry w St Edren's and Grandston etc *St D*
GRANGETOWN (St Paul) *Llan 2* **V** G J FRANCIS
GREENWAY (St Hilary) *see* Rumney *Mon*
GRESFORD (All Saints) *St As 12* **V** J T HUGHES, **NSM** D F CHILD
GRIFFITHSTOWN (St Hilda) *Mon 10* **V** C J WILCOX
GROESWEN (St David) *see* Pentyrch w Capel Llanillterne *Llan*
GRONANT (St Winifred) *see* Llanasa *St As*
GROSMONT (St Nicholas) and Skenfrith and Llangattock Lingoed and Llanfair Chapel *Mon 1* **R** T H A MASON, **OLM** J PROSSER
GUILSFIELD (St Aelhaiarn) w Buttington *St As 10* **V** R A BIRD
GUMFRESTON (St Lawrence) *see* Tenby *St D*
GWAENYSGOR *see* Meliden and Gwaenysgor *St As*
GWAUN-CAE-GURWEN *St D 13* **V** *vacant* (01269) 822430
GWEHELOG *see* Usk and Gwehelog w Llantrisant w Llanllowell *Mon*
GWENDDWR (St Dubricius) *see* Aberedw w Llandeilo Graban and Llanbadarn etc *S & B*
GWENLLI (St Mark) *see* Llanarth and Capel Cynon w Talgarreg etc *St D*
GWERNAFFIELD (Holy Trinity) and Llanferres *St As 16* **V** J P HARRIS
GWERNAMYNYDD (St Mark) *see* Mold *St As*
GWERNESNEY (St Michael) *see* Llangwm Uchaf and Llangwm Isaf w Gwernesney etc *Mon*
GWERNFFRWD (St David) *see* Llanyrnewydd *S & B*
GWERSYLLT (Holy Trinity) *St As 12* **V** S M HUYTON, **NSM** E M POWELL
GWYDDELWERN (St Beuno) *see* Betws Gwerful Goch w Llangwm, Gwyddelwern etc *St As*
GWYNFE (All Saints) *see* Llangadog and Gwynfe w Llanddeusant *St D*
GWYTHERIN (St Winifred) *see* Betws-yn-Rhos w Petryal *St As*
GYFFIN (St Benedict) *see* Conwy w Gyffin *Ban*
GYFFYLLIOG (St Mary) *see* Llanfwrog and Clocaenog and Gyffylliog *St As*
HAFOD (St John) *see* Cen Swansea *S & B*
HAKIN (St Mary) *see* Hubberston *St D*
HALKYN (St Mary the Virgin) w Caerfallwch w Rhesycae *St As 4* **R** *vacant* (01352) 711675
HANMER (St Chad) and Bronington and Bettisfield and Tallarn Green *St As 11* **P-in-c** C HUGHES
HARLECH (St Tanwg) and Llanfair-juxta-Harlech w Llanfihangel-y-Traethau and Llandecwyn *Ban 8* **V** R A BEACON
HAROLDSTON ST ISSELLS (St Issell) *see* Haverfordwest St Mary and St Thos w Haroldston *St D*
HAROLDSTON WEST (St Madog) *see* Walton W w Talbenny and Haroldston W *St D*
HAVERFORDWEST (St Martin) w Lambston *St D 5* **V** C W BOWEN
HAVERFORDWEST (St Mary) and St Thomas w Haroldston St Issells *St D 5* **R** D EVANS, **C** J K PLESSIS
HAWARDEN (St Deiniol) (Holy Spirit) *St As 13* **TR** T F L GRIFFITHS, **TV** M J BATCHELOR, C A HILL, **C** S F HILDRETH, G BECKETT, **NSM** J STEPHENS
HAY (St Mary) (St John) w Llanigon and Capel-y-Ffin *S & B 4* **V** R D WILLIAMS
HAYSCASTLE (St Mary) *see* Nolton w Roch and St Lawrence w Ford etc *St D*
HENDY (St David) *see* Llangennech and Hendy *St D*
HENEGLWYS (St Llwydian) *see* Llandrygarn w Bodwrog and Heneglwys etc *Ban*
HENFYNYW (St David) w Aberaeron and Llanddewi Aberarth w Llanbadarn Trefeglwys *St D 8* **V** A T G JOHN, **C** H Q GREGORY-SMITH, **NSM** H G LEWIS
HENLLAN (St David) *see* Llandysul w Bangor Teifi w Henllan etc *St D*
HENLLAN (St Sadwrn) and Llannefydd and Bylchau *St As 2* **R** J P P WILLIAMS
HENLLAN AMGOED (St David) *see* Whitland w Cyffig and Henllan Amgoed etc *St D*
HENLLYS (St Peter) *see* Cwmbran *Mon*

HENRY'S MOAT (St Bernard) *see* Maenclochog and New Moat etc *St D*
HEOL-Y-CYW (St Paul) *see* Llanilid w Pencoed *Llan*
HERBRANDSTON (St Mary) and Hasguard w St Ishmael's *St D 5* **R** *vacant*
HEYOPE (St David) *see* Beguildy and Heyope and Llangynllo and Bleddfa *S & B*
HIGH CROSS (St Anne) *see* Bassaleg *Mon*
HIRWAUN (St Lleurwg) (St Winifred) *Llan 9* **V** B L JONES
HODGESTON (Church) *see* Monkton *St D*
HOLT (St Chad), Rossett and Isycoed *St As 12* **V** R A SUTER, **NSM** V C T TUCKER
HOLYHEAD (St Cybi) (Morawelon) (St Ffraid) (St Gwenfaen) *Ban 3* **R** C A LLEWELLYN, **TV** N A RIDINGS
HOLYWELL (St James) (Holy Trinity) *St As 4* **V** J D P LOMAS
HOPE (Parish Church) *St As 13* **R** M K SNELLGROVE
HOWEY (St David) *see* Llandrindod w Cefnllys and Disserth *S & B*
HUBBERSTON (St David) (Holy Spirit) *St D 5* **R** A M CHADWICK, **C** I J GIRLING
HUNDLETON (St David) *see* Monkton *St D*
ILSTON (St Illtyd) w Pennard *S & B 8* **V** D J WILKINSON
IRFON VALLEY *S & B 2* **P-in-c** C M HAYNES
ISYCOED (St Paul) *see* Holt, Rossett and Isycoed *St As*
ITTON (St Deiniol) and St Arvans w Penterry and Kilgwrrwg w Devauden *Mon 2* **V** M J GOLLOP, **NSM** M E ZORAB
JAMESTON *see* Carew *St D*
JEFFREYSTON (St Jeffrey) w Reynoldston and East Williamston and Loveston *St D 4* **R** N P DAVIES
JOHNSTON (St Peter) *see* Llangwm w Freystrop and Johnston *St D*
JORDANSTON (St Cawrda) *see* Mathry w St Edren's and Grandston etc *St D*
KEMEYS COMMANDER (All Saints) *see* Bettws Newydd w Trostrey etc *Mon*
KENFIG *see* Pyle w Kenfig *Llan*
KENFIG HILL (St Theodore) (St Colman) *Llan 7* **P-in-c** P G MORRIS
KERRY (St Michael) and Llanmerewig and Dolfor *St As 7* **V** A T W REYNOLDS
KILGETTY *see* Begelly w Ludchurch and Crunwere *St D*
KILGWRRWG (Holy Cross) *see* Itton and St Arvans w Penterry and Kilgwrrwg etc *Mon*
KILLAY (St Hilary) (St Martin) *S & B 6* **V** T J WILLIAMS
KILVEY (All Saints) *see* Swansea St Thos and Kilvey *S & B*
KNELSTON *see* SW Gower *S & B*
KNIGHTON (St Edward) and Norton and Whitton and Pilleth and Cascob *S & B 5* **V** A J PEARCE, **NSM** J H STOCKER, P C F GERRARD
LALESTON (St David) w Tythegston and Merthyr Mawr *Llan 6* **V** E J EVANS, **NSM** J M LEWIS
LAMBSTON (St Ishmael) *see* Haverfordwest St Martin w Lambston *St D*
LAMPETER and Llanddewibrefi Group, The *St D 9* **V** A W WILLIAMS, **C** J G MATTHEWS, B D TIMOTHY
LAMPETER PONT STEFFAN (St Peter) *see* Lampeter and Llanddewibrefi Gp *St D*
LAMPETER VELFREY (St Peter) and Llanddewi Velfrey *St D 15* **R** M G R MORRIS
LAMPHEY (St Faith and St Tyfei) *see* Monkton *St D*
LANDORE (St Paul) *S & B 10* **P-in-c** R G JONES, **NSM** N P DOYLE
LANGSTONE (not known) *see* Bishton *Mon*
LANKNANSH (St Mary) *see* Llantwit Major *Llan*
LAUGHARNE (St Martin) w Llansadwrnen and Llandawke *St D 15* **V** D L R BROWNRIDGE
LAVERNOCK (St Lawrence) *see* Penarth and Llandough *Llan*
LAWRENNY (St Caradog) *see* Martletwy w Lawrenny and Minwear etc *St D*
LECKWITH *see* Penarth and Llandough *Llan*
LETTERSTON (St Giles) w Llanfair Nant-y-Gof and Puncheston w Little Newcastle and Castle Bythe *St D 3* **R** R GRIFFITHS, **NSM** M C CHARLES
LISVANE (St Denys) *Llan 2* **V** P N THOMPSON
LISWERRY *see* Newport St Andr *Mon*
LITTLE NEWCASTLE (St Peter) *see* Letterston w Llanfair Nant-y-Gof etc *St D*
LLAN-GAN *see* Whitland w Cyffig and Henllan Amgoed etc *St D*
LLAN-LLWCH (St Mary) w Llangain and Llangynog *St D 11* **V** R I PROTHEROE
LLAN-NON (St Non) *see* Cwm Gwendraeth *St D*
LLAN-SAINT (All Saints) *see* St Ishmael's w Llan-saint and Ferryside *St D*
LLAN-Y-BRI (Holy Trinity) *see* Llansteffan and Llan-y-bri etc *St D*
LLANABER (St Mary) (St John) (St David) w Caerdeon *Ban 8* **R** K G HORSWELL
LLANAELHAEARN (St Aelhaiarn) w Clynnog Fawr *Ban 1* **R** I THOMAS
LLANAFAN FAWR (St Afan) *see* Upper Wye *S & B*
LLANAFAN-Y-TRAWSCOED (St Afan) *see* Llanfihangel w Llanafan and Llanwnnws etc *St D*
LLANALLGO (St Gallo) *see* Llaneugrad w Llanallgo and Penrhosllugwy etc *Ban*
LLANANNO (St Anno) *see* Llanbister w Llanbadarn Fynydd w Llananno etc *S & B*
LLANARMON (St Garmon) *see* Criccieth and Treflys w Llanystumdwy etc *Ban*
LLANARMON DYFFRYN CEIRIOG (St Garmon) *see* Llansantffraid Glyn Ceirog and Llanarmon etc *St As*
LLANARMON MYNYD (St Garmon) *see* Llanrhaeadr-ym-Mochnant etc *St As*
LLANARMON YN IAL (St Garmon) *see* Llanbedr DC w Llangynhafal, Llanychan etc *St As*
LLANARTH (St David) (St Teilo) and Capel Cynon w Talgarreg and (St Mark) *St D 8* **V** C L BOLTON
LLANARTH (St Teilo) *see* Llanddewi Rhydderch w Llangattock-juxta-Usk etc *Mon*
LLANARTHNE (St David) and Llanddarog *St D 11* **P-in-c** H J DAVIES
LLANASA (St Asaph and St Cyndeyrn) (St Winifred) *St As 4* **V** G H TRIMBY
LLANBABO (St Pabo) *see* Valley w Llechylched and Caergeiliog *Ban*
LLANBADARN FAWR (St Padarn) *St D 10* **V** W S T MORGAN
LLANBADARN FAWR (St Padarn) and Llandegley and Llanfihangel Rhydithon w Abbey Cwmhir *S & B 5* **P-in-c** A C BALLARD
LLANBADARN FYNYDD (St Padarn) *see* Llanbister w Llanbadarn Fynydd w Llananno etc *S & B*
LLANBADARN ODWYN (St Padarn) *see* Lampeter and Llanddewibrefi Gp *St D*
LLANBADARN TREFEGLWYS (St Padarn) *see* Henfynyw w Aberaeron and Llanddewi Aberarth etc *St D*
LLANBADARN-Y-GARREG (St Padarn) *see* Aberedw w Llandeilo Graban and Llanbadarn etc *S & B*
LLANBADOC (St Madog) *see* Llangybi and Coedypaen w Llanbadoc *Mon*
LLANBADRIG (St Padrig) *see* Llanfechell w Bodewryd w Rhosbeirio etc *Ban*
LLANBEBLIG (St Peblig) w Caernarfon and Betws Garmon w Waunfawr *Ban 1* **R** R F DONALDSON, R J HUGHES
LLANBEDR (St Peter) *see* Llanenddwyn w Llanddwywe, Llanbedr w Llandanwg *Ban*
LLANBEDR DYFFRYN CLWYD (St Peter) w Llangynhafal, Llanychan, and Llanarmon yn Ial *St As 3* **R** H BUTLER
LLANBEDR PAINSCASTLE (St Peter) *see* Bryngwyn and Newchurch and Llanbedr etc *S & B*
LLANBEDR-Y-CENNIN (St Peter) *see* Caerhun w Llangelynin w Llanbedr-y-Cennin *Ban*
LLANBEDR YSTRAD YW (St Peter) *see* Llangenni and Llanbedr Ystrad Yw w Patricio *S & B*
LLANBEDRGOCH (St Peter) *see* Llanfair Mathafarn Eithaf w Llanbedrgoch *Ban*
LLANBEDROG (St Pedrog) w Llannor and Llangian *Ban 11* **R** A JONES
LLANBERIS (St Peris) (St Padarn) w Llanrug *Ban 1* **R** *vacant*
LLANBISTER (St Cynllo) w Llanbadarn Fynydd w Llananno and Llanddewi Ystradenni *S & B 5* **P-in-c** L A MARSHALL
LLANBLETHIAN (St Blethian) *see* Cowbridge *Llan*
LLANBOIDY (St Brynach) *see* Meidrim and Llanboidy and Merthyr *St D*
LLANBRADACH (All Saints) *see* Ystrad Mynach w Llanbradach *Llan*
LLANBRYN-MAIR (St Mary) *see* Bro Ddyfi Uchaf *Ban*
LLANCARFAN (St Cadoc) w Llantrithyd *Llan 4* **V** *vacant* (01446) 750241
LLANDAFF (Cathedral of St Peter and St Paul w St Dyfrig, St Teilo and St Euddogwy) *Llan 3* **V** J T LEWIS, **C** E F DOWLAND-OWEN
LLANDAFF North (All Saints) *Llan 3* **V** T J G S COOPER
LLANDANWG *see* Llanenddwyn w Llanddwywe, Llanbedr w Llandanwg *Ban*
LLANDAVENNY *see* Penhow, St Brides Netherwent w Llandavenny etc *Mon*
LLANDAWKE (St Odoceus) *see* Laugharne w Llansadwrnen and Llandawke *St D*
LLANDDANIEL-FAB (St Deiniolfab) *see* Llanfair-pwll and Llanddaniel-fab etc *Ban*

LLANDDAROG (St Twrog) *see* Llanarthne and Llanddarog *St D*
LLANDDEINIOL (St Deiniol) *see* Llansantffraed w Llanrhystud and Llanddeiniol *St D*
LLANDDEINIOLEN (St Deiniol) w Llanfair-is-gaer w Penisa'r-waun *Ban 1* **V** *vacant* (01248) 671967
LLANDDERFEL (St Derfel) *see* Llandrillo and Llandderfel *St As*
LLANDDEW (St David) *see* Brecon St Mary w Llanddew *S & B*
LLANDDEWI *see* Llanwrtyd w Llanddulas in Tir Abad etc *S & B*
LLANDDEWI (St David) *see* SW Gower *S & B*
LLANDDEWI ABERARTH (St David) *see* Henfynyw w Aberaeron and Llanddewi Aberarth etc *St D*
LLANDDEWI FACH (St David) *see* Bryngwyn and Newchurch and Llanbedr etc *S & B*
LLANDDEWI RHONDDA (St Barnabas) *see* Pwllgwaun and Llanddewi Rhondda *Llan*
LLANDDEWI RHONDDA (St David) *as above*
LLANDDEWI RHYDDERCH (St David) w Llangattock-juxta-Usk and Llanarth w Clytha and Llansantffraed *Mon 1* **V** M S SADLER
LLANDDEWI YSTRADENNI (St David) *see* Llanbister w Llanbadarn Fynydd w Llananno etc *S & B*
LLANDDEWIBREFI (St David) *see* Lampeter and Llanddewibrefi Gp *St D*
LLANDDEWI'R CWM (St David) *see* Builth and Llanddewi'r Cwm w Llangynog etc *S & B*
LLANDDOGET (St Doged) *see* Llanrwst and Llanddoget and Capel Garmon *St As*
LLANDDONA (St Dona) *see* Llansadwrn w Llanddona and Llaniestyn etc *Ban*
LLANDDOWROR (St Teilo) *see* St Clears w Llangynin and Llanddowror etc *St D*
LLANDDULAS (St Cynfryd) and Llysfaen *St As 6* **R** I M BROTHERSTON
LLANDDWYWE (St Ddwywe) *see* Llanenddwyn w Llanddwywe, Llanbedr w Llandanwg *Ban*
LLANDDYFNAN (St Ddyfnan) *see* Llansadwrn w Llanddona and Llaniestyn etc *Ban*
LLANDDYFNAN (St Deiniol) *as above*
LLANDECWYN (St Tecwyn) *see* Harlech and Llanfair-juxta-Harlech etc *Ban*
LLANDEFAELOG-FACH (St Maelog) *see* Cynog Honddu *S & B*
LLANDEFALLE (St Matthew) and Llyswen w Boughrood and Llanstephen w Talachddu *S & B 4* **R** I P CHARLESWORTH
LLANDEGFAN (St Tegfan) w Llandysilio *Ban 6* **V** R G R SMITH
LLANDEGLA (St Tecla) *St As 17* **R** M SQUIRES
LLANDEGLEY (St Tecla) *see* Llanbadarn Fawr, Llandegley and Llanfihangel etc *S & B*
LLANDEGVETH (St Tegfeth) *see* Llanfrechfa and Llanddewi Fach w Llandegveth *Mon*
LLANDEILO *see* Maenclochog and New Moat etc *St D*
LLANDEILO ABERCYWYN *see* Llansteffan and Llan-y-bri etc *St D*
LLANDEILO FAWR (St Teilo) and Taliaris *St D 14* **V** P J BEMENT, **C** R J DAVIES, **NSM** P C A MANSEL LEWIS
LLANDEILO GRABAN (St Teilo) *see* Aberedw w Llandeilo Graban and Llanbadarn etc *S & B*
LLANDEILO TAL-Y-BONT (St Teilo) (St Michael) *S & B 9* **V** J P H WALTERS
LLANDELOY (St Teilo) *see* Dewisland *St D*
LLANDENNY (St John the Apostle) *see* Raglan w Llandenny and Bryngwyn *Mon*
LLANDEUSSANT (St Simon and St Jude) *see* Llangadog and Gwynfe w Llanddeusant *St D*
LLANDEVAUD (St Peter) *see* Penhow, St Brides Netherwent w Llandavenny etc *Mon*
LLANDEWI FACH *see* Llanfrechfa and Llanddewi Fach w Llandegveth *Mon*
LLANDEWI SKIRRID (St David) *see* Llantilio Pertholey w Bettws Chpl etc *Mon*
LLANDEWI VELFREY (St David) *see* Lamp Velfrey and Llanddewi Velfrey *St D*
LLANDILO'R FAN (St Teilo) *see* Defynnog, Llandilo'r Fan, Llanulid, Llywel etc *S & B*
LLANDINAM (St Llonio) w Trefeglwys w Penstrowed *Ban 9* **V** *vacant* (01686) 688341
LLANDINGAT (St Dingad) w Myddfai *St D 14* **V** B T RICE
LLANDINORWIG (Christ Church) (St Mary) *Ban 1* **V** *vacant*
LLANDOGO (St Oudoceus) w Whitebrook Chapel and Tintern Parva *Mon 2* **R** J P W REES, **NSM** J W DEARNLEY, N HILL
LLANDOUGH (St Dochdwy) *see* Penarth and Llandough *Llan*
LLANDOUGH (St Dochwy) *see* Cowbridge *Llan*
LLANDOVERY *see* Llandingat w Myddfai *St D*
LLANDOW (Holy Trinity) *see* Colwinston w Llandow and Llysworney *Llan*
LLANDRILLO (St Trilio) (St Derfel) and Llandderfel *St As 17* **V** S J ROBERTS
LLANDRILLO-YN-RHOS (St Trillo) (St George) *St As 6* **V** D JACKS
LLANDRINDOD (Holy Trinity) (Old Parish Church) w Cefnllys and Disserth *S & B 5* **R** A G LOAT, **NSM** A TWEED
LLANDRINIO (St Trinio, St Peter and St Paul) *see* Llandysilio and Penrhos and Llandrinio etc *St As*
LLANDRYGARN (St Trygarn) w Bodwrog, Heneglwys, Trewalchmai and Llanerch-y-medd *Ban 4* **NSM** E D JERMAN
LLANDUDNO (St George) (St Tudno) (Holy Trinity) (Our Saviour) *Ban 2* **R** J E NICE, **TV** J R ALLEN
LLANDUDWEN (St Tudwen) *see* Nefyn w Tudweiliog w Llandudwen w Edern *Ban*
LLANDULAIS IN TIR ABAD (St David) *see* Llanwrtyd w Llanddulas in Tir Abad etc *S & B*
LLANDWROG (St Twrog) and Llanwnda *Ban 1* **V** T ROBERTS
LLANDYBIE (St Tybie) *St D 13* **V** J H GRAVELL
LLANDYFAELOG (St Maelog) *see* Cydweli and Llandyfaelog *St D*
LLANDYFAN (Church) *see* Llandybie *St D*
LLANDYFODWG (St Tyfodwg) *Llan 6* **V** *vacant*
LLANDYFRIOG (St Tyfriog) *see* Newcastle Emlyn w Llandyfriog etc *St D*
LLANDYFRYDOG (St Tyfrydog) *see* Llandrygarn w Bodwrog and Heneglwys etc *Ban*
LLANDYGAI (St Tegai) and Maes y Groes *Ban 5* **P-in-c** A W COLEMAN, **NSM** T R WILLIAMS
LLANDYGWYDD (St Tygwydd) *see* Maenordeifi and Capel Colman w Llanfihangel etc *St D*
LLANDYRNOG (St Tyrnog) (St Cwyfan) and Llangwyfan *St As 2* **R** E B THOMAS
LLANDYRY (Church) *see* Pen-bre *St D*
LLANDYSILIO (St Tysilio) *see* Llandegfan w Llandysilio *Ban*
LLANDYSILIO (St Tysilio) *see* Whitland w Cyffig and Henllan Amgoed etc *St D*
LLANDYSILIO (St Tysilio) (St Mary) and Penrhos and Llandrinio w Criggion *St As 10* **R** W K ROWELL
LLANDYSILIOGOGO (St Tysilio) *see* Llangrannog w Llandysiliogogo w Penbryn *St D*
LLANDYSSIL (St Tyssil) *see* Montgomery and Forden and Llandyssil *St As*
LLANDYSUL (St Tysul) w Bangor Teifi w Henllan and Llanfairorllwyn w Llangynllo *St D 7* **V** E ROBERTS, **C** D C LLOYD
LLANEDEYRN (All Saints) *see* Cyncoed *Mon*
LLANEDI (St Edith) w Tycroes and Saron *St D 13* **V** D G DAVIES
LLANEDWEN (St Edwen) *see* Llanfair-pwll and Llanddaniel-fab etc *Ban*
LLANEGRYN (St Mary and St Egryn) w Aberdyfi w Tywyn *Ban 12* **C** A A WHITE, **NSM** C C TEN WOLDE
LLANEGWAD (St Egwad) w Llanfynydd *St D 14* **V** P S JOHNES
LLANEILIAN (St Eilian) *see* Amlwch *Ban*
LLANELEN (St Helen) *see* Govilon w Llanfoist w Llanelen *Mon*
LLANELIAN (St Elian) w Trofarth *St As 6* **V** M JONES, **NSM** D KAY
LLANELIDAN (St Elidan) *see* Llanfair DC, Derwen, Llanelidan and Efenechtyd *St As*
LLANELLI (St Elli) *S & B 3* **V** A FRANCIS
LLANELLI (St Elli) (All Saints) (St Alban) (Christ Church) (St David) (St John) (St Peter) *St D 12* **TR** I M THOMAS, **TV** D R PAYNE, C J DAVIES, **C** R J PATTINSON
LLANELLTUD (St Illtyd) *see* Dolgellau w Llanfachreth and Brithdir etc *Ban*
LLANELWEDD (St Matthew) *see* Colwyn *S & B*
LLANENDDWYN (St Enddwyn) w Llanddwywe and Llanbedr w Llandanwg *Ban 8* **R** S K N BEACON
LLANENGAN (St Engan) *see* Llanbedrog w Llannor and Llangian *Ban*
LLANERCH AERON (St Non) w Ciliau Aeron and Dihewyd and Mydroilyn *St D 8* **R** D B DAVIES
LLANERCH-Y-MEDD (Eglwys Crist) *see* Llandrygarn w Bodwrog and Heneglwys etc *Ban*
LLANERCH-Y-MEDD (St Mair) *as above*
LLANERFYL (St Erfyl) *see* Garthbeibio w Llanerfyl w Llangadfan *St As*
LLANEUGRAD (St Eugrad) w Llanallgo and Penrhosllugwy w Llanfihangel Tre'r Beirdd *Ban 7* **R** *vacant*

LLANFABON (St Mabon) (St John the Baptist) *Llan 1* **R** C T REANEY
LLANFACHRAETH (St Machraeth) *see* Bodedern w Llanfaethlu *Ban*
LLANFACHRETH (St Machreth) *see* Dolgellau w Llanfachreth and Brithdir etc *Ban*
LLANFAELOG (St Maelog) and Llangwyfan *Ban 3* **R** M M BRADY
LLANFAELRHYS (St Maelrhys) *see* Aberdaron w Rhiw and Llanfaelrhys etc *Ban*
LLANFAES *see* Brecon St David w Llanspyddid and Llanilltyd *S & B*
LLANFAETHLU (St Maethlu) *see* Bodedern w Llanfaethlu *Ban*
LLANFAGLAN (St Mary) *see* Llandwrog and Llanwnda *Ban*
LLANFAIR (Church) *see* Gwaun-cae-Gurwen *St D*
LLANFAIR (Church) *see* Llandingat w Myddfai *St D*
LLANFAIR (St Mary) *see* Grosmont and Skenfrith and Llangattock etc *Mon*
LLANFAIR-AR-Y-BRYN (St Mary) *see* Cil-y-Cwm and Ystrad-ffin w Rhandir-mwyn etc *St D*
LLANFAIR CAEREINION (St Mary), Llanllugan and Manafon *St As 8* **V** C S WEBB
LLANFAIR CLYDOGAU (St Mary) *see* Lampeter and Llanddewibrefi Gp *St D*
LLANFAIR DISCOED (St Mary) *see* Caerwent w Dinham and Llanfair Discoed etc *Mon*
LLANFAIR DYFFRYN CLWYD (St Cynfarch and St Mary) (Jesus Chapel) and Derwen and Llanelidan and Efenechtyd *St As 3* **V** T E MART
LLANFAIR-IS-GAER (Old Parish Church) *see* Llanddeiniolen w Llanfair-is-gaer etc *Ban*
LLANFAIR-IS-GAER (St Mary) *as above*
LLANFAIR-JUXTA-HARLECH (St Mary) *see* Harlech and Llanfair-juxta-Harlech etc *Ban*
LLANFAIR KILGEDDIN *see* Bettws Newydd w Trostrey etc *Mon*
LLANFAIR MATHAFARN EITHAF (St Mary) w Llanbedrgoch *Ban 6* **R** *vacant* (01248) 852348
LLANFAIR NANT-GWYN (St Mary) *see* Nevern and Y Beifil w Eglwyswrw and Meline etc *St D*
LLANFAIR NANT-Y-GOF (St Mary) *see* Letterston w Llanfair Nant-y-Gof etc *St D*
LLANFAIR-PWLL (St Mary) and Llanddaniel-fab w Penmynydd w Llanedwen *Ban 6* **R** P HUGHES
LLANFAIR TALHAEARN (St Mary) *see* Betws-yn-Rhos w Petryal *St As*
LLANFAIR-YN-NEUBWLL *see* Valley w Llechylched and Caergeiliog *Ban*
LLANFAIR-YN-Y-CWMWD (St Mary) *see* Newborough w Llanidan and Llangeinwen etc *Ban*
LLANFAIR-YNG-NGHORNWY (St Mary) *see* Bodedern w Llanfaethlu *Ban*
LLANFAIRFECHAN (St Mary) (Christ Church) w Aber *Ban 2* **R** C M EVANS
LLANFAIRORLLWYN (St Mary) *see* Llandysul w Bangor Teifi w Henllan etc *St D*
LLANFAIRPWLLGWYNGYLLGOGERYCHW-YRND-ROBWLL-LLANTISILIOGOGOGOCH (St Mary) *see* Llanfair-pwll and Llanddaniel-fab etc *Ban*
LLANFALLTEG (St Mallteg) w Castell Dwyran *St D 15* **V** *vacant*
LLANFAREDD (St Mary) *see* Colwyn *S & B*
LLANFECHAIN (St Garmon) *see* Llansantffraid-ym-Mechain and Llanfechain *St As*
LLANFECHAN (St Afan) *see* Irfon Valley *S & B*
LLANFECHELL (St Mechell) w Bodewryd w Rhosbeirio w Llanfflewin and Llanbadrig *Ban 7* **R** G W EDWARDS
LLANFERRES (St Berres) *see* Gwernaffield and Llanferres *St As*
LLANFEUGAN (St Meugan) w Llanthetty w Llansantffraed-juxta-Usk *S & B 3* **P-in-c** A S ROBINSON
LLANFFINAN (St Ffinan) *see* Llanfihangel Ysgeifiog w Llangristiolus etc *Ban*
LLANFFLEWIN (St Fflewin) *see* Llanfechell w Bodewryd w Rhosbeirio etc *Ban*
LLANFIHANGEL (St Michael) *see* Llantwit Major *Llan*
LLANFIHANGEL ABERCYWYN (St Michael) *see* St Clears w Llangynin and Llanddowror etc *St D*
LLANFIHANGEL ABERGWESSIN *see* Llanwrtyd w Llanddulas in Tir Abad etc *S & B*
LLANFIHANGEL ABERYTHYCH (St Michael) *see* Llangathen w Llanfihangel Cilfargen etc *St D*
LLANFIHANGEL-AR-ARTH (St Michael) w Capel Dewi *St D 7* **V** *vacant* (01559) 384858
LLANFIHANGEL BRYNPABUAN (St Michael and All Angels) *see* Upper Wye *S & B*
LLANFIHANGEL CILFARGEN *see* Llangathen w Llanfihangel Cilfargen etc *St D*
LLANFIHANGEL CRUCORNEY (St Michael) w Oldcastle and Cwmyoy and Llanthony *Mon 1* **V** D J YOUNG
LLANFIHANGEL FECHAN (St Michael) *see* Cynog Honddu *S & B*
LLANFIHANGEL GENAU'R-GLYN (St Michael) and Llangorwen *St D 10* **V** D B THOMAS
LLANFIHANGEL GLYN MYFYR (St Michael) *see* Cerrigydrudion w Llanfihangel Glyn Myfyr etc *St As*
LLANFIHANGEL GOBION (St Michael) *see* Bettws Newydd w Trostrey etc *Mon*
LLANFIHANGEL HELYGEN (St Michael) *see* Upper Wye *S & B*
LLANFIHANGEL LLEDROD (St Michael) *see* Llanilar w Rhostie and Llangwyryfon etc *St D*
LLANFIHANGEL NANTBRAN (St Michael) *see* Trallwng w Bettws Penpont w Aberyskir etc *S & B*
LLANFIHANGEL NANTMELAN (St Michael) *see* New Radnor and Llanfihangel Nantmelan etc *S & B*
LLANFIHANGEL PENBEDW *see* Maenordeifi and Capel Colman w Llanfihangel etc *St D*
LLANFIHANGEL PONTYMOILE (St Michael) *see* Panteg w Llanfihangel Pontymoile *Mon*
LLANFIHANGEL RHOS-Y-CORN (St Michael) *see* Brechfa w Abergorlech etc *St D*
LLANFIHANGEL RHYDITHON (St Michael) *see* Llanbadarn Fawr, Llandegley and Llanfihangel etc *S & B*
LLANFIHANGEL ROGIET *see* Caldicot *Mon*
LLANFIHANGEL TALYLLYN (St Michael) *see* Llyn Safaddan *S & B*
LLANFIHANGEL-TOR-Y-MYNYDD (St Michael) *see* Llanishen w Trellech Grange and Llanfihangel etc *Mon*
LLANFIHANGEL TRE'R BEIRDD (St Mihangel) *see* Llaneugrad w Llanallgo and Penrhosllugwy etc *Ban*
LLANFIHANGEL-UWCH-GWILI (St Michael) *see* Abergwili w Llanfihangel-uwch-Gwili etc *St D*
LLANFIHANGEL-Y-CREUDDYN (St Michael) w Llanafan-y-Trawscoed and Llanwnnws and Ysbyty Ystwyth *St D 10* **V** H A CHIPLIN
LLANFIHANGEL-Y-PENNANT (St Michael) *see* Llanegryn w Aberdyfi w Tywyn *Ban*
LLANFIHANGEL-Y-TRAETHAU (St Michael) *see* Harlech and Llanfair-juxta-Harlech etc *Ban*
LLANFIHANGEL-YN-NHYWYN *see* Valley w Llechylched and Caergeiliog *Ban*
LLANFIHANGEL-YNG-NGHWYNFA (St Michael) *see* Llanwddyn and Llanfihangel-yng-Nghwynfa etc *St As*
LLANFIHANGEL YSGEIFIOG (St Michael) w Llangristiolus w Llanffinan *Ban 4* **R** *vacant*
LLANFIHANGEL-YSTERN-LLEWERN (St Michael) *see* Rockfield and Dingestow Gp *Mon*
LLANFIHANGEL YSTRAD (St Michael) and Cilcennin w Trefilan and Nantcwnlle *St D 8* **V** B W THOMAS
LLANFILO (St Bilo) *see* Bronllys w Llanfilo *S & B*
LLANFOIST (St Ffwyst) *see* Govilon w Llanfoist w Llanelen *Mon*
LLANFOR (St Mor and St Deiniol) w Rhosygwaliau *St As 17* **R** *vacant*
LLANFRECHFA (All Saints) and Llanddewi Fach w Llandegveth *Mon 10* **V** *vacant* (01633) 482343
LLANFROTHEN (St Brothen) *see* Penrhyndeudraeth w Llanfrothen w Beddgelert *Ban*
LLANFRYNACH (St Brynach) *see* Cowbridge *Llan*
LLANFRYNACH (St Brynach) and Cantref w Llanhamlach *S & B 3* **V** P G R SIMS
LLANFUGAIL (St Migail) *see* Valley w Llechylched and Caergeiliog *Ban*
LLANFWROG (St Mwrog and St Mary) and Clocaenog and Gyffylliog *St As 3* **R** J B DAVIES
LLANFYLLIN (St Myllin) and Bwlchycibau *St As 9* **R** M R BALKWILL
LLANFYNYDD (St Egwad) *see* Llanegwad w Llanfynydd *St D*
LLANFYNYDD (St Michael) (St Egwad) *St As 16* **R** A J POOLMAN
LLANFYRNACH (St Brynach) *see* Clydau w Egremont and Llanglydwen etc *St D*
LLANGADFAN (St Cadfan) *see* Garthbeibio w Llanerfyl w Llangadfan *St As*
LLANGADOG (St Cadog) and Gwynfe w Llanddeusant *St D 14* **V** K M D COTTAM
LLANGADWALADR (St Cadwaladr) *see* Llansilin w Llangadwaladr and Llangedwyn *St As*

LLANGADWALADR (St Cadwaladr) *see* Trefdraeth w Aberffraw, Llangadwaladr etc *Ban*
LLANGAFFO (St Caffo) *see* Newborough w Llanidan and Llangeinwen etc *Ban*
LLANGAIN (St Cain) *see* Llan-llwch w Llangain and Llangynog *St D*
LLANGAMMARCH (St Cadmarch) *see* Irfon Valley *S & B*
LLANGAN (St Canna) *see* Coychurch, Llangan and St Mary Hill *Llan*
LLANGANTEN (St Cannen) *see* Irfon Valley *S & B*
LLANGAR (St John the Evangelist) *see* Corwen w Llangar, Glyndyfrdwy etc *St As*
LLANGASTY TALYLLYN (St Gastyn) *see* Llyn Safaddan *S & B*
LLANGATHEN (St Cathen) w Llanfihangel Cilfargen and Llanfihangel Aberythych *St D 14* **V** W R HUGHES
LLANGATTOCK (St Cattwg) and Llangyndir *S & B 3* **R** K RICHARDS
LLANGATTOCK-JUXTA-USK (St Cadoc) *see* Llanddewi Rhydderch w Llangattock-juxta-Usk etc *Mon*
LLANGATTOCK LINGOED (St Cadoc) *see* Grosmont and Skenfrith and Llangattock etc *Mon*
LLANGATTOCK-VIBON-AVEL (St Cadoc) *see* Rockfield and Dingestow Gp *Mon*
LLANGEDWYN (St Cedwyn) *see* Llansilin w Llangadwaladr and Llangedwyn *St As*
LLANGEFNI (St Cyngar) w Tregaean *Ban 4* **R** P MCLEAN
LLANGEINOR (St Ceinor) and the Garw Valley *Llan 6* **P-in-c** D J MORTIMORE
LLANGEINWEN (St Ceinwen) *see* Newborough w Llanidan and Llangeinwen etc *Ban*
LLANGEITHO (St Ceitho) and Blaenpennal w Betws Leucu and Gartheli *St D 9* **P-in-c** J D E JONES
LLANGELER (St Celer) w Pen-Boyr *St D 7* **P-in-c** J N GILLIBRAND
LLANGELYNIN (St Celynnin) *see* Caerhun w Llangelynin w Llanbedr-y-Cennin *Ban*
LLANGELYNNIN (St Celynin) *see* Arthog w Fairbourne w Llangelynnin w Rhoslefain *Ban*
LLANGENNECH (St Gwynog) and Hendy *St D 12* **V** P C JONES
LLANGENNI (St Cenau) and Llanbedr Ystrad Yw w Patricio *S & B 3* **R** K J M EWEN, **NSM** R O MULLIS
LLANGENNITH (St Cenydd) *see* Reynoldston w Penrice and Llangennith *S & B*
LLANGERNYW (St Digain) *see* Betws-yn-Rhos w Petryal *St As*
LLANGEVIEW (St David) *see* Llangwm Uchaf and Llangwm Isaf w Gwernesney etc *Mon*
LLANGIAN (St Gian) *see* Llanbedrog w Llannor and Llangian *Ban*
LLANGIWG (St Ciwg) *S & B 7* **V** G H GREEN
LLANGLYDWEN (St Cledwyn) *see* Clydau w Egremont and Llanglydwen etc *St D*
LLANGOEDMOR (St Cynllo) *see* Cardigan w Mwnt and Y Ferwig w Llangoedmor *St D*
LLANGOLLEN (St Collen) (St John) w Trevor and Llantysilio *St As 14* **V** T J B PRITCHARD, **C** O B PARRY
LLANGOLMAN (St Colman) *see* Maenclochog and New Moat etc *St D*
LLANGORSE (St Paulinus) *see* Llyn Safaddan *S & B*
LLANGORWEN (All Saints) *see* Llanfihangel Genau'r-glyn and Llangorwen *St D*
LLANGOWER (St Cywair) *see* Bala *St As*
LLANGRANNOG (St Carannog) w Llandysiliogogo w Penbryn *St D 8* **V** I D FORSTER
LLANGRISTIOLUS (St Cristiolus) *see* Llanfihangel Ysgeifiog w Llangristiolus etc *Ban*
LLANGUNNOG *see* Llanishen w Trellech Grange and Llanfihangel etc *Mon*
LLANGUNNOR (St Ceinwr) w Cwmffrwd *St D 11* **V** W D A GRIFFITHS, **NSM** C M STEEL
LLANGURIG (St Curig) *see* Llanidloes w Llangurig *Ban*
LLANGWLLOG (St Cwyllog) *see* Llandrygarn w Bodwrog and Heneglwys etc *Ban*
LLANGWLLONG (St Anau) *as above*
LLANGWM (St Catherine) *see* Betws Gwerful Goch w Llangwm, Gwyddelwern etc *St As*
LLANGWM (St Jerome) w Freystrop and Johnston *St D 5* **R** *vacant* (01437) 890087
LLANGWM ISAF (St John) *see* Llangwm Uchaf and Llangwm Isaf w Gwernesney etc *Mon*
LLANGWM UCHAF (St Jerome) and Llangwm Isaf w Gwernesney and Llangeview w Wolvesnewton *Mon 5* **P-in-c** D WOOD
LLANGWNNADL (St Gwynhoedl) *see* Aberdaron w Rhiw and Llanfaelrhys etc *Ban*
LLANGWYFAN *see* Llandyrnog and Llangwyfan *St As*
LLANGWYFAN (St Cwyfan) *see* Llanfaelog and Llangwyfan *Ban*
LLANGWYFAN (St Cwyfan Old Church) *as above*
LLANGWYRYFON (St Ursula) *see* Llanilar w Rhostie and Llangwyryfon etc *St D*
LLANGYBI (St Cybi) *see* Criccieth and Treflys w Llanystumdwy etc *Ban*
LLANGYBI (St Cybi) *see* Lampeter and Llanddewibrefi Gp *St D*
LLANGYBI (St Cybi) and Coedypaen w Llanbadoc *Mon 5* **R** A E MORTON
LLANGYFELACH (St David and St Cyfelach) (St Teilo-on-the-Clase) *S & B 7* **V** R J DAVIES-HANNEN
LLANGYNDEYRN (St Cyndeyrn) *see* Cwm Gwendraeth *St D*
LLANGYNDIR (St Cynidr and St Mary) *see* Llangattock and Llangyndir *S & B*
LLANGYNFELYN (St Cynfelyn) *see* Borth and Eglwys-fach w Llangynfelyn *St D*
LLANGYNHAFAL (St Cynhafal) *see* Llanbedr DC w Llangynhafal, Llanychan etc *St As*
LLANGYNIN (St Cynin) *see* St Clears w Llangynin and Llanddowror etc *St D*
LLANGYNLLO (St Cynllo) *see* Llandysul w Bangor Teifi w Henllan etc *St D*
LLANGYNLLO (St Cynllo) *see* Beguildy and Heyope and Llangynllo and Bleddfa *S & B*
LLANGYNOG *see* Builth and Llanddewi'r Cwm w Llangynog etc *S & B*
LLANGYNOG (St Cynog) *see* Llan-llwch w Llangain and Llangynog *St D*
LLANGYNOG (St Cynog) (St Melangel) *St As 9* **P-in-c** L M EDWARDS
LLANGYNWYD (St Cynwyd) (St Stephen) (St Tydfil) w Maesteg *Llan 6* **C** K J HARMAN
LLANGYNYW (St Cynyw) *see* Meifod w Llangynyw w Pont Robert w Pont Dolanog *St As*
LLANGYSTENNIN (St Cystenin) (St Michael) (St Katherine) (St Mary) *St As 5* **R** J C HARVEY
LLANHAMLACH (St Peter and St Illtyd) *see* Llanfrynach and Cantref w Llanhamlach *S & B*
LLANHARAN (St Julius and St Aaron) w Peterston-super-Montem *Llan 6* **V** *vacant* (01443) 226307
LLANHARRY (St Illtud) *Llan 4* **P-in-c** G A BLYTH, **NSM** B J REANEY
LLANHENNOCK (St John) *see* Caerleon w Llanhennock *Mon*
LLANHILLETH (Christchurch) (St Mark) *Mon 8* **P-in-c** M T MESLEY
LLANHYWEL (St Hywel) *see* Dewisland *St D*
LLANIDAN (St Nidan) *see* Newborough w Llanidan and Llangeinwen etc *Ban*
LLANIDLOES (St Idloes) w Llangurig *Ban 9* **V** R P PITCHER
LLANIESTYN (St Iestyn) *see* Llansadwrn w Llanddona and Llaniestyn etc *Ban*
LLANIESTYN (St Iestyn) *see* Botwnnog w Bryncroes *Ban*
LLANIGON (St Eigon) *see* Hay w Llanigon and Capel-y-Ffin *S & B*
LLANILAR (St Hilary) w Rhostie and Llangwyryfon w Llanfihangel Lledrod *St D 10* **P-in-c** R W TOWNSEND
LLANILID (St Illid and St Curig) w Pencoed *Llan 6* **R** N P JONES
LLANILLTYD (St John) *see* Brecon St David w Llanspyddid and Llanilltyd *S & B*
LLANINA (St Ina) *see* Llanllwchacarn and Llanina *St D*
LLANISHEN (Christ Church) *see* Cardiff Ch Ch Roath Park *Llan*
LLANISHEN (St Dennis) w Trellech Grange and Llanfihangel Tor-y-Mynydd w Llangunnog and Llansoy *Mon 3* **P-in-c** D M OWEN
LLANISHEN (St Isan) (St Faith) *Llan 2* **V** M D WITCOMBE
LLANLLAWDDOG (St Llawddog) *see* Llanpumsaint w Llanllawddog *St D*
LLANLLAWER *see* Newport w Cilgwyn and Dinas w Llanllawer *St D*
LLANLLECHID (St Cross) *see* Llandygai and Maes y Groes *Ban*
LLANLLECHID (St Llechid) *see* Glanogwen w St Ann's w Llanllechid *Ban*
LLANLLEONFEL (Parish Church) *see* Irfon Valley *S & B*
LLANLLOWELL (St Llywel) *see* Usk and Gwehelog w Llantrisant w Llanllowell *Mon*
LLANLLUGAN (St Mary) *see* Llanfair Caereinion, Llanllugan and Manafon *St As*

LLANLLWCHAEARN (St Llwchaiarn) and Llanina *St D 8*
R M J NEEDS
LLANLLWCHAIARN (All Saints) *see* Newtown w Llanllwchaiarn w Aberhafesp *St As*
LLANLLWCHAIARN (St Llwchaiarn) *as above*
LLANLLWNI (St Luke or St Llonio) *see* Llanybydder and Llanwenog w Llanllwni *St D*
LLANLLYFNI (St Rhedyw) (St John) (Christ Church) *Ban 1*
R *vacant*
LLANLLYR-YN-RHOS (St Llyr) *see* Upper Wye *S & B*
LLANMADOC (St Madoc) *see* Llanrhidian w Llanmadoc and Cheriton *S & B*
LLANMAES (St Catwg) *see* Llantwit Major *Llan*
LLANMARTIN (St Martin) *see* Bishton *Mon*
LLANMEREWIG (St Llwchaiarn) *see* Kerry and Llanmerewig and Dolfor *St As*
LLANMILOE (St Barbara) *see* Pendine w Llanmiloe and Eglwys Gymyn w Marros *St D*
LLANNEFYDD (St Nefydd and St Mary) *see* Henllan and Llannefydd and Bylchau *St As*
LLANNOR (Holy Cross) *see* Llanbedrog w Llannor and Llangian *Ban*
LLANOVER (St Bartholomew) *see* Goetre w Llanover *Mon*
LLANPUMSAINT (Five Saints) w Llanllawddog *St D 11*
V *vacant* (01267) 253205
LLANRHAEADR-YM-MOCHNANT (St Dogfan), Llanarmon Mynydd Mawr and Penybontfawr *St As 9* **V** J H C DAVIES
LLANRHAEADR-YNG-NGHINMEIRCH (St Dyfnog) w Prion and Nantglyn *St As 2* **V** J M WILLIAMS
LLANRHEITHAN (St Rheithan) *see* Dewisland *St D*
LLANRHIAN (St Rhian) *as above*
LLANRHIDIAN (St Rhidian and St Illtyd) w Llanmadoc and Cheriton *S & B 8* **V** *vacant* (01792) 390144
LLANRHOS (St Paul) *St As 5* **V** R H GRIFFITHS,
C V A BURTON, M C PARRY, **NSM** P A WRIGHT
LLANRHUDDLAD (St Rhuddlad) *see* Bodedern w Llanfaethlu *Ban*
LLANRHWYDRUS *as above*
LLANRHYCHWYN (St Rhychwyn) *see* Caerhun w Llangelynin w Llanbedr-y-Cennin *Ban*
LLANRHYDD (St Meugan) *see* Ruthin w Llanrhydd *St As*
LLANRHYSTUD (St Restitutis) *see* Llansantffraed w Llanrhystud and Llanddeiniol *St D*
LLANRUG (St Gabriel) *see* Llanberis w Llanrug *Ban*
LLANRUG (St Michael) *as above*
LLANRUMNEY (St Dyfrig) *Mon 6* **V** M I R DOWSETT
LLANRWST (St Grwst) and Llanddoget and Capel Garmon *St As 5* **R** L D NORMAN
LLANSADWRN (St Sadwrn) w Llanddona and Llaniestyn w Pentraeth w Llanddyfnan *Ban 6* **R** D PRYS
LLANSADWRN (St Sadwrn) w Llanwrda and Manordeilo *St D 14* **V** A J LEGG
LLANSADWRNEN (St Sadwrnen) *see* Laugharne w Llansadwrnen and Llandawke *St D*
LLANSAMLET (St Samlet) (St John) (St Paul) *S & B 7*
V C M DARVILL
LLANSANNAN (St Sannan) *see* Betws-yn-Rhos w Petryal *St As*
LLANSANNOR (St Senwyr) *see* Cowbridge *Llan*
LLANSANTFFRAED (St Bridget) *see* Llanddewi Rhydderch w Llangattock-juxta-Usk etc *Mon*
LLANSANTFFRAED (St Bridget) w Llanrhystud and Llanddeiniol *St D 8* **V** J W SMITH
LLANSANTFFRAED-IN-ELWELL (St Bridget) *see* Colwyn *S & B*
LLANSANTFFRAED-JUXTA-USK (St Bride) *see* Llanfeugan w Llanthetty etc *S & B*
LLANSANTFFRAID, Bettws and Aberkenfig *Llan 6*
V R G AUSTIN, **C** G E DANIEL, **NSM** O M PARRY
LLANSANTFFRAID GLAN CONWY (St Ffraid) (St Martin) and Eglwysbach *St As 5* **R** C R OWEN
LLANSANTFFRAID GLYN CEIRIOG (St Ffraid) and Llanarmon Dyffryn Ceiriog and Pontfadog *St As 14*
V P J CLARKE
LLANSANTFFRAID-YM-MECHAIN (St Ffraid) and Llanfechain *St As 9* **V** *vacant* (01691) 828244
LLANSANTFRAID GLYN DYFRDWY (St Ffraid) *see* Corwen w Llangar, Glyndyfrdwy etc *St As*
LLANSAWEL (St Mary), Briton Ferry *Llan 8* **V** G C POWELL
LLANSAWEL (St Sawyl) *see* Cynwyl Gaeo w Llansawel and Talley *St D*
LLANSILIN (St Silin) w Llangadwaladr and Llangedwyn *St As 9*
V C F CARTER
LLANSOY (St Tysoi) *see* Llanishen w Trellech Grange and Llanfihangel etc *Mon*
LLANSPYDDID (St Cattwg) *see* Brecon St David w Llanspyddid and Llanilltyd *S & B*
LLANSTADWEL (St Tudwal) *St D 5* **V** P W D FLAVELL
LLANSTEFFAN (St Ystyffan) and Llan-y-bri and Llandeilo Abercywyn *St D 11* **V** S E JONES
LLANSTEPHEN (St Steffan) *see* Llandefalle and Llyswen w Boughrood etc *S & B*
LLANSTINAN (St Justinian) *see* Llanwnda, Goodwick w Manorowen and Llanstinan *St D*
LLANTARNAM (St Michael) *see* Cwmbran *Mon*
LLANTHETTY (St Tetti) *see* Llanfeugan w Llanthetty etc *S & B*
LLANTHONY (St David) *see* Llanfihangel Crucorney w Oldcastle etc *Mon*
LLANTILIO CROSSENNY (St Teilo) and Penrhos w Llanvetherine and Llanvapley *Mon 1* **V** C H A PRINCE
LLANTILIO PERTHOLEY (St Teilo) w Bettws Chapel and Llanddewi Skirrid *Mon 1* **Hon Par Dn** D A LEE
LLANTOOD *see* Cilgerran w Bridell and Llantwyd *St D*
LLANTRISANT (Church) *see* Ysbyty Cynfyn w Llantrisant and Eglwys Newydd *St D*
LLANTRISANT (St Afran, St Ieuan and St Sanan) *see* Valley w Llechylched and Caergeiliog *Ban*
LLANTRISANT (St Illtyd, St Gwynno and St Dyfodwg) (St Michael) (St David) *Llan 11* **V** V L PARKINSON,
C I HODGES, **NSM** R M GRIFFITHS
LLANTRISANT (St Peter, St Paul and St John) *see* Usk and Gwehelog w Llantrisant w Llanllowell *Mon*
LLANTRITHYD (St Illtyd) *see* Llancarfan w Llantrithyd *Llan*
LLANTWIT FARDRE (St Illtyd) (St Andrew) *Llan 11*
V M K JONES, **NSM** K G SIMPSON
LLANTWIT MAJOR (St Illtud) (St Donat) *Llan 4*
TR J A WEBBER, **TV** J L JONES, **C** M J DOBBS, T O HUGHES
LLANTWYD (St Illtud) *see* Cilgerran w Bridell and Llantwyd *St D*
LLANTYSILIO (St Tysilio) *see* Llangollen w Trevor and Llantysilio *St As*
LLANULID (St Ilid) *see* Defynnog, Llandilo'r Fan, Llanulid, Llywel etc *S & B*
LLANUWCHLLYN (St Deiniol) *see* Bala *St As*
LLANVACHES (St Dyfrig) *see* Penhow, St Brides Netherwent w Llandavenny etc *Mon*
LLANVAPLEY (St Mable) *see* Llantilio Crossenny w Penrhos, Llanvetherine etc *Mon*
LLANVETHERINE (St James the Elder) *as above*
LLANWDDYN (St Wyddyn) and Llanfihangel-yng-Nghwynfa and Llwydiarth *St As 9* **V** J E T YENDALL
LLANWELLWYFO (St Gwenllwyfo) *see* Amlwch *Ban*
LLANWENARTH CITRA (St Peter) *see* Abergavenny St Mary w Llanwenarth Citra *Mon*
LLANWENOG (St Gwenog) *see* Llanybydder and Llanwenog w Llanllwni *St D*
LLANWERN (St Mary) *see* Bishton *Mon*
LLANWINIO (St Gwynio) *see* Tre-lech a'r Betws w Abernant and Llanwinio *St D*
LLANWNDA (St Baglan Old Church) *see* Llandwrog and Llanwnda *Ban*
LLANWNDA (St Gwyndaf) *as above*
LLANWNDA (St Gwyndaf) and Goodwick (St Peter) w Manorowen and Llanstinan *St D 3* **V** B BARNES
LLANWNNEN (St Lucia) *see* Lampeter and Llanddewibrefi Gp *St D*
LLANWNNOG (St Gwynog) and Caersws w Carno *Ban 9*
V D J CHAPMAN
LLANWNNWS (St Gwnnws) *see* Llanfihangel w Llanafan and Llanwnnws etc *St D*
LLANWRDA (St Cwrdaf) *see* Llansadwrn w Llanwrda and Manordeilo *St D*
LLANWRIN (St Ust and St Dyfrig) *see* Machynlleth w Llanwrin and Penegoes *Ban*
LLANWRTHWL (St Gwrthwl) *see* Cwmddauddwr w St Harmon's and Llanwrthwl *S & B*
LLANWRTYD (St James) (St David) w Llanddulas in Tir Abad and Eglwys Oen Duw and Llanfihangel Abergwessin and Llanddewi *S & B 2* **P-in-c** P E N DAVID
LLANWYDDELAN (St Gwyddelan) *see* Betws Cedewain and Tregynon and Llanwyddelan *St As*
LLANWYNNO (Christ Church) *see* Pontypridd St Matt and Cilfynydd w Llanwynno *Llan*
LLANWYNNO (St Gwynno) *as above*
LLANYBYDDER (St Peter) and Llanwenog w Llanllwni *St D 9*
V W R FILLERY
LLANYCEFN (Church) *see* Llawhaden w Bletherston and Llanycefn *St D*
LLANYCHAEARN (St Llwchaiarn) *see* Aberystwyth *St D*

LLANYCHAN (St Hychan) *see* Llanbedr DC w Llangynhafal, Llanychan etc *St As*
LLANYCHAR (Church) *see* Fishguard w Llanychar and Pontfaen w Morfil etc *St D*
LLANYCHLWYDOG *as above*
LLANYCIL (St Beuno) *see* Bala *St As*
LLANYCRWYS (St David) *see* Pencarreg and Llanycrwys *St D*
LLANYMAWDDWY (St Tydecho) *see* Bro Ddyfi Uchaf *Ban*
LLANYNGHENEDL VALLEY (St Michael) *see* Valley w Llechylched and Caergeiliog *Ban*
LLANYNYS *see* Builth and Llanddewi'r Cwm w Llangynog etc *S & B*
LLANYNYS (St Saeran) *St As 3* **V** *vacant*
LLANYRE *see* Upper Wye *S & B*
LLANYRNEWYDD (St Gwynour) *S & B 8* **P-in-c** D M T WALTERS
LLANYSTYMDWY (St John the Baptist) *see* Criccieth and Treflys w Llanystumdwy etc *Ban*
LLANYWERN (St Mary the Virgin) *see* Llyn Safaddan *S & B*
LLAWHADEN (St Aidan) w Bletherston and Llanycefn *St D 2* **V** D E FAULKNER
LLAWRYBETWS (St James) *see* Betws Gwerful Goch w Llangwm, Gwyddelwern etc *St As*
LLAY (St Martin) *St As 12* **V** P A WALKER
LLECHGYNFARWY (St Cynfarwy) *see* Bodedern w Llanfaethlu *Ban*
LLECHRYD (St Tydfil) *see* Maenordeifi and Capel Colman w Llanfihangel etc *St D*
LLECHYLCHED (Holy Trinity) *see* Valley w Llechylched and Caergeiliog *Ban*
LLISWERRY *see* Newport St Andr *Mon*
LLOWES (St Meilig) *see* Glasbury and Llowes w Clyro and Betws *S & B*
LLWYDCOED (St James) *see* Aberdare St Fagan *Llan*
LLWYDIARTH (St Mary) *see* Llanwddyn and Llanfihangel-yng-Nghwynfa etc *St As*
LLWYNCELLYN (St Luke) *see* Cymmer and Porth *Llan*
LLWYNDERW (Holy Cross) (Clyne Chapel) *S & B 6* **V** G E BENNETT
LLWYNGWRIL *see* Arthog w Fairbourne w Llangelynnin w Rhoslefain *Ban*
LLWYNHENDY (St David) *St D 12* **V** A M GRAY
LLWYNYPIA *see* Ystrad Rhondda w Ynyscynon *Llan*
LLYN SAFADDAN *S & B 4* **V** R T EDWARDS
LLYS-Y-FRAN (St Meilyr) *see* Maenclochog and New Moat etc *St D*
LLYSFAEN (St Cynfran) *see* Llanddulas and Llysfaen *St As*
LLYSWEN (St Gwendoline) *see* Llandefalle and Llyswen w Boughrood etc *S & B*
LLYSWORNEY (St Tydfil) *see* Colwinston w Llandow and Llysworney *Llan*
LLYWEL (St David) *see* Defynnog, Llandilo'r Fan, Llanulid, Llywel etc *S & B*
LOUGHOR (St Michael) (St David) (St Paul) *S & B 9* **V** D ROBERTS, **NSM** K MORGAN
LOVESTON (St Leonard) *see* Jeffreyston w Reynoldston and E Williamston etc *St D*
LUDCHURCH (St Elidyr) *see* Begelly w Ludchurch and Crunwere *St D*
MACHEN (St Michael) (St John the Baptist) *Mon 6* **R** P VANN, **Par Dn** D A WRIGHT
MACHYNLLETH (St Peter) w Llanwrin and Penegoes *Ban 10* **R** E W ROWLANDS, **C** T R WEBB
MAENCLOCHOG (St Mary) and Llandeilo w Henry's Moat w Mynachlogddu w Llangolman w New Moat w Llys y Fran *St D 2* **V** *vacant* (01437) 532238
MAENORDEIFI (St David) (Old Parish Church) and Capel Colman w Llanfihangel Penbedw w Penrhydd and Castellan w Llandygwydd w Cenarth w Cilrhedyn and Llechryd *St D 6* **P-in-c** P R MACKNESS
MAENTWROG (St Twrog) w Trawsfynydd *Ban 8* **R** *vacant*
MAERDY (All Saints) *see* Rhondda Fach Uchaf *Llan*
MAESGLAS and Duffryn *Mon 9* **V** J V MOLE
MAESMYNIS AND LLANYNYS (St David) *see* Builth and Llanddewi'r Cwm w Llangynog etc *S & B*
MAESTEG (St David) *see* Llangynwyd w Maesteg *Llan*
MAESTEG (St Michael) *as above*
MAESTEILO (St John) *see* Llandeilo Fawr and Taliaris *St D*
MAESTIR (St Mary) *see* Lampeter and Llanddewibrefi Gp *St D*
MAGOR (St Mary) *Mon 4* **TR** B J PARFITT, **C** P J HAYLER, **Par Dn** A M PRICE, **NSM** N D HOWARD
MAINDEE (St John the Evangelist) (St Mary) *Mon 9* **V** D NEALE, **C** H PORTER, **NSM** J K BEARDMORE, J A WELSH
MALLYWD (St Tydecho) *see* Bro Ddyfi Uchaf *Ban*
MALPAS (St Mary) *Mon 9* **V** D G PARFITT, **C** C M MORRIS, **OLM** F M A EVANS
MAMHILAD (St Illtud) w Monkswood and Glascoed Chapel *Mon 10* **R** R G HACKETT
MANAFON (St Michael) *see* Llanfair Caereinion, Llanllugan and Manafon *St As*
MANCOT (St Michael) *see* Hawarden *St As*
MANORBIER (St James) *see* Carew *St D*
MANORDEILO (St Paul) *see* Llansadwrn w Llanwrda and Manordeilo *St D*
MANOROWEN (St Mary) *see* Llanwnda, Goodwick w Manorowen and Llanstinan *St D*
MANSELTON (St Michael and All Angels) *S & B 10* **V** T H JONES
MARCHWIEL (St Marcella) *see* Bangor Monachorum, Worthenbury and Marchwiel *St As*
MARCROSS (Holy Trinity) *see* Llantwit Major *Llan*
MARGAM (St Mary) (St David) *Llan 7* **V** T A DOHERTY
MARLOES (St Peter) *see* Dale and St Brides w Marloes *St D*
MARROS (St Lawrence) *see* Pendine w Llanmiloe and Eglwys Gymyn w Marros *St D*
MARSHFIELD (St Mary) and Peterstone Wentloog and Coedkernew w St Bride's Wentloog *Mon 6* **V** D C MATTHEWS, **Par Dn** A J JENKINS
MARTLETWY (St Marcellus) w Lawrenny and Minwear and Yerbeston w Templeton *St D 4* **V** S M TEMPLE
MATHERN (St Tewdric) and Mounton w St Pierre *Mon 2* **V** J E L WHITE
MATHRY (Holy Martyrs) w St Edren's and Grandston w St Nicholas and Jordanston *St D 3* **V** P L DAVIES
MATTHEWSTOWN (All Saints) *see* Penrhiwceiber, Matthewstown and Ynysboeth *Llan*
MAUDLAM (St Mary Magdalene) *see* Pyle w Kenfig *Llan*
MEIDRIM (St David) and Llanboidy and Merthyr *St D 15* **V** J GAINER
MEIFOD (St Tysilio and St Mary) w Llangynyw w Pont Robert w Pont Dolanog *St As 8* **V** J L W WILLIAMS
MELIDEN (St Melyd) (St Mary Magdalene) and Gwaenysgor *St As 1* **V** D P D H REES
MELINE (St Dogmael) *see* Nevern and Y Beifil w Eglwyswrw and Meline etc *St D*
MENAI BRIDGE (St Mary) *see* Llandegfan w Llandysilio *Ban*
MERLIN'S BRIDGE (St Mark) *see* Haverfordwest St Mary and St Thos w Haroldston *St D*
MERTHYR (St Martin) *see* Meidrim and Llanboidy and Merthyr *St D*
MERTHYR CYNOG (St Cynog) *see* Cynog Honddu *S & B*
MERTHYR DYFAN (St Dyfan and St Teilo) *Llan 5* **R** R C PARRISH, **NSM** B BUTLER
MERTHYR MAWR (St Teilo) *see* Laleston w Tythegston and Merthyr Mawr *Llan*
MERTHYR TYDFIL (Christ Church) (St Luke) *Llan 10* **V** S S MORGAN, **C** J E PARKIN, C M L STONE
MERTHYR TYDFIL (St David) (St Tydfil's Well) *Llan 10* **R** M J DAVIES
MERTHYR VALE (St Mary and Holy Innocents) *see* Troedyrhiw w Merthyr Vale *Llan*
MICHAELSTON-LE-PIT (St Michael and All Angels) *see* St Andrews Major w Michaelston-le-Pit *Llan*
MICHAELSTON-SUPER-AVON *see* Cwmafan *Llan*
MICHAELSTON-SUPER-ELY (St Michael) *see* St Fagans w Michaelston-super-Ely *Llan*
MICHAELSTON-Y-FEDW (St Michael) *Mon 6* **P-in-c** J A DALE
MICHEL TROY (St Michael) *see* Monmouth w Overmonnow etc *Mon*
MILFORD HAVEN (St Katherine) (St Peter) (St Thomas à Becket) *St D 5* **V** J H M DAVIES
MINERA (St Andrew) *see* Bwlchgwyn and Minera *St As*
MINERA (St David) *as above*
MINERA (St Mary) *as above*
MINERA (St Tudfil) *as above*
MINWEAR (St Womar) *see* Martletwy w Lawrenny and Minwear etc *St D*
MISKIN (St John the Baptist) *see* Mountain Ash and Miskin *Llan*
MOCHDRE (All Saints) *St As 7* **P-in-c** A R MARSHALL
MOLD (St Mary) *St As 16* **V** C I DAY
MONINGTON (St Nicholas) *see* St Dogmael's w Moylgrove and Monington *St D*
MONKSWOOD (St Matthew) *see* Mamhilad w Monkswood and Glascoed Chapel *Mon*
MONKTON (St Nicholas and St John) *St D 1* **TR** M L COX, **TV** R JONES, A J TURNER, **C** C M T WOOD

MONMOUTH (St Mary the Virgin) w Overmonnow w Wonastow w Michel Troy *Mon 3* **V** R E PAIN, **C** V I D F POWELL, **NSM** D J MCGLADDERY
MONTGOMERY (St Nicholas) and Forden and Llandyssil *St As 10* **NSM** R BRIGNELL
MORFIL *see* Fishguard w Llanychar and Pontfaen w Morfil etc *St D*
MORRISTON (St David) (St John) *S & B 7* **V** H M LERVY, **NSM** E G PHILLIPS
MOSTYN (Christ Church) *St As 4* **V** *vacant* (01745) 560513
MOUNTAIN ASH (St Margaret) (St Illtyd) and Miskin *Llan 9* **V** M L CHIPLIN, **NSM** M E MAYLOR
MOUNTON *see* Narberth w Mounton w Robeston Wathen and Crinow *St D*
MOUNTON (St Andoenus) *see* Mathern and Mounton w St Pierre *Mon*
MOYLGROVE (St Mynno, St David and St Andrew) *see* St Dogmael's w Moylgrove and Monington *St D*
MWNT (Holy Cross) *see* Cardigan w Mwnt and Y Ferwig w Llangoedmor *St D*
MYDDFAI (St Michael) *see* Llandingat w Myddfai *St D*
MYDROILYN (Holy Trinity) *see* Llanerch Aeron w Ciliau Aeron and Dihewyd etc *St D*
MYNACHLOGDDU (St Dogmael) *see* Maenclochog and New Moat etc *St D*
MYNYDD ISA *see* Bistre *St As*
MYNYDDISLWYN (St Tudor) *Mon 7* **TR** R J SUMMERS, **TV** A S HUNT, R JEFFORD, **OLM** M BARGE
NANNERCH (St Michael) *see* Cilcain and Nannerch and Rhydymwyn *St As*
NANTCWNLLE (St Cynllo) *see* Llanfihangel Ystrad and Cilcennin w Trefilan etc *St D*
NANTGLYN (St James) *see* Llanrhaeadr-yng-Nghinmeirch w Prion and Nantglyn *St As*
NANTMEL (St Cynllo) *see* Rhayader and Nantmel *S & B*
NANTYGLO (Holy Trinity and St Anne) *see* Blaina and Nantyglo *Mon*
NARBERTH (St Andrew) w Mounton w Robeston Wathen and Crinow *St D 4* **R** T P LEWIS
NASH (St Mary) *see* Carew *St D*
NASH (St Mary) *see* Magor *Mon*
NEATH (St Thomas) (St David) (St Catherine) (St Peter and St Paul) *Llan 8* **TR** S J RYAN, **C** W M T V COUGHLIN, **NSM** C A MULLIGAN
NEBO (Dewi Sant) *see* Llansantffraed w Llanrhystud and Llanddeiniol *St D*
NEFYN (St David) (St Mary) w Tudweiliog w Llandudwen w Edern *Ban 11* **V** E OWEN, **NSM** N M HAWKINS
NELSON (St John the Baptist) *see* Llanfabon *Llan*
NERCWYS (St Mary) *see* Treuddyn w Nercwys *St As*
NEVERN (St Brynach) and Y Beifil w Eglwyswrw and Meline and Eglwyswen and Llanfair Nant-gwyn *St D 6* **V** J P LEWIS
NEW HEDGES (St Anne) *see* Tenby *St D*
NEW MOAT (St Nicholas) *see* Maenclochog and New Moat etc *St D*
NEW RADNOR (St Mary) and Llanfihangel Nantmelan and Evancoyd w Gladwestry and Colva *S & B 5* **P-in-c** M K E MORGAN
NEW TREDEGAR (St Dingat) *Mon 7* **NSM** J EVANS
NEWBOROUGH (St Peter) w Llanidan, Llangeinwen, Llanfair-yn-y-Cwmwd and Llangaffo *Ban 4* **R** R L NEWALL
NEWBRIDGE (St Paul) (St Peter) *Mon 7* **V** M J JEFFORD
NEWBRIDGE-ON-WYE (All Saints) *see* Upper Wye *S & B*
NEWCASTLE (St Illtud) *Llan 6* **V** D E C LLOYD
NEWCASTLE EMLYN (Holy Trinity) w Llandyfriog and Troed-yr-aur w Brongwyn *St D 7* **V** D J L ROBERTS
NEWCHURCH (St Mary) *see* Cynwil Elfed and Newchurch *St D*
NEWCHURCH (St Mary) *see* Bryngwyn and Newchurch and Llanbedr etc *S & B*
NEWCHURCH (St Michael) *see* Cynwil Elfed and Newchurch *St D*
NEWCHURCH (St Peter) *as above*
NEWCHURCH (St Peter) *see* Caerwent w Dinham and Llanfair Discoed etc *Mon*
NEWMARKET *see* Dyserth and Trelawnyd and Cwm *St As*
NEWPORT (All Saints) *Mon 9* **V** G HOLLOWOOD
NEWPORT (Cathedral of St Woolos) (St Martin) *Mon 9* **V** R D FENWICK
NEWPORT (Christ Church) *Mon 9* **V** I S DOULL
NEWPORT (St Andrew) (St Philip) *Mon 9* **V** P MUSINDI
NEWPORT (St John Baptist) *Mon 9* **V** C D WESTBROOK
NEWPORT (St John the Evangelist) *see* Maindee *Mon*
NEWPORT St Julian (St Julius and St Aaron) *Mon 9* **V** D R WILLIAMS
NEWPORT (St Mark) *Mon 9* **V** A R WILLIE
NEWPORT (St Mary) *see* Maindee *Mon*
NEWPORT (St Mary) w Cilgwyn and Dinas w Llanllawer *St D 6* **R** *vacant*
NEWPORT (St Matthew) *Mon 9* **V** *vacant* (01633) 769453
NEWPORT St Paul *Mon 9* **P-in-c** S P TOMS
NEWPORT (St Stephen) and Holy Trinity *Mon 9* **V** E L MATHIAS-JONES
NEWPORT (St Teilo) *Mon 9* **P-in-c** T H J PALMER
NEWQUAY (St Llwchaiarn) *see* Llanllwchaearn and Llanina *St D*
NEWTON (St Peter) *S & B 6* **V** C M P JONES
NEWTON NORTH *see* Slebech and Uzmaston w Boulston *St D*
NEWTON NOTTAGE (St John the Baptist) (All Saints) (St David) *Llan 7* **R** P R MASSON, **C** P A LEYSHON
NEWTOWN (St David) w Llanllwchaiarn w Aberhafesp *St As 7* **R** A S GRIMWOOD, **NSM** E C YATES
NEYLAND (St Clement) *see* Llanstadwel *St D*
NICHOLASTON (St Nicholas) *see* Oxwich w Penmaen and Nicholaston *S & B*
NOLTON (St Madog) w Roch and St Lawrence w Ford and Hayscastle *St D 5* **R** M H ROWLANDS
NOLTON (St Mary) *see* Coity w Nolton *Llan*
NORTHOP (St Eurgain and St Peter) (St Mary) *St As 16* **V** R P BILLINGSLEY
NORTON (Mission Church) *see* Oystermouth *S & B*
NORTON (St Andrew) *see* Knighton, Norton, Whitton, Pilleth and Cascob *S & B*
NOTTAGE (St David) *see* Newton Nottage *Llan*
OAKWOOD (St John) *see* Neath *Llan*
OGMORE VALE (St John the Baptist) *see* Cwm Ogwr *Llan*
OVERMONNOW (St Thomas) *see* Monmouth w Overmonnow etc *Mon*
OVERTON (St Mary the Virgin) and Erbistock and Penley *St As 11* **R** D T B LEWIS
OXWICH (St Illtyd) w Penmaen and Nicholaston *S & B 8* **V** *vacant* (01792) 371241
OYSTERMOUTH (All Saints) *S & B 6* **V** K EVANS, **C** J ANDREW, **NSM** D J H WATKINS
PANTEG (St Mary) w Llanfihangel Pontymoile *Mon 10* **R** P K WALKER, **Par Dn** P R EVANS
PANTYFFRID (Mission Church) *see* Berriew *St As*
PATRICIO (St Issui the Martyr) *see* Llangenni and Llanbedr Ystrad Yw w Patricio *S & B*
PEMBROKE (St Daniel) *see* Monkton *St D*
PEMBROKE (St Mary) *as above*
PEMBROKE (St Michael) *as above*
PEMBROKE DOCK (St John) *see* Carew *St D*
PEMBROKE DOCK (St Patrick) *as above*
PEMBROKE DOCK (St Teilo) *as above*
PEN-BOYR (St Llawddog) *see* Llangeler w Pen-Boyr *St D*
PEN-BRE (St Illtud) *St D 12* **V** A J MEATS
PENALLT (Old Church) and Trellech *Mon 3* **V** S J HOWELLS, **NSM** J M BONE
PENALLY (St Nicholas) *see* Tenby *St D*
PENARTH (All Saints) (St Peter) (St Luke) *Llan 5* **V** P A COX, **C** E EVANS
PENARTH (St Augustine) (Holy Nativity) and Llandough *Llan 5* **R** R DONKIN, **C** S JENKYNS
PENBRYN (St Michael) *see* Llangrannog w Llandysiliogogo w Penbryn *St D*
PENCADER (St Mary) *see* Llanfihangel-ar-arth w Capel Dewi *St D*
PENCARREG (St Patrick) and Llanycrwys *St D 9* **V** B E MORRIS
PENCLAWDD *see* Llanyrnewydd *S & B*
PENCOED (St David) *see* Llanilid w Pencoed *Llan*
PENCOED (St Paul) *as above*
PENDERYN MELLTE (St Cynog) *S & B 1* **R** J H SCOTT
PENDINE (St Margaret) w Llanmiloe and Eglwys Gymyn w Marros *St D 15* **R** W P NASH
PENDOYLAN (St Cadoc) w Welsh St Donats *Llan 4* **V** E C R COUNSELL
PENEGOES (St Cadfarch) *see* Machynlleth w Llanwrin and Penegoes *Ban*
PENHOW (St John the Baptist) and St Brides Netherwent w Llandavenny and Llanvaches and Llandevaud *Mon 4* **V** J HEALES
PENISARWAEN (St Helen) *see* Llanddeiniolen w Llanfair-is-gaer etc *Ban*
PENLEY (St Mary Magdalene) *see* Overton and Erbistock and Penley *St As*
PENLLECH *see* Aberdaron w Rhiw and Llanfaelrhys etc *Ban*
PENLLERGAER (St David) *S & B 9* **V** F A BAYES
PENLLWYN (St Mary the Virgin) *see* Mynyddislwyn *Mon*
PENLLYN (Chapel of Ease) *see* Cowbridge *Llan*

PENMAEN (St David) *see* Mynyddislwyn *Mon*
PENMAEN (St John the Baptist) *see* Oxwich w Penmaen and Nicholaston *S & B*
PENMAENMAWR *see* Dwygyfylchi *Ban*
PENMARK (St Mary) w Porthkerry *Llan 5* **V** S C PARE
PENMYNYDD (St Credifael) *see* Llanfair-pwll and Llanddaniel-fab etc *Ban*
PENNAL (St Peter ad Vincula) w Corris and Esgairgeiliog *Ban 10* **R** G AP IORWERTH
PENNANT (St Thomas) *see* Llanrhaeadr-ym-Mochnant etc *St As*
PENNANT MELANGELL (St Melangel) *see* Llangynog *St As*
PENNARD (St Mary) *see* Ilston w Pennard *S & B*
PENPONT (no dedication) *see* Trallwng w Bettws Penpont w Aberyskir etc *S & B*
PENRHIWCEIBER (St Winifred), Matthewstown and Ynysboeth *Llan 9* **V** A K HOLMES
PENRHOS (Holy Trinity) *see* Llandysilio and Penrhos and Llandrinio etc *St As*
PENRHOS (St Cadoc) *see* Llantilio Crossenny w Penrhos, Llanvetherine etc *Mon*
PENRHOSLLUGWY (St Michael) *see* Llaneugrad w Llanallgo and Penrhosllugwy etc *Ban*
PENRHYDD *see* Maenordeifi and Capel Colman w Llanfihangel etc *St D*
PENRHYN-COCH (St John) *see* Elerch w Penrhyncoch w Capel Bangor and Goginan *St D*
PENRHYNDEUDRAETH (Holy Trinity) w Llanfrothen w Beddgelert *Ban 8* **V** S M OWEN
PENRHYNSIDE (St Sannan) *see* Llanrhos *St As*
PENRHYNSIDE BAY (St David) *as above*
PENRICE (St Andrew) *see* Reynoldston w Penrice and Llangennith *S & B*
PENSARN (St David) *see* Abergele *St As*
PENSTROWED (St Gwrhai) *see* Llandinam w Trefeglwys w Penstrowed *Ban*
PENTERRY (St Mary) *see* Itton and St Arvans w Penterry and Kilgwrrwg etc *Mon*
PENTIR (St Cedol) (St Elizabeth) *Ban 5* **V** *vacant* (01248) 362016
PENTRAETH (St Mary) *see* Llansadwrn w Llanddona and Llaniestyn etc *Ban*
PENTRE (St Peter) *Llan 12* **V** H H ENGLAND-SIMON
PENTRECHWYTH (St Peter) *see* Glantawe *S & B*
PENTREFOELAS (Parish Church) *see* Cerrigydrudion w Llanfihangel Glyn Myfyr etc *St As*
PENTROBIN (St John) *see* Hawarden *St As*
PENTWYN (St David) *see* Cyncoed *Mon*
PENTWYN (St Mary) *see* Penallt and Trellech *Mon*
PENTYRCH (St Cadwg) w Capel Llanillterne *Llan 3* **V** J W BINNY
PENYBONTFAWR *see* Llanrhaeadr-ym-Mochnant etc *St As*
PENYCAE (St Thomas) *see* Rhosymedre w Penycae *St As*
PENYCLAWDD (St Martin) *see* Rockfield and Dingestow Gp *Mon*
PENYDARREN (St John the Baptist) *see* Dowlais and Penydarren *Llan*
PENYFAI (All Saints) *Llan 6* **P-in-c** G AP GWILYM
PENYFFORDD (Emmanuel) *see* Hope *St As*
PENYGRAIG (St Barnabas) *see* Dinas and Penygraig w Williamstown *Llan*
PENYWAUN (St Winifred) *see* Hirwaun *Llan*
PETERSTON-SUPER-ELY (St Peter) w St Brides-super-Ely *Llan 4* **R** *vacant* (01446) 760297
PETERSTON-SUPER-MONTEM (St Peter) *see* Llanharan w Peterston-super-Montem *Llan*
PETERSTONE WENTLOOG (St Peter) *see* Marshfield and Peterstone Wentloog etc *Mon*
PILLETH (Our Lady of Pilleth) *see* Knighton, Norton, Whitton, Pilleth and Cascob *S & B*
PISTYLL (St Beuno) *see* Nefyn w Tudweiliog w Llandudwen w Edern *Ban*
PLAS POWER (St Mary) *see* Wrexham *St As*
PONT AMAN (St Thomas) *see* Betws w Ammanford *St D*
PONT DOLANOG (St John the Evangelist) *see* Meifod w Llangynyw w Pont Robert w Pont Dolanog *St As*
PONT-IETS (St Mary) *see* Cwm Gwendraeth *St D*
PONT ROBERT (St John the Evangelist) *see* Meifod w Llangynyw w Pont Robert w Pont Dolanog *St As*
PONTARDAWE (All Saints) *see* Llangiwg *S & B*
PONTARDAWE (St Peter) *as above*
PONTARDDULAIS *see* Llandeilo Tal-y-bont *S & B*
PONTARFYNACH *see* Ysbyty Cynfyn w Llantrisant and Eglwys Newydd *St D*
PONTARGOTHI (Holy Trinity) *see* Llanegwad w Llanfynydd *St D*
PONTBLYDDYN (Christ Church) *St As 16* **V** P J MACKRIELL, **NSM** C M POOLMAN
PONTERWYD *see* Ysbyty Cynfyn w Llantrisant and Eglwys Newydd *St D*
PONTFADOG (St John) *see* Llansantffraid Glyn Ceirog and Llanarmon etc *St As*
PONTFAEN (St Brynach) *see* Fishguard w Llanychar and Pontfaen w Morfil etc *St D*
PONTLLANFRAITH (St Augustine) *see* Mynyddislwyn *Mon*
PONTLLIW (St Anne) *see* Penllergaer *S & B*
PONTLOTTYN (St Tyfaelog) (St Michael) (St Aidan) w Fochriw *Llan 1* **V** P A DEROY-JONES
PONTNEATHVAUGHAN (St John) *see* Penderyn Mellte *S & B*
PONTNEWYDD (Holy Trinity) *Mon 10* **V** D J DUNN, **Par Dn** H D THOMAS, **OLM** D L THOMAS
PONTNEWYNYDD (All Saints) *see* Pontypool *Mon*
PONTRHYDFENDIGAID (St David) *see* Tregaron w Ystrad Meurig and Strata Florida *St D*
PONTSIAN (St John) *see* Llandysul w Bangor Teifi w Henllan etc *St D*
PONTYATES (St Mary) *see* Cwm Gwendraeth *St D*
PONTYBEREM (St John) *as above*
PONTYCLUN (St Paul) w Talygarn *Llan 4* **V** G P KARAMURA
PONTYCYMMER (St David) *see* Llangeinor and the Garw Valley *Llan*
PONTYGWAITH (St Mary Magdalene) *see* Rhondda Fach Uchaf *Llan*
PONTYMISTER (St Margaret) *see* Risca *Mon*
PONTYPOOL (St James) (St Matthew) *Mon 10* **R** B R PIPPEN, **TV** P A GOLLEDGE, **C** A TEMPLE-WILLIAMS
PONTYPRIDD (St Catherine) *Llan 11* **V** E M GREEN
PONTYPRIDD (St Matthew) and Cilfynydd w Llanwynno *Llan 11* **P-in-c** P BOYLE, **NSM** G TUCK
POOL QUAY (St John the Evangelist) *St As 10* **NSM** R PARKER
PORT EYNON (St Cattwg) *see* SW Gower *S & B*
PORT TALBOT (St Agnes) *see* Aberavon *Llan*
PORT TALBOT (St David) *see* Margam *Llan*
PORT TALBOT (St Theodore) (Holy Cross) (St Peter) *Llan 7* **V** C J AMOS
PORTH *see* Cymmer and Porth *Llan*
PORTH (St Paul) w Trealaw *Llan 12* **V** R A ANGEL
PORTHCAWL (All Saints) *see* Newton Nottage *Llan*
PORTHKERRY (Rhoose Mission Church) *see* Penmark w Porthkerry *Llan*
PORTHKERRY (St Curig) *as above*
PORTHMADOC (St John) (St Cyngar) and Ynyscynhaearn and Dolbenmaen *Ban 11* **V** A J WILLIAMS
PORTSKEWETT (St Mary) *see* Caldicot *Mon*
PRENDERGAST (St David) w Rudbaxton *St D 2* **R** G D GWYTHER
PRESTATYN (Christ Church) (Church of Holy Spirit) *St As 1* **V** D Q BELLAMY, **C** K A JOHNSON
PRINCES GATE (St Catherine) *see* Lamp Velfrey and Llanddewi Velfrey *St D*
PRION (St James) *see* Llanrhaeadr-yng-Nghinmeirch w Prion and Nantglyn *St As*
PUNCHESTON (St Mary) *see* Letterston w Llanfair Nant-y-Gof etc *St D*
PUNCHSTON *see* Fishguard w Llanychar and Pontfaen w Morfil etc *St D*
PWLL (Holy Trinity) *see* Burry Port and Pwll *St D*
PWLLCROCHAN *see* Monkton *St D*
PWLLGWAUN (St Mark) and Llanddewi Rhondda *Llan 11* **P-in-c** C E BURR
PWLLHELI *see* Denio w Abererch *Ban*
PYLE (St James) (St Mary Magdalene) w Kenfig *Llan 7* **P-in-c** I K REES
QUAR, THE (St Tydfil's Well) *see* Merthyr Tydfil St Dav *Llan*
QUEENSFERRY (St Andrew) *see* Shotton *St As*
RADNOR (St Mary) *see* New Radnor and Llanfihangel Nantmelan etc *S & B*
RADNOR, EAST *see* Knighton, Norton, Whitton, Pilleth and Cascob *S & B*
RADYR (St John the Baptist) (Christ Church) *Llan 3* **R** W G BARLOW, **C** A P JAMES
RAGLAN (St Cadoc) w Llandenny and Bryngwyn *Mon 5* **P-in-c** J WAKELING
REDBERTH (Church) *see* Carew *St D*
REDWICK (St Thomas) *see* Magor *Mon*
RESOLVEN (St David) *see* Vale of Neath *Llan*
REYNOLDSTON (Church) *see* Jeffreyston w Reynoldston and E Williamston etc *St D*
REYNOLDSTON (St George) w Penrice and Llangennith *S & B 8* **R** P J WILLIAMS

RHANDIRMWYN (St Barnabas) *see* Cil-y-Cwm and Ystrad-ffin w Rhandir-mwyn etc *St D*
RHAYADER (St Clement) and Nantmel *S & B 5* **V** *vacant* (01597) 810223
RHESYCAE (Christ Church) *see* Halkyn w Caerfallwch w Rhesycae *St As*
RHEWL (Church) *see* Llanbedr DC w Llangynhafal, Llanychan etc *St As*
RHIWLAS (Mission Church) *see* Llansilin w Llangadwaladr and Llangedwyn *St As*
RHONDDA FACH UCHAF *Llan 12* **P-in-c** G J R GEORGE-ROGERS
RHOS (St James) *see* Llangeler w Pen-Boyr *St D*
RHOSBEIRIO *see* Llanfechell w Bodewryd w Rhosbeirio etc *Ban*
RHOSCOLYN *see* Holyhead *Ban*
RHOSCROWTHER (St Decumanus) *see* Monkton *St D*
RHOSDDU *see* Wrexham *St As*
RHOSESEMOR *see* Halkyn w Caerfallwch w Rhesycae *St As*
RHOSILI (St Mary the Virgin) *see* SW Gower *S & B*
RHOSLEFAIN (St Mary) *see* Arthog w Fairbourne w Llangelynnin w Rhoslefain *Ban*
RHOSLLANNERCHRUGOG (St John the Evangelist) (St David) (St Mary) *St As 14* **V** J S EVANS
RHOSTIE *see* Llanilar w Rhostie and Llangwyryfon etc *St D*
RHOSYGWALIAU (Holy Trinity) *see* Llanfor w Rhosygwaliau *St As*
RHOSYMEDRE (St John the Evangelist) w Penycae *St As 14* **V** *vacant* (01978) 822125
RHUDDLAN (St Mary) *St As 1* **V** J G GRIFFITHS
RHULEN (St David) *see* Colwyn *S & B*
RHYD-Y-MWYN (St John the Evangelist) *see* Cilcain and Nannerch and Rhydymwyn *St As*
RHYDYBRIW (Capel Rhydybriw) *see* Defynnog, Llandilo'r Fan, Llanulid, Llywel etc *S & B*
RHYDYFELIN (St Luke) w Graig *Llan 11* **P-in-c** M D GABLE
RHYL (Holy Trinity) (St Thomas) (St John) (St Ann) *St As 1* **V** J GLOVER, **C** J R GAVIN, M J BENNETT
RHYMNEY (St David) *Mon 7* **V** M A ADSETTS
RISCA (St Mary) *Mon 6* **V** J BLACKBURN
ROATH (St German) *Llan 2* **V** R D DOXSEY, **C** D J ATKINS
ROATH (St Margaret) (St Anne) (St Edward) (St Teilo's School) *Llan 2* **V** G W WILLIAMS, **C** S M REES, C R DOWNS
ROATH (St Martin) *Llan 2* **V** I D HAMER, **NSM** T G WATKIN
ROATH (St Philip) *see* Tremorfa St Phil CD *Llan*
ROATH (St Saviour) *Llan 2* **V** A RABJOHNS
ROATH PARK (Christ Church) *see* Cardiff Ch Ch Roath Park *Llan*
ROBERTSTOWN (St John the Evangelist) *see* Aberdare *Llan*
ROBESTON WATHEN (Church) *see* Narberth w Mounton w Robeston Wathen and Crinow *St D*
ROBESTON WEST (St Andrew) *see* Walwyn's Castle w Robeston W *St D*
ROCH (St Mary) *see* Nolton w Roch and St Lawrence w Ford etc *St D*
ROCKFIELD (St Cenedlon) w St Maughans w Llangattock-vibon-Avel w LLanfihangel-ystern-LLewern w Dingestow w Llangovan and Penyclawdd w Tregaer w Cwmcarvan *Mon 3* **V** S L GUEST, **Hon C** J R ELLIS, **NSM** J M ELLIS, J-J S AIDLEY
ROGERSTONE (St John the Baptist) *see* Bassaleg *Mon*
ROGIET (St Mary) *see* Caldicot *Mon*
ROSEMARKET (St Ishmael) *see* Burton and Rosemarket *St D*
ROSSETT (Christ Church) *see* Holt, Rossett and Isycoed *St As*
RUABON (St Mary) (All Saints) *St As 14* **V** M A HARRISON
RUDBAXTON (St Michael) *see* Prendergast w Rudbaxton *St D*
RUDRY (St James) *see* Bedwas and Rudry *Mon*
RUMNEY (St Augustine) *Mon 6* **V** D A G HATHAWAY
RUTHIN (St Peter) w Llanrhydd *St As 3* **R** R BAYLEY
ST ANDREWS MAJOR (St Andrew) (St Peter) w Michaelston-le-Pit *Llan 5* **R** D H RHYDDERCH
ST ARVANS (St Arvan) *see* Itton and St Arvans w Penterry and Kilgwrrwg etc *Mon*
ST ASAPH (Cathedral of St Asaph and St Cyndeyrn) *St As 1* **TR** C N L POTTER, **TV** A C SULLY
ST ATHAN (St Tathan) *see* Llantwit Major *Llan*
ST BRIDES (St Bridget) *see* Dale and St Brides w Marloes *St D*
ST BRIDES MAJOR (St Bridget) *see* Ewenny w St Brides Major *Llan*
ST BRIDES MINOR (St Bride) *see* Llansantffraid, Bettws and Aberkenfig *Llan*
ST BRIDES NETHERWENT (St Bridget) *see* Penhow, St Brides Netherwent w Llandavenny etc *Mon*
ST BRIDES-SUPER-ELY (St Bride) *see* Peterston-super-Ely w St Brides-super-Ely *Llan*
ST BRIDE'S WENTLOOG *see* Marshfield and Peterstone Wentloog etc *Mon*
ST CLEARS (St Mary Magdalene) w Llangynin and Llanddowror and Llanfihangel Abercywyn *St D 15* **V** B D WITT
ST DAVIDS (Cathedral of St David and St Andrew) *see* Dewisland *St D*
ST DOGMAEL'S (St Thomas) w Moylgrove and Monington *St D 6* **V** D P DAVIES
ST DOGWELLS (St Dogfael) *see* Spittal w Trefgarn and Ambleston w St Dogwells *St D*
ST EDREN'S *see* Mathry w St Edren's and Grandston etc *St D*
ST ELVIS *see* Dewisland *St D*
ST FAGANS (St Mary) w Michaelston-super-Ely *Llan 3* **R** A R WINTLE
ST FLORENCE (St Florentius) *see* Carew *St D*
ST GEORGE (St George) *see* Towyn and St George *St As*
ST GEORGE-SUPER-ELY (St George) *see* St Nicholas w Bonvilston and St George-super-Ely *Llan*
ST HARMON'S (St Garmon) *see* Cwmddauddwr w St Harmon's and Llanwrthwl *S & B*
ST HILARY (St Hilary) *see* Cowbridge *Llan*
ST HILARY (St Hilary) Greenway *see* Rumney *Mon*
ST ISHMAEL'S (St Ishmael) *see* Herbrandston and Hasguard w St Ishmael's *St D*
ST ISHMAEL'S (St Ishmael) w Llan-saint and Ferryside *St D 12* **V** R M JENKINS
ST ISSELL'S (St Issell) and Amroth *St D 4* **V** M BUTLER
ST LAWRENCE (St Lawrence) *see* Nolton w Roch and St Lawrence w Ford etc *St D*
ST LYTHANS (St Bleiddian) *see* Wenvoe and St Lythans *Llan*
ST MARY CHURCH (St Mary) *see* Cowbridge *Llan*
ST MARY HILL (St Mary) *see* Coychurch, Llangan and St Mary Hill *Llan*
ST MAUGHEN'S (St Meugan) *see* Rockfield and Dingestow Gp *Mon*
ST MELLONS (St Mellon) *Mon 6* **V** D KELLEN, **C** J GOULD, **NSM** G R DAVIES
ST NICHOLAS (St Nicholas) *see* Mathry w St Edren's and Grandston etc *St D*
ST NICHOLAS (St Nicholas) w Bonvilston and St George-super-Ely *Llan 4* **R** E T WILSON
ST PETROX (St Pedrog) *see* Monkton *St D*
ST PIERRE (St Peter) *see* Mathern and Mounton w St Pierre *Mon*
ST THOMAS *see* Haverfordwest St Mary and St Thos w Haroldston *St D*
ST TWYNNELLS (St Gwynog) *see* Monkton *St D*
SANDFIELDS *see* Aberavon *Llan*
SANDYCROFT (Holy Spirit) *see* Hawarden *St As*
SANDYCROFT (St Francis) *as above*
SARON (St David) *see* Llanedi w Tycroes and Saron *St D*
SAUNDERSFOOT *see* St Issell's and Amroth *St D*
SEALAND (St Barth) *see* Hawarden *St As*
SEBASTOPOL (St Oswald) *see* Griffithstown *Mon*
SENGHENYDD (St Peter) *see* Eglwysilan *Llan*
SEVEN SISTERS (St David) *see* Dulais Valley *Llan*
SEVEN SISTERS (St Mary) *as above*
SHIRENEWTON (St Thomas à Becket) *see* Caerwent w Dinham and Llanfair Discoed etc *Mon*
SHOTTON (St Ethelwold) *St As 13* **V** D P MORRIS, **NSM** M F WILKINSON
SILIAN (St Sulien) *see* Lampeter and Llanddewibrefi Gp *St D*
SINAN (All Saints) *see* Cefn w Trefnant w Tremeirchion *St As*
SIX BELLS (St John) *see* Abertillery w Cwmtillery w Six Bells *Mon*
SKENFRITH (St Bride) *see* Grosmont and Skenfrith and Llangattock etc *Mon*
SKETTY (St Paul) (Holy Trinity) *S & B 6* **V** A J KNIGHT, **C** S SARAPUK
SKEWEN (St John) (All Saints) (St Mary) *Llan 8* **V** M WILLIAMS, **C** D O JONES
SLEBECH (St John the Baptist Parish Centre) and Uzmaston w Boulston *St D 2* **V** D M GRIFFITHS
SOLVA (St Aidan) *see* Dewisland *St D*
SOUTHERNDOWN (All Saints) *see* Ewenny w St Brides Major *Llan*
SOUTHSEA (All Saints) *see* Brymbo and Southsea *St As*
SPITTAL (St Mary) w Trefgarn and Ambleston w St Dogwells *St D 2* **V** D R REES
STACKPOLE ELIDOR (St James and St Elidyr) *see* Monkton *St D*
STEYNTON (St Cewydd and St Peter) *St D 5* **V** J I HOLDSWORTH, **NSM** D G DAVIES
STRATA FLORIDA (St Mary) *see* Tregaron w Ystrad Meurig and Strata Florida *St D*

SULLY (St John the Baptist) *Llan 5* **R** E B DOWDING
SWANSEA (St Barnabas) *S & B 11* **V** P C FRENCH
SWANSEA (St Gabriel) *S & B 6* **V** D M GRIFFITHS
SWANSEA (St James) *S & B 11* **V** D A WALKER
SWANSEA (St Jude) *S & B 11* **P-in-c** H V PARSELL
SWANSEA (St Luke) *S & B 10* **P-in-c** J B DAVIES
SWANSEA (St Nicholas-on-the-Hill) *S & B 11* **P-in-c** P KEOWN
SWANSEA (St Peter) *S & B 10* **V** H M WILLIAMS, **C** I DAVIES
SWANSEA (St Thomas) (St Stephen) and Kilvey *S & B 11* **V** A J M MEREDITH, **NSM** J W WEDGBURY
SWANSEA, CENTRAL (St Mary) (Holy Trinity) (Christ Church) (St Matthew) (St Mark) (St John) *S & B 11* **TR** A J VESSEY, **TV** C L WILLIAMS, **C** S M KNIGHT, K P J PADLEY
TAI'RGWAITH (St David) *see* Gwaun-cae-Gurwen *St D*
TAL-Y-LLYN (St David) *see* Llanegryn w Aberdyfi w Tywyn *Ban*
TALACHDDU (St Mary) *see* Llandefalle and Llyswen w Boughrood etc *S & B*
TALBENNY (St Mary) *see* Walton W w Talbenny and Haroldston W *St D*
TALGARREG (St David) *see* Llanarth and Capel Cynon w Talgarreg etc *St D*
TALGARTH (St Gwendoline) and Llanelieu *S & B 4* **V** *vacant* (01874) 711249
TALIARIS (Holy Trinity) *see* Llandeilo Fawr and Taliaris *St D*
TALLARN GREEN (St Mary Magdalene) *see* Hanmer, Bronington, Bettisfield, Tallarn Green *St As*
TALLEY (St Michael) *see* Cynwyl Gaeo w Llansawel and Talley *St D*
TALYBONT (St Cross) *see* Llandygai and Maes y Groes *Ban*
TALYBONT (St David) *see* Llanfihangel Genau'r-glyn and Llangorwen *St D*
TALYGARN (St Anne) *see* Pontyclun w Talygarn *Llan*
TALYLLYN *see* Pennal w Corris and Esgairgeiliog *Ban*
TALYLLYN (St Mary) *see* Llanegryn w Aberdyfi w Tywyn *Ban*
TEMPLETON (St John) *see* Martletwy w Lawrenny and Minwear etc *St D*
TENBY (St Mary) (St Julian's Chapel) *St D 4* **TR** W D JENKINS, **TV** S M JOHN, **C** D A BAXTER
TINTERN (St Michael) *see* Llandogo w Whitebrook Chpl and Tintern Parva *Mon*
TIRABAD (St David) *see* Llanwrtyd w Llanddulas in Tir Abad etc *S & B*
TIRTHIL (St Michael) *see* Pontlottyn w Fochriw *Llan*
TON-YR-YWEN (School) *see* Llanishen *Llan*
TONDU (St John) *see* Llansantffraid, Bettws and Aberkenfig *Llan*
TONDU (St Thomas) *as above*
TONGWYNLAIS (St Michael) (St James) *Llan 3* **V** V J PAYNE
TONMAWR (St Teilo) *see* Neath *Llan*
TONNA (St Anne) *Llan 8* **P-in-c** N LEA, **NSM** C GALSWORTHY
TONPENTRE *see* Ystradyfodwg *Llan*
TONYPANDY (St Andrew) w Clydach Vale *Llan 12* **V** M J GILL
TONYREFAIL (St David) (St Alban) w Gilfach Goch *Llan 12* **V** R E MOVERLEY
TOWNHILL *see* Swansea St Nic *S & B*
TOWYN (St Mary) and St George *St As 1* **V** H G A JALLAND
TRAEAN-GLAS (St Mary) *see* Defynnog, Llandilo'r Fan, Llanulid, Llywel etc *S & B*
TRALLWNG (St David) w Bettws Penpont w Aberyskir w Llanfihangel Nantbran w Battle *S & B 1* **V** N HOOK
TRAWSFYNYDD (St Madryn) *see* Maentwrog w Trawsfynydd *Ban*
TRE-GROES (St Ffraid) *see* Llandysul w Bangor Teifi w Henllan etc *St D*
TRE-LECH A'R BETWS (St Teilo) w Abernant and Llanwinio *St D 11* **P-in-c** E HOWELLS
TREALAW (All Saints) *see* Porth w Trealaw *Llan*
TREBANOS (St Michael) *see* Clydach *S & B*
TREBOETH (St Alban) (Penlan Church) *S & B 10* **P-in-c** R G JONES, **NSM** N P DOYLE
TREDEGAR (St George) (St James) *Mon 7* **V** J G DAVIS, **C** M OWEN
TREDUNNOC (St Andrew) *Mon 5* **V** *vacant*
TREFDRAETH (St Beuno) (Eglwys Crist y Brenin) w Aberffraw w Llangadwaladr w Cerrigceinwen *Ban 4* **R** A R M VAN DEN HOF
TREFEGLWYS (St Michael) *see* Llandinam w Trefeglwys w Penstrowed *Ban*
TREFGARN (St Michael) *see* Spittal w Trefgarn and Ambleston w St Dogwells *St D*
TREFILAN (St Hilary) *see* Llanfihangel Ystrad and Cilcennin w Trefilan etc *St D*
TREFLYS (St Michael) *see* Criccieth and Treflys w Llanystumdwy etc *Ban*
TREFNANT (Holy Trinity) *see* Cefn w Trefnant w Tremeirchion *St As*
TREFOR (St George) *see* Llanaelhaearn w Clynnog Fawr *Ban*
TREFRIW (St Mary) *see* Caerhun w Llangelynin w Llanbedr-y-Cennin *Ban*
TREGAEAN (St Caian) *see* Llangefni w Tregaean *Ban*
TREGAER (St Mary) *see* Rockfield and Dingestow Gp *Mon*
TREGARON (St Caron) w Ystrad Meurig and Strata Florida *St D 9* **V** P W DAVIES
TREGARTH (St Mair) *Ban 5* **I** L J PERRY, **NSM** E PARRI
TREGYNON (St Cynon) *see* Betws Cedewain and Tregynon and Llanwyddelan *St As*
TREHARRIS (St Matthias), Trelewis and Bedlinog *Llan 10* **V** P M N GULLIDGE
TREHERBERT (St Alban) *see* Treorchy and Treherbert *Llan*
TREHERBERT (St Mary Communion Centre) *as above*
TRELAWNYD (St Michael) *see* Dyserth and Trelawnyd and Cwm *St As*
TRELLECH (St Nicholas) *see* Penallt and Trellech *Mon*
TRELLECH GRANGE (not known) *see* Llanishen w Trellech Grange and Llanfihangel etc *Mon*
TREMAIN (St Michael) *see* Aberporth w Tremain w Blaenporth and Betws Ifan *St D*
TREMEIRCHION (Corpus Christi) *see* Cefn w Trefnant w Tremeirchion *St As*
TREMORFA (St Philip) Conventional District *Llan 5* **NSM** M K JONES
TREORCHY (St Matthew) and Treherbert *Llan 12* **P-in-c** P N COLEMAN
TRETHOMAS (St Thomas) *see* Bedwas and Rudry *Mon*
TRETOWER (St John the Evangelist) *see* Crickhowell w Cwmdu and Tretower *S & B*
TREUDDYN (St Mary) w Nercwys *St As 16* **V** J B JONES
TREVETHIN (St Cadoc) *see* Pontypool *Mon*
TREVETHIN (St John the Divine) *as above*
TREVOR (Church) *see* Llangollen w Trevor and Llantysilio *St As*
TREWALCHMAI (St Morhaiarn) *see* Llandrygarn w Bodwrog and Heneglwys etc *Ban*
TROED-YR-AUR (St Michael) *see* Newcastle Emlyn w Llandyfriog etc *St D*
TROEDRHIWGARTH (St Mary the Virgin) *Llan 7* **V** D G MORRIS
TROEDYRHIW (St John) w Merthyr Vale *Llan 10* **V** S J BARNES
TROFARTH (St John) *see* Llanelian w Trofarth *St As*
TROSTEY (St David) *see* Bettws Newydd w Trostrey etc *Mon*
TROWBRIDGE MAWR (St Hilary) *see* Rumney *Mon*
TUDWEILIOG (St Cwyfan) *see* Nefyn w Tudweiliog w Llandudwen w Edern *Ban*
TUMBLE (Dewi Sant) *see* Cwm Gwendraeth *St D*
TY SIGN (St David) *see* Risca *Mon*
TYCOCH (All Souls) *S & B 6* **V** P J GWYNN
TYCROES (St Edmund) *see* Llanedi w Tycroes and Saron *St D*
TYLORSTOWN (Holy Trinity) *see* Rhondda Fach Uchaf *Llan*
TYNANT (Mission Church) *see* Maentwrog w Trawsfynydd *Ban*
TYTHEGSTON (St Tydwg) *see* Laleston w Tythegston and Merthyr Mawr *Llan*
TYWYN (St Cadfan) *see* Llanegryn w Aberdyfi w Tywyn *Ban*
TYWYN (St Matthew) *as above*
UNDY (St Mary) *see* Magor *Mon*
UPPER WYE, The *S & B 2* **V** *vacant* (01597) 822472
USK (St Mary) and Gwehelog w Llantrisant w Llanllowell *Mon 10* **V** J F GRAY
UZMASTON (St Ismael) *see* Slebech and Uzmaston w Boulston *St D*
VALE OF NEATH *Llan 8* **V** P A LEWIS
VALLEY (St Michael) w Llechylched and Caergeiliog *Ban 3* **R** T BONNET
VAYNOR (St Gwynno) *see* Cefn Coed w Vaynor *S & B*
WALTON EAST (St Mary) *see* Wiston w Walton E and Clarbeston *St D*
WALTON WEST (All Saints) w Talbenny and Haroldston West *St D 5* **R** A P JOHNSON, **NSM** R M M JOHNSON
WALWYN'S CASTLE (St James the Great) w Robeston West *St D 5* **R** D J LOWEN
WATERSTON *see* Llanstadwel *St D*
WATTSTOWN (St Thomas) *see* Ynyshir *Llan*
WAUNARLLWYDD (St Barnabas) *S & B 9* **V** L J TAYLOR
WAUNFAWR (St John the Evangelist) *see* Llanbeblig w Caernarfon and Betws Garmon etc *Ban*
WAUNFELIN (St John the Divine) *see* Pontypool *Mon*
WAUNWEN (St Mark) *see* Cen Swansea *S & B*

WELSH ST DONATS (St Donat) *see* Pendoylan w Welsh St Donats *Llan*
WELSHPOOL (St Mary) (Christ Church) w Castle Caereinion *St As 10* **R** R L BROWN
WENVOE (St Mary) and St Lythans *Llan 5* **P-in-c** A C BERRY
WHISTON (not known) *see* Magor *Mon*
WHITCHURCH (St David) *see* Dewisland *St D*
WHITCHURCH (St Mary) (St Thomas) (All Saints) *Llan 3* **TR** J H L ROWLANDS, **TV** M GREENAWAY-ROBBINS, **C** M P COLTON, **Hon C** H G LEWIS, **NSM** B A SMITH
WHITEBROOK (Holy Trinity) *see* Llandogo w Whitebrook Chpl and Tintern Parva *Mon*
WHITECHURCH IN KEMES *see* Nevern and Y Beifil w Eglwyswrw and Meline etc *St D*
WHITFORD (St Mary and St Beuno) *see* Gorsedd w Brynford, Ysgeifiog and Whitford *St As*
WHITLAND (St Mary) w Cyffig and Henllan Amgoed and Llan-gan w Llandysilio and Clunderwen *St D 15* **V** K G TAYLOR
WHITTON (St David) *see* Knighton, Norton, Whitton, Pilleth and Cascob *S & B*
WICK (St James) *see* Llantwit Major *Llan*
WILCRICK (St Mary) *see* Bishton *Mon*
WILLIAMSTON, EAST (Church) *see* Jeffreyston w Reynoldston and E Williamston etc *St D*
WILLIAMSTOWN (St Illtud) *see* Dinas and Penygraig w Williamstown *Llan*
WISTON (St Mary Magdalene) w Walton East and Clarbeston *St D 2* **V** N CALE
WOLVESNEWTON (St Thomas à Becket) *see* Llangwm Uchaf and Llangwm Isaf w Gwernesney etc *Mon*
WONASTOW (St Wonnow) *see* Monmouth w Overmonnow etc *Mon*
WORTHENBURY (St Deiniol) *see* Bangor Monachorum, Worthenbury and Marchwiel *St As*
WREXHAM (St Giles's Parish Church) (St David) (St Mark) (St Mary) (All Saints) (St Margaret) (St James) (St John) *St As 18* **R** G O MARSHALL, **TV** G J OWEN, K B COLLINS, D A SLIM, S F WALKER, **C** M R J G WALKER, P POWELL, M BURNS
WYNDHAM (St David) *see* Cwm Ogwr *Llan*
Y BEIFIL (St Andrew) *see* Nevern and Y Beifil w Eglwyswrw and Meline etc *St D*
Y FERWIG (St Pedrog) *see* Cardigan w Mwnt and Y Ferwig w Llangoedmor *St D*
YERBESTON *see* Martletwy w Lawrenny and Minwear etc *St D*
YNYSBOETH *see* Penrhiwceiber, Matthewstown and Ynysboeth *Llan*
YNYSCYHAEARN (Mission Church) *see* Porthmadoc and Ynyscynhaearn and Dolbenmaen *Ban*
YNYSCYHAEARN (St Cynhaearn) *as above*
YNYSCYNON (St Cynon) *see* Ystrad Rhondda w Ynyscynon *Llan*
YNYSDDU (St Theodore) *see* Mynyddislwyn *Mon*
YNYSHIR (St Anne) (St Thomas) *Llan 12* **V** G P BIGMORE
YNYSMEUDW (St Mary) *see* Llangiwg *S & B*
YSBYTY CYNFYN (St John the Baptist) w Llantrisant and Eglwys Newydd *St D 10* **V** *vacant* (01970) 890663
YSBYTY IFAN (St John the Baptist) *see* Cerrigydrudion w Llanfihangel Glyn Myfyr etc *St As*
YSBYTY YSTWYTH (St John the Baptist) *see* Llanfihangel w Llanafan and Llanwnnws etc *St D*
YSFA (St Mark) *see* Rhayader and Nantmel *S & B*
YSGEIFIOG (St Mary) *see* Gorsedd w Brynford, Ysgeifiog and Whitford *St As*
YSTALYFERA (St David) *S & B 7* **V** G TURNER
YSTRAD-FFIN (St Paulinus) *see* Cil-y-Cwm and Ystrad-ffin w Rhandir-mwyn etc *St D*
YSTRAD MEURIG (St John the Baptist) *see* Tregaron w Ystrad Meurig and Strata Florida *St D*
YSTRAD MYNACH (Holy Trinity) w Llanbradach *Llan 1* **V** M D BROOKS
YSTRAD RHONDDA (St Stephen) w Ynyscynon *Llan 12* **V** P S GALE
YSTRAD ROAD (St Illtyd) *see* Swansea St Pet *S & B*
YSTRADFELLTE (St Mary) *see* Penderyn Mellte *S & B*
YSTRADGYNLAIS (St Cynog) *S & B 7* **R** D I DAVIES
YSTRADOWEN (St Owain) *see* Cowbridge *Llan*
YSTRADYFODWG (St John the Baptist) *Llan 12* **R** P N COLEMAN

SCOTTISH INCUMBENCIES

An index of incumbencies of the Scottish Episcopal Church. The incumbency entry gives the full legal name, followed by the diocese and the name(s) and appointment(s) of the clergy serving there (if there are none, the telephone number of the parsonage house is given where known). Church dedications are indicated in brackets. The following are the main abbreviations used; for others see the full list of abbreviations.

C	Curate
Dss	Deaconess
Hon C	Honorary Curate
NSM	Non-stipendiary Minister
P-in-c	Priest-in-charge
R	Rector

ABERCHIRDER (St Marnan) *Mor* **R** A J SIMPSON
ABERDEEN (Cathedral of St Andrew) *Ab* **R** R E KILGOUR, **NSM** R FINNIE
ABERDEEN (St Clement) *Ab* **P-in-c** D A FRENCH
ABERDEEN (St James) *Ab* **NSM** R B EDWARDS
ABERDEEN (St John the Evangelist) *Ab* **R** I M POOBALAN
ABERDEEN (St Margaret of Scotland) *Ab* **R** A E NIMMO, **Hon C** D H WRIGHT
ABERDEEN (St Mary) *Ab* **R** *vacant*
ABERDEEN (St Ninian) *Ab* **P-in-c** R E KILGOUR
ABERDEEN (St Peter) *Ab* **NSM** J DUTHIE
ABERDOUR (St Columba) - West Fife Team Ministry *St And* **R** V A NELLIST
ABERFOYLE (St Mary) *St And* **R** R W GROSSE
ABERLOUR (St Margaret of Scotland) *Mor* **R** *vacant*
ABOYNE (St Peter) *Ab* **R** J R BETTELEY
AIRDRIE (St Paul) *Glas* **R** G B FYFE
ALEXANDRIA (St Mungo) *Glas* **P-in-c** S H B GORTON
ALFORD (St Andrew) *Ab* **I** J WALKER, **P-in-c** A L JAMES, **NSM** J BURCHILL
ALLOA (St John the Evangelist) *St And* **C** S B F LOBLEY, **NSM** E FORGAN
ALYTH (St Ninian) *St And* **R** K W RATHBAND, **NSM** P S FERNANDO, D A CAMERON
ANNAN (St John the Evangelist) *Glas* **P-in-c** M P CALLAGHAN, **Hon C** J L HIGGINS
APPIN *see* W Highland Region *Arg*
ARBROATH (St Mary) *Bre* **R** J CUTHBERT
ARDBRECKNISH (St James) *Arg* **R** N D MACCALLUM
ARDCHATTAN (Holy Spirit) *Arg* **R** N D MACCALLUM
ARDROSSAN (St Andrew) *Glas* **P-in-c** S ROBERTSON, **NSM** A MONTGOMERIE
ARPAFEELIE (St John the Evangelist) *Mor* **R** R F BURKITT, **Hon C** M C ALDCROFT
ARRAN, ISLE OF *Arg* **R** *vacant*
AUCHENBLAE *see* Drumtochty *Bre*
AUCHINDOIR (St Mary) *Ab* **R** J WALKER, **NSM** J BURCHILL
AUCHMITHIE (St Peter) *Bre* **R** J CUTHBERT
AUCHTERARDER (St Kessog) *St And* **R** R G L MACALISTER
AYR (Holy Trinity) *Glas* **R** D G JONES, **NSM** J A MASON
BAILLIESTON (St John) *see* Glas E End *Glas*
BALERNO (St Mungo) *Edin* **R** M J H ROUND, **NSM** N F HALLAM
BALLACHULISH (St John) *Arg* **R** *vacant*
BALLATER (St Kentigern) *Ab* **R** J R BETTELEY
BANCHORY (St Ternan) *Ab* **R** *vacant* (01330) 822783
BANFF (St Andrew) *Ab* **P-in-c** J M PAISEY
BARROWFIELD (St John the Baptist) *Glas* **R** *vacant*
BATHGATE (St Columba) *Edin* **P-in-c** R INNES, **NSM** P F KIRK
BEARSDEN (All Saints) *Glas* **TR** K T ROACH, **TV** E M FARROW
BELLS WYND *see* Douglas *Glas*
BIELDSIDE (St Devenick) *Ab* **R** E MARQUIS-FAULKES, **NSM** P W BRUNT, **Dss** J E MACCORMACK
BIRNAM *see* Dunkeld *St And*
BISHOPBRIGGS (St James-the-Less) *Glas* **P-in-c** S R PAISLEY, **C** S L LILLIE, **Hon C** G E W SCOBIE
BLAIR ATHOLL *see* Kilmaveonaig *St And*
BLAIRGOWRIE (St Catherine) *St And* **R** K W RATHBAND, **NSM** P S FERNANDO, D A CAMERON
BO'NESS (St Catharine) *Edin* **P-in-c** D R BUNYAN, **Hon C** E J M P LENNARD
BRAEMAR (St Margaret) *Ab* **R** J R BETTELEY
BRECHIN (St Andrew) *Bre* **NSM** J G C BARR, U R SHONE, J NELSON
BRIDGE OF ALLAN (St Saviour) *St And* **R** K HOLDSWORTH
BRIDGE OF WEIR (St Mary) *Glas* **P-in-c** P J C MCGRANAGHAN
BRIDGEND *see* Islay *Arg*
BRORA (St Columba) *Mor* **P-in-c** M O LANGILLE
BROUGHTY FERRY (St Mary) *Bre* **R** R W BREADEN, **C** W S H DOCHERTY
BUCKIE (All Saints) *Ab* **P-in-c** J M PAISEY
BUCKSBURN (St Machar) *Ab* **P-in-c** D HEDDLE
BUCKSTONE (St Fillan) *see* Edin St Fillan *Edin*
BURNSIDE *see* Moffat *Glas*
BURNTISLAND (St Serf) - West Fife Team Ministry *St And* **R** V A NELLIST
BURRAVOE (St Colman) *Ab* **P-in-c** M N OXLEY, **NSM** E H MCNAB
CALLANDER (St Andrew) *St And* **R** R W GROSSE
CAMBUSLANG (St Cuthbert) *Glas* **P-in-c** D M IND, **NSM** M A DANSON
CAMPBELTOWN (St Kiaran) *Arg* **NSM** A J WILLIAMSON
CARNOUSTIE (Holy Rood) *Bre* **R** K G G GIBSON, **C** E M LAMONT, **Hon C** J B HARDIE
CASTLE DOUGLAS (St Ninian) *Glas* **P-in-c** D W BAYNE
CATTERLINE (St Philip) *Bre* **R** R K ACARNLEY
CHALLOCH (All Saints) *Glas* **P-in-c** N E H NEWTON
CHAPELHILL *see* Cruden Bay *Ab*
CLARKSTON (St Aidan) *Glas* **R** P G M FLETCHER, **NSM** C CURTIS
CLERMISTON *see* Edin Clermiston Em *Edin*
CLYDEBANK (St Columba) *Glas* **NSM** A G BOYD
COATBRIDGE (St John the Evangelist) *Glas* **R** G B FYFE
COLDSTREAM (St Mary and All Souls) *Edin* **P-in-c** M LOCKEY
COLINTON *see* Edin St Cuth *Edin*
COMRIE (St Serf) *St And* **R** C P SHERLOCK
COUPAR ANGUS (St Anne) *St And* **R** K W RATHBAND, **NSM** P S FERNANDO, D A CAMERON
COURTHILL Chapel *see* Kishorn *Mor*
COVE BAY (St Mary) *Ab* **R** *vacant* (01224) 895033
CRAIGHALL *see* Ellon *Ab*
CRIEFF (St Columba) *St And* **R** C P SHERLOCK
CROACHY *see* Strathnairn St Paul *Mor*
CROMARTY (St Regulus) *Mor* **R** R F BURKITT
CRUDEN BAY (St James the Less) *Ab* **R** G H STRANRAER-MULL, **NSM** J F F SHEPHERD, G P WHALLEY
CULLODEN (St Mary-in-the-Fields) *Mor* **P-in-c** A A SINCLAIR
CUMBERNAULD (Holy Name) *Glas* **P-in-c** A S DELAMERE
CUMBRAE (Cathedral of The Isles and Collegiate Church of the Holy Spirit) *Arg* **R** *vacant* (01475) 530353
CUMINESTOWN (St Luke) *Ab* **P-in-c** G G MACINTOSH
CUPAR (St James the Great) *St And* **R** *vacant* (01334) 653548
DALBEATTIE (Christ Church) *Glas* **R** *vacant* (01556) 610671
DALKEITH (St Mary) *Edin* **R** M A S GOODMAN, **NSM** M E JONES, E S JONES, J O GODFREY
DALMAHOY (St Mary) *Edin* **P-in-c** D L COLLINGWOOD, **NSM** J DYER, B M JOHNSON
DALRY (St Peter) *Glas* **P-in-c** S ROBERTSON
DENNISTOUN (St Kentigern) *see* Glas E End *Glas*
DINGWALL (St James the Great) *Mor* **P-in-c** I N PALLETT, **NSM** R FLOCKHART, V C SAUNDERS
DOLLAR (St James the Great) *St And* **C** R E CARMAN, **NSM** F A M LAWRY, H I SOGA
DORNOCH (St Finnbarr) *Mor* **P-in-c** M O LANGILLE
DOUGLAS (Sancta Sophia) *Glas* **R** *vacant* (01555) 663065
DOUNE (St Modoc) *St And* **NSM** S M COATES
DRUMLITHIE (St John the Baptist) *Bre* **R** M J R TURNER
DRUMTOCHTY (St Palladius) *Bre* **R** M J R TURNER
DUFFTOWN (St Michael and All Angels) *Ab* **NSM** R E TAIT
DUMBARTON (St Augustine) *Glas* **P-in-c** K L MACAULAY
DUMFRIES (St John the Evangelist) *Glas* **C** I MEREDITH
DUNBAR (St Anne) *Edin* **P-in-c** P LEWER ALLEN, **NSM** J WOOD, R B COPLETON
DUNBLANE (St Mary) *St And* **R** J I CAMERON
DUNDEE (Cathedral of St Paul) *Bre* **R** M A F BYRNE
DUNDEE (St John the Baptist) *Bre* **P-in-c** J J MORROW, **NSM** J M PRIOR
DUNDEE (St Luke) *Bre* **R** K J CAVANAGH
DUNDEE (St Margaret) *Bre* **R** J H MILNE, **C** A WALLER
DUNDEE (St Martin) *Bre* **P-in-c** D ELDER
DUNDEE (St Mary Magdalene) *Bre* **R** D SHEPHERD
DUNDEE (St Ninian) *Bre* **P-in-c** J J MORROW, **NSM** J M PRIOR
DUNDEE (St Salvador) *Bre* **P-in-c** C H CLAPSON, **Hon C** G M GREIG

DUNFERMLINE (Holy Trinity) - West Fife Team Ministry *St And* **R** D CAMPBELL
DUNKELD (St Mary) w Birnam *St And* **R** D F BROOKE
DUNOON (Holy Trinity) *Arg* **R** H G C LEE
DUNS (Christ Church) *Edin* **P-in-c** K G WEBB
DUROR (St Adamnan) *see* W Highland Region *Arg*
EAST END *see* Glas E End *Glas*
EAST KILBRIDE (St Mark) *Glas* **P-in-c** K H MARSHALL
EASTGATE (St Peter) *see* Peebles *Edin*
EASTRIGGS (St John the Evangelist) *Glas* **P-in-c** M P CALLAGHAN
EDINBURGH (Cathedral of St Mary) *Edin* **R** G J T FORBES, **TV** D J B FOSTEKEW, **C** P V P BLACKLEDGE, **NSM** G P FOSTER
EDINBURGH (Christ Church) *Edin* **R** S C JUSTICE, **TV** R H PROCTER, **C** M F CHATTERLEY, **NSM** J WILLIAMS
EDINBURGH (Emmanuel) *Edin* **R** *vacant*
EDINBURGH (Good Shepherd) *Edin* **R** T D MORRIS, **C** G J M SAUNDERS, N MOLL
EDINBURGH (Holy Cross) *Edin* **R** W D KORNAHRENS, **NSM** M F HARRISON
EDINBURGH (Old St Paul) *Edin* **R** I J PATON, **Hon C** C S DAVIES-COLE
EDINBURGH (St Andrew and St Aidan) *Edin* **R** *vacant*
EDINBURGH (St Barnabas) *Edin* **P-in-c** P D DIXON, **NSM** A C ANDERSON
EDINBURGH (St Columba) *Edin* **R** A J FULLER, **TV** R O GOULD, J S RICHARDSON, J D R WHITLEY, **C** A WAGSTAFF
EDINBURGH (St Cuthbert) *Edin* **R** S C PARSONS, **NSM** D YEOMAN
EDINBURGH (St David of Scotland) *Edin* **P-in-c** D J DURIE
EDINBURGH (St Fillan) *Edin* **R** M D ROBSON, **Hon C** M C REED
EDINBURGH (St Hilda) *Edin* **R** *vacant*
EDINBURGH (St James the Less) *Edin* **R** S I BUTLER, **NSM** M S NORTHCOTT, J P MITCHELL
EDINBURGH (St John the Evangelist) *Edin* **R** J A ARMES, **C** D REID, **NSM** P J BRAND, C A HUME
EDINBURGH (St Luke) *see* Wester Hailes St Luke *Edin*
EDINBURGH (St Margaret of Scotland) *Edin* **TV** G R HART
EDINBURGH (St Mark) *Edin* **R** *vacant*
EDINBURGH (St Martin of Tours) *Edin* **R** J A CONWAY, **NSM** S KILBEY
EDINBURGH (St Michael and All Saints) *Edin* **R** K PEARSON
EDINBURGH (St Ninian) *Edin* **P-in-c** P J D ALLEN, **C** A B SHEWAN
EDINBURGH (St Paul and St George) *Edin* **R** D G RICHARDS, **C** D A S MACLAREN, J L MACLAREN, **NSM** M J PARKER
EDINBURGH (St Peter) *Edin* **R** F W TOMLINSON, **C** J R AULD, K R MACAULAY, B A MACAULAY
EDINBURGH (St Philip and St James) *Edin* **R** K F SCOTT
EDINBURGH (St Salvador) *Edin* **P-in-c** H L WILLIAMSON, **C** C NAISMITH, G J M SAUNDERS, N MOLL
EDINBURGH (St Thomas) Private Chapel *Edin* **R** I R HOPKINS, **C** A R MACDONALD
EDINBURGH (St Vincent) Private Chapel *Edin* **P-in-c** R A GRANT
ELGIN (Holy Trinity) w Lossiemouth (St Margaret) *Mor* **R** M J STRANGE, **NSM** M A EATON, J SCLATER
ELIE AND EARLSFERRY (St Michael and All Angels) *St And* **R** *vacant* (01333) 330254
ELLON (St Mary on the Rock) *Ab* **R** G H STRANRAER-MULL, **NSM** J F F SHEPHERD, G P WHALLEY, R SPENCER, C A FOX
EORROPAIDH (St Moluag) *Arg* **P-in-c** B A MORRISON, **NSM** C P A LOCKHART
ERSKINE *see* Renfrew *Glas*
EYEMOUTH (St Ebba) *Edin* **NSM** S S COX, J M EDIE, F D J SMOUT
FALKIRK (Christ Church) *Edin* **R** J B PENMAN, **NSM** A V SMITH
FASQUE (St Andrew) *Bre* **R** M J R TURNER
FETTERCAIRN *see* Fasque *Bre*
FOCHABERS Gordon Chapel *Mor* **R** *vacant* (01343) 820337
FORFAR (St John the Evangelist) *St And* **R** J M RICHARDSON, **C** E N RAMSAY
FORRES (St John the Evangelist) *Mor* **P-in-c** C J PIPER
FORT WILLIAM (St Andrew) *Arg* **R** G A GUINNESS
FORTROSE (St Andrew) *Mor* **R** R F BURKITT
FRASERBURGH (St Peter) *Ab* **R** P J LEES
FYVIE (All Saints) *Ab* **R** *vacant*
GALASHIELS (St Peter) *Edin* **R** D I MCCOSH
GALLOWGATE *see* Aberdeen St Marg *Ab*
GARTCOSH (St Andrew) *Glas* **R** *vacant*
GATEHOUSE OF FLEET (St Mary) *Glas* **R** P J TAYLOR, **NSM** A DAWSON
GIRVAN (St John) *Glas* **R** D G JONES, **NSM** B H G COLLIE, J A MASON
GLASGOW (All Saints) *Glas* **R** A L CHESWORTH
GLASGOW (Cathedral of St Mary the Virgin) *Glas* **R** P J DINES, **Hon C** K J SHAW, **NSM** C A MCKILLOP
GLASGOW East End (St John) (St Kentigern) (St Serf) *Glas* **TV** C G WYLIE, A C SALMON
GLASGOW (Good Shepherd and Ascension) *Glas* **P-in-c** J F LYON
GLASGOW (Holy Cross) *Glas* **P-in-c** A L CHESWORTH, **NSM** D D KEEBLE
GLASGOW (St Bride) *Glas* **R** R F JONES, **NSM** I T DRAPER
GLASGOW (St Gabriel) *Glas* **R** *vacant*
GLASGOW (St George) *Glas* **Hon C** S M P MAITLAND
GLASGOW (St Margaret) *Glas* **R** T C O MONTGOMERY, **C** S-A MCDOUGALL
GLASGOW (St Matthew) *Glas* **R** *vacant*
GLASGOW (St Ninian) *Glas* **R** G D DUNCAN, **C** P R WATSON, K BOHAN
GLASGOW (St Oswald) *Glas* **P-in-c** R N O'SULLIVAN
GLASGOW (St Silas) Private Chapel *Glas* **R** D W MCCARTHY
GLENCARSE (All Saints) *Bre* **R** *vacant* (01738) 860386
GLENCOE (St Mary) *Arg* **R** *vacant* (01855) 811335
GLENROTHES (St Luke the Evangelist) - Central Fife Team Ministry *St And* **R** J W ALLAN, **TV** J D MARTIN, D N CALVIN-THOMAS
GLENURQUHART (St Ninian) *Mor* **P-in-c** H B HUTCHENS
GOUROCK (St Bartholomew) *Glas* **R** G F HOLLEY
GOVAN *see* Glas St Gabr *Glas*
GRANGEMOUTH (St Mary) *Edin* **R** D R BUNYAN, **Hon C** E J M P LENNARD
GRANTOWN-ON-SPEY (St Columba) *Mor* **P-in-c** P A THOMPSON
GREENOCK (St John the Evangelist) *Glas* **R** A R SHERIDAN, **C** D M ORR
GRETNA (All Saints) *Glas* **P-in-c** M P CALLAGHAN
GREYFRIARS *see* Kirkcudbright *Glas*
GRULINE (St Columba) *see* W Highland Region *Arg*
GULLANE (St Adrian) *Edin* **R** J C LINDSAY, **C** L A MORTIS
HADDINGTON (Holy Trinity) *Edin* **R** A J BAIN, **NSM** J WOOD, R B COPLETON
HAMILTON (St Mary the Virgin) *Glas* **R** I D BARCROFT
HARRIS, ISLE OF *see* Leverburgh *Arg*
HARRIS, ISLE OF (Christ Church) *Arg* **P-in-c** J D L DAVIES
HAWICK (St Cuthbert) *Edin* **R** I E WALTER
HAY DRIVE *see* Edin St Andr and St Aid *Edin*
HELENSBURGH (St Michael and All Angels) *Glas* **P-in-c** D A COOK
HUNTLY (Christ Church) *Mor* **R** A J SIMPSON
HYNDLAND (St Bride) *see* Glas St Bride *Glas*
INNERLEITHEN (St Andrew) *Edin* **P-in-c** R D LEE, **NSM** C B AITCHISON, C CHAPLIN
INSCH (St Drostan) *Ab* **R** *vacant*
INVERARAY (All Saints) *Arg* **P-in-c** R F F FLATT
INVERBERVIE (St David) *Bre* **P-in-c** I G STEWART
INVERGORDON (St Ninian) *Mor* **P-in-c** A H MCMICHAEL
INVERGOWRIE (All Souls) *Bre* **P-in-c** A W CUMMINS, **C** P M BALFOUR
INVERKEITHING (St Peter) - West Fife Team Ministry *St And* **R** V A NELLIST
INVERNESS (Cathedral of St Andrew) *Mor* **R** *vacant*
INVERNESS (St John the Evangelist) *Mor* **P-in-c** A A SINCLAIR
INVERNESS (St Michael and All Angels) *Mor* **R** L A BLACK
INVERURIE (St Mary) *Ab* **R** J WALKER, **NSM** J BURCHILL
IONA (St Columba) *Arg* **R** *vacant*
IRVINE (St Andrew) Local Ecumenical Project *Glas* **P-in-c** S ROBERTSON, **NSM** A MONTGOMERIE
ISLAY (St Columba) *Arg* **R** *vacant*
ISLE OF HARRIS *see* Harris Ch Ch *Arg*
JEDBURGH (St John the Evangelist) *Edin* **R** D B H HERBERT, **Hon C** W J GROVER
JOHNSTONE (St John) *Glas* **P-in-c** S A MARSH
JORDANHILL (All Saints) *see* Glas All SS *Glas*
KEITH (Holy Trinity) *Mor* **R** A J SIMPSON
KELSO (St Andrew) *Edin* **Hon C** I D L CLARK, D C MYLNE, R JONES
KEMNAY (St Anne) *Ab* **P-in-c** J WALKER, **NSM** J BURCHILL
KENTALLEN (St Moluag) *see* W Highland Region *Arg*
KESSOCK-TORE *see* Arpafeelie *Mor*
KILLIN (St Fillan) *St And* **P-in-c** J F W SYMON
KILMACOLM (St Fillan) *Glas* **P-in-c** P J C MCGRANAGHAN
KILMARNOCK (Holy Trinity) *Glas* **R** K G STEPHEN
KILMARTIN (St Columba) *Arg* **R** R F F FLATT
KILMAVEONAIG (St Adamnan) *St And* **R** *vacant*
KINCARDINE O'NEIL (Christ Church) *Ab* **R** *vacant*

KINGHORN (St Mary and St Leonard) *St And* **NSM** G N BENSON
KINLOCH RANNOCH (All Saints) *St And* **R** *vacant*
KINLOCHLEVEN (St Paul) *see* W Highland Region *Arg*
KINLOCHMOIDART (St Finian) *Arg* **R** *vacant*
KINROSS (St Paul) *St And* **P-in-c** M KESTON
KIRKCALDY (St Peter) *St And* **NSM** G N BENSON
KIRKCUDBRIGHT (St Francis of Assisi) *Glas* **R** P J TAYLOR, **NSM** A DAWSON
KIRKWALL (St Olaf) *Ab* **NSM** D DAWSON
KIRRIEMUIR (St Mary) *St And* **P-in-c** R P HARLEY, **C** E N RAMSAY
KISHORN Chapel *Mor* **NSM** H S WIDDOWS
KNIGHTSWOOD (Holy Cross) *see* Glas H Cross *Glas*
LADYBANK (St Mary) *St And* **R** *vacant*
LADYCROFT *see* Balerno *Edin*
LANARK (Christ Church) *Glas* **R** *vacant*
LANGHOLM (All Saints) *Glas* **R** *vacant* (01461) 38268
LARGS (St Columba) *Glas* **R** P M POTTER
LASSWADE (St Leonard) *Edin* **R** M A S GOODMAN, **NSM** M E JONES, E S JONES, J O GODFREY
LAURENCEKIRK (St Laurence) *Bre* **R** M J R TURNER
LEITH (St James the Less) *see* Edin St Jas *Edin*
LENZIE (St Cyprian) *Glas* **R** J E MARSBURG, **Hon C** B A OGUGUO
LERWICK (St Magnus) *Ab* **R** M N OXLEY, **NSM** E H MCNAB
LEVEN (St Margaret) - Central Fife Team Ministry *St And* **TV** J D MARTIN
LEVERBURGH *Arg* **R** *vacant*
LEWIS, ISLE OF *see* Stornoway *Arg*
LINLITHGOW (St Peter) *Edin* **P-in-c** R INNES
LIVINGSTON Local Ecumenical Project *Edin* **Min** E C THOMPSON
LOCHALSH (St Donnan) *Mor* **R** *vacant*
LOCHBUIE (St Kilda) *Arg* **R** *vacant*
LOCHEARNHEAD (St Angus) *St And* **R** C P SHERLOCK
LOCHEE (St Magaret) *see* Dundee St Marg *Bre*
LOCHGELLY (St Finnian) - Central Fife Team Ministry *St And* **TV** J D MARTIN
LOCHGILPHEAD (Christ Church) *Arg* **R** R F F FLATT
LOCHINVER (St Gilbert) *Mor* **P-in-c** A H MCMICHAEL
LOCKERBIE (All Saints) *Glas* **P-in-c** M P CALLAGHAN, **C** L M BANDS
LONGSIDE (St John) *Ab* **R** *vacant*
LOSSIEMOUTH (St Margaret) *see* Elgin w Lossiemouth *Mor*
LUNAN HEAD (St Margaret) *St And* **R** *vacant*
MARYGATE *see* Pittenweem *St And*
MAYBOLE (St Oswald) *Glas* **R** D G JONES, **NSM** B H G COLLIE, J A MASON
MELROSE (Holy Trinity) *Edin* **R** M I HOUSTON, **NSM** D W WOOD
MILLPORT *see* Cumbrae (or Millport) *Arg*
MILNGAVIE (St Andrew) *Glas* **TV** E M FARROW
MOFFAT (St John the Evangelist) *Glas* **P-in-c** M P CALLAGHAN, **C** L M BANDS
MONIFIETH (Holy Trinity) *Bre* **C** E M LAMONT
MONKLANDS *see* Airdrie *Glas*
MONKSTOWN *see* Ladybank *St And*
MONTROSE (St Mary and St Peter) *Bre* **R** I G STEWART
MOTHERWELL (Holy Trinity) *Glas* **P-in-c** A WYLIE
MUCHALLS (St Ternan) *Bre* **P-in-c** R K ACARNLEY, **C** R PATERSON, **Hon C** J A ALLARD
MULL, ISLE OF *see* Lochbuie *Arg*
MULL, ISLE OF *see* W Highland Region *Arg*
MURRAYFIELD (Good Shepherd) *see* Edin Gd Shep *Edin*
MUSSELBURGH (St Peter) *Edin* **R** R COOKE
MUTHILL (St James) *St And* **R** R G L MACALISTER
NAIRN (St Columba) *Mor* **P-in-c** D MCALISTER
NETHER LOCHABER (St Bride) *Arg* **R** *vacant*
NEW GALLOWAY (St Margaret of Scotland) *Glas* **P-in-c** J R REPATH
NEW PITSLIGO (St John the Evangelist) *Ab* **R** *vacant*
NEWBURGH (St Katherine) *St And* **R** *vacant*
NEWLANDS (St Margaret) *see* Glas St Marg *Glas*
NEWPORT-ON-TAY (St Mary) *St And* **P-in-c** A BUNNELL
NEWTON STEWART *see* Challoch *Glas*
NORTH BALLACHULISH *see* Onich *Arg*
NORTH BERWICK (St Baldred) *Edin* **R** J C LINDSAY, **C** L A MORTIS
NORTH MEARNS *see* Stonehaven *Bre*
OBAN (Cathedral of St John) *Arg* **R** N D MACCALLUM
OLD DEER (St Drostan) *Ab* **R** *vacant*
OLDMELDRUM (St Matthew) *Ab* **R** A B MACGILLIVRAY, **Hon C** D W MCHARDY
ONICH (St Bride) *Arg* **R** *vacant*
OXGANGS (St Hilda) *see* Edin St Hilda *Edin*
PAISLEY (Holy Trinity) *Glas* **R** D W MCFARLAND
PAISLEY (St Barnabas) *Glas* **R** D W MCFARLAND
PEEBLES (St Peter) *Edin* **R** R D LEE, **NSM** C B AITCHISON, C CHAPLIN
PENICUIK (St James the Less) *Edin* **R** J H BRUCE, **Hon C** G P C CROSFIELD, **NSM** N F SUTTLE, T A BRAMLEY
PERTH (Cathedral of St Ninian) *St And* **C** K HOLDSWORTH, **NSM** R F SAUNDERS, A C MAZUR
PERTH (St John the Baptist) *St And* **R** R C FYFFE, **Hon C** R H DARROCH, W F HARRIS, W L GLAZEBROOK, **NSM** F A FORSHAW
PETERHEAD (St Peter) *Ab* **P-in-c** G H STRANRAER-MULL
PINMORE *Glas* **NSM** B H G COLLIE
PITLOCHRY (Holy Trinity) *St And* **R** *vacant* (01796) 472539
PITTENWEEM (St John the Evangelist) *St And* **R** *vacant*
POLLOCKSHIELDS (St Ninian) *see* Glas St Ninian *Glas*
POLTALLOCH *see* Kilmartin *Arg*
POOLEWE (St Maelrubha) *Mor* **R** *vacant*
PORT GLASGOW (St Mary the Virgin) *Glas* **R** S D N BARRETT
PORTNACROIS (Holy Cross) *see* W Highland Region *Arg*
PORTPATRICK (St Ninian) *Glas* **P-in-c** E A TUGWELL
PORTREE (St Columba) *Arg* **R** *vacant*
PORTSOY (St John the Baptist) *Ab* **P-in-c** J M PAISEY
PRESTONPANS (St Andrew) *Edin* **R** R COOKE
PRESTWICK (St Ninian) *Glas* **R** P D NOBLE
RENFREW (St Margaret) w Erskine *Glas* **P-in-c** S A MARSH
ROSLIN (Collegiate Church of St Matthew) *Edin* **NSM** M J FASS
ROTHESAY (St Paul) *Arg* **R** *vacant*
ROTHIEMURCHUS (St John the Baptist) *Mor* **C** H K M COOK
ST ANDREWS (All Saints) *St And* **R** J P MASON, **C** M-L MOFFETT, **Hon C** G D WHITE
ST ANDREWS (St Andrew) - Central Fife Team Ministry *St And* **R** R A GILLIES, **C** P B ROBERTSON, J A RANDALL, **NSM** D A BEADLE, R T EVANS, T A HART, W R BLACKBURN
ST FILLANS (Church of the Holy Spirit) *St And* **R** *vacant*
SANDYLOAN *see* Gullane *Edin*
SELKIRK (St John the Evangelist) *Edin* **R** W B ELLIOT, **Hon C** I G D DUNLOP
SHETTLESTON (St Serf) *see* Glas E End *Glas*
SKYE, ISLE OF *see* Portree *Arg*
SOUTH QUEENSFERRY (Priory Church St Mary of Mount Carmel) *Edin* **P-in-c** T J HARKIN, **NSM** I MACROBERT
STANLEY (St Columba) *St And* **NSM** R F SAUNDERS
STIRLING (Holy Trinity) *St And* **R** A M PEDEN
STONEHAVEN (St James) *Bre* **R** R K ACARNLEY, **C** M S PATERSON, **Hon C** J A ALLARD
STORNOWAY (St Peter) *Arg* **R** S J G BENNIE
STRANRAER (St John the Evangelist) *Glas* **P-in-c** E A TUGWELL
STRATHNAIRN (St Paul) *Mor* **P-in-c** E P MOSLEY
STRATHPEFFER (St Anne) *Mor* **P-in-c** I N PALLETT, **NSM** R FLOCKHART, V C SAUNDERS
STRATHTAY (St Andrew) *St And* **R** D F BROOKE
STRICHEN (All Saints) *Ab* **NSM** G G KELMAN
STROMNESS (St Mary) *Ab* **NSM** I ST C COSBY
STRONTIAN *Arg* **R** *vacant*
TAIN (St Andrew) *Mor* **P-in-c** A H MCMICHAEL
TARFSIDE (St Drostan) *Bre* **R** *vacant*
TAYPORT (St Margaret of Scotland) *St And* **P-in-c** R G SOMMERVILLE
TEINDHILLGREEN *see* Duns *Edin*
THURSO (St Peter and Holy Rood) *Mor* **P-in-c** J STEVENSON, **Hon C** F E DAVIES, G R TYLER
TIGHNABRUAICH *Arg* **R** *vacant*
TOFTS *see* Dalry *Glas*
TORRY *see* Aberdeen St Pet *Ab*
TROON (St Ninian) *Glas* **R** D S MUNGAVIN
TURRIFF (St Congan) *Ab* **P-in-c** G G MACINTOSH, **NSM** S M DYER, R M HAINES
UDDINGSTON (St Andrew) *Glas* **P-in-c** D M IND, **NSM** M A DANSON
ULLAPOOL (St Mary the Virgin) *Mor* **R** *vacant*
WEST FIFE Team Ministry - *see* Aberdour; Burntisland; Dunfermline; Inverkeithing and Lochgelly *St And*
WEST HIGHLAND Region *Arg* **P-in-c** P L RICE, **C** D DAVIDSON
WEST LINTON (St Mungo) *Edin* **R** J H BRUCE, **Hon C** G P C CROSFIELD, **NSM** T A BRAMLEY
WESTER HAILES (St Luke) *Edin* **C** K R WHITEFIELD
WESTGATE *see* Dunbar *Edin*
WESTHILL (Trinity) *Ab* **R** I J FERGUSON
WHITERASHES (All Saints) *Ab* **R** A B MACGILLIVRAY
WHITING BAY *see* Is of Arran *Arg*
WICK (St John the Evangelist) *Mor* **P-in-c** J STEVENSON, **Hon C** F E DAVIES, G R TYLER
WISHAW (St Andrew) *Glas* **P-in-c** A WYLIE
WOODHEAD OF FETTERLETTER *see* Fyvie *Ab*
YELL *see* Burravoe *Ab*

IRISH BENEFICES AND CHURCHES

An index of benefices of the Church of Ireland (shown in bold type), together with entries for churches and other licensed places of worship. Where the church name is the same as that of the benefice (or the first place name in the benefice), the church entry is omitted. Church dedications are indicated in brackets.

The benefice entry gives the full legal name, together with the diocese and the name(s) and appointment(s) of clergy serving there (if there are none, the telephone number of the parsonage house is given). The following are the main abbreviations used; for others see the full list of abbreviations.

Bp's C	Bishop's Curate
C	Curate
C-in-c	Curate-in-charge
Hon C	Honorary Curate
I	Incumbent (includes Rector or Vicar)
NSM	Non-stipendiary Minister
P-in-c	Priest-in-charge

AASLEAGH (St John the Baptist) *see* Tuam w Cong and Aasleagh *T, K & A*
ABBEYLEIX (St Michael and All Angels) w Ballyroan, Ballinakill, Killermogh, Aughmacart, Durrow and Attanagh *C & O* **I** P A HARVEY, **NSM** A WALLACE
ABBEYSTREWRY (no dedication) w Creagh, Tullagh, Castlehaven and Caheragh *C, C & R* **I** B J HAYES
ABINGDON (no dedication) *see* Killaloe w Stradbally *L & K*
ACHILL (Holy Trinity) *see* Aughaval w Achill, Knappagh, Dugort etc *T, K & A*
ACHONRY (Cathedral of St Crumnathy) w Tubbercurry and Killoran *T, K & A* **I** K R SOUTHERTON
ACTON (no dedication) and Drumbanagher *Arm* **Bp's C** J M BARTON
ADARE (St Nicholas) *see* Adare and Kilmallock w Kilpeacon, Croom etc *L & K*
ADARE (St Nicholas) and Kilmallock w Kilpeacon, Croom, Kilflynn, Kilfinane, Knockaney, Bruff and Caherconlish *L & K* **I** R V C LEWIS
AGHABOG (no dedication) *see* Ematris w Rockcorry, Aghabog and Aughnamullan *Clogh*
AGHADE (All Saints) *see* Fenagh w Myshall, Aghade and Ardoyne *C & O*
AGHADERG (St Mellan) w Donaghmore and Scarva *D & D* **I** *vacant*
AGHADOE *see* Killarney w Aghadoe and Muckross *L & K*
AGHADOWEY (St Guaire) w Kilrea *D & R* **I** *vacant* (028) 2954 0257
AGHADOWN (Church Cross) *see* Ballydehob w Aghadown *C, C & R*
AGHADOWN (St Matthew) *as above*
AGHADRUMSEE (no dedication) w Clogh and Drumsnatt *Clogh* **I** V E KILLE
AGHALEE (Holy Trinity) *D & D* **I** S E DOOGAN, **NSM** J R CORBETT
AGHALURCHER (no dedication) w Tattykeeran, Cooneen and Mullaghfad *Clogh* **I** R T GILLIAN
AGHANAGH (no dedication) *see* Boyle and Elphin w Aghanagh, Kilbryan etc *K, E & A*
AGHANCON (no dedication) *see* Shinrone w Aghancon etc *L & K*
AGHANLOO (St Lugha) *see* Tamlaghtard w Aghanloo *D & R*
AGHAVEA (no dedication) *Clogh* **I** D W ROBINSON
AGHAVILLY (St Mary) *see* Tynan w Middletown and Aghavilly *Arm*
AGHAVOE (no dedication) *see* Rathdowney w Castlefleming, Donaghmore etc *C & O*
AGHER (no dedication) *see* Rathmolyon w Castlerickard, Rathcore and Agher *M & K*
AGHERTON (St John the Baptist) *Conn* **I** P W ROOKE, **C** N J SLOANE
AGHOLD (no dedication) *see* Tullow w Shillelagh, Aghold and Mullinacuff *C & O*
AGHOUR (St Lachtan) *see* Kilkenny w Aghour and Kilmanagh *C & O*
AHASCRAGH *see* Aughrim w Ballinasloe etc *L & K*
AHERLA *see* Moviddy Union *C, C & R*
AHOGHILL (St Colmanell) w Portglenone *Conn* **I** *vacant*
ALDERGROVE *see* Killead w Gartree *Conn*
ALMORITIA (St Nicholas) *see* Mullingar, Portnashangan, Moyliscar, Kilbixy etc *M & K*
ALTEDESERT (no dedication) *see* Kildress w Altedesert *Arm*
ANNACLONE (Christ Church) *see* Magherally w Annaclone *D & D*
ANNADUFF (St Ann) *see* Kiltoghart w Drumshambo, Annaduff and Kilronan *K, E & A*
ANNAGH (St Andrew) w Drumaloor, Cloverhill, Drumgoon, Dernakesh, Ashfield and Killesherdoney *K, E & A* **I** E R G WEST, **NSM** R W STAFFORD
ANNAGHMORE (St Francis) *Arm* **I** D S MCVEIGH
ANNAHILT (Ascension) w Magherahamlet *D & D* **I** J R HOWARD
ANNALONG (no dedication) *D & D* **I** W J PRESS
ANNESTOWN *see* Waterford w Killea, Drumcannon and Dunhill *C & O*
ANTRIM (All Saints) *Conn* **I** S R MCBRIDE, **C** E R MURRAY, **NSM** D E FERGUSON
ANTRIM (St Patrick) *see* Connor w Antrim St Patr *Conn*
ARBOE (no dedication) *see* Ballinderry, Tamlaght and Arboe *Arm*
ARDAGH (St Patrick) w Tashinny, Shrule and Kilcommick *K, E & A* **Bp's C** A W KINGSTON
ARDAMINE (St John the Evangelist) w Kiltennel, Glascarrig, Kilnamanagh, Kilmuckridge and Monamolin *C & O* **I** R J GRAY
ARDARA (St Connall) w Glencolumbkille, Inniskeel, Glenties and Lettermacaward *D & R* **I** G B FREEMAN, **NSM** M C CLASSON
ARDCARNE (no dedication) *see* Boyle and Elphin w Aghanagh, Kilbryan etc *K, E & A*
ARDCLINIS (St Mary) and Tickmacrevan w Layde and Cushendun *Conn* **P-in-c** M A HUTCHINSON
ARDCOLM (no dedication) *see* Wexford w Ardcolm and Killurin *C & O*
ARDEE (St Mary) *see* Drogheda w Ardee, Collon and Termonfeckin *Arm*
ARDGLASS (St Nicholas) *see* Lecale Gp *D & D*
ARDKEEN (Christ Church) *see* Ballyhalbert w Ardkeen *D & D*
ARDMORE (no dedication) w Craigavon *D & D* **I** *vacant* (028) 3834 0357
ARDMORE (St Paul) *see* Youghal Union *C, C & R*
ARDNAGEEHY (no dedication) *see* Fermoy Union *C, C & R*
ARDOYNE (Holy Trinity) *see* Fenagh w Myshall, Aghade and Ardoyne *C & O*
ARDOYNE (Immanuel) *see* Belfast H Trin and St Silas *Conn*
ARDQUIN (no dedication) *see* Ballyphilip w Ardquin *D & D*
ARDRAHAN *see* Aughrim w Ballinasloe etc *L & K*
ARDSTRAW (St Eugene) w Baronscourt, Badoney Lower and Badoney Upper and Greenan *D & R* **I** H HALL
ARDTREA (St Andrew) w Desertcreat *Arm* **I** D J BELL
ARKLOW (St Saviour) w Inch and Kilbride *D & G* **I** N J W SHERWOOD
ARMAGH (Cathedral of St Patrick) *Arm* **I** H CASSIDY
ARMAGH (St Mark) *Arm* **I** J W MCKEGNEY, **C** P M BARTON
ARMAGHBREAGUE (no dedication) *see* Keady w Armaghbreague and Derrynoose *Arm*
ARMOY (St Patrick) w Loughguile and Drumtullagh *Conn* **I** F M BACH
ARVAGH (no dedication) w Carrigallen, Gowna and Columbkille *K, E & A* **I** *vacant*
ASHFIELD (no dedication) *see* Annagh w Drumgoon, Ashfield etc *K, E & A*
ASKEATON (St Mary) *see* Rathkeale w Askeaton, Kilcornan and Kilnaughtin *L & K*
ATHBOY (St James) *see* Trim and Athboy Gp *M & K*
ATHLONE (St Mary) w Benown, Kiltoom and Forgney *M & K* **I** G T DOYLE
ATHY (St Michael) w Kilberry, Fontstown and Kilkea *D & G* **I** C P JEFFERS
ATTANAGH *see* Abbeyleix w Ballyroan etc *C & O*
AUGHANUNSHIN *see* Conwal Union w Gartan *D & R*
AUGHAVAL (no dedication) w Achill, Knappagh, Dugort, Castlebar and Turlough *T, K & A* **I** G L HASTINGS
AUGHAVAS (no dedication) *see* Mohill w Farnaught, Aughavas, Oughteragh etc *K, E & A*
AUGHER (no dedication) w Newtownsaville and Eskrahoole *Clogh* **I** *vacant*
AUGHMACART (St Tighernagh) *see* Abbeyleix w Ballyroan etc *C & O*
AUGHNACLIFFE *see* Arvagh w Carrigallen, Gowna and Columbkille *K, E & A*

AUGHNACLOY *see* Carnteel and Crilly *Arm*
AUGHNAMULLAN (Christ Church) *see* Ematris w Rockcorry, Aghabog and Aughnamullan *Clogh*
AUGHRIM (Holy Trinity) w Ballinasloe, Clontuskert, Ahascragh, Woodlawn, Kilmacduagh and Ardrahan *L & K* I T A SULLIVAN
AUGHRIM (St John the Evangelist) *see* Castlemacadam w Ballinaclash, Aughrim etc *D & G*
BADONEY LOWER (St Patrick) *see* Ardstraw w Baronscourt, Badoney Lower etc *D & R*
BADONEY UPPER (St Aichen) *as above*
BAGENALSTOWN *see* Dunleckney w Nurney, Lorum and Kiltennel *C & O*
BAILIEBOROUGH (no dedication) w Knockbride, Shercock and Mullagh *K, E & A* NSM A J LINDSAY
BALBRIGGAN (St George) *see* Holmpatrick w Balbriggan and Kenure *D & G*
BALGRIFFIN (St Doulagh) *see* Malahide w Balgriffin *D & G*
BALLAGHTOBIN (no dedication) *see* Kells Gp *C & O*
BALLEE (no dedication) *see* Bright w Ballee and Killough *D & D*
BALLIGAN *see* Ballywalter w Inishargie *D & D*
BALLINA *see* Killala w Dunfeeny, Crossmolina, Kilmoremoy etc *T, K & A*
BALLINACLASH (no dedication) *see* Castlemacadam w Ballinaclash, Aughrim etc *D & G*
BALLINADEE (no dedication) *see* Bandon Union *C, C & R*
BALLINAFAD *see* Boyle and Elphin w Aghanagh, Kilbryan etc *K, E & A*
BALLINALEA *see* Mostrim w Granard, Clonbroney, Killoe etc *K, E & A*
BALLINALECK *see* Cleenish w Mullaghdun *Clogh*
BALLINAMALLARD *see* Magheracross *Clogh*
BALLINAMORE *see* Mohill w Farnaught, Aughavas, Oughteragh etc *K, E & A*
BALLINASLOE (St John the Evangelist) *see* Aughrim w Ballinasloe etc *L & K*
BALLINATONE *see* Castlemacadam w Ballinaclash, Aughrim etc *D & G*
BALLINDERRY (no dedication) *Conn* I E J HARRIS
BALLINDERRY (St John), Tamlaght and Arboe *Arm* I H J W MOORE
BALLINEEN *see* Kinneigh Union *C, C & R*
BALLINGARRY (no dedication) *see* Cloughjordan w Borrisokane etc *L & K*
BALLINLOUGH *see* Roscommon w Donamon, Rathcline, Kilkeevin etc *K, E & A*
BALLINROBE (St Mary) *see* Tuam w Cong and Aasleagh *T, K & A*
BALLINTEMPLE (no dedication) *see* Kilmore w Ballintemple *K, E & A*
BALLINTEMPLE (St Mary) *see* Cashel w Magorban, Tipperary, Clonbeg etc *C & O*
BALLINTOGHER *see* Taunagh w Kilmactranny, Ballysumaghan etc *K, E & A*
BALLINTOY (no dedication) w Rathlin and Dunseverick *Conn* I *vacant*
BALLINTUBBERT (St Brigid) *see* Stradbally w Ballintubbert, Coraclone etc *C & O*
BALLISODARE (Holy Trinity) w Collooney and Emlaghfad *T, K & A* I R E DADSWELL
BALLIVOR *see* Trim and Athboy Gp *M & K*
BALLNACARGY *see* Mullingar, Portnashangan, Moyliscar, Kilbixy etc *M & K*
BALLYBAY (Christ Church) w Mucknoe and Clontibret *Clogh* I J P HEYHOE
BALLYBEEN (St Mary) *D & D* I J M HARVEY
BALLYBRACK (St Matthias) *see* Killiney Ballybrack *D & G*
BALLYBUNNION *see* Tralee w Kilmoyley, Ballymacelligott etc *L & K*
BALLYCANEW (no dedication) *see* Gorey w Kilnahue, Leskinfere and Ballycanew *C & O*
BALLYCARNEY (no dedication) *see* Ferns w Kilbride, Toombe, Kilcormack etc *C & O*
BALLYCARRY *see* Kilroot and Templecorran *Conn*
BALLYCASTLE (Holy Trinity) *see* Ramoan w Ballycastle and Culfeightrin *Conn*
BALLYCLARE *see* Ballynure and Ballyeaston *Conn*
BALLYCLOG (St Patrick) *see* Brackaville w Donaghendry and Ballyclog *Arm*
BALLYCLUG (St Patrick) *see* Ballymena w Ballyclug *Conn*
BALLYCOMMON *see* Geashill w Killeigh and Ballycommon *M & K*
BALLYCONNELL *see* Swanlinbar w Tomregan, Kinawley, Drumlane etc *K, E & A*
BALLYCOTTON *see* Youghal Union *C, C & R*
BALLYCULTER (Christ Church) *see* Lecale Gp *D & D*
BALLYDEHOB (St Matthias) w Aghadown *C, C & R* I P R DRAPER
BALLYEASTON (St John the Evangelist) *see* Ballynure and Ballyeaston *Conn*
BALLYEGLISH (St Matthias) *see* Desertlyn w Ballyeglish *Arm*
BALLYFIN (no dedication) *see* Maryborough w Dysart Enos and Ballyfin *C & O*
BALLYGAWLEY (no dedication) *see* Errigle Keerogue w Ballygawley and Killeshil *Arm*
BALLYHAISE *see* Drung w Castleterra, Larah and Lavey etc *K, E & A*
BALLYHALBERT (St Andrew) w Ardkeen *D & D* I J J HEMPHILL
BALLYHOLME (St Columbanus) *D & D* I A F ABERNETHY, C D M ACHESON
BALLYHOOLEY (no dedication) *see* Fermoy Union *C, C & R*
BALLYJAMESDUFF (no dedication) *see* Kildrumferton w Ballymachugh and Ballyjamesduff *K, E & A*
BALLYKELLY *see* Tamlaghtfinlagan w Myroe *D & R*
BALLYLESSON *see* Drumbo *D & D*
BALLYMACARRETT (St Patrick) (St Christopher) (St Martin) *D & D* I C L HALL-THOMPSON, NSM S P HOOPER
BALLYMACASH (St Mark) *Conn* I W G IRWIN, C E HENDERSON
BALLYMACELLIGOTT (no dedication) *see* Tralee w Kilmoyley, Ballymacelligott etc *L & K*
BALLYMACHUGH (St Paul) *see* Kildrumferton w Ballymachugh and Ballyjamesduff *K, E & A*
BALLYMACKEY (St Michael) *see* Nenagh *L & K*
BALLYMACORMACK (no dedication) *see* Templemichael w Clongish, Clooncumber etc *K, E & A*
BALLYMAGLASSON *see* Dunboyne Union *M & K*
BALLYMAHON *see* Ardagh w Tashinny, Shrule and Kilcommick *K, E & A*
BALLYMARTLE (no dedication) *see* Kinsale Union *C, C & R*
BALLYMASCANLAN (St Mary) w Creggan and Rathcor *Arm* I S A PRAGNELL, NSM R W R MOORE
BALLYMENA (St Patrick) w Ballyclug *Conn* I S G E LLOYD, C N D S PHAIR, D W R DUNN
BALLYMONEY *see* Kinneigh Union *C, C & R*
BALLYMONEY (St Patrick) w Finvoy and Rasharkin *Conn* I E R LAVERY, NSM W J HOLMES, R J SIMPSON
BALLYMORE *see* Clondehorkey w Cashel *D & R*
BALLYMORE (St Mark) *Arm* I S J BLACK
BALLYMORE EUSTACE (St John) *see* Blessington w Kilbride, Ballymore Eustace etc *D & G*
BALLYMOTE *see* Ballisodare w Collooney and Emlaghfad *T, K & A*
BALLYMOYER (St Luke) *see* Newtownhamilton w Ballymoyer and Belleck *Arm*
BALLYNAFEIGH (St Jude) *D & D* I N JARDINE
BALLYNAHINCH *see* Magheradroll *D & D*
BALLYNAKILL (All Saints) *see* Abbeyleix w Ballyroan etc *C & O*
BALLYNAKILL (St Thomas) *see* Omey w Ballynakill, Errislannan and Roundstone *T, K & A*
BALLYNASCREEN *see* Kilcronaghan w Draperstown and Sixtowns *D & R*
BALLYNURE (Ascension) *see* Baltinglass w Ballynure etc *C & O*
BALLYNURE (Christ Church) and Ballyeaston *Conn* I R M MCCONNELL
BALLYPHILIP (no dedication) w Ardquin *D & D* P-in-c M J HOUSTON
BALLYRASHANE (St John the Baptist) w Kildollagh *Conn* I S S HEANEY
BALLYROAN (no dedication) *see* Abbeyleix w Ballyroan etc *C & O*
BALLYSALLY (St Andrew) *see* Coleraine *Conn*
BALLYSCULLION (no dedication) *see* Drummaul w Duneane and Ballyscullion *Conn*
BALLYSCULLION (St Tida) *D & R* I *vacant*
BALLYSEEDY (no dedication) *see* Tralee w Kilmoyley, Ballymacelligott etc *L & K*
BALLYSHANNON *see* Kilbarron w Rossnowlagh and Drumholm *D & R*
BALLYSILLAN *see* Belfast St Mark *Conn*
BALLYSUMAGHAN (no dedication) *see* Taunagh w Kilmactranny, Ballysumaghan etc *K, E & A*
BALLYWALTER (Holy Trinity) w Inishargie *D & D* I J R L BOWLEY
BALLYWARD *see* Drumgath w Drumgooland and Clonduff *D & D*
BALLYWILLAN (Holy Trinity) *Conn* NSM D J STEELE
BALRATHBOYNE *see* Kells Union *M & K*

BALTEAGH (St Canice) w Carrick *D & R* **I** I E DINSMORE
BALTIMORE *see* Abbeystrewry Union *C, C & R*
BALTINGLASS (St Mary) w Ballynure, Stratford-on-Slaney and Rathvilly *C & O* **I** M A MCCULLAGH
BANAGHER (St Moresuis) *see* Cumber Lower w Banagher *D & R*
BANAGHER (St Paul) *see* Clonfert Gp *L & K*
BANBRIDGE *see* Seapatrick *D & D*
BANDON (St Peter) w Rathclaren, Innishannon, Ballinadee and Brinny *C, C & R* **I** N K DUNNE, **NSM** E C M FERGUSON
BANGOR Primacy (Christ Church) *D & D* **I** *vacant*
BANGOR (St Columbanus) *see* Ballyholme *D & D*
BANGOR (St Comgall) *D & D* **I** N H PARKER, **C** G WITHERS
BANGOR ABBEY (Bangor Abbey) *D & D* **I** R NESBITT, **C** W A BOYCE
BANNOW (no dedication) *see* Taghmon w Horetown and Bannow *C & O*
BANTRY *see* Kilmocomogue Union *C, C & R*
BARONSCOURT (no dedication) *see* Ardstraw w Baronscourt, Badoney Lower etc *D & R*
BARR (no dedication) *see* Donacavey w Barr *Clogh*
BEARA (St Peter) *C, C & R* **I** *vacant* (00353) (21) 63036
BECTIVE *see* Trim and Athboy Gp *M & K*
BELFAST (All Saints) *Conn* **I** B A FOLLIS
BELFAST (Cathedral of St Anne) *Conn* **Prec** S R MCBRIDE, **C** J K BELL
BELFAST (Christ Church) *Conn* **I** *vacant*
BELFAST (Holy Trinity) (St Silas) *Conn* **I** T R WILLIAMS, **NSM** D G BEATTIE
BELFAST Malone (St John) *Conn* **I** J O MANN, **C** A L STEWART
BELFAST (St Aidan) *Conn* **I** *vacant* (028) 9079 0977
BELFAST (St Andrew) *Conn* **NSM** S K HOUSTON
BELFAST (St Bartholomew) *Conn* **I** R ELSDON
BELFAST (St Brendan) *D & D* **I** F MCCREA, **C** J HARRIS
BELFAST (St Christopher) *see* Ballymacarrett *D & D*
BELFAST (St Clement) *D & D* **I** S D LOGAN
BELFAST (St Donard) *D & D* **I** R C MCCARTNEY
BELFAST (St George) *Conn* **I** B STEWART
BELFAST (St Jude) *see* Ballynafeigh St Jude *D & D*
BELFAST (St Katharine) *Conn* **I** W J TAGGART
BELFAST (St Mark) *Conn* **I** J C WILSON
BELFAST (St Martin) *see* Ballymacarrett *D & D*
BELFAST (St Mary) (Holy Redeemer) *Conn* **I** J P WALKER
BELFAST (St Mary Magdalene) *Conn* **Bp's C** R H MOORE
BELFAST (St Matthew) *Conn* **I** G J O DUNSTAN
BELFAST (St Michael) *Conn* **I** N B DODDS, **C** E QUIREY
BELFAST (St Nicholas) *Conn* **I** G CLUNIE
BELFAST (St Ninian) *Conn* **I** *vacant*
BELFAST (St Patrick) *see* Ballymacarrett *D & D*
BELFAST (St Paul) (St Barnabas) *Conn* **I** K M BROWN
BELFAST (St Peter) (St James) *Conn* **I** C J MCCOLLUM
BELFAST (St Simon) (St Philip) *Conn* **I** W T LONG
BELFAST (St Stephen) (St Luke) *Conn* **I** *vacant*
BELFAST (St Thomas) *Conn* **I** W A LEWIS, **NSM** J M ELSDON
BELFAST Upper Falls (St John the Baptist) *Conn* **I** T CLELAND
BELFAST Upper Malone (Epiphany) *Conn* **I** P K MCDOWELL
BELFAST Whiterock (St Columba) *Conn* **Bp's C** J T P TWOMEY
BELLAGHY *see* Ballyscullion *D & R*
BELLEEK (no dedication) *see* Garrison w Slavin and Belleek *Clogh*
BELLEEK (St Luke) *see* Newtownhamilton w Ballymoyer and Belleck *Arm*
BELLERENA *see* Tamlaghtard w Aghanloo *D & R*
BELMONT (St Peter) *see* Culmore w Muff and Belmont *D & R*
BELTURBET *see* Annagh w Drumgoon, Ashfield etc *K, E & A*
BELVOIR (Transfiguration) *D & D* **I** T KEIGHTLEY, **C** J MOULD, A A MCCARTNEY
BENOWN (no dedication) *see* Athlone w Benown, Kiltoom and Forgney *M & K*
BILBO (no dedication) *see* Castlecomer w Colliery Ch, Mothel and Bilbo *C & O*
BILLIS (no dedication) *see* Lurgan w Billis, Killinkere and Munterconnaught *K, E & A*
BILLY (no dedication) w Derrykeighan *Conn* **I** J R ANDERSON
BIRR (St Brendan) w Eglish, Lorrha, Dorrha and Lockeen *L & K* **I** R W CARNEY
BLACKLION *see* Killinagh w Kiltyclogher and Innismagrath *K, E & A*
BLACKROCK (All Saints) *see* Stillorgan w Blackrock *D & G*
BLACKROCK (St Michael) *see* Douglas Union w Frankfield *C, C & R*
BLARNEY *see* Carrigrohane Union *C, C & R*
BLESSINGTON (St Mary) w Kilbride, Ballymore Eustace and Holywood *D & G* **I** K R GOVAN
BOHO (no dedication) *see* Devenish w Boho *Clogh*
BOOTERSTOWN (St Philip and St James) *see* Dublin Booterstown *D & G*
BORNACOOLA *see* Templemichael w Clongish, Clooncumber etc *K, E & A*
BORRIS Clonagoose *see* Leighlin w Grange Sylvae, Shankill etc *C & O*
BORRIS Littleton *see* Kilcooley w Littleon, Crohane and Fertagh *C & O*
BORRIS-IN-OSSORY (no dedication) *see* Clonenagh w Offerlane, Borris-in-Ossory etc *C & O*
BORRISNAFARNEY (no dedication) *see* Cloughjordan w Borrisokane etc *L & K*
BORRISOKANE (no dedication) *as above*
BOURNEY (St Burchin) *see* Roscrea w Kyle, Bourney and Corbally *L & K*
BOVEVAGH (St Eugenius) *see* Dungiven w Bovevagh *D & R*
BOYLE (no dedication) and Elphin w Aghanagh, Kilbryan, Ardcarne and Croghan *K, E & A* **I** K A L BARRETT
BRACKAVILLE (Holy Trinity) w Donaghendry and Ballyclog *Arm* **I** K R J HALL
BRANTRY (Holy Trinity) *see* Caledon w Brantry *Arm*
BRAY (Christ Church) *D & G* **I** B T STANLEY, **C** I M CRUICKSHANK, **NSM** S A KINGSTON
BRIGHT (no dedication) w Ballee and Killough *D & D* **I** G J WHITEHEAD
BRIGOWN (St George) *see* Fermoy Union *C, C & R*
BRINNY (no dedication) *see* Bandon Union *C, C & R*
BROOKEBOROUGH *see* Aghavea *Clogh*
BROOMHEDGE (St Matthew) *Conn* **I** P J GALBRAITH
BROUGHSHANE *see* Skerry w Rathcavan and Newtowncrommelin *Conn*
BRYANSFORD *see* Castlewellan w Kilcoo *D & D*
BUNBEG *see* Gweedore, Carrickfin and Templecrone *D & R*
BUNCLODY (St Mary) w Kildavin, Clonegal and Kilrush *C & O* **I** K L J HOMFRAY
BUNCRANA *see* Fahan Lower and Upper *D & R*
BUNDORAN *see* Cloonclare w Killasnett, Lurganboy and Drumlease *K, E & A*
BUSH *see* Ballymascanlan w Creggan and Rathcor *Arm*
BUSHMILLS *see* Dunluce *Conn*
CAHERAGH (St Mary) *see* Abbeystrewry Union *C, C & R*
CAHERCONLISH (St Ailbe) *see* Adare and Kilmallock w Kilpeacon, Croom etc *L & K*
CAHIR (St Paul) *see* Clonmel w Innislounagh, Tullaghmelan etc *C & O*
CAIRNCASTLE (St Patrick) *see* Kilwaughter w Cairncastle and Craigy Hill *Conn*
CALARY (no dedication) *see* Newcastle w Newtownmountkennedy and Calary *D & G*
CALEDON (St John) w Brantry *Arm* **I** D B WILSON
CALRY (no dedication) *K, E & A* **I** M E E MCELHINNEY
CAMLOUGH (Christ the Redeemer) w Mullaglass *Arm* **I** R G HOEY, **NSM** J MOORE
CAMP *see* Dingle w Killiney and Kilgobbin *L & K*
CAMUS-JUXTA-BANN (St Mary) *D & R* **I** J J CUNNINGHAM
CAMUS-JUXTA-MOURNE (Christ Church) *D & R* **I** G S A WILSON
CAPPAGH (St Eugene) w Lislimnaghan *D & R* **I** D J QUINN
CAPPOQUIN (St Anne) *see* Lismore w Cappoquin, Kilwatermoy, Dungarvan etc *C & O*
CARBURY (no dedication) *see* Clonsast w Rathangan, Thomastown etc *M & K*
CARLOW (St Mary) w Urglin and Staplestown *C & O* **I** *vacant*
CARNALEA (St Gall) *D & D* **I** M A PARKER, **NSM** R R HARRIS
CARNALWAY (St Patrick) *see* Newbridge w Carnalway and Kilcullen *M & K*
CARNDONAGH *see* Moville w Greencastle, Donagh, Cloncha etc *D & R*
CARNEW (All Saints) *see* Crosspatrick Gp *C & O*
CARNLOUGH *see* Ardclinis and Tickmacrevan w Layde and Cushendun *Conn*
CARNMONEY (Holy Evangelists) *Conn* **I** M A MALCOLM
CARNTEEL (St James) and Crilly *Arm* **I** W R FERGUSON
CARRICK (no dedication) *see* Balteagh w Carrick *D & R*
CARRICK-ON-SHANNON *see* Kiltoghart w Drumshambo, Annaduff and Kilronan *K, E & A*
CARRICKFERGUS (St Nicholas) *Conn* **I** J A MCMASTER, **C** W S COFFEY
CARRICKFIN (St Andrew) *see* Gweedore, Carrickfin and Templecrone *D & R*

CARRICKMACROSS (St Fin Barre) w Magheracloone *Clogh* I D COLE
CARRIGALINE (St Mary) w Killanully and Monkstown *C, C & R* I S D ARMSTRONG
CARRIGALLEN (no dedication) *see* Arvagh w Carrigallen, Gowna and Columbkille *K, E & A*
CARRIGANS *see* Taughboyne, Craigadooish, Newtowncunningham etc *D & R*
CARRIGART *see* Mevagh w Glenalla *D & R*
CARRIGROHANE (St Peter) w Garrycloyne, Inniscarra and Magourney *C, C & R* I W P OLHAUSEN
CARRIGTWOHILL (St David) *see* Rathcooney Union *C, C & R*
CARROWDORE (Christ Church) w Millisle *D & D* I T K D GRAHAM
CARRYDUFF (St Ignatius) *see* Killaney w Carryduff *D & D*
CASHEL (Cathedral of St John the Baptist) w Magorban, Tipperary, Clonbeg and Ballintemple *C & O* I P J KNOWLES
CASHEL (no dedication) *see* Clondehorkey w Cashel *D & R*
CASTLEARCHDALE (St Patrick) *see* Derryvullen N w Castlearchdale *Clogh*
CASTLEBAR (Christ Church) *see* Aughaval w Achill, Knappagh, Dugort etc *T, K & A*
CASTLEBLAYNEY *see* Ballybay w Mucknoe and Clontibret *Clogh*
CASTLECOMER (St Mary) w the Colliery Church, Mothel and Bilbo *C & O* I T A SHERLOCK
CASTLECONNELL *see* Killaloe w Stradbally *L & K*
CASTLECONNOR (no dedication) *see* Killala w Dunfeeny, Crossmolina, Kilmoremoy etc *T, K & A*
CASTLEDAWSON (Christ Church) *D & R* I D S MCLEAN
CASTLEDERG *see* Derg w Termonamongan *D & R*
CASTLEDERMOT (St James) *see* Narraghmore and Timolin w Castledermot etc *D & G*
CASTLEFLEMING (no dedication) *see* Rathdowney w Castlefleming, Donaghmore etc *C & O*
CASTLEGREGORY *see* Dingle w Killiney and Kilgobbin *L & K*
CASTLEHAVEN (no dedication) *see* Abbeystrewry Union *C, C & R*
CASTLEKNOCK (St Brigid) and Mulhuddart, w Clonsilla *D & G* I A D H ORR, C E DUNNE
CASTLELOST *see* Mullingar, Portnashangan, Moyliscar, Kilbixy etc *M & K*
CASTLEMACADAM (Holy Trinity) w Ballinaclash, Aughrim and Macreddin *D & G* I G W BUTLER
CASTLEMAINE *see* Kilcolman w Kiltallagh, Killorglin, Knockane etc *L & K*
CASTLEMARTYR (St Anne) *see* Youghal Union *C, C & R*
CASTLEPOLLARD (St Michael) and Oldcastle w Loughcrew, Mount Nugent, Mayne and Drumcree *M & K* I P M RUTHERFORD
CASTLEREA *see* Roscommon w Donamon, Rathcline, Kilkeevin etc *K, E & A*
CASTLERICKARD *see* Rathmolyon w Castlerickard, Rathcore and Agher *M & K*
CASTLEROCK (Christ Church) w Dunboe and Fermoyle *D & R* I M R K FERRY, NSM A QUIGLEY
CASTLETERRA (no dedication) *see* Drung w Castleterra, Larah and Lavey etc *K, E & A*
CASTLETOWN *see* Killeshin w Cloydagh and Killabban *C & O*
CASTLETOWN *see* Rathkeale w Askeaton, Kilcornan and Kilnaughtin *L & K*
CASTLETOWN *see* Kells Union *M & K*
CASTLETOWNBERE *see* Beara *C, C & R*
CASTLETOWNROCHE (no dedication) *see* Mallow Union *C, C & R*
CASTLETOWNSEND *see* Abbeystrewry Union *C, C & R*
CASTLEVENTRY (no dedication) *see* Ross Union *C, C & R*
CASTLEWELLAN (St Paul) w Kilcoo *D & D* P-in-c G G GRAHAM
CAVAN *see* Urney w Denn and Derryheen *K, E & A*
CELBRIDGE (Christ Church) w Straffan and Newcastle-Lyons *D & G* I M A WOODERSON
CHAPELIZOD (St Laurence) *see* Dublin Crumlin w Chapelizod *D & G*
CHARLEMONT (no dedication) *see* Moy w Charlemont *Arm*
CLABBY (St Margaret) *see* Tempo and Clabby *Clogh*
CLANABOGAN (no dedication) *see* Edenderry w Clanabogan *D & R*
CLANE (St Michael and All Angels) w Donadea and Coolcarrigan *M & K* I D FRAZER, C A V STEWART
CLARA (St Brigid) w Liss, Moate and Clonmacnoise *M & K* I *vacant* (00353) (506) 31406
CLARE (no dedication) *see* Loughgilly w Clare *Arm*
CLAUDY *see* Cumber Upper w Learmount *D & R*
CLEENISH (no dedication) w Mullaghdun *Clogh* I G P BRIDLE
CLIFDEN *see* Omey w Ballynakill, Errislannan and Roundstone *T, K & A*
CLOGH (Holy Trinity) *see* Aghadrumsee w Clogh and Drumsnatt *Clogh*
CLOGHER (Cathedral of St Macartan) w Errigal Portclare *Clogh* I R C THOMPSON
CLOGHERNY (St Patrick) w Seskinore and Drumnakilly *Arm* R *vacant* (028) 8075 8219
CLONAGOOSE (St Moling) *see* Leighlin w Grange Sylvae, Shankill etc *C & O*
CLONAKILTY *see* Kilgariffe Union *C, C & R*
CLONALLON (no dedication) w Warrenpoint *D & D* P-in-c J H SIMS
CLONARD *see* Mullingar, Portnashangan, Moyliscar, Kilbixy etc *M & K*
CLONASLEE *see* Mountmellick w Coolbanagher, Rosenallis etc *M & K*
CLONBEG (St Sedna) *see* Cashel w Magorban, Tipperary, Clonbeg etc *C & O*
CLONBRONEY (St John) *see* Mostrim w Granard, Clonbroney, Killoe etc *K, E & A*
CLONBULLOGUE *see* Clonsast w Rathangan, Thomastown etc *M & K*
CLONCHA (no dedication) *see* Moville w Greencastle, Donagh, Cloncha etc *D & R*
CLONDALKIN (St John) w Rathcoole *D & G* I W P HOUSTON, NSM O BOOTHMAN
CLONDEHORKEY (St John) w Cashel *D & R* I S JOHNSON
CLONDEVADDOCK (Christ the Redeemer) w Portsalon and Leatbeg *D & R* NSM S JOHNSON
CLONDUFF (St John) *see* Drumgath w Drumgooland and Clonduff *D & D*
CLONE (St Paul) *see* Enniscorthy w Clone, Clonmore, Monart etc *C & O*
CLONEGAL (no dedication) *see* Bunclody w Kildavin, Clonegal and Kilrush *C & O*
CLONEGAM (Holy Trinity) *see* Fiddown w Clonegam, Guilcagh and Kilmeaden *C & O*
CLONENAGH (no dedication) w Offerlane, Borris-in-Ossory, Seirkieran and Roskelton *C & O* I S F MIKHAIL
CLONES (St Tighernach) w Killeevan *Clogh* P-in-c A P R WAKELY
CLONEYHURKE (no dedication) *see* Portarlington w Cloneyhurke and Lea *M & K*
CLONFADFORAN *see* Tullamore w Durrow, Newtownfertullagh, Rahan etc *M & K*
CLONFEACLE (St Patrick) w Derrygortreavy *Arm* I A J PARKHILL
CLONFERT (Cathedral of St Brendan) w Donanaughta, Banagher and Lickmolassy *L & K* I A J NEVIN, NSM E C L ROBINSON
CLONGISH (St Paul) *see* Templemichael w Clongish, Clooncumber etc *K, E & A*
CLONLARA *see* Killaloe w Stradbally *L & K*
CLONLEIGH (St Lugadius) *see* Raphoe w Raymochy and Clonleigh *D & R*
CLONMACNOISE (St Kieran) *see* Clara w Liss, Moate and Clonmacnoise *M & K*
CLONMEL (St Mary) w Innislounagh, Tullaghmelan, Fethard, Kilvemnon and Cahir *C & O* I G A KNOWD, C A CARTER
CLONMEL UNION (Christ Church) *C, C & R* I *vacant* (00353) (21) 811790
CLONMELLON *see* Trim and Athboy Gp *M & K*
CLONMORE (St John) *see* Enniscorthy w Clone, Clonmore, Monart etc *C & O*
CLONMORE (St John) *see* Kiltegan w Hacketstown, Clonmore and Moyne *C & O*
CLONOE (St Michael) *see* Tullaniskin w Clonoe *Arm*
CLONSAST (no dedication) w Rathangan, Thomastown, Monasteroris, Carbury and Rahan *M & K* I L E A PEILOW
CLONSILLA (St Mary) *see* Castleknock and Mulhuddart w Clonsilla *D & G*
CLONTARF *see* Dublin Clontarf *D & G*
CLONTIBRET (St Colman) *see* Ballybay w Mucknoe and Clontibret *Clogh*
CLONTUSKERT (St Matthew) *see* Aughrim w Ballinasloe etc *L & K*
CLOONCLARE (no dedication) w Killasnett, Lurganboy and Drumlease *K, E & A* Bp's C C J STEVENSON
CLOONCUMBER (no dedication) *see* Templemichael w Clongish, Clooncumber etc *K, E & A*
CLOONEY (All Saints) w Strathfoyle *D & R* I J C D MAYES, C P A THOMPSON
CLOUGH *see* Craigs w Dunaghy and Killagan *Conn*

CLOUGHFERN (Ascension) *Conn* **I** D LOCKHART, **C** A E STEWART
CLOUGHJORDAN (St Kieran) w Borrisokane, Ballingary, Borrisnafarney and Templeharry *L & K* **I** S M NEILL, **NSM** R M GILL
CLOUGHMILLS *see* Craigs w Dunaghy and Killagan *Conn*
CLOVERHILL (St John) *see* Annagh w Drumgoon, Ashfield etc *K, E & A*
CLOYDAGH (no dedication) *see* Killeshin w Cloydagh and Killabban *C & O*
CLOYNE (Cathedral of St Colman) w Inch, Corkbeg, Midleton and Gurranekennefeake *C, C & R* **I** A G MARLEY
COACHFORD *see* Carrigrohane Union *C, C & R*
COALISLAND *see* Brackaville w Donaghendry and Ballyclog *Arm*
COBH *see* Clonmel Union *C, C & R*
COLAGHTY *see* Lack *Clogh*
COLEBROOK *see* Aghalurcher w Tattykeeran, Cooneen etc *Clogh*
COLERAINE *see* Killowen *D & R*
COLERAINE (St Patrick) *Conn* **I** C R A EASTON, **C** D RICHARDSON
COLIN (St Andrew) *see* Derriaghy w Colin *Conn*
COLLIERY CHURCH, THE *see* Castlecomer w Colliery Ch, Mothel and Bilbo *C & O*
COLLON (no dedication) *see* Drogheda w Ardee, Collon and Termonfeckin *Arm*
COLLOONEY (St Paul) *see* Ballisodare w Collooney and Emlaghfad *T, K & A*
COLPE (St Columba) *see* Julianstown and Colpe w Drogheda and Duleek *M & K*
COLUMBKILLE (St Thomas) *see* Arvagh w Carrigallen, Gowna and Columbkille *K, E & A*
COMBER (St Mary) *D & D* **I** J P O BARRY, **NSM** R A B MOLLAN
COMERAGH *see* Lismore w Cappoquin, Kilwatermoy, Dungarvan etc *C & O*
CONARY (St Bartholomew) *see* Dunganstown w Redcross and Conary *D & G*
CONG (St Mary) *see* Tuam w Cong and Aasleagh *T, K & A*
CONNOR (St Saviour) w Antrim St Patrick *Conn* **I** S GILCHRIST
CONVOY (St Ninian) w Monellan and Donaghmore *D & R* **I** *vacant* (00353) (74) 47164
CONWAL (no dedication) w Aughanunshin and Gartan *D & R* **I** W C S WRIGHT
COOKSTOWN *see* Derryloran *Arm*
COOLBANAGHER (St John) *see* Mountmellick w Coolbanagher, Rosenallis etc *M & K*
COOLCARRIGAN (no dedication) *see* Clane w Donadea and Coolcarrigan *M & K*
COOLKELLURE (St Edmund) *see* Fanlobbus Union *C, C & R*
COOLOCK (St John) *see* Raheny w Coolock *D & G*
COONEEN (no dedication) *see* Aghalurcher w Tattykeeran, Cooneen etc *Clogh*
COOTEHILL *see* Annagh w Drumgoon, Ashfield etc *K, E & A*
CORACLONE (St Peter) *see* Stradbally w Ballintubbert, Coraclone etc *C & O*
CORBALLY (Christ Church) *see* Roscrea w Kyle, Bourney and Corbally *L & K*
CORK (Cathedral of St Fin Barre) (St Nicholas) *C, C & R* **I** M A J BURROWS, **NSM** E W HUNTER
CORK (St Ann) Shandon w St Mary *C, C & R* **I** B J G O'ROURKE
CORKBEG (St Michael and All Angels) *see* Cloyne Union *C, C & R*
CORRAWALLEN (no dedication) *see* Kildallan w Newtowngore and Corrawallen *K, E & A*
COURTMACSHERRY (St John the Evangelist) *see* Kilgariffe Union *C, C & R*
CRAIGADOOISH (no dedication) *see* Taughboyne, Craigadooish, Newtowncunningham etc *D & R*
CRAIGAVAD *see* Glencraig *D & D*
CRAIGAVON (St Saviour) *see* Ardmore w Craigavon *D & D*
CRAIGS (no dedication) w Dunaghy and Killagan *Conn* **I** W R G WILLANS
CRAIGY HILL (All Saints) *see* Kilwaughter w Cairncastle and Craigy Hill *Conn*
CREAGH *see* Abbeystrewry Union *C, C & R*
CREAGH *see* Aughrim w Ballinasloe etc *L & K*
CRECORA *see* Adare and Kilmallock w Kilpeacon, Croom etc *L & K*
CREGAGH (St Finnian) *D & D* **I** J N BATTYE, **C** A W A MAYES
CREGGAN (no dedication) *see* Ballymascanlan w Creggan and Rathcor *Arm*
CRILLY (St George) *see* Carnteel and Crilly *Arm*
CRINKEN (St James) *D & G* **I** E M VAUGHAN
CROGHAN (Holy Trinity) *see* Boyle and Elphin w Aghanagh, Kilbryan etc *K, E & A*
CROHANE (no dedication) *see* Kilcooley w Littleon, Crohane and Fertagh *C & O*
CROM (Holy Trinity) *see* Kinawley w H Trin *K, E & A*
CROOKHAVEN (St Brendan) *see* Kilmoe Union *C, C & R*
CROOM (no dedication) *see* Adare and Kilmallock w Kilpeacon, Croom etc *L & K*
CROSSGAR *see* Kilmore and Inch *D & D*
CROSSHAVEN *see* Templebreedy w Tracton and Nohoval *C, C & R*
CROSSMOLINA (no dedication) *see* Killala w Dunfeeny, Crossmolina, Kilmoremoy etc *T, K & A*
CROSSPATRICK Group (no dedication) w Kilcommon, Kilpipe, Preban and Carnew, The *C & O* **I** D P M DUNNE
CRUMLIN *see* Dublin Crumlin w Chapelizod *D & G*
CRUMLIN (St John) *see* Glenavy w Tunny and Crumlin *Conn*
CRUMLIN ROAD *see* Belfast St Mary w H Redeemer *Conn*
CULDAFF (no dedication) *see* Moville w Greencastle, Donagh, Cloncha etc *D & R*
CULFEIGHTRIN (no dedication) *see* Ramoan w Ballycastle and Culfeightrin *Conn*
CULLYBACKEY *see* Craigs w Dunaghy and Killagan *Conn*
CULMORE (Holy Trinity) w Muff and Belmont *D & R* **I** M E G MOORE
CUMBER LOWER (Holy Trinity) w Banagher *D & R* **I** *vacant*
CUMBER UPPER (no dedication) w Learmount *D & R* **I** J R D SLATER
CURRAGH (Garrison Church of St Paul) *see* Kildare w Kilmeague and Curragh *M & K*
CURRIN (St Andrew) w Drum and Newbliss *Clogh* **P-in-c** A P R WAKELY
CUSHENDALL *see* Ardclinis and Tickmacrevan w Layde and Cushendun *Conn*
CUSHENDUN (no dedication) *as above*
DALKEY (St Patrick) *D & G* **I** W B A NEILL
DARTREY *see* Ematris w Rockcorry, Aghabog and Aughnamullan *Clogh*
DELGANY (Christ Church) *D & G* **I** N J W WAUGH
DENN (no dedication) *see* Urney w Denn and Derryheen *K, E & A*
DERG (no dedication) w Termonamongan *D & R* **I** W P QUILL
DERNAKESH (Chapel of Ease) *see* Annagh w Drumgoon, Ashfield etc *K, E & A*
DERRALOSSARY *see* Rathdrum w Glenealy, Derralossary and Laragh *D & G*
DERRIAGHY (Christ Church) w Colin *Conn* **I** J C BUDD
DERRYBRUSK (St Michael) *see* Maguiresbridge w Derrybrusk *Clogh*
DERRYGONNELLY *see* Inishmacsaint *Clogh*
DERRYGORTREAVY (St Columba) *see* Clonfeacle w Derrygortreavy *Arm*
DERRYHEEN (no dedication) *see* Urney w Denn and Derryheen *K, E & A*
DERRYKIGHAN (St Colman) *see* Billy w Derrykeighan *Conn*
DERRYLANE (no dedication) *see* Killeshandra w Killegar and Derrylane *K, E & A*
DERRYLIN *see* Kinawley w H Trin *K, E & A*
DERRYLORAN (St Luran) *Arm* **I** R J N PORTEUS, **C** J EWART
DERRYNOOSE (St John) *see* Keady w Armaghbreague and Derrynoose *Arm*
DERRYVOLGIE (St Columba) *Conn* **I** D M QUIGLEY
DERRYVULLEN NORTH (St Tighernach) w Castlearchdale *Clogh* **I** *vacant*
DERRYVULLEN SOUTH (St Tighernach) w Garvary *Clogh* **I** J W STEWART
DERVOCK *see* Billy w Derrykeighan *Conn*
DESERTCREAT (no dedication) *see* Ardtrea w Desertcreat *Arm*
DESERTLYN (St John) w Ballyeglish *Arm* **I** A N STRINGER
DESERTMARTIN (St Conghall) w Termoneeny *D & R* **I** K R KINGSTON
DESERTOGHILL (no dedication) *see* Errigal w Garvagh *D & R*
DESERTSERGES (no dedication) *see* Kinneigh Union *C, C & R*
DEVENISH (St Molaise) w Boho *Clogh* **I** D P KERR
DIAMOND (St Paul) *see* Tartaraghan w Diamond *Arm*
DINGLE (St James) w Killiney and Kilgobbin *L & K* **I** *vacant*
DOAGH *see* Kilbride *Conn*
DOLLINGSTOWN (St Saviour) *see* Magheralin w Dollingstown *D & D*

DONABATE (St Patrick) *see* Swords w Donabate and Kilsallaghan *D & G*
DONACAVEY (no dedication) w Barr *Clogh* **I** F G RUTLEDGE
DONADEA (St Peter) *see* Clane w Donadea and Coolcarrigan *M & K*
DONAGH (no dedication) *see* Moville w Greencastle, Donagh, Cloncha etc *D & R*
DONAGH (St Salvator) w Tyholland and Errigal Truagh *Clogh* **I** *vacant* (00353) (47) 88277
DONAGHADEE (no dedication) *D & D* **R** I R GAMBLE, **C** G F GALWAY
DONAGHCLONEY (St Patrick) w Waringstown *D & D* **I** T D ALLEN
DONAGHEADY (St James) *D & R* **I** D H J FERRY
DONAGHENDRY (St Patrick) *see* Brackaville w Donaghendry and Ballyclog *Arm*
DONAGHMORE (no dedication) *see* Rathdowney w Castlefleming, Donaghmore etc *C & O*
DONAGHMORE (St Bartholomew) *see* Aghaderg w Donaghmore and Scarva *D & D*
DONAGHMORE (St Michael) w Upper Donaghmore *Arm* **I** T S FORSTER
DONAGHMORE (St Patrick) *see* Convoy w Monellan and Donaghmore *D & R*
DONAGHMORE, UPPER (St Patrick) *see* Donaghmore w Upper Donaghmore *Arm*
DONAGHPATRICK (St Patrick) *see* Kells Union *M & K*
DONAMON (no dedication) *see* Roscommon w Donamon, Rathcline, Kilkeevin etc *K, E & A*
DONANAUGHTA (St John the Baptist) *see* Clonfert Gp *L & K*
DONARD (no dedication) *see* Donoughmore and Donard w Dunlavin *D & G*
DONEGAL (no dedication) w Killymard, Lough Eske and Laghey *D & R* **I** R FOX
DONEGORE (St John) *see* Templepatrick w Donegore *Conn*
DONEMANA *see* Donagheady *D & R*
DONERAILE (St Mary) *see* Mallow Union *C, C & R*
DONNYBROOK (St Mary) *see* Dublin Irishtown w Donnybrook *D & G*
DONOUGHMORE (no dedication) and Donard w Dunlavin *D & G* **I** G D B SMITH
DORRHA (no dedication) *see* Birr w Lorrha, Dorrha and Lockeen *L & K*
DOUGLAS (St Luke) w Blackrock, Frankfield and Marmullane *C, C & R* **I** A M WILKINSON, **C** E V CREMIN, **NSM** P T HANNA
DOWN (Cathedral of the Holy and Undivided Trinity) *D & D* **I** *vacant*
DOWN (St Margaret) w Hollymount *D & D* **I** S M J DICKSON, **NSM** M S WALSHE
DOWNPATRICK *see* Down H Trin w Hollymount *D & D*
DOWNPATRICK *see* Down Cathl *D & D*
DRAPERSTOWN (St Columb) *see* Kilcronaghan w Draperstown and Sixtowns *D & R*
DREW MEMORIAL *see* Belfast St Simon w St Phil *Conn*
DRIMOLEAGUE (St Matthew) *see* Fanlobbus Union *C, C & R*
DRINAGH (Christ Church) *as above*
DROGHEDA (St Mary) *see* Julianstown and Colpe w Drogheda and Duleek *M & K*
DROGHEDA (St Peter) w Ardee, Collon and Termonfeckin *Arm* **I** M GRAHAM
DROMAHAIR *see* Clooncläre w Killasnett, Lurganboy and Drumlease *K, E & A*
DROMARA (St John) w Garvaghy *D & D* **I** A W MILLAR
DROMARD (Christ Church) *see* Skreen w Kilmacshalgan and Dromard *T, K & A*
DROMOD (St Michael and All Angels) *see* Kenmare w Sneem, Waterville etc *L & K*
DROMORE (Cathedral of Christ the Redeemer) *D & D* **I** S H LOWRY, **NSM** T J MCKEOWN
DROMORE (Holy Trinity) *Clogh* **I** T K HANLON
DRUM (no dedication) *see* Currin w Drum and Newbliss *Clogh*
DRUMACHOSE (Christ Church) *D & R* **I** S MCVEIGH
DRUMALOOR (St Andrew) *see* Annagh w Drumgoon, Ashfield etc *K, E & A*
DRUMANY (Christ Church) *see* Kinawley w H Trin *K, E & A*
DRUMBANAGHER (St Mary) *see* Acton and Drumbanagher *Arm*
DRUMBEG (St Patrick) *D & D* **I** R R W DEVENNEY
DRUMBO (Holy Trinity) *D & D* **I** R C NEILL
DRUMCANNON (Christ Church) *see* Waterford w Killea, Drumcannon and Dunhill *C & O*
DRUMCAR *see* Kilsaran w Drumcar, Dunleer and Dunany *Arm*
DRUMCLAMPH (no dedication) w Lower Langfield and Upper Langfield *D & R* **I** R G KEOGH
DRUMCLIFFE (St Columba) w Kilrush, Kilfenora, Kilfarboy, Kilnasoolagh, Shannon and Kilferagh *L & K* **I** R C HANNA, **NSM** P E HANNA
DRUMCLIFFE (St Columba) w Lissadell and Munninane *K, E & A* **I** A J FORSTER
DRUMCONDRA *see* Dublin Drumcondra w N Strand *D & G*
DRUMCONRATH (St Peter) *see* Kingscourt w Syddan *M & K*
DRUMCREE (Ascension) *Arm* **I** J A PICKERING
DRUMCREE (St John) *see* Castlepollard and Oldcastle w Loughcrew etc *M & K*
DRUMGATH (St John) w Drumgooland and Clonduff *D & D* **I** D SOMERVILLE
DRUMGLASS (St Anne) w Moygashel *Arm* **I** F D SWANN, **C** T A CROSS
DRUMGOOLAND (no dedication) *see* Drumgath w Drumgooland and Clonduff *D & D*
DRUMGOON (All Saints) *see* Annagh w Drumgoon, Ashfield etc *K, E & A*
DRUMHOLM (no dedication) *see* Kilbarron w Rossnowlagh and Drumholm *D & R*
DRUMINISKILL (Chapel of Ease) *see* Killesher *K, E & A*
DRUMKEERAN *see* Killinagh w Kiltyclogher and Innismagrath *K, E & A*
DRUMKEERAN (no dedication) w Templecarne and Muckross *Clogh* **I** *vacant* (028) 6863 1210
DRUMLANE (no dedication) *see* Annagh w Drumgoon, Ashfield etc *K, E & A*
DRUMLEASE (no dedication) *see* Clooncläre w Killasnett, Lurganboy and Drumlease *K, E & A*
DRUMMAUL (St Brigid) w Duneane and Ballyscullion *Conn* **I** T P KERR
DRUMMULLY (no dedication) *see* Galloon w Drummully and Sallaghy *Clogh*
DRUMNAKILLY (Holy Trinity) *see* Clogherny w Seskinore and Drumnakilly *Arm*
DRUMQUIN *see* Drumclamph w Lower and Upper Langfield *D & R*
DRUMRAGH (St Columba) w Mountfield *D & R* **I** W A SEALE, **C** L D A CRAWFORD
DRUMREILLY (no dedication) *see* Mohill w Farnaught, Aughavas, Oughteragh etc *K, E & A*
DRUMSHAMBO (St John) *see* Kiltoghart w Drumshambo, Annaduff and Kilronan *K, E & A*
DRUMSNATT (St Molua) *see* Aghadrumsee w Clogh and Drumsnatt *Clogh*
DRUMTALLAGH (no dedication) *see* Armoy w Loughguile and Drumtullagh *Conn*
DRUNG (no dedication) w Castleterra, Larah and Lavey and Killoughter *K, E & A* **I** *vacant*
DUBLIN Booterstown (St Philip and St James) *D & G* **I** G V WHARTON
DUBLIN (Christ Church Cathedral) Group: (St Andrew) (St Werburgh) (St Michan) St Paul and Grangegorman *D & G* **I** R D HARMAN, **V** D A PIERPOINT, **C** S T IRVINE
DUBLIN Clontarf (St John the Baptist) *D & G* **I** D C SARGENT
DUBLIN Crumlin (St Mary) w Chapelizod *D & G* **I** I J POWER
DUBLIN Drumcondra (no dedication) w North Strand *D & G* **I** W H BLACK, **NSM** A A SHINE
DUBLIN (Irish Church Missions) and St Thomas *D & G* **Supt** E J COULTER
DUBLIN Irishtown (St Matthew) w Donnybrook *D & G* **I** E G ARDIS, **NSM** J M GORDON
DUBLIN Mount Merrion (St Thomas) *D & G* **I** G V WHARTON
DUBLIN Rathfarnham (no dedication) *D & G* **I** E C J WOODS, **C** A E TAYLOR
DUBLIN Rathmines (Holy Trinity) w Harold's Cross *D & G* **I** N G MCENDOO
DUBLIN Sandford (no dedication) w Milltown *D & G* **I** S O GYLES
DUBLIN Sandymount (St John the Evangelist) *D & G* **P-in-c** K J MORONEY, **C** J A MCKAY
DUBLIN Santry (St Pappan) w Glasnevin and Finglas *D & G* **I** D W OXLEY, **NSM** M A GILBERT
DUBLIN (St Ann) (St Stephen) *D & G* **I** T HASKINS, **C** F E J RANKIN
DUBLIN (St Bartholomew) w Leeson Park *D & G* **I** M J THOMPSON
DUBLIN (St George and St Thomas) *D & G* **Bp's C** K M POULTON, **NSM** N MACMASTER
DUBLIN (St Patrick's Cathedral) Group: (St Catherine and St James) (St Audoen) *D & G* **TV** J W R CRAWFORD, **C** J M B KISSELL, **NSM** C E BAKER
DUBLIN Whitechurch (no dedication) *D & G* **I** A H N MCKINLEY, **NSM** P COMERFORD

DUBLIN (Zion Church) *D & G* **I** W R J GOURLEY
DUGORT (St Thomas) *see* Aughaval w Achill, Knappagh, Dugort etc *T, K & A*
DULEEK *see* Julianstown and Colpe w Drogheda and Duleek *M & K*
DUN LAOGHAIRE (Christ Church) *D & G* **I** V G STACEY
DUNAGHY (St James) *see* Craigs w Dunaghy and Killagan *Conn*
DUNANY *see* Kilsaran w Drumcar, Dunleer and Dunany *Arm*
DUNBOE (St Paul) *see* Castlerock w Dunboe and Fermoyle *D & R*
DUNBOYNE Union (St Peter and St Paul) w Kilcock, Maynooth, Moyglare, Dunshaughlin and Ballymaglasson *M & K* **I** J H AITON
DUNDALK (St Nicholas) w Heynestown *Arm* **I** S A PRAGNELL, **NSM** R W R MOORE
DUNDELA (St Mark) *D & D* **I** F J MCDOWELL, **C** C M WOODS
DUNDONALD (St Elizabeth) *D & D* **I** T G ANDERSON
DUNDRUM *see* Cashel w Magorban, Tipperary, Clonbeg etc *C & O*
DUNDRUM (St Donard) *see* Kilmegan w Maghera *D & D*
DUNEANE (no dedication) *see* Drummaul w Duneane and Ballyscullion *Conn*
DUNFANAGHY (Holy Trinity), Raymunterdoney and Tullaghbegley *D & R* **I** M S HARTE
DUNFEENY (no dedication) *see* Killala w Dunfeeny, Crossmolina, Kilmoremoy etc *T, K & A*
DUNGANNON *see* Drumglass w Moygashel *Arm*
DUNGANSTOWN (St Kevin) w Redcross and Conary *D & G* **I** J R HEANEY
DUNGARVAN (St Mary) *see* Lismore w Cappoquin, Kilwatermoy, Dungarvan etc *C & O*
DUNGIVEN (no dedication) w Bovevagh *D & R* **NSM** N I LYTTLE
DUNGLOE *see* Gweedore, Carrickfin and Templecrone *D & R*
DUNHILL (St John the Baptist) *see* Waterford w Killea, Drumcannon and Dunhill *C & O*
DUNKERRIN (no dedication) *see* Shinrone w Aghancon etc *L & K*
DUNLAVIN (St Nicholas) *see* Donoughmore and Donard w Dunlavin *D & G*
DUNLECKNEY (St Mary) w Nurney, Lorum and Kiltennel *C & O* **I** F J G WYNNE
DUNLEER (no dedication) *see* Kilsaran w Drumcar, Dunleer and Dunany *Arm*
DUNLUCE (St John the Baptist) *Conn* **I** G E GRAHAM
DUNMANWAY *see* Fanlobbus Union *C, C & R*
DUNMORE EAST *see* Waterford w Killea, Drumcannon and Dunhill *C & O*
DUNMURRY (St Colman) *Conn* **I** T H PRIESTLY
DUNNALONG (St John) *see* Leckpatrick w Dunnalong *D & R*
DUNSEVERICK (no dedication) *see* Ballintoy w Rathlin and Dunseverick *Conn*
DUNSFORD (St Mary) *see* Lecale Gp *D & D*
DUNSHAUGHLIN (St Seachnal) *see* Dunboyne Union *M & K*
DURROW (St Columba) *see* Tullamore w Durrow, Newtownfertullagh, Rahan etc *M & K*
DURROW (St Fintan) *see* Abbeyleix w Ballyroan etc *C & O*
DURRUS (St James the Apostle) *see* Kilmocomogue Union *C, C & R*
DYSART ENOS (Holy Trinity) *see* Maryborough w Dysart Enos and Ballyfin *C & O*
EASKEY (St Anne) *see* Killala w Dunfeeny, Crossmolina, Kilmoremoy etc *T, K & A*
EDENDERRY *see* Clonsast w Rathangan, Thomastown etc *M & K*
EDENDERRY (no dedication) w Clanabogan *D & R* **I** R W CLARKE
EDGEWORTHSTOWN *see* Mostrim w Granard, Clonbroney, Killoe etc *K, E & A*
EGLANTINE (All Saints) *Conn* **I** C W BELL
EGLINTON *see* Faughanvale *D & R*
EGLISH (Holy Trinity) w Killylea *Arm* **I** W QUIGLEY
ELPHIN (no dedication) *see* Boyle and Elphin w Aghanagh, Kilbryan etc *K, E & A*
EMATRIS (St John the Evangelist) w Rockcorry, Aghabog and Aughnamullan *Clogh* **I** *vacant*
EMLAGHFAD (no dedication) *see* Ballisodare w Collooney and Emlaghfad *T, K & A*
ENNIS *see* Drumcliffe w Kilnasoolagh *L & K*
ENNISCORTHY (St Mary) w Clone, Clonmore, Monart and Templescobin *C & O* **I** C W LONG, **NSM** J DEACON, P A NEILAND
ENNISKEEN *see* Kingscourt w Syddan *M & K*
ENNISKERRY *see* Powerscourt w Kilbride *D & G*
ENNISKILLEN *see* Rossory *Clogh*
ENNISKILLEN (Cathedral of St Macartin) *Clogh* **I** B J COURTNEY, **C** B I LINTON
ENNISNAG (St Peter) *see* Kells Gp *C & O*
ERRIGAL (St Paul) w Garvagh *D & R* **I** *vacant* (028) 2955 8226
ERRIGAL PORTCLARE (no dedication) *see* Clogh w Errigal Portclare *Clogh*
ERRIGAL TRUAGH (St Muadhan) *see* Donagh w Tyholland and Errigal Truagh *Clogh*
ERRIGLE KEEROGUE (no dedication) w Ballygawley and Killeshil *Arm* **I** *vacant*
ERRISLANNNAN (no dedication) *see* Omey w Ballynakill, Errislannan and Roundstone *T, K & A*
ESKRAHOOLE (no dedication) *see* Augher w Newtownsaville and Eskrahoole *Clogh*
EYRECOURT *see* Clonfert Gp *L & K*
FAHAN LOWER (Christ Church) and UPPER (St Mura) *D & R* **Bp's C** S D BARTON
FALLS, LOWER (St Luke) *see* Belfast St Steph w St Luke *Conn*
FALLS, UPPER *see* Belfast Upper Falls *Conn*
FANLOBBUS (St Mary) w Drimoleague, Drinagh and Coolkellure *C, C & R* **I** W P HEWITT
FARNAUGHT (no dedication) *see* Mohill w Farnaught, Aughavas, Oughteragh etc *K, E & A*
FAUGHANVALE (St Canice) *D & R* **I** J W BLAIR
FENAGH (All Saints) w Myshall, Aghade and Ardoyne *C & O* **I** L D D SCOTT
FERMOY (Christ Church) w Ballyhooley, Knockmourne, Ardnageehy and Brigown *C, C & R* **I** C S GIBSON
FERMOYLE (no dedication) *see* Castlerock w Dunboe and Fermoyle *D & R*
FERNS (Cathedral of St Edan) w Kilbride, Toombe, Kilcormack and Ballycarney *C & O* **I** L D A FORREST, **NSM** L R ROGERS
FERRY, EAST *see* Cloyne Union *C, C & R*
FERTAGH (no dedication) *see* Kilcooley w Littleon, Crohane and Fertagh *C & O*
FETHARD (Holy Trinity) *see* Clonmel w Innislounagh, Tullaghmelan etc *C & O*
FETHARD (St Mogue) *see* New w Old Ross, Whitechurch, Fethard etc *C & O*
FIDDOWN (no dedication) w Clonegam, Guilcagh and Kilmeaden *C & O* **I** C G CLIFFE
FINAGHY (St Polycarp) *Conn* **I** J C T SKILLEN, **C** E HENDERSON
FINGLAS (St Canice) *see* Dublin Santry w Glasnevin and Finglas *D & G*
FINNER (Christ Church) *see* Killinagh w Kiltyclogher and Innismagrath *K, E & A*
FINTONA *see* Donacavey w Barr *Clogh*
FINVOY (no dedication) *see* Ballymoney w Finvoy and Rasharkin *Conn*
FIVEMILETOWN (St John) *Clogh* **I** R J RIDDEL
FLORENCECOURT *see* Killesher *K, E & A*
FONTSTOWN (St John the Evangelist) *see* Athy w Kilberry, Fontstown and Kilkea *D & G*
FORGNEY (St Munis) *see* Athlone w Benown, Kiltoom and Forgney *M & K*
FOUNTAINS *see* Lismore w Cappoquin, Kilwatermoy, Dungarvan etc *C & O*
FOXFORD *see* Straid *T, K & A*
FOYNES *see* Rathkeale w Askeaton, Kilcornan and Kilnaughtin *L & K*
FRANKFIELD (Holy Trinity) *see* Douglas Union w Frankfield *C, C & R*
FRENCH CHURCH *see* Portarlington w Cloneyhurke and Lea *M & K*
FRENCHPARK *see* Roscommon w Donamon, Rathcline, Kilkeevin etc *K, E & A*
GALLOON (St Comgall) w Drummully and Sallaghy *Clogh* **I** *vacant*
GALWAY (St Nicholas) w Kilcummin *T, K & A* **I** P L TOWERS
GARRISON (no dedication) w Slavin and Belleek *Clogh* **I** B T KERR
GARRYCLOYNE (no dedication) *see* Carrigrohane Union *C, C & R*
GARTAN (St Columba) *see* Conwal Union w Gartan *D & R*
GARTREE (no dedication) *see* Killead w Gartree *Conn*
GARVAGH *see* Errigal w Garvagh *D & R*
GARVAGHY (no dedication) *see* Dromara w Garvaghy *D & D*
GARVARY (Holy Trinity) *see* Derryvullen S w Garvary *Clogh*
GEASHILL (St Mary) w Killeigh and Ballycommon *M & K* **I** J L CRAMPTON
GILFORD *see* Tullylish *D & D*
GILFORD (St Paul) *D & D* **I** T J CADDEN

GILNAHIRK (St Dorothea) *D & D* **I** T C KINAHAN, **NSM** E O'BRIEN
GLANDORE *see* Ross Union *C, C & R*
GLANMIRE *see* Rathcooney Union *C, C & R*
GLASCARRIG (no dedication) *see* Ardamine w Kiltennel, Glascarrig etc *C & O*
GLASLOUGH *see* Donagh w Tyholland and Errigal Truagh *Clogh*
GLASNEVIN (St Mobhi) *see* Dublin Santry w Glasnevin and Finglas *D & G*
GLENAGEARY (St Paul) *D & G* **I** G G DOWD, **C** S M E WIDERMARK
GLENALLA (St Columbkille) *see* Mevagh w Glenalla *D & R*
GLENARM *see* Ardclinis and Tickmacrevan w Layde and Cushendun *Conn*
GLENAVY (St Aidan) w Tunny and Crumlin *Conn* **I** J E C RUTTER
GLENBEIGH (St John) *see* Kilcolman w Kiltallagh, Killorglin, Knockane etc *L & K*
GLENCAIRN *see* Belfast St Andr *Conn*
GLENCAR *see* Clooncläre w Killasnett, Lurganboy and Drumlease *K, E & A*
GLENCOLUMBKILLE (St Columba) *see* Ardara w Glencolumbkille, Inniskeel etc *D & R*
GLENCRAIG (Holy Trinity) *D & D* **I** P S P HEWITT, **NSM** B W PARKER
GLENDERMOTT (no dedication) *D & R* **I** F D CREIGHTON
GLENEALY (no dedication) *see* Rathdrum w Glenealy, Derralossary and Laragh *D & G*
GLENOE *see* Glynn w Raloo *Conn*
GLENTIES (no dedication) *see* Ardara w Glencolumbkille, Inniskeel etc *D & R*
GLENVILLE *see* Fermoy Union *C, C & R*
GLYNN (St John) w Raloo *Conn* **I** S B FORDE
GORESBRIDGE *see* Leighlin w Grange Sylvae, Shankill etc *C & O*
GOREY (Christ Church) w Kilnahue, Leskinfere and Ballycanew *C & O* **I** M J J HAYDEN, **NSM** J F FORBES
GORTIN *see* Ardstraw w Baronscourt, Badoney Lower etc *D & R*
GOWNA (no dedication) *see* Arvagh w Carrigallen, Gowna and Columbkille *K, E & A*
GRACEFIELD (no dedication) *see* Woodschapel w Gracefield *Arm*
GRANARD (St Patrick) *see* Mostrim w Granard, Clonbroney, Killoe etc *K, E & A*
GRANGE (St Aidan) *see* Loughgall w Grange *Arm*
GRANGE SYLVAE (St George) *see* Leighlin w Grange Sylvae, Shankill etc *C & O*
GRANGEGORMAN (All Saints) *see* Dublin Ch Ch Cathl Gp *D & G*
GREENAN (no dedication) *see* Ardstraw w Baronscourt, Badoney Lower etc *D & R*
GREENCASTLE (St Finian) *see* Moville w Greencastle, Donagh, Cloncha etc *D & R*
GREENISLAND (Holy Name) *Conn* **I** P LYONS
GREY ABBEY (St Saviour) w Kircubbin *D & D* **I** R D SEYMOUR-WHITELEY
GREYSTONES (St Patrick) *D & G* **I** E J SWANN, **C** O H WILLIAMS
GROOMSPORT (no dedication) *D & D* **I** D J M POLLOCK
GUILCAGH (St John the Evangelist) *see* Fiddown w Clonegam, Guilcagh and Kilmeaden *C & O*
GURRANEKENNEFEAKE (no dedication) *see* Cloyne Union *C, C & R*
GWEEDORE (St Patrick), Carrickfin and Templecrone *D & R* **Bp's C** W B JOHNSTON
HACKETSTOWN (St John the Baptist) *see* Kiltegan w Hacketstown, Clonmore and Moyne *C & O*
HAROLD'S CROSS (no dedication) *see* Dublin Rathmines w Harold's Cross *D & G*
HELEN'S BAY (St John the Baptist) *D & D* **I** L J MEDHURST
HEYNESTOWN (St Paul) *see* Dundalk w Heynestown *Arm*
HIGHFIELD *see* Belfast Whiterock *Conn*
HILLSBOROUGH (St Malachi) *D & D* **I** J F DINNEN, **C** W S NIXON
HILLTOWN *see* Drumgath w Drumgooland and Clonduff *D & D*
HOLLYFORT *see* Gorey w Kilnahue, Leskinfere and Ballycanew *C & O*
HOLLYMOUNT (no dedication) *see* Down H Trin w Hollymount *D & D*
HOLMPATRICK (St Patrick) w Balbriggan and Kenure *D & G* **I** A J RUFLI
HOLYCROSS *see* Templemore w Thurles and Kilfithmone *C & O*
HOLYWOOD (St Kevin) *see* Blessington w Kilbride, Ballymore Eustace etc *D & G*
HOLYWOOD (St Philip and St James) *D & D* **I** R M ELKS, **C** C I BENNETT, D I CADDOO
HORETOWN (St James) *see* Taghmon w Horetown and Bannow *C & O*
HORSELEAP *see* Clara w Liss, Moate and Clonmacnoise *M & K*
HOWTH (St Mary) *D & G* **I** W K M BREW
INCH *see* Cloyne Union *C, C & R*
INCH (no dedication) *see* Kilmore and Inch *D & D*
INCH (no dedication) *see* Arklow w Inch and Kilbride *D & G*
INISHARGIE (St Andrew) *see* Ballywalter w Inishargie *D & D*
INISHMACSAINT (St Ninnidh) *Clogh* **I** S G BOURKE
INISTIOGE (St Mary) *see* Kells Gp *C & O*
INNISCALTRA (St Caimin) *see* Killaloe w Stradbally *L & K*
INNISCARRA (no dedication) *see* Carrigrohane Union *C, C & R*
INNISHANNON (Christ Church) *see* Bandon Union *C, C & R*
INNISKEEL (no dedication) *see* Ardara w Glencolumbkille, Inniskeel etc *D & R*
INNISLOUNAGH (St Patrick) *see* Clonmel w Innislounagh, Tullaghmelan etc *C & O*
INNISMAGRATH (no dedication) *see* Killinagh w Kiltyclogher and Innismagrath *K, E & A*
INVER *see* Larne and Inver *Conn*
INVER (St John the Evangelist) w Mountcharles, Killaghtee and Killybegs *D & R* **I** H J K MCLAUGHLIN
IRISHTOWN *see* Dublin Irishtown w Donnybrook *D & G*
IRVINESTOWN *see* Derryvullen N w Castlearchdale *Clogh*
ISLANDMAGEE (St John) *see* Whitehead and Islandmagee *Conn*
JOANMOUNT *see* Belfast H Trin and St Silas *Conn*
JOHNSTOWN *see* Kilcooley w Littleon, Crohane and Fertagh *C & O*
JORDANSTOWN (St Patrick) *Conn* **I** N P BAYLOR, **C** T S JOHNSTON
JULIANSTOWN (St Mary) and Colpe w Drogheda and Duleek *M & K* **I** P H A LAWRENCE
KEADY (St Matthew) w Armaghbreague and Derrynoose *Arm* **I** W G NEELY
KELLS (St Columba) w Balrathboyne, Moynalty, Donaghpatrick and Castletown *M & K* **I** E W RUSSELL
KELLS (St Mary) w Ballaghtobin, Kilmoganny, Ennisnag, Inistioge and Kilfane *C & O* **I** D L SANDES
KENAGH *see* Ardagh w Tashinny, Shrule and Kilcommick *K, E & A*
KENMARE (St Patrick) w Sneem, Dromod and Valentia *L & K* **NSM** A W SHAW
KENTSTOWN (St Mary) *see* Navan w Kentstown, Tara, Slane, Painestown etc *M & K*
KENURE (no dedication) *see* Holmpatrick w Balbriggan and Kenure *D & G*
KESH *see* Magheraculmoney *Clogh*
KILBARRON (St Anne) w Rossnowlagh and Drumholm *D & R* **I** B R RUSSELL
KILBERRY (no dedication) *see* Athy w Kilberry, Fontstown and Kilkea *D & G*
KILBIXY (St Bigseach) *see* Mullingar, Portnashangan, Moyliscar, Kilbixy etc *M & K*
KILBONANE (St Mark) *see* Moviddy Union *C, C & R*
KILBRIDE (Holy Trinity) *see* Ferns w Kilbride, Toombe, Kilcormack etc *C & O*
KILBRIDE (no dedication) *see* Blessington w Kilbride, Ballymore Eustace etc *D & G*
KILBRIDE (St Bride) *Conn* **I** P REDFERN
KILBRIDE (St Brigid) *see* Arklow w Inch and Kilbride *D & G*
KILBRIDE BRAY (no dedication) *see* Powerscourt w Kilbride *D & G*
KILBRONEY (no dedication) *D & D* **Bp's C** S JONES
KILBRYAN (no dedication) *see* Boyle and Elphin w Aghanagh, Kilbryan etc *K, E & A*
KILCLEAGH *see* Clara w Liss, Moate and Clonmacnoise *M & K*
KILCLIEF (no dedication) *see* Lecale Gp *D & D*
KILCLUNEY (St John) *see* Mullabrack w Markethill and Kilcluney *Arm*
KILCOCK *see* Dunboyne Union *M & K*
KILCOLMAN (no dedication) w Kiltallagh, Killorglin, Knockane and Glenbeigh *L & K* **I** M J D SHANNON, **C** J C STEPHENS
KILCOMMICK (no dedication) *see* Ardagh w Tashinny, Shrule and Kilcommick *K, E & A*
KILCOMMON (no dedication) *see* Crosspatrick Gp *C & O*

KILCOO (no dedication) see Castlewellan w Kilcoo D & D

KILCOOLEY (no dedication) w Littleton, Crohane and Fertagh C & O **I** B Y FRYDAY

KILCOOLEY (St Columba) see Bangor Abbey D & D

KILCORMACK (St Cormac) see Ferns w Kilbride, Toombe, Kilcormack etc C & O

KILCORNAN (no dedication) see Rathkeale w Askeaton, Kilcornan and Kilnaughtin L & K

KILCROHANE see Kenmare w Sneem, Waterville etc L & K

KILCRONAGHAN (no dedication) w Draperstown and Sixtowns D & R **I** D MORROW

KILCULLEN (St John) see Newbridge w Carnalway and Kilcullen M & K

KILCUMMIN (no dedication) see Galway w Kilcummin T, K & A

KILDALLAN (no dedication) w Newtowngore and Corrawallen K, E & A **NSM** G W BROWNE

KILDARE (Cathedral of St Brigid) w Kilmeague and Curragh Garrison Church M & K **I** R K TOWNLEY

KILDARTON (no dedication) see Lisnadill w Kildarton Arm

KILDAVIN (St Paul) see Bunclody w Kildavin, Clonegal and Kilrush C & O

KILDOLLAGH (St Paul) see Ballyrashane w Kildollagh Conn

KILDRESS (St Patrick) w Altedesert Arm **I** B J A CRUISE

KILDRUMFERTON (St Patrick) w Ballymachugh and Ballyjamesduff K, E & A **I** J R SIDES

KILFANE (no dedication) see Kells Gp C & O

KILFARBOY (Christ Church) see Drumcliffe w Kilnasoolagh L & K

KILFAUGHNABEG (Christ Church) see Ross Union C, C & R

KILFENORA (Cathedral of St Fachan) see Drumcliffe w Kilnasoolagh L & K

KILFERAGH (no dedication) as above

KILFINANE (St Andrew) see Adare and Kilmallock w Kilpeacon, Croom etc L & K

KILFITHMONE (no dedication) see Templemore w Thurles and Kilfithmone C & O

KILFLYNN (no dedication) see Adare and Kilmallock w Kilpeacon, Croom etc L & K

KILGARIFFE (no dedication) w Kilmalooda, Kilnagross, Timoleague and Courtmacsherry C, C & R **I** I R JONAS

KILGLASS (no dedication) see Killala w Dunfeeny, Crossmolina, Kilmoremoy etc T, K & A

KILGLASS (St Anne) see Mostrim w Granard, Clonbroney, Killoe etc K, E & A

KILGOBBIN (no dedication) see Dingle w Killiney and Kilgobbin L & K

KILHORNE see Annalong D & D

KILKEA (no dedication) see Athy w Kilberry, Fontstown and Kilkea D & G

KILKEE see Drumcliffe w Kilnasoolagh L & K

KILKEEL (Christ Church) D & D **I** G MILLAR, **NSM** S J K TEGGARTY

KILKEEVIN (Holy Trinity) see Roscommon w Donamon, Rathcline, Kilkeevin etc K, E & A

KILKENNY (Cathedral of St Canice) (St John), Aghour and Kilmanagh C & O **I** N N LYNAS, **C** E M E MURRAY

KILKENNY WEST see Athlone w Benown, Kiltoom and Forgney M & K

KILL (no dedication) D & G **I** S F GLENFIELD, **C** S MCELHINNEY

KILL (St John) see Naas w Kill and Rathmore M & K

KILL O' THE GRANGE see Kill D & G

KILLABBAN (no dedication) see Killeshin w Cloydagh and Killabban C & O

KILLADEAS (Priory Church) see Trory w Killadeas Clogh

KILLAGAN (no dedication) see Craigs w Dunaghy and Killagan Conn

KILLAGHTEE (St Peter) see Inver w Mountcharles, Killaghtee and Killybegs D & R

KILLALA (Cathedral of St Patrick) w Dunfeeny, Crossmolina, Kilmoremoy, Castleconnor, Easkey and Kilglass T, K & A **I** S M PATTERSON, **Bp's C** N J O'RAW, **NSM** D T S CLEMENTS

KILLALLON (St John) see Trim and Athboy Gp M & K

KILLALOE (Cathedral of St Flannan) w Stradbally, Clonlara, Mountshannon, Abingdon and Tuomgraney L & K **I** vacant

KILLANEY (St Andrew) w Carryduff D & D **I** J R AUCHMUTY, **NSM** R L RENNIX

KILLANNE (St Anne) w Killegney, Rossdroit and Templeshanbo C & O **I** R J HARMSWORTH

KILLANULLY see Carrigaline Union C, C & R

KILLARGUE (no dedication) see Killinagh w Kiltyclogher and Innismagrath K, E & A

KILLARNEY (St Mary) w Aghadoe and Muckross L & K **NSM** S G EVANS

KILLASHEE (St Paul) see Templemichael w Clongish, Clooncumber etc K, E & A

KILLASNETT (no dedication) see Cloonclare w Killasnett, Lurganboy and Drumlease K, E & A

KILLCONNELL see Aughrim w Ballinasloe etc L & K

KILLEA (St Andrew) see Waterford w Killea, Drumcannon and Dunhill C & O

KILLEA (St Fiach) see Taughboyne, Craigadooish, Newtowncunningham etc D & R

KILLEAD (St Catherine) w Gartree Conn **I** vacant

KILLEDMOND see Dunleckney w Nurney, Lorum and Kiltennel C & O

KILLEEVAN (no dedication) see Clones w Killeevan Clogh

KILLEGAR (no dedication) see Killeshandra w Killegar and Derrylane K, E & A

KILLEGNEY (no dedication) see Killanne w Killegney, Rossdroit and Templeshanbo C & O

KILLEIGH (no dedication) see Geashill w Killeigh and Ballycommon M & K

KILLELAGH (no dedication) see Maghera w Killelagh D & R

KILLENAULE (no dedication) see Kilcooley w Littleon, Crohane and Fertagh C & O

KILLERMOGH (no dedication) see Abbeyleix w Ballyroan etc C & O

KILLERY see Taunagh w Kilmactranny, Ballysumaghan etc K, E & A

KILLESHANDRA (no dedication) w Killegar and Derrylane K, E & A **I** vacant

KILLESHER (St John) K, E & A **I** G M S WATSON, **NSM** T J WOODS

KILLESHERDONEY (St Mark) see Annagh w Drumgoon, Ashfield etc K, E & A

KILLESHIL (St Paul) see Errigle Keerogue w Ballygawley and Killeshil Arm

KILLESHIN (no dedication) w Cloydagh and Killabban C & O **I** R H BYRNE

KILLESK (All Saints) see New w Old Ross, Whitechurch, Fethard etc C & O

KILLETER see Derg w Termonamongan D & R

KILLINAGH (no dedication) w Kiltyclogher and Innismagrath K, E & A **I** vacant

KILLINCHY (no dedication) w Kilmood and Tullynakill D & D **I** N D J KIRKPATRICK

KILLINEY Ballybrack (St Matthias) D & G **I** I P POULTON

KILLINEY (Holy Trinity) D & G **I** H C MILLS

KILLINEY (St Brendan) see Dingle w Killiney and Kilgobbin L & K

KILLINICK (no dedication) see Kilscoran w Killinick and Mulrankin C & O

KILLINKERE (no dedication) see Lurgan w Billis, Killinkere and Munterconnaught K, E & A

KILLISKEY (no dedication) see Wicklow w Killiskey D & G

KILLODIERNAN (no dedication) see Nenagh L & K

KILLOE (St Catherine) see Mostrim w Granard, Clonbroney, Killoe etc K, E & A

KILLORAN (no dedication) see Achonry w Tubbercurry and Killoran T, K & A

KILLORGLIN (no dedication) see Kilcolman w Kiltallagh, Killorglin, Knockane etc L & K

KILLOUGH (St Anne) see Bright w Ballee and Killough D & D

KILLOUGHTER (no dedication) see Drung w Castleterra, Larah and Lavey etc K, E & A

KILLOUGHY see Tullamore w Durrow, Newtownfertullagh, Rahan etc M & K

KILLOWEN see Kinneigh Union C, C & R

KILLOWEN (St John) D & R **I** D M COLLINS

KILLSALLAGHAN (St David) see Swords w Donabate and Kilsallaghan D & G

KILLUCAN (St Etchen) see Mullingar, Portnashangan, Moyliscar, Kilbixy etc M & K

KILLURIN (no dedication) see Wexford w Ardcolm and Killurin C & O

KILLYBEGS (no dedication) see Inver w Mountcharles, Killaghtee and Killybegs D & R

KILLYGARVAN (St Columb) see Tullyaughnish w Kilmacrennan and Killygarvan D & R

KILLYLEA (St Mark) see Eglish w Killylea Arm

KILLYLEAGH (St John the Evangelist) D & D **I** J C MUNYANGAJU

KILLYMAN (St Andrew) Arm **I** S R T BOYD

KILLYMARD (no dedication) see Donegal w Killymard, Lough Eske and Laghey D & R

KILMACABEA (no dedication) see Ross Union C, C & R

KILMACDUAGH (no dedication) see Aughrim w Ballinasloe etc L & K

KILMACRENNAN (St Finnian and St Mark) *see* Tullyaughnish w Kilmacrennan and Killygarvan *D & R*
KILMACSHALGAN (St Mary) *see* Skreen w Kilmacshalgan and Dromard *T, K & A*
KILMACTHOMAS (no dedication) *see* Lismore w Cappoquin, Kilwatermoy, Dungarvan etc *C & O*
KILMACTRANNY (no dedication) *see* Taunagh w Kilmactranny, Ballysumaghan etc *K, E & A*
KILMAINHAMWOOD *see* Kingscourt w Syddan *M & K*
KILMAKEE (St Hilda) *Conn* **I** D H BOYLAND, **NSM** R MOORE
KILMALLOCK (St Peter and St Paul) *see* Adare and Kilmallock w Kilpeacon, Croom etc *L & K*
KILMALOODA (All Saints) *see* Kilgariffe Union *C, C & R*
KILMANAGH (no dedication) *see* Kilkenny w Aghour and Kilmanagh *C & O*
KILMEADEN (St Mary) *see* Fiddown w Clonegam, Guilcagh and Kilmeaden *C & O*
KILMEAGUE (no dedication) *see* Kildare w Kilmeague and Curragh *M & K*
KILMEEN (Christ Church) *see* Kinneigh Union *C, C & R*
KILMEGAN (no dedication) w Maghera *D & D* **I** C J CARSON
KILMOCOMOGUE Union (no dedication) *C, C & R* **I** P M WILLOUGHBY
KILMOE (no dedication) w Teampol-na-mbocht, Schull and Crookhaven *C, C & R* **I** E E M LYNCH
KILMOGANNY (St Matthew) *see* Kells Gp *C & O*
KILMOOD (St Mary) *see* Killinchy w Kilmood and Tullynakill *D & D*
KILMORE (Cathedral of St Fethlimidh) w Ballintemple *K, E & A* **I** *vacant*
KILMORE (Christ Church) and Inch *D & D* **I** J D M PIERCE
KILMORE (no dedication) *see* Monaghan w Tydavnet and Kilmore *Clogh*
KILMORE (no dedication) *see* Kiltoghart w Drumshambo, Annaduff and Kilronan *K, E & A*
KILMORE (St Aidan) (St Saviour) *Arm* **I** *vacant*
KILMOREMOY (St Michael) *see* Killala w Dunfeeny, Crossmolina, Kilmoremoy etc *T, K & A*
KILMOYLEY *see* Tralee w Kilmoyley, Ballymacelligott etc *L & K*
KILMUCKRIDGE (no dedication) *see* Ardamine w Kiltennel, Glascarrig etc *C & O*
KILMURRY (St Andrew) *see* Moviddy Union *C, C & R*
KILNAGROSS (no dedication) *see* Kilgariffe Union *C, C & R*
KILNAHUE (St John the Evangelist) *see* Gorey w Kilnahue, Leskinfere and Ballycanew *C & O*
KILNALECK *see* Kildrumferton w Ballymachugh and Ballyjamesduff *K, E & A*
KILNAMANAGH (St John) *see* Ardamine w Kiltennel, Glascarrig etc *C & O*
KILNASOOLAGH (no dedication) *see* Drumcliffe w Kilnasoolagh *L & K*
KILNAUGHTIN (St Brendan) *see* Rathkeale w Askeaton, Kilcornan and Kilnaughtin *L & K*
KILPEACON (St Beacon) *see* Adare and Kilmallock w Kilpeacon, Croom etc *L & K*
KILPIPE (no dedication) *see* Crosspatrick Gp *C & O*
KILREA (St Patrick) *see* Aghadowey w Kilrea *D & R*
KILRONAN (St Thomas) *see* Kiltoghart w Drumshambo, Annaduff and Kilronan *K, E & A*
KILROOT (St Colman) and Templecorran *Conn* **I** M J MCCANN, **NSM** W STEWART
KILROSSANTY (no dedication) *see* Lismore w Cappoquin, Kilwatermoy, Dungarvan etc *C & O*
KILRUSH *see* Drumcliffe w Kilnasoolagh *L & K*
KILRUSH (St Brigid) *see* Bunclody w Kildavin, Clonegal and Kilrush *C & O*
KILSARAN (St Mary) w Drumcar, Dunleer and Dunany *Arm* **Bp's C** P D THORNBURY
KILSCORAN (no dedication) w Killinick and Mulrankin *C & O* **I** *vacant*
KILSKEERY (no dedication) w Trillick *Clogh* **I** W J JOHNSTON
KILTALLAGH (St Carthage) *see* Kilcolman w Kiltallagh, Killorglin, Knockane etc *L & K*
KILTEEVOGUE (St John) *see* Stranorlar w Meenglas and Kilteevogue *D & R*
KILTEGAN (St Peter) w Hacketstown, Clonmore and Moyne *C & O* **I** S E B DURAND
KILTENNEL (no dedication) *see* Ardamine w Kiltennel, Glascarrig etc *C & O*
KILTENNEL (St Peter) *see* Dunleckney w Nurney, Lorum and Kiltennel *C & O*
KILTERNAN (St Kiernan) *D & G* **I** D G MOYNAN
KILTINANLEA (no dedication) *see* Killaloe w Stradbally *L & K*
KILTOGHART (St George) w Drumshambo, Anaduff and Kilronan *K, E & A* **I** *vacant* (00353) (61) 20053
KILTOOM *see* Athlone w Benown, Kiltoom and Forgney *M & K*
KILTUBRIDE (St Brigid) *see* Mohill w Farnaught, Aughavas, Oughteragh etc *K, E & A*
KILTULLAGH (no dedication) *see* Roscommon w Donamon, Rathcline, Kilkeevin etc *K, E & A*
KILTYCLOGHER (no dedication) *see* Killinagh w Kiltyclogher and Innismagrath *K, E & A*
KILVEMNON (St Hugh) *see* Clonmel w Innislounagh, Tullaghmelan etc *C & O*
KILWARLIN UPPER (St John) w LOWER (St James) *D & D* **I** T D B PIERCE
KILWATERMOY (St Mary) *see* Lismore w Cappoquin, Kilwatermoy, Dungarvan etc *C & O*
KILWAUGHTER (no dedication) w Cairncastle and Craigy Hill *Conn* **I** R Q THOMPSON
KINAWLEY (no dedication) w Holy Trinity *K, E & A* **I** G T W DAVISON
KINAWLEY (St Paul) *see* Swanlinbar w Tomregan, Kinawley, Drumlane etc *K, E & A*
KINGSCOURT (St Ernan) w Drumconrath, Syddan and Moybologue *M & K* **I** R S J BOURKE
KINLOUGH *see* Killinagh w Kiltyclogher and Innismagrath *K, E & A*
KINNEAGH (no dedication) *see* Narraghmore and Timolin w Castledermot etc *D & G*
KINNEIGH (St Bartholomew) w Ballymoney, Kilmeen, Desertserges, Killowen and Murragh *C, C & R* **I** J F HUBBARD-JONES
KINNITTY (St Trinnian) *see* Shinrone w Aghancon etc *L & K*
KINSALE (St Multose) w Runcurran, Ballymartle and Templetrine *C, C & R* **I** D WILLIAMS
KIRCONRIOLA *see* Ballymena w Ballyclug *Conn*
KIRCUBBIN (Holy Trinity) *see* Grey Abbey w Kircubbin *D & D*
KNAPPAGH (St Thomas) *see* Aughaval w Achill, Knappagh, Dugort etc *T, K & A*
KNOCK (St Columba) *D & D* **I** G A MCCAMLEY, **NSM** J F GOWEN
KNOCKANE (no dedication) *see* Kilcolman w Kiltallagh, Killorglin, Knockane etc *L & K*
KNOCKANEY (St John) *see* Adare and Kilmallock w Kilpeacon, Croom etc *L & K*
KNOCKBREDA (no dedication) *D & D* **I** P F PATTERSON, **C** B R MARTIN
KNOCKBRIDE (no dedication) *see* Bailieborough w Knockbride, Shercock and Mullagh *K, E & A*
KNOCKLOUGHRIM *see* Desertmartin w Termoneeny *D & R*
KNOCKMOURNE (no dedication) *see* Fermoy Union *C, C & R*
KNOCKNAGONEY (Annunciation) *D & D* **Bp's C** D L BROWN
KNOCKNAMUCKLEY (St Matthias) *D & D* **I** B T BLACOE
KNOCKNAREA (St Anne) *see* Sligo w Knocknarea and Rosses Pt *K, E & A*
KYLE (no dedication) *see* Roscrea w Kyle, Bourney and Corbally *L & K*
LACK (no dedication) *Clogh* **I** W A CAPPER
LAGHEY (no dedication) *see* Donegal w Killymard, Lough Eske and Laghey *D & R*
LAMBEG (no dedication) *Conn* **I** K A MCREYNOLDS
LANESBOROUGH *see* Roscommon w Donamon, Rathcline, Kilkeevin etc *K, E & A*
LANGFIELD, LOWER (no dedication) *see* Drumclamph w Lower and Upper Langfield *D & R*
LANGFIELD, UPPER (no dedication) *as above*
LARAGH (St John) *see* Rathdrum w Glenealy, Derralossary and Laragh *D & G*
LARAH AND LAVEY (no dedication) *see* Drung w Castleterra, Larah and Lavey etc *K, E & A*
LARNE AND INVER (St Cedma) *Conn* **I** S B FORDE, **C** M W J LONEY, **NSM** R A KER
LAVEY *see* Drung w Castleterra, Larah and Lavey etc *K, E & A*
LAYDE (no dedication) *see* Ardclinis and Tickmacrevan w Layde and Cushendun *Conn*
LEA (no dedication) *see* Portarlington w Cloneyhurke and Lea *M & K*
LEAP *see* Ross Union *C, C & R*
LEARMOUNT (no dedication) *see* Cumber Upper w Learmount *D & R*
LEATBEG (no dedication) *see* Clondevaddock w Portsalon and Leatbeg *D & R*
LECALE Group *see* Down Cathl *D & D*

LECALE Group: Saul, Ardglass, Dunsford, Ballyculter and Kilclief *D & D* **I** T H HULL, **Bp's C** S M J DICKSON, **NSM** G J SAVAGE
LECKPATRICK (St Patrick) w Dunnalong *D & R* **I** E G BUNTING
LEESON PARK (Christ Church) *see* Dublin St Bart w Leeson Park *D & G*
LEIGHLIN (Catherdal of St Laserian) w Grange Sylvae, Shankill, Clonagoose and Gowran *C & O* **I** *vacant*
LEIXLIP (St Mary) *see* Lucan w Leixlip *D & G*
LESKINFERE (no dedication) *see* Gorey w Kilnahue, Leskinfere and Ballycanew *C & O*
LETTERKENNY *see* Conwal Union w Gartan *D & R*
LETTERMACAWARD (no dedication) *see* Ardara w Glencolumbkille, Inniskeel etc *D & R*
LICKMOLASSY *see* Clonfert Gp *L & K*
LIFFORD *see* Raphoe w Raymochy and Clonleigh *D & R*
LIMAVADY *see* Drumachose *D & R*
LIMAVADY *see* Tamlaghtfinlagan w Myroe *D & R*
LIMERICK CITY (Cathedral of St Mary) (St Michael) *L & K* **I** J M G SIRR
LISBELLAW (no dedication) *Clogh* **I** *vacant*
LISBURN (Christ Church) *Conn* **I** E P DUNDAS, **C** D M MATCHETT
LISBURN (Christ Church Cathedral) *Conn* **I** W S WRIGHT, **C** K D MCGRATH
LISBURN (St Paul) *Conn* **I** J I CARSON
LISLIMNAGHAN (Holy Trinity) *see* Cappagh w Lislimnaghan *D & R*
LISMORE (Cathedral of St Carthage) w Cappoquin, Kilwatermoy, Dungarvan, Kilrossanty, Stradbally and Kilmacthomas *C & O* **I** W BEARE
LISNADILL (St John) w Kildarton *Arm* **I** M C KENNEDY
LISNASKEA (Holy Trinity) *Clogh* **I** S A CROWTHER
LISS (no dedication) *see* Clara w Liss, Moate and Clonmacnoise *M & K*
LISSADELL (no dedication) *see* Drumcliffe w Lissadell and Munninane *K, E & A*
LISSAN (no dedication) *Arm* **I** R H BOYD
LISTOWEL *see* Tralee w Kilmoyley, Ballymacelligott etc *L & K*
LITTLE ISLAND (St Lappan) *see* Rathcooney Union *C, C & R*
LITTLETON (no dedication) *see* Kilcooley w Littleon, Crohane and Fertagh *C & O*
LOCKEEN (no dedication) *see* Birr w Lorrha, Dorrha and Lockeen *L & K*
LONDONDERRY *see* Templemore *D & R*
LONDONDERRY (Christ Church) *D & R* **P-in-c** W C MCNEE
LONDONDERRY (St Augustine) *D & R* **I** P L STOREY
LONGFORD *see* Templemichael w Clongish, Clooncumber etc *K, E & A*
LORRHA (St Ruadhan) *see* Birr w Lorrha, Dorrha and Lockeen *L & K*
LORUM (no dedication) *see* Dunleckney w Nurney, Lorum and Kiltennel *C & O*
LOUGH ESKE (Christ Church) *see* Donegal w Killymard, Lough Eske and Laghey *D & R*
LOUGHBRICKLAND *see* Aghaderg w Donaghmore and Scarva *D & D*
LOUGHCREW *see* Castlepollard and Oldcastle w Loughcrew etc *M & K*
LOUGHGALL (St Luke) w Grange *Arm* **I** G P MCADAM
LOUGHGILLY (St Patrick) w Clare *Arm* **I** J L WILSON
LOUGHGUILE (All Saints) *see* Armoy w Loughguile and Drumtullagh *Conn*
LOUGHINISLAND (no dedication) *D & D* **Bp's C** S M J DICKSON
LUCAN (St Andrew) w Leixlip *D & G* **I** J S PEOPLES, **C** S L HALES
LUGGACURREN (Resurrection) *see* Stradbally w Ballintubbert, Coraclone etc *C & O*
LURGAN (Christ the Redeemer) (St Andrew) *D & D* **I** M J ELLIOTT, **C** W J C ORR
LURGAN (no dedication) w Billis, Killinkere and Munterconnaught *K, E & A* **I** C W L MCCAULEY
LURGAN (St John the Evangelist) *D & D* **I** J M WHITE
LURGANBOY (Chapel of Ease) *see* Clooncläre w Killasnett, Lurganboy and Drumlease *K, E & A*
MACOSQUIN *see* Camus-juxta-Bann *D & R*
MACREDDIN *see* Castlemacadam w Ballinaclash, Aughrim etc *D & G*
MACROOM *see* Moviddy Union *C, C & R*
MAGHERA (no dedication) *see* Kilmegan w Maghera *D & D*
MAGHERA (St Lurach) w Killelagh *D & R* **I** R S MILLER
MAGHERACLOONE (St Molua) *see* Carrickmacross w Magheracloone *Clogh*
MAGHERACROSS (no dedication) *Clogh* **I** C J MATCHETT
MAGHERACULMONEY (St Mary) *Clogh* **I** W E MCGIRR
MAGHERADROLL (no dedication) *D & D* **I** W W RUSSELL
MAGHERAFELT (St Swithin) *Arm* **I** T SCOTT
MAGHERAGALL (no dedication) *Conn* **I** N J DARK
MAGHERAHAMLET (no dedication) *see* Annahilt w Magherahamlet *D & D*
MAGHERALIN (Holy and Undivided Trinity) w Dollingstown *D & D* **I** G A HARRON
MAGHERALLY (St John the Evangelist) w Annaclone *D & D* **I** E HANNA
MAGORBAN (no dedication) *see* Cashel w Magorban, Tipperary, Clonbeg etc *C & O*
MAGOURNEY *see* Carrigrohane Union *C, C & R*
MAGUIRESBRIDGE (Christ Church) w Derrybrusk *Clogh* **I** *vacant* (028) 6772 1250
MALAHIDE (St Andrew) w Balgriffin *D & G* **I** N E C GAMBLE
MALIN *see* Moville w Greencastle, Donagh, Cloncha etc *D & R*
MALLOW (St James) w Doneraile and Castletownroche *C, C & R* **I** R G KINGSTON
MALLUSK (St Brigid) *Conn* **I** I C BALLENTINE
MALONE *see* Belfast Malone St Jo *Conn*
MALONE, UPPER *see* Belfast Upper Malone (Epiphany) *Conn*
MANORCUNNINGHAM *see* Raphoe w Raymochy and Clonleigh *D & R*
MANORHAMILTON *see* Clooncläre w Killasnett, Lurganboy and Drumlease *K, E & A*
MARKETHILL (no dedication) *see* Mullabrack w Markethill and Kilcluney *Arm*
MARMULLANE (St Mary) *see* Douglas Union w Frankfield *C, C & R*
MARYBOROUGH (St Peter) w Dysart Enos and Ballyfin *C & O* **I** H A DUNGAN, **P-in-c** N G GILLESPIE
MAYNE *see* Castlepollard and Oldcastle w Loughcrew etc *M & K*
MAYNOOTH (St Mary) *see* Dunboyne Union *M & K*
MAYO (no dedication) *see* Killeshin w Cloydagh and Killabban *C & O*
MEALIFFE *see* Templemore w Thurles and Kilfithmone *C & O*
MEENGLASS (Ascension) *see* Stranorlar w Meenglas and Kilteevogue *D & R*
MEVAGH (Holy Trinity) w Glenalla *D & R* **I** *vacant*
MIDDLE CHURCH (no dedication) *see* Ballinderry *Conn*
MIDDLETOWN (St John) *see* Tynan w Middletown and Aghavilly *Arm*
MIDLETON (St John the Baptist) *see* Cloyne Union *C, C & R*
MILLISLE (St Patrick) *see* Carrowdore w Millisle *D & D*
MILLTOWN *see* Kilcolman w Kiltallagh, Killorglin, Knockane etc *L & K*
MILLTOWN (St Andrew) *Arm* **I** G W MACARTNEY
MILLTOWN (St Philip) *see* Dublin Sandford w Milltown *D & G*
MILLTOWN MALBAY *see* Drumcliffe w Kilnasoolagh *L & K*
MITCHELSTOWN *see* Fermoy Union *C, C & R*
MOATE (St Mary) *see* Clara w Liss, Moate and Clonmacnoise *M & K*
MOHILL (St Mary) w Farnaught, Aughavas, Oughteragh, Kiltubride and Drumreilly *K, E & A* **I** F W ATKINS, **NSM** C LINDSAY
MOIRA (St John) *D & D* **I** T R WEST, **C** J M MEGARRELL
MONAGHAN (St Patrick) w Tydavnet and Kilmore *Clogh* **I** I T H BERRY, **C** W H BLAIR
MONAMOLIN (St Molig) *see* Ardamine w Kiltennel, Glascarrig etc *C & O*
MONART (St Peter) *see* Enniscorthy w Clone, Clonmore, Monart etc *C & O*
MONASTEREVAN (St John the Evangelist) w Nurney and Rathdaire *M & K* **I** L T C STEVENSON
MONASTERORIS (no dedication) *see* Clonsast w Rathangan, Thomastown etc *M & K*
MONELLAN (St Anne) *see* Convoy w Monellan and Donaghmore *D & R*
MONEYMORE *see* Desertlyn w Ballyeglish *Arm*
MONEYREAGH (no dedication) *see* Orangefield w Moneyreagh *D & D*
MONKSTOWN (Good Shepherd) *Conn* **Bp's C** G R SHAW
MONKSTOWN (no dedication) *D & G* **I** K DALTON, **C** D MCCALLIG
MONKSTOWN (St John) *see* Carrigaline Union *C, C & R*
MOSSLEY (Holy Spirit) *Conn* **I** N R CUTCLIFFE, **NSM** R E COTTER
MOSTRIM (St John) w Granard, Clonbroney, Killoe, Rathaspeck and Streete *K, E & A* **P-in-c** J M CATTERALL
MOTHEL (no dedication) *see* Castlecomer w Colliery Ch, Mothel and Bilbo *C & O*

MOUNT MERRION (Pentecost) *D & D* **Bp's C** B E BIRD
MOUNT MERRION (St Thomas) *see* Dublin Mt Merrion *D & G*
MOUNT NUGENT (St Bride) *see* Castlepollard and Oldcastle w Loughcrew etc *M & K*
MOUNTCHARLES (Christ Church) *see* Inver w Mountcharles, Killaghtee and Killybegs *D & R*
MOUNTFIELD (no dedication) *see* Drumragh w Mountfield *D & R*
MOUNTMELLICK (St Paul) w Coolbanagher, Rosenallis and Clonaslee *M & K* **I** O M R DONOHOE
MOUNTRATH *see* Clonenagh w Offerlane, Borris-in-Ossory etc *C & O*
MOUNTSHANNON *see* Killaloe w Stradbally *L & K*
MOVIDDY (no dedication), Kilbonane, Kilmurry, Templemartin and Macroom *C, C & R* **I** R E B WHITE
MOVILLA (no dedication) *D & D* **I** K HIGGINS
MOVILLE (St Columb) w Greencastle, Donagh, Cloncha and Culdaff *D & R* **I** H GILMORE
MOY (St James) w Charlemont *Arm* **I** D I GILLESPIE
MOYBOLOGUE *see* Kingscourt w Syddan *M & K*
MOYDOW (no dedication) *see* Ardagh w Tashinny, Shrule and Kilcommick *K, E & A*
MOYGASHEL (no dedication) *see* Drumglass w Moygashel *Arm*
MOYGLARE (All Saints) *see* Dunboyne Union *M & K*
MOYLISCAR *see* Mullingar, Portnashangan, Moyliscar, Kilbixy etc *M & K*
MOYNALTY (St Mary) *see* Kells Union *M & K*
MOYNE (St John) *see* Kiltegan w Hacketstown, Clonmore and Moyne *C & O*
MOYNTAGHS *see* Ardmore w Craigavon *D & D*
MOYRUS *see* Omey w Ballynakill, Errislannan and Roundstone *T, K & A*
MUCKAMORE (St Jude) (St Matthias) *Conn* **I** B S CADDEN
MUCKNOE (St Maeldoid) *see* Ballybay w Mucknoe and Clontibret *Clogh*
MUCKROSS (Holy Trinity) *see* Killarney w Aghadoe and Muckross *L & K*
MUCKROSS (St John) *see* Drumkeeran w Templecarne and Muckross *Clogh*
MUFF (no dedication) *see* Culmore w Muff and Belmont *D & R*
MULHUDDART (St Thomas) *see* Castleknock and Mulhuddart, w Clonsilla *D & G*
MULLABRACK (no dedication) w Markethill and Kilcluney *Arm* **I** N J HUGHES
MULLAGH (no dedication) *see* Bailieborough w Knockbride, Shercock and Mullagh *K, E & A*
MULLAGHDUN (no dedication) *see* Cleenish w Mullaghdun *Clogh*
MULLAGHFAD (All Saints) *see* Aghalurcher w Tattykeeran, Cooneen etc *Clogh*
MULLAGLASS (St Luke) *see* Camlough w Mullaglass *Arm*
MULLAVILLY (no dedication) *Arm* **I** B J HARPER
MULLINACUFF (no dedication) *see* Tullow w Shillelagh, Aghold and Mullinacuff *C & O*
MULLINGAR (All Saints) w Portnashangan, Moyliscar, Kilbixy, Almoritia, Killucan, Clonard and Castlelost *M & K* **I** D P R CARMODY, **NSM** D HUTTON-BURY, J WYNNE
MULRANKIN (St David) *see* Kilscoran w Killinick and Mulrankin *C & O*
MUNNINANE (St Kevin) *see* Drumcliffe w Lissadell and Munninane *K, E & A*
MUNTERCONNAUGHT (no dedication) *see* Lurgan w Billis, Killinkere and Munterconnaught *K, E & A*
MURRAGH (no dedication) *see* Kinneigh Union *C, C & R*
MYROE (St John) *see* Tamlaghtfinlagan w Myroe *D & R*
MYROSS *see* Ross Union *C, C & R*
MYSHALL (Christ the Redeemer) *see* Fenagh w Myshall, Aghade and Ardoyne *C & O*
NAAS (St David) w Kill and Rathmore *M & K* **I** M G WOODERSON
NARRAGHMORE (Holy Saviour) and Timolin w Castledermot and Kinneagh *D & G* **I** K V KENNERLEY
NAVAN (St Mary) w Kentstown, Tara, Slane, Painestown and Stackallen *M & K* **I** J D M CLARKE
NENAGH (St Mary) w Ballymackey, Templederry and Killodiernan *L & K* **I** M G ROWLEY-BROOKE, **NSM** P E HANNA
NEWBLISS (no dedication) *see* Currin w Drum and Newbliss *Clogh*
NEWBRIDGE (St Patrick) w Carnalway and Kilcullen *M & K* **I** J J MARSDEN
NEWCASTLE (no dedication) w Newtownmountkennedy and Calary *D & G* **I** W L BENNETT
NEWCASTLE (St John) *D & D* **I** I M ELLIS
NEWCASTLE-LYONS (no dedication) *see* Celbridge w Straffan and Newcastle-Lyons *D & G*
NEWCESTOWN *see* Kinneigh Union *C, C & R*
NEWMARKET-ON-FERGUS *see* Drumcliffe w Kilnasoolagh *L & K*
NEWRY (St Mary) (St Patrick) *D & D* **I** K E SUTTON
NEWTOWNARDS (St Mark) *D & D* **I** K J SMYTH, **C** I G DELAMERE
NEWTOWNBARRY *see* Bunclody w Kildavin, Clonegal and Kilrush *C & O*
NEWTOWNBUTLER *see* Galloon w Drummully and Sallaghy *Clogh*
NEWTOWNCROMMELIN (no dedication) *see* Skerry w Rathcavan and Newtowncrommelin *Conn*
NEWTOWNCUNNINGHAM (All Saints) *see* Taughboyne, Craigadooish, Newtowncunningham etc *D & R*
NEWTOWNFERTULLAGH *see* Tullamore w Durrow, Newtownfertullagh, Rahan etc *M & K*
NEWTOWNFORBES *see* Templemichael w Clongish, Clooncumber etc *K, E & A*
NEWTOWNGORE (no dedication) *see* Kildallan w Newtowngore and Corrawallen *K, E & A*
NEWTOWNHAMILTON (St John) w Ballymoyer and Belleck *Arm* **I** *vacant*
NEWTOWNMOUNTKENNEDY (St Matthew) *see* Newcastle w Newtownmountkennedy and Calary *D & G*
NEWTOWNSAVILLE (no dedication) *see* Augher w Newtownsaville and Eskrahoole *Clogh*
NEWTOWNSTEWART *see* Ardstraw w Baronscourt, Badoney Lower etc *D & R*
NOHOVAL (no dedication) *see* Templebreedy w Tracton and Nohoval *C, C & R*
NURNEY (no dedication) *see* Monasterevan w Nurney and Rathdaire *M & K*
NURNEY (St John) *see* Dunleckney w Nurney, Lorum and Kiltennel *C & O*
OFFERLANE (no dedication) *see* Clonenagh w Offerlane, Borris-in-Ossory etc *C & O*
OLD LEIGHLIN *see* Leighlin w Grange Sylvae, Shankill etc *C & O*
OLDCASTLE (St Bride) *see* Castlepollard and Oldcastle w Loughcrew etc *M & K*
OMAGH *see* Drumragh w Mountfield *D & R*
OMEY (Christ Church) w Ballynakill, Errislannan and Roundstone *T, K & A* **I** A M A PREVITE
ORANGEFIELD (St John the Evangelist) w Moneyreagh *D & D* **I** W J R LAVERTY, **NSM** I M FRAZER
OSSORY *see* Kilcooley w Littleon, Crohane and Fertagh *C & O*
OUGHTERAGH (no dedication) *see* Mohill w Farnaught, Aughavas, Oughteragh etc *K, E & A*
OUGHTERARD *see* Galway w Kilcummin *T, K & A*
PACKANE *see* Nenagh *L & K*
PAINESTOWN *see* Navan w Kentstown, Tara, Slane, Painestown etc *M & K*
PALLASKENRY *see* Rathkeale w Askeaton, Kilcornan and Kilnaughtin *L & K*
PASSAGE WEST *see* Douglas Union w Frankfield *C, C & R*
PAULSTOWN *see* Leighlin w Grange Sylvae, Shankill etc *C & O*
PETTIGO *see* Drumkeeran w Templecarne and Muckross *Clogh*
PILTOWN *see* Fiddown w Clonegam, Guilcagh and Kilmeaden *C & O*
POMEROY (no dedication) *Arm* **NSM** W J A DAWSON
PORT LAOIS *see* Maryborough w Dysart Enos and Ballyfin *C & O*
PORTADOWN (St Columba) *Arm* **I** W M ADAIR, **C** J MCCLENAGHAN
PORTADOWN (St Mark) *Arm* **I** J N T CAMPBELL, **C** R E JACKSON, M T KINGSTON
PORTAFERRY *see* Ballyphilip w Ardquin *D & D*
PORTARLINGTON (St Paul) w Cloneyhurke and Lea *M & K* **I** L T C STEVENSON, **NSM** H M SCULLY
PORTGLENONE (no dedication) *see* Ahoghill w Portglenone *Conn*
PORTLAOISE *see* Maryborough w Dysart Enos and Ballyfin *C & O*
PORTLAW *see* Fiddown w Clonegam, Guilcagh and Kilmeaden *C & O*
PORTNASHANGAN *see* Mullingar, Portnashangan, Moyliscar, Kilbixy etc *M & K*
PORTRUSH *see* Ballywillan *Conn*
PORTSALON (All Saints) *see* Clondevaddock w Portsalon and Leatbeg *D & R*
PORTSTEWART *see* Agherton *Conn*
PORTUMNA (Christ Church) *see* Clonfert Gp *L & K*

POWERSCOURT (St Patrick) w Kilbride *D & G*
I R B ROUNTREE, **NSM** H E A LEW
PREBAN (St John) *see* Crosspatrick Gp *C & O*
RAHAN *see* Clonsast w Rathangan, Thomastown etc *M & K*
RAHAN (St Carthach) *see* Tullamore w Durrow, Newtownfertullagh, Rahan etc *M & K*
RAHENY (All Saints) w Coolock *D & G* **I** J T CARROLL
RALOO (no dedication) *see* Glynn w Raloo *Conn*
RAMELTON *see* Tullyaughnish w Kilmacrennan and Killygarvan *D & R*
RAMOAN (St James) w Ballycastle and Culfeightrin *Conn*
I D M PALMER
RANDALSTOWN *see* Drummaul w Duneane and Ballyscullion *Conn*
RAPHOE (Cathedral of St Eunan) w Raymochy and Clonleigh *D & R* **I** J HAY
RASHARKIN (St Andrew) *see* Ballymoney w Finvoy and Rasharkin *Conn*
RATHANGAN (no dedication) *see* Clonsast w Rathangan, Thomastown etc *M & K*
RATHASPECK (St Thomas) *see* Mostrim w Granard, Clonbroney, Killoe etc *K, E & A*
RATHBARRON *see* Achonry w Tubbercurry and Killoran *T, K & A*
RATHCAVAN (no dedication) *see* Skerry w Rathcavan and Newtowncrommelin *Conn*
RATHCLAREN (Holy Trinity) *see* Bandon Union *C, C & R*
RATHCLINE (no dedication) *see* Roscommon w Donamon, Rathcline, Kilkeevin etc *K, E & A*
RATHCOOLE (no dedication) *see* Clondalkin w Rathcoole *D & G*
RATHCOOLE (St Comgall) *Conn* **I** C D BELL
RATHCOONEY (St Mary and All Saints) w Little Island and Carrigtwohill *C, C & R* **I** D J OWEN
RATHCOR (no dedication) *see* Ballymascanlan w Creggan and Rathcor *Arm*
RATHCORE (St Ultan) *see* Rathmolyon w Castlerickard, Rathcore and Agher *M & K*
RATHDAIRE (Ascension) *see* Monasterevan w Nurney and Rathdaire *M & K*
RATHDOWNEY (no dedication) w Castlefleming, Donaghmore, Rathsaran and Aghavoe *C & O* **I** J G MURRAY
RATHDRUM (St Saviour) w Glenealy, Derralossary and Laragh *D & G* **C** O E HENDERSON
RATHFARNHAM *see* Dublin Rathfarnham *D & G*
RATHFRILAND *see* Drumgath w Drumgooland and Clonduff *D & D*
RATHGAR *see* Dublin Zion Ch *D & G*
RATHKEALE (Holy Trinity) w Askeaton, Foynes, Kilcornan and Kilnaughtin *L & K* **NSM** W M ROMER
RATHLIN (St Thomas) *see* Ballintoy w Rathlin and Dunseverick *Conn*
RATHMICHAEL (no dedication) *D & G* **I** F C APPELBE
RATHMINES *see* Dublin Rathmines w Harold's Cross *D & G*
RATHMOLYON (St Michael and All Angels) w Castlerickard, Rathcore and Agher *M & K* **P-in-c** D P R CARMODY
RATHMORE (St Columbkille) *see* Naas w Kill and Rathmore *M & K*
RATHMULLAN *see* Tullyaughnish w Kilmacrennan and Killygarvan *D & R*
RATHMULLAN (no dedication) w Tyrella *D & D*
Bp's C S M J DICKSON, **NSM** M S WALSHE
RATHOWEN *see* Mostrim w Granard, Clonbroney, Killoe etc *K, E & A*
RATHSARAN (no dedication) *see* Rathdowney w Castlefleming, Donaghmore etc *C & O*
RATHVILLY (St Mary) *see* Baltinglass w Ballynure etc *C & O*
RAYMOCHY (no dedication) *see* Raphoe w Raymochy and Clonleigh *D & R*
RAYMUNTERDONEY (St Paul) *see* Dunfanaghy, Raymunterdoney and Tullaghbegley *D & R*
REDCROSS (Holy Trinity) *see* Dunganstown w Redcross and Conary *D & G*
REDHILLS *see* Drung w Castleterra, Larah and Lavey etc *K, E & A*
RICHHILL (St Matthew) *Arm* **I** D COE
RIVERSTOWN *see* Taunagh w Kilmactranny, Ballysumaghan etc *K, E & A*
ROCHFORT BRIDGE *see* Mullingar, Portnashangan, Moyliscar, Kilbixy etc *M & K*
ROCKCORRY (no dedication) *see* Ematris w Rockcorry, Aghabog and Aughnamullan *Clogh*
ROSCOMMON (St Colman) w Donamon, Rathcline, Kilkeevin, Kiltullagh and Tybohine *K, E & A* **I** *vacant* (00353) (903) 26230
ROSCREA (St Cronan) w Kyle, Bourney and Corbally *L & K*
I J A A CONDELL, **NSM** L W RUDDOCK
ROSENALLIS (St Brigid) *see* Mountmellick w Coolbanagher, Rosenallis etc *M & K*
ROSKELTON (no dedication) *see* Clonenagh w Offerlane, Borris-in-Ossory etc *C & O*
ROSS (Cathedral of St Fachtna) w Kilmacabea, Myross, Kilfaughnabeg and Castleventry *C, C & R* **I** C L PETERS
ROSS, NEW (St Mary) w OLD (St Mary), Whitechurch, Fethard, Killesk and Tintern *C & O* **I** P G MOONEY
ROSSCARBERY *see* Ross Union *C, C & R*
ROSSDROIT (St Peter) *see* Killanne w Killegney, Rossdroit and Templeshanbo *C & O*
ROSSES POINT (no dedication) *see* Sligo w Knocknarea and Rosses Pt *K, E & A*
ROSSINVER (no dedication) *see* Killinagh w Kiltyclogher and Innismagrath *K, E & A*
ROSSMIRE *see* Lismore w Cappoquin, Kilwatermoy, Dungarvan etc *C & O*
ROSSNAKILL *see* Clondevaddock w Portsalon and Leatbeg *D & R*
ROSSNOWLAGH (St John) *see* Kilbarron w Rossnowlagh and Drumholm *D & R*
ROSSORY (no dedication) *Clogh* **I** C T PRINGLE,
NSM F I NIXON
ROSTREVOR *see* Kilbroney *D & D*
ROUNDSTONE (no dedication) *see* Omey w Ballynakill, Errislannan and Roundstone *T, K & A*
RUNCURRAN *see* Kinsale Union *C, C & R*
RUSHBROOKE *see* Clonmel Union *C, C & R*
RUTLAND *see* Carlow w Urglin and Staplestown *C & O*
RYNAGH *see* Clonfert Gp *L & K*
SAINTFIELD (no dedication) *D & D* **I** C J POLLOCK
SALLAGHY (no dedication) *see* Galloon w Drummully and Sallaghy *Clogh*
SANDFORD *see* Dublin Sandford w Milltown *D & G*
SANDHILL *see* Sligo w Knocknarea and Rosses Pt *K, E & A*
SANDYMOUNT *see* Dublin Sandymount *D & G*
SANTRY *see* Dublin Santry w Glasnevin and Finglas *D & G*
SAUL (St Patrick) *see* Lecale Gp *D & D*
SCARVA (St Matthew) *see* Aghaderg w Donaghmore and Scarva *D & D*
SCHULL (Holy Trinity) *see* Kilmoe Union *C, C & R*
SCOTSHOUSE *see* Currin w Drum and Newbliss *Clogh*
SEAFORDE *see* Lecale Gp *D & D*
SEAGOE (St Gobhan) *D & D* **C** P JACK
SEAPATRICK (Holy Trinity) (St Patrick) *D & D* **I** W J SCOTT,
C A GALLIGAN
SEIRKIERAN (St Kieran) *see* Clonenagh w Offerlane, Borris-in-Ossory etc *C & O*
SESKINORE (no dedication) *see* Clogherny w Seskinore and Drumnakilly *Arm*
SEYMOUR HILL *see* Kilmakee *Conn*
SHANDON (St Ann) *see* Cork St Ann's Union *C, C & R*
SHANKILL *see* Belfast St Matt *Conn*
SHANKILL *see* Lurgan Ch the Redeemer *D & D*
SHANKILL (St John) *see* Leighlin w Grange Sylvae, Shankill etc *C & O*
SHANNON (Christ Church) *see* Drumcliffe w Kilnasoolagh *L & K*
SHERCOCK (no dedication) *see* Bailieborough w Knockbride, Shercock and Mullagh *K, E & A*
SHILLELAGH (no dedication) *see* Tullow w Shillelagh, Aghold and Mullinacuff *C & O*
SHINRONE (St Mary) w Aghancon, Dunkerrin and Kinnitty *L & K* **I** A MINION, **NSM** J J WHITE SPUNNER
SHRULE (no dedication) *see* Ardagh w Tashinny, Shrule and Kilcommick *K, E & A*
SION MILLS (Good Shepherd) *see* Urney w Sion Mills *D & R*
SIXMILECROSS (St Michael) w Termonmaguirke *Arm*
I R C LOGUE
SIXTOWNS (St Anne) *see* Kilcronaghan w Draperstown and Sixtowns *D & R*
SKERRIES *see* Holmpatrick w Balbriggan and Kenure *D & G*
SKERRY (St Patrick) w Rathcavan and Newtowncrommelin *Conn* **I** J F A BOND
SKIBBEREEN *see* Abbeystrewry Union *C, C & R*
SKREEN (no dedication) w Kilmacshalgan and Dromard *T, K & A* **I** A M O FERGUSON
SLANE (St Patrick) *see* Navan w Kentstown, Tara, Slane, Painestown etc *M & K*
SLAVIN (no dedication) *see* Garrison w Slavin and Belleek *Clogh*
SLIGO (Cathedral of St Mary and St John the Baptist) w Knocknarea and Rosses Point *K, E & A* **I** A WILLIAMS

SNEEM (Transfiguration) *see* Kenmare w Sneem, Waterville etc *L & K*
SPANISH POINT *see* Drumcliffe w Kilnasoolagh *L & K*
STACKALLEN *see* Navan w Kentstown, Tara, Slane, Painestown etc *M & K*
STAPLESTOWN (no dedication) *see* Carlow w Urglin and Staplestown *C & O*
STEWARTSTOWN *see* Brackaville w Donaghendry and Ballyclog *Arm*
STILLORGAN (St Brigid) w Blackrock *D & G* **I** I GALLAGHER, **C** A W MATCHETT, **NSM** R D MARSHALL
STONEYFORD (St John) *Conn* **Bp's C** A MALLON
STORMONT (St Molua) *D & D* **I** W D HUMPHRIES
STRABANE *see* Camus-juxta-Mourne *D & R*
STRADBALLY (All Saints) *see* Killaloe w Stradbally *L & K*
STRADBALLY (St James) *see* Lismore w Cappoquin, Kilwatermoy, Dungarvan etc *C & O*
STRADBALLY (St Patrick) w Ballintubbert, Coraclone, Timogue and Luggacurren *C & O* **I** N G GILLESPIE
STRAFFAN (no dedication) *see* Celbridge w Straffan and Newcastle-Lyons *D & G*
STRAID (no dedication) *T, K & A* **I** *vacant*
STRAND, NORTH (no dedication) *see* Dublin Drumcondra w N Strand *D & G*
STRANGFORD *see* Lecale Gp *D & D*
STRANORLAR (no dedication) w Meenglas and Kilteevogue *D & R* **C** J DEANE
STRATFORD-ON-SLANEY (St John the Baptist) *see* Baltinglass w Ballynure etc *C & O*
STRATHFOYLE (no dedication) *see* Clooney w Strathfoyle *D & R*
STREETE (no dedication) *see* Mostrim w Granard, Clonbroney, Killoe etc *K, E & A*
SUMMER COVE *see* Kinsale Union *C, C & R*
SWANLINBAR (St Augustine) w Tomregan, Kinawley, Drumlane and Templeport *K, E & A* **C** S G WILSON
SWATRAGH *see* Maghera w Killelagh *D & R*
SWORDS (St Columba) w Donabate and Kilsallaghan *D & G* **I** R W DEANE, **NSM** K E LONG
SYDDAN (St David) *see* Kingscourt w Syddan *M & K*
SYDENHAM *see* Belfast St Brendan *D & D*
TAGHMON (St Munn) w Horetown and Bannow *C & O* **I** *vacant*
TALLAGHT (St Maelruain) *D & G* **I** W R H DEVERELL, **NSM** A E J BENNETT
TAMLAGHT *see* Derryvullen S w Garvary *Clogh*
TAMLAGHT (St Luke) *see* Ballinderry, Tamlaght and Arboe *Arm*
TAMLAGHT O'CRILLY UPPER (no dedication) w LOWER (no dedication) *D & R* **I** R J STEWART
TAMLAGHTARD (St Gedanus) w Aghanloo *D & R* **I** I E DINSMORE
TAMLAGHTFINLAGAN (St Findlunganus) w Myroe *D & R* **I** H R GIVEN
TANEY (Christ Church) (St Nahi) *D & G* **I** W D SINNAMON, **C** L J TANNER, B T DALY
TARA *see* Navan w Kentstown, Tara, Slane, Painestown etc *M & K*
TARBERT *see* Tralee w Kilmoyley, Ballymacelligott etc *L & K*
TARTARAGHAN (St Paul) w Diamond *Arm* **I** D HILLIARD
TASHINNY (no dedication) *see* Ardagh w Tashinny, Shrule and Kilcommick *K, E & A*
TATTYKEERAN (no dedication) *see* Aghalurcher w Tattykeeran, Cooneen etc *Clogh*
TAUGHBOYNE (St Baithan) w Craigadooish, Newtowncunningham and Killea *D & R* **I** D W T CROOKS
TAUNAGH (no dedication) w Kilmactranny, Ballysumaghan and Killery *K, E & A* **I** K A L BARRETT, **C** N H L REGAN
TEAMPOL-NA-MBOCHT (Altar) *see* Kilmoe Union *C, C & R*
TEMPLEBREEDY (Holy Trinity) w Tracton and Nohoval *C, C & R* **I** D R NUZUM, **NSM** H E A MINION
TEMPLECARNE (no dedication) *see* Drumkeeran w Templecarne and Muckross *Clogh*
TEMPLECORRAN (St John) *see* Kilroot and Templecorran *Conn*
TEMPLECRONE (St Crone) *see* Gweedore, Carrickfin and Templecrone *D & R*
TEMPLEDERRY (no dedication) *see* Nenagh *L & K*
TEMPLEHARRY (no dedication) *see* Cloughjordan w Borrisokane etc *L & K*
TEMPLEMARTIN (St Martin) *see* Moviddy Union *C, C & R*
TEMPLEMICHAEL (St John) w Clongish, Clooncumber, Killashee and Ballymacormack *K, E & A* **I** D A CATTERALL
TEMPLEMORE Londonderry (Cathedral of St Columb) *D & R* **I** W W MORTON
TEMPLEMORE (St Mary) w Thurles and Kilfithmone *C & O* **I** P M COLE-BAKER
TEMPLEPATRICK (St Patrick) w Donegore *Conn* **I** S A FIELDING
TEMPLEPORT (St Peter) *see* Swanlinbar w Tomregan, Kinawley, Drumlane etc *K, E & A*
TEMPLESCOBIN (St Paul) *see* Enniscorthy w Clone, Clonmore, Monart etc *C & O*
TEMPLESHANBO (St Colman) *see* Killanne w Killegney, Rossdroit and Templeshanbo *C & O*
TEMPLETRINE (no dedication) *see* Kinsale Union *C, C & R*
TEMPO (no dedication) and Clabby *Clogh* **I** M A ARMSTRONG
TERMONAMONGAN (St Bestius) *see* Derg w Termonamongan *D & R*
TERMONEENY (no dedication) *see* Desertmartin w Termoneeny *D & R*
TERMONFECKIN (St Feckin) *see* Drogheda w Ardee, Collon and Termonfeckin *Arm*
TERMONMAGUIRKE (St Columbkille) *see* Sixmilecross w Termonmaguirke *Arm*
THOMASTOWN (no dedication) *see* Clonsast w Rathangan, Thomastown etc *M & K*
THURLES (no dedication) *see* Templemore w Thurles and Kilfithmone *C & O*
TICKMACREVAN (St Patrick) *see* Ardclinis and Tickmacrevan w Layde and Cushendun *Conn*
TIMOGUE (St Mogue) *see* Stradbally w Ballintubbert, Coraclone etc *C & O*
TIMOLEAGUE (Ascension) *see* Kilgariffe Union *C, C & R*
TIMOLIN (St Mullin) *see* Narraghmore and Timolin w Castledermot etc *D & G*
TINTERN (St Mary) *see* New w Old Ross, Whitechurch, Fethard etc *C & O*
TIPPERARY (St Mary) *see* Cashel w Magorban, Tipperary, Clonbeg etc *C & O*
TOBERMORE *see* Kilcronaghan w Draperstown and Sixtowns *D & R*
TOMREGAN (no dedication) *see* Swanlinbar w Tomregan, Kinawley, Drumlane etc *K, E & A*
TOOMBE (St Catherine) *see* Ferns w Kilbride, Toombe, Kilcormack etc *C & O*
TOOMNA (no dedication) *see* Kiltoghart w Drumshambo, Annaduff and Kilronan *K, E & A*
TOORMORE *see* Kilmoe Union *C, C & R*
TRACTON *see* Templebreedy w Tracton and Nohoval *C, C & R*
TRALEE (St John the Evangelist) w Kilmoyley, Ballymacelligott, Ballyseedy, Listowel and Ballybunnion *L & K* **I** R WARREN, **NSM** M J HANLEY
TRAMORE *see* Waterford w Killea, Drumcannon and Dunhill *C & O*
TRILLICK (Christ Church) *see* Kilskeery w Trillick *Clogh*
TRIM (Cathedral of St Patrick) and Athboy Group, The *M & K* **I** R W JONES
TRORY (St Michael) w Killadeas *Clogh* **I** V E S MCKEON
TUAM (Cathedral of St Mary) w Cong and Aasleagh *T, K & A* **I** A J GRIMASON, **C** M RYAN
TUAMGRANEY (St Cronan) *see* Killaloe w Stradbally *L & K*
TUBBERCURRY (St George) *see* Achonry w Tubbercurry and Killoran *T, K & A*
TUBRID *see* Drumkeeran w Templecarne and Muckross *Clogh*
TULLAGH (no dedication) *see* Abbeystrewry Union *C, C & R*
TULLAGHBEGLEY (St Ann) *see* Dunfanaghy, Raymunterdoney and Tullaghbegley *D & R*
TULLAGHMELAN (no dedication) *see* Clonmel w Innislounagh, Tullaghmelan etc *C & O*
TULLAMORE (St Catherine) w Durrow, Newtownfertullagh, Rahan, Tyrellspass and Killoughy *M & K* **I** G G FIELD
TULLANISKIN (Holy Trinity) w Clonoe *Arm* **I** E M CULBERTSON
TULLOW (no dedication) *D & G* **I** C W BRYAN
TULLOW (St Columba) w Shillelagh, Aghold and Mullinacuff *C & O* **I** W J RITCHIE
TULLYAUGHNISH (St Paul) w Kilmacrennan and Killygarvan *D & R* **I** *vacant*
TULLYLISH (All Saints) *D & D* **I** A YOUNG
TULLYNAKILL (no dedication) *see* Killinchy w Kilmood and Tullynakill *D & D*
TUNNY (St Andrew) *see* Glenavy w Tunny and Crumlin *Conn*
TURLOUGH (no dedication) *see* Aughaval w Achill, Knappagh, Dugort etc *T, K & A*
TYBOHINE (no dedication) *see* Roscommon w Donamon, Rathcline, Kilkeevin etc *K, E & A*
TYDAVNET (St Davnet) *see* Monaghan w Tydavnet and Kilmore *Clogh*

TYHOLLAND (St Sillian) *see* Donagh w Tyholland and Errigal Truagh *Clogh*
TYNAN (St Vindic) w Middletown and Aghavilly *Arm* **I** W B PAINE
TYRELLA (St John) *see* Rathmullan w Tyrella *D & D*
TYRELLSPASS (St Sinian) *see* Tullamore w Durrow, Newtownfertullagh, Rahan etc *M & K*
UPPER DONAGHMORE (St Patrick) *see* Donaghmore w Upper Donaghmore *Arm*
URGLIN (no dedication) *see* Carlow w Urglin etc *C & O*
URNEY (Christ Church) w Sion Mills *D & R* **I** D SKUCE
URNEY (no dedication) w Denn and Derryheen *K, E & A* **I** M R LIDWILL, **NSM** R W STAFFORD
VALENTIA (St John the Baptist) *see* Kenmare w Sneem, Waterville etc *L & K*
VIRGINIA *see* Lurgan w Billis, Killinkere and Munterconnaught *K, E & A*
WARINGSTOWN (Holy Trinity) *see* Donaghcloney w Waringstown *D & D*
WARRENPOINT (no dedication) *see* Clonallon w Warrenpoint *D & D*
WATERFORD (Christ Church Cathedral) w Killea, Drumcannon and Dunhill *C & O* **I** T R LESTER, **TV** M E JOHNSTON, **NSM** J E CROWLEY
WATERVILLE *see* Kenmare w Sneem, Waterville etc *L & K*
WESTPORT *see* Aughaval w Achill, Knappagh, Dugort etc *T, K & A*
WEXFORD (St Iberius) w Ardcolm and Killurin *C & O* **I** M P JANSSON, **NSM** R G GRAHAM
WHITECHURCH *see* Dublin Whitechurch *D & G*
WHITECHURCH (no dedication) *see* New w Old Ross, Whitechurch, Fethard etc *C & O*
WHITEGATE *see* Cloyne Union *C, C & R*
WHITEHEAD (St Patrick) and Islandmagee *Conn* **I** M F TAYLOR
WHITEHOUSE (St John) *Conn* **I** T A H FOSTER
WHITEROCK *see* Belfast Whiterock *Conn*
WICKLOW (no dedication) w Killiskey *D & G* **I** J P CLARKE, **C** P TAYLOR
WILLOWFIELD (no dedication) *D & D* **I** D A MCCLAY
WOODBURN (Holy Trinity) *Conn* **I** T A G MCCANN
WOODLAWN (no dedication) *see* Aughrim w Ballinasloe etc *L & K*
WOODSCHAPEL (St John) w Gracefield *Arm* **I** *vacant* (028) 7941 8230
YOUGHAL (St Mary's Collegiate) w Ardmore, Castlemartyr and Ballycotton *C, C & R* **I** A W MCCROSKERY
ZION *see* Dublin Zion Ch *D & G*

THE DIOCESE IN EUROPE

Diocesan Office, 14 Tufton Street, London SW1P 3QZ
Tel (020) 7898 1155 Fax 7898 1166
E-mail diocesan.office@europe.c-of-e.org.uk
Web site www.europe.anglican.org

ARCHDEACONS

1. Eastern P M S CURRAN
2. France A M G WELLS
3. Gibraltar A G WOODS
4. Italy and Malta A SIDDALL
5. North West Europe D W VAN LEEUWEN
6. Germany and Northern Europe *vacant*
7. Switzerland J R WILLIAMS

Further information may be obtained from the appropriate archdeacon (the archdeaconry number is given after the name of each country), and a detailed leaflet is obtainable from the diocesan office. Mission to Seafarers chaplaincies are listed separately at the end of the section.

Albania 1

Served from Athens (Greece)

Andorra 3

Served from Barcelona (Spain)

Armenia 1

YEREVAN *vacant*

Austria 1

VIENNA (Christ Church) **Chapl** P M S CURRAN, **Asst Chapl** A P HACKL, M HALCHUK

Azerbaijan 1

BAKU *vacant*

Belgium 5

ANTWERP (St Boniface) **Chapl** D W VAN LEEUWEN, **C** J M DAY
BRUGES (St Peter) *vacant*
BRUSSELS (Pro-Cathedral of the Holy Trinity) **C** I K MENSAH
CHARLEROI **P-in-c** J-P HERMAN
GHENT (St John) **P-in-c** P R TILLEY
KNOKKE (St George) **Chapl** D W VAN LEEUWEN
LEUVEN **Chapl** J-P HERMAN
LIÈGE **P-in-c** P M YIEND
OSTEND **C** J M DAY
TERVUREN **Chapl** H T COX, **Asst Chapl** S C RIORDAN
YPRES (St George) **P-in-c** R T JONES

Bosnia and Herzegovina 1

Served from Belgrade (Serbia and Montenegro)

Bulgaria 1

Served from Bucharest (Romania)

Croatia 1

Served from Vienna (Austria)

Czech Republic 1

PRAGUE **P-in-c** J D PHILPOTT

Denmark 6

COPENHAGEN (St Alban) w Aarhus *vacant*

Estonia 6

TALLINN (St Timothy and St Titus) **P-in-c** G PIIR

Finland 6

HELSINKI w Tampere **Chapl** R R J MORETON, **Asst Chapl** M K T PAJUNEN, **C** T ALASAUKKO-OJO

France 2

AIX-EN-PROVENCE *see* Marseille w Aix-en-Provence
ANNECY Served from Geneva (Switzerland)
AQUITAINE (Bordeaux, Chapdeuil, Limeuil, Monteton, Périgueux-Chancelade and Ribérac) **Chapl** M R SELMAN, **C** C GORDON-WALKER
ARRAS *see* Pas de Calais
BEAULIEU-SUR-MER (St Michael) **P-in-c** R T GREENACRE
BIARRITZ *vacant*
BORDEAUX *see* Aquitaine
BOULOGNE-SUR-MER *see* Pas de Calais
BRILLAC *see* Poitou-Charentes
BRITTANY (Guerlesquin, Nantes, Ploërmel) **P-in-c** R W FRAY
CAEN *see* Paris St George
CAHORS *see* Toulouse
CALAIS *see* Pas de Calais
CANNES (Holy Trinity) **Chapl** P J ANDERSON
CHANTILLY (St Peter) **Chapl** J A WILKINSON
CHAPDEUIL *see* Aquitaine
CHEVRY *see* Versailles w Chevry
COGNAC (Charente) *see* Poitou-Charentes
DINARD (St Bartholomew) **P-in-c** A C CHARTERS
FONTAINEBLEAU **Asst Chapl** D G NEWSTEAD
GRAND MADIEU *see* Poitou-Charentes
GRENOBLE **Chapl** S COFFIN
GUERLESQUIN *see* Brittany
HESDIN *see* Pas de Calais
LILLE (Christ Church) **P-in-c** R A FARRAR
LIMEUIL *see* Aquitaine
LORGUES *see* St Raphaël
LYON **Chapl** C J MARTIN
MAISONS-LAFFITTE (Holy Trinity) **Chapl** T WHITFIELD, **Asst Chapl** D M R FLACH
MARSEILLE (All Saints) w Aix-en-Provence *vacant*
MENTON (St John) *vacant*
MONTETON *see* Aquitaine
NANTES *see* Brittany
NICE (Holy Trinity) w Vence **Chapl** K J LETTS
PARIS (St George) **Chapl** D J HOUGHTON, **C** B SIXTUS
PARIS (St Michael) **Chapl** A M G WELLS, **Asst Chapl** T NORMAN, **C** J C LAMBERT, E O LABOUREL
PAS DE CALAIS (Arras, Boulogne-sur-Mer, Calais, Hesdin) **P-in-c** J D D PORTER
PAU (St Andrew) **P-in-c** J A HESLOP
PÉRIGUEUX-CHANCELADE *see* Aquitaine
PLOËRMEL *see* Brittany
POITOU-CHARENTES (Brillac, Cognac (Charente), Le Grand Madieu, Salles de Villefagnan, St Léger de la Martinière, St Médard de Magné and Vendée) **P-in-c** C M A HEPPER, **C** A B DAVIES, H L DOOR
PORT GRIMAUD *see* St Raphaël
ROUEN (All Saints) *vacant*
ST LÉGER DE LA MARTINIÈRE *see* Poitou-Charentes
ST MÉDARD DE MAGNÉ *see* Poitou-Charentes
ST RAPHAËL (St John the Evangelist) w Lorgues, Port Grimaud and Sellians **P-in-c** O B EATON
SALLES DE VILLEFAGNAN *see* Poitou-Charentes

SELLIANS *see* St Raphaël
STRASBOURG Asst Chapl J L MURRAY
TOULOUSE Chapl I L MORT
VENCE (St Hugh) *see* Nice w Vence
VENDÉE *see* Poitou-Charentes
VERSAILLES (St Mark) w Chevry
Chapl P H KENCHINGTON, **Asst Chapl** J K BROWN

Georgia 1

TBILISI *vacant*

Germany 6

BERLIN (St George) Chapl C W JAGE-BOWLER, **Asst Chapl** I K E AHRENS
BONN w Cologne Chapl I WRIGHT
DÜSSELDORF (Christ Church) *vacant*
FREIBURG-IM-BREISAU P-in-c R P STOCKITT
HAMBURG (St Thomas à Becket) Chapl R I S WHITE, **C** E G ANDERS
HEIDELBERG *vacant*
LEIPZIG Chapl G M REAKES-WILLIAMS
STUTTGART *vacant*

Gibraltar 3

GIBRALTAR (Cathedral of the Holy Trinity)
Chapl A G WOODS (Dean), **Asst Chapl** W H D WATSON

Greece 1

ATHENS, GREATER Sen Chapl M M BRADSHAW, **Asst Chapl** V C AGGETT, **Hon Asst Chapl** W J BURKE
CORFU (Holy Trinity) P-in-c P C OWEN

Hungary 1

BUDAPEST Chapl D MOSS

Italy 4

FLORENCE (St Mark) w Siena (St Peter) and Bologna
Chapl L A C MACLEAN
LIGURIA w Genoa (The Holy Ghost) and Bordighera *vacant*
MILAN (All Saints) and Varese Chapl N S D GIBSON
NAPLES (Christ Church) w Sorrento, Capri and Bari
Chapl A SIDDALL
PALERMO (Holy Cross) *see* Sicily
ROME (All Saints) w Macerata Chapl J BOARDMAN, **C** S MACVANE
SICILY P-in-c R J ROGERS
TAORMINA (St George) *see* Sicily
VENICE (St George) w Trieste P-in-c J-H D BOWDEN

Latvia 6

RIGA (St Saviour) Chapl J CALITIS

Luxembourg 5

LUXEMBOURG Chapl C LYON

Macedonia 1

Served from Belgrade (Serbia and Montenegro)

Malta and Gozo 4

VALLETTA (Pro-Cathedral of St Paul) w Sliema (Holy Trinity) Chapl T O MENDEL, P G WOLFENDEN

Monaco 2

MONTE CARLO (St Paul) Chapl J T JOUSTRA

Morocco 3

CASABLANCA (St John the Evangelist) Chapl J E GOOCH
TANGIER (St Andrew) *vacant*

The Netherlands 5

AMSTERDAM (Christ Church) w Den Helder and Heiloo
Chapl M P C COLLINSON, **Asst Chapl** H K ADAN, J R ALBERS, J R BALL
ARNHEM *see* East Netherlands
EAST NETHERLANDS Chapl S W VAN LEER
EINDHOVEN Chapl F P NOORDANUS
HAARLEM P-in-c B RICHARDS
HAGUE, THE (St John and St Philip) Chapl M B SANDERS, **Asst Chapl** R K PRICE, **C** R DYMOND
NIJMEGEN *see* East Netherlands
ROTTERDAM (St Mary) P-in-c M STARK
TWENTE (St Mary) *see* East Netherlands
UTRECHT (Holy Trinity) w Zwolle Chapl J DE WIT, **Asst Chapl** P STAPLES
VOORSCHOTEN Chapl P J BOURNE

Norway 6

OSLO (St Edmund) w Bergen, Trondheim and Stavanger
Asst Chapl P R HOGARTH, **C** M STRØMMEN

Poland 1

WARSAW w Gdansk *vacant*

Portugal 3

ALGARVE (St Vincent) Chapl E S BRITT
LISBON (St George) w Estoril (St Paul)
Chapl M BULLOCK
MADEIRA (Holy Trinity) P-in-c H C SMART
PORTO (*or* OPORTO) (St James) P-in-c M SUMARES

Romania 1

BUCHAREST (The Resurrection) Chapl J A RAMSAY

Russian Federation 1

MOSCOW (St Andrew) w Vladivostock
Chapl S E STEPHENS
ST PETERSBURG *vacant*

Serbia and Montenegro 1

BELGRADE w Skopje Chapl J R FOX

Slovakia

Served from Vienna (Austria)

Slovenia

Served from Vienna (Austria)

Spain 3

BARCELONA (St George) Chapl P H JORDAN
COSTA BLANCA Chapl E LEWIS, **Asst Chapl** P C EDWARDS
COSTA DEL SOL EAST P-in-c D E C WRIGHT
COSTA DEL SOL WEST *vacant*
FUENGIROLA (St Andrew) *see* Costa del Sol East
IBIZA P-in-c R L SHORT
LANZAROTE *vacant*
LAS PALMAS (Holy Trinity) P-in-c A R WEBB
MADRID (St George) Chapl I C HUTCHINSON CERVANTES
MÁLAGA (St George) P-in-c R G TAYLOR, **C** R J TAYLER
MENORCA Chapl M J BUNCE
MOJACAR P-in-c H D BROAD
NERJA and Almuñécar *vacant*
PALMA DE MALLORCA (St Philip and St James)
Chapl R A ELLIS, **Asst Chapl** M REDFEARN
PLAYA DE LAS AMERICAS Tenerife *see* Tenerife Sur
PUERTO DE LA CRUZ Tenerife (All Saints)
Chapl D T JENKINS
PUERTO POLLENSA Mallorca *see* Palma de Mallorca
TENERIFE SUR (St Eugenio) P-in-c K A GORDON
TORREVIEJA Chapl C MCCORMACK

Sweden 6

GOTHENBURG (St Andrew) w Halmstad, Jönköping and Uddevalla P-in-c B P MOSS
MALMÖ Served from Copenhagen (Denmark)
STOCKHOLM (St Peter and St Sigfrid) w Gävle and Västerås *vacant*

Switzerland 7

BASLE Chapl G P READ, **Asst Chapl** R STOCKITT
BERNE (St Ursula) w Neuchâtel Chapl R L PAMPLIN, **Asst Chapl** L D BISIG
GENEVA (Holy Trinity) Chapl M A FRENCH
LA CÔTE P-in-c P R HOLLEY
LAUSANNE (Christ Church) P-in-c A KELHAM
LUGANO (St Edward the Confessor) P-in-c A L THOMAS
MONTREUX (St John) w Gstaad Chapl J R WILLIAMS, **C** P J PARRY
VEVEY (All Saints) w Château d'Oex and Villars Chapl C J ATKINSON
ZÜRICH (St Andrew) w Lucerne and St Moritz Chapl J K NEWSOME, **Asst Chapl** G J AMAT-TORREGROSA, **C** R HILLIARD

Turkey 1

ANKARA (St Nicholas) P-in-c G B EVANS
ISTANBUL (Christ Church) (Chapel of St Helena) w Moda (All Saints) Chapl I W L SHERWOOD
IZMIR (SMYRNA) (St John the Evangelist) w Bornova (St Mary Magdalene) Chapl R W EVANS

Ukraine 1

KIEV (Christ Church) *vacant*

MISSION TO SEAFARERS CHAPLAINCIES

Belgium 5

ANTWERP *Lay Chapl*
GHENT Chapl P R TILLEY

France 2

DUNKERQUE Chapl P G HISCOCK

The Netherlands 5

ROTTERDAM and Schiedam *vacant*
VLISSINGEN *vacant*

CHAPLAINS TO HER MAJESTY'S SERVICES

ROYAL NAVY

Chaplain of the Fleet and Archdeacon for the Royal Navy
Director General Naval Chaplaincy Service
The Ven B K HAMMETT QHC
Royal Navy Chaplaincy Service, Room 205, Victory Buildings, HM Naval Base, Portsmouth PO1 3LS
Tel (023) 9272 7900 Fax 9272 7111

Chaplains RN

D BARLOW
N A BEARDSLEY
S A R BEVERIDGE
K C BROMAGE
M BROTHERTON
A M CALLON
B R CLARKE
A S CORNESS
A J DUFF
G M ELMORE
M L EVANS
W H FRANKLIN
M J GOUGH
J GREEN
S P HALLAM
M J HARMAN
J HILL
R G HILLIARD
M J HILLS
G E D HITCHINS
C W W HOWARD
B J HUGHES
N J KELLY
S I LAMB
C J LUCKRAFT
J O MORRIS
S P PARSELLE
G S PETZER
A G PHILLIPS
M G POLL
R L PYNE
P J D S SCOTT
D J SIMPSON
S P SPRINGETT
M P M STEWART
D W W THOMAS
I J WHEATLEY
D V WYLIE

ARMY

Chaplain-General HM Land Forces
The Revd D E WILKES OBE QHC
Tel (01980) 615801
(The present Chaplain-General is a minister of the Methodist Church)

Deputy Chaplain-General
The Revd J P WHITTON QHC
Tel (01980) 615802
(The present Deputy Chaplain-General is a minister of the Church of Scotland)

Archdeacon for the Army
The Ven S ROBBINS
Tel (01980) 615804
Ministry of Defence, Chaplains (Army), Trenchard Lines, Upavon, Pewsey SN9 6BE
Tel (01980) 615802 Fax 615800

Chaplains to the Forces

D J ADAMS
W G ASHTON
D G BAILEY
J BALL
K G BARRY
K D BELL
A S F BENNETT
P R BOSHER
K M BRETEL
C S T BRODDLE
C S BUTLER
P J CABLE
M R CHRISTIAN
T A R COLE
D P CONNING
N L COOK
A J COOPER
A A COSLETT
C P CRAVEN
D P CREES
N N CROSSEY
D W DAVIES
R J DOWNES
S J H DUNWOODY
W J N DURANT
P A EAGLES
B ELLIOTT
H D EVANS
A J FELTHAM-WHITE
S A FRANKLIN
L F GANDIYA
J R B GOUGH
S E GRIFFITH
C J GROOCOCK
R A B HALL
R J HALL
R W HAYTER
R A HEMMINGS
L T J HILLARY
A W INGHAM
P A IRWIN
R C M JARVIS
M V JONES
K R JOYCE
N A KNIGHTS JOHNSON
C M LANGSTON
A M LATIFA
W B LISTER
N A LLEWELLYN
S H LODWICK
J M LOVEDAY
S T J MCCAULAY
T R MCKNIGHT
K MADDY
A C MARTLEW
K D MENTZEL
D J MERCERON
P J MILLS
B D MILLSON
R M MITCHELL
J S MOESEL
M P MORTON
F E MYATT
R OLLIFF
T R PLACE
R PLUCK
J A H POLLARD
R M PRIEST
M E REYNOLDS
R J RICHARDSON
M C ROBBINS
M P ROEMMELE
P F A SPRINGFORD
A C STEELE
M R N STEVENSON
S B THATCHER
A H THOMAS
A J TOTTEN
P VICKERS
J L VINCENT
B WALTON
H WANLISS
D C WEAVER
P S WRIGHT

ROYAL AIR FORCE

Chaplain-in-Chief
The Ven R D HESKETH CB QHC

Command Chaplains
E CORE, R J PENTLAND
Chaplaincy Service (RAF), HQ, Personnel and Training Command, RAF Innsworth, Gloucester GL3 1EZ
Tel (01452) 712612 ext 5164 Fax 510828

Chaplains RAF

N B P BARRY
J M BEACH
C W K BERRY-DAVIES
G S BROWN
J P M CHAFFEY
A T COATES
G L COLLINGWOOD
A J DAVIES
V R DUNSTAN-MEADOWS
M J ELLIOTT
J R ELLIS
A C GATRILL
A J D GILBERT
N P HERON
J C HETHERINGTON
A D HEWETT
C E HEWITT
J A HOBSON
S P IREDALE
M H JACKSON
R V JACKSON
I A JONES
M P D KENNARD
S P LAMOND
T R LEE
A B MCMULLON
C A MITCHELL
W L F MOUNSEY
D J NORFIELD
D T OSBORN
S J RADLEY
E J RANCE
P A RENNIE
J R RUSSELL
L E SPICER
J W K TAYLOR
P J M TOLLERSON
A J TURNER
A W WAKEHAM-DAWSON
I S WARD
G WILLIAMS
J K WILSON
G E WITHERS
T WRIGHT
E L WYNN

PRISON CHAPLAINS

HM PRISON SERVICE (England and Wales)

Chaplain General to HM Prisons
The Ven W A NOBLETT

Church of England members of Chaplaincy HQ staff:
P J TAYLOR (Assistant Chaplain General)
R M WILTSHIRE (Assistant Chaplain General)
W M CAREY (Training Officer)

HM Prison Service Chaplaincy, 6th Floor, Horseferry House, Dean Ryle Street, London SW1P 2AW

Tel (020) 7217 8960 *or* 7217 8678 Fax (020) 7217 8980
E-mail chaplaincy@prisons-chap-hq.demon.co.uk

Prisons

Acklington B K COOPER, M D TETLEY
Albany S C LUCAS
Altcourse M T RANDALL
Ashfield N J HAY, V ASHWORTH
Ashwell R J LUBKOWSKI, J B J SAUNDERS
Askham Grange R A CLEGG
Bedford S M WHITE
Belmarsh W J SALMON
Birmingham B J GRACIE
Blakenhurst J W GEEN
Blundeston M R RENNARD
Bristol D J H POWE, M E DESMOND
Brixton R T GREEN
Brockhill I E MCINTYRE DE ROMERO
Buckley Hall B A EATON
Bullingdon T P EDGE
Bullwood Hall J A WEEKS, S SAYERS
Camp Hill T J MANN
Canterbury C I HITCHENS, P B D CRICK
Cardiff M C JOHN
Channings Wood N R MARTIN
Chelmsford G C PEARSON
Coldingley A L FOWLER, C F HOLT, J HUNTER
Cookham Wood J E G DASH
Dartmoor W H BIRDWOOD
Doncaster P IRESON
Dorchester T A M SANKEY
Dovegate D HIGGON
Downview R A DEEDES
Drake Hall D J HOWARD
Durham F A ELTRINGHAM
East Sutton Park N FRY
Eastwood Park J M PHILLIPS
Edmunds Hill E R BELL
Elmley T G JACQUET
Everthorpe P MOORHOUSE
Exeter C V CURD, J G WITHERS
Featherstone E J POOLE
Forest Bank S A JONES
Foston Hall J C HONOUR, S BAXTER
Full Sutton M L KAVANAGH
Garth A J B KEITH
Gartree I L JOHNSON
Gloucester K A L DENNIS, D B SMALL
Grendon and Spring Hill M E BRAIN
Guys Marsh M J RIDGEWELL
Haverigg D J E CLARKE
Hewell Grange P HAMMERSLEY
Hollesley Bay R B THOMPSON
Holloway K WILKIN
Holme House T A MCCARTHY, J N GREENWOOD, S L NICHOLSON
Hull N J WHETTON
Kingston (Portsmouth) M D H JOHNSTON
Kirkham R A LANE
Lancaster Castle C WOODCOCK
Latchmere House F R BENTLEY
Leeds P TARLETON, R H BAILEY
Leicester A V HEDGES
Lewes M J ELWIS
Leyhill S BRACE
Lincoln J D BIRD
Lindholme M D J MCCREADY
Littlehey R C BUNYAN
Liverpool D W GOODWIN, E SUTHERLAND, I R SHACKLETON
Long Lartin P J KNIGHT, F L MIDDLEMISS
Low Newton A F WAKEFIELD, C M PROUSE
Lowdham Grange C KNIGHT
Maidstone G L LONG
Manchester L H COOPER, R A H MARSHALL
Moorland T M BAYFORD
Morton Hall C C MUNN
Mount, The P J ABREY
New Hall D L SMITH, E J CLAY, J T PERRY
North Sea Camp J F GLEADALL
Norwich J A WILSON
Nottingham M T PHILLIPS
Parc (Bridgend) D C TILT
Parkhurst T LANE
Pentonville R J S PEARSON
Peterborough R J SIMMONDS
Preston P C BROWNE
Ranby A HIRST
Reading D J LITTLE, M E BRAIN
Risley J SEPHTON
Rochester Y R MARCUSSEN
Rye Hill P D STELL, G D MORRIS
Send A J FORAN
Shepton Mallet G BIRD
Shrewsbury D S FARLEY, J J WADDINGTON-FEATHER
Stafford J M DIXON, R C PAYNE
Standford Hill C E N DAVIS, B I M DURKAN
Stocken E GHINN
Styal M THOMPSON
Sudbury F V G BALLENTYNE
Swaleside J H WAITE
Swansea L HOPKINS
Verne, The A M BALL
Wakefield J K HAYWARD
Wandsworth J A F GALBRAITH
Wayland N TIVEY, D N STEVENS, S G STEPHENSON
Wellingborough R M M CREIGHTON
Whatton D J BURTON, J D HENSON
Winchester P A NEWMAN
Wolds, The G F COOKE
Woodhill S C LISTON
Wormwood Scrubs A R TYLER, H K DODHIA, M P STRANGE

Young Offender Institutions

Aylesbury J M WILLIAMS
Castington C R MURRIE, E P BOSSWARD
Deerbolt D G HARTLEY, G KIRTLEY
Feltham M A WILKINSON, P FOSTER
Glen Parva J E FITZGERALD
Hatfield C D LETHBRIDGE
Huntercombe and Finnamore Wood I D THACKER
Isle of Man N D GREENWOOD
Kirklevington Grange M D ALLSOPP
Lancaster Farms B J MAYNE
Portland P THOMPSON
Stoke Heath C S SEDDON, M J NEWSOME, R C PAYNE
Swinfen Hall J BARNES
Thorn Cross N G SHAW
Usk and Prescoed N R SANDFORD
Werrington House D E KENDRICK
Wetherby G JONES, S D JONES

SCOTTISH PRISON SERVICE

Scottish Prison Service, Calton House, 5 Redheughs Rigg, Edinburgh E12 9HW
Tel (0131) 556 8400 Fax 244 8774

Aberdeen J D ALEXANDER
Edinburgh M C REED
Glenochil F A M LAWRY

NORTHERN IRELAND PRISON SERVICE

Northern Ireland Office, Dundonald House, Upper Newtownards Road, Belfast BT4 3SU
Tel (028) 9052 0700 Fax 9052 5327

Belfast N B DODDS
Maghaberry J R HOWARD
Maze, The W A MURPHY

IRISH PRISON SERVICE

Department of Justice, 72–76 St Stephen's Green, Dublin 2, Irish Republic
Tel (00353) (1) 678 9711 Fax 676 4718

Limerick J M G SIRR
Midlands Portlaoise H A DUNGAN

HOSPITAL CHAPLAINS

An index of whole-time and part-time hospital chaplains

Secretary to the Hospital Chaplaincies Council
The Revd E J LEWIS
Church House, Great Smith Street, London SW1P 3NZ
Tel (020) 7898 1894 Fax 7898 1891

At institutions with more than one chaplain the names are listed in order of senority.

ABERDEEN ROYAL INFIRMARY *see* Grampian Univ Hosp NHS Trust
ABINGDON *see* SW Oxon Primary Care Trust
ADDENBROOKE'S Cambridge *see* Cam Univ Hosps NHS Foundn Trust
ADELAIDE AND MEATH Dublin S D GREEN, M A J WILSON
AINTREE HOSPITALS NHS TRUST Liverpool I J LOVETT
AIREDALE GENERAL *see* Airedale NHS Trust
AIREDALE NHS TRUST B M WILKINSON, G L HALL, J P SMITH
ALDER HEY CHILDREN'S Liverpool *see* R Liverpool Children's NHS Trust
ALEXANDRA Redditch *see* Worcs Acute Hosps NHS Trust
ALL SAINTS Eastbourne *see* E Sussex Hosps NHS Trust
ALLINGTON NHS TRUST M R RENNARD
ALNWICK INFIRMARY *see* Northumbria Healthcare NHS Trust
ALTON COMMUNITY *see* N Hants Loddon Community NHS Trust
AMBERSTONE Hailsham *see* Eastbourne and Co Healthcare NHS Trust
ANDOVER DISTRICT COMMUNITY HEALTH CARE NHS TRUST D F KING
ANDOVER WAR MEMORIAL COMMUNITY HOSPITAL *see* Andover District Community Health Care NHS Trust
ARCHERY HOUSE Dartford *see* W Kent NHS and Soc Care Trust
ARMAGH AND DUNGANNON HEALTH AND SOCIAL SERVICES TRUST C W M ROLSTON
ASHFIELD COMMUNITY Kirkby-in-Ashfield *see* Sherwood Forest Hosps NHS Trust
ASHFORD *see* E Kent Hosps NHS Trust
ASHFORD AND ST PETER'S HOSPITAL NHS TRUST J A ROBINSON
ASHINGTON *see* Northumbria Healthcare NHS Trust
ASHWORTH Maghull C J MOON
ASTON HALL *see* S Derbyshire Community and Mental Health Trust
AYLESBURY VALE COMMUNITY HEALTHCARE NHS TRUST S L BUSHELL
BARKING HAVERING AND REDBRIDGE HOSPITALS NHS TRUST P MARTIN, T COLEMAN, M R JUDGE
BARNET *see* Barnet and Chase Farm Hosps NHS Trust
BARNET, ENFIELD AND HARINGEY MENTAL HEALTH TRUST T M BARON
BARNET AND CHASE FARM HOSPITALS NHS TRUST T M BARON, J D LINTHICUM, J D A WALKER
BARNSLEY DISTRICT GENERAL HOSPITAL NHS TRUST M P YATES
BARROW Bristol *see* United Bris Healthcare NHS Trust
BARTS AND THE LONDON NHS TRUST P J COWELL, B RHODES
BASILDON *see* S Essex Mental Health & Community Care NHS Trust
BASILDON AND THURROCK GENERAL HOSPITALS NHS TRUST M H KELLY
BASSETLAW DISTRICT GENERAL Worksop *see* Doncaster and Bassetlaw Hosps NHS Trust
BATH AND WEST COMMUNITY NHS TRUST H ANDREWES UTHWATT, M JOYCE, C T TOOKEY
BATTLE Reading *see* R Berks and Battle Hosps NHS Trust
BEBINGTON M B KELLY
BECKENHAM *see* Bromley Hosps NHS Trust
BEDFORD HOSPITAL NHS TRUST P N S GIBSON
BEIGHTON HOSPITAL Sheffield *see* Sheff Care Trust
BELFAST CITY HOSPITAL HEALTH AND SOCIAL SERVICES TRUST J K BELL
BELVOIR PARK Belfast *see* Belfast City Hosp Health and Soc Services Trust
BENENDEN Kent C F SMITH
BENNION CENTRE Leicester *see* Leics Partnership NHS Trust
BENSHAM Gateshead *see* Gateshead Health NHS Trust
BERWICK INFIRMARY *see* Northumbria Healthcare NHS Trust
BETHLEM ROYAL Beckenham *see* S Lon and Maudsley NHS Trust
BIDEFORD *see* N Devon Healthcare NHS Trust
BILLINGE *see* Wrightington Wigan and Leigh NHS Trust
BIRCH HILL *see* Pennine Acute Hosps NHS Trust
BIRMINGHAM Monyhull Learning Disabilities Service *see* S Birm Mental Health NHS Trust
BIRMINGHAM AND MIDLAND EYE *see* City Hosp NHS Trust Birm
BIRMINGHAM AND SOLIHULL MENTAL HEALTH TRUST D L HART
BIRMINGHAM CHILDREN'S HOSPITAL NHS TRUST N E BALL, P NASH
BIRMINGHAM CITY *see* City Hosp NHS Trust Birm
BIRMINGHAM HEARTLANDS AND SOLIHULL NHS TRUST A M BOYD, W E HASSALL, N E BALL
BIRMINGHAM SKIN *see* City Hosp NHS Trust Birm
BIRMINGHAM SPECIALIST COMMUNITY HEALTH NHS TRUST H A N PLATTS, L M MORRIS, R M ELLIOTT
BIRMINGHAM WOMEN'S HEALTHCARE NHS TRUST S W BARTON
BISHOP AUCKLAND GENERAL *see* S Durham Healthcare NHS Trust
BLACKBERRY HILL Bristol *see* N Bris NHS Trust
BLACKBURN ROYAL INFIRMARY *see* E Lancs Hosps NHS Trust
BLACKPOOL, FYLDE AND WYRE HOSPITALS NHS TRUST J M TURNER
BLACKPOOL, WYRE AND FYLDE COMMUNITY HEALTH SERVICES NHS TRUST P D LAW-JONES
BLYTH COMMUNITY *see* Northumbria Healthcare NHS Trust
BODMIN *see* Cornwall Partnership NHS Trust
BODMIN *see* N and E Cornwall Primary Care Trust
BOLTON GENERAL *see* Bolton Hosps NHS Trust
BOLTON HOSPITALS NHS TRUST N K GRAY, G F WEIR
BOOTH HALL CHILDREN'S Manchester *see* Cen Man/Man Children's Univ Hosp NHS Trust
BOOTHAM PARK *see* York Health Services NHS Trust
BORDERS GENERAL NHS TRUST D L MAYBURY
BOURNE Lincs *see* NW Anglia Healthcare NHS Trust
BOURNEMOUTH, ROYAL GENERAL *see* R Bournemouth and Christchurch Hosps NHS Trust
BRADFORD CITY PRIMARY CARE TRUST, A M E BROWN
BRADFORD HOSPITALS NHS TRUST C P JOHNSON, J JACKSON
BRADGATE MENTAL HEALTH UNIT Leicester *see* Leics Partnership NHS Trust
BRAMCOTE Nuneaton *see* N Warks NHS Trust
BRANDON MENTAL HEALTH UNIT Leicester *see* Leics Partnership NHS Trust
BRIDLINGTON AND DISTRICT *see* Scarborough and NE Yorks Healthcare NHS Trust
BRIDPORT COMMUNITY *see* SW Dorset Primary Care Trust
BRIGHTON AND SUSSEX UNIVERSITY HOSPITALS NHS TRUST R J ST C HARLOW-TRIGG, S UNDERDOWN
BRIGHTON GENERAL *see* Brighton and Sussex Univ Hosps NHS Trust
BRISTOL GENERAL *see* United Bris Healthcare NHS Trust
BRISTOL ROYAL FOR SICK CHILDREN *as above*
BRISTOL ROYAL INFIRMARY *as above*
BROADGREEN Liverpool *see* R Liverpool and Broadgreen Univ Hosps NHS Trust
BROADMOOR Crowthorne T W WALT
BROMLEY HOSPITALS NHS TRUST T J MERCER
BROOKLANDS Marston Green *see* N Warks NHS Trust
BROOMFIELD Chelmsford *see* Mid-Essex Hosp Services NHS Trust
BRYN Y NEUADD Llanfairfechan *see* NW Wales NHS Trust
BUCKLAND Dover *see* E Kent Hosps NHS Trust
BURNLEY GENERAL *see* E Lancs Hosps NHS Trust
CAERPHILLY DISTRICT MINERS' *see* Gwent Healthcare NHS Trust

CALDERDALE AND HUDDERSFIELD NHS TRUST S V BROOKS, M W PARROTT, M D ELLERTON
CAMBOURNE/REDRUTH COMMUNITY *see* W of Cornwall Primary Care Trust
CAMBRIDGE UNIVERSITY HOSPITALS NHS FOUNDATION TRUST A L ALDRIDGE, B M WOOLLARD, K C MORRISON, K J LOMAX
CAMBRIDGESHIRE AND PETERBOROUGH MENTAL HEALTH PARTNERSHIPS NHS TRUST J P NICHOLSON
CAMDEN AND ISLINGTON COMMUNITY HEALTH SERVICES NHS TRUST B BATSTONE
CANNOCK CHASE *see* Mid Staffs Gen Hosps NHS Trust
CANTERBURY St Martin's *see* E Kent NHS and Soc Care Partnership Trust
CARDIFF AND VALE NHS TRUST D R LLOYD-RICHARDS, L E D CLARK, E J BURKE
CARDIFF COMMUNITY HEALTHCARE NHS TRUST J H L ROWLANDS
CARDIFF ROYAL INFIRMARY *see* Cardiff and Vale NHS Trust
CASTEL *see* States of Guernsey Bd of Health
CASTLE Okehampton *see* Mid Devon Primary Care Trust
CASTLE HILL Cottingham *see* Hull and E Yorks Hosps NHS Trust
CASTLEFORD NORMANTON AND DISTRICT *see* Mid Yorks Hosps NHS Trust
CATERHAM *see* Surrey and Sussex Healthcare NHS Trust
CEFN COED Swansea *see* Swansea NHS Trust
CENTRAL CORNWALL PRIMARY CARE TRUST J C GREATBATCH, P DE GREY-WARTER
CENTRAL MANCHESTER/MANCHESTER CHILDREN'S UNIVERSITY HOSPITAL NHS TRUST S TURNER, M L T MCGONIGLE, A-M HUMPHREYS
CENTRAL MIDDLESEX NHS TRUST K N HALL, M D MOORHEAD
CENTRAL SHEFFIELD UNIVERSITY HOSPITALS NHS TRUST H C BLACKBURN
CHAILEY HERITAGE Lewes G A LAY
CHAPEL ALLERTON Leeds *see* Leeds Teaching Hosps NHS Trust
CHARING CROSS *see* Hammersmith Hosps NHS Trust
CHARLTON LANE CENTRE Leckhampton *see* Glos Hosps NHS Trust
CHASE, THE Bordon *see* N Hants Loddon Community NHS Trust
CHASE FARM Enfield *see* Barnet and Chase Farm Hosps NHS Trust
CHEDDON ROAD *see* Taunton and Somerset NHS Trust
CHELMSFORD Broomfield *see* Mid-Essex Hosp Services NHS Trust
CHELSEA AND WESTMINSTER HEALTHCARE NHS TRUST S B SMITH, C BEARDSLEY
CHELTENHAM GENERAL *see* Glos Hosps NHS Trust
CHEPSTOW COMMUNITY *see* Gwent Healthcare NHS Trust
CHERRY KNOWLE Sunderland *see* Priority Healthcare Wearside NHS Trust
CHERRY TREE Stockport *see* Stockport NHS Trust
CHESHIRE AND WIRRAL PARTNERSHIP NHS TRUST H J ALDRIDGE, D R NUGENT
CHESTERFIELD AND NORTH DERBYSHIRE NHS TRUST J K BUTTERFIELD
CHESTERTON Cambridge *see* Cam Univ Hosps NHS Foundn Trust
CHICHESTER St Richard's *see* R W Sussex Trust
CHIPPENHAM COMMUNITY *see* Wilts and Swindon Healthcare NHS Trust
CHORLEY AND SOUTH RIBBLE DISTRICT GENERAL *see* Lanc Teaching Hosps NHS Trust
CHRISTCHURCH *see* R Bournemouth and Christchurch Hosps NHS Trust
CHRISTIE HOSPITAL NHS TRUST Manchester D K PRYCE
CHURCHILL, THE Oxford *see* Ox Radcliffe Hosps NHS Trust
CIRENCESTER *see* Cotswold and Vale Primary Care Trust
CIRENCESTER *see* Glos Hosps NHS Trust
CITY GENERAL Stoke-on-Trent *see* Univ Hosp of N Staffs NHS Trust
CITY HOSPITAL York *see* York Health Services NHS Trust
CITY HOSPITAL NHS TRUST Birmingham G DOWNS
CITY HOSPITALS SUNDERLAND NHS TRUST P H WEBB, M WARNER
CLACTON GENERAL *see* Essex Rivers Healthcare NHS Trust
CLATTERBRIDGE Wirral *see* Cheshire and Wirral Partnership NHS Trust
CLAYBURY Woodford Bridge *see* Forest Healthcare NHS Trust Lon
CLAYTON Wakefield *see* Mid Yorks Hosps NHS Trust
CLEVELAND, SOUTH Middlesbrough *see* S Tees Hosps NHS Trust
CLIFTON Lytham St Annes *see* Blackpool, Fylde and Wyre Hosps NHS Trust
COLCHESTER GENERAL *see* Essex Rivers Healthcare NHS Trust
COLCHESTER MATERNITY *as above*
COLINDALE *see* Enfield Primary Care Trust
CONQUEST St Leonards-on-Sea *see* E Sussex Hosps NHS Trust
CONQUEST, THE Bexhill *see* Hastings and Rother NHS Trust
COOKRIDGE Leeds *see* Leeds Teaching Hosps NHS Trust
CORNWALL HEALTHCARE NHS TRUST J T MCCABE
CORNWALL PARTNERSHIP NHS TRUST C D NEWELL
COTSWOLD AND VALE PRIMARY CARE TRUST M J WITHEY
COUNTESS MOUNTBATTEN HOSPICE Southampton *see* Southn Univ Hosps NHS Trust
COUNTESS OF CHESTER *see* Cheshire and Wirral Partnership NHS Trust
COUNTY DURHAM AND DARLINGTON PRIORITY SERVICES NHS TRUST C JAY
COVENTRY AND WARWICKSHIRE *see* Univ Hosps Coventry and Warks NHS Trust
CROMER *see* Norfolk and Nor Univ Hosp NHS Trust
CROSSLANE Newby *see* Tees and NE Yorks NHS Trust
CROYDON MENTAL HEALTH SERVICES Warlingham *see* S Lon and Maudsley NHS Trust
CUMBERLAND INFIRMARY *see* N Cumbria Acute Hosps NHS Trust
CYNTHIA SPENCER HOUSE Northampton *see* Northants Healthcare NHS Trust
DARLINGTON MEMORIAL *see* S Durham Healthcare NHS Trust
DARTFORD AND GRAVESHAM NHS TRUST P J IVESON
DELANCEY Leckhampton *see* Glos Hosps NHS Trust
DELLWOOD Reading *see* R Berks and Battle Hosps NHS Trust
DERBY CITY GENERAL *see* S Derbyshire Acute Hosps NHS Trust
DERBY CITY GENERAL *see* S Derbyshire Community and Mental Health Trust
DERBYSHIRE CHILDREN'S *see* S Derbyshire Acute Hosps NHS Trust
DERBYSHIRE ROYAL INFIRMARY *as above*
DEREHAM *see* Norwich Primary Care Trust
DERRIFORD *see* Plymouth Hosps NHS Trust
DEVIZES COMMUNITY *see* Wilts and Swindon Healthcare NHS Trust
DEVONSHIRE ROAD Blackpool *see* Blackpool, Fylde and Wyre Hosps NHS Trust
DEWI SANT Pontypridd *see* Pontypridd and Rhondda NHS Trust
DEWSBURY AND DISTRICT *see* Mid Yorks Hosps NHS Trust
DODDINGTON COUNTY March *see* NW Anglia Healthcare NHS Trust
DONCASTER AND BASSETLAW HOSPITALS NHS TRUST M C WRIGHT, C L SMITH
DONCASTER AND SOUTH HUMBER HEALTHCARE NHS TRUST J E PALIN, L M MAGNUSSON
DONCASTER ROYAL INFIRMARY *see* Doncaster and Bassetlaw Hosps NHS Trust
DONCASTER ROYAL INFIRMARY PSYCHIATRIC UNIT *see* Doncaster and S Humber Healthcare NHS Trust
DORKING *see* Surrey and Sussex Healthcare NHS Trust
DORSET HEALTH CARE NHS TRUST K S TIMBRELL
DRYBURN Durham *see* N Dur Healthcare NHS Trust
DUCHESS OF KENT HOUSE St Andrews *see* States of Guernsey Bd of Health
DUCHY Truro H C T OLIVEY
DUDLEY GROUP OF HOSPITALS NHS TRUST P TONGUE, D J PAPWORTH
DUNSTON HILL Gateshead *see* Gateshead Health NHS Trust
DURHAM AND DARLINGTON PRIORITY SERVICES NHS TRUST *see* Co Dur and Darlington Priority Services NHS Trust
EALING HOSPITAL NHS TRUST C P GUINNESS, C L MADDOCK, J L OSBORNE, G M BERESFORD JONES, M K DAVIDGE-SMITH
EARLS HOUSE Durham *see* Co Dur & Darlington Priority Services NHS Trust

EAST AND NORTH HERTFORDSHIRE NHS TRUST F S E GIBBS, S J MANLEY-COOPER, D J PROUD, J E HATTON
EAST BERKSHIRE NHS TRUST FOR PEOPLE WITH LEARNING DISABILITIES G F THEOBALD
EAST CHESHIRE NHS TRUST J BUCKLEY
EAST HAMPSHIRE PRIMARY CARE TRUST J E HAIR, C R PRESTIDGE
EAST KENT HOSPITALS NHS TRUST P F HILL, P M KIRBY, K FAZZANI
EAST KENT NHS AND SOCIAL CARE PARTNERSHIP TRUST P J RICHMOND, G D KENDREW, R P C PODGER
EAST LANCASHIRE HOSPITALS NHS TRUST J R L CLARK, J E C PERCIVAL, R L ALLEN, D ALTHAM
EAST SOMERSET NHS TRUST E J ROTHWELL
EAST SURREY LEARNING DISABILITY AND MENTAL HEALTH SERVICES NHS TRUST C E LATHAM
EAST SURREY PRIORITY CARE NHS TRUST N J COPSEY
EAST SUSSEX HOSPITALS NHS TRUST C R GORING, J G DAVENPORT
EASTBOURNE AND COUNTY HEALTHCARE NHS TRUST M J ELWIS, A C J CORNES
EASTBOURNE GENERAL *see* E Sussex Hosps NHS Trust
EASTBOURNE HOSPITALS NHS TRUST J H KIMBERLEY, N P CHATFIELD
EDGWARE COMMUNITY *see* Barnet and Chase Farm Hosps NHS Trust
EDITH CAVELL Peterborough *see* Pet Hosps NHS Trust
ELIZABETH GARRETT ANDERSON OBSTETRIC London *see* Univ Coll Lon Hosps NHS Foundn Trust
ELLESMERE PORT *see* Cheshire and Wirral Partnership NHS Trust
ELY *see* Cardiff and Vale NHS Trust
ELY *see* Cardiff Community Healthcare NHS Trust
ENFIELD PRIMARY CARE TRUST T M BARON, T D ATKINS
EPPING FOREST PRIMARY CARE TRUST B C MORRISON
EPSOM St Ebba's *see* Surrey Oaklands NHS Trust
EPSOM AND ST HELIER NHS TRUST C VALLINS, H A SMITH, A WALFORD, D WALFORD
EPSOM GENERAL *see* Epsom and St Helier NHS Trust
ERITH AND DISTRICT *see* Qu Mary's Sidcup NHS Trust
ESSEX COUNTY *see* Essex Rivers Healthcare NHS Trust
ESSEX RIVERS HEALTHCARE NHS TRUST R SMITH, M W THOMPSON, J I SEARS, R J R HUMPHRIES
EVESHAM COMMUNITY *see* Worcs Community and Mental Health Trust
EXETER HEALTH AUTHORITY (Mental Health/Handicap) D J WALFORD
FAIRFIELD GENERAL *see* Pennine Acute Hosps NHS Trust
FALMOUTH *see* Cen Cornwall Primary Care Trust
FARNHAM ROAD Guildford *see* Surrey Hants Borders NHS Trust
FAZAKERLEY Liverpool *see* Aintree Hosps NHS Trust Liv
FIELDHEAD Wakefield *see* Wakef and Pontefract Community NHS Trust
FINCHLEY MEMORIAL *see* Enfield Primary Care Trust
FOREST HEALTHCARE NHS TRUST London M O PRITCHARD, D J DALAIS
FOREST LODGE Sheffield *see* Sheff Care Trust
FRENCHAY Bristol *see* N Bris NHS Trust
FRIARAGE Northallerton *see* Northallerton Health Services NHS Trust
FRIMLEY PARK HOSPITAL NHS TRUST J S MCARTHUR-EDWARDS
FULBOURN Cambridge *see* Cam Univ Hosps NHS Foundn Trust
FURNESS *see* Morecambe Bay Hosps NHS Trust
FURNESS *see* Morecambe Bay Primary Care Trust
GATESHEAD HEALTH NHS TRUST J R PERRY, R L FERGUSON
GEORGE ELIOT HOSPITAL NHS TRUST Nuneaton E C POGMORE, D R L WHITE, S P MOULT, P DODDS
GLENFIELD Bennion Centre *see* Leics Partnership NHS Trust
GLENFIELD Bradgate Mental Health Unit *as above*
GLENFIELD Leicester *see* Univ Hosps Leic NHS Trust
GLENSIDE Bristol R MEREDITH-JONES
GLOUCESTERSHIRE HOSPITALS NHS TRUST W B IRVINE, R T SWAIN
GLOUCESTERSHIRE PARTNERSHIP TRUST M J WITHEY
GLOUCESTERSHIRE ROYAL *see* Glos Hosps NHS Trust
GOOD HOPE HOSPITAL NHS TRUST Sutton Coldfield A T BALL
GOODALL CENTRE Bishop Auckland *see* S Durham Healthcare NHS Trust
GORSE HILL Leicester *see* Leics Partnership NHS Trust
GOSPORT WAR MEMORIAL *see* E Hants Primary Care Trust
GRAMPIAN UNIVERSITY HOSPITAL NHS TRUST S SPENCER
GREAT ORMOND STREET HOSPITAL FOR CHILDREN NHS TRUST N WALTER, D A MOORE BROOKS, J W CROSSLEY
GREENACRES Dartford *see* W Kent NHS and Soc Care Trust
GROVE, THE Shardlow *see* S Derbyshire Community and Mental Health Trust
GUILDFORD St Luke's *see* R Surrey Co Hosp NHS Trust
GUY'S AND ST THOMAS' HOSPITALS NHS TRUST London M A K HILBORN, R A SHAW, J M WATTS
GWENT COUNTY Griffithstown *see* Gwent Healthcare NHS Trust
GWENT HEALTHCARE NHS TRUST A W TYLER, M J MARSDEN, M C G LANE
HALSTEAD COMMUNITY *see* Essex Rivers Healthcare NHS Trust
HALTON GENERAL *see* N Cheshire Hosps NHS Trust
HAM GREEN Bristol *see* N Bris NHS Trust
HAMBLETON AND RICHMONDSHIRE PRIMARY CARE TRUST S R BAXTER
HAMMERSMITH HOSPITALS NHS TRUST E MORRIS
HAMPSHIRE PARTNERSHIPS NHS TRUST J E HAIR
HAROLD WOOD *see* Barking Havering and Redbridge Hosps NHS Trust
HARROGATE HEALTH CARE NHS TRUST P GREENWELL
HARROW *see* NW Lon Hosp NHS Trust
HARROW AND HILLINGDON HEALTHCARE NHS TRUST D P BYRNE
HARTLEPOOL *see* N Tees and Hartlepool NHS Trust
HARTLEPOOL *see* Tees and NE Yorks NHS Trust
HARTSHILL ORTHOPAEDIC *see* N Staffs Hosp NHS Trust
HARWICH COMMUNITY *see* Essex Rivers Healthcare NHS Trust
HASTINGS AND ROTHER NHS TRUST D J JEFFREYS
HEART HOSPITAL London *see* Univ Coll Lon Hosps NHS Foundn Trust
HEATHERWOOD AND WEXHAM PARK HOSPITAL NHS TRUST P L DEEMING, D S JONES, C E L SMITH, R A CHEEK
HELLESDON Norfolk *see* Norfolk Mental Health Care NHS Trust
HEMEL HEMPSTEAD GENERAL *see* W Herts Hosps NHS Trust
HEREFORD HOSPITALS NHS TRUST P A ROBERTS, L C RHODES
HERGEST UNIT Ysbyty Gwynedd *see* NW Wales NHS Trust
HEXHAM *see* Northumbria Healthcare NHS Trust
HIGHBURY Bulwell *see* Notts Healthcare NHS Trust
HILL HOUSE Swansea *see* Swansea NHS Trust
HILLINGDON HOSPITAL NHS TRUST R CHRISTIAN, W F WHITE
HINCHINGBROOKE HEALTH CARE NHS TRUST A-L K GARVIE, P M DUFFETT-SMITH
HITCHIN *see* E and N Herts NHS Trust
HITHER GREEN London *see* Lewisham Hosp NHS Trust
HOMERTON UNIVERSITY HOSPITAL NHS TRUST London R J OGSTON
HOPE Salford *see* Salford R Hosps NHS Trust
HORSHAM *see* W Sussex Health and Soc Care NHS Trust
HUDDERSFIELD ROYAL INFIRMARY *see* Calderdale and Huddersfield NHS Trust
HULL AND EAST RIDING COMMUNITY HEALTH NHS TRUST E ROSE
HULL AND EAST YORKSHIRE HOSPITALS NHS TRUST S E CEELY, P J NELSON, J A SHARP, A R MARSDEN
HULL MATERNITY *see* Hull and E Yorks Hosps NHS Trust
HULL ROYAL INFIRMARY *as above*
HURSTWOOD PARK Haywards Heath *see* Brighton and Sussex Univ Hosps NHS Trust
IDA DARWIN Cambridge *see* Cam Univ Hosps NHS Foundn Trust
INVICTA COMMUNITY CARE NHS TRUST S A J MITCHELL, R WARD
IPSWICH St Clements *see* Local Health Partnerships NHS Trust
IPSWICH HOSPITAL NHS TRUST S CARLSSON, G T MELVIN, R A FINCH
ISEBROOK Wellingborough *see* Northants Healthcare NHS Trust
ISLE OF MAN DEPARTMENT OF HEALTH AND SOCIAL SECURITY P S FREAR
ISLE OF WIGHT HEALTHCARE NHS TRUST G J CLIFTON-SMITH, M D H JOHNSTON, G M HURT

JAMES PAGET HEALTHCARE NHS TRUST V M STEADY, J A FAIRBAIRN
JERSEY GROUP H M A CERMAKOVA
JESSOP WOMEN'S Sheffield *see* Cen Sheff Univ Hosps NHS Trust
JOHN RADCLIFFE Oxford *see* Ox Radcliffe Hosps NHS Trust
KELLING *see* Norwich Primary Care Trust
KENT AND CANTERBURY *see* E Kent Hosps NHS Trust
KENT AND SUSSEX Tunbridge Wells *see* Maidstone and Tunbridge Wells NHS Trust
KETTERING GENERAL HOSPITAL NHS TRUST L S MCCORMACK, R G BROWN
KEYCOL Kent *see* Thames Gateway NHS Trust
KIDDERMINSTER *see* Worcs Acute Hosps NHS Trust
KIDDERMINSTER GENERAL *see* Worcs Community and Mental Health Trust
KING EDWARD VII Castel *see* States of Guernsey Bd of Health
KING EDWARD VII Midhurst D B WELSMAN
KING GEORGE Redbridge *see* Barking Havering and Redbridge Hosps NHS Trust
KING'S COLLEGE HOSPITAL NHS TRUST S T MEYER, D W RUSHTON
KING'S LYNN AND WISBECH HOSPITALS NHS TRUST A L HAIG
KINGS MILL Sutton-in-Ashfield *see* Sherwood Forest Hosps NHS Trust
KING'S WOOD CENTRE Colchester *see* N Essex Mental Health Partnership NHS Trust
KINGSBURY COMMUNITY London *see* Parkside Community NHS Trust Lon
KINGSTON HOSPITAL NHS TRUST Surrey G W HOLMES
KINGSWAY Derby *see* S Derbyshire Community and Mental Health Trust
KNEESWORTH HOUSE Royston N TAYLOR
LANCASHIRE TEACHING HOSPITALS NHS TRUST R J FISHER, J G PRYSOR-JONES
LANGBAURGH PRIMARY CARE TRUST P L BISHOP
LANSDOWNE *see* Cardiff and Vale NHS Trust
LEA CASTLE Wolverley *see* N Warks NHS Trust
LEEDS St Mary's *see* Leeds Mental Health Teaching NHS Trust
LEEDS GENERAL INFIRMARY *see* Leeds Teaching Hosps NHS Trust
LEEDS MENTAL HEALTH TEACHING NHS TRUST M I KIMBALL
LEEDS TEACHING HOSPITALS NHS TRUST, The C J SWIFT, G HANCOCKS, B J TURNER, T P LUSTY
LEICESTER GENERAL *see* Univ Hosps Leic NHS Trust
LEICESTER GENERAL Brandon Mental Health Unit *see* Leics Partnership NHS Trust
LEICESTER ROYAL INFIRMARY *see* Univ Hosps Leic NHS Trust
LEICESTERSHIRE PARTNERSHIP NHS TRUST T H GIRLING
LEIGH INFIRMARY *see* Wrightington Wigan and Leigh NHS Trust
LEIGHTON Crewe *see* Mid Cheshire Hosps Trust
LEWISHAM HOSPITAL NHS TRUST A L SHAW, K J GRANT
LIBERTON Edinburgh *see* Lothian Univ Hosps NHS Trust
LIFECARE Caterham *see* Surrey Oaklands NHS Trust
LINCOLN Witham Court ESMI Unit *see* Linc Distr Healthcare NHS Trust
LINCOLN COUNTY *see* Lincs Partnership NHS Trust
LINCOLN COUNTY *see* United Lincs Hosps NHS Trust
LINCOLN DISTRICT HEALTHCARE NHS TRUST R G WILKINSON, G P POND, D YOUNG
LINCOLNSHIRE PARTNERSHIP NHS TRUST P N MARSHALL
LINDEN CENTRE Broomfield *see* N Essex Mental Health Partnership NHS Trust
LISTER Stevenage *see* E and N Herts NHS Trust
LITTLE BROMWICH CENTRE FOR ELDERLY MENTAL HEALTH Small Heath *see* Birm and Solihull Mental Health Trust
LITTLE PLUMSTEAD *see* Norwich Primary Care Trust
LITTLEMORE Oxford *see* Oxon Mental Healthcare NHS Trust
LIVERPOOL CARDIOTHORACIC CENTRE *see* R Liverpool and Broadgreen Univ Hosps NHS Trust
LLANDOUGH *see* Cardiff and Vale NHS Trust
LLANDUDNO GENERAL *see* NW Wales NHS Trust
LLANFRECHFA GRANGE Cwmbran *see* Gwent Healthcare NHS Trust
LLANTRISANT Royal Glamorgan *see* Pontypridd and Rhondda NHS Trust
LLWYNYPIA *as above*
LOCAL HEALTH PARTNERSHIPS NHS TRUST Suffolk G T MELVIN
LONDON AND SURREY *see* R Marsden NHS Trust
LONDON CHEST *see* Barts and The Lon NHS Trust
LONGLEY CENTRE Sheffield *see* Sheff Care Trust
LOTHIAN PRIMARY HEALTHCARE NHS TRUST P D SKELTON, D YEOMAN
LOTHIAN UNIVERSITY HOSPITALS NHS TRUST C T UPTON
LOUTH COUNTY *see* United Lincs Hosps NHS Trust
LOVERSALL Doncaster *see* Doncaster and S Humber Healthcare NHS Trust
LOWESTOFT AND NORTH SUFFOLK *see* Jas Paget Healthcare NHS Trust
LUDLOW *see* Shropshire Co Primary Care Trust
LUTON AND DUNSTABLE HOSPITAL NHS TRUST E A BRADLEY
MACCLESFIELD DISTRICT GENERAL *see* E Cheshire NHS Trust
MAIDSTONE AND TUNBRIDGE WELLS NHS TRUST P J PLUMLEY, D F L PETZSCH, S J BLADE
MAINDIFF COURT Abergavenny *see* Gwent Healthcare NHS Trust
MANCHESTER AND SALFORD SKIN *see* Salford R Hosps NHS Trust
MANCHESTER ROYAL EYE *see* Cen Man/Man Children's Univ Hosp NHS Trust
MANCHESTER ROYAL INFIRMARY *as above*
MANOR Walsall *see* Walsall Hosps NHS Trust
MANSFIELD COMMUNITY *see* Sherwood Forest Hosps NHS Trust
MANSFIELD DISTRICT PRIMARY CARE TRUST P BENTLEY
MANYGATES MATERNITY Wakefield M P CROFT
MARIE CURIE CENTRE Newcastle upon Tyne R FINDLAYSON
MAUDSLEY Denmark Hill *see* S Lon and Maudsley NHS Trust
MAYDAY HEALTHCARE NHS TRUST Thornton Heath H A FIFE
MAYDAY UNIVERSITY *see* Mayday Healthcare NHS Trust Thornton Heath
MEADOWFIELD Worthing *see* W Sussex Health and Soc Care NHS Trust
MEANWOOD PARK Leeds *see* Leeds Mental Health Teaching NHS Trust
MEDWAY Gillingham *see* Thames Gateway NHS Trust
MEDWAY MARITIME Gillingham *see* W Kent NHS and Soc Care Trust
MEDWAY NHS TRUST A J AMOS, P A MCKENZIE
MELKSHAM COMMUNITY *see* Wilts and Swindon Healthcare NHS Trust
MEMORIAL Darlington *see* Co Dur & Darlington Priority Services NHS Trust
MENDIP PRIMARY CARE TRUST E J SMITH
MICHAEL CARLISLE CENTRE Sheffield *see* Sheff Care Trust
MID CHESHIRE HOSPITALS TRUST G D GEDDES, S HUGHES
MID DEVON PRIMARY CARE TRUST D J WALFORD, D M FLETCHER
MID-ESSEX HOSPITAL SERVICES NHS TRUST S M SOUTHEE
MID STAFFORDSHIRE GENERAL HOSPITALS NHS TRUST I S VAUGHAN, P J GRAYSMITH
MID YORKSHIRE HOSPITALS NHS TRUST M GASKELL, M J WINBOLT LEWIS, J P TAYLOR
MIDDLESBROUGH GENERAL *see* S Tees Hosps NHS Trust
MIDDLESEX *see* Univ Coll Lon Hosps NHS Foundn Trust
MILDMAY MISSION M F SCHLEGER
MILLBROOK MENTAL HEALTH UNIT Sutton-in-Ashfield *see* Notts Healthcare NHS Trust
MILTON KEYNES GENERAL NHS TRUST C E HOUGH, T CLAPTON
MILTON KEYNES PRIMARY CARE TRUST C E HOUGH
MONTAGU Mexborough *see* Doncaster and Bassetlaw Hosps NHS Trust
MONYHULL LEARNING DISABILITIES SERVICE Birmingham *see* S Birm Mental Health NHS Trust
MOORFIELDS EYE HOSPITAL NHS TRUST D E ALLEN
MOORGREEN West End Southampton *see* Hants Partnerships NHS Trust

MORECAMBE BAY HOSPITALS NHS TRUST J L TYRER, D V A BROWN, G GARBUTT
MORECAMBE BAY PRIMARY CARE TRUST D V A BROWN
MORPETH COTTAGE *see* Northumbria Healthcare NHS Trust
MORRISTON Swansea *see* Swansea NHS Trust
MOSELEY HALL Birmingham *see* Birm Specialist Community Health NHS Trust
MOUNT, THE Bishopstoke *see* Win and Eastleigh Healthcare NHS Trust
MUSGROVE PARK Taunton *see* Taunton and Somerset NHS Trust
NAPSBURY St Albans *see* Enfield Primary Care Trust
NATIONAL HOSPITAL FOR NEUROLOGY AND NEUROSURGERY London *see* Univ Coll Lon Hosps NHS Foundn Trust
NEVILL HALL Abergavenny *see* Gwent Healthcare NHS Trust
NEW CRAIGS Inverness *see* NHS Highland
NEW CROSS Wolverhampton *see* R Wolv Hosps NHS Trust
NEWARK *see* Sherwood Forest Hosps NHS Trust
NEWBURY AND COMMUNITY PRIMARY CARE TRUST B DAGNALL
NEWCASTLE Royal Victoria Infirmary *see* Newcastle upon Tyne Hosps NHS Trust
NEWCASTLE St Nicholas *see* Newc City Health NHS Trust
NEWCASTLE CITY HEALTH NHS TRUST F B ALLEN
NEWCASTLE GENERAL *see* Newcastle upon Tyne Hosps NHS Trust
NEWCASTLE MENTAL HEALTH UNIT A E MARR
NEWCASTLE UPON TYNE HOSPITALS NHS TRUST M J SHIPTON, A MAUDE, R FINDLAYSON
NEWHAM PRIMARY CARE TRUST N J COPSEY
NEWTON ABBOT *see* S Devon Healthcare NHS Trust
NEWTOWN Worcester *see* Worcs Community and Mental Health Trust
NHS HIGHLAND M F HICKFORD
NORFOLK AND NORWICH UNIVERSITY HOSPITAL NHS TRUST E S LANGAN, C B REED, P A ATKINSON, T W HARRIS, J M STEWART
NORFOLK MENTAL HEALTH CARE NHS TRUST W F BAZELY, M I KNOWLES, S F NUNNEY
NORTH AND EAST CORNWALL PRIMARY CARE TRUST G G C MINORS, R N STRANACK, R E B MAYNARD
NORTH BRISTOL NHS TRUST D C DAVIES, S J ORAM, N A HECTOR, A J PARKER, C A G LEGGATE, A M BUCKNALL, A J GAUNT, A R GOOD
NORTH CAMBRIDGESHIRE Wisbech *see* King's Lynn and Wisbech Hosps NHS Trust
NORTH CHESHIRE HOSPITALS NHS TRUST J E DUFFIELD
NORTH CUMBRIA ACUTE HOSPITALS NHS TRUST J D KELLY
NORTH DEVON DISTRICT Barnstaple *see* N Devon Healthcare NHS Trust
NORTH DURHAM HEALTHCARE NHS TRUST M MASTERMAN, D J WILSON
NORTH EAST LONDON MENTAL HEALTH TRUST R B WHITE
NORTH EAST WALES NHS TRUST K B COLLINS
NORTH ESSEX MENTAL HEALTH PARTNERSHIP NHS TRUST R SMITH
NORTH HAMPSHIRE HOSPITALS NHS TRUST P J GOOLD, A J ASKEW
NORTH HAMPSHIRE LODDON COMMUNITY NHS TRUST P J GOOLD
NORTH MANCHESTER GENERAL *see* Pennine Acute Hosps NHS Trust
NORTH MERSEY COMMUNITY NHS TRUST M C DAVIES
NORTH MIDDLESEX HOSPITAL NHS TRUST B D FENTON, P C ATHERTON
NORTH STAFFORDSHIRE HOSPITAL NHS TRUST J M AUSTERBERRY
NORTH STAFFORDSHIRE ROYAL INFIRMARY *see* Univ Hosp of N Staffs NHS Trust
NORTH TEES AND HARTLEPOOL NHS TRUST L PURVIS, R CUTHBERTSON
NORTH TEES GENERAL *see* Tees and NE Yorks NHS Trust
NORTH TYNESIDE GENERAL North Shields *see* Northumbria Healthcare NHS Trust
NORTH WARWICKSHIRE NHS TRUST S P MOULT, H A N PLATTS
NORTH WEST ANGLIA HEALTHCARE NHS TRUST K G PRATT, S J SMITH
NORTH WEST LONDON HOSPITALS NHS TRUST D P BYRNE
NORTH WEST WALES NHS TRUST W ROBERTS, R H GRIFFITHS
NORTHALLERTON HEALTH SERVICES NHS TRUST A H DODD
NORTHAMPTON GENERAL HOSPITAL NHS TRUST G A SARMEZEY
NORTHAMPTONSHIRE HEALTHCARE NHS TRUST C R GOODLEY, J A PARKIN, R J T FARMER, G C RUMBOLD
NORTHCROFT Erdington *see* Birm and Solihull Mental Health Trust
NORTHERN DEVON HEALTHCARE NHS TRUST K E W MATHERS, R M REYNOLDS
NORTHERN GENERAL HOSPITAL NHS TRUST Sheffield J A FRYER
NORTHGATE Great Yarmouth *see* Jas Paget Healthcare NHS Trust
NORTHGATE Morpeth *see* Northgate and Prudhoe NHS Trust
NORTHGATE AND PRUDHOE NHS TRUST D F MAYHEW
NORTHUMBERLAND MENTAL HEALTH NHS TRUST R H MCLEAN
NORTHUMBRIA HEALTHCARE NHS TRUST C F MEEHAN, D MACNAUGHTON, J WAIYAKI, R H MCLEAN
NORWICH, WEST *see* Norfolk and Nor Univ Hosp NHS Trust
NORWICH PRIMARY CARE TRUST P A ATKINSON, R D BRANSON, S F NUNNEY, M M KINGSTON
NOTTINGHAM CITY HOSPITAL NHS TRUST C BROWN, Y E GLASS
NOTTINGHAMSHIRE HEALTHCARE NHS TRUST C M J THODY, M EVANS, K R EVANS
NUFFIELD ORTHOPAEDIC CENTRE NHS TRUST J E COCKE
NUNNERY FIELDS Canterbury *see* E Kent Hosps NHS Trust
ODIHAM COTTAGE *see* N Hants Loddon Community NHS Trust
OKEHAMPTON AND DISTRICT *see* Mid Devon Primary Care Trust
OLDCHURCH Romford *see* Barking Havering and Redbridge Hosps NHS Trust
ORMSKIRK AND DISTRICT GENERAL *see* W Lancashire NHS Trust
ORSETT *see* Basildon and Thurrock Gen Hosps NHS Trust
OVERDALE St Helier *see* Jersey Gp of Hosps
OXFORD RADCLIFFE HOSPITALS NHS TRUST G A BARKER, C A SMITH, N P FENNEMORE, D E MICKLETHWAITE
OXFORDSHIRE MENTAL HEALTHCARE NHS TRUST F B STEVENSON, A C HOLMES
OXTED *see* Surrey and Sussex Healthcare NHS Trust
PADDINGTON COMMUNITY London *see* Parkside Community NHS Trust Lon
PAIGNTON *see* S Devon Healthcare NHS Trust
PAPWORTH HOSPITAL NHS TRUST J A COOMBS
PARK PREWETT *see* N Hants Loddon Community NHS Trust
PARKLANDS Basingstoke *see* Hants Partnerships NHS Trust
PARKSIDE COMMUNITY NHS TRUST London R G THOMPSON
PATRICK STEAD Halesworth *see* Allington NHS Trust
PEMBURY *see* Maidstone and Tunbridge Wells NHS Trust
PEMBURY *see* W Kent NHS and Soc Care Trust
PENDLE COMMUNITY Nelson *see* E Lancs Hosps NHS Trust
PENNINE ACUTE HOSPITALS NHS TRUST, THE K L DUNN, M R MORGAN, E J DAVIES, R R WATSON
PETER HODGKINSON CENTRE Lincoln *see* Linc Distr Healthcare NHS Trust
PETERBOROUGH HOSPITALS NHS TRUST R E HIGGINS
PETERSFIELD COMMUNITY *see* E Hants Primary Care Trust
PIERREMONT UNIT Darlington *see* Co Dur & Darlington Priority Services NHS Trust
PILGRIM Boston *see* United Lincs Hosps NHS Trust
PINDERFIELDS GENERAL Wakefield *see* Mid Yorks Hosps NHS Trust
PLAISTOW *see* Newham Primary Care Trust
PLUMSTEAD, LITTLE *see* Norwich Primary Care Trust
PLYMOUTH HOSPITALS NHS TRUST A P R KYRIAKIDES-YELDHAM, M CHURCHER
PONTEFRACT GENERAL INFIRMARY *see* Mid Yorks Hosps NHS Trust
PONTYPRIDD AND RHONDDA NHS TRUST G A BLYTH
POOLE St Ann's *see* Dorset Health Care NHS Trust
POOLE HOSPITAL NHS TRUST E J LLOYD, I R PEARCE

PORTSMOUTH HOSPITALS NHS TRUST F D HILLEBRAND, B R SMITH, A P BURR, B A MOSSE, J POWER
PRINCESS ALEXANDRA Harlow *see* N Essex Mental Health Partnership NHS Trust
PRINCESS ALEXANDRA HOSPITAL NHS TRUST Harlow G R ROWLANDS
PRINCESS ALICE Eastbourne *see* Eastbourne Hosps NHS Trust
PRINCESS ANNE Southampton *see* Southn Univ Hosps NHS Trust
PRINCESS ELIZABETH St Martin *see* States of Guernsey Bd of Health
PRINCESS LOUISE London *see* Parkside Community NHS Trust Lon
PRINCESS MARGARET Swindon *see* Swindon and Marlborough NHS Trust
PRINCESS MARGARET ROSE ORTHOPAEDIC Edinburgh *see* Lothian Univ Hosps NHS Trust
PRINCESS MARINA Northampton *see* Northants Healthcare NHS Trust
PRINCESS OF WALES COMMUNITY Bromsgrove *see* Worcs Community and Mental Health Trust
PRINCESS ROYAL Haywards Heath *see* Brighton and Sussex Univ Hosps NHS Trust
PRINCESS ROYAL Hull *see* Hull and E Yorks Hosps NHS Trust
PRIORITY HEALTHCARE WEARSIDE NHS TRUST C J WORSFOLD
PRIORITY HOUSE Maidstone *see* W Kent NHS and Soc Care Trust
PUREY CUST NUFFIELD York J A RENDALL
QUEEN ALEXANDRA Portsmouth *see* Portsm Hosps NHS Trust
QUEEN CHARLOTTE Hammersmith *see* Hammersmith Hosps NHS Trust
QUEEN ELIZABETH Birmingham *see* Univ Hosp Birm NHS Foundn Trust
QUEEN ELIZABETH Gateshead *see* Gateshead Health NHS Trust
QUEEN ELIZABETH King's Lynn *see* King's Lynn and Wisbech Hosps NHS Trust
QUEEN ELIZABETH Woolwich *see* Qu Eliz Hosp NHS Trust
QUEEN ELIZABETH HOSPITAL NHS TRUST D M FLAGG, G M HESKINS
QUEEN ELIZABETH II Welwyn Garden City *see* E and N Herts NHS Trust
QUEEN ELIZABETH PSYCHIATRIC Birmingham *see* Birm and Solihull Mental Health Trust
QUEEN ELIZABETH THE QUEEN MOTHER Margate *see* E Kent Hosps NHS Trust
QUEEN MARY'S SIDCUP NHS TRUST L A GREEN, J A PEAL
QUEEN VICTORIA Morecambe *see* Morecambe Bay Hosps NHS Trust
QUEEN VICTORIA HOSPITAL NHS TRUST East Grinstead C EVERETT-ALLEN
QUEEN VICTORIA MEMORIAL Welwyn *see* E and N Herts NHS Trust
QUEEN'S MEDICAL CENTRE NOTTINGHAM UNIVERSITY HOSPITAL NHS TRUST W P WATERS, B M S CHAMBERS, J HEMSTOCK, S M CUMMING, A M BROOKS, P S WEEDING
QUEEN'S MEDICAL CENTRE UNIVERSITY HOSPITAL Nottingham, Department of Psychiatry and Psychiatric Medicine *see* Notts Healthcare NHS Trust
QUEEN'S PARK Blackburn *see* E Lancs Hosps NHS Trust
RADCLIFFE INFIRMARY Oxford *see* Ox Radcliffe Hosps NHS Trust
RAIGMORE HOSPITAL NHS TRUST Inverness A A SINCLAIR
RAMPTON Retford *see* Notts Healthcare NHS Trust
RAMSGATE GENERAL *see* E Kent Hosps NHS Trust
RATHBONE Liverpool *see* N Mersey Community NHS Trust
REASIDE CLINIC Rednal *see* Birm and Solihull Mental Health Trust
REDBRIDGE King George *see* Barking Havering and Redbridge Hosps NHS Trust
RICHARDSON Barnard Castle *see* S Durham Healthcare NHS Trust
RIDGE LEA Lancaster *see* Morecambe Bay Primary Care Trust
RIDGEWOOD CENTRE Frimley *see* Surrey Hants Borders NHS Trust
ROBERT JONES/AGNES HUNT ORTHOPAEDIC HOSPITAL NHS TRUST Oswestry A M ROBERTS, A R BAILEY
ROCHDALE INFIRMARY *see* Pennine Acute Hosps NHS Trust
ROCHFORD *see* S Essex Mental Health & Community Care NHS Trust
ROOKWOOD Llandaff *see* Cardiff and Vale NHS Trust
ROTHERHAM GENERAL HOSPITALS NHS TRUST J E ASHTON
ROYAL ALBERT EDWARD INFIRMARY *see* Wrightington Wigan and Leigh NHS Trust
ROYAL ALEXANDRA CHILDREN'S Brighton *see* Brighton and Sussex Univ Hosps NHS Trust
ROYAL BELFAST HOSPITAL FOR SICK CHILDREN *see* R Group of Hosps Health and Soc Services Trust
ROYAL BERKSHIRE AND BATTLE HOSPITALS NHS TRUST M W SSERUNKUMA, D H LOVERIDGE
ROYAL BOURNEMOUTH AND CHRISTCHURCH HOSPITALS NHS TRUST B WILLIAMS, A SESSFORD, J R EVANS
ROYAL BROMPTON AND HAREFIELD NHS TRUST N K LEE, A J R GANDON
ROYAL CHELSEA T B F HINEY, R H WHITTINGTON
ROYAL CORNWALL HOSPITALS TRUST M A TREMBATH
ROYAL DEVON AND EXETER HEALTHCARE NHS TRUST D J WALFORD, A J COCKRAM
ROYAL EARLSWOOD Redhill *see* E Surrey Learning Disability NHS Trust
ROYAL EDINBURGH *see* Lothian Primary Healthcare NHS Trust
ROYAL FREE HAMPSTEAD NHS TRUST R H MITCHELL, P D CONRAD, N J K TEGALLY
ROYAL GLAMORGAN Llantrisant *see* Pontypridd and Rhondda NHS Trust
ROYAL GROUP OF HOSPITALS AND DENTAL HOSPITALS HEALTH AND SOCIAL SERVICES TRUST Belfast A MALLON, E HENDERSON, J K BELL
ROYAL GWENT Newport *see* Gwent Healthcare NHS Trust
ROYAL HALLAMSHIRE Sheffield *see* Cen Sheff Univ Hosps NHS Trust
ROYAL HAMPSHIRE COUNTY Winchester *see* Win and Eastleigh Healthcare NHS Trust
ROYAL HOSPITAL FOR NEURO-DISABILITY J M FARMAN
ROYAL HOSPITAL FOR SICK CHILDREN Edinburgh *see* Lothian Univ Hosps NHS Trust
ROYAL INFIRMARY OF EDINBURGH *as above*
ROYAL LANCASTER INFIRMARY *see* Morecambe Bay Hosps NHS Trust
ROYAL LIVERPOOL AND BROADGREEN UNIVERSITY HOSPITALS NHS TRUST G A PERERA, C J PETER
ROYAL LIVERPOOL CHILDREN'S NHS TRUST D J WILLIAMS
ROYAL LONDON *see* Barts and The Lon NHS Trust
ROYAL MANCHESTER CHILDREN'S *see* Cen Man/Man Children's Univ Hosp NHS Trust
ROYAL MARSDEN NHS TRUST London and Surrey D F BROWN, A R MIR, S F SEWELL, A J MCCULLOCH
ROYAL MATERNITY Belfast *see* R Group of Hosps Health and Soc Services Trust
ROYAL NATIONAL ORTHOPAEDIC HOSPITAL NHS TRUST W A BROOKER, P M REECE
ROYAL OLDHAM *see* Pennine Acute Hosps NHS Trust
ROYAL ORTHOPAEDIC HOSPITAL NHS TRUST R J FARMAN
ROYAL PRESTON *see* Lanc Teaching Hosps NHS Trust
ROYAL SHREWSBURY *see* Shrewsbury and Telford NHS Trust
ROYAL SOUTH HAMPSHIRE *see* Southn Univ Hosps NHS Trust
ROYAL SURREY COUNTY HOSPITAL NHS TRUST D N HOBDEN, J S MCARTHUR-EDWARDS
ROYAL SUSSEX COUNTY Brighton *see* Brighton and Sussex Univ Hosps NHS Trust
ROYAL UNITED HOSPITAL BATH NHS TRUST P F SUTTON, G OAKES
ROYAL VICTORIA Belfast *see* R Group of Hosps Health and Soc Services Trust
ROYAL VICTORIA Edinburgh *see* Lothian Univ Hosps NHS Trust
ROYAL VICTORIA Folkestone *see* E Kent Hosps NHS Trust
ROYAL WEST SUSSEX TRUST J P COOPER
ROYAL WOLVERHAMPTON HOSPITALS NHS TRUST S PETTY, C W FULLARD
RUNWELL *see* S Essex Mental Health & Community Care NHS Trust
RUSSELLS HALL Dudley *see* Dudley Gp of Hosps NHS Trust
ST ALBANS Napsbury *see* Enfield Primary Care Trust
ST ALBANS CITY *see* W Herts Hosps NHS Trust

ST ANDREW'S Northampton J M BOWERS
ST ANN'S Poole *see* Dorset Health Care NHS Trust
ST ANN'S Tottenham *see* Barnet, Enfield and Haringey Mental Health Trust
ST AUSTELL COMMUNITY *see* Cen Cornwall Primary Care Trust
ST BARNABAS Saltash *see* Cornwall Healthcare NHS Trust
ST BARTHOLOMEW'S London *see* Barts and The Lon NHS Trust
ST BARTHOLOMEW'S Rochester *see* Medway NHS Trust
ST BARTHOLOMEW'S Rochester *see* W Kent NHS and Soc Care Trust
ST CADOC'S Caerleon *see* Gwent Healthcare NHS Trust
ST CATHERINE'S Doncaster *see* Doncaster and S Humber Healthcare NHS Trust
ST CATHERINE'S COMMUNITY Birkenhead *see* Cheshire and Wirral Partnership NHS Trust
ST CHARLES COMMUNITY London *see* Parkside Community NHS Trust Lon
ST CROSS Rugby *see* Univ Hosps Coventry and Warks NHS Trust
ST EBBA'S Epsom *see* Surrey Oaklands NHS Trust
ST EDMUND'S Northampton *see* Northn Gen Hosp NHS Trust
ST GEORGE'S Morpeth *see* Northd Mental Health NHS Trust
ST GEORGE'S Stafford *see* S Staffs Healthcare NHS Trust
ST GEORGE'S HEALTHCARE NHS TRUST London H A JOHNSON, I M AINSWORTH-SMITH, J DEVERILL, J M FARMAN, C J CARTER
ST HELENS AND KNOWSLEY HOSPITALS NHS TRUST J E SHEPHERD, L MCCLUSKEY
ST HELIER Carshalton *see* Epsom and St Helier NHS Trust
ST HELIER GENERAL *see* Jersey Gp of Hosps
ST JAMES'S UNIVERSITY Leeds *see* Leeds Mental Health Teaching NHS Trust *and* Leeds Teaching Hosps NHS Trust
ST JOHN'S Axbridge J SMITH
ST JOHN'S Canterbury A A W DAWKINS
ST LUKE'S Armagh *see* Armagh and Dungannon Health and Soc Services
ST LUKE'S Bradford *see* Bradf Hosps NHS Trust
ST LUKE'S Middlesbrough *see* Tees and NE Yorks NHS Trust
ST MARGARET'S Epping *see* Epping Forest Primary Care Trust
ST MARTIN'S Bath *see* Bath and West Community NHS Trust
ST MARTIN'S Canterbury *see* E Kent NHS and Soc Care Partnership Trust
ST MARY'S Armley *see* Leeds Mental Health Teaching NHS Trust
ST MARY'S Kettering *see* Northants Healthcare NHS Trust
ST MARY'S Portsmouth *see* Portsm Hosps NHS Trust
ST MARY'S HOSPITAL FOR WOMEN AND CHILDREN Manchester *see* Cen Man/Man Children's Univ Hosp NHS Trust
ST MARY'S NHS TRUST Paddington S J FLATT, A H BARRON
ST MICHAEL'S Aylsham *see* Norwich Primary Care Trust
ST MICHAEL'S Bristol *see* United Bris Healthcare NHS Trust
ST MICHAEL'S Warwick *see* S Warks Combined Care NHS Trust
ST NICHOLAS Canterbury M A MORRIS
ST NICHOLAS Newcastle *see* Newc City Health NHS Trust
ST OSWALD'S Ashbourne *see* S Derbyshire Community and Mental Health Trust
ST PANCRAS *see* Camden and Islington Community Health NHS Trust
ST PETER'S Chertsey *see* Ashford and St Pet Hosp NHS Trust
ST PETER'S HOSPITAL NHS TRUST Chertsey J M ALLFORD
ST RICHARD'S Chichester *see* R W Sussex Trust
ST SAVIOUR *see* Jersey Gp of Hosps
ST THOMAS' London *see* Guy's and St Thos' Hosps NHS Trust Lon
ST THOMAS Stockport *see* Stockport NHS Trust
ST WOOLOS Newport *see* Gwent Healthcare NHS Trust
SALFORD MENTAL HEALTH SERVICES NHS TRUST D R SUTTON
SALFORD ROYAL HOSPITALS NHS TRUST I S CARTER, J B F GRANT, C J BROWN, J R WALKER
SALISBURY HEALTH CARE NHS TRUST C RENYARD, K S M FLIPPANCE, A SYMES
SALKELD DAY Chepstow *see* Gwent Healthcare NHS Trust
SALVINGTON LODGE Worthing *see* W Sussex Health and Soc Care NHS Trust
SANDWELL GENERAL West Bromwich *see* Sandwell Health Care NHS Trust
SANDWELL HEALTH CARE NHS TRUST K A DUCKETT
SANDWELL MENTAL HEALTH NHS AND SOCIAL CARE TRUST E C LOUIS
SAVERNAKE Marlborough *see* Wilts and Swindon Healthcare NHS Trust
SCARBOROUGH AND NORTH EAST YORKSHIRE HEALTHCARE NHS TRUST M C DOE
SCARBOROUGH GENERAL *see* Scarborough and NE Yorks Healthcare NHS Trust
SEACROFT Leeds *see* Leeds Teaching Hosps NHS Trust
SEDGEFIELD COMMUNITY Stockton-on-Tees *see* S Durham Healthcare NHS Trust
SELBY WAR MEMORIAL *see* York Health Services NHS Trust
SELLY OAK *see* Univ Hosp Birm NHS Foundn Trust
SEVENOAKS *see* Invicta Community Care NHS Trust
SEVERALLS Colchester *see* Essex Rivers Healthcare NHS Trust
SEVERALLS HOUSE Colchester *see* N Essex Mental Health Partnership NHS Trust
SEVERN NHS TRUST P MINALL, D E STODDART, S G RICHARDS, C CARTER
SHAROE GREEN Preston *see* Lanc Teaching Hosps NHS Trust
SHEFFIELD Royal Hallamshire *see* Cen Sheff Univ Hosps NHS Trust
SHEFFIELD CARE TRUST H G SMART, S H FAIRWEATHER
SHEFFIELD CHILDREN'S HOSPITAL NHS TRUST G L WILTON
SHEFFIELD NORTHERN GENERAL *see* N Gen Hosp NHS Trust Sheff
SHEFFIELD TEACHING HOSPITALS NHS TRUST D E R EQUEALL, J DALEY, K G LOWE, N M JOHNSON
SHELTON Bicton Heath *see* Shropshire Co Primary Care Trust
SHEPPEY COMMUNITY Minster-on-Sea *see* Thames Gateway NHS Trust
SHERWOOD FOREST HOSPITALS NHS TRUST J A S WOOD, D C PAYNE
SHOTLEY BRIDGE GENERAL Consett *see* N Dur Healthcare NHS Trust
SHREWSBURY AND TELFORD NHS TRUST A W WARNER, J DAVIES, P HRYZIUK, M I FEARNSIDE
SHREWSBURY ROYAL INFIRMARY *see* Shrewsbury and Telford NHS Trust
SHROPSHIRE COUNTY PRIMARY CARE TRUST M R GODSON, R A GREEN
SIMPSON MEMORIAL MATERNITY PAVILION Edinburgh *see* Lothian Univ Hosps NHS Trust
SINGLETON Swansea *see* Swansea NHS Trust
SIR MICHAEL SOBELL HOUSE HOSPICE *see* Ox Radcliffe Hosps NHS Trust
SIR ROBERT PEEL Tamworth *see* S Staffs Healthcare NHS Trust
SOLIHULL *see* Birm Heartlands and Solihull NHS Trust
SOUTH AND EAST DORSET PRIMARY CARE TRUST J E HOLBROOK
SOUTH BIRMINGHAM MENTAL HEALTH NHS TRUST D G JONES, J M MASON
SOUTH DEVON HEALTHCARE NHS TRUST G S KENDALL, P G LUFF, B R TUBBS
SOUTH DOWNS HEALTH NHS TRUST G S JOHNSON, D L I PERKS
SOUTH DURHAM HEALTHCARE NHS TRUST B SELMES, G G GRAHAM, R I MCTEER, V T FENTON
SOUTH ESSEX MENTAL HEALTH AND COMMUNITY CARE NHS TRUST J H DELFGOU
SOUTH LONDON AND MAUDSLEY NHS TRUST M R SUTHERLAND, A A WILSON, J H STEVENS, I A BOWMAN, R RATCLIFFE
SOUTH MANCHESTER UNIVERSITY HOSPITALS NHS TRUST J F C PERRYMAN, S GROSSCURTH, P BUTLER, S M MCLEOD
SOUTH SHORE Blackpool *see* Blackpool, Fylde and Wyre Hosps NHS Trust
SOUTH STAFFORDSHIRE HEALTHCARE NHS TRUST H J BAKER, G J CROSSLEY
SOUTH TEES HOSPITALS NHS TRUST P J CARRINGTO
SOUTH TYNESIDE DISTRICT South Shields *see* S Tyne Healthcare Trust
SOUTH TYNESIDE HEALTHCARE TRUST P R BEALI A J BEALING
SOUTH WARWICKSHIRE COMBINED CARE NHS T J A CARTWRIGHT
SOUTH WARWICKSHIRE HEALTH CARE NHS TRU P S KNIGHT

SOUTH WEST DORSET PRIMARY CARE TRUST E J WOODS
SOUTH WEST OXFORDSHIRE PRIMARY CARE TRUST P E SEAMAN
SOUTHAMPTON CITY PRIMARY CARE TRUST A R BEVIS
SOUTHAMPTON GENERAL *see* Southn Univ Hosps NHS Trust
SOUTHAMPTON UNIVERSITY HOSPITALS NHS TRUST R O L LOWNDES, F O BOOT, K A MACKINNON, J E L ALEXANDER
SOUTHEND HEALTH CARE NHS TRUST G L CROOK, R H S EASTOE, B E WEST, L M WILLIAMS
SOUTHERN DERBYSHIRE ACUTE HOSPITALS NHS TRUST K J SKIPPON, D W ASHTON, H P JONES, P A SHORT
SOUTHERN DERBYSHIRE COMMUNITY AND MENTAL HEALTH SERVICES NHS TRUST D PERKINS, J B BLACKMAN
SOUTHLANDS Shoreham-by-Sea *see* W Sussex Health and Soc Care NHS Trust
SOUTHMEAD Bristol *see* N Bris NHS Trust
SOUTHPORT AND ORMSKIRK NHS TRUST A P J GALBRAITH
STAFFORD DISTRICT GENERAL *see* Mid Staffs Gen Hosps NHS Trust
STAMFORD AND RUTLAND *see* Pet Hosps NHS Trust
STANDISH Stonehouse *see* Glos Hosps NHS Trust
STANLEY ROYD Wakefield *see* Wakef and Pontefract Community NHS Trust
STATES OF GUERNSEY BOARD OF HEALTH J LE BILLON
STEPPING HILL Stockport *see* Stockport NHS Trust
STOCKPORT NHS TRUST B J LOWE
STOKE MANDEVILLE HOSPITAL NHS TRUST G P HARRISON, S BLAGDEN
STOKE-ON-TRENT CITY GENERAL *see* Univ Hosp of N Staffs NHS Trust
STROUD GENERAL *see* Severn NHS Trust
SUNDERLAND DISTRICT GENERAL *see* City Hosps Sunderland NHS Trust
SURREY AND SUSSEX HEALTHCARE NHS TRUST J M GLASSPOOL, D G O ROBINSON, A G LOW
SURREY HAMPSHIRE BORDERS NHS TRUST A K TUCK, G E KNIFTON
SURREY OAKLANDS NHS TRUST N J COPSEY
SWAFFHAM COMMUNITY *see* NW Anglia Healthcare NHS Trust
SWANSEA NHS TRUST N R GRIFFIN, D M GRIFFITHS
SWINDON AND MARLBOROUGH NHS TRUST J M SKINNER
TAMESIDE AND GLOSSOP ACUTE SERVICES NHS TRUST J HILDITCH
TAMESIDE GENERAL *see* Pennine Acute Hosps NHS Trust
TAUNTON AND SOMERSET NHS TRUST M L GODIN, C F CRAGGS, R J ALLEN, G M KIRK, P CUFF, P A SELF, M D A WILLIAMS
TAYSIDE UNIVERSITY HOSPITALS NHS TRUST D J GORDON
TEES AND NORTH EAST YORKSHIRE NHS TRUST P L WALKER, P L BISHOP, B HARRISON
TEIGNMOUTH *see* S Devon Healthcare NHS Trust
TELFORD Princess Royal *see* Shrewsbury and Telford NHS Trust
TEWKESBURY *see* Glos Hosps NHS Trust
THAMES GATEWAY NHS TRUST P R BECKINSALE, G H SPENCER, J PEAL
THANET MENTAL HEALTH UNIT Margate *see* E Kent NHS and Soc Care Partnership Trust
THETFORD COTTAGE DAY *see* W Suffolk Hosps NHS Trust
THURROCK COMMUNITY *see* S Essex Mental Health & Community Care NHS Trust
TICKHILL ROAD Doncaster *see* Doncaster and S Humber Healthcare NHS Trust
TINDAL CENTRE Aylesbury *see* Aylesbury Vale Community Healthcare NHS Trust
TINDALE CRESCENT Bishop Auckland *see* S Durham Healthcare NHS Trust
TIVERTON AND DISTRICT *see* Mid Devon Primary Care Trust
TONE VALE *see* Taunton and Somerset NHS Trust
TORBAY DISTRICT GENERAL *see* S Devon Healthcare NHS Trust
TRANWELL UNIT Gateshead *see* Gateshead Health NHS Trust
TREDEGAR GENERAL *see* Gwent Healthcare NHS Trust
TREORCHY Ysbyty George Thomas *see* Pontypridd and Rhondda NHS Trust
TRINITY Retford A J KERSWILL
TRINITY Somerset *see* Taunton and Somerset NHS Trust
TROPICAL DISEASES *see* Camden and Islington Community Health NHS Trust
TROWBRIDGE COMMUNITY *see* Wilts and Swindon Healthcare NHS Trust
ULVERSTON *see* Morecambe Bay Hosps NHS Trust
UNITED BRISTOL HEALTHCARE NHS TRUST E A POWELL, J E NORMAN
UNITED LINCOLNSHIRE HOSPITALS NHS TRUST C M BONEYWELL, M R SAUNDERS, D C MAYLOR, D R WILLIAMS
UNIVERSITY Hartlepool *see* N Tees and Hartlepool NHS Trust
UNIVERSITY Stockton-on-Tees *as above*
UNIVERSITY COLLEGE LONDON HOSPITALS NHS FOUNDATION TRUST P ROWNTREE, M O BRACKLEY
UNIVERSITY HOSPITAL BIRMINGHAM NHS FOUNDATION TRUST E F BUXTON, R C EVANS, R FARMAN
UNIVERSITY HOSPITAL OF NORTH STAFFORDSHIRE NHS TRUST S GOODWIN
UNIVERSITY HOSPITAL OF WALES *see* Cardiff and Vale NHS Trust
UNIVERSITY HOSPITALS COVENTRY AND WARWICKSHIRE NHS TRUST H PRIESTNER, S F BETTERIDGE
UNIVERSITY HOSPITALS OF LEICESTER NHS TRUST M TURNER, M T SHARPE, R A LAMBERT, C R ROE, S C POLASHEK, R SEMEONOFF, M J MORRIS
VERRINGTON Wincanton *see* E Somerset NHS Trust
VICTORIA Blackpool *see* Blackpool, Fylde and Wyre Hosps NHS Trust
WAKEFIELD AND PONTEFRACT COMMUNITY NHS TRUST C M GARTLAND
WALSALL HOSPITALS NHS TRUST A E COLES
WALSGRAVE GENERAL Coventry *see* Univ Hosps Coventry and Warks NHS Trust
WALTON Liverpool *see* Aintree Hosps NHS Trust Liv
WANSBECK GENERAL Ashington *see* Northumbria Healthcare NHS Trust
WAREHAM *see* S and E Dorset Primary Care Trust
WARMINSTER COMMUNITY *see* Wilts and Swindon Healthcare NHS Trust
WARNEFORD Leamington Spa *see* S Warks Health Care NHS Trust
WARNEFORD PARK Oxford *see* Oxon Mental Healthcare NHS Trust
WARRINGTON *see* N Cheshire Hosps NHS Trust
WARRINGTON COMMUNITY HEALTH CARE NHS TRUST P LOVATT
WARWICKSHIRE, SOUTH *see* S Warks Health Care NHS Trust
WATFORD GENERAL *see* W Herts Hosps NHS Trust
WAYLAND Attleborough *see* Norwich Primary Care Trust
WELLS ROAD CENTRE Mapperley *see* Notts Healthcare NHS Trust
WELWYN Queen Victoria Memorial *see* E and N Herts NHS Trust
WELWYN GARDEN CITY Queen Elizabeth II *as above*
WESHAM PARK Preston *see* Blackpool, Wyre and Fylde Community NHS Trust
WEST CHESHIRE *see* Cheshire and Wirral Partnership NHS Trust
WEST CORNWALL *see* R Cornwall Hosps Trust
WEST CUMBERLAND *see* N Cumbria Acute Hosps NHS Trust
WEST DORSET GENERAL HOSPITALS NHS TRUST N D TOOTH
WEST HEATH Birmingham *see* Birm Specialist Community Health NHS Trust
WEST HERTFORDSHIRE HOSPITALS NHS TRUST G R COBB, G J A COOK
WEST HILL Dartford *see* Dartford and Gravesham NHS Trust
WEST KENT NHS AND SOCIAL CARE TRUST J G C LAWRENCE
WEST LANCASHIRE NHS TRUST R MOUGHTIN, C H JONES
WEST LONDON MENTAL HEALTH NHS TRUST D I BARNES, J L OSBORNE
WEST MIDDLESEX UNIVERSITY HOSPITAL NHS TRUST J L OSBORNE, C L MADDOCK
WEST OF CORNWALL PRIMARY CARE TRUST A N COUCH, D G MILLER
WEST PARK Macclesfield R J DOULTON
WEST SUFFOLK HOSPITALS NHS TRUST D CRAWLEY
WEST SUSSEX HEALTH AND SOCIAL CARE NHS TRUST G REEVES

WESTERN COMMUNITY Southampton *see* Hants Partnerships NHS Trust
WESTERN GENERAL Edinburgh *see* Lothian Univ Hosps NHS Trust
WESTHAVEN Weymouth P S THOMAS
WESTMINSTER MEMORIAL Shaftesbury M E HARDING
WESTMORLAND *see* Morecambe Bay Hosps NHS Trust
WESTMORLAND *see* Morecambe Bay Primary Care Trust
WESTON AREA HEALTH TRUST C ARGLES
WESTON GENERAL Weston-super-Mare *see* Weston Area Health Trust
WESTON PARK Sheffield *see* Cen Sheff Univ Hosps NHS Trust
WEXHAM PARK Slough *see* Heatherwood and Wexham Park Hosp NHS Trust
WHARFEDALE GENERAL Otley *see* Leeds Teaching Hosps NHS Trust
WHELLEY *see* Wrightington Wigan and Leigh NHS Trust
WHIPPS CROSS *see* Forest Healthcare NHS Trust Lon
WHISTON Prescot *see* St Helens and Knowsley Hosps NHS Trust
WHITBY *see* Scarborough and NE Yorks Healthcare NHS Trust
WHITCHURCH *see* Cardiff and Vale NHS Trust
WHITCHURCH *see* Cardiff Community Healthcare NHS Trust
WHITCHURCH COMMUNITY *see* Shropshire Co Primary Care Trust
WHITTINGTON HOSPITAL NHS TRUST E C M K JONES
WILLIAM HARVEY Ashford *see* E Kent Hosps NHS Trust
WILLIAM HARVEY Arundel Unit *see* E Kent NHS and Soc Care Partnership Trust
WILTSHIRE AND SWINDON HEALTHCARE NHS TRUST P F YACOMENI, R M LOWRIE, J A COUTTS
WIMBORNE *see* S and E Dorset Primary Care Trust
WINCHESTER AND EASTLEIGH HEALTHCARE NHS TRUST N R FLOOD, D J COTTRILL
WINWICK Warrington *see* Warrington Community Health Care NHS Trust
WISBECH *see* King's Lynn and Wisbech Hosps NHS Trust
WITHAM COURT ESMI UNIT Lincoln *see* Linc Distr Healthcare NHS Trust
WITHINGTON Manchester *see* S Man Univ Hosps NHS Trust
WITNEY *see* SW Oxon Primary Care Trust
WORCESTER ROYAL INFIRMARY *see* Worcs Acute Hosps NHS Trust
WORCESTERSHIRE ACUTE HOSPITALS NHS TRUST B M JONES, I SCOTT, J V THOMPSON, L A W SWABY
WORCESTERSHIRE COMMUNITY AND MENTAL HEALTH TRUST, The L L BURN, M E BARR, M E STANTON-HYDE
WORDSLEY *see* Dudley Gp of Hosps NHS Trust
WORTHING PRIORITY CARE NHS TRUST R J CASWELL
WREXHAM MAELOR *see* NE Wales NHS Trust
WRIGHTINGTON WIGAN AND LEIGH NHS TRUST R J HUTCHINSON, T D HARGREAVES-STEAD, R TOWNLEY, D J ROSCOE, A J EDWARDS
WYTHENSHAWE Manchester *see* S Man Univ Hosps NHS Trust
YEOVIL DISTRICT *see* E Somerset NHS Trust
YORK HEALTH SERVICES NHS TRUST R ROGERS, E W A CRAGG
YSBYTY GEORGE THOMAS Treorchy *see* Pontypridd and Rhondda NHS Trust
YSBYTY GWYNEDD Penrhosgarnedd *see* NW Wales NHS Trust
YSBYTY PENRHOS STANLEY Holyhead *as above*
YSTRAD MYNACH Hengoed *see* Gwent Healthcare NHS Trust

HOSPICE CHAPLAINS

BARNSLEY A PRITCHETT
BOLTON S C NEAL
CHILDREN'S SOUTH WEST Fremington P H HOCKEY
COMPTON Wolverhampton H J SMART
DOROTHY HOUSE Winsley K M CROUCH
DOUGLAS MACMILLAN Blurton J Y TILLIER, W H SMITH
DOUGLAS MACMILLAN Stoke-on-Trent D A HEWITSON, G R HARPER
EARL MOUNTBATTEN Newport G M HURT
EAST ANGLIA'S CHILDREN'S D M OSBORN
EAST HERTFORDSHIRE HOSPICE CARE G G BROWN
EAST LANCASHIRE Blackburn J R L CLARK
EDEN HALL MARIE CURIE Hampstead T J BELL
EXETER HOSPISCARE R J YEOMANS
GARDEN HOUSE Letchworth A DE C LADD
JERSEY G J HOUGHTON
KATHARINE HOUSE Banbury P C SMITH
KATHARINE HOUSE Stafford P J GRAYSMITH
KEMP Kidderminster R S MURRIN
KIRKWOOD Huddersfield M E WOOD
LECKHAMPTON COURT V J KERNER
MARIE CURIE Warren Pearl C A HIBBERD
MARTLETS Hove C G SPINKS
MARY ANN EVANS Nuneaton D R L WHITE
MEADOW HOUSE London J L OSBORNE
MOUNT EDGCUMBE A D WEST
MYTON HAMLET Warwick W S GRAHAM
OVERGATE Elland D BURROWS
PILGRIM'S Canterbury E R G HOPTHROW
ST ANDREW'S Grimsby A R MARSDEN
ST BARNABAS' Worthing J H MCCORMACK
ST CATHERINE'S Crawley J M NEVILL
ST CATHERINE'S Scarborough K D JACKSON
ST CHRISTOPHER'S London E M TOLLER
ST ELIZABETH Ipswich M CARTER
ST FRANCIS Berkhamsted E J HUGHES
ST GILES Lichfield D J SHERIDAN, P L HOLLIDAY
ST JOHN'S Wirral P B PRITCHARD
ST LEONARD'S York A G PEARSE, C W M BALDOCK
ST LUKE'S Plymouth T A SMITH
ST LUKE'S Sheffield J SANKEY
ST MARGARET'S Taunton S TUCKER
ST MARGARET'S Yeovil I G HUGHES
ST MICHAEL'S Basingstoke A EDMEADS
ST MICHAEL'S Hereford J M NEVILL
ST MICHAEL'S St Leonards-on-Sea R LANGTON
ST OSWALD'S Newcastle upon Tyne J L JACKSON
ST PETER AND ST JAMES North Chailey R A MOORE, R J ST C HARLOW-TRIGG
ST PETER'S Bristol W B M DOWIE
ST WILFRID'S Eastbourne C R BEARD
SHROPSHIRE AND MID-WALES H J EDWARDS
SPRINGHILL Rochdale E J DAVIES
STRATHCARRON Denny S M COATES
THORPE HALL Peterborough L M ELLIOTT
TRINITY London C A CLARKE
TRINITY IN THE FYLDE Blackpool J E DENNETT
WESTON C J S TURNER
WILLEN Milton Keynes S W BARNES

EDUCATIONAL CHAPLAINS

This index only lists deans and chaplains, and does not aim to provide a comprehensive list of clergy serving at educational institutions. Those institutions which do not currently have Anglican chaplains are not recorded.

General Synod Board of Education: Secretary The Reverend Canon J Hall
Church House, Great Smith Street, London SW1P 3NZ
Tel (020) 8987 1501 Fax 8987 1520

UNIVERSITIES

ABERDEEN D HEDDLE
ABERTAY D SHEPHERD
ANGLIA POLYTECHNIC N S COOPER, I R MOODY
BATH A V I BERNERS-WILSON, B F CHAPMAN
BATH SPA UNIVERSITY COLLEGE T J K BELL, J P KNOTT
BOLTON P G EDWARDS
BRIGHTON C R LAWLOR
BRISTOL J MUELLER-SCHNURR, M SCHNURR
BRUNEL *Uxbridge Campus* C E SARGENT
BUCKINGHAMSHIRE CHILTERNS UNIVERSITY COLLEGE A W DICKINSON, T A STACEY
CAMBRIDGE
Christ's P C A HARBRIDGE
Churchill J RAWLINSON
Clare R D GREEVES
Corpus Christi J B LAWSON
Downing K J EYEONS
Emmanuel J L CADDICK
Girton A M GUITE
Gonville and Caius J D MCDONALD
Jesus J COLLIS
King's R E LLOYD MORGAN
Magdalene S BARRINGTON-WARD, J T W RIGNEY
Newnham J KENNEDY
Pembroke L A ADAM, B WATCHORN
Peterhouse J B QUASH, M P WARD
Queens' J M HOLMES
Robinson M E DAWN
Selwyn J KENNEDY
Sidney Sussex P M WADDELL
St Catharine's P H RICHMOND
St John's D J DORMOR, C R HILLMAN
Trinity R H ADAMS, A S BROWNE, D G MACKENZIE MILLS
Trinity Hall (Dean) J N MORRIS
CENTRAL LANCASHIRE W E TURNER
CORK *University College* G P ST J HILLIARD, A W MCCROSKERY
COVENTRY M A J WARD
CRANFIELD H K SYMES-THOMPSON
DE MONTFORT P J LITTLEFORD, J S PARKIN
DERBY C J HODDER
DUBLIN *Trinity College* A W MCCORMACK
DUNDEE A W CUMMINS
DURHAM
Collingwood B J H DE LA MARE
Grey D J KENNEDY
Hatfield R W LAWRANCE
St Chad's C C H COOK
St Hild and St Bede J H LAWSON
St Mary's N P D CHITTENDEN
Trevelyan K S BRUCE
University A BASH
Van Mildert K S BRUCE
EAST ANGLIA D T THORNTON
EAST LONDON J A RAMSAY
EDINBURGH R O GOULD, D P WILLIAMS
ESSEX D J J EADES
EXETER C A HADLEY
GLASGOW R F JONES
GLOUCESTERSHIRE T L R MERCHANT, P D SAINSBURY
GREENWICH J E DICKER, J F GOMES
HASTINGS R J MORTIMER
HUDDERSFIELD M R POLLARD
HULL J C STEPHENSON
KEELE C M LACK
KENT S C E LAIRD
KINGSTON D BUCKLEY
LANCASTER K J HUGGETT
LEEDS METROPOLITAN D A CALDER
LEICESTER A S KASIBANTE
LINCOLN L C ACKLAM
LIVERPOOL M F BAYNHAM, M L CHAMBERLAIN
LIVERPOOL HOPE UNIVERSITY COLLEGE S SHAKESPEARE, I C STUART
LIVERPOOL JOHN MOORES R E DICKINSON
LONDON
Central Chaplaincies S G WILLIAMS
Goldsmiths' College P E COLLIER
Imperial College of Science, Technology and Medicine A W WILLSON
King's R A BURRIDGE *(Dean)* T F DITCHFIELD
London School of Economics and Political Science D T PEEBLES
Queen Mary and Westfield J E PETERSEN
Royal Free and University College Medical School G L LEGOOD
Royal Holloway and Bedford New T E F ROSE
Royal Veterinary College G L LEGOOD
University E V DANDO
Wye J S RICHARDSON
LONDON METROPOLITAN R M C LEIGH, F M WEAVER
LOUGHBOROUGH S J RICHARDSON
LUTON H D THORNTON
MANCHESTER T E BIDDINGTON, I D GOMERSALL, K A C WASEY
MANCHESTER METROPOLITAN T E BIDDINGTON, I D GOMERSALL, K A C WASEY
NEWCASTLE M R VASEY-SAUNDERS
NORTHUMBRIA AT NEWCASTLE A J SHIPTON
NOTTINGHAM J W BENTHAM, I D TARRANT
NOTTINGHAM TRENT R H DAVEY
OXFORD
All Souls J H DRURY
Balliol H D DUPREE
Brasenose P J GROVES
Christ Church C A LEWIS *(Dean)*, J A SHAW, R J WILLIAMSON
Corpus Christi J D MALTBY
Exeter M R BIRCH
Hertford L K ROBERTS
Jesus M R HODSON
Keble A K SHIN
Lady Margaret Hall A G DOIG
Lincoln G D WESTHAVER
Magdalen M J PIRET, A W M RITCHIE
Mansfield J B MUDDIMAN
Merton S M JONES
New J A SHAW
Oriel M J HARRIS
Queen's P J M SOUTHWELL
St Edmund Hall G HEGARTY
St Hilda's B W MOUNTFORD
St Hugh's J D GILPIN
St John's E D H CARMICHAEL
St Peter's A J MOORE
Trinity E M PERCY
University W G D SYKES
Wadham H A HARRIS
Worcester E L PENNINGTON
Wycliffe Hall G N MAUGHAN
OXFORD BROOKES M J WHIPP
PLYMOUTH R S WILLIAMS
PORTSMOUTH P A W JONES
QUEEN'S *Belfast (Dean of Residence)* P G MCGLINCHEY
ROYAL COLLEGE OF ART A W WILLSON
ST ANDREWS J P MASON
ST MARTIN'S *Ambleside* P WILLOX
SALFORD D J PALMER
SHEFFIELD W R S LAMB
SHEFFIELD HALLAM J A HORROCKS

SOUTH BANK F Y-C HUNG
SOUTHAMPTON S M STEVENS
STAFFORDSHIRE B H CAMBRIDGE, W G MCNAMEE
STIRLING K HOLDSWORTH
SUNDERLAND S A A FAGBEMI
SURREY J H FROST
SURREY *Roehampton* L HARKNETT
SUSSEX G R P ASHENDEN, P OESTREICHER, A N ROBINSON
ULSTER J E G BACH
ULSTER *Jordanstown and Belfast Campuses* T S JOHNSTON
WALES
Aberystwyth S R BELL
Bangor J P BUTLER
Cardiff L M CAVANAGH, D C ROBERTS
Lampeter B D B O'MALLEY
Swansea N JOHN
WARWICK M Q BRATTON
WEST OF ENGLAND R G HART
WESTMINSTER D W CHERRY
WOLVERHAMPTON G WYNNE

COLLEGES OF HIGHER EDUCATION

This index only includes those establishments known to have Anglican chaplains. It is not intended to be comprehensive.

ASHRIDGE MANAGEMENT J V M KIRKBY
ASKHAM BRYAN J H DAVIS
BISHOP GROSSETESTE *Lincoln* C A JAMES
CANTERBURY *Christ Church University College* J T LAW, S D ROWLANDS
CENTRAL LANCASHIRE A P HUTCHINSON
CHESTER A D BUCHANAN, E M BURGESS, L DIXON
COLEG GWENT A E MORTON
FAREHAM S MARTIN
GUILDHALL SCHOOL OF MUSIC AND DRAMA J BRUECK
HARPER ADAMS W E WARD
KENT INSTITUTE OF ART AND DESIGN J E DICKER
KING ALFRED'S *Winchester* J WATKINS
LONDON INSTITUTE *Chelsea College of Art and Design* A D NORWOOD
MYERSCOUGH A C A THOMASSON-ROSINGH
NEWCASTLE W E J MASH
NORTH EAST WALES INSTITUTE M R J G WALKER
NORWICH CITY C J BLACKMAN
RICHMOND-UPON-THAMES W D F VANSTONE
ROSE BRUFORD *Sidcup* G W DAVIES
ROYAL NAVAL *Greenwich* S J DAVIES
ST MARK AND ST JOHN *Plymouth* C E EDMONDS
ST MARTIN'S *Lancaster* M R PEATMAN
SPURGEON'S S J OSGOOD
UNIVERSITY COLLEGE *Chichester* H J HUGHES
UNIVERSITY COLLEGE *Worcester* S L BLOOMER
WEST ANGLIA S C STOKES
YORK ST JOHN J M S CLINES

COLLEGES OF FURTHER EDUCATION

This index only includes those establishments known to have Anglican chaplains. It is not intended to be comprehensive.

BISHOP BURTON COLLEGE OF AGRICULTURE *York* M J WESTBY
BOURNEMOUTH AND POOLE D A HART, S W MILLER
BROOKSBY MELTON A J HAMPTON
BURY P H SUMSION
CANNINGTON P MARTIN
CENTRAL LIVERPOOL J S WILLIAMS
CITY COLLEGE *Liverpool* J S WILLIAMS
CITY OF BATH A R HAWKINS
COLEG SIR GAR H J DAVIES
MERRIST WOOD COLLEGE OF AGRICULTURE AND HORTICULTURE A W BRYANT
NEW COLLEGE *Swindon* D ORMSTON
NORTH LINDSEY *Scunthorpe* S J WALKER
NORTH WARWICKSHIRE AND HINCKLEY N J NIXON
NORTH WEST LONDON F B CAPIE
NORTHUMBERLAND D P PALMER
NORTON RADSTOCK J B THICKE
ST MARTIN'S *Carlisle* A V WEST
SOMERSET COLLEGE OF ARTS AND TECHNOLOGY D ROBERTS
SOUTH TYNESIDE A RAINE
WORCESTER COLLEGE OF TECHNOLOGY P D J SWANN
YEOVIL COLLEGE D R GENT

SIXTH-FORM COLLEGES

This index only includes those colleges known to have Anglican chaplains. It is not intended to be comprehensive.

FARNBOROUGH N L SHARP
ROSSMORE COMMUNITY T F GOMM

SCHOOLS

This index only includes those schools known to have Anglican chaplains. It is not intended to be comprehensive.

ABBOTS BROMLEY P G GREEN
ABINGDON H L KIRK
ALDENHAM *Hertfordshire* W W BELL
ALLEYN'S *Dulwich* J H JONES
AMESBURY A J GREADY
ARCHBISHOP TENISON'S *Kennington* A J REID
ARDINGLY COLLEGE *Haywards Heath* I R COLSON
BANCROFT'S *Woodford Green* I MOORE
BARNARD CASTLE S J RIDLEY
BEDFORD D L LAWRENCE-MARCH
BEDGEBURY *Kent* H J CROMPTON
BERKHAMSTED COLLEGIATE *Hertfordshire* S GOLDING
BETHANY *Goudhurst* S C BATTERSBY
BISHOP RAWSTORNE *Preston* R J BRUNSWICK
BISHOP WORDSWORTH *Salisbury* J A BERSWEDEN
BISHOP'S BLUE COAT CHURCH OF ENGLAND HIGH *Chester* I J HUTCHINGS
BLOXHAM M G PRICE
BLUE COAT COMPREHENSIVE *Walsall* C M WILLIAMS
BLUE COAT *Reading* N J BENNETT
BLUECOAT *Nottingham* K W G JOHNSON
BLUNDELL'S *Tiverton* T C HUNT
BOX HILL B STEADMAN-ALLEN
BRADFIELD *Berkshire* C PYNN
BRAMCOTE *Nottinghamshire* C F ANDREWS
BRENTWOOD *Essex* D J GILCHRIST
BRIGHTON COLLEGE R P S EASTON
BRISTOL CATHEDRAL S B TAYLOR
BROMSGROVE E C REED
BRYANSTON *Dorset* A J DAYNES
CANFORD *Wimborne* C JERVIS, K K SUGDEN
CASTERTON *Lancashire* P S ATKINSON
CHARTERHOUSE *Godalming* S J HARKER, R G LLOYD
CHELTENHAM COLLEGE R DE LA BAT SMIT
CHELTENHAM LADIES' COLLEGE D T MERRY, H R WOOD
CHIGWELL *Essex* C P COLLINGWOOD
CHRIST'S COLLEGE *Brecon* R M LLEWELLYN
CHRIST'S HOSPITAL *Horsham* A MITRA, N J MITRA
CITY OF LONDON FREEMEN'S *Ashtead Park* D F P RUTHERFORD
CLAYESMORE *Blandford* A J H EDWARDS
CLIFTON COLLEGE *Bristol* K TAPLIN
COLFE'S *London* A C COLLIER
CRAIGCLOWAN *Perth* A C MAZUR
CRANBROOK *Kent* D COOK
CRANLEIGH *Surrey* P V PARKER
DAUNTSEY'S *Devizes* D R JOHNSON
DEAN CLOSE *Cheltenham* E L TALBOT
DENSTONE COLLEGE *Uttoxeter* M A SMITH
DERBY GRAMMAR P R JONES
DERBY HIGH R J A BARRETT
DUKE OF YORK'S ROYAL MILITARY *Dover* J R BROUGHTON
DULWICH COLLEGE S E YOUNG
DULWICH PREPARATORY *Cranbrook* I M BUTLER
EASTBOURNE COLLEGE C J COMYNS, C K MACDONALD
ELIZABETH COLLEGE *Guernsey* R G HARNISH
EMANUEL *Wandsworth* P M HUNT
EPSOM COLLEGE C D BROWN, C A CASE, P THOMPSON
ETON COLLEGE *Berkshire* D COOPER, P A HESS, C M JONES, C W MITCHELL-INNES
FELSTED *Essex* J HART
FETTES COLLEGE *Edinburgh* P J D ALLEN
GIGGLESWICK J J N SYKES
GLENALMOND COLLEGE E C KERR
GODOLPHIN *Salisbury* B R SEARLE-BARNES
GORDON'S *Woking* D H ROBINSON
GOSDEN HOUSE J N E BUNDOCK
GREIG CITY ACADEMY P J HENDERSON
GRESHAM'S *Holt* B R ROBERTS
HABERDASHERS' ASKE'S *Elstree* D M LINDSAY
HAILEYBURY COLLEGE *Hertfordshire* C R BRIGGS
HARROGATE LADIES' COLLEGE J CHEESEMAN
HARROW J E POWER
HEATHFIELD *Ascot* D J DUNCANSON
HEREFORD CATHEDRAL P A ROW
HIGHGATE *London* P J J KNIGHT
HOLMEWOOD HOUSE *Tunbridge Wells* R NOBLE
HURSTPIERPOINT COLLEGE *Hassocks* P L TAIT
IAN RAMSEY *Stockton* S J GILES
IPSWICH D J WARNES
KENT COLLEGE *Pembury* S M MORRELL
KIMBOLTON *Cambridgeshire* A P GOODCHILD
KING EDWARD VI *Southampton* J G POPPLETON
KING EDWARD'S *Birmingham* D H RAYNOR
KING EDWARD'S *Witley* R W E MILLINGTON
KING'S *Bruton* N H WILSON-BROWN
KING'S COLLEGE *Cambridge* P A BURT
KING'S COLLEGE SCHOOL *Wimbledon* L R F COLLINS
KING'S COLLEGE *Taunton* C L MARSHALL
KING'S *Gloucester* J B P J HADFIELD
KING'S HOSPITAL *Dublin* P R CAMPION, R H WHITESIDE
KING'S *Rochester* S R ALLSOPP, J A THACKRAY
KING'S *Tynemouth* W D MILLER
KING'S *Worcester* M R DORSETT
KING'S, THE *Canterbury* C F ARVIDSSON
KING'S, THE *Ely* T P HUMPHRY
LANCING COLLEGE R P MARSH
LORD MAYOR TRELOAR COLLEGE *Alton* E B PRUEN
LORD WANDSWORTH COLLEGE *Basingstoke* S LEYSHON
LORETTO *Musselburgh* A F C KEULEMANS
LOUGHBOROUGH GRAMMAR A J S COX
MAGDALEN COLLEGE SCHOOL *Oxford* N SEWARD
MALVERN COLLEGE A P LAW
MALVERN GIRLS' COLLEGE C GRIFFITHS
MANOR *York* M A HAND
MARLBOROUGH COLLEGE D J DALES, J G W DICKIE
MATTHEW HUMBERSTON *Grimsby* T STOTT
MERCHANT TAYLORS' *Crosby* D A SMITH
MERCHANT TAYLORS' *Northwood* R D E BOLTON
MILLFIELD *Somerset* S F BLOXAM-ROSE
MILTON ABBEY *Dorset* R W B THOMSON
MONKTON COMBE *Bath* P STEPHENS
MONMOUTH J B HENCHER, G R KNIGHT, D J MCGLADDERY
MORETON HALL A B STRATFORD
NORWICH A M R HOUSMAN
OAKHAM A C V ALDOUS
ORMSKIRK A J M WATKINSON
OUNDLE *Peterborough* I C BROWNE, D R H EDWARDSON
PANGBOURNE COLLEGE *Berkshire* B J CUNNINGHAM
PETER SYMONDS COLLEGE *Winchester* N P SEAL
PETERBOROUGH HIGH P A W COTTON
POCKLINGTON *York* M A SMITH
PORT REGIS PREPARATORY *Shaftesbury* M T P ZAMMIT
PORTSMOUTH GRAMMAR A K BURTT
PREBENDAL *Chichester* D NASON
PRIOR'S FIELD J M FELLOWS
PRIORY, THE A C JONAS
QUAINTON HALL *Harrow* N V J ROPER
QUEEN ANNE'S *Caversham* H C BENSON
QUEEN ELIZABETH GRAMMAR *Blackburn* P S J HEDWORTH
QUEEN ETHELBURGA'S COLLEGE *York* B A ARMITAGE
QUEEN MARGARET'S *York* R L OWEN
RADLEY COLLEGE *Oxfordshire* T J E FERNYHOUGH, T D MULLINS
RANBY HOUSE *Retford* S N PAUL
RAVENSCLIFFE HIGH *Halifax* A MAUDE
REED'S *Cobham* A J CLARKE
REIGATE GRAMMAR M J H FOX
RENDCOMB COLLEGE *Cirencester* C D JEFFERSON
REPTON PREPARATORY *Foremarke Hall* N A BAILEY
RIDDLESWORTH HALL *Norwich* K A HAWKES
RISHWORTH *Ripponden* N SALT
ROEDEAN *Brighton* M E SITWELL
ROSSALL *Fleetwood* S P C COOPER
ROYAL ALEXANDRA AND ALBERT *Reigate* R K HENSHALL
ROYAL MASONIC FOR GIRLS *Rickmansworth* J H D JENKINS
ROYAL RUSSELL *Croydon* S J PADFIELD
ROYAL WOLVERHAMPTON P C ATKINSON
RUGBY R M HORNER
ST AIDAN'S *Harrogate* P T ASKEW
ST ALBANS C D PINES
ST ALBANS HIGH SCHOOL FOR GIRLS D C FITZGERALD CLARK

ST BEDE'S ECUMENICAL *Reigate* J P SCOTT
ST BEDE'S *Upper Dicker* S J MORGAN
ST BEES *Cumbria* P R BRYAN
ST CATHERINE'S *Bramley* C DE F TICKNER
ST COLUMBA'S *Dublin* M R HEANEY
ST DAVID'S COLLEGE *Llandudno* T R HALL
ST DUNSTAN'S ABBEY *Plymouth* M T BAILEY
ST EDMUND'S *Canterbury* M J HORTON
ST EDWARD'S *Oxford* D S WIPPELL
ST ELPHIN'S *Matlock* A J WILLIAMS
ST GEORGE'S *Edgbaston* S G THORBURN
ST GEORGE'S *Harpenden* A P MANNING
ST GEORGE'S *Windsor* M J BOAG
ST HELEN'S AND ST KATHARINE'S *Abingdon* J M WHITE
ST HILDA'S *Whitby* M R STANFORD
ST JAMES AND THE ABBEY *Malvern* C N H ATTWOOD
ST JOHN'S *Leatherhead* M J LAWSON
ST LAWRENCE COLLEGE *Ramsgate* D J PEAT
ST MARY'S *Calne* P M O GILES
ST MARY'S HALL *Brighton* A H MANSON-BRAILSFORD
ST MARY'S *Westbrook* B D R WOOD
ST OLAVE'S GRAMMAR *Orpington* H P C BROADBENT
ST PAUL'S *Barnes* P L F ALLSOP
ST PAUL'S GIRLS' *Hammersmith* V L BARON
ST PETER'S HIGH *Exeter* S SHEPPARD
ST PETER'S *York* J DALY
ST SAVIOUR'S AND ST OLAVE'S *Newington* J G CAVALCANTI
ST SWITHUN'S *Winchester* T E HEMMING
SEAFORD COLLEGE *Petworth* P M GILBERT
SEDBERGH C D GRIFFIN
SEVENOAKS N N HENSHAW
SHERBORNE S J N GRAY
SHIPLAKE *Henley-on-Thames* R P PRANCE
SHREWSBURY G W DOBBIE
SIR THOMAS BOTELER HIGH *Warrington* J E HARRIES
SMALLWOOD MANOR PREPARATORY *Uttoxeter* C J CANN
SOLIHULL A C HUTCHINSON
STAMFORD M R RUFF
STOCKPORT GRAMMAR L E J LEAVER
STONAR *Melksham* G R J FORCE-JONES
STOWE *Buckingham* R B JACKSON
STRATHALLAN *Perth* R A M T QUICK
SUTTON VALENCE *Kent* P A KISH
TAVERHAM HALL *Norwich* R W B MASSINGBERD-MUNDY
TETTENHALL COLLEGE *Wolverhampton* J G PARRY
TONBRIDGE S M BEAUMONT, T D PAGE
TRENT COLLEGE *Nottingham* T R HAGGIS
TRINITY *Belvedere* R J IRETON
TRINITY *Teignmouth* C M S LUFF
TUDOR HALL *Banbury* J F JACKSON
UPPER CHINE *Shanklin* A W SWANBOROUGH
UPPINGHAM *Leicestershire* R K HARRISON
WAKEFIELD CATHEDRAL J M WARE
WARWICK A W GOUGH
WELLINGBOROUGH M J WALKER
WELLINGTON COLLEGE *Berkshire* K M O'BRIEN, A D T RICHARDS
WELLINGTON *Somerset* J P HELLIER
WELLS CATHEDRAL A J KEEP
WEST BUCKLAND *Barnstaple* A M KETTLE
WEST OF ENGLAND *School for those with little or no sight* P J S CROCKETT
WESTMINSTER G J WILLIAMS
WESTONBIRT P DIXON
WINCHESTER COLLEGE R G A FERGUSON, J D SMITH
WISPERS *Haslemere* N JONES
WOODBRIDGE I A WILSON
WORKSOP COLLEGE *Nottinghamshire* P FINLINSON
WORTH D M JARMY
WYCOMBE ABBEY *High Wycombe* T J WRIGHT
WYMONDHAM COLLEGE I JONES

THEOLOGICAL COLLEGES AND COURSES

This index includes the name of the principal or warden and the names of staff members who are Anglican clergy and whose appointments are at least half-time.

Theological Colleges

Church of Ireland Theological College
Braemor Park, Dublin 14, Irish Republic
Tel (00353) (1) 492 3506 Fax 492 3082
E-mail admin@citc.ie
PRIN C A EMPEY TUTORS/LECTS A S JENSEN, K J MORONEY, B T DALY, T W GORDON

College of the Resurrection
Stocks Bank Road, Mirfield WF14 0BW
Tel (01924) 490441 Fax 492738
E-mail cirvine@mirfield.org.uk
PRIN C P IRVINE DIR STUDIES P G ALLAN CR
TUTOR/LECT J GRIBBEN CR

Cranmer Hall
St John's College, 3 South Bailey, Durham DH1 3RJ
Tel 0191–334 3500 Fax 334 3501
E-mail sj-cranmer-hall@durham.ac.uk
PRIN S W SYKES WARDEN S J L CROFT
DIR MISS AND PAST STUDIES G T WAKEFIELD
DIR MIN FORMATION J HIRST
TUTORS/LECTS A B BARTLETT, M J WHIPP, C W READ

Oak Hill Theological College
Chase Side, London N14 4PS
Tel (020) 8449 0467 Fax 8441 5996
E-mail mailbox@oakhill.ac.uk
PRIN D G PETERSON VICE-PRIN C M GREEN
TUTORS/LECTS H C HENDRY, M J OVEY, J E ROBSON

The Queen's College
Somerset Road, Edgbaston, Birmingham B15 2QH
Tel 0121–454 1527 Fax 454 8171
E-mail enquire@queens.ac.uk
PRIN D J P HEWLETT
TUTORS/LECTS J L HUGHES, S BURNS

Ridley Hall
Ridley Hall Road, Cambridge CB3 9HG
Tel (01223) 741080 Fax 741081
E-mail ridley-pa@lists.cam.ac.uk
PRIN C J COCKSWORTH ASSOC PRIN J S BEGBIE
VICE-PRIN M B THOMPSON DIR PAST STUDIES M P M BOOKER
TUTORS/LECTS S M BARCLAY, R W MAYO, P S HESLAM, J B WELLS, S M GRIFFITHS, P D A WESTON

Ripon College
Cuddesdon, Oxford OX44 9EX
Tel (01865) 874404 Fax 875431
E-mail admin@ripon-cuddesdon.ac.uk
PRIN J M CLARKE VICE-PRIN AND DIR STUDIES B C CASTLE
TUTORS/LECTS M D CHAPMAN, R A FAIRHURST, A R TEAL

St John's College
Chilwell Lane, Bramcote, Beeston, Nottingham NG9 3DS
Tel 0115–925 1114 Fax 943 6438
E-mail principal@stjohns-nottm.ac.uk
PRIN C BAXTER[1] DEAN J J WITCOMBE DIR STUDIES H J WORSLEY
TUTORS/LECTS J H DARCH, M D MOYNAGH, S D DYAS, J G KELLY, P NASH

St Michael and All Angels' College
54 Cardiff Road, Llandaff, Cardiff CF5 2YJ
Tel (029) 2056 3379 *or* 2057 6377
E-mail stmichaels@nildram.co.uk
PRIN P H SEDGWICK VICE-PRIN G W WILLIAMS
TUTORS/LECTS J C CUTTELL, R G AUSTIN, J V THOMPSON, R K A THOMPSON

St Stephen's House
16 Marston Street, Oxford OX4 1JX
Tel (01865) 247874 Fax 794338
E-mail dgmoss@ermine.ox.ac.uk *or* jeremy.sheehy@ssho.ox.ac.uk
PRIN J P SHEEHY VICE-PRIN R E M DOWLER
TUTOR M F LLOYD

Theological Institute of the Scottish Episcopal Church
Old Coates House, 32 Manor Place, Edinburgh EH3 7EB
Tel 0131–220 2272 Fax 220 2294
E-mail tisec@scotland.anglican.org
PRIN M J FULLER DIR PAST STUDIES A L TOMLINSON
DIR LITURG STUDIES I J PATON COURSE DIR M KESTON
TUTOR R K ACARNLEY

Trinity College
Stoke Hill, Bristol BS9 1JP
Tel 0117–968 2803 Fax 968 7470
E-mail principal@trinity-bris.ac.uk
PRIN G I KOVOOR VICE-PRIN R H PESKETT
TUTORS/LECTS P P JENSON, J L NOLLAND, R P SYMMONS, J H S STEVEN, J M GOSNEY

Westcott House
Jesus Lane, Cambridge CB5 8BP
Tel (01223) 741000 Fax 741002
E-mail westcott-house@lists.cam.ac.uk
PRIN M G V ROBERTS VICE-PRIN A C W TILBY
DIR STUDIES V E RAYMER TUTOR S SCHOFIELD

Wycliffe Hall
54 Banbury Road, Oxford OX2 6PW
Tel (01865) 274200 Fax 274215
E-mail enquiries@wycliffe.ox.ac.uk
PRIN R D TURNBULL VICE-PRIN G S TOMLIN
DIR MIN G N MAUGHAN SEN TUTOR P J M SOUTHWELL
TUTORS A J GODDARD, C J HEADLEY, P W L WALKER, D WENHAM

Regional Courses

Carlisle and Blackburn Diocesan Training Institute
Church House, West Walls, Carlisle CA3 8UE
Tel (01228) 522573 Fax 562366
E-mail therbert@globalnet.co.uk
PRIN T D HERBERT DEP PRIN T S EVANS
TUTOR G E MARRISON

East Anglian Ministerial Training Course
EAMTC Office, 5 Pound Hill, Cambridge CB3 0AE
Tel (01223) 741026 Fax 741027
E-mail admin@eamtc.org.uk
PRIN M A BROWN DIR PAST STUDIES H J STANTON[2]
TUTORS R M MORGAN, E SHREEVE[3]

East Midlands Ministry Training Course
Room C90, School of Continuing Education,
University of Nottingham,
Jubilee Campus, Wollaton Road, Nottingham NG8 1BB
Tel 0115–951 4854 Fax 951 4817
E-mail emmtc@nottingham.ac.uk
PRIN M J TAYLOR

North East Oecumenical Course
Ushaw College, Durham DH7 9RH
Tel 0191–373 7600 Fax 373 7601
E-mail office@neoc.org.uk
PRIN T PITT DIR STUDIES M CHESTER

Northern Ordination Course
Luther King House, Brighton Grove, Rusholme,
Manchester M14 5JP
Tel 0161–249 2511 Fax 248 9201
E-mail office@thenoc.org.uk
PRIN C J BURDON TUTOR M E LEIGH, S C SPENCER, K CARVELEY[4], C MCMULLEN[5]

North Thames Ministerial Training Course
Chase Side, London N14 4PS
Tel (020) 8364 9442 Fax 8364 8889
E-mail davids@ntmtc.org.uk
PRIN D D SCEATS TUTORS A V COLEMAN, A OSBORN, D E P PALK

[1] Dr Baxter is a lay person. [2] Ms Stanton is a lay person. [3] Dr Shreeve is a Methodist. [4] Dr Carveley is a Methodist minister.
[5] Mrs McMullen is a lay person.

St Albans and Oxford Ministry Course
Diocesan Church House,
North Hinksey Lane, Botley, Oxford OX2 0NB
Tel (01865) 208260 Fax 790470
PRIN G M BUTTERWORTH VICE-PRIN G HEGARTY
DIR STUDIES S MOYISE[1] TUTORS A J P GARROW, E C CARDALE

The South East Institute for Theological Education
Ground Floor, Sun Pier House, Medway Street,
Chatham ME4 4HF
Tel (01634) 832299
E-mail principal@seite.fsnet.co.uk
PRIN J F WORTHEN TUTOR J F WORTHEN

Southern Theological Education and Training Scheme
19 The Close, Salisbury SP1 2EE
Tel (01722) 424820 Fax 424811
E-mail principal@sarum.ac.uk
DIR V P WHITE DEP DIR D A HOLGATE
MINL DEVELOPMENT OFFICER R G A RIEM TUTOR R BROWN

South West Ministry Training Course
SWMTC Office, Haighton Building,
St Luke's Campus, Heavitree Road, Exeter EX1 2LU
Tel (01392) 264737
E-mail principal@swmtc.org.uk
PRIN D G MOSS TUTORS H M ISON, S SHEPPARD

West Midlands Ministerial Training Course
The Queen's Foundation for Ecumenical Theological Education,
Somerset Road, Edgbaston, Birmingham B15 2QH
Tel 0121–454 1527
E-mail enquire@queens.ac.uk
PRIN D J P HEWLETT TUTOR C A WORSLEY

West of England Ministerial Training Course
University of Gloucestershire, Francis Close Hall,
Swindon Road, Cheltenham GL50 4AZ
Tel and fax (01242) 543382
E-mail office@wemtc.freeserve.co.uk
PRIN M W S PARSONS VICE-PRIN K M CROUCH
DIR STUDIES M DAVIES[2]

Guildford Diocesan Ministry Course
Diocesan House, Quarry Street, Guildford GU1 3XG
Tel (01483) 571826
E-mail jonscho@hotmail.com
DIR J M SCHOFIELD

Hereford Local Ministry Scheme
The Cottage, Bishop Mascall Centre, Lower Galdeford,
Ludlow SY8 1RZ
Tel (01584) 872822 Fax 877945
E-mail a.holding@hereford.anglican.org
DIR G H EARNEY

Lichfield OLM Scheme
Backcester Lane, Lichfield WS13 6JH
Tel (01543) 306225 Fax 306229
E-mail elizabeth.jordan@lichfield.anglican.org
DIR E A JORDAN

Lincoln OLM Scheme
The Forum, Church House, Lincoln LN2 1PU
Tel (01522) 529241 Fax 512717
E-mail matthew.naylor@lincoln.anglican.org
DIR D M MCCORMICK

Liverpool OLM Scheme
The Rectory, 10 Church Lane, Ormskirk L39 6SB
Tel (01695) 423204 Fax 423971
E-mail principal.olm@btopenworld.com
DIR M P ADAMS

Manchester OLM Scheme
Church House, 90 Deansgate, Manchester M3 2GJ
Tel 0161–828 1409 *or* 828 1410
E-mail annedawtry@manchester.anglican.org
DIR A F DAWTRY

Newcastle OLM Scheme
Church House, St John's Terrace, North Shields NE29 6HS
Tel 0191–270 4150 Fax 270 4101
E-mail r.bryant@lineone.net *or*
r.bryant@newcastle.anglican.org
DIR R K BRYANT

Norwich OLM Scheme
Emmaus House, 65 The Close, Norwich NR1 4DH
Tel (01603) 611196 Fax 766476
E-mail johngoodchild@norwich.anglican.org
DIR J M GOODCHILD

Oxford OLM Scheme
St Albans and Oxford Ministry Course,
Diocesan Church House,
North Hinksey Lane, Botley, Oxford OX2 0NB
Tel (01865) 208200
E-mail beren.hartless@oxford.anglican.org
PRIN B I de la T HARTLESS

St Edmundsbury and Ipswich Diocesan Ministry Course
St Mary's Bungalow, Hengrave Hall,
Hengrave, Bury St Edmunds IP28 6LZ
Tel (01284) 749435
E-mail sheila@stedmundsbury.anglican.org
PRIN C AMJAD-ALI

Salisbury OLM Scheme
Board of Ministry, Church House, Crane Street,
Salisbury SP1 2QB
Tel (01722) 411944 Fax 411990
E-mail david.heslop@salisbury.anglican.org
PRIN D A HESLOP VICE-PRIN R BROWN

Southwark OLM Scheme
Diocese of Southwark, Trinity House, 4 Chapel Court, Borough High Street, London SE1 1HW
Tel (020) 7939 9472 Fax 7939 9466
E-mail nigel.godfrey@dswark.org.uk
PRIN N P GODFREY

Wakefield Ministry Scheme
Church House, 1 South Parade, Wakefield WF1 1LP
Tel (01422) 493569 Fax (01924) 364834
E-mail ministry@wakefield.anglican.org
PRIN E M BRADNUM

Ordained Local Ministry Schemes

Blackburn OLM Scheme
Dean House, 449 Padiham Road, Burnley BB12 6TE
Tel (01282) 412291 Fax 470361
E-mail vgoddard@clara.co.uk
DIR T D HERBERT

Canterbury OLM Scheme
Diocesan House, Lady Wootton's Green, Canterbury CT1 1NQ
Tel (01227) 459401 Fax 450964
E-mail gwalker@diocant.org
PRIN *vacant* VICE-PRIN L A WALKER

Carlisle OLM Scheme
Church House, West Walls, Carlisle CA3 8UE
Tel (01228) 22573 Fax 562366
E-mail admin@cbdti.org.uk
DIR T D HERBERT

Coventry OLM Scheme
The Vicarage, 4 Hill Wootton Road, Leek Wootton,
Warwick CV35 7QL
Tel (01926) 854832 Fax 859117
E-mail brian@bwpvic.fslife.co.uk
DIR B W PEARSON

Gloucester OLM
4 College Green, Gloucester GL1 2LR
Tel (01452) 410022 ext 231 Fax 382905
E-mail dhoyle@glosdioc.org.uk
DIR D M HOYLE

[1] Dr Moyise is a lay person.
[2] Dr Davies is a Roman Catholic lay person.

BISHOPS OF ANGLICAN DIOCESES OVERSEAS

AUSTRALIA

PROVINCE OF NEW SOUTH WALES

Armidale
Peter Robert Brain
Anglican Diocesan Registry, PO Box 198, Armidale, NSW, Australia 2350
Tel (0061) (2) 6772 4491
Fax (0061) (2) 6772 9261
E-mail diocarm@northnet.com.au

Bathurst
Richard Warwick Hurford
PO Box 23, Bathurst, NSW, Australia 2795
Tel (0061) (2) 6331 1722
Fax (0061) (2) 6332 2772
E-mail bxbishop@ix.net.au

(Assistant)
Peter Thomas Danaher
PO Box 619, Dubbo, NSW, Australia 2830
Tel (0061) (2) 6882 0753
Fax (0661) (2) 6881 6740
E-mail htdiocesan@optusnet.com.au

Canberra and Goulburn
George Victor Browning
GPO Box 1981, Canberra, ACT, Australia 2601
Tel (0061) (2) 6248 0811
Fax (0061) (2) 6247 6829
E-mail george.browning@anglican.org.au

(Assistants)
Allan B. Ewing
10 Stanley Street, Wagga Wagga, NSW, Australia 2650
Tel (0061) (2) 6926 4226
Fax (0061) (2) 6921 6259
E-mail aewing@bigpond.net.au

Trevor W. Edwards,
28 McBryde Crescent, Wanniassa, ACT 2903
Tel (0061) (2) 6231 7347
Fax (0061) (2) 6231 7500
E-mail trevor@stmattswanniassa.org.au

Grafton
Keith Slater
Bishopsholme, PO Box 4, Grafton, NSW, Australia 2460
Tel (0061) (2) 6643 4122
Fax (0061) (2) 6643 1814
E-mail angdiog@nor.com.au

Newcastle
Brian George Farran
The Bishop's Registry, PO Box 817, Newcastle, NSW, Australia 2300
Tel (0061) (2) 4926 3733
Fax (0061) (2) 4936 1968 *or* 4925 2526
E-mail bishop@angdon.com

(Assistant)
Graeme Stanley Rutherford
10 Pangari Close, PO Box 9095, Wyoming, NSW, Australia 2250
Tel (0061) (2) 4329 2902
Fax (0061) (2) 4329 5501
E-mail bishopgraeme@bigpond.com

Riverina
Douglas R. Stephens
PO Box 10, Narrandera, NSW, Australia 2700
Tel (0061) (2) 6959 1648
Fax (0061) (2) 6959 2903
E-mail rivdio@dragnet.net.au

Sydney (Archbishop and Metropolitan)
Peter Frederick Jensen
PO Box Q190, Queen Victoria Buildings, Sydney, NSW, Australia 1230
Tel (0061) (2) 9265 1521
Fax (0061) (2) 9265 1504
E-mail res@sydney.anglican.asn.au

(Liverpool)
Peter Tasker
address as above
Tel (0061) (2) 9265 1530
Fax (0061) (2) 9265 1543
E-mail ptasker@sydney.anglican.asn.au

(North Sydney)
Glenn Naunton Davies
address as above
Tel (0061) (2) 9265 1533
Fax (0061) (2) 9265 1543
E-mail gdavies@sydney.anglican.asn.au

(Western Sydney, formerly Parramatta)
Ivan Yin Lee
PO Box 1443, Parramatta, NSW, Australia 2124
Tel (0061) (2) 9635 3186
Fax (0061) (2) 9689 3636
E-mail ilee@westernsydney.anglican.asn.au

(South Sydney)
Robert Charles Forsyth
PO Box Q190, Queen Victoria Buildings, Sydney, NSW, Australia 1230
Tel (0061) (2) 9265 1501
Fax (0061) (2) 9265 1543
E-mail robforsyth@sydney.anglican.asn.au

(Wollongong)
Reginald John Piper
74 Church Street, Wollongong, NSW, Australia 2500
Tel (0061) (2) 4225 2800
Fax (0061) (2) 4228 4296
E-mail rpiper@wollongong.anglican.asn.au

PROVINCE OF QUEENSLAND

Brisbane (Archbishop and Primate)
Phillip John Aspinall
PO Box 421, Brisbane, Qld, Australia 4001
Tel (0061) (7) 3835 2222
Fax (0061) (7) 3832 5030
E-mail archbishops@anglicanbrisbane.org.au

(Northern Region)
Richard Franklin Appleby
address as above
Tel (0061) (7) 3352 5053
Fax (0061) (7) 3352 4907
E-mail rappleby@anglicanbrisbane.org.au

(Southern Region)
Ronald John Chantler Williams
address and fax as above
Tel (0061) (7) 3835 2213
E-mail rwilliams@anglicanbrisbane.org.au *or* rkwill@gil.com.au

(Western Region)
Robert William Nolan
PO Box 2600, Toowomba, Qld, Australia 4350
Tel (0061) (7) 4639 1875
Fax (0061) (7) 4632 6882
E-mail rwnolan@bigpond.com

North Queensland
John Ashley Noble
PO Box 1244, Townsville, Qld, Australia 4810
Tel (0061) (7) 4771 4175
Fax (0061) (7) 4721 1756
E-mail bishopnq@anglicannq.org

(Torres Strait Islander Bishop)
Saibo Mabo
PO Box 714, Thursday Island, Qld, Australia 4875
Tel (0061) (7) 4069 1960
E-mail bishopti@bigpond.com

(National Aboriginal Bishop)
James Randolph Leftwich
129A Lake Street, Qld, Australia 4878
Fax (0061) (7) 4058 1090

Northern Territory, The
Philip Leslie Freier
GPO Box 2950, Darwin, NT, Australia 0801
Tel (0061) (8) 8941 7440
Fax (0061) (8) 8941 7446 *or* 8941 7227
E-mail pfreier@internode.on.net

Rockhampton
Godfrey Charles Fryar
PO Box 6158, Central Queensland Mail Centre, Rockhampton, Qld, Australia 4702
Tel (0061) (7) 4927 3188
Fax (0061) (7) 4922 4562
E-mail bishop@anglicanrock.org.au

PROVINCE OF SOUTH AUSTRALIA

Adelaide (Archbishop and Metropolitan)
Jeffrey William Driver
26 King William Road, North Adelaide, S Australia 5006
Tel (0061) (8) 8305 9353
Fax (0061) (8) 8305 9399
E-mail churchoffice@adelaide.anglican.com.au

The Murray
Ross Owen Davies
23 Ellendale Avenue, PO Box 394, Murray Bridge, S Australia 5253
Tel (0061) (8) 8532 2270
Fax (0061) (8) 8532 5760
E-mail registry@murray.anglican.org

Willochra	Garry John Weatherill Bishop's House, Gladstone, S Australia 5473 Tel (0061) (8) 8662 2249 Fax (0061) (8) 8662 2027 E-mail garth@tell.net.au

PROVINCE OF VICTORIA

Ballarat	Michael George Hough PO Box 89, Ballarat, Vic, Australia 3353 Tel (0061) (3) 5331 1183 Fax (0061) (3) 5332 2982 E-mail bpsec@ballaratanglican.au
Bendigo	Andrew William Curnow PO Box 2, Bendigo, Vic, Australia 3552 Tel (0061) (3) 5443 4668 Fax (0061) (3) 5441 2173 E-mail bishop@bendigoanglican.org.au
Gippsland	*vacant* PO Box 928, Sale, Vic, Australia 3850 Tel (0061) (3) 5144 2044 Fax (0061) (3) 5144 7183
Melbourne (Archbishop)	*vacant* The Anglican Centre, 209 Flinders Lane, Melbourne, Vic, Australia 3000 Tel (0061) (3) 9653 4220 Fax (0061) (3) 9650 2184 E-mail archbishop@melbourne.anglican.com.au
(Eastern Region)	Stephen John Hale *address, tel and fax as above* E-mail shale@melbourne.anglican.com.au
(Northern Region)	Philip Huggins *address, tel and fax as above* E-mail nthregbishop@melbourne.anglican.com.au
(Western Region)	Paul Raymond White *address, tel and fax as above* E-mail pwhite@melbourne.anglican.au
(Southern Region)	John Warwick Wilson *address and fax as above* Tel (0061) (3) 9653 4220
Wangaratta	Ralph David Farrer Bishop's Lodge, PO Box 457, Wangaratta, Vic, Australia 3676 Tel (0061) (3) 5721 3643 Fax (0061) (3) 5722 1427 E-mail bishop@wangaratta.anglican.org

PROVINCE OF WESTERN AUSTRALIA

Bunbury	William David Hair McCall Bishopscourt, PO Box 15, Bunbury, W Australia 6231 Tel (0061) (8) 9721 2100 Fax (0061) (8) 9791 2300 E-mail bishop@diocese.geo.net.au *or* office@diocese.geo.net.au
North West Australia	David Mulready PO Box 171, Geraldton, W Australia 6531 Tel (0061) (8) 9921 7277 Fax (0061) (8) 9964 2220 E-mail bishop@anglicandnwa.org
Perth (Archbishop and Metropolitan)	Roger Adrian Herft GPO Box W2067, Perth, W Australia 6001 Tel (0061) (8) 9325 7455 Fax (0061) (8) 9325 6741 E-mail archbishop@perth.anglican.org
Defence Force (and Hon. Asst. Bishop of Perth)	Thomas Robert Frame 12 Coghill Close, Kambah, ACT 2902 Tel (0061) (2) 6296 4465 Fax (0061) (2) 6296 4431
(Southern Region)	David Owen Murray 3rd Floor, 26 Queen Street, Fremantle, W Australia 6160 Tel (0061) (8) 9430 7224 Fax (0061) (8) 9336 3374 E-mail srbishop@iinet.net.au *or* plusdave@iinet.net.au
(Goldfields Country Region)	Tom Wilmot Bishopsbourne, 41 Ward Street, Kalgoorlie, W Australia 6433 Tel (0061) (8) 9325 7455 Fax (0061) (8) 9325 6741 E-mail kalang@westnet.com.au
(Northern Region)	*vacant* PO Box 42, Joondalup, W Australia 6919 Tel (0061) (8) 9300 0833 Fax (0061) (8) 9300 0893 *or* 9243 1751 E-mail nrbishop@nw.com.au

DIOCESE OF TASMANIA

Tasmania	John Douglas Harrower GPO Box 748H, Hobart, Tas, Australia 7001 Tel (0061) (3) 6223 8811 Fax (0061) (3) 6223 8968 E-mail bishop@anglicantas.org.au

BRAZIL

Brasilia	Maurício José Araújo de Andrade EQS 309/310, sala 1 – Asa Sul, Caixa Postal 093, 70.359–970, Brasilia, Brazil Tel (0055) (61) 443 4305 Fax (0055) (61) 443 4337 E-mail mandrade@ieab.org.br
Curitiba	Naudal Alves Gomes Rua Sete de Setembro, 3927 – Centro, 80250–010 Curitiba, PR, Brazil Tel (0055) (41) 232 0917 E-mail ngomes@ieab.org.br
Pelotas	Sebastiao Armando Gameleira Soares Rua Felix da Cunha, 425 – Centro, Caixa Postal Caixa Postal 791, 96001–970 Pelotas, RS, Brazil Tel (0055) (532) 277120 *fax as telephone*
Recife (Ecclesiastical Authority named by the Brazilian Primate)	Filadelfo Oliveira Neto, Rua Virgílio Mota, 70, Parnamirim, 52060–582, Recife, PE, Brazil Tel (0055) (81) 3441 6843 E-mail foliveira@ieab.org.br
Rio de Janeiro	Celso Franco de Oliveira Rua Fonseca Guimarães, 12 Sta.Teresa, 20240–260, Rio de Janeiro, RJ, Brazil Tel (0055) (21) 2220 2148 Fax (0055) (21) 2252 9686 E-mail coliveira@ieab.org.br
São Paulo	Hiroshi Ito Rua Borges Lagoa 172 Vila Clementino 04038–030, São Paulo, SP, Brazil Tel (0055) (11) 5549 9011 Fax (0055) (11) 5083 2619 E-mail hito@ieab.org.br
South Western Brazil	Jubal Pereira Neves Av. Rio Branco, 880 / Sub-solo – Centro, Caixa Postal 116, Santa Maria, RS, Brazil Tel (0055) (55) 223 1196 *fax as telephone* E-mail jneves@ieab.org.br
Southern Brazil	Orlando Santos de Oliveira Av. eng. Ludolfo Boehl, 278, Teresópolis, 91720–150, Porto Alegre, RS, 91.720–130, Brazil Tel (0055) (51) 318 6199 *fax as telephone* E-mail osoliveira@ieab.org.br

BURMA (MYANMAR)

Hpa-an	*vacant* c/o Church of the Province of Myanmar, 140 Pyidaungsu Yeiktha Road, Dagon PO (11191), Yangon, Myanmar Tel (0095) (1) 246 813 Fax (0095) (1) 251 405

Mandalay	J Mya Than Bishopscourt, 22nd Street, 'C' Road (between 85-86 Road), Mandalay, Myanmar Tel (0095) (2) 34110
(Assistant)	Philip Aung Khin Thein *address etc as above*
Mytikyina	David Than Lwin Diocesan Office, Tha Kin Nat Pe Road, Thida Ya, Myitkyina, Kachin State, Myanmar Tel (0095) (74) 23104
(Assistant)	Gam Dee *address etc as above*
Sittwe	Barnabas Theaung Hawi St John's Church, Paletwa, Southern Chin State, via Sittwe, Myanmar
Toungoo	Saw John Wilme Diocesan Office, Nat-shin-Naung Road, Toungoo, Myanmar Tel (0095) (54) 21519
Yangon (Archbishop)	Samuel San Si Htay 601 Pyay Road, University PO, GPO Box 1400, Yangon 11041, Myanmar Tel (0095) (1) 246 813 Fax (0095) (1) 251 405
(Assistant)	Joseph Than Pe 44 Pay Road, Dagon PO (11191), Yangon, Myanmar Tel (0095) (1) 72668 *or* 72300 Fax (0095) (1) 77512

BURUNDI

Bujumbura	Pie Ntukamazina BP 1300, Bujumbura, Burundi Tel (00257) (2) 22641 *or* 35374 Fax (00257) (2) 27496 E-mail mgrpie@cbinf.com *or* eebbuja@cbinf.com
Buye	*vacant* Eglise Episcopale du Burundi, BP 94, Ngozi, Burundi Tel (00257) (30) 2210 Fax (00257) (30) 2317 E-mail diocbuye@cbinf.com
Gitega	Jean W Nduwayo BP 23, Gitega, Burundi Tel (00257) (40) 2247 Fax (00257) (40) 2246 E-mail eebgitega@cbinf.com
Makamba	Martin Blaise Nyaboho BP 96, Makamba, Burundi Tel (00257) (9) 26493 (mobile) Fax (00257) (2) 29129 E-mail eebprov@cbinf.com
Matana (Archbishop)	Bernard Ntahoturi BP 447, Bujumbura, Burundi Tel (00257) (2) 70361 Fax (00257) (2) 29129 E-mail ntahober@cbinf.com

CANADA

Primate of Canada	Andrew S Hutchinson 80 Hayden Street, Toronto ON, Canada, M4Y 3G2 Tel (001) (416) 924 9192 Fax (001) (416) 924 0211 E-mail primate@national.anglican.ca *or* glight@national.anglican.ca

PROVINCE OF BRITISH COLUMBIA AND YUKON

British Columbia	James A J Cowan 900 Vancouver Street, Victoria BC, Canada, V8V 3V7 Tel (001) (250) 386 7781 Fax (001) (250) 386 4013 E-mail synod@bc.anglican.ca
Caledonia	William J Anderson PO Box 278, Prince Rupert BC, Canada, V8J 3P6 Tel (001) (250) 624 6013 Fax (001) (250) 624 4299 E-mail caledonia.synodofc@citytel.net
Anglican Parishes of the Central Interior (formerly Cariboo)	Gordon S Light PO Box 1979, 100 Mile House, BC, Canada, V0K 2E0 Tel (001) (250) 395 1222 Fax (001) (250) 395 1252 E-mail acpi-bishop@telus.net
Kootenay	John E Privett 1876 Richter Street, Kelowna BC, Canada, V1Y 2M9 Tel (001) (250) 762 3306 Fax (001) (250) 762 4150 *or* 862 5895 E-mail diocese_of_kootenay@telus.net
New Westminster	Michael C Ingham 580–401 W Georgia Street, Vancouver BC, Canada, V6B 5A1 Tel (001) (604) 684 6306 Fax (001) (604) 684 7017 E-mail michael_ingham@ecunet.org *or* bishop@vancouver.anglican.ca
Yukon (Archbishop and Metropolitan)	Terrence O Buckle PO Box 4247, Whitehorse YT, Canada, Y1A 3T3 Tel (001) (867) 667 7746 Fax (001) (867) 667 6125 E-mail synodoffice@klondiker.com

PROVINCE OF CANADA

Central Newfoundland	*vacant* 34 Fraser Road, Gander NF, Canada, A1V 2E8 Tel (001) (709) 256 2372 Fax (001) (709) 256 2396 E-mail bishopcentral@nfld.net
Eastern Newfoundland and Labrador	Cyrus C J Pitman 19 King's Bridge Road, St John's NF, Canada, A1C 3K4 Tel (001) (709) 576 6697 Fax (001) (709) 576 7122 E-mail cpitman@anglicanenl.nf.net
Fredericton	Claude E W Miller 115 Church Street, Fredericton NB, Canada, E3B 4C8 Tel (001) (506) 459 1801 Fax (001) (506) 460 0520 E-mail diocese@anglican.nb.ca
Montreal	Barry B Clarke 1444 Union Avenue, Montreal QC, Canada, H3A 2B8 Tel (001) (514) 843 6577 Fax (001) (514) 843 3221 *or* 843 6344 E-mail bishops.office@montreal.anglican.org
Nova Scotia and Prince Edward Island	Frederick J Hiltz 5732 College Street, Halifax NS, Canada, B3H 1X3 Tel (001) (902) 420 0717 Fax (001) (902) 425 0717 E-mail office@nspeidiocese.ca
(Suffragan)	Susan Moxley *address etc as above*
Quebec (Archbishop and Metropolitan)	A Bruce Stavert 31 rue des Jardins, Quebec QC, Canada, G1R 4L6 Tel (001) (418) 692 3858 Fax (001) (418) 692 3876 E-mail synodoffice@quebec.anglican.ca
Western Newfoundland	Percy D Coffin 25 Main Street, Corner Brook NF, Canada, A2H 1C2 Tel (001) (709) 639 8712 Fax (001) (709) 639 1636 E-mail dsown@nf.aibn.ca

PROVINCE OF ONTARIO

Algoma	Ronald C Ferris PO Box 1168, Sault Ste Marie ON, Canada, P6A 5N7 Tel (001) (705) 256 5061 *or* 256 2791 Fax (001) (705) 946 1860 E-mail dioceseofalgoma@on.aibn.com
Huron	Bruce H W Howe 190 Queens Avenue, London ON, Canada, N6A 5R8 Tel (001) (519) 434 6893 Fax (001) (519) 673 4151 E-mail bishops@huron.anglican.org
(Suffragan)	Robert F Bennett *address etc as above*
Moosonee (Archbishop and Metropolitan)	Caleb James Lawrence Box 841, Schumacher ON, Canada, P0N 1G0 Tel (001) (705) 360 1129 Fax (001) (705) 360 1120 E-mail dmoose@domaa.ca
Niagara	David Ralph Spence Cathedral Place, 252 James Street N, Hamilton ON, Canada, L8R 2L3 Tel (001) (905) 527 1316 *or* 527 1317 Fax (001) (905) 527 1281 E-mail bishop@niagara.anglican.ca
Ontario	George L R Bruce 90 Johnson Street, Kingston ON, Canada, K7L 1X7 Tel (001) (613) 544 4774 Fax (001) (613) 547 3745 E-mail gbruce@ontario.anglican.ca
Ottawa	Peter Robert Coffin 71 Bronson Avenue, Ottawa ON, Canada, K1R 6G6 Tel (001) (613) 232 7124 *or* 233 7741 ext 223 Fax (001) (613) 232 3955 E-mail ann-day@ottawa.anglican.ca
Toronto	Colin R Johnson 135 Adelaide Street East, Toronto ON, Canada, M5C 1L8 Tel (001) (416) 363 6021 Fax (001) (416) 363 3683 *or* 363 7678 E-mail cjohnson@toronto.anglican.ca *or* diocese@toronto.anglican.ca
(York-Simcoe)	George Elliott 2174 King Rd, Suite 2, King City ON, Canada, L7B 1L6 Tel (001) (905) 833 8327 Fax (001) (905) 833 8329 E-mail ysimcoe@neptune.on.ca
(Credit Valley)	M Philip Polle 256 Sheldon Avenue, Etobicoke ON, Canada M8W 4X8 Tel (001) (416) 503 9903 Fax (001) (416) 503 8299 E-mail cvalley@tap.net *or* atottenham@tap.net
(Trent-Durham)	*vacant* 63 Glen Dhu Drive, Whitby ON, Canada, L1R 1K3 Tel (001) (905) 668 1558 Fax (001) (905) 668 8216 E-mail bishopb@yesic.com
(York-Scarborough)	Michael Hugh Harold Bedford-Jones Bishop's Room, St Paul's Church, 3333 Finch Avenue East, Scarborough ON, Canada, M1W 2R9 Tel (001) (416) 497 7750 Fax (001) (416) 497 4103 E-mail mbj@total.net

PROVINCE OF RUPERT'S LAND

The Arctic	Andrew P. Atagotaaluk 4910 51st Street, PO Box 1454, Yellowknife NT, Canada, X1A 2P1 Tel (001) (867) 873 5432 Fax (001) (867) 837 8478 E-mail diocese@internorth.com
(Nunavik Region)	Benjamin T. Arreak Box 154, Kuujjuaqq, QC, Canada, J0M 1C0 Tel (001) (819) 964 2324 Fax (001) (819) 964 2113 E-mail btarreak@sympatico.ca
(Mackenzie and Kitikmeot Region)	Larry D Robertson Box 190, Yellowknife, NT, Canada, X1A 2N2 Tel (001) (867) 873 5432 Fax (001) (867) 873 8478 E-mail larryr@arcticnet.org
Athabasca (Archbishop and Metropolitan)	John Robert Clarke Box 6868, Peace River AB, Canada, T8S 1S6 Tel (001) (780) 624 2767 Fax (001) (780) 624 2365 E-mail dioath@telusplanet.net *or* bbpath@teleuplanet.net
Brandon	James D. Njegovan PO Box 21009, WE PO, Brandon MB, Canada, R7B 3W8 Tel (001) (204) 727 7550 Fax (001) (204) 727 4135 E-mail bishopbdn@mts.net *or* diobran@mts.net
Calgary	*vacant* 560 – 1207 11th Avenue SW Calgary AB, Canada, T3C 0M5 Tel (001) (403) 243 3673 Fax (001) (403) 243 2182 E-mail synod@calgary.anglican.ca *or* diocese@calgary.anglican.ca
Edmonton	Victoria Matthews 10035-103 Street, Edmonton AB, Canada, T5J 0X5 Tel (001) (403) 439 7344 Fax (001) (403) 439 6549 E-mail bishopv@telusplanet.net *or* bishopv@telusnet.net
Keewatin	David N Ashdown 915 Ottawa Street, Keewatin ON, Canada, P0X 1C0 Tel (001) (807) 547 3353 Fax (001) (807) 547 3356 E-mail keewatinbishop@gokenora.com
Qu'Appelle	*vacant* 1501 College Avenue, Regina SK, Canada, S4P 1B8 Tel (001) (306) 522 1608 Fax (001) (306) 352 6808 E-mail quappelle@sasktel.net
Rupert's Land	Donald D Phillips 935 Nesbitt Bay, Winnipeg MB, Canada, R3T 1W6 Tel (001) (204) 922 4200 Fax (001) (204) 922 4219 E-mail general@rupertsland.ca
Saskatchewan	Anthony John Burton 1308 Fifth Avenue East, Prince Albert SK, Canada, S6V 2H7 Tel (001) (306) 763 2455 Fax (001) (306) 764 5172 E-mail burton@sasktel.net *or* diosask@hotmail.com
Saskatoon	Rodney Andrews PO Box 1965, Saskatoon SK, Canada, S7K 3S5 Tel (001) (306) 244 5651 *or* 242 0837 Fax (001) (306) 933 4606 E-mail anglicanbishop@sasktel.net

CENTRAL AFRICA

Botswana	Trevor Mwamba PO Box 679, Gaborone, Botswana Tel (00267) 395 3779 Fax (00267) 391 3015 E-mail anglidiocese@info.bw

Central Zambia	Derek Gary Kamukwanba PO Box 70172, Ndola, Zambia Tel (00260) (2) 612431 Fax (00260) (2) 615954 E-mail adcznla@zamnet.zm
Central Zimbabwe	Ishmael Mukuwanda PO Box 25, Gweru, Zimbabwe Tel (00263) (54) 21030 Fax (00263) (54) 21097 E-mail diocent@telconet.co.zw
Eastern Zambia	William Muchombo PO Box 510154, Chipata, Zambia Tel (00260) (62) 21294 *fax as telephone* E-mail dioeastzm@zamtel.zm
Harare	Nolbert Kunonga Bishopsmount Close, PO Box UA7, Harare, Zimbabwe Tel (00263) (4) 702253 *or* 702254 Fax (00263) (4) 700419 E-mail angbishophre@mango.zw
Lake Malawi	Nicholas Henderson PO Box 30349, Lilongwe 3, Malawi Tel (00265) 797858 Fax (00265) 731966 *or* 731895
Luapula	Robert Mumbi PO Box 70210, Mansa, Luapula, Zambia
Lusaka	David Njovu Bishop's Lodge, PO Box 30183 Lusaka, Zambia Tel (00260) (1) 264515 Fax (00260) (1) 262379 E-mail angdiolu@zamnet.zm
Manicaland	Sebastian Bakare 115 Herbert Chitepo Street Mutare, Zimbabwe Tel (00263) (20) 64194 Fax (00262) (20) 63076 E-mail diomani@syscom.co.zw
Masvingo	Godfrey Taonezvi PO 1421, Masvingo, Zambia Tel (00263) (39) 362 536 E-mail anglicandiomsv@comone.co.zw
Matabeleland	Wilson Sitshebo PO Box 2422, Bulawayo, Zimbabwe Tel (00263) (9) 61370 Fax (00263) (9) 68353 E-mail angdiomat@telconet.co.zw
Northern Malawi	Christopher John Boyle PO Box 120, Mzuzu, Malawi Tel (00265) 334930 Fax (00265) 333805 E-mail bishopboyle@sdnp.org.mw
Northern Zambia	Albert Chama PO Box 20798, Kitwe, Zambia Tel (00260) (2) 223 264 Fax (00260) (2) 224 778 E-mail dionorth@zamnet.zm
Southern Malawi	James Tengatenga P/Bag 1, Chilema, Zomba, Malawi Tel (00265) 960143 Fax (00265) 539207 E-mail angsoma@sdnp.org.mw *or* jtengatenga@unima.wn.apc.org
Southern Malawi – Upper Shire (Archbishop)	Bernard Amos Malango Private Bag 1, Chilema, Zomba, Malawi Tel (00260) (1) 539 203 *fax as telephone* E-mail bernardmalango@hotmail.com *or* angus@malawi.net

CENTRAL AMERICA

Costa Rica	Hector Monterroso Iglesia Episcopal Costarricense, Apt 2773, 1000 San Jose, Costa Rica Tel (00506) 225 0209 *or* 253 0790 Fax (00506) 253 8331 E-mail anglicancr@racsa.co.cr
El Salvador (Primate)	Martin de Jesus Barahona 47 Avenida Sur, 723 Col Flor Blanca, Apt Postal (01), 274 San Salvador, El Salvador Tel (00503) 223 2252 *or* 224 6131 Fax (00503) 223 7952 E-mail anglican.sal@integra.com.sv
Guatemala	Armando Roman Guerra-Soria Apartado 58A, Guatemala City, Guatemala Tel (00502) 2473 0852 Fax (00502) 2472 0764 E-mail diocesis@terra.com.gt
Nicaragua	Sturdie Downs Apartado 1207, Managua, Nicaragua Tel (00505) (2) 225174 Fax (00505) (2) 226701 E-mail episcnic@cablenet.com.ni
Panama	Julio Murray Box R, Balboa, Republic of Panama Tel (00507) 212 0062 Fax (00507) 262 2097

CEYLON (SRI LANKA)

Colombo	Duleep Kamil de Chickera 368/3A Bauddhaloka Mawatha, Colombo 7, Sri Lanka Tel (0094) (1) 684810 Fax (0094) (1) 684811 E-mail bishop@eureka.lk
Kurunegala	Kumara Bandara Samuel Illangasinghe Bishop's Office, Cathedral Close, Kurunegala, Sri Lanka Tel (0094) (37) 22191 Fax (0094) (37) 26806

CONGO (formerly ZAÏRE)

Boga	Patrice Byankya Njojo PO Box 25586, Kampala, Uganda Tel (00256) (41) 273817 Mobile (00256) 77-647495 E-mail njojob2000@yahoo.com
Bukavu (Archbishop)	Balufuga Dirokpa Fidèle BP 134, Cyangugu, Rwanda Mobile (00243) 9861 1180 E-mail dirokpa1@hotmail.com *or* anglicadiobkv@yahoo.co.uk
Katanga (formerly Shaba)	Henri Isingoma Kahwa PO Box 22037, Kitwe, Zambia Tel (00243) 886533 Fax (00243) 884 6383 E-mail peac_isingoma@yahoo.fr
Kindu	Zacharie Masimango Katanda BP 5, Gisenyi, Rwanda Tel (00243) 813 286 255 Mobile (250) 841 8517 E-mail angkindu@yahoo.fr *or* angkindu@antenna.nl
Kinshasa (Missionary diocese)	Fidèle Dirokpa Balufuga (Archbishop and Bishop of Bukavu)
(Assistant)	Jean Molanga Botola EAC Kinshasa, BP 16482, Kinshasa 1, DR Congo Mobile (00243) 98 62 35 08 E-mail molanga2k@yahoo.co.uk
Kisangani	Lambert Funga Botolome PO Box 25586, Kampala, Uganda Tel (00243) 9863 3545 E-mail lambertfunga@hotmail.com
Nord Kivu	Munzenda Methusela Musababo PO Box 506, Bwera-Kasese, Uganda Tel (00243) 9838 5509 Fax (00871) 166 1121 E-mail munzenda_eac@yahoo.fr

HONG KONG

Eastern Kowloon
Louis Tsui
Diocesan Office,
4/F Holy Trinity Bradbury Centre,
139 Ma Tau Chung Road,
Kowloon, Hong Kong, China
Tel (00852) 2713 9983
Fax (00852) 2711 1609
E-mail ekoffice@ekhkskh.org.hk

Hong Kong Island (Archbishop)
Peter Kwong Kong Kit
Bishop's House, 1 Lower Albert Road,
Hong Kong, China
Tel (00852) 2526 5355
Fax (00852) 2525 2537
E-mail office1@hkskh.org

Western Kowloon
Thomas Yee-po Soo
15/F Ultragrace Commercial Building,
5 Jordan Road, Kowloon, Hong Kong, China
Tel (00852) 2783 0811
Fax (00852) 2783 0799
E-mail hkskhdwk@netvigator.com

INDIAN OCEAN

Antananarivo (Archbishop)
Remi Joseph Rabenirina
Evêché Anglican,
Lot VK57 ter, Ambohimanoro,
101 Antananarivo, Madagascar
Tel (00261) (20) 222 0827
Fax (00261) (20) 226 1331
E-mail eemdanta@dts.mg

Antsiranana
Roger Chung Po Chuen
Evêché Anglican, BP 278,
201 Antsiranana, Madagascar
Tel (00261) (20) 822 2650
fax as telephone

Fianarantsoa
Gilbert Rateloson Rakotondravelo
Évêché Anglican, Mananjary 317, Madagascar

Mahajanga
Jean-Claude Andrianjafimanana
BP 169, Mahajanga 401, Madagascar
E-mail eemdmaha@dts.mg *or*
revmctod@dts.mg

Mauritius
Ian Ernest
Bishop's House, Nallelamby Road, Phoenix,
Mauritius
Tel (00230) 686 5158
Fax (00230) 697 1096
E-mail dioang@intnet.mu

Seychelles
Santosh Marray
Bishop's House, PO Box 44, Victoria,
Seychelles
Tel (00248) 224242
Fax (00248) 224296
E-mail angdio@seychelles.net

Toamasina
Jean Paul Solo
Evêché Anglican, Rue James Seth, BP 531,
Toamasina 501, Madagascar
Tel (00261) (2) 0533 1663
Fax (00261) (2) 0533 1689

JAPAN

Chubu
Francis Toshiaki Mori
51–3 Meigetsu-cho, 2 chome,
Showa-ku, Nagoya 466–0034, Japan
Tel (0081) (52) 858 1007
Fax (0081) (52) 858 1008
E-mail office.chubu@nskk.org

Hokkaido
Nathaniel Makoto Uematsu
Kita 15 jo, Nishi 5–20,
Kita-ku, Sapporo 001–0015, Japan
Tel (0081) (11) 717 8181
Fax (0081) (11) 736 8377
E-mail hokkaido@nskk.org *or*
bishop.hok@nskk.org

Kita Kanto
Zerubbabel Katsuichi Hirota
3 10 6 Ootemachi, Maebashi, 371–0026, Japan
Tel (0081) (48) 642 2680
Fax (0081) (48) 648 0358 *or* 476 7484
E-mail kitakanto@nskk.org

Kobe
Andrew Yutaka Nakamura, 5–11–1 Yamatedori,
Chuo ku, Kobe shi 650–0011, Japan
Tel (0081) (78) 351 5469
Fax (0081) (78) 382 1095
E-mail aao52850@syd.odn.ne.jp

Kyoto
Stephen Takashi Kochi
380 Okakuen, Shimotachiuri-agaru,
Karasumadori,
Kamikyo-ku, Kyoto 602–8011, Japan
Tel (0081) (75) 431 7204
Fax (0081) (75) 441 4238 *or* 432 6723
E-mail kyoto@mse.biglobe.ne.jp

Kyushu
Gabriel Shoji Igarashi
2–9–22 Kusakae, Chuo-ku,
Fukuoka 810–0045, Japan
Tel (0081) (92) 771 2050
Fax (0081) (92) 771 9857
E-mail d-kyushu@try-net.or.jp

Okinawa
David Shoji Tani
1733 13 Aza Meada, Urasoe City,
Okinawa 910–2102, Japan
Tel (0081) (98) 942 1101
Fax (0081) (98) 942 1102
E-mail office.okinawa@nskk.org

Osaka (Primate)
James Toru Uno
2–1–8 Matsuzaki-cho, Abeno-ku,
Osaka 545–0053, Japan
Tel (0081) (6) 621 2179
Fax (0081) (6) 621 3097 *or* 6219148
E-mail office.osaka@nskk.org

Tohoku
John Hiromichi Kato
2–13–15 Kokobun-cho, Aoba-ku,
Sendai 980-0803, Japan
Tel (0081) (22) 223 2349
Fax (0081) (22) 223 2387
E-mail fujishima.tohoku@nskk.org

Tokyo
Peter Jintaro Ueda
3–6–18 Shiba Koen, Minato-ku,
Tokyo 105-0011, Japan
Tel (0081) (3) 3433 0987 *or* 3433 2417
Fax (0081) (3) 3433 8678
E-mail general sec.tko@nskk.org

Yokohama
James Satoru Endo
14–57 Mitsuzawa Shimo-cho,
Kanagawa-ku, Yokohama 221–0852, Japan
Tel (0081) (45) 321 4988
Fax (0081) (45) 323 4978
E-mail yokohama.kyouku@nskk.org

JERUSALEM AND THE MIDDLE EAST

Cyprus and the Gulf (Bishop *in*) (President)
George Clive Handford
PO Box 22075, CY 1517–Nicosia, Cyprus
Tel (00357) (22) 671220
Fax (00357) (22) 674553
E-mail bishop@spidernet.com.cy *or*
georgia@spidernet.com.cy

Egypt (Bishop *in*)
Mouneer Hanna Anis
Diocesan Office, PO Box 87,
Zamalek Distribution, 11211, Cairo, Egypt
Tel (0020) (2) 738 0829
Fax (0020) (2) 735 8941
E-mail bishopmouneer@link.net

Iran (Episcopal Vicar General)
Azad Marshall
455B Canal View Housing Society, Multan
Road, Lahore 53700, Pakistan
Tel (0092) (300) 841 0444
Fax (0092) (42) 542 0591
E-mail gulf_bishop@hotmail.com

Jerusalem (Bishop *in*)
Riah Hanna Abu El-Assal
St George's Close, PO Box 1278,
Jerusalem 91 091, Israel
Tel (00972) (2) 627 1670
Fax (00972) (2) 627 3847
E-mail ediocese-jer@j-diocese.com

KENYA

All Saints Cathedral (Archbishop)
Benjamin M. Nzimbi
PO Box 40502, 00100 Nairobi, Kenya
Tel (00254) (20) 714 755
Fax (00254) (20) 718 442/714 750
E-mail archoffice@swiftkenya.com

Bondo	Johannes Otieno Angela PO Box 240, 40601 Bondo, Kenya Tel (00254) (335) 20415 E-mail ackbondo@swiftkenya.com
Bungoma	Eliud Wabukala PO Box 2392, 50200 Bungoma, Kenya Tel (00254) (337) 30481 *fax as telephone* E-mail ackbungoma@swiftkenya.com
Butere	Horace Etemesi PO Box 54, 50101 Butere, Kenya Tel (00254) (333) 20038 E-mail ackbutere@swiftkenya.com
Eldoret	Thomas Kogo PO Box 3404, 30100 Eldoret, Kenya Tel (00254) (321) 62785 E-mail ackeldoret@africaonline.co.ke
Embu	Moses Njeru Njue PO Box 189, Embu, Kenya Tel (00254) (161) 20618 *or* 20264 Fax (00254) (161) 30468 E-mail ack-embu@maf.org.ke *or* ackembu@swiftkenya.com
Kajiado	Jeremiah John Mutua Taama PO Box 203, 01100 Kajiado, Kenya Tel (00254) (301) 21105 Fax (00254) (301) 21106 E-mail ackajiado@swiftkenya.com
Katakwa	Eluid Odera Okiring PO Box 68, 50244 Amagoro, Kenya Tel (00254) (337) 54079 Tel (00254) (337) 54017 E-mail ackatakwa@swiftkenya.com
Kirinyaga	Daniel Munene Ngoru PO Box 95, 10304 Kutus, Kenya Tel (00254) (163) 44221 *or* 44028 Fax (00254) (163) 44020 E-mail ackirinyaga@swiftkenya.com
Kitale	Stephen Kewasis Nyorsok PO Box 4176, 30200 Kitale, Kenya Tel (00254) (325) 31631 Fax (00254) (325) 31387 E-mail ack.ktl@africaonline.co.ke
Kitui	*vacant* PO Box 1054, 90200 Kitui, Kenya Tel (00254) (141) 22682 Fax (00254) (141) 22119 E-mail ackitui@swiftkenya.com
Machakos	Joseph Mutie Kanuku PO Box 282, 90100 Machakos, Kenya Tel (00254) (145) 21379 Fax (00254) (145) 20178 E-mail ackmachakos@swiftkenya.com
Maseno North	Simon Mutingole Oketch PO Box 416, 50100 Kakemega, Kenya Tel (00254) (331) 30729 Fax (00254) (331) 30752 E-mail ackmnorth@swiftkenya.com
Maseno South	Francis Mwayi Abiero PO Box 114, 40100 Kisumu, Kenya Tel (00254) (35) 43511 Fax (00254) (57) 21009 E-mail ackmsouth@swiftkenya.com
Maseno West	Joseph Otieno Wasonga PO Box 793, 40600 Siaya, Kenya Tel (00254) (334) 21075 Fax (00254) (334) 21483 E-mail ackmwest@swiftkenya.com
Mbeere	Gideon Grishon Ireri PO Box 122, 60104 Siakago, Kenya Tel (00254) (162) 21261 Fax (00254) (162) 21083 E-mail ackmbeere@swiftkenya.com
Meru	Charles Ndiga Mwendwa PO Box 427, 60200 Meru, Kenya Tel (00254) (164) 30719 E-mail ackmeru@swiftkenya.com *or* ackmeru@plansonline.net
Mombasa	Julius Robert Katoi Kalu Ukumbusho House, Nkrumah Road, PO Box 80072, 80100 Mombasa, Kenya Tel (00254) (11) 311105 Fax (00254) (11) 316361 E-mail ackmsa@swiftmombasa.com
Mt Kenya Central	Julius Gatambo Gachuche PO Box 121, 10200 Murang'a, Kenya Tel (00254) (156) 30560 *or* 30559 E-mail ackmkcentral@wananchi.com
(Assistant)	Allan Waithaka *address etc as above*
Mt Kenya South	Timothy Ranji PO Box 886, 00900 Kiambu, Kenya Tel (00254) (154) 22997 *or* 22521 Fax (00254) (154) 22408 E-mail ackmtksouth@swiftkenya.com
Mt Kenya West	Joseph M Kagunda PO Box 229, 10100 Nyeri, Kenya Tel (00254) (171) 30214 Fax (00254) (171) 4954 E-mail ackmtkwest@africaonline.co.ke
Mumias	Beneah Justin Okumu Salalah PO Box 213, 50102 Mumias, Kenya Tel: (00254) (333) 41476 Fax (00254) (333) 41232 E-mail ackmumias@swiftkenya.com
Nairobi	Peter Njagi Njoka PO Box 72846, 00200 Nairobi, Kenya Tel (00254) (2) 224 146 *or* 226 337 Fax (00254) (2) 226 259 E-mail acknairobi@swiftkenya.com
Nakuru	Stephen Njihia Mwangi PO Box 56, (Moi Road), 20100 Nakuru, Kenya Tel (00254) (37) 212155 *or* 212151 Fax (00254) (37) 44379 E-mail acknkudioc@net2000ke.com
Nambale	Josiah Makhandia Were PO Box 4, 50409 Nambale, Kenya Tel (00254) (336) 24040 *fax as telephone* E-mail acknambale@swiftkenya.com
Nyahururu	Charles Gaikia Gaita PO Box 926, 20300 Nyahururu, Kenya Tel (00254) (365) 32179 E-mail nyahu_dc@africaonline.co.ke
Southern Nyanza	James Kenneth Okiel PO Box 65, 40300 Homa Bay, Kenya Tel (00254) (385) 22127 Fax (00254) (385) 22056 E-mail acksnyanza@swiftkenya.com
Taita Taveta	Samson Mwakitawa Mwaluda PO Box 75, 80300 Voi, Kenya Tel (00254) (147) 30096 Fax (00254) (147) 30364 *or* 31387 E-mail acktaita@swiftmombasa.com
Thika	Gideon Gichuhi Githiga PO Box 214, 01000 Thika, Kenya Tel (00254) (151) 21735 *or* 31654 Fax (00254) (151) 31544 E-mail ackthika@swiftkenya.com

KOREA

Pusan	Joseph Dae-yong Lee 18 Daechengdong-2ga, Chung-Ku, Pusan 600–092, Republic of Korea Tel (0082) (51) 463 5742 Fax (0082) (51) 463 5957 E-mail bpjoseph@hanmail.net
Seoul (Primate)	Matthew Chul Bum Chung 3 Chong Dong, Chung Ku, Seoul 100–120, Republic of Korea Tel (0082) (2) 735 6157 *or* 738 6597 Fax (0082) (2) 723 2640 E-mail mcbchung@hotmail.com

Taejon	Andrew Hyun Sam Sin 87–6 Sunwha 2don, Chung-Ku, Taejon 302–823, Republic of Korea Tel (0082) (42) 256 9987 Fax (0082) (42) 255 8918 E-mail tdio@unitel.co.kr

MELANESIA

Banks and Torres (formerly North Vanuatu)	Nathan Tome c/o PO Box 19, Sola, Vanualava, Torba Province, Vanuatu Tel (00678) 38520 *fax as telephone*
Central Melanesia (Archbishop)	Sir Ellison Leslie Pogo Church of Melanesia, PO Box 19, Honiara, Solomon Islands Tel (00677) 21892 *or* 26601 Fax (00677) 21098 *or* 22072 E-mail epogo@comphq.org.sb
Central Solomons	Charles Koete Church of Melanesia, PO Box 52, Tulagi, CIP, Solomon Islands Tel (00677) 32006 Fax (00677) 32119
Hanuato'o	Jonnie Kuper PO Box 20, Kirakira, Makira/Ulawa Province, Solomon Islands Tel (00677) 50012 Fax (00677) 50128 E-mail ebiscobal@solomon.com
Malaita	Terry Michael Brown Bishop's House, PO Box 7, Auki Malaita, Solomon Islands Tel (00677) 40144, (00872) (762) 822474 *or* (00872) (762) 822426 Mobile (0066) 11 4512 1071 Fax (00677) 40027 *or* (00872) (762) 822444 E-mail terrymalaita@yahoo.com *or* domauki@solomon.com.sb
Temotu	David Vunagi Bishop's House, Lluesalo, Lata, Santa Cruz, Temotu Province, Solomon Islands Tel (00677) 53080 Fax (00677) 53092
Vanuatu	Hugh Blessing Boe Bishop's House, PO Box 238, Luganville, Santo, Vanuatu Tel (00678) 36026 *or* 36631 Fax (00678) 36631 E-mail diocese_of_vanuatu@ecunet.org
Ysabel	Richard Naramana PO Box 6, Buala, Jejevo, Ysabel Province, Solomon Islands Tel (00677) 35124 Fax (00677) 37071

MEXICO

Cuernavaca	Ramiro Delgado Vera Minerva No 1 Fracc. Delicas, CP 62431 Cuernavaca, Morelos, Mexico 62330 Tel (0052) (73) 152870 E-mail adoc@cableonline.com.mx
Mexico (Archbishop)	Carlos Touché-Porter Ave San Jeronimo 117, Col S Angel, Deleg A Obregon, 01000, Mexico Tel (0052) (55) 5616 3193 Tel (0052) (55) 5616 2205 E-mail diomex@avantel.net
Northern Mexico	Marcelino Rivera Delgado Simón Bolivar 2005 Norte, Mitras Centro CP 64460, Monterrey NL, Mexico Tel (0052) (81) 8333 0992 Fax (0052) (81) 8348 7362 E-mail diocesisdelnorte@att.net.mx
Southeastern Mexico	Benito Juárez-Martinez Avenue de Las Americas #73, Col Aguacatal 91130 Xalapa, Veracruz, Mexico Tel (0052) (228) 814 6951 Fax (0052) (228) 814 4387 E-mail dioste99@aol.com
Western Mexico	Lino Rodríguez Amaro Fco. Javier Gamboa #255, Col Sector Juarez 44100 Guadalajara, Jalisco, Mexico Tel (0052) (33) 3615 5070 Fax (0052) (3) 3616 4413 E-mail iamoccidente@prodigy.net.mx

MYANMAR *see* BURMA

NEW ZEALAND (AOTEAROA, NEW ZEALAND AND POLYNESIA)

(Primate and Archbishop)	Whakahuihui Vercoe P O Box 146, Rotorua, New Zealand Tel (0064) (7) 343 7280 Fax (0064) (7) 343 7281 E-mail pihopa.matamua@xtra.co.nz
Aotearoa (Bishop in Tai Rawhiti)	William Brown Turei PO Box 568, Gisborne, New Zealand Tel (0064) (6) 867 8856 Fax (0064) (6) 867 8859 E-mail browntmihi@xtra.co.nz
(Bishop in Te Manawa O Te Wheke)	*vacant* P O Box 146, Rotorua Tel (0064) (7) 348 6093 Fax (0064) (7) 348 6091 E-mail ha.mow@xtra.co.nz
(Bishop in Tai Tokerau)	Te Kitohi Wiremu Pikaahu PO Box 25, Paihia, Bay of Islands, New Zealand Tel (0064) (9) 402 6788 Fax (0064) (9) 402 6663 E-mail tkwp@tokerau.ang.org.nz
(Bishop in Te Waipounamu)	John Robert Kuru Gray PO Box 10086, Christchurch, New Zealand Tel (0064) (3) 389 1683 Fax (0064) (3) 389 0912 E-mail hawaipounamu@xtra.co.nz
(Bishop in Te Upoko O Te Ika)	Muru Walters 6 Rajaputana Way, Khandallah, Wellington, New Zealand Tel (0064) (4) 479 8549 Fax (0064) (4) 479 8513 E-mail muruwalters@xtra.co.nz
Auckland	John Campbell Paterson PO Box 37 242, Parnell, Auckland 1033, New Zealand Tel (0064) (9) 302 7202 Fax (0064) (9) 303 3321
(Assistant)	John Richard Randerson, P O Box 37–148, Parnell, Auckland 1033, New Zealand Tel (0064) (9) 303 9500 Fax (0064) (9) 302 7215 E-mail dean@holy-trinity.org.nz
Christchurch	David John Coles PO Box 4438, Christchurch 8001, New Zealand Tel (0064) (3) 379 5950 Fax (0064) (3) 379 5954 E-mail bishop@chch.ang.org.nz
Dunedin	George Howard Douglas Connor PO Box 5445, Dunedin, New Zealand Tel (0064) (3) 477 4931 Fax (0064) (3) 477 4932 E-mail bishop@dn.anglican.org.nz
Nelson	Derek Lionel Eaton PO Box l00, Nelson, New Zealand Tel (0064) (3) 548 3124 Fax (0064) (3) 548 2125 *or* 548 8991 E-mail bpderek@nelsonanglican.org.nz
Polynesia	Jabez Leslie Bryce Box 35, Suva, Fiji Tel (00679) 330 4716 Fax (00679) 330 2687 E-mail episcopus@is.com.fj *or* diopolynesia@is.com.fj

(Diocese of Polynesia in Aotearoa New Zealand)	Winston Halapua St John's College, Private Bag 28–907, Remuera, Auckland Tel (0064) (9) 521 2725 Fax (0064) (9) 521 2420 E-mail winstonh@stjohns.auckland.ac.nz
(Vanua Levu and Taveuni)	Apimeleki Nadoki Qiliho Diocese of Polynesia, P O Box 35, Suva, Fiji Tel (00679) 330 8539 Fax (00679) 330 2152 E-mail minoff@connect.com.fj
(Viti Levu West)	Gabriel Mahesh Prasad Sharma P O Box 117, Lautoka, Fiji Tel (00679) 666 0124 Fax (00679) 666 0124 E-mail gabsharma@yahoo.com
Waiapu	John William Bluck PO Box 227, Napier, New Zealand Tel (0064) (6) 835 8230 Fax (0064) (6) 835 0680 E-mail john.waiapu@hb.ang.org.nz
Waikato	David John Moxon PO Box 21, Hamilton, New Zealand Tel (0064) (7) 838 2309 Fax (0064) (7) 838 0052 E-mail bishop@hn-ang.org.nz
(Taranaki)	Philip Richardson Te Awhina-Bishop's House, 566 Mangorei Road New Plymouth, R01, New Zealand Tel (0064) (6) 759 1178 Fax (0064) (6) 759 1180 E-mail philip.richardson@xtra.co.nz
Wellington	Thomas John Brown PO Box 12-046, Wellington, New Zealand Tel (0064) (4) 472 1057 Fax (0064) (4) 499 1360 E-mail bishoptom@paradise.net.nz

NIGERIA

PROVINCE OF ABUJA

Abuja (Archbishop and Primate)	Peter Jasper Akinola Archbishop's Palace, PO Box 212, ADCP, Abuja, Nigeria Tel (00234) (9) 523 6950 Fax (00234((9) 523 0986 E-mail abuja@anglican-nig.org
Bida	Jonah Kolo c/o PO Box 2469, Minna, Nigeria Tel (00234) (66) 461694 E-mail bida@anglican-nig.org
Gwagwalada	Tanimu Samari Aduda Diocesan Headquarters, Secretariat Road, PO Box 287, Gwagwalada, Abuja, Nigeria Tel (00234) (9) 882 2083 E-mail gwagwalada@anglican-nig.org
Kafanchan	William Weh Diya Bishopscourt, 5B Jemma'a Street, PO Box 29, Kafanchan, Kaduna State, Nigeria Tel (00234) (61) 20634
Lafia	Miller Maza PO Box 560, Lafia, Nasarawa State, Nigeria Tel (00234) (47) 221 329
Lokoja	Emmanuel Egbunu PO Box 11, Lokoja, Kogi State, Nigeria Tel (00234) (58) 220588 Fax (00234) (58) 220 5881 E-mail lok-anglican@beta.linkserve.com
Makurdi	Nathaniel Nyitar Inyom Bishopscourt, PO Box 1, Makurdi, Benue State, Nigeria Tel (00234) (44) 533 349 *fax as telephone* E-mail makurdi@anglican-nig. org
Minna	Nathaniel Yisa Bishopscourt, Dutsen Kura, PO Box 2469, Minna, Niger State, Nigeria Tel (00234) (66) 220 035 (Office) *or* 220 514 (Home)
Oturkpo	Ityobe Ugede St John's Cathedral, Sgt Ugbade Ave, PO Box 360, Oturkpo, Benue State, Nigeria

PROVINCE OF BENDEL

Asaba	Nicholas D Okoh Bishopscourt, Cable Point, PO Box 216, Asaba, Delta State, Nigeria Tel (00234) (46) 280682 or 280043 E-mail asaba@anglican-nig.org
Benin	P O J Imasueh Bishopscourt, PO Box 82, Benin City, Edo State, Nigeria Tel (00234) (52) 250552 E-mail benin@anglican-nig.org
Esan	Friday John Imakhai Bishopscourt, Ujoelen, PO Box 921, Ekpoma, Edo State, Nigeria Tel (00234) (55) 981 079
Ika	Peter Onekpe Bishopscourt, c/o PO Box 5, Agbor, Delta State, Nigeria Tel (00234) (55) 25014
Oleh	Jonathan Francis Ekokotu Edewor PO Box 8, Oleh, Delta State, Nigeria Tel (00234) (48) 880 584
Sabongidda-Ora (Archbishop)	Albert Agbaje Bishopscourt, PO Box 13, Sabongidda-Ora, Edo State, Nigeria Tel (00234) (57) 54049
Ughelli	Vincent O Muoghereh Bishopscourt, Ovurodawanre, PO Box 760, Ughelli, Delta State, Nigeria Tel (00234) (53) 258 307 Fax (00234) (53) 250 091
Warri	Edafe Emamezi Bishopscourt, 17 Mabiaku Road, GRA, PO Box 4571, Warri, Nigeria Tel (00234) (53) 255 857 E-mail angwar@skannet.com

PROVINCE OF IBADAN

Ibadan (Archbishop)	Joseph Akinfenwa Bishopscourt, PO Box 3075, Mapo, Ibadan, Nigeria Tel (00234) (2) 810 1400 Fax (00234) (2) 810 1413 E-mail ibadan@anglican-nig.org *or* ibadan@anglican.skannet.com.ng
Ibadan North	Segun Okubadejo Bishopscourt, Moyede, PO Box 182, Dugbe, Ibadan, Nigeria Tel (00234) (2) 8107 482 E-mail ibadannorth@anglican-nig.org *or* angibn@skannet.com
Ibadan South	Jacob Ademola Ajetunmobi Bishopscourt, PO Box 166, Dugbe, Ibadan, Nigeria Tel (00234) (2) 231 9141 *fax as telephone* E-mail ibadan-south@anglican-nig.org *or* jacajet@skannet.com.ng
Ife	Gabriel B Oloniyo Bishopscourt, PO Box 312, Ife-Ife, Osun State, Nigeria Tel (00234) (36) 232 255
Igbomina	Michael Oluwakayode Akinyemi Bishopscourt, Esie, PO Box 102, Oro P.A, Kwara State, Nigeria Tel (00234) (31) 701 464
Ilesha	Olubayu Samuel Sowale Diocesan Headquarters, Muroko Road, PO Box 237, Ilesa, Nigeria Tel (00234) (36) 460 138 E-mail ilesha@anglican-nig.org
Kwara	Jeremiah Olagbamigbe A Fabuluje Bishopscourt, Fate Road, PO Box 1884, Ilorin, Kwara State, Nigeria Tel (00234) (31) 220879 E-mail kwara@anglican.skannet.com.ng

Offa	Gabriel Akinbolarin Akinbiyi PO Box 21, Offa, Kwarra State, Nigeria Tel (00234) (31) 801011 E-mail offa@anglican-nig.org
Oke-Osun	Nathaniel Fasogbon Bishopscourt, PO Box 251, Gbongan, Osun State, Nigeria Mobile: (00234) 80 335 6944
Osun	James Afolabi Popoola Bishopscourt, Isale-Aro, PO Box 285, Osogbo, Nigeria Tel (00234) (35) 230325 E-mail osun@anglican-nig.org

PROVINCE OF JOS

Bauchi	Laudamus Ereaku Bishop's House, 2 Hospital Road, PO Box 2450, Bauchi, Nigeria Tel (00234) (77) 543 460 E-mail bauchi@anglican.skannet.com.ng
Damaturu	Daniel Abu Yisa PO Box 312, Damaturu, Yobe State, Nigeria Tel (00234) (74) 522 142 E-mail damaturu@anglican-nig.org
Gombe	Henry Chukwudum Ndukuba St Peter's Cathedral, PO Box 39, Gombe, Nigeria Tel (00234) (72) 220489 or 221212 Fax (00234) (72) 221141 E-mail gombe@anglican-nig.org *or* hcndukuba@yahoo.com
Jalingo	Simon Peters Mutum PO Box 4, Jalingo, Taraba State, Nigeria Tel (00234) (79) 23312 *fax as telephone* E-mail jalingo@anglican-nig.org *or* jalingo@anglican.skannet.com.ng
Jos	Benjamin Argak Kwashi Bishopscourt, PO Box 6283, Jos, Plateau State, Nigeria Tel (00234) (73) 612221 *fax as telephone* E-mail jos@anglican-nig.org *or* jos@anglican.skannet.com.ng
Maiduguri (Archbishop)	Emmanuel K Mani Bishopscourt, Off Lagos Street, GRA PO Box 1693, Maiduguri, Borno State, Nigeria Tel (00234) (76) 234010 *fax as telephone* E-mail maiduguri@anglican-nig.org
Yola	Christian Ogochukwu Efobi PO Box 601, Jemeta-Yola, Adamawa State, Nigeria Tel (00234) (75) 624303 E-mail yola@anglican-nig.org

PROVINCE OF KADUNA

Dutse	Yusuf Ibrahim Lumu PO Box 15, Dutse, Jigawa State, Nigeria Tel (00234) (64) 721379 E-mail dutse@anglican-nig.org
Gusau	Simon Bala PO Box 64, Gusau, Zamfara State, Nigeria Tel (00234) (63) 204 747 E-mail gusau@anglican.skannet.com.ng
Kaduna (Archbishop)	Josiah Idowu-Fearon PO Box 72, Kaduna, Nigeria Tel (00234) (62) 240085 Fax (00234) (62) 244408 E-mail kaduan@anglican-nig.org
Kano	Zakka Lalle Nyam Bishopscourt, PO Box 362, Kano, Nigeria Tel (00234) (64) 647 816 *fax as telephone* E-mail kano@anglican-nig.org *or* kano@anglican.skannet.com.ng
Katsina	James Sekari Kwasu Bishop's Lodge, PO Box 904, Katsina, Nigeria Tel (00234) (65) 432718 E-mail katsina@anglican-nig.org *or* bishopkwasu@yahoo.co.uk
Kebbi	Edmund Efoyikeye Akanya PO Box 701, Birnin Kebbi, Kebbi State, Nigeria Tel (00234) (68) 321 179 *fax as telephone* E-mail kebbi@anglican.skannet.com
Sokoto	Augustine Omole Bishop's Lodge, 68 Shuni Road, PO Box 3489, Sokoto, Nigeria Tel (00234) (60) 234639 Fax (00234) (60) 232323 E-mail sokoto@anglican-nig.org
Wusasa	Ali Buba Lamido Box 28, Wusasa Zaria, Nigeria Tel (00234) (69) 334594 E-mail wusasa@anglican-nig.org *or* wusasa@anglican.skannet.com.ng

PROVINCE OF LAGOS

Egba	Matthew Oluremi Owadayo Bishopscourt, Onikolobo, PO Box 267, Ibara, Abeokuta, Nigeria Tel (00234) (39) 241 235 Fax (00234) (39) 240 933 E-mail egba@anglican-nig.org *or* mowadayo@yahoo.com
Ijebu	Ezekiel Awosoga Bishopscourt, Ejirin Road, PO Box 112, Ijebu-Ode, Nigeria Tel (00234) (37) 431 801
Lagos (Archbishop)	Ephraim Adebola Ademowo Archbishop's Palace, 29 Marina, PO Box 13, Lagos, Nigeria Tel and fax (00234) (1) 263 6026 Fax (00234) (1) 263 6536 E-mail lagos@anglican.skannet.com.ng *or* bishop@rcl.nig.com
Lagos West	Peter A Adebiyi Vining House (2nd Floor), Archbishop Vining Memorial Cathedral, Oba Akinjobi Road, G.R.A. Ikeja, Nigeria Tel (00234) (51) 493 7333 E-mail lagoswest@anglican-nig.org *or* dioceseoflagoswest@yahoo.com
On the Coast	Joshua Ogunele Bishopscourt, Ikoya Rd, P. M. B. 3, Ilutitun Osooro, Ondo State Mobile (00234) 8056 345 496
Remo	Michael O. Fape Bishopscourt, Ewusi Street, PO Box 522, Sagamu, Ogun State, Nigeria Tel (00234) (37) 640 598 E-mail remo@anglican-nig.org *or* mofape@skannet.com
Yewa	Simeon O M Adebola Bishopscourt, PO Box 484, Ilaro, Ogun State, Nigeria Tel (00234) (39) 440 695

PROVINCE OF THE NIGER

Abakaliki	Benson C B Onyeibor All Saints' Cathedral, PO Box 112, Abakaliki, Ebonyi State, Nigeria Tel (00234) (43) 20762 E-mail abakaliki@anglican-nig.org
Awka (Archbishop)	Maxwell Samuel Chike Anikwenwa Bishopscourt, Ifite Road, PO Box 130, Awka, Anambra State, Nigeria Tel (00234) (48) 550058 or 553516 E-mail awka@anglican-nig.org *or* anglawka@infoweb.abs.net *or* provoftheniger@infoweb.abs.net

Enugu	Emmanuel O Chukwuma Bishop's House, PO Box 418, Enugu, Enugu State, Nigeria Tel (00234) (42) 435 804 Fax (00234) (42) 259 808 E-mail enugu@anglican-nig.org
Nnewi	Godwin Izundu Nmezinwa Okpala c/o Bishopscourt (opposite Total filling station), PO Box 2630, Uruagu-Nnewi, Anambra State, Nigeria Tel (00234) (46) 460226 Fax (00234) (46) 462676 E-mail nnewi@anglican.skannet.com.ng
Nsukka	Jonah C Iloñuba PO Box 516, Nsukka, Enugu State, Nigeria E-mail nsukka@anglican-nig.org
Oji River	Amos Amankechinelo Madu PO Box 213, Oji River, Enugu State, Nigeria Tel (00234) (48) 881 741 E-mail ojiriver@anglican-nig.org
The Niger (Bishop *on*)	Ken Okeke PO Box 2, Onitsha, Anambra State Nigeria Tel (00234) (46) 210 337 E-mail niger@anglican-nig.org *or* kengoziokeke@yahoo.com

PROVINCE OF THE NIGER DELTA

Aba	Ugochuckwu U. Ezuoke Bishopscourt, 70/72 St Michael's Road, PO Box 212, Aba, Nigeria Tel (00234) (82) 220231 E-mail aba@anglican-nig.org
Ahoada	Clement Nathan Ekpeye Bishopscourt, St Paul's Cathedral, PO Box 4, Ahoada, Ahoada East L.G.A., Rivers State, Nigeria E-mail ahoada@anglican-nig.org
Calabar	Tunde Adeleye Bishopscourt, PO Box 74, Calabar, Cross River State, Nigeria Tel (00234) (87) 232 812 E-mail calabar@anglican-nig.org
The Niger Delta	Gabriel H Pepple Bishopcourt, 4 Harley St, Old G.R.A./ Forces Ave, Port Harcourt, Rivers State, Nigeria Tel (00234) (84) 233308 E-mail nigerdelta@anglican-nig.org
Niger Delta North	Ignatius Kattey PO Box 53, Diobu, Port Harcourt, Rivers State, Nigeria Tel (00234) (84) 231338 E-mail niger-deltanorth@anglican-nig.org *or* niger-delta-north@anglican.skannet.com.ng
Niger Delta West	Adoluphus Amabebe Bishopscourt, PO Box 10, Yenagoa, Bayelsa, Nigeria Tel (00234) (84) 490 010 E-mail nigerdelta-west@anglican-nig.org
Okrika	Tubokosemie Abere Bishopscourt, PO Box 11, Okrika, Rivers State, Nigeria Tel (00234) (84) 575 003 E-mail dioceseofokrika@yahoo.com
Ukwa	Samuel Kelechieze PO Box 20468, Aba, Nigeria E-mail ukwa@anglican-nig.org
Umuahia	Ikechi N Nwosu St Stephen's Cathedral Church Compound, PO Box 96, Umuahia, Abia State, Nigeria Tel (00234) (88) 220 311 E-mail umuahia@anglican-nig.org
Uyo (Archbishop)	Emmanuel E Nglass Bishopscourt, PO Box 70, Uyo, Akwa Ibom State, Nigeria Tel (00234) (85) 204142 E-mail uyo@anglican-nig.org

PROVINCE OF ONDO

Akoko	O O Obijole PO Box 572, Ikare-Akoko, Ondo State, Nigeria Tel (00234) (50) 670 668 akoko@anglican.skannet.com.ng
Akure	Michael Ipinmoye Bishopscourt, PO Box 1622, Akure, Nigeria Tel (00234) (34) 241 572 *fax as telephone* E-mail akdangc@akure.rcl.nig.com
Ekiti (Archbishop)	Samuel Adedayo Abe Bishopscourt, PO Box 12, Okesa Street, Ado-Ekiti, Nigeria Tel (00234) (30) 250 305 E-mail ekiti@anglican.skannet.com.ng
Ekiti-Oke	Isaac Olatunde Olubowale Bishopscourt, Temidire St, P.M.B. 207, Usi-Ekiti, Ekiti State, Nigeria E-mail ekitioke@anglican-nig.org
Ekiti West	Samuel Oludare Oke Bishop's Residence, 6 Ifaki Street, PO Box 477, Ijero-Ekiti, Nigeria Tel (00234) (30) 850 314
Kabba	S.amuel S Olayanju Bishopscourt, Obaro Way, PO Box 62, Kabba, Kogi State, Nigeria Tel (00234) (58) 300 633
Ondo	George L Lasebikan Bishopscourt, College Road, PO Box 265, Ondo, Nigeria Tel (00234) (34) 610 718 E-mail ondo@anglican-nig.org *or* angondon@skannet.com
Owo	James Adedayo Oladunjoye Bishopscourt, PO Box 472, Owo, Ondo State, Nigeria Tel (00234) (51) 241 463 E-mail owo@anglican-nig.org

PROVINCE OF OWERRI

Egbu	Emmanuel Uchechukwu Iheagwam All Saints' Cathedral, Diocese of Egbu, PO Box 1967, Owerri, Imo State, Nigeria Tel (00234) (83) 231 797 E-mail egbu@anglican-nig.org
Ideato	Caleb A Maduoma Bishopscourt, PO Box 2, Arondizuogu, Ideato North L.G.A., Imo State, Nigeria E-mail ideato@anglican-nig.org
Mbaise	Bright Joseph Egemasi Ogu Bishopscourt, PO Box 10, Ife, Ezinihitte Mbaise, Imo State, Nigeria Tel (00234) (83) 441 488 E-mail mbaise@anglican-nig.org
Okigwe North	Alfred Iheanyichukwu Sunday Nwaizuzu PO Box 156, Okigwe, Imo State, Nigeria Tel (00234) (88) 420 124 E-mail okigwenorth@anglican-nig.org *or* bishopalfred@yahoo.com
Okigwe South	David Onuoha Bishopscourt, Ezeoke Nsu, PO Box 235, Nsu, Ehime Mbano LGA, Imo State, Nigeria Mobile (00234) 8037 454 510 E-mail okigwesouth@anglican-nig.org *or* okisouth@yahoo.com
Orlu (Archbishop)	Bennett C I Okoro Bishopscourt, PO Box 260, Nkwerre, Imo State, Nigeria Tel (00234) (82) 440 538
Owerri	Cyril Chukwunonyerem Okorocha Bishop's Bourne, PO Box 31, Owerri, Imo State, Nigeria Tel (00234) (83) 230 417 Fax (00234) (82) 440 183 E-mail owerri@anglican-nig.org *or* adowe@phca.linkserve.com

PAPUA NEW GUINEA

Aipo Rongo (Archbishop)	James Simon Ayong PO Box 893, Mount Hagen, Western Highlands Province, Papua New Guinea Tel (00675) 542 1131 *or* 3727 Fax (00675) 542 1181 E-mail acpngair@global.net.pg *or* archbishopjayong@hotmail.com
Dogura	Tevita Talanoa PO Box l9, Dogura, MBP, Papua New Guinea Tel (00675) 641 1530 Fax (00675) 641 1129
New Guinea Islands, The	Allan Migi Bishop's House, PO Box 806, Kimbe, Papua New Guinea Tel (00675) 983 5917 Fax (00675) 983 5120 E-mail acpngngi@global.net.pg
Popondota	*vacant* Anglican Diocese of Popondota, PO Box 26, Popondetta, Oro Province, Papua New Guinea Tel (00675) 329 7194 Fax (00675) 329 7476 E-mail acpngpop@global.net.pg
Port Moresby	Peter John Fox PO Box 6491, Boroko, NCD Port Moresby, Papua New Guinea Tel (00675) 323 2489 Fax (00675) 323 2493 E-mail acpngpom@global.net.pg *or* foxfamily@daltron.com.pg

THE PHILIPPINES

Prime Bishop	Ignacio Capuyan Soliba PO Box 10321, Broadway Centrum 1112 Quezon City, Philippines *or* 275 E Rodriguez Sr Avenue 1102 Quezon City, Philippines Tel (0063) (2) 722 8478, 722 8481 *or* 722 9459 Fax (0063) (2) 721 1923 E-mail soliba@edsamail.com.ph ecpnational@edsamail.com.ph *or* soliba@hotmail.com.ph
Central Philippines	Dixie C Taclobao *address as above* Tel (0063) (2) 412 8561 Fax (0063) (2) 724 2143 E-mail central@i-next.net
North Central Philippines	Joel A Pachao 358 Magsaysay Avenue, Baguio City 2600, Philippines Tel (0063) (74) 443 7705 Fax (0063) (74) 442 2432 E-mail edncp@bgo.csi.com.ph
Northern Luzon	Renato M Abibico Bulanao, 3800 Tabuk, Kalinga, Philippines Tel (0063) (74) 872 2295 Fax (0063) (74) 872 2013
Northern Philippines	Edward Pacyaya Malecdan Diocesan Center, Bontoc 2616, Mountain Province, Philippines Tel (0063) (74) 602 1026 Fax (0063) (74) 462 4009 E-mail brentednp@hotmail.com
Santiago	Alexander A Wandag Sr Episcopal Diocese of Santiago, Divisoria, 3311 Santiago City, Isabela, Philippines Tel (0063) (78) 682 1256 *fax as telephone*
Southern Philippines	Danilo Labanacruz 186 Sinsuat Avenue, Rosario Heights, Cotabato City 9600, Philippines Tel (0063) (64) 421 2960 Fax (0063) (64) 421 1703 E-mail edsp-ecp@cotabato.mozcom.com

RWANDA

Butare	Venuste Mutiganda BP 255, Butare, Rwanda Tel (00250) 30710 Fax (00250) 30504
Byumba	Onesphore Rwaje BP 17, Byumba, Rwanda Tel (00250) 64242 *fax as telephone* E-mail byumba@rwandatel1.rwanda1.com
Cyangugu	Geoffrey Rwubusisi PO Box 52, Cyangugu, Rwanda Tel (00250) 53 7877 Fax (00250) 53 7878
Gahini	Alexis Bilindabagabo BP 22, Kigali, Rwanda Tel (00250) 67422 Fax (00250) 77831
Kibungo	Josias Sendegaya EER Kibungo Diocese, BP 719, Kibungo, Rwanda Tel (00250) 56 6194 E-mail peer@rwanda1.com
Kigali (Archbishop)	Emmanuel Musaba Kolini EER/DK, BP 61, Kigali, Rwanda Tel (00250) 73213 *fax as telephone* E-mail sonja914@compuserve.com
Kigeme	Augustin Mvunabandi BP 67, Gikongoro, Rwanda Tel (00250) 535 086 *or* 088 *or* 087 E-mail dkigeme@mail.rw
Shyira	John Rucyahana Kabango EER – Shyira Diocese, BP 26, Kigali, Rwanda Tel (00250) 546 449 *fax as telephone* E-mail bpjohnr@rwanda1.com
Shyogwe	Jéred Kalimba BP 27, Gitarama, Rwanda Tel (00250) 62460 Fax (00254) 62469 E-mail rds@rwandatel1.rwanda1.com

SOUTH EAST ASIA

Kuching	Made Katib Bishop's House, PO Box 347, 93704 Kuching, Sarawak, Malaysia Tel (0060) (82) 240 187 *or* 240188 Fax (0060) (82) 426 488 E-mail bkg@pc.jaring.my
(Assistant)	Bolly Anak Lapok PO Box 347, 93704 Kuching, Sarawak, Malaysia Tel (0060) (82) 429 755 Fax (0060) (82) 426 488 E-mail bollylapok@hotmail.com
Sabah (Archbishop)	Datuk Ping Chung Yong PO Box 10811, 88809 Kota Kinabalu, Sabah, Malaysia Tel (0060) (88) 245 846 Fax (0060) (88) 245 942 E-mail pcyong@pc.jaring.my
(Assistant)	Chen Fah Yong Church of the Good Samaritan, PO Box 12320, 88826 Kota Kinabalu, Sabah, Malaysia Tel (0060) (88) 212 686 Fax (0060) (89) 271862 E-mail goodsam@pd.jaring.my
Singapore	John Chew 4 Bishopsgate, Singapore 249970 Tel (0065) 6474 1661 Fax (0065) 6479 1054 E-mail bpoffice@anglican.org.sg
West Malaysia	Tan Sri Cheng Ean Ling Rumah Bishop, 14 Pesiaran Stonor, 50450 Kuala Lumpur, Malaysia Tel (0060) (3) 2031 2728 Fax (0060) (3) 2031 3225 E-mail diocese@tm.net.my

(Assistant)
Moses Elisha Ponniah
St Barnabas Church, 4 Jalan Dato Hamzah,
41000 Kelang, Selangor, Malaysia
Tel (0060) (3) 3372 8191
Fax (0060) (3) 3373 7223
E-mail stbarnak@tm.net.my

SOUTHERN AFRICA

Angola (missionary diocese)
Andre Soares
Av Lenini, Travessa D Antonia,
Saldanha N 134, CP 10 1498, Angola
Tel (00244) (2) 395 792
Fax: (00244) (2) 396 794
E-mail anglicana@ebonet.net

Cape Town (Archbishop)
Winston Hugh Njongonkulu Ndungane
16-20 Bishopscourt, Claremont 7708,
South Africa
Tel (0027) (21) 761 2531
Fax (0027) (21) 797 1298 *or* 761 4193
E-mail archbish@bishopscourt-cpsa.org.za

(Suffragan)
Garth Counsell
PO Box 1932, Cape Town 8000
Tel (0027) (21) 465 4557

(False Bay)
Merwyn Edwin Castle
PO Box 2804, Somerset West,
7129 South Africa
Tel (0027) (21) 852 9544
Fax (0027) (21) 852 9430
E-mail mcastle@cpsa.org.za

Christ the King
Peter John Lee
PO Box 1653, Rosettenville 2130 South Africa
Tel (0027) (11) 435 0097
Fax (0027) (11) 435 2868
E-mail dckpeter@corpdial.co.za

George
Donald Frederick Harker
PO Box 227, George 6530, South Africa
Tel (0027) (44) 873 5680
Mobile (0027) (82) 891 8541
Fax (0027) (44) 873 5680
E-mail diocese.g@pixie.co.za

Grahamstown
Thabo Cecil Makgoba
PO Box 181, Grahamstown 6140, South Africa
Tel (0027) (46) 636 1996
Fax (0027) (46) 622 5231
E-mail bpgtn@intekom.co.za

The Highveld (formerly South Eastern Transvaal)
David Albert Beetge
PO Box 563, Brakpan 1540, South Africa
Tel (0027) (11) 740 1154
Fax (0027) (11) 740 9156
E-mail dbeetge@iafrica.com

Johannesburg
Brian Charles Germond
PO Box 1131, Johannesburg 2000, South Africa
Tel (0027) (11) 336 8724
Fax (0027) (11) 333 3053
E-mail bgermond@cpsajoburg.org.za

Kimberley and Kuruman
Itumeleng Baldwin Moseki
PO Box 45, Kimberley 8300, South Africa
Tel (0027) (53) 833 2433
Fax (0027) (53) 831 2730
E-mail ibmoseki@telkomsa.net

Lebombo
Dinis Salomão Sengulane
CP 120, Maputo, Mozambique
Tel (00258) (1) 405 364 *or* 404 885
Fax (00258) (1) 401 093
E-mail bispo_sengulane@virconn.com

Lesotho
Joseph Mahapu Tsubella
PO Box 87, Maseru 100, Lesotho
Tel (00266) 311 974
Fax (00266) 310 161
E-mail diocese@ilesotho.com

Matlosane (formerly Klerksdorp)
David Cecil Tapi Nkwe
PO Box 11417, Klerksdorp, 2570 South Africa
Tel (0027) (18) 462 5530 *or* 464 2260
Fax (0027) (18) 462 4939
E-mail matlosane@lantic.net

Mpumalanga
Leslie Walker
PO Box 4327, White River 1240, South Africa
Tel (0027) (13) 751 1960
Fax (0027) (13) 751 3638
E-mail diompu@telkomsa.net

Namibia
vacant
PO Box 57, Windhoek 9000, Namibia
Tel (00264) (61) 238 920
Fax (00264) (61) 225 903
E-mail anglican@iafrica.com.na

Natal
Rubin Phillip
PO Box 47439, Greyville 4023, South Africa
Tel (0027) (31) 309 2066
Fax (0027) (31) 308 9316
E-mail bishop@dionatal.org.za

(Central)
Funginkosi Mbhele
Private Bag 899, Pietermaritzburg 3200,
South Africa
Tel (0027) (33) 394 1560
Fax (0027) (33) 394 8785
E-mail bishopmbhele@dionatal.org.za

(Coast)
Elijah Robert Thwala
PO Box 47439, Greyville 4023, South Africa
Tel (0027) (31) 308 9314
Fax (0027) (31) 308 9316
E-mail bishopthwala@dionatal.org.za

Niassa
Mark van Koevering
Diocese do Niassa, CP 264,
Lichinga, Niassa, Mozambique
Tel (00258) 712 0735
fax as telephone
E-mail diocese-niassa@teledata.mz

Order of Ethiopia (Bishop of the)
Sigzibo Dwane
PO Box 46803, Glosderry 7702, South Africa
Tel (0027) (21) 683 0006
Fax (0027) (21) 683 0008
E-mail sdwane@yebo.co.za

Port Elizabeth
Nceba Bethlehem Nopece
PO Box 7109, Newton Park 6055, South Africa
Tel (0027) (41) 365 1387
Fax (0027) (41) 365 2049
E-mail pebishop@iafrica.com

Pretoria
Johannes T Seoka
PO Box 1032, Pretoria, 0001 South Africa
Tel (0027) (12) 322 2218
Fax (0027) (12) 322 9411
E-mail ptabish@cpsa.org.za

(Suffragan)
Mazwi Ernest Tisani
348 General Beyers St, Pretoria North 0116,
South Africa
Tel (00264) (12) 546 6253
E-mail bishopmazwi@mweb.co.za

St Helena
John William Salt
Bishopsholme, PO Box 62,
St Helena Island, South Atlantic Ocean
Tel (00290) 4471
Fax (00290) 4728
E-mail bishop@helanta.sh

St John's
Sitembele Tobela Mzamane
PO Box 25, Umtata 5100, South Africa
Tel (0027) (47) 532 4450
Fax (0027) (47) 532 4191
E-mail diocese@intekom.co.za

St Mark the Evangelist
Martin Andre Breytenbach
PO Box 643, Pietersburg 0700, South Africa
Tel (0027) (15) 297 3297
Mobile (0027) (82) 441 2568
Fax (0027) (15) 297 0408
E-mail breytie@cpsa.org.za

Swaziland
Meshack Boy Mabuza
PO Box 118, Mbabane, Swaziland
Tel (00268) 404 3624
Fax (00268) 404 6571
E-mail bishopmabuza@africaonline.co.sz

The Free State
Elistan Patrick Glover
PO Box 411, Bloemfontein 9300, South Africa
Tel (0027) (51) 447 6053
Fax (0027) (51) 447 5874
E-mail bishoppatrick@dsc.co.za

Umzimvubu
Mlibo Mteteleli Ngewu
PO Box 644, Kokstad 4700, South Africa
Tel (0027) (39) 727 4117
fax as telephone
E-mail umzimvubu@futurenet.co.za

Zululand	Dino Gabriel PO Box 147, Eshowe, Zululand, 3815 South Africa Tel (0027) (354) 742047 *fax as telephone* E-mail bishopdino@netactive.co.za

SOUTHERN CONE OF AMERICA

Argentina (Presiding Bishop)	Gregory Venables Rioja 2995 (1636), Olivos, Provincia de Buenos Aires, Argentina Tel (0054) (11) 4342 4618 Fax (0054) (11) 4331 0234 E-mail bpgreg@ciudad.com.ar
Bolivia	Frank Lyons Inglesia Anglicana Episcopal de Bolivia, Casilla 848, Cochabamba, Bolivia Tel (00591) (4) 440 1168 *fax as telephone* E-mail BpFrank@sams-usa.org
Chile	Hector Zavala Casilla 50675, Correo Central, Santiago, Chile Tel (0056) (2) 638 3009 *or* 639 1509 Fax (0056) (2) 639 4581 E-mail tzavala@iach.cl
(Assistant)	Abelino Manuel Apeleo Casilla de Correo 26-D, Temuco, Chile Tel (0056) (45) 211 130 *fax as telephone* E-mail aapeleo@iach.cl
Northern Argentina	Humberto Edmundo Axt Iglesia Anglicana, Casilla de Correo 187, 4400 Salta, Argentina Tel (0054) (387) 431 1718 Fax (0054) (387) 431 2622 E-mail diana_epi@salnet.com.ar
(Assistant)	Mario Lorenzo Mariño Casilla 19, CP 3636 Ingeniero Juárez, FCNGB Formosa, Argentina Tel (0054) (387) 431 1718 Fal (0054) (387) 431 2622 E-mail diana.epi@salnet.com.ar
Paraguay	John Alexander Ellison Iglesia Anglicana Paraguya, Casilla de Correo 1124, Asunción, Paraguay Tel (00595) (21) 200 933 Fax (00595) (21) 214 328 E-mail jellison@pla.net.py
Peru	Harold William Godfrey Calle Alcalá 336, Urb la Castellana, Santiago de Surco, Lima 33, Peru Tel (0051) (1) 422 9160 Fax (0051) (1) 440 8540 E-mail wgodfrey@amauta.rcp.net.pe
Uruguay	Miguel Tamayo Casilla de Correos 6108, 11000 Montevideo, Uruguay Tel (00598) (2) 915 9627 Fax (00598) (2) 916 2519 E-mail mtamayo@netgate.com.uy

SUDAN

Bor	Nathaniel Garang Anyieth c/o NSCC, PO Box 52802, Nairobi, Kenya Tel (00254) (733) 855 521 *or* 855 675 E-mail ecs_dioceseofbor@yahoo.co.uk
Cueibet	Reuben Maciir Makoi c/o CEAS, PO Box 40870, Nairobi, Kenya Fax (00254) (2) 570807 E-mail eapo@cms-africa.org
El-Obeid	Ismail Abudigan Gibreil Kawo PO Box 211, El Obeid, Sudan E-mail ecsprovince@hotmail.com
Ezo	Benjamin John Ruati c/o ECS Support Office, PO Box 7576, Kampala, Uganda Tel (00256) (41) 343 497 E-mail ecs-kpa@africaonline.co.ug
Ibba	Levi Hassan Nzakora c/o ECS, PO Box 7576, Kampala, Uganda Tel (00256) (41) 343 497 *fax as telephone* E-mail ecs-kpa@africaonline.co.ug
Juba (Archbishop)	Joseph Biringi Hassan Marona PO Box 110, Juba, Sudan Tel (00249) (811) 820 065 E-mail ecsprovince@hotmail.com
Kadugli and Nuba Mountains	Andudu Adam Elnail PO Box 35, Kadugli, Sudan E-mail kadudiocese@hotmail.com
Kajo-Keji	Manasseh Benyi Dawidi PO Box 26833, Kampala, Uganda Tel (00254) (41) 343 497 E-mail ecs-kpa@africaonline.co.ug
Khartoum	Ezekiel Kondo PO Box 65, Omdurman, 35 Khartoum, Sudan Fax (00249) (15) 556931 E-mail diocofkhartoum@hotmail.com
Lainya	Peter Amidi c/o ECS Support Office, PO Box 7576, Kampala, Uganda Tel (00256) (77) 658 753 *fax as telephone* E-mail petamidi@yahoo.com
Lui	Bullen A Dolli PO Box 60837, Nairobi, Kenya Tel (00254) (2) 720 037 *or* 720 056 Fax (00249) (2) 714 420 E-mail luidiocese@wananchi.com
Malakal	Hilary Garang Aweer PO Box 604, Khartoum, Sudan E-mail ecsprovince@hotmail.com
Maridi	Justin Badi Arama c/o ECS, PO Box 7576, Kampala, Uganda Tel (00256) (41) 343 497 *fax as telephone* E-mail ecs-kpa@africaonline.co.ug
Mundri	Eluzai Gima Munda c/o ECS, PO Box 7576, Kampala, Uganda Tel (00256) (41) 343 497 *fax as telephone* E-mail ecs-kpa@africaonline.co.ug
Port Sudan	Yousif Abdalla Kuku PO Box 278, Port Sudan, Sudan Tel (00249) (311) 821 224 E-mail ecsprovince@hotmail.com
Rejaf	Michael Sokiri Lugör PO Box 110, Juba, Sudan Tel (00249) (811) 20040 Fax (00249) (811) 20065 E-mail ecsprovince@hotmail.com
Renk	Daniel Deng Bul Yak PO Box 1532, Khartoum North, Sudan Mobile (00249) (122) 99275 *fax as telephone* E-mail ecs_renk@hotmail.com
Rokon	Francis Loyo PO Box 6702, Nairobi 00100 APO, Kenya Tel (00254) (2) 568 541 *or* 568539 Fax (00254) (2) 560864 E-mail REAP@maf.or.ke (mark FOA Francis Loyo)
Rumbek	Alapayo Manyang Kuctiel c/o CMS Nairobi, PO Box 56, Nakuro, Kenya Tel (00254) (37) 43186 E-mail ecs-kpa@africaonline.co.ug
Torit	Wilson Arop PO Box 26157, Kampala, Uganda Tel (00256) (41) 230 015 E-mail ecstorit@africaonline.co.ug
Wau	Henry Cuir Riak c/o CMS Nairobi, PO Box 56, Nakuru, Kenya Tel (00254) (37) 43186 E-mail riakcuir@yahoo.com

Yambio — Peter Munde Yacoub
c/o ECS, PO Box 7576, Kampala, Uganda
Tel (00256) (41) 343 497
Mobile (00256) 77 622367
fax as telephone
E-mail ecs-kpa@africaonline.co.ug

Yei — Hilary Luate Adeba
PO Box 588, Arua, Uganda
Tel (00256) (756) 561 175
E-mail ecs-kpa@africaonline.co.ug

Yirol — Benjamin Mangar Mamur
c/o St Matthew's Church, PO Box 39, Eldoret, Kenya
E-mail eapo@cms-africa.org

TANZANIA

Central Tanganyika — Godfrey Mdimi Mhogolo
Makay House, PO Box 15, Dodoma, Tanzania
Tel (00255) (26) 232 1714
Fax (00255) (26) 232 4518
E-mail mhogolo@kicheko.com *or* mhogolo@pnc.com.au

(Assistant) — Ainea Kusenha
address etc as above

Dar-es-Salaam — Valentino Mokiwa
PO Box 25016, Ilala, Dar-es-Salaam, Tanzania
Tel (00255) (22) 286 4426
E-mail mokiwa_valentine@hotmail.com

Kagera — Aaron Kijanjali
PO Box 18, Ngara, Tanzania
Tel (00255) (28) 222 3624
Fax (00255) (28) 222 2518
E-mail act-kagera@africaonline.co.tz

Kondoa — Yohana Zakaria Mkavu
PO Box 7, Kondoa
Tel (00255) (26) 236 0312
Fax: (00255) (26) 236 0304 *or* 0324
E-mail act-kondoa@maf.or.tz

Mara — Hilkiah Deya Omindo
PO Box 131, Musoma, Tanzania
Tel (00255) (28) 262 2376
Fax (00255) (28) 262 2414
E-mail maracpt@maf.org

Masasi — Patrick Mwachiko
Private Bag, PO Masasi, Mtwara Region, Tanzania
Tel (00255) (23) 251 0016
Fax (00255) (23) 251 0351
E-mail actmasasidev@makondenet.com

Morogoro — Dudley Mageni
PO Box 320, Morogoro, Tanzania
Tel (00255) (23) 260 4602
fax as telephone
E-mail act-morogoro@africaonline.co.tz

Mount Kilimanjaro — Simon Elilekia Makundi
PO Box 1057, Arusha, Tanzania
Tel (00255) (27) 254 8396
E-mail dmk@habari.co.tz

(Assistant) — John Hayden
PO Box 74, Kibaya
Tel (00255) (27) 255 5327
E-mail dkiteto@elct.com *or* johnhayden@dsl.pipex.com

Mpwapwa — Simon E Chiwanga
PO Box 2, Mpwapwa, Tanzania
Tel (00255) (26) 232 4123
Fax (00255) (26) 232 0063
E-mail dmp@maf.or.tz

Rift Valley — Alpha Francis Mohamed
PO Box 16, Manyoni, Tanzania
Tel (00255) (26) 254 0013
Fax (00255) (26) 250 3014
E-mail act-drv@maf.or.tz

Ruaha (Archbishop) — Donald Leo Mtetemela
Box 1028, Iringa, Tanzania
Tel (00255) (26) 270 1211
Fax (00225) (26) 270 2479
E-mail ruaha@africaonline.co.tz

Ruvuma — Maternus K Kapinga
PO Box 1357, Songea, Ruvuma, Tanzania
Tel (00255) (25) 260 0090
Fax (00255) (25) 260 2987
E-mail askkapinga@peramiho.org

Southern Highlands — John Mwela
PO Box 198, Mbeya
Tel (00255) (25) 250 0216
E-mail dsh-dev@atma.co.tz

South West Tanganyika — Michael Robert Westall
Bishop's House, PO Box 32, Njombe, Tanzania
Tel (00255) (26) 278 2010
Fax (00255) (26) 278 2403
E-mail dswt@africaonline.co.tz

Southern Highlands — John Mwela
PO Box 198, Mbeya, Tanzania
Tel (00255) (25) 250 0216

Tabora — Sadock Makaya
PO Box 1408, Tabora, Tanzania
Tel (00255) (26) 260 4124
Fax (00255) (26) 260 4899
E-mail acttbr@taboraonline.com

Tanga — Philip D Baji
PO Box 35, Korogwe, Tanga, Tanzania
Tel (00255) (27) 264 0522
Fax (00255) (27) 264 0631
E-mail bajipp@yahoo.com

Victoria Nyanza — John Paul Changae
PO Box 278, Mwanza, Tanzania
Tel (00255) (28) 250 0627
Fax (00255) (28) 250 0676
E-mail mfukochangae@yahoo.com

Western Tanganyika — Gerard E Mpango
PO Box 13, Kasulu, Tanzania
Tel (00255) (28) 281 0321
fax as telephone
E-mail bpmpango@maf.org *or* askofugm@yahoo.com

(Assistants) (Lake Zone, Kigoma) — Naftali Bikaka
PO Box 1378, Kigoma, Tanzania
Tel (00255) (28) 281 0321

(Southern Zone, Rukwa in Sumbawanga) — Mark Badeleya
PO Box 226, Sumbawanga, Tanzania
Tel (00255) (25) 280 0287

Zanzibar — Douglas Toto
PO Box 5, Mkunazini, Zanzibar, Tanzania
Tel (00255) (24) 223 5348
Fax (00255) (24) 223 6772
E-mail secactznz@zanlink.com

UGANDA

Bukedi — Nicodemus Engwalas-Okille
PO Box 170, Tororo, Uganda
Mobile (00256) 77 542 164

Bunyoro-Kitara — Nathan Kyamanywa
PO Box 20, Hoima, Uganda
Tel (00256) (465) 40128
Mobile (00256) 77 648 232
E-mail bkdioces@infocom.co.ug

Busoga — Michael Kyomya
PO Box 1658, Jinja, Uganda
Mobile (00256) 75 649 102

Central Buganda — Jackson Matovu
PO Box 1200, Karoni-Gomba, Mpigi, Uganda
Mobile (00256) 77 475 640
E-mail veldhuis@africaonline.co.ug

East Ankole — Elisha Kyamugambi
PO Box 14, Mbarara, Ankole, Uganda
Tel (00256) (485) 20290
Mobile (00256) 77 525 847

Kampala (Archbishop) — Henry Luke Orombi
PO Box 14123, Kampala, Uganda
Tel (00256) (41) 270 218 *or* 270 219
Mobile (00256) 77 476 476
Fax (00256) (41) 251 925 *or* 245 597
E-mail coutr@uol.co.ug

(Assistant)	Zac Niringiye PO Box 335, Kampala, Uganda Tel (00256) (41) 290 231 Fax (00256) (41) 342601
Karamoja	Peter Lomongin PO Box 44, Moroto, Uganda Mobile (00256) 77 961 353
Kigezi	George Katwesigye PO Box 3, Kabale, Uganda Tel (00256) (486) 22003 Fax (00256) (486) 22802 Mobile (00256) 77 446 954
Kinkizi	John Ntegyereize PO Box 77, Karuhinda, Rukungiri, Uganda Tel (00873) (761) 604794 *or* 604795 Fax (00873) (761) 604796 *or* 604797
Kitgum	Benjamin Ojwang PO Box 187, Kitgum, Uganda Mobile (00256) 77 361 201
Kumi	Thomas Edison Irigei PO Box 18, Kumi, Uganda Mobile (00256) 77 659 460
Lango	John Charles Odrukami PO Box 6, Lira, Uganda Mobile (00256) 77614 000
Luwero	Evans Mukasa Kisekka PO Box 125, Luwero, Uganda Tel (00256) (41) 610 070 *or* 610 048 Fax (00256) (41) 610 132 *or* 610 070 Mobile (00256) 77 421 220
Madi and West Nile	Enock Lee Drati PO Box 370, Arua, Uganda Mobile (00256) 77 473 733
Masindi-Kitari	Stanley Ntagali PO Box 515, Masindi, Uganda Tel (00256) (41) 270 218 Fax (00256) (41) 251 925 E-mail counet_ps@Mukla.gn.apc.org
Mbale	Samwiri Namakhetsa Khaemba Wabulakha Bishop's House, PO Box 473, Mbale, Uganda Tel (00256) (45) 33533 Mobile (00256) 77 512 051
Mityana	Dunstan Bukenya PO Box 102, Mityana, Uganda Tel (00256) (46) 2017 Mobile (00256) 77 615 789
Muhabura	*vacant* Church of Uganda, PO Box 22, Kisoro, Uganda Tel (00256) (486) 30014 *or* 30058 Fax (00256) (486) 30059
Mukono	Elia Paul Luzinda PO Box 39, Mukono, Uganda Tel (00256) (41) 290 229 Mobile (00256) 77 603 348
Namirembe	Samuel Balagadde Ssekkadde PO Box 14297, Kampala, Uganda Tel (00256) (41) 271682 *or* 244347 Mobile (00256) 77 500 494 E-mail namid@infocom.co.ug
Nebbi	Alphonse Watho-kudi PO Box 27, Nebbi, Uganda Mobile (00256) 77 650 032
North Ankole	John Muhanguzi c/o PO Box 14, Rushere Mbarara, Ankole, Uganda Mobile (00256) 77 369 947
North Kigezi	Edward Muhima PO Box 23, Rukungiri, Uganda Tel (00256) (486) 42433 Mobile (00256) 77 709 387
North Mbale	*vacant* PO Box 1837, Mbale, Uganda Fax (00256) (41) 254 576
Northern Uganda	Nelson Onono-Onweng PO Box 232, Gulu, Uganda Mobile (00256) 77 587 840 E-mail dnu@bushnet.net
Ruwenzori	Benezeri Kisembo PO Box 37, Fort Portal, Uganda Mobile (00256) 77 470 671 E-mail orphans@africaonline.co.ug
Sebei	Augustine Joe Arapyona Salimo PO Box 23, Kapchorwa, Uganda Tel (00256) (45) 51072 *or* 51008 Mobile (00256) 77 550 520
Soroti	Charles Bernard Obaikol-Ebitu PO Box 107, Soroti, Uganda Tel (00256) (45) 61795 Mobile (00256) 77 557 909
South Ruwenzori	Jackson T. Nzerebende PO Box 42, Kasese, Uganda Mobile (00256) 77 713 736 Fax (00256) (483) 44450
West Ankole	William Magambo PO Box 140, Bushenyi, Uganda Tel (00256) 77 465 488 E-mail westankoladiocese@infocom.co.ug
West Buganda	Samuel Cephas Kamya PO Box 242, Masaka, Uganda Mobile (00256) 77 413 400 E-mail westbuganda@anglican.co.ug

UNITED STATES OF AMERICA

The roman numerals indicate to which of the nine provinces of ECUSA the diocese belongs

Presiding Bishop	Frank Tracy Griswold Episcopal Church Center, 815 Second Avenue, New York, NY 10017, USA Tel (001) (212) 716 6276 Fax (001) (212) 490 3298 E-mail stolley@episcopalchurch.org
(Office of Pastoral Development)	Frank Clayton Matthews 8100 Three Chopt Road, Suite 102, Richmond, VA 23229, USA Tel (001) (804) 282 6007 Fax (001) (804) 282 6008 E-mail cmatthews@episcopalchurch.org
(Bishop Suffragan for Chaplaincies and Bishop in Charge of Micronesia)	George Elden Packard Episcopal Church Center, 815 Second Avenue, New York, NY 10017, USA Tel (001) (800) 334 7626 ext 6065 Fax (001) (212) 867 1654 E-mail gpackard@episcopalchurch.org
Alabama (IV)	Henry Nutt Parsley 521 North 20th Street, Birmingham, AL 35203-2611, USA Tel (001) (205) 715 2060 Fax (001) (205) 715 2066 E-mail hparsley@dioala.org
(Suffragan)	Mark H Andrus *address etc as above* E-mail mandrus@dioala.org
Alaska (VIII)	Mark Lawrence MacDonald 1205 Denali Way, Fairbanks, AK 99701-4137, USA Tel (001) (907) 452 3040 Fax (001) (907) 456 6552 E-mail mmacdonald@gci.net
Albany (II)	Daniel William Herzog 68 South Swan Street, Albany, NY 12210, USA Tel (001) (518) 465 4737 Fax (001) (518) 436 1182 E-mail bishop@global2000.net
(Suffragan)	David John Bena *address etc as above* E-mail bishopbena@albanydiocese.org
Arizona (VIII)	Kirk Stevan Smith 114 West Roosevelt Street, Phoenix, AZ 85003-1406, USA Tel (001) (602) 254 0976 Fax (001) (602) 495 6603 Email bishop@azdiocese.org

Arkansas (VII) Larry Earl Maze
Cathedral House, PO Box 164668,
Little Rock, AR 72216-4668, USA
Tel (001) (501) 372 2168
Fax (001) (501) 372 2147
E-mail lmaze@arkansas.anglican.org

Atlanta (IV) John Neil Alexander
2744 Peachtree Road NW,
Atlanta, GA 30363-0701, USA
Tel (001) (404) 601 5320
Fax (001) (404) 601 5330
E-mail bishop@episcopalatlanta.org

Bethlehem (III) Paul Victor Marshall
333 Wyandotte Street,
Bethlehem, PA 18015-1527, USA
Tel (001) (610) 691 5655 *or* 691 5656
Fax (001) (610) 691 1682
E-mail bishop@diobeth.org

California (VIII) William Edwin Swing
1055 Taylor Street,
San Francisco, CA 94108, USA
Tel (001) (415) 673 5015
Fax (001) (415) 673 9268
E-mail bishop@diocal.org

Central Ecuador (IX) *vacant*
Avenue Amazonas 4430 Y Villalengua,
Piso 7 Oficina 708, Edificio Banco Amazonas,
Quito, Ecuador
Tel (00593) (22) 296 083
Fax (00593) (22) 813 937

Central Florida (IV) John Wadsworth Howe
Diocesan Office, 1017 E Robinson Street,
Orlando, FL 32801-2023, USA
Tel (001) (407) 423 3567
Fax (001) (407) 872 0006
E-mail jhowe@cfdiocese.org

(Assistant) Hugo Luis Pina-Lopez
address as above
Tel (001) (407) 423 3567
Fax (001) (407) 872 0006
E-mail hisporlfl@aol.com

Central Gulf Coast (IV) Philip Menzie Duncan II
201 Mo Baylen (BX13330),
Pensacola, FL 32591-3330, USA
Tel (001) (850) 434 7337
Fax (001) (850) 434 8577
E-mail bishopduncan@diocgc.org

Central New York (II) Gladstone Skip Adams
310 Montgomery Street, Suite 200,
Syracuse, NY 13202-2093, USA
Tel (001) (315) 474 6596
Fax (001) (315) 478 1632
E-mail kmcdaniel@cny.anglican.org

Central Pennsylvania (III) Michael Whittington Creighton
Box 11937, Harrisburg, PA 17108-1937, USA
Tel (001) (717) 236 5959
Fax (001) (717) 236 6448
E-mail bishopcpa@aol.com

Chicago (V) William Dailey Persell
65 East Huron Street,
Chicago, IL 60611, USA
Tel (001) (312) 751 4200 *or* 751 4217
E-mail bishop@epischicago.org

(Assistant) Victor Alfonso Scantlebury
Address and fax as above
Tel (001) (312) 751 4216
E-mail vscantlebury@epischicago.org

Colombia (IX) Francisco J. Duque Gómez
Apartado Aereo 52964, Bogota 2, Colombia
Tel (0057) (1) 288 3187 *or* 288 3167
Fax (0057) (1) 288 3248
E-mail iec@iglesiaepiscopal.org.co

Colorado (VI) Robert J. O'Neill
1300 Washington Street,
Denver, CO 80203-2008, USA
Tel (001) (303) 837 1173
Fax (001) (303) 837 1311
E-mail bishoponeill@coloradodiocese.org

Connecticut (I) Andrew Donnan Smith
1335 Asylum Avenue, Hartford,
CT 06105-2295, USA
Tel (001) (860) 233 4481
E-mail jburnep@ctdiocese.org

(Suffragans) James Elliott Curry
address etc as above
E-mail jcurry@ctdiocese.org

Wilfrido Ramos-Orench
address etc as above
E-mail wramos@ctdiocese.org

Dallas (VII) James Monte Stanton
1630 North Garrett Street, Dallas, TX 75206, USA
Tel (001) (214) 826 8310
Fax (001) (214) 826 5968
E-mail pmatson@episcopal-dallas.org *or* jmsdallas@aol.com

Delaware (III) Wayne Parker Wright
2020 Tatnall Street,
Wilmington, DE 19802, USA
Tel (001) (302) 656 5441
Fax (001) (302) 656 7342
E-mail bishop@dioceseofdelaware.net

Dominican Republic (IX) Julio Cesar Holguin
Apartado 764, Calle Santiago No 114,
Santo Domingo, Dominican Republic
Tel (001) (809) 686 6014
Fax (001) (809) 686 6364
E-mail iglepidom@codetel.net.do *or* iglepidom@verizon.net.do

East Carolina (IV) Clifton Daniel
Box 1336, Kinston, NC 27803, USA
Tel (001) (252) 522 0885
Fax (001) (252) 523 5272
E-mail diocese@diocese-eastcarolina.org

East Tennessee (IV) Charles Glen vonRosenberg
401 Cumberland Avenue,
Knoxville, TN 37902-2302, USA
Tel (001) (865) 966 2110
Fax (001) (865) 966 2535
E-mail cgvonr@etdiocese.net

Eastern Michigan (V) Edwin Max Leidel
Diocesan Office, 924 N Niagara Street,
Saginaw, MI 48602, USA
Tel (001) (989) 752 6020
Fax (001) (989) 752 6120
E-mail bishopeed@eastmich.org

Eastern Oregon (VIII) William Otis Gregg
PO Box 1548, The Dalles, OR 97058, USA
Tel (001) (541) 298 4477
Fax (001) (541) 296 0939
E-mail diocese@episdioeo.org

Easton (III) James J Shand
314 North, Easton, MD 21601–3684, USA
Tel (001) (410) 822 1919
E-mail bishopshand@dioceseofeaston.org

Eau Claire (V) Keith Bernard Whitmore
510 South Farwell Street,
Eau Claire, WI 54701, USA
Tel (001) (715) 835 3331
Fax (001) (715) 835 9212
E-mail bishokeith@dioceseofeauclaire.org

El Camino Real (VIII) *vacant*
PO Box 1903, Monterey, CA 93942, USA
Tel (001) (831) 394 4466
Fax (001) (831) 394 7133
E-mail susan@edecr.org

Europe, Convocation of American Churches in (VII) Pierre Welté Whalon
American Cathedral of the Holy Trinity,
23 Avenue George V, 75008 Paris, France
Tel (0033) (1) 47 20 02 23
fax as telephone
E-mail ecusa.eu@american-cathedral.com

Florida (IV) Samuel J. Howard
325 Market Street, Jacksonville,
FL 32202-2796, USA
Tel (001) (904) 356 1328
Fax (001) (904) 355 1934
E-mail vhaskew@diocesefl.org

Fond du Lac (V) Russell Edward Jacobus
PO Box 149, Fond du Lac, WI 54936-0149, USA
Tel (001) (920) 921 8866
Fax (001) (920) 921 8761
E-mail bishop@episcopalfonddulac.org

Fort Worth (VII) Jack Leo Iker
2900 Alemeda Street, Fort Worth, TX 76116, USA
Tel (001) (817) 244 2885
Fax (001) (817) 244 3363
E-mail jliker@fwepiscopal.org *or* diocese@fwepiscopal.org

Georgia (IV) Henry Irving Louttit
611 East Bay Street, Savannah, GA 31401-1296, USA
Tel (001) (912) 236 4279
Fax (001) (912) 236 2007
E-mail diocesega@att.net

Haiti (II) Jean Zache Duracin
Eglise Episcopale d'Haiti,
BP 1309, Port-au-Prince, Haiti
Tel (00509) 257 1624
Fax (00509) 257 3412
E-mail epihaiti@hotmail.com

Hawaii (VIII) Richard Sui On Chang
Diocesan Office, 229 Queen Emma Square,
Honolulu, HI 96813-2304, USA
Tel (001) (808) 536 7776
Fax (001) (808) 538 7194
E-mail RSOChang@episcopalhawaii.org

Honduras (IX) Lloyd Emmanuel Allen
Apartado Postal 586, San Pedro Sula, Cortés 21105, Honduras, Central America
Tel (00504) 566 6155 *or* 556 6268
Fax (00504) 556 6467
E-mail honduras@anglicano.hn

Idaho (VIII) Harry Bainbridge
PO Box 936, Boise, ID 83701, USA
Tel (001) (208) 345 4440
Fax (001) (208) 345 9735
E-mail carrolk@idahodiocese.org

Indianapolis (V) Catherine Elizabeth Maples Waynick
1100 West 42nd Street,
Indianapolis, IN 46208, USA
Tel (001) (317) 926 5454
Fax (001) (317) 926 5456
E-mail bishop@indydio.org

Iowa (VI) Alan Scarfe
225 37th Street, Des Moines,
IA 50312-4399, USA
Tel (001) (515) 277 6165
Fax (001) (515) 277 0273
E-mail diocese@iowaepiscopal.org

Kansas (VII) Dean E. Wolfe
Bethany Place, 833-35 Polk Street,
Topeka, KS 66612, USA
Tel (001) (785) 235 9255
Fax (001) (785) 235 2449
E-mail diocese@episcopal-ks.org

Kentucky (IV) Edwin Funsten Gulick
425 South Second Street,
Louisville, KY 40202-1417, USA
Tel (001) (502) 584 7148
Fax (001) (502) 587 8123
E-mail tedg@episcopalky.org

Lexington (IV) Stacy Fred Sauls
PO Box 610, Lexington, KY, 40586, USA
Tel (001) (859) 252 6527
Fax (001) (859) 231 9077
E-mail diocese@diolex.org

Litoral Diocese of Ecuador (IX) Alfredo Ulloa Morante España
Box 0901-5250,
Amarilis Fuentes entre V Trujillo,
y La 'D', Guayaquil, Equador
Tel (00593) (4) 443 050 *or* 345532
Fax (00593) (4) 443088
E-mail bishopmorante@hotmail.com

Long Island (II) Orris George Walker
36 Cathedral Avenue,
Garden City, NY 11530, USA
Tel (001) (516) 248 4800
Fax (001) (516) 248 1616
E-mail owalker@dioceseli.org

(Suffragan) Rodney Rae Michel
address etc as above
E-mail rmichel@dioceseli.org *or* rodmitre@aol.com

Los Angeles (VIII) Joseph Jon Bruno
Box 512164, Los Angeles, CA 90051-0164, USA
Tel (001) (213) 482 2040 ext 236
Fax (001) (213) 482 0844
E-mail bishop@ladiocese.org

(Suffragan) Chester Lovelle Talton
address etc as above
E-mail suffragan@ladiocese.org

Louisiana (IV) Charles Edward Jenkins
1623 Seventh Street,
New Orleans, LA 70115-4411, USA
Tel (001) (504) 895 6634
Fax (001) (504) 895 6637
E-mail vhendrickson@edola.org

Maine (I) Chilton Abbie Richardson Knudsen
Loring House, 143 State Street,
Portland, ME 04101, USA
Tel (001) (207) 772 1953
Fax (001) (207) 773 0095
E-mail info@diomaine.org *or* revcrk@aol.com *or* chilton_knudsen@ecunet.org

Maryland (III) Robert Wilkes Ihloff
4 East University Parkway,
Baltimore, MD 21218-2437, USA
Tel (001) (800) 443 1399 *or* (410) 467 1399
Fax (001) (410) 554 6387
E-mail +rihloff@ang-md.org

(Suffragan) John Leslie Rabb
address etc as above
E-mail jrabb@ang-md.org

Massachusetts (I) Marvil Thomas Shaw
Society of St John the Evangelist,
138 Tremont St, Boston, MA 02111, USA
Tel (001) (617) 482 4826 ext 407
Fax (001) (617) 451 6446
E-mail jdrapeau@diomass.org

(Suffragans) Roy F (Bud) Cederholm
address etc as above

Gayle E Harris
address etc as above
E-mail SHP@diomass.org

Michigan (V) Wendell Nathaniel Gibbs
4800 Woodward Avenue,
Detroit, MI 48201, USA
Tel (001) (313) 832 4400
Fax (001) (313) 831 0259
E-mail wgibbs@edomi.org

Milwaukee (V) Steven Andrew Miller
804 East Juneau Street,
Milwaukee, WI 53202, USA
Tel (001) (414) 272 3028
Fax (001) (414) 272 7790
E-mail info@diomil.org

Minnesota (VI) James Louis Jelinek
1730 Clifton Place, Suite 201,
Minneapolis, MN 55403, USA
Tel (001) (612) 871 5311
Fax (001) (612) 871 0552
E-mail karen.o@episcopalmn.org

Mississippi (IV) Duncan Montgomery Gray III
St Andrew's Cathedral, PO Box 23107,
Jackson, MS 39225-3107, USA
Tel (001) (601) 948 5954
Fax (001) (601) 354 3401
E-mail kathryn.weathersby@ecunet.org

Missouri (V) George Wayne Smith
1210 Locust Street,
St Louis, MO 63103, USA
Tel (001) (314) 231 1220
Fax (001) (314) 231 3373
E-mail bishop@missouri.anglican.org

Montana (VI)	C. Franklin Brookhart, Jr. 515 North Park Avenue, Helena, MT 59601, USA Tel (001) (406) 422 2230 Fax (001) (406) 442 2238 E-mail mtdiocese@qwest.net
Navajoland Area Mission (VIII)	Rustin Kimsey (Acting) PO Box 720, Farmington, NM 87499–0720, USA Tel (001) (505) 327 7549 Fax (001) (505) 327 6904
Nebraska (VIII)	Joe Goodwin Burnett 109 North 18th Street, Omaha, NE 68102-4903, USA Tel (001) (402) 341 5373 Fax (001) (402) 341 8683 E-mail diocese@episcopal-ne.org
Nevada (VIII)	Katherine Jefferts Schori 2100 South Maryland Parkway, Suite 4, Las Vegas, NV 89104, USA Tel (001) (702) 737 9190 Fax (001) (702) 737 6488 E-mail secretary@dionv.lvcoxmail.com
New Hampshire (I)	Gene Robinson 63 Green Street, Concord, NH 03301, USA Tel (001) (603) 224 1914 Fax (001) (603) 225 7884 E-mail grinnh@aol.com *or* jbarnes@nhepiscopal.org
New Jersey (II)	George E Councell 808 West State Street, Trenton, NJ 08618, USA Tel (001) (609) 394 5281 Fax (001) (609) 394 9546 E-mail diocese@newjersey.anglican.org
New York (II)	Mark Sean Sisk Synod House, 1047 Amsterdam Avenue, Cathedral Heights, New York, NY 10025, USA Tel (001) (212) 316 7400 Fax (001) (212) 316 7405 E-mail bpsisk@dioceseny.org
(Suffragan)	Catherine Scimeca Roskam Region Two Office, 55 Cedar Street, Dobbs Ferry, NY 10522, USA Tel (001) (914) 693 3848 Fax (001) (914) 693 0407 E-mail bproskam@dioceseny.org
(Assistant)	Egbert Don Taylor Synod Office, 1047 Amsterdam Avenue, Cathedral Heights, New York, NY 10025, USA Tel (001) (212) 316 7400 Fax (001) (212) 316 7405 E-mail bptaylor@dioceseny.org
Newark (II)	John Palmer Croneberger 31 Mulberry Street, Newark, NJ 07102, USA Tel (001) (973) 622 4306 Fax (001) (973) 622 3503 E-mail thebishop@dioceseofnewark.org
North Carolina (IV)	Michael Bruce Curry 200 West Morgan St., Suite 300, Raleigh, NC 27601, USA Tel (001) (919) 834 7474 Fax (001) (919) 834 7546 E-mail margo.acomb@episdionc.com
North Dakota (VI)	Michael G Smith 3600 25th St S, Fargo, ND 58104–6861, USA Tel (001) (701) 235 6688 Fax (001) (701) 232 3077 E-mail RobinsNest72176@aol.com
Northern California (VIII)	Jerry Alban Lamb Box 161268, Sacramento, CA 95816-5902, USA Tel (001) (916) 442 6918 Fax (001) (916) 442 6927 E-mail Bishopjal@dncweb.org
Northern Indiana (V)	Edward Stuart Little II 117 North Lafayette Boulevard, South Bend, IN 46601, USA Tel (001) (574) 233 6489 Fax (001) (574) 287 7914 E-mail NorthInd7@juno.com
Northern Michigan (V)	James Arthur Kelsey 131 East Ridge Street, Marquette, MI 49855, USA Tel (001) (906) 228 7160 Fax (001) (906) 228 7171 E-mail jim.kelsey@ecunet.org
Northwest Texas (VII)	Charles Wallis Ohl Jr. The Hulsey Episcopal Church Center, 1802 Broadway, Lubbock, TX 79401, USA Tel (001) (806) 763 1370 Fax (001) (804) 472 0641 E-mail diocese@nwt.org
Northwestern Pennsylvania (III)	Robert Deane Rowley 145 West 6th Street, Erie, PA 16501, USA Tel (001) (814) 456 4203 *or* (800) 643 2351 Fax (001) (814) 454 8703 E-mail rdrowleyjr@aol.com *or* dioNWPA@aol.com
Ohio (V)	Mark Hollingsworth Jr. 2230 Euclid Avenue, Cleveland, OH 44115-2499, USA Tel (001) (216) 771 4815 Fax (001) (216) 623 0735 E-mail office@dohio.org
Oklahoma (VII)	Robert Manning Moody 924 North Robinson, Oklahoma City, OK 73102, USA Tel (001) (405) 232 4820 Fax (001) (405) 232 4912 E-mail pwollenberg@episcopaloklahoma.org
Olympia (VIII)	Vincent Waydell Warner PO Box 12126, Seattle, WA 98102, USA Tel (001) (206) 325 4200 Fax (001) (206) 325 4631 E-mail vwarner@ecww.org
(Suffragan)	Bavi Edna ('Nedi') Rivera *address etc as above* E-mail nrivera@ecww.org
Oregon (VIII)	Johncy Itty 11800 S.W. Military Lane, Portland, OR 97219, USA Tel (001) (503) 636 5613 Fax (001) (503) 636 5616 E-mail johncyi@diocese oregon.org
Pennsylvania (III)	Charles Ellesworth Bennison 240 South Fourth Street, Philadelphia, PA 19106, USA Tel (001) (215) 627 6434 ext 112 *or* 131 Fax (001) (215) 627 7750 E-mail charlesb@diopa.org
(Assisting Bishop)	Clarence Coleridge *address etc as above* E-mail clarencec@diopa.org
Pittsburgh (III)	Robert William Duncan 325 Oliver Avenue, Pittsburgh, PA 15222-2467, USA Tel (001) (412) 281 6131 Fax (001) (412) 471 5591 E-mail duncan@pgh.anglican.org
(Assistant)	Henry William Scriven *address etc as above* E-mail scriven@pgh.anglican.org
Puerto Rico	David Andres Alvarez PO Box 902, St Just, PR 00978, Puerto Rico Tel (001) (787) 761 9800 Fax (001) (787) 761 0320 E-mail iep@spiderlink.net *or* davidal@coqui.net *or* obispoalvarez@spiderlink.net
Quincy (V)	Keith Lynn Ackerman 3601 N North Street, Peoria, IL 61604-1599, USA Tel (001) (309) 688 8221 Fax (001) (309) 688 8229 *or* 692 2421 E-mail doq@dioceseofquincy.org
Rhode Island (I)	Geralyn Wolf 275 North Main Street, Providence, RI 02903-1298, USA Tel (001) (401) 274 4500 Fax (001) (401) 331 9430 E-mail bishop@episcopalri.org

(Assisting Bishop)
David Joslin
address etc as above
E-mail Bp.Joslin@episcopalri.org

Rio Grande (VII)
Terence Kelshaw
4304 Carlisle Boulevard North East, Albuquerque, NM 87107-4811, USA
Tel (001) (505) 881 0636
Fax (001) (505) 883 9048
E-mail tkelshaw@aol.com *or* diocom@dioceserg.org

Rochester (II)
Jack Marston McKelvey
935 East Avenue, Rochester, NY 14607, USA
Tel (001) (585) 473 2977
E-mail BpJackM@aol.com

San Diego (VIII)
James R Mathes
2728 Sixth Avenue, San Diego, CA 92103-6397, USA
Tel (001) (619) 291 5947
Fax (001) (619) 291 8362
E-mail jmathes@edsd.org

San Joaquin (VIII)
John-David Mercer Schofield
4159 East Dakota Avenue, Fresno, CA 93726, USA
Tel (001) (559) 244 4828
Fax (001) (559) 244 4832
E-mail sjoaquin@sjoaquin.net

South Carolina (IV)
Edward Lloyd Salmon Jr.
Box 20127, Charleston, SC 29413-0127, USA
Tel (001) (843) 722 4075
Fax (001) (843) 723 7628
E-mail elsalmon@dioceseofsc.org *or* ljones@dioceseofsc.org

(Suffragan)
William Jones Skilton
address etc as above
E-mail bskilton@dioceseofsc.org

South Dakota (VI)
Creighton Leland Robertson
500 South Main Street, Sioux Falls, SD 57104-6814, USA
Tel (001) (605) 338 9751
Fax (001) (605) 336 6243
E-mail office.diocese@midconetwork.com *or* creighton_robertson@ecunet.org

Southeast Florida (IV)
Leopold Frade
525 North East 15th Street, Miami, FL 33132, USA
Tel (001) (305) 373 0881
Fax (001) (305) 375 8054
E-mail info@diosef.org

(Assistant)
James Ottley
address etc as above

Southern Ohio (V)
vacant
412 Sycamore Street, Cincinnati, OH 45202-4179, USA
Tel (001) (513) 421 0311
Fax (001) (513) 421 0315
E-mail bishop_thompson@episcopal-dso.org

(Suffragan)
Kenneth Lester Price
125 East Broad Street, Columbus, OH 43215, USA
Tel (001) (614) 461 8429
Fax (001) (614) 461 1015
E-mail bishop_price@episcopal-dso.org

Southern Virginia (III)
David Conner Bane
600 Talbot Hall Road, Norfolk, VA 23505-4361, USA
Tel (001) (757) 423 8287
Fax (001) (757) 440 5354
E-mail dcbane@diosova.org

(Suffragan)
Carol J Gallagher
112 North Union Street, Petersburg, VA 23803, USA
Tel (001) (804) 863 2095
Fax (001) (804) 863 2096
E-mail bishopcarol@verizon.net

Southwest Florida (IV)
John Bailey Lipscomb
7313 Merchant Ct, Sarasota, FL 34240–8437, USA
Tel (001) (941) 556 0315
Fax (001) (941) 556 0321
E-mail jlipscomb@dioceseswfla.org

Southwestern Virginia (III)
Frank Neff Powell
PO Box 2279, Roanoke, VA 24009-2279, USA
Tel (001) (540) 342 6797
Fax (001) (540) 343 9114
E-mail npowell@dioswva.org

Spokane (VIII)
James Edward Waggoner
245 East 13th Avenue, Spokane, WA 99202-1114, USA
Tel (001) (509) 624 3191
Fax (001) (509) 747 0049
E-mail jimw@spokanediocese.org

Springfield (VIII)
Peter Hess Beckwith
821 South 2nd Street, Springfield, IL 62704-2694, USA
Tel (001) (217) 525 1876
Fax (001) (217) 525 1877
E-mail diocese@episcopalspringfield.org *or* phbxebs@midwest.net

Taiwan (VIII)
David J H Lai
Friendship House, #7 Lane 105, Hangchow South Rd, Sec. 1, Taipei, Taiwan 10044, Republic of China
Tel (00886) (2) 2341 1265
Fax (00886) (2) 2396 2014
E-mail skh.tpe@msa.hinet.net

Tennessee (IV)
Bertram Nelson Herlong
50 Vantage Way, Suite 107, Nashville, TN 37228-1504, USA
Tel (001) (615) 251 3322
Fax (001) (615) 251 8010
E-mail info@episcopaldiocese tn.org

Texas (VII)
Don Adger Wimberly
3203 West Alabama Street, Houston, TX 77098, USA
Tel (001) (713) 520 6444
Fax (001) (713) 520 5723
E-mail dwimberly@epicenter.org

(Suffragan)
Rayford High
address etc as above
E-mail rhigh@epicenter.org

Upper South Carolina (IV)
Dorsey Felix Henderson
1115 Marion Street, Columbia, SC 29201, USA
Tel (001) (803) 771 7800
Fax (001) (803) 799 5119
E-mail diocese@edusc.org

Utah (VIII)
Carolyn Tanner Irish
80 South 300 East Street, PO Box 3090, Salt Lake City, UT 84110-3090, USA
Tel (001) (801) 322 4131
Fax (001) (801) 322 5096
E-mail cirish@episcopal-ut.org

Venezuela (IX)
Orlando Guerrero Torres
Apartado 49–143, Avenida Caroni 100, Colinas de Bello Monte, Caracas 1042 A, Venezuela
Tel (0058) (212) 753 0723
Fax (0058) (212) 751 3180
E-mail iglanglicanavzla@cantv.net

Vermont (I)
Thomas Clark Ely
Diocesan House, 5 Rock Point Road, Burlington, VT 05401-2735, USA
Tel (001) (802) 863 3431
Fax (001) (802) 860 1562
E-mail tely@dioceseofvermont.org

Virgin Islands (II)
Ambrose Gumbs
13 Commandant Gade, Charlotte Amalie, St Thomas, VI 00801, USA
Tel (001) (340) 774 1223
Fax (001) (809) 777 8485
E-mail bishop@episcovi.org

Virginia (III)
Peter James Lee
110 West Franklin Street, Richmond, VA 23220, USA
Tel (001) (804) 643 8451
Fax (001) (804) 644 6928
E-mail pjlee@thediocese.net

(Assistant)
Francis Campbell Gray
address etc as above
E-mail fcgray@thediocese.net

(Suffragan)	David Colin Jones Northern Virginia Office, Goodwin House, 4800 Fillmore Avenue, Alexandria, VA 22311, USA Tel (001) (703) 824 1325 Fax (001) (703) 824 1348 E-mail djones@thediocese.net
Washington (III)	John Bryson Chane Episcopal Church House, Mount St Alban, Washington, DC 20016, USA Tel (001) (202) 537 6555 Tel (001) (202) 364 6605 E-mail jchane@edow.org
(Assisting Bishop)	Barbara C Harris *address etc as above* E-mail bharris@edow.org
West Missouri (VII)	Barry Robert Howe PO Box 413227, Kansas City, MO 64141-3227, USA Tel (001) (816) 471 6161 Fax (001) (816) 471 0379 E-mail bphowe@earthlink.net *or* barryroberthowe@cs.com
West Tennessee (IV)	Don Edward Johnson 692 Poplar Avenue, Memphis, TN 38105, USA Tel (001) (901) 526 0023 Fax (001) (901) 526 1555 E-mail info@episwtn.org
West Texas (VII)	James Edward Folts PO Box 6885, San Antonio, TX 78209, USA Tel (001) (210) 824 5387 Fax (001) (210) 822 8779 E-mail marjorie.george@dwtx.org *or* jefh1@aol.com
(Coadjutor)	Gary R. Lillibridge *address etc as above* E-mail gary.lillibridge@dwtx.org
West Virginia (III)	William Michie Klusmeyer PO Box 5400, Charleston, WV 25361-5400, USA Tel (001) (304) 344 3597 Fax (001) (304) 343 3295 E-mail mklusmeyer@wvdiocese.org
Western Kansas (VII)	James Marshall Adams Box 2507, Salina, KS 67402-2507, USA Tel (001) (785) 825 1626 Fax (001) (785) 825 0974 E-mail marydiowksorg@sbcglobal.net
Western Louisiana (VII)	D Bruce MacPherson PO Box 2031, Alexandria, LA 71309, USA Tel (001) (318) 442 1304 Fax (001) (318) 442 8712 E-mail dbm3wla@aol.com
Western Massachusetts (I)	Gordon Scruton 37 Chestnut Street, Springfield, MA 01103, USA Tel (001) (413) 737 4786 Fax (001) (413) 746 9873 E-mail bishopwma@aol.com
Western Michigan (V)	Robert R Gepert 2600 Vincent Avenue, Portage, MI 49024-5653, USA Tel (001) (616) 381 2710 Fax (001) (616) 381 7067 E-mail rgepert@edwm.org *or* edwmorg@edwm.org
Western New York (II)	J Michael Garrison 1114 Delaware Avenue, Buffalo, NY 14209, USA Tel (001) (716) 881 0660 Fax (001) (716) 881 1724 E-mail jmgarrison@Episcopalwny.org *or* michael.garrison4@gte.net
Western North Carolina (IV)	G Porter Taylor 900B CenterPark Drive, Asheville, NC 28805, USA Tel (001) (828) 225 6656 Fax (001) (828) 225 6657 E-mail bishop@diocesewnc.org
Wyoming (VI)	Bruce Edward Caldwell 104 South Fourth Street, Laramie, WY 82070, USA Tel (001) (307) 742 6606 Fax (001) (307) 742 6782 E-mail bruce@wydiocese.org

WEST AFRICA

Accra (Archbishop)	Justice Ofei Akrofi Bishopscourt, PO Box 8, Accra, Ghana Tel (00233) (21) 662 292 *or* 663595 Fax (00233) (21) 668 822 E-mail adaccra@ghana.com *or* bishopakrofi@ghana.com
Bo	Samuel Sao Gbonda 1 A MacRobert Street, PO Box 21, Bo, Southern Province, Sierra Leone Tel (00232) (32) 648 Fax (00233) (32) 605
Cameroon (missionary area)	*vacant* BP 15705, Akwa, Duala, Cameroon Tel (00237) 408 552 *fax as telephone* E-mail camanglica-church@camnet.cm *or* agneslabep@yahoo.com
Cape Coast	Danile S A Allotey Bishopscourt, PO Box A233, Adisadel Estates, Cape Coast, Ghana Tel (00233) (42) 32 502 Fax (00233) (42) 32 637 E-mail danallotey@priest.com
Freetown	Julius Olotu Prince Lynch Bishop's Court, PO Box 537, Freetown, Sierra Leone Tel (00232) (22) 251 307 Mobile (00232) 76 620 690 Fax (00233) (22) 251 306 (via Ghana)
The Gambia	Solomon Tilewa E W Johnson Bishopscourt, PO Box 51, Banjul, The Gambia Tel (00220) 228 405 Mobile (00220) 905 227 E-mail anglican@qanet.gm *or* stilewaj@hotmail.com
Guinea	Albert D Gomez BP 187, Conakry, Guinea Tel (00224) 451 323 E-mail galbertdguillaume@yahoo.fr
Ho	Matthias K Mededues Badohu Bishopslodge, PO Box MA 300, Ho, Volta Region, Ghana Tel (00233) (91) 26644 *or* 26806 Mobile (00233) 208 162 246 E-mail matthoda@ucomgh.com
Koforidua	Francis B Quashie PO Box 980, Koforidua, Ghana Tel (00233) (81) 22 329 Fax (00233) (81) 22 060 E-mail cwpa_gh@yahoo.com
Kumasi	Daniel Yinkah Sarfo St Cyprian's Avenue, PO Box 144, Kumasi, Ghana Tel (00233) (51) 24 117 Mobile (00233) 277 890 411 *fax as telephone* E-mail anglicandioceseofkumasi@yahoo.com *or* dysarfo2000@yahoo.co.uk
Liberia	Edward W Neufville PO Box 10-0277, 1000 Monrovia 10, Liberia Tel (00231) 224 760 Mobile (00377) 47 516 440 Fax (00231) 227 519 E-mail bishop@liberia.net *or* BishopNeufville@netscape
Sekondi	*vacant* PO Box 85, Sekondi, Ghana Tel (00233) (31) 4604 E-mail angdiosek@yahoo.com
Sunyani	Thomas Ampah Brient PO Box 23, Sunyani, Ghana Tel (00233) (61) 23213 Mobile (00233) 208 121 670 Fax (00233) (61) 71230 E-mail anglicandiocese@hotmail.com

Tamale	Emmanuel Anyindana Arongo PO Box 110, Tamale NR, Ghana Tel (00233) (71) 26639 Fax (00233) (71) 22906 Mobile (00233) 277 890 878 E-mail bishopea2000@yahoo.com

WEST INDIES

The Bahamas and the Turks and Caicos Islands (Archbishop)	Drexel Wellington Gomez Church House, PO Box N-7107, Nassau, Bahamas Tel (001242) 322 3015 Fax (001242) 322 7943 E-mail primate@bahamas.net.bs
(New Providence)	Gilbert Arthur Thompson *address etc as above*
Barbados	John Walder Dunlop Holder Mandeville House, Collymore Rock, St Michael, Barbados, West Indies Tel (001246) 426 2762 Fax (001246) 426 0871 E-mail jwdh@sunbeach.net
Belize	*vacant* 25 Bishopsthorpe, Southern Foreshore, PO Box 535, Belize City, Belize, Central America Tel (00501) (2) 73029 Fax (00501) (2) 76898 E-mail bzediocese@btl.net
Guyana	Randolph Oswald George The Diocesan Office, PO Box 10949, 49 Barrack Street, Georgetown, Guyana Tel (00592) (22) 64 775 Fax (00592) (22) 76 091 E-mail dioofguy@networksgy.com
Jamaica and the Cayman Islands	Alfred Charles Reid 2 Caledonia Avenue, Kingston 5, Jamaica Tel (001876) 920 2712 Fax (001876) 960 1774 E-mail bishopja@anglicandiocese.com
(Kingston)	Robert McLean Thompson 14 Ottawa Avenue, Kingston 6, Jamaica, West Indies Tel (001876) 926 6692 Fax (001876) 960 8463 E-mail standrewch@cwjamaica.com
(Mandeville)	Harold Benjamin Daniel Bishop's Residence, 3 Cotton Tree Road, PO Box 84, Mandeville, Jamaica Tel (001876) 625 6817 Fax (001876) 625 6819 E-mail hbdaniel@cwjamaica.com
(Montego Bay)	Howard Gregory PO Box 346, Montego Bay, Jamaica, West Indies Tel (001876) 952 4963 Fax (001876) 971 8838 E-mail hkagregory@hotmail.com
North Eastern Caribbean and Aruba	Leroy Errol Brooks St Mary's Rectory, PO Box 180, The Valley, Anguilla, West Indies Tel (001264) 497 2235 Fax (001264) 497 8555 E-mail brookx@anguillanet.com
Trinidad and Tobago	Calvin Wendell Bess Hayes Court, 21 Maraval Road, Port of Spain, Trinidad, West Indies Tel (001868) 622 7387 Fax (001868) 628 1319 E-mail bessc@tstt.net.tt
Windward Islands	Sehon S. Goodridge Bishop's Court, Montrose, PO Box 502, St Vincent, West Indies Tel (001784) 456 1895 Fax (001784) 456 2591

EXTRA-PROVINCIAL DIOCESES

Bermuda (Canterbury)	Alexander Ewen Ratteray Diocesan Office, PO Box HM 769, Hamilton HM CX, Bermuda Tel (001441) 292 2967 Fax (001441) 296 0592 E-mail bishopratteray@ibl.bm *or* diocoff@ibl.bm
§Cuba	Miguel Tamayo Calle 6 No 273, Vedado, Havana 4, 10400 Cuba Tel (0053) (7) 35655, 38003, 321120 *or* 312436 Fax (0053) (7) 333293 E-mail episcopal@ip.etecsa.cu
Lusitanian Church (Canterbury)	Fernando da Luz Soares Secretaria Diocesana, Apartado 392, P-4430 Vila Nova de Gaia, Portugal Tel (00351) (22) 375 4018 Fax (00351) (22) 375 2016 E-mail centrodiocesano@igreja lusitana.org
Spanish Reformed Episcopal Church (Canterbury)	Carlos López Lozano Calle Beneficencia 18, 28004 Madrid, Spain Tel (0034) (91) 445 2560 Fax (0034) (91) 594 4572 E-mail eclesiae@arrakis.es

§ Under a Metropolitan Council of the Primate of Canada, the Archbishop of the West Indies and the President-Bishop of the Episcopal Church's Province IX.

BISHOPS OF CHURCHES WHERE ANGLICANS HAVE UNITED WITH CHRISTIANS OF OTHER TRADITIONS

NORTH INDIA

Agra	Samuel R Cutting Bishop's House, St Paul's Church Compound, 4/116-B Church Road, Civil Lines, Agra, UP, 282 002, India Tel (0091) (562) 2154 845 Fax (0091) (562) 2520 074 E-mail doacni@sancharnet.in
Amritsar	Pradeep Kumar Samantaroy 26 R B Prakash Chand Road, opp Police Ground, Amritsar, Punjab, 143 001, India Tel (0091) (183) 222 2910 *fax as telephone* E-mail bunul3@rediffmail.com
Andaman and Car Nicobar Islands	Christopher Paul Cathedral Church Compound, House No 1, Staging Post, Car Nicobar, 744 301, Andaman and Nicobar Islands Tel (0091) (3192) 267 025 Fax (0091) (3192) 231 362
Barrackpore (Deputy Moderator)	Brojen Malakar Bishop's Lodge, 86 Middle Road, Barrackpore, Parganas North, 743 101, India Tel (0091) (33) 2592 0147 Fax (0091) (33) 2561 1852
Bhopal	Laxman L Maida Bishop's House, Mission Compound, First Church, Ratlam, 457 001, MP, India Tel (0091) (7412) 238 206 Mobile (0091) 98270 04737 E-mail bhopal_diocese@rediffmail.com

Calcutta	P S P Raju Bishop's House, 51 Chowringhee Road, Calcutta, WB, 700 071, India Tel (0091) (33) 282 2426 Fax (0091) (33) 282 6340 E-mail samrajubh@vsnl.net
Chandigarh (Deputy Moderator)	Joel Vidyasagar Mal Bishop's House, Mission Compound, Brown Road, Ludhiana, Punjab, 141 008, India Tel (0091) (161) 266 5706 Fax (0091) (161) 260 9431
Chotanagpur (Moderator)	Zechariah James Terom Bishop's Lodge, PO Box 1, Church Road, Ranchi, Bihar, 834 001, India Tel (0091) (651) 235 1181 Fax (0091) (651) 235 1184
Cuttack	Reuben Senapati Bishop's House, Mission Road, Cuttack, Orissa, 753 001, India Tel (0091) (671) 301 448 E-mail diocese@vsnl.net
Delhi	Karam Masih Bishop's House, 1 Church Lane, off North Avenue, New Delhi, 110 001, India Tel (0091) (11) 2371 7471 E-mail stmartin@dels.vsnl.net.in
Durgapur	Probal Kanto Dutta St Michael's Church Compound, Aldrin Path, Bidhan Nagar, Dugapur 713 212, India Tel (0091) (343) 253 6220 E-mail probal_dutta@yahoo.com
Eastern Himalayas	Dhirendra Kumar Sahu Bishop's Lodge, PO Box 4, Darjeeling, West Bengal, 734 101, India Tel (0091) (354) 225 8183 Fax (0091) (354) 53882 E-mail bishopsahu13@sify.com
Gujarat	Vinod Kumar Mathushellah Malaviya Bishop's House, Ellis Bridge, Ahmedabad, Gujarat State, 380 006, India Tel (0091) (79) 2656 195 *fax as telephone* E-mail gujdio@wilnetonline.net
Jabalpur	Prem Chand Singh Bishop's House, 2131 Napier Town, Jabalpur, MP, 482 001, India Tel (0091) (761) 2622 109 E-mail cnijbdio@sancharnet.in
Kolhapur	Bathuel Ramchandra Tiwade Bishop's House, EP School Compound, Kolhapur, Maharashtra, 416 003, India Tel (0091) (231) 2654 832 *fax as telephone* E-mail kdccni@vsnl.com
Lucknow	Anil R Stephen Bishop's House, 25 Mahatma Gandhi Marg, Allahabad, UP, 211 001, India Tel (0091) (532) 2623 324 *fax as telephone*
Marathwada	A K Pradham Bishop's House, Mission Compound, Jalna 431 203, MS, India Tel (0091) (240) 239 687
Mumbai	Baiju F Gavit St John's House, Duxbury Lane, Colaba, Mumbai, 400 005, India Tel (0091) (22) 2215 4126 *or* 1439 Fax (0091) (22) 2206 0248 E-mail bishopbomcni@rediffmail.com
Nagpur	*vacant* Cathedral House, Sadar, Nagpur, MS, 440 001, India Tel (0091) (712) 252 3089 Fax (0091) (712) 255 6740 E-mail bishop@nagpur.dot.net.in
(Moderator's Commissary)	Baiju F Gavit
Nasik	Kamble Lemuel Pradip Bishop's House, Tarakur, 1 Outram Road, Ahmednagar, Maharashtra, 414 001, India Tel (0091) (241) 2428 746 Fax (0091) (241) 2428 682 E-mail bishopofnasik@rediffmail.com
North East India	Purely Lyngdoh Bishop's Kuti, Shillong 1, Meghalaya, 793 001, India Tel (0091) (364) 2223 155 Fax (0091) (364) 2501 178 E-mail bishopnei15@hotmail.com
Patna	Philip Phembuar Marandih Bishop's House, Christ Church Compound, Bhagalpur, Bihar, 812 001, India Tel (0091) (641) 2400 314 *fax as telephone* E-mail cnipatna@rediffmail.com
Phulbani	*vacant* Bishop's House, G Udaigiri, Phulbani, Kandhamal, Orissa, 762 100, India Tel (0091) (680) 242 333
(Moderator's Commissary)	P P Marandhi Mobile (0091) 94312 13138
Pune	Vijay Bapurao Sathe 1A Steveley Road (General Bhagat Marg), Pune, MS, 411 001, India Tel (0091) (20) 2633 4371
Rajasthan	Collin Theodore 2/10 CNI Social Centre, Civil Lines, Opp. Bus Stand, Jaipur Rd, Ajmer 305 001, India Tel (0091) (145) 2420 633 Fax (0091) (145) 2621 627
Sambalpur	Christ Kiron Das Mission Compound, Bolangir, Orissa, 767 001, India Tel (0091) (6652) 233 340 Fax (0091) (6652) 230 625

SOUTH INDIA

Chennai	V Devasahayam Diocesan Office, PO Box 4914, Chennai, TN, 600 086, India Tel (0091) (44) 811 3933 *or* 811 3929 Fax (0091) (44) 811 0608
Coimbatore	M Dorai Bishop's House, 204 Race Course Road, Coimbatore, TN1, 641018, India Tel (0091) (422) 213 605 Fax (0091) (442) 200 400
Dornakal	Allu Rajarathnam Bishop's House, Cathedral Compound, Dornakal, Andhra Pradesh 506 381, India Tel (0091) (8719) 25747 *or* 27376 E-mail bishoprajarathnam@usa.net
East Kerala	Kunnumpurathu Joseph Samuel Bishop's House, Melukavumattom, Kottayam, Kerala State, 686 652, India Tel (0091) (482) 291 026 Fax (0091) (482) 291 044
Jaffna	*vacant* 17 Francis Lane, Colombo 6, Sri Lanka Tel (0094) (75) 511 233 Fax (0094) (1) 584 836
Kanyakumari	G. Devakadasham CSI Diocesan Office, 71A Dennis Street, Nagercoil, 629 001, India Tel (0091) (4652) 31 539 Fax (0091) (4652) 31 295
Karimnagar	Sanki John Theodore Bishop's House, PO Box 40, Mukarampura Post, Karimnagar, Andhra Pradesh, 505 001, India Tel (0091) (8722) 42 229
Karnataka Central (Deputy Moderator)	Vasanthkumar Suputhrappa Diocesan Office, 20 Third Cross, CSI Compound, Bangalore, Karnataka, 560 027, India Tel (0091) (80) 222 3766

Karnataka North	*vacant* Bishop's House, Haliyal Road, Dharwad, Karnataka State, 580 008, India Tel (0091) (836) 745 593 Fax (0091) (836) 745 461
Karnataka South	Devaraj Bangera Bishop's House, Balmatta, Mangalore, Karnataka, 575 001, India Tel (0091) (824) 429 657 Fax (0091) (824) 425 042
Krishna-Godavari	G Dyvasirvadam CSI St Andrew's Cathedral Campus, Main Rd, Machilipatnam 521 002, AP, India Tel (0091) (8672) 220 623 E-mail bishopkrishna@yahoo.com
Madhya Kerala	Thomas Samuel Bishop's House, Cathedral Road, Kottayam, Kerala State, 686 018, India Tel (0091) (481) 566 536 Fax (0091) (481) 566 531
Madurai-Ramnad	Christopher Asir CSI Diocesan Office, 162 East Veli Street, AVH Building 1st Floor, Madurai District, Tamil Nadu, 625 001, India Tel (0091) (452) 732 541 *fax as telephone*
Medak (Moderator)	Badda Peter Sugandhar Bishop's Annexe, 145 MacIntyre Road, Secunderabad, Andhra Pradesh, 500 003, India Tel (0091) (40) 783 3151 Fax (0091) (40) 782084 E-mail bishopsugandhar@csimedakdiocese.com
Nandyal	Abraham Theodore Gondi Bishop's House, Nandyal RS, Kurnool District, Andhra Pradesh, 518 502, India Tel (0091) (8514) 45731 Fax (0091) (8514) 42255
North Kerala	George Isaac Bishop's House, Shoranur, Kerala State, 679 121, India Tel (0091) (4921) 622 545 Fax (0091) (4921) 622 798
Rayalaseema	Chowtipalle Bellam Moses Frederick Bishop's House, CSI Compound, Gooty, Ananthapur District, Andhra Pradesh, 515 401, India Tel (0091) (855) 242 375 Fax (0091) (855) 242 668
South Kerala	John Wilson Gladstone Bishop's House, LMS Compound, Trivandrum 695 033, Kerala State, India Tel (0091) (471) 318 662 Fax (0091) (471) 316 439 E-mail bishopgladstone@yahoo.com
Tirunelveli	Jeyapaul David Bishopstowe, PO Box 118, Tirunelveli, Tamil Nadu, 627 002, India Tel (0091) (462) 572 744 Fax (0091) (462) 574 525 E-mail bpcsitvl@pronet.in
Trichy-Tanjore	Daniel James Srinivasan PO Box 31, 8 Racquet Court Lane, Tiruchirapalli, Tamil Nadu, 620 001, India Tel (0091) (431) 771254 Fax (0091) (431) 418485 E-mail csittd@tr.net.in
Thoothukudi-Nazareth (Bishop in Charge)	B P Sughandar (Bishop in Medak)
Vellore	Yesurathnam William CSI Diocesan Office, 1/A Officer's Lane, Vellore, North Arcot District, 632 001, India Tel (0091) (416) 232 160 Fax (0091) (416) 223 835

BANGLADESH

Dhaka (Moderator)	Michael S Baroi St Thomas's Church, 54 Johnson Road, Dhaka-1, Bangladesh Tel (00880) (2) 711 6546 Fax (00880) (2) 711 8218 E-mail cbdacdio@bangla.net
Kushtia	Paul S Sarkar 94 NS Road, Thanapara, Kushtia, Bangladesh Tel (00880) (71) 61892 *fax as telephone* E-mail cob@citechco.net

PAKISTAN

The Arabian Gulf (Bishop *for*) (Area Bishop within the Diocese of Cyprus)	Azad Marshall PO Box 3192, Gulberg-1, Lahore, Punjab, 54660, Pakistan Tel (0092) (42) 522 0286 *or* 541 5529 Fax (0092) (42) 522 0591
Faisalabad	John Samuel Bishop's House, PO Box 27, Mission Road, Gojra, Distt Toba Tek Sing, Faisalabad, Pakistan Tel (0092) (4651) 511 290 *fax as telephone* E-mail jsamuel@brain.net.pk
Hyderabad	Raffique Masih 27 Liaquat Road, Civil Lines, Hyderabad, Sind, 71000, Pakistan Tel (0092) (221) 780 221 Fax (0092) (221) 28 772 E-mail hays@hyd.infolink.net.pk
Karachi (Deputy Moderator)	Sadiq Daniel Holy Trinity Cathedral, Jinnah Rd, Karachi 75530, Pakistan Tel (0092) (21) 521 8112 Fax (0092) (21) 565 3175 E-mail sadiqdaniel@hotmail.com
Lahore	Alexander John Malik Bishopsbourne, Cathedral Close, The Mall, Lahore, 54000, Pakistan Tel (0092) (42) 723 3560 Fax (0092) (42) 722 1270 E-mail bishop_Lahore@hotmail.com
Multan	John Victor Mall 113 Qasim Road, PO Box 204, Multan Cantt, Pakistan Tel (0092) (61) 588 799 *fax as telephone* E-mail bishopmd@mul.paknet.com.pk
Peshawar	*vacant* St John's Cathedral, 1 Sir-Syed Road, Peshawar, NWFP, 25000, Pakistan Tel (0092) (91) 276 519 Fax (0092) (91) 277 499
Raiwind (Moderator)	Samuel Azariah 17 Warris Road, PO Box 2319, Lahore 54000, Pakistan Tel (0092) (42) 758 8950 Fax (0092) (42) 757 7255 E-mail azariahs@lhr.comsats.net.pk
Sialkot	Samuel Pervez Lal Kothi, Barah Patthar, Sialkot 2, Punjab, Pakistan Tel (0092) (432) 264 895 Fax (0092) (432) 264 828

PROVINCIAL OFFICES

From which further information may be sought

Anglican Communion Office St Andrew's House, 16 Tavistock Crescent, Westbourne Park, London W11 1AP, UK
Tel (020) 7313 3900 E-mail aco@anglicancommunion.org

Australia PO Box Q190, Queen Victoria PO, Sydney, NSW, Australia 1230
Fax (0061) (2) 9264 6552 E-mail gsoffice@anglican.org.au

Bangladesh St Thomas's Church, 54 Johnson Road, Dhaka 1100, Bangladesh
Fax (00880) (2) 238218

Brazil Caixa Postal 11510, Teresópolis, Cep 90841-970, Porto Alegre, RS, Brazil
Fax (0055) (51) 3318 6200 E-mail cwinnischofer@ieab.org.br

Burundi BP 2098, Bujumbura, Burundi
Fax (00257) 229 129 E-mail eebprov@cbinf.com

Canada 80 Hayden St, Toronto ON, M4Y 3G2
Fax (001) (416) 968 7983 E-mail general.secretary@national.anglican.ca

Central Africa Private Bag 1, Chilema, Malawi
E-mail bernardmalango@hotmail.com

Central America Iglesia Episcopal Costarricense, Apartado 10520–1000, San José, Costa Rica
Fax (00506) 253 8331 E-mail iarca@amnet.co.cr

Ceylon Bishop's House, 368/3A Bauddhaloka Mawatha, Colombo 7, Sri Lanka
Fax (0094) (1) 684811 E-mail diocol@eureka.lk

Congo (formerly Zaïre) PO Box 25586, Kampala, Uganda
Tel (00256) 7764 7495 E-mail eac-mags@infocom.co.ug

England Church House, Great Smith Street, London SW1P 3NZ, UK
Tel (020) 7898 1000 Fax (020) 7898 1001 E-mail feedback@c-of-e.org.uk

Hong Kong 1 Lower Albert Road, Hong Kong
Fax (00852) 2525 2537 E-mail office1@hkskh.org

Indian Ocean Evêché Anglican, Ambohimanoro, 101-Antananarivo, Madagascar
Fax (00261) (20) 226 1331 E-mail eemdanta@dts.mg

Ireland Church of Ireland House, Church Avenue, Rathmines, Dublin 6, Irish Republic
Fax (00353) (1) 497 8821 E-mail office@rcbdub.org

Japan 65-3 Yarai-cho, Shinjuku-ku,Tokyo 162-0805, Japan
Fax (0081) (52) 283175 E-mail province@nskk.org

Jerusalem and the Middle East PO Box 22075, Nicosia 1517, Cyprus
Fax 357 2 22 674553 E-mail: georgia@spidernet.com.cy / bishop@spidernet.com.cy

Kenya PO Box 40502, 00100 Nairobi, Kenya
Fax (00254) (2) 718 442 E-mail archoffice@swiftkenya.com

Korea 3 Chong-dong, Chung-ku, Seoul 100-120, Korea
Fax (0082) (2) 723 2640 E-mcbchung@hotmail.com

Melanesia Provincial Headquarters, PO Box 19, Honiara, Solomon Islands
Fax (0067) 21 890 E-mail gkiriau@comphq.org.sb

Mexico Calle La Otra Banda 40, Col. San Angel, Delegación Alvaro Obregón, 01000 México, DF, Mexico
Fax (0052) (55) 5616 4063 E-mail ofipam@att.net.mx

Myanmar (formerly Burma) 140 Pyidaungsu-Yeiktha Road, Dagon PO (11191), Yangon, Myanmar
Fax (0095) (1) 251 405 E-mail cpm.140@mptmail.net.mm

New Zealand (Aotearoa, New Zealand and Polynesia) PO Box 885, Hastings, New Zealand
Fax (0064) (6) 878 7905 E-mail gensec@ang.org.nz

Nigeria Episcopal House, PO Box 212, AD CP, Abuja, Nigeria
E-mail gensec@anglican-nig.org

North India CNI, 16 Pandit Pant Marg, New Delhi 110001, India
Fax (0091) (11) 2371 6901 *or* 2371 3710 E-mail gscni@ndb.vsnl.net.in

Pakistan St John's Cathedral, 1 Sir Syed Road, Peshawar, Pakistan
Fax (0092) (91) 277 499

Papua New Guinea Box 673, Lae, MP, Papua New Guinea
Fax (00675) 472 1852 E-mail acpng@global.net.pg

Philippines PO Box 10321, Broadway Centrum, 1112 Quezon City, Philippines
Fax (0063) (2) 721 1923 E-mail ecpiadmn@info.com.ph

Rwanda BP 2487, Kigali, Rwanda
Tel and fax (00250) 51 4160 E-mail peer@ rwanda1.com

Scotland 21 Grosvenor Crescent, Edinburgh EH12 5EE, UK
Tel 0131-255 6357 Fax 0131-346 7247 E-mail secgen@scotland.anglican.org

South East Asia PO Box 347, Kuching, 93704 Sarawak, Malaysia
Fax (0060) (82) 426488 E-mail denwee@tm.net.my

South India CSI Centre, 5 Whites Road, Royapettah, Chennai 600 041, India
E-mail csi@vsnl.com

Southern Africa 20 Bishopscourt Dr, Bishopscourt, Claremont, Western Cape 7708, South Africa
Fax (0027) (21) 797 1329 E-mail peocpsa@mail.ngo.za

South America A. Gallinal 1852, Montevideo, Uruguay
E-mail lego@adinet.co.uy

Sudan PO Box 604, Khartoum, Sudan
E-mail ecsprovince@hotmail.com

Tanzania PO Box 899, Dodoma, Tanzania
Tel (00255) (26) 232 4565 E-akiri@anglican.or.tz

Uganda PO Box 14123, Kampala, Uganda
Fax (00256) (41) 251 925 E-mail ankundarev@yahoo.com

USA Episcopal Church Center, 815 Second Avenue, New York, NY 10017, USA
Fax (001) (212) 490 3298 E-mail stolley@episcopalchurch.org

Wales 39 Cathedral Road, Cardiff CF11 9XF, UK
Tel (029) 2034 8218 Fax (029) 2038 7835 E-mail: information@churchinwales.org.uk

West Africa PO Box Lt 226, Lartebiokorshie, Accra, Ghana
E-mail cpwa@ghana.com

West Indies PO Box N-7107, Nassau, Bahamas
Fax (001) (242) 322 7943 E-mail: primate@bahamas.net.bs

DIRECTORIES OF THE ANGLICAN PROVINCES

The following provinces of the Anglican Communion are known to publish directories of their clergy.

Australia *The Australian Anglican Directory* Published annually
Angela Grutzner & Associates Pty Ltd, PO Box 306, Malvern, Vic, Australia 3144
Fax (0061) (3) 9822 5927

Canada *The Anglican Year Book* Published annually
Anglican Book Centre, 600 Jarvis Street, Toronto ON, Canada, M4Y 2J6
Tel (001) (416) 924 9192 Fax (001) (416) 924 270

Ireland *Church of Ireland Directory* Published annually
Styletype Publishing Co (Ireland) Ltd, Sheldon House, 60 Pembroke Road, Dublin 4, Irish Republic

Japan (in Japanese) *Seikokai Yearbook* Published annually
Nippon Sei Ko Kai Provincial Office, 65 Yarai-cho, Shinijuku, Tokyo 162-0805, Japan

Jerusalem and the Middle East *A Provincial Directory*
Provincial Office, Box 1248, 20 Nablus Road, Jerusalem

New Zealand *Clerical Directory* Published annually
General Synod Office, PO Box 885, Hastings, New Zealand
Tel (0064) (6) 878 7902 Fax (0064) (6) 878 7905

Nigeria *Nigeria Churchman's Year Book*
Church House, 29 Marina, PO Box 78, Lagos, Nigeria

Scotland *Scottish Episcopal Church Directory* Published annually
Synod Office, 21 Grosvenor Crescent, Edinburgh EH12 5EE

Southern Africa *Clerical Directory* Published annually
Provincial Office, PO Box 61394 Marshalltown, Johannesburg, 2107, South Africa
Tel (0027) (11) 836 5825 Fax (0027) (11) 836 5782 E-mail publish@mail.ngo.za

Southern Cone of America *Directorio Provincial* Published every three years
Casilla 50675, Correo Central, Santiago, Chile

United States of America *Episcopal Clerical Directory* Published every two years
Church Publishing Incorporated, 445 Fifth Avenue, New York, NY 100016-0109, USA
Tel (001) (800) 242 1918 Fax (001) (212) 779 3392 E-mail *via website* www.ecdplus.org

Diocesan lists are the source of information for the Churches of Brazil, Central Africa and Ceylon. In the West Indies, the Diocese of Jamaica (fax (001) (876) 968 0618) publishes a *Clerical Directory*. For the provinces not listed above, information should be sought from the provincial secretary or from dioceses.

Close links with many overseas provinces are maintained by the following missionary organizations:

Church Mission Society
Partnership House, 157 Waterloo Road, London SE1 8UU
Tel (020) 7928 8681 Fax (020) 7401 3215 E-mail info@cms-uk.org

Crosslinks (formerly the Bible Churchmen's Missionary Society)
251 Lewisham Way, London SE4 1XF
Tel (020) 8691 6111 Fax (020) 8694 8023 E-mail info@crosslinks.org

Mission to Seafarers (formerly The Missions to Seamen)
St Michael Paternoster Royal, College Hill, London EC4R 2RL
Tel (020) 7248 5202 Fax (020) 7248 4761 E-mail depsecgen@missiontoseafarers.org

Mothers' Union
Mary Sumner House, 24 Tufton Street, London SW1P 3RB
Tel (020) 7222 5533 Fax (020) 7222 1591 E-mail mu@themothersunion.org

Society for Promoting Christian Knowledge
36 Causton Street, London SW1P 4ST
Tel (020) 7592 3900 Fax (020) 7592 3939 E-mail spck@spck.org.uk

South American Mission Society
Allen Gardiner Cottage, Pembury Road, Tunbridge Wells, Kent YN2 3QU
Tel 01892 538 647 Fax 01892 525 797 E-mail finsec@samsgb.org

United Society for the Propagation of the Gospel
Partnership House, 157 Waterloo Road, London SE1 8XA
Tel (020) 7928 8681 Fax (020) 7928 2371 E-mail enquiries@uspg.org.uk

ADDRESSES UNKNOWN

The following are clergy whose addresses are currently unknown. Fuller details are contained in the biographical section. We should be grateful for any information to help us complete our records in respect of these clergy.

ACKROYD, David Andrew. b 66. **d** 97. C Ogley Hay *Lich* 02-03
AGGREY, Solomon Samuel. b 49. **d** 80. Miss Partner CMS from 88
ANDERSON, Olaf Emanuel. b 64. **d** 87. Australia from 94
ANTONY-ROBERTS, Gelert Roderick. b 43. **d** 90. C Alton St Lawr *Win* 90-94
ARRANDALE, Richard Paul Matthew. b 63. **d** 90. C Crawley *Chich* 94
ASBURY, William. b 35. **d** 97. Perm to Offic *Liv* from 00
ASHDOWN, Barry Frederick. b 42. **d** 68. C Southwick St Mich *Chich* 91-93
ATHERLEY, Keith Philip. b 56. **d** 80. CF 89-03
ATHERTON, Philip Andrew. b 51. **d** 84
BAILEY, Norman Gerald. b 25. **d** 83. Perm to Offic *Bris* from 97
BAKER, Stephen Anthony. b 55. **d** 91. Chapl Eliz Coll Guernsey 97-01
BAKER, William Alfred Douglas. b 21. **d** 75. Perm to Offic *Heref* 97-00
BAMBER, David Beverley. b 51. **d** 77. C E Retford *S'well* 91-92
BANFIELD, Andrew Henry. b 48. **d** 73. Soc Services Development Officer Glos Co Coun from 89; Perm to Offic *Glouc* from 02
BANNER, Prof Michael Charles. b 61. **d** 86. NSM Balsham, Weston Colville, W Wickham etc *Ely* from 01
BARBER, Charles William Walters. b 60. **d** 86. V Bowling St Steph *Bradf* 96-04
BARNES, Stephen Martin Leonard. b 60. **d** 87. NSM Kingstanding St Mark *Birm* 98-04
BARON, Peter Murray. b 56. **d** 93. V Northwood H Trin *Lon* 98-04
BARRETT, Graham Crichton. b 51. **d** 90. P-in-c St Issey w St Petroc Minor *Truro* 95-00; Dioc Children's Adv 95-00
BARTLE, Alan. b 45. **d** 84. P-in-c Thorney Abbey *Ely* 93-95
BENFORD, Brian. b 47. **d** 85. NSM Gawber *Wakef* 90-02
BENTHAM, Philip John (Ben). b 55. **d** 96. Zimbabwe from 00
BERGER, Otto. b 19. **d** 83. Perm to Offic *Chelmsf* from 93
BISHOP, Huw Daniel. b 49. **d** 73. CF (TA) from 85
BODKIN, Thomas Patrick Joseph. b 45. **d** 80
BOOKER, James Howard. b 57. **d** 90 Chapl HM Pris Peterhead 93-00
BOSSOM, Peter Emery. b 28. **d** 82. rtd 86
BOULT, Geoffrey Michael. b 56. **d** 80. Perm to Offic *Sarum* 95-98
BOWCOTT, Jonathan Michael William. b 67. **d** 01. C Cricklewood St Gabr and St Mich *Lon* 01-04
BOWLES, David Anthony. b 44. **d** 68. Perm to Offic *Derby* 93-95 and *Roch* 95-98
BRIDGER, Francis William. b 51. **d** 78. Prin Trin Coll Bris 99-05
BROWN, Jonathan Alexander Iain. b 75. **d** 00. P-in-c Cynog Honddu *S & B* 03-05; Min Can Brecon Cathl 03-05
BROWN, Julian Keith. b 57. **d** 85. Asst Chapl Versailles *Eur* from 94
BRYAN, Leslie Harold. b 48. **d** 73. CF 79-03
BURGESS, Paul Christopher James. b 41. **d** 68. TV Livingston LEP *Edin* 88-92
CAMPBELL, William George. b 31. **d** 57. Canada 57-96, 01-03 and from 04
CARPENTER, David James. b 52. **d** 76. V Staincliffe and Carlinghow *Wakef* 00-05
CARTER, Colin John. b 56. **d** 93. St Geo Healthcare NHS Trust Lon from 00
CHALK, Miss Susan Christine. b 50. **d** 93. NSM Bradford Peverell, Stratton, Frampton etc *Sarum* 93-03
CHANDRA, Kevin Douglas Naresh. b 65. **d** 96. TV Erdington *Birm* 02-05
CHILDS, Martin James. b 63. **d** 99. C Mountain Ash and Miskin *Llan* 99-04
CLARKE, Daniel. b 17. **d** 41. rtd 97
CLARKE, Denis John. b 23. **d** 87. rtd 98
CLAYTON, George Hamilton. b 42. **d** 93. NSM Send *Guildf* 93-99
COCKBILL, Douglas John. b 53. **d** 78. USA from 05
CONSTABLE, Mrs Sharon Joanne. b 57. **d** 98. Hong Kong from 04
COOK, Helen. b 50. **d** 96. C Rothiemurchus *Mor* from 96
COOPER, Ms Gillian Anne. b 55. **d** 87. New Zealand from 01
CORDINER, Alan Dobson. b 61. **d** 92. P-in-c Bootle, Corney, Whicham and Whitbeck *Carl* 98-05
CRUTTENDEN, Leslie Roy. b 39. **d** 84. NSM River *Cant* 90-01
DAVEY, Andrew John. b 57. **d** 83. Pilsdon Community 94-04
DAY, Paul Geoffrey. b 56. **d** 89. Lic to Adn Loughb *Leic* 98
DE VERNY, David Dietrich. b 55. **d** 83. Gen Sec Fellowship of St Alb and St Sergius 90-92
DICKSON, Anthony Edward. b 59. **d** 88. R Fownhope w Mordiford, Brockhampton etc *Heref* 94-99
DICKSON, Richard Arthur. b 67. **d** 93. Sweden from 96
DOWN, Peter Michael. b 54. **d** 79. Hon C Westfield *B & W* 01-02
ELLIOTT, Charles Middleton. b 39. **d** 64. Dean and Chapl Trin Hall Cam 90-01
ELLIOTT, David Reed. b 62. **d** 93. Dioc Communications Dept 98-00
ENGLER, Mrs Margaret Dorothy. b 44. **d** 93. rtd 04
EVANS, Claire Elizabeth Phoebe. b 78. **d** 02. Lic to Offic *Llan* from 04
EVANS, Miss Daphne Gillian. b 41. **d** 87. rtd 88
EVANS, Geoffrey David. b 44. **d** 70
EVENSON, Bruce John. b 46. **d** 98. Stockholm w Gävle and Västerås *Eur* 02-05
EVES, Barry. b 51. **d** 88. V Bubwith w Skipwith *York* 93-04
FLETCHER, Steven John Carylon. b 60. **d** 92. C Newquay *Truro* 92-93
FORDHAM, Richard George. b 34. **d** 91
FOX, Jonathan Alexander. b 56. **d** 81. TV Madeley *Heref* 97-02
FOX, Mrs Lynn. b 51. **d** 92. TM Clifton *S'well* 96-98
FRANK, Derek John. b 49. **d** 85. Vevey w Château d'Oex and Villars *Eur* 93-02
GADD, Bryan Stephen Andrew. b 56. **d** 81. Chapl Summer Fields Sch Ox 90-02
GALLON, Mrs Audrey Kay. b 41. **d** 97. Perm to Offic *Cant* 04-05
GERRY, Ulric James. b 67. **d** 97. Tanzania from 02
GIBBS, Darryl. b 73. **d** 98. V Llanwynno *Llan* 03-04
GILBERT, Caroline Margaret. b 62. **d** 90. Hon C Aston SS Pet and Paul *Birm* 90-93
GILBERT, Christopher Anthony. b 60. **d** 89. TV Cannock *Lich* 97-01
GODDARD, Mrs Doris. b 48. **d** 96. NSM Blackdown *B & W* from 05
GOLDSTONE-CREASEY, Graham. b 51. **d** 83. P-in-c Gleadless Valley *Sheff* 95-98
GRAY, Dale Armitage. b 42. **d** 92. rtd 98
GREEN, Gareth David. b 60. **d** 97. V W Ardsley *Wakef* 00-03
GRIMSDALE, Mrs Margaret. b 24. **d** 87. rtd 90
GRÜNEWALD, Gottfried Johannes. b 38. **d** 69. rtd 05
GUILLAN, Miss Barbara Doris. b 19. **d** 87. rtd 89
HALL, Edwin George. b 40. **d** 91. rtd 97
HAMMOND, Frank. b 49. **d** 77. C Blundellsands St Nic *Liv* 80-83
HAMMOND, Canon Jacob Aryee. b 47. **d** 84. Merthyr Tydfil 97-04
HANDLEY, Terence Anthony. b 55. **d** 87
HARDING, John Stuart Michael. b 45. **d** 81. V Broxtowe *S'well* 87-98; Perm to Offic *M& K* 01-02
HARRIES, Malcolm David. b 44. **d** 96. P-in-c Godley cum Newton Green *Ches* 00-04
HARRIS, David. b 52. **d** 77. Perm to Offic *Lon* 85-88
HART, Colin Edwin. b 45. **d** 74. Lect St Jo Coll Nottm 87-01; Public Preacher *S'well* 87-01; Hon C Trowell 91-01
HAYES, Michael John. b 52. **d** 78. NSM Norwood St Mary *Lon* 00-03
HAYNES, Cyril Michael. b 26. **d** 84. Perm to Offic *Heref* 96-99
HENSON, Richard Clive. b 41. **d** 88. rtd 99
HERBERT, Graham Paul. b 54. **d** 81. C Claygate *Guildf* 99-01
HILL, Mrs Anne Doreen. b 40. **d** 88. rtd 04
HOGG, William Ritson. b 47. **d** 72.V Catterick *Ripon* 88-97
HOLLIS, Anthony Wolcott Linsley. b 40. **d** 64. Bermuda from 92
HORTON, Andrew Charles. b 50. **d** 73. TR Selsdon St Jo w St Fran *S'wark* 98-03
HUGHES, John William George. b 48. **d** 72. Chapl RAF 86-02
HUGHES, Robert Guy. b 64. **d** 93. Chapl K Sch Ely 96-99; Min Can Ely Cathl *Ely* 96-99
HULME, Ms Juliette Mary. b 57. **d** 94. CF 02-05
HUNT, Andrew Collins. b 54. **d** 00. NSM Cainscross w Selsley *Glouc* 00-02
HUNT, Paul Firth. b 62. **d** 89. V Leeds Richmond Hill *Ripon* 95-01
HURLEY, Mark Tristan. b 57. **d** 91. V Bicker *Linc* 00-02
HUXTABLE, Christopher Michael Barclay. b 61. **d** 95. Chapl St Mary's Sch Wantage 04-05
HYSON, Peter Raymond. b 51. **d** 87. TV Whitton *Sarum* 92-99
JACOBS, Michael David. b 41. **d** 65. Leic Univ *Leic* 84-02
JAMES, David Henry. b 45. **d** 98. rtd 00
JELLEY, David. b 25. **d** 87. rtd 97; Perm to Offic *Leic* from 00

JENKINS, Frederick Llewellyn. b 14. **d** 37. rtd 77
JONES, Helen Alison. b 59. **d** 96. C Brocklesby Park *Linc* 97-98
JONES, Michael. b 49. **d** 85. V Hamer *Man* 93-05
JORDAN, Anthony John. b 50. **d** 83. NSM Bournemouth St Fran *Win* 88-03
KEMP, Barry. b 48. **d** 74. Chapl Ld Wandsworth Coll Basingstoke 92-02
KING, Timothy William. b 52. **d** 81. R Farncombe *Guildf* 95-00
KNIGHT, Jonathan Morshead. b 59. **d** 88. OCF from 99; CF (TAVR) from 00; Hon Lect Th Kent Univ from 00
LA TOUCHE, Francis William Reginald. b 51. **d** 76. V Burstwick w Thorngumbald *York* 91-02
LANGRIDGE, Molly Deirdre. b 48. **d** 98. NSM King's Lynn St Marg w St Nic *Nor* 98-03
LENNOX, Joan Baxter. b 50. **d** 96. C Baillieston *Glas* 96-97
LEWIS, Timothy John. b 56. **d** 86. Chapl RN 89-02
LICHTENBERGER, Miss Ruth Eileen. b 34. **d** 96. rtd 05
LYNAS, Mrs Judith. b 53. **d** 92. Hon C Longfleet *Sarum* 97-99
McCREADY, Maurice Shaun. b 55. **d** 83
MacDONALD, Alastair Douglas. b 48. **d** 74. Chapl Hants Partnerships NHS Trust 01-04
MACDONALD, Cameron. b 51. **d** 90. CF 95-05
McMAHON, Brian Richard. b 39. **d** 87. NSM Colney Heath St Mark *St Alb* 87-03
MacVANE, Sara. **d** 05. C Rome *Eur* from 05
MALDOOM, Ms Julie Marilyn. b 65. **d** 96. C Chinnor w Emmington and Sydenham etc *Ox* 96-99
MANN, Ms Angela. b 58. **d** 94. Perm to Offic *Sarum* 97-99
MARAJH, Brian Melvin. **d** 86. S Africa from 99
MARTIN, Miss Marion. b 47. **d** 87. rtd 88
MASON, Francis Robert Anthony. b 56. **d** 90. R Jersey Grouville *Win* 98-04
MATTHEWS, Canon Royston Peter. b 39. **d** 64. rtd 05
MAYES, Suzanne Janette. b 55. **d** 98. Chapl HM Pris Wellingborough 02-04
MILLER, Stephen Michael. b 63. **d** 91. Miss to Seafarers from 99
MITCHELL, Christopher Derek. b 61. **d** 89. C Brookfield St Mary *Lon* 92-96
MORDECAI, Thomas Huw. b 59. **d** 87. PV Westmr Abbey 98-01
✠MPALANYI-NKOYOYO, The Rt Revd Livingstone. b 37. **d** 69. rtd 02
MULLER, Anton Michael. b 61. **d** 99. TV Penrith w Newton Reigny and Plumpton Wall *Carl* 03-04; P-in-c Dacre 03-04; Chapl N Cumbria Mental Health NHS Trust 03-04
NUNN, Stephen Robert. b 64. **d** 92. Chapl HM Pris Kingston (Portsm) 01-03
O'REILLY, Ms Eileen Catherine. b 47. **d** 96. USA from 00
OAKES, Robert. b 47. **d** 82. R S Hill w Callington *Truro* 88-03; P-in-c Linkinhorne 88-03; Hon Can Truro Cathl 01-03
ORCHIN, Robert Andrew. b 71. **d** 95. P-in-c Portsea St Geo *Portsm* 00-02
OTTO, Andrew James. b 63. **d** 01. C Trowbridge H Trin *Sarum* 01-05
OTTO, Francis James Reeve. b 42. **d** 69. Perm to Offic *Ox* from 04
PALMER, Malcolm Leonard. b 46. **d** 82. Canada from 01
PARFITT, Neil. **d** 99. V Ferndale w Maerdy *Llan* 03-04
PARKE, Simon Frederick Fenning. b 57. **d** 84. V Tufnell Park St Geo and All SS *Lon* 93-03
PEARCE, Valerie Olive. b 46. **d** 97. Sisters of the Ch 77-04; Lic to Offic *S'wark* 97-04
PEEK, John Richard. b 51. **d** 76. Chapl Bearwood Coll Wokingham 96-98
PERRICONE, Vincent James. b 50. **d** 89. P-in-c Glas H Cross *Glas* 95-03
PETERSON, Canon John Louis. b 42. **d** 76. Sec Gen Acc 95-04
PHILLIPS, Geoffrey Clarke. b 50. **d** 96. Chapl HM Pris Shepton Mallet 01-03
PORTER, Miss Joy Dove. b 50. **d** 91. Rouen Miss to Seamen *Eur* 97-00; Dn-in-c Rouen All SS 97-00
POTTER, John Dennis. b 39. **d** 94. NSM Box w Hazlebury and Ditteridge *Bris* 94-98
PRICE, Alun Huw. b 47. **d** 70. CF 77-03
QUILL, John Stephen. b 51. **d** 79. Adv to Bd of Soc Resp *Worc* 90-95
RADLEY, Stephen Gavin. b 62. **d** 89. P-in-c Marley Hill *Dur* 96-01
RAYNER, David. b 49. **d** 78. Perm to Offic *Lon* from 99
REEVE, Kenneth Robert. b 23. **d** 68
ROBERTS, John Charles. b 50. **d** 73. Lic to Offic *Bris* 93-95
ROBINSON, William Pitchford. b 50. **d** 75. Australia from 86
ROPER, Douglas. b 72. **d** 00. C Mancetter *Cov* 03-04
ROSOMAN, Richard John. b 59. **d** 92. V Malvern H Trin and St Jas *Worc* 00-04
ROWLANDS, Marc Alun. b 62. **d** 99. P-in-c Llanpumsaint w Llanllawddog *St D* 02-05
RUSSELL, David Edward. **d** 52. Perm to Offic *Chich* and *Roch* from 98
SALENIUS, Richard Mark. b 57. **d** 80. V Brightlingsea *Chelmsf* 96-05
SHARPLES, Ms Susan Margaret. b 58. **d** 94. USA from 01
SHENTON, David. b 57. **d** 95. TV Melton Mowbray *Leic* 99-01
SIMPSON, Mrs June Hall. b 31. **d** 87. rtd 01
SMITH, David Charles Stuart. **d** 61. Australia 61-72, 75-89 and from 90; rtd 96
SMITH, Gary Russell. b 56. **d** 96. C Southampton Maybush St Pet *Win* 96-00
SMITH, Lewis Shand. b 52. **d** 77. Miss to Seafarers from 80
SMITH, Mark Richard Samuel. b 63. **d** 89. TV Stockport SW *Ches* 01-02
SMITH, Michael. b 54. **d** 89. V Ashbourne w Mapleton *Derby* 98-04
SOKOLOWSKI, Mrs Stephanie Mary. b 56. **d** 94. C Godstone and Blindley Heath *S'wark* 97-04
SPARROW, Michael Kenneth. **d** 75. Schiedam Miss to Seafarers *Eur* 93-03
SPENCE, Elizabeth. **d** 05. NSM Cowley St Jas *Ox* from 05
SPEYER, Nicholas Anthony. b 48. **d** 79. Australia from 84
STACKPOLE, Robert Aaron. b 59. **d** 90. Canada from 93
STEVENS, Alan Robert. b 55. **d** 89. P-in-c N w S Kilworth and Misterton *Leic* 97-00
STEVENSON, Ms Jan. b 65. **d** 94. C Coleraine *Conn* 99-04
STEWART, William James. b 58. **d** 83. Min Dublin Ch Ch Cathl Gp *D & G* 93-04; CORE (St Cath Ch) 93-04; Chapl Dub Coll of Catering 94-04; Min Can St Patr Cathl Dublin 00-04
STOCK-HESKETH, Jonathan Philip. b 49. **d** 83. Lect Nottm Univ 95-04
SUSTINS, Nigel. b 46. **d** 88. Perm to Offic *S'wark* 96-02
TARRANT, Paul John. b 57. **d** 82. R Edin Old St Paul *Edin* 96-97
TEE, John. b 59. **d** 82. CF 89-03
THACKER, James Robert. b 40. **d** 66. Japan 99-04
THRALL, Canon Margaret Eleanor. b 28. **d** 82. rtd 98; Perm to Offic *Ban* from 98
TOWNSEND, Derek William (Bill). b 52. **d** 91. V Banbury St Paul *Ox* 98-01
TRIMBLE, Mrs Anne Inman. b 40. **d** 92. rtd 94
TURAY, Prince Eddie Solomon. b 60. **d** 85. Perm to Offic *Lon* 01-02
VILLAGE, Andrew. b 54. **d** 92. Univ of Wales (Ban) *Ban* from 04
WALKER, Christopher James Anthony. b 43. **d** 87. rtd 98
WALTERS, Mrs Sheila Ann Beatrice. b 37. **d** 89. NSM Packington w Normanton-le-Heath *Leic* 02-05
WARD, Prof Graham John. b 55. **d** 90. Prof Contextual Th Man Univ *Man* from 99
WARKE, Alistair Samuel John. b 66. **d** 92. I Killyman *Arm* 95-04; Hon V Choral Arm Cathl 95-04
WATKINS, Miss Lorna Ann Francis Charles. b 59. **d** 84. R Herbrandston and Hasguard w St Ishmael's *St D* 99-05
WATSON, Miss Violet Hazel. b 29. **d** 87. Perm to Offic *St Alb* 88-90
WEBSTER, John Bainbridge. b 55. **d** 83. Lady Marg Prof Div Ox Univ 96-04; Can Res Ch Ch *Ox* 96-04
WELSH, Jennifer Lee. b 59. **d** 87. Perm to Offic *Win* 94-02 and *Lon* from 03
WHATMOUGH, Michael Anthony (Tony). b 50. **d** 81. V Bris St Mary Redcliffe w Temple etc *Bris* 93-04
WHITING, Antony Gerald Stroud. b 26. **d** 86. rtd 98
WICKHAM, Nicholas John. b 27. **d** 87. rtd 92
WILLIAMS, Robert Edward. b 50. **d** 74. CF 88-05
WILLIS, Andrew Lyn. b 48. **d** 74. Chapl RAF 83-02
WITTING, Anna Brynhild Marianne. b 48. Sweden from 04
WOODSIDE, David. b 60. **d** 90. C Stoke Newington St Mary *Lon* 90-92
WORRALL, Peter Henry. b 62. **d** 95. P-in-c Hartlebury *Worc* 99-04
WRIST-KNUDSEN, Svend Michael. b 61. **d** 91. P-in-c Penzance St Jo *Truro* 95-97
WYLIE, Nigel Bruce. b 62. **d** 91. C Selly Park St Steph and St Wulstan *Birm* 91-94
YEO, Mrs Jennifer Marjorie. b 40. **d** 90. Perm to Offic *Ex* from 98
YEO, Richard Ellery. b 25. **d** 89. Perm to Offic *Ex* from 95

CLERGY WHO HAVE DIED SINCE THE LAST EDITION

A list of clergy who have died since 4 August 2003, when the compilation of the 2004/05 edition was completed. The month and year of death (if known) are recorded with each entry.

ACKERLEY, Herbert 07/04
ACKROYD, Peter Runham 01/05
ADAMS, George Ernest 01/04
AIZLEWOOD, John David 04/05
ALLEN, Michael Tarrant 10/04
ALLEN, Stanley Leonard Sidney 02/04
AMBROSE, Edgar 05/04
ANDREWS, Jennifer Wendy 12/04
ANSCOMBE, Thomas 12/04
ARBUCKLE, James Hugh 10/03
ARBUTHNOT, James 08/04
ARDLEY, John Owen 02/04
ARMSTRONG, John James 12/04
ARNOLD, Alan Roy 12/04
ARRANTASH, Reginald Thomas 05/04
ARTISS, Joseph Sturge 07/05
ASHTON, Joseph Patrick Bankes (Pat) 10/03
ATHERTON, Albert 07/05
ATKINS, Graham Anthony Hazlewood 04/04
ATKINSON, Peter Geoffrey 07/04
AVES, John Albert 01/04
AYAD, Karl 12/03
BACON, Lionel William Rupert 01/04
BAGGALEY, Dennis 02/05
BAGLEY, Richard Alexander 05/04
BAINBRIDGE, Norman Harold 10/04
BAIRD, Edward Simpson 11/04
BAKER, Henry Blandford Benedict 08/04
BAKER, Robin Henry 01/04
BALL, Glynne Howell James 10/04
BANNISTER, Simon Monro 09/04
BANNON, Richard Babington 02/05
BARBER, William Ewart Worsley 12/04
BARKER, Francis Howard 10/03
BARKER, Leonard Roy 10/04
BARKER, Stephen Luke Remington 01/04
BARKER, Walter Frederick 05/04
BARNARD, John Stuart 12/03
BARNARD, William Henry 01/05
BARRY, Herbert Brian 03/05
BARTLETT, Alan 07/05
BARTON, Cyril Albert 01/04
BATY, Ernest John 02/05
BEAVAN, Charles Kenneth 09/03
BEDDOW, Arthur Josiah Comyns 06/04
BEECH, Harold 11/04
BELLINGHAM, Charles Eric William 09/04
BENCE, Roy 03/05
BENFIELD, Gordon 08/04
BENNET, Gordon Duncan Affleck 08/04
BENNETT, Michael Edgar 03/05
BERRY, Geoffrey Wilbur Ronald 03/04
BEUKES, Douglas 08/04
BICKERDYKE, James Clifford 06/05
BIDDELL, John Herman 06/05
BIDDLE, Rodney William Dennis 04/05
BIDDLESTONE, Joseph 11/03
BIDE, Peter William 09/03
BIGGS, Laurence Walter 05/05
BILL, Denis Aubrey 12/03
BILLINGHAM, Peter Charles Geoffrey 11/04
BIRCH, Arthur Kenneth 08/04
BIRKETT, Peter 10/03
BIRLEY, John Lindsay 10/03
BLACKSHAW, Alfred 11/04
BLAGDON-GAMLEN, Peter Eugène 03/04
BLAKE, Derek Gordon 01/04
BLAKE, Roy Harold David 02/05
BLAND, Thomas 11/04
BLOOMFIELD, Gillian 10/03
BLUNDELL, Derek George 11/03
BOFF, Charles Roy 11/04
BOGGIS, Christine Louise 09/03
BOND, Clifford Frank 02/04
✠BONSER, David 03/05
BOOCOCK, John Walter 04/05
BOOTH, James Roger 10/04
BORRILL, John 04/05
BOWLER, Denis Charles Stanley 01/05
BRACK, Edward James 05/04
BRADBURY, Roy Albert 08/04
BRADLEY, Cecil Robert Jones 09/03
BRADLEY, Donald John Walter 08/04
BRADSHAW, Jolyon Anthony 03/05
BRAITHWAITE, Wilfrid 09/03
BRANWELL, Edward Bruce 09/04
BRAY, Thomas Chadwick 01/04
BRETTELL, Robert Michael 05/05
BRIDGLAND, Cyril John Edwin 12/03
✠BRIGGS, George Cardell 03/04
BROADHURST, Kenneth 10/04
BROCKBANK, Leslie David 01/04
BROOKSTEIN, Royston 10/03
BROWN, Glenys 07/04
BROWN, Michael Rene Warneford 02/04
BRUMWELL, Francis John Thomas 09/04
BRUNSDON, Thomas Kenneth 12/03
BRUTON, Keith Leslie 11/04
BUCKLEY, Michael Richard 07/05
BUFFEE, Leslie John 12/03
BURCH, Cyril John 01/04
BURGESS, Derek Mark 02/04
BURGESS, Henry James 12/03
BURGIN, Henry Kenneth 06/04
BURR, Brian Gilbert 12/04
BURROWS, George Henry Jerram 10/03
BURT, Noel Bryce 04/05
BURTON, Edward Arthur 10/03
BUSBY, Jack Wright 12/04
BUTCHER, David John 06/04
BYRNE, Robert James Matthew 11/03
CAMIER, James 04/05
CANHAM, Philip Edward 05/04
CARR, Douglas Nicholson 02/05
CARRE, John Trenchard 05/04
CARSON, Herbert Moore 10/03
CARTWRIGHT, John Walter Deryk 06/05
CASEY, Ernest George 06/04
CHALMERS, Robert Alan 12/03
CHALONER, Stephen Mason 12/04
CHANTRY, Richard Michael 09/03
CHAPMAN, Albert Aidan 10/04
CHAPMAN, David John 12/03
CHAPMAN, William Howard Dale 11/04
CHAPPELL, Eric Richardson 10/03
CHARE, Frederic Keith 09/04
CHEALL, Henry Frederick Knowles 03/04
CHILDS, Leonard Neil 02/04
CHISHOLM, David Whitridge 12/04
CHIVERS, William Herbert 05/05
CHRISTIAN, Ronald George 05/05
CLARK, Russell John 09/04
CLARKE, David George Alexander 07/04
CLAYTON-JONES, Roger Francis 01/04
CLENDON, David Arthur 08/04
COATES, Francis Gustav 10/04
COGMAN, Frederick Walter 07/05
COLBY, Robert James 03/04
COLEMAN, John Edward Noel 03/04
COLEMAN, Robert William Alfred 04/05
COLLINS, George Martyn 08/04
COLLINS, James Frederick 01/05
CONWAY, Owen Arnott 09/04
COOK, Derek Edward 11/04
COOPER, Sydney Bernard Nikon 10/04
CORNELL, John Lister 07/05
CORNISH, Philip Gordon Pym 04/05
CORRADINE, John 07/05
COWIE, Leonard Wallace 01/04
COWLING, Wilfred Edmund 12/03
COX, Alan 06/04
CRABTREE, Eric 03/05
CRAWFORD, John 10/03
CRESSWELL, Kenneth Benjamin 05/04
CRIPPS, Harold Ernest 12/03
CROOKS, Frederick Walter (Mike) 09/03
CROWSON, Richard Charles Marriott 12/04
CULL, Ernest Geoffrey 08/03
CUMBERLAND, Leslie Hodgson 12/03
CUMING, Mark Alexander 04/05
CURSON, James Desmond 01/04
CURTIS, Wilfred Frank 05/05
DABBS, Roger Stevens 10/03
DAGGER, John Henry Kynaston 03/04
DAMMERS, Alfred Hounsell 08/04
DAND, Robert William Scrymgour 02/05
DANIELS, Norman 05/05
DAUBUZ, Michael Claude 05/05
DAVIES, Arthur Cadwaladr 11/04
DAVIES, Clifford Morgan 09/03
DAVIES, Dewi Caradog 12/03
DAVIES, Ivor Llewelyn 06/05
DAVIES, James Owen 10/04
DAVIES, John Gwyn 06/05
DAVIES, Laurence Gordon 06/04
DAVIES, Philip Bertram 02/05
DAVIES, Walter Hugh 05/05
DAWSON, William John 12/03
DAY, John Nathaniel 10/04

DAY, Terence Patrick 12/03
DEAN, Francis John Michael 12/03
DENHAM, Thomas William 07/04
DERBYSHIRE, Alan George 12/04
DICKENSON, Geoffrey 11/03
DIL, Pierre Joseph 03/05
DINES, Anthony Bernard 08/04
DISNEY, Peter James 11/04
DOBSON, John Haselden 01/05
DODDS, Arthur Whitfield 01/04
DOTY, Joseph Bonn 09/03
DOUGLAS, Archibald Sholto 02/04
DOWNIE, James Hubert 05/04
DOWNS, Ivan Frederick 03/05
DUDLEY, John Rea 12/04
DUFOUR, Prudence Elaine 08/04
DUFTON, Francis Trevor 12/04
DUNHILL, Robin Arnold 01/05
DUNSTAN, Alan Leonard 09/04
DUNSTAN, Gordon Reginald 01/04
DURIE, Ian Geoffrey Campbell 04/05
DURRANS, Anthony 08/04
EAST, Reginald Walter 08/04
ECCLES, Ernest Pattison 03/04
EDMONDS, Joseph William 01/04
EDWARDS, Dudley James Milne 08/04
EDWARDS, John Gregory 10/03
EDWARDS, Thomas Harold David 04/04
EKE, Robert Foord Stansfield 04/04
ELCOAT, George Alastair 02/04
ELIOT, Whately Ian 03/05
ELLIOTT, John George 10/04
ELLMORE, Geoffrey Richard 03/04
ELSEY, Cyril 10/04
EMMET, Herbert Gerald 05/04
ENGLAND, Robert Gordon 02/05
ERSON, William Kingston 07/05
ESTDALE, Francis Albert 05/04
ETHERIDGE (née ROBERTS), Marjorie 03/04
ETTLINGER, Max Brian 06/04
EVANS, Donald Henry 02/04
EVANS, Frederick Albert 02/04
EVANS, Lewys Thomas Gareth 11/04
EVANS, Trefor Rhys 01/04
EXALL, John Aubrey 07/04
FAIR, Richard Francis 06/04
FARNWORTH, Michael Godfrey Frankland 10/03
FAULKNER, Peter Charles 07/05
FELIX, Donald Cameron 11/04
FERGUSON, John Richard Preston 06/05
FIELDER, Arthur John 11/03
FINNEMORE, Ernest Harold 05/05
FIRTH, Ronald Mahlon 12/04
✠FISHER, Reginald Lindsay (Brother Michael) 12/03
FITZWILLIAMS, Mark Morshead 12/03
FLETCHER, Francis Cecil 04/04
FORD, Lionel Peter 09/04
FORSYTH, William 07/05
FOTHERGILL, Anthony Page 05/04
FOWKE, Thomas Randall 09/03
FRANCE, Geoffrey Charles 10/03
FRANCIS, Donald 04/05
FRANCIS, Edward Reginald 05/04
FRANCIS, Ernest Walter 01/04
FRANCIS (or ROOSE FRANCIS), Leslie 11/04
FROSTICK, Alan Norman 04/04
FRYER, Anthony Charles 05/04
FRYER, Peter Hugh 05/04
FULLER, Frank William 12/03
GALBRAITH, John Watson Joseph Denham 09/04
GALLAGHER, Hubert 07/04
GARRATT, John William 12/04
GAUNT, Arthur Raymond 02/05
GEORGE, Alec 06/05
GILL, Donald Maule Harvell 08/04
GILMAN, Charles Philip 04/04
GLASS, Edward Eric Ivor 01/05
GLENDINING, Alan 08/04
GLENN, Michael David 12/04
GOATER, Charles Frederick 09/03
GOLDSPINK, Robert William 01/04
GOTT, Joseph Desmond 07/05
GOVER, Michael Sydney Richard 12/03
GRACE, Juliet Christine 04/05
GRAHAM, Douglas Wrixon 04/04
GRAHAM, John Francis Ottiwell Skelton 02/04
GRAIN, Anthony Ernest 03/04
GRAIN, Keith Charles 01/04
GRANGER, Ronald Harry 01/05
GRANT, Edward Francis 06/05
GRAY, Hugh Henry James 11/03
GREEN, Alan Thomas 12/04
GREEN, Vivian Hubert Howard 01/05
GREEN, William Lewis 11/03
GREEN, William John 03/04
GREENWOOD, Hilary Peter Frank 09/03
GREGORY, Ivan Henry 10/04
GRIFFIN, William George 09/04
GRIFFITH, Geoffrey Grenville 06/04
GRIMWADE, Eric Peter 01/05
GUILLOTEAU, Claude 04/04
GURNEY, Richmond Harptree 06/04
HACK, Alison Ruth 06/05
HAIGH, Owen Quentin 04/05
HALE, John 02/05
HALL, Ernest 06/05
HALL, William Norman 03/05
HALLETT, Roy 10/03
HALLIBURTON, Robert John 09/04
HAMMERSLEY, John Goodwin 11/04
HAMMOND, Mary 09/03
HANCOCK, Douglas Charles 03/05
HANDLEY, Harold 11/04
HANNAH, Richard 01/05
HARDING, David Anthony 01/04
HARKNESS, Verney Austin Barnett 12/03
HARPER, Horace Frederic 05/05
HARRAP, William Charles 02/04
HARRISON, Alan William 04/05
HARRISON, Colin Charles 03/05
HARRISON, David Robert 10/04
HARROP, Joseph Blakemore (Blake) 01/05
HART, Henry St John 10/04
HARTLEY, William Reginald (Rex) 02/04
HARVEY, Brian 01/05
HAWES, Clive 06/04
HAWES, George Walter 03/04
HAWORTH, John Luttrell 06/04
HAYTER, Michael George 05/05
HAYWARD, Alfred Ross 03/04
HAWKINS, John Henry 05/05
✠HEAVENER, Robert William 03/05
HECKINGBOTTOM, John Michael 05/05
HEDLEY, Ronald 06/04
HELLIWELL, Zena Mary 08/04
HEMS, Richard Brian 03/04
HERBERT, Alan 11/04
HERON, Alexander Francis 10/04
HEWER, Sidney Eric 06/04
✠HEYWARD, Oliver Spencer 12/03
HIBBS, Lawrence Winston 11/03
HICKIN, Maurice Whitehouse 01/05
HICKLEY, Peter Michael 05/04
HILDAGE, James Francis 09/04
HILL, Derek Ingram 10/03
HILLMAN, Jesse James 11/04
HILLS, John Bucknell 04/04
HIRST, Wilfrid 10/03
HITCHINSON, William Henry 11/03
HOBBS, Philip Bertram 04/05
HOBSON, Herbert Leslie 01/05
HODGSON, Matthew William 01/04
HOLMES, Judith Ella 03/05
HOPKINSON, Alfred Stephan 08/04
HOROBIN, Hector Stanley 01/04
HOUGH, Edward Lewis 12/03
HOUGHTON, Edward Johnson 01/05
HOUSE, Francis Harry 09/04
HOWARD, Michael Paul Penrose 02/05
HOWARTH, Jack Raymond 09/04
HOWELLS, Donald Lockwood 04/05
HUMPHREYS, William Haydn 09/03
HUMPHRIES, Harold Joseph 06/04
HUMPLEBY, Peter 11/03
HUNTER, David 06/05
HUNTER, David Matheson 10/04
HUNTER-BAILEY, James Ralph 01/05
HUSSEY, William Kenneth Alfred 07/05
HUTCHINSON, Harold 05/04
HUTTON, Brian Allan 12/04
INMAN, John Phillip 09/03
IORNS, Derrick John 06/04
JACKSON, Derrick Raymond 05/05
JACKSON, George 01/04
JACKSON, Kenneth Evans 01/05
JACKSON, Stanley 07/04
JAMES, David Walter Skyrme 10/04
JAMES, Gordon Cecil (Jimmy) 12/03
JAMES, Lewis John 10/03
JAMES, Peter Heppell 02/04
JAMES, William Arthur 10/04
JARVIS, Eric Thomas Noel 10/04
JEE, Colin Scott 03/05
JENKINS, Cyril 03/04
JENKINS, Ernest Dennis 09/04
JEPHSON, Douglas Ronald Shipstone 12/04
JOBSON, Paul 10/03
JOHNSON, Walter 03/04
JOHNSTON, James 04/04
JONES, Alban Vaughan 02/05
JONES, Alfred Albert 09/03
JONES, David Noel 06/05
JONES, Derek John 12/04
JONES, Glyn Owen 02/05
JONES, Humphrey Ingham 11/03
JONES, John Morgan 06/04
JONES, John Samuel 05/05
JONES, Kenneth John 02/05
JONES, Kenneth William 08/03
JONES, Robert Dwyfor 06/05
JONES, William Alexander 04/05
JONES, William Glyndwr 09/03
JONES, William Lloyd 08/04
JOWETT, Alfred 07/04
JOY, Leslie John Clifton 02/04
JUDGE, James Arthur 06/05
KAYE, Norman 06/05
KEANE, James Goldsworthy 02/05
KEELING, Michael John 02/04
KELLETT, Colin 01/04
KEMP, Jack Noel 02/04
KENNY, Thomas Percival Robert 05/05
KING, John Michael Stuart 10/03
KINGS, Peter Robert 04/04
KIRBY, John Patrick 10/04

KNAPMAN, Hugh William Hartly 11/04
KNIGHT, Donald 01/04
KONING, Hendrik Bernadus 09/04
LANE, David John 01/05
LANGTON, Maurice Charles 12/03
LASHBROOKE, John 07/04
LAVILLE, Jocelyn Roger (Jo) 12/03
LAW, Herbert James Wentworth 01/05
LAWRENCE, George Leslie 02/04
LAWRENSON, James Percival 02/04
LAZONBY, Alan Frederick 01/04
LE FEUVRE, Henry Mauger 10/03
LEE, Frederick Roydon 10/04
LEE, John Foden 11/03
LEFEVER, Henry Charles 08/04
LEMMON, Rowland 02/04
LENNARD, Thomas Jay 06/04
LENTON, Robert Vincent 12/03
LEWIS, David Roy 08/04
LEWIS, Edward John 11/04
LEWIS, Peter Goulstone 04/05
LEWIS, Robert Hugh Cecil 11/04
LEWIS, Trevor Charlton Haselden 04/04
LINTON, Sydney 10/03
LLOYD, Charles Henry 01/05
LLOYD, John James 06/04
LOCKHART, Antony William Castleton 01/04
LOCKLEY, Harold 09/04
LOCKWOOD, David Nicholas 03/05
LOCKYER, Maurice David 04/04
LONGBOTHAM, Richard Ashley 08/04
LOOSEMORE, James Clive 07/05
LOPDELL-BRADSHAW, Humphrey Maitland 12/04
LOVEJOY, Geoffrey William 04/04
LOVELAND, John Michael 07/04
LOVEWELL, Robert Antony 07/04
LOWE, Eric 02/05
LUCAS, Kenneth Ashley 01/04
LUCAS, Raymond Charles Henry 07/05
LUMB, Dennis 09/04
LURKINGS, Edward Henry 03/05
✠LYTH, Richard Edward 02/05
McCLAUGHRY, Victor Thomas 04/05
McCLOUGHLIN, Joshua 02/05
McCULLOCH, Geoffrey Kenneth 11/04
MACKAY, Ian Stuart Reay 12/03
McKELVIE, Alfred 06/05
MACKENZIE, George 12/03
MACLAREN, Grant 05/04
MACNAUGHTON, Donald Allan 10/03
MACONACHIE, Alwyn 11/04
MALLETT, Pamela Joan 01/05
MANCE, Herbert William 11/03
MANN, Gary 01/05
✠MARCUS, Justus Mauritius 12/03
MARKLAND, Vincent Hilton 08/04
MARTIN, David Geoffrey 07/05
MARTIN, John Albert 05/04
MARTIN, John Keith 02/05
MARTIN, Kenneth Cyril 04/04
MARTIN, Sara Galloway 11/03
MARTIN, William Henry Blyth 01/04
MASLEN, Trevor 02/04
MASTERS, Raymond Austin 02/05
MATHEWS, Ronald Peel Beresford 05/05
MATTHIAS, Edwin 01/05
MAWSON, Frank 01/04
MAXWELL, Richard Renwick 11/03
MAYES, Leonard Harry 07/04
MAYO, Gordon Edwin 11/03
MEAKIN, John Ernest 04/04
MEASEY, George 11/03
MENZIES, Alastair Charles Vass 03/05
✠MERCER, Eric Arthur John 11/03
MEREDITH, James Noel Michael Creed 06/05
MEREDITH, Ronald Duncan d'Esterre 10/04
MERWOOD, Raymond George 04/05
MESSOM, Alan George 11/03
MILES, Ruth Cecilia 07/04
MILLARD, Albert George 01/04
MILLS, Leslie 02/04
MILNER, Leslie 10/03
MITCHELL, Cecil Robert 07/04
MITCHELL, Frank 07/05
MITCHELL, Josephine Dorothy 04/04
MOLL, David Henry 10/04
✠MONTEFIORE, Hugh William 05/05
MONTGOMERY, Charles George Greathead 02/05
MONTGOMERY, John Alexander 04/04
MOODY, Aubrey Rowland 03/04
MOODY, Derek Frank 04/05
✠MOORE, James Edward 03/05
MOORE, Peter 05/04
MOORE, Robert George Chaffey 05/04
MORGAN, Brian 04/04
MORGAN, Robert Hugh 02/05
MOSEDALE, Hugh Alfred 02/04
MOSELEY, Arthur William 02/04
MOSFORD, Denzil Joseph 12/03
MOSS, Stephen 2005
MOSS, Wilfrid Maurice 01/05
MOXLEY, Cyril Edward 03/04
MULCOCK, Edward John 11/03
MURENZI, François Xavier 11/03
MYERS, Arnold George 04/05
NASH, Richard Edward 11/04
NELSON, Kenneth Edmund 03/04
NESBITT, Charles Howard 12/03
NEWCOMBE, Kenneth Harry 02/05
NEWHAM, Jill 09/03
NICHOLS, Albert Percival 09/04
NICKALLS, Frederick William 12/03
NOBLE, Arthur 10/03
NOEL, Frank Arthur 10/04
NUNN, Geoffrey William John 02/05
NUTTALL, Wilfrid (Bill) 05/05
O'BRIEN, John 10/03
ODLUM, Michael Julian 11/04
OLDALE, Harry 09/04
OLDROYD, James Healey 04/05
OLHAUSEN, William John 03/04
OLIVER, Arthur Norman 10/03
O'LOUGHLIN, Gordon Raymond 06/04
OLYOTT, Leonard Eric 04/05
✠OWEN, Edwin 04/05
OWEN, Ethelston John Charles 03/05
OWEN, Gerald 03/04
PALMER, John Russell 11/03
PARISH, George Richard 12/04
PARKES, Robert Stephen 06/05
PARKINSON, John Fearnley 12/03
PARRY, Brychan Vaughan 04/05
PARSONS, Jeffrey Michael Langdon 08/04
PATIENT, Peter Leslie 02/04
PATTON, Desmond Hilton 11/03
PAYNE, Alan Frank 11/03
PEACE, Geoffrey 06/04
PEACOCK, David Christopher 07/04
PEARCE, Denis William Wilfrid 04/05
PEARCE, Frank 11/03
PEARSON, Brian 12/03
PELLANT, Walter Reginald Guy 05/04
PELTOR, Lawrence Frank 04/04
PESKETT, Osmond Fletcher 03/04
PETT, Douglas Ellory 02/05
PETTITT, Mervyn Francis 11/04
PEYTON JONES, Donald Lewis 12/04
PHAROAH, Donald James 12/03
PHILLIPS, Frederick Wallace (Ferdie) 06/05
PHILLIPSON, Christopher Quintin 07/04
PIACHAUD, François Allen 04/05
PIKE, Roger Walter 01/05
PILKINGTON, Margaret 08/03
PILLING, Neville 01/04
PIPER, Leonard Arthur 09/03
POLLOCK, Jennifer Susan 12/04
POOLE, Denis Tom 07/04
POTTER, Colin Michael 05/05
POUNTAIN, Eric Gordon 10/04
POWELL, Richard Michael Wheler 03/05
PRICE, Alec John 02/05
PRICE, Roy Ernest 05/04
PRIOR, Christopher 09/04
PUGH, David 05/05
PUTMAN, Nina Maude Elaine 08/04
QUINNEY, William Elliot 07/05
RALPH, Charles 06/05
RAYBOULD, Norman William 08/04
READ, Christopher Holditch 03/05
READ, Jack 07/05
READ, John Hanson 07/04
REARDON, Martin Alan 01/05
REDGRAVE, Ronald Oliver 02/04
REED, Bruce Douglas 11/03
REID, William Frederick (Eric) 12/03
REITH, Ivor Stuart Weston 12/03
RENNISON, Walter Patrick 11/03
RENOUF, Peter Mark 10/03
RENOUF, Robert Wilson 01/04
RESTALL, Gerald Dalton 10/04
REVELL, Arthur 01/04
REVETT, Graham Francis 05/04
REYNOLDS, Stanley Kenneth 04/05
✠RICHARDS, John 11/03
RICHARDS, William Antony 03/04
RICHARDSON, Charles 06/04
RICHARDSON, Jack Cyril 11/03
RITCHIE, John Young Wylie 12/03
RIVETT-CARNAC, Sir Thomas Nicholas 05/04
ROBERTS, Elwyn 09/04
ROBERTSON, George Edward 08/03
ROBERTSON, James Smith 03/04
ROBINSON, Hugh Stanley 04/04
ROBINSON, John Howard 12/04
ROBINSON, Stuart 03/05
ROBSON, Irwin 05/04
✠ROGERS, Alan Francis Bright 10/03
ROGERS, Donovan Charles Edgar 01/05
ROGERSON, Derek Russell 03/05
ROOKE, Henry John Warburton 03/05
ROSCAMP, Alan Nicholas Harrison 02/05
ROSE, Roy 02/04
ROTHWELL, Eric 05/05
ROUNDS, Philip Rigby 09/04
ROWLANDS, Daniel John 09/04
ROWLANDSON, Gary Clyde 06/04
ROYCROFT, James Gordon Benjamin 07/04
ROYSTON-BALL, Peter 05/05

RUDDY, Denys Henry 02/04
RUSSELL, Eric 04/05
RUTHERFORD, John Allarton Edge 01/05
RYAN, Christopher John 02/04
RYLANDS, Thomas Michael 10/03
SALTER, Samuel 05/05
SAMUEL, Theophilus 03/04
SANDERSON, Harold 02/04
SAUNDERS, Edward George Humphrey 08/04
SAWYERS, Thomas Adam Barton 05/04
SCOTT, Patrick Henry Fowlis 02/05
SCRIVEN, Paul Michael 11/04
SEELEY, John Frederick 01/04
SELBY, Sydney Arthur 02/05
SHANNON, Francis Thomas 03/04
SHEA, Guy Roland John 01/05
SHEILD, Edward Oscar 05/05
✠SHEPPARD, (David Stuart) 03/05
SHORTEN, Richard Deering 06/04
SILKSTONE, Harry William James 03/05
SIMMONS, Raymond Agar 09/03
SIMPSON, William Thomas 02/04
SIMPSON, William Vaughan 07/04
SINGLETON, James Richard 05/04
SISSON, Trevor 06/05
SKELDING, Donald Brian 01/05
SKEMP, Stephen Rowland 06/04
SKIPWITH, Osmund Humberston 12/03
SLADEN, Philip 10/03
SLATER, John 06/04
SLATOR, William Thompson Howard 09/03
SLY, Harold Kenneth 01/05
SMITH, Anthony Adam Dalziel 03/04
SMITH, David John 05/05
SMITH, Dennis Peter 10/03
SMITH, Esmond Ernest Carrington 05/05
SMITH, Gilbert 05/04
SMITH, John Stewart 01/04
SMITH, John David Elliott 02/05
SMITH, Laurence Kenneth Powell 07/04
SMITH, Thomas Robert Selwyn 12/03
SMYTHE, Harry Reynolds 07/05
SNELL, William Graham Brooking 07/05
SNOW, Edward Brian 05/04
SOUTHWOOD, Robert Alfred 05/04
SPARLING, Harold William 10/03
STAGG, Charles Roy 12/03
STANNARD, Harold Frederick David 10/03
STEARE, Peter Douglas 10/03
STEPHENS, John James Frederick 02/04
STEVENS, David Johnson (Brother David Stephen) 09/03
STEVENS, David Leonard 01/04
STEVENS, Ralph Samuel Osborn 03/05
STEVENS, Trevor 05/04
STEWART, Maurice Evan 10/04
STIRRUP, Roger 11/04
STOBART, Judith Audrey 06/05
STOCKLEY, Michael Ian 04/04
STONE, Ernest Arthur 08/04
STONE, Noel Alfred William 05/04
STONE, Rodney Cameron 06/04
STRATFIELD, Robert John 11/04
STRICKLAND, Ernest Armitage 12/03
STRIDE, Desmond William Adair 04/04
STRONG, Stephen Charles 02/05
STRUDWICK, Donald Frank 07/05
STUART, James Douglas Maxwell 10/03
STUBBS, Anthony Richard Peter (Ælred) 10/04
STUDD, Christopher Sidney 01/04
STURDY, William David Mark 03/05
SULLIVAN, Bernard George 01/05
SWINDLEY, Geoffrey 09/03
SWINNERTON, Edward 10/03
SWINSON, Kenneth Anthony 12/03
SYMONDS, Edward George 04/04
TAGGART, Justin Paul 02/05
TANNER, Frederick James 11/03
TATE, Harold Richard 01/04
TATTERSALL, James 05/05
TAYLOR, John Frederick 09/03
TAYLOR, Kenneth Charles 05/05
TAYLOR, Neville Patrick 01/05
TAYLOR, Thomas Fish 12/03
TENNANT, Osmond Roy 04/05
THIEDE, Carsten Peter 12/04
THOMAS, Alan 12/04
THOMAS, Alan William Charles 01/05
THOMAS, Peter 03/05
THOMAS, Ralph Pilling 10/04
THOMAS, Richard 09/03
THOMPSON, David Frank 04/04
✠THOMPSON, James Lawton 09/03
THOMPSON, Robert 09/04
THORBURN, Austin Noel 06/04
THORNLEY, Arthur Richard 02/04
THREADGILL, Alan Roy 01/04
TIDMARSH, Philip Reginald Wilton 07/05
TOMLINSON, John Coombes 01/05
TOWNEND, Noel Alexander Fortescue 12/03
TRAVERSE, Ernest 01/05
TREBLE, Harry 10/03
TRIGG, John Alfred 07/05
TWYCROSS, Stephen Jervis 06/05
TYERS, Gerald Seymour 06/04
TYMMS, Wilfrid Widdas 11/04
TYNDALE-BISCOE, William Francis (Brother Francis) 12/03
TYRRELL, Frank Englefield (Peter) 01/05
UNWIN, Christopher Philip 12/04
VALE, David Phipps 06/05
VAUGHAN, Ronald Alfred 02/05
VEAZEY, Harry Christopher Hurford 11/03
VENABLES, Dudley James 08/04
VEVAR, John Harvard 01/04
VIGAR, Gilbert Leonard 11/04
VILLIERS, Tony 03/05
VIRJI, Elizabeth Jane 03/04
VOUT, Victor Alan 03/05
WACKWITZ-MARSHALL, Alan John 09/04
WADDY, Richard Patteson Stacy 11/03
WAGHORN, Geoffrey Brian 06/05
WAGSTAFF, Alan Robert Joseph 10/04
WAINWRIGHT, Frank Alan 07/05
WAKEFIELD, Kenneth Eyles 05/05
✠WAKELING, John Denis 10/04
WALDEN, Samuel 05/04
WALDRON, Laurence Charles 04/05
WALKER, Alan David 11/03
WALKER, Barry Donovan 12/04
WALKER, Ernest Alwyn 12/03
WALKER, Jack 10/03
WALKER, William 02/04
WALTERS, John Morgan 11/04
WARD, Louis Arthur 04/05
WARDLE, Edward Christian 01/05
WARLAND, Cyril John 02/05
WARRINER, Leonard 02/04
WARRINGTON, Gwynfa Lewis Jones 01/05
WATERER, Anthony Tatham 12/04
WATHEN, Sydney Gordon 06/05
WATSON, Basil Alderson 10/04
WATSON, John 10/04
WATTHEY, Arthur Edward 07/04
WATTON, Robert Newman Kingsley 08/04
WATTS, Ronald Horace 05/05
WAYTE, Alleyn Robert 09/04
WEAVER, Raymond Alexander 09/04
WEBB, Richard Lacey 11/04
WEBBER, Peter Cecil 09/04
WEDGWOOD, Charles Mervyn 11/03
WELLS, Stephen Glossop 01/05
WEST, Gerald Eric 04/04
WESTLAKE, Peter Alan Grant 12/03
WHITE, Jonathan Roger 07/05
WHITE, Kenneth Charles 11/04
WHITE, Noel Louis 01/04
WHITEHEAD, Denys Gordon 02/05
WHITLOW, Brian William 08/04
WHITTAKER, Arthur 06/05
WHITTAKER, Arthur George 11/04
WHYTE, Malcolm Dorrance 09/03
WILDING, Joseph 07/05
WILES, Maurice Frank 06/05
WILLETT, Michael John Farquhar 03/04
WILLIAMS, David Albert 08/04
WILLIAMS, Edward Bryan 02/05
WILLIAMS, Glyn Alun 12/03
WILLIAMS, Harold Edgar 10/04
WILLIAMS, Ieuan Merchant 05/05
WILLIAMS, John Edward 01/05
WILLIAMS, John Elwyn Askew 04/05
WILLIAMS, John Herbert 12/03
WILLIAMS, Malcolm Kendra 03/04
WILLIAMS, Robert David 11/04
WILLIAMS, Robert George Dibdin 12/03
WILLS, Herbert Ashton Peter 09/04
WILSON, Brian Arthur 08/03
WILSON, David Merritt 07/04
WILSON, John Walter 01/05
WILSON, Michael 11/03
WILTSHIRE, Albert 07/05
WINTER, Henry David 03/04
WINTERBOTHAM, Anthony James Marshall 10/03
WOOD, Eric Basil 10/04
WOOD, Philip Hervey 01/05
WOOD, Reginald John 07/05
WOOD, Thomas Patrick Scarborough 05/05
WOODHAMS, Kathryn Asma Patricia 09/03
WOODLAND, Robert Alan 01/05
WOOLLEY, Christopher Andrew Lempriere 05/04
WOULDHAM, Ralph Douglas Astley 02/04
WRIGHT, Graham Ewen 01/05
WRIGHT, Peter Gordon 04/04
WYNNE, James Arthur Hill 03/04
YOUNG, Henry Lawrence 10/03
YOUNG, Roger Edward 07/05
YOUNG, Stanley 02/04
YOUNG, Walter Howlett 12/04

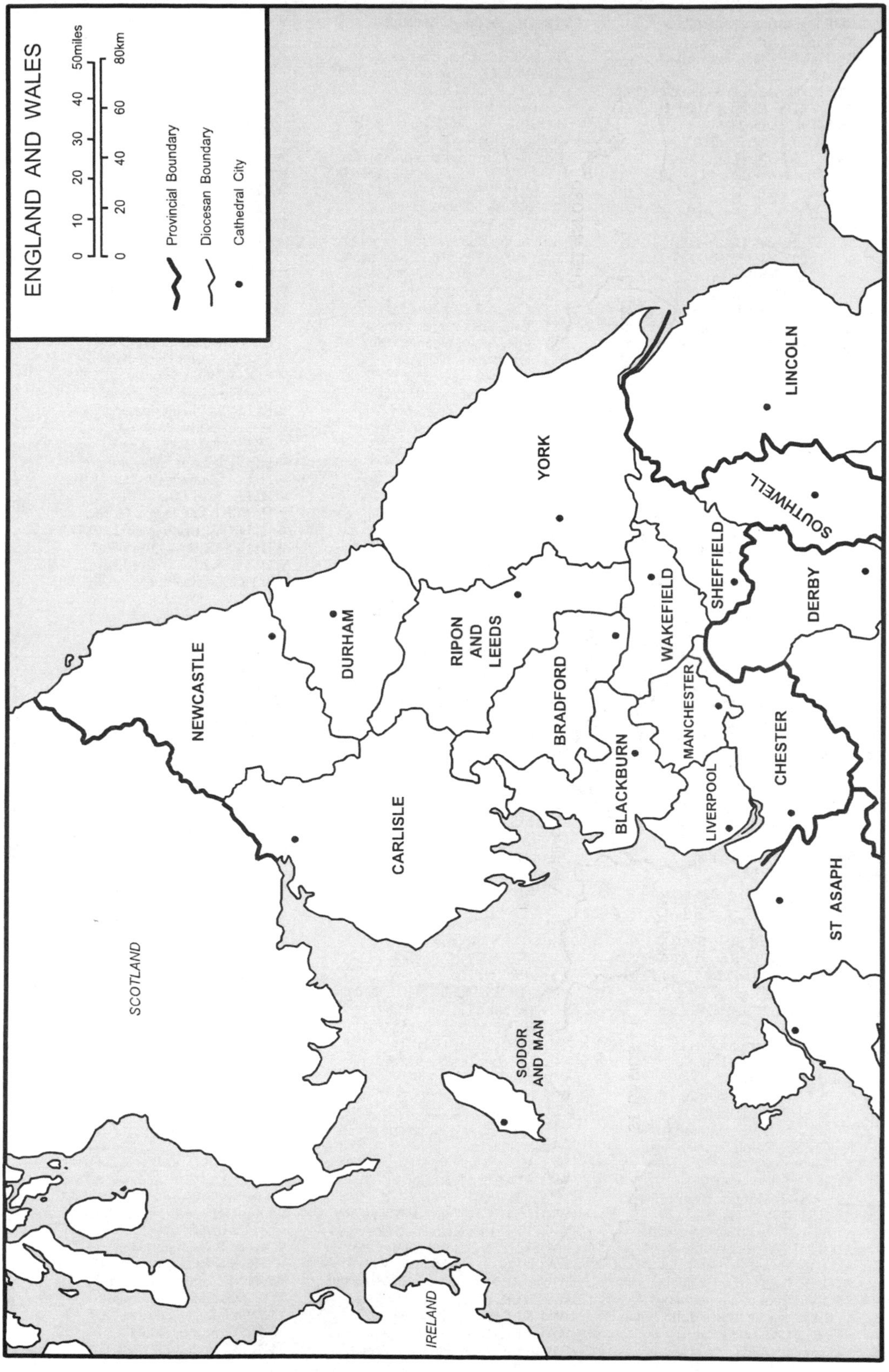
ENGLAND AND WALES
0 10 20 30 40 50miles
0 20 40 60 80km
Provincial Boundary
Diocesan Boundary
Cathedral City
NEWCASTLE
DURHAM
YORK
RIPON AND LEEDS
BRADFORD
WAKEFIELD
SHEFFIELD
LINCOLN
SOUTHWELL
DERBY
BLACKBURN
MANCHESTER
LIVERPOOL
CHESTER
CARLISLE
ST ASAPH
SODOR AND MAN
SCOTLAND
IRELAND

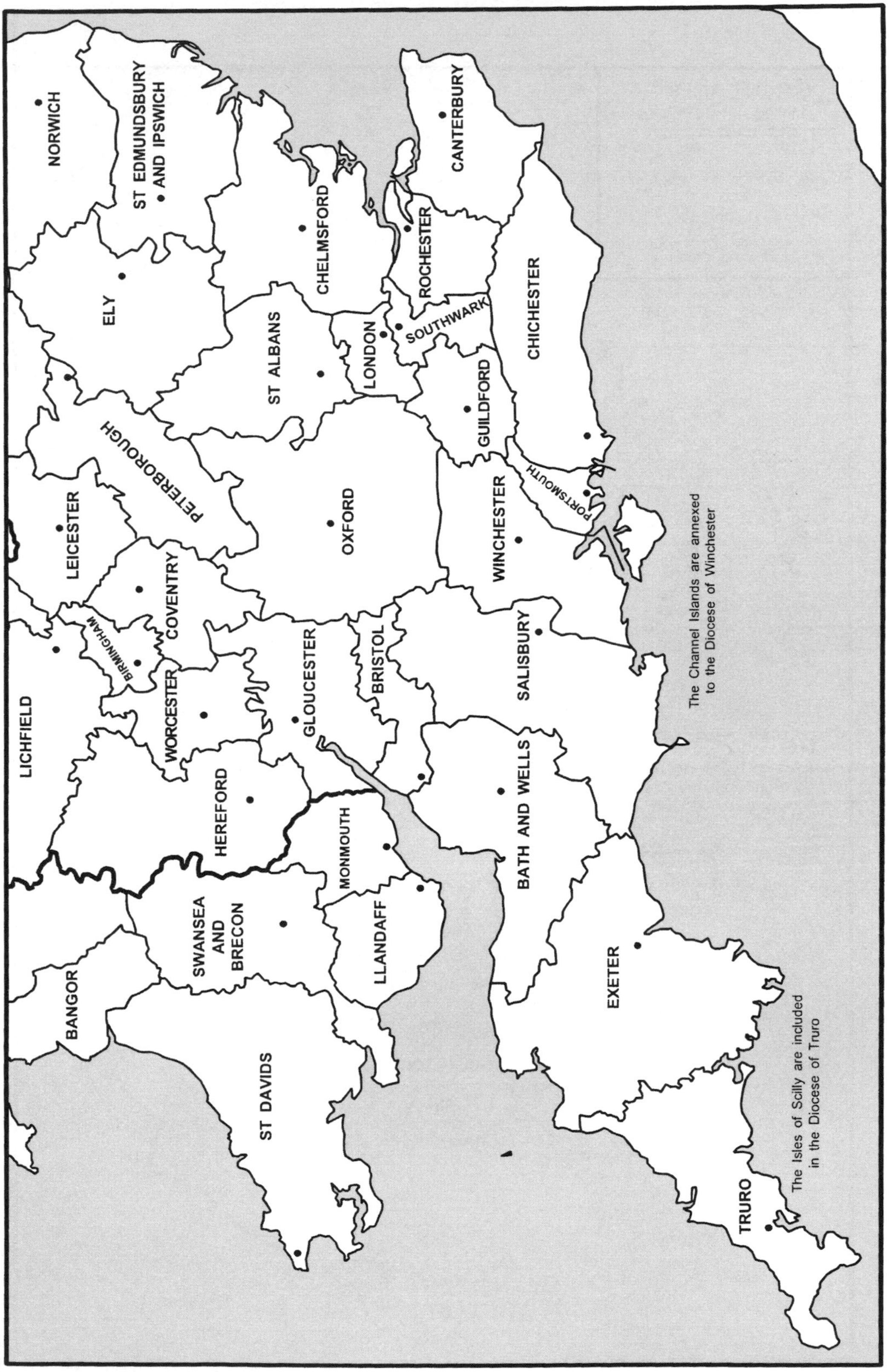
NORWICH
ST EDMUNDSBURY AND IPSWICH
CANTERBURY
CHELMSFORD
ROCHESTER
ELY
SOUTHWARK
LONDON
CHICHESTER
ST ALBANS
GUILDFORD
PETERBOROUGH
PORTSMOUTH
OXFORD
LEICESTER
WINCHESTER
COVENTRY
BIRMINGHAM
SALISBURY
BRISTOL
GLOUCESTER
LICHFIELD
WORCESTER
The Channel Islands are annexed to the Diocese of Winchester
HEREFORD
BATH AND WELLS
MONMOUTH
SWANSEA AND BRECON
LLANDAFF
EXETER
BANGOR
ST DAVIDS
The Isles of Scilly are included in the Diocese of Truro
TRURO

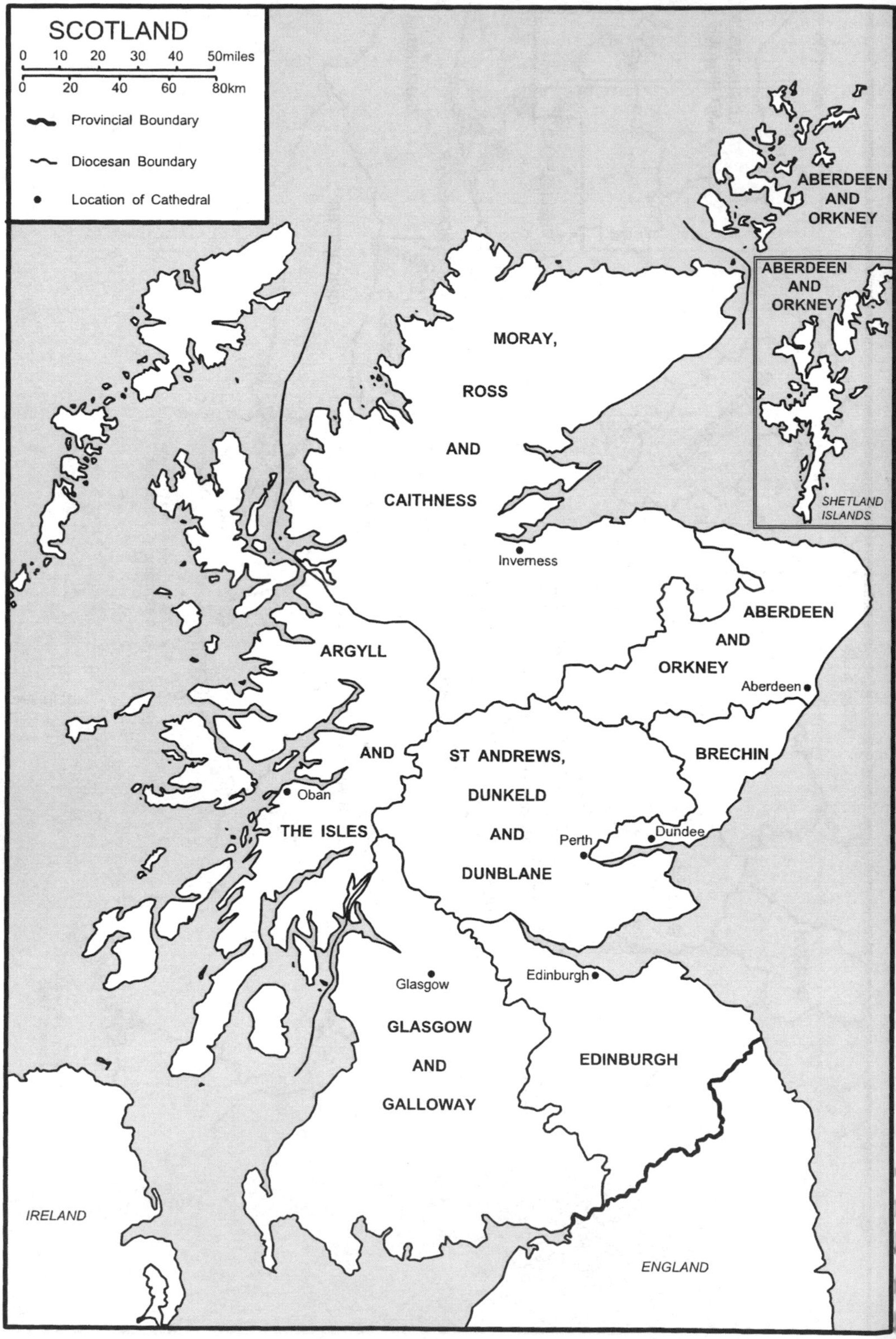
SCOTLAND
0 10 20 30 40 50miles
0 20 40 60 80km
Provincial Boundary
Diocesan Boundary
Location of Cathedral
ABERDEEN AND ORKNEY
ABERDEEN AND ORKNEY
SHETLAND ISLANDS
MORAY, ROSS AND CAITHNESS
Inverness
ABERDEEN AND ORKNEY
Aberdeen
ARGYLL AND THE ISLES
Oban
BRECHIN
ST ANDREWS, DUNKELD AND DUNBLANE
Perth
Dundee
Glasgow
Edinburgh
GLASGOW AND GALLOWAY
EDINBURGH
IRELAND
ENGLAND

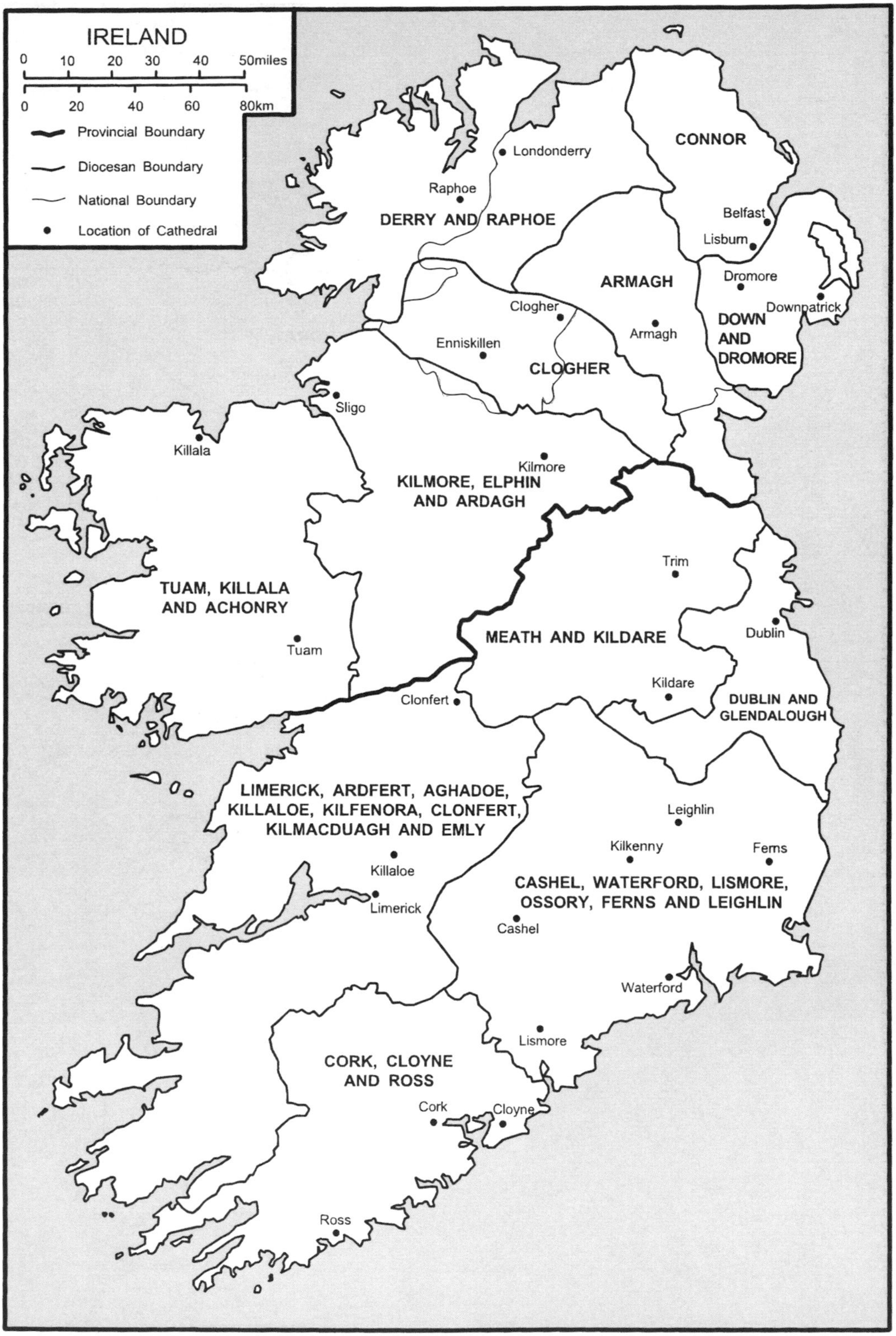
IRELAND
0 10 20 30 40 50miles
0 20 40 60 80km
Provincial Boundary
Diocesan Boundary
National Boundary
Location of Cathedral
Londonderry
Raphoe
DERRY AND RAPHOE
CONNOR
Belfast
Lisburn
Dromore
Downpatrick
DOWN AND DROMORE
ARMAGH
Armagh
Clogher
Enniskillen
CLOGHER
Sligo
Killala
Kilmore
KILMORE, ELPHIN AND ARDAGH
TUAM, KILLALA AND ACHONRY
Tuam
Trim
Dublin
MEATH AND KILDARE
Kildare
Clonfert
DUBLIN AND GLENDALOUGH
LIMERICK, ARDFERT, AGHADOE, KILLALOE, KILFENORA, CLONFERT, KILMACDUAGH AND EMLY
Killaloe
Limerick
Leighlin
Kilkenny
Ferns
CASHEL, WATERFORD, LISMORE, OSSORY, FERNS AND LEIGHLIN
Cashel
Waterford
Lismore
CORK, CLOYNE AND ROSS
Cork
Cloyne
Ross

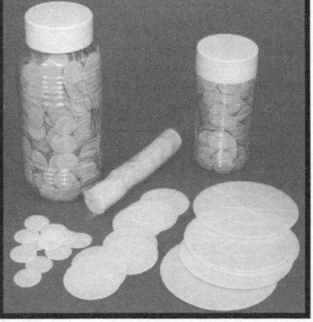

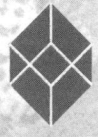

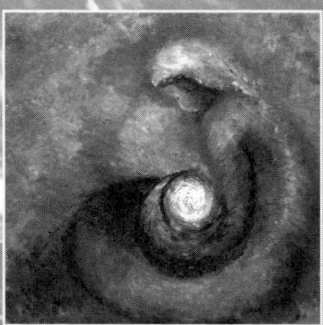

sovereign account
it's not
what you give,
it's the way
that you give it
stewardship
The one account for all your charitable giving
• Fund through your payroll
• Regular and one-off gifts
• Charity 'cheque' book
• Give to Christian and secular charities
• Give to Christian workers and bible college students
• Option to remain anonymous
Join over 21,000 others and open an account with the leading Christian provider of charitable giving services
Stewardship is the Christian financial support services charity formed by the merger of Stewardship Services and Sovereign Giving. A registered charity no. 234714.
Call us on
08452 26 26 27
or visit
www.sovereignaccount.org

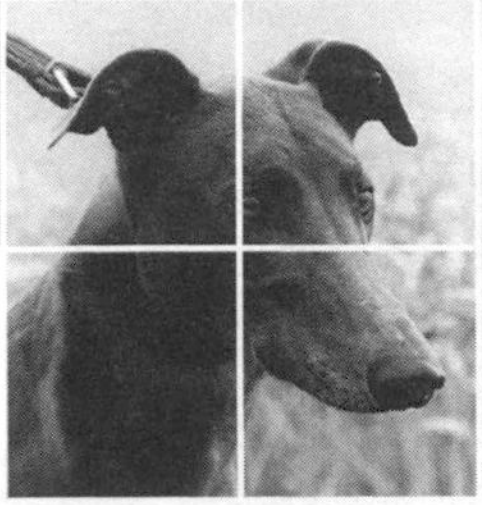

JAMES CHASE
Heavenly furniture...........
for Heavenly buildings
Thornton Road,Bradford BD1 2JT
T : 08457 125 488 (local rate)
E : sales@james-chase.co.uk
W : www.james-chase.co.uk

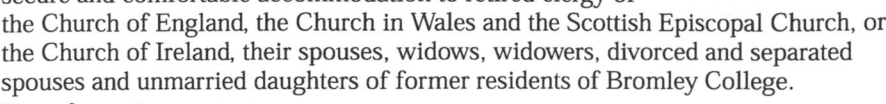